Y0-BVR-193

The
HAMMOND ALMANAC
of a
million facts records forecasts
1982

Martin A. Bacheller,
Editor in Chief

A Gift from the Estate of
Michael Hart
www.gutenberg.org

Hammond Almanac, Inc.
Maplewood, N.J. 07040

CURRENT EVENTS & FUTURE TRENDS	9
U.S. HISTORY & GOVERNMENT	66
MONEY & ECONOMICS	184
TRAVEL & TRANSPORTATION	217
FACTS ABOUT SOCIETY	244
HEALTH, EARTH, SPACE & SCIENCE	269
STATES, PROVINCES CITIES	351
WORLD NATIONS & ATLAS	504
EDUCATION & COMMUNICATION	736
WORLD HISTORY & BIOGRAPHY	783
CELEBRITIES THE ARTS, AWARDS	835
SPORTS	910

Martin A. Bacheller, Editor in Chief
Dorothy C. Bacheller, Ernest J. Dupuy, Jonathan F. Erway,
   Charles G. Lees, Jr. (Sports), **Maria Maggi, W. Z. Myers, Ulrike Wiede,** Editors
   Anita Diamond, Charity Dobbins, Editorial Assistants
Harvey Brittle, Director of Production
Drew Kuber, Director of Creative Operations

William B. Cummings, William A. DeGregorio, Walter Fox, Bob Perlongo,
   John D. Tedford, Contributing Editors

Laurence Urdang, Contributing Editor
Alan Isaacs, Advisory Editor, Science
John Daintith, Editor, Science
Elizabeth Martin, Editor, Earth Sciences
Helen Swallow, Editor, Medicine
John Landry, Editor, Current Events

Bill Carter, *Television Review*
Robert Dahlin, *Book Review*
Mel Gussow, *Theatre Review*
Stephen Handzo, *Film Review*
Henry T. Wallhauser, *Music Review*

THE FUTURE *section appearing on pages 9–37 was prepared by the World Future Society,*
4916 St. Elmo Avenue, Washington, D.C. 20014; Edward S. Cornish, President.

Data for the Index of U.S. Colleges and Universities found on pages 739–757 were supplied
by Peterson's Guides, P.O. Box 2123, Princeton, N.J. 08540, a communications company special-
izing in higher educational data.

The Hammond Almanac is the successor to
The New York Times Encyclopedic Almanac.

Copyright © 1969, 1970, 1971 by The New York Times Company. Copyright © 1972 by Quadrangle
Books, Inc. and Almanac Publishing Company, Inc. Copyright © 1973, 1974, 1975, 1976, 1977,
1978, 1979, 1980, 1981 by Hammond Almanac, Inc. All rights reserved. No part of this book
may be reproduced in any form, by Photostat, microfilm, xerography, or any other means, or
incorporated into any information retrieval system, electronic or mechanical, without the writ-
ten permission of the copyright owner.

Library of Congress Catalog Card Number: 79-642716
Published simultaneously in the United States and Canada   ISBN 0-441-31603-4 495 (Softcover)
Printed in the United States of America   ISBN 0-8437-4028-0 (Hardcover)

HAMMOND ALMANAC, INC.
Maplewood, New Jersey 07040
HUGH JOHNSON, *President*

CONTENTS

THE FUTURE —
CAREERS OF TOMORROW:
EXCITING CHANGES IN THE WORLD OF WORK 9–37
NEWS MAPS 38–48
'80/'81 MONTH-BY-MONTH CHRONOLOGY 49–65
LATE CHANGES 65
U.S. HISTORY 66–165
    Outline of United States History 66
    Declaration of Independence 72
    Constitution 74
    Administrations, Cabinets, and Congresses since 1789 83
    Presidential Biographies 99
    Lincoln's Gettysburg Address 139
    U.S. Presidential Index 140
    Vice-Presidents 142
    First Ladies 146
    U.S. Presidential Elections since 1789 153
    1976 Presidential Election Results 164
    1980 Presidential Election Results 165
U.S. GOVERNMENT: 1981 166–183
    White House Office–1981 166
    U.S. Cabinet–1981 167
    Heads of Federal Departments and Agencies–1981 168
    1980 House of Representatives Election Results 170
    1976, 1978, 1980 Senatorial Election Results 172
    Congressional Representatives Under Each Apportionment 173
    Members of the House of Representatives 174
    Members of the Senate 177
    Standing Congressional Committees 178
    U.S. Courts 180
TAXES/EXPENDITURES 184–194
    State and Local Government Expenditures: Per Capita 184
    The Budget Dollar 185
    Federal Grants to States 185
    Expenditure of Federal Tax Dollars 185
    U.S. Budget 186
    State Per Capita Income 186
    Internal Revenue Taxes 187
    Addresses of U.S. Internal Revenue Offices 187
    Tax Tips 188
    Federal Tax Collections 190
    Tax Burden: Selected Countries 190
    State Income Tax Rates and Exemptions 191
    State Sales and Use Tax Rates 194
    City Sales and Income Tax Rates 194
FINANCE/INDUSTRY/LABOR 195–216
    Facts about U.S. Money 195
    Compound Interest Table 196
    Gold Production 197
    Companies with the Largest Number of Common Stockholders 197
    U.S. Corporate Profits 197
    Foreign Exchange Rates 198
    Money Depreciation: Annual Rates 198
    Central Bank Discount Rates 198
    Gross National Product: U.S. and World 199
    U.S. Oil Imports 200

Largest U.S. Corporations 200
Leading U.S. Farm Crops 202
U.S. Farm Payments 202
U.S. Livestock Population 202
U.S. Passenger Car Production 203
World Motor Vehicle Production 203
Passenger Car Imports to U.S. 203
Largest Foreign Car Producers 203
U.S. Labor Force 204
Unemployment Rates: By Sex and Race 204
Minority Group Employment 204
U.S. Labor Unions 205
Average Union Hourly Scale 205
Unemployment Insurance Benefits 206
Employment Outlook to 1985 206
U.S. Nuclear Power Plants 207
U.S. Fuel Production 208
World Nuclear Power 208
Energy Consumption 208
Largest Foreign Companies 209
World Oil Producers 209
U.S. Metals Production 209
World Mineral Production Leaders 210
U.S. Exports and Imports 210
World Trade of the United States 211
World Economic Summary 211
Wall Street Glossary 212
Leading Stocks in Market Value 214
Regular Dividend Payers 215
U.S. Energy Supply/Demand Balance 216

TRAVEL/TRANSPORTATION **217–243**

Major U.S. Vehicular Tunnels 217
Railroad Passenger Service 217
Intercity Bus Lines 218
Amtrak, Conrail 218
Longest Railway Tunnels 218
Automobile Registrations and Drivers by State 219
World Motor Vehicle Fatality Rates 219
U.S. Intercity Road Mileage 220
U.S. Air Distances 221
U.S. Railroad Distances 222
Toll-Free Telephone Numbers 223
National Parks 225
U.S. Passport 227
Foreign City Weather 228
Customs Hints 230
Health Hints for Travelers 231
World Cities' Cost-of-Living Index 232
Customs Duties 232
Commercial Passenger Planes 233
Air Distances Between Major Cities 234
World Aviation Records 236
Major International Airports 238
Airline Traffic Volume 238
Air Safety Records 239
World's Fastest Trains 239
Selected World Merchant Fleets 240
Foreign Commerce at Selected U.S. Ports 240
Major World Ship Canals 241
World Cities: Time Differences 241
Major Passenger Liners 242
World's Leading Bridges 242

CENSUS/SOCIAL SERVICES **244–260**

U.S. Population and Area 244
Resident U.S. Population by State and Rank 244

Largest U.S. Metropolitan Areas 245
Voter Participation: Presidential Elections 246
Immigration to the United States 246
World Population Facts 247
Most Populous Cities and Countries 247
Leading Counties and Cities Ranked by Median Family Income 248
U.S. Metropolitan Area Per Capita Income 248
Urban Family Budget 249
Worldwide Cost of Living 249
The American Consumer: Personal Expenditures 249
Consumer Price Index 250
Average U.S. Retail Food Prices 250
American Family Characteristics 251
Sex Ratio of U.S. Population 251
U.S. Marriage and Divorce Rates 251
Illegitimate Births in America 251
U.S. Divorce Laws 252
Median Duration of U.S. Marriages . . . 253
U.S. Marriage Laws 254
Social Security and Medicare 255
Poverty in America 259
Aid to Families with Dependent Children 260
Drug Law Enforcement 260

U.S. CRIME SUMMARY 261–263

Drugs: Uses and Abuses 261
Crimes in U.S. Cities 262
Capital Punishment 263
Executions in the United States 263

CIVIL RIGHTS/RACE 264–268

Civil Rights Legislation 264
U.S. Population by Race and Spanish Origin—1980 264
Employment in Urban Poverty Areas 265
Women's Rights: Social History 266
Black Population of U.S. Cities 266
Black American History 266

PUBLIC HEALTH/MEDICINE 269–283

Biological and Medical Science Review 269
U.S. Expectation of Life 271
Death Rates in America 272
U.S. Homicides and Suicides 273
International Suicide Rates 273
Venereal Disease 273
Cancer 274
Hospital Costs 275
Abortion and the Law 275
Pollution in U.S. 276
Medical Care Indexes 276
Milestones of Medicine 277
Medical Glossary 278
Modern Drug Advances 280
Psychiatric Terms 281
Patient Care in Mental Health Facilities 282
Recommended Daily Diets 283
Desirable Weights for Adult Men and Women 283

EARTH: FACTS/FIGURES 284–313

Earth: Third Planet from the Sun 284
The Continents 286
Prehistoric Creatures 287
Fossil Man 288
Animal Kingdom 289

Endangered Wildlife 290
Long Foreign Rivers 291
Oceans and Seas 291
Major World Glaciers 292
Large Lakes of the World 292
Great World Deserts 292
High Mountain Peaks of the World 293
Dams, Man-made Lakes, and Hydroelectric Plants 294
Volcanoes 295
World Waterfalls 295
Worldwide Weather Extremes 296
World's Highest Buildings 297
Earth's Geographic Extremes 298
Principal World Islands 298
Geographic Extremes and Centers of the United States 299
Average and Extreme U.S. Elevations 300
Principal U.S. Rivers, Lakes and Mountain Peaks 301
U.S. Temperature Extremes 302
U.S. City Weather 304
National Weather Service 306
Meteorological Glossary 306
National Oceanic and Atmospheric Administration 307
Standard Time Zones 307
Latitude and Longitude of U.S. Cities 308
Sunrise and Sunset 308
Perpetual Calendar 310
Holidays and Commemorated Days 312
New World Explorers 313

STARS/PLANETS/SPACE 314–335

Origin and Evolution of the Universe 314
Stellar and Galactic Terms 315
Constellations 317
Major Astronomical Facilities 319
The Sun, Our Nearest Star 321
Planets 322
Spectral Sequence 324
Planetary Space Probes 324
Moon 326
Satellites of the Solar System 327
Asteroids 327
Comets and Meteors 328
Astronomical Phenomena: 1981 329
U.S. Space Program 330
Manned Space-Flight Programs 332

SCIENCE: PAST/PRESENT 336–350

Engineering Achievements 336
Periodic Table of Elements 336
Elements and Their Discoverers 337
Landmarks of Science 338
Metric Weights and Measures 340
Table of Equivalents 340
Roman Numerals 341
Binary Numbers 341
Unit Conversions 342
U.S. Customary Weights and Measures 343
Temperature Conversions 343
Science Glossary 344
Multiplication and Division Table 346
Foreign Weights and Measures 347
Squares, Cubes, Square Roots and Cube Roots 348
Decimal Equivalents of Common Fractions 348
Inventors and Inventions 349

U.S. STATES/CITIES/TERRITORIES 351–457

The Fifty States: Alabama–Wyoming 352

REPRESENTATIVE AMERICAN CITIES 458–475

TERRITORIES 476–479

CANADA 480–503

WORLD NATIONS 504–710
Territories and Dependencies 704

THE ATLAS 513–528

DIPLOMATIC AFFAIRS 711–727
The United Nations 711
Representative International Organizations 719
U.S. Contributions to International Organizations 720
U.S. Foreign Economic Assistance 721
Selected Foreign Embassies and Ambassadors 722
American Diplomats Abroad 723
British Prime Ministers 724
The Commonwealth 725
World Communist Party Strength 726
Soviet Leaders and Rulers of China 727

MILITARY AFFAIRS 728–735
U.S. Wars and Casualties 728
U.S. Veterans 728
National Guard 729
U.S. Military Pay Scales 729
American Military Cemeteries on Foreign Soil 730
Joint Chiefs of Staff 731
U.S. Casualties in Vietnam 731
Cost Estimates of American Wars 731
Veterans Benefits 732
U.S. Military Aid 733
Nuclear Armaments 733
Warplanes 734
Active U.S. Military Forces 734
Blacks in U.S. Armed Forces 735
Military-Industrial Complex 735
Armed Forces of the World 735

EDUCATION: FACTS/FIGURES 736–759
Expenditures for Public Education 736
High School Graduates 736
College and University Graduates 736
Education and Income 736
Level of Education: White and Black Adults 737
U.S. Educational Expenditures 737
Elementary and Secondary Schools 738
U.S. Public Libraries 738
Index of U.S. Colleges and Universities 739
Large U.S. University Libraries 758
List of Reference Books 758

COMMUNICATIONS/LANGUAGE 760–767
Current Words and Phrases 760
Most Common American Surnames 762
Major World Languages 762
Leading American Magazines 763
U.S. Advertising Volume 763
U.S. and World Newspapers 764
Leading TV Advertisers 764
Forms of Address 765
U.S. Postal Information and Regulations 766

ZIP CODES AND 1980 POPULATIONS OF
U.S. TOWNS AND CITIES 768–782

HISTORY: ANCIENT/MODERN 783–808
Present Monarchs and Dynasties 783
Selected Past Rulers and Dynasties 785
Family History is for Everyone 787
Outline of World History 788
Seven Wonders of the Ancient World 808

WORLD BIOGRAPHY 808–842
World Figures 808
Scientists and Mathematicians 818
Philosophers, Theologians, and Religionists 819
Men of Medicine and Physiology 820
Notables of Art and Architecture 822
Novelists, Dramatists, Poets, and Other Writers 825
Notables of the Musical World 829
Film Directors 832
Celebrities: Past and Present 835

ARTS: POPULAR/CLASSICAL 843–857
All-time Movie Moneymakers 843
Longest Broadway Runs 844
Major World Dance Groups 844
Popular Discography 845
Classical Discography 846
Leading Opera Companies 847
Symphony Orchestras of the U.S. and Canada 848
Professional Resident and Repertory Theatres 849
Art Museums 850
The Reviews:
Books 852
Theatre 854
Music 855
Television 856
Films 857

PRIZES/AWARDS 858–876
Nobel Prize Winners 858
Pulitzer Prizes 864
Other Awards 871
Academy Award Winners 874

THE DIRECTORY 877–881

RELIGION: FAITHS/FOLLOWERS 882–897
Major World Religions 882
Principal Religions of the World: Estimated Membership 886
The Popes 887
Calendar of Religious Holidays 888
College of Cardinals 889
U.S. Religious Bodies 891

DISASTERS/CATASTROPHES 898–909

SPORTS: FACTS/FIGURES 910–999
(See special sports index page 910)

OBITUARIES 1000–1007

INDEX 1008–1040

THE FUTURE

IBM

Careers of Tomorrow
Exciting Changes in the World of Work

A special report prepared for the
HAMMOND ALMANAC by the staff
of the *WORLD FUTURE SOCIETY*

What's been happening recently in the
world of jobs and careers — with special
focus on what the future holds for:

- The Economy and Jobs
- Occupational Outlook
- Career Counseling
- New Occupations
- Productivity
- The Workweek
- Unions
- The Work Ethic
- Jobs and Family Life
- Where the Jobs Will Be
- Fast-Growing and Slow-
    Growing Occupations

Goodyear

New Jersey Bell

*Top: Computer graphics display
system aids auto designer.*

*Above: Older production worker
trims mold for rubber tires.*

*Left: Telephone installer at
work checking a circuit.*

The World Future Society is a nonprofit,
nonpartisan association of scholars, scientists and others interested in forecasts of
what may happen in technology, society,
human values and other fields during the
coming years. The Society's headquarters
are at 4916 St. Elmo Avenue, Washington,
D.C. 20014.

Work in the 1980s

Will the Economy Do Its Job?

by Edward Cornish

President of the
World Future Society
Washington, D.C.

In the minds of the average citizen, the economy has two tasks: first, to produce the goods and services that people want, and second, to provide jobs so that people can earn the money to buy the things they want. Providing jobs often seems more important than providing goods because people tend to assume that if they earn enough money they will usually be able to obtain whatever they need.

The economy has performed its job-producing function reasonably well in the past few years, if viewed from the long-term perspective. Back in the 1940s, Vice-President Henry Wallace dreamed of an economy that would offer sixty million jobs. Today the U.S. economy employs about 100 million workers. Dissatisfaction persists, however. Many people seem to be left out of the system, apparently unable to find jobs even though thousands of employers complain that they can't find the people to fill the available positions, and newspapers routinely publish large numbers of help-wanted advertisements. The unemployment rate during the first half of 1981 exceeded 7 percent—a far higher rate than the average for the 1950s and 1960s.

In July 1981, when the unemployment rate dropped slightly to 7 percent, many government officials expressed relief. Their worries continued, however, because that level is still high enough to cause concern. The figure is almost certain to go higher if the nation moves into a recession. During the 1973-75 recession, the unemployment rate climbed to 9 percent—the highest since the incredible 25 percent rate reached during the Great Depression. The Reagan Administration's cutbacks in government programs and the Federal Reserve Board's tight money policies seemed likely to bring about more unemployment in the short run. The Administration argues, nevertheless, that the private sector would be able to provide many new jobs to replace those lost through cutbacks in government programs.

Despite the worries, the economy was producing an almost incredibly high standard of living for most of the American people, if viewed from a historical perspective. People who complained that they could not afford to buy a house or an automobile could usually console themselves with a pleasure trip, a restaurant meal, a sunbath at a swimming pool, or a bit of entertainment from a videotape recorder. Compared to the hardships of the pioneer days or even the early 1950s, Americans were enjoying an affluent life-style in the 1980s. Even the unemployed were fed and housed in reasonable comfort for the most part, often because other family members were working or because government and private programs offered substantial compensation.

Still, the unemployed couldn't help worrying—and a lot of economists worried along with them. Two critically important industries—home building and automobile manufacturing—had slumped to Depressionlike depths, victims of soaring interest rates and the high prices of their products. Other industries such as steel, rubber and textiles seemed mired permanently in such troubles as falling demand, pressure from unions and competition from overseas producers. Even the new information industries such as computers and microprocessors could no longer be viewed as oases of blissful prosperity. In 1981, more than one semiconductor manufacturer laid off workers.

The uneasiness about the economy has led to talk about "revitalizing" industry in the United States. Part of the uneasiness arises from the observation of certain statistical indicators that suggest the U.S. no longer is progressing as rapidly as in the past. Overall economic growth was 4.1 percent a year in the 1960s, but slipped in the 1970s to 2.9 percent. On the international level, the U.S. standard of living—highest in the world in 1972—dropped to fifth place.

In the years following World War II, the U.S. dominated world trade, but its share has steadily declined over the past decades. In the 1970s the U.S. lost 23 percent of its share of the world market. In addition, U.S. products are also losing out in domestic markets. No radios are being made in the U.S. "American-made" television sets are assembled largely from components made elsewhere. "U.S. industry's loss of competitiveness over the past two decades has been nothing short of an economic disaster," lamented *Business Week* in June 1980. "Even sectors where the U.S. still racks up tremendous trade surpluses have been losing their share of the world market steadily."

To pay for heavy imports of petroleum, natural gas and manufactured goods, the U.S. has been selling off many of its assets to foreign countries and their nationals. The U.S. has also been borrowing substantially from other nations to finance the national debt as well as corporate bond issues. In effect, the U.S., once the rich uncle in the family of nations, must get its economic house in order or wind up as a poor relation.

Reindustrialization

Amid the concern about the U.S. economy, there has been a lot of discussion of "reindustrialization"—a term which became highly popular in some circles. The concept seems to offer something to everyone—more government help for ailing industries, more jobs for workers in steel and automobiles, better U.S. products for consumers and more contracts for government consultants. Yet for all its appeal, reindustrialization seems more of a catchword than a solution.

New York Stock Exchange

Bethlehem Steel

The action on the floor of the New York Stock Exchange reflects how investors view the economy.

The U.S. steel industry must make massive investments in new plant equipment if it is to survive.

"I have great difficulty with understanding what reindustrialization really is," confessed U.S. Senator William Proxmire. "We suffer from a whole series of problems. We suffer from declining productivity, high unemployment, painfully high interest rates and high trade deficits. We also have a surplus of proposals for what to do about these problems. Reindustrialization is the one that is getting the most press."

Proxmire, a Democrat from Wisconsin, went on to say that he thinks reindustrialization includes such things as federal loans, federal government export subsidies and tax credits.

"The common denominator of all these proposals is that they would have the government help with the problems. I am very sensitive to this because, as Chairman of the Senate Banking Committee, I sat in on the rescue of Lockheed and Chrysler—both of which I thought were very serious mistakes. The marketplace is a better gauge than the bureaucrats. And most business groups are telling us to get off their backs."

Proxmire pointed out a dilemma: People are demanding less government—but keep finding more tasks for government to carry out. "If the federal government is going to take on a welfare role for our industries, it will just get bigger than it is now," he said.

Expressing doubt that government officials are likely to make wiser decisions than the marketplace, the Senator also said, "Money will go where the political power is; it will go where unions are mobilized, where mayors and governors, representatives and senators have the power to push it. Anybody who thinks that the government resources will be allocated on the basis of merit hasn't been in Washington very long."

But if the money for modernizing America's obsolescent industries does not come from the government, what will be its source? The industries most desperately in need of modernization typically have the least amount of capital with which to work. Nor can they easily attract capital from the American people, who have been spending their money rather than saving it, thanks in part to inflation. Why put money in a savings account paying 5 percent or 6 percent interest when the money is losing its value at a rate of perhaps 10 percent? To avoid the erosion of their purchasing power, many people spend their money immediately on things that bring temporary satisfaction. Others buy real estate or objects expected to go up in value as the dollar goes down. But purchases of old coins, antiques, rare postage stamps and gold do not provide the funds needed by industry to modernize its plants.

The Reagan Administration hopes that its policies will reduce inflation drastically, thereby restoring people's confidence in U.S. money and their willingness to save. The savings would then become the capital needed to modernize industry. At the same time, the Administration believes the big tax cuts approved by Congress during the summer of 1981 will increase the incentives of both industry and individuals to work harder and produce more. The tax cuts may also help reduce the hidden economies which, by some accounts, are growing rapidly as people seek to escape government taxes and regulations.

The Hidden Economies

The notion of an "underground," or "subterranean," economy has come to prominence to explain such anomalies as the very large number of $100 bills in circulation at a time when most people rarely see one. The experts believe that many of the big greenbacks are used in the drug trade and in all kinds of "off-the-books" transactions.

As economists began probing into the underground economy, it became clear that a vast amount of economic activity is not recorded by the various systems of national accounts and so never figures in the GNP. There is the waitress who pockets a tip but fails to report it to the Internal Revenue Service and the teen-ager who mows a lawn for pay but does not tell the government about his earnings. There is also the growing business of "garage sales" or "yard sales" in which goods are bought and sold but taxes are rarely paid, and the flourishing of barter transactions in which taxes are avoided because no money changes hands.

Another highly important hidden economy operates in the privacy of each homestead—the so-called household economy. Do-it-yourselfers grow vegetables, prepare meals, provide sleeping accommodations for others, and so on. Despite the fact that these services add up to hundreds of

Harbourfront Communications Dept.

Bell Labs

Outdoor flea markets and garage sales are a way of adding to a household's income.

Testing this advanced telephone switching system is part of growing service industry.

billions of dollars in value, they are not figured into the economic life of the nation.

What is disturbing today is that high taxes and government regulations may be encouraging more people to move into the hidden economies, thus forcing the rest of the economy to bear increasingly heavy burdens. In some countries, such as Sweden and Italy, economists have noted a general retreat from the heavily taxed, legitimate economy to the underground world, where "black work" is performed and the government collects nothing for taxes and social services.

By reducing the burden of taxes and regulations, the Reagan Administration hopes to slow, if not halt, the spread of the hidden economies. If people can keep more of what they earn, they should have less reason to operate in the subterranean economy.

The Service Economy

Not everyone is worried about the decline of U.S. industry. Some observers believe it is part of a natural and generally desirable process and can be likened to the decline of agriculture as the dominant occupation in America. Agriculture today provides employment for less than 4 percent of the workforce, in contrast to the 90 percent it employed in the 18th century. In the years ahead, manufacturing may decline until it, too, occupies only a tiny percentage of the population.

Where, then, will the rest of the jobs be?

In the services—especially the rapidly growing information area, which includes financial planning, legal services, computer repair, and so on. With affluence, Americans have demanded more and more services. Medical care cannot be manufactured in a factory, and neither hairstyling nor groundskeeping can be packaged and sold. Over the past 30 years, most of the new jobs have been in service occupations. For every new job in manufacturing, more than five were created in the service-producing industries. Today, three of every five working Americans are employed in service jobs.

The development of the service sector has provided many jobs of all kinds for factory workers displaced by automated equipment on the assembly line. But transferring workers from manufacturing to services is not always easy. For one thing, manufacturing jobs tend to be highly paid, unionized positions; a worker forced off the assembly line in Detroit may not find a service job to match the pay in the automobile industry.

Three Views of the Economic Outlook

A balanced assessment of the U.S. economy in the early 1980s would have to recognize that it is performing reasonably well if judged by past standards, but not as well as people feel it should. Furthermore, signs of deterioration loom large for the years ahead. With inexpensive energy no longer available, how can the U.S. earn the foreign exchange needed to buy energy overseas? Energy will still be available, but it probably will not be as cheap as it was in the years before 1973. A more worrisome problem is inflation. How can the nation curb its persistent inflation without triggering a job-destroying recession?

Time will tell whether or not the concerns about the economy were well grounded. Today professional economists and other experts offer widely different forecasts. Generally speaking, U.S. government officials take an optimistic view, while private economists are more worried. The darkest views come from a group of authors who have written books with titles such as *How to Cope with the Developing Financial Crisis* (Ashby Bladen, 1980) and *How to Prosper During the Coming Bad Years* (Howard Ruff, 1979).

Let's look at each of these views in turn:

Optimistic View: President Reagan, who surprised observers with his success in getting Congress to approve reductions in both federal spending and in taxes, has suggested that the tax cuts will stimulate new economic activity. In the Administration's view, the economy should respond strongly in 1982 as inflation winds down, business increases its capital investment, and workers—allowed to keep more of their earnings—respond by producing more goods and services. With business booming, more job opportunities of all kinds will be available for people who want to work. Because the economy is producing more goods, there will be more of everything for everybody.

Cautious View: Less optimistic than the Reagan Administration, private economic forecasters generally appear uncertain about the impact of the Administration's policies on the economy. As tax cuts are phased in, how will people use the extra money they have available? Will they spend it, causing prosperity for retailers and manufacturers of consumer goods in the short run, but not easing the nation's capital shortage problem? Or will they save it, thereby reducing interest rates and helping industry to modernize? Maybe it will work, but a quick solution to our economic problems probably cannot be expected in either case.

Pessimistic View: The pessimists anticipate a major slump during the 1980s, with waves of failures among businesses and financial institutions. Inflation might come to an abrupt end as deflation sets in, or a terrible hyperinflation as that which took place in Germany in 1923 could occur. Either alternative could cause a rapid rise in unemployment.

Advocates can cite evidence to support each of these views because the U.S. economy is extraordinarily complex and exhibits a variety of symptoms, each of which can be interpreted in manifold ways. Even a single statistic can be viewed from many different angles: If the unemployment rate in March is 8.3 percent, that single statistic may be seen as "a marked improvement over the 8.8 percent in February" or "far worse than the 7 percent that most observers expected." The figure may remain the same, but the interpretation varies with the interpreter. The Howard Ruffs and Ashby Bladens worry about a depression, but other writers scoff. For example, the Kiplinger editors in their 1979 report *The Exciting '80s*, edited by Austin H. Kiplinger and Arnold B. Barach, state flatly that "the fear of a devastating bust is unwarranted. It's not going to happen." Kiplinger and Barach offer a rosy picture of the 1980s economy—sustained business growth, more jobs in most fields, bigger profits, higher living standards, and so on.

Under the circumstances, and with all the division of opinion, the most surprising thing that could happen to the economy in the years just ahead would be for it to fail to offer a lot of surprises.

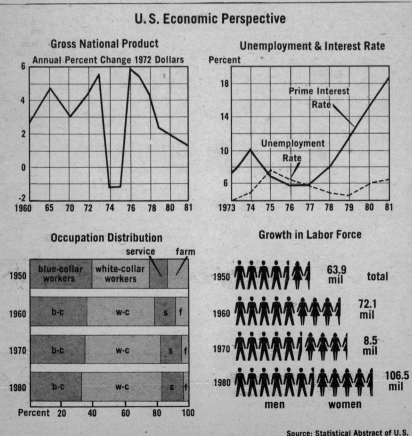

U.S. Economic Perspective

Gross National Product
Annual Percent Change 1972 Dollars

Unemployment & Interest Rate
Percent

Prime Interest Rate

Unemployment Rate

Occupation Distribution

Growth in Labor Force

Source: Statistical Abstract of U.S.

The Occupational Outlook

Major Trends in the Job Market

Perhaps never before in history has choosing a career been so difficult. More occupations can be pursued, and more new options spring up every day. At the same time, traditional occupations are changing radically.

There is one consolation, however. Because so many job choices are available, and because they change in character so rapidly, a lifelong career commitment is unnecessary. An increasing number of people who believed they had made lifetime career decisions now are switching to something else. A dentist wakes up one morning, decides he never wants to look into another mouth again and enrolls in a computer course. An actress decides that the glamour of the theatre is not what she wanted after all and goes into a nunnery. A plumber decides he would rather be a merchant and uses an unexpected inheritance to buy a convenience store.

Choosing a career is not something new, but it used to be a lot easier. In the past, a boy would naturally follow the occupation of his father, learning the needed skills at an early age. By the time he reached adulthood, he would be fully trained in the occupation. A girl would become a wife and mother, learning the necessary homemaking skills from her mother in the same way that a boy learned skills from his father. Thus a smooth transition from childhood play into the adult world of work took place.

The Industrial Revolution Made New Jobs

But the situation changed radically as the Industrial Revolution, which began in England about 1750, spread across Europe and North America. Economic activity moved out of the home, into factories and later into offices. Work moved away from the homestead because the machines required a power source not available in the home, and the many workers needed to tend the operation could not be accommodated in a single household.

As factories and machines increased in size and complexity, worker specialization and the level of training required grew steadily. When steam power replaced waterpower, the degree of complexity soared. Steam power led to new occupations such as boilermaker, steam fitter and steam engineer, and expanded the demand for millwrights and mining engineers.

© 1973 Time Inc.

Since efficiency increased as the operations expanded, the scale of production grew. Increasingly complex transportation systems were developed to bring raw materials to factories and to carry finished products to customers. The burgeoning transportation requirements stimulated a demand for naval architects, railroad engineers and crane operators, among others. Since the sources of raw materials and the customers were now located thousands of miles apart, it became increasingly important to improve communications. No significant gains over transporting messages by a rider on horseback were made until the advent of the telegraph in the early 1800s and the telephone in the 1870s. These inventions—the first electronic communications systems—made possible effective coordination of activities over a much larger geographic area. The inventions also created a demand for telegraphers, telephone operators, line maintenance workers and telephone assemblers.

Thanks to the improvements in transportation and communications, companies could manufacture products on a colossal scale, carry huge quantities of goods by rail and ship across long distances and sell them to a growing number of customers. The scale of these operations demanded increasingly large companies employing thousands of workers, each of whom was highly specialized, performing a single function with maximum efficiency.

To collect the capital required for expansion, companies issued shares of stock, which could be bought and sold through brokerages and exchanges. To protect their growing capital, they began buying insurance, hiring guards and putting their valuables in bank vaults. Each new field almost inevitably subdivided into smaller fields and new specialties. The insurance business created a demand for actuaries and statisticians. Maintaining security required safe manufacturers, alarm systems firms, bonding companies and fingerprint specialists.

In the simple world of the 18th century, a farmer grew wheat, took it to a nearby miller to be ground into flour and took the flour back to the farm for baking into bread. In the more complex world of the 19th century, a farmer might still grow wheat, but there might be no

A.T. & T. Co.

![Primitive blacksmith toolmaking operations.]

Primitive blacksmith toolmaking operations.

Communications center, circa 1917.

miller nearby to turn the wheat into flour. So the farmer might have to sell the grain to a grain merchant and use the money to buy flour to make bread, or buy bread from a local baker who used flour made from some other farmer's wheat. In the still more complex world of the 20th century, the farmer sells grain to a grain company and buys packaged bread from a supermarket, having no contact either with the consumer of the grain or the producers of the finished product. Although it is still possible to make bread at home from flour ground from wheat grown in a field outside the kitchen window, the procedure now involves thousands of workers, and the grain travels hundreds of miles on a circuitous route from field to dinner table.

Career-switching

As the industrial revolution becomes the super industrial revolution, specialization continues to grow and more and more occupations are available from which to choose. But a strange thing has happened along the way: The specialization is exasperating the specialist. It may be more efficient to do the same thing all day long, but it is also likely to be very boring. An airline reservations clerk gets tired of taking reservations day in and day out and resigns to become a bartender; the physician wearies of listening to patients and decides to become a choir director; the scientist chucks it all to become a real estate agent. Today an increasing number of people are leaving their area of specialization. Mid-life career-switching has become a national pastime, partly because affluence makes possible living without a regular income for extended periods of time.

One encouragement to career-switching for couples is the working spouse, whose income makes it less essential to work at a distasteful job simply to make money. In one instance, an economist with a high-paying but demanding job with a business concern decided to become a college professor after his wife went to work. The position gave him far less money but much more freedom to pursue personal interests. A childless couple in their thirties discovered that they could live comfortably on what they made by working only part-time. Now they have adopted a semi-retired life-style long before the usual retirement age. Significantly, perhaps, the husband did not start working on a part-time basis until long after his wife had adopted such a schedule.

Merck Sharp & Dohme Pharmaceutical Labs

Computer control room for a modern drug firm.

For Some, Why Work?

The declining need to work in order to meet one's basic needs has led to both a romanticization of work and a casualness toward the job at hand. The general affluence of society has made it possible for governments to provide substantial benefits for the unemployed; as a result, many find that the financial difference between working and not working is very small or even negative. Accepting welfare payments instead of working has appeal if one's take-home pay is small and it is reduced further by payments for child care, transportation to the job, etc. It may also make sense to collect unemployment compensation without looking seriously for other work when another household member is employed and the free time can be used to perform more satisfying and economically beneficial household tasks. Thus unemployment no longer holds the terrors that it once did, and many people feel they don't have to worry about losing their jobs. This has led to an increased freedom among employees to reorganize the workplace so as to make it more comfortable for themselves. The resulting changes have made working conditions far more pleasant and have encouraged the development of the "career" mystique.

Before the 1960s, a job was generally viewed as a necessary evil. Only the rare individual could have a career—that is, could hold a succession of posts offering increasing power, prestige and money. Ordinary people had to be content with performing necessary but disagreeable functions day in and day out with little hope of any real improvement in their lot. For most people, work was and always would be without much satisfaction or joy.

Changes in the Workplace

The surge of affluence in the 1950s and 1960s changed many people's attitudes toward work partly because many jobs became much less disagreeable than in the past. With labor in short supply and the economy booming, employers readily cooperated with workers in making jobs more pleasant. Working hours were shortened, and in many places, formality and rigid rules governing such things as lunch hours and coffee breaks were relaxed. In addition, many amenities began to embellish the work environment: piped-in music, modish decor, stylish cafeterias and recreation facilities (sometimes even including swimming pools, bowling alleys and golf courses). The more progressive employers became highly imaginative in granting workers privileges unknown to the workforce of the 1930s and 1940s. These included educational benefits or time away from the workplace to participate in civic activities. Oftentimes the company contributed funding for such projects. Employees could also participate in "professional" activities, have three-martini lunches and occasionally attend conventions at luxury resorts at company expense.

The atmosphere of the workplace probably reached its headiest level about 1967. At this time, President Lyndon Johnson's "Great Society" programs had been launched and a general sense pervaded Washington and elsewhere that such ancient problems as poverty, racism, ignorance and ill health could be swiftly and permanently banished. Many believed this could be achieved in a relaxed work environment characterized by sociable brainstorming unfettered by the traditional discipline of the workplace. During this halcyon era, all problems seemed solvable, and solving them was expected to create fun jobs that were also "meaningful" and highly rewarding financially.

The Bubble Bursts

But things began to fall apart in 1968, a year marked by the assassinations of the Rev. Dr. Martin Luther King, Jr., and Senator Robert F. Kennedy. Following Dr. King's assassination, rioting mobs rampaged through Washington's ghetto, burning, looting and forcing the city into a state of martial law. Violence also broke out at the Democratic National Convention in Chicago. Throughout the nation, people disrupted communities with demonstrations and bombings. Meanwhile, mounting inflation—caused in large measure by the heavy cost of the accelerated war in Southeast Asia—eroded the nation's economic base. During the 1970s, the rise in the U.S. standard of living came to a virtual standstill: All things considered, the average American was hardly better off in 1980 than in 1970.

The 1960s had been a period of "liberation." College students were liberated from the parietal rules and tough academic discipline; women were freed from many of the constraints associated with their roles as wives and mothers; and everyone was freed from God—attendance at religious observances dropped sharply during the 1960s. One result of these trends toward liberation was that many institutions that once provided meaning for people's lives began to decline in importance. For centuries, people dreamed of heaven as a reward for the pains of earthly existence, but after God "died" in the 1960s, the decline in religious observances resulted in a decline in spiritual sustenance. Family life, another mainstay of human existence, also declined as the divorce rate soared. National pride, an emotional support, declined in the aftermath of Vietnam and Watergate. It would, of course, be a wild exaggeration to suggest that religion or family life disappeared during the tumultuous 1960s, but both were shaken.

As the old dreams faded—the dreams of heaven, a warm and secure family life and participation in an invincible and noble nation-state—a new dream asserted itself. This was the dream of having a successful career. The successful career would lead to the realization of a second dream, that of having a carefree, pleasurable life-style. Both of these dreams focus on the self and probably derive much of their force from television, which greatly extended its domain over American minds and souls during the 1960s and 1970s. In the theology of the television commercial, one should work and live for one's own self—not for one's family, one's nation, or one's God.

The Dream of a "Career"

And so the dream of an ideal career developed: Typically, the career would include a period of training, during which one's merit was established and one gained the tools to perform tasks that would win admiration—and money—as

Cathy Abramson

Computer-assisted typesetting has created new jobs while displacing skilled compositors.

one moved steadily up the ladder of success. During this ascent one would, of course, enjoy all the creature comforts, live in luxurious surroundings, consume gourmet edibles and potables, have an abundance of admiring friends and adoring lovers—just like the people in the television commercials. And, like the people on television, one would not have to do much tedious work.

In the 1970s, the material affluence which developed so strongly in the 1960s received a series of shocks. The price of petroleum quadrupled in 1973, triggering steep increases in the costs of such basic items as fuel oil and gasoline. Prices for almost everything else rose, too, since every business in America had to pay more for its energy. In addition to the arrival in 1974 of double-digit inflation, the unemployment rate jumped that year to 9 percent—the highest level since the Great Depression. For the automobile and housing industries, conditions would have been truly Depressionlike had not generous governmental and union benefits been available to the unemployed.

In the 1980s, the world of work has become baffling indeed. In addition to the increasing number of jobs from which to choose, the arrival of the baby-boom generation in the job market means that competition for most desirable occupations has become extremely keen. For many young people in the 1980s, the world of work no longer seems to offer highly attractive "careers." Instead, it has again become a world of jobs, and even the jobs are no longer so easily obtained. Hence, for many young people uncertainty grows. Even when they know what they want to do, they often question their possible success in their chosen fields. Doubtless many would approve the advice offered by Frank Endicott, former director of placement at Northwestern University and author for 35 years of an annual report on employment trends. Endicott suggested that students should prepare for two careers: one that they really want to pursue and one that is readily marketable. Such advice still does not solve the perplexities of today's job market, however.

The attitude of a typical young person today might be something like this:

"I'd like to get a master's degree in business administration so I have a solid foundation and can get a job. Then I would like to get into computers, because I think there will be a lot of jobs in that area. But I really don't like business and computers at all. What I really like—I think—is teaching. But I hear that there are no good teaching jobs available, so it makes better sense to go into computers. Maybe after I have made some money, I could go into teaching—or, better yet—into forestry. I have always liked the outdoors and being on my own. I also like wood carving and would like to try that for a while even though I wouldn't make much money at it. Maybe somewhere there is a job for me teaching foresters how to whittle wood."

Occupations Forecast

If it were possible to know the structure of the job market in the years ahead, it would be relatively easy to direct people to those areas where they are most likely to find jobs. In addition, schools and universities would find it much easier to train young people for the jobs that would be available. But making such forecasts is extraordinarily difficult, because new technology is constantly changing the nature of the skills that are wanted, making some occupations obsolete and creating others in a manner that seems to be totally unforeseeable.

In addition, the job market will be heavily influenced by the overall prosperity of the economy. During boom times, people send their children to ballet schools and their dogs to poodle parlors, thereby providing jobs for ballet masters and poodle groomers. During hard times, the children forego ballet lessons and the poodles go unshorn.

Assuming increasing prosperity in the 1980s, the following businesses are likely to prosper: airlines, hotels and motels, nightclubs, gourmet restaurants, country clubs, ski resorts, automobile dealerships, real estate agencies, travel bureaus, furniture stores, swimming pool and tennis court construction firms, art galleries, plastic surgery clinics, interior decorating studios and fashion boutiques.

But if times are hard, the businesses just mentioned are likely to decline, and others will do well: used automobile sales lots, secondhand clothing stores, pawnshops, sewing centers, door-to-door selling enterprises, fertilizer stores, secondhand bookstores and junk shops.

The most serious attempt at occupational forecasting is made by the U.S. Department of Labor's Bureau of Labor Statistics (BLS), which publishes biennially the *Occupational Outlook Handbook*, describing the prospects for hundreds of occupations. The Bureau's forecasts are based primarily on recent trends which are projected into the future. Such forecasting does not always prove accurate, however. For many, a trend may reverse. For example the abrupt rise in the price of petroleum in 1973 caused an unexpected demand for firewood; the woodcutter's trade, long in decline, suddenly revived. At the same time the petroleum price rise, followed by erratic waves in the supply and demand of gasoline, forced thousands of gasoline stations out of business.

According to the BLS, fast-growing occupations in the period to 1990 include: bank and financial managers—up 36.7 percent; cashiers—up 49.7 percent; guards—up 49.6 percent; and food-service workers—up 33.1 percent.

Declining occupations are expected to be: bus drivers—down 5.7 percent; farmers—down 15.1 percent; bakers—down 7.1 percent; postal clerks —down 19.2 percent; keypunch operators—down 26.7 percent; and stenographers—down 27.7 percent.

The Bureau anticipates that the proportion of white-collar workers in the labor force will grow at the expense of blue-collar workers—especially people with little training. Among white-collar occupations, openings in the broad category of *professional, technical and kindred workers* will go up 40.4 percent. Within that category, openings for engineers will rise 22.5 percent; life and physical scientists, 24.7 percent; computer specialists, 30.8 percent; social scientists, 36.1 percent; and lawyers, 23.2 percent. But not every group in the category will increase: Openings for college and university teachers will decline by 14.3 percent and those for secondary schoolteachers by 26.5 percent.

A good outlook for a given field does not, of course, mean that any given individual will be successful in it—but it is generally easier to succeed in an expanding field rather than a contracting one.

The Job Potential in New Fields

One way to get into an expanding area is to look for a pioneering field. During the 1980s, innumerable new businesses will start and many of these will constitute new fields. Often these will be offshoots of scientific and technical research that has been done over past decades. Military, space, medical and other research programs have spurred the development of new goods and services not yet applied to human needs. The potential for innovations from the thousands of recent scientific discoveries is mind-boggling, but realizing that potential will take time, imagination and work. The possibilities for utilizing space technology are almost as vast as space itself, yet private enterprise has only begun to move into this incredibly vast realm. By the end of the 1980s, there may be scores, even hundreds of space laboratories and perhaps the first space factories. By about 1990 the first space colony will be under construction, and several bases may have been built on the moon. By the year 2000, developments in space may suggest a real-life version of *Star Wars*.

The oceans will offer many thousands of new jobs during the 1980s. A few decades ago, petroleum engineers and geologists never dreamed that they might be sailing the oceans or working on artificial islands built on steel piers anchored to the sea floor. Now such "Texas Towers" are only part of a growing exploitation of the oceans' resources. The oceans have other

Consumers' Gas Company

Oil drillers and geologists have gone to sea.

riches, such as potato-shaped nodules containing manganese and other metals, that literally are lying on the ocean floor, waiting to be picked up and processed. The arctic regions, the great deserts and the jungles, too, will provide a growing number of jobs during the 1980s as those areas are increasingly exploited.

Various new technical fields such as electronic information technology and genetic engineering are rapidly expanding. The vast computer field, which barely existed before 1950, continues to grow. In July 1981, the Bureau of Labor Statistics confirmed that graduates of computer science programs "should have highly favorable job opportunities throughout the 1980s."

"Despite an overall surplus of college graduates," the BLS said, "colleges are not producing enough computer specialists to meet present demand, and training programs must be expanded considerably if future needs are to be met.

"Even after doubling in the 1970s, overall employment in the field is expected to almost double again by 1990, and all computer occupations except keypunch operator will grow rapidly. Topping the list of fast-growing jobs is computer service technician, with a projected growth rate of 154 percent between 1978 and 1990. That of systems analyst will grow by 120 percent. The largest occupational group in the computer field—computer and peripheral equipment operator—will more than double: job openings should average 46,200 a year."

Many scholars believe that the information fields will be increasingly important in the years ahead and that the best way to get a good job is to get a good education. This view is clearly in line with the general trend in the 20th century. The information fields—science, teaching, research, law, government, business administration, etc.—have grown rapidly, while agriculture and manufacturing have declined. The typical worker before the Industrial Revolution was a farmer; the typical worker after the Industrial Revolution was a laborer. Today, the typical worker is perhaps a clerk—a manipulator of information.

It now appears, however, that long years spent getting an education do not guarantee a good job. One problem is the frequent mismatch between the educational courses that attract students and the training that employers seek in applicants for jobs. Then, too, jobs are not

Goodyear

Growing interest in crops of guayule as a source of rubber is part of new look at agriculture.

created arbitrarily by employers, but reflect the choices of their customers—government, other businesses and consumers. A governmental decision to explore space creates jobs for astronautical engineers and space scientists. A consumer's decision to buy a house creates jobs in construction trades. The employers act largely as a result of customers' decisions to purchase certain types of goods or services. And it is very hard to forecast just what people will be buying in the years ahead.

Thus the future job market must remain a mystery. In 1985, employers may be offering lucrative salaries to anyone who knows anything about genetic engineering. On the other hand, virtually no demand could occur, either because the field did not develop as well as people today believe it will or because so many people choose to train as genetic engineers and the field becomes glutted. The same caveats apply to most other fields. Today, physicians are in very short supply and command huge salaries, but already it appears that the medical profession may be overcrowded by the late 1980s—partly because the lure of large salaries has attracted so many people to medicine.

As to the shrinking areas of employment, the long, steady decline of agriculture could come to a halt in the 1980s and possibly even experience a reversal. The explosion in the price of energy in the 1970s has changed the economics of farming, which had become increasingly energy-intensive. With energy far more expensive and human labor perhaps a little less so, relatively speaking, more farmers may be planting crops for energy as well as food. Gasohol can be made from a variety of crops, and oils from a number of plants can substitute in many instances for petroleum products. Instead of disappearing, farming may prove to be an expanding occupation as harvesting takes place on the desert, in the oceans, and perhaps in space colonies.

The 1980s are likely to be a period of economic turbulence, but the chance for success will remain for people who can see opportunities where others see only problems. During the Great Depression, a young man made millions of dollars while some of his contemporaries were losing everything.

One day in 1929, William Benton, an advertising man, was walking down a street in Chicago. Since it was a hot day, most of the windows were open, and he could hear the radios in the apartments. What he heard most often were the voices of the actors in *Amos 'n' Andy*, a comedy program. So Benton walked back down the same street, counting the radios he could hear. Of the 23 receivers, 21 were tuned in to that program. Benton rushed back to his advertising firm and suggested they broadcast their commercials for Pepsodent toothpaste on *Amos 'n' Andy*. His superiors agreed, and the product's sales boomed. Though nobody knew it at the time, Benton had conducted what may have been the first audience survey of radio broadcasting.

Benton's career offers a powerful lesson for the 1980s. His day, as now, was a time of both economic troubles and new technologies offering many opportunities for people with imagination.

Fast-Growing vs. Slow-Growing Occupations

The U.S. Department of Labor expects the economy to create more than 20 million new jobs during the 1980s. In addition, about 47 million jobs will open up as workers retire, die, or leave the labor force.

The Department's Bureau of Labor Statistics makes its projections for specific occupations on the basis of its model of the economy in 1990. Bureau officials caution that the projections are based on generally optimistic assumptions about the nation's economy in the decade ahead (see below).

Using the forecasting tools available, here are some of the occupations that the Department of Labor thinks will grow *faster* than average and others that will grow *slower*.

Faster-than-Average Growth

Accountants • assemblers • automobile painters • automobile repairers • automobile sales workers • bank clerks, officers and tellers • bartenders • biochemists • boilermakers • business machine repairers • cement masons and terrazzo workers • clerical workers • computer programmers • computer technicians • construction glaziers • cooks and chefs • corrections officers • dental assistants • dental lab technicians • dieticians • dispensing opticians • display workers • dry wall workers • EKG and EEC technicians • engineers: agricultural, biomedical, industrial, metallurgical, mining • engineering and science technicians • floor covering installers • floral designers • food counter workers • geologists • geophysicists • government construction inspectors • guards • health services administrators • hotel housekeepers • industrial machinery repairers • insulation workers • insurance claims representatives • iron workers • landscape architects • lithographers • maintenance electricians • medical lab workers • medical record technicians • nursing: RNs, LPNs, aides • occupational health and safety workers • occupational therapists and aides • operating engineers • optometrists • osteopathic physicians • pest controllers • podiatrists • purchasing agents • range managers • real estate agents and brokers • receptionists • respiratory therapy workers • retail sales • secretaries • sheet metal workers • speech pathologists • statisticians • systems analysts • teacher aides • tilesetters • travel agents • truck mechanics • wastewater treatment plant operators • welders

Note: The Bureau of Labor Statistics projections for specific occupations are based on the following assumptions about the economy:

1. Inflation will decelerate to 5.2 percent annually during the 1980s.
2. Unemployment will stabilize at about 4.5 percent by the mid-1980s.
3. Higher energy prices will not constrain growth of the gross national product.
4. There will be no radical changes in U.S. economic institutions.

Slower-than-Average Growth

Blacksmiths • bookbinders and bindery workers • bowling-pin machine mechanics • bricklayers • compositors • coremakers • credit managers • electrotypers and stereotypers • forge shop occupations • food technologists • foundry patternmakers • historians • hotel managers • keypunch operators • locomotive engineers • mathematicians • molders • motion picture projectionists • office machine operators • painters and paperhangers • parking attendants • photoengravers • piano and organ tuners • plasterers • postal clerks • political scientists • press operators • railroad conductors • railroad signal workers • school counselors • securities sales workers • sociologists • stationary engineers • telegraphers, telephoners and tower operators

Fast Growing But Competitive

The Bureau believes the following occupations will grow faster than the average, but are so attractive that there is likely to be keen competition, especially for entry level positions:

Actors • actuaries • architects • city managers • dancers • emergency medical technicians • forestry technicians • labor relations workers • lawyers • musicians • physical therapists • pilots and flight attendants • radiologic technicians • urban and regional planners

5. Current social, technological and scientific trends will continue.
6. There will be no major event such as a war or widespread, long-lasting energy shortages that would alter the economic growth rate or the industrial structure.

For more information, see the *Occupational Outlook Handbook*, published by the Bureau of Labor Statistics, U.S. Department of Labor, 200 Constitution Avenue N.W., Washington, D.C. 20210.

The Strange New Occupations

New career fields of all sorts will develop during the 1980s because of emerging technological possibilities and changes in human needs and social attitudes.

Developments in technology make it possible to do what was previously impossible or simply too expensive. The new products and systems create, first of all, jobs for scientists and engineers, who have the task of implementing the development, whether it is a drug, a new method of cooling or a new bug killer. After the technologists are finished, other workers are needed to manufacture the product and sell it. And still other workers are needed later to install, repair and use the equipment.

Occasionally a major technological breakthrough creates a whole new industry. This happened, for example, when computers were developed after World War II. At first, it appeared that only a few organizations could use the mechanical brains, which were, by today's standards, big, stupid and frightfully expensive. Thanks to a rapid succession of important improvements, however, prices came down and computers became faster, smaller and more useful. Today millions of people are using computers, performing tasks that could not have existed without the invention of the "electronic brain."

The 1970s saw the arrival of "personal" computers—small, inexpensive machines that are "friendly" (easy for the nontechnician to learn to use). In the past five years, hundreds of computer stores have opened to supply the needs of both hobbyists and the growing number of people who are using a small computer in their work. One offshoot of the computer industry is the electronic game. At a good location, an electronic game may gross $20,000 or more in a single year. Servicing the games and operating the establishments where they are located now provide jobs for thousands of people.

Many other jobs appear as new needs emerge and make it possible for new businesses to flourish. For example, the sudden rise in the price of petroleum and natural gas created thousands of new jobs, many of which seem unrelated to energy. It is easy to understand why the ancient craft of the woodcutter revived—a cord of firewood may now bring $100 or $200 in some areas. But other impacts of higher petroleum prices require explanation.

Take, for instance, guayule, a desert shrub with spiky, blue-gray leaves. About 10 percent to 20 percent rubber by weight, guayule was long used as a source of natural rubber. Synthetic rubber, which constitutes about 70 percent of the rubber used around the world, is made principally from petroleum. When petroleum prices soared, synthetic rubber also went up in price. Natural rubber plantations overseas could not meet the demand; furthermore, natural rubber has many qualities that make it more desirable than synthetic rubber for many uses. As a result, many people are now scrambling to develop guayule plantations on the western deserts. Thanks to this "guayule rush," the seeds of the plant often sell for $800 to $1,000 a pound.

The surge in the divorce rate since the mid-1960s has not only led to a lot of work for lawyers and psychiatrists, but has spawned a whole new profession—that of "divorce planner," or "divorce mediator." Assuming a couple is determined to obtain a divorce, the mediator can help them decide how to divide the property and can make arrangements that will be in their joint interest. Generally the couple is emotionally overwrought and ignorant of the important issues that need to be settled. A divorce mediator can help them make the best of the situation and, unlike a divorce lawyer, the mediator considers the interests of both parties.

Here is a sampling of other occupational fields that have recently emerged or appear likely to develop during the 1980s:

Videodating services: The videotape recorder makes it possible for an amateur to make a short motion picture at relatively modest cost. One of the new services available through the new technology is the ancient art of matchmaking. Commercial videodating services compile a library of videotapes of their customers as well as biographical data. The opportunity to review a large number of biographies and see selections on videotape makes it much easier for a customer to meet the right kind of person. The rise of divorce and the mobility of today's society have helped make videodating services successful.

Services for the handicapped: Many educational and business institutions are currently making their facilities more accessible to people with physical handicaps. The impetus came from federal regulations requiring institutions receiving federal funds or contracts to make their programs accessible to the handicapped. Accessibility means installing elevators so that people in wheelchairs can reach all floors, hiring sign-language translators for the deaf, and providing tape recorders for the blind.

Draft horses and equipment: The rise in the price of fuel has greatly increased the cost of operating tractors. As a result, some farmers are going back to using horses in their work. In England, Charles Pinney, operator of Cart Horse Company Limited, turned to horses and carts 10 years ago. He says that the horse is "one of the most efficient machines known to man." Pinney sells, for $2,000, a package that includes a horse, cart, and harness along with lessons in how to use the equipment. By contrast, a tractor costs between $13,000 and $15,000. Pinney says a good draft horse has a working life of 15 to 20 years and can handle rocky slopes that prove difficult for tractors. With land as well as fuel becoming more expensive, the economics may increasingly favor the horse.

Phobia fighting: About one million people suffer from some severe form of phobia. They may be afraid of heights, airplanes, insects, public washrooms, or crowds, and many are paying to rid themselves of their fears. Phobia therapists accompany fearful subjects to the situation they most dread—highways, tall buildings, airplanes or whatever—and offer support until they overcome their phobia. Fear of flying is one of the most common phobias today, and air travelers occasionally see large groups of phobiacs traveling with a therapist who is gently trying to get them to forget their fears.

Arctic drilling: Drilling for oil in Alaska's Beaufort Sea is another result of the increase in petroleum prices. The job of an arctic driller is not everybody's cup of tea; the job is lonely, boring, dirty and dangerous, but the oil-short world is willing to pay well to see that it is done. A driller may make $90,000 a year, and since no local opportunities exist for spending, return to civilization with a small fortune.

Electric car service station: The United States today has only about 2,000 electric vehicles in use, but the Department of Energy projects that as many as nine million such vehicles will be operating by the year 2000, constituting about 5 percent of the total U.S. vehicle fleet. Electric cars currently cost more than gasoline- or diesel-powered cars and have a range of only about 50 or 60 miles before their batteries need recharging. But they are inexpensive to operate—perhaps as little as six cents per mile—and research continues to improve on battery life and power output. With the continued rise in the cost of petroleum, the future of the electric car looks bright.

Erotic boutiques: The liberalization of sexual mores has opened the way for stores that specialize in erotic goods. Offerings may include anything from brass-framed Persian and Indian erotic prints, "happy anniversary" underwear, body paints, X-rated greeting cards, can-can dolls to gold lamé g-strings for men. For customers too staid to browse in an erotic boutique, merchandisers now organize erotica parties for selling to groups in the home.

New security devices: Electronics has made possible a variety of devices to protect homes and business establishments. One such device is a machine that can scan people's fingertips and decide whether or not they should be admitted to a bank vault, a computer file or a nuclear missile site. As the finger is placed on the plate of a Fingermatrix machine, a laser scans the image of the print, and a computer compares the print with records stored in its memory. Manufacturing and marketing such devices has become one of the major growth industries.

Brain food stores: All over North America, health food stores have blossomed in recent years. For example, in Bethesda, Maryland, the Low Sodium Pantry caters to people who must avoid salt and foods containing sodium. In the future, special stores may serve those people who want to improve their mental functioning. Research is now in progress to determine the efficacy of various bodily chemicals such as lecithin in improving human memory. Richard Wurtman, a researcher at the Massachusetts Institute of Technology, has spent nearly a decade examining the effects of nutrition on brain function. The brain, Wurtman says, "is intimately affected by what we eat. For this reason, memory may be affected by what we had for breakfast." In the years ahead, there may be jobs for people to service machines dispensing mind-improving drugs in schools and elsewhere.

Genetic engineering: The excitement in genetic research is almost as great as that generated

Univ. of Wisconsin

Laboratory technician measures density of a bacterial extract carrying the gene which causes bean seeds to produce storage protein. Genetic engineering is an important new field.

during the birth of solid state electronics. The new technology could lead to a number of important new industries, each of which might eventually employ thousands, possibly even millions of workers. Genetic engineering began when researchers in California found that by introducing new genes into a "host" organism, the host could be made to express the new trait. In 1978 scientists succeeded in introducing bacteria to produce insulin identical to that made by the human body, thus opening the possibility of using bacteria to produce many kinds of drugs. Genetic engineering now offers an extraordinarily powerful approach toward many human goals. Already work is underway to produce bacteria to eat oil spills, custom-made plants that are herbicide resistant or carry their own insect repellant, organisms to improve the process for making gasohol, new drugs to ward off the common cold, chemicals to break down industrial wastes, etc. The prospects are so exciting that genetic engineering firms have become the darlings of Wall Street financiers.

Truffle nurseries: Gourmets have long sung the praises of the truffle, a black fungus that enhances cuisine in the best French restaurants. Truffles grow in the south of France and are harvested by 6,000 professional trufflers who work with dogs and pigs that sniff out the underground delicacy from around the tree roots where it grows. Though it looks like a black, badly deteriorated golf ball, the truffle is the world's costliest vegetable, retailing for about $50 each. The truffle defied cultivation until 1977, when agronomist Jean Grente at the French National Institute of Agronomic Research grafted the germinating seeds of truffles to the roots of oak and hazelnut seedlings, planted the saplings in chalky soil, and waited until—voilà! a truffle! In the years ahead, truffle-growing may become a viable occupation.

Talking signs: Microprocessors have made possible the synthesis of human speech, and this capability is now being built into signs. A talking sign may announce: "FIRE IN THE BUILDING—EXIT THIS WAY, EXIT THIS WAY, PLEASE," or "DANGER! GO BACK! SENSORS INDICATE THIS EXIT UNSAFE. SEEK ALTERNATE EXIT." Manufacturing and selling such signs will likely become one of the new occupations in the years ahead.

The Great Productivity Mystery

Americans typically blame "inflation" for their economic problems, failing to realize that inflation is caused in great measure by the failure of productivity to grow as before. Productivity refers to the amount of goods and services that a worker produces per hour. It is often hard to measure, but almost all the statistics seem to agree that the productivity of U.S. workers is no longer increasing as rapidly as it did during the 1950s and 1960s. In those decades, productivity surged upward and living standards rose rapidly. During the 1970s and early 1980s, productivity growth has slowed and at times even actually declined. As a result, U.S. living standards failed to improve in the 1970s at the strong rate of the two previous decades.

A review of current writing shows that economists and other observers have turned up many suspects in the productivity mystery, but few agree on which suspects are the most guilty. Business tends to blame government regulations and the decline of the work ethic among employees. Workers tend to blame management insensitivity and errors. Consumers blame short-sighted managers and lazy workers.

Here are some of the suspects and the charges against them.

Suspect 1: The Workers

If the workers are no longer producing goods and services at the rapidly improving rate of previous years, it is natural to wonder if they have stopped putting forth their best efforts. Polls indicate that today's workers are less oriented toward working hard and saving their money than were yesterday's. Workers now appear to be more interested in enjoying their leisure than in obtaining merit by work. Given the choice, today's workers often will sacrifice earnings in order to have more leisure. On the job, they may be less diligent than in the past. According to one recent survey, the average worker spends only 55 percent of an eight-hour workday actually producing. The rest of the worktime is spent in chatting, personal projects, daydreaming, etc. The more relaxed attitude toward work is attributed to the general affluence in the society and the absence of sufficiently strong incentives for hard work. "Nobody's hungry any more," one observer said.

The changing composition of the workforce is also cited by many economists as an underlying reason for lagging productivity. During the 1970s, large numbers of women, young people and minorities moved into the workforce. These workers generally were less experienced than the older white male workers who have long been the core group in the employment ranks. In addition, many of the new entrants into the workforce have traditionally lacked the strong commitment to work that characterized the average worker in the past. Women who are mothers of small children, for example, may feel that they need to place their children's welfare ahead of their duties as employees. Young people often have difficulty adjusting to the discipline of the workplace. Coming from loosely structured schoolrooms, many teen-agers lack the same work ethic and self-discipline acquired by earlier generations.

As the new groups of workers gain greater experience in the workplace, their productivity is expected to improve. Some evidence suggests, however, that the entry of these new groups of workers has adversely affected the performance of adult white males. In many instances, workplace rules are relaxed to accommodate the new groups of workers, and in these situations it is difficult not to relax rules for all workers in a given category. Employers frequently are fearful of disciplining a minority worker lest they face charges of bias, which can lead to time-consuming lawsuits. And if they cannot discipline minority workers for failing to measure up to work requirements, it becomes more difficult to punish nonminority workers for violations.

In many instances, employers have been required by governmental and other pressure groups to hire and promote women and members of minority groups, and this has meant in practice that some people are given jobs for which they are poorly qualified. Political pressure to hire and promote teen-agers does not appear to be nearly as great as that to hire and promote women and minority workers; in fact there has been growing pressure during the 1970s to hire older workers. New laws now protect individuals between the ages of 40 and 70 from age discrimination.

Efforts to make the workplace more accessible to handicapped people may also have reduced productivity. In many jobs, handicapped workers outperform the nonhandicapped, but employers pressured to hire the handicapped may put them in jobs beyond their capabilities simply to satisfy governmental regulations.

Workers are frequently accused of hurting efficiency by refusing to accept new equipment or changes in work rules designed to improve efficiency. There is little question that workers through history have occasionally resisted new equipment—perhaps the most celebrated instance being the Luddite attacks on new weaving machinery introduced into Britain in the early 19th century—but resistance to new equipment among today's workers seems minimal. Workers generally seem to recognize that new equipment is needed for their employers to remain competitive in the marketplace, and they have accepted new equipment so long as labor shared in the benefits. Often workers express genuine liking of the new machines that help them to do their jobs more efficiently. This appears to be the case, for example, with supermarket employees using new optical scanners to read the Universal Price Codes on articles and record automatically the price and type of goods on the sales slip. Thanks to the new machines, the Giant supermarket chain, based in Landover, Maryland, has reported that the lines of customers at the checkout counters move much more quickly, and fewer personnel are needed.

Suspect 2: The Managers

Steel industry executives are charged with a short-sighted refusal to make timely investments in new efficient steel mills. The automobile manufacturers are faulted for not anticipating the public demand for small, fuel-efficient cars, and for failing to upgrade their plants.

The automobile and steel managements contend, however that they have been making enormous investments in improving their plants' efficiency, but government environmental regulations, tax codes, etc., have critically hampered their efforts. They argue that the Japanese, Canadian, and other governments have provided better incentives to their industries than has the American government.

Management is also accused of failing to support research on new and improved products and methods that would enhance productivity. Management's usual response to this criticism is that they are in fact making a great effort in research and development, but again point to difficulties imposed by various government regulations.

Many other charges are leveled at management. Writing in the July/August 1980 issue of the *Harvard Business Review,* management professors Robert H. Hayes and William J. Abernathy argue that U.S. management now is excessively dominated by accountants and lawyers. They cite figures indicating that lawyers and accountants now head about one third of America's largest corporations—a 50 percent increase over the past quarter of a century. These "professional managers" aim for quick results with short-term profits and avoid long-term gambles on new technology that might produce major gains in productivity.

Inside the corporation, according to Hayes and Abernathy, the number of performance indicators and regular reports has steadily multiplied. Middle-level managers are expected to show demonstrable progress, usually on a quarterly basis. Outside the companies, Wall Street analysts and investment fund managers demand rapidly rising profits. As a result, U.S. companies may achieve short-term gains through mergers, cutting costs (including investment and research costs), and "hyping" sales with undue product promotion. But the short-term orientation leads to lagging effectiveness over the long term.

Management is also accused of harming productivity by failing to provide adequate rewards for worker performance as opposed to educational credentials. If management pays more attention to college and university degrees than to on-the-job performance, the message to employees is "productivity doesn't count."

Management is also faulted for not giving greater weight to workers' suggestions for improving productivity. Much interest has been

expressed in Japan and its "quality circles"—groups of workers assigned to improve the quality of work in their areas. Ironically, Japan imported the productivity movement from the United States and other Western countries, but gave it a twist of their own.

The managing director of the Japan Productivity Center in Tokyo, Masichiro Muto, recently gave this answer when asked, "What is the secret of Japan's high productivity?"

"In the past we overlooked or ignored a Japanese trait that is now being reevaluated as an important ingredient for improving the nation's productivity. Thirty-five years ago when we lost World War II, we had to scrap old customs, old-style management and old values and seek technological innovation. But we soon discovered new merit in our old ways and used them to enhance productivity. The Japanese, for instance, often act in groups rather than as separate individuals. We seek to work together in groups."

Group-oriented thinking and behavior has contributed to improving industrial productivity in Japan, Muto says. The groups tend to be small, he explains, because in a small group each member feels more responsibility for maintaining product quality and is in a better position to use his originality to improve quality control.

Suspect 3: Government

Businesses often blame government policies for lagging productivity. The Goodyear Tire and Rubber Company of Akron, Ohio, reported in 1980 that in a single week its computer center had cranked out 345,000 pages of reports to meet a single new regulation of the Occupational Safety and Health Administration. The company estimated that filling out the required reports of six federal agencies required 34 employee-years. Another company, TRW, Inc., has reported that productivity gains in its factories were largely offset by the lawyers, accountants and other office workers who were added to its workforce to cope with the growing burden of regulations.

Managers argue that they have to spend more time worrying about what the government might do next than on improving products and efficiency. Top executives who spend several weeks a year in Washington to find out how they can best comply with new regulations do not then have that time to spend on improving productivity. This does not mean, of course, that the regulations are necessarily bad: They may be desirable as steps toward various social goals such as protecting workers from injury in the workplace, preventing pollution of the environment, etc.

Some government regulations may harm productivity in the short term but improve it in the long run—in theory, at least. Government regulations to protect the physical well-being of workers could mean healthier workers in the future; these healthier workers would be more productive than workers physically harmed by their jobs. Coal miners suffering from black lung disease are unlikely to be productive workers.

The federal government is also blamed by many economists for causing inflation by running huge budget deficits and covering them, in

Tenneco Inc.

Production line of tractor transmission cases.

part, by enlarging the money supply. These economists note that inflation began soaring in 1973 about the time that statistics began signalling a major slowdown in productivity gains. Inflation makes it more profitable to speculate than to produce. People who are producing goods and services find their generally low-profit return diminished further by the double effect of inflation itself and the fact that inflation puts them in higher tax brackets.

Inflation also shortens the time perspective of business. In inflation, changing prices create uncertainty and interest rates are forced up. As interest rates rise, capital costs for a long-term project become extraordinarily heavy. For example, if the interest rate is 5 percent, the total amount of the interest will equal the amount of the loan after about 14 years. But if interest rates reach 20 percent, the borrower must pay interest totaling as much as the loan itself after about three and a half years. Under such circumstances, a new plant or improvement project that will not yield a return for 10 to 20 years is not likely to be undertaken.

4. Other Suspects

Energy. The U.S. energy problem became acute in 1973. While the OPEC countries were quadrupling the price of petroleum, American productivity in general began to slip, making energy a logical suspect in the productivity puzzle.

It is possible to point to clear-cut examples of the impact of increased fuel costs. A truck driver can deliver goods faster by driving 70 miles an hour down the highways than a driver averaging 55 miles per hour. When the 55-mile-per-hour limit was imposed to alleviate the fuel problem, the productivity of truck drivers declined.

Unquestionably, efforts to conserve fuel by using less light and heat can trim the productivity of workers somewhat. So, too, may other hard-to-measure effects of the rising costs of energy. Farmers, for example, have had to pay much higher costs for fertilizers and weedkillers as well as for fuel to operate farm machinery. In many instances, farmers may choose to substitute people for energy-consuming machinery. When this happens, the output per fieldworker inevitably drops.

The energy crisis has made it necessary to extract petroleum from low-grade, relatively inaccessible sources, which inevitably requires extra efforts. A worker can "produce" a barrel of oil from a rich pool just under the earth's surface much more quickly than a barrel produced by building a huge metal tower out in the ocean and sending a drill down thousands of feet to the sea floor. The growing shortage of natural resources in relation to the world's burgeoning population means that more work is often required for a given amount of raw material.

Spendthrift Society. Many economists and business leaders believe that the failure of Americans to increase savings is an important underlying reason for the decline in productivity growth. "Our expectations for the 'good life' have exceeded our ability to pay for it, causing us to dip into reserves," says Willard C. Butcher, president of the Chase Manhattan Bank. "On the consumer level, inflation has spawned strong anti-saving habits by creating a buy-now mentality—spend, borrow, but buy today for tomorrow you'll pay more."

Thomas R. Wilcox, chairman of the Crocker National Bank in California, concurs.

"We don't worry too much about 'rainy days' anymore," says Wilcox, "since our politicians keep telling us that our 'good samaritan' society is ready to help all those in need. So our savings go down."

Since people are spending more and saving less, the banks and other financial institutions have less money to loan. This shortage of investment capital has led to soaring interest rates, and thus made business reluctant to make the capital investments that could lead to greater productivity.

Economic Cycle. Some economic thinkers believe that the decline in productivity is a symptom of the current low phase in the long-term economic cycle.

Productivity increased rapidly during the 1950s and 1960s because the capital equipment per worker was increasing rapidly to make up for the lack of capital investment during the 1930s and 1940s. Making additional capital investment in plants now, given the current technology, will not significantly increase productivity and does not pay for itself. For that reason, business finds that adding more workers is more economical than increasing productivity through new plant equipment. Therefore, according to proponents of cyclical theory, increased productivity for the economy as a whole cannot be expected until the next wave of new technology.

Possible Solutions

With so many suspects, there is no agreement as to what should be done to correct the nation's lagging productivity, but here are a few currently popular suggestions for reinvigorating the growth of the U.S. economy and the productivity of U.S. workers.

1. *Increase workers' incentives to improve productivity.* Cut income taxes so workers can keep more of what they earn. Give bonuses to the more productive workers. Get workers more involved in efforts to raise productivity.

2. *Reduce government regulations and taxes on business.* In 1981 the Reagan Administration successfully prodded Congress into cutting taxes for both business and individuals and providing faster tax write-offs for plant and equipment—incentives for modernization. Reducing the number of regulatory requirements would free busi-

UPI

Automated auto assembly line in Japan uses robots.

ness from paperwork and other burdens that hold productivity down.

3. *Stimulate innovation.* New inventions and other technological and social innovations can greatly improve productivity. The typesetting machines developed in the 19th century, for example, enabled a compositor to set far more type per hour than was previously possible. Today typesetting is being linked to computers that make it far easier to make corrections and thus enhance productivity still further.

To stimulate innovation, interest rates need to be reduced from their present high levels. When capital for new investment is not easily

obtained, businesses continue to use their old equipment and buy only those new systems that have a quick payoff. Longer-term projects often give the greatest hope for improving productivity.

Clearly, there is no agreement either on the causes of the recent decline in productivity growth or on the way to reverse it. But there is one consolation: The U.S. workforce continues to produce an extraordinary abundance of goods and services and Americans still enjoy one of the highest standards of living in the world. Somewhere somebody must be doing at least *some* work.

Workers Trade Money for Time —and Vice Versa

The old equation—"time is money"—may still apply as far as employers are concerned, but a growing number of employees now place a higher value on nonworking hours and are willing to accept smaller wages if they can have more time to themselves. According to a recent U.S. Department of Labor survey, an overwhelming majority of today's workers would now forego pay raises in favor of more free time—and a voice in determining how that free time is scheduled. In response to employee demands for increased free time, a number of alternatives to the standard nine-to-five, 40-hour workweek are gaining momentum.

• *Flexitime* (or *flextime* or *gliding time*). New flexible work scheduling allows employees to start and quit work at times that best meet their personal schedules. In general, flexitime maintains a certain "core" period when all or most employees are expected to be present—typically in the late morning and early afternoon.

Workers on flexitime can avoid evening rush-hour traffic jams, shop, schedule morning workouts, or get a haircut on a long lunch hour. Companies are finding that flexitime is a good recruiting asset. In addition it cuts productivity losses caused by tardiness and sick leave and also improves morale.

• *Compressed workweek.* The traditional five-day workweek is shortened to four or fewer days by lengthening the work day. A few employers now offer a nine-hour day, four-day week as an option.

• *Job sharing.* Opportunities for job sharing are also increasing as employers find that "two halves" often equal more than one whole in terms of creativity, productivity and morale, with the bonus of adding slots for fulfilling affirmative action goals. For two people who share one position, it often combines the advantages of both part-time and full-time employment, with salaries and fringe benefits prorated. An "empty nester" attempting to ease back into the working world can alternate weeks with a young mother who needs time out from the demands of the home. At a large medical center, two women share a single public affairs

slot: One works two days a week and the other three, but they serve as a team for meetings and during peak periods.

• *Part-time shifts.* One out of every five persons now has a part-time job, and experts predict even greater numbers of part-time workers in the years ahead. Employers find that part-timers supplement their full-time workers and allow fuller utilization of expensive plant equipment. In Athens, Georgia, a large percentage of full-time workers at a textile plant believes that weekends are "for God, family and some good fun," so students from a nearby college constitute most of the Saturday, Sunday shift.

• *Gliding retirement.* Increased flexibility in working hours is proving to be a blessing to older workers about to retire. Some organizations now provide phased retirement programs that ease employees into their leisure years. Longer vacations and a reduced workweek at the approach of the end of a career helps make for an easy transition.

Not all workers prefer more time to more money. For those who want more money, a second job offers a popular option. Professionals who want to supplement their incomes are now joining the moonlighters' ranks, once the almost exclusive domain of lower-income or blue-collar workers. In one large East Coast city, a young lawyer exchanges his three-piece suit for painter's pants on the weekends.

In the past, virtually all multiple job holders were men, but the picture has changed as an increasing number of women are living alone or heading households. In New York City, the single mother of two college-age sons moonlights as an editor after leaving her full-time position of foundation administrator.

Whither Unions?

Organized labor in the United States today faces a very uncertain future. Membership is dropping, public opinion is cool, and the Reagan Administration appears less sympathetic to union demands than the preceding Carter officeholders. Many newspaper pundits and academic observers suggest that organized labor is fading as a force in American life. New strategies may be required if the labor movement is to resume the vigorous growth of earlier times.

Rumors of organized labor's approaching demise are clearly exaggerated, but the statistics look bleak, suggesting that labor now faces a period of soul-searching. Labor union membership as a percentage of the total U.S. workforce has declined over the past quarter century; in the past two years there has been an actual loss of union members while the total workforce has grown. The U.S. Department of Labor reports that the number of union members in the U.S. dropped to 22,228,000 workers, a decline of 552,000 between 1978 and 1980. Labor's share of the nation's workforce is now only 20.8 percent; only about one worker in five is a union member.

The largest recent declines occurred in the machinists and aerospace workers union and the automobile workers union, both in economically depressed manufacturing fields. The auto workers posted a loss of 142,000 members; as a result, the union had to cut back its staff. Moving against the general trend, the carpenter's union scored a gain of 63,000 members, the biggest advance among five unions that expanded their membership.

"The state of the union movement today is murky at best, as viewed both by the unions themselves and their political and economic adversaries," says James H. Jordan, vice-president —Employee Relations of ICA Americas, Inc. "A major question is: Can they continue to grow?"

Yes, says Lane Kirkland, president of the AFL-CIO. Kirkland anticipates "substantial gains in union membership over the next decade." He says that membership growth will continue in those fields currently gaining members and expansion will occur in industries and geographic areas where progress has been slow.

Although many observers predict a bumpy period for the national economy in the 1980s, unions may not fare poorly. During the Great Depression of the 1930s, unions were encouraged and protected as a matter of deliberate government policy, and the great mass production industries were organized. During the depression, unions won wide public support for their activities. They were viewed as defenders of the "common man" rather than as groups interested in gaining more privileges for their own members irrespective of the national interest. Thanks in large measure to this favorable climate, union membership sextupled between 1933 and 1956, reaching 18,477,000. Since then, membership has increased, but not nearly as fast as the overall growth of the workforce.

What has caused the slowdown in union growth?

First, the number of workers in manufacturing in the United States—the traditional base of union strength—stopped its rapid growth. Instead, employment has grown primarily in the service industries, which have always been more difficult to organize. One reason for the decline of manufacturing in the United States has been the success of unions in raising the wages of American workers, which has had the effect of making U.S. goods less competitive in the marketplace. As columnist Joseph Kraft put it, "The troubles of heavy industry arise in no small part from ludicrously generous wage settlements that priced American firms out of markets for autos, steel, tires, and other such items."

Second, large numbers of women have entered the workforce. Women workers have tended to leave the workforce when they get married or bear children and have not developed the strong commitment to unionism found among male workers.

Third, union members have found themselves with interests that conflict sharply with members of other unions. Members of private-sector unions, for example, are taxpayers and therefore have a vested interest in opposing the large wage increases granted to public employees. The strike of the air traffic controllers in 1981 led to layoffs for thousands of workers in other unions; thus their support for the strikers was often lukewarm.

Fourth, the past successes of unions in obtaining benefits have left many employers in a disadvantageous position against competition. For example, the wages of postal workers have increased the price of postage to a point at which the postal system is losing potential business to private carriers, electronic information systems, and other substitute services. The increased cost of labor has encouraged managers to use as little as possible through such strategies as automation, exporting labor-intensive operations to regions or nations where labor is cheaper, or even having the customer perform much of the labor himself. Examples of the latter strategy are cafeterias, where customers carry their food to their tables, and unassembled furniture, which the customer must assemble and finish the product.

Fifth, past successes have made many union members complacent. The large wages and other fringe benefits enjoyed by most union members have put many of them in a specially privileged class: Their compensation is far higher than the average for nonunionized workers doing similar work. With cost-of-living adjustments written into many contracts, negotiations and the resulting contract now tend to be relatively unexciting compared to the "cliffhangers" of the past. Many union leaders now have to face the question, "But what have you done for me lately?"

Sixth, suspicion of unions and their leaders. Rampant corruption in certain unions encourages suspicion of unions in general. Tales of extravagance among union executives arouse the suspicions of the rank and file, who regard their leaders as being out of touch with the workers' economic problems. A deeper mistrust of unionism in general exists among many workers. For example, Southern textile workers fear that unions threaten their jobs: Mill owners facing union agitation and the possibility of having to pay wages that will make their products uncompetitive, frequently close factories and move elsewhere—sometimes out of the United States. Workers, especially in rural areas or small towns, know that if their local factories close, few jobs will be available.

Seventh, individualism has increased greatly in recent years. "Americans, more than ever, conceive of themselves and their society in highly individualistic terms," says labor expert James Jordan. "Unions, on the other hand, are built on a foundation of group control and their behavior is predicated on a notion of group action which contradicts and appears to violate the central tenets of individualism. Consider the strike, the most effective trade union mechanism. When a majority votes to strike, it means that 'none shall work.' "

In short, the same individualistic, self-oriented attitudes that make today's worker difficult for an employer also make him difficult for a union leader, and today's union organizers must struggle hard to develop the united spirit needed for effective collective action. In recent instances, union leaders have faced highly restive memberships ready to reject any leader who does not fit their mood of the moment.

Possible Future Developments

The future of unions appears to hinge on a variety of forces—the general state of the economy, technological advances, political developments, etc.—that are difficult to forecast. It is possible, however, to point to a few things that might happen in the years ahead.

• *Pink-collar unionism:* One dream of the unions is the organization of some 14 million secretaries, file clerks, keypunch operators, and other overwhelmingly female clerical workers. In times past, office workers typically earned more than factory workers, but their relative pay has slipped, partly because a very large number of people have the skills needed for office work. Office clerical workers have been hard to bring into the union movement because they work in small units, tend to drop out of the workforce for family reasons, and frequently work only on a part-time basis. As women remain for longer periods in the labor force, the unionization of office workers may become easier, but a new potential obstacle has arisen from technologies that are making many job functions unnecessary. Just as new photocopiers made many routine typing jobs unnecessary, new word-processing equipment may make it possible for increasing amounts of information to be produced and transmitted with little human labor.

• *Electronic intelligence:* A new round of automation promises to make many tasks in factories and offices unnecessary. Robots in automobile factories, word-processors in offices, and computers in homes will greatly reduce the need for certain types of work now being performed by human beings. Jobs that are threatened include those of welders, typists, bank tellers, postal workers, etc.

• *Multinational unions:* The development of multinational corporations and their proven ability to move operations away from places where labor is expensive (often because of unions) to where it is cheap presents a major challenge to unions. Until now unions have fought the export of jobs by agitating to keep out foreign goods. This tactic often brings them into conflict with pro-consumer forces and free trade advocates. Can unions develop effective multinational unions that can raise wages simultaneously for all workers in an industry, wherever the factories may be? What tactics can be used to keep jobs from slipping away to nonunion workers and robots?

Despite the many unanswered questions, unions could be entering a period of new growth rather than decline. The present unsatisfactory state of today's economy and the possibility of further deterioration implies that economic issues may again become of prime importance to people. If so, workers might increasingly turn to unions as the best hope for finding economic security.

UPI

UPI

The strike of air traffic controllers in August 1981 led to layoffs of workers elsewhere in the industry.

Unionization of textile mills in the South has met with resistance and increased automation.

The Decline of the Work Ethic in America

Dept. of Energy   U.S. Small Business Admin.

The deep coal mines near Marissa, Illinois, require young workers in large numbers, willing to work.

The need for jobs by some less-advantaged workers overshadows concerns for workplace amenities.

Throughout history work was generally accepted as an essential part of life: If you didn't work, you didn't eat. The close connection between work and material well-being continued after the Industrial Revolution, even though the worker was less likely to be engaged directly in food production. During the mid-20th century, however, the link between production of goods and services and their consumption has weakened. Many jobs today bear little resemblance to the backbreaking toil in fields and factories that typified work in the past. Work has become far more pleasant. In spite of that fact, people seem less willing to accept the inevitability of work.

Some societies have looked on work as having positive value. Sociologists, following Germany's Max Weber, have suggested that the development of Protestantism, which emphasized individual responsibility in religion, fostered the development of an ethic that dignified—even glorified—work. This work ethic nurtured the growth of the industrial societies in northern Europe. Weber and his followers suggest that when work receives an ecclesiastical or moral blessing, an overproduction of goods and services results. This surplus creates the capital needed for industrial expansion.

The work ethic thrived in many areas during the first half of the 20th century. The German recovery from World War II—often described as an economic miracle—was frequently attributed to the strong work ethic of the German people. In 1959, a Krupp worker explained that work for the average German at that time had a deep meaning: "To look back on a day's work well done is as uplifting [to the worker] as a painting of a good picture to an artist."

The work ethic was also strong in the U.S. at the time, and the U.S. economy prospered as never before. Since the 1960s, however, the work ethic seems to have been rejected even as work itself has become more pleasant. Employers have boosted wages, added amenities and provided fringe benefits; yet people's attitudes toward work appear to have become more negative, at least in some respects. Without the con-

viction that work expresses one's devotion to family, nation and God, many people are left feeling that work is a nasty, boring imposition on their freedom.

Why the Work Ethic Has Declined

Factors contributing to the apparent decline of the work ethic include:

1. *Affluence.* The American economy now produces such an abundance of food, clothing and other goods that many people find it easy to satisfy their most pressing needs with little or no work. A large nation could be fed with the food that winds up in U.S. garbage pails. Since food is so plentiful in the U.S., the threat of starvation no longer forces many people into working.

2. *Entitlements.* Modern societies have taken increasing responsibility for maintaining a minimum standard of living for their populations. Mere residency is widely viewed as enough to entitle a person to food, shelter and medical care. These goods and services now are provided to large numbers of people who have not worked to earn the money to buy them.

3. *Women in the workforce.* The recent flood of married women into the labor force has decreased the pressure on men to remain working. As more women have entered the job market, an increasing percentage of working-age men have left it. Many decide to retire early or take extended leaves from regular employment because their wives can now support them.

4. *Fewer children.* Since the 1960s, people have had fewer children, hence there is less pressure on workers to provide economic support for their progeny.

5. *Television.* Entertainment is the main role of television in the average person's life, and since work is usually not as entertaining as various nonwork activities, television tends to stress leisure. Most of the people in television programs enjoy amenities of all kinds while doing very little that resembles the nitty-gritty work of the assembly line or typing pool. Television commercials are especially rich in images of play rather than those of work. The old-time minister

may have glorified the redeeming value of hard work, but television preaches that it's more fun to play.

6. *Decline of religion.* Church attendance has dropped substantially since the 1960s, and religious support for hard work appears to have waned. Religion traditionally emphasized the duties that people have to others—duties which often were expressed through work.

7. *Prolonged education.* Schools appear to have contributed in a variety of ways to the decline of the work ethic. First, schools have generally relaxed their own requirements. Many schools demand little homework from their students and allow students to pass courses without having met previous standards of proficiency. Second, the prolongation of schooling has kept many young people out of the workforce, and thus has kept them from experiencing work through much of their lives. Third, the educational system emphasizes talk rather than action.

8. *Credentialism.* Many employers now depend heavily on the academic system to select their workers. An executive may be hired, not on the basis of superior performance as a worker but for having an academic degree or other certification.

9. *Unrealistic image.* Television and other media have given people the idea that work should be fun and prestigious. Professionals and executives are exalted; blue-collar workers, clerks and farmers are often given little credit for their contributions to society. If the media suggest that people are chumps for doing the ordinary work of society, it is hardly surprising that many workers do not feel good about their jobs.

10. *Anti-authority attitudes.* Most jobs require the establishment of goals and rules as well as evaluations of employees' performance by supervisors. People resent having to submit their wills to another person, especially if they had not learned to respond to authority at home and in the educational system. Workers not accustomed to discipline at an earlier age find it difficult to accept as adults.

11. *Extensive use of credit.* The use of credit—credit cards, mortgages, department store accounts, automobile loans, etc.—has tended to blur the close connection between production (effort) and consumption (enjoyment). Thanks to credit, one can fly to Las Vegas for the weekend without having worked and saved the money to do so. In principle, work remains connected to the enjoyments provided by earnings, but the use of credit makes the connection a bit vague.

12. *Inflation.* By destroying the purchasing power of savings that have resulted from hard work, inflation does its bit to undermine the work ethic. Perhaps more insidiously, inflation rewards those people who spend their time figuring out schemes for speculation and tax avoidance rather than in producing goods.

13. *Social Security and retirement benefits.* Before the U.S. Government instituted the Social Security System in the 1930s, most workers were prodded by the knowledge that they were building savings for the time when they would no longer be able to work. Savings would keep them from the poorhouse or from dependence on their children. As Social Security benefits have increased, more and more people have felt that they no longer needed to save for their retirement years, and therefore did not need to work as hard as they might otherwise.

14. *Divorce.* Divorce has conflicting impacts on people's desire to work. On the one hand, divorce often forces a nonworking wife to get a salaried job, and it may make her ex-husband earn more in order to pay alimony and child support to his former wife in addition to meeting financial obligations to a new wife. In some cases, however, the divorced husband may find that little earnings remain after paying taxes and making payments to his ex-wife; he thus loses his incentive to work.

15. *Crime.* Workers naturally become discouraged if thieves deprive them of their earnings or possessions acquired through hard work. This situation occurs with increasing frequency as the crime rate rises.

16. *Resentment.* Wide publicity is given to the salaries paid to a fortunate few—professional athletes, television personalities, etc. Employment agencies often advertise positions offering 50 percent more than the usual rate for a given category of workers in order to attract the attention of prospects. Workers may not realize that they are seeing exceptional or unreal salary offers and may, in consequence, become disillusioned with the salaries they themselves receive.

17. *Shortage of workers.* When workers are scarce, their wages tend to rise. This does not necessarily mean that they will work more hours, however. Many will work less, since less work is needed to earn the same income.

18. *Decline of "macho" character of work.* One reason many people take pride in their work is that they feel they are doing something that other people cannot. The entry of new groups of workers into many job categories often diminishes the old cadre's feelings of being "special."

Dissatisfaction With Work

The job dissatisfaction among American workers increased substantially in the 1970s, according to a study by the University of Michigan's Institute for Social Research. The Institute found that discontent is most pronounced among college graduates but extends to virtually all occupations and population groups in the workforce. Comparison among surveys made in 1969, 1973 and 1977 indicate that workers have become increasingly less satisfied with their pay, their job security and their hours. More employees now feel their work is uninteresting, and not as many believe that they have the opportunity to develop their own special abilities. They have begun to feel "locked in" their present jobs, with opportunities for mobility decreasing, and they are becoming apprehensive about the future value of their job skills. A major emerging problem today is the mismatch between the jobs available and the jobs that people want. This problem has intensified as more and more young people receive university degrees.

Whether or not they attended college, workers today generally want "meaningful" rather than "menial" jobs. To satisfy the demand for "good" positions rather than just "dead-end" jobs, politicians have created a wide variety of taxpayer-supported work programs to provide work experience; at the same time, tasks that urgently need workers are left undone. Henry Marien, a resident of Washington, D.C., reported in the *Washington Star* in 1979 on his experience with the city's trash problem. Outraged by the trash littering much of the nation's capital, Marien contacted city officials; he was told no funds were available for a cleanup. Money was available, Marien reported, for various job-training programs but not for a job that didn't require any training!

The "Me" Generation

Social critics have recently focused much attention on the phenomenon of the "me" generation. More than in the past, people today focus on their own needs and show little real concern about the needs of others or of society as a whole. The phenomenon is often described as "narcissism," a term derived from the legendary Narcissus, who fell in love with his own reflection. Unlike workers who feel they have a duty to hold their personal desires in check while employed by someone else, narcissists demand those things they want for themselves.

In the past, workers were prepared to sacrifice their wants for the sake of their children and future rewards, and they felt morally bound to follow their employer's wishes while at work. Members of the "me" generation feel entitled to do what they themselves want and *now*—even when on the job.

Dilemma in the Workplace

Sociologist Daniel Bell has explained in his book *The Cultural Contradictions of Capitalism* that the U.S. economy seeks people who are ideal producers to be workers, and people who are ideal consumers to be customers. Unfortunately, the mentality desired in a customer comes into conflict with the mentality desired in a worker. Workers need to develop strong self-discipline, work hard and postpone pleasure. On the other hand, customers, ideally, are people who indulge their immediate desires for gratification—people who will immediately run out to buy a television sponsor's product.

Capitalist society, Bell argues, is undermined on the one hand by cultural values that encourage workers to seek instant gratification rather than to work hard and save their money, and on the other, by a political system which emphasizes equality in the distribution of goods and services. Without strong rewards for industriousness, many employees choose not to work hard and production suffers.

One irony of today's workplace is that as conditions have grown better, workers have become increasingly unhappy. Many highly educated professionals in the U.S. now feel "trapped" in positions that appear from the outside to be pinnacles of success. At the same time, many young people entering the job market feel alienated by job situations that they view as restricting their freedom to "grow," tying them to fixed hours of work and patterns of daily activity and depriving them of opportunities to meet new people and encounter unexpected situations.

The frustrations in the workplace have led to the partial or total abandonment of work by large numbers. Their options are many.

How the Nonworking Exist

1. *Welfare.* If one can qualify for welfare by being disabled or having small children and exhibiting no means of support, one may apply to receive welfare payments, which provide unearned income.

2. *Unemployment compensation.* Workers who have paid unemployment insurance while employed and are laid off or have an acceptable reason for resigning are eligible to collect unemployment compensation. An extended period of compensated unemployment can be economically advantageous to an unemployed worker who can use the time to catch up on household chores or other projects.

3. *Financial support from relatives.* In many circumstances, being supported by relatives is socially approved. One half of a married couple can earn enough for both, and offspring may continue to live with their families after reaching adulthood. Older adults may also live with and be supported by their children.

4. *Begging.* Soliciting money or food from strangers is an ancient custom. Despite the existence of public and private agencies established to give assistance, some needy prefer the anonymity of begging.

5. *Theft.* For the amoral person with no desire to work, there is perhaps nothing so potentially rewarding as theft. The soaring crime rate in U.S. cities attests to the growing numbers of people resorting to this method.

6. *Hustling.* Dealing in drugs, trafficking in stolen goods, and other activities that are illegal or socially unacceptable offer another means of escaping work. The ambitious hustler, however, can turn these underground activities into something approximating real work.

7. *Early retirement and disability pensions.* Many corporations and government agencies allow workers to retire before reaching an established mandatory retirement age and to collect a substantial proportion of their previous salaries. Social Security benefits can be collected as early as age 62 in some cases. Oftentimes workers can retire with a generous pension because of a disability even though they are employable in another capacity.

Partial Escapes

1. *Idling at work.* The average employee is estimated to spend about 55 percent of the work day actually producing. Some workers may receive full pay while in fact working less than 25 percent of their work day.

2. *Avoiding hard jobs.* In today's workplace, employees are often given a wide choice of work assignments. It is often possible for a worker to dodge any work that is difficult or unpleasant.

3. *Turning a hard job into an easy job.* This can be done in a variety of ways: delegating the tasks to an assistant or a new employee; suggesting that the job be subcontracted; doing the job in a perfunctory way.

4. *Working part-time.* In today's relaxed workplace, there is rarely a time clock. By coming late, taking extended breaks and leaving early, a worker can greatly reduce the actual amount of productive time.

5. *Downward mobility.* Both management and unions have been surprised to find in recent years that some simple tasks at the bottom of the occupational hierarchy are prized by many

workers. These jobs offer good pay, considering the undemanding character of the work. Many prefer these easy jobs to better-paying but more demanding positions.

6. *Being "sick."* Illness is a generally accepted excuse that can be used to escape work.

Return of the Work Ethic?

The work ethic may at least have a partial comeback in the 1980s—at least there are a few signs indicating such a change. One is the apparently growing realization of American workers that they can no longer take for granted an ever-expanding economy. The soaring cost of energy and inflation in general have forced Americans to work harder in order to enjoy the same life-style. There has also been increasing resentment and rebellion against high taxes, which are used, in part, to provide payments to people who are not working or not working very diligently.

The growing number of college graduates in the job market no longer are prized for simply having a degree. Increasingly, emphasis may be placed on the actual work performed. Also to be noted are the increasing numbers of workaholics, people who are driven to perform in their jobs (see box below). These people commit a major share of their waking moments to their jobs and they feel uncomfortable when idle. Despite their addiction, they seem to be generally happy and normal people—so long as they are working.

Workaholics: The People Who Say, "Thank God It's Monday"

In today's leisure-oriented society, people who like to work and feel lost when not doing so are said to suffer from a dread disease—workaholism. The disease is described in *Workaholics: Living With Them, Working With Them,* by psychologist Marilyn Machlowitz, a self-confessed workaholic. As evidence of her credentials for writing the book, Machlowitz reports that after her freshman year in college, she got *three* summer jobs. Her father accused her of being a "workaholic," and thus she was off on a major investigation of the subject.

Machlowitz estimates that workaholics comprise no more than 5 percent of the population. She discovered a heavy concentration of them during New York City's blackout in 1977: Hundreds of people had gone to work in Manhattan despite radio requests to stay home. The workaholics paced impatiently outside their office buildings, demanding entry even if a thirty-flight climb was required to reach their desks.

Among the many workaholics she uncovered were heart surgeon Denton Cooley, who isn't happy unless he can perform operations all day, and author Isaac Asimov, who admits that he has an anxiety attack if he spends as much as three hours away from his typewriter.

The bias against workaholics arises from the fact that people who work to live cannot understand those who live to work and love it. Machlowitz says, "They watch in amazement and wonder about those who delight in what they do. Workaholics' unorthodox attitude—that their work is so much 'fun they'd probably do it for free—causes nonworkaholics to question their own situation. The latter group begins to worry, 'What's wrong with my job?' or, worse, 'What's wrong with me?'"

To resolve their misgivings about workaholics, nonworkaholics say to themselves, "Sure, workaholics are successful at work, but aren't they really ruining the rest of their lives?" Machlowitz found, however, that, ". . . workaholics are surprisingly happy. They are doing exactly what they love—work—and they can't get enough of it."

The dark side of workaholism is the suffering often experienced by the people who work and live with workaholics. Coworkers experience "envy and anxiety" about getting half as far as those who work twice as hard. Wives, husbands and children of workaholics must cope with and compensate for the workaholics' failure to do things at home.

Machlowitz identified four distinct types of workaholics:

• *The dedicated workaholic* — single-minded and one-dimensional; no interests other than work; hates vacations, sports and amusements.

• *The integrated workaholic* — incorporates outside activities into the job itself; considers a wide variety of activities to be part of the job.

• *The diffuse workaholic* — "has fingers in lots of pies"; has a short attention span—excited by a lot of things and will work intensely at them, but loses interest after a short period of time.

• *The intense workaholic* — pursues leisure activities with the same passion, sense of purpose and pace as work; hobbies become just "a job of a different kind"; likely to become a marathon runner, applying the same energy and exactitude toward training, clocking times and completing difficult courses as one does toward a career.

Psychiatrist Lawrence Susser treats workaholics with outdoor play therapy, starting with a six- to eight-hour hike. "I bring my dog along; that usually brings out the child in them," explains Susser. Another part of the therapy is a two-hour lunch: "Have you ever seen a workaholic take two hours for lunch?"

Jobs and Family Life

The Home: Workplace of the Future?

The idea of working at home rather than going to a distant workplace strikes most people as an attractive but strange and impractical idea. In times past, however, the home and its surroundings were the usual labor site. The current practice of going elsewhere to work is an innovation brought on by the Industrial Revolution, but indications now suggest that work may return to the home.

The evolution of the workplace may explain why futurists anticipate a back-to-the-home movement. Through most of American history, the homestead was the normal workplace for most people. As late as 1790 about 90 percent of the American people lived on farms and had their homes near the fields they tilled. As industry developed in the 19th century and early 20th century, large numbers of men, women and children left the farms to work in factories, often in towns far distant from their homes.

Social reformers at the beginning of the 20th century sought to free women and children from the need to work by achieving the passage of legislation on their behalf. Prevailing attitudes at the time dictated that no self-respecting husband would allow his wife to work for wages. Lower-class women worked out of necessity, but middle-class women were free to take care of their homes and children. The meaning of "female emancipation" has changed completely as the result of recent attitudinal changes. During most of the 20th century, the phrase meant freeing women *from* paid work; in recent years it has come to mean freeing women *for* paid work.

During both world wars, women were pressed into a variety of jobs; after each war women tended to move out of the workforce. During the Great Depression, efforts were sometimes made to discourage married women from working; since positions were scarce, job openings should go to single women or, better, to men who were supporting women and children.

In the late 1960s, a new women's movement developed, demanding equality in the workplace. Feminist ideologues argued that men and women have the same rights and duties—an equal responsibility for earning the money needed by the family coupled with shared responsibility for doing the housework and taking care of the children.

But ambivalence about "equality" persists. Even those who subscribe intellectually to anti-sexist theories often find them difficult to accept emotionally. Columnist Jane Bryant Quinn pointed out recently that it is common today for a working woman to believe that her husband's income is "ours" but her own income is "mine."

"When she pays a grocery bill or buys shoes for the children," says Quinn, "she has a sense of giving up something that should be hers. These feelings date to the day when women were said to be working for pin money—defined as money earned for their own amusement rather than for economic need.

"Nowadays, the incomes of most working wives are an essential prop to the family's standard of living. Yet a woman's pin-money thinking may lead her to feel that her paycheck is really hers alone. Deep down, she may resent that it must be shared."

Even the most anti-sexist men find it difficult to accept their wives making more money than they themselves earn. "It's unbelievable the self-doubt that comes along when she starts getting that monthly check," says one man with a wife earning $65,000 annually. "You keep losing male identity. You become expendable, more expendable as time goes by." One possible solution in such a situation is for the man to assume the traditional woman's role. Men who drop out of the workforce to become "househusbands" experience the same problems that housewives do when they try to rejoin it, with the added problem that people denigrate them. One househusband reported, "I'm black and blue from being fended off by personnel managers with ten-foot poles." Executives engaged in hiring personnel will rarely accept childrearing as a legitimate excuse for a man's not working for several years.

Work Breaks Up Family

Work in today's industrial society breaks up the family in several distinct ways. Most obviously, work forces family members to leave their homes in order to labor elsewhere. But separation is not the only problem: If men and women worked apart they would not be exposed to the temptations that exist in today's unisex workplaces. In the past, men normally worked with other men when they were away from home, and women workers typically worked separately from the men. The barriers were not always impermeable, but they tended to keep the sexes apart on the job.

In today's work environment, however, the sexes mingle freely and constantly, and married people are constantly exposed to temptation. Some large establishments may be likened to sexual marketplaces where merchandise of all types is constantly on display and can be freely inspected without risk. Under such circumstances, a husband or wife is very likely to meet someone that he or she will find attractive.

The unisex workplace may also intensify emotional buildups. When the sexes work separately, especially among males, there is often much ribald joshing which provides an outlet for sexual as well as aggressive feelings. The combining of men and women in one work area changes the atmosphere, with both sexes suppressing primitive sexual and aggressive urges. Unable to vent anger and sexual feeling easily and safely at frequent intervals, a worker may seek the sympathy and emotional release that a lover can provide. Additionally, people working together develop common interests and understandings that draw them together emotionally. Office parties are notorious for being occasions where, under the influence of alcohol, sexual attractions find expression.

Perhaps nowhere have the sexual temptations of the workplace been more publicized than in police work. Police customarily work in pairs, and a strong emotional attachment builds up between police officer and partner. In addition to the close physical contact and interaction during the normal working day, frequent emo-

UPI

Women on police teams are a break from the past.

tionally tense, high-risk situations occur in which partners are heavily dependent on each other's performance.

Distant Career Opportunities

The business world frequently creates attractive opportunities requiring a family member to relocate. Corporations move their executives from place to place based on business requirements, with little concern for the families of the executives being moved. From the corporation's standpoint, transfers are often essential, and refusal to accept a transfer may be fatal to an executive's career advancement. But the impact of moves on a family are often traumatic.

Frequent moves may weaken a family by forcing its individual members to become overly dependent on each other. A nonworking woman who goes with her husband into a new community often finds that her husband has a ready-made system of social contacts through his work while she is totally stripped of her identity and is without friends in the new location.

Children, having lost their former companions, are forced to depend more heavily on their parents and on each other. Resentments and frustrations generated by forced moves offer one explanation for the heavy incidence of physical abuse within military families.

If only one spouse is pursuing an active career, the family may be reasonably expected to survive when transfers are required. If both marriage partners have careers, the family is at high risk of disintegrating. If the husband's career forces him to work in Boston and the wife's career requires that she work in Houston, the family is almost certain to suffer. A lot of imaginative adjustments are worked out to try to meet such situations. Some companies will provide a job for the spouse when an executive is transferred, but in a very large number of cases, a divorce eventually results. The United States now has more than a million divorces a year, and the time seems to be fast approaching when more than half of all marriages will end in divorce. Clearly a lot of family trouble begins with the nature of work in today's society.

Working at Home

As factories become increasingly automated and require fewer workers, a growing number of people may find themselves working at home. Spurring the move of work back to the home is the computer communications revolution, which enables people to stay in constant touch with their offices, supervisors and clients while at home.

The amount of office-oriented work being done at home appears to be increasing dramatically. For example, the Continental Illinois Bank is conducting a major experiment in having its staff type letters, memos and statistical work using word processors linked to the bank's office in Chicago. One clerical worker reports that the system enables her to work while caring for her baby.

A management consultant in Palo Alto found that his computer terminal enabled him to continue working after he contracted pneumonia and was forced to stay at home for nearly two weeks. He also found the device handy for working at irregular times, day or night.

Another employee, who also operates a 50-acre farm in Massachusetts, spends about five hours a day at the company-linked terminal. A commodities trader listens to Beethoven while looking at the prices of wheat and soybeans on his home computer screen. He finds that his detachment from the hurly-burly on the exchange floor in Chicago helps him to make rational judgments.

People generally like working at home, but they have discovered a few disadvantages. For one thing, it is often difficult for supervisors in the workplace and workers who are at home to communicate with each other, because much information is passed during brief meetings in hallways and around the water cooler. In addition, the computer does not pick up the vast amount of nonverbal information that can be crucial in many situations. For example, body language can be important in gauging the degree of interest a prospective customer may have in a particular product.

Though many people benefit from the lack of distractions at home, others have difficulty disciplining themselves. The presence of other people at work stimulates and encourages certain types of people to work. Many stay-at-home workers complain of loneliness and deliberately go out on trips that bring them into contact with other people. In the opposite situation, a busy household can have too much distraction for effective work.

Yet the advantages of working at home are enormous. For one thing, much time and energy could be saved if people did not have to commute to and from the workplace. Professor Jack M. Nilles, director of interdisciplinary programs at the University of Southern California, says the need for oil imports could be eliminated if urban commuting were reduced appreciably.

Many handicapped people, as well as mothers with small children, can rejoin the workforce if they can work at home. People in isolated areas where there are few paid jobs may also be able to work in their homes.

Already many categories of employees appear to be performing more work at home: college professors, insurance agents, lawyers, public relations directors, salespersons, editors and, of course, computer programmers. In the future more and more people may follow their lead—communicating with, rather than commuting to, their jobs. If so, perhaps families will again be united rather than separated by work.

Where the Jobs Will Be

Since the grass always seems greener somewhere else, people are constantly on the move in a never-ending search for better opportunities.

Americans have, historically, tended to move westward, finding employment, first in the rich agricultural lands of the Midwest, and later in the mines and grazing lands of the Far West. Decade after decade, the center of population has shifted steadily to the west. Then during the 1970s, population began to shift southward from "frost belt" to the "sun belt." Despite the widely held impression that the North and Midwest are losing jobs, employment in those areas has continued to grow over the past decade. The loss of jobs in the manufacturing sector has been more than offset by expansion in services. New England, often considered to be an industrial "basket case," enjoyed an economic rebound during the past decade, thanks in part to its high-technology industries.

In 1981 the depressed automobile industry made Detroit a poor place to look for work, and pockets of high unemployment appeared in other regions. In contrast, the revival of mining in the West—brought about by higher metal prices and new cost-effective methods of extraction—is revitalizing localities that had been virtual ghost towns. Nevada's Virginia City, which burst into prominence after the big gold and silver strikes along the Comstock Lode more than a century ago, is one of the new boom towns of the West.

Economic prosperity is not always welcomed by local residents, however. People in small Nevada towns are afraid the new mining operations will destroy the picturesque, peaceful rural life they have long enjoyed. Similarly, in the Pacific Northwest people worry that an influx of newcomers may destroy their pleasant lifestyles. Oregon Secretary of State Norma Paulus has been quoted as saying, "Oregonians are paranoid about Californians moving in and Californicating Oregon." Former Oregon Governor Tom McCall pioneered his state's "visit-but-don't-stay" inhospitality movement. A Seattle newspaper columnist urged readers to "fight them off" by advertising the region's persistent rainfall.

Where will jobs be most plentiful in the years ahead? No one knows, but experts generally

agree that during the 1980s, economic growth will continue to be greater in the West and South than in the Northeast and Midwest for a number of reasons. Energy costs for both business and home will be cheaper in areas with both a less severe climate and local sources of petroleum and natural gas. New transportation hubs have grown rapidly outside the Northeast and Midwest—Atlanta, Fort Lauderdale, Houston, Denver, Dallas-Fort Worth, Memphis, etc. Land is often more plentiful and regulations fewer outside the Northeast. An increase in automation may reduce the number of workers needed in the established industries of the Northeast and Midwest.

Back to the Country

Historically, Americans have tended to move not only westward, but from farms to cities as manufacturing concentrated in urban areas. The latter trend partially reversed itself when suburban areas developed rapidly after World War II. During the early 1970s, the cityward migration pattern reversed completely for the first time in U.S. history; migration to nonmetropolitan areas actually exceeded migration to metropolitan areas. The migration from urban centers left many older cities in a precarious economic position. According to a survey conducted for the Joint Economic Committee of the U.S. Congress, half the nation's cities had operating deficits in 1980. More than three quarters of the cities expected their budgets to be in the red in 1981.

"There's something like a crisis ahead," said committee chairman Henry S. Reuss, a Wisconsin Democrat. Reasons for the financial troubles include the high rate of inflation, inept city management, and state governments' frequent refusal to offer substantial help. The committee report suggested that without federal aid cities will be forced to increase taxes in order to maintain the existing level of services, which in turn, could cause more businesses and middle-class residents to move to the suburbs. People leave cities to escape high taxes, crime, expensive real estate, and overcrowding. As city dwellers move into the suburbs, jobs develop nearby, often leaving a decaying core in the center of a metropolitan region. All movement does not trend away from the city however. Urban centers have compelling attractions—employment opportunities, medical services, educational facilities, cultural attractions, and often inexpensive housing left behind by the people escaping the city. Here is what a booster for each of the three types of residences, urban, rural, and suburban might say:

City dweller. "The city has everything; I can walk from my home to supermarkets, clothing stores, hairstylists, restaurants, and almost anything else I might need. I can get on a bus and ride to a concert, an opera, a theatre, etc. Whatever you want, the city has. And it's easy to get to my job."

Rural dweller. "Nobody bothers me here. I can do whatever I like. The air and water are pure. The people are friendly. There are no major crime or parking problems. In the country we have real peace."

UPI

The Houston skyline, like that of other magnet cities, seems to have shot up overnight.

Suburbanite. "We have the best of both worlds. We are close enough to the city to enjoy the best that it offers. On the other hand, we are far enough away to be protected from most of the problems. On weekends we can easily drive into rolling country, yet we don't have to worry about being buried for weeks under the snow in the country or living in an asphalt jungle in the city."

Americans have long been highly mobile, quickly pulling up roots and moving to new locations when job opportunities presented themselves. Recently, however, people have become much more reluctant to accept transfers.

This phenomenon was encountered by the General Dynamics Corporation, which builds submarines in Groton, Connecticut. Needing skilled workers a few years ago, the company sent a recruiting team to Youngstown, Ohio, where a steel mill had recently closed. Virtually none of the steelworkers accepted an employment offer. The workers were unwilling to move because they were receiving substantial benefits under the nation's trade adjustment assistance program and because they thought their plant might reopen. In Youngstown and elsewhere workers are reluctant to move if they have low mortgages on their homes—a major consideration since interest rates have soared. Other important reasons for people not wanting to transfer were that spouses may not be able to find an appropriate job in the new location; they didn't want to take their children out of school; they didn't want to leave friends and relatives. All of these factors have resulted in a decline in the proportion of Americans who move each year. In the 1950s, about 20 percent of the population moved during a typical year. Currently the figure is about 18 percent. (In an interesting aside, when Americans do move today, most do the moving themselves. Of the 22 million people who changed residence in 1980, 84 percent moved their own household goods instead of hiring a professional mover.)

Alternative Work-Residence Arrangements

Some people resolve the rural-urban question of where to work and live by having homes in more than one environment—an apartment in the city and a cottage on a mountain lake; a suburban home and a condominium apartment at an oceanside resort. Some entertainers, politicians and people in other occupations have become "bicoastals"—living and working part of the time on the West Coast and part on the East Coast. The bicoastals report a number of curious problems arising from their mobile life-style. They must duplicate everything from golf clubs to phonograph records; they must change airlines frequently to avoid seeing the same in-flight films; and they often forget which coast they are on and wear the wrong clothes (for example, arriving in an open-necked shirt when calling on government officials in Washington). They even have trouble keeping their watches set for the correct time zone.

Modern transportation and communications systems have freed Americans from geographical limitations when they look for places to work and live. This new freedom may play an important role in determining both where people work and where they live. Rural living may get a boost from the new communications systems technologies such as satellite television and computer networks. The latter makes it possible for people to stay in close touch with their offices even though they may be thousands of miles away. If people can get a job *anywhere*, where will they want that job to be? Does it really matter if they can simply communicate with their jobs rather than having to actually go to them?

Famous People and Their Dead-end Jobs

A menial job isn't necessarily a one-way ticket to a dead-end life. Famous people who started out at the low end of the totem pole include:

Carl Sandburg, poet and biographer worked as a dishwasher.

Glenn Seaborg, Nobel Prize-winning atomic scientist, mowed lawns, delivered newspapers and picked apricots.

Eugene O'Neill, playwright, served as a sailor.

Alvin Toffler, futurist and author, drove a truck.

Abraham Lincoln, 16th President of the United States, worked as a dirt farmer and as a hired hand on a flatboat.

Herman Kahn, physicist and policy analyst, clerked in a supermarket.

John Steinbeck, novelist, worked as a carpenter and ranch hand.

Anton van Leeuwenhoek, discoverer of microbes, was a janitor.

Ronald Reagan, 40th U.S. President, worked as a lifeguard.

Many show business luminaries once put bread on the table by toiling away at routine jobs far from the stage or screen.

Robert Conrad picked up dirty diapers door-to-door for a diaper service.

Della Reese drove a taxi.

Ed Asner delivered groceries.

Dyan Cannon set pins in a bowling alley.

Patrick Duffy pulled nails out of old boards for a salvage company.

Sally Struthers cleaned the ladies' restroom and sold popcorn at a movie theater.

Sonny Bono delivered meat for a butcher.

Loretta Lynn picked strawberries sunrise to sundown for 25 cents a day.

Engelbert Humperdinck operated a lathe in a boot factory.

Career Counseling

The abundance of career options available today has helped to promote the development of a relatively new occupation, career counseling.

Career counseling has its roots in the vocational guidance movement of the first quarter of the 20th century, but not until the late 1960s and early 1970s did it come to be viewed as a vital part of education. While many other occupations may fall victim to automation or economic conditions in the 1980s, career counseling will probably continue to grow, partly because it has come to be thought of as a near-necessity for success in the complex world of work and careers.

"In spite of the fact that opportunities for job and career changes are more prevalent now than in the past, systems for finding jobs have scarcely improved," writes H. Lee Rust in his book, *Jobsearch: The Complete Manual for Job Seekers.*

Career counselors may be on the staffs of high schools or colleges, helping young people plan and prepare for a career, or they may work for independent firms, assisting clients with the complexities and strategies of looking for work. Career counseling in educational institutions emphasizes a general awareness of career options and the preparation needed for a specific career. Counselors in independent firms, on the other hand, tend to be more pragmatic and result-oriented.

"Career education encourages early tryout and exploration in order to give new meaning and motivation to study and other worthwhile experiences," says one school administrator. "At the same time, it promotes the idea that hard choices should be delayed until all basic facts are gathered about the person and the changing world of work."

Independent career counselors, sometimes called career coaches, will often have very specific, practical strategies for job hunters. Among them are ways to present oneself to a superior in order to upgrade a job and methods of securing a higher salary at the outset in a new position.

"When the interviewer mentions salary ranges," explains career counselor Richard LeFante in the *Wall Street Journal,* "take the top figure and repeat it. Say 'Hmmm.' Think about it; count to 30 and look at the person." If the interviewer really wants to hire you, he will raise the offer. "After 45 seconds, most people can't stand the silence." LeFante has heard of people getting $3,000 to $5,000 more using this technique.

Career Changing

Career changing is fairly commonplace today and may become more so through the '80s. Some career changes are forced by such factors as job obsolescence, but other switches are matters of choice. Many people with successful high-paying jobs are forgoing security, prestige and substantial salaries in favor of "the good life."

Beale Rodgers, a former accountant, and his wife had a combined income of $50,000, company cars and an expensive home. But Rodgers "just hated accounting." So he packed up his family and bought a general store in rural Virginia. "The pressures of the large corporation just got to be too much," he commented.

The economic security that many people enjoy today often makes it relatively easy to change careers. Working wives, who more and more often are receiving salaries comparable to their husbands', are frequently able to support their families while their husbands go back to school, retraining for a new career in such fields as law, forestry or music.

Increased education seems to have popularized the idea that work should be meaningful and satisfying. Monetary gains are less and less the motivating factors for many people in choosing careers.

"The 'now' generation appears no longer motivated by extrinsic rewards alone," comments S. Norman Feingold, president of the National Careers and Counseling Service. The primary thrust of young people, Feingold maintains, is personal growth and self-actualization, and that implies career switching when a chosen occupation fails to meet personal goals.

"Job dissatisfaction is likely to become more commonplace in the next two decades, simply because there aren't enough top jobs in the economy to satisfy all the drive and ambition of the post-World War II baby-boom population that is moving up the workforce promotion ladder," comments the *Washington Post.* "Many of these persons probably will shift careers abruptly once or twice in their working lives after going as far as they can."

Younger people and women tend to change jobs more readily than older men, who are often tied down by economic needs and less likely to think that they can afford to make a major career switch.

Job redundancy is also causing many people to change careers. The introduction of electronics into industry has changed the nature of some occupations; long-established jobs are being replaced by new ones requiring new technological skills. Many workers in printing and publishing, the auto industry, steel manufacturing and other areas find that their traditional skills are no longer needed, and they are not trained in the skills required for the new jobs. A variety of programs and ideas are being put forth to deal with the involuntary career changes.

"There is a shortage of skilled workers on the horizon," states a Labor Department official. "These displaced workers are an asset. They are at least disciplined, if not skilled. The big problem ahead of us is going to be to fit them to the jobs out there."

One difficulty in preparing workers for jobs is that the positions that workers prepare for may not exist or may be on the decline by the time the workers have finished their training. W. Clyde Helms, a former Defense Department employee and now president of Occupational Forecasting, a futurist firm in Arlington, Virginia, has studied this problem in some depth.

Unknown numbers of jobs are obsolete or becoming so, Helms says, yet schools and government programs persist in training people for those jobs. In some cases, the jobs simply won't be there next year. In other instances, the jobs

Los Angeles Community College · UPI

Training to be a welder may not make sense if welding jobs are being eliminated.

A mock job interview is videotaped to help a graduate at the Univ. of North Carolina.

may still be there, but will employ equipment that is totally different from what the prospective workers trained on. Helms proposes a national occupational assessment center in order to predict what jobs will be in demand and what jobs will be obsolete.

"We spend hundreds of millions of dollars to create new technology," says Helms, but invest very little ". . . to study its impact on employment—what jobs will be outmoded, what new ones will be needed."

Pension reforms are also contributing to career changes by removing economic penalties that often accompany leaving a firm. The Pension Reform Act of 1974, which entitles employees to pension benefits after 10 years of employment, has enabled many people to switch careers and make a fresh start while still receiving pension payments. Futurist David Pearce Snyder believes there is a 90 percent chance that Congress will mandate five-year pension vesting and portability by 1986 in response to the desires of an increasingly mobile population.

Other government action could also help job changers. Education and training programs for disadvantaged workers and for workers who are left without jobs by the shrinking economy are often funded by federal, state and local governments.

Psychologist Seymour B. Sarason has suggested that governments might institute an "educare" program similar to Medicare. Under an educare plan, every citizen would be entitled, at some point after entering the workforce, to return to school for a specified length of time at public expense to receive further education and training in any given area.

The program would be open to workers regardless of whether or not a career change was a matter of choice or a result of changing employment patterns. Many career changes, Sarason believes, are brought on by the recognition of how far the reality of work and adult life fall below people's expectations. Loneliness is a common element in this dissatisfaction, affecting even successful people. People seek a sense of community—the ability to identify with a small congenial group of familiar individuals. The real

motivation for changing careers in mid-life, he finds, is often the desire to seek out and become part of such a small group.

West Germany has provided a type of educare program with the hopes that the overall economy will improve as it gains more skilled workers. Every adult, whether employed or unemployed, is entitled to two years of full-time training plus an income subsidy, which can be as high as 90 percent of the last salary earned.

The income subsidy is primarily intended for low-wage workers. The maximum subsidy allowed may nearly equal the income of low-wage workers, so they lose little income while upgrading their skills. Thus the workers needing the most training receive the strongest encouragement to seek it out.

Counseling for Retirement and Leisure

People can get too much of a good thing, and leisure is no exception. When people are not required to work, they may lose their sense of importance, their sense of value to the world.

"Increasing leisure time before and after retirement is something about which people need professional counseling," says counselor Feingold.

There are signs that many elderly people are resisting retirement. A combination of longer life expectancy for older persons, better health, declining physical demands of most work, and financial considerations appears to be fostering a desire on the part of many persons for gradual or intermittent retirement rather than complete mandatory retirement at a comparatively early age.

Early retirement, part-time work, work-sharing programs, the four-day workweek, and a host of other alternatives to the 40-hour, five-day workweek will likely leave people with more time on their hands in the future. Community action projects, local politics and other unpaid occupations may become a more important part of people's lives. By the 1990s choosing an avocation may become as important as choosing a vocation. Similar counseling techniques may be needed, and that is expected to lead to the development of a whole new career area—leisure counseling.

NEWS MAPS

NORWEGIAN SEA

ICELAND

Prince Charles and Lady Diana Spencer married (July 29, 1981).

Rioting by youths sweeps British cities (July 1981).

Ten IRA hunger strikers die in Belfast prison by mid-August 1981.

SWEDEN

FINLAND

Helsinki ★

NORWAY

Oil

Oil

Stockholm ★

UNITED

No. Ire.

NORTH SEA

DENMARK

U.S.S.R.

KINGDOM

BALTIC SEA

IRELAND

Garret FitzGerald becomes prime minister in coalition government (June 1981).

Marc Eyskens is named premier (April 6, 1981) following fall of Martens' government.

Socialist François Mitterrand elected president, defeating Giscard d'Estaing (May 10, 1981). Socialists capture absolute majority in National Assembly in parliamentary elections (June 14 & 21, 1981).

NETHERLANDS

London ★

WEST

Berlin

EAST

★

Following a long period of labor unrest, the Polish government recognizes Rural Solidarity, the Polish farmers' union (May 10, 1981). Food shortage crisis develops during 1981.

BELGIUM

GERMANY

Rhine

Paris ★

LUX.

POLAND

GERMANY

CZECHOSLOVAKIA

SWITZERLAND

AUSTRIA

HUNGARY

FRANCE

ROMANIA

Belgrade ★

Danube

BLACK SEA

YUGOSLAVIA

BULGARIA

PORTUGAL

Lisbon ★

Madrid ★

SPAIN

Pope John Paul II is wounded by Turkish terrorist at Vatican City (May 13, 1981).

Giovanni Spadolini, leader of the Republican party, is appointed premier (June 28, 1981).

ITALY

★ Rome

ALBANIA

GREECE

TURKEY

Athens ★

MEDITERRANEAN

Premier Francisco Sá Carneiro is killed in plane crash (Dec. 4, 1980). He is succeeded by Francisco Pinto Balsemão (Jan. 10, 1981).

Rightists seize Cortes in abortive coup attempt (Feb. 23-24, 1981). Following resignation of Adolfo Suárez (Jan. 29, 1981), Leopoldo Calvo Sotelo is sworn in as premier (Feb. 26).

MALTA

SEA

Greece becomes full member of the European Community (Jan. 1, 1981).

Albanian separatists riot in Yugoslavia's Kosovo province (March-May 1981).

MOROCCO

TUNISIA

EGYPT

ALGERIA

LIBYA

EUROPE

European Community members are underlined   © Copyright HAMMOND INCORPORATED, Maplewood, N.J.

U.S.S.R.

PACIFIC OCEAN

BERING SEA

ARCTIC OCEAN

SEA OF OKHOTSK

Vladivostok

SEA OF JAPAN

JAPAN

N. KOR.

S. KOR.

S i b e r i a

S.F.S.R.

BAM R.R. (under construction)

L. Baykal

R.R.

Trans-Siberian

MONGOLIA

CHINA

Natural gas production at Urengoi field to be increased for possible export to Western Europe (reported Aug. 1, 1981).

Gas

Oil

Novosibirsk

Premier of Kirgiz Republic is murdered in sleep (Dec. 4, 1980).

Afghan guerrillas tie down 100,000 Soviet occupation troops during 1981.

Premier Aleksey Kosygin resigns (Oct. 23, 1980) and is succeeded by Nikolai A. Tikhanov. Kosygin dies (Dec. 19).

Oil

Gas

RUSSIAN

Oil

Underground press reports that Kiev workers staged three successful strikes in April 1981.

KAZAKH

Aral Sea

KIRGIZ

TADZHIK

UZBEK

TURKMEN

Gas

AFGHANISTAN

Caspian Sea

Oil

Oil

Oil

IRAN

SWEDEN

NOR.

FINLAND

Leningrad

EST.

LAT.

LITH.

WHITE

RUSS.

Moscow

Gas

Kiev

UKRAINE

Gas

Oil

ARM.

AZER.

GEOR.

BLACK SEA

IRE.

UNITED KINGDOM

NETH.

DEN.

W. GER.

E. GER.

POLAND

CZECH.

AUS.

HUN.

ROM.

MOLD.

BUL.

Gas

TURKEY

SYRIA

IRAQ

SAUDI ARABIA

© Copyright HAMMOND INCORPORATED, Maplewood, N. J.

MIDDLE EAST

U. S. to provide Pakistan with $3 billion in military and economic aid (June 1981).

Anti-Soviet guerrilla resistance continues during 1981. USSR troop commitment rises to 100,000 personnel.

American hostages are released and flown to U. S. (Jan. 20, 1981). Bani-Sadr is ousted as president (June 22); Premier Rajai is elected in his place (July 24). Ayatollah Beheshti and 71 fundamentalist leaders are killed when bomb explodes at meeting (June 28). President Rajai and new Premier Bahonar are killed in Aug. 30 bomb explosion.

Sporadic fighting between Iran and Iraq continues during 1981.

Israeli warplanes destroy Iraqi nuclear plant near Baghdad (June 7, 1981).

Over 100 passengers are released from hijacked Pakistani plane, when Pakistan government agrees to release 54 political prisoners (March 12, 1981).

Israeli jets bomb PLO headquarters in Beirut, killing 300 (July 17, 1981).

President Anwar el-Sadat is assassinated at military parade grounds near Cairo (Oct. 6, 1981).

© Copyright HAMMOND INCORPORATED, Maplewood, N.J.

SOUTHERN ASIA

U.S. to provide Pakistan with $3 billion in military and economic aid (June 1981).

President Ziaur Rahman is assassinated in abortive coup (May 30, 1981).

Initial reports indicate 215 killed in Bihar train wreck (June 6, 1981). Many more feared dead.

Coup attempt against Prem government fails (April 1-3, 1981).

U. S. backs Cambodian factions fighting Vietnamese-dominated government in Phnom Penh (May 2, 1981).

Pope John Paul II visits Philippines (Feb. 17-22, 1981). President Marcos is re-elected (June 16).

Inter-island ship sinks, drowning 580 passengers and crew (Jan. 27, 1981).

© Copyright HAMMOND INCORPORATED, Maplewood, N.J.

EAST ASIA

© Copyright HAMMOND INCORPORATED, Maplewood, N.J.

Japanese government agrees to limit auto exports to U.S. for two years (May 1, 1981).

U.S. nuclear submarine accidentally sinks Japanese freighter (April 9, 1981).

Jetliner explodes and crashes, killing 110 passengers (Aug. 22, 1981).

New constitution is promulgated (Oct. 27, 1980).

President Kim Il Sung's son, Kim Jong Il, is appointed to second-ranking post in North Korean Communist party Secretariat (October 1980).

Sixteen members of the "Gang of Four," including Mao's widow, Jiang Jing, are given suspended death sentences and long imprisonment (Jan. 25, 1981). Hu Yaobang replaces Hua Guofeng as Politburo chairman (June 29, 1981).

Severe drought cripples farm production in Hubei and Hebei provinces. Floods sweep Sichuan province (1981).

PACIFIC OCEAN

Hokkaido

★ Tokyo

N J A P A N

Honshu

Shikoku

Kyushu

SEA OF JAPAN

NORTH KOREA

★ Seoul
SOUTH KOREA

YELLOW SEA

EAST CHINA SEA

TAIWAN

★ Taipei

PHILIPPINES

• Harbin

Shenyang •

• Shanghai

Peking ★ (Beijing)

HEBEI

He (R.)

Huang (R.)/Yellow

Xi'an •

HUBEI

• Wuhan

(Yangtze)

Chongqing •

Jiang

Chiang

SICHUAN

• Lanzhou

• Canton   HONG KONG (U.K.)

Macau (Port.)

Hainan

C H I N A

U.S.S.R.

★ Ulaanbaatar

M O N G O L I A

Ürümqi •

X I N J I A N G

(S I N K I A N G)

• Lhasa

T I B E T

U.S.S.R.

VIETNAM

LAOS

THAILAND

BURMA

BHUTAN

BANGLADESH

NEPAL

I N D I A

KASHMIR

PAK.

AFGH.

BAY OF BENGAL

AUSTRALIA AND THE PACIFIC

U.S. | MEXICO

CHINA

JAPAN

TAIWAN

Hong Kong

SOUTH CHINA SEA

PHILIPPINE SEA

★ Manila

PHILIPPINES

MALAYSIA

INDONESIA

INDIAN OCEAN

NORTHERN MARIANAS

Guam

Pope John Paul II visits Guam (Feb. 23, 1981).

BELAU

CAROLINE ISLANDS

FED. STATES OF MICRONESIA

TERRITORY OF THE PACIFIC ISLANDS

PAPUA NEW GUINEA

AUSTRALIA

Perth

Prime Minister Fraser's Liberal-Country party coalition reelected to the House with reduced majority (Oct. 18, 1980).

Canberra ★ Sydney

Melbourne

CORAL SEA

SOLOMON IS.

NAURU

New Caledonia (Fr.)

VANUATU

Secessionist leader, Jimmy Stevens, is sentenced to 14 years in prison (Nov. 1980).

NEW ZEALAND

TUVALU

W. SAMOA

AMER.

TONGA

KIRIBATI

OCEAN

Cook Is.

Midway Is.

Wake I.

MARSHALL ISLANDS

U.S. signs agreements with the Marshall Islands, the Federated States of Micronesia and the Republic of Belau, establishing "free association status" for the new states (Oct.-Nov. 1980).

Tarawa

Line Islands

HAWAIIAN ISLANDS

Honolulu ●

UNITED STATES

P A C I F I C

Tahiti

FRENCH POLYNESIA

MARQUESAS IS.

Pitcairn I.

Easter I.

© Copyright HAMMOND INCORPORATED, Maplewood, N.J.

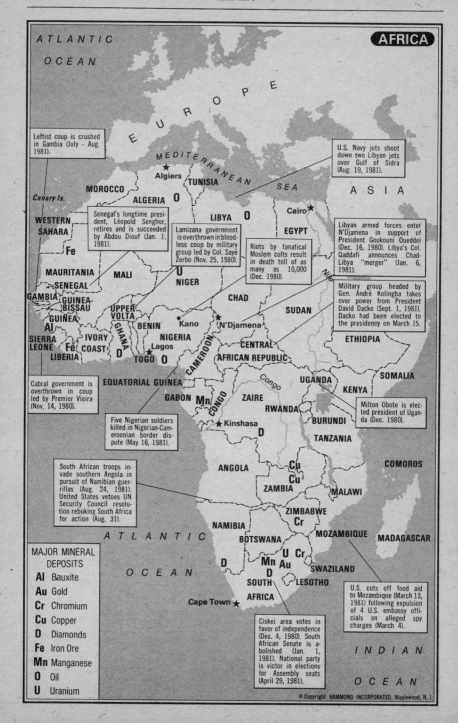

ATLANTIC

OCEAN

AFRICA

Leftist coup is crushed
in Gambia (July - Aug.
1981).

U.S. Navy jets shoot
down two Libyan jets
over Gulf of Sidra
(Aug. 19, 1981).

E U R O P E

MEDITERRANEAN   SEA

Algiers ★ TUNISIA

Canary Is.

MOROCCO

WESTERN
SAHARA

ALGERIA   O

Fe

MAURITANIA

SENEGAL

GAMBIA GUINEA-
BISSAU

GUINEA

SIERRA   Al
LEONE   Fe   IVORY
LIBERIA   COAST   GHANA

MALI

UPPER
VOLTA

BENIN

TOGO   O

LIBYA   O

Cairo ★

EGYPT

ASIA

Senegal's longtime presi-
dent, Léopold Senghor,
retires and is succeeded
by Abdou Diouf (Jan. 1,
1981).

Lamizana government
is overthrown in blood-
less coup by military
group led by Col. Sayé
Zerbo (Nov. 25, 1980).

U
NIGER

• Kano

NIGERIA
Lagos
D   ★

CHAD

N'Djamena

Riots by fanatical
Moslem cults result
in death toll of as
many as 10,000
(Dec. 1980).

SUDAN

Nile

Libyan armed forces enter
N'Djamena in support of
President Goukouni Oueddei
(Dec. 16, 1980). Libya's Col.
Qaddafi announces Chad-
Libya "merger" (Jan. 6,
1981).

Military group headed by
Gen. André Kolingba takes
over power from President
David Dacko (Sept. 1, 1981).
Dacko had been elected to
the presidency on March 15.

ETHIOPIA

CENTRAL
AFRICAN REPUBLIC

CAMEROON

Cabral government is
overthrown in coup
led by Premier Vieira
(Nov. 14, 1980).

EQUATORIAL GUINEA

GABON   Mn

CONGO

★ Kinshasa

D

Five Nigerian soldiers
killed in Nigerian-Cam-
eroonian border dis-
pute (May 16, 1981).

Congo

ZAIRE

RWANDA

BURUNDI

UGANDA

KENYA

SOMALIA

Milton Obote is elec-
ted president of Ugan-
da (Dec. 1980).

South African troops in-
vade southern Angola in
pursuit of Namibian guer-
rillas (Aug. 24, 1981).
United States vetoes UN
Security Council resolu-
tion rebuking South Africa
for action (Aug. 31).

ANGOLA

ZAMBIA

Cu
Cu

TANZANIA

COMOROS

MALAWI

ATLANTIC

ZIMBABWE
Cr

NAMIBIA

BOTSWANA

MOZAMBIQUE

MADAGASCAR

OCEAN

D

Mn
D

U Cr
Au

SWAZILAND

SOUTH   LESOTHO
AFRICA

Cape Town ★

MAJOR MINERAL
DEPOSITS

Al Bauxite
Au Gold
Cr Chromium
Cu Copper
D   Diamonds
Fe Iron Ore
Mn Manganese
O   Oil
U   Uranium

U.S. cuts off food aid
to Mozambique (March 13,
1981) following expulsion
of 4 U.S. embassy offi-
cials on alleged spy
charges (March 4).

INDIAN

OCEAN

Ciskei area votes in
favor of independence
(Dec. 4, 1980). South
African Senate is a-
bolished (Jan. 1,
1981). National party
is victor in elections
for Assembly seats
(April 29, 1981).

© Copyright HAMMOND INCORPORATED, Maplewood, N.J.

QUEEN ELIZABETH ISLANDS

ARCTIC OCEAN

Ellesmere I.

GREENLAND

Baffin Island

Victoria I.

NORTHWEST TERRITORIES

Yellowknife

BEAUFORT SEA

Mackenzie R.

YUKON TERRITORY

ALASKA

UNITED STATES

BRITISH COLUMBIA

Vancouver

ALBERTA

Edmonton

SASKATCH-EWAN

MANITOBA

Winnipeg

HUDSON BAY

Labrador

NEWFOUNDLAND

ONTARIO

QUÉBEC

Québec

Montréal

Ottawa

Montebello

Toronto

P.E.I.

NEW BRUNSWICK

NOVA SCOTIA

Halifax

ST. PIERRE & MIQUELON (Fr.)

UNITED STATES

PACIFIC OCEAN

CANADA

> 1981 Census taken across Canada (June 3).
> Postal workers' strike of 43 days ends on Aug. 10, 1981.

> Progressive Conservative party of Premier Davis gains 12 provincial legislature seats in March 18, 1981, Ontario elections.

> Premier René Levesque's Parti Québecois wins 80 seats in provincial legislature elections on April 13, 1981, a gain of 13.

> Government leaders of seven top industrial nations meet to discuss world economic issues (July 19-21, 1981).

> Nova Scotian offshore waters opened to oil exploration (April 1981).

> Federal government and Alberta reach accord on oil prices (Sept. 1, 1981).

© Copyright HAMMOND INCORPORATED, Maplewood, N.J.

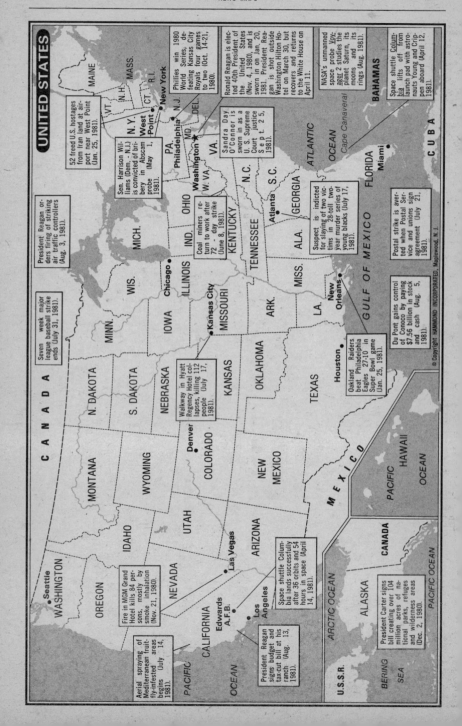

UNITED STATES

52 freed U.S. hostages from Iran land at airport near West Point (Jan. 25, 1981).

Sen. Harrison Williams (Dem. - N.J.) is convicted of bribery in Abscam probe (May 1, 1981).

Ronald Reagan is elected 40th President of the United States (Nov. 4, 1980), and is sworn in on Jan. 20, 1981. President Reagan is shot outside Washington Hilton Hotel on March 30, but recovers and returns to the White House on April 11.

Phillies win 1980 World Series, defeating Kansas City Royals four games to two (Oct. 14-21, 1980).

Sandra Day O'Connor is sworn in as a U. S. Supreme Court justice (Sept. 25, 1981).

NASA's unmanned space probe Voyager 2 studies the planet Saturn, its moons and its rings (Aug. 1981).

Space shuttle Columbia lifts off from launch pad with astronauts Young and Crippen aboard (April 12, 1981).

President Reagan orders firing of striking air traffic controllers (Aug. 3, 1981).

Coal miners return to work after 72 - day strike (June 8, 1981).

Seven week major league baseball strike ends (July 31, 1981).

Suspect is indicted for slaying of two victims in 28-toll two-year murder series of young blacks (July 17, 1981).

Postal strike is averted when Postal Service and unions sign agreement (July 21, 1981).

Walkway in Hyatt Regency Hotel collapses, killing 112 people (July 17, 1981).

Du Pont gains control of Conoco by paying $7.56 billion in stock and cash (Aug. 5, 1981).

Oakland Raiders beat Philadelphia Eagles 27-10 in Super Bowl game (Jan. 25, 1981).

Fire in MGM Grand Hotel kills 84 persons, mostly by smoke inhalation (Nov. 21, 1980).

Space shuttle Columbia lands successfully after 36 orbits and 54 hours in space (April 14, 1981).

President Reagan signs budget and tax-cut bill at his ranch (Aug. 13, 1981).

Aerial spraying of Mediterranean fruit-fly-infested areas begins (July 14, 1981).

President Carter signs bill creating over 104 million acres of national parks, refuges and wilderness areas (Dec. 2, 1980).

© Copyright HAMMOND INCORPORATED, Maplewood, N.J.

Map labels

CANADA

WASHINGTON
Seattle

OREGON

PACIFIC OCEAN

CALIFORNIA
Edwards A.F.B.
Los Angeles

NEVADA
Las Vegas

IDAHO

MONTANA

WYOMING

UTAH

ARIZONA

COLORADO
Denver

NEW MEXICO

N. DAKOTA

S. DAKOTA

NEBRASKA

KANSAS

OKLAHOMA

TEXAS

MINN.

IOWA

MISSOURI
Kansas City

ARK.

LA.
New Orleans
Houston

WIS.

ILLINOIS
Chicago

MICH.

IND.

OHIO

KENTUCKY

TENNESSEE

MISS.

ALA.

GEORGIA
Atlanta

MAINE

VT. N.H.

MASS.

CT. R.I.

N.Y.
New York
West Point

PA.
Philadelphia

N.J.

DEL.

MD.

W. VA.

VA.

N.C.

S.C.

Washington

ATLANTIC OCEAN

FLORIDA
Miami

Cape Canaveral

GULF OF MEXICO

BAHAMAS

CUBA

MEXICO

HAWAII
PACIFIC OCEAN

ARCTIC OCEAN

ALASKA
CANADA

U.S.S.R.

BERING SEA

PACIFIC OCEAN

MIDDLE AMERICA

© Copyright HAMMOND INCORPORATED, Maplewood, N.J.

Government workers' strike cripples tourist industry (April - May 1981).

Thousands of Haitian economic refugees flee in small boats to U.S. (1980-81).

American FBI agents arrest 10 American and Canadian mercenaries in New Orleans before they can launch coup to take over Dominican government (April 27, 1981).

Bahamian police deport 102 Haitian refugees, shipwrecked on island in an attempt to reach Miami (Nov. 13, 1980).

Following election defeat of Michael Manley's People's National party, Philip Seaga of the moderate Jamaica Labour party is sworn in as prime minister (Nov. 1, 1980).

Eric Eustace Williams, Trinidad & Tobago's P.M. since independence in 1962, dies on March 29, 1981. He is succeeded by George M. Chambers.

Ecuadoran embassy is held by 29 Cubans in unsuccessful attempt to leave country (Feb. 13-21, 1981).

Britain and Guatemala sign treaty settling century-old Belize dispute (March 11, 1981). Belize becomes independent (Sept. 21).

Political violence continues.

Panamanian leader, Gen. Omar Torrijos Herrera, killed in plane crash (Aug. 1, 1981).

José Napoleón Duarte Fuentes becomes president (Dec. 13, 1980). Four-year violence continues.

U.S. withholds aid to Nicaragua as a result of Nicaraguan provision of staging areas for Salvadoran rebels (April 1, 1981).

Leftists kidnap an American missionary (Jan. 19, 1981) and kill him (March 7), claiming he served the CIA.

Prime Minister Forbes Burnham assumes presidency under new constitution (Oct. 6, 1980).

A three-man military junta takes over from President Garcia Meza (Aug. 4, 1981).

Ecuador and Peru briefly clash in border dispute (Jan. 28 - Feb. 2, 1981). President Roldos is killed in airplane crash (May 24).

Chilean voters approve new constitution (Sept. 11, 1980) which took effect in March 1981. President Pinochet takes oath of office under new charter on March 11, 1981, for eight-year term.

Electorate rejects draft constitution (Nov. 30, 1980). Gen. Gregorio Alvarez is selected as president (Aug. 1, 1981).

Gen. Roberto Eduardo Viola takes office as president (March 29, 1981). Ex-president Isabel Perón is sentenced to eight years in prison but is later released on parole (July 6).

CARIBBEAN SEA
WEST INDIES
ATLANTIC OCEAN
Caracas ★
VENEZUELA
Bogotá ★
COLOMBIA
GUYANA
SURINAME
FRENCH GUIANA
ECUADOR
Amazon
Belém
BRAZIL
Recife
PERU
Lima ★
La Paz ★
Brasília ★
BOLIVIA
PACIFIC
PARAGUAY
São Paulo
Rio de Janeiro
CHILE
OCEAN
Santiago ★
URUGUAY
Buenos Aires ★
ARGENTINA
ATLANTIC OCEAN
FALKLAND IS.

© Copyright HAMMOND INCORPORATED, Maplewood, N. J.

SOUTH AMERICA

'80/'81 MONTH-BY-MONTH CHRONOLOGY

OCTOBER 1980

NATIONAL

1 / Republican Ronald Reagan woos Democrats in New York City with moral support for federal aid to help rebuild the West Side Highway.

2 / The U.S. House of Representatives expels Rep. Michael Joseph (Ozzie) Myers (D.-Pa.) by a vote of 376-30 following his conviction Aug. 30 for bribery and conspiracy in the Abscam probe by the Federal Bureau of Investigation. It is the first such ouster since 1861, when three representatives were expelled for supporting the Confederacy during the Civil War.

Larry Holmes, 30, World Boxing Council heavyweight champion, easily retains his title when former three-time champion Muhammad Ali, 38, cannot answer the bell for the 11th round in a bout at Las Vegas.

3 / Republican Ronald Reagan affirms his support for permitting voluntary prayer in public schools while addressing a forum of the National Religious Broadcasters Association at Liberty Baptist College in Lynchburg, Va.

4 / The College Entrance Examination Board reports Scholastic Aptitude Test scores of college-bound high school students continue to drop, with the most obvious declines in mathematical and verbal skills.

5 / President Carter makes five temporary appointments to the board of the U.S. Synthetic Fuels Corporation.

6 / The U.S. Supreme Court refuses to review an appeals court ruling that an economic boycott against Missouri by the National Organization for Women did not violate the Sherman Anti-trust Act.

7 / Rep. John W. Jenrette, Jr. (D.-S.C.) and businessman John R. Stowe of Richmond, Va., are convicted of bribery and conspiracy in the Abscam probe by the Federal Bureau of Investigation.

8 / President Carter signs the Housing and Community Development Act of 1980 and creates a task force to evaluate the housing industry's prospects for the next 10 years.

10 / The Kansas City Royals clinch the American League baseball pennant by winning the third game against the New York Yankees by a score of 4-2 at Yankee Stadium in a best-of-five game series. The Royals swept the first and the second games, Oct. 8 and 9 at Kansas City, by scores of 7-2 and 3-2, respectively.

President Carter signs a bill providing federal grants to states to educate and aid Cuban, Haitian and Indochinese children.

12 / The Philadelphia Phillies beat the Houston Astros 8-7 in the final game of a five-game series and win the National League baseball pennant.

14 / The first public sale of one million shares of Genentech Inc. makes market history in New York. Minutes after trading started, the price per share for the genetic-engineering stock shot from $35 to $89.

15 / The White House dissociates itself from remarks made by Andrew Young, former U.S. representative to the United Nations, during a campaign speech for President Carter at Ohio State University.

16 / Ronald Reagan and running mate George Bush are endorsed by black civil rights leaders Rev. Ralph David Abernathy and Hosea Williams, leaders of the Southern Christian Leadership Conference.

17 / The nation's "real" adjusted gross national product shows a one percent growth in the third quarter, reports the Commerce Department. Real GNP, measured in 1972 dollars, increased to an annual rate of $1.412 trillion.

19 / A 17-year textile labor battle wanes in a 2½-year agreement reached by Stevens and Co. and the AFL-CIO Amalgamated Clothing and Textile Workers. The pact covers workers at 10 plants where the union won representation rights and will cover workers at 70 more plants if the union wins the same rights in the next 18 months.

20 / The U.S. Supreme Court refuses to review, thus letting stand, an Illinois court decision that a divorced mother must give up custody of her three children because she was living with a man who was not the children's natural father. The case was Jarrett v. Jarrett.

The Court also declines to review a challenge to the Food and Drug Administration's ban on the interstate sale and shipment of the purported cancer-curing drug Laetrille. The case was U.S. v. Rutherford.

21 / The Philadelphia Phillies of the National League win their first world championship, defeating the Kansas City Royals of the American League by a score of 4-1 in the sixth game of the 1980 World Series at Philadelphia. The Phillies took the best four-of-seven series by winning the first two and last two games.

22 / Republican Ronald Reagan declines further comment on the holding of 52 Americans by Iran. Reagan says lives of the hostages are at stake and should not become a political issue.

23 / The Screen Actors Guild and the American Federation of Television and Radio Artists end a three-month strike, approving a new three-year contract by a five-to-one margin.

24 / Workers in four of the nation's major copper-mining companies remain on strike despite settlements by Kennecott Corp. and Phelps Dodge Corp., the nation's largest and second-largest producers, respectively. Still negotiating are Anaconda Copper Co., Anamax Mining Co., Sarco Inc. and Newmont Mining Co.

The Labor Department reports the Consumer Price Index rose a seasonally adjusted one percent in September.

U.S. Supreme Court Justice William J. Brennan, Jr., temporarily enjoins the government from transferring about 2,000 Cuban and Haitian refugees in Florida to a military base in Puerto Rico.

27 / General Motors Corp. reports a third-quarter net loss of $567 million. The announcement is followed Oct. 28 by a similar report from Ford Motor Co., claiming a $595-million loss, and Oct. 29 by a $489.7-million third-quarter loss statement from Chrysler Corp.

29 / The U.S. Treasury Dept. and the Office of Management and Budget report the federal deficit for fiscal 1980 is $59.96 billion, twice that at the end of 1979 and the second-largest deficit in U.S. history.

30 / Sen. Harrison A. Williams, Jr. (D.-N.J.) and three associates are indicted on charges of bribery, conspiracy and related counts for allegedly seeking a loan and titanium mining stock in return for for political favors.

INTERNATIONAL

2 / The People's Republic of China denounces as "unacceptable" an agreement of reciprocal nondiplomatic immunity, signed in Washington, D.C., by members of the American Institute in Taiwan and the Coordination Council for North American Affairs.

3 / West German Chancellor Helmut Schmidt wins the chancellorship as the coalition of Social Democrats (SPD) and Free Democrats (FDP) increases its majority in the Bundestag from 10 to 45 seats.

4 / Four thousand people die in two earthquakes that devastate El Asnam in northern Algeria. The first quake registered 7.7 on the Richter scale and hit shortly after noon. The second quake, four hours later, registered 6.5.

13 / The UN General Assembly votes 74-35, with 32 abstentions against a resolution that would have ousted the UN representative of the Pol Pot regime that ruled Cambodia before it was toppled by guerrillas backed by Vietnamese troops. Approving the resolution, say its opponents, would recognize a puppet government in Phnom Penh headed by Heng Samrin.

14 / Most of Canada's 47,000 striking federal government clerks end their 15-day walkout after the government grants wage hikes of about 25 percent over a two-year period but no cost-of-living increases or shorter workweek.

15 / French President Valéry Giscard d'Estaing arrives in China to visit Communist Party Chairman Hua Guofeng, Vice Chairman Deng Xiaoping, and Premier Zhao Ziyang just two days before it is announced China would purchase two 900-Mw nuclear atomic reactors from France at a cost of about $950 million each.

Fiat auto manufacturing company reaches an agreement with its striking workers in Turin, Italy, after a month's shutdown. The strike started over the planned dismissal of 14,500 employees and cost Fiat about $580 million in lost production, the workers about $70 million in lost wages.

16 / The Sri Lanka Parliament votes 139-18 to expel former prime minister Sirimavo Bandaranaike and revoke her civil rights for seven years. She keeps her post as nominal head of the Sri Lanka Freedom Party.

China detonates a nuclear device in the atmosphere at the Lop Nor test site, the first such test since December 1978 and much smaller than the November 1976 explosion, estimated to have equaled about four million tons of TNT.

18 / Australian Prime Minister Malcolm Fraser is returned to power for a second time as the coalition of his Liberal Party and the National Country Party retains a majority in the lower house of Parliament. The opposing Labour Party gains more seats but not enough for control.

19 / A convention of the American Society of Travel Agents is aborted in Manila when 20 people are injured from a bomb explosion shortly after Philippine Pres. Ferdinand Marcos addresses 5,000 delegates. The April 6 Liberation Movement had warned several agents to cancel the convention. On Oct. 30 Marcos orders the arrest of 30 persons, most of them living in the U.S.

20 / NATO's Defense Planning Committee unanimously approves Greece's return to the alliance's integrated military organization. Greece had withdrawn in protest from NATO in 1974 when Turkey, also a NATO member, sent combat forces into Cyprus to take control of the northern section of the island.

21 / Soviet President Leonid Brezhnev reports to the Communist Party Central Committee that food shortages in Russia are an increasing problem and that the 1980 grain harvest was a poor one.

22 / South Korean voters approve constitutional changes that guarantee human rights, reinstate habeas corpus, outlaw torture of prisoners and limit the president to one seven-year term.

23 / Soviet Premier Aleksey N. Kosygin, 76, resigns because of ill health and is succeeded by his first deputy, Nikolai A. Tikhonov, 75, an economic planner.

24 / A three-judge Warsaw court grants legal status to Solidarity, Poland's new independent federation of trade unions; but notes an amendment to the federal charter that declares the Polish Communist Party plays a "leading role" in national affairs and cites socialism as the keystone of Polish society.

27 / Cuba pardons and releases 30 U.S. prisoners in an apparent goodwill gesture by Cuban President Fidel Castro. Five of those freed were arrested when they landed in Miami, Fla., four on charges of plane hijacking, one on a charge of violating parole. Three others facing serious charges in the U.S. elected to stay in Cuba.

28 / Saudi Arabia severs diplomatic relations with Libya following a series of speeches by Libyan leader Col. Muammar el Qaddafi, who criticized Saudis for accepting four radar surveillance planes from the U.S.

29 / Nine persons die and 81 are injured when a bomb explodes inside the main Beijing (Peking) railway terminal. China's news agency reports "an unknown person" was responsible.

30 / The Jamaica Labour Party, led by Edward Seaga, captures 51 of 60 seats in the House of Representatives and topples Jamaican Prime Minister Michael Manley, leader of the People's National Party. Manley was head of government for eight years.

31 / Muhammad Jawad Baqir Tunguyan, Iran's prime minister of petroleum, and several other officials are captured by Iraqi troops near the Iranian oil refining center of Abadan. Iran protests the capture as a violation of international law, but Iraq maintains those captured are prisoners of war, not hostages like the U.S. citizens Iran seized in November 1979.

NOVEMBER 1980

NATIONAL

3 / The U.S. Supreme Court refuses to review appeal by former U.S. Rep. Michael J. Myers (D.-Pa.) of his indictment and conviction in first Abscam trial. Myers was convicted Aug. 31 for bribery and conspiracy and expelled Oct. 2 from House of Representatives.

Court lifts its temporary ban on the opening of a refugee camp in Puerto Rico and clears way for transferring Haitian and Cuban refugees from Florida to the island.

4 / Ronald Wilson Reagan, a conservative Republican and former governor of California, is elected the 40th President of the United States, soundly defeating incumbent Democratic Pres. Jimmy Carter. Reagan receives more than 43.6 million votes, Carter just over 35.5 million. The electoral vote score is 489 to 49, representing a Reagan victory in all but six states and the District of Columbia. Election also gives Republicans control of Senate for first time since 1956. Democrats lose 34 seats in House of Representatives but retain their majority. John Anderson, Republican running as an Independent, receives about 5.3 million votes.

5 / Federal judge in Washington awards $4.9 million to families of former Chilean ambassador Orlando Letelier and his aide, Ronni Moffitt, both killed in bomb blast in Washington Sept. 21. Judge says Chile should pay $2.9 million of the award because agents of the Chilean secret police, DINA, were the assassins. The remaining $2 million, judge rules, should come from Juan Manuel Contreras, former head of DINA, and five assassins, including an American, Michael Vernon Townley.

6 / W. Mark Felt, former acting associate director of the Federal Bureau of Investigation, and Edward S. Miller, former chief of the FBI's intelligence division, are convicted by a jury in federal district court at Washington, D.C., of conspiring to violate constitutional rights of American citizens by authorizing federal agents to break into homes and offices, without warrants, during 1972-73 in search of fugitive members of Weather Underground. Among those testifying were former President Richard M. Nixon and five former U.S. attorneys general.

Five top homicide investigators from throughout nation sent to Atlanta, Ga., to aid investigation of unsolved abductions and slayings there of at least 15 black children during previous fifteen months.

7 / American Motors Corp. reports third-quarter loss of $84.9 million, compounding similar loss in the second quarter. Company ended 1980 fiscal year Sept. 30 with record loss of $155.7 million on sales of $2.68 billion.

8 / Steelworkers union at Kellogg, Idaho, ends eight-month strike against Sunshine Mining Co., assuring resumed production at nation's richest silver mine. New four-year contract with Kellogg members of AFL-CIO United Steelworkers of America boosts hourly wage during life of agreement from $8.86 to $10.51 for about 550 miners and clerical workers.

10 / FMC Corp. pleads guilty to obstructing Environmental Protection Agency in its search for source of pollution in drinking water at Huntington, W. Va. Court orders FMC to pay $35,000 fine and contribute $1 million to water pollution research fund.

Company was charged with dumping 3,000 pounds of carbon tetrachloride into Kanawha River every day from South Charleston plant but admitted to daily disposal of only few hundred pounds.

14 / Federal Reserve Board announces it is hiking its discount rate from 11 percent to 12 percent because of a rapid rise in demand for bank credit.

U.S. Supreme Court drops title "Mr. Justice" for all members but doesn't explain why. Conjecture is that deletion is prelude to appointment of first woman justice.

17 / An all-white jury in Greensboro, N.C., acquits six Ku Klux Klansmen and Nazis of murder and of felonious rioting at anti-Klan rally in Greensboro, Nov. 3, 1979. Dead included five Communist Worker Party demonstrators, four white men, and one black woman, all preparing a "Death to the Klan" rally when fighting broke out with Klansmen and Nazis.

18 / U.S. Air Force narrows preferred selection of bases for proposed MX nuclear missile to two locations in Nevada and Utah. Governors of Nevada, Utah, Texas and New Mexico had all protested situating bases in their states.

President-elect Reagan tells reporters he agrees with critics of busing for school desegregation that the program has failed and he supports legislation that would prohibit Justice Department from taking up cases that would promote such court-ordered programs.

19 / Airlift of Cuban refugees begins as first plane carrying 120 refugees arrives in Miami from Havana. New arrivals are some of approximately 600 Cubans stranded at port of Mariel when Cuban government closed port, ending boatlift of refugees to U.S. in September.

20 / Congress approves a Fiscal 1981 budget of $632.4 billion, including a deficit of $27.4 billion, based on projected revenue of $605 billion for fiscal year, which started Oct. 1.

President-elect Reagan and wife, Nancy, visit President Carter and wife, Rosalynn, at the White House. Visit lasts about 90 minutes.

Reagan meets privately with West German Chancellor Helmut Schmidt.

21 / Second-worst hotel fire in U.S. history sweeps through the lower floors of the MGM Grand Hotel in Las Vegas just after dawn, killing 84 persons and injuring at least 500. Most victims were trapped between 19th and 30th floors of luxury hotel and apparently died of smoke inhalation as poisonous fumes and billowing smoke shot upwards.

23 / Caspar W. Weinberger, chairman of Reagan's Economic Policy Coordinating Committee, urges "severe cuts" in federal spending; says he believes Reagan favors holding federal spending in 1981 to $620 billion or less.

24 / Senate approves bill to establish fund for cleaning up chemical dumps and toxic waste spills; votes for $1.6 billion "superfund" to finance effort. Most of the money would come from new taxes on chemical industry.

25 / Ford Motor Co. and federal government announce settlement of job discrimination case involving women employees and members of minorities. Company agrees to spend $23 million for special training programs, set aside $10 million more for developing skills required for better jobs, make hourly rate and salary adjustment awards totaling $13 million, and hire 200 minority men, 170 white women and 90 minority women for craft positions by 1982.

INTERNATIONAL

2 / Iranian Majlis (parliament) approves conditions for release of 52 U.S. hostages. Proposed terms are basically the same as those demanded Sept. 12 by Ayatollah Ruhollah Khomeini but move negotiations closer to resolution.

6 / Representative of 23 Islamic states conclude three-day meeting in Ankara, Turkey, after approving 10-point program for improved cooperation in science, technology, industry, agriculture, communications, health, and finance.

7 / Tanzanian Pres. Julius Nyerere names new Cabinet following election Oct. 26 to a fourth five-year term; appoints Cleopa David Msuya prime minister and Salim Ahmed Salim foreign minister.

8 / Sadegh Ghotbzadeh, former Iranian foreign minister, is arrested for alleging that state broadcasting system is controlled by Islamic fundamentalists. Ayatollah Ruhollah Khomeini ordered Ghotbzadeh's release Nov. 10.

Israel's Labor Party causes furor by endorsing proposed Jordanian-Palestinian state that would extend beyond Jordan into West Bank and include Gaza Strip.

10 / Warren Christopher, U.S. deputy secretary of state, arrives in Algeria as head of team of U.S. government officials carrying U.S. response to conditions demanded by Iranian Majlis for release of 52 U.S. hostages.

Michael Foot, British MP for 30 years, elected by his Labour Party colleagues to lead his constituency. Foot defeated Denis Healey in runoff election and took over post vacated in October by former prime minister James Callaghan.

U.S. International Trade Commission rules that serious financial problems of U.S. car manufacturers do not warrant restricting importation of cars and light trucks into U.S.

12 / U.S. unmanned spacecraft Voyager I comes within 125,000 kilometers (77,000 miles) of planet Saturn and reveals planet has many more rings than suspected. Photographs made by spacecraft also show three more moons, increasing total known to 15.

Political Renovation Committee of South Korea releases names of 811 politicians banned from political activities until end of 1988 as part of purge for start of Fifth Republic. By Nov. 25 government clears and reinstates 268 of 586 on list who filed appeals.

14 / Lech Walesa, head of Solidarity, Poland's independent federation of trade unions, meets for 90 minutes with Communist Party Leader Stanislaw Kania; next day urges an end to wildcat strikes.

Luis de Almeida Cabral, president of small African nation of Guinea-Bissau since independence in 1974, is ousted by Premier Joao Bernardo Vieira. The black socialist opposed Cabral's plan to unite Guinea-Bissau with racially mixed Cape Verde.

15 / Pope John Paul II arrives in Cologne, West Germany, for five-day religious pilgrimage to bolster Roman Catholic Church and improve relations with Protestant churches; first visit to Germany by a pope since 1782. Pontiff quotes Martin Luther several times, expresses a willingness to study ways for reconciliation with Lutheran churches, and hears young Catholics in Munich challenge Roman Catholic teachings on sexual behavior and role of women in church.

20 / Beijing (Peking) court opens trial of Jiang Jing (Chiang Ch'ing), leader of the Gang of Four, and nine of her associates, five of them former high-ranking military officers. Jiang Jing is widow of the late Chinese Communist Party chairman Mao Zedong (Mao Tse-tung) and with others is accused of trying to overthrow dictatorship of proletariat.

23 / Earthquake measuring 6.9 on Richter scale devastates southern Italy, killing more than 3,000 people; hardest hit are provinces of Naples, Salerno, Potenza and Avelino.

24 / Democratic Action Congress party wins eight of 12 seats in Tobago's first parliamentary election. Victors favored autonomy from Trinidad, the relatively rich island that had dominated Tobago since 1889. Great Britain granted the two Caribbean islands independence in 1962 and they formed one nation.

25 / Government of Sangoule Lamizana, president of Upper Volta in northwest Africa, tumbles in military coup by Col. Saye Zerbo. Upper Volta is one of world's poorest nations. Lamizana seized power in 1966 but was elected president in 1978.

27 / Arab League ends three-day summit meeting in Amman, Jordan, despite a boycott by Algeria, Lebanon, Libya, Southern Yemen, Syria and Palestine Liberation Organization. Syria had asked League to postpone conference until internal conflicts among Arab countries (divided loyalties in Iran-Iraq war) were resolved.

28 / Haitian police begin arrest of about 200 persons, labeled as Communist agitators, in largest roundup of critics of the government since Jean-Claude

Duvalier became president in 1971. Included were many journalists, politicians, teachers, students and human rights activists.

DECEMBER 1980

NATIONAL

1 / President-elect Ronald Reagan assures National League of Cities that his first priority is national economy: cities will have more control over use of federal funds during his administration.

2 / President Carter signs Alaska land bill, designating more than 104 million acres of national parks, wildlife refuges and wilderness areas.

State Republicans name Sen. Howard Baker, Jr. (Tenn.), majority leader for incoming 97th Congress.

3 / Reps. Frank Thompson, Jr. (D.-N.J.), and John M. Murphy (D.-N.Y.) are found guilty of charges arising from Abscam investigation. Thompson is convicted of bribery and conspiracy, conflict of interest and accepting an unlawful gratuity, but is found innocent of bribery.

House votes 274-94 to accept Senate-passed bill that establishes a $1.6 billion fund for cleaning up chemical dumps and toxic-waste spills.

4 / Gov. Ella Grasso (D.-Conn.), 61, announces she will resign Dec. 31 because ill health has reduced stamina needed to continue in office. Medical tests following surgery for ovarian cancer previous spring reveal malignancy has spread to her liver. She is succeeded Dec. 31 by Lt. Gov. William A. O'Neill, elected on ticket with her in 1978.

Federal Reserve Board raises discount rate from 12 percent to 13 percent.

Stuart E. Eizenstat, chief domestic policy adviser to President Carter, urges greater role in party affairs for Democratic members of Congress and governors. Many Democratic leaders, he says, feel party has lost touch with middle class.

5 / AFL-CIO president Lane Kirkland says federation may break tradition and endorse political candidates at start of campaigns rather than waiting for official nominations.

Chrysler Corp. and Ford Motor Co. announce plans to promote sales of their 1981 model cars. Chrysler will give sliding-scale rebates ranging from $300-800 per car. Ford will provide direct interest subsidies to customers buying certain Ford models on credit, assuring carrying charges no greater than 12 percent.

Physician, journalist and author Dr. Michael J. Halberstam is shot and killed after surprising burglar in the physician's apartment in Washington, D.C. Dr. Halberstam bled to death while undergoing surgery. Charged with shooting was a convicted burglar, Bernard Charles Welch, Jr., of Great Falls, Va.

7 / Select Commission on Immigration and Refugee Policy recommends illegal aliens in U.S. be granted legal status and permanent immigration quota be raised from 270,000 to 350,000 annually.

Mass transit service in Boston and eastern Massachusetts ends one-day shutdown when Gov. Edward J. King signs bill assuring funds to keep system operating through Dec. 31.

8 / Former Beatles rock musician and composer John Lennon, 40, is shot and killed in New York City by man arrested by police and identified as Mark David Chapman, 25, of Honolulu, a former suicidal psychiatric patient. Lennon was hit five times by bullets from a .38-caliber handgun as he stepped from a limousine into archway of Dakota apartment building on New York's West Side.

9 / Chrysler Corp. announces plans to close two plants manufacturing K-cars the week before start of automotive industry's annual shutdown.

New York Stock Exchange reports 18.1 percent increase in shareholders from June 1975 to June 1980, listing a current total of 29.8 million individual shareholders.

10 / Rep. John W. Jenrette, Jr. (D.-S.C.), resigns from House to avoid expulsion following conviction in October on charges of bribe-taking and conspiracy in the Abscam investigation.

Federal jury in Chicago indicts 11 members of FALN, Puerto Rican terrorist group, on charges of terrorism and violence in connection with 28 bombings in Chicago area between June 1975 and November 1979.

11 / U.S. District Court Judge William B. Bryant dismisses 2½-year-old charges that attorney L. Patrick Gray approved illegal break-ins when he was acting director of Federal Bureau of Investigation during Nixon Administration.

President-elect Ronald Reagan announces eight Cabinet-level appointments: Donald T. Regan, Secretary of the Treasury; Caspar W. Weinberger, Secretary of Defense; Malcolm Baldridge, Secretary of Commerce; Sen. Richard S. Schweiker (R.-Pa.), Secretary of Health and Human Services; Andrew L. (Drew) Lewis, Jr., Secretary of Transportation; Rep. David A. Stockton (R.-Mich.), Director of the Office of Management and Budget; William French Smith, Attorney General; William J. Casey, Director of Central Intelligence.

12 / Union representing 6,400 Los Angeles city employees announces ratification of new two-year contract with 19 percent pay raise.

Golden Nugget, operator of casinos in Las Vegas, opens new $160-million hotel-casino in Atlantic City, bringing to six the number of such operations in the New Jersey resort.

14 / Former workers of Darlington Manufacturing Co., in Florence, S.C., which closed in 1956, approve a $5-million settlement of dispute over back pay. Workers are members of the AFL-CIO Amalgamated Clothing and Textile Workers Union.

16 / For first time in 30 years Export-Import Bank decides not to pay a dividend to U.S. Treasury and keeps all its 1980 proceeds, which amount to $109.6 million.

17 / Federal jury in San Antonio, Texas, acquits Charles Veverka, Jr., white former Dade County, Fla., police officer, of conspiring to cover up fatal beating of Arthur McDuffie, black insurance executive, in 1979.

18 / Gov. Carlos Romero Barcelo is declared winner of Puerto Rico's Nov. 4 gubernatorial election in which Rafael Hernandez Colon had originally been reported victor. Final totals gave Romero 759,540 votes, Hernandez, 756,037.

19 / Most large U.S. banks raise prime interest rate to record 21.5 percent.

20 / Flight attendants for Continental Airlines end two-week strike with settlement calling for 20.5 percent increase over 27 months.

22 / Federal Bureau of Land Management announces plan to manage and protect 12.1 million acres of California desert.

24 / Environmental Protection Agency issues final regulations limiting noise on new motorcycles after Jan. 1, 1983, to 83 decibels, scaling down to 80 decibels by Jan. 1, 1986.

27 / President Jimmy Carter breaks his collarbone while cross-country skiing near Camp David, Md.

29 / Advisory panel to President Carter recommends helping residents of declining cities to move to suburbs or sun belt in search of jobs. Recommendation contradicts President's national urban policy.

INTERNATIONAL

2 / President Carter warns Russia that U.S.-Soviet relations would be seriously affected by a Soviet invasion of Poland. All nine members of European Economic Community express same view.

4 / UNESCO estimates one third of world's population can neither read nor write, forecasts that total number of such persons will increase by 70 million during next decade, and India will have largest number of uneducated persons at turn of century.

Portuguese Premier Francisco Sá Carneiro and eight others are killed in plane crash near Lisbon.

5 / Fears of a Soviet invasion of Poland wane slightly as members of Warsaw Pact, including Russia, express confidence that Poland will retain its socialist government without damage.

6 / In first Taiwan election of Legislative Yuan and the National Assembly since 1977, ruling Kuomintang (KMT) members capture 57 of 70 contested seats in 360-seat legislature and 63 of 76 contested seats in National Assembly.

8 / Edgar Z. Tekere, head of Zimbabwe's manpower, planning and development ministry, is freed by a Salisbury court despite his conviction for murdering white farmer in early August; court's decision is based on 1975 law protecting government officials from antiterrorist activities.

10 / Soviet Pres. Leonid Brezhnev addresses Indian Parliament with proposal of "peace and security" for Persian Gulf. Brezhnev seeks pledge from all major powers not to use or threaten to use force against countries around Persian Gulf and not to interfere in their internal affairs.

Tension between Jordan and Syria abates as both countries agree to withdraw troops from border separating the two nations.

11 / U.S. rejects Russian request for pledges of non-intervention in Persian Gulf area saying there can be no security in region while Soviet troops remain in Afghanistan.

13 / Uganda's state electoral commission announces election victory of Uganda People's Congress and second term for Pres. Milton Obote but Democratic Party charges four-party race was tainted by fraud and intimidation and demands new election supervised by independent commission.

16 / Libyan troops, at request of Goukouni Oueddei president of Chad, drive troops loyal to Premier Hissene Habre out of the nation's capital with artillery and aircraft. Habre flees to Cameroon and signs a cease-fire agreement worked out by the Organization of African Unity.

18 / Aleksey N. Kosygin, chairman of Soviet Union's Council of Ministers for 16 years, dies in Moscow. Ill health forced 76-year-old leader to relinquish premiership in late October. An elaborate state funeral honors Kosygin, whose ashes are placed in wall of Kremlin.

21 / Iranian minister of state for executive affairs declares during a news conference in Tehran that "it is very easy" for U.S. to meet Iran's demand for $24 billion as ransom for 52 American hostages. U.S. Secretary of State Edmund Muskie calls demand "unreasonable."

25 / Iraqi Pres. Saddam Hussein announces Iraqi forces had moved into Iran's Kurdistan province the previous week.

26 / Abdelkarim Gheraieb, Algerian ambassador to Iran, announces he visited all 52 U.S. hostages in Tehran and found "the conditions of their present existence satisfactory." The ambassador and an official from Algerian Foreign Ministry were allowed to visit hostages to counter rumors that some were in jail and others in poor health.

27 / About 5,000 Afghans attack Soviet embassy in Tehran, Iran, on first anniversary of Soviet invasion of their country. Some Afghans climb over embassy walls and smash windows until driven off by Iranian security guards. Crowd then demonstrates at the Afghan embassy. Two days later, in Kabul, capital of Afghanistan, anti-Soviet and antigovernment demonstrators stone vehicles until Soviet tanks and soldiers take control of streets.

28 / Mexico announces it will terminate all existing fishing agreements with U.S. Decision follows several years of unsuccessful negotiations to determine each country's fishing rights. In July, U.S. embargoed Mexican tuna imports after Mexico arrested six San Diego (Calif.)-based tuna seiners for fishing in Mexican waters.

29 / The most important criminal trials in modern Chinese history end in Beijing (Peking), but sentencing of 10 defendants is delayed; central figure in trial was Jiang Jing (Chiang Ch'ing), 67-year-old widow of party chairman Mao Zedong (Mao Tse-tung). She and other defendants are accused of trying to take control of government.

JANUARY 1981

NATIONAL

1 / Administrators regain control after 600 inmates at Washington state prison go on New Year's Eve rampage.

Officials at Lafayette Parish (La.) prison quell six-hour riot by inmates.

2 / Federal officials probe claim by Florida state prison inmate that he routinely beat fellow inmates with approval of prison guards. One victim died.

Washington, D.C., Superior Court Judge Nicholas S. Nunzio frees Abdul Hamin, one of 12 Hanafi Muslims convicted in 1977 takeover of three Washington buildings and holding of 149 hostages. Hamin had served three years of 36-to-108-year prison term.

7 / President Carter asks Congress to raise pay of 34,000 top federal officials by 16.8 percent and pay of all civilian workers 5.5 percent; proposal would raise yearly salaries of Cabinet members from $69,630 to $81,328, of members of Congress from $60,662 to $70,853.

8 / Baltimore (Md.) judge sentences former U.S. intelligence agent David H. Barnett to 18 years in prison after conviction on charges of passing U.S. secrets and names of 30 U.S. agents to the KGB, Soviet intelligence agency.

Power failure hits Utah and parts of Idaho and Wyoming; more than 1.5 million people lose electrical service for six hours.

9 / Rep. Raymond F. Lederer (D.-Pa.), only representative indicted in Abscam to be reelected in 1980, found guilty of bribery and conspiracy in accepting $50,000 bribe in 1979 from U.S. agents posing as Arab sheiks.

12 / Supreme Court rules Tax Reform Act of 1975 can be applied retroactively.

14 / Record three-day freeze ends in Florida after wide damage to citrus and vegetable crops from temperatures as low as 8° Fahrenheit.

15 / Rallies throughout nation commemorate birthday of Rev. Martin Luther King, Jr., slain civil rights leader. Congress criticized for not declaring Jan. 15 national holiday to honor memory of Rev. King.

Four-state Delaware River Basin Commission bans nonessential use of water in 462 communities to counter growing water shortage. Commission includes governors of New York, New Jersey, Pennsylvania and Delaware.

Congress receives President Carter's final budget proposal for 1982, which includes an 11.5 percent increase in federal spending for the year to start Oct. 1. Projected is a federal outlay of $739.3 billion based on anticipated receipts of $711.8 billion; budget leaves an anticipated deficit of $27.5 billion.

16 / President Carter opposes presidential commission's recommendation favoring migration of people from older Northern cities to the sun belt.

19 / Pre-inaugural festivities for President-elect Ronald Wilson Reagan draw about 18,000 persons to Washington's Capital Centre sports arena.

New York City Mayor Edward Koch declares drought emergency and orders fines of up to $1,000 for violations of ban on nonessential uses of water.

20 / Ronald Wilson Reagan is sworn in as the 40th President of the United States, at age 69 the oldest man ever to assume the office. George Herbert Walker Bush is sworn in as Vice President.

As President Reagan concludes his inaugural address, detention of 52 American hostages by Iran comes to an end; the first of two Algerian airliners carrying the hostages leaves Tehran's Mehabad Airport.

21 / Senate votes 93-6 to confirm Alexander Haig as secretary of state, opponents objecting to what they consider his moral insensitivity, backers praising what they view as "Haig grit."

Supreme Court votes 7-2 to revoke citizenship of Feodor Federenko, 73, Ukrainian who entered the U.S. in 1949, after learning he served as a Nazi prison guard in WW II. He became a naturalized citizen in 1970.

23 / U.S. State Department lawyers assure U.S. companies and individuals with claims against Iran that compensation procedures will be part of hostage accord.

25 / Oakland Raiders win National Football League championship, beating Philadelphia Eagles 27-10 in Super Bowl XV at Louisiana Superdome in New Orleans before 75,000 fans and national TV audience.

The 52 former hostages from Iran fly from Wiesbaden, Germany, to a military airport outside West Point, N.Y.; President Reagan gives White House reception for hostages' relatives.

26 / Former Rep. Richard Kelly (R.-Fla.) and two co-defendants are convicted in Abscam probe of

bribery, conspiracy and interstate travel to further illegal activity. The co-defendants: Eugene Ciuzio, Longwood, Fla., businessman, and Stanley Weiz, Smithtown, N.Y., accountant.

29 / President Reagan, in his first news conference since assuming office, announces 60-day freeze on pending government regulations and new steps to fight inflation, denounces Soviet intentions and renounces revenge on Iran for taking U.S. hostages as unworthy of America.

30 / Ticker-tape parade in New York City draws millions of people celebrating return of 52 hostages from Iran.

INTERNATIONAL

1 / Israeli army report claims attacks in 1980 against Palestine Liberation Organization, especially in Lebanon, "paralyzed" PLO and sharply cut Israeli casualties from PLO raids.

2 / Syria denies Jordanian charges that Syrian troops machine-gunned to death 200 civilians in Aleppo during the previous week. Syria says troops killed nine terrorists.

Group calling itself Secret Army for Liberation of Armenia threatens to attack all Swiss diplomats in retaliation for alleged Swiss mistreatment of two Armenian prisoners.

3 / World Bank reports it canceled $250-million loan to India. Prime Minister Indira Gandhi protests.

4 / Sources in New York and Moscow report the number of Jews allowed to leave the Soviet Union in 1980 was almost 60 percent less than in 1979 and the number of Armenians allowed to leave almost doubled.

Israeli Cabinet upholds Dec. 31, 1980, removal of Herzl Shafir as national police chief by approving appointment of Aryeh Izvan as Shafir's replacement.

5 / Nigerian government expels Libyan diplomatic mission in Lagos after Libyan embassy changed to "People's Bureau."

6 / Libya announces merger with Chad three weeks after Libyan troops helped victorious faction in Chad's prolonged civil war enter the capital city of Ndjamena.

Canada announces it will reluctantly provide C$900 million over a three-year period in special low-rate export financing under a policy of "credit mixte."

7 / Australia's Victorian State Electricity Commission discloses A$3.5 billion plans for two 2,000 megawatt coal-fired power plants in the Latrobe Valley.

Poland's Solidarity receives $160,000 donation for office equipment and supplies from AFL-CIO workers in U.S.

U.S. Department of State, in response to protest from Canadian government, reports it has ordered U.S. consulates in Canada to stop using private American citizens living in Canada as selective service registrars for the military draft.

9 / Size of new Soviet attack submarine "Oscar" stuns U.S. Navy and intelligence communities, *Washington Post* reports; "Oscar" said to be twice as large as any U.S. attack sub—and fast.

10 / Zimbabwe Prime Minister Robert Mugabe demotes Home Foreign Affairs Minister Joshua Nkomo and dismisses Edgar Z. Tekere, manpower and planning minister.

Millions of Polish workers defy government and take the day off to demonstrate demand for five-day, 40-hour work week.

11 / British seamen strike to support demand for 16 percent wage hike; stall ferry services and other shipping.

12 / Bedouin member of Israeli Knesset (parliament), Hammad Abu Rabia, is shot to death in Jerusalem.

Bombs destroy nine U.S. military jets and damage two others at the Muniz Air National Guard base near San Juan, Puerto Rico. A pro-independence group called the Macheteros claims responsibility.

13 / About 100 guerrillas of unknown nationality land on a beach in eastern El Salvador and are intercepted by Salvadoran troops. Fighting continues throughout the day.

14 / Marshal Victor Kulikov, Soviet commander-in-chief of Warsaw Pact armies, meets with Polish Communist Party and military leaders in Warsaw.

Philip Alston, U.S. ambassador to Australia, tells the Australian government the U.S. is suspending

talks on the use of U.S. Australian bases by U.S. B-52 bombers.

15 / Giovanni D'Urso, an Italian justice official, is released unharmed in Rome by the Red Brigade after being kidnapped Dec. 1980.

Iran's exports of oil return to 800,000 barrel-a-day level that prevailed before start of war with Iraq, according to *New York Times*.

16 / Italy's largest petrochemical group, Montedison S.p.A., announces it will dismiss 8,500, about 19 percent of its workforce, because of reorganization.

17 / Philippines President Ferdinand E. Marcos lifts martial law, which he imposed in September 1972.

18 / Bahamian government monitors its Jan. 18 midnight deadline for illegal Haitian refugees to leave the country. Haitians who remain after midnight would be subject to arrest and deportation.

20 / Workers at Ford Motor Company's British unit vote to accept a 9.5 percent pay increase offer in polls at 24 plants. Only three plants had majorities opposed to the offer.

21 / The newspaper *Australian* reports the U.S. is secretly enlarging a communications base near Woomera in South Australia.

22 / Canadian Secretary of State for External Affairs Mark MacGuigan says his country's foreign policy will be more selective in forging new ties with centers of wealth and power; specified are Nigeria, Algeria, Indonesia and the oil-producing states of the Middle East.

23 / U.S. suspends payments to Nicaragua from $75-million economic aid fund because of alleged support of guerrillas in El Salvador by Sandinista government.

25 / Four former British Labour Cabinet ministers object to what they view as a drift of the party to the left and say they will form a "Council for Social Democracy."

26 / Great Britain approves new £990-million ($2.38 billion) two-year aid package for British Leyland, the ailing state-owned automaker.

28 / Jamaican Prime Minister Edward P.G. Seaga emerges from two-hour luncheon with President Ronald Reagan at the White House and says he hopes the session signals new thrust in U.S. foreign policy toward Latin America and the Caribbean.

30 / South African commandos destroy three guerrilla command centers in Maputo, Mozambique.

FEBRUARY 1981

NATIONAL

2 / Wells Fargo National Bank claims clique of California sports promoters and firms defrauded the bank of $21.3 million in arranging boxing event publicized by using name of Muhammad Ali, former heavyweight champion.

3 / Senate votes 80-17 to confirm appointment of Raymond Donovan as Secretary of Labor.

Jury of five Marine Corps officers at Camp Lejeune, N.C., convicts Marine Corps Pfc. Robert R. Garwood of collaborating with enemy and assaulting fellow soldier while Vietnam prisoner of war.

4 / President Reagan meets with Republican and Democratic leaders of the House and Senate to discuss national economy.

5 / President Reagan in first TV address from Oval Office claims "economic calamity" will befall U.S. unless Congress adopts Reagan tax cut package and recommended budget controls.

6 / Labor Department reports national unemployment rate was 7.4 percent in January; national unemployment rising .4 percent from December to 97.7 million workers.

7 / President Reagan signs legislation permitting rise in ceiling on national debt from $935.1 billion to $985 billion.

8 / Chief Justice Warren E. Burger warns that violent crime is causing "reign of terror" in U.S.; urges tighter crime control.

9 / Federal Reserve System Open Market Committee reduces U.S. monetary growth targets and votes to allow interest banks charge each other to vary between 15 and 20 percent.

10 / George P. Schultz, former Treasury secretary, and 11 other prominent Republicans are appointed by President Reagan to Economic Policy Advisory Board.

Fire at 20-story Las Vegas Hilton kills eight people and injures 20 more; arson suspected.

11 / Federal jury in Trenton, N.J., convicts General Electric Co. of bribing Carlos Velasquez Toro, former operations manager for Puerto Rico's Water Resources Authority, with $1 million in 1974, to assure $92 million contract award for new electric plant. Toro died in 1979.

Seatrain Lines Inc. declares bankruptcy with debts exceeding $400 million. Three-year delay in building Alaska pipeline and 1973-74 Arab oil embargo were factors in Seatrain failure.

13 / Mergers and acquisitions decreased 11 percent in 1980, reports financial expert W.T. Grimm & Co.

17 / General Motors Corp. and Ford Motor Co. announce the biggest cash rebate programs in automotive history to stimulate flagging car sales.

18 / President Reagan urges $41.4 billion cut in 1982 spending proposed by former President Jimmy Carter.

19 / Entertainer Frank Sinatra receives gaming license from Nevada after being barred from Nevada's gambling trade since 1963 because of alleged connections with organized crime.

20 / Three Democratic congressmen criticize tax cuts proposed by President Reagan as counterproductive in trying to reduce inflation. NBC and ABC provide free time to air the views of House Majority Leader Jim Wright (Tex.), and Senators Lawton Chiles (Fla.) and Gary Hart (Colo.).

Sunkist Growers Inc. agrees to sell its Arizona Products division in Yuma to settle federal antitrust charges and accepts 10-year ban against acquiring any commercial citrus-processing plants in California or Arizona without FTC approval.

21 / U.S. District Judge Sylvia Rambo, in Harrisburg, Pa., tentatively approves $20 million in claim settlements arising from accident at Three Mile Island nuclear plant in 1979; requires two insurers to improve radiation monitoring and emergency planning and to provide an additional $5 million in public health funds to study accident's psychological impact.

23 / Chrysler Corp. authorizes continuation of 7 percent rebate program for buyers of new Chrysler cars; dealers to pay first $200 of rebate.

26 / Nation's governors at conference in Washington, D.C., vote 36-2 in support of President Reagan's economic recovery program but stand opposed to any shift of tax burdens from federal level to state and local governments.

Vietnam veteran, former Army Master Sgt. Roy P. Benavidez of El Campo, Texas, receives Medal of Honor from President Reagan for saving lives of eight Green Berets in battle near Loc Ninh May 2, 1968.

Jury in White Plains, N.Y., deliberates 48 hours and convicts Jean S. Harris of second-degree murder in March 19, 1980, slaying of Dr. Herman Tarnower, prominent cardiologist and author of The Complete Scarsdale Diet.

25 / Labor Department reports government's consumer price index rose seasonally adjusted 0.7 percent in January, or at 9.1 percent annual rate.

26 / Corporation for Public Broadcasting receives $150 million donation (over 15 years), a record CPB windfall, from publisher Walter H. Annenberg to develop college-level home study TV curriculum.

27 / Chrysler Corp. assured of $400 million in additional loan guarantees by Chrysler Loan Guarantee Board, bringing drawn-down on $1.5 billion authorized by Congress in 1980 to $1.2 billion.

Charles T. Manatt, 44, of Los Angeles, elected chairman of the Democratic National Committee to replace John C. White, who will retire.

28 / National League of Cities pledges to support President Reagan's economic goals; expresses concern about skimpy federal programs for inner-city industry.

INTERNATIONAL

1 / Tehran radio reports Iran has severed diplomatic relations with Morocco and Jordan because they supported Iraq in its war with Iran.

Jia Ruoyu, former mayor of Shenyang in the 1950s, replaces Lin Huija (Huchia) as mayor of Beijing (Peking). Lin reportedly failed to improve conditions in the capital and was also replaced as first secretary of the Communist Party for Beijing by Duan Junyi.

2 / South African businessman Harry Oppenheimer, chairman of Anglo-American Corp. and DeBeers Consolidated Mines Ltd., charges that Prime Minister Pieter W. Botha's "total strategy" for combating Marxism, black nationalism and Western pressures is a threat to South Africa's parliamentary system.

3 / Petro-Canada, state-owned oil company, confirms plan to buy control of Petrofina Canada Ltd. from Belgian parent company in public tender offer of C$120 per share for all 12.2 million outstanding shares of Petrofina Canada stock.

4 / Chinese news broadcast mentions Communist Party Chairman Hua Guofeng, who appears on TV broadcast Feb. 6 after prolonged silence about him led Western observers to believe he had been ousted.

5 / Paris talks between French President Valéry Giscard d'Estaing and West German Chancellor Helmut Schmidt focus on East-West issues. A joint statement Feb. 5 urges moderation and declares West will respond resolutely to crises.

6 / Twenty gunmen kidnap Hisham al-Mohaisen, Jordanian chargé d'affaires, and his maid, killing a guard and a passing motorist outside Mohaisen's Beirut home. Jordan accuses Syria of planning the abduction.

7 / Myall Creek floodwaters rush through Dalby, Australia, and leave 1,000 people homeless. Prime Minister Malcolm Fraser promises the victims federal aid.

8 / Overseas Development Council reports gains in life expectancy are leveling off in the world's poorer nations after a generation of fast improvement.

9 / Polish Communists oust Premier Josef Pinkowski and replace him with Poland's defense minister, Gen. Wojciech Jaruzelski, 57, a moderate on domestic issues.

10 / Polish Supreme Court rejects farmers' application for official union registration but considers allowing "producer associations" without collective bargaining rights.

11 / In letter to Secretary of State Alexander M. Haig, Jr., Soviet Foreign Minister Andrei A. Gromyko strongly rejects U.S. criticism of recent Soviet foreign policy.

12 / Asian Wall Street Journal reports 1980 trade between South Korea and China totaled about $300 million despite lack of official ties between the two countries.

13 / Three former American hostages sue Iran for $30 million each, claiming the Iranian government failed to protect U.S. personnel in the embassy in Tehran.

14 / Australia withdraws diplomatic recognition of Pol Pot regime in Cambodia.

Forty-four persons die and 129 others are injured in fire that sweeps discotheque in Dublin, Ireland.

15 / Pope John Paul II embarks on 12-day pilgrimage to the Philippines, Guam and Japan.

16 / Palestine Liberation Organization confirms it receives Soviet military aid and training.

17 / Egyptian President Anwar Sadat says he would recognize Palestinian government-in-exile and permit such a government in Cairo but would oppose a leadership role for Palestine Liberation Organization's Yasir Arafat.

18 / Students at Poland's University of Lodz and many other Polish schools end a 26-day sit-in protesting central government control of curricula; students win concessions.

19 / Poland, with new premier, Gen. Wojciech Jaruzelski, eases labor problems and builds support of students, workers, and independent trade union, Solidarity.

20 / Netherlands Premier Andreas A.M. van Agt approves sale of two submarines to Taiwan; Beijing protests.

Moslem and Communist raiders kill 27 persons in Thailand; victims include passengers of downed Thai helicopter.

21 / Soviet Defense Minister Dimitri F. Ustinov charges U.S. and Western European allies are renewing Cold War and planning for armed combat with Russia.

23 / Spanish civil guards, led by Lt. Col. Antonio Tejero Molina, seize parliament building in Madrid, hold Cabinet and about 350 legislators hostage. Coup collapses next day.

24 / Buckingham Palace announces engagement of Prince Charles, 32, and Lady Diana Spencer, 19; July wedding planned.

25 / Soviets deny supplying leftist guerrillas in El Salvador.

26 / U.S. State Department rejects proposal from leftists seeking part in talks to end conflict in El Salvador.

27 / Soviet Premier Nikolai A. Tikhonov presents 1981-85 five-year plan to party congress; plan accents "Communist construction and consolidation of peace."

28 / China's Deputy Premier Yao Yilin reports government plan to cut spending by $9.8 billion for 1981 balanced budget of $64.6 billion.

MARCH 1981

NATIONAL

2 / Exxon Corp. netted $5.67 billion profit on 1980 revenues of $110.47 billion and leads oil business as most lucrative U.S. enterprise, reports *New York Times*.

3 / Alderman Vincent Schoemehl, Jr., 34, upsets Mayor James Conway in Democratic mayoral primary in St. Louis.

4 / Federal Trade Commission ends 4½-year antitrust probe of auto industry.

5 / Report shows U.S. car sales in February fell 2.1 percent from 1980 levels; U.S.-built units drop 4.6 percent, from 588,531 to 539,277.

President Reagan announces $1 million in federal aid for mental and social programs in Atlanta, Ga., in wake of slayings of 22 black children.

6 / President Reagan replaces hiring freeze for federal civilian employees with new permanent ceiling; 37,000 federal workers to be cut by 1982 in addition to jobs ordered dropped by Carter Administration.

9 / Convicted murderer Steven T. Judy is executed in Indiana State Prison at Michigan City for April 1979 rape-slaying of Terry Lee Chasteen and drowning of her three children.

10 / Federal spending cuts totaling $48.6 billion proposed by President Reagan for fiscal budget.

11 / Utah House of Representatives defeats bill that would restrict money market funds offering third-party checking; Utah Senate had passed bill.

12 / United States Conference of Mayors rebuffs Reagan budget program as "disaster for the cities."

Standard Oil Co. of Ohio (Sohio) reports agreement to purchase Kennecott Corp., nation's largest copper producer, for $1.77 billion, $62 per share. Sohio, 13th largest U.S. refiner, is 53 percent-owned by British Petroleum Co.

13 / Money market fund report shows over $100 billion assets from pooled investment funds, bank certificates, commercial paper, and government debt obligations. Bankers blame money market funds for draining deposits.

14 / Manhattan's Westway highway project gets federal approval and $1.7 billion book with announcement by President Reagan after meeting in New York with Mayor Edward Koch.

15 / Crime boss Philip C. (Chicken Man) Testa killed by bomb blast as he enters son's home in South Philadelphia. Testa was allegedly connected with Philadelphia and New Jersey crime family.

16 / Congressional Budget Office reports Reagan Administration underestimated federal budget for Fiscal 1982 by $20 billion to $25 billion; defense costs said to be $6 billion to $7 billion more than estimate.

Mandatory busing program halted by Los Angeles Board of Education after 18-year legal fight over desegregation in nation's second-largest school district.

17 / "Phony" is initial characterization of Congressional Budget Office analysis by President Reagan, answering CBO's claim of Reagan Administration budget deficiencies. Reagan later modifies initial

reaction by describing budget disagreement as containing "differing assumptions."

18 / Secretary of State Alexander M. Haig, Jr., addresses congressional committeess to explain Administration's $6.87 billion security assistance request for 1982 and urges creation of strategic "consensus" in Middle East that would include Arab nations and Israel as best protection against Soviet threat.

19 / Arkansas Gov. Frank White signs into law a bill requiring balanced treatment of "creation science" and Darwinian evolutionary theory in Arkansas public schools.

Senate Budget Committee approves $36.4 billion cut in 1982 budget.

20 / Government responsive to the people is what President Reagan assures Conservative Political Action Conference the nation needs and will get under his Administration. Haunting President are March 18 Gallup Poll results showing his ratings by public after eight weeks of office are lower than those of other recent newly elected presidents.

23 / Supreme Court rules 6-3 that states can make it criminal offense for physician to perform abortion on teen-age girl without first talking with her parents.

Supreme Court rules 5-4 that statutory rape laws that only punish males are constitutional. Case involved teen-agers in California, one of 11 states that punish only males in statutory rape convictions; 37 states punish both males and females.

24 / Consumer price index rose seasonally adjusted one percent in February, or at 12 percent rate, reports Labor Department. Two thirds of increase attributed to rising costs of energy products.

25 / Roger B. Smith, chairman of General Motors Corp., says GM still wants to renegotiate current contract with United Auto Workers despite recent UAW refusal. Smith says GM labor costs are as much as $8 per hour higher than those in certain countries. Ford Motor Co. also seeks renegotiation.

26 / Delayed action by Senate Republicans on controversial social issues like abortion and school prayer explained by Senate Majority Leader Howard H. Baker, Jr., as postponement of key problems to assure passage of Reagan economic package.

27 / Actress Carol Burnett wins $1.6 million libel judgment against *National Enquirer* from Los Angeles Superior Court jury.

30 / President Reagan shot in chest by assailant identified as John Warnock Hinckley, Jr., 25, of Evergreen, Colorado, as Reagan walks to limousine outside Washington Hilton Hotel. President rushed to hospital, undergoes surgery, recovers enough to sit up in bed March 31 and sign bill into law eliminating proposed hike in dairy price supports. Also shot by one or more of the bullets fired by the assailant were President's press secretary James S. Brady, 40, and two security officers.

31 / Eastern coal miners reject proposed new three-year contract; strike started March 27 continues in Appalachian and Midwestern coal fields.

INTERNATIONAL

1 / Protesting Canada's energy policy, provincial government in Alberta limits production of light and medium crude oil.

British Prime Minister Margaret Thatcher visits U.S. to discuss economic and strategic issues with President Reagan.

2 / U.S. expands aid to El Salvador with $25-million grant and 20 additional military advisers to help battle leftist forces.

3 / President Reagan in interview with CBS' Walter Cronkite says U.S. doesn't intend to send combat troops to El Salvador but hopes to end violence there by diplomacy.

4 / Mozambique accuses four U.S. embassy officials of spying and expels them. U.S. denies charge.

5 / El Salvadoran President Jóse Napoleon Duarte announces creation of three-man electoral commission as prelude to 1982 election of Constitutional Assembly.

6 / U.S. reports it will sell Saudi Arabia new equipment to enhance combat capability of previously purchased F-15 jet fighters.

7 / West German Defense Minister Hans Apel announces cancellation of planned arms programs for budgetary reasons.

8 / Fundamentalist Islamic Republican Party attacks Iranian President Abolhassan Bani-Sadr and demands his ouster on treason charges because of his alleged part in violence March 5 at Tehran University. Ayatollah Ruhollah Khomeini pleads for conciliation.

9 / Afghan rebels might receive arms from U.S. if they request them, says President Reagan.

10 / Poland rocks under walkout of more than 300,000 workers in Lodz following a series of arrests and detentions of Polish dissidents. Solidarity leader Lech Walesa had tried to prevent the walkout.

11 / Stalled fishing treaty between U.S. and Canada mars visit to Canada by President Reagan, who ends trip with promises to Prime Minister Pierre Trudeau that U.S. Coast Guard won't enforce jurisdictional claims against Canadian vessels.

12 / Pakistan agrees to free 55 political prisoners in exchange for more than 100 passengers held hostage on a hijacked Pakistani jetliner in Damascus, Syria.

13 / Soviet Soyuz T-4 spacecraft with cosmonauts aboard docks with Salyut 6 space station after March 12 launch; cosmonauts are Vladimir Kovalyonok and Viktor Savinykh.

14 / Iraqi Pres. Saddam Hussein offers to arm Iranian factions opposed to central government in Tehran; especially cited as possible arms recipients were the Kurds and Persian people of Khuzistan, Baluchistan and Azerbaijan.

15 / Central African Republic President David Dacko elected to new six-year term, winning 377,027 votes, or 50 percent of ballots cast.

16 / U.S. accuses Soviet Union of ignoring American appeals to end hijacking of Pakistani jetliner during its stay in Kabul, Afghanistan, March 2-7.

18 / Soviet "imperial foreign policy" and terrorist training camps are key points in remarks to U.S. congressional committees by Secretary of State Alexander M. Haig, Jr., in seeking $6.87 billion military assistance appropriation for 1982.

19 / Riot policemen in Bydgoszcz, Poland, break up farmers' demonstration in assembly; farmers promised but denied opportunity to speak.

20 / Nigerian Pres. Shehu Shagari visits London and gives U.S. President Reagan "benefit of the doubt" in developing policy toward South Africa but warns tough policy needed to deal with "evil system of apartheid."

21 / Israel sells Kfir jet fighters with American engines to Ecuador after receiving U.S. approval.

22 / Soviet Union launches Soyuz 39 spacecraft with two-man team of a Soviet and a Mongolian to dock March 23 with Salyut 6 space station.

23 / U.S. State Department admits that Jeane J. Kirkpatrick, U.S. ambassador to United Nations, met secretly March 15 in New York with Lt. Gen. P.W. van der Westhuizen, South African military intelligence officer.

24 / Solidarity union commission in Poland calls for national warning strike March 27 and indefinite general strike four days later if no agreement is reached with government on key issues.

25 / Lebanon decides to send 900 troops to bolster 600 others already serving with United Nations Interim Force in Lebanon (UNIFIL); decision follows death of three soldiers in shelling of Qantara village by Christian militia March 16.

26 / Tension rises between Polish authorities and Solidarity, cancelling last-minute efforts to avoid strike. Warsaw Pact military exercises expand in Poland.

27 / Biggest organized protest in history of Communist Poland involves most of 13 million workers in country, snarling traffic, communications and health services in four-hour warning strike protesting March 19 beatings of union activists at Bydgoszcz.

29 / Argentina swears in Gen. Roberto Eduardo Viola as 37th president.

Alleged 1968 conspiracy plot to overthrow former Labour government headed by Prime Minister Harold Wilson reported by *Sunday Times* in London. Wilson admits several people approached key leaders, including Earl Mountbatten, but were rebuffed.

31 / Solidarity National Commission votes to accept agreement with government negotiated by Lech Walesa.

Indonesian commandos kill four of five hijackers and rescue 55 hostages aboard Indonesian airliner in Bangkok, Thailand.

APRIL 1981

NATIONAL

1 / Handwritten confession made public in San Francisco placing "full responsibility" with former People's Temple aide Larry J. Layton for the slayings of Rep. Leo J. Ryan and four others Nov. 18, 1978, on airstrip near Jonestown, Guyana; confession reportedly taken by Guyanese officials four days after killings.

2 / Senate endorses $36.9 billion spending cut for 1982, almost $3 billion more than requested by Reagan Administration.

FBI reports explosive bullets were used in assassination attempt March 30 on life of President Reagan.

3 / Jobless rate in March was seasonably adjusted 7.3 percent, Labor Dept. reports.

Producer price index for finished goods in March rose seasonably adjusted 1.3 percent, says Labor Dept.

Chrysler Corp. permanently closes Lynch Road assembly plant in Detroit, and 2,200 workers lose jobs.

4 / San Antonio, Texas, elects Mayor Henry Gabriel Cisneros, first Mexican-American mayor of major U.S. city. Cisneros, who has Ph.D. in public administration, won 62 percent of vote.

6 / Supreme Court rules 8-1 states cannot deny unemployment benefits to workers leaving jobs for religious reasons.

U.S. car sales in March increased 7.4% from previous year, report says.

Reagan Administration eases rules for eliminating proposed automotive environmental and safety hazards.

7 / Attacks on Pres. Reagan's economic program punctuate comments by House Speaker O'Neill at a news conference and by Democratic National Chairman Charles Manatt to the National Press Club.

Ex-Yippie leader Abbie Hoffman is sentenced to three years in prison on charges of possessing and selling cocaine.

8 / Private and parochial schools provide better education than public institutions, reports Dr. James S. Coleman of University of Chicago.

9 / Democratic alternative to Reagan budget would spend $714.6 billion; House Budget Committee approves it 17-13.

Reagan budget resolution for fiscal years 1981-84 rejected by Senate Budget Committee 12-8.

11 / President Reagan returns to White House after 12 days recuperating from wounds of assassination attempt.

12 / Astronauts John W. Young, 50, and Robert L. Crippen, 43, aboard U.S. space shuttle *Columbia* lift off Cape Canaveral, Fla., launch pad at 7 a.m. (Eastern Standard Time) for world's first flight of reusable spacecraft.

13 / Metropolitan Edison Co., operator and 50 percent owner of Three Mile Island nuclear power plant, gets new line of credit; Met Ed bankruptcy threatened since 1979 nuclear accident at the plant.

14 / U.S. space shuttle *Columbia* lands successfully, 1:21 p.m. (Eastern Standard Time) at Edwards Air Force Base in Mojave Desert in California, after 36 orbits of earth and 54 hours in space. Astronauts John W. Young and Robert L. Crippen get heroes' welcome.

15 / President Reagan unconditionally pardons two former FBI officials convicted of authorizing illegal break-ins, W. Mark Felt, former acting FBI associate director, and Edward W. Miller, former chief of FBI intelligence division.

16 / Commerce Dept. says housing starts in March increased 5.8 percent to seasonably adjusted annual rate of 1.24 million.

17 / Faster licensing of nuclear reactors proposed by Nuclear Regulatory Commission.

20 / Italian financier Michele Sindona convicted of jumping bail in 1979 in New York to avoid bank fraud trial; also convicted of conspiracy and bail jumping—Sindona associate Antonio Caruso.

21 / Justice Dept. clears federal officals of any illegal action during 1980 investigation of Billy Carter's relations with Libya.

23 / Tornadoes in Missouri kill at least three persons and wreak heavy damage.

24 / Grain sales embargo on Soviet Union removed after 15 months by President Reagan. President Carter had imposed the embargo Jan. 4, 1980, in protest against Soviet intervention in Afghanistan.

26 / Federal Home Loan Bank Board reports record withdrawals of savings in March at nation's savings and loan associations, withdrawals exceeding deposits by $2.26 billion. Previous record withdrawals occurred in April 1979 and in July 1966.

27 / Spiro T. Agnew took thousands of dollars in bribes while he was governor of Maryland and U.S. vice president, rules Maryland court; orders Agnew to repay state $248,735.

29 / Grand jury in Buffalo, N.Y., indicts U.S. Army Pvt. Joseph G. Christopher, of Buffalo, stationed at Fort Benning, Ga., on second-degree murder charges in connection with series of racially motivated slayings of three black men in September 1980.

30 / President Reagan stresses international human rights during "Day of Remembrance" for six million Jews killed in German death camps and vows to use presidency as pulpit to condemn injustice and persecution.

INTERNATIONAL

1 / Israeli army leaders warn United Nations of impending clashes between United Nations Interim Forces in Lebanon (UNIFIL) and Christian militiamen if UN expands Lebanese army in south.

Purges of Islamic courts and revolutionary guards ordered by Ayatollah Ruhollah Khomeini on the second anniversary of Iran's Islamic revolution. Revolutionary guards were allegedly adding to political turmoil in Iran, ignoring Khomeini rules.

2 / Anthony Wedgewood Benn, a leader of British Labour Party's left wing, says he will seek the party's deputy leadership, held by Denis Healey, former Chancellor of the Exchequer and a rightwing leader. Benn ignores pleas from party leader Michael Foot to abandon bid for Healey's post.

Norwegian researchers have discovered that a drug called timolol greatly cuts risk of second and fatal heart attacks, reports New England Journal of Medicine.

3 / Nine-member mission of Islamic Conference makes second visit to Tehran seeking ways to end Iranian-Iraqi war. Mission visited Baghdad March 31 and April 4 for same reason.

4 / U.S. Secretary of Defense Caspar Weinberger warns that Soviet intervention in Poland might move U.S. to sell arms to China.

U.S. Secretary of State Alexander M. Haig, Jr., meets in Cairo with Egyptian President Anwar Sadat and other leaders to discuss proposed multinational force for Sinai.

5 / Swiss voters reject by a ratio of five-to-one a proposed constitutional amendment that would give more rights to foreigners working on a seasonal basis in Switzerland. About 110,000 such workers would have been affected.

6 / Belgium swears in Mark Eyskens as premier to replace Wilfried Martens, who resigned March 31 because of disagreement over economic policy.

7 / Warsaw Pact forces end "Soyuz '81" maneuvers which had involved 60,000 troops and spilled over into Poland; Western leaders remain concerned about Soviet intentions.

Poland says it cannot meet April through July payments on its $23-billion debts to West and notifies 400 Western banks holding Polish notes.

El Salvadoran security forces slay as many as 30 unarmed civilians in Soyopango, shantytown suburb of San Salvador.

8 / Soviet President Leonid I. Brezhnev addresses Czechoslovak Communist Party in Prague and says Poland can solve its own problems without aid from Warsaw Pact. Leaders of North Atlantic Treaty Organization still worry about Soviet intervention in

Poland's labor and union affairs, and Soviet military presence.

9 / West German Chancellor Helmut Schmidt criticizes the Soviet Union for marching into Afghanistan.

Syria's government newspaper charges that U.S. Secretary of State Alexander M. Haig, Jr., came to the Middle East earlier in the week with plans contrary to Arab recovery of usurped rights.

10 / Poland's Sejm (parliament) votes to suspend right to strike for next two months, despite objection of independent trade unions.

11 / U.S. Secretary of State Alexander Haig, Jr., says U.S. fears about Warsaw Pact military action against Poland have eased.

13 / Leaders of French and Italian Communist Parties warn against outside intervention in Poland, convinced Poland can settle its own affairs.

Premier René Lévesque's Parti Québecois wins second consecutive five-year term, capturing 80 of 122 seats in provincial election.

15 / Suriname government announces it quelled coup attempt about 40 miles west of capital city of Paramaribo; second try to overthrow government since junior army officers seized power in February 1980 from elected civilian officials.

16 / U.S.-French peace plan for Lebanon drowns in objections from Soviet and East German delegates of the United Nations Security Council, who insist that Israel be singled out as responsible for recent increase in fighting in Lebanon.

17 / Rural Solidarity, Polish union claiming to represent 3.5 million private farmers, wins recognition from Polish government; signed agreement assures right to operate "without hindrance" until official recognition May 10.

19 / Iraq expands war aims by declaring it wants to dismember Iran, reports Washington Post after interview with Deputy Premier Tareq Aziz; Iraq had wanted peace with united Iran but had changed policy and would now offer help to Iranian splinter groups.

20 / U.S. Navy accepts liability for sinking of 2,350-ton Japanese freighter Nissho Maru April 9 in collision with American nuclear submarine George Washington in East China Sea. Accident occurred about 110 miles off southern tip of Japan and split hull of freighter, which sank in 15 minutes; captain and first mate lost at sea. Damages and claims total $4.2 million.

21 / U.S. announces decision made earlier in month to sell Saudi Arabia billions of dollars worth of arms, including five Advanced Warning and Command Systems (AWACS), electronic surveillance aircraft worth $2 billion each.

India confirms U.S. has offered five-year military and economic aid program, $500 million in first year, to counter Soviet moves in Afghanistan. Previous week, India protested sale of American arms to Pakistan.

22 / Israeli Prime Minister Menachem Begin protests sale of Advanced Warning and Command Systems (AWACS) aircraft to Saudi Arabia; AWACS will jeopardize Israel's security, says Begin.

23 / Rioting and violence erupt in four cities in Northern Ireland in protest against British presence and condition of hunger-striker Robert Sands, imprisoned Irish Republican Army guerrilla who had been elected to Parliament April 10.

24 / U.S. announces plans for permanent major military command with 200,000 troops to protect Persian Gulf region that would replace year-old Rapid Deployment Force which could not start formal operations for three to five years. Tentative plans call for basing new command in U.S., then shifting headquarters to Navy ship in Persian Gulf.

26 / Delay of AWACS sale to Saudi Arabia is confirmed by Senate Majority Leader Howard H. Baker, Jr., on CBS-TV's Face the Nation. Baker says Reagan Administration decided to delay the sale of the AWACS surveillance planes until Congress is better informed about total Saudi arms package.

27 / Poland receives an extension from 15 Western creditor nations on $2.5-billion loan payment due in 1981.

28 / Australian Prime Minister Malcolm Fraser survives parliamentary no-confidence vote 712-47 after opposition Labour Party presses for his ouster.

30 / U.S., Britain and France veto four UN Security Council resolutions to block economic and political sanctions against South Africa; resolutions were designed to press South Africa for early independence settlement for South-West Africa (Namibia).

MAY 1981

NATIONAL

1 / Auto industry learns that Japanese government agrees to limit automobile imports to U.S. for two years and will consider third year of restraint. Agreement limits Japan's auto exports to U.S. to 1.68 million units during Japan's current fiscal year, April 1, 1981, to March 31, 1982.

3 / Thousands of protesters in Washington, D.C., demonstrate against U.S. military aid to El Salvador and proposed increases in defense spending; largest demonstration in capital since protest to end Vietnam War.

4 / Federal Reserve Board raises bellwether interest rate from 13 to 14 percent in effort to control money supply.

5 / Mormon church leaders oppose deployment of MX missile in Utah and Nevada; send announcement to President Reagan.

Navy should build its own submarines, says Adm. Hyman G. Rickover, outspoken developer of nuclear warships, at House hearing.

Reagan Administration modifies plans for welfare data bank; abandons plans to ask Congressional approval for U.S. welfare master file.

6 / Explosion and crash of military tracking plane kills all 21 persons aboard; plane from Wright Patterson Air Force Base in Dayton, Ohio, was on training mission when it exploded and plummeted into field 45 miles west of Baltimore, Md.

Collision of Staten Island ferryboat and Norwegian freighter injures more than 60 of approximately 2,340 ferryboat passengers. Crash occurs in heavy fog near Statue of Liberty in Upper New York Bay.

Treasury Secretary Donald T. Regan predicts higher interest rates and terms year's budget a "disaster."

7 / President Reagan gains budget victory as Democratic-controlled House adopts Reagan-endorsed $689-billion budget for 1982; projected deficit is $31 billion.

Plot to overthrow tiny Caribbean island of Dominica cited by New Orleans federal jury issuing indictments against 10 alleged mercenaries, including six men linked to Ku Klux Klan.

8 / Leaders of 150 American Indian nations demand resignation of Secretary of Interior James G. Watt.

Los Angeles investigates unexplained deaths of 27 elderly patients at two hospitals.

10 / St. Phillip's Church at 134th St. in New York's Harlem receives Archbishop of Canterbury, the Most Rev. Robert Runcie, spiritual leader of the Anglican church; St. Phillip's is one of several Episcopal churches archbishop visited on tour of U.S.

11 / Guest-worker program for Mexicans being considered by Reagan Administration to cut illegal immigrations.

Blackjack players who memorize cards can't be barred from Atlantic City casinos, a New Jersey appellate court rules in upholding argument of Kenneth S. Uston.

12 / Rural America changing dramatically, 1980 census reveals; two distinct rural Americas are created by declining family farms and by manufacturing jobs exported from cities.

13 / Largest seizure of illegal weapons in the U.S., reported by federal agents who purchased $1.2 million worth of arms from manufacturer; arms were used as bait to arrest six persons in Texas preparing to fly guns to South Africa.

14 / Michael Reagan, son of President Reagan admits he used his father's name in seeking Air Force contracts for California company and says he will resign from the firm.

15 / Second flight of U.S. space shuttle *Columbia* is scheduled for Sept. 30 by National Aeronautics and Space Administration.

International Brotherhood of Teamsters elects Roy L. Williams as interim head of the union to replace Frank E. Fitzsimmons, who died May 6.

17 / President Reagan delivers commencement address at University of Notre Dame affirming his faith in the future of freedom and recalling his acting part in the 1940 film, "Knute Rockne."

18 / Coal talks halt in Washington about two hours after they start; Sam M. Church, Jr., president and chief negotiator of United Mine Workers, refuses industry offer.

19 / Busing of 3,000 more Buffalo pupils ordered by federal judge in completing school desegregation plan.

20 / Massachusetts General Hospital, teaching and research arm of Harvard Medical School, accepts contract involving $50-million grant from Hoechst A.G. of Frankfurt, West Germany.

22 / Southern Michigan Prison inmates riot, seize two cell blocks and burn a prison store.

24 / Body of black male found in Chattahoochee River near Atlanta, Ga.; police may add victim to the case of Atlanta's missing or murdered children.

26 / Record $10.6 million legal fee awarded three lawyers for work in obtaining more than $100 million for eight tribes of Sioux Indians deprived of land in Black Hills, South Dakota.

27 / Navy jet crash kills 14 sailors and injures 45 aboard U.S. nuclear carrier *Nimitz* off coast of North Florida.

28 / President Reagan accuses Wall Street of misinterpreting his economic program.

29 / Striking United Mine Workers present second proposal for ending 64-day walkout.

30 / New York pianist Andre Michel Schub, 22, wins International Piano Competition and $12,000 cash prize.

INTERNATIONAL

1 / Millions of workers throughout the world observe May Day, international holiday for organized labor. In Moscow, military regiments march through Red Square. In Poland, crowds parade and mingle with party leaders.

2 / Carl Duckett, former deputy director for U.S. Central Intelligence Agency, confirms CIA concluded that Israel had developed nuclear weapons.

4 / Gunmen kill a general and a policeman in Madrid.

Syria resists pressure to withdraw missiles from Lebanon.

Military aid to Guatemala considered by U.S.

5 / Irish Republican Army leader Bobby Sands dies from starvation on 66th day of hunger strike. Britain reaffirms its policy on Northern Ireland amid new violence in streets.

6 / U.S. closes Libyan mission in Washington and expels diplomats because of alleged attempts to murder Libyan dissidents in America.

8 / Averting Syrian-Israeli war is main effort of special American envoy Philip C. Habib in Beirut discussion; Syria rejects Israeli demand to remove Syrian antiaircraft missiles from Lebanon.

10 / Israel vows air strikes against Syria unless Syria withdraws missiles from Lebanon; Israeli Prime Minister Menachem Begin schedules talks with U.S. envoy Philip Habib.

11 / Financial turmoil in France follows May 10 election of President François Mitterrand, Socialist Party leader who defeated incumbent Valéry Giscard d'Estaing. Mitterrand is first Socialist president since Fifth Republic was formed in 1958.

12 / Independent Polish farmers' union granted legal status by Warsaw court, ending eight-month confrontation.

13 / Pope John Paul II shot and rushed to hospital from St. Peter's Square, where he was hit by two bullets. Man arrested in shooting identified as 24-year-old Turkish terrorist, Mehmet Ali Agca, who had been convicted of the murder of an editor in Turkey and escaped from prison in 1979.

14 / Pope's condition remains critical after five hours of surgery at Gemelli Hospital in Rome for bullet wounds suffered May 13.

Syrian missile hits pilotless Israeli reconnaissance plane over eastern Lebanon.

15 / African issues discussed at White House by President Reagan and South Africa's Foreign Minister Roelof F. Botha.

U.S. State Department believes Israeli attack on Syrian missile sites in Lebanon imminent, orders evacuation of U.S. embassy in Beirut and evacuation of American dependents.

17 / West German Chancellor Helmut Schmidt says he may resign because opponents reject NATO proposal to modernize middle-range nuclear missiles in Western Europe.

Leaders of Western news organizations oppose proposal by United Nations group that new World Information Group regulate flow of news and information around the globe.

18 / Referendum in Italy upholds abortion law allowing termination of pregnancy in first 90 days for women over 18 years of age.

Soviet oil production in 1980s will be sufficient to keep Soviet Union independent of imported petroleum, says U.S. Central Intelligence Agency.

20 / U.S. votes against World Health Organization code that would ban promotion of infant formulas as discouraging breast feeding. Committee adopted code by vote of 93-3, with nine abstentions.

Leaders of Israel and Syria criticize opposing policies but urge Philip C. Habib, special American envoy, to continue efforts to ease tensions.

21 / U.S. should continue embargo of arms and investments in South Africa until black majority there significantly shares political power, says report of 11 prominent Americans in private study sponsored by Rockefeller Foundation.

Two U.S. military patrols into Laos probed "hints" that American prisoners of war were still alive there, Reagan Administration reveals.

22 / Syria shoots down second pilotless Israeli reconnaissance plane over Lebanon; first one downed May 14.

Moneyed French citizens switch investments abroad, displaying lack of confidence in government of President François Mitterrand; on first full day in office, Mitterrand dissolves National Assembly and names Cabinet without any Communist members. French Central Bank says it will raise interest rate to record 22 percent.

24 / Spanish police commandos rescue about 200 hostages and kill one of the gunmen holding them in a bank headquarters.

Four gunmen hijack Turkish jetliner to Bulgaria and threaten to kill all 110 passengers.

25 / Turkey announces recapture of hijacked jet and rescue of all passengers in Bulgarian resort of Burgas.

26 / Two Soviet cosmonauts land Soyuz spacecraft in Central Asia after final mission to earth-orbiting Salyut 6 space station, base for record-setting human endurance tests during past four years.

27 / Italy's Prime Minister Arnaldo Forlani and Cabinet resign in scandal over secret Masonic Lodge headed by alleged Fascist and Mafia-connected Licio Gelli as grandmaster.

Riot police storm university campus at Johannesburg as protests mark South Africa's observation of 20 years as republic.

28 / Israeli jets destroy antiaircraft missile batteries in Lebanon.

29 / Lebanese Christian militiamen and Syrian forces exchange rocket fire in Zahle, 20 miles east of Beirut.

30 / Rocket fire blasts Beirut beach, killing at least eight sunbathers.

JUNE 1981

NATIONAL

2 / Justice Department says Air Force "botched" inquiry of Second Lieut. Christopher M. Cooke, accused of making unauthorized visits to Soviet Union, by promising him immunity for cooperation in probe.

Democrats on House Ways and Means Committee challenge President Reagan's tax-relief program with proposed plan for two years instead of three.

Stringent curbs on Medicaid abortions approved by House and Senate conferees, who reject House-passed measure that would extend abortion restrictions to federal workers.

3 / Cities with rent controls would lose some federal housing funds under bill approved by Senate; House not expected to approve provision.

4 / Atlanta police examine evidence from 23-year-old black man's house and car in effort to link him with slaying of 28 young blacks in area in last 22 months.

James Earl Ray stabbed 22 times in Tennessee prison where he is serving 99-year sentence for murder of Rev. Dr. Martin Luther King, Jr.

5 / National unemployment rate jumps to 7.6 percent in May from 7.3 percent in April; first significant increase in one year.

Mass deportation hearings start in Miami for newly arrived Haitians; Justice Department says it will order hearings in open court after Naturalization Service started proceedings behind closed doors and barred private attorneys.

6 / Opposition to MX missile mounts in Utah and Nevada after Mormon church announces publicly it will fight deployment of missile defense system in Great Basin.

Proposal for ethics panel vetoed by International Brotherhood of Teamsters; dissidents suggested panel in claiming new general President Roy L. Williams unfit for office because of indictment on charges of bribery and conspiracy.

7 / Haitians being deported again by Federal Government as detention center in Miami tightens security and Naturalization Service orders confinement for all Haitians who arrived illegally on planes after Feb. 23.

8 / Women paid less than men can sue employers, regardless of whether jobs are identical for both sexes, Supreme Court rules.

9 / Busing to achieve school desegregation suffers setback as House votes 265-122 to prohibit Justice Department from pursuing cases that could lead to busing as means of racial integration.

10 / Tighter college loan restrictions urged by House Education and Labor Committee in approving stricter plan than that of Senate Committee on Labor and Human Resources.

11 / President Reagan pushes hard for tax-cut plan, asking 350 backers to help win Congressional approval.

12 / Major league baseball players strike for second time in history after negotiations fail in 18-month-old labor dispute.

15 / Farmland shortage may develop early in next century, reports Agriculture Department, noting current conversion of three million acres of farmland annually.

16 / Victims of Agent Orange may receive medical treatment, Congress decides for first time in 98-0 vote authorizing medical care for Vietnam veterans affected by defoliation chemical.

17 / Cost-benefit considerations irrelevant in protecting workers from toxins, rules Supreme Court; maximum protection required.

18 / Anti-abortion bill hearings end on highly emotional pitch.

White House warns threatened air-traffic controller strike would be illegal and would reap strong antistrike measures. Controllers seek $10,000 raise and 32-hour instead of 40-hour week.

19 / Greater lung cancer risk not proven among non-smoking wives of smokers, reports American Cancer Society in contradicting Japanese study.

21 / Eleven of 29 climbers on Mt. Rainier, Washington, believed dead in ice avalanche.

Murder of one of 28 blacks slain or missing in Atlanta, Ga., charged to Wayne B. Williams, 23-year-old talent scout and free-lance cameraman.

22 / Air-traffic controllers reach tentative agreement, scratch scheduled strike.

25 / Male-only military draft upheld by Supreme Court 6-3.

26 / Sun Myung Moon, founder of Unification Church, faces deportation on Justice Department claim of illegal immigration.

28 / Sale of U.S. weapons information to Polish intelligence service charged by Federal Bureau of Investigation to William H. Bell, 61, former employee

of Hughes Aircraft Co., in El Segundo, Calif., and Marian W. Zacharski, 29, head of Polish American Machinery Co., Elk Grove Village, Ill.

29 / President Reagan receives cool welcome in Denver from National Association for Advancement of Colored People.

INTERNATIONAL

2 / Libyan interventionism scored by Reagan Administration with promise to support African countries that want to resist it.

3 / Minimum wage in France increased 10 percent and pension benefits rise in one of first actions by new Socialist government; President François Mitterrand announces plans to nationalize some French industries.

Pope John Paul II leaves hospital three weeks after being shot; blesses crowds on his way to Vatican apartment.

4 / Sales of advanced weapons to China reported under serious consideration by Reagan Administration.

Salvadoran military reported directing new repressions of civilians; military junta unable to control local commanders.

5 / Four anti-Communist dissidents in Poland ordered released from jail by Warsaw court.

Preliminary arms discussions between U.S. and Soviet Union agreed upon as preliminary to September meeting between U.S. Secretary of State Alexander M. Haig, Jr., and Soviet Foreign Minister Andrei A. Gromyko, when limitation of medium-range nuclear missiles in Europe will be discussed.

7 / Mexican President José López Portillo arrives in Washington for talks with President Reagan about Central America.

Attempts to end bloodletting in Lebanon mark emergency meeting of Arab League at presidential palace near Beirut.

Israeli jet fighters bomb Iraqi nuclear reactor near Baghdad; United States and Arab governments protest.

9 / Israel defends bombing of Iraqi nuclear reactor; Prime Minister Menachem Begin says facility was producing material for nuclear weapons.

United States grain sale offer to Russians proposes six million metric tons by Sept. 30.

10 / Abolhassan Bani-Sadr dismissed by Ayatollah Ruhollah Khomeini as commander-in-chief of Iranian armed forces.

Stanislaw Kania survives challenge to his Communist party leadership in Poland during heated session of Central Committee.

11 / Earthquake in Iran kills at least 1,500 people in southeastern province of Kerman.

Israel protests suspended delivery of F-16 jet fighters by U.S. as unfair reaction to Israeli bombing of Iraqi nuclear reactor; Israel says her security was in jeopardy.

12 / F-16 fighter planes for Pakistan considered by Reagan Administration to offset Soviet threat in Afghanistan.

15 / Equality amendment to Swiss constitution, stressing equal rights for women as well as men, approved by referendum.

France's Socialist party wins landslide victory in National Assembly in first round of voting.

16 / Israel apparently violated arms accord with U.S. by bombing Iraqi nuclear reactor, says President Reagan.

17 / Sales of American weapons to China approved in principle, reports U.S. Secretary of State Alexander M. Haig, Jr., after visit to Peking.

18 / France admits secret accord with Iraq on nuclear reactor near Baghdad but says installation bombed by Israeli jets June 7 could not have supplied nuclear explosives in sufficient quantity to threaten Israel.

19 / United Nations Security Council strongly condemns Israel for destroying Iraqi nuclear reactor.

Western Europe launches two communications satellites expected to compete with American system.

21 / President Abolhassan Bani-Sadr impeached by Iranian Parliament, which declares him politically incompetent.

22 / Abolhassan Bani-Sadr dismissed as president of Iran by Ayatollah Khomeini; Moslem clergy and secular followers take complete control of post-revolutionary government; Bani-Sadr goes into hiding.

Delay in arms negotiations indicated by Eugene V. Rostow, President Reagan's nominee to head Arms Control and Disarmament Agency.

24 / Proposed arms sale to Saudi Arabia divides U.S. White House and Congress; bipartisan Congressional majority opposes plan to sell radar aircraft, but White House will push transaction.

25 / Joint military maneuvers of Hungarian and Russian troops reported to be increasing military pressure on Poland.

New Sinai peace force announced as part of accord between Egypt, Israel, and United States; forces would patrol desert after Israel withdraws from Egyptian territory on April 25, 1982.

26 / Executions of dissidents in Iran reported continuing in relentless drive urged by close aide of Ayatollah Ruhollah Khomeini, Hojatolislam Ali Khameini.

28 / Bomb explosion in Tehran kills 72 people including 18 members of Parliament and an Iranian Cabinet minister, and injures Iranian Prime Minister Mohammad Ali Rajai; blast occurred at headquarters of governing Islamic Republican party.

Italy's Christian Democrats lose control of prime minister's office for first time in 36 years as Giovanni Spadolini, secretary of Republican party, is sworn in to head 27-member coalition government.

29 / Peking's strongest leader, Deng Xiaoping, named chairman of Communist party to replace Hua Guofeng, who lost support because of alleged "leftist errors."

U.S. State Department announces American-Egyptian nuclear accord will allow Cairo to buy two large atomic reactors and fuel to generate electricity.

Iran's Ayatollah Khomeini vows that Iranian revolution will continue despite deaths of 72 high public figures in bomb explosion June 28 at Tehran.

30 / Early returns in Israeli elections indicate close race between Prime Minister Menachem Begin and Shimon Peres, Labor party leader.

JULY 1981

NATIONAL

1 / Television stations must sell "reasonable" amounts of time to candidates for federal office, Supreme Court rules.

Supreme Court rules that police generally need warrant to open closed container found in car trunk but don't need warrant to search passenger area of car after passengers are arrested; decision reverses rulings by state appellate courts.

2 / Montana's 30 percent tax on coal production is legal and doesn't unconstitutionally interfere with interstate commerce, rules Supreme Court.

3 / Government rests case in 14-week bribery and conspiracy trial in New Orleans of reputed crime leader Carlos Marcellos, accused of authorizing kickbacks for Louisiana state insurance business.

6 / Record merger sought by E. I. Du Pont de Nemours in offer of $7.3 billion for Conoco, nation's ninth largest oil company.

7 / Sandra Day O'Connor will be named to Supreme Court, announces President Reagan; 51-year-old judge on Arizona Court of Appeals would be first woman on High Court. Controversy boils over her views on abortion and proposed equal rights amendment.

9 / Antiabortion bill approved by Senate subcommittee in first significant Congressional action toward reversing 1973 Supreme Court ruling that gave American women right to terminate pregnancy.

10 / Aerial spraying of California's fruitfly infestation ordered by Gov. Edmund G. Brown, Jr., as alternative to federal quarantine that would require fumigation of all produce leaving state.

Florida announces lawsuit against federal government for actions associated with Haitian and Cuban refugees in Miami area but does not disclose nature of complaint.

12 / Challenge to Du Pont-Conoco merger raised by Joseph E. Seagram & Sons, offering to pay Conoco stockholders $85 per share, almost $3.8 billion in cash, for 51 percent interest in Conoco.

13 / Mobil vies with Seagram & Sons to own Conoco and negotiates for $5-billion loan to buy the company amid reports that Texaco, Inc. and Standard Oil of California have also joined the fray.

14 / Top C.I.A. official, Max C. Hugel, suddenly resigns amid claims he helped wrangle fraudulent securities deals in the 1970s as manager of an electronics firm.

16 / Costliest military bill in U.S. history, $136 billion for Fiscal 1982, approved by House in 354-to-63 vote.

17 / Pregnant women warned by Surgeon General that alcohol they may consume raises risk of miscarriage and birth defects.

Five southern states warn they will reject much California produce if it is not sprayed to protect it from Mediterranean fruitfly. Florida, Mississippi, South Carolina, and Texas issue the ultimatum.

Lobby walkway collapses at Hyatt Regency Hotel in Kansas City, killing 111 people.

20 / Prosecution of draft evaders foreseen as Selective Service System sends Justice Department list of 134 names of youths who failed to register.

21 / U.S. mail strike averted by new three-year contract featuring 11 percent wage hike, bonuses, and improved cost-of-living benefits for 600,000 postal workers.

22 / Chrysler Corp. reports first profit in more than two years but financial experts remain skeptical about Chrysler future.

Psychiatrists say John W. Hinckley, Jr., is competent to stand trial for the shooting of President Reagan and was probably sane at the time of the assassination attempt March 30.

23 / The 128-year-old *Washington Star* announces it will close Aug. 7 because of steady drop in daily circulation and financial losses of $20 million annually.

24 / Surgeons at St. Luke's Hospital in Houston remove man's damaged heart and replace it with artificial one but appeal for donation of human heart. Two days later, human heart donated and transplanted, but man dies Aug. 2.

29 / Flight controllers veto tentative labor agreement reached June 22 but don't say if strike will follow.

30 / New policy on illegal aliens announced by Reagan Administration would ban them from employment in U.S., halt influx of Haitian "boat people" in Florida, and set quota of 50,000 Mexican workers as two-year experiment.

31 / Major league baseball players end seven-week strike after losing estimated $28 million in salaries but winning concessions in free-agent compensation dispute and collective bargaining rights.

INTERNATIONAL

1 / Chinese leaders pledge improved prosperity for country under Communist rule.

2 / Iranian leaders urge citizens to report suspicious activities in effort to stem attacks on officials of revolution.

3 / Polish Cabinet reorganizes to deal more effectively with country's economic crisis.

5 / Tension reported easing in Beirut and Zahle as special Arab League committee adjourns peace talks.

6 / Isabel Perón granted conditional freedom by court in Argentina; former Argentinian president and widow of Juan Perón had been under house arrest for past five years.

Iranian leaders have 27 people, described as leftists, executed.

7 / Bishop Jozef Glemp named new primate of Poland; pledges to continue dialogue with authorities started by his predecessor Stefan Cardinal Wyszynski.

9 / Israel-Jordan border closed to tourists by order of Prime Minister Menachem Begin.

10 / Blacks riot in south London after local businessman was arrested for intervening in behalf of friend being questioned by police; most black rioters of West Indian background.

12 / Stronger Western Europe needed, agree West German Chancellor Helmut Schmidt and French President François Mitterrand as they start two-day meeting.

13 / Protestors demanding jobs hurl tomatoes at Prime Minister Margaret Thatcher as she calls for unity among Britons during visit to riot-torn Liverpool.

15 / Communists set precedent in Poland by agreeing to elect entire membership of Polish Communist party by secret ballot that includes choice of contenders.

16 / New American nuclear policy committed to preventing spread of nuclear weapons and to promoting safe, peaceful nuclear programs, says President Reagan.

17 / Israeli jets bomb Beirut; Israeli Prime Minister Menachem Begin warns attacks will continue, even if Palestinian camps in Lebanon are in civilian areas; U.S. calls for cease-fire in Israeli-Lebanese area.

19 / Poland needs 110 percent rise in prices and wage freeze to solve economic problems, says Prime Minister Wojciech Jaruzelski.

High U.S. interest rates and their effect abroad criticized by leaders of industrial democracies at opening of economic conference at Ottawa.

20 / Yasir Arafat, head of Palestine Liberation Organization, vows to fight back against barbaric war he claims Israel started with Lebanon.

21 / Israel agrees to authorize American special envoy Philip C. Habib to act as its intermediary in peace talks with Lebanon.

22 / Turkish terrorist Mehmet Ali Agca sentenced to life imprisonment for trying to kill Pope John Paul II and wounding two American women May 13, in St. Peter's Square.

23 / New shipments of F-16 jets to Israel urged by leaders of 34 American Jewish organizations; suspension of shipments seen as "one-sided punishment of Israel."

24 / Israel offers and P.L.O. accepts cease-fire, reportedly with condition laid down by Israelis that Palestine guerrillas halt further military buildup in southern Lebanon.

Reagan Administration officials stress need to follow up Israeli-P.L.O. cease-fire with firm steps to end civil war in Lebanon and renewed commitment to peace negotiations started with Camp David accords.

26 / Palestinian guerrilla leaders censure faction refusing to honor tenuous cease-fire with Israel.

Nigeria may use "oil weapon" against U.S. in retaliation against Reagan Administration's policies on South Africa, says Nigerian official.

28 / Earthquake strikes Iran and kills at least 8,000 people; Iranian leader Ayatollah Khomeini calls disaster "test sent by God."

29 / Wedding of British Prince Charles and Lady Diana Spencer in St. Paul's Cathedral attended by 2,500 guests and watched by 700 million television viewers around world.

30 / Protests over food scarcity and prices spread through Poland; Warsaw local of national trade union calls for two-hour strike in first days of August as warning to government.

31 / Plan to open passion play in Jerusalem draws objection from Jews claiming such presentations are anti-Semitic because they seem to blame Jews for death of Jesus.

Poland reorganizes Cabinet with appointment of two generals to the legislative body by Prime Minister Wojciech Jaruzelski, bringing total number of generals in Cabinet to four. Jaruzelski also replaces Deputy Prime Minister Mieczylslaw Jagielski with former Labor Minister Janusz Obodowski.

AUGUST 1981

NATIONAL

1 / U.S. House backs Social Security minimum benefit of $122 monthly, rejecting President Reagan's plan to abolish it.

2 / Air traffic controllers threatening strike warned by federal employer that no amnesty will be granted if controllers violate federal laws against walkout.

3 / Air traffic controllers strike, grounding half of 14,200 daily flights across nation; President Reagan warns strikers will lose jobs unless they return to work in 48 hours.

5 / Du Pont gains control of Conoco Inc., one of the nation's largest oil corporations, by paying $7.56 billion in stock and cash; Du Pont wins bidding battle against Mobil Corporation and Seagram.

6 / Confession of accused spy reported by U.S. Air Force; military court reveals Second Lieut. Christopher M. Cooke admits photocopying secret information and giving it to Soviets.

7 / Air traffic controllers seek support from other labor organizations for strike; military personnel ordered to man control stations at civilian airports.

9 / New education bill for men recruited into ground combat divisions of military services planned by Reagan Administration.

11 / Labor Department probe of teamster union pension fund criticized by Senate investigators claiming probe poorly managed.

13 / Historic tax and budget cuts assured as President Reagan signs new bill into law, warning Congressional changes in his initial tax cut plan may create big deficit.

14 / Mediterranean fruitfly invasion of California spreads to San Joaquin Valley.

Tennessee's former Gov. Ray Blanton sentenced to three years in prison and fined $11,000 for extortion and conspiracy in selling liquor licenses while in office; two former aides, James Allen and Clyde Hood, also sentenced and fined; all three freed on bond pending outcome of appeals.

16 / Immediate threat to continued life of *Philadelphia Bulletin* eliminated as eight unions grant $4.9 million in concessions to keep paper alive.

17 / Federal government accepts applications from air traffic controllers to replace those striking.

Release of 322 Cuban refugees ordered by federal judge in Atlanta; refugees spent more than year in federal prison because they lacked proper entry papers.

18 / Tropical storm "Dennis" moves into Atlantic after deluging Florida for three days.

19 / Japan agrees to continue accepting produce exports from California if state certifies produce carries no Mediterranean fruitflies.

20 / Federal government rejects air traffic controllers' request to renew negotiations as strike enters thirteenth day.

21 / Nationwide protests by Immigration and Naturalization workers seeking higher pay and more staff.

23 / Steepest inflation in 16 months lifted Consumer Price Index 1.2 percent during July, reports federal government.

27 / Voyager 2 camera platform malfunction cripples spacecraft on trek behind Saturn after closest approach to planet.

28 / Justice Department reverses July position and assures Chicago it is satisfied with city's school desegregation plans.

Not guilty plea entered by John W. Hinckley, Jr., at arraignment in Washington on charges of trying to kill President Reagan and three other men last March.

31 / Pay increase of 4.8 percent for federal workers earning less than $50,112 recommended to Congress by President Reagan.

INTERNATIONAL

2 / Kiernan Doherty, 25, member of the Irish Republican Army, dies in Northern Ireland's Maze Prison on 73rd day of hunger strike to protest lack of political status for fellow IRA hunger strikers in British prison; Doherty is eighth hunger striker to die at Maze Prison in last five months.

3 / Food shortages in Poland trigger confrontation between members of Solidarity union and police.

Pact for Sinai peace force signed by Israel and Egypt; United States to provide half of 2,500-member international patrol on Sinai peninsula.

4 / New coalition government in Israel announced after compromises by Prime Minister Menachem Begin with three major religious parties. Begin starts second term of office with only a 61-member majority in 120-member Parliament.

5 / American-Egyptian talks open in Washington; Egyptian President Anwar Sadat urges United States to negotiate with Palestine Liberation Organization to help achieve peace in Middle East.

Tehran orders French ambassador to leave Iran, and Paris urges French citizens living in Iran to depart as Iranians protest political asylum granted by Paris to Abolhassan Bani-Sadr, former Iranian president.

6 / Iran holds 62 French nationals who tried to leave Iran after warnings from Paris that anti-French feelings were mounting in Tehran.

7 / Polish government attacks Solidarity trade union for "aggressive, arrogant behavior" following four-hour strike to protest food shortages.

European air traffic controllers in Finland, France, Norway and Italy start scattered job actions to support strike by American controllers.

9 / United States draws strong censure from Soviets over plans to produce neutron bomb.

12 / Trans-Atlantic air travel resumes after Canadian air traffic controllers end boycott of flights to and from United States in support of American controllers' strike.

Colombia severs relations with Cuba because, say Colombian authorities, Cuba is training guerrillas to fight in Colombia.

13 / U.S. President Reagan defends decision to produce neutron bombs, saying neutron weapons are defensive and won't be deployed in Europe without consulting America's allies.

14 / Poland's Solidarity leader, Lech Walesa, and Polish hierarchy of Roman Catholic Church urge moderation in union's drive to improve lives of workers.

16 / Yasir Arafat supports peace plan for Middle East proposed by Saudi Arabia's Crown Prince Fahd, who urges Israel to withdraw from West Bank.

17 / Shipments of F-16 and R-15 jet fighters to Israel will resume, says U.S. State Department after 10-week delay because Israel bombed Iraqi nuclear reactor in June.

Execution of 23 Iranian leftists reported by Iranian state radio during continuing purge of anti-revolutionary activists in Tehran.

18 / Printers strike in Poland and demand more access to state-run media.

Hijackers of Iranian gunboat seized off coast of Spain threaten to destroy craft in Marseille, where French officials refuse to refuel the boat; French spurn demands of Iran to arrest hijackers and return craft.

19 / United States reports two Navy jets shot down two Libyan jets over disputed waters near Libya's coast. Libya says one U.S. Navy jet shot down and accuses United States of aggression.

23 / Moscow demands support of Soviet-style Communism from Eastern bloc allies; Soviet concern mounts over turmoil in Poland.

24 / United States reports North Koreans fired missile at U.S. reconnaissance aircraft. Missile missed plane, which U.S. protests was in international territory, by five miles.

25 / South African troops enter Angola in campaign against guerrillas.

27 / Angola demands immediate withdrawal of South African troops and requests emergency meeting of United Nations Security Council.

28 / U.S. Secretary of State Alexander M. Haig, Jr., accuses Cuba and Russia of supporting civil war in El Salvador; joint Mexican-French statement to United Nations Security Council recognizes guerrillas in El Salvador as "representative political force."

30 / Bombing in Iran kills five people, including President Mohammad Ali Rajai and Prime Minister Mohammad Javad Bahonar.

31 / American general and 19 other persons injured in bomb explosion at European headquarters of U.S. Air Force in Ramstein, West Germany.

American support for South Africa indicated at United Nations as Reagan Administration vetoes Security Council resolution condemning South African raid on Angola.

SEPTEMBER 1981

NATIONAL

1 / Slower rise in military spending predicted by Congressional sources and confirmed by Pentagon;

cut from $15 billion to $10 billion said to be assured by Reagan Administration in coming fiscal year.

John W. Hinckley, Jr., denied bail by federal judge, who says Hinckley, accused of trying to kill President Reagan and assaulting three other men March 30, would probably flee if released.

2 / U.S. economy may not recover as fast as predicted by Reagan Administration, say some Administration members.

3 / Federal government announces formation of special unit to coordinate investigation of any large-scale fraud in food-stamp program; unit to include officials of the Departments of Agriculture and Justice, and the Postal Service; Justice Department officials estimate $1 billion lost to food-stamp fraud annually, say evidence of cheating is increasing.

4 / Smaller federally subsidized school lunches proposed by Department of Agriculture.

6 / Labor and White House battle over Administration's handling of air traffic controllers' strike; AFL-CIO President Lane Kirkland calls federal tactics "hardfisted."

8 / Philadelphia teachers strike to protest widespread dismissals of teachers and canceled raise.

9 / Drug abuse rising again in Northeast after 8-year decline, notes federal report.

Wall Street warned by Republican leaders to lower interest rates or GOP will seek federal restrictions.

10 / President Reagan orders members of Cabinet to propose $75 billion in additional budget cuts for Fiscal 1983 and 1984 and urges support for his economic program.

11 / Federal water rights curbed and primacy of state water management assured in new policy announced by Secretary of Interior James G. Watt.

Large military pay raises for noncommissioned officers provided in bill passed by Senate 81-0; House must approve.

13 / John McEnroe wins U.S. Tennis Open, defeating Bjorn Borg at National Tennis Center in Flushing Meadow, New York, for his third consecutive singles title; scores were 4-6, 6-2, 6-4, 6-3.

14 / Reagan Administration agrees to compromise that would raise farm price supports $4.1 billion above projected budget over next four years.

15 / Sandra Day O'Connor's nomination as Associate Justice of Supreme Court approved by Senate Judiciary Committee.

16 / Eleven more protesters arrested at Diablo Canyon nuclear plant in California; total arrests rise to 558 in demonstration against building nuclear plant close to undersea fault.

Restriction on school busing for racial integration foreseen as U.S. Senate votes 61-36 to end three-month filibuster against busing legislation.

17 / Warnings of race riots cancel scheduled rugby match at Albany, N.Y., between South African national Springboks and soccer stars from East Coast.

Opponents of proposed $8.5-billion sale of Airborne Warning and Control Systems (AWACS) aircraft to Saudi Arabia claim majority of U.S. Senate is against transaction.

18 / President Reagan defends economic recovery program and vows to fight for new round of spending cuts.

Full-scale investigation of former American intelligence agent Edwin P. Wilson announced by House Select Committee on Intelligence; Wilson charged with illegally exporting explosives to Libya.

19 / Reunion concert of Paul Simon and Art Garfunkel draws more than 100,000 people to Central Park in New York City.

More than 240,000 members of organized labor and civil rights groups demonstrate in Washington, D.C., to protest federal cuts in social programs and changes in job safety rules.

20 / Tubing at Indian Point, N.Y., nuclear plant of Consolidated Edison Company said to be rusting faster than expected; one-year shutdown and $100 million in repairs foreseen; condition similar to that affecting 16 other such plants across country.

21 / Sandra Day O'Connor confirmed by U.S. Senate as Associate Justice of Supreme Court; confirmation vote is 99-0.

Rugby game ban lifted by federal judge, allowing South African Springboks to play Eastern Rugby Union team at Albany, N.Y.

22 / New York City Mayor Edward I. Koch wins both Democratic and Republican nominations for reelection in primary election that had been delayed 12 days because of legal problems involving reapportionment of City Council districts.

South African Springboks beat Eastern Rugby Union team 41-0 in mud and heavy rain at Albany, N.Y.; contest heavily policed and watched by only 300 spectators; about 1,000 demonstrators heckle players following morning bomb blast that damaged Rugby Union's office in Schenectady, N.Y.

Former American hostages of Iran should receive $12.50 a day for their 444 days in captivity, presidential commission says; $5,550 total per hostage much less than $1,000 per day sought by lawyer for hostage group; commission proposes unlimited health and medical benefits in addition to $5,550 lump sum per hostage.

Increase from 5½ to 6 percent in interest on passbook savings with savings and loan associations allowed by federal regulators; 5¼ to 5¾ percent increase allowed for commercial banks.

23 / House votes 354-56 to make it a crime to disclose identity of American intelligence agents working undercover.

White House tape recordings from 1971 reveal President Nixon endorsed "thug" tactics to quell anti-Vietnam War demonstrators; no proof that tactics suggested by presidential aide H.R. Haldeman were ever used.

24 / Additional $13 billion cut in spending and $3 billion in tax revenue increase for 1982 proposed by President Reagan in his fifth prime-time television speech.

Consumer price index rose 0.8 percent in August, reports Labor Department.

25 / Sandra Day O'Connor sworn in as 102nd justice and first woman on U.S. Supreme Court; oath administered by Chief Justice Warren E. Burger.

30 / Two-cent hike in price of first-class domestic stamp announced by Postal Service, overruling independent Postal Rate Commission for first time. New price of 20 cents to become effective Nov. 1.

Five key safety systems at Diablo Canyon nuclear power plant in California become suspect as federal government broadens scope of inquiry.

INTERNATIONAL

1 / Oil accord reached by Canadian government with Alberta, its major petroleum producing province, after year of bitter debate; agreement provides for gradual price increases over a period of five years.

2 / Iran announces appointment of Muhammad Reza Mahdavi Kani as provisional prime minister to replace Muhammad Javad Bahonar, killed with President Muhammad Ali Rajai in August 30 bomb explosion.

Central African Republic regime of President David Dacko is overthrown by General Kalingba.

3 / Iranian Parliament overwhelmingly supports appointment of Mahdavi Kani as new prime minister; Tehran radio reports 55 more leftists killed by firing squads in 10 cities.

4 / Roundup of dissidents in Cairo results in arrest of 1,000 critics of President Anwar el-Sadat.

5 / Gunmen in Beirut assassinate Louis Delamare, French ambassador to Lebanon.

6 / Bomb blast in Tehran kills Iran's revolutionary prosecutor general, Hojatolislam Ali Qoddousi, fourth senior government official killed in one week.

Egypt's Coptic Pope Shenuda III deposed by President el-Sadat, who vows to replace pope with five bishops and dissolve militant Moslem Brotherhood.

7 / Solidarity must provide programs to lead Poland out of economic crisis, say leaders during second day of union's first anniversary convention in Gdansk.

Israeli Prime Minister Menachem Begin arrives in U.S. for first talks with President Reagan on Middle East; officials indicate talks will review possibility of stronger strategic ties between U.S. and Israel, including sharing of American spy satellite data.

8 / Two-day prison uprising at Bydgoszcz, Poland, ends calmly after 150 inmates barricade themselves inside main detention center.

Sale of special advanced bomb racks to improve Saudi Arabia's bombing capability with F-15 jet fighters being considered by Reagan Administration.

9 / Defiance of Poland's leaders expressed by Solidarity union as 80 delegates at union's first annual convention ask authorities to sponsor referendum on right of workers to manage factories.

Biggest loan in history of International Monetary Fund, $5.68 billion for India, tentatively approved by I.M.F. officials.

11 / Joint U.S.-Israeli naval maneuvers and stockpiling of American medical supplies in Israel may be part of future strategy accords between U.S. and Israel, says U.S. Secretary of State Alexander M. Haig, Jr.

12 / Grenade explosion kills leading Iranian clergyman, Ayatollah Assadollah Madani, and six other persons at outdoor prayer meeting in Tabriz.

Police in Cairo use tear gas to dispel Moslem demonstrators protesting repression of religious sects by Egyptian President Anwar el-Sadat.

13 / Evidence of chemical warfare employed by Soviets in Southeast Asia cited by U.S. Secretary of State Alexander M. Haig, Jr., in speech in West Berlin; police battle demonstrators protesting Haig's visit and U.S. foreign policy.

14 / Iran announces 44 people have registered to run for special election Oct. 2; dominant candidate is 42-year-old Hojatolislam Ali Khameini, leader of Islamic Republican Party, recovering from throat wounds suffered in June 27 bomb explosion.

15 / Terrorist ambush in Heidelberg, West Germany, wounds U.S. Army European Commander, Gen. Frederick J. Kroesen and wife.

Egypt expels Soviet ambassador and staff members for stimulating religious conflicts.

Pope John Paul II issues encyclical declaring labor unions important element of modern industrial society and vehicle for social justice.

16 / Polish government in strongest attack on Solidarity accuses union of political opposition that could evoke "national tragedy."

Gradual deployment of MX missile and other new arms announced by Reagan Administration at suggestion of U.S. Secretary of Defense Caspar W. Weinberger.

17 / Bomb explosion in Beirut, Lebanon, kills 23 people, mostly civilians, at guerrilla command center of Palestine-Lebanese leftist alliance.

18 / Death penalty abolished in France by 369-116 vote of National Assembly; vote ends 190-year history of guillotine and makes France last country in Western Europe to abolish death sentence.

19 / Moscow confirms deaths of two Soviet military advisers in South African attack in Angola earlier in month.

20 / Bomb explosion in cinema at Beirut, Lebanon, kills three people and wounds 28 others; Front for Liberation of Lebanon claims responsibility.

21 / Soviet workers in open letter to Polish workers invoke Warsaw Pact obligations of Soviet and Polish governments to defend Communism from any encroachment.

Third-world countries advised by U.S. Secretary of State Alexander M. Haig, Jr., not to expect large increases in resources from rich nations but to rely on free markets, private initiative and foreign capital; Haig addresses United Nations.

22 / United Nations speech by Soviet Foreign Minister Andrei A. Gromyko accuses United States of promoting nuclear arms race to counter what Gromyko says is nonexistent Soviet threat; Gromyko addresses United Nations on eve of talks with U.S. Secretary of State Alexander M. Haig, Jr.

24 / Four armed Armenian nationalists seize Turkish consulate in Paris and hold 20 hostages, demand that all Armenian prisoners in Turkish jails be released within 12 hours; one Turkish guard is killed, two other people are wounded during takeover.

25 / Armenian nationalists who seized Turkish consulate in Paris surrender; 20 hostages released unharmed.

27 / Fierce fighting erupts in Tehran between Mujahedeen guerrillas and revolutionary guard of Ayatollah Ruhollah Khomeini, according to report from Beirut.

Solidarity union delegates at national convention in Gdansk, Poland, assail union leaders for compromising with government to win autonomy; AFL-CIO president Lane Kirkland refused visa to attend convention as union guest.

29 / Four top Iranian military leaders killed in air crash near Tehran: Col. Musa Namju, defense minister; Maj. Gen. Valiollah Falahi, acting chief of staff; Col. Javad Fahouri, former defense minister and air force commander; Gen. Mohson Kalahdoz head of airborne division and commander of revolutionary guards.

LATE CHANGES (To October 21, 1981)

WORLD NATIONS

Egypt. Hosni Mubarak, 53, was sworn in as President on October 14, 1981, succeeding Anwar el-Sadat who was assassinated on Oct. 6 (see obituary on page 1006).

Greece. Andreas Papandreou, born 1919, was sworn in as Premier on October 21, 1981, following the election victory of his Panhellenic Socialist party over the New Democracy party of Premier George Rallis on Oct. 18.

Iran. Hojatolislam Ali Khamenei, born 1939, was sworn in as President on October 13, 1981, following his election on Oct. 2. On Oct. 19 it was announced that Ali Akbar Vellayati, 36, would become Iran's Prime Minister.

Netherlands. The coalition government of Premier Andries van Agt resigned on October 16, 1981.

Norway. Kare Willoch succeeded to the premiership on October 14, 1981, following the resignation of the government of Gro Harlem Brundtland on Oct. 13.

Poland. Premier Wojciech Jaruzelski succeeded Stanislaw Kania as First Secretary of the Central Committee of the United Workers' party (Communist) on October 18, 1981.

U.S. HOUSE OF REPRESENTATIVES

Representative Eugene V. Atkinson of Pennsylvania's 25th Congressional District announced on October 14, 1981, that he was switching from the Democratic party to the Republican party.

OBITUARIES

Dayan, Moshe, 66, Israeli general, statesman and diplomat who led his nation's armed forces to victory in the conflicts of 1956, 1967 and 1973; he played a key role in the Israeli-Egyptian peace negotiations of 1978-79; in Tel Aviv, Oct. 16, 1981.

NOBEL PRIZE WINNERS—1981

Physiology and Medicine

Roger W. Sperry, born 1913, American
David H. Hubel, born 1926, American (born in Canada)
Torsten N. Wiesel, born 1924, Swedish

Chemistry

Kenichi Fukui, born 1918, Japanese
Roald Hoffmann, born 1937, American (born in Poland)

Physics

Kai M. Siegbahn, born 1918, Swedish
Nicolaas Bloembergen, born 1920, American (born in the Netherlands)
Arthur L. Schawlow, born 1921, American

Economic Science

James Tobin, born 1918, American

Literature

Elias Canetti, born 1905 in Bulgaria, resides in Britain, writes in German

Peace

Office of the UN High Commissioner for Refugees

THE UNITED STATES

OUTLINE OF UNITED STATES HISTORY

16TH CENTURY

1564 French Huguenots failed in attempts to establish settlements in present-day South Carolina and Florida.

1565 Spaniards built fort at St. Augustine, Florida, first permanent white colony in present-day United States.

1585 Sir Walter Raleigh dispatched expedition to Roanoke Island, Virginia; settlement abandoned (1586).

1590 No traces found of second Roanoke settlement—the Lost Colony (established 1587)—and birthplace of Virginia Dare, first English child born (1587) in America.

1598 Juan de Oñate began settlement in New Mexico.

17TH CENTURY

1607 Colony established at Jamestown, Virginia; Captain John Smith elected (1608) head of group. Pocahontas, daughter of Powhatan, head of an Indian confederacy in that region, rescued John Smith after Indian capture.

1612 John Rolfe developed effective method of curing tobacco; later (1614) married Pocahontas.

1614 Dutch established trading post in what is now New York State.

1619 House of Burgesses, first representative assembly in America, met at Jamestown.
The first 20 blacks arrived in Virginia as indentured servants.

1620 Pilgrims arrived from England in *Mayflower* and founded colony at Plymouth, Massachusetts; signed Mayflower Compact, first written constitution in colonies.

1626 Peter Minuit bought Manhattan Island from Indians for the equivalent of $24 and named it New Amsterdam.

1629 Massachusetts Bay Company formed; John Winthrop elected governor.

1630 Settlement established at Boston, Massachusetts.

1630–1640 "Great Migration" of Puritans from England settled Massachusetts and Connecticut.

1632 Cecilius Calvert, 2d Lord Baltimore, established Roman Catholic colony in Maryland.

1636 Banished (1635) from Massachusetts Bay colony, Roger Williams founded Providence, Rhode Island, first English colony to grant religious freedom.
Harvard College founded.

1638 First printing press established in Cambridge, Massachusetts; printed (1640) *Bay Psalm Book*.

1647 Peter Stuyvesant became head of New Netherlands; his dictatorial rule was resented.

1655 Stuyvesant seized Swedish forts on Delaware, ending Swedish rule in North America.

1662 Virginia became the first colony to declare slavery hereditary,

1664 English took New Amsterdam, changing name to New York.

1676 Nathaniel Bacon led Virginia frontiersmen against raiding Indians and then against Governor Berkeley; Bacon's death virtually ended rebellion.

1677 William Penn framed first charter separating church and state at the Quaker colony of West Jersey.

1680 New Hampshire became separate province.

1682 La Salle reached mouth of Mississippi and claimed area from Quebec to Gulf Coast—Louisiana—for France.
William Penn founded Philadelphia for Quakers.

1686 New England made a royal dominion; tyrannical rule of Edmund Andros ended in 1689 when England's "Glorious Revolution" spread to the colonies.

1689 King William's War between French and English began as part of greater European war; Treaty of Ryswick (1697) restored prewar positions.

1690 Benjamin Harris published first newspaper, in Boston, that was suppressed after one issue for criticizing conduct of war.

1692 Witch trials began in Salem, Massachusetts; 20 "witches" executed before hunt ended (1693).

1693 William and Mary College founded in Williamsburg, Virginia.

1699 Sieur d'Iberville founded Old Biloxi (now Ocean Springs) on Biloxi Bay, first permanent settlement in Louisiana Territory.

18TH CENTURY

1700 By this date, shipbuilding and whaling industries had developed in New England; plantation system in Virginia, Maryland, and Carolina fully established.

1704 Boston *News-Letter*, first continuous colonial newspaper, was started.

1716 First American theater built, in Williamsburg.

1724 English established Fort Dummer near site of Brattleboro, considered first permanent Vermont settlement.

1732–1757 Benjamin Franklin annually published *Poor Richard's Almanack*.

1733 James Oglethorpe founded colony in Savannah, Georgia, last of the original 13 colonies to be settled.

1734–1735 John Peter Zenger, editor and publisher of *New-York Weekly Journal*, tried for sedition; acquittal was landmark in assuring freedom of press in America.

1734–1750 Jonathan Edwards, in New England, and George Whitefield, in Georgia, led Great Awakening, a series of religious revivals.

1741 Captain Vitus Bering discovered Alaska and claimed it for Russia.

1744 King George's War, extension in America of War of the Austrian Succession in Europe, began; Treaty of Aix-la-Chapelle (1748) restored prewar position.

1754 French erected Fort Duquesne, on site of Pittsburgh, Pennsylvania.
George Washington's fight with French in Ohio territory became first skirmish of French and Indian War, which spread (1756) to Europe and became known as the Seven Years War.

1763 Treaty of Paris ended French control east of Mississippi; Spain ceded Florida to England in return for Cuba.

1764 Parliament passed the Sugar Act, first law to raise money for crown in the colonies, and Currency Act, which forbade all colonies to issue paper money.
James Otis denounced acts in pamphlet, noting British offense of taxation without representation.

1765 College of Philadelphia (later part of University of Pennsylvania) offered first professional medical training in colonies.
Parliament issued Stamp Act, first direct tax levied by crown on American colonies.
Colonials convoked Stamp Act Congress; organized Sons of Liberty.

1766 Stamp Act repealed, but Parliament passed Declaratory Act, affirming its right to legislate for colonies.

1767 Townshend Acts passed by Parliament, imposing import duties; many colonies enacted nonimportation agreements.

1769–1782 Fray Junípero Serra founded nine Franciscan missions in California.

1770 In Boston, several colonists were killed by English soldiers in a melee, later known as the Boston Massacre.
Townshend Acts repealed, except for tea tax; colonial merchants worked for conciliation.

1773 Parliament passed Tea Act granting East India Company full remission of all tea duties.
Boston Tea Party occurred, when patriots dressed

as Indians dumped tea shipment into Boston Harbor.

1774 First Continental Congress met in Philadelphia, with representatives from all colonies except Georgia.

1775 Patrick Henry made his "Liberty or Death" speech before Virginia Assembly.

Parliament passed New England Restraining Act, forbidding colonies to trade with any nation except Britain and British West Indies.

Minutemen fought British at Lexington and Concord, signaling start of American Revolution's military phase.

Second Continental Congress met in Philadelphia and appointed Washington chief of Continental forces.

The first abolitionist society in America was established in Philadelphia.

British defeated Americans at Bunker Hill and attacked Boston; city under siege until March 1776.

1776 Thomas Paine's *Common Sense* published, calling for American independence.

Declaration of Independence adopted by Congress.

Nathan Hale ("I only regret that I have but one life to lose for my country") executed by British as American spy.

Washington, leading troops across Delaware River, made surprise attack on British at Trenton, New Jersey.

1777 General Burgoyne's defeat at Saratoga was major American victory.

Articles of Confederation adopted by Congress (ratified by all colonies by 1781).

Congress recommended that colonial governments appropriate Loyalist property.

Washington and troops took up winter quarters at Valley Forge, Pennsylvania.

1778 Americans and French signed Treaty of Alliance.

British took Savannah, Georgia.

1779 John Paul Jones ("I have not yet begun to fight"), commanding *Bon Homme Richard*, defeated British frigate *Serapis*, off coast of England.

1780 Washington's troops mutinied at Morristown, New Jersey, because of sparse supplies and delayed salaries.

Benedict Arnold's treason exposed.

1781 Washington and Rochambeau planned joint Franco-American Yorktown (Va.) campaign, which brought surrender of Cornwallis and virtually ended hostilities.

Congress chartered Bank of North America to supply government with money.

1782 John Adams, Benjamin Franklin, and John Jay negotiated peace treaty with British in Paris.

1783 Treaty of Paris acknowledged independence of the United States.

Almost the entire American army disbanded without authority and Congress fled Philadelphia to escape discontented soldiers.

Last of 100,000 Loyalists fled country.

General Washington bade farewell to his officers at Fraunces Tavern, New York City.

1786 Daniel Shays led discontented Massachusetts farmers in armed rebellion; insurrection crushed (1787) and later Massachusetts enacted more liberal legislation.

1787 Constitutional Convention held in Philadelphia.

Congress adopted the Northwest Ordinance creating and providing a government for the Northwest Territory; slavery in region was prohibited.

Alexander Hamilton, James Madison, and John Jay began writing *The Federalist Papers*, which urged acceptance of Constitution.

Delaware was first state to ratify Constitution.

1788 New Hampshire ratified the Constitution, thereby achieving the necessary nine-state acceptance.

1789 George Washington elected nation's first President and John Adams became Vice-President.

First Congress met in New York, nation's first capital.

Federal Judiciary Act provided for organization of Supreme Court, 13 district courts, and three circuit courts; John Jay became first Chief Justice.

1790 Hamilton organized national fiscal program.

First census recorded American population as 3,929,214.

Capital temporarily moved to Philadelphia.

1791 Bill of Rights became part of Constitution.

Bank of the United States established.

1793 Washington declared American neutrality vis-à-vis France and Britain.

Citizen Genêt, Minister of French Republic to the United States, asked to leave because of his conduct; later became American citizen.

The Fugitive Slave Act was passed, making it illegal to give comfort to or prevent the arrest of a runaway slave.

Eli Whitney invented cotton gin.

1794 Federal troops put down Whisky Rebellion in western Pennsylvania.

Jay's treaty with Britain concluded; provision included British agreement to withdraw from Northwest posts; ratified (1795).

1795 11th Constitutional Amendment is ratified: a state cannot be sued by citizen of another state.

1796 In his Farewell Address, Washington warned of permanent foreign alliances and encouraged temporary ones in times of emergency.

John Adams (Federalist) elected President; Thomas Jefferson (Democratic-Republican) elected Vice-President.

1797 Affairs with France deteriorated, especially after the XYZ Affair: Talleyrand's agents tried to extort bribes from American commissioners in Paris.

1798-1800 Americans fought undeclared naval war with France; Convention of 1800 released United States from alliance with France.

1798 Alien and Sedition Acts passed by Federalists to repress political opposition.

Kentucky and Virginia Resolutions maintained unconstitutionality of Alien and Sedition Acts; expressed early states rights theory.

1799 Washington died at Mount Vernon.

19TH CENTURY

1800 Washington, D.C., became nation's capital.

1801 House of Representatives chose Jefferson for President and Aaron Burr Vice-President after electoral tie; Jefferson was first President inaugurated in new capital.

1802 Congress established U.S. Military Academy at West Point, New York.

1803 In *Marbury* v. *Madison*, Chief Justice Marshall established principle of judicial review.

United States purchased Louisiana from France for about $15 million, doubling nation's area.

Meriwether Lewis and William Clark began their westward expedition.

1804 Hamilton killed in duel with Aaron Burr.

1807 Congress enacted law prohibiting importation of slaves after January 1, 1808.

Embargo enacted because of British harassment on seas; repealed (1809), but trade with France and Great Britain still prohibited.

1808 Congress prohibited the admission of any new slaves into the United States.

1809 James Madison sworn in as President with George Clinton as Vice-President.

1811 General William Henry Harrison defeated Tecumseh's forces at Battle of Tippecanoe.

1812 War declared on Great Britain for impressing U.S. seamen, blockading, and violating neutrality; Americans suffered setbacks on land, but naval successes boosted low morale.

1813 British blockaded coast, but Captain Oliver Hazard Perry's naval victory secured Lake Erie for United States.

1814 British took offensive, capturing and burning Washington, but suffered losses in attempt to invade New York from Canada.

Francis Scott Key wrote lyrics of "Star-spangled Banner."

At Hartford Convention, New England delegates met to revise Constitution and oppose war.

Treaty of Ghent ended war.

1815 Andrew Jackson defeated British at New Orleans before news of peace arrived.

Fleet under Stephen Decatur ended Barbary states' imposition of tribute on American merchant vessels.

1816 James Monroe elected President and Daniel D. Tompkins, Vice-President.

First protective tariff enacted.

68   THE UNITED STATES

1817 New York State legislature authorized construction of Erie Canal; it opened in 1825.

1818 U.S.-Canadian boundary to Rockies fixed; United States and Britain agreed to occupy Oregon Territory jointly.

1819 Financial panic seized nation.
Adams-Onís Treaty, ceding Spain's Florida holding to the United States, signed; Andrew Jackson became (1821) Florida's first governor.

1820 Missouri Compromise prohibited slavery in Louisiana Territory north of Missouri's southern border; Missouri admitted to Union as slave state and Maine as free state.
First American missionaries arrived in Hawaii.

1821 Spain granted Moses Austin land in Texas for settlement.

1822–1826 U.S. government recognized newly independent Latin American republics.

1823 Monroe Doctrine promulgated: any further European effort to colonize the Americas or interfere in their affairs would be considered a hostile act.

1824–1825 Presidential election resulted in no candidate having a majority; House chose John Quincy Adams President after much bargaining between candidates.

1828 Congress passed protectionist "Tariff of Abominations."
Andrew Jackson elected first Democratic President; introduced spoils system on national level; Calhoun reelected Vice-President.

1829 David Walker, a free black, published his famous "Appeal," one of the most militant antislavery documents.

1830 Senators Daniel Webster (Mass.) and Robert Y. Hayne (S.C.) engaged in historic states' rights debate.

1831 William Lloyd Garrison began to publish *The Liberator*.
Nat Turner led major slave insurrection in Virginia.

1832 President Jackson vetoed renewal of National Bank.
South Carolina nullified U.S. tariff laws; Jackson declared action was rebellion and ordered Forts Moultrie and Sumter reinforced.

1833 Jackson began second term; ordered public deposits withdrawn from Bank of the United States and put into state banks; Secretary of the Treasury Taney deposited funds in "pet banks."
American Anti-Slavery Society founded at Philadelphia as abolitionist movement grew more vocal.

1834 Whig party had come into being; Henry Clay led group formed by National Republicans, states' righters, and dissident Democrats.

1835 Seminoles in Florida resisted forced transportation West; despite capture (1837) of their leader Osceola, resistance continued until 1842.

1836 Mexican leader Santa Anna captured fort of Alamo at San Antonio, Texas; Sam Houston later led American victory at Battle of San Jacinto.
Texas declared its independence from Mexico; Houston became president of independent republic.

1837 Martin Van Buren inaugurated as President.
Panic of 1837 depressed economy.

1840 By this time, Underground Railroad was fully organized to rescue fugitive slaves.

1841 President William Henry Harrison died a month after inauguration; John Tyler became first Vice-President to succeed to Presidency as a result of incumbent's death.
Horace Greeley founded the New York *Tribune*.

1842 Webster-Ashburton Treaty with Britain settled northeastern U.S. boundary.

1843 United States recognized independence of Hawaii.

1844 James K. Polk elected President; George M. Dallas elected Vice-President.

1845 Texas agreed to join Union and was annexed.
Mexico broke off diplomatic relations with United States.
U.S. Naval Academy established at Annapolis, Maryland.

1846 Mexican War broke out after Mexican troops crossed Rio Grande; Zachary Taylor led American victory at Battles of Palo Alto, Resaca de la Palma, Monterrey, and Buena Vista.
Oregon boundary established by treaty with Great Britain.

Wilmot Proviso, banning slavery in territory acquired from Mexican War, failed to pass (1846, 1847) Congress.

1847 General Winfield Scott captured Mexico City.
Led by Brigham Young, the Mormons settled at Salt Lake City, Utah.

1848 Treaty of Guadalupe Hidalgo signed by the United States and Mexico; established Rio Grande as boundary; Mexico recognized U.S. claim to Texas and ceded New Mexico and California in return for $15 million.
First Women's Rights Convention, led by Lucretia Mott and Elizabeth Cady Stanton, held at Seneca Falls, New York.
Discovery of gold in California touched off "Gold Rush."

1849 Zachary Taylor (Whig) was inaugurated.
The first school integration lawsuit was filed by Benjamin Roberts against the City of Boston. The Massachusetts Supreme Court rejected the suit, setting the groundwork for the "separate but equal" doctrine.

1850 Vice-President Millard Fillmore (Whig) succeeded to the Presidency after Taylor died of cholera.
Congress passed Henry Clay's Compromise of 1850: California admitted as free state; remainder of Mexican territory divided into New Mexico and Utah, without prior decision on slavery; more effective Fugitive Slave Law enacted; slave trade abolished in capital.
Clayton-Bulwer Treaty, concerning freedom of future canal zone, signed with Britain; abrogated (1901).

1852 Harriet Beecher Stowe's *Uncle Tom's Cabin* published.

1853 Commodore Matthew C. Perry visited Japan and obtained (1854) trade agreement.
Gadsden Purchase: land now included in New Mexico and Arizona purchased from Mexico.

1854 Congress enacted Kansas and Nebraska Act, sponsored by Stephen A. Douglas: repealed Missouri Compromise and provided that people in states would decide slavery issue.

1854–1856 Settlement of Kansas brought bloody fighting; U.S. Senate engaged in violent debates.

1856 Republican party, formed in large part by Northern Whigs, held its first convention.

1857 Supreme Court's Dred Scott decision ruled Missouri Compromise unconstitutional, holding that a slave's residence in free territory did not make him free and denying citizenship rights to descendants of slaves.

1858 Abraham Lincoln debated Senator Douglas on slavery issue and became national figure.

1859 John Brown, Kansas abolitionist, unsuccessfully tried to seize federal arsenal at Harpers Ferry, Virginia, to start slave insurrection; captured, he was hanged for treason.
First oil well drilled at Titusville, Pa., by Col. Edwin L. Drake.

1860 Lincoln elected President; South Carolina passed ordinance of secession.

1861 Mississippi, Florida, Alabama, Georgia, Louisiana, and Texas seceded from Union; Confederate States of America formed with Jefferson Davis (Miss.) as president; constitution based on states' rights doctrine.
South Carolina troops fired on Fort Sumter (April 12), forcing Union troops to evacuate; signaled start of Civil War.
Lincoln proclaimed blockade of Confederate states.
Virginia, Arkansas, Tennessee, and North Carolina joined Confederacy.
Robert E. Lee and Joseph E. Johnston resigned from U.S. Army.
West Virginia broke away from Virginia; admitted to Union in 1863.

1862 Lincoln issued Emancipation Proclamation to take effect January 1863.
Major Civil War battles of Shiloh, *Monitor* and *Merrimack*, Peninsular Campaign, Second Bull Run, Antietam, and Fredericksburg occurred.

1863 First national conscription act enacted; draft riots exploded in New York City.
General George Meade's Union forces defeated General Lee's army at Gettysburg; Lincoln delivered famous address at dedication of Gettysburg Cemetery.

1864 General Ulysses S. Grant became commander of Union armies.

General William Tecumseh Sherman marched through Georgia to the sea; captured Atlanta and Savannah.

1865 13th Amendment abolishing slavery was ratified.

Lee surrendered (April 9) at Appomattox (Va.) Courthouse.

Lincoln assassinated (April 14) by John Wilkes Booth at Ford's Theater, Washington, D.C.; Vice-President Andrew Johnson became President.

1866 Ku Klux Klan formed in Tennessee.

Civil Rights Act, bestowing citizenship on blacks passed over Johnson's veto.

Congress adopted the 14th Amendment containing "due process" and "equal protection" clauses guaranteeing civil rights of blacks.

1867 Three Reconstruction Acts passed over Johnson's vetoes; divided South into military districts and abolished qualifications for Confederate States' readmission to Union.

Secretary of State William H. Seward purchased Alaska from Russia for $7.2 million.

Northerners, called "carpetbaggers," participated in Southern Reconstruction; Southern whites allying themselves with Radicals were called "scalawags."

1868 Andrew Johnson was impeached by House and tried by Senate; two-thirds vote required for conviction failed by one vote.

Seven former Confederate states readmitted to Union.

14th Amendment was ratified.

The transcontinental railroad was completed.

1869 15th Amendment, giving blacks right to vote, proposed; ratified (1870).

1870 *New York Times* began exposé of Tammany Hall corruption; led to eventual imprisonment of Boss Tweed.

Joseph H. Rainey of South Carolina became the first black to sit in the House of Representatives after election to the 41st Congress; he subsequently was reelected four times.

General Robert E. Lee died.

The 15th Amendment was adopted, guaranteeing the right to vote to all U.S. citizens.

1871 Civil service reform began with establishment of first Civil Service Commission.

Disastrous fire destroyed most of Chicago.

1872 New York *Sun* charged prominent Republicans with taking bribes in Crédit Mobilier scandal (corruption in building Union Pacific railroad); resulted (1873) in Congressional investigation.

1873 Financial panic developed into five-year depression, worst to date.

1875 Civil Rights Act was passed forbidding discrimination against blacks in public facilities.

1876 General Custer and his troops were massacred by Sitting Bull's Sioux Indians at the Little Bighorn.

Presidential election contest between Samuel Tilden and Rutherford B. Hayes disputed; special electoral commission declared (1877) Hayes President.

1877 Reconstruction Era officially ended.

Federal troops put down a series of railroad strikes.

1878 Bland-Allison Act, passed over Hayes's veto, required government to purchase silver.

1881 President James A. Garfield was shot; succeeded by Chester A. Arthur.

1882 Chinese Exclusion Act barred immigration of Chinese laborers for 10 years; later legislation continued policy until 1943.

1883 Pendleton Act established civil service system.

Supreme Court ruled antidiscrimination portions of 1875 Civil Rights Act invalid, opening the way for repassage of Jim Crow laws.

1886 American Federation of Labor organized with Samuel Gompers as first president.

Statue of Liberty unveiled in New York harbor.

Capture of Apache chief Geronimo ended Southwest Indian warfare.

Anarchists convicted of Haymarket Massacre.

1889 Oklahoma "land rush" opened all but panhandle of Oklahoma Territory for settlement.

U.S.-Latin American conference established (1890) body later called Pan American Union.

1890 Sherman Anti-Trust Act became law.

Highly protective McKinley Tariff adopted.

1891 Populist party formed as part of agrarian protest movement.

1893 Financial panic caused partly by severe gold drain began; thousands of banks and commercial institutions failed before economy recovered (1897).

World's Columbian Exposition held in Chicago.

1894 Unemployment became widespread; "Coxey's Army" of the jobless marched on Washington to demand public works program.

Pullman strike brought federal intervention.

1895 Southern states inaugurated "grandfather" clauses as part of program (including literacy tests and poll taxes) to disfranchise blacks.

U.S. involvement in British-Venezuelan dispute led to broad construction of Monroe Doctrine, stressing right of the United States to intercede in hemispheric disputes.

1896 Supreme Court in *Plessy* v. *Ferguson* upheld Louisiana law requiring segregated railroad facilities, under "separate but equal" doctrine.

1897 Gold rush in Klondike began.

1898 Spanish-American War broke out after battleship *Maine* exploded in harbor of Havana, Cuba; in Treaty of Paris Spain granted Cuba independence, ceded Puerto Rico, Guam, and Philippines to United States in return for payment of $20 million; Cuba came under U.S. military control, headed by General Leonard Wood.

United States annexed Hawaii.

1899 United States participated in first Hague Conference, which established Permanent Court of Arbitration.

20TH CENTURY

1900 United States expressed its commitment to Chinese Open Door policy.

U.S. troops helped relieve Peking during Boxer Rebellion.

Samoan Islands were divided between the United States and Germany.

1901 U.S. military rule of Philippines ended and civil government organized; islands became territory (1902).

Platt amendment, which Cubans had to incorporate (1902) in their constitution and recognize (1903) in treaty, made island virtual American protectorate; abrogated (1934).

Second Hay-Pauncefote Treaty gave Americans free hand in Isthmian canal.

President McKinley was shot in Buffalo; Theodore Roosevelt became President.

1902 Roosevelt pledged "Square Deal" for both labor and industry; began "trust-busting" with prosecution of the Northern Securities Company.

1903 Wright brothers flew first successful heavier-than-air machine.

1904 Roosevelt's annual message contained his "Corollary" to the Monroe Doctrine: United States' obligation to maintain order in Latin America.

1905 Russo-Japanese peace treaty signed at Portsmouth, New Hampshire; Roosevelt's role of mediator brought him (1906) Nobel Peace Prize.

Industrial Workers of the World, radical labor organization, founded in Chicago.

1906 Earthquake and fire destroyed San Francisco.

Pure Food and Drug and Meat Inspection Acts signed.

1907 "Gentlemen's Agreement": Japan agreed not to allow laborers to migrate to America.

1908 William Howard Taft elected President.

1909 Payne-Aldrich Tariff set high protective rates.

Robert E. Peary discovered North Pole.

1912 Roosevelt bolted Republican party and was Progressive (Bull Moose) party's candidate for President.

Woodrow Wilson won three-way Presidential race.

U.S. marines landed in Nicaragua to protect American interests during revolt.

1913 The 16th (income tax) and 17th (popular election of U.S. Senators) Amendments ratified.

Federal Reserve System established national banking and currency system.

United States began intervention in Mexican Revolution.

1914 Federal Trade Commission established.

Clayton Anti-Trust Act supplemented and strength-

ened Sherman Anti-Trust Act.
United States proclaimed its neutrality in World War I.
U.S. naval forces bombarded and occupied Vera Cruz, Mexico.
Panama Canal opened.

1915 *Lusitania* and *Arabic* sinkings brought strong protest notes from Wilson and modification of German submarine warfare.

1916 General John J. Pershing's troops pursued Pancho Villa 200 miles into Mexico without success.

1916–1924 U.S. troops occupied Santo Domingo.

1917 United States severed relations with Germany.
Publication of secret Zimmermann note, proposing German-Mexican alliance, helped Wilson gain House approval for arming merchantmen.
Congress declared war on Germany (April 6); General Pershing appointed head of American Expeditionary Force (AEF).
Congress passed Selective Service Act; Espionage Act; and Trading with the Enemy Act, forbidding commerce with enemy nations.
United States purchased Virgin Islands from Denmark.

1918 Wilson announced his "Fourteen Points" for peace.
Germany surrendered and armistice signed (November 11); U.S. war deaths, 112,432, many from disease.
Sedition Act passed; many Socialist and pacifist leaders imprisoned during next few years.

1919 Wilson toured country on behalf of League of Nations; awarded Nobel Peace Prize; suffered stroke.
18th Amendment (Prohibition) ratified.

1920 19th Amendment (women's suffrage) ratified.
Socialist Presidential candidate Eugene Debs, in prison, polled almost a million votes.
A. Mitchell Palmer ordered mass arrests of agitators during "Red scare" period.
Senate refused to ratify Versailles Treaty, ending World War I.
Warren G. Harding (Republican) and Calvin Coolidge elected President and Vice-President.

1922 Leading powers agreed to limit naval forces at Washington Arms Conference.

1923 Harding died; Coolidge became President.

1923–1924 Knowledge that Secretary of the Interior Albert B. Fall had secretly leased Teapot Dome oil reserves to Harry F. Sinclair was one of many Harding administration scandals made public.

1924 Soldiers Bonus Act compensated veterans for overseas duty.

1925 John Scopes, Tennessee schoolteacher, was defended by Clarence Darrow and prosecuted by William Jennings Bryan; Bryan secured the conviction of Scopes for teaching evolution.

1926 Richard Byrd and Floyd Bennett became first men to fly over North Pole.
U.S. troops landed in Nicaragua to quell rebellion; troops finally withdrawn in 1933.

1927 Charles A. Lindbergh made first nonstop solo flight from New York to Paris, becoming an international hero overnight.

1928 Kellogg-Briand Pact, outlawing war, signed by the United States; ratified by Senate (1929).
Al Smith, a Roman Catholic, ran as Democratic Presidential candidate.
Herbert C. Hoover and Charles Curtis elected President and Vice-President.

1929 Stock Market crash grew into worldwide Great Depression; low point came 1932–1933.
St. Valentine's Day massacre in Chicago marked peak of gangster wars.

1930 United States, Great Britain, and Japan agreed to limit navies at London Naval Conference.
Hawley-Smoot Tariff brought duty level to an all-time high.

1931 Hoover proposed one-year moratorium on interallied debts and reparations because of worldwide economic crisis.

1932 Reconstruction Finance Corporation established.
Lindbergh's son kidnapped and slain.
"Bonus Army," camped in Washington seeking early payment of veterans' benefits, was dispersed by Army troops led by Douglas MacArthur.
Franklin Delano Roosevelt and John Nance Garner were elected President and Vice-President.

1933 Roosevelt's "New Deal" began with bank holiday

to lessen severe economic crisis; later he took nation off gold standard and delivered his radio "fireside chats."
"Hundred Days" session of Congress produced Emergency Banking Relief Act, Agricultural Adjustment Act, Federal Emergency Relief Act, and established Civilian Conservation Corps, Civil Works Administration, and Federal Bank Deposit Insurance Corporation. Supreme Court later declared several New Deal Acts unconstitutional.
Congress created Tennessee Valley Authority and established Commodity Credit Corporation.
21st Amendment repealed Prohibition.
Roosevelt's "Good Neighbor Policy" included opposition to armed intervention in Latin America.

1933–1936 Severe drought converted Great Plains into "Dust Bowl."

1934 Export-Import Bank established.
Congress passed Securities Exchange Act and established Federal Communications Commission and Federal Housing Administration.
John Dillinger slain by FBI agents in Chicago.

1935 Additional New Deal agencies created included Works Progress Administration, with Harry L. Hopkins as head; Resettlement Administration, directed by Rexford G. Tugwell; Rural Electrification Administration; and a new National Labor Relations Board.
Social Security Act created federal-state system of unemployment and old-age compensation.

1937 Supreme Court upheld New Deal legislation such as N.L.R.A. and Social Security; Roosevelt allowed "Court packing" plan to drop.
Relations with Japan started to deteriorate after sinking of U.S. gunboat *Panay*.

1938 Congress voted billion-dollar naval building program.
Fair Labor Standards Act (Wages and Hours Law) set up minimum wage and maximum hours for companies connected with interstate commerce.
Mexican expropriation of U.S. oil property caused long controversy.

1939 American neutrality pledged after war broke out in Europe; but "cash and carry" policy allowed for exports of arms to belligerent powers.
Albert Einstein and other scientists told Roosevelt of possibilities of developing atomic bomb.

1940 Smith Act (Alien Registration Act) included provisions that made it unlawful to advocate or teach the overthrow or destruction of any government in the United States by force and to be a member of any group dedicated to such a policy.
Selective Training and Service Act (Burke-Wadsworth Bill), nation's first peacetime program of compulsory military service was enacted.

1941 Roosevelt delivered Four Freedom's speech.
Lend-Lease Act allowed friendly nations to secure arms without cash.
Atlantic Charter, joint statement of postwar aims, issued by Roosevelt and Prime Minister Churchill.
Japanese attacked (December 7) Pearl Harbor; Congress declared war on Japan.
Germany and Italy declared war (December 11) on United States.

1942 Pacific Coast Japanese-Americans were relocated to Western detention camps; released in 1944; action upheld by Supreme Court.
In Pacific, Bataan and Corregidor fell to Japanese; U.S. Marines won major victory at Guadalcanal; U.S. planes, led by Major General James H. Doolittle, raided Tokyo.
First self-sustaining nuclear reaction achieved at the University of Chicago.
United Nations Pact signed by 26 nations at Washington.

1943 American forces helped drive Germans from North Africa and invaded Italy, which surrendered to Allies.
U.S. troops in the Pacific began island-hopping operations and combined with ANZAC troops to force retreat of Japanese in New Guinea.
Roosevelt attended conferences in Casablanca, Quebec, Cairo, and Teheran.

1944 Dwight D. Eisenhower became Supreme Commander of American Expeditionary Forces.

Allies invaded Europe and liberated France, Belgium, and Luxembourg.

Roosevelt defeated Thomas E. Dewey and won fourth term; Harry S. Truman elected Vice-President.

1945 U.S. troops recaptured Philippines from Japanese.

Churchill, Roosevelt, and Stalin met at Yalta.

Roosevelt died (April 12); succeeded by Truman.

United Nations established in San Francisco.

Germany surrendered (May 7) unconditionally.

United States dropped atomic bombs on Japanese cities of Hiroshima and Nagasaki; Japan surrendered (August 14).

Potsdam Conference, to plan occupation and settlement of Europe, attended by Truman, Churchill (succeeded by Clement Attlee), and Stalin.

1946 Philippines gained independence from U.S.

United States set up Atomic Energy Commission for civilian control of atomic energy.

United Nations established permanent headquarters in New York City.

Churchill delivered his "Iron Curtain" speech at Fulton, Missouri; marked beginning of Cold War.

1947 "Truman Doctrine," economic and military assistance, began with aid to Greece and Turkey.

General George C. Marshall proposed plan for European recovery.

Taft-Hartley Act, limiting power of labor, passed over Truman's veto.

1948 Whittaker Chambers accused Alger Hiss of transmitting documents to Russians; Hiss denied charges, was indicted for perjury, and convicted (1950).

Truman issued Executive Order ending segregation in the armed forces.

U.S. airlift frustrated Soviet blockade of Berlin.

Truman defeated Dewey in upset election.

1949 Truman outlined his Point Four program of technical assistance to aid world peace.

North Atlantic Treaty Organization approved.

1950 South Korea invaded by North Korean troops; Truman ordered U.S. forces into area.

Senator Joseph McCarthy charged that the State Department was infiltrated by Communists.

1951 22d Amendment, limiting President to two terms, ratified.

Truman recalled General MacArthur from Korea for insubordination.

1952 Supreme Court declared Truman's seizure of steel mills during strike unconstitutional.

McCarran-Walter Bill restricted immigration.

General Dwight D. Eisenhower became first Republican to win Presidency since 1928.

1953 Korean armistice signed.

1954 *Brown v. Board of Education of Topeka:* Supreme Court outlawed racial segregation in public schools, as "inherently unequal."

United States commitment in Southeast Asia began with formation of SEATO and financial aid to Indo-China (Vietnam, Laos, and Cambodia).

1955 Supreme Court ordered school desegregation to proceed "with all deliberate speed."

AFL and CIO merged into one labor organization.

1956 Arrest of seamstress Rosa Parks for refusing to give her seat to a white man on a bus in Montgomery, Alabama, resulted in a bus boycott led by Martin Luther King, Jr.

1957 Eisenhower extended Truman Doctrine to Middle East with aid to Jordan.

Governor Orval Faubus called out Arkansas National Guard to prevent integration of Little Rock schools; Eisenhower sent federal troops to protect rights of black students.

Civil Rights Act was passed—the first such legislation since Reconstruction.

1958 First U.S. Earth satellite was launched.

Eisenhower sent marines to Lebanon during civil insurrection.

1959 Alaska and Hawaii admitted to Union.

Soviet Premier Khrushchev met with Eisenhower at Camp David, Maryland.

1960 American U-2 reconnaissance plane shot down over Soviet territory; Francis Gary Powers, pilot, exchanged for Rudolf Abel in 1962.

John F. Kennedy elected President with Lyndon B. Johnson as Vice-President.

1961 Anti-Castro invasion at Bay of Pigs failed.

Kennedy established Peace Corps and proposed Alliance for Progress.

Alan B. Shepard, Jr.; first American in space.

1962 After bloody campus clashes, James H. Meredith became the first black to enter the University of Mississippi.

John H. Glenn, Jr.; first American to orbit Earth.

Kennedy protested presence of Russian missiles on Cuba; danger of nuclear war ended with Soviet dismantling of weapons.

1963 Racial violence broke out in Birmingham, Ala.

United States, Britain, and Soviet Union signed treaty barring atmospheric nuclear testing.

Washington and Moscow opened "hot line" phone connection to reduce risk of accidental war.

Martin Luther King led "March on Washington."

Kennedy assassinated in Dallas; Lyndon B. Johnson became President.

1964 Civil Rights Act strengthened voting guarantee, prohibited segregation in public facilities.

24th Amendment, abolishing poll tax, ratified.

Johnson won landslide victory over Barry Goldwater in Presidential election.

1965 Large-scale antiwar demonstrations developed after Johnson announced Vietnam troop build-up.

Race riot erupted in Watts section of Los Angeles.

Johnson sent troops to Dominican Republic.

1966 Medicare program went into effect.

Chicago, Cleveland, and other Northern cities experienced major race riots.

1967 Antiwar, antidraft, and race riots increased.

Johnson and Premier Kosygin met at Glassboro, New Jersey.

25th Amendment, providing continuity in case of Presidential disability, ratified.

Treaty pledging peaceful uses of outer space signed with Soviet Union and Great Britain.

1968 North Korea seized U.S. Navy intelligence ship *Pueblo;* men released 11 months later.

Reverend Martin Luther King, Jr. and Senator Robert F. Kennedy assassinated.

Delegates from Washington and Hanoi met in Paris for preliminary Vietnam peace talks.

Richard M. Nixon won Presidential election; Spiro Agnew became Vice-President.

1969 Americans Neil A. Armstrong and Edwin E. Aldrin, Jr., were first men to land on Moon.

1970 U.S. and South Vietnamese troops enter Cambodia.

1971 26th Amendment grants voting rights to 18-year-olds. Nixon froze wages and prices; devalued dollar by 8.57%.

1972 Nixon visited Russia and China.

"Watergate Burglars" caught inside Democratic party's national headquarters.

Richard M. Nixon and Spiro T. Agnew reelected President and Vice-President.

1973 "Watergate" dominated American political scene. Spiro T. Agnew resigned vice-presidency; Gerald R. Ford replaced him.

1974 President Nixon resigned and Gerald Ford became the 38th president.

1975 The Vietnam war ended. Unemployment reached 9.2%, highest since 1941.

1976 Jimmy Carter defeated Ford in Presidential election; Walter F. Mondale elected Vice-President.

1977 Carter established "human rights" as a key element in U.S. foreign policy.

1978 U.S. dollar fell in value against Western European and Japanese currencies.

1979 U.S. recognized the People's Republic of China.

Gasoline and fuel oil prices rose sharply.

Canal Zone ceded to Panama.

U.S. Embassy personnel taken hostage in Iran.

1980 Over 125,000 refugees fled Cuba for U.S.

Ronald W. Reagan defeated Carter in Presidential election; George H. W. Bush elected Vice-President.

1981 Iran returned hostages to U.S.

President Reagan shot in Washington, but recovered successfully.

Astronauts Young and Crippen piloted space shuttle *Columbia* around earth in 36 orbits.

In CONGRESS, July 4, 1776

A DECLARATION

By the REPRESENTATIVES of the UNITED STATES OF AMERICA,

In GENERAL CONGRESS assembled.

WHEN in the Course of human Events, it becomes necessary for one People to dissolve the Political Bands which have connected them with another, and to assume among the Powers of the Earth, the separate and equal Station to which the Laws of Nature and of Nature's God entitle them, a decent Respect to the Opinions of Mankind requires that they should declare the causes which impel them to the Separation.

WE hold these Truths to be self-evident, that all Men are created equal, that they are endowed by their Creator with certain unalienable Rights, that among these are Life, Liberty, and the Pursuit of Happiness—That to secure these Rights, Governments are instituted among Men, deriving their just Powers from the Consent of the Governed, that whenever any Form of Government becomes destructive of these Ends, it is the Right of the People to alter or to abolish it, and to institute new Government, laying its Foundation on such Principles, and organizing its Powers in such Form, as to them shall seem most likely to effect their Safety and Happiness. Prudence, indeed, will dictate that Governments long established should not be changed for light and transient Causes; and accordingly all Experience hath shewn, that Mankind are more disposed to suffer, while Evils are sufferable, than to right themselves by abolishing the Forms to which they are accustomed. But when a long Train of Abuses and Usurpations, pursuing invariably the same Object, evinces a Design to reduce them under absolute Despotism, it is their Right, it is their Duty, to throw off such Government, and to provide new Guards for their future Security. Such has been the patient Sufferance of these Colonies; and such is now the Necessity which constrains them to alter their former Systems of Government. The History of the present King of Great-Britain is a History of repeated Injuries and Usurpations, all having in direct Object the Establishment of an absolute Tyranny over these States. To prove this, let Facts be submitted to a candid World.

HE has refused his Assent to Laws, the most wholesome and necessary for the public Good.

HE has forbidden his Governors to pass Laws of immediate and pressing Importance, unless suspended in their Operation till his Assent should be obtained; and when so suspended, he has utterly neglected to attend to them.

HE has refused to pass other Laws for the Accommodation of large Districts of People, unless those People would relinquish the Right of Representation in the Legislature, a Right inestimable to them, and formidable to Tyrants only.

HE has called together Legislative Bodies at Places unusual, uncomfortable, and distant from the Depository of their public Records, for the sole Purpose of fatiguing them into Compliance with his Measures.

HE has dissolved Representative Houses repeatedly, for opposing with manly Firmness his Invasions on the Rights of the People.

HE has refused for a long Time, after such Dissolutions, to cause others to be elected; whereby the Legislative Powers, incapable of Annihilation, have returned to the People at large for their exercise; the State remaining in the mean time exposed to all the Dangers of Invasion from without, and Convulsions within.

HE has endeavoured to prevent the Population of these States; for that Purpose obstructing the Laws for Naturalization of Foreigners; refusing to pass others to encourage their Migrations hither, and raising the Conditions of new Appropriations of Lands.

HE has obstructed the Administration of Justice, by refusing his Assent to Laws for establishing Judiciary Powers.

HE has made Judges dependent on his Will alone, for the Tenure of their Offices, and the Amount and Payment of their Salaries.

HE has erected a Multitude of new Offices, and sent hither Swarms of Officers to harass our People, and eat out their Substance.

HE has kept among us, in Times of Peace, Standing Armies, without the consent of our Legislatures.

HE has affected to render the Military independent of and superior to the Civil Power.

HE has combined with others to subject us to a Jurisdiction foreign to our Constitution, and unacknowledged by our Laws; giving his Assent to their Acts of pretended Legislation:

FOR quartering large Bodies of Armed Troops among us:

FOR protecting them, by a mock Trial, from Punishment for any Murders which they should commit on the Inhabitants of these States:

FOR cutting off our Trade with all Parts of the World:

FOR imposing Taxes on us without our Consent:

FOR depriving us, in many Cases, of the Benefits of Trial by Jury:

FOR transporting us beyond Seas to be tried for pretended Offences:

FOR abolishing the free System of English Laws in a neighbouring Province, establishing therein an arbitrary Government, and enlarging its Boundaries, so as to render it at once an Example and fit Instrument for introducing the same absolute Rule into these Colonies:

FOR taking away our Charters, abolishing our most valuable Laws, and altering fundamentally the Forms of our Governments:

FOR suspending our own Legislatures, and declaring themselves invested with Power to legislate for us in all Cases whatsoever.

HE has abdicated Government here, by declaring us out of his Protection and waging War against us.

HE has plundered our Seas, ravaged our Coasts, burnt our Towns, and destroyed the Lives of our People.

HE is, at this Time, transporting large Armies of foreign Mercenaries to compleat the Works of Death, Desolation, and Tyranny, already begun with circumstances of Cruelty and Perfidy, scarcely paralleled in the most barbarous Ages, and totally unworthy the Head of a civilized Nation.

HE has constrained our fellow Citizens taken Captive on the high Seas to bear Arms against their Country, to become the Executioners of their Friends and Brethren, or to fall themselves by their Hands.

HE has excited domestic Insurrections amongst us, and has endeavoured to bring on the Inhabitants of our Frontiers, the merciless Indian Savages, whose known Rule of Warfare, is an undistinguished Destruction of all Ages, Sexes and Conditions.

IN every stage of these Oppressions we have Petitioned for Redress in the most humble Terms: Our repeated Petitions have been answered only by repeated Injury. A Prince, whose Character is thus marked by every act which may define a Tyrant, is unfit to be the Ruler of a free People.

NOR have we been wanting in Attentions to our British Brethren. We have warned them from Time to Time of Attempts by their Legislature to extend an unwarrantable Jurisdiction over us. We have reminded them of the Circumstances of our Emigration and Settlement here. We have appealed to their native Justice and Magnanimity, and we have conjured them by the Ties of our common Kindred to disavow these Usurpations, which, would inevitably interrupt our Connections and Correspondence. They too have been deaf to the Voice of Justice and of Consanguinity. We must, therefore, acquiesce in the Necessity, which denounces our Separation, and hold them, as we hold the rest of Mankind, Enemies in War, in Peace, Friends.

WE, therefore, the Representatives of the UNITED STATES OF AMERICA, in GENERAL CONGRESS, Assembled, appealing to the Supreme Judge of the World for the Rectitude of our Intentions, do, in the Name, and by Authority of the good People of these Colonies, solemnly Publish and Declare, That these United Colonies are, and of Right ought to be, FREE AND INDEPENDENT STATES; that they are absolved from all Allegiance to the British Crown, and that all political Connection between them and the State of Great-Britain, is and ought to be totally dissolved; and that as FREE AND INDEPENDENT STATES, they have full Power to levy War, conclude Peace, contract Alliances, establish Commerce, and to do all other Acts and Things which INDEPENDENT STATES may of right do. And for the support of this Declaration, with a firm Reliance on the Protection of divine Providence, we mutually pledge to each other our Lives, our Fortunes, and our sacred Honor.

Signed by ORDER and in
BEHALF of the CONGRESS,
JOHN HANCOCK, PRESIDENT

ATTEST.
CHARLES THOMSON, SECRETARY.

SIGNERS OF THE DECLARATION OF INDEPENDENCE: 1776

Name	Age	Occupation	Education	Representing	Birthplace	Born	Died
John Adams	40	Lawyer	Harvard	Massachusetts	Braintree, Mass.	1735	1826
Samuel Adams	53	Politician	Harvard	Massachusetts	Boston, Mass.	1722	1803
Josiah Bartlett	46	Physician	Private tutors	New Hampshire	Amesbury, Mass.	1729	1795
Carter Braxton	39	Planter	William & Mary	Virginia	Newington, Va.	1736	1797
Charles Carroll	38	Planter	Educated in Europe	Maryland	Annapolis, Md.	1737	1832
Samuel Chase	35	Lawyer	Private tutors	Maryland	Somerset Co., Md.	1741	1811
Abraham Clark	40	Lawyer-Farmer	Self-educated	New Jersey	Elizabethtown, N.J.	1726	1794
George Clymer	37	Merchant	Self-educated	Pennsylvania	Philadelphia, Pa.	1739	1813
William Ellery	48	Lawyer	Harvard	Rhode Island	Newport, R.I.	1727	1820
William Floyd	41	Farmer	Private tutors	New York	Brookhaven, N.Y.	1734	1821
Benjamin Franklin	71	Public servant	Grammar school	Pennsylvania	Boston, Mass.	1706	1790
Elbridge Gerry	31	Merchant	Harvard	Massachusetts	Marblehead, Mass.	1744	1814
Button Gwinnett	c. 41	Planter	Preparatory studies	Georgia	Gloucestershire, England	c. 1735	1777
Lyman Hall	52	Physician	Yale	Georgia	Wallingford, Conn.	1724	1790
John Hancock	39	Merchant	Harvard	Massachusetts	Braintree, Mass.	1737	1793
Benjamin Harrison	c. 50	Planter	Attended William & Mary	Virginia	Charles City Co., Va.	c. 1726	1791
John Hart	c. 65	Farmer	Self-educated	New Jersey	Stonington, Conn.	c. 1711	1779
Joseph Hewes	46	Merchant	Grammar school	North Carolina	Kingston, N.J.	1730	1779
Thomas Heyward	29	Lawyer	Studied law in England	South Carolina	St. Helena's Parish, S.C.	1746	1809
William Hooper	34	Lawyer	Harvard	North Carolina	Boston, Mass.	1742	1790
Stephen Hopkins	70	Public servant	Self-educated	Rhode Island	Providence, R.I.	1707	1785
Francis Hopkinson	38	Lawyer	College of Philadelphia[1]	New Jersey	Philadelphia, Pa.	1737	1791
Samuel Huntington	45	Lawyer	Self-educated	Connecticut	Windham, Conn.	1731	1796
Thomas Jefferson	33	Lawyer-Planter	William & Mary	Virginia	Goochland Co., Va.	1743	1826
Richard Henry Lee	44	Planter	Private tutors	Virginia	Westmoreland Co., Va.	1732	1794
Francis Lightfoot Lee	41	Planter	Private tutors	Virginia	Westmoreland Co., Va.	1734	1797
Francis Lewis	63	Merchant	Grammar school	New York	Llandaff, Wales	1713	c. 1802
Philip Livingston	60	Merchant	Yale	New York	Albany, N.Y.	1716	1778
Thomas Lynch	26	Planter	Studied law in England	South Carolina	Prince George's Parish, S.C.	1749	1779
Thomas McKean	42	Lawyer	Preparatory studies	Delaware	New London Township, Pa.	1734	1817
Arthur Middleton	34	Planter	Studied law in England	South Carolina	near Charlestown, S.C.	1742	1787
Lewis Morris	50	Landowner	Yale	New York	Morrisania, N.Y.	1726	1798
Robert Morris	42	Merchant	Self-educated	Pennsylvania	Liverpool, England	1734	1806
John Morton	c. 42	Surveyor	Private tutors	Pennsylvania	Ridely, Pa.	c. 1724	1777

Name	Age	Occupation	Education	Representing	Birthplace	Born	Died
Thomas Nelson	41	Planter	Educated in England	Virginia	Yorktown, Va.	1738	1789
William Paca	37	Lawyer	College of Phila-delphia;[1] attended schools in England	Maryland	near Abingdon, Md.	1740	1799
Robert Treat Paine	45	Lawyer	Harvard	Massachusetts	Boston, Mass.	1731	1814
John Penn	c. 36	Lawyer	Self-educated	North Carolina	Caroline Co., Va.	c. 1740	1788
George Read	42	Lawyer	Preparatory studies	Delaware	near Northeast, Cecil Co., Md.	1733	1798
Caesar Rodney	48	Landowner	Private tutors	Delaware	near Dover, Del.	1728	1784
George Ross	46	Lawyer	Preparatory studies	Pennsylvania	New Castle, Del.	1730	1779
Benjamin Rush	30	Physician	College of New Jersey;[2] medical education, Univ. of Edinburgh	Pennsylvania	Byberry, Pa.	1745	1813
Edward Rutledge	26	Lawyer	Studied law in England	South Carolina	Charleston, S.C.	1749	1800
Roger Sherman	55	Merchant	Self-educated	Connecticut	Newton, Mass.	1721	1793
James Smith	c. 57	Lawyer-Iron master	Preparatory studies	Pennsylvania	Ireland	c. 1719	1806
Richard Stockton	46	Lawyer	College of New Jersey[2]	New Jersey	Princeton, N.J.	1730	1781
Thomas Stone	c. 33	Lawyer-Planter	Private tutors	Maryland	Charles Co., Md.	1743	1787
George Taylor	c. 60	Iron master	Preparatory studies	Pennsylvania	Ireland	1716	1781
Matthew Thornton	c. 62	Physician	Preparatory studies	New Hampshire	Ireland	c. 1714	1803
George Walton	c. 35	Lawyer	Self-educated	Georgia	Prince Edward Co., Va.	c. 1741	1804
William Whipple	46	Merchant	Grammar school	New Hampshire	Kittery, Me.	1730	1785
William Williams	45	Public servant-Merchant	Harvard	Connecticut	Lebanon, Conn.	1731	1811
James Wilson	33	Lawyer	Educated in Scotland	Pennsylvania	near St. Andrews, Scotland	1742	1798
John Witherspoon	53	College presi-dent-Clergyman	Univ. of Edinburgh	New Jersey	Gifford, Hadding-tonshire, Scotland	1723	1794
Oliver Wolcott	49	Lawyer	Yale	Connecticut	Windsor, Conn.	1726	1797
George Wythe	c. 50	Lawyer	Attended William & Mary	Virginia	Elizabeth City Co., Va.	1726	1806

[1] now University of Pennsylvania. [2] now Princeton University.

THE CONSTITUTION

WE, the People of the United States, in order to form a more perfect union, establish justice, insure domestic tranquility, provide for the common defence, promote the general welfare, and secure the blessings of liberty to ourselves and our posterity, do ordain and establish this Constitution for the United States of America.

ARTICLE I.

Sect. 1. ALL legislative powers herein granted shall be vested in a Congress of the United States, which shall consist of a Senate and House of Representatives.

Sect. 2. The House of Representatives shall be composed of members chosen every second year by the people of the several states, and the electors in each state shall have the qualifications requisite for electors of the most numerous branch of the state legislature.

No person shall be a representative who shall not have attained to the age of twenty-five years, and been seven years a citizen of the United States, and who shall not, when elected, be an inhabitant of that state in which he shall be chosen.

[1][Representatives and direct taxes shall be apportioned among the several states which may be included within this Union, according to their respective numbers, which shall be determined by adding to the whole number of free persons, including those bound to service for a term of years, and excluding Indians not taxed, three-fifths of all other persons.] The actual enumeration shall be made within three years after the first meeting of the Congress of the United States, and within every subsequent term of ten years, in such manner as they shall by law direct. The number of representatives shall not exceed one for every thirty thousand, but each state shall have at least one representative; and until such enumeration shall be made, the state of New-Hampshire shall be entitled to chuse three, Massachusetts eight, Rhode-Island and Providence Plantations one, Connecticut five, New-York six, New-Jersey four, Pennsylvania eight, Delaware one, Maryland six, Virginia ten, North-Carolina five, South-Carolina five, and Georgia three.

When vacancies happen in the representation from any state, the Executive authority thereof shall issue writs of election to fill such vacancies.

The House of Representatives shall chuse their Speaker and other officers; and shall have the sole power of impeachment.

Sect. 3. The Senate of the United States shall be composed of two senators from each state, [2][chosen by the legislature thereof,] for six years; and each senator shall have one vote.

Immediately after they shall be assembled in consequence of the first election, they shall be divided as equally as may be into three classes. The seats of the senators of the first class shall be vacated at the expiration of the second year, of the second class at the expiration of the fourth year, and of the third class at the expiration of the sixth year, so that one-third may be chosen every second year; [3][and if vacancies happen by resignation, or otherwise, during the recess of the

[1] The part enclosed by brackets was changed by section 2 of Amendment XIV. [2] The clause enclosed by brackets was changed by clause 1 of Amendment XVII. [3] The part enclosed by brackets was changed by clause 2 of Amendment XVII.

Legislature of any state, the Executive thereof may make temporary appointments until the next meeting of the Legislature, which shall then fill such vacancies.]

No person shall be a senator who shall not have attained to the age of thirty years, and been nine years a citizen of the United States, and who shall not, when elected, be an inhabitant of that state for which he shall be chosen.

The Vice-President of the United States shall be President of the Senate, but shall have no vote, unless they be equally divided.

The Senate shall chuse their other officers, and also a President pro tempore, in the absence of the Vice-President, or when he shall exercise the office of President of the United States.

The Senate shall have the sole power to try all impeachments. When sitting for that purpose, they shall be on oath or affirmation. When the President of the United States is tried, the Chief Justice shall preside: And no person shall be convicted without the concurrence of two-thirds of the members present.

Judgment in cases of impeachment shall not extend further than to removal from office and disqualification to hold and enjoy any office of honor, trust or profit under the United States; but the party convicted shall nevertheless be liable and subject to indictment, trial, judgment and punishment, according to law.

Sect. 4. The times, places and manner of holding elections for senators and representatives, shall be prescribed in each state by the legislature thereof; but the Congress may at any time by law make or alter such regulations, except as to the places of chusing Senators.

The Congress shall assemble at least once in every year, and such meeting shall ⁴[be on the first Monday in December,] unless they shall by law appoint a different day.

Sect. 5. Each house shall be the judge of the elections, returns and qualifications of its own members, and a majority of each shall constitute a quorum to do business; but a smaller number may adjourn from day to day, and may be authorized to compel the attendance of absent members, in such manner, and under such penalties as each house may provide.

Each house may determine the rules of its proceedings, punish its members for disorderly behaviour, and, with the concurrence of two-thirds, expel a member.

Each house shall keep a journal of its proceedings, and from time to time publish the same, excepting such parts as may in their judgment require secrecy; and the yeas and nays of the members of either house on any question shall, at the desire of one-fifth of those present, be entered on the journal.

Neither house, during the session of Congress shall, without the consent of the other, adjourn for more than three days, nor to any other place than that in which the two houses shall be sitting.

Sect. 6. The senators and representatives shall receive a compensation for their services, to be ascertained by law, and paid out of the treasury of the United States. They shall in all cases, except treason, felony and breach of the peace, be privileged from arrest during their attendance at the session of their respective houses, and in going to and returning from the same; and for any

speech or debate in either house, they shall not be questioned in any other place.

No senator or representative shall, during the time for which he was elected, be appointed to any civil office under the authority of the United States, which shall have been created, or the emoluments whereof shall have been encreased during such time; and no person holding any office under the United States, shall be a member of either house during his continuance in office.

Sect. 7. All bills for raising revenue shall originate in the house of representatives; but the senate may propose or concur with amendments as on other bills.

Every bill which shall have passed the house of representatives and the senate, shall, before it become a law, be presented to the president of the United States; if he approve he shall sign it, but if not he shall return it, with his objections to that house in which it shall have originated, who shall enter the objections at large on their journal, and proceed to reconsider it. If after such reconsideration two-thirds of that house shall agree to pass the bill, it shall be sent, together with the objections, to the other house, by which it shall likewise be reconsidered, and if approved by two-thirds of that house, it shall become a law. But in all such cases the votes of both houses shall be determined by yeas and nays, and the names of the persons voting for and against the bill shall be entered on the journal of each house respectively. If any bill shall not be returned by the President within ten days (Sundays excepted) after it shall have been presented to him, the same shall be a law, in like manner as if he had signed it, unless the Congress by their adjournment prevent its return, in which case it shall not be a law.

Every order, resolution, or vote to which the concurrence of the Senate and House of Representatives may be necessary (except on a question of adjournment) shall be presented to the President of the United States; and before the same shall take effect, shall be approved by him, or, being disapproved by him, shall be repassed by two-thirds of the Senate and House of Representatives, according to the rules and limitations prescribed in the case of a bill.

Sect. 8. The Congress shall have power

To lay and collect taxes, duties, imposts and excises, to pay the debts and provide for the common defence and general welfare of the United States; but all duties, imposts and excises shall be uniform throughout the United States;

To borrow money on the credit of the United States;

To regulate commerce with foreign nations, and among the several states, and with the Indian tribes;

To establish an uniform rule of naturalization, and uniform laws on the subject of bankruptcies throughout the United States;

To coin money, regulate the value thereof, and of foreign coin, and fix the standard of weights and measures;

To provide for the punishment of counterfeiting the securities and current coin of the United States;

To establish post offices and post roads;

To promote the progress of science and useful arts, by securing for limited times to authors and inventors the exclusive right to their respective writings and discoveries;

---

⁴ The clause enclosed by brackets was changed by section 2 of Amendment XX.

To constitute tribunals inferior to the supreme court;

To define and punish piracies and felonies committed on the high seas, and offences against the law of nations;

To declare war, grant letters of marque and reprisal, and make rules concerning captures on land and water;

To raise and support armies, but no appropriation of money to that use shall be for a longer term than two years;

To provide and maintain a navy;

To make rules for the government and regulation of the land and naval forces;

To provide for calling forth the militia to execute the laws of the union, suppress insurrections and repel invasions;

To provide for organizing, arming, and disciplining, the militia, and for governing such part of them as may be employed in the service of the United States, reserving to the States respectively, the appointment of the officers, and the authority of training the militia according to the discipline prescribed by Congress;

To exercise exclusive legislation in all cases whatsoever, over such district (not exceeding ten miles square) as may, by cession of particular States, and the acceptance of Congress, become the seat of the government of the United States, and to exercise like authority over all places purchased by the consent of the legislature of the states in which the same shall be, for the erection of forts, magazines, arsenals, dock-yards, and other needful buildings;—And

To make all laws which shall be necessary and proper for carrying into execution the foregoing powers, and all other powers vested by this constitution in the government of the United States, or in any department or officer thereof.

Sect. 9. The migration or importation of such persons as any of the states now existing shall think proper to admit, shall not be prohibited by the Congress prior to the year one thousand eight hundred and eight, but a tax or duty may be imposed on such importation, not exceeding ten dollars for each person.

The privilege of the writ of habeas corpus shall not be suspended, unless when in cases of rebellion or invasion the public safety may require it.

No bill of attainder or ex post facto law shall be passed.

No capitation, or other direct, tax shall be laid, unless in proportion to the census or enumeration herein before directed to be taken.[5]

No tax or duty shall be laid on articles exported from any state. No preference shall be given by any regulation of commerce or revenue to the ports of one state over those of another: nor shall vessels bound to, or from, one state, be obliged to enter, clear, or pay duties in another.

No money shall be drawn from the treasury, but in consequence of appropriations made by law; and a regular statement and account of the receipts and expenditures of all public money shall be published from time to time.

No title of nobility shall be granted by the United States:—And no person holding any office of profit or trust under them, shall, without the consent of the Congress, accept of any present, emolument, office, or title, of any kind whatever, from any king, prince, or foreign state.

Sect. 10. No state shall enter into any treaty, alliance, or confederation; grant letters of marque and reprisal; coin money; emit bills of credit; make any thing but gold and silver coin a tender in payment of debts; pass any bill of attainder, ex post facto law, or law impairing the obligation of contracts, or grant any title of nobility.

No state shall, without the consent of the Congress, lay any imposts or duties on imports or exports, except what may be absolutely necessary for executing its inspection laws; and the net produce of all duties and imposts, laid by any state on imports or exports, shall be for the use of the Treasury of the United States; and all such laws shall be subject to the revision and controul of the Congress. No state shall, without the consent of Congress, lay any duty of tonnage, keep troops, or ships of war in time of peace, enter into any agreement or compact with another state, or with a foreign power, or engage in war, unless actually invaded, or in such imminent danger as will not admit of delay.

II.

Sect. 1. The executive power shall be vested in a president of the United States of America. He shall hold his office during the term of four years, and, together with the vice-president, chosen for the same term, be elected as follows.

Each state shall appoint, in such manner as the legislature thereof may direct, a number of electors, equal to the whole number of senators and representatives to which the state may be entitled in the Congress: but no senator or representative, or person holding an office of trust or profit under the United States, shall be appointed an elector.

[6][The electors shall meet in their respective states, and vote by ballot for two persons, of whom one at least shall not be an inhabitant of the same state with themselves. And they shall make a list of all the persons voted for, and of the number of votes for each; which list they shall sign and certify, and transmit sealed to the seat of the government of the United States, directed to the president of the senate. The president of the senate shall, in the presence of the senate and house of representatives, open all the certificates, and the votes shall then be counted. The person having the greatest number of votes shall be the president, if such number be a majority of the whole number of electors appointed; and if there be more than one who have such majority, and have an equal number of votes, then the house of representatives shall immediately chuse by ballot one of them for president; and if no person have a majority, then from the five highest on the list the said house shall in like manner chuse the president. But in chusing the president, the votes shall be taken by states, the representation from each state having one vote; a quorum for this purpose shall consist of a member or members from two-thirds of the states, and a majority of all the states shall be necessary to a choice. In every case, after the choice of the president, the person having the greatest number of votes of the electors shall be the vice-president. But if there should remain two or more who have equal votes, the senate shall chuse from them by ballot the vice-president.]

The Congress may determine the time of chusing the electors, and the day on which they shall give their votes; which day shall be the same throughout the United States.

[5] See also Amendment XVI. [6] This paragraph has been superseded by Amendment XII.

No person except a natural born citizen, or a citizen of the United States, at the time of the adoption of this constitution, shall be eligible to the office of president; neither shall any person be eligible to that office who shall not have attained to the age of thirty-five years, and been fourteen years a resident within the United States.

[7]In case of the removal of the president from office, or of his death, resignation, or inability to discharge the powers and duties of the said office, the same shall devolve on the vice-president, and the Congress may by law provide for the case of removal, death, resignation or inability, both of the president and vice-president, declaring what officer shall then act as president, and such officer shall act accordingly, until the disability be removed, or a president be elected.

The president shall, at stated times, receive for his services, a compensation, which shall neither be encreased nor diminished during the period for which he shall have been elected, and he shall not receive within that period any other emolument from the United States, or any of them.

Before he enter on the execution of his office, he shall take the following oath or affirmation:

"I do solemnly swear (or affirm) that I will faithfully execute the office of president of the United States, and will to the best of my ability, preserve, protect and defend the constitution of the United States."

Sect. 2. The president shall be commander in chief of the army and navy of the United States, and of the militia of the several States, when called into the actual service of the United States; he may require the opinion, in writing, of the principal officer in each of the executive departments, upon any subject relating to the duties of their respective offices, and he shall have power to grant reprieves and pardons for offences against the United States, except in cases of impeachment.

He shall have power, by and with the advice and consent of the senate, to make treaties, provided two-thirds of the senators present concur; and he shall nominate, and by and with the advice and consent of the senate, shall appoint ambassadors, other public ministers and consuls, judges of the supreme court, and all other officers of the United States, whose appointments are not herein otherwise provided for, and which shall be established by law. But the Congress may by law vest the appointment of such inferior officers, as they think proper, in the president alone, in the courts of law, or in the heads of departments.

The president shall have power to fill up all vacancies that may happen during the recess of the senate, by granting commissions which shall expire at the end of their session.

Sect. 3. He shall from time to time give to the Congress information of the state of the union, and recommend to their consideration such measures as he shall judge necessary and expedient; he may, on extraordinary occasions, convene both houses, or either of them, and in case of disagreement between them, with respect to the time of adjournment, he may adjourn them to such time as he shall think proper; he shall receive ambassadors and other public ministers; he shall take care that the laws be faithfully executed, and shall commission all the officers of the United States.

Sect. 4. The president, vice-president and all civil officers of the United States, shall be removed from office on impeachment for, and con-

victim of, treason, bribery, or other high crimes and misdemeanors.

III.

Sect. 1. The judicial power of the United States, shall be vested in one supreme court, and in such inferior courts as the Congress may from time to time ordain and establish. The judges, both of the supreme and inferior courts, shall hold their offices during good behaviour, and shall, at stated times, receive for their services, a compensation, which shall not be diminished during their continuance in office.

Sect. 2. The judicial power shall extend to all cases, in law and equity, arising under this constitution, the laws of the United States, and treaties made, or which shall be made, under their authority; to all cases of admiralty and maritime jurisdiction; to controversies to which the United States shall be a party; to controversies between two or more States, between a state and citizens of another state,[8] between citizens of different States, between citizens of the same state claiming lands under grants of different States, and between a state, or the citizens thereof, and foreign States, citizens or subjects.

In all cases affecting ambassadors, other public ministers and consuls, and those in which a state shall be party, the supreme court shall have original jurisdiction. In all the other cases before mentioned, the supreme court shall have appellate jurisdiction, both as to law and fact, with such exceptions, and under such regulations as the Congress shall make.

The trial of all crimes, except in cases of impeachment, shall be by jury; and such trial shall be held in the state where the said crimes shall have been committed; but when not committed within any state, the trial shall be at such place or places as the Congress may by law have directed.

Sect. 3. Treason against the United States, shall consist only in levying war against them, or in adhering to their enemies, giving them aid and comfort. No person shall be convicted of treason unless on the testimony of two witnesses to the same overt act, or on confession in open court.

The Congress shall have power to declare the punishment of treason, but no attainder of treason shall work corruption of blood, or forfeiture except during the life of the person attainted.

IV.

Sect. 1. Full faith and credit shall be given in each state to the public acts, records, and judicial proceedings of every other state. And the Congress may by general laws prescribe the manner in which such acts, records and proceedings shall be proved, and the effect thereof.

Sect. 2. The citizens of each state shall be entitled to all privileges and immunities of citizens in the several states.

A person charged in any state with treason, felony, or other crime, who shall flee from justice, and be found in another state, shall, on demand of the executive authority of the state from which he fled, be delivered up, to be removed to the state having jurisdiction of the crime.

[9][No person held to service or labour in one state, under the laws thereof, escaping into another, shall, in consequence of any law or regulation therein, be discharged from such service or labour, but shall be delivered up on claim of

---

[7] Affected by Amendment XXV. [8] Affected by Amendment XI. [9] Superseded by Amendment XIII.

the party to whom such service or labour may be due.]

Sect. 3. New states may be admitted by the Congress into this union; but no new state shall be formed or erected within the jurisdiction of any other state; nor any state be formed by the junction of two or more states, or parts of states, without the consent of the legislatures of the states concerned as well as of the Congress.

The Congress shall have power to dispose of and make all needful rules and regulations respecting the territory or other property belonging to the United States; and nothing in this Constitution shall be so construed as to prejudice any claims of the United States, or of any particular state.

Sect. 4. The United States shall guarantee to every state in this union a Republican form of government, and shall protect each of them against invasion; and on application of the legislature, or of the executive (when the legislature cannot be convened) against domestic violence.

V.

The Congress, whenever two-thirds of both houses shall deem it necessary, shall propose amendments to this constitution, or, on the application of the legislatures of two-thirds of the several states, shall call a convention for proposing amendments, which, in either case, shall be valid to all intents and purposes, as part of this constitution, when ratified by the legislatures of three-fourths of the several states, or by conventions in three-fourths thereof, as the one or the other mode of ratification may be proposed by Congress; Provided, that no amendment which may be made prior to the year one thousand eight hundred and eight shall in any manner affect the first and fourth clauses in the ninth sec-

tion of the first article; and that no state, without its consent, shall be deprived of its equal suffrage in the senate.

VI.

All debts contracted and engagements entered into, before the adoption of this Constitution, shall be as valid against the United States under this Constitution, as under the confederation.

This constitution, and the laws of the United States which shall be made in pursuance thereof; and all treaties made, or which shall be made, under the authority of the United States, shall be the supreme law of the land; and the judges in every state shall be bound thereby, any thing in the constitution or laws of any state to the contrary notwithstanding.

The senators and representatives beforementioned, and the members of the several state legislatures, and all executive and judicial officers, both of the United States and of the several States, shall be bound by oath or affirmation, to support this constitution; but no religious test shall ever be required as a qualification to any office or public trust under the United States.

VII.

The ratification of the conventions of nine States, shall be sufficient for the establishment of this constitution between the States so ratifying the same.

[Done in Convention, by the unanimous consent of the States present, the seventeenth day of September, in the year of our Lord one thousand seven hundred and eighty-seven, and of the Independence of the United States of America the twelfth. In witness whereof we have hereunto subscribed our Names.]

SIGNERS OF THE CONSTITUTION: 1787

Name	Age	Occupation	Education	Representing	Birthplace	Born	Died
Abraham Baldwin	32	Lawyer	Yale	Georgia	Guilford, Conn.	1754	1807
Richard Bassett	42	Lawyer	Private tutors	Delaware	Cecil Co., Md.	1745	1815
Gunning Bedford	c. 40	Lawyer	College of New Jersey[1]	Delaware	Philadelphia, Pa.	1747	1812
John Blair	c. 55	Jurist	Studied law in England	Virginia	Williamsburg, Va.	1732	1800
William Blount	38	Public servant	Private tutors	North Carolina	Bertie Co., N.C.	1749	1800
David Brearley	42	Jurist	Private tutors	New Jersey	Spring Grove, N.J.	1745	1790
Jacob Broom	35	Businessman	Preparatory studies	Delaware	Wilmington, Del.	1752	1810
Pierce Butler	43	Planter	Private tutors	South Carolina	Co. Carlow, Ireland	1744	1822
Daniel Carroll	57	Planter-Businessman	Educated at Jesuit schools in Maryland and France	Maryland	Upper Marlboro, Md.	1730	1796
George Clymer	48	Merchant	Self-educated	Pennsylvania	Philadelphia, Pa.	1739	1813
Jonathan Dayton	26	Lawyer	College of New Jersey[1]	New Jersey	Elizabeth-Town, N.J.	1760	1824
John Dickinson	55	Public servant	Studied law in England	Delaware	Talbot Co., Md.	1732	1808
William Few	39	Lawyer	Self-educated	Georgia	near Baltimore, Md.	1748	1828
Thomas Fitzsimons	c. 46	Businessman	Self-educated	Pennsylvania	Ireland	1741	1811
Benjamin Franklin	81	Public servant	Grammar school	Pennsylvania	Boston, Mass.	1706	1790
Nicholas Gilman	32	Public servant	Grammar school	New Hampshire	Exeter, N.H.	1755	1814
Nathaniel Gorham	49	Businessman	Private tutors	Massachusetts	Charlestown, Mass.	1738	1796
Alexander Hamilton	32	Lawyer	King's College[2]	New York	West Indies	1755	1804
Jared Ingersoll	37	Lawyer	Yale; studied law in England	Pennsylvania	New Haven, Conn.	1749	1822
Daniel of St. Thomas Jenifer	c. 64	Planter-Public servant	Preparatory studies	Maryland	Charles Co., Md.	1723	1790
William Samuel Johnson	59	Lawyer-College president	Yale; A.M., Harvard	Connecticut	Stratford, Conn.	1727	1819
Rufus King	32	Lawyer	Harvard	Massachusetts	Scarboro, Mass.	1755	1827
John Langdon	46	Businessman	Grammar School	New Hampshire	Portsmouth, N.H.	1741	1819
William Livingston	53	Public servant	Yale	New Jersey	Albany, N.Y.	1723	1790
James Madison	36	Lawyer	College of New Jersey[1]	Virginia	Port Conway, Va.	1751	1836
James McHenry	c. 34	Businessman	Educated in Ireland and Delaware; studied medicine under Benjamin Rush	Maryland	Ireland	c. 1753	1816
Thomas Mifflin	33	Merchant	College of Philadelphia[3]	Pennsylvania	Philadelphia, Pa.	1744	1800
Gouverneur Morris	35	Lawyer	King's College[2]	Pennsylvania	Morrisania, N.Y.	1752	1816
Robert Morris	53	Merchant	Self-educated	Pennsylvania	Liverpool, England	1734	1806
William Paterson	31	Lawyer	College of New Jersey[1]	Maryland	Co. Antrim, Ireland	1745	1806

Name	Age	Occupation	Education	Representing	Birthplace	Born	Died
Charles Pinckney	29	Lawyer	Preparatory studies	South Carolina	Charleston, S.C.	1757	1824
Charles Cotesworth Pinckney	41	Lawyer	Oxford	South Carolina	Charleston, S.C.	1746	1825
George Read	53	Lawyer	Preparatory studies	Delaware	near Northeast, Cecil Co., Md.	1733	1798
John Rutledge	c. 58	Public servant	Studied law in England	South Carolina	Charleston, S.C.	1739	1800
Roger Sherman	66	Businessman	Self-educated	Connecticut	Newton, Mass.	1721	1793
Richard Dobbs Spaight	29	Planter	Educated in Ireland and Scotland	North Carolina	New Bern, N.C.	1758	1802
George Washington ...	55	Planter	Private tutors	Virginia	Westmoreland Co., Va.	1732	1799
Hugh Williamson	41	Businessman-Physician	College of Philadelphia;[3] M.D., Univ. of Utrecht	North Carolina	West Nottingham, Pa.	1735	1819
James Wilson	44	Lawyer	Educated in Scotland	Pennsylvania	Scotland	1742	1798

[1] now Princeton University. [2] now Columbia University. [3] now University of Pennsylvania.

THE CONSTITUTIONAL AMENDMENTS

The first ten amendments* to the original Constitution are known as the Bill of Rights.

AMENDMENT [I]

Congress shall make no law respecting an establishment of religion, or prohibiting the free exercise thereof; or abridging the freedom of speech, or of the press; or the right of the people peaceably to assemble, and to petition the Government for a redress of grievances.

AMENDMENT [II]

A well regulated Militia, being necessary to the security of a free State, the right of the people to keep and bear Arms, shall not be infringed.

AMENDMENT [III]

No Soldier shall, in time of peace be quartered in any house, without the consent of the Owner, nor in time of war, but in a manner to be prescribed by law.

AMENDMENT [IV]

The right of the people to be secure in their persons, houses, papers, and effects, against unreasonable searches and seizures, shall not be violated, and no Warrants shall issue, but upon probable cause, supported by Oath or affirmation, and particularly describing the place to be searched, and the persons or things to be seized.

AMENDMENT [V]

No person shall be held to answer for a capital, or otherwise infamous crime, unless on a presentment or indictment of a Grand Jury, except in cases arising in the land or naval forces, or in the Militia, when in actual service in time of War or public danger; nor shall any person be subject for the same offence to be twice put in jeopardy of life or limb; nor shall be compelled in any criminal case to be a witness against himself, nor be deprived of life, liberty, or property, without due process of law; nor shall private property be taken for public use, without just compensation.

AMENDMENT [VI]

In all criminal prosecutions, the accused shall enjoy the right to a speedy and public trial, by an impartial jury of the State and district wherein the crime shall have been committed, which district shall have been previously ascertained by law, and to be informed of the nature and cause of the accusation; to be confronted with the witnesses against him; to have compulsory process for obtaining witnesses in his favor, and to have the Assistance of Counsel for his defence.

AMENDMENT [VII]

In Suits at common law, where the value in controversy shall exceed twenty dollars, the right of trial by jury shall be preserved, and no fact tried by a jury, shall be otherwise re-examined in any Court of the United States, than according to the rules of the common law.

AMENDMENT [VIII]

Excessive bail shall not be required, nor excessive fines imposed, nor cruel and unusual punishments inflicted.

AMENDMENT [IX]

The enumeration in the Constitution, of certain rights, shall not be construed to deny or disparage others retained by the people.

AMENDMENT [X]

The powers not delegated to the United States by the Constitution, nor prohibited by it to the States, are reserved to the States respectively, or to the people.

AMENDMENT [XI][1]

The Judicial power of the United States shall not be construed to extend to any suit in law or equity, commenced or prosecuted against one of the United States by Citizens of another State, or by Citizens or Subjects of any Foreign State.

AMENDMENT [XII][2]

The Electors shall meet in their respective states, and vote by ballot for President and Vice-President, one of whom, at least, shall not be an inhabitant of the same state with themselves; they shall name in their ballots the person voted for as President, and in distinct ballots the person voted for as Vice-President, and they shall make distinct lists of all persons voted for as President, and

* The first 10 amendments, together with 2 others that failed of ratification, were proposed to the several States by resolution of Congress on September 25, 1789. The ratifications were transmitted by the Governors to the President and by him communicated to Congress from time to time. The first 10 amendments were ratified by 11 of the 14 States. Virginia completed the required three fourths by ratification on December 15, 1791, and its action was communicated to Congress by the President on December 30, 1791. The legislatures of Massachusetts, Georgia, and Connecticut ratified them on March 2, 1939, March 18, 1939, and April 19, 1939, respectively.

[1] The Eleventh Amendment was proposed by resolution of Congress on March 4, 1794. It was declared by the President, in a message to Congress dated January 8, 1798, to have been ratified by three fourths of the several States. Records of the National Archives show that the 11th Amendment was ratified by 13 of the 16 States. It was not ratified by New Jersey or Pennsylvania.
[2] The Twelfth Amendment was proposed in lieu of the original third paragraph of section I of article II, by resolution of Congress on December 9, 1803. It was declared in a proclamation of the Secretary of State, dated September 25, 1804, to have been ratified by three fourths of the States. Records of the National Archives show that it was ratified by 14 States and rejected by Connecticut and Delaware.

of all persons voted for as Vice-President, and of the number of votes for each, which lists they shall sign and certify, and transmit sealed to the seat of the government of the United States, directed to the President of the Senate;—The President of the Senate shall, in the presence of the Senate and House of Representatives, open all the certificates and the votes shall then be counted;—The person having the greatest number of votes for President, shall be the President, if such number be a majority of the whole number of Electors appointed; and if no person have such majority, then from the persons having the highest numbers not exceeding three on the list of those voted for as President, the House of Representatives shall choose immediately, by ballot, the President. But in choosing the President, the votes shall be taken by states, the representation from each state having one vote; a quorum for this purpose shall consist of a member or members from two-thirds of the states, and a majority of all the states shall be necessary to a choice. ³[And if the House of Representatives shall not choose a President whenever the right of choice shall devolve upon them, before the fourth day of March next following, then the Vice-President shall act as President, as in the case of the death or other constitutional disability of the President.]—The person having the greatest number of votes as Vice-President, shall be the Vice-President, if such number be a majority of the whole number of Electors appointed, and if no person have a majority, then from the two highest numbers on the list, the Senate shall choose the Vice-President; a quorum for the purpose shall consist of two-thirds of the whole number of Senators, and a majority of the whole number shall be necessary to a choice. But no person constitutionally ineligible to the office of President shall be eligible to that of Vice-President of the United States.

AMENDMENT [XIII]⁴

Section 1. Neither slavery nor involuntary servitude, except as a punishment for crime whereof the party shall have been duly convicted, shall exist within the United States, or any place subject to their jurisdiction.

Section 2. Congress shall have power to enforce this article by appropriate legislation.

AMENDMENT [XIV]⁵

Section 1. All persons born or naturalized in the United States, and subject to the jurisdiction thereof, are citizens of the United States and of the State wherein they reside. No State shall make or enforce any law which shall abridge the privileges or immunities of citizens of the United States; nor shall any State deprive any person of life, liberty, or property, without due process of

law; nor deny to any person within its jurisdiction the equal protection of the laws.

Section 2. Representatives shall be apportioned among the several States according to their respective numbers, counting the whole number of persons in each State, excluding Indians not taxed. But when the right to vote at any election for the choice of electors for President and Vice President of the United States, Representatives in Congree, the Executive and Judicial officers of a State, or the members of the Legislature thereof, is denied to any of the male inhabitants of such State, being twenty-one years of age, and citizens of the United States, or in any way abridged, except for participation in rebellion, or other crime, the basis of representation therein shall be reduced in the proportion which the number of such male citizens shall bear to the whole number of male citizens twenty-one years of age in such State.

Section 3. No person shall be a Senator or Representative in Congress, or elector of President and Vice President, or hold any office, civil or military, under the United States, or under any State, who, having previously taken an oath, as a member of Congress, or as an officer of the United States, or as a member of any State legislature, or as an executive or judicial officer of any State, to support the Constitution of the United States, shall have engaged in insurrection or rebellion against the same, or given aid or comfort to the enemies thereof. But Congress may by a vote of two-thirds of each House, remove such disability.

Section 4. The validity of the public debt of the United States, authorized by law, including debts incurred for payment of pensions and bounties for services in suppressing insurrection or rebellion, shall not be questioned. But neither the United States nor any State shall assume or pay any debt or obligation incurred in aid of insurrection or rebellion against the United States, or any claim for the loss or emancipation of any slave; but all such debts, obligations and claims shall be held illegal and void.

Section 5. The Congress shall have power to enforce, by appropriate legislation, the provisions of this article.

AMENDMENT [XV]⁶

Section 1. The right of citizens of the United States to vote shall not be denied or abridged by the United States or by any State on account of race, color, or previous condition of servitude.

Section 2. The Congress shall have power to enforce this article by appropriate legislation.

AMENDMENT [XVI]⁷

The Congress shall have power to lay and collect taxes on incomes, from whatever source de-

---

³ The part enclosed by brackets has been superseded by section 3 of Amendment XX.
⁴ The Thirteenth Amendment was proposed by resolution of Congress on January 31, 1865. It was declared in a proclamation of the Secretary of State, dated December 18, 1865, to have been ratified by 27 States. Subsequent records of the National Archives show that the 13th Amendment was ratified by 7 additional States. It was rejected by Kentucky and Mississippi.
⁵ The Fourteenth Amendment was proposed by resolution of Congress on June 13, 1866. By a concurrent resolution of Congress adopted July 21, 1868, it was declared to have been ratified by "three fourths and more of the several States of the Union," and the Secretary of State was required duly to promulgate the amendment as a part of the Constitution. He accordingly issued a proclamation, dated July 28, 1868, declaring the amendment to have been ratified by 30 States, "being more than three fourths." Records of the National Archives show that the 14th Amendment was subsequently ratified by 8 additional States. It was rejected by Kentucky.
⁶ The Fifteenth Amendment was proposed by resolution of Congress on February 26, 1869. It was declared in a proclamation of the Secretary of State, dated March 30, 1870, to have been ratified by 29 States, which "constitute three fourths." Records of the National Archives show that the 15th Amendment was subsequently ratified by 6 more of the States. It was rejected by Kentucky, Maryland, and Tennessee.
⁷ The Sixteenth Amendment was proposed by resolution of Congress on July 12, 1909. It was declared in a proclamation of the Secretary of State, dated February 25, 1913, to have been ratified by 38 States, which "constitute three fourths." Subsequent records of the National Archives show that the 16th Amendment was ratified by 4 additional States. It was rejected by Connecticut, Florida, Rhode Island, and Utah.

rived, without apportionment among the several States, and without regard to any census or enumeration.

AMENDMENT [XVII][8]

The Senate of the United States shall be composed of two Senators from each State, elected by the people thereof, for six years; and each Senator shall have one vote. The electors in each State shall have the qualifications requisite for electors of the most numerous branch of the State legislatures.

When vacancies happen in the representation of any State in the Senate, the executive authority of such State shall issue writs of election to fill such vacancies: *Provided,* That the legislature of any State may empower the executive thereof to make temporary appointments until the people fill the vacancies by election as the legislature may direct.

This amendment shall not be so construed as to affect the election or term of any Senator chosen before it becomes valid as part of the Constitution.

AMENDMENT [XVIII][9]

[Section 1. After one year from the ratification of this article the manufacture, sale, or transportation of intoxicating liquors within, the importation thereof into, or the exportation thereof from the United States and all territory subject to the jurisdiction thereof for beverage purposes is hereby prohibited.

[Sec. 2. The Congress and the several States shall have concurrent power to enforce this article by appropriate legislation.

[Sec. 3. This article shall be inoperative unless it shall have been ratified as an amendment to the Constitution by the legislatures of the several States, as provided in the Constitution, within seven years from the date of the submission hereof to the States by the Congress.]

AMENDMENT [XIX][10]

The right of citizens of the United States to vote shall not be denied or abridged by the United States or by any State on account of sex.

Congress shall have power to enforce this article by appropriate legislation.

AMENDMENT [XX][11]

Section 1. The terms of the President and Vice President shall end at noon on the 20th day of January, and the terms of Senators and Representatives at noon on the 3d day of January, of the years in which such terms would have ended if this article had not been ratified; and the terms of their successors shall then begin.

Sec. 2. The Congress shall assemble at least once in every year, and such meeting shall begin at noon on the 3d day of January, unless they shall by law appoint a different day.

Sec. 3. If, at the time fixed for the beginning of the term of the President, the President elect shall have died, the Vice President elect shall become President. If a President shall not have been chosen before the time fixed for the beginning of his term, or if the President elect shall have failed to qualify, then the Vice President elect shall act as President until a President shall have qualified; and the Congress may by law provide for the case wherein neither a President elect nor a Vice President elect shall have qualified, declaring who shall then act as President, or the manner in which one who is to act shall be selected, and such person shall act accordingly until a President or Vice President shall have qualified.

Sec. 4. The Congress may by law provide for the case of the death of any of the persons from whom the House of Representatives may choose a President whenever the right of choice shall have devolved upon them, and for the case of the death of any of the persons from whom the Senate may choose a Vice President whenever the right of choice shall have devolved upon them.

Sec. 5. Sections 1 and 2 shall take effect on the 15th day of October following the ratification of this article.

Sec. 6. This article shall be inoperative unless it shall have been ratified as an amendment to the Constitution by the legislatures of three-fourths of the several States within seven years from the date of its submission.

AMENDMENT [XXI][12]

Section 1. The eighteenth article of amendment to the Constitution of the United States is hereby repealed.

Sec. 2. The transportation or importation into any State, Territory, or possession of the United States for delivery or use therein of intoxicating liquors, in violation of the laws thereof, is hereby prohibited.

Sec. 3. This article shall be inoperative unless it shall have been ratified as an amendment to the Constitution by conventions in the several States, as provided in the Constitution, within seven

[8] The Seventeenth Amendment was proposed by resolution of Congress on May 13, 1912. It was declared in a proclamation of the Secretary of State, dated May 31, 1913, to have been ratified by 36 States, which "constitute three fourths." Records of the National Archives show that the 17th Amendment was subsequently ratified by 1 additional State. It was rejected by Utah and Delaware.

[9] The Eighteenth Amendment was proposed by resolution of Congress on December 18, 1917. It was declared in a proclamation of the Acting Secretary of State, dated January 29, 1919, to have been ratified by 36 States, which "constitute three fourths." Subsequent records of the National Archives show that the 18th Amendment was ratified by 10 additional States. It was rejected by Rhode Island. By its own terms the 18th Amendment became effective one year after its ratification, which was consummated on January 16, 1919, and therefore went into effect on January 16, 1920.
Repeal of the 18th Amendment on December 5, 1933, was proclaimed by the President in his proclamation of that date, when the ratification of the 21st Amendment was certified by the Acting Secretary of State.

[10] The Nineteenth Amendment was proposed by resolution of Congress on June 4, 1919. It was declared in a proclamation of the Secretary of State, dated August 26, 1920, to have been ratified by 36 States, which "constitute three fourths." Subsequent records of the National Archives show that the 19th Amendment was ratified by 5 additional States. It was rejected by Georgia, South Carolina, Mississippi, Delaware, and Louisiana.

[11] The Twentieth Amendment was proposed by resolution of Congress on March 2, 1932. It was declared in a proclamation of the Secretary of State, dated February 6, 1933, to have been ratified by 39 States, which "constitute more than the requisite three fourths." Subsequent records of the National Archives show that the 20th Amendment was ratified by all 48 States before sections 1 and 2 became effective on October 15, 1933. The other sections of the amendment became effective on January 23, 1933, when its ratification was consummated by three fourths of the States.

[12] The Twenty-first Amendment was proposed by resolution of Congress on February 20, 1933. It was certified in a proclamation of the Acting Secretary of State dated December 5, 1933, to have been ratified by conventions of 36 States, which "constitute the requisite three fourths of the whole number of States." Subsequent records of the National Archives show that the 21st Amendment was ratified by 2 additional States. It was rejected by the convention of South Carolina. North Carolina voted against holding a convention.

years from the date of the submission hereof to the States by the Congress.

AMENDMENT [XXII][13]

Section 1. No person shall be elected to the office of the President more than twice, and no person who has held the office of President, or acted as President, for more than two years of a term to which some other person was elected President shall be elected to the office of the President more than once. But this Article shall not apply to any person holding the office of President when this Article was proposed by the Congress, and shall not prevent any person who may be holding the office of President, or acting as President, during the term within which this Article becomes operative from holding the office of President or acting as President during the remainder of such term.

Sec. 2. This article shall be inoperative unless it shall have been ratified as an amendment to the Constitution by the legislatures of three-fourths of the several States within seven years from the date of its submission to the States by the Congress.

AMENDMENT [XXIII][14]

Section 1. The District constituting the seat of Government of the United States shall appoint in such manner as the Congress may direct:

A number of electors of President and Vice President equal to the whole number of Senators and Representatives in Congress to which the District would be entitled if it were a State, but in no event more than the least populous State; they shall be in addition to those appointed by the States, but they shall be considered, for the purposes of the election of President and Vice President, to be electors appointed by a State; and they shall meet in the District and perform such duties as provided by the twelfth article of amendment.

Section 2. The Congress shall have power to enforce this article by appropriate legislation.

AMENDMENT [XXIV][15]

Section 1. The right of citizens of the United States to vote in any primary or other election for President or Vice President, for electors for President or Vice President, or for Senator or Representative in Congress, shall not be denied or abridged by the United States or any State by reason of failure to pay any poll tax or other tax.

Section 2. The Congress shall have power to enforce this article by appropriate legislation.

AMENDMENT [XXV][16]

Section 1. In case of removal of the President from office or of his death or resignation, the Vice President shall become President.

Sec. 2. Whenever there is a vacancy in the office of the Vice President, the President shall nominate a Vice President who shall take office upon confirmation by a majority vote of both Houses of Congress.

Sec. 3. Whenever the President transmits to the President pro tempore of the Senate and the Speaker of the House of Representatives his written declaration that he is unable to discharge the powers and duties of his office, and until he transmits to them a written declaration to the contrary, such powers and duties shall be discharged by the Vice President as Acting President.

Sec. 4. Whenever the Vice President and a majority of either the principal officers of the executive departments or of such other body as Congress may by law provide, transmit to the President pro tempore of the Senate and the Speaker of the House of Representatives their written declaration that the President is unable to discharge the powers and duties of his office, the Vice President shall immediately assume the powers and duties of the office as Acting President.

Thereafter, when the President transmits to the President pro tempore of the Senate and the Speaker of the House of Representatives his written declaration that no inability exists, he shall resume the powers and duties of his office unless the Vice President and a majority of either the principal officers of the executive department or of such other body as Congress may by law provide, transmit within four days to the President pro tempore of the Senate and the Speaker of the House of Representatives their written declaration that the President is unable to discharge the powers and duties of his office. Thereupon Congress shall decide the issue, assembling within forty-eight hours for that purpose if not in session. If the Congress, within twenty-one days after receipt of the latter written declaration, or, if Congress is not in session, within twenty-one days after Congress is required to assemble, determines by two-thirds vote of both Houses that the President is unable to discharge the powers and duties of his office, the Vice President shall continue to discharge the same as Acting President; otherwise, the President shall resume the powers and duties of his office.

AMENDMENT [XXVI][17]

Section 1. The right of citizens of the United States, who are eighteen years of age or older, to vote shall not be denied or abridged by the United States or by any State on account of age.

Sec. 2. The Congress shall have power to enforce this article by appropriate legislation.

---

[13] The Twenty-second Amendment was proposed by resolution of Congress on March 24, 1947. Ratification was completed on February 27, 1951, when the thirty-sixth State (Minnesota) approved the amendment. On March 1, 1951, the Administrator of General Services certified that "the States whose Legislatures have so ratified the said proposed Amendment constitute the requisite three-fourths of the whole number of States in the United States." Records of the National Archives show that the 22d Amendment was subsequently ratified by 5 additional States.

[14] The Twenty-third Amendment was proposed by resolution of Congress on June 16, 1960. The Administrator of General Services certified the ratification and adoption of the amendment by three-fourths of the States on April 3, 1961. It was rejected by Arkansas.

[15] The Twenty-fourth Amendment was proposed by resolution of Congress on August 27, 1962. It was declared in a Proclamation of the Administrator of General Services dated February 4, 1964, to have been ratified by three-fourths of the States. It was rejected by the legislature of Mississippi on December 20, 1962.

[16] The Twenty-fifth Amendment to the Constitution was proposed by the Congress on July 6, 1965. It was declared in a certificate of the Administrator of General Services, dated February 23, 1967, to have been ratified by the legislatures of 39 of the 50 States. Ratification was completed on February 10, 1967.

[17] The Twenty-sixth Amendment was proposed by resolution of Congress on March 23, 1971. On July 5, 1971, the Administrator of General Services certified the ratification and adoption of the amendment by three fourths of the states.

ADMINISTRATIONS, CABINETS, AND CONGRESSES

SOURCE: *Biographical Directory of the American Congress* and other sources

A cabinet officer is not appointed for a fixed term and does not necessarily go out of office with the President who appointed him; while it is customary to tender his resignation at the time a change of administration takes place, he remains formally at the head of his department until a successor is appointed. Subordinates acting temporarily as heads of departments are not considered cabinet officers; in the earlier period of the nation's history, not all cabinet officers were heads of departments.

The dates immediately following the names of executive officers are those upon which commissions were issued, unless otherwise specifically noted. Where periods of time are indicated by dates as, for instance, March 4, 1793–March 3, 1797, both such dates are included as portions of the time period.

The National Security Act of 1947 (Pub. Law 253, 80th Cong., 1st sess.), approved July 26, 1947, created the office of Secretary of Defense and merged the War and Navy Departments into the National Military Establishment. The act was subsequently amended (Pub. Law 216, 81st Cong., 1st sess.): Section 201. (a) There is hereby established, as an executive department of the Government, the **Department of Defense.**

The Reorganization Plan Number 1 of 1953 (Pub. Law 13, 83d Cong., 1st sess.), approved April 1, 1953, abolished the Federal Security Agency and created the **Department of Health, Education, and Welfare,** which was renamed the **Department of Health and Human Services** in 1979.

The **Department of Housing and Urban Development** was established by the Department of Housing and Urban Development Act of September 9, 1965 (79 Stat. 667; 5 U.S.C. 642).

The **Department of Transportation** was established by the Department of Transportation Act of October 15, 1966 (80 Stat. 931; 49 U.S.C. 1681).

As of July 1, 1971, the Post Office Department became **The U.S. Postal Service,** a quasi-independent nonprofit corporation. The Postmaster General ceased to be a member of the cabinet.

The **Department of Energy** was established by Public Law 95-91, August 4, 1977.

The **Department of Education** was established by Public Law 96-88, October 17, 1979.

Congressional vacancies are not noted below.

First Administration of GEORGE WASHINGTON
APRIL 30, 1789, TO MARCH 3, 1793

PRESIDENT—George Washington, of Virginia (No party). VICE-PRESIDENT—John Adams, of Massachusetts. SECRETARY OF STATE—John Jay, of New York, was Secretary for Foreign Affairs under the Confederation, and continued to act, at the request of Washington, until Jefferson took office. Thomas Jefferson, of Virginia, September 26, 1789; entered upon duties March 22, 1790. SECRETARY OF THE TREASURY—Alexander Hamilton, of New York, September 11, 1789. SECRETARY OF WAR—Henry Knox, of Massachusetts, September 12, 1789. ATTORNEY GENERAL—Edmund Randolph, of Virginia, September 26, 1789; entered upon duties February 2, 1790. POSTMASTER GENERAL—Samuel Osgood, of Massachusetts, September 26, 1789. Timothy Pickering, of Pennsylvania, August 12, 1791; entered upon duties August 19, 1791.

1st Congress

1st Session: Mar. 4, 1789–Sept. 29, 1789[1]; 2d Session: Jan. 4, 1790–Aug. 12, 1790; 3d Session: Dec. 6, 1790–Mar. 3, 1791.

President pro tempore of the Senate: John Langdon, of New Hampshire (elected Apr. 6, 1789). Speaker of the House: Frederick A. C. Muhlenberg, of Pennsylvania (elected Apr. 1, 1789).

Senate: 17 pro-administration; 9 opposition

House: 38 pro-administration; 26 opposition

2d Congress

1st Session: Oct. 24, 1791–May 8, 1792; 2d Session: Nov. 5, 1792–Mar. 2, 1793; Special Session of the Senate: Mar. 4, 1791.

President pro tempore of the Senate: Richard H. Lee, of Virginia (elected Apr. 18, 1792); John Langdon, of New Hampshire (elected Nov. 5, 1792 and Mar. 1, 1793). Speaker of the House: Jonathan Trumbull, of Connecticut (elected Oct. 24, 1791).

Senate: 16 Federalist; 13 Democratic-Republican

House: 37 Federalist; 33 Democratic-Republican

Second Administration of GEORGE WASHINGTON
MARCH 4, 1793, TO MARCH 3, 1797

PRESIDENT—George Washington, of Virginia (No party). VICE-PRESIDENT—John Adams, of Massachusetts. SECRETARY OF STATE—Thomas Jefferson, of Virginia, continued from preceding administration. Edmund Randolph, of Virginia, January 2, 1794. Timothy Pickering, of Pennsylvania (Secretary of War), ad interim, August 20, 1795. Timothy Pickering, of Pennsylvania, December 10, 1795. SECRETARY OF THE TREASURY—Alexander Hamilton, of New York, continued from preceding administration. Oliver Wolcott, Jr., of Connecticut, February 2, 1795. SECRETARY OF WAR—Henry Knox, of Massachusetts, continued from preceding administration. Timothy Pickering, of Pennsylvania, January 2, 1795. Timothy Pickering, of Pennsylvania (Secretary of State), ad interim, December 10, 1795, to February 5, 1796. James McHenry, of Maryland, January 27, 1796; entered upon duties February 6, 1796. ATTORNEY GENERAL—Edmund Randolph, of Virginia, continued from preceding administration. William Bradford, of Pennsylvania, January 27, 1794; entered upon duties January 29, 1794. Charles Lee, of Virginia, December 10, 1795. POSTMASTER GENERAL—Timothy Pickering, of Pennsylvania, continued from preceding administration. Timothy Pickering, of Pennsylvania, recommissioned June 1, 1794. Joseph Habersham, of Georgia, February 25, 1795.

3d Congress

1st Session: Dec. 2, 1793–June 9, 1794; 2d Session: Nov. 3, 1794–Mar. 3, 1795; Special Session of the Senate: Mar. 4, 1793.

President pro tempore of the Senate: Ralph Izard, of South Carolina (elected May 31, 1794); Henry Tazewell, of Virginia (elected Feb. 20, 1795). Speaker of the House: Frederick A. C. Muhlenberg, of Pennsylvania (elected Dec. 2, 1793).

Senate: 17 Federalist; 13 Democratic-Republican

House: 57 Democratic-Republican; 48 Federalist

4th Congress

1st Session: Dec. 7, 1795–June 1, 1796; 2d Session: Dec. 5, 1796–Mar. 3, 1797; Special Session of the Senate: June 8, 1795–June 26, 1795.

President pro tempore of the Senate: Henry Tazewell, of Virginia (elected Dec. 7, 1795), Samuel Livermore, of New Hampshire (elected May 6, 1796), William Bingham, of Pennsylvania (Feb. 16, 1797). Speaker of the House: Jonathan Dayton, of New Jersey (elected Dec. 7, 1795).

Senate: 19 Federalist; 13 Democratic-Republican

House: 54 Federalist; 52 Democratic-Republican

Administration of JOHN ADAMS
MARCH 4, 1797, TO MARCH 3, 1801

PRESIDENT—John Adams, of Massachusetts (Federalist). VICE-PRESIDENT—Thomas Jefferson, of Virginia. SECRETARY OF STATE—Timothy Pickering, of Pennsylvania, continued from preceding administration; resignation requested May 10, 1800, but declining to resign, he was dismissed May 12, 1800. Charles Lee, of Virginia (Attorney General), ad interim, May 13, 1800. John Marshall, of Virginia, May 13, 1800; entered upon duties June 6, 1800. John Marshall, of Virginia (Chief Justice of the United States), ad interim, February 4, 1801, to March 3, 1801. SECRETARY OF THE TREASURY—Oliver Wolcott, Jr., of Connecticut, continued from preceding administration. Samuel Dexter, of Massachusetts, January 1, 1801. SECRETARY OF WAR—James McHenry, of Maryland, continued from preceding administration. Benjamin Stoddert, of Maryland (Secretary of the Navy), ad interim, June 1, 1800, to June 12, 1800. Samuel Dexter, of Massachusetts, May 13, 1800; entered upon duties June 12, 1800. Samuel Dexter, of Massachusetts (Secretary of the Treasury), ad interim, January 1, 1801. ATTORNEY GENERAL—Charles Lee, of Virginia, continued from preceding administration. POSTMASTER GENERAL—Joseph Habersham, of Georgia, continued from preceding administration. SECRETARY OF THE NAVY—Benjamin Stoddert, of Maryland, May 21, 1798; entered upon duties June 18, 1798.

5th Congress

1st Session: May 15, 1797–July 10, 1797; 2d Session: Nov. 13, 1797–July 16, 1798; 3d Session: Dec. 3, 1798–Mar. 3, 1799; Special Sessions of the Senate: Mar. 4, 1797; July 17, 1798–July 19, 1798.

President pro tempore of the Senate: William Bradford, of Rhode Island (elected July 6, 1797); Jacob Read, of South Carolina (elected Nov. 22, 1797); Theodore Sedgwick, of Massachusetts (elected June 27, 1798); John Laurence, of New York (elected Dec. 6, 1798); James Ross of Pennsylvania (elected Mar. 1, 1799). Speaker of the House: Jonathan Dayton, of New Jersey (reelected May 15, 1797); George Dent, of Maryland served as Speaker pro tempore Apr. 20, 1798, and May 28, 1798.

Senate: 20 Federalist; 12 Democratic-Republican

House: 58 Federalist; 48 Democratic-Republican

[1] Both houses met for the first time on Mar. 4, 1789, but each lacked a quorum. They met from day to day until the House attained a quorum on Apr. 1, 1789, and the Senate on Apr. 6, 1789.

6th Congress

1st Session: Dec. 2, 1799–May 14, 1800; 2d Session: Nov. 17, 1800–Mar. 3, 1801.

President pro tempore of the Senate: Samuel Livermore, of New Hampshire (elected Dec. 2, 1799); Uriah Tracy, of Connecticut (elected May 14, 1800); John E. Howard, of Maryland (elected Nov. 21, 1800); James Hillhouse, of Connecticut (elected Feb. 28, 1801). Speaker of the House: Theodore Sedgwick, of Massachusetts (elected Dec. 2, 1799).

Senate: 19 Federalist; 13 Democratic-Republican

House: 64 Federalist; 42 Democratic-Republican

First Administration of THOMAS JEFFERSON
MARCH 4, 1801, TO MARCH 3, 1805

PRESIDENT—Thomas Jefferson, of Virginia (Democratic-Republican). VICE-PRESIDENT—Aaron Burr, of New York. SECRETARY OF STATE—John Marshall, of Virginia (Chief Justice of the United States), for one day (March 4, 1801), and for a special purpose. Levi Lincoln, of Massachusetts (Attorney General), ad interim, March 5, 1801. James Madison, of Virginia, March 5, 1801; entered upon duties May 2, 1801. SECRETARY OF THE TREASURY—Samuel Dexter, of Massachusetts, continued from preceding administration to May 6, 1801. Albert Gallatin, of Pennsylvania, May 14, 1801. SECRETARY OF WAR—Henry Dearborn, of Massachusetts, March 5, 1801. ATTORNEY GENERAL—Levi Lincoln, of Massachusetts, March 5, 1801, to December 31, 1804. POSTMASTER GENERAL—Joseph Habersham, of Georgia, continued from preceding administration. Gideon Granger, of Connecticut, November 28, 1801. SECRETARY OF THE NAVY—Benjamin Stoddert, of Maryland, continued from preceding administration. Henry Dearborn, of Massachusetts (Secretary of War), ad interim, April 1, 1801. Robert Smith, of Maryland, July 15, 1801; entered upon duties July 27, 1801.

7th Congress

1st Session: Dec. 7, 1801–May 3, 1802; 2d Session: Dec. 6, 1802–March 3, 1803; Special Session of the Senate: Mar. 4, 1801–Mar. 5, 1801.

President pro tempore of the Senate: Abraham Baldwin, of Georgia (elected Dec. 7, 1801; Apr. 17, 1802); Stephen R. Bradley, of Vermont (elected Dec. 14, 1802; Feb. 25, 1803; Mar. 2, 1803). Speaker of the House: Nathaniel Macon, of North Carolina (elected Dec. 7, 1801).

Senate: 18 Democratic-Republican; 14 Federalist

House: 69 Democratic-Republican; 36 Federalist

8th Congress

1st Session: Oct. 17, 1803–Mar. 27, 1804; 2d Session: Nov. 5, 1804–Mar. 3, 1805.

President pro tempore of the Senate: John Brown, of Kentucky (elected Oct. 17, 1803; Jan. 23, 1804); Jesse Franklin, of North Carolina (elected Mar. 10, 1804); Joseph Anderson, of Tennessee (elected Jan. 15, 1805; Feb. 28, 1805; Mar. 2, 1805). Speaker of the House: Nathaniel Macon, of North Carolina (reelected Oct. 17, 1803).

Senate: 25 Democratic-Republican; 9 Federalist

House: 102 Democratic-Republican; 39 Federalist

Second Administration of THOMAS JEFFERSON
MARCH 4, 1805, TO MARCH 3, 1809

PRESIDENT—Thomas Jefferson, of Virginia (Democratic-Republican). VICE-PRESIDENT—George Clinton, of New York. SECRETARY OF STATE—James Madison, of Virginia, continued from preceding administration. SECRETARY OF THE TREASURY—Albert Gallatin, of Pennsylvania, continued from preceding administration. SECRETARY OF WAR—Henry Dearborn, of Massachusetts, continued from preceding administration. John Smith (chief clerk), ad interim, February 17, 1809. ATTORNEY GENERAL—John Breckinridge, of Kentucky, August 7, 1805 (died December 14, 1806). Caesar A. Rodney, of Delaware, January 20, 1807. POSTMASTER GENERAL—Gideon Granger, of Connecticut, continued from preceding administration. SECRETARY OF THE NAVY—Robert Smith, of Maryland, continued from preceding administration.

9th Congress

1st Session: Dec. 2, 1805–Apr. 21, 1806; 2d Session: Dec. 1, 1806–Mar. 3, 1807; Special Session of the Senate: Mar. 4, 1805.

President pro tempore of the Senate: Samuel Smith, of Maryland (elected Dec. 2, 1805; Mar. 18, 1806; Mar. 2, 1807). Speaker of the House: Nathaniel Macon, of North Carolina (reelected Dec. 2, 1805).

Senate: 27 Democratic-Republican; 7 Federalist

House: 116 Democratic-Republican; 25 Federalist

10th Congress

1st Session: Oct. 26, 1807–Apr. 25, 1808; 2d Session: Nov. 7, 1808–Mar. 3, 1809.

President pro tempore of the Senate: Samuel Smith, of Maryland (elected Apr. 16, 1808); Stephen R. Bradley, of Vermont (elected Dec. 28, 1808); John Milledge, of Georgia (elected Jan. 30, 1809). Speaker of the House: Joseph B. Varnum, of Massachusetts (elected Oct. 26, 1807).

Senate: 28 Democratic-Republican; 6 Federalist

House: 118 Democratic-Republican; 24 Federalist

First Administration of JAMES MADISON
MARCH 4, 1809, TO MARCH 3, 1813

PRESIDENT—James Madison, of Virginia (Democratic-Republican). VICE-PRESIDENT—George Clinton, of New York. (Died April 20, 1812.) SECRETARY OF STATE—Robert Smith, of Maryland, March 6, 1809. James Monroe, of Virginia, April 2, 1811; entered upon duties April 6, 1811. SECRETARY OF THE TREASURY—Albert Gallatin, of Pennsylvania, continued from preceding administration. SECRETARY OF WAR—John Smith (chief clerk), ad interim, continued from preceding administration. William Eustis, of Massachusetts, March 7, 1809; entered upon duties April 8, 1809; served to December 31, 1812. James Monroe, of Virginia (Secretary of State), ad interim, January 1, 1813. John Armstrong, of New York, January 13, 1813; entered upon duties February 5, 1813. ATTORNEY GENERAL—Caesar A. Rodney, of Delaware, continued from preceding administration; resigned December 5, 1811. William Pinkney, of Maryland, December 11, 1811; entered upon duties January 6, 1812. POSTMASTER GENERAL—Gideon Granger, of Connecticut, continued from preceding administration. SECRETARY OF THE NAVY—Robert Smith, of Maryland, continued from preceding administration. Charles W. Goldsborough (chief clerk), ad interim, March 8, 1809. Paul Hamilton, of South Carolina, March 7, 1809; entered upon duties May 15, 1809; served to December 31, 1812. Charles W. Goldsborough (chief clerk), ad interim, January 7, 1813, to January 18, 1813. William Jones, of Pennsylvania, January 12, 1813; entered upon duties January 19, 1813.

11th Congress

1st Session: May 22, 1809–June 28, 1809; 2d Session: Nov. 27, 1809–May 1, 1810; 3d Session: Dec. 3, 1810–Mar. 3, 1811; Special Session of the Senate: Mar. 4, 1809–Mar. 7, 1809.

President pro tempore of the Senate: Andrew Gregg, of Pennsylvania (elected June 26, 1809); John Gaillard, of South Carolina (elected Feb. 28, 1810; Apr. 17, 1810); John Pope, of Kentucky (elected Feb. 23, 1811). Speaker of the House: Joseph B. Varnum, of Massachusetts (reelected May 22, 1809).

Senate: 28 Democratic-Republican; 6 Federalist

House: 94 Democratic-Republican; 48 Federalist

12th Congress

1st Session: Nov. 4, 1811 to July 6, 1812; 2d Session: Nov. 2, 1812–Mar. 3, 1813.

President pro tempore of the Senate: William H. Crawford, of Georgia (elected Mar. 24, 1812). Speaker of the House: Henry Clay, of Kentucky (elected Nov. 4, 1811).

Senate: 30 Democratic-Republican; 6 Federalist

House: 108 Democratic-Republican; 36 Federalist

Second Administration of JAMES MADISON
MARCH 4, 1813, TO MARCH 3, 1817

PRESIDENT—James Madison, of Virginia (Democratic-Republican). VICE-PRESIDENT—Elbridge Gerry, of Massachusetts (died November 23, 1814). SECRETARY OF STATE—James Monroe, of Virginia, continued from preceding administration. James Monroe, of Virginia (Secretary of War), ad interim, October 1, 1814. James Monroe, of Virginia, February 28, 1815. SECRETARY OF THE TREASURY—Albert Gallatin, of Pennsylvania, continued from preceding administration. William Jones, of Pennsylvania (Secretary of the Navy), performed the duties of the Secretary of the Treasury during the absence of Mr. Gallatin in Europe (April 21, 1813, to February 9, 1814). George W. Campbell, of Tennessee, February 9, 1814. Alexander J. Dallas, of Pennsylvania, October 6, 1814; entered upon duties October 14, 1814. William H. Crawford, of Georgia, October 22, 1816. SECRETARY OF WAR—John Armstrong, of New York, continued from preceding administration. James Monroe, of Virginia (Secretary of State), ad interim, August 30, 1814. James Monroe, of Virginia, September 27, 1814; entered upon duties October 1, 1814. James Monroe, of Virginia (Secretary of State), ad interim, March 1, 1815. Alexander J. Dallas, of Pennsylvania (Secretary of the Treasury), ad interim, March 14, 1815, to August 8, 1815. William H. Crawford, of Georgia, August 1, 1815; entered upon duties August 8, 1815. George Graham (chief clerk), ad interim, October 22, 1816, to close of administration. ATTORNEY GENERAL—William Pinkney, of Maryland, continued from preceding administration. Richard Rush, of Pennsylvania, February 10, 1814; entered upon duties the day following. POSTMASTER

GENERAL—Gideon Granger, of Connecticut, continued from preceding administration. Return J. Meigs, Jr., of Ohio, March 17, 1814; entered upon duties April 11, 1814. SECRETARY OF THE NAVY—William Jones, of Pennsylvania, continued from preceding administration. Benjamin Homans (chief clerk), ad interim, December 2, 1814. Benjamin W. Crowninshield, of Massachusetts, December 19, 1814; entered upon duties January 16, 1815.

13th Congress
1st Session: May 24, 1813–Aug. 2, 1813; 2d Session: Dec. 6, 1813–Apr. 18, 1814; 3d Session: Sept. 19, 1814–Mar. 3, 1815.

President pro tempore of the Senate: Joseph B. Varnum, of Massachusetts (elected Dec. 6, 1813); John Gaillard, of South Carolina (elected Apr. 18, 1814; Nov. 25, 1814). Speaker of the House: Henry Clay, of Kentucky (reelected May 24, 1813); Langdon Cheves, of South Carolina (elected Jan. 19, 1814).

Senate: 27 Democratic-Republican; 9 Federalist
House: 112 Democratic-Republican; 68 Federalist

14th Congress
1st Session: Dec. 4, 1815–Apr. 30, 1816; 2d Session: Dec. 2, 1816–Mar. 3, 1817.

President pro tempore of the Senate: John Gaillard, of South Carolina (continued from preceding Congress). Speaker of the House: Henry Clay, of Kentucky (reelected Dec. 4, 1815).

Senate: 25 Democratic-Republican; 11 Federalist
House: 117 Democratic-Republican; 65 Federalist

First Administration of JAMES MONROE
MARCH 4, 1817, TO MARCH 3, 1821

PRESIDENT—James Monroe, of Virginia (Democratic-Republican). VICE-PRESIDENT—Daniel D. Tompkins, of New York. SECRETARY OF STATE—John Graham (chief clerk), ad interim, March 4, 1817. Richard Rush, of Pennsylvania (Attorney General), ad interim, March 10, 1817. John Quincy Adams, of Massachusetts, March 5, 1817; entered upon duties September 22, 1817. SECRETARY OF THE TREASURY—William H. Crawford, of Georgia, continued from preceding administration. William H. Crawford, of Georgia, recommissioned March 5, 1817. SECRETARY OF WAR—George Graham (chief clerk), ad interim, March 4, 1817. John C. Calhoun, of South Carolina, October 8, 1817; entered upon duties December 10, 1817. ATTORNEY GENERAL—Richard Rush, of Pennsylvania, continued from preceding administration to October 30, 1817. William Wirt, of Virginia, November 13, 1817; entered upon duties November 15, 1817. POSTMASTER GENERAL—Return J. Meigs, Jr., of Ohio, continued from preceding administration. SECRETARY OF THE NAVY—Benjamin W. Crowninshield, of Massachusetts, continued from preceding administration. John C. Calhoun, of South Carolina (Secretary of War), ad interim, October 1, 1818. Smith Thompson, of New York, November 9, 1818; entered upon duties January 1, 1819.

15th Congress
1st Session: Dec. 1, 1817–Apr. 20, 1818; 2d Session: Nov. 16, 1818–Mar. 3, 1819; Special Session of the Senate: Mar. 4, 1817–Mar. 6, 1817.

President pro tempore of the Senate: John Gaillard, of South Carolina (continued from preceding Congress; elected Mar. 6, 1817; Mar. 31, 1818). James Barbour, of Virginia (elected Feb. 15, 1819). Speaker of the House: Henry Clay, of Kentucky (reelected Dec. 1, 1817).

Senate: 34 Democratic-Republican; 10 Federalist
House: 141 Democratic-Republican; 42 Federalist

16th Congress
1st Session: Dec. 6, 1819–May 15, 1820; 2d Session: Nov. 13, 1820–Mar. 3, 1821.

President pro tempore of the Senate: James Barbour, of Virginia (continued from preceding Congress); John Gaillard, of South Carolina (elected Jan. 25, 1820). Speaker of the House: Henry Clay, of Kentucky (reelected Dec. 6, 1819), John W. Taylor, of New York (elected Nov. 15, 1820).

Senate: 35 Democratic-Republican; 7 Federalist
House: 156 Democratic-Republican; 27 Federalist

Second Administration of JAMES MONROE
MARCH 4, 1821, TO MARCH 3, 1825

PRESIDENT—James Monroe, of Virginia (Democratic-Republican). VICE-PRESIDENT—Daniel D. Tompkins, of New York. SECRETARY OF STATE—John Quincy Adams, of Massachusetts, continued from preceding administration. SECRETARY OF THE TREASURY—William H. Crawford, of Georgia, continued from preceding administration. SECRETARY OF WAR—John C. Calhoun, of South Carolina, continued from preceding administration. ATTORNEY GENERAL—William Wirt, of Virginia, continued

from preceding administration. POSTMASTER GENERAL—Return J. Meigs, Jr., of Ohio, continued from preceding administration. John McLean, of Ohio, commissioned June 26, 1823, to take effect July 1, 1823. SECRETARY OF THE NAVY—Smith Thompson, of New York, continued from preceding administration. John Rodgers (commodore, United States Navy, and President of the Board of Navy Commissioners), ad interim, September 1, 1823. Samuel L. Southard, of New Jersey, September 16, 1823.

17th Congress
1st Session: Dec. 3, 1821–May 8, 1822; 2d Session: Dec. 2, 1822–Mar. 3, 1823.

President pro tempore of the Senate: John Gaillard, of South Carolina (elected Feb. 1, 1822; Feb. 19, 1823). Speaker of the House: Philip P. Barbour, of Virginia (elected Dec. 4, 1821).

Senate: 44 Democratic-Republican; 4 Federalist
House: 158 Democratic-Republican; 25 Federalist

18th Congress
1st Session: Dec. 1, 1823–May 27, 1824; 2d Session: Dec. 6, 1824–Mar. 3, 1825.

President pro tempore of the Senate: John Gaillard, of South Carolina (elected May 21, 1824). Speaker of the House: Henry Clay, of Kentucky (elected Dec. 1, 1823).

Senate: 44 Democratic-Republican; 4 Federalist
House: 187 Democratic-Republican; 26 Federalist

Administration of JOHN QUINCY ADAMS
MARCH 4, 1825, TO MARCH 3, 1829

PRESIDENT—John Quincy Adams, of Massachusetts (Democratic-Republican). VICE-PRESIDENT—John C. Calhoun, of South Carolina. SECRETARY OF STATE—Daniel Brent (chief clerk), ad interim, March 4, 1825. Henry Clay, of Kentucky, March 7, 1825. SECRETARY OF THE TREASURY—Samuel L. Southard, of New Jersey (Secretary of the Navy), ad interim, March 7, 1825. Richard Rush, of Pennsylvania, March 7, 1825; entered upon duties August 1, 1825. SECRETARY OF WAR—James Barbour, of Virginia, March 7, 1825. Samuel L. Southard, of New Jersey (Secretary of the Navy), ad interim, May 26, 1828. Peter B. Porter, of New York, May 26, 1828; entered upon duties June 21, 1828. ATTORNEY GENERAL—William Wirt, of Virginia, continued from preceding administration. POSTMASTER GENERAL—John McLean, of Ohio, continued from preceding administration. SECRETARY OF THE NAVY—Samuel L. Southard, of New Jersey, continued from preceding administration.

19th Congress
1st Session: Dec. 5, 1825–May 22, 1826; 2d Session: Dec. 4, 1826–Mar. 3, 1827; Special Session of the Senate: Mar. 4, 1825–Mar. 9, 1825.

President pro tempore of the Senate: John Gaillard, of South Carolina (elected Mar. 9, 1825). Nathaniel Macon, of North Carolina (elected May 20, 1826; Jan. 2, 1827; Mar. 2, 1827). Speaker of the House: John W. Taylor, of New York (elected Dec. 5, 1825).

Senate: 26 pro-administration; 20 opposition
House: 105 pro-administration; 97 opposition

20th Congress
1st Session: Dec. 3, 1827–May 26, 1828; 2d Session: Dec. 1, 1828–Mar. 3, 1829.

President pro tempore of the Senate: Samuel Smith, of Maryland (elected May 15, 1828). Speaker of the House: Andrew Stevenson, of Virginia (elected Dec. 3, 1827).

Senate: 20 pro-administration; 26 opposition
House: 94 pro-administration; 119 opposition

First Administration of ANDREW JACKSON
MARCH 4, 1829, TO MARCH 3, 1833

PRESIDENT—Andrew Jackson, of Tennessee (Democratic). VICE-PRESIDENT—John C. Calhoun, of South Carolina (resigned December 28, 1832). SECRETARY OF STATE—James A. Hamilton, of New York, ad interim, March 4, 1829. Martin Van Buren, of New York, March 6, 1829; entered upon duties March 28, 1829. Edward Livingston, of Louisiana, May 24, 1831. SECRETARY OF THE TREASURY—Samuel D. Ingham, of Pennsylvania, March 6, 1829. Asbury Dickins (chief clerk), ad interim, June 21, 1831. Louis McLane, of Delaware, August 8, 1831. SECRETARY OF WAR—John H. Eaton, of Tennessee, March 9, 1829. Philip G. Randolph (chief clerk), ad interim, June 20, 1831. Roger B. Taney, of Maryland (Attorney General), ad interim, July 21, 1831. Lewis Cass, of Ohio, August 1, 1831; entered upon duties August 8, 1831. ATTORNEY GENERAL—John M. Berrien, of Georgia, March 9, 1829, to June 22, 1831. Roger B. Taney, of Maryland, July 20, 1831. POSTMASTER GENERAL—John McLean, of Ohio, continued from preceding administration. William T. Barry, of Kentucky, March 9, 1829; entered upon duties April 6, 1829. SECRETARY OF THE NAVY—Charles Hay (chief clerk), ad interim, March 4, 1829. John Branch, of North Carolina, March 9, 1829. John Boyle (chief clerk), ad interim, May 12, 1831. Levi Woodbury, of New Hampshire, May 23, 1831.

21st Congress
1st Session: Dec. 7, 1829–May 31, 1830; 2d Session: Dec. 6, 1830–Mar. 3, 1831; Special Session of the Senate: Mar. 4, 1829–Mar. 17, 1829.

President pro tempore of the Senate: Samuel Smith, of Maryland (elected Mar. 13, 1829; May 29, 1830; Mar. 1, 1831). Speaker of the House: Andrew Stevenson, of Virginia (reelected Dec. 7, 1829).

Senate: 26 Democratic; 22 National Republican
House: 139 Democratic; 74 National Republican

22d Congress
1st Session: Dec. 5, 1831–July 16, 1832; 2d Session: Dec. 3, 1832–Mar. 2, 1833.

President pro tempore of the Senate: Littleton W. Tazewell, of Virginia (elected July 9, 1832); Hugh L. White, of Tennessee (elected Dec. 3, 1832). Speaker of the House: Andrew Stevenson of Virginia (reelected Dec. 5, 1831).

Senate: 25 Democratic; 21 National Republican
House: 141 Democratic; 58 National Republican

Second Administration of ANDREW JACKSON
MARCH 4, 1833, TO MARCH 3, 1837

PRESIDENT—Andrew Jackson, of Tennessee (Democratic). VICE-PRESIDENT—Martin Van Buren, of New York. SECRETARY OF STATE—Edward Livingston, of Louisiana, continued from preceding administration. Louis McLane of Delaware, May 29, 1833. John Forsyth, of Georgia, June 27, 1834; entered upon duties July 1, 1834. SECRETARY OF THE TREASURY—Louis McLane, of Delaware, continued from preceding administration. William J. Duane, of Pennsylvania, May 29, 1833; entered upon duties June 1, 1833. Roger B. Taney, of Maryland, September 23, 1833. McClintock Young (chief clerk), ad interim, June 25, 1834. Levi Woodbury, of New Hampshire, June 27, 1834; entered upon duties July 1, 1834. SECRETARY OF WAR—Lewis Cass, of Ohio, continued from preceding administration. Carey A. Harris, of Tennessee (Commissioner of Indian Affairs), ad interim, October 5, 1836. Benjamin F. Butler, of New York (Attorney General), ad interim, October 26, 1836. Benjamin F. Butler, of New York, commissioned March 3, 1837, ad interim, "during the pleasure of the President, until a successor, duly appointed, shall accept such office and enter upon the duties thereof." ATTORNEY GENERAL—Roger B. Taney, of Maryland, continued from preceding administration to September 23, 1833. Benjamin F. Butler, of New York, November 15, 1833; entered upon duties November 18, 1833. POSTMASTER GENERAL—William T. Barry, of Kentucky, continued from preceding administration. Amos Kendall, of Kentucky, May 1, 1835. SECRETARY OF THE NAVY—Levi Woodbury, of New Hampshire, continued from preceding administration. Mahlon Dickerson, of New Jersey, June 30, 1834.

23d Congress
1st Session: Dec. 2, 1833–June 30, 1834; 2d Session: Dec. 1, 1834–Mar. 3, 1835.

President pro tempore of the Senate: Hugh L. White, of Tennessee (continued from the previous Congress); George Poindexter, of Mississippi (elected June 28, 1834); John Tyler, of Virginia (elected Mar. 3, 1835). Speaker of the House: Andrew Stevenson, of Virginia (reelected Dec. 2, 1835); John Bell, of Tennessee (elected June 2, 1834); Henry Hubbard, of New Hampshire served as Speaker pro tem May 16, 1834.

Senate: 20 Democratic; 20 National Republican
House: 147 Democratic; 113 various parties

24th Congress
1st Session: Dec. 7, 1835–July 4, 1836; 2d Session: Dec. 5, 1836–Mar. 3, 1837.

President pro tempore of the Senate: William R. King, of Alabama (elected July 1, 1836; Jan. 28, 1837). Speaker of the House: James K. Polk, of Tennessee (elected Dec. 7, 1835).

Senate: 27 Democratic; 25 Whig
House: 145 Democratic; 98 Whig

Administration of MARTIN VAN BUREN
MARCH 4, 1837, TO MARCH 3, 1841

PRESIDENT—Martin Van Buren, of New York (Democratic). VICE-PRESIDENT—Richard M. Johnson, of Kentucky. SECRETARY OF STATE—John Forsyth, of Georgia, continued from preceding administration. SECRETARY OF THE TREASURY—Levi Woodbury, of New Hampshire, continued from preceding administration. SECRETARY OF WAR—Benjamin F. Butler, of New York, ad interim, continued from preceding administration. Joel R. Poinsett, of South Carolina, March 7, 1837; entered upon

duties March 14, 1837. ATTORNEY GENERAL—Benjamin F. Butler, of New York, continued from preceding administration. Felix Grundy, of Tennessee, July 5, 1838, to take effect September 1, 1838. Henry D. Gilpin, of Pennsylvania, January 11, 1840. POSTMASTER GENERAL—Amos Kendall, of Kentucky, continued from preceding administration. John M. Niles, of Connecticut, May 19, 1840, to take effect May 25, 1840; entered upon duties May 26, 1840. SECRETARY OF THE NAVY—Mahlon Dickerson, of New Jersey, continued from preceding administration. James K. Paulding, of New York, June 25, 1838, to take effect "after the 30th instant"; entered upon duties July 1, 1838.

25th Congress
1st Session: Sept. 4, 1837–Oct. 16, 1837; 2d Session: Dec. 4, 1837–July 9, 1838; 3d Session: Dec. 3, 1838–Mar. 3, 1839; Special Session of the Senate: Mar. 4, 1837–Mar. 10, 1837.

President pro tempore of the Senate: William R. King, of Alabama (elected Mar. 7, 1837; Oct. 13, 1837; July 2, 1838; Feb. 25, 1839). Speaker of the House: James K. Polk, of Tennessee (reelected Sept. 4, 1837).

Senate: 30 Democratic; 18 Whig; 4 other
House: 108 Democratic; 107 Whig; 24 other

26th Congress
1st Session: Dec. 2, 1839–July 21, 1840; 2d Session: Dec. 7, 1840–Mar. 3, 1841.

President pro tempore of the Senate: William R. King, of Alabama (continued from the preceding Congress; reelected July 3, 1840; Mar. 3, 1841). Speaker of the House: Robert M. T. Hunter, of Virginia (elected Dec. 16, 1839).

Senate: 28 Democratic; 22 Whig
House: 124 Democratic; 118 Whig

Administration of WILLIAM HENRY HARRISON
MARCH 4, 1841, TO APRIL 4, 1841

PRESIDENT—William Henry Harrison, of Ohio (Whig) (died April 4, 1841). VICE-PRESIDENT—John Tyler, of Virginia. SECRETARY OF STATE—J. L. Martin (chief clerk), ad interim, March 4, 1841. Daniel Webster, of Massachusetts, March 5, 1841. SECRETARY OF THE TREASURY—McClintock Young (chief clerk), ad interim, March 4, 1841. Thomas Ewing, of Ohio, March 5, 1841. SECRETARY OF WAR—John Bell, of Tennessee, March 5, 1841. ATTORNEY GENERAL—John J. Crittenden, of Kentucky, March 5, 1841. POSTMASTER GENERAL—Selah R. Hobbie, of New York (First Assistant Postmaster General), ad interim, March 4, 1841. Francis Granger, of New York, March 6, 1841; entered upon duties March 8, 1841. SECRETARY OF THE NAVY—John D. Simms (chief clerk), ad interim, March 4, 1841. George E. Badger, of North Carolina, March 5, 1841.

Administration of JOHN TYLER
APRIL 6, 1841, TO MARCH 3, 1845

PRESIDENT—John Tyler, of Virginia (Whig). SECRETARY OF STATE—Daniel Webster, of Massachusetts, continued from preceding administration. Hugh S. Legaré, of South Carolina (Attorney General), ad interim, May 9, 1843. William S. Derrick (chief clerk), ad interim, June 21, 1843. Abel P. Upshur, of Virginia (Secretary of the Navy), ad interim, June 24, 1843. Abel P. Upshur, of Virginia, July 24, 1843 (killed by the explosion of a gun on the U.S.S. Princeton February 28, 1844). John Nelson, of Maryland (Attorney General), ad interim, February 29, 1844. John C. Calhoun, of South Carolina, March 6, 1844; entered upon duties April 1, 1844. SECRETARY OF THE TREASURY—Thomas Ewing, of Ohio, continued from preceding administration. McClintock Young (chief clerk), ad interim, September 13, 1841. Walter Forward, of Pennsylvania, September 13, 1841. McClintock Young (chief clerk), ad interim, March 1, 1843. John C. Spencer, of New York, March 3, 1843; entered upon duties March 8, 1843. McClintock Young (chief clerk), ad interim, May 2, 1844. George M. Bibb, of Kentucky, June 15, 1844; entered upon duties July 4, 1844. SECRETARY OF WAR—John Bell, of Tennessee, continued from preceding administration. Albert M. Lea, of Maryland (chief clerk), ad interim, September 12, 1841. John C. Spencer, of New York, October 12, 1841. James M. Porter, of Pennsylvania, March 8, 1843. William Wilkins, of Pennsylvania, February 15, 1844; entered upon duties February 20, 1844. ATTORNEY GENERAL—John J. Crittenden, of Kentucky, continued from preceding administration. Hugh S. Legaré, of South Carolina, September 13, 1841; entered upon duties September 20, 1841 (died June 20, 1843). John Nelson, of Maryland, July 1, 1843. POSTMASTER GENERAL—Francis Granger, of New York, continued from preceding administration. Selah R. Hobbie, of New York (First Assistant Postmaster General) ad interim, September 14, 1841. Charles A. Wickliffe, of Kentucky, September 13, 1841; entered upon duties October 13, 1841. SECRETARY OF THE NAVY—George E. Badger, of North Carolina, continued from preceding administration. John D. Simms (chief clerk), ad interim, September 11, 1841. Abel P. Upshur, of Virginia, September 13, 1841; entered upon duties October 11, 1841. David Henshaw, of Massachusetts, July 24, 1843. Thomas W. Gilmer, of Virginia, February 15, 1844; entered upon duties February 19, 1844 (killed by the explosion of a gun on the U.S.S. Princeton February 28, 1844). Lewis Warrington (captain, United States Navy), ad interim, February 29, 1844. John Y. Mason, of Virginia, March 14, 1844; entered upon duties March 26, 1844.

27th Congress

1st Session: May 31, 1841–Sept. 13, 1841; 2d Session: Dec. 6, 1841–Aug. 31, 1842; 3d Session: Dec. 5, 1842–Mar. 3, 1843; Special Session of the Senate: Mar. 4, 1841–Mar. 15, 1841.

President pro tempore of the Senate: William R. King, of Alabama (elected Mar. 4, 1841); Samuel L. Southard, of New Jersey (elected Mar. 11, 1841); Willie P. Mangum, of North Carolina (elected May 31, 1842). Speaker of the House: John White, of Kentucky (elected May 31, 1841).

Senate: 28 Whig; 22 Democratic; 2 other
House: 133 Whig; 102 Democratic; 6 other

28th Congress

1st Session: Dec. 4, 1843–June 17, 1844; 2d Session: Dec. 2, 1844–Mar. 3, 1845.

President pro tempore of the Senate: Willie P. Mangum, of North Carolina (continued from the preceding Congress). Speaker of the House: John W. Jones, of Virginia (elected Dec. 4, 1843); George Hopkins acted as Speaker for part of the day Feb. 28, 1845.

Senate: 28 Whig; 25 Democratic; 1 other
House: 115 Whig; 108 Democratic; 4 other

Administration of JAMES K. POLK
MARCH 4, 1845, TO MARCH 3, 1849

PRESIDENT—James K. Polk, of Tennessee (Democratic). VICE-PRESIDENT—George M. Dallas, of Pennsylvania. SECRETARY OF STATE—John C. Calhoun, of South Carolina, continued from preceding administration. James Buchanan, of Pennsylvania, March 6, 1845; entered upon duties March 10, 1845. SECRETARY OF THE TREASURY—George M. Bibb, of Kentucky, continued from preceding administration. Robert J. Walker, of Mississippi, March 6, 1845; entered upon duties March 8, 1845. SECRETARY OF WAR—William Wilkins, of Pennsylvania, continued from preceding administration. William L. Marcy, of New York, March 6, 1845; entered upon duties March 8, 1845. ATTORNEY GENERAL—John Nelson, of Maryland, continued from preceding administration. John Y. Mason, of Virginia, March 6, 1845; entered upon duties March 11, 1845. Nathan Clifford, of Maine, October 17, 1846, to March 18, 1848, when he resigned. Isaac Toucey, of Connecticut, June 21, 1848; entered upon duties June 29, 1848. POSTMASTER GENERAL—Charles A. Wickliffe, of Kentucky, continued from preceding administration. Cave Johnson, of Tennessee, March 6, 1845. SECRETARY OF THE NAVY—John Y. Mason, of Virginia, continued from preceding administration. George Bancroft, of Massachusetts, March 10, 1845. John Y. Mason, of Virginia, September 9, 1846.

29th Congress

1st Session: Dec. 1, 1845–Aug. 10, 1846; 2d Session: Dec. 7, 1846–Mar. 3, 1847; Special Session of the Senate: Mar. 4, 1845–Mar. 20, 1845.

President pro tempore of the Senate: Ambrose H. Sevier, of Arkansas (under designation of the Vice-President served Dec. 27, 1845); David R. Atchison, of Missouri (elected Aug. 8, 1846; Jan. 11, 1847; Mar. 3, 1847). Speaker of the House: John W. Davis, of Indiana (elected Dec. 1, 1845).

Senate: 31 Democratic; 25 Whig
House: 143 Democratic; 77 Whig; 6 other

30th Congress

1st Session: Dec. 6, 1847–Aug. 14, 1848; 2d Session: Dec. 4, 1848–Mar. 3, 1849.

President pro tempore of the Senate: David R. Atchison, of Missouri (elected Feb. 2, 1848; June 1, 1848; June 26, 1848; July 29, 1848; Dec. 26, 1848; Mar. 2, 1849). Speaker of the House: Robert C. Winthrop, of Massachusetts (elected Dec. 6, 1847); Armistead Burt served as Speaker pro tem June 19–22, 1848.

Senate: 36 Democratic; 21 Whig; 1 other
House: 115 Whig; 108 Democratic; 4 other

Administration of ZACHARY TAYLOR
MARCH 4, 1849, TO JULY 9, 1850

PRESIDENT—Zachary Taylor, of Louisiana (Whig). (Oath administered March 5, 1849. Died July 9, 1850.) VICE-PRESIDENT

—Millard Fillmore, of New York. SECRETARY OF STATE—James Buchanan, of Pennsylvania, continued from preceding administration. John M. Clayton, of Delaware, March 7, 1849. SECRETARY OF THE TREASURY—Robert J. Walker, of Mississippi, continued from preceding administration. William M. Meredith, of Pennsylvania, March 8, 1849. SECRETARY OF WAR—William L. Marcy, of New York, continued from preceding administration. Reverdy Johnson, of Maryland (Attorney General), ad interim, March 8, 1849. George W. Crawford, of Georgia, March 8, 1849; entered upon duties March 14, 1849. ATTORNEY GENERAL—Isaac Toucey, of Connecticut, continued from preceding administration. Reverdy Johnson, of Maryland, March 8, 1849. POSTMASTER GENERAL—Cave Johnson, of Tennessee, continued from preceding administration. Selah R. Hobbie, of New York (First Assistant Postmaster General), ad interim, March 6, 1849. Jacob Collamer, of Vermont, March 8, 1849. SECRETARY OF THE NAVY—John Y. Mason, of Virginia, continued from preceding administration. William B. Preston, of Virginia, March 8, 1849. SECRETARY OF THE INTERIOR—Thomas Ewing, of Ohio, March 8, 1849.

Administration of MILLARD FILLMORE
JULY 10, 1850, TO MARCH 3, 1853

PRESIDENT—Millard Fillmore, of New York (Whig). SECRETARY OF STATE—John M. Clayton, of Delaware, continued from preceding administration. Daniel Webster, of Massachusetts, July 22, 1850 (died October 24, 1852). Charles M. Conrad, of Louisiana (Secretary of War), ad interim, October 25, 1852. Edward Everett, of Massachusetts, November 6, 1852. SECRETARY OF THE TREASURY—William M. Meredith, of Pennsylvania, continued from preceding administration. Thomas Corwin, of Ohio, July 23, 1850. SECRETARY OF WAR—George W. Crawford, of Georgia, continued from preceding administration. Samuel J. Anderson (chief clerk), ad interim, July 23, 1850. Winfield Scott (major general, U.S. Army), ad interim, July 24, 1850. Charles M. Conrad, of Louisiana, August 15, 1850. ATTORNEY GENERAL—Reverdy Johnson, of Maryland, continued from preceding administration, served to July 22, 1850. John J. Crittenden, of Kentucky, July 22, 1850; entered upon duties August 14, 1850. POSTMASTER GENERAL—Jacob Collamer, of Vermont, continued from preceding administration. Nathan K. Hall, of New York, July 23, 1850. Samuel D. Hubbard, of Connecticut, August 31, 1852; entered upon duties September 14, 1852. SECRETARY OF THE NAVY—William B. Preston, of Virginia, continued from preceding administration. Lewis Warrington (captain, U.S. Navy), ad interim, July 23, 1850. William A. Graham, of North Carolina, July 22, 1850; entered upon duties August 2, 1850. John P. Kennedy, of Maryland, July 22, 1852; entered upon duties July 26, 1852. SECRETARY OF THE INTERIOR—Thomas Ewing, of Ohio, continued from preceding administration. Daniel C. Goddard (chief clerk), ad interim, July 23, 1850. Thomas M. T. McKennan, of Pennsylvania, August 15, 1850. Daniel C. Goddard (chief clerk), ad interim, August 27, 1850. Alexander H. H. Stuart, of Virginia, September 12, 1850; entered upon duties September 16, 1850.

31st Congress

1st Session: Dec. 3, 1849–Sept. 30, 1850; 2d Session: Dec. 2, 1850–Mar. 3, 1851; Special Session of the Senate: Mar. 5, 1849–Mar. 23, 1849.

President pro tempore of the Senate: David R. Atchison, of Missouri (elected Mar. 5, 1849; Mar. 16, 1849). William R. King, of Alabama (elected May 6, 1850, July 11, 1850). Speaker of the House: Howell Cobb, of Georgia (elected Dec. 22, 1849), Robert C. Winthrop, of Massachusetts, served as Speaker pro tem April 19, 1850.

Senate: 35 Democratic; 25 Whig; 2 other
House: 112 Democratic; 109 Whig; 9 other

32d Congress

1st Session: Dec. 1, 1851–Aug. 31, 1852; 2d Session: Dec. 6, 1852–Mar. 3, 1853; Special Session of the Senate: Mar. 4, 1851–Mar. 13, 1851.

President pro tempore of the Senate: William R. King, of Alabama (continued from preceding Congress); David R. Atchison, of Missouri (elected Dec. 20, 1852). Speaker of the House: Linn Boyd, of Kentucky (elected Dec. 1, 1851).

Senate: 35 Democratic; 24 Whig; 3 other
House: 140 Democratic; 88 Whig; 5 other

Administration of FRANKLIN PIERCE
MARCH 4, 1853, TO MARCH 3, 1857

PRESIDENT—Franklin Pierce, of New Hampshire (Democratic). VICE-PRESIDENT—William R. King, of Alabama (died April 18, 1853). SECRETARY OF STATE—William Hunter (chief clerk), ad interim, March 4, 1853. William L. Marcy, of New York,

March 7, 1853. SECRETARY OF THE TREASURY—Thomas Corwin, of Ohio, continued from preceding administration. James Guthrie, of Kentucky, March 7, 1853. SECRETARY OF WAR—Charles M. Conrad, of Louisiana, continued from preceding administration. Jefferson Davis, of Mississippi, March 7, 1853. Samuel Cooper (Adjutant General, U.S. Army), ad interim, March 3, 1857. ATTORNEY GENERAL—John J. Crittenden, of Kentucky, continued from preceding administration. Caleb Cushing, of Massachusetts, March 7, 1853. POSTMASTER GENERAL—Samuel D. Hubbard, of Connecticut, continued from preceding administration. James Campbell, of Pennsylvania, March 7, 1853. SECRETARY OF THE NAVY—John P. Kennedy, of Maryland, continued from preceding administration. James C. Dobbin, of North Carolina, March 7, 1853. SECRETARY OF THE INTERIOR—Alexander H. H. Stuart, of Virginia, continued from preceding administration. Robert McClelland, of Michigan, March 7, 1853.

33d Congress

1st Session: Dec. 5, 1853–Aug. 7, 1854; 2d Session: Dec. 4, 1854–Mar. 3, 1855; Special Session of the Senate: Mar. 4, 1853–Apr. 11, 1853.

President pro tempore of the Senate: David R. Atchison, of Missouri (elected Mar. 4, 1853); Lewis Cass, of Michigan (elected Dec. 4, 1854); Jesse D. Bright, of Indiana (elected Dec. 5, 1854). Speaker of the House: Linn Boyd, of Kentucky (re-elected Dec. 5, 1853).

Senate: 38 Democratic; 22 Whig; 2 other
House: 159 Democratic; 71 Whig; 4 other

34th Congress

1st Session: Dec. 3, 1855–Aug. 18, 1856; 2d Session: Aug. 21, 1856–Aug. 30, 1856; 3d Session: Dec. 1, 1856–Mar. 3, 1857.

President pro tempore of the Senate: Jesse D. Bright, of Indiana (continued from preceding Congress; elected June 11, 1856); Charles E. Stuart, of Michigan (served June 5, 1856; elected June 9, 1856); James M. Mason, of Virginia (served Jan. 5, 1857; elected Jan. 6, 1857). Speaker of the House: Nathaniel P. Banks, of Massachusetts (elected Feb. 2, 1856).

Senate: 40 Democratic; 15 Republican; 5 other
House: 108 Republican; 83 Democratic; 43 other

Administration of JAMES BUCHANAN
MARCH 4, 1857, TO MARCH 3, 1861

PRESIDENT—James Buchanan, of Pennsylvania (Democratic). VICE-PRESIDENT—John C. Breckinridge, of Kentucky. SECRETARY OF STATE—William L. Marcy, of New York, continued from preceding administration. Lewis Cass, of Michigan, March 6, 1857. William Hunter (chief clerk), ad interim, December 15, 1860. Jeremiah S. Black, of Pennsylvania, December 17, 1860. SECRETARY OF THE TREASURY—James Guthrie, of Kentucky, continued from preceding administration. Howell Cobb, of Georgia, March 6, 1857. Isaac Toucey, of Connecticut (Secretary of the Navy), ad interim, December 10, 1860. Philip F. Thomas, of Maryland, December 12, 1860. John A. Dix, of New York, January 11, 1861; entered upon duties January 15, 1861. SECRETARY OF WAR—Samuel Cooper (Adjutant General, U.S. Army), ad interim, March 4, 1857. John B. Floyd, of Virginia, March 6, 1857. Joseph Holt, of Kentucky (Postmaster General), ad interim, January 1, 1861. Joseph Holt, of Kentucky, January 18, 1861. ATTORNEY GENERAL—Caleb Cushing, of Massachusetts, continued from preceding administration. Jeremiah S. Black, of Pennsylvania, March 6, 1857; entered upon duties March 11, 1857. Edwin M. Stanton, of Pennsylvania, December 20, 1860; entered upon duties December 22, 1860. POSTMASTER GENERAL—James Campbell, of Pennsylvania, continued from preceding administration. Aaron V. Brown, of Tennessee, March 6, 1857 (died March 8, 1859). Horatio King, of Maine (First Assistant Postmaster General), ad interim, March 9, 1859. Joseph Holt, of Kentucky, March 14, 1859. Horatio King, of Maine (First Assistant Postmaster General), ad interim, January 1, 1861. Horatio King, of Maine, February 12, 1861. SECRETARY OF NAVY—James C. Dobbin, of North Carolina, continued from preceding administration. Isaac Toucey, of Connecticut, March 6, 1857. SECRETARY OF THE INTERIOR—Robert McClelland, of Michigan, continued from preceding administration. Jacob Thompson, of Mississippi, March 6, 1857; entered upon duties March 10, 1857. Moses Kelly (chief-clerk), ad interim, January 10, 1861.

35th Congress

1st Session: Dec. 7, 1857–June 14, 1858; 2d Session: Dec. 6, 1858–Mar. 3, 1859; Special Sessions of the Senate: Mar. 4, 1857–Mar. 14, 1857; June 15, 1858–June 16, 1858.

President pro tempore of the Senate: James M. Mason, of Virginia (elected Mar. 4, 1857); Thomas J. Rusk, of Texas (elected Mar. 14, 1857); Benjamin Fitzpatrick, of Alabama (elected Dec. 7, 1857; Mar. 29, 1858; June 14, 1858; Jan. 25, 1859). Speaker of the House: James L. Orr, of South Carolina (elected Dec. 7, 1857).

Senate: 36 Democratic; 20 Republican; 8 other
House: 118 Democratic; 92 Republican; 26 other

36th Congress

1st Session: Dec. 5, 1859–June 25, 1860; 2d Session: Dec. 3, 1860–Mar. 3, 1861: Special Sessions of the Senate: Mar. 4, 1859–Mar. 10, 1859; June 26, 1860–June 28, 1860.

President pro tempore of the Senate: Benjamin Fitzpatrick, of Alabama (elected Mar. 9, 1859; Dec. 19, 1859; Feb. 20, 1860; June 26, 1860); Jesse D. Bright, of Indiana (June 12, 1860); Solomon Foot, of Vermont (elected Feb. 16, 1861). Speaker of the House: William Pennington, of New Jersey (elected Feb. 1, 1860).

Senate: 36 Democratic; 26 Republican; 4 other
House: 114 Republican; 92 Democratic; 31 other

First Administration of ABRAHAM LINCOLN
MARCH 4, 1861, TO MARCH 3, 1865

PRESIDENT—Abraham Lincoln, of Illinois (Republican). VICE-PRESIDENT—Hannibal Hamlin, of Maine. SECRETARY OF STATE—Jeremiah S. Black, of Pennsylvania, continued from preceding administration. William H. Seward, of New York, March 5, 1861. SECRETARY OF THE TREASURY—John A. Dix, of New York, continued from preceding administration. Salmon P. Chase, of Ohio, March 5, 1861; entered upon duties March 7, 1861. George Harrington, of the District of Columbia (Assistant Secretary), ad interim, July 1, 1864. William P. Fessenden, of Maine, July 1, 1864; entered upon duties July 5, 1864. SECRETARY OF WAR—Joseph Holt, of Kentucky, continued from preceding administration. Simon Cameron, of Pennsylvania, March 5, 1861; entered upon duties March 11, 1861. Edwin M. Stanton, of Pennsylvania, January 15, 1862; entered upon duties January 20, 1862. ATTORNEY GENERAL—Edwin M. Stanton, of Pennsylvania, continued from preceding administration. Edward Bates, of Missouri, March 5, 1861. James Speed, of Kentucky, December 2, 1864; entered upon duties December 5, 1864. POSTMASTER GENERAL—Horatio King, of Maine, continued from preceding administration. Montgomery Blair, of the District of Columbia, March 5, 1861; entered upon duties March 9, 1861. William Dennison, of Ohio, September 24, 1864; entered upon duties October 1, 1864. SECRETARY OF THE NAVY—Isaac Toucey, of Connecticut, continued from preceding administration. Gideon Welles, of Connecticut, March 5, 1861; entered upon duties March 7, 1861. SECRETARY OF THE INTERIOR—Moses Kelly (chief clerk), ad interim, March 4, 1861. Caleb B. Smith, of Indiana, March 5, 1861. John P. Usher, of Indiana (Assistant Secretary), ad interim, January 1, 1863. John P. Usher, of Indiana, January 8, 1863.

37th Congress

1st Session: July 4, 1861–Aug. 6, 1861; 2d Session: Dec. 2, 1861–July 17, 1862; 3d Session: Dec. 1, 1862–Mar. 3, 1863; Special Session of the Senate: Mar. 4, 1861–Mar. 28, 1861.

President pro tempore of the Senate: Solomon Foot, of Vermont (elected Mar. 23, 1861; July 18, 1861; Jan. 15, 1862; Mar. 31, 1862; June 19, 1862; Feb. 18, 1863). Speaker of the House: Galusha A. Grow, of Pennsylvania (elected July 4, 1861).

Senate: 31 Republican; 10 Democratic; 8 other
House: 105 Republican; 43 Democratic; 30 other

38th Congress

1st Session: Dec. 7, 1863–July 4, 1864; 2d Session: Dec. 5, 1864–Mar. 3, 1865; Special Session of the Senate: Mar. 4, 1863–Mar. 14, 1863.

President pro tempore of the Senate: Solomon Foot, of Vermont (elected Mar. 4, 1863; Dec. 18, 1863; Feb. 23, 1864; Mar. 11, 1864; Apr. 11, 1864); Daniel Clark, of New Hampshire (elected Apr. 26, 1864; Feb. 9, 1865). Speaker of the House: Schuyler Colfax, of Indiana (elected Dec. 7, 1863).

Senate: 36 Republican; 9 Democratic; 5 other
House: 102 Republican; 75 Democratic; 9 other

Second Administration of ABRAHAM LINCOLN
MARCH 4, 1865, TO APRIL 15, 1865

PRESIDENT—Abraham Lincoln, of Illinois (Republican) (died April 15, 1865). VICE-PRESIDENT—Andrew Johnson, of Tennessee. SECRETARY OF STATE—William H. Seward, of New York, continued from preceding administration. SECRETARY OF THE TREASURY—George Harrington, of the District of Columbia (Assistant Secretary), ad interim, March 4, 1865. Hugh McCulloch, of Indiana, March 7, 1865; entered upon duties March 9, 1865. SECRETARY OF WAR—Edwin M. Stanton, of Pennsylvania, continued from preceding administration. ATTORNEY GENERAL—James Speed, of Kentucky, continued from preceding administration. POSTMASTER GENERAL—William Dennison, of Ohio, continued from preceding administration. SECRETARY OF THE NAVY—Gideon Welles, of Connecticut, continued from preceding administration. SECRETARY OF THE INTERIOR—John P. Usher, of Indiana, continued from preceding administration.

Administration of ANDREW JOHNSON
APRIL 15, 1865, TO MARCH 3, 1869

PRESIDENT—Andrew Johnson, of Tennessee (Republican). SEC-RETARY OF STATE—William H. Seward, of New York, continued from preceding administration. SECRETARY OF THE TREASURY —Hugh McCulloch, of Indiana, continued from preceding administration. SECRETARY OF WAR—Edwin M. Stanton, of Pennsylvania, continued from preceding administration; suspended August 12, 1867. Ulysses S. Grant (General of the Army), ad interim, August 12, 1867. Edwin M. Stanton, of Pennsylvania, reinstated January 13, 1868, to May 26, 1868. John M. Schofield, of Illinois, May 28, 1868; entered upon duties June 1, 1868. ATTORNEY GENERAL—James Speed, of Kentucky, continued from preceding administration. J. Hubley Ashton, of Pennsylvania (Assistant Attorney General), acting, July 17, 1866. Henry Stanbery, of Ohio, July 23, 1866. Orville H. Browning, of Illinois (Secretary of the Interior), ad interim, March 13, 1868. William M. Evarts, of New York, July 15, 1868; entered upon duties July 20, 1868. POSTMASTER GENERAL—William Dennison, of Ohio, continued from preceding administration. Alexander W. Randall, of Wisconsin (First Assistant Postmaster General), ad interim, July 17, 1866. Alexander W. Randall, of Wisconsin, July 25, 1866. SECRETARY OF THE NAVY—Gideon Welles, of Connecticut, continued from preceding administration. SECRETARY OF THE INTERIOR—John P. Usher, of Indiana, continued from preceding administration. James Harlan, of Iowa, May 15, 1865. Orville H. Browning, of Illinois, July 27, 1866, to take effect September 1, 1866.

39th Congress
1st Session: Dec. 4, 1865–July 28, 1866; 2d Session: Dec. 3, 1866–Mar. 3, 1867; Special Session of the Senate: Mar. 4, 1865–Mar. 11, 1865.

President pro tempore of the Senate: Lafayette S. Foster, of Connecticut (elected Mar. 7, 1865); Benjamin F. Wade, of Ohio (elected Mar. 2, 1867). Speaker of the House: Schuyler Colfax, of Indiana (reelected Dec. 4, 1865).

Senate: 42 Union; 10 Democratic
House: 149 Union; 42 Democratic

40th Congress
1st Session: Mar. 4, 1867–Mar. 30, 1867; July 3, 1867–July 20, 1867; Nov. 21, 1867–Dec. 1, 1867; 2d Session: Dec. 2, 1867–July 27, 1868; Sept. 21, 1868; Oct. 16, 1868; Nov. 10, 1868; 3d Session: Dec. 7, 1868–Mar. 3, 1869; Special Session of the Senate: Apr. 1, 1867–Apr. 20, 1867.

President pro tempore of the Senate: Benjamin F. Wade, of Ohio (continued from the preceding Congress). Speaker of the House: Schuyler Colfax, of Indiana (reelected Mar. 4, 1867); Theodore M. Pomeroy, of New York (elected Mar. 3, 1869).

Senate: 42 Republican; 11 Democratic
House: 143 Republican; 49 Democratic

First Administration of ULYSSES S. GRANT
MARCH 4, 1869, TO MARCH 3, 1873

PRESIDENT—Ulysses S. Grant, of Illinois (Republican). VICE-PRESIDENT—Schuyler Colfax, of Indiana. SECRETARY OF STATE —William H. Seward, of New York, continued from preceding administration. Elihu B. Washburne, of Illinois, March 5, 1869. Hamilton Fish, of New York, March 11, 1869; entered upon duties March 17, 1869. SECRETARY OF THE TREASURY—Hugh McCulloch, of Indiana, continued from preceding administration. John F. Hartley, of Maine (Assistant Secretary), ad interim, March 5, 1869. George S. Boutwell, of Massachusetts, March 11, 1869. SECRETARY OF WAR—John M. Schofield, of Illinois, continued from preceding administration. John A. Rawlins, of Illinois, March 11, 1869. William T. Sherman, of Ohio, September 9, 1869; entered upon duties September 11, 1869. William W. Belknap, of Iowa, October 25, 1869; entered upon duties November 1, 1869. ATTORNEY GENERAL—William M. Evarts, of New York, continued from preceding administration. J. Hubley Ashton, of Pennsylvania (Assistant Attorney General), acting, March 5, 1869. Ebenezer R. Hoar, of Massachusetts, March 5, 1869; entered upon duties March 11, 1869. Amos T. Akerman, of Georgia, June 23, 1870; entered upon duties July 8, 1870. George H. Williams, of Oregon, December 14, 1871, to take effect January 10, 1872. POSTMASTER GENERAL—St. John B. L. Skinner, of New York (First Assistant Postmaster General), ad interim, March 4, 1869. John A. J. Creswell, of Maryland, March 5, 1869. SECRETARY OF THE NAVY—William Faxon, of Connecticut (Assistant Secretary), ad interim, March 4, 1869. Adolph E. Borie, of Pennsylvania, March 5, 1869; entered upon duties March 9, 1869. George M. Robeson, of New Jersey, June 25, 1869. SECRETARY OF THE INTERIOR—William T. Otto, of Indiana (Assistant Secretary), ad interim, March 4, 1869. Jacob D. Cox, of Ohio, March 5, 1869; entered upon duties March 9, 1869. Columbus Delano, of Ohio, November 1, 1870.

41st Congress
1st Session: Mar. 4, 1869–Apr. 10, 1869; 2d Session: Dec. 6, 1869–July 15, 1870; 3d Session: Dec. 5, 1870–Mar. 3, 1871; Special Session of the Senate: Apr. 12, 1869–Apr. 22, 1869.

President pro tempore of the Senate: Henry B. Anthony, of Rhode Island (elected Mar. 23, 1869; Apr. 9, 1869; May 28, 1870; July 1, 1870; July 14, 1870). Speaker of the House: James G. Blaine, of Maine (elected Mar. 4, 1869).

Senate: 56 Republican; 11 Democratic
House: 149 Republican; 63 Democratic

42d Congress
1st Session: Mar. 4, 1871–Apr. 20, 1871; 2d Session: Dec. 4, 1871–June 10, 1872; 3d Session: Dec. 2, 1872–Mar. 3, 1873; Special Session of the Senate: May 10, 1871–May 27, 1871.

President pro tempore of the Senate: Henry B. Anthony, of Rhode Island (elected Mar. 10, 1871; Apr. 17, 1871; May 23, 1871; Dec. 21, 1871; Feb. 23, 1872; June 8, 1872; Dec. 4, 1872; Dec. 13, 1872; Dec. 20, 1872; Jan. 24, 1873). Speaker of the House: James G. Blaine, of Maine (reelected Mar. 4, 1871).

Senate: 52 Republican; 17 Democratic; 5 other
House: 134 Democratic; 104 Republican; 5 other

Second Administration of ULYSSES S. GRANT
MARCH 4, 1873, TO MARCH 3, 1877

PRESIDENT—Ulysses S. Grant, of Illinois (Republican). VICE-PRESIDENT—Henry Wilson, of Massachusetts (died November 22, 1875). SECRETARY OF STATE—Hamilton Fish, of New York, continued from preceding administration. Hamilton Fish, of New York, recommissioned March 17, 1873. SECRETARY OF THE TREASURY—George S. Boutwell, of Massachusetts, continued from preceding administration. William A. Richardson, of Massachusetts, March 17, 1873. Benjamin H. Bristow, of Kentucky, June 2, 1874; entered upon duties June 4, 1874. Charles F. Conant, of New Hampshire (Assistant Secretary), ad interim, June 21, 1876, to June 30, 1876. Lot M. Morrill, of Maine, June 21, 1876; entered upon duties July 7, 1876. SECRETARY OF WAR— William W. Belknap, of Iowa, continued from preceding administration. William W. Belknap, of Iowa, recommissioned March 17, 1873. George M. Robeson, of New Jersey (Secretary of the Navy), ad interim, March 2, 1876. Alphonso Taft, of Ohio, March 8, 1876; entered upon duties March 11, 1876. James D. Cameron, of Pennsylvania, May 22, 1876; entered upon duties June 1, 1876. ATTORNEY GENERAL—George H. Williams, of Oregon, continued from preceding administration. George H. Williams, of Oregon, recommissioned March 17, 1873. Edwards Pierrepont, of New York, April 26, 1875, to take effect May 15, 1875. Alphonso Taft, of Ohio, May 22, 1876; entered upon duties June 1, 1876. POSTMASTER GENERAL—John A. J. Creswell, of Maryland, continued from preceding administration. John A. J. Creswell, of Maryland, recommissioned March 17, 1873. James W. Marshall, of Virginia, July 3, 1874; entered upon duties July 7, 1874. Marshall Jewell, of Connecticut, August 24, 1874; entered upon duties September 1, 1874. James N. Tyner, of Indiana, July 12, 1876. SECRETARY OF THE NAVY—George M. Robeson, of New Jersey, continued from preceding administration. George M. Robeson, of New Jersey, recommissioned March 17, 1873. SECRETARY OF THE INTERIOR—Columbus Delano, of Ohio, continued from preceding administration. Columbus Delano, of Ohio, recommissioned March 17, 1873. Benjamin R. Cowen, of Ohio (Assistant Secretary), ad interim, October 1, 1875. Zachariah Chandler, of Michigan, October 19, 1875.

43d Congress
1st Session: Dec. 1, 1873–June 23, 1874; 2d Session: Dec. 7, 1874–Mar. 3, 1875; Special Session of the Senate: Mar. 4, 1873–Mar. 26, 1873.

President pro tempore of the Senate: Mathew H. Carpenter, of Wisconsin (elected Mar. 12, 1873; Mar. 26, 1873; Dec. 11, 1873; Dec. 23, 1874); Henry B. Anthony, of Rhode Island (elected Jan. 25, 1875; Feb. 15, 1875). Speaker of the House: James G. Blaine (reelected Dec. 1, 1873).

Senate: 49 Republican; 19 Democratic; 5 other
House: 194 Republican; 92 Democratic; 14 other

44th Congress
1st Session: Dec. 6, 1875–Aug. 15, 1876; 2d Session: Dec. 4, 1876–Mar. 3, 1877; Special Session of the Senate: Mar. 5, 1875–Mar. 24, 1875.

President pro tempore of the Senate: Thomas W. Ferry, of Michigan (elected Mar. 9, 1875; Mar. 19, 1875; Dec. 20, 1875). Speaker of the House: Michael C. Kerr, of Indiana (elected Dec. 6, 1875); Samuel J. Randall, of Pennsylvania (elected Dec. 4, 1876).

Senate: 45 Republican; 29 Democratic; 2 other
House: 169 Democratic; 109 Republican; 14 other

Administration of RUTHERFORD B. HAYES
MARCH 4, 1877, TO MARCH 3, 1881

PRESIDENT—Rutherford B. Hayes, of Ohio (Republican) (oath administered March 5, 1877). VICE-PRESIDENT—William A. Wheeler, of New York. SECRETARY OF STATE—Hamilton Fish, of

New York, continued from preceding administration. William M. Evarts, of New York, March 12, 1877. SECRETARY OF THE TREASURY—Lot M. Morrill, of Maine, continued from preceding administration. John Sherman, of Ohio, March 8, 1877; entered upon duties March 10, 1877. SECRETARY OF WAR—James D. Cameron, of Pennsylvania, continued from preceding administration. George W. McCrary, of Iowa, March 12, 1877. Alexander Ramsey, of Pennsylvania, December 10, 1879; entered upon duties December 12, 1879. ATTORNEY GENERAL—Alphonso Taft, of Ohio, continued from preceding administration. Charles Devens, of Massachusetts, March 12, 1877. POSTMASTER GENERAL—James N. Tyner, of Indiana, continued from preceding administration. David M. Key, of Tennessee, March 12, 1877; resigned June 1, 1880; served to August 24, 1880. Horace Maynard, of Tennessee, June 2, 1880; entered upon duties August 25, 1880. SECRETARY OF THE NAVY—George M. Robeson, of New Jersey, continued from preceding administration. Richard W. Thompson, of Indiana, March 12, 1877. Alexander Ramsey, of Minnesota (Secretary of War), ad interim, December 20, 1880. Nathan Goff, Jr., of West Virginia, January 6, 1881. SECRETARY OF THE INTERIOR—Zachariah Chandler, of Michigan, continued from preceding administration. Carl Schurz, of Missouri, March 12, 1877.

45th Congress
1st Session: Oct. 15, 1877–Dec. 3, 1877; 2d Session: Dec. 3, 1877–June 20, 1878; 3d Session: Dec. 2, 1878–Mar. 3, 1879; Special Session of the Senate: Mar. 5, 1877–Mar. 17, 1877.

President pro tempore of the Senate: Thomas W. Ferry of Michigan (elected Mar. 5, 1877; Feb. 26, 1878; Apr. 17, 1878; Mar. 3, 1879). Speaker of the House: Samuel J. Randall, of Pennsylvania (reelected Oct. 15, 1877).

Senate: 39 Republican; 36 Democratic; 1 other
House: 153 Democratic; 140 Republican

46th Congress
1st Session: Mar. 18, 1879–July 1, 1879; 2d Session: Dec. 1, 1879–June 16, 1880; 3d Session: Dec. 6, 1880–Mar. 3, 1881.

President pro tempore of the Senate: Allen G. Thurman, of Ohio (elected Apr. 15, 1879; Apr. 7, 1880, May 6, 1880). Speaker of the House: Samuel J. Randall, of Pennsylvania (reelected Mar. 18, 1879).

Senate: 42 Democratic; 33 Republican; 1 other
House: 149 Democratic; 130 Republican; 14 other

Administration of JAMES A. GARFIELD
MARCH 4, 1881, TO SEPTEMBER 19, 1881

PRESIDENT—James A. Garfield, of Ohio (Republican) (died September 19, 1881). VICE-PRESIDENT—Chester A. Arthur, of New York. SECRETARY OF STATE—William M. Evarts, of New York, continued from preceding administration. James G. Blaine, of Maine, March 5, 1881; entered upon duties March 7, 1881. SECRETARY OF THE TREASURY—Henry F. French, of Massachusetts (Assistant Secretary), ad interim, March 4, 1881. William Windom, of Minnesota, March 5, 1881; entered upon duties March 8, 1881. SECRETARY OF WAR—Alexander Ramsey, of Minnesota, continued from preceding administration. Robert T. Lincoln, of Illinois, March 5, 1881; entered upon duties March 11, 1881. ATTORNEY GENERAL—Charles Devens, of Massachusetts, continued from preceding administration. Wayne MacVeagh, of Pennsylvania, March 5, 1881; entered upon duties March 7, 1881. POSTMASTER GENERAL—Horace Maynard, of Tennessee, continued from preceding administration. Thomas L. James, of New York, March 5, 1881; entered upon duties March 8, 1881. SECRETARY OF THE NAVY—Nathan Goff, Jr., of West Virginia, continued from preceding administration. William H. Hunt, of Louisiana, March 5, 1881; entered upon duties March 7, 1881. SECRETARY OF THE INTERIOR—Carl Schurz, of Missouri, continued from preceding administration. Samuel J. Kirkwood, of Iowa, March 5, 1881; entered upon duties March 8, 1881.

Administration of CHESTER A. ARTHUR
SEPTEMBER 20, 1881, TO MARCH 3, 1885

PRESIDENT—Chester A. Arthur, of New York. SECRETARY OF STATE—James G. Blaine, of Maine, continued from preceding administration. Frederick T. Frelinghuysen, of New Jersey, December 12, 1881; entered upon duties December 19, 1881. SECRETARY OF THE TREASURY—William Windom, of Minnesota, continued from preceding administration. Charles J. Folger, of New York, October 27, 1881; entered upon duties November 14, 1881 (died September 4, 1884). Charles E. Coon, of New York (Assistant Secretary), ad interim, September 4, 1884. Henry F. French, of Massachusetts (Assistant Secretary), ad interim, September 8, 1884. Charles E. Coon, of New York (Assistant Secretary), ad interim, September 15, 1884. Walter Q. Gresham, of Indiana, September 24, 1884. Henry F. French, of Massachusetts (Assistant Secretary), ad interim, October 29, 1884. Hugh McCulloch, of Indiana, October 28, 1884; entered upon duties

October 31, 1884. SECRETARY OF WAR—Robert T. Lincoln, of Illinois, continued from preceding administration. ATTORNEY GENERAL—Wayne MacVeagh, of Pennsylvania, continued from preceding administration. Samuel F. Phillips, of North Carolina (Solicitor General), ad interim, November 14, 1881. Benjamin H. Brewster, of Pennsylvania, December 19, 1881; entered upon duties January 3, 1882. POSTMASTER GENERAL—Thomas L. James, of New York, continued from preceding administration. Thomas L. James, of New York, recommissioned October 27, 1881. Timothy O. Howe, of Wisconsin, December 20, 1881; entered upon duties January 5, 1882 (died March 25, 1883). Frank Hatton, of Iowa (First Assistant Postmaster General), ad interim, March 26, 1883. Walter Q. Gresham, of Indiana, April 3, 1883; entered upon duties April 11, 1883. Frank Hatton, of Iowa (First Assistant Postmaster General), ad interim, September 25, 1884. Frank Hatton, of Iowa, October 14, 1884. SECRETARY OF THE NAVY—William H. Hunt, of Louisiana, continued from preceding administration. William E. Chandler, of New Hampshire, April 12, 1882; entered upon duties April 17, 1882. SECRETARY OF THE INTERIOR—Samuel J. Kirkwood, of Iowa, continued from preceding administration. Henry M. Teller, of Colorado, April 6, 1882; entered upon duties April 17, 1882.

47th Congress
1st Session: Dec. 5, 1881–Aug. 9, 1882; 2d Session: Dec. 4, 1882–Mar. 3, 1883; Special Sessions of the Senate: Mar. 4, 1881–May 20, 1881; Oct. 10, 1881–Oct. 29, 1881.

President pro tempore of the Senate: Thomas F. Bayard, of Delaware (elected Oct. 10, 1881); David Davis, of Illinois (elected Oct. 13, 1881); George F. Edmunds, of Vermont (elected Mar. 3, 1883). Speaker of the House: J. Warren Keifer, of Ohio (elected Dec. 5, 1881).

Senate: 37 Republican; 37 Democratic; 1 other
House: 147 Republican; 135 Democratic; 11 other

48th Congress
1st Session: Dec. 3, 1883–July 7, 1884; 2d Session: Dec. 1, 1884–Mar. 3, 1885.

President pro tempore of the Senate: George F. Edmunds, of Vermont (reelected Jan. 14, 1884). Speaker of the House: John G. Carlisle, of Kentucky (elected Dec. 3, 1883).

Senate: 38 Republican; 36 Democratic; 2 other
House: 197 Democratic; 118 Republican; 10 other

First Administration of GROVER CLEVELAND
MARCH 4, 1885, TO MARCH 3, 1889

PRESIDENT—Grover Cleveland, of New York (Democratic). VICE-PRESIDENT—Thomas A. Hendricks, of Indiana (died November 25, 1885). SECRETARY OF STATE—Frederick T. Frelinghuysen, of New Jersey, continued from preceding administration. Thomas F. Bayard, of Delaware, March 6, 1885. SECRETARY OF THE TREASURY—Hugh McCulloch, of Indiana, continued from preceding administration. Daniel Manning, of New York, March 6, 1885; entered upon duties March 8, 1885. Charles S. Fairchild, of New York, April 1, 1887. SECRETARY OF WAR—Robert T. Lincoln, of Illinois, continued from preceding administration. William C. Endicott, of Massachusetts, March 6, 1885. ATTORNEY GENERAL—Benjamin H. Brewster, of Pennsylvania, continued from preceding administration. Augustus H. Garland, of Arkansas, March 6, 1885; entered upon duties March 9, 1885. POSTMASTER GENERAL—Frank Hatton, of Iowa, continued from preceding administration. William F. Vilas, of Wisconsin, March 6, 1885. Don M. Dickinson, of Michigan, January 16, 1888. SECRETARY OF THE NAVY—William E. Chandler, of New Hampshire, continued from preceding administration. William C. Whitney, of New York, March 6, 1885. SECRETARY OF THE INTERIOR—Merritt L. Joslyn, of Illinois (Assistant Secretary), ad interim, March 4, 1885. Lucius Q. C. Lamar, of Mississippi, March 6, 1885. Henry L. Muldrow, of Mississippi (First Assistant Secretary), ad interim, January 11, 1888. William F. Vilas, of Wisconsin, January 16, 1888. SECRETARY OF AGRICULTURE—Norman J. Colman, of Missouri, February 13, 1889.

49th Congress
1st Session: Dec. 7, 1885–Aug. 5, 1886; 2d Session: Dec. 6, 1886–Mar 3, 1887; Special Session of the Senate: Mar. 4, 1885–Apr. 2, 1885.

President pro tempore of the Senate: John Sherman, of Ohio (elected Dec. 7, 1885); John J. Ingalls, of Kansas (elected Feb. 25, 1887). Speaker of the House: John G. Carlisle, of Kentucky (reelected Dec. 7, 1885).

Senate: 43 Republican; 34 Democratic
House: 183 Democratic; 140 Republican; 2 other

50th Congress
1st Session: Dec. 5, 1887–Oct. 20, 1888; 2d Session: Dec. 3, 1888–Mar. 3, 1889.

President pro tempore of the Senate: John J. Ingalls, of Kansas (continued from the preceding Congress). Speaker of the House: John G. Carlisle, of Kentucky (reelected Dec. 5, 1887).

Senate: 39 Republican; 37 Democratic
House: 169 Democratic; 152 Republican; 4 other

Administration of BENJAMIN HARRISON

MARCH 4, 1889, TO MARCH 3, 1893

PRESIDENT—Benjamin Harrison, of Indiana (Republican). VICE-PRESIDENT—Levi P. Morton, of New York. SECRETARY OF STATE—Thomas F. Bayard, of Delaware, continued from preceding administration. James G. Blaine, of Maine, March 5, 1889; entered upon duties March 7, 1889. William F. Wharton, of Massachusetts (Assistant Secretary), ad interim, June 4, 1892. John W. Foster, of Indiana, June 29, 1892. William F. Wharton, of Massachusetts (Assistant Secretary), ad interim, February 23, 1893. SECRETARY OF THE TREASURY—Charles S. Fairchild, of New York, continued from preceding administration. William Windom, of Minnesota, March 5, 1889; entered upon duties March 7, 1889 (died January 29, 1891). Allured B. Nettleton, of Minnesota (Assistant Secretary), ad interim, January 30, 1891. Charles Foster, of Ohio, February 24, 1891. SECRETARY OF WAR—William C. Endicott, of Massachusetts, continued from preceding administration. Redfield Proctor, of Vermont, March 5, 1889. Lewis A. Grant, of Minnesota (Assistant Secretary), ad interim, December 6, 1891. Stephen B. Elkins, of West Virginia, December 22, 1891; entered upon duties December 24, 1891. ATTORNEY GENERAL—Augustus H. Garland, of Arkansas, continued from preceding administration. William H. H. Miller, of Indiana, March 5, 1889. POSTMASTER GENERAL—Don M. Dickinson, of Michigan, continued from preceding administration. John Wanamaker, of Pennsylvania, March 5, 1889. SECRETARY OF THE NAVY—William C. Whitney, of New York, continued from preceding administration. Benjamin F. Tracy, of New York, March 5, 1889. SECRETARY OF THE INTERIOR—William F. Vilas, of Wisconsin, continued from preceding administration. John W. Noble, of Missouri, March 5, 1889; entered upon duties March 7, 1889. SECRETARY OF AGRICULTURE—Norman J. Colman, of Missouri, continued from preceding administration, Jeremiah M. Rusk, of Wisconsin, March 5, 1889; entered upon duties March 7, 1889.

51st Congress

1st Session: Dec. 2, 1889–Oct. 1, 1890; 2d Session: Dec. 1, 1890–Mar. 2, 1891; Special Session of the Senate: Mar. 4, 1889–Apr. 2, 1889.

President pro tempore of the Senate: John J. Ingalls, of Kansas (reelected Mar. 7, 1889; Apr. 2, 1889; Feb. 28, 1890; Apr. 3, 1890); Charles F. Manderson, of Nebraska (elected Mar. 2, 1891). Speaker of the House: Thomas B. Reed, of Maine (elected Dec. 2, 1889).

Senate: 39 Republican; 37 Democratic
House: 166 Republican; 159 Democratic

52d Congress

1st Session: Dec. 7, 1891–Aug. 5, 1892; 2d Session: Dec. 5, 1892–Mar. 3, 1893.

President pro tempore of the Senate: Charles F. Manderson, of Nebraska (continued from preceding Congress). Speaker of the House: Charles F. Crisp, of Georgia (elected Dec. 8, 1891).

Senate: 47 Republican; 39 Democratic; 2 other
House: 235 Democratic; 88 Republican; 9 other

Second Administration of GROVER CLEVELAND

March 4, 1893, TO MARCH 3, 1897

PRESIDENT—Grover Cleveland, of New York (Democratic). VICE-PRESIDENT—Adlai E. Stevenson, of Illinois. SECRETARY OF STATE—William F. Wharton, of Massachusetts (Assistant Secretary), ad interim, continued from preceding administration. Walter Q. Gresham, of Illinois, March 6, 1893 (died May 28, 1895). Edwin F. Uhl, of Michigan (Assistant Secretary), ad interim, May 28, 1895. Alvey A. Adee, of the District of Columbia (Second Assistant Secretary), ad interim, May 31, 1895. Edwin F. Uhl, of Michigan (Assistant Secretary), ad interim, June 1, 1895. Richard Olney, of Massachusetts, June 8, 1895; entered upon duties June 10, 1895. SECRETARY OF THE TREASURY—Charles Foster, of Ohio, continued from preceding administration. John G. Carlisle, of Kentucky, March 6, 1893. SECRETARY OF WAR—Stephen B. Elkins, of West Virginia, continued from preceding administration. Daniel S. Lamont, of New York, March 6, 1893. ATTORNEY GENERAL—William H. H. Miller, of Indiana, continued from preceding administration. Richard Olney, of Massachusetts, March 6, 1893. Judson Harmon, of Ohio, June 8, 1895; entered upon duties June 11, 1895. POSTMASTER GENERAL—John Wanamaker, of Pennsylvania, continued from preceding administration. Wilson S. Bissell, of New York, March 6, 1893. William L. Wilson, of West Virginia, March 1, 1895; entered upon duties April 4, 1895. SECRETARY OF THE NAVY—Benjamin F. Tracy, of New York, continued from preceding administration. Hilary A. Herbert, of Alabama, March 6, 1893. SECRETARY OF THE INTERIOR—John W. Noble, of Missouri, continued from preceding administration. Hoke Smith, of Georgia, March 6, 1893. John M. Reynolds, of Pennsylvania (Assistant Secretary), ad interim, September 1, 1896. David R. Francis, of Missouri, September 1, 1896; entered upon duties September 4, 1896. SECRETARY OF AGRICULTURE—

Jeremiah M. Rusk, of Wisconsin, continued from preceding administration. Julius Sterling Morton, of Nebraska, March 6, 1893.

53d Congress

1st Session: Aug. 7, 1893–Nov. 3, 1893; 2d Session: Dec. 4, 1893–Aug. 28, 1894; 3d Session: Dec. 3, 1894–Mar. 3, 1895; Special Session of the Senate: Mar. 4, 1893–Apr. 15, 1893.

President pro tempore of the Senate: Charles F. Manderson, of Nebraska (continued from preceding Congress); Isham G. Harris, of Tennessee (elected Mar. 22, 1893; Jan. 10, 1895); Matt W. Ransom, of North Carolina (elected Jan. 7, 1895). Speaker of the House: Charles F. Crisp, of Georgia (reelected Aug. 7, 1893).

Senate: 44 Democratic; 38 Republican; 3 other
House: 218 Democratic; 127 Republican; 11 other

54th Congress

1st Session: Dec. 2, 1895–June 11, 1896; 2d Session: Dec. 7, 1896–Mar. 3, 1897.

President pro tempore of the Senate: William P. Frye, of Maine (elected Feb. 7, 1896). Speaker of the House: Thomas B. Reed, of Maine (elected Dec. 2, 1895).

Senate: 43 Republican; 39 Democratic; 6 other
House: 244 Republican; 105 Democratic; 7 other

First Administration of WILLIAM McKINLEY

MARCH 4, 1897, TO MARCH 3, 1901

PRESIDENT—William McKinley, of Ohio (Republican). VICE-PRESIDENT—Garret A. Hobart, of New Jersey (died November 21, 1899). SECRETARY OF STATE—Richard Olney, of Massachusetts, continued from preceding administration. John Sherman, of Ohio, March 5, 1897. William R. Day, of Ohio, April 26, 1898; entered upon duties April 28, 1898. Alvey A. Adee (Second Assistant Secretary), ad interim, September 17, 1898. John Hay, of the District of Columbia, September 20, 1898; entered upon duties September 30, 1898. SECRETARY OF THE TREASURY—John G. Carlisle, of Kentucky, continued from preceding administration. Lyman J. Gage, of Illinois, March 5, 1897. SECRETARY OF WAR—Daniel S. Lamont, of New York, continued from preceding administration. Russell A. Alger, of Michigan, March 5, 1897. Elihu Root, of New York, August 1, 1899. ATTORNEY GENERAL—Judson Harmon, of Ohio, continued from preceding administration. Joseph McKenna, of California, March 5, 1897; entered upon duties March 7, 1897. John K. Richards, of Ohio (Solicitor General), ad interim, January 26, 1898. John W. Griggs, of New Jersey, January 25, 1898; entered upon duties February 1, 1898. POSTMASTER GENERAL—William L. Wilson, of West Virginia, continued from preceding administration. James A. Gary, of Maryland, March 5, 1897. Charles Emory Smith, of Pennsylvania, April 21, 1898. SECRETARY OF THE NAVY—Hilary A. Herbert, of Alabama, continued from preceding administration. John D. Long, of Massachusetts, March 5, 1897. SECRETARY OF THE INTERIOR—David R. Francis, of New York, March 5, 1897. Ethan A. Hitchcock, of Missouri, December 21, 1898; entered upon duties February 20, 1899. SECRETARY OF AGRICULTURE—Julius Sterling Morton, of Nebraska, continued from preceding administration. James Wilson, of Iowa, March 5, 1897.

55th Congress

1st Session: Mar. 15, 1897–July 24, 1897; 2d Session: Dec. 6, 1897–July 8, 1898; 3d Session: Dec. 5, 1898–Mar. 3, 1899; Special Session of the Senate: Mar. 4, 1897–Mar. 10, 1897.

President pro tempore of the Senate: William P. Frye, of Maine (continued from preceding Congress). Speaker of the House: Thomas B. Reed, of Maine (reelected Mar. 15, 1897).

Senate: 47 Republican; 34 Democratic; 7 other
House: 204 Republican; 113 Democratic; 40 other

56th Congress

1st Session: Dec. 4, 1899–June 7, 1900; 2d Session: Dec. 3, 1900–Mar. 3, 1901.

President pro tempore of the Senate: William P. Frye, of Maine (continued from preceding Congress). Speaker of the House: David B. Henderson, of Iowa (elected Dec. 4, 1899).

Senate: 53 Republican; 26 Democratic; 8 other
House: 185 Republican; 163 Democratic; 9 other

Second Administration of WILLIAM McKINLEY

MARCH 4, 1901, TO SEPTEMBER 14, 1901

PRESIDENT—William McKinley, of Ohio (Republican) (died September 14, 1901). VICE-PRESIDENT—Theodore Roosevelt, of New York. SECRETARY OF STATE—John Hay, of the District of Columbia, continued from preceding administration. John Hay, of the District of Columbia, recommissioned March 5, 1901. SECRETARY OF THE TREASURY—Lyman J. Gage, of Illinois, continued from preceding administration. Lyman J. Gage, of

Illinois, recommissioned March 5, 1901. SECRETARY OF WAR—Elihu Root, of New York, continued from preceding administration. Elihu Root, of New York, recommissioned March 5, 1901. ATTORNEY GENERAL—John W. Griggs, of New Jersey, continued from preceding administration. John W. Griggs, of New Jersey, recommissioned March 5, 1901. John K. Richards, of Ohio (Solicitor General), ad interim, April 1, 1901. Philander C. Knox, of Pennsylvania, April 5, 1901; entered upon duties April 10, 1901. POSTMASTER GENERAL—Charles Emory Smith, of Pennsylvania, continued from preceding administration. Charles Emory Smith, of Pennsylvania, recommissioned March 5, 1901. SECRETARY OF THE NAVY—John D. Long, of Massachusetts, continued from preceding administration. John D. Long, of Massachusetts, recommissioned March 5, 1901. SECRETARY OF THE INTERIOR—Ethan A. Hitchcock, of Missouri, continued from preceding administration. Ethan A. Hitchcock, of Missouri, recommissioned March 5, 1901. SECRETARY OF AGRICULTURE—James Wilson, of Iowa, continued from preceding administration. James Wilson, of Iowa, recommissioned March 5, 1901.

First Administration of THEODORE ROOSEVELT
SEPTEMBER 14, 1901, TO MARCH 3, 1905

PRESIDENT—Theodore Roosevelt, of New York (Republican). SECRETARY OF STATE—John Hay, of the District of Columbia, continued from preceding administration. SECRETARY OF THE TREASURY—Lyman J. Gage, of Illinois, continued from preceding administration. Leslie M. Shaw, of Iowa, January 9, 1902; entered upon duties February 1, 1902. SECRETARY OF WAR—Elihu Root, of New York, continued from preceding administration. William H. Taft, of Ohio, January 11, 1904, to take effect February 1, 1904. ATTORNEY GENERAL—Philander C. Knox, of Pennsylvania, continued from preceding administration. Philander C. Knox, of Pennsylvania, recommissioned December 16, 1901. William H. Moody, of Massachusetts, July 1, 1904. POSTMASTER GENERAL—Charles Emory Smith, of Pennsylvania, continued from preceding administration. Henry C. Payne, of Wisconsin, January 9, 1902. Robert J. Wynne, of Pennsylvania, October 10, 1904. SECRETARY OF THE NAVY—John D. Long, of Massachusetts, continued from preceding administration. William H. Moody, of Massachusetts, April 29, 1902; entered upon duties May 1, 1902. Paul Morton, of Illinois, July 1, 1904. SECRETARY OF THE INTERIOR—Ethan A. Hitchcock, of Missouri, continued from preceding administration. SECRETARY OF AGRICULTURE—James Wilson, of Iowa, continued from preceding administration. SECRETARY OF COMMERCE AND LABOR—George B. Cortelyou, of New York, February 16, 1903. Victor H. Metcalf, of California, July 1, 1904.

57th Congress
1st Session: Dec. 2, 1901–July 1, 1902; 2d Session: Dec. 1, 1902–Mar. 3, 1903; Special Session of the Senate: Mar. 4, 1901–Mar. 9, 1901.

President pro tempore of the Senate: William P. Frye, of Maine (reelected Mar. 7, 1901). Speaker of the House: David B. Henderson, of Iowa (reelected Dec. 2, 1901).

Senate: 55 Republican; 35 Democratic; 4 other
House: 197 Republican; 151 Democratic; 9 other

58th Congress
1st Session: Nov. 9, 1903–Dec. 7, 1903; 2d Session: Dec. 7, 1903–Apr. 28, 1904; 3d Session: Dec. 5, 1904–Mar. 3, 1905; Special Session of the Senate: Mar. 5, 1903–Mar. 19, 1903.

President pro tempore of the Senate: William P. Frye, of Maine (continued from preceding Congress). Speaker of the House: Joseph G. Cannon, of Illinois (elected Nov. 9, 1903).

Senate: 57 Republican; 33 Democratic
House: 208 Republican; 178 Democratic

Second Administration of THEODORE ROOSEVELT
MARCH 4, 1905, TO MARCH 3, 1909

PRESIDENT—Theodore Roosevelt, of New York (Republican). VICE-PRESIDENT—Charles Warren Fairbanks, of Indiana. SECRETARY OF STATE—John Hay, of the District of Columbia, continued from preceding administration. John Hay, of the District of Columbia, recommissioned March 6, 1905 (died July 1, 1905). Francis B. Loomis, of Ohio (Assistant Secretary), ad interim, July 1, 1905, to July 18, 1905. Elihu Root, of New York, July 7, 1905; entered upon duties July 19, 1905. Robert Bacon, of New York, January 27, 1909. SECRETARY OF THE TREASURY—Leslie M. Shaw, of Iowa, continued from preceding administration. Leslie M. Shaw, of Iowa, recommissioned March 6, 1905. George B. Cortelyou, of New York, January 15, 1907, to take effect March 4, 1907. SECRETARY OF WAR—William H. Taft, of Ohio, continued from preceding administration. William H. Taft, of Ohio, recommissioned March 6, 1905. Luke E. Wright, of Tennessee, June 29, 1908; entered upon duties July 1, 1908. ATTORNEY GENERAL—William H. Moody, of Massachusetts, continued from preceding administration. William H. Moody, of Massachusetts, recommissioned March 6, 1905. Charles J. Bonaparte, of Maryland, December 12, 1906; entered upon duties December 17, 1906. POSTMASTER GENERAL—Robert J.

Wynne, of Pennsylvania, continued from preceding administration. George B. Cortelyou, of New York, March 6, 1905. George von L. Meyer, of Massachusetts, January 15, 1907, to take effect March 4, 1907. SECRETARY OF THE NAVY—Paul Morton, of Illinois, continued from preceding administration. Paul Morton, of Illinois, recommissioned March 6, 1905. Charles J. Bonaparte, of Maryland, July 1, 1905. Victor H. Metcalf, of California, December 12, 1906; entered upon duties December 17, 1906. Truman H. Newberry, of Michigan, December 1, 1908. SECRETARY OF THE INTERIOR—Ethan A. Hitchcock, of Missouri, continued from preceding administration. Ethan A. Hitchcock, of Missouri, recommissioned March 6, 1905. James R. Garfield, of Ohio, January 15, 1907, to take effect March 4, 1907. SECRETARY OF AGRICULTURE—James Wilson, of Iowa, continued from preceding administration. James Wilson, of Iowa, recommissioned March 6, 1905. SECRETARY OF COMMERCE AND LABOR—Victor H. Metcalf, of California, continued from preceding administration. Victor H. Metcalf, of California, recommissioned March 6, 1905. Oscar S. Straus, of New York, December 12, 1906; entered upon duties December 17, 1906.

59th Congress
1st Session: Dec. 4, 1905–June 30, 1906; 2d Session: Dec. 3, 1906–Mar. 3, 1907; Special Session of the Senate: Mar. 4, 1905—Mar. 18, 1905.

President pro tempore of the Senate: William P. Frye, of Maine (continued from preceding Congress). Speaker of the House: Joseph G. Cannon, of Illinois (reelected Dec. 4, 1905).

Senate: 57 Republican; 33 Democratic
House: 250 Republican; 136 Democratic

60th Congress
1st Session: Dec. 2, 1907–May 30, 1908; 2d Session: Dec. 7, 1908–Mar. 3, 1909.

President pro tempore of the Senate: William P. Frye, of Maine (reelected Dec. 5, 1907). Speaker of the House: Joseph G. Cannon, of Illinois (reelected Dec. 2, 1907).

Senate: 61 Republican; 31 Democratic
House: 222 Republican; 164 Democratic

Administration of WILLIAM H. TAFT
March 4, 1909, TO MARCH 3, 1913

PRESIDENT—William H. Taft, of Ohio (Republican). VICE-PRESIDENT—James S. Sherman, of New York (died October 30, 1912). SECRETARY OF STATE—Robert Bacon, of New York, continued from preceding administration. Philander C. Knox, of Pennsylvania, March 5, 1909. SECRETARY OF THE TREASURY—George B. Cortelyou, of New York, continued from preceding administration. Franklin MacVeagh, of Illinois, March 5, 1909; entered upon duties March 8, 1909. SECRETARY OF WAR—Luke E. Wright, of Tennessee, continued from preceding administration. Jacob M. Dickinson, of Tennessee, March 5, 1909; entered upon duties March 12, 1909. Henry L. Stimson, of New York, May 16, 1911; entered upon duties May 22, 1911. ATTORNEY GENERAL—Charles J. Bonaparte, of Maryland, continued from preceding administration. George W. Wickersham, of New York, March 5, 1909. POSTMASTER GENERAL—George von L. Meyer, of Massachusetts, continued from preceding administration. Frank H. Hitchcock, of Massachusetts, March 5, 1909. SECRETARY OF THE NAVY—Truman H. Newberry, of Michigan, continued from preceding administration. George von L. Meyer, of Massachusetts, March 5, 1909. SECRETARY OF THE INTERIOR—James R. Garfield, of Ohio, continued from preceding administration. Richard A. Ballinger, of Washington, March 5, 1909. Walter Lowrie Fisher, of Illinois, March 7, 1911. SECRETARY OF AGRICULTURE—James Wilson, of Iowa, continued from preceding administration. James Wilson, of Iowa, recommissioned March 5, 1909. SECRETARY OF COMMERCE AND LABOR—Oscar S. Straus, of New York, continued from preceding administration. Charles Nagel, of Missouri, March 5, 1909.

61st Congress
1st Session: Mar. 15, 1909–Aug. 5, 1909; 2d Session: Dec. 6, 1909–June 25, 1910; 3d Session: Dec. 5, 1910–Mar. 3, 1911; Special Session of the Senate: Mar. 4, 1909–Mar. 6, 1909.

President pro tempore of the Senate: William P. Frye, of Maine (continued from preceding Congress). Speaker of the House: Joseph G. Cannon, of Illinois (reelected Mar. 15, 1909).

Senate: 61 Republican; 32 Democratic
House: 219 Republican; 172 Democratic

62d Congress
1st Session: Apr. 4, 1911–Aug. 22, 1911; 2d Session: Dec. 4, 1911–Aug. 26, 1912; 3d Session: Dec. 2, 1912–Mar. 3, 1913.

President pro tempore of the Senate: William P. Frye, of Maine (continued from preceding Congress). Charles Curtis, of Kansas (elected to serve Dec. 4–12, 1911). Augustus O. Bacon, of Georgia (elected to serve Jan. 15–17, 1912; Mar. 11–12, 1912; Apr. 8, 1912; May 10, 1912; May 30–June 3, 1912; June 13–July 5, 1912; Aug. 1–10, 1912; Aug. 27–Dec. 15, 1912; Jan. 5–18, 1913; Feb. 2–15, 1913). Jacob H. Gallinger, of New

Hampshire (elected to serve Feb. 12–14, 1912; April 26–27, 1912; May 7, 1912; July 6–31, 1912; Aug. 12–26, 1912; Dec. 16, 1912–Jan. 4, 1913; Jan. 19–Feb. 1, 1913; Feb. 16–Mar. 3, 1913). Henry C. Lodge, of Massachusetts (elected to serve Mar. 25–26, 1912). Frank B. Brandegee, of Connecticut (elected to serve May 25, 1912). Speaker of the House: James B. Clark, of Missouri (elected Apr. 4, 1911).

Senate: 51 Republican; 41 Democratic
House: 228 Democratic; 161 Republican; 1 other

First Administration of WOODROW WILSON
MARCH 4, 1913, TO MARCH 3, 1917

PRESIDENT—Woodrow Wilson, of New Jersey (Democratic). VICE-PRESIDENT—Thomas R. Marshall, of Indiana. SECRETARY OF STATE—Philander C. Knox, of Pennsylvania, continued from preceding administration. William Jennings Bryan, of Nebraska, March 5, 1913. Robert Lansing, of New York (counselor), ad interim, June 9, 1915. Robert Lansing, of New York, June 23, 1915. SECRETARY OF THE TREASURY—Franklin MacVeagh, of Illinois, continued from preceding administration. William Gibbs McAdoo, of New York, March 5, 1913; entered upon duties March 6, 1913. SECRETARY OF WAR—Henry L. Stimson, of New York, continued from preceding administration. Lindley M. Garrison, of New Jersey, March 5, 1913. Hugh L. Scott (United States Army), ad interim, February 12, 1916; served from February 11 to March 8, 1916. Newton D. Baker, of Ohio, March 7, 1916; entered upon duties March 9, 1916. ATTORNEY GENERAL—George W. Wickersham, of New York, continued from preceding administration. James Clark McReynolds, of Tennessee, March 5, 1913; entered upon duties March 6, 1913. Thomas Watt Gregory, of Texas, August 29, 1914; entered upon duties September 3, 1914. POSTMASTER GENERAL—Frank H. Hitchcock, of Massachusetts, continued from preceding administration. Albert Sidney Burleson, of Texas, March 5, 1913. SECRETARY OF THE NAVY—George von L. Meyer, of Massachusetts, continued from preceding administration. Josephus Daniels, of North Carolina, March 5, 1913. SECRETARY OF THE INTERIOR—Walter Lowrie Fisher, of Illinois, continued from preceding administration. Franklin Knight Lane, of California, March 5, 1913. SECRETARY OF AGRICULTURE—James Wilson, of Iowa, continued from preceding administration. David Franklin Houston, of Missouri, March 5, 1913; entered upon duties March 6, 1913. SECRETARY OF COMMERCE—Charles Nagel, of Missouri (Secretary of Commerce and Labor), continued from preceding administration. William C. Redfield, of New York, March 5, 1913. SECRETARY OF LABOR—Charles Nagel, of Missouri (Secretary of Commerce and Labor), continued from preceding administration. William Bauchop Wilson, of Pennsylvania, March 5, 1913.

63d Congress
1st Session: Apr. 7, 1913–Dec. 1, 1913; 2d Session: Dec. 1, 1913–Oct. 24, 1914; 3d Session: Dec. 7, 1914–Mar. 3, 1915; Special Session of the Senate: Mar. 4, 1913–Mar. 17, 1913.

President pro tempore of the Senate: James P. Clarke, of Arkansas (elected Mar. 13, 1913). Speaker of the House: James B. Clark, of Missouri (reelected Apr. 7, 1913).

Senate: 51 Democratic; 44 Republican; 1 other
House: 291 Democratic; 127 Republican; 17 other

64th Congress
1st Session: Dec. 6, 1915–Sept. 8, 1916; 2d Session: Dec. 4, 1916–Mar. 3, 1917.

President pro tempore of the Senate: James P. Clarke, of Arkansas (reelected Dec. 6, 1915); Willard Saulsbury, of Delaware (elected Dec. 14, 1916). Speaker of the House: James B. Clark, of Missouri (reelected Dec. 6, 1915).

Senate: 56 Democratic; 40 Republican
House: 230 Democratic; 196 Republican; 9 other

Second Administration of WOODROW WILSON
MARCH 4, 1917, TO MARCH 3, 1921

PRESIDENT—Woodrow Wilson, of New Jersey (Democratic). (Oath administered March 5, 1917.) VICE-PRESIDENT—Thomas R. Marshall, of Indiana. SECRETARY OF STATE—Robert Lansing, of New York, continued from preceding administration. Frank L. Polk, of New York (Under Secretary), ad interim, February 14, 1920, to March 13, 1920. Bainbridge Colby, of New York, March 22, 1920; entered upon duties March 23, 1920. SECRETARY OF THE TREASURY—William Gibbs McAdoo, of New York, continued from preceding administration. Carter Glass, of Virginia, December 6, 1918; entered upon duties December 16, 1918. David F. Houston, of Missouri, January 31, 1920; entered upon duties February 2, 1920. SECRETARY OF WAR—Newton D. Baker, of Ohio, continued from preceding administration. ATTORNEY GENERAL—Thomas Watt Gregory, of Texas, continued from preceding administration. A. Mitchell Palmer, of Pennsylvania, March 5, 1919. POSTMASTER GENERAL—Albert Sidney Burleson, of Texas, continued from preceding administration. Albert Sidney Burleson, of Texas, recommissioned January 24, 1918. SECRETARY OF THE NAVY—Josephus Daniels, of North Carolina, con-

tinued from preceding administration. SECRETARY OF THE INTERIOR—Franklin Knight Lane, of California, continued from preceding administration. John Barton Payne, of Illinois, February 28, 1920; entered upon duties March 13, 1920. SECRETARY OF AGRICULTURE—David Franklin Houston, of Missouri, continued from preceding administration. Edwin T. Meredith, of Iowa, January 31, 1920; entered upon duties February 2, 1920. SECRETARY OF COMMERCE—William C. Redfield, of New York, continued from preceding administration. Joshua Willis Alexander, of Missouri, December 11, 1919; entered upon duties December 16, 1919. SECRETARY OF LABOR—William Bauchop Wilson, of Pennsylvania, continued from preceding administration.

65th Congress
1st Session: Apr. 2, 1917–Oct. 6, 1917; 2d Session: Dec. 3, 1917–Nov. 21, 1918; 3d Session: Dec. 2, 1918–Mar. 3, 1919; Special Session of the Senate: Mar. 5, 1917–Mar. 16, 1917.

President pro tempore of the Senate: Willard Saulsbury, of Delaware (continued from preceding Congress). Speaker of the House: James B. Clark, of Missouri (reelected Apr. 2, 1917).

Senate: 53 Democratic; 42 Republican
House: 216 Democratic; 210 Republican; 6 other

66th Congress
1st Session: May 19, 1919–Nov. 19, 1919; 2d Session: Dec. 1, 1919–June 5, 1920; 3d Session: Dec. 6, 1920–Mar. 3, 1921.

President pro tempore of the Senate: Albert B. Cummins, of Iowa (elected May 19, 1919). Speaker of the House: Frederick H. Gillett, of Massachusetts (elected May 19, 1919).

Senate: 49 Republican; 47 Democratic
House: 240 Republican; 190 Democratic; 3 other

Administration of WARREN G. HARDING
MARCH 4, 1921, TO AUGUST 2, 1923

PRESIDENT—Warren G. Harding, of Ohio (Republican) (died August 2, 1923). VICE-PRESIDENT—Calvin Coolidge, of Massachusetts. SECRETARY OF STATE—Bainbridge Colby, of New York, continued from preceding administration. Charles Evans Hughes, of New York, March 4, 1921; entered upon duties March 5, 1921. SECRETARY OF THE TREASURY—David F. Houston, of Missouri, continued from preceding administration. Andrew W. Mellon, of Pennsylvania, March 4, 1921; entered upon duties March 5, 1921. SECRETARY OF WAR—Newton D. Baker, of Ohio, continued from preceding administration. John W. Weeks, of Massachusetts, March 5, 1921. ATTORNEY GENERAL—A. Mitchell Palmer, of Pennsylvania, continued from preceding administration. Harry M. Daugherty, of Ohio, March 5, 1921. POSTMASTER GENERAL—Albert Sidney Burleson, of Texas, continued from preceding administration. Will H. Hays, of Indiana, March 5, 1921. Hubert Work, of Colorado, March 4, 1922. Harry S. New, of Indiana, February 27, 1923; entered upon duties March 5, 1923. SECRETARY OF THE NAVY—Josephus Daniels, of North Carolina, continued from preceding administration. Edwin Denby, of Michigan, March 5, 1921. SECRETARY OF THE INTERIOR—John Barton Payne, of Illinois, continued from preceding administration. Albert B. Fall, of New Mexico, March 5, 1921. Hubert Work, of Colorado, February 27, 1923; entered upon duties March 5, 1923. SECRETARY OF AGRICULTURE—Edwin T. Meredith, of Iowa, continued from preceding administration. Henry C. Wallace, of Iowa, March 5, 1921. SECRETARY OF COMMERCE—Joshua Willis Alexander, of Missouri, continued from preceding administration. Herbert C. Hoover, of California, March 5, 1921. SECRETARY OF LABOR—William Bauchop Wilson, of Pennsylvania, continued from preceding administration. James J. Davis, of Pennsylvania, March 5, 1921.

First Administration of CALVIN COOLIDGE
AUGUST 3, 1923, TO MARCH 3, 1925

PRESIDENT—Calvin Coolidge, of Massachusetts (Republican). SECRETARY OF STATE—Charles Evans Hughes, of New York, continued from preceding administration. SECRETARY OF THE TREASURY—Andrew W. Mellon, of Pennsylvania, continued from preceding administration. SECRETARY OF WAR—John W. Weeks, of Massachusetts, continued from preceding administration. ATTORNEY GENERAL—Harry M. Daugherty, of Ohio, continued from preceding administration. Harlan F. Stone, of New York, April 7, 1924; entered upon duties April 9, 1924. POSTMASTER GENERAL—Harry S. New, of Indiana, continued from preceding administration. SECRETARY OF THE NAVY—Edwin Denby, of Michigan, continued from preceding administration. Curtis D. Wilbur, of California, March 18, 1924. SECRETARY OF THE INTERIOR—Hubert Work, of Colorado, continued from preceding administration. SECRETARY OF AGRICULTURE—Henry C. Wallace, of Iowa, continued from preceding administration (died October 25, 1924). Howard M. Gore, of West Virginia (Assistant Secretary), ad interim, October 26, 1924, to November 22, 1924. Howard M. Gore, of West Virginia, November 21, 1924; entered upon duties November 22, 1924. SECRETARY OF COMMERCE—

Herbert C. Hoover, of California, continued from preceding administration. SECRETARY OF LABOR—James J. Davis, of Pennsylvania, continued from preceding administration.

67th Congress

1st Session: Apr. 11, 1921–Nov. 23, 1921; 2d Session: Dec. 5, 1921–Sept. 22, 1922; 3d Session: Nov. 20, 1922–Dec. 4, 1922; 4th Session: Dec. 4, 1922–March 3, 1923; Special Session of the Senate: Mar. 4, 1921–Mar. 15, 1921.

President pro tempore of the Senate: Albert B. Cummins, of Iowa (reelected Mar. 7, 1921). Speaker of the House: Frederick H. Gillett, of Massachusetts (reelected Apr. 11, 1921).

Senate: 59 Republican; 37 Democratic
House: 303 Republican; 131 Democratic; 1 other

68th Congress

1st Session: Dec. 3, 1923–June 7; 1924; 2d Session: Dec. 1, 1924–Mar. 3, 1925.

President pro tempore of the Senate: Albert B. Cummins, of Iowa (continued from preceding Congress). Speaker of the House: Frederick H. Gillett, of Massachusetts (reelected Dec. 3, 1923).

Senate: 51 Republican; 43 Democratic; 2 other
House: 225 Republican; 205 Democratic; 5 other

Second Administration of CALVIN COOLIDGE

MARCH 4, 1925, TO MARCH 3, 1929

PRESIDENT—Calvin Coolidge, of Massachusetts (Republican). VICE-PRESIDENT—Charles G. Dawes, of Illinois. SECRETARY OF STATE—Charles Evans Hughes, of New York, continued from preceding administration. Frank B. Kellogg, of Minnesota, February 16, 1925; entered upon duties March 5, 1925. SECRETARY OF THE TREASURY—Andrew W. Mellon, of Pennsylvania, continued from preceding administration. SECRETARY OF WAR —John W. Weeks, of Massachusetts, continued from preceding administration. Dwight F. Davis, of Missouri, October 13, 1925; entered upon duties October 14, 1925. ATTORNEY GENERAL—James M. Beck, of Pennsylvania (Solicitor General), ad interim, March 4, 1925, to March 16, 1925. John G. Sargent, of Vermont, March 17, 1925; entered upon duties March 18, 1925. POSTMASTER GENERAL—Harry S. New, of Indiana, continued from preceding administration. Harry S. New, of Indiana, recommissioned March 5, 1925. SECRETARY OF THE NAVY—Curtis D. Wilbur, of California, continued from preceding administration. SECRETARY OF THE INTERIOR—Hubert Work, of Colorado, continued from preceding administration. Roy O. West, of Illinois, ad interim, July 25, 1928, to January 21, 1929. Roy O. West, January 21, 1929. SECRETARY OF AGRICULTURE—Howard M. Gore, of West Virginia, continued from preceding administration. William M. Jardine, of Kansas, February 18, 1925; entered upon duties March 5, 1925. SECRETARY OF COMMERCE—Herbert C. Hoover, of California, continued from preceding administration. William F. Whiting, of Massachusetts, ad interim, August 21, 1928, to December 11, 1928. William F. Whiting, December 11, 1928. SECRETARY OF LABOR—James J. Davis, of Pennsylvania, continued from preceding administration.

69th Congress

1st Session: Dec. 7, 1925–July 3, 1926; Nov. 10, 1926; 2d Session: Dec. 6, 1926–Mar. 3, 1927; Special Session of the Senate: Mar. 4, 1925–Mar. 18, 1925.

President pro tempore of the Senate: Albert B. Cummins, of Iowa (continued from preceding Congress); George H. Moses, of New Hampshire (elected Mar. 6, 1925). Speaker of the House: Nicholas Longworth, of Ohio (elected Dec. 7, 1925).

Senate: 56 Republican; 39 Democratic; 1 other
House: 247 Republican; 183 Democratic; 4 other

70th Congress

1st Session: Dec. 5, 1927–May 29, 1928; 2d Session: Dec. 3, 1928–Mar. 3, 1929.

President pro tempore of the Senate: George H. Moses, of New Hampshire (reelected Dec. 15, 1927). Speaker of the House: Nicholas Longworth, of Ohio (reelected Dec. 15, 1927).

Senate: 49 Republican; 46 Democratic; 1 other
House: 237 Republican; 195 Democratic; 3 other

Administration of HERBERT C. HOOVER

MARCH 4, 1929, TO MARCH 3, 1933

PRESIDENT—Herbert C. Hoover, of California (Republican). VICE-PRESIDENT—Charles Curtis, of Kansas. SECRETARY OF STATE —Frank B. Kellogg, of Minnesota, continued from preceding administration. Henry L. Stimson, of New York, March 4, 1929; entered upon duties March 29, 1929. SECRETARY OF THE TREASURY—Andrew W. Mellon, of Pennsylvania, continued from preceding administration. Ogden L. Mills, of New York, February 10, 1932; entered upon duties February 13, 1932. SECRETARY OF WAR—Dwight F. Davis, of Missouri, continued from preceding administration. James W. Good, of Illinois, March 5, 1929; entered upon duties March 6, 1929. Patrick J. Hurley, of Oklahoma, December 9, 1929. ATTORNEY GENERAL—John G. Sar-

gent, of Vermont, continued from preceding administration. James DeWitt Mitchell, of Minnesota, March 5, 1929; entered upon duties March 6, 1929. POSTMASTER GENERAL—Harry S. New, of Indiana, continued from preceding administration. Walter F. Brown, of Ohio, March 5, 1929; entered upon duties March 6, 1929. SECRETARY OF THE NAVY—Curtis D. Wilbur, of California, continued from preceding administration. Charles F. Adams, of Massachusetts, March 5, 1929. SECRETARY OF THE INTERIOR—Roy O. West, of Illinois, continued from preceding administration. Ray L. Wilbur, of California, March 5, 1929. SECRETARY OF AGRICULTURE—William M. Jardine, of Kansas, continued from preceding administration. Arthur M. Hyde, of Missouri, March 5, 1929; entered upon duties March 6, 1929. SECRETARY OF COMMERCE—William F. Whiting, of Massachusetts, continued from preceding administration. Robert P. Lamont, of Illinois, March 5, 1929. Roy D. Chapin, of Michigan, ad interim, August 8, 1932; to December 14, 1932. Roy D. Chapin, of Michigan, December 14, 1932. SECRETARY OF LABOR—James J. Davis, of Pennsylvania, continued from preceding administration. William N. Doak, of Virginia, December 8, 1930; entered upon duties December 9, 1930.

71st Congress

1st Session: Apr. 15, 1929–Nov. 22, 1929; 2d Session: Dec. 2, 1929–July 3, 1930; 3d Session: Dec. 1, 1930–Mar. 3, 1931; Special Sessions of the Senate: Mar. 4, 1929–Mar. 5, 1929; July 7, 1930–July 21, 1930.

President pro tempore of the Senate: George H. Moses, of New Hampshire (continued from preceding Congress). Speaker of the House: Nicholas Longworth, of Ohio (reelected Apr. 15, 1929).

Senate: 56 Republican; 39 Democratic; 1 other
House: 267 Republican; 167 Democratic; 1 other

72d Congress

1st Session: Dec. 7, 1931–July 16, 1932; 2d Session: Dec. 15, 1932–Mar. 3, 1933.

President pro tempore of the Senate: George H. Moses, of New Hampshire (continued from preceding Congress). Speaker of the House: John N. Garner, of Texas (elected Dec. 7, 1931).

Senate: 48 Republican; 47 Democratic; 1 other
House: 220 Democratic; 214 Republican; 1 other

First Administration of FRANKLIN DELANO ROOSEVELT

MARCH 4, 1933, TO JANUARY 20, 1937

PRESIDENT—Franklin Delano Roosevelt, of New York (Democratic). VICE-PRESIDENT—John N. Garner, of Texas. SECRETARY OF STATE—Cordell Hull, of Tennessee, March 4, 1933. SECRETARY OF THE TREASURY—William H. Woodin, of New York, March 4, 1933. Henry Morgenthau, Jr., of New York (Under Secretary), ad interim, January 1, 1934, to January 8, 1934. Henry Morgenthau, Jr., of New York, January 8, 1934. SECRETARY OF WAR—George H. Dern, of Utah, March 4, 1933. ATTORNEY GENERAL—Homer S. Cummings, of Connecticut, March 4, 1933. POSTMASTER GENERAL—James A. Farley, of New York, March 4, 1933. SECRETARY OF THE NAVY—Claude A. Swanson, of Virginia, March 4, 1933. SECRETARY OF THE INTERIOR—Harold L. Ickes, of Illinois, March 4, 1933. SECRETARY OF AGRICULTURE—Henry A. Wallace, of Iowa, March 4, 1933. SECRETARY OF COMMERCE—Daniel C. Roper, of South Carolina, March 4, 1933. SECRETARY OF LABOR—Frances Perkins, of New York, March 4, 1933.

73d Congress

1st Session: March 9, 1933–June 15, 1933; 2d Session: Jan. 3, 1934–June 18, 1934; Special Session of the Senate: Mar. 4, 1933–Mar. 6, 1933.

President pro tempore of the Senate: Key Pittman, of Nevada (elected Mar. 9, 1933). Speaker of the House: Henry T. Rainey, of Illinois (elected Mar. 9, 1933).

Senate: 60 Democratic; 35 Republican; 1 other
House: 310 Democratic; 117 Republican; 5 other

74th Congress

1st Session: Jan. 3, 1935–Aug. 26, 1935; 2d Session: Jan. 3, 1936–June 20, 1936.

President pro tempore of the Senate: Key Pittman, of Nevada (reelected Jan. 7, 1935). Speaker of the House: Joseph W. Byrnes, of Tennessee (elected Jan. 3, 1935); William Bankhead, of Alabama (elected June 4, 1936).

Senate: 69 Democratic; 25 Republican; 2 other
House: 319 Democratic; 103 Republican; 10 other

Second Administration of FRANKLIN DELANO ROOSEVELT

JANUARY 20, 1937, TO JANUARY 20, 1941

PRESIDENT—Franklin Delano Roosevelt, of New York (Democratic). VICE-PRESIDENT—John N. Garner, of Texas. SECRETARY OF STATE—Cordell Hull, of Tennessee, continued from preceding administration. SECRETARY OF THE TREASURY— Henry Morgenthau, Jr., of New York, continued from preceding administration. SECRETARY OF WAR—George H. Dern, of Utah, continued from preceding administration (died August 27, 1936). Harry H. Woodring, of Kansas (Assistant Secretary), ad interim, September 25, 1936, to May 6, 1937. Harry H. Woodring, of Kansas, May 6, 1937. Henry L. Stimson, of New York, July 10, 1940. ATTORNEY GENERAL—Homer S. Cummings, of Connecticut, continued from preceding administration. Frank Murphy, of Michigan, ad interim, January 2, 1939, to January 17, 1939. Frank Murphy, of Michigan, January 17, 1939. Robert H. Jackson, of New York, January 18, 1940. POSTMASTER GENERAL—James A. Farley, of New York, continued from preceding administration. James A. Farley, of New York, recommissioned January 22, 1937. Frank C. Walker, of Pennsylvania, September 10, 1940. SECRETARY OF THE NAVY—Claude A. Swanson, of Virginia, continued from preceding administration (died July 7, 1939). Charles Edison, of New Jersey, Acting Secretary from August 5, 1939, to December 30, 1939. Charles Edison, of New Jersey (Assistant Secretary), ad interim, December 30, 1939, to January 11, 1940. Charles Edison, of New Jersey, January 11, 1940. Frank Knox, of Illinois, July 10, 1940. SECRETARY OF THE INTERIOR—Harold L. Ickes, of Illinois, continued from preceding administration. SECRETARY OF AGRICULTURE—Henry A. Wallace, of Iowa, continued from preceding administration. Claude R. Wickard, of Indiana, August 27, 1940; entered upon duties September 5, 1940. SECRETARY OF COMMERCE—Daniel C. Roper, of South Carolina, continued from preceding administration. Harry L. Hopkins, of New York, ad interim, December 24, 1938, to January 23, 1939. Harry L. Hopkins, of New York, January 23, 1939. Jesse H. Jones, of Texas, September 16, 1940; entered upon duties September 19, 1940. SECRETARY OF LABOR—Frances Perkins, of New York, continued from preceding administration.

75th Congress

1st Session: Jan. 5, 1937–Aug. 21, 1937; 2d Session: Nov. 15, 1937–Dec. 21, 1937; 3d Session: Jan. 3, 1938–June 16, 1938.

President pro tempore of the Senate: Key Pittman, of Nevada (continued from preceding Congress). Speaker of the House: William B. Bankhead, of Alabama (reelected Jan. 5, 1937).

Senate: 76 Democratic; 16 Republican; 4 other
House: 331 Democratic; 89 Republican; 13 other

76th Congress

Jan. 3, 1939–Aug. 5, 1939; 2d Session: Sept. 21, 1939–Nov. 3, 1939; 3d Session: Jan. 3, 1940–Jan. 3, 1941.

President pro tempore of the Senate: Key Pittman, of Nevada (continued from preceding Congress); William H. King, of Utah (elected Nov. 19, 1940). Speaker of the House: William B. Bankhead, of Alabama (reelected Jan. 3, 1940); Sam Rayburn, of Texas (elected Sept. 16, 1940).

Senate: 69 Democratic; 23 Republican; 4 other
House: 261 Democratic; 164 Republican; 4 other

Third Administration of FRANKLIN DELANO ROOSEVELT
JANUARY 20, 1941, TO JANUARY 20, 1945

PRESIDENT—Franklin Delano Roosevelt, of New York (Democratic). VICE-PRESIDENT—Henry A. Wallace, of Iowa. SECRETARY OF STATE—Cordell Hull, of Tennessee, continued from preceding administration. Edward R. Stettinius, of Virginia, November 30, 1944; entered upon duties December 1, 1944. SECRETARY OF THE TREASURY—Henry Morgenthau, Jr., of New York, continued from preceding administration. SECRETARY OF WAR—Henry L. Stimson, of New York, continued from preceding administration. ATTORNEY GENERAL—Robert H. Jackson, of New York, continued from preceding administration. Francis Biddle, of Pennsylvania, September 5, 1941. POSTMASTER GENERAL—Frank C. Walker, of Pennsylvania, continued from preceding administration. Frank C. Walker, of Pennsylvania, recommissioned January 27, 1941. SECRETARY OF THE NAVY—Frank Knox, of Illinois, continued from preceding administration (died April 28, 1944). James V. Forrestal, of New York, May 18, 1944. SECRETARY OF THE INTERIOR—Harold L. Ickes, of Illinois, continued from preceding administration. SECRETARY OF AGRICULTURE—Claude R. Wickard, of Indiana, continued from preceding administration. SECRETARY OF COMMERCE—Jesse H. Jones, of Texas, continued from preceding administration. SECRETARY OF LABOR—Frances Perkins, of New York, continued from preceding administration.

77th Congress

1st Session: Jan. 3, 1941–Jan. 2, 1942; 2d Session: Jan. 5, 1942–Dec. 16, 1942.

President pro tempore of the Senate: Pat Harrison, of Mississippi (elected Jan. 6, 1941); Carter Glass, of Virginia (elected July 10, 1941). Speaker of the House: Sam Rayburn, of Texas (reelected Jan. 3, 1941).

Senate: 66 Democratic; 28 Republican; 2 other
House: 268 Democratic; 162 Republican; 5 other

78th Congress

1st Session: Jan. 6, 1943–Dec. 21, 1943; 2d Session: Jan. 10, 1944–Dec. 19, 1944.

President pro tempore of the Senate: Carter Glass, of Virginia (continued from preceding Congress). Speaker of the House: Sam Rayburn, of Texas (reelected Jan. 6, 1943).

Senate: 57 Democratic; 38 Republican; 1 other
House: 222 Democratic; 208 Republican; 5 other

Fourth Administration of FRANKLIN DELANO ROOSEVELT
JANUARY 20, 1945, TO APRIL 12, 1945

PRESIDENT—Franklin Delano Roosevelt, of New York (Democratic) (died April 12, 1945). VICE-PRESIDENT—Harry S. Truman, of Missouri. SECRETARY OF STATE—Edward R. Stettinius, of Virginia, continued from preceding administration. SECRETARY OF THE TREASURY—Henry Morgenthau, Jr., of New York, continued from preceding administration. SECRETARY OF WAR—Henry L. Stimson, of New York, continued from preceding administration. ATTORNEY GENERAL—Francis Biddle, of Pennsylvania, continued from preceding administration. POSTMASTER GENERAL—Frank C. Walker, of Pennsylvania, continued from preceding administration. Frank C. Walker, of Pennsylvania, recommissioned February 6, 1945. SECRETARY OF THE NAVY—James V. Forrestal, of New York, continued from preceding administration. SECRETARY OF THE INTERIOR—Harold L. Ickes, of Illinois, continued from preceding administration. SECRETARY OF AGRICULTURE—Claude R. Wickard, of Indiana, continued from preceding administration. SECRETARY OF COMMERCE—Jesse H. Jones, of Texas, continued from preceding administration. Henry A. Wallace, of Iowa, March 1, 1945; entered upon duties March 2, 1945. SECRETARY OF LABOR—Frances Perkins, of New York, continued from preceding administration.

First Administration of HARRY S TRUMAN
APRIL 12, 1945, TO JANUARY 20, 1949

PRESIDENT—Harry S Truman, of Missouri (Democratic). SECRETARY OF STATE—Edward R. Stettinius, of Virginia, continued from preceding administration. James F. Byrnes, of South Carolina, July 2, 1945; entered upon duties July 3, 1945. George C. Marshall, of Pennsylvania, January 8, 1947; entered upon duties January 21, 1947. SECRETARY OF THE TREASURY—Henry Morgenthau, Jr., of New York, continued from preceding administration. Fred M. Vinson, of Kentucky, July 18, 1945; entered upon duties July 23, 1945. John W. Snyder, of Missouri, June 12, 1946; entered upon duties June 25, 1946. SECRETARY OF DEFENSE—James Forrestal, of New York, July 26, 1947; entered upon duties September 17, 1947. SECRETARY OF WAR—Henry L. Stimson, of New York, continued from preceding administration. Robert Porter Patterson, of New York, September 26, 1945; entered upon duties September 27, 1945. Kenneth C. Royall, of North Carolina, July 21, 1947; entered upon duties July 25, 1947, and served until September 17, 1947. ATTORNEY GENERAL—Francis Biddle, of Pennsylvania, continued from preceding administration. Tom C. Clark, of Texas, June 15, 1945; entered upon duties September 27, 1945. POSTMASTER GENERAL—Frank Walker, of Pennsylvania, from preceding administration. Robert E. Hannegan, of Missouri, May 8, 1945; entered upon duties July 1, 1945. Jesse M. Donaldson, of Missouri, December 16, 1947. SECRETARY OF THE NAVY—James V. Forrestal, of New York, continued from preceding administration; served until September 17, 1947. SECRETARY OF THE INTERIOR—Harold L. Ickes, of Illinois, continued from preceding administration. Julius A. Krug, of Wisconsin, March 6, 1946; entered upon duties March 18, 1946. SECRETARY OF AGRICULTURE—Claude R. Wickard, of Indiana, continued from preceding administration. Clinton P. Anderson, of New Mexico, June 2, 1945; entered upon duties June 30, 1945. Charles F. Brannan, of Colorado, May 29, 1948; entered upon duties June 2, 1948. SECRETARY OF COMMERCE—Henry A. Wallace, of Iowa, continued from preceding administration. William Averell Harriman, of New York, ad interim, September 28, 1946, to January 28, 1947. William Averell Harriman, of New York, January 28, 1947. Charles Sawyer, of Ohio, May 6, 1948. SECRETARY OF LABOR—Frances Perkins, of New York, continued from preceding administration. Lewis B. Schwellenbach, of Washington, June 1, 1945; entered upon duties July 1, 1945 (died June 10, 1948). Maurice J. Tobin, of Massachusetts, ad interim, August 13, 1948.

79th Congress

1st Session: Jan. 3, 1945–Dec. 21, 1945; 2d Session: Jan. 14, 1946–Aug. 2, 1946.

President pro tempore of the Senate: Kenneth McKellar, of Tennessee (elected Jan. 6, 1945). Speaker of the House: Sam Rayburn, of Texas (reelected Jan. 3, 1945).

Senate: 56 Democratic; 38 Republican; 1 other
House: 242 Democratic; 190 Republican; 2 other

80th Congress

1st Session: Jan. 3, 1947–Dec. 19, 1947; 2d Session: Jan. 6, 1948–Dec. 31, 1948.

President pro tempore of the Senate: Arthur H. Vandenberg, of Michigan (elected Jan. 4, 1947). Speaker of the House: Joseph W. Martin, Jr., of Massachusetts (elected Jan. 3, 1947).

Senate: 51 Republican; 45 Democratic

House: 245 Republican; 188 Democratic; 1 other

Second Administration of HARRY S TRUMAN

JANUARY 20, 1949, TO JANUARY 20, 1953

PRESIDENT—Harry S Truman, of Missouri (Democratic). VICE-PRESIDENT—Alben W. Barkley, of Kentucky. SECRETARY OF STATE—Dean G. Acheson, of Connecticut, January 19, 1949; entered upon duties January 21, 1949. SECRETARY OF THE TREASURY—John W. Snyder, of Missouri, continued from preceding administration. SECRETARY OF DEFENSE—James V. Forrestal, of New York, continued from preceding administration. Louis A. Johnson, of West Virginia, March 23, 1949; entered upon duties March 28, 1949. George C. Marshall, of Pennsylvania, September 20, 1950; entered upon duties September 21, 1950. Robert A. Lovett, of New York, September 14, 1951; entered upon duties September 17, 1951. ATTORNEY GENERAL —Tom C. Clark, of Texas, continued from preceding administration. J. Howard McGrath, of Rhode Island, August 19, 1949; entered upon duties August 24, 1949. James P. McGranery, of Pennsylvania, May 21, 1952; entered upon duties May 27, 1952. POSTMASTER GENERAL—Jesse M. Donaldson, of Missouri, continued from preceding administration. Jesse M. Donaldson, of Missouri, recommissioned February 8, 1949. SECRETARY OF THE INTERIOR—Julius A. Krug, of Wisconsin, continued from preceding administration. Oscar L. Chapman, of Colorado (Under Secretary), ad interim, December 1, 1949, to January 19, 1950. Oscar L. Chapman, of Colorado, January 19, 1950. SECRETARY OF AGRICULTURE—Charles F. Brannan, of Colorado, continued from preceding administration. SECRETARY OF COMMERCE—Charles Sawyer, of Ohio, continued from preceding administration. SECRETARY OF LABOR—Maurice J. Tobin, of Massachusetts, ad interim, continued from preceding administration. Maurice J. Tobin, of Massachusetts, recommissioned February 1, 1949.

81st Congress

1st Session: Jan. 3, 1949–Oct. 19, 1949; 2d Session: Jan. 3, 1950–Jan. 2, 1951.

President pro tempore of the Senate: Kenneth D. McKellar, of Tennessee (elected Jan. 3, 1949). Speaker of the House: Sam Rayburn, of Texas (elected Jan. 3, 1949).

Senate: 54 Democratic; 42 Republican

House: 263 Democratic; 171 Republican; 1 other

82d Congress

1st Session: Jan. 3, 1951–Oct. 20, 1951; 2d Session: Jan. 8, 1952—July 7, 1952.

President pro tempore of the Senate: Kenneth D. McKellar, of Tennessee (continued from preceding Congress). Speaker of the House: Sam Rayburn, of Texas (reelected Jan. 3, 1951).

Senate: 49 Democratic; 47 Republican

House: 234 Democratic; 199 Republican; 1 other

First Administration of DWIGHT D. EISENHOWER

JANUARY 20, 1953, TO JANUARY 20, 1957

PRESIDENT—Dwight D. Eisenhower, of New York (Republican). VICE-PRESIDENT—Richard M. Nixon, of California. SECRETARY OF STATE—John Foster Dulles, of New York, January 21, 1953. SECRETARY OF THE TREASURY—George M. Humphrey, of Ohio, January 21, 1953. SECRETARY OF DEFENSE—Charles E. Wilson, of Michigan, January 26, 1953; entered upon duties January 28, 1953. ATTORNEY GENERAL—Herbert Brownell, Jr., of New York, January 21, 1953. POSTMASTER GENERAL—Arthur E. Summerfield, of Michigan, January 21, 1953. SECRETARY OF THE INTERIOR—Douglas McKay, of Oregon, January 21, 1953. Frederick A. Seaton, of Nebraska, June 6, 1956; entered upon duties June 8, 1956. SECRETARY OF AGRICULTURE— Ezra Taft Benson, of Utah, January 21, 1953. SECRETARY OF COMMERCE—Sinclair Weeks, of Massachusetts, January 21, 1953. SECRETARY OF LABOR—Martin P. Durkin, of Maryland, January 21, 1953. James P. Mitchell, of New Jersey, ad interim, October 9, 1953, to January 19, 1954. James P. Mitchell, of New Jersey, January 19, 1954. SECRETARY OF HEALTH, EDUCATION, AND WELFARE—Oveta Culp Hobby, of Texas, April 10, 1953; entered upon duties April 11, 1953. Marion B. Folsom, of New York, July 20, 1955; entered upon duties August 1, 1955.

83d Congress

1st Session: Jan. 3, 1953—Aug. 3, 1953; 2d Session: Jan. 6, 1954–Dec. 2, 1954.

President pro tempore of the Senate: Styles Bridges, of New Hampshire (elected Jan. 3, 1953). Speaker of the House: Joseph W. Martin, Jr., of Massachusetts (elected Jan. 3, 1953).

Senate: 48 Republican; 47 Democratic; 1 other

House: 221 Republican; 211 Democratic; 1 other

84th Congress

1st Session: Jan. 5, 1955–Aug. 2, 1955; 2d Session: Jan. 3, 1956–July 27, 1956.

President pro tempore of the Senate: Walter F. George, of Georgia (elected Jan. 5, 1955). Speaker of the House: Sam Rayburn, of Texas (elected Jan. 5, 1955).

Senate: 48 Democratic; 47 Republican; 1 other

House: 232 Democratic; 203 Republican

Second Administration of DWIGHT D. EISENHOWER

JANUARY 20, 1957, TO JANUARY 20, 1961

PRESIDENT—Dwight D. Eisenhower, of Pennsylvania (Republican). VICE-PRESIDENT—Richard M. Nixon, of California. SECRETARY OF STATE—John Foster Dulles, of New York, continued from preceding administration. Christian A. Herter, of Massachusetts, April 21, 1959; entered upon duties April 22, 1959. SECRETARY OF THE TREASURY—George M. Humphrey, of Ohio, continued from preceding administration. Robert Bernerd Anderson, of Connecticut, July 2, 1957; entered upon duties July 29, 1957. SECRETARY OF DEFENSE—Charles E. Wilson, of Michigan, continued from preceding administration. Neil H. McElroy, of Ohio, August 19, 1957; entered upon duties October 9, 1957. Thomas S. Gates, Jr., of Pennsylvania, ad interim, December 1, 1959, to January 26, 1960. Thomas S. Gates, Jr., of Pennsylvania, January 26, 1960. ATTORNEY GENERAL— Herbert Brownell, Jr., of New York, continued from preceding administration. William P. Rogers, of Maryland, ad interim, November 8, 1957, to January 27, 1958. William P. Rogers, of Maryland, January 27, 1958. POSTMASTER GENERAL—Arthur E. Summerfield, of Michigan, continued from preceding administration. Arthur E. Summerfield, of Michigan, recommissioned February 4, 1957. SECRETARY OF THE INTERIOR—Frederick A. Seaton, of Nebraska, continued from preceding administration. SECRETARY OF AGRICULTURE—Ezra Taft Benson, of Utah, continued from preceding administration. SECRETARY OF COMMERCE—Sinclair Weeks, of Massachusetts, continued from preceding administration. Lewis L. Strauss, of New York, ad interim, November 13, 1958, to June 27, 1959. Frederick H. Mueller, of Michigan (Under Secretary), ad interim, July 21, 1959, to August 6, 1959. Frederick H. Mueller, of Michigan, August 6, 1959. SECRETARY OF LABOR—James P. Mitchell, of New Jersey, continued from preceding administration. SECRETARY OF HEALTH, EDUCATION, AND WELFARE—Marion B. Folsom, of New York, continued from preceding administration. Arthur S. Flemming, of Ohio, July 9, 1958; entered upon duties August 1, 1958.

85th Congress

1st Session: Jan. 3, 1957–Aug. 30, 1957; 2d Session: Jan. 7, 1958–Aug. 24, 1958.

President pro tempore of the Senate: Carl Hayden, of Arizona (elected Jan. 3, 1957). Speaker of the House: Sam Rayburn, of Texas (reelected Jan. 3, 1957).

Senate: 49 Democratic; 47 Republican

House: 233 Democratic; 200 Republican

86th Congress

1st Session: Jan. 7, 1959–Sept. 15, 1959; 2d Session: Jan. 6, 1960–Sept. 1, 1960.

President pro tempore of the Senate: Carl Hayden, of Arizona (continued from preceding Congress). Speaker of the House: Sam Rayburn, of Texas (reelected Jan. 7, 1959).

Senate: 64 Democratic; 34 Republican

House: 283 Democratic; 153 Republican

Administration of JOHN F. KENNEDY

JANUARY 20, 1961, TO NOVEMBER 22, 1963

PRESIDENT—John F. Kennedy, of Massachusetts (Democratic) (died November 22, 1963). VICE-PRESIDENT—Lyndon B. Johnson, of Texas. SECRETARY OF STATE—Dean Rusk, of New York, January 20, 1961. SECRETARY OF THE TREASURY—C. Douglas Dillon, of Washington, D.C., January 20, 1961. SECRETARY OF DEFENSE—Robert S. McNamara, of Michigan, January 20, 1961. ATTORNEY GENERAL—Robert F. Kennedy, of Massachusetts, January 20, 1961. POSTMASTER GENERAL—J. Edward Day, of California, January 20, 1961, to August 9, 1963. John A. Gronouski of Wisconsin, September 10, 1963. SECRETARY OF THE INTERIOR—Stewart L. Udall, of Arizona, January 20, 1961. SECRETARY OF AGRICULTURE—Orville L. Freeman, of Minnesota, January 20, 1961. SECRETARY OF COMMERCE—Luther H. Hodges, of North Carolina, January 20, 1961. SECRETARY OF LABOR—Arthur J. Goldberg, of Washington, D.C., January 20, 1961. W. Willard Wirtz, of Illinois, September 25, 1962. SECRETARY OF HEALTH, EDUCATION, AND WELFARE—Abraham A. Ribicoff, of Connecticut, January 21, 1961, to July 13, 1962. Anthony J. Celebrezze, of Ohio, July 31, 1962.

First Administration of LYNDON B. JOHNSON
NOVEMBER 22, 1963, TO JANUARY 20, 1965

PRESIDENT—Lyndon B. Johnson, of Texas (Democratic). SECRETARY OF STATE—Dean Rusk, of New York, continued from preceding administration. SECRETARY OF THE TREASURY—C. Douglas Dillon, of Washington, D.C., continued from preceding administration. SECRETARY OF DEFENSE—Robert S. McNamara, of Michigan, continued from preceding administration. ATTORNEY GENERAL—Robert F. Kennedy, of Massachusetts, continued from preceding administration. Nicholas Katzenbach, of Illinois, ad interim, Sept. 4, 1964. POSTMASTER GENERAL—John S. Gronouski, of Wisconsin, continued from preceding administration. SECRETARY OF THE INTERIOR—Stewart L. Udall, of Arizona, continued from preceding administration. SECRETARY OF AGRICULTURE—Orville L. Freeman of Minnesota, continued from preceding administration. SECRETARY OF COMMERCE—Luther H. Hodges, of North Carolina, continued from preceding administration to January 15, 1965. John T. O'Connor, of New Jersey, January 15, 1965. SECRETARY OF LABOR—W. Willard Wirtz, of Illinois, continued from preceding administration. SECRETARY OF HEALTH, EDUCATION, AND WELFARE—Anthony J. Celebrezze, of Ohio, continued from preceding administration.

87th Congress
1st Session: Jan. 3, 1961–Sept. 27, 1961; 2d Session: Jan. 10, 1962–Oct. 13, 1962.
President pro tempore of the Senate: Carl Hayden, of Arizona (continued from preceding Congress). Speaker of the House: Sam Rayburn, of Texas (reelected Jan. 3, 1961); John W. McCormack, of Massachusetts (elected Jan. 10, 1962).
Senate: 65 Democratic; 35 Republican
House: 263 Democratic; 174 Republican

88th Congress
1st Session: Jan. 9, 1963–Dec. 30, 1963; 2d Session: Jan. 7, 1964–Oct. 3, 1964.
President pro tempore of the Senate: Carl Hayden, of Arizona (continued from preceding Congress). Speaker of the House: John W. McCormack (reelected Jan. 9, 1963).
Senate: 67 Democratic; 33 Republican
House: 258 Democratic; 177 Republican

Second Administration of LYNDON B. JOHNSON
JANUARY 20, 1965 TO JANUARY 20, 1969

PRESIDENT—Lyndon B. Johnson, of Texas (Democratic). VICE-PRESIDENT—Hubert H. Humphrey, of Minnesota. SECRETARY OF STATE—Dean Rusk, of New York, continued from preceding administration. SECRETARY OF THE TREASURY—C. Douglas Dillon, of Washington, D.C., continued from preceding administration to March 31, 1965. Henry H. Fowler, of Virginia, April 1, 1965 to December 20, 1968. Joseph W. Barr, of Indiana, December 23, 1968. SECRETARY OF DEFENSE—Robert S. McNamara, continued from preceding administration. Clark Clifford, of Maryland, January 19, 1968. ATTORNEY GENERAL—Nicholas Katzenbach, of Illinois, ad interim, continued from preceding administration, confirmed on Feb. 10, 1965. Ramsey Clark, of Texas, March 2, 1967. POSTMASTER GENERAL—John A. Gronouski, of Wisconsin, continued from preceding administration. Lawrence O'Brien, of Massachusetts, August 29, 1965, to April 10, 1968. Marvin Watson, of Texas, April 10, 1968. SECRETARY OF THE INTERIOR—Stewart L. Udall, of Arizona, continued from preceding administration. SECRETARY OF AGRICULTURE—Orville L. Freeman, of Minnesota, continued from preceding administration. SECRETARY OF COMMERCE—John T. O'Connor, of New Jersey, continued from preceding administration to January 18, 1967. Alexander B. Trowbridge, of New York, May 23, 1967, to February 16, 1968. C. R. Smith, of New York, March 1, 1968. SECRETARY OF LABOR—W. Willard Wirtz, of Illinois, continued from preceding administration. SECRETARY OF HEALTH, EDUCATION, AND WELFARE—Anthony J. Celebrezze, of Ohio, continued from preceding administration. John W. Gardner, of New York, July 27, 1965. Wilbur J. Cohen, of Michigan, May 16, 1968. SECRETARY OF HOUSING AND URBAN DEVELOPMENT—Robert C. Weaver, of Washington, D.C., January 18, 1966 to January 1, 1969. Robert C. Wood, of Massachusetts, January 2, 1969. SECRETARY OF TRANSPORTATION—Alan S. Boyd, of Florida, January 16, 1967.

89th Congress
1st Session: Jan. 4, 1965–Oct. 23, 1965; 2d Session: Jan. 10, 1966–Oct. 22, 1966.
President pro tempore of the Senate: Carl Hayden, of Arizona (continued from preceding Congress). Speaker of the House: John W. McCormack, of Massachusetts (reelected Jan. 4, 1965).
Senate: 68 Democratic; 32 Republican
House: 295 Democratic; 140 Republican

90th Congress
1st Session: Jan. 10, 1967–Dec. 15, 1967; 2d Session: Jan. 15, 1968–Oct. 14, 1968.
President pro tempore of the Senate: Carl Hayden, of Arizona (continued from preceding Congress). Speaker of the House: John W. McCormack, of Massachusetts (reelected Jan. 10, 1967).

Senate: 64 Democratic; 36 Republican
House: 248 Democratic; 187 Republican

First Administration of RICHARD M. NIXON
JANUARY 20, 1969, TO JANUARY 20, 1973

PRESIDENT—Richard M. Nixon, of California (Republican). VICE-PRESIDENT—Spiro T. Agnew, of Maryland. SECRETARY OF STATE—William P. Rogers, of New York, January 22, 1969. SECRETARY OF THE TREASURY—David M. Kennedy, of Illinois, January 22, 1969 to February 10, 1971. John B. Connally, of Texas, February 11, 1971. George P. Shultz of Illinois, June 12, 1972. SECRETARY OF DEFENSE—Melvin R. Laird, of Wisconsin, January 22, 1969. ATTORNEY GENERAL—John N. Mitchell, of New York, January 22, 1969. Richard G. Kleindienst, of Arizona, ad interim, Feb. 15, 1972; took office June 12, 1972. POSTMASTER GENERAL—Winton M. Blount, of Alabama, January 22, 1969 to July 1, 1971. This office was then abolished as a cabinet post. SECRETARY OF THE INTERIOR—Walter J. Hickel, of Alaska, January 23, 1969. Fred J. Russell, of California, ad interim, Nov. 26, 1970. Rogers C. B. Morton, of Maryland, Jan. 29, 1971. SECRETARY OF AGRICULTURE—Clifford M. Hardin, of Nebraska, Jan. 22, 1969. Earl L. Butz, of Indiana, Dec. 2, 1971. SECRETARY OF COMMERCE—Maurice H. Stans, of New York, Jan. 22, 1969. Peter G. Peterson, of Illinois, Feb. 21, 1972. SECRETARY OF LABOR—George P. Shultz, of New York, Jan. 22, 1969. James D. Hodgson, of California, July 2, 1970. SECRETARY OF HEALTH, EDUCATION, AND WELFARE—Robert H. Finch, of California, Jan. 22, 1969. Elliot L. Richardson, of Massachusetts, June 15, 1970. SECRETARY OF HOUSING AND URBAN DEVELOPMENT—George W. Romney, of Michigan, Jan. 22, 1969. SECRETARY OF TRANSPORTATION—John A. Volpe, of Massachusetts, Jan. 22, 1969.

91st Congress
1st Session: Jan. 3, 1969–Dec. 23, 1969; 2d Session: Jan. 19, 1970–Jan. 2, 1971.
President pro tempore of the Senate: Richard B. Russell, of Georgia (elected Jan. 3, 1969). Speaker of the House: John W. McCormack, of Massachusetts (reelected Jan. 3, 1969).
Senate: 57 Democratic; 43 Republican
House: 244 Democratic; 191 Republican

92d Congress
1st Session: Jan. 21, 1971–Dec. 17, 1971; 2d Session: Jan. 18, 1972–Oct. 18, 1972
President pro tempore of the Senate: James O. Eastland of Mississippi (elected July 28, 1972). (Richard B. Russell, continued from preceding Congress, died in office. Allen J. Ellender of Louisiana, who was elected Jan. 22, 1971, died in office.) Speaker of the House: Carl Albert, of Oklahoma (elected Jan. 21, 1971).
Senate: 54 Democratic; 44 Republican; 1 Independent-Democratic; 1 Conservative-Republican.
House: 255 Democratic; 180 Republican

Second Administration of RICHARD M. NIXON
JANUARY 20, 1973, TO AUGUST 9, 1974

PRESIDENT—Richard M. Nixon, of California (Republican). Resigned August 9, 1974. VICE PRESIDENT—Spiro T. Agnew, of Maryland. Resigned October 10, 1973. Gerald R. Ford, Jr., of Michigan, December 6, 1973. SECRETARY OF STATE—William P. Rogers, of Maryland, continued from preceding administration. Kenneth Rush, of New York (Deputy Secretary of State), ad interim, September 4, 1973. Henry A. Kissinger, of the District of Columbia, September 21, 1973. SECRETARY OF THE TREASURY—George P. Shultz, of Illinois, continued from preceding administration. William E. Simon, of New Jersey, April 30, 1974. SECRETARY OF DEFENSE—Melvin R. Laird, of Wisconsin, continued from preceding administration. Elliot L. Richardson, of Massachusetts, January 29, 1973. William P. Clements, Jr., of Texas, ad interim, May 26, 1973. James R. Schlesinger, of Virginia, June 28, 1973. ATTORNEY GENERAL—Richard G. Kleindienst, of Arizona, continued from preceding administration. Elliot L. Richardson, of Massachusetts, May 23, 1973. Robert H. Bork, of Pennsylvania (Solicitor General), ad interim, October 20, 1973. William B. Saxbe, of Ohio, Feb. 4, 1974. SECRETARY OF THE INTERIOR—Rogers C. B. Morton, of Maryland, continued from preceding administration. SECRETARY OF AGRICULTURE—Earl L. Butz, of Indiana, continued from preceding administration. SECRETARY OF COMMERCE—Frederick B. Dent, of South Carolina, ad interim, Jan. 18, 1973; took office Feb. 2, 1973. SECRETARY OF LABOR—James D. Hodgson, of California, continued from preceding administration. Peter J. Brennan, of New York, January 31, 1973. SECRETARY OF HEALTH, EDUCATION, AND WELFARE—Elliot L. Richardson, of Massachusetts, continued from preceding administration. Caspar W. Weinberger, of California, February 8, 1973. SECRETARY OF HOUSING AND URBAN DEVELOPMENT—George Romney, of Michigan, continued from preceding administration. James T. Lynn, of Ohio, January 31, 1973. SECRETARY OF TRANSPORTATION—John A. Volpe, of Massachusetts, continued from preceding administration.

Claude S. Brinegar, of California, January 18, 1973.

93rd Congress

1st Session: Jan. 3, 1973-Dec. 22, 1973; 2nd Session: Jan. 21, 1974-Dec. 20, 1974.

President pro tempore of the Senate: James O. Eastland of Mississippi (continued from preceding Congress). Speaker of the House: Carl Albert, of Oklahoma (continued from preceding Congress).

Senate: 56 Democratic; 42 Republican; 1 Conservative-Republican; 1 Independent

House: 244 Democratic; 191 Republican; 1 Independent

Administration of GERALD R. FORD, JR.

AUGUST 9, 1974 TO JANUARY 20, 1977

PRESIDENT—Gerald R. Ford, Jr., of Michigan. VICE PRESIDENT—Nelson A. Rockefeller, of New York, December 19, 1974. SECRETARY OF STATE—Henry A. Kissinger, of the District of Columbia, continued from preceding administration. SECRETARY OF THE TREASURY—William E. Simon, of New Jersey, continued from preceding administration. SECRETARY OF DEFENSE—James R. Schlesinger, of Virginia, continued from preceding administration. Donald H. Rumsfeld, of Illinois, November 18, 1975. ATTORNEY GENERAL—William B. Saxbe, of Ohio, continued from preceding administration. Edward H. Levi, of Illinois, February 5, 1975. SECRETARY OF THE INTERIOR—Rogers C.B. Morton, of Maryland, continued from preceding administration. D. Kent Frizzell, of Kansas (Solicitor), ad interim, May 1, 1975. Stanley K. Hathaway of Wyoming, June 11, 1975. D. Kent Frizzell, of Kansas (Solicitor), ad interim, July 25, 1975. Thomas S. Kleppe, of North Dakota, October 9, 1975. SECRETARY OF AGRICULTURE—Earl L. Butz, of Indiana, continued from preceding administration. John A. Knebel, of Oklahoma, ad interim, October 4, 1976. John A. Knebel, November 5, 1976. SECRETARY OF COMMERCE—Frederick B. Dent, of South Carolina, continued from preceding administration. John K. Tabor, of Pennsylvania (Under Secretary), ad interim, March 12, 1975. Rogers C.B. Morton, of Maryland, April 25, 1975. Elliot L. Richardson, of Massachusetts, December 11, 1975. SECRETARY OF LABOR—Peter J. Brennan, of New York, continued from preceding administration. John T. Dunlop, of Massachusetts, March 6, 1975. Willie J. Usery, Jr., of Georgia, February 4, 1976. SECRETARY OF HEALTH, EDUCATION, AND WELFARE—Caspar W. Weinberger, of California, continued from preceding administration. Forrest David Mathews, of Alabama, June 26, 1975. SECRETARY OF HOUSING AND URBAN DEVELOPMENT—James T. Lynn, of Ohio, continued from preceding administration. Carla A. Hills, of California, March 5, 1975. SECRETARY OF TRANSPORTATION—Claude S. Brinegar, of California, continued from preceding administration. William T. Coleman, Jr., of Pennsylvania, March 3, 1975.

94th Congress

1st Session: Jan. 14, 1975-Dec. 19, 1975; 2nd Session: Jan. 19, 1976-Oct. 1, 1976.
President pro tempore of the Senate: James O. Eastland, of Mississippi (continued from preceding Congress). Speaker of the House: Carl Albert, of Oklahoma (continued from preceding Congress).
Senate: 61 Democratic; 37 Republican; 1 Conservative-Republican; 1 Independent
House: 291 Democratic; 144 Republican

Administration of JIMMY CARTER

JANUARY 20, 1977 TO JANUARY 20, 1981

PRESIDENT—Jimmy (James E.) Carter, of Georgia, VICE PRESIDENT—Walter F. Mondale, of Minnesota. SECRETARY OF STATE—Cyrus R. Vance, of New York, January 23, 1977. Edmund S. Muskie, of Maine, May 8, 1980. SECRETARY OF THE TREASURY—W. Michael Blumenthal, of Michigan, January 23, 1977. G. William Miller, of Oklahoma, August 6, 1979. SECRETARY OF DEFENSE—Harold Brown, of California, January 21, 1977. ATTORNEY GENERAL—Griffin B. Bell, of Georgia, January 26, 1977. Benjamin R. Civiletti, of Maryland, August 16, 1979.

SECRETARY OF THE INTERIOR—Cecil R. Andrus, of Idaho, January 23, 1977. SECRETARY OF AGRICULTURE—Robert S. Bergland, of Minnesota, January 23, 1977. SECRETARY OF COMMERCE—Juanita M. Kreps, of North Carolina, January 23, 1977. Philip M. Klutznick, of Illinois, January 2, 1980. SECRETARY OF LABOR—F. Ray Marshall, of Texas, January 27, 1977. SECRETARY OF HEALTH AND HUMAN SERVICES—Joseph A. Califano, Jr., of the District of Columbia, January 25, 1977. Patricia R. Harris, of the District of Columbia, August 3, 1979. (On Sept. 27, 1979 Congress gave final approval to a bill establishing a cabinet-level Department of Education; the Department of Health, Education and Welfare is to be renamed the Department of Health and Human Resources) SECRETARY OF HOUSING AND URBAN DEVELOPMENT—Patricia R. Harris, of the District of Columbia, January 23, 1977. Moon Landrieu, of Louisiana, September 24, 1979. SECRETARY OF TRANSPORTATION—Brockman Adams, of Washington, January 23, 1977. Neil E. Goldschmidt, of Oregon, August 15, 1979. SECRETARY OF ENERGY—James R. Schlesinger, of Virginia, August 5, 1977. Charles W. Duncan, of Texas, August 24, 1979. SECRETARY OF EDUCATION—Shirley M. Hufstedler, of California, December 6, 1979.

95th Congress

1st Session: Jan. 4, 1977-Dec. 15, 1977; 2nd Session: Jan. 19, 1978-Oct. 15, 1978
President pro tempore of the Senate: James O. Eastland, of Mississippi (continued from preceding Congress). Deputy President pro tempore of the Senate: Hubert H. Humphrey,[1] of Minnesota. Speaker of the House: Thomas P. O'Neill, Jr., of Massachusetts.
Senate: 61 Democratic; 38 Republican; 1 Independent
House: 290 Democratic; 145 Republican

96th Congress

1st Session: Jan. 3, 1979-Jan. 3, 1980[2];
2nd Session: Jan. 3, 1980-Dec. 16, 1980
President pro tempore of the Senate: Warren G. Magnuson, of Washington. Speaker of the House: Thomas P. O'Neill, Jr., of Massachusetts. (continued from preceding Congress) Senate: 58 Democratic; 41 Republican; 1 Independent. House: 276 Democratic; 159 Republican.

[1]Office of Deputy President pro tempore was established January 5, 1977, pursuant to Senate Resolution 17, Ninety-fifth Congress. This office no longer exists since the death of Hubert H. Humphrey, Jan. 13, 1978. [2]The Senate adjourned sine die Dec. 20, 1979.

Administration of RONALD W. REAGAN

FROM JANUARY 20, 1981

PRESIDENT—Ronald W. Reagan, of California, VICE PRESIDENT—George H. W. Bush, of Texas, SECRETARY OF STATE—Alexander M. Haig, Jr., of Pennsylvania, January 21, 1981, SECRETARY OF THE TREASURY—Donald T. Regan, of New York, January 22, 1981, SECRETARY OF DEFENSE—Caspar W. Weinberger, of California, January 21, 1981, ATTORNEY GENERAL—William F. Smith, of California, January 23, 1981, SECRETARY OF THE INTERIOR—James G. Watt, of Colorado, January 23, 1981, SECRETARY OF AGRICULTURE—John R. Block, of Illinois, January 22, 1981, SECRETARY OF COMMERCE—Malcolm Baldrige, of Connecticut, January 23, 1981, SECRETARY OF LABOR—Raymond J. Donovan, of New Jersey, February 4, 1981, SECRETARY OF HEALTH AND HUMAN SERVICES—Richard S. Schweiker, of Pennsylvania, January 22, 1981, SECRETARY OF HOUSING AND URBAN DEVELOPMENT—Samuel R. Pierce, Jr., of New York, January 23, 1981, SECRETARY OF TRANSPORTATION—Andrew L. Lewis, Jr., of Pennsylvania, January 23, 1981, SECRETARY OF ENERGY—James B. Edwards, of South Carolina, January 23, 1981, SECRETARY OF EDUCATION—Terrell H. Bell, of Utah, January 23, 1981.

97th Congress

1st Session: Jan. 5, 1981
President pro tempore of the Senate: Strom Thurmond of South Carolina Speaker of the House: Thomas P. O'Neill, Jr., of Massachusetts (continued from preceding Congress) Senate: 53 Republican; 46 Democratic; 1 Independent-Democrat. House: 243 Democratic; 191 Republican; 1 Vacant.

THE PRESIDENTIAL BIOGRAPHIES

George Washington

George Washington, 1st President (1789–1797), son of Augustine and Mary (Ball) Washington, was born on February 22, 1732, in Westmoreland County, Virginia. Of a family that migrated from England in 1658, George's father was a moderately well-to-do planter. He died when George was 11, and young Washington was brought up by his half-brother, Lawrence, whom he idolized and who took over the estate and functioned as a surrogate father.

George received a simple education at the parish church and at 16 entered the employ of Lord Thomas Fairfax as a land surveyor. Adept at mathematics and athletics, Washington in surveying Fairfax's vast holdings in mountainous western Virginia, learned to live in the wilderness, govern his helpers, and maintain accurate survey records on which land titles were based. In 1752, Lawrence Washington died. George inherited a share of Lawrence's lands, and he was commissioned (1753) a major and put in charge of training militia in southern Virginia. He immediately began to study histories of wars and books on military tactics.

Soon after, Washington emerged into public view when he volunteered for a hazardous and vital mission. Governor Robert Dinwiddie of Virginia was eager to warn the French that they must withdraw their troops from the Ohio River Valley, which the British hoped to settle. Bearing Dinwiddie's message, Washington, prudent and an excellent horseman, led a small party through the snow-covered wilderness to the successful completion of the mission.

At 22, Washington was promoted to lieutenant colonel as the French and Indian Wars commenced and was assigned as aide to British General Edward Braddock, a respected professional soldier, who led a disastrous expedition against the French at Fort Duquesne. Washington's personal skill in the battle was widely praised, and he was appointed (1755) colonel and entrusted with the defense of Virginia's 350-mile western frontier. At his urging, a new attack was made upon Fort Duquesne, and he again distinguished himself by capturing the French stronghold. With the French retreating into Canada, the fighting ceased, and Washington, now the most famous American-born soldier, retired to private life.

At Mount Vernon, which initially he leased from Lawrence's widow, he became at the age of 26, a country gentleman and successful businessman. He also commenced his political career by serving from 1759 to 1774 as a member of Virginia's House of Burgesses. This legislative background stood him well. A leader in opposition to British policy, Washington was a delegate to the First Continental Congress (1774-75) and, with the outbreak of the Revolutionary War, he was named commander-in-chief of the Continental forces.

Beset with obstacles seldom faced by military commanders, Washington described his troops as "raw militia, badly officered, and with no government." Since his troops preferred short-term enlistments and summer fighting to winter, he seldom commanded 10,000 men at one time. Weak in power, Congress supported Washington poorly, sometimes leaving him without adequate funds to pay his troops. Many subordinate officers were preoccupied with jealousies and intrigues. Yet by ingenious retreats and thrusts, Washington kept his army afield, survived defeat at Germantown, a cruel winter at Valley Forge, and built up an able force that entrapped Cornwallis's army at Yorktown and forced its surrender. Washington emerged from the Revolution as the unrivaled hero and symbol of the new nation.

In 1783, he again retired to Mount Vernon, where life was pleasantly calm. However, by 1786, he like other leaders was distressed by the weaknesses of American government under the Articles of Confederation. When the Constitutional Convention gathered at Philadelphia in 1787, Washington received a hero's welcome as head of the Virginia delegation, and he was promptly elected president of the convention. In fashioning a strong Presidency, the convention, Pierce Butler wrote, "cast their eyes toward General Washington . . ."

After the Constitution was ratified, the first Electoral College met on February 4, 1789, and unanimously elected Washington President. On April 30, he was inaugurated at Federal Hall, in New York City, the capital. "I walk on untrodden ground," Washington said soon after beginning his new responsibilities. "There is scarcely any part of my conduct that may not hereafter be drawn into precedent."

Facing times that overflowed with crises, Washington left the republic far stronger and more confident than when he took office. An output of measures, highly impressive by today's standards, flowed from his administration. The Revolutionary debts of the states were assumed by the national government, a national currency was issued, and a Bank of the United States established to provide credit. Manufacture and trade were promoted by tariffs and bounties; inventions were protected by patent and copyright laws. A postal system was established; national security was improved by the reorganization of the army and the navy, the founding of West Point, and the construction of fortifications on the eastern seaboard and in the West. In the development of many of these measures, Washington was aided by his brilliant Secretary of the Treasury, Alexander Hamilton.

Hamilton's advocacy of a Bank of the United States touched off a dispute with Secretary of State Thomas Jefferson and Attorney General Edmund Randolph, who considered the bank unconstitutional because express authorization was not provided in the fundamental law. Washington sided with Hamilton, who argued that the national government could use all powers, except those denied by the Constitution. Time and again, where the Constitution was unclear, Washington exercised executive authority.

The President truly dominated the executive branch. With few exceptions, he prescribed the duties of his department heads and kept abreast of daily detail. So confident was he of his mastery that he brought together two of the most gifted and assertive department heads the nation has ever known—Jefferson and Hamilton. Washington succeeded outstandingly, where many of his successors have failed, in relations with Congress. He converted his popularity into major laws without tarnishing his prestige in political struggles. He prized the intrinsic dignity of the Presidency and gave the office a regal quality.

In 1793, Washington was reelected again by a unanimous electoral vote; his second term was to be more difficult than the first. War now raged between England and France, growing out of the French Revolution. Hamilton and Jefferson, in conflict over domestic questions, were also bitterly divided over the war. Each led a party reflecting his views: Hamilton—the Federalists, Jefferson—the Anti-Federalists (Democratic-Republicans). Hamilton's party sympathized with Britain and Jefferson's with France. As usual, Washington tried to be a moderating influence between his two strong secretaries. In weighing policy toward the war, he found convenience in meeting with all his secretaries simultaneously: and the institution known as the Cabinet was born.

On April 22, 1793, Washington issued a neutrality proclamation calling for "conduct friendly and impartial" to the warring nations. American vessels were barred from carrying war supplies to the belligerents. When the French minister to the United States, Citizen Genêt, attempted to outfit warships in American ports and to send them against the British, Washington requested that France recall its representative, because of his threat to American neutrality.

American relations with Britain also were badly deteriorating. British warships intercepted United States' vessels bearing food supplies to France, seizing their cargoes and impressing their seamen into the British navy. The British also refused to give up western frontier forts as they were obligated to under the treaty ending the Revolutionary War; instead, they stirred up the Indians in the surrounding area. To resolve these prickly questions, Washington dispatched Chief Justice John Jay to Britain. The resulting Jay Treaty dealt with trade and the frontier forts, but not with Britain's halting of American ships and seizure of seamen. Senate consideration of the treaty occasioned a bitter fight between the Federalists who supported it and the Anti-Federalists. Hostile newspapers called for Washington's impeachment. And some denounced him as an aristocrat and an enemy of true democracy. The Senate eventually approved the treaty.

In 1794, Washington demonstrated that he could enforce federal laws in the states when he put down the Whisky Rebellion by dispatching troops against farmers in western Pennsylvania who refused to pay federal taxes on whisky.

Declining to serve a third term, Washington issued his Farewell Address in 1796, announcing his retirement and warning against "permanent alliances" with foreign powers. Washington had gotten the U.S. Presidency off to a strong start, perhaps most fundamentally because of the bold, enterprising view he took of his office and his inspiring personal qualities. Washington retired to Mount Vernon, where he died on December 14, 1799.

John Adams

John Adams, 2d President (1797-1801), was born October 30, 1735, in Braintree (now Quincy), Massachusetts. The son of a Puritan farmer, Adams was graduated (1755) from Harvard College. After teaching briefly, he read law, was admitted (1758) to the bar.

An opponent of the Stamp Act, he was elected (1771) to the Massachusetts colonial legislature. There he steadily resisted British colonial policies and in 1774, just prior to the American Revolution, he was chosen a delegate to the First Continental Congress. At the Second Continental Congress (1775), he pressed for American independence and persuaded Congress to organize the Continental Army and to appoint George Washington as commander-in-chief. Adams helped draft and defend the Declaration of Independence amid turbulent Congressional debates.

In 1778 Adams was dispatched to Paris to build ties between France and the struggling new nation, but his impatience, ready candor, and pride served him ill in diplomacy, and he returned home. A year later, he was elected to the convention that prepared the important Massachusetts state constitution. He returned (1780) to diplomacy as minister to the Netherlands, where he won recognition for the United States and, more important, negotiated a loan. With John Jay and Benjamin Franklin, Adams negotiated (1782) the Treaty of Paris with Great Britain that ended the American Revolution. Three years later, Congress named him the first United States minister to Britain. He was rebuffed by the British, and in 1788 he asked to be recalled.

Soon after his return to America, he was elected Vice-President under George Washington. Despite his characterization of his new post as "the most insignificant office that ever the invention of man contrived or his imagination conceived," Adams was a constructive influence in filling his duties in the Senate.

When Washington declined (1796) to serve a third Presidential term, the Federalists, led by Alexander Hamilton, supported Adams for the Presidency, while the Democratic-Republicans turned to Thomas Jefferson. Adams won by three votes.

At the outset, Adams stressed that his Presidency would be an extension of Washington's. He retained his predecessor's entire cabinet and, in his inaugural address, promised to continue the Washington policies. Despite these reassurances, Federalists became distrustful when Adams, deeming it necessary to improve relations with France, offered the ministry to that country to Jefferson.

When Jefferson declined, Adams was on the point of conferring the post upon another Democratic-Republican leader, James Madison. However, a cabinet upheaval loomed over the step, and Adams reconsidered. Although President, Adams was not leader of his party. Alexander Hamilton, who held no government post was the Federalist leader, and the loyalties of some cabinet members ran to him rather than to Adams.

The central problems and policies of the Adams administration derived from the French Revolution and the ensuing war between France and Britain. Both countries claimed the right to seize American vessels, and the French Directory went so far as to declare that all Americans serving on British vessels were pirates. Adams sought to steer a middle course between Hamilton and his strong partiality toward Britain and Jefferson's similar disposition toward France.

The President called Congress into special session to consider ways of keeping peace. To his cabinet he distributed a series of questions on the Franco-British situation, seeking advice before framing his message to Congress. The questions were leaked to Hamilton, who prepared replies that were submitted through the cabinet to Adams, who accepted their substance, proposing that defenses be strengthened.

Simultaneously, the President dispatched ministers to France to arrange a treaty. The French representatives demanded a bribe and a loan, touching off the sensational episode that became known as the XYZ Affair. Adams again asked his cabinet for advice, and again Hamilton surreptitiously supplied it, proposing a more vigorous policy toward France and closer ties with Britain. Adams accepted the former, but not the latter. Congress responded with actions just short of war, by declaring all treaties with France null and void, creating a Navy Department, and increasing the army and authorizing new ships.

Eager to keep peace, Adams moved to restore diplomatic relations with France. (Adams first nominated W. Vans Murray to become minister to France. The President acted without consulting the cabinet, which enraged the Hamiltonians in it. Federalists in the Senate raised various objections as a prelude to rejecting it. In a bold move, Adams replaced the Murray nomination with the proposal of a three-member peace commission. The step brought press and public opinion so strongly to the President's side that the commission was approved.) Fearful of an Anglo-American alliance, the French this time were cooperative and war was averted. Adams achieved his supreme goal of maintaining peace, but at the high price of alienating his ardently pro-British Federalist party.

In 1798, smarting under criticism of their opposition to France, the Federalists passed the repressive Alien and Sedition laws that were designed to limit and punish criticism of the government and its officers. Adams neither supported the laws' passage nor applied them. Nevertheless, anti-Federalist journalists were arrested and sentiment turned against the administration.

His successful avoidance of war with France alienated Federalist leaders who deemed Adams a traitor to his party. Jefferson, leader of the Democratic-Republicans, observed that the followers of Hamilton were only "a little less hostile" to Adams than to himself. After long, calculated delay, Adams dealt with his cabinet secretaries who, in effect, were Hamilton's spies. One, James McHenry, resigned after a stormy confrontation with Adams, and another, Timothy Pickering, was dismissed.

Without a party behind him, Adams made a poor showing in seeking reelection in 1800. Both Jefferson and Aaron Burr exceeded him in electoral votes (73 each), while Adams received 65. The election was ultimately decided by the House of Representatives.

So aggrieved was Adams by his defeat that he refused to remain in Washington for Jefferson's inauguration and returned home to Quincy. Subsequently the two Presidents—Jefferson and Adams—renewed their friendship. Adams lived longer than any other President, dying on July 4, 1826, a few months before his 91st birthday.

Thomas Jefferson

Thomas Jefferson, 3d President (1801–1809), was born at Shadwell in Goochland County, Virginia, on April 13, 1743. His father was a planter, scholar, militia colonel, and a member of the House of Burgesses; his mother was a Virginia Randolph. Something of Jefferson's democratic impulse doubtless derived from the frontier influences of the Blue Ridge region in which he was reared. Educated by tutors and in local schools, Jefferson studied at William and Mary College, from which he was graduated (1762).

After leaving college, Jefferson studied law under George Wythe and was admitted (1767) to the bar. His practice was soon very successful, and in 1769, his political career began with his election to the House of Burgesses, in which he served until 1774. Not a brilliant speaker (later, as President, he abandoned the practice of delivering Congressional messages in person), Jefferson was brilliant at drafting laws and resolutions. As relations with the British deteriorated, Jefferson on the eve of the Revolution was a busy draftsman of protest documents. A triumph of revolutionary logic was his pamphlet "A Summary View of the Rights of British America," printed in 1774.

A year later, Jefferson was sent as a delegate to the Continental Congress. Always standing with those who were resolved to resist Great Britain, he was deputed to draft the Declaration of Independence, which with few changes Congress adopted on July 4, 1776.

Two months later, Jefferson resigned from Congress and returned to the Virginia House of Delegates, in which he served until 1779 when he was elected governor of Virginia, succeeding Patrick Henry. Disinclined toward the military life, he did not fight in the Revolutionary War. As a Virginia lawmaker, Jefferson was a powerful democratizing influence who moved his state away from virtual control by a few wealthy slaveholders. By amendment of the Virginia land laws, he effected a more equitable land distribution, which was the key to voting rights and educational opportunity. Even more important were his bills to assure religious freedom. Although he failed in his attempt to pass laws that would have gradually abolished slavery in Virginia, he remained opposed to that institution.

Jefferson resigned (1781) as governor, believing that the British army's threat to his state necessitated a military man to serve as chief executive. During a brief interval of private life, Jefferson began writing his Notes on Virginia, an extended statement of his beliefs.

He served (1784–89) in several diplomatic assignments and replaced Benjamin Franklin as minister to France. Jefferson sympathized openly with the French Revolution, believing it similar in essence to the American rebellion. His wide travel in Europe broadened his interests, particularly in architecture and agriculture.

Jefferson was abroad and did not participate in the Constitutional Convention of 1787, but his influence was felt in the quick preparation of the Bill of Rights; its omission from the original Constitution he had considered intolerable. He served as Secretary of State in Washington's first administration.

Jefferson was soon sharply at odds with the Secretary of the Treasury, Alexander Hamilton. After supporting several of Hamilton's early financial measures for the sake of unity, Jefferson, preferring an agricultural society, opposed Hamilton's plans to encourage manufacturing and trade and to found a national bank. In resisting Hamilton's broad interpretation of the Constitution to justify these measures, Jefferson advocated states' rights and "strict construction" of the Constitution, limiting the federal government's powers to those that the document specifically granted. Jefferson and Hamilton fought bitterly over foreign policy. Jefferson and the "Democratic-Republicans" who gathered as a party around him (and who were precursors of today's Democratic party) favored France, while Hamilton and the Federalists favored England. Late in 1793 their differences became so acute that Jefferson resigned.

He was elected (1796) Vice-President, with the Federalist John Adams as President. After four years of bitter party strife, Jefferson was elected (1800) President. His Vice-Presidential running mate, Aaron Burr, received the same number of electoral votes, and the election was referred to the House of Representatives. Thanks to the intervention of Hamilton, who advised Federalists to support Jefferson, the sage of Monticello won.

The first President to be inaugurated in Washington, Jefferson quickly set an example of simplicity. His inaugural address was an appeal for bipartisan cooperation—"We are all Republicans —we are all Federalists"—and his conception of government was largely negative, in the sense that he believed the federal government should deal chiefly with foreign affairs, leaving local matters to the states. Jefferson's view was that government should restrain men from harming one another, but otherwise leave them to their own concerns. Federal expenditures should be curtailed and excise taxes repealed.

Although Jefferson appointed followers such as James Madison as Secretary of State and Albert Gallatin as Secretary of the Treasury, he found the lesser offices, the infant bureaucracy, filled with Federalists. Noting that vacancies "by death are few; by resignations none," Jefferson foreshadowed the spoils system by replacing some Federalists in lesser offices with Democratic-Republicans. He refused to honor the Federalist appointment of "midnight judges" in the outgoing Adams' administration. Near the close of his Presidential tenure, Republicans held a majority of executive-branch appointments.

Through his party, Jefferson exerted strong control over Congress and accomplished the repeal of major Federalist statutes, including the Judiciary Act of 1801. His action was rebuked in *Marbury* v. *Madison,* the principle of which was that the Supreme Court may invalidate an act of Congress; Jefferson never accepted this principle. In pardoning those convicted of violating the Alien and Sedition laws, he asserted Presidential power over Congressional law. Heartily approving the use of the impeachment power against partisan Federalist judges, he was regretful of its failure when it was directed against Justice Samuel Chase, who had been impeached (1804) for discrimination against Jeffersonians.

The extraordinary diplomatic achievement of Jefferson's Presidency was the Louisiana Purchase (1803), which was negotiated by Robert Livingston and James Monroe. The temptation of acquiring a vast territory under favorable terms and of protecting the Mississippi's freedom of navigation overwhelmed Jefferson's devotion to strict Constitutional construction. Observing later that he "stretched the Constitution till it cracked," Jefferson submitted the purchase treaty to the Senate which readily approved it.

Jefferson was unsuccessful in seeking to acquire West Florida, chiefly because his lack of candor offended Congress. His reliance on diplomacy collapsed against the depredations of the Barbary pirates off North Africa. Ultimately, he dispatched a naval force and blockaded ports, and later he ordered frigates into action against the sultan of Morocco.

Aided by economic prosperity as well as political achievement, Jefferson was reelected in 1804 by an overwhelming majority. A major event in the second term was the trial of former Vice-President Aaron Burr, who was suspected by Jefferson of having politicked for the Presidency and now was accused of treasonable plottings. Burr's trial became a contest of wits between Jefferson and Chief Justice John Marshall. The latter's definition of treason made Burr's conviction impossible, to Jefferson's disgust.

Jefferson's diplomatic skill at peace-keeping was severely tested by the pressures of European war upon American neutrality. The Napoleonic decrees, British impressment of American seamen, and the audacity of a British frigate in firing on the United States' *Chesapeake,* combined to drive Jefferson to issue a proclamation denying British armed vessels the hospitality of United States waters.

In December 1807, Jefferson forced the Embargo Act through Congress; it prohibited exporting any produce from an American port or sailing any American ship to a foreign port. Enforcement of the act cast the administration in the role of exercising arbitrary power against key rights of the individual. Ironically, the exigencies of the Presidency brought Jefferson to violate the very values with which he was so long and so thoroughly identified—the sanctity of individual rights against governmental encroachment.

The embargo fell more heavily and injuriously upon the United States than upon France and England. Idle ships, unsold goods, and commercial unemployment fired opposition in New England, embittered the sections most loyal to Jefferson, and brought Congress to rebel against the President. Ultimately, Jefferson retreated by approving the Non-Intercourse Act of 1809 under which the embargo was partially raised.

Despite the rocky conclusion of his tenure, Jefferson handpicked his successor, Madison. He retired to Monticello, pursued scientific farming, counseled Presidents Madison and Monroe, and kept in touch with public affairs through a large correspondence. He died on July 4, 1826, on the same day as John Adams and on the 50th anniversary of the adoption of the Declaration of Independence.

James Madison

James Madison, 4th President (1809–1817), was born on March 16, 1751, in Port Conway, Virginia, the son of a planter and justice of the peace, whose forebears had settled in Virginia in the 1600s. A frail and sickly child, Madison was educated by private tutors and graduated (1771) from the College of New Jersey (now Princeton). A year of postgraduate study there was devoted to Hebrew, history, and law.

Torn between the ministry and politics, he chose the latter and was elected (1774) to the Committee of Safety in Orange County, Virginia, an important organ of local government in the twilight of the colonial period. In 1776, Madison was a delegate to the Williamsburg convention that declared for independence and established a state government. Serving in Virginia's first legislative assembly, Madison met Thomas Jefferson and began a lifelong friendship. In 1778, Madison was a member of the executive council, and in 1779 the state legislature elected him to the Continental Congress.

Until 1788, Madison served either in the Virginia legislature or in Congress, where he quickly became convinced that the Continental Congress needed more power, particularly in financial affairs. Although only 36 years old, Madison represented (1787) Virginia at the Constitutional Convention in Philadelphia and took a leading part in the deliberations. Champion of a strong central government, he drafted the "Virginia Plan" on which the Constitution was based. Known as the "Father of the Constitution," Madison kept a journal of the convention—the most complete record available of the proceedings—and his knowledge of past governments and the inherent problems of federalism was invaluable. Madison was a member of the Virginia ratifying convention and, with John Jay and Alexander Hamilton, wrote *The Federalist*, a series of newspaper essays that are regarded as the best explanation of the American constitutional system.

In 1789, Madison defeated James Monroe for election to the new U.S. House of Representatives. One of its most able members, Madison drafted key legislation and played a leading part in preparing the first 10 amendments to the Constitution, known as the Bill of Rights. Soon convinced that Hamilton's policies were hurtful to farmers in the South and West, Madison joined Jefferson in founding the Democratic-Republican party. In 1797, Madison retired, briefly, from politics; however, outraged by the repressive Alien and Sedition Acts (1798), he drafted the Virginia Resolutions, condemning the acts and holding that the states could declare them unconstitutional.

Upon becoming President in 1801, Jefferson appointed Madison Secretary of State. He passed a busy apprenticeship in an administration that, like his own would be, was preoccupied with foreign affairs and the problems of European war. In 1808, after two Presidential terms, Jefferson, following the tradition of George Washington, declined a third term. He chose Madison to be his successor. Madison received 122 electoral votes to 47 for Federalist C. C. Pinckney.

Small and unimpressive in person, Madison at his inaugural, wrote Washington Irving, looked like "a withered little apple-John."

In its early months, Madison's administration was largely an inherited Presidency. He made no changes in Jefferson's cabinet, except to move Robert Smith from the Navy to the State Department. The cabinet, however, had an additional heritage, an old feud between Smith and Treasury Secretary Albert Gallatin. Eventually, Madison dismissed Smith and made Monroe his Secretary of State.

The war between Britain and France was continuing as were their depredations upon American shipping, despite Jefferson's policy of neutrality. In 1810, an act of Congress called for the resumption of trade with both France and Britain, but warned of American withdrawal if either power resumed shipping violations. France soon began

such violations, and Britain stirred up the Indians in the West. In the House of Representatives, "hawks" such as Henry Clay and John Calhoun clamored for a war which, they believed would result in the annexation of Canada and Spanish Florida. New England was opposed to war; the rest of the nation demanded it; ultimately Madison called for war against Great Britain, and Congress declared it on June 18, 1812.

Later that year Madison was reelected President by 128 electoral votes to 89 for Mayor De Witt Clinton of New York City.

Both by his contemporaries and by historians, Madison is not rated as a good war President. Calhoun wrote of him, "Our President though a man of amiable manners and great talents has not we I fear those commanding talents, which are necessary to control those about him." Madison was handicapped by poor field commanders and by acute sectional and factional differences. Northern Republicans hobbled his efforts to seize the remainder of the Floridas, and Southern Republicans were unenthusiastic about conquering Canada. Each party faction feared that out of conquered territory might come new states favoring the other. Federalists generally opposed "Mr. Madison's War."

In its early stage the war went badly for the United States. For two years, every thrust into Canada was foiled. Britain clamped a tight blockade upon the eastern coast. On August 24, 1814, British forces occupied and burned Washington, and the Madisons fled the White House. But then American fortunes brightened. A British thrust down Lake Champlain was repulsed, and Andrew Jackson won a thrilling victory at New Orleans. In the Treaty of Ghent, however, signed December 24, 1814, not a single U.S. war aim was achieved. At Madison's direction, the demand upon Britain to renounce impressments was dropped. The only demand imposed was that Britain leave occupied American territory.

The war's close saw the decline of the Federalist party, a decline speeded by Madison's adopting its key principles. He approved a new bank of the United States, a tariff act of 1816 to protect "infant industries," and the establishment of substantial military and naval forces on a permanent basis. However, Madison did not accept the Federalist plank of internal domestic improvements to be undertaken by the national government. Such ventures, he thought, necessitated a constitutional amendment.

After leaving the Presidency, Madison lived in retirement on his estate at Montpelier, Virginia. He was a member of the Virginia Constitutional Convention of 1829 and occasionally offered counsel to his successor, James Monroe. Madison died at Montpelier on June 28, 1836, and is buried nearby.

James Monroe

James Monroe, 5th President (1817–1825), was born April 28, 1758, in Westmoreland County, Virginia, the eldest of five children of a circuit judge and planter. A student at William and Mary College when the Revolution broke out, Monroe joined the army, fought in major battles, and was wounded at Harlem Heights in New York and at the Battle of Trenton.

After the Revolution, Monroe studied law under Thomas Jefferson, then the governor of Virginia, and an important friendship between the
two began. Monroe's political career commenced
with his election (1780) to the Virginia legislature. Three years later he was elected to the
Continental Congress, in which he opposed a
highly centralized government but supported
tariff-making by Congress. In 1786, he returned
from Congress to serve in the Virginia Assembly.

Monroe was a state delegate to the Virginia
convention that was called to ratify the new U.S.
Constitution. So strong was his admiration for
Jefferson that he moved to Charlottesville, Vir-
ginia, where he built Ash Lawn, not far from
Jefferson's estate, Monticello.

Monroe ran unsuccessfully against James Madison for the first U.S. House of Representatives;
however, the Virginia legislature elected him
(1790) to the U.S. Senate. Allied with Jefferson
and Madison, Monroe opposed the centralizing
policies of Alexander Hamilton and, aided by
Albert Gallatin and Aaron Burr, shared in the
founding of the Democratic-Republican party. In
1794, Washington appointed Monroe minister to
France, a country he deeply admired. He criticized Jay's (Anglo-American) Treaty so severely,
however, that Washington, with whom he had
previously clashed, recalled him in 1796.

From 1799 to 1802, Monroe was governor of
Virginia. During Jefferson's Presidency, he was
dispatched (1802) to Paris to help Robert R.
Livingston arrange the Louisiana Purchase; the
next year in Spain he aided in the unsuccessful
negotiations for the purchase of the Floridas. In
1803 Jefferson named Monroe minister to Britain.
From 1811 to 1816, he was Madison's Secretary
of State.

In 1816, Monroe was elected President, winning easily over his Federalist opponent, Senator
Rufus King of New York. He was reelected in
1820, with only one electoral vote cast against
him.

Monroe's Presidency coincided with "the era
of good feeling." After the election of 1816, the
Federalist party disappeared and the Democratic-
Republicans flourished as the country's only party.
Thanks to fast developing industry and western
settlement, the country prospered. Not even the
depression of 1818 dampened the good feeling.

Few disturbing domestic political issues troubled Monroe's first Presidential years. He opposed
"the American System" of House Speaker Henry
Clay, who demanded internal domestic improvements and a protective tariff. A strict construc-
tionist, Monroe in his first annual message declared that Congress lacked the constitutional
power to establish a system of internal improvements. Subsequently, however, he modified his
position by granting an appropriation to repair
the Cumberland Road and approving the first
harbor act. He also approved the 1824 tariff act
and moved to a middle-of-the-road position on
tariffs and domestic improvements.

In 1819, Missouri applied for admission to the
Union as a slave state. A bitter legislative struggle followed on the questions of limiting slavery
in Missouri and in the remainder of the Louisiana
Purchase. Although sympathetic to the South,
Monroe, in keeping with his view of the Presidency, did not involve himself in the struggle
until a bill reached him. It provided for the admission of Missouri as a slave state, while banning

slavery from much of the rest of the Louisiana
Purchase.

Monroe doubted that Congress could constitutionally impose such a ban. His cabinet also had
doubts but, ultimately, he decided to leave the
question unresolved, signing the act that became
known as the Missouri Compromise of 1820.

Attentive to the public's attitude toward his
administration, Monroe traveled through the
Northeast—a venture that increased his popularity
—and later toured the South and Southwest.
Monroe demonstrated unusual personal growth in
the Presidency by moving away from the evident
sectionalism of his first years toward national per-
spectives. With breadth of vision and a talent for
conciliation, Monroe led a cabinet of strong personalities drawn from the country's major regions: John Quincy Adams (Secretary of State),
John Calhoun (War), William Wirt (Attorney
General), and William H. Crawford (Treasury).

In foreign affairs, the Monroe administration
arranged with Great Britain to limit armaments
on the Great Lakes and resolved a long-standing
dispute with Newfoundland and Labrador over
fishing rights. Monroe acquired (1819) Florida
from Spain by the Adams-Onís Treaty, even
though midway in the negotiations Andrew Jackson had invaded Florida (1818). Monroe also approved of the American Colonization Society
settling Liberia; Monrovia was named for him.

A triumph of skillful Presidential leadership,
the Monroe Doctrine began its evolution with the
clamors for recognition by Spain's former Latin
American colonies. Monroe dispatched special
agents to those emerging countries and sought to
associate Congress with his eventual policy. He
recognized the former colonies and, on learning
that European powers contemplated a reconquest
of them, he and his cabinet developed the message to Congress of December 2, 1823, that set
forth the doctrine. In effect, it threatened war
against European powers that attempted to "extend their system to any portion of this hemisphere." Although Secretary of State Adams
played an important part in the formulation of
the doctrine, Monroe conceived the idea of a
legislative message to convey it and drafted its
central paragraphs.

After leaving office, Monroe retired to his estate
near Leesburg, Virginia. He served as regent of
the University of Virginia and was presiding officer of the Virginia Constitutional Convention in
1829. Financial distress, stemming from long
years of public service, forced Monroe to move
(1830) to New York City to live with his married
daughter. He died there on July 4, 1831. Subsequently his remains were moved to Richmond,
Virginia.

John Quincy Adams

John Quincy Adams, 6th President (1825–1829),
was born July 11, 1767, in Braintree (now
Quincy), Massachusetts, the eldest son of the 2d
President of the United States. Because his father
had served as American diplomatic representative
to several European countries during the Revolution, Adams received his early schooling abroad.
His advanced learning enabled him to enter Harvard College as a junior and graduate in 1787.
After reading law for three years, he was admitted
to the bar.

But having few clients, Adams took up political journalism. He wrote articles replying to Tom Paine's *The Rights of Man*, which he considered too radical, and attacked the French Minister Edmond Genêt, who during the Washington administration urged the United States to join France in her war with Great Britain. In 1794, George Washington appointed the 27-year-old Adams minister to the Netherlands and, two years later, to Portugal. He served as minister to Prussia after his father became (1797) President.

With the advent (1801) of the Jefferson administration, Adams abandoned diplomacy and turned to politics as a Federalist; he was elected (1802) to the Massachusetts Senate but the Federalist leader there soon considered Adams "too unmanageable." A year later he was elected to the U.S. Senate from Massachusetts. In the Senate, he often voted with the Democratic-Republicans, although a Federalist, and he supported Jefferson's embargo policy to which other New England Federalists were bitterly opposed. When the end of Adams' term approached, the Federalists, feeling betrayed, elected (1808) another man to his place, and Adams immediately resigned.

He returned (1809) to diplomacy under James Madison, who appointed him minister to Russia. Near the end of his service there (1814), he became one of the U.S. commissioners who negotiated the Treaty of Ghent ending the War of 1812. In 1815 Madison appointed Adams minister to Britain; in 1817 James Monroe named him Secretary of State. Adams was a leading influence in the formulation of the Monroe Doctrine.

Just as Madison and Monroe had risen to the Presidency from the post of Secretary of State, Adams considered himself qualified for a similar ascent in the election of 1824. Proud, high-minded, and an independent in politics (which made party men look askance at him), Adams made little effort to obtain votes. Moreover, he faced formidable opponents: John Calhoun, Henry Clay, Andrew Jackson, and William Crawford. Calhoun soon withdrew from the Presidential race and was elected Vice-President. For President, Jackson received 99 electoral votes; Adams, 84; Crawford, 41; and Clay, 37. Since none of the candidates had won a majority, the House of Representatives had to choose among the three leading candidates.

Before the House voted, however, Jackson's followers charged that Adams had promised Clay a cabinet post in exchange for his support. Following his election, Adams appointed Clay Secretary of State, prompting Jacksonians in Congress to cry that Adams and Clay had made "a corrupt bargain." These circumstances assured Adams of unrelenting Jacksonian hostility.

In his inaugural address, Adams advocated an ambitious program of domestic improvements and, in his first annual message, he called for federal promotion of the arts and sciences, establishment of a national university and astronomical observatories, and support for scientific enterprises. Strict Northern constructionists were distressed by Adams' liberal interpretations of the Constitution, while Southerners were fearful that the logic of these Constitutional views might lead to federal abolition of slavery.

Neither by personality nor by circumstance was Adams sufficiently endowed to excel in two critical Presidential roles: as party leader and as legislative leader. Although his party controlled the House, the opposition ruled the Senate. Adams himself had little faith in his ability to command success in Congress. A simple proposal, such as his request for authority to dispatch a mission to the Panama Congress of Latin American states, encountered rough trouble in the legislature. A master of diatribe, John Randolph, launched a pointed attack on the supposed Adams-Clay "deal." Worse than Randolph's attack was the failure of anyone in the President's own party to defend him.

Adams made no attempt to soften Congressional opposition by the adroit use of patronage. Seemingly self-obstructive, his principles took precedence over party claims. His administration made only 12 removals from office, a degree of restraint that alienated friends and encouraged enemies. In other ways, too, Adams demonstrated that he was very little of a politician. His cabinet contained no one who had openly supported him for President. He even countenanced the aid openly given by one cabinet secretary to the future Presidential candidacy of Jackson.

The midterm Congressional elections went against Adams' interests, and for the first time in the history of the Presidency a large majority of Congress opposed the administration.

Adams' chief legislative success was the enactment (1828) of the "tariff of abominations," the high rates of which favored New England manufacturers and hurt Southern farmers, who had to pay more for imports. Southern resentment endangered Adams' chances for reelection.

The 1828 Presidential campaign was one of unparalleled bitterness. Adams did not answer—although his supporters did—the attacks of Jackson and his followers. Adams believed it beneath the dignity of the President to engage in political debate. Adams had no party of his own to cope with the well-organized opposition, and Jackson won an overwhelming victory: 178 electoral votes to 83 for Adams. But Adams did not regret leaving the Presidency.

After his Presidential term, Adams briefly enjoyed political retirement, until his election to the House of Representatives. Taking his seat in 1831, he served there for 17 years. He was the first Congressman to argue that slaves could be freed in time of war, an argument that Lincoln was to utilize in the Emancipation Proclamation.

Adams died of a paralytic stroke in the Speaker's Room of the House of Representatives on February 23, 1848. He is buried in Quincy, Massachusetts.

Andrew Jackson

Andrew Jackson, 7th President (1829–1837), was born on March 15, 1767, in Waxhaw, South Carolina, the son of a linen weaver who, upon migrating to the United States from Ireland, became a farmer. Jackson's mother, too, was born in Ireland. In the frontier wilderness of the Carolinas, Jackson grew up with little education or refinement, and with a combative nature. But he was also energetic, self-confident, honest, and straightforward. He was genuinely the first of the "log-cabin" Presidents.

In the American Revolution, Jackson at 13 joined the South Carolina militia and was captured (1781) by the British. After the war, he read law and was admitted (1787) to the bar at the age of 20. In 1788, he became solicitor of the western district of North Carolina (now Tennessee) and soon excelled at sending law violators and debtors to jail. His success in public office rapidly enlarged his private law practice. Through successful land speculation, Jackson also increased his fortune, and he acquired the Hermitage, a plantation near Nashville.

Later that year, he was elected to the U.S. House of Representatives. His rough frontier manners won him attention and popularity, and he was appointed (1797) to the U.S. Senate at the age of 30. But impatient of the slow pace of life in Philadelphia (then the capital) and eager to care for his private affairs, Jackson resigned from the Senate the following year. The Tennessee legislature made his political retirement short lived by making him justice of the state supreme court (July 1798), and he served in that capacity until 1804. The pressures of creditors forced him to resign and devote himself to private affairs. By selling off land and winning steadily on his horses, Jackson withstood his creditors.

His already substantial public service had not compensated for his scanty formal education. A critic said that "his letters, with their crudities in spelling and grammar, would make the better educated angels weep." Nor did his temper diminish; he was party to many duels.

His service in the War of 1812 established him as a national military hero and a popular idol of the West. His best-known victory, at New Orleans, was gained after the treaty of peace had been signed, but before he had learned of it. In 1817 Jackson led a military expedition to Florida to guard the border, but he engaged and defeated the Seminole Indians in battle, pursuing them into northwest Florida. He ordered two British subjects, accused of inciting the Seminoles, hanged, thus precipitating diplomatic crises with Britain and Spain.

As a war hero, Jackson was attractive to politicians, and they began to talk of electing him President. In 1822 the Tennessee legislature nominated him to run for President in 1824 and, as a step in that direction, the legislature elected him to the U.S. Senate in 1823. Jackson again favorably impressed the Washington political community.

In the bitterly fought Presidential election of 1824, Jackson was one of five major candidates. Although he received more electoral votes than any of his rivals, he lacked a majority and the choice went to the House of Representatives. Supporters of Henry Clay in the House gave their votes to John Quincy Adams, who was elected. When Adams appointed Clay as Secretary of State, Jackson was convinced that he had been cheated out of the Presidency by "a corrupt bargain" between his two rivals.

The Presidential election of 1828 was even more bitter. It was the first election in which each Presidential nomination was made by state legislatures and mass meetings, instead of the traditional Congressional caucuses. Seeking reelection, Adams was the "National Republican" or Whig candidate. Jackson won easily, with 178 electoral votes to 83 for Adams.

His inaugural address was a true harbinger of Jackson's future policies. "The Federal Constitution," he said, "must be obeyed, state rights preserved, our national debts must be paid, direct taxes and loans avoided, and the Federal Union preserved." Jackson, who expressed and believed in the phrase "Let the people rule," invited the inaugural crowd into the White House. The results were disastrous: people grabbed up food and punch, stood on chairs, tore draperies, and broke china. The crowd's pressure endangered Jackson, who gladly escaped through a window.

Consistent with his desire for popular rule, Jackson became the first President to use the spoils system on a substantial scale. To Jackson's friend, Senator William L. Marcy of New York, is credited the slogan, "to the victor belong the spoils." Under the Jacksonian conception of spoils, experts were unnecessary for the conduct of government. The people could do its tasks and, best of all, members of the victorious party.

Although Jackson extolled popular rule, he also maximized his own personal rule as President, sometimes to the point of arbitrary power. He developed what became known as the "kitchen cabinet," a small group of personal advisers who were not in the cabinet but, in some cases, occupied subcabinet positions. The kitchen cabinet advised on policies and helped implement them; it tended to supplant the regular cabinet with which Jackson was chronically dissatisfied.

Jackson's revulsion to anything smacking of class privilege led him to attack the Bank of the United States. Although privately owned and managed, the bank, as chartered by Congress, had control over the nation's currency system. Jackson considered the act of Congress that had created the bank unconstitutional. On economic grounds, also, he opposed the bank. Jackson criticized it for failing to establish a "uniform and sound" currency, since he favored a "hard money" policy—one in which paper money would be based on specie (gold and silver).

In 1832 when Congress passed a bill rechartering the bank, Jackson vetoed it. Hitherto Presidents had restricted their use of the veto to constitutional grounds, but Jackson broke new ground by elaborating on the policy considerations prompting his action.

The election of 1832 was a landmark in Presidential history. For the first time, Presidential nominees were chosen by national conventions. The Democratic-Republican party broke into two parties. Jackson's opponents, who called themselves "National Republicans," nominated Henry Clay, while Jackson's followers continued to style themselves as "Republicans" or "Democratic-Republicans." The election was fought on the issue "Jackson or the Bank," and Jackson again won easily, with 219 electoral votes to 49 for Clay.

Spurred by his victory, Jackson continued to move against the Bank of the United States. He directed that government funds deposited with it be removed and placed in state banks, which opponents called "pet banks." "The dying monster," as Jackson called the Bank of the United States, was defeated after a savage fight and transformed itself into a state bank of Pennsylvania.

Meanwhile, banks having the use of government funds issued paper money in enormous quantities, prompting wild speculation. In 1836, Jackson suddenly issued his "specie circular," declaring that the government would accept only gold or silver in payment for public lands. He also required these banks to give up the money deposited with them, so that he might lend it to the states. The result was a disastrous panic that reached full force in the administration of his successor, Martin Van Buren.

Jackson also enhanced Presidential influence by his firm handling of the nullification crisis. In November 1832, South Carolina declared the high tariff acts of 1828 and 1832 null and void and threatened to secede. By proclamation, Jackson warned South Carolina that the law would be enforced and ordered troops and warships concentrated near Charleston. Congress passed a force bill, authorizing the President to employ the armed forces to collect tariffs. Eventually a new compromise tariff law was passed, and South Carolina withdrew its nullification of the tariff laws.

Jackson took a different course when Georgia disregarded the authority of the United States, as expressed by the Supreme Court. The Court had held unconstitutional a Georgia law concerning lands which by treaties had been given to the Indians. When Georgian authorities imprisoned a violator of the state law, Jackson refused to use the executive power to uphold the decision of the Supreme Court, and merely remarked, "John Marshall has made the decision; now let him enforce it." Some explain Jackson's position as one motivated by his long-standing distaste for Indians and for Marshall.

The audacious, enterprising, politically skillful Jackson remade the Presidency. His unprecedented use of spoils and the national nominating convention made it a party office. As a popular President and effective party leader, he became the first President to appeal to the people over the heads of their legislative representatives.

After leaving the Presidency, Jackson retired to the Hermitage and supported the Presidencies of his protégés—Van Buren and Polk. He died on June 8, 1845, and is buried at the Hermitage.

Martin Van Buren

Martin Van Buren, 8th President 1837–1841), was born on December 5, 1782, in Kinderhook, New York, the son of a truck-farmer who was also tavern keeper. As a child, Van Buren enjoyed listening to his father's patrons discuss politics. At the age of 14, he left school to serve an apprenticeship in law offices at Kinderhook and Albany and was admitted to the bar in 1803.

While practicing in Kinderhook, he gained (1808) his first public office, being appointed surrogate of Columbia County by Gov. Daniel D. Tompkins. Van Buren rose rapidly in his New York political career, serving as state senator, attorney general, U.S. Senator, and delegate to the New York constitutional convention of 1821. An admirer of the ideas of Thomas Jefferson, Van Buren was a Democratic-Republican. As U.S. Senator (1821–28), he led in the fight against imprisonment for debt and the extension of the slave trade.

In 1828, Van Buren was elected governor of New York and gave invaluable support to the Presidential race of Andrew Jackson. A grateful Jackson named him Secretary of State but, more important, Van Buren rose to primacy among Jackson's advisers. Completely in accord with Jackson's policies, Van Buren in 1832 ran successfully for Vice-President, Jackson being re-elected. As Jackson's chosen successor, Van Buren received the Democratic Presidential nomination in 1836 and won the election virtually unopposed.

Van Buren entered office pledged to follow the footsteps of his predecessor. The new President inherited not only policies but a legacy of problems as well. The worst of these was the feverish speculation in public lands that had developed in the latter days of the Jackson administration. Rich and poor alike, banks and their branches had all indulged in speculation. To check it, Jackson had issued the Specie Circular of July 1, 1836, that stipulated the government need only accept gold and silver in payment for public lands. Despite this restraint and others, a financial crash occurred (May 10, 1837) on Van Buren's 36th day in office. Bank closings and failures spread like plague, the nation having begun its first great depression.

Van Buren perceived neither the power nor the duty of the Presidency to help the people in their economic plight. Despite loud clamors of opposition, Van Buren held to Jackson's Specie Circular. His financial policies alienated conservative (or "bank") Democrats, especially in the politically important states of Virginia and New York. The rival Whig party denounced Van Buren for indifference and "heartlessness," pointing to his failure to issue paper money and resort to other relief measures that might have benefited the people and the economy. Van Buren, whose talents lay more in political manipulation than in persuasive public leadership, followed the practice of ignoring his critics. At this time, as throughout his political career, he was confident that "the sober second thought" of the people would support him.

Another Jacksonian inheritance was America's fiercest and costliest Indian war, the Seminole War in Florida. The great treasure of lives and money required to prosecute the eight-year war further diminished Van Buren's popularity. Even more costly, politically, was his policy toward Canada, since Americans sympathized with the Canadian rebellion of 1837. When British authorities seized an insurgent vessel in American waters, Van Buren resisted vociferous opinion that the country go to war with Great Britain. The President and his administration were derided as "tools of Victoria." In 1839, a border dispute between Maine and New Brunswick erupted, threatening war again, but Van Buren prevailed for peace with patience and tact.

Foreign policy, however, damaged his standing with the Southern base of his party. Facing pressures to annex the now independent Texas, he resisted because he did not want war with Mexico. He also opposed the extension of slavery, which the acquisition of Texas augured.

Dignified, courtly, and given to dandified dress and expensive tastes, Van Buren was a cartoonist's delight. But he was a leader with principles and convictions that he held to at the price of unpopularity and failure of reelection. His party bravely renominated him in 1840. In the boisterous "hard-cider" campaign of 1840, the Whigs delighted to chant that "Little Van" was "a used-up man." In his overwhelming defeat, Van Buren even lost his own state of New York.

Although driven from the Presidency, Van Buren remained active in politics for the next two decades. He continued to oppose annexation of Texas and approved the Wilmot Proviso, which barred slavery in territory acquired from Mexico. In 1848, he was the Presidential nominee of the Free-Soil party. Although defeated, he took so many votes in New York from the Democratic nominee, Lewis Cass, that the Whigs' Zachary Taylor was elected. Van Buren supported Democratic Presidents Pierce and Buchanan, as well as the prosecution of the Civil War. He died at his country estate of Lindenwald, near his birthplace, July 24, 1862.

William Henry Harrison

William Henry Harrison, 9th President (March 4–April 4, 1841), was born at Berkeley, Charles City County, Virginia, on February 9, 1773. His father, a plantation owner and member of the Virginia aristocracy, was a signer of the Declaration of Independence.

Harrison attended Hampden-Sydney College and studied medicine in Philadelphia. Unattracted by the medical profession, he accepted an appointment by President Washington to the army as ensign in 1791.

Harrison served with distinction in the Indian campaigns of the Northwest Territory, rose to a captaincy, and in 1798 resigned his commission to settle at North Bend, Ohio, near Cincinnati. President John Adams appointed him secretary of the Northwest Territory. In 1799, he became the first territorial delegate to Congress.

For 12 years Harrison was territorial governor of Indiana and superintendent of Indian affairs. By negotiating vast land cessions from the Indians, he opened Ohio and Indiana to American settlement. When Tecumseh, a chieftain of the Shawnee Indians, and his brother the Shawnee Prophet objected to the land cessions, Harrison in November 1811 defeated the Indians in a formidable battle at Tippecanoe on the Wabash River. The battle made Harrison a national hero, admiringly called "Old Tippecanoe."

In the War of 1812, Harrison was commissioned a major general in command of forces in the Northwest. He took Detroit in September 1813, and in early October he established American hegemony in the West, when he defeated the combined Indian and British forces at the Thames River in Ontario, where Tecumseh was finally killed.

Harrison resigned his commission and as a war hero was elected in 1816 to the U.S. House of Representatives. He subsequently served in the Ohio Senate and in the U.S. Senate. Appointed minister to Colombia by President John Quincy Adams, Harrison was recalled when Andrew Jackson came to power. He retired to his farm at North Bend, and, to supplement his income, served as county recorder and clerk of the county court.

In 1836, Harrison's political fortunes recovered dramatically when the Whigs nominated him for President. Although defeated by Martin Van Buren, the Democratic candidate, Harrison ran an impressive race, carrying seven states. In 1840, the Whigs, including Daniel Webster and Henry Clay, nominated Harrison for President and John Tyler for Vice-President.

The 1840 Presidential campaign, famous for its slogan "Tippecanoe and Tyler too," is a classic of political demagoguery. Harrison's standing as a war hero, the absence of a platform, and diversionary political propaganda, enabled the Whigs to avoid the emerging issue of slavery. Van Buren, the incumbent, was portrayed drinking champagne from a crystal goblet at a table laden with costly viands and dinnerware. Harrison was seen content with a log cabin and hard cider. Aided also by the suffering of the Panic of 1837, Harrison scored an overwhelming victory.

His inaugural stirred enormous enthusiasm. His address, partly the work of Webster, prolix and abounding in classical allusions, was an extended statement of the Whig doctrine of the Presidency. Deferential to Congress, it viewed the legislators as the center of decision.

Harrison appointed a cabinet of high quality, headed by Daniel Webster as Secretary of State. On March 17, the President called a special session of Congress to meet on May 31 to act on the country's continuing financial distress. A week later, he took ill, developed pneumonia, and died, a month after his inauguration. Harrison was the first of our Presidents to die in office.

John Tyler

John Tyler, 10th President (1841–1845), was born on March 29, 1790, in Charles City County, Virginia, the son of Judge John Tyler, a distinguished lawyer and governor of Virginia. Young Tyler graduated from William and Mary College at 17, was admitted to the bar at 19, and at 21 his public career began with his election to the Virginia House of Delegates.

Tyler moved steadily through a political career of remarkable breadth, as U.S. Congressman, Senator, governor of Virginia, and delegate to the important Virginia constitutional conventions of 1829 and 1830. In 1836, he was an unsuccessful candidate for the Vice-Presidency, but in the "Tippecanoe and Tyler too" campaign of 1840, with William Henry Harrison heading the Whig ticket, he ran again, this time successfully. Harrison died a month after his inauguration, and on April 4, 1841, Tyler became the first Vice-President to succeed to the Presidency.

Some chose to interpret the succession provision of the Constitution to mean that Tyler was only "Acting President," but he insisted upon the office's full title and powers. The reluctance to grant Tyler recognition was partly rooted in the unusual circumstances of his nomination. Tyler was an ex-Democrat who, as a legislator, had been a stubborn advocate of states' rights and consequently opposed to nationalistic Whig policies. The Whigs had nonetheless nominated him for the Vice-Presidency to attract Southern votes. They reasoned that, as Vice-President, Tyler would command no influence in the Harrison administration.

After Tyler became President, his ambiguous situation was further complicated by the presence in the Senate of Henry Clay, the heavy-handed but powerful leader of the Whig party. Clay was soon scornfully speaking of Tyler as "a President without a party." Tyler was also an obstacle to Clay's driving ambition to become President; if Tyler could be discredited to the point of being denied renomination, Clay might himself seize the prize.

Tyler, in a conciliatory step, retained the entire Harrison cabinet, which presumably should have satisfied the Whigs and Clay, but they were irreconcilable. A rift quickly developed over the Whig measure to reestablish a national bank. Twice Tyler vetoed the national bank bill. As a strict constitutionalist, he argued that a national bank must not be permitted to establish branches in the states without their prior consent. After the second bank veto, Tyler's entire cabinet resigned, with the exception of Daniel Webster, the Secretary of State. Webster remained only long enough to complete a treaty with Canada setting the northeast boundary of the United States.

With Clay now openly saying of the President that "I'll drive him before me," Tyler's own measures encountered rough treatment in Congress and his nominations to office were usually blocked.

Despite the deadlock with his own party, Tyler brought off some substantial achievements. He was adept at seizing upon issues that by their merit or popularity transcended partisanship. He was not unskilled at political maneuver and when a favorite project to annex Texas by treaty was lost—with every Whig but one voting against it —Tyler outmaneuvered his opponents and arranged for annexation by joint resolution.

A cultivated Southern gentleman, master of the good story and easy conversation, Tyler was attractive to Congressmen and, as a veteran legislator, experienced in dealing with them. Under his evident influence Congress passed a number of constructive laws. The Navy was thoroughly reorganized. A bureau was established for nautical charts and instruments, which later developed into the Naval Observatory. An act opening the way to initiating a national telegraphic system was passed, a step leading to the development of the Weather Bureau.

As President, Tyler excelled as an administrator and in employing his powers in foreign affairs. He conducted the government with a minimum of waste, although Congress provided no system for controlling public funds. Tyler brought the Seminole War to an end, entered into a treaty with China opening the doors of the Orient for the first time, and applied the Monroe Doctrine to Texas and Hawaii.

Despite his achievements, Tyler could muster only minor factional support for renomination in 1844. Withdrawing from the Presidential race, he retired to his estate, Sherwood Forest, in Virginia on the James River. There he lived in virtual retirement for 14 years, except for service as chancellor of the College of William and Mary from 1859 to 1861. In 1861, he proposed and presided over the secret North-South Conference held at Washington in an eleventh-hour effort to prevent the Civil War. When this failed, he advocated immediate secession and was elected a member of the congress of the Confederacy, but he died on January 18, 1862, before he could take his seat in that body.

James Knox Polk

James Knox Polk, 11th President (1845–1849) was born on November 2, 1795, near Pineville in Mecklenburg County, North Carolina. Polk was of Scots-Irish stock, and his father soldiered in the Revolution. In 1806, the large and growing Polk family moved to central Tennessee, and Polk's schooling in that frontier district was fragmentary. Nevertheless, he entered the University of North Carolina at the age of 20, compiled an impressive record, and graduated in 1818. He studied law under Felix Grundy, the politician

and noted criminal lawyer, was admitted to the bar, and practiced in Columbia, Tennessee.

An able orator in demand at political meetings, Polk became known as "the Napoleon of the Stump." This talent, as well as his friendship with Andrew Jackson, propelled him into a political career. In 1823 he was elected to the Tennessee House of Representatives, and in 1825 to the U.S. Congress, where he served seven consecutive terms, the last two as Speaker.

In 1839, he was elected governor of Tennessee. Although an ardent Jacksonian Democrat, he was defeated for reelection in 1841 and again in 1843.

Polk then turned to national politics, and when the Democratic national convention gathered in Baltimore in 1844, he was considered a serious candidate for the Vice-Presidency, but was unthought of for the Presidency. Circumstances, however, brought him an unexpected Presidential nomination: the first successful "dark horse" candidate in the history of the office.

Just before the convention met, former President Martin Van Buren issued a statement opposing the annexation of Texas, which offended both Western and Southern interests. This position eliminated Van Buren, the leading contender for the Democratic nomination. Polk's stand on Texas and the disputed territory of Oregon—"Reannexation of Texas and Reoccupation of Oregon" —won him the nomination and the election. Since Polk lacked national prominence, the rival Whig party's campaign slogan was, "Who is James Polk?" The Democrats countered with "54-40 or Fight!", a reference to the entire Oregon territory, which the United States, it was felt, should possess even at the price of war with Great Britain. In the election Polk narrowly defeated Henry Clay, the Whig candidate, by winning New York State.

His inaugural address exalted the Union and deplored sectional discord. More specifically, he opposed a tariff "for protection merely" and asserted uncompromisingly that the United States' title to Oregon was "clear and unquestionable."

The independent treasury bill of 1846, which he adroitly shepherded through Congress, reestablished a financial system that endured, with only minor modification, until the Federal Reserve System was established during Woodrow Wilson's administration.

The Walker Tariff Act of 1846, true to Polk's purpose, put most tariff duties on a revenue basis and used ad valorem in place of specific duties. Polk prevailed against political foes who foresaw only ruination for manufacturing and the public treasury.

Oregon proved a more difficult issue. Aided by Secretary of State James Buchanan and after long negotiations with Great Britain, Polk won a settlement that was something less than his campaign slogan had demanded. Buchanan proposed that the Oregon Territory be divided by extending to the Pacific coast the boundary provided by the 49th parallel. When Britain rejected the compromise, Polk boldly reasserted his claim to the entire Oregon Territory. Britain then acquiesced to the 49th parallel line, except for Vancouver Island, and the treaty that was signed (1846) incorporated this division.

The acquisition of California was a severe test of Polk's political skills. Aiming to secure the territory by purchases, he reasserted some longstanding damage claims against Mexico. Certain that Mexico could not pay her debt, he expected her to cede the territory. Mexico rejected any kind of bargain, and American troops under Gen. Zachary Taylor provoked hostilities along the Rio Grande. Polk asked Congress on May 9, 1846, for a declaration of war because of the unpaid claims and because Mexico had invaded American soil. The treaty at the end of the Mexican War ceded California and New Mexico to the United States, for which Mexico was paid $15 million, and the old damage claims were assumed by the United States. Polk's opponents charged that he had forced the war upon Mexico to extend slavery.

To induce Mexico to accept the treaty, Polk had asked Congress for $2 million to be used for "diplomatic purposes." The sum was to be devoted to paying the Mexican army, a step that was indispensable to acceptance of the treaty. David Wilmot offered a proviso to the appropriation, directing that slavery be excluded from any territory acquired through use of the funds made available to the President. Polk angrily termed Wilmot's proviso "a mischievous and foolish amendment," aimed at diplomatic embarrassment. After Polk threatened to veto it, the proviso was defeated, but it brought the building conflict between North and South into the open.

In foreign affairs, Polk extended the reach of the Monroe Doctrine from a prohibition of forcible foreign interference to any kind of interference in American affairs. He effectively opposed an invitation by the people of Yucatán in Mexico for Britain or Spain to exert sovereignty over their territory.

Polk was an exacting administrator who closely supervised the affairs of his departments. He bore ungladly the less palatable aspects of politics. He was contemptuous of the spoils system and, in a rare act for a President, vetoed two river-and-harbor bills, Congress's traditional and politically sacred pork-barrel method of legislation.

Serious and diligent almost to a fault, Polk had little time for pleasure and small talk. Secretive, particularly in dealing with Congress, he offended many by his reticence and sly maneuvers. He was lacking in personal magnetism and had few intimate friends, although Bancroft deemed him "generous and benevolent."

Just before taking office, Polk declared he would not be a candidate for reelection. He died on June 15, 1849, shortly after leaving office.

Zachary Taylor

Zachary Taylor, 12th President (March 4, 1849–July 9, 1850) was born November 24, 1784, at Montebello, Orange County, Virginia. His father was a farmer and a colonel in the Revolution. When he was less than a year old, Taylor and his family migrated to Kentucky. There on the frontier, schools were little known, and Taylor absorbed a sketchy education from tutoring.

In 1808, he obtained a commission as first lieutenant in the army. During 40 years of military service, which ended when he was nominated for President, Taylor fought in the War of 1812, against the Indians in the Northwest and in Florida, and in the Mexican War. In the Seminole Indian War in Florida, the muscular, stocky Taylor became known as "Old Rough and Ready" to troops who admired his valor and candor. His dis-

tinction at the battle of Okeechobee against the Seminoles won him the rank of brevet brigadier general.

Taylor commanded the army in Texas, and a Mexican attack upon his forces in 1846 was used by Congress as justification for declaring war. After Taylor's victory at Monterrey, Mexico, President James K. Polk, distrustful of Taylor's independent spirit and his potential as a political rival, turned over most of Taylor's troops to a new commander. Santa Anna, the Mexican commander, learning of Taylor's weakened forces, attacked him at Buena Vista with troops that were numerically far superior. A stunning victory in an all-day battle made Taylor a national hero and immediately inspired both leading parties, the Democrats and the Whigs, to consider him as a candidate for the Presidential election of 1848.

As a lifelong soldier, Taylor had never voted, and his political views, if any existed, were unknown. Mindful of their victory with another military hero, W. H. Harrison in 1840, the Whigs in 1848 chose Taylor as their nominee over such other formidable contenders as Henry Clay and Daniel Webster.

Stressing that his administration would be nonpartisan and free from party pledges, Taylor defeated his Democratic opponent, Lewis Cass, and the Free-Soil nominee, Martin Van Buren, in the first election to be held simultaneously in all the states.

As President, Taylor was a potential force to check the widening breach between the North and South over slavery. He was a slave owner, but numbered among his closest counselors the antislavery Whig, Senator William H. Seward of New York. In addition, his electoral victory was fashioned by substantial support from both sections; he carried seven Northern and eight Southern states. His inaugural address urged Congress to work for conciliation of sectional controversies and offered a program no one could criticize: friendly relations in foreign affairs, an efficient army and navy, and encouragement of agriculture, commerce, and manufacture.

For all of this political insulation, Taylor had to face the fiery issue of the admission of new states to the Union on a free or slave basis. Thanks largely to his overriding nationalistic sentiment, Taylor quickly took an antislavery position, for above all he wanted to annex the territories won in the Mexican War. He wrote to Jefferson Davis that nature had excluded slavery from the new Southwest, and, in a Pennsylvania address, he assured Northerners they "need have no apprehension of the further extension of slavery."

Taylor dispatched a special emissary, Thomas Butler King, to counsel Californians in forming a constitution and applying for statehood. Similar assistance was given New Mexico. In special messages to Congress in 1850, he urged unconditional admission for California and statehood for New Mexico.

In a counterthrust, Southern legislators filibustered against the admission of California and insisted that all measures concerning territories ceded by Mexico be taken up in a single bill. Southern Whigs withdrew their support of Taylor, and such Southern leaders as Alexander Stephens and Robert Tombs threatened the President with secession.

In Congress, Henry Clay framed a series of bills known collectively as the Compromise of 1850 in an effort to placate both the North and the South. Taylor would doubtless have opposed the compromise, but following ceremonies connected with building the Washington Monument, he was stricken with cholera and died after a Presidential tenure of only 16 months.

In foreign affairs, Taylor's Secretary of State, John M. Clayton, negotiated the Clayton-Bulwer Treaty with Great Britain which guaranteed the neutrality of an isthmian canal. (The previous Polk administration had secured rights to build a canal across Nicaragua.)

Millard Fillmore

Millard Fillmore, 13th President (July 10, 1850–March 3, 1853), was born in Locke (now Summerhill) in Cayuga County, New York, on January 7, 1800. The son of a frontier farmer who had migrated from Vermont, young Fillmore had scant schooling and was apprenticed to a wool carder. Intent upon studying law, he migrated to Buffalo, where he worked in a lawyer's office for room and board. In 1823, he was admitted to the bar and began practice in East Aurora, New York.

Fillmore's political career began with his election in 1828 to the New York State Assembly on an Anti-Mason ticket. He secured the passage of a law that abolished imprisonment for debt and formed a friendship with the Albany publisher and political leader, Thurlow Weed. In 1830, Fillmore moved back to Buffalo and a year later was elected to the first of four terms in the U.S. Congress. He supported the emerging Whig party and the nationalistic policies of Henry Clay. As chairman of the powerful Ways and Means Committee, he oversaw the 1842 tariff act that raised duties on manufactured goods. On the burning issue of slavery, he was a moderate.

In 1844, Fillmore ran as the Whig candidate for governor of New York but was unsuccessful and returned to his law practice. In 1846, he became the first chancellor of the University of Buffalo. A year later, he was elected comptroller of New York.

Fillmore's acceptability to both Northern and Southern Whigs and his backing by Henry Clay resulted in his election as Vice-President with Zachary Taylor in 1848. As Vice-President, he presided over the bitter Senate debates on the slavery compromise measures of 1850 with notable fairness. Midway in this political turbulence President Taylor died, and Fillmore became the second "accidental President."

The Taylor Cabinet promptly resigned. Fillmore's nomination of Daniel Webster of New Hampshire as Secretary of State and John Crittenden of Kentucky as Attorney General was indicative of the new President's preference for a moderate Whig position and his readiness to compromise in the growing conflict between North and South. In his message to Congress of August 6, 1850, Fillmore made a compelling plea for settlement by compromise. An opponent, Salmon Chase, credited the Presidential message with winning over six New England votes in the Senate and moving Congress down the compromise road.

Clay's "omnibus" compromise bill, unable to be passed as a whole, was separated into its several parts. These sections were soon enacted, and the President approved them believing that only through them could the Union be saved. Fillmore and Clay led not a united party, but rather one that represented a bipartisan coalition of Northern Democrats and Southern Whigs. To Southerners, a key element of the compromise was the new Fugitive Slave Law; Fillmore's approval of it cost him the support of Northern Whigs. Since the Presidency was Whig and Congress Democratic, little important legislation was passed, other than the Compromise of 1850.

In seeking renomination as the Whig standard-bearer in 1852, Fillmore enjoyed support from Southern Whigs. His rival, Webster, was backed by New Englanders, and another rival, General Winfield Scott, by an extreme antislavery group. When the Fillmore-Webster factions failed to unite, the nomination passed to Scott. Like other Presidents from Jackson to Lincoln, Fillmore was limited to one Presidential term by the slavery dispute, which prevented the Chief Executive from satisfying both the Northern and Southern wings of his party.

As President, Fillmore presented an image of cool-headedness and caution. His paramount political value was preservation of the Union, a goal to which he subordinated any specific interest or issue in the slavery controversy. From his deathbed, Henry Clay urged Fillmore's renomination, while Webster hailed his administration as one of the ablest.

Fillmore's advent to politics coincided with the emergence of the Whig party, and his departure with its demise. The 1852 elections were the last national campaign in which the Whigs were active. In 1856, Fillmore was the Presidential nominee of the American, or Know-Nothing, party. Stressing the value of unity and the dangers of sectionalism, he ran last in a three-way race. Always preferring conciliation to coercion, Fillmore opposed Lincoln's policies in the Civil War and supported Andrew Johnson's stand against radical reconstruction.

For all his lack of early advantages, Fillmore, according to a contemporary, possessed "a grace and polish of manner which fitted him for the most refined circles of the metropolis." Fillmore's political activities ended with the Reconstruction. He died on March 8, 1874. In 1969, a substantial body of Fillmore papers was discovered.

Franklin Pierce

Franklin Pierce, 14th President (1853–1857), was born on November 23, 1804, in Hillsboro, New Hampshire. His father, Benjamin Pierce, served in the Revolution and later was a brigadier general in the state militia. He was also a two-term governor of New Hampshire and left a valuable heritage of political connections for his son, who, after study at nearby academies and at Phillips Exeter, entered Bowdoin College in Maine.

After graduating from Bowdoin in 1824, Pierce read law and was admitted to the bar in 1827. He began practice in Hillsboro and two years later commenced his political career by winning election as a Jacksonian Democrat to the New Hampshire House of Representatives. Reelected two years later, he also became Speaker. In 1833, he began a term in the U.S. House of Representatives and after a second term was elected to the U.S. Senate. He was the youngest member of that body, which then included such giants as Webster, Clay, and Calhoun. Because of his wife's poor health, Pierce resigned from the Senate in 1842 and resumed law practice in Concord, New Hampshire.

When the Mexican War broke out, Pierce, a staunch nationalist, inspired by his father's record in the Revolution, enlisted as a private. He advanced rapidly to brigadier general and served in key battles. In 1848, he resigned from the army, and two years later he became president of New Hampshire's Fifth State Constitutional Convention.

In 1852, Pierce became the Democratic Presidential nominee, a classic instance of a successful "dark horse" candidate. He received no votes until the 35th ballot and won on the 49th, as an acceptable compromise candidate in the deepening North-South split over slavery. An advocate of the Compromise of 1850, Pierce was regarded as a Northerner with Southern sympathies. Pierce was victorious over his Whig opponent, General Winfield Scott, by carrying every state but four, although with less than a 50,000 plurality.

By having avoided issues in his campaign, Pierce hoped to make his administration one of harmony. His cabinet was a perfect political balance of two conservative Southerners, two conservative Northerners, an antislavery Northerner, a states' rights Southerner, and a New England Whig. His inaugural address and early actions stressed objectives of general appeal. He promised a vigorous foreign policy and an economical and efficient administration. He called for a larger and better army and navy and reduction of the debt through use of the Treasury surplus. But Pierce's strategy of harmony was bedeviled by rising Northern sentiment against slavery and its expansion.

In foreign affairs, Pierce was an expansionist. His policies reflected his nationalism and, presumably, were designed to divert attention from domestic issues and gratify Southern hopes of introducing the slave economy into new territories. Accordingly, Pierce sought to convince Great Britain that under the Clayton-Bulwer Treaty she ought to withdraw from Nicaragua and Honduras. When negotiations failed, he tacitly supported a proslavery "filibustering" expedition against Nicaragua.

Pierce negotiated to acquire Hawaii, but the venture failed when the king of the islands died. Pierce's overtures to the Russians for the purchase of Alaska were unavailing. His administration's most brazen move was the Ostend Manifesto, a declaration by three proslavery American ministers calling for the annexation of Cuba. The public, the Senate, and the President's own party reacted indignantly to this move.

Pierce's foreign policies were not altogether blanketed with failure. A treaty was made with Japan in 1854, opening that country to American trading interests. James Gadsden, a special Presidential emissary, negotiated the purchase of land from Mexico that settled a boundary dispute and secured right-of-way for a southern railroad to the Pacific.

The President's preoccupation with foreign policy could not forestall a sudden, unexpected upsurge of the slavery issue. Leading Democratic Senators brought up a bill to organize Kansas and Nebraska as new territories out of the Indian lands, thus threatening the slender slavery truce.

When the Kansas-Nebraska Bill became law in 1854, both proslavery and antislavery settlers poured into the territory, and trouble quickly developed as both factions vied for control. Civil war erupted in Kansas when a free-soil group organized a government independent of the President's. Ultimately, Pierce ordered the free-soil government to cease and put federal troops at the disposal of the governor of Kansas. The Kansas experience served to reinforce the Democratic party's identification with slavery and to spur the rise of the new Republican party and the Know-Nothing party.

Pierce strove energetically to restore his crumbling popularity and win renomination. He launched an anti-British drive and demanded the recall of the British Minister Crampton for illegally recruiting troops in the United States for the Crimean War. But the Democratic national convention of 1856, apprehensive of rising Republican strength, looked for a "safer" man; it found him in James Buchanan, who, by having been abroad, had been untouched by the controversies of the Pierce era.

Although humiliated by his rejection for renomination, Pierce labored diligently to reduce and master problems before leaving office. He established a regular (proslavery) government in Kansas and, thanks to the continued presence of troops, he could proclaim that "peace now reigns in Kansas." A treaty was negotiated under which Britain agreed to abandon its interests in Central America except those in Honduras. The Senate, however, withheld its approval. Upon leaving office, Pierce at least had the satisfaction of seeing his party retain control of the Presidency and regain Congress.

After leaving the Presidency, Pierce traveled abroad to aid his wife's health. In the Civil War, having returned to Concord, he was an outspoken critic of Lincoln's, holding that war could have been averted by better leadership. The increasing unpopularity of his views relegated him to obscurity. His death on October 8, 1869, was almost unnoticed.

James Buchanan

James Buchanan, 15th President (1857–1861), was born April 23, 1791, in Cove Gap, Pennsylvania, the second of 11 children and the son of a merchant-farmer. After graduation (1809) from Dickinson College in Carlisle, Pennsylvania, Buchanan studied law in Lancaster and began practice there in 1812. He volunteered for duty in the War of 1812 and helped defend the city of Baltimore.

Originally a Federalist, Buchanan was elected (1814) to the Pennsylvania House of Representatives. In 1816 he ran unsuccessfully for the U.S. Congress but, four years later, he won and began 10 years of service in that body. Joining the Democratic party, he supported the Presidential race of Andrew Jackson in 1824 and again in 1828, when Jackson won. Grateful for Buchanan's continued support, President Jackson appointed him (1831) minister to Russia. After negotiating America's first trade treaty with Russia, Buchanan returned to the United States, and in 1834 he was elected U.S. Senator.

Buchanan was a favorite-son candidate for the Democratic Presidential nomination of 1844, but he withdrew his name before the convention met. James K. Polk, who was elected, made Buchanan his Secretary of State in 1845. In this post,

Buchanan oversaw the negotiations that secured the southern half of the Oregon country and the vast territory in the Southwest from Mexico. His support of the annexation of Texas and the acquisition of Cuba led to the charge that he was a pro-slavery politician.

When the Whigs recaptured the Presidency in 1849, Buchanan retired to Wheatland, his estate near Lancaster. He was an unsuccessful aspirant for the Presidency in 1852. Franklin Pierce, who was nominated and elected, appointed Buchanan minister to Great Britain. By serving abroad, Buchanan avoided the fierce domestic political struggle over the Kansas-Nebraska Act and was, therefore, highly available in 1856 for the Democratic Presidential nomination. As the eventual nominee, Buchanan stressed the necessity of pre-serving the Union and avoided taking a stand on the slavery question. In a three-cornered race, Buchanan won only a popular plurality, although he secured a large majority of the electoral vote. He was a bachelor and the only Pennsylvanian to have become President.

Buchanan's plan for halting the worsening schism over slavery was revealed in his inaugural address and in the formation of his cabinet. In choosing his department heads, he preserved "the sacred balance," giving equal representation to slaveholding and nonslaveholding states. In his inaugural address, he declared that the question of slavery in the territories was a matter for the courts to determine, a view that he asserted confi-dently after learning how the pending Dred Scott case would be decided.

Buchanan hoped to deflect national attention from grievous domestic problems by fostering a dynamic foreign policy. He moved to acquire Cuba, but Congress failed to provide the neces-sary appropriations to begin negotiations. To avoid European intervention, he proposed to bolster the Benito Juarez government in Mexico, but Congress again would not lend financial support to the scheme.

Buchanan's image as a Northern man with Southern sympathies was affirmed by his accept-ing the Dred Scott decision as final and by his support of the proslavery Kansas constitution. Buchanan stressed that this constitution was re-publican in form and properly left the question of slavery up to popular determination once Kansas became a state. The President's stand divided the Democratic party into two great fac-tions. It identified the administration with the Southern wing and ignited a revolt by the fol-lowers of Stephen A. Douglas.

The growing crisis of disunion was magnified when South Carolina moved toward secession. Buchanan rejected the advice of his military com-manders to garrison Southern ports. (In his an-nual legislative message, however, he had emphatically denied the right of secession.) Si-multaneously, he admitted an inability to deal with actual secession, since federal officers in South Carolina, through whom he enforced the law, had resigned. In a close construction of Pres-idential authority, Buchanan held that except for defending U.S. property in South Carolina and collecting customs, the Chief Executive lacked authority to act. Congress alone could decide whether existing laws were amendable for carry-ing out the Constitution.

Buchanan dispatched a personal agent, Caleb Cushing, to dissuade the South Carolinians from secession and again rejected military advice to reinforce the forts in Charleston harbor. A South Carolina convention, nevertheless, voted to se-cede and Major Robert Anderson moved his Federal troops from indefensible Fort Moultrie to Fort Sumter, a step that South Carolina spokes-men said violated a Presidential commitment to keep the status quo.

In the quickening tension, Buchanan's cabi-net collapsed, with both Northern and Southern members resigning. The President filled the va-cancies with Northern and border-state members, a harbinger of firmer policies. Buchanan sent re-inforcements to Fort Sumter and announced his intent to hold it and keep peace until "the ques-tion shall have been settled by competent author-ity." Buchanan proposed new legislation to deal with the crisis, but Congress was unresponsive.

Buchanan retired into obscurity at Wheatland and died on June 1, 1868.

Abraham Lincoln

Abraham Lincoln, 16th President (March 4, 1861–April 14, 1865), was born in a dirt-floor log cabin in Hardin (now Larue) County, Kentucky, on February 12, 1809. His father, Thomas, was a migratory frontier farmer and carpenter, who was nearly always poor and moved from Ken-tucky to Indiana and, eventually, to Illinois. Of Lincoln's mother, Nancy Hanks of Rockingham County, Virginia, little is known. She died when young Lincoln was nine, and his home seemed empty and lonely after her death, until his father married Sarah (Bush) Johnston, a widow, who brought affection to the family. Lincoln may have spoken of her when he said: "God bless my mother; all that I am or ever hope to be I owe to her."

Lincoln absorbed a scanty frontier education (his formal education probably totaled less than one year). Books were scarce, but Lincoln taught himself to read and was a close student of the family Bible. His boyhood readings in it pro-vided the store of Biblical quotations and refer-ences that later abounded, with great effect, in his addresses and writings.

As a strong, large-boned youth of 6 feet, 4 inches, Lincoln was admirably suited for hard work, which he experienced in the full. He split logs for fence rails, plowed fields, cut corn, threshed wheat, and took a flat boat loaded with farm produce to New Orleans. As a boy, he showed talent as a speaker; his knack for telling stories and imitating local personalities made people gather to hear him, often at a store in which he was a clerk. His homely face and black coarse hair added fascination to what he said.

From 1831 to 1837, Lincoln was settled in New Salem, Illinois, a log-cabin community near Springfield. For a time he clerked in a store (which soon failed). As unemployment threat-ened, the Black Hawk War commenced, and Lincoln volunteered for service. His company elected him captain, but he saw no fighting ex-cept, he said, "with the mosquitoes."

Returning (1832) from the war, Lincoln groped for a way to make a livelihood. With a partner, he bought a grocery store in New Salem on credit. When the store failed and the partner died, Lincoln paid off the debts, an accomplishment that won him the nickname "Honest Abe." In 1833, Lincoln was appointed postmaster of New Salem, and eked out a living as a deputy to the county surveyor and from other odd-job fees.

Trying for the state legislature in 1834, Lincoln won as a Whig and served four successive two-year terms. His ready stories and sharp wit enabled him to excel in debate, and his leadership gifts were recognized in his selection as the Whig's floor leader. Simultaneous with his young political career, Lincoln read law and won (1836) his license to practice. In Springfield, he experienced a succession of partnerships, including one with William H. Herndon, who later became his biographer.

Lincoln "traveled the circuit," accompanying judges and fellow lawyers through the counties to try cases. The cases were heard in inns, which permitted Lincoln to indulge his talent for strong, effective argument when he thought his client was right.

Lincoln emerged in national politics when he was elected as a Whig to the U.S. House of Representatives and on December 6, 1847, took his seat in Congress where, to the displeasure of his constituents, he opposed President Polk and his conduct of the Mexican War. When his term ended on March 4, 1849, Lincoln did not dare run again because of the general unpopularity of his war views among his constituency. Convinced that his political career was ended, he returned to Springfield where, through hard work and a fast-growing practice, he became one of the best-known lawyers in Illinois in the 1850s.

In 1855, agitated by the national political issue of slavery, Lincoln again turned to politics. Opposed to slavery, although he was never an abolitionist, Lincoln spoke against the principal author of the Kansas-Nebraska Act, Illinois Senator Stephen A. Douglas, and supported the candidacies of legislators opposed to the act. In that same year, Lincoln ran unsuccessfully for the U.S. Senate. Believing that slavery was the negation of the nation's commitment to freedom and equality, he left the Whigs and joined the antislavery Republican party.

In 1858, Lincoln was nominated to run against Douglas for the U.S. Senate. In his speech at the Illinois Republican convention, Lincoln said that "I believe this government cannot endure permanently half slave and half free." The Senatorial contest included a series of debates between Lincoln and Douglas centered on the extension of slavery into free territory. Holding that he was not an abolitionist, Lincoln condemned slavery "as a moral, social, and political evil." Douglas won the election, but the debates gained Lincoln national attention.

In May 1860, the Republican national convention nominated Lincoln for President on the third ballot, after William H. Seward of New York had led on the first two ballots. Considered a moderate on the slavery question, Lincoln received 180 electoral votes to 72 for Breckinridge, 39 for Bell, and 12 for Douglas. Lincoln, elected President, was pledged not to abolish slavery, but to preserve the Union and to prevent the spread of slavery.

However, Southern secession began as soon as Lincoln's election was assured. On December 20, 1860, South Carolina passed a secession ordinance. By the time Lincoln was inaugurated (March 4, 1861), seven states had seceded and formed the Confederate government. Denying in his inaugural address that the federal government would interfere with slavery in states in which the Constitution protected it, he warned that he would use the full power of the nation to "hold, occupy, and possess" the "property and places belonging to the Federal government."

With the coming of war, Lincoln acted boldly and energetically. He called out the militia to suppress the "insurrection," expanded the regular army and navy, raised a volunteer army, closed the post office to "treasonable correspondence," imposed a blockade on Southern ports, and suspended the writ of habeas corpus in areas where Southern sympathizers were active. He also ordered the spending of unappropriated funds for purposes unauthorized by Congress.

For Lincoln's wartime Presidency, the Civil War was a severe test of the human spirit. A succession of battlefield defeats afflicted the North, and a substantial body of Northern opinion demanded peace. Many were willing to fight to preserve the Union, but not to destroy slavery. Others urged the destruction of slavery as the war's supreme goal. Lincoln had to keep the antislavery extremists in check to prevent the secession of the border states. Jealousies and frictions unsettled his cabinet. He appointed and removed a succession of field commanders in the vain hope of securing a major military victory.

In mid-1862, Lincoln decided to drop his reserve on the slavery question and issue a proclamation of emancipation. On the advice of Secretary of State Seward, he awaited a Northern victory. Seizing upon the dubious success of Union forces at Antietam (September 1862), Lincoln issued the proclamation on September 22. He declared that slaves in states in rebellion on January 1, 1863, would be free. Lincoln's action gave a clear-cut moral purpose to the war, setting the stage for the 13th Amendment to the Constitution (adopted in December 1865) that ended slavery throughout the United States.

The tide of the war ran strongly in the Union's favor in 1863 and 1864. Lincoln was renominated (1864), and easily defeated his Democratic opponent, General George B. McClellan, by an electoral vote of 212 to 21 and a popular majority that exceeded 400,000 votes. When Lincoln again took the oath of office (March 4, 1865), the end of the war was in sight, and his inaugural address outlined a postwar policy. He urged that, instead of vengeance, there be "malice toward none" and "charity for all." Pressed to decide if seceded states were in or out of the Union, Lincoln, in his last public address (April 11, 1865), said that the question was unimportant: the Southern states "finding themselves safely at home, it would be utterly immaterial whether they had ever been abroad."

On April 14, five days after Lee's surrender, Lincoln was mortally shot by John Wilkes Booth—an actor and fanatical supporter of the Confederacy—at Ford's Theater in Washington and died the next morning.

Lincoln as President withstood the trials of war with a granitic self-confidence. Yet he was a man of the purest humility, extraordinary wisdom, and shrewd judgment—a master politician in understanding and shaping public opinion. His lean, beautiful, moving prose brought to his Presidency an eloquence that no other incumbent has matched.

Andrew Johnson

Andrew Johnson, 17th President (April 15, 1865–March 3, 1869), was born on December 29, 1808, at Raleigh, North Carolina. His father, who was a sexton, porter, and constable, died when Johnson was four, and at 10 he was apprenticed to a tailor. Thanks to the tailor's practice of employing someone to read aloud as his workmen stitched, and to the local newspaper and a few books, Johnson became familiar with American history and politics.

In 1826, Johnson moved to Greeneville, Tennessee, where he set up his own tailor shop. His efforts in organizing a workingman's party led to his election as alderman in opposition to the local slave-holding aristocracy's candidate. In 1830, he became mayor of Greeneville, and five years later he was elected to the Tennessee legislature and served continuously until 1843. Although formally unschooled, Johnson continued his political rise when elected (1843) to the U.S. House of Representatives in which he served for 10 years.

In Congress Johnson staunchly represented the interests of the "common people" and, in 1845, he introduced the first homestead bill for providing farms for landless citizens from public lands. Johnson's political beliefs were influenced by his fellow Tennessean, Andrew Jackson. Johnson's powerful voice and quick mind enhanced his popularity while provoking concern among Southern aristocrats who opposed his homestead policy. Johnson was elected (1853) Tennessee governor and U.S. Senator (1857), thus becoming one of the few major Southern officeholders of the time who had supported himself by manual labor. Although a slaveholder and a Democrat, Johnson defended the Union. In fact, he was the only Southern Senator not to resign and secede with his state. When Union armies won back (1862) control of western Tennessee, Lincoln appointed Johnson military governor of the state and, by 1864, he had organized a loyal government. This achievement won Johnson the Vice-Presidential nomination on Lincoln's Republican ticket in 1864.

Upon Lincoln's assassination, Johnson assumed the office of President in an atmosphere of grief and rage. Quickly moving to restore conditions of peace after the Civil War, Johnson disbanded most of the Federal army, revoked the blockade of the South, and restored peace. For the difficult problem of reestablishing local government in the seven states of the former Confederacy, Johnson faced rival Presidential and Congressional plans that had been formulated under Lincoln.

Although claiming to assert Lincoln's plan, Johnson actually altered it in some particulars. Unlike Lincoln, who had offered a general amnesty, Johnson required that 14 classes of persons —particularly the well-to-do—apply for pardon. But in judging the loyalty of a state government, Johnson required neither that there be a stipulated proportion of loyal voters nor that state legislatures or conventions take specific steps.

Under Johnson's stimulation, new state governments were organized, secession ordinances were repealed, and slavery abolished. The 13th Amendment was ratified (1865) by all Southern states, except Mississippi. The new governments, however, failed to extend suffrage to qualified blacks, as Johnson suggested. The President did not curb Southern police regulations that were aimed, presumably, at keeping order among blacks but quickened Northern suspicions of an attempt to restore slavery.

Congress, which had not been in session, met in December 1865. The Radical Republicans, who favored harsh reconstruction terms for the South, realized that they would be outnumbered if Southern legislators were seated. As a result, the Radicals refused to seat the Southerners, arguing that they had been illegally elected. Led by Congressman Thaddeus Stevens of Pennsylvania, the Radicals further contended that the Southern states had to come in as new states or continue to be regarded as conquered territory. However, in his message to Congress, Johnson viewed the states and the Constitution as intertwined: since the act of secession was null and void under the Constitution to begin with, Southern state functions had been in his view simply suspended, not destroyed.

In the conflict that developed, Congress' lawmaking powers were pitted against the President's veto power. Congress passed an act extending the Freedmen's Bureau, but Johnson vetoed it. His veto of the Civil Rights Act, however, failed. The act aimed to guarantee the rights of freedmen against violation by state law. Congress also passed (1868) the 14th Amendment, which was designed to incorporate the substance of the act into the Constitution.

With the Congressional elections of 1866 in prospect, Johnson decided to present his case to the people and made his "swing around the circle," as it was known, through the East and Midwest in August and September. Although the venture began well, Johnson was provoked into making some ill-tempered remarks when goaded by Radical hecklers, and a hostile press ran biased accounts of his conduct. The election results imperiled Johnson: Congressional foes increased and, consequently, his veto power deteriorated.

Emboldened by its ability to overwhelm the President's veto power, Congress now began to encroach seriously on his domain. It circumvented the Presidential pardoning power, which Johnson had used on behalf of prominent Confederates, by excluding Confederates from office until Congress granted amnesty. The Tenure of Office Act (1867), which was passed despite Presidential veto, prohibited the Chief Executive from removing, without Senate consent, any officer appointed with the Senate's consent. The Supreme Court declined to review the act.

On August 12, 1867, Johnson suspended Secretary of War Edwin M. Stanton, a Radical informer, and appointed General Ulysses S. Grant as temporary secretary. But Grant was also a Radical sympathizer and, in January 1868, he returned his office to Stanton. On February 21, Johnson, formally removing Stanton, made General Lorenzo Thomas Secretary ad interim. Stanton, however, locked himself in his office to prevent Thomas from taking over, and the Senate refused to confirm Thomas' nomination.

A few days later, the House of Representatives voted 128 to 47 to impeach Johnson on 11 counts. A garish extravaganza of 11½ weeks' duration, the trial was presided over by Chief Justice Salmon P. Chase who, although wanting to be President with an intensity that Lincoln had once likened to insanity, proved to be a model of fairness. If the President was convicted, the new President was to be one of the Senate's own, Ben Wade of Ohio, its president pro tempore, who stood first in the line of succession under a law that dated back to 1792.

As the proceedings moved on, the case against Johnson proved thin and revealed that some Senators were more intent upon punishing him than seeing justice done. Fierce pressure was brought to bear on undecided Senators to build up the two-thirds vote required for conviction.

On May 16, the Senate voted on the eleventh charge, the one that Johnson's opponents believed the most likely to pass. As the vote proceeded, it became clear that the outcome would depend on the vote of Senator Edmund G. Ross of Kansas, who said "not guilty" and saved Johnson by a single vote. Votes were taken on only two other articles with identical results, and the trial ended.

In foreign affairs, Johnson and Secretary of State Seward achieved (1867) the purchase of Alaska from Russia and in 1865, by threat of force, they induced Napoleon III to withdraw his troops from Mexico. Maximilian, who was installed (1864) by Napoleon III as Mexico's emperor while the United States was distracted by the Civil War, was overthrown by Juarez.

For all of his travail, Johnson nonetheless aspired to be the Democratic nominee for President in 1868, but the party chose Governor Horatio Seymour of New York.

After leaving the White House, Johnson ran unsuccessfully for Congress in 1869 and 1872. In 1874, however, he was elected to the U.S. Senate, the only former President to become a Senator. Johnson served only in a special short session in March 1875. After returning to Tennessee, he suffered a paralytic stroke and died on July 31, 1875.

Ulysses Simpson Grant

Ulysses Simpson Grant, 18th President (1869–1877), was born on April 27, 1822, in Point Pleasant, Ohio, the eldest son of a farmer and tanner. An excellent horseman but disinclined toward farm work, Grant applied to West Point.

An average student at West Point, Grant impressed his classmates as academically lazy and careless in dress. Graduating in 1843, he served with distinction in the Mexican War and attained the rank of first lieutenant.

After the war, Grant served in western posts and drank excessively, until his commanding officer ordered him either to reform or to resign. In 1854 he did resign and took up farming near St. Louis. Handicapped by poor land, Grant sold the farm in 1859 and became employed in a real estate office, but performed his main duty—collecting rents—poorly. He next worked, briefly, in the U.S. Customhouse, and in 1860 joined his father's hardware store in Galena, Illinois. As a storekeeper, he was unsuccessful, too.

At the outbreak of the Civil War, Grant, now 40 years old and unsettled, drilled a company of volunteers in Galena and then went to Springfield to work for the Illinois adjutant general. His request to the War Department for a colonelcy was ignored; however, in May 1861 the governor of Illinois appointed him colonel of the 21st Illinois Volunteers. By August, he was a brigadier general of volunteers and was given command of southwestern Missouri. An aggressive field commander, he swept through victories in Missouri, Kentucky, and Tennessee. In 1862, he gave

the Union its first major victory when he captured Forts Henry and Donelson. At the latter fort he specified, "No terms other than an unconditional and immediate surrender can be accepted."—This earned him the nickname "Unconditional Surrender Grant."

Grant moved on to larger commands and greater victories at Shiloh, Vicksburg, and Chattanooga. In March 1864, Lincoln made him a lieutenant-general, placed him in command of all the Union armies, and said of Grant that "he makes things git." Grant took personal command of the Army of the Potomac to confront the Confederates under General Robert E. Lee. Relentlessly applying superior manpower and force, Grant wore down the enemy and brought Lee to surrender at Appomattox, April 9, 1865. Generous in victory, Grant permitted the vanquished Confederates to keep their horses "for the spring plowing." Lavishly hailed in the victorious Union, Grant was made a full general in 1866, the first such designation since George Washington.

In 1868, Grant the military hero won the Republican nomination for President and triumphed easily over his Democratic opponent, Governor Horatio Seymour of New York. A newcomer to politics, Grant accepted the nomination in a note the brevity of which was unheard of in for Presidential candidates, but it did contain the apt sentiment, "Let us have peace." Always a man of opinions, Grant declined to ride in the inaugural with the outgoing President, Andrew Johnson, owing to an estrangement that stemmed from Johnson's imbroglio with the War Department.

Unfamiliar and uneasy with politics, Grant conducted business in the executive mansion in a military style. Military aides did much of the work of the administration and Grant, upon issuing orders, expected battle-command compliance. To his misfortune, he did not readily perceive the subtle resistances and manipulations of civilian administrators.

Cabinet appointments, often used by a President to build support within his party, were devoted by Grant to the indulgence of his personal preferences. As Secretary of State he named his close friend Elihu Washburne. His military aide, John A. Rawlins, became Secretary of War. Grant sought to implant in the Treasury his friend, the merchant Alexander T. Stewart, who proved legally ineligible. Grant also made appointments with little regard to actual job fitness and soon had to redesign his Cabinet to recognize both party considerations and competence.

Aided by a distinguished Secretary of State, Hamilton Fish (Washburne's successor), Grant cleared up the serious controversies with Great Britain over the *Alabama* claims (when the United States claimed damages for British-supported Confederate cruisers) and carefully preserved the neutrality of the United States in Spain's suppression of Cuban insurrection. Grant made a bold, but embarrassingly futile, attempt to annex Santo Domingo, and when Charles Sumner, a powerful Republican leader, denounced Grant, he was removed as chairman of the Foreign Relations Committee; this break with Sumner was perhaps Grant's worst disaster in foreign affairs.

The Civil War left a heritage of bonds and other securities that were easy prey to manipulation by speculators. To foil them, Grant approved legislation establishing the policy of ultimate redemption of legal tender notes in coin. But the speculators and gamblers—especially Jim Fisk and Jay Gould—struck back by cornering gold on the market and by "buying" cronies and administrative associates of the President with favors. Grant, to whom defeat and submission were alien, released a flood of gold from the Treasury to overwhelm the corner. The victory was costly, resulting in the "Black Friday" of 1869, when thousands were ruined.

Never vindictive toward the South, Grant declined to enforce the 14th amendment, which had granted Negro rights. His detachment coincided with the beginnings of intimidation in the old Confederacy of Negro voters.

In 1872, Grant was unanimously renominated and won reelection against Horace Greeley, nominee of the Democrats as well as the Liberal Republicans, who were seeking both a more radical Reconstruction policy and a more competent administration.

Grant's second term was dominated by scandals. His private secretary, Orville Babcock, was implicated in the notorious Whisky Ring and suspected of wrongdoing in the Santo Domingo negotiations. Secretary of War William Belknap was revealed to have accepted bribes from a trader at an Indian post. Through the loyalty of Grant, both escaped punishment. Grant himself was criticized for coarse tastes, excessive appetite for material enjoyment, and low associations. He was seen in public with the "robber baron" Jim Fisk and offered the post of Chief Justice to the notorious political boss Roscoe Conkling.

Although Grant is rated as one of the worst Presidents, he nevertheless piloted the country and the Presidency through the difficult aftermath of Andrew Johnson's confrontation with Congress. He also overcame a severe financial crisis and brought Anglo-American relations into a new era of harmony and mutual respect.

In 1880 Grant was the candidate of Roscoe Conkling and the powerful Stalwart faction for the Republican Presidential nomination, but he was defeated on a late ballot by Garfield.

After leaving office, Grant settled in New York City and lost (1884) his savings in a fraudulent banking firm. A merciful Congress appointed him general at full pay and subsequently added retirement pay. While suffering from throat cancer, Grant wrote his memoirs. Published (2 vols., 1885–86) by Mark Twain, they were a remarkable financial success and rank among the great military narratives of history. Grant soon died, on July 23, 1885, but his courage and indomitable spirit in the face of grave illness had restored his family's security.

Rutherford Birchard Hayes

Rutherford Birchard Hayes, 19th President (1877–1881), was born on October 4, 1822, in Delaware, Ohio. His father, a storekeeper from Vermont, died the year he was born. Raised by an uncle, Hayes graduated from Kenyon College (Ohio) as valedictorian. After study at Harvard Law School, he began the practice of law at Lower Sandusky (now Fremont), Ohio, and in 1849 he moved to Cincinnati.

Upon the outbreak of the Civil War, Hayes volunteered and was commissioned a major. Wounded four times, he advanced to the rank of major general. While on the battlefield, he was nominated for the U.S. House of Representatives and elected. A staunch Republican, he supported the Radical postwar reconstruction program and was reelected. However, he resigned from Congress to become governor of Ohio. Reelected twice, he ran on a platform in 1875 calling for "sound money" in opposition to Democratic monetary policy.

Hayes's hard-money position helped win him the Republican Presidential nomination in 1876 over the better-known James G. Blaine. Hayes defeated the Democratic nominee, Samuel J. Tilden, in a fiercely disputed election that threatened the country with civil war. Although Hayes received only a minority of the popular votes, a partisan election commission awarded him the office.

Hayes became President under a cloud of resentment over the dubious legitimacy of his incumbency. So restive was the country's mood that he took the oath of office privately, and the inaugural parade and ball were omitted. His shadowed Presidency coincided with a critical juncture in the nation's affairs. Wise statesmanship was needed to bring the stormy Reconstruction Period to an end.

Despite his electoral handicap, Hayes bravely faced problems and justified the boast of a forebear that "the name of Hayes began by valor." Days after his inauguration, Hayes removed federal troops from the South, thereby ending the period of Reconstruction. Wade, Blaine, and other leading Republicans angrily protested the step which imperiled the Republican "carpetbag" governments. These had made Hayes's election possible and could not exist without military protection. The wisdom of Hayes's policy was demonstrated by the end of violence and by the emergence of normalcy in the South.

Like other Presidents of his era, Hayes grappled with the problem of civil service reform. He offended the Stalwarts, the spoils-minded faction of his party, by declaring that appointments to office must be made on the basis of ability and tenure must be protected. Beginning with Secretary of the Interior Carl Schurz, Hayes's department heads applied these principles widely.

Hayes won admiration from "sound money" advocates for his devotion to the resumption of specie payments. The farmers of the Midwest and city workingmen, beset by the severe economic depression of 1876–77, widely favored soft money—"an irredeemable paper currency," and the "free coinage of silver." The House of Representatives passed bills for both in 1877. In a vigorous message of opposition to Congress, Hayes insisted upon resumption and payment of the public debt in gold. Hayes's action forestalled the Senate from passing a bill to postpone resumption. His veto, however, could not defeat the Bland-Allison bill calling upon the government to coin each month from $2 million to $4 million in silver dollars to be full legal tender.

Despite the business depression and political opposition, Hayes continued to accumulate a gold reserve, and on January 1, 1879, for the first time since the Civil War, the government declared that it would pay out gold, or "specie," in exchange for paper money.

Just as he showed little sympathy for the economically embattled farmer, Hayes was insensitive to the plight of labor in the economic depression. In 1877, with a railroad strike raging in 10 states, Hayes furnished state authorities with arms from national arsenals and, as commander-in-chief, transferred Federal troops from remote posts to the scenes of trouble.

Assertive toward Congress, Hayes vetoed a Chinese exclusion bill because it violated a treaty with China. He fought Congress successfully on "riders" to two appropriation bills. In an uncommon achievement for a President, he brought Congress to remove the riders.

Convinced that a President performed better if he served for only one term, Hayes in accepting the nomination in 1876 expressed his resolve to be a single-term President. Party leaders, dismayed by his bursts of independence, encouraged him to keep that resolve.

Hayes left office with the satisfaction of seeing the resentment over his flawed Presidential victory evaporate. His hard work, efficiency, and tough moral fiber impressed the public. After leaving office, he devoted his final years to education and philanthropy. He died in Fremont, Ohio, on January 17, 1893.

James Abram Garfield

James Abram Garfield, 20th President (March 4, 1881–September 19, 1881), was born on November 19, 1831, in Orange, Ohio, the son of a frontier farmer. Fatherless at two, Garfield became "a self-made man," who supported his widowed mother by working on farms and as a carpenter.

At 18, Garfield began study at Hiram (Ohio) College and later transferred to Williams College, Williamstown, Massachusetts. Graduating in 1856, Garfield returned to Ohio and rose to a professorship of ancient languages and literature at Hiram College and served as president from 1857 to 1861.

With the outbreak of the Civil War, Garfield was commissioned a lieutenant colonel of an Ohio volunteer regiment. Serving at Chickamauga and as chief of staff to General Rosecrans, he rose to the rank of major general. In 1863 when he was elected to the U.S. House of Representatives, Garfield resigned from the army.

Serving for 17 years in the House, Garfield was a regular Republican of antislavery convictions and a firm advocate of Radical reconstruction. He was an influential member of key House committees on finance and military affairs and in 1876 was minority leader. Garfield was also a member of the Electoral Commission created by Congress to decide state contests in the disputed election of 1876.

In the Republican National Convention of 1880, Garfield, a compromise candidate, was nominated for President on the 36th ballot. A "dark horse," he had defeated ex-President Grant, whom the Stalwarts, a party faction, were promoting for a third term. Because Garfield was a member of a rival Republican faction, Chester A. Arthur, a Stalwart, was nominated for Vice-President.

The Stalwarts, headed by Senator Roscoe Conkling of New York, remained unappeased. Upon becoming President, Garfield became embroiled with Conkling in a war over patronage. Garfield sent to the Senate the nominations of men of his own choice for minor posts in the New York Custom House. Conkling felt the step violated pledges given in return for his acceptance of Gar-

field as Presidential nominee and invoked Senatorial courtesy to defeat the nominations.

Garfield's conflict with leading Republican personalities spread to the Post Office, where the "star route" frauds were uncovered. The Post Office scandalously overpaid certain persons operating these mail routes, including the chairman of the Republican National Committee. Despite intimidation, Garfield had prosecutions launched against offenders. He also withdrew all nominations for New York appointments, except for the Custom House, to stress Presidential independence and integrity in the appointive process.

Since Republican control of the Senate was insecure, the Republican caucus chose not to break with the President and supported his New York Custom House appointments. An outraged Conkling resigned from the Senate and invited the New York legislature to vindicate him.

Garfield approved the proposal of his Secretary of State James G. Blaine to call a conference of Latin-American nations to review the Clayton-Bulwer Treaty with Great Britain, entered into in 1850. Garfield and Blaine were eager to advance a proposed isthmian canal and to shake off the treaty's provision that called for Anglo-American control of the waterway.

Before the conference could take place, Garfield was shot on July 2, 1881, by Charles Guiteau, a Stalwart and an office-seeker disappointed by the deadlock over patronage. Garfield lingered on until September 19, 1881, when he died.

Chester Alan Arthur

Chester Alan Arthur, 21st President (1881–1885), was born on October 5, 1830, at Fairfield, Vermont, the son of a Baptist clergyman. Arthur graduated from Union College, Schenectady, in 1848, where he was elected to Phi Beta Kappa. After teaching school in Vermont and serving as school principal in Cohoes, New York, Arthur moved to New York City to study law, and in 1854 was admitted to the bar.

A brilliant lawyer, Arthur won fame in two civil liberties lawsuits. One, a pre-Civil War case, held that a slave brought into New York became free. The other established that Negroes enjoyed the same rights on New York streetcars as whites.

Arthur, a staunch Republican, was rewarded in 1861 with the post of engineer-in-chief of New York State, and in the Civil War, he held further political positions as inspector general of New York troops and quartermaster of New York State. As such he helped organize the New York militia. After the war, in 1871, President Grant appointed him to the well-paid office of collector of the Port of New York, one of the choicest of political plums.

Competent and honest as the collector, Arthur, in the fashion of the day, ran the Custom House as an adjunct of Roscoe Conkling's New York Republican machine. Patronage was openly distributed, clerks freely attended party caucuses and conventions, got out the vote, and slacked on the job. Eventually, Arthur was removed by his fellow Republican, reform-minded President Rutherford Hayes.

At the Republican national convention of 1880, James Garfield was nominated for the Presidency, after the Conkling clique of New York Republicans, the Stalwarts, failed to nominate Grant for a third term. To sweeten the defeat, the convention chose Arthur, a leading Stalwart, for the Vice-Presidency.

Garfield's assassination soon after his inauguration made Arthur President.

Arthur is a classic instance of a man who became a better President than was generally expected. Forebodings of the day saw Arthur running the Presidency as a machine politician and spoilsman, and opening the hospitality of the White House to the Custom House loafers. Many ridiculed Arthur as a "dude" and "Gentleman Boss," owing to his courtly manners and dandified dress. But Arthur proved otherwise. His bearing as President was dignified, honorable, and constructive. His devotion to principle in the manner of his younger days as a civil liberties attorney quickly transformed his image into that of a man well capable of being President.

In addressing himself to the emerging problems of the day, especially the shabby morality of post-Civil War politics, Arthur suffered imposing handicaps; his cabinet was inherited from the rival Garfield faction, and he lacked a working majority in Congress. Matters worsened after the 1882 elections, when the Democrats won control of the House of Representatives.

Nevertheless, Arthur built a commendable record of effort and achievement. When he recommended the Civil Service Reform Act of 1883—the basis of the present-day personnel system—his former friends and colleagues felt betrayed because it drastically limited patronage.

He demonstrated courage and conscience in vetoing a Chinese exclusion bill that violated a treaty with China. Congress, however, overrode his veto. He also vetoed a river and harbor appropriation bill of 1882, contending that it wastefully committed public funds for improper local purposes. Congress again defeated his veto. His several defeats weakened his standing with professional politicians.

Arthur extracted from Congress laws to build a modern navy to replace the obsolete fleet dating back to the Civil War. He worked for tariff reform, and secured a new protective tariff act, with little reform. The Alaska Territory was organized. A treaty of friendship, commerce, and navigation was signed with Korea; a treaty for the construction of a canal with Nicaragua; and an agreement for a coaling and repair station at Pearl Harbor with Hawaii. Although lacking in drama, Arthur's administration was marked by growing prosperity in the country.

Arthur aspired to renomination for the Presidency in 1884, but his candidacy withered at an early stage. Professional politicians, bitter over his support of the civil service law, widely opposed him and reformers failed to support him.

At the end of his Presidential term, he returned to New York City where he resumed his law practice. He died on November 18, 1886, a little more than a year after leaving office, and was buried in Albany, New York.

Grover Cleveland

Grover Cleveland, 22d (1885–1889) and 24th President (1893–1897), was born in Caldwell,

New Jersey, on March 18, 1837. He was the fifth of nine children of a Presbyterian country minister and a relative of Moses Cleaveland, founder of Cleveland, Ohio. While a child, his family moved to Fayetteville and then to Clinton, in upstate New York. His father's death barred Cleveland from a college education. Heading west to seek his fortune, he proceeded no farther than Buffalo, where an uncle secured him a clerkship in a law office. In 1859, at the age of 22, he was admitted to the bar. When the Civil War erupted, Cleveland could not enlist because of the necessity of supporting his mother and sisters, and he borrowed money to hire a conscription substitute.

The industrious Cleveland entered politics as a ward worker for the Democratic party in Buffalo. In 1862, he was elected ward supervisor, and a year later he was appointed assistant district attorney of Erie County. His political career remained uneventful until 1871, when he was elected sheriff of Erie County, and in 1882, he was elected mayor of Buffalo. His efficiency and rigorous honesty ("Public office is public trust," he once said) won him rapid fame. After one year as mayor, he was chosen governor of New York.

In their national convention of 1884, the Democrats nominated Cleveland for President. His Republican opponent was the glamorous James G. Blaine and, in the ensuing campaign, the character of the candidates was viciously assailed. The Democratic party was described by the opposition as the party of "Rum, Romanism, and Rebellion." Offended Catholic voters supported Cleveland, and the "mugwumps," a reform wing of the Republican party, backed him, impressed by his reform record. Winning in a close race, Cleveland became the first Democratic President since the Civil War.

An awaiting question for his Presidency was whether Cleveland could transfer to the larger, more complex arena of national politics the atmosphere of probity and reform he so successfully cultivated in state and local officeholding. He was quickly tested by the new Civil Service Reform Law passed in the twilight of the previous administration. His "mugwump" supporters pressed for civil service reform, but from Cleveland's own party came a long line of Democratic office seekers, hungry for reward after 24 years of exclusion from Presidential patronage.

Pledged to "practical reform," Cleveland gave slow and reserved recognition to partisan demands. Simultaneously, he lent steady support to the new Civil Service Commission and induced Congress to repeal the Tenure of Office Act, a shadow upon the Presidency since 1867. He skillfully preserved Presidential independence in appointments, but his sturdy middle course served to offend both the politicians and the reformers.

Cleveland also championed the cause of tariff reform. Embarrassed by the substantial surplus in the Treasury, and convinced that it was fostered by excessive tariff rates, Cleveland called for tariff revision to diminish what he regarded as improper favoritism to protected industries.

Cleveland was renominated in 1888, and although he won a larger popular vote than his Republican opponent, Benjamin Harrison, the latter mustered a majority of the electoral vote to win the election.

In 1892, Cleveland regained the Presidency, a popular figure in the face of wide disgruntlement over the McKinley Tariff Act of 1890 and its high-rate structure. But the pleasure of victory was quickly displaced by the storms of economic crisis. From the Harrison administration, Cleveland inherited the forces that produced the Panic of 1893; bank failures, bankruptcies, and massive unemployment seized the economy. Cleveland resisted demands for inflation by Western and Southern Democrats and Populists and, instead, chose to combat the crisis through sound money policies and orthodox economic measures. Cleveland won a long, bitter fight only by receiving substantial Republican support, since the Democratic party was characterized by a cleavage between sound money and inflationary factions.

The animosities raised by the fight crippled Cleveland's chances for tariff reform. The Wilson-Gorman bill that finally passed so reflected the views of protectionist Democrats that Cleveland termed the legislation "party perfidy and party dishonor." Unwilling to sign the Wilson bill, Cleveland permitted it to become law without his signature.

Cleveland's sound money policy was beset by sharp declines in Treasury holdings of gold, and he was forced to replenish the reserves through large bond issues arranged with a syndicate of Eastern financiers. His vocal Democratic opponents charged the President with being in alliance with Wall Street.

In the wake of the Panic of 1893, strikes were widespread, and in 1894 striking employees of the Pullman Company and Eugene V. Debs' American Railway Union halted trains across the country. Violence erupted in Chicago, the center of the strike. In a historic intervention, the President declared that the strikers had interfered with the free flow of the mails, and regular army troops were dispatched to Chicago to enforce the laws. Governor J. P. Altgeld of Illinois, who did not want the troops, demanded their recall in vain.

In foreign affairs, Cleveland rejected the imperialist tendencies of recent American policy. He refused to deal with a new government in Hawaii, established by a revolution managed by American residents. Cleveland rejected domestic pressures to intervene in behalf of Cuban insurrectionists and make war with Spain; he ignored a Congressional resolution recognizing Cuba.

Cleveland was assertive in foreign affairs when what he regarded as legitimate American interests were at stake. In Venezuela's boundary dispute with Britain, he gave new precision to the Monroe Doctrine by articulating the hegemony of the United States in the Americas and our specific interest in the boundary dispute.

By the end of Cleveland's term, the "silver" or inflationary Democrats dominated his party and, at the national convention of 1896, they nominated—to Cleveland's great distress—William Jennings Bryan, the silver orator. Cleveland preferred the Republican nominee, William McKinley, and his sound-money policies, but he took no part in the campaign.

After leaving the Presidency, Cleveland lived in Princeton, New Jersey. He lectured at the University, served as a trustee, and in 1904 published *Presidential Problems*, one of the most penetrating books by a former President about the office. He died June 24, 1908, and fittingly, his last words were: "I have tried so hard to do right."

Benjamin Harrison

Benjamin Harrison, 23d President (1889–1893), was born on August 20, 1833, at North Bend, Ohio. Of distinguished ancestry, he was the great-grandson of a signer of the Declaration of Independence, a grandson of President William Henry Harrison, and the son of a congressman. He studied at Miami University (Ohio), graduating in 1852, and was admitted to the bar the following year. In 1854 he moved to Indianapolis, where he practiced law and politics.

During the Civil War Harrison served with distinction on the battlefield and was brevetted brigadier general. A prosperous corporation lawyer in Indianapolis after the war, he was active in Republican politics and held various local and party offices. In 1876 he ran unsuccessfully for governor, but five years later he won a seat in the United States Senate.

His distinguished background, war record, and the importance of Indiana to Republican electoral strategy gained him the Presidential nomination in 1888. He received a majority of the electoral vote, although Grover Cleveland, running for re-election, won a plurality of the popular vote.

In the White House, Harrison and his Secretary of State, James G. Blaine, conducted an assertive foreign policy as the United States moved toward a posture of imperialism. A Pan-American Congress was highly successful. The United States established its claims in Samoa and checked German expansion there. Harrison was less successful, however, in a controversy with Great Britain over the killing of fur seals in the Bering Sea. Aggressive efforts to establish American rights to Mole St. Nicholas in Haiti failed. The Harrison administration also engaged in bitter negotiations with Chile following an attack on American sailors in Valparaiso; the United States demanded an apology and ultimately received it.

One of Harrison's fondest projects was the annexation of Hawaii. In his administration's closing days, he sent a treaty for that purpose to the Senate. His successor, Grover Cleveland, however, withdrew the treaty before the Senate voted.

In domestic affairs, Harrison was torn between the demands of the Civil Service Reform Act of 1883 and the more traditional spoils system. He followed a moderate course that displeased both the reformers and the organization politicians. On balance, his civil service record was statesmanlike. He appointed and retained Theodore Roosevelt as civil service commissioner, and angered the spoilsmen by adding 11,000 civil service positions to the classified list.

In legislation, Harrison was disinclined to oppose policies his party advocated in Congress. Since the party was in the hands of leaders he could not control, his impact upon the laws of the day was minor. Congress passed the McKinley Tariff Act, imposing the highest duties up to that time. Harrison, however, secured the insertion of a reciprocity provision, the act's only popular feature.

Harrison approved the Sherman Silver Purchase Act to help the silver industry. He signed a rivers and harbors act, a giant pork-barrel measure, and an act markedly increasing pension expenditures. He supported a federal elections bill, embodying several reforms, but it failed. Harrison also aided the Sherman Anti-Trust Act, passed to counteract popular feeling that the Republicans were the party of big business. However, this was insufficient to forestall the Democrats from winning control of the House in 1890, which further diminished Harrison's influence on legislation.

Opposed by party leaders and bosses, such as Quay, Platt, and "Czar" Reed, Harrison secured renomination in 1892 only with difficulty. They and other politicians were offended by his limited patronage policy and cold personality. His reserve, a frigid look darting from steel-gray eyes, and his brevity of response wore badly with politicians. Despite his manner, Harrison was a remarkably effective public speaker, bringing one observer to note: "Harrison can make a speech to 10,000 men, and every man of them will go away his friend. Let him meet the same 10,000 men in private, and every one will go away his enemy."

Party apathy, labor hostility to an administration heavily partial to business, and other factors caused Harrison's defeat in his race for reelection in 1892 against Cleveland.

After leaving the Presidency, Harrison continued to gain distinction as a lawyer, and in 1898 he represented Venezuela in her boundary dispute with Great Britain. He died in Indianapolis on March 13, 1901.

William McKinley

William McKinley, 25th President (March 4, 1897–September 14, 1901), was born on January 29, 1843, at Niles, Ohio, the son of an iron-founder. After attending Poland Seminary (Ohio) and Allegheny College (Pennsylvania), McKinley taught school.

Following service in the Union Army in the Civil War, where he rose to the rank of major, McKinley studied at Albany (New York) Law School and was admitted to the bar in 1867; he soon moved to Canton, Ohio, where he began practice.

McKinley began his political career in 1869 by election as prosecuting attorney for Stark County, Ohio. In 1876, he was elected as a Republican to the U.S. House of Representatives, where he remained, except for one term, until 1891. As Congressman, McKinley sponsored the McKinley Tariff Act, which set record-high protective duties, and voted for the Bland-Allison (silver purchase) act.

Defeated for reelection in 1890, McKinley attracted the friendship and support of Mark Hanna, a powerful, wealthy Ohio Republican. Their lasting political partnership helped McKinley win election as governor in 1891 and reelection in 1893.

In 1896, McKinley's popularity and Hanna's shrewd management brought the Republican Presidential nomination to the governor. Pitted against him as the Democratic nominee was the colorful William Jennings Bryan whose free silver doctrines and Populist ties alarmed the business community and alienated many Democratic conservatives. Bryan, a superb orator, made a record number of speaking appearances. McKinley and Hanna, in contrast, perfected the "front porch" campaign; instead of the candidate going to the people, the people came to the candidate. Cooperating railroads gave excursion rates so low that one newspaper said that visiting McKinley was "cheaper than staying home."

McKinley's election was interpreted as a mandate for a high protective tariff and for a gold monetary standard, as opposed to a silver standard. Promptly after his inauguration, McKinley called a special session of Congress to act on the tariff; the Dingley Tariff Act resulted, the high duties of which delighted business. Not until 1900 was a monetary law enacted. It established the gold dollar as the United States standard and strictly limited the coinage of silver.

The monetary law was delayed by the Spanish-American War. When McKinley was inaugurated, Cuba was in revolt against Spain. The United States battleship *Maine* was blown up in Havana harbor, and McKinley was pressed to intervene. He did not want to go to war, nor fight legislators who were demanding war. Ultimately, he referred the problem to Congress, knowing that it favored war; Congress directed the President to intervene in Cuba to establish Cuban independence.

As a war President, McKinley was handicapped by an inadequate war department and army. Disease was more deadly and inefficiency more harassing than the Spanish enemy. Although the navy performed creditably, McKinley was fortunate in facing a weak enemy.

McKinley did not want to annex territory, but as in the coming of the war, his political style prevailed over his political ends. As a politician, he eschewed conflict. His natural kindliness and his background as a tariff negotiator adept at conciliating everyone ruled his approach to foreign affairs. As a public leader, famous for "keeping his ear close to the ground," he was seldom more than a half-step ahead of his constituents. Convinced from a tour of the Midwest that the people favored annexation, he instructed his peace negotiators accordingly. The Philippines, Guam, and Puerto Rico were ceded to the United States. Cuba was placed under American control until it could establish a government of its own. During the war, the Hawaiian Islands were annexed by joint resolution of Congress.

McKinley guided the country through its initial experiences as an imperial nation. A law to govern the new insular possessions was passed. The war department was reorganized. Rebellious Filipinos, seeking independence, were fought, and a commission headed by William Howard Taft was dispatched to the islands to set up the government of the United States there. In 1899 Secretary of State John Hay negotiated the Open Door policy with European nations with interests in China. But the Boxer Rebellion in China soon prompted intervention by many powers, including the United States.

In 1900, McKinley was reelected, upon defeating Bryan, this time to the cry of "a full dinner-pail for four years more." The war had turned the McKinley era into one of booming prosperity, and the election returns showed that the benign McKinley had the support of the people. The electorate also approved the new imperialism.

McKinley was at the crest of popularity and political vindication when he was shot by an anarchist, Leon Czolgosz, on September 6, 1901, at Buffalo, New York. He died on September 14.

McKinley's term, divided between the 19th century and the 20th, aptly symbolizes his contribution as a bridge between the old and the modern Presidency. With him ended the line of Presidents who had fought in the Civil War, and his popularity throughout the country signified that the breach between the North and South had been healed and was no longer a preoccupation of the Chief Executive. Likewise, he presided over the advent of a new era, in which the United States, through war with Spain, first took rank as a world power.

Theodore Roosevelt

Theodore Roosevelt, 26th President (September 14, 1901–March 3, 1909), was born on October 27, 1858, in New York City, the son of a wealthy merchant of Dutch ancestry and of a mother of distinguished Georgian family whose brother served in the Confederate navy. Endowed with great energy, curiosity, and grit, Roosevelt was handicapped by frail health; however, by careful exercise, he built up unusual strength. He traveled widely and was educated by tutors until he entered Harvard (1876). After graduating (1880), he enrolled in Columbia Law School but, legal studies not proving of interest, turned to politics.

In 1881, at the age of 23, Roosevelt, as a Republican, was elected to the New York State Assembly. At first his fellow legislators looked askance at his expensive dress and pronounced sideburns, but his vitality and intelligence won their respect to the point that they elected (1882) him Republican minority leader. His disinclination to follow orders, however, prompted the party bosses to remove him. Roosevelt, nevertheless, remained highly influential in the assembly, working closely with Democratic Governor Grover Cleveland for the advancement of civil service reform.

In 1884, Roosevelt abandoned his political career in remorse over the deaths of his wife and mother, passing the next two years on his ranches in the Dakota Territory. There he developed his skills at riding and hunting and acquired Western flairs. In 1886, he remarried and returned to his home at Sagamore Hill (Oyster Bay) on Long Island. That year he also returned to politics, running unsuccessfully for mayor of New York City against overwhelming Democratic strength.

Roosevelt's speech-making for the Presidential candidacy of Benjamin Harrison was rewarded by Harrison's appointing him (1889) a member of the U.S. Civil Service Commission. Shrewd in cultivating publicity, Roosevelt brought the commission out of the shadows, interested the public in its work, and accomplished remarkable gains against the spoils system. As police commissioner of New York City (1895–97), he again used the power of publicity to restore discipline and stamp out police dishonesty.

In 1897 President William McKinley, for whom Roosevelt had campaigned the year before, appointed him Assistant Secretary of the Navy. Roosevelt worked to strengthen the navy but, when the United States and Spain went to war in 1898, Roosevelt resigned at once and organized the spectacular volunteer cavalry regiment that won fame as the "Rough Riders."

Roosevelt returned from Cuba a military hero and, with the Republican party in New York State besmirched by scandal, his nomination for governor was supported even by Boss Tom Platt, who was personally averse to the reform-minded Roosevelt. Elected, Roosevelt promoted reform legislation and forced through a law taxing the franchises of public service corporations. Large business interests were angered, and "Boss" Platt and other Republican leaders resolved to rid New York of Roosevelt by moving him into the 1900 national election as McKinley's running mate for the Vice-Presidency, presuming that in that office Roosevelt would be harmless and forgotten. Against his own inclinations, the governor accepted.

Ten months after the Republican victory that ensued, McKinley was assassinated, and Roosevelt became President at the early age of 42. Although he kept all members of McKinley's cabinet and said reassuringly that he would continue the late President's policies "absolutely unbroken," Roosevelt's zest and political skill soon broke the confines of this heritage, and business leaders, recalling his state reform policies, quavered.

In his first message to Congress (December 1901), Roosevelt addressed himself to the growing problem of business trusts, proposing not their prohibition, but regulation. His policy was illustrated by the government's suit (1902) against the Northern Securities Company, which J. P. Morgan interests had formed to control major railroads in the West. The company was charged with reducing competition, and the Supreme Court, upholding the government, ordered its dissolution. In all, the administration filed suits against 43 other corporations and achieved triumphs against the tobacco and oil trusts.

Roosevelt was the first President conspicuously friendly to labor. In 1902, facing a widespread anthracite coal strike and lacking express legal authority, Roosevelt nonetheless intervened, urging the disputants to arbitrate. When the miners agreed, but the mine-owners balked, Roosevelt threatened to have the army seize and operate the pits. Eventually a settlement was reached favorable to the miners, to whom public opinion was sympathetic. At Roosevelt's recommendation, Congress established (1903) a Department of Commerce and Labor.

In the foreign policy of his first term, Roosevelt used "the big stick"—the threat of force to advance his purposes. In 1902, he had applied the Monroe Doctrine when German and British naval forces threatened Venezuelan ports, trying to force payments of debts. Roosevelt warned Germany that the United States might use force if any Venezuelan territory was occupied. As a result, Germany withdrew her vessels, and a settlement was negotiated. In 1904, when Santo Domingo was staggering under European debts, the "Roosevelt Corollary" of the Monroe Doctrine was born. Under it, the United States announced that it was prepared to exercise "an international police power" in instances "of wrongdoing or impotence."

While negotiating (1903) to secure a strip of land across Panama—a prelude to the eventual construction of the canal—Roosevelt supported and recognized a revolutionary Panamanian government that signed the necessary treaty, and American troops protected this new government from Colombian rule.

Roosevelt was reelected (1904) by a record popular majority over the Democratic nominee, Judge Alton B. Parker. At the President's initiative, his often reluctant Congress passed a pure food law, a meat inspection law, and the Hepburn law that conferred on the Interstate Commerce Commission the power of railroad rate-making. Roosevelt promoted an aggressive conservation policy, which added enormous acreage to the national forests, and also promoted the reclamation and irrigation of arid lands.

Foreign affairs continued to be demanding during Roosevelt's second term. His mediation and strong personal influence brought the Russo-Japanese War to an end in 1905, an achievement that brought him the Nobel Peace Prize. Roosevelt, however, retained faith in the efficacy and value of a show of force. When relations with Japan deteriorated and possible attack on the Philippines was feared, he dispatched (1908) the fleet to the Far East and around the world. This step prompted several diplomatic agreements with Japan.

Roosevelt was the first President whose administration was continuously involved in major foreign policy, and his Square Deal program of social justice—he called his office "a bully pulpit" —was also the first of its kind. He was extraordinarily skillful at rallying public opinion; however, a contemporary cartoon that depicted him with large clenched teeth, a thick spiked club, and a belt full of pistols also tells much of his style. Audacious and innovative in legislative relations, he began the practice of supplementing his messages with actual drafts of bills, and he was the first of modern Presidents to appeal to public opinion to advance his measures in Congress.

After his election in 1904, Roosevelt declared that "under no circumstances" would he run again for President. He chose his Secretary of War, William Howard Taft, as his successor, and Taft was both nominated and elected.

After leaving office, Roosevelt went big-game hunting in Africa and, when he returned (1910) to the United States, he was approached by disgruntled progressive Republicans who felt that Taft had betrayed them. Failing to bring Taft around to his own progressive ways, Roosevelt broke with his protégé and, in 1912, he ran for a Presidential third term. After winning in Republican primaries, he was denied the nomination in the Taft-controlled convention. Roosevelt and his supporters bolted and formed the Bull Moose party. In the tumultuous campaign, Roosevelt survived an attempted assassination to run second in the three-way race that was easily won by the Democratic candidate: Woodrow Wilson.

In 1913 and 1914, Roosevelt made pioneering explorations in the Brazilian jungle. After the outbreak of World War I, he was an early advocate of preparedness against Germany and critical of Wilson's caution. When America entered the war, Roosevelt wanted to raise and lead an army division, but Wilson refused. Roosevelt opposed American entry into the League of Nations, which he considered an excessive limitation on national sovereignty. He would probably have been a leading contender for the Republican Presidential nomination in 1920 but for his unexpected death on January 6, 1919. He is buried at Sagamore Hill.

William Howard Taft

William Howard Taft, 27th President (1909–1913), was born on September 15, 1857, in Cincinnati. His father, Alphonso Taft, had served as a judge in Ohio, as a cabinet officer under President Grant, and as U.S. minister to Austria and Russia. A huge, studious youth, William graduated (1878) with honors from Yale and (1880) from the Cincinnati Law School.

Admitted to the bar, he promptly moved into public service. He served (1881–82) as assistant prosecuting attorney for Hamilton County, Ohio. In 1882, President Chester Arthur appointed Taft, a Republican, collector of internal revenue for the first district, with headquarters in Cincinnati. Within a year he resigned, because he could not in good conscience discharge competent employees to open up jobs for Republicans.

After a brief return to private law practice, Taft resumed (1885) his public career as assistant solicitor for Hamilton County. He filled out a vacancy on the Superior Court in 1887, and the following year was elected for a five-year term. Except for the Presidency, this was the only office to which he was ever elected. He moved on to national prominence in 1890 when President Benjamin Harrison appointed him U.S. Solicitor General. Two years later, he became a United States Circuit Court judge, and his rulings occasionally displeased labor unions.

In 1900, Taft was thrust into a totally new endeavor—both for himself and for the nation—when President McKinley appointed him chairman of a commission to govern the Philippine Islands, which had been acquired in the Spanish-American War. Designated governor the following year, Taft was a model administrator, building roads and harbors, establishing civil courts, and installing organs of self-government. In 1904, President Theodore Roosevelt appointed Taft Secretary of War. In addition to presiding with marked competence over a complex department, he also became a kind of trouble-shooter, assisting in Roosevelt's Panamanian policies and in negotiations for concluding the Russo-Japanese War.

When Roosevelt declined (1908) to run, he recommended that Taft become his successor. Preferring appointment to the Supreme Court, Taft acquiesced after some hesitation. He easily defeated the Democratic Presidential nominee, William Jennings Bryan. The ponderous, good-humored Taft, cautious in action and conservative in temperament, illustrates the type of public figure who diminishes his exceptional record as administrator and judge in the Presidency.

At a disadvantage by being the heir to the scintillating Roosevelt, Taft suffered in the inevitable comparison. Almost immediately, he was confronted with a profound struggle in the House of Representatives, in which progressive Republicans, led by George Norris of Nebraska, overthrew "Cannonism"—the almost unlimited power wielded by House Speaker "Uncle Joe" Cannon. Taft declined to support the Norris forces, and they, after their victory, declined to cooperate with the President.

Taft had been elected on a platform pledged to revise the tariff. A believer in protection, he felt that somewhat reduced duties would help control the trusts. Summoning Congress into special session to deal with the tariff, he seemed highly restrained in promoting his views on Capitol Hill. Although the House enacted a bill with big tariff reductions, the Senate, led by the devoted protectionist Nelson W. Aldrich of Rhode Island worked to keep duties high. Although the eventual Payne-Aldrich Tariff Act lowered some rates slightly, the general rate level was undisturbed. Taft disapproved of the bill, but he signed it, deeming it the best that could be then secured.

Taft further damaged his standing with progressive Republicans in the dispute between Chief Forester Gifford Pinchot and Secretary of the Interior Richard Ballinger. Pinchot charged that Roosevelt's conservation policies were being desecrated by the Interior Department, which he accused of selling land concessions too cheaply to water and power companies, as well as of illegal transactions in the sale of Alaskan coal lands. Taft backed Ballinger, whose conduct was investigated and upheld by a Congressional committee. Taft then dismissed Pinchot, and angered progressive Republicans moved back toward Theodore Roosevelt.

Despite its political troubles, the Taft administration made solid accomplishments. The 16th Amendment (income tax) and the 17th (direct election of Senators) were added to the Constitution—the first new amendments since the aftermath of the Civil War. At Taft's initiative, Congress enlarged the powers of the Interstate Commerce Commission and created a commerce court, a children's bureau, the Postal Savings system, and a parcel post. The Department of Labor was also established, and Alaska achieved full territorial government. Taft took the first steps toward establishing a federal budget, by requesting his department heads to submit detailed reports of their financial needs.

Although the Theodore Roosevelt administration tends to be identified with an aggressive antitrust policy, Taft well outdid his predecessor. In four years, the Taft administration launched almost twice as many "trust-busting" prosecutions for violations of the Sherman Anti-Trust Act than Roosevelt had in almost eight years.

In foreign affairs, Secretary of State Philander Knox played a large part in promoting "dollar diplomacy," by which trade, finance, and commerce were used to increase America's diplomatic influence. The U.S. government negotiated loans with China, Honduras, Nicaragua, and other countries, as a step toward encouraging private bankers to make additional loans to these nations.

In 1910, Roosevelt returned from a hunting trip to Africa and hustled into the political arena. His speeches advocating a "new nationalism" attracted Republican progressives, while Republican conservatives moved behind Taft to win him renomination. The conservatives, or "Stand-Patters," proved too strong for the progressives, or insurgents, and the President defeated Roosevelt in 1912 by being renominated on the first ballot. Roosevelt and his followers then left the convention and organized the new Progressive, or "Bull Moose," party, with Roosevelt as its Presidential nominee. With the Republican vote so divided, the Democratic nominee, Woodrow Wilson, was elected. Taft received only 8 electoral votes, Roosevelt 88, and Wilson 435.

Upon leaving the Presidency, Taft became a Yale law professor in 1913, and that year he was also elected president of the American Bar Association. In World War I, he was joint chairman of the National War Labor Board. President Harding appointed him (1921) Chief Justice of the United States, which he deemed his greatest public honor. Taft served with distinction until 1930, when declining health forced his retirement. He died on March 8, 1930, and is buried in Arlington National Cemetery.

Woodrow Wilson

Woodrow Wilson, 28th President (1913–1921), was born on December 28, 1856, at Staunton, Virginia. The son of a Presbyterian minister, Thomas Woodrow Wilson (his full name) was reared in an atmosphere of religious piety and respect for scholarship. Wilson entered Davidson College in North Carolina at the age of 17, transferring after a year to Princeton University, from which he was graduated (1879). He studied law at the University of Virginia, but withdrew (1881) from the school because of poor health.

In 1882, Wilson began to practice law in Atlanta; however, after a year of few clients and a discovered distaste for the commercial world, he returned to academic life and studied political science at Johns Hopkins University, where his thesis, *Congressional Government*, earned wide acclaim. After taking his Ph.D., he taught at Bryn Mawr College and Wesleyan University. In 1890, he became professor of jurisprudence and political economy at Princeton University. His reputation as a teacher and scholar having grown steadily, Wilson was named (1902) president of Princeton. Highly innovative as an administrator and tenacious in purpose against the most formidable odds, Wilson reorganized the curriculum, but suffered defeats in attempting to reform the eating clubs and revamp the graduate school.

Wilson's Princeton controversies resulted in his resignation as president, but the attendant publicity cast him as a fighter for democracy against the snobbery of privilege. New Jersey Democratic boss James Smith, Jr., and Colonel George Harvey, a party leader and publisher of *Harper's Weekly*, were both impressed with Wilson's political potential and secured (1910) his nomination for governor of New Jersey.

Once elected, Wilson fought Smith and his conservative organization and pushed through a primary election law, a corrupt practices act, an employer's liability law, an improved education law, and other legislation that suddenly placed New Jersey in the vanguard of progressivism.

Wilson's gubernatorial achievements also won national attention and established him in the confidence of William Jennings Bryan, who, despite three defeats for the Presidency, was still a dominant force in the Democratic party. At the 1912 national convention in Baltimore, Wilson won the Presidential nomination on the 46th ballot. Bryan's support was invaluable, and Wilson proved acceptable to the party's large progressive wing. With Republicans divided between Taft and Theodore Roosevelt, Wilson won the election easily.

His inaugural address (March 4, 1913) sounded progressive themes: "Here muster not the forces of party, but the forces of humanity." He immediately set a swift pace of initiative and activity, calling Congress into special session and addressing the two houses in person, thus breaking a century-long precedent. Wilson moved through Congress an extraordinary body of legislation that comprised his "New Freedom" program. A new tariff law lowered duties and removed them altogether on such commodities as wool, sugar, and iron ore. The Clayton Anti-Trust Act was passed (1914), and the Federal Trade Commission was established (also 1914) to regulate trusts and interstate trade. The Federal Reserve System was created (1913)—in effect, a central banking system empowered to provide a new currency and to facilitate the flow of capital through 12 reserve banks.

Wilson promoted this extraordinary legislative output with a generous investment of his own energies and skills. He worked closely with Democratic legislative leaders and the powerful committee chairmen. Adroit in using patronage, he was indefatigable in employing his own impressive powers of personal persuasion. He encouraged the revival of the long-dormant Congressional caucus as a forum in which his program might be presented to legislators for the purpose of organizing support. His exceptional gifts of articulation rallied attention to his program.

Wilson's early Presidential years were also preoccupied with foreign policy. He made amends for the recently assertive, if not highhanded, policies of the United States toward its Latin-American neighbors, assuring them (Mobile, Alabama, in 1913) that "the United States would never again seek one additional foot of territory by conquest." When the reform government of Francisco Madero in Mexico was overthrown, Wilson declined to recognize the new master, Victoriano Huerta, who had caused Madero's murder. Against raging turmoil within Mexico and intense pressure at home to intervene because of endangered American interests, Wilson nonetheless held to a policy of "watchful waiting" to permit the Mexican people to choose a government for themselves.

In August 1914, foreign policy compounded its demands on Wilson when World War I exploded. The President echoed the dominant sentiment of the nation when he proclaimed its neutrality. He was continuously buffeted in seeking to hold to this policy by the ravages of German submarines, by Britain's close administration of her blockade that often proved detrimental to American shipping interests, and by the solidifying of different segments of domestic opinion toward the belligerents. In 1915, neutrality was severely tested by the heavy loss of American life suffered when a German submarine sank the British passenger vessel *Lusitania*. Secretary of State William Jennings Bryan resigned, deeming Wilson's protest notes to Germany too strong; other Americans considered Wilson too detached and neutral by stating that there was such a thing as being "too proud to fight."

With Democrats promoting the slogan: "He kept us out of war," Wilson won reelection in 1916. However, he had declined to use neutrality as a campaign promise, and the defeat of Wilson's Republican opponent, Charles Evans Hughes, was a close race. Weeks before Wilson's second inauguration, Germany resumed unrestricted submarine warfare against all shipping, including American vessels. On April 2, 1917, Wilson went before Congress to request a declaration of war, averring that "the world must be made safe for democracy."

Wilson was an impressive war leader. Both for the United States and the world, he more than anyone articulated the purposes and the issues of the war. He infused the conflict with moral aspiration and harmonized its goals with his previous progressive domestic program. In a speech (January 8, 1918), he set forth the Fourteen Points that were his framework for a peace settlement. Among other things, he called for "a general association of nations," "open covenants of peace openly arrived at," freedom of the seas,

arms reduction, and independence for various territories and countries. Wilson's guidelines afforded Germany a basis on which to appeal for peace.

Wilson personally headed the American delegation to the peace conference at Paris. Eager to make his Fourteen Points the center of the settlement, he believed that the United States should be represented by its head of government as the other major allies were. In the hard bargaining at the conference table, Wilson, to win acceptance of his plan for the League of Nations, and other of the Fourteen Points, had to make concessions and compromises.

He encountered more difficulty on his return to the United States, where he faced the task of securing Senate approval of the peace treaty and the League of Nations, for not only had Wilson been under criticism for excluding senators in the United States' delegation to the peace conference, but his general political position in the nation had weakened. He had asked for the election of Democrats to Congress in 1918 as a demonstration of popular confidence, but the voters responded by increasing Republican strength.

In the Senate, the peace treaty met fierce resistance from isolationists, such as Senators Hiram W. Johnson, James A. Reed, and William E. Borah as well as from many others, led by Henry Cabot Lodge, who were ready to approve the treaty but with important changes.

Deciding to take his fight for the league to the people, Wilson began (September 4, 1919) an ambitious speaking tour of the Midwest and Far West. Always frail in health, he had been weakened by the recent demands of office, and his doctors had advised against the trip. On September 25, following a speech at Pueblo, Colorado, Wilson collapsed from fatigue and tension aboard his train. The remainder of his tour was abandoned, and he returned to Washington. On October 3, he suffered a paralytic stroke.

The Presidency now sustained its longest and most difficult experience with an invalided Chief Executive. Seldom leaving his bed, Wilson did not call a cabinet meeting for more than six months, until April 13, 1920. The President's second wife, Mrs. Edith Bolling Wilson, not only guided his hand as he signed documents, but selected and digested the matters that were submitted for his personal attention.

From his sickbed, the President waged a losing fight for the peace treaty. The Senate Foreign Relations Committee, led by its chairman Senator Lodge, added 14 reservations, including one that declared the United States undertook no obligation to support the League of Nations. Wilson requested his Senate supporters to vote against the decimated treaty, but his term of office closed without its approval.

Repudiated at home, Wilson nevertheless was honored abroad as the recipient of the Nobel Peace Prize in 1920. He died in Washington on February 3, 1924, and is buried in the National Cathedral.

Warren Gamaliel Harding

Warren Gamaliel Harding, 29th President (1921–1923), was born on November 2, 1865, in Blooming Grove, Ohio; he was the son of a homeopathic doctor and descended from an English family that had landed at Plymouth and migrated (1820) to Ohio. After study at local schools, Harding entered Ohio Central College, when he was only 14 years old and graduated three years later.

Harding moved (1882) with his parents to Marion, Ohio, where he taught briefly in a one-room schoolhouse; he also read law, sold insurance, and eventually turned to journalism. He soon became editor and part owner of the Marion *Star.* As editor, he was drawn into local political life and gained prominence as an orator. He was elected to the Ohio senate in 1900 and to the lieutenant governorship in 1904. He was the unsuccessful Republican candidate for governor in 1910, but five years later he was elected to the U.S. Senate. In Ohio politics, Harding became the close friend of Harry M. Daugherty, an astute political manager who desired to make Harding President, just as Mark Hanna in an earlier day had charted the course to the White House of his fellow Ohioan, William McKinley.

As Senator, Harding was a member of the Foreign Relations Committee and supported approval of the peace treaty of World War I, with reservations "sufficient to safeguard" American interests. Genial and good-looking, Harding enjoyed the fellowship of the Senate, but introduced no important legislation.

His emergence as a dark-horse, compromise nominee for the Presidency in 1920 was the outcome of deliberations by leading Republican Senators and party bosses in what Harry Daugherty called a "smoke-filled room" in Chicago's Blackstone Hotel. Conducting a "front-porch" campaign, Harding took no clear-cut stand on the leading issue: the League of Nations. He attacked it, but at the same time promised support for an "association of nations." He sidestepped domestic issues by promising a restoration of "normalcy." Harding easily defeated the Democratic nominee, James M. Cox.

Few Presidents have come into office facing more difficult tasks than Harding. The Versailles peace treaty was suspended uncertainly in the political air, having failed to win the Senate's approval under President Wilson. Powerful Republican Senators wanted to scrap the league; other legislators, who were eager to avoid future war, sought to salvage it. Substantial unemployment attended the changeover from a wartime to a peacetime economy. Harding approached these problems with a Presidential theory that looked to Congress and the cabinet for leadership; he rejected Wilson's performance as representing an encroachment on the powers of Congress.

Aided by a strong Secretary of State, Charles Evans Hughes, Harding was assertive in foreign affairs. The President moved quickly and energetically to break the impasse on the League of Nations. He made peace treaties with Germany and other enemy powers that omitted the league covenant. Harding's most conspicuous achievement in foreign policy was the Washington Disarmament Conference (1921), which resulted in treaties among the United States, Britain, France, Japan, and Italy that limited naval armament, restricted submarine use, and banned the use of poison gas in warfare.

The Harding era was marked by a surge of isolation; legislation was passed that for the first time placed quotas on immigration, and the Fordney-McCumber tariff act (1922) raised duties to record highs. Remaining aloof from European politics, the administration declined to take part in conferences at Geneva and The Hague. Unofficial American representatives on the Reparations Commission were withdrawn, and American troops stationed on the Rhine were gradually reduced. Harding himself, however, was a non-isolationist, and he repeatedly urged the promotion of peace through international friendship, as well as advocating American participation in the Permanent Court of International Justice at The Hague.

In domestic affairs, Harding largely acquiesced to what cabinet officers, Congress, and assertive group interests put forward for public policy. The excess profits tax was repealed, to the delight of business. The "farm bloc"—legislators of both parties devoted to agricultural interests—put through measures responsive to their needs.

Harding's cabinet included such strong and highly regarded public personalities as Secretary of State Hughes and Secretary of Commerce Herbert Hoover, as well as appointees who brought the administration into deep discredit. In addition, Harding had about him what became known as "the Ohio gang," whom he enjoyed as social companions and favored with responsible appointments.

Corruption set in and spread widely. Harding suffered a drastic shrinkage of political popularity not only because of betrayal by friends, but also due to deepening agricultural depression that brought heavy losses to Republicans in the 1922 Congressional elections, in which the Republican House majority fell from 165 to 15 and the Senate from 24 to 10.

In June 1923, Harding moved to restore his administration to public approval by embarking on a speaking tour through the West and Alaska. En route he received distressing news concerning the Senate investigation of oil leases, or what soon fanned out as the Teapot Dome scandal. Secretary of the Interior Albert B. Fall was subsequently convicted of accepting a bribe for leasing naval oil reserves to private oil interests. Harding's political manager, Attorney General Harry M. Daugherty, was implicated (but not convicted) in malfeasance in the Alien Property Custodian's Office. A friend and aide of Daugherty, Jesse W. Smith, committed suicide following revelations of settlements that Smith had arranged between the justice department and law violators.

In Seattle, Harding developed an illness that was attributed to food poisoning. His tour was suspended in San Francisco, where doctors said he was suffering from pneumonia. After a brief gain, Harding died there on August 2, 1923. There was no autopsy, and the precise cause of his death remains unknown. He was spared the humiliation of experiencing the trials of his two cabinet officials, Fall and Daugherty.

Historians generally rank Harding as one of the weakest of Presidents. But the qualities that made him weak also made him appealing to the bosses in the "smoke-filled room" and to a nation weary of Wilsonian zeal.

Calvin Coolidge

Calvin Coolidge, 30th President (1923–1929), was born John Calvin Coolidge on July 4, 1872, in Plymouth Notch, Vermont. He was the son of John Calvin Coolidge, a farmer and shrewd, experienced politician who served in the Vermont legislature and held local offices. The son was graduated (1895) from Amherst College. He read law with a firm in Northampton, Massachusetts, was admitted (1897) to the bar, and soon opened his own office in Northampton.

In the tradition of the young smalltown lawyer, Coolidge entered politics as a Republican campaign worker in 1896. Three years later, he was elected a member of the Northampton City Council and, over the next five years, served as city solicitor and clerk of county courts. He was elected (1906) to the Massachusetts House of Representatives and reelected (1907).

Remarkable for his taciturnity—the very opposite of the stereotype extrovert politician—Coolidge moved up a career line of city and state politics with electoral invincibility. He was elected (1909) mayor of Northampton and reelected (1910). From 1912 to 1915, he served in the Massachusetts Senate, of which he was president for two terms. He was elected (1915) lieutenant governor and twice reelected. In 1918, he v as elected governor.

In that office, Coolidge became a national figure by his resolute handling of the 1919 Boston police strike, declaring with cryptic force, "There is no right to strike against the public safety by anybody, anywhere, any time." By his firm action of calling in the militia, Coolidge suppressed the strike and won reelection overwhelmingly. The strike also helped boost him into the 1920 Vice-Presidential nomination. The Harding-Coolidge ticket won easily.

Upon Harding's death in 1923, Coolidge became President and the following year was elected to a full term. He commenced his tenure under extraordinarily difficult political circumstances. Scarcely had he declared his intention to carry out policies begun by Harding, when the Teapot Dome and other scandals of the previous administration were exposed. In this test, too, Coolidge was resolute, acting with fearless probity. He eluded the political temptation to shield the Harding administration against scandalous disclosure by bringing about the resignations of Harding's Attorney General, Harry Daugherty, and other important officials. Only three members of the Harding cabinet continued in office throughout the Coolidge administration.

Coolidge continued Harding's policy of responsiveness to the needs and interests of business. Declaring that "the business of America is business," Coolidge promoted a program of what he called "constructive economy." His principal policies were high tariffs, reduced income taxes, lowering the national debt, and strict governmental economy. So devoted was Coolidge to public thrift that he committed the rare political act of vetoing a (World War I) veterans' bonus bill, although Congress overrode him.

Paradoxically, Coolidge's bent for economy in government was enormously popular at a time when society, thanks to a soaring economy, was spendthrift. It was the era of rampant stock market speculation, freely countenanced Prohibition violations, "flaming youth," and the "jazz age." Champion of a rejected code of thrift and propriety, the President was a beloved figure—a reminder of old values that, although discarded, were still respected. In public addresses, Coolidge's pithy, apt expression of the old philosophy was widely appreciated. For example: "Let men

in public office substitute the light that comes from the midnight oil for the limelight."

Distrustful of progressivism and opposed to legislation favoring any interest but business, Coolidge employed the veto in important instances where Congress transgressed his principles. For example, he vetoed legislation authorizing government operation of Muscle Shoals (Tennessee River rapids) for the production of electric power. Agriculture did not share in the booming prosperity, but suffered from falling prices and declining exports. Coolidge nonetheless twice vetoed legislation affording relief for farmers through government purchase of surplus products and sale abroad.

In foreign affairs, Coolidge, aided by Secretary of State Frank B. Kellogg, moved the country away from its isolationist tendencies. The secretary negotiated the Kellogg-Briand Pact, to which many nations subscribed, that sought to outlaw war. Although Coolidge opposed United States membership in the League of Nations, he favored joining the World Court. But when the Senate imposed unacceptable conditions, Coolidge dropped the project. A plan worked out by Vice-President Dawes and an international committee provided a new basis on which Germany might pay her World War I reparations.

Under Coolidge, relations with Mexico improved when Ambassador Dwight Morrow negotiated the settlement of old issues and obtained important concessions for American oil interests. With Japan, however, relations declined following Congress's passage of an immigration law that completely excluded Japanese; the President signed it under protest.

As the expected Republican Presidential nominee in 1928, Coolidge astounded the nation on August 2, 1927, by handing the press a slip of paper on which was written: "I do not choose to run for President in 1928." In his autobiography, he stated his conviction that "the chances of having wise and faithful public service are increased by a change in the Presidential office after a moderate length of time."

After leaving the Presidency, Coolidge returned to Northampton, where he wrote an autobiography and a series of daily newspaper articles that dealt mainly with political and economic topics. He was distressed by the coming of the depression in 1929, and it was reported that he felt he should have used the Presidency more assertively to have prevented it. He died on January 5, 1933.

Herbert Clark Hoover

Herbert Clark Hoover, 31st President (1929–1933) and the first President from west of the Mississippi River, was born in West Branch, Iowa, on August 10, 1874. His father was a farmer and village blacksmith, and the family was strong in the Quaker faith. Orphaned at eight years of age, Hoover was raised by relatives in the West.

After graduation (1895) from Stanford University, Hoover became a successful mining engineer and businessman, with offices in New York, San Francisco, and London. His work took him all over the world and won him a fortune, as well as an international engineering and administrative reputation. In World War I, driven by his Quaker principles, he put aside his business affairs and administered to human suffering as chairman of the American Relief Commission with exceptional success that made him an international public figure.

In 1919, both the Republican and Democratic parties pressed Hoover to become their candidate for President the following year. Hoover clarified the question of his party affiliation by announcing that he was a Republican and that he would not be a candidate. In 1921, President Harding appointed him Secretary of Commerce, a post that Hoover continued in under President Coolidge.

As secretary, Hoover again functioned as a dynamic administrator with wide-ranging concerns. Under his hand, the Department of Commerce dramatically expanded its activities, and he oversaw conferences on foreign trade, industrial production, labor affairs, child welfare, and housing. The new industries of radio communication and aviation also came under his regulation.

When President Coolidge declined to run for reelection in 1928, Hoover easily won the Republican Presidential nomination. In a hard-fought campaign against his Democratic opponent, Governor Alfred E. Smith of New York, Hoover envisaged the day when poverty would be eliminated, and Americans would have "two chickens in every pot and a car in every garage." Impressed with Republican prosperity, voters expected even more of it from Hoover because of his genius for economic success. Elected overwhelmingly, he won 40 of the 48 states, with 444 electoral votes to Smith's 87.

Hoover's inaugural address sounded the notes of optimism. "In no nation," he said, "are the fruits of accomplishment more secure." He moved to help depression-ridden farmers by calling Congress into special session (April 1929) and bringing it to create a Federal Farm Board to encourage the growth of farm cooperatives and to absorb agricultural surpluses. Hoover also proposed an increase of tariff duties on farm imports to protect domestic markets. The resulting Hawley-Smoot Tariff Act not only incorporated Hoover's recommendations, but raised duties on many nonagricultural items. As a result, American foreign trade dropped, a contributing factor to the oncoming depression.

Seven months after Hoover's inaugural, the stock market crashed, and the upheaval of the Great Depression, which had long been building in the Harding-Coolidge era, exploded with devastating fury. Stocks collapsed in value, thousands became unemployed, fortunes evaporated overnight. The depression's root cause, in Hoover's view, was not material or political, but psychological: an erosion of confidence. Consequently, Hoover organized conferences with businessmen and labor leaders to spread reassurance and to secure their help in keeping wages and prices stable and avoiding strikes. The President aimed to improve confidence both by paring back federal expenditure and balancing the budget.

But the depression not only persisted but deepened. Unemployment reached a peak of one-fourth of the labor force. Bank failures rocketed, and mortgage foreclosures became commonplace. Reflecting his political philosophy, Hoover stressed the initiation of public works by states and localities to aid the unemployed. The Federal government, he believed, could help indirectly and, in 1932 at Hoover's request, Congress established the Reconstruction Finance Corporation (RFC), which made loans to banks to save them from bankruptcy and supported state relief programs.

Hoover also promoted conservation and federally administered public works programs to reduce unemployment. Federal flood control and navigation improvement projects were undertaken, and construction of Boulder (now Hoover) Dam on the Colorado River was begun. The Hoover administration substantially increased the acreage of national parks and forests, and it also launched major programs of public buildings and major highway construction.

In June 1932, some 15,000 veterans marched on Washington to pressure Congress into passing a bonus law. Opposing the bonus as financially unsound, Hoover eventually employed troops to drive the veterans out of the capital.

Under Hoover, American foreign policy tended toward forbearance and cooperation. He brought Congress to agree to a moratorium on war debt and reparation payments and also stressed goodwill in relations with Latin America. Following his election, he toured Latin America and as President removed the marines from an extended presence in Nicaragua. Hoover also concluded an agreement with Haiti that looked to the withdrawal of American troops in 1934.

Eager to promote disarmament, Hoover proposed that the principles of the London Naval Treaty of 1930 be extended to reduce land weapons; however, the proposal was declined by other nations. In 1931, when the Japanese invaded Manchuria and the League of Nations condemned Japan as an aggressor, Hoover announced that the United States would not recognize territorial aggrandizement that violated the Kellogg-Briand Pact.

A man whose motto was "Work is life," Hoover put in long hours at his desk and drove his staff hard. "He has the greatest capacity for assimilating and organizing information of any man I ever knew," said his Secretary of State, Henry L. Stimson. Yet a solution to the depression eluded this brilliant administrator. Hoover's critics contended that he overrelied on state, local, and private action, and was handicapped by a philosophical indisposition to exploit federal opportunities and resources.

With the nation still deep in depression, the Republicans dutifully renominated Hoover in 1932; however, his Democratic opponent, Franklin D. Roosevelt, promising a "new deal," defeated him by carrying 42 of the 48 states and by collecting 472 electoral votes to Hoover's 59.

After leaving the Presidency, Hoover was a vigorous critic of Roosevelt's New Deal, and later President Truman named Hoover chairman of the Famine Emergency Commission to report on the needs of many nations suffering from the ravages of World War II. Hoover made a similar study of Germany and Austria. In 1947, Truman appointed Hoover chairman of the Commission on Organization of the Executive Branch of the Government. Better known as "the Hoover Commission," the group proposed important changes in governmental organization and management. A second Hoover Commission was created in 1953. Hoover died on October 20, 1964, at age 90.

Franklin Delano Roosevelt

Franklin Delano Roosevelt, 32d President (March 4, 1933–April 12, 1945), was born on January 30, 1882, at Hyde Park, New York, into a wealthy family which in the 1640s had migrated from Holland to New Amsterdam (later New York City). He was a fifth cousin of Theodore Roosevelt.

After studying at Groton and graduating from Harvard, Franklin extended his studies for another year and entered (1904) Columbia Law School. Admitted to the bar in 1907, Roosevelt evidenced little interest in the practice of law, but he soon discovered a keen taste for politics and won election (1910) as a Democrat to the New York Senate against great odds. As state senator, he demonstrated extraordinary adroitness as a political leader by thwarting party bosses who were bent on boosting a Tammany nominee into the U.S. Senate.

Following his vigorous campaign for Presidential aspirant Woodrow Wilson in 1912, Roosevelt was appointed Assistant Secretary of the Navy. Tammany secured its revenge two years later by helping defeat his quest in a primary for nomination to the U.S. Senate. Roosevelt's full emergence into national prominence was betokened by his nomination for the Vice-Presidency in 1920, with James M. Cox heading the ticket in an unsuccessful race.

Roosevelt returned to private life as vice-president of the Fidelity and Deposit Company of Maryland. A year later, he succumbed to poliomyelitis, which paralyzed him from the waist down. By great courage and effort, Roosevelt in time managed to walk a little by wearing braces on his legs and using crutches. In 1924, he surged back into national politics by nominating Alfred E. Smith for the Presidency, as a thrilled convention watched him master his crippling illness by walking slowly to the podium.

At Smith's insistence, Roosevelt ran (1928) for governor of New York and was barely elected. Reelected in 1930, Roosevelt won acclaim for his broad attack on the Great Depression with measures that were to find their counterparts in his subsequent program as President.

He received the Democratic Presidential nomination in 1932 and became the first nominee to make an acceptance speech at a national convention. Promising a "new deal" to bring the nation out of the depression, he easily defeated his Republican opponent, President Herbert Hoover.

At the moment of Roosevelt's inaugural, the depression was at its worst: breadlines of unemployed, mounting mortgage foreclosures, closed banks, and the widespread, gray despair that the country's complex paralyzing economic forces might never be fathomed and overcome.

Roosevelt created an immediate impression of action and initiative. He declared a "bank holiday," closing down the banks for federal inspection; those in good financial condition were permitted to reopen. The confidence of depositors, which had been shaken by rampant bank failures, was restored. He summoned Congress into special session, and between March 9 and June 16, 1933, the famous "100 Days," more legislation of major impact was passed than ever before.

The New Deal, as these accumulated economic and social measures became known, included relief for the unemployed, aid for farm mortgages, a civilian conservation corps, a Tennessee Valley Authority, a National Industrial Recovery Act, and an Agricultural Adjustment Act under which a price subsidy was provided to farmers who agreed to limit their output. Roosevelt's measures were directed to the unemployed, the farmer, labor, the young, the aged, and the Negro, all of whom suffered most acutely from the depression.

In advancing his program, Roosevelt gave a bravura performance as Presidential leader and politician. In "fireside chats," as his national radio addresses were called, he explained his purposes, actions, and plans. His press conferences were remarkably newsworthy and conducted with a skill and charm that left many reporters warmly disposed toward his administration. As legislative leader, Roosevelt was adept at attracting bipartisan support, at timing his measures well, and at exploiting his political opportunities. To the country, he appeared a confident leader whose easy humor and ready laughter were marks of self-possession in the face of national crisis.

In 1936, Roosevelt was overwhelmingly reelected, defeating the Republican nominee, Governor Alfred M. Landon of Kansas. Roosevelt's political fortunes now went into something of a tailspin, to the delight of his many foes and detractors, who considered him a "traitor to his class." The Supreme Court held such key measures as the National Industrial Recovery Act, the Agricultural Adjustment Act, and other laws unconstitutional. Roosevelt moved in 1937 to "pack the court." Although rebuffed, he did slow the pace of hostile court decisions.

Foreign policy was largely preoccupied with the war clouds gathering over Europe and the Pacific, culminating in Germany's invasion of Poland on September 1, 1939. Although restricted by neutrality legislation, Roosevelt sought to give "all aid short of war" to nations fighting the Axis. The neutrality laws were modified in the directions that Roosevelt urged. Isolationists, who believed the United States should remain uninvolved, attacked Roosevelt as bent upon bringing the United States into the struggle. When he shattered precedent by running for the Presidency for a third time, he was severely attacked and was driven to promise to try to keep the nation out of war. He prevailed over his Republican opponent, Wendell Willkie, but with reduced majorities.

Following France's surrender to Germany in June 1940, Roosevelt undertook bold initiatives to aid embattled Britain. He exchanged old American destroyers for American assumption of leases on several British bases in the Western Hemisphere. He promoted the Lend-Lease Act that authorized the provision of war supplies to any nation fighting the Axis. In a meeting with Winston Churchill in August 1941 on the high seas, the two leaders adopted the Atlantic Charter that attested to the ideals of freedom of the seas, the territorial integrity of nations, peaceful trade, freedom of choice of governmental form. Earlier in a speech on January 6, 1941, Roosevelt had declared that all men are entitled to at least four freedoms: freedom from want, freedom of worship, freedom of speech, and freedom from fear. The two documents provided a foundation of ideals and aims for the war.

With America's deepening commitment to the Allies, relations with Germany, Italy, and Japan deteriorated rapidly. On December 7, 1941, Japan attacked the United States fleet at Pearl Harbor and the nation found itself quickly at war with the Axis. Decisions of the utmost magnitude faced the President. After conferring with Churchill in Washington, for example, Roosevelt chose to concentrate on the defeat of Germany first, after which the full force of war was to be directed against Japan.

As commander-in-chief, Roosevelt was the chief architect of the North African invasion, which commenced on November 7, 1942. This was followed by invasions of Sicily and Italy, and finally the cross-channel, D-Day invasion of Normandy. In the latter enterprise, Roosevelt was under pressure from Joseph Stalin to create a second front quickly to relieve German pressure on the Russians. Stalin wanted the Normandy venture to begin before the President was convinced the Allies were prepared for it. Churchill preferred a thrust up through the Balkans to check the western surge of the Russians. Roosevelt remained the master of the decision.

The President furthered war diplomacy in a 1943 meeting with Churchill at Casablanca, where they agreed to accept only unconditional surrender by the Axis.

With the war at its peak, Roosevelt reluctantly ran (1944) for a fourth Presidential term, and he easily defeated his Republican opponent, Thomas E. Dewey. Roosevelt began his new term in obviously failing health, yet journeyed to Yalta in the Crimea to confer with Churchill and Stalin. The Crimea Declaration, which emerged from the conference, affirmed the principles of the Atlantic Charter and the objectives of the Casablanca conference. Plans for the defeat and occupation of Germany were drawn, and a future meeting at San Francisco was agreed on at which the United Nations would be organized as an enduring international structure. In return for Far East concessions, Russia agreed to enter the war against Japan.

In the weeks following the Yalta meeting, Roosevelt, whose wartime policies had assumed the continued goodwill and cooperation of the Soviet Union, grew restive with doubts over Soviet attitudes.

On April 12, 1945, about a month before Germany surrendered, Roosevelt suddenly died at Warm Springs, Georgia. He was buried at Hyde Park.

As President, Roosevelt employed the resources of his office with boldness and initiative. He delighted to break precedents and embark on new ways. His cabinet appointees were lively and resourceful, and he was given to employing both "Brain Trusters," who were usually academicians fertile in ideas, and wide-ranging White House assistants. Adroit in political controversy, he impressed fellow politicians with his canny sense of timing. Although given to deviousness, he unfailingly projected an air of rectitude. In the age of radio, he excelled at stirring public opinion, and as party leader he solidified the loyalties of such groups as labor and blacks to the Democratic party. These groups, joined with the South, city party organizations, and farmers constituted "the Roosevelt coalition," which endured for decades after its creator's death.

Harry S Truman

Harry S Truman, 33d President (April 12, 1945- January 20, 1953), was born on May 8, 1884, in Lamar, Missouri. The oldest of three children of a farmer and livestock dealer, Truman was raised on a farm near Independence. A voracious reader of military history, he hoped to attend West Point, but was rejected because of unsatisfactory vision. After finishing high school, he worked as a timekeeper for a railroad construction gang, as a mail clerk for a Kansas City newspaper, and as a bookkeeper in Kansas City banks. In World War I, Truman helped recruit a field artillery regiment. He saw action in France, was discharged (1919) as a major, and later rose to colonelcy in the reserves.

After the war, Truman invested in a men's clothing store, in Kansas City, but it failed in the farm depression of 1921. At this bleak moment, Truman turned to politics and secured an introduction to "Big Tom" Pendergast, Democratic boss of Kansas City. Impressed with Truman's political promise, Pendergast supported (1922) Truman's successful campaign for administrator of Jackson County; however, after a two-year term, Truman was defeated for reelection because of factional strife within his party. In his free time, Truman studied law at Kansas City Law School, and in 1926, he was elected presiding judge, serving in that capacity until 1934. Overseeing large projects of public works construction, he earned a reputation for probity and efficiency.

With Pendergast's backing, Truman was elected (1934) to the U.S. Senate. During a decade in the Senate, Truman strongly supported the New Deal, and during World War II he achieved national renown as chairman of the Senate's Special Committee to investigate the National Defense Program. The Truman Committee, as it was known, excelled at uncovering waste and inefficiency in war production.

In 1944, Truman won the Democratic Vice Presidential nomination as a compromise choice in a spirited contest between several contenders. When President Roosevelt suddenly died, Truman became President at a critical moment in the nation's history. Within his first weeks as President, Germany surrendered and the United Nations was launched at the San Francisco conference as a postwar international organization. He met with the British and Soviet leaders at Potsdam, and made the grave decision to employ the atomic bomb against Japan to bring World War II to a quick conclusion.

Truman now had to lead the nation's reconversion from its wartime mobilization to a peacetime footing. In a message to Congress (September 6, 1945), he proposed a sweeping program (the "Fair Deal,") that was an extension of the New Deal. His proposals included an expanded social security system, a higher minimum wage, a permanent fair employment practices commission to protect minority rights, comprehensive housing legislation, government aid for scientific research, and public power projects on the Missouri, Columbia, and Arkansas rivers.

Few of Truman's proposals were enacted. In 1946, the Republicans gained control of both houses of Congress, and the President's program was blocked by a coalition of conservative Republicans and Democrats. His chief success was legislation for public housing that was passed with substantial help from the Senate Republican leader, Robert A. Taft. In 1947, Congress approved Truman's plan to unify the armed forces by creating the U.S. Department of Defense. In that same year, Congress passed the Taft-Hartley Labor Act, a far-ranging measure for regulating labor unions and labor-management relations. In a bitterly worded message, Truman vetoed the act but was overridden by Congress.

In foreign affairs, United States relations with the Soviet Union swiftly deteriorated as the Communists gained control in the nations of Eastern Europe. To check the Communist tide, Truman advanced a doctrine of American aid to nations that resisted either direct or indirect Communist aggression. The Truman Doctrine, as it became known, was prompted by Britain's inability to continue her aid to Greece and Turkey in their struggle against Communist actions, and American aid checked a Communist-supported civil war in Greece and bolstered Turkey's military strength.

In 1947, the Marshall Plan (European Recovery Program) extended the Truman Doctrine to speed the recovery of Western European economies from the devastation resulting from World War II. The Marshall Plan was a combination of European self-help supported by massive American outlays. The Soviet Union was invited to join the plan, but declined.

The continuing decline in American-USSR relations became known as "The Cold War," and the Truman administration's policy of applying counterforce—political, economic, or military—corresponding to the shifts and maneuvers of the Soviet Union was spoken of as the policy of "containment." Congress generously supported the President through appropriations and statutory authority.

While coping with the Cold War, Truman faced sharp political strife at home in the 1948 election. A segment of liberal Democrats formed the Progressive party and nominated Henry A. Wallace for President. Other liberal Democrats sought unsuccessfully to deny Truman the Democratic nomination. Conservative Southern Democrats formed the Dixiecrat party and nominated J. Strom Thurmond. Against mountainous odds and almost miraculously, Truman defeated the Republican nominee, Governor Thomas E. Dewey. Truman relied upon a "whistle-stop" campaign and rousing oratory that was directed at the Republican 80th Congress, which he characterized as "do-nothing" and "the worst in memory."

Foreign affairs dominated Truman's new term. A 1948 Communist coup in Czechoslovakia prompted Western European nations to draw together in their defenses and led to the creation of the North Atlantic Treaty Organization (NATO) under which the United States and other pact nations agreed that an attack on one member would be regarded as an attack on all member nations. An Anglo-American airlift thwarted the Communist blockade of Berlin in 1948.

In his inaugural address, Truman proposed 'a bold new program" by which American technical and production skills could help "underdeveloped" areas. Implementation of the proposal began (1950) when Congress established the Point Four Program. In 1951, Truman initiated a foreign-aid program for Southeast Asian countries threatened by Communism. A Mutual Security program was also instituted to improve military defenses in many countries worldwide.

The Cold War became hot (June 25, 1950), when Communist North Korea invaded South Korea. Truman quickly responded by committing United States forces to South Korea's defense under UN auspices. Commanded by General Douglas MacArthur, UN forces overran most of North Korea, only to have Communist China enter the war. MacArthur proposed to bomb Communist bases in Manchuria, but Truman, who did not wish to extend the war, rejected the plan. When MacArthur publicly criticized the administration, Truman removed him from his command, igniting a furor of debate and criticism.

In domestic affairs, Truman fared little better with the new Democratic Congress than he had with the former Republican one. The Truman administration faced charges of Communist infiltration into the U.S. Department of State that were lodged by Senator Joseph McCarthy of Wisconsin. A House investigating committee made similar accusations about other agencies. As a result, Truman set up a federal loyalty board to deal with the problem, and the justice department launched prosecutions of American Communist leaders. The administration was hobbled by exposures of corruption among subordinates, who were generously defended by the President for reasons of friendship or party necessity.

On March 29, 1952, Truman announced that he would not seek reelection. Nevertheless, he campaigned strenuously for the unsuccessful Democratic nominee, Adlai E. Stevenson. After leaving office, Truman wrote his memoirs, which were published in two volumes, commented occasionally on national issues, and remained interested in the Democratic party. He died on December 26, 1972, and is buried at Independence, Missouri.

Winston Churchill credited President Truman with making "great and valiant decisions." Other admirers of his administration cited his courage and his gift of seeing issues divested of complication and of stating them in plain, blunt terms. His critics felt that his candor and affinity for strong language were undignified. Others considered him a man of the people, and Truman acknowledged these differences of opinion by once saying that he expected to be "cussed and discussed" for years to come.

Dwight David Eisenhower

Dwight David Eisenhower, 34th President (1953–1961), was born in Denison, Texas, on October 14, 1890 as David Dwight Eisenhower. Of Swiss and German ancestry, Eisenhower's parents belonged to the River Brethren religious sect, which was opposed to war and violence. While young, Eisenhower moved to Abilene, Kansas; after graduating from high school, he worked in the local creamery where his father was engineer.

To the disappointment of his parents, Eisenhower entered West Point at the age of 21 and graduated in the 1915 class that included Omar Bradley and James Van Fleet. In World War I, he was commander of a tank training center near Gettysburg, Pennsylvania. His postwar career included service in the Canal Zone; study at the General Staff School at Fort Leavenworth, Kansas, and at the U.S. Army War College. Eisenhower became (1933) an aide of General Douglas MacArthur in the Philippines. Brilliance in field maneuvers won him assignment to the war plans division of the war department, and he became (1942) head of the operations division. At mid-year, Eisenhower was named U.S. commander of the European Theater of Operations.

Eisenhower oversaw the North African invasion (November 1942) and directed the invasions of Sicily and Italy. He was named (1943) supreme commander of the Allied Expeditionary Force (AEF) that was organized for the Normandy invasion. He excelled at bringing proud, independent generals of various nations into working harmony and directing the military operations of an unprecedented scale that achieved (1945) the unconditional surrender of Germany. Made a five-star general (1944) and chief of staff of the U.S. Army (1945), Eisenhower played a leading part in the "unification" of the armed services under the newly established U.S. Department of Defense. He retired (1948) from active duty to become president of Columbia University.

After soundings made by both Democratic and Republican sources, Eisenhower announced (1948) his unavailability as a Presidential candidate. After 30 months he left his Columbia post to serve as NATO commander and to organize the forces of that alliance.

The approaching 1952 elections brought new pressures on Eisenhower to run for the Presidency, and he responded. He retired from the army to campaign successfully for the Republican nomination against Senator Robert A. Taft. Promising to "clean up the mess in Washington" and that "I shall go to Korea" to help end the war, the enormously popular "Ike" Eisenhower easily defeated his Democratic opponent, Adlai E. Stevenson. Eisenhower also helped his party win control of both houses of Congress. Soon after the election, he journeyed to Korea to observe the war first-hand.

From long observation of the Presidency during his military career, Eisenhower considered that the office was administered with excessive informality. As a result, he installed a staff system comparable to the military's and designated Sherman Adams, former governor of New Hampshire, as his chief White House aide. For the first time, the cabinet worked regularly according to a prearranged agenda, records of cabinet proceedings were kept, and each cabinet officer was responsible for monitoring problems and taking initiatives in his area of affairs.

Eisenhower was an apostle of what he termed Modern Republicanism, which, in its most ambitious projection, looked for major policy changes in his party. It called for the strengthening of federal social programs, and the President secured an expanded coverage of the social security system—its largest extension since its beginning under FDR. The minimum wage was also increased. Eisenhower was watchful that new measures did not encroach on state jurisdictions.

The President's domestic program included a 13-year highway building program that was urgently needed, because of a construction backlog that had accumulated during World War II. Eisenhower also succeeded in bringing Congress to modify the traditional rigid price supports of certain staple farm products.

In national security, the Eisenhower administration introduced "the new look" that shifted the emphasis of military expenditure from conventional forces and weapons to atomic weapons, which were regarded as more economical. In for-

eign affairs, an agreement was reached between the United States and Canada for joint development of the St. Lawrence Seaway.

More than most Presidents, Eisenhower faced substantial encroachment (or its threat) on his office and the functioning of the executive branch. Senator John Bricker of Ohio sponsored an amendment to curb the President's power to make treaties and executive agreements. After a strenuous fight, the President and his Secretary of State, John Foster Dulles, defeated the amendment.

Another Republican Senator, Joseph R. McCarthy of Wisconsin, steadily confronted the administration with accusations of subversion and Communist infiltration of the executive branch. Eisenhower, who declined to deal "in terms of personality," refrained from directly attacking McCarthy, a stand that prompted criticism. But when McCarthy charged that the United States Information Agency had Communist books in its European libraries, Eisenhower counseled students in an address at Dartmouth College: "Don't join the bookburners. . . . Don't be afraid to go to the library and read every book."

In foreign affairs, Eisenhower made important gains for peace and guided the Korean war to a close. He advanced (1953) the "Atoms for Peace" program, under which the world nations were to pool atomic energy information and output for peaceful purposes. The proposal led to the creation (1957) of the International Atomic Agency. The President proposed (1955) that the United States and the Soviet Union permit air inspection of each other's military installations, but the USSR declined.

On September 24, 1955, Eisenhower suffered a heart attack, the first of several illnesses with which he was afflicted during his years in office. His good recovery enabled him to run for a second term in 1956, when he again easily defeated Adlai Stevenson.

In his second term, Eisenhower sent (1957) Federal troops to Little Rock, Arkansas, to enforce school desegregation that was being resisted by Governor Orval Faubus. The nation suffered an economic recession in 1957 and 1958, but business improved markedly during the latter half of 1958. Eisenhower lost his chief assistant, Sherman Adams, in 1958, when Congressional investigations revealed that he had accepted gifts from a businessman who was under scrutiny by government agencies. Adams denied any wrongdoing, but resigned his White House post.

Eisenhower's hopes to develop a more peaceful international climate were defeated by repeated difficulties with the Communist world. The Soviet's launching (1957) of Sputnik I—the first manmade satellite—emboldened the Russians. Crisis in the Middle East evoked the "Eisenhower Doctrine," pledging American military aid to any Middle East nation that requested it to repel Communist aggression, and Eisenhower applied (1958) the doctrine to Lebanon. When Chinese Communists shelled Nationalist-held Quemoy island in 1958, the President committed American naval aid to protect Chinese Nationalist convoys.

Eisenhower met (1959) with Soviet Premier Nikita Khrushchev in a summit conference in the United States; however, a further summit conference at Paris (1960) was broken up by Khrushchev, because of an American U-2 reconnaissance aircraft that had been shot down over Russian territory. Following many provocations by Fidel Castro, Eisenhower broke off diplomatic relations with Cuba in 1961.

Eisenhower was the first President to be limited to two terms by the 22d Constitutional Amendment. Retiring to his farm in Gettysburg, Pennsylvania, Eisenhower wrote memoirs of his Presidential years and other books, supported Richard Nixon's Presidential campaigns, and discussed various political questions. He died on March 28, 1969, and is buried at Abilene, Kansas.

John Fitzgerald Kennedy

John Fitzgerald Kennedy, 35th President (January 20, 1961–November 22, 1963) was born into a political family on May 29, 1917, in Brookline, Massachusetts. His paternal grandfather was a state senator and Boston ward boss, and his maternal grandfather was John F. ("Honey Fitz") Fitzgerald—Boston mayor, state senator, and U.S. Representative. Kennedy's father, Joseph P. Kennedy, was a self-made millionaire and ambassador to Great Britain during World War II.

After studies at the London School of Economics and Princeton, Kennedy graduated (1940) from Harvard, where he majored in political science and international relations. His senior thesis, *Why England Slept*, became a best-selling book.

At the outbreak of World War II, Kennedy enlisted in the Navy and served as commander of a PT boat in the South Pacific. In action off the Solomon Islands, a Japanese destroyer sank his boat. Kennedy heroically saved an injured member of his crew. After release from the Navy, Kennedy worked briefly as a reporter for the Hearst newspapers.

The World War II death of his older brother Joe, who had been expected to become the family politician, devolved that function on John Kennedy. He was elected (1946) to the U.S. House of Representatives, defeating eight opponents in the Democratic primary of the Massachusetts 11th district and easily overcoming his Republican opponent. As Congressman, Kennedy voted regularly for Truman's Fair Deal program. Reelected twice, Kennedy became (1952) Senator in an upset defeat of the popular Henry Cabot Lodge. Kennedy underwent (1954–55) operations to correct a spinal injury that he had sustained in the war; while recovering, he wrote *Profiles in Courage*, for which he won the Pulitzer Prize.

In 1956, Kennedy was a strong contender for the Vice-Presidential nomination, losing to Estes Kefauver in a close race. Kennedy was easily reelected (1958) to the Senate. From 1956 onward, however, he was busily preparing to make a Presidential race and eventually won the 1960 Democratic nomination, after scoring several crucial primary victories. In a hard-fought contest with his Republican opponent, Richard M. Nixon, Kennedy—a youthful, handsome, and wealthy figure with an attractive wife and a highly persuasive television style—won the election in the closest race of the century. Vital to his success were his televised debates with Nixon. At the age of 43, Kennedy became the youngest man ever elected President, and he was also the first Roman Catholic to occupy the office.

Kennedy's Presidential campaign had been geared largely to the industrial and urban states. On attaining office, he promoted legislative measures that he had promised to support if elected. Included in his recommendations to Congress were major educational legislation, medical aid for the aged, the creation of a Department of Urban Affairs, and an increase in the minimum wage.

He suffered severe resistance in the House of Representatives, where a conservative coalition of Republicans and Democrats thwarted much of his program. Because of this opposition, he long held back the promotion of major civil rights legislation. He sustained defeats on his farm bill, the urban department, health care for the aged, and education. His chief legislative triumph was the passage (1962) of the Trade Expansion Act, which gave the President broad powers to reduce tariffs to enable the United States to trade freely with the European Common Market.

In a rare step, President Kennedy sought to break the legislative logjam by seeking, with Speaker Sam Rayburn's help, to enlarge the House Rules Committee, at which point much legislation was stopped. The administration's position in the committee became somewhat improved following the fight, but not sufficiently to push key measures through.

Although blocked on Capitol Hill on civil rights legislation, Kennedy was diligent and ingenious in advancing civil rights policies through executive initiatives and actions. The Kennedy administration, with Robert Kennedy as Attorney General, was aggressive in prosecuting violations of the Supreme Court's school desegregation decisions; it directed U.S. marshals, the regular army, and the federalized National Guard to quell (1961) rioting against black and white "freedom riders" in Montgomery, Alabama; it employed the government contract to improve the civil rights standards of private employers; and it demanded that the civil service improve black recruitment and promotion. In televised appeals, the President promoted understanding of civil rights problems.

More than most modern Presidents, Kennedy was preoccupied with crisis, both foreign and domestic. In 1962, certain steel companies raised their prices, after Kennedy had induced labor to scale down its demands to check inflation. Outraged by management's action, the President moved forcefully against the companies involved and denounced them publicly. The companies withdrew the price rises, but the stock market soon underwent its sharpest drop since 1929. Within weeks, Kennedy faced a civil rights crisis in Mississippi, when the governor refused to obey a federal court order requiring that James Meredith, a black, be enrolled at the University. The President dispatched Federal troops and marshals, and Meredith was enrolled.

In foreign affairs, the President seemed never without crisis. Prepared and outfitted under American auspices, Cuban rebels invaded their homeland to overthrow the Communist-backed leader (1961), Fidel Castro. The assault was savagely repulsed, and Kennedy publicly took responsibility for the disaster. Berlin was a constant concern of the President. Aiming to end the Allied participation in control of the city, the Soviet Union and East Germany engaged in a series of maneuvers that culminated in the erection of the Berlin Wall, which sealed off escape from East to West Berlin. The President called up army reserves and dispatched military units to the border until the tense situation eased.

Kennedy faced (1961–62) spreading Communist penetration in Southeast Asia and made substantial commitments of American troops and matériel to the defense of South Vietnam and Thailand. Military advisers were sent to Laos.

Late in 1962, Kennedy became the first President to engage in a confrontation with another nuclear power. The Soviet Union built missile sites in Cuba from which it would have been possible to launch attacks on American cities. Kennedy imposed a blockade or "quarantine," barring the introduction of any offensive missiles to Cuba. The President also made clear that the United States would respond to any nuclear attack from Cuba on a Western Hemisphere nation by retaliating against the Soviet Union. After 14 days of intense deliberations by the President and his counselors and exchanges of messages with Russia, the crisis was resolved by Premier Khrushchev's ordering that the Cuban bases be dismantled and the missiles returned to Russia. In world eyes, Kennedy emerged from this crisis as a well-poised, rational, and resolute leader who had thoroughly excelled his Soviet opponent.

The Kennedy years were an era when young men were in charge of Presidential institutions. In his inaugural address, the President noted that a new generation was coming into power. Himself the first President born in the 20th century, Kennedy filled his chief posts with men in their 30s and early 40s. His administration he described as the "New Frontier." In foreign affairs, its chief innovations were establishment of the Peace Corps and the Latin-American Alliance for Progress and the nuclear test-ban treaty. In domestic affairs, he demonstrated new "vigor" in attacking urban problems. The Kennedy administration was also marked by new attention to American culture. Not since the days of Theodore Roosevelt did so many musicians, artists, writers, and scientists visit the White House.

For all of the power and majesty of his office, Kennedy displayed a remarkable gift for self-depreciation. A master of irony, both keen and gentle, he directed it at himself as well as at others. A capacity for self-criticism helped Kennedy maintain exceptional composure in crisis, to keep his assessments of problems and people in balance, and to question the well-settled responses of the past.

On November 22, 1963, the Kennedy era was suddenly ended in Dallas, Texas, where Lee Harvey Oswald murdered the President. An appalled nation and world mourned his death. He is buried at a simple site in Arlington National Cemetery.

Lyndon Baines Johnson

Lyndon Baines Johnson, 36th President (November 22, 1963–January 20, 1969), was born on a farm near Stonewall, Texas, on August 27, 1908, the son of a state legislator and school teacher. The family moved (1913) to Johnson City, Texas, where young Johnson was educated in the local public schools. He taught (1928) grade school in Cotulla, Texas, and graduated (1930) from South-west Texas State Teachers College. For the next two years, he taught public school in Houston.

Johnson began his political career in 1932 as secretary to a Texas Congressman and attended Georgetown University Law School in Washington. An enthusiastic supporter of the New Deal, Johnson became (1935) state director of the National Youth Administration in Texas. His first attempt at elective office was successful, when voters chose him to fill a vacancy in 1937 in the U.S. House of Representatives, and he was continuously reelected until 1948.

Immediately after the Japanese attack on Pearl Harbor, Johnson became the first member of Congress to go into uniform, entering active service in the U.S. Navy. He rose to lieutenant commander before being called back to Congress.

Johnson was elected (1948) to the U.S. Senate after winning the Democratic primary election by a hairline margin of 87 votes. Proving himself well-endowed with the gifts for legislative leadership and steeped in knowledge of Congressional procedures, Johnson rose rapidly in the Senate. He became (1951) Democratic whip, and he was elected (1953) Democratic leader, serving until 1960. He was reelected (1954) to the Senate and suffered a serious heart attack a year later. As Senate leader, Johnson was moderate in policy, extraordinarily persuasive, and skillful in effecting compromise. He was a top contender for the Democratic Presidential nomination in 1960, but it was won by John F. Kennedy, who chose him to be his Vice-President.

Kennedy's assassination on November 22, 1963, suddenly brought Johnson into the Presidency. Under these tragic circumstances, he quickly administered the office with a skill and self-possession that reassured the nation and the world. He guided through Congress the Civil Rights Act of 1964, a major education bill, a new tax law, and an economic opportunity act that declared "war on poverty."

In the 1964 Presidential elections, Johnson won an overwhelming victory over his Republican opponent, Barry M. Goldwater. Johnson received the largest percentage of popular votes ever accorded a President and perhaps, more important, he won lop-sided Democratic majorities in Congress.

Against this extraordinarily favorable legislative background, Johnson, with shrewd strategy and relentless drive, pushed legislation through Congress in 1965 and 1966 that instituted more innovations in domestic affairs than any other President in any other single session of Congress in this century. The "Great Society" program, as his platform became known, included medical care for the aged under social security, the first comprehensive aid-to-education law, a voting rights bill, a broad housing program, immigration reform, programs for highway beautification and for combating heart disease and cancer, and water and air pollution measures. After the 1966 Congressional elections that resulted in a loss of Democratic strength, the legislative output fell significantly.

The Presidential Succession Constitutional Amendment (25th) was adopted (1967) with Johnson's strong backing, and Congress passed (1968) a strong civil rights bill that included guarantees of open housing.

Crisis flared (1965) in the Dominican Republic, when the President dispatched U.S. marines to thwart a take-over by what he termed "a band of Communist conspirators."

The dominant preoccupation, however, of the Johnson administration was the Vietnamese war, which was already large in scale by the time that Johnson took office. When U.S. warships were alleged to have been attacked (1964) in the Gulf of Tonkin, Johnson ordered a bombing of North Vietnamese PT-boat bases, and Congress expressed approval in a broadly stated resolution. The President increased (1965) the numbers of American fighting men in Vietnam, although he encouraged the North Vietnamese to begin "unconditional negotiations."

In late 1967, additional U.S. troops were committed to the conflict. In the face of heavy Vietcong offensives in 1968 against South Vietnam cities, the President was criticized by "hawks" for restricting bombing in North Vietnam and by "doves" for not ending the bombing altogether. On March 31, the President announced a partial end to the bombing of North Vietnam and simultaneously appointed representatives to negotiate with the North Vietnamese in Paris. On October 31, Johnson ordered a complete halt to the bombing and shelling of North Vietnam.

Johnson pursued policies aiming toward improved relations with Eastern Europe and the Soviet Union, proposed treaties barring military activity in outer space and the proliferation of nations producing nuclear weapons, conducted a summit conference with Soviet Premier Kosygin at Glassboro, New Jersey, in 1967, and sought to prevent and terminate the Arab-Israeli war of 1967. In 1968, North Korea seized the U.S.S. *Pueblo*, precipitating a potentially major crisis that Johnson contained with diplomacy.

In a televised address (March 31, 1968), announcing a partial halt to the bombing of North Vietnam, Johnson also disclosed that he would "not accept the nomination of my party as your President."

Johnson's forte in the Presidency was clearly in the area of legislative relations, toward which his previous career was so strongly directed. "I am a compromiser and a manipulator," he once described himself. His perceptions of the nature of power moved him more to the backstage than to the frontstage of politics. "In every town," he once said, "there's some guy on top of the hill in a big white house who can get things done. I want to get that man on my side." As a public leader, he was handicapped by the unfriendliness toward him of many academics, the press, and American youth. Johnson did not have the great strength in the national party organization that Franklin D. Roosevelt enjoyed, nor did he have the personal organization for party affairs of John F. Kennedy. These deficiencies undoubtedly added to the troubles involved in his possible renomination in 1968. With roots in Populism and the Southwest, Johnson had difficulty winning national acceptance, particularly in the East. He died Jan. 22, 1973 and is buried near Johnson City, Texas.

Richard Milhous Nixon

Richard Milhous Nixon, 37th President (January 20, 1969–August 9, 1974), was born of Quaker parentage in Yorba Linda, California, on January 9, 1913. When he was nine years old, the Nixon family moved to Whittier, California, where his father ran a combination grocery store and gas station. After graduating from Whittier College (1934) and Duke University Law School (1937), he practiced law in Whittier and worked briefly as an attorney for the Office of Price Administration in Washington, D. C. Following United States entry into World War II, he served (1942–46) as a naval officer.

Nixon's political career began in 1946, when a group of California Republicans urged him to run for Congress. He won a hard-fought contest (during which he accused his opponent, a New Deal Democrat, of being soft on Communism) and was reelected in 1948. In the House of Representatives, he contributed importantly to the development of the Marshall Plan and the Taft-Hartley act. He gained national prominence in 1948–49 by pressing an investigation by the House Un-American Activities Committee into charges that Alger Hiss, a former State Department official, had passed government information to Russian agents in the 1930s. In 1950, a federal district court convicted Hiss of perjury.

On the crest of the prominence attained by the Hiss case, Nixon was elected (1950) to the Senate from California. Two years later, Republicans nominated Nixon as the Vice-Presidential running mate of Dwight D. Eisenhower.

In 1960 Nixon was defeated by John F. Kennedy in a close race for the Presidency. The campaign witnessed the first televised debate between Presidential candidates. Turning to authorship, Nixon published (1962) *Six Crises,* a personal account of major interludes in his career. That year he also ran unsuccessfully against incumbent Edmund (Pat) Brown for governor of California.

He entered a crowded field of contestants for the 1968 Republican Presidential nomination, excelled in the primaries, and by forestalling defection of Southern delegates to his rival, Governor Ronald Reagan of California, won a first-ballot nomination. His selection of Governor Spiro T. Agnew of Maryland as a running mate and the firm adherence of Southern delegates, led by Strom Thurmond of South Carolina, to his nomination, prompted discussion that Nixon was pursuing a "Southern strategy."

Projecting a "New Nixon" image, he appealed to the nation's discontent with the Vietnam War and its concern for preserving law and order. In a close race, he defeated Hubert H. Humphrey, who led a divided Democratic party, and George C. Wallace, nominee of the American Independent party.

Nixon was engrossed, during his first term, in the Indo-China war. He sought a negotiated settlement, but despite both private and public talks in Paris, the war continued to drag on. In August, 1972, the American ground combat role ended in Vietnam as the last combat infantry unit was returned to the U.S. To replace the departing forces, the President depended on a policy of "Vietnamization," and American warplanes based throughout Southeast Asia.

To offset criticism that the United States was absorbed in Vietnam to the neglect of other parts of the world, the President visited several West European capitals in 1969, and he became the first President in nearly 25 years to visit a

Communist nation (Romania). His 1972 visits to Russia and China were hailed as historic moments in American diplomacy.

In domestic affairs Nixon was less successful in combating inflation. In August 1971, he instituted price and wage controls. It was the first time such constraints had been applied to the U.S. economy during peacetime, but by the time he left office in 1974, the economy was in a recession.

The President was reelected in 1972 by one of the greatest margins in U.S. history. He was helped by a disorganized Democratic party that was deeply split when old-line party leaders were routed in their effort to block the nomination of Sen. George McGovern of South Dakota.

Allegations of major scandals broke before the election, but apparently had little effect on the outcome. Not until the following year, when the bugging of Democratic headquarters in the Watergate Hotel was fully understood, did public opinion turn sharply downward.

In 1973 peace negotiations in Paris finally bore fruit, at least for the United States. Peace accords were signed in January which called for the end of all fighting and the withdrawal of American and other foreign troops from Vietnam and the rest of Indochina. What the President called "peace with honor" did not bring a halt in the fighting between North and South Vietnam or between Communist insurgents and government forces in Cambodia. U.S. bombing was halted with the peace treaty in Vietnam but continued in Cambodia until August when Nixon halted the bombing under heavy congressional pressure.

For the first time in years, Vietnam and other foreign crises were completely eclipsed by events in Washington. Although the White House initially wrote off the Watergate incident as of no major significance, the combined forces of the press, a Senate investigating committee, and a special prosecutor, eventually forced Nixon to resign in disgrace and left many of his former top assistants accused of obstruction of justice.

Gerald R. Ford

Gerald Rudolph Ford, 38th President (August 9, 1974-January 20, 1977), is unique in American history. He was neither elected president nor vice president, but rather, was first appointed vice president under a new Constitutional amendment, when Vice President Agnew resigned in disgrace, and then became President when Nixon resigned.

Prior to becoming vice president, Ford had spent his entire political career in the U.S. House of Representatives, where he was the respected Republican House Minority Leader. After assuming the Presidency, Ford's popularity was initially very high, but continuing inflation, the pardon of former President Nixon, and the granting of limited amnesty to Vietnam-era draft evaders and deserters, quickly brought this "honeymoon" to an end.

President Ford was born in Omaha, Neb., on July 14, 1913. His mother and father were divorced shortly after his birth, and when his mother remarried, her second husband adopted the future president, renaming Leslie Lynch King, Jr., Gerald R. Ford, Jr.

Ford was raised in Grand Rapids, Mich.; was graduated from the University of Michigan, where he was captain of the football team; and received his law degree from Yale University.

In 1942 he entered the U.S. Navy, serving 47 months and participating for two years in 3d and 5th Fleet Carrier operations with the U.S.S. Monterey. After discharge, in 1946, Ford resumed his law practice briefly in Grand Rapids before being elected, in 1948, to the U.S. House of Representatives, a seat he retained for 25 years, through the election of 1972. In 1963, Ford was appointed by President Lyndon Johnson as a member of the Warren Commission to investigate the assassination of President Kennedy.

From the time of his entry into Congress, Gerald Ford's views tended toward the conservative. He voted against most social welfare legislation, in favor of weakened minimum wage bills, and he opposed forced school busing. He supported, however, key civil rights bills at the time of their final passage.

By 1959, Ford was gaining increasing party support for leadership of the House Republicans. In 1960, he was endorsed by Michigan Republicans as the state's favorite son for the G.O.P. vice-presidential nomination. By 1964, he had gained sufficient support to challenge successfully Rep. Charles R. Halleck for the post of House Minority Leader. Generally content with Ford's noncombative, middle-of-the-road approach to issues in his years as Minority Leader, his contituency continued to return him to Congress with majorities of over 60 per cent.

When, on October 12, 1973, Ford was nominated to succeed Spiro T. Agnew as Vice President, he willingly offered to make public any personal information or documentation asked for, including a full statement of net worth, as a way of removing any stigma attached to the office by the departed Vice President.

Richard M. Nixon resigned as President of the United States on August 9, 1974, and Gerald R. Ford was sworn in as his successor on the same day. Ford immediately moved to assure a stable transition of power, retaining Henry Kissinger as Secretary of State, meeting with foreign envoys to reaffirm the Nixon Administration's foreign policies, and conferring with members of the Cabinet, the National Security Council, and the government's economic advisors.

In 1975 President Ford twice escaped death at the hands of would-be assassins. In May when a U.S. merchant ship, the "Mayaguez", was fired on, boarded and seized by Cambodians, Ford reminded the world of his enormous power by ordering a swift attack by Marines which resulted in the rescue of the ship and its crew.

The nomination of an incumbent president by his own party is traditionally assured, but Ford had to meet a strong challenge from former Governor of California, Ronald Reagan. In August 1976, Ford was nominated on the first ballot as the Republican presidential candidate at the Republican National Convention in Kansas City, Missouri. In the November election, he was defeated by his Democratic opponent, Jimmy Carter.

Jimmy Carter

Jimmy Carter, 39th President (January 20, 1977-January 20, 1981) was born in the small farming town of Plains, Georgia, on October 1, 1924. His father, James Earl Carter, had managed a dry goods store and brokered in peanuts; his mother Lillian, was a registered nurse. The Carter family roots in Georgia go back 150 years for eight generations.

The first member of his family to be graduated from high school, Jimmy Carter attended Georgia Southwestern College and Georgia Institute of Technology prior to his entrance into the U.S. Naval Academy at Annapolis. He graduated 59th in a class of 820 and for six years had a series of assignments which took him from battleships to submarines. In 1952 he was selected by Adm. Hyman G. Rickover to be a part of the Navy's nuclear submarine program. When his father died in 1953, Carter left the Navy and returned to Plains, where he took over the family's peanut warehousing business and built it into a thriving operation.

A deacon in the Plains Baptist Church and member of the local school board, Carter entered politics in 1962. He won a seat in the Georgia Senate that year, but it took a court suit to reverse irregularities that at first gave the primary to his opponent. He easily won a second term in 1964. In his bid for the governorship in 1966, he was third in a six-man primary contest. Encouraged by his showing, he campaigned again in 1970, winning the primary nomination and the election by a comfortable margin.

As governor, Carter reorganized that state's government, consolidating agencies and introducing a system of zero-based budgeting. He extended state hospital services and was a strong advocate of environmental protection. His stand on equal rights for "the poor, rural, black or not influential" brought Carter his first nationwide attention.

Barred by state law from a second term as governor, he announced in December 1974, one month before the end of his term, that he would run for President. For over a year, almost unnoticed by the press, Jimmy Carter was on the road. A good showing in the Iowa caucus in mid-January brought media attention; and his win in the New Hampshire primary launched a series of victories which eliminated the opposition and earned him the nomination on the first ballot at the Democratic convention. Carter won the close election against President Gerald Ford by holding together enough of the basic old Democratic coalition, namely labor, blacks and liberals.

One of Carter's first acts as President was to grant a pardon to almost all Vietnam draft evaders. A reorganization of the complex structure of departments and agencies was begun, and a new, Cabinet-level Department of Energy was created. A separate Department of Education was spun off from the Department of Health, Education and Welfare which has been renamed the Department of Health and Human Services.

Carter's program on energy was designed largely to reduce America's dependency on foreign oil. The President asked for a limit on imported oil, gradual price decontrol of domestically produced oil, and development of alternative sources of energy. He requested a tax on "gas guzzlers" and incentives for the purchase of small cars. Increases in coal production, greater use of solar energy and effective insulation were other key elements in the package. After long delays, significant portions of Carter's energy program were passed by Congress. Missing from the bills passed were penalties on heavy energy consumption.

In the area of foreign affairs, the effect of President Carter's policies and methods was immediate. Carter set his own course, giving a moral content to American foreign policy that had been missing in earlier years. He won respect in some quarters for concluding treaties that would turn the Panama Canal over to Panama by the year 2000 and for the restraint shown in coping with troubles in Iran, Afghanistan and Nicaragua. Carter strengthened ties between the United States and the Communist government of China, and after a lapse of almost 30 years, full diplomatic relations between the two nations were resumed in 1979.

The President's forthright championing of human rights and his outspoken defense of Soviet dissidents caused an immediate negative reaction in Moscow. Relations became increasingly strained by Western suspicions concerning a Soviet arms buildup and moves by Moscow in Africa. In spite of these differences, Carter and Soviet President Brezhnev negotiated to limit the nuclear arms race. Long, arduous sessions of the Strategic Arms Limitations Talks (SALT II) produced an agreement signed on June 15, 1979. The treaty got a mixed reaction in the U.S. Senate and it eventually was placed in limbo when the Soviets invaded Afghanistan.

In defense matters, Carter served notice on the Pentagon that he was in charge. He scrapped the B-1 bomber program, used his veto to block construction of a new nuclear aircraft carrier, and deferred production of the neutron bomb, although he reserved the option to produce it later. The President approved the development of the MX mobile ICBM in June 1979.

In the Middle East, the Carter Administration gained much in bringing Israel and Egypt to the 1978 Camp David peace negotiations. Some of the bloom came off Carter's Middle East success with the seizure of the American hostages in Tehran in November 1979 and the Soviet takeover of Afghanistan two months later. Carter called for a boycott of the Moscow Olympics and a cutback of exports to the USSR, thus cooling off U.S.-Soviet relations, but neither diplomatic pressure nor an aborted military rescue mission could free the U.S. hostages.

The events of late 1979 were working against Carter's chances of securing a second term. Part of the erosion of Carter's popularity came from the nation's sagging economy. Inflation was running in double-digit figures, interest rates were at an all-time high and the predictions were for a long-term recession. However, the President was able to defeat his Democratic challenger, Senator Edward Kennedy, in the primaries and win renomination.

In the three-man contest in November, Carter was overwhelmingly defeated by his Republican opponent, former Governor Ronald Reagan. The entry of John Anderson as an independent did not affect the outcome.

Ronald Wilson Reagan

Ronald Wilson Reagan, 40th President (January 20, 1981-   ), was born in the small, north-western Illinois town of Tampico on February 6, 1911, and spent the period from his ninth to his 21st years in nearby Dixon. The area was a white Protestant, Republican stronghold in which his father, John Edward Reagan, eked out a living as an Irish Catholic Democrat who worked intermittently as a shoe salesman and who, during the Great Depression, held positions administering federal welfare programs at the local level. His wife, Nelle, is remembered as a strong woman who held the family unit intact despite five moves in 14 years, her operative Scottish Protestant credo being "God will pro-vide"; Reagan's older brother, Neil, remembers, "you could draw a pretty close parallel with Huck Finn and Tom Sawyer. We never had a worry in the world that I can remember."

After graduation from high school, where extracurricular activities included football, act-ing and a stint as a lifeguard, Reagan attended nearby Eureka College, graduating in 1932 with a bachelor's degree in economics and sociology. Settling on show business as a career, he worked as a sportscaster for radio stations in Davenport and Des Moines, Iowa, until 1937, when on a vacation trip to Hollywood he made a successful screen test for Warner Brothers. His ensuing film career encompassed 50 movies in a quarter-century span that was interrupted during World War II by three years' service in the Army Air Force in California, where he worked on train-ing films. His commercial feature film credits include King's Row, Dark Victory and Knute Rockne—All American. In 1940 he married actress Jane Wyman.

After the War, Reagan, then a Democrat, was active in liberal causes and served six one-year terms as chairman of the Motion Picture In-dustry Council. An outspoken anti-Communist, he testified as a friendly witness, along with Robert Taylor and other actors, in the con-troversial House Un-American Activities Com-mittee hearings. In 1952 he married actress Nancy Davis, his first marriage having ended in divorce four years earlier.

In the 1950s, Reagan's political philosophy became increasingly conservative; in his auto-biography, Where's the Rest of Me?, he credits actor George Murphy as being at this time key influence on his political thinking. Reagan began a television career in 1954 as host and an oc-casional performer on General Electric Theater, also becoming a spokesman for the company and, increasingly, for a variety of conservative viewpoints. From 1962 to 1965 he served as host for the TV series, Death Valley Days; the series' theme of rugged but decent individualists vic-toriously pursuing manifest destiny along the western frontier was perfectly attuned to the philosophy and image he was then developing.

During the 1960s, Reagan became ever more active in politics, joining the Republican party in 1962 and two years later delivering a notable speech in support of GOP presidential candidate Barry Goldwater. "We can," he said, "preserve for our children this, the last best hope of man on earth, or we can sentence them to take the first step into a thousand years of darkness."

Encouraged by California businessmen, Reagan launched his own political career by running for governor of California in 1966. He defeated the incumbent Edmund B. ("Pat") Brown by a margin of nearly one million votes. After being reelected in 1970, Reagan chose not to run for a third term. In an era of unusual political ferment and polarization, and faced with an unfriendly Democratic legislature, Reagan as governor achieved limited success in implementing his conservative ideas on tax and spending cuts, welfare reform and higher educa-tion. The California budget increased from $4.6 billion to $10.2 billion, but by the time Reagan left office there was a large surplus. Higher education funding was cut in the earlier years, but after the student protest movement had sub-sided, funding for the state university system was doubled. Reagan did achieve reductions of welfare case loads.

After his eight years as California governor, Reagan continued espousing his political views via a nationally syndicated radio commentary program, a newspaper column and an extensive speaking schedule that brought him into contact with many civic, business and political groups. In 1968 he made an unsuccessful, eleventh-hour attempt for the GOP presidential nomination. In November 1975 Reagan announced his can-didacy for the 1976 GOP presidential nomina-tion; his forceful attacks on détente with the Soviets and on excessive federal spending and regulation reaped impressive wins in the pri-maries, but he lost on the first ballot by a squeaky-thin, 1,181-1,070 margin to incumbent President Gerald R. Ford. Four years later, widespread impatience with persistent inflation and with President Jimmy Carter's handling of the Iranian hostage situation helped set the stage for Reagan's resounding victories at the GOP presidential nominating convention and later at the polls.

Reagan's presidency had hardly begun when an unsuccessful assassination attempt occurred on March 30, 1981; Reagan suffered a bullet wound in the chest from which he made a quick recovery.

After eight months in office, the Reagan Ad-ministration has shown a tough posture in its relations with the Soviet Union and toward potential Communist expansion in Central America. The less-than smooth-running Reagan team had to learn quickly to deal with the realities of the Middle East political tangles and to sort out the pluses and minuses of new nuclear and conventional weapons systems for an expanded military. On the domestic side, Reagan has demonstrated impressive political skills in getting his economic program of budget and tax cuts through Congress. In the first test of will involving labor, the Reagan Administration appears to have won a critical battle against striking air traffic controllers.

MINORITY PRESIDENTS

SOURCE: U.S. Library of Congress and other sources

Under the Electoral College System, 15 Presidents have been elected who did not receive a majority of the popular votes cast. Three of them—John Quincy Adams, Rutherford B. Hayes, and Benjamin Harrison—actually trailed their opponents in the popular vote. The table shows the percentage of the popular vote received by the candidates.

Year	Elected		Opponents	
1824	Adams 30.54	Jackson 43.13	Clay 13.24	Crawford 13.09
1844	Polk 49.56	Clay 48.13	Birney 2.30	—
1848	Taylor 47.35	Cass 42.52	Van Buren 10.13	—
1856	Buchanan 45.63	Frémont 33.27	Fillmore 21.08	Smith .01
1860	Lincoln 39.79	Douglas 29.40	Breckinridge 18.20	Bell 12.60
1876	Hayes 48.04	Tilden 50.99	Cooper .97	—
1880	Garfield 48.32	Hancock 48.21	Weaver 3.35	Others .12
1884	Cleveland 48.53	Blaine 48.24	Butler 1.74	St. John 1.49
1888	Harrison 47.86	Cleveland 48.66	Fisk 2.19	Streeter 1.29
1892	Cleveland 46.04	Harrison 43.01	Weaver 8.53	Others 2.42
1912	Wilson 41.85	Roosevelt 27.42	Taft 23.15	Others 7.58
1916	Wilson 49.26	Hughes 46.12	Benson 3.16	Others 1.46
1948	Truman 49.51	Dewey 45.13	Thurmond 2.40	H. Wallace 2.38
1960	Kennedy 49.71	Nixon 49.55	Unpledged .92	Others .27
1968	Nixon 43.16	Humphrey 42.73	G. Wallace 13.63	Others .48

UNCOMPLETED TERMS OF PRESIDENTS AND VICE-PRESIDENTS

President	Term	Succeeded by
William H. Harrison	Mar. 4, 1841—Apr. 4, 1841	John Tyler
Zachary Taylor	Mar. 5, 1849—July 9, 1850	Millard Fillmore
Abraham Lincoln	Mar. 4, 1865—Apr. 15, 1865 (2d term)	Andrew Johnson
James A. Garfield	Mar. 4, 1881—Sept. 19, 1881	Chester A. Arthur
William McKinley	Mar. 4, 1901—Sept. 14, 1901 (2d term)	Theodore Roosevelt
Warren G. Harding	Mar. 4, 1921—Aug. 2, 1923	Calvin Coolidge
Franklin D. Roosevelt	Jan. 20, 1945—Apr. 12, 1945 (4th term)	Harry S Truman
John F. Kennedy	Jan. 20, 1961—Nov. 22, 1963	Lyndon B. Johnson
Richard M. Nixon	Jan. 20, 1973—Aug. 9, 1974 (2d term)	Gerald R. Ford

Vice-President	Term	Vice-President	Term
George Clinton	Mar. 4, 1809—Apr. 20, 1812 (2d term)	Thomas A. Hendricks	Mar. 4, 1885—Nov. 25, 1885
Elbridge Gerry	Mar. 4, 1813—Nov. 23, 1814	Garret A. Hobart	Mar. 4, 1897—Nov. 21, 1899
John C. Calhoun[1]	Mar. 4, 1829—Dec. 28, 1832	James S. Sherman	Mar. 4, 1909—Oct. 30, 1912
William R. King	Mar. 4, 1853—Apr. 18, 1853	Spiro T. Agnew[2]	Jan. 20, 1973—Oct. 10, 1973
Henry Wilson	Mar. 4, 1873—Nov. 22, 1875		

[1] Calhoun resigned to become a U.S. Senator. [2] Agnew resigned after pleading "no contest" to a charge of income tax evasion. He was succeeded by Gerald R. Ford, the first man to succeed to the office.

LINCOLN'S GETTYSBURG ADDRESS

Four score and seven years ago our fathers brought forth on this continent, a new nation, conceived in Liberty, and dedicated to the proposition that all men are created equal.

Now we are engaged in a great civil war, testing whether that nation, or any nation so conceived and so dedicated, can long endure. We are met on a great battle-field of that war. We have come to dedicate a portion of that field, as a final resting place for those who here gave their lives that that nation might live. It is altogether fitting and proper that we should do this.

But, in a larger sense, we can not dedicate—we can not consecrate—we can not hallow—this ground. The brave men, living and dead, who struggled here, have consecrated it, far above our poor power to add or detract. The world will little note, nor long remember what we say here, but it can never forget what they did here. It is for us the living, rather, to be dedicated here to the unfinished work which they who fought here have thus far so nobly advanced. It is rather for us to be here dedicated to the great task remaining before us—that from these honored dead we take increased devotion to that cause for which they gave the last full measure of devotion—that we here highly resolve that these dead shall not have died in vain—that this nation, under God, shall have a new birth of freedom—and that government of the people, by the people, for the people, shall not perish from the earth.

U.S. PRESIDENTIAL INDEX

(F) = Federal Party; (D-R) = Democratic-Republican Party; (W) = Whig Party; (D) = Democratic Party; (R) = Republican Party.

President and Political Party	Place and Date of Birth	Parents	Ancestry	Religious Affiliation
1. George Washington (favored F)	Westmoreland Co., Va.; Feb. 22, 1732	Augustine and Mary (Ball) Washington	English	Episcopalian
2. John Adams (F)	Braintree, Mass.; Oct. 19, 1735	John and Susanna (Boylston) Adams	English	Unitarian
3. Thomas Jefferson (D-R)	Goochland Co., Va.; Apr. 13, 1743	Peter and Jane (Randolph) Jefferson	Welsh	No formal affiliation
4. James Madison (D-R)	Port Conway, Va.; Mar. 16, 1751	James and Eleanor (Conway) Madison	English	Episcopalian
5. James Monroe (D-R)	Westmoreland Co., Va.; Apr. 28, 1758	Spence and Elizabeth (Jones) Monroe	Scottish, Welsh	Episcopalian
6. John Quincy Adams (D-R)	Braintree, Mass.; July 11, 1767	John and Abigail (Smith) Adams	English	Unitarian
7. Andrew Jackson (D)	Waxhaw, S.C.; Mar. 15, 1767	Andrew and Elizabeth (Hutchinson) Jackson	Scots-Irish	Presbyterian
8. Martin Van Buren (D)	Kinderhook, N.Y.; Dec. 5, 1782	Abraham and Maria (Hoes) Van Buren	Dutch	Dutch Reformed
9. William H. Harrison (W)	Charles City Co., Va.; Feb. 9, 1773	Benjamin and Elizabeth (Bassett) Harrison	English	Episcopalian
10. John Tyler (W)	Charles City Co., Va.; Mar 29, 1790	John and Mary (Armistead) Tyler	English	Episcopalian
11. James Knox Polk (D)	Mecklenburg Co., N.C.; Nov. 2, 1795	Samuel and Jane (Knox) Polk	Scots-Irish	Presbyterian
12. Zachary Taylor (W)	Orange Co., Va.; Nov. 24, 1784	Richard and Sarah (Strother) Taylor	English	Episcopalian
13. Millard Fillmore (W)	Locke, N.Y.; Jan. 7, 1800	Nathaniel and Phoebe (Millard) Fillmore	English	Unitarian
14. Franklin Pierce (D)	Hillsboro, N.H.; Nov. 23, 1804	Benjamin and Anna (Kendrick) Pierce	English	Episcopalian
15. James Buchanan (D)	Cove Gap, Pa.; Apr. 23, 1791	James and Elizabeth (Speer) Buchanan	Scots-Irish	Presbyterian
16. Abraham Lincoln (R)	Hardin Co., Ky.; Feb. 12, 1809	Thomas and Nancy (Hanks) Lincoln	English	No formal affiliation
17. Andrew Johnson (D)	Raleigh, N.C.; Dec. 29, 1808	Jacob and Mary (McDonough) Johnson	Scottish, Irish, English	No formal affiliation
18. Ulysses Simpson Grant (R)	Point Pleasant, Ohio; Apr. 27, 1822	Jesse and Hannah (Simpson) Grant	Scottish, English	Methodist
19. Rutherford B. Hayes (R)	Delaware, Ohio; Oct. 4, 1822	Rutherford and Sophia (Birchard) Hayes	English, Scottish	No formal affiliation
20. James Abram Garfield (R)	Orange, Ohio; Nov. 19, 1831	Abram and Eliza (Ballou) Garfield	English, French, Huguenot	Disciples of Christ
21. Chester Alan Arthur (R)	Fairfield, Vt.; Oct. 5, 1830	William and Malvina (Stone) Arthur	Scots-Irish, English	Episcopalian
22., 24. Grover Cleveland (D)	Caldwell, N.J.; Mar. 18, 1837	Richard and Ann (Neal) Cleveland	English, Scots-Irish	Presbyterian
23. Benjamin Harrison (R)	North Bend, Ohio; Aug. 20, 1833	John and Elizabeth (Irwin) Harrison	English	Presbyterian
25. William McKinley (R)	Niles, Ohio; Jan. 29, 1843	William and Nancy (Allison) McKinley	Scots-Irish, English	Methodist
26. Theodore Roosevelt (R)	New York, N.Y.; Oct. 27, 1858	Theodore and Martha (Bulloch) Roosevelt	Dutch, Scottish, English, Huguenot	Dutch Reformed
27. William Howard Taft (R)	Cincinnati, Ohio; Sept. 15, 1857	Alphonso and Louise (Torrey) Taft	English, Scots-Irish	Unitarian
28. Woodrow Wilson (D)	Staunton, Va.; Dec. 28, 1856	Joseph and Jessie (Woodrow) Wilson	Scots-Irish, Scottish	Presbyterian
29. Warren G. Harding (R)	Blooming Grove, Ohio; Nov. 2, 1865	George and Phoebe (Dickerson) Harding	English, Scots-Irish	Baptist
30. Calvin Coolidge (R)	Plymouth Notch, Vt.; July 4, 1872	John and Victoria (Moor) Coolidge	English	Congregationalist
31. Herbert Clark Hoover (R)	West Branch, Iowa; Aug. 10, 1874	Jesse and Huldah (Minthorn) Hoover	Swiss-German, English	Quaker
32. Franklin D. Roosevelt (D)	Hyde Park, N.Y.; Jan. 30, 1882	James and Sara (Delano) Roosevelt	Dutch, Huguenot, English	Episcopalian
33. Harry S Truman (D)	Lamar, Mo.; May 8, 1884	John and Martha (Young) Truman	English, Scots-Irish	Baptist
34. Dwight D. Eisenhower (R)	Denison, Tex.; Oct. 14, 1890	David and Ida (Stover) Eisenhower	Swiss-German	Presbyterian
35. John F. Kennedy (D)	Brookline, Mass.; May 29, 1917	Joseph and Rose (Fitzgerald) Kennedy	Irish	Roman Catholic
36. Lyndon Baines Johnson (D)	Near Stonewall, Tex.; Aug. 27, 1908	Samuel and Rebekah (Baines) Johnson	English	Disciples of Christ
37. Richard Milhous Nixon (R)	Yorba Linda, Calif.; Jan. 9, 1913	Frank and Hannah (Milhous) Nixon	English, Scots-Irish	Quaker
38. Gerald R. Ford (R)	Omaha, Neb.; July 14, 1913	Gerald R. and Dorothy (Gardner) Ford	English	Episcopalian
39. Jimmy Carter (D)	Plains, Ga.; Oct. 1, 1924	James Earl and Lillian (Gordy) Carter	English	Baptist
40. Ronald W. Reagan (R)	Tampico, Ill.; Feb. 6, 1911	John and Nelle (Wilson) Reagan	Irish, Scottish, English	Disciples of Christ

Occupation Prior to Politics	Elected From	Age at Inauguration	Date of Death and Place of Burial	Presidential Terms	Vice-President
Surveyor, Soldier, Planter	Virginia	57	Dec. 14, 1799; "Mount Vernon," Va.	Apr. 30, 1789–Mar. 3, 1793 Mar. 4, 1793–Mar. 3, 1797	John Adams John Adams
Teacher, Lawyer	Massachusetts	61	July 4, 1826; Quincy, Mass.	Mar. 4, 1797–Mar. 3, 1801	Thomas Jefferson
Planter, Lawyer	Virginia	57	July 4, 1826; "Monticello," Va.	Mar. 4, 1801–Mar. 3, 1805 Mar. 4, 1805–Mar. 3, 1809	Aaron Burr George Clinton
Planter	Virginia	57	June 28, 1836; "Montpelier," Va.	Mar. 4, 1809–Mar. 3, 1813 Mar. 4, 1813–Mar. 3, 1817	George Clinton Elbridge Gerry
Lawyer	Virginia	58	July 4, 1831; Richmond, Va.	Mar. 4, 1817–Mar. 3, 1821 Mar. 4, 1821–Mar. 3, 1825	Daniel Tompkins Daniel Tompkins
Lawyer	Massachusetts	57	Feb. 23, 1848; Quincy, Mass.	Mar. 4, 1825–Mar. 3, 1829	John Calhoun
Planter, Lawyer, Soldier	Tennessee	61	June 8, 1845; "Hermitage," Tenn.	Mar. 4, 1829–Mar. 3, 1833 Mar. 4, 1833–Mar. 3, 1837	John Calhoun Martin Van Buren
Lawyer	New York	54	July 24, 1862; Kinderhook, N.Y.	Mar. 4, 1837–Mar. 3, 1841	Richard Johnson
Soldier, Planter	Ohio	68	Apr. 4, 1841; North Bend, Ohio	Mar. 4, 1841–Apr. 4, 1841	John Tyler
Lawyer	Virginia	51	Jan. 18, 1862; Richmond, Va.	Apr. 6, 1841–Mar. 3, 1845	——
Lawyer	Tennessee	49	June 15, 1849; Nashville, Tenn.	Mar. 4, 1845–Mar. 3, 1849	George Dallas
Soldier, Planter	Louisiana	64	July 9, 1850; near Louisville, Ky.	Mar. 4, 1849–July 9, 1850	Millard Fillmore
Lawyer	New York	50	Mar. 8, 1874; Buffalo, N.Y.	July 10, 1850–Mar. 3, 1853	——
Lawyer	New Hampshire	48	Oct. 8, 1869; Concord, N.H.	Mar. 4, 1853–Mar. 3, 1857	William King
Lawyer	Pennsylvania	65	June 1, 1868; Lancaster, Pa.	Mar. 4, 1857–Mar. 3, 1861	John Breckinridge
Lawyer	Illinois	52	Apr. 15, 1865; Springfield, Ill.	Mar. 4, 1861–Mar. 3, 1865 Mar. 4, 1865–Apr. 15, 1865	Hannibal Hamlin Andrew Johnson
Tailor	Tennessee	56	July 31, 1875; Greeneville, Tenn.	Apr. 15, 1865–Mar. 3, 1869	
Soldier, Farmer, Clerk	Illinois	46	July 23, 1885; New York, N.Y.	Mar. 4, 1869–Mar. 3, 1873 Mar. 4, 1873–Mar. 3, 1877	Schuyler Colfax Henry Wilson
Lawyer	Ohio	54	Jan. 17, 1893; Fremont, Ohio	Mar. 4, 1877–Mar. 3, 1881	William Wheeler
Laborer, Professor	Ohio	49	Sept. 19, 1881; Cleveland, Ohio	Mar. 4, 1881–Sept. 19, 1881	Chester Arthur
School Teacher, Lawyer	New York	50	Nov. 18, 1886; Albany, N.Y.	Sept. 19, 1881–Mar. 3, 1885	——
Lawyer	New York	47, 55	June 24, 1908; Princeton, N.J.	Mar. 4, 1885–Mar. 3, 1889 Mar. 4, 1893–Mar. 3, 1897	Thomas Hendricks Adlai Stevenson
Lawyer	Indiana	55	Mar. 13, 1901; Indianapolis, Ind.	Mar. 4, 1889–Mar. 3, 1893	Levi Morton
School Teacher, Clerk, Lawyer	Ohio	54	Sept. 14, 1901; Canton, Ohio	Mar. 4, 1897–Mar. 3, 1901 Mar. 4, 1901–Sept. 14, 1901	Garret Hobart Theodore Roosevelt
Historian, Rancher	New York	42	Jan. 6, 1919; Oyster Bay, N.Y.	Sept. 14, 1901–Mar. 3, 1905 Mar. 4, 1905–Mar. 3, 1909	Charles Fairbanks
Lawyer	Ohio	51	Mar. 8, 1930; Arlington, Va.	Mar. 4, 1909–Mar. 3, 1913	James Sherman
Lawyer, University President	New Jersey	56	Feb. 3, 1924; Washington, D.C.	Mar. 4, 1913–Mar. 3, 1917 Mar. 4, 1917–Mar. 3, 1921	Thomas Marshall Thomas Marshall
Newspaper Editor and Publisher	Ohio	55	Aug. 2, 1923; Marion, Ohio	Mar. 4, 1921–Aug. 2, 1923	Calvin Coolidge
Lawyer	Massachusetts	51	Jan. 5, 1933; Plymouth, Vt.	Aug. 3, 1923–Mar. 3, 1925 Mar. 4, 1925–Mar. 3, 1929	Charles Dawes
Engineer, Relief Administrator	California	54	Oct. 20, 1964; West Branch, Iowa	Mar. 4, 1929–Mar. 3, 1933	Charles Curtis
Lawyer	New York	51	April 12, 1945; Hyde Park, N.Y.	Mar. 4, 1933–Jan. 20, 1937 Jan. 20, 1937–Jan. 20, 1941 Jan. 20, 1941–Jan. 20, 1945 Jan. 20, 1945–Apr. 12, 1945	John Garner John Garner Henry Wallace Harry Truman
Clerk, Haberdasher, Farmer	Missouri	60	Dec. 26, 1972; Independence, Mo.	Apr. 12, 1945–Jan. 20, 1949 Jan. 20, 1949–Jan. 20, 1953	Alben Barkley
Soldier	New York	62	Mar. 28, 1969; Abilene, Kan.	Jan. 20, 1953–Jan. 20, 1957 Jan. 20, 1957–Jan. 20, 1961	Richard Nixon Richard Nixon
Author, Reporter	Massachusetts	43	Nov. 22, 1963; Arlington, Va.	Jan. 20, 1961–Nov. 22, 1963	Lyndon Johnson
School Teacher	Texas	55	Jan. 22, 1973; near Johnson City, Texas	Nov. 22, 1963–Jan. 20, 1965 Jan. 20, 1965–Jan. 20, 1969	Hubert Humphrey
Lawyer	New York	55	—	Jan. 20, 1969–Jan. 20, 1973 Jan. 20, 1973–Aug. 9, 1974	Spiro Agnew Gerald R. Ford
Lawyer	—	61	—	Aug. 9, 1974–Jan. 20, 1977	Nelson Rockefeller
Businessman, Farmer	Georgia	52	—	Jan. 20, 1977–Jan. 20, 1981	Walter Mondale
Actor, Broadcaster, Lecturer	California	69	—	Jan. 20, 1981	George H. W. Bush

THE VICE-PRESIDENTS

For those Vice-Presidents who became Presidents—John Adams, Thomas Jefferson, Martin Van Buren, John Tyler, Millard Fillmore, Andrew Johnson, Chester A. Arthur, Theodore Roosevelt, Calvin Coolidge, Harry S. Truman, Lyndon B. Johnson, Richard M. Nixon, and Gerald R. Ford—see the Presidential biographies.

Aaron Burr

Vice-President (1801–1805) to Thomas Jefferson *Political Party:* Democratic-Republican *Born:* Newark, New Jersey, February 6, 1756 *Ancestry:* English *Religious Affiliation:* Presbyterian *Education:* College of New Jersey (now Princeton University), 1772; thereafter briefly studied theology *Wives:* Married Mrs. Theodosia Prevost in 1782; she died in 1794. Married Mrs. Stephen Jumel in 1833; she petitioned for divorce a year later *Children:* Two by first wife *Home:* New York *Occupations before Vice-Presidency:* Revolutionary soldier, lawyer, politician, U.S. Senator (1791–1797) *Age at Inauguration:* 44 *Outstanding Facts:* In the Presidential election of 1800, an electoral vote tie between Aaron Burr and Thomas Jefferson threw the election into the House of Representatives, where, mainly through the efforts of Alexander Hamilton, the Presidency was finally won by Jefferson, with the Vice-Presidency going to Burr. In 1804, after Burr had been nominated for the governorship of New York, Hamilton again contributed to his defeat. Burr challenged Hamilton to a duel and killed him. This, as well as President Jefferson's suspicions that Burr had intrigued for the Presidency, effectively ended his political career. As Vice-President, Burr presided over the Senate with impartiality *Occupation after Vice-Presidency:* He became involved in a political conspiracy, the aims of which still remain unclear, and was tried for treason but acquitted. He left the country and schemed abroad but, frustrated in his plans, returned to the United States, where he again took up the practice of law *Died:* Sept. 14, 1836 *Place of Burial:* Princeton, N.J.

George Clinton

Vice-President (1805–1812) to Thomas Jefferson and James Madison *Political Party:* Democratic-Republican *Born:* Little Britain (now Ulster County), New York, July 26, 1739 *Ancestry:* English, Scots-Irish *Religious Affiliation:* Presbyterian *Education:* Private tutoring *Wife:* Married Cornelia Tappen in 1770 *Children:* Six *Home:* New York *Occupations before Vice-Presidency:* Lawyer, Revolutionary soldier, politician, governor of New York (1777–1795, 1801–1804) *Age at Inauguration:* 65 *Outstanding Facts:* An advocate of state sovereignty, Clinton was one of the chief opponents of the Constitution. He hoped to be President but lost out to James Madison, to whom he was openly hostile. He spent much time in New York and was a poor presiding officer of the Senate. Clinton was the first Vice-President to die in office *Died:* April 20, 1812 *Place of Burial:* Washington, D.C.; reinterred (1908) in Kingston, Ulster County, N.Y.

Elbridge Gerry

Vice-President (1813–1814) to James Madison *Political Party:* Democratic-Republican *Born:* Marblehead, Massachusetts, July 17, 1744 *Ancestry:* English *Religious Affiliation:* Episcopalian *Education:* Harvard College, 1762 *Wife:* Married Ann Thompson in 1786 *Children:* Nine *Home:* Massachusetts *Occupations before Vice-Presidency:* Merchant, politician, signer of the Declaration of Independence, governor of Massachusetts (1810–1812) *Age at Inauguration:* 63 *Outstanding Facts:* He socialized a great deal during his brief tenure and is now chiefly remembered for *gerrymander,* the term given to his attempt while governor of Massachusetts to redistrict the state in his party's favor *Died:* November 23, 1814 *Place of Burial:* Washington, D.C.

Daniel D. Tompkins

Vice-President (1817–1825) to James Monroe *Political Party:* Democratic-Republican *Born:* Fox Meadow (now Scarsdale), New York, June 21, 1774 *Ancestry:* Scottish, English *Religious Affiliation:* Presbyterian *Education:* Columbia College, 1795 *Wife:* Married Hannah Minthorne in 1798 *Children:* Eight *Home:* New York *Occupations before Vice-Presidency:* Lawyer, politician, governor of New York (1807–1817) *Age at Inauguration:* 42 *Outstanding Facts:* He spent much time contesting court cases arising out of actions he took over expenditures made while he was governor of New York during the War of 1812 *Occupation after Vice-Presidency:* He continued contesting various court actions *Died:* June 11, 1825 *Place of Burial:* New York City

John Caldwell Calhoun

Vice-President (1825–1832) to John Quincy Adams and Andrew Jackson *Political Party:* Democratic *Born:* Abbeville, South Carolina, March 18, 1782 *Ancestry:* Scots-Irish *Religious Affiliation:* Presbyterian *Education:* Yale College, 1804, studied (1805–1806) at Litchfield (Conn.) Law School *Wife:* Married Floride Calhoun in 1811 *Children:* Nine *Home:* South Carolina *Occupations before Vice-Presidency:* Lawyer, planter, U.S. Congressman (1811–1817), Secretary of War (1817–1825) *Age at Inauguration:* 42 *Outstanding Facts:* A strong supporter of Jackson, he opposed Adams throughout the latter's administration. In 1828 in his *South Carolina Exposition,* he set forth the principles of states' rights and nullification. Originally thought of as Jackson's successor, he broke with the President over a variety of issues, including the very nature of the federal union. Calhoun resigned as Vice-President upon being elected to the Senate in 1832. In the Senate he eloquently defended his states' rights principles and proslavery viewpoint in dramatic debates with Daniel Webster *Occupations after Vice-Presidency:* Senator (1832–1844, 1845–1850), Cabinet officer (Secretary of State, 1844–1845) *Died:* March 31, 1850 *Place of Burial:* Charleston, South Carolina

Richard Mentor Johnson

Vice-President (1837–1841) to Martin Van Buren *Political Party:* Democratic *Born:* Beargrass Creek (a frontier settlement on the present location of Louisville), Kentucky, autumn of 1780 *Ancestry:* English *Religious Affiliation:* Baptist *Education:* Preparatory school and private instruction *Wife:* Johnson was a bachelor *Home:* Kentucky *Occupations before Vice-Presidency:* Lawyer, soldier, educator, politician, U.S. Congressman (1814–1819, 1829–1837), Senator (1819–1829) *Age at Inauguration:* 56 *Outstanding Facts:* A hero of the War of 1812, Johnson was said to be the slayer of Chief Tecumseh at the Battle of the Thames. Johnson has been the only Vice-President ever elected by the Senate; he failed to get enough electoral votes. *Occupations after Vice-Presidency:* Businessman, state legislator (1841-1842, 1850) *Died:* Nov. 19, 1850 *Place of Burial:* Frankfort, Ky.

George Mifflin Dallas

Vice-President (1845–1849) to James K. Polk *Political Party:* Democratic *Born:* Philadelphia, July 10, 1792 *Ancestry:* Scottish, English *Religious Affiliation:* Presbyterian *Education:* Princeton College, 1810 *Wife:* Married Sophia Chew in 1816 *Children:* Eight *Home:* Pennsylvania *Occupations before Vice-Presidency:* Lawyer, politician, diplomat *Age at Inauguration:* 52 *Outstanding Facts:* Although nominated as a protectionist, he cast (1846) the deciding vote for a lower tariff *Occupations after Vice-Presidency:* Lawyer, diplomat, writer *Died:* December 31, 1864 *Place of Burial:* Philadelphia

William Rufus Devane King

Vice-President (1853) to Franklin Pierce *Political Party:* Democratic *Born:* Sampson County, North Carolina, April 7, 1786 *Ancestry:* Scots-Irish, Huguenot *Religious Affiliation:* Presbyterian *Education:* University of North Carolina, 1803 *Wife:* King was a bachelor *Home:* Alabama *Occupations before Vice-Presidency:* Lawyer, politician, U.S. Congressman (1811–1816), Senator (1819–1844; 1848–1852), diplomat *Age at Inauguration:* 66 *Outstanding Facts:* Elected while recovering from tuberculosis in Cuba, he died shortly after his return. *Died:* April 18, 1853 *Place of Burial:* "Kings Bend," Ala.; reinterred in Selma, Ala.

John Cabell Breckinridge

Vice-President (1857–1861) to James Buchanan *Political Party:* Democratic *Born:* "Cabell's Dale" (near Lexington), Kentucky, January 21, 1821 *Ancestry:* English, Scots-Irish *Religious Affiliation:* Presbyterian *Education:* Centre College (Ky.), 1838; thereafter he studied law at Transylvania University *Wife:* Married Mary Cyrene Burch in 1843 *Children:* Five *Home:* Kentucky *Occupations before Vice-Presidency:* Lawyer, soldier, politician, U.S. Congressman (1851–1855) *Age at Inauguration:* 36 *Outstanding Facts:* The youngest man ever to become Vice-President, he was dignified beyond his years and ably presided over the Senate. Breckinridge tried to achieve some kind of compromise during the years prior to the Civil War. *Occupations after Vice-Presidency:* U.S. Senator (1861), Confederate soldier, Confederate Secretary of War (1865), lawyer, businessman *Died:* May 17, 1875 *Place of Burial:* Lexington, Kentucky

Hannibal Hamlin

Vice-President (1861–1865) to Abraham Lincoln *Political Party:* Republican *Born:* Paris, Maine, August 27, 1809 *Ancestry:* English *Religious Affiliation:* Unitarian *Education:* Preparatory studies *Wives:* Married Sarah Jane Emery in 1833; she died in 1855. Married her half-sister Ellen Vesta Emery in 1856 *Children:* Five by first wife, two by second wife *Home:* Maine *Occupations before Vice-Presidency:* Farmer, printer, lawyer, politician, U.S. Senator (1857–1861) *Age at Inauguration:* 51 *Outstanding Facts:* Hamlin was a staunch advocate of emancipation *Occupations after Vice Presidency:* Political appointee, lawyer, businessman, U.S. Senator (1869–1881), diplomat *Died:* July 4, 1891 *Place of Burial:* Bangor, Maine

Schuyler Colfax

Vice-President (1869–1873) to Ulysses S. Grant *Political Party:* Republican *Born:* New York City, March 23, 1823 *Ancestry:* English, Huguenot *Religious Affiliation:* Dutch Reformed *Education:* Grade school *Wives:* Married Evelyn Clark in 1844; she died in 1862. Married Ellen Wade in 1868 *Children:* One by second wife *Home:* Indiana *Occupations before Vice-Presidency:* Political appointee, journalist, U.S. Congressman (1855–1869), speaker of the House (1863–1869) *Age at Inauguration:* 45 *Outstanding Facts:* In 1870, midway through his term, he announced his retirement from political life, hoping that the public would demand that he remain. No such clamor developed, and Colfax rescinded his decision. Colfax failed of renomination. Later it was revealed that Colfax had been involved in the Credit Mobilier railroad scandal, which effectively ended his public career *Occupation after Vice-Presidency:* Lecturer *Died:* January 13, 1885 *Place of Burial:* South Bend, Indiana

Henry Wilson

Vice-President (1873–1875) to Ulysses S. Grant *Political Party:* Republican *Born:* Farmington, New Hampshire, February 16, 1812 *Ancestry:* Scots-Irish *Religious Affiliation:* Congregationalist *Education:* Little formal schooling *Wife:* Married Harriet Malvina Howe in 1840 *Children:* One *Home:* Massachusetts *Occupations before Vice-Presidency:* Indentured worker, school teacher, cobbler, businessman, newspaperman, politician, U.S. Senator (1855–1873) *Age at Inauguration:* 61 *Outstanding Facts:* As Vice-President ill health made his attendance in presiding over the Senate irregular, and he died in office *Died:* November 22, 1875 *Place of Burial:* Natick, Massachusetts

William Almon Wheeler

Vice-President (1877–1881) to Rutherford B. Hayes *Political Party:* Republican *Born:* Malone, New York, June 30, 1819 *Ancestry:* English *Religious Affiliation:* Presbyterian *Education:* Attended (1838–1840) the University of Vermont *Wife:* Married Mary King in 1845 *Children:* None *Home:* New York *Occupations before Vice-Presidency:* Lawyer, banker, businessman, politician, U.S. Congressman (1861–1863, 1869–1877) *Age at Inauguration:* 57 *Outstanding Facts:* Little known nationally when nominated for the office, he performed its major function, presiding over the Senate, with faithfulness *Occupation after Vice-Presidency:* Poor health resulted in general inactivity; unsuccessfully nominated for U.S. Senator in 1881 *Died:* June 4, 1887 *Place of Burial:* Malone, N.Y.

Thomas Andrews Hendricks

Vice-President (1885) to Grover Cleveland *Political Party:* Democratic *Born:* Zanesville, Ohio, September 7, 1819 *Ancestry:* Scottish, English, Huguenot *Religious Affiliation:* Episcopalian *Education:* Hanover College (Indiana), 1841 *Wife:* Married Eliza Morgan in 1845 *Children:* One *Home:* Indiana *Occupations before Vice-Presidency:* Lawyer, politician, defeated candidate for Vice-President in 1876 *Age at Inauguration:* 65 *Outstanding Fact:* He died 8 months after taking office. *Died:* Nov. 25, 1885 *Place of Burial:* Indianapolis, Ind.

Levi Parsons Morton

Vice-President (1889–1893) to Benjamin Harrison *Political Party:* Republican *Born:* Shoreham, Vermont, May 16, 1824 *Ancestry:* English *Religious Affiliation:* Episcopalian *Education:* Preparatory schools *Wives:* Married Lucy Young Kimball in 1856; she died in 1871 Married Anna Livingston Read Street in 1873 *Children:* One by first wife; six by second wife *Home:* New York *Occupations before Vice-Presidency:* Clerk, school teacher, businessman, U.S. Congressman (1879–1881), diplomat *Age at Inauguration:* 64 *Outstanding Fact:* He was passed over for renomination as Vice-President *Occupations after Vice-Presidency:* Real estate investor, banker, Governor of New York (1895–1897) *Died:* May 16, 1920 *Place of Burial:* Rhinebeck, N.Y.

Adlai Ewing Stevenson

Vice-President (1893–1897) to Grover Cleveland *Political Party:* Democratic *Born:* Christian County, Kentucky, October 23, 1835 *Ancestry:* Scots-Irish *Religious Affiliation:* Presbyterian *Education:* Attended Centre College (Kentucky) two years *Wife:* Married Letitia Green in 1866 *Children:* Four *Home:* Illinois *Occupations before Vice-Presidency:* Lawyer, politician, U.S. Congressman (1875–1877, 1879–1881) *Age at Inauguration:* 57 *Outstanding Facts:* He presided with fairness over a Senate that had recently turned him down for a District of Columbia judicial post. A "soft money" advocate, he was unsympathetic to President Cleveland's monetary views but never embarrassed the administration with open disagreement *Occupations after Vice-Presidency:* Lawyer and politician *Died:* June 14, 1914 *Place of Burial:* Bloomington, Illinois

Garret Augustus Hobart

Vice-President (1897–1899) to William McKinley *Political Party:* Republican *Born:* Long Branch, New Jersey, June 3, 1844 *Ancestry:* English, Dutch, Huguenot *Religious Affiliation:* Presbyterian *Education:* Rutgers College, 1863 *Wife:* Married Jennie Tuttle in 1869 *Children:* Two *Home:* New Jersey *Occupations before Vice-Presidency:* Lawyer, businessman, banker, politician *Age at Inauguration:* 52 *Outstanding Facts:* He presided over the Senate with ability. Hobart cast the deciding vote against granting the Philippine Is. independence *Died:* In office, Nov. 21, 1899 *Place of Burial:* Paterson, N.J.

Charles Warren Fairbanks

Vice-President (1905–1909) to Theodore Roosevelt *Political Party:* Republican *Born:* Near Unionville Center, Ohio, May 11, 1852 *Ancestry:* English *Religious Affiliation:* Methodist *Education:* Ohio Wesleyan, 1872 *Wife:* Married Cornelia Cole in 1874 *Children:* Five *Home:* Indiana *Occupations before Vice-Presidency:* Newspaperman, railroad lawyer, politician, U.S. Senator (1897–1905) *Age at Inauguration:* 52 *Outstanding Facts:* Although Fairbanks and President Roosevelt represented opposite wings of the Republican Party, they maintained cordial relations *Occupations after Vice-Presidency:* Lawyer, unsuccessful candidate for Vice-Pres. in 1916 *Died:* June 4, 1918 *Place of Burial:* Indianapolis, Ind.

James Schoolcraft Sherman

Vice-President (1909–1912) to William Howard Taft *Political Party:* Republican *Born:* Utica, New York, October 24, 1855 *Ancestry:* English *Religious Affiliation:* Dutch Reformed *Education:* Hamilton College, 1878 *Wife:* Married Carrie Babcock in 1881 *Children:* Three *Home:* New York *Occupations before Vice-Presidency:* Lawyer, banker, politician, U.S. Congressman (1887–1891, 1893–1909) *Age at Inauguration:* 53 *Outstanding Facts:* An affable man known as "Sunny Jim," he presided well over the Senate. Renominated but died before the election *Died:* October 30, 1912 *Place of Burial:* Utica, N.Y.

Thomas Riley Marshall

Vice-President (1913–1921) to Woodrow Wilson *Political Party:* Democratic *Born:* North Manchester, Indiana, March 14, 1854 *Ancestry:* English *Religious Affiliation:* Presbyterian *Education:* Wabash College, 1873 *Wife:* Married Lois Irene Kimsey in 1895 *Children:* None *Home:* Indiana *Occupations before Vice-Presidency:* Lawyer, politician, governor of Indiana (1909–1913) *Age at Inauguration:* 58 *Outstanding Facts:* Marshall was the first Vice-President in nearly a century to succeed himself. While President Wilson was ill, Marshall acted as ceremonial head of state, but he refused to accept any of the President's powers. He was well known for his quip, "What this country needs is a good five-cent cigar" *Occupations after Vice-Presidency:* Lawyer, lecturer, political appointee *Died:* June 1, 1925 *Place of Burial:* Indianapolis, Ind.

Charles Gates Dawes

Vice-President (1925–1929) to Calvin Coolidge *Political Party:* Republican *Born:* Marietta, Ohio, August 27, 1865 *Ancestry:* English *Religious Affiliation:* Congregationalist *Education:* Marietta College, 1884; Cincinnati Law School, 1886 *Wife:* Married Caro D. Blymer in 1889 *Children:* Four (two adopted) *Home:* Illinois *Occupations before Vice-Presidency:* Lawyer, banker, businessman, soldier, politician *Age at Inauguration:* 59 *Outstanding Facts:* Dawes shared the Nobel Peace Prize in 1925 for his work in attempting to settle through the Dawes Plan the problem of German reparations. A short-tempered man, he infuriated the Senate by telling that body it was time to change its antiquated rules *Occupations after Vice-Presidency:* Diplomat, public servant, banker, businessman *Died:* April 23, 1951 *Place of Burial:* Chicago

Charles Curtis

Vice-President (1929–1933) to Herbert Hoover *Political Party:* Republican *Born:* Topeka, Kansas, January 25, 1860 *Ancestry:* American Indian, English, French *Religious Affiliation:* Episcopalian *Education:* High school *Wife:* Married Annie E. Baird in 1884 *Children:* Three *Home:* Kansas *Occupations before Vice-Presidency:* Lawyer, politician, U.S. Congressman (1893–1907), Senator (1907–1913, 1915–1929) *Age at Inauguration:* 69 *Outstanding Facts:* Lacking a close relationship with President Hoover, Curtis had little to say or do *Occupations after Vice-Presidency:* Lawyer, businessman *Died:* February 8, 1936 *Place of Burial:* Topeka, Kansas

John Nance Garner

Vice-President (1933–1941) to Franklin D. Roosevelt *Political Party:* Democratic *Born:* Blossom Prairie, Texas, November 22, 1868 *Ancestry:* English, Welsh, Scottish *Religious Affiliation:* Methodist *Education:* High school *Wife:* Married Elizabeth Rheiner in 1895 *Children:* One *Home:* Texas *Occupations before Vice-Presidency:* Lawyer, businessman, banker, politician,

U.S. Congressman (1903–1933), Speaker of the House of Representatives (1931–1933) *Age at Inauguration:* 63 *Outstanding Facts:* Garner retained much of his influence with Congress while Vice-President and during his first term helped to obtain passage of much New Deal legislation. During his second term, he increasingly found himself out of sympathy with President Roosevelt's programs, and he was not renominated *Occupations after Vice-Presidency:* Businessman, banker, cattle rancher *Died:* November 7, 1967 *Place of Burial:* Uvalde, Texas

Henry Agard Wallace

Vice-President (1941–1945) to Franklin D. Roosevelt *Political Party:* Democratic *Born:* Near Orient, Iowa, October 7, 1888 *Ancestry:* Scots-Irish *Religious Affiliation:* Episcopalian *Education:* Iowa State College, 1910 *Wife:* Married Ilo Browne in 1914 *Children:* Three *Home:* Iowa *Occupations before Vice-Presidency:* Editor, farmer, Secretary of Agriculture (1933–1940) *Age at Inauguration:* 52 *Outstanding Facts:* President Roosevelt cast the Vice-Presidency under Wallace into its most active role up to that time. Wallace served as good-will ambassador to Latin America, the Soviet Union, and the Far East. He also undertook various defense duties. However, his political and social views caused him to be viewed suspiciously by the Democratic Party and he failed of renomination *Occupations after Vice-Presidency:* Secretary of Commerce (1945–1946), author, farmer, defeated candidate for President in 1948 *Died:* November 18, 1965 *Place of Burial:* Des Moines, Iowa

Alben William Barkley

Vice-President (1949–1953) to Harry S Truman *Political Party:* Democratic *Born:* Near Lowes, Kentucky, November 24, 1877 *Ancestry:* Scots-Irish *Religious Affiliation:* Methodist *Education:* Marvin College (Kentucky), 1897; attended University of Virginia Law School *Wives:* Married Dorothy Brower in 1903; she died in 1947. Married Mrs. Carleton S. Hadley in 1949 *Children:* Three by first wife *Home:* Kentucky *Occupations before Vice-Presidency:* Lawyer, politician, U.S. Senator (1927–1949) *Age at Inauguration:* 71 *Outstanding Facts:* Very popular, he was nicknamed "Veep" during his tenure. He was the only Vice-President to marry while in office. After President Truman announced he would not run again, Barkley attempted to win the Presidential nomination but failed *Occupations after Vice-Presidency:* Lawyer, U.S. Senator (1955–1956) *Died:* April 30, 1956 *Place of Burial:* Paducah, Kentucky

Hubert Horatio Humphrey

Vice-President (1965–1969) to Lyndon B. Johnson *Political Party:* Democratic *Born:* Wallace, South Dakota, May 27, 1911 *Ancestry:* Welsh, Norwegian *Religious Affiliation:* Congregationalist *Education:* University of Minnesota, 1939; M.A., Louisiana State, 1940; began work for a Ph.D. *Wife:* Married Muriel Fay Buck in 1936 *Children:* Four *Home:* Minnesota *Occupations before Vice-Presidency:* Pharmacist, teacher, politician, U.S. Senator (1949–1965) *Age at Inauguration:* 53 *Outstanding Facts:* Humphrey was an energetic Vice-President and traveled widely as a spokesman of the United States. He was a vigorous defender of the Johnson administration. Humphrey ran unsuccessfully for the Presidency in 1968. *Occupations after Vice-Presidency:* College teaching, U.S. Senator (1971-1978) *Died:* January 13, 1978 *Place of Burial:* Minneapolis, Minnesota

Spiro Theodore Agnew

Vice-President (1969–1973) to Richard M. Nixon *Political Party:* Republican *Born:* Baltimore, Maryland, November 9, 1918 *Ancestry:* Greek, English *Religious Affiliation:* Episcopalian *Education:* University of Baltimore Law School, 1947 *Wife:* Married Eleanor Isabel Judefind in 1942 *Children:* Four *Home:* Maryland *Occupations before Vice-Presidency:* Lawyer, politician, governor of Maryland (1967–1969) *Age at Inauguration:* 50 *Outstanding Facts:* Agnew resigned his office and pleaded "no contest" to one charge of income tax evasion after being implicated in a kickback scheme. He was the first Vice-President in history to resign under duress.

Nelson Aldrich Rockefeller

Vice-President (1974-1977) to Gerald R. Ford *Political Party:* Republican *Born:* Bar Harbor, Maine, July 8, 1908 *Ancestry:* English, Scottish, German *Religious Affilation:* Baptist *Education:* Dartmouth College, 1930 *Wives:* Mary Todhunter Clark, June 23, 1930 (div. 1962), Margaretta Fitler Murphy, May 1963 *Home:* New York and Bar Harbor, Maine *Occupation before Vice-Presidency:* various government posts, four-term governor of New York *Age at Inauguration:* 66 *Outstanding Facts:* Nominated under the 25th Amendment by President Ford following resignation of Richard M. Nixon as President and Ford's assumption of the presidency *Occupations after Vice Presidency:* Art interests *Died:* January 26, 1979 *Place of Burial:* Pocantico Hills, New York

Walter Frederick Mondale

Vice-President (1977-1981) to Jimmy Carter *Political Party:* Democratic *Born:* Ceylon, Minnesota, January 5, 1928 *Ancestry:* Norwegian *Religious Affiliation:* Methodist *Education:* University of Minnesota Law School, 1956 *Wife:* Married Joan Adams in 1955 *Children:* Three *Home:* Minnesota *Occupation before Vice-Presidency:* Lawyer, state attorney general, U.S. Senator (1965-1977) *Age at Inauguration:* 49 *Outstanding Facts:* His untraditional role as the President's personal international emissary added new responsibility and power to the previously passive, ceremonial role of the Vice-President *Occupation after Vice-Presidency:* Lawyer.

George Herbert Walker Bush

Vice-President (1981-   ) to Ronald W. Reagan *Political Party:* Republican *Born:* Milton, Massachusetts, June 12, 1924 *Ancestry:* English *Religious Affiliation:* Episcopal *Education:* Yale University, 1948 *Wife:* Married Barbara Pierce in 1945 *Children:* Five *Home:* Houston, Texas *Occupation before Vice-Presidency:* Oil industry businessman; member of US House of Representatives 1967-1971; U.S. Ambassador to the United Nations, 1971-1973; Chairman of the Republican National Committee 1973-1974; Head of U.S. Liaison Office in Beijing, China, 1974-1977; Director of the Central Intelligence Agency, 1975-1977; Chairman of bank in Houston, 1977-1980 *Age at Inauguration:* 56 *Outstanding Facts:* 1980 Republican presidential candidate from 1979 until 1980, when he withdrew from the race.

THE FIRST LADIES

Mrs. George Washington—Born Martha Dandridge, daughter of a planter, in New Kent County, Virginia, on June 21, 1731. At 18, she married Daniel Parke Custis, heir to a large estate, and she bore him four children, two of whom died in infancy. After Custis died on July 8, 1757, leaving her reputedly the richest widow in Virginia, she married Colonel George Washington on January 6, 1759; at 27, she was eight months older than her second husband.

Besides adding substantially to his property (she provided 17,000 acres and 300 slaves, compared with his own estate of 5,000 acres and 49 slaves), she also gave him a happy domestic life. Small, plump, and cheerful, she was amply blessed with common sense, if not brilliance. When Washington became President, many contemporaries thought she humanized her austere husband—"Mrs. Washington is one of those unassuming characters which create love and esteem," Mrs. John Adams wrote to a sister.

In New York, then Philadelphia, where "Lady" Washington held sway in makeshift mansions while the new capital of Washington was being planned, she made an amiable hostess at the formal receptions and dinners her husband instituted as the social side of his official duties.

There were no children of her second marriage, but she was a doting mother to the offspring of her first husband, who were treated as his own by Washington. Although her daughter, Martha (Patsy) Parke Custis, died at 17, her son, John Parke Custis, married and had three daughters and a son. Mrs. Washington survived her husband two years, dying on May 22, 1802, at Mount Vernon, where she was buried.

Mrs. John Adams—Born Abigail Smith on November 11, 1744, in Weymouth, Massachusetts, the daughter of a Congregational minister. Although she had no formal schooling, she read much more widely than most girls, and first attracted the notice of her future husband by the breadth of her intellectual interests. But before they married on October 25, 1764, they were deeply in love, and theirs was a devoted union.

Shrewd, witty, and warm-hearted, Mrs. Adams was of inestimable help in furthering the careers of both her husband and her son, John Quincy Adams, the nation's sixth President: she is the only woman in American history to have been the wife of one President and the mother of another. She also won celebrity in her own right as a gifted letter-writer with a keen political instinct.

Mrs. Adams was the first First Lady to live in the Executive Mansion in Washington, moving there in November 1800 when most of the rooms were still unfinished; she gained lasting fame in American folklore by having her laundry set out to dry before the fire in the East Room, one of the few chambers where some warmth could be obtained. During the brief period before her husband's term expired on March 3, 1801, she had the distinction, too, of holding the first formal gathering in the Mansion—a reception on New Year's Day of 1801, when 135 callers were greeted in the crimson-hung Oval Room. Besides John Quincy, she had two other sons and a daughter; another daughter died in infancy. Mrs. Adams died at the Adams home in Quincy, Massachusetts, on October 28, 1818, and was buried there.

Mrs. Thomas Jefferson—Born Martha Wayles on October 30, 1748, in Charles City County, Virginia, the daughter of a wealthy lawyer and planter. At 18, she married a young Virginian, Bathurst Skelton, who died on September 30, 1768, leaving her with an infant son. No portrait or reliable facts about her have survived, but she was said to be musically inclined and well-off when she married Thomas Jefferson on January 1, 1772. Her firstborn child, and four of the six children she bore her second husband, died in early childhood. After just 10 years as Mrs. Jefferson, she died on September 6, 1782, and was buried at Monticello; so Jefferson had been a widower for 18 years when he became President.

Being opposed to elaborate state entertaining, he held such functions to a minimum, but when he did receive guests, often his hostess was Mrs. James (Dolley) Madison, the wife of his Secretary of State, or one of his two surviving daughters—Mrs. John Wayles Eppes and Mrs. Thomas Mann Randolph, whose eighth child, James Madison Randolph, was the first baby born in the Executive Mansion (on January 17, 1806).

Mrs. James Madison—Born Dolley Paine on May 20, 1768, the daughter of Virginia Quakers temporarily settled in North Carolina. When she was 15, her family moved to Philadelphia, and on January 7, 1790, she married John Todd, a Quaker lawyer who died three years later, leaving her with one son; another had already died. Strikingly handsome despite her plain garb, the young widow quickly attracted new suitors, among them "the great little Madison," as she described him in a letter. They were married on September 15, 1794, when he was 43 and she 26.

She soon blossomed forth in elegant dress, but with a warmth and simplicity of manner that made her one of the best loved figures of her day. As White House hostess during the Jefferson administration, then as First Lady, she reigned socially supreme in Washington from 1801 to 1817. The first Inaugural Ball, on March 4, 1809, marked her husband's assumption of the Presidency, and she appeared there in queenly yellow velvet, set off by a plumed satin headdress.

Dolley Madison put much effort into furnishing the Executive Mansion suitably, but her fine draperies were destroyed when the British burned the building on August 24, 1814. Mrs. Madison is supposed to have saved the famous Gilbert Stuart portrait of Washington from the flames and also her husband's invaluable notes describing the Constitutional Convention of 1787.

While the White House was being rebuilt, the Madisons lived in Octagon House, a private mansion. They had no children, and her one son grew up a ne'er-do-well. Upon leaving Washington, Mrs. Madison continued entertaining on a grand scale at Montpelier, her husband's Virginia plantation. She returned to Washington following his death, and took up residence in 1837 in a small house across Lafayette Square from the White House. Here she received homage till she died on July 12, 1849, and was buried at Montpelier.

Mrs. James Monroe—Born Elizabeth Kortright in New York City on June 30, 1768, the daughter of a former British Army captain. At 17, on February 16, 1786, she married James Monroe, 10 years her senior. Succeeding the popular Dolley Madison as First Lady, Mrs. Monroe precipitated a social storm.

Reserved and regal in manner, she refused to follow Mrs. Madison's custom of paying calls on capital hostesses, and she added to the outrage felt by much of Washington society by declining to make the White House's first wedding into an elaborate official ceremony; only relatives and close friends were invited to the marriage of the younger of the Monroes' two daughters, Maria, to Samuel L. Gouverneur on March 9, 1820. But during her husband's second term, Mrs. Monroe's policy of restricting the social obligations of the Presidential family to the receiving of guests, without any ritual paying of calls, won general approval, and it has been followed ever since. Mrs. Monroe died on September 23, 1830, at Oak Hill, her husband's Virginia plantation, and she was buried in Richmond.

Mrs. John Quincy Adams—Born Louisa Catherine Johnson in London on February 12, 1775, the daughter of a Marylander serving as a financial agent in England. In London, on July 27, 1797, she became the wife of John Quincy Adams, then serving his first diplomatic tour of duty abroad. The mother of three sons—the youngest, Charles Francis Adams, was the highly regarded American Minister to Great Britain during the Civil War—Mrs. Adams was plagued by ill health but made a gracious First Lady.

Much less stiff in manner than her husband, she was noted for her ornate headdresses and fashionable gowns when she received at the fortnightly levees held in the White House during her regime there. Besides her own sons and one daughter, her family during her years in the Executive Mansion also included the three orphaned children of one of her sisters, and many nieces and nephews paid frequent visits. Mrs. Adams died in the family's private residence in Washington on May 15, 1852, and was buried in Quincy, Massachusetts.

Mrs. Andrew Jackson—Born Rachel Donelson in 1767, the daughter of Colonel John Donelson of Virginia. When she was 13, her family moved to Kentucky, where she married Captain Lewis Robards in 1785. He proved a suspicious husband, and five years later he sought permission from the legislature to divorce her.

Mistakenly believing a divorce had been granted, she and Andrew Jackson were married near Natchez in 1791; then on discovering two years afterward that Robards had just obtained the divorce, they were remarried on January 17, 1794. As Jackson's fame spread, gossip about this unfortunate episode hurt his wife increasingly. He fought at least one duel to defend her honor (killing Charles Dickinson in Kentucky in 1806), but when the slander was revived in the scurrilous Presidential campaign of 1828, he could not protect her. Her death of a heart attack on December 22, 1828, just as he was preparing to leave for Washington, was widely blamed on scandalmongers. She was buried at The Hermitage, Jackson's home near Nashville.

A kindly woman fond of smoking a corncob pipe, though by no means illiterate as often charged, Mrs. Jackson had no children, but she and her husband adopted a nephew. During Jackson's administration, Mrs. Andrew Jackson Donelson, wife of his nephew, often served as his hostess.

Mrs. Martin Van Buren—Born Hannah Hoes on March 8, 1783, in Kinderhook, New York, where she knew her future husband from early childhood. Distant relatives on his mother's side, they were married February 21, 1807, and had four sons before she died in Albany on February 5, 1819; she was buried at Kinderhook. A widower for 18 years when he entered the Executive Mansion, Van Buren had as his official hostess Mrs. Abraham Van Buren, the South Carolina-born wife of his oldest son.

Mrs. William Henry Harrison—Born Anna Tuthill Symmes on July 25, 1775, near Morristown, New Jersey, the daughter of Colonel John Cleves Symmes, who later became a judge and large landholder in the Northwest Territory. When Lieutenant William Henry Harrison asked Colonel Symmes for his daughter's hand, the application was rejected on the ground that an Army officer could not support a wife. As a result, the couple ran off to be married by a justice of the peace on November 25, 1795.

While her husband advanced militarily and politically, Mrs. Harrison brought up 10 children. Because she had only recently recovered from an illness, she did not attend her husband's inauguration on March 4, 1841. She remained at the Harrison home in North Bend, Ohio, to complete her convalescence, expecting to be well enough by May to assume her duties as First Lady in Washington. But her husband took cold and died exactly one month after assuming office, and Mrs. Harrison never did move into the Executive Mansion. Surviving until February 25, 1864, when she died and was buried at North Bend, she outlived all but one of her children—John Scott Harrison, whose son Benjamin became President in 1889.

Mrs. John Tyler—The first Mrs. Tyler was born Letitia Christian in New Kent County, Virginia, on November 12, 1790. Married on March 29, 1813, she had eight children, one of whom died in infancy. Partially paralyzed by a stroke in 1839, she was unable to assume any social duties when her husband became President two years later. Her only appearance downstairs at the Executive Mansion came at the wedding of her daughter, Elizabeth, to William Nevison Waller on January 31, 1842. Mrs. Tyler died on September 10, 1842, in the White House and was buried at Cedar Grove, Virginia.

The role of official hostess during most of Tyler's administration was taken by his daughter-in-law, Mrs. Robert Tyler, a former actress born Priscilla Cooper in Bristol, Pennsylvania. But on June 26, 1844, the 54-year-old President married the 24-year-old Julia Gardiner, who in the nine months remaining to his term established herself as one of the nation's most flamboyant First Ladies. Born May 4, 1820, on Gardiner's Island, New York, she belonged to a wealthy society family, and she surrounded herself with a "court" of elegant young ladies when she began entertaining lavishly in Washington. The mother of seven children, she survived her husband 27 years; she died on July 10, 1889, in Richmond and was buried there beside him.

Mrs. James Knox Polk—Born Sarah Childress on September 4, 1803, in Murfreesboro, Tennessee, the daughter of a wealthy merchant. After attending the Female Academy in Salem, North Carolina, considered then to be the South's outstanding school for girls, she married James Polk on January 1, 1824.

A shrewd and ambitious woman, she had no children and devoted herself to advancing her husband's political career. As First Lady, she opened the Executive Mansion to the public two evenings a week, besides holding formal receptions and dinners frequently. Under her direction, the building received its first complete redecorating since Monroe's administration. Though a strict Presbyterian who frowned on dancing and Sunday visiting, she allowed wine to be served and was fond of showy clothes. Mrs. Polk survived her husband 42 years, dying on August 14, 1891, in Nashville, where she was buried.

Mrs. Zachary Taylor—Born Margaret Mackall Smith on September 21, 1788, in Calvert County, Maryland, the daughter of a planter. On June 21, 1810, she married Lieutenant Zachary Taylor and spent most of the next 35 years at frontier Army posts. She had six children, two of whom died in infancy. By the time her husband was elected President, ill health prevented her taking an active role as First Lady, and her youngest daughter, Mrs. William Wallace Bliss, acted as her father's official hostess. Mrs. Taylor died on August 18, 1852, near Pascagoula, Louisiana, and was buried beside her husband in Springfield, Kentucky.

Mrs. Millard Fillmore—The first Mrs. Fillmore was born Abigail Powers on March 13, 1798, in Stillwater, New York. The daughter of a Baptist minister, she met her future husband at a nearby academy when he appeared as a fellow pupil. Two years older than he, and much more cultivated, she helped him with his studies. They were married on February 5, 1826, and had two children.

In poor health when she became First Lady, she assigned her official duties to her daughter, Mary Abigail, her own contribution being her successful effort to secure funds from Congress for setting up a small library in the White House. At the inauguration ceremonies for her husband's successor, she caught a cold which developed into pneumonia, and she died in Washington on March 30, 1853. She was buried in Buffalo.

Five years later, on February 10, 1858, former President Fillmore married Mrs. Caroline C. McIntosh, the 44-year-old widow of a Troy, New York, merchant. The second Mrs. Fillmore, who had no children, survived her husband seven years, dying in Buffalo on August 11, 1881.

Mrs. Franklin Pierce—Born Jane Means Appleton on March 12, 1806, in Hampton, New Hampshire, the daughter of Jesse Appleton, who later became president of Bowdoin College. After the death of her father, she married Franklin Pierce on November 10, 1834. Frail and shy but with strict ideas of propriety, she had a tragic life. Two of her three sons died of infant ailments, and eight weeks before her husband's inauguration as President, their only remaining child—an 11-year-old boy whom she idolized—was killed in a train accident. She never recovered from this blow and spent her years in the White House secluded in her own room, pitifully writing pencil notes to her lost son.

For the limited official entertaining carried on during her husband's administration, her girlhood friend, Mrs. Abby L. Means, who had come to Washington as her companion, served as hostess. Mrs. Pierce died on December 2, 1863, in Andover, Massachusetts, and was buried in Concord, New Hampshire.

Buchanan Administration—James Buchanan, the nation's only bachelor President, had as his official hostess his orphaned niece, Miss Harriet Lane. A charming young woman with a taste for splendor, she entertained elaborately during her uncle's administration. Five years after leaving the White House, in 1866, she married Henry E. Johnson, a Baltimore banker.

Mrs. Abraham Lincoln—Born Mary Ann Todd on December 13, 1818, in Lexington, Kentucky, the daughter of a prosperous merchant. At 22, while visiting a married sister, Mrs. Ninian Edwards, in Springfield, Illinois, she became engaged to one of her brother-in-law's fellow legislators, the backwoods lawyer Abraham Lincoln. Under controversial circumstances—some say Lincoln failed to appear the first time the wedding was scheduled—the engagement was broken; but the marriage finally took place on November 4, 1842.

Lively and intelligent, Mrs. Lincoln was also quick-tempered to the point of emotional instability. In the White House, she aroused widespread criticism for her grasping attitude toward money and her poor judgment in choosing friends. She was so shocked by her husband's assassination that her behavior became increasingly erratic.

After leaving Washington, she brought about a new wave of newspaper abuse by attempting to sell her old clothes and jewelry. On May 19, 1875, a Chicago court adjudged her insane, and she was confined in a private sanitorium at Batavia, Illinois, for four months. Thereafter, she lived quietly abroad or with relatives until she died on July 16, 1882, in Springfield, where she was buried beside her husband. Of their four sons, only the oldest, Robert Todd Lincoln, survived her.

Mrs. Andrew Johnson—Born Eliza McCardle on October 4, 1810, in Leesburg, Tennessee, the daughter of a shoemaker. She was a 16-year-old schoolgirl living with her widowed mother in the Tennessee town of Greeneville when Andrew Johnson arrived to take up tailoring there; a few months later, on May 5, 1827, they were married. Finding he could hardly read and not write at all, she taught him these skills during the next several years. Mrs. Johnson had five children, one of whom died in infancy.

When her husband unexpectedly became President, she was a frail grandmother who told a White House visitor: "We are plain people from Tennessee temporarily in a high place, and you must not expect too much of us in a social way." During her husband's administration, the role of official hostess was shared by their two daughters, Mrs. David Patterson and Mrs. Daniel Stover. Mrs. Johnson died on January 15, 1876, in Greene County, Tennessee and was buried beside her husband in Greeneville.

Mrs. Ulysses S. Grant—Born Julia Boggs Dent on January 26, 1826, in St. Louis, Missouri, the daughter of Colonel Frederick Dent. She met her future husband while he was stationed at the nearby Jefferson Barracks, and they were married on August 22, 1848. The mother of three sons and a daughter, she took the hardships of being an Army wife cheerfully, even living in a tent at times when she joined her husband in the field during the Civil War, but she also enjoyed the glitter of capital society and entertained elaborately as First Lady. Her daughter, Nellie, became Mrs. Algernon Sartoris in a splendid White House wedding on May 21, 1874. Mrs. Grant died on December 14, 1902, in Washington and was buried beside her husband in Grant's Tomb in New York City.

Mrs. Rutherford Birchard Hayes—Born Lucy Ware Webb on August 28, 1831, in Chillicothe, Ohio, the daughter of a physician. A sweet-tempered and devout Methodist, she met her future husband while attending Wesleyan Female College in Cincinnati. He was a lawyer, eight years her senior, who called on her at the urging of his mother, who had already chosen Lucy Webb as the ideal candidate for her son's wife. Rutherford Hayes agreed, the marriage took place on December 30, 1852, and he gained a devoted companion who bore him one daughter and seven sons (three died in infancy). He also gave his country its first First Lady with a college diploma.

But for all her gentle submissiveness, Mrs. Hayes had strong temperance convictions. To please her, President Hayes banished wine from the White House during his administration, thereby inadvertently subjecting her to widespread ridicule as "Lemonade Lucy." Yet Mrs. Hayes was no hard-eyed reformer. She was a warm, friendly woman whose most lasting contribution in the White House was her initiation of annual Easter egg-rolling contests in 1878. She died of a stroke on June 25, 1889, at the Hayes home in Fremont, Ohio, and she was buried there.

Mrs. James Abram Garfield—Born Lucretia Rudolph on April 19, 1832, the daughter of the leading merchant in Hiram, Ohio. She met her future husband while attending a local academy her father had helped to found; after teaching a few years, she married James Garfield on November 11, 1858. They had seven children, two of whom died in infancy. Her tenure as First Lady was brief, but made memorable by tragedy. "The wife of the President is the bravest woman in the Universe," the New York *Herald* said of her. For she had only just recovered from a near-fatal attack of malaria and was convalescing at a seaside cottage in Elberon, New Jersey, when she received word on July 2, 1881, that her husband had been shot.

She immediately returned to Washington and displayed remarkable composure during the 80 days that he lingered on the brink of death. She traveled back to Elberon with him when he was moved there on September 6, and she was at his bedside when he died on September 19, 1881. Mrs. Garfield survived her husband 36 years. She died on March 14, 1918, in Pasadena, California, and was buried beside her husband in Cleveland.

Mrs. Chester Alan Arthur—Born Ellen Lewis Herndon on August 30, 1837, in Fredericksburg, Virginia, the daughter of Captain William Lewis Herndon of the U.S. Navy and explorer of the Amazon. Brought up in gracious Southern style, she was taken on a European tour at 16 and, while visiting New York City a few years later, met Chester Arthur; they were married on October 25, 1859. She had three children, one dying in infancy.

Beautiful and cultivated, she helped her Vermont-born husband develop a taste for elegance but did not live to reign as First Lady. She died of pneumonia in New York on January 12, 1880, ten months before her husband's nomination to the Vice-Presidency, and she was buried in Albany. Arthur's widowed sister, Mrs. John McElroy, served as his hostess while he was in the White House.

Mrs. Grover Cleveland—Born Frances Folsom on July 21, 1864, in Buffalo, New York, the daughter of Oscar Folsom, a lawyer who was killed in a buggy accident in 1875. Her father's partner, Grover Cleveland, then assumed responsibility for her. A tall, attractive young woman, she was attending Wells College when he became President in 1885. He was 48 years old and a bachelor. On June 2, 1886, they were married in the Blue Room of the White House, and this first Presidential wedding in the Executive Mansion was celebrated by the pealing of every church bell in Washington. (John Tyler, the only other President to marry while in office, had been wed at the Church of the Ascension in New York City.)

The 22-year-old Mrs. Cleveland won immediate popularity and was considered the most charming First Lady since Dolley Madison. Her friendliness drew large crowds to her public receptions. She had five children, the second—Esther, who later became Mrs. William Bosanquet—being the only 'Presidential child to be born in the White House (on September 9, 1893). Mrs. Cleveland survived her husband 39 years and, five years after his death, on February 10, 1913, she became the first Presidential widow to remarry. Her second husband was Thomas J. Preston, a Princeton professor of archaeology. She died on October 29, 1947, in Baltimore and was buried in Princeton.

Mrs. Benjamin Harrison—The first Mrs. Harrison was born Caroline (Carrie) Scott, on October 1, 1832, in Oxford, Ohio. She was the daughter of a Presbyterian minister who also conducted a school for girls. After teaching briefly, she married Benjamin Harrison on October 20, 1853; they had two children. As First Lady, she became the first President General of the National Society of the Daughters of the American Revolution. Prevented by ill health from taking an active social role, she died in the White House on October 25, 1892, and was buried in Indianapolis. The duties of official hostess during much of the Harrison administration were assumed by Mrs. Mary Scott Dimmick, a widowed niece of Mrs. Harrison's.

After leaving office, former President Harrison married Mrs. Dimmick in New York City on April 6, 1896; she was 37, and he was then 62. They had one child. The second Mrs. Harrison, a native of Honesdale, Pennsylvania, survived her husband 46 years, dying in New York on January 5, 1948.

Mrs. William McKinley—Born Ida Saxton on June 8, 1847, the daughter of a leading banker in Canton, Ohio. Charming but high-strung, she was, unconventionally, working as a cashier in her father's bank when she met a handsome newcomer to town, Major William McKinley; they were married on January 25, 1871. A year later, she gave birth to a daughter, then became pregnant again soon afterward. Before the birth of her second baby, her mother died, and Mrs. McKinley became severely depressed. The subsequent death of both her infant daughters left her a nervous invalid subject to frequent epileptic fits. Nevertheless, as her husband rose politically, she insisted on appearing with him at all social functions, and he became adept at shielding her when she suffered a seizure.

The nature of her illness was not generally known when she became First Lady, and her delicate health required many innovations in official entertaining. Despite protocol, she was seated beside the President at state dinners, and Mrs. Garret Hobart, wife of McKinley's Vice-

President during his first term, assisted her in many ceremonial duties. Mrs. McKinley survived her slain husband five years, dying on May 26, 1907, in Canton, where she was buried beside him.

Mrs. Theodore Roosevelt—The first Mrs. Roosevelt was born Alice Hathaway Lee on July 29, 1861, in Chestnut Hill, Massachusetts. As a charming girl of 17, she met her future husband while he was attending Harvard. They were married on October 27, 1880, soon after his graduation, when he was 22 and she 19. But two days after the birth of their first child—a daughter, also named Alice—she died (on February 14, 1884) of a previously unsuspected case of Bright's disease. Roosevelt lost his beloved young wife on the same day his mother died of typhoid fever.

He gradually recovered from the shock of this double tragedy after renewing his childhood friendship with Edith Kermit Carow. They were married in London, where she was temporarily living, on December 2, 1886. The daughter of a New York merchant, she had been born in Connecticut on August 6, 1861. The second Mrs. Roosevelt, who gave her husband four sons and another daughter, made an unusually poised and capable First Lady.

Besides coping with the antics of her high-spirited youngsters, she supervised an extensive remodeling of the White House which changed the mansion, her husband said, from "a shabby likeness of the ground floor of the Astor House into a simple and dignified dwelling for the head of a republic." In addition, she arranged an elegant East Room wedding when "Princess Alice" married Congressman Nicholas Longworth of Ohio on February 17, 1906. Mrs. Roosevelt died on September 30, 1948, at the family's summer home in Oyster Bay, New York, and she was buried there.

Mrs. William Howard Taft—Born Helen Herron on June 2, 1861, in Cincinnati, but always called Nellie. The daughter of Judge John Williamson Herron, she visited the White House at 17 as the guest of her father's former law partner, President Rutherford B. Hayes, and decided then that she would like to be First Lady. Studious as well as ambitious, she taught a few years before marrying William Howard Taft on June 19, 1886.

Two months after she did move into the White House, she suffered a stroke which prevented her from taking part in social activities for more than a year; then after her recovery, she and her husband celebrated their 25th wedding anniversary with an evening garden party for which the grounds of the Executive Mansion were spectacularly illuminated. Mrs. Taft left a lasting physical impression on Washington by sponsoring the planting of the capital's famous Japanese cherry trees, which she admired from the time of a diplomatic trip to Japan with her husband. The eldest of her three children, Robert A. Taft, became the distinguished Senator from Ohio. Mrs. Taft died on May 22, 1943, in Washington and was buried beside her husband in Arlington National Cemetery.

Mrs. Woodrow Wilson—The first Mrs. Wilson was born Ellen Louise Axson in Rome, Georgia, on May 15, 1860. Daughter of a Presbyterian minister, she married Wilson on June 24, 1885. An art student with a fondness for music and literature, she had a great influence on her husband; from their marriage to her death, they were never separated a day. They had three daughters, two

of whom were married in the White House—Jessie, who became Mrs. Francis Bowes Sayre in an elaborate East Room ceremony on November 25, 1913, and Eleanor, who became Mrs. William Gibbs McAdoo at a smaller wedding in the Blue Room on May 7, 1914. The latter occasion was marred by the increasing weakness of Mrs. Wilson, who died in the White House on August 6, 1914.

Her death left the President so depressed by grief and loneliness that his physician, Dr. Cary T. Grayson, became alarmed until he, perhaps inadvertently, provided a cure. Dr. Grayson introduced Mrs. Edith Bolling Galt, an attractive 42-year-old widow, to Wilson's cousin, Miss Helen Woodrow Bones, who was temporarily serving as White House hostess. Miss Bones invited Mrs. Galt to tea in March of 1915. Just two months later, the President proposed marriage to Mrs. Galt, and they were married at her Washington home on December 18, 1915.

Born in Wytheville, Virginia, on October 15, 1872, the second Mrs. Wilson had been married to Norman Galt, a Washington jeweler, in 1896, then widowed twelve years later. As First Lady during World War I, she kept official entertaining to a minimum. After her husband was partly paralyzed by a stroke on October 2, 1919, she shielded him from visitors to the extent that she was called "the nation's first Lady President." She survived him 36 years, dying in Washington on December 28, 1961.

Mrs. Warren Gamaliel Harding—Born Florence Kling on August 15, 1860, the daughter of a banker who was the richest man in the small Ohio city of Marion. At 19, she eloped with Henry De-Wolfe, the black sheep in an old local family. A year later, he abandoned her and an infant son, and she was forced to return to her stern father whose rule she had sought to escape.

After being divorced, she married Warren Harding on July 8, 1891; she was five years his senior. Then she took over the business side of the Marion *Star*, which Harding had recently acquired. Mrs. Harding was sometimes credited with inspiring her husband's political career, and in Ohio political circles she was known as "The Duchess." In the White House, failing health limited her social activities, but she survived her husband by a year, dying on November 21, 1924, in Marion, where she was buried.

Mrs. Calvin Coolidge—Born Grace Goodhue in Burlington, Vermont, on January 3, 1879, the daughter of a mechanical engineer. After graduating from the University of Vermont in 1902, she became a teacher at the Clarke Institute for the Deaf in Northampton, Massachusetts. An exceptionally warm person, she married the silent Calvin Coolidge on October 4, 1905, and was sometimes described as his most important asset.

In the White House, despite her husband's frugal management of menu planning, her charm won her wide popularity. She had two sons, but the younger, Calvin Jr., died at 16 of blood poisoning on July 7, 1924, less than a year after his father succeeded to the Presidency. Mrs. Coolidge died on July 8, 1957, in Northampton, and she was buried in Plymouth, Vermont.

Mrs. Herbert Clark Hoover—Born Lou Henry in Waterloo, Iowa, on March 29, 1874, the daughter of a banker who subsequently moved his family to Monterey, California. She entered Stanford University in 1894, planning to become a geology teacher, but she married Hoover, a fellow student, on February 10, 1899, and went to China with him. After living in many foreign lands, while her husband pursued his career, and raising two sons, Mrs. Hoover enjoyed settling in Washington in 1921, when her husband entered President Harding's Cabinet.

By the time she moved into the White House on March 4, 1929, she had a large circle of friends in the capital, and she entertained extensively as First Lady. But on January 1, 1930, she held what proved to be the last of the annual New Year's Day receptions in the Executive Mansion. When Mrs. John Adams had started the custom in 1801, 135 guests appeared to be greeted by the President and his wife; in 1930, more than 9,000 people sought admission, causing Mr. and Mrs. Hoover to make a point of being out of Washington over New Year's during the rest of his term. (His successor, President Franklin Roosevelt, formally discontinued these gatherings which had grown so unwieldy.) Mrs. Hoover died in New York City on January 7, 1944. The gravesite is located at West Branch, Iowa.

Mrs. Franklin Delano Roosevelt—Born Anna Eleanor Roosevelt on October 11, 1884, in New York City, the daughter of Theodore Roosevelt's younger brother, Elliott. Owing to the early death of both her parents, she was brought up by her maternal grandmother, Mrs. V. G. Hall. A shy and solitary child, she was educated in Europe; then on March 17, 1905, she married her fifth cousin, Franklin Roosevelt. They had six children, one son dying in infancy. After her husband's crippling attack of infantile paralysis in 1921, she took an increasingly active part in politics, serving as his eyes and ears at meetings he could not attend.

In the White House, she continued this role on a much broader scale, traveling thousands of miles to inspect coal mines and prisons and American military installations everywhere. A controversial figure as First Lady because of her outspoken support for humanitarian and civil rights causes, Mrs. Roosevelt broke with tradition by holding regular press conferences, lecturing widely, and writing a syndicated newspaper column, "My Day."

She won worldwide esteem as one of the century's outstanding women. President Truman, after her husband's death, appointed her to the United States delegation to the United Nations. She also served the world organization as chairman of its Commission for Human Rights. She died on November 7, 1962, in New York City, and was buried beside her husband at Hyde Park, New York.

Mrs. Harry S Truman—Born Elizabeth Virginia Wallace in Independence, Missouri, on February 13, 1885, but always called Bess. Her maternal grandparents owned a flour mill. As a little girl with blond curls, she captivated her future husband at Sunday school in the First Presbyterian Church. Married on June 28, 1919, she had one daughter.

Unassuming and not fond of ceremony, Mrs. Truman tried to avoid personal publicity as First Lady. She was helped in her effort to live quietly by the fact that serious structural weaknesses were discovered in the White House during her residence there; and from November 1948 until March 1952, the Trumans lived across Pennsylvania Avenue in Blair House. After her husband left office, Mrs. Truman was happy to retire with him to the family home in Independence.

Mrs. Dwight David Eisenhower—Born Mamie Geneva Doud on November 14, 1896, the daughter of a prosperous meat packer in Boone, Iowa. When she was 10, her family moved to Denver, but usually spent the colder months visiting San Antonio. Early in the winter of 1915, while at San Antonio, a young second lieutenant stationed at nearby Fort Sam Houston was introduced to the pretty and popular Miss Doud; on Valentine's Day, they became engaged, and they were married on July 1, 1916. For the next several decades, she lived at Army posts all over the world. She had two sons, but the older died at three.

A warm and friendly woman, Mrs. Eisenhower became accustomed to official entertaining during her Army years. But she described herself as "nonpolitical." After leaving the White House, she enjoyed retirement at the Gettysburg farm that was their first home.

After a massive stroke in late September 1979, she was hospitalized at Walter Reed Army Medical Center in Washington, D.C., where she died in her sleep on November 11, 1979. She was buried beside her husband in Abilene, Kansas.

Mrs. John Fitzgerald Kennedy—Born Jacqueline Lee Bouvier on July 28, 1929, in Southampton, New York, the daughter of John Vernon Bouvier 3d, a wealthy stockbroker. With generations of social prominence on both sides of her family, she attended private schools, had her own pony, and made a glittering début at Newport in 1947. (After the divorce of her parents in 1940, her mother married Hugh D. Auchincloss of Washington and Newport.) Then she went on to further study at Vassar, the Sorbonne, and George Washington University, from which she graduated in 1951. As the "Inquiring Camera Girl" for the Washington *Times-Herald*, she interviewed a young senator whom she had recently met at a dinner party; they were married on September 12, 1953, in St. Mary's Roman Catholic Church at Newport.

The nation's third youngest First Lady, she was 31 on moving into the White House. She won admiration everywhere for her tasteful redecoration of the White House and the glamorous receptions she arranged; this "Kennedy style" to which she contributed so much was a major ingredient in her husband's popularity.

With her two children, she lived in New York City after leaving the White House until her marriage on October 20, 1968, to Aristotle Socrates Onassis, the Greek shipping multimillionaire who died on March 15, 1975.

Mrs. Lyndon Baines Johnson—Born Claudia Alta Taylor on December 22, 1912, in Karnack, Texas, the daughter of Thomas Jefferson Taylor, a prosperous landowner and merchant. When she was two, a nursemaid called her Lady Bird—because she was "as purty as a lady bird"—and the nickname stuck. Brought up by an aunt after her mother died when she was five, she grew into a shy and nature-loving girl with an interest in studying.

Shortly after receiving a journalism degree from the University of Texas, she met the tall secretary to a Texas Congressman; and Lyndon Johnson proposed to her the next day. They were married two months later, on November 17, 1934. Mrs.

Johnson helped her husband along every step of his career. She provided the money for his first Congressional campaign (by borrowing against the $67,000 she was due to inherit from her mother), and she ran his Washington office while he took military leave during World War II.

In the White House, Mrs. Johnson's personal warmth was often credited with smoothing over difficulties caused by her husband's more abrasive personality. She showed a broader concern about public questions than any First Lady with the exception of Mrs. Franklin Roosevelt. Mrs. Johnson was particularly interested in promoting efforts to beautify the nation's cities and towns.

Mrs. Richard Milhous Nixon—Born Thelma Ryan on March 16, 1912, in Ely, Nevada, the daughter of a miner who took up farming a year later, and moved his family to Artesia, California. Her father always called her Pat, and the nickname stayed with her.

After graduating with honors from the University of Southern California in 1937, she taught commercial subjects at Whittier High School in Whittier, California, where she met her future husband in a local amateur theater group; they were married on June 21, 1940. Throughout his career, she has tirelessly supported him at every step. She gained valuable experience toward meeting her responsibilities while her husband was Vice-President under President Eisenhower.

Poised and imperturbable, she has brought up two daughters, the younger of whom, Julie, married David Eisenhower, grandson of the former President, in December 1968. Although she fulfilled her role of official hostess with grace, she generally shunned the limelight while in the White House. In 1976 she suffered a partial stroke.

Mrs. Gerald R. Ford—Born Elizabeth Anne Bloomer on April 8, 1918, in Chicago, Illinois, but moved to Grand Rapids, Michigan at the age of three. Mrs. Ford attended the Bennington School of Dance in Vermont and studied modern dance with Martha Graham. She spent two years in New York as a dancer in the Martha Graham Concert Group. In 1942, she returned to Grand Rapids and married William Warren. They were divorced in 1947. While in Grand Rapids she organized her own dance group and, in addition, became a model and fashion coordinator for a Grand Rapids department store. On October 15, 1948, she married Gerald R. Ford. The Fords have four children.

In Washington, Betty Ford was active in the Republican Wives Club, on the Board of Directors of the League of Republican Women in the District of Columbia, and as President of the Senate Red Cross Club. Mrs. Ford is noted for her candor in expressing her opinions and beliefs and is concerned with promoting equal opportunities for women.

Mrs. Jimmy Carter—Born Eleanor Rosalynn Smith on August 18, 1927, on her maternal grand-father's farm in Plains, Georgia, the daughter of town garage mechanic, Edgar Smith. While attending Georgia Southwestern College, Rosalynn studied interior decorating. She lived at home and helped her family from age 15 when she first went to work in a local beauty parlor. When 18-year-old Rosalynn married Jimmy Carter on July 7, 1946, she had known the U.S. Naval Academy midshipman five years as her best friend's brother. The Carters have four children. Rosalynn enjoyed travelling from base to base until the death of Carter's father caused the couple's return to Plains in 1953 and catalyzed their first team effort in the family peanut business. Rosalynn deftly managed bookkeeping, office work, tax returns and helped to create a thriving business. Rosalynn profoundly influenced Carter's key presidential campaign strategy: to run in all possible primaries.

In the White House, Rosalynn demonstrated extraordinary determination and drive. She went along on presidential junkets both at home and abroad. On her own, she toured the U.S. in support of her favorite causes, campaigning and acting as observer for her husband; abroad she represented him at a presidential inauguration and a papal funeral. But more importantly, Rosalynn maintained her position as advisor to the President, a position which grew in both importance and visibility during the second half of the one-term Carter presidency.

Mrs. Ronald Wilson Reagan—Born Anne Frances Robbins on July 6, 1921, in New York City, the daughter of a New Jersey car salesman who left home soon after her birth. At the age of two, she was sent to live with relatives in Maryland to enable her mother, actress Edith Luckett, to pursue her career. Five years later, her mother married Dr. Loyal Davis, a prominent neurosurgeon in Chicago, who legally adopted Nancy when she was 14. Nancy has always been her nickname.

A leader in student government and dramatics at Girls' Latin School in Chicago, Nancy Davis also played forward on the field hockey team, while gaining a reputation for propriety. Upon graduation from Smith College, where she majored in drama, she pursued a career as a film actress in Hollywood. She became acquainted with Ronald Reagan after consulting with him on a Screen Actors Guild-related problem, and on March 1, 1952, they were married. They have two grown children, Patricia Ann and Ronald Prescott; President Reagan has two other children, a daughter, Maureen, and an adopted son, Michael, from a previous marriage.

Upon moving to Washington, Nancy Reagan arranged for a refurbishing of the Executive Mansion's public rooms and a complete redecorating of the family quarters. She and her husband are credited with bringing back to White House receptions a grand style of entertaining, with limousines, white tie and tails, and couturier gowns. Some of that glamorous world came close to being shattered in the ordeal of the attempted assassination of the President two months after the inauguration.

U.S. PRESIDENTIAL ELECTIONS: 1789—1972

The first four Presidential elections (1789, 1792, 1796, and 1800) were held under Article II, Section 1, of the Constitution, which provided for the College of Electors to vote for two candidates —the one with the majority of votes was elected President, and the next highest became Vice-President. A tie in the Electoral College in 1800 led to the passage of the Twelfth Amendment, which provides for separate ballots for President and Vice-President.

Prior to the election of 1824, records of popular vote are scanty and inaccurate.

ELECTION OF 1789

The Political Scene: The struggle over the ratification of the Constitution had led to the emergence of two political factions, the Federalists, who supported the new Constitution, and the Anti-Federalists, who opposed it.

Nominations and Campaign: George Washington, although identified with the Federalists, was unopposed for the Presidential nomination and received a unanimous vote from the 69 electors.

Results of 1789 Election:

Presidential Candidate	Party	Electoral Votes
George Washington	None	69
John Adams	None	34
Other candidates	None	35
Votes not cast	—	4

Comments: Rhode Island and North Carolina had not yet ratified the Constitution when the electors cast their ballots, and a deadlock between the Federalist Senate and the Anti-Federalist Assembly in New York prevented the choosing of any electors.

ELECTION OF 1792

The Political Scene: Thomas Jefferson and James Madison in Virginia and George Clinton and Aaron Burr in New York provided the leadership of the Democratic-Republican party, which emerged in opposition to Alexander Hamilton's financial policy, to the Federalist emphasis on a strong central government, and to a loose or flexible interpretation of the Constitution.

Nominations: Both parties urged that Washington accept another term, but the Jeffersonians opposed Adams' re-election with Clinton's candidacy.

The Campaign: Adams was accused of being antidemocratic and a secret monarchist, but the real target of the Democratic-Republicans was Hamilton.

Results of 1792 Election:

Presidential Candidate	Party	Electoral Votes
George Washington	Federalist	132
John Adams	Federalist	77
George Clinton	Democratic-Republican	50
Other candidates	—	5
Votes not cast	—	3

ELECTION OF 1796

The Political Scene: Washington, who deplored partisan politics, refused to consider another term, thus insuring the first real contest for the Presidency.

Nominations: Jefferson was the logical candidate for the Democratic-Republicans, but Hamilton was less than

ELECTION OF 1796 (cont.)

happy about the candidacy of John Adams of Massachusetts for the Federalists and hoped that Thomas Pinckney, the ostensible Federalist Vice-Presidential candidate, might win if Federalist electors in the South withheld their votes from Adams.

The Campaign: Adams electors in New England countered Hamilton's scheme by omitting Pinckney from their ballots. The unexpected result of the Federalist bickering was the election of Jefferson to the Vice-Presidency.

Results of 1796 Election

Presidential Candidate	Party	Electoral Votes
John Adams	Federalist	71
Thomas Jefferson	Democratic-Republican	68
Thomas Pinckney	Federalist	59
Aaron Burr	Democratic-Republican	30
Other candidates	—	48

ELECTION OF 1800

The Political Scene: The wars of the French Revolution had created another area of disagreement between the Federalists, who favored Great Britain, and the Democratic-Republicans, who tended to support France. The apparent desire of some Federalist leaders for a war with France alarmed the nation.

Nominations: Congressional caucuses of each party chose the candidates: Adams and Pinckney for the Federalists and Jefferson and Burr for the Democratic-Republicans.

The Campaign: The Federalists gave their opponents a powerful campaign issue in the repressive Alien and Sedition Acts that Jefferson and Madison eloquently denounced in the Virginia and Kentucky Resolutions.

Results of 1800 Election:

Presidential Candidate	Party	Electoral Votes
Thomas Jefferson	Democratic-Republican	73
Aaron Burr	Democratic-Republican	73
John Adams	Federalist	65
Charles C. Pinckney	Federalist	64
John Jay	Federalist	1

Comments: Because the candidates for President and Vice-President were not separately nominated, Jefferson and Burr ended in a tie. The House of Representatives elected Jefferson on the 36th ballot after seven days of balloting. To prevent the situation from arising again, the Twelfth Amendment, ratified in 1804, provided for separate balloting for President and Vice-President. Jefferson's triumph ended the Federalist era and ushered in a quarter century of Democratic-Republican control of the Presidency.

ELECTION OF 1804

The Political Scene: Jefferson's efficient administration and the acquisition of the vast Louisiana Territory gained his party almost universal support and led the more extreme Federalist leaders into the Essex Junto, an abortive scheme to separate the northeastern states from the Union.

Nominations: The Congressional caucuses of each party chose the candidates. A falling-out between Jefferson and Burr led to the latter's replacement as Vice-Presidential candidate by George Clinton of New York. Charles C. Pinckney of South Carolina and Rufus King of New York comprised the Federalist ticket.

The Campaign: The machinations of the Essex Junto all but destroyed the Federalist party; the only question remaining was the size of Jefferson's victory.

Results of 1804 Election:

Presidential Candidate	Party	Electoral Votes	Vice-Presidential Candidate	Party	Electoral Votes
Thomas Jefferson	Democratic-Republican	162	George Clinton	Democratic-Republican	162
Charles C. Pinckney	Federalist	14	Rufus King	Federalist	14

Comments: Jefferson won every electoral vote but those of Connecticut and Delaware and two in Maryland.

ELECTION OF 1808

The Political Scene: The disastrous effects of the Embargo of 1808 on American commerce revived the Federalist party in New England and caused dissension among the Jeffersonians.

Nominations: It took considerable pressure by Jefferson to get the rebellious factions within his party to accept his choice of James Madison of Virginia to succeed him. Clinton of New York was again the Vice-Presidential candidate. Federalist leaders engineered the renomination of the 1804 ticket of Pinckney and King.

The Campaign: Running primarily on the Embargo issue, the Federalists considerably improved their showing over the previous election, but could not overcome the solid Democratic-Republican majority that had been created.

Results of 1808 Election:

Presidential Candidate	Party	Electoral Votes	Vice-Presidential Candidate	Party	Electoral Votes
James Madison	Democratic-Republican	122	George Clinton	Democratic-Republican	113
Charles C. Pinckney	Federalist	47	Rufus King	Federalist	47
George Clinton	Democratic-Republican	6	Other candidates	—	15
Votes not cast	—	1	Votes not cast	—	1

ELECTION OF 1812

The Political Scene: Conflict with Great Britain over maritime rights and alleged incitement of Indian rebellion caused Madison to request a declaration of war in June 1812.

Nominations: The Republican congressional caucus, dominated by young "War Hawk" representatives from the frontier states, renominated Madison, a month before the war message. Elbridge Gerry of Massachusetts received the Vice-Presidential nomination. Insurgent Republicans in New York put up DeWitt Clinton, who thereupon received Federalist support but not an official endorsement. Jared Ingersoll of Pennsylvania ran with him.

The Campaign: Although Clinton tried to avoid running as a Peace-Federalist candidate, his strength clearly lay in the Northeast, the section most unenthusiastic about the war.

Results of 1812 Election:

Presidential Candidate	Party	Electoral Votes	Vice-Presidential Candidate	Party	Electoral Votes
James Madison	Democratic-Republican	128	Elbridge Gerry	Democratic-Republican	131
DeWitt Clinton	Federalist	89	Jared Ingersoll	Federalist	86
Votes not cast	—	1	Votes not cast	—	1

Comments: The vote of Pennsylvania together with the solid backing of the South and West elected Madison.

ELECTION OF 1816

The Political Scene: The end of the War of 1812 and an economic boom assured the continued ascendancy of the Democratic-Republicans.

Nominations: The congressional caucus chose James Monroe of Virginia over William H. Crawford of Georgia in a close contest. The choice of Daniel D. Tompkins for the Vice-Presidency renewed the Virginia-New York alliance. Rufus King of New York, although not selected by any formal process, was considered the Federalist nominee.

The Campaign: King, the last Federalist candidate, received only the votes of Massachusetts, Connecticut, and Delaware in a campaign he hardly contested at all.

Results of 1816 Election:

Presidential Candidate	Party	Electoral Votes	Vice-Presidential Candidate	Party	Electoral Votes
James Monroe	Democratic-Republican	183	Daniel D. Tompkins	Democratic-Republican	183
Rufus King	Federalist	34	John E. Howard	Federalist	22
Votes not cast	—	4	Other candidates	—	12
			Votes not cast	—	4

Comments: Following Washington, Jefferson, and Madison, Monroe was the last of the Virginia dynasty and the last of the men of the revolutionary era to hold the Presidency.

ELECTION OF 1820

The Political Scene: No great national issue disturbed the country enough for anyone to oppose Monroe's reelection.

Nomination and Campaign: Monroe received every electoral vote except that of William Plumer of New Hampshire.

Results of 1820 Election:

Presidential Candidate	Party	Electoral Votes	Vice-Presidential Candidate	Party	Electoral Votes
James Monroe	Democratic-Republican	231	Daniel D. Tompkins	Democratic-Republican	218
John Quincy Adams	Independent	1	Other candidates	—	14
Votes not cast	—	3	Votes not cast	—	3

Comments: The tradition that Plumer voted for John Quincy Adams in order to preserve for Washington alone the honor of a unanimous selection is of dubious validity; Plumer simply disliked Monroe and his policies.

ELECTION OF 1824

The Political Scene: The "Era of Good Feelings" ended as the Democratic-Republican organization dissolved into sectional groupings.

Nominations: A poorly attended congressional caucus selected William H. Crawford of Georgia, while various state legislatures nominated Henry Clay of Kentucky, Andrew Jackson of Tennessee, John Quincy Adams of Massachusetts, and John C. Calhoun of South Carolina. Calhoun subsequently withdrew to run for the Vice-Presidency on Jackson's ticket.

The Campaign: Clay put forward his celebrated plan calling for a strong protective tariff, domestic improvements, and a national bank—policies that Adams also endorsed. Jackson relied on his popular appeal as a military hero.

Results of 1824 Election:

Presidential Candidate	Party	Electoral Votes	Popular Vote Total	Percentage	Vice-Presidential Candidate and Electoral Votes	Party
John Quincy Adams	None	84	115,696	31.9	John C. Calhoun ... 182	None
Andrew Jackson	None	99	152,933	42.2	Nathan Sanford ... 30	None
William H. Crawford	None	41	46,979	12.9	Nathaniel Macon ... 24	None
Henry Clay	None	37	47,136	13.0	Other candidates ... 25	

Comments: Since no candidate had gained a majority of the electoral vote, the House of Representatives, voting by states and with each state having one vote, chose Adams on the first ballot.

ELECTION OF 1828

The Political Scene: More than two-thirds of the electorate had voted against Adams in 1824. This circumstance negated his hopes for a successful administration, and the Jacksonians commenced their plans to unseat him.

Nominations: The Tennessee legislature renominated Jackson in 1825, and the incumbent Vice-President Calhoun once again agreed to be his running mate. This is considered the first ticket of the modern Democratic party. Adams ran for reelection as a National Republican.

The Campaign: Although important differences on national questions divided Adams and Jackson, these issues disappeared in a welter of vituperative personal attacks against each standard-bearer.

Results of 1828 Election:

Presidential Candidate	Party	Electoral Votes	Popular Vote Total	Percentage	Vice-Presidential Candidate and Electoral Votes		Party
Andrew Jackson	Democratic	178	647,292	56.0	John C. Calhoun	171	Democratic
John Quincy Adams	National Republican	83	507,730	44.0	Richard Rush	83	National Republican
					William Smith	7	Democratic

Comments: The election of Jackson, the frontier hero, represented a triumph for the West and the South. It also symbolized the arrival of the common people to political power.

ELECTION OF 1832

The Political Scene: Internal disputes within Jackson's cabinet and the President's strong stand against nullification caused a break between Jackson and Calhoun. Jackson's veto of a bill rechartering the Bank of the United States, however, created the major issue in the campaign.

Conventions and Nominees: For the first time the national nominating convention was employed by the three parties in the field. All met at Baltimore, with the Anti-Masonic party holding the first convention (September 26, 1831) and choosing William Wirt of Maryland. The National Republicans nominated the legislative champion of the Bank of the United States—Henry Clay of Kentucky, while the Democrats unanimously endorsed Jackson and replaced Calhoun for the Vice-Presidency with Martin Van Buren of New York. The Democratic convention adopted a rule requiring a two-thirds vote of the whole convention for nomination. This remained in effect until 1936.

The Campaign: Clay attacked Jackson's veto of the bank bill and his opposition to internal improvements. He misjudged the popular temper; to the average voter, Jackson's bank policy was a blow against monopoly and privilege.

Results of 1832 Election:

Presidential Candidate	Party	Electoral Votes	Popular Vote Total	Percentage	Vice-Presidential Candidate and Electoral Votes		Party
Andrew Jackson	Democratic	219	688,242	54.5	Martin Van Buren	189	Democratic
Henry Clay	National Republican	49	473,462	37.5	John Sergeant	49	National Republican
John Floyd	Independent	11	—	—	Henry Lee	11	Independent
William Wirt	Anti-Masonic	7	101,051	8.0	Amos Ellmaker	7	Anti-Masonic
Votes not cast	—	2	—	—	William Wilkins	30	Independent
					Votes not cast	2	—

Comments: The Anti-Masonic party, opposed to the Masons and other secret societies, was the first third party in American history. On December 28, 1832, following the election, Vice-President Calhoun resigned his office.

ELECTION OF 1836

The Political Scene: Opponents of "King Andrew" Jackson formed the Whig party, taking the name of the antimonarchial English political party to emphasize Jackson's alleged autocratic tendencies.

Conventions and Nominees: Jackson desired his Vice-President Martin Van Buren of New York to succeed him, and the Democratic convention at Baltimore (May 20–22, 1835) unanimously ratified his choice. Richard M. Johnson of Kentucky was the Vice-Presidential candidate. The Whigs, lacking a leader with national appeal, nominated three sectional candidates (Daniel Webster of Massachusetts, Hugh L. White of Tennessee, and William Henry Harrison of Ohio) in an effort to throw the election into the House of Representatives.

The Campaign: Jackson's personality and the record of his administration provided the issues for the campaign. The influence of "Old Hickory" was probably decisive, since Van Buren received a bare majority of the popular vote. The Senate, for the only time in history, elected the Vice-President with 33 votes for Johnson, 16 for Granger.

Results of 1836 Election:

Presidential Candidate	Party	Electoral Votes	Popular Vote Total	Percentage	Vice-Presidential Candidate and Electoral Votes		Party
Martin Van Buren	Democratic	170	764,198	50.9	Richard M. Johnson	147	Democratic
William H. Harrison	Whig	73	549,508	36.6	Francis Granger	77	Whig
Hugh L. White	Whig	26	145,352	9.7	John Tyler	47	Democratic
Daniel Webster	Whig	14	41,287	2.7	William Smith	23	Independent
W. P. Mangum	Independent	11	—	—			

ELECTION OF 1840

The Political Scene: The Panic of 1837, which had been caused mainly by Jackson's erratic financial policies, fell with full force during Van Buren's administration, hurting his prospects for reelection.

Conventions and Nominees: The Whigs in Pennsylvania met at Harrisburg (May 4–5, 1840) to name William Henry Harrison of Ohio and John Tyler of Virginia as their ticket, while the Democrats convening at Baltimore (May 5–7) unanimously renominated Van Buren. The antislavery Liberty party in a convention at Albany, New York, nominated James G. Birney of New York and Thomas Earle of Pennsylvania.

The Campaign: The Whigs avoided any divisive issues and conducted a campaign of parades and ballyhoo, complete with the first memorable political slogan, "Tippecanoe and Tyler too."

Results of 1840 Election:

Presidential Candidate	Party	Electoral Votes	Popular Vote Total	Percentage	Vice-Presidential Candidate and Electoral Votes		Party
William H. Harrison	Whig	234	1,275,612	52.9	John Tyler	234	Whig
Martin Van Buren	Democratic	60	1,130,033	46.8	Richard Johnson	48	Democratic
James G. Birney	Liberty	—	7,053	.3	Thomas Earle	—	Liberty
					L. W. Tazewell	11	Independent
					James K. Polk	1	Democratic

Comments: Barely a month after his inauguration, Harrison became the first President to die in office and was succeeded by Tyler on April 6, 1841.

ELECTION OF 1844

The Political Scene: In his one term Tyler managed to disrupt the Whig party and to secure the annexation of Texas, but he failed to settle the Oregon question.

Conventions and Nominees: The Whigs convened at Baltimore (May 1) to nominate Henry Clay for President and Senator Theodore Frelinghuysen of New Jersey for Vice-President. Later in the month at the same city, the Democrats chose the first "dark horse" nominee for the Presidency. Ex-President Van Buren had a clear majority on the early ballots but could not reach the required two-thirds vote. On the ninth ballot, the convention chose James K. Polk of Tennessee with George M. Dallas of Pennsylvania as the Vice-Presidential candidate. The Liberty party meeting at Buffalo, New York (August 1843), again named James G. Birney with Thomas Morris of Ohio as his running mate.

The Campaign: Polk, an ardent expansionist, favored the Texas annexation and the acquisition of Oregon with the slogan "Fifty-four forty or fight." Clay was hurt in the South by his wavering on Texas, and in the North by the defection of antislavery Whigs to the Liberty party.

Results of 1844 Election:

Presidential Candidate	Party	Electoral Votes	Popular Vote Total	Percentage	Vice-Presidential Candidate
James K. Polk	Democratic	170	1,339,368	49.6	George M. Dallas
Henry Clay	Whig	105	1,300,687	48.1	Theodore Frelinghuysen
James G. Birney	Liberty	—	62,197	2.3	Thomas Morris

Comments: Although far from conclusive, Polk's victory was regarded as a popular endorsement of a vigorous policy of expansion.

ELECTION OF 1848

The Political Scene: Polk settled the Oregon dispute with Great Britain, led the nation through a successful war with Mexico, and secured a vast accretion of territory. Yet he left office immensely unpopular and with the question of the extension of slavery into the new territories threatening to divide the country.

Conventions and Nominees: Polk had renounced a second term and the Democratic convention meeting at Baltimore (May 1848) picked a ticket of Lewis Cass of Michigan and William O. Butler of Kentucky. Although most Whigs had opposed the Mexican War, it provided them with their party's two leading Presidential candidates, Generals Zachary Taylor and Winfield Scott. The convention at Philadelphia named Taylor of Louisiana with Millard Fillmore of New York. Antislavery dissidents from both parties formed the Free Soil party and, meeting at Buffalo (August 1848), nominated ex-President Martin Van Buren with Charles Francis Adams of Massachusetts as his running mate.

The Campaign: On the paramount issue, the Free Soilers opposed extension of slavery into the newly acquired territories, while Cass endorsed the concept of popular sovereignty, or letting the settlers decide. Taylor refused to take any stand at all, correctly counting on his war popularity to carry him to victory.

Results of 1848 Election:

Presidential Candidate	Party	Electoral Votes	Popular Vote Total	Percentage	Vice-Presidential Candidate
Zachary Taylor	Whig	163	1,362,101	47.3	Millard Fillmore
Lewis Cass	Democratic	127	1,222,674	42.4	William O. Butler
Martin Van Buren	Free Soil	—	291,616	10.1	Charles Francis Adams

Comments: Taylor died on July 9, 1850. The succession of Fillmore to the Presidency made possible the Compromise of 1850.

ELECTION OF 1852

The Political Scene: Moderates in both parties had been alarmed by threats of disunion and vainly hoped the Compromise of 1850 would stifle the slavery agitation.

Conventions and Nominees: President Fillmore desired another term, but the Whigs again turned to a military hero, selecting General Winfield Scott of Virginia on the 53d ballot. The convention then named William A. Graham of North Carolina for the Vice-Presidency. The Democrats, who like the Whigs met at Baltimore in June, had a number of potential nominees, but none of the leaders could gain the necessary two-thirds majority. On the 99th ballot, "dark horse" Franklin Pierce of New Hampshire was named with William R. King of Alabama as the party's Vice-Presidential candidate. The remnants of the Free Soil party met in Pittsburgh in August to choose a ticket of John P. Hale of New Hampshire and George W. Julian of Indiana.

The Campaign: Both sides avoided the slavery question, and personalities dominated a rather listless campaign.

Results of 1852 Election:

Presidential Candidate	Party	Electoral Votes	Popular Vote Total	Percentage	Vice-Presidential Candidate
Franklin Pierce	Democratic	254	1,609,038	50.8	William R. King
Winfield Scott	Whig	42	1,386,629	43.8	William A. Graham
John P. Hale	Free Soil	—	156,297	4.9	George Julian

Comments: Scott was the last Presidential candidate of the Whig party.

ELECTION OF 1856

The Political Scene: Despite their overwhelming victory in 1852, the Democrats found it more and more difficult to reconcile their Northern and Southern wings, while the Whigs disintegrated entirely. The passage of the Kansas-Nebraska Act led to the founding of the Republican party.

Conventions and Nominees: In their first national convention at Philadelphia in June, the Republicans nominated John C. Frémont of California and William L. Dayton of New Jersey. Although widely considered to be the ablest leader in the party, Stephen A. Douglas' sponsorship of the Kansas-Nebraska Act prevented his nomination by the Democratic convention at Cincinnati in June. On the 17th ballot a Northerner acceptable to the South, James Buchanan of Pennsylvania, was named with John C. Breckinridge of Kentucky as his running mate. The anti-immigrant, anti-Catholic, American (or Know-Nothing) party had nominated ex-President Fillmore and Andrew J. Donelson at its convention in Philadelphia in February.

The Campaign: The Republicans endorsed a protective tariff and condemned the extension of slavery into the territories. The Democratic platform supported the Kansas-Nebraska Act and the principle of popular sovereignty for the territories.

Results of 1856 Election:

Presidential Candidate	Party	Electoral Votes	Popular Vote Total	Percentage	Vice-Presidential Candidate
James Buchanan	Democratic	174	1,839,237	45.6	John C. Breckinridge
John C. Frémont	Republican	114	1,341,028	33.3	William L. Dayton
Millard Fillmore	American	8	849,872	21.1	Andrew J. Donelson

Comments: Frémont's 114 electoral votes—all from free states—demonstrated the sectional nature of the new Republican party.

ELECTION OF 1860

The Political Scene: The Dred Scott decision, bloody fighting between sectional partisans in Kansas, and John Brown's raid on Harpers Ferry had widened the gulf between the free and slave states. Politicians in the states of the Deep South openly threatened secession if a Republican President was elected.

Conventions and Nominations: The Democrats meeting at Charlest..r (April 23–May 3, 1860) failed to nominate a candidate after 57 ballots, because the delegations of eight southern states withdrew in protest against the platform statement on slavery in the territories. Reassembling in Baltimore (June 18–23), the party nominated Stephen A. Douglas of Illinois and Benjamin Fitzpatrick of Alabama after further Southern defections. When Fitzpatrick declined to run, the national committee chose Herschel V. Johnson of Georgia. The Southern seceders, calling themselves the National Democratic party, convened in Baltimore on June 28 and nominated John Breckinridge of Kentucky and Joseph Lane of Oregon on a platform that endorsed slavery in the territories. The Constitutional Union party, which was composed chiefly of former Whigs and was strongest in the border states, had met in Baltimore (May 9) to choose John Bell of Tennessee and Edward Everett of Massachusetts. Abraham Lincoln of Illinois required only three ballots to defeat preconvention favorite William H. Seward at the Republican convention in Chicago (May 18–20).

The Campaign: The Republicans promised congressional action to preserve freedom in the territories. Slavery and the sectional issues dominated the scene.

Results of 1860 Election:

Presidential Candidate	Party	Electoral Votes	Popular Vote Total	Percentage	Vice-Presidential Candidate
Abraham Lincoln	Republican	180	1,867,198	39.8	Hannibal Hamlin
Stephen A. Douglas	Democratic	12	1,379,434	29.4	Herschel V. Johnson
John C. Breckinridge	National Democratic	72	854,248	18.2	Joseph Lane
John Bell	Constitutional Union	39	591,658	12.6	Edward Everett

Comments: The division among his opponents seemed to insure Lincoln's election. Curiously, however, if all the popular votes cast for his opponents had been given to one man, Lincoln still would have won the electoral vote, because of the heavy distribution of his vote among the more populous states. A little more than a month after the election, South Carolina seceded from the Union.

ELECTION OF 1864

The Political Scene: The apparent inability of the Union armies to end Confederate resistance increased the sentiment for peace, causing many leading Republicans to oppose Lincoln's renomination.

Conventions and Nominees: The Republicans (styling themselves the National Union party) met at Baltimore in June and renominated Lincoln. War-Democrat Andrew Johnson of Tennessee became the Vice-Presidential candidate. The Democrats meeting at Chicago in August nominated a ticket of General George B. McClellan of New Jersey and George H. Pendleton of Ohio.

The Campaign: The Democratic platform pronounced the war a failure and demanded a cessation of hostilities and the restoration of peace on the basis of the Federal Union of States. But spectacular Union victories at Mobile Bay, Atlanta, and in the Shenandoah Valley destroyed this peace platform, and insured Lincoln's victory.

Results of 1864 Election:

Presidential Candidate	Party	Electoral Votes	Popular Vote Total	Percentage	Vice-Presidential Candidate
Abraham Lincoln	Republican	212	2,219,362	55.1	Andrew Johnson
George McClellan	Democratic	21	1,805,063	44.9	George Pendleton
Votes not cast		—	1	—	—	Votes not cast

Comments: John Wilkes Booth assassinated Lincoln, who was succeeded on April 15, 1865, by Andrew Johnson.

ELECTION OF 1868

The Political Scene: President Johnson and the Republican leadership fell out over Reconstruction policies. The Senate failed by one vote of removing the President by impeachment in May 1868.

Conventions and Nominees: The Republicans met (as the Union Republican party) at Chicago in May and selected General Ulysses S. Grant of Illinois with Schuyler Colfax of Indiana as his running mate. The Democrats meeting in Tammany Hall, New York City, in July drafted Horatio Seymour of New York after 21 ballots and complex maneuverings had failed to produce a candidate. The Vice-Presidential nod went to Francis P. Blair of Missouri.

The Campaign: In 1868 and for a generation thereafter, the Republicans used the "bloody shirt" tactic, attempting to label the Democrats as the party of secession and treason.

Results of 1868 Election:

Presidential Candidate	Party	Electoral Votes	Popular Vote Total	Percentage	Vice-Presidential Candidate
Ulysses S. Grant	Republican	214	3,013,313	52.7	Schuyler Colfax
Horatio Seymour	Democratic	80	2,703,933	47.3	Francis P. Blair, Jr.

Comments: Texas, Virginia, and Mississippi were not readmitted to the Union until 1870, therefore they cast no votes in this election. Grant greatly benefited from black votes in the South.

ELECTION OF 1872

The Political Scene: Evidence of corruption within his administration and disagreement with his Southern policy led many Republicans to oppose Grant's renomination.

Conventions and Nominees: When it became apparent, however, that Grant would be renominated, a group of dissenters calling themselves the Liberal Republican party met at Cincinnati in May and nominated a ticket of Horace Greeley of New York and B. Gratz Brown of Missouri. Greeley's nomination provided a dilemma for the Democrats. Greeley had consistently criticized their party, but to nominate someone else would serve only to reelect Grant. Accordingly, the Democrats in convention at Baltimore in July accepted Greeley and Brown. The Republicans at Philadelphia in June had unanimously renominated Grant.

The Campaign: Although tariff and currency questions were debated to some extent, the Republicans relied on Grant's war record to overcome the scandals. Most Democratic voters reacted unenthusiastically to Greeley.

Results of 1872 Election:

Presidential Candidate	Party	Electoral Votes	Popular Vote Total	Percentage	Vice-Presidential Candidate	Electoral Votes
Ulysses S. Grant	Republican	286	3,597,375	55.6	Henry Wilson	286
Horace Greeley	Democratic, Liberal Republican	—	2,833,711	43.8	B. Gratz Brown	47
Thomas A. Hendricks	Democratic	42	—	—	Other candidates	19
B. Gratz Brown	Democratic, Liberal Republican	18	—	—	Votes not cast	14
Other candidates		—	3	—	—	—
Votes not cast		—	17	—	—	—

Comments: Greeley died after the election and his electoral votes went to other candidates.

ELECTION OF 1876

The Political Scene: Growing national indignation at the scandals of Grant's second administration caused both parties to seek Presidential candidates associated with reform government.

Conventions and Nominees: The Republicans met at Cincinnati in June to select Rutherford B. Hayes of Ohio on the seventh ballot after the reform element had blocked the nomination of James G. Blaine. William A. Wheeler of New York was the Vice-Presidential candidate. Samuel J. Tilden of New York, who was acclaimed for his part in breaking up the notorious Tweed Ring, received a first-ballot nomination from the Democrats at St. Louis in June. Thomas A. Hendricks of Indiana was named for the Vice-Presidency. The inflationary Greenback party named Peter Cooper of New York and Samuel F. Carey of Ohio.

The Campaign: Hayes's good record as governor of Ohio somewhat blunted Democratic efforts to capitalize on the corruption of the Grant regime. Tilden waged a very cautious campaign and probably did not pay enough attention to the "solid South."

Results of 1876 Election:

Presidential Candidate	Party	Electoral Votes	Popular Vote Total	Percentage	Vice-Presidential Candidate
Rutherford B. Hayes	Republican	185	4,035,924	47.9	William A. Wheeler
Samuel J. Tilden	Democratic	184	4,287,670	50.9	Thomas A. Hendricks
Peter Cooper	Greenback	—	82,797	1.0	Samuel F. Carey

Comments: When the returns came in, the 19 electoral votes of South Carolina, Florida, and Louisiana were in dispute. After months of controversy over rival sets of returns, Congress established an electoral commission composed of five senators, five representatives, and five members of the Supreme Court to determine the valid returns. The commissioners—eight Republicans and seven Democrats—voted along strict party lines to award the 19 votes and the Presidency to Hayes.

ELECTION OF 1880

The Political Scene: Throughout the entire period of the "Gilded Age," few significant issues divided the two parties. This was particularly true in 1880 when, appealing to the veteran vote, both Republicans and Democrats nominated former generals.

Conventions and Nominees: The Republicans met in Chicago in June to choose "dark horse" James A. Garfield of Ohio on the 36th ballot, after reform or "Mugwump" delegates had blocked a proposed third term for Grant and a drive for James G. Blaine had collapsed. Chester A. Arthur of New York was named for the Vice-Presidency. Winfield S. Hancock of Pennsylvania and William H. English of Indiana comprised the ticket selected by the Democrats at Cincinnati in June. The Greenback party nominated a third general, James B. Weaver of Iowa, with B. J. Chambers of Texas named for the Vice-Presidency.

The Campaign: Personal attacks on the candidates characterized the campaign. The Democrats emphasized Garfield's involvement in the Crédit Mobilier Scandal, while the Republicans harped on Hancock's inexperience and naiveté.

Results of 1880 Election:

Presidential Candidate	Party	Electoral Votes	Popular Vote Total	Percentage	Vice-Presidential Candidate
James A. Garfield	Republican	214	4,454,433	48.3	Chester A. Arthur
Winfield S. Hancock	Democratic	155	4,444,976	48.2	William English
James B. Weaver	Greenback	—	308,649	3.3	B. J. Chambers

Comments: In July 1881 Charles J. Guiteau, a deranged and disappointed office-seeker, shot Garfield, who died on September 19, 1881. Arthur succeeded to the Presidency the following day.

ELECTION OF 1884

The Political Scene: Although President by accident, Arthur made a respectable record in the office. He failed, however, to build up enough support for a nomination in his own right.

Conventions and Nominees: Despite a challenge from Arthur, James G. Blaine of Maine succeeded in this his third try for the Republican nomination. The Chicago convention meeting in June then picked John A. Logan of Illinois as his running mate. The Democrats convening in Chicago on July 8 nominated Grover Cleveland of New York and Thomas A. Hendricks of Indiana.

The Campaign: In what has been remembered as the dirtiest campaign in American history, Cleveland was charged with fathering an illegitimate child, and Blaine was abused for alleged shady practices while Speaker of the House. Many prominent "Mugwump" Republicans refused to support Blaine and endorsed Cleveland.

Results of 1884 Election:

Presidential Candidate	Party	Electoral Votes	Popular Vote Total	Percentage	Vice-Presidential Candidate
Grover Cleveland	Democratic	219	4,875,971	48.5	Thomas A. Hendricks
James G. Blaine	Republican	182	4,852,234	48.3	John A. Logan
Benjamin F. Butler	Greenback	—	175,066	1.7	A. M. West
John P. St. John	Prohibition	—	150,957	1.5	William Daniel

Comments: Just prior to election day, one of Blaine's supporters referred to the Democrats as the party of "Rum, Romanism and Rebellion," a slur on Irish Catholic voters that probably caused Blaine to lose New York State and, hence, the election.

ELECTION OF 1888

The Political Scene: Cleveland's firm, honest, and conservative administration gained him a great deal of respect, but at the same time offended powerful pressure groups such as the Grand Army of the Republic and the tariff protectionists.

Conventions and Nominees: The Democrats renominated Cleveland by acclamation in St. Louis in June. Allen G. Thurman of Ohio joined him on the ticket. In a convention marked with much intrigues and bargaining, the Republicans named Benjamin Harrison of Indiana and Levi P. Morton of New York at Chicago in June.

The Campaign: The Democrats condemned the inequities of the high protective tariff. The Republicans replied that the system of protection served the interests of America over those of Europe.

Results of 1888 Election:

Presidential Candidate	Party	Electoral Votes	Popular Vote Total	Percentage	Vice-Presidential Candidate
Benjamin Harrison	Republican	233	5,445,269	47.8	Levi P. Morton
Grover Cleveland	Democratic	168	5,540,365	48.6	Allen G. Thurman
Clinton B. Fisk	Prohibition	—	250,122	2.2	John A. Brooks
Aaron J. Streeter	Union Labor	—	147,606	1.3	C. E. Cunningham

Comments: The Republicans managed to turn part of the Irish vote against Cleveland, when, on a pretext, a foolish letter favoring Cleveland over Harrison was obtained from the British Minister in Washington.

ELECTION OF 1892

The Political Scene: Popular anger with veteran and tariff legislation combined with a growing militancy among farmers to hand the Republicans a stunning defeat in the midterm elections of 1890 and brighten Democratic prospects for regaining the Presidency.

Conventions and Nominees: Both parties met in June, the Democrats at Chicago and the Republicans at Minneapolis, to renominate their standard-bearers of 1888—Cleveland and Harrison. For the Vice-Presidency, the Democrats chose Adlai E. Stevenson of Illinois; the Republicans, Whitelaw Reid of New York. The Populist or People's party held its first national nominating convention at Omaha in July, endorsing James B. Weaver of Iowa and James G. Field of Virginia.

Campaign Issues: Debate centered on controversial measures of the Harrison administration together with the demand for the free and unlimited coinage of silver and the general agrarian unrest.

Results of 1892 Election:

Presidential Candidate	Party	Electoral Votes	Popular Vote Total	Percentage	Vice-Presidential Candidate
Grover Cleveland	Democratic	277	5,556,982	46.0	Adlai E. Stevenson
Benjamin Harrison	Republican	145	5,191,466	43.0	Whitelaw Reid
James B. Weaver	Populist	22	1,029,960	8.5	James G. Field
John Bidwell	Prohibition	—	271,111	2.2	James B. Cranfill

Comments: The Populists became the first third party since 1860 to win any electoral votes.

ELECTION OF 1896

The Political Scene: The Panic of 1893 struck with full force after Cleveland's inauguration, and the subsequent "hard times" were blamed on the Democrats. It appeared possible that the Populists could replace the Democrats as the second major party.

Conventions and Nominees: The Republican convention at St. Louis in June nominated William McKinley of Ohio on the first ballot and Garrett Hobart of New Jersey as his running mate. The Democrats meeting at Chicago in July named William Jennings Bryan of Nebraska on the fifth ballot. Arthur Sewall of Maine was selected for the Vice-Presidential nomination. The Populists at their St. Louis convention in July accepted Bryan, but named Thomas E. Watson of Georgia for the Vice-Presidency.

The Campaign: Bryan's stand for the "free and unlimited coinage of silver" brought down on him the fury of the country's conservative interests. McKinley conducted a "front porch" campaign, but a strenuous and expensive effort was carried on in his behalf under the direction of Mark Hanna.

Results of 1896 Election:

Presidential Candidate	Party	Electoral Votes	Popular Vote Total	Percentage	Vice-Presidential Candidate
William McKinley	Republican	271	7,113,734	51.0	Garret Hobart
William J. Bryan	Democratic-Populist	176	6,516,722	46.7	Arthur Sewall / Thomas E. Watson
John M. Palmer	National Democratic	—	135,456	.97	Simon Buckner
Joshua Levering	Prohibition	—	131,285	.94	Hale Johnson

Comments: Bryan, whose "Cross of Gold" speech is perhaps the most famous ever made at a convention, failed to win any of the nation's industrial states, indicating the limited appeal of the free-silver issue.

ELECTION OF 1900

The Political Scene: The successful conclusion of the Spanish-American War and returning prosperity buoyed Republican hopes for another Presidential victory.

Conventions and Nominees: At the Republicans' Philadelphia convention in June, McKinley was unanimously renominated and war hero Theodore Roosevelt of New York was selected for the Vice-Presidency. The Democrats met at Kansas City, Missouri, in July to choose Bryan again. Adlai E. Stevenson of Illinois was named for Vice-President. This year Eugene V. Debs of Indiana received the first of his five Presidential nominations by the Socialist party.

The Campaign: Theodore Roosevelt did most of the campaigning for the Republican ticket, stressing the "full dinner pail" of McKinley prosperity and the national pride in territories acquired from Spain. Bryan once more endorsed free silver, but called imperialism the paramount issue. He also criticized the growth of the giant trusts.

Results of 1900 Election:

Presidential Candidate	Party	Electoral Votes	Popular Vote Total	Percentage	Vice-Presidential Candidate
William McKinley	Republican	292	7,219,828	51.7	Theodore Roosevelt
William J. Bryan	Democratic	155	6,358,160	45.5	Adlai E. Stevenson
John C. Wolley	Prohibition	—	210,200	1.5	Henry B. Metcalf
Eugene V. Debs	Socialist	—	95,744	.7	Job Harriman

Comments: McKinley, who was shot by anarchist Leon Czolgosz at the Pan-American Exposition in Buffalo, died on September 14, 1901. At the age of 42, Roosevelt became the youngest President in history.

ELECTION OF 1904

The Political Scene: Roosevelt's moderately progressive policies, his energetic regimen, and his obvious relish of the Presidency made him the most popular President since Lincoln.

Conventions and Nominees: Mark Hanna's death early in 1904 removed the only man capable of challenging Roosevelt for the Presidential nomination. The Republican convention meeting at Chicago in June gave "T.R." its unanimous vote and chose Charles W. Fairbanks of Indiana to run with him. Having lost twice with the progressive Bryan, the Democrats turned to a more conservative candidate, Judge Alton B. Parker of New York. The convention, which met at St. Louis in July, then named Henry G. Davis of West Virginia for Vice-President.

The Campaign: Parker, who endorsed the gold standard, was portrayed by the Democrats as a safe, conservative candidate. A colorless figure, he could not hope to match Roosevelt's popular appeal.

Results of 1904 Election:

Presidential Candidate	Party	Electoral Votes	Popular Vote Total	Percentage	Vice-Presidential Candidate
Theodore Roosevelt	Republican	336	7,628,831	56.4	Charles W. Fairbanks
Alton B. Parker	Democratic	140	5,084,533	37.6	Henry G. Davis
Eugene V. Debs	Socialist	—	402,714	3.0	Benjamin Hanford
Silas C. Swallow	Prohibition	—	259,163	1.9	George W. Carroll

Comments: After his great victory, Roosevelt announced that he would not be a candidate for a third term, a pledge that was to haunt him in 1912.

ELECTION OF 1908

The Political Scene: Roosevelt, the unchallenged leader of his party, determined to pick his successor. Following Parker's decisive defeat, the Democrats were ready to return to Bryan.

Conventions and Nominees: The Republican conclave at Chicago in June ratified Roosevelt's choice of his Secretary of War William Howard Taft of Ohio and named James S. Sherman of New York to run with him. The Democrats meeting at Denver in July picked a ticket of Bryan and John W. Kern of Indiana.

The Campaign: In a dull campaign, Bryan promised to revise the tariff downward; Taft replied that he also intended to work for a downward revision.

Results of 1908 Election:

Presidential Candidate	Party	Electoral Votes	Popular Vote Total	Percentage	Vice-Presidential Candidate
William H. Taft	Republican	321	7,679,114	51.6	James S. Sherman
William J. Bryan	Democratic	162	6,410,665	43.0	John W. Kern
Eugene V. Debs	Socialist	—	420,858	2.8	Benjamin Hanford
Eugene W. Chafin	Prohibition	—	252,704	1.7	Aaron S. Watkins

Comments: Bryan was the only major party candidate in American history to run three unsuccessful races for the Presidency.

ELECTION OF 1912

The Political Scene: The opposition of progressive Republicans to Taft's policies led to an open rupture of the party, with Theodore Roosevelt leading the insurgents.

Conventions and Nominees: When the Republican convention meeting at Chicago in June decided a contest for disputed delegate seats in favor of Taft, Roosevelt ordered his delegates to abstain from voting. Taft and Sherman were renominated on the first ballot, but Roosevelt's delegates became the nucleus of the Progressive or "Bull Moose" party, which met in Chicago in August to nominate Roosevelt and Hiram Johnson of California. The Democrats convening in Baltimore (June 25–July 2) produced a drawn-out but exciting contest. Champ Clark of Missouri obtained a majority on the 10th ballot but could not reach the necessary two thirds. On the 46th ballot, the delegates chose Woodrow Wilson of New Jersey. Thomas R. Marshall of Indiana was selected for the Vice-Presidency.

The Campaign: With Wilson, Roosevelt, and Socialist nominee Eugene V. Debs all campaigning as reform candidates, the voters were asked to decide which man could best implement progressive policies. Wilson's New Freedom program emphasized dissolution of the great trusts and the return to free competition. Roosevelt's New Nationalism stressed regulation of big business by the federal government.

Results of 1912 Election:

Presidential Candidate	Party	Electoral Votes	Popular Vote Total	Percentage	Vice-Presidential Candidate
Woodrow Wilson	Democratic	435	6,301,254	41.8	Thomas R. Marshall
Theodore Roosevelt	Progressive	88	4,127,788	27.4	Hiram Johnson
William H. Taft	Republican	8	3,485,831	23.1	{ James S. Sherman { Nicholas M. Butler
Eugene V. Debs	Socialist	—	901,255	6.0	Emil Seidel
Eugene Chafin	Prohibition	—	209,644	1.4	Aaron S. Watkins

Comments: Three-quarters of the popular vote went to the reform candidates, indicating the strength of the progressive movement in the country. The Republican split insured Wilson's election.

ELECTION OF 1916

The Political Scene: The question of possible American involvement in World War I overshadowed the domestic controversies of the Wilson administration.

Conventions and Nominees: The Republicans nominated Charles Evans Hughes of New York and Charles W. Fairbanks of Indiana at their convention at Chicago in June. The Progressive party disintegrated when Theodore Roosevelt refused to be its candidate again. The Democrats at St. Louis in June renominated Wilson and Marshall.

The Campaign: The Democrats went before the electorate as the party of peace, using the slogan "Wilson and Peace with Honor, or Hughes with Roosevelt and War." Hughes had the difficult task of reconciling the belligerent Theodore Roosevelt with his antiwar supporters among German-Americans and other groups.

Results of 1916 Election:

Presidential Candidate	Party	Electoral Votes	Popular Vote Total	Percentage	Vice-Presidential Candidate
Woodrow Wilson	Democratic	277	9,131,511	49.3	Thomas R. Marshall
Charles E. Hughes	Republican	254	8,548,935	46.1	Charles W. Fairbanks
Allan L. Benson	Socialist	—	585,974	3.2	George R. Kirkpatrick
J. Frank Hanly	Prohibition	—	220,505	1.2	Ira Landrith

Comments: Wilson's carrying of California's electoral vote proved decisive.

ELECTION OF 1920

The Political Scene: An immense reaction against the idealism of the Wilson years and the sacrifices entailed by World War I characterized the mood of the American people, who were anxious to return to normalcy.

Conventions and Nominees: The Republican choice fell upon "dark horse" Warren G. Harding, an Ohio editor, whose selection on the 10th ballot at Chicago on June 12, came after a meeting of party leaders in the famous "smoke-filled room" of the Blackstone Hotel. Calvin Coolidge of Massachusetts, who had won popular acclaim for his opposition to the Boston police strike, received the Vice-Presidential nod.

For the Democrats, Wilson probably desired a third nomination, but his physical incapacity and political unpopularity made this impossible. The San Francisco convention chose a relative unknown in James M. Cox of Ohio on the 44th ballot on July 6th and Franklin D. Roosevelt of New York, the possessor of a magnetic name, as his running mate.

The Campaign: The League of Nations was the most debated campaign topic, with Cox supporting American entry into the world body and Harding straddling the issue.

Results of 1920 Election:

Presidential Candidate	Party	Electoral Votes	Popular Vote Total	Percentage	Vice-Presidential Candidate
Warren G. Harding	Republican	404	16,153,115	60.3	Calvin Coolidge
James M. Cox	Democratic	127	9,133,092	34.1	Franklin D. Roosevelt
Eugene V. Debs	Socialist	—	915,490	3.4	Seymour Stedman
Parley P. Christensen	Farmer-Labor	—	265,229	1.0	Max S. Hayes

Comments: The massive Republican victory represented more of a rejection of Wilson and the Democrats than a personal mandate for Harding, who died in office after a scandal-marred administration and was succeeded by Calvin Coolidge on August 3, 1923.

ELECTION OF 1924

The Political Scene: The cautious conservatism and New England frugality of Calvin Coolidge reduced the political capital the Democrats hoped to make out of the Harding administration's scandals.

Conventions and Nominees: The Republican convention at Cleveland in June chose Coolidge with Charles G. Dawes of Illinois. The Democratic convention in New York City lasted from June 24 until July 29, and the resulting contest between Alfred E. Smith and William Gibbs McAdoo led to the most ballots ever taken in a Presidential nominating convention. Finally after Smith and McAdoo had withdrawn, the delegates nominated John W. Davis of West Virginia on the 103d ballot. Charles W. Bryan of Nebraska was the Vice-Presidential selection. Dissident farm and labor elements in both parties formed the Progressive party, which named a ticket of Robert M. LaFollette of Wisconsin and Burton K. Wheeler of Montana at a convention held in Cleveland in July.

The Campaign: The bitter Democratic convention destroyed what little chance the party had of unseating Coolidge. Both major candidates concentrated their fire on LaFollette rather than each other.

Results of 1924 Election:

Presidential Candidate	Party	Electoral Votes	Popular Vote Total	Percentage	Vice-Presidential Candidate
Calvin Coolidge	Republican	382	15,719,921	54.0	Charles G. Dawes
John W. Davis	Democratic	136	8,386,704	28.8	Charles W. Bryan
Robert M. LaFollette	Progressive	13	4,832,532	16.6	Burton K. Wheeler

Comments: LaFollette won the electoral vote of Wisconsin.

ELECTION OF 1928

The Political Scene: In the summer of 1927, Coolidge announced "I do not choose to run for President . . ." Despite the efforts of a "draft Coolidge" movement, most Republicans were willing to turn to another candidate.

Conventions and Nominees: The Republicans met at Kansas City, Missouri, in June and nominated a ticket of Herbert Hoover of California and Charles Curtis of Kansas. The Democrats meeting at Houston in June needed only one ballot to name Alfred E. Smith of New York for the Presidency and Joseph T. Robinson of Arkansas for the Vice-Presidency.

The Campaign: Smith, who differed with Hoover on the issues of prohibition, public power, and agriculture, found it difficult to make a dent in the public satisfaction with Republican prosperity.

Results of 1928 Election:

Presidential Candidate	Party	Electoral Votes	Popular Vote Total	Percentage	Vice-Presidential Candidate
Herbert C. Hoover	Republican	444	21,437,277	58.22	Charles Curtis
Alfred E. Smith	Democratic	87	15,007,698	40.8	Joseph T. Robinson
Norman M. Thomas	Socialist	—	265,583	.7	James Maurer

Comments: Smith, the first Roman Catholic candidate nominated by a major party, lost many votes particularly in the South because of his religion, but gained many others for the same reason in the Northeast and Midwest.

ELECTION OF 1932

The Political Scene: The Wall Street crash of 1929 and the subsequent economic depression made a Democratic victory almost certain and quickened the race for the party's nomination.

Conventions and Nominees: The Republicans meeting at Chicago in June renominated Hoover and Curtis. The Democrats held their convention during the same month in the same city. Franklin D. Roosevelt of New York, who had outdistanced a large field of contenders in the preconvention maneuvering, was nominated on the fourth ballot with John N. Garner of Texas as his running mate.

The Campaign: Roosevelt promised the country a New Deal and a willingness to experiment with different approaches in an effort to end the economic crisis. Hoover warned of even greater difficulties if the Democrats won.

Results of 1932 Election:

Presidential Candidate	Party	Electoral Votes	Popular Vote Total	Percentage	Vice-Presidential Candidate
Franklin D. Roosevelt	Democratic	472	22,829,501	57.4	John Nance Garner
Herbert C. Hoover	Republican	59	15,760,684	39.6	Charles Curtis
Norman M. Thomas	Socialist	—	884,649	2.2	James Maurer

Comments: Roosevelt's landslide victory carried into office many Democratic Congressmen who were to help implement his program.

ELECTION OF 1936

The Political Scene: New Deal policies enraged political conservatives, but gained the Democrats many new supporters.

Conventions and Nominees: Delegates convening in Cleveland in June named a Republican ticket of Alfred M. Landon of Kansas and Frank Knox of Illinois. The Democrats met later in the month at Philadelphia to renominate Roosevelt and Garner by acclamation. The convention also abolished the two-thirds rule for choosing candidates, making a simple majority sufficient. Father Charles E. Coughlin, Dr. Francis Townsend, and Gerald L. K. Smith, all radical critics of the New Deal, formed the Union party at Cleveland in August and nominated William Lemke of North Dakota and Thomas C. O'Brien of Massachusetts.

The Campaign: The Republicans attacked Roosevelt and the New Deal for allegedly building a giant and wasteful bureaucracy. Roosevelt was content to run on his record.

Results of 1936 Election:

Presidential Candidate	Party	Electoral Votes	Popular Vote Total	Percentage	Vice-Presidential Candidate
Franklin D. Roosevelt	Democratic	523	27,757,333	60.8	John Nance Garner
Alfred M. Landon	Republican	8	16,684,231	36.5	Frank Knox
William Lemke	Union	—	892,267	2.0	Thomas C. O'Brien

Comments: Roosevelt won the most sweeping electoral victory in modern history, carrying every state but Maine and Vermont.

ELECTION OF 1940

The Political Scene: With the outbreak of World War II in 1939, American neutrality once again became the dominant political issue in an election year.

Conventions and Nominees: The Republicans convened in Philadelphia in June. A tremendous groundswell of public opinion for Wendell L. Willkie of New York enabled him to overcome the early lead of Thomas E. Dewey and Robert A. Taft and win the nomination on the sixth ballot. His running mate was Charles L. McNary of Oregon. Roosevelt won his third nomination from the Democratic convention held in Chicago in July. At his insistence, Henry Wallace of Iowa replaced Garner for the Vice-Presidency.

The Campaign: The Democratic platform and Roosevelt were pledged against participation in foreign wars, except in case of attack. Willkie endorsed most New Deal measures and did not differ substantially from Roosevelt on foreign policy, but he stressed that Roosevelt's attempt to win a third term threatened democratic government.

Results of 1940 Election:

Presidential Candidate	Party	Electoral Votes	Popular Vote Total	Percentage	Vice-Presidential Candidate
Franklin D. Roosevelt	Democratic	449	27,313,041	54.7	Henry A. Wallace
Wendell L. Willkie	Republican	82	22,348,480	44.8	Charles L. McNary

Comments: Roosevelt, destined to win a fourth term as well, was the only man to win more than two elections or to serve more than eight years as President.

ELECTION OF 1944

The Political Scene: In the nation's third wartime election, Roosevelt benefited from the general reluctance "to change horses in midstream."

Conventions and Nominees: The Republicans held their convention at Chicago in June. Thomas E. Dewey of New York received all but one vote on the first ballot, and John W. Bricker of Ohio was the unanimous choice as his running mate. The Democrats convening at Chicago in July once again chose Roosevelt, but Wallace had earned the enmity of many party leaders, and the delegates turned to Harry S. Truman of Missouri for the Vice-Presidency.

The Campaign: The Republicans called for new political leadership for the work of peace and reconstruction, but agreed with the Democrats in the necessity of American participation in a postwar international organization.

Results of 1944 Election:

Presidential Candidate	Party	Electoral Votes	Popular Vote Total	Percentage	Vice-Presidential Candidate
Franklin D. Roosevelt	Democratic	432	25,612,610	53.3	Harry S Truman
Thomas E. Dewey	Republican	99	22,017,617	45.9	John W. Bricker

Comments: On April 12, 1945, Roosevelt died and was succeeded on the same day by Truman.

ELECTION OF 1948

The Political Scene: Deep splits within the Democratic party and an apparent public desire for a change portended a Republican victory.

Conventions and Nominees: The Republicans meeting at Philadelphia in June again nominated Thomas E. Dewey. Earl Warren of California was the Vice-Presidential choice. The Democrats met in the same city the following month and unenthusiastically nominated a ticket of Truman and Alben W. Barkley of Kentucky. Several Southern delegations that were opposed to the party's civil rights platform bolted the convention and named a States' Rights or "Dixiecrat" ticket of Strom Thurmond of South Carolina for President and Fielding L. Wright of Mississippi for Vice-President. A fourth party, the Progressive, which was composed largely of liberal and left-wing Democrats critical of Truman's foreign policy, ran Henry A. Wallace of Iowa and Glenn Taylor of Idaho.

The Campaign: A distinct underdog because of the Dixiecrat and Progressive tickets, Truman undertook a vigorous campaign in which he castigated the Republican-controlled 80th Congress as a "do nothing" one. Dewey, who was indicated the certain winner in the public opinion polls, conducted a very cool and careful campaign.

Results of 1948 Election:

Presidential Candidate	Party	Electoral Votes	Popular Vote Total	Percentage	Vice-Presidential Candidate
Harry S Truman	Democratic	303	24,179,345	49.6	Alben W. Barkley
Thomas E. Dewey	Republican	189	21,991,291	45.1	Earl Warren
J. Strom Thurmond	States' Rights	39	1,176,125	2.4	Fielding L. Wright
Henry A. Wallace	Progressive	—	1,157,326	2.4	Glenn Taylor

Comments: Truman's upset victory reflected his ability to hold almost the entire labor and Negro vote and to carry the key Midwestern farm states of Ohio, Iowa, and Wisconsin.

ELECTION OF 1952

The Political Scene: Truman announced early in the year that he would not be a candidate for a third term. In any case, the Korean War had dimmed his prospects of reelection.

Conventions and Nominees: General Dwight D. Eisenhower beat off the strong challenge of Robert A. Taft to win the nomination of the Republican convention that was held in Chicago in July. Richard M. Nixon of California received the Vice-Presidential designation. The Democrats convened in Chicago later in the same month and named a ticket of Adlai E. Stevenson of Illinois and John J. Sparkman of Alabama.

The Campaign: The Republicans used the slogan "Communism, Korea, and corruption," and Eisenhower promised a personal visit to Korea. Stevenson, a first-rate campaigner, was nonetheless forced on the defensive.

Results of 1952 Election:

Presidential Candidate	Party	Electoral Votes	Popular Vote Total	Percentage	Vice-Presidential Candidate
Dwight D. Eisenhower	Republican	442	33,936,234	55.1	Richard M. Nixon
Adlai E. Stevenson	Democratic	89	27,314,992	44.4	John J. Sparkman

Comments: Eisenhower carried the Republicans to victory in both houses of Congress, marking the only time since 1931 or after that the party has controlled the executive and legislative branches of government at the same time.

ELECTION OF 1956

The Political Scene: Suffering a serious heart attack in September 1955, Eisenhower waited until the end of February 1956 before announcing that he would run for a second term.

Conventions and Nominees: Senator Estes Kefauver of Tennessee conducted an extensive primary campaign; however, he withdrew in favor of Stevenson a week before the Democrats met in Chicago in August. Kefauver then won a spirited contest with John F. Kennedy for the Vice-Presidency. The Republicans meeting in San Francisco in August renominated Eisenhower and Nixon.

The Campaign: Stevenson proposed the possibility of ending the draft system and an agreement with the Soviet Union on Cold War issues. In addition, the Democrats referred to Eisenhower's health and the possibility of Nixon's succession to the Presidency. The Republicans emphasized the "peace and prosperity" of the Eisenhower years.

Results of 1956 Election:

Presidential Candidate	Party	Electoral Votes	Popular Vote Total	Percentage	Vice-Presidential Candidate
Dwight D. Eisenhower	Republican	457	35,590,472	57.4	Richard M. Nixon
Adlai E. Stevenson	Democratic	73	26,022,752	42.0	Estes Kefauver
Walter B. Jones	No party	1	—	—	—

Comments: Eisenhower became the first winning Presidential candidate since Zachary Taylor in 1848 to fail to carry his party to victory in either the House of Representatives or the Senate.

ELECTION OF 1960

The Political Scene: The mood of the country was somewhat restive, primarily because of economic recessions in 1953, 1957, and 1960, but also because of increasing disquiet over issues relating to civil rights and race relations.

Conventions and Nominations: John F. Kennedy of Massachusetts entered several Presidential primaries to disprove alleged liabilities of his youth and his Roman Catholic religion; victories in key contests in Wisconsin and West Virginia assured his first ballot victory at the Democratic Convention in Los Angeles (July 11-15), where he chose Lyndon B. Johnson of Texas as his running mate. Vice-President Richard Nixon of California easily overcame a challenge from Nelson Rockefeller of New York to win a first ballot endorsement from the Republican National Convention at Chicago (July 25-28).

The Campaign: Nixon emphasized the unity, strength, and stability that he claimed the Republicans had given the country during the previous eight years. Kennedy complained of stagnation and apathy in Washington and decline of American prestige abroad, promising to get the country moving again and, particularly, to revitalize the economy.

Results of 1960 Election:

Presidential Candidate	Party	Electoral Votes	Popular Vote Total	Percentage	Vice-Presidential Candidate
John F. Kennedy	Democratic	303	34,226,731	49.7	Lyndon B. Johnson
Richard M. Nixon	Republican	219	34,108,157	49.5	Henry Cabot Lodge
Harry F. Byrd	No party	15	440,298	.6	—

Comments: Kennedy built his victory on the large industrial states of the Northeast and key states in the South, where Johnson's candidacy helped. Kennedy was assassinated on November 22, 1963, in Dallas by Lee Harvey Oswald.

ELECTION OF 1964

The Political Scene: In less than a year in office, Lyndon Johnson had compiled a record of legislative achievements that put him in excellent position for the campaign.

Conventions and Nominees: The Republican convention meeting at San Francisco in July witnessed the first victory for the conservative wing of the party in over a generation with the nomination of Barry M. Goldwater of Arizona. William Miller of New York was selected as his running mate. The Democrats convened at Atlantic City in August to nominate Johnson and Hubert H. Humphrey of Minnesota, both of whom were named by acclamation.

The Campaign: The Democrats were happy to run on the record of the Kennedy-Johnson administration, while depicting Goldwater as a dangerous reactionary, Goldwater assailed the Johnson administration for permitting a decline in government morality and efficiency and a deterioration of national prestige abroad.

Results of 1964 Election:

Presidential Candidate	Party	Electoral Votes	Popular Vote Total	Percentage	Vice-Presidential Candidate
Lyndon B. Johnson	Democratic	486	43,129,484	61.1	Hubert H. Humphrey
Barry M. Goldwater	Republican	52	27,178,188	38.5	W. E. Miller

Comments: Johnson gained a larger percentage of the popular vote than any candidate in modern times. Only Franklin Roosevelt in 1936 received more electoral votes.

ELECTION OF 1968

The Political Scene: On March 31, Johnson announced he would not seek reelection following repeated attacks on his Vietnam war policy. Sen. Robert F. Kennedy was assassinated in June following his victory in the California primary. Ronald Reagan and Nelson Rockefeller challenged Richard Nixon for the Republican nomination.

Conventions and Nominees: The Republicans met in Miami in August and nominated Richard Nixon on the first ballot. Spiro T. Agnew was chosen for the Vice-Presidency. At a Chicago convention marred by much turbulence, the Democrats chose Hubert H. Humphrey of Minnesota; Edmund S. Muskie of Maine was the Vice-Presidential nominee. George C. Wallace of Alabama ran as Presidential candidate of the American Independent Party among other designations.

The Campaign: Nixon promised an honorable conclusion of the Vietnam war and the restoration of law and order throughout the country. Humphrey pledged to seek a political solution to the struggle in Vietnam and promised to work toward ending divisiveness in American life. Wallace, an extreme conservative, appeared to hope to force the election into the House of Representatives, where his electors might hold the balance of power.

Results of 1968 Election:

Presidential Candidate	Party	Electoral Votes	Popular Vote Total	Percentage	Vice-Presidential Candidate
Richard M. Nixon	Republican	301	31,785,480	43.4	Spiro T. Agnew
Hubert H. Humphrey	Democratic	191	31,275,165	42.7	Edmund S. Muskie
George C. Wallace	American Independent	46	9,906,473	13.5	Curtis E. LeMay

Comments: Nixon received the lowest percentage of the popular vote for a successful candidate since 1912.

ELECTION OF 1972

The Political Scene: The first Nixon administration reveled in its diplomatic gains abroad, while attempting to diminish the domestic problems of unemployment and inflation. The Democrats attacked Nixon's record on domestic affairs, along with hurling charges against the Committee to Reelect the President, accused of masterminding a break-in at the Democratic headquarters in the Watergate complex.

Conventions and Nominees: The Democrats met in Miami, Florida, in July and nominated Sen. George McGovern on the first ballot. His choice for Vice-President, Sen. Thomas F. Eagleton of Missouri, was endorsed by the convention's acclamation. Eagleton resigned from the ticket in late August, however, and was replaced by R. Sargent Shriver of Maryland. The Republicans met in Miami in August, and the incumbents were nominated without opposition.

The Campaign: Nixon did little active campaigning, using his spectacular trips to Moscow and Peking to give him exposure. McGovern had come from behind to win the Democratic nomination, but his campaign never regained its momentum when his first running mate, Sen. Thomas Eagleton, withdrew following disclosures that he had undergone shock treatment for depression. The Democrats were defeated in a near-record landslide.

Results of 1972 Election:

Presidential Candidates	Party	Electoral Votes	Popular Vote Total	Percentage	Vice-Presidential Candidate
Richard M. Nixon	Republican	520	47,167,319	60.7	Spiro T. Agnew
George S. McGovern	Democratic	17	29,169,504	37.5	R. Sargent Shriver
John G. Schmitz	American	—	1,102,963	1.4	Thomas J. Anderson
John Hospers	Libertarian	1	2,691	—	Theodora Nathan

Comments: Division among the Democrats, with many party conservatives turning to Nixon, contributed to the Republican victory, along with apparent voter apathy regarding the Watergate issue.

1976 PRESIDENTIAL ELECTION RESULTS

State	Electoral Vote	Popular Vote				Percentages			
		Carter	Ford	McCarthy	Other	Carter	Ford	McCarthy	Other
Alabama	9	659,170	504,070	—	19,610	56	43	—	1
Alaska	3	44,058	71,555	—	7,961	36	58	—	6
Arizona	6	295,602	418,642	19,229	9,246	40	56	3	1
Arkansas	6	498,604	267,903	639	389	65	35	—	—
California	45	3,742,284	3,882,244	26,047	10,314	48	50	—	2
Colorado	7	460,801	584,278	—	179,242	43	54	2	1
Connecticut	8	647,895	719,261	—	19,199	47	52	—	1
Delaware	3	122,461	109,780	2,432	969	52	47	1	—
Dist. Columbia	3	137,818	27,873	—	3,139	82	17	—	1
Florida	17	1,636,000	1,469,531	23,643	21,457	52	47	1	—
Georgia	12	979,409	483,743	—	—	67	33	—	—
Hawaii	4	147,375	140,003	—	3,923	51	48	—	1
Idaho	4	126,549	204,151	—	10,232	37	60	—	3
Illinois	26	2,271,295	2,364,269	55,939	29,779	48	50	1	1
Indiana	13	1,014,714	1,185,958	—	21,690	46	53	—	1
Iowa	8	619,931	632,863	20,051	6,461	48	49	2	1
Kansas	7	430,421	502,752	13,185	11,487	45	53	1	1
Kentucky	9	615,717	531,852	6,837	12,736	53	46	—	1
Louisiana	10	661,365	587,446	6,490	22,082	52	46	—	2
Maine	4	232,279	236,320	10,874	3,495	48	49	2	1
Maryland	10	759,612	672,661	—	—	53	47	—	—
Massachusetts	14	1,429,475	1,030,276	65,637	22,170	56	40	3	1
Michigan	21	1,696,714	1,893,742	47,905	13,229	47	52	1	—
Minnesota	10	1,070,440	819,395	35,490	24,606	55	42	2	1
Mississippi	7	381,329	366,846	4,074	16,141	50	48	—	2
Missouri	12	998,387	927,443	24,029	3,741	51	48	1	—
Montana	4	149,259	173,703	—	5,772	45	53	—	2
Nebraska	5	233,293	359,219	9,383	4,854	38	59	2	1
Nevada	3	92,479	101,273	—	8,124	46	50	—	4
New Hampshire	4	147,645	185,935	4,095	1,952	43	55	1	1
New Jersey	17	1,444,653	1,509,688	32,717	27,414	48	50	1	1
New Mexico	4	201,148	211,419	—	4,023	48	51	—	1
New York	41	3,389,558	3,100,791	—	177,913	51	46	—	3
North Carolina	13	927,365	741,960	—	8,581	55	44	—	1
North Dakota	3	136,078	153,684	2,952	4,594	46	52	—	2
Ohio	25	2,009,959	2,000,626	58,267	41,604	49	49	1	1
Oklahoma	8	532,442	545,708	14,101	—	49	50	1	—
Oregon	6	490,407	492,120	40,207	7,142	48	48	4	—
Pennsylvania	27	2,328,677	2,205,604	50,584	35,922	50	48	1	1
Rhode Island	4	227,636	181,249	—	1,699	55	44	—	1
South Carolina	8	450,807	346,149	—	5,627	56	43	—	1
South Dakota	4	147,068	151,505	—	2,105	49	50	—	1
Tennessee	10	825,879	633,969	5,004	11,494	56	43	—	1
Texas	26	2,082,319	1,953,300	20,118	16,147	51	48	1	—
Utah	4	182,110	337,908	3,907	17,293	34	62	1	3
Vermont	3	77,798	100,387	4,001	1,716	42	55	2	1
Virginia	12	813,896	836,554	—	46,644	48	49	—	3
Washington	12	717,323	777,732	36,986	23,493	46	50	2	2
West Virginia	6	435,864	314,726	—	—	58	42	—	—
Wisconsin	11	1,040,232	1,004,987	34,943	21,174	49	48	2	1
Wyoming	3	62,239	92,717	624	763	40	59	—	1
Total Popular Votes		**40,825,839**	**39,147,770**	**680,390**	**949,348**				
Total Popular Votes, all candidates		**81,603,346**							

Minor candidates: Roger McBride (Libertarian Party), 171,627; Lester G. Maddox (American Independent Party), 168,264; Thomas Anderson (American Party), 152,513; Peter Camejo (Socialist Workers Party), 90,287; Gus Hall (Communist Party), 58,692; Margaret Wright (People's Party), 49,014; Lyndon H. LaRouche (U.S. Labor Party), 40,043; Benjamin C. Bubar (Prohibition Party), 15,902; Jules Levin (Socialist Labor Party), 9,322; Frank P. Zeidler (Socialist Party), 5,991; Others, 187,693.

ELECTION OF 1976

The Political Scene: Following the turmoil of the second Nixon administration, with the resignation of Spiro T. Agnew and then Nixon himself, Gerald R. Ford hoped to retain the Presidency, a position to which he had never been elected. The Democrats saw an opportunity to regain the White House by stressing the need for a return to "moral" government, while Eugene J. McCarthy of Minnesota, an independent, campaigned on a platform which called for the abolition of the two-party system, one which he felt made the government less responsive to the will of the people.

Conventions and Nominees: In July the Democrats met in New York City, with Jimmy Carter of Georgia virtually assured a first-ballot nomination after a string of primary victories. Walter F. Mondale of Minnesota was chosen the Vice-Presidential nominee. Incumbent Gerald R. Ford of Michigan successfully fought off a conservative challenge by Ronald W. Reagan

of California in the Republicans' August convention in Kansas City, Missouri. Robert J. Dole of Kansas was selected by Ford to be his running mate. McCarthy picked Willam Clay Ford of Michigan to share his independent ticket.

The Campaign: Ford, as an appointed incumbent, hampered by the aftermath of the Watergate scandals and the 1974 economic recession, was unable to generate enthusiasm and loyalty within the Republican Party, even though he campaigned hard. Carter, an outsider from the Washington political scene, charged Ford with dealing ineffectively with high unemployment, and pledged to create more jobs, consider pardons for Vietnam draft evaders, reorganize the federal government, and develop a national energy policy. His televised debates with Ford helped convince many voters he was of presidential stature.

RESULTS OF 1976 ELECTION

Presidential Candidate	Party	Electoral Votes	Popular Vote		Vice-Presidential Candidates
			Total	Percentage	
Jimmy Carter	Democratic	297	40,825,839	50.0+	Walter F. Mondale
Gerald R. Ford	Republican	240	39,147,770	47.9	Robert J. Dole
Ronald Reagan	No Party	1			

Comments: Carter was the first President elected from a southern state since Zachary Taylor in 1848.

FINAL 1980 PRESIDENTIAL ELECTION RESULTS

State	Electoral Vote	Popular Vote Reagan	Carter	Anderson	Other	Percentages Reagan	Carter	Anderson	Other
Alabama	9	654,192	636,730	16,481	34,526	49	47	1	3
Alaska	3	86,112	41,842	11,155	19,336	55	26	7	12
Arizona	6	529,688	246,843	76,952	20,462	61	28	9	2
Arkansas	6	403,164	398,041	22,468	13,909	48	47	3	2
California	45	4,522,994	3,082,943	739,618	237,383	52	36	9	3
Colorado	7	652,264	368,009	130,633	33,544	55	31	11	3
Connecticut	8	677,210	541,732	171,807	15,536	47	39	12	1
Delaware	3	111,252	105,754	16,288	2,374	47	45	7	1
District of Columbia	3	23,313	130,231	16,131	4,214	14	75	9	2
Florida	17	2,046,951	1,419,475	189,692	30,809	56	38	5	1
Georgia	12	654,168	890,955	36,055	15,627	41	56	2	1
Hawaii	4	130,112	135,879	32,021	5,275	43	45	10	2
Idaho	4	290,699	110,192	27,058	9,482	67	25	6	2
Illinois	26	2,358,049	1,981,413	346,754	63,505	50	42	7	1
Indiana	13	1,255,656	844,197	111,639	30,541	56	38	5	1
Iowa	8	676,026	508,672	115,633	17,330	51	39	9	1
Kansas	7	566,812	326,150	68,231	18,602	58	33	7	2
Kentucky	9	635,274	617,417	31,127	11,809	49	48	2	1
Louisiana	10	792,853	708,453	26,345	20,940	51	46	2	1
Maine	4	238,522	220,974	53,327	10,188	46	42	10	2
Maryland	10	680,606	726,161	119,537	14,192	44	47	8	1
Massachusetts	14	1,057,631	1,053,802	382,539	30,118	42	42	15	1
Michigan	21	1,915,225	1,661,532	275,223	57,745	49	43	7	1
Minnesota	10	873,268	954,173	174,997	49,478	43	47	8	2
Mississippi	7	441,089	429,281	12,036	9,344	50	48	1	1
Missouri	12	1,074,181	931,182	77,920	16,541	51	44	4	1
Montana	4	206,814	118,032	29,281	9,825	57	32	8	3
Nebraska	5	419,214	166,424	44,854	9,041	66	26	7	2
Nevada	3	155,017	66,666	17,651	4,358	64	27	7	2
New Hampshire	4	221,705	108,864	49,693	3,728	58	28	13	1
New Jersey	17	1,546,557	1,147,364	234,632	47,131	52	39	8	2
New Mexico	4	250,779	167,826	29,459	8,173	55	37	6	2
New York	41	2,888,831	2,728,372	467,801	116,955	46	44	8	2
North Carolina	13	915,018	875,635	52,800	12,380	49	47	3	1
North Dakota	3	193,695	79,189	23,640	4,592	64	26	8	2
Ohio	25	2,206,545	1,752,414	254,472	70,172	52	41	6	1
Oklahoma	8	695,570	402,026	38,284	13,828	61	35	3	1
Oregon	6	571,044	456,890	112,389	41,193	48	39	10	3
Pennsylvania	27	2,261,872	1,937,540	292,921	69,168	50	42	6	2
Rhode Island	4	154,793	198,342	59,819	3,013	37	48	14	1
South Carolina	8	439,277	428,220	13,868	6,893	49	48	2	1
South Dakota	4	198,343	103,855	21,431	4,074	61	32	6	1
Tennessee	10	787,761	783,051	35,991	10,813	49	48	2	1
Texas	26	2,510,705	1,881,147	111,613	38,171	55	42	2	1
Utah	4	439,687	124,266	30,284	9,915	73	20	5	2
Vermont	3	94,628	81,952	31,761	4,958	44	39	15	2
Virginia	12	989,609	752,174	95,418	28,831	53	40	5	2
Washington	9	865,244	650,193	185,073	41,884	50	37	11	2
West Virginia	6	334,206	367,462	31,691	4,356	45	50	4	1
Wisconsin	11	1,088,845	981,584	160,657	42,135	48	43	7	2
Wyoming	3	110,700	49,427	12,072	4,514	63	28	7	2
Total Popular Votes		**43,893,770**	**35,480,948**	**5,719,222**	**1,402,911**				
Total Popular Votes, all candidates		**86,496,851**							

Minor candidates: John B. Anderson (Independent Party), 5,719,222; Ed Clark (Libertarian), 920,049; Barry Commoner (Citizens Party), 232,533; Andrew Pulley (Socialist Workers), 48,650; Guss Hall (Communist Party), 43,896; John R. Rarick (American Independent Party), 41,157; Percy L. Greaves, Jr. (American Party), 14,230; Deirdre Griswold (Workers World Party), 13,213; Benjamin C. Bubar (National Statesman Party), 7,127; David McReynolds (Socialist Party), 6,720; Maureen Smith (Peace and Freedom Party), 18,106; Ellen McCormack (Right to Life Party but known as Respect for Life Party in Kentucky), 32,319; Kurt Lynen (Middle Class Candidate Party), 3,694; Bill Gahres (Down with Lawyers Party), 1,718; Martin Wendelken (Independent [Wendelken] Party), 923; Harley J. McLain (Natural Peoples' League Party), 296.

ELECTION OF 1980

The Political Scene: The Carter Administration was beset with the domestic problems of rampant inflation, high interest rates, and increasing unemployment, and on the foreign scene by the American hostages in Iran and the troublesome Middle East unrest despite the Camp David accords. Republicans and some elements in the Democratic Party criticized Carter for his ineptitude and lack of leadership, and in July 1980 he received a very low rating in a public opinion poll as a president.

Conventions and Nominees: The Republicans nominated Ronald Reagan on the first ballot at their convention in Detroit in July. In a surprise move Reagan picked George Bush, who as a presidential contender released his delegates shortly before the convention, as his vice presidential candidate, although mo-

mentum had built up behind former President Gerald Ford for the nomination. In August, incumbent Jimmy Carter easily won the nomination at the Democratic convention in New York City (after Edward M. Kennedy ended his candidacy only hours into the convention). Walter F. Mondale was again chosen as Carter's running mate.

The Campaign: The Reagan-Bush team campaigned feverishly throughout the states, while Carter, beleaguered by the Iranian hostage problem, campaigned little, leaving it mostly to Mondale, cabinet members and aides. The Reagan-Carter TV debates appeared to enhance Reagan's election chances. John B. Anderson, having lost his bid for the Republican presidential nomination, chose Democrat Patrick J. Lucey to share his Independent ticket.

RESULTS OF 1980 ELECTION Presidential Candidate	Party	Electoral Votes	Popular Vote Total	Percentage	Vice-Presidential Candidates
Ronald W. Reagan	Republican	489	43,893,770	50.7+	George H.W. Bush
Jimmy Carter	Democrat	49	35,480,948	41.0+	Walter F. Mondale
John B. Anderson	Independent*	0	5,719,222	6.6	Patrick J. Lucey

* In New York, Anderson was the presidential candidate of the Liberal Party.

Comments: Carter became the third president (after Hoover and Ford) in modern times to be voted out of office after a single term.

THE WHITE HOUSE OFFICE—1981

Counselor to the President . . . . Edwin Meese III
Chief of Staff and
  Assistant to the President . . . . James A. Baker III
Deputy Chief of Staff and
  Assistant to the President . . . . Michael K. Deaver
Assistant to the President for
  National Security Affairs . . . . Richard V. Allen
Assistant to the President for
  Policy Development . . . . Martin Anderson
Assistant to the President and
  Press Secretary . . . . James S. Brady
Assistant to the President for
  Public Liaison . . . . Elizabeth H. Dole
Counsel to the President . . . . Fred F. Fielding
Assistant to the President for
  Legislative Affairs . . . . Max L. Friedersdorf
Assistant to the President for
  Communications . . . . David R. Gergen
Assistant to the President . . . . Edwin L. Harper
Assistant to the President for
  Presidential Personnel . . . . E. Pendleton James
Assistant to the President for
  Political Affairs . . . . Franklyn C. Nofziger
Assistant to the President for
  Intergovernmental Affairs . . . . Richard S. Williamson
Deputy Counselor to the President . . Robert M. Garrick
Deputy Assistant to the President and
  Assistant to the Deputy Chief
  of Staff . . . . Joseph W. Canzeri
Deputy Assistant to the President for
  Public Liaison . . . . Red Cavaney
Deputy Assistant to the President and
  Deputy to the Chief of Staff . . . . . Richard G. Darman
Deputy Assistant to the President for
  Legislative Affairs . . . . Kenneth M. Duberstein
Deputy Assistant to the President and
  Director of the Office of
  Cabinet Administration . . . . Craig L. Fuller
Deputy Assistant to the President and
  Director of the Office of
  Policy Development . . . . Edwin J. Gray
Deputy Assistant to the President and
  Director of Special Support
  Services . . . . Edward V. Hickey, Jr.
Deputy Assistant to the President for
  Communications . . . . Larry M. Speakes
Deputy Assistant to the President and
  Deputy to the Chief of Staff . . . . . Francis S. M. Hodsoll
Deputy Assistant to the President for
  Intergovernmental Affairs . . . . Alan F. Holmer
Deputy Assistant to the President and
  Director of Staff for the First Lady Peter McCoy

Deputy Assistant to the President for
  Legislative Affairs . . . . Powell A. Moore
Deputy Assistant to the President for
  National Security Affairs . . . . James W. Nance
Deputy Assistant to the President for
  Political Affairs . . . . Edward Rollins
Deputy Assistant to the President and
  Deputy Press Secretary . . . . Karna S. Stringer
Deputy Assistant to the President for
  Communications and
  Director of the Office of
  Communications . . . . Frank A. Ursomarso
Assistant Counselor to the President Edwin W. Thomas, Jr.
Deputy Counsel to the President. . . . Herbert E. Ellingwood
Deputy Counsel to the President . . . Richard A. Hauser
Special Assistant to the President for
  Policy Development . . . . Douglas L. Bandow
Special Assistant to the President for
  Public Liaison . . . . Aram Bakshian, Jr.
Special Assistant to the President. . . Richard S. Beal
Special Assistant to the President for
  Public Liaison . . . . Morton C. Blackwell
Special Assistant to the President for
  Public Liaison . . . . Robert F. Bonitati
Special Assistant to the President for
  Public Liaison . . . . John F. Burgess
Special Assistant to the President. . . David C. Fischer
Special Assistant to the President for
  Policy Development . . . . Kevin R. Hopkins
Special Assistant to the President for
  Public Liaison . . . . Virginia H. Knauer
Special Assistant to the President and
  Deputy Director of Special
  Support Services . . . . Dennis E. LeBlanc
Special Assistant to the President for
  Public Liaison . . . . Diana L. Lozano
Special Assistant to the President for
  Intergovernmental Affairs . . . . J. Steven Rhodes
Special Assistant to the President for
  Intergovernmental Affairs . . . . Judy F. Peachee
Special Assistant to the President for
  Administration . . . . John F. W. Rogers
Special Assistant to the President and
  Director of the Advance Office . . . Stephen M. Studdert
Special Assistant to the President for
  Public Liaison . . . . Wayne H. Valis
Special Assistant to the President. . . Helene A. von Damm
Special Assistant for Scheduling. . . . Gregory Newell
Curator . . . . Clement E. Conger
Physician to the President . . . . Daniel Ruge, M.D.
Chief Usher . . . . Rex W. Scouten

U.S. GOVERNMENT OFFICIALS: ANNUAL SALARIES SOURCE: Office of Personnel Management

Executive Branch		Legislative Branch		Judicial Branch	
President	$200,000	Speaker of the House	$79,125	Chief Justice	$92,400
Vice-President	84,700	President Pro Tem		Associate Justices	88,700
Top Executive		(Senate)	68,575	Judges of the U.S. Court of	
Positions[1]		Majority and Minority		Appeals	70,900
I	69,630	Leaders	68,575	Judges of the U.S. District	
II	60,662.50	Members of Congress	60,662.50	Court	67,100
III	55,387.50	Comptroller General	60,662.50	Director of the	
IV	52,750	Heads of Other		Administrative Office of the	
V	50,112.50	Legislative Agencies	52,750	United States Courts	67,100

[1] Top Executive positions are in levels I-V, ranging from Secretaries of Executive departments at level I to heads of major bureaus at level V; for a listing, see Sections 5312-5316 of Title 5, United States Code.

THE U.S. CABINET: 1981

Secretary of State: Alexander M. Haig, Jr.; b. Dec. 2, 1924, Philadelphia, Pa.; ed. U.S. Military Academy (B.S., 1947), Georgetown University (M.S., 1961), graduate of U.S. Naval War College in 1960 and Army War College in 1966. He served in the U.S. Army (1947-1979), holding various positions in the Pentagon; battalion and brigade commander in the 1st Infantry Division, Vietnam (1966-67); and regimental commander and deputy commandant, U.S. Military Academy (1967-69). In 1973 he became the military assistant in the National Security Council; he was assistant to the president and chief of the White House staff (1973-74); commander-in-chief, U.S. European Command and supreme allied commander, Europe (SHAPE) (1974-79). For six months in 1979, he was professor of political science at an eastern university (July-Dec. 1979); corporate executive of a conglomerate (1979-1981). He assumed his cabinet post on Jan. 21, 1981.

Secretary of the Treasury: Donald T. Regan; b. Dec. 21, 1918, Cambridge, Mass.; ed. Harvard University (B.A., 1940). U.S. Marine Corps (1940-45); investment firm in 1946 as a trainee and then became its chief executive in 1971. Member of the policy committee of the Business Roundtable, the Council on Foreign Affairs, and the Committee for Economic Development. He assumed his cabinet post on Jan. 22, 1981.

Secretary of Defense: Caspar W. Weinberger; b. Aug. 18, 1917, San Francisco; ed. Harvard College (A.B., 1938), Harvard Law School (LL.B., 1941). U.S. Army (1941-45); law clerk in the U.S. Court of Appeals (1945-47); attorney (1947-59 and 1959-1969); elected delegate to the Assembly of the California State Legislature (1952-58); California's director of finance (1968-1970); chairman of the Federal Trade Commission (Jan.-July 1970); deputy director then director of the Office of Management and Budget (1970-73); U.S. Secretary of Health, Education and Welfare (1973-75); corporate officer in an engineering firm (1975-1980). He assumed his cabinet post on Jan. 21, 1981.

Attorney General: William F. Smith; b. Aug. 26, 1917, Wilton, N.H.; ed. University of California (A.B., 1939), Harvard Law School (LL.B., 1942). U.S. Naval Reserve (1942-46); attorney (1946-1980). Member, board of trustees of a number of colleges, universities, educational institutes, and a member of several law organizations. Chairman and vice chairman of the California delegation to the Republican National Convention, in 1968, 1972, 1976 and 1980. He assumed his cabinet post on Jan. 23, 1981.

Secretary of the Interior: James G. Watt; b. Jan. 31, 1938, Lusk, Wyo.; ed. College of Commerce and Industry, University of Wyoming (1960). University of Wyoming Law School (J.D., 1962). Personal assistant, legislative assistant and counsel to the former U.S. Senator Simpson of Wyoming; secretary of the National Resources Committee and the Environmental Pollution Advisory Counsel; U.S. Chamber of Commerce (1966-69); special assistant, deputy assistant secretary, and then director of the Bureau of Outdoor Recreation, U.S. Department of the Interior (1969-1975); commissioner of the Federal Power Commission (1975-77), vice chairman of the Federal Power Commission (1977); president and chief legal officer of a legal foundation (1977). He assumed his cabinet post on Jan. 23, 1981.

Secretary of Agriculture: John R. Block; b. Feb. 15, 1935, Gilson, Ill.; ed. U.S. Military Academy (1957). U.S. Army (1957-1960); operated the family owned farms ever since. Illinois state director of agriculture (1977-1980), during which time he conducted a number of surveys on agriculture in Eastern Europe and the Far East; held offices in a variety of agriculture-related groups and advisory councils. He assumed his cabinet post on Jan. 22, 1981.

Secretary of Commerce: Malcolm Baldridge; b. Oct. 4, 1922, Omaha, Neb.; ed. Yale University (B.A., 1944). U.S. Army during World War II. Ranch hand and rodeo circuit rider; foundry foreman in a manufacturing company in 1947 and moved up the ranks before becoming the president in 1960. Corporate officer of another manufacturing company (1962-1980); member of boards of directors of several large corporations; member of the Business Council, the Council on Foreign Relations and the International Chamber of Commerce. He assumed his cabinet post on Jan. 23, 1981.

Secretary of Labor: Raymond J. Donovan; b. Aug. 31, 1930, Bayonne, N.J.; ed. Notre Dame Seminary (B.A., 1952). Associated with an insurance company (1953-58); joined construction company beginning in 1959 with primary responsibility for labor relations; member of several labor unions; advisor to several charitable organizations. He assumed his cabinet post on Feb. 4, 1981.

Secretary of Health and Human Services: Richard S. Schweiker; b. June 1, 1926, Norristown, Pa.; ed. Pennsylvania State University (B.A., 1950). U.S. Navy (1944-46). Businessman, then president of a construction materials company, beginning in 1950. Elected to the U.S. House of Representatives (1960-69); U.S. Senate (1969-1981). In Congress he was a member of many committees dealing with health matters; delegate or an alternate delegate to the Republican National Conventions in 1962, 1966, 1972, and Republican vice presidential nominee in 1976. He assumed his cabinet post on Jan. 22, 1981.

Secretary of Housing and Urban Development: Samuel R. Pierce, Jr.; b. Sept. 8, 1922, Glen Cove, Long Island, N.Y.; ed. Cornell University (1947), Cornell University (LL.B., 1949), New York University School of Law (M.A., 1952). U.S. Army during World War II. Assistant district attorney for New York County (1949); assistant U.S. attorney for the Southern District of New York (1953-55); assistant to the under secretary of the Department of Labor (1955-56); associate counsel and counsel with the Subcommittee on Antitrust of the Committee on the Judiciary of the U.S. House of Representatives (1956-57); judge of the New York Court of General Sessions (1959-60); private law practice (1960-1970) and (1973-1981); general counsel in the U.S. Department of Treasury (1970-73). He assumed his cabinet post on Jan. 23, 1981.

Secretary of Transportation: Andrew L. Lewis, Jr; b. Nov. 3, 1931, Philadelphia, Pa.; ed. Haverford College (B.S., 1953), Harvard Graduate School of Business (M.B.A., 1955). Production manager in 1955, then on the board of directors of a manufacturing company; until 1974, he held positions as a corporate officer in several construction materials manufacturing companies, and personnel placement company; trustee of a railroad company (1971-1980). Delegate to the Republican Nat'l Conventions in 1968, 1972, 1976, and 1980; deputy chairman of the Republican Nat'l Comm. (1980). He assumed his cabinet post on Jan. 23, 1981.

Secretary of Energy: James B. Edwards; b. June 24, 1927, Hawthorne, Fla.; ed. College of Charleston (B.S., 1950), University of Louisville School of Dentistry (D.M.D., 1955). U.S. Maritime Service during World War II, U.S. Navy (1955-57), U.S. Naval Reserve (1957-1967). Practiced oral and maxillofacial surgery; elected for one term as a member of the South Carolina Senate in 1972; governor of South Carolina (1975-79); chairman of the National Governors' Association Subcommittee on Nuclear Energy (1978); chairman of the Southern Governors' Conference (1978). Member of several national dental organizations. He assumed his cabinet post on Jan. 23, 1981.

Secretary of Education: Terrell H. Bell; b. Nov. 11, 1921, Lava Hot Springs, Idaho; ed. Southern Idaho College of Education (B.A., 1946), University of Idaho (M.S., 1954), University of Utah (Ph.D.-educational administration, 1961). U.S. Marine Corps (1942-46). Athletic coach and teacher in a public high school (1946-47); superintendent of public schools at various times between 1947 and 1976; interim positions as professor and chairman of the Department of Educational Administration and superintendent of public instruction (1962-1970); deputy commissioner for school systems, U.S. Office of Education (1970-71); commissioner of higher education and chief executive officer for the State of Utah (1976-1980). He assumed his cabinet post on Jan. 23, 1981.

FEDERAL EMPLOYMENT†

SOURCE: Office of Personnel Management

	Employees
Total, All Agencies	**2,899,480**
LEGISLATIVE BRANCH	40,898
Congress	20,871
Architect of the Capitol	2,083
General Accounting Office	5,434
Government Printing Office	6,552
Library of Congress	5,321
JUDICIAL BRANCH	15,178
EXECUTIVE BRANCH	2,843,404
Executive Office of the President	1,783
White House Office	346
Office of the Vice-President	20
Office of Management and Budget	615
Council of Economic Advisors	34
Executive Departments:	
State (Includes AID)	23,521
Treasury	131,637
Defense:	
Military, Total	960,704
Department of the Army	346,548
Department of the Navy	317,163
Department of the Air Force	231,667
Civilian, Total	76,578
Justice	56,867
Interior	79,546
Agriculture	122,889
Commerce	47,010
Labor	23,544
Health and Human Services	159,945
Housing and Urban Development	16,726
Transportation	71,641
Energy	21,692
Education	7,538
ACTION	1,992
Environmental Protection Agency	14,927
Equal Employment Opportunity Commission	3,815
Federal Communications Commission	2,183
Federal Deposit Insurance Corporation	3,443
Federal Trade Commission	1,882
General Services Administration	37,240
International Communication Agency	8,084
Interstate Commerce Commission	1,971
National Aeronautics and Space Administration	23,696
National Labor Relations Board	2,964
Nuclear Regulatory Commission	3,334
Office of Personnel Management	8,530
Securities and Exchange Commission	2,216
Small Business Administration	5,936
Smithsonian Institution	4,516
Tennessee Valley Authority	51,841
U.S. Postal Service	655,748
Veterans Administration	235,480

† List includes selected federal agencies with 1,500 or more employees. The total, however, represents all paid civilian employees of the U.S. government. Employees of the CIA, National Security Agency, and Special Youth Programs are not included. Data as of January 1981.

HEADS OF FEDERAL DEPARTMENTS AND AGENCIES[1] (as of October 1, 1981)

Departments and Agencies	Head
ACTION	Thomas W. Pauken
806 Connecticut Avenue N.W.	Director
20525	
Central Intelligence Agency	William J. Casey
Washington, D.C. 20505	Director
Civil Aeronautics Board	Clinton McKinnon**
1825 Connecticut Ave. N.W.	Chairman
20428	
Commission on Civil Rights	Dr. Arthur S. Flemming
1121 Vermont Ave. N.W. 20425	Chairman
Consumer Product Safety	Nancy H. Steorts
Commission	Chairwoman
1111 18th St. N.W. 20207	
Council of Economic Advisors	Murray L. Weidenbaum
Executive Office Bldg. 20506	Director
Council on Environmental	A. Alan Hill
Quality	Chairman
722 Jackson Pl. N.W. 20006	
Department of Agriculture	John R. Block
14th St. and Independence	Secretary of Agriculture
Ave. S.W. 20250	
Deputy Secretary	Richard E. Lyng
Department of Commerce	Malcolm Baldridge
14th St. between Constitution	Secretary of Commerce
Ave. and E St. N.W. 20230	
Deputy Secretary	Joseph R. Wright, Jr.
Patent & Trademark Office	Gerald J. Mossinghoff
Crystal Plaza, Arlington, Va.	Commissioner
Bureau of Economic Analysis	George Jaszi
1401 K St. N.W. 20230	Director
Bureau of the Census	Bruce K. Chapman
Suitland, Md. 20233	Director
National Bureau of Standards	Ernest Ambler
I-270 & Quince Orchard Rd.,	Director
Gaithersburg, Md. 20234	
National Oceanic and Atmo-	John V. Byrne
spheric Administration	Administrator
6001 Executive Blvd.,	
Rockville, Md. 20852	
Department of Defense	Caspar W. Weinberger
The Pentagon 20301	Secretary of Defense
Deputy Secretary of Defense	Frank C. Carlucci
Joint Chiefs of Staff	Gen. David C. Jones
USAF Chairman	
Department of the	Verne Orr
Air Force	Secretary of the Air Force
The Pentagon 20330	
Department of the Army	John O. Marsh, Jr.
The Pentagon 20310	Secretary of the Army
Department of the Navy	John F. Lehman, Jr.
The Pentagon 20350	Secretary of the Navy
Commandant of the	Gen. Robert H. Barrow
Marine Corps	
Department of Education	Dr. Terrel H. Bell
400 Maryland Ave. S.W. 20202	Secretary of Education
Under Secretary	William C. Clohan, Jr.
Department of Energy	James B. Edwards
1110 Independence Ave. S.W.	Secretary of Energy
20314	
Deputy Secretary	W. Kenneth Davis
Federal Energy Regulatory	Charles M. Butler, III
Commission	Chairman
Department of Health	Richard S. Schweiker
and Human Services	Secretary of Health
200 Independence Ave. S.W.	and Human Services
20201	
Under Secretary	David B. Swoap
Office of Human Develop-	Dorcas R. Hardy
ment Services	Ass't Sec. for Human
	Development Services
Food and Drug Administrations	Dr. Arthur Hayes
5600 Fishers Lane, Rockville,	Commissioner
Md. 20857	

Departments and Agencies	Head
National Institutes of Health	Dr. Thomas E. Malone*
9000 Rockville Pike,	Director
Bethesda, Md. 20205	
Public Health Service	Edward N. Brandt
5600 Fishers Lane,	Ass't Sec. for Health
Rockville, Md. 20857	
Social Security	John A. Svahn
Administration	Commissioner
330 Indiana Ave. S.W.	
20201	
Department of Housing and	Samuel R. Pierce, Jr.
Urban Development	Secretary of Housing and
451 7th St. S.W. 20410	Urban Development
Under Secretary	Donald I. Hovde
Department of the Interior	James G. Watt
C St. between 18th and 19th	Secretary of the Interior
Sts. N.W. 20240	
Under Secretary	Donald P. Hodel
Bureau of Indian Affairs	Ken Payton
	Acting Deputy
	Ass't Sec.-Indian
	Affairs
Bureau of Mines	Robert C. Horton
	Director
Geological Survey	Dallas L. Peck
	Director
National Park Service	Russell E. Dickenson
	Director
Department of Justice	William F. Smith
Constitution Ave. and 10th	Attorney General
St. N.W. 20530	
Deputy Attorney General	Edward C. Schmults
Solicitor General	Rex E. Lee
F.B.I.	William H. Webster
	Director
Immigration and Natural-	Norman Braman**
ization Service	Commissioner
Drug Enforcement Administration	Francis M. Mullen, Jr.*
1405 I St. N.W.20537	Administrator
Department of Labor	Raymond J. Donovan
200 Constitution Ave.	Secretary of Labor
N.W. 20210	
Under Secretary	Malcolm R. Lovell, Jr.
Department of State	Alexander M. Haig, Jr.
2201 C St. N.W. 20520	Secretary of State
Deputy Secretary of State	William P. Clark
Chief of Protocol	Leonore Annenberg
Department of Transportation	Andrew L. Lewis, Jr.
400 7th St. S.W. 20590	Secretary of Transportation
Deputy Secretary	Darrell M. Trent
U.S. Coast Guard	Adm. John B. Hayes, USCG
	Commandant
Federal Aviation	J. Lynn Helms
Administration	Administrator
Federal Highway	Ray A. Barnhart
Administration	Administrator
Federal Railroad	Robert W. Blanchette
Administration	Administrator
Department of the Treasury	Donald T. Regan
15th St. and Pennsylvania	Secretary of the Treasury
Ave. N.W. 20220	
Deputy Secretary	Richard T. McNamar
Commissioner of Customs	William Von Raab**
Bureau of Engraving	Harry R. Clements
and Printing	Director
Bureau of the Mint	Donna Pope
	Director
Internal Revenue Service	Roscoe L. Egger, Jr.
	Commissioner
Comptroller of the	C. Todd Conover**
Currency	
Treasurer of the U.S.	Angela M. Buchanan
U.S. Secret Service	H. Stuart Knight
	Director
Bureau of Alcohol,	George R. Dickerson
Tobacco & Firearms	Director

[1]All addresses are Washington, D.C., unless otherwise noted.* Acting ** Named or nominated but without Senate confirmation.

District of Columbia.............. Marion Barry
District Building, 14th &   Mayor of the District
E Sts. N.W. 20004   of Columbia

Environmental Protection .... Anne McG. Gorsuch
Agency   Administrator
401 M St. S.W. 20460

Equal Employment............... William M. Bell**
Opportunity Commission   Chairman
2401 E St. N.W. 20506

Export-Import Bank of the.......... William H. Draper III
United States   President & Chairman
811 Vermont Ave. N.W. 20571

Farm Credit Administration......... Donald E. Wilkinson
490 L'Enfant Plaza East S.W.   Governor
20578

Federal Communications........... Mark S. Fowler
Commission   Chairman
1919 M St. N.W. 20554

Federal Deposit .... Irvine Sprague
Insurance Corporation   Chairman
550 17th St. N.W. 20429

Federal Election Commission .... John W. McGarry
1325 K St. N.W. 20463   Chairman

Federal Maritime Commission ...... Alan Green, Jr.
1100 L St. N.W. 20573   Chairman

Federal Mediation and .... Kenneth E. Moffett*
Conciliation Service   Director
2100 K St. N.W. 20427

Federal Reserve System, ... Paul A. Volcker
Board of Governors of the   Chairman
Constitution Ave. and 20th
St. N.W. 20551

Federal Trade Commission .... James C. Miller III
Pennsylvania Ave. and 6th   Chairman
St. N.W. 20580

Foreign Claims Settlement .... Richard W. Yarborough
Commission of the U.S.   Chairman
1111 20th St. N.W. 20579

General Accounting Office......... Charles A. Bowsher
441 G St. N.W. 20548   Comptroller General

General Services Administration .... Gerald P. Carmen
18th and F Sts. N.W. 20405   Administrator
Archivist of the U.S.............. Robert M. Warner

Government Printing Office........ Danford L. Sawyer
North Capitol and H Sts. N.W.   Public Printer
20401

Interstate Commerce Commission ... Reese H. Taylor, Jr.
12th St. and Constitution   Chairman
Ave. N.W. 20423

Library of Congress............... Daniel J. Boorstin
10 First St. S.E. 20540   Librarian of Congress

Copyright Office ....,........... David L. Ladd
Crystal Mall Annex,   Register of Copyrights
Arlington, Va. 20559

National Aeronautics and .... James M. Beggs
Space Administration   Administrator
400 Maryland Ave. S.W. 20546

National Credit Union .... Lawrence Connell
Administration   Administrator
1776 G St. N.W. 20456

National Foundation on
the Arts and the Humanities
National Endowment............. Livingston L. Biddle, Jr.[2]
for the Arts   Chairman
2401 E St. N.W. 20520

National Endowment............, Joseph D. Duffey[2]
for the Humanities   Chairman
806 15th St. N.W. 20506

National Labor Relations Board .... John Van de Water**
1717 Pennsylvania Ave. N.W.   Chairman
20570

National Mediation Board.......... George S. Ives
1425 K St. N.W. 20572   Chairman

National Science Foundation .... John B. Slaughter
1800 G St. N.W. 20550   Director

National Security Council .... Richard V. Allen
Executive Off. Bldg. 20506   Ass't to the
                                  President

National Transportation Safety ...... James B. King
Board   Chairman
800 Independence Ave. S.W.
20594

Nuclear Regulatory Commission..... Joseph M. Hendrie
1717 H St. N.W. 20555   Chairman

Occupational Safety and Health ..... Timothy F. Cleary
Review Commission   Chairman
1825 K St. 20006

Office of Management and .... David A. Stockman
Budget   Director
Executive Office Building 20503

Office of Personnel Management .... Donald J. Devine
1900 E. St. N.W. 20415   Director

Office of Policy Development .... Martin Anderson
1600 Pennsylvania Ave. N.W.   Ass't to the Pres. for
20500   Development Policy

Office of Technology Assessment .... John H. Gibbons
600 Pennsylvania Ave. S.E.   Director
20510

Office of the United States .... William E. Brock
Trade Representative   United States Trade
1800 G St. N.W. 20506   Representative

Panama Canal Commission .... Michael Rhode, Jr.
425 13th St. N.W. 20004   Secretary

Postal Rate Commission .... Janet D. Steiger*
2000 L St. N.W. 20268   Chairman

Securities and Exchange........... John S. R. Shad
Commission   Chairman
500 N. Capitol St. N.W.
20549

Selective Service System .... Thomas K. Turnage
600 E St. N.W. 20435   Director

Small Business Administration...... Michael Cardenas
1441 L St. N.W. 20416   Administrator

Smithsonian Institution .... S. Dillon Ripley
1000 Jefferson Drive S.W.   Secretary
20560

Synthetic Fuels Corporation U.S. .... Edward E. Noble
                                  Chairman

Tennessee Valley Authority......... S. David Freeman
412 1st St. S.E.   Chairman
Knoxville, Tenn. 20444

United States Arms Control......... Eugene V. Rostow
and Disarmament Agency   Director
320 21st St. N.W. 20451

United States Information Agency ... Charles Z. Wick
1750 Pennsylvania Ave. N.W.   Director

United States International Develop- . M. Peter McPherson*
ment Cooperation Agency   Director
320 21st St. N.W. 20523

United States International Trade.... Bill Alberger
Commission   Chairman
701 E St. N.W. 20436

United States Postal Service........ William F. Bolger
475 L'Enfant Plaza West S.W.   Postmaster General
20260

Veterans Administration .... Robert Nimmo
810 Vermont Ave. N.W. 20420   Administrator

---

* Acting ** Named or nominated but without Senate confirmation. [2] Term ends in fall of 1981, but no replacement has been nominated and confirmed by the Senate as of Oct.1, 1981.

VOTES CAST FOR MEMBERS OF THE U.S. HOUSE OF REPRESENTATIVES IN 1980 BY DISTRICT

SOURCE: Statistics of the Presidential and Congressional Election of November 4, 1980

State and district	Vote cast in 1980 Democrat	Republican
Alabama:		
1st	......	111,089
2d	63,447	104,796
3d	107,654	......
4th	129,365	......
5th	117,626	......
6th	87,536	95,019
7th	122,505	43,320
Alaska:		
At large	39,922	114,089
Arizona:		
1st	40,045	136,961
2d	127,736	88,653
3d	141,448	65,845
4th	85,046	142,565
Arkansas:		
1st	NA	......
2d	42,278	159,148
3d	......	NA
4th	NA	......
California:		
1st	107,682	145,098
2d	109,789	141,698
3d	170,670	64,215
4th	133,853	60,935
5th	101,105	89,624
6th	93,400	34,500
7th	142,044	70,479
8th	108,380	76,580
9th	90,504	67,265
10th	102,231	45,987
11th	85,823	80,100
12th	37,009	143,817
13th	132,246	79,766
14th	79,883	133,979
15th	108,072	37,895
16th	158,360	54,675
17th	53,780	129,159
18th	51,415	126,046
19th	36,990	162,849
20th	43,024	199,674
21st	73,898	74,674
22d	57,477	115,241
23d	126,020	62,742
24th	93,569	39,744
25th	49,080	21,116
26th	40,099	116,715
27th	100,061	109,807
28th	108,725	23,179
29th	80,095	10,282
30th	74,119	24,136
31st	69,146	38,203
32d	84,057	39,260
33d	50,365	122,439
34th	46,351	138,024
35th	88,279	100,743
36th	88,628	73,247
37th	58,091	165,371
38th	91,880	66,256
39th	54,504	175,228
40th	66,512	213,999
41st	101,101	123,187
42d	69,936	79,713
43d	46,361	298,815
Colorado:		
1st	107,364	67,804
2d	153,550	111,868
3d	105,820	84,292
4th	76,849	178,221
5th	62,003	177,319
Connecticut:		
1st	137,849	80,816
2d	119,176	104,107
3d	103,903	117,024
4th	74,326	124,285

State and district	Vote cast in 1980 Democrat	Republican
5th	117,316	115,614
6th	142,685	98,331
Delaware:		
At large	81,227	133,842
Florida:		
1st	119,829	75,939
2d	138,252	57,588
3d	104,672	31,208
4th	147,775	76,924
5th	140,903	177,603
6th	......	NA
7th	132,529	52,138
8th	151,613	61,820
9th	139,468	58,734
10th	72,646	272,393
11th	201,713	137,520
12th	107,164	128,561
13th	127,828	42,830
14th	95,820	32,027
15th	132,952	70,433
Georgia:		
1st	82,145	......
2d	92,264	33,107
3d	89,040	......
4th	117,091	51,546
5th	101,646	35,640
6th	66,606	96,071
7th	115,892	54,242
8th	91,103	31,033
9th	115,576	54,341
10th	102,177	25,194
Hawaii:		
1st	98,256	19,819
2d	141,477	......
Idaho:		
1st	100,697	116,845
2d	81,364	116,196
Illinois:		
1st	119,562	5,660
2d	129,771	17,428
3d	137,283	61,955
4th	71,814	152,377
5th	106,142	27,136
6th	60,951	123,593
7th	80,056	14,041
8th	98,524	17,845
9th	106,543	39,244
10th	89,008	137,707
11th	121,166	52,417
12th	64,729	185,080
13th	52,000	131,448
14th	61,224	202,583
15th	45,721	150,898
16th	64,224	132,905
17th	65,305	125,806
18th	76,471	125,561
19th	51,753	142,616
20th	96,950	123,427
21st	63,476	132,186
22d	66,065	146,014
23d	107,786	59,644
24th	112,134	110,176
Indiana:		
1st	112,016	43,537
2d	122,326	103,957
3d	85,136	103,972
4th	77,542	120,055
5th	80,378	129,474
6th	99,089	98,302
7th	69,051	137,604
8th	97,059	119,415
9th	136,574	75,601
10th	103,083	90,051
11th	105,468	78,743

State and district	Vote cast in 1980 Democrat	Republican
Iowa:		
1st	72,602	133,349
2d	93,175	111,587
3d	101,735	107,869
4th	117,896	100,335
5th	127,895	84,472
6th	129,460	71,866
Kansas:		
1st	73,586	121,545
2d	78,859	92,107
3d	82,414	109,294
4th	124,014	55,899
5th	45,676	141,029
Kentucky:		
1st	118,565	......
2d	99,670	52,110
3d	85,873	46,681
4th	62,138	126,049
5th	54,027	112,093
6th	72,473	105,376
7th	117,665	......
Louisiana:		
1st	8,277	81,777
2d	48,662	25,521
3d	94,529	......
4th	162,330	......
5th	105,267	......
6th	12,149	118,540
7th	NA	......
8th	75,433	34,059
Maine:		
1st	86,819	188,667
2d	51,026	186,406
Maryland:		
1st	97,743	91,143
2d	121,017	89,961
3d	102,293	32,074
4th	47,375	120,985
5th	106,035	25,693
6th	146,101	62,913
7th	97,104	12,650
8th	148,301	101,659
Massachusetts:		
1st	52,457	156,514
2d	120,711	38,672
3d	141,560	54,213
4th	103,466	95,898
5th	136,758	70,547
6th	111,393	103,192
7th	155,759	......
8th	128,689	35,477
9th	104,010	......
10th	85,629	131,794
11th	137,066	......
12th	195,791	71,620
Michigan:		
1st	123,286	6,244
2d	83,550	115,562
3d	113,080	102,591
4th	47,777	148,950
5th	101,737	118,061
6th	108,548	111,272
7th	147,280	......
8th	124,155	77,009
9th	......	168,713
10th	126,962	111,496
11th	75,515	146,205
12th	112,698	90,931
13th	79,719	6,473
14th	90,362	78,395
15th	113,492	53,046
16th	105,844	42,735
17th	127,525	44,313
18th	135,705	68,575
19th	60,100	168,530

N.A. = Not Available

State and district	Vote cast in 1980 Democrat	Republican
Minnesota:		
1st	67,279	171,099
2d	102,586	158,082
3d	57,868	179,393
4th	119,182	82,537
5th	126,451	48,200
6th	126,173	140,402
7th	124,026	135,084
8th	182,228	72,350
Mississippi:		
1st	104,269	61,292
2d	96,750	42,300
3d	128,035	......
4th	52,303	69,321
5th	46,416	131,559
Missouri:		
1st	91,272	38,667
2d	148,227	81,762
3d	143,132	41,277
4th	151,459	71,869
5th	110,957	47,309
6th	62,048	149,281
7th	76,844	161,668
8th	95,751	127,675
9th	135,905	104,835
10th	94,465	116,167
Montana:		
1st	112,866	70,874
2d	63,370	91,431
Nebraska:		
1st	43,605	160,705
2d	88,843	107,736
3d	34,967	182,887
Nevada:		
At large	165,107	63,163
New Hampshire:		
1st	114,061	73,565
2d	63,350	113,304
New Jersey:		
1st	147,352	42,154
2d	135,437	97,072
3d	106,269	104,184
4th	68,480	95,447
5th	41,269	156,016
6th	92,227	125,792
7th	99,737	108,760
8th	95,493	44,625
9th	75,321	116,128
10th	76,154	11,778
11th	106,155	57,772
12th	36,577	134,973
13th	56,251	152,862
14th	86,921	45,606
15th	92,457	75,812
New Mexico:		
1st	120,903	125,910
2d	55,085	61,564
New York:		
1st	85,629	91,647
2d	84,035	51,256
3d	75,389	74,868
4th	54,607	97,064
5th	73,032	88,945
6th	74,319	71,838
7th	73,785	19,280
8th	79,150	20,970
9th	63,796	34,453
10th	57,804	35,089
11th	69,922	19,128
12th	34,611	3,372
13th	77,704	16,813
14th	42,929	7,154
15th	49,684	37,709
16th	64,536	13,860
17th	46,178	57,810
18th	62,598	87,286
19th	72,995	7,335
20th	79,356	15,350
21st	29,731	1,883
22d	63,178	9,943
23d	85,749	54,866
24th	100,182	52,921
25th	37,369	136,619
26th	34,906	137,159
27th	103,863	75,892
28th	164,088	37,504
29th	65,562	124,156
30th	50,635	101,496
31st	37,266	128,397
32d	52,407	98,498
33d	36,941	119,489
34th	37,883	133,278
35th	39,214	127,623
36th	115,334	41,756
37th	90,119	14,701
38th	35,681	141,763
39th	93,839	69,194
North Carolina:		
1st	108,738	......
2d	99,297	35,946
3d	84,862	39,393
4th	97,167	84,631
5th	99,117	94,894
6th	76,957	80,275
7th	88,564	40,270
8th	95,013	67,317
9th	71,504	101,156
10th	52,485	120,777
11th	90,789	104,485
North Dakota:		
At large	166,437	124,707
Ohio:		
1st	38,529	124,080
2d	103,423	72,693
3d	95,558	66,698
4th	51,150	133,795
5th	57,704	137,003
6th	84,235	101,288
7th	38,952	124,137
8th	44,162	139,590
9th	68,728	96,927
10th	49,433	143,403
11th	51,224	128,507
12th	108,690	98,110
13th	113,439	64,296
14th	103,336	55,962
15th	48,708	129,025
16th	39,219	149,960
17th	47,900	128,870
18th	134,835	42,354
19th	77,272	107,032
20th	96,217	......
21st	83,188	11,103
22d	108,137	80,836
23d	144,371	......
Oklahoma:		
1st	115,381	82,293
2d	101,516	86,544
3d	NA	......
4th	74,245	71,339
5th	36,815	90,053
6th	111,694	60,980
Oregon:		
1st	203,532	105,083
2d	138,089	141,854
3d	156,371	60,940
4th	158,745	130,861
Pennsylvania:		
1st	111,693	37,893
2d	127,106	......
3d	67,942	40,866
4th	73,895	127,475
5th	47,092	148,898
6th	117,965	57,844
7th	99,381	87,643
8th	99,593	103,585
9th	......	157,241
10th	43,152	145,703
11th	86,703	93,621
12th	106,750	72,999
13th	57,745	138,212
14th	102,545	44,071
15th	66,626	99,874
16th	38,891	129,765
17th	97,995	63,790
18th	127,641	58,821
19th	41,584	136,873
20th	122,100	46,313
21st	112,427	51,821
22d	118,084	50,020
23d	41,033	122,855
24th	86,567	86,687
25th	119,817	58,768
Rhode Island:		
1st	120,756	57,844
2d	92,970	115,057
South Carolina:		
1st	76,743	81,988
2d	73,353	92,306
3d	87,680	57,840
4th	......	90,941
5th	99,773	......
6th	70,747	75,964
South Dakota:		
1st	109,910	57,155
2d	63,447	88,991
Tennessee:		
1st	......	130,296
2d	46,578	147,947
3d	117,355	74,761
4th	137,612	35,954
5th	118,506	62,746
6th	......	127,945
7th	133,606	39,227
8th	110,139	......
Texas:		
1st	137,665	......
2d	142,496	60,742
3d	49,667	218,228
4th	102,787	93,915
5th	70,892	67,848
6th	144,816	59,503
7th	48,594	242,810
8th	67,921	72,856
9th	103,225	......
10th	135,618	88,940
11th	128,520	......
12th	99,104	65,005
13th	98,779	80,819
14th	93,884	71,495
15th	105,325	45,090
16th	104,734	......
17th	130,465	......
18th	71,985	16,128
19th	126,632	......
20th	84,113	17,725
21st	58,425	196,424
22d	101,094	106,797
23d	104,595	45,139
24th	93,690	59,172
Utah:		
1st	144,459	157,111
2d	87,967	194,885
Vermont:		
At large	......	154,274
Virginia:		
1st	......	130,130
2d	......	97,319
3d	60,962	96,524
4th	59,930	92,557
5th	112,143	......
6th	......	123,125
7th	......	139,957
8th	94,530	95,624
9th	52,636	119,196
10th	105,883	110,840

N.A. = Not Available

State and district	Vote cast in 1980 Democrat	Republican	State and district	Vote cast in 1980 Democrat	Republican	State and district	Vote cast in 1980 Democrat	Republican
Washington:			West Virginia:			4th	146,437	61,027
1st	41,830	180,475	1st	107,471	61,438	5th	129,574	37,267
2d	162,002	82,639	2d	80,940	102,805	6th	98,628	143,980
3d	155,906	92,872	3d	84,980	94,583	7th	164,340	89,745
4th	100,114	134,691	4th	117,595	36,020	8th	81,043	169,664
5th	120,530	111,705				9th	56,838	206,227
6th	122,903	106,236	Wisconsin:					
7th	112,848	84,218	1st	126,222	96,047	Wyoming:		
			2d	142,037	119,514	At large	53,338	116,361
N.A. = Not Available			3d	126,859	132,001			

VOTES CAST FOR SENATORS IN 1976, 1978, AND 1980

(The figures show the vote for the Democratic and Republican nominees, except as otherwise indicated. Compiled from official statistics)

VOTE

STATE	1976 Democrat	Republican	1978 Democrat	Republican	1980 Democrat	Republican	Total vote cast in 1980
Alabama			{ 401,852[1] / 547,054	316,170[1]	610,175	650,362	1,296,757[2]
Alaska			29,574	92,783	72,007	84,159	156,762
Arizona	400,334	321,236			422,972	432,371	874,238[2]
Arkansas			395,506	84,308	477,905	330,576	808,812[2]
California	3,502,862	3,748,973			4,704,098	3,091,671	8,324,012[2]
Colorado			330,148	480,801	590,501	571,295	1,173,142[2]
Connecticut	561,018	785,683			763,969	581,884	1,356,075[2]
Delaware	98,042	125,454	93,930	66,479			
Florida	1,799,518	1,057,886			1,705,409	1,822,460	3,528,028[2]
Georgia	162,305	122,724	536,320	108,808	776,143	803,686	1,579,829[2]
Hawaii					224,485	53,068	288,006[2]
Idaho			89,635	194,412	214,439	218,701	439,647[2]
Illinois			1,448,187	1,698,711	2,565,302	1,946,296	4,580,029[2]
Indiana	868,522	1,275,833			1,015,962	1,182,414	2,198,376
Iowa			395,066	421,598	581,545	683,014	1,276,986[2]
Kansas			317,602	403,354	340,271	598,686	938,957
Kentucky			290,730	175,766	720,891	386,029	1,106,920
Louisiana			(b)	(b)	810,692	23,947	841,013
Maine	292,704	193,489	127,327	212,294			
Maryland	772,101	530,439			435,118	850,970	1,286,088
Massachusetts	1,726,657	722,641	1,093,283	890,584			
Michigan	1,831,031	1,635,087	1,484,193	1,362,165			
Minnesota	1,290,736	478,602	{ 538,675[4] / 638,375	957,908[4] / 894,092			
Mississippi	554,433		187,541	267,302			
Missouri	813,571	1,090,064			1,074,859	985,399	2,066,965[2]
Montana	206,232	115,213	160,353	127,589			
Nebraska	313,805	279,284	334,096	159,706			
Nevada	127,214	63,471			92,129	144,224	243,273[2]
New Hampshire			127,945	133,745	179,455	195,559	375,060[2]
New Jersey	1,681,140	1,054,508	1,082,960	844,200			
New Mexico	176,382	234,681	160,045	183,442			
New York	3,422,594[3]	2,836,633[3]			2,618,661	2,272,082	6,014,914[2]
North Carolina			516,663	619,151	887,653	898,064	1,797,665[2]
North Dakota	175,772	103,466			86,658	210,347	299,272[2]
Ohio	1,941,113	1,823,774			2,770,786	1,137,695	4,027,303[2]
Oklahoma			493,953	247,857	478,283	587,252	1,098,294[2]
Oregon			341,616	550,165	501,963	594,290	1,140,494[2]
Pennsylvania	2,126,977	2,381,891			2,122,391	2,230,404	4,418,042[2]
Rhode Island	167,665	230,329	229,557	76,061			
South Carolina			280,146	351,917	612,554	257,946	870,500
South Dakota			84,767	170,832	129,018	190,594	327,478[2]
Tennessee	751,180	673,231	466,228	642,644			
Texas	2,199,956	1,636,370	1,139,149	1,151,376			
Utah	223,948	290,221			151,454	437,675	594,298[2]
Vermont	85,682	94,481			104,176	101,421	209,124[2]
Virginia	(a)	(a)	608,511	613,232			
Washington	1,071,219	361,546			792,052	936,317	1,728,369
West Virginia	566,359		249,034	244,317			
Wisconsin	1,396,970	521,902			1,065,487	1,106,311	2,204,202[2]
Wyoming	70,558	84,810	50,456	82,908			

(a) Harry F. Byrd, Jr., Independent, had 890,778 votes; E. R. Zumwalt, Democrat, had 596,009 votes; Martin H. Perper, Independent, had 70,559 votes.
(b) Figures not available.
[1] For unexpired term ending Jan. 3, 1981.
[2] Includes the vote for various other candidates.
[3] Total vote received as candidate had one or more other party endorsements.
[4] For unexpired term ending Jan. 3, 1983.

U.S. CONGRESSIONAL REPRESENTATIVES UNDER EACH APPORTIONMENT: 1790-1980

State	1790	1800	1810	1820	1830	1840	1850	1860	1870	1880	1890	1900	1910[1]	1930	1940	1950	1960	1970	1980
Alabama			[2]1	3	5	7	7	6	8	8	9	9	10	9	9	9	8	7	7
Alaska																[2]1	1	1	1
Arizona													[2]1	1	2	2	3	4	5
Arkansas					[2]1	1	2	3	4	5	6	7	7	7	7	6	4	4	4
California						[2]2	2	3	4	6	7	8	11	20	23	30	38	43	45
Colorado									[2]1	1	2	3	4	4	4	4	4	5	6
Connecticut	5	7	7	7	6	4	4	4	4	4	4	5	5	6	6	6	6	6	6
Delaware	1	1	1	2	1	1	1	1	1	1	1	1	1	1	1	1	1	1	1
Florida						[2]1	1	1	2	2	2	3	4	5	6	8	12	15	19
Georgia	3	2	4	6	7	9	8	8	7	9	10	11	11	12	10	10	10	10	10
Hawaii																[2]1	2	2	2
Idaho											[2]1	1	1	2	2	2	2	2	2
Illinois			[2]1	1	3	7	9	14	19	20	22	25	27	27	26	25	24	24	22
Indiana			[2]1	3	7	10	11	11	13	13	13	13	13	12	11	11	11	11	10
Iowa						[2]2	2	6	9	11	11	11	11	9	8	8	7	6	6
Kansas								1	3	7	8	8	8	7	6	6	5	5	5
Kentucky	2	6	10	12	13	10	10	9	10	11	11	11	11	9	9	8	7	7	7
Louisiana			[2]1	3	3	4	4	5	6	6	6	7	8	8	8	8	8	8	8
Maine			[3]7	7	8	7	6	5	5	4	4	4	4	3	3	3	2	2	2
Maryland	6	8	9	9	9	8	6	6	5	6	6	6	6	6	6	6	7	8	8
Massachusetts	8	14	17	[3]13	13	12	10	11	10	11	12	13	14	16	15	14	14	12	11
Michigan					[2]1	3	4	6	9	11	12	12	13	17	17	18	19	19	18
Minnesota							[2]2	2	3	5	7	9	10	9	9	9	8	8	8
Mississippi			[2]1	1	2	2	5	5	6	7	7	8	8	7	7	6	5	5	5
Missouri				1	2	5	7	9	13	14	15	16	16	13	13	11	10	10	9
Montana										[2]1	1	1	2	2	2	2	2	2	2
Nebraska								[2]1	1	3	6	6	6	5	4	4	3	3	3
Nevada								[2]1	1	1	1	1	1	1	1	1	1	1	2
New Hampshire	3	4	5	6	6	5	4	3	3	2	2	2	2	2	2	2	2	2	2
New Jersey	4	5	6	6	6	5	5	5	7	7	8	10	12	14	14	14	15	15	14
New Mexico													[2]1	1	2	2	2	2	3
New York	6	10	17	27	34	40	34	33	31	33	34	34	37	43	45	43	41	39	34
North Carolina	5	10	12	13	13	13	9	8	7	8	9	9	10	10	11	12	12	11	11
North Dakota											[2]1	2	3	2	2	2	2	1	1
Ohio		[2]1	6	14	19	21	21	19	20	21	21	21	22	24	23	23	24	23	21
Oklahoma												[2]5	8	9	8	6	6	6	6
Oregon								[2]1	1	2	3	3	3	3	4	4	4	4	5
Pennsylvania	8	13	18	23	26	28	24	25	24	27	28	30	32	36	34	33	30	27	25
Rhode Island	1	2	2	2	2	2	2	2	2	2	2	2	3	2	2	2	2	2	2
South Carolina	5	6	8	9	9	9	7	6	4	5	7	7	7	7	6	6	6	6	6
South Dakota											[2]2	2	3	2	2	2	2	2	1
Tennessee		[2]1	3	6	9	13	11	10	8	10	10	10	10	10	9	10	9	9	8
Texas						[2]2	2	4	6	11	13	16	18	21	21	22	23	24	27
Utah												[2]1	1	2	2	2	2	2	3
Vermont	2	4	6	5	5	4	3	3	3	2	2	2	2	1	1	1	1	1	1
Virginia	10	19	22	23	22	21	15	13	11	10	10	10	10	9	9	10	10	10	10
Washington										[2]1	2	3	5	6	6	7	7	7	8
West Virginia								3	4	4	5	6	6	6	6	6	5	4	4
Wisconsin						[2]2	3	6	8	9	10	11	11	10	10	10	10	9	9
Wyoming										[2]1	1	1	1	1	1	1	1	1	1
Total	65	106	142	186	213	242	232	237	243	293	332	357	391	435	435	435	437	435	435

[1] No apportionment was made in 1920. [2] The following representation was added after the several census apportionments indicated when new States were admitted and is included in the above table: First. Tennessee, 1. Second. Ohio, 1. Third. Alabama, 1; Illinois, 1; Indiana, 1; Louisiana, 1; Mississippi, 1. Fifth. Arkansas, 1; Michigan, 1. Sixth. California, 2; Florida, 1; Iowa, 2; Texas, 2; Wisconsin, 2. Seventh. Minnesota, 2; Oregon, 1. Eighth. Nebraska, 1; Nevada, 1. Ninth. Colorado, 1. Tenth. Idaho, 1; Montana, 1; North Dakota, 1; South Dakota, 2; Washington, 1; Wyoming, 1. Eleventh. Utah, 1. Twelfth. Oklahoma, 5. Thirteenth. Arizona, 1; New Mexico, 1. Seventeenth. Alaska, 1; Hawaii, 1. [3] Twenty Members were assigned to Massachusetts, but 7 of these were credited to Maine when that area became a State.

THE HOUSE OF REPRESENTATIVES
Democratic members are in roman, Republicans in *italics.*

Ninety-Seventh Congress, First Session January 5, 1981

Democrats 243; *Republicans* 191; 1 Vacant; Total: 435

Speaker: Thomas P. O'Neill, Jr., Mass.
Majority Leader: James C. Wright, Jr., Texas
Majority Whip: Thomas S. Foley, Wash.
Minority Leader: *Robert H. Michel,* Ill.
Minority Whip: *Trent Lott,* Miss.
Clerk: Edmund L. Henshaw, Jr.

Sergeant at Arms: Benjamin J. Guthrie
Parliamentarian: William Holmes Brown
Doorkeeper: James T. Molloy
Postmaster: Robert V. Rota
Press Gallery Superintendent: Benjamin C. West
Chaplain: Rev. James David Ford, B.D.

HOUSE MEMBERS BY STATE AND DISTRICT (1st Session, 97th Congress)

Democratic members are in roman, Republicans in *italics*.

Dist.	Representative	Residence
Alabama		
1.	Jack Edwards	Mobile
2.	*William L. Dickinson*	Montgomery
3.	Bill Nichols	Sylacauga
4.	Tom Bevill	Jasper
5.	Ronnie G. Flippo	Florence
6.	Albert L. Smith, Jr.	Birmingham
7.	Richard C. Shelby	Tuscaloosa
Alaska		
	*Don Young	Fort Yukon
Arizona		
1.	*John J. Rhodes*	Mesa
2.	Morris K. Udall	Tucson
3.	*Bob Stump*	Tolleson
4.	*Eldon Rudd*	Scottsdale
Arkansas		
1.	Bill Alexander	Osceola
2.	*Edwin R. Bethune, Jr.*	Searcy
3.	*John P. Hammerschmidt*	Harrison
4.	Beryl F. Anthony, Jr.	El Dorado
California		
1.	*Eugene A. Chappie*	Roseville
2.	*Don H. Clausen*	Crescent City
3.	Robert T. Matsui	Sacramento
4.	Vic Fazio	Sacramento
5.	John L. Burton	San Francisco
6.	Phillip Burton	San Francisco
7.	George Miller	Martinez
8.	Ronald V. Dellums	Berkeley
9.	Fortney H. Stark, Jr.	Oakland
10.	Don Edwards	San Jose
11.	Thomas P. Lantos	San Mateo
12.	*Paul N. McCloskey, Jr.*	Menlo Park
13.	Norman Y. Mineta	San Jose
14.	Norman D. Shumway	Stockton
15.	Tony Coelho	Merced
16.	Leon E. Panetta	Carmel Valley
17.	*Charles Pashayan, Jr.*	Fresno
18.	*William Thomas*	Bakersfield
19.	*Robert J. Lagomarsino*	Ventura
20.	*Barry M. Goldwater, Jr.*	Woodland Hills
21.	*Bobbi Fiedler*	Northridge
22.	*Carlos J. Moorhead*	Glendale
23.	Anthony C. Beilenson	Los Angeles
24.	Henry A. Waxman	Los Angeles
25.	Edward R. Roybal	Los Angeles
26.	*John H. Rousselot*	San Marino
27.	*Robert K. Dornan*	Santa Monica
28.	Julian C. Dixon	Culver City
29.	Augustus F. Hawkins	Los Angeles
30.	George E. Danielson	Monterey Park
31.	Mervyn M. Dymally	Compton
32.	Glenn M. Anderson	Harbor City
33.	*Wayne Grisham*	La Mirada
34.	Daniel E. Lungren	Long Beach
35.	*David T. Dreier*	La Verne
36.	George E. Brown, Jr.	Riverside
37.	*Jerry Lewis*	Highland
38.	*Jerry M. Patterson*	Santa Ana
39.	*William E. Dannemeyer*	Fullerton
40.	*Robert E. Badham*	Newport Beach
41.	*William D. Lowery*	San Diego
42.	*Duncan L. Hunter*	Coronado
43.	*Clair W. Burgener*	La Jolla
Colorado		
1.	Patricia Schroeder	Denver
2.	Timothy E. Wirth	Denver
3.	Ray Kogovsek	Pueblo
4.	*Hank Brown*	Greeley
5.	*Ken Kramer*	Colorado Springs
Connecticut		
1.	(Vacant)	
2.	Samuel Gejdenson	Bozrah
3.	*Lawrence J. DeNardis*	Hamden
4.	*Stewart B. McKinney*	Fairfield
5.	William Ratchford	Danbury
6.	Toby Moffett	Unionville
Delaware		
	*Thomas B. Evans, Jr.	Wilmington

* Representative at large.

Dist.	Representative	Residence
Florida		
1.	Earl Hutto	Panama City
2.	Don Fuqua	Altha
3.	Charles E. Bennett	Jacksonville
4.	*William V. Chappell, Jr.*	Ocala
5.	*Bill McCollum, Jr.*	Altamonte Springs
6.	*C. W. Young*	St. Petersburg
7.	Sam M. Gibbons	Tampa
8.	Andrew P. Ireland	Winter Haven
9.	Bill Nelson	Melbourne
10.	*L. A. Bafalis*	Fort Myers Beach
11.	Dan Mica	West Palm Beach
12.	*E. Clay Shaw, Jr.*	Fort Lauderdale
13.	William Lehman	North Miami Beach
14.	Claude D. Pepper	Miami
15.	Dante B. Fascell	Miami
Georgia		
1.	Ronald "Bo" Ginn	Millen
2.	Charles F. Hatcher	Albany
3.	Jack T. Brinkley	Columbus
4.	Elliott H. Levitas	Atlanta
5.	Wyche Fowler, Jr.	Atlanta
6.	*Newt Gingrich*	Carrollton
7.	Larry P. McDonald	Marietta
8.	Billy Lee Evans	Macon
9.	Edgar L. Jenkins	Jasper
10.	D. Douglas Barnard, Jr.	Augusta
Hawaii		
1.	Cecil Heftel	Honolulu
2.	Daniel K. Akaka	Honolulu
Idaho		
1.	*Larry E. Craig*	Midvale
2.	*George V. Hansen*	Pocatello
Illinois		
1.	Harold Washington	Chicago
2.	Gus Savage	Chicago
3.	Martin A. Russo	South Holland
4.	*Edward J. Derwinski*	Flossmoor
5.	John G. Fary	Chicago
6.	*Henry J. Hyde*	Bensenville
7.	Cardiss Collins	Chicago
8.	Dan Rostenkowski	Chicago
9.	Sidney R. Yates	Chicago
10.	*John E. Porter*	Evanston
11.	Frank Annunzio	Chicago
12.	*Philip M. Crane*	Mount Prospect
13.	*Robert McClory*	Lake Bluff
14.	*John N. Erlenborn*	Glen Ellyn
15.	Tom Corcoran	Ottawa
16.	Lynn M. Martin	Rockford
17.	*George M. O'Brien*	Joliet
18.	*Robert H. Michel*	Peoria
19.	*Tom Railsback*	Moline
20.	Paul Findley	Pittsfield
21.	*Edward R. Madigan*	Lincoln
22.	Daniel B. Crane	Danville
23.	Charles Melvin Price	East St. Louis
24.	Paul Simon	Carbondale
Indiana		
1.	Adam Benjamin, Jr.	Hobart
2.	Floyd J. Fithian	Lafayette
3.	John P. Hiler	La Porte
4.	*Daniel R. Coats*	Fort Wayne
5.	*Elwood H. Hillis*	Kokomo
6.	David W. Evans	Indianapolis
7.	*John T. Myers*	Covington
8.	*H. Joel Deckard*	Evansville
9.	Lee H. Hamilton	Columbus
10.	Philip R. Sharp	Muncie
11.	Andrew Jacobs, Jr.	Indianapolis
Iowa		
1.	*Jim Leach*	Davenport
2.	*Thomas J. Tauke*	Dubuque
3.	*Cooper Evans*	Grundy Center
4.	Neal Smith	Altoona
5.	Tom Harkin	Ames
6.	Berkley W. Bedell	Spirit Lake

Dist.	Representative	Residence
Kansas		
1.	*Charles P. Roberts*	Dodge City
2.	*Jim Jeffries*	Atchison
3.	*Larry Winn, Jr.*	Overland Park
4.	Daniel R. Glickman	Wichita
5.	*Robert Whittaker*	Augusta
Kentucky		
1.	Carroll Hubbard, Jr.	Mayfield
2.	William H. Natcher	Bowling Green
3.	Romano L. Mazzoli	Louisville
4.	*M. Gene Snyder*	Jefferson Co.
5.	*Harold D. Rogers*	Somerset
6.	*Larry Hopkins*	Lexington
7.	Carl D. Perkins	Hindman
Louisiana		
1.	*Robert L. Livingston, Jr.*	New Orleans
2.	Corinne "Lindy" Boggs	New Orleans
3.	Wilbert J. Tauzin	Thibodaux
4.	Charles E. Roemer III	Bossier Parish
5.	Thomas J. Huckaby	Ringgold
6.	*W. Henson Moore*	Baton Rouge
7.	John B. Breaux	Crowley
8.	Gillis W. Long	Alexandria
Maine		
1.	*David F. Emery*	Rockland
2.	*Olympia J. Snowe*	Auburn
Maryland		
1.	Roy P. Dyson	Great Mills
2.	Clarence D. Long	Ruxton
3.	Barbara A. Mikulski	Baltimore
4.	*Marjorie S. Holt*	Severna Park
5.	Steny H. Hoyer	District Heights
6.	Beverly Byron	Frederick
7.	Parren J. Mitchell	Baltimore
8.	Michael D. Barnes	Kensington
Massachusetts		
1.	*Silvio O. Conte*	Pittsfield
2.	Edward P. Boland	Springfield
3.	Joseph D. Early	Worcester
4.	Barney Frank	Newton
5.	James M. Shannon	Lawrence
6.	Nicholas Mavroules	Peabody
7.	Edward J. Markey	Malden
8.	Thomas P. O'Neill, Jr.	Cambridge
9.	John "Joe" Moakley	Boston
10.	Margaret M. Heckler	Wellesley
11.	Brian J. Donnelly	Dorchester
12.	Gerry E. Studds	Cohasset
Michigan		
1.	John Conyers, Jr.	Detroit
2.	Carl D. Pursell	Plymouth
3.	Howard Wolpe	Lansing
4.	*Mark D. Siljander*	Three Rivers
5.	*Harold S. Sawyer*	Rockford
6.	*Jim Dunn*	East Lansing
7.	Dale E. Kildee	Flint
8.	M. Robert Traxler	Bay City
9.	*Guy A. Vander Jagt*	Luther
10.	Don Albosta	St. Charles
11.	*Robert W. Davis*	Gaylord
12.	David E. Bonior	Mount Clemens
13.	George W. Crockett, Jr.	Detroit
14.	Dennis M. Hertel	Detroit
15.	William D. Ford	Taylor
16.	John D. Dingell	Trenton
17.	William M. Brodhead	Detroit
18.	James J. Blanchard	Pleasant Ridge
19.	*William S. Broomfield*	Birmingham
Minnesota		
1.	*Arlen Erdahl*	West St. Paul
2.	*Thomas M. Hagedorn*	Truman
3.	*Bill Frenzel*	Golden Valley
4.	Bruce F. Vento	St. Paul
5.	Martin O. Sabo	Minneapolis
6.	*Vin Weber*	Slayton
7.	*Arlan Stangeland*	Barnesville
8.	James L. Oberstar	Chisholm
Mississippi		
1.	Jamie L. Whitten	Charleston
2.	David R. Bowen	Cleveland
3.	G. V. Montgomery	Meridian
4.	Wayne Dowdy	McComb
5.	*Trent Lott*	Pascagoula

Dist.	Representative	Residence
Missouri		
1.	William L. Clay	St. Louis
2.	Robert A. Young	Maryland Heights
3.	Richard A. Gephardt	St. Louis
4.	Ike Skelton	Lexington
5.	Richard Bolling	Kansas City
6.	E. Thomas Coleman	Kansas City
7.	*Gene Taylor*	Sarcoxie
8.	Wendell Bailey	Willow Springs
9.	Harold L. Volkmer	Hannibal
10.	*William Emerson*	De Soto
Montana		
1.	Pat Williams	Helena
2.	*Ronald C. Marlenee*	Scobey
Nebraska		
1.	*Douglas K. Bereuter*	Utica
2.	*Hal Daub*	Omaha
3.	*Virginia Smith*	Chappell
Nevada		
°James D. Santini		Las Vegas
New Hampshire		
1.	Norman E. D'Amours	Manchester
2.	*Judd Gregg*	Greenfield
New Jersey		
1.	James J. Florio	Camden
2.	William J. Hughes	Ocean City
3.	James J. Howard	Spring Lake Heights
4.	*Christopher H. Smith*	Old Bridge
5.	*Millicent H. Fenwick*	Bernardsville
6.	Edwin B. Forsythe	Moorestown
7.	*Margaret S. Roukema*	Ridgewood
8.	Robert A. Roe	Wayne
9.	Harold C. Hollenbeck	E. Rutherford
10.	Peter W. Rodino, Jr.	Newark
11.	Joseph G. Minish	West Orange
12.	*Matthew J. Rinaldo*	Union
13.	*James A. Courter*	Hackettstown
14.	Frank J. Guarini	Jersey City
15.	Bernard J. Dwyer	Edison
New Mexico		
1.	*Manuel Lujan, Jr.*	Albuquerque
2.	*Joseph R. Skeen*	Picacho
New York		
1.	*William Carney*	Hauppauge
2.	Thomas J. Downey	West Islip
3.	*Gregory W. Carman*	Farmingdale
4.	*Norman F. Lent*	East Rockaway
5.	Raymond J. McGrath	Valley Stream
6.	*John LeBoutillier*	Westbury
7.	Joseph P. Addabbo	Ozone Park
8.	Benjamin S. Rosenthal	Elmhurst
9.	Geraldine A. Ferraro	Forest Hills
10.	Mario Biaggi	Bronx
11.	James H. Scheuer	Neponsit
12.	Shirley A. Chisholm	Brooklyn
13.	Stephen J. Solarz	Brooklyn
14.	Frederick W. Richmond	Brooklyn
15.	Leo C. Zeferetti	Brooklyn
16.	Charles E. Schumer	Brooklyn
17.	*Guy V. Molinari*	Staten Island
18.	S. William Green	Manhattan
19.	Charles B. Rangel	New York
20.	Theodore S. Weiss	New York
21.	Robert Garcia	Bronx
22.	Jonathan B. Bingham	Bronx
23.	Peter A. Peyser	Irvington
24.	Richard L. Ottinger	Pleasantville
25.	Hamilton Fish, Jr.	Millbrook
26.	Benjamin A. Gilman	Middletown
27.	Matthew F. McHugh	Ithaca
28.	Samuel S. Stratton	Amsterdam
29.	Gerald B. Solomon	Glens Falls
30.	*David O'B. Martin*	Canton
31.	Donald J. Mitchell	Herkimer
32.	*George C. Wortley*	Fayetteville
33.	*Gary A. Lee*	Dryden
34.	*Frank J. Horton*	Rochester
35.	*Barber B. Conable, Jr.*	Alexander
36.	John J. LaFalce	Tonawanda
37.	Henry J. Nowak	Buffalo
38.	*Jack F. Kemp*	Hamburg
39.	Stanley N. Lundine	Jamestown

° Representative at large.

Dist.	Representative	Residence
	North Carolina	
1.	Walter B. Jones	Farmville
2.	L. H. Fountain	Tarboro
3.	Charles O. Whitley, Sr.	Mount Olive
4.	Ike F. Andrews	Siler City
5.	Stephen L. Neal	Winston-Salem
6.	Walter E. Johnston III	Greensboro
7.	Charles G. Rose	Fayetteville
8.	W. G. Hefner	Concord
9.	James G. Martin	Davidson
10.	James T. Broyhill	Lenoir
11.	Bill Hendon	Asheville

North Dakota
*Byron L. Dorgan .... Bismarck

Dist.	Representative	Residence
	Ohio	
1.	Willis D. Gradison, Jr.	Cincinnati
2.	Thomas A. Luken	Cincinnati
3.	Tony P. Hall	Dayton
4.	Michael G. Oxley	Findlay
5.	Delbert L. Latta	Bowling Green
6.	Bob McEwen	Hillsboro
7.	Clarence J. Brown	Urbana
8.	Thomas N. Kindness	Hamilton
9.	Edward F. Weber	Toledo
10.	Clarence E. Miller	Lancaster
11.	J. William Stanton	Painesville
12.	Robert N. Shamansky	Bexley
13.	Donald J. Pease	Oberlin
14.	John F. Seiberling	Akron
15.	Chalmers P. Wylie	Columbus
16.	Ralph S. Regula	Navarre
17.	John M. Ashbrook	Johnstown
18.	Douglas Applegate	Steubenville
19.	Lyle Williams	Lordstown
20.	Mary Rose Oakar	Cleveland
21.	Louis Stokes	Cleveland
22.	Dennis E. Eckart	Euclid
23.	Ronald M. Mottl	Parma

Dist.	Representative	Residence
	Oklahoma	
1.	James R. Jones	Tulsa
2.	Mike Synar	Muskogee
3.	Wesley W. Watkins	Ada
4.	Dave McCurdy	Norman
5.	Marvin H. Edwards	Oklahoma City
6.	Glenn English	Cordell

Dist.	Representative	Residence
	Oregon	
1.	Les AuCoin	Forest Grove
2.	Denny Smith	Salem
3.	Ronald L. Wyden	Portland
4.	James Weaver	Eugene

Dist.	Representative	Residence
	Pennsylvania	
1.	Thomas M. Foglietta	Philadelphia
2.	William H. Gray III	Philadelphia
3.	Joseph F. Smith	Philadelphia
4.	Charles F. Dougherty	Philadelphia
5.	Richard T. Schulze	Malvern
6.	Gus Yatron	Reading
7.	Robert W. Edgar	Broomall
8.	James K. Coyne	Wash. Crossing
9.	E. G. Shuster	Everett
10.	Joseph M. McDade	Scranton
11.	James L. Nelligan	Forty-Fort
12.	John P. Murtha	Johnstown
13.	Lawrence Coughlin	Villanova
14.	William J. Coyne	Pittsburgh
15.	Donald L. Ritter	Coopersburg
16.	Robert S. Walker	E. Petersburg
17.	Allen E. Ertel	Montoursville
18.	Douglas Walgren	Pittsburgh
19.	William F. Goodling	Jacobus
20.	Joseph M. Gaydos	McKeesport
21.	Don Bailey	Greensburg
22.	Austin J. Murphy	Charleroi
23.	William F. Clinger, Jr.	Warren
24.	Marc L. Marks	Sharon
25.	Eugene V. Atkinson	Aliquippa

Dist.	Representative	Residence
	Rhode Island	
1.	Fernand J. St Germain	Woonsocket
2.	Claudine Schneider	Narragansett

* Representative at large.

Dist.	Representative	Residence
	South Carolina	
1.	Thomas F. Hartnett	Mount Pleasant
2.	Floyd D. Spence	Lexington
3.	Butler C. Derrick, Jr.	Edgefield
4.	Carroll A. Campbell, Jr.	Greenville
5.	Kenneth L. Holland	Gaffney
6.	John L. Napier	Bennettsville

Dist.	Representative	Residence
	South Dakota	
1.	Thomas A. Daschle	Aberdeen
2.	Clint R. Roberts	Presho

Dist.	Representative	Residence
	Tennessee	
1.	James H. Quillen	Kingsport
2.	John J. Duncan	Knoxville
3.	Marilyn L. Bouquard	Chattanooga
4.	Albert Gore, Jr.	Carthage
5.	Bill Boner	Nashville
6.	Robin L. Beard, Jr.	Franklin
7.	Ed Jones	Yorkville
8.	Harold E. Ford	Memphis

Dist.	Representative	Residence
	Texas	
1.	Sam B. Hall, Jr.	Marshall
2.	Charles Wilson	Lufkin
3.	James M. Collins	Dallas
4.	Ralph M. Hall	Rockwall
5.	James A. Mattox	Dallas
6.	Phil Gramm	College Station
7.	Bill Archer	Houston
8.	Jack M. Fields	Humble
9.	Jack Brooks	Beaumont
10.	J. J. Pickle	Austin
11.	J. Marvin Leath	Marlin
12.	James C. Wright, Jr.	Fort Worth
13.	Jack E. Hightower	Vernon
14.	William N. Patman	Ganado
15.	Eligio de la Garza	Mission
16.	Richard C. White	El Paso
17.	Charles Stenholm	Stamford
18.	George T. Leland	Houston
19.	Kent Hance	Lubbock
20.	Henry B. Gonzalez	San Antonio
21.	Tom Loeffler	Hunt
22.	Ron Paul	Lake Jackson
23.	Abraham Kazen, Jr.	Laredo
24.	Martin Frost	Dallas

Dist.	Representative	Residence
	Utah	
1.	James V. Hansen	Farmington
2.	David D. Marriott	Salt Lake City

Vermont
*James M. Jeffords .... Rutland

Dist.	Representative	Residence
	Virginia	
1.	Paul S. Trible, Jr.	Newport News
2.	G. William Whitehurst	Virginia Beach
3.	Thomas J. Bliley, Jr.	Richmond
4.	Robert W. Daniel, Jr.	Spring Grove
5.	W.C. (Dan) Daniel	Danville
6.	M. Caldwell Butler	Roanoke
7.	J. Kenneth Robinson	Winchester
8.	Stan Parris	Woodbridge
9.	William C. Wampler	Bristol
10.	Frank R. Wolf	Vienna

Dist.	Representative	Residence
	Washington	
1.	Joel Pritchard	Seattle
2.	Al Swift	Bellingham
3.	Don L. Bonker	Olympia
4.	Sid W. Morrison	Zillah
5.	Thomas S. Foley	Spokane
6.	Norman D. Dicks	Port Orchard
7.	Mike Lowry	Mercer Island

Dist.	Representative	Residence
	West Virginia	
1.	Robert H. Mollohan	Fairmount
2.	Cleveland K. Benedict	Lewisburg
3.	David M. Staton	South Charleston
4.	Nick Joe Rahall II	Beckley

Dist.	Representative	Residence
	Wisconsin	
1.	Les Aspin	Racine
2.	Robert W. Kastenmeier	Sun Prairie
3.	Steven C. Gunderson	Osseo
4.	Clement J. Zablocki	Milwaukee
5.	Henry S. Reuss	Milwaukee
6.	Thomas E. Petri	Fond du Lac
7.	David R. Obey	Wausau
8.	Tobias Roth	Appleton
9.	F. James Sensenbrenner	Shorewood

Wyoming
*Richard Cheney .... Casper

THE SENATE
Democrats are in roman type, Republicans in *italics*

Ninety-Seventh Congress, First Session
Democrats 53; *Republicans 46;* Independents-Democrat 1
President: *George H. W. Bush*
President Pro Tempore: *Strom Thurmond,* S.C.
Majority Leader: *Howard H. Baker, Jr.,* Tenn.
Assistant Majority Leader: *Theodore F. Stevens,* Alaska

Minority Leader: Robert C. Byrd, W. Va.
Minority Whip: Alan Cranston, Calif.
Secretary: William F. Hildenbrand
Assistant Secretary: William A. Ridgely
Sergeant at Arms: Howard S. Liebengood
Secretary for the Majority: Howard O. Greene, Jr.
Secretary for the Minority: Terrence E. Sauvain
Chaplain: The Rev. Richard C. Halverson

State	Senator	Service From	Term Expires	State	Senator	Service From	Term Expires
Alabama	Howell T. Heflin	Jan. 3, 1979	Jan. 3, 1985	Kansas	*Robert J. Dole*	Jan. 3, 1969	Jan. 5, 1987
	Jeremiah A. Denton, Jr.	Jan. 3, 1981	Jan. 5, 1987		*Nancy Landon Kassebaum*	Dec. 23, 1978	Jan. 3, 1985
Alaska	*Theodore F. Stevens*	Dec. 24, 1968	Jan. 3, 1985	Kentucky	Walter D. Huddleston	Jan. 3, 1973	Jan. 3, 1985
	Frank H. Murkowski	Jan. 5, 1981	Jan. 5, 1987		Wendell H. Ford	Dec. 28, 1974	Jan. 5, 1987
Arizona	*Barry M. Goldwater*	Jan. 3, 1969	Jan. 5, 1987	Louisiana	Russell B. Long	Dec. 31, 1948	Jan. 5, 1987
	Dennis DeConcini	Jan. 3, 1977	Jan. 3, 1983		J. Bennett Johnston, Jr.	Nov. 14, 1972	Jan. 3, 1985
Arkansas	Dale Bumpers	Jan. 3, 1975	Jan. 5, 1987	Maine	*William S. Cohen*	Jan. 3, 1979	Jan. 3, 1985
	David H. Pryor	Jan. 3, 1979	Jan. 3, 1985		George J. Mitchell	May 17, 1980	Jan. 3, 1983
California	Alan Cranston	Jan. 3, 1969	Jan. 5, 1987	Maryland	*Charles McC. Mathias, Jr.*	Jan. 3, 1969	Jan. 5, 1987
	S. I. Hayakawa	Jan. 3, 1977	Jan. 3, 1983		Paul S. Sarbanes	Jan. 3, 1977	Jan. 3, 1983
Colorado	Gary W. Hart	Jan. 3, 1975	Jan. 5, 1987	Massachusetts	Edward M. Kennedy	Nov. 7, 1962	Jan. 3, 1983
	William L. Armstrong	Jan. 3, 1979	Jan. 3, 1985		Paul Tsongas	Jan. 3, 1979	Jan. 3, 1985
Connecticut	*Lowell P. Weicker, Jr.*	Jan. 3, 1971	Jan. 3, 1983	Michigan	Donald W. Riegle, Jr.	Dec. 30, 1976	Jan. 3, 1983
	Christopher J. Dodd	Jan. 3, 1981	Jan. 5, 1987		Carl Levin	Jan. 3, 1979	Jan. 3, 1985
Delaware	*William V. Roth, Jr.*	Jan. 1, 1971	Jan. 3, 1983	Minnesota	*David F. Durenberger*	Nov. 8, 1978	Jan. 3, 1983
	Joseph R. Biden, Jr.	Jan. 3, 1973	Jan. 3, 1985		*Rudy Boschwitz*	Dec. 30, 1978	Jan. 3, 1985
Florida	Lawton M. Chiles, Jr.	Jan. 3, 1971	Jan. 3, 1983	Mississippi	John C. Stennis	Nov. 5, 1947	Jan. 3, 1983
	Paula Hawkins	Jan. 3, 1981	Jan. 5, 1987		*Thad Cochran*	Dec. 27, 1978	Jan. 3, 1985
Georgia	Sam Nunn	Nov. 8, 1972	Jan. 3, 1985	Missouri	Thomas F. Eagleton	Dec. 28, 1968	Jan. 5, 1987
	Mack Mattingly	Jan. 3, 1981	Jan. 5, 1987		*John C. Danforth*	Dec. 27, 1976	Jan. 3, 1983
Hawaii	Daniel K. Inouye	Jan. 3, 1963	Jan. 5, 1987	Montana	John Melcher	Jan. 3, 1977	Jan. 3, 1983
	Spark M. Matsunaga	Jan. 3, 1977	Jan. 3, 1983		Max Baucus	Dec. 15, 1978	Jan. 3, 1985
Idaho	*James A. McClure*	Jan. 3, 1973	Jan. 3, 1985	Nebraska	Edward Zorinsky	Dec. 28, 1976	Jan. 3, 1983
	Steve Symms	Jan. 3, 1981	Jan. 5, 1987		John J. Exon, Jr.	Jan. 3, 1979	Jan. 3, 1985
Illinois	*Charles H. Percy*	Jan. 3, 1967	Jan. 3, 1985	Nevada	Howard W. Cannon	Jan. 3, 1959	Jan. 3, 1983
	Alan J. Dixon	Jan. 3, 1981	Jan. 5, 1987		*Paul Laxalt*	Dec. 18, 1974	Jan. 5, 1987
Indiana	*Richard G. Lugar*	Jan. 3, 1977	Jan. 3, 1983	New Hampshire	*Gordon J. Humphrey*	Jan. 3, 1979	Jan. 3, 1985
	Dan Quayle	Jan. 3, 1981	Jan. 5, 1987		*Warren B. Rudman*	Jan. 3, 1981	Jan. 5, 1987
Iowa	*Roger W. Jepsen*	Jan. 3, 1979	Jan. 3, 1985	New Jersey	Harrison A. Williams	Jan. 3, 1959	Jan. 3, 1983
	Charles E. Grassley	Jan. 3, 1981	Jan. 5, 1987		Bill Bradley	Jan. 3, 1979	Jan. 3, 1985

State	Senator	Service From	Term Expires	State	Senator	Service From	Term Expires
New Mexico	Pete V. Domenici	Jan. 3, 1973	Jan. 3, 1985	South Dakota	Larry Pressler	Jan. 3, 1979	Jan. 3, 1985
	Harrison Schmitt	Jan. 3, 1977	Jan. 3, 1983		James Abdnor	Jan. 3, 1981	Jan. 5, 1987
New York	Daniel P. Moynihan	Jan. 3, 1977	Jan. 3, 1983	Tennessee	Howard H. Baker, Jr.	Jan. 3, 1967	Jan. 3, 1985
	Alfonse M. D'Amato	Jan. 3, 1981	Jan. 5, 1987		James R. Sasser	Jan. 3, 1977	Jan. 3, 1983
North Carolina	Jesse A. Helms	Jan. 3, 1973	Jan. 3, 1985	Texas	John G. Tower	June 15, 1961	Jan. 3, 1985
	John P. East	Jan. 3, 1981	Jan. 5, 1987		Lloyd M. Bentsen	Jan. 3, 1971	Jan. 3, 1983
North Dakota	Quentin N. Burdick	Aug. 8, 1960	Jan. 3, 1983	Utah	Edwin J. Garn	Dec. 21, 1974	Jan. 5, 1987
	Mark Andrews	Jan. 3, 1981	Jan. 5, 1987		Orrin G. Hatch	Jan. 3, 1977	Jan. 3, 1983
Ohio	John H. Glenn, Jr.	Dec. 24, 1974	Jan. 5, 1987	Vermont	Robert T. Stafford	Sept. 16, 1971	Jan. 4, 1983
	Howard M. Metzenbaum	Jan. 3, 1977	Jan. 3, 1983		Patrick J. Leahy	Jan. 3 1975	Jan. 5, 1987
Oklahoma	David L. Boren	Jan. 3, 1979	Jan. 3, 1985	Virginia	Harry F. Byrd, Jr.†	Nov. 12, 1965	Jan. 3, 1983
	Donald L. Nickles	Jan. 3, 1981	Jan. 5, 1987		John W. Warner	Jan. 2, 1979	Jan. 3, 1985
Oregon	Mark O. Hatfield	Jan. 10, 1967	Jan. 3, 1985	Washington	Henry M. Jackson	Jan. 3, 1953	Jan. 3, 1983
	Robert W. Packwood	Jan. 3, 1969	Jan. 5, 1987		Slade Gorton	Jan. 3, 1981	Jan. 5, 1987
Pennsylvania	H. John Heinz III	Jan. 3, 1977	Jan. 3, 1983	West Virginia	Jennings Randolph	Nov. 5, 1958	Jan. 3, 1985
	Arlen Specter	Jan. 5, 1981	Jan. 5, 1987		Robert C. Byrd	Jan. 3 1959	Jan. 3 1983
Rhode Island	Claiborne Pell	Jan. 3, 1961	Jan. 3, 1985	Wisconsin	William Proxmire	Aug. 28, 1957	Jan. 3, 1983
	John H. Chafee	Dec. 29, 1976	Jan. 3, 1983		Robert W. Kasten, Jr.	Jan. 3, 1981	Jan. 5, 1987
South Carolina	Strom Thurmond	Nov. 7, 1956	Jan. 3, 1985	Wyoming	Malcolm Wallop	Jan. 3, 1977	Jan. 3, 1983
	Ernest F. Hollings	Nov. 9, 1966	Jan. 5, 1987		Alan K. Simpson	Jan. 1, 1979	Jan. 3, 1985

†Independent-Democrat

STANDING CONGRESSIONAL COMMITTEES

HOUSE OF REPRESENTATIVES

Agriculture: Agriculture and forestry in general, including price stabilization, farm credit and security, crop insurance, meat and livestock inspections, soil conservation, and rural electrification.

Appropriations: Appropriation of money for the support of the government, examination of operations of any executive department or agency (including agencies of which the majority stock is government owned).

Armed Services: Matters relating to the national military establishment, including military space activities; conservation of naval petroleum resources; strategic materials; scientific research and development for military purposes; Selective Service.

Banking, Finance and Urban Affairs: Financial matters other than taxes and appropriations, including price, commodity, rent, or services controls; deposit insurance, the Federal Reserve System; the valuation of the dollar; public and private housing.

Budget: To set ceilings for overall government spending, giving Congress a coordinated approach to the federal budget for the first time; to study effects of legislation on budget outlays and tax expenditures.

District of Columbia: Municipal affairs (except appropriations) of the District.

Education and Labor: Measures relating to education and labor, including child labor and convict labor; wages and hours; arbitration of labor disputes; the school-lunch program.

Foreign Affaris: U.S. relations with other governments; the UN and international monetary organizations; the diplomatic service, foreign loans, protection of American citizens abroad; interventions and declarations of war.

Government Operations: Budget and accounting measures other than appropriations; relationships of federal government with states and municipalities; reorganizations of executive branch; studies of all levels of government operations; reports of Comptroller General.

House Administration: General administration of the House, including employment of clerks and reporters; federal elections; corrupt practices; contested elections; and the Library of Congress.

Interior and Insular Affairs: Public lands in general; forest reserves and national parks created from the public domain; the Geological Survey; public mineral resources; irrigation; insular possessions; and American Indian affairs.

Interstate and Foreign Commerce: Commerce, communications, and transportation (except water transportation that is not subject to the Interstate Commerce Commission); interstate power transmission (except installation of connections between government waterpower projects); railroad commerce and labor; civil aeronautics; inland waterways; interstate oil compacts; petroleum and natural gas (except on public lands); securities and exchanges; public health; and the Weather Bureau.

Judiciary: Judicial proceedings in general; federal courts and judges; Constituitional amendments; civil rights; interstate compacts; immigration and naturalization; apportionment of representatives; meetings of Congress and attendance of members; Presidential succession; the Patent Office; claims against the United States; bankruptcy, mutiny, espionage, and counterfeiting; protection of trade and commerce.

Merchant Marine and Fisheries: The merchant marine in general; navigation and pilotage laws; regulation of common carriers by water (except matters falling under the jurisdiction of the Interstate Commerce Commission); the Coast Guard; the National Ocean Survey; oversees the activities of the Panama Canal Commission; and fisheries and wildlife, including research and conservation.

Post Office and Civil Service: Postal service and federal civil service; the census and collection of statistics; and the National Archives.

Public Works and Transportation: Public buildings and roads; flood control; improvement of rivers and harbors; public works for navigation, including bridges and dams (other than international); water power; and pollution of navigable waters.

Rules: Rules and order of business of the House; recesses and final adjournments of Congress; creation of committees.

Science and Technology: Scientific and astronautical research and development in general; the National Aeronautics and Space Administration; the National Aeronautics and Space Council; the National Science Foundation; the Bureau of Standards; science scholarships.

Small Business: Assistance to and protection of small businesses; participation of small business enterprises in federal procurement and government contracts.

Standards of Official Conduct: Regulations and standards for members, officers, and employees of the House.

Veterans' Affairs: Veterans' measures in general; pensions, armed forces life insurance, rehabilitation and education; and veterans' hospitals.

Ways and Means: Revenue and tax measures in general; customs; transportation of dutiable goods; federal Social Security; reciprocal trade agreements; U.S. bonded debt; and deposit of public moneys.

SENATE

Agriculture, Nutrition, and Forestry: Agriculture in general, including meat and livestock inspection, farm credit and security, soil conservation, crop insurances, and rural electrification; domestic and foreign matters relating to food, nutrition and hunger; forestry and forest reserves (excluding those created from the public domain) in general.

Appropriations: Appropriation of money for the support of the government.

Armed Services: Matters relating to the national military establishment, including military space activities; oversees activities of the Panama Canal Commission; conservation of naval petroleum resources; and strategic materials.

Banking, Housing, and Urban Affairs: Financial matters other than appropriations and taxes; deposit insurance; Federal Reserve System; valuation of the dollar; price control; public and private housing; and financial aid to industry on matters assigned to other committees.

Budget: To set ceilings for overall government spending, giving Congress a coordinated approach to the federal budget for the first time; to study effects of legislation on budget outlays and tax expenditures.

Commerce, Science, and Transportation: Interstate and foreign commerce; interstate railroads, buses, trucks, and pipelines; communications; civil aeronautics; non-military aeronautical and space sciences; merchant marine and navigation, both inland and oceanic; Coast Guard; oceans, weather, and atmospheric activities; fish and wildlife conservation; consumer product regulation; Bureau of Standards; science, engineering, and technology research and development.

Energy and Natural Resources: Energy policy, regulation, conservation, research and development; nuclear and solar energy; production, distribution and utilization of energy sources; public lands and forests; national parks; territorial possessions.

Environment and Public Works: Environmental policy, research and development; water resources; flood control; public works; pollution control; regional economic development; highway construction and maintenance; public buildings and their grounds.

Finance: Revenue and tax matters in general; deposit of public moneys; U.S. bonded debt; customs; transportaion of dutiable goods; reciprocal trade agreements; tariffs; import quotas; Social Security.

Foreign Relations: Relations with foreign nations, as well as treaties; protection of American citizens abroad; interventions and declarations of war; diplomatic service; American business interests abroad; the U.N. and international monetary organizations; foreign loans.

Governmental Affairs: Budget and accounting measures other than appropriations; executive branch reorganizations; Comptroller General reports; studies of all levels of government operations; study of relations between the U.S. and states, municipalities, and international organizations of which the U.S. is a member; postal service; census. Judiciary: Judicial proceedings; federal courts and judges; Constitutional amendments; the Patent Office; claims against the U.S.; civil liberties; protection of trade and commerce; meetings of Congress and attendance of members; immigration and naturalization; bankruptcy, mutiny, espionage, counterfeiting; apportionment of representatives; interstate compacts.

Labor and Human Resources: Education, health, and public welfare; labor, including foreign laborers; private pension plans; aging; arts and humanities.

Rules and Administration: General administration of the Senate; federal elections; corrupt practices; contested elections; management of Library of Congress; reorganization acts; creation of new standing committees.

Veterans' Affairs: Veterans' hospitals, education, compensation, and welfare.

CONGRESSIONAL JOINT COMMITTEES, COMMISSIONS AND BOARDS

Joint Committees on:
  Library, Printing, Taxation
Joint Economic Committee
Commission on Art and Antiquities of U.S. Senate
Commission on Security and Cooperation in Europe
Commission on Wartime Relocation and Internment of Civilians
Commission on the West Central Front of the U.S. Capital
Consumer Product Safety Commission
Distric of Columbia Law Revision Commission
Franklin Delano Roosevelt Memorial Commmission
House Commission on Congressional Mailing Standards
House Office Building Commission
Japan United States Friendship Commission
Migratory Bird Conservation Commission
National Commission on Alcoholism and Other Alcohol-Related Problems

National Commission for Employment Policy
Permanent Committee for the Oliver Wendell Holmes Devise Fund
President's Commission on Mental Retardation
Senate Office Building Commission
Temporary Commission on Financial Oversight of the District of Columbia
Environmental Study Conference
Members of Congress for Peace Through Law
North Atlantic Assembly
The Interparliamentary Union
Board for International Broadcasting
Board of Visitors to the Air Force Academy
Board of Visitors to the Coast Guard Academy
Board of Visitors to the Merchant Marine Academy
Board of Visitors to the Military Academy
Board of Visitors to the Naval Academy

MEMBERS OF THE U.S. SUPREME COURT

Source: Supreme Court of the United States and other sources

CHIEF JUSTICES	Place of Birth	Year of Birth	Education	Appointed by President	Date Oath Taken	Age at Oath	Date Service Ended	Service Ended By	Years of Service Term	Age at End of Service Term	Date of Death
Jay, John	New York	1745	King's College (now Columbia University), grad. 1764	Washington	Oct. 1789	44	June 1795	resigned	5	49	May 1829
Rutledge, John†	South Carolina	1739	Studied law at Middle Temple, London	Washington				rejected	0	56	June 1800
Ellsworth, Oliver	Connecticut	1745	Attended Yale College; College of New Jersey (now Princeton University), grad. 1766	Washington	Mar. 1796	50	Dec. 1800	resigned	4	55	Nov. 1807
Marshall, John	Virginia	1755	Attended College of William and Mary	Adams	Feb. 1801	45	July 1835	death	34	79	July 1835
Taney, Roger Brooke	Maryland	1777	Dickinson College, Penn., grad. 1795	Jackson	Mar. 1836	59	Oct. 1864	death	28	87	Oct. 1864
Chase, Salmon Portland	New Hampshire	1808	Attended Cincinnati College; Dartmouth College, grad. 1826	Lincoln	Dec. 1864	56	May 1873	death	8	65	May 1873
Waite, Morrison Remick	Connecticut	1816	Yale College, grad. 1837	Grant	Mar. 1874	57	Mar. 1888	death	14	71	Mar. 1888
Fuller, Melville Weston	Maine	1833	Bowdoin College, grad. 1853; attended Harvard Law School	Cleveland	Oct. 1888	55	July 1910	death	21	77	July 1910
White, Edward Douglass*	Louisiana	1845	Attended Mount St. Mary's College, Md.; Jesuit College in New Orleans, La.; and Georgetown College, Washington, D.C.	Taft	Dec. 1910	65	May 1921	death	10	75	May 1921
Taft, William Howard	Ohio	1857	Yale College, grad. 1878; Cincinnati Law School, LL.B. 1880	Harding	July 1921	63	Feb. 1930	retired	8	72	Mar. 1930
Hughes, Charles Evans*	New York	1862	Attended Colgate University; Brown University, Rhode Island, grad. 1881; M.A. 1884; Columbia Law School, LL.B. 1884	Hoover	Feb. 1930	67	June 1941	retired	11	79	Aug. 1948
Stone, Harlan Fiske*	New Hampshire	1872	Amherst College, Mass., grad. 1894; M.A. 1897; Columbia Law School, LL.B. 1898	Roosevelt, F.	July 1941	68	Apr. 1946	death	4	73	Apr. 1946
Vinson, Frederick Moore	Kentucky	1890	Kentucky Normal College, grad.; Centre College, Ky., grad. 1909; LL.B. 1911	Truman	June 1946	56	Sept. 1953	death	7	63	Sept. 1953
Warren, Earl	California	1891	University of California, LL.B. 1912; J.D. 1914	Eisenhower	Oct. 1953	62	June 1969	retired	16	78	July 1974
Burger, Warren Earl	Minnesota	1907	Attended University of Minnesota; St. Paul College of Law, LL.B. 1931	Nixon	June 1969	61	—	—	—	—	—
ASSOCIATE JUSTICES											
Cushing, William	Massachusetts	1732	Harvard College, grad. 1751	Washington	Sept. 1789	57	Sept. 1810	death	20	77	Sept. 1810
Wilson, James	Scotland	1742	Attended University of St. Andrews (Scotland)	Washington	Sept. 1789	47	Aug. 1798	death	8	56	Aug. 1798
Blair, John Jr.	Virginia	1732	College of William and Mary, grad. 1754; studied law at Middle Temple, London	Washington	Sept. 1789	57	Jan. 1796	resigned	6	63	Aug. 1800
Iredell, James	England	1751	Private tutoring	Washington	Feb. 1790	39	Oct. 1799	death	8	48	Oct. 1799
Johnson, Thomas	Maryland	1732	No formal education	Washington	Nov. 1791	59	Sept. 1793	resigned	1	61	Oct. 1819
Paterson, William	Ireland	1745	College of New Jersey (now Princeton University), grad. 1763; M.A. 1766	Washington	Mar. 1793	47	Sept. 1806	death	13	61	Sept. 1806
Chase, Samuel	Maryland	1741	Private tutoring	Washington	Jan. 1796	55	June 1811	death	15	70	June 1811
Washington, Bushrod	Virginia	1762	College of William and Mary, grad. 1778	Adams, J.	Dec. 1798	36	Nov. 1829	death	31	67	Nov. 1829
Moore, Alfred	North Carolina	1755	Attended private schools	Adams, J.	Apr. 1800	44	Feb. 1804	resigned	4	48	Oct. 1810
Johnson, William	South Carolina	1771	College of New Jersey (now Princeton University), grad. 1778	Jefferson	Apr. 1804	32	Aug. 1834	death	30	63	Aug. 1834
Livingston, Brockholst	New York	1757	College of New Jersey (now Princeton University), grad. 1774	Jefferson	Sept. 1806	49	Mar. 1823	death	16	65	Mar. 1823
Todd, Thomas	Virginia	1765	Private tutoring	Jefferson	Mar. 1807	42	Feb. 1826	death	18	60	Feb. 1826
Duvall, Gabriel	Maryland	1752	Dartmouth College, graduation date unknown	Madison	Nov. 1811	59	? 1835	resigned	23	81	Mar. 1844
Story, Joseph	Massachusetts	1779	Harvard College, grad. 1798	Madison	Feb. 1812	32	Sept. 1845	death	33	65	Sept. 1845
Thompson, Smith	New York	1768	College of New Jersey (now Princeton University), grad. 1798	Monroe	Dec. 1823	55	Dec. 1843	death	20	75	Dec. 1843
Trimble, Robert	Virginia	1776	Attended Kentucky Academy (now Transylvania College)	Adams, J. Q.	Apr. 1826	49	Aug. 1828	death	2	51	Aug. 1828
McLean, John	New Jersey	1784	Private tutoring	Jackson	? 1829	44	Apr. 1861	death	32	76	Apr. 1861

* Also served as associate justice: Rutledge (1789—91); White (1894—1910); Hughes (1910—16); Stone (1925—41).

† Presided at Aug. 1795 term, but Senate refused to confirm him in December.

Associate Justices	Place of Birth	Year of Birth	Education	Appointed by President	Date Oath Taken	Age at Oath	Date Service Ended	Service Ended By	Years of Service	Age at End of Term	Date of Death
Baldwin, Henry	Connecticut	1780	Yale College, grad. 1797	Jackson	? 1830	50	Apr. 1844	death	14	64	Apr. 1844
Wayne, James M.	Georgia	1790	College of New Jersey (now Princeton University), grad. 1808	Jackson	Jan. 1835	45	July 1867	death	32	77	July 1867
Barbour, Philip P.	Virginia	1783	No record of formal education	Jackson	Mar. 1836	53	Feb. 1841	death	5	58	Feb. 1841
Catron, John	Pennsylvania	1786	No record of formal education	Jackson	Mar. 1837	51	May 1865	death	28	79	May 1865
McKinley, John	Virginia	1780	No record of formal education	Van Buren	? 1837	57	July 1852	death	15	72	July 1852
Daniel, Peter V.	Virginia	1784	Attended College of New Jersey (now Princeton Univ.)	Van Buren	Feb. 1841	57	May 1860	death	19	76	May 1860
Nelson, Samuel	New York	1792	Middlebury College, grad. 1813	Tyler	Mar. 1845	53	Nov. 1872	resigned	27	80	Dec. 1873
Woodbury, Levi	New Hampshire	1789	Dartmouth College, grad. 1809	Polk	May 1845	56	Sept. 1851	death	5	61	Sept. 1851
Grier, Robert C.	Pennsylvania	1794	Dickinson College, grad. 1812	Polk	Aug. 1846	52	Feb. 1870	resigned	23	75	Aug. 1870
Curtis, Benjamin	Massachusetts	1809	Harvard College, grad. 1829	Fillmore	Dec. 1851	42	Sept. 1857	resigned	6	48	Sept. 1874
Campbell, John A.	Georgia	1811	University of Georgia, grad. 1826; Attended West Point, 1826-28	Pierce	Mar. 1853	42	Apr. 1861	resigned	8	50	Mar. 1889
Clifford, Nathan	New Hampshire	1803	Attended private schools	Buchanan	Jan. 1858	55	July 1881	death	23	78	July 1881
Swayne, Noah Haynes	Virginia	1804	No record of formal education	Lincoln	Jan. 1862	57	Jan. 1881	retired	18	76	June 1884
Miller, Samuel Freeman	Kentucky	1816	Transylvania University, Ky., grad. 1838	Lincoln	July 1862	46	Oct. 1890	death	28	74	Oct. 1890
Davis, David	Maryland	1815	Kenyon College, Ohio, grad. 1832; Yale Law School, LL.B. 1835	Lincoln	Dec. 1862	47	Mar. 1877	resigned	14	61	June 1886
Field, Stephen Johnson	Connecticut	1816	Williams College, Mass., grad. 1837	Lincoln	May 1863	46	Dec. 1897	retired	34	81	Apr. 1899
Strong, William	Connecticut	1808	Yale College, grad. 1828; M.A. 1831; attended Yale Law School	Grant	Mar. 1870	61	Dec. 1880	retired	10	72	Aug. 1895
Bradley, Joseph P.	New York	1813	Rutgers College, grad. 1836	Grant	Mar. 1870	57	Jan. 1892	death	21	78	Jan. 1892
Hunt, Ward	New York	1810	Union College, N.Y., grad. 1828	Grant	Jan. 1873	62	Jan. 1882	disabled	9	71	Mar. 1886
Harlan, John Marshall	Kentucky	1833	Centre College, Ky., grad. 1850; studied law at Transylvania College, Ky.	Hayes	Dec. 1877	44	Oct. 1911	death	33	78	Oct. 1911
Woods, William Burnham	Ohio	1824	Yale College, grad. 1845	Hayes	Jan. 1881	56	May 1887	death	6	62	May 1887
Matthews, Stanley	Ohio	1824	Kenyon College, Ohio, grad. 1840	Garfield	May 1881	56	Mar. 1889	death	7	64	Mar. 1889
Gray, Horace	Massachusetts	1828	Harvard College, grad. 1845; Harvard Law School, LL.B. 1849	Arthur	Jan. 1882	53	Sept. 1902	death	20	74	Sept. 1902
Blatchford, Samuel	New York	1820	Columbia College, grad. 1837	Arthur	Apr. 1882	62	July 1893	death	11	73	July 1893
Lamar, Lucius Quintus C.	Georgia	1825	Emory College, Ga., grad. 1845	Cleveland	Jan. 1888	62	Jan. 1893	death	5	67	Jan. 1893
Brewer, David Josiah	Asia Minor	1837	Yale College, grad. 1856; M.A. 1859; Albany (N.Y.) Law School, LL.B. 1858	Harrison	Jan. 1890	52	Mar. 1910	death	20	72	Mar. 1910
Brown, Henry Billings	Massachusetts	1836	Yale College, grad. 1856	Harrison	Jan. 1891	54	May 1906	retired	15	70	Sept. 1913
Shiras, George, Jr.	Pennsylvania	1832	Yale College, grad. 1853; Yale Law School, LL.B. 1854	Harrison	Oct. 1892	60	Feb. 1903	retired	10	71	Aug. 1924
Jackson, Howell Edmunds	Tennessee	1832	West Tennessee College, grad. 1849; attended University of Virginia; Cumberland University, Tenn., LL.B. 1856	Harrison	Dec. 1893	61	Aug. 1895	death	2	63	Aug. 1895
Peckham, Rufus Wheeler	New York	1838	Attended Albany (N.Y.) Academy	Cleveland	Jan. 1896	57	Oct. 1909	death	13	70	Oct. 1909
McKenna, Joseph	Pennsylvania	1843	Benicia Collegiate Institute, Calif., grad. 1865	McKinley	Jan. 1898	54	Jan. 1925	retired	26	81	Nov. 1926
Holmes, Oliver Wendell	Massachusetts	1841	Harvard College, grad. 1861; LL.B. 1866	Roosevelt, T.	Dec. 1902	61	Jan. 1932	retired	29	90	Mar. 1935
Day, William Rufus	Ohio	1849	University of Michigan, grad. 1870	Roosevelt, T.	Mar. 1903	53	Nov. 1922	retired	19	73	July 1923
Moody, William Henry	Massachusetts	1853	Harvard College, grad. 1876; att. Harvard Law School	Roosevelt, T.	Dec. 1906	52	Nov. 1910	disabled	3	56	July 1917
Lurton, Horace Harmon	Kentucky	1844	Attended Douglas University, Chicago (now University of Chicago); Cumberland University, Tenn., LL.B. 1867	Taft	Jan. 1910	65	July 1914	death	4	70	July 1914
Van Devanter, Willis	Indiana	1859	Attended Indiana Asbury (now De Pauw) University; Cincinnati Law School, LL.B. 1881	Taft	Jan. 1911	51	June 1937	retired	26	78	Feb. 1941
Lamar, Joseph Rucker	Georgia	1857	Bethany College, W. Va., grad. 1877; studied law, Washington and Lee University, Va.	Taft	Jan. 1911	53	Jan. 1916	death	5	58	Jan. 1916
Pitney, Mahlon	New Jersey	1858	College of New Jersey (now Princeton University), grad. 1879	Taft	Mar. 1912	54	Dec. 1922	resigned	10	64	Dec. 1924

Associate Justices (cont.)	Place of Birth	Year of Birth	Education	Appointed by President	Date Oath Taken	Age at Oath	Date Service Ended	Service Ended By	Years of Service Term	Age at End of Service Term	Date of Death
McReynolds, James Clark	Kentucky	1862	Vanderbilt University, Tenn., grad. 1882; University of Virginia Law School, LL.B. 1884	Wilson	Oct. 1914	52	Jan. 1941	retired	26	78	Aug. 1946
Brandeis, Louis Dembitz	Kentucky	1856	Harvard Law School, LL.B. 1877	Wilson	June 1916	59	Feb. 1939	retired	22	82	Oct. 1941
Clarke, John Hessin	Ohio	1857	Western Reserve University, Ohio, grad. 1877	Wilson	Oct. 1916	59	Sept. 1922	resigned	5	65	Mar. 1945
Sutherland, George	England	1862	Studied law at the University of Michigan	Harding	Oct. 1922	60	Jan. 1938	retired	15	75	July 1942
Butler, Pierce	Minnesota	1866	Carleton College, Minn., grad. 1887	Harding	Jan. 1923	56	Nov. 1939	death	16	73	Nov. 1939
Sanford, Edward Terry	Tennessee	1865	University of Tennessee, grad. 1883; Harvard University, M.A. 1889; Harvard Law School, LL.B. 1889	Harding	Feb. 1923	57	Mar. 1930	death	7	64	Mar. 1930
Roberts, Owen Josephus	Pennsylvania	1875	University of Pennsylvania, grad. 1895; LL.B. 1898	Hoover	June 1930	55	July 1945	resigned	15	70	May 1955
Cardozo, Benjamin Nathan	New York	1870	Columbia University, grad. 1889; M.A. 1890; attended Columbia Law School	Hoover	Mar. 1932	61	July 1938	death	6	68	July 1938
Black, Hugo Lafayette	Alabama	1886	University of Alabama, Law School, LL.B. 1906	Roosevelt, F.	Aug. 1937	51	Sept. 1971	retired	34	85	Sept. 1971
Reed, Stanley Forman	Kentucky	1884	Kentucky Wesleyan College, grad. 1902; also Yale University, grad. 1906; studied law at Columbia University	Roosevelt, F.	Jan. 1938	53	Feb. 1957	retired	19	72	Apr. 1980
Frankfurter, Felix	Austria	1882	City College of New York, grad. 1902; Harvard Law School, LL.B. 1906	Roosevelt, F.	Jan. 1939	56	Aug. 1962	retired	23	79	Feb. 1965
Douglas, William Orville	Minnesota	1898	Whitman College, Wash., grad. 1920; Columbia Law School, LL.B. 1925	Roosevelt, F.	Apr. 1939	40	Nov. 1975	retired	36	77	Jan. 1980
Murphy, Frank	Michigan	1890	University of Michigan, LL.B. 1914; studied law at Lincoln's Inn, London, and Trinity College, Dublin	Roosevelt, F.	Feb. 1940	49	July 1949	death	9	59	July 1949
Byrnes, James Francis	South Carolina	1879	No record of formal education	Roosevelt, F.	July 1941	62	Oct. 1942	resigned	1	63	Apr. 1972
Jackson, Robert Houghwout	New York	1892	Attended Albany (N.Y.) Law School	Roosevelt, F.	July 1941	49	Oct. 1954	death	13	62	Oct. 1954
Rutledge, Wiley Blount	Kentucky	1894	University of Wisconsin, grad. 1914; University of Colorado, LL.B. 1922	Roosevelt, F.	Feb. 1943	48	Sept. 1949	death	6	55	Sept. 1949
Burton, Harold Hitz	Massachusetts	1888	Bowdoin College, Me., grad. 1909; Harvard Law School, LL.B. 1912	Truman	Oct. 1945	57	Oct. 1958	retired	13	70	Oct. 1964
Clark, Thomas Campbell	Texas	1899	University of Texas, grad. 1921; LL.B. 1922	Truman	Aug. 1949	49	June 1967	retired	18	67	June 1977
Minton, Sherman	Indiana	1890	Indiana University, LL.B. 1915	Truman	Oct. 1949	58	Oct. 1956	retired	7	65	Apr. 1965
Harlan, John Marshall	Illinois	1899	Princeton University, grad. 1920; Rhodes Scholar to Oxford University, 1921–23; New York Law School, LL.B. 1924	Eisenhower	Mar. 1955	55	Sept. 1971	retired	16	72	Dec. 1971
Brennan, William Joseph, Jr.	New Jersey	1906	University of Pennsylvania, grad. 1928; Harvard Law School, LL.B. 1931	Eisenhower	Oct. 1956	50					—
Whittaker, Charles Evans	Kansas	1901	University of Kansas City, LL.B. 1924	Eisenhower	Mar. 1957	56	Apr. 1962	retired	5	61	Nov. 1973
Stewart, Potter	Michigan	1915	Yale University, grad. 1937; attended Cambridge University, England; Yale Law School, LL.B. 1941	Eisenhower	Oct. 1958	43	July 1981	retired	23	66	—
White, Byron Raymond	Colorado	1917	University of Colorado, grad. 1938; Rhodes Scholar, Oxford, England, 1939; Yale Law School, LL.B. 1946	Kennedy	Apr. 1962	44					—
Goldberg, Arthur Joseph	Illinois	1908	Northwestern University, grad. 1929; J.D. 1930	Kennedy	Oct. 1962	54	July 1965	resigned	3	56	—
Fortas, Abe	Tennessee	1910	Southwestern College, grad. 1930; Yale Law School, LL.B. 1933	Johnson	Oct. 1965	55	May 1969	resigned	4	58	—
Marshall, Thurgood	Maryland	1908	Lincoln University, grad. 1929; Howard University, LL.B. 1933	Johnson	Oct. 1967	59					—
Blackmun, Harry Andrew	Minnesota	1908	Harvard College, grad. 1929; Harvard Law School, LL.B. 1932	Nixon	June 1970	61					—
Powell, Lewis Franklin, Jr.	Virginia	1907	Washington and Lee University, grad. 1929, LL.B. 1931; Harvard University, LL.M. 1932	Nixon	Jan. 1972	64					—
Rehnquist, William Hubbs	Wisconsin	1924	Stanford University, grad. 1948; M.A. Harvard University 1950; LL.B. Stanford 1952	Nixon	Jan. 1972	47					—
Stevens, John Paul	Illinois	1920	Univ. of Chicago, grad. 1941; Northwestern Univ. School of Law, J.D. 1947	Ford	Dec. 1975	55					—
O'Connor, Sandra Day	Texas	1930	Stanford University, grad. 1950; Stanford Univ. Law School, LL.B. 1952	Reagan	Sept. 1981	51					—

THE U.S. COURTS SOURCE: Administrative Office of the U.S. Courts

SUPREME COURT OF THE UNITED STATES
Washington, D.C.

Chief Justice (Salary: $92,400): Warren E. Burger of Virginia.

Associate Justices (Salaries: $88,700): William J. Brennan, Jr., of New Jersey; Byron R. White of Colorado; Thurgood Marshall of New York; Harry A. Blackmun of Minnesota; Lewis F. Powell, Jr., of Virginia; William H. Rehnquist of Arizona; John P. Stevens of Illinois; Sandra Day O'Connor of Arizona.

U.S. COURT OF APPEALS
(Salaries: $70,900)

District of Columbia Circuit: Carl McGowan, Chief Judge; J. Skelly Wright, Edward Allen Tamm, Spottswood W. Robinson III, Roger Robb, George E. MacKinnon, Malcolm Richard Wilkey, Patricia M. Wald, Abner J. Mikva, Harry T. Edwards, Ruth B. Ginsburg, James A. Belson.

First Circuit (Maine, Massachusetts, New Hampshire, Rhode Island, Puerto Rico): Frank M. Coffin, Chief Judge, Portland, Maine; Levin H. Campbell, Boston, Mass.; Hugh H. Bownes, Concord, N.H.; Stephen G. Breyer, Boston, Mass.

Second Circuit (Connecticut, New York, Vermont): Wilfred Feinberg, Chief Judge, New York, N.Y.; Irving R. Kaufman, New York, N.Y.; James L. Oakes, Brattleboro, Vt.; William H. Timbers, Bridgeport, Ct.; Thomas J. Meskill, New Britain, Ct.; Walter R. Mansfield, Amalya L. Kearse, both of New York, N.Y.; Ellsworth Van Graafeiland, Rochester, N.Y.; Jon O. Newman, Hartford, Ct.

Third Circuit (Delaware, New Jersey, Pennsylvania, Virgin Islands): Collins J. Seitz, Chief Judge, Wilmington, Del.; James Hunter III, Camden, N.J.; A. Leon Higginbotham, Arlin M. Adams, Dolores Korman Sloviter, all of Philadelphia, Pa.; Ruggero J. Aldisert, Joseph F. Weis, Jr., both of Pittsburgh, Pa.; John J. Gibbons, Leonard I. Garth, both of Newark, N.J.

Fourth Circuit (Maryland, North Carolina, South Carolina, Virginia, West Virginia): Harrison L. Winter, Chief Judge, Baltimore, Md.; John D. Butzner, Jr., Richmond, Va.; Donald Stuart Russell, Spartanburg, S.C.; H. Emory Widener, Jr., Abingdon, Va.; Kenneth K. Hall, James M. Sprouse, both of Charleston, W. Va.; James Dickson Phillips, Jr., Durham, N.C.; Francis D. Murnaghan, Jr., Baltimore, Md.; Samuel J. Ervin III, Asheville, N.C.; Robert F. Chapman of Columbia, S.C.

New Fifth Circuit[1*][2] (Louisiana, Mississippi, Texas, and the Canal Zone): Charles Clark, Chief Judge, Jackson, Miss.; James P. Coleman, Ackermann, Miss.; Alvin B. Rubin, Baton Rouge, La.; Robert A. Ainsworth, Jr., Albert Tate, Jr., both of New Orleans, La.; Thomas G. Gee, Thomas M. Reavley, Samuel D. Johnson, Jr., and Jerre S. Williams, all of Austin, Tex.; Henry A. Politz, Shreveport, La.; John R. Brown, Carolyn D. Randall, both of Houston, Tex.; Reynaldo G. Garza, Brownsville, Tex.; Irving L. Goldberg, Dallas, Tex.

Sixth Circuit (Kentucky, Michigan, Ohio, Tennessee): George Clifton Edwards, Jr., Chief Judge, Cincinnati, Ohio; Paul C. Weick, Akron, Ohio; Pierce Lively, Danville, Ky.; Albert J. Engel, Grand Rapids, Mich.; Gilbert S. Merritt, Nashville, Tenn.; Damon J. Keith, Cornelia Kennedy, both of Detroit, Mich.; Bailey Brown, Memphis, Tenn.; Boyce F. Martin, Jr., Louisville, Ky.; Nathaniel R. Jones, Cincinnati, Ohio.

Seventh Circuit (Illinois, Indiana, Wisconsin): Thomas E. Fairchild, Chief Judge, Chicago, Ill.; Luther M. Swygert,

Walter J. Cummings, Richard D. Cudahy, Wilbur F. Pell, Jr., Robert A. Sprecher, William J. Bauer, Harlington Wood, Jr., all of Chicago, Ill.

Eighth Circuit (Arkansas, Iowa, Minnesota, Missouri, Nebraska, North Dakota, South Dakota): Donald Lay, Chief Judge, Omaha, Nebr.; Gerald W. Heaney, Duluth, Minn.; Myron H. Bright, Fargo, N. Dak.; Donald R. Ross, Omaha, Nebr.; Roy L. Stephenson, Des Moines, Iowa; J. Smith Henley, Harrison, Ark.; Richard S. Arnold, Little Rock, Ark.; Theodore McMillian, St. Louis, Mo.

Ninth Circuit (Arizona, California, Idaho, Montana, Nevada, Oregon, Washington, Alaska, Hawaii, Guam): James R. Browning, Chief Judge, San Francisco, Calif.; Euguene A. Wright, Betty B. Fletcher, Jerome J. Farris, all of Seattle, Wash.; Thomas Tang, Mary M. Schroeder, William C. Canby, Jr., all of Phoenix, Ariz.; Herbert Y.C. Choy, Honolulu, Hawaii; Alfred T. Goodwin, Otto R. Skopil, Jr., both of Portland, Oregon; J. Clifford Wallace, San Diego, Calif.; Joseph T. Sneed, Cecil F. Poole, both of San Francisco, Calif.; Anthony M. Kennedy, Sacramento, Calif.; J. Blaine Anderson, Boise, Idaho; Procter Hug, Jr., Reno, Nevada; Harry Pregerson, Arthur L. Alarcon, Warren J. Ferguson, Dorothy W. Nelson, William A. Norris, Stephen R. Reinhardt, Walter Ely, all of Los Angeles, Calif.; Robert Boochever, Juneau, Alaska.

Tenth Circuit (Colorado, Kansas, New Mexico, Oklahoma, Utah, Wyoming): Oliver Seth, Chief Judge, Santa Fe, N. Mex.; William J. Holloway, Jr., Oklahoma City, Okla.; James E. Barrett, Cheyenne, Wyo.; William E. Doyle and Robert H. McWilliams, both of Denver, Colo.; Monroe McKay, Salt Lake City, Utah; James K. Logan, Olathe, Kansas; Stephanie K. Seymour, Tulsa, Okla.

New Eleventh Circuit[1*] (Alabama, Florida, and Georgia): John C. Godbold, Chief Judge, Montgomery, Ala.; Frank M. Johnson, Jr., Montgomery, Ala.; Gerald B. Tjoflat, Jacksonville, Fla.; Phyllis A. Kravitch, Albert J. Henderson, James C. Hill, all of Atlanta, Ga.; Paul H. Roney, St. Petersburg, Fla.; Peter T. Fay, Miami, Fla.; Robert S. Vance, Birmingham, Ala.; Joseph W. Hatchett, Tallahassee, Fla.; R. Lanier Anderson III, Macon, Ga.; Thomas A. Clark, Tampa, Fla.

U.S. DISTRICT COURTS

Judges of U.S. District Courts and the Chief Judge of the District of Columbia receive annual salaries of $67,100.

U.S. TERRITORIAL JUDGES

The District Judges earn annual salaries of $67,100.

U.S. COURT OF CLAIMS

717 Madison Place, N.W., Washington, D.C.
(Salaries: $70,900)

Chief Judge: Daniel M. Friedman, Associate Judges: Oscar H. Davis, Philip Nichols, Jr., Shiro Kashiwa, Robert L. Kunzig, Marion T. Bennett and Edward S. Smith.

U.S. COURT OF CUSTOMS AND PATENT APPEALS

717 Madison Place, N.W., Washington, D.C.
(Salaries: $70,900)

Chief Judge: Howard T. Markey, Associate Judges: Giles S. Rich, Jack R. Miller, Philip B. Baldwin, Helen W. Nies.

U.S. COURT OF INTERNATIONAL TRADE

1 Federal Plaza, New York, N.Y.
(Salaries: $67,100)

Chief Judge: Edward D. Re, Judges: Paul P. Rao, Morgan Ford, Scovel Richardson, Frederick Landis, James L. Watson, Herbert N. Maletz, Bernard Newman, Nils A. Boe.

[1*]At the end of September 1980, Congress passed legislation to split the Fifth Circuit judicial district, which becomes effective October 1, 1981. The new Eleventh Circuit will consist of Alabama, Florida, and Georgia, with its seat in Atlanta, Ga. The new Fifth Circuit will consist of Louisiana, Mississippi, Texas, and the Canal Zone, with its seat in New Orleans, La. A tentative list of the membership for the two new circuit courts was derived from their current residence location. [2] In accordance with the Panama Canal Treaty between the United States and Panama, which became effective October 1, 1979, 40% of the former Panama Canal Zone remains in the control of the U.S. Panama Canal Commission until December 31, 1999. The present Fifth Circuit continues its jurisdiction for this area.

STATE AND LOCAL GOVERNMENT EXPENDITURES: PER CAPITA
Source: U.S. Bureau of the Census

Year	Total general	Education	Highways	Public welfare	Health and hospitals	Police and fire
1902	$ 12.80	$ 3.22	$ 2.21	$ .47	$ .75	$ 1.14
1913	21.23	5.93	4.31	.53	1.11	1.70
1922	47.41	15.49	11.76	1.08	2.35	3.17
1932	62.15	18.50	13.93	3.55	3.65	4.23
1936	59.63	16.98	11.12	6.45	3.64	4.05
1940	69.85	19.97	11.91	8.75	4.61	4.54
1944	64.04	20.18	8.67	8.19	4.74	4.80
1946	78.00	23.74	11.83	9.97	5.79	5.47
1948	120.60	36.68	20.71	14.31	8.38	7.16
1950	150.22	47.31	25.07	19.38	11.52	8.34
1952	166.29	53.00	29.63	17.76	13.92	9.71
1954	189.06	65.01	34.04	18.84	14.83	10.98
1956	219.42	79.02	41.56	18.76	16.57	12.35
1958	258.76	91.84	49.43	22.03	19.97	14.33
1960	288.21	104.00	52.38	24.47	21.08	15.35
1961	307.01	112.39	53.78	25.78	22.32	16.96
1962	324.00	119.56	55.74	27.36	23.37	17.51
1963	339.19	125.81	59.11	28.74	24.59	17.99
1964	362.20	137.38	60.96	30.13	25.66	18.74
1965	385.30	147.37	63.05	32.58	27.66	19.89
1966	422.97	169.95	65.20	34.50	30.17	21.19
1967	471.79	191.64	70.41	41.53	33.56	22.99
1968	512.41	205.93	72.46	49.32	37.76	25.18
1969	578.14	233.94	76.35	59.97	42.19	28.19
1970	646.20	259.39	80.83	72.23	47.57	32.07
1971	730.52	288.05	87.73	88.36	54.32	36.50
1972	801.38	311.60	91.29	101.18	61.79	41.07
1973	863.60	332.21	88.70	112.37	65.97	45.18
1974	941.19	358.74	94.36	118.67	75.43	48.85
1975	1082.58	412.24	105.71	132.11	88.43	56.54
1976	1195.99	452.89	111.37	151.89	96.37	62.56
1977	1268.37	475.22	106.80	166.14	104.20	67.82
1978	1361.90	507.91	112.85	179.49	114.41	73.87
1979	1488.05	542.70	129.22	183.64	128.20	78.84

U.S. — BUDGET: 1789-1981
Source: U.S. Office of Management and Budget (in millions of dollars)

Fiscal Year	Receipts	Outlays	Surplus or Deficit (—)	Fiscal Year	Receipts	Outlays	Surplus or Deficit (—)
1789–1849	1,160	1,090	+70	1941	8,621	13,634	—5,013
1850–1900	14,462	15,453	—991	1942	14,350	35,114	—20,764
1901	588	525	+63	1943	23,649	78,533	—54,884
1902	562	485	+77	1944	44,276	91,280	—47,004
1903	562	517	+45	1945	45,216	92,690	—47,474
1904	541	584	—43	1946	39,327	55,183	—15,856
1905	544	567	—23	1947	38,394	34,532	+3,862
1906	595	570	+25	1948	41,774	29,773	+12,001
1907	666	579	+87	1949	39,437	38,834	+603
1908	602	659	—57	1950	39,485	42,597	—3,112
1909	604	694	—89	1951	51,646	45,546	+6,100
1910	676	694	—18	1952	66,204	67,721	—1,517
1911	702	691	+11	1953	69,574	76,107	—6,533
1912	693	690	+3	1954	69,719	70,890	—1,170
1913	714	715	—*	1955	65,469	68,509	—3,041
1914	725	726	—*	1956	74,547	70,460	+4,087
1915	683	746	—63	1957	79,990	76,741	+3,249
1916	761	713	+48	1958	79,636	82,575	—2,939
1917	1,101	1,954	—853	1959	79,249	92,104	—12,855
1918	3,645	12,677	—9,032	1960	92,492	92,223	+269
1919	5,130	18,493	—13,363	1961	94,389	97,795	—3,406
1920	6,649	6,358	+291	1962	99,676	106,813	—7,137
1921	5,571	5,062	+509	1963	106,560	111,311	—4,751
1922	4,026	3,289	+736	1964	112,662	118,584	—5,922
1923	3,853	3,140	+713	1965	116,833	118,430	—1,596
1924	3,871	2,908	+963	1966	130,856	134,652	—3,796
1925	3,641	2,924	+717	1967	149,552	158,254	—8,702
1926	3,795	2,930	+865	1968	153,671	178,833	—25,161
1927	4,013	2,857	+1,155	1969	187,784	184,548	+3,236
1928	3,900	2,961	+939	1970	193,743	196,588	—2,845
1929	3,862	3,127	+734	1971	188,392	211,425	—23,033
1930	4,058	3,320	+738	1972	208,649	232,021	—23,373
1931	3,116	3,577	—462	1973	232,225	247,074	—14,849
1932	1,924	4,659	—2,735	1974	264,932	269,620	—4,688
1933	1,997	4,598	—2,602	1975	280,997	326,185	—45,188
1934	3,015	6,645	—3,630	1976	300,005	366,439	—66,434
1935	3,706	6,497	—2,791	TQ	81,773	94,729	—12,956
1936	3,997	8,422	—4,425	1977	357,762	402,725	—44,963
1937	4,956	7,733	—2,777	1978	401,997	450,836	—48,839
1938	5,588	6,765	—1,177	1979	465,940	493,673	—27,733
1939	4,979	8,841	—3,862	1980	520,000	658,800	—138,800
1940	6,361	9,456	—3,095	1981 est.[1]	605,600	717,600	—112,000
				1982[1]	662,400	779,500	—117,100

* Less than $500,000. [1] Based on the 1982 budget from the Mid-Session Review in July 1981. [2] Fiscal years through 1976 began on July 1 and ended on the following June 30. Beginning with fiscal year 1977, each fiscal year begins on October 1 and ends on the following September 30. The Transition Quarter (TQ) refers to the 3-month period from the end of fiscal year 1976 on June 30, 1976, to the beginning of fiscal year 1977 on October 1, 1976.
Note: Data for 1789–1939 are for the administrative budget; 1940 and thereafter are for the unified budget.

THE BUDGET DOLLAR

SOURCE: Office of Management and Budget
Fiscal Year 1982

Where it comes from . . .

Excise Taxes 7¢
Other 4¢
Borrowing 6¢
Corporation Income Taxes 9¢
Individual Income Taxes 43¢
Social Insurance Receipts 30¢

Direct Benefit Payments to Individuals 42¢
National Defense 27¢
Net Interest 11¢
Grants to States and Localities 12¢
Other Federal Operations 8¢

Where it goes . . .

FEDERAL GRANTS TO STATES[1]

SOURCE: Tax Foundation, Inc.

These comparisons of Federal tax burdens for aid payments per $1.00 of assistance do not actually indicate the entire costs which state and local governments incur for obtaining Federal grants. The comparisons, with few exceptions, do not take into account the costs to these governments of administering the programs for which the aid is granted, nor the amounts of matching funds which the state and local governments must make available out of their own revenue in order to qualify as recipients of these grants. In the last few years, it is estimated that state and local governments provided approximately $1.00 of matching funds for each $2.50 of Federal aid.

"PAYING STATES"[1]

Twenty-three states paid more in U.S. taxes to support grant programs than they received in aid in fiscal year 1980.

State	Grants (millions)	Estimated tax burden for grants (millions)	Tax Burden for $1 of Aid All Grants	Tax Burden for $1 of Aid Rev. Sharing
Texas	$3,961.2	$5,539.8	$1.40	$1.35
Conn.	1,156.8	1,560.0	1.35	1.50
Ind.	1,608.1	2,153.9	1.34	1.25
Ohio	3,433.3	4,352.1	1.27	1.22
Fla.	2,851.1	3,501.2	1.23	1.39
N.J.	2,832.9	3,439.1	1.21	1.17
Kansas	816.7	983.9	1.20	1.26
Colo.	965.3	1,161.1	1.20	1.21
Calif.	8,723.0	10,450.3	1.20	1.00
Ill.	4,476.1	5,300.5	1.18	1.23
Va.	1,807.9	2,056.4	1.14	1.14
Iowa	994.4	1,125.7	1.13	1.00
Ariz.	823.0	930.7	1.13	.88
Wyo.	190.8	212.7	1.11	1.22
Nebr.	545.8	602.7	1.10	1.03
Wash.	1,632.3	1,799.3	1.10	1.47
Nev.	322.0	354.5	1.10	1.66
Mo.	1,698.2	1,852.5	1.09	1.17
Okla.	1,057.9	1,108.0	1.05	1.15
Mich.	3,926.1	4,041.8	1.03	1.07
N.H.	345.4	354.5	1.03	1.19
Oregon	1,015.1	1,037.1	1.02	1.00
Penn.	4,514.5	4,609.1	1.02	1.06

"RECEIVING STATES"

Twenty-seven states and the District of Columbia paid less in taxes to support grant programs than they received in aid.

State	Grants (millions)	Estimated tax burden for grants (millions)	Tax Burden for $1 of Aid All Grants	Tax Burden for $1 of Aid Rev. Sharing
Md.	$1,886.2	$1,843.6	$.98	$1.07
Minn.	1,664.8	1,595.5	.96	.88
Del.	275.3	257.0	.93	.95
N.C.	1,927.5	1,772.7	.92	.76
La.	1,563.3	1,418.2	.91	.79
Tenn.	1,623.7	1,453.6	.90	.83
Wis.	2,023.4	1,799.3	.89	.85
Hawaii	463.2	390.0	.84	.88
S.C.	1,065.4	877.5	.82	.69
Mass.	2,886.5	2,313.4	.80	.83
Utah	547.5	434.3	.79	.72
Idaho	369.6	292.5	.79	.82
Ky.	1,462.3	1,143.4	.78	.77
R.I.	477.4	363.4	.76	.93
N.Y.	9,569.4	7,277.1	.76	.75
N.M.	563.6	416.6	.74	.77
Ala.	1,556.2	1,134.6	.73	.75
Ga.	2,370.3	1,701.8	.72	.84
Ark.	934.7	629.3	.67	.66
N.D.	342.6	230.5	.67	.88
W. Va.	949.5	602.7	.63	.74
Maine	522.5	328.0	.63	.59
Mont.	459.7	274.8	.60	.73
Miss.	1,177.8	629.3	.53	.47
Alaska	441.9	230.5	.52	.76
S.D.	439.5	212.7	.48	.68
Vt.	355.4	159.5	.45	.57
D.C.	1,019.6	328.0	.32	.92

[1]Excludes shared revenues; includes general revenue sharing and trust fund aids.

EXPENDITURE OF FEDERAL TAX DOLLARS (FISCAL YEAR 1981)*

SOURCE: Tax Foundation, Inc.; Revised Budget for Fiscal Year 1981 (May 1981)

Item	Worker's Share Amount	% of Total	Item	Worker's Share Amount	% of Total
Total	$6,339	100.00	Natural resources and environment	$127	2.00
Income security	2,127	33.55	International affairs	105	1.65
National defense	1,501	23.68	Community and regional development	95	1.50
Interest	716	11.29	Energy	86	1.35
Health	618	9.75	General purpose fiscal assistance	63	1.00
Education, training, employment and social services	283	4.47	General science, space, & technology	58	.91
			General government	47	.74
Transportation	222	3.51	Administration of justice	44	.69
Veterans' benefits	207	3.27	Commerce and housing credit	30	.47
			Agriculture	11	.17

*Based on worker earning $22,000 a year as sole source of support for wife and two dependent children.

THE U.S. BUDGET: RECEIPTS AND OUTLAYS (in billions of dollars)

SOURCE: U.S. Office of Management and Budget

Description	1977 Actual	1978 Actual	1979 Actual	1980 Actual	1981[1] Est	1982[1] Est
Receipts by source:						
Individual income taxes	157.6	181.0	217.8	244.1	285.6	302.9
Corporation income taxes	54.9	60.0	65.7	64.6	63.3	66.8
Social insurance taxes and contributions	108.7	123.4	141.6	160.7	186.8	214.2
Excise taxes	17.5	18.4	18.7	24.3	41.7	48.1
Estate and gift taxes	7.3	5.3	5.4	6.4	6.9	7.6
Customs duties	5.2	6.6	7.4	7.2	7.6	7.9
Miscellaneous receipts	6.5	7.4	9.2	12.7	13.9	14.9
Total receipts:	**357.8**	**402.0**	**465.9**	**520.0**	**605.6**	**662.4**
Outlays by function:						
National defense[2]	97.5	105.2	117.7	145.8	179.9	225.7
International affairs	4.8	5.9	6.1	15.5	23.6	17.7
General science, space, and technology	4.7	4.7	5.0	6.1	6.5	7.2
Energy	4.2	5.9	6.9	36.4	6.4	9.1
Natural resources and environment	10.0	10.9	12.1	13.1	10.7	7.9
Agriculture	5.5	7.7	6.2	4.9	5.7	5.3
Commerce and housing credit	*	3.3	2.6	10.5	6.6	8.3
Transportation	14.6	15.4	17.5	20.2	25.1	20.7
Community and regional development	6.3	11.0	9.5	10.1	8.5	6.7
Education, training, employment, and social services	21.0	26.5	29.7	30.6	30.5	25.4
Health	38.8	43.7	49.6	58.8	71.9	83.3
Income security	137.9	146.2	160.2	224.2	250.7	262.6
Veterans benefits and services	18.0	19.0	19.9	21.2	23.2	24.7
Administration of justice	3.6	3.8	4.2	4.4	4.4	4.2
General government	3.3	3.7	4.2	4.6	5.0	5.1
General purpose fiscal assistance	9.5	9.6	8.4	8.7	6.2	6.5
Interest	38.0	44.0	52.6	64.5	83.1	92.3
Allowances[3]						0.7
Undistributed offsetting receipts	−15.1	−15.8	−18.5	−21.9	−30.2	−33.7
Total outlays:	**402.7**	**450.8**	**493.7**	**658.8**	**717.6**	**779.5**
Budget deficit:	**−44.9**	**−48.8**	**−27.8**	**−138.8**	**−112.0**	**−117.1**

[1]Based on estimates of the 1982 Budget of the Mid-Session Review in July 1981. [2]Includes civilian and military pay raises for Department of Defense. [3]Includes allowances for civilian agency pay raises.

FEDERAL, STATE & LOCAL GOVERNMENT FINANCES: 1929—1980

SOURCE: U.S. Department of Commerce, Bureau of Economic Analysis

	(Billions of Dollars)						
	1929	1939	1949	1959	1978	1979	1980*
Total Government**							
Receipts	11.3	15.4	55.9	129.4	681.6	765.2	836.8
Expenditures	10.3	17.6	59.3	131.0	681.9	753.2	869.0
Federal Government							
Receipts	3.8	6.7	38.7	89.8	431.5	494.4	540.8
Expenditures	2.6	8.9	41.3	91.0	460.7	509.2	602.0
State and Local Government							
Receipts	7.6	9.6	19.5	46.4	327.4	351.2	384.0
Expenditures	7.8	9.6	20.2	46.9	298.4	324.4	355.0

*Preliminary. ** Total government is after subtraction of Federal grants-in-aid to state and local governments.

STATE PER CAPITA INCOME: 1979 and 1980

SOURCE: U.S. Department of Commerce, Bureau of Economic Analysis

Rank	State	1979 Income	1980 Income	Percent of National Average 1980	Rank	State	1979 Income	1980 Income	Percent of National Average 1980
	United States	$ 8,637	$ 9,521	100	24.	Iowa	8,666	9,358	98
					25.	Wisconsin	8,646	9,348	98
	States				26.	Oregon	8,652	9,317	98
1.	Alaska	11,355	12,790	134	27.	New Hampshire	8,162	9,131	96
2.	Connecticut	10,368	11,720	123	28.	Oklahoma	8,150	9,116	96
—	District of Columbia	10,691	12,039	126	29.	Florida	8,053	8,996	94
3.	California	9,825	10,938	115	30.	Missouri	8,232	8,982	94
4.	New Jersey	9,756	10,924	115	31.	Indiana	8,365	8,936	94
5.	Wyoming	9,840	10,898	114	32.	Arizona	7,949	8,791	92
6.	Nevada	9,731	10,727	113	33.	North Dakota	8,355	8,747	92
7.	Illinois	9,683	10,521	111	34.	Montana	7,894	8,536	90
8.	Maryland	9,404	10,460	110	35.	Louisiana	7,491	8,458	89
9.	Delaware	9,159	10,339	109	36.	Georgia	7,309	8,073	85
10.	Washington	9,477	10,309	108	37.	Idaho	7,462	8,056	85
11.	New York	9,166	10,260	108	38.	Maine	7,051	7,925	83
12.	Massachusetts	8,998	10,125	106	39.	New Mexico	7,150	7,841	82
13.	Hawaii	9,129	10,101	106	40.	Vermont	7,105	7,827	82
14.	Colorado	8,939	10,025	105	41.	North Carolina	7,110	7,819	82
15.	Kansas	9,223	9,983	105	42.	South Dakota	7,511	7,806	82
16.	Michigan	9,343	9,950	105	43.	West Virginia	7,191	7,800	82
17.	Minnesota	8,927	9,724	102	44.	Tennessee	7,084	7,720	80
18.	Texas	8,493	9,545	100	45.	Utah	7,042	7,649	80
19	Ohio	8,703	9,462	99	46.	Kentucky	7,052	7,613	80
20.	Rhode Island	8,387	9,444	99	47.	Alabama	6,819	7,488	79
21	Pennsylvania	8,555	9,434	99	48.	Arkansas	6,756	7,428	76
22.	Virginia	8,447	9,392	99	49.	South Carolina	6,577	7,266	76
23.	Nebraska	8,651	9,365	98	50.	Mississippi	6,070	6,580	69

INTERNAL REVENUE TAXES

Source: U.S. Internal Revenue Service

Year	Collections	Cost of Collecting $100	Tax per Capita	Year	Collections	Cost of Collecting $100	Tax per Capita
1866	$310,120,448	$2.47	$8.49	1932	$1,557,729,043	$2.17	$12.47
1868	190,374,926	4.90	4.98	1934	2,672,239,195	1.08	21.13
1870	184,302,828	4.47	4.62	1935	3,299,435,572	1.29	25.91
1873	113,504,013	5.83	2.64	1937	4,653,195,315	1.12	36.08
1875	110,071,515	4.83	2.44	1939	5,181,573,953	1.13	39.55
1876	116,768,096	4.09	2.53	1941	7,370,108,378	0.89	55.04
1878	110,654,163	3.67	2.30	1942	13,047,868,518	0.58	96.39
1880	123,981,916	3.63	2.47	1943	22,371,385,497	0.44	163.00
1881	135,229,912	3.74	2.62	1944	40,121,760,233	0.32	288.82
1883	144,553,345	3.53	2.67	1945	43,800,387,576	0.33	311.82
1885	112,421,121	3.96	1.98	1946	40,672,096,998	0.43	286.55
1886	116,902,896	3.68	2.02	1948	41,864,542,295	0.44	284.39
1888	124,326,475	3.20	2.05	1950	38,957,131,768	0.59	255.84
1890	142,594,697	2.87	2.26	1951	50,445,686,315	0.49	325.71
1891	146,035,416	2.88	2.27	1952	65,009,585,560	0.42	412.62
1893	161,004,990	2.62	2.40	1954	69,919,990,791	0.38	428.89
1895	143,246,078	2.88	2.06	1955	66,288,692,000	0.42	399.50
1896	146,830,616	2.78	2.07	1957	80,171,971,000	0.38	466.16
1898	170,866,819	2.29	2.32	1958	79,978,476,484	0.42	457.33
1900	295,316,108	1.58	3.88	1959	79,797,972,806	0.44	448.73
1901	306,871,669	1.55	3.95	1960	91,774,802,823	0.40	507.96
1903	230,740,925	2.07	2.86	1961	94,401,086,398	0.44	513.91
1905	234,187,976	2.01	2.79	1962	99,440,839,245	0.45	533.09
1906	249,102,738	1.90	2.92	1963	105,925,395,281	0.47	559.74
1908	251,665,950	1.92	2.84	1964	112,260,257,115	0.49	585.03
1910	289,957,220	1.74	3.14	1965	114,434,633,721	0.52	588.95
1911	322,526,300	1.68	3.44	1966	128,879,961,342	0.48	655.68
1913	344,424,454	1.59	3.54	1967	148,374,814,552	0.45	746.68
1915	415,681,024	1.64	4.13	1968	153,636,837,665	0.46	765.48
1916	512,723,288	1.40	5.03	1969	187,919,559,668	0.40	927.19
1917	809,393,640	0.95	7.83	1970	195,722,096,497	0.45	955.31
1918	3,698,955,821	0.33	35.38	1971	191,647,198,138	0.51	925.63
1919	3,850,150,079	0.53	36.65	1972	209,855,736,878	0.54	1,004.83
1921	4,595,357,062	0.72	42.34	1973	237,787,204,058	0.49	1,130.11
1925	2,584,140,268	1.44	22.31	1974	268,952,253,663	0.49	1,269.24
1926	2,835,999,892	1.23	24.16	1975	293,822,725,772	0.54	1,375.96
1928	2,790,535,538	1.17	23.16	1976	302,519,791,922	0.56	1,406.30
1929	2,939,054,375	1.17	24.14	1977	358,139,416,730	0.50	1,647.91
1930	3,040,145,733	1.13	24.68	1978	399,776,389,362	0.49	1,826.61
				1979	460,412,185,013	0.46	2,083.82
				1980	519,375,273,361	0.44	2,325.04

ADDRESSES OF U.S. INTERNAL REVENUE OFFICES

If you are located in:	Send your return to:
Alabama, Florida, Georgia, Mississippi, South Carolina	Internal Revenue Service Center Atlanta, Georgia 31101
Delaware, District of Columbia, Maryland, Pennsylvania	Internal Revenue Service Center Philadelphia, Pennsylvania 19255
Michigan, Ohio	Internal Revenue Service Center Cincinnati, Ohio 45999
Arkansas, Kansas, Louisiana, New Mexico, Oklahoma, Texas	Internal Revenue Service Center Austin, Texas 73301
Illinois, Iowa, Missouri, Wisconsin	Internal Revenue Service Center Kansas City, Missouri 64999
Connecticut, Maine, Massachusetts, New Hampshire, New York (except N.Y.C. and Nassau, Rockland, Suffolk, and Westchester counties), Rhode Island, Vermont	Internal Revenue Service Center Andover, Massachusetts 05501
Indiana, Kentucky, North Carolina, Tennessee, Virginia, West Virginia	Internal Revenue Service Center Memphis, Tennessee 37501
Alaska, Arizona, Colorado, Idaho, Minnesota, Montana, Nebraska, Nevada, North Dakota, Oregon, South Dakota, Utah, Washington, Wyoming	Internal Revenue Service Center Ogden, Utah 84201
California, Hawaii	Internal Revenue Service Center Fresno, California 93888

If you are located in:	Send your return to:
New York City and N.Y. counties of Nassau, Rockland, Suffolk, and Westchester; New Jersey	Internal Revenue Service Center Holtsville, New York 00501
American Samoa	Internal Revenue Service Center Philadelphia, Pennsylvania 19255
Guam	Commissioner of Revenue and Taxation Agana, Guam 96910
Puerto Rico (or if excluding income under section 933), Virgin Islands: Non permanent residents	Internal Revenue Service Center Philadelphia, Pennsylvania 19255
Virgin Islands: Permanent residents	Department of Finance, Tax Division Charlotte Amalie, St. Thomas Virgin Islands 00801

U.S. citizens with foreign addresses (except A.P.O. and F.P.O.) and those excluding income under sec. 911 or 931: file with Internal Revenue Service, Philadelphia, Pa. 19255

	U.S. citizens with A.P.O. or F.P.O. address of:
Miami	Internal Revenue Service Center Atlanta, Georgia 31101
New York	Internal Revenue Service Center Holtsville, New York 00501
San Francisco	Internal Revenue Service Center Fresno, California 93888
Seattle	Internal Revenue Service Center Ogden, Utah 84201

TAX TIPS

Prepared by **H&R BLOCK**
THE INCOME TAX PEOPLE

The tax tips discussed here are based on current tax law as of August 13, 1981. New tax legislation could result in changes.

INVESTMENTS, CAPITAL GAINS

For 1981, up to $200 ($400 on a joint return) of qualifying dividends and interest may be excluded from income. In years after 1981, the dividend exclusion will be $100 ($200 on a joint return). There will be no interest exclusion until 1985; but up to $1,000 ($2,000 on a joint return) interest earned on specified, one-year savings certificates will be tax exempt. These savings certificates may be purchased between October 1, 1981 and December 31, 1982. Beginning in 1985, an exclusion of 15% of net interest up to $3,000 ($6,000 on a joint return) will be allowed.

U.S. series EE bonds may be a worthwhile investment. Interest earned is not taxable until the bonds mature (plus extensions) or are cashed. Or, you may elect to report the interest each year as it accrues. If the latter choice is made, all such interest in all future years is taxable as it accrues. This election may be wise when it is expected that gross income will be greater in the year(s) the bonds will be cashed than in the intervening years (such as bonds purchased for a child which will be used for his or her future). The first year the election is made, a return must be filed with a statement on the option chosen. Thereafter a return is filed or not, based on the usual filing requirements.

You may open a savings account or purchase stock to save for your child's college education or future without paying tax on the earnings. The security or savings must be in the child's name and neither the principal nor earnings can be used for the child's support or in any way used by you. You may be custodian of the investment. The child is not required to file a return for any year in which his or her investment income is less than $1,000 or gross income is less than $3,300. If the child is required to file, his or her tax on this income would most likely be less than the adult would have paid.

Sales of capital assets should be planned to gain the greatest possible tax advantage without sacrificing economic results. Try to avoid sales at a loss in the same year in which you will have a long-term gain. Only 40% of a net long-term capital gain is taxable, but gains and losses must be combined to determine the net gain or loss. To realize 100% of a long-term loss, sell short-term assets at a gain. (Only 50% of a net long-term loss is deductible against ordinary income.) Generally, property owned over one year is long term. Commodity futures are long term if held over 6 months.

SELLING YOUR PRINCIPAL RESIDENCE

If you sell your home, all or part of any gain will not be taxed immediately if, within 18 months, you buy and occupy another home. For sales after January 20, 1980, the replacement period is 24 months. The deferred gain reduces the basis of the new home. A taxpayer age 55 or over on the date of sale may exclude up to $100,000 ($125,000 on sales after July 20, 1981) gain from sale of his or her principal residence. To qualify, you must have owned and lived in the home three of the five years ending on the date of sale. This election may be made only once in a lifetime.

If you sell your home on contract and cannot defer all or part of the gain, you may use the installment method. Gain is reported in the years that payments are received instead of all in the year of sale.

END-OF-YEAR TAX PLANNING

It will generally be advantageous to defer receipt of income to later years, if possible. The tax rates are being reduced over a three-year period. The highest tax rate for all types of income will be 50%. The cumulative reduction will be 23%.

Married couples who have been discussing the pros and cons of both spouses working may decide yes more often. Beginning in 1982, a "marriage penalty" deduction will be allowed that will reduce the difference in tax paid by a married couple on their combined income and the tax each would pay on his or her separate income if they were not married. This deduction is allowed regardless of whether you itemize. In 1982, 5%, up to $1,500 (10%, up to $3,000, in years after 1982), of the qualified earned income of the spouse having the lower earned income may be deducted.

Beginning in 1982, the amount of estimated unpaid tax at which estimated tax payments are required increases $100 each year until it reaches $500 for 1985 and later years. The interest rate on underpayments will increase to 100% of the prime bank rate and will be adjusted annually. No more "low-interest loans" from the government.

Before the end of the year, you should estimate whether the total of your itemized deductions will exceed your zero bracket amount. If it will, it may be beneficial to pay any outstanding obligations that are deductible before the end of the year. If the total itemized deductions will not exceed the zero bracket amount, it will be better to postpone (if possible) payment of deductible obligations until the beginning of the new tax year.

ADOPTION EXPENSES

Beginning in 1981, up to $1,500 of unreimbursed expenses incurred to adopt a child with special needs may be deducted on Schedule A. A qualified child is one for whom adoption assistance payments are made under section 473 of the Social Security Act.

CHARITABLE CONTRIBUTIONS

You may deduct actual transportation expenses incurred in performing volunteer work for a charitable organization. In lieu of actual costs, you may deduct nine cents a mile plus parking fees and tolls. Also deductible are the cost and upkeep of uniforms required to be worn and equipment or supplies purchased to perform volunteer work. All items must be used solely for the charitable work.

You may deduct up to 50 percent of adjusted gross income for cash contributions made to churches, educational organizations, certain medical organizations, public organizations such as libraries and symphony orchestras, and other charities that receive most of their support from the general public or the government.

In 1982 through 1986, a portion of your charitable contributions will be deductible even if you don't itemize.

CASUALTY LOSS

Loss or damage to your property resulting from a sudden or unusual event such as severe weather, fire, accident or theft may be deductible. If you sustained such a loss in an area determined by the President to warrant federal disaster assistance, the loss may be claimed on your tax return for the year of the loss or the preceding year, whichever is more advantageous.

AGE 65 BRINGS TAX BENEFITS

You are allowed an additional personal exemption if you are 65 or older on the last day of the year. For tax purposes, you are considered 65 on the day before your 65th birthday.

You may be eligible for a tax credit if you are age 65 or older or are under age 65 and receive a pension or annuity from a public retirement system. The maximum credit is $375 for single individuals, $562.50 for married individuals filing a joint return, and $281.25 for married individuals filing a separate return. Married individuals must file a joint return to claim the credit unless they lived apart for the entire year.

CLAIMING DEPENDENTS

It is not always necessary to provide more than half of the support for a relative to claim him or her as a dependent. If you and one or more persons could claim the relative as a dependent, except for the support test and together contribute more than 50 percent of the support, you can agree to let any one who individually furnishes more than 10 percent of the support claim the dependent. The other contributors must sign Multiple Support Declarations (Form 2120) which are to be attached to the return of the individual who claims the exemption.

Parents who provide over half the total support of their working child (who is under 19 or is a student) may claim a dependent exemption regardless of the amount the child earns.

DIVORCED TAXPAYERS

Generally, the parent who has custody of the child for the greater part of the year is entitled to claim the exemption. There are two exceptions to this rule. The noncustodial parent is entitled to the exemption if he or she:

1) contributed at least $600 toward each child's support during the year and the divorce decree or other agreement specifies that this parent is entitled to the exemption. Any agreement must be in writing. OR

2) provided $1,200 (or more) support for each child during the year and the parent having custody cannot prove that he or she provided more support.

Child support payments are neither deductible by the payer nor taxable to the recipient. If the decree does not specify an amount as child support, the entire payment is alimony. Alimony payments, generally, are deductible by the payer and taxable to the recipient. Deductible alimony is claimed as an adjustment, deductible regardless of whether deductions are itemized.

EARNED INCOME CREDIT

Some individuals will qualify for the earned income credit. If both your adjusted gross income and your earned income are less than $10,000 and you maintain your home for a qualifying child you may be eligible for this credit. Maximum credit is $500.

OTHER CREDITS

An investment credit is available when qualified business property is purchased. Employees may be able to claim this credit if required to use their own vehicles, tools, etc. in their work.

Residential energy credit is available for insulation, storm or thermal windows and certain energy saving devices installed in your home. Also for solar, wind or geothermal equipment. Energy investment credit is available to businesses for energy-conserving expenditures.

You may be able to claim a credit if you pay for the care of your child or disabled dependent that enables you to be gainfully employed. Beginning in 1982, both the maximum amount of qualified expenses and the maximum percentage have increased. Away from home care of a disabled spouse or dependent will qualify for the credit if certain conditions are met.

INDIVIDUAL RETIREMENT ACCOUNTS

An employee who is not covered by a pension, profit-sharing, or other qualified plan may establish an Individual Retirement Account (IRA). If eligible, you may contribute and deduct up to the lesser of 15 percent of your compensation or $1,500 each year. In addition, the amount earned on the contributions is not taxable until it is withdrawn. Generally, no amount may be withdrawn until you reach age 59 1/2.

If you and your spouse are eligible to establish an IRA and your spouse received no earned income during the year, you may contribute to spousal IRAs. The maximum deduction and contribution for spousal IRAs is the lesser of 15% of compensation or $1,750, one-half to each account. You have until the due date of your tax return to establish and contribute to an IRA for that year.

Beginning in 1982, all workers, including those covered by an employer's qualified plan, can contribute to an IRA. The new law allows people to put as much as 100% of their earned income into an IRA, with a limit of $2,000 ($2,250 for a spousal IRA). There will no longer be a requirement that equal amounts be contributed to each spousal account.

DEPRECIABLE ASSETS

In years after 1980, recovery of the cost of property used for business or employment purposes will generally be more rapid and the computation more simple. In general, a larger investment credit will be earned in fewer years.

Beginning in 1982, an election will be available to deduct up to $5,000 of the cost of tangible personal property used for business or employment purposes. The allowable deduction increases to $10,000 by 1986. It is allowed in place of the recovery deduction (depreciation) and investment credit.

INCOME EARNED ABROAD

Income earned abroad by U.S. citizens and residents will be excludable up to $75,000 in 1982 increasing to $95,000 by 1986. Excessive housing costs will also be deductible.

ESTATE AND GIFT TAXES

The gift and estate tax laws have been revised. Beginning in 1982, you can give up to $10,000 per year per recipient without incurring gift tax, unlimited amounts may be transferred between spouses without incurring gift or estate taxes, and by 1987 only estates valued in excess of $600,000 will be taxed.

FEDERAL TAX COLLECTIONS

Source: Tax Foundation, Inc. Based on official U.S. Government figures.

SELECTED FISCAL YEARS 1959-1981
(Figures in millions)

SOURCE	1959	1969	1978	1979	1980	1981*
Total	$77,520	$182,575	$389,164	$450,817	$500,950	$586,255
Income and profits taxes	54,028	123,927	240,940	283,518	308,666	350,022
Individual income	36,719	87,249	180,988	217,841	244,069	284,013
Corporate income and profits	17,309	36,678	59,952	65,677	64,600	66,009
Excise taxes	10,675	15,222	18,376	18,745	24,329	44,393
Alcoholic beverages	2,979	4,482	5,492	5,531	—	—
Tobacco products	1,793	2,136	2,446	2,492	—	—
Manufacturers' excises	3,928	6,243	6,328	5,901	—	—
Gasoline	1,687	3,053	4,296	4,383	—	—
Passenger automobiles[1]	1,031	1,858	—	—	—	—
Tires and tubes	277	582	803	852	—	—
Automobile and truck parts and accessories	165	90	183	221	—	—
Trucks and buses	214	516	834	927	—	—
Lubricating oils	73	93	104	107	—	—
Other manufacturers' excises	481	51	108	117	—	—
Retailers' excises	353	—[2]	526[3]	552[3]	—	—
Miscellaneous excises	1,624	2,361	3,584	3,563	—	—
Telephone and telegraph	685	1,304	1,642	1,340	—	—
Transportation of persons	225	222	1,107	1,282	—	—
Other miscellaneous excises	714	835	835[4]	941[4]	—	—
Estate and gift taxes	1,333	3,491	5,285	5,411	6,389	6,909
Employment taxes	8,526	34,236	103,893	120,074	138,765	161,051
Unemployment taxes[5]	2,024	3,328	13,850	15,387	15,336	16,338
Customs	925	2,319	6,573	7,439	7,174	7,439
Miscellaneous	9	52	247	243	288	103

*Data for 1981 are estimated. [1]Repealed as of July 15, 1971. [2]Repealed as of June 22, 1965. [3]Includes taxes on noncommercial aviation fuels and diesel fuels used on highways. [4]Includes Black Lung disability fund taxes and undistributed tax deposits and unapplied collections. [5]Includes state unemployment taxes deposited with the Treasury.

PER CAPITA PROPERTY TAX COLLECTIONS

Source: Bureau of the Census and the Tax Foundation

State	Amount 1969	1979	Percent Increase	State	Amount 1969	1979	Percent Increase	State	Amount 1969	1979	Percent Increase
U.S. Avg.	$152	$295	94	Ky.	$ 64	$131	103	Ohio	$146	$260	78
Ala.	36	73	100	La.	60	102	68	Okla.	89	149	68
Alaska	104	826	696	Maine	149	302	103	Oreg.	181	366	102
Ariz.	155	353	128	Md.	145	276	90	Pa.	106	230	117
Ark.	58	125	115	Mass.	225	546	143	R.I.	157	399	154
Calif.	249	266	7	Mich.	165	376	127	S.C.	49	151	205
Colo.	171	326	91	Minn.	156	311	99	S.D.	204	343	68
Conn.	210	456	117	Miss.	60	138	130	Tenn.	68	155	127
Del.	77	165	116	Mo.	122	205	68	Texas	118	274	131
Fla.	114	247	117	Mont.	194	408	110	Utah	130	230	77
Ga.	82	209	156	Nebr.	201	389	93	Vt.	151	360	139
Hawaii	87	191	118	Nev.	165	355	115	Va.	83	223	170
Idaho	117	245	110	N.H.	185	426	129	Wash.	135	308	128
Ill.	173	350	102	N.J.	227	506	123	W.Va.	64	131	105
Ind.	165	247	49	N.M.	77	131	71	Wisc.	193	346	79
Iowa	177	339	91	N.Y.	211	482	128	Wy.	196	513	162
Kansas	179	357	99	N.C.	68	163	140	D.C.	151	323	115
				N.D.	163	257	58				

TAX BURDEN: SELECTED COUNTRIES

Source: Tax Foundation, Inc. Based on OECD data

Country	TAXES* AS % OF GROSS DOMESTIC PRODUCT 1968	1973	1978	Country	TAXES* AS % OF GROSS DOMESTIC PRODUCT 1968	1973	1978
Australia	24.57	26.68	28.81	Japan	17.86	22.35	24.06
Austria	35.30	37.58	41.43	Luxembourg	29.77	35.55	49.88
Belgium	34.32	37.39	44.18	Netherlands	38.81	43.73	46.79
Canada	29.61	31.33	31.13	New Zealand	25.93	27.88	30.36
Denmark	36.14	42.33	43.59	Norway	37.69	45.29	46.94
Finland	33.66	34.59	36.54	Portugal	19.94	22.04	26.15
France	35.38	35.66	39.67	Spain	16.41	18.98	22.76
Germany, West	32.08	36.27	37.82	Sweden	39.81	43.45	53.50
Greece	24.32	22.71	28.12[1]	Switzerland	22.58	26.27	31.47
Ireland	29.13	31.49	33.38	Turkey	17.06	21.40	22.53
Italy	28.83	26.28	32.58	United Kingdom	34.77	31.96	34.45
				United States	27.51	29.70	30.19

*In U.S. dollars. [1]Data for 1977.

STATE INCOME TAX RATES AND EXEMPTIONS: 1982

SOURCE: Reprinted with permission from the *State Tax Guide*, published by Commerce Clearing House, Inc.

Five states have neither personal nor corporate income tax; they are Nevada, South Dakota, Texas, Washington, and Wyoming.

Under personal exemptions, additional exemptions for aged and/or blind are not included. All figures are as of May 1981

State	Personal Exemptions		Individual Rates				Corporation Rates
ALABAMA	Single	$1,500	1st	$1,000 .... 1.5%	Next	$2,000 .... 4.5%	5%. Financial institutions
	Married	3,000	Next	2,000 3	Over	5,000 5	6%
	Dependent	300					
ALASKA			The Alaska personal income tax was repealed by the state legislature and signed into law in late September 1980. Refunds are due all persons who paid taxes for the year 1979 and during 1980.				5.4% plus 4% surtax.

ARIZONA	Single	$1,000	1st	$1,000 .... 2%	Next	$1,000 .... 6%	1st	$1,000	2.5%
	Married	2,000	Next	1,000 3	Next	1,000 7	2nd	1,000	4
	Dependent	600	Next	1,000 4	Over	6,000 8	3rd	1,000	5
			Next	1,000 5			4th	1,000	6.5
							5th	1,000	8
							6th	1,000	9
			Joint returns may split their income.				Over	6,000	10.5

ARKANSAS	From tax:						1st	$3,000	1%
	Single	$17.50	1st	$2,999 .... 1%	Next	$6,000 .... 4.5%	2nd	3,000	2
	Married	35.00	Next	3,000 .... 2.5	Next	10,000 6	Next	5,000	3
	Dependent	6.00	Next	3,000 .... 3.5	$25,000 and over. 7		Next	14,000	5
							Over	25,000	6

CALIFOR- NIA	From tax:		0-$ 2,630 .... 1%	$12,540-$14,510 .... 7%	9.6%.
	Single	$25.00	2,630- 4,610 2	14,510- 16,500 8	Financial institutions, other than banks, are allowed lim-
	Married	50.00	4,610- 6,590 3	16,500- 18,470 9	ited offset for personal
	Dependent	8.00	6,590- 8,580 4	18,470- 20,450 10	property taxes and license
			8,580- 10,560 5	20,450 and over 11	fees.
			10,560- 12,540 6		

Tax rates for heads of households range from 1% of taxable income not over $4,000 to 11% of taxable income over $23,750.

COLORADO	Single	$ 850	0- $1,236 .... 2.5%	$ 6,181-$ 7,418 .... 5%	5%.
	Married	1,700	1,236- 2,473 3	7,418- 8,654 .... 5.5	
	Dependent	850	2,473- 3,709 .... 3.5	8,654- 9,890 6	
			3,709- 4,945 4	9,890- 11,127 .... 6.5	
			4,945- 6,181 .... 4.5	11,127- 12,363 .... 7.5	
				12,363 and over. 8	

Surtax on intangible income over $5,000. .... 2%
Tax reduction credit applies to reduce the effective rate of tax ½ of 1% in each bracket up to $9,000.

CONNECTI- CUT	Single	$100	Rates ranging from 1% on the net capital gains and dividends of at least $20,000, up to 9% on $100,000 and over.	10%, $50 min., or .31 of 1 mill per dollar of net income, whichever is greatest. $100,000 maximum.
	Married, filing jointly	200		
	Married, filing separately	100		

DELAWARE	Single	$ 600	1st	$1,000 .... 1.4%	Next	$ 5,000 .... 8.2%	8.7%.
	Married	1,200	Next	1,000 2	Next	5,000 .... 8.4	
	Dependent	600	Next	1,000 3	Next	5,000 .... 8.8	
			Next	1,000 .... 4.2	Next	5,000 .... 9.4	
			Next	1,000 .... 5.2	Next	10,000 11	
			Next	1,000 .... 6.2	Next	10,000 .... 12.2	
			Next	2,000 .... 7.2	Over	50,000 .... 13.5	
			Next	2,000 8			

D. OF COLUMBIA	Single	$1,000	1st	$1,000 .... 2%	Next	$ 5,000 .... 7%	9% plus 10% surtax. Mini- mum $25.
	Married	2,000	Next	1,000 3	Next	3,000 8	
	Dependent	1,000	Next	1,000 4	Next	4,000 9	
			Next	1,000 5	Next	8,000 10	
			Next	1,000 6	Over	25,000 11	

FLORIDA	No personal in- come tax.			5%.

GEORGIA	Single	$1,500	1st	$1,000 .... 1%	Next	$ 2,000 .... 4%	6%.
	Married	3,000	Next	2,000 2	Next	3,000 5	
	Dependent	700	Next	2,000 3	Over	10,000 6	
			Rates are for married persons filing jointly.				

HAWAII	Single	$1,000	1st	$ 500 .... 2.25%	Next	$ 5,000 .... 8.5%	1st	$25,000	5.85%
	Married	2,000	Next	500 .... 3.25	Next	4,000 .... 9.5	Over	25,000	6.435
	Dependent	1,000	Next	500 .... 4.5	Next	6,000 10			
			Next	500 5	Next	10,000 .... 10.5			
			Next	1,000 .... 6.5	Over	30,000 11			
			Next	2,000 .... 7.5					

IDAHO	Single	$1,000	1st	$1,000 .... 2%	Next	$1,000 .... 5.5%	6.5%. Additional tax $10.
	Married	2,000	Next	1,000 4	Next	1,000 .... 6.5	
	Dependent	1,000	Next	1,000 .... 4.5	Over	5,000 .... 7.5	
			Additional $10 due from each person (joint returns deemed one person) filing return. Joint returns may split their income.				

ILLINOIS	Single	$1,000	2.5% of taxable net income.	4%.
	Married	2,000		
	Dependent	1,000		

INDIANA	Single	$1,000	1.9% of federal adjusted gross income.	3% + 3% supplemental in- come tax.
	Married	2,000		
	Dependent	500		

IOWA	From tax:		0- $1,023 .... 0.5%	$ 4,092-$ 7,161 .... 5%	1st	$ 25,000	6%
	Single	$17.00	1,023- 2,046 .... 1.25	7,161- 9,207 6	Next	75,000	8
	Married	34.00	2,046- 3,069 .... 2.75	9,207- 15,345 7	Over	100,000	10
	Dependent	12.00	3,069- 4,092 .... 3.5	15,345- 20,460 8			

State	Personal Exemptions	Individual Rates	Corporation Rates

IOWA (cont'd)

Individual Rates:
$20,460-$25,575 .... 9%
25,575- 30,690 10
30,690- 40,920 11
$40,920-$76,725 12
76,725 and over 13

Corporation Rates:
Financial institutions:
5% of taxable income.

KANSAS

Personal Exemptions:
Single $1,000
Married 2,000
Dependent 1,000

Individual Rates:
1st $2,000 ...... 2%
Next 1,000 ...... 3.5
Next 2,000 4
Next 2,000 5
Next $ 3,000 .... 6.5%
Next 10,000 .... 7.5
Next 5,000 .... 8.5
Over 25,000 .... 9.0

Corporation Rates:
4.5% + 2¼% surtax over $25,000.

KENTUCKY

Personal Exemptions: None

Individual Rates:
1st $3,000 ...... 2%
Next 1,000 3
Next 1,000 4
Next $3,000 .... 5%
Over 8,000 6

Corporation Rates:
1st $25,000 3%
Next 25,000 4
Next 50,000 5
Over 100,000 6

LOUISIANA

Personal Exemptions:
Single .... $ 6,000
Married 12,000
Dependent 1,000

Individual Rates:
1st $10,000 ...... 2%
Next 40,000 4
Over 50,000 6
Joint returns may split their income.

Corporation Rates:
Up to $ 25,000 4%
Next 25,000 4%
Next 50,000 6
Next 100,000 7
Over 200,000 8

MAINE

Personal Exemptions:
Single $1,000
Married 2,000
Dependent 1,000

Individual Rates:
1% on the first $2,000 to 10% of taxable income over $25,000.

Corporation Rates:
1st $25,000 4.95%
Over 25,000 6.93

MARYLAND

Personal Exemptions:
Single .... $ 800
Married 1,600
Dependent 800

Individual Rates:
1st $1,000 ...... 2%
Next 1,000 3
Next $1,000 .... 4%
Over 3,000 5

Corporation Rates:
7%.

MASSACHUSETTS

Personal Exemptions:
From earned income:
Single $2,000
Married (joint return) 2,000
plus up to $2,000 for spouse with lower income plus $800 if that spouse's income was under $2,000.
Dependent 700

Individual Rates:
Interest, dividends, net capital gains 10%
Earned income, annuities 5
(Plus 7.5% surtax)

Corporation Rates:
8.33% of net income plus $2.60 per $1,000 of tangible property, or $200 (whichever is greater), plus 14% surtax.

MICHIGAN

Personal Exemptions:
Single $1,500
Married 3,000
Dependent 1,500

Individual Rates:
4.6% of adjusted gross income.

Corporation Rates:
2.35%.

MINNESOTA

Personal Exemptions:
From tax:
Single ...... $ 60
Married 120
Dependent 60

Individual Rates:
0- $ 599 .... 1.6%
599- 1,198 ...... 2.2
1,198- 2,394 ...... 3.5
2,394- 3,590 ...... 5.8
3,590- 4,786 ...... 7.3
4,786- 5,982 ...... 8.8
$ 5,982-$ 8,374 ...... 10.2%
8,374- 10,766 ...... 11.5
10,766- 14,952 ...... 12.8
14,952- 23,921 ...... 14.0
23,921- 32,890 ...... 15.0
Over 32,890 ...... 16.0

Corporation Rates:
12%. Minimum, $100.

MISSISSIPPI

Personal Exemptions:
Single $6,000
Married 9,500
Dependent 1,500

Individual Rates:
1st $5,000 ...... 3%
Over 5,000 4

Corporation Rates:
1st $5,000 3%
Over 5,000 4

MISSOURI

Personal Exemptions:
Single $1,200
Married 2,400
Dependent 400

Individual Rates:
1st $1,000 ...... 1.5%
2nd 1,000 2
3rd 1,000 ...... 2.5
4th 1,000 3
5th 1,000 ...... 3.5
6th $1,000 .... 4%
7th 1,000 .... 4.5
8th 1,000 .... 5.0
9th 1,000 .... 5.5
Over 9,000 .... 6.0

Corporation Rates:
5%.

MONTANA

Personal Exemptions:
Single .... $ 800
Married 1,600
Dependent 800

Individual Rates:
1st $1,000 ...... 2%
Next 1,000 3
Next 2,000 4
Next 2,000 5
Next 2,000 6
Next 2,000 7
Next $ 4,000 .... 8%
Next 6,000 9
Next 15,000 10
Over 35,000 11
(Plus 10% surtax.)

Corporation Rates:
6.75%. Minimum tax for corporations, $50, except $10 for small business corporations.

NEBRASKA

Personal Exemptions:
Single $1,000
Married 2,000
Dependent 1,000

Individual Rates:
15% of adjusted federal income tax liability.

Corporation Rates:
1st $25,000 3.75%
Over 25,000 4.125

NEW HAMPSHIRE

Personal Exemptions:
$600 (Interest and dividend tax).

Individual Rates:
5% on income from interest and dividends.

Corporation Rates:
8%.

NEW JERSEY

Personal Exemptions:
Single $1,000
Married 2,000
Dependent 1,000

Individual Rates:
1st $20,000 ...... 2%
Over $20,000 ...... 2.5%
New York and Pennsylvania residents working in New Jersey are taxed at the same respective rate of their state of residence.

Corporation Rates:
7.25% on allocated net income of interstate corporations, plus additional tax on net worth.

NEW MEXICO

Personal Exemptions:
Single $1,000
Married 2,000
Dependent 1,000

Individual Rates:
Rates range from 0.6% of net income for 1st $2,000 to 6.7% of net income over $100,000.

Corporation Rates:
1st $1 million 4%
2nd $1 million 5%
Over $2 million 6%

State	Personal Exemptions	Individual Rates		Corporation Rates

NEW YORK
Single $ 750
Married 1,500
Dependent 750

1st	$1,000	2%	Next	$ 2,000	9%
Next	2,000	3	Next	2,000	10
Next	2,000	4	Next	2,000	11
Next	2,000	5	Next	2,000	12
Next	2,000	6	Next	2,000	13
Next	2,000	7	Over	23,000	14
Next	2,000	8			

10% of net income, min. $250 or a tax on three alternative bases, whichever produces the greatest tax.

NORTH CAROLINA
Single $1,100
Married 2,200
Dependent 700

1st	$2,000	3%	Next	$ 4,000	6%
Next	2,000	4	Over	10,000	7
Next	2,000	5			

6%.

NORTH DAKOTA
Single $1,000
Married 2,000
Dependent 1,000

1st	$3,000	1%	Next	$ 4,000	4%
Next	2,000	2	Next	18,000	5
Next	3,000	3	Over	30,000	7.5

1st	$ 3,000	2%
Next	5,000	3
Next	12,000	4
Next	10,000	5
Next	20,000	6
Over	50,000	7

OHIO
Single $ 650
Married 1,300
Dependent 650

1st	$5,000	0.5%	Next	$ 5,000	2.5%
Next	5,000	1	Next	20,000	3
Next	5,000	2	Over	40,000	3.5

4% of first $25,000 of net value; 8% of value over $25,000; or 5 mills per dollar of value, whichever is greater. Min., $50.

OKLAHOMA
Single $ 750
Married 1,500
Dependent 750

1st	$2,000	0.5%	Next	$2,500	4%
Next	3,000	1	Next	2,500	5
Next	2,500	2	Remainder	2,500	6
Next	2,500	3			

4%.

OREGON
Single $1,000
Married 2,000
Dependent 1 000

1st	$ 500	4%	Next	$1,000	8%
Next	500	5	Next	1,000	9
Next	1,000	6	Over	5,000	10
Next	1,000	7			

7½%; minimum $10.

PENNSYLVANIA
None

No personal income tax. 2.2% of specified classes of income.

10.5%.

RHODE ISLAND
Single $1,000
Married 2,000
Dependent 1 000

19% of modified federal income tax liability.

8% of net income or 40¢ per $100 of corporate net worth, whichever is the greater.

SOUTH CAROLINA
Single $ 800
Married 1,600
Dependent 800

1st	$2,000	2%	Next	$ 2,000	5%
Next	2,000	3	Next	2,000	6
Next	2,000	4	Over	10,000	7

6%; banks 4.5%.

TENNESSEE
None

6% on dividends and interest.

6%.

UTAH
Single $1,000
Married 2,000
Dependent 1,000

1st	$1,500	2.25%	Next	1,500	$169 + 5.75%
Next	1,500	$41 + 3.75	Next	1,500	255 + 6.75
Next	1,500	98 + 4.75	Over	7,500	356 + 7.75

Rates are for married taxpayers filing jointly.

4%. Minimum $25.

VERMONT
Single $1,000
Married 2,000
Dependent 1,000

23% of federal income tax liability.

1st	$ 10,000	5%
Next	15,000	6
Next	225,000	7
Next	250,000	7.5
Min. $50.		

VIRGINIA
Single $ 600
Married 1,200
Dependent 600

1st	$3,000	2%	Over	$12,000	5¾%
Next	2,000	3			
Next	7,000	5			

6%.

WEST VIRGINIA
Single $ 600
Married 1,200
Dependent 600

1st	$2,000	2.1%	Next	$ 6,000	$1,126 + 6.5%
2nd	2,000	42 + 2.3	Next	6,000	1,516 + 6.8
3rd	2,000	88 + 2.8	Next	6,000	1,924 + 7.2
4th	2,000	144 + 3.2	Next	6,000	2,356 + 7.5
5th	2,000	208 + 3.5	Next	10,000	2,806 + 7.9
6th	2,000	278 + 4.0	Next	10,000	3,596 + 8.2
7th	2,000	350 + 4.6	Next	10,000	4,416 + 8.6
8th	2,000	450 + 4.9	Next	10,000	5,276 + 8.8
9th	2,000	548 + 5.3	Next	10,000	6,156 + 9.1
10th	2,000	654 + 5.4	Next	50,000	7,066 + 9.3
11th	2,000	762 + 6.0	Next	50,000	11,716 + 9.5
Next	4,000	882 + 6.1	Over	200,000	16,466 + 9.6

6%.

WISCONSIN
From tax:
Single $20
Married 40
Dependent 20

1st	$3,300	3.4%	Next	$ 3,300	8.7%
Next	3,300	5.2	Next	5,500	9.1
Next	3,300	7.0	Next	22,000	9.5
Next	3,300	8.2	Over	44,000	10.0

1st	$1,000	2.3%
Next	1,000	2.8
Next	1,000	3.4
Next	1,000	4.5
Next	1,000	5.6
Next	1,000	6.8
Over	6,000	7.9

STATE SALES AND USE TAX RATES

SOURCE: *State Tax Guide*, Commerce Clearing House, Inc.

State	Sales	Use*	State	Sales	Use*	State	Sales	Use*
Alabama[1]	4%	4%	Kentucky[1]	5%	5%	Ohio[1]	4%	4%
Arizona[1]	4%	4%	Louisiana[1]	3%	3%	Oklahoma[1]	2%	2%
Arkansas[1]	3%	3%	Maine	5%	5%	Pennsylvania[1]	6%	6%
California[1]	4¾%	4¾%	Maryland	5%	5%	Rhode Island	6%	6%
Colorado[1]	3%	3%	Massachusetts	5%	5%	South Carolina	4%	4%
Connecticut	7½%[2]	7½%[2]	Michigan	4%	4%	South Dakota[1]	5%	5%
D.C.	6%	6%	Minnesota[1]	4%	4%	Tennessee[1]	4½%	4½%
Florida	4%	4%	Mississippi	5%	5%	Texas[1]	4%	4%
Georgia[1]	3%	3%	Missouri[1]	3⅛%	3⅛%	Utah[1]	4%	4%
Hawaii	4%	4%	Nebraska[1]	3%	3%	Vermont	3%	3%
Idaho	3%	3%	Nevada[1]	5¾%	5¾%	Virginia[1]	3%	3%
Illinois[1]	4%	4%	New Jersey	5%	5%	Washington [1]	4½%	4½%
Indiana	4%	4%	New Mexico[1]	3¾%	3¾%	West Virginia[1]	3%	3%
Iowa	3%	3%	New York[1]	4%	4%	Wisconsin[1]	4%	4%
Kansas[1]	3%	3%	North Carolina[1]	3%	3%	Wyoming[1]	3%	3%
			North Dakota	3%	3%			

*As of May 1980. The list of states imposing sales and use taxes does not include Alaska and Delaware. Alaska imposes a business license (gross receipts) tax, and Delaware imposes a merchants' and manufacturers' license tax and a use tax on leases. Other states impose occupation, admission, license, or gross receipts taxes in addition to sales and use taxes. [1] Local tax rates are additional.

CITY SALES TAX RATES

SOURCE: *All-State Sales Tax Reports*, published by Commerce Clearing House, Inc.

For these selected U.S. cities, the first rate given is the state sales tax applicable in the city. The second is the city or county rate. The third is the additional sales and use tax. The rates added together give total city sales tax rate.

City	Sales Tax Rate	City	Sales Tax Rate	City	Sales Tax Rate	City	Sales Tax Rate
Atlanta	3% + 1%	Greensboro, N.C.	3% + 1%	New York City	4% + 4%	Salt Lake	
Birmingham	4% + 1%	Houston	4% + 1%	Norfolk	3% + 1%	City	4% + ¾% + ¼%
Buffalo	4% + 3%	Kansas City,		Oklahoma City	2% + 2%	San Antonio	4% + 1%
Chicago	4% + 1%	Mo.	3⅛% + ½%	Omaha	3% + 1½%	San Diego	
Cincinnati	4% + ½%	Los Angeles		Phoenix	4% + 1%		4¾% + 1¼% + 1%
Cleveland	4% + ½%		4¾% + 1¼% + 1%	Richmond	3% + 1%	San Francisco	
Dallas	4% + 1%	Memphis	4½% + 1½%	St. Louis	3⅛% + 1%		4¾% + 1¼% + 1%
Denver	3% + 3%	New Orleans				Seattle	4½% + ½%
			3% + 2½% + 2%				

CITY INCOME TAXES

SOURCE: Commerce Clearing House, Inc.

CITIES (500,000 OR MORE)	Present rate	Date of Introduction
Alabama		
Birmingham	1.0%	1970
Maryland		
Baltimore	50% of state income tax[1]	1966
Michigan		
Detroit	2.0	1962
Missouri		
St. Louis	1.0	1948
New York		
New York	0.9 to 4.3	1966
Ohio		
Cleveland	2.0	1967
Columbus	1.5	1947
Pennsylvania		
Philadelphia	4⁵⁄₁₆	1939
Pittsburgh	1.25	1976

CITIES (125,000 TO 499,000)	Present rate	Date of Introduction
Kentucky		
Louisville	2.2%	1948
Missouri		
Kansas City	1.0	1964
Michigan		
Flint	1.0	1965
Grand Rapids	1.0	1967
Lansing	1.0	1968
Ohio		
Akron	1.8	1962
Canton	1.5	1954
Cincinnati	2.0	1954
Dayton	1.75	1949
Toledo	1.5	1967
Youngstown	1.5	1948
Pennsylvania		
Erie	1.0	1948

[1]Individual income tax only.

FINANCE/INDUSTRY/LABOR

FACTS ABOUT U.S. MONEY

SOURCE: U.S. Treasury Department

In the early days of our nation, before United States money was issued, there were in circulation English shillings, French louis d'ors, and Spanish doubloons, along with other units of those nations' money. This caused confusion and slowed up trade. The dollar was adopted (1785) by the Congress existing under the Articles of Confederation as the unit of our money, and the decimal system as the method of reckoning. In 1792 the United States monetary system was established, and the U.S. Mint began coining money at Philadelphia in 1793.

Many changes in the laws governing coinage and the denominations themselves have been made since the original 1792 act. Coins no longer in use include the half-cent, two-cent, three-cent, and 20-cent pieces, as well as the silver half dime. The five-cent nickel coin was introduced in 1866. Gold coins were struck from 1795 through 1933, in denominations ranging from $1 to $20. The minting and issuance of gold coins were terminated by Section 5 of the Gold Reserve Act of 1934.

President Johnson signed (July 23, 1965) an historic bill providing for the first major change in U.S. coinage in more than a century. Silver was eliminated altogether from the dime and quarter and substantially reduced in the half dollar.

On Dec. 31, 1970, President Nixon signed the Bank Holding Company Act calling for the removal of all silver from silver dollars and half dollars. This legislation also authorized a silver dollar with a design emblematic of the symbolic eagle of the Apollo 11 landing on the Moon. Once adopted, a coin design may not be changed more often than once in 25 years without specific legislation.

The selection of coin designs is usually made by the Director of the Mint, with the approval of the Secretary of the Treasury. However, Congress has, in a few instances, prescribed them. For example, as a part of the bicentennial celebration of Washington's birth in 1932, Congress declared that the likeness of our first President should appear on the quarter dollar.

The Lincoln penny was the first portrait coin of a regular series minted by the United States. The 100th anniversary of Lincoln's birth aroused sentiment sufficiently strong to overcome a long-prevailing popular prejudice against the use of portraits on coins. A new reverse design was adopted in 1959, when the sesquicentennial of Lincoln's birth was observed. The familiar likeness on the obverse remains unchanged. Others which followed are the 25-cent coin, with Washington's profile, first minted in 1932; the five-cent piece honoring Jefferson, adopted in 1938; the FDR dime, introduced in 1946, and in 1971 the Eisenhower silver dollar, manufacture of which was discontinued in December 1978.

In July 1979, a new, smaller dollar coin was introduced whose size is between the half dollar and the quarter; its smaller size will save in the cost of dollar bill production and help the circulation of the little-used dollar coin. This coin bears the likeness of women's suffrage leader Susan B. Anthony.

Portraits of living persons on American coins are extremely rare and confined to a few commemorative issues of limited minting.

The year 1976 marked the 200th anniversary of American Independence. One of the most far-reaching Government observances was the issuance of specially designed dollars, half dollars, and quarters. Circulation commenced on July 4, 1975, and production ended on December 31, 1976.

The design selection used for American paper currency, including the selection of portraits, is a responsibility of the Secretary of the Treasury, who acts with the advice of the Director of the Bureau of Engraving and Printing, the Treasurer of the United States, and others. By tradition, portraits used on present paper money are those of deceased statesmen of assured historical significance.

The first regular issue of United States currency, the Demand notes that were issued in 1861, carried the portraits of Alexander Hamilton (first Secretary of the Treasury) on the $5 denomination and of Abraham Lincoln on the $10 denomination.

Those design features of U.S. paper currency that have historical or idealistic significance, as distinct from purely ornamental or security implications, include the following:

(1) The New Treasury Seal: Approved on January 29, 1968, the seal of the Department of the Treasury is found on the face of each note. Balance scales, a key, and a chevron with 13 stars appear on the seal, along with the date "1789," the year the Department was created.

(2) The obverse and reverse of the Great Seal of the United States are reproduced on the backs of $1 bills.

(3) Portraits of great Americans used on the face of currency.

(4) Pictures of famous buildings, monuments or events used on the back of currency.

All notes of the same denomination bear the same portrait. Designs on U.S. currency (Federal Reserve Notes) now in circulation are as follows:

Denomination and Class	Portrait	Back
$1 Fed. Reserve Note	Washington	Obverse and reverse of Great Seal of U.S.
$2 Fed. Reserve Note	Jefferson	John Trumbull's "Declaration of Independence"
$5 Fed. Reserve Note	Lincoln	Lincoln Memorial
$10 Fed. Reserve Note	Hamilton	U.S. Treasury Building
$20 Fed. Reserve Note	Jackson	White House
$50 Fed. Reserve Note	Grant	U.S. Capitol
$100 Fed. Reserve Note	Franklin	Independence Hall

Notes of the higher denominations ($500, $1,000, $5,000, and $10,000) have not been printed for many years. As they are returned to Federal Reserve banks, they are removed from circulation and destroyed. The portraits selected for these small-sized notes were McKinley for the $500, Cleveland for the $1,000, Madison for the $5,000, and Chase for the $10,000.

The motto "In God We Trust" owes its presence on U.S. coins largely to the increased religious sentiment existing during the Civil War. Salmon P. Chase, then Secretary of the Treasury, received a number of appeals from devout persons throughout the country urging that the Deity be suitably recognized on our coins as it was on the coins of other nations.

The approved motto first made its appearance on the two-cent coin, authorized by Act of Congress (April 22, 1864), but its use has not been uninterrupted. In 1866 the motto was introduced on the double eagle, eagle, and half eagle gold coins and on the silver dollar, half dollar, and the quarter dollar pieces. It was included in the nickel five-cent design from 1866 to 1883, when it was dropped and not restored until the introduction of the Jefferson nickel in 1938. The motto has been in continuous use on the penny since 1909 and on the dime since 1916.

A law passed by the 84th Congress and approved by the President on July 11, 1955, provides that "In God We Trust" shall appear on all United States paper currency and coins.

By a joint resolution of the 84th Congress, approved by the President on July 30, 1956, "In God We Trust" was declared to be the official motto of the United States.

COMPOUND INTEREST TABLE

What a $1 deposit, compounded monthly, grows to over a thirty-year period.

Interest Rates

Years	5%	5¼%	5½%	5¾%	6%	6¼%	6½%	6¾%	7%	7¼%	7½%	7¾%	8%
1	1.0512	1.0538	1.0564	1.0590	1.0617	1.0643	1.0670	1.0696	1.0723	1.0750	1.0776	1.0803	1.0830
1½	1.0778	1.0812	1.0858	1.0899	1.0939	1.0980	1.1021	1.1062	1.1104	1.1145	1.1187	1.1229	1.1270
2	1.1049	1.1105	1.1160	1.1216	1.1272	1.1328	1.1384	1.1441	1.1498	1.1555	1.1613	1.1671	1.1729
2½	1.1329	1.1399	1.1470	1.1542	1.1614	1.1686	1.1759	1.1833	1.1906	1.1981	1.2055	1.2130	1.2206
3	1.1615	1.1702	1.1789	1.1878	1.1967	1.2056	1.2147	1.2238	1.2329	1.2422	1.2514	1.2608	1.2702
3½	1.1908	1.2012	1.2117	1.2223	1.2330	1.2438	1.2547	1.2657	1.2767	1.2879	1.2991	1.3105	1.3219
4	1.2209	1.2331	1.2455	1.2579	1.2705	1.2832	1.2960	1.3090	1.3221	1.3353	1.3486	1.3621	1.3757
4½	1.2517	1.2658	1.2801	1.2945	1.3091	1.3238	1.3387	1.3538	1.3690	1.3844	1.4000	1.4157	1.4316
5	1.2834	1.2994	1.3157	1.3322	1.3489	1.3657	1.3828	1.4001	1.4176	1.4354	1.4533	1.4715	1.4898
5½	1.3158	1.3339	1.3523	1.3709	1.3898	1.4090	1.4284	1.4480	1.4680	1.4882	1.5087	1.5214	1.5504
6	1.3490	1.3693	1.3899	1.4108	1.4320	1.4536	1.4754	1.4976	1.5201	1.5429	1.5661	1.5896	1.6135
6½	1.3831	1.4057	1.4286	1.4519	1.4755	1.4996	1.5240	1.5489	1.5741	1.5997	1.6258	1.6522	1.6791
7	1.4180	1.4430	1.4683	1.4941	1.5204	1.5471	1.5742	1.6019	1.6300	1.6586	1.6877	1.7173	1.7474
7½	1.4539	1.4813	1.5092	1.5376	1.5666	1.5961	1.6261	1.6567	1.6879	1.7196	1.7520	1.7849	1.8185
8	1.4906	1.5206	1.5511	1.5823	1.6141	1.6466	1.6797	1.7134	1.7478	1.7829	1.8187	1.8552	1.8925
8½	1.5282	1.5609	1.5943	1.6284	1.6631	1.6987	1.7350	1.7721	1.8099	1.8485	1.8880	1.9283	1.9694
9	1.5668	1.6023	1.6386	1.6758	1.7137	1.7525	1.7922	1.8327	1.8742	1.9166	1.9599	2.0042	2.0495
9½	1.6064	1.6449	1.6842	1.7245	1.7658	1.8080	1.8512	1.8954	1.9407	1.9871	2.0346	2.0832	2.1329
10	1.6470	1.6885	1.7311	1.7747	1.8194	1.8652	1.9122	1.9603	2.0097	2.0602	2.1121	2.1652	2.2196
10½	1.6886	1.7333	1.7792	1.8263	1.8747	1.9243	1.9752	2.0274	2.0810	2.1361	2.1925	2.2505	2.3099
11	1.7313	1.7793	1.8287	1.8795	1.9316	1.9852	2.0402	2.0968	2.1549	2.2147	2.2760	2.3391	2.4039
11½	1.7750	1.8266	1.8796	1.9342	1.9903	2.0480	2.1075	2.1686	2.2315	2.2962	2.3627	2.4312	2.5016
12	1.8198	1.8750	1.9319	1.9904	2.0508	2.1129	2.1769	2.2428	2.3107	2.3807	2.4527	2.5269	2.6034
12½	1.8658	1.9248	1.9856	2.0483	2.1130	2.1798	2.2486	2.3196	2.3928	2.4683	2.5462	2.6265	2.7093
13	1.9130	1.9759	2.0408	2.1079	2.1772	2.2488	2.3227	2.3990	2.4778	2.5591	2.6431	2.7299	2.8195
13½	1.9613	2.0283	2.0976	2.1693	2.2434	2.3200	2.3992	2.4811	2.5658	2.6533	2.7438	2.8374	2.9341
14	2.0108	2.0821	2.1560	2.2324	2.3115	2.3934	2.4782	2.5660	2.6569	2.7509	2.8483	2.9491	3.0535
14½	2.0616	2.1374	2.2159	2.2974	2.3817	2.4692	2.5599	2.6538	2.7512	2.8522	2.9568	3.0653	3.1777
15	2.1137	2.1941	2.2776	2.3642	2.4541	2.5474	2.6442	2.7447	2.8489	2.9572	3.0695	3.1860	3.3069
15½	2.1671	2.2524	2.3409	2.4330	2.5286	2.6280	2.7313	2.8386	2.9501	3.0660	3.1864	3.3115	3.4414
16	2.2218	2.3121	2.4061	2.5038	2.6055	2.7112	2.8213	2.9358	3.0549	3.1788	3.3077	3.4419	3.5814
16½	2.2780	2.3735	2.4730	2.5766	2.6846	2.7971	2.9142	3.0363	3.1634	3.2958	3.4337	3.5774	3.7271
17	2.3355	2.4365	2.5418	2.6516	2.7662	2.8856	3.0102	3.1402	3.2757	3.4171	3.5645	3.7183	3.8786
17½	2.3945	2.5011	2.6125	2.7288	2.8502	2.9770	3.1094	3.2477	3.3921	3.5429	3.7003	3.8647	4.0364
18	2.4550	2.5675	2.6852	2.8082	2.9368	3.0712	3.2118	3.3588	3.5125	3.6732	3.8413	4.0169	4.2006
18½	2.5170	2.6357	2.7598	2.8899	3.0260	3.1685	3.3176	3.4738	3.6373	3.8084	3.9876	4.1751	4.3714
19	2.5806	2.7056	2.8366	2.9739	3.1179	3.2688	3.4269	3.5927	3.7665	3.9486	4.1395	4.3395	4.5492
19½	2.6458	2.7774	2.9155	3.0605	3.2126	3.3723	3.5398	3.7157	3.9002	4.0939	4.2971	4.5104	4.7342
20	2.7126	2.8511	2.9966	3.1495	3.3102	3.4790	3.6564	3.8429	4.0387	4.2446	4.4608	4.6880	4.9268
20½	2.7812	2.9268	3.0800	3.2412	3.4108	3.5892	3.7769	3.9744	4.1822	4.4008	4.6037	4.8727	5.1272
21	2.8514	3.0045	3.1657	3.3355	3.5144	3.7028	3.9013	4.1104	4.3307	4.5627	4.8071	5.0646	5.3357
21½	2.9235	3.0842	3.2537	3.4325	3.6211	3.8200	4.0298	4.2511	4.4845	4.7306	4.9902	5.2640	5.5527
22	2.9973	3.1660	3.3442	3.5324	3.7311	3.9410	4.1626	4.3966	4.6438	4.9047	5.1803	5.4173	5.7786
22½	3.0730	3.2501	3.4373	3.6352	3.8445	4.0658	4.2997	4.5471	4.8087	5.0852	5.3776	5.6868	6.0136
23	3.1507	3.3663	3.5329	3.7410	3.9613	4.1945	4.4134	4.7028	4.9795	5.2724	5.5825	5.9017	6.2582
23½	3.2302	3.4249	3.6311	3.8498	4.0816	4.3273	4.5877	4.8637	5.1563	5.4664	5.7951	6.1435	6.5127
24	3.3118	3.5157	3.7321	3.9618	4.2056	4.4643	4.7388	5.0302	5.3394	5.6676	6.0159	6.3854	6.7776
24½	3.3955	3.6090	3.8360	4.0771	4.3333	4.6056	4.8949	5.2024	5.5291	5.8762	6.2450	6.6369	7.0533
25	3.4813	3.7048	3.9427	4.1957	4.4650	4.7514	5.0562	5.3804	5.7254	6.0924	6.4829	6.8983	7.3402
25½	3.5692	3.8031	4.0523	4.3178	4.6006	4.9019	5.2228	5.5646	5.9288	6.3166	6.7928	7.1699	7.6387
26	3.6594	3.9041	4.1651	4.4434	4.7404	5.0570	5.3948	5.7551	6.1393	6.5491	6.9862	7.4523	7.9494
26½	3.7518	4.0077	4.2809	4.5727	4.8844	5.2172	5.5725	5.9521	6.3573	6.7901	7.2523	7.7458	8.2727
27	3.8466	4.1141	4.4000	4.7058	5.0327	5.3823	5.7561	6.1558	6.5831	7.0400	7.5285	8.0508	8.6092
27½	3.9438	4.2232	4.5224	4.8427	5.1856	5.5527	5.9457	6.3665	6.8169	7.2991	7.8153	8.3679	8.9594
28	4.0434	4.3353	4.6482	4.9836	5.3431	5.7285	6.1416	6.5844	7.0590	7.5677	8.1130	8.6974	9.3238
28½	4.1456	4.4504	4.7775	5.1286	5.5055	5.9099	6.3439	6.8098	7.3097	7.8462	8.4220	9.0399	9.7030
29	4.2503	4.5685	4.9104	5.2778	5.6727	6.0970	6.5529	7.0429	7.5693	8.1350	8.7428	9.3959	10.0976
29½	4.3577	4.6897	5.0467	5.4314	5.8450	6.2900	6.7688	7.2839	7.8381	8.4344	9.0758	9.7659	10.5083
30	4.4677	4.8192	5.1874	5.5894	6.0226	6.4872	6.9918	7.5332	8.1165	8.7448	9.4215	10.1505	10.9357

GOLD PRODUCTION

Source: U.S. Bureau of Mines (figures in millions of dollars at $35 per fine ounce through 1971, $38 per fine ounce in 1972 and 1973, and $42.22 per fine ounce beginning in 1974)

	1960	1965	1970	1974	1975	1976	1977	1978	1979	1980[1]
South Africa	784.4	1,069.0	1,128.0	1,029.7	968.4	968.4	950.0	956.3	954.9	914.9
Canada	162.0	125.6	84.3	71.7	69.8	71.2	72.5	71.8	66.4	67.6
United States	58.8	58.6	63.5	47.6	44.4	44.2	46.5	42.2	40.9	39.3
Other Africa	67.7	74.6	48.9	49.4	44.8	54.9	43.0	38.5	38.2	34.6
Ghana	30.8	26.7	24.6	25.9	22.1	22.5	20.3	17.0	17.3	15.1
Zimbabwe	19.7	19.2	15.3	14.1	14.9	16.3	17.0	16.8	16.3	15.2
Zaire	11.1	2.3	6.2	5.5	4.4	4.3	3.4	3.2	3.4	3.2
Latin America	50.2	39.8	32.4	42.4	52.4	61.0	57.3	57.2	65.1	86.4
Colombia	15.2	11.2	7.1	11.2	13.0	12.6	10.9	10.4	11.4	12.2
Mexico	10.5	7.6	6.9	5.7	6.1	6.9	9.0	8.5	8.0	13.4
Nicaragua	6.9	5.4	4.0	3.5	3.0	3.2	2.8	2.5	2.5	2.3
Peru	4.9	3.7	3.3	4.2	3.3	3.4	4.1	4.4	5.0	6.5
Asia	35.6	41.8	44.2	47.3	44.8	45.7	49.4	50.5	51.6	56.0
Philippines	14.4	15.4	21.1	22.7	21.2	21.2	23.6	25.7	23.1	27.2
Japan	11.8	18.1	24.8	5.9	6.1	5.8	7.2	3.5	5.4	5.3
India	5.6	4.6	3.6	4.3	3.8	4.3	3.9	3.7	3.6	3.7
Europe*	12.2	—	10.4	25.2	21.5	28.3	27.2	23.0	23.7	24.7
Oceania	43.3	36.1	26.7	53.0	51.1	76.1	59.7	60.8	55.9	52.6
Australia	38.0	30.7	21.9	21.6	22.2	21.0	26.2	27.4	24.7	24.9
World Total	1,214	1,446	1,438	1,366	1,297	1,350	1,306	1,301	1,417	1,405

[1]Estimated.   * Data exclude USSR.

COMPANIES WITH THE LARGEST NUMBER OF COMMON STOCKHOLDERS

Source: New York Stock Exchange (Figures rounded to nearest thousand)

EARLY 1981

Company	Stockholders	Company	Stockholders
American Tel. & Tel.	3,026,000	duPont de Nemours	213,000
General Motors	1,191,000	Niagara Mohawk Power	211,000
International Business Machines	737,000	Chrysler Corporation	209,000
Exxon Corporation	697,000	Atlantic Richfield	203,000
General Electric	524,000	Northeast Utilities	196,000
General Tel. & Electronics	486,000	Southern California Edison	193,000
Texaco Incorporated	394,000	Standard Oil (Indiana)	188,000
Sears, Roebuck	350,000	Ohio Edison	183,000
Ford Motor Co.	346,000	Virginia Electric & Power	183,000
Southern Company	345,000	Westinghouse Electric	176,000
American Electric Power	338,000	Middle South Utilities	175,000
Gulf Oil	312,000	Consumers Power	172,000
Mobil Corporation	272,000	BankAmerica	171,000
Commonwealth Edison	269,000	Union Electric	169,000
Pacific Gas & Electric	261,000	Union Carbide Corp.	164,000
Philadelphia Electric	253,000	Occidental Petroleum	161,000
RCA	252,000	Long Island Lighting	160,000
U. S. Steel	248,000	Pennsylvania Power	157,000
Standard Oil of California	247,000	General Public Utilities	151,000
Detroit Edison	242,000	Columbia Gas System	144,000
Consolidated Edison	237,000	Pan American World Airways	140,000
Eastman Kodak	234,000	Bethlehem Steel	139,000
Tenneco Inc.	232,000	Transamerica Corporation	138,000
Public Service Electric & Gas	231,000	Duquesne Light	138,000
International Tel. & Tel.	214,000	Greyhound Corporation	137,000

U.S. CORPORATE PROFITS (In billions of dollars)

Source: U.S. Department of Commerce, Bureau of Economic Analysis

	Total pre-tax profits	Tax liability	After-tax profits	Dividends	Undistributed profits
1929	10.0	1.4	8.6	5.8	2.8
1930	3.7	.8	2.9	5.5	− 2.6
1931	− .4	.5	− .9	4.1	− 4.9
1932	− 2.3	.4	− 2.7	2.5	− 5.2
1933	1.0	.5	.4	2.0	− 1.6
1935	3.6	1.0	2.6	2.8	− .2
1940	10.0	2.8	7.2	4.0	3.2
1945	19.8	10.7	9.1	4.6	4.5
1950	42.9	18.0	25.0	8.8	16.2
1955	49.2	22.0	27.2	10.3	16.9
1960	49.8	22.7	27.1	12.8	14.3
1965	77.2	30.9	46.3	19.1	27.2
1969	86.7	39.5	47.2	22.5	24.7
1970	75.4	34.2	41.3	22.5	18.8
1971	86.6	37.5	49.0	22.9	26.1
1972	100.6	41.6	58.9	24.4	34.5
1973	125.6	49.0	76.6	27.0	49.6
1974	136.7	51.6	85.1	29.9	55.2
1975	132.1	50.6	81.5	30.8	50.7
1976	166.3	63.8	102.5	37.4	65.1
1977	192.6	72.6	120.0	39.9	80.1
1978	223.3	83.0	140.3	44.6	95.7
1979	255.4	87.6	167.8	50.2	117.6
1980	210.4	80.7	129.7	37.5	92.2

FOREIGN EXCHANGE RATES: 1949-1981   Source: Federal Reserve Bulletin (in U.S. cents)

Year	United Kingdom (pound)	Canada (dollar)	Nether-lands (guilder)	West Germany* (deutsche mark)	Switzer-land (franc)	France† (franc)	Belgium (franc)	Japan‡ (yen)	Italy (lira)
1949	368.72	92.88	34.53	NA	23.31	.3017	2.20	NA	.1699
1950	280.07	91.47	26.25	23.84	23.14	.2858	1.99	NA	.1601
1951	279.96	94.94	26.26	23.84	23.06	.2856	1.99	NA	.1600
1953	281.27	101.65	26.34	23.84	23.32	.2856	2.00	NA	.1600
1956	279.57	101.60	26.11	23.79	23.33	.2855	2.00	.2779	.1600
1958	280.98	103.03	26.42	23.85	23.33	.2858	2.00	.2779	.1601
1960	280.76	103.12	26.51	23.98	23.15	20.39	2.00	.2778	.1610
1962	280.78	93.56	27.76	25.01	23.12	20.41	2.01	.2771	.1611
1964	279.21	92.69	27.72	25.16	23.15	20.40	2.01	.2763	.1601
1966	279.30	92.81	27.63	25.01	23.11	20.35	2.01	.2760	.1601
1968	239.35	92.80	27.63	25.05	23.17	20.19	2.00	.2774	.1604
1970	239.59	95.80	27.65	27.42	23.20	18.09	2.01	.2792	.1595
1972	250.08	100.94	31.15	31.36	26.19	19.83	2.27	.3300	.1713
1974	234.03	102.26	37.27	38.72	33.69	20.81	2.57	.3430	.1537
1976	180.48	101.41	37.85	39.74	40.01	20.94	2.59	.3374	.1204
1977	174.49	94.11	40.75	43.08	41.71	20.34	2.79	.3734	.1133
1978	191.84	87.73	46.28	49.87	56.28	22.22	3.18	.4798	.1178
1979	212.24	85.39	49.84	54.56	60.12	23.50	3.41	.4583	.1204
1980	232.58	85.53	50.37	55.09	59.70	23.69	3.42	.4431	.1169
1981 (March)	223.19	83.94	42.91	47.50	52.04	20.15	2.90	.4790	.0970

*Beginning with June 1950. †Beginning with 1960, 100 old francs = 1 new franc. ‡Beginning with November 1956. NA = Not Available.

MONEY DEPRECIATION: ANNUAL RATES   Source: International Monetary Fund

The value of money is here measured by reciprocals of official cost-of-living or consumer price indexes. (1970 = 100)

	INDEXES: VALUE OF MONEY 1979	1980	RATE OF DEPRECI-ATION 1970-80		INDEXES: VALUE OF MONEY 1979	1980	RATE OF DEPRECI-ATION 1970-80		INDEXES: VALUE OF MONEY 1979	1980	RATE OF DEPRECI-ATION 1970-80
Switzerland	64	62	5.0	Dominican				Spain	29	25	15.0
Germany, West	64	61	5.1	Republic	43	37	10.3	Korea, South	29	22	16.3
Austria	58	54	6.3	Australia	41	37	10.5	Mexico	27	21	16.7
Egypt	63	51	6.9	South Africa	42	37	10.6	Indonesia	23	19	17.8
Netherlands	53	49	7.2	Syria	43	36	10.8	Jamaica	25	19	17.9
Belgium	53	49	7.4	Jordan	38	36	11.0	Portugal	22	19	18.2
United States	53	47	7.8	Finland	39	34	11.2	Yugoslavia	24	19	18.2
India	53	47	7.8	Kenya	36	32	12.0	Colombia	19	15	20.0
Canada	51	46	8.0	Saudi Arabia	33	32	12.2	Peru	11	7	30.1
Norway	50	44	8.4	Ecuador	35	30	12.6	Turkey	14	7	31.0
Venezuela	54	44	8.4	New Zealand	36	31	12.5	Brazil	9	5	35.4
Japan	46	42	9.0	Trinidad & Tobago	34	29	13.0	Ghana	5	3	41.2
Sweden	47	41	9.2	Philippines	33	28	13.5	Israel	7	3	41.7
Guatemala	44	40	9.5	Ireland	33	28	13.7	Uruguay	*	*	62.5
France	45	40	9.6	United Kingdom	33	28	13.7	Argentina	*	*	119.2
Denmark	44	39	9.6	Italy	33	27	13.8	Chile	*	*	130.2
				Greece	33	26	14.3				

*Less than 1.

CENTRAL BANK DISCOUNT RATES

Source: International Monetary Fund (end of period quotations in percent per annum)

	1963	1965	1967	1969	1971	1973	1975	1977	1978	1979	1980	1981[1]
United States	3.50	4.50	4.50	6.00	4.50	7.50	6.00	6.00	9.50	12.00	13.00	13.00
United Kingdom	4.00	6.00	8.00	8.00	5.00	13.00	11.25	7.00	12.50	17.00	14.00	14.00
Industrial Europe												
Austria	4.50	4.50	3.75	4.75	5.00	7.75	6.00	5.50	4.50	3.75	6.75	6.75
Belgium	4.25	4.75	4.00	7.50	5.50	9.00	6.00	9.00	6.00	10.50	12.00	12.00
France	4.00	3.50	3.50	8.00	6.50	11.00	8.00	9.50	9.50	9.50	9.50	9.50
Germany	3.00	4.00	3.00	6.00	4.00	7.00	3.50	3.00	3.00	6.00	7.50	7.50
Italy	3.50	3.50	3.50	3.50	3.50	6.50	6.00	11.50	10.50	15.00	16.50	16.50
Netherlands	3.50	4.50	4.50	6.00	5.00	8.00	4.50	4.50	6.50	9.50	8.00	8.00
Norway	3.50	3.50	3.50	4.50	4.50	4.50	5.00	6.00	7.00	9.00	9.00	9.00
Sweden	4.00	5.50	6.00	7.00	5.00	5.00	6.00	8.00	6.50	9.00	10.00	12.00
Switzerland	2.00	2.50	3.00	3.75	3.75	4.50	3.00	1.50	1.00	2.00	3.00	3.00
Canada	4.00	4.75	6.00	8.00	4.75	7.25	9.00	7.50	10.75	14.00	17.26	17.11
Japan	5.84	5.48	5.84	6.25	4.75	9.00	6.50	4.25	3.50	6.25	7.25	7.25

[1]January.

MONETARY TERMS

Balance of Payment—A nation's transactions with other nations, for trade, investment, tourism, foreign aid, and the like. A deficit occurs when more is paid out than a nation earns.

Balance of Trade—That part of the balance of payments covering exports and imports of goods.

Devalue or Devaluation—The act of changing a currency's par value downward.

Exchange Control—Government controls on purchase of foreign currencies for various purposes, aimed at protecting a nation's reserves.

Foreign Exchange—The term applied to foreign currencies.

Foreign Exchange Market—The market in which foreign currencies are

bought and sold and the daily trading price in terms of dollars is set. It is not a specific place but rather a series of trading "desks," usually at banks.

Par Value—The international value of a currency, expressed as so many ounces of gold or so many U.S. dollars and cents.

Reserves—A nation's holdings of gold plus certain foreign currencies.

Reserve Currency—A currency in which other nations hold part of their reserves.

"Run" or "Attack"—A mass wave of selling of a particular currency on the foreign exchange markets.

Support—Official intervention in the foreign exchange market by a nation's central bank to hold up the price of the nation's currency.

U.S. GROSS NATIONAL PRODUCT†

SOURCE: U.S. Department of Commerce, Bureau of Economic Analysis

	1929	1933	1945	1955	1965	1975	1979	1980
Gross National Product	103.4	55.8	212.3	399.3	688.1	1528.8	2413.9	2626.5
GNP in Constant (1972) Dollars	314.7	222.1	559.0	654.8	925.9	1202.1	1483.0	1480.9
Personal Consumption Expenditures	77.3	45.8	119.5	253.7	430.2	980.4	1510.9	1672.3
Durable goods	9.2	3.5	8.0	38.6	62.8	132.9	212.3	211.9
Nondurable goods	37.7	22.3	71.9	122.9	188.6	409.3	602.2	675.4
Services	30.3	20.1	39.6	92.1	178.7	438.2	696.3	785.1
Gross Private Domestic Investment	16.2	1.4	10.6	68.4	112.0	189.1	415.8	395.4
Fixed Investment	14.5	3.0	11.7	62.4	102.5	200.6	398.3	400.8
Nonresidential	10.5	2.4	10.1	38.3	71.3	149.1	279.7	295.4
Structures	5.0	0.9	2.8	14.4	26.1	52.9	96.3	108.6
Producers' durable equipment	5.5	1.4	7.3	23.9	45.1	96.3	183.4	186.8
Residential	4.0	0.6	1.6	24.1	31.2	51.5	118.6	105.3
Nonfarm structures	3.8	0.5	1.4	23.0	29.9	49.5	113.9	100.3
Farm structures	0.2	*	0.1	0.6	0.6	0.9	1.8	2.0
Producers' durable equipment	*	*	*	0.4	0.7	1.1	2.9	3.0
Change in business inventories	1.7	−1.6	−1.0	6.0	9.5	−11.5	17.5	−5.3
Net exports of goods and services	1.1	0.4	−0.6	2.2	7.6	20.4	13.4	24.2
Government purchases	8.8	8.2	82.8	75.0	136.4	338.9	473.8	534.6
Federal	1.4	2.1	74.6	44.5	67.3	123.3	167.9	198.9
National defense	—	—	73.5	38.4	49.4	83.9	111.2	131.7
Non-defense	—	—	1.1	6.0	17.8	39.4	56.7	67.2
State and local	7.4	6.1	8.2	30.6	71.1	215.6	305.9	335.7

†In billions of dollars. * Less than $0.1 billion.

GROSS DOMESTIC OR NATIONAL PRODUCT: SELECTED NATIONS 1980

SOURCE: Dr. Herbert Block, The Planetary Product

	GNP Total ($ Millions)	GNP Per Capita (Dollars)	Population Mid-1980 (Millions)		GNP Total ($ Millions)	GNP Per Capita (Dollars)	Population Mid-1980 (Millions)
North America				Israel	18,995	5,052	3.76
†Canada	235,333	9,864	23.86	Jordan	2,592	1,112	2.33
UNITED STATES	2,626,500	11,596	226.51	Kuwait	17,532	12,920	1.36
Western Europe				Qatar	5,508	31,838	0.17
†Austria	53,358	7,127	7.49	Saudi Arabia	83,891	12,521	7.00
†Belgium	85,064	8,619	9.87	Syria	8,570	988	8.68
†Denmark	50,745	9,878	5.14	†Turkey	39,530	865	45.70
†Finland	33,423	7,004	4.77	United Arab Emirates	9,556	10,600	0.90
†France	508,085	9,479	53.60	**East Asia**			
Germany, West	642,422	10,509	61.13	China, Rep. of (Taiwan)	32,510	1,826	17.81
†Greece	29,311	3,089	9.49	Hong Kong	19,194	3,952	4.86
†Iceland	1,600	7,018	0.23	Indonesia	63,111	417	151.20
†Ireland	12,423	3,770	3.30	†Japan	986,053	8,426	117.03
†Italy	302,982	5,300	57.17	Korea, South	42,439	1,067	39.77
†Luxembourg	3,221	8,972	0.36	Malaysia	18,977	1,355	14.01
†Netherlands	99,421	7,048	14.11	Philippines	28,809	589	48.88
†Norway	40,437	9,887	4.09	Singapore	10,932	4,580	2.39
†Portugal	19,960	2,009	9.93	Thailand	28,504	601	47.42
†Spain	114,825	3,022	38.00	**Oceania**			
†Sweden	92,335	11,111	8.31	†Australia	132,676	9,115	14.56
†Switzerland	64,613	10,245	6.31	†New Zealand	19,496	6,227	3.13
†United Kingdom	297,978	5,340	55.80	**Latin America**			
Africa (Excluding Egypt)				Argentina	56,778	2,089	27.18
Algeria	27,914	1,483	18.83	Bolivia	3,704	692	5.36
Ethiopia	3,846	118	32.59	Brazil	251,500	2,067	121.65
Gabon	2,470	4,186	0.59	Chile	20,710	1,880	11.01
Ghana	6,084	501	12.13	Colombia	26,297	983	26.75
Ivory Coast	7,483	932	8.03	Dominican Republic	6,067	1,066	5.69
Kenya	4,597	288	15.94	Ecuador	8,437	1,052	8.02
Libya	22,020	7,357	2.99	Guatemala	7,529	1,067	7.06
Morocco	12,691	605	20.97	Jamaica	3,631	1,602	2.27
Nigeria	54,271	704	77.09	Mexico	138,006	2,045	67.50
South Africa	47,982	1,690	28.39	Panama	3,212	1,680	1.91
Sudan	6,458	346	18.67	Peru	21,082	1,200	17.61
Tanzania	3,532	197	17.91	Uruguay	4,990	1,704	2.93
Tunisia	7,811	1,207	6.47	Venezuela	51,044	3,398	15.02
Uganda	3,505	256	13.69	**Communist Countries**			
Zaire	4,140	142	28.92	Albania	2,160	805	2.68
Zambia	2,654	455	5.83	Bulgaria	29,889	3,370	8.87
Zimbabwe	3,784	509	7.44	China, People's Rep.	592,000	576	1,027.00
South Asia				Cuba	13,985	1,407	9.94
Afghanistan	3,115	207	15.03	Czechoslovakia	85,000	5,542	15.34
Bangladesh	11,116	123	90.49	Germany, East	99,619	5,945	16.76
Burma	6,416	186	34.41	Hungary	39,373	3,665	10.74
India	137,363	202	680.06	Korea, North	15,914	824	19.32
Pakistan	20,688	239	86.47	Mongolia	1,324	782	1.69
Sri Lanka	4,803	324	14.85	Poland	124,905	3,513	35.56
Near East				Romania	89,328	4,017	22.24
Egypt	24,102	573	42.04	USSR	1,280,616	4,820	265.71
Iran	43,661	1,128	38.72	Vietnam	6,000	113	53.00
Iraq	35,615	2,666	13.36	Yugoslavia	72,302	3,232	22.37
				WORLD	10,490,220	2,338	4,486.92

†Gross Domestic Product

OIL IMPORTS: 1979-1980 Source: Social and Economic Statistics Administration, U.S. Dept. of Commerce

(Quantity in barrels, value in dollars.)

	General Imports Calendar Year 1979		General Imports Calendar Year 1980	
Country of Origin	Net Quantity	F.a.s. Value	Net Quantity	F.a.s. Value
Canada	104,674,468	$ 1,887,827,000	75,691,312	$ 2,207,042,980
Mexico	162,740,395	3,040,753,000		
Guatemala			640,229	19,633,968
Mexico			194,172,141	5,926,624,931
Trinidad	45,204,148	884,336,000	43,668,377	1,495,584,999
Colombia	219,911	2,570,000		
Argentina			355,423	9,162,400
Ecuador	12,927,052	281,385,000		
Brazil			342,807	10,101,492
Peru	16,193,100	399,973,000		
Ecuador			7,985,722	276,422,612
Venezuela	133,032,215	2,127,676,000		
Peru			14,885,543	541,971,949
Italy	180,616	8,610,000		
Venezuela			70,984,862	1,694,829,171
Norway	34,274,840	713,127,000		
Norway			61,628,643	2,075,375,629
United Kingdom	68,442,200	1,391,133,000	56,779,053	1,922,460,779
Iran	119,928,183	2,565,097,000	8,475,152	285,188,277
Iraq	33,745,076	612,941,000		
Iraq			11,508,933	347,482,145
Kuwait	2,485,385	55,351,000		
Kuwait			12,509,186	445,467,150
Oman	14,030,808	248,768,000	9,745,283	330,478,599
Qatar	13,104,486	278,896,000		
Oman			7,091,334	236,265,427
Saudi Arabia	490,353,252	7,855,478,000		
Qatar			452,951,677	12,231,167,618
Syria	5,763,620	152,883,000		
Saudi Arabia			603,797	20,761,556
United Arab Emirates	109,991,603	1,963,047,000		
Syria			66,101,253	1,971,678,898
Brunei	2,279,941	40,335,000		
United Arab Emirates			5,293,232	185,200,284
China (PRC)	4,109,411	71,789,000		
Brunei			763,970	18,808,941
Indonesia	136,981,450	2,404,511,000		
China (PRC)			120,916,467	3,698,759,377
Malaysia	18,705,323	393,327,000		
Indonesia			19,972,628	705,158,245
Australia	424,949	8,170,000		
Malaysia			162,754,345	5,680,525,847
Algeria	218,292,361	4,282,415,000		
Algeria			13,996,799	440,837,230
Angola	14,660,865	288,529,000		
Angola			15,352,284	537,086,927
Cameroon	7,059,179	150,652,000		
Cameroon			2,565,713	83,098,648
Congo (Brazzaville)	3,774,570	67,596,000		
Congo (Brazzaville)			12,406,854	400,159,288
Egypt	17,209,337	344,633,000		
Egypt			7,768,262	264,094,171
Gabon	16,775,758	313,649,000		
Gabon			299,010	10,273,046
Ghana	461,211	7,406,000		
Ghana			197,487,324	7,010,060,598
Libya	251,780,242	5,162,444,000		
Libya			311,659,797	10,625,616,660
Nigeria	401,659,051	7,973,608,000		
Nigeria			1,774,505	51,894,424
Tunisia	4,243,416	90,318,000		
Tunisia			4,642,173	157,498,349
Zaire	1,606,361	30,743,000		
Zaire			21	779
Other Countries	259	7,000		
Other Countries			21	779
Total	**2,467,315,042**	**$46,099,983,000**	**1,974,774,111**	**$61,916,773,394**

LARGEST U.S. COMMERCIAL BANKS Source: Fortune Magazine

Bank	Assets[1] ($000)	Rank '80	'79	Deposits ($000)	Rank	Loans[2] ($000)	Rank
Citicorp (New York)	114,920,000	1	2	71,771,000	2	69,915,000	1
BankAmerica Corp. (San Francisco)	111,617,291	2	1	88,426,156	1	62,482,124	2
Chase Manhattan Corp. (New York)	76,189,567	3	3	56,846,002	3	46,506,335	3
Manufacturers Hanover Corp. (New York)	55,522,249	4	4	41,744,624	4	30,348,158	4
J.P. Morgan & Co. (New York)	51,990,646	5	5	35,593,807	5	25,972,414	6
Continental Illinois Corp. (Chicago)	42,089,408	6	7	27,313,667	7	27,120,625	5
Chemical New York Corp.	41,342,220	7	6	30,067,000	6	22,159,068	7
Bankers Trust New York Corp.	32,325,603	8	8	23,942,285	9	15,990,717	11
Western Bancorp. (Los Angeles)	32,110,327	9	10	24,863,703	8	17,707,309	9
First Chicago Corp.	28,699,441	10	9	21,361,154	10	16,788,573	10
Security Pacific Corp. (Los Angeles)	27,794,208	11	11	21,168,617	11	18,147,918	8
Wells Fargo & Co. (San Francisco)	23,638,063	12	12	16,207,468	12	15,969,283	12
Crocker National Corp. (San Francisco)	19,062,665	13	14	14,908,644	13	12,402,443	13
Irving Bank Corp. (New York)	18,089,818	14	13	14,163,187	14	8,416,288	16
Marine Midland Banks (Buffalo)	17,479,565	15	15	14,163,018	15	9,588,419	14

[1] As of December 31, 1980. [2] Net of unearned discount and loan loss reserve.

LARGEST DIVERSIFIED FINANCIAL COMPANIES Source: Fortune Magazine

Company	Assets[1] ($000)	Rank '80	'79	Revenues ($000)	Rank	Net Income ($000)	Rank
Federal National Mortgage Assn. (Washington, D.C.)	58,470,003	1	*	5,202,910	5	14,208	39
Aetna Life & Casualty (Hartford)	35,752,700	2	1	13,318,000	1	561,600	1
Travelers Corp. (Hartford)	21,637,986	3	2	8,790,092	2	362,739	3
American Express (New York)	19,709,000	4	3	5,504,000	3	376,000	2
Merrill Lynch & Co. (New York)	13,245,784	5	5	3,022,473	9	203,349	11
H.F. Ahmanson (Los Angeles)	13,109,603	6	4	1,317,119	22	54,322	28
INA (Philadelphia)	10,604,000	7	8	5,255,000	4	292,738	4
Great Western Financial (Beverly Hills)	10,252,838	8	7	997,222	27	39,172	33
First Charter Financial (Beverly Hills)	9,676,378	9	6	955,093	29	39,206	32
Loews (New York)	9,125,112	10	9	4,535,098	6	206,099	10
Transamerica (San Francisco)	8,887,023	11	10	4,384,055	7	244,979	7
Lincoln National (Fort Wayne, Ind.)	8,470,373	12	11	2,692,901	11	175,697	12
Continental (New York)	8,215,970	13	12	3,419,046	8	269,192	6
Imperial Corp. of America (San Diego)	7,347,443	14	14	713,703	34	40,659	31
American General Corp. (Houston)	7,293,328	15	13	2,291,716	12	229,906	8

[1] As of December 31, 1980. * Not on last year's list.

LARGEST INDUSTRIAL CORPORATIONS

SOURCE: *Fortune* Magazine

Company	Sales ($000)	Rank '80	Rank '79	Assets ($000)	Rank	Net Income ($000)	Rank
Exxon (New York)	103,142,834	1	1	56,576,558	1	5,650,090	1
Mobil (New York)	59,510,000*	2	3	32,705,000	3	3,272,000	3
General Motors (Detroit)	57,728,500	3	2	34,581,000	2	(762,500)	490
Texaco (Harrison, N.Y.)	51,195,830	4	5	26,430,355	5	2,642,542	4
Standard Oil of California (San Francisco)	40,479,000	5	6	22,162,000	7	2,401,000	5
Ford Motor (Dearborn, Mich.)	37,085,500	6	4	24,347,600	6	(1,543,300)	491
Gulf Oil (Pittsburgh)	26,483,000*	7	7	18,638,000	9	1,407,000	11
International Business Machines (Armonk, N.Y.)	26,213,000	8	8	26,703,000	4	3,562,000	2
Standard Oil (Ind.) (Chicago)	26,133,080	9	10	20,167,474	8	1,915,314	6
General Electric (Fairfield, Conn.)	24,959,000	10	9	18,511,000	10	1,514,000	10
Atlantic Richfield (Los Angeles)	23,744,302	11	12	16,604,844	12	1,651,423	8
Shell Oil (Houston)	19,830,000	12	13	17,615,000	11	1,542,000	9
International Telephone & Telegraph (New York)	18,529,655	13	11	15,417,183	13	894,326	15
Conoco (Stamford, Conn.)	18,325,400	14	15	11,036,275	18	1,026,195	14
E.I. du Pont de Nemours (Wilmington, Del.)	13,652,000	15	16	9,560,000	22	716,000	21

*Does not include excise taxes.

LARGEST UTILITIES

SOURCE: *Fortune* Magazine

Company	Assets[1] ($000)	Rank '80	Rank '79	Operating Revenues ($000)	Rank	Net Income[2] ($000)	Rank
American Telephone & Telegraph (New York)	125,450,800	1	1	50,791,200	1	6,079,700	1
General Telephone & Electronics (Stamford, Conn.)	19,720,457	2	2	9,978,875	2	477,876	3
Southern Company (Atlanta)	11,466,555	3	3	3,763,483	6	344,395	6
Pacific Gas & Electric (San Francisco)	11,295,203	4	4	5,258,899	3	524,770	2
American Electric Power (Columbus)	10,951,984	5	6	3,756,464	7	348,377	5
Commonwealth Edison (Chicago)	10,177,142	6	5	3,324,043	12	382,003	4
Southern California Edison (Rosemead, Calif.)	7,733,898	7	8	3,661,117	8	317,536	8
Consolidated Edison (New York)	7,459,681	8	7	3,947,165	5	334,676	7
Middle South Utilities (New Orleans)	7,334,879	9	9	2,342,228	22	195,907	20
Public Service Electric & Gas (Newark)	6,724,860	10	10	2,994,054	16	281,717	11
Texas Utilities (Dallas)	6,552,972	11	12	2,174,553	24	297,844	10
Virginia Electric & Power (Richmond)	6,491,464	12	11	2,119,774	26	241,620	12
Duke Power (Charlotte)	6,328,174	13	13	1,682,822	32	311,091	9
Consumers Power (Jackson, Mich.)	6,276,596	14	14	2,303,983	23	223,798	14
Detroit Edison	5,741,686	15	16	1,812,514	29	188,566	21

[1] As of December 31, 1980. [2] After extraordinary items.

LARGEST RETAILING COMPANIES

SOURCE: *Fortune* Magazine

Company	Sales[1] ($000)	Rank '80	Rank '79	Assets ($000)	Rank	Net Income ($000)	Rank
Sears, Roebuck (Chicago)	25,194,900	1	1	28,053,800	1	606,000	1
Safeway Stores (Oakland)	15,102,673	2	2	3,338,832	6	119,368	8
K-Mart (Troy, Mich.)	14,204,381	3	3	6,102,462	2	260,527	3
J.C. Penney (New York)	11,353,000	4	4	5,863,000	3	233,000	4
Kroger (Cincinnati)	10,316,741	5	5	1,997,545	11	94,386	14
F.W. Woolworth (New York)	7,218,176	6	7	3,171,894	7	160,915	6
Great Atlantic & Pacific Tea (Montvale, N.J.)	6,684,179	7	6	1,230,522	23	(3,807)	48
Lucky Stores (Dublin, Calif.)	6,468,682	8	8	1,400,601	18	90,458	16
American Stores Co. (Salt Lake City)	6,419,884	9	14	1,292,992	20	51,553	26
Federated Department Stores (Cincinnati)	6,300,686	10	9	3,575,513	5	277,727	2
Montgomery Ward (Chicago)	5,496,907	11	10	3,942,230	4	(137,122)	50
Winn-Dixie Stores (Jacksonville)	5,388,979	12	11	903,709	27	91,950	15
Southland (Dallas)	4,758,656	13	13	1,495,385	17	77,672	18
City Products (Des Plaines, Ill.)	4,462,378	14	12	1,283,236	22	43,015	28
Jewel Companies (Chicago)	4,267,922	15	15	1,288,901	21	55,893	22

[1] All figures are for the fiscal year ending January 31, 1981.

LARGEST LIFE INSURANCE COMPANIES

SOURCE: *Fortune* Magazine

Company	Assets[1] ($000)	Rank '80	Rank '79	Premium & Annuity Receipts ($000)	Rank	Life Insurance in Force ($000)	Rank
Prudential (Newark)*	59,778,470	1	1	8,668,858	1	406,571,823	1
Metropolitan (New York)*	48,309,771	2	2	6,010,574	2	349,192,320	2
Equitable Life Assurance (New York)*	34,599,737	3	3	4,163,345	4	197,338,258	3
Aetna Life (Hartford)	22,270,634	4	4	5,412,032	3	144,214,809	4
New York Life*	19,725,325	5	5	2,682,329	6	122,764,294	6
John Hancock Mutual (Boston)*	18,760,598	6	6	2,436,403	7	133,703,479	5
Connecticut General Life (Bloomfield)	13,776,921	7	7	1,861,488	8	80,402,921	8
Travelers (Hartford)	13,351,227	8	8	3,955,025	5	104,402,349	7
Northwestern Mutual (Milwaukee)*	11,350,786	9	9	1,193,496	12	61,308,461	10
Teachers Insurance & Annuity (New York)*	9,748,371	10	11	1,315,944	10	7,587,077	43
Massachusetts Mutual (Springfield)*	9,145,484	11	10	1,239,769	11	50,934,797	13
Mutual of New York*	8,005,708	12	12	891,919	18	37,968,654	15
Bankers Life (Des Moines)*	7,988,996	13	13	1,536,613	9	35,051,210	17
New England Mutual (Boston)*	6,823,015	14	14	991,410	17	31,672,479	19
Mutual Benefit (Newark)*	5,872,814	15	15	1,093,035	15	40,241,181	14

[1] As of December 31, 1980. * Mutual company.

LEADING U.S. FARM CROPS

Source: U.S. Department of Agriculture, Crop Reporting Board, ESCS

Crop	Unit	PRODUCTION (in 1,000 units) 1979	1980	YIELD PER ACRE[4] 1979	1980
Corn for grain	Bushels	7,938,819	6,647,534	109.7	91.0
Sorghum for grain	Bushels	808,862	587,997	62.7	46.2
Oats	Bushels	526,551	457,593	54.4	53.0
Barley	Bushels	382,798	358,544	50.9	49.6
Wheat, total	Bushels	2,134,060	2,369,666	34.2	33.4
Winter	Bushels	1,601,234	1,891,251	36.9	36.8
Durum	Bushels	106,654	108,395	27.1	22.4
Other spring	Bushels	426,172	370,020	28.2	25.3
Rice	Cwt.	131,947	145,063	4,599.0[3]	4,403.0[3]
Rye	Bushels	22,389	16,265	25.8	24.5
Soybeans for beans	Bushels	2,267,901	1,817,097	32.1	26.8
Flaxseed	Bushels	12,014	8,128	13.7	11.6
Peanuts for nuts	Pounds	3,968,485	2,296,250	2,611.0	1,633.0
Sunflower seeds	Pounds	7,296,110	3,804,090	1,349.0	1,015.0
Popcorn	Pounds	536,560	528,300	2,993.0	2,465.0
Cotton, total	Bales	14,629.3	11,124.5	547.0[3]	411.0[3]
Hay	Tons	147,847	131,070	2.4	2.21
Beans, dry edible	Cwt.	20,476	26,100	1,480.0[3]	1,422.0[3]
Peas, dry edible	Cwt.	2,039	3,285	1,499.0[3]	2,433.0[3]
Potatoes	Cwt.	342,497	301,006	270.0	261.0
Sweetpotatoes	Cwt.	13,370	10,948	117.0	106.0
Tobacco	Pounds	1,526,549	1,772,001	1,845.0	1,936.0
Sugarbeets	Tons	21,996	23,275	19.6	19.6
Sugarcane	Tons	26,532	28,235	36.2	38.4
Coffee	Pounds	2,190	1,450	1,220.0	850.0
Hops	Pounds	54,929	75,560	1,727.0	2,037.0
Cranberries	Barrels	2,475.5	2,692.5	106.7	116.1
Apples, Com'l	Pounds	8,143,100	8,706,500		
Peaches	Pounds	2,951,200	3,073,600		
Pears	Tons	854.7	885.8		
Grapes	Tons	4,989.0	5,576.1		
Oranges	Boxes	210,600[1]	273,830[2]		
Grapefruit	Boxes	67,380[1]	73,200[2]		
Lemons	Boxes	19,600[1]	20,750[2]		
Limes	Boxes	720[1]	1,100[2]		

[1]1978-79 production figures. [2]1979-80 production figures. [3]Yield in pounds. [4]Yield per acre figures not available for fruit.

INCLUSIVE STATE—FARM PAYMENT TOTALS: 1980

Source: U.S. Department of Agriculture, Agricultural Stabilization Conservation Service

State	Amount	State	Amount	State	Amount
Alabama	$ 23,029,461	Maine	$ 3,442,879	Oregon	$ 5,896,910
Alaska	193,369	Maryland	3,515,152	Pennsylvania	8,333,061
Arizona	5,081,366	Massachusetts	742,001	Rhode Island	94,827
Arkansas	34,513,335	Michigan	10,665,356	South Carolina	13,430,062
California	14,111,283	Minnesota	69,592,604	South Dakota	63,592,130
Colorado	16,148,472	Mississippi	18,769,163	Tennessee	18,680,287
Connecticut	940,706	Missouri	78,907,535	Texas	227,255,133
Delaware	1,035,473	Montana	57,136,636	Utah	5,088,718
Florida	7,042,744	Nebraska	81,518,011	Vermont	1,322,000
Georgia	28,865,821	Nevada	1,341,150	Virginia	13,301,863
Hawaii	711,013	New Hampshire	702,684	Washington	9,457,756
Idaho	7,900,967	New Jersey	869,316	West Virginia	2,489,228
Illinois	35,733,584	New Mexico	19,869,929	Wisconsin	12,373,192
Indiana	15,024,292	New York	5,821,511	Wyoming	6,506,186
Iowa	44,563,603	North Carolina	13,187,094	Puerto Rico	862,900
Kansas	92,418,627	North Dakota	115,715,304	Virgin Islands	39,858
Kentucky	10,003,916	Ohio	9,402,801	Undistributed	2,863,442
Louisiana	19,980,854	Oklahoma	33,516,045	Total	$1,273,601,610

LIVESTOCK POPULATION ON U.S. FARMS AND RANCHES (as of January 1)

Source: U.S. Department of Agriculture, Crop Reporting Board, ESCS

Year	CATTLE AND CALVES	SHEEP AND LAMBS	HOGS AND PIGS	CHICKENS[2]
1959	92,322,000	32,606,000	58,045,000	387,002,000
1961[3]	97,700,000	32,725,000	55,560,000	366,082,000
1963	104,488,000	29,176,000	62,726,000[1]	375,575,000
1965	109,000,000	25,127,000	56,106,000	394,118,000
1967	108,783,000	23,953,000	57,125,000	425,571,000
1969	110,015,000	21,350,000	60,829,000	413,287,000
1971	114,578,000	19,731,000	67,285,000	433,280,000[1]
1973	121,539,000	17,641,000	59,017,000	404,191,000
1975	132,028,000	14,515,000	54,693,000	384,101,000
1977	122,810,000	12,722,000	54,934,000	378,361,000
1978	116,375,000	12,421,000	56,539,000	386,518,000
1979	110,864,000	12,365,000	60,356,000	396,933,000
1980	111,192,000	12,687,000	67,353,000	400,585,000
1981	115,013,000	12,942,000	64,520,000	392,200,000

[1]Begins inventory as of December 1 preceding year. [2]Excludes commercial broilers. [3]Includes Alaska and Hawaii beginning 1961.

U.S. PASSENGER CAR PRODUCTION: 1980

SOURCE: Motor Vehicle Manufacturers Association of the United States, Inc.

Company	Automobile Production	Company	Automobile Production	Company	Automobile Production
AMERICAN MOTORS CORP.	164,725	Pinto	68,179	Grand Prix	76,030
Spirit	54,223	Mustang	232,507	LeMans	64,870
Concord	68,344	Total Ford	929,627	Firebird	79,570
Eagle	42,158	Marquis	55,524	Phoenix	136,210
		Cougar XR7	42,927	Sunbird	149,239
CHRYSLER CORP.	638,974	Cougar/Monarch	41,264	Total Pontiac	556,431
Horizon	145,036	Zephyr	66,657	Oldsmobile	233,845
Reliant	75,822	Lynx	37,641	Toronado	37,923
Volaré	51,735	Bobcat	12,445	Cutlass	395,785
Gran Fury	14,472	Capri	68,070	Omega	115,674
Caravelle	6,277	Lincoln	22,781	Total Oldsmobile	783,227
Total Plymouth	293,342	Mark	28,146	Buick	149,668
LeBaron	62,592	Versailles	1,866	Riviera	44,525
Chrysler	19,871	Total Lincoln-Mercury	377,321	Century/Regal	370,880
Total Chrysler-Plymouth	375,805			Skylark	218,502
Omni	121,703			Total Buick	783,575
Aries	60,666	GENERAL MOTORS CORP.	4,064,566	Cadillac	115,424
Aspen	36,881	Chevrolet	134,909	Eldorado	54,267
Diplomat	30,733	Corvette	44,190	Seville	34,300
St. Regis	13,186	Monte Carlo	125,474	Total Cadillac	203,991
Total Dodge	263,169	Malibu	231,594		
		Camaro	118,212	CHECKER MOTORS CORP.	3,197
FORD MOTOR CO.	1,306,948	Citation	459,393		
LTD	91,135	Monza	150,544	VOLKSWAGEN OF AMERICA	197,106
Thunderbird	117,856	Chevette	454,068		
Granada	113,281	Acadian	18,958	TOTAL PASSENGER CARS	6,375,516
Fairmont	198,219	Total Chevrolet	1,737,342		
Escort	108,450	Pontiac	50,512		

WORLD MOTOR VEHICLE PRODUCTION: 1980

SOURCE: U.N. *Monthly Bulletin of Statistics,* © United Nations, July 1981

Country	Passenger Cars	Commercial Vehicles	Total	Country	Passenger Cars	Commercial Vehicles	Total
Japan	7,041,800	4,004,200	11,046,000	Australia[3]	318,000	47,000	365,000
United States	6,372,000	1,667,000	8,039,000	Sweden[1]	309,600	50,400	360,000
France	3,487,600	515,200	4,002,800	Argentina[3]	220,600	61,200	281,800
Germany, West	3,512,800	380,700	3,893,500	Czechoslovakia	183,700	88,000	271,100
USSR[1]	1,314,000	780,000[2]	2,094,000	Yugoslavia	187,200	64,100	251,300
Italy[1]	1,476,000	151,200	1,627,200	Germany, East	176,000	37,000	213,000
Canada	846,948	527,500	1,374,300	India	47,800	65,400	113,200
United Kingdom	923,600	389,200	1,312,800	Romania	67,200	33,600	100,800
Spain[1]	973,200	165,600	1,138,800	Netherlands	80,900	15,300	96,200
Brazil[1]	553,200	574,800	1,128,000	Austria	7,600	7,800	15,400
Mexico[3]	311,700	132,100	443,800	Hungary	—	11,700	11,700
Poland	351,300	60,000	411,300				

[1]1979 figures.   [2]Excluding wheeled tractors.   [3]Including assembly.

NEW PASSENGER CARS, TRUCKS AND BUSES IMPORTED INTO THE UNITED STATES: 1979

SOURCE: Motor Vehicle Manufacturers Association of the United States, Inc.

Japan	1,624,963	Italy	72,458	France	27,890
Canada	944,740	Sweden	65,909	Belgium	87
Germany, West	495,686	United Kingdom	46,964	OTHERS	2,390
				TOTAL	3,281,087

LARGEST PASSENGER CAR PRODUCER FOR EACH COUNTRY: 1979†

SOURCE: Motor Vehicle Manufacturers Association of the United States, Inc.

Country	Producer	1979 Production	Country	Producer	1979 Production
Argentina	Ford Motor Argentina S.A.	54,895	Mexico	Volkswagen de Mexico	98,918
Australia	Ford	120,000	Netherlands	Daf & Volvo	89,112
Belgium	General Motors Continental S.A.	340,673	Peru	Toyota	1,780
			Poland	Fabryka Samochodow Malolitrazowych	243,175
Brazil	Volkswagen	293,483			
Canada	General Motors	558,405	Spain	S.E.A.T.-Fiat	288,103
France	Renault	1,403,949	Sweden	Volvo	212,782
West Germany	Volkswagen	1,156,455	Turkey	Fiat (Tofas)	21,597
India	Hindustan Motors	17,523	United Kingdom	British Leyland	503,767
Italy	Fiat	1,480,991	Venezuela	General Motors de Venezuela	35,699
Japan	Toyota Motor	2,111,302	Yugoslavia	Zavodi Crvena Zastava	208,582

†Excluding United States.

THE U.S. LABOR FORCE

SOURCE: U.S. Department of Labor, Bureau of Labor Statistics

TOTAL LABOR FORCE*

Year	Number	% of popula-tion	Total Civilian Employed
1948	62,080,000	60.4	60,254,000
1950	63,858,000	59.4	58,344,000
1952	65,730,000	59.9	58,920,000
1954	66,993,000	60.0	60,110,000
1956	69,409,000	61.0	63,802,000
1958	70,275,000	60.4	63,036,000
1959	70,921,000	60.2	64,630,000
1960	72,142,000	60.2	65,778,000
1961	73,031,000	60.2	65,746,000
1962	73,442,000	59.7	66,702,000
1963	74,571,000	59.6	67,762,000
1964	75,830,000	59.6	69,305,000
1965	77,178,000	59.7	71,088,000
1966	78,893,000	60.1	72,895,000
1967	80,793,000	60.6	74,372,000
1968	82,272,000	60.7	75,920,000
1969	84,239,000	61.1	77,902,000
1970	85,903,000	61.3	78,627,000
1971	86,929,000	61.0	79,120,000
1972	88,991,000	61.0	81,702,000
1973	91,040,000	61.4	84,409,000
1974	93,240,000	61.8	85,936,000
1975	94,793,000	61.8	84,783,000
1976	96,917,000	62.1	87,485,000
1977	99,534,000	62.8	90,546,000
1978	102,537,000	63.7	94,373,000
1979	104,996,000	64.2	96,945,000
1980	106,821,000	64.3	97,270,000

*Persons 16 years of age and over; includes members of the armed forces.

UNEMPLOYMENT RATES: BY SEX AND RACE

SOURCE: U.S. Department of Labor, Bureau of Labor Statistics

Year	Unemployment Rate Total	Male	Fe-male	White Total	Male	Fe-male	Black and other Total	Male	Fe-male
1948	3.8	3.6	4.1	3.5	3.4	3.8	5.9	5.8	6.1
1950	5.3	5.1	5.7	4.9	4.7	5.3	9.0	9.4	8.4
1952	3.0	2.8	3.6	2.8	2.5	3.3	5.4	5.2	5.7
1954	5.5	5.3	6.0	5.0	4.8	5.6	9.9	10.3	9.3
1956	4.1	3.8	4.8	3.6	3.4	4.2	8.3	7.9	8.9
1958	6.8	6.8	6.8	6.1	6.1	6.2	12.6	13.8	10.8
1959	5.5	5.3	5.9	4.8	4.6	5.3	10.7	11.5	9.4
1960	5.5	5.4	5.9	4.9	4.8	5.3	10.2	10.7	9.4
1961	6.7	6.4	7.2	6.0	5.7	6.5	12.4	12.8	11.8
1962	5.5	5.2	6.2	4.9	4.6	5.5	10.9	10.9	11.0
1963	5.7	5.2	6.5	5.0	4.7	5.8	10.8	10.5	11.2
1964	5.2	4.6	6.2	4.6	4.1	5.5	9.6	8.9	10.6
1965	4.5	4.0	5.5	4.1	3.6	5.0	8.1	7.4	9.2
1966	3.8	3.2	4.8	3.3	2.8	4.3	7.3	6.3	8.6
1967	3.8	3.1	5.2	3.4	2.7	4.6	7.4	6.0	9.1
1968	3.6	2.9	4.8	3.2	2.6	4.3	6.7	5.6	8.3
1969	3.5	2.8	4.7	3.1	2.5	4.2	6.4	5.3	7.8
1970	4.9	4.4	5.9	4.5	4.0	5.4	8.2	7.3	9.3
1971	5.9	5.3	6.9	5.4	4.9	6.3	9.9	9.1	10.8
1972	5.6	4.9	6.6	5.0	4.5	5.9	10.0	8.9	11.3
1973	4.9	4.1	6.0	4.3	3.7	5.3	8.9	7.6	10.5
1974	5.6	4.8	6.7	5.0	4.3	6.1	8.9	9.1	10.7
1975	8.5	7.9	9.3	7.8	7.2	8.6	13.9	13.7	14.0
1976	7.7	7.0	8.6	7.0	6.4	7.9	13.1	12.7	13.6
1977	7.0	6.2	8.2	6.2	5.5	7.3	13.1	12.4	14.0
1978	6.0	5.2	7.2	5.2	4.5	6.2	11.9	10.9	13.9
1979	5.8	5.1	6.8	5.1	4.4	5.9	11.3	10.3	12.3
1980	7.1	6.9	7.4	6.3	6.1	6.5	13.2	13.3	13.1

MINORITY GROUP PARTICIPATION IN THE U.S. LABOR MARKET: 1979 Preliminary

SOURCE: Equal Employment Opportunity Commission

% OF MINORITY WORKERS IN PARTICULAR CATEGORY[1]

	Total	WHITE COLLAR Total	Professional	Technical	Clerical	Blue Collar	Service Workers
Black, Total[1]	11.6%	7.2%	4.1%	8.5%	11.0%	14.6%	22.4%
Male	6.3	2.4	1.9	3.6	2.0	10.0	10.1
Female	5.3	4.8	2.2	4.9	9.0	4.6	12.3
Hispanic, Total	5.2	3.2	1.8	3.3	4.3	7.1	7.6
Male	3.2	1.4	1.2	2.1	0.9	5.1	4.4
Female	2.0	1.8	0.6	1.3	3.4	2.0	3.2
Asian or Pacific Islander, Total	1.4	1.7	3.4	2.3	1.6	0.9	1.8
Male	0.7	0.9	2.1	1.4	0.4	0.5	0.9
Female	0.7	0.8	1.3	0.9	1.2	0.4	0.9
American Indian or Alaskan Native, Total	0.4	0.3	0.3	0.4	0.4	0.5	0.4
Male	0.3	0.2	0.2	0.2	0.1	0.4	0.2
Female	0.1	0.1	0.1	0.1	0.3	0.1	0.2
All Minorities, Total	18.6	12.4	9.6	14.5	17.3	23.1	32.2
Male	10.5	4.9	5.3	7.3	3.4	16.0	15.5
Female	8.1	7.5	4.2	7.1	13.8	7.1	16.6

[1]Percent of total employment in given occupational category.

MINORITY GROUP EMPLOYEES IN U.S. LABOR MARKET: 1979 Preliminary

SOURCE: Equal Employment Opportunity Commission

Figures are in thousands	Total	WHITE COLLAR Total	Professional	Technical	Clerical	Blue Collar	Service Workers
All U.S. Employees	33,862	16,751	2,993	1,736	5,301	14,181	2,929
Male	20,264	8,405	1,922	1,054	932	10,540	1,318
Female	13,598	8,346	1,071	682	4,370	3,641	1,612
All Black Employees	3,932	1,207	121	148	581	2,069	656
Male	2,124	410	56	63	106	1,420	295
Female	1,808	798	65	85	476	649	361
All Hispanics	1,761	529	55	58	230	1,010	222
Male	1,082	232	35	36	49	721	129
Female	678	297	19	22	181	289	93
All Asian or Pacific Islander	463	286	102	39	84	126	52
Male	241	145	63	24	20	70	26
Female	222	140	39	15	64	55	26
All American Indian or Alaskan Native	139	57	8	6	21	69	12
Male	92	33	5	4	8	53	6
Female	47	24	2	2	13	17	6
All Minority Employees	6,295	2,079	286	252	916	3,274	942
Male	3,539	820	160	128	183	2,264	455
Female	2,755	1,259	126	124	734	1,010	487

PRINCIPAL U.S. LABOR UNIONS AND EMPLOYEE ASSOCIATIONS, 1980
SOURCE: U.S. Department of Labor, Bureau of Labor Statistics

The following is a list of selected labor unions with a 1980 membership of more than 100,000.

International Brotherhood of Teamsters, Chauffeurs, Warehousemen, and Helpers of America, * 25 Louisiana Avenue, N.W., Washington, D.C. 20001; **Membership:** 1,891,000

National Education Association, * 1201 16th St., N.W., Washington, D.C. 20036; **Membership:** 1,684,000

International Union, United Automobile, Aerospace and Agricultural Implement Workers of America, 8000 East Jefferson Ave., Detroit, Mich. 48214; **Membership:** 1,357,000

United Food and Commercial Workers Union, 1775 K St., N.W., Washington, D.C. 20006; **Membership:** 1,300,000

United Steelworkers of America, Five Gateway Center, Pittsburgh, Pa. 15222; **Membership:** 1,238,000

American Federation of State, County and Municipal Employees, 1625 L Street, N.W., Washington, D.C. 20036; **Membership:** 1,238,000

International Brotherhood of Electrical Workers, 1125 15th St., N.W., Washington, D.C. 20005; **Membership:** 1,041,000

United Brotherhood of Carpenters and Joiners of America, 101 Constitution Ave., N.W., Washington, D.C. 20001; **Membership:** 832,000

International Association of Machinists and Aerospace Workers, 1300 Connecticut Ave., N.W., Washington, D.C. 20036; **Membership:** 745,000

Service Employees' International Union, 2020 K St., N.W., Washington, D.C. 20006; **Membership:** 650,000

Laborers' International Union of North America, 905 16th St., N.W., Washington, D.C. 20006; **Membership:** 608,000

Communications Workers of America, 1925 K St., N.W., Washington, D.C. 20006; **Membership:** 551,000

American Federation of Teachers, 11 Dupont Circle, Washington, D.C. 20036; **Membership:** 502,000

Amalgamated Clothing and Textile Workers of America, 15 Union Square, New York, N.Y. 10003; **Membership:** 455,000

International Union of Operating Engineers, 1125 17th St., N.W., Washington, D.C. 20036; **Membership:** 423,000

Hotel and Restaurant Employees and Bartenders International Union, 120 E. Fourth St., Cincinnati, Oh. 45202; **Membership:** 400,000

United Association of Journeymen and Apprentices of the Plumbing and Pipefitting Industry of the United States and Canada, 901 Massachusetts Ave., N.W., Washington, D.C. 20001; **Membership:** 352,000

International Ladies' Garment Workers Union, 1710 Broadway, New York, N.Y. 10019; **Membership:** 323,000

American Federation of Musicians, 1500 Broadway, New York, N.Y. 10036; **Membership:** 299,000

American Federation of Government Employees, 1325 Massachusetts Avenue, N.W., Washington, D.C. 20005; **Membership:** 255,000

American Postal Workers Union, 817 Fourteenth Street, N.W., Washington, D.C. 20005; **Membership:** 251,000

United Mine Workers of America, * 900 15th Street, N.W., Washington, D.C. 20005; **Membership:** 245,000

International Union of Electrical, Radio, and Machine Workers, 1126 16th St., N.W., Washington, D.C. 20036; **Membership:** 233,000

National Association of Letter Carriers, 100 Indiana Ave., N.W., Washington, D.C. 20001; **Membership:** 230,000

United Paperworkers International Union, 702 Church St., Nashville, Tenn. 37202; **Membership:** 219,000

Retail, Wholesale, and Department Store Union, 30 East 29th St., New York, N.Y. 10016; **Membership:** 215,000

National Association of Government Employees, * 285 Dorchester Ave., Boston, Mass. 02127; **Membership:** 200,000

United Transportation Union, 14600 Detroit Avenue, Cleveland, Ohio, 44107; **Membership:** 190,000

International Association of Bridge and Structural Iron Workers, 1750 New York Ave., N.W., Suite 400, Washington, D.C. 20006; **Membership:** 184,000

American Nurses Association, * 2420 Pershing Rd., Kansas City, Mo. 64108; **Membership:** 180,000

Brotherhood of Railway, Airline, and Steamship Clerks, Freight Handlers, Express and Station Employees, 3 Research Place, Rockville, Md. 20850; **Membership:** 180,000

International Association of Firefighters, 1750 New York Avenue, N.W., Washington, D.C. 20006; **Membership:** 178,000

International Brotherhood of Painters and Allied Trades of the United States and Canada, 1750 New York Avenue, N.W., Washington, D.C. 20006; **Membership:** 164,000

Amalgamated Transit Union, 5025 Wisconsin Ave., N.W., Washington, D.C. 20016; **Membership:** 162,000

United Electrical, Radio, and Machine Workers of America, * 11 East 51st St., New York, N.Y. 10022; **Membership:** 162,000

Bakery, Confectionary, and Tobacco Workers' International Union of America, 10401 Connecticut Ave., Kensington, Md. 20795; **Membership:** 160,000

Oil, Chemical, and Atomic Workers International Union, P.O. Box 2812, 1636 Champa St., Denver, Colo. 80201; **Membership:** 154,000

Sheet Metal Workers' International Association, 1750 New York Ave., N.W., Washington, D.C. 20006; **Membership:** 154,000

United Rubber, Cork, Linoleum, and Plastic Workers of America, 87 South High St., Akron, Ohio 44308; **Membership:** 151,000

Fraternal Order of Police, * G—3136 Pasadena Ave., Flint, Mich. 48504; **Membership:** 150,000

International Brotherhood of Boilermakers, Iron Ship Builders, Blacksmiths, Forgers, and Helpers, 8th St. at State Ave., Kansas City, Kansas 66101; **Membership:** 145,000

International Union of Bricklayers and Allied Craftsmen, 815 15th St., N.W., Washington, D.C. 20005; **Membership:** 135,000

Transport Workers Union of America, 1980 Broadway, New York, New York 10023; **Membership:** 130,000

National Alliance of Postal and Federal Employees, * 1644 11th St., N.W., Washington, D.C. 20001; **Membership:** 125,000

International Printing and Graphic Communications Union, 1730 Rhode Island Avenue, N.W., Washington, D.C. 20036; **Membership:** 122,000

International Woodworkers of America, 1622 North Lombard St., Portland, Oregon 97217; **Membership:** 112,000

Office and Professional Employees International Union, 265 West 14th St., New York, N.Y. 10011; **Membership:** 107,000

California State Employees Association, * 1108 0 Street, Sacramento, Calif. 95814; **Membership:** 105,000

Brotherhood of Maintenance of Way Employees, 12050 Woodward Ave., Detroit, Mich. 48203; **Membership:** 102,000

* Independent—not members of AFL-CIO

AVERAGE UNION HOURLY SCALE
SOURCE: U.S. Department of Labor, Bureau of Labor Statistics

| Year | Building | | Printing | | Local trucking | | | Year | building | | Printing | | Local trucking | | |
	Journeymen	Helpers and laborers	Book and job	Newspapers	Drivers	Helpers	Local transit workers		Journeymen	Helpers and laborers	Book and job	Newspapers	Drivers	Helpers	Local transit workers
1960	$3.86	$2.88	$3.08	$3.48	$2.68	$2.38	$2.37	1975	$9.32	$7.06	$6.86	$7.57	$6.87	$6.27	$6.25
1965	4.64	3.54	3.58	3.94	3.26	2.90	2.88	1976	9.92	7.54	7.41	8.17	7.42	6.67	6.63
1970	6.54	4.86	4.65	5.13	4.41	3.91	4.03	1977	0.44	8.03	7.91	8.74	8.09	7.28	7.12
1972	7.69	5.68	5.49	6.09	5.49	4.90	4.68	1978	11.05	8.54	8.51	9.23			7.53
1974	8.55	6.53	6.34	7.01	6.39	5.84	5.62	1979	11.80	9.15	—	—	9.61	8.60	8.17

UNION CONTRACTS OF 1980
SOURCE: U.S. Department of Labor, Bureau of Labor Statistics

Major collective bargaining settlements in the private sector during 1980 provided average first-year wage adjustments of 9.5 percent, higher than the 7.5 percent average negotiated throughout 1979. Annual wage adjustments over the life of the contracts in this sector averaged 7.1 pecent in 1980 and 6.0 percent in 1979. About 61 percent of the workers under 1980 settlements were covered by contracts with cost-of-living adjustment (COLA) clauses, slightly higher than the 58 percent for all major contracts negotiated in 1979.

First-year wage adjustments in contracts with COLA provisions averaged 8.0 percent, compared with 11.8 percent for contracts without such provisions. (Corresponding averages were 6.2 and 9.1 percent in 1979.) When negotiated wage adjustments are averaged over the life of the contracts, the annual rates in 1980 were 5.0 percent for contracts with COLA clauses and 10.4 percent for those without (compared with 4.6 and 8.0 percent in 1979).

In manufacturing, negotiated wage adjustments averaged 7.3 percent in the first contract year and 5.4 percent annually over the life of the agreements. In nonmanufacturing, the averages were higher, 11.0 and 8.3 percent, respectively. In the construction industry, without COLA provisions, first-year wage adjustments averaged 13.6 and 10.2 percent in all other industries combined. When negotiated wage changes for these contracts are averaged over the life of the agreements, the annual rate for construction was 12.0 percent, higher than the 9.1 percent for all other industries combined.

UNEMPLOYMENT INSURANCE BENEFITS (1980 Calendar year)

SOURCE: U.S. Department of Labor

State unemployment insurance benefits for the totally unemployed are listed below. Where two figures are given for legal minimum and maximum benefits, the larger figures include dependents' allowances.

State	Average Unemployment Benefit[1]	Legal Minimum[2]	Legal Maximum[2]	Actual Average[1]	Legal Range[2]	State	Average Unemployment Benefit[1]	Legal Minimum[2]	Legal Maximum[2]	Actual Average[1]	Legal Range[2]
U.S. Avg.	$ 98.86†	—	—	14.9†	—	Mont.	$ 98.11	$33	$131	12.7	8-26
Ala.	76.76	$15	$ 90	12.0	11-26	Nebr.	93.78	12	106	11.3	17-26
Alaska	85.13	34-58	150-222	17.8	16-26	Nev.	100.09	16	123	12.0	11-26
Ariz.	83.44	25	95	12.5	12-26	N.H.	84.82	21	114	8.1	26-26
Ark.	88.95	15	136	12.1	10-26	N.J.	100.69	20	133	16.1	15-26
Calif.	86.41	30	120	15.7	12-26*	N.M.	82.74	24	117	15.0	18-26
Colo.	110.99	25	160	10.8	7-26*	N.Y.	94.12†	25	125	20.0†	26-26
Conn.	102.73	15-22	140-190	12.5	26-26*	N.C.	87.09	15	139	9.4	13-26
Del.	108.47	20	150	13.7	11-26	N.D.	105.94	39	143	13.4	12-26
D.C.	122.22	13-14	196*	20.7	17-34	Ohio	124.95	10	136-215	16.2	20-26
Fla.	74.49	10	105	12.0	10-26	Okla.	99.75	16	156	11.7	20-26
Ga.	78.68	27	90	9.9	4-26	Oreg.	98.86	38	138	13.7	6-26
Hawaii	106.11	5	157	13.5	26-26*	Pa.	115.56	35-40	175-183	16.7	26-30
Idaho	97.46	36	132	12.4	10-26	P.R.	53.29†	7	84	23.6†	20-20*
Ill.	114.60	43	142-189	18.6	26-26	R.I.	89.04	32-37	130-150	14.0	12-26
Ind.	84.73†	40	84-141	13.2†	9-26	S.C.	82.19	10	114	9.4	10-26
Iowa	117.02	17-18	134-162	11.9	15-26	S.D.	96.87†	28	119	11.2	13-26
Kans.	105.84	34	136	12.8	10-26	Tenn.	78.04	20	110	13.8	12-26
Ky.	101.33	22	128	15.0	15-26	Texas	86.22	21	126	12.3	9-26
La.	108.52	10	164	15.1	12-28	Utah	105.70	10	150	13.7	10-26*
Maine	85.55	18-23	104-156	10.8	7-26*	Vt.	90.13	18	125	13.7	26-26
Md.	91.72	25-28	120*	14.1	26-26	Va.	95.54	38	122	12.1	12-26
Mass.	97.38	12-18	142-213	15.0	9-30*	Wash.	110.43	41	150	14.6	16-30*
Mich.	101.87	16-18*	97-136	18.1	11-26	W.Va.	105.92	18	184	13.2	28-28
Minn.	117.72	30	162	15.3	11-26	Wis.	117.47	31	166	14.2	1-34*
Miss.	69.26	10	90	12.8	12-26	Wyo.	107.51	24	146	10.8	12-26*
Mo.	88.41	15	105	13.4	10-26*						

†Preliminary.   *Provisional.   [1]1980 Calendar year.   [2]1981 Calendar year.

EMPLOYMENT OUTLOOK TO 1990

Occupation	Average Annual Openings 1978 through 1990
Accountants	61,000
Actors and actresses	850
Airplane pilots	3,800
All-round mechanics	22,500
Anthropologists	350
Architects	4,000
Astronomers	40
Bank clerks	45,000
Bank officers and managers	28,000
Bank tellers	17,000
Barbers	9,700
Blacksmiths	300
Bookkeeping workers	96,000
Bricklayers, stonemasons, etc.	6,200
Local transit busdrivers	3,100
Carpenters	58,000
Chemists	6,100
Chiropractors	1,500
Computer operating personnel	12,500
Construction laborers	49,000
Cooks and chefs	86,000
Cosmetologists	28,500
Dentists	5,500
Dietitians	3,300
Drafters	11,000
Economists	7,800
Electricians (construction)	12,900
Engineers	46,500
Firefighters	7,500
Furniture upholsterers	1,100
Gasoline station attendants	5,200
Geographers	500
Geologists	1,700
Geophysicists	600
Health services administrators	18,000
Historians	700
Hotel managers and assistants	8,900
Industrial designers	550
Insurance agents, brokers, and underwriters	30,000
Interior designers	3,600
Landscape architects	1,100
Lawyers	37,000
Librarians	8,000
Locomotive engineers	2,000

Occupation	Average Annual Openings 1978 through 1990
Mail carriers	7,000
Mathematicians	1,000
Mechanics and repairers— Central office craft occupations	1,000
Line installers and cable splicers	600
Telephone and PBX installers and repairers	3,000
Airconditioning, refrigeration and heating	8,200
Appliance repairers	6,900
Automobile body repairers	7,800
Automobile mechanics	37,000
Business machine repairers	4,200
Computer service technicians	5,400
Farm equipment mechanics	3,500
Industrial machinery repairers	58,000
Maintenance electricians	15,500
Piano and organ tuners and repairers	700
Shoe repairers	1,600
Television and radio service technicians	6,100
Truck and bus mechanics	6,800
Medical laboratory workers	14,800
Meteorologists	300
Newspaper reporters	2,400
Licensed practical nurses	60,000
Registered nurses	85,000
Oceanographers	150
Office machine operators	9,700
Optometrists	1,600
Painters and paperhangers	27,500
Personnel and labor relations workers	17,000
Pharmacists	7,800
Photographers	3,800
Physicians and osteopathic physicians	19,000
Physicists	1,000
Plasterers	1,100

Occupation	Average Annual Openings 1978 through 1990
Plumbers and pipefitters	20,000
Podiatrists	600
Police officers	16,500
Political scientists	500
Postal clerks	2,000
Printing occupations Bookbinders and bindery workers	2,600
Compositors	3,900
Lithographers	2,300
Photoengravers	150
Printing press operators and assistants	5,000
Private household workers	45,000
Programmers	9,200
Psychologists	6,700
Public relations workers	7,500
Purchasing agents	13,400
Radiologic (X-ray) technologists	9,000
Radio and Television announcers	850
Real estate agents and brokers	50,000
Retail trade sales workers	226,000
Wholesale trade sales workers	40,000
School counselors	1,700
Secretaries and stenographers	305,000
Social workers	22,000
Sociologists	600
Statisticians	1,500
Surveyors	2,300
Systems analysts	7,900
College and university teachers	11,000
Kindergarten and elementary school teachers	86,000
Secondary school teachers	7,200
Telephone operators	9,900
Occupational therapists	1,300
Physical therapists	2,700
Local truck drivers	64,000
Long distance truck drivers	21,500
Typists	59,000
Urban planners	800
Veterinarians	1,700
Welders	35,000

U.S. LICENSED COMMERCIAL NUCLEAR POWER PLANTS AS OF APRIL 1, 1981

SOURCE: Nuclear Regulatory Commission

State	Name of Facility	Operating Company	Authorized Power Level (MWe)	Type*
Alabama	Farley 1	Alabama Power Company	829	PWR
Alabama	Farley 2	Alabama Power Company	829	PWR
Alabama	Browns Ferry 1	TVA	1,065	BWR
Alabama	Browns Ferry 2	TVA	1,065	PWR
Alabama	Browns Ferry 3	TVA	1,065	BWR
Arkansas	Arkansas 1	Arkansas Power & Light Company	850	PWR
Arkansas	Arkansas 2	Arkansas Power & Light Company	912	PWR
California	Rancho Seco	Sacramento Municipal Utility District	918	PWR
California	San Onofre 1	Southern California Edison Company	430	PWR
Colorado	Ft. St. Vrain	Public Service Company of Colorado	330	HTGR
Connecticut	Connecticut Yankee	Connecticut Yankee Atomic Power Company	575	PWR
Connecticut	Millstone 1	Northeast Nuclear Energy Company	660	BWR
Connecticut	Millstone 2	Northeast Nuclear Energy Company	830	PWR
Florida	Crystal River 3	Florida Power Corporation	825	PWR
Florida	St. Lucie 1	Florida Power & Light Company	802	PWR
Florida	Turkey Point 3	Florida Power & Light Company	693	PWR
Florida	Turkey Point 4	Florida Power & Light Company	693	PWR
Georgia	Edwin I. Hatch 1	Georgia Power Company	786	BWR
Georgia	Edwin I. Hatch 2	Georgia Power Company	795	BWR
Illinois	Dresden 1†	Commonwealth Edison Company	200	BWR
Illinois	Dresden 2	Commonwealth Edison Company	794	BWR
Illinois	Dresden 3	Commonwealth Edison Company	794	BWR
Illinois	Quad-Cities 1	Commonwealth Edison Company	789	BWR
Illinois	Quad-Cities 2	Commonwealth Edison Company	789	BWR
Illinois	Zion 1	Commonwealth Edison Company	1,040	PWR
Illinois	Zion 2	Commonwealth Edison Company	1,040	PWR
Iowa	Duane Arnold	Iowa Electric Light & Power Company	538	BWR
Maine	Maine Yankee	Maine Yankee Atomic Power Company	790	PWR
Maryland	Calvert Cliffs 1	Baltimore Gas & Electric Company	845	PWR
Maryland	Calvert Cliffs 2	Baltimore Gas & Electric Company	845	PWR
Massachusetts	Pilgrim 1	Boston Edison Company	655	BWR
Massachusetts	Yankee-Rowe	Yankee Atomic Electric Company	175	PWR
Michigan	Big Rock Point	Consumers Power Company	72	BWR
Michigan	Palisades	Consumers Power Company	805	PWR
Michigan	D.C. Cook 1	Indiana & Michigan Electric Company	1,054	PWR
Michigan	D.C. Cook 2	Indiana & Michigan Electric Company	1,060	PWR
Minnesota	Monticello	Northern States Power Company	545	BWR
Minnesota	Prairie Island 1	Northern States Power Company	530	PWR
Minnesota	Prairie Island 2	Northern States Power Company	530	PWR
Nebraska	Cooper Station	Nebraska Public Power District	778	BWR
Nebraska	Ft. Calhoun	Omaha Public Power District	457	PWR
New Jersey	Oyster Creek 1	Jersey Central Power & Light Company	650	BWR
New Jersey	Salem 1	Public Service Electric & Gas Company	1,090	PWR
New Jersey	Salem 2	Public Service Electric & Gas Company	1,115	PWR
New York	Indian Point 2	Consolidated Edison Company of New York	873	PWR
New York	Nine Mile Point 1	Niagara Mohawk Power Corporation	610	BWR
New York	Indian Point 3	Power Authority of the State of New York	873	PWR
New York	Fitzpatrick	Power Authority of the State of New York	821	PWR
New York	R.E. Ginna 1	Rochester Gas & Electric. Corporation	490	PWR
North Carolina	Brunswick 1	Carolina Power & Light Comnpany	821	BWR
North Carolina	Brunswick 2	Carolina Power & Light Company	821	BWR
North Carolina	McGuire 1	Duke Power Company	Zero Power	PWR
Ohio	Davis-Besse 1	Toledo Edison Company	906	PWR
Oregon	Trojan	Portland General Electric Company	1,130	PWR
Pennsylvania	Beaver Valley 1	Duquesne Light Company	852	PWR
Pennsylvania	Three Mile I. 1	Metropolitan Edison Company	819	PWR
Pennsylvania	Three Mile I. 2†	Metropolitan Edison Company	906	PWR
Pennsylvania	Peach Bottom 2	Philadelphia Electric Company	1,065	BWR
Pennsylvania	Peach Bottom 3	Philadelphia Electric Company	1,065	BWR
South Carolina	H.B. Robinson 2	Carolina Power & Light Company	700	PWR
South Carolina	Oconee 1	Duke Power Company	887	PWR
South Carolina	Oconee 2	Duke Power Company	887	PWR
South Carolina	Oconee 3	Duke Power Company	887	PWR
Tennessee	Sequoyah 1	TVA	1,140	PWR
Vermont	Vermont Yankee	Vermont Yankee Nuclear Power Corporation	514	BWR
Virginia	North Anna 1	Virginia Electric & Power Company	850	PWR
Virginia	North Anna 2	Virginia Electric & Power Company	898	PWR
Virginia	Surry 1	Virginia Electric & Power Company	822	PWR
Virginia	Surry 2	Virginia Electric & Power Company	822	PWR
Wisconsin	Lacrosse	Dairyland Power Cooperative	50	BWR
Wisconsin	Point Beach 1	Wisconsin Electric Power Company	497	PWR
Wisconsin	Point Beach 2	Wisconsin Electric Power Company	497	PWR
Wisconsin	Kewaunee	Wisconsin Public Service Corporation	535	PWR

*PWR—Pressurized Water Reactor; BWR—Boiling Water Reactor; HTGR—High Temperature Gas Cooled Reactor † Shut down indefinitely.

U.S. PRODUCTION OF ENERGY BY TYPE

SOURCE: Energy Information Administration

Fuel	Unit	1977	1978	1979[1]	1980[1]
Coal[2]	million short tons	697.2	670.2	781.1	835.4
	quadrillion Btu	15.83	15.04	17.65	18.88
Natural gas[3]	trillion cubic feet	19.16	19.12	19.66	19.30
	quadrillion Btu	19.57	19.49	20.08	19.70
Petroleum[4]	million barrels	3.009	3.178	3.121	3.146
	quadrillion Btu	17.45	18.43	18.10	18.25
Natural Gas	million barrels	590	572	578	573
Plant Liquids	quadrillion Btu	2.33	2.25	2.29	2.27
Hydropower[5]	billion kilowatt hours	223.6	283.5	283.1	279.2
	quadrillion Btu	2.33	2.96	2.95	2.91
Nuclear Power	billion kilowatt hours	250.9	276.4	255.2	251.1
	quadrillion Btu	2.70	2.98	2.75	2.70
Geothermal	billion kilowatt hours	3.6	3.0	3.9	5.1
	quadrillion Btu	0.08	0.06	0.08	0.11
Wood & Waste[6]	billion kilowatt hours	0.5	0.3	0.5	.04
	quadrillion Btu	0.01	[7]	0.01	[7]
Total Energy Production	quadrillion Btu	60.29	61.20	63.91	64.82

[1]Preliminary. [2]Bituminous coal, lignite, and anthracite. [3]Marketed production. [4]Crude oil and lease condensate. [5]Electric utility and industrial generation of hydropower. [6]Wood, refuse, and other vegetal fuels consumed by electric utilities. [7]Less than 0.005 quadrillion Btu.

NUCLEAR POWER

SOURCE: International Atomic Energy Agency

During the 25 years which have lapsed since the 1955 Geneva Conference, a tremendous development effort has taken place in the nuclear power field. Roughly speaking, the first decade from 1955-1965 was marked by the emergence of several promising nuclear power systems which bridged the gap between prototypes and industrial plants. The second period from 1965 to the present witnessed the rapid introduction of large nuclear stations in the electric systems of industrial countries and the commissioning of a few nuclear power plants in some developing countries.

In 1956 there were in the world two power reactors with a total capacity of 0.6 MWe in two countries. By 1965, these members had risen to 44 reactors operating in 9 countries and with a total capacity of 4.9 MWe. By 1981, we find 261 stations with a capacity of over 144,483 MWe operating in 21 countries, and by 1995, 601 plants with close to 464,049 MWe in 33 states.

ESTIMATED WORLD NUCLEAR POWER GROWTH*

Country	1981 No. Reactors	1981 Capacity (1000 MWe)	1995 est. No. Reactors	1995 est. Capacity (1000 MWe)	Country	1981 No. Reactors	1981 Capacity (1000 MWe)	1995 est. No. Reactors	1995 est. Capacity (1000 MWe)
Argentina	1	0.3	5	2.8	Korea, South	1	0.6	9	7.4
Belgium	3	1.7	7	5.5	Mexico	—	—	2	1.3
Brazil	—	—	3	3.1	Netherlands	2	0.5	2	0.5
Bulgaria	3	1.2	8	5.6	Pakistan	1	0.1	1	0.1
Canada	11	5.5	25	15.2	Philippines	—	—	1	0.6
Cuba	—	—	2	0.8	Poland	—	—	4	1.6
Czechoslovakia	2	0.8	20	12.2	Romania	—	—	2	1.3
Egypt	—	—	1	0.6	South Africa	—	—	2	1.8
Finland	4	2.2	5	3.2	Spain	4	2.0	18	15.1
France	26	18.1	74	73.2	Sweden	9	6.4	12	9.4
Germany, East	5	1.7	15	5.9	Switzerland	4	1.9	5	2.9
Germany, West	14	8.6	32	29.2	Turkey	—	—	1	0.7
Hungary	—	—	4	1.6	USSR	35	14.0	72	50.9
India	4	0.8	8	1.7	U.K.	31	7.0	42	14.3
Israel	—	—	1	0.6	United States	73	54.7	169	160.7
Italy	4	1.4	9	5.3	Yugoslavia	—	—	2	1.6
Japan	24	15.0	38	27.2	Total*	261	144.5	601	464.0

*Does not include People's Republic of China, for which no information is available.

ENERGY CONSUMPTION PER CAPITA IN 1976 (Kg of coal equivalent per capita)

SOURCE: U.N. Statistical Yearbook 1978; © United Nations

Country	1976	Country	1976	Country	1976
World	2,069	Greece	2,250	Poland	5,253
Algeria	729	Hungary	3,553	Portugal	1,050
Argentina	1,804	Iceland	4,556	Romania	4,036
Australia	6,657	India	218	Saudi Arabia	1,901
Austria	4,013	Iran	1,490	South Africa	2,985
Belgium	6,049	Ireland	3,170	Spain	2,399
Brazil	731	Israel	2,541	Sweden	6,036
Bulgaria	4,710	Italy	3,284	Switzerland	3,340
Canada	9,950	Japan	3,679	Thailand	308
China	706	Korea, North	3,072	Tunisia	456
Cuba	1,225	Korea, South	1,020	Turkey	743
Czechoslovakia	7,397	Libya	1,589	United Kingdom	5,268
Denmark	5,320	Mexico	1,227	UNITED STATES	11,554
Egypt	473	Netherlands	6,224	USSR	5,259
Finland	5,177	New Zealand	3,617	Uruguay	1,000
France	4,380	Nigeria	94	Venezuela	2,838
Germany, East	6,789	Norway	5,263	Yugoslavia	2,016
Germany, West	5,992	Philippines	329	Zimbabwe	634

LARGEST FOREIGN INDUSTRIAL COMPANIES: 1980
SOURCE: *Fortune* magazine, August 10, 1981

Rank '80	'79	Company	Country	Industry	Sales ($000)
1	1	Royal Dutch/Shell Group	Netherlands-Britain	Petroleum	77,114,243
2	2	British Petroleum	Britain	Petroleum	48,035,941
3	4	ENI	Italy	Petroleum	27,186,939
4	5	Fiat	Italy	Motor vehicles	25,155,000
5	6	Française des Pétroles	France	Petroleum	23,940,355
6	3	Unilever	Britain-Netherlands	Food products	23,607,516
7	10	Renault	France	Motor vehicles	18,979,278
8	16	Petróleos de Venezuela	Venezuela	Petroleum	18,818,931
9	19	Elf-Aquitaine	France	Petroleum	18,430,074
10	9	Phillips' Gloeilampenfabrieken	Netherlands	Electronics, appliances	18,402,818
11	8	Volkswagenwerk	Germany	Motor vehicles	18,339,046
12	11	Siemens	Germany	Electronics, appliances	17,950,253
13	12	Daimler-Benz	Germany	Motor vehicles	17,108,100
14	7	Peugeot-Citroën	France	Motor vehicles and parts	16,846,434
15	13	Hoechst	Germany	Chemicals	16,480,551
16	14	Bayer	Germany	Chemicals	15,880,596
17	15	BASF	Germany	Chemicals	15,277,348
18	18	Thyssen	Germany	Steel and industrial products	15,235,998
19	27	Petrobrás (Petróleo Brasileiro)	Brazil	Petroleum	14,836,326
20	39	Pemex (Petróleos Mexicanos)	Mexico	Petroleum	14,813,514
21	20	Nestlé	Switzerland	Food products, beverages	14,615,187
22	17	Toyota Motor	Japan	Motor vehicles	14,233,779
23	21	Nissan Motor	Japan	Motor vehicles	13,853,503
24	25	Imperial Chemical Industries	Britain	Chemicals	13,290,347
25	23	Nippon Steel	Japan	Metal refining—steel	13,104,996
26	22	Hitachi	Japan	Electronics, appliances	12,871,328
27	26	Matsushita Electric Industrial	Japan	Electronics, appliances	12,684,404
28	24	Mitsubishi Heavy Industries	Japan	Motor vehicles, industrial equipment	10,997,586
29	28	B.A.T. Industries	Britain	Tobacco	10,987,175
30	32	Général d'Electricité	France	Electronics, appliances	10,847,129

WORLD CRUDE PETROLEUM PRODUCERS
SOURCE: U.N. *Monthly Bulletin of Statistics*, © United Nations, July 1981

The list below is a compilation of the latest available figures on the oil production of selected countries. The figures for Communist countries are generally estimates. All figures are given in thousands of metric tons per average calendar month.

Region and Country	1973	1979	1980
North America:			
Canada	7,336	6,104	5,867
Mexico	1,938	6,156	8,080.
Trinidad and Tobago	734	924	915
United States	37,849	35,069	35,332
South America:			
Argentina	1,790	2,022	2,100
Bolivia	183	107	95
Brazil *	690*	692*	760*
Chile	106	70[1]	N.A.
Colombia	791	534	539[2]
Ecuador	885	910	879
Peru	290	788	804
Venezuela	14,648	10,336	9,533
Europe:			
Austria	215	144	123
Czechoslovakia	14	9	8
Denmark	6	37	28[2]
France	105	100	118
Germany, West	553	398	386
Hungary	166	169	169
Italy	87	136	150
Netherlands	124	106	107
Norway	132	1,524	2,034
Romania	1,191	1,027	N.A.
Spain	64	75	102
United Kingdom	31*	6,478*	6,706*
USSR	35,753*	49,243*	50,250*
Yugoslavia	278	345	352

Region and Country	1973	1979	1980
Africa:			
Algeria	4,229	4,475	3,952
Angola	680	558	619
Congo	174	217	220
Egypt	707	2,217	2,454
Gabon	633	899	823
Libya	8,740	8,405	7,177
Nigeria	8,480	9,542	8,473[3]
Tunisia	324	461	469
Zaire	N.A.	86	85
Asia:			
Bahrain	284	213	202
Burma	81	129	N.A.
India	600	1,069	783
Indonesia	5,579	6,511	6,482
Iran	24,403	12,772	6,148
Iraq	8,295	14,037	10,822
Japan	58	40	36
Kuwait	12,702	10,500	7,128
Malaysia	362	1,127	1,096
Oman	1,219	1,233	1,180
Pakistan	36	41	40
Qatar	2,292	2,042	1,908
Saudi Arabia	31,482	39,664	41,310
Syria	462	708	708
Turkey	293	237	194
United Arab Emirates	6,813	7,486	7,015
Oceania:			
Australia	1,595	1,805	1,539

*Includes natural gas liquids. N.A.: Data insufficient or not available. [1]1978 Average. [2]Average of 10 months of 1980. [3]Average for 11 months of 1980.

U.S. METALS PRODUCTION
SOURCE: American Iron & Steel Institute; U.S. Bureau of Mines; Zinc Institute Inc. (figures in short tons)

Year	Pig Iron and Ferroalloys	Steel Ingots[2]	Rolled Iron and Steel Products	Aluminum[2]	Copper[3]	Zinc[4]	Lead[3]
1961	66,565,063	98,014,492	73,411,563	1,903,200	1,165,155	896,900	261,921
1965	90,918,000	131,461,601	99,304,221	2,754,500	1,351,734	1,078,300	301,147
1970	93,851,000	131,514,000	N.A.	3,976,148	1,719,657	961,153	571,767
1972	91,338,000	133,241,000	N.A.	4,122,452	1,664,840	706,898	618,915
1973	103,089,000	150,799,000	N.A.	4,529,116	1,717,940	687,861	603,024
1974	98,332,000	145,720,000	N.A.	4,903,000	1,597,000	590,181	663,870
1975	81,850,000	116,642,000	N.A.	3,879,000	1,413,000	445,916	621,464
1976	88,874,000	128,000,000	N.A.	4,251,000	1,606,000	535,953	609,546
1977	82,968,000	125,330,000	N.A.	4,539,000	1,504,000	434,054	592,491
1978	87,679,000	137,031,000	N.A.	4,804,000	1,496,000	445,879	583,845
1979	87,003,000	136,341,000	N.A.	5,023,000	1,591,000	537,427	579,334
1980	68,721,000[2]	111,835,000[2]	N.A.	5,130,000	1,175,000	398,751	634,000

[1]Plus castings. [2]Primary. [3]Recoverable from domestic mines. [4]Primary slab smelter output.

WORLD MINERAL-PRODUCTION LEADERS: 1980

SOURCE: U.N. *Monthly Bulletin of Statistics*, July 1981, © United Nations (data in thousands of metric tons per calendar month.)

ITEM	COUNTRY AND PRODUCTION		
Bauxite .... Australia (2,337)	Guinea (1,017)	Jamaica (964.5)[1]	Suriname (397.4)[1]
Coal...................... U.S. (59,539)	USSR (58,892)	Poland (16,993)	U.K. (10,845)
Coal, Lignite & Brown .... E. Germany (21,339)[1]	USSR (13,429)[1]	W. Germany (10,819)	Czechoslovakia (8,017)
Copper Ore .... U.S. (117.5)	Chile (87.7)	Zambia (61.4)	Canada (58.8)
Crude Oil .... USSR (50,250)	Saudi Arabia (41,310)	U.S. (35,332)	Iraq (10,822)
Iron Ore .... USSR (20,500)	Australia (8,082)	U.S. (5,867)	Canada (4,151)
Lead Ore.................. U.S. (45.9)	Australia (34.0)	Canada (24.7)	Mexico (12.1)
Natural Gas[2] .... U.S. (1,732,816)	USSR (1,264,040)	Netherlands (240,096)	Canada (231,998)
Tin Concentrates .... Malaysia (5,140)[3]	Thailand (3,588)[3]	Indonesia (2,657)	Bolivia (2,353)[4]
Zinc Ore .... Canada (88.2)	Australia (42.3)	U.S. (26.0)	Japan (19.8)

[1]1979 figures. [2]In terajoules. [3]Average for 11 months of 1980. [4]Average for 3 months of 1980.

U.S. EXPORTS AND IMPORTS: GEOGRAPHIC AREAS

SOURCE: U.S. Dept. of Commerce, International Trade Administration

Area	Exports (millions of $)			Imports (millions of $)			Trade Balance
	1978	1979	1980	1978	1979	1980	1980
Total	$143,663	$181,816	$220,705	$171,978	$206,327	$240,843	$ − 20,138
Developed Countries................	85,585	110,579	130,849	98,909	111,514	125,104	+ 5,745
Developing Countries...............	52,895	62,983	81,125	71,230	92,345	113,236	− 32,111
Communist Areas in Europe..........	4,503	5,684	3,860	1,502	1,865	1,433	+ 2,427
Canada	28,374	33,096	35,860	33,525	38,099	41,455	− 5,595
Latin American Republics...........	20,185	26,259	36,030	18,556	24,782	29,851	+ 6,179
Other Western Hemisphere	1,835	2,200	2,688	4,392	5,701	7,183	− 4,495
Western Europe	39,929	53,514	67,512	36,483	41,684	46,416	+ 21,096
Japan	12,885	17,581	20,790	24,458	26,243	30,701	− 9,911
Near East	12,412	11,030	11,900	11,919	14,988	17,280	− 5,380
East and South Asia...............	13,509	18,436	23,722	21,665	24,913	29,811	− 6,089
Australia and Oceania	3,464	4,319	4,876	2,350	3,072	3,392	+ 1,484
Africa	5,887	6,299	9,060	16,799	24,377	32,251	− 23,191

U.S. EXPORTS AND IMPORTS: PRINCIPAL COMMODITIES

SOURCE: U.S. Dept. of Commerce, International Trade Administration

	Exports (millions of $)			Imports (millions of $)			Trade Balance
	1978	1979	1980	1978	1979	1980	1980
Total...........................	$141,065	$178,436	$216,434	$173,276	$207,086	$241,297	$ − 24,863
Excluding military grant aid	140,980	178,271	216,278	—	—	—	—
Crude foods	12,723	15,787	19,362	7,240	7,689	7,735	+ 11,627
Manufactured foods	6,648	7,581	9,516	8,128	9,624	10,245	− 729
Crude materials	15,654	20,088	23,765	40,123	56,003	76,135	− 52,370
Agricultural.....................	10,470	11,893	12,779	1,971	2,339	2,307	+ 10,472
Semimanufactures	18,907	30,983	37,638	29,171	34,298	33,865	+ 3,773
Finished manufactures	87,133	103,997	126,152	88,614	99,473	111,963	+ 14,189
Excluding military grant aid	87,048	103,832	125,996	—	—	—	—

U.S. EXPORTS AND IMPORTS: SELECTED MERCHANDISE

SOURCE: U.S. Dept. of Commerce, International Trade Administration

Exports (millions of $)	1978	1979	1980	Imports (millions of $)	1978	1979	1980
Food and live animals...............	$19,311	$22,251	$27,744	Food and live animals...............	$13,522	$15,171	$15,763
Grains and preparations	11,634	14,454	18,079	Meat	1,856	2,539	2,346
Wheat	4,335	5,265	6,374	Fish	2,212	2,639	2,612
Corn	5,301	7,025	8,570	Coffee	3,728	3,820	3,872
Beverages and Tobacco	2,293	2,337	2,663	Beverages and Tobacco	2,221	2,566	2,772
Crude Inedible Materials (nonfuel)	15,555	20,756	23,791	Crude Inedible Materials (nonfuel)	9,294	10,651	10,496
Mineral Fuels.....................	3,881	5,621	7,982	Mineral Fuels.....................	42,096	60,061	79,058
Animal and Vegetable Oils	1,521	1,845	1,946	Chemicals	6,430	7,458	8,582
Chemicals	12,623	17,308	20,740	Machinery and Transport Equipment ..	47,590	53,678	60,546
Machinery and Transport Equipment ..	59,268	70,495	84,629	Electrical Apparatus	11,307	12,763	14,779
Electronic Computers	4,359	3,604	4,791	Automobiles and Parts	20,579	22,075	24,134
Electrical Apparatus	6,967	8,635	10,485	Other Manufactured Goods...........	46,296	51,098	55,902
Transport Equipment	21,163	25,750	28,839	Paper.........................	2,293	3,356	3,587
Road Motor Vehicles & Parts	12,148	15,077	14,590	Metals........................	15,714	17,457	20,107
Aircraft, Parts and Accessories ...	8,203	9,719	12,816	Textiles & Clothing	7,857	8,921	8,867
				Footware	2,585	2,859	2,808

LEADING U.S. TRADING PARTNERS: 1980

SOURCE: U.S. Department of Commerce, International Trade Administration (figures in millions of dollars)

Export Trade

COUNTRY	VALUE	COUNTRY	VALUE
Canada	$35,395	Netherlands	$8,669
Japan	20,790	France	7,485
Mexico	15,145	Belg. and Lux.	6,661
United Kingdom	12,694	Saudi Arabia	5,769
West Germany	10,960		

Import Trade

COUNTRY	VALUE	COUNTRY	VALUE
Canada	$41,455	United Kingdom	9,755
Mexico	12,520	Libya	7,124
Japan	12,509	China (Taiwan)	6,850
West Germany	11,681	Algeria	6,577
Nigeria	10,905		

VALUE OF U.S. EXPORTS AND IMPORTS

SOURCE: U.S. Department of Commerce, International Trade Administration (figures in millions of dollars)

Year	Total Exports*	Total Imports	Trade Balance	Year	Total Exports*	Total Imports	Trade Balance	Year	Total Exports*	Total Imports	Trade Balance
1980	220,549	240,834	−20,286	1971	43,573	45,784	−2,210	1962	20,986	16,464	+4,522
1979	181,651	206,256	−24,605	1970	42,664	40,114	+2,550	1961	20,226	14,761	5,465
1978	143,577	171,978	−28,535	1969	37,332	36,043	1,289	1960	19,659	15,073	4,586
1977	121,150	147,685	−26,535	1968	34,063	33,226	837	1959	16,426	15,690	736
1976	115,150	121,009	−5,859	1967	31,030	26,889	4,141	1958	16,375	13,392	2,983
1975	107,589	96,570	+11,019	1966	29,490	25,618	3,872	1957	19,516	13,418	6,098
1974	97,997	100,648	−2,650	1965	26,742	21,427	5,315	1956	17,343	12,905	4,438
1973	70,873	69,832	+1,041	1964	25,832	18,749	7,083	1955	14,298	11,566	2,732
1972	49,227	55,940	−6,714	1963	22,467	17,207	5,260	1954	12,857	10,371	2,486

*Excluding aid in the form of military grants.

U.S. SHARE OF WORLD TRADE: 1938-1980

SOURCE: United Nations *Monthly Bulletin of Statistics*, June 1981, © United Nations (figures in millions of dollars)

Year	Total World Exports*	U.S. Exports	Year	Total World Imports*	U.S. Imports
1980	1,825,800	216,668	1980	1,887,500	255,643
1979	1,488,900	178,578	1979	1,527,400	217,664
1978	1,175,100	141,154	1978	1,211,600	182,787
1977	1,018,200	119,042	1977	1,045,700	156,758
1976	896,400	113,323	1976	910,500	128,872
1975	788,000	106,157	1975	801,000	102,984
1974	767,900	97,144	1974	773,300	107,112
1973	517,900	70,223	1973	528,600	68,656
1972	372,300	48,968	1972	383,600	55,282
1971	314,100	43,492	1971	328,300	45,516
1970	280,000	42,590	1970	294,100	39,756
1969	243,500	37,462	1969	256,400	35,863
1968	212,500	34,199	1968	224,700	33,066
1967	189,900	31,243	1967	201,500	26,813
1966	180,600	29,998	1966	192,000	25,439
1965	164,800	27,189	1965	174,800	21,348
1964	152,200	26,300	1964	161,000	18,666
1963	135,400	23,104	1963	143,500	17,072
1962	141,400	21,446	1962	149,800	16,317
1960	128,000	20,412	1960	135,500	15,071
1958	108,100	17,755	1958	114,100	13,298
1953	82,700	15,661	1953	84,200	10,915
1948	57,500	12,545	1948	63,600	7,183
1938	23,500	3,064	1938	25,400	2,180

*Excluding trade of the Centrally Planned Economies.

WORLD ECONOMIC SUMMARY: 1976-1980

SOURCE: United Nations *Monthly Bulletin of Statistics*, June 1981, © United Nations

Item	Unit*	1976	1980	Item	Unit*	1976	1980
Agricultural production:				Sugar	Mil. tons	83.6	85.1
Barley	Mil. tons	187	179	Sawnwood[1]	1,000 cu.m.	431	443†
Coffee	1,000 tons	3,553	4,574	Woodpulp	Mil. tons	87.2	92.9†
Corn	Mil. tons	333	359	Newsprint	Mil. tons	22.5	23.9‡
Cotton (lint)	Mil. tons	12.1	13.8	Cement[2]	Mil. tons	711	760
Eggs	Mil. tons	23.9	27.3	Pig iron and ferroalloys[2]	Mil. tons	495	499
Meat	Mil. tons	127	142	Crude steel[2]	Mil. tons	648	702
Milk	Mil. tons	438	468	Tin[2 4 5]	1,000 tons	182	182
Potatoes	Mil. tons	263	252	Merchant vessels,			
Rice	Mil. tons	350	391	launched[2 3 4]	Mil. gr.tons	33.92	13.57
Tea	1,000 tons	1,586	1,927	Motor vehicles (passenger)[2]	Millions	23.93	28.81
Tobacco	1,000 tons	5,669	5,531	Electric energy[2]	Bil. kw.-hr.	6,775	7,693
Wheat	Mil. tons	425	434	**External trade:**[1 2 4]			
Wool, greasy	1,000 tons	2,596	2,766	Imports, c.i.f.	Bil. U.S. dol.	910.4	1,856.2
Rubber (natural)	1,000 tons	3,565	3,745	Exports, f.o.b.	Bil. U.S. dol.	896.5	1,857.0
Fish catches	Mil. tons	72.1	72.4†				
Industrial Production:				**Transport:**			
Coal[2]	Mil. tons	1,940	2,106	Railway freight	Bil. tons-km	6,143	6,618‡
Crude petroleum[2]	Mil. tons	2,786	2,869	Merchant shipping, loaded	Mil. tons	3,346	3,778‡
Wheat flour[2]	Mil. tons	128.7	132.3†	Civil aviation, km flown[4 6]	Millions	7,830	9,060‡

*Data are in metric units.   †Latest available figures are from 1978.   ‡Latest available figures are from 1979. [1] Excludes Eastern Europe. [2] Excludes China. [3] Excludes East Germany. [4] Excludes USSR. [5] Excludes North Korea. [6] Includes ICAO members.

WALL STREET GLOSSARY

SOURCE: New York Stock Exchange

Assets: Everything a corporation owns or has outstanding: cash, investments, money due it, materials and inventories (current assets); buildings and machinery (fixed assets); and patents and good will (intangible assets).

Averages: Various ways of measuring the trend of securities prices, the most popular of which is the Dow-Jones average of 30 industrial stocks listed on the New York Stock Exchange. The numbers are not true numerical averages, but take into account such factors as past splits, etc.

Balance Sheet: A condensed statement showing the nature and amount of a company's assets, liabilities, and capital on a given date. In dollar amounts, the balance sheet shows what the company owned, what it owed, and the ownership interest in the company of its stockholders.

Bear: Someone who believes the market will decline.

Blue Chip: Common stock in a company known nationally for the quality and wide acceptance of its products or services and its ability to make money and pay dividends.

Bond: Basically an IOU or promissory note of a corporation, usually issued in multiples of $1,000 or $5,000. A bond is evidence of a debt on which the issuing company usually promises to pay the bondholders a specified amount of interest for a specified length of time, and to repay the loan on the expiration date. In every case a bond represents debt—its holder is a creditor of the corporation and not a part owner as is the shareholder.

Book Value: An accounting term. Book value of a stock is determined from the company's records, by adding all assets (generally excluding intangibles), then deducting all debts and other liabilities, plus the liquidation price of any preferred issues. The sum arrived at is divided by the number of common shares outstanding and the result is book value per common share. Book value may have little or no significant relationship to market value.

Bull: One who believes the market will rise.

Capital Gain or Capital Loss: Profit or loss from the sale of a capital asset. Under current federal income tax laws, a capital gain may be either short-term (12 months or less) or long-term (more than 12 months). A short-term capital gain is taxed at the reporting individual's full income tax rate. A long-term capital gain is subject to a lower tax.

Capitalization: Total amount of the various securities issued by a corporation. Capitalization may include bonds, debentures, preferred and common stock. Bonds and debentures are usually carried on the books of the issuing company in terms of their par or face value. Preferred and common shares may be carried in terms of par or stated value. Stated value may be either an arbitrary figure decided upon by the directors, or may represent the amount received by the company from the sale of the securities at the time of issuance.

Cash Flow: Reported net income of a corporation *plus* amounts charged off for depreciation, depletion, amortization, extraordinary charges to reserves, which are bookkeeping deductions and not paid out in actual dollars and cents.

Common Stock: Securities that represent an ownership interest in a corporation. If the company has also issued preferred stock, both common and preferred have ownership rights, but the preferred normally has prior claim on dividends and, in the event of liquidation, assets. Claims of both common and preferred stockholders are junior to claims of bondholders or other creditors of the company. Common-stock holders assume greater risk but, as preferred-stock holders, but generally exercise greater control and may gain greater reward.

Conglomerate: A corporation that has diversified its operations usually by acquiring enterprises in widely varied industries.

Convertible: A bond, debenture, or preferred share that may be exchanged by the owner for common stock or another security, usually of the same company, in accordance with the terms of the issue.

Dealer: An individual or firm in the securities business acting as a principal rather than as an agent. Typically, a dealer buys for his own account and sells to a customer from his own inventory. The dealer's profit or loss is the difference between the price he pays and the price he receives for the same security.

Discretionary Account: An account in which the customer gives the broker or someone else discretion, which may be complete or within specific limits, as to the purchase and sales of securities or commodities including selection, timing, amount and price to be paid or received.

Dollar Cost Averaging: A system of buying securities at regular intervals with a fixed dollar amount. Under this system the investor buys by the dollars' worth rather than by the number of shares. If each investment is of the same number of dollars, payments buy more when the price is low and fewer when it rises. Thus temporary downswings in price benefit the investor if he continues periodic purchases in both good times and bad and the price at which the shares are sold is more than their average cost.

Dow Theory: A theory of market analysis based upon the performance of the Dow-Jones industrial and transportation stock price averages. The Theory says that the market is in a basic upward trend if these averages advance above a previous important high. When the averages dip, there is said to be a downward trend.

Fiscal Year: A corporation's accounting year. Due to the nature of their particular business, some companies do not use the calendar year for their bookkeeping.

Growth Stock: Stock of a company with prospects for future growth—a company whose earnings are expected to increase at a relatively rapid rate.

Investment Banker: Also known as an underwriter. He is the middleman between the corporation issuing new securities and the public. One or more investment bankers buy outright from a corporation a new issue of stocks or bonds. The group forms a syndicate to sell the securities to individuals and institutions. Investment bankers also distribute very large blocks of stocks or bonds.

Investment Company: A company or trust which uses its capital to invest in other companies. There are two principal types: the closed-end and the open-end, or mutual fund. Closed-end shares are readily transferable in the open market and are bought and sold like other shares. Open-end funds sell their own new shares to investors, stand ready to buy back their old shares, and are not listed.

Legal List: A list of investments selected by various states in which certain institutions and fiduciaries, such as insurance companies and banks, may invest.

Liquidity: The ability of the market in a particular security to absorb a reasonable amount of buying or selling at reasonable price changes. Liquidity is one of the most important characteristics of a good market.

Listed Stock: The stock of a company that is traded on a securities exchange and for which a listing application and a registration statement, giving detailed information about the company and its operations, have been filed with the Securities & Exchange Commission (SEC), unless otherwise exempted, and the exchange itself. The various stock exchanges have different standards for listing.

Load: The portion of the offering price of shares of open-end investment companies in excess of the value of the underlying assets which cover sales commissions and all other costs of distribution. The load is incurred only on purchase, there being, in most cases, no charge when the shares are sold (redeemed).

Margin: The amount paid by the customer when he uses his broker's credit to buy a security. Under Federal Reserve regulations, the initial margin required in the past years has ranged from 50 percent of the purchase price all the way to 100 percent.

NASD: The National Association of Securities Dealers, Inc., an association of brokers and dealers in the over-the-counter securities business.

NYSE Common Stock Index: A composite index covering price movements of all common stocks listed on the "Big Board." It is based on the close of the market December 31, 1965, as 50.00 and is weighted according to the number of shares listed for each issue. The index is computed continuously by the Exchange's Market Data System and printed on the ticker tape each half hour. Point changes in the index are converted to dollars and cents so as to provide a meaningful measure of changes in the average price of listed stocks. The composite index is supplemented by separate indexes for four industry groups: industrials, transportation, utilities, and finances.

Option: A right to buy (call) or sell (put) a fixed amount of a given stock at a specified price within a limited period of time. The purchaser hopes that the stock's price will go up (if he bought a call) or down (if he bought a put) by an amount sufficient to provide a profit greater than the cost of the contract and the commission and other fees required to exercise the contract. If the stock price holds steady or moves in the opposite direction, the price paid for the option is lost entirely.

Over-the-Counter: A market for securities made up of securities dealers who may or may not be members of a securities exchange. Thousands of companies have insufficient shares outstanding, stockholders, or earnings to warrant application for listing on a stock exchange. Securities of these companies are traded in the over-the-counter market between dealers who act either as principals or as brokers for customers. The over-the-counter market is the principal market for U.S. Government bonds and municipals.

Par: In the case of a common share, a dollar amount assigned to the share by the company's charter. Par value may also be used to compute the dollar amount of the common shares on the balance sheet. Par value has little significance so far as market value of common stock is concerned. Many companies today issue no-par stock, but give a stated per share value on the balance sheet. In the case of preferred shares and bonds, however, par is important. It often signifies the dollar value upon which dividends on preferred stocks and interest on bonds are figured. The issuer of a 6% bond promises to pay that percentage of the bond's par value annually.

Point: In the case of shares of stock, a point means $1. In the case of bonds, a point means $10.

Portfolio: Holdings of securites by an individual or institution. A portfolio may contain bonds, preferred stocks and common stocks of various types of enterprises.

Preferred Stock: A class of stock with a claim on the company's earnings before payment may be made on the common stock, usually also entitled to priority over common stock if the company liquidates. It is usually entitled to dividends at a specified rate before payment of a dividend on the common stock.

Price-Earnings Ratio: The price of a share of stock divided by earnings per share for a twelve-month period.

Principal: The person for whom a broker executes an order, or a dealer buying or selling for his own account. The term "principal" may also refer to a person's capital or to the face amount of a bond.

Puts and Calls: see Option

Quotation: Often shortened to "quote." The highest bid to buy and the lowest offer to sell a security in a given market at a given time. A "quote" on a stock might

be "45¼ to 45½." This means that $45.25 is the highest price any buyer would pay at the time the quote was given on the floor of the Exchange, and that $45.50 was the lowest price that any seller would take at the same time.

REIT: Real Estate Investment Trust, an organization similar to an investment company but concentrating its holdings in real estate. The yield is generally liberal since REIT's are required to distribute as much as 90% of their income.

Registration: Before a public offering may be made of new securities by a company, or of outstanding securities by controlling stockholders—through the mails or in interstate commerce—the securities must be registered under the Securities Act of 1933. Registration statement is filed with the SEC by the issuer. It must disclose pertinent information relating to the company's operations, securities, management, and purpose of the public offering. Securities of railroads under jurisdiction of the Interstate Commerce Commission (ICC), and certain other types of securities, are exempted.

Round Lot: A unit of trading or a multiple thereof. On the New York Stock Exchange, the unit of trading is generally 100 shares in stocks and $1,000 par value in the case of bonds. In some inactive stocks, the unit of trading is 10 shares.

Short Sale: A person who believes a stock will decline and and sells it though he does not own any has made a short sale. Your broker borrows the stock so he can deliver the 100 shares to the buyer. The money value of the shares borrowed is deposited by your broker with the lender. Sooner or later you must cover your short sale by buying the same amount of stock you borrowed for return to the lender. If you are able to buy at a lower price than you sold it for, your profit is the difference between the two prices—not counting commissions and taxes. Stock exchange and federal regulations govern and limit the conditions under which a short sale may be made on a national securities exchange.

Specialist: A member of the New York Stock Exchange who has two functions: First, to maintain an orderly market in the stocks in which he is registered as a specialist. The Exchange expects the specialist to buy or sell for his own account, to a reasonable degree, when there is a temporary disparity between supply and demand. Second, the specialist acts as a broker's broker. When a commission broker on the exchange floor receives a limit order, he cannot wait at the particular post where the stock is traded until the price reaches the specified level. He leaves the order with the specialist, who will try to execute it in the market if and when the stock declines to the specified price. The specialist must always put his customers' interests first.

Split: The division of the outstanding shares of a corporation into a larger number of shares. A 3-for-1 split by a company with 1 million shares outstanding would result in 3 million shares outstanding. After the 3-for-1 split, each holder of 100 shares would have 300 shares.

Take-Over: The acquiring of one corporation by another — usually in a friendly merger but sometimes marked by a "proxy fight."

Yield: Also known as return. The dividends or interest paid by a company expressed as a percentage of the current price. A stock with a current market value of $40 a share paying dividends at the rate of $2.00 is said to return 5% ($2.00 - $40.00).

WALL STREET INDEXES

Dow Jones Industrial Average: The addition of closing prices for 30 stocks divided by the current divisor. The divisor is never the number of stocks listed, but by reflecting splits, mergers, and bankruptcies, it is constantly revised.

NASDAQ Composite Index: The measure of all domestic common issues traded over-the-counter included in the NASDAQ System, exclusive of those listed on an exchange and those with only one market maker. The index is market value-weighted, in that the importance of each stock is proportional to its price times the number of shares outstanding.

New York Stock Exchange Common Stock Index: The current aggregate market value (sum of all shares times the price per share) divided by the adjusted base market value and multiplied by 50. The adjusted value reflects additions or deletions of listings, but remains unaffected by stock splits and dividends.

Standard and Poor's Index: The aggregate market value (price of each share times the number of shares) for 425 industrial stocks, expressed as one-tenth the percentage of the average market value relative to the average market value during the years 1941-43.

THE AMERICAN SHAREHOLDER

The latest NYSE shareownership survey, conducted during 1975, revealed that almost 1 out of 5 shareowners had left the stock market since early 1970. U.S. shareowners numbered 25.3 million and included 1 out of 6 adult Americans in mid-1975. In this five-and-one-half-year period, the median age of shareowners increased by 5 years, from 48 to 53. For the first time since the Exchange began conducting shareownership surveys in 1952, the number of shareowners in the U.S. did not increase.

These 25 million shareowners held shares in some 11,000 publicly owned corporations and investment companies, which had 40.7 billion shares of stock outstanding at a total market value of $800 billion. While the number of shares of stock outstanding increased 12.6% from 36.2 billion in 1970, depressed economic conditions reduced the total market value of stocks outstanding, which declined 21.3% from $1.1 trillion in 1970.

Although the total number of U.S. shareowners declined 18.1%, the number of shareowners of NYSE-listed stocks declined only 1.9% to 18.0 million. Adult female shareowners slightly outnumbered adult males.

The average shareowner's income rose from $13,500 in early 1970 to $19,000 in mid-1975, paralleling changes in purchasing power. The incidence of shareowners with household incomes below $10,000 declined from 28.8% of all U.S. shareowners in 1970 to 14.6% in mid-1975.

Year	Number of Shareowners (millions)	Percent of U.S. Population
1952	6.5	4%
1959	12.5	7
1962	17.0	9
1965	20.1	10
1971	31.9	17
1972	32.5	17
1973	31.7	15
1974	30.9	14
1975	25.3	12
1980	29.8	—

INSTITUTIONAL FAVORITES

Source: Standard & Poor's Corporation

The Standard & Poor's Corporation issues most favored by institutional investors are ranked here by the number of companies owning them.

Issue	Ind. Div. Rate $	% Yld. on Div.	P-E Ratio	Issue	Ind. Div. Rate $	% Yld. on Div.	P-E Ratio	Issue	Ind. Div. Rate $	% Yld. on Div.	P-E Ratio
Int'l Bus. Mach.	3.44	5.6	11	Johnson & Johnson	2.30	2.2	16	American Express	2.00	4.4	9
American Tel. & Tel.	5.40	10.6	6	Citicorp	1.56	6.9	6	Weyerhaeuser Co.	1.30	3.4	16
Exxon Corp.	6.00	8.7	5	Tenneco, Inc.	2.60	5.5	8	Smith Kline Corp.	1.92	2.5	17
General Electric	3.00	4.5	10	Procter & Gamble	3.80	5.4	9	BankAmerica Corp.	1.44	5.4	6
Eastman Kodak	3.50	4.3	11	Gen'l Tel. & Elect.	2.72	9.9	7	Alcan Aluminum Ltd.	1.80	4.9	6
Atlantic Richfield	2.20	4.2	8	K-Mart	.92	4.8	9	Georgia-Pacific	1.20	3.9	13
General Motors	2.40	4.5	*	Union Oil of Calif.	.80	2.1	10	Warner-Lambert	1.32	5.9	9
Mobil Corp.	4.00	6.2	5	Union Carbide	3.20	5.2	6	Emerson Electric	1.76	4.1	12
Xerox Corp.	3.00	5.4	8	Reynolds (R.J.) Indus.	2.40	5.5	7	Getty Oil	2.00	2.7	7
Schlumberger, Ltd.	1.00	1.0	21	Coca-Cola	2.32	6.3	11	Morgan (J.P.)	3.10	6.3	6
Standard Oil (Ind.)	2.60	3.6	11	Pfizer, Inc.	1.60	3.0	15	Schering-Plough	1.60	4.4	8
Texaco Inc.	2.60	7.1	4	Union Pacific	1.60	2.2	17	Dart & Kraft	3.40	6.9	7
Standard Oil of Cal.	2.00	4.9	6	Bristol-Myers	1.84	3.3	14	Int'l Paper	2.40	4.9	8
Merck & Co.	2.60	3.1	15	Standard Oil (Ohio)	1.80	3.4	7	Monsanto Co.	3.60	5.1	10
Minnesota Mng./Mfg.	3.00	4.8	11	Texas Utilities	1.88	10.7	5	Boeing Co.	1.60	4.6	6
Phillips Petroleum	2.20	4.7	7	Eli Lilly & Co.	2.30	3.6	14	Central & So. West	1.58	11.7	5
Halliburton Co.	1.20	1.6	18	Pepsico Inc.	1.30	3.9	11	Deere & Co.	1.90	4.1	14
Dow Chemical	1.80	4.8	9	Int'l Tel. & Tel.	2.60	8.1	6	J.C. Penney	1.84	6.5	8
Conoco Inc.	2.60	4.7	6	Digital Equipment			16	Hewlett-Packard	.40	.4	20
Amer. Home Prods.	1.80	5.4	12	Raytheon Co.	2.40	2.3	15	Aluminum Co. of Amer.	1.80	5.1	5
Philip Morris	2.00	3.9	11	Abbott Laboratories	1.44	2.4	17	McDonald's Corp.	.80	1.3	11
Gulf Oil	2.50	7.1	5	Burroughs Corp.	2.60	5.0	10	Commonwealth Edison	2.60	13.8	6
Caterpillar Tractor	2.40	3.7	10	Avon Products	3.00	8.1	9	United Technologies	2.40	4.3	8
Sears, Roebuck & Co.	1.36	7.4	9	Dresser Indus.	.68	1.4	14	Aetna Life & Casual.	2.32	6.6	6
du Pont (E.I.) de Nem.	2.40	4.8	10	Marathon Oil	2.00	3.7	9	Ford Motor	1.20	5.2	*

* = Deficit

THE 50 LEADING STOCKS IN MARKET VALUE (AS OF DEC. 31, 1980)

Source: New York Stock Exchange

Issue	Listed Shares (in millions)	Market Value (in millions)	Issue	Listed Shares (in millions)	Market Value (in millions)
Int'l Business Machines	584.1	$ 39,648	Johnson & Johnson	61.9	$ 6,172
Exxon Corp.	453.2	36,540	du Pont de Nemours	146.6	6,155
American Tel. & Tel.	740.6	35,457	Tenneco Inc.	118.4	6,142
Standard Oil Co. (Ind.)	304.3	24,308	Sun Company	123.3	6,009
Schlumberger, N.V.	200.7	23,483	Procter & Gamble	82.7	5,698
Shell Oil	308.9	17,993	Philip Morris Inc.	124.8	5,396
Mobil Corp.	212.6	17,167	Hewlett-Packard Co.	60.0	5,367
Standard Oil of Calif.	171.1	17,020	Smith Kline Corp.	66.5	5,317
Atlantic Richfield	236.3	15,037	Superior Oil	26.6	5,257
General Electric	231.5	14,177	Xerox Corp.	84.3	5,045
General Motors	297.3	13,415	Caterpillar Tractor	86.5	5,017
Texaco Inc.	274.3	13,132	Sears, Roebuck & Co.	325.3	5,002
Eastman Kodak	161.6	11,269	Raytheon Co.	44.5	4,894
Halliburton Co.	118.0	9,854	Eli Lilly & Co.	75.8	4,820
Gulf Oil	211.9	9,245	Reynolds (R.J.) Indus.	104.4	4,761
Phillips Petroleum	154.4	9,074	American Home Products	168.4	4,737
Standard Oil (Ohio)	120.8	8,697	BankAmerica Corp.	147.8	4,471
Getty Oil	88.5	8,134	Weyerhaeuser Co.	128.6	4,389
Union Oil of Calif.	173.5	7,742	Digital Equipment	45.9	4,360
Union Pacific	96.0	7,557	Marathon Oil	61.5	4,354
Conoco Inc.	113.5	7,417	Boeing Co.	97.6	4,318
Teledyne, Inc.	32.3	6,985	Dresser Industries	79.7	4,263
Minnesota Mining & Mfg.	118.0	6,962	General Tel. & Electronics	154.8	4,199
Dow Chemical	202.0	6,489	Coca-Cola Co.	124.0	4,138
Merck & Co.	75.9	6,432	Cities Service	84.7	4,025
			TOTAL	8,305.9	$497,540

REGULAR DIVIDEND PAYERS
SOURCE: Standard & Poor's Corporation

The following companies have paid quarterly, semi-annual, or annual dividends for 60 years or more. Dividends are for 1980.

Company	Dividends Began	Dividend	Company	Dividends Began	Dividend	Company	Dividends Began	Dividend
Allied Chemical	1887	2.200	Eastman Kodak	1902	3.500	Oklahoma Gas & Electric	1908	1.680
Amerada Hess	1922	1.100	Emhart Corporation	1902	2.400	Orange/Rockland Util	1908	1.600
American Brands	1905	6.200	Equifax Incorporated	1913	2.400	Owens-Illinois	1907	1.560
American District Teleg	1903	1.400	Equimark Corporation	1872	.960	Pacific Gas & Electric	1919	2.720
American Electric Power	1909	2.260	Exxon Corporation	1882	6.000	Pacific Lighting	1909	2.440
American Express	1870	2.000	Fidelity Union Banc	1893	2.800	Peavey Company	1915	1.140
American Home Products	1919	1.800	First Int'l Bancshares	1875	1.800	J.C. Penney	1922	1.840
American Natural Res	1904	3.440	First National Boston	1784	2.500	Pennwalt Corporation	1863	2.200
American Sterilizer	1914	.340	First Nat'l St. Bancorp	1812	2.200	Pfizer, Incorporated	1901	1.600
American Tel. & Tel	1881	5.400	Fisher Scientific	1907	.520	Philadelphia Electric	1902	1.800
Amfac, Incorporated	1898	1.440	Foxboro Company	1916	1.400	Potomac Electric Power	1904	1.520
Anchor Hocking	1914	1.360	Gatx Corporation	1919	2.400	PPG Industries	1899	2.160
Arizona Public Service	1920	2.120	General Bancshares	1913	.800	Procter & Gamble	1891	3.800
Atlantic City Electric	1919	1.960	General Electric	1899	3.000	Pub. Service of Colorado	1907	1.680
Avon Products	1919	3.000	General Mills	1898	1.480	Pub. Serv. Elec. & Gas	1907	2.440
Baltimore Gas & Electric	1910	2.560	General Motors	1915	2.400	Quaker Oats	1906	1.600
Bancal Tri-State	1875	1.200	Gillette Company	1906	1.900	Raybestos-Manhattan	1895	1.600
Bank of N.Y. Company	1785	3.000	Great Lakes Internatl	1920	1.020	Reece Corporation	1882	.600
Bankers Trust N.Y.	1904	1.850	Great Northern Nekoosa	1910	1.800	Republic Financial Serv	1906	1.200
Bay State Gas	1853	2.320	Hackensack Water	1886	2.200	Republic of Texas	1920	1.400
Bell & Howell	1915	.960	Handy & Harman	1905	.500	Rexnord, Incorporated	1894	1.080
Bell Telephone of Canada	1881	1.800	Harris Bank Corporation	1908	2.000	Reynolds (RJ) Industries	1900	2.400
Borden, Incorporated	1899	1.900	Hawaiian Electric	1901	2.640	San Diego Gas & Electric	1909	1.600
Boston Edison	1890	2.800	Heinz (H.J.)	1911	2.600	Scott Paper	1915	1.000
Bristol-Myers	1900	1.840	Heller (WE) Int'l	1921	1.300	Scoville Incorporated	1856	1.520
British Petroleum	1917	2.240	Hercules, Incorporated	1913	1.200	Security Pacific	1881	2.000
Burroughs Corporation	1895	2.600	Houghton Mifflin	1908	1.600	Shell Transport/Trade	1898	2.310
Campbell Soup	1902	2.100	Household Finance	1917	1.600	Sierra Pacific Power	1916	1.460
Cannon Mills	1890	1.200	Hydraulic Company	1903	1.680	Singer Company	1863	.100
Carpenter Technology	1907	2.000	Idaho Power	1917	2.520	Southeast Banking	1908	1.000
Carter-Wallace	1883	.400	Ideal Basic Industries	1911	1.700	Southern Calif. Edison	1909	2.960
Castle & Cooke	1896	.800	INA Corporation	1874	2.400	Southern New Eng. Tel	1891	4.080
Caterpillar Tractor	1914	2.400	Industrial National	1791	1.760	Springs Mills	1898	1.360
Ceco Corporation	1921	.900	Ingersoll-Rand	1910	3.400	Squibb Corporation	1902	1.200
Central Hudson G. & E	1903	2.360	Interco, Incorporated	1913	2.880	Standard Brands	1899	1.640
Central Illinois Light	1921	1.820	IBM	1916	3.440	Standard Oil of Calif.	1912	2.000
Champion Spark Plug	1919	.800	Iowa Resources	1909	2.720	Standard Oil, Indiana	1894	2.600
Chase Manhattan	1848	3.100	Irving Bank Corporation	1865	3.040	Stanley Works	1877	.680
Chemical New York	1827	3.840	Jefferson-Pilot	1913	1.400	Stauffer Chemical	1915	1.200
Chesebrough-Pond's	1883	1.520	Johnson Controls	1901	1.300	Sterling Drug	1902	.920
Cincinnati Bell	1879	2.520	Johnson & Johnson	1905	2.300	Sun Company, Inc.	1904	1.800
Cincinnati Gas & Elec	1853	2.040	JWT Group	1917	1.440	Tampa Electric	1900	1.560
Citicorp	1813	1.560	Kansas City Power & Light	1921	2.780	Texaco Incorporated	1903	2.600
Cleveland Elec. Ill.	1901	2.080	K-Mart	1913	.920	Texas Commerce Bankshare	1920	.920
Coca-Cola	1893	2.320	Kroger Company	1902	1.520	Texas Gulf Incorporated	1921	2.000
Colgate-Palmolive	1895	1.120	Lilly (Eli) & Company	1885	2.300	Texas Utilities	1917	1.880
Combustion Engineer	1911	1.500	Lincoln National	1920	3.000	Times Mirror	1892	1.720
Commonwealth Edison	1890	2.600	Louisville Gas & Elec	1913	2.140	Timken Company	1921	3.650
Cone Mills	1914	2.200	Ludlow Corporation	1872	.800	Tokheim Corporation	1920	.540
Conn. General Insurance	1867	1.760	Manhattan Life Corp	1851	.320	Towle Manufacturing	1917	.440
Connecticut Natural Gas	1851	1.800	Manufacturers Hanover	1852	2.720	Travelers Corporation	1864	2.880
Consolidated Edison	1885	2.960	May Department Stores	1911	1.700	Tucson Electric Power	1918	1.720
Consumers Power	1913	2.360	Melville Corporation	1916	1.800	UGI Corporation	1885	1.880
Continental Corporation	1854	2.400	Minn. Mining/Mfg	1916	3.000	Union Carbide	1918	3.200
Conwood Corporation	1903	2.200	Mirro Corporation	1902	.960	Union Electric	1906	1.520
Corning Glass Works	1881	2.320	Mobil Corporation	1902	4.000	Union Oil of California	1916	.800
CPC International	1920	3.840	Monarch Machine Tool, Co	1913	.800	Union Pacific	1900	1.600
Dayton Power & Light	1919	1.820	Morgan (J.P.) & Company	1892	3.100	United Illuminating	1900	2.760
Delmarva Power and Light	1921	1.520	Murphy (G.C.)	1913	1.280	U.S. Gypsum	1919	2.400
De Luxe Check Print	1921	1.560	Nabisco, Incorporated	1899	1.800	U.S. Tobacco	1912	2.400
Dentsply International	1900	.880	National Fuel Gas	1903	2.700	UpJohn Company	1909	2.000
Detroit Edison	1909	1.600	National-Standard	1916	1.240	Walker (H) Cons Hm	1848	1.320
Diamond International	1882	2.200	National Steel	1907	2.000	Washington Gas Light	1852	2.640
Dome Mines, Ltd	1920	.900	NCNB Corporation	1903	.800	Washington Water Power	1899	2.240
Donnelley (RR) & Sons	1911	1.280	New York St. Elec. & Gas	1910	1.880	West Pt.-Pepperell	1888	3.200
Dow Chemical	1911	1.800	NL Industries	1906	1.600	Westvaco Corporation	1892	1.800
Dow Jones & Company	1906	1.840	NLT Corporation	1920	1.320	Wickes Corporation	1895	1.040
du Pont (EI) de Nemours	1904	2.400	Norfolk & Western Ry	1901	2.600	Woolworth, (F.W.)	1912	1.800
Duquesne Light	1913	1.800	Northern States Power	1910	2.420	Wrigley, (Wm) Jr.	1913	2.090

ENERGY: THE NATION'S FUTURE

U.S. ENERGY SUPPLY/DEMAND BALANCE: HISTORY AND PROJECTIONS FOR THREE BASE SCENARIOS, 1965-1995
(Quadrillion Btu per Year)

Source: U.S. Department of Energy, Energy Information Administration

	History			Projections								
				1985			1990			1995		
	1965	1973	1978	Low	Mid	High	Low	Mid	High	Low	Mid	High
World Oil Price (1979 dollars per barrel)	6.00	6.50	15.50	27.00	32.00	39.00	27.00	37.00	44.00	27.00	41.00	56.00
Domestic Energy Supply												
Oil	18.4	22.1	20.7	18.5	18.7	19.0	18.1	19.6	20.3	16.5	19.4	21.0
Gas	15.8	22.2	19.5	18.1	18.2	18.2	18.3	18.7	18.7	17.0	17.8	18.1
Coal	13.4	14.4	15.0	24.9	25.0	24.9	28.5	29.3	29.5	34.3	36.7	36.8
Nuclear	(a)	0.9	3.0	5.6	5.6	5.6	8.1	8.2	8.1	9.6	9.6	9.6
Other	2.1	2.9	3.0	3.4	3.4	3.4	3.7	3.7	3.7	4.1	4.1	4.1
Subtotal, Domestic Production	49.7	62.4	61.2	70.6	70.9	71.1	76.7	79.4	80.3	81.5	87.6	89.5
Net Oil Imports	5.0	13.0	17.1	14.2	12.1	11.0	17.0	11.7	9.5	21.2	11.8	7.7
Net Gas Imports[b]	0.5	1.0	0.9	0.8	0.8	0.8	1.8	0.8	0.8	2.5	0.8	0.8
Net Coal Imports	-1.4	-1.4	-0.9	-2.2	-2.2	-2.2	-2.8	-2.7	-2.7	-3.6	-3.6	-3.6
Subtotal, Net Imports[c]	4.1	12.6	17.2	12.8	10.7	9.6	16.0	9.7	7.6	20.1	9.0	4.9
Total Supply	53.8	75.0	78.4	83.4	81.6	80.7	92.7	89.1	87.9	101.6	96.5	94.4
Energy Demand[d]												
Refined Petroleum Products	22.5	31.2	34.2	31.0	29.4	28.7	32.8	29.9	28.7	36.0	31.3	29.1
Natural Gas	13.4	18.8	16.7	16.6	16.2	16.1	17.7	16.8	16.7	18.3	17.3	17.4
Coal	6.1	4.6	3.7	6.8	6.9	6.9	7.4	7.6	7.6	7.9	8.2	7.7
Electricity	3.3	5.8	6.8	8.3	8.3	8.3	10.0	10.0	10.0	11.4	11.6	11.7
Total End-Use Consumption	45.2	60.4	61.4	62.7	60.9	60.0	67.9	64.3	63.0	73.7	68.3	65.9
Conversion Losses[e]	7.8	14.1	16.6	20.7	20.7	20.7	24.8	24.8	24.9	27.9	28.2	28.5
Total Consumption	53.0	74.5	78.0	83.4	81.6	80.7	92.7	89.1	87.9	101.6	96.5	94.4

[a] Less than .05 quadrillion Btu.
[b] Includes Canadian and Mexican natural gas imports and liquefied natural gas imports under projects currently approved.
[c] Includes .05 quadrillion Btu of electricity imports in 1973 and .07 quadrillion Btu in 1978. Includes imports for the Strategic Petroleum Reserve which began in 1977.
[d] Includes refinery consumption of refined petroleum products and natural gas.
[e] Includes losses or gains from electricity generation, synthetics production, and petroleum refining.

MAJOR U.S. VEHICULAR TUNNELS Source: Federal Highway Administration

UNDERWATER TUNNELS

State or City	Name and Location	Length Portal to Portal (Feet)
Alabama	Bankhead Tunnel at Mobile, Mobile River	3,109
Alabama	George C. Wallace Tunnel, Interstate 10, Mobile River	3,000
California	Posey Tube, Oakland Estuary	3,500
California	Webster St. Tube, Oakland Estuary	3,350
Louisiana	Harvey Tunnel Intracoastal Canal	1,080
Maryland	Baltimore Harbor Tunnel	7,650
Massachusetts	Sumner Tunnel, Boston Harbor	5,650
Massachusetts	Lt. Wm. F. Callahan, Jr. Tunnel, Boston Harbor	5,047
Michigan	Detroit-Windsor Tunnel	5,160
New York City	Holland Tunnel, Hudson River	8,557
New York City	Lincoln Tunnel, Hudson River	8,215
New York City	Lincoln Tunnel (3d Tube), Hudson River	8,013
New York City	Queens Midtown Tunnel, East River	6,414
New York City	Brooklyn-Battery Tunnel, Upper New York Bay	9,117*
Texas	Baytown Tunnel, Houston Ship Channel	3,009
Texas	Washburn Tunnel, Houston Ship Channel	2,936
Virginia	Elizabeth River, near Norfolk	3,920
Virginia	2d Elizabeth River, near Norfolk	4,194
Virginia	Hampton Roads, near Norfolk, I-64	7,479
Virginia	2d Hampton Roads Tunnel near Norfolk, Interstate 64	7,500
Virginia	Chesapeake Bay Crossing (Cape Charles to Cape Henry):	
Virginia	Baltimore Channel Tunnel	5,450
Virginia	Thimble Shoal Tunnel	5,738

LAND TUNNELS

State or City	Name and Location	Length Portal to Portal (Feet)
Arizona	Mule Pass, Benson Douglas Highway	1,400
Arizona	Queen Creek Tunnel, Superior-Miami	1,200
California	Wawona, Yosemite Nat'l Park	4,233
California	Big Oak Flat, Yosemite Nat'l Park	2,083
California	Broadway, Low Level Twin Bore, Oakland	2,944
California	Caldecott (New) Tunnel No. 3, Oakland	3,371
California	Broadway, San Francisco	1,616
California	Park Presidio, San Francisco	1,300
California	Waldo Tunnel, Marin County	1,000
California	Elephant Butte, Plumas	1,187
California	International Airport Underpass, Los Angeles	1,910
Colorado	SN-WPH 81 G(1), near Idaho Springs—U.S. 6	1,036
Colorado	1-F Entrance Road, Mesa Verde Nat'l Park	1,470
Colorado	Eisenhower Memorial Tunnel, I-70 (2 bores)	8,950†
Colorado	Interstate 70, near Glenwood Springs	1,045
Connecticut	West Rock Tunnel, near New Haven	1,200
D. C.	9th Street Expressway	1,600
D. C.	Center Leg Air Rights Tunnel, I-95	1,200
D. C.	Center Leg Air Rights Tunnel, I-395 (not open to traffic)	1,200

LAND TUNNELS (Cont.)

State or City	Name and Location	Length Portal to Portal (Feet)
Hawaii	Kalihi Tunnel, Honolulu	2,780
Hawaii	Nuuanu-Pali Tunnel No. 1	1,000
Massachusetts	John F. Fitzgerald Expressway, Boston	2,335
Massachusetts	Prudential Passageway, Boston	1,980
Minnesota	Lowry Hill Tunnel at Minneapolis—Interstate 94	1,500
Nevada	Carlin Canyon Tunnel, near Elko on Interstate 80	1,400
New York City	Battery Park	2,300
New York City	First Avenue	1,377
New York City	F.D.R. Drive (42–48 Sts.)	1,600
New York City	F.D.R. Drive (81–89 Sts.)	2,400
New York City	Park Avenue	1,400
New York City	178–179 Sts., Cross-Town	2,414
North Carolina	Beaucatcher Tunnel, Asheville	1,100
North Carolina	Along Pigeon River, Haywood County	1,035
North Carolina	Along Pigeon River, Haywood County	1,122
North Carolina	Blue Ridge Parkway, near Waynesville	820
Ohio	Lytle Park Tunnel in Cincinnati—Interstate 71	850
Oregon	Arch Cape, U.S. 101	1,228
Oregon	Elk Creek Umpqua Highway, State Rt. 58	1,102
Oregon	U.S. Route 26, Vista Ridge, Portland	1,100
Oregon	Sunset Tunnel	779
Oregon	Tooth Park, Route 30	837
Pennsylvania	Squirrel Hill Tunnel, Pittsburgh	4,225
Pennsylvania	Armstrong Hill Tunnel, Pittsburgh	1,325
Pennsylvania	Liberty Tubes, Pittsburgh	6,336
Pennsylvania	Fort Pitt, Pittsburgh	3,550
Pa. Turnpike	Allegheny Tunnel	6,070
—	Tuscarora Tunnel	5,326
—	Kittatinny Tunnel	4,727
—	Blue Mountain	4,339
—	Evans Tunnel, NE Extensions	4,379
Rhode Island	Providence Reconverted Streetcar Tunnel	1,793
Tennessee	Bachman Tunnel, U.S. Route 41, Chattanooga	1,027
Tennessee	Wilcox Tunnel, Chattanooga	1,312
Utah	Copperfield Tunnel, Copperfield	6,989
Utah	Zion Nat'l Park Tunnel, Rt. 1, State Rt. 15	5,766
Virginia	Colonial Parkway, Project 1D3	1,200
Virginia	Route I-77, Big Walker Mountain	4,200
Washington	State Rt. 1-AW-3, Battery Street Tunnel, Seattle	2,140
Washington	State Rt. 2–639, U.S. 10—approach to Lake Washington, Seattle	1,466
Washington	Cayuse Pass Tunnel, Mt. Rainier	510
West Virginia	West Virginia Turnpike	2,669
West Virginia	I-70, Wheeling	1,485
West Virginia	East River Mountain Tunnel, near Bluefield—Interstate 77	5,700
Wyoming	I-80, Green River	1,137

VEHICULAR TUNNELS UNDER CONSTRUCTION

State or City	Name and Location	
Maryland	Fort McHenry Tunnel, Baltimore, I-95 under Patapsco River	

* Longest underwater U.S. vehicular tunnel. † Longest U.S. land vehicular tunnel.

RAILROAD PASSENGER SERVICE
Source: Interstate Commerce Commission

Year ended Dec. 31[1]	Average miles of road operated	Passengers carried (Thousands)	Total passenger-miles (Millions)	Revenues per passenger per mile* (Cents)	Revenues per passenger per mile† (Cents)	Passenger train-miles (Thousands)	Train-miles per train-hour	Percent passenger cars unserviceable
1960	94,117	325,872	21,258	3.01	3.03	209,367	40.7	8.7
1965	76,993	298,877	17,389	3.18	3.14	172,344	41.3	7.9
1969	56,484	295,880	13,120	3.38	3.33	122,591	41.0	8.3
1970	49,533	283,970	12,169	3.60	3.63	107,106	41.0	7.8
1971[2]	40,261	272,401	8,833	4.27	4.64	69,127	37.1	9.6
1972[2]	29,398	261,099	8,560	4.76	5.31	60,993	38.3	15.3
1973[2]	28,286	254,506	9,298	4.76	5.19	60,768	37.6	17.4
1974[2]	31,344	274,298	10,337	5.22	5.85	64,368	38.2	17.1
1975[2]	31,576	269,394	9,735	5.50	6.31	65,766	39.2	17.9
1976[2]	34,474	271,581	10,307	5.72	6.30	66,487	31.2	16.9
1977[2]	31,903	275,322	10,295	5.91	6.64	66,237	33.0	20.4
1978[2]	30,369	281,069	10,223	5.95	6.62	64,190	32.3	19.6
1979[3]	28,200	301,300	11,306	5.65	6.50	61,679	34.3	N.A.
1980[3]	29,113	300,183	10,995	7.34	8.60	60,460	31.3	N.A.

[1] Effective Jan. 1, 1965, the revenue qualification of a Class I railroad was increased from average annual operating revenues of $3 million or more to $5 million or more; effective Jan. 1, 1976, this was again raised to $10 million or more. [2] Includes National Railroad Passenger Corp. (AMTRAK). [3] Preliminary. * Includes commutation. † Excludes commutation.

INTERCITY BUS LINES   Source: American Bus Association

Summary of Operations	1960	1964	1968	1972	1979	1980[5]
Operating companies	1,150	1,100	1,050	1,000	1,200	1,330
Buses	20,974	20,500	21,000	21,400	20,680	21,900
Miles of highway served[1]	265,000	260,000	260,000	270,000	280,000	280,000
Employees[2]	45,000	46,800	47,300	49,100	47,000	50,000
Total bus miles (millions)	1,092	1,183	1,190	1,182	1,135	1,182
Fare-paying passengers (millions)	366	360	398	393	359	373
Fare-paying passenger-miles (millions)	19,300	23,300	24,500	25,600	27,200	27,700
Operating revenue, all services ($ millions)	556.2	686.7	797.6	974.4	1,654.8	1,946.5
Operating expenses ($ millions)	494.8	594.9	708.7	882.1	1,564.6	1,813.0
Net operating revenue before income taxes ($ millions)	61.4	91.8	88.9	92.3	90.2	133.5
Operating ratio[4]	89.0	86.6	88.9	90.5	94.6	93.1
Taxes assigned to operations ($ millions)[3]	53.2	63.5	67.9	84.1	101.2	112.6

[1]Includes duplication between carriers. [2]Operating companies only. [3]Excludes income taxes. [4]Operating expenses divided by operating revenues. [5]Preliminary.

AMTRAK

On May 1, 1971, Amtrak was established as the National Railroad Passenger Corporation. Amtrak had several basic objectives: to reverse the downward trend in passenger ridership, to provide modern, efficient intercity rail passenger service and to develop fully the potential of modern intercity rail service.

The Corporation operates trains through contractual agreements with existing railroads outside of the Northeast. In 1976, Amtrak assumed full ownership and operating control of the Boston-Washington Northeast Corridor.

In Fiscal Year 1980, Amtrak operated an average of 217 trains daily, serving 525 stations, and carried 21.2 million passengers while grossing $429 million. During the fiscal year, the Corporation placed 103 new bi-level cars in service, built or rehabilitated 18 stations and continued its rebuilding program for hundreds of its older steam-equipped cars.

CONRAIL

A private, for-profit corporation created by an Act of Congress, the Consolidated Rail Corporation (Conrail) began operations on April 1, 1976. It was conveyed most of the rail properties of the Central of New Jersey, Erie Lackawanna, Lehigh and Hudson River, Lehigh Valley, Penn Central, and Reading lines. Conrail operates over a 17,700 route-mile system (39,988 track miles, including 32,408 track miles owned by Conrail) in 16 eastern and midwestern states, the District of Columbia and two provinces of Canada.

Conrail is primarily a freight railroad, operating more than 1,200 trains a day. In addition, Conrail operates certain rail commuter services under contract with local, regional or state authorities, and some intercity passenger trains under contract with Amtrak.

Conrail's purpose is to create a viable, private-sector rail freight system in the Northeast and Midwest, providing efficient and essential rail service to customers.

LONGEST RAILWAY TUNNELS   Source: Railway Directory and Yearbook

There are considerable discrepancies in figues given by various authorities on precise tunnel lengths.

		Length			
Tunnel	Date of Opening	Miles	Yards	Operating Railway	Country
Seikan	U.C.	33	810	Japanese National	Japan
Dai-shimizu	U.C.	13	1,403	Japanese National	Japan
Simplon No. II	Oct. 16, 1922	12	559	Swiss Federal & Italian State	Switzerland-Italy
Simplon No. I	June 1, 1906	12	537	Swiss Federal & Italian State	Switzeraind-Italy
New Kanmon	March 10, 1975	11	1,059	Japanese National	Japan
Appenine	Apr. 22, 1934	11	892	Italian State	Italy
Rokko	March 15, 1972	10	132	Japanese National	Japan
Gotthard	Jan. 1, 1882(a)	9	562	Swiss Federal	Switzerland
Lötschberg	July 15, 1913	9	140	Bern-Lötschberg-Simplon	Switzerland
Hokuriku	June 10, 1962	8	1,055	Japanese National	Japan
Mont Cenis (Fréjus)	Sept. 17, 1871	8	855	Italian State	France-Italy
New Shimizu	Oct. 1, 1967	8	651	Japanese National	Japan
Aki	March 10, 1975	8	141	Japanese National	Japan
Cascade	Jan. 12, 1929	7	1,397	Great Northern	United States
Kita-Kyushu	March 10, 1975	7	493	Japanese National	Japan
Kubiki	Oct. 1, 1969	7	70	Japanese National	Japan
Flathead	November 1970	6	5,275	Great Northern	United States
Arlberg	Sept. 20, 1884	6	650	Austrian Federal	Austria
Moffat	Feb. 27, 1928	6	373	Denver & Rio Grande Western	United States
Shimizu	Sept. 1, 1981	6	35	Japanese National	Japan
Kvineshei	Dec. 17, 1943(b)	5	1,112	Norwegian State	Norway
Bingo	March 10, 1975	5	915	Japanese National	Japan
Rimutaka	Nov. 3, 1955	5	821	New Zealand Government	New Zealand
Ricken	Oct. 1, 1910	5	608	Swiss Federal	Switzerland
Grenchenberg	Oct. 1, 1915	5	581	Swiss Federal(c)	Switzerland
Otira	Aug. 4, 1923	5	564	New Zealand Government	New Zealand
Tauern	July 7, 1909	5	551	Austrian Federal	Austria
Haegebostad	Dec. 17, 1943(b)	5	467	Norwegian State	Norway
Fukouka	March 10, 1975	5	458	Japanese National	Japan
Ronco	Apr. 4, 1889	5	277	Italian State	Italy
Hauenstein (Lower)	Jan. 8, 1916	5	95	Swiss Federal	Switzerland
Connaught	Dec. 6, 1916	5	39	Canadian Pacific	Canada
Karawanken	Oct. 1, 1906	4	1,683	Austrian Federal	Austria-Yugoslavia
New Tanna	Oct. 1, 1964	4	1,663	Japanese National	Japan
Somport	July 18, 1928	4	1,572	French National	France-Spain
Tanna	Dec. 1, 1934	4	1,493	Japanese National	Japan
Ulrikken	Aug. 1, 1964	4	1,338	Norwegian State	Norway
Hoosac	Feb. 9, 1875	4	1,230	Boston & Maine	United States
Monte Orso	Oct. 28, 1927	4	1,230	Italian State	Italy
Lupacino	Sept. 24, 1958	4	1,178	Italian State	Italy
Vivola	Oct. 28, 1927	4	1,004	Italian State	Italy
Monte Adone	Apr. 22, 1934	4	760	Italian State	Italy
Jungfrau	Aug. 1, 1912	4	750	Jungfrau	Switzerland
Borgallo	Aug. 1, 1894	4	700	Italian State	Italy
Severn	Sept. 1, 1886	4	628	Western Region	Great Britain
Lusse (Vosges)	Aug. 9, 1937	4	474	French National	France
Marianopoli	Aug. 1, 1885	4	42	Italian State	Italy

(a) For goods traffic; passengers: June 1, 1882. (b) These were wartime openings under German Occupation. Full traffic began March 1, 1944. (c) The Gronchenberg tunnel is owned but not worked by the Bern-Lötschberg-Simplon Railway.

ESTIMATED AUTOMOBILE REGISTRATIONS: 1980 (in thousands)
SOURCE: U.S. Federal Highway Administration

State	Registrations	State	Registrations	State	Registrations	State	Registrations
Alabama	2,115	Illinois	7,534	Montana	588	Rhode Island	514
Alaska	156	Indiana	2,941	Nebraska	874	South Carolina	1,542
Arizona	1,325	Iowa	1,755	Nevada	422	South Dakota	374
Arkansas	1,017	Kansas	1,393	New Hampshire	543	Tennessee	2,373
California	12,852	Kentucky	1,833	New Jersey	4,324	Texas	7,389
Colorado	1,764	Louisiana	1,976	New Mexico	680	Utah	686
Connecticut	2,060	Maine	531	New York	7,162	Vermont	260
Delaware	326	Maryland	2,373	North Carolina	3,492	Virginia	3,060
Dist. of Col.	238	Massachusettts	3,325	North Dakota	366	Washington	2,310
Florida	6,429	Michigan	5,241	Ohio	6,254	West Virginia	970
Georgia	3,038	Minnesota	2,459	Oklahoma	1,845	Wisconsin	2,530
Hawaii	516	Mississippi	1,166	Oregon	1,513	Wyoming	289
Idaho	479	Missouri	2,454	Pennsylvania	5,811	**Total**	**123,467**

ESTIMATED LICENSED DRIVERS, BY SEX: 1980 (in thousands)
SOURCE: Federal Highway Administration

State	Male Drivers	Female Drivers	Total Drivers	State	Male Drivers	Female Drivers	Total Drivers
Alabama	1,180	1,068	2,248	Montana	322	266	588
Alaska	124	97	221	Nebraska	570	525	1,095
Arizona	1,012	824	1,836	Nevada	315	270	585
Arkansas	767	685	1,452	New Hampshire	346	315	661
California	8,302	7,333	15,635	New Jersey	2,211	2,210	4,421
Colorado	1,067	985	2,052	New Mexico	449	418	867
Connecticut	1,055	1,093	2,148	New York	5,154	4,133	9,287
Delaware	213	201	414	North Carolina	1,973	1,821	3,794
Dist. of Col.	190	159	349	North Dakota	223	201	424
Florida	4,017	3,492	7,509	Ohio	4,574	2,999	7,573
Georgia	1,740	1,593	3,333	Oklahoma	961	941	1,902
Hawaii	298	241	539	Oregon	1,002	871	1,873
Idaho	339	305	644	Pennsylvania	4,100	3,315	7,415
Illinois	3,731	3,282	7,013	Rhode Island	305	282	587
Indiana	1,888	1,770	3,658	South Carolina	1,030	932	1,962
Iowa	1,151	1,024	2,175	South Dakota	251	229	480
Kansas	984	901	1,885	Tennessee	1,466	1,348	2,814
Kentucky	1,133	966	2,099	Texas	4,870	4,389	9,259
Louisiana	1,252	1,076	2,328	Utah	407	405	812
Maine	377	343	720	Vermont	180	164	344
Maryland	1,399	1,271	2,670	Virginia	1,715	1,689	3,404
Massachusetts	1,893	1,877	3,770	Washington	1,398	1,239	2,637
Michigan	3,361	3,091	6,452	West Virginia	845	637	1,482
Minnesota	1,217	1,115	2,332	Wisconsin	1,578	1,434	3,012
Mississippi	855	741	1,596	Wyoming	184	157	344
Missouri	1,703	1,572	3,275	**Total**	**77,677**	**68,295**	**145,972**

WORLD MOTOR VEHICLE FATALITY RATES
(per 100,000 population)

SOURCE: U.N. Demographic Yearbook 1978, © United Nations

Nation	Rate
Kuwait (1977)	36.0
Venezuela (1977)	34.2
Austria (1976)	28.8
Australia (1977)	27.2
Italy (1972)	25.9
Belgium (1976)	25.1
France (1970)	23.5
Germany, West (1976)	23.5
Canada (1976)	22.5
UNITED STATES (1976)	21.9
Costa Rica (1977)	21.3
New Zealand (1976)	21.1
Switzerland (1977)	20.2
Czechoslovakia (1976)	19.5
Netherlands (1977)	18.6
Greece (1976)	17.9
Hungary (1977)	17.6
Iceland (1977)	17.6
Denmark (1976)	17.1
Germany, East (1976)	16.4
Mexico (1975)	16.4
Argentina (1977)	16.1
Israel (1977)	15.7
Spain (1975)	15.1
Sweden (1975)	15.1
Jordan (1976)	14.1
Bulgaria (1976)	12.6
England Wales (1976)	12.3
Norway (1977)	11.6
Singapore (1977)	11.4
Japan (1977)	10.6

AUTO CASUALTY RATES
SOURCE: International Road Federation

	Vehicles per 1,000 pop.	Rates per million vehicle-kilometers Injuries	Deaths
Australia (1979)	394	85[3]	3.5[3]
Belgium (1979)	312	202[2]	6.0[2]
Canada (1978)	413	109[3]	2.9[3]
Denmark (1979)	277	60	2.7
Finland (1979)	245	38[2]	3.0[2]
France (1979)	344	129	4.6
Iceland (1978)	338	61	2.3
Italy (1979)	308	86[2]	3.3[2]
Japan (1979)	195	176[1]	2.7[1]
Netherlands (1978)	293	95[2]	3.5[2]
New Zealand (1979)	411	87[2]	3.8[2]
Norway (1979)	292	71[1]	2.6[1]
United Kingdom (1979)	268	117	2.3
United States (1978)	534	127	2.0
West Germany (1979)	368	149	4.0

[1]1977. [2]1978. [3]1976.

U.S. DEATHS AND DEATH RATES FROM MOTOR VEHICLE ACCIDENTS
SOURCE: National Center for Health Statistics

Year	Number	Rate per 100,000 population
1978	52,411	24.0
1977	49,510	22.9
1976	47,038	21.9
1975	45,853	21.5
1974	46,402	22.0
1972	56,278	27.0
1970	54,633	26.9

U.S. ROAD MILEAGE

	Atlanta	Baltimore	Birmingham	Boston	Buffalo	Chicago	Cincinnati	Cleveland	Dallas	Denver	Des Moines	Detroit	Houston	Indianapolis
Akron	672	331	702	653	207	366	230	33	1173	1385	707	190	1270	295
Albuquerque	1396	1889	1266	2194	1767	1289	1378	1381	639	422	994	1538	814	1299
Atlanta		669	152	1068	877	695	461	686	805	1401	894	727	798	1272
Baltimore	669		787	399	345	695	484	351	1458	1701	1025	511	1449	580
Birmingham	152	787		1185	902	636	476	716	654	1282	808	449	662	480
Boston	1068	399	1185		449	975	840	632	1819	1989	1311	699	1916	905
Buffalo	877	345	902	449		529	430	186	1373	1282	865	252	1543	541
Chicago	695	687	656	975	529		295	343	936	1016	338	275	1085	187
Cincinnati	461	494	476	840	430	295		244	943	1373	571	265	1085	108
Cleveland	686	351	716	632	186	343	244		1187	1357	679	167	1234	309
Columbus	549	408	579	769	323	359	107	137	1050	1233	695	189	1147	172
Dallas	805	1458	653	1819	1373	936	943	1187		784	679	1284	242	882
Denver	1401	1701	1282	1989	1282	1016	1373	1357	784		679	1284	1026	1061
Des Moines	894	1025	808	1311	865	338	571	679	679	679		606	946	483
Detroit	726	511	741	699	252	275	265	167	1284	1284	606		1686	277
El Paso	1427	2034	1275	2391	1945	1434	1526	1759	622	654	1139	1686	755	1423
Hartford	972	303	1090	102	342	902	752	562	1690	1858	1232	731	1752	822
Houston	814	1449	662	1916	1470	1085	1040	1234	242	1026	946	1686		997
Indianapolis	508	580	480	905	541	187	108	309	882	1061	483	277	997	
Jacksonville	314	793	426	1191	1067	775	570	793	994	1708	1208	911	822	822
Kansas City, Mo.	810	1099	706	1483	1099	499	590	644	499	600	213	896	2080	484
Little Rock	505	1086	386	1494	1048	644	618	824	325	957	573	896	441	548
Los Angeles	394	386	366	386	986	2095	286	301	1403	1120	1801	375	930	822
Louisville	366	947	247	980	540	544	110	73	464	1035	608	550	741	114
Memphis	394	1355	297	1644	723	479	464	713	454	1095	713	896	787	436
Mexico City	1800	1355	1648	2902	2456	1360	2270	1249	1309	2046	1754	2337	986	437
Miami	665	1144	765	1542	1418	1126	921	1144	1309	2046	1559	1847	1198	1173
Milwaukee	784	776	745	1064	618	91	384	432	1015	1040	361	364	1174	276
Minneapolis/St. Paul	1105	1097	1066	1385	979	412	705	753	956	922	252	698	1198	597
Montgomery	169	832	92	1236	748	1085	568	793	498	1374	900	1184	659	885
Montreal	1230	562	1289	324	448	848	762	578	1763	1862	1584	573	1860	1235
Nashville	256	729	205	1165	719	451	290	533	686	1158	638	555	789	294
New Orleans	493	1138	351	1536	1165	925	820	1010	498	1303	989	1085	555	885
New York City	855	187	974	216	445	820	659	451	1607	1851	1173	667	1636	729
Oklahoma City	845	1321	726	1684	1308	797	843	1052	215	615	740	1052	458	743
Omaha	1012	1163	911	1449	1003	476	691	817	656	540	139	744	898	583
Philadelphia	766	97	884	304	365	762	578	426	1526	1092	1092	586	1546	648
Phoenix	1810	2335	1658	2682	2236	1722	1816	2050	1005	818	1430	2050	1155	1710
Pittsburgh	697	231	742	599	205	461	284	125	1232	1482	804	289	1233	354
Portland, Ore.	2654	2816	2552	3085	2639	2112	2405	2453	2043	1278	1819	2385	2233	2297
Providence	1003	464	1249	30	562	956	918	626	1751	1944	1296	785	1813	883
Reno	2408	2613	2288	2919	2444	1965	2173	2226	1677	856	1623	2218	1867	2065
St. Louis	558	817	481	1178	848	291	336	543	645	856	336	543	867	237
Salt Lake City	1900	2118	1781	2393	2716	2189	2402	2530	1806	521	1094	1852	1731	1536
San Francisco	2523	2689	2403	3163	2718	2630	2620	2530	1955	1270	1806	2530	1955	1752
Seattle	2427	2756	2590	3070	2404	2356	2189	2427	1773	1347	1773	1740	2302	2245
Toledo	668	454	683	742	296	241	207	110	1154	1250	572	276	814	745
Topeka	897	1162	730	1619	2073	562	653	740	693	693	471	814	945	547
Tulsa	783	1219	664	1650	1204	693	740	948	271	856	691	1057	513	641
Washington, D.C.	630	39	748	437	359	687	492	351	1372	1696	1018	511	1410	564

	Kansas City, Mo.	Los Angeles	Memphis	Milwaukee	Minneapolis	Montreal	Nashville	New Orleans	New York City	Philadelphia	Phoenix	Pittsburgh	St. Louis
Akron	779	2368	709	455	776	597	519	1049	487	406	2003	105	532
Albuquerque	790	806	1030	1370	1247	2111	1289	1289	2001	1918	454	1626	1040
Atlanta	779	2197	367	784	1097	1289	205	493	855	97	1810	697	558
Baltimore	1099	2695	947	776	1097	562	725	1138	187	97	2325	230	817
Birmingham	1056	2056	247	745	1066	1289	138	351	974	884	2130	598	476
Boston	1456	3052	1355	1064	1385	324	1165	1536	216	304	2682	598	1178
Buffalo	1010	2606	909	618	939	393	719	1253	445	365	2236	217	802
Chicago	499	2095	544	91	412	848	451	929	820	762	1722	461	291
Cincinnati	599	2186	459	384	705	820	290	820	659	578	1816	284	338
Cleveland	824	2420	723	432	753	576	533	1063	557	507	2050	125	546
Columbus	499	2245	586	448	769	713	396	926	557	476	1882	182	409
Dallas	499	1403	464	1040	956	1763	760	498	1601	1526	1005	1232	645
Denver	751	1134	1105	1040	841	1862	686	1601	1851	1092	1430	1482	856
Des Moines	201	1801	608	361	252	1862	498	989	1171	1171	1871	804	336
Detroit	751	2347	713	364	685	573	555	1114	667	667	1430	285	543
El Paso	935	798	1086	1513	1339	2280	1184	1085	2173	2173	400	1872	1180
Hartford	1423	2895	1226	1226	1317	317	1308	1114	121	121	2545	477	1050
Houston	822	1553	561	1098	1198	1934	783	359	1636	1546	1153	1319	794
Indianapolis	484	2080	436	276	597	885	294	572	648	648	1313	354	237
Jacksonville	1123	2397	673	1098	1419	2920	359	490	890	890	1999	865	872
Kansas City, Mo.		1596	459	516	441	1438	570	416	1319	1201	1330	937	250
Little Rock	405	1701	139	624	825	1438	361	282	1238	1238	1330	897	353
Los Angeles	1596		1831	2107	1940	2920	2017	1940	2790	2721	400	2533	264
Louisville	516	2107	369	390	711	1299	180	710	769	688	1757	394	264
Memphis	459	1831		624	840	622	222	401	1170	1057	1466	460	758
Mexico City	1647	2017	1547	2164	2104	2846	1769	1345	2846	2532	1625	2314	284
Miami	1470	2712	624	1449	1770	1705	921	862	1330	1241	2300	1216	1223
Milwaukee	580	2176	624		326	937	540	1013	875	851	1806	550	370
Minneapolis/St. Paul	441	1940	840	326		1258	937	1013	1241	1253	1330	871	572
Montgomery	798	2920	401	540	1241	1299	297	324	1253	1172	1640	611	1116
Montreal	1524	2920	1547	937	1258		1109	1640	388	467	2550	611	1116
Nashville	524	1901	222	540	937	1109		530	949	868	1725	394	302
New Orleans	824	1901	401	1013	1013	1640	530		1325	1235	1593	1093	673
New York City	1319	2915	1170	875	1241	388	949	1325		92	2459	386	966
Oklahoma City	1319	1357	478	932	1253	1678	868	1235	1472	1472	987	1097	506
Omaha	205	1662	664	358	358	1630	756	1026	1312	1312	1335	942	459
Philadelphia	1201	2721	1057	851	1253	467	868	1235	92		2430	305	885
Phoenix	1330	400	1466	1806	1330	2550	1725	1593	2459	2430		2163	1478
Pittsburgh	937	2533	820	550	871	611	394	1093	386	305	2163		591
Portland, Ore.	1846	970	2305	2026	1990	2746	2305	2541	2953	2872	1366	2571	2096
Providence	1367	2956	1287	1056	1381	342	1088	1506	182	268	2591	538	1120
Reno	1252	477	2011	1732	1773	2803	2192	2175	2765	2685	221	2394	1890
St. Louis	250	1848	294	370	546	2192	302	695	966	885	1478	591	
Salt Lake City	1874	734	2157	1455	1239	2273	2410	2303	3025	3025	759	1890	1368
San Francisco	1874	403	2157	2213	2227	1670	2512	2303	2944	2944	1943	2522	2126
Seattle	2038	1145	686	1977	1962	1739	2610	3421	966	2186	2209	2209	2126
Toledo	63	2313	686	330	651	497	459	610	884	529	1943	228	509
Topeka	63	1537	522	520	653	1387	459	889	1382	884	1091	1000	160
Tulsa	258	1461	417	772	715	1518	634	689	1370	1301	1091	995	404
Washington, D.C.	1048	2644	908	776	1097	600	686	1099	225	136	2274	230	801

	Salt Lake City	San Francisco	Seattle	Washington, D.C.
Akron	1800	2541	2427	331
Albuquerque	611	1127	1482	1838
Atlanta	1900	2523	2756	630
Baltimore	2218	2876	2748	39
Birmingham	1781	2393	2575	748
Boston	2405	3163	3050	437
Buffalo	1958	2716	2590	359
Chicago	1431	2189	2063	687
Cincinnati	1644	2189	2356	492
Cleveland	1772	2530	2404	351
Columbus	1701	2459	2420	392
Dallas	1241	1806	2112	1372
Denver	512	1852	1347	1696
Des Moines	1270	1852	1773	1018
Detroit	1700	2458	2336	511
El Paso	869	1200	1740	1983
Hartford	2326	1955	2955	342
Houston	1431	1955	2302	1410
Indianapolis	1536	2294	2245	564
Jacksonville	2207	2799	3070	754
Kansas City, Mo.	1116	1874	1874	1048
Little Rock	1456	2027	2277	1047
Los Angeles	734	403	1145	2644
Louisville	1632	2390	2362	596
Memphis	1534	2390	2331	908
Mexico City	2100	2419	2948	2396
Miami	2545	2213	3421	1105
Milwaukee	1455	2213	1977	776
Minneapolis/St. Paul	1239	2456	1641	1097
Montgomery	1873	2456	2667	799
Montreal	2273	1670	2697	600
Nashville	1670	2410	2512	686
New Orleans	1739	2410	2610	1099
New York City	2303	3025	2904	225
Oklahoma City	1108	1678	1962	1307
Omaha	955	1713	1667	1156
Philadelphia	2186	2944	1541	136
Phoenix	653	2648	2524	2274
Pittsburgh	1890	2410	2512	230
Portland, Ore.	802	3140	175	2797
Providence	2390	3140	3019	403
Reno	530	221	742	2618
St. Louis	1368	2126	2109	801
Salt Lake City		759	871	2111
San Francisco	759		827	2869
Seattle	871	827		2748
Toledo	1670	2428	2302	454
Topeka	1053	1811	1831	1205
Tulsa	1191	1776	2038	
Washington, D.C.	2111	2869	2748	

* via Canadian routes.

U.S. AIR DISTANCES   (See also, AIR DISTANCES BETWEEN MAJOR WORLD CITIES, pp. 234–235)

	Atlanta	Birmingham	Boston	Buffalo	Charleston, S.C.	Chicago	Cincinnati	Cleveland	Dallas	Denver	Des Moines	Detroit	Houston	Indianapolis	Jacksonville	Kansas City, Mo.	Los Angeles	Louisville	Miami	Minneapolis	Nashville	New Orleans	New York City	Omaha	Philadelphia	Phoenix	Pittsburgh	Portland, Ore.	St. Louis	Salt Lake City	San Francisco	Seattle	Tulsa	Washington, D.C.
Albuquerque	1272	1138	1972	1580	1539	1129	1251	1421	588	334	754	1364	754	1006	1488	718	647	1042	1674	915	1073	1006	1815	721	1753	330	1499	1107	942	484	896	1184	604	1653
Amarillo	999	866	1722	1338	1266	894	992	1173	334	358	533	1124	533	915	1219	481	937	848	1560	776	833	915	1604	526	1494	598	1244	1304	685	668	1157	1359	335	1391
Atlanta		140	867	719	267	587	392	554	721	1199	738	596	694	432	270	676	1936	321	604	907	214	424	760	817	666	1592	521	2172	467	1583	2139	2182	678	543
Billings	1519	1425	1861	1473	1761	1073	1304	1369	1092	454	790	1283	1315	1204	1796	846	959	1220	2085	742	1275	1484	1760	703	1727	872	1304	608	959	387	904	668	930	1669
Birmingham	140		1052	776	402	578	406	618	581	1095	691	641	567	433	374	578	1802	326	665	862	182	312	864	732	783	1456	608	2066	400	1466	2013	2082	552	661
Boston	937	1052		400	820	851	740	551	1551	1769	1159	613	1605	807	1017	1251	2596	826	1255	1123	943	1359	188	1282	271	2300	483	2540	1038	2099	2699	2493	1398	393
Buffalo	776	776	400		699	454	393	173	1205	1370	760	216	1286	435	879	861	2198	483	1181	731	627	1086	292	881	279	1906	178	2156	662	1699	2300	2117	1023	292
Burlington, Vt.	957	1049	182	304	881	699	609	476	1510	1654	1049	516	1580	760	1079	1361	2685	985	1347	985	916	1361	260	1171	328	2220	445	2385	662	1699	2568	2333	1027	432
Charleston, S.C.	227	361	721	538		760	516	560	976	1474	1049	681	936	560	197	928	2119	500	482	1104	455	630	641	1058	562	1857	562	2425	727	1845	2405	2428	945	453
Charlotte	227	361	721	538	177	587	335	435	967	1441	819	509	981	428	341	803	2119	343	660	933	340	649	533	918	451	1783	362	2290	568	1727	2301	2295	853	330
Cheyenne	1229	1119	1735	1286	1486	891	1082	1199	726	96	558	1082	947	947	1493	560	831	1032	1763	642	1032	1131	1604	410	1556	586	1298	947	795	371	967	973	588	1477
Chicago	587	578	851	454	757		252	308	803	920	309	238	940	180	863	410	1745	269	1187	333	397	833	713	432	666	1453	410	1758	289	1260	1858	1737	598	597
Cincinnati	369	406	740	393	516	252		222	814	1094	461	229	892	98	770	541	1897	77	952	605	238	706	570	603	503	1581	257	1985	309	1453	2043	1972	661	404
Cleveland	554	618	551	173	609	308	222		1025	1227	617	90	1114	263	770	700	1987	311	1087	622	459	924	405	739	360	1749	114	2055	492	1568	2166	2026	853	306
Dallas	721	581	1551	1198	981	803	814	1025		663	632	999	225	763	908	451	1240	726	1111	852	631	443	1374	586	1299	887	1070	1633	547	999	1483	1681	236	1185
Denver	1212	1095	1769	1307	1474	920	1094	1227	663		610	1156	879	1000	1467	558	831	1017	1723	632	1010	1082	1631	483	1579	586	1320	982	796	371	949	1021	550	1494
Des Moines	738	691	1159	760	967	309	461	617	632	610		546	879	410	1023	166	1438	476	1420	246	546	831	1082	123	973	973	1155	443	316	833	1550	1469	396	896
Detroit	596	641	613	216	681	238	229	90	999	1156	546		1105	240	831	645	1983	316	1152	528	457	939	482	578	443	1690	205	1969	455	1479	2079	1938	813	396
El Paso	1291	1152	2072	1692	1552	1252	1335	1525	571	557	983	1479	662	1183	1473	745	701	1164	1643	1157	1160	983	1907	839	1836	346	1590	1286	1034	674	995	1395	674	1728
Fargo	1060	1060	1300	910	1317	569	820	835	972	642	390	745	1183	725	1399	549	1447	660	1806	214	806	1222	1210	390	1184	1204	949	1239	660	863	1446	1197	741	1140
Houston	701	567	1605	1286	936	940	892	1114	225	879	879	1105		865	821	644	1374	803	968	1056	665	318	1420	794	1341	1017	1137	1836	679	1199	1645	1891	442	1220
Indianapolis	426	433	807	435	594	165	107	263	763	1000	410	240	865		699	453	1809	107	1024	499	251	712	646	525	585	1499	330	1885	231	1356	1949	1872	551	494
Jacksonville	285	374	1017	879	197	863	770	770	908	1467	1023	831	821	699		826	2147	594	326	1191	473	480	841	937	758	1872	625	2574	758	1982	2451	2455	745	647
Kansas City, Mo.	676	578	1251	861	928	414	541	700	451	558	166	645	644	453	826		1356	480	1241	414	473	680	1097	166	1038	1046	919	1484	238	925	1506	1426	217	945
Knoxville	155	235	861	516	344	454	316	316	767	1259	913	745	723	453	552	547	1983	188	756	1794	161	547	633	745	552	1607	375	2115	291	1457	2121	2114	642	430
Little Rock	456	325	1259	913	679	552	524	524	293	831	723	722	388	388	723	325	1480	435	968	831	277	355	1181	492	1007	1137	779	1759	291	1148	1688	1785	251	892
Los Angeles	1936	1802	2596	2203	2119	1745	1897	1983	1240	831	1438	1983	1374	1809	2147	1356		1829	2339	1536	1769	1673	2451	1315	2394	357	2136	825	1589	579	347	959	1266	2300
Louisville	319	331	826	483	500	269	77	311	726	1017	476	316	803	107	594	480	1829		919	605	154	623	657	581	582	1508	344	1950	242	1402	1986	1943	550	476
Memphis	337	217	1137	803	681	491	461	623	420	879	485	528	484	384	590	369	1809	367	872	699	197	358	957	619	881	1263	663	1849	240	1402	1867	1867	341	765
Miami	604	665	1255	1181	482	1187	952	1087	1111	1726	1420	1152	968	1024	326	1241	2339	919		1511	809	669	1092	1397	1010	1982	1010	2708	1061	2089	2594	2734	1176	923
Minneapolis	907	862	1123	731	1104	355	605	622	862	700	246	528	1056	466	1191	414	1524	605	1511		697	1051	1018	290	985	1280	743	1427	466	987	1584	1395	626	934
Nashville	214	182	943	627	455	397	238	459	617	1023	525	457	665	251	470	473	1809	154	809	697		469	761	697	685	1446	472	1969	254	1393	1963	1975	515	569
New Orleans	424	312	1359	1086	455	833	706	924	443	1082	1022	939	318	453	480	680	1673	623	669	1051	469		1171	847	1089	1316	919	2101	598	1434	1926	2101	548	966
New York City	748	864	188	292	641	713	570	405	1374	1631	1022	482	1420	646	838	1097	2451	657	1092	1018	761	1171		1144	83	2145	317	2435	888	1972	2571	2408	1181	205
Omaha	817	732	1282	883	1058	432	603	739	586	483	123	578	794	525	937	166	1315	581	1397	290	697	847	1144		1094	1036	835	2145	354	833	1429	1369	392	1014
Philadelphia	666	783	271	279	562	666	503	360	1299	1579	973	443	1341	585	758	1038	2394	582	1397	985	685	1089	83	1094		2083	259	2412	811	1925	2523	2380	1163	123
Phoenix	1592	1456	2300	1906	1857	1453	1581	1749	887	586	1155	1690	1017	1499	1872	1049	357	1508	1982	1280	1446	1316	2145	1036	2083		1828	1005	1272	559	653	1114	937	1848
Pittsburgh	521	608	483	178	528	410	257	115	1070	1320	715	205	1137	330	703	781	2136	344	1010	743	472	919	317	835	259	1828		2165	559	1668	2264	2138	917	192
Portland, Ore.	2172	2066	2540	2156	2425	1758	1985	2055	1633	982	1155	1969	1836	1885	2574	1484	825	1950	2708	743	1969	2101	2435	2145	2412	1005	2165		1723	636	534	145	1531	2354
Raleigh	356	491	609	490	242	642	396	405	1057	1463	842	510	968	483	414	905	2237	426	789	1008	457	776	426	1008	345	1903	330	2377	667	1823	2410	2367	972	233
St. Louis	467	400	1038	662	704	262	309	492	547	796	316	455	679	231	751	238	1589	242	1061	466	254	598	875	354	811	1272	559	1723		1162	1744	1724	361	712
Salt Lake City	1583	1466	2099	1699	1845	1051	1453	1568	999	371	833	1479	1199	1356	1982	925	579	1402	2089	987	1393	1434	1972	833	1925	504	1668	636	1162		600	701	917	1848
San Antonio	882	744	1766	1430	1122	1051	1039	1256	252	872	882	1238	189	949	1011	702	1206	949	1148	1081	856	507	1584	828	1291	792	1087	1720	504	600	1490	1787	486	1388
San Francisco	2139	2013	2699	2300	2540	1858	2043	2166	1483	949	1550	2079	1645	1949	2451	1506	347	1986	2594	1584	1963	1926	2571	1429	2523	653	2264	534	1744	600		678	1461	2442
Seattle	2182	2082	2493	2117	2485	1737	1972	2026	1681	1021	1469	1938	1891	1872	2455	1426	959	1943	2734	1395	1975	2101	2408	1369	2380	1114	2138	145	1724	701	678		1550	2329
Spokane	1961	1865	2266	1888	2204	1508	1742	1809	1489	826	1240	1709	1709	1641	2251	1198	940	1717	2521	1166	1752	1898	2179	1146	2151	1015	1908	290	1500	550	727	229	1353	2101
Syracuse	781	875	264	138	592	514	403	257	1308	1473	863	320	1413	541	928	984	2291	567	1212	861	591	1187	194	1021	220	2044	205	2281	592	1831	2435	2295	1115	290
Tulsa	678	552	1398	1003	945	598	626	853	236	550	396	813	442	551	745	217	1206	550	1176	626	515	548	1231	352	1163	937	917	1531	361	917	1461	1560		1058
Washington, D.C.	543	661	393	292	453	597	481	306	1185	1494	896	396	1220	494	647	945	2300	476	923	934	569	966	205	1008	123	1903	192	2354	712	1848	2442	2329	1058	
Wichita	776	658	1424	1104	1039	591	702	873	340	437	334	821	559	620	1031	177	1197	620	1266	546	594	677	1266	257	1266	879	950	1411	394	808	1369	1437	130	1106

U.S. RAILROAD DISTANCES

	Albuquerque	Atlanta	Baltimore	Birmingham	Boston	Buffalo	Chicago	Cincinnati	Cleveland	Dallas	Denver	Des Moines	Detroit	El Paso	Houston	Indianapolis	Jacksonville	Kansas City, Mo.	Los Angeles	Memphis	Miami	Mobile	New Orleans	New York City	Oklahoma City	Philadelphia	Pittsburgh	Portland, Ore.	St. Louis	St. Paul	Salt Lake City	San Francisco	Seattle	Washington, D.C.
Albuquerque		1554	2102	1388	2356	1862	934	1338	1528	1678	723	477	1108	1610	253	925	1430	1819	887	889	1135	2185	1229	967	1605	648	2124	1776	2014	1190	1363	985	2356	2047
Amarillo	374		1181	1728	1014	2028	1534	634	1016	1154	370	444	780	1282	444	465	1056	1466	559	761	832	1559	876	493	1832	328	1775	1427	2798	816	1039	973	2028	1690
Atlanta	2102	676		167	799	1091	416	799	734	490	748	825	952	748	856	585	350	907	862	420	716	353	493	716	907	771	806	2798	612	1130	1854	2718	2824	638
Baltimore	2356	1181	676		734	395	734	490	750	1448	1526	1154	582	1471	1755	585	716	1051	2285	746	1058	1016	1154	187	1394	95	328	3030	890	1130	2051	3059	2937	38
Billings	1862	1728	799	734		2296	796	1339	1618	1822	656	582	1550	1386	1491	1386	2226	1051	1452	1535	2592	1958	1924	2096	1394	2094	1747	961	1310	882	669	1418	903	2043
Birmingham	1388	1014	167	734	2296		494	651	459	658	1154	459	681	1194	650	481	459	741	2095	253	804	479	266	797	35	894	797	2665	479	882	669	1906	2551	761
Boston	934	1215	799	395	796	494		481	741	968	1414	1376	678	1304	746	258	524	882	252	444	1418	1576	1444	229	1743	321	415	2723	1202	1414	1906	2551	2665	454
Buffalo	935	925	734	734	1339	651	481		358	639	1418	698	272	1266	882	358	639	1252	1258	258	1150	1266	1155	415	1174	366	247	2038	396	920	1713	2787	2665	434
Butte	1369	2157	2305	2024	2296	494	524	524	2032	1519	738	468	694	738	746	252	258	114	2499	252	168	374	746	229	867	778	494	2038	489	668	1786	2535	2438	2273
Cheyenne	583	1181	1471	2095	2414	1215	494	494	1519	995	1259	1335	1396	2130	827	1300	1581	1031	1931	1031	1903	1569	1447	1903	845	1811	1463	1266	921	855	433	1182	667	1759
Chicago	1338	734	796	651	1018	524	281	281	340	968	1026	358	284	1396	1205	188	1083	451	2092	527	1449	921	908	908	816	816	468	2199	284	396	1514	2263	2141	764
Cincinnati	1528	582	481	481	938	144	260	260	260	975	1262	639	257	1543	1026	109	840	616	2370	494	1341	769	747	747	664	664	316	2470	338	617	1778	2527	2656	486
Cleveland	1678	750	459	459	741	184	340	340		1234	1356	698	184	1736	1370	283	1100	811	2538	758	1466	1007	1096	571	1065	479	131	2325	523	736	1854	2603	2481	427
Columbia, S.C.	1801	254	515	420	930	846	867	586		1078	1747	1173	844	2200	1327	730	264	1096	2550	673	646	646	747	610	1160	610	772	3019	833	1479	2344	2989	3045	476
Dallas	723	825	1448	658	1864	1418	968	975	1234	835		968	1352	697	713	636	1353	517	1460	481	1462	646	506	506	1635	610	1543	3237	711	997	1343	1930	2394	1410
Denver	477	1526	1822	739	2044	1266	1026	1262	1356	1747	835	683	1200	646	1096	264	1098	617	1353	739	1842	1341	1039	1039	1494	1842	1494	1301	1497	997	886	570	1374	1554
Des Moines	1108	957	1210	1376	1550	882	358	639	698	835	683		646	1200	730	630	1266	254	1934	645	1667	752	494	645	739	1266	826	1918	340	295	1653	2299	2438	1192
Detroit	1610	748	624	746	678	272	284	257	184	1149	1200	646		1668	1340	372	1098	723	2499	489	1464	1005	1094	648	1031	550	296	2305	489	706	1751	2500	2413	592
Duluth	1515	1202	1265	739	746	1376	188	639	698	1038	1298	411	740	1577	1413	652	1551	623	2306	686	1906	991	1425	1391	1425	726	810	2496	726	152	1526	2175	1762	1233
El Paso	253	1471	2095	1304	2414	1192	1396	1561	1736	646	730	1166	1668		827	1500	1764	945	831	1128	2130	1152	1152	2190	566	2190	1834	2496	1283	1845	1283	2710	3355	2056

(Remaining rows of the distance matrix — Fargo, Houston, Indianapolis, Jacksonville, Kansas City Mo., Knoxville, Los Angeles, Louisville, Memphis, Miami, Mobile, Nashville, New Orleans, New York City, Oklahoma City, Omaha, Philadelphia, Pittsburgh, Portland Ore., Richmond, St. Louis, St. Paul, Salt Lake City, San Antonio, San Francisco, Seattle, Spokane, Tucson, Washington D.C., Wichita — continue below with their respective distances in the same column order.)

	Albuquerque	Atlanta	Baltimore	Birmingham	Boston	Buffalo	Chicago	Cincinnati	Cleveland	Dallas	Denver	Des Moines	Detroit	El Paso	Houston	Indianapolis	Jacksonville	Kansas City, Mo.	Los Angeles	Memphis	Miami	Mobile	New Orleans	New York City	Oklahoma City	Philadelphia	Pittsburgh	Portland, Ore.	St. Louis	St. Paul	Salt Lake City	San Francisco	Seattle	Washington, D.C.
Fargo	1605	1372	1435	1289	1656	1162	638	1139	1546	1239	1128	358	1121	2087	1121	910	1667	451	2092	921	2306	1515	1546	1454	1017	1061	1454	1601	816	242	1988	2058	2861	1403
Houston	925	856	1569	718	1933	1554	1205	1110	1268	264	1099	1206	1368	827		1206	975	560	1641	616	1341	471	363	1703	699	1703	1426	2872	648	1063	1222	1988	2553	991
Indianapolis	1430	585	355	205	1933	1205	184	109	283	951	1261	1110	372	1561	1301		935	518	2181	394	1366	647	717	811	782	856	617	2511	324	580	1680	2422	2656	1115
Jacksonville	1819	350	750	503	1210	283	1083	840	1100	1096	1811	542	1098	1764	975	935		1175	2578	691	366	472	612	981	1329	1080	1153	3107	781	1479	2344	3171	3049	653
Kansas City, Mo.	887	580	794	986	1091	779	451	616	811	517	636	254	723	945	781	518	1175		1776	484	1534	691	873	1329	343	1492	1152	2131	278	538	1501	2171	2422	1424
Knoxville	1556	197	545	254	961	737	574	296	494	903	1454	683	551	1945	781	518	547	818	2363	422	913	520	679	1330	891	1062	1068	3015	414	956	1776	2420	3171	507
Los Angeles	889	2285	1908	1376	3244	2750	2092	2227	2499	1460	1353	1934	2499	831	1641	2181	2578	1776		1942	2944	2106	1966	3082	1556	3082	2643	1187	1809	2330	732	470	1370	2906
Louisville	1463	476	392	392	1052	869	527	114	374	861	1188	645	494	1667	616	111	824	484	2306	380	1190	658	747	869	719	890	778	2739	274	691	1713	2462	2486	133
Memphis	1135	420	742	482	1570	913	532	494	758	481	1258	494	481	1128	616	394	691	484	1942		1153	380	394	1191	487	1062	810	2496	305	879	1653	2298	2438	296
Miami	2185	832	1206	447	1376	1736	1449	1341	1466	1462	2177	1667	1464	2130	1341	1366	366	1534	2944	1153		1057	838	1347	1544	1256	1418	3514	1283	1845	2710	3355	3495	1122
Mobile	1229	353	1016	744	1376	1266	921	769	1007	646	1341	752	1005	1152	471	647	472	691	2106	380	1057		658	747	869	1302	1206	2872	648	1222	1273	1848	2422	991
Nashville	1374	288	761	205	1117	745	446	301	559	720	1238	548	560	1357	560	140	637	560	2181	239	1003	363	560	948	726	856	871	2511	324	859	1824	2581	2861	723
New Orleans	985	490	1154	503	1569	1517	921	491	769	506	1341	1096	1094	1152	363	717	612	873	1966	394	838	140		978	742	1068	1152	2732	699	1221	1355	1848	2436	1115
New York City	2051	1130	187	986	794	395	908	811	571	1635	1811	636	648	2190	1703	811	981	1329	3082	1191	1347	869	978		1365	91	439	3107	1051	1204	2147	3171	3042	225
Oklahoma City	985	1066	545	907	1120	1174	816	664	1065	236	1160	739	1031	566	699	782	1329	343	1556	487	1544	869	742	1365		1451	1153	2422	542	813	1811	1906	3079	1681
Omaha	1209	1130	794	928	1210	975	488	610	698	1096	537	130	628	1718	1612	519	1544	196	1809	617	366	1152	1062	1360	538	1304	1181	1850	414	348	1404	2137	718	1492
Philadelphia	2124	771	95	892	488	366	816	664	479	1543	1719	637	550	2100	1703	856	1080	1237	3082	1062	1256	1302	1068	91	1451		346	3049	959	1212	2139	3079	2957	133
Pittsburgh	1776	800	328	894	593	247	468	316	131	1842	1494	780	296	1834	1426	617	1153	1152	2643	810	1418	1206	1152	439	1153	348		2739	611	803	2731	2610	296
Portland, Ore.	1849	2798	3030	2665	3217	2732	2199	2470	2750	2227	1373	1918	2505	2496	2491	2427	3148	1968	1188	2496	3514	2872	2732	3107	2422	3049	2739		2187	1803	884	718	182	3025
Richmond	2038	579	155	735	570	550	862	581	544	1385	1833	1120	708	2031	1435	903	640	1390	3016	903	919	932	413	341	1390	250	413	3095	919	1258	2359	3108	3003	117
St. Louis	1190	612	1193	479	1202	396	284	338	523	711	914	340	489	1283	648	324	781	278	2032	305	1283	648	699	1051	542	959	611	2187		574	1440	2189	2213	882
St. Paul	1363	1039	816	395	1414	920	396	617	736	997	886	295	706	1845	1063	580	1479	538	2330	879	1845	1222	1221	1204	813	1212	803	1803	574		1374	2213	1745	1161
Salt Lake City	985	2051	1854	669	1906	1713	1514	1778	1854	1343	570	1653	1751	1283	1222	1680	2344	1501	732	1653	2710	991	1355	2147	1811	2139	2731	884	1440	1374		821	1066	2278
San Antonio	2051	1268	2422	1247	2330	1892	2247	2330	2603	247	1268	1115	2589	713	201	1811	1426	821	1430	1464	2456	1115	1273	2300	573	2300	2586	2146	924	1268	1614		900	3028
San Francisco	1209	1066	2937	2551	3159	2665	2263	2527	2610	1930	1374	2199	2500	2600	1811	3079	3171	2171	470	2298	3355	1848	1848	3171	1906	3079	2610	718	2189	2213	821		821	2906
Seattle	2031	904	3145	894	3159	2665	2141	2656	2481	2394	1554	2438	2413	3355	2553	2656	3049	2422	1370	2438	3495	2422	2436	3042	3079	2957	2610	182	2213	1745	1066	821		2906
Spokane	1726	2514	2628	2381	2849	2355	1831	2112	2171	2084	1249	1634	2103	1979	2348	2015	2819	1644	1086	1903	1435	1572	1737	1285	972	1285	310	2596
Tucson	565	1783	2407	1616	2726	2232	1708	1873	2048	958	1042	1478	1980	312	1139	1775	2076	1257	502	1440	2442	1464	2586	1030	2494	2146	1690	1737	1285	972	1872	2368
Washington, D.C.	2047	638	38	761	454	764	544	427	1410	1790	592	2065	1478	653	756	1062	991	1115	225	1424	133	296	3025	882	1161	3028	2906
Wichita	721	986	1401	819	1681	1187	663	819	1003	408	580	433	791	672	721	1257	212	1563	566	1623	913	1053	481	692	1087	1884	2139	1363

TOLL-FREE TELEPHONE NUMBERS

The following lists contain the toll-free telephone numbers for airlines, hotels, motels, and car rental companies. Airline companies often have local telephone numbers for reservations and information. If no local number is listed, dial 800 followed by the number given in the first column. In Atlanta and New York precede all 800 numbers with "1." EN (Enterprise) numbers require operator assistance.

AIRLINES	800 Toll-Free Number	ATLANTA	CHICAGO	LOS ANGELES	NEW YORK	WASHINGTON, D.C.
Aer Lingus Irish	223-6292		800 223-6537	800 223-6537	212 557-1110	800 223-6537
Aerocondor						800 327-0743
Aeroflot					212 661-4050	202 296-8060
Aerolineas Argentinas	327-0276	800 223-5450	312 922-0707	213 683-1633	212 974-3370	202 296-3863
Aeromexico	223-9780	800 223-9780		213 380-6030	212 391-2900	
Aero Perú	327-4363[2]		800 327-4363	800 327-4363	212 765-2200	
Air Canada		800 621-6464	312 527-3900	213 776-7000	212 869-1900	202 638-2132
Air Florida		800 327-2971			212 265-6140	202 783-5390
Air France		800 221-2110	312 782-6181	213 625-7171	212 247-0100	202 337-8711
Air India	223-7776			213 380-4481	212 751-6200	
Air Jamaica		800 523-5585	312 527-3923	800 523-5618	212 421-9750	
Air New Zealand		800 421-5540		213 776-8790	800 421-5540	800 421-5540
Air Panama Internacional	327-2417				800 329-2417	
Alaska Airlines	426-0333					
Alitalia		800 223-9770	312 427-4720	800 223-5730	212 582-8900	202 393-2829
American	433-7300[1]	404 521-2655	312 372-8000	213 937-6811	212 661-4242	202 393-2345
Avianca	327-9899[2,3]	800 221-2200	312 346-8252	800 327-9899	212 586-6040	202 347-3626
Aviateca International	1 800-327-9832[2]					
Bahamasair		404 766-0351	800 327-8080	800 327-8080	800 327-8080	800 327-8080
Braniff International	527-4000[1]	404 577-7700	312 372-8900	213 680-2202	212 687-8200	202 296-2400
British Airways		800 327-9722	312 332-7744	213 272-8866	212 687-1600	202 393-5300
B.W.I.A. International	327-7401			800 327-7401	212 581-3200	800 221-6874
CP Air		800 426-7007	800 426-7000	213 625-0131	800 426-7000	800 426-7000
Capitol International		404 261-5477	800 223-6365		212 883-0750	800 223-6365
Cathay Pacific				213 627-3253	212 541-9750	202 833-9393
China Airlines		0-WX-6935	312 427-2920	213 624-6160	212 581-6500	202 833-1760
Commuter Airlines					800 252-1490	800 847-1462
Continental	525-0280[4]		312 686-6500	213 772-6000	212 974-0028	202 628-6666
Czechoslovak Air Lines			312 372-1551		212 682-5833	
Delta Air Lines		404 765-5000	312 346-5300	213 386-5510	212 239-0700	202 920-5500
Eastern Air Lines		404 435-1111	312 467-2900	213 380-2070	(D) 212 986-5000 (I) 212 661-3500	202 393-4000
Ecuatoriana Airlines	327-1337					
El Al Israel Airlines	223-6280			800 223-6700	212 486-2600	
Ethiopian Airlines		404 588-9476	312 663-4100	213 462-7291	212 867-0095	202 363-0207
Finnair		800 223-5308	800 223-5308	800 223-5700	212 889-7070	800 223-5260
Frontier Airlines		404 523-5487	312 686-6294			
Gulf Air	223-1740		312 861-0117	213 879-3645	212 986-4500	202 296-2910
Hawaiian Airlines		404 237-2885	312 236-5196	213 640-1040	212 355-4843	800 367-5320
Iberia Air Lines of Spain		800 221-9640	800 221-9640	800 221-9741	212 793-3300	800 221-9640
Icelandair		800 223-5390		800 223-5500	212 757-8585	800 223-5190
Japan Air Lines		800 223-5405	312 263-1384	213 620-9580	212 759-9100	800 223-5405
KLM Royal Dutch Airlines		800 223-5322	312 346-3635	213 776-6300	212 759-3600	800 223-5322
Korean Airlines		404 522-7461	312 558-9300	213 484-1900	212 244-8330	800 223-5262
Kuwait Airlines			312 263-3858	213 627-1485	212 581-9412	202 296-4644
Lacsa	1 800 327-7700[2]			213 385-2272	212 245-6370	
Laker Skytrain		800 221-0374	800 221-0374	800 221-0374	212 459-6092	800 221-0374
Lan-Chile Airlines	327-3614					
Lot Polish Airlines	223-0593		312 236-3388		212 869-1074	
Lufthansa German Airlines	645-3880		800 645-3880	800 645-3880	212 357-8400	800 645-3880
Mexicana Airlines	421-2150[5]	404 237-8661	800 421-2150	213 646-9500		800 531-7921
Midway Airlines		800 626-4321	312 471-4710	800 231-0270	800 231-0270	800 231-0270
National Airlines	see Pan Am					
New York Air					212 426-4710	
Northwest Orient		404 577-3271	312 346-4900	213 380-1511	(D) 212 564-2300 (I) 212 563-7200	(D) 202 337-0611 (I) 202 337-0666
Olympic Airways	223-1226[3]	212 838-3600	212 838-3600	213 624-6441	212 838-3600	212 838-3600
Ozark Air Lines		404 686 9565	312 726-4680		212 586-3612	202 347-4744

[1]except Texas. [2]except Florida. [3]except NYC. [4]except Col., Ill., Tex., Alaska, Hawaii. [5]except Calif. (D) domestic. (I) international.

AIRLINES	800 Toll-Free Number	ATLANTA	CHICAGO	LOS ANGELES	NEW YORK	WASHINGTON, D.C.
Pakistan International			312 263-3082	213 628-0245	212 949-0488	202 296-1755
Pan Am		404 688-9830	312 332-4900	213 670-7301	(D) 212 697-9000	202 833-1000
					(I) 212 973-4000	
People Express					212 772-0344	
Philippine Airlines				800 652-1555	800 227-4600	800 227-4600
Piedmont Airlines		404 681-3100	312 263-3656		212 489-1460	202 347-1800
Qantas Airways . . . .:.	227-4500			800 622-0850		
Republic Airlines		404 762-5561	312 346-9860		212 581-8851	202 347-0448
Sabena Belgian World Airlines	645-3790			800 645-1382	212 961-6200	800 645-3933
SAS Scandinavian Airlines		800 231-2350		213 652-8600	212 657-7700	
Singapore Airlines	227-3314			800 632-2767	800 227-3314	202 466-3747
South African Airways		0-WX-6477	312 467-1186	800 223-9870	212 826-1245	
Swissair.	221-4750	800 221-4743			212 995-8400	
TAN-SAHSA Honduras Airlines . . . . 1 800 327-1225[2]			312 236-3246	213 485-0261	212 730-0800	800 327-1225
TAP The Airline of Portugal.		800 221-2061		800 221-7370	212 944-2100	800 221-2061
Thai Airways International		800 426-5204	312 855-3930	1 800 426-5030	800 426-5204	800 426-5204
Trans Australian Airlines . .			312 329-1266	213 849-2151	800 227-4500	
Trans World Airlines		404 522-5738	312 332-7600	213 483-1100	212 290-2121	212 239-0270
Transamerica Airlines		404 681-0588		800 228-5800	212 239-0270	
UTA French Airlines.		404 581-0520	312 782-6181	213 625-7171	212 247-0100	800 221-2110
United Airlines.		404 394-2234	312 569-3000	213 772-2121	212 867-3000	202 893-3400
U.S. Air.	223-5720[3]	800 245-1640	312 726-1201		212 736-3200	202 783-4500
Varig Brazilian Airlines . . .					212-682-3100	
Viasa Venezuela International Airways. . .		800 327-5454	800 327-5454	800 327-5454	800 221-2150	800 221-2150
Western Airlines			312 782-8296	213 776-2311	212 966-1646	202 737-4825
World Airways			312 663-5433	213 646-9404	800 526-8320	202 298-7155
Yugoslav (JAT) Airlines . . .			312 782-1322	213 388-0379	212 785-4050	

HOTELS and MOTELS	Telephone Number
Admiral Benbow Inns.	800 238-6877
Best Western Motels.	800 528-1234
Days Inns.	800 241-2340 (except Ga.)
Econo Travel.	1 800 446-6900 (except Va.)
Guest Quarters.	800 424-2900
Holiday Inns.	800 238-8000
Howard Johnson Motor Lodges.	800 654-2000
Hyatt Hotels.	800 228-9000
Marriott Hotels.	800 228-9290
Omni International Hotels.	800 241-5500
Pick-Americana Hotels.	800 228-3278
Playboy Club-Hotels.	800 621-1116
Princess Hotels.	800 223-1818
Quality Inns.	800 228-5151
Ramada Inns.	800 228-2828
Rockresorts	
In Atlanta:.	404 939-4896
In Boston:.	617 542-0202
In Chicago:.	312 266-0609
In Los Angeles:.	213 846-9611

HOTELS and MOTELS	Telephone Number
In New York:.	212 586-4459
Sheraton Hotels.	800 325-3535
Sonesta Hotels.	800 225-1372
Stouffer Hotels.	800 321-6888
Travelodge Motels.	800 255-3050
Treadway Inns.	800 631-0182
Trust Houses Forte Hotels.	800 223-5672
Western International Hotels.	800 228-3000

CAR RENTAL COMPANIES

Agency Rent-a-Car.	800 321-1972
Ajax Rent-A-Car.	800 421-0896
Avis Rent a Car.	800 331-1212
Budget Rent A Car.	800 228-9650
Dollar Rent-a-Car.	800 421-6868
Econo-Car.	800 228-1000
Greyhound Rent-a-Car.	800 327-2501
Hertz Rent A Car.	800 654-3131
National Car Rental. . . . .,.	800 328-4567
Sears Rent a Car.	800 228-2800
Thrifty Rent A Car.	800 331-4200

THE NATIONAL PARK SYSTEM

Source: National Park Service, U.S. Department of the Interior

Park Service Areas	Number	Park Service Areas	Number	Park Service Areas	Number	Park Service Areas	Number
National Parks	48	National Battlefield Parks	3	National Capital Parks	1	National Scenic Trail	1
National Historical Parks	26	National Battlefield Sites	1	White House	1	National Preserves	12
National Monuments	78	National Historic Sites	63	National Recreation Areas	17	"Other" Parks	10
National Military Parks	10	National Memorials	22	National Lakeshores	4	National Mall	1
National Battlefields	10	National Parkways	4	National Rivers (wild and scenic)	10	National Visitor Center	1
National Seashores	10						

Total 333

OUR NATIONAL PARKS

Acadia National Park, Maine; (gross acreage, 38,970.86). Rugged coastal area on Mount Desert Island, highest elevation on eastern seaboard; picturesque Schoodic peninsula on mainland. Includes Isle au Haut. Sieur de Monts Nat'l Mon. est. 1916; est. as Lafayette Nat'l Park 1919; changed to Acadia Nat'l Park 1929. Visits (1980): 3,273,100

Arches National Park, Utah; (gross acreage, 73,378.98). Extraordinary products of erosion in the form of giant arches, windows, pinnacles, and pedestals. Proclaimed as a nat'l mon. 1929; est. as a nat'l park 1971. Visits (1980): 290,500

Badlands National Park, South Dakota; (gross acreage, 243,302.33). Carved by erosion, this scenic landscape contains animal fossils of 40 million years ago, and supports bison, bighorn sheep, deer, and antelope. Authorized 1929; wilderness designated 1976; renamed nat'l park 1978. Visits (1980): 964,700

Big Bend National Park, Texas; (gross acreage, 708,118.40) Spectacular mountain and desert scenery; variety of unusual geological formations in the great bend of the Rio Grande. Authorized 1935; est. 1944. Visits (1980): 209,700

Biscayne National Park, Florida; (gross acreage, 180,127.65) Part of the only coral reefs in North America, this aquatic park contains a chain of islands, Biscayne Bay, and rare marine species. Authorized as a nat'l mon. 1968; est. as a nat'l park 1980. Visits (1980): 248,071

Bryce Canyon National Park, Utah; (gross acreage, 35,835.08). Along the edge of the Paunsaugunt Plateau of southern Utah stand innumerable highly colored and grotesque pinnacles, walls, and spires. Bryce Canyon Nat'l Mon. est. 1923; Utah Nat'l Park authorized 1924; changed to Bryce Canyon Nat'l Park 1928. Est. 1928. Visits (1980): 573,500

Canyonlands National Park, Utah; (gross acreage, 337,570.43). Geological wonderland of rock, spires, and mesas rising more than 7,800 feet. Extensive and sometimes large petroglyphs (stone carvings) chipped by prehistoric Indians about 1,000 years ago. Est. 1964. Visits (1980): 57,000

Capitol Reef National Park, Utah; (gross acreage, 241,904.26). Sixty-mile uplift of sandstone cliffs, with highly colored sedimentary formations dissected by narrow high-walled gorges. Dome-shaped white rock along the Fremont River accounts for the name. Proclaimed as a nat'l mon. 1937; est. as a nat'l park 1971. Visits (1980): 377,400

Carlsbad Caverns National Park, New Mexico; (gross acreage, 46,755.33). A series of connected caverns with countless magnificent and curious formations. Carlsbad Cave Nat'l Mon. est. 1923; Carlsbad Caverns Nat'l Park est. 1930. Visits (1980): 673,000

Channel Islands National Park, California; (gross acreage, 249,353.77). Est. as a nat'l mon. in 1938, and as a nat'l park in 1980, Channel Islands Nat'l Park is rich in marine life and aquatic recreation, and has the only northern fur seal breeding colony south of Alaska. Visits (1980): 135,600

Crater Lake National Park, Oregon; (gross acreage, 160,290.33). Lake of deepest blue in heart of once-active volcano, Mt. Mazama; encircled by multicolored lava walls 500 to 2,000 feet high. Est. 1902. Visits (1980): 484,300

Denali National Park, Alaska; (gross acreage, 4,065,493). Mount McKinley, highest mountain (20,320 feet) in North America; large glaciers of the Alaska Range; caribou, Dall sheep, moose, grizzly bears, wolves. Est. 1917. Visits (1980): 514,200

Everglades National Park, Florida; (gross acreage, 1,398,800.00). Largest remaining subtropical wilderness in conterminous United States; extensive fresh-and salt-water areas, open Everglades prairies, mangrove forests; abundant wildlife, including rare birds. Authorized 1934. Est. 1947. Visits (1980): 802,400

Gates of the Arctic National Park, Alaska; (gross acreage, 7,052,000) Contains broad valleys, meandering rivers, and the jagged peaks of the Central Brooks Range. Caribou, wolves, grizzly bears and Dall sheep share the habitat. Proclaimed a nat'l mon. 1978; est. as a nat'l park 1980.

Glacier Bay National Park, Alaska (gross acreage, 3,878,269) Noted for its glaciers, whales, brown bears, mountain goats, seals and eagles. Mount Fairweather is the highest peak in southeast Alaska. Proclaimed a nat'l mon. 1925; est. as a nat'l park 1980. Visits (1980): 130,571

Glacier National Park, Montana; (gross acreage, 1,013,594.67). Superb Rocky Mountain scenery, with numerous glaciers and lakes nestling among the highest peaks; forms part of Waterton-Glacier International Peace Park. est. 1932. Est. 1910. Visits (1980): 1,475,500

Grand Canyon National Park, Arizona; (gross acreage, 1,218,375.24). Most spectacular part of the Colorado River's greatest canyon; exposure of rocks representing vast geologic time. First Grand Canyon Nat'l Mon. est. 1908; nat'l park est. 1919. Marble Canyon and second Grand Canyon Nat'l Mons. and other lands absorbed 1975. Visits (1980): 2,526,200

Grand Teton National Park, Wyoming; (gross acreage, 310,516.23). Series of peaks comprising the most impressive part of the Teton range; once a noted landmark of Indians and "Mountain Men." Includes part of Jackson Hole; winter feeding ground of largest American elk herd. Est. 1929. Visits (1980): 3,489,000

Great Smoky Mts. National Park, N.C.-Tenn.; (gross acreage, 520,269.44). Loftiest range east of the Black Hills and one of the oldest uplands on earth. Diversified and luxuriant plant life, often of extraordinary size. Authorized 1926; est. for administration and protection only 1930; est. for full development 1934. Visits (1980): 11,900,800

Guadalupe Mts. National Park, Texas; (gross acreage, 76,293.06). Mountain mass rising from desert contains portions of the world's most extensive and significant Permian limestone fossil reef. Also features a tremendous earth fault, lofty peaks, unusual flora and fauna. Authorized 1966. Visits (1980): 113,800

Haleakala National Park, Hawaii; (gross acreage, 28,655.25). World-famous 10,023-foot Haleakala volcano (dormant), with one of the largest and most colorful craters known, in which grows a species of the rare silversword; native and migratory birdlife. Authorized 1960; est. 1961. Visits (1980): 577,100

Hawaii Volcanoes National Park, Hawaii; (gross acreage, 229,177.03). Scene of impressive active volcanism on the island of Hawaii; luxuriant vegetation at lower elevations; rare plants and animals. Est. as Hawaii Nat'l Park 1916; changed to Hawaii Volcanoes Nat'l Park 1961. Visits (1980): 2,367,900

Hot Springs National Park, Arkansas; (gross acreage, 5,826.26). Mineral hot springs (47), used in the treatment of certain ailments. Set aside as Hot Springs Reservation by federal government 1832; nat'l park est. 1921. Visits (1980): 5,269,600

Isle Royale National Park, Michigan; (gross acreage, 571,796.18). Forested island, distinguished for its wilderness character; moose and wolves; pre-Columbian copper mines. Authorized 1931; est. 1940. Visits (1980): 15,000

Katmai National Park, Alaska; (gross acreage, 4,430,125) Enlarged to provide more denning territory for the Alaska brown bear, this area was proclaimed a nat'l mon. in 1918 as a result of a 1912 volcanic eruption (Valley of Ten Thousand Smokes). Est. as a nat'l park 1980.Visits (1980): 11,868

Kenai Fjords National Park, Alaska; (gross acreage, 567,000) Rich in scenery and wildlife, this park has mountain goats, sea otters, Steller sea lions and seabirds, such as puffins. Proclaimed a nat'l mon. 1978; est. as a nat'l park 1980.

Kings Canyon National Park, California; (gross acreage, 460,136.20). Mountain wilderness dominated by two enormous canyons of the Kings River and by the summit peaks of the High Sierra. The former General Grant Nat'l Park, with its giant sequoias, is a detached section of the park. General Grant Nat'l Park est. 1890, abolished 1940, and its lands made part of Kings Canyon Nat'l Park; est. 1940. Visits (1980): 823,800

Kobuk Valley National Park, Alaska; (gross acreage, 1,710,000) The park, lying in northwest Alaska, includes the Salmon River, boreal forest, tundra and a 25 square-mile expanse of sand, the Great Kobuk Sand Dunes. Archeological sites reveal more than 10,000 years of human use. Proclaimed a nat'l mon. 1978, est. as a nat'l park 1980.

Lake Clark National Park, Alaska; (gross acreage, 2,439,000) The park contains the headwaters of the world's most important source of red salmon, two active volcanoes, lakes, glaciers and waterfalls; populated by a broad variety of wildlife. Proclaimed a nat'l mon. 1978; est. as a nat'l park 1980.

Lassen Volcanic National Park, California; (gross acreage, 106,372.36). Lassen Peak, which erupted between 1914 and 1921, exhibits volcanic phenomena. Lassen Peak and Cinder Cone Nat'l Mons. est. 1907; made part of Lassen Volcanic Nat'l Park 1916, when it was est. Visits (1980): 394,400

Mammoth Cave National Park, Kentucky; (gross acreage, 52,452.22). Series of underground passages, 146 miles explored; beautiful limestone, gypsum and cave onyx formations; deep pits and high domes; river 360 feet below surface. Authorized 1926; provided for minimum park area 1934; minimum area accepted for administration 1936; fully est. 1941. Visits (1980): 1,668,900

Mesa Verde National Park, Colorado; (gross acreage, 52,085.14). Best preserved prehistoric cliff dwellings in the United States. Est. 1906. Visits (1980): 540,800

Mount Rainier National Park, Washington; (gross acreage, 235,404.00). Greatest single-peak glacial system in the conterminous United States, radiating from the summit and slopes of an ancient volcano; dense forests, flowered meadows. Est. 1899. Visits (1980): 2,001,000

North Cascades National Park, Washington; (gross acreage, 504,780.94). Wild alpine region of jagged peaks, mountain lakes, and numerous glaciers. Est. 1968. Visits (1980): 819,200*

Olympic National Park, Washington; (gross acreage, 914,889.90). Mountain wilderness containing finest remnant of Pacific Northwest rain forest; active glaciers; rare Roosevelt elk. Mount Olympus Nat'l Mon. est. 1909; transferred from U.S. Dept. of Agriculture 1933; Olympic Nat'l Park est. 1938. Visits (1980): 2,482,300

Petrified Forest National Park, Arizona; (gross acreage, 93,492.57). Extensive natural exhibit of petrified wood; Indian ruins and petroglyphs; portion of colorful Painted Desert. Est. as a nat'l mon. 1906; changed to nat'l park 1962. Visits (1980): 686,700

Redwood National Park, California; (gross acreage, 109,414.65). Coastal redwood forests contain virgin groves of ancient trees. Park includes 40 miles of scenic Pacific coastline. Est. 1968. Visits (1980): 539,400

Rocky Mountain National Park, Colorado; (gross acreage, 263,808.71). One of the most diversified sections of the Front Range of the Rocky Mountains with 107 named peaks in excess of 11,000 feet. Est. 1915. Visits (1980): 2,654,200

Sequoia National Park, California; (gross acreage, 402,487.83). Great groves of giant sequoias, world's largest and among the oldest living things; magnificent High Sierra scenery, including Mount Whitney, highest mountain (14,494 feet) in conterminous United States. Est. 1890. Visits (1980): 862,800

Shenandoah National Park, Virginia; (gross acreage, 194,826.30). Outstanding portion of Blue Ridge with Skyline Drive traversing crest; magnificent vistas of historic Shenandoah Valley, Piedmont; hardwood forests; wealth of wildflowers. Authorized 1926; est. 1935. Visits (1980): 1,769,700

Theodore Roosevelt National Park, North Dakota; (gross acreage, 70,416.39). The park includes scenic badlands along the Little Missouri River, some original prairie grasslands, and part of Theodore Roosevelt's Elkhorn Ranch. Memorial park est. 1947; renamed 1978. Visits (1980): 603,200

Virgin Islands National Park, V.I.; (gross acreage, 14,695.33). St. John, an island of lush green hills and white sandy beaches; rich in tropical plant and animal life; pre-historic Carib Indian relics; remains of Danish colonial sugar plantations. Authorized 1956; est. 1956. Visits (1980): 808,700

Voyageurs National Park, Minnesota; (gross acreage, 219,128.00). Beautiful lakes and forests, interesting geology; historically used as passage between Great Lakes and Northwest Territory by French fur traders. Land area, 144,891.16 acres. Authorized 1971. Visits (1980): 272,400

Wind Cave National Park, South Dakota; (gross acreage, 28,292.08). Limestone caverns in scenic Black Hills, decorated by beautiful boxwork and calcite crystal formations; elk, deer, pronghorn, prairie dog towns and bison herd. Est. 1903. Visits (1980): 969,800

Wrangell-St. Elias National Park, Alaska; (gross acreage; 8,147,000) This park contains the largest collection of glaciers and peaks over 16,000 feet in North America. Wildlife includes caribou, Dall sheep, glacier bear, and trumpeter swans. Proclaimed a nat'l mon. 1978; est. a nat'l park 1980.

Yellowstone National Park, Wyo.-Mont.-Idaho; (gross acreage, 2,219,822.70). World's greatest geyser area; spectacular falls and canyons of the Yellowstone River; one of the world's greatest wildlife sanctuaries. First and largest nat'l park. Est. 1872. Visits (1980): 2,018,800

Yosemite National Park, California; (gross acreage, 760,917.18). Mountainous region of unusual beauty; Yosemite and other inspiring gorges with sheer granite cliffs; spectacular waterfalls; three groves of giant sequoias. Est. 1890. El Portal administrative site, 991.19 acres of federal land adjacent to the park, authorized 1958. Visits (1980): 2,583,200

Zion National Park, Utah; (gross acreage, 146,551 .10). Outstanding colorful canyon and mesa scenery; erosion and faulting patterns that create phenomenal shapes and landscapes; former volcanic activity. Zion Canyon, a vertical-walled chasm, readily accessible. Est. as Munkuntuweap Nat'l Mon. 1909; changed to Zion Nat'l Mon. 1918; est. as a nat'l park (including the Nat'l Mon. 1937) 1919. Visits (1980): 1,233,700

* Acreage and visitor figures include those for Lake Chelan and Ross Lake National Recreation Areas

THE U.S. PASSPORT

SOURCE: Department of State, Passport Services

A passport is your official identification as a citizen of the United States. Application for a passport should be made, in person, before a passport agent at one of the passport agencies located in Boston; Chicago; Detroit; Honolulu; Houston; Los Angeles; Miami; New Orleans; New York; Philadelphia; San Francisco; Seattle; Stamford, Conn.; and Washington, D.C.; or a clerk of any federal court or state court of record or a judge or clerk of any probate court accepting applications; or a postal employee designated by the postmaster at a post office which has been selected to accept passport applications.

When you apply for a passport you must present the following items: proof of U.S. citizenship (a previously issued passport, birth certificate, or naturalization papers); two identical photographs taken within six months of the date of your application (have them taken by a professional photographer who knows the requirements concerning pose and size of prints); identification—a document such as a driver's license with your signature and your photograph or physical description on it. The fee for a passport is $10[1], plus a $5 execution fee. Allow about two to three weeks for processing of your application, longer if you apply during peak travel periods.

A passport is valid for five years[1] from the date of issue unless specifically limited to a shorter period by the Secretary of State. A new passport will be required for travel after expiration of the five-year period.

Application for a new passport must be made in person at the places listed above, or—under certain circumstances—a person who is the bearer of a passport issued within eight years prior to the date of his or her new application may apply for a subsequent passport by mail.

The applicant must submit completed form DSP-82 (Application for Passport by Mail), which is available from travel agents and the places listed above, the previous passport, two new signed passport photographs, and a fee of $10. The applicant should carefully read the instructions on the application to determine his or her eligibility to use this form.

Loss or theft of a valid passport is a serious matter and should be reported in writing immediately to Passport Services, Department of State, Washington, D.C. 20524 or the nearest Passport Agency. If the passport holder is abroad when the loss occurs, he or she should notify the nearest U.S. consulate. Theft of a passport should also be reported to local police authorities.

Visas

A visa is official permission to visit a country granted by the government of that country. An American who plans to go abroad can check the general visa requirements for each country he or she plans to visit in a booklet entitled "Visa Requirements of Foreign Governments," which is available at any office accepting passport applications. Specific details should be obtained from the nearest embassy or consulate of the country in which you wish to do any traveling.

[1]Congressional approval has been requested to increase the passport fee and to extend the validity of the passport beyond five years.

FOREIGN GOVERNMENT TOURIST OFFICES

Australian Tourist Commission
1270 Ave. of the Americas, Rm. 2908
New York, NY 10020

Austrian National Tourist Office
545 Fifth Avenue
New York, NY 10017

Bahamas Tourist Office
30 Rockefeller Plaza
New York, NY 10020

Belgian National Tourist Office
745 Fifth Avenue
New York, NY 10022

Bermuda Government Official Travel
Information Office
630 Fifth Avenue
New York, NY 10020

British Tourist Authority
680 Fifth Avenue
New York, NY 10019

Canadian Government Office of Tourism
1251 Ave. of the Americas
New York, NY 10020

(Cedok) Czechoslovak Travel Bureau
10 East 40th Street
New York, NY 10016

Dominican Tourist Information Center, Inc.
485 Madison Avenue
New York, NY 10022

Egyptian Government Tourist Office
630 Fifth Avenue
New York, NY 10020

Finland National Tourist Office
75 Rockefeller Plaza
New York, NY 10020

French Travel Board
610 Fifth Avenue
New York, NY 10020

German National Tourist Office
630 Fifth Avenue
New York, NY 10022

Greek National Tourist Organization
645 Fifth Avenue
New York, NY 10022

Haiti Government Tourist Bureau
30 Rockefeller Plaza
New York, NY 10020

India Government Tourist Office
30 Rockefeller Plaza
New York, NY 10020

Irish Tourist Board
590 Fifth Avenue
New York, NY 10036

Israel Government Tourism Administration
350 Fifth Avenue
New York, NY 10016

Italian Government Travel Office
630 Fifth Avenue
New York, NY 10020

Jamaica Tourist Board
2 Hammarskjöld Plaza
New York, NY 10017

Japan National Tourist Organization
45 Rockefeller Plaza
New York, NY 10020

Kenya Tourist Office
60 East 56th Street
New York, NY 10022

Korea National Tourism Corp.
Suite 323 510 Building
510 West 6th Street
Los Angeles, CA 90014

Malaysian Tourist Center
420 Lexington Avenue
New York, NY 10017

Mexican National Tourist Council
405 Park Avenue
New York, NY 10022

Moroccan National Tourist Office
521 Fifth Avenue
New York, NY 10017

Panama Government Tourist Bureau
630 Fifth Avenue
New York, NY 10020

Polish National Tourist Office
500 Fifth Avenue
New York, NY 10036

Romanian National Tourist Office
573 Third Avenue
New York, NY 10016

Scandinavian National Tourist Office
75 Rockefeller Plaza
New York, NY 10020

South African Tourist Corporation
610 Fifth Avenue
New York, NY 10020

Spanish National Tourist Office
665 Fifth Avenue
New York, NY 10022

Sri Lanka Ceylon Tourist Board
609 Fifth Avenue
New York, NY 10017

Suriname Tourist Bureau
1 Rockefeller Plaza
New York, NY 10020

Swiss National Tourist Office
608 Fifth Avenue
New York, NY 10020

Thailand Tourist Organization
20 East 82nd Street
New York, NY 10028

Turkish Government Tourism Office
821 United Nations Plaza
New York, NY 10017

Yugoslav State Tourist Office
630 Fifth Avenue
New York, NY 10020

Zambia National Tourist Bureau
150 East 58th Street
New York, NY 10022

FOREIGN CITY WEATHER

Two figures are given for each of the months, thus 88/73. The first figure is the average daily high temperature (°F) and the second is the average daily low temperature (°F) for the month. The boldface figures indicate the average number of days with rain for each month.

City	January	February	March	April	May	June	July	August	September	October	November	December
ABIDJAN, Ivory Coast	88/73 3	90/75 4	90/75 6	90/75 8	88/75 16	85/73 18	83/73 8	82/71 7	83/73 8	85/74 13	87/74 13	88/74 6
ACAPULCO, Mexico	85/70 0	87/70 0	87/70 0	87/71 0	89/74 4	89/76 15	89/75 14	89/75 14	88/75 18	88/74 12	88/72 4	87/70 1
ACCRA, Ghana	88/73 1	88/75 2	88/76 4	88/76 6	89/74 9	84/74 10	81/73 4	80/71 3	81/73 4	85/74 6	87/75 5	88/75 2
ADDIS ABABA, Ethiopia	75/43 2	76/47 5	77/50 8	77/50 10	77/50 10	74/49 20	69/50 28	69/50 27	72/49 21	75/45 3	73/43 2	73/41 2
ALGIERS, Algeria	59/43 11	61/49 9	63/52 9	68/55 5	73/59 5	79/65 2	83/70 1	85/71 1	81/69 4	74/63 7	66/56 11	60/51 12
AMSTERDAM, Netherlands	40/34 19	41/34 15	46/37 13	52/43 14	60/50 12	65/55 12	69/59 14	68/59 14	64/56 15	56/48 18	47/41 19	41/35 19
ANKARA, Turkey	39/24 8	42/26 8	51/31 7	63/40 7	73/49 7	78/53 5	86/59 1	87/59 1	78/52 3	69/44 5	57/37 6	43/29 9
APIA, Western Samoa	86/75 22	85/76 19	86/74 19	86/75 14	85/74 12	85/74 7	84/75 9	84/75 9	84/74 11	85/75 14	86/74 16	85/74 19
ATHENS, Greece	54/42 7	55/43 6	60/46 5	67/52 3	77/60 3	85/67 2	90/72 1	90/72 1	83/66 2	74/60 4	64/52 6	57/46 7
BAGHDAD, Iraq	60/39 4	64/42 4	71/48 4	85/57 3	97/67 1	105/73 0	110/76 0	110/76 0	104/70 0	92/61 1	77/51 3	64/42 5
BALI, Indonesia	88/74 19	88/74 14	88/73 11	88/74 7	88/73 5	87/71 3	87/70 1	87/70 1	89/71 2	90/73 2	90/75 6	88/74 14
BANGKOK, Thailand	89/68 1	91/72 1	93/75 3	95/77 3	93/77 7	91/76 10	90/76 13	90/76 15	89/76 13	88/75 14	87/72 5	87/68 1
BARCELONA, Spain	56/42 5	57/44 7	62/51 7	65/50 5	71/57 5	78/63 5	81/69 1	84/71 5	78/65 7	69/55 6	62/50 7	57/44 6
BEIRUT, Lebanon	62/51 15	63/51 12	66/54 9	72/58 5	78/64 2	84/74 1	87/74 0	89/74 0	84/74 1	81/69 1	73/60 7	65/54 15
BELFAST, Northern Ireland	45/34 18	47/34 18	50/35 13	53/39 14	59/43 17	65/47 13	65/51 13	65/51 13	62/48 17	55/41 8	50/37 15	46/35 25
BELGRADE, Yugoslavia	37/27 8	41/27 8	53/35 10	64/45 6	74/53 13	79/59 14	84/61 11	84/61 11	76/55 8	65/47 8	52/39 7	40/30 9
BERLIN, Germany	35/26 10	38/27 8	46/32 8	55/38 9	65/46 8	72/52 0	74/55 10	74/54 10	66/48 9	55/41 8	43/33 8	37/29 11
BIARRITZ, France	54/40 16	52/38 11	57/43 11	62/44 8	66/51 11	72/56 9	76/61 7	77/61 7	77/58 9	74/55 11	58/44 12	53/41 14
BOGOTA, Colombia	67/48 6	68/49 7	67/49 14	67/51 20	66/51 17	66/51 16	66/50 18	65/50 16	66/49 13	66/50 20	66/50 16	66/49 15
BOMBAY, India	83/67 1	83/67 1	86/72 1	89/76 1	91/80 1	89/79 14	85/77 21	85/76 19	85/76 13	89/76 5	89/73 1	87/69 1
BONN, West Germany	39/30 7	37/26 6	51/35 7	60/40 7	67/46 13	73/52 10	73/56 16	72/55 17	67/50 10	57/43 8	47/37 8	44/36 15
BRASILIA, Brazil	80/65 17	81/64 20	80/64 12	82/62 10	79/56 5	77/52 0	78/51 0	82/55 0	80/65 5	80/65 5	82/64 16	78/64 16
BRINDISI, Italy	55/43 10	57/43 8	62/47 7	63/41 6	73/57 5	81/58 4	86/61 1	86/60 3	80/60 4	73/53 6	64/52 7	58/46 8
BUCHAREST, Romania	33/20 6	38/24 5	54/35 7	62/44 6	74/51 8	81/58 8	86/60 5	86/60 4	87/60 5	65/44 5	49/35 6	38/26 9
BUDAPEST, Hungary	35/26 7	40/28 7	52/35 5	62/44 8	72/52 9	79/57 7	82/61 7	81/59 7	73/53 5	61/45 8	47/37 8	38/31 9
BUENOS AIRES, Argentina	85/63 7	83/63 6	79/60 7	72/53 8	64/47 7	57/41 7	57/42 8	60/43 9	64/46 8	69/50 9	76/56 9	82/61 8
CAIRO, Egypt	65/47 1	69/48 1	75/52 2	83/57 1	91/63 1	95/68 0	96/70 0	95/71 0	90/68 0	86/65 1	78/58 1	68/50 1
CALCUTTA, India	80/55 1	84/59 2	93/69 2	97/75 3	96/77 7	92/79 13	89/79 18	89/78 13	90/78 13	89/74 6	84/64 1	79/55 1
CAPE TOWN, South Africa	78/60 3	79/60 2	77/58 3	73/53 6	67/49 9	65/46 9	63/45 10	64/46 8	65/49 7	70/52 5	73/55 3	76/58 3
CARACAS, Venezuela	75/56 6	77/56 2	79/58 3	80/62 4	80/65 11	78/62 14	78/62 11	79/61 13	80/61 13	79/61 12	77/60 13	78/58 10
CHARLOTTE AMALIE, Virgin Islands	82/73 18	81/72 13	82/73 12	84/74 13	85/76 15	87/77 8	88/77 11	88/77 11	87/77 13	87/77 18	85/76 19	83/74 18
COLOMBO, Sri Lanka	86/72 7	87/72 6	88/74 7	88/76 14	87/78 15	85/77 18	85/77 12	85/77 11	85/77 13	85/75 19	85/75 19	85/72 10
COPENHAGEN, Denmark	36/29 9	36/28 7	41/31 9	50/37 7	61/44 8	67/51 8	72/55 9	69/54 12	63/49 9	53/42 9	43/35 10	38/32 11
DARWIN, Australia	90/77 20	90/77 18	90/77 17	92/76 6	93/73 1	88/69 1	87/63 0	89/70 0	91/74 2	93/77 5	94/78 10	92/78 15
DJAKARTA, Indonesia	84/74 18	84/74 11	86/74 15	87/75 11	87/75 11	87/74 7	87/73 5	87/73 4	88/74 5	87/74 12	86/74 12	85/74 14
DUBLIN, Ireland	47/35 13	47/35 11	51/36 10	54/38 11	59/41 11	65/48 11	67/51 13	67/51 13	63/47 12	57/43 12	51/38 12	47/36 13
EDINBURGH, Scotland	43/35 18	43/35 15	47/36 15	50/39 16	55/43 15	62/48 15	65/52 17	64/52 17	60/48 16	53/44 18	47/39 18	44/36 17
FLORENCE, Italy	49/35 9	53/36 9	59/40 7	68/46 7	75/53 9	74/58 5	89/63 4	88/62 4	81/58 6	69/51 9	58/42 10	50/37 9
GENEVA, Switzerland	39/29 10	43/30 9	51/35 10	58/41 9	66/48 12	73/55 11	77/58 9	76/57 10	69/52 10	58/44 11	47/37 11	40/31 10
GUAYAQUIL, Ecuador	88/70 10	87/71 25	88/72 24	88/72 14	88/68 9	87/68 4	84/67 2	84/67 2	87/66 2	88/68 3	88/68 4	88/70 10
HAMBURG, West Germany	35/28 12	37/30 10	42/33 10	51/39 11	60/47 11	66/53 10	70/57 13	69/56 13	63/51 10	53/44 11	44/36 11	38/31 12
HAMILTON, Bermuda	68/58 14	68/57 13	68/57 12	71/59 9	76/64 8	81/69 8	85/73 10	86/74 13	85/72 11	79/69 12	74/63 13	70/60 15
HAVANA, Cuba	79/65 6	79/65 4	81/67 4	84/69 4	86/72 7	88/73 10	89/75 10	89/75 11	88/75 11	85/73 11	81/69 7	79/67 6
HELSINKI, Finland	27/17 11	26/15 8	32/22 8	43/30 8	55/41 8	63/49 5	71/57 9	66/55 11	57/46 11	45/37 12	37/30 11	31/22 11
HONG KONG	64/56 4	63/55 5	67/60 7	75/67 8	82/74 13	85/78 18	87/78 17	87/78 15	85/77 13	81/73 6	74/65 2	68/59 3
JERUSALEM, Israel	55/41 9	56/42 11	65/46 3	73/50 4	81/57 1	85/60 0	87/63 0	87/64 0	85/62 1	81/59 1	70/53 4	59/45 7
JOHANNESBURG, South Africa	78/58 12	77/58 9	75/55 5	72/50 4	66/43 3	63/41 1	63/39 1	68/43 1	73/48 2	77/55 10	77/55 10	77/55 11
KARACHI, Pakistan	77/55 1	79/58 1	85/67 1	90/73 1	93/79 1	93/82 1	91/81 2	88/79 2	88/77 1	91/72 1	87/64 5	80/57 1
KINGSTON, Jamaica	86/67 3	86/67 2	86/68 2	87/72 4	87/72 4	89/74 5	89/74 4	90/73 10	89/73 6	87/73 7	87/71 6	87/69 4
LAGOS, Nigeria	88/74 2	89/77 3	89/78 7	89/77 10	87/76 16	85/74 20	83/74 16	82/73 10	83/74 14	85/74 16	88/75 7	88/75 2
LA PAZ, Bolivia	63/43 21	63/43 18	64/42 16	65/40 9	64/37 5	62/34 2	62/33 2	63/35 4	64/38 9	66/40 9	67/42 11	65/42 18

	January	February	March	April	May	June	July	August	September	October	November	December
LAS PALMAS, Canary Is.	70/58 8	71/58 5	71/59 5	71/61 3	73/62 1	75/65 1	77/67 1	79/70 1	79/69 1	79/67 5	76/64 7	72/60 8
LENINGRAD, USSR	23/12 17	24/12 15	33/18 13	45/31 11	58/42 12	66/51 12	71/57 13	66/55 12	57/45 14	45/37 15	34/27 17	26/18 18
LIMA, Peru	82/66 9	83/67 1	83/66 1	80/63 1	74/60 1	68/58 1	67/57 1	66/56 2	68/57 1	71/58 1	74/60 1	78/62 1
LISBON, Portugal	56/46 9	58/47 8	61/49 10	64/52 7	69/56 6	75/60 2	79/63 1	80/64 1	76/62 4	69/57 7	62/52 10	57/47 10
LIVERPOOL, England	44/36 18	44/36 13	48/38 13	52/41 14	58/46 14	63/51 13	66/55 15	65/55 16	61/51 15	55/46 17	48/41 17	45/37 18
LONDON, England	44/35 17	45/35 13	51/37 11	56/40 14	63/45 13	69/51 11	72/55 13	72/54 13	67/51 13	58/44 14	49/39 16	45/36 16
MADRID, Spain	47/33 9	51/35 9	57/40 11	64/44 9	71/50 9	80/57 4	87/62 3	86/62 2	77/56 6	66/48 8	54/40 10	48/35 9
MANILA, Philippines	86/69 6	88/69 3	91/71 4	93/73 4	93/75 12	91/75 17	87/75 24	87/75 23	87/74 19	88/74 19	87/72 14	86/70 11
MARACAIBO, Venezuela	89/73 1	90/73 1	91/74 1	92/76 4	92/77 7	93/75 5	94/76 3	94/77 7	92/76 8	90/74 14	91/76 8	91/75 2
MARSEILLE, France	53/38 10	55/38 8	59/43 8	64/49 8	71/55 6	79/62 4	84/66 2	83/65 3	77/60 5	68/53 8	58/45 8	53/39 9
MELBOURNE, Australia	78/57 8	78/57 7	75/55 9	68/51 13	62/47 14	57/44 16	56/42 17	59/43 17	63/46 14	67/48 14	71/50 13	75/54 11
MEXICO CITY, Mexico	66/42 4	69/43 5	75/47 9	77/51 14	78/54 17	76/55 21	73/53 27	73/54 27	74/53 23	70/50 13	68/46 6	66/43 4
MILAN, Italy	40/29 7	47/33 6	56/38 8	66/46 8	74/54 9	80/61 6	84/64 6	82/63 6	74/58 5	64/49 7	51/39 7	42/33 7
MONTEVIDEO, Uruguay	83/62 6	82/61 5	78/59 5	71/53 6	64/48 6	59/43 7	58/43 6	59/43 7	63/46 6	64/49 6	74/54 6	79/59 7
MOSCOW, USSR	21/9 11	23/10 9	32/17 8	47/31 9	65/44 9	73/51 10	76/55 12	72/52 12	61/43 9	46/34 11	31/23 10	23/13 9
MUNICH, West Germany	33/23 10	37/25 9	45/31 10	54/37 13	63/45 13	69/51 14	72/54 14	71/53 13	64/48 11	53/40 10	42/31 9	36/26 11
NAIROBI, Kenya	77/54 5	79/55 6	77/57 11	75/58 16	72/56 7	70/53 9	69/51 6	70/52 7	75/52 6	76/55 9	74/56 15	74/55 11
NAPLES, Italy	54/42 11	55/43 11	60/46 6	67/50 6	73/56 6	81/62 3	86/67 1	86/67 3	81/63 6	72/56 9	63/49 11	57/45 11
NASSAU, Bahamas	77/65 6	77/64 4	79/64 5	81/69 6	84/71 9	87/74 12	88/76 14	89/76 14	88/75 15	85/73 13	81/70 9	79/67 6
NEW DELHI, India	70/44 2	75/49 2	87/58 1	97/68 1	105/79 2	102/83 4	96/81 8	93/79 8	93/75 4	93/65 1	84/52 1	73/46 1
NICE, France	56/44 8	56/41 6	59/45 8	64/52 7	69/55 6	76/62 5	81/66 2	81/66 5	77/62 6	70/55 7	62/48 7	58/43 8
NOUMEA, New Caledonia	86/72 10	85/73 12	85/72 16	83/70 13	79/66 15	77/64 13	76/62 13	76/61 12	78/63 8	80/65 7	83/68 7	86/70 6
ODESSA, USSR	28/22 7	31/26 4	39/32 5	52/41 6	67/55 6	74/62 7	79/65 5	78/65 5	68/58 5	57/47 5	43/35 9	33/27 8
OSLO, Norway	30/20 8	32/20 7	40/32 7	50/34 7	62/43 7	69/51 8	73/56 10	69/53 11	60/45 8	49/37 10	37/29 9	31/24 10
PALERMO, Sicily, Italy	58/47 14	59/43 8	62/49 7	66/53 5	73/59 5	80/66 3	85/72 1	87/72 1	83/69 4	75/62 10	67/55 9	61/50 11
PALMA, Majorca, Spain	57/42 16	59/43 8	62/49 7	66/49 5	72/54 6	80/61 3	84/66 1	86/67 2	81/64 6	74/57 7	65/50 6	59/44 10
PAPEETE, Tahiti	89/72 16	89/73 16	89/72 15	89/72 10	87/70 10	86/69 6	86/68 5	86/67 6	86/69 5	87/70 8	88/72 14	88/72 14
PARIS, France	42/32 15	45/33 13	52/36 15	60/41 14	67/47 14	73/52 11	76/55 12	75/55 12	69/50 11	59/44 14	49/38 15	43/33 17
PEKING, China	35/15 3	41/20 3	54/30 3	69/46 6	80/56 5	88/65 9	89/71 16	86/69 12	80/58 7	69/44 4	50/30 2	37/19 2
PHNOM PENH, Cambodia	87/70 1	90/72 1	93/74 2	94/76 6	92/76 14	91/76 15	89/75 16	89/76 17	88/76 17	87/76 17	86/74 9	86/71 4
PORT-AU-PRINCE, Haiti	87/68 3	88/68 5	89/69 7	88/69 7	90/72 14	92/73 8	94/74 7	93/73 11	91/73 12	90/72 12	88/71 10	87/69 3
PORT OF SPAIN, Trinidad	85/67 14	86/67 8	89/69 7	88/69 7	89/70 10	87/71 17	88/71 20	88/71 21	88/71 15	87/70 17	87/70 17	86/69 16
PRAGUE, Czechoslovakia	34/25 12	38/28 11	46/33 13	55/40 12	65/49 13	72/55 14	74/58 14	73/57 12	65/52 11	54/44 11	41/35 12	34/29 13
RANGOON, Burma	89/65 1	92/67 1	96/71 1	97/76 2	92/77 14	86/76 23	85/76 26	85/76 25	86/76 20	89/76 13	88/73 7	88/67 1
RIO DE JANEIRO, Brazil	84/73 13	85/73 11	83/72 12	80/69 10	77/66 10	76/64 7	75/63 7	76/64 4	75/65 11	77/66 13	79/68 13	82/71 14
ROME, Italy	54/39 8	56/39 11	62/42 11	68/46 6	74/55 6	82/60 3	88/64 2	88/64 3	83/61 6	73/53 9	63/46 8	56/41 9
SAIGON (HO CHI MINH CITY), Vietnam	87/70 2	89/71 1	93/74 2	95/76 4	92/76 14	89/75 21	88/75 23	88/75 20	88/74 21	88/74 20	88/73 11	87/71 7
SAN JUAN, Puerto Rico	80/70 20	80/70 15	81/70 10	82/72 14	84/74 16	85/75 17	85/75 19	85/76 20	86/75 18	85/75 18	84/73 11	81/72 21
SANTIAGO, Chile	85/53 0	84/52 0	80/49 1	74/45 1	65/41 5	58/37 6	59/37 6	62/39 5	66/42 3	72/45 7	78/48 4	83/51 0
SAO PAULO, Brazil	81/63 19	82/64 17	81/62 15	78/58 10	74/51 9	71/51 8	71/50 6	73/51 8	74/54 11	76/55 11	78/59 14	80/61 13
SEOUL, South Korea	32/15 8	37/20 8	47/29 7	62/41 8	72/51 10	80/61 10	84/70 16	87/71 14	78/59 9	67/45 7	51/32 9	37/20 8
SEVILLE, Spain	59/41 9	62/44 9	67/48 7	73/51 8	80/57 5	89/63 2	96/67 1	97/68 1	89/63 3	78/57 5	67/49 6	60/44 8
SHANGHAI, China	46/33 9	47/34 9	55/40 9	66/50 9	77/59 9	82/67 11	91/74 7	90/74 8	82/66 9	74/57 4	63/45 6	53/36 9
SINGAPORE, Singapore	86/73 17	88/73 11	88/75 14	88/75 15	89/75 15	88/75 13	88/75 13	87/75 14	87/75 14	87/74 16	87/74 18	87/74 19
SOFIA, Bulgaria	34/22 8	39/25 7	51/32 8	62/41 8	70/49 9	76/54 9	82/57 7	82/56 6	74/50 4	63/42 7	48/35 9	37/26 9
STOCKHOLM, Sweden	31/23 14	30/22 10	37/26 9	47/32 6	58/41 5	68/51 7	71/57 8	68/53 10	58/46 8	48/39 9	38/31 9	33/26 13
SYDNEY, Australia	78/65 14	78/65 13	76/63 14	71/58 14	66/52 13	61/49 12	60/46 12	63/48 11	67/51 12	71/56 12	74/60 12	77/63 13
TAIPEI, Taiwan, China	66/54 9	65/53 13	70/57 12	77/63 14	83/69 12	89/73 13	92/76 10	91/75 12	88/73 10	81/67 9	75/62 7	69/57 8
TEHRAN, Iran	45/27 4	50/32 4	59/39 5	71/49 9	82/58 2	93/66 1	99/72 1	97/71 1	90/64 0	76/53 1	63/43 3	51/33 4
TEL AVIV, Israel	65/48 10	65/48 8	67/50 9	74/54 2	81/61 1	84/65 0	87/69 0	87/70 0	86/68 1	84/64 2	77/59 7	66/52 11
TOKYO, Japan	47/29 5	48/31 6	54/36 10	63/46 10	71/54 10	76/63 12	83/70 10	86/70 8	79/66 12	69/55 11	60/43 7	52/33 5
VALPARAISO, Chile	72/56 1	72/56 1	70/54 4	67/52 5	63/50 2	60/48 7	60/47 8	61/47 8	62/48 6	65/50 2	69/52 1	71/54 1
VENICE, Italy	43/33 6	46/35 5	54/41 6	63/49 7	71/57 8	79/63 8	82/67 7	82/67 7	78/62 6	65/52 7	54/43 9	46/37 7
VIENNA, Austria	34/26 8	38/28 7	47/34 7	58/41 8	67/50 11	73/56 14	76/59 13	75/58 12	66/52 9	55/44 8	44/36 9	37/30 9
WELLINGTON, New Zealand	69/56 10	69/56 9	67/54 11	63/51 13	58/47 14	55/44 17	53/42 18	54/43 17	57/46 15	60/48 14	63/50 13	67/54 12
ZURICH, Switzerland	48/14 11	52/15 11	62/22 14	70/32 14	77/39 14	83/47 15	86/51 15	84/49 11	78/42 11	68/32 14	57/25 12	49/16 13

CUSTOMS HINTS

SOURCE: U.S. Customs Service

Customs exemptions: These apply only to articles brought back at the time of your return to the United States. You have a $300 exemption (subject to limitations on cigars, cigarettes, and liquor), if you are returning from a stay abroad of at least 48 hours (no minimum time limit for Mexico and American Virgin Islands), and you have not used the $300 exemption or any part of it within the preceding 30 days. Articles in excess of the $300 exemption up to $600 in value, based on the fair retail price of each item in the country of purchase, may be entered at a flat rate of 10% , if accompanying you at the time of your return, if acquired as an incident to your trip, if for personal or household use, and if properly declared to customs.

Cigars and Cigarettes—Not more than 100 cigars and 200 cigarettes (one carton) may be included in your exemption. Your cigarettes, however, may be subject to a tax imposed by state and local authorities.

Liquor—One liter of alcoholic beverages may be included in the exemption if you are 21 years old or older.

Articles imported in excess of your customs exemption: Will be subject to duty unless the items are entitled to free entry or prohibited. After deducting your exemption and the value of any articles duty free, a flat rate of duty will be applied to the next $600 worth (fair retail value) of merchandise. Any dollar amount of an article over $600 will be dutiable at various rates of duty based on wholesale value. The flat rate of duty is 10% of fair retail value in the country of acquisition; 5% for articles purchased in certain U.S. Territories.

Traveling back and forth across border: If you cross the border at one point and then swing back into the United States to enter the foreign country at another point, you might lose your exemption unless certain requirements are met. Ask a customs officer about these.

American Virgin Islands, American Samoa, Guam: If you return either directly or indirectly from these places, you have a $600 customs exemption provided that not more than $300 of it is applied to merchandise obtained elsewhere than these insular possessions. (The American Virgin Islands are exempt from the 48-hour-minimum time requirement.) Articles whose value exceeds $600 and were acquired in the insular possessions will be assessed at a rate of 5%, and they may accompany you or be shipped home. These articles must be for your own use or for gifts. Four liters of alcoholic beverages may be included in this exemption provided that not more than one liter is acquired elsewhere than in these islands.

Customs declarations: All articles acquired abroad and in your possession at the time of your return must be declared to U.S. customs, either orally or in writing. Declaration lists are distributed on planes and ships and should be prepared well in advance. Your declaration must include items that you are bringing back for another person at his request, any article that you intend to use or sell in your business, alterations or repairs of articles taken abroad, and gifts given to you while abroad. Wearing or using an article acquired abroad does not exempt it from duty, and it must be declared at the price you paid for it. The customs officer may make a reduction in value for wear and use.

Necessary written declarations: All articles acquired abroad must be declared in writing when their total value (including alterations and repairs) exceeds $300, when more than one liter of alcoholic beverages or more than 100 cigars or cigarettes are included, when some of the items are intended for other than personal or household use, or when a customs duty or internal revenue tax is collectible on any article in your possession, or unaccompanied tourist purchases are being sent from U.S. insular possessions.

Family declarations: A family head may make a joint declaration for all members residing in the same household and returning with him as a group. A family may bring in articles free of duty valued up to $300 for each member (e.g., a family of seven: $2,100), even if the articles acquired by some members exceed their $300 exemptions. Returning minors and children are entitled to the same exemptions as adults (except for alcoholic beverages). Children born abroad who have never resided in the United States are not eligible for the exemption, but may claim Customs exemption as a nonresident.

Value of articles: You must declare the price actually paid for each article. If you do not know the price, say so. If an article was not purchased, state its fair value in the country where it was acquired. If you understate the value of an article or misrepresent an article, you may have to pay a penalty in addition to payment of duty.

Preparation for customs: It is helpful to make a list of items obtained abroad before reaching the port of entry. Retain sales slips and have these readily available for examination. Pack articles acquired abroad separately.
Foreign-made articles taken abroad: These are dutiable each time they are brought into our country unless you have acceptable proof of prior possession. Documents which fully describe the article, such as a bill of sale or an insurance policy may be considered. Items which may be readily identified by serial number or permanently affixed markings may be taken to the Customs office nearest you and registered before your departure to expedite free entry of these items when you return.

Gifts: These are considered to be for your personal use and may be included in your exemption. This proviso includes both gifts given to you while abroad and those you intend to give to others after your return. Gifts intended for business or pomotional purposes may not be included. While abroad you may send gifts totaling $25 ($40 from U.S. insular possessions) retail value to people in the United States without duty or tax, provided that the addressee does not receive 'n a single day (at the customs processing station) gift parcels exceeding the $25 limitation. Write "unsolicited gift–Value under $25" in large letters on the outside of package as well as the retail value of the contents. Alcoholic beverages and tobacco products may not be sent, nor alcoholic perfumes valued at more than $5.

Personal belongings sent home: Personal belongings of U.S. origin taken abroad may be sent back by mail duty free if, on the outside wrapper or enclosed in the package, it is stated that the articles were taken out of the U.S. as personal effects and are being returned without having been repaired or altered while abroad.

Automobiles, boats, airplanes: Vehicles taken abroad for noncommercial use may be returned duty free by proving they were taken out of this country. Proof may be the state registration for an automobile, the Federal Aviation Agency certificate of registration for an airplane, a yacht license or motorboat identification, or a customs registration certificate for any vehicle. Dutiable repairs or accessories acquired abroad must be declared. A leaflet entitled "Importing a Car" is available from any customs office for those considering purchase abroad of a foreign car.

Household effects: If you plan to reside overseas for more than one year, household effects may be sometimes duty free. Check with a customs office or U.S. consulate.

$25 exemption: If you are not entitled to the $300 exemption because of the 30-day or 48-hour limitations, you may bring in free of duty or tax articles that were acquired abroad for your personal or household use, if their total retail value does not exceed $25. This is an individual exemption that cannot be grouped on a family declaration. You may include any of the following in this exemption: 50 cigarettes, 10 cigars, four ounces of alcoholic beverages, or four ounces of alcoholic perfume. If the value of any article (or articles) exceeds $25, no article may be exempted from duty or tax.

GSP: Generalized System of Preferences (GSP) is designed to help improve the economy of 107 developing nations and 32 dependent territories by exempting certain items from import duty when brought into the U.S. from these areas. The brochure "GSP & The Traveler" or a customs office can provide further information.

PROHIBITED AND RESTRICTED ARTICLES

Articles considered injurious to the general welfare are prohibited entry. Among these items are obscene publications, lottery tickets, wild birds, their eggs and feathers, endangered wildlife and items made from them, protected marine mammals, liquor-filled candies, switchblade knives.

Narcotics are also prohibited. If your medical condition requires drugs containing narcotics, you should carry a prescription or written statement from your doctor.

Trademarked articles: Foreign-made TM articles may be limited as to the quantity which may be brought into the U.S. if the registered TM has been recorded by an American trademark owner with U.S. Customs. Persons arriving in the U.S. with a TM article are allowed an exemption, usually one article, unless the TM owner allows a quantity over this amount.

Fruits, plants, vegetables: These, with cuttings, seeds, and unprocessed plant products, are either prohibited from entry or require an import license. Address applications to: Quarantines, U.S.D.A., Federal Center Bldg., Hyattsville, Md. 20782.

Meats, livestock, poultry: These items and their by-products (such as sausage, paté), are prohibited or restricted from entering the U.S., depending on the animal disease condition in the country of origin. Fresh meat is generally prohibited; canned meat is permited if the inspector can determine that it is commercially canned, hermetically sealed, and can be kept without refrigeration. Other canned, cured, and dried meat is severely restricted from most countries. Cheese, except cottage cheese, may be brought into the country.

Money or all types of negotiable instruments: Any amount may be brought into or taken out of the United States. Persons importing or exporting an amount of more than $5,000 are required to file a report of the transaction with U.S. Customs. Ask a customs officer for the form at the time you arrive or depart with such amounts.

Pets: There are controls, restrictions and prohibitions on the entry if animals, birds, turtles, wildlife and all endangered species. Cats and dogs must be free of evidence of diseases communicable to man. Vaccination against rabies is not required for cats or dogs arriving from rabies-free countries. Personally owned pet birds may be entered (limit of two if of the Psittacine family), but APHIS and Public Health Service requirements must be met. This includes quarantine at any APHIS facility at specified locations, at the owner's expense. Advance reservations are required. For more information write: Veterinary Services, APHIS, U.S.D.A., Hyatsville, Md. 20782.

Monkeys—Live monkeys and other non-human primates may not be imported into the United States except by a registered importer for scientific, educational, or exhibition purposes.

Biological materials: Disease organisms and vectors for research and educational purposes require a permit. Write the Foreign Quarantine Program, Center for Disease Control, Atlanta, Ga. 30333.

Prohibited merchandise: Tourists may import items for their personal use up to a value of $100 from the following countries: Cuba, North Korea, Vietnam, and Cambodia. This allowance may only be used once every six months, and the articles must accompany the visitor upon his return.

Firearms and ammunition: Up to three nonautomatic firearms may be taken out of the country and returned if they are registered with customs or field office of the Bureau of Alcohol, Tobacco and Firearms. Firearms and ammunition are subject to import restrictions. Contact the Bureau of Alcohol, Tobacco and Firearms, Department of the Treasury, Washington, D.C. 20226.

HEALTH HINTS FOR TRAVELERS

SOURCE: U.S. Public Health Service

Under the International Health Regulations adopted by the World Health Organization a country, under certain conditions, may require International Certificates of Vaccination against Smallpox, Cholera, or Yellow Fever. For *direct* travel from the U.S. to many countries, no vaccinations are required—certain vaccinations are required by some countries in Africa and Asia. Some countries require vaccination against yellow fever or cholera if you arrive from an area infected with these diseases. **No vaccinations are required to return to the U.S. from any country.**

Required immunizations must be recorded in the International Certificates of Vaccination, form PHS-731. You can obtain this form with your passport application, from your local health department, or from the Superintendent of Documents, Government Printing Office, Washington, D.C. 20402, for 50 cents.

The Certificates must be signed by you and your physician or by a person under his supervision and be validated with an approved stamp. Validation of Cholera Certificates can be obtained at most health departments or from vaccinating physicians who possess a validation stamp. Yellow Fever Vaccinations must be given at an officially designated Yellow Fever Vaccination Center and the Certificate validated by the Center that administers the vaccine. Information on the location of Yellow Fever Vaccination Centers is available from state and local health departments.

Smallpox has been eradicated. If you plan to travel to a country that requires vaccination as a condition for entry, you should consult your physician concerning a written statement that smallpox vaccination is contraindicated for health reasons.

The Cholera Certificate is valid for 6 months beginning 6 days after 1 injection of vaccine or on the date of revaccination if within 6 months of the first injection.

The Yellow Fever Certificate is valid for 10 years beginning 10 days after primary vaccination or on the date of revaccination if within 10 years of the first injection.

Military personnel and their dependents, as well as other persons traveling under the auspices of the Department of Defense, are required to receive the immunizations as set forth by current service regulations.

RECOMMENDED VACCINATIONS

Recommendations on the use of certain vaccines and prophylactic measures depend upon your immunization status, itinerary, the areas of the world to be visited, and the nature and duration of travel. Most international travelers probably do not need any additional vaccination or prophylaxis if their routine immunization status is up to date. In most developed countries such as Canada, Australia, New Zealand, and Europe, the risk to the health of the traveler will be no greater than that incurred while traveling throughout the United States. In the countries of Africa, Asia, South America, and in the countries of southern North America, the South Pacific, Middle East and Far East, living conditions and standards of sanitation and hygiene vary greatly. For travel to primarily tourist areas on itineraries which do not include travel in rural areas and consequently less risk of exposure to food or water of questionable quality, the risk of disease remains quite small. Travelers to smaller cities off the usual tourist routes and those who visit small villages or rural areas for extended periods are at greater risk of acquiring infectious diseases because of exposure to water and food of uncertain quality and closer contact with local residents who may harbor the organisms that cause such diseases. Typhoid is prevalent in many countries of Africa, Asia, and Central America. Vaccination is recommended for travel to areas off the usual tourist itinerary. The risk of contacting hepatitis-A varies with living conditions, the prevalence of hepatitis in the areas visited, and particularly the length of stay. Vaccination against plague is not indicated for most travelers to countries reporting cases, particularly if their travel is limited to urban areas with modern lodgings.

There is a risk of acquiring malaria when traveling to parts of the Caribbean, Central and South America, Africa, the Middle East, the Indian subcontinent, and the Far East. You are strongly advised to seek information from your health department or private physician concerning the need for protection against malaria and for instructions on how the prophylactic drugs should be taken.

You are advised to contact your local health department, physician or agency two weeks prior to departure to obtain current information on vaccinations required by and recommended for the countries to be visited.

Unvaccinated Travelers: A traveler who does not have the required vaccinations upon entering a country may be subject to vaccination, medical follow-up, and/or isolation.

Exemption from Vaccination: If a physician thinks vaccination should not be performed on medical grounds, the traveler should be given a signed, dated statement of the reasons on the physician's letterhead stationery.

HEALTH PROTECTION HINTS

If you wear glasses, take along your lens prescription.

If you need medications regularly, take an adequate supply with you. Because of possible serious consequences to your health, do not buy medications "over the counter" unless you are familiar with the product.

If you have diabetes, are allergic to penicillin, or have any physical condition that may require emergency care, have some identification–a tag or bracelet or card–on your person at all times indicating this. Diabetics should take along an extra supply of medication. Drugs or medicines which must be taken should be accompanied by a letter from the traveler's physician.

Water can be considered safe only if it is obtained from adequately chlorinated sources, if boiled for ten minutes, or if treated with liquid chlorine laundry bleach or tincture of iodine.

Swimming in contaminated water may result in eye, ear, and certain intestinal infections. Generally only chlorinated pools can be considered safe places to swim.

Take it easy in unaccustomed conditions of heat and high altitudes.

It is wise to check with the local American Embassy or consulate for a list of acceptable doctors and dentists, and hospitals, if needed.

WORLD CITIES: COST-OF-LIVING INDEX: 1980

Source: *U.N. Monthly Bulletin of Statistics* (Special Table K), March 1981, © United Nations

Note: This table shows the relative cost-of-living comparison, based on prices for goods, services and housing for international UN officials stationed in various cities of the world. In the following table, the cost-of-living is based on New York City = 100.

City	Index	City	Index	City	Index
Afghanistan, Kabul	89	Greece, Athens	108	Nicaragua, Managua	67
Argentina, Buenos Aires	216	Guatemala, Guatemala	99	Pakistan, Islamabad	89
Australia, Sydney	104	Guinea, Conakry	125	Panama, Panama City	93
Austria, Vienna	130	Guyana, Georgetown	86	Paraguay, Asunción	107
Bangladesh, Dacca	95	Haiti, Port-au-Prince	88	Peru, Lima	100
Barbados, Bridgetown	99	Hungary, Budapest	83	Philippines, Manila	100
Belgium, Brussels	137	India, New Delhi	86	Poland, Warsaw	69
Benin, Cotonou	99	Indonesia, Jakarta	109	Romania, Bucharest	82
Brazil, Rio de Janeiro	88	Iran, Tehran	99	Senegal, Dakar	124
Bulgaria, Sofia	97	Iraq, Baghdad	93	Singapore, Singapore	93
Burma, Rangoon	79	Italy, Rome	100	Spain, Madrid	114
Canada, Montréal	79	Jamaica, Kingston	70	Sri Lanka, Colombo	74
Chile, Santiago	116	Japan, Tokyo	160	Sudan, Khartoum	127
Colombia, Bogotá	93	Kenya, Nairobi	103	Swaziland, Mbabane	71
Cuba, Havana	81	Korea, South, Seoul	113	Switzerland, Geneva	142
Cyprus, Nicosia	84	Kuwait, Kuwait	105	Syria, Damascus	134
Czechoslovakia, Bratislava	68	Liberia, Monrovia	115	Thailand, Bangkok	89
Denmark, Copenhagen	134	Libya, Tripoli	145	Togo, Lomé	95
Dominican Rep., Santo Domingo	89	Madagascar, Antananarivo	111	Tunisia, Tunis	128
Ecuador, Quito	86	Malaysia, Kuala Lumpur	93	Turkey, Ankara	79
Egypt, Cairo	86	Malta, Valletta	77	United Kingdom, London	140
El Salvador, San Salvador	100	Mauritius, Port Louis	81	United States, Washington, DC	95
Ethiopia, Addis Ababa	95	Mexico, Mexico City	95	Uruguay, Montevideo	115
Fiji, Suva	94	Morocco, Rabat	126	Venezuela, Caracas	138
France, Paris	139	Nepal, Kathamandu	86	Yemen, San'a	133
Germany, West, Bonn	134	Netherlands, The Hague	134	Yugoslavia, Belgrade	92

RATES OF CUSTOMS DUTY: 1981 Source: U.S. Customs Service

This abbreviated list of popular items imported by tourists is intended to be used as an advisory guide only. The customs officer examining baggage at the point of entry determines the rates of duty on dutiable articles. Rates are often higher for items imported from certain Communist-controlled countries. These rates apply to those articles brought in after the $600 maximum has been reached and the 10% flat rate (5% for insular possessions) no longer applies.

Item	Rate
Antiques: produced prior to 100 years before the date of entry	Free
Automobiles, passenger	2.9%
Beads:	
imitation precious, and semi-precious stones	4.7 to 11.4%
ivory	8.5%
Binoculars, prism	Free
Books, foreign author or foreign language	Free
Cameras:	
motion picture, over $50 each	5.6%
still, over $10 each	6.4%
cases, leather	9.5%
lenses	10.6%
China:	
bone	16.3%
nonbone, other than tableware	20.8 to 26%
China tableware, nonbone, available in 77-piece sets:	
valued not over $56 per set	35.5%
valued over $56 per set	15.8%
Cigarette lighters:	
pocket, valued at over 42 cents each	19.1%
table	10.2%
Clocks, valued over $5 but not over $10	63¢ + 13.6% + 5.3¢ for each jewel
valued over $10 each	95¢ + 13.6% + 5.3¢ for each jewel
Drawings (done all by hand)	Free
Earthenware tableware, household available in 77-piece sets:	
valued not over $38 per set	20.5%

Item	Rate
valued over $38 per set	9.7%
Figurines, china	3.1 to 19.1%
Fur: wearing apparel	7.1 to 15.7%
other manufactures of	3.4 to 12.5%
Furniture:	
wood, chairs	7.2 to 7.7%
wood, other than chairs	4.9%
Gloves:	
wool, over $4 per dozen	37.5¢ lb. + 18.5%
horsehide or cowhide	15%
Handkerchiefs, cotton, plain	25% to 5¢ lb. + 35%
Ivory, manufactures of	5.8%
Jade, cut but not set	2.9%
other articles of jade	21%
Jewelry, precious metal or stone: silver chief value, valued not over $18 per doz	27.5%
other	10.6%
Leather:	
pocketbooks, bags	7.7 to 10%
other manufactures of	3.8 to 11%
Motorcycles	4.7%
Musical instruments:	
music boxes, wood	6.8%
woodwind, except bagpipes	6.9%
Paintings (done all by hand)	Free
Pearls, loose or temporarily strung and without clasp:	
genuine	Free
cultured	2.4%
imitation	17%
permanently or temporarily strung (with clasp attached or separate)	10.6 to 23.4%
Perfume	6¢ lb. + 6.9%
Postage stamps	Free
Radios:	

Item	Rate
transistors	9.3 to 9.8%
other	6%
Rattan:	
furniture	16%
other manufactures of	11.7%
Records, phonograph	4.8%
Shaver, electric	6.2%
Shell, manufactures of	3.4%
Shoes, leather	2.5 to 20%
Sterling flatware and tableware:	
knives and forks	3.5¢ each + 8.1%
spoons and tableware	11%
Stereo equipment	5.1 to 7.8%
Stones, cut but not set:	
diamonds not over one-half carat	Free
diamonds over one-half carat	Free to 4.4%
Sweaters, of wool, over $5 per pound	37.5¢ lb. + 20%
Tape recorders	5.1 to 6.9%
Toys	14.9%
Watches, on $100 watch, duty varies	from $6 to $13
Wearing apparel:	
embroidered or ornamented	21 to 42.5%
not embroidered, not ornamented	
cotton, knit	21%
cotton, not knit	8 to 21%
linen, not knit	7.5%
manmade fiber, knit	25¢ lb. + 32.5%
manmade fiber, not knit	25¢ lb. + 27.5%
silk, knit	10%
silk, other	16%
wool, knit	37.5¢ lb. + 15.5 to 32%
Wood, carvings and articles of	7.3%

ALCOHOLIC BEVERAGES IMPORT RESTRICTIONS

State laws: Liquor may not be imported in violation of state law.
Mail Importations: United States postal laws prohibit the shipment of alcoholic beverages by mail.
Gift packages: Alcoholic beverages may not be included in gift parcels sent to persons in the U.S.A. and are not entitled to free entry under the $25 gift exemption.

Customs Exemption: A returning resident 21 years or older may include in his $300 customs exemption one liter of alcoholic beverages free of duty and internal revenue tax. The importation must be for his own use or for a gift and not in violation of the laws of the state of arrival.

MAJOR COMMERCIAL PASSENGER PLANES

Country Company and Type	Maximum Number of Passengers	Maximum Speed (MPH)	Wingspan (Feet)	Length (Feet)	Height (Feet)
International Europe					
Airbus Industrie A300	345	576	147.1	175.1	54.2
France					
Dassault Mercure	134	575	100.3	114.3	37.3
Aerospatiale Caravelle IIR	50	498	112.5	107.3	28.6
Aerospatiale Caravelle III	99	500	112.5	105.0	28.6
Aerospatiale Super Caravelle	118	498	112.5	108.3	28.6
Aerospatiale Concorde	140	1300	84.0	203.9	37.1
United Kingdom					
BAC 111-475	89	541	93.6	93.6	24.6
BAC 111-500	119	541	93.6	107.0	24.6
British Aerospace 1150 Super VC 10	163	600	146.2	171.8	39.5
British Aerospace Trident 1E	139	605	95.0	115.8	27.0
British Aerospace Comet 4	83	530	115.0	111.5	29.5
British Aerospace Avro 748	60	281	98.6	67.0	24.1
British Aerospace Concorde	140	1300	84.0	203.9	37.1
Handley Page HPR 7-200	56	275	94.8	75.5	24.1
Hawker Siddeley Comet 4	81	530	115.0	111.5	29.5
Hawker Siddeley Trident 1E	139	605	95.0	114.8	27.0
Japan					
Nihon YS-11	60	297	105.0	86.3	29.5
Netherlands					
Fokker F27 MK500	60	298	95.2	82.2	28.6
Fokker F27 MK600	48	298	95.2	77.3	27.9
Fokker F28 MK3000	65	524	82.25	89.9	27.8
Fokker F28 MK4000	85	524	82.25	97.1	27.8
Fokker F28 MK6000	85	524	82.25	97.1	27.8
USSR					
Ilyushin IL-18V	110	425	122.7	117.8	—
Ilyushin IL-62	186	560	142.0	174.2	40.5
Tupolev TU-134	72	621	95.2	114.5	29.7
Tupolev TU-144	130	M.2.3	81.0	180.0	—
Tupolev TU-154	164	559	123.3	157.2	37.5
United States					
Boeing 707-120	181	600	130.9	144.5	42.0
Boeing 707-320	219	600 plus	145.7	152.9	42.5
Boeing 707-420RWL	189	593	142.7	152.9	42.5
Boeing 720	167	600	130.9	136.2	41.8
Boeing 727-200	189	600 plus	108.0	153.2	34.0
Boeing 737-100	103	580 plus	93.0	94.0	37.0
Boeing 737-200	130	573	93.0	100.0	37.0
Boeing 747	550	640	195.6	231.3	63.4
Boeing 757	233	600	124.5	155.25	44.5
Boeing 767	289	600	155.07	159.1	52.0
Fairchild Hiller F-27	48	275	95.2	77.2	27.5
Fairchild Hiller FH-227	52	300	95.2	83.1	27.5
General Dynamics 240	40	304†	91.8	74.8	26.9
General Dynamics Metropolitan 440	44	310	105.3	81.5	28.2
General Dynamics Convair 580	53	342†	105.3	81.5	29.1
General Dynamics 600	46	317	91.8	74.8	26.9
General Dynamics Convair 880	107	600	120.0	129.0	42.0
General Dynamics Convair 990	130	500	131.0	141.0	42.0
Lockheed TriStar L-1011	400	620	155.4	178.7	55.4
McDonnell Douglas DC-9 Series 10	90	586	89.3	104.3	27.5
McDonnell Douglas DC-9 Series 20	90	586	93.3	104.3	27.5
McDonnell Douglas DC-9 Series 30	139	586	93.3	119.25	27.5
McDonnell Douglas DC-9 Series 40	139	576	93.3	125.5	28.0
McDonnell Douglas DC-9 Series 50	139	576	93.3	133.5	28.0
McDonnell Douglas DC-9 Super 80	172	576	107.8	147.9	29.3
McDonnell Douglas DC-10 Series 10	380	600 plus	155.3	182.25	58.1
McDonnell Douglas DC-10 Series 30	380	600 plus	165.3	181.6	58.1
McDonnell Douglas DC-10 Series 40	380	600 plus	165.3	182.25	58.1

† Best cruising speed.

OPERATIONS AT 30 TOP-RANKING U.S. AIRPORTS: FISCAL YEAR 1979
Source: Federal Aviation Administration

Tower	Rank	1979 Operations†	Tower	Rank	1979 Operations†
Chicago O'Hare Int'l, Ill.	1	735,524	Torrance Municipal, Calif.	16	408,506
Long Beach, Calif.	2	646,401	Phoenix Sky Harbor Int'l, Ariz.	17	394,731
Santa Ana, Claif.	3	616,870	Fort Worth Meacham, Tex.	18	383,184
Atlanta International, Ga.	4	594,410	Miami International, Fla.	19	378,939
Van Nuys, Calif.	5	586,037	San Jose Reid Hillview, Calif.	20	372,389
Los Angeles Int'l, Calif.	6	547,960	Las Vegas McCarran Int'l, Nev.	21	369,211
Opa Locka, Fla.	7	527,579	Memphis International, Tenn.	22	369,069
Oakland International, Calif.	8	523,453	San Francisco, Calif.	23	363,791
Denver Stapleton Int'l, Colo.	9	482,389	Boston Logan, Mass.	24	355,959
Tamiami, Fla.	10	456,101	La Guardia, N.Y.	25	353,968
San Jose Municipal, Calif.	11	452,102	Washington National, D.C.	26	351,485
Dallas Ft. Worth Regional, Tex.	12	436,362	Pittsburgh Greater Int'l, Pa.	27	346,838
Denver Arapahoe County, Colo.	13	428,649	Philadelphia Int'l, Pa.	28	344,630
Seattle Boeing, Wash.	14	426,711	St. Louis Int'l, Mo.	29	341,854
Honolulu, Hawaii	15	411,376	Fort Lauderdale, Fla.	30	338,780

†Takeoffs and landings.

AIR DISTANCES BETWEEN MAJOR WORLD CITIES (See also, U. S. AIR DISTANCES, p. 221)
Source: USAF Aeronautical Chart and Information Center (in statute miles)

	Bangkok	Berlin	Cairo	Cape Town	Caracas	Chicago	Hong Kong	Honolulu	Istanbul	Lima	London	Madrid	Melbourne
Accra	6,850	3,330	2,672	2,974	4,576	5,837	7,615	10,052	3,039	5,421	3,169	2,412	9,325
Amsterdam	5,707	360	2,015	5,997	4,883	4,118	5,772	7,254	1,372	6,538	222	921	10,286
Anchorage	6,022	4,545	6,116	10,478	5,353	2,858	5,073	2,778	5,388	6,385	4,491	5,181	7,729
Athens	4,930	1,121	671	4,957	5,815	5,447	5,316	8,353	352	7,312	1,488	1,474	9,297
Auckland	4,645	9,995	8,825	6,574	9,620	9,507	4,625	5,346	9,203	7,989	10,570	10,884	1,610
Baghdad	3,756	2,029	798	4,924	7,020	6,430	4,260	8,399	1,006	8,487	2,547	2,675	8,105
Bangkok	—	5,351	4,521	6,301	10,558	8,569	1,076	6,610	4,648	12,241	5,929	6,334	4,579
Beirut	4,272	1,689	341	4,794	6,520	6,097	4,756	8,536	614	7,972	2,151	2,190	8,579
Belgrade	5,073	623	1,147	5,419	5,587	5,000	5,327	7,882	500	7,169	1,053	1,263	9,578
Berlin	5,351	—	1,768	5,958	5,242	4,415	5,443	7,323	1,075	6,893	580	1,162	9,929
Bombay	1,870	3,915	2,717	5,103	9,034	8,066	2,679	8,036	3,000	10,389	4,478	4,689	6,101
Buenos Aires	10,490	7,395	7,360	4,285	3,155	5,582	11,478	7,554	7,608	1,945	6,907	6,236	7,219
Cairo	4,521	1,768	—	4,510	6,337	6,116	5,057	8,818	741	7,725	2,158	2,069	8,700
Cape Town	6,301	5,958	4,510	—	6,361	8,489	7,377	11,534	5,204	6,074	5,988	5,306	6,428
Caracas	10,558	5,242	6,337	6,361	—	2,500	10,171	6,024	6,050	1,699	4,662	4,351	9,703
Chicago	8,569	4,415	6,116	8,489	2,500	—	7,797	4,256	5,485	3,772	3,960	4,192	9,667
Copenhagen	5,361	222	1,964	6,179	5,215	4,263	5,392	7,101	1,252	6,886	595	1,289	9,936
Denver	8,409	5,092	6,846	9,331	3,078	920	7,476	3,346	6,164	3,986	4,701	5,028	8,755
Frankfurt (W. Germany)	5,581	270	1,817	5,815	5,022	4,344	5,709	7,450	1,160	6,660	408	885	10,133
Helsinki	4,903	689	2,069	6,490	5,658	4,442	4,867	6,818	1,330	7,349	1,135	1,835	9,448
Hong Kong	1,076	5,443	5,057	7,377	10,171	7,797	—	5,557	4,989	11,415	5,986	6,556	4,605
Honolulu	6,610	7,323	8,818	11,534	6,024	4,256	5,557	—	8,118	5,944	7,241	7,874	5,501
Houston	9,261	5,337	7,005	8,608	2,262	942	8,349	3,902	6,400	3,123	4,860	5,014	8,979
Istanbul	4,648	1,075	741	5,204	6,050	5,485	4,989	8,118	—	7,593	1,551	1,701	9,100
Karachi	2,305	3,365	2,222	5,153	8,502	7,564	2,977	8,059	2,457	9,943	3,928	4,152	6,646
Keflavik	6,300	1,505	3,267	7,107	4,269	2,942	6,044	6,085	2,578	5,965	1,188	1,802	10,552
Kinshasa	5,974	3,916	2,618	2,047	5,752	7,085	6,904	11,178	3,241	6,322	3,951	3,305	8,112
Leningrad	4,718	826	2,034	6,500	5,843	4,589	4,687	6,816	1,306	7,534	1,307	1,985	9,263
Lima	12,241	6,893	7,725	6,074	1,699	3,772	11,415	5,944	7,593	—	6,316	5,907	8,052
Lisbon	6,651	1,442	2,352	5,301	4,040	4,001	6,862	7,835	2,015	5,591	989	317	11,049
London	5,929	580	2,158	5,988	4,662	3,960	5,986	7,241	1,551	6,316	—	786	10,508
Madrid	6,334	1,162	2,069	5,306	4,351	4,192	6,556	7,874	1,701	5,907	786	—	10,766
Melbourne	4,579	9,929	8,700	6,428	9,703	9,667	4,605	5,501	9,100	8,052	10,508	10,766	—
Mexico City	9,793	6,054	7,677	8,516	2,234	1,688	8,789	3,791	7,106	2,635	5,558	5,642	8,420
Montreal	8,337	3,740	5,403	7,920	2,443	746	7,736	4,919	4,798	3,967	3,256	3,449	10,390
Moscow	4,394	1,001	1,770	6,277	6,176	4,984	4,443	7,049	1,087	7,855	1,556	2,140	8,965
Nairobi	4,481	3,947	2,217	2,543	7,179	8,012	5,447	10,740	2,957	7,821	4,229	3,840	7,159
New Delhi	1,812	3,598	2,752	5,769	8,837	7,486	2,339	7,413	2,837	10,430	4,178	4,528	6,340
New York City	8,669	3,980	5,598	7,801	2,124	714	8,061	4,969	5,022	3,635	3,473	3,596	10,352
Oslo	5,395	523	2,243	6,477	5,167	4,050	5,342	6,801	1,518	6,857	718	1,485	9,934
Panama City	10,871	5,856	7,118	7,021	867	2,321	10,089	5,254	6,756	1,454	5,285	5,081	9,027
Paris	5,877	549	1,973	5,782	4,735	4,145	5,992	7,452	1,400	6,367	215	652	10,442
Peking	2,027	4,600	4,687	8,034	8,978	6,625	1,195	5,084	4,407	10,365	5,089	5,759	5,632
Rabat	6,652	1,623	2,230	4,954	4,111	4,282	6,954	8,177	2,008	5,590	1,254	474	10,856
Rio de Janeiro	9,987	6,207	6,153	3,773	2,805	5,288	11,002	8,295	6,378	2,351	5,751	5,045	8,218
Rome	5,493	735	1,305	5,231	5,198	4,823	5,773	8,040	853	6,748	892	849	9,940
Saigon (Ho Chi Minh City)	467	5,771	4,987	6,534	10,905	8,695	938	6,302	5,102	12,180	6,345	6,779	4,168
San Francisco	7,930	5,673	7,436	10,248	3,908	1,860	6,904	2,397	6,711	4,516	5,369	5,806	7,850
Santiago	10,967	7,772	7,967	4,947	3,033	5,295	11,615	6,861	8,135	1,528	7,241	6,639	7,017
Seattle	7,455	5,060	6,809	10,205	4,096	1,737	6,481	2,681	6,077	4,961	4,799	5,303	8,176
Shanghai	1,797	5,231	5,188	8,062	9,508	7,071	760	4,947	4,975	10,665	5,728	6,386	4,991
Shannon	6,256	940	2,534	6,188	4,320	3,583	6,246	7,006	1,938	5,992	387	884	10,826
Singapore	887	6,167	5,143	6,007	11,408	9,376	1,608	6,728	5,379	11,689	6,747	7,079	3,767
St. Louis	8,763	4,676	6,370	8,549	2,414	265	7,949	4,134	5,744	3,589	4,215	4,426	9,476
Stockholm	5,141	505	2,084	6,422	5,422	4,288	5,115	6,873	1,347	7,109	892	1,613	9,693
Tehran	3,392	2,184	1,220	5,240	7,322	6,502	3,844	8,072	1,274	8,850	2,739	2,974	7,838
Tokyo	2,865	5,557	5,937	9,155	8,813	6,313	1,792	3,860	5,574	9,628	5,956	6,704	5,070
Vienna	5,252	323	1,455	5,656	5,374	4,696	5,432	7,632	791	6,990	767	1,124	9,802
Warsaw	5,032	322	1,588	5,934	5,563	4,679	5,147	7,368	858	7,212	901	1,425	9,609
Washington D.C.	8,807	4,182	5,800	7,892	2,051	2,598	8,157	4,839	5,225	3,504	3,676	3,794	10,174

Mexico City	Montreal	Moscow	Nairobi	New Delhi	New York	Paris	Peking	Rio de Janeiro	Rome	San Francisco	Singapore	Stockholm	Tehran	Tokyo	Vienna	Warsaw
6,677	5,146	4,038	2,603	5,279	5,126	2,988	7,359	3,501	2,624	7,688	7,183	3,835	3,874	8,594	3,100	3,440
5,735	3,426	1,337	4,136	3,958	3,654	271	4,890	5,938	807	5,465	6,526	701	2,533	5,788	581	681
3,776	3,133	4,364	8,287	5,709	3,373	4,697	3,997	8,145	5,263	2,005	6,678	4,102	5,654	3,463	4,856	4,601
7,021	4,737	1,387	2,827	3,120	4,938	1,305	4,757	6,030	654	6,792	5,629	1,498	1,539	5,924	801	996
8,274	10,231	9,018	7,315	6,420	10,194	10,519	5,626	8,259	10,048	7,692	3,848	9,732	7,935	5,017	9,886	9,676
8,082	5,768	1,583	2,431	1,966	6,007	2,405	3,925	6,938	1,836	7,466	4,427	2,164	431	5,199	1,781	1,752
9,793	8,337	4,394	4,481	1,812	8,669	5,877	2,027	9,987	5,493	7,930	887	5,141	3,392	2,865	5,252	5,032
7,707	5,405	1,514	2,420	2,479	5,622	1,987	4,352	6,478	1,368	7,302	4,935	1,931	913	5,598	1,401	1,459
6,610	4,305	1,066	3,328	3,270	4,526	902	4,634	6,145	449	6,296	5,833	1,010	1,741	5,720	309	516
6,054	3,740	1,001	3,947	3,598	3,980	549	4,600	6,207	735	5,673	6,167	505	2,184	5,557	323	322
9,739	7,524	3,132	2,811	722	7,811	4,367	2,953	8,334	3,846	8,406	2,427	3,880	1,743	4,196	3,725	3,601
4,580	5,597	8,369	6,479	9,823	5,279	6,857	11,994	1,231	6,925	6,455	9,870	7,799	8,565	11,411	7,334	7,656
7,677	5,403	1,770	2,217	2,752	5,598	1,973	4,687	6,153	1,305	7,436	5,143	2,084	1,220	5,937	1,455	1,588
8,516	7,920	6,277	2,543	5,769	7,801	5,782	8,034	3,773	5,231	10,248	6,007	6,422	5,240	9,155	5,656	5,934
2,234	2,443	6,176	7,179	8,837	2,124	4,735	8,978	2,805	5,198	3,908	11,408	5,422	7,322	8,813	5,374	5,563
1,688	746	4,984	8,012	7,486	714	4,145	6,625	5,288	4,823	1,860	9,376	4,288	6,502	6,313	4,696	4,679
5,918	3,605	971	4,156	3,640	3,857	642	4,503	6,321	953	5,473	6,195	325	2,287	5,415	540	417
1,438	1,639	5,501	8,867	7,730	1,631	4,900	6,385	5,866	5,887	953	9,079	4,879	7,033	5,815	5,395	5,322
5,945	3,650	1,261	3,865	3,811	3,857	295	4,853	5,932	595	5,700	6,386	745	2,346	5,831	388	559
6,101	3,845	554	4,282	3,247	4,126	1,192	3,956	6,872	1,370	5,435	5,759	248	2,062	4,872	895	569
8,789	7,736	4,443	5,447	2,339	8,061	5,992	1,195	11,002	5,773	6,904	1,608	5,115	3,844	1,792	5,432	5,147
3,791	4,919	7,049	10,740	7,413	4,969	7,452	5,084	8,295	8,040	2,397	6,728	6,873	8,072	3,860	7,632	7,368
749	1,605	5,925	8,746	8,388	1,419	5,035	7,244	5,015	5,702	1,648	9,954	5,227	7,442	6,685	5,609	5,609
7,106	4,798	1,087	2,957	2,837	5,022	1,400	4,407	6,378	853	6,711	5,379	1,347	1,274	5,574	791	858
9,249	6,997	2,600	2,708	678	7,277	3,817	3,020	8,082	3,306	8,078	2,942	3,340	1,194	4,313	3,175	3,052
4,614	2,317	2,083	5,404	4,749	2,597	1,402	4,951	6,090	2,068	4,196	7,181	1,352	3,568	5,497	1,813	1,745
7,915	6,378	4,328	4,234	4,692	6,378	3,742	7,002	4,105	3,186	8,920	6,132	4,388	3,612	8,307	3,619	3,910
6,276	4,005	396	4,230	3,069	4,291	1,350	3,789	7,028	1,460	5,523	5,575	431	1,926	4,733	986	642
2,635	3,967	7,855	7,821	10,430	3,635	6,367	10,365	2,351	6,748	4,516	11,689	7,109	8,850	9,628	6,990	7,212
5,396	3,255	2,433	4,013	4,844	3,377	904	6,040	4,777	1,163	5,679	7,393	1,862	3,288	6,943	1,432	1,720
5,558	3,256	1,556	4,229	4,178	3,473	215	5,089	5,751	892	5,369	6,747	892	2,739	5,956	767	901
5,642	3,449	2,140	3,840	4,528	3,596	652	5,759	5,045	849	5,806	7,079	1,613	2,974	6,704	1,124	1,425
8,420	10,390	8,965	7,159	6,340	10,352	10,442	5,632	8,218	9,940	7,850	3,767	9,693	7,838	5,070	9,802	9,609
—	2,315	6,671	9,218	9,119	2,086	5,723	7,772	4,769	6,374	1,889	10,331	5,965	8,182	7,036	6,316	6,335
2,315	—	4,397	7,267	7,012	333	3,432	6,541	5,082	4,102	2,544	9,207	3,667	5,879	6,470	4,007	4,021
6,671	4,397	—	3,928	2,703	4,680	1,550	3,627	7,162	1,477	5,884	5,236	764	1,534	4,663	1,039	716
9,218	7,267	3,928	—	3,371	7,365	4,020	5,720	5,556	3,340	9,598	4,636	4,299	2,709	6,996	3,625	3,800
9,119	7,012	2,703	3,317	—	7,319	4,103	2,350	8,747	3,684	7,691	2,574	3,466	1,584	3,638	3,467	3,277
2,086	333	4,680	7,365	7,319	—	3,638	6,867	4,805	4,293	2,574	9,539	3,939	6,141	6,757	4,233	4,271
5,722	3,418	1,024	4,446	3,726	3,686	838	4,395	6,462	1,248	5,196	6,249	260	2,462	5,238	839	661
1,496	2,542	6,720	8,043	9,422	2,213	5,388	8,939	3,296	5,916	3,326	11,692	5,956	8,011	8,441	6,031	6,175
5,723	3,432	1,550	4,020	4,103	3,638	—	5,138	5,681	688	5,579	6,676	964	2,624	6,054	643	853
7,772	6,541	3,627	5,720	2,350	6,867	5,138	—	10,778	5,076	5,934	2,754	4,197	3,496	1,305	4,664	4,340
5,612	3,537	2,579	3,733	4,841	3,636	1,125	6,206	4,589	1,184	5,995	7,348	2,084	3,263	7,174	1,546	1,866
4,769	5,082	7,162	5,556	8,747	4,805	5,681	10,778	—	5,704	6,621	9,776	6,638	7,368	11,535	6,124	6,453
6,374	4,102	1,477	3,340	3,684	4,293	688	5,076	5,704	—	6,259	6,231	1,229	2,126	6,140	476	819
9,718	8,558	4,798	4,874	2,268	8,889	6,303	2,072	10,290	5,943	7,829	682	5,534	3,851	2,689	5,687	5,454
1,889	2,544	5,884	9,598	7,691	2,574	5,579	5,934	6,621	6,259	—	8,449	5,372	7,362	5,148	5,992	5,854
4,094	5,436	8,770	7,180	10,518	5,106	7,224	11,859	1,820	7,391	5,926	10,190	8,120	9,185	10,711	7,760	8,059
2,340	2,289	5,217	9,006	7,046	2,409	5,012	5,432	6,890	5,680	679	8,074	4,731	6,686	4,793	5,381	5,222
8,033	7,067	4,248	5,951	2,646	7,384	5,772	645	11,339	5,679	6,150	2,363	4,837	3,974	1,097	5,281	4,963
5,172	2,873	1,863	4,563	4,529	3,086	563	5,398	5,597	1,247	5,040	7,089	1,135	3,117	6,064	1,153	1,258
10,331	9,207	5,236	4,636	2,574	9,539	6,676	2,754	9,776	6,231	8,449	—	5,993	4,106	3,304	6,039	5,846
1,425	978	5,248	8,231	7,736	878	4,398	6,792	5,218	5,073	1,744	9,544	4,552	6,766	6,407	4,955	4,942
5,965	3,667	764	4,299	3,466	3,939	964	4,197	6,638	1,229	5,372	5,993	—	2,217	5,091	771	504
8,182	5,879	1,534	2,709	1,584	6,141	2,624	3,496	7,386	2,126	7,362	4,106	2,217	—	4,775	1,983	1,878
7,036	6,479	4,663	6,996	3,638	6,757	6,054	1,305	11,535	6,140	5,148	3,304	5,091	4,775	—	5,689	5,346
6,316	4,007	1,039	3,625	3,467	4,233	643	4,664	6,124	476	5,992	6,039	771	1,983	5,689	—	347
5,336	4,021	716	3,800	3,277	4,271	853	4,340	6,453	819	5,854	5,846	504	1,878	5,346	347	—
1,883	490	4,873	7,550	7,500	203	3,841	6,965	4,783	4,496	2,444	9,667	4,135	6,340	6,792	4,436	4,471

WORLD AVIATION RECORDS

SOURCE: National Aeronautic Association

JET AND ROCKET AIRPLANES

Date Record

1/10-11/62 Distance in a Straight Line
U.S.: 12,532.28 miles
Major Clyde P. Evely, USAF
Boeing B52-H
Kadena, Okinawa, to Madrid, Spain

6/6-7/62 Distance over a Closed Circuit
U.S.: 11,336.92 miles
Captain William Stevenson, USAF
Boeing B52-H
Seymour-Johnson, North Carolina;
Kindley, Bermuda; Sondrestrom,
Greenland; Anchorage, Alaska;
March AFB, California; Key West,
Florida; Seymour-Johnson, N.C.

8/31/77 Altitude
USSR: 123,523.58 feet
Alexander Fedotov
E-226M Airplane
Podmoskovnoye, USSR

7/17/62 Altitude (Rocket Powered)
U.S.: 314,750 feet
Major Robert M. White, USAF
North American X-15-1 (NASA Aircraft)
Edwards Air Force Base, California

7/28/76 Altitude in Horizontal Flight
U.S.: 85,068,997 feet
Capt. Robert C. Helt, USAF
Lockheed SR-71

7/28/76 Speed over a Straight Course
U.S.: 2,193.16 miles per hour
Capt. Eldon W. Joersz, USAF
Lockheed SR-71
Beale Air Force Base, California

7/27/76 Speed over a Closed Circuit
U.S.: 2,092.294 miles per hour
Major Adolphus H. Bledsoe, Jr., USAF
Lockheed SR-71
Beale Air Force Base, California

PROPELLER-DRIVEN AIRPLANES

Date Record

9/29/46 Distance in a Straight Line
U.S.: 11,235.6 miles
Commander T. D. Davies, USN
Lockheed P2V-1 Monoplane
Perth, Australia to Columbus, Ohio

11/7-9/69 Distance in a Closed Circuit
U.S.: 8,974.0 miles
James R. Bede
BD-2 Airplane
Columbus, Ohio, to Kansas City Course

10/22/38 Altitude
ITALY: 56,046 feet
Mario Pezzi
Caproni 161 Biplane
Montecelio, Italy

8/14/79 Speed over a 3-Km. Course
U.S.: 499.04 miles per hour
Steve Hinton
P-51D
Tonopah, Nevada

4/9/51 Speed over a 15/25-Km. Course
U.S.: 464.374 miles per hour
Jacqueline Cochran
North American P-51
Indio, California

7/20-25/75 Speed around the World
AUSTRALIA: 203.64 miles per hour
Pilot: D. N. Dalton; Copilot: T. Gwynne-Jones
Beechcraft Duke
Brisbane, Tarawa, Honolulu, San Jose, Toronto, Gander, Gatwick, Damascus, Dubai, Madras, Singapore, Darwin, Brisbane
Elapsed Time: 5 days, 2 hours, 19 minutes, 57 seconds

TURBOPROP AIRPLANES

Date Record

2/20/72 Distance in a Straight Line
U.S.: 8,732.09 miles
Lt. Col. Edgar L. Allison, Jr., USAF
Lockheed HC-130 Hercules
Ching-Chuan Kang, Taiwan to Scott AFB, Ill.

11/4/72 Distance in a Closed Circuit
U.S.: 6,278.05 miles
Cdr. Philip R. Hite, U.S. Navy
Lockheed RP-3D
NAS Patuxent River, Md.

1/27/71 Speed over a 15/25-Km Course
U.S.: 501.44 miles per hour
Commander D. H. Lilienthal, USN
Lockheed P3C Orion
NAS Patuxent River, Md.

3/27/72 Altitude
U.S.: 51,014 feet
Donald R. Wilson
LTV-L450F Airplane
Greenville, Texas

WORLD COMMERCIAL AIRCRAFT SPEEDS

Date Record

11/2/77 Barbados/London
ENGLAND: 1,134.85 miles per hour
Captain Norman Todd
Concorde
Elapsed time: 3 h, 42 m, 5 s

9/6/62 Chicago/Mexico City
U.S.: 534.15 miles per hour
Captain D. W. Ledbetter
Boeing 720B
Elapsed time: 3 h, 10 m, 6.3 s

4/30/60 London/Athens
GREECE: 506.29 miles per hour
Captain P. Ioanides (Olympic Airways)
Comet DH-106-4B (SXDAK)
Elapsed time: 3 h, 13 m, 42 s

6/5/62 London/Miami
ENGLAND: 321.02 miles per hour
Captain G. N. Henderson (Cunard Eagle Airways); Captain P. Wilson
Boeing 707-465
Elapsed time: 13 h, 46 m, 38 s

12/1/66 Los Angeles/Mexico City
MEXICO: 597.88 miles per hour
Captain Rafael T. Zapata (Mexicana de Aviacion)
Boeing 727-64
Elapsed time 2 h, 36 m

12/8/61 Los Angeles/New York
U.S.: 636.8 miles per hour
Captain William Miller (American Airlines, Inc.)
Boeing 707B-123
Elapsed time: 3 h, 52 m, 43 s

9/6/62 Mexico City/Chicago
U.S.: 558.28 miles per hour
Captain E. Schlanser (American Airlines, Inc.)
Boeing 720B
Elapsed time: 3 h, 1 m, 53.2 s

5/6/62 Miami/London
ENGLAND: 419.94 miles per hour
Captain P. Wilson (Cunard Eagle Airways)
Captain M. Gudmundsson
Boeing 707-465
Elapsed time: 10 h, 31 m, 55 s

5/28/60 Montreal/London
CANADA: 565.29 miles per hour
Captain R. M. Smith (Trans-Canada Air Lines)
Douglas DC 8-40
Elapsed time: 5 h, 44 m, 42 s

6/2/63 New York/Bergen
NORWAY: 533.13 miles per hour
Captain B. Bjornstad (Scandinavian Airlines Systems)
Douglas DC-8
Elapsed time: 6 h, 32 m, 20 s

11/26/54 New York/Madrid
SPAIN: 379.624 miles per hour
Captain C. I. Batida (Iberian Airlines)
Lockheed Super Constellation L-1049E
Elapsed time: 9 h, 29 m

2/19/74 New York/Rio de Janeiro
U.S.: 594.28 miles per hour
Capt. Theodore C. Patecell
(Pan American World Airways)
Boeing 707-300 B/A
Elapsed time: 8 h, 5 m, 30 s

6/3/60 New York/San Francisco
AUSTRALIA: 510.092 miles per hour
Captain A. Yates (Quantas Empire Airways)
Boeing 707-138 VH-EBE
Elapsed time: 5 h, 3 m, 48.35 s

8/18/78 Paris/Washington, D.C.
FRANCE: 1,071.86 miles per hour
Captain Pierre Chanoine (Air France)
Concorde
Elapsed time: 3 h, 35 m, 15 s

12/8/61 San Francisco/New York
U.S.: 658 miles per hour
Captain T. E. Jonson (American Airlines, Inc.)
Boeing 707B-123
Elapsed time: 3 h, 55 m, 50 s

NATIONAL COMMERCIAL AIRCRAFT SPEEDS

Date Record

4/10/63 West to East Transcontinental: 680.90 miles per hour
Captain Wylie H. Drummond (American Airlines, Inc.)
Boeing 707-123
Los Angeles International Airport/Idlewild Airport
Distance: 2,474 statute miles
Elapsed time: 3 h, 38 m

8/15/62 East to West Transcontinental: 575.52 miles per hour
Captain Gene Kruse (American Airlines, Inc.)
Boeing 707-720B
Idlewild Airport/Los Angeles International Airport
Distance: 2,474 statute miles
Elapsed time: 4 h, 19 m, 15 s

8/5/47 Atlanta/Chicago: 290.501 miles per hour
Captain H. T. Merrill (Eastern Air Lines)
Lockheed Constellation
Atlanta Municipal Airport/Chicago Municipal Airport
Distance: 590 miles; 2 hours, 1 minute, 55 seconds

7/19/63 Atlanta/Los Angeles: 566.82 miles per hour
Captain L. L. Caruthers (Delta Air Lines)
Douglas DC-8
Atlanta Municipal Airport/Los Angeles International Airport
Distance: 1,946 miles; 3 hours, 25 minutes, 59 seconds

1/21/63 Atlanta/New York: 589.64 miles per hour
Captain Michael Winicki (Delta Air Lines)
Douglas DC-8-51
Atlanta Municipal Airport/Idlewild Int'l Airport
Distance: 760 miles; 1 hour, 17 minutes, 20 seconds

10/30/62 Baltimore/Los Angeles: 563.46 miles per hour
Captain Howard U. Morton (American Airlines)
Boeing 707
Friendship Int'l Airport/Los Angeles Int'l Airport

Date	Record
4/29/65	**Boston/Los Angeles: 562.57** miles per hour

Captain George C. Dent (American Airlines)
Boeing 707
Logan Int'l Airport/Los Angeles Int'l Airport
Distance: 2,610 miles; 4 hours, 38 minutes, 21 seconds

7/20/63 Boston/New York: 414.61 miles per hour
Captain Peter C. Bals (American Airlines)
Convair 990
Logan Int'l Airport/Idlewild Int'l Airport
Distance: 186 miles; 00 hours, 26 minutes, 55 seconds

8/5/47 Chicago/Atlanta: 326.925 miles per hour
Captain H. T. Merrill (Eastern Air Lines)
Lockheed Constellation
Chicago Municipal Airport/Atlanta Municipal Airport
Distance: 590 miles; 1 hour, 48 minutes, 20 seconds

2/16/65 Chicago/Boston: 692.28 miles per hour
Captain Alden Young (American Airlines)
Convair 990
Chicago O'Hare Airport/Logan Int'l Airport
Distance: 865 miles; 1 hour, 14 minutes, 58 seconds

4/20/65 Chicago/Fort Worth: 548.85 miles per hour
Captain Glen L. Stockwell (American Airlines)
Boeing 727
O'Hare Int'l Airport/Greater Southwest Int'l Airport
Distance: 809 miles; 1 hour, 28 minutes, 26 seconds

4/9/65 Chicago/Indianapolis: 494.93 miles per hour
Captain P. G. Cook (American Airlines)
Boeing 707
O'Hare Int'l Airport/WEIR Cook Int'l Airport
Distance: 179 miles; 00 hours, 21 minutes, 42 seconds

1/2–3/62 Chicago/Miami: 588 miles per hour
Captain Dean Clifton (Delta Air Lines)
Convair 880
Chicago O'Hare Airport/Miami Int'l Airport
Distance: 1,184 miles; 2 hours, 1 minute

10/28/65 Chicago/New York: 644.36 miles per hour
Captain W. J. Callahan (American Airlines)
Boeing 727
O'Hare Int'l Airport/LaGuardia Airport
Distance: 733 miles; 1 hour, 8 minutes, 15 seconds

2/3/65 Chicago/Washington, D.C.: 510.58 miles per hour
Captain A. B. Perriello (American Airlines)
Lockheed Electra L-188
O'Hare Int'l Airport/Washington National Airport
Distance: 612 miles; 1 hour, 11 minutes, 5 seconds

3/12/65 Dallas/New York: 686.73 miles per hour
Captain William F. Bonnell (American Airlines)
Boeing 707/720
Love Field/John F. Kennedy Int'l Airport
Distance: 1,384 miles; 2 hours, 6 minutes

Date	Record
2/18/65	**Dallas/San Francisco:** 580.46 miles per hour

Captain W. R. Swain (American Airlines)
Boeing 707/720
Love Field/San Francisco Int'l Airport
Distance: 1,477 miles; 2 hours, 32 minutes, 40 seconds

3/12/65 Dallas/Washington, D.C.: 643.06 miles per hour
Captain W. T. Fleming (American Airlines)
Boeing 707/720
Love Field/Dulles Int'l Airport
Distance: 1,162 miles; 1 hour, 48 minutes, 25 seconds

12/7/61 Los Angeles/Baltimore: 657.68 miles per hour
Captain Stan Smith (American Airlines)
Boeing 707/123B
Los Angeles Int'l Airport/Friendship Airport
Distance: 2,329 miles; 3 hours, 32 minutes, 28 seconds

11/26/65 Los Angeles/Boston: 666.61 miles per hour
Captain Simon P. Bittner (American Airlines)
Boeing 707
Los Angeles Int'l Airport/Logan Int'l Airport
Distance: 2,610 miles; 3 hours, 54 minutes, 55 seconds

4/9/63 Los Angeles/Chicago: 672.80 miles per hour
Captain George R. Russon (American Airlines)
Boeing 707/123
Los Angeles Int'l Airport/O'Hare Int'l Airport
Distance: 1,746 miles; 2 hours, 35 minutes, 42 seconds

3/9/65 Los Angeles/Dallas: 689.00 miles per hour
Captain W. R. Hunt (American Airlines)
Boeing 707/123
Los Angeles Int'l Airport/Love Field
Distance: 1,245 miles; 1 hour, 48 minutes, 25 seconds

7/16/47 Miami/Chicago: 300.390 miles per hour
Captain H. T. Merrill (Eastern Air Lines)
Lockheed Constellation
36th Street Airport/Chicago Municipal Airport
Distance: 1,183 miles; 3 hours, 56 minutes, 22 seconds

5/28/47 Miami/New York: 314.477 miles per hour
Captain E. R. Brown (Eastern Air Lines)
Lockheed Constellation
36th Street Airport/LaGuardia Airport
Distance: 1,096 miles; 3 hours, 29 minutes, 11.4 seconds

MAN-POWERED AIRCRAFT

Date	Record
6/12/79	**Duration, Distance**

U.S.: 2 hours, 49 minutes; 22.26 miles
Bryan Allen
Gossamer Albatross
Folkestone, England to Cap Gris-Nez, France

BALLOONS (LARGE)

Date	Record
8/12-17/78	**Duration, Distance**

U.S.: 137 hrs., 5 min., 50 secs.; 3,107.61 miles
Ben L. Abruzzo, Maxie L. Anderson, Larry M. Newman; Double Eagle II
Presque Isle, Maine to Miserey, France

Date	Record
5/4/61	**Altitude**

U.S.: 113,739.9 feet
Commander Malcolm D. Ross, USNR
"Lee Lewis Memorial"
Gulf of Mexico

GLIDERS

Date	Record
4/25/72	**Distance in a Straight Line**

W. GERMANY: 907.7 miles
Hans Werner Grosse
ASK 12 Sailplane
Luebeck, W. Ger. to Biarritz, France.

1/14/78 Distance to a Goal 779.36 miles
NEW ZEALAND: Group Flight; David Wapier Speight, S. H. Georgeson, Bruce Lindsay Drake
Tower Peak Station to TeAraroa
Nimbus 2

5/9/77 Distance to a Goal and Return
U.S.: 1,015.81 miles
Karl Striedieck
ASW 17 Sailplane
Lock Haven, Pennsylvania

2/25/61 Altitude above Sea Level
U.S.: 46,267 feet
Paul F. Bikle
Schweizer SCG 123 E. Sailplane
Mojave, Lancaster, California

2/25/61 Altitude Gained
U.S.: 42,303 feet
Paul F. Bikle
Schweizer SGA 123 E. Sailplane
Mojave, Lancaster, California

HELICOPTERS

Date	Record
4/6–7/66	**Distance in a Straight Line**

U.S.: 2,213.04 miles
Robert G. Ferry
Hughes YOH 6A helicopter
Culver City, California to Daytona Beach, Florida

3/26/66 Distance in a Closed Circuit
U.S.: 1,739.96 miles
Jack Schweibold
Hughes YOH-6A helicopter
Edwards AFB, California

6/21/72 Altitude
FRANCE: 40,820 feet
Jean Boulet
Alouette SA 315-001 "Lama" Helicopter
Istres, France

11/4/71 Altitude in Horizontal Flight
U.S.: 36,122 feet
CWO James K. Church, USA
Sikorsky CH-54B Helicopter
Stratford, Connecticut

12/14/70 Speed over a 3 Km Course
U.S.: 216.839 miles per hour
Byron Graham
Sikorsky S-67 Helicopter
Windsor Locks, Connecticut

9/21/78 Speed over a 15/25 Km Course
USSR: 228.91 miles per hour
Gourguen Karapetyan
Helicopter A-10
Podmoskovnoye Aerodrome

HANG GLIDING

Date	Record
7/23/80	**Distance in a Straight Line**

U.S.: 104.28 miles
George Worthington
Mitchell Wing
Cerro Gordo Peak, Calif.

7/22/78 Gain in Altitude
U.S.: 11,700 feet
George D. Worthington
Seagull 10 Meter
Cerro Gordo Peak, California

7/21/77 Straight Distance to Goal
U.S.: 95.44 miles
George D. Worthington
ASG-21 Albatross Sails
Cerro Gordo Peak, Calif. to Benton Station, Calif.

BUSIEST WORLD AIRPORTS Source: International Civil Aviation Organization

Airports are ranked here according to their total passenger traffic (embarked plus disembarked) for 1979. USSR airports opened to domestic traffic exclusively are not included.

Airport	Passengers (in millions)	Airport	Passengers (in millions)	Airport	Passengers (in millions)	Airport	Passengers (in millions)
Chicago (O'Hare)	47.8	New York		Pittsburgh	11.1	Copenhagen	9.3
Atlanta	41.7	(La Guardia)	18.4	Houston	10.9	Minneapolis	9.3
Los Angeles	34.9	Osaka	16.8	Madrid	10.7	New York (Newark)	9.3
London (Heathrow)	27.9	Frankfurt (Main)	16.6	Las Vegas	10.6	Athens	9.1*
New York (Kennedy)	27.0	Boston (Logan)	15.2	Rome (Fiumicino)	10.5	Saint Louis	9.1
San Francisco	23.1	Paris (Orly)	14.5	Philadelphia	10.4	London (Gatwick)	8.7
Dallas/Fort Worth	22.6	Honolulu	14.5	Mexico City	10.2	Tampa	8.2
Tokyo	20.7*	Washington (Nat'l)	14.3	Seattle	9.8	Sydney	8.0
Denver	20.5	Toronto	14.1	Paris (De Gaulle)	9.8	Palma de Mallorca	8.0
Miami	19.6	Detroit	11.2	Amsterdam	9.7	Cleveland	7.7

*Estimate

MAJOR INTERNATIONAL AIRPORTS Source: International Civil Aviation Organization

Airports on the list are ranked according to the total international passenger traffic for 1979. *Estimated data.

Airport	City	PASSENGERS (000) International	Domestic	Total	COMMERCIAL OPERATIONS (000) International	Domestic	Total
Heathrow	London	23,791	4,137	27,929	212.9	63.3	276.2
J.F. Kennedy	New York	13,333	13,638	26,971	91.8	151.8	243.6
Frankfurt-Main	Frankfurt	11,602	4,964	16,566	137.9	70.2	208.1
Schiphol	Amsterdam	9,593	110	9,703	138.9	5.2	144.1
De Gaulle	Paris	8,668	1,095	9,763	91.6	12.3	103.9
Orly	Paris	8,470	6,076	14,546	95.3	73.6	168.9
Gatwick	London	7,767	927	8,695	85.8	29.1	114.9
Miami Int'l	Miami	7,484	12,144	19,628	.....	.....	305.4
Kastrup	Copenhagen	7,215	2,100	9,316	120.9	35.3	156.2
Zürich	Zürich	7,161	359	7,520	105.5	8.0	113.5
New Tokyo Int'l	Tokyo	6,624	638	7,262	.....	.....	62.6
Toronto Int'l	Toronto	6,568	7,562	14,130	66.3	109.4	175.7
Fiumicino	Rome	6,468	4,076	10,544	.....	.....	143.9
Hong Kong Int'l	Hong Kong	6,230	0	6,230	55.9	.2	56.1
Tokyo Int'l	Tokyo	6,003*	14,697*	20,700*	.....	.....	142.0*
Palma de Mallorca	Palma de Mallorca	5,896	2,055	7,951	52.8	24.2	77.0
Athinai	Athens	5,459*	3,672*	9,131*	70.1*	41.4*	111.5*
Singapore Int'l	Singapore	5,430	.....	5,430	66.4	.....	66.4
Bruxelles Nat'l	Brussels	5,130	6	5,136	86.0	.2	86.2
Los Angeles Int'l	Los Angeles	4,997	29,859	34,857	41.5	346.1	387.6
Düsseldorf	Düsseldorf	4,916	1,917	6,832	49.3	32.9	82.2
Cairo Int'l	Cairo	4,671	856	5,527	57.8	13.8	71.6
Linate	Milan	3,956	1,983	5,940	61.6	29.9	91.5
Barajas	Madrid	3,948	6,722	10,670	49.9	74.4	124.3
Bangkok	Bangkok	3,658	398	4,056	45.2	7.1	52.3
Arlanda	Stockholm	3,533	1,134	4,667	52.5	21.5	74.0
Benito Juarez	Mexico City	3,420*	6,786*	10,206	.....	.....	118.7
Cointrin	Geneva	3,344	666	4,010	55.8	14.9	70.7
München	Munich	3,222	2,510	5,732	43.9	38.8	82.7
O'Hare Int'l	Chicago	2,941	44,839	47,780	29.8	639.5	669.3
Sheremetievo	Moscow	2,868	1,027	3,896	44.6	16.1	60.7
Ben Gurion	Tel Aviv	2,746	.....	.....	21.3	.....	.....
Schwechat	Vienna	2,720	41	2,760	49.6	.9	50.5

AIRLINE TRAFFIC VOLUME Source: International Civil Aviation Organizaion

According to estimates released in March 1981 by the International Civil Aviation Organization for its 145 member states*, in 1980 the airlines carried 634 million passengers for a total of 904,000 million kilometers (562,000 million passenger miles on scheduled services), representing increases of 0.5 percent over 1979.

Year	Miles Flown	Hours Flown	Passengers Carried	Passenger-Miles	Average Number of Passengers per Aircraft	Miles Flown per Passenger	Miles Flown per hr.
	(In Millions)						
1980†	5,790	15.2	634	562,000	97	886	381
1979	5,630	14.8	633	559,000	99	883	380
1978	5,280	14.0	581	495,000	94	852	377
1977	5,030	13.4	517	429,000	85	830	377
1976	4,870	13.0	475	393,000	81	828	374
1975	4,670	12.6	436	356,000	76	817	371
1974	4,580	12.5	424	340,000	74	802	366
1973	4,660	12.7	405	323,000	69	798	367
1972	4,480	12.2	368	288,500	64	784	367
1971	4,390	12.2	333	253,500	58	771	360
1970	4,355	12.1	311	237,500	55	762	360
1969	4,170	11.8	293	218,000	52	744	354
1968	3,730	11.0	262	192,500	52	736	339
1967	3,290	10.2	233	169,500	52	727	320
1966	2,790	9.3	200	142,000	51	711	301
1965	2,550	8.7	177	123,000	48	696	292
1964	2,300	8.2	155	106,000	46	687	280
1963	2,130	7.9	135	91,500	43	674	270
1962	2,015	7.8	121	80,500	40	668	261
1961	1,940	8.0	111	72,500	38	656	242
1960	1,930	8.6	106	67,500	35	640	224
1959	1,920	9.0	99	61,000	32	615	214
1958	1,820	8.8	88	53,000	29	603	208
1957	1,765	8.7	86	51,000	29	590	202
1955	1,425	7.3	68	38,000	27	562	196

SAFETY RECORD: U.S. CERTIFICATED AND SUPPLEMENTAL AIR CARRIERS*

SOURCE: National Transportation Safety Board

Year	Number of Accidents		Fatalities				Aircraft Miles Flown	Accident Rate per Million Aircraft Miles Flown	
	Total	Fatal	Passg.	Crew	Others	Total		Total Accidents	Fatal Accidents
1960	90	17	429	57	13	499	1,130,069,000	.078	.011
1965	83	9	226	35	0	261	1,536,395,000**	.054	.006
1968	71	15	306	37	6	349	2,498,848,000**	.028	.005
1969	63	10	132	22	4	158	2,736,596,000**	.023	.003
1970	55	8	118	24	4	146	2,684,552,000**	.020	.003
1971	48	8	174	23	6	203	2,660,731,000**	.018	.002
1972	50	8	160	17	13	190	2,619,043,000**	.019	.003
1973	43	9	200	26	1	227	2,646,669,000**	.016	.003
1974	47	9	421	46	0	467	2,464,295,000**	.019	.003
1975	45	3	113	11	0	124	2,477,764,000**	.018	.001
1976	28	4	39	6	0	45	2,568,113,000**	.011	.002
1977	26	5	381	17	257	655	2,684,072,000**	.010	.002
1978	24	6	141	12	10	163	2,793,697,000	.009	.002
1979	32	6	323	29	3	355	2,899,131,000	.011	.002
1980[1]	20	2	11	2	1	14	3,035,600,000	.007	.001

*Beginning in 1975, accidents involving commercial operators of large aircraft are included. Beginning in 1979, accidents of deregulated all-cargo carriers are included.
** Nonrevenue miles of the supplemental air carriers are not reported.
[1]Preliminary.

SAFETY RECORD: WORLD SCHEDULED AIRLINES[1]

SOURCE: International Civil Aviation Organization

Year	Number of Accidents: Passenger-carrying Aircraft	Number of Passengers Killed	Fatality Rate (per 100 million Pass.-mi.)	Fatal Accidents (per 100 million Mi. Flown)	Fatal Accidents[†]	Year	Number of Accidents: Passenger-carrying Aircraft	Number of Passengers Killed	Fatality Rate (per 100 million Pass.-mi.)	Fatal Accidents (per 100 million Mi. Flown)	Fatal Accidents[†]
1950	27	581	3.15	3.02	0.54	1970	28	687	0.29	0.64	0.23
1952	21	386	1.54	1.90	0.34	1971	31	867	0.34	0.71	0.26
1954	28	443	1.36	2.19	0.42	1972	42	1,210	0.42	0.94	0.34
1956	27	552	1.25	1.71	0.34	1973	36	862	0.27	0.77	0.28
1958	30	609	1.15	1.65	0.34	1974	29	1,299	0.38	0.62	0.23
1960	34	873	1.29	1.71	0.38	1975	20	443	0.13	0.43	0.16
1962	29	778	1.97	1.44	0.37	1976	20	734	0.19	0.41	0.15
1964	25	616	0.58	1.09	0.30	1977	24	516	0.11	0.48	0.18
1966	31	1,001	0.70	1.12	0.33	1978	25	755	0.15	0.47	0.18
1968	35	912	0.47	0.94	0.32	1979	31	879	0.16	0.55	0.21
						1980*	20	747	0.13	0.34	0.13

[†]Per 100,000 aircraft hours. [1] Excluding USSR. *Preliminary figures.

WORLD'S FASTEST TRAINS[1]

SOURCE: Donald M. Steffee

Railroad	Train	From	To	Miles	Time (min.)	Speed (mph)
Passenger						
French National	TGV	Macon	Monchanin	39.2	20	117.6
Japanese National	Hikari Train	Nagoya	Yokohama	196.5	105	112.3
German Federal	Three Trains	Hamm	Bielefeld	41.7	24	104.2
British Rail	High Speed Trains (3 runs)	London	Bristol Pkwy.	111.7	65 1/2	102.3
Italian State	Rapido (2 runs)	Rome[2]	Chiusi	91.9	65	84.8
Amtrak	Four trains	Rensselaer	Hudson	28.0	20	84.0
VIA (Canada)	Turbotrain	Guildwood	Dorval	310.9	223	83.6
Swedish State	No. 142	Skvode	Laxa	52.2	41	77.4
Freight						
British Rail	Freightliner	Carlisle	Wigan	105.1	95 1/2	66.2
Union Pacific	BASV	North Platte	Cheyenne	225.4	205	66.0
French National	Freight Express	Orange	St. Rambert de Albon	87.6	81	64.9

[1]Fastest run in each country. [2]Runs listed in both directions.

FASTEST AMERICAN PASSENGER TRAINS

SOURCE: Donald M. Steffee

Railroad	Train	From	To	Miles	Time (min.)	Speed (mph)
Amtrak	Four Trains	Rensselaer	Hudson	28.0	20	84.0
Amtrak	Bankers	Wilmington	Baltimore	68.4	50	82.1
Amtrak	Southwest Limited	Syracuse	Lamar	99.9	73	82.1
Amtrak	Colonial	Metro Park	Trenton	33.9	25	81.4
Amtrak	Seven trains	Wilmington[1]	Baltimore	68.4	51	80.5
Amtrak	Palmetto	New Brunswick	Trenton	25.4	19	80.2
Amtrak	Metroliners (2 runs)	Newark	Trenton	48.1	36	80.2
Amtrak	Minute Man	Wilmington	Aberdeen	38.7	29	80.1
Amtrak	Southwest Limited	Dodge City	Hutchinson	120.1	90	80.1
Conrail	Jersey Arrow	Princeton Jct.	Newark	38.4	29	79.4
Amtrak	Seventeen trains	Wilmington[1]	Baltimore	68.4	52	78.9
Amtrak	Four trains	Metro Park[1]	Trenton	33.9	26	78.2
Amtrak	Merchants Limited	Newark	Trenton	48.1	37	78.0
Amtrak	Southwest Limited	Lamar	Garden City	99.9	77	77.8
Amtrak	Three trains	Wilmington	Baltimore	68.4	53	77.4
Amtrak	San Francisco Zephyr	Akron	McCook	142.9	111	77.2
Amtrak	Eight trains	Trenton[1]	No. Philadelphia	27.9	22	76.2
Amtrak	Liberty Express	Metro Park	Princeton Jct.	24.1	19	76.1
Amtrak	Six trains	Wilmington	Baltimore	68.4	54	76.0
Amtrak	Three trains	Newark	Trenton	48.1	38	75.9
Amtrak	Palmetto	Trenton	Metro Park	33.0	27	75.3

[1]Runs listed in both directions.

SELECTED MERCHANT FLEETS OF THE WORLD   Source: U.S. Maritime Administration

Country of Registry	Number	Gross Tons	Dead-weight Tons
TOTAL—ALL COUNTRIES	24,798	382,649	650,902
United States	865	15,564	23,589
Privately-Owned	569	12,967	20,540
Government-Owned	296	2,596	3,049
Reserve Fleet	255	2,183	2,577
Other	41	413	472
Algeria	69	1,198	1,814
Argentina	201	2,167	3,280
Australia	76	1,412	2,193
Austria	12	81	125
Bangladesh	29	251	363
Belgium	69	1,639	2,589
Brazil	294	3,935	6,556
British Colonies	216	3,312	5,272
Bulgaria*	114	1,147	1,685
Canada	101	593	909
Chile	49	533	846
China (People's Rep.)*	645	6,227	9,372
China (Republic of)*	170	1,859	2,937
Colombia	44	282	368
Cuba*	87	664	897
Cyprus	457	2,053	2,991
Czechoslovakia	17	155	232
Denmark	290	4,801	8,090
Ecuador	29	231	311
Egypt	89	461	624
Finland	179	2,221	3,591
France	359	11,196	19,884
Germany, East*	157	1,307	1,808
Germany, West	502	7,735	12,485
Ghana	26	148	198
Greece	2,876	37,359	63,542
Honduras	40	185	223
Hungary*	22	75	105
Iceland	34	66	100
India	363	5,598	9,100
Indonesia	239	968	1,343
Iran	54	1,000	1,658
Iraq	35	1,217	2,245
Ireland	26	141	211
Israel	37	416	558
Italy	624	10,941	18,489
Ivory Coast	18	165	214
Japan	1,751	35,980	61,192
Korea, North*	23	136	202
Korea, South	362	3,748	6,218
Kuwait	99	2,484	4,158
Lebanon	73	201	267
Liberia	2,380	81,559	158,702
Libya	27	836	1,530
Malaysia	62	573	848
Maldives	31	103	134
Mexico	63	806	1,236
Morocco	44	324	536
Netherlands	450	4,999	8,165
New Zealand	26	208	255
Nigeria	28	381	575
Norway	632	22,068	39,494
Pakistan	48	424	570
Panama	2,347	21,590	35,257
Peru	46	478	753
Philippines	200	1,400	2,166
Poland	303	3,119	4,631
Portugal	81	1,198	2,020
Romania*	184	1,673	2,498
Saudi Arabia	73	1,371	2,397
Singapore	667	7,505	12,341
Somalia	11	57	77
South Africa	33	614	775
Spain	506	7,134	12,656
Sweden	233	4,112	6,899
Switzerland	26	240	364
Thailand	62	337	506
Tunisia	21	112	161
Turkey	168	1,259	1,931
USSR¹*	2,514	16,347	21,612
United Arab Emirates	12	109	197
United Kingdom	1,110	25,330	41,937
Venezuela	71	700	1,029
Vietnam	35	173	264
Yugoslavia	253	2,315	3,540
Zaire	8	77	116

† Oceangoing ships (1,000 gross tons and more) as of December 31, 1979. Tonnage in thousands. * Source material limited. ¹ Includes 2 U.S. Government-owned ships transferred to USSR under lend-lease agreements.

FOREIGN COMMERCE AT SELECTED U.S. PORTS: 1978

Source: U.S. Corps of Engineers (figures in thousands of short tons of cargo)

Port	Imports	Exports
ATLANTIC COAST PORTS		
New Haven Harbor, Conn.	1,495	174
New Castle and vicinity, Del.	4,025	16
Wilmington Harbor, Del.	1,271	239
Canaveral Harbor, Fla.	1,919	189
Jacksonville Harbor, Fla.	3,833	1,975
Miami Harbor, Fla.	955	1,184
Port Everglades Harbor, Fla.	1,826	162
Savannah Harbor, Ga.	5,138	2,585
Portland Harbor, Maine	17,205	18
Baltimore Harbor and Channels, Md.	17,508	14,339
Fall River Harbor, Mass.	1,969	24
Port of Boston, Mass.	6,712	794
Salem Harbor, Mass.	784	—
Portsmouth Harbor, N.H.	1,880	85
Camden-Gloucester, N.J.	1,856	385
Paulsboro and vicinity, N.J.	12,296	102
Port of Albany, N.Y.	1,628	1,099
Port of New York, N.Y. and N.J.	55,923	6,093
Port of Wilmington, N.C.	2,997	340
Marcus Hook and vicinity, Pa.	15,981	146
Penn Manor and vicinity, Pa.	3,869	40
Philadelphia Harbor, Pa.	26,390	4,338
Providence River and Harbor, R.I.	1,438	527
Charleston Harbor, S.C.	3,313	1,956
Norfolk Harbor, Va.	6,027	16,926
Port of Newport News, Va.	499	5,217
San Juan Harbor, P.R.	3,245	364
GULF COAST PORTS		
Mobile Harbor, Ala.	10,679	5,190
Tampa Harbor, Fla.	4,845	17,058
Baton Rouge, La.	16,900	11,432
Lake Charles (Calcasieu R. & Pass), La.	6,625	1,626
New Orleans, La.	23,298	40,481
Pascagoula Harbor, Miss.	8,237	3,899
Beaumont, Texas	25,434	4,192
Brownsville, Texas	786	375
Corpus Christi, Texas	20,463	5,862
Freeport Harbor, Texas	14,975	1,289
Galveston Channel, Texas	1,542	3,918
Harbor Island, Texas	5,604	0.6
Houston Ship Channel, Texas	42,197	20,050
Matagorda Ship Channel, Texas	3,698	194
Port Arthur, Texas	17,027	2,163
Texas City Channel, Texas	14,396	745
PACIFIC COAST PORTS		
Skagway Harbor, Alaska	328	558
Long Beach Harbor, Calif.	9,286	6,983
Los Angeles Harbor, Calif.	12,659	3,697
Oakland Harbor, Calif.	1,877	2,617
Richmond Harbor, Calif.	3,425	425
San Francisco Harbor, Calif.	869	734
Stockton, Calif.	424	691
Barbers Point Harbor, Hawaii	3,871	133
Honolulu Harbor, Hawaii	1,154	98
Coos Bay, Oreg.	67	4,371
Port of Astoria, Oreg.	78	1,040
Port of Portland, Oreg.	2,035	9,596
Anacortes Harbor, Wash.	6,426	122
Everett Harbor & Snowhomish R., Wash.	601	1,549
Grays Harbor & Chehalis R., Wash.	1	2,558
Port Angeles Harbor, Wash.	820	1,849
Port of Longview, Wash.	695	5,146
Port of Vancouver, Wash.	1,010	509
Seattle Harbor, Wash.	5,196	2,701
Tacoma Harbor, Wash.	2,396	5,715

MAJOR WORLD SHIP CANALS

Name	Location	Year Opened	Length (Miles)	Minimum Depth (Feet)	Minimum Width (Feet)
Baltic-White Sea	USSR: Povenets on Lake Onega to Belmorsk on White Sea	1933	140	16	NA
Cape Cod	U.S.: Buzzards Bay to Cape Cod Bay, Mass.	1914	17.4	32	450
Chesapeake and Delaware	U.S.: Delaware River to Chesapeake Bay	1927	19	35	450
Chicago Sanitary and Ship	U.S.: Lake Michigan to Des Plaines River, Ill.	1900	33.8	20	160
Corinth	Greece: Gulf of Athens to Gulf of Corinth	1893	3.5	26.25	69
Houston Ship	U.S.: Houston, Texas, to Gulf of Mexico	1914	50	36	300
Kiel (Nord-Ostsee)	Germany: North Sea to Baltic Sea	1895	53.2	38	144
Manchester Ship	England: Manchester to Mersey River	1894	35.5	28	90
Moscow	USSR: Moscow to Volga River	1937	80	18	280
North Sea	Netherlands: Amsterdam to IJmuiden	1876	17.5	45	443
Panama	Panama: Cristóbal on Atlantic Ocean to Balboa on Pacific Ocean	1914	50.72	41.6	300
St. Lawrence Seaway	U.S.-Canada: Atlantic Ocean to Great Lakes system	1959	2,347*	27	450
Sault Sainte Marie (Canadian)	U.S.-Canada: Lake Huron to Lake Superior	1895	1.38	27	150
Sault Sainte Marie (American)	U.S.-Canada: Lake Huron to Lake Superior	1855	1.8	27	80
Suez	Egypt: Port Said on Mediterranean Sea to Suez on Gulf of Suez	1869	100.76	42	196
Terneuzen-Ghent	Belgium-Netherlands: Ghent to Scheldt Estuary at Terneuzen	1827	11	29	164
Volga-Baltic	USSR: Caspian Sea to Leningrad on Baltic Sea	1964	225	NA	NA
Volga-Don	USSR: Volga River to Don River, as linking waterway for Baltic-Black Sea route	1952	62	NA	NA
Welland	Canada: Lake Erie to Lake Ontario	1932	27.6	27	80

* Distance from Strait of Belle Isle to Duluth, Minnesota. NA = Not Available.

PANAMA CANAL USERS: 1979
SOURCE: *Statistical Abstract of the U.S.*, 1980

Commercial Ocean Traffic

Nationality of vessel	Transits	Net tons (1,000)	Cargo (1,000 long tons)
UNITED STATES	1,633	28,200	24,800
United Kingdom	967	12,300	10,800
Greece	1,338	17,000	21,600
Japan	1,074	15,400	10,200
Liberia	1,864	30,200	33,500
Norway	401	7,400	6,700
Panama	1,145	11,200	9,300
U.S.S.R.	587	3,300	2,200
All Others	3,926	42,300	35,000

PANAMA CANAL TRAFFIC, 1950-1979
SOURCE: *Statistical Abstract of the U.S.*, 1980

	Total Transits	Commercial Ocean Traffic Transits	Commercial Ocean Traffic Cargo (long tons)
1950	5,900	5,400	28,900,000
1955	8,300	8,000	40,600,000
1960	12,100	10,800	59,300,000
1965	12,900	11,800	76,600,000
1970	15,500	13,700	114,300,000
1973	15,100	13,800	126,100,000
1974	15,300	14,000	147,900,000
1975	14,700	13,600	140,100,000
1976	13,200	12,200	117,200,000
1977	13,100	11,900	123,000,000
1978	13,800	12,700	142,500,000
1979	14,400	12,900	154,100,000

WORLD CITIES: STANDARD TIME DIFFERENCES

When it is 12 noon in New York (Eastern Standard Time), the standard time in other cities is as follows:

City	Time	City	Time	City	Time	City	Time
Alexandria	7:00 p.m.	Delhi	10:30 p.m.	Ketchikan	9:00 a.m.	Rome	6:00 p.m.
Amsterdam	6:00 p.m.	Denver	10:00 a.m.	Kinshasa	6:00 p.m.	Salt Lake City	10:00 a.m.
Anchorage	7:00 a.m.	Jakarta	12:00 Midnight	Lima	12:00 Noon	San Fran-	
Athens	7:00 p.m.			Lisbon	5:00 p.m.	cisco	9:00 a.m.
Auckland	5:00 a.m.*	Dublin	5:00 p.m.	London		San Juan	1:00 p.m.
Baghdad	8:00 p.m.	Fairbanks	7:00 a.m.	(Greenwich)	5:00 p.m.	Santiago	1:00 p.m.
Bangkok	12:00 Midnight	Frankfurt	6:00 p.m.	Los Angeles	9:00 a.m.	Seattle	9:00 a.m.
		Frobisher		Madrid	6:00 p.m.	Seoul	2:00 a.m.*
Barcelona	6:00 p.m.	Bay	1:00 p.m.	Manila	1:00 a.m.*	Shanghai	1:00 a.m.*
Basra	8:00 p.m.	Gander	1:30 p.m.	Melbourne	3:00 a.m.*	Singapore	12:30 a.m.*
Beirut	7:00 p.m.	Geneva	6:00 p.m.	Miami	12:00 Noon	Stockholm	6:00 p.m.
Berlin	6:00 p.m.	Glasgow	5:00 p.m.	Monrovia	5:00 p.m.	Suva	5:00 a.m.*
Bogotá	12:00 Noon	Halifax	1:00 p.m.	Montevideo	2:00 p.m.	Sydney	3:00 a.m.*
Bombay	10:30 p.m.	Hamilton		Moscow	8:00 p.m.	Tehran	8:30 p.m.
Boston	12:00 Noon	(Bermuda)	1:00 p.m.	New Orleans	11:00 a.m.	Tel Aviv	7:00 p.m.
Brussels	6:00 p.m.	Havana	12:00 Noon	Nome	6:00 a.m.	Tokyo	2:00 a.m.*
Bucharest	7:00 p.m.	Helsinki	7:00 p.m.	Nouméa	4:00 a.m.*	Tucson	10:00 a.m.
Budapest	6:00 p.m.	Ho Chi		Oslo	6:00 p.m.	Valparaíso	1:00 p.m.
Buenos		Minh City	12:00	Papeete	7:00 a.m.	Vancouver	9:00 a.m.
Aires	2:00 p.m.	(Saigon)	Midnight	Paris	6:00 p.m.	Vienna	6:00 p.m.
Cairo	7:00 p.m.	Hong Kong	1:00 a.m.*	Peking	1:00 a.m.*	Vladivostok	3:00 a.m.*
Calcutta	10:30 p.m.	Honolulu	7:00 a.m.	Phoenix	10:00 a.m.	Warsaw	6:00 p.m.
Cape Town	7:00 p.m.	Houston	11:00 a.m.	Portland	9:00 a.m.	Washington,	
Caracas	1:00 p.m.	Istanbul	8:00 p.m.	Rangoon	11:30 p.m.	D.C.	12:00 Noon
Chicago	11:00 a.m.	Jerusalem	7:00 p.m.	Recife	2:00 p.m.	Whitehorse	8:00 a.m.
Copenhagen	6:00 p.m.	Johannes-		Reykjavík	5:00 p.m.	Yokohama	2:00 a.m.*
Dakar	5:00 p.m.	burg	7:00 p.m.	Rio de		Zürich	6:00 p.m.
Damascus	7:00 p.m.	Juneau	9:00 a.m.	Janeiro	2:00 p.m.		
		Karachi	10:00 p.m.				

* = following day.

LARGE PASSENGER LINERS

Source: Cruise Lines International Association

Ship Name	Line	Flag	Length, ft.	Tonnage	Max. No. Passengers
Norway	Norwegian Caribbean Lines	Norwegian	1,035	70,202	2,000
Queen Elizabeth 2	Cunard Line, Ltd.	British	963	67,140	1,909
Canberra	P & O Cruises, Ltd.	British	818	45,000	1,800
Oriana	P & O Cruises, Ltd.	British	804	42,000	1,800
Oceanic	Home Lines Cruises	Panamanian	774	39,241	1,034
Festivale	Carnival Cruise Lines	Panamanian	760	38,175	1,400
Rotterdam	Holland America Cruises	Netherlands	748	38,000	1,111
Italis	Chandris, Inc.	Panamanian	723	26,353	2,258
Oceanic Independence	American Hawaii Lines	USA	682	20,300	1,000
Eugenio C.	Costa Cruises	Italian	713	30,000	1,100
Sea Princess	P & O Cruises, Ltd.	British	660	27,670	844
Mardi Gras	Carnival Cruise Lines	Panamanian	650	27,250	1,240
Britanis	Chandris, Inc.	Greek	642	25,245	1,545
Ellinis	Chandris, Inc.	Greek	642	18,564	1,552
Statendam	Holland America Cruises	Netherlands	642	24,500	893
Carnivale	Carnival Cruise Lines	Panamanian	640	27,250	1,350
Maxim Gorki	Black Sea Shipping Co.	USSR	639	25,000	728
Song of Norway	Royal Caribbean Cruise Line	Norwegian	635	23,005	1,170
Nordic Prince	Royal Caribbean Cruise Line	Norwegian	635	23,000	1,168
Navarino	Karageorgis Cruises	Greek	631	23,000	772
Doric	Home Lines Cruises	Panamanian	629	25,300	750
Vistafjord	Norwegian American Cruises	Norwegian	628	25,000	660
Emerald Seas	Eastern Steamship Lines	Panamanian	622	24,458	920
Sagafjord	Norwegian American Cruises	Norwegian	620	25,000	500
Veendam	Holland America Cruises	Panamanian	617	23,500	713
Volendam	Holland America Cruises	Panamanian	617	23,500	717
Fairsea	Sitmar Cruises	Liberian	608	25,000	1,467
Fairwind	Sitmar Cruises	Liberian	608	25,000	1,467
Federico C.	Costa Cruises	Italian	606	20,416	689
Azure Seas	Western Lines	Panamanian	603	20,000	800

WORLD'S LEADING BRIDGES

Source: American Society of Civil Engineers

Bridges listed here are grouped by type of construction and ranked by the length of their spans.

SUSPENSION BRIDGES

Bridge	Main Span Meters	Feet	Completion Date	Location
Humber	1,410	4,626	1981	Hull, England
Verrazano-Narrows	1,298	4,260	1964	New York City
Golden Gate	1,280	4,200	1937	San Francisco
Mackinac Straits	1,158	3,800	1957	Mackinaw City, Michigan
Bosporus	1,074	3,524	1973	Istanbul, Turkey
George Washington	1,067	3,500	1931	New York City
Tagus	1,013	3,323	1966	Lisbon, Portugal
Forth Road	1,006	3,300	1964	Scotland
Severn	988	3,240	1966	England/Wales
Tacoma Narrows	853	2,800	1950	Washington
Angostura	712	2,336	1967	Ciudad Bolivàr, Venezuela
Kanmon Strait	712	2,336	1973	Honshu, Japan
San Francisco-Oakland	704	2,310	1936	San Francisco
Bronx-Whitestone	701	2,300	1939	New York City
Quebec	668	2,190	1970	Quebec, Canada
Delaware Memorial I & II	655	2,150	1951 1968	Wilmington, Delaware
Melville Gas Pipe	610	2,000	1951	Louisiana
Walt Whitman	610	2,000	1957	Philadelphia
Tancarville	608	1,995	1959	Le Havre, France
Lillebaelt	600	1,968	1970	Lillebaelt Strait, Denmark
Ambassador	564	1,850	1929	Detroit, Michigan
Throgs Neck	549	1,800	1961	New York City
Benjamin Franklin	533	1,750	1926	Philadelphia
Skojmen	525	1,722	1972	Narvik, Norway

*Under construction.

Bridge	Main Span Meters	Feet	Completion Date	Location
Kvalsund	525	1,722	1976	Kvalsund, Norway
Kleve-Emmerich	500	1,640	1965	Emmerich, West Germany
Bear Mountain	497	1,632	1924	New York
Newport	487	1,600	1969	Rhode Island
Chesapeake	487	1,600	1952	Maryland
Williamsburg	487	1,600	1903	New York City
Brooklyn	486	1,595	1883	New York City
Lion's Gate	472	1,550	1938	British Columbia, Canada
Hirado	465		1977	Nagasaki, Japan
Mid-Hudson	457	1,500	1930	New York
Manhattan	448	1,470	1909	New York City
Triborough	420	1,380	1937	New York City

CABLE-STAYED BRIDGES
Orthotropic Steel Deck

Bridge	Main Span Meters	Feet	Completion Date	Location
Hooghly River	457	1,500	*	Calcutta, India
Saint Nazaire	404	1,325	1975	Brittany, France
Stretto di Rande	400	1,312	1978	Vigo, Spain
Luling	376	1,235	*	Louisiana
Dusseldorf	367	1,204	1978	Fleke, West Germany
Yamatogawa	355		*	Osaka, Japan
Duisburg-Neuenkamp	350	1,148	1970	West Germany
West Gate	336	1,102	1974	Melbourne, Australia
Brazo Largo	330	1,083	1977	Guazu, Argentina
Zarate	330	1,083	1977	Palmas, Argentina
Kohlbrand	325	1,066	1974	Hamburg, West Germany
Knee	320	1,050	1969	Dusseldorf, West Germany

Prestressed Concrete Deck

Bridge	Main Span Meters	Feet	Completion Date	Location
Pasadas	330	1,082	*	Argentina—Paraguay
Brotonne	320	1,050	1976	Caudebec, France
Pasco, Kennewick	299	981	1979	Washington
Wadi-Kuf	282	925	1972	Beida, Libya
Tiel	267	876	1975	Waal, Netherlands
Manuel Belgrano	245	804	1973	Corrientes, Argentina
Rafael Urdaneta	235	771	1962	Maracaibo, Venezuela
Poleevera	208	682	1967	Genoa, Italy

STEEL TRUSS BRIDGES

Bridge	Main Span Meters	Feet	Completion Date	Location
Cantilever				
Quebec	549	1,800	1918	St. Lawrence River, Canada
Forth	521	1,710	1889	Scotland
Minato	510	1,673	1974	Osaka, Japan
Commodore J.J. Barry	501	1,644	1974	Pennsylvania
Greater New Orleans	480	1,575	1958	Louisiana
Howrah	457	1,500	1943	Calcutta, India
East Bay	427	1,400	1936	Oakland, Calif.
Baton Rouge	376	1,235	1968	Louisiana
Astoria	376	1,235	1966	Oregon
Tappan Zee	369	1,212	1956	New York
Longview	366	1,200	1930	Washington
Baltimore	366	1,200	1976	Maryland
Queensboro	360	1,182	1908	New York City
Continuous				
Astoria	376	1,235	1966	Oregon
Oshima	325	1,066	1976	Japan
Tenmon	300	984	1966	Japan
Kuronoseto	300	984	1974	Japan
Dubuque	258	945	1943	Iowa
Braga Memorial	256	840	1966	Massachusetts
Earle	252	825	1956	Kentucky
Lincoln Trail	252	825	1966	Indiana
Cairo	250	820	1975	Illinois
Simple Span				
Metropolis	219	720	1917	Illinois
Municipal	204	668	1910	St. Louis, Missouri
Elizabethtown	179	586	1906	Ohio

LONGEST ARCHES

Bridge	Main Span Meters	Feet	Completion Date	Location
Steel				
New River Gorge	518	1,700	1977	West Virginia
Bayonne	510	1,675	1931	New Jersey
Sydney Harbor	509	1,670	1932	Sydney, Australia
Fremont	383	1,255	1971	Oregon
Zdakov	380	1,244	1967	Orlik, Czechoslovakia
Port Mann	366	1,200	1964	B.C., Canada
Runcorn	330	1,082	1961	Mersey, England
Birchenough	329	1,080	1935	Sabi, Zimbabwe
Glen Canyon	313	1,028	1959	Arizona
Lewiston-Queenston	305	1,000	1962	Niagara River, U.S.A.-Canada
Hellgate	298	978	1916	New York City
Concrete				
KRK	390	1,280	1974	Zagreb, Yugoslavia
Gladesville	305	1,000	1964	Sydney, Australia
Amizade	290	951	1964	Foz do Ignacu, Brazil
Arrabida	270	885	1963	Oporto, Portugal
Sando	264	866	1943	Kramfors, Sweden

LONGEST BRIDGES IN THE WORLD

SOURCE: American Society of Civil Engineers

Measurements that determine the longest bridges in the world include the bridge span or spans, as well as its approach roads.

Name of Bridge	Length in Feet	Completed	Location
Lake Pontchartrain Causeway II	126,055	1969	New Orleans-Lewisburg, La.
Lake Pontchartrain Causeway I	125,827	1956	New Orleans-Lewisburg, La.
Chesapeake Bay Bridge-Tunnel	93,203	1964	Cape Henry-Cape Charles, Va.
Presidente Costa e Silva Bridge	45,866	1974	Rio de Janeiro—Niteroi, Brazil
Marathon Key-Bahia Honda Key Bridge	38,915	1910	Florida Keys
San Mateo-Hayward Bridge I	37,183	1929	San Francisco Bay
San Mateo-Hayward Bridge II	35,708	1967	San Francisco Bay
Lake Maracaibo Bridge	28,473	1962	Punta Piedras-Punta Iguana, Venezuela
Transbay Bridge	27,286	1936	San Francisco-Oakland
Lake Pontchartrain Trestle	24,927	1927	Blind Bayou-Slidell, La.
Mackinac Straits Bridge	23,390	1957	Mackinaw City-St. Ignace, Mich.
James River Bridge	23,177	1928	Chuckatuck Creek-Newport News, Va.
Huey P. Long Bridge	22,996	1935	New Orleans
Sunshine Skyway (Structure C)	22,373	1954	St. Petersburg-Palmetto, Fla.
Richmond-San Rafael Bridge	21,965	1957	San Pablo Bay, Calif.
Astoria Bridge	21,697	1966	Pt. Ellice, Wash.-Astoria, Ore.
Chesapeake Bay Bridge	21,286	1952	Sandy Point-Kent Island, Md.
Öland Island Bridge	19,882	1972	Svinö-Möllstorp, Sweden
Oosterschelde Bridge	16,475	1965	Middelburg-Zierikzee, Netherlands
Tappan Zee Bridge	16,013	1955	South Nyack—Tarrytown, N.Y.

U.S. POPULATION AND AREA: 1790–1980

SOURCE: Bureau of the Census (Series P–25)

POPULATION

Year	Number (1,000)	Percent Increase	Per Square Mile[1]	AREA (1,000 sq. mi.) Land	AREA (1,000 sq. mi.) Water
1790	3,929	(X)	4.5	865	24
1800	5,308	35.1	6.1	865	24
1810	7,240	36.4	4.3	1,682	34
1820	9,638	33.1	5.6	1,749	39
1830	12,866	33.5	7.4	1,749	39
1840	17,069	32.7	9.8	1,749	39
1850	23,192	35.9	7.9	2,940	53
1860	31,443	35.6	10.6	2,970	53
1870	39,818	26.6	13.4	2,970	53
1880	50,156	26.0	16.9	2,970	53
1890	62,948	25.5	21.2	2,970	53
1900	75,995	20.7	25.6	2,970	53
1910	91,972	21.0	31.0	2,970	53
1920	105,711	14.9	35.6	2,969	53
1930	122,775	16.1	41.2	2,977	45
1940	131,669	7.2	44.2	2,977	45
1950	150,697	14.5	50.7	2,975	48
1960	179,323	18.5	50.5	3,541	74
1970	203,235	13.3	57.5	3,537	78
1971*	206,219	1.5	58.3	3,537	78
1972*	208,234	1.0	58.9	3,537	78
1973*	209,860	0.8	59.3	3,537	78
1975*	213,121	0.8	60.3	3,537	78
1976*	214,659	0.7	60.7	3,537	78
1978*	218,228	1.7	61.7	3,537	78
1979*	220,099	0.9	62.2	3,537	78
1980²	226,505	2.9	64.0	3,537	78

(X) Not applicable. [1] Land area only. [2] As of April 1980 census.
* As of July 1.

CENTER OF POPULATION OF THE UNITED STATES: 1790 TO 1970

SOURCE: Bureau of the Census

Census Year	Approximate location
Conterminous United States*	
1790 ..	23 miles east of Baltimore, Md.
1800 ..	18 miles west of Baltimore, Md.
1810 ..	40 miles northwest by west of Washington, D.C. (in Virginia)
1820 ..	16 miles east of Moorefield, W. Va.
1830 ..	19 miles west-southwest of Moorefield, W. Va.
1840 ..	16 miles south of Clarksburg, W. Va.
1850 ..	23 miles southeast of Parkersburg, W. Va.
1860 ..	20 miles south by east of Chillicothe, Ohio
1870 ..	48 miles east by north of Cincinnati, Ohio
1880 ..	8 miles west by south of Cincinnati, Ohio (in Kentucky)
1890 ..	20 miles east of Columbus, Ind.
1900 ..	6 miles southeast of Columbus, Ind.
1910 ..	In the city of Bloomington, Ind.
1920 ..	8 miles south-southeast of Spencer, Owen County, Ind.
1930 ..	3 miles northeast of Linton, Greene County, Ind.
1940 ..	2 miles southeast by east of Carlisle, Haddon township, Sullivan County, Ind.
1950 ..	8 miles north-northwest of Olney, Richland County, Ill.
United States	
1950 ..	3 miles northeast of Louisville, Clay County, Ill.
1960 ..	In Clinton County, Ill. 6½ miles northwest of Centralia
1970 ..	In St. Clair County, Ill. 5 miles east-southeast of Mascoutah

* Conterminous United States excludes Alaska and Hawaii.

RESIDENT U.S. POPULATION BY STATE AND RANK, APRIL 1980 CENSUS

SOURCE: U.S. Bureau of the Census (Population in thousands)

Rank	State	Population
1 ..	California	23,669
2 ..	New York	17,557
3 ..	Texas	14,228
4 ..	Pennsylvania	11,867
5 ..	Illinois	11,418
6 ..	Ohio	10,797
7 ..	Florida	9,740
8 ..	Michigan	9,258
9 ..	New Jersey	7,364
10 ..	North Carolina	5,874
11 ..	Massachusetts	5,737
12 ..	Indiana	5,490
13 ..	Georgia	5,464
14 ..	Virginia	5,346
15 ..	Missouri	4,915
16 ..	Wisconsin	4,705
17 ..	Tennessee	4,591
18 ..	Maryland	4,216
19 ..	Louisiana	4,204
20 ..	Washington	4,130
21 ..	Minnesota	4,077
22 ..	Alabama	3,890
23 ..	Kentucky	3,661
24 ..	South Carolina	3,119
25 ..	Connecticut	3,108
26 ..	Oklahoma	3,025
27 ..	Iowa	2,913
28 ..	Colorado	2,889
29 ..	Arizona	2,718
30 ..	Oregon	2,633
31 ..	Mississippi	2,521
32 ..	Kansas	2,363
33 ..	Arkansas	2,286
34 ..	West Virginia	1,950
35 ..	Nebraska	1,570
36 ..	Utah	1,461
37 ..	New Mexico	1,300
38 ..	Maine	1,125
39 ..	Hawaii	965
40 ..	Rhode Island	947
41 ..	Idaho	944
42 ..	New Hampshire	921
43 ..	Nevada	799
44 ..	Montana	787
45 ..	South Dakota	690
46 ..	North Dakota	653
47 ..	District of Columbia	638
48 ..	Delaware	595
49 ..	Vermont	511
50 ..	Wyoming	471
51 ..	Alaska	400

STANDARD CONSOLIDATED STATISTICAL AREAS (SCSA's)

SOURCE: U.S. Bureau of the Census

Rank 1980	Standard Consolidated Statistical Area	1980 Population	1970 Population
1.	New York-Newark-Jersey City, N.Y.-N.J.-Conn.	16,120,023	17,035,270
2.	Los Angeles-Long Beach-Anaheim, Calif.	11,496,206	9,980,859
3.	Chicago-Gary-Kenosha, Ill.-Ind.-Wis.	7,868,246	7,726,039
4.	Philadelphia-Wilmington-Trenton, Pa.-Del.-N.J.	5,548,789	5,627,719
5.	San Francisco-Oakland-San Jose, Calif.	5,182,021	4,630,576
6.	Detroit-Ann Arbor, Mich.	4,617,510	4,669,154
7.	Boston-Lawrence-Lowell, Mass.-N.H.	3,448,122	3,526,349
8.	Houston-Galveston, Tex.	3,101,290	2,169,128
9.	Cleveland-Akron-Lorain, Ohio	2,833,957	2,999,811
10.	Miami-Fort Lauderdale, Fla.	2,640,022	1,887,892
11.	Seattle-Tacoma, Wash.	2,092,348	1,836,949
12.	Cincinnati-Hamilton, Ohio-Ky.-Ind.	1,660,190	1,613,414
13.	Milwaukee-Racine, Wis.	1,570,275	1,574,722
14.	Indianapolis-Anderson, Ind.	1,306,265	1,249,874
15.	San Juan-Caguas, Puerto Rico	1,260,337	1,078,398
16.	Providence-Fall River, R.I.-Mass.	1,096,047	1,078,436
17.	Dayton-Springfield, Ohio	1,013,955	1,040,137

LARGEST U.S. METROPOLITAN AREAS (Rank by 1980 Census)

SOURCE: U.S. Bureau of the Census

Rank 1980	Standard Metropolitan Statistical Area	1980 Population	1970 Population	Rank 1980	Standard Metropolitan Statistical Area	1980 Population	1970 Population
1	New York, N.Y.-N.J.	9,119,737	9,973,716	74	Springfield-Chicopee-Holyoke, Mass.-Conn.	530,668	541,752
2	Los Angeles-Long Beach, Calif.	7,477,657	7,041,980	75	Oxnard-Simi Valley-Ventura, Calif.	529,899	378,497
3	Chicago, Ill.	7,102,328	6,974,755	76	Wilmington, Del.-N.J.-Md.	524,108	499,493
4	Philadelphia, Pa.-N.J.	4,716,818	4,824,110	77	Flint, Mich.	521,589	508,664
5	Detroit, Mich.	4,352,762	4,435,051	78	Fresno, Calif.	515,013	413,329
6	San Francisco-Oakland, Calif.	3,252,721	3,109,249	79	Long Branch-Asbury Park, N.J.	503,173	461,849
7	Washington, D.C.-Md.-Va.	3,060,240	2,910,111	80	Baton Rouge, La.	493,973	375,628
8	Dallas-Fort Worth, Tex.	2,974,878	2,377,623	81	Tacoma, Wash.	485,643	412,344
9	Houston, Tex.	2,905,350	1,999,316	82	El Paso, Tex.	479,899	359,291
10	Boston, Mass.	2,763,357	2,899,101	83	Knoxville, Tenn.	476,517	409,409
11	Nassau-Suffolk, N.Y.	2,605,813	2,555,868	84	Lansing-East Lansing, Mich.	468,482	424,271
12	St. Louis, Mo.-Ill.	2,355,276	2,410,884	85	Las Vegas, Nev.	461,816	273,288
13	Pittsburgh, Pa.	2,263,894	2,401,362	86	Albuquerque, N. Mex.	454,499	333,266
14	Baltimore, Md.	2,174,023	2,071,016	87	Paterson-Clifton-Passaic, N.J.	447,585	460,782
15	Minneapolis-St. Paul, Minn.-Wis.	2,114,256	1,965,391	88	Harrisburg, Pa.	446,072	410,505
16	Atlanta, Ga.	2,029,618	1,595,517	89	Mobile, Ala.	442,819	376,690
17	Newark, N.J.	1,965,304	2,057,468	90	Johnson City-Kingsport-Bristol, Tenn.-Va.	433,638	373,591
18	Anaheim-Sta. Ana-Garden Grove, Calif.	1,931,570	1,421,233	91	Charleston-North Charleston, S.C.	430,301	336,036
19	Cleveland, Ohio	1,898,720	2,063,729	92	Chattanooga, Tenn.-Ga.	426,540	370,857
20	San Diego, Calif.	1,861,846	1,357,854	93	New Haven-West Haven, Conn.	417,592	411,287
21	Miami, Fla.	1,625,979	1,267,792	94	Wichita, Kans.	411,313	389,352
22	Denver-Boulder, Colo.	1,619,921	1,239,545	95	Columbia, S.C.	408,176	322,880
23	Seattle-Everett, Wash.	1,606,765	1,424,605	96	Canton, Ohio	404,421	393,789
24	Tampa-St. Petersburg, Fla.	1,569,492	1,088,549	97	Bakersfield, Calif.	403,089	330,234
25	Riverside-San Bernardino-Ontario, Calif.	1,557,080	1,139,149	98	Bridgeport, Conn.	395,455	401,752
26	Phoenix, Ariz.	1,508,030	971,228	99	Little Rock-N. Little Rock, Ark.	393,494	323,296
27	Cincinnati, Ohio-Ky.-Ind.	1,401,403	1,387,207	100	Davenport-Rock Island-Moline, Iowa-Ill.	383,958	362,638
28	Milwaukee, Wis.	1,397,143	1,403,884	101	Fort Wayne, Ind.	382,961	361,984
29	Kansas City, Mo.-Kans.	1,327,020	1,273,926	102	York, Pa.	381,255	329,540
30	San Jose, Calif.	1,295,071	1,065,313	103	Shreveport, La.	376,646	336,000
31	Buffalo, N.Y.	1,242,573	1,349,211	104	Beaumont-Port Arthur, Tex.	375,497	347,568
32	Portland, Ore.-Wash.	1,242,187	1,007,130	105	Worcester, Mass.	372,940	372,144
33	New Orleans, La.	1,186,725	1,046,470	106	Peoria, Ill.	365,864	341,979
34	Indianapolis, Ind.	1,166,929	1,111,352	107	Newport News-Hampton, Va.	364,449	333,140
35	Columbus, Ohio	1,093,293	1,017,847	108	Lancaster, Pa.	362,346	320,079
36	San Antonio, Tex.	1,071,954	888,179	109	Stockton, Calif.	347,342	291,073
37	Fort Lauderdale-Hollywood, Fla.	1,014,043	620,100	110	Spokane, Wash.	341,835	287,487
38	Sacramento, Calif.	1,014,002	803,793	111	Des Moines, Iowa	338,048	313,562
39	Rochester, N.Y.	971,879	961,516	112	Vallejo-Fairfield-Napa, Calif.	334,402	251,129
40	Salt Lake City-Ogden, Utah	936,255	705,458	113	Augusta, Ga.-S.C.	327,372	275,787
41	Providence-Warwick-Pawtucket, R.I.-Mass	919,216	908,887	114	Corpus Christi, Tex.	326,228	284,832
42	Memphis, Tenn.-Ark.-Miss.	912,887	834,103	115	Madison, Wis.	323,545	290,272
43	Louisville, Ky.-Ind.	906,240	867,330	116	Lakeland-Winter Haven, Fla.	321,652	228,515
44	Nashville-Davidson, Tenn.	850,505	699,271	117	Jackson, Miss.	320,425	258,906
45	Birmingham, Ala.	847,360	767,230	118	Utica-Rome, N.Y.	320,180	340,477
46	Oklahoma City, Okla.	834,088	699,092	119	Lexington-Fayette, Ky.	318,136	266,701
47	Dayton, Ohio	830,070	852,531	120	Colorado Springs, Colo.	317,458	239,288
48	Greensboro-Winston-Salem-High Point, N.C.	827,385	724,129	121	Reading, Pa.	312,509	296,382
49	Norfolk-Virginia Beach-Portsmouth, Va.-N.C.	806,691	732,600	122	Huntington-Ashland, W. Va.-Ky.-Ohio	311,350	286,935
50	Albany-Schenectady-Troy, N.Y.	795,019	777,977	123	Evansville, Ind.-Ky.	309,408	284,959
51	Toledo, Ohio-Mich.	791,599	762,658	124	Huntsville, Ala.	308,593	282,450
52	Honolulu, Hawaii	762,874	630,528	125	Trenton, N.J.	307,863	304,116
53	Jacksonville, Fla.	737,519	621,827	126	Binghamton, N.Y.-Pa.	301,336	302,672
54	Hartford, Conn.	726,114	720,581	127	Santa Rosa, Calif.	299,827	204,885
55	Orlando, Fla.	700,699	453,270	128	Santa Barbara-Santa Maria-Lompoc, Calif.	298,660	264,324
56	Tulsa, Okla.	689,628	549,154	129	Appleton-Oshkosh, Wis.	291,325	276,948
57	Akron, Ohio	660,328	679,239	130	Salinas-Seaside-Monterey, Calif.	290,444	247,450
58	Gary-Hammond-E. Chicago, Ind.	642,781	633,367	131	Pensacola, Fla.	289,782	243,075
59	Syracuse, N.Y.	642,375	636,596	132	McAllen-Pharr-Edinburg, Tex.	283,229	181,535
60	Northeast Pennsylvania	640,396	621,882	133	Lawrence-Haverhill, Mass.-N.H.	281,981	258,564
61	Charlotte-Gastonia, N.C.	637,218	557,785	134	South Bend, Ind.	280,772	279,813
62	Allentown-Bethlehem-Easton, Pa.-N.J.	636,714	594,382	135	Erie, Pa.	279,780	263,654
63	Richmond, Va.	632,015	547,542	136	Rockford, Ill.	279,514	272,063
64	Grand Rapids, Mich.	601,680	539,225	137	Kalamazoo-Portage, Mich.	279,192	257,723
65	New Brunswick-Perth Amboy-Sayreville, N.J.	595,893	583,813	138	Eugene-Springfield, Ore.	275,226	215,401
66	West Palm Beach-Boca Raton, Fla.	573,125	348,993	139	Lorain-Elyria, Ohio	274,909	256,843
67	Omaha, Nebr.-Iowa	570,399	542,646	140	Melbourne-Titusville-Cocoa, Fla.	272,959	230,006
68	Greenville-Spartanburg, S.C.	568,758	473,454	141	Montgomery, Ala.	272,687	225,911
69	Jersey City, N.J.	556,972	607,839	142	Charleston, W. Va.	269,595	257,140
70	Austin, Tex.	536,450	360,463	143	Duluth-Superior, Minn.-Wis.	266,650	265,350
71	Youngstown-Warren, Ohio.	531,350	537,124	144	Modesto, Calif.	265,902	194,506
72	Tucson, Ariz.	531,263	351,667	145	Ann Arbor, Mich.	264,748	234,103
73	Raleigh-Durham, N.C.	530,673	419,254	146	Johnstown, Pa.	264,506	262,822
				147	Hamilton-Middletown, Ohio	258,787	226,207
				148	Daytona Beach, Fla.	258,762	169,487
				149	Macon, Ga.	254,623	226,782
				150	Salem, Ore.	249,895	186,658

VOTER PARTICIPATION: PRESIDENTIAL ELECTIONS PERCENTAGE OF VOTING AGE POPULATION; AND PERCENTAGE IN THE 25 LARGEST STATES

Source: U.S. Bureau of the Census

Sex:	1980 election	1976 election	1972 election	Age:	1980 election	1976 election	1972 election
Male	59.1	59.6	64.1	18–20	44.7	38.0	48.3
Female	59.4	58.8	62.0	21–24	52.7	45.6	50.7
				25–34	62.0	55.4	59.7
				35–44	70.6	63.3	66.3
Race:				45–54	74.0	67.9	70.9
White	60.9	60.9	64.5	55–64	77.0	69.7	70.7
Black	50.5	48.7	52.1	65–74	77.2	54.8	68.1
Spanish origin*	29.9	31.8	37.5	75 and over	69.2	54.8	55.6

25 Largest States in Population

Voter Participation:	1980 election	1976 election	1972 election	Voter Participation:	1980 election	1976 election	1972 election
Alabama	56.4	54.6	N.A.	Minnesota	73.3	75.4	N.A.
California	53.8	54.8	66.0	Missouri	67.3	63.1	65.4
Connecticut	67.6	64.4	N.A.	New Jersey	59.6	59.1	66.7
Florida	55.5	54.7	59.0	New York	54.8	56.4	63.5
Georgia	53.5	54.1	49.2	North Carolina	52.2	48.7	49.0
Illinois	66.4	65.6	71.1	Ohio	60.7	59.5	65.6
Indiana	61.6	64.8	68.9	Pennsylvania	54.9	57.3	61.0
Iowa	67.7	67.6	N.A.	Tennessee	56.7	55.2	N.A.
Kentucky	56.9	55.6	N.A.	Texas	51.1	53.2	55.0
Louisiana	63.9	59.9	N.A.	Virginia	55.2	55.2	49.3
Maryland	58.6	58.7	N.A.	Washington	61.2	64.4	N.A.
Massachusetts	65.6	68.9	68.7	Wisconsin	74.5	72.4	N.A.
Michigan	64.1	64.0	65.1				

* Persons of Spanish origin can be of any race. NA = Not available.

IMMIGRATION TO THE UNITED STATES   Source: U.S. Immigration and Naturalization Service

Years	Number	Years	Number	Years	Number	Years	Number
1820	8,385	1881–1890	5,246,613	1961–1965	1,450,312	1973	400,063
1821–1830	143,439	1891–1900	3,687,564	1966	323,040	1974	394,861
1831–1840	599,125	1901–1910	8,795,386	1967	361,972	1975	386,194
1841–1850	1,713,251	1911–1920	5,735,811	1968	454,448	1976	398,613
1851–1860	2,598,214	1921–1930	4,107,209	1969	358,579	1977	462,315
1861–1870	2,314,824	1931–1940	528,431	1970	373,326	1978	601,442
1871–1880	2,812,191	1941–1950	1,035,039	1971	370,478	1979	460,348
		1951–1960	2,515,479	1972	384,685		

IMMIGRATION BY COUNTRIES: 1820–1979   Source: U.S. Immigration and Naturalization Service

Countries	1979	Total (1820 to 1979)	Countries	1979	Total (1820 to 1979)
All countries	460,348	49,125,313	Romania	1,180	172,071
Europe	64,173	36,267,136	Spain	3,285	262,836
Albania	25	2,581	Sweden [2]	764	1,272,689
Austria [1]	507	4,316,149	Switzerland	774	349,877
Hungary [1]	528		USSR	1,919	3,375,233
Belgium	646	203,064	Yugoslavia [4]	1,861	115,410
Bulgaria [4]	127	67,954	Other Europe	434	56,039
Czechoslovakia	494	137,523			
Denmark	378	364,538	Asia	182,970	3,036,730
Estonia	9	1,137	China	2,944	518,494
Finland	284	33,725	India	18,625	182,323
France	2,905	753,329	Japan	4,496	410,934
Germany [1]	7,166	6,984,909	Turkey	1,306	386,861
Great Britain			Other Asia	155,599	1,538,118
England	14,336	3,192,894			
Scotland	803	820,866			
Wales	128	95,255	America	197,123	9,247,834
Not specified	270	805,092	Canada & Newfoundland	20,181	4,125,038
Greece	5,942	660,828	Mexico	52,479	2,176,206
Ireland	808	4,724,352	West Indies	71,029	1,757,830
Italy	5,969	5,300,387	Central America	17,709	330,572
Latvia	13	2,568	South America	35,715	748,739
Lithuania	23	3,875	Other America	10	109,449
Luxembourg	42	2,909			
Netherlands	1,184	360,825	Africa	11,212	143,271
Norway [2]	438	856,912	Australia & New Zealand	2,476	120,984
Poland [3]	3,863	518,359	Pacific Islands	135	24,706
Portugal	7,068	452,422	Not specified	2,259	284,652

[1] Data for Austria-Hungary were not reported until 1861; Austria and Hungary have been recorded separately since 1905. From 1938 to 1945 inclusive, Austria was included with Germany. [2] From 1820 to 1868, the figures for Norway and Sweden were combined. [3] Poland was recorded as a separate country from 1820 to 1898 and again since 1920. [4] Bulgaria, Serbia, and Montenegro were first reported in 1899. Bulgaria has been reported separately since 1920, while the Serb, Croat, and Slovene Kingdom has been recorded as Yugoslavia since 1922. Data collected from country of last residence.

WORLD POPULATION FACTS

Source: U.N. Demographic Yearbook 1978, Population and Vital Statistics Report April 1, 1981, © United Nations

Regions	1950	Midyear Estimates (in Millions) 1970	1975	1980	Annual % increase (1970-80)
WORLD	2,513	3,678	4,033	4,415	1.8
Africa	219	354	406	469	2.8
Americas	330	509	559	615	1.9
Asia*	1,380	2,091	2,319	2,558	2.0
Europe*	392	460	474	484	0.5
Oceania	13	19	21	23	1.9
USSR	180	244	254	267	0.9

* Excluding USSR.

MOST POPULOUS URBAN AREAS

Source: Various statistical reports

City	Population	Year	City	Population	Year
New York, U.S.	16,120,023	1980	Lüda, China	4,000,000	1970 (E)
Mexico City, Mexico	13,993,866	1980	Istanbul, Turkey	3,864,493	1975 (E)
São Paulo, Brazil	12,578,045	1980	Chengdu, China	3,850,000	1979 (E)
Los Angeles, U.S.	11,496,206	1980	Wuhan, China	3,832,487	1979 (E)
Shanghai, China	11,320,000	1979 (E)	Santiago, Chile	3,691,548	1978 (E)
Paris, France	9,878,524	1975	Nanjing, China	3,551,000	1979 (E)
Buenos Aires, Argentina	9,749,000	1978 (E)	Madrid, Spain	3,520,320	1975 (E)
Rio de Janeiro, Brazil	9,018,981	1980	Chongqing, China	3,500,000	1970 (E)
Peking (Beijing), China	8,706,000	1979 (E)	Karachi, Pakistan	3,498,634	1972
Tokyo, Japan	8,646,520	1975	Boston, U.S.	3,448,122	1980
Moscow, U.S.S.R.	8,011,000	1979	Ho Chi Minh City (Saigon),		
Jakarta, Indonesia	7,916,000	1981 (E)	Vietnam	3,419,978	1979
Chicago, U.S.	7,868,246	1980	Delhi, India	3,287,883	1971
Seoul, South Korea	7,500,000	1977 (E)	Jinan, China	3,202,000	1979 (E)
Tianjin, China	7,390,000	1979 (E)	Houston, U.S.	3,101,290	1980
Calcutta, India	7,031,382	1971	Washington, U.S.	3,060,240	1980
London, U.K.	7,028,200	1976 (E)	Sydney, Australia	3,021,300	1976
Bombay, India	5,970,575	1971	Dallas-Ft. Worth, U.S.	2,974,878	1980
Philadelphia, U.S.	5,548,789	1980	Rome, Italy	2,897,505	1977
Canton, China	5,350,000	1979 (E)	Toronto, Canada	2,864,700	1979 (E)
San Francisco-Oakland, U.S.	5,182,021	1980	Cleveland, U.S.	2,833,957	1980
Cairo, Egypt	5,084,463	1976	Montréal, Canada	2,818,300	1979 (E)
Detroit, U.S.	4,617,510	1980	Manila-Quezon City,		
Leningrad, U.S.S.R.	4,588,000	1979	Philippines	2,792,239	1980
Tehran, Iran	4,496,159	1976	Osaka, Japan	2,778,987	1975
Bogotá, Colombia	4,324,000	1978 (E)	Xi'an, China	2,760,000	1979 (E)
Bangkok, Thailand	4,178,000	1975 (E)	Harbin, China	2,750,000	1970 (E)
Lima, Peru	4,000,000	1972	Birmingham, U.K.	2,743,300	1976 (E)

(E) Estimated data.

MOST POPULOUS COUNTRIES

Source: Population and Vital Statistics Report April 1, 1981, © United Nations

Country	Midyear 1979 Estimate (in Millions)	Annual % Increase 1975-79	Density per Sq. Mi.	Area in Sq. Mi.	Country	Midyear 1979 Estimate (in Millions)	Annual % Increase 1975-79	Density per Sq. Mi.	Area in Sq. Mi.
China	945.02	1.3	256.0	3,691,000	Thailand	46.14	2.5	232.5	198,455
India	650.98	2.0	512.9	1,269,339	Turkey	44.24	2.3	147.0	300,946
USSR	263.43	0.9	30.5	8,649,490	Egypt	40.98	2.5	106.0	386,659
UNITED STATES	220.58	0.8	61.0	3,615,123	Korea, South	37.61	1.6	985.1	38,175
Indonesia	148.47	2.4	188.3	788,430	Spain	37.18	1.1	189.7	195,988
Brazil	118.65	2.8	36.1	3,286,470	Iran	36.94	2.9	58.1	636,293
Japan	115.87	1.0	795.1	145,730	Poland	35.23	0.9	291.8	120,725
Bangladesh	86.64	2.6	1,571.7	55,126	Burma	32.91	2.2	125.7	261,789
Nigeria	84.50	—	222.6	379,628	Ethiopia	30.42	2.6	64.5	471,776
Pakistan	79.84	3.3	257.2	310,403	South Africa	28.48	2.8	60.3	472,359
Mexico	69.38	3.7	91.1	761,600	Zaire	27.87	2.9	30.3	918,962
Germany, West	61.34	− 0.2	640.9	95,704	Argentina	26.73	1.3	25.0	1,068,296
Italy	56.91	0.5	489.3	116,303	Colombia	26.36	2.8	59.9	439,735
United Kingdom	55.88	− 0.0	592.0	94,399	Canada	23.69	1.0	6.2	3,851,809
France	53.48	0.4	254.6	210,038	Yugoslavia	22.16	0.9	224.3	98,766
Vietnam	51.08	—	397.8	128,405	Romania	22.05	0.9	240.4	91,699
Philippines	46.58	2.6	402.6	115,707	Morocco	19.47	3.0	112.9	172,413

LARGEST COUNTRIES, BY GEOGRAPHICAL AREA

Source: Various official reports

Rank	Country	Area in Sq. Mi.	Rank	Country	Area in Sq. Mi.
1	USSR	8,649,490	15	Libya	679,358
2	Canada	3,851,809	16	Iran	636,293
3	China (People's Rep.)	3,691,000	17	Mongolia	606,163
4	UNITED STATES	3,615,123	18	Peru	496,222
5	Brazil	3,286,470	19	Chad	495,752
6	Australia	2,967,909	20	Niger	489,189
7	India	1,269,339	21	Angola	481,351
8	Argentina	1,068,296	22	South Africa	472,359
9	Sudan	967,494	23	Ethiopia	471,776
10	Algeria	919,591	24	Mali	464,873
11	Zaire	918,962	25	Mauritania	452,702
12	Saudi Arabia	829,995	26	Colombia	439,735
13	Indonesia	788,430	27	Bolivia	424,163
14	Mexico	761,600			

NATION'S 50 LEADING COUNTIES* IN MEDIAN FAMILY INCOME: 1969†

SOURCE: U.S. Bureau of the Census, 1970 Census of Population: Characteristics of Population

Rank	County	Income	Rank	County	Income	Rank	County	Income
1.	Montgomery, Md.	$16,710	18.	Fairfield, Conn.	$13,086	35.	Suffolk, N.Y.	$12,084
2.	Fairfax, Va.	15,707	19.	Lake, Ill.	13,009	36.	Baltimore, Md.	12,081
3.	Nassau, N.Y.	14,632	20.	Waukesha, Wis.	12,795	37.	Arapahoe, Colo.	12,063
4.	Du Page, Ill.	14,458	21.	Norfolk, Mass.	12,749	38.	Hartford, Conn.	12,057
5.	Marin, Calif.	13,935	22.	Montgomery, Pa.	12,747	39.	Jefferson, Colo.	12,045
6.	Oakland, Mich.	13,826	23.	Ozaukee, Wis.	12,620	40.	Honolulu, Hawaii	12,035
7.	Westchester, N.Y.	13,784	24.	Union, N.J.	12,593	41.	Putnam, N.Y.	11,996
8.	Rockland, N.Y.	13,753	25.	Santa Clara, Calif.	12,456	42.	Middlesex, N.J.	11,982
9.	Arlington, Va.	13,743	26.	Prince Georges, Md.	12,450	43.	McHenry, Ill.	11,965
10.	Bergen, N.J.	13,597	27.	Monroe, N.Y.	12,423	44.	Lake, Ohio	11,964
11.	Anchorage, Alaska	13,593	28.	Contra Costa, Calif.	12,423	45.	Kane, Ill.	11,947
12.	Howard, Md.	13,472	29.	Geauga, Ohio	12,411	46.	Richmond, N.Y.	11,894
13.	Somerset, N.J.	13,433	30.	St. Louis, Mo.	12,392	47.	King, Wash.	11,886
14.	Morris, N.J.	13,421	31.	Washtenaw, Mich.	12,294	48.	Tolland, Conn.	11,874
15.	Johnson, Kans.	13,384	32.	Orange, Calif.	12,245	49.	Middlesex, Mass.	11,860
16.	San Mateo, Calif.	13,222	33.	De Kalb, Ga.	12,137	50.	Delaware, Pa.	11,822
17.	Macomb, Mich.	13,110	34.	Dakota, Minn.	12,120			

* With 50,000 or more population.   † Figures are for calendar year 1969, as gathered in 1970 census.

NATION'S 50 LARGEST CITIES* RANKED BY MEDIAN FAMILY INCOME: 1970 CENSUS

SOURCE: U.S. Department of Commerce, Bureau of Economic Analysis

Rank	City	SMSA*	City Only	Rank	City	SMSA*	City Only
1.	Honolulu, Hawaii	$12,035	$12,539	26.	Oakland, Calif.	$ 9,626	$9,626
2.	San Jose, Calif.	12,456	11,927	27.	Washington, D.C.	12,933	9,583
3.	Seattle, Wash.	11,676	11,037	28.	Nashville-Davidson, Tenn.	9,187	9,473
4.	Indianapolis, Ind.	10,754	10,754	29.	Philadelphia, Pa.	10,783	9,366
5.	St. Paul, Minn.	11,682	10,544	30.	Fort Worth, Texas	10,101	9,271
6.	Los Angeles, Calif.	10,972	10,535	31.	Boston, Mass.	11,449	9,133
7.	San Francisco, Calif.	11,802	10,503	32.	Cleveland, Ohio	11,407	9,107
8.	Toledo, Ohio	10,932	10,474	33.	Oklahoma City, Okla.	9,345	9,106
9.	Long Beach, Calif.	10,282	10,282	34.	Cincinnati, Ohio	10,257	8,894
10.	Milwaukee, Wis.	11,338	10,262	35.	Baltimore, Md.	10,577	8,815
11.	Chicago, Ill.	11,931	10,242	36.	Buffalo, N.Y.	11,430	8,804
12.	Omaha, Nebr.	10,204	10,208	37.	Pittsburgh, Pa.	9,737	8,800
13.	San Diego, Calif.	10,133	10,166	38.	Jacksonville, Fla.	8,671	8,671
14.	Detroit, Mich.	12,117	10,045	39.	Memphis, Tenn.	8,542	8,646
15.	Dallas, Tex.	10,405	10,019	40.	Louisville, Ky.	9,814	8,564
16.	Rochester, N.Y.	11,969	10,002	41.	Atlanta, Ga.	10,695	8,399
17.	Minneapolis, Minn.	9,960	9,960	42.	St. Louis, Mo.	10,504	8,182
18.	Phoenix, Ariz.	9,856	9,956	43.	El Paso, Tex.	7,792	7,963
19.	Kansas City, Mo.	10,588	9,910	44.	Norfolk, Va.	8,705	7,821
20.	Houston, Tex.	10,191	9,876	45.	Birmingham, Ala.	8,295	7,737
21.	Tulsa, Okla.	9,286	9,870	46.	Newark, N.J.	11,847	7,735
22.	Portland, Oreg.	10,463	9,799	47.	San Antonio, Tex.	7,981	7,734
23.	Columbus, Ohio	10,460	9,731	48.	Tampa, Fla.	7,883	7,678
24.	New York, N.Y.	10,870	9,682	49.	New Orleans, La.	8,670	7,445
25.	Denver, Colorado	10,777	9,654	50.	Miami, Fla.	9,245	7,304

* Standard Metropolitan Statistical Areas (city plus outlying areas).

U. S. METROPOLITAN AREA PER CAPITA INCOME: 1979

SOURCE: U.S. Department of Commerce, Bureau of Economic Analysis

SMSA'S WITH HIGHEST INCOMES		SMSA'S WITH LOWEST INCOMES	
Standard Metropolitan Statistical Area	Income	Standard Metropolitan Statistical Area	Income
Reno, Nevada	$12,317	Monroe, Louisiana	$6,945
Bridgeport-Stamford-Norwalk-Danbury, Connecticut	12,266	Albany, Georgia	6,943
Anchorage, Alaska	12,200	Killeen-Temple, Texas	6,935
San Francisco-Oakland, California	11,741	Johnson City-Kingsport-Bristol, Tennessee-Virginia	6,878
Midland, Texas	11,712	Pensacola, Florida	6,859
Washington, DC-Maryland-Virginia	11,313	Bryan-College Station, Texas	6,817
San Jose, California	11,064	Fort Smith, Arkansas-Oklahoma	6,810
Salinas-Seaside-Monterey, California	10,838	Tuscaloosa, Alabama	6,767
Seattle-Everett, Washington	10,788	Columbus, Georgia-Alabama	6,758
Houston, Texas	10,638	Clarksville-Hopkinsville, Tennessee-Kentucky	6,678
Los Angeles-Long Beach, California	10,606	St. Cloud, Minnesota	6,620
Anaheim-Santa Ana-Garden Grove, California	10,547	Bloomington, Indiana	6,571
West Palm Beach-Boca Raton, Florida	10,520	Panama City, Florida	6,487
Newark, New Jersey	10,500	Fayetteville, North Carolina	6,448
Nassau-Suffolk, New York	10,468	Biloxi-Gulfport, Mississippi	6,436
Chicago, Illinois	10,455	Pascagoula-Moss Point, Mississippi	6,343
Detroit, Michigan	10,433	Anniston, Alabama	6,251
Sarasota, Florida	10,425	Alexandria, Louisiana	6,236
Peoria, Illinois	10,295	El Paso, Texas	6,207
Ann Arbor, Michigan	10,275	Las Cruces, New Mexico	6,091
Las Vegas, Nevada	10,175	Lawton, Oklahoma	6,089
Cleveland, Ohio	10,167	Brownsville-Harlingen-San Benito, Texas	5,731
Denver-Boulder, Colorado	10,133	Provo-Orem, Utah	5,721
Portland, Oregon-Washington	10,067	Laredo, Texas	5,106
Cedar Rapids, Iowa	10,037	McAllen-Pharr-Edinburg, Texas	5,024

URBAN INTERMEDIATE BUDGET FOR A 4-PERSON FAMILY IN SELECTED METROPOLITAN AREAS: 1980 (in dollars)

SOURCE: U.S. Bureau of Labor Statistics, Autumn 1980 Urban Family Budgets and Comparative Indexes for Selected Urban Areas (USDL: 81-195)

Metropolitan Areas	All Items	Food	Metropolitan Areas	All Items	Food
Anchorage Alaska	$29,682	$6,513	St. Louis, Mo.-Ill.	$22,248	$5,828
Atlanta, Ga.	21,131	5,291	San Diego, Calif.	22,727	5,345
Baltimore, Md.	23,389	5,386	San Francisco-Oakland, Calif.	24,704	5,645
Boston, Mass.	27,029	5,818	Seattle-Everett, Wash.	23,392	5,550
Buffalo, N.Y.	23,995	5,676	Washington, D.C.-Md.-Va.	25,203	5,864
Chicago, Ill.-N.W. Ind.	23,387	5,633			
Cincinnati, Ohio-Ky.-Ind.	22,681	5,673	Metropolitan Area Average	23,597	5,642
Cleveland, Ohio	23,429	5,605			
Dallas, Texas	20,766	5,304	**Nonmetropolitan Areas**		
Denver, Colo.	22,813	5,212			
Detroit, Mich.	23,168	5,520	Northeast	23,319	5,557
Honolulu, Hawaii	28,488	6,952	North Central	21,288	5,199
Houston, Texas	21,572	5,484	South	19,769	5,157
Kansas City, Mo.-Kans	22,504	5,528	West	21,933	5,238
Los Angeles-Long Beach, Calif.	22,500	5,411			
Milwaukee, Wis.	24,028	5,391	Nonmetropolitan Area Average	21,070	5,257
Minneapolis-St. Paul, Minn.	23,630	5,510			
New York, N.Y.-N.E. N.J.	26,749	6,187	**URBAN U.S. AVERAGE**	**23,134**	**5,571**
Philadelphia, Pa.-N.J.	24,364	6,227			
Pittsburgh, Pa.	24,492	5,741			

WORLDWIDE COST OF LIVING—1980 (1970 = 100)

SOURCE: U.N. *Monthly Bulletin of Statistics*, June 1981

Country	All Items	Food	Country	All items	Food
Argentina (Buenos Aires)	259,090.0	62,163.0	Ivory Coast (Abidjan)	312.7	360.6
Australia	269.2	271.3	Japan	236.6	234.3
Austria	183.9	170.3	Jordan[4]	173.3	159.2
Bahamas (Nassau)[1]	183.4	202.2	Korea, South	450.7	514.2
Bangladesh (Dacca)[1]	401.6	383.4	Liberia	258.2	255.0
Barbados[2]	104.5	104.9	Luxembourg	190.2	180.8
Belgium	203.5	178.8	Madagascar (Antananarivo)	242.7	261.5
Canada	216.7	263.5	Malawi (Blantyre)	243.9	269.9
Chile (Santiago)	419,601.0	500,946.0	Malaysia (Peninsular)	177.2	190.0
Costa Rica (San Jose)	279.4	303.9	Morocco	171.4	168.1
Cyprus[3]	133.5	129.2	Netherlands	202.9	124.1
Czechoslovakia	112.3	106.1	New Caledonia (Noumea)	225.8	227.5
Denmark[3]	255.6	163.0	New Zealand	324.6	340.1
El Salvador[3]	117.5	119.3	Norway	224.0	216.7
Fiji	260.8	271.4	Pakistan[5]	305.1	307.1
Finland	292.5	300.3	Panama (Panama City)[4]	139.2	137.6
France	251.3	254.0	Papua New Guinea[5]	220.7	230.4
Gambia (Banjul-Kambo St. Mary)	267.1	290.1	Paraguay (Asuncion)	342.7	386.5
Germany, West	164.3	153.3	Philippines[1]	294.7	275.7
Ghana (Accra)[3]	377.8	360.2	Saint Lucia	362.6	400.5
Gibraltar	401.5	385.1	Spain	414.1	372.6
Greece	379.7	425.2	Sri Lanka (Colombo)	230.2	248.8
Guadeloupe (Basse-Terre)	267.7	288.5	Sweden	241.5	248.9
Guatemala[4]	166.1	156.1	Switzerland	162.5	162.8
Haiti (Port-au-Prince)	277.3	312.9	Thailand (Bangkok, Metropolis)	248.9	271.0
Honduras (Tegucigalpa)	211.0	233.1	Trinidad and Tobago	339.7	358.2
Hong Kong[6]	160.0	156.0	Tunisia (Tunis)[3]	124.9	131.9
Hungary	155.4	165.3	United Kingdom	360.8	395.8
Ireland	360.0	367.1	UNITED STATES[6]	212.4	216.4
Israel	3,235.7	3,784.6	Venezuela (Caracas)	226.8	313.0
Italy	369.1	355.6	Yugoslavia	558.7	592.3
			Zimbabwe	207.6	203.5

[1] 1972 = 100. [2] March 1980 = 100. [3] 1977 = 100. [4] 1975 = 100. [5] 1971 = 100. [6] Beginning 1978, the series has been linked to the new urban wage earners-clerical workers, unadjusted. (CPI-W)

THE AMERICAN CONSUMER: PERSONAL EXPENDITURES (1980)

SOURCE: U.S. Department of Commerce, Bureau of Economic Analysis

	Personal Consumption Expenditures by Type of Product (Billions of Dollars)		Personal Consumption Expenditures by Type of Product (Billions of Dollars)
Total personal consumption expenditures	1,672.3	Other nondurable goods	136.1
		Fuel oil and coal	19.7
Durable goods	**211.9**	Other	116.4
Motor vehicles and parts	89.9	**Services**	**785.1**
Furniture and household equipment	84.6	Housing	272.0
Other	37.4	Household operation	111.7
Nondurable goods	**675.4**	Electricity and gas	55.7
Food	345.5	Other	56.0
Clothing and shoes	104.8	Transportation	63.8
Gasoline and oil	89.0	Other	337.5

CONSUMER PRICE INDEX* AND PURCHASING POWER OF THE CONSUMER DOLLAR
(1967=100) Source: Bureau of Labor Statistics

Year	All Items	Food & Beverages	Housing	Rent	Apparel & Upkeep	Trans- portation	Medical Care	Enter- tain- ment	Other Goods and Services	Purchasing power of the consumer dollar
1968	104.2	103.6	104.0	102.4	105.4	103.2	106.1	105.7	105.2	.960
1970	116.3	114.7	118.2	110.1	116.1	112.7	120.6	116.7	116.8	.860
1971	121.3	118.3	123.4	115.2	119.8	118.6	128.4	122.9	122.4	.824
1972	125.3	123.2	128.1	119.2	122.3	119.9	132.5	126.5	127.5	.799
1973	133.1	139.5	133.7	124.3	126.8	123.8	137.7	130.0	132.5	.752
1974	147.7	158.7	148.8	130.6	136.2	137.7	150.5	139.8	142.0	.678
1975	161.2	172.1	164.5	137.3	142.3	150.6	168.6	152.2	153.9	.621
1976	170.5	177.4	174.6	144.7	147.6	165.5	184.7	159.8	162.7	.587
1977	181.5	188.0	186.5	153.5	154.2	177.2	202.4	167.7	172.2	.551
1978	195.4	206.3	202.8	164.0	159.6	185.5	219.4	176.6	183.3	.512
1979	217.4	228.5	227.6	176.0	166.6	212.0	239.7	188.5	196.7	.461
1980	246.8	248.0	263.3	191.1	178.4	249.7	265.9	205.3	214.5	.406

* Consumer Price Index for All Urban Consumers (CPI-U)

AVERAGE U.S. RETAIL FOOD PRICES Source: Bureau of Labor Statistics (in cents)

Year	Flour, wheat 10 lbs.	Rice lb.	White bread lb.	Round steak lb.	Rib roast lb.	Chuck roast lb.	Pork chops lb.	Bacon sliced lb.	Milk[1] qt.	Butter lb.	Cheese lb.	Pota- toes 15 lbs.	Sugar lb.	Eggs doz.	Coffee lb.
1913	33	8.7	5.6	22.3	19.8	16.0	21.0	27.0	8.9	38.3	22.1	25.5	5.5	34.5	29.8
1918	67	12.9	9.8	36.9	30.7	26.6	39.0	52.9	13.9	57.7	35.9	48.0	9.7	56.9	30.5
1919	72	15.1	10.0	38.9	32.5	27.0	42.3	55.4	15.5	67.8	42.6	57.0	11.3	62.8	43.3
1920	81	17.4	11.5	39.5	33.2	26.2	42.3	52.3	16.7	70.1	41.6	94.5	19.4	68.1	47.0
1927	55	10.7	9.2	38.7	34.1	25.2	37.2	47.8	14.1	56.3	38.6	57.0	7.2	48.7	47.4
1930	46	9.5	8.6	42.6	36.4	28.6	36.2	42.5	14.1	46.4	36.6	54.0	6.1	44.5	39.5
1932	32	6.6	7.0	29.7	25.6	18.5	21.5	24.2	10.7	27.8	24.4	25.5	5.0	30.2	29.4
1934	49	8.0	8.3	28.1	23.6	17.5	25.5	29.1	11.2	31.5	25.0	34.5	5.5	32.5	26.9
1937	47.9	8.4	8.6	39.1	32.8	25.7	36.7	41.3	12.5	40.7	29.4	41.9	5.6	36.2	25.5
1939	37.9	7.7	7.9	36.0	29.5	23.4	30.4	31.9	12.2	32.5	25.3	37.1	5.4	32.1	22.4
1941	45.2	8.7	8.1	39.1	31.1	25.5	34.3	34.3	13.6	41.1	30.0	35.2	5.7	39.7	23.6
1942	52.8	12.1	8.7	43.5	34.0	29.3	41.4	39.4	15.0	47.3	34.8	51.3	6.8	48.4	28.3
1944	64.7	12.8	8.8	41.4	33.4	28.8	37.3	41.1	15.6	50.0	36.0	69.8	6.7	54.5	30.1
1946	70.8	14.0	10.4	52.1	43.1	36.6	48.5	53.3	17.6	71.0	50.1	70.2	7.7	58.6	34.4
1948	98.0	20.8	13.9	90.5	73.7	64.4	77.2	76.9	21.8	86.7	65.6	83.8	9.4	72.3	51.4
1950	98.2	16.8	14.3	93.6	74.3	61.6	75.4	63.7	20.6	72.9	51.8	69.2	9.7	60.4	79.4
1954	107.2	19.6	17.2	90.7	70.3	51.4	86.3	81.7	23.0	72.4	57.6	78.9	10.5	58.5	110.8
1956	106.6	17.2	17.9	88.2	70.1	48.4	78.2	57.3	24.2	72.1	57.2	101.6	10.6	60.2	103.4
1958	110.4	18.4	19.3	104.2	81.6	63.3	91.8	79.3	25.3	74.2	58.0	93.9	11.3	60.4	90.7
1960	110.8	18.6	20.3	105.5	81.7	61.6	85.8	65.5	26.0	74.9	68.6	107.7	11.6	57.3	75.3
1962	114.0	19.1	21.2	107.8	84.1	62.3	89.8	70.3	26.1	75.2	72.4	94.8	11.7	54.0	70.8
1964	113.4	18.8	20.7	103.9	82.8	56.8	88.0	66.7	26.4	74.4	73.4	113.6	12.8	53.9	81.6
1965	116.2	19.0	20.9	108.4	89.7	59.5	97.3	81.3	26.3	75.4	75.4	140.6	11.8	52.7	83.3
1966	118.8	19.0	22.2	110.7	93.2	62.2	106.3	95.4	27.8	82.2	84.4	112.4	12.0	59.9	82.3
1967	119.2	18.6	22.2	110.3	94.0	60.7	100.4	83.7	28.7	83.0	87.2	112.1	12.1	49.1	76.9
1968	116.8	18.8	22.4	114.3	98.8	63.5	102.9	81.4	30.3	83.6	88.8	114.5	12.2	52.9	76.4
1969	116.2	18.8	23.0	126.7	109.3	70.4	112.2	87.8	31.5	84.6	94.0	122.4	12.4	62.1	76.5
1970	117.9	19.1	24.3	130.2	111.7	72.5	116.2	94.9	33.0	86.6	100.7	134.5	13.0	61.4	91.1
1971	119.9	19.6	25.0	136.1	118.0	75.0	108.1	80.0	33.9	87.6	105.5	129.2	13.6	52.9	93.4
1972	119.2	19.6	24.7	147.7	129.5	82.1	124.6	96.2	34.5	87.1	108.6	138.9	13.9	52.4	92.7
1973	151.2	26.0	27.6	174.6	152.2	102.8	155.9	132.5	37.6	91.6	120.8	205.4	15.1	78.1	104.0
1974	205.0	44.0	34.5	179.8	158.5	102.1	156.5	132.0	39.2	94.6	145.8	249.6	32.3	78.3	122.9
1975	198.8	41.1	36.0	188.5	179.6	102.8	185.6	175.6	39.3	102.5	153.6	201.6	37.2	77.0	133.4
1976	185.2	37.5	35.3	178.3	177.4	96.9	184.8	171.1	41.4	126.1	173.0	219.0	24.0	84.1	187.3
1977	169.2	35.3	35.5	176.1	182.1	92.0	181.2	156.2	42.0	133.1	172.0	224.6	21.6	82.3	347.2
1978[2]	169.0	40.2	35.8	189.5	200.2	103.3	193.2	173.2	42.8	139.6	92.3[3]	198.0	23.9	81.5	339.5
1979	Prices not available														
1980	209.1	51.2[4]	50.9	276.9	294.5	181.9	195.3	146.5	52.5	187.8	N.A.	286.6	41.7[5]	84.4[6]	310.6[7]

1) Milk — 1933 through 1973 = delivered milk; after 1973 milk purchased in grocery stores. 2) Data for 1978 are averages only for January through April. 3) American Process cheese. 4) White, long grain, uncooked rice. 5) White sugar, 33-80 oz. package. 6) Grade A large eggs. 7) Coffee, 100%, ground roast, 13.1-20 oz. can.

THE CHANGING AMERICAN FOOD BASKET: 1914—1980 Source: U.S. Department of Agriculture
The table indicates the amount of food that could be purchased through the years with one hour of labor.

Item	Unit	1914	1919	1929	1939	1949	1959	1969	1977	1980
Bread, white	Lb.	3.5	4.7	6.4	7.9	9.8	11.1	13.9	15.9	14.3
Round steak	Lb.	0.9	1.2	1.2	1.7	1.6	2.0	2.5	3.2	2.6
Pork chops	Lb.	1.0	1.1	1.5	2.1	1.9	2.6	2.8	3.1	3.7
Sliced bacon	Lb.	0.8	0.9	1.3	2.0	2.1	3.3	3.6	3.6	5.0
Butter	Lb.	0.6	0.7	1.0	1.9	1.9	2.9	3.8	4.2	3.9
Cheese	Lb.	1.0	1.1	1.4	2.5	2.4	3.8	3.4	3.3	N.A.
Milk, fresh	Qt.[2]	—	—	—	5.6	7.0	9.1	11.6	13.5	6.9
Eggs, fresh	Doz.	0.6	0.8	1.1	2.0	2.0	4.1	5.1	6.8	8.7
Oranges	Doz.[3]	—	0.9	1.3	2.2	2.7	3.3	3.8	4.4	19.7
Potatoes	Lb.	12.3	12.4	17.0	25.1	25.1	34.8	38.9	37.6	38.3
Tomatoes[1] (canned)		—	2.9	4.4	7.3	9.1	14.1	16.2	15.0	17.3
Margarine	Lb.	—	1.1	2.1	3.8	4.5	7.8	11.5	9.8	10.0

1) #2 can from 1914 to Sept. 1954; #303 can beginning Oct. 1954; 1 pound beginning in 1980.
2) ½ gallon beginning in 1980. 3) 1 pound beginning in 1980.

AMERICAN FAMILY CHARACTERISTICS: 1980

SOURCE: U.S. Bureau of Census

Characteristic	Families	Percent	Characteristic	Families	Percent
All families	58,426,000	100.0	Nonmetropolitan	19,377,000	33.2
White	51,389,000	88.0	Headed by Women	8,540,000	14.6
Black and Other	7,037,000	12.0	Age of Family Head:		
Family Size:			Under 25 years	3,725,000	6.4
2 persons	22,913,000	39.2	25–34 years	13,743,000	23.5
3 persons	13,332,000	22.8	35–44 years	12,159,000	20.8
4 persons	12,180,000	20.8	45–54 years	10,709,000	18.3
5 persons	5,871,000	10.0	55–64 years	9,298,000	15.9
6 persons	2,439,000	4.2	65 years or older	8,792,000	15.0
7 persons or more	1,691,000	2.9	Marital Status of Household Heads:		
Own Children under 18 Years Old:			All Households	79,108,000	100.0
No children	27,909,000	47.8	Married	51,867,000	65.6
1 child	12,231,000	20.9	Separated	2,944,000	3.7
2 children	11,280,000	19.3	Widowed	10,462,000	13.2
3 children	4,616,000	7.9	Divorced	7,421,000	9.4
4 children or more	2,390,000	4.1	Single	9,359,000	11.8
Residence:					
Metropolitan	39,049,000	66.8			

SEX RATIO OF U.S. POPULATION

SOURCE: U.S. Bureau of the Census (males per 100 females). Figures relate to July 1, and include Armed Forces overseas

Year	All ages	Under 15 years	15 to 24 years	25 to 44 years	45 to 64 years	65 or older	Year	All ages	Under 15 years	15 to 24 years	25 to 44 years	45 to 64 years	65 or older
1979	95.0	104.3	102.4	97.3	92.2	68.4	1968	96.2	103.7	102.2	96.9	92.4	73.8
1978	95.1	104.3	102.3	97.4	92.1	68.5	1966	96.7	103.7	102.1	96.9	93.2	75.7
1977	95.1	104.2	102.3	97.3	92.0	68.7	1964	97.1	103.6	101.8	97.0	94.1	77.9
1976	95.1	104.2	102.3	97.3	91.9	69.0	1962	97.5	103.4	101.5	97.0	94.9	80.2
1974	95.4	104.1	102.2	97.3	91.6	69.7	1960	97.8	103.4	101.4	96.9	95.7	82.6
1972	95.6	104.0	102.1	97.2	91.6	70.8	1956	98.4	103.7	100.6	97.2	97.0	85.8
1970	95.9	103.9	102.2	96.9	91.7	72.0	1950	99.3	103.8	100.0	97.2	100.1	89.5

MARITAL STATUS OF ADULTS (Persons 14 years old and over)

SOURCE: U.S. Bureau of Census

Marital Status and Sex	1955*	1960	1970	1980	Marital Status and Sex	1955*	1960	1970	1980
Total (millions)	107	114	147	168	Male, total (cont.)				
Single millions	16	17	37	43	Widowed	4.6	4.1	3.0	2.5
Married (millions)	79	84	94	104	Divorced	1.9	2.1	2.2	4.8
Widowed (millions)	10	11	11	12	Female, total (millions)	56	59	77	88
Divorced (millions)	2	3	5	10	Percent distribution	100.0	100.0	100.0	100.0
Male, total (millions)	51	55	70	80	Single	12.0	11.8	22.1	22.4
Percent distribution	100.0	100.0	100.0	100	Married	71.9	71.3	62.0	59.0
Single	17.4	17.8	28.2	29.3	Husband separated	2.5	2.2	2.2	2.8
Married	76.1	76.0	66.6	63.4	Widowed	13.6	14.0	12.5	11.9
Wife separated	1.5	1.7	1.3	1.8	Divorced	2.4	2.9	3.5	6.6

* Excludes Alaska and Hawaii.

U.S. MARRIAGE AND DIVORCE RATES

SOURCE: National Center for Health Statistics

Year	Marriages/Divorces Number (thousands)		Rate (per thousand)		Year	Marriages/Divorces Number (thousands)		Rate (per thousand)	
1910	948	83	10.3	0.9	1965	1,800	479	9.3	2.5
1915	1,008	104	10.0	1.0	1966	1,857	499	9.5	2.5
1920	1,274	171	12.0	1.6	1967	1,927	523	9.7	2.6
1925	1,188	175	10.3	1.5	1968	2,069	584	10.4	2.9
1930	1,127	196	9.2	1.6	1969	2,145	639	10.6	3.2
1935	1,327	218	10.4	1.7	1970	2,159	708	10.6	3.5
1940	1,596	264	12.1	2.0	1971	2,190	773	10.6	3.7
1945	1,613	485	12.2	3.5	1972	2,282	845	11.0	4.1
1950	1,667	385	11.1	2.6	1973	2,284	915	10.9	4.4
1955	1,531	377	9.3	2.3	1974	2,230	977	10.5	4.6
1960	1,523	393	8.5	2.2	1975	2,153	1,036	10.1	4.9
1962	1,577	413	8.5	2.2	1976	2,155	1,083	10.0	5.0
1963	1,654	428	8.8	2.3	1977	2,178	1,091	10.0	5.0
1964	1,725	450	9.0	2.4	1978*	2,282	1,130	10.5	5.2

* Provisional figures.

ILLEGITIMATE BIRTHS IN AMERICA

SOURCE: National Center for Health Statistics (Figures in thousands)

Categories	1940	1950	1960	1965	1970	1975	1976	1977	1978
Total Illegitimate Live Births	89.5	141.6	224.3	291.2	398.7	447.9	468.1	515.7	543.9
By age of mother:									
Under 15 years	2.1	3.2	4.6	6.1	9.5	11.0	10.3	10.1	9.4
15 to 19 years	40.5	56.0	87.1	123.1	190.4	222.5	225.0	239.7	239.7
20 to 24 years	27.2	43.1	68.0	90.7	126.7	134.0	145.4	168.6	186.5
25 to 29 years	10.5	20.9	32.1	36.8	40.6	50.2	55.4	62.4	70.0
30 to 34 years	5.2	10.8	18.9	19.6	19.1	19.8	21.0	23.7	26.5
35 to 39 years	3.0	6.0	10.6	11.4	9.4	8.1	8.6	8.8	9.4
40 and over	1.0	1.7	3.0	3.7	3.0	2.3	2.3	2.3	2.3
By color of mother:									
White	40.3	53.5	82.5	123.7	175.1	186.4	197.1	220.1	233.6
Nonwhite	49.2	88.1	141.8	167.5	215.1	261.6	271.0	295.5	310.2

DIVORCE LAWS 1980

SOURCE: Women's Bureau, U.S. Department of Labor and *The Book of the States* (1980-81) by the Council of State Governments

State or other Jurisdiction	Residence required before filing suit for divorce(c)	"No fault" divorce (a)			"Traditional" Grounds for Absolute Divorce (b)												Period before parties may remarry after final decree (f)	
		Marriage breakdown (d)	Separation	Prior decree of limited divorce	Adultery	Mental and/or physical cruelty	Desertion	Alcoholism and/or drug addiction	Impotency	Non-support by husband	Insanity	Pregnancy at marriage	Bigamy	Unexplained absence	Felony conviction or imprisonment	Other	Plaintiff	Defendant
Alabama	6 mos.(g)	•	2 yrs.(h)	2 yrs.	•	•	1 yr.	•	•	•	5 yrs.	•	•		•	(i)	60 days(i)	60 days(i)
Alaska					•	•	1 yr.	•	•		18 mos.							
Arizona	90 days	•					1 yr.											
Arkansas	60 days(k)		3 yrs.		•	•	1 yr.	•			3 yrs.							
California	(m)	•									(q)				•	(p)		
Colorado	90 days	•														(p)		
Connecticut	1 yr.(o)	•			•	•	1 yr.	•	•	•	5 yrs.		•	7 yrs.	•	(q)		(u)
Delaware	6 mos.		18 mos.								(q)					(p,s,t)		
Florida	6 mos.	•					1 yr.				3 yrs.(r)							
Georgia	6 mos.	•									2 yrs.						(u)	(u)
Hawaii	3 mos.	•	2 yrs.(h)	(v)												(p,s,t)		
Idaho	6 wks.	•	5 yrs.		•	•	1 yr.	•			3 yrs.				•	(w,x)		
Illinois	90 days				•	•	1 yr.	2 yrs.	•		2 yrs.		•		•		1 yr.(i)	1 yr.(i)
Indiana	6 mos.	•					1 yr.		•		3 yrs.						30 days	30 days
Iowa	1 yr.	•																
Kansas	60 days	•			•	•	1 yr.	•	•	•	3 yrs.	•	•		•	(ad)		
Kentucky	180 days(y)	•															6 mos.(i)	6 mos.(i) (ag)
Louisiana	(z)		2 yrs.	(aa)	•		1 yr.								•			
Maine	6 mos.(o)	•			•	•		•	•	•	3 yrs.							
Maryland	(ab)		(ac)		•		3 yrs.	•	•	•	3 yrs.			2 yrs.	•			
Massachusetts	(ae)				•	•	1 yr.	•	•	•					•	(ad)		
Michigan	180 days(o)	•					1 yr.											
Minnesota	1 yr.(o)	•	180 days															
Mississippi	1 yr.				•	•	1 yr.	•	•		3 yrs.	•	•		•	(s,af)	6 mos.(i)	6 mos.(i) (ag)
Missouri	90 days	•					1 yr.			(al)						(s,af)		
Montana	90 days	•																
Nebraska	1 yr.	•					2 yrs.				2 yrs.					(ah,ai)		
Nevada	6 wks.(o)	•	1 yr.(u)								2 yrs.			2 yrs.		(aj)		
New Hampshire	1 yr.(o)	•			•	•	2 yrs.	•	•	(al)			•		•	(an,ai)		
New Jersey	1 yr.		18 mos.		•	•	1 yr.	•			2 yrs.				•	(aj)		
New Mexico	6 mos.	•			•	•	1 yr.				5 yrs.(ak)					(i)		(u)
New York	1 yr.(o)		1 yr.(h)	1 yr.	•	•	1 yr.		(ak)	(al)					(ak)			
North Carolina	6 mos.		1 yr.		•		1 yr.	•	•		3 yrs.							
North Dakota	1 yr.	•			•	•	1 yr.	•	•	•	4 yrs.				•			
Ohio	6 mos.		2 yrs.		•	•	1 yr.	•	•	(al)	5 yrs.	•	•		•	(p,an)	6 mos.	6 mos.
Oklahoma	6 mos.(ao)	•			•	•	1 yr.	•	•		5 yrs.	•	•		•	(p,an)	60 days	60 days
Oregon	6 mos.	•															6 mos.	6 mos. (aq)
Pennsylvania	1 yr.				•	•	2 yrs.		•	(al)	3 yrs.		•		•	(j,s,ap)		
Rhode Island	2 yrs.		3 yrs.		•	•	5 yrs.	•		•			•		•	(as,at)		
South Carolina	3 mos.(au)		3 yrs.		•	•	1 yr.	•		1 yr.					•			
South Dakota					•	•	1 yr.	•	•				•	7 yrs.	•			
Tennessee	6 mos.				•	•	1 yr.	1 yr.	•		5 yrs.				•	(x,av)		
Texas	6 mos.	•	3 yrs.		•	•	1 yr.				3 yrs.		•		•	(x,av)	30 days(i)	30 days(i)
Utah	3 mos.		3 yrs.(h)		•	•	1 yr.	•	•	1 yr.	(aw)				•			
Vermont	6 mos.(ax)		6 mos.	2 yrs.(u)	•	•	1 yr.				5 yrs.							

"Traditional" Grounds for Absolute Divorce

State or other Jurisdiction	Residence required before filing suit for divorce(c)	"No fault" divorce (a) Marriage breakdown (d)	Separation	Prior decree of limited divorce	Adultery	Mental and/or physical cruelty	Desertion	Alcoholism and/or drug addiction	Impotency	Non-support by husband	Insanity	Pregnancy at marriage	Un-explained absence	Bigamy	Felony conviction or imprisonment	Other	Plaintiff	Defendant
Virginia	6 mos.	•	1 yr.	(ay)	•	—	1 yr.	—	—	—	—	—	—	—	•	—	—	—
Washington	—	•	2 yrs.	—	•	•	1 yr.	—	—	—	3 yrs.	—	—	—	•	—	—	—
West Virginia	1 yr.(o)	—	1 yr.	—	•	•	1 yr.	1 yr.	—	—	—	—	—	—	•	—	—	—
Wisconsin	6 mos.	—	2 yrs.(az)	—	—	—	—	—	—	—	1 yr.	—	—	—	—	—	6 mos.	6 mos.
Wyoming	60 days(o)	—	—	—	•	•	1 yr.	—	—	—	2 yrs.	—	10 yrs.	—	•	(ba,bb)	—	—
District of Columbia	6 mos.	*(bc)	6 mos.(bc)	*(bd)	—	—	—	—	—	—	—	—	—	—	—	—	—	—
Puerto Rico	1 yr.(o)	—	2 yrs.	—	•	•	1 yr.	—	•	—	7 yrs.	—	—	—	•	(bf)	—	(bg)

Period before parties may remarry after final decree (f) — last two columns: Plaintiff, Defendant.

(a) "No fault" includes all proceedings where it is not necessary to prove one of the "traditional" grounds for divorce. In some states divorce can be obtained by the agreement of both parties; in others, unilaterally. (b) "Traditional" grounds enacted into English and American law during mid-1800s. (c) Local residence may also be required. (d) Expressed in statutes as irreconcilable breakdown of marriage relationship, irreconcilable differences, incompatibility, marriage insupportable because of discord, etc. (e) By another man; unknown to husband. (f) In contested divorce cases, many lawyers advise no remarriage until time for appeal has passed. (g) Two years for wife filing on grounds of nonsupport. (h) Under decree of separate maintenance and/or written separation agreement. (i) Crime against nature. (j) Except to each other. In Iowa, court can waive ban. (k) Three-month residency required before final judgment. (l) Grounds available to both party is resident for 6 months. (n) Incurable. (o) In some cases, a lesser period of time may be allowed. (p) Fraud, force, or duress. (q) Grounds indicated, along with basis for finding of marriage breakdown. (r) Mental incompetence. (s) Parties related by marriage or blood contrary to statute. (t) Mental incapacity at time of marriage. (u) In the discretion of the court. (v) After expiration of term of separation decree. (w) Loathsome disease. (x) Attempt on life of spouse by poison or other means showing malice. (y) No decree until parties have lived apart for 60 days. (z) Must be permanent residents (domiciliaries) of state and grounds must have occurred in state. (aa) Spouse who obtained separation may obtain absolute divorce 1 year after decree becomes final. One party may obtain divorce 1 year and 60 days from date of separation decree. (ab) One year if cause occurred out of state; 2 years for insanity. (ac) Voluntary living apart for 1 year and no reasonable expectation of reconciliation, or living separate and apart without cohabitation or interruption for 3 years. (ad) Any cause which renders marriage null and void from the outset. (ae) One year if grounds occurred outside of Commonwealth. (af) Insanity or idiocy at time of marriage not known to other party. (ag) When divorce is granted on grounds of adultery, court may prohibit remarriage. Disability may be removed after 1 year upon satisfactory evidence of reformation. (ah) Membership in religious sect not believing in marriage. (ai) Wife out of state 10 years without husband's consent. (aj) Deviant sexual contact without consent. (ak) Grounds for annulment. (al) Grounds for separation. (am) On petition of both spouses, accompanied by separation agreement executed and confirmed by both spouses in court appearance not less than 90 days after filing of petition. (an) Defendant obtained divorce from plaintiff in another state. (ao) Five years for insanity and spouse in out-of-state facility. (ap) Remarriage after 2 years upon false but well-founded rumor of death of spouse. (If first spouse reappears, he or she may seek divorce for bigamy within 6 months.) (aq) If divorce is granted for adultery, the guilty party cannot marry the accomplice in adultery during lifetime of former spouse. (ar) Shorter period in court's discretion. (as) Void or voidable marriage; in case party is deemed civilly dead from crime or other circumstances, party may be presumed dead. (at) Gross misbehavior or wickedness. (au) If both parties residents; 1 year if one is a nonresident. (av) Refusal by wife to move to state with husband. (aw) Adjudication of permanent and incurable insanity. (ax) Two years if grounds are insanity. (ay) Limited divorce granted on the grounds of cruelty, reasonable apprehension of bodily hurt, willful desertion, or abandonment may be merged into an absolute divorce after 1 year. (az) Two years' separation without material fault by plaintiff. (ba) Husband guilty of conduct constituting vagrancy. (bb) Conviction of felony before marriage. (bc) Voluntary separation, involuntary separation, 1 year. (bd) Granted for 6 months' voluntary separation, 1 year involuntary separation, adultery, or cruelty. (be) By mutual consent. (bf) Attempt by either parent to corrupt son or prostitute daughter, or proposal to prostitute wife. (bg) If remarriage before 301 days, she must present certificate showing pregnancy or nonpregnancy if she has given birth. If pregnant, former spouse presumed to be father.

MEDIAN DURATION OF U.S. MARRIAGES PRIOR TO DIVORCE OR ANNULMENT (in years)

SOURCE: National Center for Health Statistics

State*	1950	1960	1970	1978
Reporting States Average	5.3	7.1	6.7	6.6
Alabama	(NA)	5.3	5.3	4.9
Alaska	5.0	6.2	5.4	5.3
California	(NA)	6.8	6.6	8.4
Connecticut	(NA)	8.6	8.6	5.6
Georgia	(NA)	5.4	5.4	5.5
Hawaii	(NA)	6.3	7.2	5.5
Idaho	4.2	4.8	6.3	4.8
Illinois	(NA)	(NA)	6.6	6.3
Iowa	4.5	5.7	5.6	5.9
Kansas	(NA)	5.8	5.1	5.0
Kentucky	(NA)	(NA)	5.7	5.8
Maryland	(NA)	9.0	8.8	8.5
Michigan	(NA)	(NA)	7.0	7.0
Missouri	6.6	(NA)	5.4	5.1
Montana	5.2	(NA)	5.1	5.1
Nebraska	5.7	5.1	6.0	6.4
New York	(NA)	6.3	9.3	8.3
Ohio	(NA)	(NA)	6.3	6.0
Oregon	4.7	5.9	5.9	6.2
Pennsylvania	(NA)	9.2	8.1	7.7
Rhode Island	(NA)	(NA)	9.2	8.2
South Carolina	(NA)	6.3	5.6	6.9
South Dakota	4.8	6.3	5.5	5.6
Tennessee	4.6	4.7	5.6	5.5
Utah	(NA)	(NA)	5.0	5.0
Vermont	(NA)	8.3	8.3	7.7
Virginia	8.2	8.3	7.9	7.1
Wisconsin	(NA)	8.2	6.3	6.0
Wyoming	4.2	5.4	4.6	4.7

(NA) Not Available. *By reporting states only.

MARRIAGE LAWS: 1980

Source: Women's Bureau, U.S. Department of Labor and The Book of States, (1980-81), by the Council of State Governments

State	Age at Which Marriage Can be Contracted without Parental Consent		Age at Which Marriage Can be Contracted With Parental Consent		Blood Test and Other Medical Requirements Period between Examination and Issuance of License (days)	Scope of Medical Examination	Waiting Period Before Issuance of License	After Issuance of License
	Male	Female	Male	Female				
Alabama	18	18	17(a)	14(a)	30	(b)	—	—
Alaska	18	18	16(c)	16(c)	30	(b)	3 da.	—
Arizona	18	18	16(c)	16(c)	30	(b)	(d)	—
Arkansas	18	18	17(c)	16(c)	30	(b)	3 da.	—
California	18	18	18(a,c)	16(a,c)	30	(b,f,g,h)	—	—
Colorado	18	18	16(c)	16(c)	30	(b,g,i)	—	—
Connecticut	18	18	16(c)	16(c)	35	(b)	4 da.	—
Delaware	18	18	18(c)	16(c)	30	(b)	—	(k)
Florida	18	18	16(a,c)	16(a,c)	30	(b)	3 da.	—
Georgia	18(l)	18(l)	16(c,l)	16(c,l)	30	(b,f)	3 da.(m)	—
Hawaii	18	18	16	16(c)	30	(b)	—	—
Idaho	18	18	16(c)	16(c)	—	(g)	(o)	—
Illinois	18	18	16(c)	16(c)	15	(b,f)	3 da.	—
Indiana	18	18	17(c)	17(c)	30	(b,f)	3 da.	—
Iowa	18	18	16	16	20	(b)	3 da.	—
Kansas	18	18	18(c)	18(c)	30	(b)	3 da.	—
Kentucky	18	18	(a,q)	(a,q)	15	(b,f)	3 da.	—
Louisiana	18	18	18(c)	16(c)	10	(b)	—	72 hrs.
Maine	18	18	16(c)	16(c)	60	(b)	5 da.	—
Maryland	18	18	16(c)	16(c)	—	—	48 hrs.	—
Massachusetts	18	18	18(c)	18(c)	30	(b,g)	3 da.	—
Michigan	18	18	(r)	16	30	(b)	3 da.	—
Minnesota	18	18	18	16(s)	—	—	5 da.	—
Mississippi	21	21	17(c)	15(c)	30	(b)	3 da.	—
Missouri	18	18	15(c)	15(c)	15	(b)	3 da.	—
Montana	18	18	18(c)	18(c)	20	(b)	5 da.	3 da.
Nebraska	19	19	17	17	30	(b,g)	2 da.	—
Nevada	18	18	16(a,c)	16(a,c)	—	—	—	—
New Hampshire	18	18	14(s)	13(s)	30(t)	(b)	3 da.	—
New Jersey	18	18	16(c)	16(c)	30	(b)	72 hrs.	—
New Mexico	18	18	16(c)	16(c)	30	(b)	72 hrs.	—
New York	18	18	16	14(u)	30	(b,f)	—	24 da.(v)
North Carolina	18	18	16	16(c)	30	(b,g,w,x)	—	—
North Dakota	18	18	16	16	30	(b,y)	—	—
Ohio	18	18	18(c)	16(c)	30	(b)	5 da.	—
Oklahoma	18	18	16(c)	16(c)	30	(b)	(o)	—
Oregon	18	18	17	17	30	(b)	—	(z)
Pennsylvania	18	18	16(c)	16(c)	30	(b,aa)	3 da.	—
Rhode Island	18	18	18(c)	16(c)	40	(b,g,x)	—	—
South Carolina	18	18	16(c)	14(c)	—	—	24 hrs.	—
South Dakota	18	18	16(c)	16(c)	20	(b)	—	—
Tennessee	18	18	16(c)	16(c)	30	(b)	3 da.(ab)	—
Texas	18	18	14(c)	14(c)	21	(b)	—	—
Utah	18	18	16(a)	14(a)	30	(b)	—	—
Vermont	18	18	16(c)	16(c)	30	(b)	—	5 da.
Virginia	18	18	16(a,c)	16(a,c)	30	(b)	—	—
Washington	18	18	17(c)	17(c)	—	(b,x,ac)	3 da.	—
West Virginia	18	18	(q)	(q)	30	(b)	3 da.	—
Wisconsin	18	18	16	16	20	(b)	5 da.	—
Wyoming	19	19	17(c)	16(c)	30	(b)	—	—
District of Columbia	18	18	16(a)	16(a)	30	(b)	3 da.	—
Puerto Rico	21	21	18(c)	16(c)	10(ad)	(b,ac)	—	—

Note: Common law marriage is recognized in Alabama, Colorado, Georgia, Idaho, Iowa, Kansas, Montana, Ohio, Oklahoma, Pennsylvania, Rhode Island, South Carolina, Texas, and the District of Columbia. (a) Parental consent not required if previously married. (b) Venereal diseases. (c) Legal procedure for younger persons to obtain license. (d) Blood test must be on record at least 48 hours before issuance of license. (f) Sickle cell anemia. (g) Rubella immunity. (h) Tay-Sachs disease. (i) Rh factor (k) Residents, 24 hours; nonresidents, 96 hours. (l) Parental consent is not needed regardless of age in cases of pregnancy or when couple has a living child born out of wedlock. (m) Unless parties are 18 years of age or over, or woman is pregnant, or applicants are the parents of a living child born out of wedlock. (o) Three days if parties are under 18 years of age. (q) Non minimum age. (r) No provision in the law for parental consent for males. (s) Permission of judge also required. (t) Maximum period between blood test and date of intended marriage. (u) If under 16 years of age, consent of family court judge also required. (v) However, marriage may not be solemnized within 3 days of date on which specimen for blood test was taken. (w) Mental competence. (x) Tuberculosis. (y) Some marriages prohibited if a party is severely retarded. (z) License valid 3 days after application signed and valid for 30 days thereafter. (aa) Court order needed if party is weakminded, insane, or of unsound mind. (ab) May be waived if certain conditions are met. (ac) Affidavit of mental competence required. Also, no epilepsy in Puerto Rico. (ad) Maximum time from blood test to expiration of license.

SOCIAL SECURITY AND MEDICARE
SOURCE: U.S. Social Security Administration

The basic idea of social security is a simple one: during working years employees, their employers, and self-employed people pay social security contributions which are pooled in special trust funds. When earnings stop or are reduced because the worker retires, becomes disabled, or dies, monthly cash benefits are paid to replace part of the earnings the family has lost.

Part of the contributions made go into a separate hospital insurance trust fund so that when workers and their dependents reach 65 they will have help in paying their hospital bills. Medicare is available also to people under 65 who have been entitled to social security disability benefits for 2 years or more and to insured people of any age and their dependents who need a kidney transplant or dialysis treatment because of permanent kidney failure. Medical insurance, also available, helps pay doctors' bills and other medical expenses. This program is financed out of premiums partially paid for by those who are enrolled with the majority of the cost paid for by the Federal Government. Under present law, the Federal share can never be less than one-half the cost of the program. Starting July 1, 1981, enrollees pay $11.00 a month for this protection.

Nine out of 10 working people in the United States are now building protection for themselves and their families under social security.

FINANCING THE PROGRAMS

Federal retirement, survivors, and disability benefits and hospital insurance benefits are paid for by contributions based on earnings covered under social security.

If you are employed, you and your employer share the contributions. If you are self-employed, you pay contributions for retirement, survivors, and disability insurance at about 1½ times the rate for an employee. However, the hospital insurance contribution rate is the same for the employer, the employee, and the self-employed person.

As long as you have earnings that are covered by the law, you pay contributions regardless of your age and even if you are receiving social security benefits.

How Contributions Are Paid

If you are employed, your contribution is deducted from your wages each payday. Your employer sends it, with an equal amount as his own share of the contribution, to the Internal Revenue Service.

If you are self-employed and your net earnings are $400 or more in a year, you must report your earnings and pay your self-employment contribution each year when you file your individual income tax return. This is true even if you owe no income tax.

Your wages and self-employment income are entered on your individual record by the Social Security Administration. This record of your earnings will be used to determine your eligibility for benefits and the amount of cash benefits you will receive.

The maximum amount of earnings that can count for social security and on which you pay social security contributions is shown in the following table:

Year	Amount	Year	Amount
1937-50	$3,000	1974	13,200
1951-54	3,600	1975	14,100
1955-58	4,200	1976	15,300
1959-65	4,800	1977	16,500
1966-67	6,600	1978	17,700
1968-71	7,800	1979	22,900
1972	9,000	1980	25,900
1973	10,800	1981	29,700

Earnings over the maximums have been reported to your social security record, but cannot be used to figure your benefit rate.

When you work for more than one employer in a year and pay social security contributions on wages over the social security maximum, you may claim a refund of the excess contributions on your income tax return for that year.

If you work for only one employer and he deducts too much in contributions, you should apply to the employer for a refund. A refund is made only when more than the required amount of contributions has been paid. Questions about contributions or refunds should be directed to the Internal Revenue Service. These tables show the schedule of contributions rates now in the law:

SOCIAL SECURITY TAX RATES (in percent)

Year	OASI[*1]	DI[*2]	HI[3]	Total
Employers & employees, each				
1977	4.375	0.575	0.90	5.85
1978	4.275	.775	1.00	6.05
1979	4.330	.750	1.05	6.13
1980	4.520	.560	1.05	6.13
1981	4.700	.650	1.30	6.65
1982-84	4.575	.825	1.30	6.70
1985	4.750	.950	1.35	7.05
1986-89	4.750	.950	1.45	7.15
1990 & later	5.100	1.100	1.45	7.65
Self-employed				
1977	6.1850	0.8150	0.90	7.90
1978	6.0100	1.0900	1.00	8.10
1979	6.0100	1.0400	1.05	8.10
1980	6.2725	0.7750	1.05	8.10
1981	7.0250	0.9750	1.30	9.30
1982-84	6.8125	1.2375	1.30	9.35
1985	7.1250	1.4250	1.35	9.90
1986-89	7.1250	1.4250	1.45	10.00
1990 & later	7.6500	1.6500	1.45	10.75

*By allocation in law. [1]Old Age, Survivors Insurance. [2]Disability Insurance. [3]Hospital Insurance.

Social Security Cash Benefits

To get monthly cash payments for yourself and your family, or for your survivors to get payments in case of your death, you must first have credit for a certain amount of work under social security. This is measured in quarters of coverage. Credit may have been earned at any time after 1936.

In 1981, all employees and self-employed people earn one quarter of coverage for each $310 of their covered annual earnings. This quarter of coverage measure is increased each year to reflect increases in average wages. No more than 4 quarters can be earned for any year, regardless of total earnings.

For years before 1978, employees earned one quarter of coverage for a 3-month calendar quarter in which they were paid covered wages of $50 or more. Four quarters were counted for any year in which a person had $400 or more in self-employment income or in cash wages from farm work, or for any year a person had the maximum earnings that counted for social security.

You can be either fully or currently insured or both, depending on the total amount of credit you have for work under social security and the amount you have in the last 3 years.

If you stop working under social security before you have earned enough credit to be insured, no cash benefits will be payable to you. The earnings already credited to you will remain on your social security record; if you later return to work, regardless of your age, all your covered earnings will be considered.

Fully Insured

Just how much credit you must have to be fully insured depends upon the year you reach 62 or upon the date of your death or disability.

The amount of credit you will need is measured in quarters of coverage; but for convenience, the table on this page is given in years. The people in your social security office will be glad to give you further details if you have questions.

You are fully insured if you have credit for at least as many years as shown on the appropriate line of the following chart.

When you reach 62 or become disabled	You will be fully insured if you have credit for this much work
1975	6
1977	6½
1979	7
1981	7½
1983	8
1987	9
1991 or later	10

If you become disabled or die before reaching 62 you are fully insured if you have credit for ¼ year of work for each year after 1950 and up to the year of your disability or death. In counting the number of years after 1950, omit years before you were 22.

No one is fully insured with credit for less than 1½ years of work and no one needs more than 10 years of work to be fully insured.

Currently Insured

You will be currently insured if you have social security credit for at least 1½ years of work within the 3 years before you die. If you leave a widow or widower and young children, they are eligible for monthly benefits if you were currently insured.

AMOUNTS OF MONTHLY PAYMENTS

The amount of monthly social security benefits due you or your dependents or survivors is based on your average earnings under social security over a period of years.

The exact amount of your benefit cannot be figured until there is an application for benefits, and all of your earnings up to the time of the application are considered.

A worker who doesn't get any benefits before 65 and who delays his retirement past age 65 will get a special credit that can mean a larger benefit. The credit adds 1 percent for each year (¹⁄₁₂ of 1 percent for each month) from age 65 to age 72 (3 percent for people reaching 65 after 1981).

The law provides a special minimum benefit at retirement for some people who worked under social security more than 20 years. This provision helps people who had low incomes, but above a specified amount, in their working years. The amount of the special minimum depends on the number of years of coverage. For a worker retiring at 65 with 30 or more years of coverage, the minimum would be $289.00.

DISABILITY PAYMENTS

If you become disabled before 65, you and certain members of your family may be eligible for benefits.

Do not wait too long after you are disabled to apply for benefits; if you wait more than a year, you may lose benefits. Payments may begin with the 6th full month of disability.

If you are found eligible for disability insurance benefits, you will remain eligible as long as you are disabled. When you reach 65, your benefit will be changed to retirement payments at the same rate.

Who Is Considered Disabled?

A person is considered disabled only if he has a severe physical or mental condition which—

prevents him from working, and
is expected to last (or has lasted) for at least 12 months or is expected to result in death.

A person with a severe medical condition could be eligible even if he manages to do a little work.

How Much Work Credit Is Required for a Disabled Worker?

If you become disabled before you are 24, you need credit for 1½ years of work in the 3 years before you become disabled.

If you become disabled between 24 and 31, you need social security credits for half the time after you are 21 and before you become disabled.

To get disability benefits if you become disabled at 31 or later, you must be fully insured and have credit for 5 years of work out of the 10 years ending when you become disabled.

People who become disabled because of blindness can get benefits without having to meet the requirement of substantial recent work.

FAMILY PAYMENTS

Monthly payments can be made to certain dependents: *When the worker gets retirement or disability benefits; When the worker dies.*

These dependents are:

Unmarried children under 18, or between 18 and 22 if they are full-time students;

Unmarried children 18 or over who were severely disabled before they reached 22 and who continue to be disabled;

A wife, husband, widow, or widower regardless of age, if caring for a child under 18 or disabled and the child gets payments based on the worker's record;

A wife 62 or widow 60 or older, even if there are no children entitled to payments;

A widow 50 or older (or widower 50 or older) who becomes disabled not later than 7 years after the death of the worker or not later than 7 years after the end of entitlement to benefits as a widow or widower with a child;

A husband 62 or over or widower 60 or over;

Dependent parents 62 or over after a worker dies.

In addition to monthly benefits, a lump-sum payment of $255 may be made after the worker's death.

Payments may also be made to a divorced wife or husband at 62 or a surviving divorced wife or husband at 60 (or a disabled surviving divorced wife or husband 50 or older) if the marriage lasted at least 10 years.

Benefits also can be paid a dependent surviving divorced wife or husband at any age if she is caring for her deceased former husband's child under 18 or disabled who is entitled to benefits.

For more information about this provision, get in touch with your social security office.

Generally, a marriage must have lasted at least 1 year before dependents of a retired or disabled worker can get monthly benefits; survivors can get benefits in most cases if the marriage lasted at least 9 months.

Examples of monthly social security retirement payments for workers who reach 65 before 1980 (effective June 1980)

Average yearly earnings after 1950 covered by social security

Benefits can be paid to:	$923 or less	$3,000	$4,000	$5,000	$6,000	$8,000	$10,000*
Retired worker at 65	153.10	316.40	372.20	431.60	487.80	606.30	671.80
Wife or husband at 65	76.60	158.20	186.10	215.80	243.90	303.20	335.90
Wife under 65 and one child in her care	76.60	167.20	263.80	364.90	406.80	454.70	503.70
Maximum family payment	229.70	483.60	636.00	796.30	894.60	1061.00	1175.50

*The maximum retirement benefit generally payable to a worker who is 65 in 1981 is $677.00.

Amount of Your Family's Benefits

Cash benefits to your dependents, and to your survivors in case of your death, are figured from the amount of your retirement or disability benefit.

Permanently reduced benefits are received by:

Workers and their wives who choose to start receiving retirement benefits while they are between 62 and 65;
Widows and widowers who choose to start receiving benefits between 60 and 65 and
Disabled widows and disabled widowers 50 or older who receive benefits before they reach 65.

The amount of the reduction depends on the number of months they receive benefits before they reach 65. On the average, people who choose to get benefits early will collect about the same value in total benefits over the years, but in smaller installments to take account of the longer period during which they will be paid.

If a person is entitled to monthly benefits based on the social security records of two or more workers, he will receive no more than the largest of the benefits.

The lump-sum payment at a worker's death is $255.

Benefits Not Taxable

Social security benefits you receive are not subject to Federal income tax.

AN APPLICATION IS NECESSARY

Before payments can start, an application must be filed. When you are nearing 65 or if you become disabled, get in touch with your social security office.

It is important for you to inquire at your social security office 2 or 3 months before you reach 65, not only for the possibility of retirement benefits, but also for Medicare benefits, which are available whether or not you retire. If you wait until the month you reach 65 to apply for the medical insurance part of Medicare, you will lose at least one month of protection.

If you plan to retire *before* you reach 65, it is important to apply for benefits no later than the last day of the month you want benefits to begin. Generally, benefits payable for months before age 65 can start no earlier than the month you apply.

When a person who has worked under the social security law dies, some member of his family should get in touch with the social security office.

If you cannot come to the social security office write or telephone. A representative can arrange to visit you.

Long delay in filing an application can cause loss of some benefits, since back payments for monthly cash retirement or survivor benefits can be made for no more than 6 months.

An application for a lump-sum death payment must usually be made within 2 years of the worker's death.

HEALTH INSURANCE (MEDICARE)

Nearly all people 65 and over are eligible for health insurance protection under Medicare, including some people who do not have enough credit for work covered by social security to qualify for monthly cash benefits.

Medicare also covers people who have been getting disability checks for 2 years or more and insured people and their dependents who need a kidney transplant or dialysis treatment because of permanent kidney failure.

There are two parts to Medicare: hospital insurance and, for those who choose, medical insurance.

Eligibility for Hospital Insurance

If you are 65 or over and are entitled to social security or railroad retirement benefits or if you are disabled and have been getting disability for 2 consecutive years or more, you are automatically eligible for hospital insurance; if you are not entitled to either of these benefits, you should ask about hospital insurance and medical insurance at your social security office.

People 65 or older who are not automatically entitled to hospital insurance can buy this protection for a monthly premium of $89 for the 12-month period starting July 1, 1981, although you will also have to purchase medical insurance.

After you establish your eligibility, you receive a health insurance card, which shows that you have hospital insurance, medical insurance, or both.

YOUR HOSPITAL INSURANCE

. Hospital insurance will help pay the cost of covered services for the following hospital and follow-up care:

Up to 90 days of hospital care in a participating hospital during a "benefit period."[1] For the first 60 days of care in 1981, your hospital insurance will pay all but the first $204 of expenses. For the 61 through the 90th day of care, your hospital insurance will pay all but $51 daily for covered services. (There is a lifetime limit of payment for 190 days of care in mental hospitals.)
You also have 60 reserve days which can be used after you have exhausted your 90 days of hospital care in a "benefit period." Reserve days are not replaced after you use them. Hospital insurance pays all but $102 a day of your covered expenses during the reserve days.

Hospital insurance in many cases also pays for up to 100 days of care in a participating skilled nursing facility after a hospital stay. Hospital insurance pays for all covered services for the first 20 days of care and all but $25.50 per day for up to 80 more days.

Up to 100 home health "visits" from a participating home health agency when prescribed by your physician may also be covered (effective July 1981, number of visits unlimited).

WHAT YOUR MEDICAL INSURANCE PAYS

Anyone who is 65 or older *or* entitled to hospital insurance is eligible for medical insurance. People who get monthly social security or railroad retirement benefits are automatically enrolled in medical insurance—unless they say they don't want it—at the same time they become entitled to hospital insurance. Other eligible people must apply for medical insurance at a social security office.

You will have protection at the earliest possible time if you enroll during the 3-month period just before the month you first become eligible for medical insurance. You may also enroll the month you become eligible and during the 3 following months, but your protection will not start until 1 to 3 months after that.

Anyone who declines enrollment in Medicare medical insurance during the initial enrollment period can enroll at any time. The premium will be 10 percent higher for each full year a person could have had medical insurance but didn't choose to.

Medical insurance is financed with monthly premiums paid by those who are enrolled and by the Federal Government. The basic medical insurance premium is currently $11.00 a month for the 12-month period starting July 1, 1981.

If you wish to drop your medical insurance, you may give notice to do so at any time. You can re-enroll at any time.

YOUR MEDICAL INSURANCE

Generally, your medical insurance will pay 80 percent of the reasonable charges for the following services after the first $60 in a calendar year.

Physicians' and surgeons' services, no matter where you receive the services—in the doctor's office, in a clinic, in a hospital, or at home. (You do not have to meet the $60 deductible before your medical insurance will pay for X-ray or laboratory services of physicians when you are a bed patient in a hospital. The full reasonable charge will be paid, instead of 80 percent only if the physician accepts assignment.) Home health services even if you have not been in a hospital—effective July 1981, the number of visits is unlimited. (Medical insurance pays the reasonable cost after you meet the $60 deductible.)

A number of other medical and health services, such as diagnostic tests, surgical dressings and splints, and rental or purchase of medical equipment.

Outpatient physical therapy services—whether or not you are homebound—furnished under supervision of a participating hospital, skilled nursing facility, home health agency, approved clinic, rehabilitation agency, or public health agency. All outpatient services of a participating hospital, including diagnostic tests or treatments.

Certain services by podiatrists (but not routine foot care or treatment of flat feet or partial dislocation). Limited services by chiropractors.

---

[1] A "benefit period" begins the first time you enter a hospital after your hospital insurance starts. It ends after you have not been an inpatient for 60 days in a row in any hospital or in any facility that mainly provides skilled nursing or rehabilitation services.

For More Medicare Information

For more information on the health insurance programs, get in touch with your social security office and ask for a copy of the leaflet, "A brief explanation of Medicare."

MEDICAID

Both Medicare and Medicaid are part of the Social Security Act. They differ, however, in that the former is an insurance program intended to help those 65 (and some disabled people under 65), while Medicaid is designed for certain kinds of needy and low-income people: the aged (65 or older), the blind, the disabled, members of families with dependent children, and other cases involving children.

Medicaid programs, paid for by money from federal, state, and local taxes, were available in all states except Arizona as of April 1974. Under these programs, payment is made for at least the following services: inpatient hospital care; outpatient hospital services; other laboratory and X-ray services; skilled nursing home services; physicians' services; the screening, diagnosis, and treatment of children; and home health care services.

Medicaid can pay what Medicare does not pay for people who are eligible for both programs. For example, Medicaid can pay the $204 deductible amount for the first 60 days of hospital care under hospital insurance, and the $51 a day for the next 30 days of care. Medicaid also can pay the $60 deductible and the monthly premium for medical insurance.

OLD-AGE, SURVIVORS, AND DISABILITY INSURANCE PROGRAM

PROJECTED EXPENDITURES, INCOME, AND LEVEL OF THE COMBINED OASI AND DI TRUST FUNDS AFTER THE SOCIAL SECURITY AMENDMENTS OF 1977
(in billions)

Calendar Year	Expenditures	Income	Net increase in funds	Funds at beginning of year	Funds at beginnning of year as a percentage of outgo during year
1977	$ 87.6	$ 82.1	$ −5.5	$ 41.1	47%
1978	97.2	92.4	− 4.8	35.6	37
1979	106.9	106.5	− 0.4	30.8	29
1980	117.1	119.1	2.0	30.4	26
1981	127.4	137.1	9.6	32.4	25
1982	138.3	150.2	11.9	42.0	30
1983	149.2	161.3	12.1	53.9	36
1984	161.2	172.9	11.7	66.0	41
1985	174.0	194.2	20.1	77.7	45
1986	187.6	209.0	21.4	97.9	52
1987	202.0	223.7	21.7	119.3	59

SOCIAL SECURITY: 1985-2050 A.D.

SOURCE: Social Security Administration

Note: Social Security is not true insurance because reserves are not built up against all future liabilities. Due to its governmental status the administrators try only to insure that income for a given year is enough to pay all expenses and to add a certain percentage to the Social Security trust fund (they try to keep the fund equal to the sum of all payments the previous year).

In order to keep payments and the trust fund at the proper levels over a long period, the administrators compute probable benefit payments (outgo) and then determine what income will be necessary to make the payments. Because of fluctuations in employment, inflation, and population rates, both figures are very difficult

to compute, but the table below shows the product of all the administrators' computations. In essence it shows the percentage of taxable payroll required to pay off Social Security obligations in any year. This may sound complicated, but it is not. In order to clarify it, let's look at one year; 1985: in that year it will take a total of 11.16 percent of the taxable payroll (roughly $1,116 for a worker earning $10,000) to keep the system solvent. (This means that for everyone receiving $4,000 in benefits, there will be 4 workers earning $10,000 and paying a tax of $1,000.)

NOTE: each worker would not pay entire $1,000; it is divided equally between employee and employer. The table takes into account how many workers there will be, how much they'll be making, the effects of population change on the number of people eligible for benefits, etc.

OLD-AGE, SURVIVORS, AND DISABILITY INSURANCE AND MEDICARE PROGRAMS

PROJECTED EXPENDITURES, TAX INCOME, AND NET DIFFERENCES EXPRESSED AS A PERCENTAGE OF TAXABLE PAYROLL[1]

Year	Old-Age and Survivors Insurance Expend.	Income	Disability Insurance Expend.	Income	Medicare Hospital Insurance Expend.	Income	Total for OASDHI Expend.	Income	Medicare Supplementary Medical Ins. Expenditures[2]
1977	9.39	8.75	1.50	1.15	1.99	1.80	12.88	11.70	0.85
1980	8.63	8.66	1.48	1.50	2.22	2.10	12.33	12.26	0.96
1985	8.79	9.50	1.66	1.90	2.98	2.70	13.43	14.10	1.28
1990	8.71	10.20	1.87	2.20	3.76	2.90	14.34	15.30	1.64
1995	8.68	10.20	2.07	2.20	4.52	2.90	15.27	15.30	1.90
2000	8.63	10.20	2.34	2.20	5.27	2.90	16.24	15.30	2.00
2025	13.49	10.20	2.91	2.20	7.44[3]	2.90	23.84	15.30	2.63
2050	13.35	10.20	2.82	2.20	7.61[3]	2.90	23.78	15.30	2.52

[1]The effective taxable payroll is slightly different for OASDI and HI because of the tax treatment of self-employed persons; however, it does not materially affect the comparisons. In 1977, taxable payroll represented about 85 percent of total earnings in covered employment; in 1981 and later the corresponding percentage will be approximately 91 percent.

[2]Expenditures are approximately equal to total income from premiums and general revenue for the Medicare-SMI program. Although the Medicare-SMI program is not financed by payroll taxes, its cost is shown for comparison as a percentage of payroll which is taxable for HI purposes. Figures after 1977 are based upon unpublished estimates.

[3]Based upon unpublished estimates. For the purpose of this comparison, it was assumed that after the year 2000 medical care unit cost increases would be equal to average wage increases in covered employment.

DISADVANTAGED: A DEFINITION

The level of family income used to determine whether or not a person is poor has been raised an average of $920 by the U.S. Department of Labor to reflect increases in consumer prices over the past year.

The revised poverty-level guidelines for metropolitan area and farm families became effective March 11, 1981, based on the Office of Management and Budget (OMB) recommendations.

Income levels for families of one through six persons are:

Family Size	Income: Nonfarm*	Income: Farm*
1	$ 4,310	$3,680
2	5,690	4,850
3	7,070	6,020
4	8,450	7,190
5	9,830	8,360
6	11,210	9,530

* For Continental U.S.

Income limits for families of more than six persons may be determined by adding for the nonfarm and farm levels these amounts for each additional person: $1,380 and $1,170 for the Continental U.S.

The OMB poverty levels, in conjunction with the Lower Living Standard Income Levels for local areas set by the Bureau of Labor Statistics and based on family income data, are used by CETA administrators to determine eligibility for CETA programs. The higher figure is the one used. The revised Lower Living Standard Income Levels will be issued for localities later.

The eligibility requirements for most CETA programs include the definition of "economically disadvantaged" containing provisions incorporating the OMB income poverty levels and the Lower Living Standard income levels.

The Labor Department's Employment and Training Administration (ETA) partially defines an economically disadvantaged person as one who is a member of a family whose income during the previous six months on an annualized basis does not exceed the poverty level or 70 percent of the lower living standard income level—whichever is higher.

POVERTY IN THE UNITED STATES

SOURCE: Bureau of the Census (numbers in millions)

	Number below Poverty Level				Percent below Poverty Level			
Year	Total	White	Black and Other Races	Black Only	Total	White	Black and Other Races	Black Only
1979	25.3	16.8	8.5	7.6	11.6	8.9	28.6	30.9
1978	24.5	16.3	8.2	7.6	11.4	8.7	22.8	30.6
1977	24.7	16.4	8.3	7.7	11.6	8.9	29.0	31.3
1976	25.0	16.7	8.3	7.6	11.8	9.1	29.4	31.1
1975	25.9	17.8	8.1	7.5	12.3	9.7	29.3	31.3
1974	23.4	15.7	7.6	7.2	11.2	8.6	28.3	30.3
1973	23.0	15.1	7.8	7.4	11.1	8.4	29.6	31.4
1972	24.5	16.2	8.3	7.7	11.9	9.0	31.9	33.3
1971	25.6	17.8	7.8	7.4	12.5	9.9	30.9	32.5
1970	25.4	17.5	7.9	7.5	12.6	9.9	32.0	33.5
1965	33.2	22.5	10.7	NA	17.3	13.3	47.1	NA

FACTS ABOUT THE POOR

SOURCE: Community Services Administration

Based on 1980 population and 1979 income, there were 25,214,000 poor persons. Despite the fact that two out of every three poor persons are white, the incidence of poverty among non-whites was 28.6% as compared to 8.9% for whites. Children under 18 years of age make up 39.9% of the poor.

Between 1978 and 1979 the number of poor persons increased by 717,000. At the same time the number of poor persons aged 65 years and over increased by 351,000. (These are included in the 717,000.)

For the 5,292,000 poor families, the average income deficit in 1979 was $2,697. For the 5,575,000 poor unrelated individuals, the deficit averaged $1,488. (Average income deficit is the amount of income below the income poverty level, which for 1980 for a non-farm family of four was $7,450 and for a farm family of four was $6,340.) In order to bring all the poor to the poverty income level, a total direct payment would be required of $22,568,124,000.

POVERTY IN AMERICA BY STATES

SOURCE: Bureau of Census

State	Thousands of Poor Persons 1969*	1975	State	Thousands of Poor Persons 1969*	1975	State	Thousands of Poor Persons 1969*	1975
Total	27,125	23,991	Kentucky	718	596	North Dakota	93	66
Alabama	857	587	Louisiana	933	720	Ohio	1,041	997
Alaska	35	23	Maine	131	126	Oklahoma	465	370
Arizona	264	314	Maryland	387	313	Oregon	235	204
Arkansas	523	392	Massachusetts	473	408	Pennsylvania	1,228	1,133
California	2,153	2,192	Michigan	819	821	Rhode Island	100	80
Colorado	263	230	Minnesota	398	324	South Carolina	595	478
Connecticut	212	204	Mississippi	767	607	South Dakota	120	88
Delaware	58	47	Missouri	672	565	Tennessee	836	660
District of Columbia	123	86	Montana	92	86	Texas	2,047	1,870
Florida	1,068	1,225	Nebraska	188	147	Utah	118	103
Georgia	924	883	Nevada	43	53	Vermont	52	63
Hawaii	69	67	New Hampshire	65	126	Virginia	691	513
Idaho	92	85	New Jersey	574	586	Washington	336	299
Illinois	1,112	1,150	New Mexico	227	223	West Virginia	380	270
Indiana	493	424	New York	1,986	1,671	Wisconsin	421	352
Iowa	319	225	North Carolina	996	788	Wyoming	38	33
Kansas	275	178						

*Source: 1970 Census Fourth Count Summary Tapes

AID TO FAMILIES WITH DEPENDENT CHILDREN

Source: U.S. Department of Health, Education and Welfare (Data for December 1980)

State	NUMBER OF RECIPIENTS			PAYMENTS TO RECIPIENTS	Average per–		Percentage change from Dec. 1979	
	Families	Total	Children	Total	Family	Recipient	Recipients	Amount
Total[1]	3,841,208	11,101,556	7,600,455	$1,106,656,020	$288.10	$ 99.68	7.0	14.8
Ala.	63,246	178,322	127,684	6,967,928	110.17	39.07	– .4	.9
Alaska	6,606	15,931	10,882	2,590,514	392.15	162.61	5.5	31.3
Ariz.	21,573	59,809	43,589	3,809,666	176.59	63.70	19.7	26.8
Ark.	29,822	85,008	61,667	4,360,856	146.23	51.30	.4	3.1
Calif.	511,486	1,498,216	996,054	220,451,580	431.00	147.14	10.1	27.8
Colo.	29,467	81,031	55,415	7,591,646	257.63	93.69	8.9	17.8
Conn.	49,407	139,685	96,240	18,308,524	370.57	131.07	2.9	14.7
Del.	12,404	34,243	23,555	2,817,520	227.15	82.28	5.1	5.9
D.C.	30,278	81,985	56,556	7,661,257	253.03	93.45	– 5.1	– 4.4
Fla.	103,315	279,392	199,015	18,229,236	176.44	65.25	12.8	16.0
Ga.	89,912	233,730	168,813	12,591,009	140.04	53.87	8.5	23.4
Guam	1,492	5,311	3,877	316,333	212.02	59.56	12.4	15.6
Hawaii	20,046	61,342	40,802	7,731,955	385.71	126.05	2.2	3.7
Idaho	7,503	20,326	13,845	2,064,949	275.22	101.59	– .9	3.0
Ill.	222,937	691,434	482,773	62,903,873	282.16	90.98	4.6	8.4
Ind.	60,229	170,239	119,431	12,351,154	205.07	72.55	11.8	23.5
Iowa	40,476	111,287	73,907	12,553,542	310.15	112.80	13.6	15.3
Kans.	27,720	71,956	50,828	7,817,479	282.02	108.64	11.3	19.3
Ky.	67,159	175,071	122,437	12,478,662	185.81	71.28	6.7	22.5
La.	72,163	218,966	160,212	11,254,465	155.96	51.40	4.1	19.1
Maine	21,466	57,700	39,504	4,954,190	230.79	85.86	– 5.1	– .9
Md.	80,823	220,316	148,989	19,304,624	238.85	87.62	5.0	17.5
Mass.	125,232	347,830	226,570	43,793,572	349.70	125.91	– 1.2	7.2
Mich.	246,648	752,578	494,459	96,243,119	390.20	127.88	16.4	21.3
Minn.	53,856	145,634	96,383	18,582,462	345.04	127.60	11.9	20.0
Miss.	59,814	176,253	129,704	5,257,257	87.89	29.83	2.8	5.8
Mo.	73,506	215,682	144,865	16,795,310	228.49	77.87	12.9	24.1
Mont.	7,136	19,883	13,621	1,646,790	230.77	82.82	8.7	12.0
Nebr.	13,573	37,541	25,900	3,890,757	286.65	103.64	10.6	24.8
Nev.	5,114	13,827	9,524	1,096,034	214.32	79.27	23.9	35.7
N.H.	8,647	23,648	15,636	2,377,068	274.90	100.52	9.7	17.2
N.J.[1]	152,383	469,010	322,034	49,908,100	327.52	106.41	2.8	13.1
N.M.	19,550	56,157	38,657	3,705,145	189.52	65.98	7.8	21.9
N.Y.	367,628	1,109,601	762,672	136,745,976	371.97	123.24	1.3	1.9
N.C.	80,074	201,828	142,638	13,014,235	162.53	64.48	4.3	5.5
N.D.	4,859	13,111	9,045	1,413,489	290.90	107.81	3.2	9.9
Ohio	200,243	572,347	380,365	50,348,940	251.44	87.97	16.9	16.9
Okla.	31,543	91,984	66,752	7,880,651	249.84	85.67	5.5	6.4
Oreg.	35,440	93,993	60,731	9,315,930	262.86	99.11	– 4.3	– 23.5
Pa.[1]	218,713	637,387	435,408	64,712,837	295.88	101.53	2.6	9.1
P.R.	46,245	169,697	118,368	2,812,545	60.82	16.57	– 2.9	14.9
R.I.	18,772	53,950	36,563	7,613,825	405.59	141.13	7.3	8.7
S.C.	57,643	156,080	110,573	6,685,505	115.98	42.83	4.5	21.8
S.D.	6,946	18,753	13,120	1,555,186	223.90	82.93	– 7.1	– 1.8
Tenn.	65,958	173,854	122,637	7,448,916	112.93	42.85	10.2	10.7
Texas	106,104	320,002	232,384	11,490,205	108.29	35.91	4.5	4.6
Utah	13,954	43,710	27,335	4,504,653	322.82	103.06	25.9	33.8
Vt.	8,129	24,251	15,379	2,839,074	349.25	117.07	14.7	21.2
V.I.	1,165	3,441	2,721	228,534	196.17	66.41	13.3	57.6
Va.	65,272	175,927	121,821	14,487,213	221.95	82.35	7.8	19.1
Wash.	61,639	173,339	108,234	23,434,682	380.19	135.20	20.9	27.2
W. Va.	28,026	79,971	60,820	4,970,373	177.35	62.15	3.8	5.6
Wis.	85,129	231,979	154,465	32,026,663	376.21	138.06	15.2	26.7
Wyo.	2,737	7,008	4,996	720,012	263.07	102.74	6.5	8.3

[1] Estimated data.

DRUG LAW ENFORCEMENT   Source: Drug Enforcement Administration (DEA)

Item	STATE AND LOCAL ARRESTS				DEA FEDERAL ARRESTS			
	1976	1977	1978	1979	1976	1977	1978	1979
Number of Arrests	500,540	569,293	596,940	519,377	9,240	9,369	7,433	7,943
Arrest Rate per 100,000	285.2	298.4	283.3	253.8				
Estimated % by Drug								
Narcotics (heroin, cocaine)	9.9%	13.2%	13.2%	12.2%	56.8%	64.8%	61.2%	55.3%
Cannabis	72.4%	71.2%	70.9%	70.0%	29.5%	18.2%	20.9%	21.3%
Dangerous Drug	3.0%	15.6%	15.9%	17.8%	13.3%	16.5%	17.2%	21.2%
Other	14.7%	–	–	–	0.4%	.5%	.7%	2.2%
Estimated % by Race								
White	77.0%	77.0%	76.5%	76.7%	82.5%	80.6%	80.1%	81.2%
Nonwhite	22.9%	22.9%	23.5%	23.3%	17.1%	19.4%	19.9%	18.8%
Estimated % by Age								
Under 21	52.4%	50.7%	50.4%	48.3%	9.3%	8.2%	5.6%	6.2%
21-24	76.1%	23.2%	23.0%	23.6%	29.8%	26.5%	16.7%	18.2%
25-29	14.0%	14.5%	14.3%	15.0%	27.3%	28.4%	27.6%	26.7%
30-39	7.2%	8.4%	6.3%	9.6%	22.6%	25.2%	34.1%	32.9%
40 or Older	2.5%	3.2%	6.0%	3.5%	10.9%	12.1%	16.0%	16.0%
Estimated % by Sex								
Male	86.4%	86.1%	86.3%	85.5%	85.6%	85.8%	87.2%	87.7%
Female	13.6%	13.9%	13.7%	13.5%	14.4%	14.2%	12.8%	14.3%

DRUGS: USES AND ABUSES
Source: Smith Kline & French

Drugs	Pharmacologic Classification	Federal Controls	Medical Use	Potential for Physical Dependence	How Taken When Abused	Comments
Morphine (an opium derivative)	Central Nervous System Depressant	Narcotic: Schedule II Controlled Substances Act of 1970	To relieve pain	Yes	Orally or by injection	Morphine is the standard against which other narcotic analgesics are compared. Legally available on prescription only.
Heroin (a morphine derivative)	Depressant	Narcotic: Schedule I C. S. A. of 1970	To relieve pain	Yes	Sniffed or by injection	Not legally available in the United States. Used medically in some countries for relief of pain.
Codeine (an opium derivative)	Depressant	Narcotic C. S. A. of 1970	To relieve pain and coughing	Yes	Orally (usually as cough syrup)	Preparations containing specified minimal amounts of codeine are classified as "exempt" narcotics (Schedule V) and can be obtained without prescription in some states.
Paregoric (preparation containing opium)	Depressant	Narcotic: Schedule II C. S. A. of 1970	For sedation and to counteract diarrhea	Yes	Orally or by injection	Paregoric is often boiled to concentrate narcotic content prior to injection. Prescription only.
Meperidine (synthetic morphine-like drug)	Depressant	Narcotic: Schedule II C. S. A. of 1970	To relieve pain	Yes	Orally or by injection	Shorter acting than morphine. Frequent cosing required. Withdrawal symptoms appear quickly. Prescription only.
Methadone (synthetic morphine-like drug)	Depressant	Narcotic: Schedule II C. S. A. of 1970	To relieve pain	Yes	Orally or by injection	Longer acting than morphine. Withdrawal symptoms develop more slowly and are less intense and more prolonged. Prescription only.
Cocaine	Central Nervous System Stimulant	Schedule II C. S. A. of 1970	Local anesthetic	No	Sniffed or by injection	Available legally only for research.
Marijuana	Hallucinogen	Schedule I	No	No	Smoked or orally	
Barbiturates (e.g., amobarbital, pentobarbital, secobarbital)	Depressant	Schedule II and III C. S. A. of 1970	For sedation, sleep-producing, epilepsy, high blood pressure	Yes	Orally or by injection	Written prescription only. No refills for Schedule II barbiturates. For Schedule III barbiturates original prescription expires after 6 months. Only 5 refills permitted within this period. Dependence generally occurs only with the use of high doses for a protracted period of time.
Amphetamine drugs (e.g., amphetamine, dextroamphetamine, methamphetamine—also known as desoxyephedrine)	Stimulant	Schedule II C. S. A. of 1970	For antiappetite, narcolepsy, hyperkinetic behavior disorders	No	Orally or by injection	Written prescription only. No refills permitted.
LSD (also mescaline, peyote, psilocybin, DMT, STP, THC)	Hallucinogen	Schedule I C. S. A. of 1970	Medical research only	No	Orally or by injection	

U.S. INDEX OF CRIME Source: Federal Bureau of Investigation

	Total	Violent	Property	Murder	Forcible Rape	Robbery	Aggravated Assault	Burglary	Larceny-Theft	Motor Vehicle Theft
TRENDS BY GEOGRAPHIC REGION (Percent change, 1980 over 1979)										
Northeastern States	+ 8	+12	+ 8	+ 5	+ 5	+19	+ 5	+14	+ 5	+ 3
North Central States	+ 9	+12	+ 8	+ 4	+ 5	+23	+ 5	+14	+ 8	− 3
Southern States	+11	+13	+11	+ 6	+12	+19	+ 9	+16	+10	+ 4
Western States	+10	+14	+ 9	+15	+12	+19	+10	+12	+ 9	+ 3
TOTAL	+10	+13	+ 9	+ 7	+ 9	+20	+ 8	+14	+ 8	+ 2
TRENDS BY YEARS (Percent change 1968-1980, each year over previous year)										
1970/1969	+ 9	+12	+ 9	+ 8	+ 2	+17	+ 8	+11	+ 9	+ 6
1971/1970	+ 6	+11	+ 6	+11	+11	+11	+10	+ 9	+ 5	+ 2
1972/1971	− 4	+ 2	− 5	+ 5	+11	− 3	+ 7	− 1	− 6	− 6
1973/1972	+ 6	+ 5	+ 6	+ 5	+10	+ 2	+ 7	+ 8	+ 5	+ 5
1974/1973	+18	+11	+18	+ 5	+ 8	+15	+ 8	+18	+21	+ 5
1975/1974	+10	+ 5	+10	− 1	+ 1	+ 5	+ 6	+ 7	+14	+ 2
1976/1975	0	− 4	+ 1	− 8	+ 1	−10	+ 1	− 5	+ 5	− 4
1977/1976	− 3	+ 2	− 4	+ 2	+11	− 4	+ 6	− 1	− 6	+ 1
1978/1977	+ 2	+ 5	+ 2	+ 2	+ 7	+ 3	+ 7	+ 2	+ 1	+ 2
1979/1978	+ 9	+11	+ 9	+10	+13	+12	+10	+ 6	+10	+11
1980/1979	+10	+13	+ 9	+ 7	+ 9	+20	+ 8	+14	+ 8	+ 2

CRIME: U.S. CITIES (Offenses Known to the Police, 1979 and 1980)
Source: Federal Bureau of Investigation

Preliminary figures for cities over 100,000 population reporting more than 11,000 incidents.

City	Crime Index 1979	Crime Index 1980	City	Crime Index 1979	Crime Index 1980
Akron, Ohio	16,258	18,448	Miami, Fla.	37,180	52,540
Albuquerque, N. Mex.	27,341	29,326	Milwaukee, Wis.	38,370	41,446
Anaheim, Calif.	17,009	17,131	Minneapolis, Minn.	32,406	35,820
Anchorage, Alaska	11,848	11,724	Mobile, Ala.	16,580	21,034
Arlington, Texas	9,979	11,341	Montgomery, Ala.	11,196	12,852
Atlanta, Ga.	58,724	55,949	Nashville, Tenn.	28,612	34,886
Austin, Texas	27,237	30,067	New Haven, Conn.	17,602	17,834
Baltimore, Md.	73,744	76,704	New Orleans, La.	52,479	53,575
Baton Rouge, La.	23,924	26,226	New York, N.Y.	621,110	710,153
Beaumont, Texas	10,050	11,346	Norfolk, Va.	19,907	20,183
Berkeley, Calif.	12,765	13,000	Oklahoma City, Okla.	33,577	36,191
Birmingham, Ala.	31,862	35,403	Omaha, Nebr.	24,352	24,430
Bridgeport, Conn.	12,358	15,627	Orlando, Fla.	14,022	17,532
Buffalo, N.Y.	26,975	29,086	Paterson, N.J.	10,988	14,260
Charlotte, N.C.	22,984	26,196	Peoria, Ill.	12,054	12,129
Chattanooga, Tenn.	13,362	16,098	Philadelphia, Pa.	82,586	101,145
Chicago, Ill.	186,728	196,605	Phoenix, Ariz.	75,147	88,523
Cincinnati, Ohio	33,120	32,987	Pittsburgh, Pa.	27,958	30,399
Cleveland, Ohio	51,994	57,602	Portland, Ore.	36,078	40,833
Colorado Springs, Colo.	14,871	16,910	Providence, R.I.	12,652	14,317
Columbia, S.C.	10,931	13,944	Richmond, Va.	18,828	21,493
Columbus, Ohio	50,605	55,362	Riverside, Calif.	13,675	15,626
Corpus Christi, Texas	17,544	19,385	Rochester, N.Y.	28,287	28,990
Dallas, Texas	93,761	106,010	Rockford, Ill.	11,594	12,751
Dayton, Ohio	25,036	26,593	Sacramento, Calif.	31,652	34,699
Denver, Colo.	51,990	58,745	St. Louis, Mo.	57,213	64,631
Des Moines, Iowa	17,424	19,369	St. Paul, Minn.	21,001	22,134
Detroit, Mich.	110,725	127,423	St. Petersburg, Fla.	18,021	21,067
El Paso, Texas	26,439	27,065	Salt Lake City, Utah	17,453	19,086
Flint, Mich.	20,147	21,208	San Antonio, Texas	54,981	57,873
Fort Lauderdale, Fla.	19,309	20,955	San Bernardino, Calif.	14,196	16,392
Fort Wayne, Ind.	13,611	15,101	San Diego, Calif.	72,093	70,505
Fort Worth, Texas	42,690	48,492	San Francisco, Calif.	70,745	70,424
Fresno, Calif.	23,265	24,806	San Jose, Calif.	43,309	51,831
Gary, Ind.	11,660	12,446	Santa Ana, Calif.	16,992	19,033
Grand Rapids, Mich.	14,624	16,185	Savannah, Ga.	14,204	14,656
Greensboro, N.C.	10,301	12,470	Seattle, Wash.	46,339	53,294
Hartford, Conn.	20,643	23,392	Shreveport, La.	15,376	18,784
Hollywood, Fla.	11,547	12,810	South Bend, Ind.	10,161	11,433
Honolulu, Hawaii	52,926	57,718	Spokane, Wash.	15,685	16,437
Huntsville, Ala.	11,936	13,044	Springfield, Mass.	13,397	14,410
Indianapolis, Ind.	35,105	37,220	Springfield, Mo.	12,504	13,472
Jacksonville, Fla.	39,349	42,890	Stockton, Calif.	13,753	16,502
Jersey City, N.J.	16,670	19,245	Syracuse, N.Y.	14,963	13,828
Kansas City, Kansas	16,199	17,495	Tacoma, Wash.	14,324	16,516
Kansas City, Mo.	42,065	49,275	Tampa, Fla.	31,687	38,903
Knoxville, Tenn.	11,237	12,423	Tempe, Ariz.	9,397	11,046
Las Vegas, Nev.	34,133	41,405	Toledo, Ohio	32,603	34,047
Lexington, Ky.	13,537	15,562	Tucson, Ariz.	30,799	35,945
Lincoln, Nebr.	9,601	11,261	Tulsa, Okla.	27,431	32,016
Long Beach, Calif.	28,957	32,314	Virginia Beach, Va.	13,540	15,069
Los Angeles, Calif.	258,635	293,838	Washington, D.C.	56,430	63,666
Louisville, Ky.	18,892	20,072	Wichita, Kans.	20,391	24,562
Lubbock, Texas	13,332	13,492	Winston-Salem, N.C.	12,221	12,973
Madison, Wis.	13,663	14,796	Worcester, Mass.	12,573	12,978
Memphis, Tenn.	44,499	50,921	Yonkers, N.Y.	10,420	11,522
Mesa, Ariz.	10,948	12,098			

CAPITAL PUNISHMENT

ABOLITION COUNTRIES*

Australia		Israel**	1954
Federal**	1945	Italy***	1944
New South Wales**	1955	Liechtenstein	(1798)
Queensland**	1922	Luxembourg	1979
Tasmania**	1968	Mexico†	1970
Austria	1968	Monaco	1962
Belgiumª	1867	Nepal	1950
Bolivia	1962	Netherlands	1886
Brazil	1979	New Zealand	1961
Canada	1976	Nicaragua	1979
Colombia	1910	Norway	1905
Costa Rica	1870	Panama	1915
Denmark	1978	Portugal	1867
Dominican Republic	1924	San Marino	1848
Ecuador	1897	Spain	1978
Finland***	1949	Sweden***	1921
West Germany	1949	Switzerland	1942
Honduras	1957	United Kingdom	1969
Iceland	1940	Uruguay	1907
India (Travencore)	1944	Vatican City State	1969
		Venezuela	1864

*Capital punishment abolished de jure as of year indicated; if abolished only de facto, date in parentheses indicates year of last execution. **Death penalty retained for certain exceptional crimes other than murder, rape, burglary, robbery, arson, and kidnapping. ***Death penalty retained for use in wartime or under military law. ªOne murderer executed during World War I in 1918. †Death penalty retained in 3 of 32 states.

Death Penalty States	Year of Last Execution	Death Penalty States	Year of Last Execution
Ala.	1965	Mont.	1943
Ariz.	1963	Nebr.	1959
Ark.	1964	Nev.	1979
Calif.	1967	N.H.	1939
Colo.	1967	N.M.	1960
Conn.	1960	N.C.	1961
Del.	1946	Ohio‡	1963
Fla.	1979	Oklahoma	1966
Ga.	1964	Penn.	1962
Idaho	1957	S.C.	1962
Ill.	1962	S.D.	NA
Ind.	1981	Tenn.	1960
Ky.	1962	Texas	1964
La.	1961	Utah	1977
Md.	1961	Vt.	1950
Miss.	1964	Va.	1962
Mo.	1965	Wash.	1963
		Wyo.	1965

‡Death penalty reinstituted July 1981.

UNITED STATES

In the United States, 15 states and the District of Columbia have no laws authorizing the use of the death penalty: Alaska, Hawaii, Iowa, Kansas, Maine, Massachusetts, Michigan, Minnesota, New Jersey, New York (except for murder committed while serving a life sentence), North Dakota, Oregon, Rhode Island, West Virginia and Wisconsin.

Except for a few special cases, all states have abolished the mandatory death penalty for murder, rape, and other crimes, leaving the decision between death or life imprisonment to the discretion of the jury or the court. This is the result of the U.S. Supreme Court decision, known as the "Furman" decision, which ruled by a 5-to-4 vote in 1972 that the death penalty for murder and for rape, when imposed mandatorily by the jury, constitutes cruel and unusual punishment and is in violation of the U.S. Constitution's 8th and 14th amendments.

In 1976, the U.S. Supreme Court affirmed that the death penalty did not violate the Constitution's ban on "cruel and unusual" punishment. However, "mandatory" death sentences for crimes such as murder are held not valid. At the same time, the Court upheld state statutes passed in Georgia, Florida, and Texas, while striking down those of Louisiana and North Carolina. Since this 1976 "Gregg" ruling, 35 states have enacted capital punishment laws which have not been successfully challenged in the courts.

Although no executions took place in 1980, there were 714 persons on death row as of Dec. 31—the highest year-end total ever recorded. In contrast, the number of prisoners relieved of the death sentence was the smallest in over a decade.

In late 1980 and early 1981, capital punishment was eliminated in two states. On Oct. 23, the Massachusetts law was struck down in a decision that implied that capital punishment is unconstitutional in theory. Oregon's law was voided on Jan. 20.

On May 4, 1981, the U.S. Supreme Court ruled that protection against "double jeopardy" applies to capital punishment. Thus, a convict once sentenced to imprisonment could not later be sentenced to death for the same crime.

However, the trend in favor of capital punishment continued in the first half of 1981, with reports of a death row population of 780. On Feb. 17, the N.Y. Assembly approved a death penalty bill for some cases of murder, although the majority vote was not enough to override Gov. Carey's veto. On Mar. 9, Steven T. Judy was executed in Indiana. In mid-June, the U.S. Senate Judiciary Committee approved a bill facilitating the use of capital punishment for such crimes as treason, espionage, and presidential assassinations. Ohio restored its death penalty on July 1.

Prisoners on Death Row as of December 31, 1980

State	Total	Law	State	Total	Law
Ala.	44	post-Furman[1]	Nebr.	10	post-Furman
Ariz.	34	post-Furman	Nev.	10	post-Gregg
Ark.	15	post-Furman	N.H.	—	post-Gregg
Calif.	44	post-Gregg	N.M.	1	post-Gregg
Colo.	—	post-Furman	N.C.	15	post-Furman
Conn.	—	post-Furman	Okla.	30	post-Gregg
Del.	3	post-Gregg	Oreg.[2]	3	post-Gregg
Fla.	153	post-Furman	Pa.	7	post-Furman
Ga.	80	post-Furman	S.C.	14	post-Gregg
Idaho	1	post-Gregg	S.D.	—	post-Gregg
Ill.	32	post-Gregg	Tenn.	15	post-Gregg
Ind.	6	post-Gregg	Tex.	139	post-Furman
Ky.	5	post-Gregg	Utah	4	post-Gregg
La.	7	post-Furman	Vt.	—	pre-Furman
Md.	2	post-Gregg	Va.	12	post-Gregg
Miss.	12	post-Gregg	Wash.	5	post-Gregg
Mo.	7	post-Gregg	Wyo.	1	post-Gregg
Mont.	3	post-Gregg			

[1]Pre-Furman law for homicide by a person serving a life sentence only. [2]Death penalty voided 1981.

EXECUTIONS IN THE UNITED STATES SOURCE: U.S. Dept. of Justice, Bureau of Justice Statistics

Year	Prisoners Executed				Year	Prisoners Executed			
	Total	White	Black	Other		Total	White	Black	Other
Total (1930-80)	3,862	1,754	2,066	42	1952	83	36	47	—
Percent	100.0	45.4	53.5	1.1	1951	105	57	47	1
1980	—	—	—	—	1950	82	40	42	—
1979	2	2	—	—	1949	119	50	67	2
1978	—	—	—	—	1948	119	35	82	2
1977	1	1	—	—	1947	153	42	111	—
1967	2	1	1	—	1946	131	46	84	1
1966	1	1	—	—	1945	117	41	75	1
1965	7	6	1	—	1944	120	47	70	3
1964	15	8	7	—	1943	131	54	74	3
1963	21	13	8	—	1942	147	67	80	—
1962	47	28	19	—	1941	123	59	63	1
1961	42	20	22	—	1940	124	49	75	—
1960	56	21	35	—	1939	160	80	77	3
1959	49	16	33	—	1938	190	96	92	2
1958	49	20	28	1	1937	147	69	74	4
1957	65	34	31	—	1936	195	92	101	2
1956	65	21	43	1	1935	199	119	77	3
1955	76	44	32	—	1934	168	65	102	1
1954	81	38	42	1	1932	140	62	75	3
1953	62	30	31	1	1930	155	90	65	—

CIVIL RIGHTS/RACE

CIVIL RIGHTS LEGISLATION

SOURCE: Congressional Quarterly Inc.

Six major civil rights bills have been passed by Congress since 1957. Highlights of these bills are:

1957—The Civil Rights Act of 1957 (HR 6127-PL 85-315) was the first civil right legislation passed by Congress since the Reconstruction period. It prohibited action to prevent persons from voting in federal elections, authorizing the Attorney General to bring suit when a person was deprived of his voting rights. It also created a Civil Rights Commission and set up a Civil Rights Division in the Department of Justice.

1960—The Civil Rights Act of 1960 (HR 8601-PL 86-449) strengthened provisions of the 1957 Act for court enforcement of voting rights and required that voting records be preserved. It also contained limited criminal penalty provisions relating to bombing and to obstruction of federal court orders.

1964—The Civil Rights Act of 1964 (HR 7152-PL 88-352) prohibited discrimination on the basis of race, sex, or national origin in public accommodations and in federally assisted programs. It also prohibited discrimination by employers and unions.

1965—The Voting Rights Act of 1965 (S 1564-PL 89-110) authorized the Attorney General to appoint federal examiners to register voters in certain areas.

1968—A civil rights bill (HR 2516-PL 90-284) prohibited discrimination in the sale or rental of about 80 percent of all housing. It also protected persons exercising specified rights, such as attending school.

1970—A bill (HR 4249-PL 91-285) amended and extended the Voting Rights Act of 1965. It extended its application to Northern cities or counties where literacy tests are required.

1975—The Voting Rights Act was extended for seven years.

U.S. POPULATION BY RACE AND SPANISH ORIGIN: 1980

SOURCE: Bureau of the Census

REGIONS AND STATES	White	Black	American Indian, Eskimo, and Aleut			Chinese	Filipino	Japanese
			American Indian	Eskimo	Aleut			
United States, total	188,340,790	26,488,218	1,361,869	42,149	14,177	806,027	774,640	700,747
Northeast Region	42,328,154	4,848,786	76,574	890	718	217,730	75,104	46,930
Maine	1,109,850	3,128	4,057	17	13	484	666	336
N.H.	910,099	3,990	1,297	41	14	790	314	448
Vt.	506,736	1,135	968	8	8	271	101	227
Mass.	5,362,836	221,279	7,483	129	131	25,015	3,073	4,483
R.I.	896,692	27,584	2,872	14	12	1,718	1,218	474
Conn.	2,799,420	217,433	4,431	68	34	4,691	3,132	1,864
N.Y.	13,961,106	2,401,842	38,117	330	285	148,104	33,956	24,524
N.J.	6,127,090	924,786	8,176	130	88	23,366	24,377	9,905
Pa.	10,654,325	1,047,609	9,173	153	133	13,291	8,267	4,669
North Central Region	52,183,794	5,336,542	246,456	1,286	763	72,905	79,945	44,426
Ohio	9,597,266	1,076,734	11,986	167	87	9,911	7,435	5,479
Ind.	5,004,567	414,732	7,681	107	47	3,974	3,625	2,356
Ill.	9,225,575	1,675,229	15,833	242	196	28,590	43,839	18,550
Mich.	7,868,956	1,198,710	39,702	208	128	10,993	11,162	5,859
Wis.	4,442,598	182,593	29,318	110	69	4,097	2,698	2,237
Minn.	3,936,948	53,342	34,841	118	67	4,835	2,675	2,790
Iowa	2,838,805	41,700	5,367	59	27	2,110	1,225	1,049
Mo.	4,346,267	514,274	12,127	119	73	4,290	4,029	2,651
N.D.	625,536	2,568	20,119	32	6	305	446	230
S.D.	638,955	2,144	45,081	17	3	269	282	262
Nebr.	1,490,569	48,389	9,147	26	24	1,106	867	1,378
Kans.	2,167,752	126,127	15,254	81	36	2,425	1,662	1,585
South Region	58,944,057	14,041,374	369,497	1,580	1,046	90,616	82,596	44,636
Del.	488,543	95,971	1,309	13	8	1,004	813	426
Md.	3,158,412	958,050	7,823	113	85	14,485	10,965	4,805
D.C.	171,796	448,229	996	19	16	2,475	1,297	752
Va.	4,229,734	1,008,311	9,093	156	87	9,360	18,901	5,207
W. Va.	1,874,751	65,051	1,555	37	18	881	1,313	404
N.C.	4,453,010	1,316,050	64,519	57	59	3,170	2,542	3,186
S.C.	2,145,122	948,146	5,666	70	22	1,388	3,697	1,414
Ga.	3,948,007	1,465,457	7,444	108	67	4,324	2,792	3,370
Fla.	8,178,387	1,342,478	18,981	199	136	13,471	14,212	5,565
Ky.	3,379,648	259,490	3,518	59	33	1,318	1,443	1,056
Tenn.	3,835,078	725,949	5,012	62	29	2,909	1,901	1,657
Ala.	2,869,688	995,623	7,483	50	28	1,503	960	1,394
Miss.	1,615,190	887,206	6,131	28	21	1,835	1,442	687
Ark.	1,890,002	373,192	9,346	48	17	1,275	921	754
La.	2,911,243	1,237,263	11,950	59	55	3,298	2,614	1,482
Okla.	2,597,783	204,658	169,297	107	60	2,461	1,687	1,975
Texas	11,197,663	1,710,250	39,374	395	305	25,459	15,096	10,502
West Region	34,884,785	2,261,516	669,342	38,393	11,650	424,776	536,995	564,755
Mont.	740,148	1,786	37,153	79	38	346	458	754
Idaho	901,641	2,716	10,418	76	27	905	680	2,585
Wyo.	447,716	3,364	7,088	27	10	392	253	600
Colo.	2,570,615	101,702	17,726	235	98	3,897	2,901	9,858
N. Mex.	976,465	24,042	104,634	88	55	1,441	1,182	1,280
Ariz.	2,240,033	75,034	152,610	138	109	6,820	3,363	4,074
Utah	1,382,550	9,225	19,158	81	17	2,730	928	5,474
Nev.	699,377	50,791	13,201	74	29	2,978	4,037	2,308
Wash.	3,777,296	105,544	58,159	1,251	1,361	18,113	24,363	26,369
Oreg.	2,490,192	37,059	26,587	407	315	8,033	4,257	8,429
Calif.	18,031,689	1,819,282	198,095	1,734	1,482	322,340	357,514	261,817
Alaska	308,455	13,619	21,849	34,135	8,063	521	3,095	1,589
Hawaii	318,608	17,352	2,664	68	46	56,260	133,964	239,618

EMPLOYMENT IN URBAN POVERTY AREAS   Source: Bureau of Statistics

U.S. Employment Status	TOTAL 1979	TOTAL 1980	WHITE 1979	WHITE 1980	BLACK AND OTHER 1979	BLACK AND OTHER 1980
Total United States						
Civilian labor force	102,908,000	104,719,000	90,602,000	92,171,000	12,306,000	12,548,000
Unemployed	5,963,000	7,448,000	4,577,000	5,790,000	1,386,000	1,658,000
Unemployment rate (percent)	5.8	7.1	5.1	6.3	11.3	13.2
Poverty Areas						
Civilian labor force	16,195,000	16,394,000	11,695,000	11,918,000	4,500,000	4,476,000
Unemployed	1,318,000	1,626,000	697,000	899,000	621,000	727,000
Unemployment rate (percent)	8.1	9.9	6.0	7.5	13.8	16.2

Asian and Pacific Islander

Indian	Korean	Vietnamese	Hawaiian	Samoan	Guamanian	Spanish Origin	REGIONS AND STATES
361,544	354,529	261,714	167,253	42,050	32,132	14,605,883	United States, total
120,761	68,152	24,855	3,786	804	1,637	2,604,261	Northeast Region
392	481	465	58	16	49	5,005	Maine
563	515	209	64	13	13	5,587	N.H.
343	288	85	18	8	14	3,304	Vt.
8,387	4,655	3,172	374	145	197	141,043	Mass.
851	592	314	71	14	51	19,707	R.I.
4,995	2,116	1,825	177	69	101	124,499	Conn.
60,511	34,157	6,644	1,566	296	773	1,659,245	N.Y.
29,507	12,845	2,884	632	92	234	491,867	N.J.
15,212	12,503	9,257	826	151	205	154,004	Pa.
85,119	62,149	36,633	5,174	1,242	2,154	1,276,405	North Central Region
13,105	7,257	3,509	768	117	232	119,880	Ohio
4,290	3,253	2,338	475	54	123	87,020	Ind.
35,711	23,980	7,025	1,063	187	606	635,525	Ill.
14,680	8,700	4,208	798	105	226	162,388	Mich.
3,657	2,643	2,249	383	48	153	62,981	Wis.
3,669	6,318	5,866	243	40	97	32,124	Minn.
2,147	2,259	2,476	182	59	70	25,536	Iowa
4,099	3,519	3,179	633	478	230	51,667	Mo.
294	342	283	46	13	20	3,903	N.D.
182	258	378	45	24	28	4,028	S.D.
928	993	1,432	160	27	105	28,020	Nebr.
2,357	2,627	3,690	378	90	264	63,333	Kans.
83,586	70,375	80,240	10,500	2,154	5,059	4,473,172	South Region
1,075	495	205	65	6	43	9,671	Del.
13,705	15,087	4,131	616	82	400	64,740	Md.
950	338	505	237	15	66	17,652	D.C.
8,483	12,550	10,000	903	270	535	79,873	Va.
1,641	587	253	74	14	27	12,707	W. Va.
4,718	3,581	2,391	839	241	500	56,607	N.C.
2,143	1,390	1,072	438	77	188	33,414	S.C.
4,347	5,970	2,294	778	177	409	61,261	Ga.
9,138	4,673	7,592	1,377	252	476	857,898	Fla.
2,226	2,102	1,090	342	129	265	27,403	Ky.
3,195	2,237	1,391	432	83	158	34,081	Tenn.
1,992	1,782	1,333	516	69	146	33,100	Ala.
1,163	576	1,281	330	22	76	24,731	Miss.
832	583	2,042	257	6	62	17,873	Ark.
2,873	1,729	10,877	563	121	214	99,105	La.
2,879	2,698	4,671	515	87	301	57,413	Okla.
22,226	13,997	29,112	2,218	503	1,193	2,985,643	Texas
72,078	153,853	119,986	147,793	37,850	23,282	6,252,045	West Region
162	301	275	135	24	48	9,974	Mont.
310	610	429	318	59	52	36,615	Idaho
176	235	167	102	15	29	24,499	Wyo.
2,298	5,316	4,026	861	173	567	339,300	Colo.
805	705	1,043	217	61	82	476,089	N. Mex.
2,101	2,446	1,989	804	147	354	440,915	Ariz.
830	1,319	2,108	844	763	80	60,302	Utah
622	2,044	1,123	609	135	253	53,786	Nev.
4,002	13,077	9,833	2,974	1,830	1,942	119,986	Wash.
1,938	4,427	5,564	1,488	244	387	65,833	Oreg.
57,989	103,891	89,587	23,091	20,096	17,662	4,543,770	Calif.
241	1,534	383	388	135	149	9,497	Alaska
604	17,948	3,459	115,962	14,168	1,677	71,479	Hawaii

WOMEN'S RIGHTS: SOCIAL HISTORY OF AMERICAN WOMEN

1821 Emma Willard founds the Troy Female Seminary, the first endowed school for girls in America.

1848 Seneca Falls Convention held; Elizabeth Cady Stanton, Lucretia Mott and others draft the "Declaration of Sentiments," the first public protest against the inequality of the economic, political, and social positions of women in America.

1849 Elizabeth Blackwell completes her training at Geneva Medical College and becomes the first woman ever to receive an M.D. degree.

1868 New York women form the Working Women's Association to fight for better working conditions.

1868 Susan B. Anthony and Elizabeth Cady Stanton found *The Revolution*, a newspaper with the motto; "Men, their rights and nothing more; women, their rights and nothing less!"

1869 National Woman Suffrage Association founded; American Woman Suffrage Association founded; two organizations merge in 1890 to work for a voting rights amendment to the Constitution.

1873 State of Illinois passes the first women's equal employment legislation.

1890 Wyoming, the first territory to grant political equality to women, joins the Union.

1917 Miss Jeannette Rankin of Montana becomes the first woman to serve in Congress.

1920 Nineteenth Amendment to the Constitution adopted, giving women the right to vote.

1963 Congress passes the Equal Pay Act which stipulates that equal pay must be given for equal work.

1964 Under Title VII of the Civil Rights Act passed by Congress, discrimination based on sex by employers of 15 or more employees is prohibited.

1972 Ms. magazine, written and edited by women, begins publication.

1973 The Supreme Court issues two decisions rendering all state abortion laws unconstitutional.

1973 The Senate July 23 passes a bill to protect consumers against unfair billing practices and to prohibit lenders from discriminating on the basis of sex or marital status in all credit transactions.

1974 Little League Baseball allows girls to play.

1976 The military academies of the Army, Air Force and Navy admit women to their freshman classes.

1977 The National Women's Conference meets in Houston, Texas, in observance of International Women's Year.

1978 Congress passes the Pregnancy Disability Bill, making pregnancy an insurable disability.

1978 Congress passes a bill extending the time by three years three months for ratification of the Equal Rights Amendment.

THE EQUAL RIGHTS AMENDMENT (Pending)

SOURCE: National Organization for Women, 425 13th St. NW, Suite 1001, Washington, D.C. 20004

The Equal Rights Amendment, which would be Amendment XXVII to the U.S. Constitution, was proposed by Congress on March 22, 1972. A total of 38 states must ratify the ERA for its adoption. As of January 18, 1977, 35 states had done so. The current deadline for ratification by the states is June 30, 1982. The text follows:

Section 1. Equality of rights under the law shall not be denied or abridged by the United States or by any state on account of sex.

Section 2. The Congress shall have the power to enforce, by appropriate legislation, the provisions of this article.

Section 3. This amendment shall take effect two years after the date of ratification.

BLACK POPULATION OF LARGE U.S. CITIES SOURCE: Bureau of the Census

Cities by Rank	Black Population 1970	1980	% of Total Population
New York City, N.Y.	1,668,115	1,784,124	25.2
Chicago, Ill.	1,102,620	1,197,000	39.8
Detroit, Mich.	660,428	758,939	63.1
Philadelphia, Pa.	653,791	638,878	37.8
Los Angeles, Calif.	503,606	505,208	17.0
Washington, D.C.	537,712	448,229	70.3
Houston, Texas	316,551	440,257	27.6
Baltimore, Md.	420,210	431,151	54.8
New Orleans, La.	267,308	308,136	55.3
Memphis, Tenn.	242,513	307,702	47.6
Dallas, Texas	210,238	265,594	29.4
Cleveland, Ohio	287,841	251,347	43.8
St. Louis, Mo.	254,191	206,386	45.6
Newark, N.J.	207,458	191,743	58.2
Oakland, Calif.	124,710	159,234	46.9
Birmingham, Ala.	126,388	158,223	55.6
Indianapolis, Ind.	134,320	152,626	21.8
Milwaukee, Wis.	105,088	146,940	23.1
Jacksonville, Fla.	118,158	137,324	25.4
Cincinnati, Ohio	125,070	130,467	33.8
Boston, Mass.	104,707	126,229	22.4
Columbus, Ohio	99,627	124,880	22.1
Kansas City, Mo.	112,005	122,699	27.4
Richmond, Va.	104,766	112,357	51.3
Gary, Ind.	92,695	107,644	70.8
Nashville-Davidson, Tenn.	87,851	105,942	23.3
Pittsburgh, Pa.	104,904	101,813	24.0
Charlotte, N.C.	72,972	97,627	31.0
Jackson, Miss.	61,063	95,357	47.0
Buffalo, N.Y.	94,329	95,116	26.6
Norfolk, Va.	87,261	93,987	35.2
Fort Worth, Texas	78,324	87,723	22.8
Miami, Fla.	76,156	87,110	25.1
San Francisco, Calif.	96,078	86,414	12.7
Shreveport, La.	62,152	84,627	41.1
Louisville, Ky.	86,040	84,080	28.2
Baton Rouge, La.	81,781	80,119	36.5
San Diego, Calif.	52,961	77,700	8.9
Dayton, Ohio	74,284	75,031	36.9
Mobile, Ala.	67,356	72,568	36.2
Montgomery, Ala.	44,523	69,765	39.2
Flint, Mich.	54,237	66,124	41.4
East Orange, N.J.	40,099	64,354	83.5
Tampa, Fla.	54,720	63,835	23.5
Rochester, N.Y.	49,647	62,332	25.8
Jersey City, N.J.	54,595	61,954	27.7
Toledo, Ohio	52,915	61,750	17.4
Compton, Calif.	55,781	60,812	74.8
Denver, Colo.	47,011	59,252	12.1
Oklahoma City, Okla.	50,103	58,702	14.6
San Antonio, Texas	50,041	57,654	7.3
Inglewood, Calif.	10,066	54,010	57.3
Chattanooga, Tenn.	42,610	53,716	31.7
Winston-Salem, N.C.	45,533	52,968	40.2
East St. Louis, Ill.	48,368	52,751	95.6
Akron, Ohio	48,205	52,719	22.2
Greensboro, N.C.	40,633	51,373	33.0
Little Rock, Ark.	33,396	51,091	32.2

BLACK-AMERICAN HISTORY

Year   Event

1619 The first Negroes to be brought to the American colonies arrived in Virginia as indentured servants.

1661 Virginia passed the first law making Negroes slaves.

1663 Slavery was legally recognized in Maryland.

1688 Quakers in Germantown, Pa., issued the first formal antislavery protest in the Western Hemisphere.

1770 Crispus Attucks, a runaway slave, was killed in the Boston Massacre.

1775 The Pennsylvania Abolition Society, the first anti-slavery society in America, was founded.

1776 The Declaration of Independence was signed, the final version omitting an attack on slavery by Thomas Jefferson contained in the draft version.

The Continental Congress approved a proposal by General George Washington to permit the enlistment of free Negroes in the Continental Army. About 5,000 Negroes served in the War of Independence.

1787 Congress barred the extension of slavery into the Northwest Territory.

1791 Eli Whitney invented the cotton gin, spurring the expansion of cotton plantations and the demand for slaves.

1800 Gabriel Prosser, a Virginia slave, led an unsuccessful insurrection and was hanged with 24 conspirators.

1807 British Parliament abolished the slave trade.
Congress barred the importation of new slaves into U.S. territory.

1816 The American Colonization Society was formed to resettle free American Negroes in Africa.

1820 Congress adopted the Missouri Compromise providing for the admission of Missouri into the Union as a slave state, and Maine's entry as a free state. All territory north of 36°30' was declared free; all territory south of that line was left open to slavery.

1827 The first Negro newspaper, *Freedom's Journal*, began publication in New York City.
Slavery was abolished in New York State.

1830 The U.S. Census Bureau reported that 3,777 Negro heads of families owned slaves.

1831 Federal and state troops crushed a slave rebellion in Southampton County, Va., led by Nat Turner. The rebellion, in which more than 50 whites and more than 100 slaves were killed, ended in the capture and execution of Turner and led to the adoption of more rigid slave codes.

1847 Frederick Douglass, a former slave and a lecturer with the Massachusetts Anti-Slavery Society, began publishing *North Star*, an abolitionist newspaper.

1849 Harriet Tubman escaped from slavery in Maryland. She became one of the most venturesome conductors on the Underground Railroad, leading over 300 slaves to freedom.
Benjamin Roberts filed the first school integration suit on behalf of his daughter. The Massachusetts Supreme Court rejected the suit and established a "separate but equal" precedent.

1850 The Compromise of 1850 admitted California to the Union as a free state but strengthened the Fugitive Slave Law, giving greater inducement for the apprehension of runaway slaves.

1852 Harriet Beecher Stowe's novel *Uncle Tom's Cabin*, a vastly popular antislavery work, was published.

1853 *Clotelle: or the President's Daughter* by historian William Wells Brown was published—the first novel by an American Negro.

1854 James A. Healy was ordained a priest in Notre Dame cathedral, Paris. He later became America's first Negro Roman Catholic bishop.
The first Negro college, Lincoln University, was founded as Ashmun Institute in Oxford, Pa.

1855 The first Negro to win elective office in the United States, John Mercer Langston, was elected clerk of Brownhelm Township, Lorain Co., O.

1863 The Draft Riots took place in New York City. Blacks and abolitionists were attacked and killed.

1865 By the end of the Civil War, some 186,000 Negroes had served with the Union forces.
The Thirteenth Amendment, freeing all slaves, was passed by Congress.
The Freedman's Bureau was organized to aid and protect newly freed blacks in the South.
Dr. John S. Rock, a Boston physician and lawyer, was the first Negro admitted to the bar of the United States Supreme Court.
Southern states passed the "Black Codes" in an attempt to restrict the freedom of emancipated slaves.

1866 Charles L. Mitchell and Edward G. Walker were elected to the Massachusetts House of Representatives, becoming the first Negroes to serve in a U.S. legislature.

1867 Morehouse College, Atlanta, Ga., and Howard University, Washington, D.C., were founded.

1868 Oscar J. Dunn attained the highest elective office held by an American Negro up to that time, becoming lieutenant governor of Louisiana.

1869 Ebenezer Don Carlos Basset was appointed minister to Haiti, the first Negro diplomat to represent the United States.

1870 Hiram Revels was elected to fill the unexpired U.S. Senate term of Jefferson Davis of Mississippi, becoming the first Negro Senator. He served a year.
Joseph H. Rainey of South Carolina became the first Negro in the House of Representatives. He was subsequently reelected four times.

1875 Congress passed a civil rights act prohibiting discrimination in such public accommodations as hotels and theaters.

1877 Henry O. Flipper became the first Negro to graduate from West Point.

1881 Tennessee passed a "Jim Crow" law instituting segregated railroad travel that set a trend among other states in the South.
Booker T. Washington opened Tuskegee Institute in Alabama.

1883 The Supreme Court declared the 1875 Civil Rights Act unconstitutional.

1890 Mississippi instituted restrictions on voting, including a poll tax and literacy tests, which were designed to disenfranchise Negroes. During the decade, other Southern states followed. Louisiana added (1898) the exclusionary device of the "grandfather clause," which set educational and property qualifications for voting but exempted those whose ancestors had been eligible to vote as of Jan. 1, 1867.

1891 The Provident Hospital in Chicago—the first such interracial institution in America—was founded by Negro surgeon Daniel Hale Williams.

1895 Frederick Douglass, the Negro abolitionist whom Lincoln had called "the most meritorious man of the 19th century," died.

1896 The National Association of Colored Women was organized in Washington, D.C.; Mary Church Terrell served as its first president.

1898 Four Negro regiments in the regular army compiled an excellent combat record during the Spanish-American War. Dismounted elements of the black Ninth and Tenth Cavalry rescued the Rough Riders from near annihilation.

1905 Twenty-nine Negro intellectuals from 14 states, headed by Dr. W. E. B. DuBois, organized the Niagara Movement, which demanded the abolition of all racial distinctions. The meeting took place at Fort Erie, N.Y.

1909 Matthew Henson, a Negro member of Admiral Peary's expedition, placed the American flag at the North Pole.

1910 The National Association for the Advancement of Colored People (NAACP) was founded in New York. The "Great Migration" of more than 2 million Southern blacks began.

1911 The National Urban League was founded. It was originally made up of two groups: The Committee for Improving the Industrial Conditions of Negroes and The League for the Protection of Colored Women.

1915 The Association for the Study of Negro Life and History was established by the "father of Negro history," Dr. Carter G. Woodson.

1917 Ten thousand Negroes marched down Fifth Avenue in New York to protest the many lynchings in the South. The parade was led by W. E. B. DuBois. Race riots broke out in East St. Louis, Illinois.

1920 The pioneer black nationalist Marcus Garvey inaugurated the International Convention of the Universal Negro Improvement Association (UNIA) in Harlem. UNIA reached its greatest influence during the following two years.

1928 Oscar De Priest of Illinois was the first black Congressman from a northern state.

1935 Mary McLeod Bethune organized the National Council of Negro Women.

1936 Negro track star Jesse Owen won four gold medals in the Olympics at Berlin.

1937 William H. Hastie became the first Negro to serve as a U.S. Federal judge.

Joe Louis became heavyweight boxing champion of the world, defeating Jim Braddock for the title.

1939 Contralto Marian Anderson, denied the use of Constitution Hall in Washington by the Daughters of the American Revolution, sang on Easter Sunday before 75,000 people at the Lincoln Memorial.

1940 Benjamin O. Davis, Sr., was appointed the first black general in the U.S. armed forces.

Dr. Charles R. Drew did notable research into blood preservation and discovered blood plasma.

1941 A Negro threat to stage a massive protest march on Washington resulted in the issuance of Executive Order 8802 prohibiting racial discrimination in defense industries or the government (but not the armed forces).

1942 The Congress of Racial Equality (CORE), an action-oriented civil rights group, was founded by James Farmer in Chicago.

1947 Statistics amassed by Tuskegee Institute indicated that in the period 1882–1947 3,426 Negroes were lynched in the United States. Of these, 1,217 were lynched in the 1890–1900 decade.

1948 President Truman issued Executive Order 9981 calling for "equality of treatment and opportunity" in the armed forces.

1949 William L. Dawson became the first Negro to head a Congressional committee.

1951 Ralph J. Bunche, who won a Nobel Peace Prize in 1950, was appointed Under-Secretary of the United Nations, the highest ranking American employed by the international body.

Private First Class William Thompson was awarded the Congressional Medal of Honor for bravery in the Korean War, the first Negro to win it since the Spanish-American War.

1952 A Tuskegee Institute report indicated that for the first time in 71 years of compilation, no lynchings were reported in the United States.

1954 In "Brown v. Board of Education of Topeka" the U.S. Supreme Court held that segregation in public education denied equal protection of the laws.

1955 A bus boycott in Montgomery, Ala., was led by Dr. Martin Luther King, Jr., after Rosa Parks was arrested for refusing to give up her seat to a white man.

1957 Central High School in Little Rock, Ark., was integrated by nine Negro children, but not until President Eisenhower had called in troops to keep order.

1960 Four Negro North Carolina A & T College freshmen occupied places at a Woolworth lunch counter, launching a wave of nonviolent sit-ins.

1961 CORE began "Freedom Rides" that rolled through the South, protesting segregation.

1962 The Albany (Ga.) Movement—a citywide attempt, supported by the Southern Christian Leadership Conference, Student Nonviolent Coordinating Committee, NAACP, and CORE, to abolish discrimination in all public facilities—was formed.

James Meredith desegregated the University of Mississippi, after President Kennedy dispatched troops and riots killed two persons.

1963 NAACP leader Medgar Evers was murdered in the doorway of his home in Jackson, Miss.

Birmingham, Ala.: The plight of Negroes in the South and throughout the nation was dramatized here as fire hoses, police dogs, and rough handling by the police, followed by bomb blasts in the black ghetto, became the order of the day. September 15: A bomb blast at the Sixteenth Street Baptist Church killed four girls.

June 11: President Kennedy declared that the black struggle for civil rights is a "moral issue."

August 28: The March on Washington in which more than 200,000 Americans from all walks of life converged on the nation's capital constituted one of the largest single protests in American history. The marchers gathered on the steps of the Lincoln Memorial to dramatize discontent with the Negro's plight.

1964 Three young civil-rights workers—Michael Schwerner, Andrew Goodman, and James E. Chaney—were murdered in Mississippi.

Riots exploded in Harlem and elsewhere.

1965 Malcolm X., former Black Muslim and advocate of black nationalism, was assassinated in New York City.

Thurgood Marshall was named as the first Negro Solicitor General of the United States.

President Johnson signed the Voting Rights Act, under which federal examiners are authorized to register black voters who have been refused by state officials.

Riots erupted in the Watts section of Los Angeles; 35 people were killed, 883 others were injured, and 3,598 were arrested. Damage totaled more than $220 million.

1966 Robert Weaver was appointed head of the Department of Housing and Urban Development (HUD), the first Negro ever to serve at cabinet level.

Constance Baker Motley, former borough president of Manhattan, became the first Negro woman to become a federal judge in American history.

The U.S. Supreme Court outlawed all poll taxes.

The concept of "Black Power" was adopted by CORE.

1967 Solicitor General Thurgood Marshall became the first Negro Supreme Court Justice.

At a four-day Black Power conference—the largest of its kind in American history—more than 400 people representing 45 civil rights groups from 36 cities convened in Newark, N.J., expressing viewpoints that ranged from moderate to militant.

1968 April 4: While standing on the balcony of a Memphis motel, Dr. Martin Luther King, Jr., was shot and killed by a sniper.

The Kerner Commission reported that "our nation is moving toward two societies, one black, one white—separate and unequal."

1969 Educational institutions acceded to demands by black students for more black studies.

James Earl Ray pleaded guilty to the assassination of Martin Luther King; sentenced to 99 years in prison.

1970 The killing in December 1969 of a Black Panther leader, Fred Hampton, led to a federal investigation and the subsequent conclusion that the Chicago police had exercised undue force.

1971 Samuel L. Gravely, Jr., was made the first black admiral in the U.S. Navy.

Thirteen Black Panthers, including two who fled to Algeria during the trial, were acquitted in New York City on charges of conspiring to bomb department stores and police stations and to murder policemen.

The six-month trial in New Haven of Bobby G. Seale, chairman of the Black Panther party, and Mrs. Ericka Huggins, a New Haven Panther, for crimes arising from the death of Alex Rackley, ended in a mistrial as the jury was unable to reach a verdict. Rackley, a Panther, died in May 1969.

1972 Over 8,000 delegates and observers met in Gary, Indiana as the first National Black Political Convention voted to set up a permanent representative body to set the direction for black political and social actions.

Angela Davis, accused of conspiracy to kidnap and murder, was acquitted.

The busing of children, both black and white, from one neighborhood school district to another became an important political issue. The Nixon administration supported and signed into law a bill which prohibited busing solely to achieve racial integration.

1975 Black Muslims agreed to accept white members.

1976 U.S. Supreme Court outlawed discrimination in commercially operated nonsectarian private schools.

1977 The TV dramatization of Alex Haley's book Roots was seen by the largest audience ever. The story chronicled the black author's family history from mid-eighteenth century African beginnings.

1978 U.S. Supreme Court ruled that the University of California Medical School at Davis must admit Allan P. Bakke, a 38-year-old white engineer, as the school's minority-admissions plan was inflexible and racially biased. The justices ruled, however, that race could be considered as a university admission factor. Black leaders expressed concern regarding the decision.

PUBLIC HEALTH/MEDICINE

BIOLOGICAL AND MEDICAL SCIENCE REVIEW: 1980/81

Helen H. Swallow, C.N.M., Member, American Medical Writers Association, and W. J. Morse, Jr., M.D.

Changing birth practices: The number of Caesarean births in the United States is increasing rapidly, but so, too, are the number of out-of-hospital births.

In the past year, approximately one of every six babies born in the United States was delivered by Caesarean section—a tripling in the percentage of Caesarean births in just one decade. In some hospitals, Caesareans accounted for more than one quarter of all births.

In 1980, an NIH (National Institute of Health) task force made up of doctors, lawyers, ethicists, and consumers studied the matter of increasing Caesarean births and concluded that the chief reasons for the rise are repeat Caesareans, abnormal labor, fetal distress, and breech position of the fetus.

Repeat Caesareans are performed in accordance with a seventy-year-old obstetrical dictum stating that once a woman has had a Caesarean birth she should always have a Caesarean birth. Although 99% of women who have undergone Caesarean sections are delivered in like fashion for subsequent births, a number of recent studies indicate that the subsequent Caesareans are probably not necessary. It is thought that the uterus is not necessarily severely weakened by Cæsarean section and that the conventional apprehension that labor is likely to cause rupture of a scarred uterus is probably not well founded. The NIH task force recommends that the expectant mothers who are otherwise normal be offered a trial of labor for births subsequent to a Caesarean delivery.

The task force was unable to determine whether abnormal labor is actually occurring more frequently among American women—perhaps as the result of better nourished, larger babies—or whether it is merely being diagnosed more readily than it has been in the past.

Fetal distress necessitating Caesarean delivery is being diagnosed much more often because of the widespread use of electronic fetal monitoring (EFM). The task force determined, however, that neither the increase in EFM nor the increase in Caesarean births has resulted in a decrease in perinatal mortality.

Breech position of the fetus has long been known to be associated with greater risk of complication in vaginal birth. The task force found that obstetricians feel increasingly hard pressed to justify subjecting their patients to those risks, but it concluded that more discrimination in the management of breech birth is warranted. The group advised experienced obstetricians to deliver breech babies vaginally if the mother's pelvis is normal and if the baby is not premature and weighs less than eight pounds.

Helen I. Marieskind, a Seattle health administrator who has also investigated the increasing frequency of Caesarean sections, has suggested that fear of malpractice suits may be another reason why obstetricians choose to perform more Caesarean sections. Whether or not it is absolutely necessary, a surgical delivery offers virtual certainty of a good result. Doctors may be less inclined to expose themselves to the possible consequences of a complicated vaginal birth, and, as Marieskind points out, fees for Caesarean deliveries are higher than that for vaginal deliveries.

Coincident with the increasing application of medical technology to births in a hospital, there has been a growing disaffection among consumers with hospital birth and conventional obstetric practices. In 1976, according to the American College of Obstetricians and Gynecologists, 99.6% of all births in the United States occurred in hospitals. In the past year, however, in some districts, more than 10% of births took place out of hospital. The Maternity Center Association in New York City, the first out-of-hospital birth center in the East, reports that many states now have units run, as theirs is, by nurse midwives. Obstetricians generally deplore these divergences from the conventional practices and predict dire consequences. Results of recent investigations do not seem to bear them out: In December

1980, in the *Journal of the American Association,* Claude A. Burnitt III, M.D., and his co-workers reported their study of homebirths in North Carolina. Among medically screened low-risk mothers for whom home delivery was planned, the neonatal death rate was 3 per 1,000 live births—lower than the statewide rate for hospital births. Though the researchers did not advocate homebirth, they did conclude that "For prenatally screened low-risk women, delivery by a trained nurse midwife under physician supervision, perhaps in a birthing center with hospital backup, may have a cost advantage over physician-hospital delivery without unacceptable risk of maternal or neonatal mortality."

A safe, effective hepatitis B vaccine: The first clinical trials of a vaccine to prevent hepatitis B infection were completed in New York early in 1981. Hepatitis B (formerly called serum hepatitis or post-transfusion hepatitis) is the most severe and debilitating form of hepatitis viral infection. It is characterized by hepatomegaly (swelling of the liver), fever, weakness, jaundice, loss of appetite, abdominal discomfort, and general malaise. Chronic liver disease may follow infection. The symptoms develop within a few weeks of exposure to the virus, usually through a transfusion of blood or blood components, or by entry of the virus into the bloodstream from contaminated needles or other equipment. An estimated 80,000 to 100,000 cases occur each year in the United States.

The breakthrough was made possible by the work of Baruch S. Blumberg, M.D., Nobel Laureate of the Institute for Cancer Research. In 1964, he identified an antigen on the protein coat of the hepatitis B virus (the Australia antigen or HBsAg), enabling researchers to identify the virus and to distinguish it from hepatitis A and other causes of liver inflammation. In 1972, Saul Krugman, M.D., of New York University Medical Center, devised a crude vaccine to protect children who were at great risk of becoming infected when admitted to Willowbrook Hospital in Staten Island, where hepatitis B was epidemic. Dr. Krugman took blood samples from carriers of the disease who had an excess of the antigen, separated the HBsAg, purified it, diluted it, heated the diluted vaccine to weaken the virus, and administered it to children before they were admitted to the hospital. Only 30% of the children contracted the disease instead of the nearly 100% that might have been expected to contract it had the vaccine not been given.

This year's trials were performed by Wolf Szumness, M.D., of the New York Blood Center, to evaluate a commercially prepared vaccine made possible by Dr. Krugman's work. A series of three injections of the vaccine were given to one half of a group of 1,000 homosexual, male volunteers; the other half of this especially susceptible group received placebo injections. Neither the volunteers nor the people giving the injections knew which subjects were receiving the vaccine and which were being given the placebo. A small number of the men receiving the vaccine developed soreness or pruritus around the site of the injection, but no other adverse effects were noted. Of the vaccinated men, over 96% were shown to have antibodies to the virus within six months of the vaccination. None of them contracted hepatitis B. Of the 500 men given placebo injections, 27% contracted the disease.

Dr. Blumberg, who discovered the antigen that allowed identification of the virus, observes in *Science* that in areas of the world where primary hepatocellular carcinoma (PHC) is common, hepatitis B infection is also common and that in people who have this virulent form of liver cancer, a great many carry the antigen HBsAg in their blood. It is his hope that a vaccine that prevents hepatitis B will also prevent PHC, thereby becoming the first anticancer vaccine.

New bone being grown from a powder: A team from Harvard Medical School is using a new technique that may revolutionize the treatment of major bone defects, especially of the face and skull. Bone from a cadaver is crushed to powder and the minerals are extracted by a chemical process. The remaining demineralized bone is washed, dried, and sterilized. The powder is placed where the growth of bone is desired. One of the patients treated by the team had had most of his skull removed surgically. A few weeks after the operation, the powdered, demineralized bone was applied to the tough membrane surrounding the brain (the dura). In a little over a year, a hard, bony skull had developed. An infant born without a nose or with a cleft palate may also be treated effectively with this new bone-growing technique. A nose may be formed, and the space between the sides of the palate on the roof of the mouth may be filled in.

Prior to the development of this technique, it was necessary to transplant bone from a donor or from another site in the patient's body. Bone transplantation works by a process called osteoconduction; cells from surrounding bone migrate to the borders of the transplanted bone, knitting the two surfaces together. Possibly owing to the minerals contained in the whole bone used for transplantation, the bone is often partially or entirely absorbed. After infancy, many operations are sometimes necessary and the results may include prolonged pain and dysfunction.

In the new technique, bone grows by a process called osteoinduction in which fibroblasts (cells of the body that are usually active in forming scar tissue in the healing process) cause the formation of cartilage as they come in contact with the demineralized, powdered bone. In the experiments in rats that preceded the human trials, cartilage began to form within three days, and a week later the new cartilage was developing capillaries. Four days after that, normal-appearing bone with a good vascular supply had formed.

The Harvard team is trying to discover what causes the fibroblasts to make cartilage instead of scar tissue. If that process can be understood, it may be possible to stop the growth at the cartilage stage, as might be desirable, for instance, in fashioning the auricle of the ear or parts of the nose normally made of cartilage. Sufficient time has not yet elapsed to be certain that the new technique provides bone strong and durable enough for permanent correction. During the next two years, patients who have undergone the treatment will continue to be observed, and the procedures required for FDA approval of powdered bone for general use will be followed.

Vasectomy and atherosclerosis: During the past year, approximately half a million men in the United States have undergone voluntary sterilization by vasectomy. The operation has generally been considered to be safe and effective and to cause no lasting harm. It is inexpensive, comparatively simple to perform under local anesthesia, and commonly judged to be the best procedure for permanent contraception.

Studies in the past year suggest the possibility that vasectomy may cause an autoimmune reaction that may, in turn, promote the development of atherosclerosis during the years following the procedure. A theory based on one study, suggests that in early life, during the time in which the immune system develops the ability to differentiate between self and nonself, mature sperm are not present to be identified as "self" and that during sexual maturation, the genital system is able to prevent maturing sperm and their antigens from interacting with the immune system. With the cutting of the ducts at vasectomy, a "leakage" of sperm antigens occurs, and the immune system reacts with the antigens to form an immune complex that becomes part of the atherosclerotic plaques that build up on the insides of arteries, thus making vasectomized men more susceptible to heart attack.

Critics fault the theory for three reasons: the data supporting the theory are derived from studies of vasectomized and nonvasectomized monkeys and may not be applicable to men; the number of monkeys studied was small and the association of vasectomy with atherosclerosis may have occurred by chance; and retrospective studies have not found that significantly greater numbers of vasectomized men have developed atherosclerosis. Further studies on large populations of men are necessary to prove or disprove the association. Such studies are currently under way at several centers.

In response to the growing number of queries from men who have had the operation, Ruth Crozier, advisor

in the biological sciences at the National Institute of Child Health and Human Development (NICHD) offers the following reassurance: "I don't think worry is warranted at this time. If vasectomy is a risk factor it is minor compared to smoking, hypertension, and elevated cholesterol levels."

Venereal diseases: An epidemic of venereal diseases has been traced to one common, previously unsuspected organism—Chlamydia trachomitis. It is a small, parasitic organism that is found throughout the world. It cannot live outside the cells of a host, and it is spread easily from person to person. There are several immunotypes that have for years been known to cause a variety of infectious diseases, including trachoma (the leading cause of blindness in the world), lymphogranuloma venerum, psittacosis, and inclusion conjunctivitis of the newborn. Until recently it was not recognized as the cause of many common, sexually transmitted infections, including nongonococcal urethritis (NGU) and epididymitis in men, and salpingitis, pelvic inflammatory disease (PID), cervicitis, and vaginitis in women. It had been thought to be a normal part of the flora of the reproductive tract in women, not the pathogen in an epidemic of venereal diseases.

In women chlamydial infection of the cervix and vagina may be chronic and asymptomatic. Unknowingly, the woman may transmit the infection to a sexual partner or to a baby during delivery. Early symptoms include a mildly inflamed cervix and a vaginal discharge, but these are such common findings that unless the woman or the person examining her is looking for C. trachomitis, the infection will not be diagnosed or properly treated. If it grows more severe, the internal pelvic organs may become inflamed (pelvic inflammatory disease [PID]), and the Fallopian tubes may swell. Marked abdominal pain increases as the lining of the tubes becomes inflamed (salpingitis). In men chlamydial infection is not as likely to be asymptomatic. Men tend to develop epididymitis (inflammation of the long, narrow ducts that carry sperm to the vas deferens). Fever, chills, inguinal pain, and swelling of the epididymis are usual. Infection of the urethra (nongonoccocal urethritis) may result in inflammation of the urethra and discharge and pain with urination. The infection is easily passed back and forth between infected people. While the organism may sometimes grow on ordinary culture media in the laboratory, it cannot be reliably grown following routine procedures. (Methods exist for growing C. trachomitis, but they are slow, cumbersome, and expensive. Further, C. trachomitis is not easily identifiable under the microscope, even when properly stained with iodine and examined by an expert.) Specialized techniques are being developed to allow definitive and rapid identification of the organism, as is already possible for gonorrhea and syphilis.

Recent studies show that in Sweden and in England C. trachomitis causes more salpingitis than do the other venereal diseases. In some cities in the United States chlamydial PID is three times as common as gonoccocal PID. In pregnancy there is evidence that some cases of spontaneous abortion (miscarriage), premature labor, and fetal death are associated with chlamydial infection. After an episode of salpingitis and PID the Fallopian tubes may be scarred, increasing the chances that the woman will be unable to conceive because the tubes are blocked with scar tissue or that she will have a pregnancy in one of the scarred and narrowed tubes, an event that always ends in fetal death. Roughly 20% of women who have severe salpingitis will become infertile. Among other conditions caused by C. trachomitis are paratrachoma, urethral syndrome, Fitz-Hugh and Curtis syndrome, Bartholinitis, postpartum endometritis, proctitis, Reiter's syndrome, adult and newborn pneumonia, otitis media, vaginitis in children, and, in very young infants, sudden infant death syndrome (SIDS).

Of the men and women who are diagnosed as being infected with C. trachomitis, 20% remain infected after treatment. The usual recommended treatment is fourteen days of oral tetracycline. If given in adequate dosage to the infected person and simultaneously to the sexual partner or partners, the incidence of the disease could be drastically reduced. King K. Holmes, M.D., of the United States Public Health Service Hospital in Seattle writes in the Journal of the American Medical Society that hospitalization and intravenous treatment with more than one antibiotic may be necessary, especially for those who have severe symptoms or who are not cured after treatment with tetracycline.

LONGEVITY IN THE UNITED STATES

Source: 1979 and 1980 data from Statistical Bureau, Metropolitan Life Insurance Company; earlier years from the National Center for Health Statistics

The expectation of life at birth for the resident population of the United States increased to an all-time high in 1979 and then decreased slightly in 1980. Preliminary life tables indicate that the average length of life for the total population rose from 73.3 years in 1978 to 74.1 years in 1979 and decreased to 73.8 years in 1980—a gain of 3.1 years since 1969-71 and of 14.6 years since 1929-31, when the average was only about 59 years.

The expected lifetime was 70.1 years for the male newborn and 77.7 years for the female. The infant mortality rate in 1980 declined to a new low of 12.5 per 1,000 live births.

EXPECTATION OF LIFE IN THE U.S.: 1949-51 to 1980

Age	1949-51	1959-61	1969-71	1976	1978	1979*	1980†
0-1	68.1	69.9	70.7	72.8	73.3	74.1	73.8
1	69.2	70.7	71.2	72.9	73.3	74.0	73.7
15	55.9	57.3	57.7	59.3	59.7	60.4	60.1
25	46.6	47.9	48.4	50.0	50.4	51.1	50.7
35	37.3	38.5	39.1	40.6	41.0	41.7	41.4
45	28.5	29.5	30.1	31.5	31.9	32.5	32.2
55	20.6	21.4	22.0	23.2	23.5	24.1	23.8
65	13.8	14.4	15.0	16.0	16.3	16.9	16.4

*Provisional (revised estimate based on results of the 1980 census). †Preliminary.

EXPECTATION OF LIFE—UNITED STATES: 1978
Source: National Center for Health Statistics

AGE	Total (years)	White Male	White Female	All Other Male	All Other Female	Age	Total (years)	White Male	White Female	All other Male	All other Female
Birth	73.3	70.2	77.8	65.0	73.6	43	33.7	30.8	37.1	28.1	34.4
1	73.3	70.1	77.6	65.5	74.0	44	32.8	29.9	36.1	27.3	33.5
2	72.4	69.2	76.7	64.6	73.1	45	31.9	29.1	35.2	26.5	32.7
3	71.5	68.3	75.7	63.7	72.1	46	31.0	28.2	34.3	25.8	31.8
4	70.5	67.3	74.8	62.8	71.2	47	30.1	27.3	33.4	25.0	31.0
5	69.5	66.3	73.8	61.8	70.2	48	29.3	26.5	32.5	24.3	30.2
6	68.6	65.4	72.8	60.8	69.3	49	28.4	25.6	31.6	23.5	29.3
7	67.6	64.4	71.8	59.9	68.3	50	27.6	24.8	30.7	22.8	28.5
8	66.6	63.4	70.8	58.9	67.3	51	26.7	24.0	29.8	22.1	27.8
9	65.6	62.4	69.9	57.9	66.3	52	25.9	23.2	29.0	21.4	27.0
10	64.6	61.5	68.9	57.0	65.4	53	25.1	22.4	28.1	20.8	26.2
11	63.7	60.5	67.9	56.0	64.4	54	24.3	21.6	27.3	20.1	25.5
12	62.7	59.5	66.9	55.0	63.4	55	23.5	20.8	26.4	19.5	24.7
13	61.7	58.5	65.9	54.0	62.4	56	22.7	20.1	25.6	18.9	24.0
14	60.7	57.5	64.9	53.1	61.4	57	22.0	19.3	24.7	18.3	23.3
15	59.7	56.6	64.0	52.1	60.4	58	21.2	18.6	23.9	17.7	22.5
16	58.8	55.6	63.0	51.1	59.5	59	20.5	17.9	23.1	17.1	21.8
17	57.8	54.7	62.0	50.2	58.5	60	19.7	17.2	22.3	16.5	21.2
18	56.9	53.8	61.1	49.3	57.5	61	19.0	16.5	21.5	16.0	20.5
19	56.0	52.9	60.1	48.3	56.6	62	18.3	15.8	20.7	15.5	19.9
20	55.0	52.0	59.1	47.4	55.6	63	17.6	15.2	19.9	15.1	19.3
21	54.1	51.1	58.2	46.5	54.7	64	17.0	14.6	19.2	14.6	18.6
22	53.2	50.2	57.2	45.7	53.7	65	16.3	14.0	18.4	14.1	18.0
23	52.2	49.3	56.2	44.8	52.8	66	15.7	13.4	17.7	13.6	17.3
24	51.3	48.4	55.3	43.9	51.8	67	15.0	12.8	16.9	13.1	16.7
25	50.4	47.5	54.3	43.1	50.9	68	14.4	12.2	16.2	12.5	16.0
26	49.5	46.5	53.3	42.2	49.9	69	13.7	11.6	15.5	12.0	15.4
27	48.5	45.6	52.4	41.4	49.0	70	13.1	11.1	14.8	11.6	14.8
28	47.6	44.7	51.4	40.5	48.1	71	12.5	10.6	14.1	11.1	14.2
29	46.6	43.8	50.4	39.7	47.1	72	12.0	10.1	13.4	10.7	13.7
30	45.7	42.8	49.5	38.8	46.2	73	11.4	9.6	12.7	10.4	13.2
31	44.8	41.9	48.5	37.9	45.2	74	10.9	9.1	12.1	10.0	12.8
32	43.8	41.0	47.5	37.1	44.3	75	10.4	8.6	11.5	9.8	12.5
33	42.9	40.0	46.6	36.2	43.4	76	9.8	8.2	10.9	9.5	12.2
34	41.9	39.1	45.6	35.4	42.5	77	9.4	7.8	10.3	9.3	11.9
35	41.0	38.2	44.6	34.5	41.5	78	9.0	7.4	9.8	9.1	11.7
36	40.1	37.2	43.7	33.7	40.6	79	8.5	7.1	9.3	8.9	11.6
37	39.1	36.3	42.7	32.9	39.7	80	8.1	6.7	8.8	8.8	11.5
38	38.2	35.4	41.8	32.0	38.8	81	7.8	6.4	8.3	8.7	11.3
39	37.3	34.5	40.8	31.2	37.9	82	7.4	6.1	7.9	8.6	11.1
40	36.4	33.6	39.9	30.4	37.0	83	7.1	5.8	7.5	8.5	10.9
41	35.5	32.6	38.9	29.6	36.1	84	6.7	5.5	7.1	8.2	10.5
42	34.6	31.7	38.0	28.9	35.3	85 over	6.4	5.3	6.7	7.8	9.9

INFANT AND NEONATAL DEATH RATES IN THE UNITED STATES: 1978

Source: National Center for Health Statistics (Deaths per 1,000 live births)

State	Infant Deaths[1]	Neonatal Deaths[2]	State	Infant Deaths[1]	Neonatal Deaths[2]	State	Infant Deaths[1]	Neonatal Deaths[2]	State	Infant Deaths[1]	Neonatal Deaths[2]
Ala.	16.1	11.0	Ill.	15.7	10.9	Mont.	11.6	7.3	R.I.	13.6	10.6
Alaska	14.4	9.4	Ind.	13.1	8.6	Nebr.	13.0	9.1	S.C.	18.6	12.4
Ariz.	13.1	9.0	Iowa	12.6	8.9	Nev.	12.5	8.6	S.D.	13.5	9.4
Ark.	16.4	10.5	Kans.	12.5	8.7	N.H.	10.4	8.0	Tenn.	14.8	10.5
Calif.	11.8	7.7	Ky.	12.7	8.6	N.J.	13.0	9.3	Texas	14.3	9.8
Colo.	11.2	6.9	La.	17.3	12.0	N.M.	14.1	9.0	Utah	11.4	7.8
Conn.	11.6	9.3	Maine	10.4	6.1	N.Y.	14.0	10.1	Vt.	10.4	8.0
Del.	13.2	9.6	Md.	14.7	11.1	N.C.	16.6	11.4	Va.	13.8	9.7
D.C.	27.3	20.2	Mass.	11.1	8.1	N.D.	13.5	9.6	Wash.	12.5	7.9
Fla.	14.1	9.3	Mich.	13.8	9.2	Ohio	13.3	9.2	W.Va.	15.1	10.3
Ga.	15.4	10.3	Minn.	12.0	8.3	Okla.	14.3	9.0	Wis.	11.2	7.6
Hawaii	11.1	7.6	Miss.	18.7	12.3	Oreg.	12.9	7.7	Wyo.	13.0	8.1
Idaho	11.7	7.3	Mo.	14.8	10.8	Pa.	13.7	10.5	U.S. avg.	13.8	9.5

[1] Under 1 yr.   [2] Under 28 days.

PUBLIC HEALTH/MEDICINE

LEADING CAUSES OF DEATH IN THE UNITED STATES: 1978
SOURCE: National Center for Health Statistics

Rank	Cause of Death	Number of Deaths	Death Rate per 100,000 Population	Rank	Cause of Death	Number of Deaths	Death Rate per 100,000 Population
	ALL CAUSES	1,927,788	883.4	5.	Influenza & Pneumonia	58,319	26.7
1.	Heart Diseases	729,510	334.3	6.	Diabetes Mellitus	33,841	15.5
2.	Cancer	396,992	181.9	7.	Cirrhosis of Liver	30,066	13.8
3.	Cerebrovascular			8.	Arteriosclerosis	28,940	13.3
	diseases	175,629	80.5	9.	Suicide	27,294	12.5
4.	Accidents	105,561	48.4	10.	Diseases of Early Infancy	22,033	10.1
	Motor Vehicular	52,411	24.0		All Other Causes	319,603	146.5
	All Other	53,150	24.4				

DEATH RATES FOR SPECIFIED CAUSES, BY COLOR AND SEX: UNITED STATES, 1978
SOURCE: National Center for Health Statistics

(Rate per 100,000 population in specified group)

	Total			White			All Other		
	Both sexes	Male	Female	Both sexes	Male	Female	Both sexes	Male	Female
All causes	883.4	994.4	778.3	895.7	999.8	796.5	805.1	959.7	664.5
Major cardiovascular diseases	442.7	472.8	414.2	459.5	489.2	431.2	335.5	365.6	308.1
Diseases of heart	334.3	375.3	295.5	348.6	390.8	308.4	242.8	273.8	214.7
Hypertension	2.5	2.4	2.6	2.3	2.2	2.4	3.7	3.8	3.6
Cerebrovascular diseases	10.4	9.6	20.3	18.4	15.3	21.4	13.5	13.2	13.7
Arteriosclerosis	13.3	10.9	9.7	12.8	15.7	10.1	8.0	8.7	7.3
Cancer	181.9	203.5	161.4	186.6	206.4	167.7	152.0	184.9	122.1
Accidents	48.4	69.6	28.3	47.9	68.3	28.5	51.3	78.2	26.8
Motor vehicle accidents	24.0	35.9	12.7	24.4	36.2	13.1	21.8	34.1	10.6
All other accidents	24.4	33.7	15.5	23.5	32.1	15.4	29.5	44.1	16.3
Influenza and pneumonia	1.9	1.6	2.1	2.0	1.7	2.3	0.9	0.9	0.9
Cirrhosis of liver	13.8	18.6	9.3	13.2	17.8	8.8	17.5	23.3	12.3
Diabetes mellitus	15.5	13.1	17.8	15.0	12.9	17.0	18.7	14.7	22.5
Suicide	12.5	19.0	6.3	13.4	20.2	6.9	6.9	11.1	3.1
Homicide	9.4	14.9	4.1	5.9	9.2	2.9	31.2	52.6	11.8
Bronchitis, emphysema, and asthma	10.0	14.4	5.9	10.8	15.5	6.4	5.0	7.3	2.9
Tuberculosis, all forms	1.3	1.8	0.9	1.1	1.4	0.7	3.0	4.3	1.7

DEATH RATES IN AMERICA 1978 (per 100,000)
SOURCE: National Center for Health Statistics

Age Group	Total			White			All Other		
	Both sexes	Male	Female	Both sexes	Male	Female	Both sexes	Male	Female
All ages[1]	883.4	994.4	778.3	895.7	999.8	796.5	805.1	959.7	664.5
Under 1 year	1,434.4	1,591.7	1,269.6	1,218.3	1,359.6	1,069.7	2,456.7	2,708.5	2,206.5
1-4	69.2	78.2	59.9	62.7	71.7	53.3	99.0	108.1	89.7
5-9	33.4	38.9	27.8	31.4	36.3	26.3	43.0	51.5	34.4
10-14	34.3	43.7	24.6	33.0	41.8	23.7	40.9	53.1	28.6
15-19	100.9	145.3	55.3	101.8	146.9	55.2	96.0	136.1	55.9
20-24	134.7	203.1	66.5	126.3	190.8	61.0	184.0	278.4	97.2
25-29	131.8	192.2	72.5	115.7	168.3	63.0	233.7	356.7	128.5
30-34	139.7	192.9	87.8	120.6	165.0	76.4	270.5	402.3	159.7
35-39	189.4	254.0	127.9	161.7	215.3	109.6	381.6	548.8	244.8
40-44	296.1	382.8	213.8	257.2	329.1	187.5	562.6	784.7	380.9
45-49	471.6	608.5	341.4	428.5	553.8	307.8	779.7	1,021.3	570.1
50-54	742.4	980.9	520.5	683.7	906.6	474.5	1,216.8	1,610.3	877.4
55-59	1,115.9	1,490.1	774.3	1,046.0	1,404.8	716.5	1,734.2	2,266.7	1,271.5
60-64	1,774.2	2,411.5	1,212.8	1,695.2	2,318.2	1,143.4	2,537.7	3,339.1	1,867.3
65-69	2,463.0	3,439.3	1,685.2	2,412.7	3,394.5	1,628.2	2,878.3	3,814.8	2,150.3
70-74	3,787.4	5,241.5	2,724.9	3,684.9	5,166.9	2,612.5	4,877.9	5,984.5	3,980.1
75-79	6,024.2	8,065.8	4,713.2	5,393.8	7,996.2	4,564.3	7,547.7	8,724.1	6,620.7
80-84	8,954.0	11,597.1	7,509.4	9,080.7	11,821.8	7,606.7	7,573.2	9,419.8	6,372.9
85 and over	14,700.7	17,258.9	13,541.2	15,316.0	18,100.3	14,079.0	9,228.7	10,678.2	8,449.0

[1]Figures for age not stated included in "All ages" but not distributed among age groups.

U.S. DEATHS FROM ACCIDENTS
SOURCE: National Center for Health Statistics

Type of Accident	Deaths per 100,000 Population			Type of Accident	Deaths per 100,000 Population		
	1970	1973	1978		1970	1973	1978
All Accidents	56.4	55.2	48.4	Unspecified falls	5.6	5.5	4.3
Railway Accidents	0.4	0.4	0.3	Accidents caused			
Motor vehicle accidents	26.9	26.5	24.0	By fire and flames	3.3	3.1	2.8
Motor vehicle traffic	26.3	25.9	23.5	By firearms	1.2	1.2	0.8
Vehicle pedestrian	4.4	4.3	3.7	Accidents mainly of industrial type			
Other road vehicle accidents	0.1	0.1	0.1	Cutting or piercing instruments	0.1	0.1	0.1
Water transport accidents	0.8	0.8	0.7	Explosive material	0.3	0.2	0.2
Air and space transport accidents	0.8	0.8	0.9	Hot substances, etc.	0.1	0.1	0.1
Accidental poisoning				Electric current	0.6	0.5	0.5
By solid and liquid substances	1.8	1.8	1.4	Other	1.9	1.8	1.6
By gases and vapors	0.8	0.8	0.8	Inhalation and ingestion of objects	1.4	1.4	1.4
Accidental falls	8.3	7.9	6.3	Accidental drowning	3.1	3.4	2.7
Fall from one level to another	2.4	2.0	1.8	Complications due to medical procedures	1.8	1.7	1.4
Fall on the same level	0.4	0.3	0.2	All other accidents	2.8	2.5	2.5

U.S. HOMICIDES AND SUICIDES Source: National Center For Health Statistics

Item	1960 Male	1960 Female	1965 Male	1965 Female	1970 Male	1970 Female	1978 Male	1978 Female
Homicide	6,269	2,195	8,148	2,564	13,278	3,570	15,838	4,594
Assault by:								
Firearms and explosives	3,460	1,167	4,807	1,351	9,209	2,004	10,997	2,389
Cutting and piercing instruments	1,442	394	1,847	445	2,229	551	2,729	783
Other means	1,069	631	1,216	768	1,512	1,010	1,854	1,414
Intervention of police	242	3	271	—	328	5	257	8
Execution	56	—	7	—	1	—	1	—
Suicide	14,539	4,502	15,490	6,017	16,629	6,851	20,188	7,106
Poisoning	2,631	1,699	3,179	2,816	3,299	3,285	3,105	2,912
Hanging and strangulation	2,576	79	2,453	744	2,422	831	2,759	753
Firearms and explosives	7,879	1,138	8,457	1,441	9,704	2,068	12,830	2,557
Other	1,453	875	1,401	1,016	1,204	667	1,494	884

—Represents zero.

ACCIDENTAL DEATH RATES: BY NATIONS
Source: U.N. Demographic Yearbook, 1978 (Table 21), © United Nations

Nation	Latest Year Available	Accidental Deaths per 100,000 Population*	Nation	Latest Year Available	Accidental Deaths per 100,000 Population*
South Africa			Switzerland	1977	46.8
Nonwhite	1971	88.0	Norway	1977	46.0
White	1971	70.9	Ireland	1975	45.2
Zimbabwe (European)	1977	75.0	Mexico	1975	45.1
France	1970	74.8	Greece	1976	44.7
Austria	1976	69.8	Yugoslavia	1975	43.9
Hungary	1977	63.3	Costa Rica	1977	42.9
Portugal	1975	63.3	Bulgaria	1976	40.4
Luxembourg	1976	62.6	Uruguay	1976	39.7
Belgium	1976	60.5	Spain	1975	38.6
Kuwait	1977	59.1	Netherlands	1977	37.3
Czechoslovakia	1976	58.7	Denmark	1976	37.0
Venezuela	1977	57.9	Israel	1977	33.4
Finland	1974	56.8	Jordan	1976	31.4
Iceland	1977	54.1	England Wales	1976	30.6
Ecuador	1975	53.1	Canada	1976	30.0
Germany, East	1976	52.4	Japan	1977	26.6
Germany, West	1976	51.5	Chile	1976	24.8
New Zealand	1976	51.2	Singapore	1977	21.8
Italy	1972	48.9	Paraguay	1977	20.1
Australia	1977	48.0	Malta	1977	19.8
Sweden	1975	48.0	Argentina	1977	19.5
UNITED STATES	1976	46.9	Hong Kong	1977	19.5

*Based on population estimates for the designated year.

INTERNATIONAL SUICIDE RATES (per 100,000 population)
Source: United Nations Demographic Yearbook, 1978 (Table 21), © United Nations

Nation	Year	Rate	Nation	Year	Rate
Hungary	1977	40.3	Australia	1977	11.1
Finland	1974	25.1	Uruguay	1976	10.8
Denmark	1976	23.9	Singapore	1977	9.7
Switzerland	1977	23.8	Netherlands	1977	9.2
Austria	1976	22.7	New Zealand	1976	9.2
Germany, West	1976	21.7	Trinidad Tobago	1976	8.9
Czechoslovakia	1976	20.8	Portugal	1975	8.5
Iceland	1977	20.4	Argentina	1977	7.8
Sweden	1975	19.4	England Wales	1976	7.8
Japan	1977	17.8	Israel	1977	6.5
Belgium	1976	16.6	Mauritius	1977	6.4
France	1970	15.4	Italy	1972	5.8
Cuba	1971	15.0	Chile	1976	5.7
Luxembourg	1976	14.6	Ireland	1975	4.7
Zimbabwe (European)	1977	14.6	Venezuela	1977	4.6
South Africa			Costa Rica	1977	4.4
White	1971	14.5	Spain	1975	3.9
Nonwhite	1971	5.6	Greece	1976	2.8
Bulgaria	1976	14.1	Paraguay	1977	1.8
Yugoslavia	1975	13.4	Mexico	1975	1.7
Canada	1976	12.8	Kuwait	1977	0.4
UNITED STATES	1976	12.5	Guyana	1976	0.3
Hong Kong	1977	12.3	Jordan	1976	0.2
Norway	1977	11.4	Egypt	1975	0.1

VENEREAL DISEASE Source: American Social Health Association

Venereal disease, or more accurately, sexually transmissible disease, encompasses 20 conditions of which gonorrhea, nongonococcal urethritis/cervicitis, genital herpes, syphilis, cytomegalovirus and group B streptococcal disease are the most dangerous. It is estimated that over ten million persons were affected with some form of VD this year. Complications from prolonged and untreated infection with some forms of VD can lead to serious medical conditions, some of which can be permanently debilitating and even fatal.

Most venereal diseases can be completely cured although at least two are viral and cannot. Genital herpes is spreading at an alarming rate, and is associated with cervical cancer in women and brain damage in newborn babies. With vaccines for any of the venereal diseases still some way off, major attention is given to educating the public. The American Social Health Association produces and distributes, films, literature and other material suited for home, classroom or clinic. Additionally, the VD National Hotline, an information and referral service in the continental U.S. is 800-227-8922 (Calif., 800-982-5883), provides service 8 AM-8 PM, M-F, 10 AM-6 PM, S/Sun.

REFERENCE CHART: LEADING CANCER SITES, 1981 (ESTIMATED)

SOURCE: American Cancer Society. All figures rounded to nearest 1,000.

Site	Estimated New Cases 1981	Estimated Deaths 1981	Warning Signal: If you have one, see your doctor	Safeguards	Comment
BREAST	111,000	37,000	Lump or thickening in the breast or unusual discharge from nipple.	Regular checkup. Monthly breast self-examination.	The leading cause of cancer death in women.
COLON AND RECTUM	120,000	55,000	Change in bowel habits; bleeding.	Regular checkup, including digital, occult blood and proctoscopic exams, especially after age 40.	Because of accuracy of available tests, is potentially a highly curable disease.
LUNG	122,000	105,000	Persistent cough, or lingering respiratory ailment cigarettes.	80% of lung cancer would be prevented if no one smoked	The leading cause of cancer death among men and rising mortality among women.
ORAL (INCLUDING PHARYNX)	27,000	9,000	Sore that does not heal. Difficulty in swallowing.	Regular checkup.	Many more lives should be saved because the mouth is easily accessible to visual examination by physicians and dentists.
SKIN	14,000[1]	7,000	Sore that does not heal, or change in wart or mole.	Regular checkup, avoidance of over-exposure to sun.	Skin cancer is readily detected by observation, and diagnosed by simple biopsy.
UTERUS	54,000[2]	10,000	Unusual bleeding or discharge.	Regular checkup, including pelvic examination with Pap test.	Uterine cancer mortality has declined 70% during the last 40 years with wider application of the Pap test. Postmenopausal women with abnormal bleeding should be checked.
KIDNEY AND BLADDER	55,000	19,000	Urinary difficulty bleeding, in which case consult doctor at once	Regular checkup with urinalysis.	Protective measures for workers in high-risk industries are helping to eliminate one of the important causes of these cancers.
LARYNX	11,000	4,000	Hoarseness—difficulty in swallowing.	Regular checkup, including larygoscopy.	Readily curable if caught early.
PROSTATE	70,000	23,000	Urinary difficulty	Regular checkup, including palpation.	Occurs mainly in men over 60, the disease can be detected by palpation at regular checkup.
STOMACH	24,000	14,000	Indigestion	Regular checkup.	An 80% decline in mortality in 50 years, for reasons yet unknown.
LEUKEMIA	23,000	16,000	Leukemia is cancer of blood-forming tissues and is characterized by the abnormal production of immature white blood cells. Acute lymphocytic leukemia strikes mainly children and is treated by drugs which have extended life from a few months to as much as ten years. Chronic leukemia strikes usually after age 25 and progresses less rapidly.		
LYMPHOMAS	40,000	22,000	These cancers arise in the lymph system and include Hodgkin's Disease and lymphosarcoma. Some patients with lymphatic cancers can lead normal lives for many years. Five-year survival rate for Hodgkin's Disease increased from 25% to 54% in 20 years.		

[1]Only melanoma. Estimate new cases of non-melanoma skin cancer over 400,000. [2]If carcinoma in situ is included, cases total over 98,000.

PROGRESS AGAINST CANCER

Category	1937	1980
Saved (alive five years after treatment)	Fewer than one in five	One in three
Uterine cancer	Chief cause of cancer death in women	Death rate cut more than 70% since 1930 Could be reduced more
Lung cancer	Mounting: no prospect of control	Still mounting: but upward of 80% could be prevented
Research support	Less than $1,000,000	Over $1,000,000,000
Cancer clinics and registries approved by American College of Surgeons	240 in United States and Canada	Over 800, plus expansion of teaching, research, treatment centers
State control measures	Seven states	All 50 states
Chemotherapy	Almost no research	Major research attack has produced more than 40 useful drugs

One in two patients could be saved today by early diagnosis and prompt treatment.

CANCER DEATH RATES AROUND THE WORLD   SOURCE: American Cancer Society

Death Rates per 100,000 Population—1974-75.

Male Cancer Death Rates		Male Cancer Death Rates		Female Cancer Death Rates		Female Cancer Death Rates	
Czechoslovakia*	213.2	New Zealand	174.5	Ireland	132.3	Iceland	115.4
Scotland	205.0	Northern Ireland	170.3	Hungary	129.0	Belgium	115.2
Belgium	200.4	Hong Kong	169.4	Scotland	128.7	Netherlands	113.8
Hungary	195.2	Italy*	169.2	Denmark	127.2	Sweden	112.3
France*	194.5	Denmark	165.5	Austria	123.4	Canada*	109.3
Netherlands	193.4	Ireland	165.1	England & Wales	123.0	UNITED STATES	106.1
Luxembourg*	193.4	Australia	163.2	Uruguay*	122.9	Luxembourg*	106.1
Uruguay*	192.9	Singapore	162.1	New Zealand	121.8	Costa Rica	106.0
England & Wales	189.7	Poland	160.4	Chile	121.4	Switzerland	103.5
Austria	189.4	UNITED STATES	159.4	Germany, West	121.3	Trinidad & Tobago*	102.9
Germany, West	182.4	Canada*	157.6	Israel	118.5	Australia	102.0
Finland*	182.0	Chile	147.0	Northern Ireland	118.1	Norway	101.8
Switzerland	175.2	Sweden	146.6	Czechoslovakia*	118.0	Poland	101.2

*1974 only.

ADJUSTED HOSPITAL EXPENSE PER INPATIENT DAY: COMMUNITY HOSPITALS, 1968-1979   Source: American Hospital Association

Expenses per day related to inpatient care adjusted to exclude those expenses incurred for outpatient care.

Hospital Size All Community	1968	1970	1972	1974	1976	1977	1978	1979
Hospitals	$55.80	$73.73	$94.87	$113.55	$151.79	$173.98	$194.34	$217.34
6-24 Beds	41.98	59.68	75.76	83.44	117.46	132.19	152.34	176.19
25-49 Beds	41.10	54.15	68.68	82.73	113.42	132.33	151.68	172.05
50-99 Beds	45.24	58.85	72.98	86.58	117.95	134.53	149.68	170.12
100-199 Beds	51.11	65.87	84.31	101.06	135.04	154.64	172.50	193.55
200-299 Beds	56.22	74.32	92.43	111.35	148.37	169.76	186.94	206.90
300-399 Beds	59.24	77.96	99.34	116.80	155.99	177.72	200.70	223.27
400-499 Beds	60.67	79.68	100.23	122.11	160.35	183.55	208.78	234.15
500 or more Beds	66.27	87.37	115.34	136.73	179.80	206.40	228.53	254.17

HOSPITAL COSTS IN COMMUNITY HOSPITALS   Source: American Hospital Association

Year	Adjusted Expenses per Inpatient Day	Average Length of Stay (Days)	Average Adjusted Expense per Patient Stay	Year	Adjusted Expenses per Inpatient Day	Average Length of Stay (Days)	Average Adjusted Expense per Patient Stay
1963	$35.11	7.7	$270.35	1973	$102.44	7.8	$ 799.03
1965	40.56	7.8	316.37	1974	113.55	7.8	885.69
1967	49.46	8.3	410.52	1975	133.81	7.7	1030.34
1969	64.26	8.3	533.36	1976	151.79	7.7	1168.78
1970	73.73	8.2	604.59	1977	173.98	7.6	1322.25
1971	83.43	8.0	667.44	1978	194.34	7.6	1474.41
1972	94.87	7.9	749.47	1979	217.34	7.6	1641.48

ABORTION AND THE LAW

On January 22, 1973, the U.S. Supreme Court issued two landmark rulings in *Roe v. Wade* and *Doe v. Bolton* which declared the abortion laws of Texas and Georgia, respectively, unconstitutional. As a result of these decisions, state abortion laws are subject to the Court's three-fold guidelines (each of which determines the states' power to regulate abortion based on the trimester of pregnancy in question).

Since that time, state legislatures and the Congress have set up parental and spousal consent requirements or funding regulations pursuant to their legitimate interests "in the health of the mother and the potential life of the fetus." In a 1976 decision, the Court ruled that the State cannot, in all cases, require parental consent to abortions for minors. The Court did decide, however, that statutory provisions requiring written consent of the aborting mother, and requiring recordkeeping and reporting which "are reasonably directed to the preservation of maternal health and that properly respect a patient's confidentiality and privacy," are constitutional. During 1981, the High Court decided that a statute which requires a physician to notify an immature, unemancipated minor's parents of her intent to abort was unconstitutional. The Court also affirmed an Indiana federal court decision upholding the constitutionality of an Indiana law requiring that all second trimester abortions be performed in hospitals.

In two 1977 decisions, *Maher v. Roe* and *Beal v. Doe*, the Court ruled that states have no Constitutional or statutorial obligation to provide Medicaid funding for elective nontherapeutic abortion. The Court maintained that "the State unquestionably has a 'strong and legitimate interest in encouraging normal childbirth...' an interest honored over the centuries." Such "sensitive" issues, declared the Court, are properly decided by the legislature in a democratic society. In June 1980, the Supreme Court, in *Harris v. McRae* and *Williams v. Zbarag*, extended its ruling by determining that neither Congress nor the States need provide funding for medically necessary abortions. Resolving a much contested element in the abortion controversy, the Court further declared that such funding restrictions are not violative of the First Amendment's Establishment Clause just because it "may coincide with the religious tenets of the Roman Catholic Church."

ABORTION DEBATE: 1981

Since 1973, opponents of abortion have sought to reverse the Court's decisions through legislation and litigation. Their major efforts have been directed in these areas:

Constitutional Amendments: "Right-to-life" and "states rights" amendments have been proposed. The former would accord personhood to the unborn child, while the latter would return abortion regulation to the states. As an alternative means to amending the Constitution, abortion opponents are pursuing, at the state level, the route that would require Congress to convene a Constitutional Convention to adopt a "Human Life Amendment." As of August 1981, 19 state legislatures—of a required 34—have passed resolutions to attain this end.

Human Life Statute: Abortion opponents added another approach to changing the present law by introducing a Human Life Bill which would, instead of directly amending the Constitution, make a legislative finding that human life "begins at conception," that "the Fourteenth Amendment ... protects all human beings," and declare that due process of law must therefore be accorded to unborn children. The states and the federal government would then be free to prohibit abortions. Constitutional scholars are divided on the constitutionality of such a proposal.

Funding Restrictions: In 1976, Congress enacted the "Hyde Amendment" to the Labor-HEW Appropriations bill to cut off, in most cases, federal funds for abortion provided through the Medicaid program. Various versions, more or less restrictive than the 1976 bill, had been enacted by each successive Congress. A number of states had also continued to prohibit the use of public funds for abortion. Court challenges were brought against the Hyde Amendment and some of the state laws which restricted government funding of abortions. In two 1977 decisions, the U.S. Supreme Court held that funding of non-medically necessary abortions is not mandated by either the Constitution or the Medicaid provisions of the Social Security Act. Subsequently, two federal judges, one each from Illinois and New York, declared the Hyde Amendment unconstitutional. The Illinois judge also ruled unconstitutional an Illinois statute prohibiting state funding of medically necessary abortions. Federal funding of abortion was then resumed pending action by the Supreme Court. In June 1980, the Court, extending the reasoning of the 1977 cases, decided that neither Congress nor the States was constitutionally compelled, nor were the States required by the Medicaid statute, to provide funding for medically necessary abortions. Its opinion also affirmed that "abortion is inherently different from other medical procedures because no other medical procedure involves the purposeful termination of a potential life." In order to circumvent the effect of permitting states to prohibit abortion funding, abortion advocates sued in California and Massachusetts to have abortion funding restrictions declared violative of their *state* constitutions. Both courts decided that their respective state constitutions, as compared with the United States Constitution, afford a greater degree of protection to a woman's decision to have an abortion. Hence, California, with regard to all abortions, and Massachusetts, with respect to medically necessary abortions, held that where the state funds childbirth it must also contribute to abortions. Similar arguments are under consideration by a New Jersey appellate court.

Consent Requirements: The Supreme Court has ruled that parental and spousal vetoes of a woman's choice to abort are unconstitutional. However, in 1981 in *H.L. v. Matheson* the highest tribunal declared that a law which mandates "possible" notification of parents of a minor who is seeking an abortion, and is a dependent, unemancipated child making "no claim or showing as to her maturity or as to her relation with her parents" is constitutional. The Court voted that such a statute serves to preserve "family integrity and [protect] adolescents."

"Informed Consent" Provisions: Laws mandating counseling procedures such as detailing fetal development and possible physical and psychological complications subsequent to abortion have been passed by several state legislatures.

AIR POLLUTION IN U.S. AIR QUALITY CONTROL AREAS: 1978
SOURCE: Environmental Protection Agency

OZONE/OXIDANT
Note: The new ozone standard is 235 $\mu g/m^3$, daily maximum hour.

Number of Stations

Metropolitan Area	Total Valid	Exceeding 1-hour Average of 160$\mu g/m^3$	Range of Max. 1-Hr. Values ($\mu g/m^3$*)
New York	13	13	216–392
Los Angeles	22	19	176–686
Chicago	27	15	137–451
Philadelphia	16	14	216–392
Detroit	8	6	216–353
San Francisco	18	10	176–333
Boston	3	3	255–274
Washington, D.C.	14	11	216–372
Cleveland	11	8	137–412
St. Louis	16	13	157–412

*$\mu g/m^3$ = micrograms per cubic meter.

CARBON MONOXIDE
Note: The 8-hour standard is 10 milligrams per cubic meter of air ($\mu g/m^3$) arithmetic mean.

Number of Stations

Metropolitan Area	Total Valid	Exceeding 8-Hour Standard	Range of Max. 8-Hour Values ($\mu g/m^3$)*
New York	23	11	4.1–18.7
Los Angeles	24	12	6.2–22.6
Chicago	18	5	4.3–18.1
Philadelphia	20	7	4.1–16.1
Detroit	9	3	6.8–13.6
San Francisco	15	3	5.8–16.5
Boston	6	5	9.9–15.6
Washington, D.C.	14	10	15.8–24.4
Cleveland	3	1	6.5–13.1
St. Louis	13	7	5.0–16.0

* $\mu g/m^3$ = milligrams per cubic meter.

SULFUR DIOXIDE
Note: The primary annual standard is 80 $\mu g/m^3$, arithmetic mean.

Number of Stations

Metropolitan Area	Total Valid	Exceeding Annual Standard	Range of Annual Mean ($\mu g/m^3$)*
New York	25	0	15–56
Los Angeles	1	0	4–4
Chicago	20	0	11–79
Philadelphia	15	0	24–70
San Francisco	8	0	5–11
Detroit	7	0	20–44
Boston	3	0	21–51
Washington, D.C.	5	0	12–58
Cleveland	4	0	57–72
St. Louis	10	0	30–47

*$\mu g/m^3$ = micrograms per cubic meter.

TOTAL SUSPENDED PARTICULATES
Note: Th primary annual standard is 75 $\mu g/m^3$, geometric mean.

Number of Stations

Metropolitan Area	Total Valid	Exceeding Annual Standard	Range of Annual Mean ($\mu g/m^3$)*
New York	91	6	26– 95
Los Angeles	15	12	62–153
Chicago	91	27	38–138
Philadelphia	46	5	29–94
Detroit	40	13	39–151
San Francisco	14	1	40–114
Boston	16	1	37–82
Washington, D.C.	44	1	32–79
Cleveland	87	15	43–146
St. Louis	26	10	25–176

*$\mu g/m^3$ = micrograms per cubic meter.

WORLDWIDE TANKER* CASUALTIES, 1973 TO 1979
SOURCE: Tanker Advisory Center, New York, N.Y.

Accidental Tanker Oil Spills

Year	Number	Amount (tons)
1973	36	84,458
1974	48	67,114
1975	45	188,042
1976	29	204,235
1977	49	213,080
1978	35	260,488
1979	65	723,533

*Includes tankers, ore/oil and bulk/oil ships of 6,000 deadweight tons

Tanker Casualties by Flag of Registry, 1978

Country	total	Percent of Total
U.S.	76	11.1
U.K.	87	12.7
Greek	96	14.0
Japanese	12	1.8
Liberian	187	27.3
Norwegian	18	2.6
Panamanian	33	4.8
USSR	8	1.2
Other nations	168	24.5 and over.
Total, 66 nations	685	100.0

MEDICAL CARE INDEXES
SOURCE: U.S. Bureau of Labor Statistics

Year	All medical care items*	Physicians' services	Dental services	Optometric examination and eyeglasses	Hospital daily service charges	Prescriptions and drugs
1935	36.1	39.2	40.8	56.7	11.9	70.7
1945	42.1	46.0	49.6	63.9	16.2	74.8
1955	64.8	65.4	73.0	77.0	41.5	94.7
1960	79.1	77.0	82.1	85.1	56.3	104.5
1962	83.5	81.3	84.7	89.2	64.9	101.7
1964	87.3	85.2	89.4	90.9	72.4	100.5
1965	89.5	88.3	92.2	92.8	76.6	100.2
1966	93.4	93.4	95.2	95.3	84.0	100.5
1967	100.0	100.0	100.0	100.0	100.0	100.0
1968	106.1	105.6	105.5	103.2	113.2	100.2
1969	113.4	112.9	112.9	107.6	127.9	101.3
1970	120.6	121.4	119.4	113.5	143.9	103.6
1971	128.4	129.8	127.0	120.3	160.8	105.4
1972	132.5	133.8	132.3	124.9	102.0†	105.6
1973	137.7	138.2	136.4	129.5	105.6†	105.9
1974	150.5	150.9	146.8	138.6	115.1†	109.6
1975	168.6	169.4	161.9	149.6	132.3†	118.8
1976	184.7	188.5	172.2	158.9	148.7†	126.0
1977	202.4	206.0	185.1	168.2	164.1†	134.1
1978	219.4	223.1	198.1	—	—	143.5
1979	239.7	243.6	214.8	—	—	153.8
1980	265.9	269.3	240.2	—	—	186.1

*1967 = 100 †Hospital Service Charges (January 1972 = 100)

MILESTONES OF MEDICINE

Date	Milestone	Discoverer	Nationality
6th cent. B.C.	First recorded dietary and sanitary laws	Book of Leviticus	Hebrew
5th–4th cent. B.C.	Medicine moves from realm of superstition to that of observation; emergence of the idea of nature as healer	Hippocrates	Greek
4th cent. B.C.	Beginning of a systematic study of anatomy	Herophilus	Greek
2d cent. A.D.	Correlation of extant medical knowledge into a single great system that influenced medical thought until the 16th century	Clarissimus Galen	Greco-Roman
9th or 10th cent.	First-known description of smallpox and differentiation between that disease and measles; the approach was used until the 18th century	Rhazes or Rasis	Persian
16th cent.	Reaffirmation of nature as prime healer; also, beginning of chemotherapy	Paracelsus	Swiss
1543	Publication of De humani corporis fabrica, first anatomy textbook based entirely on observation, rather than on Galen's writings	Andreas Vesalius	Flemish
c. 1590	Invention of the microscope	Zacharias Janssen	Dutch
1628	Discovery of blood circulation	William Harvey	English
c. 1648	Founding of biochemistry	Jan Baptista van Helmont	Flemish
1661	Discovery that capillaries are vein-artery junctions, thus completing the explanation of blood circulation	Marcello Malpighi	Italian
1736	First successful appendectomy	Claudius Amyand	French
1757–66	Established physiology as a branch of science	Albrecht von Haller	Swiss
1796	First successful antitoxin vaccination (for smallpox)	Edward Jenner	English
1800	Founding of histology—the study of tissues	Marie F. X. Bichat	French
1816	Invention of the stethoscope	René Laënnec	French
1822	Description of the process of digestion	William Beaumont	American
1838–39	Establishment of cell theory founding of cytology	Matthias Schleiden, Theodor Schwann	German
1842	Use of ether as an anesthetic during surgery	Crawford W. Long	American
1844	Use of nitrous oxide as anesthetic during surgery	Horace Wells	American
1857	Development of the pasteurization process began	Louis Pasteur	French
1860	Experiments that finally destroyed the idea of spontaneous generation	Louis Pasteur	French
1865	Introduction of surgical antisepsis	Joseph Lister	English
1866	Invention of the clinical thermometer	Thomas C. Allbut	English
1870–1909	Founding of neuroanatomy	Camillo Golgi	Italian
c. 1872	Founding of bacteriology	Ferdinand Cohn	German
1877	Publication of postulates for determining the etiology of diseases	Robert Koch	German
1883–84	Discovery of the bacillus that causes diphtheria	Edwin Klebs, Friedrich Löffler	German
1890–95	Founding of serology and immunology	Paul Ehrlich, Emil von Behring	German
1894	Discovery of bubonic plague's causative bacillus	Alexandre Yersin	French
		S. Kitasato	Japanese
1892, 1895	Founding of virology	Dmitri Ivanovski	Russian
		(Independently, M. Beijerinck)	Dutch
1895	Publication of Studies in Hysteria; founding of psychoanalysis	Sigmund Freud	Austrian
1895	Discovery of X rays	Wilhelm Roentgen	German
1897	Development of method for making a differential blood count	Paul Ehrlich	German
1901	Establishment of etiology of yellow fever	Walter Reed and others	American
1906	Development of specific test for syphilis	August Wassermann and others	German
		(Independently, Lazlo Detre)	Hungarian
1906	Passage of U.S. Pure Food Law—the first legislation of its kind	Harvey W. Wiley	American
1912	Discovery of vitamins	Casimir Funk	American, b. Poland
1915	Discovery of pellagra cure	Joseph Goldberger	American, b. Austria-Hungary
1921	Isolation of insulin for use in diabetic therapy	Frederick Banting, Charles Best	Canadian
1926	Discovery of liver extract (vitamin B_1)	George Minot, William Murphy	American
1928	Invention of artificial respirator ("iron lung")	Philip Drinker, Louis Shaw	American
1928	Discovery of penicillin	Alexander Fleming	Scottish
c. 1932	First use of sulfa drugs in therapy	Gerhard Domagk	German
1940	Discovery of the Rh factor	Karl Landsteiner	American, b. Austria
1943	Discovery of streptomycin and its use in treating tuberculosis	Selman Waksman	American
1944	Introduction of corrective heart surgery to enable survival of "blue babies"	Alfred Blalock, Helen Taussig	American
1949	Cortisone introduced into medical therapy	Philip Hench and others	American
1953	Establishment of cryosurgery in which body temperature is lowered to slow circulation, allowing dry-heart surgery	Henry Swan	American
1954	Introduction of open-heart surgery	C. Walton Lillehei	American
1954	Development of hypodermic poliomyelitis vaccine	Jonas Salk	American
1955	Development of oral poliomyelitis vaccine	Albert Sabin	American
1963	First use of artificial heart for circulating blood during heart surgery	Michael De Bakey	American
1967	First surgical transplant of a human heart	Christiaan Barnard	South African
1969	Deciphering of structure of gamma globulin—one of the body's chief defenders against diseases	Gerald Edelman and others	American
1972	Research into the structure of antibodies	Gerald Edelman	American
		Rodney R. Porter	English
1978	First "test-tube" baby born	Patrick Steptoe, Robert Edwards	English
1979	First synthesis of a biologically active human protein, Interferon	Kari Cantell	Finnish
		Charles Weissmann	Swiss
		Walter Gilbert	American

MEDICAL GLOSSARY

Abscess: Collection of pus in a tissue cavity resulting from a localized infection associated with cellular disintegration.

Anemia: Decrease in the number of circulating red blood cells or in their hemoglobin (oxygen-carrying pigment) content. Can result from excessive bleeding or blood destruction (either inherited or disease caused) or from decreased blood formation (either nutritional deficiency or disease). In one form, sickle-cell anemia, it is inherited, occurring almost wholly among blacks. Pernicious anemia is caused by inability to absorb vitamin B_{12}.

Angina: Choking pain. Angina pectoris: chest pain resulting from insufficient blood circulation through the vessels supplying blood to the heart, precipitated by exertion or emotion and usually relieved by a vasodilator drug.

Arteriosclerosis: Generalized thickening, loss of elasticity, and hardening of the body's small and medium-size arteries.

Atherosclerosis: Arteriosclerosis in which fatty plaques build up in the lining of the arteries, narrowing the passageway and making the arterial walls thick and stiff.

Asthma: Disease characterized by repeated attacks of shortness of breath, with wheezing, cough, and choking feeling due to a spasmodic narrowing of the small bronchi.

Biopsy: Removal of a small piece of tissue from the living body for microscopic or chemical examination to assist in disease diagnosis.

Bronchitis: Inflammation of the bronchi (tubular passages leading to lung cavities).

Cancer: Malignant disease in which abnormal tissue develops. The tumor may grow, invade nearby tissues and organs, and spread through the body via the lymph and blood vessels.

Cataract: Opacity of the normally transparent eye lens; this condition leads to impaired vision and stems from hereditary, nutritional, inflammatory, toxic, traumatic, or degenerative causes.

Catheterization: Introduction of a tubular instrument called a catheter into a body cavity for purposes of injecting fluids (as in intravenous therapy), of withdrawing fluids (as in bladder catheterization), or for observing body functions (as in cardiac catheterization).

Cerebrospinal Fluid Examination: Chemical, miscroscopic, and bacteriological examination of a sample of the usually clear and colorless liquid bathing the brain and spinal cord. The sample is usually removed by needle puncture of the lumbar spine.

Cirrhosis: Chronic liver ailment that results in a progressive destruction of liver cells and impairment of the organ's functions.

Computerized Axial Tomography (CAT Scan): The use of serial X-ray beams, recorders, and a computer to construct a visual, 3-dimensional description of any portion of the body for identification of abnormal structures or processes.

Conjunctivitis: Acute or chronic inflammation of the conjunctiva—the delicate transparent membrane lining the eyelids and covering the exposed surface of the eyeball. It results from the action of bacteria, allergens, and physical or chemical irritants.

Cyst: Any normal or abnormal sac in the body, especially one containing a liquid or semiliquid material.

Cystic Fibrosis: An inherited disease of the mucous-secreting glands that appears in infancy. Respiratory, excretory, and digestive functions are impaired by the copious production of thick secretions. There is no cure, but modern antibiotics and respiratory therapy enable children to live into adulthood.

Cystitis: Acute or chronic inflammation of the urinary bladder, caused by infection or irritation. The symptoms are frequent voiding accompanied by burning sensation and, sometimes, blood in the urine.

Diabetes (Mellitus): Hereditary or acquired disease of the insulin-secreting cells of the pancreas. Symptoms are thirst, weight loss, and frequent urination. Diabetes is diagnosed by use of urine and blood sugar tests. It is treated by regulating the sugar in the blood with diet, oral drugs, or, when necessary, with regular injections of insulin. Severe diabetes, if untreated, will result in kidney failure, blindness, and death.

Eczema: Inflammatory skin disease that produces a great variety of lesions, such as vesicles, thickening of skin, watery discharge, and scales and crusts, with itching and burning sensations. Eczema is caused by allergy, infections, and nutritional, physical, and sometimes unknown factors.

Edema: Excessive accumulation of water and salt in the tissue spaces, caused by kidney or heart disease (generalized edema) or by local circulatory impairment stemming from inflammation, trauma, or neoplasm (localized edema).

Electrocardiogram (ECG or EKG): Graphic tracing of the electric current that is produced by the rhythmic contraction of the heart muscle. Visually, a periodic wave pattern is produced. Changes in the wave pattern may appear in the course of various heart diseases; the tracing is obtained by applying electrodes on the skin of the chest and limbs.

Electroencephalogram (EEG): Graphic recording of the electric current created by the activity of the brain. The electrodes are placed on the scalp.

Embolism: Blocking of a blood vessel by a dislodged blood clot (after surgery), a fat globule (after a fracture), gas bubbles (after sudden decompression), clumps of bacteria (in certain infections), or by other matter.

Emphysema (Pulmonary): Lung disease characterized by over distention of the air sacs of the lungs (alveoli), their loss of elasticity, and destruction of the walls separating them. It results in a reduction of the respiratory surface, chronic shortness of breath, wheezing, and cough.

Epilepsy: Disease characterized by sudden and brief (in some forms momentary) convulsions, which are associated with impairment or loss of consciousness, psychic or sensory disturbances, and autonomic nervous system perturbations.

Gangrene: A form of necrosis (tissue death) due to an inadequate blood supply. Infection may also occur.

Gastritis: Acute or chronic inflammation of the lining of the stomach. It may be caused by the ingestion of alcohol, spices, medicines, chemicals, foods, as well as by infections or allergy.

Gastroscopy: Direct visualization of the stomach interior by means of an optical instrument called a gastroscope.

Gastrointestinal Series (G.I. Series): Serial X-ray examination of the stomach and intestines.

Glaucoma: Eye disease characterized by an increase in the internal pressure in the eye, caused by alteration of the intraocular fluid flow and resulting in visual impairment, and if untreated, blindness.

Goiter: Enlargement of the thyroid gland that shows as a swelling at the base of the neck. Goiter is often associated with iodine deficiency (endemic goiter), or with excessive secretion of thyroid hormones (exophthalmic goiter).

Gout: A disturbance of body chemistry, manifested by elevated uric acid blood levels and excessive deposits in tissues, particularly joints and cartilages. It is characterized by repeated attacks of acute and very painful inflammation of joints, especially those of the big toe but also of ankles, knees, wrists, and elbows.

Hematoma: Swelling produced by a collection of blood escaping from a ruptured blood vessel, resulting from trauma or injury. It is generally located under the skin and subcutaneous tissue, or under the bony structure of the skull.

Hemorrhage (Bleeding): Any copious blood loss from the circulation. If sufficiently severe or unchecked, it will lead to anemia, shock, and death.

Hemorrhoids (Piles): Abnormal dilatation of the veins of the rectum and anus, causing local swelling, pain, itching, bleeding, and induration.

Hepatitis: Liver inflammation, caused by infection or toxic substances. It is characterized by clay-colored stools, dark urine, fever, and jaundice (yellow coloration of the skin and white of the eye).

Hernia: Protrusion of a portion of an organ or tissue through an abnormal body opening. Inguinal hernia is one of the most common and consists of an intestinal loop protruding at the groin.

Hypertension: Disease characterized by elevated blood pressure, resulting from the functional or pathological narrowing of the peripheral small arteries. Except in limited instances, its cause is generally unknown.

Immunotherapy: A method of treating certain diseases by stimulating the body's natural immune response, resulting in partial or total immunization.

Intestinal Obstruction: Blocking of the normal flow of the intestinal contents, caused by twisting of a gut loop, benign tumor, cancer, or foreign body.

Kidney Failure (Renal Failure): Severe impairment of the excretory function of the kidney. The acute form occurs most frequently after crushing injuries, transfusion of mismatched blood, severe burns or shock, generalized infections, obstetric accidents, and certain chemical poisoning.

Laboratory Procedures: Laboratory tests performed to assist in disease diagnosis and treatment. Usually these tests are carried out on samples of blood, urine, or other body fluids. The most common are:

Blood Count: Determination of the number and percentage of red and white blood cells from a blood sample that is obtained by puncturing a vein or the skin. It consists of a red blood cell count (RBC), white blood cell count (WBC), and platelet count.

Blood Grouping: Classification of red blood cells by the demonstration of specific antigens in the blood. Always done prior to transfusion.

Blood Chemistry: Determination of the content of various blood chemicals; the most usual are: sugar, for diabetes; urea nitrogen (BUN), for kidney or liver disease; uric acid, for gout; and cholesterol, for vascular and liver disease.

Blood Culture: Investigation to detect the presence of pathogenic germs by special culturing in artificial media.

Urinalysis (Urine Analysis): Examination of urine constituents, both normal (urea, uric acid, total nitrogen, ammonia, chlorides, phosphate, and others) and abnormal (albumin, glucose, acetone, bile, blood, cells, and bacteria).

Meningitis: Inflammation of the enveloping membranes of the brain or spinal cord, caused by virus, bacteria, yeasts, fungi, or protozoa. It is frequently a serious complication of another infection.

Metabolism: The total of the physical and chemical processes occurring in the living organism by which its substance is produced, maintained, and exchanged with transformation of energy; this energy itself provides fuel for all body functions and heat production.

Metastasis: Transfer of a disease (usually cancer) or the causative agent of a disease (e.g. bacteria or cancer cells) from one organ or part of the body to another, through the blood or lymph vessels.

Multiple Sclerosis: A chronic and slowly progressive disease of unknown cause that is characterized by patches of fibrous tissue degeneration in brain and spinal cord, causing various nervous system symptoms. The disease's course is marked by occasional periods of worsening or improvement.

Muscular Dystrophy: An inherited disease that involves the progressive weakness and degeneration of voluntary skeletal muscle fibers without nerve involvement.

Myocarditis: Inflammation of the heart muscle that is associated with or caused by a number of infectious diseases, toxic chemicals, drugs, and traumatic agents.

Necrosis: Localized death of tissue, following interruption of the blood supply to the area.

Nephritis: Inflammatory, acute or chronic disease of the kidneys, which usually follows some form of infection or toxic chemical poisoning. It impairs renal function, causing headache, edema, elevated blood pressure, and appearance of albumin in urine.

Neuralgia: Brief attack of acute and severe shooting pain along the course of one or more peripheral nerves, usually without clear cause.

Neuritis: Inflammation or degeneration of one or more peripheral nerves, causing pain, tenderness, tingling sensations, numbness, paralysis, muscle weakness, and wasting and disappearance of reflexes in the area involved. The cause may be infectious, toxic, nutritional (vitamin B_1 deficiency), or unknown.

Pancreatitis: Inflammation of the pancreas, either mild or acute and fulminating. The chronic form is character-

ized by recurrent attacks of diverse severity. Symptoms are sudden abdominal pain, tenderness and distention, vomiting and, in severe cases, shock and circulatory collapse.

Pap Smears (Papanicolau Smears): Method of staining smears of various body secretions—especially cervical but also respiratory, digestive, or genitourinary—to detect cancer by examining the normally shed cells in the smear. The procedure is named for its developer.

Parkinsonism (Paralysis Agitans): A usually chronic condition, marked by muscular rigidity, immobile face, excessive salivation, and tremor. These symptoms characterize Parkinson's disease; however, they are also observed in the course of treatment with certain psychotropic drugs or following encephalitis, or trauma.

Pericarditis: Acute or chronic inflammation of the pericardium (fibrous sac surrounding the heart), caused by infection, trauma, myocardial infarction, cancer, or complication from other diseases.

Peritonitis: Acute or chronic inflammation of the serous membrane lining abdominal walls and covering the contained viscera. Its symptoms are abdominal pain and tenderness, nausea, vomiting, moderate fever, and constipation. It is usually caused by infectious agents or foreign matter entering the abdominal cavity from the intestinal tract (perforation), female genital tract, blood stream, or the outside (wounds, surgery).

Phlebitis: Condition caused by inflammation of a vein wall, usually resulting in the formation of a blood clot inside its cavity. Phlebitis produces pain, swelling, and stiffness of the affected part, generally a limb.

Pleurisy: Acute or chronic inflammation of the pleura (serous membranes lining the thoracic cavity and covering the lungs). It often accompanies inflammatory lung diseases and may be caused by infection, cancer, or cardiac infarct.

Pneumonia: An acute inflammation of the lungs, usually caused by bacterial or viral infection. Chills, sharp chest pain, shortness of breath, cough, rusty sputum, fever, and headache are primary symptoms.

Pneumothorax: Accumulation of air or gas in the space between the lungs and the chest wall, resulting in collapse of the lung.

Polycythemia: An abnormal increase in the number of circulating red blood cells.

Polyp: A protruding excrescence or growth from a mucous membrane, usually of the nasal passages but also of the uterine cervix, alimentary tract, or vocal cords.

Psoriasis: Chronic, occasionally acute, recurrent skin disease of unknown cause, characterized by thickened red skin patches that are covered with whitish shiny scales (plaques). Psoriasis usually affects the scalp, elbows, knees, back, and buttocks.

Pulmonary Edema: An acute condition in which there is a waterlogging of the lung tissue, including its alveolar cavities. Respiration is impaired. If inadequately treated, it may lead to rapid death; it is often a complication of chronic heart disease.

Rheumatic Fever: Disease characterized by initial sore throat, chills, high fever, and painful inflammation of large joints. Frequently cardiac complications follow, leading to permanent organic heart disease.

Rickets: Generally a disease of infants and young children caused by vitamin D deficiency. There is defective bone calcification that causes skeletal deformities, such as bow legs, knock knees, and pigeon chest.

Sciatica: A severe pain along the sciatic nerve, which extends from the buttocks along the back of the thigh and leg to the ankle.

Spinal Curvature: A marked displacement of the normally straight vertical spine, which may be caused by disease or mechanical deviation of the bones or muscles of the spine, hips, or legs.

Septicemia: Presence of bacteria or bacterial toxins in the circulating blood caused by the breakdown of local defenses, permitting a circumscribed infection to spread.

Silicosis: Occupational disease, usually chronic, causing fibrosis of the lungs. It results from inhalation of the dust of stone, flint, or sand that contains silica (quartz).

Slipped Disk: An acute or chronic condition, caused by the traumatic or degenerative displacement and protrusion of the softened central core of an intervertebral disk (cartilagenous disk between the spine bones), especially of the lower back. Symptoms are low back pain, which frequently extends to the thigh; muscle spasm; and tenderness.

Spastic Paralysis (Cerebral Palsy): A condition probably stemming from various causes present since birth. Associated with nonprogressive brain damage, cerebral palsy is characterized by spastic, jerky voluntary movements, or constant involuntary and irregular writhing.

Stroke (Cerebral Apoplexy): A sudden attack of paralysis, with disturbance of speech and thought. It is caused by the destruction of brain substance, as the result of brain hemorrhage, vascular damage, intravascular clotting, or local circulatory insufficiency.

Tardive Dyskinesia (TD): A condition in which there are repeated involuntary movements of the extremities, face, jaw, and tongue. TD afflicts many people who have taken antipsychotic medications for prolonged periods of time. It is disfiguring and usually not reversible.

Thermography: A diagnostic technique for locating the presence of underlying tumors by recording infrared radiations that emanate from the body surface: tumors radiate more heat than the surrounding tissues.

Thrombophlebitis: Condition caused by the inflammation of a vein complicated by the formation of an intravascular blood clot (thrombus). Circulation is obstructed in the affected area, usually the legs.

Thrombosis: Formation, development, or presence of a blood clot inside an artery or vein. This condition can be serious, if it affects the blood vessels of vital organs, such as the brain, heart, or lungs.

Toxic Shock Syndrome: A severe, life-threatening systemic infection caused by staphylococcal organisms. The infection may be associated with the use of "high-absorbency" tampons.

Tumor: A swelling or growth of new tissue; it develops independently of surrounding structures and serves no specific function of its own.

Uremia: Toxic clinical condition in which renal insufficiency allows the retention of urinary waste products in the circulating blood.

Varicose Veins: Abnormally distended and lengthened superficial veins caused by slowing and obstruction of the normal blood backflow. Varicose veins are most commonly observed in the legs, anus and rectum (hemorrhoids), and scrotum (varicocele).

MODERN DRUG ADVANCES

Acyclovir—Antiviral drug effective in preliminary studies for treatment of herpes infections.

Adrenocorticosteroids—More than 20 synthetic adrenal hormones and their chemical derivatives. They are used primarily in the treatment of "collagen diseases" (e.g., rheumatoid arthritis) and in the suppression of certain inflammatory diseases or immunological processes.

Allopurinol—An oral drug used in suppressing the symptoms of gout.

Ampicillin—A "broad-spectrum" semisynthetic penicillin effective in the treatment of many infections.

Antithyroid Agents—A group of unrelated compounds, ranging from propylthiouracil to radio-iodide; used for treating hyperthyroidism.

BCG (Bacille Calmette-Guérin)—A nonvirulent strain of tubercle bacillus used in vaccines for immunization against tuberculosis and experimentally in controlling some forms of cancer.

Chloramphenicol—An important broad-spectrum antibiotic that is used to treat typhoid fever, certain types of food poisoning, and other infections caused by microorganisms that are resistant to other antibiotics.

Chloroquin Compounds—Antimalarial and antiamebic.

Chlorpromazine and Other Tranquilizers—Over 30 compounds with mild depressant action on the brain, used in certain mental illnesses and anxiety states, and for antinauseant and sedative effects.

Clomiphene Citrate—A drug that improves fertility, sometimes causing multiple births.

Diphenhydramine and 30 Other Antihistaminics—Employed mainly in treating certain allergic conditions and also for antiemetic and sedative effects.

Estrogen-Progestogen Contraceptives—Oral contraceptive agents.

Ganglionic Blocking Agents, Mostly Quaternary Ammonium Compounds—Used in the treatment of certain types of hypertension.

Griseofulvin—A drug taken orally that is effective against many fungal infections of the skin and fingernails and toenails.

Halogenated Hydrocarbon Anesthetics—Volatile liquids that are used for inhalation anesthesia.

Hydantoins—Used to prevent or reduce seizures in epilepsy and other conditions.

Hypnotic Barbiturates—Sedatives and sleeping pills.

Immune Globulins—A protein derived from human blood that, when injected into persons exposed to certain infectious diseases, confers temporary immunity.

Interferon—A protein, produced by the white blood cells, that activates immune systems, prevents an invading virus from reproducing itself within the host cell, and changes membranes of the invaded cell to interfere with the virus's ability to infect other cells. It was recently synthesized and is being used experimentally in the treatment of certain cancers and viruses.

Isoniazid—The most important drug in the treatment and prophylaxis of tuberculosis.

Isoproterenol—Used in the treatment of bronchial asthma, particularly to relieve the bronchial-tube spasm.

Lidocaine and Other Local Anesthetics—Injected locally to anesthetize tissues prior to minor surgical operations.

Lithium—A drug found effective in the treatment of manic-depressive psychoses.

Meperidine—A powerful pain-relieving drug.

Methantheline and Other Anticholinergics—Parasympatholytic agents used in cases of peptic ulcer and to decrease hypermotility (or spasm) of the gastrointestinal tract.

Methicillin—The first penicillin effective against staph (staphylococcus) infections that are resistant to ordinary penicillin.

Oral Antidiabetes Agents—Drugs that stimulate the pancreas to produce more insulin, given to treat mild diabetes.

Propranolol—A drug for heart-rhythm disorders.

Rauwolfia and Veratrum Alkaloids—Principles of plant origin used in treating hypertension or as a tranquilizer.

Streptomycin—An important antibiotic, and one of the primary drugs for treating tuberculosis.

Sulfonamides—Used in the treatment of infections of the respiratory and urinary tracts and in certain types of meningitis.

Surgical Skeletal Muscle Relaxants (About seven surgical, peripherally acting preparations)—These drugs are used to relax muscles during surgery.

Synthetic Anticoagulants—Used to prevent formation or extension of blood clots within arteries and veins.

Ten Basic Penicillins, Plus Salts and Esters—Antibacterial drugs that are used primarily to treat infections of the skin, respiratory tract, and of the genitourinary tract.

Tetracycline Derivatives, Plus Salts and Esters—Used in the treatment of a wide variety of infections caused by many different types of micro-organisms.

Thiazide Organomercurial and Diuretics—To remove excess fluid from the body in certain types of heart and kidney diseases. Also used in the treatment of hypertension (high blood pressure).

Trihexyphenidyl, Amantadine Hydrochloride, L-Dopa, and Other Anti-Parkinsonism Agents—Used to relieve the muscle symptoms in patients with Parkinson's disease.

Vaccines—For the prevention or modification of infectious diseases, such as poliomyelitis, measles, and mumps.

PSYCHIATRIC TERMS

Source: American Psychiatric Association

Alienation: The estrangement felt in cultural settings one views as foreign, unpredictable, or unacceptable.

Anal Character: In psychoanalysis a pattern of behavior in an adult that originates in the anal eroticism of infancy and is characterized by such traits as excessive orderliness, miserliness, and obstinacy.

Anorexia Nervosa: A disorder marked by severe and prolonged refusal to eat, resulting in significant weight loss, amenorrhea or impotence, disturbance of body image, and an intense fear of becoming obese. Most frequently encountered in girls and young women.

Anxiety: Apprehension, the source of which is largely unknown or unrecognized. It is different from fear, which is the emotional response to a consciously recognized and usually external danger.

Autistic Child: In child psychiatry, a child who responds chiefly to inner thoughts, who does not relate to his environment, and whose overall functioning is immature and often appears retarded.

Blocking: Difficulty in recollection, or interruption of a train of thought or speech, caused by unconscious emotional factors.

Catatonic State (catatonia): A state characterized by immobility with muscular rigidity or inflexibility and at times by excitability. Virtually always a symptom of schizophrenia.

Community Mental Health Center (CMHC): A mental health delivery system providing community-based services. Regulations require that the following services be provided: inpatient, outpatient, partial hospitalization, services for children and the elderly, half-way houses, alcohol and drug abuse programs, emergency services, follow-up care, assistance to the courts and other public agencies, and consultation and education.

Compensation: (1) A defense mechanism, operating unconsciously, by which the individual attempts to make up for (i.e., to compensate for) real or fancied deficiencies; (2) a conscious process in which the individual strives to make up for real or imagined defects in such areas as physique, performance, skills, or psychological attributes.

Complex: A group of associated ideas that have a common emotional tie. These are largely unconscious and significantly influence attitudes and associations. Examples are:

Inferiority complex: Feelings of inferiority stemming from real or imagined physical or social inadequacies that may cause anxiety or other adverse reactions. The individual may overcompensate by excessive ambition or by the development of special skills, often in the very field in which he was originally handicapped.

Oedipus complex: Attachment of the child for the parent of the opposite sex, accompanied by envious and aggressive feelings toward the parent of the same sex. These feelings are largely repressed (i.e., made unconscious) because of the fear of displeasure or punishment by the parent of the same sex. In its original use, the term applied only to the male child.

Compulsion: An insistent, repetitive, and unwanted urge to perform an act that is contrary to the person's ordinary conscious wishes or standards. Failure to perform the compulsive act results in overt anxiety.

Defense Mechanism: A specific process, operating unconsciously, that is employed to seek relief from emotional conflict and freedom from anxiety.

Depression: Psychiatrically, a morbid sadness, dejection, or melancholy; to be differentiated from grief, which is realistic and proportionate to what has been lost. A depression may be a symptom of any psychiatric disorder or may constitute its principal manifestation.

Ego: In psychoanalytic theory, one of the three major divisions of human personality, the others being the *id* and *superego*. The ego, commonly identified with consciousness of self, is the mental agent mediating among three contending forces: the external demands of social pressure or reality; the primitive instinctual demands arising from the *id* imbedded as it is in the deepest level of the unconscious; and the claims of the *superego*, born of parental and social prohibitions and functioning as an internal censor or "conscience."

Empathy: An objective awareness of the feelings, emotions, and behavior of another person. To be distinguished from sympathy, which is usually nonobjective and noncritical.

Epilepsy: A disorder characterized by periodic seizures, and sometimes accompanied by a loss of consciousness. May be caused by organic or emotional disturbances.

Major epilepsy (grand mal): Characterized by gross convulsive seizures, with loss of consciousness.

Minor epilepsy (petit mal): Minor nonconvulsive epileptic seizures; may be limited to only momentary lapses of consciousness.

Euphoria: An exaggerated feeling of physical and emotional well-being inconsonant with reality.

Extroversion: A state in which attention and energies are largely directed outward from the self, as opposed to interest primarily directed toward the self, as in introversion.

Family Therapy: Psychiatric treatment of a family, usually begun when one member develops a mental disorder that may, in turn, reflect disease in another member.

Free Association: In psychoanalytic therapy, spontaneous, uncensored verbalization by the patient of whatever comes to mind.

Fugue: A major state of personality dissociation characterized by amnesia and actual physical flight from the immediate environment.

Homosexuality: Sexual attraction or relationship between members of the same sex.

Latent homosexuality: A condition characterized by unconscious homosexual desires.

Overt homosexuality: Homosexuality that is consciously recognized or practiced.

Hypnosis: A state of increased receptivity to suggestion and direction, initially induced by the influence of another person. The degree may vary from mild suggestibility to a trance state so profound as to be used in surgical operations.

Hypochondriasis: Overconcern with the state of physical or emotional health, accompanied by various bodily complaints without demonstrable organic pathology.

Hysterical Personality: A personality type characterized by shifting emotional feelings, susceptibility to suggestion, impulsive behavior, attention seeking, and immaturity.

Id: See Ego.

Inhibition: Interference with or restriction of activities; the result of an unconscious defense against forbidden instinctual drives.

Insight: Self-understanding. A major goal of psychotherapy. The extent of the individual's understanding of the origin, nature, and mechanisms of his attitudes and behavior.

Mania: A suffix denoting a pathological preoccupation with some desire, idea, or activity; a morbid compulsion. Some frequently encountered manias are *dipsomania*, compulsion to drink alcoholic beverages; *egomania*, pathological preoccupation with self; *kleptomania*, compulsion to steal; *pyromania*, morbid compulsion to set fires.

Manic-Depressive Reaction (bi-polar disorder): A group of psychiatric disorders marked by conspicuous mood swings, ranging from normal to elation or to depression, or alternating. Officially regarded as a psychosis but may also exist in milder form.

Depressed phase: Characterized by depression of mood with retardation and inhibition of thinking and physical activity.

Manic phase: Characterized by heightened excitability, acceleration of thought, speech, and bodily motion, and by elation or grandiosity of mood, and irritability.

Masochism: Pleasure derived from undergoing physical or psychological pain inflicted by oneself or by others. It may be consciously sought or unconsciously arranged or invited. Present to some degree in all human relations and to greater degrees in all psychiatric disorders. It is the converse of sadism, in which pain is inflicted on another, and the two tend to coexist in the same individual.

Narcissism (narcism): Self-love, as opposed to object-love (love of another person). Some degree of narcissim is considered healthy and normal, but an excess interferes with relations with others.

Obsession: Persistent, unwanted idea or impulse that cannot be eliminated by logic or reasoning.

Overcompensation: A conscious or unconscious process in which a real or fancied physical or psychological deficit inspires exaggerated correction.

Paranoid State: Characterized by delusions of persecution. A paranoid state may be of short duration or chronic.

Phobia: An obsessive, unrealistic fear of an external object or situation. Some of the common phobias are *acrophobia,* fear of heights; *agoraphobia,* fear of open places; *claustrophobia,* fear of closed spaces; *mysophobia,* fear of dirt and germs; *xenophobia,* fear of strangers.

Projective Tests: Psychological tests used as a diagnostic tool. Among the most common projective tests is the Rorschach (inkblot) test.

Psychoanalysis: A theory of human development and behavior, a method of research, and a system of psychotherapy, originally described by Sigmund Freud (1856–1939). Through analysis of free associations and interpretation of dreams, emotions and behavior are traced to the influence of repressed instinctual drives in the unconscious. Psychoanalytic treatment seeks to eliminate or diminish the undesirable effects of unconscious conflicts by making the patient aware of their existence, origin, and inappropriate expression.

Psychoneurosis: One of the two major categories of emotional illness, the other being the psychoses. It is usually less severe than a psychosis, with minimal loss of contact with reality.

Psychosis: A major mental disorder of organic and/or emotional origin in which there is a departure from normal patterns of thinking, feeling, and acting. Commonly characterized by loss of contact with reality, distortion of perception, regressive behavior and attitudes, diminished control of elementary impulses and desires, and delusions and hallucinations. Chronic and generalized personality deterioration may occur. A majority of patients in public mental hospitals are psychotic.

Psychosomatic: Adjective to denote the constant and inseparable interdependence of the psyche (mind) and the soma (body). Most commonly used to refer to illnesses in which the manifestations are primarily physical with at least a partial emotional cause.

Psychotherapy: The term for any type of mental treatment that is based primarily upon verbal or nonverbal communication with the patient, in distinction to the use of drugs, surgery, or physical measures such as electric or insulin shock.

Regression: The partial or symbolic return to more infantile patterns of reacting.

Repression: A defense mechanism, operating unconsciously, that banishes unacceptable ideas, emotions, or impulses from consciousness or that keeps out of consciousness what has never been conscious.

Sadism: *See* Masochism.

Schizophrenia: A severe emotional disorder of psychotic depth characteristically marked by a retreat from reality with delusion formation, hallucinations, emotional disharmony, and regressive behavior. Formerly called dementia praecox. Its prognosis has improved in recent years.

Shock Treatment: A form of psychiatric treatment in which electric current, insulin, or carbon dioxide is administered to the patient and results in a convulsive reaction to alter favorably the course of mental illness.

Sublimation: A defense mechanism, operating unconsciously, by which instinctual but consciously unacceptable drives are diverted into personally and socially acceptable channels.

Superego: *See* Ego.

Unconscious: That part of the mind the content of which is only rarely subject to awareness. It is the repository for knowledge that has never been conscious or that may have been conscious briefly and was then repressed.

PATIENT CARE EPISODES IN MENTAL HEALTH FACILITIES

SOURCE: National Institute for Mental Health

Patient care episodes are defined as the number of residents in inpatient facilities at the beginning of the year (or the number of persons on the rolls of noninpatient facilities) plus the total additions to these facilities during the year. Total additions during the year include new admissions, readmissions, and returns from long-term leave. The index, patient care episodes, therefore, is not equal to a true annual prevalence rate nor the annual prevalence of treated mental disorder, since episodes of care are counted rather than cases. This index does present useful measures of the volume of services utilized by persons with mental disorders and as such are useful in describing the distribution of episodes by age, sex, modality and type of facility.

While trend data on day care episodes by type of facility are not available for more than a few years, such data are available for inpatient and outpatient episodes as illustrated below. The number of inpatient and outpatient care episodes in mental health facilities in 1977 — 6.6 million — was almost four times greater than the approximately 1.7 million episodes in 1955.

Number and percent distribution of inpatient and outpatient care episodes[1], in selected mental health facilities, by type of facility: United States, 1955, 1965, 1975 and 1977 (Provisional)

Year	Total All[1] Facilities	Inpatient Services of: State & County Mental Hospitals	Private Mental[2] Hospitals	Gen. Hosp. Psychiatric Service (non-VA)	VA Psychiatric Inpatient Services	Outpatient Psychiatric Services of: Federally Assisted Comm. Men. Health Cen.	Federally Assisted Comm. Men. Health Cen.	Other
Number of Patient Care Episodes
1977	6,639,278	574,226	184,189	571,725	217,507	268,966	1,741,729	3,080,936
1975	6,409,447	598,993	165,327	265,934	88,355	—	—	379,000
1965	2,636,525	804,926	125,428	542,642	176,800	130,088	622,906	1,693,848
1955	1,675,352	818,832	123,231	519,328	115,843	—	—	1,071,000
Percent Distribution
1977	100.0	8.6	2.8	8.6	3.3	4.1	26.2	46.4
1975	100.0	9.3	2.6	8.8	3.3	3.9	24.7	47.4
1965	100.0	30.5	4.8	19.7	4.4	—	—	40.6
1955	100.0	48.9	7.3	15.9	5.3	—	—	22.6

[1] In order to present trends on the same set of facilities over this interval, it has been necessary to exclude from this table the following: private psychiatric office practice; psychiatric service modes of all types in hospitals or outpatient clinics of Federal agencies other than the VA (e.g., Public Health Service, Indian Health Service, Department of Defense Bureau of Prisons, etc.); inpatient service modes of multiservice facilities not shown in this table; all partial care episodes, and outpatient episodes of VA hospitals. [2] Includes estimates of episodes of care in residential treatment centers for emotionally disturbed children.

Source (All years except 1977): The National Institute of Mental Health, Statistical Note 139—Provisional data on patient care—episodes in mental health facilities, August 1977.

Source (1977): Unpublished provisional data from the National Institute of Mental Health.

RECOMMENDED DAILY DIETARY ALLOWANCES FOR AMERICANS

The schedule is designed for the maintenance of good nutrition of normally active Americans in a temperate climate. The following abbreviations are used: Gm. for gram; Mg. for milligram; I.U. for International Unit.

Family Members	Weight (Pounds)	Height Feet Inches	Calories	Protein (Gms.)	Calcium (Gms.)	Iron (Mg.)	Vitamin A (I.U.)	Thiamine (Mg.)	Riboflavin (Mg.)	Niacin (Mg. Equiv.)	Ascorbic Acid (Mg.)	Vitamin D (I.U.)
MEN												
18–35 years	154	5–9	2,900	70	0.8	10	5,000	1.2	1.7	19	70	—
35–55 years	154	5–9	2,600	70	0.8	10	5,000	1.0	1.6	17	70	—
55–75 years	154	5–9	2,200	70	0.8	10	5,000	0.9	1.3	15	70	—
WOMEN												
18–35 years	128	5–4	2,100	58	0.8	15	5,000	0.8	1.3	14	70	—
35–55 years	128	5–4	1,900	58	0.8	15	5,000	0.8	1.2	13	70	—
55–75 years	128	5–4	1,600	58	0.8	10	5,000	0.8	1.2	13	70	—
CHILDREN												
1–3 years	29	2–10	1,300	32	0.8	8	2,000	0.5	0.8	9	40	400
3–6 years	40	3–6	1,600	40	0.8	10	2,500	0.6	1.0	11	50	400
6–9 years	53	4–1	2,100	52	0.8	12	3,500	0.8	1.3	14	60	400
BOYS												
9–12 years	72	4–7	2,400	60	1.1	15	4,500	1.0	1.4	16	70	400
12–15 years	98	5–1	3,000	75	1.4	15	5,000	1.2	1.8	20	80	400
15–18 years	134	5–8	3,400	85	1.4	15	5,000	1.4	2.0	22	80	400
GIRLS												
9–12 years	72	4–7	2,200	55	1.1	15	4,500	0.9	1.3	15	80	400
12–15 years	103	5–2	2,500	62	1.3	15	5,000	1.0	1.5	17	80	400
15–18 years	117	5–4	2,300	58	1.3	15	5,000	0.9	1.3	15	70	400

DESIRABLE WEIGHTS FOR ADULT MEN AND WOMEN

MEN
WEIGHT (LB.) IN INDOOR CLOTHING*

Height (in shoes, 1-in. heels) FT. IN.	Small Frame	Medium Frame	Large Frame
5 2	112–120	118–129	126–141
5 3	115–123	121–133	129–144
5 4	118–126	124–136	132–148
5 5	121–129	127–139	135–152
5 6	124–133	130–143	138–156
5 7	128–137	134–147	142–161
5 8	132–141	138–152	147–166
5 9	136–145	142–156	151–170
5 10	140–150	146–160	155–174
5 11	144–154	150–165	159–179
6 0	148–158	154–170	164–184
6 1	152–162	158–175	168–189
6 2	156–167	162–180	173–194
6 3	160–171	167–185	178–199
6 4	164–175	172–190	182–204

WOMEN
WEIGHT (LB.) IN INDOOR CLOTHING*

Height (in shoes, 2-in. heels) FT. IN.	Small Frame	Medium Frame	Large Frame
4 10	92–98	96–107	104–119
4 11	94–101	98–110	106–122
5 0	96–104	101–113	109–125
5 1	99–107	104–116	112–128
5 2	102–110	107–119	115–131
5 3	105–113	110–122	118–134
5 4	108–116	113–126	121–138
5 5	111–119	116–130	125–142
5 6	114–123	120–135	129–146
5 7	118–127	124–139	133–150
5 8	122–131	128–143	137–154
5 9	126–135	132–147	141–158
5 10	130–140	136–151	145–163
5 11	134–144	140–155	149–168
6 0	138–148	144–159	153–173

* For nude weight, deduct 5–7 lbs. (male) or 2–4 lbs. (female).

RECOMMENDED FOOD QUANTITIES IN TERMS OF SERVINGS

Source: U.S. Department of Agriculture

Here follows a table of food groups and approximate amounts of foods as served per person per day, according to low-cost and moderate-cost plans. Servings allow for some plate waste. In addition to the food groups mentioned, some fats and oils (available in butter and margarine) and sugar (in its own form or in sweets and preserves) should be included in most diets.

NUMBER OF SERVINGS PER PERSON PER DAY

Food Group	Unit	Plan	Child 1–6 years[1]	Child 6–12 years[1]	Girl 12–20 years	Boy 12–20 years	Woman 20–55 years	Woman 55 years and over	Man 20–55 years	Man 55 years and over
Meat, poultry, fish or alternates	1 oz. cooked lean meat, 1 egg, ½ cup cooked dry beans, or 2 tbsp. peanut butter	Low Cost	3–3½	4–4½	4½–5	4½–6	5½–6	3½–4½	5½–6	4½–5½
		Moderate	3½–4½	5–7	7	7–8	7½	5½–6½	7½–8	7
Milk, cheese, ice cream, ice milk	1 8-oz. cup of milk as beverage or in cooking or cheese or ice cream	Low Cost	2¼	2¼–3	4	4	2	2	2	2
		Moderate	3	3	4	4	2	2	2	2
Vegetables and fruits	½ cup or equivalent vegetable or fruit as served	Low Cost	2–3½	4½–5½	5–6	5½–6½	4½–5½	3½–4½	5–6	4–5
		Moderate	2½–4½	4½–6	5½–6½	6–7½	5–6	4–4½	5½–7	5–6
Cereal and bakery products	1 slice of bread or other bakery products with equal flour; 1 oz. ready-to-eat cereal; or ¾ cup cooked cereal or cereal product	Low Cost	5–7	8–9	8–9	14–16	7–8	5–7	12–14	8–9
		Moderate	4–6	8–9	7–8	13–15	7–8	4–5	11–13	7–8

[1] Smaller amount is for younger children.

EARTH: FACTS/FIGURES

EARTH: THIRD PLANET FROM THE SUN

The Earth, our planet, is located at an average distance of 93 million miles from the Sun, which it orbits 365.2564 days, the "sidereal year," when measured in one way or in 365.2422 days, the "tropical year," by another way. (The calendar year of 365.2425 days was chosen to agree closely with the latter.) The Earth completes one rotation on its axis in 23 hours, 56 minutes, and 4 seconds, and its equator is inclined 23 degrees and 27 minutes to the plane of the ecliptic. The equatorial diameter of the Earth is 7,926 miles; its polar diameter is 7,900 miles. The Earth's average density is 5.52 grams/cm^3.

The circumference of the Earth around the equator has been estimated at 24,900 miles, while its circumference around the poles is thought to be about 24,820 miles. From these dimensions, it is obvious that the Earth is not a true sphere, but rather a *geoid*—a triaxial ellipsoid that is nearly spherical but flattened at the poles. Small bulges produce four "corners"—at Ireland, off Peru, south of Africa, and near New Guinea. Space-satellite measurements have further indicated two "dimples" in the Northern Hemisphere, giving the Earth a slightly pearlike appearance.

The Earth has an average density of 5.52 grams/cm^3 and an estimated mass of 5.883 X 10^{21} tons and an estimated volume of 2.6 X 10^{11} cubic miles. Its total surface area is approximately 197,272,000 square miles, of which the land area makes up only about 57,200,000 square miles. The average land elevation is 2,700 feet; the average ocean depth is 12,500 feet.

It is generally believed that the Earth and the other planets are 4.6 billion years old, although the oldest rocks found on the Earth are only 3.7 billion years old. Scientists have given names to the various geological time periods of Earth's history.

The largest segments of geologic time are called eras and are named according to the type of life that then existed. Eras are divided into periods, which are further divided into epochs. The period names usually refer to locations where rocks of the specific period were first studied (e.g., Devonian signifies Devonshire, England; Cretaceous, the chalk deposits that are found on both sides of the English Channel). Other names, such as Ordovician and Silurian, are actually the names of Celtic tribes that inhabited parts of Wales where rocks from this time interval were first studied.

Era	Period, Epoch	Age (Millions of Years Ago)	Evolution of Life
Cenozoic	Quaternary, Recent & Pleistocene	0 to 2.5	Man
	Tertiary, Pliocene	2.5 to 12	Higher Mammals
	Tertiary, Miocene	12 to 25	
	Tertiary, Oligocene	25 to 36	
	Tertiary, Eocene	36 to 58	
	Tertiary, Paleocene	58 to 63	
Mesozoic	Cretaceous	63 to 135	Modern Vegetation
	Jurassic	135 to 200	Birds
	Triassic	200 to 230	Mammals
Paleozoic	Permian	230 to 280	
	Carboniferous	280 to 345	Reptiles
	Devonian	345 to 405	Amphibians
	Silurian	405 to 425	Land Plants
	Ordovician	425 to 500	Agnathans, Fishes
	Cambrian	500 to 570	Invertebrate Animals
Pre-Cambrian	Late Pre-Cambrian	570 to 700	Higher Algae
	Upper Pre-Cambrian	700 to 1600	
	Middle Pre-Cambrian	1600 to 2700	Unicellular Organisms
	Lower Pre-Cambrian	2700 to 3500	Blue-green Algae
	Archaean	3500+	Bacteria

THE EARTH'S INTERIOR

The core at the Earth's center is the least-known part of the interior; our knowledge of it stems mostly from study of seismic (earthquake) waves and their propagation. However, it is known that the solid inner core of iron is surrounded by a liquid outer core of iron. The inner core, which has a radius of about 850 miles, is believed to have a very high pressure and high temperature (about 10,000° F) and a density of about 13.5 grams/cm^3 (13.5 times the density of water). The outer core has a thickness of about 1,200 miles. Surrounding the outer core is the mantle, which is 1,800 miles thick. The boundary between the mantle and the core is called the Gutenberg-Wiechert Discontinuity.

The mantle has an average density of 5 grams/cm^2 and consists of three layers: the plastic inner mantle that surrounds the liquid core, a transition region, and the outer solid mantle. The uppermost region of the Earth's interior is called the crust and is separated from the outer mantle by the Mohorovicic Discontinuity (or M-Discontinuity). The crust consists of continental crust and oceanic crust. The continental crust is composed of relatively light silicon rocks, such as granite, andesite, and various grades of metamorphic rocks known under the general name of *sial* (aluminum silicate, with silicon oxide comprising 60%) which has an average density of 2.7 grams/cm^3. The continental crust has an average thickness of 23 miles, reaching 40 to 45 miles under high mountain chains. The oceanic crust is composed of heavier basaltic rocks that contain greater proportions of metallic oxides, such as magnesium and iron, under the general name of *sima* (magnesium silicate, with silicon oxide comprising only 46%) which has an average density of 3.0 grams/cm^2. The oceanic crust has an average thickness of 4 miles. As well as being lighter and much thicker, the continental crust is considerably older than the ocean crust.

EARTH'S WATER-COVERED SURFACE

The oceans (hydrosphere) cover some 140 million square miles—70 percent of the Earth's total surface area—to an average depth of 12,500 feet. There are 340 million cubic miles of liquid water on the Earth's surface—making our planet a truly water-covered one. The greatest ocean depth is found in the Marianas Trench in the Western Pacific, being more than 37,500 feet deep.

Chemically, the ocean consists of water (96.5%) and numerous dissolved salts (3.5%), of which common salt (2.8%) is easily the most abundant. The principal elements in seawater are chlorine, sodium, magnesium, sulfur, oxygen, calcium, potassium, bromine, strontium, boron, and smaller amounts of carbon, fluorine, and iodine.

The features of the ocean floor, which result from deformations of the Earth's crust, are either elevations—ridges, rises, seamounts, and sills—or depressions—troughs, trenches, basins, and deeps. For example, the Atlantic Ocean is divided into two troughs by a north-south ridge, the Mid-Atlantic Ridge, which extends into both hemispheres. On either side of the ridge, depths exceeding 16,000 feet exist.

THE EARTH'S ATMOSPHERE

For its first 60 miles, the Earth's atmosphere has a nearly homogeneous composition consisting of the following gases:

Constituent	Percent by Volume
Nitrogen (N$_2$)	78.084
Oxygen (O$_2$)	20.946
Argon (Ar)	0.934
Carbon dioxide (CO$_2$)	0.033
Neon (Ne)	0.000018
Helium (He)	0.000005
Methane (CH$_4$) & Krypton (Kr)	0.000001

Water vapor (H$_2$O) varies within the lower atmosphere (the lowest 7 miles) from 0 to 4 percent, but it generally is present in concentrations of 0.1 to 1 percent. Water vapor is rarely found above the lower atmosphere.

Above 60 miles, the atmosphere is no longer homogeneous, but rather successive layers consisting of atomic oxygen (O), helium (He), and hydrogen (H).

Incoming solar radiation reaching our planet heats up the Earth's surface to about $-18°$ F. At this temperature, the Earth emits infrared radiation into space in all directions; however, the carbon dioxide and water vapor molecules in the Earth's lower atmosphere absorb and then reemit this infrared radiation. Part of the reemitted infrared radiation is directed downward and strikes the Earth's surface, increasing the surface temperature to a value of about 60° F, which is the Earth's actual mean temperature, averaged over the entire year. The absorption and reemission of infrared radiation by CO_2 and H_2O is known as the "Greenhouse Effect" or greenhouse temperature enhancement.

The Earth's neutral atmosphere can be divided into five distinct regions, depending on the region's temperature gradient, which is the variation of temperature with height within a particular atmospheric region. That is, a positive temperature gradient means that temperature increases with height; a negative temperature gradient means that temperature decreases with height; an undefined temperature gradient means that the density of molecules is too low to give a meaningful value to the temperature.

Atmospheric Region	Height	Temperature Gradient
Troposphere	0 to 7 miles	... Negative
Stratosphere	7 to 30 miles	... Positive
Mesosphere	30 to 50 miles	... Negative
Thermosphere ...	50 to 300 miles	... Positive
Exosphere	Above 300 miles	... Undefined

The troposphere contains about two-thirds of the total mass of the atmosphere. Within this layer, the temperature decreases with increasing height at a "lapse rate" of about 3.5° F per 1,000 feet. The decrease of temperature with height results from the atmosphere's being heated by solar radiation mainly from below. Whenever there is warmer below cooler air, vertical motions in the atmosphere result, since warm air is lighter than cool air. Such a condition causes vertical wind motions or convective currents within the troposphere. All of our weather, such as clouds and precipitation, occurs in the troposphere.

At the top of the troposphere, the temperature (about $-75°$ F) stops decreasing with height, and the stratosphere begins. Within the stratosphere, the temperature increases

with height from heating that is caused by the absorption of solar ultraviolet radiation by the stratospheric ozone layer. Since ozone absorbs most of the incoming solar ultraviolet radiation, this lethal radiation does not reach the surface, where it would adversely affect life.

At the top of the stratosphere, the temperature reaches its maximum of about 35° F, and the mesosphere begins. Within the mesosphere, the temperature decreases approximately 1.5° F per 1,000 feet. The temperature minimum of the entire atmosphere, about $-130°$ F, is found at the top of the mesosphere.

Above this mesopause, the thermosphere begins. This is a region in which the temperature increases with height because of the absorption and subsequent heating of solar X rays and short wavelength ultraviolet radiation. The temperature of the higher layers of the thermosphere can reach about 2000° F. However, at the extremely low density prevailing in this region temperature is a somewhat meaningless concept. Above the thermosphere is the exosphere, which is the top of the Earth's neutral atmosphere.

In addition to the neutral atmosphere of Earth, there are several regions consisting of large amounts of positive atomic nuclei or ions and negative electrons. The absorption of solar X rays and ultraviolet radiation results in the ionization of the air, which, in turn, results in several ionized layers known as the ionosphere. Another region of charged particles—protons and electrons—comprises the Van Allen Radiation belts, which surround the Earth at distances from about 1250 to 3000 miles and 8000 to 12,000 miles. The protons and electrons are held within the radiation belts by the Earth's magnetic field. Most of the electrons and protons in the belt's outer portion come from the Sun in the form of the solar wind.

There is evidence to suggest that the Earth originally had an atmospheric composition similar to that of Jupiter: mostly hydrogen and helium, some methane and ammonia, and no oxygen. It is possible that life began in this atmosphere. However, at some point in the past, the entire original atmosphere was lost and the present one developed. It is believed that nitrogen came from the Earth's interior via volcanic outgassing, as did the carbon dioxide and water vapor in the present atmosphere. Most of the oxygen in our atmosphere was probably produced by plant photosynthesis. Atmospheric argon was produced by the decay of radioactive potassium in rocks and minerals in the Earth's interior.

ORIGIN OF LIFE ON EARTH

The Earth and the other planets are thought to be about 4.6 billion years old. The earliest known fossil records of living organisms on our planet are about 3 billion years old. It is estimated that life existed on our planet some 3.5 to 4 billion years ago, suggesting that up to 1 billion years elapsed before life evolved on Earth from the material then available. Fundamental to an understanding of the origin of life is knowledge of the chemical makeup of living cells.

Two types of molecules—proteins and nucleic acids—play basic functional roles in living cells. Proteins are large complex molecules consisting of a number of amino acids that are joined together to form a long chain. An amino acid is a carbon compound containing an acid group (—COOH) and a basic amino group (—NH2). Some 21 different amino acids have been found in proteins. Enzymes are the biochemical catalysts that control many metabolic processes. Enzymes are proteins in which the amino-acid chain has been folded into a very specific shape.

Nucleic acids are formed in the cell nucleus, but some are produced in other cell parts. Like proteins, nucleic acids are complex molecules composed of chains of simpler units. The fundamental unit of nucleic acids is a complex molecule called a nucleotide, which consists of three separate parts: residues of a nitrogenous base, a sugar with five carbon atoms, and phosphoric acid.

In a given nucleic acid, all of the sugar residues are the same. They are either all ribose or all deoxyribose. When the sugar residues are all ribose, the nucleic acids are called ribonucleic acids (RNA) and, when they all are deoxyribose, the nucleic acids are called deoxyribonucleic acids (DNA). Both DNA and RNA are produced

in the nuclei of nearly all living cells but, whereas RNA leaves the nucleus and enters the surrounding cytoplasm, essentially all the DNA remains within the nucleus.

Nucleic acids are the key materials for all terrestrial life forms, their presence being fundamental to life processes. DNA is the principal component of genes and chromosomes, passed from parents to offspring. The sequence of nucleotides in DNA comprises the genetic code, which determines the type and amount of protein synthesized in a particular living cell. Hence, it appears that the formation of nucleic acids is related to the origin of life. It has been suggested that viruses, which are larger than a single molecule but smaller than a cell nucleus, represent an intermediate stage between nonliving and living systems. However, the modern virus, which needs to inhabit a cell in order to live, is presumed to be a development of a more primitive precursor.

The probable inorganic elements and conditions on Earth during its first billion years, which together combined to form life, were first discussed by the Russian biochemist A. I. Oparin in his 1924 publication The Origin of Life. Oparin described the gradual step-by-step evolution of life from the simple inorganic elements of hydrogen, carbon, nitrogen, and oxygen. A somewhat similar view was expressed (1928) independently by the English biochemist J. B. S. Haldane. The first attempts to simulate early conditions on Earth and produce biological compounds in the laboratory were largely failures. Although oxygen is now the second most abundant gas in the Earth's atmosphere, accounting for some 21% by volume, it was probably not always so abundant.

If oxygen were as abundant in the past as it is today, then carbon would be present mainly as carbon dioxide. Oparin suggested that atmospheric carbon probably existed originally in the reduced form—methane (CH_4)—and not in oxidized form—carbon dioxide (CO_2). Similarly, nitrogen, now present in free state and accounting for some 78% by volume of the atmosphere, would have been in the reduced form of ammonia (NH_3). Like Oparin, but for entirely different reasons, Haldane also concluded that the Earth's primitive atmosphere probably contained little if any free oxygen but consisted mainly of carbon dioxide, ammonia, and water vapor.

In 1952, the American chemist H. C. Urey showed that the Earth's primitive atmosphere should have consisted of methane, ammonia, water vapor, and free hydrogen gas. Urey and S. Miller began a series of lab experiments attempting to synthesize the gases of his theoretical atmosphere into complex organic molecules. After exposing gases to ultraviolet radiation, to simulate the sun's radiation, Urey and Miller reported (1953) that they had successfully produced several amino acids, as well as other organic compounds of biological interest.

From similar laboratory experiments made by P. H. Abelson (1956) and by Pavlovskaya and A. G. Pasinsky (1957) in the USSR, it has been established that amino acids can be produced by passing an electrical discharge (simulating lightning discharges in the Earth's primitive atmosphere) through various gas mixtures other than those used by Urey and Miller. Provided the gaseous system has overall reducing characteristics, amino acids are always formed. Other experiments have shown that amino acids can even be formed in aqueous solutions.

As life evolved on Earth, it appears certain that later stages took place in a liquid water environment. This is evidenced by the presence of large amounts of water in all living organisms and the fact that the calcium/potassium ratio in seawater and blood is roughly similar. Furthermore the earliest organisms would have required the protection of the oceans from the damaging solar ultraviolet radiation. It seems likely that the primitive organisms in the oceans started to obtain hydrogen necessary for the synthesis of amino acids and other organic molecules by dissociating water using light energy. This is an important stage in the evoluton of life since free oxygen was released into the atmosphere. Once oxygen and then ozone built up in the atmosphere, the land was effectively shielded from solar ultraviolet. At this stage organisms appear to have emerged from the sea and colonized land.

Laboratory experiments have shown that amino acids and nucleic acids could have been synthesized in a reducing atmosphere of hydrogen, methane, ammonia, and water vapor. It is now believed that the Earth originally had such an atmosphere when life originated.

ANCIENT SUPERCONTINENTS

American scientists of the Environmental Science Services Administration reported in 1969 that they had established that Australia and Antarctica, which are now separated by about 2,000 miles of water, were once part of an ancient supercontinent.

The scientists, Walter Sproll and Dr. Robert S. Dietz, having processed oceanographic data obtained in 1967 by U.S. and Australian scientists during a global cruise of the Coast and Geodetic Survey Ship *Oceanographer*, relate that there was a fit between the two continents.

Sproll and Dietz are supporters of the continental-drift theory: that the continents constantly drift about 1-6 in. each year in the earth's mantle—the part of the earth's interior that rests between the molten central core and the crust. Among the scientists who espouse this theory, some believe that there was once a single supercontinent they call Pangaea; others, including Sproll and Dietz, contend that there were two supercontinents, which they refer to as Gondwana and Laurasia.

Supporters of the two-continent theory believe that Gondwana was composed of Australia, Antarctica, Africa, India, South America, Madagascar, and various submerged fragments, while Laurasia is thought to have consisted of North America and Eurasia.

It was generally believed of the two continents that southern Australia was once linked with another land mass, but opinions differed as to which one. Antarctica was the popular choice, but some thought it was Madagascar; others contended that it was the east coast of Africa, while still others believed it to have been the southwestern coast of South America.

Sproll and Dietz reported that their study shows that the south coast of Australia once joined Antarctica and identifies the exact position of fit: the SE end of Australia —including Tasmania—fitted into Antarctica's Ross Sea, while the SW end reached to just off Antarctica's Knox Coast; the concave Great Bight of Australia fitted against the convex outline of Wilkes Land.

"Recent geophysical findings on the ocean floor have demonstrated to the satisfaction of most earth scientists that the continents were once together," the ESSA scientists said. "About 200 to 250 million years ago, they commenced to separate and slowly drifted to their present scattered locations around the globe. One of the last units to be sundered—the Australia-Antarctica split—may have occurred as late as 40 million years ago.

The fit of continents is not the only evidence of continental drift. There is a very significant fit of rock formations and other geological structures in landmasses now separated by oceans. Studies of the past positions of the magnetic poles also indicate relative movement between continents. Again the scattered distribution of certain animals and plants in the distant past as well as that of ancient climatic zones can only be satisfactorily explained by continental drift: the discovery in Antarctica of a fossilized bone of an extinct amphibian points to a much milder Antarctic climate in the past.

Continental drift is now explained in terms of plate tectonics. The earth's outer shell is divided into at least 15 rigid rock segments, known as plates, that extend downward through the earth's crust and float on a semi-molten layer of the upper mantle. Seven of the plates are of major size and in most cases carry a continental landmass with surrounding ocean floor and island arcs. The plates are slowly moving relative to each other, driven by powerful forces within the earth's mantle. The movements of the plates have produced the present continent locations. At their boundaries plates are either slowly separating with new material added from the mantle, or converging with one plate being ground down and consumed under another, or are gliding past each other. Almost all earthquake, volcanic, and mountain-building activity closely follows these boundaries and is related to movements between them.

THE CONTINENTS

Name	Area (in square miles)	Percent of World's Land	Highest Point (in feet)	Lowest Point (in feet)
Asia	17,129,000	29.7	Mount Everest (29,028), Nepal-China	Dead Sea (1,296 below sea level), Israel-Jordan
Africa	11,707,000	20.0	Kibo (19,340), a peak of Mount Kilimanjaro, Tanzania	Lake Assal, Djibouti (510 below sea level)
North America	9,363,000	16.3	Mount McKinley (20,320), Alaska	Death Valley (282 below sea level), California
South America	6,886,000	12.0	Aconcagua (22,831), Argentina	Salinas Grandes (131 below sea level), Valdés Pen., Argentina
Europe	4,057,000	7.0	El'brus (18,510), USSR	Caspian Sea (92 below sea level), USSR
Australia	2,942,000	5.1	Mount Kosciusko (7,316), New South Wales	Lake Eyre (52 below sea level), South Australia
Antarctica	5,500,000	9.6	Vinson Massif (16,864)	Sea level

PREHISTORIC CREATURES

Allosaurus: This predator of 125 million years ago was the giant of its day: 34-feet long, more than eight feet high, and with a reach of about 15 feet above the ground. It had a massive skull that was nearly a yard long and a lower jaw hinged far back, enabling it to swallow food in unchewed lumps. Allosaurus remains have been found in Utah, Wyoming, and other Rocky Mountain states.

Anatosaurus *(Trachodon):* This 30-foot, duck-billed dinosaur lived in North America about 100 million years ago. It had a long narrow skull, a ducklike bill, and at the back of the jaws up to 2,000 grinding teeth, which were continuously replaced as they wore out. The anatosaurus could swim and wade, as evidenced by its webbed feet and deep oarlike tail.

Apatosaurus *(Brontosaurus):* This quadruped dinosaur probably grew to more than 70 feet in length and 30 tons in weight. Because of its size, the apatosaurus (as well as the brachiosaurus) had a huge pelvis and long, heavy shoulder blades. It had a short but deep body, a long neck, a massive tail, and a relatively tiny brain weighing about one pound. The apatosaurus was herbivorous and semiaquatic; as its nostrils were situated high on its head it could stand almost fully submerged. It lived about 125 million years ago in Colorado, Wyoming, Texas, and other Western states.

Archaeopteryx: Appearing about 150 million years ago, the archaeopteryx was the earliest known bird and was about the size of our crow. Although it had feathers, its bony tail, toothed jaws, and the claws on its forelimbs were reptilian. But its hindlimbs were birdlike, thus it could walk and run like a chicken. The archaeopteryx was probably warm-blooded, had weak flying muscles, and a gliding flight.

Baluchitherium: The largest land mammal ever to have lived. Found in Oligocene (circa 28–30 million years ago) deposits of Western and Central Asia, it was over 16 feet tall and weighed several tons; its head alone was over 4 feet long. Baluchitherium was related to the modern rhinoceros, but unlike the rhino it had no horns, long limbs, and a long neck, which would have suited it for swift running and browsing on leaves on the higher branches of trees.

Brachiosaurus: Ranging from 60 to 80 feet in length and weighing up to 80 tons, the brachiosaurus was one of the largest land animals that ever lived. The dinosaur's front legs were massive; consequently, its shoulders were high and sloped giraffe-fashion to the hips. Since its nostrils were located on a raised area of the head, the creature could breathe while standing in deep water. The brachiosaurus, which fed on vegetation, lived in Colorado, adjacent areas, and eastern Africa more than 125 million years ago.

Camptosaurus: Appearing in North America about 125 million years ago, the camptosaurus ranged between four and 15 feet in length. It had strong hind limbs; small, stout forelimbs; and a broad hand with full fingers. Its femur was curved, suggesting that this dinosaur sometimes walked on all fours. The camptosaurus was a nonpredatory planteater, with a flat, beak-like mouth.

Coelacanth: This subgroup of lobe-finned fishes ranged in weight from 125 to 150 pounds and were strong, armed with sharp teeth, and active. Early coelacanths were freshwater fish, but later forms were marine. They first appeared about 350 million years ago and were thought to have become extinct about 65 million years ago. However, in 1938 a fisherman caught a 4½-foot coelacanth off the coast of South Africa, and since then several other specimens have been caught.

Compsognathus: This dinosaur was no larger than a big fowl, and two-thirds of its body was neck and tail. Its toes were long and clawed, and its small jaws were lined with sharp teeth. This slender bipedal creature preyed on small reptiles, on the Baltic coast of what is now Germany, about 125 million years ago.

Eohippus *(Hyracotherium):* As its name implies, the "dawn (eo) horse (hippus)" was the earliest-known horse, appearing about 60 million years ago on the Great Plains of North America. The species varied from 10 to 20 inches high; all of these horses had four toes on each front foot and three on each hind foot. The eohippus was lightly built; its hindquarters were high and its simple teeth were suited for browsing on leaves. Some species of the eohippus migrated to Europe about 50 million years ago, becoming ancestors of the Old World horse. By the time that the Indians reached North America, the New World horse had become extinct.

Hesperornis: This flightless water bird ranged from Europe to North America about 100 million years ago. The hesperornis had an elongated body, about 6 feet long, with feet that enabled it to swim. It had a long bill, possibly toothed, and preyed on fish. Although its ancestors probably had wings, those of the hesperornis were useless evolutionary remnants.

Iguanodon: This genus of herbivorous dinosaurs varied in length from 15 to 30 feet and reached a height of 15 feet. All specimens had narrow bodies. They walked on hind feet, which had three large toes and one small one, and used their long heavy tails for balancing. Their small "forefeet" were five-fingered and had a thumb that was shaped into a bony spike. Iguanodon remains have been found in Europe and North Africa; the genus flourished between 100 and 140 million years ago.

Kronosaurus: Similar to the sperm whale of today, the kronosaurus paddled through Australian seas about 70 million years ago. Its neck was comparatively short, and its elongated skull measured 12 feet. The kronosaurus had large eyes and temporal openings, nostrils in front of the eyes, an almost solid palate, and long sharp teeth.

Lystrosaurus: A member of the dicynodont group of mammal-like reptiles, this animal is dated from the early Triassic Age (circa 220 million years ago) of both South Africa and Asia. It is believed that the dicynodonts may in general have preferred to live in marshy country, but Lystrosaurus is the only one which may have been aquatic to any extent. All dicynodonts were herbivorous and were the most common land animals of their time.

Megatherium: The largest of the extinct giant ground sloths, it flourished in both North and South America during the Pleistocene (circa 1.5 million to 10,000 years ago). This early mammal was slightly larger than the modern elephant and possessed extremely massive limbs. Its teeth grew continually throughout life and were adapted for a leaf-eating diet. It had a short, massive neck and tail, but a relatively long trunk. Its hands possessed powerful claws, which probably served to draw branches down towards its extensible tongue; the animal appears to have walked on the outside of its knuckles.

Pteranodon: This flying reptile lived between 85 and 100 million years ago, ranging from present-day Kansas to Europe and possibly around the world. Its body was small, bulking to about that of a small turkey. Its jaws formed a long toothless beak, and the back of the skull extended into a bony crest that was between about four and six feet long. The pteranodon's large wingspread, about 25 feet, and pelicanlike gular pouch gave it a most unreptilian appearance.

Stegosaurus: This "plated dinosaur" was a quadruped, about 20 feet long and weighing about 2 tons. It had short forelegs, two rows of bony plates down its back, and long pointed spikes on its tail. The brain of the stegosaurus, about the size of a walnut, weighed only about 2½ ounces. The bony plates, together with its tail spikes, may have been used for defense against predators; alternatively they may have functioned as heat exchangers. This herbivorous dinosaur roamed the American West about 125 million years ago.

Triceratops: This dinosaur was also herbivorous and also lived in the American West, about 100 million years ago. The head of the triceratops was about eight feet long and sheltered a two-pound brain. Its body, which was about 20 feet long, was bulky and shaped like a barrel. The dinosaur's four legs were of equal size. The name *triceratops* is derived from the creature's three horns: one on the nose and one over each eye.

Tyrannosaurus: The "tyrant" dinosaur was a flesh-eater and well equipped for predation with six-inch teeth that were housed in a four-foot-long skull. Existing for a short time, about 85 million years ago, this dinosaur was 40 feet long and 19 feet tall. It weighed up to eight tons. Its forelimbs were reduced to such a degree that it is believed that they were not utilitarian; therefore, the creature's predation was probably restricted to its use of its jaws and powerful clawed hind legs.

Uintatherium: The uintatheres were primitive rhinoceros-like ungulates of late Paleocene and Eocene times (circa 50 to 60 million years ago), and are distantly related to the elephants. Their long, low skulls were characterized by a number of large, horn-like bony swellings; they possessed large, saber-like upper canine teeth which were presumably very effective as defensive weapons.

FOSSIL MAN

Remains of what may be man's earliest ancestors were found on two continents in 1934 and in 1961. Fossil bones from sites in India and Africa indicate that these creatures (Ramapithecus and Kenyapithecus), in spite of having lived more than 14 million years ago, were more manlike than apelike.

However, the oldest bones to be placed with certainty in the category "Hominidae," or the family of Man, are about 4 million years old. Hominid remains have been found in several locations. Many archaeologists have given their finds a different name (e.g., Zinjanthropus, Paranthropus, Plesianthropus), but today we recognize that all of these individuals who lived between 2 million and 4 million B.C. have the same general characteristics and can be called by the general genus name, Australopithecus, or "southern ape."

The different genus and species names are given in the chart below to indicate that they probably represent different branches of the same group.

The brain of Australopithecus was about the same size as that of a modern large ape—half that of modern man. In spite of his apelike traits, Australopithecus walked erect.

Some of the specimens found by L. S. B. Leakey in 1960 have been given the classification name Homo, the genus to which modern man belongs. Homo habilis was only 3½ to 4½ feet tall but had a larger brain and more manlike features.

Homo erectus, sometimes called Pithecanthropus or "ape man" (e.g., Java Man, Peking Man), was probably the direct ancestor of modern man, Homo sapiens. He appeared at least 1½ million years ago and was structurally similar to us although he lacked a forehead and possessed a bony shelf over his eyes and a small chin. He made tools and knew how to use fire.

The next major evolutionary advance came approximately 100,000 years ago with the appearance of Neanderthal Man; he, too, was short in stature and had low brows, but his brain was equal in size to that of modern man, and he possessed a language. He was not a settler, but instead hunted widely.

At about 35,000 B.C., as the Neanderthals were disappearing, modern man, Homo sapiens (e.g., Cromagnon), appeared. He was taller and more delicate, and he fashioned intricate tools and clothing and drew paintings of his environment. However, it was not until 9,000 years ago that Homo sapiens became a domesticator of animals, a farmer, and a settler.

MAJOR FOSSIL MAN DISCOVERIES

Year	Scientific Name	Period and Estimated Date (B.C.)	Location	Remains	Discoverer
1848	Homo calpicus (Gibraltar Man)	Upper Pleistocene 50,000–120,000	Forbes Quarry, Gibraltar	skull	Lieutenant Flint
1856	Homo neanderthalensis (Neanderthal Man)	Upper Pleistocene 50,000	Neander Valley, nr. Dusseldorf, Germany	skull, bones	Johann C. Fuhlrott
1868	Homo sapiens (Cromagnon)	Upper Pleistocene 35,000	Cromagnon, France	4 skeletons, 1 fetus	Louis Lartet
1891	Pithecanthropus erectus (Java Man)	Lower Pleistocene 700,000	Trinil, Java	skull, femur	Eugene Dubois
1907	Homo heidelbergensis (Heidelberg Man)	Middle Pleistocene 450,000	Mauer, nr. Heidelberg, Germany	lower jaw	Otto Schoetensack
1909–13	Eoanthropus dawsoni* (Piltdown Man)	Holocene (Recent)	Piltdown, Sussex, England	composite skull	Charles Dawson
1924	Australopithecus africanus (Southern Ape)	Pleistocene c. 3,000,000	Taung, South Africa	skull	M. de Bruyn
1921–37	Sinanthropus pekinensis (Peking Man)	Middle Pleistocene 450,000	Choukoutien, nr. Peking, China	skulls, teeth, bones	Davidson Black
1929–34	Mt. Carmel Man	Upper Pleistocene 50,000	Tabun and Skhul, Israel	parts of 16 skeletons	Dorothy Garrod
1934	Ramapithecus	Upper Miocene 10,000,000	NW India	parts of jaws	G. E. Lewis
1935–55	Early Homo sapiens (Swanscombe Skull)	Middle Pleistocene 250,000	Swanscombe, Kent, England	parts of skull	A. T. Marston
1938	Paranthropus robustus	Lower Pleistocene c. 2,000,000	Kromdraai, Transvaal	skull part, bones	G. Terblanche
1947	Australopithecus prometheus (Southern Ape)	Lower Pleistocene c. 3,000,000	Makapansgat, Transvaal	skull fragments	J. Kitching
1953–60	Neanderthal Man	Upper Pleistocene 50,000	Shanidar, Iraq	skeletons	Ralph Solecki
1959	Zinjanthropus boisei (Nutcracker Man)	Lower Pleistocene c. 1,750,000	Olduvai, Tanzania	skull	Mary D. Leakey
1960	Homo habilis	Lower Pleistocene c. 1,750,000	Olduvai, Tanzania	skull fragments	Louis S. B. Leakey
1961	Kenyapithecus wickeri	Middle Miocene c. 14,000,000	Fort Ternan, Kenya	palate, teeth	Louis S. B. Leakey
1965	Homo erectus palaeohungaricus	Middle Pleistocene 450,000	Vertesszollos, Hungary	occipital bone	Laszlo Vertes
1967–72	Australopithecus boisei, Australopithecus africanus, Homo habilis	Upper Pliocene 4,000,000–1,500,000	Omo Valley, Ethiopa	various remains	Y. Coppens, F. C. Howell, and teams
1968–80	Australopithecus boisei, Homo habilis, Homo erectus	Pleistocene 2,200,000–1,300,000	Koobi Fora (formerly East Rudolf), Kenya	150 specimens	Richard Leakey and team
1971	Early Homo sapiens? (Arago Man)	Middle Pleistocene 300,000	Arago, France	skull, jaws, pelvis	H. de Lumley
1973–80	Australopithecus afarensis	Upper Pliocene c. 3,000,000	Afar, Ethiopia	various remains, including partial skeleton "Lucy"	Y. Coppens, M. Taieb, D. Johanson, and teams
1975–80	Australopithecus afarensis	Upper Pliocene c. 3,500,000	Laetoli, Tanzania	footprints, jaws, teeth, 8 adults, 3 children	Mary Leakey and team

MAXIMUM LIFE-SPANS OF ANIMALS
The list below reflects the maximum life-span of various animals while in captivity.

Years	Animal	Years	Animal	Years	Animal	Years	Animal
190	Giant Tortoise	37	Chimpanzee	25	Tiger	17	Goat
138	Eastern Box Turtle	36	Toad	25	Zebra	16	Bullfrog
84	Elephant	33	Gorilla	23	Leopard	16	Cheetah
80	Freshwater Oyster	31	Gibbon	23	Domestic Cat	16	Kangaroo
68	Owl	31	Grizzly Bear	22	Domestic Dog	15	Pronghorn
55	Eagle	30	Dolphin	20	Cougar	15	Reindeer
51	Pelican	30	Lion	20	Cow	15	Timber Wolf
50	Domestic Horse	28	Giraffe	20	Moose	14	Chicken
46	Jackass	28	Sea Lion	20	Rattlesnake	14	Coyote
45	Baboon	25	Black Bear	20	Sheep	13	Rabbit
41	Polar Bear	25	Camel	19	Beaver	10	Pig

THE ANIMAL KINGDOM

This classification system of living animals is one of many types available. Subphyla are included only for phylum Chordata, subclasses only for class Mammalia, and orders only for Eutheria in class Mammalia.

SUBKINGDOM PROTOZOA—one-celled animals
Phylum Protozoa—acellular animals (protozoans)
    Class Mastigophora (Flagellata)—flagellates
    Class Sarcodina (Rhizopoda)—sarcodines
    (Amoeba)
    Class Sporozoa—spore-forming parasites
    Class Ciliophora (Ciliata)—ciliates (Paramecium)
SUBKINGDOM MESOZOA—certain wormlike parasites
  Phylum Mesozoa—mesozoans
SUBKINGDOM PARAZOA—pore-perforated bodies
  Phylum Porifera—sponges
    Class Calcarea—chalky sponges
    Class Hexactinellida—glass sponges
    Class Demospongiae—horny sponges
SUBKINGDOM METAZOA—multi-cellular animals
  Phylum Coelenterata (Cnidaria)—coelenterates
    Class Hydrozoa—hydroids (Portuguese man-of-war)
    Class Scyphozoa—jellyfish
    Class Anthozoa—sea anemones and corals
  Phylum Ctenophora—ctenophores
    Class Tentaculata—with tentacles
    Class Nuda—without tentacles
  Phylum Platyhelminthes—flatworms
    Class Turbellaria—free-living flatworms
    Class Trematoda—flukes
    Class Cestoda—tapeworms
    Class Gnathostomulida—gnathostomulids
  Phylum Nemertea—nemertines (ribbon worms)
    Class Anopla—unarmed proboscis
    Class Enopla—armed proboscis
  Phylum Acanthocephala—thorny-headed worms
  Phylum Aschelminthes—aschelminths
    Class Rotifera (Rotatoria)—rotifers
    Class Gastrotricha—gastrotrichs
    Class Kinorhyncha (Echinodera)—kinorhynchs
    Class Nematoda—nematodes (roundworms)
    Class Nematomorpha—horsehair worms
    Class Priapulida—priapulids
  Phylum Sipunculida—sipunculids
  Phylum Bryozoa (Ectoprocta)—bryozoans
    Class Phylactolaemata—fresh-water
    Class Gymnolaemata—salt-water
  Phylum Entoprocta—entoprocts
  Phylum Phoronida—phoronids
  Phylum Brachiopoda—brachiopods
    Class Inarticulata—without teeth
    Class Articulata—with teeth
  Phylum Mollusca—mollusks
    Class Amphineura—chitons
    Class Monoplacophora—monoplacophs
    Class Gastropoda—gastropods (snails, slugs)
    Class Scaphopoda—tooth shells
    Class Bivalvia (Lamellibranchia)—bivalve mollusks
    Class Cephalopoda—cephalopods (squids, octopi)
  Phylum Echiurida—echiuroid marine worms
  Phylum Annelida—segmented worms
    Class Polychaeta—sand-and bristleworms
    Class Mysostomaria—mysostomarians
    Class Oligochaeta—earthworms
    Class Hirudinea—leeches
    Class Archiannelida—no external segments
  Phylum Onychophora—velvet worms
  Phylum Tardigrada—tardigrades (water bears)

Phylum Pentastomida—tongue worms
Phylum Arthropoda—arthropods
    Class Merostomata—horseshoe & king crabs
    Class Arachnida—spiders, ticks, mites, scorpions
    Class Pycnogonida (Pantopoda)—sea spiders
    Class Crustacea—crustaceans
    Class Chilopoda—centipedes
    Class Diplopoda—millipedes
    Class Pauropoda—pauropods
    Class Symphyla—symphylids (garden centipede)
    Class Insecta—insects
Phylum Chaetognatha—arrowworms
Phylum Pogonophora—beard worms
Phylum Hemichordata—hemichordates
    Class Enteropneusta—acorn worms
    Class Pterobranchia—pterobranchs
    Class Planctosphaeroidea—planctosphaera
Phylum Echinodermata—echinoderms
    Class Echinoidea—sea urchins, sand dollars
    Class Holothuroidea—sea cucumbers
    Class Crinoidea—crinoids (sea lilies, feather stars)
    Class Asteroidea—starfish
    Class Ophiuroidea—brittle & basket stars
Phylum Chordata—chordates
  Subphylum Urochordata (Tunicata)—tunicates
    Class Ascidiacea—sea squirts
    Class Thaliacea—salps
    Class Larvacea—larvaceans
  Subphylum Cephalochordata—lancelets
  Subphylum Vertebrata (Craniata)—vertebrates
    Class Agnatha—jawless vertebrates
    Class Chondrichthyes (Elasmobranchii)—cartilaginous fish (sharks, rays)
    Class Osteichthyes—bony fish
    Class Amphibia—amphibians
    Class Reptilia—reptiles
    Class Aves—birds
    Class Mammalia—mammals
      Subclass Prototheria—egg laying mammals (monotremes)
      Subclass Theria—viviparous (live-bearing) mammals
        Infraclass Metatheria—pouched mammals (marsupials)
        Infraclass Eutheria—placental mammals
          Order Insectivora—moles, shrews, hedgehogs
          Order Dermoptera—flying lemurs (colugos)
          Order Chiroptera—bats
          Order Primates—lemurs, monkeys, apes, man
          Order Edentata—sloths, anteaters, armadillos
          Order Pholidota—pangolins
          Order Lagomorpha—rabbits, hares, pikas
          Order Rodentia—rodents
          Order Cetacea—whales, dolphins, porpoises
          Order Carnivora—carnivores (dogs, cats)
          Order Pinnipedia—seals, sea lions, walruses
          Order Tubulidentata—aardvark
          Order Proboscidea—elephants
          Order Hyracoidea—hyraxes (coneys)
          Order Sirenia—sea cows (manatee, dugong)
          Order Perissodactyla—odd-toe ungulates (horses, zebras, tapirs, rhinoceroses)
          Order Artiodactyla—even-toed ungulates (cattle, deer, sheep, goats, pigs, camels)

ANIMAL GESTATION PERIODS AND LITTERS

SOURCE: Grace Davall, Assistant Curator, Mammals and Birds, New York Zoological Society

Animal	Gestation Period	Litter Size	Animal	Gestation Period	Litter Size
AMERICAN BUFFALO (BISON)	270–285 days	1	HORSE	11 months	1
BABOON	6 months	1–2	KANGAROO	38–39 days	1–2
BLACK BEAR	7 months	1–4	LION	108 days	1–4
CAMEL	12–13 months	1	MACAQUE	160–170 days	1–2
CAT	63 days	1–6	MINK	48–51 days	4–8
CHIMPANZEE	226 days	1–2	MOUSE	19–21 days	1–9
CHINCHILLA	105–111 days	1–4	OPOSSUM	12–13 days	4–13
COW	280 days	1–2	OTTER	9½–12½ months	1–4
DEER (WHITE-TAIL)	7 months	2	PIG	112–115 days	4–6
DOG	61 days	1–12	RABBIT	1 month	1–13
DOLPHIN	9 months	1	RACCOON	63 days	1–6
ELEPHANT	21 months	1	SHEEP	150 days	1–3
FOX	49–55 days	1–8	SKUNK	52 days	4–7
GERBIL	14 days	1–7	SQUIRREL	44 days	2–5
GIRAFFE	14–15 months	1	TIGER	100–108 days	2–4
GORILLA	8½ months	1	WOLF	60–63 days	1–13
HAMSTER	16–19 days	2–12	YAK	just over 9 months	1
			ZEBRA	11–12 months	1

ENDANGERED WILDLIFE SOURCE: Office of Endangered Species, U.S. Dept. of the Interior

Anyone wishing to know the status of any animal should contact the Office of Endangered Species, Dept. of the Interior, Washington, D.C. 20240. Below is a selection from official List of Endangered Fauna, including the 109 native to the United States.

BONY FISHES (Class *Osteichthyes/Phylum Chordata*)
Sturgeons & Paddlefishes (Order: *Acipenseriformes*): 1. Sturgeon, Shortnose.

Trout, Salmon & Relatives (Order: *Salmoniformes*): 1. Ala Balik; 2. Cisco, Longjaw; 3. Trout, Arizona (Apache); 4. Trout, Gila; 5. Trout, Greenback cutthroat; 6. Trout, Lahontan cutthroat; 7. Trout, Paiute cutthroat.

Carps, Minnows & Relatives (Order: *Cypriniformes*): 1. Ayumodoki; 2. Bonytail, Pahranagat; 3. Chub, Humpback; 4. Chub, Mohave; 5. Cicek; 6. Cui-ui; 7. Dace, Kendall Warm Springs; 8. Dace, Moapa; 9. Squawfish, Colorado River; 10. Tanago, Miyako; 11. Woundfin.

Sticklebacks (Order: *Solenichthyiformes*): 1. Stickleback, Unarmored threespine.

Silversides, Topminnows & Relatives (Order: *Atheriniformes*): 1. Gambusia, Big Bend; 2. Gambusia, Clear Creek; 3. Gambusia, Pecos; 4. Killifish, Pahrump; 5. Pupfish, Comanche Springs; 6. Pupfish, Devil's Hole; 7. Pupfish, Owens River; 8. Pupfish, Tecopa; 9. Pupfish, Warm Springs; 10. Topminnow, Gila.

Perches & Relatives (Order: *Perciformes*): 1. Darter, Fountain; 2. Darter, Maryland; 3. Darter, Okaloosa; 4. Darter, Watercress; 5. Pike, Blue.

AMPHIBIANS (Class *Amphibia/Phylum Chordata*)
Salamanders (Order: *Urodela*): 1. Salamander, Desert slender; 2. Salamander, Santa Cruz long-toed; 3. Salamander, Texas blind. Frogs (Order: *Anura*): 1. Frog, Stephen Island; 2. Frog, Israel painted; 3. Toad, Houston.

REPTILES (Class *Reptilia/Phylum Chordata*)
Turtles (Order: *Testudinata*): 1. Terrapin, River (Tuntong); 2. Tortoise, Galapagos; 3. Tortoise, Madgascar radiated; 4. Tortoise, Short-necked (swamp); 5. Turtle, Aquatic box; 6. Turtle, Atlantic Ridley; 7. Turtle, Hawksbill; 8. Turtle, Leatherback.

Crocodiles (Order: *Crocodilia*): 1. Alligator, American; 2. Crocodile, Cuban; 3. Crocodile, Morelet's.

Lizards & Snakes (Order: *Squamata*): 1. Lizard, Day gecko; 2. Lizard, Round Island day gecko; 3. Lizard, Anegada ground iguana; 4. Lizard, Barrington land iguana; 5. Lizard, Blunt-nosed leopard; 6. Snake, Jamaica boa; 7. Snake, Puerto Rican boa; 8. Snake, San Francisco garter.

BIRDS (Class *Aves/Phylum Chordata*)
Albatrosses, Petrels & Relatives (Order: *Procellariiformes*): 1. Albatross, Short-tailed; 2. Cahow (Bermuda petrel); 3. Petrel, Hawaiian dark-rumped.

Pelicans (Order: *Pelecaniformes*): 1. Pelican, Brown.

Ducks, Geese, Swans & Relatives (Order: *Anseriformes*): 1. Duck, Hawaiian (koloa); 2. Duck, Laysan; 3. Duck, Mexican; 4. Duck, White-winged wood; 5. Goose, Aleutian Canada; 6. Goose, Hawaiian (nene).

Eagles, Falcons, Vultures & Relatives (Order: *Falconiformes*): 1. Condor, Andean; 2. Condor, California; 3. Eagle, Monkey-eating; 4. Eagle, Southern bald; 5. Eagle, Spanish imperial; 6. Falcon, American peregrine; 7. Falcon, Arctic peregrine; 8. Goshawk, Christmas Island; 9. Hawk, Anjouan Island sparrow; 10. Hawk, Galapagos; 11. Hawk, Hawaiian (io); 12. Kite, Florida Everglade.

Pheasants, Grouse, Curassows & Relatives (Order: *Galliformes*): 1. Curassow, Red-billed; 2. Curassow, Trinidad white-headed; 3. Guan, Horned; 4. Megapode, Maleo; 5. Megapode, LaPerouse's; 6. Pheasant, Bar-tailed; 7. Pheasant, Blyth's tragopan; 8. Pheasant, Brown-eared; 9. Pheasant, Cabot's tragopan; 10. Pheasant, Chinese monal; 11. Pheasant, Edward's; 12. Pheasant, Imperial; 13. Pheasant, Mikado; 14. Pheasant, Palawan peacock; 15. Pheasant, Sclater's monal; 16. Pheasant, Swinhoe's; 17. Pheasant, Western tragopan; 18. Pheasant, White-eared; 19. Prairie Chicken, Attwater's greater; 20. Quail, Masked bobwhite.

Cranes, Rails, Bustards & Relatives (Order: *Gruiformes*): 1. Bustard, Great Indian; 2. Coot, Hawaiian; 3. Crane, Hooded; 4. Crane, Japanese; 5. Crane, Mississippi sandhill; 6. Crane, Siberian white; 7. Crane, Whooping; 8. Gallinule, Hawaiian; 9. Kagu (rail); 10. Rail, Auckland Island; 11. Rail, California clapper; 12. Rail, Light-footed clapper; 13. Rail, Yuma clapper; 14. Wanderer, Plains; 15. Takahe.

Plovers, Snipes, Gulls & Relatives (Order: *Charadriiformes*): 1. Curlew, Eskimo; 2. Gull, Audouin's; 3. Stilt, Hawaiian; 4. Tern, California least.

Pigeons, Doves, Sandgrouse & Relatives (Order: *Columbiformes*): 1. Dove, Cloven-feathered; 2. Dove, Grenada; 3. Dove, Palau ground; 4. Pigeon, Azores wood; 5. Pigeon, Chatham Island; 6. Pigeon, Puerto Rican plain.

Parrots (Order: *Psittaciformes*): 1. Parrot, Puerto Rican; 2. Parakeet, Splendid.

Owls (Order: *Strigiformes*): 1. Owl, Anjouan scops; 2. Owl, Palau; 3. Owl, New Zealand laughing.

Goatsuckers & Relatives (Order: *Caprimulgiformes*): 1. Whip-poor-will, Puerto Rican.

Woodpeckers, Puffbirds, Barbets & Relatives (Order: *Piciformes*): 1. Woodpecker, Imperial; 2. Woodpecker, Ivory-billed; 3. Woodpecker, Red-cockaded.

Perching Birds—Sparrows, Larks, Thrushes & Relatives (Order: *Passeriformes*): 1. Bulbul, Mauritius olivaceous; 2. Crow, Hawaiian (alala); 3. Cuckoo-Shrike, Mauritius; 4. Cuckoo-Shrike, Reunion; 5. Finch, Sao Miguel bullfinch; 6. Flycatcher, Chatham Island robin; 7. Flycatcher, Eyrean grass-wren; 8. Flycatcher, Grey-necked rock-fowl; 9. Flycatcher, Palau fantail; 10. Flycatcher, Seychelles black; 11. Flycatcher, Tahiti; 12. Flycatcher, Western bristlebird; 13. Flycatcher, White-necked rock-fowl; 14. Flycatcher (Tyrant), Euler's; 15. Flycatcher (Tyrant), Scarlet-breasted robin; 16. Flycatcher (Tyrant), Tinian monarch; 17. Grackle, Slender-billed; 18. Honeycreeper, Akiapolaau; 19. Honeycreeper, Crested (akohekohe); 20. Honeycreeper, Hawaii akepa (akepa); 21. Honeycreeper, Kauai akialoa; 22. Honeycreeper, Maui parrotbill; 23. Honeycreeper, Maui akepa (akepuie); 24. Honeycreeper, Molokai creeper (kakawahie); 25. Honeycreeper, Oahu creeper (alauwahio); 26. Honeycreeper, Ou; 27. Honeycreeper, Palila; 28. Honeycreepers, Laysan & Nihoa finches; 29. Honeycreepers, Kauai & Maui nukupuus; 30. Honey-eater, Helmeted; 31. Honey-eater, Kauai Oo (oo aa); 32. Scrub-bird, Noisy; 33. Sparrow, Cape Sable; 34. Sparrow, Dusky seaside; 35. Sparrow, Santa Barbara song; 36. Starling, Ponape Mountain; 37. Starling, Rothschild's (myna); 38. Thrasher, White-breasted; 39. Thrush, Large Kauai; 40. Thrush, Molokai (olomau); 41. Thrush, Seychelles magpie-robin; 42. Thrush, Small Kauai (puaiohi); 43. Thrush, Western whipbird; 44. Warbler, Nihoa millerbird; 45. Warbler, Bachman's; 46. Warbler, Kirtland's.

MAMMALS (Class *Mammalia/Phylum Chordata*)
Bats (Order: *Chiroptera*): 1. Bat, Indiana; 2. Bat, Hawaiian hoary.

Primates (Order: *Primates*): 1. Avahis; 2. Aye-aye; 3. Colobus, Red; 4. Colobus, Zanzibar red; 5. Gibbon, Kloss; 6. Gibbon, Pileated; 7. Gorilla; 8. Indris; 9. Langur, Douc; 10. Langur, Pagi Island; 11. Lemurs; 12. Lemurs, Gentle; 13. Lemurs, Sportive & Weasel; 14. Lemurs, Dwarf; 15. Lemurs, Mouse; 16. Lemurs, Fork-marked; 17. Macaque, Lion-tailed; 18. Mangabey, Tana River; 19. Marmoset, Goeldi's; 20. Monkey, Spider; 21. Monkey, Spider; 22. Orangutan; 23. Sifakas; 24. Tamarins, Golden-rumped; (Golden Marmosets); 25. Uakari.

Rodents (Order: *Rodentia*): 1. Rat, Morro Bay kangaroo; 2. Mouse, Salt marsh harvest; 3. Prairie dog, Utah; 4. Squirrel, Delmarva fox.

Whales, Dolphins & Porpoises (Order: *Cetacea*): 1. Whale, Blue; 2. Whale, Bowhead; 3. Whale, Finback; 4. Whale, Gray; 5. Whale, Humpback; 6. Whale, Right; 7. Whale, Sei; 8. Whale, Sperm.

Carnivores (Order: *Carnivora*): 1. Bear, Mexican grizzly; 2. Cat, Tiger; 3. Cheetah; 4. Cougar, Eastern; 5. Dog, Asiatic wild; 6. Ferret, Black-footed; 7. Fox, Northern kit; 8. Fox, San Joaquin kit; 9. Hyaena, Barbary; 10. Hyaena, Brown; 11. Jaguar; 12. Leopard; 13. Leopard, Formosan clouded; 14. Leopard, Snow; 15. Lion, Asiatic; 16. Lynx, Spanish; 17. Margay; 18. Marten, Formosan yellow-throated; 19. Ocelot; 20. Otter, Cameroon clawless; 21. Otter, Giant; 22. Otter, La Plata; 23. Panther, Florida; 24. Serval, Barbary; 25. Tiger; 26. Wolf, Eastern timber; 27. Wolf, Northern Rocky Mountain; 28. Wolf, Red; 29. Wolf, Maned.

Sirenians (Order: *Sirenia*): 1. Manatee, Florida.

Even-Toed Ungulates (Order: *Artiodactyla*): 1. Anoa; 2. Banteng; 3. Bison, Wood; 4. Deer, Columbian white-tailed; 5. Deer, Key; 6. Deer, Marsh; 7. Deer, McNeill's; 8. Deer, Swamp; 9. Gazelle, Cuviers; 10. Pronghorn, Sonoran; 11. Hartebeest, Swayne's; 12. Ibex, Pyrenean; 13. Impala, Black-faced.

LONG FOREIGN RIVERS

River	Empties Into	Length (in miles)	River	Empties Into	Length (in miles)
Amazon	Atlantic Ocean	3,915	Nile-Kagera	Mediterranean Sea	4,145
Amu-Dar'ya	Aral Sea	1,616	Ob'-Irtysh-Black Irtysh	Gulf of Ob' (Kara Sea)	3,362
Amur-Shilka-Onon	Tatar Strait	2,744	Oder	Baltic Sea	538
Angara	Yenisey River	1,135	Oka	Volga River	918
Araguaia	Tocantins River	1,367	Olenek	Laptev Sea	1,411
Athabasca	Lake Athabasca	765	Orange	Atlantic Ocean	1,350
Belaya	Kama River	889	Orinoco	Atlantic Ocean	1,600
Brahmaputra	Bay of Bengal	1,700	Ottawa	St. Lawrence River	790
Chang Jiang (Yangtze)	East China Sea	3,900	Paraguay	Paraná River	1,584
Churchill	Hudson Bay	1,000	Paraná-La Plata	Atlantic Ocean	2,450
Congo (Zaire)	Atlantic Ocean	2,718	Peace-Finlay	Slave River	1,195
Cubango-Okovango	Okovango Swamps	994	Pechora	Pechora Sea	1,124
Danube	Black Sea	1,775	Pilcomayo	Paraguay River	1,000
Darling	Murray River	1,160	Po	Adriatic Sea	420
Dnieper	Black Sea	1,368	Purus	Amazon River	1,995
Dniester	Black Sea	876	Rhine	North Sea	820
Don	Sea of Azov	1,222	Rhone	Gulf of Lions	505
Dvina, Northern	White Sea	809	Rio Grande	Gulf of Mexico	1,885
Ebro	Mediterranean Sea	565	St. Lawrence	Gulf of St. Lawrence	1,900
Elbe	North Sea	724	Salween	Gulf of Martaban	1,770
Euphrates	Persian Gulf	1,700	São Francisco	Atlantic Ocean	1,811
Fraser	Strait of Georgia	850	Saskatchewan	Lake Winnipeg	1,205
Ganges	Bay of Bengal	1,550	Seine	English Channel	482
Huang He (Yellow)	Yellow Sea	2,877	Selenga	Lake Baykal	920
Indigirka	East Siberian Sea	1,228	Si	South China Sea	1,650
Indus	Arabian Sea	1,800	Sungari	Amur River	1,130
Irrawaddy	Bay of Bengal	1,325	Syr-Dar'ya—Naryn	Aral Sea	1,859
Japurá	Amazon River	1,500	Tagus (Tajo, Tejo)	Atlantic Ocean	565
Kama	Volga River	1,262	Tigris	Euphrates River	1,181
Kasai	Congo River	1,338	Tisza	Danube River	800
Kolyma	East Siberian Sea	1,562	Tocantins	Pará River	1,677
Lena	Laptev Sea	2,734	Ural	Caspian Sea	1,509
Limpopo	Indian Ocean	995	Uruguay	Río de La Plata	994
Loire	Bay of Biscay	628	Vistula	Gulf of Gdańsk	664
Mackenzie-Peace-Finlay	Beaufort Sea	2,635	Volga	Caspian Sea	2,194
Madeira	Amazon River	2,013	Volta	Atlantic Ocean	710
Magdalena	Caribbean Sea	1,000	Yangtze (Chang Jiang)	East China Sea	3,900
Mekong	South China Sea	2,610	Yellow (Huang He)	Yellow Sea	2,877
Meuse	North Sea	590	Yenisey	Kara Sea	2,543
Murray-Darling	Indian Ocean	2,310	Yenisey-Angara	Kara Sea	3,100
Negro	Amazon River	1,400	Yukon	Bering Sea	1,979
Nelson-Saskatchewan	Hudson Bay	1,600	Zambezi	Indian Ocean	1,600
Niger	Gulf of Guinea	2,548			

OCEANS AND SEAS

Ocean	Area (in square miles)	Percent of World's Water	Greatest Depth (in feet)	Sea	Area (in square miles)	Greatest Depth (in feet)
Pacific	64,186,000	46	Mariana Trench, off the Mariana Islands, 36,198	Caribbean	970,000	24,720
				Mediterranean Sea	969,000	16,896
				South China Sea	895,000	15,000
Atlantic	31,862,000	22.9	Puerto Rico Trench, (Milwaukee Deep), off Puerto Rico, 28,374	Bering Sea	875,000	15,800
				Gulf of Mexico	600,000	12,300
				Sea of Okhotsk	590,000	11,070
Indian	28,350,000	20.3	Java Trench, off Java, 25,344	East China Sea	482,000	9,500
				Sea of Japan	389,000	12,280
				Hudson Bay	317,500	846
Arctic	5,427,000	3.9	Eurasia Basin, north of Svalbard, 17,880	North Sea	222,000	2,200
				Black Sea	185,000	7,365
				Red Sea	169,000	7,200
				Baltic Sea	163,000	1,506

ELEMENTS IN SEAWATER

SOURCE: U.S. Office of Saline Water

Element	Milligrams per Kilogram*	Element	Milligrams per Kilogram*	Element	Milligrams per Kilogram*
Chlorine	18,980	Aluminum	0.5	Cesium	0.002
Sodium	10,561	Rubidium	0.2	Uranium	0.0015
Magnesium	1,272	Lithium	0.1	Molybdenum	0.0005
Sulfur	884	Phosphorus	0.001–0.10	Thorium	0.0005
Calcium	400	Barium	0.05	Cerium	0.0004
Potassium	380	Iodine	0.05	Silver	0.0003
Bromine	65	Arsenic	0.01 –0.02	Vanadium	0.0003
Carbon	28	Iron	0.002–0.02	Lanthanum	0.0003
Strontium	13	Manganese	0.001–0.01	Yttrium	0.0003
Boron	4.6	Copper	0.001–0.01	Nickel	0.0001
Silicon	0.02–4.0	Zinc	0.005	Scandium	0.00004
Fluorine	1:4	Lead	0.004	Mercury	0.00003
Nitrogen (compound)	0.01–0.7	Selenium	0.004	Gold	0.000006

* Parts per million.

MAJOR GLACIERS OF THE WORLD

Based on statistics from "Fluctuation of Glaciers 1965-70," © IAHS/UNESCO, 1973, and other sources.

Name	Locality	*Area (sq. mi.)	*Length (mi.)	Name	Locality	*Area (sq. mi.)	*Length (mi.)
Aletsch	Swiss Alps	45	15	Langjökull†	Iceland	265	40
Amundsen	Antarctica	—	60	Logan	Alaska-Yukon	—	70
Baltoro	Asia (Karakoram)	290	35	Malaspina	Alaska-Yukon	1,350	75
Beardmore	Antarctica	130	100	Muir	Alaska	400	15
Bering	Alaska	—	125	Muldrow	Alaska	735	45
Bivachnyy	Asia (Pamir)	75	15	Mýrdalsjökull†	Iceland	180	30
Chisana	Alaska	135	30	Nabesna	Alaska	775	50
Columbia	Alaska	110	40	Petermann	Greenland	—	90
Denman	Antarctica	—	70	Rennick	Antarctica	185	160
Fedchenko	Asia (Pamir)	350	45	Rider	Greenland	125	—
Gangotri	Asia (Himalaya)	115	20	Rimo	Asia (Karakoram)	200	30
Garmo	Asia (Pamir)	60	15	Robert Scott	Antarctica	—	90
Geographical Society	Asia (Pamir)	50	15	Shackleton	Antarctica	—	90
Grum-Grzhimaylo	Asia (Pamir)	60	25	Shamrock	Alaska	40	15
Hispar	Asia (Karakoram)	240	35	Siachen	Asia (Karakoram)	450	50
Hofsjökull†	Iceland	260	—	Svartisen	Norway	200	20
Hubbard	Alaska-Yukon	—	75	Tasman	New Zealand	50	20
Humboldt	Greenland	—	70	Temir-su	Asia (Tien Shan)	45	25
Inyl'chek, Yuzh.	Asia (Tien Shan)	110	40	Totten	Antarctica	—	45
Jostedalsbreen†	Norway	485	60	Triumvirate	Alaska	170	30
Kahiltna	Alaska	—	45	Vatnajökull†	Iceland	2,200	90
Lambert	Antarctica	—	270	Zemu	Asia (Himalaya)	50	20
				Zeravshan	Asia (Turkestan)	45	15

* Approximate, subject to continuous revision. † Icefield.

LARGE LAKES OF THE WORLD

Lake	Continent	Area (in sq. miles)	Length (in miles)	Max. Depth (in ft.)	Lake	Continent	Area (in sq. miles)	Length (in miles)	Max. Depth (in ft.)
Caspian Sea	Asia-Europe	143,243	746	3,264	Reindeer	N. America	2,568	143	—
Superior	N. America	31,700	383	1,301	Tonle Sap	Asia	2,500–1,000*	85	40–5
Victoria	Africa	26,724	250	270	Turkana (Rudolf)	Africa	2,463	160	240
Aral Sea	Asia	25,676	266	256	Issyk-Kul'	Asia	2,425	114	2,303
Huron	N. America	23,010	247	748	Urmia	Asia	2,300–1,500*	90	50
Michigan	N. America	22,300	321	923	Torrens	Australia	2,230*	120	—
Tanganyika	Africa	12,650	420	4,700	Vänern	Europe	2,156	85	328
Baykal	Asia	12,162	395	5,316	Winnipegosis	N. America	2,075	125	38
Great Bear	N. America	12,096	190	1,356	Albert	Africa	2,075	100	160
Nyasa (Malawi)	Africa	11,555	360	2,320	Kariba	Africa	2,050	175	295
Great Slave	N. America	11,269	300	2,015	Nettilling	N. America	1,956	65	—
Chad	Africa	10,000–4,000*	175–125	25–15	Chany	Asia	1,931–965*	56	39–23
Erie	N. America	9,910	241	209	Nipigon	N. America	1,872	70	540
Winnipeg	N. America	9,417	265	60	Gairdner	Australia	1,825–0*	100	—
Ontario	N. America	7,340	193	775	Mweru	Africa	1,800	75	60
Ladoga	Europe	7,104	124	738	Manitoba	N. America	1,794	140	12
Balkhash	Asia	7,027	376	87	Taymyr	Asia	1,737	125	85
Maracaibo	S. America	5,120	110	100	Kyoga	Africa	1,700	75	25
Bangweulu	Africa	4,500–1,900*	50	—	Khanka	Asia	1,700	59	33
Dongting	Asia	4,500–1,500*	80	—	Lake of the Woods	N. America	1,679	70	70
Onega	Europe	3,710	154	377	Peipus	Europe	1,400	87	50
Eyre	Australia	3,500–0*	110	—	Qinghai	Asia	1,625	70	125
Titicaca	S. America	3,200	120	1,000	Nasser-Nubia	Africa	1,550	350	—
Nicaragua	N. America	3,100	100	230	Dubawnt	N. America	1,480	70	—
Athabasca	N. America	3,064	200	400	Van	Asia	1,470	80	—
					Wollaston	N. America	1,035	70	—
					Great Salt	N. America	940	75	27

* Max. and min. of fluctuating water area.

GREAT WORLD DESERTS

Desert	Location	Size	Desert	Location	Size
Arabian (Eastern)	North Africa-Red Sea coast	c. 70,000 sq. mi.	Mojave	Southern California	c. 15,000 sq.mi.
Atacama	Northern Chile	c. 140,000 sq. mi.; c. 600 mi. long	Namib	South-West African coast	c. 800 mi. long; c. 60 mi. wide
Colorado	Southern California	c. 2,500 sq. mi.	Nefud (An Nafud)	Northern Arabia	c. 180 mi. long; c. 140 mi. wide
Dasht-i-Kavir	Iran	c. 450 mi. long; c. 175 mi. wide	Negev	Southern Israel	c. 5,000 sq. mi.
Dasht-i-Lut	Iran	c. 300 mi. long; c. 175 mi. wide	Nubian	Northern Sudan	c.150,000 sq. mi.
Death Valley	California	c. 140 mi. long; c. 10 mi. wide	Rub al Khali	Southern Arabia	c. 235,000 sq.mi.
Gibson	Western Australia	c. 250,000 sq. mi.	Sahara	Northern Africa	c. 3,500,000 sq. mi; c. 3,100 mi. long; c. 1,100 mi. wide
Gobi	China and Mongolia	c. 500,000 sq. mi.; c. 1,000 mi. long	Sechura	Peruvian coast	c. 10,000 sq. mi.
Great Salt Lake	Utah	c.125 mi. long; c. 80 mi. wide	Simpson	Central Australia	c. 45,000 sq. mi.
Great Sandy	Western Australia	c. 150,000 sq. mi.	Syrian (El Hamad)	Northern Arabia, Iraq, Jordan & Syria	c. 450 mi. long; c. 350 mi. wide
Great Victoria	Western and South Australia	c. 250,000 sq. mi.	Taklamakan	Xinjiang Uygur Aut. Reg., China	c. 180,000 sq. mi.; c. 500 mi. long; c. 300 mi. wide
Kalahari	Southern Africa	c. 225,000 sq. mi.	Thar (Great Indian)	India and Pakistan	c. 500 mi. long; c. 275 mi.wide
Kara-Kum	Turkmen SSR, USSR	c. 115,000 sq. mi.; c. 650 mi. long	Vizcaíno	Baja California Sur, Mexico	c. 6,000 sq. mi.
Kyzyl-Kum	Uzbek & Kazakh SSR, USSR	c. 100,000 sq. mi.			

HIGH MOUNTAIN PEAKS (See page 301 for U. S. peaks over 14,000 feet)

Name	Location	Feet
ASIA		
Everest (Chomolungma)	Nepal-China (Tibet)	29,028
K2 (Godwin-Austen)	Pakistan-China	28,250
Kanchenjunga I	Nepal-India	28,208
Lhotse	Nepal-China (Tibet)	27,923
Makalu	Nepal-China (Tibet)	27,824
Kanchenjunga II	Nepal-India	27,803
Lhotse Shar	Nepal-China (Tibet)	27,504
Dhaulagiri I	Nepal	26,810
Manaslu I (Kutang)	Nepal	26,760
Cho Oyu I	Nepal-China (Tibet)	26,750
Nanga Parbat I	Pakistan	26,660
Annapurna I	Nepal	26,504
Gasherbrum I	Pakistan	26,470
Broad Peak	Pakistan	26,400
Gasherbrum II	Pakistan	26,362
Gosainthan (Shisha Pangma)	China (Tibet)	26,291
Gasherbrum IV	Pakistan	26,181
Gasherbrum III	Pakistan	26,090
Annapurna II	Nepal	26,041
Gyachung Kang	Nepal-China (Tibet)	25,990
Nanga Parbat II	Pakistan	25,953
Himalchuli	Nepal	25,895
Disteghil Sar	Pakistan	25,868
Nuptse	Nepal	25,850
Khinyang Chhish	Pakistan	25,760
Masherbrum	Pakistan	25,660
Nanda Devi	India	25,645
Cho Oyu II	Nepal-China (Tibet)	25,611
Chomo Lönzo	China (Tibet)	25,558
Rakaposhi	Pakistan	25,550
Batura Muztagh I	India (Kashmir)	25,540
Kanjut Sar	India (Kashmir)	25,460
Kamet	India-China (Tibet)	25,447
Namzha Parwa	China (Tibet)	25,445
Dhaulagiri II	Nepal	25,429
Saltoro Kangri	Pakistan	25,400
Batura Muztagh II	Pakistan	25,361
Gurla Mandhada	China (Tibet)	25,355
Ulu Muztag	China (Sinkiang-Tibet)	25,340
Trivor	Pakistan	25,330
Kungur	China (Sinkiang)	25,325
Jannu	Nepal	25,294
Dhaulagiri III	Nepal	25,271
Tirich Mir	Pakistan	25,230
Saser Kangri I	India (Kashmir)	25,170
Chogolisa	Pakistan	25,148
Dhaulagiri IV	Nepal	25,135
Kangchungtse (Makalu II)	Nepal-China (Tibet)	25,128
Dhaulagiri V	Nepal	24,992
Rathong	Nepal-India	24,912
Gongga Shan	China	24,790
Annapurna III	Nepal	24,787
Kula Kangri	Bhutan-China (Tibet)	24,784
Changtse	China (Tibet)	24,780
Muztagata	China (Sinkiang)	24,757
Annapurna IV	Nepal	24,688
Communism Peak	USSR	24,590
Noshaq	Pakistan-Afghanistan	24,581
Jongsong Peak	India-China (Tibet)	24,472
Malubiting	Pakistan	24,470
Pobeda Peak	USSR	24,406
Chomo Lhari	Bhutan-China (Tibet)	23,997
Muztag	China (Sinkiang)	23,891
Anyêmaqên	China	23,490
Demavend	Iran	18,376
Ararat	Turkey	16,946
Djaja (Carstensz)	Indonesia (New Guinea)	16,503
Klyuchevskaya Sopka	USSR	15,584
Kinabalu	Malaysia (Sabah)	13,455
Kerintji	Indonesia (Sumatra)	12,484
Fuji	Japan	12,389
Semeru	Indonesia (Java)	12,060
AFRICA		
Kilimanjaro (Kibo)	Tanzania	19,340
Kenya (Batian)	Kenya	17,058
Kilimanjaro (Mawenzi)	Tanzania	16,896
Margherita (Ruwenzori)	Uganda-Zaire	16,795
Ras Dashan	Ethiopia	15,157
Meru	Tanzania	14,979
Karisimbi	Rwanda-Zaire	14,787
Elgon (Wagagai)	Kenya-Uganda	14,178
Toubkal	Morocco	13,665
Cameroon (Fako Peak)	Cameroon	13,350
Teide	Canary Is.	12,198
AUSTRALIA and OCEANIA		
Wilhelm	Papua New Guinea	14,793
Mauna Kea	US (Hawaii)	13,796
Mauna Loa	US (Hawaii)	13,680
Cook (Aorangi)	New Zealand	12,349
Kosciusko	Australia	7,316
ANTARCTICA		
Vinson Massif	16,864	Markham	14,285
Tyree	16,289	Bell	14,117
Gardner	15,374	Mackellar	14,098
Kirkpatrick	14,856	Anderson	13,990
Elizabeth	14,698	Bentley	13,934
EUROPE (including Caucasus)		
El'brus	USSR	18,510
Shkhara	USSR	17,064
Dykh-Tau	USSR	17,054
Koshtan-Tau	USSR	16,877
Dzhangi-Tau	USSR	16,565
Kazbek	USSR	16,558
Mont-Blanc	France	15,771
Dufourspitze (Mte. Rosa)	Switz.-Italy	15,203
Dom (Mischabel)	Switz.	14,911
Lyskamm	Switz.-Italy	14,852
Weisshorn	Switz.	14,780
Täschhorn	Switz.	14,733
Matterhorn	Switz.	14,692
Mont-Maudit	France-Italy	14,649
Dent-Blanche	Switz.	14,293
Nadelhorn	Switz.	14,196
Grand-Combin	Switz.	14,154
Lenzspitze	Switz.	14,098
Finsteraarhorn	Switz.	14,022
Rimpfischhorn	Switz.	13,776
Aletschhorn	Switz.	13,763
Jungfrau	Switz.	13,642
Gran Paradiso	Italy	13,323
Piz Bernina	Switz.-Italy	13,284
Grossglockner	Austria	12,457
Mulhacén	Spain	11,411
Etna	Italy	11,053
Zugspitze	Germany-Austria	9,721
Olympus (Mytikas)	Greece	9,570
Glittertind	Norway	8,110
Ben Nevis	UK (Scotland)	4,406
Vesuvius	Italy	4,190
NORTH AMERICA		
Logan	Canada	19,524
Citlaltépetl (Orizaba)	Mexico	18,855
St. Elias	Canada-US	18,008
Popocatépetl	Mexico	17,887
Iztaccíhuatl	Mexico	17,343
Lucania	Canada	17,147
King Peak	Canada	16,971
Steele	Canada	16,644
Wood	Canada	15,885
Vancouver	Canada-US	15,700
Fairweather	Canada-US	15,300
Toluca (Zinantécatl)	Mexico	15,015
Walsh	Canada	14,780
La Malinche	Mexico	14,635
Nevada de Colima	Mexico	14,205
Cofre de Perote	Mexico	14,050
Tajumulco	Guatemala	13,845
Robson	Canada	12,972
Chirripó Grande	Costa Rica	12,530
Parícutin	Mexico	10,400
SOUTH AMERICA		
Aconcagua	Argentina	22,831
Ojos del Salado	Argentina	22,546
Bonete	Argentina-Chile	22,572
Tupungato	Argentina-Chile	22,310
Pissis	Argentina	22,245
Mercedario	Argentina	22,211
Huascarán	Peru	22,205
Llullaillaco	Argentina-Chile	22,057
Cumbre del Libertador Gen. San Martín	Argentina	22,047
Ancohuma	Bolivia	21,489
Sajama	Bolivia	21,391
Nacimiento	Argentina	21,302
Illampu	Bolivia	21,276
Illimani	Bolivia	21,184
Coropuna	Peru	21,079
Nevados de Huandoy	Peru	20,981
Toro	Argentina-Chile	20,932
Chimborazo	Ecuador	20,561
Cotopaxi	Ecuador	19,347
El Misti	Peru	19,199

EARTH: FACTS/FIGURES

DAMS, MAN-MADE LAKES, HYDROELECTRIC PLANTS

SOURCE: Water and Power Resources Service, Dept. of the Interior

HIGHEST DAMS

A = Arch; E = Earth or Rockfill; G = Gravity; M = Multi-Arch; UC = Under Construction

Name of Dam		Height Meters	Feet	Year Completed	Name of Dam		Height Meters	Feet	Year Completed
1. Rogunsky, USSR	E	325	1,066	UC	15. Hoover, U.S.A.	A/G	221	726	1936
2. Nurek, USSR	E	317	1,040	UC	16. Contra, Switzerland	A	220	722	1965
3. Grand Dixence, Switzerland	G	285	935	1962	17. Piva (Mratinje), Yugoslavia	A	220	722	1975
4. Inguri, USSR	A	272	892	UC	18. Dworshak, U.S.A.	G	219	717	1974
5. Chicoasen, Mexico	E	265	869	UC	19. Glen Canyon, U.S.A.	A	216	710	1964
6. Vaiont, Italy	A	265	869	1961	20. Daniel Johnson, Canada	M	214	703	1968
7. Mica, Canada	E	242	794	1974	21. Toktogul, USSR	G	213	699	UC
8. Sayanskaya, USSR	A	242	794	UC	22. Auburn, U.S.A.	A	209	685	UC
9. Chivor, Colombia	E	237	778	1975	23. Luzzone, Switzerland	A	208	682	1963
10. Mauvoisin, Switzerland	A	237	777	1957	24. Keban, Turkey	E/G	207	679	1974
11. Oroville, U.S.A.	E	235	770	1968	25. Dez, Iran	A	203	666	1963
12. Chirkey, USSR	A	233	764	1975	26. Almendra, Spain	A	202	662	1970
13. Bhakra, India	G	226	742	1963	27. Koelbrein, Austria	A	200	656	1977
14. El Cajon, Honduras	A	226	741	UC					

LARGEST DAMS

Based on total volume of dam structure.

Name of Dam	Volume (Thousands) Cubic Meters	Cubic Yards	Year Completed
1. New Cornelia Tailings, U.S.A.	209,500	274,026	1973
2. Tarbela, Pakistan	121,000	158,268	1975
3. Fort Peck, U.S.A.	96,034	125,612	1940
4. Raul Leoni, Venezuela	78,000	102,014	UC
5. Ataturk, Turkey	73,700	96,400	UC
6. Oahe, U.S.A.	70,343	92,008	1963
7. Oosterschelde, Netherlands	70,000	91,560	UC
8. Yacyreta-Apipe, Argentina-Paraguay	70,000	91,560	UC
9. Mangla, Pakistan	65,651	85,872	1967
10. Gardiner, Canada	65,440	85,596	1968
11. Afsluitdijk, Netherlands	63,400	82,927	1932
12. Oroville, U.S.A.	59,639	78,008	1968
13. San Luis, U.S.A.	59,378	77,666	1967
14. Garrison, U.S.A.	50,846	66,506	1956
15. Cochiti, U.S.A.	49,417	64,631	1975
16. Tabka, Syria	46,000	60,168	1975
17. Kiev, USSR	44,000	57,552	1964
18. W.A.C. Bennett, Canada	43,733	57,203	1967
19. High Aswan (Sadd-el-Aali), Egypt	41,733	57,203	1970
20. Dantiwada Left Earthenbank, India	41,040	53,680	1965
21. Saratov, USSR	40,400	52,843	1967
22. Mission Tailings #2, U.S.A.	40,088	52,435	1973
23. Fort Randall, U.S.A.	38,383	50,205	1956
24. Kanev, USSR	37,860	49,520	1974
25. Kakhova, USSR	35,640	46,617	1955
26. Lauwerszee, Netherlands	35,575	46,532	1969
27. Beas, India	35,019	45,800	1975

GREATEST MAN-MADE LAKES

Name of Dam	Capacity Millions of Cubic Meters	Thousands of Acre-Feet	Year Completed
1. Owen Falls, Uganda	204,800	166,000	1954
2. Bratsk, USSR	169,270	137,220	1964
3. High Aswan (Sadd-el-Aali), Egypt	169,000	137,000	1970
4. Kariba, Zimbabwe-Zambia	160,368	130,000	1959
5. Akosombo, Ghana	148,000	120,000	1965
6. Daniel Johnson, Canada	141,852	115,000	1968
7. Raul Leoni, Venezuela	136,000	110,000	UC
8. Krasnoyarsk, USSR	73,300	59,425	1972
9. W.A.C. Bennett, Cananda	70,309	57,006	1967
10. Zeya, USSR	68,400	55,452	1975
11. Cabora Bassa, Mozambique	64,000	51,900	1974
12. LaGrande, Canada	62,260	50,475	UC
13. Ust-Ilimsk, USSR	59,300	48,100	UC
14. Volga-V.I.Lenin, USSR	58,000	47,020	1955
15. Bukhtarma, USSR	53,000	42,970	1960
16. Ataturk, Turkey	48,700	39,481	UC
17. Irkutsk, USSR	46,000	37,290	1956
18. Hoover, U.S.A.	36,703	29,755	1936
19. Vilyui, USSR	35,900	29,104	1967
20. Sobradinho, Brazil	34,200	27,700	1978
21. Tucurui, Brazil	34,000	27,564	UC
22. Volgograd-22nd Congress, USSR	33,500	27,160	1958
23. Glen Canyon, U.S.A.	33,305	27,000	1964
24. Keban, Turkey	31,000	25,110	1974
25. Garrison, U.S.A.	30,000	24,321	1956
26. Iroquois, Canada	29,960	24,288	1958
27. Oahe, U.S.A.	29,100	23,591	1963

LARGEST HYDROELECTRIC PLANTS

MW = Megawatts

Name of Dam	Rated Capacity MW Present	MW Ultimate	Year of Initial Operation
1. Italpu, Brazil-Paraguay	—	12,870	UC
2. Grand Coulee, U.S.A.	6,263	6,494	1941/80
3. Guri, Venezuela	524	7,300	1967
4. Sayanskaya, USSR	—	6,400	UC
5. Krasnoyarsk, USSR	6,096	6,096	1968
6. LaGrande 2, Canada	—	5,328	UC
7. Churchill Falls, Canada	5,225	5,225	1971
8. Bratsk, USSR	4,100	4,600	1964
9. Sukhovo, USSR	—	4,500	UC
10. Ust-Ilimsk, USSR	720	4,320	1974
11. Cabora Bassa, Mozambique	2,425	4,000	1975
12. Tucurui, Brazil	—	3,960	UC
13. Rogunsky, USSR	—	3,600	UC
14. Paulo Afonso, Brazil	1,524	3,409	1955
15. Solteira, Brazil	3,200	3,200	1973
16. Inga I, Zaire	360	2,820	1974
17. John Day, U.S.A.	2,160	2,700	1968
18. Nurek, USSR	—	2,700	UC
19. Sao Simao, Brazil	—	2,680	UC
20. Volgograd-22nd Congress, USSR	2,560	2,560	1958
21. Chicoasen, Mexico	—	2,400	1980
22. Volga-V.I. Lenin, USSR	2,300	2,300	1955
23. Iron Gates I, Romania-Yugoslavia	2,300	2,300	1970
24. W.A.C.Bennett, Canada	1,816	2,270	1969
25. Foz Do Areia, Brazil	2,511	—	1980
26. High Aswan (Sadd-el-Aali), Egypt	2,100	2,100	1967
27. Bath County, U.S.A.	—	2,100	UC
28. Tarbela, Pakistan	700	2,100	1977
29. Itumbiara, Brazil	—	2,124	UC
30. Chief Joseph, U.S.A.	1,879	2,069	1956
31. Salto Santiago, Brazil	—	2,031	1979
32. Robert Moses-Niagara, U.S.A.	1,950	1,950	1961
33. Salto Grande, Argentina-Uruguay	—	1,890	1979
34. Dinorwic, U.K.	—	1,880	1981
35. Ludington, U.S.A.	1,872	1,872	1973
36. St. Lawrence Power Dam, U.S.A.-Canada	1,824	1,824	1958
37. The Dalles, U.S.A.	1,807	1,807	1957
38. Karakaya, Turkey	—	1,800	UC
39. Grand Maison, France	1,200	1,800	UC
40. Mica, Canada	—	1,740	UC
41. Itaparica, Brazil	—	2,500	UC
42. Kemano, Canada	813	1,670	1954
43. Blue Ridge, U.S.A.	—	1,600	UC
44. Beauharnois, Canada	1,021	1,574	1950
45. Kariba, Zimbabwe-Zambia	1,266	1,566	1959
46. San Carlos, Colombia	—	1,550	UC

VOLCANOES

Key to letters: (E) Last eruption, with year in parentheses; (R) Rumbling; (St) Steaming; (D) Dormant.

Name	Location	Height (in feet)
AFRICA		
Kibo (Kilimanjaro) (D)	Tanzania	19,340
Cameroon Mt. (E-1959)	Cameroon	13,350
El Teide (St)	Canary Is.	12,172
Nyiragongo (E-1977)	Zaire	11,385
Nyamulagira (E-1976)	Zaire	10,028
Fogo (E-1951)	Cape Verde Is.	9,281
Piton de la Fournaise (E-1977)	Réunion	8,632
Tristan da Cunha (E-1961)	South Atlantic	6,760
Teneguia (D)	Canary Is.	2,006
ANTARCTICA		
Deception Island (E-1970)		—
Erebus (E-1978)		12,450
Melbourne (St)		8,500
ASIA and AUSTRALASIA		
Klyuchevskaya (E-1962)	USSR	15,584
Kerintji (St)	Indonesia	12,484
Fuji (D)	Japan	12,389
Rindjani (E-1964)	Indonesia	12,224
Tolbachik (E-1941)	USSR	12,080
Semeru (E-1981)	Indonesia	12,060
Ichinskaya (St)	USSR	11,880
Kronotskaya (D)	USSR	11,575
Koryakskaya (E-1957)	USSR	11,339
Slamet (E-1953)	Indonesia	11,247
Raung (St)	Indonesia	10,932
Shiveluch (E-1964)	USSR	10,771
Dempo (St)	Indonesia	10,364
Welirang (D)	Indonesia	10,354
Agung (E-1964)	Indonesia	10,308
Sundoro (D)	Indonesia	10,285
Tjareme (E-1938)	Indonesia	10,098
Gede (E-1949)	Indonesia	9,705
Apo (D)	Philippines	9,369
Merapi (E-1969)	Indonesia	9,551
Bezymyannaya (E-1961)	USSR	9,514
Marapi (D)	Indonesia	9,485
Tambora (D)	Indonesia	9,353
Mayon (E-1978)	Philippines	7,940
Alaid (E-1981)	USSR	7,674
Ulawun (E-1980)	Papua New Guinea	7,546
Sinila (E-1979)	Indonesia	c. 7,000
Gamalama (E-1980)	Indonesia	5,625
Bulosan (E-1978)	Philippines	5,140
Usu (E-1978)	Japan	2,390
Taal (E-1977)	Philippines	990
MID-PACIFIC		
Mauna Kea (D)	Hawaii	13,796
Mauna Loa (E-1975)	Hawaii	13,680
Kilauea (E-1977)	Hawaii	4,077
EUROPE		
Etna (E-1981)	Sicily, Italy	11,053
Askja (E-1961)	Iceland	4,954
Hekla (E-1981)	Iceland	4,892
Vesuvius (St)	Italy	4,190
Stromboli (E-1971)	Lipari Is., Italy	3,038

Name	Location	Height (in feet)
Surtsey (E-1967)	Iceland	570
Eldfell (E-1973)	Iceland	327
NORTH AMERICA		
Popocatépetl (St)	Mexico	17,887
Colima (St)	Mexico	14,205
Wrangell (St)	Alaska	14,163
Torbert (E-1953)	Alaska	11,413
Spurr (E-1953)	Alaska	11,069
Lassen (D)	California	10,457
Paricutín (D)	Mexico	10,400
Redoubt (E-1966)	Alaska	10,197
Iliamna (St)	Alaska	10,016
Shishaldin (St)	Aleutians	9,387
St. Helens (E-1980-81)	Washington	8,364
Pavlof (E-1980)	Alaska	8,261
Veniaminof (D)	Alaska	8,225
Griggs (St)	Alaska	7,600
Mageik (St)	Alaska	7,250
Douglas (St)	Alaska	7,064
Chiginagak (D)	Alaska	6,900
Katmai (E-1962)	Alaska	6,715
Kukak (St)	Alaska	6,700
Makushin (D)	Aleutians	6,680
Pogromni (E-1964)	Aleutians	6,568
Martin (E-1960)	Alaska	6,050
Trident (E-1963)	Alaska	6,010
Augustine (E-1976)	Alaska	3,999
CENTRAL AMERICA and CARIBBEAN		
Tajumulco (R)	Guatemala	13,845
Tacaná (R)	Guatemala	13,428
Acatenango (R)	Guatemala	12,992
Fuego (E-1978)	Guatemala	12,582
Santa Maria (R)	Guatemala	12,362
Atitlan (R)	Guatemala	11,565
Irazú (E-1964)	Costa Rica	11,260
San Pedro (R)	Guatemala	9,921
Poás (St)	Costa Rica	8,930
Pacaya (E-1970)	Guatemala	8,346
Izalco (E-1967)	El Salvador	6,184
Soufrière (E-1979)	St. Vincent	4,048
SOUTH AMERICA		
Guallatiri (E-1959)	Chile	19,882
Lascar (E-1951)	Chile	19,652
Cotopaxi (St)	Ecuador	19,347
Misti (D)	Peru	19,199
Cayambe (D)	Ecuador	18,996
Tupungatito (E-1959)	Chile	18,504
Sangay (E-1946)	Ecuador	17,159
Tungurahua (R)	Ecuador	16,512
Cotacachi (E-1955)	Ecuador	16,204
Pichincha (D)	Ecuador	15,696
Purace (E-1950)	Colombia	15,604
Lautaro (St)	Chile	11,090
Llaima (E-1955)	Chile	10,239
Villarrica (E-1964)	Chile	9,318
Osorno (D)	Chile	8,730
Shoshuenco (E-1960)	Chile	7,743

WORLD WATERFALLS

Location and Name		Height[1] (in feet)
AFRICA		
Aughrabies[3]	S. Africa	482
Baratieri	Ethiopia	460
Chirombo[2]	Zambia	880
Dianzundu (Duque de Bragança)	Angola	344
Finca	Ethiopia	508
Howick	S. Africa	358
Kalambo[2][3]	Tanz.-Zambia	726
Karkloof[2]	S. Africa	350
Livingstone[2]	Zaire	875
Lofoi	Zaire	1,115
Magwa	S. Africa	450
Maletsunyane	Lesotho	630
Murchison[2]	Uganda	400
Ruacana	Angola	406
Stanley[2]	Zaire	200
Tisisat[3]	Ethiopia	140
Tsitsa	S. Africa	375
Tugela[2]	S. Africa	3,110
Verme	Ethiopia	229
Victoria[2][3]	Zimbabwe-Zambia	355

Location and Name		Height[1] (in feet)
ASIA		
Diyaluma	Sri Lanka	600
Jog (Gersoppa)[2][3]	India	830
Kegon	Japan	330
Kirindi Ela	Sri Lanka	347
Kurundu Oya	Sri Lanka	620
Laksapana	Sri Lanka	377
Nachi	Japan	430
Ramboda	Sri Lanka	329
Ratna Ella	Sri Lanka	305
Sivasamudram (Kaveri)[2]	India	320
Yudaki	Japan	335
OCEANIA		
Akaka	Hawaii (US)	420
Barron	Australia	770
Bowen[2]	New Zealand	540
Helena	New Zealand	860
Leura[2]	Australia	308
Stirling	New Zealand	505
Sutherland[2]	New Zealand	1,904

Location and Name		Height[1] (in feet)
Tully[2]	Australia	972
Wentworth[2]	Australia	518
Wollomombi[2]	Australia	1,580
EUROPE		
Aurstapet[2]	Norway	794
Gastein[2]	Austria	486
Gavarnie	France	1,385
Giessbach[2]	Switz.	1,312
Glomach	UK (Scotland)	370
Golling[2]	Austria	203
Iffigen	Switz.	394
Kile[2]	Norway	1,840
Krimml[2]	Austria	1,246
Låtefoss[2]	Norway	541
Mardalsfoss (E.)[2]	Norway	1,696
Mardalsfoss (W.)	Norway	1,535
Marmore[2]	Italy	525
Mongefossen[2]	Norway	2,539
Reichenbach[2]	Switz.	656
Rjoandefoss[2]	Norway	1,847
Rjukenfoss	Norway	983

[1] Height means total drop whether in one or more leaps. [2] Falls consisting of more than one leap.
[3] Falls that diminish greatly seasonally.

Location and Name		Height[1] (in feet)
Simme[2]	Switz.	459
Skjeggedalsfoss	Norway	525
Skykkjedalsfoss	Norway	820
Søtefoss	Norway	896
Stalheimsfoss	Norway	413
Staubbach	Switz.	984
Stäuber	Switz.	590
Stigfoss	Norway	590
Toce[2]	Italy	470
Trümmelbach[2]	Switz.	1,312
Tyssefoss[2]	Norway	1,749
Tyssestrengene[2]	Norway	2,795
Vermafoss	Norway	1,248
Vettisfoss[2]	Norway	1,214
Vøringfoss	Norway	597

NORTH AMERICA

Basaseachic	Mexico	1,000
Bridalveil	US (Calif.)	620
Chequaga	US (N.Y.)	156
Churchill	Canada (Newf.)	245
Comet	US (Wash.)	320
Cumberland	US (Ky.)	68
Della	Canada (B.C.)	1,443
Fairy	US (Wash.)	700
Fall Creek	US (Tenn.)	256
Feather	US (Calif.)	640
Grand	Canada (N. Br.)	75
Grand	Canada (Ont.)	150
Granite	US (Wash.)	350
Illilouette	US (Calif.)	370
Juanacatlán, Salto de[3]	Mexico	70
Jumatán	Mexico	394

Location and Name		Height[1] (in feet)
Manitou	US (Wis.)	165
Minnehaha[3]	US (Minn.)	52
Missouri (Great Falls)[2]	US (Mont.)	90
Montmorency	Canada (Que.)	274
Multnomah[2]	US (Oreg.)	620
Narada	US (Wash.)	168
Necaxa	Mexico	540
Nevada	US (Calif.)	594
Niagara[2]:		
American	US (N.Y.)	167
Canadian (Horseshoe)	U.S.-Canada	158
Palouse	US (Wash.)	198
Panther	Canada (Alta.)	600
Passaic (Great Falls)[3]	US (N.J.)	70
Potomac (Great Falls)[2]	US (Md.-Va.)	90
Ribbon[3]	US Calif.)	1,612
Saint Anthony	US (Minn.)	60
Seven	US (Colo.)	266
Shawinigan	Canada (Que.)	150
Shoshone[2 3]	US (Idaho)	210
Silver Strand	US (Calif.)	1,170
Sluiskin	US (Wash.)	300
Snoqualmie	US (Wash.)	270
Tahquamenon[2]	US (Mich.)	88
Takakkaw[2]	Canada (B.C.)	1,650
Taughannock	US (N.Y.)	215
Tower	US (Wyo.)	132
Twin[2 3]	US (Idaho)	125
Vernal	US (Calif.)	317
Virginia	Canada (N.W.T.)	315
Xico	Mexico	256

Location and Name		Height[1] (in feet)
Yellowstone[2]		
Upper	US (Wyo.)	109
Lower		308
Yosemite[2]	US (Calif.)	2,425
Upper		1,430

SOUTH AMERICA

Angel[2]	Venezuela	3,212
Upper		2,648
Anta, Cascada da	Brazil	665
Candelas, Cataratas de	Colombia	984
Glass	Brazil	1,325
Grande	Arg.-Uruguay	75
Grande	Brazil	140
Great	Guyana	500
Iguazú (Iguaçu)[2]	Brazil	237
Itiquira	Brazil	395
Kaieteur[2]	Guyana	822
highest		741
King Edward VIII	Guyana	850
King George VI	Guyana	1,600
Kukenaam[3]	Venezuela	2,000
Marina[2]	Guyana	500
Papagaio	Brazil	350
Patos-Maribondo	Brazil	115
Paulo Afonso[2]	Brazil	275
Roraima[3]	Guyana	1,500
Sete Quedas (Guairá)	Brazil-Parag.	360
Tequendama	Colombia	482
Urubupungá	Brazil	33

[1] Height means total drop whether in one or more leaps. [2] Falls consisting of more than one leap. [3] Falls that diminish greatly seasonally.

OUTSTANDING WORLDWIDE WEATHER EXTREMES

SOURCE: National Oceanic & Atmospheric Administration

TEMPERATURE EXTREMES

Temperature extremes for any place on Earth are determined by a number of factors, including altitude, latitude, and physical characteristics. For an extreme to be recorded, an observation must be made at the precise time and place of occurrence; consequently, more extreme temperatures undoubtedly have occurred.

THE HOTTEST

Area	Max. (°F.)	Place	Elevation (Ft.)	Date
Africa	136	Al'Aziziyah, Libya	380	Sept. 13, 1922
North America	134	Death Valley, California	−178	July 10, 1913
Asia	129	Tirat Tsvi, Israel	−722	June 21, 1942
Australia	128	Cloncurry, Queensland	622	Jan. 16, 1889
Europe	122	Seville, Spain	26	Aug. 4, 1881
South America	120	Rivadavia, Argentina	676	Dec. 11, 1905
Oceania	108	Tuguegarao, Philippines	72	Apr. 29, 1912
Antarctica	58	Esperanza, Palmer Peninsula	26	Oct. 20, 1956

THE COLDEST

Area	Min. (°F.)	Place	Elevation (Ft.)	Date
Antarctica	−127	Vostok Station	11,220	Aug. 24, 1960
Asia	− 90	Oymyakon, USSR	2,625	Feb. 6, 1933
Greenland	− 87	Northice Station	7,690	Jan. 9, 1954
North America	− 81	Snag, Yukon, Canada	1,925	Feb. 3, 1947
Europe	− 67	Ust'-Shchugor, USSR	279	date unknown
South America	− 27	Sarmiento, Argentina	879	June 1, 1907
Africa	− 11	Ifrane, Morocco	5,364	Feb. 11, 1935
Australia	− 8	Charlotte Pass, New South Wales	NA	July 22, 1947

RAINFALL EXTREMES

The total annual precipitation recorded at a place may vary greatly from year to year. The rainiest places show the greatest variations from year to year in actual amounts. The drier places show the greatest variation taken as a percentage of the mean value. At Cherrapunji, India, for example, the greatest amount of precipitation in a calendar year was 905.1 inches. The least was 282.6 inches, a difference of over 600 inches. At Arica, Chile, half of the total rainfall recorded from 1931 through 1960 fell in the single year of 1959. No rain at all fell in 19 of the 30 years. Because of such fluctuations, the average annual precipitation may be greatly influenced by the available years of record; the longer the record, the more reliable is the average.

THE WETTEST

Area	Average Annual Rainfall (Inches)	Place	Elevation (Ft.)	Years of Record
Oceania	460.0	Mt. Waialeale, Hawaii	5,075	33
Asia	450.0	Cherrapunji, India	4,309	75
Africa	404.6	Debundscha, Cameroon	30	33
South America	354.0	Quibdó, Colombia	240	11–17
North America	262.1	Henderson Lake, Br. Col.	12	15
Europe	182.8	Crkvice, Yugoslavia	3,337	23
Australia	179.0	Tully, Queensland	220	32

THE DRIEST

Area	Average Annual Rainfall (Inches)	Place	Elevation (Ft.)	Years of Record
South America	0.03	Arica, Chile	95	60
Africa	0.1	Wadi Halfa, Sudan	410	40
Antarctica	0.8	South Pole Station	9,186	11
North America	1.2	Bataques, Mexico	16	15
Asia	1.8	Aden, P.D.R. Yemen	22	51
Australia	4.05	Mulka, South Australia	NA	35
Europe	6.4	Astrakhan, USSR	45	26
Oceania	8.93	Puako, Hawaii	5	14

WORLD'S TALLEST BUILDINGS

*Under construction. SOURCE: American Society of Civil Engineers

Building	Location	Height (in feet)	Stories
Sears Tower	Chicago	1,454	110
World Trade Center (Twin Towers)	New York City	1,350	110
Empire State	New York City	1,250	102
Standard Oil (Indiana)	Chicago	1,136	80
John Hancock	Chicago	1,127	100
Texas Commerce Plaza	Houston	1,049	75
Chrysler	New York City	1,046	77
American International	New York City	950	66
First Bank Tower	Toronto	935	72
40 Wall Tower	New York City	927	71
Citicorp Center	New York City	914	59
Water Tower Place	Chicago	859	74
United California Bank	Los Angeles	858	62
United California Bank	New York City	851	66
RCA Rockefeller Center	New York City	850	70
First National Bank	Chicago	844	60
Transamerica	San Francisco	843	48
U. S. Steel	Pittsburgh	841	64
One Chase Manhattan Plaza	New York City	813	60
Pan American	New York City	808	59
Woolworth	New York City	792	57
Palace of Science and Culture	Warsaw	790	42
John Hancock Tower	Boston	790	60
M.L.C. Centre	Sydney, Australia	786	70
Commerce Court West	Toronto	784	57
Bank of America	San Francisco	778	32
3 First National Plaza	Chicago	775	58
IDS Center	Minneapolis	772	57
One Penn Plaza	New York City	766	57
Maine Montparnasse	Paris	751	64
Prudential Center	Boston	750	52
Federal Reserve	Boston	750	32
Exxon	New York City	750	54
First International Plaza	Houston	748	55
1 Liberty Plaza (U.S. Steel)	New York City	743	54
Ikebukuro Office Tower	Tokyo	742	60
20 Exchange Place (Citibank)	New York City	741	55
Renaissance 1	Detroit	739	73
Security Pacific National Bank	Los Angeles	738	57
Toronto Dominion Bank Tower	Toronto	736	56
One Astor Plaza	New York City	730	54
9 West 57th Street	New York City	725	50
Peachtree Center Plaza	Atlanta	723	71
Carlton Centre	Johannesburg	722	50
Detroit Plaza Hotel	Detroit	720	73
One Shell Plaza	Houston	714	52
First International	Dallas	710	56
Shinjuku Center	Tokyo	709	55
Terminal Tower	Cleveland	708	52
Union Carbide	New York City	707	52
General Motors	New York City	705	50
Metropolitan Life	New York City	700	50
Atlantic Richfield Plaza A & B	Los Angeles	699	52
One Shell Square	New Orleans	697	51
500 Fifth Avenue	New York City	697	58
Shinjuku Mitsui	Tokyo	696	55
IBM	Chicago	695	52
Neiman-Marcus	Chicago	690	65
55 Water Street	New York City	687	53
Chemical Bank Trust	New York City	687	50
Three Allen Center*	Houston	685	50
One Houston Center	Houston	681	46
Chanin	New York City	680	55
Gulf+Western	New York City	679	44
Marine Midland Bank	New York City	677	52
Southern Bell	Atlanta	677	46
Metropolitan Tower	New York City	675	50
Lincoln Building	New York City	673	55
Georgia Pacific Tower*	Atlanta	673	52
McGraw-Hill	New York City	670	51
1633 Broadway	New York City	670	48
Bank of Oklahoma Tower	Tulsa	667	50
Shinjuku Nomura	Tokyo	666	53
Civic Center	Chicago	662	38
First City Tower	Houston	662	49
Overseas-Chinese Banking Corp.	Singapore	660	52
Shinjuku Sumitomo	Tokyo	656	52
Parque Central Torre Oficinas	Caracas	656	56
1100 Milam	Houston	651	47
One Miracle Mile	Chicago	650	60
Ukraine Hotel	Moscow	650	34
American Brands	New York City	648	47
Lake Point Towers	Chicago	645	70
A.T.&T.	New York City	645	37
1000 Lakeshore Plaza	Chicago	640	60
Irving Trust	New York City	640	53

SELECTED WORLD STRUCTURES

SOURCE: Amer. Society of Civil Engineers

Structure	Location	Height in Feet
Polish National TV Service Tower	Plock, Poland	2,120
KTHI-TV	Fargo, N.D.	2,063
CN Communication Tower	Toronto	1,815
Ostankino TV tower	Near Moscow, USSR	1,762
Moscow TV tower	USSR	1,732
B.R.E.N. Tower	Nevada	1,527
Loran Mast	Snaefellsnes, Iceland	1,378
Danish Government Navigational Mast	Thule, Greenland	1,345
Peking Radio Antenna	China	1,312
Tower Zero	N.W. Cape, Western Australia	1,271
TV antenna	Emley Moor, England	1,265
TV antenna	Belmont, England	1,265
Zender Lopik TV Antenna	Near Lopik, Netherlands	1,253
American Electric Power smokestack	Cresap, W. Va.	1,206
Utah Copper Div. of Kennecott Copper Corp. Magna Smelter Chimney	Great Salt Lake, Utah	1,200
East Berlin Antenna	East Germany	1,185
Television Center	Moscow	1,179
TV tower	Vinnitsa, Ukraine, USSR	1,150
Loran Tower	Tomil, Yap Island	1,100
CHCHTV Antenna	Hamilton, Canada	1,093
TV tower	Tokyo	1,092
Leningrad antenna	USSR	1,065
TV Antenna	Kojál, Czechoslovakia	1,033
Weather tower	Obninsk, USSR	1,027
Lakihegg Antenna	Lakihegg, Hungary	1,006
ITA Antenna	Brynychain, Wales	1,000
Conemaugh Station Chimney (pair)	Johnstown, Pa.	1,000
TV antenna	Black Hill, Scotland	1,000
TV antenna	Durris, Scotland	1,000
TV antenna	Anglia-Mendlesham, England	1,000
ITA Antenna	Strabane, Northern Ireland	1,000
Factory chimney	Cracow, Poland	985
Eiffel Tower (with TV antenna, 1052)	Paris	984
TV Tower	Munich	951
Exxon Co. Oil Platform.	Santa Barbara, Calif.	945
TV Tower	Hamburg, Germany	856
Ohio Edison Company Chimney	Stratton, Ohio	853
General Post Office Antennae (pair)	Rugby, England	820
TV antenna	Stuttgart, Germany	767
Radio tower	Transvaal, Rep. of So. Africa	760
BBC Antenna, Crystal Palace	London	710
TV antenna	West Berlin	696
National Cathedral Tower	Washington, D.C.	660
Gateway Arch	St. Louis	630
Tour du Maine	Paris	607
Space Needle	Seattle	606
Donauturm	Vienna	597
Radio Luxembourg Antenna	Junglinster	591
Post Office Tower	London	580
San Jacinto Column	Houston	570
Tower of the First Methodist Church	Chicago	568
Washington Monument	Washington, D.C.	555
American Smelting and Refining smokestack	Tacoma, Wash.	535
Ulm Cathedral	West Germany	530
Vertical Assembly Building	Cape Canaveral, Fla.	525
Cathedral of Learning	Pittsburgh	523
Blackpool Tower	England	519
Cologne Cathedral	West Germany	515
Mole Antonelliana	Turin, Italy	510
Kaknastornet Tower	Stockholm	502

EARTH'S EXTREMES   SOURCE: National Geographic Society

Wettest spot	Mt. Waialeale, Hawaii; greatest annual average, 460 inches (12-month record, Cherrapunji, India: 1,042 inches between Aug. 1860 and July 1861)
Driest spot	Atacama Desert, Chile; rainfall barely measurable
Coldest spot	Vostok, Antarctica; −127°F. recorded in 1960; Plateau Station, Antarctica; annual average; −70°F.
Hottest spot	Al'Aziziyah, Libya; 136°F. recorded in 1922. Dalol, Danakil Depression, Ethiopia; annual average temperature; 94°F.

Northernmost town ...	Ny Alesund, Spitsbergen, Norway
Southernmost town ...	Puerto Williams, Chile
Highest town	Aucanquilcha, Chile; 17,500 feet
Lowest town	Villages along the Dead Sea; 1,299 feet below sea level
Largest gorge	Grand Canyon, Colorado River, Arizona; 277 miles long, 600 feet to 18 miles wide, 1 mile deep
Deepest gorge	Hells Canyon, Snake River, Idaho; 7,900 feet deep
Strongest surface wind .	231 mph; recorded in 1934 at Mount Washington, New Hampshire
Greatest tides	Bay of Fundy, Nova Scotia; 53 feet

PRINCIPAL WORLD ISLANDS

Island	Area (in sq. miles)	Island	Area (in sq. miles)	Island	Area (in sq. miles)
Greenland	840,000	New Caledonia (France)	6,530	Savaii (W. Samoa)	662
New Guinea	305,000	Hawaiian (U.S.)	6,450	Zanzibar (Tanzania)	641
Borneo	290,000	Nordaustlandet (Norway)	6,409	Oahu (Hawaii, U.S.)	608
Madagascar	226,400	Franz Josef Land (USSR)	6,216	Guadeloupe (France)	584
Baffin (Canada)	195,928	Kuriles (USSR)	6,025	Alands (Finland)	581
Sumatra (Indonesia)	164,000	Bahamas	5,382	Kauai (Hawaii, U.S.)	553
Japan	145,730	Samar (Philippines)	5,050	Shetlands (U.K.)	552
Philippines	115,707	New Hebrides (Vanuatu)	5,700	Rhodes (Greece)	542
New Zealand	103,736	Negros (Philippines)	4,906	Faeroes (Denmark)	540
Great Britain (U.K.)	88,764	Falklands (U.K.)	4,618	Marquesas (France)	492
Honshu (Japan)	88,000	Palawan (Philippines)	4,550	Carolines (Pacific Is.)	463
Victoria (Canada)	83,896	Panay (Philippines)	4,446	Okinawa (Japan)	454
Ellesmere (Canada)	75,767	Jamaica	4,232	Upolu (W. Samoa)	433
Celebes (Indonesia)	72,986	Aleutians (Alaska, U.S.)	4,201	Martinique (France)	425
South (N.Z.)	58,393	Hawaii (U.S.)	4,038	Tahiti (France)	402
Java (Indonesia)	48,842	Viti Levu (Fiji)	4,010	Pemba (Tanzania)	380
North (N.Z.)	44,187	Cape Breton (Canada)	3,981	Orkneys (U.K.)	372
Newfoundland (Canada)	42,031	Mindoro (Philippines)	3,759	Madeiras (Portugal)	307
Cuba	40,533	Kodiak (Alaska, U.S.)	3,670	Dominica	290
Luzon (Philippines)	40,420	Cyprus	3,572	Tonga	270
Iceland	39,768	Puerto Rico (U.S.)	3,435	Molokai (Hawaii, U.S.)	261
Mindanao (Philippines)	36,537	Corsica (France)	3,352	Bahrain	240
Moluccas (Indonesia)	32,307	New Ireland (PNG)	3,340	St. Lucia	238
Novaya Zemlya (USSR)	31,900	Crete (Greece)	3,218	Corfu (Greece)	229
Ireland	31,743	Galápagos (Ecuador)	3,075	Isle of Man (U.K.)	227
Sakhalin (USSR)	29,500	Anticosti (Canada)	3,066	Bornholm (Denmark)	227
Hispaniola (Haiti and Dominican Rep.)	29,399	Wrangel (USSR)	2,819	Singapore	226
Hokkaido (Japan)	28,983	Hebrides (U.K.)	2,812	Guam (U.S.)	212
Banks (Canada)	27,038	Canaries (Spain)	2,808	Isle Royale (Mich., U.S.)	196
Tasmania (Australia)	26,383	Leyte (Philippines)	2,786	Virgins (U.S.-U.K.)	192
Ceylon (Sri Lanka)	25,332	Kerguélen (France)	2,700	Marianas (excluding Guam) (Pacific Is.)	184
Svalbard (Norway)	23,957	Andamans (India)	2,448	Curacao (Neth. Antilles)	182
Devon (Canada)	21,331	Guadalcanal (Solomon Islands)	2,180	Barbados	166
Bismarck Arch. (PNG)	18,976	Bali (Indonesia)	2,171	Isle of Wight (U.K.)	145
Marajó (Brazil)	17,991	Prince Edward (Canada)	2,170	Lanai (Hawaii, U.S.)	140
Tierra del Fuego (Chile and Argentina)	17,900	Balearics (Spain)	1,936	St. Vincent	131
Axel Heiberg (Canada)	16,671	Trinidad (Trinidad & Tobago)	1,864	Maltese	122
Melville (Canada)	16,274	Ryukyus (Japan)	1,767	Grenada	120
Southampton (Canada)	15,913	Madura (Indonesia)	1,752	Tobago (Trinidad & Tobago)	116
Solomons	15,600	Cape Verde	1,557	Antigua	108
New Siberian Is. (USSR)	14,672	South Georgia (U.K.)	1,450	Martha's Vineyard (Mass., U.S.)	93
Severnaya Zemlya (USSR)	14,285	Euboea (Greece)	1,411	Elba (Italy)	87
New Britain (PNG)	14,100	Long (N.Y., U.S.)	1,401	Seychelles	85
Taiwan (Formosa) (China)	13,836	Socotra (PDR Yemen)	1,400	Channel (U.K.)	74
Kyushu (Japan)	13,770	Samoa	1,209	Marshalls (Pacific Is.)	70
Hainan (China)	13,127	Gotland (Sweden)	1,153	Easter (Chile)	63
Prince of Wales (Canada)	12,872	Western Samoa	1,133	Staten (N.Y., U.S.)	58
Spitsbergen (Norway)	12,355	Manitoulin (Canada)	1,068	Tutuila (Amer. Samoa)	53
Vancouver (Canada)	12,079	Réunion (France)	969	St. Helena (U.K.)	47
Timor	11,527	Azores (Portugal)	902	Nantucket (Mass., U.S.)	46
		Juventud (I. of Pines) (Cuba)	849	Hong Kong	30
Sicily (Italy)	9,926	Bioko (Fernando Po) (Equat. Guinea)	779	Manhattan (N.Y., U.S.)	22
Somerset (Canada)	9,570	Tenerife (Spain)	745	Bermudas	21
Sardinia (Italy)	9,301	Maui (Hawaii, U.S.)	729	Iwo Jima (Japan)	7.8
Fiji	7,055	Mauritius	720	Nauru	7.7
Shikoku (Japan)	6,860	Skye (U.K.)	670	Governors (N.Y., U.S.)	180 acres

GEOGRAPHIC CENTERS OF THE UNITED STATES

Source: U.S. Geological Survey

Because there is neither a generally accepted definition of a geographic center nor a completely satisfactory method for determining it, there may be as many geographic centers of a state or country as there are definitions of the term.

No marked or monumented point has been established by any government agency as the geographic center of either the 50 states, the conterminous United States, or the North American Continent. However, a monument was erected in Lebanon, Kansas, by a group of citizens who had hired engineers to determine the "geographic center" of the United States.

Sometimes confused with the geographic center of the United States is the reference point for all property lines and city, county, State, and international boundaries on the North American Continent that are tied to the National Triangulation networks of the United States, Canada, Mexico, and Central America. This point

is Meades Ranch Triangulation station located at latitude 39°13'26.686", longitude 98°32'30.506", about 12 miles north of Lucas, Kansas. It is the base point or origin of geodetic positions and directions in the triangulation net of the United States because it is at the junction of the main east-west transcontinental triangulation arc stretching from the Atlantic to the Pacific Coasts and the main north-south arc, which follows approximately the 98th meridian from the Canadian border to the Rio Grande.

In determining the centers of the states, islands adjacent to their coastlines and large bodies of water on their boundaries were excluded.

The geographic centers and positions listed below should be considered as estimates. The center of the United States (without Alaska and Hawaii) is approximately Lebanon, Kansas.

Center	Latitude (N)	Longitude (W)
Conterminous United States (48 States) Near Lebanon, Smith County, Kansas	39°50'	98°35'
Continental United States (49 States) Near Castle Rock, Butte County, South Dakota	44°59'	103°38'

Center	Latitude (N)	Longitude (W)
The United States (50 States) West of Castle Rock, Butte County, South Dakota	44°58'	103°46'
North American Continent 6 miles west of Balta, Pierce County, North Dakota	48°10'	100°10'

State	Geographic Center
Alabama	12 miles southwest of Clanton
Alaska	63°50'N., 152°00'W., 60 miles northwest of Mt. McKinley
Arizona	55 miles east-southeast of Prescott
Arkansas	12 miles northwest of Little Rock
California	35 miles east of Madera
Colorado	30 miles northwest of Pikes Peak
Connecticut	at East Berlin
Delaware	11 miles south of Dover
District of Columbia	near Fourth and L Streets NW
Florida	12 miles north-northwest of Brooksville
Georgia	18 miles southeast of Macon
Hawaii	20°15'N., 156°20'W., off Maui Island
Idaho	at Custer, southwest of Challis
Illinois	28 miles northeast of Springfield
Indiana	14 miles north-northwest of Indianapolis
Iowa	5 miles northeast of Ames
Kansas	15 miles northeast of Great Bend
Kentucky	3 miles north-northwest of Lebanon
Louisiana	3 miles southeast of Marksville
Maine	18 miles north of Dover-Foxcroft
Maryland	4½ miles northwest of Davidsonville
Massachusetts	north part of city of Worcester
Michigan	5 miles north-northwest of Cadillac
Minnesota	10 miles southwest of Brainerd
Mississippi	9 miles west-northwest of Carthage

State	Geographic Center
Missouri	20 miles southwest of Jefferson City
Montana	12 miles west of Lewistown
Nebraska	10 miles northwest of Broken Bow
Nevada	26 miles southeast of Austin
New Hampshire	3 miles east of Ashland
New Jersey	5 miles southeast of Trenton
New Mexico	12 miles south-southwest of Willard
New York	12+ miles south of Oneida and 26+ miles southwest of Utica
North Carolina	10 miles northwest of Sanford
North Dakota	5 miles southwest of McClusky
Ohio	25 miles north-northeast of Columbus
Oklahoma	8 miles north of Oklahoma City
Oregon	25 miles south-southeast of Prineville
Pennsylvania	2½ miles southwest of Bellefonte
Rhode Island	1 mile south-southwest of Crompton
South Carolina	13 miles southeast of Columbia
South Dakota	8 miles northeast of Pierre
Tennessee	5 miles northeast of Murfreesboro
Texas	15 miles north of Brady
Utah	3 miles north of Manti
Vermont	3 miles east of Roxbury
Virginia	5 miles southwest of Buckingham
Washington	10 miles west-southwest of Wenatchee
West Virginia	4 miles east of Sutton
Wisconsin	9 miles southeast of Marshfield
Wyoming	58 miles east-northeast of Lander

EXTREME POINTS OF THE UNITED STATES

Source: U.S. Geological Survey

The geographic center of an area may be defined as the center of gravity of the surface, or that point on which the surface of the area would balance if it were a cardboardlike plane of uniform thickness. Extreme points are measured from the various

centers of the U.S. Because many factors, such as curvature of the earth, large bodies of water, and irregular surfaces, affect the determination of centers of gravity, the following positions should be considered as approximations only.

Location	Direction from Geographic Center	Coordinates		Distance from Geographic Center (in miles)
		Latitude (N)	Longitude (W)	
From geographic center of United States near Lebanon, Smith County, Kansas, 39°50', 98°35' to—				
Lake of the Woods, Minnesota	Northeast	49°23'	95°09'	680
Key West, Florida	Southeast	24°33'	81°48'	1,436
West Quoddy Head, Maine	East	44°49'	66°57'	1,640
Cape Alava, Washington	West	48°10'	124°44'	1,412
From geographic center of United States (including Alaska) near Castle Rock, Butte County, S.D., 44°59', 103°38' to—				
Point Barrow, Alaska	Northwest	71°23'	156°29'	2,504
Key West, Florida	Southeast	24°33'	81°48'	1,865
West Quoddy Head, Maine	East	44°49'	66°57'	1,779
Cape Wrangell, Attu Island, Alaska	Northwest	52°55'	172°27'(E)	3,623
From geographic center of United States (including Alaska and Hawaii) west of Castle Rock, S.D., 44°58', 103°46' to—				
Point Barrow, Alaska	Northwest	71°23'	156°29'	2,502
Ka Lae (South Cape), Hawaii Island, Hawaii	Southwest	18°56'	155°41'	3,456
West Quoddy Head, Maine	East	44°49'	66°57'	1,785
Cape Wrangell, Attu Island, Alaska	Northwest	52°55'	172°27'(E)	3,620

U.S. COASTLINE & SHORELINE SOURCE: National Ocean Survey, National Oceanic and Atmospheric Administration

General coastline figures represent lengths of the seacoast outline. The coastlines of sounds and of bays are included to a point where they narrow to the width of 30 minutes of latitude, and the distance across at such point is included. Tidal shorelines include the outer coast, offshore islands, sounds, bays, and rivers to the head of tidewater or to a point where tidal waters narrow to a width of 100 feet.

	Coastline	Shoreline		Coastline	Shoreline
UNITED STATES	12,383	88,633	Pacific	7,623	40,298
(without Alaska and Hawaii)	4,993	53,677	California	840	3,427
Atlantic	2,069	28,673	Oregon	296	1,410
Maine	228	3,478	Washington	157	3,026
New Hampshire	13	131	Hawaii	750	1,052
Massachusetts	192	1,519	Alaska (Pacific only)	5,580	31,383
Rhode Island	40	384	Alaska (Arctic only)	1,060	2,521
Connecticut	—	618			
New York	127	1,850	EXTRATERRITORIAL		
New Jersey	130	1,792	Atlantic		
Pennsylvania	—	89	Navassa	5	5
Delaware	28	381	Puerto Rico	311	700
Maryland	31	3,190	Virgin Islands	117	175
Virginia	112	3,315			
North Carolina	301	3,375	Pacific		
South Carolina	187	2,876	Baker Island	3	3
Georgia	100	2,344	Guam Islands	78	110
Florida (Atlantic only)	580	3,331	Howland Island	4	4
Gulf of Mexico	1,631	17,141	Jarvis Island	5	5
Florida (Gulf only)	770	5,095	Johnston Island	5	5
Alabama	53	607	Midway Island	20	33
Mississippi	44	359	Palmyra Island	9	16
Louisiana	397	7,721	Samoa Islands	76	126
Texas	367	3,359	Wake Island	12	20

AVERAGE AND EXTREME U.S. ELEVATIONS SOURCE: U.S. Geological Survey

State or Territory	Mean Elevation (feet)	HIGH Point	Mean Elevation (feet)	LOW Point	Mean Elevation (feet)
Alabama	500	Cheaha Mountain	2,407	Gulf of Mexico	(1)
Alaska	1,900	Mount McKinley	20,320	Pacific Ocean	(1)
American Samoa	1,300	Lata Mountain (Tau I.)	3,160	Pacific Ocean	(1)
Arizona	4,100	Humphreys Peak	12,633	Colorado River	70
Arkansas	650	Magazine Mountain	2,753	Ouachita River	55
California	2,900	Mount Whitney	14,494	Death Valley	—282
Colorado	6,800	Mount Elbert	14,433	Arkansas River	3,350
Connecticut	500	Mount Frissell (So. Slope)	2,380	Long Island Sound	(1)
Delaware	60	On Ebright Road (New Castle County)	442	Atlantic Ocean	(1)
District of Columbia	150	Tenleytown (NW part)	410	Potomac River	1
Florida	100	Sec. 30, T. 6N., R. 20W.	345	Atlantic Ocean	(1)
Georgia	600	Brasstown Bald	4,784	Atlantic Ocean	(1)
Guam	330	Mount Lamlam	1,329	Pacific Ocean	(1)
Hawaii	3,030	Mauna Kea	13,796	Pacific Ocean	(1)
Idaho	5,000	Borah Peak	12,662	Snake River	710
Illinois	600	Charles Mound	1,235	Mississippi River	279
Indiana	700	Franklin Township (Wayne County)	1,257	Ohio River	320
Iowa	1,100	Sec. 29, T. 100 N., R. 41 W.	1,670	Mississippi River	480
Kansas	2,000	Mount Sunflower	4,039	Verdigris River	680
Kentucky	750	Black Mountain	4,145	Mississippi River	257
Louisiana	100	Driskill Mountain	535	New Orleans	—5
Maine	600	Mount Katahdin	5,268	Atlantic Ocean	(1)
Maryland	350	Backbone Mountain	3,360	Atlantic Ocean	(1)
Massachusetts	500	Mount Greylock	3,491	Atlantic Ocean	(1)
Michigan	900	Mount Curwood	1,980	Lake Erie	572
Minnesota	1,200	Eagle Mountain	2,301	Lake Superior	602
Mississippi	300	Woodall Mountain	806	Gulf of Mexico	(1)
Missouri	800	Taum Sauk Mountain	1,772	St. Francis River	230
Montana	3,400	Granite Peak	12,799	Kootenai River	1,800
Nebraska	2,600	Johnson Township (Kimball County)	5,426	SE corner of state	840
Nevada	5,500	Boundary Peak	13,143	Colorado River	470
New Hampshire	1,000	Mount Washington	6,288	Atlantic Ocean	(1)
New Jersey	250	High Point	1,803	Atlantic Ocean	(1)
New Mexico	5,700	Wheeler Peak	13,161	Red Bluff Reservoir	2,817
New York	1,000	Mount Marcy	5,344	Atlantic Ocean	(1)
North Carolina	700	Mount Mitchell	6,684	Atlantic Ocean	(1)
North Dakota	1,900	White Butte	3,506	Red River	750
Ohio	850	Campbell Hill	1,550	Ohio River	433
Oklahoma	1,300	Black Mesa	4,973	Little River	287
Oregon	3,300	Mount Hood	11,239	Pacific Ocean	(1)
Pennsylvania	1,100	Mount Davis	3,213	Delaware River	(1)
Puerto Rico	1,800	Cerro de Punta	4,389	Atlantic Ocean	(1)
Rhode Island	200	Jerimoth Hill	812	Atlantic Ocean	(1)
South Carolina	350	Sassafras Mountain	3,560	Atlantic Ocean	(1)
South Dakota	2,200	Harney Peak	7,242	Big Stone Lake	962
Tennessee	900	Clingmans Dome	6,643	Mississippi River	182
Texas	1,700	Guadalupe Peak	8,749	Gulf of Mexico	(1)
Utah	6,100	Kings Peak	13,528	Beaverdam Creek	2,000
Vermont	1,000	Mount Mansfield	4,393	Lake Champlain	95
Virginia	950	Mount Rogers	5,729	Atlantic Ocean	(1)
Virgin Islands	750	Crown Mountain (St. Thomas)	1,556	Atlantic Ocean	(1)
Washington	1,700	Mount Rainier	14,410	Pacific Ocean	(1)
West Virginia	1,500	Spruce Knob	4,863	Potomac River	240
Wisconsin	1,050	Timms Hill	1,951	Lake Michigan	581
Wyoming	6,700	Gannett Peak	13,804	Belle Fourche River	3,100

(1) = Sea level.

PRINCIPAL U.S. RIVERS

Source: U.S. Geological Survey

River	Empties Into:	Length (in miles)	River	Empties Into:	Length (in miles)
Mississippi-Missouri-Red Rock	Gulf of Mexico	3,741	Cumberland	Ohio River	687
Missouri-Red Rock	Mississippi River	2,564	White (Mo.-Ark.)	Mississippi River	685
Mississippi	Gulf of Mexico	2,348	North Platte	Platte River	680
Missouri	Mississippi River	2,315	Yellowstone	Missouri River	671
Yukon (U.S.-Canada)	Bering Sea	1,979	Tennessee	Ohio River	652
St. Lawrence (U.S.-Canada)	Atlantic Ocean	1,900	Mobile-Alabama-Coosa	Gulf of Mexico	639
Rio Grande (U.S.-Mexico)	Gulf of Mexico	1,885	Gila	Colorado River	630
Arkansas	Mississippi River	1,450	Washita	Red River	626
Colorado (U.S.-Mexico)	Gulf of California	1,450	Ouachita	Red River	605
Brazos	Gulf of Mexico	1,309	Little Missouri	Missouri River	560
Ohio-Allegheny	Mississippi River	1,306	Smoky Hill	Kansas River	560
Columbia (U.S.-Canada)	Pacific Ocean	1,243	Porcupine (U.S.-Canada)	Yukon River	555
Red (Okla.-Tex.-Ark.-La.)	Mississippi River	1,222	Koyukuk	Yukon River	554
Mississippi, Upper	to mouth of Missouri River	1,171	Red River of the North (U.S.-Canada)	Lake Winnipeg	545
Snake	Columbia River	1,000	Tombigbee	Mobile River	525
Ohio	Mississippi River	981	Apalachicola-Chattahoochee	Gulf of Mexico	524
Pecos	Rio Grande	926	White (S. Dak.-Nebr.)	Missouri River	507
Canadian	Arkansas River	906	Osage-Marais des Cygnes	Missouri River	496
Tennessee-N. Fk. Holston	Ohio River	900	Pend Oreille-Clark Fork	Columbia River	490
Colorado (Texas)	Gulf of Mexico	894	Pearl	Gulf of Mexico	490
Columbia, Upper (U.S.-Canada)	to mouth of Snake River	890	Powder	Yellowstone River	486
Kuskokwim	Bering Sea	800	Kootenai (U.S.-Canada)	Columbia River	485
Tanana	Yukon River	800	Wabash	Ohio River	475
North Canadian	Canadian River	784	Innoko	Yukon River	463
Kansas-Republican-Arikaree	Missouri River	743	Susquehanna	Chesapeake Bay	458
Green (Wyo.-Colo.-Utah)	Colorado River	730	Neosho	Arkansas River	450
Milk (U.S.-Canada)	Missouri River	729	South Platte	Platte River	442
Trinity	Gulf of Mexico	715	Santee-Wateree-Catawba	Atlantic Ocean	438
James (N. Dak.-S. Dak.)	Missouri River	710	Pee Dee-Yadkin	Atlantic Ocean	435
Cimarron	Arkansas River	698	Niobrara	Missouri River	431
			Wisconsin	Mississippi River	430

LARGE U.S. LAKES

Source: U.S. Geological Survey and Statistics Canada

Natural U.S. lakes with areas of 100 sq. mi. or more are listed

Lake	State	Area (sq. mi.)	Lake	State	Area (sq. mi.)
Superior	Canada, Minnesota, Wisconsin, and Michigan	31,700	Teshekpuk	Alaska	315
Huron	Canada and Michigan	23,010	Naknek	Alaska	242
Michigan	Wisconsin, Illinois, Indiana, and Michigan	22,400	Winnebago	Wisconsin	215
			Mille Lacs	Minnesota	207
Erie	Canada, Michigan, Ohio, Pennsylvania, and New York	9,910	Flathead	Montana	197
			Tahoe	California and Nevada	193
Ontario	Canada and New York	7,340	Leech	Minnesota	176
Lake of the Woods	Minnesota and Canada	1,679	Pyramid[a]	Nevada	168[b]
Great Salt[a]	Utah	1,361[b]	Pend Oreille	Idaho	148
Iliamna	Alaska	1,000	Ugashik (Upper and Lower)	Alaska	147
Okeechobee	Florida	700	Upper Klamath	Oregon	142
Pontchartrain[a]	Louisiana	625	Utah	Utah	140
Becharof	Alaska	458	Bear (including Mud Lake)	Idaho and Utah	136
Red Lake (Upper and Lower)	Minnesota	451	Yellowstone	Wyoming	134
Champlain	New York, Vermont, and Canada	435	Moosehead	Maine	117
St. Clair	Michigan and Canada	432	Tustumena	Alaska	117
Salton Sea[a]	California	374[b]	Clark	Alaska	110
Rainy	Minnesota and Canada	360	Winnibigoshish	Minnesota	109
			Dall	Alaska	100

[a] Salty. [b] Variable.

HIGHEST U.S. MOUNTAIN PEAKS

Source: U.S. Geological Survey

Peak	State	Elevation	Peak	State	Elevation	Peak	State	Elevation
Mt. McKinley	Alaska	20,320	La Plata Peak	Colorado	14,336	Mt. Shasta	California	14,162
Mt. St. Elias	Alaska	18,008	Uncompahgre Peak	Colorado	14,309	Mt. Sill	California	14,162
Mt. Foraker	Alaska	17,400				El Diente Peak	Colorado	14,159
Mt. Bona	Alaska	16,421	Crestone Peak	Colorado	14,294	Maroon Peak	Colorado	14,156
Mt. Blackburn	Alaska	16,390	Mt. Lincoln	Colorado	14,286	Tabeguache Mtn.	Colorado	14,155
Mt. Sanford	Alaska	16,237	Grays Peak	Colorado	14,270	Mt. Oxford	Colorado	14,153
South Buttress	Alaska	15,885	Mt. Antero	Colorado	14,269	Mt. Sneffels	Colorado	14,150
Mt. Vancouver	Alaska	15,700	Torreys Peak	Colorado	14,267	Mt. Democrat	Colorado	14,148
Mt. Churchill	Alaska	15,638	Castle Peak	Colorado	14,265	Capitol Peak	Colorado	14,130
Mt. Fairweather	Alaska	15,300	Quandary Peak	Colorado	14,265	Pikes Peak	Colorado	14,110
Mt. Hubbard	Alaska	15,015	Mt. Evans	Colorado	14,264	Snowmass Mtn.	Colorado	14,092
Mt. Bear	Alaska	14,831	Longs Peak	Colorado	14,255	Windom Peak	Colorado	14,087
East Buttress	Alaska	14,730	Mt. Wilson	Colorado	14,246	Mt. Russell	California	14,086
Mt. Hunter	Alaska	14,573	White Mtn.	California	14,246	Mt. Eolus	Colorado	14,084
Mt. Alverstone	Alaska	14,565	North Palisade	California	14,242	Mt. Columbia	Colorado	14,073
Browne Tower	Alaska	14,530	Shavano Peak	Colorado	14,229	Mt. Augusta	Alaska	14,070
Mt. Whitney	California	14,494	Mt. Belford	Colorado	14,197	Missouri Mtn.	Colorado	14,067
Mt. Elbert	Colorado	14,433	Mt. Princeton	Colorado	14,197	Humboldt Peak	Colorado	14,064
Mt. Massive	Colorado	14,421	Crestone Needle	Colorado	14,197	Mt. Bierstadt	Colorado	14,060
Mt. Harvard	Colorado	14,420	Mt. Yale	Colorado	14,196	Sunlight Peak	Colorado	14,059
Mt. Rainier	Washington	14,410	Mt. Bross	Colorado	14,172	Handies Peak	California	14,058
Mt. Williamson	California	14,375	Kit Carson Mtn.	Colorado	14,165	Split Mt.	Colorado	14,048
Blanca Peak	Colorado	14,345	Mt. Wrangell	Alaska	14,163	Culebra Peak	Colorado	14,047

U.S. TEMPERATURE EXTREMES

SOURCE: National Oceanic and Atmospheric Administration

HIGHEST TEMPERATURES

Greenland Ranch, Calif., with 134° on July 10, 1913, holds the record for the highest temperature ever officially recorded in the United States. This station is located in Death Valley, which is about 140 miles long, four to 16 miles wide, and runs north and south in southeastern California and southwestern Nevada. Death Valley is below sea level and flanked by towering mountain ranges with Mt. Whitney, rising to 14,495 feet, less than 100 miles to the west. It has the hottest summers in the Western Hemisphere and is the only known place in the United States where nighttime temperatures sometimes remain above 100°.

In the United States the station normally having the highest annual average is Key West, Fla., 78.2°; the highest summer average, Death Valley, Calif., 98.2°; and the highest winter average, Key West, Fla., 70.2°.

Amazing temperature rises of 40° to 50° in a few minutes occasionally may be brought about by Chinook winds. Some outstanding extreme temperature rises in short periods are:

12 hours: 83°, Granville, N. Dak., Feb. 21, 1918, from —33° to 50° from early morning to late afternoon.

15 minutes: 42°, Fort Assiniboine, Mont., Jan. 19, 1892, from —5° to 37°.

7 minutes: 34°, Kipp, Mont., Dec. 1, 1896; observer also reported that a total rise of 80° occurred in a few hours and that 30 inches of snow disappeared in one-half day.

2 minutes: 49°, Spearfish, S. Dak., Jan. 22, 1943, from —4° at 7:30 a.m. to 45° at 7:32 a.m.

HIGHEST TEMPERATURES IN CONTERMINOUS UNITED STATES BY MONTHS

Month	Temp. (°F.)	Year	Day	State	Place	Elevation Feet	Month	Temp. (°F.)	Year	Day	State	Place	Elevation Feet
Jan.	98	1936	17	Texas	Laredo	421	July	134	1913	10	Calif.	Greenland Ranch	—178
Feb.*	105	1963	3	Ariz.	Montezuma	735	Aug.†	127	1933	12	Calif.	Greenland Ranch	—178
Mar.*	108	1954	31	Texas	Rio Grande City	168	Sept.	126	1950	2	Calif.	Mecca	—175
Apr.	118	1898	25	Calif.	Volcano Springs	—220	Oct.*	116	1917	5	Ariz.	Sentinel	685
May°	124	1896	27	Calif.	Salton	—263	Nov.*	105	1906	12	Calif.	Craftonville	1,759
June°†	127	1896	15	Ariz.	Ft. Mohave	555	Dec.	100	1938	8	Calif.	La Mesa	539

* Two or more occurrences, most recent given. † Slightly higher temperatures in old records are not used owing to lack of information.

RECORD HIGHEST TEMPERATURES BY STATES

State	Temp. (°F.)	Date	Station	Elevation Feet	State	Temp. (°F.)	Date	Station	Elevation Feet
Ala.	112	Sept. 5, 1925	Centerville	345	Mo.	118	July 14, 1954*	Warsaw & Union	687–560
Alaska	100	June 27, 1915	Fort Yukon	—	Mont.	117	July 5, 1937	Medicine Lake	1,950
Ariz.	127	July 7, 1905*	Parker	345	Nebr.	118	July 24, 1936*	Minden	2,169
Ark.	120	Aug. 10, 1936	Ozark	396	Nev.	122	June 23, 1954*	Overton	1,240
Calif.	134	July 10, 1913	Greenland Ranch	—178	N.H.	106	July 4, 1911	Nashua	125
Colo.	118	July 11, 1888	Bennett	—	N.J.	110	July 10, 1936	Runyon	18
Conn.	105	July 22, 1926	Waterbury	400	N. Mex.	116	July 14, 1934*	Orogrande	4,171
Del.	110	July 21, 1930	Millsboro	20	N.Y.	108	July 22, 1926	Troy	35
D.C.	106	July 20, 1930*	Washington	112	N.C.	109	Sept. 7, 1954*	Weldon	81
Fla.	109	June 29, 1931	Monticello	207	N. Dak.	121	July 6, 1936	Steele	1,857
Ga.	112	July 24, 1952	Louisville	337	Ohio	113	July 21, 1934*	Gallipolis (near)	673
Hawaii	100	Apr. 27, 1931	Pahala	850	Okla.	120	July 26, 1943*	Tishomingo	670
Idaho	118	July 28, 1934	Orofino	1,027	Oreg.	119	Aug. 10, 1898*	Pendleton	1,074
Ill.	117	July 14, 1954	E. St. Louis	410	Pa.	111	July 10, 1936*	Phoenixville	100
Ind.	116	July 14, 1936	Collegeville	672	R.I.	102	July 30, 1949	Greenville	420
Iowa	118	July 20, 1934	Keokuk	614	S.C.	111	June 28, 1954*	Camden	170
Kans.	121	July 24, 1936*	Alton (near)	1,651	S. Dak.	120	July 5, 1936	Gannvalley	1,750
Ky.	114	July 28, 1930	Greensburg	581	Tenn.	113	Aug. 9, 1930*	Perryville	377
La.	114	Aug. 10, 1936	Plain Dealing	268	Tex.	120	Aug. 12, 1936	Seymour	1,291
Maine	105	July 10, 1911*	North Bridgton	450	Utah	116	June 28, 1892	Saint George	2,880
Md.	109	July 10, 1936*	Cumberland & Frederick	623–325	Vt.	105	July 4, 1911	Vernon	310
					Va.	110	July 15, 1954	Balcony Falls	725
Mass.	106	July 4, 1911*	Lawrence	51	Wash.	118	Aug. 5, 1961*	Ice Harbor Dam	475
Mich.	112	July 13, 1936	Mio	963	W. Va.	112	July 10, 1936*	Martinsburg	435
Minn.	114	July 6, 1936*	Moorhead	904	Wis.	114	July 13, 1936	Wisconsin Dells	900
Miss.	115	July 29, 1930	Holly Springs	600	Wyo.	114	July 12, 1900	Basin	3,500

* Also on earlier dates at the same or other places.

LOWEST TEMPERATURES

In the United States, the lowest temperature on record, —79.8°, was recorded at Prospect Creek Camp, which is located in the Endicott Mountains of northern Alaska. The lowest temperature in the 48 states, —69.7°, occurred at Rogers Pass (Lewis and Clark County, Montana), which is mountainous and heavily forested terrain, about a half mile east of and 140 feet below the summit of the Continental Divide.

The lowest average annual temperature recorded in the United States is 9.3° at Barrow, Alaska, on the Arctic coast. Barrow also has the coolest summers (June, July, August) with an average of 36.4°. The lowest average winter (December, January, February) temperature is —15.7° at Barter Island on the Arctic coast of northeast Alaska. In Hawaii, average annual temperatures range from 44.0° at Mauna Loa Slope Observatory (elevation 11,146 feet) on the island of Hawaii to 76.6° at Honolulu on the island of Oahu.

In the 48 states, Mt. Washington, N.H. (elevation 6 262 feet) has the lowest mean annual temperature, 26.9° F, and the lowest mean summer (June, July, August) temperature, 46.8°. A few stations in the Northeast and upper Rockies have mean annuals in the high 30's, and at the same stations in the latter

area summers may average in the high 40's. Winter (December, January, February) mean temperatures are lowest in northeastern North Dakota where the average is 5.9° at the Langdon Experiment Farm and northwestern Minnesota where the average is 6.1° at Hallock.

In continental areas of the Temperate Zone, 40° to 50° temperature falls in a few hours caused by advection (horizontal shifting) of cold air masses are not uncommon. Following these large drops, radiation sometimes may cause a further temperature fall resulting in remarkable changes. Some outstanding extreme temperature falls are:

24 hours: 100°, Browning, Mont., Jan. 23–24, 1916, from 44° to —56°.

12 hours: 84°, Fairfield, Mont., Dec. 24, 1924, from 63° at noon to —21° at midnight.

2 hours: 62°, Rapid City, S. Dak., Jan. 12, 1911, from 49° at 6 a.m., to —13° at 8 a.m.

27 minutes: 58°, Spearfish, S. Dak., Jan. 22, 1943, from 54° at 9 a.m., to —4° at 9:27 a.m.

15 minutes: 47°, Rapid City, S. Dak., Jan. 10, 1911, from 55° at 7 a.m. to 8° at 7:15 a.m.

LOWEST TEMPERATURES IN CONTERMINOUS UNITED STATES BY MONTHS

Month	Temp. (°F.)	Year	Day	State	Place	Elevation Feet	Month	Temp. (°F.)	Year	Day	State	Place	Elevation Feet
Jan.	−70	1954	20	Mont.	Rogers Pass	5,470	July*	10	1911	21	Wyo.	Painter	6,800
Feb.	−66	1933	9	Mont.	Riverside	6,700	Aug.*	5	1910	25	Mont.	Bowen	6,080
Mar.	−50	1906	17	Wyo.	Snake River	6,862	Sept.*	−9	1926	24	Mont.	Riverside	6,700
Apr.	−36	1945	5	N. Mex.	Eagle Nest	8,250	Oct.	−33	1917	29	Wyo.	Soda Butte	6,600
May	−15	1964	7	Calif.	White Mtn. 2	12,470	Nov.	−53	1959	16	Mont.	Lincoln 14 NE	5,130
June	2	1907	13	Calif.	Tamarack	8,000	Dec.*	−59	1924	19	Mont.	Riverside	6,700

* Two or more occurrences, most recent given.

RECORD LOWEST TEMPERATURES BY STATES

State	Temp. (°F.)	Date	Station	Elevation Feet	State	Temp. (°F.)	Date	Station	Elevation Feet
Ala.	−24	Jan. 31, 1966	Russellville	880	Nebr.	−47	Feb. 12, 1899	Camp Clarke	3,700
Alaska	−80	Jan. 23, 1971	Prospect Creek Camp	1,100	Nev.	−50	Jan. 8, 1937	San Jacinto	5,200
Ariz.	−40	Jan. 7, 1971	Hawley Lake	8,180	N.H.	−46	Jan. 28, 1925	Pittsburg	1,575
Ark.	−29	Feb. 13, 1905	Pond	1,250	N.J.	−34	Jan. 5, 1904	River Vale	70
Cal.	−45	Jan. 20, 1937	Boca	5,532	N. Mex.	−50	Feb. 1, 1951	Gavilan	7,350
Colo.	−60	Feb. 1, 1951	Taylor Park	9,206	N.Y.	−52	Feb. 9, 1934	Stillwater Reservoir	1,670
Conn.	−32	Feb. 16, 1943	Falls Village	585	N.C.	−29	Jan. 30, 1966	Mt. Mitchell	6,525
Del.	−17	Jan. 17, 1893	Millsboro	20	N. Dak.	−60	Feb. 15, 1936	Parshall	1,929
D.C.	−15	Feb. 11, 1899	Washington	112	Ohio	−39	Feb. 10, 1899	Milligan	800
Fla.	− 2	Feb. 13, 1899	Tallahassee	193	Okla.	−27	Jan. 18, 1930*	Watts	958
Ga.	−17	Jan. 27, 1940	CCC Camp F−16	—	Oreg.	−54	Feb. 10, 1933*	Seneca	4,700
Hawaii	14	Jan. 2, 1961	Haleakala, Maui Island	9,750	Pa.	−42	Jan. 5, 1904	Smethport	—
Idaho	−60	Jan. 18, 1943	Island Park Dam	6,285	R.I.	−23	Jan. 11, 1942	Kingston	100
Ill.	−35	Jan. 22, 1930	Mount Carroll	817	S.C.	−13	Jan. 26, 1940	Longcreek (near)	1,631
Ind.	−35	Feb. 2, 1951	Greensburg	954	S. Dak.	−58	Feb. 17, 1936	McIntosh	2,277
Iowa	−47	Jan. 12, 1912	Washta	1,157	Tenn.	−32	Dec. 30, 1917	Mountain City	2,471
Kans.	−40	Feb. 13, 1905	Lebanon	1,812	Tex.	−23	Feb. 8, 1933*	Seminole	3,275
Ky.	−34	Jan. 28, 1963	Cynthiana	684	Utah	−50	Jan. 5, 1913*	Strawberry Tunnel east portal	7,650
La.	−16	Feb. 13, 1899	Minden	194					
Maine	−48	Jan. 19, 1925	Van Buren	510	Vt.	−50	Dec. 30, 1933	Bloomfield	915
Md.	−40	Jan. 13, 1912	Oakland	2,461	Va.	−29	Feb. 10, 1899	Monterey	—
Mass.	−34	Jan. 18, 1957	Birch Hill Dam	840	Wash.	−48	Dec. 30, 1968	Mazama	2,120
Mich.	−51	Feb. 9, 1934	Vanderbilt	785				Winthrop	1,765
Minn.	−59	Feb. 16, 1903*	Pokegama Dam	1,280	W. Va.	−37	Dec. 30, 1917	Lewisburg	2,200
Miss.	−19	Jan. 30, 1966	Corinth	420	Wis.	−54	Jan. 24, 1922	Danbury	908
Mo.	−40	Feb. 13, 1905	Warsaw	700	Wyo.	−63	Feb. 9, 1933	Moran	6,770
Mont.	−70	Jan. 20, 1954	Rogers Pass	5,470					

* Also on earlier dates at the same or other places.

WIND CHILL

Source: National Oceanic and Atmospheric Administration

A very strong wind combined with a temperature slightly below freezing can have the same chilling effect as a temperature nearly 50°F lower in a calm atmosphere. Arctic explorers and military experts have developed what is called the "wind-chill factor," which shows the combined effects of wind and temperature as equivalent calm-air temperatures. In effect, the index describes the cooling power of the air on exposed flesh. The wind-chill table here shows this cooling power for various combinations of wind and temperature, and will help you gauge how much protection you really need.

Directions: 1) Find actual (calm) air temperature across top of table. 2) Determine wind speed and follow across to correct calm-air temperature. Number given is equivalent temperature.

For example, a 10° temperature with a 20 mph wind equals the equivalent of −24 degrees.

WIND CHILL

Equivalent Temperatures (°F)

Calm	35	30	25	20	15	10	5	0	−5	−10	−15	−20	−25	−30	−35	−40	−45
5	33	27	21	16	12	7	1	−6	−11	−15	−20	−26	−31	−35	−41	−47	−54
10	21	16	9	2	−2	−9	−15	−22	−27	−31	−38	−45	−52	−58	−64	−70	−77
15	16	11	1	−6	−11	−18	−25	−33	−40	−45	−51	−60	−65	−70	−78	−85	−90
20	12	3	−4	−9	−17	−24	−32	−40	−46	−52	−60	−68	−76	−81	−88	−96	−103
25	7	0	−7	−15	−22	−29	−37	−45	−52	−58	−67	−75	−83	−89	−96	−104	−112
30	5	−2	−11	−18	−26	−33	−41	−49	−56	−63	−70	−78	−87	−94	−101	−109	−117
35	3	−4	−13	−20	−27	−35	−43	−52	−60	−67	−72	−83	−90	−98	−105	−113	−123
40	1	−4	−15	−22	−29	−36	−45	−54	−62	−69	−76	−87	−94	−101	−107	−116	−128
45	1	−6	−17	−24	−31	−38	−46	−54	−63	−70	−78	−87	−94	−101	−108	−118	−128
50	0	−7	−17	−24	−31	−38	−47	−56	−63	−70	−79	−88	−96	−103	−110	−120	−128

Windspeed (Miles per hour)

VERY COLD

BITTER COLD

EXTREME COLD

U.S. CITY WEATHER I   Source: National Climatic Center

City	Record Temperature High (F°)	Record Temperature Low (F°)	Precip. (Water equiv.) (in.)	Snow and Sleet (in.)	Wind Speed (mph)	First Freeze Date 32 F° or less Average	First Freeze Date 32 F° or less Earliest on record	Last Freeze Date 32 F° or less Average	Last Freeze Date 32 F° or less Latest on record	Elevation of Station (feet)
Albany	104	—28	36.46	65.7	8.8	Oct. 13	Sept. 23	Apr. 27	May 20	292
Albuquerque	105	—17	8.33	10.7	9.0	Oct. 29	Oct. 11	Apr. 16	May 18	5,314
Atlanta	103	— 9	48.66	1.5	9.1	Nov. 12	Oct. 24	Mar. 24	Apr. 15	1,034
Baltimore	107	— 7	41.62	21.9	9.5	Oct. 26	Oct. 8	Apr. 15	May 11	155
Birmingham	107	—10	53.46	1.2	7.4	Nov. 10	Oct. 17	Mar. 17	Apr. 21	630
Bismarck	114	—45	16.15	38.4	10.6	Sept. 22	Sept. 6	May 11	May 30	1,660
Boise	111	—23	11.97	21.7	9.0	Oct. 12	Sept. 9	May 6	May 31	2,868
Boston	104	—18	41.55	41.9	12.6	Nov. 7	Oct. 5	Apr. 8	May 3	29
Buffalo	99	—21	35.19	88.6	12.3	Oct. 25	Sept. 23	Apr. 30	May 24	706
Burlington, Vt.	101	—30	32.54	78.4	8.8	Oct. 3	Sept. 13	May 10	May 24	340
Charleston, W. Va.	108	—24	43.66	28.8	6.5	Oct. 28	Sept. 29	Apr. 18	May 11	951
Charlotte	104	— 5	45.00	5.6	7.6	Nov. 4	Oct. 15	Apr. 2	Apr. 16	769
Cheyenne	100	—38	14.48	52.0	13.3	Sept. 27	Aug. 25	May 18	June 18	6,141
Chicago	105	—23	33.47	40.7	10.3	Oct. 26	Sept. 25	Apr. 20	May 14	623
Cincinnati	102	—19	40.40	23.2	9.1	Oct. 25	Sept. 28	Apr. 15	May 25	877
Cleveland	103	—19	34.15	51.5	10.8	Nov. 2	Sept. 29	Apr. 21	May 14	805
Columbia, S.C.	107	— 2	45.23	1.8	6.9	Nov. 3	Oct. 4	Mar. 30	Apr. 21	225
Columbus, Ohio	106	—20	36.98	27.7	8.7	Oct. 31	Oct. 7	Apr. 16	May 9	833
Concord, N.H.	102	—37	38.13	64.1	6.7	Sept. 24	Sept. 13	May 17	June 6	346
Dallas-Ft. Worth, Tex.	112	— 8	32.11	2.7	11.1	Nov. 21	Oct. 27	Mar. 16	Apr. 13	596
Denver	105	—30	14.60	60.1	9.0	Oct. 14	Sept. 16	May 2	May 28	5,332
Des Moines	110	—30	31.49	33.2	11.1	Oct. 10	Sept. 28	Apr. 20	May 11	963
Detroit	105	—24	31.49	31.7	10.2	Oct. 21	Sept. 23	Apr. 23	May 12	626
El Paso	109	— 8	8.47	4.4	9.6	Nov. 11	Oct. 31	Mar. 13	Apr. 11	3,916
Great Falls	107	—49	14.83	57.7	13.1	Sept. 26	Sept. 7	May 14	June 8	3,657
Hartford	102	—26	43.00	53.1	9.0	Oct. 15	Sept. 27	Apr. 22	May 10	179
Houston	108	5	47.07	0.4	7.6	Dec. 11	Oct. 25	Feb. 5	Mar. 27	108
Indianapolis	107	—25	39.98	21.3	9.7	Oct. 22	Sept. 27	Apr. 23	May 27	808
Jackson	107	— 5	50.96	0.8	7.7	Nov. 8	Oct. 9	Mar. 18	Apr. 25	331
Jacksonville	105	10	51.75	Trace	8.6	Dec. 16	Nov. 3	Feb. 6	Mar. 31	31
Juneau	90	—22	53.95	109.1	8.5	Oct. 21	Sept. 9	Apr. 22	June 8	24
Kansas City, Mo.	113	—22	36.66	19.7	10.2	Oct. 26	Sept. 30	Apr. 7	May 6	1,025
Little Rock	110	—13	48.17	5.3	8.2	Nov. 15	Oct. 23	Mar. 16	Apr. 13	265
Los Angeles	110	23	11.94	Trace	7.4	—	Dec. 9	—	Jan. 21	104
Louisville	107	—20	42.94	17.3	8.4	Oct. 25	Oct. 15	Apr. 10	Apr. 19	488
Memphis	106	—13	48.74	5.7	9.2	Nov. 5	Oct. 17	Mar. 20	Apr. 15	284
Miami	100	26	59.21	—	9.1	—	—	—	Feb. 6	12
Milwaukee	105	—25	30.18	45.2	11.8	Oct. 23	Sept. 20	Apr. 25	May 27	693
Minneapolis-St. Paul	108	—34	26.62	45.8	10.6	Oct. 13	Sept. 3	Apr. 29	May 24	838
Mobile	104	— 1	63.26	0.4	9.3	Dec. 12	Nov. 15	Feb. 17	Mar. 20	221
Nashville	107	—15	46.61	10.9	7.9	Oct. 31	Oct. 7	Apr. 3	Apr. 24	605
New Orleans	102	7	58.93	0.2	8.4	Dec. 3	Nov. 11	Feb. 15	Apr. 8	30
New York City	106	—15	43.56	29.1	9.4	Nov. 12	Oct. 19	Apr. 7	Apr. 24	87
Norfolk	105	2	45.22	7.2	10.6	Nov. 21	Nov. 7	Mar. 22	Apr. 14	30
Oklahoma City	113	—17	31.71	9.2	12.9	Nov. 7	Oct. 7	Apr. 1	May 3	1,304
Omaha	114	—32	28.48	32.5	10.9	Oct. 20	Sept. 24	Apr. 14	May 11	982
Philadelphia	106	—11	41.18	20.3	9.6	Nov. 17	Oct. 19	Mar. 30	Apr. 20	28
Phoenix	118	16	7.41	Trace	6.1	Dec. 11	Nov. 4	Jan. 27	Mar. 3	1,107
Pittsburgh	103	—20	36.21	45.5	9.4	Oct. 20	Oct. 10	Apr. 21	May 4	1,225
Portland, Me.	103	—39	42.15	74.3	8.8	Sept. 27	Sept. 17	May 12	May 31	63
Portland, Ore.	107	— 3	37.98	7.5	7.8	Dec. 1	Oct. 26	Feb. 25	May 4	39
Providence	104	—17	40.90	37.8	10.8	Oct. 26	Oct. 3	Apr. 14	Apr. 24	62
Reno	106	—19	7.65	26.8	6.4	Oct. 2	Aug. 30	May 14	June 25	4,400
Richmond	107	—12	43.77	14.3	7.6	Nov. 8	Oct. 5	Apr. 2	May 11	177
Sacramento	115	17	17.33	Trace	8.3	Dec. 11	Nov. 4	Jan. 24	Mar. 14	25
St. Louis	115	—23	36.70	17.8	9.5	Oct. 20	Sept. 28	Apr. 15	May 10	564
Salt Lake City	107	—30	15.63	58.1	8.7	Nov. 1	Sept. 25	Apr. 12	Apr. 30	4,227
San Francisco	106	20	18.88	Trace	10.5	—	Dec. 11	—	Jan. 21	18
Seattle	100	0	40.30	15.2	9.3	Dec. 1	Oct. 19	Feb. 23	Apr. 3	450
Spokane	108	—30	16.19	54.0	8.7	Oct. 12	Sept. 13	Apr. 20	May 16	2,365
Washington, D.C.	106	—15	40.00	16.8	9.2	Nov. 10	Oct. 2	Mar. 29	May 12	65
Wichita	114	—22	30.06	16.3	12.6	Nov. 1	Sept. 27	Apr. 5	Apr. 21	1,340
Wilmington, Del.	107	—15	43.63	20.1	9.1	Oct. 26	Sept. 27	Apr. 18	May 9	80

U.S. CITY WEATHER II

SOURCE: National Climatic Center (data based on normals for 1936-1975)

AVERAGE MONTHLY TEMPERATURES (in °F)

City	Jan.	Feb.	Mar.	April	May	June	July	Aug.	Sept.	Oct.	Nov.	Dec.	ANNUAL
Albany	23.0°	23.7°	33.5°	46.5°	58.4°	67.7°	72.5°	70.2°	62.7°	51.4°	39.7°	27.7°	48.1°
Albuquerque	34.5	39.5	46.3	54.8	63.8	73.3	77.1	75.1	68.4	56.8	43.9	35.1	55.7
Atlanta	43.5	45.6	52.6	61.3	69.6	76.4	78.5	77.8	73.1	62.9	52.0	44.7	61.5
Baltimore	33.2	35.0	42.6	53.6	63.1	72.1	76.8	75.3	68.5	57.3	46.0	36.4	55.0
Birmingham	45.6	47.1	55.0	62.9	70.7	77.8	79.9	79.6	75.2	64.6	53.4	46.3	63.2
Bismarck	8.1	12.2	25.3	42.9	54.6	64.1	70.6	68.5	57.9	45.7	28.6	15.4	41.1
Boise	29.9	35.5	42.3	49.6	57.8	65.4	74.5	72.5	62.7	52.3	40.6	32.1	51.3
Boston	28.9	29.1	36.9	46.9	57.7	67.0	72.6	70.7	64.0	54.2	43.5	32.6	50.3
Buffalo	25.1	24.5	32.3	43.3	54.6	64.7	70.3	68.9	62.6	51.8	40.0	29.5	47.3
Burlington, Vt.	18.0	18.4	29.3	42.6	55.2	64.8	69.7	67.3	59.6	48.8	36.6	23.3	44.5
Charleston, W. Va.	36.6	38.0	46.0	56.0	64.8	72.3	76.0	74.8	69.3	58.0	46.7	38.2	56.4
Charlotte	42.0	43.9	51.0	60.0	68.9	76.0	78.7	77.4	72.2	61.6	50.9	43.1	60.5
Cheyenne	26.1	27.7	32.4	41.4	51.0	61.0	67.7	66.4	57.3	46.4	35.2	28.6	45.1
Chicago	24.7	27.1	36.4	47.8	58.2	68.4	73.8	72.5	65.6	54.5	40.4	29.4	49.9
Cincinnati	30.8	33.6	41.7	53.5	63.3	71.9	75.5	74.2	67.3	56.3	43.6	34.4	53.9
Cleveland	27.5	27.8	35.9	47.0	58.3	67.9	72.2	70.6	64.6	53.8	41.6	31.3	49.9
Columbia, S.C.	46.6	48.1	55.1	63.5	71.9	78.5	80.8	79.9	75.1	64.5	54.4	47.2	63.8
Columbus, Ohio	29.4	30.8	40.0	51.1	61.9	70.9	74.8	72.9	66.6	55.0	42.3	32.4	52.3
Concord, N.H.	21.3	22.8	31.9	44.4	56.2	64.9	70.0	67.3	59.7	49.2	37.5	25.6	45.9
Dallas-Ft. Worth, Tex.	45.6	48.8	56.9	65.2	72.7	80.9	84.5	84.6	77.8	67.8	56.1	47.7	65.7
Denver	30.1	32.8	38.7	47.4	56.7	66.6	72.6	71.3	62.6	51.6	39.6	32.3	50.2
Des Moines	20.8	24.7	36.3	50.4	61.5	71.1	76.1	73.7	65.3	54.2	38.5	26.1	49.9
Detroit	25.3	25.8	34.5	46.7	58.1	68.2	73.0	71.1	64.2	53.1	40.1	29.5	49.2
El Paso	44.7	49.3	55.6	63.8	72.2	80.8	81.9	80.2	74.8	64.7	52.5	45.2	63.8
Great Falls	21.2	26.1	31.4	43.3	53.3	60.9	69.7	67.9	57.6	48.3	34.8	27.1	45.1
Hartford	27.1	27.7	36.9	47.9	59.0	67.9	73.1	70.9	63.7	53.3	42.1	30.4	50.0
Houston	53.2	54.6	62.0	67.9	74.3	79.8	82.4	81.3	77.5	70.2	59.6	55.5	68.2
Indianapolis	28.5	30.8	40.1	52.0	62.5	71.8	75.7	73.7	66.9	55.5	42.0	31.9	52.6
Jackson	48.4	50.9	57.3	65.3	72.6	79.6	81.8	81.5	76.9	66.5	55.7	49.5	65.5
Jacksonville	55.0	56.6	61.8	67.5	73.7	78.5	80.4	80.1	77.1	68.9	60.6	54.9	67.9
Juneau	22.2	27.3	31.2	38.4	46.4	52.8	55.5	54.1	49.0	41.5	32.0	26.9	39.8
Kansas City, Mo.	29.7	33.1	43.2	55.5	65.3	74.7	79.5	78.0	70.0	59.1	44.7	33.6	55.6
Little Rock	41.7	44.8	52.9	62.5	70.1	78.2	81.3	80.5	74.1	63.8	51.9	43.8	62.1
Los Angeles	54.6	55.9	56.9	59.3	62.1	64.9	68.3	69.5	68.5	65.2	60.4	56.4	61.8
Louisville	34.7	36.8	45.6	56.3	66.0	74.6	78.3	76.8	70.4	58.9	46.4	37.2	56.9
Memphis	41.3	44.1	52.2	62.1	70.5	78.2	81.2	80.0	74.1	63.5	51.6	43.6	61.9
Miami	67.5	68.0	71.3	74.9	78.0	80.9	82.2	82.7	81.6	77.8	72.3	68.5	75.5
Milwaukee	20.9	23.2	32.6	44.3	54.3	64.5	70.7	69.7	62.5	51.5	37.7	26.1	46.5
Minneapolis-St. Paul	13.2	16.7	29.6	45.7	57.9	67.8	73.1	70.7	61.5	50.0	33.0	19.5	44.9
Mobile	51.9	54.4	60.1	67.1	74.3	80.3	81.8	81.5	78.1	68.9	58.9	53.1	67.6
Nashville	39.1	41.0	49.5	59.5	68.2	76.3	79.4	78.3	72.2	61.1	48.9	41.1	59.6
New Orleans	54.3	56.5	61.7	68.9	75.4	80.8	82.2	82.0	78.8	70.7	60.7	55.6	69.0
New York City	32.3	32.7	40.6	51.1	61.9	70.9	76.1	74.6	68.0	58.0	46.7	35.7	54.1
Norfolk	41.6	42.3	48.8	57.4	66.7	74.7	78.6	77.5	72.4	62.2	52.1	43.6	59.8
Oklahoma City	37.2	40.8	49.8	60.2	68.2	77.0	81.4	81.1	73.7	62.7	49.4	39.9	60.1
Omaha	22.0	26.5	37.5	51.7	62.7	72.3	77.4	75.1	66.3	55.0	39.3	27.5	51.1
Philadelphia	33.1	33.8	41.6	52.2	63.0	71.8	76.6	74.7	68.4	57.5	46.2	36.2	54.6
Phoenix	51.6	55.4	60.5	67.7	76.0	85.2	90.8	89.0	83.6	71.7	59.8	52.4	70.3
Pittsburgh	30.7	31.3	39.9	51.1	62.0	70.6	74.6	72.8	66.6	55.2	43.2	33.6	52.7
Portland, Me.	22.4	23.4	32.3	42.8	53.2	62.4	68.2	66.6	59.6	49.6	38.6	26.9	45.5
Portland, Ore.	38.5	43.0	45.9	50.6	57.0	60.2	65.8	65.3	62.7	54.0	45.7	41.1	52.5
Providence	29.4	29.3	37.6	47.5	57.8	66.9	72.7	71.0	63.9	54.0	43.4	32.6	50.5
Reno	31.8	36.6	41.2	47.4	54.9	62.5	70.2	68.5	60.7	50.9	41.0	33.4	49.9
Richmond	38.0	39.4	46.9	56.9	66.1	74.0	77.6	76.1	69.9	58.9	48.7	39.7	57.7
Sacramento	44.9	49.8	53.1	58.1	64.5	70.8	75.4	74.3	71.6	63.4	52.9	45.7	60.4
St. Louis	31.7	34.8	44.3	56.1	65.9	75.1	79.3	77.5	70.1	59.0	45.3	35.3	56.2
Salt Lake City	28.0	33.2	40.7	49.0	58.3	68.1	77.2	75.4	65.1	53.1	40.5	31.4	51.7
San Francisco	48.0	50.9	52.9	54.6	57.3	60.3	61.5	62.0	62.9	60.0	54.3	49.3	56.2
Seattle	38.2	42.2	43.9	48.1	55.0	59.9	64.4	63.8	59.6	51.8	44.6	40.5	51.0
Spokane	26.8	31.7	39.4	47.6	55.8	62.5	70.2	68.7	59.5	48.7	37.0	30.4	48.2
Washington, D.C.	36.1	37.7	45.7	56.1	65.8	74.3	78.4	76.9	70.3	59.6	48.4	38.4	57.3
Wichita	31.6	35.2	44.7	56.3	65.4	75.3	80.3	79.3	70.9	59.6	45.2	35.0	56.5
Wilmington, Del.	32.6	33.1	41.9	52.2	62.7	71.4	76.0	74.1	67.9	56.8	45.7	35.2	54.2

THE NATIONAL WEATHER SERVICE

Although people are critical of the weather forecaster's failures, they seldom generously acknowledge his successes. Employing a vast network of radar stations, professional and amateur weather observers, orbiting satellites, and other sources of data on a regular basis, the National Weather Service, a major program element of the National Oceanic and Atmospheric Administration (in the Department of Commerce) has the impressive record of 87% accurate rain predictions for the same day and 80% for the next. The national average of success in forecasting shows that today's and tonight's temperatures are correct within about 3½ degrees and tomorrow's to within about 4½ degrees.

The National Weather Service employs about 5000 full-time people at 400 facilities within the 50 states and at 14 overseas stations. Its physical facilities are valued at approximately $75 million.

The National Meteorological Center receives the following observational reports daily: 20,000 synoptic and 29,000 hourly from surface observation; 3,000 synoptic from ships; 4,100 atmospheric soundings; 3,200 aircraft reports; and all available cloud and temperature data from weather satellites.

HURRICANE NAMES: 1982

Atlantic Ocean, Caribbean Sea, Gulf of Mexico
Alberto, Beryl, Chris, Debby, Ernesto, Florence, Gilbert, Helene, Isaac, Joan, Keith, Leslie, Michael, Nadine, Oscar, Patty, Rafael, Sandy, Tony, Valarie, William.

Eastern North Pacific
Aletta, Bud, Carlotta, Daniel, Emilia, Fabio, Gilma, Hector, Iva, John, Kristy, Lane, Miriam, Norman, Olivia, Paul, Rosa, Sergio, Tara, Vicente, Willa.

METEOROLOGICAL GLOSSARY

Anticyclone—An area of high pressure from which air spirals in all directions, usually accompanied by good weather. Anticyclones circulate in a clockwise direction in the northern hemisphere and in a counterclockwise direction in the southern (as seen from above).

Blizzard—A fall of fine, powdery snow accompanied by low temperatures and strong winds, often with low visibility and large accumulations.

Blizzard warning—Considerable amounts of snow will fall, with winds of at least 35 mph and temperatures not higher than 20°F.

Blowing snow—Snow lifted from the ground by the wind enough to restrict visibility.

Cold wave warning—A rapid and dramatic drop in temperature during the following 24 hrs requiring substantially increased protection for agricultural, industrial, commercial and social activities.

Convection—Motion of air produced by thermal or mechanical instability in the atmosphere.

Coriolis force—The force, apparently resulting from the earth's rotation, that causes high-pressure weather systems to circulate in a clockwise direction in the northern hemisphere and in a counterclockwise direction in the southern.

Cyclone—A rotary, usually columnar or funnel-shaped atmospheric system having its lowest pressure at the center of a circulating mass of air and water vapor. Cyclones circulate in a counterclockwise direction in the northern hemisphere and in a clockwise direction in the southern (as seen from above).

Drifting snow—Snow blown into significant drifts by strong winds either during or after a snowfall.

Eddy—(Within a fluid mass) a circulation pattern independent of the surrounding fluid.

Freezing drizzle—A light freezing rain.

Freezing rain—Another name for an ice storm.

Gale warning—Winds of 38–55 mph may be expected, with attendant strong wave action at sea.

Hail—Precipitation in the form of ice (hailstones) formed by the accumulation of sub-freezing water on a growing ice particle either by repeated circulation aloft or by long descent through layers of super-cooled water in clouds.

Hazardous driving (travelers') warning—Falling, blowing, or drifting snow, freezing rain or drizzle, sleet or strong winds will make driving dangerous.

Heavy snow warning—A fall of four inches or more in a 12-hr period or of six inches or more in a 24-hr period.

Hurricane—A well-defined weather system with winds of more than 74 mph and pronounced rotary circulation at the surface.

Hurricane warning—Winds of 74 mph or more may be expected within 24 hrs or high water or high waves may endanger life and property.

Hurricane watch—A hurricane that is nearby may affect the area: prepare for action if a hurricane warning is issued.

Ice storm—A winter storm in which falling rain rapidly freezes on all surfaces, causing hazardous driving conditions.

Inversion—A meteorological system in which temperature increases with an increase in altitude, the reverse of a normal system at lower altitudes.

Lightning—A discharge of electricity between clouds or between clouds and the earth resulting from an equalization between positively and negatively charged masses.

Livestock (stockmen's) warnings—Livestock will require protection from snow or ice accumulations, from a rapid drop in temperature, or from strong winds.

Neutercane—A storm, similar to and formerly identified as a cyclone or tropical storm, observed by weather satellites in areas of the oceans where hurricanes do not usually occur.

Ridge—An elongated high-pressure atmospheric system.

Seeding—The sprinkling of crystals, usually of silver iodide, into clouds and tropical storm formations in order to induce sudden freezing of super-cooled water vapor with a resultant release of latent heat of fusion, raising of cloud temperatures, and attendant reduction in maximum wind speeds. In some experiments, the intention of seeding is to increase the height and volume of storm clouds, thus dissipating the storm's energy over a wider area.

Severe blizzard warning—Considerable amounts of snow will fall, with winds of at least 45 mph and temperature not higher than 10°F.

Sleet storm—A winter storm in which falling rain freezes before striking the surface, usually bouncing on the ground.

Small-craft warning—Wind and water action may threaten the safety of small boats, which are best advised to remain in or return to port.

Snow flurries—Intermittent light snow for short periods with minimal accumulations.

Snow squalls—Brief, heavy snowfalls accompanied by gusty winds.

Storm warning—Winds of 55–74 mph may be expected, with attendant dangerous wave action at sea.

Thunder—A sound produced when lightning suddenly heats the surrounding air and causes it to expand with explosive force.

Thunderstorm—An atmospheric disturbance of varying severity, often accompanied by rain and characteristically by lightning. Thunderstorms are caused by unstable thermal convection currents of air that carry water vapor aloft creating a chimney-like effect. Exchanges of heated and cooled air and water increase and accelerate the effect, with attendant formation of ice and snow at upper altitudes and precipitation as water on the ground.

Tornado—A violently rotating column of air, moving counterclockwise at an estimated 300 mph, descending from a thunderstorm cloud system in a characteristically funnel-shaped form.

Tornado warning—A tornado has been sighted and all are advised to seek shelter.

Tornado watch—Tornadoes are expected to develop.

Tropical depression—A weather system with winds of not more than 39 mph and some circulation at the surface.

Tropical disturbance—Ill-defined weather phenomenon without strong wind and little or no circulation, sometimes better developed at higher altitudes.

Tropical storm—A well-defined weather system with winds of 39–73 mph and strong circulation at the surface.

Trough—An elongated low-pressure atmospheric system.

Waterspout—A tornado over water, in which water vapor is sucked skyward in a funnel-shaped vortex.

Wind-chill factor—The combined effect of temperature and wind velocity as compared with equivalent temperature in calm air.

NATIONAL OCEANIC AND ATMOSPHERIC ADMINISTRATION

The National Oceanic and Atmospheric Administration (NOAA) was formed on October 3, 1970, to explore, map and chart the ocean and its resources; to manage, use, and conserve those resources; and to describe, monitor, and predict conditions in all environments. It also is to issue warnings against impending destructive natural events while developing beneficial methods and assessing the consequences of environmental modification.

Among its principal functions and activities, NOAA reports the weather of the U.S. and provides weather forecasts to the general public, issues warning bulletins against destructive natural events, and provides services for such weather-sensitive activities as aviation, marine activities, and agriculture.

NOAA prepares and issues nautical and aeronautical charts and geodetic surveys. It conducts a broad range of research programs on the environment, including the use of satellites. The agency promotes wise and balanced management of the Nation's coastal zone, including the awarding of grants to states for their own development of their coastal zones. The agency also administers the Marine Mammal Protection Act of 1972.

The National Sea Grant program, which provides grants to institutions for marine research, education, and advisory services, is administered by the NOAA. It is also developing a system of data buoys for obtaining and disseminating marine environment data. Additionally, it tests and evaluates oceanographic instruments and maintains a national reference center for their specifications and characteristics.

DAYLIGHT SAVING TIME

In enacting the Uniform Time Act of 1966 (amended in 1972), the Congress made the observance of advanced (daylight) time automatic throughout the country for the six-month period extending from the last Sunday of April to the last Sunday of October.

That law, however, allows a state which falls in one time zone to exempt itself as a whole, and a state which falls in more than one time zone to exempt itself as a whole, or only that part in the most easterly zone, from the observance of advanced time. In 1977, in addition to the territories, only Arizona, Hawaii and the eastern time zone of Indiana did not observe daylight saving time from April 27 to October 26.

Faced with the energy crisis in 1974, the U.S. government required the use of daylight saving time throughout the year and, as amended later in 1974, it was temporarily observed from January 6 to October 27, 1974, and from February 23 to October 26, 1975.

Time-zone boundaries in the United States have been defined—and from time to time relocated—since 1918 by the Interstate Commerce Commission and by the Department of Transportation beginning in 1967. Prior to 1966, however, a number of communities in the vicinity of the defined boundaries chose not to recognize them. When the Uniform Time Act became effective in 1967 those communities were confronted with a problem. With its automatic advanced (daylight) feature, the 1966 act required a far greater degree of nationwide recognition of the boundaries defined by DOT. The result has been active urging by state, local, and municipal governments, as well as hundreds of requests from private citizens, for the relocation of time zones boundaries.

STANDARD TIME ZONES

Time zone boundaries for the United States are defined by the Secretary of Transportation under the Standard Time Act (1918) as amended by the Uniform Time Act (1966). In the map below, reading from east to west, when it is 5:00 P.M. Atlantic Time (a zone that runs along the Maine-New Brunswick border, and includes Puerto Rico and the Virgin Islands in the Caribbean), it is 4:00 P.M. Eastern Time; 3:00 P.M. Central Time; 2:00 P.M. Mountain Time; 1:00 P.M. Pacific Time; 12 noon Yukon Time; 11:00 A.M. Alaska-Hawaii Time; and 10:00 A.M. Bering Time (which includes Nome and Western Alaska). Thus, there is a seven-hour time difference between Nome, Alaska, and San Juan, Puerto Rico.

U. S. STANDARD TIME ZONES
Established by the Uniform Time Act
SCALE OF MILES

LATITUDE AND LONGITUDE OF U.S. CITIES

SOURCE: National Ocean Survey

City and State	Lat. ° '	Long. ° '	City and State	Lat. ° '	Long. ° '	City and State	Lat. ° '	Long. ° '
Akron, Ohio	41 05	81 31	Durham, N.C.	36 00	78 54	Nashville, Tenn.	36 10	86 47
Albany, N.Y.	42 39	73 45	El Paso, Tex.	31 46	106 29	Newark, N.J.	40 44	74 10
Albuquerque, N.M.	35 05	106 39	Eugene, Ore.	44 03	123 05	New Haven, Conn.	41 18	72 55
Allentown, Pa.	40 36	75 28	Fairbanks, Alaska	64 48	147 51	New Orleans, La.	29 57	90 04
Amarillo, Tex.	35 12	101 50	Fargo, N.D.	46 53	96 47	New York, N.Y.	40 45	74 00
Anchorage, Alaska	61 12	149 48	Flagstaff, Ariz.	35 11	111 39	Niagara Falls, N.Y.	43 05	79 03
Ann Arbor, Mich.	42 17	83 45	Fort Wayne, Ind.	41 04	85 08	Nome, Alaska	64 30	165 25
Asheville, N.C.	35 35	82 33	Fort Worth, Tex.	32 45	97 20	Norfolk, Va.	36 51	76 17
Atlanta, Ga.	33 45	84 24	Gainesville, Fla.	29 39	82 19	Oakland, Calif.	37 48	122 16
Augusta, Ga.	33 28	81 58	Galveston, Tex.	29 18	94 48	Oklahoma City, Okla.	35 28	97 31
Austin, Tex.	30 16	97 45	Gary, Ind.	41 36	87 20	Omaha, Nebr.	41 16	95 56
Baltimore, Md.	39 17	76 37	Grand Rapids, Mich.	42 58	85 40	Peoria, Ill.	40 41	89 35
Bangor, Me.	44 48	68 46	Green Bay, Wisc.	44 30	88 00	Philadelphia, Pa.	39 57	75 09
Baton Rouge, La.	30 27	91 11	Greenville, S.C.	34 50	82 24	Phoenix, Ariz.	33 27	112 04
Biloxi, Miss.	30 23	88 53	Harrisburg, Pa.	40 15	76 52	Pittsburgh, Pa.	40 26	80 00
Birmingham, Ala.	33 31	86 49	Hartford, Conn.	41 46	72 40	Pocatello, Idaho	42 52	112 27
Bismarck, N.D.	46 48	100 47	Honolulu, Hawaii	21 20	158 00	Portland, Me.	43 39	70 15
Boise, Idaho	43 37	116 12	Houston, Tex.	29 45	95 22	Portland, Ore.	45 31	122 41
Boston, Mass.	42 21	71 03	Indianapolis, Ind.	39 46	86 10	Providence, R.I.	41 50	71 25
Brattleboro, Vt.	42 51	72 33	Iowa City, Iowa	41 39	91 31	Provo, Utah	40 14	111 39
Bridgeport, Conn.	41 11	73 11	Jacksonville, Fla.	30 19	81 39	Reno, Nev.	39 31	119 48
Buffalo, N.Y.	42 52	78 52	Joplin, Mo.	37 05	94 30	Richmond, Va.	37 32	77 26
Butte, Mont.	46 01	112 32	Juneau, Alaska	58 18	134 24	Rochester, N.Y.	43 09	77 36
Casper, Wyo.	42 51	106 19	Kalamazoo, Mich.	42 17	85 35	St. Louis, Mo.	38 38	90 12
Charleston, S.C.	32 47	79 56	Kansas City, Mo.	39 05	94 35	Salt Lake City, Utah	40 45	111 53
Charlotte, N.C.	35 14	80 51	Knoxville, Tenn.	35 58	83 55	San Francisco, Calif.	37 47	122 25
Chattanooga, Tenn.	35 03	85 19	Lancaster, Pa.	40 02	76 18	Santa Fe, N.M.	35 41	105 56
Cheyenne, Wyo.	41 08	104 49	Las Vegas, Nev.	36 10	115 09	Savannah, Ga.	32 04	81 05
Chicago, Ill.	41 52	87 38	Lincoln, Nebr.	40 49	96 42	Seattle, Wash.	47 37	122 20
Cincinnati, Ohio	39 06	84 31	Little Rock, Ark.	34 45	92 17	Shreveport, La.	32 30	93 44
Cleveland, Ohio	41 30	81 42	Los Angeles, Calif.	34 03	118 14	Sioux Falls, S.D.	43 32	96 43
Columbus, Ohio	39 58	83 00	Louisville, Ky.	38 14	85 45	Syracuse, N.Y.	43 03	76 09
Concord, N.H.	43 12	71 32	Macon, Ga.	32 50	83 37	Tallahassee, Fla.	30 26	84 16
Dallas, Tex.	32 47	96 48	Madison, Wisc.	43 04	89 23	Texarkana, Tex.	33 25	94 02
Dayton, Ohio	39 45	84 11	Memphis, Tenn.	35 09	90 03	Topeka, Kans.	39 03	95 40
Daytona Beach, Fla.	29 12	81 01	Miami, Fla.	25 47	80 12	Tulsa, Okla.	36 09	96 00
Denver, Colo.	39 45	104 59	Milwaukee, Wisc.	43 02	87 54	Tucson, Ariz.	32 13	110 58
Des Moines, Iowa	41 35	93 37	Minneapolis, Minn.	44 59	93 16	Utica, N.Y.	43 07	75 13
Detroit, Mich.	42 20	83 03	Mobile, Ala.	30 42	88 03	Washington, D.C.	38 54	77 01
Dubuque, Iowa	42 30	90 40	Montgomery, Ala.	32 23	86 19	Wichita, Kans.	37 41	97 20
Duluth, Minn.	46 47	92 06	Montpelier, Vt.	44 16	72 35	Wilmington, Del.	39 45	75 33

SUNRISE AND SUNSET: 1982

SOURCE: U.S. Naval Observatory

Note: To determine Daylight Saving Time, add one hour to all times; e.g., sunrise at 20° latitude on January 2 is 7:35 D.S.T.

To determine sunrise or sunset for any location, follow these directions:

(1) From the table directly above, determine the latitude and longitude of the city closest to you;

(2) From the tables below, read the sunrise or sunset time for the desired date at the correct latitude (given in degrees at the top of the table);

(3) Determine your time zone:

(a) **Eastern Time Zone:** If longitude is less than 75°, subtract four minutes from the time on the table for each degree. If it is greater than 75°, add four minutes for each degree.

(b) **Central Time Zone:** If longitude is less than 90°, subtract four minutes from the time on the table for each degree. If it is greater, add four minutes for each degree.

(c) **Rocky Mountain Time:** If longitude is less than 105°, subtract four minutes from the time on the table for each degree. If it is greater, add four minutes for each degree.

(d) **Pacific Time:** If longitude is less than 120°, subtract four minutes from the time on the table for each degree. If it is greater, add four minutes for each degree.

			Latitude								Latitude			
Date	+20°	+30°	+35°	+40°	+46°	+50°	Date	+20°	+30°	+35°	+40°	+46°	+50°
					SUNRISE (UPPER LIMB)									
	h m	h m	h m	h m	h m	h m		h m	h m	h m	h m	h m	h m
Jan. −2	6 34	6 55	7 07	7 21	7 42	7 59	Mar. 23	6 02	6 01	6 00	5 59	5 58	5 57
2	6 35	6 56	7 08	7 22	7 42	7 59	27	5 58	5 56	5 55	5 53	5 50	5 49
6	6 37	6 57	7 09	7 22	7 42	7 58	31	5 55	5 51	5 49	5 46	5 43	5 40
10	6 37	6 57	7 09	7 22	7 41	7 56							
14	6 38	6 57	7 08	7 21	7 39	7 54	Apr. 4	5 51	5 46	5 43	5 40	5 35	5 31
18	6 38	6 56	7 07	7 19	7 36	7 51	8	5 48	5 42	5 38	5 34	5 28	5 23
22	6 38	6 55	7 05	7 17	7 33	7 47	12	5 45	5 37	5 33	5 27	5 20	5 14
26	6 37	6 54	7 03	7 14	7 30	7 42	16	5 42	5 33	5 27	5 21	5 13	5 06
30	6 36	6 52	7 01	7 11	7 25	7 37	20	5 39	5 28	5 22	5 16	5 06	4 58
							24	5 36	5 24	5 18	5 10	4 59	4 50
Feb. 3	6 35	6 49	6 58	7 07	7 20	7 31	28	5 33	5 20	5 13	5 04	4 52	4 43
7	6 33	6 47	6 54	7 03	7 15	7 25							
11	6 32	6 44	6 51	6 58	7 09	7 18	May 2	5 30	5 17	5 09	4 59	4 46	4 35
15	6 29	6 40	6 46	6 53	7 03	7 11	6	5 28	5 13	5 05	4 55	4 40	4 29
19	6 27	6 37	6 42	6 48	6 57	7 04	10	5 26	5 10	5 01	4 50	4 35	4 22
23	6 24	6 33	6 37	6 43	6 50	6 56	14	5 24	5 07	4 58	4 46	4 30	4 16
27	6 22	6 29	6 33	6 37	6 43	6 48	18	5 23	5 05	4 55	4 42	4 25	4 11
							22	5 22	5 03	4 52	4 39	4 21	4 06
Mar. 3	6 19	6 24	6 27	6 31	6 36	6 40	26	5 21	5 01	4 50	4 37	4 17	4 01
7	6 15	6 20	6 22	6 25	6 29	6 32	30	5 20	5 00	4 48	4 34	4 14	3 58
11	6 12	6 15	6 17	6 19	6 21	6 23							
15	6 09	6 10	6 11	6 12	6 14	6 15	June 3	5 20	4 59	4 47	4 33	4 12	3 55
19	6 05	6 06	6 06	6 06	6 06	6 05	7	5 20	4 58	4 46	4 31	4 10	3 52

SUNRISE (UPPER LIMB)

Date		+20°	+30°	+35°	+40°	+46°	+50°
June	11	5 20	4 58	4 45	4 31	4 09	3 51
	15	5 20	4 58	4 45	4 30	4 08	3 50
	19	5 21	4 59	4 46	4 31	4 09	3 50
	23	5 22	5 00	4 47	4 32	4 09	3 50
	27	5 23	5 01	4 48	4 33	4 11	3 52
July	1	5 24	5 02	4 49	4 35	4 13	3 55
	5	5 25	5 04	4 51	4 37	4 15	3 57
	9	5 27	5 06	4 53	4 39	4 18	4 01
	13	5 28	5 08	4 56	4 42	4 22	4 05
	17	5 30	5 10	4 58	4 45	4 25	4 09
	21	5 31	5 12	5 01	4 48	4 29	4 14
	25	5 33	5 14	5 04	4 52	4 34	4 19
	29	5 34	5 17	5 07	4 55	4 38	4 24
Aug.	2	5 36	5 19	5 10	4 59	4 43	4 30
	6	5 37	5 22	5 13	5 03	4 48	4 36
	10	5 38	5 24	5 16	5 06	4 53	4 42
	14	5 39	5 26	5 19	5 10	4 58	4 47
	18	5 41	5 29	5 22	5 14	5 03	4 53
	22	5 42	5 31	5 25	5 18	5 08	4 59
	26	5 43	5 33	5 28	5 22	5 13	5 05
	30	5 44	5 36	5 31	5 25	5 18	5 11
Sept.	3	5 45	5 38	5 34	5 29	5 23	5 17
	7	5 46	5 40	5 37	5 33	5 28	5 23
	11	5 46	5 42	5 40	5 37	5 32	5 29
	15	5 47	5 44	5 42	5 40	5 37	5 35
	19	5 48	5 46	5 45	5 44	5 43	5 41
	23	5 49	5 49	5 48	5 48	5 48	5 47

Date		+20°	+30°	+35°	+40°	+46°	+50°
Sept.	27	5 50	5 51	5 51	5 52	5 53	5 53
Oct.	1	5 51	5 53	5 54	5 56	5 58	5 59
	5	5 52	5 55	5 57	6 00	6 03	6 05
	9	5 53	5 58	6 01	6 04	6 08	6 12
	13	5 54	6 00	6 04	6 08	6 14	6 18
	17	5 55	6 03	6 07	6 12	6 19	6 24
	21	5 57	6 06	6 11	6 16	6 24	6 31
	25	5 58	6 08	6 14	6 21	6 30	6 37
	29	6 00	6 11	6 18	6 25	6 36	6 44
Nov.	2	6 02	6 14	6 22	6 30	6 41	6 51
	6	6 04	6 17	6 25	6 34	6 47	6 57
	10	6 06	6 21	6 29	6 39	6 53	7 04
	14	6 08	6 24	6 33	6 44	6 58	7 11
	18	6 10	6 27	6 37	6 48	7 04	7 17
	22	6 13	6 31	6 41	6 53	7 10	7 23
	26	6 15	6 34	6 45	6 57	7 15	7 29
	30	6 18	6 37	6 48	7 01	7 20	7 35
Dec.	4	6 20	6 40	6 52	7 05	7 24	7 40
	8	6 23	6 43	6 55	7 09	7 29	7 45
	12	6 25	6 46	6 58	7 12	7 32	7 49
	16	6 28	6 49	7 01	7 15	7 36	7 52
	20	6 30	6 51	7 03	7 18	7 38	7 55
	24	6 32	6 53	7 05	7 20	7 40	7 57
	28	6 34	6 55	7 07	7 21	7 41	7 58
	32	6 35	6 56	7 08	7 22	7 42	7 59
	36	6 36	6 57	7 09	7 22	7 42	7 58

SUNSET (UPPER LIMB)

Date		+20°	+30°	+35°	+40°	+46°	+50°
Jan.	−2	17 30	17 09	16 57	16 43	16 23	16 06
	2	17 33	17 12	17 00	16 46	16 26	16 10
	6	17 35	17 15	17 03	16 50	16 30	16 14
	10	17 38	17 18	17 07	16 54	16 35	16 19
	14	17 40	17 21	17 10	16 58	16 40	16 25
	18	17 43	17 25	17 14	17 02	16 45	16 31
	22	17 46	17 28	17 18	17 07	16 50	16 37
	26	17 48	17 32	17 22	17 12	16 56	16 44
	30	17 51	17 35	17 26	17 16	17 02	16 50
Feb.	3	17 53	17 39	17 30	17 21	17 08	16 57
	7	17 55	17 42	17 34	17 26	17 14	17 04
	11	17 57	17 45	17 38	17 31	17 20	17 11
	15	17 59	17 48	17 42	17 35	17 26	17 18
	19	18 01	17 52	17 46	17 40	17 31	17 25
	23	18 03	17 55	17 50	17 45	17 37	17 31
	27	18 04	17 57	17 54	17 49	17 43	17 38
Mar.	3	18 06	18 00	17 57	17 54	17 49	17 45
	7	18 07	18 03	18 01	17 58	17 54	17 51
	11	18 08	18 06	18 04	18 02	18 00	17 58
	15	18 10	18 08	18 07	18 06	18 05	18 04
	19	18 11	18 11	18 11	18 11	18 11	18 11
	23	18 12	18 13	18 14	18 15	18 16	18 17
	27	18 13	18 15	18 17	18 19	18 21	18 23
	31	18 14	18 18	18 20	18 23	18 27	18 30
Apr.	4	18 15	18 20	18 23	18 27	18 32	18 36
	8	18 16	18 23	18 27	18 31	18 37	18 42
	12	18 17	18 25	18 30	18 35	18 42	18 48
	16	18 18	18 28	18 33	18 39	18 48	18 55
	20	18 20	18 30	18 36	18 43	18 53	19 01
	24	18 21	18 33	18 39	18 47	18 58	19 07
	28	18 22	18 35	18 43	18 51	19 03	19 13
May	2	18 24	18 38	18 46	18 55	19 09	19 20
	6	18 25	18 40	18 49	18 59	19 14	19 26
	10	18 27	18 43	18 52	19 03	19 19	19 32
	14	18 28	18 45	18 56	19 07	19 24	19 37
	18	18 30	18 48	18 59	19 11	19 28	19 43
	22	18 32	18 50	19 02	19 14	19 33	19 48
	26	18 33	18 53	19 04	19 18	19 37	19 53
	30	18 35	18 55	19 07	19 21	19 41	19 58
June	3	18 36	18 57	19 10	19 24	19 45	20 02
	7	18 38	18 59	19 12	19 26	19 48	20 05
	11	18 39	19 01	19 14	19 29	19 50	20 08
	15	18 40	19 02	19 15	19 30	19 52	20 11
	19	18 41	19 04	19 17	19 32	19 54	20 12
	23	18 42	19 04	19 17	19 33	19 55	20 13
	27	18 43	19 05	19 18	19 33	19 55	20 13
July	1	18 43	19 05	19 18	19 33	19 54	20 13

Date		+20°	+30°	+35°	+40°	+46°	+50°
July	5	18 44	19 05	19 18	19 32	19 53	20 11
	9	18 43	19 04	19 17	19 31	19 52	20 09
	13	18 43	19 03	19 15	19 29	19 49	20 06
	17	18 42	19 02	19 14	19 27	19 46	20 02
	21	18 41	19 00	19 11	19 24	19 43	19 58
	25	18 40	18 58	19 09	19 21	19 39	19 53
	29	18 39	18 56	19 06	19 17	19 34	19 48
Aug.	2	18 37	18 53	19 02	19 13	19 29	19 42
	6	18 35	18 50	18 58	19 09	19 23	19 35
	10	18 32	18 46	18 54	19 04	19 17	19 28
	14	18 30	18 42	18 50	18 59	19 11	19 21
	18	18 27	18 39	18 45	18 53	19 04	19 13
	22	18 24	18 34	18 40	18 47	18 57	19 05
	26	18 21	18 30	18 35	18 41	18 50	18 57
	30	18 17	18 25	18 30	18 35	18 43	18 49
Sept.	3	18 14	18 21	18 25	18 29	18 35	18 41
	7	18 10	18 16	18 19	18 23	18 28	18 32
	11	18 07	18 11	18 13	18 16	18 20	18 23
	15	18 03	18 06	18 08	18 09	18 12	18 14
	19	17 59	18 01	18 02	18 03	18 04	18 06
	23	17 56	17 56	17 56	17 56	17 57	17 57
	27	17 52	17 51	17 50	17 50	17 49	17 48
Oct.	1	17 48	17 46	17 45	17 43	17 41	17 39
	5	17 45	17 41	17 39	17 37	17 33	17 31
	9	17 42	17 36	17 34	17 30	17 26	17 22
	13	17 38	17 32	17 28	17 24	17 18	17 14
	17	17 35	17 28	17 23	17 18	17 11	17 06
	21	17 32	17 23	17 18	17 12	17 04	16 58
	25	17 30	17 19	17 14	17 07	16 58	16 50
	29	17 27	17 16	17 09	17 02	16 51	16 43
Nov.	2	17 25	17 13	17 05	16 57	16 45	16 36
	6	17 23	17 10	17 02	16 53	16 40	16 29
	10	17 22	17 07	16 58	16 48	16 35	16 23
	14	17 21	17 05	16 55	16 45	16 30	16 18
	18	17 20	17 03	16 53	16 42	16 26	16 13
	22	17 19	17 01	16 51	16 39	16 22	16 08
	26	17 19	17 00	16 50	16 37	16 19	16 05
	30	17 19	17 00	16 49	16 36	16 17	16 02
Dec.	4	17 20	17 00	16 48	16 35	16 16	16 00
	8	17 21	17 00	16 48	16 35	16 15	15 59
	12	17 22	17 01	16 49	16 35	16 15	15 58
	16	17 23	17 02	16 50	16 36	16 15	15 58
	20	17 25	17 04	16 52	16 37	16 17	16 00
	24	17 27	17 06	16 54	16 39	16 19	16 02
	28	17 29	17 08	16 56	16 42	16 22	16 05
	32	17 32	17 11	16 59	16 45	16 25	16 08
	36	17 34	17 14	17 02	16 48	16 29	16 13

CALENDARS: 1801-2000

Select the desired year from the table below. The number shown with each year tells you the calendar to use for that year.

Year	Cal.	Year	Cal.	Year	Cal.	Year	Cal.	Year	Cal.
1801	5	1841	6	1881	7	1921	7	1961	1
1802	6	1842	7	1882	1	1922	1	1962	2
1803	7	1843	1	1883	2	1923	2	1963	3
1804	8	1844	9	1884	10	1924	10	1964	11
1805	3	1845	4	1885	5	1925	5	1965	6
1806	4	1846	5	1886	6	1926	6	1966	7
1807	5	1847	6	1887	7	1927	7	1967	1
1808	13	1848	14	1888	8	1928	8	1968	9
1801	1	1849	2	1889	3	1929	3	1969	4
1810	2	1850	3	1890	4	1930	4	1970	5
1811	3	1851	4	1891	5	1931	5	1971	6
1812	11	1852	12	1892	13	1932	13	1972	14
1813	6	1853	7	1893	1	1933	1	1973	2
1814	7	1854	1	1894	2	1934	2	1974	3
1815	1	1855	2	1895	3	1935	3	1975	4
1816	9	1856	10	1896	11	1936	11	1976	12
1817	4	1857	5	1897	6	1937	6	1977	7
1818	5	1858	6	1898	7	1938	7	1978	1
1819	6	1859	7	1899	1	1939	1	1979	2
1820	14	1860	8	1900	2	1940	9	1980	10
1821	2	1861	3	1901	3	1941	4	1981	5
1822	3	1862	4	1902	4	1942	5	1982	6
1823	4	1863	5	1903	5	1943	6	1983	7
1824	12	1964	13	1904	13	1944	14	1984	8
1825	7	1865	1	1905	1	1945	2	1985	3
1826	1	1866	2	1906	2	1946	3	1986	4
1827	2	1867	3	1907	3	1947	4	1987	5
1828	10	1868	11	1908	11	1948	12	1988	13
1829	5	1869	6	1909	6	1949	7	1989	1
1830	6	1870	7	1910	7	1950	1	1990	2
1831	7	1871	1	1911	1	1951	2	1991	3
1832	8	1872	9	1912	9	1952	10	1992	11
1833	3	1873	4	1913	4	1953	5	1993	6
1834	4	1874	5	1914	5	1954	6	1994	7
1835	5	1875	6	1915	6	1955	7	1995	1
1836	13	1876	14	1916	14	1956	8	1996	9
1837	1	1877	2	1917	2	1957	3	1997	4
1838	2	1878	3	1918	3	1958	4	1998	5
1839	3	1879	4	1919	4	1959	5	1999	6
1840	11	1880	12	1920	12	1960	13	2000	14

Calendar 1

JANUARY
```
S  M  T  W  T  F  S
         1  2  3  4
 5  6  7  8  9 10 11
12 13 14 15 16 17 18
19 20 21 22 23 24 25
26 27 28 29 30 31
```
FEBRUARY
```
S  M  T  W  T  F  S
                  1
 2  3  4  5  6  7  8
 9 10 11 12 13 14 15
16 17 18 19 20 21 22
23 24 25 26 27 28
```
MARCH
```
S  M  T  W  T  F  S
                  1
 2  3  4  5  6  7  8
 9 10 11 12 13 14 15
16 17 18 19 20 21 22
23 24 25 26 27 28 29
30 31
```
APRIL
```
S  M  T  W  T  F  S
       1  2  3  4  5
 6  7  8  9 10 11 12
13 14 15 16 17 18 19
20 21 22 23 24 25 26
27 28 29 30
```
MAY
```
S  M  T  W  T  F  S
             1  2  3
 4  5  6  7  8  9 10
11 12 13 14 15 16 17
18 19 20 21 22 23 24
25 26 27 28 29 30 31
```
JUNE
```
S  M  T  W  T  F  S
 1  2  3  4  5  6  7
 8  9 10 11 12 13 14
15 16 17 18 19 20 21
22 23 24 25 26 27 28
29 30
```
JULY
```
S  M  T  W  T  F  S
ияние
 1  2  3  4  5
 6  7  8  9 10 11 12
13 14 15 16 17 18 19
20 21 22 23 24 25 26
27 28 29 30 31
```
AUGUST
```
S  M  T  W  T  F  S
                1  2
 3  4  5  6  7  8  9
10 11 12 13 14 15 16
17 18 19 20 21 22 23
24 25 26 27 28 29 30
31
```
SEPTEMBER
```
S  M  T  W  T  F  S
    1  2  3  4  5  6
 7  8  9 10 11 12 13
14 15 16 17 18 19 20
21 22 23 24 25 26 27
28 29 30
```
OCTOBER
```
S  M  T  W  T  F  S
          1  2  3  4
 5  6  7  8  9 10 11
12 13 14 15 16 17 18
19 20 21 22 23 24 25
26 27 28 29 30 31
```
NOVEMBER
```
S  M  T  W  T  F  S
                  1
 2  3  4  5  6  7  8
 9 10 11 12 13 14 15
16 17 18 19 20 21 22
23 24 25 26 27 28 29
30
```
DECEMBER
```
S  M  T  W  T  F  S
             1  2  3
 4  5  6  7  8  9 10
11 12 13 14 15 16 17
18 19 20 21 22 23 24
25 26 27 28 29 30 31
```

(Calendars 2 through 6 follow the same twelve-month layout for the remaining calendar types.)

7

JANUARY	FEBRUARY	MARCH	APRIL
S M T W T F S	S M T W T F S	S M T W T F S	S M T W T F S
1	1 2 3 4 5	1 2 3 4 5	1 2
2 3 4 5 6 7 8	6 7 8 9 10 11 12	6 7 8 9 10 11 12	3 4 5 6 7 8 9
9 10 11 12 13 14 15	13 14 15 16 17 18 19	13 14 15 16 17 18 19	10 11 12 13 14 15 16
16 17 18 19 20 21 22	20 21 22 23 24 25 26	20 21 22 23 24 25 26	17 18 19 20 21 22 23
23 24 25 26 27 28 29	27 28	27 28 29 30 31	24 25 26 27 28 29 30
30 31			

MAY	JUNE	JULY	AUGUST
S M T W T F S	S M T W T F S	S M T W T F S	S M T W T F S
1 2 3 4 5 6 7	1 2 3 4	1 2	1 2 3 4 5 6
8 9 10 11 12 13 14	5 6 7 8 9 10 11	3 4 5 6 7 8 9	7 8 9 10 11 12 13
15 16 17 18 19 20 21	12 13 14 15 16 17 18	10 11 12 13 14 15 16	14 15 16 17 18 19 20
22 23 24 25 26 27 28	19 20 21 22 23 24 25	17 18 19 20 21 22 23	21 22 23 24 25 26 27
29 30 31	26 27 28 29 30	24 25 26 27 28 29 30	28 29 30 31
		31	

SEPTEMBER	OCTOBER	NOVEMBER	DECEMBER
S M T W T F S	S M T W T F S	S M T W T F S	S M T W T F S
1 2 3	1	1 2 3 4 5	1 2 3
4 5 6 7 8 9 10	2 3 4 5 6 7 8	6 7 8 9 10 11 12	4 5 6 7 8 9 10
11 12 13 14 15 16 17	9 10 11 12 13 14 15	13 14 15 16 17 18 19	11 12 13 14 15 16 17
18 19 20 21 22 23 24	16 17 18 19 20 21 22	20 21 22 23 24 25 26	18 19 20 21 22 23 24
25 26 27 28 29 30	23 24 25 26 27 28 29	27 28 29 30	25 26 27 28 29 30 31
	30 31		

8

JANUARY	FEBRUARY	MARCH	APRIL
S M T W T F S	S M T W T F S	S M T W T F S	S M T W T F S
1 2 3	1 2 3	1 2 3	1 2 3 4 5 6 7
4 5 6 7			

(Perpetual calendar tables numbered 7 through 14 continue across the page — calendars 9, 10, 11, 12, 13, 14 each containing the twelve months January through December arranged in four columns and three rows, in the same format as calendars 7 and 8.)

HOLIDAYS AND COMMEMORATED DAYS FOR 1982

Days in parentheses are not legal holidays. *—Holiday observed on following Monday; **—Holiday observed on preceding Friday. Note: applies to all states immediately following symbol.

January

1/ New Year's Day (All states & Canada)
8/ (Battle of New Orleans Day) (LA)
15/ Martin Luther King Day (AL, CT, DC, FL, IL, MD, MA, MI, NJ, PA, SC)
17/ Dr. Martin Luther King, Jr. Day (NY)
18/ Martin Luther King's Birthday (OH)
18/ Lee-Jackson Day (VA)
19/ Robert E. Lee's Birthday (AL, AR, FL, GA, MS, NC, SC)
    Confederate Heroes Day (TX)

February

1/ Abraham Lincoln's Birthday (DE, OR)
2/ (Groundhog Day)
8/ Abraham Lincoln's Birthday (AZ)
12/ Abraham Lincoln's Birthday (AK, CA, CO, CT, FL, IL, IN, IA, KS, MD, MO, MT, NJ, NM, NY, UT, VT, WA, WV)
14/ (St. Valentine's Day)
15/ Susan B. Anthony's Birthday (FL)
15/ George Washington's Birthday (All states except HI, KY, MI, MN, NE, OH, PA, SD, WI, WY)
    Combined celebration of birthdays of George Washington & Abraham Lincoln (OH, WI); called Presidents' Day (HI, ID, KY, MI, MN, NE, OH, PA, SD, WY)
23/ Mardi Gras Day (AL, LA)

March

2/ Texas Independence Day (TX)
2/ Town Meeting Day (VT)
17/ (St. Patrick's Day)
25/ Maryland Day (MD)
26/ Prince Jonah Kuhio Kalanianaole Day (HI)
29/ Seward's Day (AK)

April

2/ Pascua Florida Day (FL)
9/ Good Friday (CT, DE, FL, HI, IN, LA, MD, NJ, ND, TN) (Canada)
    Good Friday Afternoon (KY, WI)
12/ Easter Monday (NC)
12/ Anniversary of signing of Halifax Resolves (NC)
13/ Thomas Jefferson's Birthday (AL)
19/ Patriot's Day (ME, MA)
21/ San Jacinto Day (TX)
22/ Arbor Day (NE)
22/ Oklahoma Day (OK)
26/ Confederate Memorial Day (AL, FL, GA, MS)
26/ Fast Day (NH)
30/ (Arbor Day)

May

1/ (May Day)
4/ Rhode Island Independence Day (RI)
8/ Harry S Truman's Birthday (MO)
9/ (Mother's Day)
10/ Confederate Memorial Day (*—NC, SC)
15/ (Armed Forces Day)
18/ Primary Election Day (PA)
20/ Anniversary of Mecklenburg Declaration of Independence (NC)
24/ Victoria Day (Canada)
30/ Memorial Day (MI, NH, NM, OH, SD; *—DE, MD, VT)
31/ Confederate Memorial Day (VA); Decoration Day (TN)
31/ Memorial Day (All states except AL, MI, MS, NH, NM, OH, SC, SD)

June

3/ Jefferson Davis' Birthday (FL, GA, SC)
7/ Jefferson Davis' Birthday (AL, MS)
11/ King Kamehameha I Day (HI)
14/ (Flag Day)
19/ Emancipation Day (TX)
20/ (Father's Day)
20/ West Virginia Day (WV)

July

1/ Dominion Day (Canada)
4/ Independence Day (All states); (*—AK, AZ, AR, CO, CT, DE, DC, FL, HI, ID, IL, IN, IA, KY, LA, ME, MD, MA, MI, MN, MO, NE, NV, NJ, NM, NY, OH, OK, PA, SC, SD, UT, VT, VA, WI)
4/ (Indian Rights Day) (WI)
24/ Pioneer Day (UT)

August

1/ American Family Day (AZ)
2/ Colorado Day (CO)
9/ Victory Day (RI)
16/ Bennington Battle Day (VT)
20/ Admission Day (HI)
27/ Lyndon B. Johnson's Birthday (TX)
30/ Huey P. Long Day (LA)

September

6/ Labor Day (All states & Canada)
9/ Admission Day (CA)
12/ Defenders' Day (*—MD)
12/ (Grandparents' Day)
18/ (Rosh Hashanah)
27/ (Indian Day) (OK)
27/ Yom Kippur (NC)

October

9/ (Leif Ericson Day)
11/ Columbus Day (All states except AK, AR, HI, IA, KY, LA, MI, MS, NV, ND, OR, SC, SD, WA)
11/ Discoverers' Day (HI)
11/ Farmers' Day (FL)
11/ Pioneer's Day (SD)
11/ Thanksgiving Day (Canada)
18/ Alaska Day (AK)
24/ (United Nations Day)
31/ (Halloween)
31/ Nevada Day (*—NV)

November

1/ (All Saints' Day) (LA)
2/ Election Day (CO, FL, IL, IN, LA, MD, NH, NJ, NY, PA, RI, SC, TN, TX, VA, WI, WY)
9/ Veterans Day (MI, OK)
11/ Veterans Day (All states except KY); Armistice Day (MS, RI): Remembrance Day (Canada)
25/ Thanksgiving Day (All states)
26/ Thanksgiving Friday (IL, IN, IA, KY, MI, MN, NE, NH, OK, TX, WA, WY)

December

24/ Christmas Eve (AR, OK, SC, VT)
25/ Christmas Day (All states & Canada)(**—AK, AR, AZ, CT, DC, HI, ID, IL, IN, IA, LA, MD, MI, MN, MT, NE, NV, NJ, NM, OK, PA, SC, SD, TX, VT, VA)
26/ Day after Christmas (KY, SC, TX); Boxing Day (*—Canada)
31/ New Year's Eve (KY, MN, OK, PA, SD)

NEW WORLD EXPLORERS

NORTH AMERICA

c. 1000 ... Leif Ericsson (Norway) possibly sailed to Labrador and Newfoundland, from Greenland; others theorize that he reached Virginia, Nova Scotia, or New England

c. 1010 ... Thorfinn Karlsefni (Iceland) sailed from Greenland to North America, probably Labrador or New England

1497–98 ... John Cabot (England) sailed to North America, probably Cape Breton Island or Newfoundland

1513 ... Juan Ponce de León (Spain) sailed to near St. Augustine, Florida, and south to Miami Bay

1519 ... Alonso de Pineda (Spain) explored the Gulf of Mexico from Florida to the mouth of the Rio Grande

1524 ... Giovanni da Verrazano (France) explored North American coast, probably from North Carolina to Maine, entering New York Bay

1528 ... Pánfilo de Narváez (Spain) explored Florida from Tampa Bay as far as Tallahassee

1534–36 ... Jacques Cartier (France) sailed to Strait of Belle Isle, Newfoundland, and discovered Prince Edward Island; he also discovered St. Lawrence River as far as Quebec and Montreal (1535–36)

1536 ... Alvar Nuñez Cabeza de Vaca (Spain), shipwrecked on Texas coast, traveled as far as New Mexico, Arizona, and possibly California

1538–39 ... Francisco de Ulloa (Spain) explored Gulf of California to its head, proving that present-day Baja California is a peninsula

1538–41 ... Hernando de Soto (Spain) began (1539) exploring southern coast of United States, as far inland as Mississippi River, Arkansas, and Oklahoma

1539 ... Marcos de Niza (Spain) explored southeastern Arizona and perhaps New Mexico

1540–42 ... Francisco Vásquez de Coronado (Spain) explored New Mexico, Texas Panhandle, Oklahoma, and Kansas

1542 ... Juan Rodríguez Cabrillo (Spain) discovered California mainland, landing at San Diego Bay

1565 ... Pedro Menéndez de Avilés (Spain) founded St. Augustine, Florida, and explored Gulf Coast

1576–78 ... Sir Martin Frobisher (England) explored Frobisher Bay, South Baffin Island, and Hudson Strait in northeastern Canada

1577–79 ... Sir Francis Drake (England) sailed from Chile to Washington, stopping at San Francisco Bay

1585–87 ... John Davis (England) discovered Cumberland Sound off Baffin Island in northeastern Canada

1598–1605 ... Juan de Oñate (Spain) explored New Mexico (1598), Oklahoma, and the plains around Wichita, Kansas (1601), and went down the Colorado River to the Gulf of California (1605)

1602 ... Bartholomew Gosnold (England) explored eastern coast from Maine to Narragansett Bay, naming Cape Cod

1603–9 ... Samuel de Champlain (France) explored St. Lawrence River as far as Lachine (1603), New England south to Martha's Vineyard (1603–6); founded Quebec (1608); and discovered Lake Champlain (1609)

1607–9 ... John Smith (England) helped to found (1607) Jamestown, Virginia, and explored adjacent areas

1609–10 ... Henry Hudson (Netherlands) sailed up Chesapeake, Delaware, and New York Bays; under English flag, he sailed through Greenland, Labrador, Hudson Strait and Bay (1610)

1634 ... Jean Nicolet (France) explored Lake Michigan, Green Bay, and Fox River, Wisconsin

1673 ... Louis Jolliet, Father Jacques Marquette (France) navigated Mississippi, Arkansas, and Illinois Rivers to Chicago; first to establish the existence of a waterway from St. Lawrence River to the Gulf of Mexico

1678–79 ... Frère Louis Hennepin (France) explored Great Plains and the upper Mississippi River region

1678–80 ... Daniel Greysolon Duluth (Du Lhut) (France) claimed Lake Superior and upper Mississippi region for France; his treatment of the Indians gained their lasting friendship

1679–82 ... Robert Cavalier de La Salle (France) crossed Great Lakes and navigated Mississippi River to its mouth

1691–92 ... Henry Kelsey (England) explored the area around Reindeer Lake in western Canada

1692 ... Arnout Viele (France) explored the area from the Great Lakes to the Ohio River

1701 ... Antoine de la Mothe Cadillac (France) explored upper Michigan; founded Detroit

1710–18 ... Jean Baptiste le Moyne, sieur de Bienville (France), founded Mobile (1710) and New Orleans (1718)

1731–43 ... Pierre Gautier de Varennes, sieur de la Vérendrye (Canada), explored central Canada, Red River country, and the Missouri River (1731–34); discovered Lake Manitoba (1739) in central Canada; and traveled probably as far as the Black Hills in north central United States (1742–43)

1769–79 ... Daniel Boone (United States) explored Kentucky territory (1769–71) and blazed the Wilderness Road (1775)

1770–72 ... Samuel Hearne (England) opened areas of north central Canada, around Great Slave Lake and Coppermine River

1775–76 ... Silvestre Vélez de Escalante (Spain) explored Arizona and Colorado; first white man known to travel in Utah

1792 ... Robert Gray (United States) discovered Columbia River in northwestern United States

1789–93 ... Sir Alexander Mackenzie (Canada) followed Mackenzie River in Canada to Arctic Ocean (1789); explored elsewhere in Canada, making first overland crossing of North America to the Pacific, north of Mexico (1793)

1797–1810 ... David Thompson (Canada) explored Rocky Mountains and all of the Columbia River system

1803–6 ... Meriwether Lewis, William Clark (United States) navigated Missouri River to Bismarck, North Dakota, traveled west through the mountains to the Clearwater, Snake, and Columbia Rivers as far as the Pacific Ocean

1805–7 ... Zebulon Pike (United States) explored Minnesota (1805) and southwestern United States, sighted Pikes Peak (1806)

c. 1807 ... John Colter (United States) crossed Teton Range in the Rocky Mountains, and discovered Yellowstone area

1819–27 ... Sir John Franklin (England) explored northern Canada to the Arctic

1825 ... James Bridger (United States) discovered Great Salt Lake in Utah

1825–27 ... Jedediah Smith (United States) traveled from Great Salt Lake to Colorado River and San Diego, California; on return trip, he crossed Sierra Nevada and Great Salt Desert

1832–35 ... Benjamin Bonneville (United States) helped open Rocky Mountain territory

1842–45 ... John Frémont, Kit Carson (United States) explored Oregon, Nevada, and California

SOUTH AND CENTRAL AMERICA

1492–1502 ... Christopher Columbus (Spain) discovered America: Bahamas, Cuba, and Hispaniola in the Caribbean (1492); Venezuela (1498); and Honduras (1502)

1499 ... Alonso de Ojeda (Spain) explored northeastern coast of South America

1499–1509 ... Vicente Pinzón (Spain) explored coast of Brazil and discovered mouth of the Amazon River in Brazil (1499–1500); skirted along Yucatán, Honduras, and Venezuela (1508–9)

1500 ... Pedro Alvarez Cabral (Portugal) reached coast of Brazil, possibly before Pinzón

1501–2 ... Amerigo Vespucci (Portugal) discovered Rio de la Plata, explored about 6,000 miles of South American coast; he was the first to suggest that America was not part of Asia

1513 ... Vasco Núñez de Balboa (Spain) discovered the Pacific Ocean by crossing Isthmus of Panama

1516 ... Juan Díaz de Solís (Spain) sailed up Río de la Plata and explored Uruguay

1517 ... Francisco Fernández de Córdoba (Spain) discovered Yucatán in Mexico

1519 ... Gil González Dávila and Andrés Niño (Spain) explored Pacific coast of Central America from Panama to Nicaragua

1519–21 ... Hernán Cortés (Spain) discovered Aztec capital Tenochtitlán (now Mexico City) and conquered Mexico

1520 ... Ferdinand Magellan (Spain) explored Rio de la Plata and Patagonia in Argentina, and discovered the strait at the tip of South America that bears his name

1524–33 ... Francisco Pizarro (Spain) explored the San Juan River between Colombia and Ecuador; conqueror of Peru (1532–33)

1526–30 ... Sebastian Cabot (Spain) explored Río de la Plata country along Paraguay, Plata, and Paraná Rivers

1530–35 ... Nikolaus Federmann (Germany) explored northwestern Venezuela and interior of Colombia through the Andes

1533 ... Sebastián de Belalcázar (Spain) explored and conquered Ecuador and southeastern Colombia

1535–37 ... Diego de Almagro (Spain) explored from Peru south through the Andes as far as Coquimbo and the Atacama Desert in Chile

1535–37 ... Pedro de Mendoza (Spain) explored Río de la Plata and founded Buenos Aires (1536)

1536 ... Gonzalo Jiménez de Quesada (Spain) founded Bogotá, Colombia, and explored the Magdalena River, Colombia

1541 ... Francisco de Orellana (Spain) floated down the Amazon's entire length

1549–52 ... Pedro de Valdivia (Spain) explored Chile, founding Concepción and Valdivia (1552)

1595 ... Sir Walter Raleigh (England) explored Orinoco River, penetrating 300 miles into Guiana's interior

1616 ... Willem C. Schouten (Netherlands) rounded and named Cape Horn at the tip of South America, avoiding the Strait of Magellan

1799–1804 ... Alexander von Humboldt (Germany) explored source of Orinoco and Amazon Rivers, establishing the connecting systems of the two

STARS/PLANETS/SPACE

ORIGIN AND EVOLUTION OF THE UNIVERSE

One of the major and perhaps most fundamental problems in astronomy is to develop a theory of the origin and evolution of the universe, based on actual observations of stars and galaxies and on known physical laws, in the attempt to determine how the universe changes with time. Cosmology deals with the physical structure of the universe, and with the origin of the universe and of its subsystems—that is, galaxies and systems of galaxies. Several different theories of the origin and evolution of the universe have been suggested.

The Einstein-Friedmann relativistic theories of cosmology, which were first formulated (1922) by Alexander Friedmann, a Russian physicist, are based on Einstein's theory of general relativity. The relativistic theorists postulate a universe that is in constant motion and originated from one infinitesimal point and subsequently expanded. The expansion of the universe refers to the mutual recession of galaxies from each other, with a recessional velocity proportional to their distance from one another. The observational evidence for the recession of galaxies from one another was first discovered by the American astronomer Edwin Hubble in the late 1920s.

Most astronomers believe that the whole universe originated in a cataclysmic explosion. This is the basis of the "big-bang" theory. From the moment of the big bang the universe has expanded and as the galaxies formed they shared in this expansion. At the very beginning, the temperature in the universe was extremely high. As it decreased, particles of radiation (photons) and of matter were created. Within only a few minutes electrons and the nuclei of hydrogen, deuterium, and helium had been produced. Matter and radiation continued to cool and after many thousands of years the immense clouds of matter that had formed were able to condense into galaxies and stars.

According to the relativistic concept, the geometry of space determines the kind of expansion of the universe. If the curvature of space is positive, which means that space is finite, the relativistic equations predict that the expansion of the universe will come to a halt at some finite time. Thereafter, the universe will begin to contract with increasing velocity until it reaches its initial primordial state of very high density and very high temperature. This concept is sometimes referred to as a "closed" universe. If the curvature of space is negative, the expansion could be permanent; the universe could expand forever. In this "open" universe idea, even after the last star has stopped shining and the entire universe is in total darkness, the universe will still be expanding.

According to the "steady-state" or "continuous creation" theory of cosmology, galaxies recede from one another, but their spatial density remains constant. According to this theory, there is a continuous creation of new matter (hydrogen atoms) throughout space. The newly created matter subsequently condenses to form new stars and galaxies between the older galaxies, and a steady state or constant spatial density with time is maintained. In the steady-state concept, the universe had no beginning and has no end.

However, we can determine an upper limit for the age of the universe, since its rate of expansion has been continually slowing up. This is considered evidence of the primordial explosion postulated as first putting the universe in motion. Based on the present rate of the expansion, it appears that the age of the universe is between about 10 and 20 billion years.

The big-bang theory predicts that the radiation originally created in the big bang should by now have cooled to a very low temperature. It should in fact be observed as black-body radiation characteristic of a temperature of about 3 kelvin ($-270°C$), i.e., as very high frequency radio waves (microwaves) of very low intensity. In 1965, A. A. Penzias and R. W. Wilson of the Bell Telephone Laboratories in New Jersey, made an accidental discovery of major cosmological importance. They detected a background microwave emission of uniform intensity coming from all parts of the sky that corresponded to a temperature of about 3 kelvin. This is believed to be the relic radiation from the original big bang of the universe. Molecules found in interstellar space can be used as a cosmic thermometer: spectral measurements of CN absorption confirm the existence of the 3-kelvin universal background radiation.

Further evidence for the big bang comes from studies on the abundance of helium in the universe. Most of the helium in the universe is thought to have formed within minutes of the big bang. The amount predicted by theory is very close to what has been observed: helium forms about 25% (by mass) of the matter in the universe, hydrogen about 73%, with oxygen, carbon and other elements making up the balance.

According to the big-bang theory, the number of galaxies per volume of space should have been much greater in the early stages of the universe's evolution than it is today. The steady-state model holds that the number of galaxies per volume of space should be statistically the same everywhere at all times. Martin Ryle, the British Astronomer Royal, has presented very substantial radio astronomical evidence against the steady-state theory, based on counts of the numbers of radio galaxies that are very distant in space (looking farther out into space is really like looking back into time).

At present it appears that the balance of the observational evidence is against the steady-state concept and in favor of the big-bang theory.

STARS AND GALAXIES

Stars are the basic elements in the universe. More than 90 percent of the mass of our own galaxy—the Milky Way—is in the form of stars; the rest of the matter is interstellar hydrogen gas and dust that form stars. The mass of the Sun—the star of our solar system—is 2×10^{30} kg. The range of masses observed for most stars varies from 0.05 of the Sun's mass to 60 times the Sun's mass. The range of luminosity or absolute magnitude (brightness) varies from a tiny fraction of the Sun's luminosity for white dwarf stars to over a million times the Sun's luminosity for the most luminous stars. The range of stellar radii varies from 1/70,000 of the Sun's radius for neutron stars to over 1,000 times the Sun's radius for supergiants. The Sun's density is about 1.4

grams/cm^3 (a little heavier than water). White dwarfs may be over 1 million times as dense as the Sun and neutron stars even more dense; supergiants can be only one-millionth as dense as the Sun.

Multiple star systems consist of more than two stars linked by gravitational forces. Galactic or open clusters are loosely bound stellar systems with up to a few hundred stars. Globular or closed clusters are tightly bound spherical star clusters with maybe over a million stars. Galaxies are the largest stellar systems and are regarded as the basic mass elements of the universe. Galaxies, which occur in clusters, contain from a billion to a thousand billion stars each. It has been estimated that there are at least 10 billion galaxies in the universe. From observations, it appears that there are three distinct types. In spiral galaxies, spiral arms of gas and dust are distinctly visible. In elliptical galaxies, there are no visible spiral arms or gas, and the exterior shape is either elliptical or spherical. Irregular galaxies have no definite shape.

In 1944 Walter Baade reported that stars in the nucleus of spiral galaxies are different from the stars in the arms of the galaxy. Stars within the spiral arms are called Population I stars and are young and bluish in color. Population II stars are found in the galactic nucleus and galactic halo and are old and reddish in color.

Red giants are cool red stars that have undergone expansion; their luminosity may be well over 1,000 times the Sun's luminosity, and their radius several hundred times the Sun's radius. The red giant has already converted about 50 percent of its hydrogen into helium by thermonuclear processes. As this energy source becomes exhausted, expansion halts and contraction to a white dwarf may occur. White dwarfs have low luminosity, relatively high surface temperature and extremely high density. They are dying stars and are gradually cooling to become "black dwarfs" or nonluminous chunks of mass. The Sun will become a white dwarf in billions of years time.

The process by which a star dies depends on its mass. When its energy is exhausted, a star with a mass below 1.4 times the Sun's mass will become a white dwarf. One with a mass between 1.4 and about 3 times the Sun's mass will contract through the white-dwarf stage and become a tiny immensely dense neutron star. Supernovae are stars that suddenly increase their luminosity by more than 10 million times. The supernova luminosity increase reflects the fact that the star is exploding—literally blowing itself up. It is believed that the remnant of at least one supernova (the Crab Nebula) is a neutron star, which forms the pulsating radio source or "pulsar" observed in that region of the sky.

QUASARS

Quasars ("quasi-stellar radio sources") were first discovered in 1961 as starlike objects emitting extremely intense radio radiation. In 1963 optical astronomers identified these objects with faint sources of light. Since then hundreds of quasars have been found, all well beyond our galaxy. Over 99% are undetectable radio sources and are sometimes referred to as QSOs ("quasistellar objects"). It is still a most challenging problem to understand the physical process that leads to the tremendous radio emission in some quasars and the lack of it in others. The discovery that most quasars emit intense infrared radiation and X-rays must also now be explained.

In 1963, Maarten Schmidt, of the California Institute of Technology, discovered one of the main characteristics of quasars: a large red shift in the location of the emission lines in their spectra. It is generally accepted that these large red shifts are caused by the cosmological expansion of the universe. The red shift is used to determine the distance of receding extragalactic objects. The measured red shift of quasars would place them at a few billion light years—in fact, the most distant objects in the universe.

This interpretation also implies that to be detectable on Earth quasars must emit a thousand times more energy than entire galaxies, each containing about 100 billion stars. The radiative emission from quasars in the visible and in the short radio-wavelength region varies with time. The time scale and amplitude of these brightness variations place a limit on the geometrical size of the emitting object. Thus, the center of activity in a quasar is in the order of a few light months or less in diameter, compared to 100,000 light years for a galaxy. Detailed studies have been made of the complex emission lines and absorption lines that occur in the spectra of quasars. These studies indicate that the compact active region lies at the center of a group of dense, rapidly moving clouds of gas, which are enveloped in low density gas.

Despite the theories advanced, the actual origin of the tremendous energy output of quasars remains unknown. One theory is that the energy is generated in a compact cluster of stars by supernova explosions, numerous collisions between the closely packed stars, and by pulsars. In another theory the active center contains a supermassive black hole of a billion solar masses; the energy is released when gas and stars are drawn into the black hole.

Of late, there has been a growing awareness that quasars show similarities to Seyfert galaxies, which are a galaxy class characterized by the small size and high luminosity of their nuclei. Their outer parts, however, are inconspicuous. Since quasars appear photographically similar and have similar emission spectra to Seyfert galaxies, it appears that these two celestial phenomena may somehow be related.

PULSARS

In 1967 a new class of astronomical object was discovered by a Cambridge University group: a rapidly pulsating radio source, or "pulsar." The radio signals from this object, located in the constellation Vulpecula, were periodic in nature, consisting of brief radio pulses that were separated by about 1.3 seconds. Since then, more than 300 pulsars have been discovered.

The most interesting property of pulsars is the extreme regularity of their radio-emission period, which ranges from 0.033 to over 4 seconds. It was believed that this time period between radio pulses was remarkably constant, varying by not more than a few parts per million annually; however, recently it has been found that the periods of most pulsars are lengthening very slightly due to the transfer of internal rotational energy to the surroundings. Two of these pulsars have been identified with the remnants of exploding stars, the Crab Nebula and one in the constellation of Vela. These two pulsars have the shortest periods of any known—0.033 and 0.089 second, respectively—but their periods are increasing more rapidly than those of any other pulsars. A pulsar's radio pulses are of very short duration compared to the time periods between those pulses, which typically are some thousandths of a second.

Optical astronomers have gone to considerable lengths to determine if pulsars emit optical pulses as well as radio pulses. At the present time, only the Crab Nebula pulsar and the very faint Vela pulsar have been observed to emit periodic pulses of light. The former also emits X-rays, ultraviolet, and infrared radiation.

A pulsar is assumed to be a rapidly rotating neutron star, which is a very dense star with an intense magnetic field. The gravitational collapse of a massive dying star causes it to implode as a supernova and vast quantities of energy are given off. Any remaining core could be a pulsar, with a mass between 1.4 and about 3 times the Sun's mass but a diameter of only about 10 miles (the Sun's diameter is 865,000 miles). This kind of star rotates so rapidly that it can complete one rotation on its axis in less than a thousandth of a second.

STELLAR AND GALACTIC TERMS

Absolute Magnitude—Apparent magnitude that a star would have at a distance of 10 parsecs.

Albedo—Reflecting power of a nonluminous body.

Apparent Magnitude—A measure of the observed light flux received from a star or other object at Earth.

Astronomical Unit (AU)—The average distance between the Sun and the Earth. It is equal to 92,957,000 miles and is often used as a unit of measurement.

Bands (in spectra)—Emission or absorption lines, usually in the spectra of chemical compounds or radicals, coalesced into broad emission or absorption bands.

Binary Star—System of two stars revolving about a common center of gravity.

Black Body—A hypothetical perfect radiator that absorbs and reemits all radiation incident upon it.

Clouds of Magellan—Two neighboring galaxies visible to the naked eye from southern latitudes.

Cosmic Rays—Atomic nuclei (mostly protons) that are observed to strike the Earth's atmosphere with exceedingly high energies, probably from supernovae.

Cosmological Red Shift—Red shift of spectral lines in celestial objects arising from the expansion of the universe which, when interpreted with a cosmological model, indicates the distance of those objects.

Cosmology—The study of the organization and evolution of the universe.

Dark Nebula—A cloud of interstellar dust that obscures the light of more distant stars and appears as an opaque curtain.

Diffuse Nebula—A reflection or emission nebula produced by interstellar matter (not a planetary nebula).

Emission Nebula—A gaseous nebula that derives its visible light from the fluorescence of ultraviolet light from a star in or near the nebula.

Extragalactic—Beyond the galaxy.

Gamma Rays—Photons (of electromagnetic radiation) of energy higher than that of X rays—the most energetic form of electromagnetic radiation.

Gravitational Force—Force of attraction between two bodies, directly proportional to product of their masses, inversely proportional to square of distance between them.

"Heavy" Elements—In astronomy, usually those elements of greater atomic number than helium.

Hertzsprung-Russell Diagram—A basic classification of the properties of stars in which luminosity is related to effective surface temperature or star color.

Infrared Radiation—Electromagnetic radiation of wavelength longer than the longest visible (red) wavelengths but shorter than radio wavelengths.

Interstellar Dust—Microscopic solid grains, believed to be mostly dielectric compounds of hydrogen and other common elements, in interstellar space.

Interstellar Gas—Sparse gas in interstellar space.

Kelvin Temperature Scale—An absolute temperature scale, the zero point of which is −273.15° C; temperature in kelvin = temperature in °C − 273.15.

Law of the Red Shifts—The relation between the radial velocity and distance of a remote galaxy: the radial velocity is proportional to the galaxy distance.

Light-year—The distance light travels in a vacuum in one year; 1 LY = 9.46×10^{12} km, or about 6×10^{12} mi.

Luminosity—The rate of radiation of electromagnetic energy into space by a star or other object.

Magnitude—A measure of the amount of light flux received from a star or other luminous object.

Nebula—Cloud of interstellar gas or dust.

Neutron Stars—A near-final stage in stellar evolution at which nuclear energy sources are exhausted, central densities are nuclear densities, and the stars are supported by degenerate neutron pressure. Rotating neutron stars are of current interest as pulsar models.

Nova—Suddenly exploding or erupting star gradually fading to original brightness.

Nuclear Transformation—Transformation of one atomic nucleus into another.

Occultation—An eclipse of a star or planet by the moon or some other celestial body, as seen from Earth.

Parsec—The distance of an object that would have a stellar parallax of one second of arc; 1 parsec = 3.26 light-years.

Planetary Nebula—A shell of gas ejected from, and enlarging about, a certain kind of extremely hot star.

Population I and II—Two classes of stars (and star systems) classified according to their spectral characteristics, chemical compositions, radial velocities, ages, and galaxy locations.

Proton-Proton Reaction—A chain of thermonuclear reactions by which hydrogen nuclei are built up into nuclei of helium, so producing huge amounts of energy.

Radio Waves—The lowest-energy electromagnetic radiation, lying beyond the infrared region of the spectrum. Narrow bands that can pass through the Earth's atmosphere are used in radio astronomy.

Recurrent Nova—A nova that has been known to erupt more than once.

Red Shift, Redshift—A shift to longer wavelengths of the light from a celestial body; produced by Doppler shift due to body's recession from Earth.

Seyfert Galaxies—Galaxies having very bright nuclei and inconspicuous spiral arms. Their spectra show strong emission lines.

Solar Wind—Flow of high-energy particles (mainly protons and electrons) from the Sun.

Spectral Class (or Type)—A classification of a star according to the characteristics of its spectrum.

Spectrograph—An instrument for photographing a spectrum; usually attached to a telescope to photograph the spectrum of a star.

Spectroscope—An instrument for directly viewing the spectrum of a light source.

Spectrum—The array of colors or wavelengths obtained when light from a source is dispersed, as in passing it through a prism or grating.

Stellar Evolution—The changes that take place in the sizes, luminosities, structures, and the like of stars as they age.

Supergiants—Very bright stars that have undergone considerable expansion.

Ultraviolet Radiation—Electromagnetic radiation of wavelengths shorter than the shortest visible (violet) wavelengths and in the approximate range 10 to 300 nanometers.

X rays—Electromagnetic radiation lying between gamma rays and ultraviolet radiation in energy: totally absorbed by Earth's atmosphere.

THE TWENTY BRIGHTEST STARS*

The 20 brightest stars—stars with smallest apparent magnitude—contain one triple-star system and nine binary systems. The table gives the stars, their distance in parsecs, and the apparent and absolute magnitude of the stars and their components.

Star	Distance (Parsecs)	APPARENT VISUAL MAGNITUDES OF COMPONENTS			ABSOLUTE VISUAL MAGNITUDES OF COMPONENTS		
		1st	2d	3d	1st	2d	3d
Sirius	2.7	−1.47	+ 8.5	—	+1.4	+11.4	—
Canopus	34	−0.73	—	—	−3.3	—	—
Arcturus	11	−0.06	—	—	−0.3	—	—
α Centauri	1.3	−0.00	+ 1.4	+10.7	+4.4	+ 5.8	+15
Vega	8.0	+0.04	—	—	+0.6	—	—
Rigel	261	+0.08	+ 6.6	—	−7.0	− 0.4	—
Capella	14	+0.09	+ 0.5	—	+0.1	+ 0.4	—
Procyon	3.4	+0.34	+10.8	—	+2.6	+13.0	—
Betelgeuse	199	+0.41v	—	—	−5.5	—	—
Achernar	23	+0.47	—	—	−1.6	—	—
β Centauri	101	+0.59	+ 4	—	−4.4	− 0.8	—
Altair	4.9	+0.77	—	—	+1.9	—	—
α Crucis	86	+0.79	+ 1.9	—	−3.9	− 3.5	—
Aldebaran	20	+0.86	+13	—	−0.3	+12	—
Spica	80	+0.96	—	—	−3.5	—	—
Antares	132	+1.08	+ 5.1	—	−4.5	− 0.3	—
Pollux	11	+1.15	—	—	+0.2	—	—
Fomalhaut	7.0	+1.16	+ 6.5	—	+1.7	+ 7.3	—
β Crucis	175	+1.24v	—	—	−5.0	—	—
Deneb	460	+1.26	—	—	−7.0	—	—

* For information about the Sun, see page 321. v = variable magnitude.

THE NEAREST STARS*

The following list gives the star, its distance in parsecs (a parsec is equal to 3.26 light-years), and the apparent and absolute magnitudes of the star and its components. The apparent magnitude is the brightness of the star as observed from Earth, while the absolute magnitude is the brightness that the star

would have at a distance of 10 parsecs. The larger the magnitude, the fainter the star. A first-magnitude star appears roughly 2.5 times as bright as a second-magnitude star. A zero magnitude star is 2.5 times as bright as a first-magnitude star, and a —1 star is 2.5 times as bright as a zero-magnitude star.

Star	Distance (Parsecs)	APPARENT VISUAL MAGNITUDES OF COMPONENTS			ABSOLUTE VISUAL MAGNITUDES OF COMPONENTS		
		1st	2d	3d	1st	2d	3d
Proxima	1.31	10.7	—		15.1	—	—
α Centauri	1.31	0.00	+ 1.4	+10.7	+ 4.4	+ 5.8	+15
Barnard's Star	1.80	+ 9.54	—	—	+13.2	—	—
Wolf 359	2.33	+13.5	—	—	+16.7	—	—
Lalande 21185	2.48	+ 7.48	—	—	+10.5	—	—
Sirius	2.67	— 1.47	+ 8.5	—	+ 1.4	+11.4	—
Luyten 726–8	2.73	+12.5	+12.9	—	+15.4	+15.8	—
Ross 154	2.91	+10.6	—	—	+13.3	—	—
Ross 248	3.16	+12.24	—	—	+14.7	—	—
ε Eridani	3.28	+ 3.68	—	—	+ 6.1	—	—
Ross 128	3.31	+11.13	—	—	+13.5	—	—
Luyten 789–6	3.31	+12.28	—	—	+14.6	—	—
Procyon	3.37	+ 0.34	+10.7	—	+ 2.6	+13.0	—
61 Cygni	3.43	+ 5.19	+ 6.02	—	+ 7.5	+ 8.4	—
ε Indi	3.43	+ 4.71	—	—	+ 7.0	—	—
Σ 2398	3.53	+ 8.90	+ 9.69	—	+11.1	+11.9	—
BD+43°44	3.56	+ 8.07	+11.04	—	+10.3	+13.2	—
Lac 9352	3.59	+ 7.43	—	—	+ 9.6	—	—
τ Ceti	3.65	+ 3.49	—	—	+ 5.7	—	—
BD+5°1668	3.77	+10.9	—	—	+13.0	—	—
Lac 8760	3.83	+ 6.76	—	—	+ 8.8	—	—
Kapteyn's Star	3.90	+ 8.81	—	—	+10.8	—	—
Kruger 60	3.93	+ 9.85	+11.3	—	+11.9	+13.3	—
Ross 614	4.03	+11.13	+14.8	—	+13.1	+16.8	—
BD—12°4523	4.10	+10.13	—	—	+12.0	—	—
v. Maanen's Star	4.24	+12.36	—	—	+14.3	—	—

* For information about the Sun, see page 321.

THE CONSTELLATIONS

Constellations are areas of the sky with configurations of stars supposedly resembling a particular object, person, or animal. The bright stars within a given constellation are named with a Greek letter plus the genitive of the constellation, with the

brightest star getting the first Greek letter, alpha; the second brightest getting the second Greek letter, beta; and the like. The following table gives the constellation, its genitive, its English name or description, and the abbreviation for it.

Constellation	Genitive	English name or description	Abbreviation
Andromeda	Andromedae	Chained Maiden	And
Antlia	Antliae	Air pump	Ant
Apus	Apodis	Bird of Paradise	Aps
Aquarius	Aquarii	Water bearer	Aqr
Aquila	Aquilae	Eagle	Aql
Ara	Arae	Altar	Ara
Aries	Arietis	Ram	Ari
Auriga	Aurigae	Charioteer	Aur
Boötes	Boötis	Herdsman	Boo
Caelum	Caeli	Chisel	Cae
Camelo-pardalis	Camelopar-dalis	Giraffe	Cam
Cancer	Cancri	Crab	Cnc
Canes Venatici	Canum Venaticorum	Hunting dogs	CVn
Canis Major	Canis Majoris	Great dog	CMa
Canis Minor	Canis Minoris	Little dog	CMi
Capricornus	Capricorni	Sea goat	Cap
•Carina	Carinae	Keel of Argonauts' ship	Car
Cassiopeia	Cassiopeiae	Queen of Ethiopia	Cas
Centaurus	Centauri	Centaur	Cen
Cepheus	Cephei	King of Ethiopia	Cep
Cetus	Ceti	Whale	Cet
Chamaeleon	Chamae-leontis	Chameleon	Cha
Circinus	Circini	Compasses	Cir
Columba	Columbae	Dove	Col
Coma Berenices	Comae Berenices	Berenice's hair	Com
Corona Australis	Coronae Australis	Southern crown	CrA
Corona Borealis	Coronae Borealis	Northern crown	CrB
Corvus	Corvi	Crow	Crv
Crater	Crateris	Cup	Crt
Crux	Crucis	Cross (southern)	Cru
Cygnus	Cygni	Swan	Cyg
Delphinus	Delphini	Dolphin	Del
Dorado	Doradûs	Swordfish	Dor
Draco	Draconis	Dragon	Dra
Equuleus	Equulei	Little horse	Equ
Eridanus	Eridani	River	Eri
Fornax	Fornacis	Furnace	For
Gemini	Geminorum	Twins	Gem
Grus	Gruis	Crane	Gru
Hercules	Herculis	Hercules	Her
Horologium	Horologii	Clock	Hor
Hydra	Hydrae	Sea serpent	Hya
Hydrus	Hydri	Water snake	Hyi
Indus	Indi	Indian	Ind
Lacerta	Lacertae	Lizard	Lac
Leo	Leonis	Lion	Leo
Leo Minor	Leonis Minoris	Little lion	LMi
Lepus	Leporis	Hare	Lep
Libra	Librae	Balance	Lib
Lupus	Lupi	Wolf	Lup
Lynx	Lyncis	Lynx	Lyn
Lyra	Lyrae	Lyre	Lyr
Mensa	Mensae	Table Mountain	Men
Micro-scopium	Microscopii	Microscope	Mic
Monoceros	Monocerotis	Unicorn	Mon
Musca	Muscae	Fly	Mus
Norma	Normae	Rule	Nor
Octans	Octantis	Octant	Oct
Ophiuchus	Ophiuchi	Serpent bearer	Oph
Orion	Orionis	Orion, the hunter	Ori
Pavo	Pavonis	Peacock	Pav
Pegasus	Pegasi	Pegasus, the winged horse	Peg
Perseus	Persei	Perseus, hero who saved Andromeda	Per
Phoenix	Phoenicis	Phoenix	Phe
Pictor	Pictoris	Easel	Pic

Constellation	Genitive	English name or description	Abbreviation	Constellation	Genitive	English name or description	Abbreviation
Pisces	Piscium	Fishes	Psc	Sextans	Sextantis	Sextant	Sex
Piscis Austrinus	Piscis Austrini	Southern fish	PsA	Taurus	Tauri	Bull	Tau
				Telescopium	Telescopii	Telescope	Tel
*Puppis	Puppis	Stern of the Argonauts' ship	Pup	Triangulum	Trianguli	Triangle	Tri
*Pyxis	Pyxidis	Compass on the Argonauts' ship	Pyx	Triangulum Australe	Trianguli Australis	Southern triangle	TrA
Reticulum	Reticuli	Net	Ret	Tucana	Tucanae	Toucan	Tuc
Sagitta	Sagittae	Arrow	Sge	Ursa Major	Ursae Majoris	Great bear	UMa
Sagittarius	Sagittarii	Archer	Sgr	Ursa Minor	Ursae Minoris	Little bear	UMi
Scorpius	Scorpii	Scorpion	Sco	*Vela	Velorum	Sails of the Argonauts' ship	Vel
Sculptor	Sculptoris	Sculptor's tools	Scl	Virgo	Virginis	Virgin	Vir
Scutum	Scuti	Shield	Sct	Volans	Volantis	Flying fish	Vol
Serpens	Serpentis	Serpent	Ser	Vulpecula	Vulpeculae	Fox	Vul

* The four constellations Carina, Puppis, Pyxis, and Vela originally formed the single constellation Argo Navis.

SUPERNOVAE, "BLACK HOLES" AND THE GUM NEBULA

Astronomers have recently added two new objects to the growing list of strange and puzzling objects speculated about or found in the universe. A "black hole" is the hypothetical result of a runaway or uncontrolled gravitational collapse of a star or collection of stars. Eventually, if its contraction is not halted, a collapsing object will reach a limiting size, called the Schwarzschild radius, which depends upon the mass of the object. For the Sun the Schwarzschild radius would be under two miles. As the object continues to contract to less than its Schwarzschild radius it becomes a black hole. The gravitational forces exerted by this object are so strong that no matter or radiation can escape from it. The light emanating from this object is trapped and effectively removed from the "observable universe."

A supernova occurs when a star has evolved to such an unstable state that it blows itself up. The energy released in the holocaust is almost beyond comprehension. The material ejected with immense force from the exploding star forms a huge shell of gas which sweeps up interstellar gas as it expands. This is known as a supernova remnant. What remains of the star is possibly its dense central core. Astrophysicists have speculated that the core of a supernova can become either a neutron star or a black hole. The final mass of the remnant star determines whether gravitational collapse will stop at the stable neutron star

stage, instead of running away and becoming a black hole. It is believed that if the star's mass is greater than about 3.0 times the Sun's mass a black hole should readily form. (Neutron stars should form for stars whose mass is above 1.4 times the Sun's mass.) A black hole almost certainly exists in the binary star Cygnus X-1 and maybe in other X-ray binaries. There is also possible evidence of massive black holes at the centers of certain galaxies, notably M87, that would tear apart and swallow stars in the immediate surroundings.

Nebulae are extended bright luminosities in the sky. Some nebulae are the glowing remnants of supernovae. Other nebulae are clouds of ionized hydrogen surrounding hot stars, which cause them to glow continuously. Such objects surrounding hot stars are called Stromgren spheres. The Gum Nebula (discovered by the Australian astronomer, Colin S. Gum, in 1952) combines certain characteristics of the other two types of nebulae. It is about 2,600 light-years across in its longest dimension and appears to be somewhat elliptical in shape. A group of astronomers from NASA and Kitt Peak National Observatory proposes that the Gum Nebula is a fossil Stromgren sphere produced by a supernova that exploded 11,000 years ago, giving off a tremendous blast of ultraviolet radiation, which ionized interstellar hydrogen clouds for hundreds of light years around. What is now glowing is not the material that was originally ejected from the supernova, but the interstellar hydrogen gas that was there before the supernova explosion. Unlike Stromgren spheres that are continuously being ionized by hot stars, the fossil Gum Nebula is gradually decaying, as the ionized hydrogen gas recombines in the absence of a new ionizing source.

INTERSTELLAR MOLECULES

Within the last 25 years astronomers have found that there is a continuous exchange of material between stars and the interstellar medium. Stars are continually being formed from interstellar hydrogen and other gas, mixed with dust: diffuse interstellar material somehow collects into cool dense clouds which may eventually contract under gravitational forces forming stars and, possibly, planetary systems. As stars evolve, material is ejected from them to again become part of the interstellar medium.

The first interstellar molecules ever found—CH, CH+, and CN (cyanogen)—were diatomic (consisting of only two atoms) and were found more than 40 years ago by optical astronomers.

In March 1951 radio astronomers detected interstellar atomic hydrogen (H) and in 1963 they discovered the hydroxyl radical (OH) in the interstellar medium. Up to this time no one had ever detected a polyatomic molecule (consisting of three or more atoms). The formation of molecules more complex than diatomic molecules in interstellar space was believed to be rare, since interstellar densities and temperatures are so low that molecule formation is very difficult.

This idea was upset in 1968 when radio astronomers detected interstellar ammonia (NH_3). In early 1969 radio astronomers detected interstellar water vapor (H_2O). In March 1969 interstellar formaldehyde (H_2CO)—the first polyatomic organic molecule—was discovered by radio

astronomers. On March 13, 1970, a Naval Research Laboratory Aerobee rocket detected molecular hydrogen (H_2) in interstellar space.

Interstellar atomic hydrogen (H) has been observed by radio astronomers since 1951, but molecular hydrogen had previously eluded detection. In 1970 radio astronomers also found interstellar carbon monoxide (CO), hydrogen cyanide (HCN), cyanoacetylene (HC_3N), formic acid (HCOOH), and methanol or wood alcohol (CH_3OH). Another molecule, originally called "X-ogen" has since been identified as HCO+. At present over 50 interstellar molecules have been detected, including deuterium (heavy hydrogen), hydrogen sulfide (H_2S), acetaldehyde (CH_3CHO), and silicon monoxide (SiO). Large numbers are found in massive dense interstellar clouds, known as "giant molecular complexes", associated with dense clumps of dust.

Additional evidence for the existence of extraterrestrial organic molecules was given in December 1970, when it was announced that a meteorite that fell near Murchison, Victoria, Australia, on September 28, 1969, is believed to contain five of the 20 most common amino acids—glycine, alanine, glutamic acid, valine, and proline. This finding demonstrates that complex amino acids, the basic building blocks of proteins, can be and have been formed outside the Earth by natural chemical processes.

Hence, in recent years, astronomers have found that the interstellar medium is interspersed with molecules, a proportionately high fraction of which are organic compounds. As star and planet formation take place, these organic compounds may play an important role in the chemical evolution and origin of life.

OUR LOCAL GROUP OF GALAXIES

Our local group of galaxies contains over 30 members that cover a region about 3 million light-years in diameter. The largest members are both spiral galaxies—our Milky Way galaxy and the Andromeda galaxy (M31). All together, there are three spirals, four irregulars, 11 ellipticals, and many dwarf irregulars and dwarf ellipticals. Some of our local galaxies are listed below, with apparent magnitude, distance in thousand parsecs (kiloparsecs), distance in thousand parsecs (kilopcs), galactic diameter in kiloparsecs, and absolute magnitude.

Galaxy	Visual magnitude	Distance (kilopcs)	Diameter (kilopcs)	Absolute magnitude
The Milky Way	—	—	30	(−21)
Large Magellanic Cloud	0.9	48	10	−17.7
Small Magellanic Cloud	2.5	56	8	−16.5
Ursa Minor system	—	70	1	(−9)
Sculptor system	8.0	83	2.2	−11.8
Draco system	—	100	1.4	(−10)
Fornax system	8.3	190	6.6	−13.3
Leo II system	12.04	230	1.6	−10.0
Leo I system	12.0	280	1.5	−10.4

Galaxy	Visual magnitude	Distance (kilopcs)	Diameter (kilopcs)	Absolute magnitude
NGC 6822	8.9	460	2.7	−14.8
NGC 147	9.73	570	3	−14.5
NGC 185	9.43	570	2.3	−14.8
NGC 205	8.17	680	5	−16.5
NGC 221 (M32)	8.16	680	2.4	−16.5
IC 1613	9.61	680	5	−14.7
Andromeda galaxy	3.47	680	40	−21.2
NGC 598 (M33)	5.79	720	17	−18.9
Maffei 1	11.0	1000	—	−19.0

ASTRONOMICAL INSTRUMENTATION

The most important property of a telescope is its ability to gather light so that objects that are too remote or too faint to be seen with the naked eye are detectable. The light-gathering power of a telescope varies according to the total surface area of either the objective lens or the mirror in the telescope.

There are two main classes of telescopes that gather visible light: reflectors and refractors. In a reflector, a large curved mirror gathers the light; in a refractor, a large objective lens accomplishes this feat. The largest reflecting telescope now in operation has a 236″ mirror; the largest refracting telescope has a 40″ objective lens. The Schmidt camera is an optical system that utilizes both a mirror and a lens; it produces excellent star images over a large area of the sky and is in widespread use around the world.

In 1931, K. G. Jansky encountered interference in the form of radio radiation coming from an unknown source, which subsequent investigation showed was the Milky Way. In 1936, Grote Reber built the first antenna that was specifically designed to receive these cosmic radio waves. In 1942, radio radiation was first received from the Sun. After World War II, the technique of making radio astronomical observations was rapidly developed, especially in Australia, England, the Netherlands, and more recently in the United States. The 328-foot radio telescope at Bonn, West Germany is the world's largest fully steerable radio telescope.

In a radio telescope, the radiowave gathering is done by a parabolic metallic reflector, called a "dish," which focuses waves onto an antenna, or by a dipole antenna. Sensitivity is increased by using an array of such antennas.

Radio signals have been observed to come from the Sun, the Moon, certain planets, from the center of our galaxy, and from other galaxies. In addition, strong radio signals are given off by quasars while rapidly pulsating radio signals are received from pulsars. Radio signals can be used to determine both the surface and lower-atmosphere temperatures of the planets.

Other types of radio emission offer insight into the physical processes within the upper atmosphere of the planets and the Sun, as well as certain physical processes within galaxies. Signals at certain discrete radio wavelengths are caused by the presence of certain interstellar molecules. The amount and distribution of these molecules in space are determinable by using radio telescopes.

Radar astronomy systems consist of a powerful radio transmitter, capable of transmitting high-power radio signals out into space over long distances, and a sensitive antenna, with which the return radar echo is detectable. This returning radar echo can provide information about lunar and planetary surfaces, planetary atmospheres and rotation periods, and the precise values of the distances of different solar system objects. X-ray astronomy gains data from satellites and from rocket and balloon flights, X-rays being absorbed by the atmosphere. Since 1962 over 3,000 X-ray sources have been detected inside and outside our Galaxy and include supernova remnants, quasars, binary systems, and possible black holes.

Only a few bands of infrared wavelengths from space can penetrate the atmosphere. Special detectors of this radiation, on the ground and in rockets, have shown that huge quantities of infrared rays are emitted from dying stars and from stars being born.

MAJOR ASTRONOMICAL FACILITIES

This list includes the world's major astronomical observing facilities: reflecting and refracting optical telescopes, radio telescopes, and radar astronomy systems. UC = Under construction.

REFLECTING OPTICAL AND INFRARED (IR) TELESCOPES AND SCHMIDT CAMERAS

Mirror Diameter (Inches)	Observatory	In Operation Since
236	Special Astrophysical Observatory, Mount Pastukhov, USSR	1976
200	Palomar Observatory, Mount Palomar, California	1948
176*	Smithsonian Astrophysical Observatory, Mount Hopkins, Arizona	1979
165	Roque de los Muchachos Observatory, La Palma, Canaries	UC
158	Kitt Peak National Observatory, Tucson, Arizona	1974
158	Cerro Tololo Observatory, La Serena, Chile	1976
153	Siding Spring Observatory, Siding Spring, NSW, Australia	1975
153	(IR) Unit of Royal Obs., Edinburgh, Mauna Kea, Hawaii	1979
142	Canada-France-Hawaii Telescope, Mauna Kea, Hawaii	1979
142	European Southern Observatory, La Silla, Chile	1976
138	National Astronomical Observatory, Calar Alto, Spain	UC

Mirror Diameter (Inches)	Observatory	In Operation Since
126	(IR) Mauna Kea Observatory, Mauna Kea, Hawaii	1979
120	Lick Observatory, Mount Hamilton, California	1959
107	McDonald Observatory, Fort Davis, Texas	1968
102	Crimean Astrophysical Observatory, Nauchnyy, Ukrainian SSR	1960
100	Las Campanas Observatory, La Serena, Chile	1977
100	Hale Observatory, Mount Wilson, California	1917
98	Roque de los Muchachos Observatory, Canaries; originally at Royal Greenwich Observatory, England	1967
95	Space Telescope for Earth orbit, NASA/ESA	UC
90	Steward Observatory, University of Arizona, Tucson, Arizona	1969
88	Mauna Kea Observatory, University of Hawaii, Mauna Kea, Hawaii	1970
84	Kitt Peak National Observatory, Tucson, Arizona	1961

* Light-gathering power of the six 72″ mirrors in the Multiple Mirror Telescope.

Mirror Diameter (Inches)	Observatory	In Operation Since
83	McDonald Observatory, ... Fort Davis, Texas	1938
83	National Astronomical Observatory, ... Nat. Univ. of Mexico, Baja California	1977
79	(53″ Schmidt) Karl Schwarzschild Obs., . Tautenburg, East Germany	1960
77	Observatoire de Haute-Provence, ... Saint Michel, France	1958
74	David Dunlap Observatory, ... Richmond Hill, Ontario, Canada	1935
74	South African Astronomical Observatory, Sutherland, South Africa	1948
74	Mount Stromlo Observatory, ... Canberra, Australia	1955
74	Kottamia Observatory, c/o .... Helwan Observatory, Helwan, Egypt	1960
74	Okayama Astrophysical Observatory, ... Kamogata-Cho, Japan	1960
72	Dominion Astrophysical Observatory, ... Victoria, British Columbia	1918
72	Astrophysical Observatory, University ... of Padua, Asiago, Italy	1973
72	(48″ Schmidt) Palomar Observatory, ... Mount Palomar, California	1948
72	(48″ Schmidt) Unit of Royal Obs., ... Edinburgh, Siding Spring Obs., New South Wales	1973
72	Lowell Observatory, ... Flagstaff, Arizona	1965
64	(39″ Schmidt) European Southern Obs., . La Silla, Chile	1972
61	Agassiz Station, ... Harvard College Observatory, Cambridge, Massachusetts	1934
61	Cordoba Astronomical Observatory, ... Bosque Alegre Station, Argentina	1942
61	U.S. Naval Observatory, ... Flagstaff, Arizona	1963
61	Lunar and Planetary Laboratory, ... Tucson, Arizona	1965
60	Hale Observatory, ... Mount Wilson, California	1908
60	Boyden Observatory, ... Bloemfontein, South Africa	1930
60	Steward Observatory, ... Tucson, Arizona	1964
60	Lunar and Planetary Laboratory, ... Tucson, Arizona	1967
60	Palomar Observatory, ... Mount Palomar, California	1970
60	Cerro Tololo Observatory, ... La Serena, Chile	1967
60	(39″ Schmidt) Uppsala University Obs., . Kvistaberg, Sweden	1963
59	(41″ Schmidt) Tokyo Astronomical Obs., . Kiso, Japan	1976

REFRACTING TELESCOPES

Lens Diameter (Inches)	Observatory	In Operation Since
40	Yerkes Observatory, ... Williams Bay, Wisconsin	1897
36	Lick Observatory, ... Mount Hamilton, California	1888
33	Observatory of Physical Astronomy, ... Meudon, France	1893
32	Astrophysical Observatory, ... Potsdam, Germany	1899
30	Nice Observatory, ... Nice, France	1880
30	Allegheny Observatory, ... Pittsburgh, Pennsylvania	1914
28	Old Royal Greenwich Observatory, ... Greenwich, England	1894
26.5 ...	University Observatory, ... Vienna, Austria	1878
26	U.S. Naval Observatory, ... Washington, D.C.	1873
26	Leander-McCormick Observatory, ... Charlottesville, Virginia	1883
26	Royal Greenwich Observatory, ... Herstmonceux, England	1897

RADIO TELESCOPES

Antenna Diameter (Feet)	Observatory	In Operation Since
1000	Arecibo Observatory, ... Arecibo, Puerto Rico	1963
400	University of California, ... Hat Creek, California	1960
360 × 70	Ohio State-Ohio Wesleyan Radio .. Observatory, Delaware, Ohio	1962
328 × 131(2) ..	Lebedev Physics Institute, ... Serpukhov, USSR	1963
328	Max Planck Institute, ... Bonn, West Germany	1971
300	National Radio Astronomy Observatory, ... Green Bank, West Virginia	1962
250	Nuffield Radio Ast. Lab., ... Jodrell Bank, England	1957
210	Australian Nat. Radio Astron. .... Observatory (CSIRO), Parkes New South Wales	1961
210	Jet Propulsion Laboratory, ... Goldstone, California	1968
150	Naval Research Laboratory, ... Sugar Grove, West Virginia	
150	Algonquin Radio Observatory, ... Lake Traverse, Ontario	1967
140	National Radio Astronomy Observatory, ... Green Bank, West Virginia	1964
130	California Institute of Technology, . Owens Valley, California	1968
125 × 85	Nuffield Radio Astronomy Lab., . Jodrell Bank, England	1964
120	Haystack Observatory, ... NE Radio Observatory Corp., Westford, Massachusetts	1963
120	University of Illinois, ... Danville, Illinois	1971
118	Heinrich Hertz Institute, ... Berlin-Adlershof, Germany	1958
90(2)	California Institute of Technology, . Owens Valley, California	1958
88	Stanford Research Institute ..... Chatanika, Alaska	
85	University of Michigan, ... Dexter, Michigan	1959
85(3)	Jet Propulsion Laboratory, ... Goldstone, California	1960
85	Harvard Radio Astronomy Station, . Fort Davis, Texas	1961
85	University of California, ... Hat Creek, California	1962
85(2)	National Radio Astronomy Observatory, ... Green Bank, West Virginia	1964
17 mile array ..	National Radio Astronomy Obs., . Socorro, New Mexico	1980
3.1 mile array ..	Mullard Radio Astronomy Obs., . Cambridge, England	1972
1.9 mile radio-heliograph	Culgoora Solar Radio Obs., ... (CSIRO), Narrabri, New South Wales	1968
1 mile array	Westerbork Radio Observatory,..... Westerbork, Netherlands	1970
1 mile array ...	Mullard Radio Astron. Observatory, Cambridge, England	1964
1 mile array ...	Molonglo Radio Observatory, ... Sydney University, Hoskinstown, New South Wales	1960

RADAR ASTRONOMY SYSTEMS

Antenna Diameter (Feet)	Observatory	Peak Power (Kilowatts)
1000	Arecibo Observatory, ... Arecibo, Puerto Rico	2,500
250	Nuffield Radio Ast. Lab., ... Jodrell Bank, Macclesfield, England	60
120	Haystack Observatory, ... NE Radio Observatory Corp, Westford, Massachusetts	400
85	Jet Propulsion Laboratory, ... Goldstone, California	100
84	Millstone Lincoln Laboratory, ... Massachusetts Institute of Technology, Westford, Massachusetts	5,000

THE SUN, OUR NEAREST STAR

The Sun is of great importance because of its dominant influence on the Earth and the other planets and its role in the beginning and maintenance of life on our planet. But it is also important because the Sun is the only star near enough to be observed in any detail. Astronomers have inferred that physical processes on other stars are similar to those processes observed on the Sun.

This star is directly responsible for many phenomena on our planet, including the origin and survival of life, clouds, atmospheric motion and weather, and the thermal structure and composition of the Earth's atmosphere and the atmospheres of the other planets. Several billion years ago solar ultraviolet radiation supplied the energy needed to synthesize inorganic elements into the first organic molecules that formed the basis for life on Earth.

The average surface temperature of our planet, which must be within certain limits if life is to flourish and evolve, is determined by the amount of visible solar radiation the Earth's surface receives. Visible solar radiation causes water to evaporate from our oceans, and this atmospheric water vapor eventually condenses to form clouds and precipitation. Solar heating is responsible for the large-scale motions of the atmosphere and ocean, as well as small-scale phenomena, such as cumulus cloud formation. Solar X rays and ultraviolet radiation determine the temperature of the upper atmospheres of the planets, as well as the structure of planetary ionospheres.

Solar electrons and protons reaching the vicinity of the Earth, via solar wind or solar flares, are trapped by the Earth's magnetic field, forming the Van Allen radiation belts. Solar-emitted particles that collide with the atoms in our upper atmosphere cause auroral displays.

Solar particles are also responsible for radio and short-wave communication fadeouts, since clouds of these solar particles embedded in the Earth's upper atmosphere interfere with the radio reflection characteristics of the ionosphere. Sudden increases in the emission of solar X rays and energetic particles, during periods of high solar activity, may prove dangerous to astronauts orbiting above the protective blanket of atmosphere that shields life at the Earth's surface from the lethal solar radiation and particle flux.

It is believed that the formation of the Sun, the planets, and other stars began with the condensation of an interstellar gas cloud; this cloud consisted almost completely of pure hydrogen with a very small percentage of heavier elements that were produced during the explosion and ejections of exploding stars (supernovae). In fact, the interstellar medium is constantly being supplied with material rich in heavy elements that have been ejected from supernovae.

As a star contracts out of the interstellar cloud under gravitational forces, the temperature and pressure at the star's center (core) increase until the temperature reaches about 10 million degrees. At this temperature, four hydrogen nuclei in the star's core fuse together to form a single helium nucleus. However, four hydrogen nuclei weigh a little more than one helium nucleus. This small amount of mass has been converted to energy. Every second the Sun converts some 616 million tons of hydrogen into 612 million tons of helium. This thermonuclear reaction provides the tremendous amount of energy that the Sun radiates out in all directions into space in the form of electromagnetic radiation: X rays; ultraviolet, visible, and infrared rays; and radio waves. Every square meter of the Sun's surface emits 64 million watts into space.

Its high temperature causes the Sun to be a gaseous body or, more precisely, a plasma—the fourth state of matter that is attained when electrically neutral atoms break up into positively charged nuclei and negatively charged electrons. The diameter of the Sun is about 864,900 miles—more than 109 times that of the Earth. The Sun's mass is 2×10^{30} kg—or approximately 333,-000 times the mass of the Earth. The mean density of the Sun is 1.4 grams/cm³—only about one-quarter of the Earth's density—suggesting that the Sun primarily consists of very light elements. The period of the Sun's rotation on its axis depends on the solar latitude, being least (25 days) at the equator; its average rotation period is 27 days.

It is difficult to obtain any evidence that is based on direct observation about the core of the Sun. All of our knowledge of the solar core reflects theoretical considerations: it is a region of very high pressure and temperature, and thermonuclear reactions occur there. The solar energy is transported from the core by radiative processes, in which atoms absorb, reemit, and scatter the radiation. Close to the surface the energy is carried by large looping convection currents in the unstable region known as the convective zone. Shock waves from this zone carry energy into the solar atmosphere.

The solar surface (photosphere or "sphere of light") is what we see when looking up at the Sun. By using high-resolution telescopes, the convection currents' tops can actually be observed on the photosphere. The solar surface is not as smooth as had been thought; it is actually covered with a fine cellular structure (granulation), which is caused by the top of the convection cells breaking across the photosphere. Spectacular gaseous eruptions (prominences) from the surface can extend up to an altitude of 500,000 miles in great arching filaments.

Other photospheric features include sunspots and solar flares, which are discussed below. The convective motions are very important, because they appear to be the source of the mechanical energy that is responsible for heating and the observed temperature increase within the solar atmosphere. The immense temperature—2,000,-000°C—of the outer layer of the atmosphere (the corona) has no dependence on the heat flowing from the photosphere.

The solar atmosphere consists of two regions: the chromosphere and the corona. The chromosphere is 6,000 to 9,000 miles thick, and its lower part is simply an extension of the photosphere at about 6,000° C, the density decreasing very considerably. The upper chromosphere has a temperature that approaches 100,000° C.

The corona, which surrounds the chromosphere, is the region that is observed during a total solar eclipse, when the Moon, which has the same angular size in the sky as the Sun, passes directly in front of it, blocking out the photospheric radiation and permitting the fainter light of the corona to be observed.

The solar atmosphere permeates through the interplanetary medium via a constant stream of solar protons and electrons ("solar wind"). The protons and electrons have enough energy by virtue of the high temperature of the solar atmosphere to escape from the Sun's gravitational field. The solar wind streams radially outward from the Sun, and is a regular feature of the Sun. Study of the X-ray emissions from the corona have revealed large low-density regions, known as coronal holes, usually extending as winding structures from the polar regions. They appear to be the source of the high-speed particles of the solar wind.

Complicated magnetic fields occur in the region extending from the convective zone to the corona and beyond. There is much evidence that magnetic fields are of considerable importance on the Sun. Their most spectacular manifestations are related to photospheric solar activity, particularly prominences, sunspots and solar flares. Sunspots are complicated hydromagnetic phenomena displaying very strong magnetic fields; they appear dark against the bright photosphere because their temperatures are several thousand degrees lower.

Associated with sunspots are solar flares, energetic phenomena that produce both electromagnetic radiation and solar particle emission. These flares occur because their material has gained enough energy—via solar magnetic fields—to be ejected from the Sun and shot into space. One of the remarkable features of both sunspots and solar flares is that they increase then decrease in number in an 11-year cycle of solar activity. Also associated with this cycle are increased emissions of solar X rays and centimeter radio waves.

In recent years, it has been shown from studies of the frictional atmospheric drag on orbiting satellites and from direct in situ measurements with instruments on board rockets and satellites that the temperature, composition, and density of the Earth's upper atmosphere is strongly responsive to changes in solar geometry and the level of solar activity. Some of these responses follow diurnal, 27-day (solar rotation period), and 11-year (sunspot cycle) variations.

THE PLANETS

It is thought that about 4.6 billion years ago, the Earth was formed from the same interstellar gas cloud that gave birth to the other planets of the solar system and the Sun. The gas cloud was mostly hydrogen, with heavier elements making up only a small fraction of its composition. As the gas cloud contracted under gravitational forces, the temperature and pressure of the central core increased tremendously until thermonuclear reactions—the conversion of hydrogen into helium with the accompanying release of huge amounts of light and heat energy—began, and a star, the Sun, formed. Dust grains in the now disk-shaped cloud constantly collided and coalesced into ever larger bodies, which in turn consolidated into planets surrounded by gaseous atmospheres.

During the following 4.6 billion years, the planets and their atmospheres have changed and evolved significantly. The following is a brief survey of the planets in our solar system, with the exception of the Earth, which is discussed in the section *Earth: Facts/Figures.*

MERCURY is the second smallest planet in the solar system and the closest to the Sun. This combination provides for a hot and gravitationally "weak" planet that cannot retain a gaseous atmosphere. Mercury rotates within a period of 58.65 days, or exactly two thirds of its period of revolution around the Sun: 88 days.

The U.S. Mariner 10 space probe has relayed to Earth invaluable information and photographs as it flew within 500 miles of Mercury. The surface resembles that of the Moon in being heavily cratered, little eroded, and with smooth areas similar but smaller than the lunar *maria*. The surface material has a low density. Thus the average density, measured accurately by Mariner 10, of 5.5 grams/cc implies a large core of heavy material, possibly iron. The planet could therefore be similar in composition to the Earth. An iron core would mean that Mercury has a magnetic field and in fact a very weak magnetic field was detected by the probe.

No gaseous atmosphere greater than 100-billionths that of the Earth was revealed. Traces of helium were detected but this gas would be rapidly boiled off. Measurements of surface temperature gave a daytime maximum of 350°C (660°F) and a night-time minimum of −170°C (−270°F). Mercury therefore has a greater surface temperature range than any other planet, although its maximum is less than that of Venus.

VENUS, "Earth's twin" in size and mass, is otherwise unlike it. Its surface is hot (about 890°F on dark and light side and from pole to pole), waterless, corrosive and lifeless, with a pressure averaging 90 terrestrial atmospheres (equivalent to an ocean depth of 1/2 mile) and gentle surface winds of 1 to 2 mph. It has no moon, no magnetic field, no auroras and no radiation belts. Only about 2% of incident solar radiation reaches its surface, while 75% is reflected; the rest is absorbed in atmosphere and clouds. A "greenhouse effect" makes the surface abnormally hot. Atmospherically absorbed heat drives convective currents and strong winds aloft, creating wind speeds in excess of 400 mph in the middle of the cloud zone and about 200 mph atop the clouds.

Although no liquid or solid particles exist below about 21 miles, surface visibility is probably less than 1/2 mile (molecular light scattering) and a bright Venusian midday would compare to one heavily overcast on Earth. From 21 to about 31 miles there is smog and haze. The cloud layer lies at 31-41 miles and consists of tiny liquid droplets of sulfuric acid, tinged yellow with tiny grains of sulfur.

US and Soviet Space missions to Venus by Mariner, Pioneer Venus, and Venera craft have greatly increased our knowledge, especially of surface and atmospheric features. Venera probes first descended through the opaque clouds to transmit data from the surface of Venus in 1970. Pictures of a rocky landscape were returned in 1975. Densities compatible with basaltic rock have been measured and a soil analysis is planned for the 1982 Venera mission.

Radar images of an extensive area of the surface have been obtained by Earth-bound radio telescopes but now almost the entire surface has been mapped using a radar altimeter aboard the orbiting Pioneer Venus 1. This has revealed that the surface of Venus is remarkably flat: 60% of its surface lies within 500 m (1640 ft.) above or below the average surface level; the comparable figure for Earth is 25%.

Most of the surface consists of rolling upland plains in which shallow circular features, up to 500 miles across, appear. These are assumed to be impact craters produced in the very distant past. Rising well above the upland plains are two large "continents" and some smaller "islands," with jagged mountain ranges and extensive high plateaus. The highest feature on Venus, Maxwell Montes, lies on the northern continent and towers 36,000 ft above the mean surface level. It is probably a shield volcano. There is other evidence of past volcanism on Venus, although no current activity has been observed. The remainder of the surface is smooth lowland plains, equivalent to Earth's ocean-basin floors but much shallower and less extensive. Several tectonically disturbed regions have been found, including a giant 1400-mile-long rift valley near the equator.

Venus condensed too close to the Sun ever to have possessed much water. The ambient surface temperature of 890°F is too hot for water-bearing minerals such as micas and amphiboles to be stable. Probably there have never been oceans, or sedimentary rocks such as limestone. It is also doubtful that there has ever been life. Water and life have greatly altered Earth's primitive atmosphere, locking up most of its CO_2 in the hydrosphere and carbonate rocks. Were this CO_2 released on Earth our atmosphere would be much like that of Venus in bulk, pressure and composition.

The atmosphere of Venus is about 97% CO_2, 3% N_2, with traces of H_2O, O_2, noble gases, CO, SO_2, and others. In its lesser gases it is inhomogeneous in its upper reaches where photochemical reactions occur, but is homogeneous below about 21 miles, where no liquid or solid particles condense. Both Earth and Venus lost their original hydrogen and helium in the "protoplanet" stage. Were all of the atmospheric water of Venus to condense onto a level, cool surface, its depth would be about 1.5 feet.

Like Earth, Venus has an ionosphere. Unlike Earth's it persists at night, and there is an ionopause—i.e., a sharp *upper* boundary where the ionosphere reacts with the solar wind, in the absence of a magnetosphere. The atmosphere of Venus is very dynamic in its upper reaches, driven by the solar energy absorbed. At both poles there is a huge zone of down-flowing air.

The cause of the anomalous 243-day *retrograde* rotation of Venus is unknown. The once suspected spin-orbit resonance control by Earth has been discounted. Venus' spin vector is apparently aligned with the angular momentum vector of the solar system.

The slow rotation means that, unlike Earth, Venus is quite round with no equatorial bulge and no flattening at the poles. The planet probably has a molten iron core but its slow rotation precludes the existence of a magnetic field.

MARS, in direct contrast to Venus, with its hot, heavy, and opaque atmosphere, has one that is cold, thin, and transparent and readily permits observation of the planet's surface features. As observed from Earth, Mars's main surface features include white polar caps and bright and dark regions all of which show seasonal variations.

The bright areas, which constitute almost three-quarters of the total Martian surface area, give the planet its familiar ruddy color. The bright areas are believed to be siliceous, as was found from data sent back in 1971 from the Soviet probe Mars III. The dark areas cover roughly one third of the planet's surface.

Infrared observations have shown that the average temperature of the whole planet is −45° F, with a maximum equatorial noon temperature of 80° F. The daily temperature variation from noon to midnight at the equator is about 180° F, suggesting that the Martian atmosphere is very thin and thus does not retain heat. With an atmosphere much thinner than ours, the atmospheric surface pressure is only 7.7 mbar (Viking readings). Because the Martian atmosphere is so thin, it changes temperature rapidly, thus bringing about the large temperature contrasts that play a major role in driving the high Martian winds.

In 1971 three orbiting Mars probes were launched: two Russian (Mars II and III) and one American (Mariner 9). Mars III deposited a transmitter on the surface of the planet, but this failed almost immediately after arrival. Mariner 9 remained in orbit for almost a year and sent back photographs and scientific information that drastically altered man's ideas about the planet. Only half of the surface, mainly in the southern hemisphere, is substantially cratered. In the northern hemisphere, observed by Mariner 9, four immense volcanic mountains were found as well as a vast system of canyons, tributary gullies, and narrow channels. These features are far greater in scale than anything seen on earth. The largest volcanic mountain, Olympus Mons, the biggest known in the solar system, is more than 300 miles in diameter at the base and about 16 miles high. The sparsely cratered northern regions, strewn with wind-blown debris, are plains of lava that flooded the surface at different times after its earliest history. The heavily cratered southern terrain was also modified by volcanic activity.

Apparently, contrary to earlier ideas, there has been internal activity in the planet, maybe quite recently. This is also suggested by the series of huge canyons, 50 to 75 miles wide and 3 to 4 miles deep stretching along the equator to the east of the volcanic regions.

At the eastern extreme of the canyons lies a large area of chaotic terrain, first observed by Mariner 6 and 7. It is an irregular jumble of topographic forms, possibly the result of some kind of collapse related to that of the canyons. Channels, hundreds of miles long, extend from this terrain in a northwesterly direction. They also appear in other areas on the planet's surface. The channels may have been cut by large amounts of flowing water. The Viking spacecraft have since shown that in Mars' earliest history flowing water was significant in shaping its features. Since then, although surface dust and other debris have been extensively and continuously redistributed by high-speed winds, wind erosion of the surface has been negligible, leaving features sharply defined.

The bright circular region, Hellas, roughly 1000 miles across, is an example of basinlike depressions seen in several regions of the Martian surface. Mariner 7 showed it to be almost devoid of topographical features. It is exceptionally low—over a mile below the mean Martian elevation. Mariner 9 indicated that Hellas probably serves as a collection center for dust and may also be a source of dust.

The lower atmosphere can become filled with dust when the Martian winds become really strong. The dust storms are phenomena whose explanation may be similar to that of the initial stages of a hurricane. When Mariner 9 and the Soviet Mars probes reached Mars, the greatest dust storm in more than a century was raging. The mapping of the Martian surface was consequently delayed for almost three months.

The polar caps appear as a white cover over the north and south poles. This cover grows and recedes with seasonal regularity, alternating from one hemisphere to the other once every Martian year (687 Earth days). The Mariner 7 photographs showed snow-filled craters of the southern polar cap in sharp relief with snow-covered crater rims. The Viking orbiters have indicated that the residual (summer) northern and probably the southern caps are predominantly water ice not frozen carbon dioxide as hitherto suspected. The amount of water vapor in the atmosphere, although very small, was found to increase with latitude, reaching a peak at the edge of the polar caps. In addition infrared measurements showed that the surface temperature (about –70°C) is not cold enough for solid carbon dioxide to form.

The landings of Viking 1 and 2 on Mars on July 20 and September 3, 1976, respectively, have greatly increased our store of Martian information. The mission's purpose was to probe the planet's interior, surface properties, weather, atmosphere and biology. Photographs from the two Viking orbiters and the two landers have shown Mars as a planet that, like Earth, has been shaped by great forces, and have revealed Mars' characteristics to a greater degree than any other unmanned exploration of Mars has been able to accomplish.

Landing site locales were finalized only after the two spacecraft went into orbit around Mars. Viking 1 landed near a region heavily scoured by what are believed to have been ancient floods, while Viking 2 is on a vast flat plain pocked by fewer craters. The color pictures transmitted to earth showed a bright faintly pink sky and a salmon-pink surface. The dry pink dust covering most of the rock-strewn desert-like surface is composed of a mixture of iron-rich clay minerals and carbonate minerals, iron oxide probably giving Mars its red appearance.

The inorganic analysis of Martian soil showed the presence of silicon, iron, calcium, aluminum, titanium, and sulfur (in order of abundance). Analysis of the atmosphere found it to contain 95% carbon dioxide, 2.7% nitrogen, 1.6% argon, and traces of oxygen and water vapor. The presence of argon showed that there was probably a much denser atmosphere and hence a very different climate from today's. The discovery of nitrogen increases the possibility of some form of life having evolved.

Viking landers are the first spacecraft ever sent to another planet with equipment specifically designed to search for alien life forms. Information from biology experiments on Mars are inconclusive but could suggest "the possibility of biological activity in the samples being incubated." Life on Mars has of yet been neither confirmed nor ruled out, but if it does exist, it has made a different adaptation than life forms on Earth.

JUPITER has a dense, cloudy atmosphere of hydrogen and helium, with about 90% hydrogen and 2% CH_4 and NH_3 and traces of ethane and acetylene. It rotates rapidly (in approximately 9 hours 50 minutes), is flattened 1/15, has a low mean density, great mass, a large fraction of the solar system's angular momentum and 16 satellites. Its interior has a small rock-metal core, a liquid monatomic hydrogen "metallic" mantle 28,000 miles thick, and a liquid diatomic hydrogen mantle overlying that. Parallel clouds characterize its visible surface, divided into white-yellowish zones and reddish-brown belts. They probably consist of H_2O, ammonia, and NH_4SH crystals. Cloud-top temperatures average about –220°F.

Jupiter's central temperature theoretically is about 54,000°F and the planet radiates about two times as much energy as it receives, due possibly to continuing contraction.

The Great Red Spot — 24,000 × 9,000 miles — is an immense hurricane-like atmospheric disturbance, poorly understood. Other smaller, ephemeral spots are known. Since 1954 radio astronomers have detected radio signals, arising in strong magnetic fields and in Jupiter's magnetosphere. This magnetosphere is huge, complex and interacts with the solar wind, Jupiter's atmosphere, and the surface of Io (one of the planet's satellites). A "plasma torus" near Io's orbit surrounds Jupiter, containing ionized sulfur, with a temperature of 180,000°F. A "flux tube" connects Jupiter's magnetic poles and Io, and a powerful electric current flows (possibly as great as 5 million amperes). A system of rings lies in the equatorial plane.

The elongated satellite, Amalthea, is dark like an asteroid (166 × 88 miles). Io is fantastic! Seven currently active volcanoes were found spewing umbrella-shaped plumes up to 180 miles. Its surface is orange-red with no impact craters, but over 100 huge caldera-like depressions and lava flows—a "young" surface, renewed about every 10 million years.

Io and Europa are composed of rock; Ganymede and Callisto are composed of mixtures of "water-ice" and rock. Europa has few craters, Ganymede more, and craters are "shoulder-to-shoulder" on Callisto. Europa has a cracked, ice-encrusted surface. Ganymede, larger than Mercury, is also ice-encrusted, with a contorted, involuted and faulted pattern of lines and ridges. Icy Callisto has a huge bull's-eye formation (1,600 miles across), with concentric mountain ridges around a 200-mile central basin.

SATURN, the second largest planet in the solar system, has an internal and atmospheric structure similar to that of Jupiter. But it may have a greater amount of hydrogen and methane, as well as a smaller amount of ammonia in its atmosphere. The density of Saturn is very low.

First discovered by Galileo, the superb rings of Saturn have the appearance of a large, extremely thin, and flat circular sheet, lying centered on the planet in the equatorial plane. There are three prominent rings; the outer ring A is separated from the brightest ring, B, by a narrow gap called Cassini's Division. Interior to ring B is a faint, semitransparent one known as the "Crepe," or ring C. The rings are only about five miles thick and are probably composed of innumerable particles of ice.

Our knowledge of Saturn, its satellites, and ring system increased dramatically with the Pioneer 11 (1979) and Voyager 1 and 2 encounters (1980, 1981). Voyager 1 found considerable internal structure in the rings. Ring B in particular has numerous individual ringlets of particles and also some bizarre dark "spokes" that rotate with the rings around the planet. Several fainter rings exist. The narrow 300-mile-wide F ring, discovered by Pioneer 11, lies just outside the A ring. Voyager 1 pictures of this ring showed strands of material, not concentric but kinked and apparently intertwined. A highly tenuous belt, the G ring, is thought to lie beyond the F ring while evidence was found for the D and E rings, previously reported as lying inside (D) and outside the bright trio. The rings of Saturn are very large in extent. Ring A has an outer radius of 85,000 miles; that of ring G could be 95,000 miles.

Saturn has at least 16 satellites, five of the smallest and most recently discovered lying within the ring system. The largest satellite, Titan, is about the size of Mercury; it is the only satellite in the solar system observed to date that has an appreciable atmosphere, mainly of nitrogen and some methane, with a surface pressure which may be similar to that of Earth.

URANUS and **NEPTUNE** are the third- and fourth-largest planets, respectively, in the solar system. Because of their great distance from the Sun, little is known about either of them. Their mass can be calculated from the orbital period of their satellites. Their diameters have recently been recalculated by balloon measurement (Uranus: 32,-200 miles) and by a stellar occultation (Neptune: 30,800 miles).

Uranus was the first planet to be discovered with the aid of a telescope. It was discovered in 1781 by William Herschel. Neptune was telescopically discovered in 1846 by J. G. Galle; this discovery was based on orbital changes of Uranus brought about by the gravitational pull of Neptune. These gravitational perturbations were calculated by J. C. Adams and U. J. Leverrier.

Spectroscopic observations of their atmospheres have established the presence of molecular hydrogen and helium, as in the atmospheres of Jupiter and Saturn, and an increased proportion of methane.

Uranus has a system of five known moons, Neptune has two. Neptune's larger moon, Triton, Jupiter's Ganymede and Callisto, and Saturn's Titan comprise the four largest moons of the solar system.

Observations in 1977 and 1978 indicate that Uranus is surrounded by at least eight rings lying in its equatorial plane, similar to but much narrower than Saturn's rings.

PLUTO, the most distant and smallest planet in the solar system, was discovered in 1930 by C. W. Tombaugh. Although little is yet known about Pluto, it appears to be a small low-density body, too cold and small to retain an appreciable atmosphere and probably covered in a layer of methane ice.

Pluto has the most eccentric orbit in the solar system, bringing it at times closer to the Sun than Neptune. Because of its orbit, some theorists have suggested that Pluto may in fact be a runaway moon of Neptune.

In 1978 a moon was discovered in orbit around Pluto. The orbital distance and period of this moon has led to the first reasonably accurate measurement of Pluto's mass (0.2% of Earth's mass). Additional measurements now indicate a diameter of 1,500–2,000 miles.

THE SPECTRAL SEQUENCE

The spectral class or spectral type of a star is a classification that depends on the star's color or surface temperature. The spectral class and corresponding star color, approximate surface temperature, and principal features of the star's spectrum are:

Spectral Class	Color	Approximate Surface Temperature (K)	Principal Features of Spectrum
O	blue	>30,000	Relatively few absorption lines in observable spectrum. Lines of ionized helium, nitrogen, silicon, and other atoms. Weak hydrogen lines.
B	blue-white	11,000–30,000	Lines of neutral helium, ionized silicon, oxygen, and magnesium. Hydrogen lines more pronounced.
A	white	7,500–11,000	Strong lines of hydrogen. Weak lines of ionized magnesium, silicon, iron, titanium, calcium, and others. Weak lines of some neutral metals.
F	white to yellowish	6,000–7,500	Hydrogen lines still conspicuous. Lines of ionized calcium, iron, and chromium, and of neutral iron and chromium. Lines of other neutral metals.
G	yellow	5,000–6,000	Very strong lines of ionized calcium. Many lines of ionized and neutral metals. Hydrogen lines weaker.
K	orange to red	3,500–5,000	Lines of neutral metals predominate. Hydrogen lines are quite weak. Bands of molecular titanium oxide.
M	red	<3,500	Strong lines of neutral metals and strong bands of titanium oxide dominate.

IMPORTANT PLANETARY PROBES

Name of probe	Launching Local date	Launching Rocket	Weight, lbs.	Period, min.	Inclination, degrees	Perigee, miles	Apogee, miles	Results of mission—Remarks
					SOVIET UNION			
Venera I	12 Feb. 1961	—	1,417	300 days	0.58	0.7183 A.U.	1.0190 A.U.	In solar orbit; Venus probe; radio contact lost at 4.6 million miles.
Mars I	1 Nov. 1962	—	1,965	519 days	2.683	0.9237 A.U.	1.604 A.U.	In solar orbit; Mars probe; radio contact lost at 66 million miles.
Zond I	2 Apr. 1964	—	1,700		solar orbit			In solar orbit; probe aimed at Venus; failed to send back information on its target.
Zond II	30 Nov. 1964	—			solar orbit			In orbit; probe aimed at Mars; failed to send back information on its target.
Venera II	12 Nov. 1965	—	2,123		solar orbit			In solar orbit; failed to send back data.
Venera III	16 Nov. 1965	—	2,116	duration of flight: 105 days				First space probe to impact on a planet; entry capsule sent back no data after landing.
Venera IV	12 June 1967	—	2,439	duration of flight: 128 days				Instrumented capsule deployed parachute 18.10.67.

Venera V	5 Jan. 1969	—	2,500	—				Instrumented capsule deployed parachute 16.5.69.
Venera VI	10 Jan. 1969	—	2,500	—				Instrumented capsule deployed parachute 17.5.69.
Venera VII	16 Aug. 1970	—	2,500	—				Instrumented capsule transmitted data for 23 minutes 15.12.70.
Mars II	19 May 1971	—	—	duration of flight: 18 hrs.				Orbited Mars 27.11.72; sent back close-range photos.
Mars III	28 May 1971	—	—	duration of flight: 11 days				Instrumented capsule televised signals from surface.
Venera VIII	26 Mar. 1972	—	—	—				Ceased transmitting on entering atmosphere.
Mars IV	21 July 1973	—	10,250	—				Failed to go into Martian orbit.
Mars V	25 July 1973	—	10,250	—				Went into orbit March 1974.
Mars VI	5 Aug. 1973	—	10,250	—				Released descent module: ceased functioning.
Mars VII	9 Aug. 1973	—	10,250	—				Failed to go into orbit.
Venera IX	6 June 1975	—	—	duration of flight: 139 days				Descent modules landed on Venus at sites of different terrain, relaying data and clear photos of surface.
Venera X	14 June 1975	—	—	duration of flight: 134 days				
Venera XI	9 Sept. 1978	—	—	duration of flight: 108 days				Descent modules relayed detailed data and photographs.
Venera XII	14 Sept. 1978	—	—	duration of flight: 99 days				
UNITED STATES								
Pioneer 5	11 Mar. 1960	Thor-Able	95	312 days	3.55	0.8161 A.U.	0.995 A.U.	In solar orbit; launched toward Venus; studied interplanetary space.
Mariner 2	26 Aug. 1962	Atlas-Agena B	446	348 days	1.66	0.7046 A.U.	1.299 A.U.	In solar orbit; passed within 22,000 miles of Venus.
Mariner 3	5 Nov. 1964	Atlas-Agena D	575	448.7 days	0.524	0.6150 A.U.	0.8155 A.U.	In solar orbit; final speed too low.
Mariner 4	28 Nov. 1964	Atlas-Agena D	575	567.2 days	2.540	1.1089 A.U.	1.5730 A.U.	In solar orbit; highly successful; 22 photographs of Mars sent back in mid-July 1965.
Pioneer 6	16 Dec. 1965	TAID	139	311.3 days	0.1695	0.814 A.U.	0.985 A.U.	In solar orbit; studied Sun and interplanetary space.
Pioneer 7	17 Aug. 1966	TAID	130	402.9 days	0.097	1.010 A.U.	1.125 A.U.	In solar orbit; studied Sun and interplanetary space.
Mariner 5	14 June 1967	Atlas-Agena D	540	duration of flight: 127 days				In solar orbit; Venus probe; fly-by on 19.10.67.
Pioneer 8	13 Dec. 1967	TAID	145	—	—	1.0 A.U.	1.1 A.U.	In solar orbit; studied Sun and interplanetary space.
Mariner 6	24 Feb. 1969	Atlas-Agena D	—	duration of flight: 156 days				Passed within 2,000 miles of Mars on 31.7.69; relayed data and photos.
Mariner 7	27 Mar. 1969	Atlas-Agena D	—	duration of flight: 130 days				Passed within 2,000 miles of Mars on 5.8.69; sent photographs back to Earth.
Mariner 9	30 May 1971	Atlas Centaur	2,200	12 hrs.	65	800	11,000	Entered Mars orbit 14.11.71; sent photographs and instrument readings to Earth.
Pioneer 10	2 Mar. 1972	Atlas Centaur	570	—	—	—	—	Flew past Jupiter 4.12.73 relaying data and photos of planets and satellites.
Pioneer 11	6 Apr. 1973	Atlas Centaur	570	—	—	—	—	Investigated asteroid belt; passed Jupiter 3.12.74; passed Saturn 1.9.79.
Mariner 10	3 Nov. 1973	Atlas Centaur	—	—	—	—	—	Relayed data and photos of Venus, photos of Mercury.
Viking 1	20 Aug. 1975	Titan 3E/Centaur	7,550	entered Mars orbit 6/19/76; landed July 20, 1976				Orbiters studied atmosphere, photographed surface; landers studied surface geology and chemistry, testing soil for signs of life.
Viking 2	9 Sept. 1975	Titan 3E/Centaur	7,550	entered Mars orbit 8/7/76; landed Sept. 3, 1976				
Voyager 1	5 Sept. 1977	Titan 3 E/Centaur	1,820	—	flew by Jupiter March 1979, Saturn Nov. 1980			Studied and photographed atmospheres, ring systems and surfaces of main satellites in great detail.
Voyager 2	20 Aug. 1977	Titan 3 E/Centaur	1,820	—	flew by Jupiter July 1979, Saturn Aug. 1981			
Pioneer Venus 1	20 May 1978	Atlas Centaur	—	entered Venus orbit 4/12/78				Orbiter plus multiprobe atmospheric entry craft studied Venusian atmosphere and surface.
Pioneer Venus 2	8 Aug. 1978	Atlas Centaur	—	entered atmosphere 9/12/78; following payload of probes				

THE MOON

The Moon is the closest celestial body to the Earth, at a mean distance of 238,857 miles. Because of its elliptical orbit, the Moon reaches a minimum distance—or perigee —of 221,463 miles and a maximum distance—apogee—of 252,710 miles. The Moon revolves around the Earth in 27 days 7 hours 43 minutes. The Moon's rotation about its axis is equal to its period of revolution, hence the Moon always shows the Earth the same face. However, since its revolution around the Earth is not uniform, speeding up at perigee and slowing down at apogee, and because its equator is inclined 6 degrees to the plane of its orbit, about 59 percent of the Moon's surface is visible at different times from the Earth. The Moon's mass is 1/81 of the Earth's mass, and its radius of 1,080 miles makes it about one-fourth of the Earth's radius. The mean density of the Moon is 3.34 grams/cm³.

The Moon is visible, as are the Earth and the other planets, by virtue of its reflection of solar radiation. However, the Moon is a relatively poor reflector, with an albedo, or reflectivity, of only 7 percent. At full moon, the Earth is between the Sun and the Moon (although usually not in the same plane), and the whole lunar disk facing the Earth is completely illuminated. At new moon, the Moon is between the Sun and the Earth (usually not in the same plane), and the Sun's rays illuminate only the hemisphere facing it, leaving the side facing the Earth in complete darkness, making it invisible from Earth. After new moon, the waxing thin crescent turns into first quarter. Following full moon, the waning gibbous turns into last quarter, then into new moon again.

The origin of the Moon is still a major area of debate. Three different mechanisms have been suggested for its origin: independent formation in Earth orbit, formation via fission of the Earth, and capture by Earth's gravitational field after formation elsewhere.

In the independent-formation theory, the Moon is supposed to have been formed by accretion of small masses from the original interstellar gas cloud that gave birth to the Sun, the Earth, and other planets. The major difficulty with this hypothesis is the disparity in mean density between the Earth and the Moon. This density difference, which is generally believed to represent a difference in the composition—specifically in the proportion of metallic iron and silicates—makes it difficult to explain why objects accumulating in the same part of the gas cloud should have such different compositions.

In 1898, G. H. Darwin, the astronomer son of Sir Charles Darwin, concluded that the Earth and the Moon might have once formed one body that rotated at high speed (about five hours). This rapid rotation might have led to fission into one large and one or more smaller bodies, the latter eventually forming the Moon. However, mathematical objections to this theory have led modern astronomers to abandon it.

According to some hypotheses, the first large solid bodies to form in the solar system were approximately the size of the Moon. These bodies collided, forming the planets. The Moon is considered to be one of these bodies, which escaped destruction by accretion and was later gravitationally captured by the Earth.

The lunar surface is divided into bright highland areas (comprising about two thirds of the total surface) and dark lowland areas, called *maria*, because they were originally thought to be seas. Craters are the most conspicuous and most plentiful of all lunar surface features. The near side of the Moon has more *maria* than the far side, which is almost entirely covered with highland regions. The major mechanisms believed to be responsible for crater formation are meteoritic impact and lunar volcanism. Impact craters appear to be of two types. Primary craters stem from the actual impact of meteoritic material; secondary craters result in part from the rain of heavy debris ejected from the primary ones. Craters may also be formed by collapse triggered by seismic quakes, which result from the impact of a large meteorite. The frequency with which craters are found on the bright highland areas is more than 15 times that of their incidence on the dark lowland *maria*. It is known that the Moon, and also possibly Mars, Mercury, and Earth, suffered very intense bombardment by massive bodies (planetesimals) about 4 billion years ago. Shortly after this, volcanic lava flooded gigantic basins on the Moon's surface, covering many craters and creating the *maria*. Seismic waves indicate activity (moonquakes) still occurring in the Moon's core but its present thick rigid outer layers prevent any surface fracturing.

Lunar rilles, or deep canyons, some of them more than 100 miles long, were thought to be remnants of long-dried-out rivers on the Moon but are probably collapse features. One of them, the Hadley Rille, was studied at close range by the astronauts of Apollo 15 in 1971.

Mascons—dense lunar mass concentrations—were accidentally discovered in 1968 during analysis of small changes in the motion of Langley Research Center's Lunar Orbiter 5 during 80 consecutive orbits around the Moon. Five conspicuous mascons, ranging from 25 to 100 miles in extent and perhaps 25 miles below the lunar surface, were detected under all five large circular *maria* on the side of the Moon facing the Earth —Mare Imbrium, Mare Serenitatis, Mare Crisium, Mare Nectaris, and Mare Humorum. A sixth mascon is located in the central part of the lunar disk, between Sinus Aestuum and Sinus Medii. There is also some evidence that a large mascon exists under Mare Orientale. Mascons are absent from the bright lunar highlands and from the irregularly shaped *maria*. Both the presence of these features under every ringed *mare*, except Sinus Iridum, and their relative absence elsewhere, suggest a physical relationship.

In 1969, six more mascons were discovered—in Mare Smythii, Mare Humboldtianum, Mare Orientale, the ringed plain Grimaldi, and in two unnamed *maria*. As with the other mascons, the new mascons were discovered as lunar-orbiting spacecraft speeded up in passing over certain areas, which were revealed as places where the lunar gravitational attraction was stronger than average.

Due to the Moon's smaller mass, its gravitational attraction is only one sixth of the Earth's. Since the Moon is a weak gravitational body, it is believed that it could not retain any atmosphere it may have originally had for any length of time, since the atoms and molecules of the lunar atmosphere could easily drift off the planet. Observations first made with Apollo instruments have, however, revealed the presence of helium, neon, argon, and radon in very minute quantities.

The large day-to-night temperature variation observed on the Moon also suggests that it does not have an appreciable atmosphere. A planetary atmosphere acts as a heat insulator that keeps the planet's surface from experiencing wide temperature extremes from day to night. The day-to-night temperature variations on the Moon range from 300° F in the lunar equatorial region at noon to −220° F before sunrise—a daily change of over 500° F.

The samples of lunar material brought back by the Apollo astronauts consist of basaltic igneous rocks; breccias, which are composed of soil and rock fragments compacted into coherent rock; and lunar soil. The soil is a mixture of crystalline and glassy fragments with a variety of interesting shapes; it also contains fragments of iron meteorites. Most of the breccia rock fragments are similar to the larger igneous rocks and apparently were derived from them; the rocks in turn were probably once part of the underlying lunar bedrock.

The igneous rocks from the Moon contain the minerals pyroxene, plagioclase, ilmenite, olivine, and cristobalite. Three new minerals were found in these igneous rocks: pyroxmanganite, ferropseudobrookite, and a chromium-titanium compound. All of the lunar rocks were found to have unusually high concentrations of chromium, titanium, scandium, zirconium, hafnium, and yttrium, and very low concentrations of sodium. Many elements such as potassium, rubidium, cesium, chlorine, and thallium, which exist in great abundance in Earth rocks, were found to be very deficient in the lunar rocks.

Radioactive isotopic dating of the igneous rocks brought back by the astronauts shows that they were formed 3.3 to 3.7 billion years ago. In May 1970, G. Wasserburg reported that an Apollo 12 rock was found to be 4.6 billion years old, making it the oldest rock yet found on the Moon or Earth. For the soil and breccia such dating gives an age of 4.4 to 4.6 billion years. The existence of complex biological molecules in the lunar samples would be of tremendous significance, but some of the most sophisticated and sensitive analytical techniques ever devised failed to detect any. Lacking an atmosphere and an appreciable magnetic field, the moon is exposed to ultraviolet radiation as well as high-energy cosmic rays and the solar wind.

MODERN PLANETARY DATA

	Distance from Sun in Astronomical Units[1]	Period of Revolution Around Sun	Diameter[2]	Mass[3]	Density[6] (grams/cm³)
MERCURY	0.387	87.97 Days	0.38	0.055	5.5
VENUS	0.723	224.70 Days	0.95	0.815	5.25
EARTH	1.000	365.25 Days	1.00	1.00	5.517
MARS	1.524	1.88 Years	0.53	0.107	3.94
JUPITER	5.203	11.86 Years	11.20	317.9	1.330
SATURN	9.539	29.45 Years	9.36	95.2	0.706
URANUS	19.18	84.01 Years	4.06	14.6	1.21
NEPTUNE	30.06	164.79 Years	3.88	17.2	1.67
PLUTO	39.44	247.7 Years	0.23(?)	0.002	0.8(?)

	Period of Rotation (H = hours; M = minutes)	Amount of Incident Solar Radiation[4]	Albedo[5]	Observed Surface Temp.	Number of Satellites
MERCURY	58.65 Days	6.7	0.06	660°F (Dayside)	0
VENUS	243 Days (retrograde)	1.9	0.76	890°F	0
EARTH	23H 56M 4S	1.0	0.36	70°F	1
MARS	24H 37M 23S	0.43	0.16	— 45°F	2
JUPITER	9H 50M*	0.04	0.73	—220°F (Cloud-top)	16
SATURN	10H 14M**	0.01	0.76	—290°F (Cloud-top)	16
URANUS	10H 49M (retrograde)	0.003	0.93	—350°F (Cloud-top)	5
NEPTUNE	15H 48M	0.001	0.84	—360°F (Cloud-top)	2
PLUTO	6.39 Days	0.0006	0.8(?)	—380°F	1

[1] The astronomical unit, defined as the mean distance from the Earth to the Sun, is approximately 93 million miles. [2] Diameter in terms of the Earth's diameter: 7,926 miles. [3] Mass in terms of the Earth's mass: 1.3×10^{25} pounds. [4] Amount of solar radiation falling on the planet in terms of the solar radiation the Earth receives: about 1.4 kilowatts falling on every square meter of the upper atmosphere per second. [5] The albedo is the percentage of the incoming solar radiation that is reflected back to space by the planet and its atmosphere. [6] Density of water is 1.0 gram/cm³. * For the latitudes greater than 12°, the rotation period is 9H 55M. ** For temperate latitudes, the rotation period is 10H 38M.

SATELLITES OF THE SOLAR SYSTEM

Planet		Satellites	Distance from the Planet (Miles)	Period of Revolution* (Days)	Radius (Miles)	Mass (Pounds)
Earth	1	Moon	238,850	27.32	1,080	162×10^{21}
‡Mars	1	Phobos	5,810	0.32	8.4×6.5×6	—
	2	Deimos	14,595	1.26	4.7×3.7×3.4	—
†Jupiter	1	Io	262,075	1.77	1,137	160×10^{21}
	2	Europa	416,980	3.55	900	104×10^{21}
	3	Ganymede	665,130	7.15	1,550	339×10^{21}
	4	Callisto	1,169,820	16.69	1,400	209×10^{21}
	5	Amalthea	112,470	0.50	60	—
	6	Hestia	7,131,940	250.57	30	—
	7	Hera	7,292,940	259.7	9	—
	8	Poseidon	14,594,300	739	6	—
	9	Hades	14,687,200	758	6	—
	10	Demeter	7,282,700	259	6	—
	11	Pan	14,036,000	692	6	—
	12	Adrastea	13,199,000	631	6	—
	13	Leda	6,906,700	240	—	—
††Saturn	1	Mimas	115,320	0.94	150	0.09×10^{21}
	2	Enceladus	147,950	1.37	180	0.15×10^{21}
	3	Tethys	183,150	1.89	310	0.14×10^{21}
	4	Dione	234,580	2.74	310	2.20×10^{21}
	5	Rhea	327,590	4.52	400	5.06×10^{21}
	6	Titan	759,090	15.95	1,500	301×10^{21}
	7	Hyperion	921,340	21.28	150	0.68×10^{21}
	8	Iapetus	2,212,200	79.33	340	2.20×10^{21}
	9	Phoebe	8,047,700	550.34	60	—
Uranus	1	Ariel	119,200	2.52	250	2.64×10^{21}
	2	Umbriel	166,020	4.14	190	1.10×10^{21}
	3	Titania	272,390	8.70	340	8.80×10^{21}
	4	Oberon	364,270	13.46	310	5.72×10^{21}
	5	Miranda	81,000	1.41	90	$.02 \times 10^{21}$
Neptune	1	Triton	220,700	5.88	1,150	308×10^{21}
	2	Nereid	3,456,000	360	90	0.07×10^{21}
Pluto	1	1978-P-1 (Charon)	—	6.39	c.400	—

* Around planets. ‡ Satellites are roughly ellipsoidal: principal radii are given.
† A 14th satellite of Jupiter was discovered in 1979 and a 15th and 16th in 1980.
†† An additional 7 satellites of Saturn were discovered 1979, 1980; one is identified with Janus, reported 1966.

THE ASTEROIDS OR MINOR PLANETS

Between the orbits of Mars and Jupiter are found several thousand small rocky bodies, density 2–2.5 grams/cm³, orbiting the Sun. Ceres was the first to be discovered in 1801, and is also the largest (620 miles in diameter). Some 2,000 asteroids—minor planets—have now been catalogued and their orbits determined. However, there may be as many as 50,000 asteroids in the asteroid belt, most of which probably have diameters of less than a mile.

Because of their large number and planetary positions, it was originally thought that asteroids were the remnants of an exploded planet; however, since the total mass of the asteroids is less than 1/1000 of the Earth's mass, it is unlikely. Evidence shows that most asteroids have a surface consisting of very primitive material (carbonaceous chondrites) so that they may be the solid primordial remnants of the original dust from which the Sun and Earth and other planets condensed.

Many asteroids are not confined to the zone between Mars and Jupiter but have highly eccentric orbits. Hermes and Icarus pass close to Earth's orbit, Hidalgo close to Saturn's. Chiron, discovered 1977 by C. Kowall, orbits between Saturn and Uranus and has been recognized as an asteroid rather than a comet.

COMETS

Comets are bodies that move around the Sun, most of them in highly elliptical orbits. As a comet approaches the Sun, a somewhat transparent envelope of gas and dust called the *coma* appears around the small compact icy nucleus. The nucleus and coma comprise the comet's head. If the comet comes within two astronomical units of the Sun, it may develop a luminous tail—a long straight gaseous one that always points away from the Sun and a shorter broad dust tail that also curves away from the Sun.

Spectroscopic analysis of the comet's head shows the existence of the following neutral molecules and atoms: H_2O, OH, C, O, CO, CH, CN, NH, NH_2, Fe, and Ni. The following ionized molecules are found in the comet's tail: CH^+, CO^+, CO_2^+, and N_2^+. In addition, large amounts of dust are found in both the head and tail.

The comet's head may be as large as 500,000 miles across, and some comet tails are more than 10 million miles long. Comets circle the Sun in one of three types of orbits: elliptical, parabolic, or hyperbolic. Comets with elliptical orbits are periodic comets: they will continually orbit the Sun, as do the planets. Parabolic or hyperbolic orbits are probably caused by strong planetary perturbation.

The exact origin of comets is unknown. There may be hundreds of millions of comet nuclei in a huge region (Oort cloud) centered on the Sun but way beyond the orbit of Pluto. Occasionally, one may become perturbed and enter into close orbit around the Sun. Comet nuclei, which are only a few miles in diameter, are believed to consist of rocky fragments and frozen gases. As it approaches the Sun, solar radiation and heat cause the frozen gases in the nucleus to vaporize, forming the coma and later, as it comes still closer to the Sun, the tail.

The coma and head shine as sunlight is scattered by the dust and is also reradiated by fluorescent gas molecules. The gas is ionized by the solar wind streaming out radially from the Sun, carrying the gas ions with it and forming the long gaseous tail.

An enormous cloud of hydrogen, 10 times as large as the Sun, was discovered around comet Bennett in April 1970 by the National Aeronautics and Space Administration's Orbiting Geophysical Observatory (OGO) 5 satellite during a special maneuver to view the comet with a hydrogen-sensing device. Comet Bennett had become visible over portions of the United States and Britain late in March. Its huge hydrogen gas envelope—not visible from Earth—is about 8 million miles across and is probably the largest entity ever observed orbiting the Sun.

The existence of large amounts of hydrogen around comets was first discovered in January 1970 by Orbiting Astronomical Observatory (OAO) 2 when it observed a cloud around the comet Tago-Sato-Kosaka. Hydrogen is the most abundant element in the universe, and the vast amounts of it measured by the OAO and OGO satellites clearly show it to be a major constituent of comets. So it now appears that the newly discovered hydrogen clouds are a fourth feature to be added to the classical three components of a comet: the center, or nucleus; the coma; and the tail, which streams out thousands, sometimes millions of miles, always in a direction away from the Sun.

SOME PERIODIC COMETS

Comet	Period (Years)	Perihelion Distance*	Average Distance from Sun*
Encke	3.3	0.339	2.21
Grigg-Skjellerup	5.12	0.855	2.89
Tempel-2	5.27	1.37	3.0
Giacobini-Zinner	6.3	0.94	3.4
Faye	7.42	1.644	3.8
Whipple	7.44	2.47	3.8
Comas Solá	8.94	1.87	4.3
Väisälä	11.28	1.745	4.79
Neujmin-1	17.9	1.54	6.8
Crommelin	27.9	0.744	9.2
Olbers	69.6	1.18	16.9
Pons-Brooks	70.9	0.775	17.2
Halley	76.0	0.587	17.9

* In astronomical units.

METEORS

Meteors are small, usually highly fragile particles that enter the Earth's atmosphere at great speeds. A meteor will burn up or vaporize from frictional heating as it enters the atmosphere. A burning meteor is popularly referred to as a "shooting star" or "falling star." A meteor is called a *meteoroid* before it enters the earth's atmosphere; meteors the size of dust particles are called *micrometeorites*. A *fireball* is a bright glowing meteor that is brilliant enough to cast shadows on the ground. A *bolide* is a fireball that explodes in the atmosphere.

In general, an observer at any one location may observe between five and 10 meteors an hour; however, worldwide, there are some 200,000 visible meteors a day that collectively represent a mass influx of about 10 tons. In addition micrometeorites may account for some 100 tons of extraterrestrial matter that falls to Earth each day.

Meteors usually become visible at about 70 miles above the Earth's surface. Larger bodies may not completely burn up in the Earth's atmosphere and survive the trip through the atmosphere to Earth. These survivors are called *meteorites*, and may weigh as much as 60 tons; they are fundamentally different from meteors both in their origin and in their composition, which is stony, or iron-nickel, or a mixture of these.

Meteor showers occur each year as the Earth runs into patches of particle swarms that are scattered about in the Earth's orbit. When the Earth runs into one of these swarms, meteors appear to burst out in all directions from a particular radiant point. The Leonid meteor showers of November 12, 1799, and November 13, 1833, produced some 300,000 meteors per hour. The Leonid shower on the morning of November 17, 1966, may have produced as many as 2,500 meteors per minute.

Analysis of orbits and periods indicates that meteor showers may be associated with the disintegration of comets. Meteorites are probably closely related to asteroids. Meteor showers, which are named after the constellations in which their radiant point appears to lie, usually are visible for several days before and after their date of maximum occurrence. Meteors associated with meteor showers are usually completely disintegrated within the Earth's upper atmosphere.

PRINCIPAL METEOR SHOWERS

Meteor Stream	Date of Maximum Occurrence	Maximum Hourly Rate	Associated Comet
Quadrantids	Jan. 3	110	
Lyrids	Apr. 22	12	1861 I
η Aquarids	May 5	21	Halley?
Arietids	June 8*	40	
ε Perseids	June 9*	30	
β Taurids	June 30*	20	Encke
δ Aquarids	July 28	35	
Perseids	Aug. 12	68	1862 III
Draconids	Oct. 10	—	1933 III, Giacobini-Zinner
Orionids	Oct. 21	30	Halley?
Taurids	Nov. 8	12	Encke
Andromedids	Nov. 10	—	Biela
Leonids	Nov. 17	10	1866 I
Geminids	Dec. 14	58	
Ursids	Dec. 22	5	Tuttle

* Daytime showers.

ASTRONOMICAL PHENOMENA: 1982   Source: U.S. Naval Observatory

The times in the following tables, dealing with the Moon, with eclipses, and with the seasons, are all given in Greenwich (England) Mean Time (GMT); the new day "begins" at 00 hours 00 minutes (midnight) at the Greenwich meridian and lasts 23 hours and 59 minutes, until one minute before the next day begins. In the United States, there are eight standard time zones, which differ from the Greenwich Mean Time by a fixed number of hours.

To convert any GMT value to that of a particular time zone, subtract from the GMT the number of hours in the table below. If the number of hours to be subtracted is greater than the GMT value, then add 24 hours to the GMT before subtracting. This will then give the time for the preceding day. If the difference is between 00 and 11 hours, the time is A.M.; if the difference is between 12 and 23 hours the time is P.M.

Local Time Zone	To Convert from GMT
Eastern Daylight	Subtract 4 hours
Eastern Standard/Central Daylight	Subtract 5 hours
Central Standard/Mountain Daylight	Subtract 6 hours
Mountain Standard/Pacific Daylight	Subtract 7 hours

Local Time Zone	To Convert from GMT
Pacific Standard/Yukon Daylight	Subtract 8 hours
Yukon Standard/Alaska and Hawaii Daylight	Subtract 9 hours
Alaska and Hawaii Standard	Subtract 10 hours
Bering Standard	Subtract 11 hours

PHASES OF THE MOON: 1982   d = day; h = hour; m = minute (Universal Time or GMT)

	New Moon				First Quarter				Full Moon				Last Quarter		
	d	h	m		d	h	m		d	h	m		d	h	m
Jan.	25	04	56	Jan.	3	04	45	Jan.	9	19	53	Jan.	16	23	58
Feb.	23	21	13	Feb.	1	14	28	Feb.	8	07	57	Feb.	15	20	21
Mar.	25	10	17	Mar.	2	22	15	Mar.	9	20	45	Mar.	17	17	15
Apr.	23	20	29	Apr.	1	05	08	Apr.	8	10	18	Apr.	16	12	42
May	23	04	40	Apr.	30	12	07	May	8	00	45	May	16	05	11
June	21	11	52	May	29	20	07	June	6	15	59	June	14	18	06
July	20	18	57	June	28	05	56	July	6	07	32	July	14	03	47
Aug.	19	02	45	July	27	18	22	Aug.	4	22	34	Aug.	12	11	08
Sept.	17	12	09	Aug.	26	09	49	Sept.	3	12	28	Sept.	10	17	19
Oct.	17	00	04	Sept.	25	04	07	Oct.	3	01	08	Oct.	9	23	26
Nov.	15	15	10	Oct.	25	00	08	Nov.	1	12	57	Nov.	8	06	38
Dec.	15	09	18	Nov.	23	20	05	Dec.	1	00	21	Dec.	7	15	53
				Dec.	23	14	17	Dec.	31	11	33				

PERIGEE (Moon closest to Earth)

	d	h		d	h		d	h
Jan.	8	12	May	24	03	Oct.	9	01
Feb.	5	14	June	21	12	Nov.	4	10
Mar.	4	05	July	19	21	Dec.	2	11
Mar.	29	06	Aug.	17	02	Dec.	30	22
Apr.	25	21	Sept.	13	18			

APOGEE (Moon farthest from Earth)

	d	h		d	h		d	h
			Dec.	23	23	May	11	15	Sept.	25	19
Jan.	20	12	June	7	23	Oct.	23	15
Feb.	17	08	July	5	01	Nov.	20	11
Mar.	17	05	Aug.	1	10	Dec.	18	02
Apr.	14	00	Aug.	29	00			

SEASONS 1982

Spring begins — Mar. 20: 22 h: 56 m
Summer begins — June 21: 17 h: 23 m
Autumn begins — Sept. 23: 08 h: 46 m
Winter begins — Dec. 22: 04 h: 39 m

SUN DISTANCES 1982

Perihelion (Earth closest to sun) — Jan. 4
Aphelion (Earth farthest from sun) — July 4

ECLIPSES: 1982   h = hour; m = minute

JANUARY 9 — TOTAL ECLIPSE OF THE MOON
Visible in Asia, Australasia, Europe, and Africa.

Moon enters penumbra	Jan. 9: 17 h: 14.8 m
Middle of the eclipse	Jan. 9: 19 h: 55.8 m
Moon leaves penumbra	Jan. 9: 22 h: 36.9 m

JANUARY 25 — PARTIAL ECLIPSE OF THE SUN
Visible in Antarctica, New Zealand except northern part.

Eclipse begins	Jan. 25: 02 h: 49.8 m
Greatest eclipse	Jan. 25: 04 h: 42.0 m
Eclipse ends	Jan. 25: 06 h: 34.3 m

JUNE 21 — PARTIAL ECLIPSE OF THE SUN
Visible in extreme South of Africa.

Eclipse begins	June 21: 10 h: 27.8 m
Greatest eclipse	June 21: 12 h: 03.7 m
Eclipse ends	June 21: 13 h: 39.6 m

JULY 6 — TOTAL ECLIPSE OF THE MOON
Visible in New Zealand, Antarctica, the Pacific Ocean, South America, southern North America, the Atlantic Ocean, extreme western Africa.

Moon enters penumbra	July 6: 04 h: 22.2 m
Middle of the eclipse	July 6: 07 h: 30.9 m
Moon leaves penumbra	July 6: 10 h: 39.6 m

JULY 20 — PARTIAL ECLIPSE OF THE SUN
Visible in extreme north of Asia, northwest Europe, northwest of North America, Greenland, Iceland, arctic regions.

Eclipse begins	July 20: 17 h: 18.7 m
Greatest eclipse	July 20: 18 h: 43.8 m
Eclipse ends	July 20: 20 h: 09.1 m

DECEMBER 15 — PARTIAL ECLIPSE OF THE SUN
Visible in Europe except extreme north, western Asia, and extreme northeast Africa.

Eclipse begins	Dec. 15: 07 h: 21.9 m
Greatest eclipse	Dec. 15: 09 h: 31.2 m
Eclipse ends	Dec. 15: 11 h: 40.7 m

DECEMBER 30 — TOTAL ECLIPSE OF THE MOON
Visible in North America, Asia and Australasia.

Moon enters penumbra	Dec. 30: 08 h: 51.9 m
Middle of the eclipse	Dec. 30: 11 h: 28.7 m
Moon leaves penumbra	Dec. 30: 14 h: 05.5 m

CONFIGURATIONS OF THE BRIGHT PLANETS: 1982

To locate the bright planets, their location in degrees north or south of the Moon is given. All times are GMT.

	d	h			d	h			d	h	
Jan.	15	19	Mars 3° S	May	4	05	Mars 3° S	Aug.	17	14	Venus 1.4° S
	16	13	Saturn 3° S		5	13	Saturn 3° S		20	15	Mercury 5° S
	17	20	Jupiter 4° S		6	21	Jupiter 4° S		22	20	Saturn 3° S
Feb.	12	16	Mars 2° S		20	02	Venus 3° N		24	01	Jupiter 4° S
	12	22	Saturn 3° S		31	13	Mars 5° S		24	15	Mars 6° S
	14	09	Jupiter 4° S	June	1	16	Saturn 3° S	Sept.	18	22	Mercury 10° S
	20	16	Venus 7° N		2	21	Jupiter 4° S		19	10	Saturn 3° S
	21	15	Mercury 2° N		18	23	Venus 2° N		20	19	Jupiter 4° S
Mar.	11	22	Mars 2° S		20	02	Mercury 1.1° S		22	14	Mars 5° S
	12	05	Saturn 3° S		28	12	Mars 6° S	Oct.	15	11	Mercury 4° S
	13	17	Jupiter 4° S		28	21	Saturn 3° S		18	15	Jupiter 3° S
	21	14	Venus 5° N		30	01	Jupiter 4° S		21	17	Mars 3° S
	24	01	Mercury 2° N	July	18	19	Venus 0.6° N	Nov.	13	15	Saturn 3° S
Apr.	7	13	Mars 2° S		26	07	Saturn 3° S		19	21	Mars 0.5° S
	8	10	Saturn 2° S		26	22	Mars 6° S	Dec.	11	02	Saturn 3° S
	9	21	Jupiter 3° S		27	10	Jupiter 4° S		13	05	Jupiter 2° S
	20	06	Venus 4° N						19	01	Mars 1.6° N

U.S. SPACE PROGRAM   Source: National Aeronautics and Space Administration

SCIENTIFIC AND APPLICATIONS SATELLITES

Applications Technology Satellites—The Applications Technology Satellites (ATS) are designed to test in space promising techniques and equipment for use in future meteorological, navigation, and communications satellite systems. The satellites also carry scientific experiments such as instruments to measure radiation in space. The approximately 1,600-pound spacecraft was designed to include from 100 to 300 pounds of experimental equipment. A larger model, ATS-6, launched in 1974, weighs 3,000 pounds. Its transmitter was turned off in 1979. Orbits are at synchronous (approximately 22,235-mile) altitude.

Biosatellites—The biosatellites carried into space a wide variety of plants and animals ranging from microorganisms to primates. The experiments were aimed primarily at studying the biological effects of zero gravity—or weightlessness—weightlessness combined with a known source of radiation, and removal of living things from the influence of the Earth's rotation. They have contributed to knowledge in genetics, evolution, and physiology, and have provided new information about the effects of prolonged flight in space.

Discoverer—Discoverer is a U.S. military satellite program that, since its inception (February 28, 1959), has provided valuable data in such areas as radiation, meteoroids, and air density in space near Earth, as well as in aerospace medicine. A major contribution of the program was the development of the technology for midair recovery or sea recovery of packages sent from an orbiting satellite to Earth.

Early Bird—Early Bird (launched April 6, 1965) was the world's first operational commercial communications satellite. Its owner, the International Telecommunications Satellite Organization (INTELSAT), reimbursed NASA for costs involved in launching, tracking, and monitoring the satellite. Early Bird was guided by Earth stations into a nearby stationary position (relative to Earth's surface) over the Atlantic. From that point, it was able to furnish communications service (including telecasts) between Europe and North America.

Earth Resources Technology Satellites (LANDSAT)—LANDSAT is a technology development program designed to provide comprehensive observation of the Earth's surface. The spacecraft carry television cameras and radiometric scanners which collect global data on the earth's environment: the condition of the atmosphere and oceans, major ecological changes, and variations in weather systems. The 2,100-pound satellite circles the Earth four times a day and has a lifetime of more than a year to cover all four seasons and to account for seasonally-induced variations in the Earth's surface. The satellite's cameras view a 115-mile swath running north to south as the satellite orbits the Earth. This broad synoptic scanning shows more detail and contrast than the mosaic-like maps made from airplane surveys. The first spacecraft was launched in 1972, the second in 1975 and the third in 1978. Only the third is still transmitting.

Echo—Echo 1 (orbited August 12, 1960) proved that it is possible to communicate between distant areas on Earth by reflecting radio microwaves from a manmade satellite. Echo 1 was fabricated of aluminum-vapor-coated polyester film 0.0005 inch thick (about half the thickness of cellophane wrapping on a cigarette package). It was 100 feet in diameter and weighed 123½ pounds. Radio signals were literally bounced off the satellite from one point on the Earth to another.

Echo 2 (launched January 25, 1964) was 135 feet in diameter—as tall as a 13-story building—and weighed 565 pounds. Made up of a laminate of aluminum foil and polymer plastic about 0.00075 inch thick, it was 20 times as rigid as Echo 1.

Explorers—Explorers comprise the largest group of satellites in the United States space program. Explorer 1 (launched February 1, 1958) was the nation's first satellite. It made one of the most significant contributions of the Space Age, confirming existence of the previously theorized Van Allen radiation belts—a zone of intense radiation surrounding the Earth.

Generally, Explorers are small satellites carrying a limited number of experiments. Their orbits vary to serve the particular purposes of the experiments. Their designs also differ.

Explorers have been put into orbit to measure the thin wisps of air in the upper atmosphere; determine air density by latitude and altitude; provide data on the composition of Earth's ionosphere, including the presence of electrons, which enable the ionosphere to bounce back certain radio waves, thus making possible long-range radio communications on Earth; study the composition, density, pressure, and other properties of the upper atmosphere; provide information on micrometeoroids (small particles of matter in space), and measure the small variations in Earth's gravity field and fix more precisely the locations of points on Earth.

High Energy Astronomy Observatory (HEAO)—The HEAO program studies some of the most intriguing mysteries of the universe — pulsars, black holes, neutron stars, quasars and supernovae. HEAO 1, launched Aug. 12, 1977, and HEAO 3, launched September 20, 1979, were designed to perform celestial surveys, mapping the sky for sources and background of X-rays. HEAO 2, launched Nov. 13, 1978, a celestial pointing mission, was to spend one year studying individual X-ray objects in detail by using an advanced X-ray telescope.

Interplanetary Explorers—Interplanetary Explorers are a special class of Explorers to provide data on radiation and magnetic fields between the Earth and Moon. The information has been of value to science and contributed to planning for the Apollo program that landed American explorers on the Moon.

Nimbus—Advanced equipment intended for use in future operational weather satellites is tested in Nimbus, a research and development project. Nimbus 1 (launched August 28, 1964) was equipped with advanced television cameras and with a high-resolution infrared observation system. The cameras provided daylight pictures; the infrared equipment, night pictures. Nimbus 1 ceased operation about a month after operation.

The thousands of day and night pictures taken by Nimbus 1 have contributed significantly not only to study and tracking of hurricanes and other weather phenomena but also to geology, geography, oceanography, and other earth sciences.

Nimbus 2 (launched May 15, 1966) contained equipment not only for providing day and night pictures of the Earth and its clouds but also for measuring the Earth's heat balance. Heat balance refers to how much of the Sun's radiation the Earth absorbs and how much it reflects back into the atmosphere. The Nimbus 2 experiment represents the first time such information was obtained on a global basis. Study of heat balance data may increase understanding of how storms are born, develop, and die.

Nimbus 3 (launched April 14, 1969), and Nimbus 4 (launched April, 1970), were both powered by a nuclear system, contained equipment to determine the variation of temperature with height within the atmosphere. Nimbus 5 (launched December 1972) carries instruments to measure temperature in clouds as an indicator of their height. Nimbus 6 was launched on June 12, 1975, and Nimbus 7, an advanced pollution-monitoring satellite, was lofted on October 24, 1978.

Orbiting Astronomical Observatory (OAO)—Man's study of the universe has been narrowly circumscribed because the atmosphere blocks or distorts much electromagnetic radiation (X-rays, infrared rays, ultraviolet rays) from space. These emissions can tell much about the structure, evolution, and composition of celestial bodies. OAO has made it possible to observe the universe in ultraviolet wavelengths for extended periods from a vantage point above the haze of the atmosphere that contains 99 percent of Earth's air.

Orbiting Geophysical Observatory (OGO)—Orbiting Geophysical Observatories are designed to broaden significantly knowledge about the Earth and space and how the Sun influences and affects both. The approximately 1,000-pound OGO furnishes many times the data provided by smaller satellites such as the Explorers.

The principal advantage of OGO is that it makes possible the observation of numerous phenomena simultaneously for prolonged periods of time. This permits study in depth of the relationships between the phenomena. For example, while some OGO experiments report on the erratic behavior of the Sun, others may describe concurrent fluctuations in Earth and interplanetary magnetic fields, space radiation, and properties of the Earth's atmosphere.

Orbiting Solar Observatory (OSO)—OSO is a series of satellites intended for intensive study of the Sun and solar phenomena from a point above the disruptive effects of the atmosphere. The observatory is designed to carry such instruments as X-ray and Lyman Alpha spectrometers, neutron flux sensors, and gamma-ray monitors. OSO scientific equipment is supplied to NASA by leading astronomers as it is to OAO.

Data from OSO have provided deeper insight into the functioning of the Sun, and suggest that techniques could be developed for forecasting the major solar flares that flood space with intensities of radiation lethal to man and detrimental to instruments.

Pegasus—Named for the winged horse of Greek mythology, Pegasus satellites are among the heaviest and largest of U.S. spacecraft. Deployed in space, the great wings of the Pegasus satellites span 96 feet while the center section, resembling the fuselage of an airplane, is 71 feet long. The wings are designed to report punctures by micrometeoroids, tiny particles of matter speeding through space. Data from Pegasus satellites not only have advanced man's understanding of space but are aiding him in design of large craft intended for prolonged missions in space.

Relay—Project Relay demonstrated the feasibility of intercontinental and transoceanic transmission of telephone, television, teleprint, and facsimile radio signals via a medium-altitude (several thousand to 12,000 miles) active-repeater (radio-equipped) satellite.

Solar Maximum Mission—This 5,000-pound spacecraft was launched on a Delta rocket on February 14, 1980, to study solar phenomena during the period of maximum solar flares and related phenomena.

Syncom—NASA's Project Syncom (for synchronous communication) demonstrated the feasibility of employing synchronous-orbit active-repeater satellites for global communication. Syncom satellites have been used in many experiments and public demonstrations.

Telstar—Telstar-like Relay—was an experiment using active-repeater satellites in medium-altitude orbits. Because the two satellites differed in important structural and other features, they permitted comparison of different designs. This contributed to the acquisition of information needed to develop equipment for an operational communications satellite system.

TIROS—Originally a research and development project, TIROS has evolved into an operational weather observation system. TIROS stands for Television and Infra-Red Observation Satellite. The first TIROS satellite was launched on April 1, 1960. Since then, TIROS 1 and subsequent satellites have proved themselves the most effective storm detection system known. They have provided meteorologists with more than half a million usable cloud-cover pictures, enabling them to track, forecast, and analyze storms. Through TIROS observations, the U.S. Weather Service has issued thousands of storm bulletins to countries throughout the world.

Continued progress has been made in improving the observations made by TIROS and in making these observations available to weather services of other nations. TIROS satellites now provide almost global coverage as compared to the coverage of about 25 percent of the Earth's surface at the program's inception. They can provide high-quality pictures of Earth's cloud cover. Some are equipped with an automatic picture transmission (APT) system that permits receipt of TIROS cloud-cover photographs on the ground with relatively inexpensive ground equipment.

In addition to contributing significantly to the discovery and tracking of hurricanes and other weather phenomena, TIROS satellites are providing valuable data for meteorological research. Such research may lead to long-range weather forecasts and perhaps greater understanding of how hurricanes and other destructive storms breed and how their development can be curbed. TIROS pictures of the Earth are proving useful in geography and geology, in showing the magnitude of river and sea ice, and in furnishing information on snowcover and thus spring flooding.

TOS and NOAA—NASA's research and development work with meteorological satellites has led to the world's first operational weather satellite system, called TOS (for TIROS Operational Satellite). The TOS system is furnishing weathermen daily with pictures of the weather over nearly the whole Earth. TOS and an improved version called ITOS are financed, managed, and operated by the Weather Service, a part of the National Oceanic and Atmospheric Administration (NOAA) of the United States Department of Commerce. A new advanced TIROS-N satellite was launched on October 13, 1978. After the first spacecraft, the remainder of this series received NOAA designations: NOAA-6 was launched in 1979 and NOAA-7 in 1980.

Transit and the Navy Navigation Satellite System—Transit was a Department of Defense experimental navigation satellite program designed to lead to a worldwide operational navigation-satellite system for American military ships. The operational system, consisting of four satellites that are properly positioned relative to each other, is intended to provide accurate data for navigational fixes on an average of once every 1¾ hours. The system is designed to allow users to determine their precise position on Earth regardless of weather and time of day.

Vanguard—Project Vanguard was inaugurated as part of the American program for the International Geophysical Year. The first Vanguard satellite went into orbit on March 17, 1958. Among the valuable data acquired from this satellite was information regarding the relatively slight but significant distortion referred to as the "pear shape" of the Earth. Two other Vanguards were successfully launched in 1959 in this now completed program. The Vanguards provided valuable information on Earth and its space environment, including such phenomena as Earth's magnetic field, the Van Allen radiation belts, and micrometeoroids.

UNMANNED INTERPLANETARY MISSIONS

Lunar Orbiter—Lunar Orbiter 1 (launched August 10, 1966) was the first of a series of spacecraft designed to orbit the Moon and return closeup pictures and other information about Earth's only natural satellite. The photographs and other information returned to Earth by Lunar Orbiter spacecraft contributed to manned landings on the Moon and added immeasurably to knowledge. Analysis of Lunar Orbiter 5's motions around the Moon led to the surprise discovery of lunar mascons.

Mariner—Mariner 9 orbited Mars in 1971–72, sending back via television 7,000 photographs of the Martian surface. Mariner 10, launched in November 1973, flew by Venus and Mercury in February and March 1974, returning the first close-up pictures of those planets. After orbiting around the Sun, Mariner 10 again flew by Mercury on September 21, 1974, and for a third time on March 16, 1975.

Pioneer—Pioneer was the designation of NASA's first series of long-distance spacecraft. Of these, the most notable was Pioneer 5 (launched March 11, 1960), with which radio communication was maintained until June 26, 1960, when the craft was about 22.5 million miles from Earth—a record for the period.

NASA opened a new series of Pioneer experiments with the launch of Pioneer 6 (December 16, 1965). The series is designed to monitor on a continuing basis phenomena of interplanetary space such as radiation, magnetic fields, and the solar wind.

Some Pioneers are investigating space between Earth and Venus; others, between Earth and Mars. The knowledge gained is expected to advance scientific understanding and contribute to planning for manned interplanetary space flights.

Pioneer 10 (launched March 2, 1972) observed Jupiter close up in December, 1973 after passing beyond the orbit of Mars and through the Asteroid belt. Ultimately it should escape the solar system. Pioneer 11, launched March 6, 1973, followed a similar flight path, with a Jupiter encounter Dec. 4, 1974. Pioneer 11 flew past Saturn's rings in Sept. 1979.

Pioneer Venus 1 (launched May 20, 1978) and Pioneer Venus 2 (launched Aug. 8, 1978) began the most extensive study ever made of Venus upon arrival at the planet in December 1978. Swinging into orbit on Dec. 4, Pioneer Venus 1 was to sample upper atmospheric composition, make radar measurements of the surface elevations and roughness, and take daily ultraviolet and infrared pictures of the atmosphere for one Venusian year (225 Earth days) or more. On December 9, the four probes and transporter bus that comprised Pioneer Venus 2 plunged into the Venusian clouds at widely separated points for detailed measurements of the atmosphere from top to bottom.

Ranger—NASA's Project Ranger made possible the greatest single advance in lunar knowledge since Galileo first studied the Moon through a telescope more than three centuries ago. In the program, Ranger spacecraft telecast to Earth 17,255 closeups of the Moon. Features as small as 10 inches across on the lunar surface were made visible to man for the first time.

Ranger 7 through Ranger 9, the last of the Ranger series, began telecasting pictures when they were about 20 minutes away from the Moon and continued to telecast until crashing onto the surface. The Rangers with the television packages were about 5 feet in diameter at their hexagonal base and approximately 8¼ feet long. Cruising in space with appendages extended, Ranger spanned 15 feet across its winglike solar panels and measured 10¼ feet to the far edge of its dish-shaped antenna.

Surveyor—Surveyor was designed to decelerate from the lunar approach velocity of 6,000 mph (or 9,000 feet per second) to a touchdown speed of about 3½ mph.

The first Surveyors were designed as engineering test spacecraft intended primarily to test soft-landing techniques. Their legs were instrumented to return data on the Moon's surface hardness, and each carried a single scanning television camera which have transmitted over 90,000 photos of the lunar surface.

Viking—A decade of planning and work came to fruition with the landing of robot spacecraft on Mars to conduct detailed scientific investigation of the planet, including the search for life. After an 11-month journey, Viking 1 touched down on the boulder-strewn Martian plain called Chryse on July 20, 1976. On Sept. 3, its sister ship, Viking 2, landed at Utopia, about 1,600 km (1,000 mi.) nearer to Mars' polar cap.

Specially designed cameras on the craft took closeup pictures of the planet; miniature weather stations monitored the thin Martian air; other instruments noted magnetism, radiation; and Martian soil was analyzed in miniaturized biology laboratories aboard the spacecraft. The "life" experiments data both satisfied and puzzled scientists. The presence of compounds which were conceivably of biological origin was indicated by the data but the organic analysis data did not support that conclusion.

The end of the normal missions of the two spacecraft occurred in mid-November when solar conjunction produced a blackout of Viking-to-Earth communications. By mid-December, there was a return to post-conjunction operations, and the beginning of the "extended missions" which ended in 1978. The landers continued to operate during a "continued mission" phase through February 1979 and mission planners have advocated a plan to keep Viking Lander 1 operating on a reduced schedule through 1989.

Voyager—Two Voyager spacecraft, carrying instruments to conduct 11 science experiments, were launched on Aug. 20 and Sept. 5, 1977, toward Jupiter, Saturn and the outer reaches of the solar system. Voyager 1, launched on the later date, reached Jupiter on March 5, 1979, and almost immediately made two major discoveries — a ring around Jupiter and active volcanoes on Io, the planet's closest satellite. Boosted toward Saturn, Voyager 1 also examined three other satellites — Europa, Ganymede and Callisto; Voyager 2 made its closest approach to Jupiter on July 9, 1979, also surveyed Callisto, Ganymede, Europa and Amalthea. Both spacecraft continued to observe Jupiter as they headed for Saturn.

Voyager 1 explored Saturn and its ring and moon system in November 1980. Voyager 2 followed in turn in August 1981. Voyager 2 is now heading for Uranus and should reach the distant planet in January 1986.

MANNED SPACE-FLIGHT PROGRAMS

Project Mercury—Project Mercury placed the first Americans into space. The pioneering project was organized (October 5, 1958) to orbit a manned spacecraft, investigate man's reaction to, and abilities in, space flight, and recover both man and spacecraft.

Project Mercury experiments demonstrated that the high-gravity forces of launch and of atmosphere entry as well as weightlessness in orbit for as much as 34 hours do not impair man's ability to control a spacecraft. It proved that man not only augments the reliability of spacecraft controls but also can conduct scientific observations and experiments that expand and clarify information from instruments.

Project Gemini—Project Gemini markedly extended the technology and experience gained through Project Mercury and vastly increased knowledge about space, Earth, and man. The last of the Gemini missions was Gemini 12 (completed November 15, 1966). In achieving all of its major objectives, the Gemini project demonstrated that man can maneuver his craft in space; leave his craft and do useful work in space if he is properly clothed and equipped; rendezvous (find and come near) and dock (link up) his craft with another vehicle in space; function effectively during prolonged space flight of a least two weeks and return to Earth in good physical condition; and control his spacecraft during its descent from orbit and land it within a selected area on Earth.

Project Apollo—Its goals: land American explorers on the Moon and bring them safely back to Earth (which was successfully accomplished by Apollo 11 in July 1969), and establish the technology to meet other national interests in space. The Apollo spacecraft is made up of three sections or modules:

1. COMMMAND MODULE—The command module is designed to accommodate three astronauts in a "shirtsleeve" environment; i.e., the astronauts are able to work, eat, and sleep in the module without pressure suits. The command module, like the crew compartment of an airliner, has windows, and contains controls and instruments (including a computer) of various kinds to enable the astronauts to pilot their craft. The command module weighs about 5 tons. It stands 11 feet tall and has a base diameter of about 13 feet.

2. SERVICE MODULE—The service module is equipped with rocket engines and fuel supplies to enable the astronauts to propel their craft into and out of lunar orbit and to change their course in space. The service module weighs 24 tons. It is 23 feet long and 13 feet in diameter.

3. LUNAR MODULE—The lunar module (LM) is the space ferry that takes two Apollo astronauts down to the Moon and carries them from the Moon's surface into lunar orbit and rendezvous with the Apollo command and service modules in lunar orbit. At launch from Earth, the LM weighs about 14½ tons. It is some 20 feet high and has a base diameter of 13 feet. After the two-man crew of the LM returns to the command module, the LM is jettisoned in lunar orbit.

Skylab—Skylab was America's first orbiting space laboratory, launched by NASA on May 14, 1973. Eleven days later, the first of three scheduled manned missions made a rendezvous with the space station, activating its extensive facilities to conduct solar astronomy experiments, to relay informaton on Earth's ecological systems and to study the effects of weightlessness on industrial processes. Most important, however, was the medical and life sciences information obtained from observation of the three-man crews as they lived in space for prolonged periods of time. The Skylab II (actually the first manned Skylab) mission lasted 28 days; its success prompted NASA to extend Skylab III's mission (launched July 28, 1973 to 59 days. A fourth (third manned) and final Skylab mission was launched on November 16, 1973, and the crew spent 84 days in space. Skylab descended from orbit and broke up over Australia on July 11, 1979.

Apollo Soyuz Test Project—The first international manned space flight was made by United States and U.S.S.R. spacecraft July 15-24, 1975. Its objective was to accomplish spacecraft rendezvous, docking, undocking, crew transfer, interaction of control centers, and interaction of spacecraft crews. The planned joint activities were carried out successfully and the many ceremonial activities were televised as were many of the other activities.

Space Shuttle—The key element in the United States' future Space Transportation System made its first appearance as the first Space Shuttle orbiter, the Enterprise, was rolled out at the NASA/Rockwell International facility at Palmdale, Calif., in September 1976. The spacecraft successfully completed a series of approach and landing flight tests in 1977. The second Space Shuttle orbiter, Columbia, was launched from the Kennedy Space Center, Florida on April 12, 1981 and after 36 orbits of the earth landed successfully at Edwards Air Force Base in California on April 14, 1981.

The agency has 83 active astronauts, of which 19 are in candidate status. Of the 83, 26 are mission specialists and the remainder are pilots.

MANNED SPACE FLIGHTS

Spacecraft	Launching Date	Astronauts	Revolutions	Flight Time	Flight Highlights
USSR Vostok I	Apr. 12, 1961	Yuri A. Gagarin	1	1 hr. 48 mins.	First manned flight.
U.S. Mercury-Redstone 3	May 5, 1961	Alan B. Shepard, Jr.	Suborbital	0 hrs. 15 mins.	First American in space.
U.S. Mercury-Redstone 4	July 21, 1961	Virgil I. Grissom	Suborbital	0 hrs. 16 mins.	Evaluated spacecraft functions.
USSR Vostok II	Aug. 6, 1961	Gherman S. Titov	16	25 hrs. 18 mins.	More than 24 hours in space.
U.S. Mercury-Atlas 6	Feb. 20, 1962	John H. Glenn	3	4 hrs. 55 mins.	First American in orbit.
U.S. Mercury-Atlas 7	May 24, 1962	M. Scott Carpenter	3	4 hrs. 56 mins.	Landed 250 miles from target.
USSR Vostok III	Aug. 11, 1962	Andrian G. Nikolayev	60	94 hrs. 22 mins.	First group flight (Vostok III and IV).
USSR Vostok IV	Aug. 12, 1962	Pavel R. Popovich	45	70 hrs. 57 mins.	Came within 3.1 miles of Vostok III on first orbit.
U.S. Mercury-Atlas 8	Oct. 3, 1962	Walter M. Schirra, Jr.	6	9 hrs. 13 mins.	Landed 5 miles from target.
U.S. Mercury-Atlas 9	May 15, 1963	L. Gordon Cooper, Jr.	22	34 hrs. 20 mins.	First long flight by an American.
USSR Vostok V	June 14, 1963	Valery F. Bykovsky	76	119 hrs. 6 mins.	Second group flight (Vostok V and VI).
USSR Vostok VI	June 16, 1963	Valentina V. Tereshkova	45	70 hrs. 50 mins.	Passed within 3 miles of Vostok V; first woman in space.
USSR Voskhod I	Oct. 12, 1964	Komarov; Feoktistov; Yegorov	15	24 hrs. 17 mins.	First 3-man craft.
USSR Voskhod II	Mar. 18, 1965	Leonov; Belyayev	16	26 hrs. 2 mins.	First man outside spacecraft in 10-minute "walk" (Leonov).
U.S. Gemini 3	Mar. 23, 1965	Virgil I. Grissom John W. Young	3	4 hrs. 53 mins.	First manned orbital maneuvers.
U.S. Gemini 4	June 3, 1965	James A. McDivitt Edward H. White, II	62	97 hrs. 48 mins.	21-minute "space walk" (White).
U.S. Gemini 5	Aug. 21, 1965	L. Gordon Cooper, Jr. Charles Conrad, Jr.	120	190 hrs. 56 mins.	First extended manned flight.
U.S. Gemini 7	Dec. 4, 1965	Frank Borman James A. Lovell, Jr.	206	330 hrs. 35 mins.	Longest space flight at the time.
U.S. Gemini 6-A	Dec. 15, 1965	Walter M. Schirra, Jr. Thomas P. Stafford	16	25 hrs. 52 mins.	World's first successful space rendezvous.
U.S. Gemini 8	Mar. 16, 1966	Neil A. Armstrong David R. Scott	6.5	10 hrs. 42 mins.	World's first docking (to Agena target); mission cut short.
U.S. Gemini 9-A	June 3, 1966	Thomas P. Stafford Eugene A. Cernan	44	72 hrs. 21 mins.	Rendezvous, extravehicular activity, precision landing.
U.S. Gemini 10	July 18, 1966	J. W. Young; M. Collins	43	70 hrs. 47 mins.	Rendezvous with 2 targets; Agena package retrieved.
U.S. Gemini 11	Sept. 12, 1966	C. Conrad, Jr.; R. F. Gordon, Jr.	44	71 hrs. 17 mins.	Rendezvous and docking.
U.S. Gemini 12	Nov. 11, 1966	J. A. Lovell, Jr., E. E. Aldrin, Jr.	59	94 hrs. 35 mins.	3 successful extravehicular trips.

MANNED SPACE FLIGHTS (Cont.)

Spacecraft	Launching Date	Astronauts	Revolutions	Flight Time	Flight Highlights
USSR Soyuz 1	Apr. 23, 1967	Vladimir M. Komarov	17	26 hrs. 40 mins.	Heaviest manned craft; crashed, killing Komarov.
U.S. Apollo 7	Oct. 11, 1968	W. M. Schirra, Jr.; D. F. Eisele; R. Walter Cunningham	163	260 hrs. 9 mins.	First manned flight of Apollo spacecraft.
USSR Soyuz 3	Oct. 26, 1968	Georgi T. Beregovoi	60	94 hrs. 51 mins.	Rendezvous with unmanned Soyuz 2.
U.S. Apollo 8	Dec. 21, 1968	F. Borman; Wm. A. Anders; James A. Lovell, Jr.	Moon orbital (10 revolutions)	147 hrs.	First manned voyage around Moon.
USSR Soyuz 4	Jan. 14, 1969	Vladimir A. Shatalov	45	71 hrs. 14 mins.	Rendezvous with Soyuz 5.
USSR Soyuz 5	Jan. 15, 1969	Volynov; Khrunov; Yeliseyev	46	72 hrs. 46 mins.	Cosmonauts transfer to Soyuz 4.
U.S. Apollo 9	Mar. 3, 1969	J. A. McDivitt; D. R. Scott; Russell L. Schweickart	151	241 hrs. 1 min.	First docking with Lunar Module within Earth's atmosphere.
U.S. Apollo 10	May 18, 1969	Stafford; Cernan; Young	31 (Moon)	192 hrs. 3 mins.	Descent to within 9 miles of Moon.
U.S. Apollo 11	July 16, 1969	Neil A. Armstrong Edwin E. Aldrin, Jr. Michael Collins	Moon orbital for Command Module (31 revolutions)	195 hrs. 18 mins.	Armstrong and Aldrin, in Lunar Module, land in Sea of Tranquility. Collins remained in lunar orbit in Command Module. Remained on Moon for 21 hours, 36 minutes.
USSR Soyuz 6	Oct. 11, 1969	G. S. Shonin; V. N. Kubasow	79	118 hrs. 42 mins.	Welding of metals in space.
USSR Soyuz 7	Oct. 12, 1969	Filipchenko; Volkov; Gorbatko	79	118 hrs. 41 mins.	Tests for building an orbiting space laboratory.
USSR Soyuz 8	Oct. 13, 1969	V. A. Shatalov; A. S. Yeliseyev	79 *	118 hrs. 50 mins.	Test for building an orbiting space laboratory.
U.S. Apollo 12	Nov. 14, 1969	Charles Conrad, Jr.; A. L. Bean; R. F. Gordon, Jr.	Moon orbital for Command Module (45 revolutions)	244 hrs. 36 mins.	Conrad and Bean, in Lunar Module, land in Sea of Storms. Gordon remained in lunar orbit in Command Module.
U.S. Apollo 13	Apr. 11, 1970	J. A. Lovell, Jr.; F. W. Haise, Jr.; John L. Swigert, Jr.	Swung around Moon; returned to Earth	142 hrs. 52 mins.	Power failure en route to Moon led to the termination of the scheduled lunar landing of Lovell and Haise.
USSR Soyuz 9	June 1, 1970	Nikolayev; Sevastyanov	286	424 hrs. 59 mins.	Studied physical reactions to extended space travel.
U.S. Apollo 14	Jan. 31, 1971	Alan B. Shepard, Jr.; Stuart A. Roosa; Edgar D. Mitchell	Moon orbital for Command Module (34 revolutions)	216 hrs. 0.2 mins.	Shepard and Mitchell, in Lunar Module, land in Fra Mauro area. Roosa remained in lunar orbit in Command Module.
USSR Soyuz 10	Apr. 22, 1971	Shatalov; Yeliseyev; Rukavishnikov	32	47 hrs. 46 mins.	Aborted after linking up with unmanned satellite Salyut 1.
USSR Soyuz 11	June 6, 1971	Dobrovolsky; Volkov; Patsayev	360	570 hrs. 22 mins.	Docked with Salyut 1; dead on return.
U.S. Apollo 15	July 26, 1971	David R. Scott; Alfred M. Worden; James B. Irwin	Moon orbital for Command Module (64 revolutions)	295 hrs. 12 mins.	Scott and Irwin, in Lunar Module, landed in Hadley Rille and explored in Lunar Rover. Worden, from Command Module, performed experiments and first deep space walk.
U.S. Apollo 16	Apr. 16, 1972	Charles M. Duke, Jr.; Thomas K. Mattingly; John W. Young	Moon orbital for Command Module (74 revolutions)	265 hrs. 51 mins.	Young and Duke spent 71 hours, two minutes on the Moon's surface. They returned with 214 pounds of lunar rock and soil.
U.S. Apollo 17	Dec. 7, 1972	Eugene A. Cernan; Ronald E. Evans; Harrison H. Schmitt	Moon orbital for Command Module (75 revolutions)	301 hrs. 51 mins.	Cernan and Schmitt spent a record 74 hours and 59 mins. on Moon and returned with 250 pounds of lunar material.
U.S. Skylab 2	May 25, 1973	Charles "Pete" Conrad, Jr.; J. P. Kerwin; P. J. Weitz	393	672 hrs. 49 mins.	First manned flight to Skylab space station.
U.S. Skylab 3	July 28, 1973	Alan L. Bean, Owen K. Garriott, Jack R. Lousma	852	1427 hrs. 9 mins.	Second manned flight to space station demonstrating man's ability to function for long periods in space.

Mission	Date	Crew	Orbits	Duration	Description
USSR Soyuz 12	Sept. 27, 1973	V. G. Lazarev; O. G. Makarov	29	47 hrs. 16 mins.	Testing of modifications in spacecraft.
USSR Soyuz 13	Dec. 18, 1973	P. I. Klimuk; V. V. Lebedev	119	188 hrs. 55 mins.	Cosmonauts grew nutritive protein samples.
U.S. Skylab 4	Nov. 16, 1973	G. P. Carr; Wm. R. Pogue; Edward G. Gibson	1,214	2017 hrs. 17 mins.	Weightless for 84 days, the astronauts each "grew" an inch.
USSR Soyuz 14	July 3, 1974	Popovich; Artyukhin	N.A.	377 hrs. 30 mins.	Occupied Salyut 3.
USSR Soyuz 15	Aug. 26, 1974	Sarafanov; Demin	N.A.	48 hrs. 12 mins.	Failed to achieve a link-up with Salyut 3.
USSR Soyuz 16	Dec. 2, 1974	Filipchenko; Rukavishnikov	96	142 hrs. 24 mins.	ASTP precursor flight to check out new Soyuz designs.
USSR Soyuz 17	Jan. 11, 1975	Grechko; Gubarev	N.A.	709 hrs. 20 mins.	Occupied Salyut 4 and set Soviet duration record.
USSR Soyuz 18	May 24, 1975	Klimuk; Sevastyanov	N.A.	1512 hrs. (est.)	Conducted experiments with Salyut 4.
USSR Soyuz 19 / U.S. Apollo 18	July 15, 1975 / July 15, 1975	Leonov; Kubasov / Stafford; Slayton; Brand	96 Earth orbits / 136 Earth orbits	143 hrs. 31 mins. / 217 hrs. 30 mins.	ASTP joint flight. U.S. and USSR link up in space and hold a joint news conference.
USSR Soyuz 21	July 6, 1976	Volynov; Zholobov	N.A.	50 days	Conducted experiments with Salyut 5.
USSR Soyuz 22	Sept. 15, 1976	Bykovsky; Aksenov	N.A.	8 days	Photographed Earth's surface.
USSR Soyuz 23	Oct. 14, 1976	Zudov; Rozhdestvensky	N.A.	2 days	Failed to achieve link-up with Salyut 5.
USSR Soyuz 24	Feb. 7, 1977	Gorbatko; Glazkov	N.A.	425 hrs. 23 mins.	Conducted experiments with Salyut 5.
USSR Soyuz 25	Oct. 9, 1977	Kovalenak; Ryumin	N.A.	48 hrs. 46 mins.	Failed to dock with Salyut 6.
USSR Soyuz 26	Dec. 10, 1977	Romanenko; Grechko	1600 (approx.)	96 days, 10 hrs.	Docked with Salyut 6. Returned to Earth March 16, 1978.
USSR Soyuz 27	Jan. 10, 1978	Dzhanibekov; Makarov	N.A.	6 days	Docked with Salyut 6. Returned to Earth Jan. 16.
USSR Soyuz 28	March 2, 1978	Gubarev; Remek (Czech)	N.A.	7 days	Docked with Salyut 6. Returned to Earth, March 10.
USSR Soyuz 29	June 15, 1978	Kovalenak; Ivanchenkov	N.A.	139 days, 15 hrs.	Docked with Salyut 6. Returned to Earth Nov. 2.
USSR Soyuz 30	June 27, 1978	Klimuk; Hermaszewski (Pole)	N.A.	8 days	Docked with Salyut 6. Returned to Earth, July 5.
USSR Soyuz 31	Aug. 26, 1978	Bykovsky; Jaehn (E. Ger.)	N.A.	8 days	Docked with Salyut 6. Returned to Earth Sept. 3.
USSR Soyuz 32	Feb. 25, 1979	Lyakhov; Ryumin	N.A.	175 days	Docked with Salyut 6 space station; resupplied three times. Returned to Earth on Aug. 19, in Soyuz 34.
USSR Soyuz 33	Apr. 10, 1979	Rukavishnikov; Ivanov (Bulgarian)	N.A.	2 days	Aborted attempt to ferry two cosmonauts to the Salyut 6 space station. Returned to Earth, Apr. 12.
USSR Soyuz 35	Apr. 9, 1980	Ryumin; Popov	N.A.	185 days	Docked with Salyut 6 space station. In orbit for record endurance space flight. Returned to Earth, Oct. 11.
USSR Soyuz 36	May 25, 1980	Kubasov; Farkas (Hungarian)	N.A.	7 days	Link-up with Salyut 6. Returned to Earth, June 3.
USSR Soyuz T2	June 5, 1980	Malyshev; Aksenov	N.A.	4 days	Link-up with Salyut 6. Returned to Earth, June 9.
USSR Soyuz 37	July 23, 1980	Gorbatko; Tuan (Vietnamese)	N.A.	8 days	Link-up with Salyut 6. Returned to Earth, July 31.
USSR Soyuz 38	Sept. 18, 1980	Romanenko; Mendez (Cuban)	N.A.	8 days	Link-up with Salyut 6. Returned to Earth, Sept. 26.
USSR Soyuz T-3	Nov. 27, 1980	Kizim; Makarov; Strekalov	N.A.	13 days	Link-up with Salyut 6. Test of upgraded Soyuz. Returned to Earth, Dec. 10.
USSR Soyuz T-4	Mar. 12, 1981	Kovalyonok; Savinykh	N.A.	75 days	Link-up with Salyut 6. Returned to Earth, May 26.
USSR Soyuz 39	Mar. 22, 1981	Dzhanibekov; Gurragcha (Mongolian)	N.A.	8 days	Link-up with Salyut 6. Returned to Earth, Mar. 30.
U.S. Columbia (STS-1)	Apr. 12, 1981	J.W. Young; R.L. Crippen	36	54 hrs. 22 mins.	Space shuttle test flight. Returned to Earth, Apr. 14.
USSR Soyuz 40	May 14, 1981	Popov; Prunariu (Romanian)	N.A.	8 days	Link-up with Salyut 6. Returned to Earth May 22.

SCIENCE: PAST/PRESENT

ENGINEERING ACHIEVEMENTS

The following is a list of engineering projects that have received the American Society of Civil Engineers' Outstanding Civil Engineering Achievement Award.

St. Lawrence Seaway and Power Project. A swath for ocean-going vessels from the Atlantic to the Great Lakes, serving America's and Canada's energy and navigational needs.

John F. Kennedy International Airport, 1961—Designed to handle nearly all of the New York area's international air traffic, one-half of its domestic long-haul traffic, and one-quarter of its domestic short and medium air traffic.

Intercontinental Ballistic Missile Program, 1962—This program involved ICBM installations in 14 states.

Ohio River Basin Clean Streams Program, 1963—This complex of facilities for pollution control affected the economy of more than 1,500 municipalities in eight states adjacent to 1,000 miles of waterways in the Ohio River Basin.

The Glen Canyon Unit of the Colorado River Project, 1964—Rising 710 feet, the dam is only 16 feet less than Hoover Dam in height; its concrete volume is greater.

Chesapeake Bay Bridge-Tunnel, 1965 — This engineering achievement crosses over and under the open sea and links the Eastern Shore of Virginia with the mainland. Its 12.5 miles of low-level trestle, four man-made islands, two mile-long tunnels, a high and medium-level bridge and several miles of approach roads make up the project.

NASA Complex 39, 1966—This huge complex, the Apollo-Saturn assembly and launch facility at Cape Kennedy (Merritt Island), Florida, is dominated by the world's second largest building: the Vehicle Assembly Building.

St. Louis Gateway Arch, 1967—This 630-foot stainless steel arch commemorates the role of St. Louis as the historic "Gateway to the West."

San Mateo Hayward Bridge, 1968—Spans San Francisco Bay, is located 17 miles south of the city, accommodates 50,000 vehicles daily, and is 6.7 miles long.

Oroville Dam and Powerplant, 1969—This dam on California's Feather River is the highest (770 ft.) in the Western Hemisphere and the world's third largest.

Middletown, Ohio, Armco Steelworks, 1970—This steelmaking complex was cited for construction innovations, techniques, materials, and pollution control.

World Trade Center, 1971—When built, these twin towers were the world's two tallest buildings (110 stories, 1,350 feet high).

California State Water Project, 1972—The project to deliver 4.23 million acre-feet of water throughout California. Its major aqueduct extends 444 miles.

Ludington Pumped Storage Project, 1973—Water from Lake Michigan is pumped up to a reservoir from which it rushes through the turbines of the power plant, with a generating capacity of over 1.8 million kw of electricity.

Land Reclamation Program of Fulton County, Ill., 1974 — Sludge is barged down the Illinois River to Fulton County, and pumped 11 miles underground until converted into liquid fertilizer.

The Keowee-Toxaway Project, 1975 — of the Duke Power Co., in the western part of North and South Carolina, a 700-million-dollar power generating complex that includes two hydroelectric projects and a major nuclear generating station, generating over 3.4 million kw of electricity.

Lower Snake River Project, 1976 — a 140-mile development in southeastern Washington, is designed to facilitate navigation and generate power through the construction of four dams and the Lewiston levee and parkway system.

Superior, Wis., Midwest Energy Terminal, 1977—The nation's largest western coal transshipment terminal, this complex was designed to receive, store, and load coal from rail cars onto Great Lakes carriers for Detroit's fuel needs.

Trans-Alaska Pipeline, 1978 — An 800-mile system of highway, 48-inch steel pipeline from Prudhoe Bay to Valdez, eight pump stations along the route, and storage and tanker facilities at Valdez harbor.

Nation's Capital Metro Transit System, 1979—Some 30 miles of subway connecting suburban Maryland and Virginia with various sections of Washington, D.C.

Shell Oil's Cognac offshore drilling platform, 1980—Located off the coast of Louisiana, this is the tallest oil rig—1,265 ft. tall—and is capable of a daily peak oil production of 50,000 barrels and 150 mil. cu. ft. of gas.

Industry Hills Civic-Recreation-Conservation Area, 1981—(City of Industry, Calif.)—A badly scarred 600-acre hill formation was transformed into an impressive multi-purpose area to meet vital needs of the community.

PERIODIC TABLE OF ELEMENTS

The periodic table, first devised by the Russian chemist Dmitri I. Mendeleev (1834–1907) in 1869, is shown here in its present form. It is an orderly classification of the elements based on physical and chemical similarities. The atomic number of each element denotes the number of protons (positive charge) in the nucleus of its atoms as well as the number of electrons (negative charge) in its orbital shells when the atoms are neutral. In general, the higher the atomic number, the heavier the element. The table is arranged so that elements in the same vertical column possess similar properties (this similarity is related to the number of outer or valence electrons). Elements in the same horizontal row have the same number of electron shells. Numbers in brackets are atomic numbers of undiscovered elements.

	Group I A	II A	III B	IV B	V B	VI B	VII B	VIII			I B	II B	III A	IV A	V A	VI A	VII A	Inert Gases
1	H 1																	He 2
2	Li 3	Be 4											B 5	C 6	N 7	O 8	F 9	Ne 10
3	Na 11	Mg 12											Al 13	Si 14	P 15	S 16	Cl 17	Ar 18
4	K 19	Ca 20	Sc 21	Ti 22	V 23	Cr 24	Mn 25	Fe 26	Co 27	Ni 28	Cu 29	Zn 30	Ga 31	Ge 32	As 33	Se 34	Br 35	Kr 36
5	Rb 37	Sr 38	Y 39	Zr 40	Nb 41	Mo 42	Tc 43	Ru 44	Rh 45	Pd 46	Ag 47	Cd 48	In 49	Sn 50	Sb 51	Te 52	I 53	Xe 54
6	Cs 55	Ba 56	La 57	Hf 72	Ta 73	W 74	Re 75	Os 76	Ir 77	Pt 78	Au 79	Hg 80	Tl 81	Pb 82	Bi 83	Po 84	At 85	Rn 86
7	Fr 87	Ra 88	Ac 89	104	105	106	107	(108)	(109)	(110)	(111)	(112)	(113)	(114)	(115)	(116)	(117)	(118)

LANTHANIDE SERIES	Ce 58	Pr 59	Nd 60	Pm 61	Sm 62	Eu 63	Gd 64	Tb 65	Dy 66	Ho 67	Er 68	Tm 69	Yb 70	Lu 71
ACTINIDE SERIES	Th 90	Pa 91	U 92	Np 93	Pu 94	Am 95	Cm 96	Bk 97	Cf 98	Es 99	Fm 100	Md 101	No 102	Lr 103

ELEMENTS AND THEIR DISCOVERERS

Element and Symbol	Atomic Number	Atomic Weight	Discoverer and Date
Actinium (Ac)	89	(227)*	A. Debierne (1899)
Aluminum (Al)	13	27.0	F. Wöhler (1827)
Americium (Am)	95	(243)	G. Seaborg et al. (1944)
Antimony (Sb)	51	121.8	B. Valentine (1604)
Argon (Ar)	18	39.9	W. Ramsay and J. Rayleigh (1894)
Arsenic (As)	33	74.9	A. Magnus (1250) (?)
Astatine (At)	85	(210)	E. Segrè et al. (1940)
Barium (Ba)	56	137.3	H. Davy (1808)
Berkelium (Bk)	97	(247)	S. Thompson et al. (1949)
Beryllium (Be)	4	9.0	N. Vauquelin (1798)
Bismuth (Bi)	83	209.0	C. Geoffroy the Younger (1753)
Boron (B)	5	10.8	H. Davy et al. (1808)
Bromine (Br)	35	79.9	A. Balard (1826)
Cadmium (Cd)	48	112.4	F. Stromeyer (1817)
Calcium (Ca)	20	40.1	H. Davy (1808)
Californium (Cf)	98	(251)	S. Thompson et al. (1950)
Carbon (C)	6	12.0	Prehistoric
Cerium (Ce)	58	140.1	J. Berzelius and W. d'Hisinger (1803)
Cesium (Cs)	55	132.9	R. Bunsen and G. Kirchhoff (1860)
Chlorine (Cl)	17	35.5	K. Scheele (1774)
Chromium (Cr)	24	52.0	N. Vauquelin (1797)
Cobalt (Co)	27	58.9	G. Brandt (c.1735)
Copper (Cu)	29	63.5	Prehistoric
Curium (Cm)	96	(247)	G. Seaborg et al. (1944)
Dysprosium (Dy)	66	162.5	L. de Boisbaudran (1886)
Einsteinium (Es)	99	(254)	A. Ghiorso et al. (1952)
Erbium (Er)	68	167.3	C. Mosander (1843)
Europium (Eu)	63	152.0	E. Demarçay (1896)
Fermium (Fm)	100	(257)	A. Ghiorso et al. (1952)
Fluorine (F)	9	19.0	H. Moissan (1886)
Francium (Fr)	87	(223)	M. Perey (1939)
Gadolinium (Gd)	64	157.3	J. C. de Marignac (1880)
Gallium (Ga)	31	69.7	L. de Boisbaudran (1875)
Germanium (Ge)	32	72.6	C. Winkler (1886)
Gold (Au)	79	197.0	Prehistoric
Hafnium (Hf)	72	178.5	D. Coster and G. von Hevesy (1923)
Helium (He)	2	4.0	J. C. P. Janssen and N. Lockyer (1868)
Holmium (Ho)	67	164.9	J. Soret and M. Delafontaine (1878)
Hydrogen (H)	1	1.0	H. Cavendish (1766)
Indium (In)	49	114.8	F. Reich and T. Richter (1863)
Iodine (I)	53	126.9	B. Courtois (1811)
Iridium (Ir)	77	192.2	S. Tennant (1803)
Iron (Fe)	26	55.8	Prehistoric
Krypton (Kr)	36	83.8	W. Ramsay and M. Travers (1898)
Lanthanum (La)	57	138.9	C. Mosander (1839)
Lawrencium (Lr)	103	(257)	A. Ghiorso et al. (1961)
Lead (Pb)	82	207.2	Prehistoric
Lithium (Li)	3	6.9	A. Arfvedson (1817)
Lutetium (Lu)	71	175.0	G. Urbain (1907)
Magnesium (Mg)	12	24.3	Recognized by J. Black (1755)
Manganese (Mn)	25	54.9	Recognized by K. Scheele et al. (1774)
Mendelevium (Md)	101	(258)	A. Ghiorso et al. (1955)
Mercury (Hg)	80	200.6	Prehistoric
Molybdenum (Mo)	42	95.9	K. Scheele (1778)
Neodymium (Nd)	60	144.2	C. von Welsbach (1885)
Neon (Ne)	10	20.2	W. Ramsay and M. Travers (1898)
Neptunium (Np)	93	(237)	E. McMillan and P. Abelson (1940)
Nickel (Ni)	28	58.7	A. Cronstedt (1751)
Niobium (Columbium) (Nb)	41	92.9	C. Hatchett (1801)
Nitrogen (N)	7	14.0	D. Rutherford (1772)
Nobelium (No)	102	(255)	A. Ghiorso et al. (1958)
Osmium (Os)	76	190.2	S. Tennant (1803)
Oxygen (O)	8	16.0	J. Priestley (1774)
Palladium (Pd)	46	106.4	W. Wollaston (1803)
Phosphorus (P)	15	31.0	H. Brand (1669)
Platinum (Pt)	78	195.1	D. de Ulloa (1735)
Plutonium (Pu)	94	(244)	G. Seaborg et al. (1940)
Polonium (Po)	84	(209)	P. and M. Curie (1898)
Potassium (K)	19	39.1	H. Davy (1807)
Praseodymium (Pr)	59	140.9	C. von Welsbach (1885)
Promethium (Pm)	61	(145)	J. Marinsky et al. (1947)
Protactinium (Pa)	91	231.0	K. Fajans and A. H. Göhring (1913)
Radium (Ra)	88	226.1	P. and M. Curie (1898)
Radon (Rn)	86	(222)	E. Rutherford (thoron) (1899)
			E. Dorn (radon) (1900)
Rhenium (Re)	75	186.2	W. Noddack et al. (1925)
Rhodium (Rh)	45	102.9	W. Wollaston (1803)
Rubidium (Rb)	37	85.5	R. Bunsen and G. Kirchhoff (1861)
Ruthenium (Ru)	44	101.1	K. Claus (or Klaus) (1844)
Samarium (Sm)	62	150.4	L. de Boisbaudran (1879)
Scandium (Sc)	21	45.0	L. Nilson (1879)
Selenium (Se)	34	79.0	J. Berzelius (1817)
Silicon (Si)	14	28.1	J. Berzelius (1824)
Silver (Ag)	47	107.9	Prehistoric
Sodium (Na)	11	23.0	H. Davy (1807)
Strontium (Sr)	38	87.6	H. Davy (1808)
Sulfur (S)	16	32.1	Prehistoric
Tantalum (Ta)	73	180.9	A. Ekeberg (1802)
Technetium (Tc)	43	(97)	E. Segrè and C. Perrier (1937)
Tellurium (Te)	52	127.6	M. von Reichenstein (1782)
Terbium (Tb)	65	158.9	C. Mosander (1843)
Thallium (Tl)	81	204.4	W. Crookes (1861)
Thorium (Th)	90	232.0	J. Berzelius (1828)
Thulium (Tm)	69	168.9	P. Cleve (1879)
Tin (Sn)	50	118.7	Prehistoric
Titanium (Ti)	22	47.9	W. Gregor (1791)
Tungsten (Wolfram) (W)	74	183.9	J. and F. d'Elhuyar (1783)
Uranium (U)	92	238.0	E. M. Peligot (1841)
Vanadium (V)	23	51.0	A. del Rio (1801)
Xenon (Xe)	54	131.3	W. Ramsay and M. Travers (1898)
Ytterbium (Yb)	70	173.0	C. Marignac (1878)
Yttrium (Y)	39	88.9	J. Gadolin (1794)
Zinc (Zn)	30	65.4	Prehistoric
Zirconium (Zr)	40	91.2	M. Klaproth (1789)
Unnilquadium	104	(257)	A. Ghiorso et al.
Unnilpentium	105	(262)	G. Flerov et al.
Unnilhexium	106	(262)	
Unnilseptium	107	(261)	G. Flerov et al. (1976)

* A number in parentheses under "Atomic Weight" is the mass number of the longest-lived isotope.

SELECTED NATIONAL ACADEMIES OF SCIENCE

Institution	Founded
National Academy of Sciences (Rome)	1603
The Royal Society (London)	1660
Academy of Sciences (Paris)	1666
The Royal Danish Academy of Sciences and Letters (Copenhagen)	1742
Royal Academy of Sciences, Letters, and Fine Arts of Belgium (Brussels)	1772
Royal Society of Edinburgh	1783
Royal Irish Academy (Dublin)	1786
Hungarian Academy of Sciences (Budapest)	1825
Austrian Academy of Science (Vienna)	1847
The Norwegian Academy of Science and Letters in Oslo	1857
National Academy of Sciences (Washington, D. C.)	1863
Yugoslav Academy of Sciences and Arts (Zagreb)	1867
Japan Academy (Tokyo)	1879
Royal Society of Canada (Ottawa)	1882
National Academy of Science (Mexico City)	1884
Brazilian Academy of Sciences (Rio de Janeiro)	1916
Academy of Athens	1926
Academia Sinica (Taipei)	1928
National Academy of Sciences of Buenos Aires	1937
Academy of the Socialist Republic of Rumania (Bucharest)	1948
Academy of Finland (Helsinki)	1947
Chinese Academy of Sciences (Peking)	1949
Czechoslovak Academy of Sciences (Prague)	1952
Polish Academy of Sciences (Warsaw)	1952
Australian Academy of Science (Canberra)	1954
Israel Academy of Sciences and Humanities (Jerusalem)	1961
Academy of Sciences of Cuba (Havana)	1962

LANDMARKS OF SCIENCE

Date	Landmark	Discoverer	Nationality
5th cent. B.C.	The atomic structure of matter postulated	Democritus	Greek
5th cent. B.C.	Postulation of causality in nature: the belief that every natural event has a natural cause	Leucippus	Greek
c. 300 B.C.	Compilation of **Elements:** the first formal statement of geometric principles	Euclid	Greek
3d cent. B.C.	Discovery of the laws of floating bodies, establishing the discipline of hydrostatics	Archimedes	Greek
c. 230 B.C.	First measurement of the Earth's circumference (accomplished without astronomical instruments)	Eratosthenes	Greek
3d cent. B.C.	Observations and calculations leading to the conclusions that the Earth is smaller than the Sun, rotates on an inclined axis, and revolves around the Sun; also, explanation of the seasons	Aristarchus of Samos	Greek
2d cent. B.C.	Measurement of size and distance of the Sun and the Moon	Hipparchus	Greek
2d cent. A.D.	Synthesis of current astronomical knowledge in the **Almagest,** which provided a system of celestial mechanics	Claudius Ptolemaeus (Ptolemy)	Greek
9th cent. A.D.	Establishment of the theory of numbers	Al-Khowarizmi	Arabian
1530	Publication of **De re metallica,** establishing the science of mineralogy	Georg Bauer (Agricola)	German
1543	Publication of **De revolutionibus orbium coelestium;** the solar system described as heliocentric	Mikolaj Kopernik (Copernicus)	Polish
1559	First cylindrical-projection map (commonly known as Mercator's projection), establishing mapmaking	Gerhard Kremer (Mercator)	Flemish
1589–92	Discovery of the laws of motion concerning falling bodies, the pendulum, and the inclined plane	Galileo Galilei	Italian
1600	Publication of **De magnete:** the basis for future work on magnetism and electricity	William Gilbert or Gylberde	English
1609/1619	Discovery of the three fundamental laws of planetary motion	Johannes Kepler	German
1614	Invention of logarithms as a powerful method of arithmetical calculation	John Napier	Scottish
1619	Formulation of analytic geometry	René Descartes	French
1620	Publication of **Novum Organum,** elucidating first formal theory of inductive logic	Francis Bacon	English
1643	Proof that air has weight; invention of the barometer	Evangelista Torricelli	Italian
1661	Formulation of the modern concept of the distinction between chemical elements and compounds	Robert Boyle	Anglo-Irish
1662	Discovery of law (Boyle's law) governing relation between pressure and volume of a gas	Robert Boyle	Anglo-Irish
c. 1670	Discovery of the calculus: the most powerful mathematical tool	Isaac Newton [Independently (1675–76) by Gottfried Leibniz, German]	English
1676	First measurement of the velocity of light	Olaus Römer	Danish
1687	Publication of **Philosophiae naturalis principia mathematica,** establishing the laws of gravitation and universal laws of motion	Isaac Newton	English
1690	Propounding of the wave theory of light	Christiaan Huygens	Dutch
1729	Distinction between electrical conductors and nonconductors (insulators)	Stephen Gray	English
1733	Distinction between two kinds of electricity (later called positive and negative); establishment of the fundamental law of electric charges	C. F. Du Fay	French
1735	Publication of **Systema naturae:** the foundation of taxonomy	Karl von Linné (Carolus Linnaeus)	Swedish
c. 1789	Discovery of true nature of combustion	Antoine Lavoisier	French
1795	Publication of **Theory of the Earth,** which paved the way to modern geological science	James Hutton	Scottish
1799	Discovery of the law of definite proportions of elements by weight in chemical compounds	Joseph Proust	French
1801	**Disquisitiones Arithmeticae** advances number theory	Karl F. Gauss	German
1802	Discovery of the dark lines in the solar spectrum	William Wollaston [Independently (1814) by Joseph von Fraunhofer, German]	English
1803	Proposal of an atomic theory of matter to explain the laws of chemical combination	John Dalton	English
1815	Establishment of stratigraphic geology for dating geological formations	William Smith	English
1820	Discovery of electromagnetism	Hans Christian Oersted	Danish
1825–26	Formulation of non-Euclidean geometry	Nikolai I. Lobachevski [Independently (1825–26) by Janos Bolyai, Hungarian]	Russian
1827	Statement of the law (Ohm's law) of electric conduction	Georg S. Ohm	German
1828	First synthesis of an organic compound from inorganic material	Friedrich Wöhler	German
1831	Discovery of electromagnetic induction	Michael Faraday [Independently (c. 1830) by Joseph Henry, American]	English
1840s	Formulation of the law of the conservation of energy (also known as the first law of thermodynamics)	Julius R. von Mayer	German
		James P. Joule	English
		Hermann L. F. von Helmholtz	German
1850	Formulation of the concept of entropy: the second law of thermodynamics	Rudolf J. E. Clausius	German
1850s	Establishment of the science of spectroscopy	Gustav R. Kirchhoff	German
		Robert W. Bunsen	German

LANDMARKS OF SCIENCE (Continued)

Date	Landmark	Discoverer	Nationality
1852	Formulation of the concept of chemical valence	Edward Frankland	English
1854	Invention of Boolean algebra: the mathematization of logic	George Boole	English
1855	Founding of the science of oceanography	Matthew F. Maury	American
1859	Publication of **Origin of Species**, setting forth the idea of natural selection of living things	Charles Darwin [Independently (1858) by A. R. Wallace, English]	English
1861	Establishment of organic chemistry as the chemistry of carbon compounds	Friedrich A. Kekulé	German
1864	Formulation of the mathematical theory of electromagnetic radiation	James C. Maxwell	Scottish
1865	Formulation of the fundamental laws of genetics	Gregor J. Mendel	Austrian
1869	Formulation of the periodic law and periodic table of elements	Dmitri I. Mendeleev	Russian
1884	Formulation of the concepts of transfinite mathematics and the development of set theory, the basis of modern mathematical analysis	Georg Cantor	German
1884	Establishment of the concept of ionic dissociation in solution (ionization)	Svante A. Arrhenius	Swedish
1887	Propagation of electromagnetic waves (radio waves): demonstration that these waves travel at the velocity of light	Heinrich R. Hertz	German
1895	Discovery of X-rays	Wilhelm K. Roentgen	German
1896	Discovery of radioactivity in uranium	Antoine H. Becquerel	French
1897	Discovery of the electron	Joseph J. Thomson	English
1900	Postulation of quantum theory	Max Planck	German
1901	Enunciation of the idea of evolution by mutation	Hugo Marie De Vries	Dutch
	Established nature of radioactive disintegration	Ernest Rutherford	English, b. New Zealand
1905–15	Postulation of the special and general theories of relativity	Albert Einstein	American, b. Germany
1905–16	Completion of first cloud chamber for observing nuclear particles	Charles T. R. Wilson	Scottish
1911	Discovery of superconductivity	Heike Kammerlingh-Onnes	Dutch
1911	Formulation of the concept of the planetary atom	Niels H. D. Bohr	Danish
1913	Establishment of the concept of atomic number and that it is equal to the charge on the nucleus	Henry G. J. Moseley	English
1913	Completion of **Principia Mathematica**, a major contribution to symbolic logic	Bertrand A. W. Russell	English
		Alfred North Whitehead	English
1916	First relativistic theory of "black holes" formed by high-density matter	Karl Schwarzschild	German
1924–26	Formulation of wave mechanics	Louis V. de Broglie	French
		Erwin Schroedinger	German
1925	Formulation of matrix mechanics	Werner Heisenberg	German
1926	Publication of **Conditioned Reflexes**	Ivan Petrovich Pavlov	Russian
1931	Postulation of existence of the neutrino	Wolfgang Pauli	German
1932	Discovery of the neutron	James Chadwick	English
1932	Discovery of the positron	Carl D. Anderson	American
1934	Neutron bombardment of uranium leading to the production of transuranium elements	Enrico Fermi	American, b. Italy
1938	First nuclear fission of uranium	Lise Meitner	Austrian-Swedish
		Otto Hahn	German
		Fritz Strassmann	German
1942	Controlled nuclear fission of uranium	Enrico Fermi and others	American, b. Italy
1945	Explosion of first atomic bomb	J. Robert Oppenheimer and others	American
1947	Development of carbon-14 dating	Willard F. Libby	American
1948	Construction of the transistor	John Bardeen, Walter H. Brattain, & William Shockley	American
1951	First power-producing, nuclear-fission reactor	Atomic Energy Commission	American
1951	Explosion of first nuclear-fusion (hydrogen) bomb	Atomic Energy Commission	American
1953	Deciphering the double-helix structure of deoxyribonucleic acid (DNA) in the chromosome	Francis Crick, Maurice Wilkins, & James Watson	English American
1954	Construction of first maser	Charles H. Townes	American
1955	Production and detection of the antiproton	Emilio G. Segré	American, b. Italy
		Owen Chamberlain	American
1958	Discovery of belts of high-energy radiation surrounding the Earth	James A. Van Allen	American
1960	First demonstration of laser action	Theodore H. Maiman	American
1967	Deciphering the structure of ribonucleic acid (RNA)	David Harker and others	American
1968	Synthesizing of ribonuclease molecule	R. Bruce Merrifield and others	American
		Ralph F. Hirschman and others	American
1969	First men on the moon	Neil Armstrong	American
		Edwin Aldrin	American
1971	Discovery of reverse transcriptase for synthesizing DNA from RNA	H. Temin	American
1974	Detection of psi particle	Sam Ting and others	American
		Burt Richter and others	American
1976	Discovery of a charmed particle	Leon Lederman and others	American
	Completion of gene synthesis	Har Gobind Khorana	American, b. India
1978	Discovery that some animal genes are interrupted in structure with genetic material of unknown function	P. Chambon and others	French
1981	Successful launch of reusable space shuttle	NASA	American

THE BASIS OF MEASUREMENT

The International System of Units (Système International, SI) is the modernized version of the metric system, established by international agreement to provide a logical and interconnected framework for all measurements in science, industry, and commerce. The seven base units here given are the foundation for the entire system, and all other units are derived from them. (Use of metric weights and measures was legalized in the United States in 1866, and our customary units of weights and measures are defined in terms of the meter and kilogram.)

Length—Meter. The meter is defined as 1,650,763.73 wavelengths in vacuum of the orange-red line of the spectrum of krypton-86.

Time—Second. The second is defined as the duration of 9,192,631,770 cycles of the radiation associated with a specified transition of the cesium atom.

Mass—Kilogram. The standard for the kilogram is a cylinder of platinum-iridium alloy kept by the International Bureau of Weights and Measures at Paris. A duplicate at the National Bureau of Standards serves as the mass standard for the United States. The kilogram is the only base unit still defined by an artifact.

Temperature—Kelvin. The Kelvin scale has its base at absolute zero and has a fixed point at the triple point of water defined as 273.16 kelvins. This triple point, at which water forms an interface of solid, liquid, and vapor, is defined as 0. 01° C on the Celsius or centigrade scale, and 32.02° F on the Fahrenheit scale.

Electric Current—Ampere. The ampere is defined as the magnitude of the current that, when flowing through each of two long parallel wires separated by one meter in free space, results in a force between the two wires (due to their magnetic fields) of 2×10^{-7} newton for each meter of length. (A newton is the unit of force of such size that a body of one kilogram mass would experience an acceleration of one meter per second per second.)

Luminous Intensity—Candela. The candela is defined as the luminous intensity of 1/600,000 of a square meter of a radiating cavity at the temperature of solidifying platinum (2,042 K).

Amount of Substance—Mole. The mole is defined as the amount of a substance containing as many elementary units (specified as atoms, molecules, ions, electrons, photons, and so forth) as there are carbon atoms in 0.012 kilogram of carbon-12.

TABLES OF METRIC WEIGHTS AND MEASURES

LINEAR MEASURE

10 millimeters (mm)	= 1 centimeter (cm)	
10 centimeters	= 1 decimeter (dm)	= 100 millimeters
10 decimeters	= 1 meter (m.)	= 1,000 millimeters
10 meters	= 1 dekameter (dam)	
10 dekameters	= 1 hectometer (hm)	= 100 meters
10 hectometers	= 1 kilometer (km)	= 1,000 meters

AREA MEASURE

100 square millimeters	= 1 square centimeter	
10,000 square centimeters	= 1 square meter	= 1,000,000 square millimeters
100 square meters	= 1 are (a)	
100 ares	= 1 hectare (ha)	= 10,000
100 hectares	= 1 square kilometer	= 1,000,000 square meters

VOLUME MEASURE

one liter	= 0.001 cubic meter
10 milliliters (ml)	= 1 centiliter (cl)
10 centiliters	= 1 deciliter (dl) = 100 milliliters
10 deciliters	= 1 liter (l) = 1,000 milliliters

VOLUME MEASURE (Cont.)

10 liters	= 1 dekaliter (dal)
10 dekaliters	= 1 hectoliter (hl) = 100 liters
10 hectoliters	= 1 kiloliter (kl) = 1,000 liters

WEIGHT

10 milligrams (mg)	= 1 centigram (cg)
10 centigrams	= 1 decigram (dg) = 100 milligrams
10 decigrams	= 1 gram (g) = 1,000 milligrams
10 grams	= 1 dekagram (dag)
10 dekagrams	= 1 hectogram (hg) = 100 grams
10 hectograms	= 1 kilogram (kg) = 1,000 grams
1,000 kilograms	= 1 metric ton (t)

CUBIC MEASURE

1,000 cubic millimeters	= 1 cubic centimeter
1,000 cubic centimeters	= 1 cubic decimeter = 1,000,000 cubic millimeters
1,000 cubic decimeters	= 1 cubic meter = 1 stere
	= 1,000,000 cubic centimeters
	= 1,000,000,000 cubic millimeters

TABLES OF EQUIVALENTS

The name of a unit enclosed in brackets [1 chain] indicates (1) that the unit is not in current use in the United States, or (2) that the unit is believed to be based on "custom and usage" rather than on formal definition. Equivalents involving decimals are, in most instances, rounded off to the third decimal place except where exact equivalents are so designated.

1 angstrom[1]	0.1 millimicron (exactly).
	0.000 1 micron (exactly).
	0.000 000 1 millimeter (exactly).
	0.000 000 004 inch.
1 cable's length	120 fathoms.
	720 feet.
	219.456 meters (exactly).
1 centimeter	0.393 7 inch.
1 chain (Gunter's or surveyor's)	66 feet.
	20.1168 meters (exactly).
[1 chain] (engineer's)	100 feet.
	30.48 meters (exactly).
1 decimeter	3.937 inches.
1 dekameter	32.808 feet.
1 fathom	6 feet.
	1.8288 meters (exactly).
1 foot	0.3048 meter (exactly).
1 furlong	10 chains (surveyor's).
	660 feet.
	220 yards.
	⅛ statute mile.
	201.168 meters (exactly).
[1 hand]	4 inches.
1 inch	2.54 centimeters (exactly).
1 kilometer	0.621 mile.
1 league (land)	3 statute miles.
	4.828 kilometers.
1 link (Gunter's or surveyor's)	7.92 inches (exactly).
	0.201 168 meter (exactly).
[1 link (engineer's)]	1 foot.
	0.3048 meter (exactly).
1 meter	39.37 inches.
	1.094 yards.
1 micron (μ [the Greek letter mu])	0.001 millimeter (exactly).
	0.000 039 37 inch.
1 mil	0.001 inch (exactly).
	0.025 4 millimeter (exactly).

1 mile (statute or land)	5,280 feet.
	1.609 kilometers.
1 mile (nautical, international)	1.852 kilometers (exactly).
	1.151 statute miles.
	0.999 U.S. nautical miles.
1 millimeter	0.039 37 inch.
1 millimicron (mμ [the English letter m in combination with the Greek letter mu])	0.001 micron (exactly).
	0.000 000 039 37 inch.
1 point (typography)	0.013 837 inch (exactly).
	1/72 inch (approximately).
	0.351 millimeter.
1 rod, pole, or perch	16½ feet.
	5½ yards.
	5.0292 meters (exactly).
1 yard	0.9144 meter (exactly).

AREAS OR SURFACES

1 acre	43,560 square feet.
	4,840 square yards.
	0.405 hectare.
1 are	119.599 square yards.
	0.025 acre.
1 hectare	2.471 acres.
[1 square (building)]	100 square feet.
1 square centimeter	0.155 square inch.
1 square decimeter	15.500 square inches.
1 square foot	929.030 square centimeters.
1 square inch	6.4516 square centimeters (exactly).
1 square kilometer	0.386 square mile.
	247.105 acres.
1 square meter	1.196 square yards.
	10.764 square feet.
1 square mile	258.999 hectares.
1 square millimeter	0.002 square inch.
1 square rod, sq. pole, or sq. perch	25.293 square meters.
1 square yard	0.836 square meter.

CAPACITIES OR VOLUMES

1 barrel, liquid	31 to 42 gallons.[2]
1 barrel, standard for fruits, vegetables, and other dry commodities except cranberries	7,056 cubic inches. / 105 dry quarts. / 3.281 bushels.
1 barrel, standard, cranberry	5,286 cubic inches. / 86 45/64 dry quarts. / 2.709 bushels, struck measure.
1 bushel (U.S.), struck measure	2,150.42 cubic inches. / 35.239 liters.
[1 bushel, heaped (U.S.)]	2,747.715 cubic inches. / 1.278 bushels, struck measure.[3]
[1 bushel (British Imperial) (struck measure)]	1.032 U.S. bushels. / 2,219.36 cubic inches.
1 cord (firewood)	128 cubic feet.
1 cubic centimeter	0.061 cubic inch.
1 cubic decimeter	61.024 cubic inches.
1 cubic foot	7.481 gallons. / 28.316 cubic decimeters.
1 cubic inch	0.554 fluid ounce. / 4.433 fluid drams. / 16.387 cubic centimeters.
1 cubic meter	1.308 cubic yards.
1 cubic yard	0.765 cubic meter.
1 cup, measuring	8 fluid ounces. / ½ liquid pint.
1 dram, fluid or liquid (U.S.)	⅛ fluid ounce. / 0.226 cubic inch. / 3.697 milliliters. / 1.041 British fluid drachms.
1 dekaliter	2.642 gallons. / 1.135 pecks.
1 gallon (U.S.)	231 cubic inches. / 3.785 liters. / 0.833 British gallon. / 128 U.S. fluid ounces.
[1 gallon (British Imperial)]	277.42 cubic inches. / 1.201 U.S. gallons. / 4.546 liters. / 160 British fluid ounces.
1 gill	7.219 cubic inches. / 4 fluid ounces. / 0.118 liter.
1 hectoliter	26.418 gallons. / 2.838 bushels.
1 liter	1.057 liquid quarts. / 0.908 dry quart. / 61.024 cubic inches.
1 milliliter	0.271 fluid dram. / 16.231 minims. / 0.061 cubic inch.
1 ounce, fluid or liquid (U.S.)	1.805 cubic inches. / 29.574 milliliters. / 1.041 British fluid ounces.
[1 ounce, fluid (British)]	0.961 U.S. fluid ounce. / 1.734 cubic inches. / 28.412 milliliters.
1 peck	8.810 liters.
1 pint, dry	33.600 cubic inches. / 0.551 liter.
1 pint, liquid	28.875 cubic inches (exactly). / 0.473 liter.
1 quart, dry (U.S.)	67.201 cubic inches. / 1.101 liters. / 0.969 British quart.
1 quart, liquid (U.S.)	57.75 cubic inches (exactly). / 0.946 liter. / 0.833 British quart.
[1 quart (British)]	69.354 cubic inches. / 1.032 U.S. dry quarts. / 1.201 U.S. liquid quarts.
1 tablespoon	3 teaspoons. / 4 fluid drams. / ½ fluid ounce.
1 teaspoon	⅓ tablespoon. / 1⅓ fluid drams.

WEIGHTS OR MASSES

1 assay ton[4]	29.167 grams.
1 carat	200 milligrams. / 3.086 grains.
1 dram, apothecaries	60 grains. / 3.888 grams.
1 dram, avoirdupois	27 11/32 (= 27.344) grains. / 1.772 grams.
1 grain	64.798 91 milligrams (exactly).
1 gram	15.432 grains. / 0.035 ounce, avoirdupois.
1 hundredweight, gross or long[5]	112 pounds. / 50.802 kilograms.
1 hundredweight, net or short	100 pounds. / 45.359 kilograms.
1 kilogram	2.205 pounds.
1 microgram (μg [the Greek letter mu in combination with the letter g])	0.000 001 gram (exactly).
1 milligram	0.015 grain.
1 ounce, avoirdupois	437.5 grains (exactly). / 0.911 troy or apothecaries ounce. / 28.350 grams.
1 ounce, troy or apothecaries	480 grains. / 1.097 avoirdupois ounces. / 31.103 grams.
1 pennyweight	1.555 grams.
1 point	0.01 carat. / 2 milligrams.
1 pound, avoirdupois	7 000 grains. / 1.215 troy or apothecaries pounds. / 453.592 37 grams (exactly).
1 pound, troy or apothecaries	5 760 grains. / 0.823 avoirdupois pound. / 373.242 grams.
1 ton, gross or long[5]	2,240 pounds. / 1.12 net tons (exactly). / 1.016 metric tons.
1 ton, metric	2,204.623 pounds. / 0.984 gross ton. / 1.102 net tons.
1 ton, net or short	2,000 pounds. / 0.893 gross ton. / 0.907 metric ton.

[1] The angstrom is basically defined as 10⁻¹⁰ meter. [2] There are a variety of "barrels," established by law or usage. For example, federal taxes on fermented liquors are based on a barrel of 31 gallons; many state laws fix the "barrel for liquids" at 31½ gallons; one state fixes a 36-gallon barrel for cistern measurement; federal law recognizes a 40-gallon barrel for "proof spirits"; by custom, 42 gallons comprise a barrel of crude oil or petroleum products for statistical purposes, and this equivalent is recognized "for liquids" by four states. [3] Frequently recognized as 1¼ bushels, struck measure. [4] The assay ton bears the same relation to the milligram that a ton of 2,000 pounds avoirdupois bears to the ounce troy; hence the weight in milligrams of precious metal obtained from one assay ton of ore gives directly the number of troy ounces to the net ton. [5] The gross or long ton and hundredweight are used commercially in the United States to only a limited extent, usually in restricted industrial fields. These units are the same as the British "ton" and "hundredweight."

ROMAN NUMERALS

These are letter symbols used to represent numbers. The seven basic letters and their number equivalents are: I=1, V=5, X=10, L=50, C=100, D=500, M=1,000. All other numbers (there is no zero) are formed using combinations of these letters (reading left to right, highest to lowest) which, when added together, produce the desired total: MCLX=1,160; LXXI=71; XVIII=18, etc.

In most cases a subtraction principle is used to show numbers containing 4's and 9's. Thus, instead of using four consecutive similar letters (IIII, XXXX or CCCC), only one letter is shown, followed by a larger value letter from which the smaller is to be subtracted. Examples of these cases are: IV=4, IX=9, XL=40, XC=90, CD=400, CM=900. 494 is written CDXCIV, 1979 becomes MCMLXXIX.

The addition of a bar line over the Roman numeral increases its value 1,000 times. V̄ represents 5,000, X̄IX is 19,000, L̄V̄I is 56,000. A large number such as 145,262 converts to C̄X̄L̄V̄C̄C̄LXII.

BINARY NUMBERS

This number system utilizes only two symbols, 1 and 0. The location of these symbols in the binary number indicates the presence (1) or absence (0) of a certain number of units which, when added together, produce a total numerical value. The number of units to be added is determined by the length of the binary number and the location(s) of the 1 symbol. The extreme right-hand place stands for one unit; each successive place to the left represents double (2 times) the quantity of the place to its right.

Number of Units	32	16	8	4	2	1	Add	Total Value
BINARY						1	1	1
NUMBERS 10=			1		1	0	2+0	2
101=			1		0	1	4+0+1	5
1010=			1	0	1	0	8+0+2+0	10
11001=		1	1	0	0	1	16+8+0+0+1	25
101110=1	0	1	1	1	0	32+0+8+4+2+0	46

UNIT CONVERSIONS

To Convert	Into	Multiply By
Acre	hectare	0.4047
Acres	square feet	43,560.0
Acres	square miles	1.562×10^{-3}
Ampere-hours	coulombs	3,600.0
Angstrom unit	inch	3.937×10^{-9}
Angstrom unit	micron	1×10^{-4}
Astronomical unit	kilometers	1.495×10^8
Atmospheres	cms of mercury	76.0
Bolt (U.S. cloth)	meters	36.576
BTU	horsepower-hrs	3.931×10^{-4}
BTU	kilowatt-hrs	2.928×10^{-4}
BTU/hr	watts	0.2931
Bushels	cubic inches	2,150.4
Calories, gram (mean)	BTU (mean)	3.9685×10^{-3}
Centares	square meters	1.0
Centimeters	kilometers	1×10^{-5}
Centimeters	meters	1×10^{-2}
Centimeters	millimeters	10.0
Centimeters	feet	3.281×10^{-2}
Centimeters	inches	0.3937
Chain	inches	792.0
Circumference	radians	6.283
Coulombs	faradays	1.036×10^{-5}
Cubic centimeters	cubic inches	0.06102
Cubic centimeters	pints (U.S. liq.)	2.113×10^{-3}
Cubic feet	cubic meters	0.02832
Cubic feet/min	pounds water/min.	62.43
Cubic feet/sec	gallons/min.	448.831
Cubits	inches	18.0
Days	seconds	86,400.0
Degrees (angle)	radians	1.745×10^{-2}
Degrees/sec.	revolutions/min.	0.1667
Dynes	grams	1.020×10^{-3}
Dynes	joules/meter (newtons)	1×10^{-5}
Ell	inches	45.0
Em, pica	inch	0.167
Ergs	BTU	9.480×10^{-11}
Ergs	foot-pounds	7.3670×10^{-8}
Ergs	kilowatt-hours	2.778×10^{-14}
Faradays/sec.	amperes (absolute)	96,500
Fathoms	feet	6.0
Feet	centimeters	30.48
Feet	meters	0.3048
Feet	miles (nautical)	1.645×10^{-4}
Feet	miles (statute)	1.894×10^{-4}
Feet/min.	centimeters/sec.	0.5080
Feet/sec.	knots	0.5921
Feet/sec.	miles/hour	0.6818
Foot-pounds	BTU	1.286×10^{-3}
Foot-pounds	kilowatt-hours	3.766×10^{-7}
Furlongs	miles (U.S.)	0.125
Furlongs	feet	660.0
Gallons	liters	3.785
Gallons of water	pounds of water	8.3453
Gallons/min.	cubic feet/hour	8.0208
Grams	ounces (avoirdupois)	3.527×10^{-2}
Grams	ounces (troy)	3.215×10^{-2}
Grams	pounds	2.205×10^{-3}
Hand	centimeters	10.16
Hectares	acres	2.471
Hectares	square feet	1.076×10^5
Horsepower	BTU/min.	42.44
Horsepower	kilowatts	0.7457
Horsepower	watts	745.7
Hours	days	4.167×10^{-2}
Hours	weeks	5.952×10^{-3}
Inches	centimeters	2.540
Inches	miles	1.578×10^{-5}
International ampere	ampere (absolute)	0.9998
International volt	volts (absolute)	1.0003
Joules	BTU	9.480×10^{-4}
Joules	ergs	1×10^7
Kilograms	pounds	2.205
Kilometers	feet	3,281.0
Kilometers	meters	1,000.0
Kilometers	miles	0.6214
Kilometers/hr.	knots	0.5396
Kilowatts	horsepower	1.341
Kilowatt-hours	BTU	3,413.0
Knots	feet/hour	6,080.0
Knots	nautical miles/hr.	1.0
Knots	statute miles/hr.	1.151
League	miles (approximately)	3.0
Light year	miles	5.9×10^{12}
Links (surveyor's)	inches	7.92
Liters	cubic centimeters	1,000.0
Liters	cubic inches	61.02
Liters	gallons (U.S. liq.)	0.2642
Liters	milliliters	1,000.0
Liters	pints (U.S. liq.)	2.113
Meters	centimeters	100.0
Meters	feet	3.281
Meters	kilometers	1×10^{-3}
Meters	miles (nautical)	5.396×10^{-4}
Meters	miles (statute)	6.214×10^{-4}
Meters	millimeters	1,000.0
Microns	meters	1×10^{-6}
Miles (nautical)	feet	6,080.27
Miles (statute)	feet	5,280.0
Miles (nautical)	kilometers	1.853
Miles (statute)	kilometers	1.609
Miles (nautical)	miles (statute)	1.1516
Miles (statute)	miles (nautical)	0.8684
Miles/hour	feet/min.	88.0
Milligrams/liter	parts/million	1.0
Milliliters	liters	1×10^{-3}
Millimeters	inches	3.937×10^{-2}
Newtons	dynes	1×10^5
Ohms (international)	ohms (absolute)	1.0005
Ounces	grams	28.349527
Ounces	pounds	6.25×10^{-2}
Ounces (troy)	ounces (avoirdupois)	1.09714
Parsec	miles	19×10^{12}
Parsec	kilometers	3.084×10^{13}
Pints (liq.)	cubic centimeters	473.2
Pints (liq.)	cubic inches	28.87
Pints (liq.)	gallons	0.125
Pints (liq.)	quarts (liq.)	0.5
Pounds	kilograms	0.4536
Pounds	ounces	16.0
Pounds	ounces (troy)	14.5833
Pounds	pounds (troy)	1.21528
Pounds/sq. inch	grams/sq. cm.	70.31
Quarts (dry)	cubic inches	67.20
Quarts (liq.)	cubic inches	57.75
Quarts (liq.)	gallons	0.25
Quarts (liq.)	liters	0.9463
Quires	sheets	25.0
Radians	degrees	57.30
Radians	minutes	3,438.0
Reams	sheets	500.0
Revolutions	degrees	360.0
Revolutions/min.	degrees/sec.	6.0
Rods	meters	5.029
Rods	feet	16.5
Rods (surveyor's measure)	yards	5.5
Seconds	minutes	1.667×10^{-2}
Slug	pounds	32.17
Tons (long)	kilograms	1,016.0
Tons (short)	kilograms	907.1848
Tons (long)	pounds	2,240.0
Tons (short)	pounds	2,000.0
Tons (long)	tons (short)	1.120
Tons (short)	tons (long)	0.89287
Volt (absolute)	statvolts	3.336×10^{-3}
Watts	BTU/hour	3.4129
Watts	horsepower	1.341×10^{-3}
Watts (international)	watts (absolute)	1.0002
Yards	meters	0.9144
Yards	miles (nautical)	4.934×10^{-4}
Yards	miles (statute)	5.682×10^{-4}

MULTIPLES AND SUBMULTIPLES

Prefix	Symbol	Equivalent	Factor
atto-	a	quintillionth part	$\times 10^{-18}$
femto-	f	quadrillionth part	$\times 10^{-15}$
pico-	p	trillionth part	$\times 10^{-12}$
nano-	n	billionth part	$\times 10^{-9}$
micro-	μ	millionth part	$\times 10^{-6}$
milli-	m	thousandth part	$\times 10^{-3}$
centi-	c	hundredth part	$\times 10^{-2}$
deci-	d	tenth part	$\times 10^{-1}$
deca-	da	tenfold	$\times 10$
hecto-	h	hundredfold	$\times 10^2$
kilo-	k	thousandfold	$\times 10^3$
mega-	M	millionfold	$\times 10^6$
giga-	G	billionfold	$\times 10^9$
tera-	T	trillionfold	$\times 10^{12}$

TABLES OF UNITED STATES CUSTOMARY WEIGHTS AND MEASURES

LINEAR MEASURE

12 inches (in.)	= 1 foot (ft.)
3 feet	= 1 yard (yd.)
5½ yards	= 1 rod (rd.), pole, or perch (16½ ft.)
40 rods	= 1 furlong (fur.) = 220 yards = 660 feet
8 furlongs	= 1 statute mile (mi.) = 1,760 yards = 5,280 feet
3 land miles	= 1 league
5,280 feet	= 1 statute or land mile
6,076.11549 feet	= 1 international nautical mile

AREA MEASURE

Squares and cubes of units are sometimes abbreviated by using "superior" figures. For example, ft² means square foot, and ft³ means cubic foot.

144 square inches	= 1 square foot
9 square feet	= 1 square yard = 1,296 square inches
30¼ square yards	= 1 square rod = 272¼ square feet
160 square rods	= 1 acre = 4,840 square yards = 43,560 square feet
640 acres	= 1 square mile
1 mile square	= 1 section (of land)
6 miles square	= 1 township = 36 sections = 36 square miles

CUBIC MEASURE

1,728 cubic inches	= 1 cubic foot
27 cubic feet	= 1 cubic yard

LIQUID MEASURE

When necessary to distinguish the liquid pint or quart from the dry pint or quart, the word "liquid" or the abbreviation "liq." should be used in combination with the name or abbreviation of the liquid unit.

4 gills (gi.)	= 1 pint (pt.) (= 28.875 cubic inches)
2 pints	= 1 quart (qt.) (= 57.75 cubic inches)
4 quarts	= 1 gallon (gal.) (= 231 cubic inches) = 8 pints = 32 gills

APOTHECARIES FLUID MEASURE

60 minims (min.)	= 1 fluid dram (fl. dr.) (= 0.2256 cubic inch)
8 fluid drams	= 1 fluid ounce (fl. oz.) (= 1.8047 cubic inches)
16 fluid ounces	= 1 pint (= 28.875 cubic inches) = 128 fluid drams
2 pints	= 1 quart (= 57.75 cubic inches) = 32 fluid ounces = 256 fluid drams
4 quarts	= 1 gallon (= 231 cubic inches) = 128 fluid ounces = 1,024 fluid drams

DRY MEASURE

When necessary to distinguish the dry pint or quart from the liquid pint or quart, the word "dry" should be used in combination with the name or abbreviation of the dry unit.

2 pints	= 1 quart (= 67.2006 cubic inches)
8 quarts	= 1 peck (pk.) (= 537.605 cubic inches) = 16 pints
4 pecks	= 1 bushel (bu.) (= 2,150.42 cubic inches) = 32 quarts

AVOIRDUPOIS WEIGHT

When necessary to distinguish the avoirdupois dram from the apothecaries dram, or to distinguish the avoirdupois dram or ounce from the fluid dram or ounce, or to distinguish the avoirdupois ounce or pound from the troy or apothecaries ounce or pound, the word "avoirdupois" or the abbreviation "avdp." should be used in combination with the name or abbreviation of the avoirdupois unit.

(The "grain" is the same in avoirdupois, troy, and apothecaries weights.)

27 11/32 grains	= 1 dram (dr.)
16 drams	= 1 ounce (oz.) = 437½ grains
16 ounces	= 1 pound (lb.) = 256 drams = 7,000 grains
100 pounds	= 1 hundredweight (cwt.)*
20 hundredweights	= 1 ton (tn.) = 2,000 pounds*

In "gross" or "long" measure, the following values are recognized:

112 pounds	= 1 gross or long hundredweight*
20 gross or long hundredweights	= 1 gross or long ton = 2,240 pounds*

TROY WEIGHT

24 grains	= 1 pennyweight (dwt.)
20 pennyweights	= 1 ounce troy (oz. t.) = 480 grains
12 ounces troy	= 1 pound troy (lb. t.) = 240 pennyweights = 5,760 grains

APOTHECARIES WEIGHT

20 grains	= 1 scruple (s. ap.)
3 scruples	= 1 dram apothecaries (dr. ap.) = 60 grains
8 drams apothecaries	= 1 ounce apothecaries (oz. ap.) = 24 scruples = 480 grains
12 ounces apothecaries	= 1 pound apothecaries (lb. ap.) = 96 drams apothecaries = 288 scruples = 5,760 grains

GUNTER'S OR SURVEYOR'S CHAIN MEASURE

7.92 inches	= 1 link (li.)
100 links	= 1 chain (ch.) = 4 rods = 66 ft.
80 chains	= 1 statute mile = 320 rods = 5,280 ft.

* When the terms "hundredweight" and "ton" are used unmodified, they are commonly understood to mean the 100-pound hundredweight and the 2,000-pound ton, respectively; these units may be designated "net" or "short" when necessary to distinguish them from the corresponding units in gross or long measure.

TEMPERATURE CONVERSIONS

The table offers temperature conversions that range from the freezing point of water (32° F., 0° C.) to its boiling point (212° F., 100° C.). For conversions below or beyond that range, apply these formulas: to convert Fahrenheit degrees into Celsius, subtract 32, multiply by 5, and divide by 9; to convert Celsius into Fahrenheit, multiply by 9, divide by 5, and add 32. A Fahrenheit degree is smaller than a Celsius degree, one Fahrenheit degree being 5/9 of a Celsius degree.

°F	°C	°F	°C	°F	°C	°F	°C	°F	°C
32	0	72	22.2	89.6	32	103	39.4		
33.8	1	54	12.2	73	22.8	90	32.2	104	40
35.6	2	55	12.8	74.3	23	91	32.8	105	40.6
36.5	2.5	56	13.3	74	23.3	91.4	33	105.8	41
37.4	3	57	13.9	75	23.9	92	33.3	106	41.1
38	3.3	57.2	14	75.2	24	93	33.9	107	41.7
39	3.9	58	14.4	76	24.4	94	34.4	107.6	42
39.2	4	59	15	77	25	95	35	108	42.2
40	4.4	60	15.6	78	25.6	96	35.6	109	42.8
41	5	61	16.1	79	26.1	96.8	36	110	43.3
42	5.6	62	16.7	80	26.7	97	36.1	111	43.9
43	6.1	63	17.2	80.6	27	97.3	36.3	112	44.4
44	6.7	64	17.8	81	27.2	98	36.7	113	45
45	7.2	65	18.3	82	27.8	98.6	37	114	45.6
46	7.8	66	18.9	82.4	28	99	37.2	115	46.1
46.4	8	66.2	19	83	28.3	99.5	37.5	116	46.7
47	8.3	67	19.4	84	28.9	100	37.8	117	47.2
48	8.9	68	20	85	29.4	100.4	38	118	47.8
48.2	9	69	20.6	86	30	101	38.3	118.4	48
50	10	69.8	21	87	30.6	101.8	38.8	119	48.3
51	10.6	70	21.1	88	31.1	102	38.9	120	48.9
52	11.1	71	21.7	89	31.7	102.2	39	121	49.4

°F	°C	°F	°C	°F	°C	°F	°C	°F	°C
122	50	140	60	160	71.1	180	82.2	197	91.7
123	50.6	141	60.6	161	71.7	181	82.8	198	92.2
124	51.1	142	61.1	161.6	72	182	83.3	199	92.8
125	51.7	143	61.7	162	72.2	183	83.9	199.4	93
125.6	52	144	62.2	163	72.8	183.2	84	200	93.3
126	52.2	145	62.8	164	73.3	184	84.4	201	93.9
127	52.8	146	63.3	165	73.9	185	85	202	94.4
128	53.3	147	63.9	166	74.4	186	85.6	203	95
129	53.9	148	64.4	167	75	186.8	86	204	95.6
130	54.4	149	65	168	75.6	187	86.1	204.8	96
131	55	150	65.6	168.8	76	188	86.7	205	96.1
132	55.6	151	66.1	169	76.1	188.6	87	206	96.7
133	56.1	152	66.7	170	76.7	189	87.2	207	97.2
134	56.7	152.6	67	171	77.2	190	87.8	208	97.8
134.6	57	153	67.2	172	77.8	190.4	88	208.4	98
135	57.2	154	67.8	173	78.3	191	88.3	209	98.3
136	57.8	155	68.3	174	78.9	192	88.9	210	98.9
136.4	58	156	68.9	175	79.4	193	89.4	210.2	99
137	58.3	156.2	69	176	80	194	90	211	99.4
138	58.9	157	69.4	177	80.6	195	90.6	212	100
138.2	59	158	70	178	81.1	195.8	91		
139	59.4	159	70.6	179	81.7	196	91.1		

SCIENCE GLOSSARY

PHYSICS AND ATOMIC ENERGY

Absolute temperature—Temperature scale on which the zero point is absolute zero ($-273.15°$ C).

Acceleration—Rate of change of velocity; increase or decrease in velocity per unit of time.

Alpha particle—Low-speed, low-penetration helium nucleus emitted during disintegration of radioactive elements.

Anode—The positive electrode in an electric cell or an electron tube.

Angstrom—A unit of length: 1/100,000,000 centimeter.

Atom—Smallest part of a chemical element that takes part in a chemical change.

Atomic number—Number of protons in an atomic nucleus.

Atomic weight—Ratio of the average mass per atom of an element to 1/12 of the mass of an atom of carbon 12.

Beta particle—High-speed, high-penetration electron emitted during radioactive disintegration.

British thermal unit (BTU)—The amount of heat required to raise the temperature of one pound of water through one Fahrenheit degree.

Calorie—The amount of heat required to raise the temperature of one gram of water through 1° C.

Cathode—The negative electrode in an electric cell or an electron tube.

Celsius scale—A temperature scale on which the range between the freezing point of water, 0°, and the boiling point, 100°, is divided into 100 equal degrees. Also called the *Centigrade* scale.

Centrifugal force—The apparent force experienced by a body moving in a curved path that acts outward from the center of the path.

Doppler effect—Apparent change in frequency of sound waves or light waves caused by relative motion of the source toward or away from an observer, and by motion of an observer toward or from a stationary source.

Electron—Negatively charged, stable elementary particle.

Fission—Specifically, the splitting of an atomic nucleus into two parts of approximately the same size, accompanied by the release of great amounts of energy.

Fusion, nuclear—Union of two light atomic nuclei to form a heavier, more complex one, accompanied by the release of great amounts of energy. Also called *thermonuclear fusion*.

Gamma rays—Shortwave, high-frequency electromagnetic radiation emitted during disintegration of radioactive elements.

Gravity—Attraction of the earth or a celestial body for other bodies at or near its surface.

Half life—The time required for half of a radioactive substance to decay.

Hertz—Unit of frequency equal to 1 cycle per second.

Infrared—Electromagnetic radiation with wavelengths longer than visible red.

Ion—Charged atom or group of atoms produced by loss or gain of electrons from the outer orbits.

Ionization—Any process resulting in the formation of ions from atoms or molecules.

Joule—Unit of energy equal to the work done when a force of one newton moves through one meter.

Kinetic energy—Energy due to motion.

Liquid—Fluid phase of matter in which the surface is free, the volume is definite, and the shape is determined by the container.

Magnetic field—Space permeated by magnetic lines of force.

Magnetic pole—One of the two points in a magnet or a celestial body where magnetism seems to concentrate.

Mass Number—Sum of the numbers of protons and neutrons in the nucleus of an atom.

Matter—Anything that has mass and occupies space.

Meson—Any of a group of elementary particles of small mass and very short life.

Neutron—Neutral particle found in the nuclei of atoms with a mass number greater than 1.

Newton—Unit of force equal to the force required to give a mass of 1 kilogram an acceleration of 1 meter per second per second.

Nuclear reactor—Device for starting and regulating nuclear fission for the purpose of producing heat.

Nucleon—Particle found in the structure of an atom's nucleus; a proton or neutron.

Nucleus—Central, positively charged part of an atom.

Ohm—Unit of electrical resistance.

Photoelectric effect—Emission of electrons by certain substances when struck by light or other radiation.

Photon—A quantum of radiation.

Physical change—An alteration that includes no change in the molecular composition of a substance.

Physics—The study of matter and energy and the interchange of energy among material things.

Positron—Positive electron.

Proton—Positively charged, stable particle found in the nuclei of all atoms.

Quantum mechanics—Modern mathematical form of the quantum theory.

Quantum theory—Theory that all energy is lost or gained in discrete amounts (quanta).

Quark—Type of particle with fractional electron charge, postulated to be components of other particles.

Radar—Electronic system for detecting distant objects by means of transmitted high-frequency radio waves and their reflection from the objects.

Radiation—Electromagnetic waves, or particles emitted from nuclei.

Radioactivity—Disintegration of the nuclei of the atoms of certain elements, during which electromagnetic waves and elementary particles are emitted.

Relative density—Ratio of density of a substance to the density of water. Formerly *specific gravity*.

Relativity—(1) Einstein's special theory: All motion is relative to observer, and velocity of light in space is constant regardless of motion of light source or observer. Mass may be changed into energy and vice versa according to the law $E = mc^2$ (2) Einstein's general theory: gravitation is a consequence of curved space.

Resistance—Opposition to passage of electric current offered by an electrical conductor.

Spectroscope—Optical instrument for the study of spectra.

Spectrum—Band of electromagnetic radiation in which the constituent parts are arranged according to their wavelengths or their frequencies.

Transformer—Device for changing the voltage of alternating current.

Transistor—Device made of semiconductor materials for the control of the flow of electric current.

Ultrasonic—Having a frequency above that audible to human beings: above about 20,000 hertz (cycles per second).

Ultraviolet—Electromagnetic radiation with wavelengths shorter than visible violet but longer than X-rays.

Velocity—Rate of motion in a given direction.

Watt hour—The energy of 1 watt acting for 1 hour.

Wavelength—Distance between two successive points of a wave in the same phase, such as crest to crest.

X-rays—Electromagnetic radiations of short wavelength and high penetration of matter.

MATHEMATICS

Additive inverse of a number—A number with its sign changed to minus if originally plus, or vice versa.

Algorism (Algorithm)—In modern mathematics, any systematic method or procedure for computation.

Analog computer—A calculating device in which magnitudes are determined by measurement along scales rather than by digital counting, e.g., slide rule.

Analytic geometry—The technique of dealing with geometry in terms of algebra.

Antilogarithm—The number corresponding to a given logarithm, e.g., 2 is the logarithm of 100, therefore, 100 is the antilogarithm of 2.

Axiom—In a system of mathematics or logic, a proposition or statement from which secondary propositions or statements are derived.

Binary arithmetic—A system of calculation in which the only numerals used are 0 and 1, and all real numbers are represented as powers of 2.

Bit—Condensation of *binary digit*. In computer and information theory, a single binary digit, either 0 or 1.

Boolean algebra—An algebra obeying special laws that make it suitable for such uses as the study of logic and planning switching circuits.

Calculus—Generally, any system of mathematical calculation, or any system of operations involving symbols, e.g., calculus of finite differences, calculus of probabilities, and the like. Specifically, a method of mathematical analysis (developed independently by Isaac Newton and Gottfried Leibniz) involving the rate of change of a variable function.

Cardinal number—Zero and the counting numbers 1, 2, 3, 4, . . . , as distinguished from the ordinal numbers.

Cartesian coordinates—Two or three lines intersecting at right angles and providing a reference system for locating points in two or three dimensional space; used in analytic geometry.

Compound interest—Interest paid periodically on the sum of a given principle and its accruing interest.

Decimal number system—The ordinary number system (sometimes called the Arabic system) that denotes real numbers according to the place values for multiples of 10 plus the digits 0 through 9.

Derivative—A measure of the rate at which one mathematical variable changes in response to changes in a related variable.

Digital computer—A calculating machine in which mathematical operations are performed by individually tallying every digit.

Duodecimal system—A system of numeration in which the base is 12. The numbers 10 and 11 of the decimal system are rendered in the duodecimal system by arbitrary symbols, two of which in use are t (called dek) and e (called el).

Function—In classical algebra, a variable y so related to another variable x, that for each value given to x there is a value that may be determined for y.

Hardware—The electronic equipment used in a computer system, in contrast to the software.

Infinity—A quantity that is greater than any assignable quantity.

Integral—Mathematical function used in calculus for finding the area under a curve.

Intersection—That portion of two or more sets common to all the sets considered.

Iterative procedure—A means of approximating the solution to an equation by repeating a given procedure several times to get successively closer answers, each based on the preceding approximation.

Logarithm—The exponent of the power to which a number is to be raised to produce a given number. Thus, using the base 10, the logarithm of 100 is 2, because the exponent of the power to which 10 must be raised in order to equal 100 is 2 ($10^2 = 100$).

Machine language—The characters and symbols and the rules for combining them that convey information and instruction to a computer for processing.

Matrix—Usually a rectangular array of numbers, including several columns and rows, that can be manipulated as though it were a single quantity.

Modular arithmetic—A form of arithmetic dealing with the remainders left over when all the numbers considered are divided by a single number, the modulus.

Multiplicative inverse of a number—The reciprocal of that number; for example, 1/5 is the reciprocal of 5.

Non-Euclidean geometry—Any of several geometries that substitute other postulates for Euclid's fifth postulate (in effect, through a point outside a given line, only one line may be drawn parallel to the given line).

Open sentence—An equation containing one or more unknown quantities.

Ordinal number—A number that indicates position or relation; thus, 2d, 3d, 8th.

Postulate—An unproved assumption accepted as basic to a mathematical system, and from which, in combination with other postulates, the propositions of the system are derived, or in terms of which the propositions are proved.

Problem language—The language used by a programmer to state the problem to be solved by a computer.

Program—A sequence of steps to be executed by a computer to solve a given problem.

Reciprocal—The number that results when 1 is divided by a given number. Thus, the reciprocal of 2 is ½; the reciprocal of 4 is ¼; and the reciprocal of a fraction is the fraction inverted, thus the reciprocal of ⅘ is ⅚.

Repeating decimal—A nonterminating decimal in which a pattern of numbers is established and is followed by a continuous repetition of the digit or pattern of digits, thus: .22222222222, .77777777777, .1515151515-15, .234523452345; a repeating decimal is also called a recurring decimal, periodic decimal, or circulating decimal.

Scalar—A quantity indicating magnitude but not direction, in contrast to a vector.

Set—A collection of objects, symbols, or ideas with some common property or attribute.

Slide rule—A computing device usually consisting of a frame and a horizontal slide, on both of which are printed scales graduated logarithmically. Also, usually, a transparent runner, or indicator, containing a hairline that is used to enable accurate reading of the results obtained by manipulation of the slide within the frame.

Software—Programs, procedures, and routines that support and augment a computer system.

Symbolic logic—Logic performed with the use of symbols subject to certain predetermined rules.

Topology—The study of those properties of geometric figures that remain unchanged despite radical distortions of considered figures.

Transformation—A rule for transforming one set of values into another; for example, $y = 2x$ transforms each x into a y twice as large.

Truth set—A set of solutions to an equation or group of equations.

Union—The total of all the members of all the sets of the union being considered.

Vector—A quantity having direction as well as magnitude. Thus, velocity is a vector because it is specified by its direction as well as its magnitude.

CHEMISTRY

Acid—A substance that in aqueous solution turns blue litmus red, furnishes hydrogen ions, and contains hydrogen, which can be replaced by a metal.

Alkali—A water-soluble base that ionizes strongly to form hydroxide ions.

Anion—A negative ion.

Base—A substance that in aqueous solution turns red litmus blue, furnishes hydroxyl ions, and reacts with an acid to form a salt and water only.

Buffer—A solution containing either a weak acid and its salt or a weak base and its salt, thereby resisting changes in acidity or basicity.

Carbohydrate—A compound of carbon, hydrogen, and oxygen, usually having hydrogen and oxygen in the proportion of 2 to 1.

Catalyst—A substance that alters the rate at which a chemical reaction takes place, but which itself remains unchanged.

Cation—A positive ion.

Chemical change—Change in a substance involving a change in its identity due to an increase, decrease, or rearrangement of the atoms within its molecules; opposed to physical change, in which the substance keeps its identity.

Colloid—Dispersion in a medium of particles that are very small aggregates of molecules. Also called colloidal suspension.

Combustion—Any chemical change that produces heat and, usually, light. Most commonly, the combination of the oxygen of the air with a substance: burning.

Compound—A homogeneous substance composed of two or more chemical elements, the proportions of which by weight are fixed and invariable.

Cracking—A method of changing the constituents of petroleum, using pressure, heat, and catalysts, in which the hydrocarbons of high molecular weight are broken down into those of lower molecular weight.

Crystal—A solid in which the component molecules, atoms, or ions are oriented in a definite and repeated geometric pattern.

Deliquescent substance—A substance that absorbs moisture from the air and dissolves in the water so absorbed.

Deuterium—An isotope of hydrogen of mass number 2.

Distillation—Vaporization of a liquid, followed by condensation of the vapor.

Electrolysis—Chemical decomposition of a substance by an electric current passed through the substance in dissolved or molten state.

Element—A substance which cannot be decomposed by ordinary types of chemical change, or made by chemical union.

Emulsion—Dispersion of minute droplets of one liquid (that does not dissolve) in another.

Ester—Organic compounds corresponding to inorganic salts, derived by replacing hydrogen of an acid by an organic group.

Fixation of nitrogen—The combination of atmospheric nitrogen with other elements to form chemical compounds.

Formula—The combination of chemical symbols showing the composition of a chemical element or compound.

Hard water—Water that contains chemicals in solution that react with soap to form a precipitate and which therefore only lathers with difficulty.

Hydrocarbon—A compound containing only carbon and hydrogen.

Hydrolysis—Chemical reaction of a substance with water.

Ion—An atom or group of atoms possessing an electrical charge.

Isomers—Molecules that have the same number and kinds of atoms but different molecular configurations.

Isotopes—Atoms of the same atomic number which differ in the number of neutrons in the nucleus.

Molecular weight—Relative weight of a molecule compared to the weight of an atom of carbon taken as exactly 12.00; the sum of the atomic weights of the atoms in a molecule.

Molecule—The smallest unit of a substance that can exist free, and retain all the chemical properties of that substance.

Osmosis—Diffusion of a solvent through a semipermeable membrane into a more concentrated solution.

Oxidation—A process in which an atom or group of atoms loses electrons; combination with oxygen.

pH—A symbol for the logarithm of the reciprocal of the hydrogen ion concentration of a solution; thus, an indication of the acidity or basicity of a solution. A neutral solution has a pH of 7; an acid solution has a pH lower than seven, an alkaline, higher.

Photosynthesis—A chemical change that utilizes light energy; e.g., the production in plants of starch from carbon dioxide and water in sunlight.

Polymorphism—The ability of a substance to exist in two or more crystalline forms.

Precipitate—An insoluble solid deposited from a solution.

Protein—Complex organic compounds of very high molecular weight that compose a large part of all living matter; protein molecules invariably contain the elements of carbon, hydrogen, oxygen, and nitrogen.

Radical—A group of atoms that functions as a unit in chemical change.

Reduction—A process in which an atom or group of atoms gains electrons: loss of oxygen or combination with hydrogen.

Salt—A compound made up of the positive ion of a base and the negative ion of an acid.

Solution—A homogeneous mixture of two or more substances of dissimilar molecular structure. In a solution there is a dissolving medium—solvent—and a dissolved substance—solute.

Standard conditions—0° C and 1 atmosphere (760 mm, or 29.92 in. of mercury) pressure.

Synthesis—The formation of a compound from its elements or from simpler compounds.

Tritium—An isotope of hydrogen of mass number 3.

Valence—A number that represents the combining power of an atom or radical referred to hydrogen as a standard.

MULTIPLICATION AND DIVISION TABLE

A number in the top line (14) multiplied by a number in the extreme left hand column (13) produces the number where the top line and side line meet (182).

A number in the table (208) divided by the number at the top of the same column (13) results in the number (16) in the extreme left hand column. A number in the table (208) divided by the number at the extreme left (16) results in the number (13) at the top of the column.

1	2	3	4	5	6	7	8	9	10	11	12	13	14	15	16	17	18	19	20	21	22	23	24	25
2	4	6	8	10	12	14	16	18	20	22	24	26	28	30	32	34	36	38	40	42	44	46	48	50
3	6	9	12	15	18	21	24	27	30	33	36	39	42	45	48	51	54	57	60	63	66	69	72	75
4	8	12	16	20	24	28	32	36	40	44	48	52	56	60	64	68	72	76	80	84	88	92	96	100
5	10	15	20	25	30	35	40	45	50	55	60	65	70	75	80	85	90	95	100	105	110	115	120	125
6	12	18	24	30	36	42	48	54	60	66	72	78	84	90	96	102	108	114	120	126	132	138	144	150
7	14	21	28	35	42	49	56	63	70	77	84	91	98	105	112	119	126	133	140	147	154	161	168	175
8	16	24	32	40	48	56	64	72	80	88	96	104	112	120	128	136	144	152	160	168	176	184	192	200
9	18	27	36	45	54	63	72	81	90	99	108	117	126	135	144	153	162	171	180	189	198	207	216	225
10	20	30	40	50	60	70	80	90	100	110	120	130	140	150	160	170	180	190	200	210	220	230	240	250
11	22	33	44	55	66	77	88	99	110	121	132	143	154	165	176	187	198	209	220	231	242	253	264	275
12	24	36	48	60	72	84	96	108	120	132	144	156	168	180	192	204	216	228	240	252	264	276	288	300
13	26	39	52	65	78	91	104	117	130	143	156	169	182	195	208	221	234	247	260	273	286	299	312	325
14	28	42	56	70	84	98	112	126	140	154	168	182	196	210	224	238	252	266	280	294	308	322	336	350
15	30	45	60	75	90	105	120	135	150	165	180	195	210	225	240	255	270	285	300	315	330	345	360	375
16	32	48	64	80	96	112	128	144	160	176	192	208	224	240	256	272	288	304	320	336	352	368	384	400
17	34	51	68	85	102	119	136	153	170	187	204	221	238	255	272	289	306	323	340	357	374	391	408	425
18	36	54	72	90	108	126	144	162	180	198	216	234	252	270	288	306	324	342	360	378	396	414	432	450
19	38	57	76	95	114	133	152	171	190	209	228	247	266	285	304	323	342	361	380	399	418	437	456	475
20	40	60	80	100	120	140	160	180	200	220	240	260	280	300	320	340	360	380	400	420	440	460	480	500
21	42	63	84	105	126	147	168	189	210	231	252	273	294	315	336	357	378	399	420	441	462	483	504	525
22	44	66	88	110	132	154	176	198	220	242	264	286	308	330	352	374	396	418	440	462	484	506	528	550
23	46	69	92	115	138	161	184	207	230	253	276	299	322	345	368	391	414	437	460	483	506	529	552	575
24	48	72	96	120	144	168	192	216	240	264	288	312	336	360	384	408	432	456	480	504	528	552	576	600
25	50	75	100	125	150	175	200	225	250	275	300	325	350	375	400	425	450	475	500	525	550	575	600	625

FOREIGN WEIGHTS AND MEASURES

Name of Unit	Country	U.S. Equivalent
Ardeb	Egypt	43.55 gals.
Arroba	Costa Rica	25.35 lbs.
Bak (opium)	Laos	57.9 grains
Barril	Mexico	16.72 gals.
Batman	Iran	6.546 lbs.
Beswa	Afghanistan	116.8 sq. yds.
Bhara	Malaysia	400.0 lbs.
Bocoy	Cuba	18.214 bu.
Botella	Honduras	1.216 pts.
Bu	Japan	.011930 in.
Caballería	El Salvador	111.11 acres
Cable (nautical)	United Kingdom	200.0 yds.
Cajuela	Costa Rica	3.74 gals.
Căn	South Vietnam	1.333 lbs.
Candy	Burma	18,000.0 lbs.
Caneca	Cuba	4.784 gals.
Cántaro (wine)	Spain	3.572 gals.
Cape inch	South Africa	1.033 ins.
Capicha	Iran	2.32 qts.
Carga	El Salvador	200.0 lbs.
Carga	Mexico	308.6 lbs.
Case (bananas)	Western Samoa	72.0 lbs.
Catty	Indonesia	1.3616 lbs.
Centner	Denmark	110.231 lbs.
Chang	Mongolia	3.50 yds.
Cheung	Hong Kong	4.063 yds.
Chi	South Korea	1.423 sq. ins.
Cho	Japan	119.30 yds.
Chum	Malaysia	1.475 ins.
Chupak	Malaysia	1.0 qt.
Cuadra	Ecuador	91.9 yds.
Cuadra	Peru	2.47 acres
Cuarta	Costa Rica	8.228 ins.
Cuartilla	Ecuador	50.7 lbs.
Cuartillo (oil)	Mexico	.890 pt.
Cubito	Somalia	22.0 ins.
Cuerdo	Puerto Rico	.971 acre
Dariba	Egypt	43.55 bu.
Dawulla	Ethiopia	220.46 lbs.
Dékare	Bulgaria	.247 acre
Dhira	Syria	29.5 ins.
Dira	Saudi Arabia	17.3 ins.
Djuim	Byelorussian SSR	1.0 in.
Dönüm	Cyprus	1,600.0 sq. yds.
Dönüm, metric	Israel	1,196.0 sq. yds.
Doppelzentner	West Germany	220.462 lbs.
Dra (textiles)	Jordan	26.8 ins.
Du	Mongolia	5.72 qts.
El	Surinam	2.26 ft.
Fan che	Mainland China	1.19599 sq. ft.
Fanega	Paraguay	63.4 gals.
Farsakh-song	Iran	3.88 mi.
Fatar	Muscat and Oman	Span from first finger to thumb
Fen	Mainland China	.1312 in.
Frasila	Tanzania	36.0 lbs.
Fuder	West Germany	220.0 gals.
Fun	Hong Kong	.14625 in.
Fuss	West Germany	12.36 ins.
Gallon	Haiti	.8326 gal.
Gang	South Vietnam	.4306 sq. ft.
Gantang	Sabah	1.0 gal.
Gaz	Iran	1.14 yds.
Gazi jerib	Afghanistan	29.0 ins.
Gian sheng	Mainland China	27.4961 bu.
Gong qing	Mainland China	2.471054 acres
Grain, colonial	Mauritius	.819 grain
Gun	Hong Kong	1.333 lbs.
Gurraf	Libya	2.03 qts.
Habba (gold)	Sudan	1.543 grains
Hand (height of horses)	United Kingdom	4.0 ins.
Heml	Egypt	550.3 lbs.
Hold (agriculture)	Hungary	1.422 acres
Izenbi	Morocco	2,153.0 sq. yds.
Jemba	Malaysia	144.0 sq. ft.
Jin	Mainland China	1.1023 lbs.
Jutro, katastarsko	Yugoslavia	1.422 acres
Kala	Morocco	19.69 ins.
Kantang	Cambodia	1.650 gals.
Kantar	Lebanon	565.3 lbs.
Kantar	Egypt	99.05 lbs.
Ken	Japan	1.988 yds.
Kettle	Sierra Leone	8.79 qts.
Kilates (troy)	Philippines	3.09 grains
Kin	Japan	1.32 lbs.
Koku	Japan	39.68 gals.
Kosh	Nepal	2.0 mi.
Kung chang	China (Taiwan)	10.9361 yds.
Kwien	Thailand	440.0 gals.
Kwintal	Poland	220.46 lbs.
Legua	Cuba	2.635 mi.
Legua	Uruguay	3.2 mi.
Leaguer	South Africa	127.0 gals.
Lei (Chinese mi.)	Hong Kong	706–745.0 yds.
Lelong	Malaysia	2,400.0 sq. ft.
Li	Mainland China	546.8 yds.
Li	South Korea	2.440 mi.
Libra	Spain	1.014 lbs.
Livre, colonial	Seychelles	1.079 lbs.
Load (cocoa)	Sierra Leone	60.0 lbs.
Ma (Chinese yd.)	Hong Kong	35.10 ins.
Manzana	Guatemala	1.74 acres
Marco	Mexico	1.015 oz.
Marco real	Spain	1.591 acres
Maund (Imperial)	Aden	82.28 lbs.
Mecate	Costa Rica	21.942 yds.
Medida	Honduras	2.527 qts.
Meripeninkulma	Finland	1.15 mi.
Mid (oil)	Jordan	15.8 qts.
Mil	Sweden	6.214 mi.
Mile (geographical)	Indonesia	4.60 mi.
Milla legal	Argentina	1.0 mi.
Misura	Libya	4.36 gals.
Mu	Mainland China	.16474 acre
Mud	Netherlands	2.471 acres
Mudu (rice)	Nigeria	2.5 lbs.
Nim-man	Iran	3.272 lbs.
Oke	Saudi Arabia	2.8 lbs.
Onza	Honduras	1.014 oz.
Ounce, Amsterdam	Indonesia	1.089 oz.
Peninkulma (mil)	Finland	6.21 mi.
Phân	South Vietnam	2.583 sq. ft.
Pié	Argentina	1.0 ft.
Pied anglais	Haiti	1.0 ft.
Pipa	Dominican Republic	15.75 bu.
Pond	Surinam	1.102 lbs.
Poud (grain)	USSR	36.11 lbs.
Pulgada	Philippines	1.0 in.
Quintal	Angola	220.5 lbs.
Quintal	El Salvador	100.0 lbs.
Raummeter	Austria	1.308 cu. yds.
Ri	Japan	2.440 mi.
Roupi (textiles)	Cyprus	3.00 ins.
Rute	West Germany	4.12 yds.
Sâa	Libya	26.13 gals.
Saco (coffee)	Colombia	137.8 lbs.
Saco (coffee)	Peru	152.1 lbs.
Seer	Nepal	2.057 lbs.
Shaku	Japan	.635 fl. oz.
Shō	Japan	1.587 qts.
Sildarmál (herring)	Iceland	4.12 bu.
Solar	Ecuador	.43 acre
Stone	United Kingdom	14.0 lbs.
Stoop (beer)	Netherlands	1.32 gals.
Sun	Japan	1.19303 ins.
Tael	Cambodia	1.323 avoir. oz.
Tanan	Thailand	.880 qt.
Tartous	Syria	1,099.0 sq. yds.
Tercia	El Salvador	1.0 ft.
Thail (opium)	Indonesia	1.241 avoir. oz.
Thôn	South Vietnam	2.870 sq. yds.
To	Japan	3.968 gals.
Tola (standard)	Pakistan	180.0 grains
Tomme	Denmark	1.030 ins.
Tondeland	Denmark	1.363 acres
Tonne	Schleswig-Holstein, W. Ger.	1.35 acres
Tonneau de mer	Belgium	100.0 cu. ft.
Topo (usual)	Peru	.86 acre
Tuuma	Finland	1.0 in.
Ud	Sudan	2.54 yds.
Uyên (rice)	South Vietnam	.880 qt.
Vara	Chile	32.91 ins.
Vara	Paraguay	2.84 ft.
Vara	Spain	2.74 ft.
Voet, Amsterdam	Netherlands	.928 ft.
War	Aden	1.0 yd.
Wari	Kenya	1.0 yd.
Wine gallon	Barbados	.83267 gal.
Wizna	Malta	8.750 lbs.
Yang	South Korea	1.32 oz.
Yarda	Colombia	35.43 ins.
Yen	South Vietnam	13.33 lbs.
Zentner	Austria	220.46 lbs.
Zoll	West Germany	1.03 ins.

SQUARES, CUBES, SQUARE ROOTS, AND CUBE ROOTS

No.	Squares	Cubes	Square roots	Cube roots	No.	Squares	Cubes	Square roots	Cube roots
1	1	1	1.0000000	1.0000000	51	2601	132651	7.1414284	3.7084298
2	4	8	1.4142136	1.2599210	52	2704	140608	7.2111026	3.7325111
3	9	27	1.7320508	1.4422496	53	2809	148877	7.2801099	3.7562858
4	16	64	2.0000000	1.5874011	54	2916	157464	7.3484692	3.7797631
5	25	125	2.2360687	1.7099759	55	3025	166375	7.4161985	3.8029525
6	36	216	2.4494896	1.8171206	56	3136	175616	7.4833148	3.8258624
7	49	343	2.6457513	1.9129312	57	3249	185193	7.5498344	3.8485011
8	64	512	2.8284271	2.0000000	58	3364	195112	7.6157731	3.8708766
9	81	729	3.0000000	2.0800837	59	3481	205379	7.6811457	3.8929965
10	100	1000	3.1622777	2.1544347	60	3600	216000	7.7459667	3.9148676
11	121	1331	3.3166248	2.2239801	61	3721	226981	7.8102497	3.9364972
12	144	1728	3.4641016	2.2894286	62	3844	238328	7.8740079	3.9578915
13	169	2197	3.6055513	2.3513347	63	3969	250047	7.9372539	3.9790571
14	196	2744	3.7416574	2.4101422	64	4096	262144	8.0000000	4.0000000
15	225	3375	3.8729833	2.4662121	65	4225	274625	8.0622577	4.0207256
16	256	4096	4.0000000	2.5198421	66	4356	287496	8.1240384	4.0412401
17	289	4913	4.1231056	2.5712816	67	4489	300763	8.1853528	4.0615480
18	324	5832	4.2426407	2.6207414	68	4624	314432	8.2462113	4.0816551
19	361	6859	4.3588989	2.6684016	69	4761	328509	8.3066239	4.1015661
20	400	8000	4.4721360	2.7144177	70	4900	343000	8.3666003	4.1212853
21	441	9261	4.5825757	2.7589243	71	5041	357911	8.4261498	4.1408178
22	484	10648	4.6904158	2.8020393	72	5184	373248	8.4852814	4.1601676
23	529	12167	4.7958315	2.8438670	73	5329	389017	8.5440037	4.1793390
24	576	13824	4.8989795	2.8844991	74	5476	405224	8.6023253	4.1983364
25	625	15625	5.0000000	2.9240177	75	5625	421875	8.6602540	4.2171633
26	676	17576	5.0990195	2.9624960	76	5776	438976	8.7177979	4.2358236
27	729	19683	5.1961524	3.0000000	77	5929	456533	8.7749644	4.2543210
28	784	21952	5.2915026	3.0365889	78	6084	474552	8.8317609	4.2726586
29	841	24389	5.3851648	3.0723168	79	6241	493039	8.8881944	4.2908404
30	900	27000	5.4772256	3.1072325	80	6400	512000	8.9442719	4.3088695
31	961	29791	5.5677644	3.1413806	81	6561	531441	9.0000000	4.3267487
32	1024	32768	5.6568542	3.1748021	82	6724	551368	9.0553851	4.3444815
33	1089	35937	5.7445626	3.2075343	83	6889	571787	9.1104336	4.3620707
34	1156	39304	5.8309519	3.2396118	84	7056	592704	9.1651514	4.3795191
35	1225	42875	5.9160798	3.2710663	85	7225	614125	9.2195445	4.3968296
36	1296	46656	6.0000000	3.3019272	86	7396	636056	9.2736185	4.4140049
37	1369	50653	6.0827625	3.3322218	87	7569	658503	9.3273791	4.4310476
38	1444	54872	6.1644140	3.3619754	88	7744	681472	9.3808315	4.4479602
39	1521	59319	6.2449980	3.3912114	89	7921	704969	9.4339811	4.4647451
40	1600	64000	6.3245553	3.4199519	90	8100	729000	9.4868330	4.4814047
41	1681	68921	6.4031242	3.4482172	91	8281	753571	9.5393920	4.4979414
42	1764	74088	6.4807407	3.4760266	92	8464	778688	9.5916630	4.5143574
43	1849	79507	6.5574385	3.5033981	93	8649	804357	9.6436508	4.5306549
44	1936	85184	6.6332496	3.5303483	94	8836	830584	9.6953597	4.5468359
45	2025	91125	6.7082039	3.5568933	95	9025	857375	9.7467943	4.5629026
46	2116	97336	6.7823300	3.5830479	96	9216	884736	9.7979590	4.5788570
47	2209	103823	6.8556546	3.6088261	97	9409	912673	9.8488578	4.5947009
48	2304	110592	6.9282032	3.6342411	98	9604	941192	9.8994949	4.6104363
49	2401	117649	7.0000000	3.6593057	99	9801	970299	9.9498744	4.6260650
50	2500	125000	7.0710678	3.6840314	100	10000	1000000	10.0000000	4.6415888

DECIMAL EQUIVALENTS OF COMMON FRACTIONS

8ths	16ths	32ds	64ths	Equivalent
			1	.015625
		1	2	.031250
			3	.046875
	1	2	4	.062500
			5	.078125
		3	6	.093750
			7	.109375
1	2	4	8	.125000
			9	.140625
		5	10	.156250
			11	.171875
	3	6	12	.187500
			13	.203125
		7	14	.218750
			15	.234375
2	4	8	16	.250000
			17	.265625
		9	18	.281250
			19	.296875
	5	10	20	.312500
			21	.328125
		11	22	.343750
			23	.359375
3	6	12	24	.375000
			25	.390625
		13	26	.406250
			27	.421875
	7	14	28	.437500
			29	.453125
		15	30	.468750
			31	.484375
4	8	16	32	.500000
			33	.515625
		17	34	.531250
			35	.546875
	9	18	36	.562500
			37	.578125
		19	38	.593750
			39	.609375
5	10	20	40	.625000
			41	.640625
		21	42	.656250
			43	.671875
	11	22	44	.687500
			45	.703125
		23	46	.718750
			47	.734375
6	12	24	48	.750000
			49	.765625
		25	50	.781250
			51	.796875
	13	26	52	.812500
			53	.828125
		27	54	.843750
			55	.859375
7	14	28	56	.875000
			57	.890625
		29	58	.906250
			59	.921875
	15	30	60	.937500
			61	.953125
		31	62	.968750
			63	.984375
8	16	32	64	1.000000

INVENTORS AND INVENTIONS

Invention	Date	Inventor	Country	Invention	Date	Inventor	Country
abacus	c. 500 B.C.	unknown	China (?)	computer (differential analyzer)	1928	Vannevar Bush	U.S.
achromatic lens	1758	John Dolland	England	computer (electronic)	1946	J. Presper Eckert John W. Mauchly	U.S.
adding machine	1642	Blaise Pascal	France	condensed milk	1853	Gail Borden	U.S.
adding machine (commercial)	1885	William Burroughs	U.S.	cotton gin	1793	Eli Whitney	U.S.
addressing machine	1893	J. S. Duncan	U.S.	cylinder lock	1865	Linus Yale, Jr.	U.S.
aerosol spray	1941	Lyle D. Goodhue	U.S.	cultivator	1820	Henry Burden	U.S.
air brake	1869	George Westinghouse	U.S.	daguerrotype	1837	Louis J. M. Daguerre	France
air conditioning	1911	Willis H. Carrier	U.S.	dictating machine	1885	Charles S. Taintor	U.S.
air-cushion vehicle	1877	J. I. Thornycroft	England	diesel engine	1892	Rudolf C. K. Diesel	Germany
airplane	1903	Orville and Wilbur Wright	U.S.	disc brake	1902	Ferdinand W. Lanchester	England
airplane (multi-motored)	1913	Igor Sikorsky	Russia	dynamite	1866	Alfred B. Nobel	Sweden
airship (nonrigid)	1852	Henri Giffard	France	electric flatiron	1882	Henry W. Seely	U.S.
airship (rigid)	1900	Ferdinand von Zeppelin	Germany	electric generator	1832	Hippolyte Pixii	France
automatic pilot	1929	William Green	U.S.	electric motor	1822	Michael Faraday	England
automobile (electric)	1891	William Morrison	U.S.	electric shaver	1928	Jacob Schick	U.S.
automobile (internal combustion)	1887	Gottlieb Daimler Karl Benz (independently)	Germany Germany	electric stove	1896	William S. Hadaway, Jr.	U.S.
				electric vacuum cleaner	1907	James M. Spangler	U.S.
Babbitt metal	1839	Isaac Babbitt	U.S.	electromagnet	1824	William Sturgeon	England
Bakelite	1907	Leo H. Baekeland	U.S.	electron microscope	1939	Vladimir K. Zworykin	U.S.
balloon	1783	J. M. and J. E. Montgolfier	France	electroplating	1805	Luigi Brugnatelli	Italy
barbed wire	1874	Joseph F. Glidden	U.S.	electrotype	1839	Moritz-Hermann Jacobi	Russia
barometer	1643	Evangelista Torricelli	Italy	elevator (passenger)	1852	Elisha G. Otis	U.S.
battery (electric)	1800	Alessandro Volta	Italy	evaporated milk	1880	John B. Meyenberg	U.S.
benday process	1879	Benjamin Day	U.S.	firearm magazine	1854	Horace Smith and Daniel B. Wesson	U.S.
Bessemer converter	1856 1857	Henry Bessemer William Kelly (independently)	England U.S.	flanged railway rail	1831	Robert L. Stevens	U.S.
betatron	1939	Donald W. Kerst	U.S.	flying shuttle	1733	John Kay	England
bicycle	1816	Karl D. von Sauerbronn	Germany	frequency-modulation (FM) broadcasting	1933	Edwin H. Armstrong	U.S.
bifocal lens	1780	Benjamin Franklin	U.S.	galvanometer	1819	Johann S. C. Schweigger	Germany
blast furnace	1828	J. B. Neilson	Scotland	gas engine (four-cycle)	1876	Nikolaus August Otto	Germany
bottlemaking machine	1903	Michael Owens	U.S.	geiger counter	1913	Hans W. Geiger	England
Braille	1829	Louis Braille	France	glider	1853	George Cayley	England
breech-loading rifle	1810	John Hall	U.S.	gramophone (disc record)	1887	Emile Berliner	U.S.
bubble chamber	1952	Donald A. Glaser	U.S.	gyrocompass	1911	Elmer A. Sperry	U.S.
bulldozer	1923	unknown	U.S.	halftone engraving process	1886	Frederic E. Ives	U.S.
bullet (rifle)	1849	Claude E. Minié	France	helicopter (man-carrying)	1907	Paul Cornu	France
Bunsen burner	1855	Robert W. Bunsen	Germany	holography	1949	Denis Gabor	England
calculating machine (digital)	1823	Charles Babbage	England	hydraulic press	1795	Joseph Brahmah	England
camera (photographic)	1822	Joseph N. Niepce	France	hydrometer	1768	Antoine Baumé	France
carburetor	1892	Gottlieb Daimler	Germany	hydroplane	1911	Glenn H. Curtis	U.S.
cash register	1879	James Ritty	U.S.	internal combustion engine	1859	Jean J. E. Lenoir	France
cathode-ray tube	1878	William Crookes	England	internal combustion engine (high speed)	1880	Gottlieb Daimler	Germany
cellophane	c. 1900	Jacques Brandenberger	Switzerland	iron lung	1928	Philip Drinker and Louis A. Shaw	U.S.
celluloid	1855	Alexander Parkes	England	jet engine	1937	Frank Whittle	England
cement (portland)	1824	Joseph Aspdin	England	kaleidoscope	1816	David Brewster	Scotland
chronometer	1735	John Harrison	England	knitting machine	c. 1589	William Lee	England
clock (pendulum)	1656	Christiaan Huygens	Holland	lamp (incandescent)	1879	Thomas A. Edison	U.S.
cloud chamber	1911	Charles T. R. Wilson	Scotland	lamp (mercury vapor)	1901	Peter C. Hewitt	U.S.
color photography	1881	Frederic E. Ives	U.S.	lamp (neon)	1910	Georges Claude	France
combine (harvesting, threshing, cleaning)	1911	Benjamin Holt	U.S.				
compressed-air rock drill	1871	Simon Ingersoll	U.S.				

Invention	Date	Inventor	Country
laser	1960	Theodore H. Naiman	U.S.
lathe (engine-driven)	1800	Henry Maudslay	England
Leyden jar	1746	John Bevis / Pieter van Musschenbroek	England / Holland
life preserver	1805	John Edwards	England
lightning rod	1752	Benjamin Franklin	American colonies
linoleum	1860	Frederick Walton	England
linotype	1884	Ottmar Mergenthaler	U.S.
lithography	1798	Aloys Senefelder	Germany
long-playing (LP) record	1948	Peter C. Goldmark	U.S.
machine gun	1862	Richard J. Gatling	U.S.
match (friction)	1827	John Walker	England
match (safety)	1855	J. E. Lundstrom	Sweden
metronome	1816	Johann N. Mälzel	Austria
micrometer	1636	William Gascoigne	England
microphone	c. 1877	Thomas A. Edison	U.S.
microscope	1590	Zacharias Janssen	Holland
miner's lamp	1815	Humphry Davy	England
monotype	1887	Tolbert Lanston	U.S.
motion pictures	1872	Eadweard Muybridge and John D. Isaacs	U.S.
motorcycle	1885	Edward Butler	England
mowing machine	1810	Peter Gaillard	U.S.
multiplying machine	1671	Gottfried W. von Leibniz	Germany
nitroglycerine	c. 1846	Ascanio Sobrero	Italy
nylon	1935	Wallace H. Carothers	U.S.
oleomargarine	1868	Hippolyte Mége-Mouriz	France
parachute	1783	Louis S. Lenormand	France
parking meter	1935	Carlton C. Magee	U.S.
percussion cap	1816	Joshua Shaw	U.S.
phonograph (cylindrical record)	1877	Thomas A. Edison	U.S.
photocell	1895	Julius Elster and Hans Geitel	Germany
phototype-setting machine	1945	E. G. Klingberg, Fritz Stadelmann, H. R. Freund	U.S.
plow, iron	1784	James Small	England
plow (wooden)	c. 2500 B.C.	unknown	Egypt
polarizing glass (Polaroid)	1932	Edwin H. Land	U.S.
printing press (screw type)	c. 1450	Johann Gutenberg	Germany
printing with movable type	11th century	Pi-sheng	China
prism spectroscope	1859–60	Gustave Kirchhoff and Robert Bunsen	Germany
pump (air)	1650	Otto von Guericke	Germany
radar	1935	Robert A. Watson-Watt	England
radio-telegraph	1895	Guglielmo Marconi	Italy
radio-telephone	1902	Reginald A. Fessenden	U.S.
railway (electric)	1881	Werner von Siemens	Germany
railway signal (block)	1863	Ashbel Welch and Robert Stewart	U.S.
railway sleeping car	1859	George M. Pullman	U.S.
reaper	1826	Patrick Bell	Scotland
refrigerator	1858	Ferdinand Carré	France
revolver	1831	Samuel Colt	U.S.
rifle	1520	August Kotter	Germany
roller bearings	c. 1496	Leonardo da Vinci	Italy
rolling mill	c. 1496	Leonardo da Vinci	Italy
safety pin	1849	Walter Hunt	U.S.
sail	c. 3000 B.C.	unknown	Egypt
saw (circular)	1777	Samuel Miller	England
screw propeller	1804	John C. Stevens	U.S.
self-starter (automobile)	1911	Charles F. Kettering	U.S.
sewing machine	1790	Thomas Saint	England
shrapnel shell	1784	Henry Shrapnel	England
silencer (firearm)	1908	Hiram P. Maxim	U.S.
slide rule	c. 1620	William Oughtred	England
spinning machine	1764	James Hargreaves	England
sprinkler (fire)	1723	Ambrose Godfrey	England
steamboat	1783	Marquis de Jouffroy d'Abbans	France
steam engine	1628	Edward Somerset	England
steam engine (condensing)	1765	James Watt	Scotland
steam hammer	1839	James Nasmyth	Scotland
stereoscope	1838	Charles Wheatstone	England
stereotyping	1725	William Ged	Scotland
stock ticker	1870	Thomas A. Edison	U.S.
storage battery	1803	Johann W. Ritter	Germany
street car	1834	Thomas Davenport	U.S.
submarine detector	1917	Max Mason	U.S.
switchboard	1877	Edgar T. Holmes	U.S.
tank, military	1914	Ernest D. Swinton	England
tape recorder (magnetic)	1899	Valdemar Poulsen	Denmark
telegraph (multiwire)	1809	Samuel T. von Soemmering	Germany
telegraph (single wire)	1835	Samuel F. B. Morse	U.S.
telegraph cable (submarine)	1866	Cyrus W. Field	U.S.
telephone	1876	Alexander G. Bell	U.S.
telescope	1608	Hans Lippershey	Holland
telescope (reflecting)	1661	James Gregory	Scotland
television	1926	James Logie Baird	Scotland
television iconoscope scanner	1938	Vladimir K. Zworykin	U.S.
thermometer (air and water)	c. 1592	Cornelius Drebbel	Holland
thermometer (mercury)	1714	Gabriel D. Fahrenheit	Germany
threshing machine	1732	Michael Menzies	Scotland
tire (pneumatic)	1843	Robert W. Thompson	England
toaster (automatic)	1918	Charles Strite	U.S.
tractor	1825	Robert Keeley	England
transformer (electric)	1885	William Stanley	U.S.
transistor	1948	J. Bardeen, W. H. Brattain, W. Shockley	U.S.
typecasting machine	1836	David Bruce	U.S.
typewriter	1714	Henry Mill	England
vacuum bottle	1873	James Dewar	England
vacuum tube (diode)	1904	John A. Flemming	England
vacuum tube (triode)	1906	Lee De Forest	U.S.
vulcanized rubber	1839	Charles Goodyear	U.S.
Wankel engine	1957	Felix Wankel	Germany
warship (steam)	c. 1860	John Ericsson	U.S.
washing machine	1858	Hamilton E. Smith	U.S.
weaving machine	1733	John Kay	England
wirephoto	1881	Shelford Bidwell	England
xerography	1948	Chester Carlson	U.S.
X-ray tube (hot-filament)	1913	William D. Coolidge	U.S.
zipper	1893	Whitcomb L. Judson	U.S.

UNITED STATES
POLYCONIC PROJECTION

SCALE OF MILES

SCALE OF KILOMETRES

Capitals of Countries ──── ⊛
International Boundaries ──── State Capitals ⊛
                          State Boundaries ─────

Copyright by C. S. HAMMOND & Co., N.Y.

ALABAMA

MILES

KILOMETERS

State Capitals
County Seats

© Copyright HAMMOND INCORPORATED, Maplewood, N.J.

THE FIFTY STATES

ALABAMA

Site of the first Confederate capital in the prover-
bial "Heart of Dixie," Alabama is a traditionally
agricultural state in the Southern mold. A continuing concerted drive toward greater economic
diversification in the state began in the 1930s,
after costly boll weevil infestations and other problems demonstrated that the state was relying too
heavily on cotton. Today, Birmingham has become
the South's largest iron and steel producing center,
while the Redstone Arsenal and George C. Marshall Space Flight Center in Huntsville have
emerged as important research installations; in a
single decade (1950-60), Huntsville's population
more than quadrupled.

Hydroelectric power provided by the Tennessee
Valley Authority has been a key factor in Ala-
bama's growing industrialization. Tourist attrac-
tions include the Alabama Space and Rocket
Center at Huntsville, Bellingrath Gardens near
Mobile, the famed Mardi Gras celebration held in
Mobile, the Mound State Monument (Moundsville)
and the George Washington Carver Museum at
Tuskegee Institute, a school founded by Booker T.
Washington, a former slave.

The state's diverse topography ranges from the
Appalachian highlands in the northeast to the
broad coastal plain comprising about two-thirds of
the total area; in the plain's central region is the
fertile "Black Belt." Swamps, bayous, and sandy
beaches also mark the varied terrain. The state's
abbreviated coastline is dominated by Mobile Bay;
Dauphin Island lies at the bay's entrance. About 65
percent of the state is forested.

Mound Builders, who lived in the Alabama region in prehistoric times, were followed by a number of Indian tribes, including the Chickasaws,
Cherokees, and Creeks. Spaniards Cabeza de Vaca
and Hernando De Soto were among the region's
early European explorers. The first permanent European settlement was made (1702) by Frenchmen
at Fort Louis near present-day Mobile; it served as
the capital of the Louisiana Territory until 1722.
Other French settlements followed, but in 1763
France lost the region to the British.

After the American Revolution, England ceded
to the United States all of the Alabama region
except the southernmost British West Florida area
that included Mobile; this region, together with
East Florida, went to Spain.

In 1817, after a short period as part of the Territory of Mississippi, the region was organized as the
Alabama Territory. Settlers spurred by the virtual
ending of Indian troubles in the area helped the
new territory's growth; statehood came in 1819.
Slave-supported plantation farming, aided by the
recent invention of the cotton gin, soon emerged as
the main factor in the state's economy.

Alabama seceded from the Union and joined the
Confederacy in 1861; Montgomery was briefly the
Confederate capital. The state suffered a great deal
from both the Civil War and the harsh, chaotic
Reconstruction.

In the middle of the twentieth century, there
were spectacular and sometimes bloody confrontations between supporters and opponents of racial
segregation. Martin Luther King, Jr., led opponents of segregation in a boycott of Montgomery
buses in 1955-56, in the 1963 demonstrations in
Birmingham, and in a march from Selma to
Montgomery in 1965. In 1978, a suspect in the 1963
bombing of a black church in Birmingham was

convicted. Democratic Governor George Wallace
retired from politics in 1979 and was succeeded by
Forrest James, a Democrat with no segregationist
identity.

The U.S. Supreme Court in a nationally important 1980 decision ruled that the city of Mobile
could select its officials through *at-large* elections.

Full name: State of Alabama. **Origin of name:** From the Indian,
Alba Amo meaning "I Clear the Thicket." **Inhabitant:** Alabamian.
Capital: Montgomery. **State motto:** Andemus Jura Nostra Defen-
dere (We Dare Defend Our Rights). **Flag:** Red cross of St. Andrew
on white field. **Seal:** A circled map of Alabama with boundaries &
rivers. **Flower:** Camellia. **Bird:** Yellowhammer. **Tree:** Southern
pine. **Song:** "Alabama." **Nickname:** Yellowhammer State and The
Heart of Dixie.

Governor: Forrest James, Jr. **Annual salary:** $50,000. **Term:** 4
years. **Current term expires:** Jan. 1983. **Voting requirements:** 18
yrs. old & U.S. citizen; resident of state 10 days. **U.S. Congressmen:** 7 **Entered Union:** 1819 (22nd state).

Location & boundaries: Southeastern state; bounded on the north
by Tennessee; on the east by the Chattahoochee River & Georgia; on
the south by Florida & the Gulf of Mexico; & on the west by
Mississippi. **Total area:** 51,609 sq. mi. (ranks 29th). **Extreme
length:** 330 mi. **Extreme breadth:** 200 mi. **Coastline:** 53 mi. **Chief
rivers:** Mobile, Alabama, Tombigbee, Coosa. **Major lakes:**
Wheeler, Guntersville, Wilson, Martin, Mitchell. **No. of counties:**
67.

Population (1980 census): 3,890,061 (ranks 22nd). **Pop. increase
(1970-80):** 12.9%. **Largest cities:** Birmingham, Mobile, Montgomery, Huntsville. **Pop. density:** 75.3 per sq. mi. (ranks 26th). **Pop.
distribution:** White—2,869,688; Black—995,623; **Am. Indian,
Eskimo and Aleut**—7,561; **Asian and Pacific Islander**—9,695;
Other—7,494; **Spanish origin**—33,100. **Marriage rate (1978):**
12.8 per 1,000 people. **Divorce rate:** 6.7 per 1,000 people.

State finances (1979). Revenue: $3,771,000,000. **Expenditures:**
$3,558,000,000. **State taxes:** $463.61 per capita. **State personal
income tax:** Yes. **Public debt (1979):** $279.49 per capita. **Federal
aid (1980):** $400.04 per capita. **Personal income (1980):** $7,484.

Sectors of the economy (% of labor force employed in 1970):
Manufacturing (29%), Wholesale & retail trade (19%), Government
(17%), Services (9%), Educational Services (7%), Construction
(7%). **Leading products:** primary & fabricated metals, transportation equipment, machinery, food, textiles, apparel, paper, chemicals. **Minerals:** coal, cement, stone, petroleum. **Agricultural
products:** broilers, cattle, eggs, corn, soybeans, peanuts. **Fishing:**
shrimp, red snappers, blue crabs. **Avg. farm (1980):** 243 acres.
Avg. value of farm per acre (1980): $639.

Highway expenditures per capita (1979): $109.72. Persons per
motor vehicle: 1.34. **Minimum age for driver's license:** 16. **Gasoline tax:** 11¢ per gallon. **Diesel tax:** 12¢ per gallon. **Motor vehicle
deaths (1978):** 30.7 per 100,000 people.

Birthrate (1978): 16.2 per 1,000 people. **Infant mortality rate per
1,000 births (1978):** 16.1. **Physicians per 100,000 pop. (1978):** 122.
Dentists per 100,000 pop. (1978): 35. **Acceptable hospital beds
(1978):** 6.47 per 1,000 people. **State expenditures per capita for
health and hospitals (1979):** $76.49.

Education expenditures (1976-77): $394.28 per capita annually.
No. of pupils in public schools (1979): 746,000. **No. of institutions
of higher learning (1978-79):** 58. **Public school expenditure per
pupil in attendance (1977-78):** $1,498. **Avg. salary of public
school teachers (1978-79):** $13,223. **No. full-time teachers
(1979):** 43,800. **Educational attainment of adult population
(1976):** 12.2 median yrs. of school completed: 6.8% with less than
5 years of education; 10.3% with 4 yrs. of college.

Telephones (1978): 50 per 100 people. **State Chamber of Commerce:** Alabama Chamber of Commerce, 468 South Perry Street,
P.O. Box 76, Montgomery, Alabama 36101.

ALASKA

Alaska is a land of great extremes: first among the
states in area, last in population. One of the nation's biggest bargains (Alaska's purchase price
was less than 2¢ an acre), it is potentially one of the
richest states—particularly in view of the spec-

tacular oil strikes in Prudhoe Bay off the state's frigid Arctic (or North) Slope. Many believe that these strikes will fulfill the century-long promise of "The Last Frontier"; the find has already been called "one of the largest petroleum accumulations known to the world today." In 1969 about $900 million was bid for oil-land leases.

During the next decade, oil revenues so glutted state coffers that in April 1980 the state enacted a plan to share the wealth directly with Alaska's 400,000 residents. The state income tax was virtually abolished and each Alaskan was to receive annually at least $50 for every year he lived in the state since 1959. In early September 1980, the Alaska Supreme Court struck down the tax-exemption portion of the these plans to fruition. Governor Hammond countered the decision by an April law. Later that month the State Legislature voted overwhelmingly to repeal the state personal income tax. In October 1980, the Alaskan Supreme Court upheld the royalty sharing plan, but a challenge is now being reviewed by the U.S. Supreme Court.

Alaska's awesome terrain has long challenged explorers and settlers. The state, which entered the Union in 1959, is cut into isolated areas by its craggy coast and high mountains, principally the Brooks Range in the north (an extension of the Rocky Mountains) and the Alaska Range in the south, which includes Mount McKinley, the highest peak in North America. Alaskans are attempting to have the famed mountain renamed Mount Denali.

Sticking out into the sea in the northwest is the Seward Peninsula. Off the peninsula, in the Bering Strait, is U.S.-owned Little Diomede Island, separated from the USSR's Big Diomede by about two miles. Alaska is separated from the nearest state, Washington, by about 500 miles.

The Alaskan climate is widely variable. The southeast coast, protected by mountains from the north winds and influenced by the warm Japan Current, is generally temperate and rainy, while interior summers are short and very hot (with exceptionally long days), and the winters very cold.

Major tourist attractions include Denali National Park, site of Mount McKinley, Glacier Bay National Park, with its awesome ice sheet and the magnificent Inland Passage in the southeast Panhandle region.

Captain Vitus Bering, a Dane who explored for Russia, is thought to have been the first white man to visit Alaska (1741), after passing close to it on an earlier voyage. At this time there were about 75,000 Indians, Eskimos, and Aleuts in Alaska; some prehistoric campsites date back to the Ice Age.

Though several nations tried to get a foothold in the region, mainly for the trade in sea otter pelts it might support, Russia prevailed, establishing Alaska's first white settlement on Kodiak Island in 1784. By the 1850s, Russia, facing increased competition from Americans, British, and Canadians, plus a dwindling supply of fur-bearing animals, wanted to sell. In 1867, U.S. Secretary of State William H. Seward agreed to buy—for $7.2 million—thereby becoming a target of ridicule. Many Americans dubbed Alaska "Seward's Folly" or "Seward's Icebox," considering it a frozen wasteland that was relatively valueless.

But gold was discovered (1896) at Klondike in neighboring Yukon Territory, and in Alaska itself at Nome (1899) and at Fairbanks (1902). Settlement was spurred as prospectors poured in and the economy was strengthened—but the lasting gains were few.

During World War II, the region's importance as a military outpost was dramatized when the Japanese briefly occupied some of the Aleutians—the war's only North American enemy occupation. Today, Alaska contains the Distant Early Warning system (DEW line) and other defense installations, including military bases. Roughly half the state's personal income is from government sources, and 97 percent of the land is Federally owned.

With a long coastline punctuated by many bays and fjords, Alaska is a leading state in commercial fishing. Forest products account for a considerable share of the state's revenue, while the value of agricultural products remains for more potential than actual. Only a small fraction of the state's potential cropland of 2 to 3 million acres has so far been developed. Tourism is a major industry.

On Good Friday, March 27, 1964, an exceptionally powerful earthquake struck the south-central part of the state, killing 114 and causing property damage estimated at $750 million.

In 1971 Congress passed the Alaska Native Land Claims Settlement Act to extinguish the nearly 100-year old claims of Alaska's 64,000 Eskimos, Indians and Aleuts by providing 40 million acres of land and approximately $925 million in compensation. An enrollment of eligible natives began in 1972.

Construction on the $4.5 billion Trans-Alaska pipeline project, first proposed in 1969 and delayed by legal suits brought by environmentalists finally began in 1974. In June 1977 oil began to flow from Prudhoe Bay on the Arctic Ocean through the 799-mile, 48-inch hot-oil pipeline to the Gulf of Alaska port of Valdez. To get that oil the American consumer, President Carter in January 1980 announced plans for a pipeline to extend from a Washington state port, where it was to receive oil from Alaska by sea, to Minnesota.

A proposed trans-Canadian pipeline to deliver natural gas from the Alaskan North Slope to the lower forty-eight states has been approved by the United States and Canada. In January 1980 the Alberta Gas Trunk Line Co., Ltd. announced plans to begin construction of a segment of the pipeline from Calgary to the U.S. border, while the Pacific Gas and Electric Co. was expected to extend the line to Oregon.

On December 2, 1980, President Carter signed into law a bill designating over 104 million acres of Alaskan land as national parks, monuments and preserves. Among the new national parks created are Gates of the Arctic, Kenai Fjords, Kobuk Valley, Lake Clark and Wrangell-St. Elias. In certain areas oil, gas and mineral exploration and exploitation would be permitted.

Plans begun in 1974 to move the capital of Alaska from Juneau to Willow, a site chosen in 1977, have been delayed by the Alaska Legislature. State Senator Bill Ray and his supporters have blocked the move, citing the high cost to the Alaskans.

Full name: State of Alaska. **Origin of name:** From Aleutian word meaning "Great Land." **Inhabitant:** Alaskan. **Capital:** Juneau. **State motto:** North to the Future. **Flag:** Blue field with seven gold stars, representing the Big Dipper; eighth star represents the North Star. **Seal:** Rising sun shines on lake, fishing boat, merchant ship, forests, mining & agricultural activities, symbols of Alaskan resources & occupations. **Flower:** Forget-me-not. **Bird:** Willow ptarmigan. **Tree:** Sitka spruce. **Song:** "Alaska's Flag." **Nickname:** The Great Land.

Governor: Jay S. Hammond. **Annual salary:** $74,196. **Term:** 4 years. **Current term expires:** Dec. 1982. **Voting requirements:** 19 yrs. old & U.S. citizen; resident of state 10 days. **U.S. Congressman:** 1. **Entered Union:** 1959 (49th state).

ARIZONA

MILES
0 20 40 60 80
KILOMETERS
0 20 40 60 80

⊛ State Capital ⊙ County Seats

© Copyright HAMMOND INCORPORATED, Maplewood, N.J.

Longitude West of Greenwich

Location & boundaries: Pacific state: bounded on the north by the Arctic Ocean; on the east by Canada; on the south by the Pacific Ocean; & on the west by the Bering Sea & Arctic Ocean. **Total area:** 586,412 sq. mi. (ranks 1st). **Extreme length:** 2,200 mi. **Extreme breadth:** 1,200 mi. **Coastline:** 6,640 mi. **Chief rivers:** Yukon, Tanana, Kuskokwim. **Major lakes:** Iliamna, Becharof, Tustumena. **No. of boroughs:** 10.

Population (1980 census): 400,481 (ranks 50th). **Pop. increase (1970-80):** 32.4%. **Largest cities:** Anchorage, Fairbanks, Juneau. **Pop. density:** 0.68 per sq. mi. (ranks 50th). **Pop. distribution:** White—308,455; Black—13,619; Am. Indian, Eskimo and Aleut—64,047; Asian and Pacific Islander—8,035; Other—6,325; Spanish origin—9,497. **Marriage rate (1978):** 12.4 per 1,000 people. **Divorce rate:** 8.4 per 1,000 people.

State finances (1979). Revenue: $1,699,000,000. **Expenditures:** $1,466,000,000. **State taxes:** $2,011.60 per capita. **State personal income tax:** No. (In 1980, Alaska eliminated all state taxes.) **Public debt (1979):** $3,355.98 per capita. **Federal aid (1980):** $1,103.42 per capita. **Personal income (1980):** $12,406.

Sectors of the economy (% of labor force employed in 1970): Government (37%), Wholesale & retail trade (19%), Educational Services (11%), Construction (9%), Services (8%), Manufacturing (7%). **Leading products:** seafood, timber, pulp, oil, gas, petrochemicals. **Minerals:** petroleum & natural gas, coal, sand & gravel. **Agricultural products:** dairy items, eggs, cattle, hay, vegetables, wool. **Fishing:** salmon, halibut, crab, shrimp, scallops. **Avg. farm (1980):** 5,484 acres. **Avg. value of farm per acre:** Not available.

Highway expenditures per capita (1979): $352.32. **Persons per motor vehicle:** 1.57. **Minimum age for driver's license:** 16. **Gasoline tax:** 8¢ per gallon. **Diesel tax:** 8¢ per gallon. **Motor vehicle deaths (1978):** 31.5 per 100,000 people.

Birthrate (1978): 21.6 per 1,000 people. **Infant mortality rate per 1,000 births (1978):** 14.4. **Physicians per 100,000 pop. (1978):** 138. **Dentists per 100,000 pop. (1978):** 55. **Acceptable hospital beds (1978):** 4.2 per 1,000 people. **State expenditures per capita for health and hospitals (1979):** $111.39.

Education expenditures (1976-77): $1,072.57 per capita annually. **No. of pupils in public schools (1979):** 89,000. **No. of institutions of higher learning (1978-79):** 16. **Public school expenditure per pupil in attendance (1977-78):** $4,113. **Avg. salary of public school teachers (1978-79):** $22,185. **No. full-time teachers (1979):** 5,300. **Educational attainment of adult population (1976):** 12.7 median yrs. of school completed: 2.8% with less than 5 years of education; 17.6% with 4 yrs. of college.

Telephones (1978): 35 per 100 people. **State Chamber of Commerce:** Alaska State Chamber of Commerce, 310 Second Street, Juneau, Alaska 99801.

ARIZONA

Arizona, the last mainland state to join the Union (1912), lies west of the Continental Divide and consists of three general areas: the desert in the southwest, the central highlands, and the Colorado Plateau in the northwest. Almost all of the state is within the Colorado drainage basin. Its principal tourist attraction, the awesome Grand Canyon, is one of the world's natural wonders: a multicolored fissure 217 miles long, four to eight miles wide at the brim, and about a mile deep.

The warm, dry, and reputedly health-restoring climate of the state's southern region—which includes Arizona's two largest cities, Phoenix and Tucson—has made it a popular winter resort area (as well as the site of many senior citizen retirement communities). Tourism is one of the leading industries in Arizona.

In addition to the Grand Canyon, state attractions include Hoover Dam, Lake Mead, 15 national monuments, various Indian villages and reservations (the state has the nation's largest Indian population: about 152,800), Oak Creek Canyon, legendary Tombstone, the Petrified Forest, and the Painted Desert. A new addition to the list is legendary London Bridge, which a private group has re-erected at Lake Havasu City.

Bolstered by defense contracts, manufacturing has lately become the state's leading industry, followed by mining and agriculture. Arizona produces a number of metals, including more than half of the country's supply of copper.

Mummies and ancient human relics—such as baskets and cloth—have been found in a strikingly well-preserved condition in Arizona. Several Indian cultures lived there from about 25,000 to 10,000 B.C., and the ancestors of the modern Navajos (or Navahos) and Apaches lived in northern Arizona. One of the oldest continuously inhabited settlements in the country, the community of Oraibi was built sometime in the 1100s by Hopi Indians, over 5,000 of whom presently live on a reservation in northeast Arizona. The first white men were 16th-century Spanish explorers. The United States obtained (1848) most of the land from Mexico following the Mexican War; the rest was included in the Gadsden Purchase (1853).

Arizona was organized as a territory in 1863, with the capital at Prescott (1865-67), then Tucson (1867-77), Prescott again (1877-89), and finally at Phoenix. Over many years, various bloody conflicts raged in Arizona—between the whites and the Apaches, whose leaders included the fabled fighters Cochise and Geronimo, between Confederate and Union troops during the Civil War, between labor and management during violent strikes in the mining communities, and between cattlemen and sheepmen in the range wars that continued until the turn of the century. Yet another subject of contention through the years has been the water rights along the Colorado River claimed not only by Arizona but by Nevada and California as well; distribution now follows a 1963 U.S. Supreme Court ruling.

Hopi and Navajo Indians of northeastern Arizona have been feuding for years over ownership of 1.8 million acres of desert plateau which acts as a buffer between the much smaller Hopi reservation and the Navajo nation which surrounds it. The U.S. Supreme Court ruled in the early 1960s that the two tribes should share the land equally. However, following congressional action, the tract was divided between the Hopi and the Navajo in 1981.

In 1979 Governor Babbitt declared a state emergency after it was discovered that a Tucson plant manufacturing tritium (used to make illuminated watch dials and signs) was leaking radioactivity. National Guardsmen seized the plant and confiscated more than 1,000 gallons of tritium.

Full name: State of Arizona. **Origin of name:** From the Indian, Alekzon, meaning "Small Spring." **Inhabitant:** Arizonan. **Capital:** Phoenix. **State motto:** Ditat Deus (God Enriches). **Flag:** A copper-colored star centered on radiating red & yellow stripes & a horizontal blue bar. **Seal:** Miner standing in mountains symbolizes state's mineral industry; irrigated fields & cow represent agriculture. **Flower:** Saguaro cactus. **Bird:** Cactus wren. **Tree:** Paloverde. **Song:** "Arizona." **Nickname:** Grand Canyon State.

Governor: Bruce E. Babbitt. **Annual salary:** $50,000. **Term:** 4 years. **Current term expires:** Jan. 1983. **Voting requirements:** 18 yrs. old & U.S. citizen; resident of state 50 days; registered. **U.S. Congressmen:** 4 (1980 reapportionment: 5). **Entered Union:** 1912 (48th state).

Location & boundaries: Southwestern state: bounded on the north by Utah; on the east by New Mexico; & on the south by Mexico; & on the west by Baja California (Mexico), the Colorado River, California & Nevada. **Total area:** 113,909 sq. mi. (ranks 6th). **Extreme length:** 395 mi. **Extreme breadth:** 340 mi. **Chief rivers:** Colorado, Little Colorado, Gila. **Major lakes:** Mohave, Theodore Roosevelt, Lake Mead. **No. of counties:** 14.

ARKANSAS

State Capital ⊛ County Seats ⊛

MILES
10 20 30 40 50 60
KILOMETERS
10 20 30 40 50 60

© Copyright by HAMMOND INCORPORATED, Maplewood, N.J.

Population (1980 census): 2,717,866 (ranks 29th). **Pop. increase (1970-80):** 53.1%. **Largest cities:** Phoenix, Tucson, Mesa. **Pop. density:** 23.8 per sq. mi. (ranks 40th). **Pop. distribution:** White—2,240,033; Black—75,034; **Am. Indian, Eskimo and Aleut**—152,857; **Asian and Pacific Islander**—22,098; **Other**—227,844; **Spanish origin**—440,915. **Marriage rate (1978):** 11.7 per 1,000 people. **Divorce rate:** 7.3 per 1,000 people.

State finances (1979). Revenue: $2,817,000,000. **Expenditures:** $2,133,000,000. **State Taxes:** $618.70 per capita. **State personal income tax:** Yes. **Public debt (1979):** $39.25 per capita. **Federal aid (1980):** $302.81 per capita. **Personal income (1980):** $8,649.

Sectors of the economy (% of labor force employed in 1974): Wholesale & retail trade (21%), Government (19%), Services (15%), Manufacturing (14%), Educational Services (8%), Construction (7%). **Leading products:** electrical & other machinery; transportation equipment; food; primary metals; printing & publishing; stone, clay & glass products. **Minerals:** copper, sand & gravel, molybdenum, silver, cement. **Agricultural products:** cattle, dairy products, cotton lint, hay, lettuce. **Avg. farm (1980):** 7,088 acres. **Avg. value of farm per acre:** $150.

Highway expenditures per capita (1979): $122.61. **Persons per motor vehicle:** 1.45. **Minimum age for driver's license:** 16. **Gasoline tax:** 8¢ per gallon. **Diesel tax:** 8¢ per gallon. **Motor vehicle deaths (1978):** 43.6 per 100,000 people.

Birthrate (1978): 18.2 per 1,000 people. **Infant mortality rate per 1,000 births (1978):** 13.1. **Physicians per 100,000 pop. (1978):** 194. **Dentists per 100,000 pop. (1978):** 49. **Acceptable hospital beds (1978):** 4.0 per 1,000 people. **State expenditures per capita for health and hospitals (1979):** $56.95.

Education expenditures (1976-77): $561.14 per capita annually. **No. of pupils in public schools (1979):** 498,000. **No. of institutions of higher learning (1978-79):** 23. **Public school expenditure per pupil in attendance (1977-78):** $1,966. **Avg. salary of public school teachers (1978-79):** $17,750. **No. full-time teachers (1979):** 27,500. **Educational attainment of adult population (1976):** 12.6 median yrs. of school completed: 3.3% with less than 5 years of education; 15.7% with 4 yrs. of college.

Telephones (1978): 55 per 100 people. **State Chamber of Commerce:** Arizona State Chamber of Commerce, 3216 N. Third Street, Suite 103, Phoenix, Arizona 85012.

ARKANSAS

Gracing the Arkansas terrain are rugged hills, scenic valleys and streams, and impressive hardwood and pine forests. In the south and east are the generally flat West Gulf Coastal and Mississippi Alluvial Plains, while highlands make up the northwestern region. Magazine Mountain (2,853 feet) is the state's highest point. About three-fifths of the land is wooded, forming the basis for a sizable timber industry. Resources include two large national forests, the Ozark and Ouachita.

Arkansas ranks among the national leaders in cotton, rice, soybean and livestock production; it also contains one of the world's most famous spas (Hot Springs), as well as North America's first diamond mine, near Murfreesboro. No longer commercially operative, the mine is today a state park, popular among tourists; anyone finding a diamond there (up to five carats) is allowed to keep it. Another tourist attraction is the old health resort town of Eureka Springs in the Ozark region of northwestern Arkansas. Excellent hunting and fishing also contribute to the state's increasingly significant tourism business as do such attractions as the Old Arsenal in Little Rock's MacArthur Park, which marks the birthplace of one of the most famous of Arkansans, General Douglas MacArthur.

The production of oil, the state's major mineral, is another important element in the economy. Arkansas is the nation's chief producer of bauxite ore, from which aluminum is extracted. A further vital asset is an abundant water supply, convertible to hydroelectric power. A modern navigational system on the Arkansas River connects the Gulf of Mexico and Little Rock, now a foreign trade zone, the 14th such zone established in the United States, and the only one on an inland waterway.

The so-called Bluff Dwellers of about A.D. 500 are considered to have been the first inhabitants of the Arkansas region, followed by the culturally superior Mound Builders and, later, by Quapaw, Osage, and Caddo Indians.

The first Europeans to visit (1541) the area were Spanish explorers led by Hernando De Soto. Frenchmen arrived more than a century later: Marquette and Jolliet exploring (1673) the land around the mouth of the Arkansas River, and La Salle claiming (1682) for France the Arkansas region and the rest of the Mississippi Valley. In 1686, Henri de Tonti, established Arkansas Post, the first permanent settlement. The United States obtained all of what is now Arkansas as part of the Louisiana Purchase (1803).

Much of the region's early history is shared with Louisiana, of which it was a part until 1812, when it was attached to the Territory of Missouri. Settlement was spurred by the cotton boom of 1818, and a year later Arkansas Territory, incorporating part of present-day Oklahoma, was created. The 1830s saw the emergence of the slavery-supported plantation system as the state's primary economic force. The virtual absence of Indian troubles encouraged immigration, and between 1830 and 1840 population tripled.

Statehood came (1836) at a time when the slavery issue was more and more seriously dividing the nation. In March 1861, the Arkansas convention voted to remain in the Union, but when President Lincoln asked for troops, the state refused and two months later decided to secede. Many relatively small battles were fought in the state, and from 1864-65 there existed two separate state governments: one at Little Rock controlled by the Union and a Confederate one at Washington, Arkansas. Recovery in the postwar period was slow in coming, and not helped by the violence-engendering struggle (1872-74) for the governorship between Republicans Elisha Baxter and Joseph Brooks, a struggle won by Baxter only after Presidential intervention.

On the cultural scene, the Arkansas Arts Center in Little Rock offers exhibits, plays, and classes in painting, sculpture, dance, photography, music and drama. The Arkansas Symphony Orchestra was established in 1966.

In addition to a fine public school system, there is the Arkansas School for the Deaf, established about 1866 as the Arkansas Deaf-Mute Institute, and the Arkansas School for the Blind. Arkansas Enterprises for the Blind opened in 1947 a rehabilitation center providing personal adjustment, pre-vocational and vocational training for the blind and visually impaired. It has served persons from the fifty states and over twenty-four foreign countries.

In 1966 the state made political history by electing a transplanted New Yorker, Winthrop Rockefeller (now deceased), governor on the Republican ticket, climaxing a six-year effort on his part to build a two-party system in this traditionally Democratic state. Rockefeller served two terms, but lost to a political unknown, Dale Bumpers, in a third term bid in 1970.

In November 1978, Pine Bluff was chosen for the location of a proposed nerve gas plant. According to the plan, production of nerve gas shells and bombs probably would not begin before 1982.

In May and June 1980 thousands of Cuban refugees were housed at Fort Chaffee near Barling. On two occasions rioting broke out and scores of

CALIFORNIA

Cubans escaped temporarily into the surrounding area. Most of the refugees had been resettled throughout the nation by July 1981.

Full name: State of Arkansas. **Origin of name:** From Algonquian name of the Quapaw Indians. **Inhabitant:** Arkansan. **Capital:** Little Rock. **State motto:** Regnat Populus (The People Rule). **Flag:** Star-studded blue & white diamond on a red field; diamond shape represents Arkansas, the only diamond-producing state. **Seal:** Shield design has steamboat, plow, beehive & sheaf of wheat, symbolizing industry & agriculture; angel of mercy & sword of justice guard American eagle; goddess of liberty stands above. **Flower:** Apple blossom. **Bird:** Mockingbird. **Tree:** Pine. **Song:** "Arkansas." **Nickname:** Land of Opportunity.

Governor: Frank D. White. **Annual salary:** $35,000. **Term:** 2 years. **Current term expires:** Jan. 1983. **Voting requirements:** 18 yrs. old & U.S. citizen; registered in county of residence. **U.S. Congressmen:** 4. **Entered Union:** 1836 (25th state).

Location & boundaries: South Central state: bounded on the north by Missouri; on the east by the Mississippi River & the states of Missouri, Tennessee & Mississippi; on the south by Louisiana; & on the west by Texas & Oklahoma. **Total area:** 53,104 sq. mi. (ranks 27th). **Extreme length:** 275 mi. **Extreme breadth:** 240 mi. **Chief rivers:** Mississippi, Arkansas, Ouachita, White. **Major lakes:** Bull Shoals, Ouachita, Beaver, Norfork. **No. of counties:** 75.

Population (1980 census): 2,285,513 (ranks 33rd). **Pop. increase (1970-80):** 18.8%. **Largest cities:** Little Rock, Fort Smith, N. Little Rock, Pine Bluff. **Pop. density:** 43.0 per sq. mi. (ranks 35th). **Pop. distribution:** White—1,890,002; Black—373,192; Am. Indian, Eskimo and Aleut—9,411; Asian and Pacific Islander—6,732; Other—6,176; Spanish origin—17,873. **Marriage rate (1978):** 11.6 per 1,000 people. **Divorce rate:** 9.2 per 1,000 people.

State finances (1979). Revenue: $1,968,000,000. **Expenditures:** $1,897,000,000. **State taxes:** $456.22 per capita. **State personal income tax:** Yes. **Public debt (1979):** $112.04 per capita. **Federal aid (1980):** $408.96 per capita. **Personal income (1980):** $7,180.

Sectors of the economy (% of labor force employed in 1970): Manufacturing (26%), Wholesale and retail trade (19%), Government (15%), Services (8%), Educational Services (8%), Construction (7%). **Leading products:** food, lumber & wood, paper products, electrical machinery, chemicals, furniture & fixtures, apparel. **Minerals:** petroleum, natural gas, bauxite, stone, bromine, sand & gravel. **Agricultural products:** broilers, cattle, eggs, soybeans, rice, cotton lint. **Avg. farm (1980):** 295 acres. **Avg. value of farm per acre:** $829.

Highway expenditures per capita (1979): $137.51. **Persons per motor vehicle:** 1.47. **Minimum age for driver's license:** 16. **Gasoline tax:** 9.5¢ per gallon. **Diesel tax:** 10.5¢ per gallon. **Motor vehicle deaths (1978):** 26.2 per 100,000 people.

Birthrate (1978): 16.1 per 1,000 people. **Infant mortality rate per 1,000 births (1978):** 10.5. **Physicians per 100,000 pop. (1978):** 116. **Dentists per 100,000 pop. (1978):** 32. **Acceptable hospital beds (1978):** 5.5 per 1,000 people. **State expenditures per capita for health and hospitals (1979):** $56.27.

Education expenditures (1976-77): $353.71 per capita annually. **No. of pupils in public schools (1979):** 446,000. **No. of institutions of higher learning (1978-79):** 34. **Public school expenditure per pupil in attendance (1977-78):** $1,347. **Avg. salary of public school teachers (1978-79):** $11,448. **No. full-time teachers (1979):** 23,900. **Educational attainment of adult population (1976):** 12.2 median yrs. of school completed: 6.0% with less than 5 years of education; 9.1% with 4 yrs. of college.

Telephones (1978): 48 per 100 people. **State Chamber of Commerce:** Arkansas State Chamber of Commerce, 911 Wallace Building, Little Rock, Arkansas 72201.

CALIFORNIA

California, the most populous of the states, is the national leader in agriculture, commercial fishing, and motor vehicle ownership. It ranks first in manufacturing and third in land area and oil production.

The heart of the state is the fertile Central Valley, fenced in by two long north-south mountain ranges: the Sierra Nevada (on the east) and the

Coast Range. Several small forested ranges of the Klamath Mountains cover the northwestern corner of the state, while below the Coast Range are the Los Angeles Ranges, and below these, the San Diego Ranges. More than 40 percent of the land is forested. Other important land areas are the Cascade Mountains extending northward from the Central Valley and the Basin and Range Region of the southeast and extreme northeast; within the southeastern part of this region are the Mojave and Colorado deserts.

Both the highest mountain peak in the conterminous United States, Mt. Whitney (14,494 feet) and the lowest point in the hemisphere (282 feet below sea level) can be seen from Dante's View, 5,475 feet high and about 3 miles east of that lowest point. Two island groups lie off the coast: the Santa Barbara (or Channel) Islands, consisting of eight major islands 20 to 60 miles from the southern mainland, and the six small rugged Farallon Islands, about 30 miles west of San Francisco. California's main harbors are San Francisco and San Diego Bays and the man-made Los Angeles harbor, San Pedro Bay. Great extremes mark the climate, with many areas enjoying generally mild and sunny weather, partially befouled in urban areas by palls of smog.

There were about 130,000 Indians living in the California region when Juan Rodriguez Cabrillo, a Portuguese in Spanish employ, discovered it in 1542. English interest in the area began with Sir Francis Drake, who claimed (1579) it for Queen Elizabeth I, but the first permanent European settlement was made by Spaniards, who established 21 missions northward along the coast from San Diego (1769) to Sonoma (1823). In 1812, Russian fur-traders from Alaska came down and established Fort Ross on the state's northern coast, but they did not prevail. In 1822, after Mexico won its independence from Spain, California became a Mexican province, and its social, economic, and political life was centered around large cattle ranches. The first organized group of American settlers came to the region by land in 1841; the United States offered to buy the province, but Mexico refused to sell. U.S. forces occupied the area early in the Mexican War, with Mexico formally ceding its claims in 1848.

Less than two weeks before the treaty was signed, an event of massive importance occurred at John A. Sutter's sawmill near Coloma: the discovery of gold, which set off the famous Gold Rush of '49. In the following seven years, the region produced $450 million worth of gold, while the population jumped from about 15,000 to almost 300,000. This influx virtually secured American possession of the territory. San Francisco, for example, grew from an outpost to a great city, in a turbulent, often lawless, atmosphere. Vigilante groups filled the "law-and-order" gap until more stable government was established, beginning with admission of California into the Union as a free state, under terms of the Compromise of 1850. Meanwhile, California's mountain-walled isolation was rapidly ending: the telegraph reached the area in 1861, and eight years later direct rail connection was made with the rest of the country.

The late 19th and early 20th centuries were marked by continued population growth, soaring land values, and economic-rooted social tensions between American-born Californians, Mexican-Americans and Oriental immigrants. Manufacturing, especially the canning and packing of food, increased greatly; and Hollywood became the world motion picture capital.

More recently, defense-contract industries, electronics and senior citizen retirement communities

have played particularly large roles in the state's economy. Tourist attractions include Disneyland (in Anaheim), San Francisco's Golden Gate Bridge, scenic Lake Tahoe on the Nevada border, the Napa Valley wine-producing district, the Monterey-Carmel area with its renowned Seventeen Mile Drive, William Randolph Hearst's estate at San Simeon, the coastal highway between Big Sur and Morro Bay, 17 national forests, six national parks, and many scenic beaches.

With 20 million residents in 1970, California overtook New York as the most populous state. The 1980 census reported a population of 23,668,562, representing an increase of eighteen and a half percent for the decade. As a result, California will gain two additional seats in the U.S. House of Representatives.

During the 1960s, California's migrant farm workers, mostly Mexican-Americans, were organized by the United Farm Workers Organizing Committee (the union is now the United Farm Workers of America). The long, and sometimes bitterly resisted struggle was led by Cesar Chavez. In the mid-1970s, the United Farm Workers competed for worker loyalty with the Teamsters Union. The two groups settled their dispute in 1977 with a five-year agreement.

In the spring of 1978 a taxpayers' revolt against heavy government spending and high tax rates culminated in the adoption, by 65% of the vote, of Proposal 13, a state constitutional amendment mandating a 57% reduction in property taxes, and limiting the authority of state and local governments to raise taxes. No drastic reduction in government services followed—largely because the state was able to divide a huge surplus with local governments. In 1980, however, California voters rejected by a 3-2 margin another initiative (Proposition 9) which sought to reduce state income tax rates by half. Howard Jarvis, author of both propositions, has suggested he would continue his efforts in this matter by mounting an assault on state pension funds.

In the early summer of 1981 an infestation of the Mediterranean fruit fly appeared in Santa Clara County. During August the "Medfly," which is extremely destructive to fruit crops, spread to the Central Valley despite aerial spraying with insecticides and the destruction of infected fruit.

Full name: State of California. **Origin of name:** From an imaginary island in a 16th-century Spanish romance. **Inhabitant:** Californian. **Capital:** Sacramento. **State motto:** Eureka (I Have Found It). **Flag:** a bear & a red star on white field with red horizontal bar at the bottom. **Seal:** Grizzly bear stands near seated figure of Minerva; a miner, ships & peaks of Sierra Nevada in background; state motto. **Flower:** Golden poppy. **Bird:** California Valley quail. **Tree:** California redwood. **Song:** "I Love You, California." **Nickname:** Golden State.

Governor: Edmund G. Brown, Jr. **Annual salary:** $49,100. **Term:** 4 years. **Current term expires:** Jan. 1983. **Voting requirements:** 18 yrs. old & U.S. citizen; state resident 29 days. **U.S. Congressmen:** 43 (1980 reapportionment): 45. **Entered Union:** 1850 (31st state).

Location & boundaries: Pacific state: bounded on the north by Oregon; on the east by Nevada & Arizona; on the southeast by the Colorado River; on the south by Mexico; & on the west by the Pacific Ocean. **Total area:** 158,693 sq. mi. (ranks 3rd). **Extreme length:** 1775 mi. **Extreme breadth:** 1360 mi. **Coastline:** 1,264 mi. **Chief rivers:** Sacramento, San Joaquin, Klamath. **Major lakes:** Salton Sea, Tahoe, Goose. **No. of counties:** 58.

Population (1980 census): 23,668,562 (ranks 1st). **Pop. increase (1970-80):** 18.5%. **Largest cities:** Los Angeles, San Diego, San Francisco, San Jose. **Pop. density:** 149.1 per sq. mi. (ranks 15th). **Pop. distribution:** White—18,031,689; Black—1,819,262; Am. Indian, Eskimo and Aleut—201,311; Asian and Pacific Islander—1,253,987; Other—2,362,293; Spanish origin—4,543,770. **Marriage rate (1978):** 8.4 per 1,000 people. **Divorce rate:** 6.0 per 1,000 people.

State finances (1979). Revenue: $31,058,000,000. **Expenditures:** $28,319,000,000. **State taxes:** $720.54 per capita. **State personal income tax:** Yes. **Public debt (1979):** $338.24 per capita. **Federal aid (1980):** $368.54 per capita. **Personal income (1980):** $10.856

Sectors of the economy (% of labor force employed in 1970): Manufacturing (22%), Wholesale and retail trade (21%), Government (18%), Services (9%), Educational Services (8%), Construction (5%). **Leading products:** transportation equipment, food, machinery, ordnance & accessories, fabricated metals, printing & publishing. **Minerals:** petroleum, natural gas, cement, sand & gravel. **Agricultural products:** cattle, dairy items, hay, tomatoes, cotton lint. **Fishing:** tuna, salmon, crabs. **Avg. farm (1980):** 538 acres. **Avg. value of farm per acre:** $1,123.

Highway expenditures per capita (1979): $52.07. **Persons per motor vehicle:** 1.40. **Minimum age for driver's license:** 16. **Gasoline tax:** 7¢ per gallon. **Diesel tax:** 7¢ per gallon. **Motor vehicle deaths (1978):** 23.8 per 100,000 people.

Birthrate (1978): 16.0 per 1,000 people. **Infant mortality rate per 1,000 births (1978):** 11.8. **Physicians per 100,000 pop. (1978):** 228. **Dentists per 100,000 pop. (1978):** 62. **Acceptable hospital beds (1978):** 4.8 per 1,000 people. **State expenditures per capita for health and hospitals (1979):** $57.16.

Education expenditures (1976-77): $557.99 per capita annually. **No. of pupils in public schools (1979):** 4,088,000. No. of institutions of higher learning (1978-79): 262. **Public school expenditure per pupil in attendance (1977-78):** $2,004. **Avg. salary of public school teachers (1978-79):** $18,172. **No. full-time teachers (1979):** 228,200. **Educational attainment of adult population (1976):** 12.7 median yrs. of school completed: 3.3% with less than 5 years of education; 16.8% with 4 yrs. of college.

Telephones (1978): 61 per 100 people. **State Chamber of Commerce:** California Chamber of Commerce, P.O. Box 1736, 455 Capitol Mall, Sacramento, California 95808.

COLORADO

Colorado, the Centennial State, is the state with the highest overall elevation; it has more than 1,000 peaks that soar at least 10,000 feet, including legendary Pikes Peak. In the east are the high plains, while the Rockies' peaks and ranges make up the central region; and in the west is the Colorado Plateau. The Continental Divide runs generally north and south through the west-central part of the state. As is typical of mountainous areas, there are great extremes of climate, yet a surprisingly diverse agriculture.

This state is part of the *real* Old West, not the West of romanticized Westerns. Ruthlessly competitive gold mining (starting in 1858) and silver mining (1875) and the decades-long wresting of crops from the arid land shaped Colorado and defined its character.

Many metals are mined in the mountains. Molybdenum, which hardens steel and is used in rocketry, is the state's most valuable: Colorado holds over half of the world's supply. Oil shale is the state's most important undeveloped resource.

Food and machinery are the state's two main industries. Only California has more irrigated acreage; however, two-thirds of Colorado's farm output consists of livestock and livestock products. It leads in the refining of beet sugar.

Cliff-dwelling Indians are believed to have built (c. A.D. 100) Colorado's first civilization in the Mesa Verde plateau, which lies in the southwest corner of the state; they carved irrigation ditches and built many-storied pueblos.

In the 1500s, Spanish explorers became the first Europeans to visit the region but, not finding gold, they did not stay. The United States got the eastern and central areas of Colorado as part of the Louisiana Purchase and the western part as a result of the Mexican War.

The gold rush of the late 1850s was followed by the Civil War. With fewer Federal troops in the

CONNECTICUT

area, the intense fighting between whites and the Arapaho and Cheyenne Indians posed the very real threat of general lawlessness.

The establishment (1861) of the Colorado Territory was a step toward unity and stability, and the advent of the railroads in the 1870s was another. Statehood came in 1876. This was the era in which the New York journalist Horace Greeley sponsored a Colorado farming colony and advised, "Go West, young man!"

The 1880s brought fiscal health and early growth as a state, but trouble and renewed bloodshed characterized the next decade.

Silver prices dropped badly after the repeal of the Sherman Silver Purchase Act (1893), and many great mines closed, leaving behind ghost towns with colorful names such as Cripple Creek and Eureka. Range warfare was rife, and bitter hassles took place over railway franchises. Long-simmering labor-management conflict came to a head in 1914 in a battle near Trinidad between striking coal miners and the militia in which innocent women and children were killed. Subsequent reforms included regular government inspection of mines.

The state's economy advanced sharply after both World Wars. In between were more years of struggle: the great Wall Street fiasco of 1929 was accompanied, in Colorado, by drought and high winds which created a disastrous dust bowl.

Today, Colorado is prosperous. Denver is an important business center, missile-plant site, and headquarters for Federal agencies. In addition, U.S. coins are minted there, while the National Bureau of Standards laboratory at Boulder has expanded greatly in recent years. Scientists at an observation station near Climax are studying the earth's atmosphere and conducting space research.

Because of the state's magnificent scenery, tourism has developed into a major industry. Tourist attractions include Rocky Mountain and Mesa Verde National Parks, a dozen national forests, hunting and fishing, Balanced Rock in the Garden of the Gods, Royal Gorge on the Arkansas River, the ski center of Vail, Buffalo Bill's Grave on Lookout Mountain, and cultural festivals at Aspen and Central City.

The U.S. Air Force Academy, founded in 1958, is located at Colorado Springs. In 1976 the academy admitted the first female cadets.

In 1979 the Interior Department proposed stricter air quality standards for the 50-mile-long Black Canyon of the Gunnison River in the western part of the state.

Full name: State of Colorado. **Origin of name:** From Spanish for "Colored Red." **Inhabitant:** Coloradan. **Capital:** Denver. **State motto:** Nil Sine Numine (Nothing Without Providence). **Flag:** A red letter C encloses gold ball & rests against blue, white & blue bars. **Seal:** A triangular figure, representing "all seeing" eye of God, bound rods, three mountains & pick & hammer. **Flower:** Rocky Mountain columbine. **Bird:** Lark bunting. **Tree:** Blue spruce. **Song:** "Where the Columbines Grow." **Nickname:** Centennial State.

Governor: Richard D. Lamm. **Annual salary:** $50,000. **Term:** 4 years. **Current term expires:** Jan. 1983. **Voting requirements:** 18 yrs. old & U.S. citizen; resident of state and precinct, 32 days. **U.S. Congressmen:** 5 (1980 reapportionment: 6). **Entered Union:** 1876 (38th state).

Location & boundaries: Rocky Mountain state: bounded on the north by Wyoming & Nebraska; on the east by Nebraska & Kansas; on the south by Oklahoma & New Mexico; & on the west by Utah. **Total area:** 104,247 sq. mi. (ranks 8th). **Extreme length:** 387 mi. **Extreme breadth:** 276 mi. **Chief rivers:** Colorado, Arkansas, South Platte, Rio Grande. **Major lakes:** Blue Mesa; Dillon, John Martin, Granby. **No. of counties:** 63.

Population (1980 census): 2,888,834 (ranks 28th). **Pop. increase (1970-80):** 30.7%. **Largest cities:** Denver, Colorado Springs,

Pueblo. **Pop. density:** 27.7 per sq. mi. (ranks 38th). **Pop. distribution:** White—2,570,615; Black—101,702; Am. Indian, Eskimo and Aleut—18,059; Asian and Pacific Islander—29,897; Other—168,561; Spanish origin—339,300. **Marriage rate (1978):** 11.5 per 1,000 people. **Divorce rate:** 6.9 per 1,000 people.

State finances (1979). Revenue: $3,050,000,000. **Expenditures:** $2,518,000,000. **State taxes:** $519.78 per capita. **State personal income tax:** Yes. **Public debt (1979):** $153.75 per capita. **Federal aid (1980):** $334.20 per capita. **Personal income (1980):** $9,964.

Sectors of the economy (% of labor force employed in 1970): Wholesale and retail trade (22%), Government (20%), Manufacturing (15%), Educational Services (10%), Services (8%), Construction (7%). **Leading products:** food; machinery; transportation equipment; electrical equipment; printing & publishing; stone, clay & glass items; fabricated metals; chemicals; lumber. **Minerals:** molybdenum, petroleum, coal, sand & gravel. **Agricultural products:** cattle, hay, dairy items, wheat, sugar beets, sheep. **Avg. farm (1980):** 1,478 acres. **Avg. value of farm per acre:** $388.

Highway expenditures per capita (1979): $97.98. **Persons per motor vehicle:** 1.20. **Minimum age for driver's license:** 21. **Gasoline tax:** 9¢ per gallon. **Diesel tax:** 9¢ per gallon. **Motor vehicle deaths (1978):** 26.0 per 100,000 people.

Birthrate (1978): 16.3 per 1,000 people. **Infant mortality rate per 1,000 births (1978):** 11.2. **Physicians per 100,000 pop. (1978):** 212. **Dentists per 100,000 pop. (1978):** 62. **Acceptable hospital beds (1978):** 5.1 per 1,000 people. **State expenditures per capita for health and hospitals (1979):** $63.23.

Education expenditures (1976-77): $605.96 per capita annually. **No. of pupils in public schools (1979):** 545,000. **No. of institutions of higher learning (1978-79):** 41. **Public school expenditure per pupil in attendance (1977-78):** $2,258. **Avg. salary of public school teachers (1978-79):** $15,500. **No. full-time teachers (1979):** 31,700. **Educational attainment of adult population (1976):** 12.8 median yrs. of school completed: 1.3% with less than 5 years of education; 19.4% with 4 yrs. of college.

Telephones (1978): 57 per 100 people. **State Chamber of Commerce:** Colorado Association of Commerce and Industry, 1390 Logan Street, Suite 308, Denver, Colorado 80203.

CONNECTICUT

Connecticut, one of the smallest states in area, is one of the most varied and most prosperous. Generally rectangular in shape, the state is divided by the Connecticut River and its fertile valley into two almost equal regions. Gently rolling hills rise from the southern coastal plain to an average elevation of about 1,000 feet at the northern boundary.

Highly industrialized cities contrast with the scenic, typically New England countryside, 60 percent of which is forested. The southern shore has a number of excellent harbors, and several small islands lie off the coast. The southern section, particularly Fairfield County, is home for many who work in New York City.

Among Connecticut's attractions are Yale University at New Haven, the American Dance Festival at Connecticut College in New London, and this hemisphere's first school for the deaf, at Hartford.

About 7,000 members of the Algonquian Indian family were living in Connecticut before the Europeans came; of these, the Pequot were most powerful. Uncas, chief of the Mohican branch of the Pequots, was immortalized by James Fenimore Cooper in The Last of the Mohicans. Relations between the Indians and early settlers were mostly friendly, except for the brief Pequot War (1637) and the more serious King Philip's War (1675-76).

Dutch navigator Adriaen Block was the first European of record to visit the state (1614), sailing up the Connecticut River. In 1633, colonists from Holland set up a trading post (near present-day Hartford), but the Dutch lost control of the area to the English; Puritans from the Massachusetts Bay

Colony established the first permanent settlement at the site of modern Windsor that same year, and another at Wethersfield in 1634. English settlements at Hartford and Saybrook began in 1635, and representatives of the three "River Towns" of Windsor, Wethersfield, and Hartford united to form the Connecticut Colony and adopt (1639) the "Fundamental Orders" that gave citizens the right to elect government officials and omitted the religious test for citizenship; the document thus anticipated the U.S. Constitution and is considered the world's first written constitution.

Meanwhile, a wholly new colony came into being with the establishment of New Haven (1638) and other communities in the southern part of Connecticut; called the New Haven Colony, it was more rigidly Puritan than the older colony. In 1662, the Connecticut Colony procured an unusually democratic royal charter resembling the "Fundamental Orders" and providing for the incorporation (1665) of the New Haven Colony, which strongly opposed absorption but reluctantly acquiesced under threat of an alternative take-over by New York. Sir Edmund Andros, who had been named British governor of New England by James II, demanded surrender of the colony's charter; he arrived in Hartford in 1687 to seize the document, but the townspeople are said to have hidden it in the legendary Charter Oak tree.

Connecticut patriots, including Nathan Hale and Governor Jonathan Trumbull, took on a leading role in the Revolutionary War, and the colony served as the Continental Army's major supply area. After the war Connecticut gave up its claims to all western land except the so-called "Western Reserve." Statehood dates from 1788, but boundary disputes with New York, Massachusetts, and Rhode Island persisted until the present borders were established in 1799. Jefferson's Embargo Act of 1807 was highly unpopular in Connecticut, as it was elsewhere in New England. The state's contribution to the Union cause in the Civil War was exceptional; five times the quota of men volunteered.

Most early Connecticut colonists wrested their living from the land and made their own clothes and tools. Enterprising "Yankee peddlers" with horse and rig toured the nation, hawking well-turned wares. During and after the Civil War, better transportation and sharply increased immigration served to shift the economic focus from agriculture to industry. The state, sometimes called "The Arsenal of the Nation," became one of the most industrialized in the country. Its business pioneers included revolver inventor Samuel Colt, rubber magnate Charles Goodyear, and Eli Whitney, who innovated mass production of firearms and manufactured (1793) the cotton gin that proved a boon to the textile industry.

Often called the Insurance Capital of the World, Hartford is the headquarters city for nearly 40 firms in that field.

Connecticut is a leader in the production of such vital items as ball and roller bearings, electronic goods, chemicals and plastics, jet engines, helicopters, and nuclear submarines. United Technologies Corp., the state's largest employer with ten divisions and subsidiaries, and the Electric Boat Division of General Dynamics in Groton are important contributors to the nation's aerospace and submarine production. Electric Boat launched the world's first nuclear submarine in 1954. Shifting emphasis to commercial production has helped the state's numerous defense contractors withstand military cutbacks in the 1970s.

In the southwest section the industrial base is shifting from traditional skilled industry and manufacturing. A number of major companies have established headquarters facilities in the state, including Xerox, IBM, General Electric, Pepsico and Union Carbide. Connecticut ranks very high among the states in per capita income, and in the proportionate number of white-collar and professional workers in the work force.

Full name: State of Connecticut. **Origin of name:** From the Indian, Quinnehtukqut, meaning "Beside the Long Tidal River." **Inhabitant:** Nutmegger. **Capital:** Hartford. **State motto:** Qui Transtulit Sustinet (He Who Transplanted Still Sustains). **Flag:** State seal on blue field. **Seal:** Three grapevines symbolize transplanting of culture & traditions of Europe to the colony. **Flower:** Mountain laurel. **Bird:** Robin. **Tree:** White oak. **Song:** "Yankee Doodle." **Nickname:** Constitution State.

Governor: William A. O'Neill **Annual salary:** $42,000. **Term:** 4 years. **Current term expires:** Jan. 1983. **Voting requirements:** 18 yrs. old & U.S. citizen; resident of state. **U.S. Congressmen:** 6. **Entered Union:** 1788 (5th state).

Location & boundaries: New England state: bounded on the north by Massachusetts; on the east by Rhode Island; on the south by Long Island Sound; & on the west by New York. **Total area:** 5,009 sq. mi. (ranks 48th). **Extreme length:** 100 mi. **Extreme breadth:** 50 mi. **Coastline:** 253 mi. **Chief rivers:** Connecticut, Housatonic, Thames. **Major lake:** Candlewood. **No. of counties:** 8.

Population (1980 census): 3,107,576 (ranks 25th). **Pop. increase (1970-80):** 2.5%. **Largest cities:** Bridgeport, Hartford, New Haven. **Pop. density:** 620.4 per sq. mi. (ranks 4th). **Pop. distribution:** White—2,799,420; Black—217,433; **Am. Indian, Eskimo and Aleut**—4,533; **Asian and Pacific Islander**—18,970; **Other**—67,220; Spanish origin—124,499. **Marriage rate (1978):** 7.7 per 1,000 people. **Divorce rate:** 4.1 per 1,000 people.

State finances (1979). Revenue: $3,173,000,000. **Expenditures:** $2,963,000,000. **State taxes:** $551.56 per capita. **State personal income tax:** No, except on capital gains and dividends. **Public debt (1979):** $1,152.79 per capita. **Federal aid (1980):** $372.25 per capita. **Personal income (1980):** $11,445

Sectors of the economy (% of labor force employed in 1973): Manufacturing (34%), Wholesale & retail trade (22%), Services (14%), Government (14%), Educational Services (8%), Construction (5%). **Leading products:** transportation equipment, electrical and other machinery, primary and fabricated metals, chemicals, instruments. **Agricultural products:** dairy items, eggs, tobacco, forest and nursery truck crops. **Avg. farm (1980):** 118 acres. **Avg. value of farm per acre:** $2,331.

Highway expenditures per capita (1979): $67.44. **Persons per motor vehicle:** 1.38. **Minimum age for driver's license:** 16. **Gasoline tax:** 11¢ per gallon. **Diesel tax:** 11¢ per gallon. **Motor vehicle deaths (1978):** 14.5 per 100,000 people.

Birthrate (1978): 12.0 per 1,000 people. **Infant mortality rate per 1,000 births (1978):** 9.3. **Physicians per 100,000 pop. (1978):** 239. **Dentists per 100,000 pop. (1978):** 71. **Acceptable hospital beds (1978):** 6.0 per 1,000 people. **State expenditures per capita for health and hospitals (1979):** $75.72.

Education expenditures (1976-77): $416.99 per capita annually. **No. of pupils in public schools (1979):** 580,000. **No. of institutions of higher learning (1978-79):** 47. **Public school expenditure per pupil in attendance (1977-78):** $2,056. **Avg. salary of public school teachers (1978-79):** $15,939. **No. full-time teachers (1979):** 40,900. **Educational attainment of adult population (1976):** 12.6 median yrs. of school completed: 2.1% with less than 5 years of education; 18.3% with 4 yrs. of college.

Telephones (1977): 62 per 100 people. **State Chamber of Commerce:** Connecticut Business & Industry Association, Inc., 60 Washington Street, Suite 1202, Hartford, Connecticut 06106.

DELAWARE

Although only Rhode Island is smaller in size and few states are less populous, Delaware has a disproportionate worth because of its natural assets and strategic proximity to New York, Philadelphia, Baltimore, and Washington. This location and the state's convenient incorporation laws have made Delaware the home of about 70,000 char-

DELAWARE

Copyright HAMMOND INCORPORATED, Maplewood, N.J.

tered firms, including some of the country's largest.

The state is part of the Delmarva Peninsula separating Delaware and Chesapeake Bays, the peninsula being shared with Maryland and Virginia. Almost all of the state consists of a part of the Atlantic Coastal Plain extending from Florida to New Jersey; the exception is that part of the Piedmont Plateau crossing the state's northern tip and having a maximum width of about 10 miles. Rolling hills in the north slope to a nearly sea-level plain. The state has the nation's lowest mean elevation, and along the southern border is a 30,000-acre swamp. The climate is moderate though humid, with few prolonged periods of extreme temperature.

Before the Europeans arrived, the region was inhabited by the Lenni-Lenape (later called Delaware) Indians, of Algonquian linguistic stock. Although others from Europe may have preceded him, explorer Henry Hudson is credited with Delaware's discovery (1609). A year later, Captain Samuel Argall of Virginia named Delaware Bay for his colony's governor, Thomas West, Baron De La Warr. Several countries vied for control of the state; Swedes made the first permanent settlement (1638) at Fort Christina (now Wilmington); but New Sweden, as the colony as a whole was called, gave way (1655) to Dutch forces led by New Netherland Governor Peter Stuyvesant. The English seized the colony in 1664, administering it under the Duke of York until 1682. It was then annexed to Pennsylvania as The Three Lower Counties. In 1704 it became semiautonomous, and fought in the American Revolution as a separate state. It later became (1787) the first state to ratify the U.S. Constitution.

Meanwhile, the Wilmington area developed into the hub of the flour-milling business and, in 1802, Eleuthère Irénée du Pont established a gunpowder mill on nearby Brandywine Creek that was the foundation of the state's enormous chemical industry. British ships shelled Lewes during the War of 1812, but there was little damage. Great tensions were created in Delaware by the advent of the Civil War, for it was a border state, condoning slavery but remaining loyal to the Union. Antiadministration and neutralist views were common; true secessionists were rare throughout the conflict.

Aided by fertile soil and an abundant water supply, agriculture has long been an important part of Delaware's economy, although far superseded over the years by manufacturing, chiefly of chemicals, transportaion equipment, and food and food products. The Chrysler Corporation maintains a large manufacturing facility in Newark. In the 1950s, there was a new surge of industrial expansion, while the population increased by about 40 percent. Among historical attractions are Fort Christina Monument, Hagley Museum, and Winterthur Museum, in and near Wilmington; central New Castle, a unique survival of a colonial capital, almost unchanged; Dover, with notable public and private buildings; and Lewes, site of the first attempted settlement. Recreation areas include Cape Henlopen, Delaware Seashore, and Trap Pond State Parks. Rehoboth Beach and Bethany Beach are popular seashore resort areas.

Because the Delaware Bay contains a deep natural channel, a sheltered area, and a convenient route to major east coast oil refineries, the state has frequently been mentioned as a prime site for construction of a deepwater terminal. In 1971, under former Republican Gov. Russell W. Peterson, who later was named chairman of the President's Council on Environmental Quality, the state enacted a broad zoning law which flatly prohibited

off-shore ports in state waters and refineries and other heavy industry in its coastal zone.

Supporters argue that the law spells out a policy of moderate growth and is needed to protect Delaware's environment and tourist industry. Environmentalists have introduced amendments to clarify the language of the 1971 acts which remain intact despite continuing opposition from petroleum companies and industrially related groups.

In November 1978, Dover Air Force Base was the scene of the return of the 913 bodies from Jonestown, Guyana, after the mass murder-suicides there. The base's mortuary staff, plus military pathologists and graves registration experts from the Washington area, undertook the difficult task of identifying and embalming the corpses. Base personnel took on a more pleasant mission in early 1980, as they hosted the six U.S. diplomats spirited out of Iran by Canadian embassy officials in Tehran. The diplomats spent two days in seclusion at Dover before returning to their homes.

Full name: State of Delaware. **Origin of name:** From Lord De La Warr, English governor of Virginia. **Inhabitant:** Delawarean. **Capital:** Dover. **State motto:** Liberty & Independence. **Flag:** State seal in a buff diamond on a blue field with date Delaware ratified Constitution. **Seal:** A sheaf of wheat, an ear of corn, an ox, a soldier & a farmer under the crest of a ship. **Flower:** Peach blossom. **Bird:** Blue Hen Chicken. **Tree:** American holly. **Song:** "Our Delaware." **Nicknames:** Blue Hen State; Diamond State; First State.

Governor: Pierre S. du Pont IV. **Annual salary:** $35,000. **Term:** 4 years. **Current term expires:** Jan. 1985. **Voting requirements:** 18 yrs. old & U.S. citizen; state resident, 1 year; county, 3 mos.; district, 30 days. **U.S. Congressmen:** 1. **Entered Union:** 1787 (1st state).

Location & boundaries: Middle Atlantic state: bounded on the north by Pennsylvania; on the east by New Jersey, Delaware Bay & the Atlantic Ocean; & on the south & west by Maryland. **Total area:** 2,057 sq. mi. (ranks 49th). **Extreme length:** 96 mi. **Extreme breadth:** 35 mi. **Coastline:** 28 mi. **Chief rivers:** Delaware, Nanticoke, Christina. **Major lakes:** None, but many small lakes and ponds. **No. of counties:** 3.

Population (1980 census): 595,225 (ranks 47th). **Pop. increase (1970-80):** 8.6%. **Largest cities:** Wilmington, Newark, Dover. **Pop. density:** 289.3 per sq. mi. (ranks 7th). **Pop. distribution:** White—488,543; Black—95,971; **Am. Indian, Eskimo and Aleut**—1,330; **Asian and Pacific Islander**—4,132; **Other**—52,49; **Spanish origin**—9,671. **Marriage rate (1978):** 7.4 per 1,000 people. **Divorce rate:** 5.6 per 1,000 people.

State finances (1979). Revenue: $869,000,000. **Expenditures:** $762,000,000. **State taxes:** $294.63 per capita. **State personal income tax:** Yes. **Public debt (1979):** $1,469.00 per capita. **Federal aid (1980):** $462.51 per capita. **Personal income (1980):** $9,280.

Sectors of the economy (% of labor force employed in 1970): Manufacturing (30%), Wholesale and retail trade (19%), Government (15%), Services (8%), Educational Services (8%), Construction (8%). **Leading products:** chemicals & related items, food, apparel, primary & fabricated metals, textile mill items, automobiles, paper. **Agricultural products:** broilers, dairy items, corn, soybeans, potatoes. **Fishing:** clams, crabs. **Avg. farm (1980):** 207 acres. **Avg. value of farm per acre:** $2,018.

Highway expenditures per capita (1979): $106.58. **Persons per motor vehicle:** 1.47. **Minimum age for driver's license:** 16. **Gasoline tax:** 9¢ per gallon. **Diesel tax:** 9¢ per gallon. **Motor vehicle deaths (1978):** 21.6 per 100,000 people.

Birthrate (1978): 14.9 per 1,000 people. **Infant mortality rate per 1,000 births (1978):** 13.2. **Physicians per 100,000 pop. (1978):** 163. **Dentists per 100,000 pop. (1978):** 44. **Acceptable hospital beds (1978):** 6.8 per 1,000 people. **State expenditures per capita for health and hospitals (1979):** $79.20.

Education expenditures (1976-77): $594.33 per capita annually. **No. of pupils in public schools (1979):** 108,000. **No. of institutions of higher learning (1978-79):** 10. **Public school expenditure per pupil in attendance (1977-78):** $2,271. **Avg. salary of public school teachers (1978-79):** $15,555. **No. full-time teachers (1979):** 7,100. **Educational attainment of adult population (1976):** 12.5 median yrs. of school completed: 1.8% with less than 5 years of education; 15.5% with 4 yrs. of college.

Telephones (1978): 63 per 100 people. **State Chamber of Commerce:** Delaware State Chamber of Commerce, Inc., 1102 West Street, Wilmington, Delaware 19801.

FLORIDA

Florida, southernmost of the continental states, is a low-lying peninsula with a coastline second in length only to Alaska's, measuring 1,350 miles—580 on the Atlantic coast and 770 on the Gulf. The state has an average elevation of 100 feet. Curving southwestward for about 200 miles off the southern coast are the Florida Keys, including Elliott Key and Key Largo at the north and Key West at the south.

Indians are thought to have inhabited this region about 10,000 years ago. In 1513 Juan Ponce de León, a Spanish explorer said to be searching for the legendary Fountain of Youth, landed on the east coast and mistakenly thought his find was an island. He named it and claimed it for Spain. Except for an interlude of British rule (1763-1783), Spain kept a tenuous hold until 1819, when the United States bought the Spanish claim. Florida became a state in 1845, seceded from the Union in 1861, and was readmitted in 1868.

Florida's early development was severely hampered by two bloody and costly wars with the Seminole Indians, who were not defeated until 1842. Many never surrendered, but fled instead to the Everglades wilderness, became the core of a new tribe, and, eventually, were settled on reservations. In May 1970, the Seminoles were awarded $12,347,500 for land taken from them by U.S. military forces. The Indians estimate there are now 1,500 Seminoles in Florida and 3,500 in Oklahoma.

Among the fastest-growing states in the nation, Florida has risen in population from 2.8 million in 1950 to over 9.7 million today. Land values and industry have grown proportionately, but rapid expansion has created such problems for the state as attempting to keep pace with the spiraling demand for new facilities.

Tourism, with 34 million visitors in 1978, is the state's leading industry, thanks to one of the mildest and most comfortable climates east of the Mississippi and an abundance of swimming, fishing, and other recreational resources. Resort centers along the "Gold Coast" include Miami Beach (a suburb of Miami), Palm Beach, Daytona Beach, and Fort Lauderdale. Formerly a winter industry, tourism is now significant all year round. Disney World, built on a 27,400-acre site near Orlando, is the state's newest attraction; eight times as large as California's Disneyland, it is the world's largest non-governmental construction project.

Everglades National Park, at Florida's southern tip, draws many visitors. The 2,185-square-mile preserve contains the country's largest remaining tropical wilderness and a multitude of plant and animal types. Other attractions include Cypress Gardens near Winter Haven, Monkey Jungle near Goulds (a Miami suburb), and the Ringling Museum of Art in Sarasota.

Commercial fishing is a major industry in the state, although much of the water is given over to sport fishermen. There are more kinds of fish in the waters in or off Florida than anywhere else in the country. The state is also important agriculturally; its leading crop—oranges—is worth over $500 million a year. Mining of phosphate is also significant.

An important connection point for North, Central, and South American air traffic, Florida has about 330 airports; Miami International is one of the busiest in the world in passenger traffic.

Natural dangers the state faces include crop damage by droughts and early frosts, and seasonal (July-October) hurricanes. Destructive hurricanes struck Florida in 1926, 1928, 1935, 1941, and 1964. Today, many Federal programs have been implemented to help arm the state against these tropical storms.

Cape Canaveral (called Cape Kennedy from 1963 to 1973) was the launching site of most U.S. space vehicles, including the first manned vehicle to land on the moon (1969), the first orbiting laboratory (Skylab 1973), the first joint venture with the Soviet Union (1975), and first orbiting of the reusable space shuttle, the Columbia (1981).

All Florida courts were open in 1977 to news coverage by television and still picture cameras, thus making the state's judicial system the most open to media coverage in the nation.

John A. Spenkelink was put to death in the electric chair on May 25, 1979, at the Florida State Prison. He was the first person to be executed in the U.S. since 1977. His case attracted nationwide attention from those both for and against capital punishment, thereby paving the way for the reconsideration of death penalty sentences.

In 1980, Florida voters adopted a constitutional amendment to increase from $5,000 to $25,000 the homestead exemption from property taxes. The state compensated local governments for lost revenue out of a large surplus.

Tens of thousands of Cuban refugees journeyed in small boats from Mariel, Cuba, to Key West in May 1980. Many were then transferred to Eglin Air Force Base, near Fort Walton Beach in Florida's Panhandle region, before being sent to permanent settlement sites throughout the nation.

Full name: State of Florida. **Origin of name:** From Spanish, Pascua Florida, meaning "Feast of Flowers." **Inhabitant:** Floridian. **Capital:** Tallahassee. **State motto:** In God We Trust. **Flag:** State seal lies on white field crossed by diagonal red bars. **Seal:** Sun, steamboat & Indian girl strewing flowers. **Flower:** Orange blossom. **Bird:** Mockingbird. **Tree:** Sabal palm. **Song:** "Old Folks at Home." **Nickname:** Sunshine State.

Governor: Robert Graham. **Annual salary:** $59,098. **Term:** 4 years. **Current term expires:** Jan. 1983. **Voting requirements:** 18 yrs. old & U.S. citizen; resident of state and county. **U.S. Congressmen:** 15 (1980 reapportionment: 19). **Entered Union:** 1845 (27th state).

Location & boundaries: South Atlantic state: bounded on the north by Alabama, the Chattahoochee River, Georgia & St. Mary's River; on the east by the Atlantic Ocean; on the south by the Straits of Florida; & on the west by the Gulf of Mexico, the Perdido River & Alabama. **Total area:** 58,560 sq. mi. (ranks 22nd). **Extreme length:** 447 mi. **Extreme breadth:** 361 mi. **Coastline:** 399 mi. on Atlantic; 798 mi. on Gulf Coast. **Chief rivers:** St. Johns, Apalachicola, Suwannee. **Major lakes:** Okeechobee, George, Kissimmee. **No. of counties:** 67.

Population (1980 census): 9,739,992 (ranks 7th). **Pop. increase (1970-80):** 43.4%. **Largest cities:** Jacksonville, Miami, Tampa, St. Petersburg. **Pop. density:** 165.5 per sq. mi. (ranks 11th). **Pop. distribution:** White—8,178,387; Black—1,342,478; Am. Indian, Eskimo and Aleut—19,316; Asian and Pacific Islander—56,756; Other—143,055; Spanish origin—857,898. **Marriage rate (1978):** 11.0 per 1,000 people. **Divorce rate:** 7.6 per 1,000 people.

State finances (1979). Revenue: $7,286,000,000. **Expenditures:** $6,462,000,000. **State taxes:** $484.31 per capita. **State personal income tax:** No. **Public debt (1979):** $301.47 per capita. **Federal aid (1980):** $292.72 per capita. **Personal income (1980):** $8,987.

Sectors of the economy (% of labor force employed in 1970): Wholesale and retail trade (24%), Government (16%), Manufacturing (14%), Services (12%), Construction (9%), Educational Services (7%). **Leading products:** apparel products; transportation equipment; fabricated metal products; chemicals; paper items; food; printing & publishing; electrical machinery; limestone, clay &

FLORIDA

glass items; fabricated metals. **Minerals:** phosphate rock, stone, clay. **Agricultural products:** dairy items, cattle, citrus, tomatoes, sugarcane for sugar & seed, winter vegetables. **Fishing:** oysters and scallops, crabs, lobsters, shrimp. **Avg. farm (1980):** 394 acres. **Avg. value of farm per acre:** $1,097.

Highway expenditures per capita (1979): $87.34. **Persons per motor vehicle:** 1.23. **Minimum age for driver's license:** 16. **Gasoline tax:** 8¢ per gallon. **Diesel tax:** 8¢ per gallon. **Motor vehicle deaths (1978):** 26.3 per 100,000 people.

Birthrate (1978): 13.1 per 1,000 people. **Infant mortality rate per 1,000 births (1978):** 14.1. **Physicians per 100,000 pop. (1978):** 189. **Dentists per 100,000 pop. (1978):** 50. **Acceptable hospital beds (1978):** 5.5 per 1,000 people. **State expenditures per capita for health and hospitals (1979):** $61.66.

Education expenditures (1976-77): $406.79 per capita annually. **No. of pupils in public schools (1979):** 1,004,000. **No. of institutions of higher learning (1978-79):** 77. **Public school expenditure per pupil in attendance (1977-78):** $1,693. **Avg. salary of public school teachers (1978-79):** $14,590. **No. full-time teachers (1979):** 82,400. **Educational attainment of adult population (1976):** 12.4 median yrs. of school completed: 3.7% with less than 5 years of education; 13.7% with 4 yrs. of college.

Telephones (1978): 62 per 100 people. **State Chamber of Commerce:** Florida State Chamber of Commerce, P.O. Box 5497, 311 S. Calhoun Street, Tallahassee, Florida 32301.

GEORGIA

The largest state east of the Mississippi, and the last of the 13 Colonies to be founded, Georgia consists of three main land regions: in the north is a small section of the Appalachian Mountains; the Piedmont Plateau constitutes the middle; and in the south, coastal flatlands make up about three-fifths of the state's total area. Landmarks include the Okefenokee Swamp, one of the country's largest.

Mound Builders were the first known inhabitants of the Georgia region, followed in modern times by Creek and Cherokee Indians. Spanish explorer De Soto is thought to have been the first European to visit (1540) the area, but British claims soon conflicted with those of Spain; in 1733, English philanthropist James Oglethorpe led a group of his countrymen in launching the first permanent settlement at Savannah as an asylum for debtors. England ended the Spanish threat in 1742, as forces under Oglethorpe defeated their rivals in the battle of Bloody Marsh.

The sale of rum and the introduction of Negro slaves into the region were at first outlawed, but by about 1750 new legislation ended these restrictions. Many foreigners were among the early immigrants, soon followed by settlers mainly from Virginia and the Carolinas.

After the American Revolution, Georgia became a stronghold of slavery and cotton culture—fostered by the invention of the cotton gin, in 1793, by Eli Whitney, who was living near Savannah. Georgia seceded in 1861, and suffered great damage in the Civil War. The war ended slavery, but black Georgians suffered many disabilities until the civil rights movement of the 1950s and 1960s.

Changes in social patterns are evident. Public accommodations throughout the state are generally desegregated, in accordance with law, as are most school systems, although residential housing patterns in many areas limit the amount of actual school integration. In 1980 violence occurred between blacks and whites in rural Wrightsville.

As in many other parts of the country, Georgians expressed concern over busing pupils to achieve racial balance in schools. In February, 1972, classroom boycotts to protest busing cut into school attendance at Augusta. There were efforts to promote a statewide boycott, but they failed.

Georgia, the first state (1943) to grant 18-year-olds the right to vote, in 1973 lowered from 21 to 18 the legal age for adults.

Georgia is today involved in the same agriculture-to-industry transformation which the South as a whole is undergoing. Its extensive resources include a wealth of largely untapped hydroelectric power and some of the most valuable marble and gravel deposits in the country. Favorable climate, natural resources and an abundant labor supply have caused many industries to establish plants in the state. Industrialization has brought efforts at unionization, and resistance to these efforts. In 1980, the mayor and police chief of Milledgeville settled out of court with a union which had sued them for alleged illegal surveillance of union organizers. Georgia is the nation's largest supplier of peanuts and poultry, and also ranks high in textiles, egg production, lumber, cotton, peaches, and tobacco production, while Atlanta has become one of the South's most important transportation and distributing centers.

Tourism is another significant revenue source, and is aided by such attractions as the Chattahoochee and Oconee National Forests, picturesque Savannah, the Sea Island beach resorts, FDR's "Little White House" at Warm Springs, and Andersonville Prison Park and National Cemetery on the site of the infamous Confederate prison. A major attraction is the enormous Confederate Memorial carving, the world's largest single piece of sculpture, cut into the sheer north face of historic Stone Mountain, near Atlanta; the work, centerpiece of a 3,200-acre park, depicts General Robert E. Lee, Confederate President Jefferson Davis, and General Stonewall Jackson.

Former Gov. Jimmy Carter, often hailed as one of the South's "new breed" of young progressive chief executives, was inaugurated as President of the United States in 1977, the first Southern president since the Civil War.

Full name: State of Georgia. **Origin of name:** In honor of King George II of England. **Inhabitant:** Georgian. **Capital:** Atlanta. **State motto:** Wisdom, Justice & Moderation. **Flag:** State seal on a vertical blue bar; Confederate flag to the right. **Seal:** Arch representing state constitution; three columns with Georgia's motto; date 1776 is year Georgia signed Declaration of Independence. **Flower:** Cherokee rose. **Bird:** Brown thrasher. **Tree:** Live oak. **Song:** "Georgia." **Nickname:** Peach State and The Empire State of the South.

Governor: George D. Busbee. **Annual salary:** $60,000. **Term:** 4 years. **Current term expires:** Jan. 1983. **Voting requirements:** 18 yrs. old & U.S. citizen. **U.S. Congressmen:** 10. **Entered Union:** 1788 (4th state).

Location & boundaries: South Atlantic state: bounded on the north by Tennessee & North Carolina; on the east by South Carolina, the Atlantic Ocean & the Savannah, Tugaloo & Chattooga Rivers; on the south by St. Mary's River & Florida; & on the west by Florida, Alabama & the Chattahoochee River. **Total area:** 58,876 sq. mi. (ranks 21st). **Extreme length:** 315 mi. **Extreme breadth:** 250 mi. **Coastline:** 100 mi. **Chief Rivers:** Altamaha, Chattahoochee, Savannah. **Major lakes:** Lanier, Allatoona, Seminole. **No. of counties:** 159.

Population (1980 census): 5,464,265 (ranks 13th). **Pop. increase (1970-80):** 19.1%. **Largest cities:** Atlanta, Columbus, Savannah, Macon. **Pop. density:** 92.8 per sq. mi. (ranks 21st). **Pop. distribution:** White—3,948,007; Black—1,465,457; Am. Indian, Eskimo and Aleut—7,619; Asian and Pacific Islander—24,461; Other—18,721; Spanish origin—61,261. **Marriage rate (1978):** 11.0 per 1,000 people. **Divorce rate:** 6.2 per 1,000 people.

State finances (1979). Revenue: $4,605,000,000. **Expenditures:** $6,462,000,000. **State taxes:** $478.43 per capita. **State personal income tax:** Yes. **Public debt (1979):** $267.87 per capita. **Federal aid (1980):** $433.78 per capita. **Personal income (1980):** $8,000.

GEORGIA

MILES

KILOMETERS

State Capitals ⊕   County Seats ⊙

© Copyright HAMMOND INCORPORATED, Maplewood, N.J.

Counties indicated by numbers:

1 BALDWIN	10 GLASCOCK
2 BARROW	11 MONTGOMERY
3 CATOOSA	12 OCONEE
4 CHEROKEE	13 ROCKDALE
5 CLAYTON	14 SCHLEY
6 DADE	15 TALIAFERRO
7 DE KALB	16 TOWNS
8 DOUGLAS	17 WALTON
9 FAYETTE	18 WHITFIELD

Longitude West of Greenwich

Sectors of the economy (% of labor force employed in 1970): Manufacturing (27%), Wholesale and retail trade (20%), Government (16%), Services (9%), Educational Services (7%), Construction (7%). **Leading products:** textile mill items, apparel, food, transportation equipment, lumber, pulp & paper products, chemicals. **Minerals:** clays, stone, cement, sand & gravel. **Agricultural products:** broilers, eggs, cattle, peanuts, tobacco, corn. Fishing: shrimp. **Avg. farm (1980):** 296 acres. **Avg. value of farm per acre:** $682.

Highway expenditures per capita (1979): $111.97. **Persons per motor vehicle:** 1.41. **Minimum age for driver's license:** 16. **Gasoline tax:** 7.5¢ per gallon.* **Diesel tax:** 7.5¢ per gallon.* **Motor vehicle deaths (1978):** 28.9 per 100,000 people. * Plus 3% of retail sales price.

Birthrate (1978): 16.6 per 1,000 people. **Infant mortality rate per 1,000 births (1978):** 15.4. **Physicians per 100,000 pop. (1978):** 147. **Dentists per 100,000 pop. (1978):** 41. **Acceptable hospital beds (1978):** 5.7 per 1,000 people. **State expenditures per capita for health and hospitals (1979):** $73.92.

Education expenditures (1976-77): $368.56 per capita annually. **No. of pupils in public schools (1979):** 1,067,000. **No. of institutions of higher learning (1978-79):** 72. **Public school expenditure per pupil in attendance (1977-78):** $1,507. **Avg. salary of public school teachers (1978-79):** $13,432. **No. full-time teachers (1979):** 57,600. **Educational attainment of adult population (1976):** 12.3 median yrs. of school completed: 8.0% with less than 5 years of education; 12.3% with 4 yrs. of college.

Telephones (1978): 57 per 100 people. **State Chamber of Commerce:** Georgia Chamber of Commerce, 1200 Commerce Building, Atlanta, Georgia 30303.

HAWAII

Hawaii, 50th state to join (1959) the Union, is a chain of 132 islands near the center of the North Pacific Ocean, about 2,400 miles from San Francisco. The islands were formed by volcanoes erupting from the ocean floor; there are some still-active volcanoes at the easterly end of the island chain, which extends 1,523 miles, and may be divided into three groups: the sand and coral islands of the northwest, rock islets in the center, and the eight major islands at the southeast end.

The eight major islands make up all except three square miles of the entire area: Hawaii, Oahu, Maui, Kahoolawe, Lanai, Molokai, Kauai, and Niihau. Hawaii is the largest of these islands (4,038 sq. mi.), while Oahu has the highest population (over 80 percent of the state's total). On Oahu are Honolulu and Pearl Harbor. Of these eight islands, only Kahoolawe is uninhabited; it is used as a target island for bombing and artillery training. The coastline of the islands is approximately 750 miles long. Cooling trade winds make for a pleasantly mild climate all year round. Rainfall varies from hundreds of inches in the mountains to less than 10 inches in the lowlands.

A melting pot of nationalities and racial groups, Hawaii was first settled by seagoing Polynesians, most likely from the Marquesas Islands, during the eighth century. The early Hawaiians, who practiced a religion that included human sacrifice and idolatry, developed a feudal form of government. Europe learned of the islands after British explorer Captain James Cook came upon them (1778); he named them the "Sandwich Islands" in honor of the Earl of Sandwich.

Local chieftain King Kamehameha I took control (1795) of the main islands—except Kauai and Niihau—after thirteen years of warfare with other aspirants. The other two islands accepted his rule in 1810.

Missionaries were active on the islands in the 1800s. In 1840, the Kingdom of Hawaii adopted its first constitution. The growth of the vital sugar and pineapple industries increased U.S. business and political involvement, leading to the establishment (1900) of Hawaii as a United States Territory following annexation (1898). The present population includes significant numbers of Polynesians, Chinese, Filipinos, and Japanese, as well as Caucasians.

The "date which will live in infamy"—Dec. 7, 1941—saw the Japanese attack on Pearl Harbor, which drew the nation into World War II.

Hawaii has since consolidated its importance as a strategic U.S. military outpost: Army, Navy, and Air Force units of the Pacific are under a single command located there. The salaries of military personnel and civilians employed at this command constitute one of Hawaii's principal sources of income. Tourism is the major revenue source. Sugar and pineapple are still exported but are diminishing in the face of foreign competition.

The building boom which critics say created a "concrete jungle" in Waikiki to provide for the tourists is now shifting toward housing for local residents, giving rise to cries of "urban sprawl." There is considerable focus on environmental quality control, with frequent calls for preserving the land. In addition, there is growing concern over the traditional land development pattern. Most of the undeveloped land has been in the hands of a few owners who in the past leased but would not sell to private individuals, who then built homes on their leaseholds. With pressure on landowners to sell rather than lease, and with escalating land values, the future of the real estate market is uncertain.

In addition to such pleasures as swimming, boating and surfing, the islands have much to offer the scientist, historian and general sightseer, including the Bishop Museum in Honolulu—an important center for Polynesian studies; Iolani Palace in Honolulu, the only royal palace in the United States; the world's most active volcano, Kilauea, on Hawaii Island; the extinct Haleakala Crater on Maui Island; and the Waimea Canyon on Kauai Island, often called the "Grand Canyon of the Pacific." The cliff Nuuanu Pali (1,188 feet high) offers a fine view of Oahu's northeast coast.

In 1979, blue-collar state employees went on a six-week strike, causing accumulation of trash and school closings, and there was a three-day work stoppage by most of the state's police officers.

Full name: State of Hawaii. **Origin of name:** Perhaps from native name of the Polynesians' original home. **Inhabitant:** Hawaiian. **Capital:** Honolulu. **State motto:** Ua Mau Ke Ea O Ka Aina I Ka Pono (The Life of the Land Is Perpetuated in Righteousness). **Flag:** Eight alternating white, red & blue bars, representing main islands of state; Union Jack in upper left. **Seal:** Coat of arms of Hawaiian monarchy with King Kamehameha I on right & goddess of liberty on left. **Flower:** Hibiscus. **Bird:** Hawaiian goose. **Tree:** Candlenut (kukui). **Song:** "Hawaii Ponoi." **Nickname:** Aloha State.

Governor: George R. Ariyoshi. **Annual salary:** $50,000. **Term:** 4 years. **Current term expires:** Dec. 1982. **Voting requirements:** 18 yrs. old & U.S. citizen. **U.S. Congressmen:** 2. **Entered Union:** 1959 (50th state).

Location & boundaries: Pacific state composed of a chain of 132 islands, located about 2,397 miles SW of San Francisco; major islands from east to west are Hawaii, Maui, Kahoolawe, Lanai, Molokai, Oahu, Kauai & Niihau. **Total area:** 6,450 sq. mi. (ranks 47th). **Coastline:** 750 mi. **No. of counties:** 5 (inc. Kalawao County— a leprosy settlement).

Population (1980 census): 965,000 (ranks 39th). **Pop. increase (1970-80):** 25.3%. **Largest cities:** Honolulu, Kailua. **Pop. density:** 149.6 per sq. mi. (ranks 14th). **Pop. distribution: White**—318,608; **Black**—17,352; **Am. Indian, Eskimo and Aleut**—2,778; **Asian and Pacific Islander**—583,660; **Other**—42,602; **Spanish origin**—71,479. **Marriage rate (1978):** 11.9 per 1,000 people. **Divorce rate:** 5.4 per 1,000 people.

State finances (1979). Revenue: $1,670,000,000. **Expenditures:** $1,524,000,000. **State taxes:** $957.33 per capita. **State personal**

HAWAII

MILES
0 10 20 30 40 50 60
KILOMETERS
0 10 20 30 40 50 60

State Capital ⊛   County Seats ⊙

income tax: Yes. **Public debt (1979):** $1,854.48 per capita. **Federal aid (1980):** $484.51 per capita. **Personal income (1980):** $9,787.

Sectors of the economy (% of labor force employed in 1975): Wholesale and retail trade (24%), Government (23%), Services (21%), Construction (8%), Manufacturing (7%). **Leading products:** food, printing & publishing, stone, clay, glass items, fabricated metals, lumber & wood. **Agricultural products:** dairy items, cattle, hogs, sugarcane, pineapples, vegetables. **Fishing:** Aku, Ahi, Akule, tuna, big-eyed scad, marlin. **Avg. farm (1980):** 573 acres. **Avg. value of farm per acre:** Not available.

Highway expenditures per capita (1979): $99.11. **Persons per motor vehicle:** 1.66. **Minimum age for driver's license:** 15. **Gasoline tax:** 13.5¢ per gallon in Hawaii Cty., 15¢ in Honolulu Cty., 12.5¢ in Kauai Cty., 13.5¢ in Maui Cty. **Diesel tax:** 13.5¢ per gallon in Hawaii Cty., 15¢ in Honolulu Cty., 12.5¢ in Kauai Cty., 13.5¢ in Maui Cty. **Motor vehicle deaths (1978):** 21.6 per 100,000 people.

Birthrate (1978): 18.6 per 1,000 people. **Infant mortality rate per 1,000 births (1978):** 11.1. **Physicians per 100,000 pop. (1978):** 211. **Dentists per 100,000 pop. (1978):** 67. **Acceptable hospital beds (1978):** 3.9 per 1,000 people. **State expenditures per capita for health and hospitals (1979):** $133.41.

Education expenditures (1976-77): $534.32 per capita annually. **No. of pupils in public schools (1979):** 167,000. **No. of institutions of higher learning (1978-79):** 12. **Public school expenditure per pupil in attendance (1977-78):** $2,172. **Avg. salary of public school teachers (1978-79):** $18,875. **No. full-time teachers (1979):** 9,800. **Educational attainment of adult population (1976):** 12.7 median yrs. of school completed: 5.5% with less than 5 years of education; 16.8% with 4 yrs. of college.

Telephones (1978): 48 per 100 people. **State Chamber of Commerce:** Chamber of Commerce of Hawaii, Dillingham Building, 735 Bishop Street, Honolulu, Hawaii 96813.

IDAHO

Idaho is a rugged, mountainous state that does not yield its resources easily. It has the nation's deepest canyon (Hells Canyon, on the Oregon border), as well as 50 mountain peaks more than 10,000 feet high. There are three main regions: the southern, dominated by the Snake River plains and desolate volcanic terrain; the central, a primitive area of craggy mountains and canyons, dominated by the Salmon River Mountains; and the northern region, featuring the Cabinet Mountains and the Selkirk Mountains lying on the Canadian border. Forests of fir, pine, spruce, and other varieties cover about 40 percent of the state. Many peaceful, relatively unspoiled lakes set off the rough beauty of these areas and of the snow-capped mountains.

Indians are thought to have been living in the area 10,000 years ago. The region was acquired by the United States in the Louisiana Purchase (1803) and explored two years later by Lewis and Clark, who crossed the Bitterroot Range and camped near the present site of Lewiston (founded 1861). Throughout the 1860s, Idaho experienced a gold rush that drew scores of prospectors but left a legacy of ghost towns. Mining, however, is still important; Idaho ranks first nationally in the production of silver, antimony, garnets, and cobalt.

In the 1870s, the growing white occupation of Indian lands—particularly for cattle ranging—led to a series of battles between U.S. forces and the Nez Percé, Bannock, and Sheepeater tribes. Idaho gained statehood in 1890.

During the 1890s, disputes between miners and mineowners often resulted in violence and bloodshed. In 1892, in the Coeur d'Alene area, unionized miners used dynamite and guns to fight nonunion men and mineowners. There was violence again in 1899. Governor Frank Steunenberg declared martial law then and called in Federal troops to restore order. Six years later, Steunenberg, no longer in office, was murdered by a member of the Western Federation of Miners; the confessed killer, de-

fended by Clarence Darrow in a famous trial, was sentenced to life imprisonment.

Despite recent ravages by forest fires (including a 78,000-acre blaze in 1967) and troublesome mountain pine beetle infestations, agriculture is still the state's leading industry; crops include potatoes, wheat, apples, corn, barley, and hops. In 1979, the state's small poultry industry was devastated by the discovery of PCBs in chicken feed.

Irrigation, which has been crucially important, was begun on a large scale under the Federal government's Carey Act (1894) and Reclamation Act (1902). By 1950, Idaho had more than 5,000 diversion dams, 360 reservoirs (with 5 million acre-feet of water capacity), and more than 15,000 miles of irrigation canals and ditches. In 1968, the Idaho Power Company completed Hells Canyon Dam in the Snake River Valley, which also includes Oxbow and Brownlee dams. In recent years thousands of acres of new land have been brought into cultivation on high desert plateaus in the Boise area, largely possible through increased water pumping efficiency. With the completion of the Snake River navigation project in 1975, Idaho now has water access to the Pacific Ocean.

Manufacturing has been steadily increasing, particularly the dehydrating and freezing of potatoes of which Idaho produces about one-fourth of the nation's yield. Nearly 75 percent of this crop is now processed before it goes to the consumer.

Tourism, now the third-ranked industry, is also on the rise, with an estimated 6 million yearly visitors.

Soda Springs, Champagne Springs, Steamboat Spring, and Hooper Spring boast ice-cold, as well as hellishly hot, water discharges. Lava Hot Springs, the site of a state park, has yielded mineral-rich waters since Indian times.

Other attractions of Idaho include the Craters of the Moon National Monument; scenic Coeur d'Alene, Pend Oreille and Priest Lakes in the Panhandle country of northern Utah; Sun Valley that offers skating, swimming, skiing and other attractions; and the Sawtooth Mountains in central Idaho, where a new national recreation area was created in 1972. In 1978 Federal legislation established the large new Gospel-Hump Wilderness Area in north-central Idaho.

In June 1976 the Teton dam burst in the eastern part of the state, causing an estimated one billion dollars damage. Loss of human life was relatively light, but thousands of acres of farmland were destroyed and much of the Idaho cattle industry was temporarily wiped out by floodwaters. Reports indicate the collapse was in part due to poor design.

The eruption of Mount St. Helens in the neighboring state of Washington dumped volcanic ash on northern Idaho in May 1980.

Full name: State of Idaho. **Origin of name:** Probably from the Indian word meaning "Gem of the Mountains." **Inhabitant:** Idahoan. **Capital:** Boise. **State motto:** Esto Perpetua (It Is Forever). **Flag:** State seal centered on blue field. **Seal:** Woman holding scales & a spear; miner; trees & river; elk's head; horns of plenty & sheaves of grain. **Flower:** Syringa. **Bird:** Mountain bluebird. **Tree:** Western pine. **Song:** "Here We Have Idaho." **Nickname:** Gem State.

Governor: John V. Evans. **Annual salary:** $40,000. **Term:** 4 years. **Current term expires:** Jan. 1983. **Voting requirements:** 18 yrs. old & U.S. citizen; registered 5 days with county clerk or 10 days with registrar. **U.S. Congressmen:** 2. **Entered Union:** 1890 (43rd state).

Location & boundaries: Rocky Mountain state: bounded on the north by Canada; on the east by Montana & Wyoming; on the south by Utah & Nevada; & on the west by Oregon, the Snake River & Washington. **Total area:** 83,557 sq. mi. (ranks 13th). **Extreme length:** 483 mi. **Extreme breadth:** 310 mi. **Chief rivers:** Snake, Salmon, Clearwater. **Major lakes:** Pend Oreille, Coeur d'Alene, Priest. **No. of counties:** 44.

IDAHO

MILES
0   20   40   60   80

KILOMETERS
0   20   40   60   80

State Capitals ⊛   County Seats ○

© Copyright HAMMOND INCORPORATED, Maplewood, N.J.

Longitude West 114° of Greenwich

Population (1980 census) 943,935 (ranks 41st). **Pop. increase (1970-80):** 32.4%. **Largest cities:** Boise, Pocatello, Idaho Falls. **Pop. density:** 11.3 per sq. mi. (ranks 43rd). **Pop. distribution:** White—901,641; Black—2,716; **Am. Indian, Eskimo and Aleut—** 10,521; **Asian and Pacific Islander—**5,948; **Other—**23,109; **Spanish origin—**36,615. **Marriage rate (1978):** 15.4 per 1,000 people. **Divorce rate:** 7.2 per 1,000 people.

State finances (1979). Revenue: $995,000,000. **Expenditures:** $891,000,000. **State taxes:** $515.33 per capita. **State personal income tax:** Yes. **Public debt (1979):** $244.04 per capita. **Federal aid (1980):** $391.55 per capita. **Personal income (1980):** $8,126.

Sectors of the economy (% of labor force employed in 1970): Wholesale and retail trade (23%), Government (17%), Manufacturing (15%), Educational Services (9%), Services (8%), Construction (7%). **Leading products:** food; lumber & chemicals; electronics; printing & publishing; stone, clay & pumice. **Minerals:** silver, phosphate rock, lead, zinc. **Agricultural products:** potatoes, cattle, sheep, dairy items, wheat, hay, sugar beets. **Avg. farm (1980):** 660 acres. **Avg. value of farm per acre:** $553.

Highway expenditures per capita (1979): $148.97. **Persons per motor vehicle:** 1.16. **Minimum age for driver's license:** 16. **Gasoline tax:** 11.5¢ per gallon. **Diesel tax:** 11.5¢ per gallon. **Motor vehicle deaths (1978):** 37.2 per 100,000 people.

Birthrate (1978): 22.0 per 1,000 people. **Infant mortality rate per 1,000 births (1978):** 7.3. **Physicians per 100,000 pop. (1978):** 111. **Dentists per 100,000 pop. (1978):** 55. **Acceptable hospital beds (1978):** 3.9 per 1,000 people. **State expenditures per capita for health and hospitals (1979):** $46.03.

Education expenditures (1976-77): $437.65 per capita annually. **No. of pupils in public schools (1979):** 199,000. **No. of institutions of higher learning (1978-79):** 9. **Public school expenditure per pupil in attendance (1977-78):** $1,584. **Avg. salary of public school teachers (1978-79):** $13,080. **No. full-time teachers (1979):** 10,100. **Educational attainment of adult population (1976):** 12.6 median yrs. of school completed: 1.5% with less than 5 years of education; 13.5% with 4 yrs. of college.

Telephones (1978): 55 per 100 people. **State Chamber of Commerce:** Idaho Association of Commerce & Industry, 805 Idaho St., Rm. 414, P.O. Box 389, Boise, Idaho 83701.

ILLINOIS

Illinois, the nation's fifth most populous state, consists almost entirely of gently rolling plains that slope gradually from north to south, although there is a range of relatively small hills, known as the Shawnee Hills (or the "Illinois Ozarks"), in the southern part of the state. In the north is Chicago, with 28.8 miles of shoreline along Lake Michigan; it is the state's largest city by far, and the country's second largest after New York. More than 60 percent of the state's population lives in or around Chicago.

Fertile soil, excellent drainage, and a long growing season have made Illinois one of the nation's major agricultural states, despite a climate that also includes spring and summer tornadoes and wide temperature extremes. The state is usually first or second (to Iowa) in corn production, first in soybeans, and a leading producer of hogs.

Manufacturing and mining are other important revenue sources for the state, which ranks high in oil and coal production and has the nation's largest soft coal reserves. Since 1842, Illinois has been the country's leading producer of fluorspar, or fluorite, which is used in making steel.

Transportation has been a key factor in the state's growth, thanks to its strategic position between the two seaboards and its proximity to important waterways, including Lake Michigan (and the Saint Lawrence Seaway) and the Mississippi River. Canals and an extensive highway system have also helped. Chicago has been the nation's railroad hub for many years, and today is a leading air travel center.

Prehistoric Indians called Mound Builders lived in the Illinois region and left a legacy of more than 10,000 burial and temple mounds. Later inhabitants included a union of Indian tribes known as the "Illinois Confederacy." The Frenchmen Marquette and Jolliet were the first Europeans of record (1673) to visit the region and, two years later, Marquette founded a mission at the Indian town of Kaskaskia, near the present site of Utica. The first permanent European settlement, founded (1699) by French priests of the Seminary of Foreign Missions, was at Cahokia. The territory was ceded by France to Britain in 1763. In 1779, during the Revolutionary War, the Commonwealth of Virginia set up the "County of Illinois." The area passed to the Northwest Territory in 1787. The first county, St. Clair, was established in 1790. Illinois became a territory in 1809 and entered the Union as a state in 1818.

Early landmarks in the state's history included the growing migration of eastern settlers following the opening (1825) of the Erie Canal; the Black Hawk War (1832), which virtually ended Indian troubles in the area; and the "Lincoln" years (1831-60), during which Abraham Lincoln rose from New Salem laborer to Springfield lawyer and president-elect. Lincoln's seven 1858 debates on the slavery issue with prominent Democrat Stephen A. Douglas, which were held in seven different Illinois towns, did not win him the Senate seat both men were seeking, but instead won him the national attention that led to his becoming the nation's Civil War President.

Illinois made great economic advances after the Civil War, despite such setbacks as the Chicago fire (October 1871) and a number of serious labor disputes, particularly the Haymarket Square Riot (1886) and the Pullman strike (1894).

Industry boomed during World War II, which also served to put the state into the vanguard of the Atomic Age: in 1942, at the University of Chicago, Enrico Fermi and other scientists set off the world's first controlled atomic reaction.

The state's current problems are many but not unique. There have been racial tensions in the major cities, and critical unemployment in some southern cities. In recent years, Chicago has been plagued by civil unrest and corruption, and there have been violence, security problems and a number of escapes from Illinois prisons.

The state's tourist attractions include Old Town, the Art Institute, the Sears Tower, the world's tallest building, and the Museum of Science and Industry in Chicago; the reconstructed state park in New Salem, where Lincoln lived (1831-37); the Lincoln home and tomb in Springfield; the Dickson Indian Mounds near Havana; historic Galena, site of the Ulysses S. Grant home; the former Mormon settlement of Nauvoo; and Shawnee National Forest. Chain O'Lakes, a group of lakes in the northeastern part of the state, is a popular summer resort area.

Full name: State of Illinois. **Origin of name:** From Indian name meaning "The Men." **Inhabitant:** Illinoisan. **Capital:** Springfield. **State motto:** State Sovereignty—National Union. **Flag:** Adaptation of state seal centered on white field. **Seal:** An American eagle holds shield with stars & stripes, representing 13 original states; olive branch stands for peace; prairies & rising sun represent plains of Illinois. **Flower:** Native violet. **Bird:** Cardinal. **Tree:** Oak. **Song:** "Illinois." **Nickname:** Prairie State.

Governor: James R. Thompson. **Annual salary:** $58,000. **Term:** 4 years. **Current term expires:** Jan. 1983. **Voting requirements:** 18 yrs. old & U.S. citizen; resident of state, county, and district 30 days. **U.S. Congressmen:** 24 (1980 reapportionment: 22). **Entered Union:** 1818 (21st state).

Location & boundaries: Midwestern state: bounded on the north by Wisconsin; on the east by Lake Michigan, Indiana & the Wabash

ILLINOIS

MILES
0 10   20   30   40   50   60
KILOMETERS
0 10 20 30 40 50 60

State Capital ✪
County Seats ○

River; on the southeast by Kentucky; on the southwest by Missouri; & on the west by the Mississippi River, Missouri & Iowa. **Total area:** 56,400 sq. mi. (ranks 24th). **Extreme length:** 381 mi. **Extreme breadth:** 211 mi. **Shoreline:** 63 mi. **Chief rivers:** Mississippi, Illinois, Kaskaskia. **Major lakes:** Michigan, Chain O'Lakes. **No. of counties:** 102.

Population (1980 census): 11,418,461 (ranks 5th). **Pop. increase (1970-80):** 2.8%. **Largest cities:** Chicago, Rockford, Peoria. **Pop. density:** 202.5 per sq. mi. (ranks 10th). **Pop. distribution:** White—9,225,575; Black—1,675,229; **Am. Indian, Eskimo and Aleut**—16,271; **Asian and Pacific Islander**—159,551; **Other**—341,835; Spanish origin—635,525. **Marriage rate (1978):** 9.4 per 1,000 people. **Divorce rate:** 4.5 per 1,000 people.

State finances (1979). Revenue: $11,202,000,000. **Expenditures:** $10,418,000,000. **State taxes:** $563.07 per capita. **State personal income tax:** Yes. **Public debt (1979):** $509.21 per capita. **Federal aid (1980):** $392.00 per capita. **Personal income (1980):** $10,658.

Sectors of the economy (% of labor force employed in 1970): Manufacturing (30%), Wholesale and retail trade (20%), Government (13%), Services (7%), Educational Services (7%), Construction (5%). **Leading products:** machinery, food, electrical machinery, primary & fabricated metals, chemicals, printing & publishing. **Minerals:** coal; petroleum; stone, sand & gravel. **Agricultural products:** hogs, cattle, dairy items, corn, soybeans, wheat. **Acreage per farm (1980):** 272 acres. **Avg. value of farm per acre:** $1,929.

Highway expenditures per capita (1979): $93.00. **Persons per motor vehicle:** 1.30. **Minimum age for driver's license:** 16. **Gasoline tax:** 7.5¢ per gallon. **Diesel tax:** 7.5¢ per gallon. **Motor vehicle deaths (1978):** 19.0 per 100,000 people.

Birthrate (1978): 15.5 per 1,000 people. **Infant mortality rate per 1,000 births (1978):** 15.7. **Physicians per 100,000 pop. (1978):** 181. **Dentists per 100,000 pop. (1978):** 53. **Acceptable hospital beds (1978):** 6.6 per 1,000 people. **State expenditures per capita for health and hospitals (1979):** $51.99.

Education expenditures (1976-77): $476.40 per capita annually. **No. of pupils in public schools (1978):** 2,050,000. **No. of institutions of higher learning (1978-79):** 154. **Public school expenditure per pupil in attendance (1977-78):** $2,118. **Avg. salary of public school teachers (1978-79):** $16,976. **No. full-time teachers (1979):** 128,100. **Educational attainment of adult population (1976):** 12.5 median yrs. of school completed: 2.6% with less than 5 years of education; 13.7% with 4 yrs. of college.

Telephones (1978): 65 per 100 people. **State Chamber of Commerce:** Illinois State Chamber of Commerce, 20 North Wacker Drive, Chicago, Illinois 60606.

INDIANA

Although it is the smallest state in the continental United States west of the Alleghenies, Indiana ranks among the national leaders in population, agriculture, and manufacturing. Huge steel mills and oil refineries make the state's 45-mile Lake Michigan waterfront one of the world's great industrial centers, while the fertile plains of the central region produce an abundance of food (especially grain crops) for market and livestock. Mining, especially of coal and oil, is also significant; and the state's vast southern quarries produce two-thirds of the nation's building limestone. The automotive industry maintains a large number of plants in the state.

There are three main land regions: the Great Lakes Plain in the north, the central Till Plains (the largest single area), and, in the south, the Interior Low Plateau, characterized by hills, ridges, knolls, caves, and waterfalls. (The two plains regions are subdivisions of the Central Lowlands.) The generally mild, humid climate is marked by occasional temperature extremes.

The first inhabitants of the Indiana region were the prehistoric Mound Builders, followed by a number of Indian tribes, chiefly the Miamis. Many of the Indians came into the area from the east after losing their land to the white settlers. The first European of record to visit the region was Robert Cavelier, Sieur de La Salle, who made two explorations (1679, 1681) and paved the way for French fur-trading posts (in the 1720s) and the first European permanent settlement at Vincennes (fortified 1732). The English sharply challenged French control, however, and by the 1763 Treaty of Paris they gained dominance in the area; in 1774 the British government attached the territory to the province of Quebec.

During the American Revolution, George Rogers Clark and a small army financed by Virginia Governor Patrick Henry captured (1778) Vincennes from the British, lost it, and then in the following year recaptured it. Virginia relinquished (1784) its claim to the Northwest Territory, of which Indiana was the south central part; three years later, the Northwest Ordinance provided for the territory's government, the permanent exclusion of slavery, and basic individual rights. Indiana Territory was created as an entity separate from Ohio in 1800 and initially included the present states of Indiana, Illinois, and Wisconsin, as well as parts of Michigan and Minnesota. After Michigan and Illinois became separate territories (1805, 1809), Indiana had almost the same boundaries as it has today. (The present boundaries were finally established when statehood was attained, in 1816.)

Indian troubles in the area were serious and persistent during the whole early period of white settlement. Anthony Wayne's victory at Fallen Timbers in Ohio (1794) brought peace but it was short-lived. Governor William Henry Harrison, who played a primary role in Indiana's early development, purchased (1809) for the Federal Government nearly 3 million acres of Indian lands in southern Indiana; this outraged the Shawnee chief Tecumseh, who led several tribes on the warpath. Troops led by Harrison won (1811) the Battle of Tippecanoe (near present-day Lafayette) and, during the War of 1812, defeated combined Indian and British forces in the Battle of the Thames, at Moraviantown, Ontario. Thus was British influence in the region ended, and the Indian threat virtually broken.

Indiana's famous "Hoosier" personality was forged in the first half of the 19th century, and its hallmarks were rustic simplicity, self-sufficient isolation, and an almost reflexive conservatism. Attempts were made, most notably at New Harmony (1814), to reorganize society fundamentally along idealistic lines; although the experiments failed, they were the basis for the eventual development in the state of enlightened social and legal institutions and practices. The Hoosier spirit has been immortalized by such authors as Edward Eggleston, James Whitcomb Riley, Booth Tarkington, and George Ade, as well as songwriter Paul Dresser ("On the Banks of the Wabash") and artist John T. McCutcheon, whose cartoon "Injun Summer" has become a classic of its kind. And although his themes were more universal, novelist Theodore Dreiser (*Sister Carrie, An American Tragedy*) was also a Hoosier, and the brother of Paul Dresser.

Internal strife, led by the proslavery Knights of the Golden Circle, marked the Civil War period in Indiana, which, however, largely supported the Union cause. Except for occasional raids, the state saw little action.

Indiana's first public port opened in 1970 on Lake Michigan near Portage after a prolonged battle between proponents of industrial expansion and environmentalists over destruction of the unique dunelands between Gary and Michigan City. A compromise produced the Dunes National Lakeshore.

INDIANA

MILES

State Capital
County Seats

While the port permits worldwide waterborne trade via the St. Lawrence Seaway, much greater tonnage moves on the Ohio River, where there is a port at Mount Vernon; another port is planned near Jeffersonville.

Railroads and trucks remain the most important transport in Indiana, where Indianapolis is favored by being the crossroads of five interstate highways. Virtually all livestock now moves by truck, and there have been forecasts that Indianapolis will become the largest collecting point in the nation for meat animals.

Hoosiers also brag of the Army Finance Center at Ft. Benjamin Harrison, largest U.S. military building aside from the Pentagon.

Indiana's major tourist attractions include the Dunes National Lakeshore near Gary; the Motor Speedway and Hall of Fame at Indianapolis; the Lincoln Boyhood National Memorial, the Lincoln State Park near Lincoln City; the well-preserved Indian earthworks at Mounds State Park near Anderson; the Rappite and Owenite communal settlements at New Harmony; and the George Rogers Clark National Historical Park at Vincennes. Claremont is the site of Raceway Park, home of drag racing.

In 1980, the United States Supreme Court ruled that the boundary between Indiana and Kentucky was the high-water mark of the Ohio River as it was in 1792—not, as Kentucky claimed, the contemporary high-water mark. The ruling made it impossible for Kentucky to sue to stop construction of a nuclear power plant at Marble Hill, Indiana, but Kentucky gained jurisdiction over some land on the Indiana side of the river.

Full name: State of Indiana. **Origin of name:** Denoted that state was domain of Indians. **Inhabitant:** Hoosier. **Capital:** Indianapolis. **State motto:** The Crossroads of America. **Flag:** Gold torch & 19 gold stars on blue field. **Seal:** Pioneer scene represents westward expansion. **Flower:** Peony. **Bird:** Cardinal. **Tree:** Tulip poplar. **Song:** "On the Banks of the Wabash Far Away." **Nickname:** Hoosier State.

Governor: Robert D. Orr. **Annual salary:** $48,000. **Term:** 4 years. **Current term expires:** 1985. **Voting requirements:** 18 yrs. old & U.S. citizen; resident of state 30 days; township 60 days; precinct 30 days. **U.S. Congressmen:** 11 (1980 reapportionment; 10). **Entered Union:** 1816 (19th state).

Location & boundaries: Midwestern state: bounded on the north by Lake Michigan & Michigan; on the east by Ohio; on the southeast & south by the Ohio River & Kentucky; & on the west by the Wabash River & Illinois. **Total area:** 36,291 sq. mi. (ranks 38th). **Extreme length:** 280 mi. **Extreme breadth:** 160 mi. **Shoreline:** 45 mi. **Chief rivers:** Wabash, Ohio, White. **Major lakes (other than border-forming):** Monroe Reservoir, Mississinewa Reservoir, Wawasee. **No. of counties:** 92.

Population (1980 census): 5,490,179 (ranks 12th). **Pop. increase (1970-80):** 5.7%. **Largest cities:** Indianapolis, Fort Wayne, Gary. **Pop. density:** 151.3 per sq. mi. (ranks 13th). **Pop. distribution:** White—5,004,567; Black—414,732; Am. Indian, Eskimo and Aleut—7,835; Asian and Pacific Islander—20,488; Other—42,557; Spanish origin—87,000. **Marriage rate (1978):** 10.8 per 1,000 people. **Divorce rate:** 7.5 per 1,000 people.

State finances (1979). Revenue: $4,612,000,000. **Expenditures:** $4,089,000,000. **State taxes:** $494.18 per capita. **State personal income tax:** Yes. **Public debt (1979):** $107.49 per capita. **Federal aid (1980):** $292.90 per capita. **Personal income (1980):** $8,978.

Sectors of the economy (% of labor force employed in 1970): Manufacturing (36%), Wholesale and retail trade (19%), Government (13%), Educational Services (8%), Services (6%), Construction (5%). **Leading products:** electrical & other machinery, transportation equipment, food, chemicals, primary & fabricated metals. **Minerals:** coal, cement, stone, petroleum. **Agricultural products:** hogs, cattle, dairy items, corn, soybeans, wheat. **Acreage per farm (1980):** 192 acres. **Avg. value of farm per acre:** $1,723.

Highway expenditures per capita (1979): $99.20. **Persons per motor vehicle:** 1.40. **Minimum age for driver's license:** 16. **Gasoline tax:** 10.5¢ per gallon. **Diesel tax:** 10.5¢ per gallon. **Motor vehicle deaths (1978):** 24.3 per 100,000 people.

Birthrate (1978): 15.5 per 1,000 people. **Infant mortality rate per 1,000 births (1978):** 13.1. **Physicians per 100,000 pop. (1978):** 100. **Dentists per 100,000 pop. (1978):** 42. **Acceptable hospital beds (1978):** 6.1 per 1,000 people. **State expenditures per capita for health and hospitals (1979):** $53.38.

Education expenditures (1976-77): $429.01 per capita annually. **No. of pupils in public schools (1979):** 1,087,000. **No. of institutions of higher learning (1978-79):** 66. **Public school expenditure per pupil in attendance (1977-78):** $1,657. **Avg. salary of public school teachers (1978-79):** $14,726. **No. full-time teachers (1979):** 58,200. **Educational attainment of adult population (1976):** 12.4 median yrs. of school completed: 1.9% with less than 5 years of education; 11.0% with 4 yrs. of college.

Telephones (1978): 58 per 100 people. **State Chamber of Commerce:** Indiana State Chamber of Commerce, Inc., 201-212 Board of Trade Building, Indianapolis, Indiana 46204.

IOWA

With about two-thirds of its land mass between 800 and 1,400 feet above sea level, Iowa is a gently rolling plain quilted almost entirely by farms. The border-forming Mississippi and Missouri Rivers provide an abundant water supply and transportation routes.

The soil of Iowa is considered the finest in America and accounts for the fact that Iowa produces a tenth of the nation's food supply. It alternately shares the lead with Illinois in corn production, is second in soybeans and is a major producer of oats. The state's high crop yield supports the country's largest livestock industry; Iowa is the leading hog state and ranks high in cattle. It is also a leader in the production of butter and cheese.

Because of the soil's economic importance, floods and the quest of greater productivity have made Iowans conservation conscious. In fact, in 1960 it was recognized that only a quarter of the state's water supply was being effectively harnessed.

As impressive as Iowa's agriculture is, manufacturing income is greater. Farm machinery, electronic equipment, mobile homes and home appliances are important products of the state's industries. The chief industrial centers are Des Moines; Cedar Rapids, site of its first nuclear power plant (1974); Dubuque and Waterloo. Except for gypsum—Iowa is the nation's third-largest producer—mining is not significant.

The state's climate is of the continental, long-summer type, marked by great extremes; there is generally less precipitation in the western regions than in the eastern.

A civilization of Mound Builders—sedentary farmers who lived in permanent villages—predated the Indians in Iowa; the Effigy Mounds National Monument contains numerous examples of their building in bird, animal, and serpentine forms. The first Europeans to visit the region were Jacques Marquette and Louis Jolliet (1673); almost a century later (1788), the Indians allowed Julien Dubuque, a French-Canadian, to mine lead in the area of the city named for him. The United States obtained control of the state under the Louisiana Purchase (1803). Formation of Iowa Territory dates from 1838.

There was much fighting between white settlers and Indians of the area. A rich strip of land 50 miles wide along the Mississippi was won from the Sauk and Fox in 1832, after Black Hawk and his braves were defeated in battle. Other areas were taken from the Indians in 1836 and 1837. The

IOWA

Sioux ceded their claims in 1851, although an outlaw band of their numbers six years later killed 33 settlers in the Spirit Lake Massacre.

When Iowa became (1846) a state, its capital was at Iowa City; the more centrally located Des Moines became the capital in 1857. It was at this time, too, that the state's present boundaries were drawn up.

Iowa was strongly anti-slavery during the antebellum period and was a center for abolitionist activity. The state was staunchly pro-Union during the Civil War and provided a large number of troops for the Union cause.

From the beginning, the character of Iowa has been a paradoxical amalgam of free-thinking liberalism and close-to-the-vest conservatism. Education has long had a high priority in the state, resulting in the nation's lowest illiteracy rate. Iowa has 3 state-supported universities, over 30 private colleges and approximately 10 private junior colleges. In 1965 a system of 15 area community colleges and vocational-technical schools was established.

Iowa's tourist attractions include the Amana, 20 miles southwest of Cedar Rapids; the Effigy Mounds National Monument, famed for its Indian mounds in the shapes of birds and animals; and the Herbert Hoover National Historic Site east of Iowa City.

Full name: State of Iowa. **Origin of name:** From name of Sioux tribe—the Ioways or Aiouez—meaning "Sleepy Ones." **Inhabitant:** Iowan. **Capital:** Des Moines. **State motto:** Our Liberties We Prize & Our Rights We Will Maintain. **Flag:** Vertical blue, white & red bars; flying eagle carrying state motto. **Seal:** Prairie scene represents Iowa's pioneer days; an eagle flies over scene carrying streamer with state motto. **Flower:** Wild rose. **Bird:** Eastern goldfinch. **Tree:** Oak. **Song:** "The Song of Iowa." **Nickname:** Hawkeye State.

Governor: Robert D. Ray. Annual salary: $60,000. **Term:** 4 years. Current term expires: Jan. 1983. **Voting requirements:** 18 yrs. old & U.S. citizen; resident of state; registration 10 days before election. U.S. Congressmen: 6. Entered Union: 1846 (29th state).

Location & boundaries: Midwestern state: bounded on the north by Minnesota; on the east by the Mississippi River, Wisconsin & Illinois; on the south by the Des Moines River & Missouri; & on the west by the Missouri River, Nebraska, the Big Sioux River & South Dakota. Total area: 56,290 sq. mi. (ranks 25th). Extreme length: 324 mi. Extreme breadth: 210 mi. Chief rivers: Des Moines, Mississippi, Missouri, Big Sioux. Major lakes: Clear, Spirit, Storm Red Rock. No. of counties: 99.

Population (1980 census): 2,913,387 (ranks 27th). Pop. increase (1970-80): 3.1%. Largest cities: Des Moines, Cedar Rapids, Davenport. Pop. density: 51.7 per sq. mi. (ranks 32nd). Pop. distribution: White—2,838,805; Black—41,700; Am. Indian, Eskimo and Aleut—5,453; Asian and Pacific Islander—11,577; Other—15,852; Spanish origin—25,536. Marriage rate (1978): 9.6 per 1,000 people. Divorce rate: 3.8 per 1,000 people.

State finances (1979): Revenue: $3,056,000,000. Expenditures: $3,011,000,000. State taxes: $540.78 per capita. State personal income tax: Yes. Public debt (1979): $128.45 per capita. Federal aid (1980): $341.32 per capita. Personal income (1980): $9,178.

Sectors of the economy (% of labor force employed in 1976): Wholesale and retail trade (22%), Manufacturing (20%), Government (14%), Educational Services (9%), Services (7%), Construction (5%). **Leading products:** food; electrical & other machinery; chemicals; printing & publishing; primary & fabricated metals; stone, clay & glass items. **Minerals:** cement; stone, sand & gravel; gypsum. **Agricultural products:** cattle, hogs, dairy items, corn, soybeans, hay. Avg. farm (1980): 286 acres. Avg. value of farm per acre: $1,706.

Highway expenditures per capita (1979): $164.45. Persons per motor vehicle: 1.22. Minimum age for driver's license: 16. Gasoline tax: 10¢ per gallon. Diesel tax: 11.5¢ per gallon. Motor vehicle deaths (1978): 22.1 per 100,000 people.

Birthrate (1978): 15.3 per 1,000 people. Infant mortality rate per 1,000 births (1978): 12.6. Physicians per 100,000 pop. (1978): 122.

Dentists per 100,000 pop. (1978): 49. **Acceptable hospital beds** (1978): 7.4 per 1,000 people. **State expenditures per capita for health and hospitals** (1978): $68.81.

Education expenditures (1976-77): $520.91 per capita annually. **No. of pupils in public schools** (1979): 555,000. **No. of institutions of higher learning** (1978-79): 62. **Public school expenditure per pupil in attendance** (1977-78): $1,990. **Avg. salary of public school teachers** (1978-79): $14,589. **No. full-time teachers** (1979): 36,300. **Educational attainment of adult population** (1976): 12.5 median yrs. of school completed: .9% with less than 5 years of education; 12.8% with 4 yrs. of college.

Telephones (1978): 57 per 100 people. **State Chamber of Commerce:** Iowa Manufacturers Association, 706 Employers Mutual Building, 717 Mulberry Street, Des Moines, Iowa 50309.

KANSAS

The popular notion that Kansas consists wholly of flat prairie land is false; the land, in fact, rises from an elevation of about 700 feet in the southeast to more than 4,000 feet in the northwest, where the foothills of the Rockies begin. Three main land regions make up the state: the Great Plains, covering the western two-thirds; the Dissected Till Plains, covering a small area in the northeast corner; and the Southeastern Plains, often subdivided by geographers into the Osage Plains in the east and the Flint Hills in the west. Thousands of rolling hills between 100 and 400 feet high dot the state's terrain, which also features many valleys and picturesque chalk and sandstone formations. The relatively small natural water area is augmented by more than a hundred artificial lakes.

The eastern half of Kansas contains the overwhelmingly larger part of the population: the three largest cities—Wichita, Kansas City, and Topeka—are all in this section. Kansas City, on the eastern border, adjoins Kansas City, Missouri, but the two are separate municipalities.

A number of Indian tribes—including the Kansa, Wichita, Pawnee, and Comanche—were living in the Kansas region before the coming (1541) of the first European, Spanish explorer Francisco Vásquez de Coronado; he and his men were seeking the gold of a land called Quivira and, finding none, departed without establishing settlements. La Salle's far-reaching land claims (1682) on behalf of France included the Kansas region but, although French fur traders dealt with area Indians in the years immediately following, the Indians retained actual possession of the land. France yielded its claim to West Louisiana (including Kansas) to Spain in 1763, and Spain retroceded it to France (1800), which three years later sold it in the Louisiana Purchase to the United States.

Lewis and Clark, Zebulon M. Pike, and Major Stephen H. Long made (1803-19) the first serious explorations of the area, but their reports were incomplete and such as to discourage immediate American settlement. Erroneously considered a part of the "Great American Desert," the Kansas region was primarily used (1825-42) as a resettlement area for uprooted Indian tribes.

With the establishment of the Santa Fe Trail (1821), which cut across the region diagonally from northeast to southwest, and the Oregon Trail (c. 1830), which traversed part of the northeastern region, the first permanent non-Indian settlements (Fort Leavenworth-1827, Fort Scott-1842, and Fort Riley-1853) were founded as outposts to protect travelers against Indian raids.

The passage of the Kansas-Nebraska Act (1854), repealing the slavery-prohibiting Missouri Compromise of 1821 in favor of "squatter sovereignty," thrust Kansas into a bloody tug-of-war between proslavery and antislavery forces who rushed into

KANSAS

he territory and fought savagely for political con-
rol. This was the era of "Bleeding Kansas," which
aw the free-state "Jayhawkers" (including famed
bolitionist John Brown) pitted against the advo-
ates of slavery; the Jayhawkers ultimately won
ut and, in 1861 Kansas entered the Union as a free
tate.

Often called the Nation's Breadbasket, Kansas is
he leading wheat producer and flour miller as well
s one of the most important mining states. Today,
Kansas is moving toward economic diversification,
nd manufacturing has now surpassed agriculture
s the primary revenue source. The massive wheat
nd cattle raising operations have spawned an im-
ressive manufacturing segment producing farm
nd heavy equipment. Hesston Corporation is now
. world leader in farm machinery and exemplifies
Kansas' growth in this area.

The production of transportation equipment is
he major industrial activity. Wichita produces
nore than half of the nation's aircraft, while To-
eka is a center for the manufacture and repair of
ailroad cars, and is also a major tire production
enter. Kansas' strategic location in the center of
America makes it attractive to industries with na-
ionwide distribution.

Occasional periods of drought or flood have
rompted a massive program of flood control, water
onservation and utilization. More than 30 federal
eservoirs have been constructed or authorized
long with dozens of watershed districts.

The reservoirs and lesser impoundments assure
ities and industries of a stable water supply and
rovide facilities for camping, fishing, swimming,
oating and water skiing. There are state park
icilities at many of the reservoirs and an out-
tanding system of roadside parks.

Among the top tourist attractions is the Dwight
). Eisenhower Center at Abilene, featuring the
oyhood home, Museum, Presidential Library, and
hapel where the former President and World War
I commander is buried. Reconstruction of Early
ay Front Street at Dodge City and Old Ft. Larned
re other tourist attractions.

As a result of the food shortage of recent years,
housands of acres of Kansas farmland were
ressed back into production. Bumper crops of
vheat, corn and sorghum were harvested in 1976
nd 1977, both here and abroad, with the result
hat U.S. stockpiles were at their highest level in
nany years and prices dropped sharply in the face
f a lessening demand for American grains abroad.
Kansas farmers were among the leaders of the
American Agriculture movement, which withheld
rain and influenced the price support increases of
978. Corn and wheat production in 1979 again hit
ecord highs.

In the fall of 1979, a controversial Federal court
rder requiring the Wichita public schools to reas-
ign thousands of pupils in order to improve racial
alance was implemented with no serious inci-
ents. However, a violent racial confrontation be-
ween blacks and the Wichita police, unrelated to
he school reassignment order, took place on April
22, 1980.

Full name: State of Kansas. **Origin of name:** From name of Sioux
ribe, meaning "People of the South Wind." **Inhabitant:** Kansan.
apital: Topeka. **State motto:** Ad Astra per Aspera (To the Stars
hrough Difficulties). **Flag:** Blue field with wreath & yellow sunflower
ver state seal. **Seal:** Rising sun represents east; buffalo, log cabin,
iverboat, wagon & plowing farmer suggest early history of region.
lower: Sunflower. **Bird:** Western meadowlark. **Tree:** Cottonwood.
ong: "Home on the Range." **Nickname:** Sunflower State.

overnor: John Carlin. **Annual salary:** $45,000. **Term:** 4 years.
urrent term expires: Jan. 1983. **Voting requirements:** 18 yrs. old
. U.S. citizen; resident of state and voting area; registration 20 days

before election. **U.S. Congressmen:** 5. **Entered Union:** 1861 (34th
state).

Location & boundaries: Midwestern state: bounded on the north by
Nebraska; on the east by the Missouri River & Missouri; on the
south by Oklahoma; & on the west by Colorado. **Total area:** 82,264
sq. mi. (ranks 14th). **Extreme length:** 411 mi. **Extreme breadth:** 208
mi. **Chief rivers:** Arkansas, Missouri, Kansas. **Major lakes:** Tuttle
Creek, Cedar Bluff, Cheney, Perry. **No. of counties:** 105.

Population (1980 census): 2,363,208 (ranks 32nd). **Pop. increase
(1970-80):** 5.1%. **Largest cities:** Wichita, Kansas City, Topeka.
Pop. density: 28.7 per sq. mi. (ranks 37th). **Pop. distribution:**
White—2,167,752; Black—126,127; **Am. Indian, Eskimo and Aleut**—15,371; **Asian and Pacific Islander**—15,078; **Other**—38,880
Spanish origin—63,333. **Marriage rate (1978):** 10.2 per 1,000
people. **Divorce rate:** 5.4 per 1,000 people.

State finances (1979). Revenue: $2,178,000,000. **Expenditures:**
$2,012,000,000. **State taxes:** $501.34 per capita. **State personal
income tax:** Yes. **Public debt (1979):** $193.81 per capita. **Federal
aid (1980):** $345.59 per capita. **Personal income (1980):** $9,958.

Sectors of the economy (% of labor force employed in 1975):
Wholesale and retail trade (18.7%), Government (16.9%), Manufacturing (15.8%), Services (13.1%). **Leading products:** aerospace
equipment, food, chemicals, crude oil & natural gas items, machinery, printing & publishing. **Minerals:** petroleum, helium, natural
gas & gas liquids. **Agricultural products:** cattle, hogs, dairy items,
wheat, sorghum grain, hay. **Avg. farm (1980):** 669 acres. **Avg.
value of farm per acre:** $498.

Highway expenditures per capita (1979): $123.30. **Persons per
motor vehicle:** 1.00. **Minimum age for driver's license:** 16. **Gasoline tax:** 8¢ per gallon. **Diesel tax:** 8¢ per gallon. **Motor vehicle
deaths (1978):** 24.4 per 100,000 people.

Birthrate (1978): 15.7 per 1,000 people. **Infant mortality rate per
1,000 births (1978):** 12.5. **Physicians per 100,000 pop. (1978):** 151.
Dentists per 100,000 pop. (1978): 45. **Acceptable hospital beds
(1978):** 7.6 per 1,000 people. **State expenditures per capita for
health and hospitals (1979):** $77.74.

Education expenditures (1976-77): $473.76 per capita annually.
No. of pupils in public schools (1979): 423,000. **No. of institutions
of higher learning (1978-79):** 52. **Public school expenditure per
pupil in attendance (1977-78):** $1,777. **Avg. salary of public
school teachers (1978-79):** $13,197. **No. full-time teachers
(1979):** 28,100. **Educational attainment of adult population (1976):**
12.6 median yrs. of school completed: 1.0% with less than 5 years
of education; 14.6% with 4 yrs. of college.

Telephones (1978): 60 per 100 people. **State Chamber of Commerce:** Kansas Assn. of Commerce and Industry, 500 First National
Tower, One Townsite Plaza, Topeka, Kansas 66603.

KENTUCKY

Kentucky, renowned for the quality of its tobacco,
whiskey, and racehorses, was the first state west of
the Alleghenies to be settled by pioneers. A state of
sometimes bizarre contrasts, Kentucky has the nation's gold reserves (at Fort Knox) and many fine
farms and estates, yet much of its land has been
devastated by reckless lumbering and strip-min-
ing practices, and in some eastern areas chronic
unemployment prevails. Two Kentuckians, Abraham Lincoln and Jefferson Davis, were the opposing presidents in the Civil War.

Roughly triangular in shape, the state consists
of the Appalachian Plateau (known locally as the
Cumberland Plateau and constituting the largest
single area—more than a fourth of the total), the
northcentral Bluegrass Region, the Pennyroyal
Region (or Southwestern Mississippian Embay-
ment), the Western Coal Field, and the East Gulf
Coastal Plain (or Jackson Purchase Region), which
makes up the state's western tip. A double hairpin
turn in the Mississippi River separates a small bit
of extreme southwestern Kentucky from the rest of
the state. Most of the state's surface is a much-
furrowed plain sloping gently to the west. The
state's northern boundary, the Ohio River, has been

shifting gradually north- and westward for centuries. Kentucky thus had stood to gain territory with the border's expansion, but the Supreme Court ruled in January 1980 that the boundary remains fixed at its original position regardless of the movement of the Ohio River.

About half the land is farmed, and agriculture (especially tobacco) is still important, although it has been surpassed in recent years by manufacturing. Commercial fishing is limited, while mining continues as a major activity; Kentucky ranks as the country's leading coal producer. Spurred by the building of new roads, tourism is also a significant revenue source; attractions include Mammoth Cave National Park, Abraham Lincoln Birthplace National Historical Site, Daniel Boone National Forest, Natural Bridge, Cumberland Gap National Historic Park, the Bluegrass Region around Lexington, historic Harrodsburg, and the annual Kentucky Derby at Louisville.

Indians are thought to have lived in the forests of what is now western Kentucky as long as 15,000 years ago. Although other Europeans visited the region during the latter part of the 17th century, the first serious exploration of record was conducted (1750) by Dr. Thomas Walker, who passed through, and named, Cumberland Gap. About this time, a number of Indian tribes—including the Cherokee, Iroquois, and Shawnee—who were using the region as hunting grounds strongly resisted the advance of the white man. Daniel Boone explored eastern Kentucky (1767) and later spent two years in the Bluegrass Region. In 1773 he led a group of settlers into Kentucky, but Indians forced him out. James Harrod established (1774) the first permanent non-Indian settlement at Harrodsburg; in the following year Daniel Boone, acting as an agent for the Transylvania Company, returned to hack out the Wilderness Road and establish Boonesboro.

Indian raids were a continuing menace until General Anthony Wayne's victory in the Battle of Fallen Timbers in Ohio (1794) virtually ended them. Kentucky was originally a county of Virginia known as Fincastle before gaining statehood in 1792. The 1795 Pinckney's Treaty with Spain and the 1803 Louisiana Purchase made travel on the Mississippi more secure and aided development.

Kentucky's growth has been marked by conflict and violence. Kentuckians fought hard against the Alien and Sedition Acts (1798), vigorously supported the War of 1812 and the Mexican War (1846-48), and, although neutral in the Civil War, supplied each side with thousands of troops. The slavery issue, a particularly contentious one for a slaveholding state containing many abolitionists, was officially resolved in 1865 with the adoption of the 13th Constitutional Amendment. Lesser conflicts included the Hatfield-McCoy wrangle (1882-96), troubles surrounding the assassination of Democratic gubernatorial candidate William Goebel (1900), the so-called Black Patch War (1904-09) between tobacco farmers and buyers, and frequent strife between mine owners and the United Mine Workers.

In response to the energy crisis forced in the early 1970s by the oil shortage and rising prices, coal mines were reopened, resulting in a drop in the state's unemployment. After two methane gas explosions which claimed 26 lives in 1976, a mine safety bill was passed.

Full name: Commonwealth of Kentucky. **Origin of name:** From Wyandot name, Ken-tah-teh, meaning "Land of Tomorrow." **Inhabitant:** Kentuckian. **Capital:** Frankfort. **State motto:** United We Stand, Divided We Fall. **Flag:** State seal on a blue field. **Seal:** Two

men greeting each other; state motto. **Flower:** Goldenrod. **Bird** Cardinal. **Tree:** Kentucky coffee tree. **Song:** "My Old Kentucky Home." **Nickname:** Bluegrass State.

Governor: John Y. Brown, Jr. **Annual salary:** $45,000. **Term:** 4 years. **Current term expires:** Dec. 1983. **Voting requirements:** 18 yrs. old & U.S. citizen; resident of state and precinct, 30 days. **U.S. Congressmen:** 7. **Entered Union:** 1792 (15th state).

Location & boundaries: Southeastern state; bounded on the north by the Ohio River, Illinois, Indiana & Ohio; on the east by the Big Sandy & Tug Fork Rivers, West Virginia & Virginia; on the south by Tennessee; & on the west by the Mississippi River & Missouri. **Total area:** 40,395 sq. mi. (ranks 37th). **Extreme length:** 350 mi. **Extreme breadth:** 175 mi. **Chief rivers:** Ohio, Kentucky, Tennessee. **Major lakes:** Kentucky, Barkley & Cumberland Reservoirs. **No. of counties:** 120.

Population (1980 census): 3,661,433 (ranks 23rd). **Pop. increase (1970-80):** 13.7%. **Largest cities:** Louisville, Lexington Owensboro, Covington. **Pop. density:** 90.6 per sq. mi. (ranks 22nd). **Pop. distribution:** White—3,379,648; Black—259,490 Am. Indian, Eskimo and Aleut—3,610; Asian and Pacific Islander—9,971; Other—8,714; Spanish Origin—27,403. **Marriage rate (1978):** 29.5 per 1,000 people. **Divorce rate:** 3.9 per 1,000 people.

State finances (1979). Revenue: $3,842,000,000. **Expenditures:** $3,880,000,000. **State taxes:** $588.53 per capita. **State personal income tax:** Yes. **Public debt (1979):** $796.85 per capita. **Federal aid (1980):** $399.38 per capita. **Personal income (1980):** $7,718.

Sectors of the economy (% of labor force employed in 1970): Manufacturing (26%), Wholesale and retail trade (19%), Government (16%), Educational Services (8%), Services (7%), Construction (7%). **Leading products:** food, chemicals, tobacco items machinery, primary & fabricated metals, transportation equipment **Minerals:** coal, petroleum, stone, natural gas. **Agricultural products:** cattle, hogs, tobacco, dairy items, corn, hay. **Avg. farm (1980):** 152 acres. **Avg. value of farm per acre:** $879.

Highway expenditures per capita (1979): $211.37. **Persons per motor vehicle:** 1.37. **Minimum age for driver's license:** 16. **Gasoline tax:** 10.4¢ per gallon. **Diesel tax:** 10.4¢ per gallon. **Motor vehicle deaths (1978):** 25.1 per 100,000 people.

Birthrate (1978): 16.4 per 1,000 people. **Infant mortality rate per 1,000 births (1978):** 12.7. **Physicians per 100,000 pop. (1978):** 133. **Dentists per 100,000 pop. (1978):** 42. **Acceptable hospital beds (1978):** 5.1 per 1,000 people. **State expenditures per capita for health and hospitals (1979):** $52.53.

Education expenditures (1976-77): $393.23 per capita annually. **No. of pupils in public schools (1979):** 676,000. **No. of institutions of higher learning (1978-79):** 42. **Public school expenditure per pupil in attendance (1977-78):** $1,394. **Avg. salary of public school teachers (1978-79):** $13,625. **No. full-time teachers (1979):** 36,000. **Educational attainment of adult population (1976):** 12.1 median yrs. of school completed: 5.7% with less than 5 years of education; 10.0% with 4 yrs. of college.

Telephones (1978): 48 per 100 people. **State Chamber of Commerce:** Kentucky Chamber of Commerce, Versailles Rd., P.O. Box 817, Frankfort, Kentucky 40602.

LOUISIANA

With its French and Spanish background, Louisiana is rich in history and among the nation's leaders in oil and natural gas, salt, sulphur, commercial fishing, fur trapping and rice, sugar cane and sweet potato production. The Michoud plant at New Orleans was a vital rocket-assembly installation during NASA's earth orbit and Apollo moon shots, contributing to the emergence of manufacturing as a major industry in the state.

New Orleans lies 100 miles up the Mississippi River from the Gulf of Mexico. It has been the nation's second-busiest seaport since 1840 but is perhaps better known as the site of the annual Mardi Gras. The world's longest bridge, the 24-mile Lake Pontchartrain Causeway, connects New Orleans to Mandeville. A sizeable timber industry is fed by extensive forest lands.

KENTUCKY

In the north are low rolling hills, and in the east many bluffs dot the river plain. Coastal marshes and sluggish streams (bayous) are features of the southern terrain. The Mississippi Delta, a fertile sedimentary deposit, comprises a third of the state's total area.

Indians are thought to have lived in the northern part of the Louisiana region over 3,000 years ago. Spanish explorer Cabeza de Vaca may have visited the area about 1530, and Hernando De Soto did so (1540-42). Approximately 12,000 Indians were then living in the region.

In 1682 Robert Cavelier, Sieur de La Salle, reached the mouth of the Mississippi and claimed all the land drained by it and its tributaries for King Louis XIV of France.

Permanent French settlement of the Louisiana region began (1699) with its founding as a royal colony and the establishment of a community near present-day Biloxi, Mississippi. In 1717 the area was granted to a company headed by John Law, who initially centered his development in the region that is now Arkansas, but then moved south. New Orleans was founded in 1718 and four years later became the capital. Law's venture spurred immigration, but eventually failed.

French control of the region gave way (1762) to Spanish; France regained possession in 1800. Three years later, Napoleon Bonaparte, seeking funds to support his European military activities, sold the land to the United States, as part of the vast Louisiana Purchase. In 1804 the territory was divided at the state's present northern border: the northern portion, now made up of other states, was at first called the District of Louisiana, then the Territory of Louisiana, and later Missouri Territory; the southern portion, originally the Territory of Orleans, became the present state of Louisiana. The period between 1760 and 1790 was marked by an influx of French-speaking Acadians, or Cajuns, from what is now Nova Scotia, who settled mainly in the southern region.

In the early 19th century, the natives of Louisiana were a heterogeneous mixture of French, Spanish, Isleños from the Canary Islands, and Germans. Although the Louisianians generally did not welcome the coming of the Americans, they did unite behind Andrew Jackson to defeat (1815) the British in the Battle of New Orleans at the end of the War of 1812. The state, which entered the Union in 1812, was enlarged by the settlement of the West Florida Controversy, which had stemmed from conflicting Spanish and American land claims involving portions of Florida, Alabama, Mississippi, and Louisiana; the Transcontinental Treaty of 1819 gave control of the disputed regions to the United States.

Early statehood was marked by the advent of the Mississippi steamboat trade and its attendant prosperity, and by the rise of plantation agriculture. The Civil War and the Reconstruction period brought considerable hardship and chaos. White rule was ultimately reestablished and farm tenancy and sharecropping replaced the plantation system. The discovery of oil (1901) and natural gas (1916) greatly aided the state's economic recovery.

The 1927 Mississippi flood, which forced 300,000 people from their homes, remains the worst on record. But the 1973 high water flooded nearly four million acres of Louisiana for months before the crisis ebbed away into the Gulf. Enormous damage was averted by the levee system.

Huey P. Long, elected governor in 1927 and assassinated in 1935, remains the state's most renowned political figure. His term as governor launched a political dynasty that continued even after he was killed. As governor and later (1930) as

U.S. senator, Long was an advocate of a "Share the Wealth" program that challenged powerful Louisiana oil interests. He was responsible for much material progress but also was blamed for considerable political corruption. His brother Earl served three terms as governor, and his son Russell was a United States senator.

Louisiana today is becoming increasingly industrialized, often to the detriment of its tradition-ripe picturesqueness. One reason for the spurt is that the state grants 10-year tax exemptions to new industries. Tourism also has grown, and today accounts for over $1 billion annually. Those seeking to preserve the traces of the past were heartened by the Federal government's refusal (July 1969) to grant funds for part of a highway system that would have "seriously impaired the historic quality of New Orleans' famed French Quarter." An alternate route was not acceptable because of its disruptive effects on the city, excessive costs, and construction hazards to the city's river levee. The ruling was believed to be the first denial of Federal funds for a highway on the basis of preserving a historic area.

The Louisiana Offshore Oil Port (Loop) has been constructed 18 miles off Grand Isle. Tankers too large to dock at any existing U.S. ports will unload their cargo at the superport, and the oil will be sent to the mainland by pipeline. The port was completed in mid-1981 and is now in the process of being certified for use (Sept. 1981).

On March 10, 1980, David C. Treen was inaugurated as Louisiana's first Republican governor in 103 years. He had been elected by a slim margin in a run-off on Dec. 8, 1979, having promised to end the state's notorious political corruption.

Full name: State of Louisiana. **Origin of name:** In honor of King Louis XIV of France. **Inhabitant:** Louisianian. **Capital:** Baton Rouge. **State motto:** Union, Justice & Confidence. **Flag:** State seal & motto on a blue field. **Seal:** Mother pelican feeding brood. **Flower:** Magnolia. **Bird:** Brown pelican. **Tree:** Bald cypress. **Song:** "Give Me Louisiana." **Nickname:** Pelican State.

Governor: David C. Treen. **Annual salary:** $68,000. **Term:** 4 years. **Current term expires:** Mar. 1984. **Voting requirements:** 18 yrs. old & U.S. citizen; resident of state 1 yr.; county, 6 mos.; district, 3 mos.; valid I.D. **U.S. Congressmen:** 8. **Entered Union:** 1812 (18th state).

Location & boundaries: Gulf state: bounded on the north by Arkansas; on the east by the Mississippi & Pearl Rivers & Mississippi; on the southeast & south by the Gulf of Mexico; on the west by Texas & the Sabine River. **Total area:** 48,523 sq. mi. (ranks 31st). **Extreme length:** 237 mi. **Extreme breadth:** 236.5 mi. **Coastline:** 397 mi. **Chief rivers:** Mississippi, Atchafalaya, Red, Ouachita. **Major lakes:** Pontchartrain, Grand, White. **No. of parishes (counties):** 64.

Population (1980 census): 4,203,972 (ranks 19th). **Pop. increase (1970-80):** 15.3%. **Largest cities:** New Orleans, Baton Rouge, Shreveport. **Pop. density:** 86.6 per sq. mi. (ranks 24th). **Pop. distribution:** White—2,911,243; Black—1,237,263; Am. Indian, Eskimo and Aleut—12,064; Asian and Pacific Islander—23,771; Other—19,631; Spanish origin—99,105. **Marriage rate (1978):** 10.0 per 1,000 people. **Divorce rate:** 3.3 per 1,000 people.

State finances (1979). Revenue: $4,589,000,000. **Expenditures:** $4,123,000,000. **State taxes:** $557.55 per capita. **State personal income tax:** Yes. **Public debt (1979):** $656.28 per capita. **Federal aid (1980):** $371.82 per capita. **Personal income (1980):** $8,282.

Sectors of the economy (% of labor force employed in 1970): Wholesale & retail trade (21%), Government (17%), Manufacturing (16%), Services (10%), Educational Services (9%), Construction (8%). **Leading products:** chemicals, food, petroleum and paper items, transportation equipment, lumber, primary metals. **Minerals:** petroleum, natural gas, sulfur. **Agricultural products:** cattle, dairy items, rice, sugar cane, soybeans. **Fishing:** shrimp, menhaden, oysters. **Avg. farm (1980):** 296 acres. **Avg. value of farm per acre:** $984.

Highway expenditures per capita (1979): $114.76. **Persons per motor vehicle:** 1.50. **Minimum age for driver's license:** 15. **Gas-**

LOUISIANA

oline tax: 8¢ per gallon. **Diesel tax:** 8¢ per gallon. **Motor vehicle deaths (1978):** 27.2 per 100,000 people.

Birthrate (1978): 18.1 per 1,000 people. **Infant mortality rate per 1,000 births (1978):** 17.3. **Physicians per 100,000 pop. (1978):** 150. **Dentists per 100,000 pop. (1978):** 39. **Acceptable hospital beds (1978):** 5.97 per 1,000 people. **State expenditures per capita for health and hospitals (1979):** $89.45.

Education expenditures (1976-77): $400.48 per capita annually. **No. of pupils in public schools (1979):** 797,000. **No. of institutions of higher learning (1978-79):** 32. **Public school expenditure per pupil in attendance (1977-78):** $1,648. **Avg. salary of public school teachers (1978-79):** $13,254. **No. full-time teachers (1979):** 48,900. **Educational attainment of adult population (1976):** 12.3 median yrs. of school completed: 8.7% with less than 5 years of education; 11.5% with 4 yrs. of college.

Telephones (1978): 52 per 100 people. **State Chamber of Commerce:** Louisiana Association of Business & Industry, P.O. Box 3988, Baton Rouge, Louisiana 70821.

MAINE

Four-fifths of Maine is covered by forests that feed an enormous wood-processing industry. There are three general land areas: the White Mountains region in the northwest, the New England Uplands extending through the heart of the state, and the coastal lowlands of the southeast. Many bays and harbors dot the craggy, convoluted coastline. Southwest of Portland, the rockbound coast is supplanted by sandy beaches. Sailors coasting downwind from Boston gave the shore its nickname, "Down East." Fishermen are attracted by the state's 2,500 lakes and ponds and 5,000 rivers and streams. Waterpower availability is correspondingly excellent. Ten mountains rise more than 4,000 feet; undersea peaks form 400 offshore islands.

The climate is marked by generally severe winters, and summer evenings occasionally so cool that people heat their homes. Yet this very ruggedness of terrain and climate has proved an asset in drawing tourists. Skiing, camping, and other outdoor activities are especially popular, and many city-worn visitors seek out the unspoiled Allagash wilderness, the 92-mile-long Allagash Wilderness Waterway, and Mount Katahdin (5,268 ft.), which is the first place in the nation to catch the rays of the rising sun. Other attractions include Bar Harbor on Mount Desert Island, most of which is part of Acadia National Park and the many historic and picturesque towns, such as Bath, Kennebunk and Searsport, which dot the coast.

Maine may have been sighted by Norse explorer Leif Ericsson as early as A.D. 1000, and English-employed Italian sea captain John Cabot is considered to have been the first European to reach the area, in 1498. Thousands of Abnaki and Etchemin Indians were living there at the time. They peaceably coexisted with the earliest settlers but occasionally joined together to fight off raiding Iroquois. The legendary city of Norumbega, thought to have contained vast riches, drew adventurers up the Penobscot River, upon which the city was said to have been located.

Maine lands were granted (1622) by the Council for New England (successor to the Plymouth Company) to two wealthy Englishmen, Sir Ferdinando Gorges and Captain John Mason. Gorgeana (now York) became (1641) the first chartered English city in the New World. After Gorges' death (1647), Maine was largely neglected. Its settlers came under the jurisdiction of Massachusetts, which later bought (1677) the proprietary rights of Gorges' heirs for about $6,000. French efforts to control the region ended with the Treaty of Paris (1763), termi-

nating the French and Indian Wars that had begun in 1689.

Revolt against England was in the air in the 1760s because of taxes and restrictions. In 1774, Maine men followed Boston's example of a year earlier and burned a supply of British tea (York Tea Party). The first naval encounter of the American Revolution took place (June 1775) off Machias, as patriots captured the British ship *Margaretta*. The eastern part of the state passed under British control during the War of 1812.

Maine stayed a part of Massachusetts until 1820, when it was admitted to the Union as a free state under the terms of the Missouri Compromise, thus balancing Missouri's admission as a slave state. A long-simmering boundary dispute with New Brunswick was settled by the Webster-Ashburton Treaty (1842), which ended the bloodless Aroostook War.

Maine was the first state to outlaw (1851) alcohol, which remained illegal until 1934. From 1909 to 1955, to keep the state's hydroelectric power within its borders and thus attract new industries, the sale of such power outside the state was prohibited. The state's textile business has declined since the 1920s, while the food-processing industry has grown significantly. Lobsters, canned sardines, potatoes, and blueberries are among the state's most famous products, as well as shoes, beet sugar and wood pulp and paper. Mining is limited, despite large deposits of granite, limestone, and slate. The communications satellite station near Andover (completed 1962) is part of a worldwide satellite communications system.

The New York Mercantile Exchange, the only market for the round, white Maine potatoes, suspended trading in 1979, on contracts for delivery in March, April, and May. While the NYME said it acted to prevent a collapse of the market which could have resulted from the shortage of high-quality Maine potatoes, Maine farmers, who lost millions of dollars because of the halt, contended that the supply problems were caused by manipulation of the market by a few big traders. In March 1980 Maine farmers blockaded Canadian border crossings to protest the flooding of U.S. markets by Canadian potato imports.

In March 1980 members of the Penobscot Indian tribe approved an $81 million settlement proposal for their claims to half of Maine's territory.

In a referendum in March 1980, Maine voters strengthened a five-year-old ban on slot machines operated for profit to eliminate even those gambling devices operated for charity.

Full name: State of Maine. **Origin of name:** From name of ancient province in France. **Inhabitant:** Mainer. **Capital:** Augusta. **State motto:** Dirigo (I Guide). **Flag:** State seal on a blue field. **Seal:** Farmer & seaman represent two chief occupations; pine tree symbolizes forests; moose, wildlife; northern star stands for northern location. **Flower:** White pine cone & tassel. **Bird:** Chickadee. **Tree:** White pine. **Stone:** Tourmaline. **Song:** "State of Maine Song." **Nickname:** Pine Tree State.

Governor: Joseph E. Brennan. **Annual salary:** $35,000. **Term:** 4 years. **Current term expires:** Jan. 1983. **Voting requirements:** 18 yrs. old & U.S. citizen; resident of state and municipality of registration. **U.S. Congressmen:** 2. **Entered Union:** 1820 (23rd state).

Location & boundaries: New England state: bounded on the north & east by Canada; on the south by New Hampshire & the Atlantic Ocean; & on the west by New Hampshire & Canada. **Total area:** 33,215 sq. mi. (ranks 39th). **Extreme length:** 332 mi. **Extreme breadth:** 207 mi. **Coastline:** 228 mi. **Chief rivers:** Androscoggin, Kennebec, Penobscot, St. Croix. **Major lakes:** Moosehead, Chesuncook, Sebago, Rangeley. **No. of counties:** 16.

Population (1980 census): 1,124,660 (ranks 38th). **Pop. increase (1970-80):** 13.2%. **Largest cities:** Portland, Lewiston, Bangor. **Pop.**

MAINE

density: 33.8 per sq. mi. (ranks 36th). **Pop. distribution:** White—1,109,850; Black—3,128; Am Indian, Eskimo and Aleut—4,087; Asian and Pacific Islander—2,947; Other—4,648; **Spanish origin**—5,005. **Marriage rate (1978):** 10.7 per 1,000 people. **Divorce rate:** 5.7 per 1,000 people.

State finances (1979). Revenue: $1,234,000,000. **Expenditures:** $1,183,000,000. **State taxes:** $505.36 per capita. **State personal income tax:** Yes. **Public debt (1979):** $634.05 per capita. **Federal aid (1980):** $464.58 per capita. **Personal income (1980):** $7,734.

Sectors of the economy (% of labor force employed in 1970): Manufacturing (32%), Wholesale and retail trade (20%), Government (15%), Educational Services (8.2%) Services (7%), Construction (6%). **Leading products:** paper items, leather items, food, textile items, lumber & wood, transportation equipment, printing & publishing. **Minerals:** sand & gravel, cement, stone, peat. **Agricultural products:** broilers, dairy items, potatoes, hay, apples. **Fishing:** lobster, ocean perch, clams. **Avg. farm (1980):** 205 acres. **Avg. value of farm per acre:** $524.

Highway expenditures per capita (1979): $121.33. **Persons per motor vehicle:** 1.56. **Minimum age for driver's license:** 15. **Gasoline tax:** 9¢ per gallon. **Diesel tax:** 9¢ per gallon. **Motor vehicle deaths (1978):** 21.8 per 100,000 people.

Birthrate (1978): 14.5 per 1,000 people. **Infant mortality rate per 1,000 births (1978):** 10.4. **Physicians per 100,000 pop. (1978):** 149. **Dentists per 100,000 pop. (1978):** 45. **Acceptable hospital beds (1978):** 7.93 per 1,000 people. **State expenditures per capita for health and hospitals (1979):** $47.11.

Education expenditures (1976-77): $373.64 per capita annually. **No. of pupils in public schools (1979):** 234,000. **No. of institutions of higher learning (1978-79):** 27. **Public school expenditure per pupil in attendance (1977-78):** $1,551. **Avg. salary of public school teachers (1978-79):** $12,588. **No. full-time teachers (1979):** 14,900. **Educational attainment of adult population (1976):** 12.5 median yrs. of school completed: 1.2% with less than 5 years of education; 13.6% with 4 yrs. of college.

Telephones (1978): 54 per 100 people. **State Chamber of Commerce:** Maine State Chamber of Commerce, One Canal Plaza, Box 65, Portland, Maine 04112.

MARYLAND

Maryland has been called "America in Miniature" because, although small in area, it is uncommonly diverse and rich in history. Hills, valleys, rolling plains, swamps, and plateaus are all found there, and contrasting life-styles abound: from tobacco farmers in the southern part of the state to the missile makers of the highly industrialized Baltimore area, where more than half of the state's population lives. It was from Maryland that Washington, D.C. received (1791) part of its land (the rest was ceded by Virginia); when the capital was threatened by Confederate forces, Maryland became the scene of much fighting, including one of the bloodiest Civil War battles of all: Antietam (1862). Earlier, during the War of 1812, Marylander Francis Scott Key, watching the British bombardment of Baltimore's Fort McHenry, was inspired to write "The Star-Spangled Banner."

Maryland's coastline along the Atlantic Ocean is short, but Chesapeake Bay, which divides the state into an Eastern and Western Shore, provides many fine harbors, and a number of important islands dot the bay. A section of the Atlantic Coastal Plain, sometimes called "Tidewater Maryland," makes up all of the low-lying Eastern Shore. Fishing is a significant industry, and wild fowl abound.

Indians, mainly of the Algonquian family, were living in what is now Maryland before John Cabot, probably the region's first European explorer, sailed along the eastern coast in 1498. Virginian William Claiborne established the first settlement, a fur-trading post, on Kent Island.

The Maryland region was named for Henrietta Maria, queen consort of Charles I, who granted it (1632) to George Calvert, first Baron Baltimore.

But Calvert died the same year, and his son Cecilius, second Baron Baltimore, was given the grant. He soon began developing the colony as both an income source and a religious haven for persecuted fellow Catholics. The Act of Toleration (1649) was passed in behalf of the Catholics, but when the Puritans gained control of the area they repealed this instrument (1654). A short civil war followed (1655), from which the Puritans emerged victors. In 1657 a compromise briefly restored the proprietorship to Lord Baltimore.

The English government eventually (1691) made Maryland a royal province. Commercial development proceeded rapidly in the next century, particularly in the Baltimore area. Indian troubles were infrequent and comparatively mild. Boundary quarrels with Pennsylvania were settled by the drawing of the Mason-Dixon Line (1767). Marylanders staged (1774) a Boston-style "tea party" in Annapolis, protesting British rule, and fought so well in the American Revolution that George Washington nicknamed Maryland "The Old Line State," in honor of its dependable "troops of the line." The state, which entered the Union in 1788, prospered early, thanks largely to the famous Baltimore clipper ships and the opening (1830) of the Baltimore and Ohio Railroad, first in the hemisphere to carry both passengers and freight.

During the Civil War, Maryland was a sharply divided slave state that remained loyal to the Union under great pressure; the state's inherited racial problems are compounded by such factors as inadequate urban housing and public apathy.

Maryland becomes increasingly less a part of the Old South and seems to grow smaller every year. Expressways now link all areas of the state; two of them serve the rapidly developing Baltimore-Washington corridor, while Interstate 70 reaches into Western Maryland and the dual-lane U.S. 50 and U.S. 13 funnel traffic through the Eastern Shore. The Francis Scott Key Bridge opened in 1977. It is Baltimore's second harbor crossing and teams with the Harbor Tunnel. A second span of the Chesapeake Bay Bridge opened in 1973.

Maryland's tourist attractions include a wide variety of parks and forests stretching from Appalachia to the Atlantic Ocean. Annapolis is the site of the U.S. Naval Academy, with the nation's oldest statehouse in use and more original colonial buildings than any other U.S. city. Ocean City is the state's seashore resort. Columbia, the planned city built by James Rouse halfway between Baltimore and Washington, is renowned among urbanologists throughout the world.

In 1975 Maryland's Governor Mandel and five associates were indicted by a Federal grand jury on charges of mail fraud and "racketeering" activity. The trial ended abruptly in 1976 with two separate cases of tampering. A second trial held in 1977 resulted in conviction, and Mandel was sentenced to four years in prison. The sentence was voided when the 4th U.S. Circuit Court of Appeals set aside his conviction on technical grounds on January 11, 1979, but, following a review, it was reinstated on July 20. Mandel entered prison on May 19, 1980. In a separate charge filed in January 1980, the state alleged that Governor and Mrs. Mandel, upon leaving the governor's mansion in 1977, had illegally removed such state property as furniture and liquor.

Full name: State of Maryland. **Origin of name:** From Queen Henrietta Maria of England, wife of Charles I. **Inhabitant:** Marylander. **Capital:** Annapolis. **State motto:** "Fatti maschi, parole femine" ("Manly deeds, womanly words"). **Flag:** Geometric black & gold pattern in opposite quarters; red & white crosses in the others. **Seal:** Shield with coats of arms of Calvert & Crossland families; farmer represents Maryland; fisherman, Lord Baltimore's

MARYLAND

Avalon colony in Newfoundland. **Flower:** Black-eyed Susan. **Bird:** Baltimore oriole. **Tree:** White oak. **Song:** "Maryland, My Maryland." **Nickname:** Old Line State.

Governor: Harry R. Hughes. **Annual salary:** $60,000. **Term:** 4 years. **Current term expires:** Jan. 1983. **Voting requirements:** 18 yrs. old & U.S. citizen; resident of state and county 30 days. **U.S. Congressmen:** 8. **Entered Union:** 1788 (7th state).

Location & boundaries: Middle Atlantic seaboard state: bounded on the north by Pennsylvania; on the east by Delaware & the Atlantic Ocean; on the south by the Potomac River, Virginia & West Virginia; & on the west by West Virginia. **Total area:** 10,577 sq. mi. (ranks 42nd). **Extreme length:** 198.6 mi. **Extreme breadth:** 125.5 mi. **Coastline:** 31 mi. (coastline including Chesapeake Bay, 3,190 mi.). **Chief rivers:** Potomac, Susquehanna, Patuxent. **Major lakes:** Deep Creek Lake (man-made). **No. of counties:** 23, plus 1 independent city.

Population (1980 census): 4,216,446 (ranks 18th). **Pop. increase (1970-80):** 7.5%. **Largest cities:** Baltimore, Rockville, Hagerstown. **Pop. density:** 398.6 per sq. mi. (ranks 5th). **Pop. distribution:** White—3,158,412; Black—958,050; **Am. Indian, Eskimo and Aleut**—8,021; **Asian and Pacific Islander**—64,276; **Other**—27,687; **Spanish origin**—64,740. **Marriage rate (1978):** 10.9 per 1,000 people. **Divorce rate:** 4.0 per 1,000 people.

State finances (1979). Revenue: $4,977,000,000. **Expenditures:** $4,678,000,000. **State taxes:** $638.18 per capita. **State personal income tax:** Yes. **Public debt (1979):** $889.64 per capita. **Federal aid (1980):** $447.34 per capita. **Personal income (1980):** $10,322.

Sectors of the economy (% of labor force employed in 1970): Manufacturing (20%), Government (26%), Wholesale and retail trade (19%), Educational Services (8%), Services (7%), Construction (7%). **Leading products:** food and kindred products, primary metals, electrical equipment and supplies, transportation equipment, chemical and allied products, apparel, printing. **Agricultural products:** dairy items, broilers, cattle, corn, hay, tobacco. **Fishing:** oysters, crabs, clams. **Avg. farm (1980):** 170 acres. **Avg. value of farm per acre:** $2,249.

Highway expenditures per capita (1979): $127.42 **Persons per motor vehicle:** 1.46. **Minimum age for driver's license:** 16. **Gasoline tax:** 9¢ per gallon. **Diesel tax:** 9¢ per gallon. **Motor vehicle deaths (1978):** 17.1 per 100,000 people.

Birthrate (1978): 13.3 per 1,000 people. **Infant mortality rate per 1,000 births (1978):** 14.7. **Physicians per 100,000 pop. (1978):** 282. **Dentists per 100,000 pop. (1978):** 58. **Acceptable hospital beds (1978):** 5.98 per 1,000 people. **State expenditures per capita for health and hospitals (1979):** $93.91.

Education expenditures (1976-77): $568.68 per capita annually. **No. of pupils in public schools (1979):** 790,000. **No. of institutions of higher learning (1978-79):** 54. **Public school expenditure per pupil in attendance (1977-78):** $2,360. **Avg. salary of public school teachers (1978-79):** $17,403. **No. full-time teachers (1979):** 48,600. **Educational attainment of adult population (1976):** 12.6 median yrs. of school completed: 2.1% with less than 5 years of education; 18.6% with 4 yrs. of college.

Telephones (1978): 61 per 100 people. **State Chamber of Commerce:** Maryland Chamber of Commerce, 60 West Street, Annapolis, Maryland 21401.

MASSACHUSETTS

Today a key New England state, Massachusetts was also one of the most important of the 13 Colonies. It was at Plymouth in 1620 that the Pilgrims landed. And the Boston Massacre (1770) and Tea Party (1773) were major, irreversible steps on the road to the American War of Independence, which began at Lexington and Concord in 1775. Statehood dates from 1788.

The topography of the state is unusually varied. The eastern third is a low coastal plain that includes the Cape Cod peninsula and the islands due south: the Elizabeth Islands, Martha's Vineyard, and Nantucket. The New England Uplands, part of a high plateau stretching from Maine to New Jersey, extend westward for roughly 50 miles. Due

west of this area is the Connecticut Valley, which extends from Massachusetts to southern Connecticut; the Connecticut River flows through it, providing fine soil for farming. Farther west lies the Berkshire Valley, surrounded by the Berkshire Hills and, near the northwestern border, the Taconic Mountains.

Besides its historic sites, the state's attractions include the Museum of Fine Arts and Symphony Hall in Boston, Sturbridge Village with its reconstructed early 19th-century community, the summer Tanglewood music festival in the Berkshires, and literary landmarks, such as the homes of Emerson, Hawthorne and Thoreau in Concord. Cape Cod is a leading Eastern summer resort area, with long, sandy beaches and picturesque towns. To the south, the islands of Martha's Vineyard and Nantucket are vacationers' favorites because of their beauty and charm. North of Boston, the art colony town of Rockport and the fishing port of Gloucester are visited by many tourists.

Norsemen including Leif Ericsson may have visited the region about A.D. 1000, but this remains more conjecture than fact. In 1602 English explorer Bartholomew Gosnold landed on Cuttyhunk Island in the Elizabeth chain and gave Cape Cod its name, and Captain John Smith explored the coast in 1614. Oddly enough, the arrival of the Pilgrims at Plymouth six years later, after a brief stop at what is now Provincetown, was purely accidental; the *Mayflower's* destination was a point south of the Hudson River, but a severe storm diverted the ship north. Because this area was beyond the bounds of the sponsoring company in London, a provisional instrument of government called the "Mayflower Compact" was drawn up. Designed to serve until more permanent institutions could be established, this covenant of the Massachusetts Bay Colony, as the settlement was called, formed the foundation of American democracy. But it was not originally a very democratic democracy, because while the Puritans insisted on religious freedom for themselves, they denied it to others, and some they banished from the colony. Roger Williams and the Reverend Thomas Hooker were exiled in 1636, and settled in Rhode Island and Connecticut respectively. Puritan oppression climaxed with the Salem witch trials at the end of the seventeenth century; about 20 persons accused of witchcraft were put to death.

Indian troubles began with an engagement with the Pequot Indians in 1637. In 1675-76, settlers and Wampanoag Indians, led by Metacom, who was known as King Philip, battled in "King Philip's War," which the colonists won at great expense. At various times from 1689 to 1763, the colonists fought against the French and their Indian allies, and ultimately prevailed. Soon after, they began resisting the royal tax laws, setting the stage for general revolt. In 1775 General George Washington arrived in Cambridge to assume command of the Continental Army. A year later, he routed the redcoats from Boston in the war's first major American victory. Then the scene of battle shifted to New York, New Jersey, and Pennsylvania.

The American Revolution was followed in Massachusetts by hard times. There came a business depression, and friction between the legislature and farmers, many of whom suffered foreclosures for debts and taxes; an insurrection (1786-87) led by former army captain Daniel Shays became known as Shays' Rebellion. But prosperity gradually returned, only to fade away again as Jefferson's 1807 Embargo Act, intended to keep the country from involvement in European wars, seriously hurt the state's sea-oriented economy. As it

MASSACHUSETTS

happened, the precaution was a failure: war came anyway in 1812, and Massachusetts turned to manufacturing for its principal livelihood.

Over the years, steady influxes of immigrants provided a plentiful source of labor, and workers were often exploited. Labor unions fought hard for recognition, and there were strikes, occasionally marked by violence as in the 1912 textile strike at Lawrence. Governor Calvin Coolidge gained national prominence when he broke a policemen's strike in Boston in 1919.

Today Massachusetts still ranks among the national leaders in manufacturing, as well as commercial fishing. The electronics industry, tourism, and its many private colleges and universities are important to the state's economy.

Full name: Commonwealth of Massachusetts. **Origin of name:** From Algonquian name, Massa-dchu-es-at, meaning "Great-Hill-Small-Place." **Inhabitant:** Bay Stater. **Capital:** Boston. **State motto:** Ense Petit Placidam Sub Libertate Quietem (By the Sword We Seek Peace, but Peace Only under Liberty). **Flag:** State seal on white field is on one side; other side has green pine tree on blue field. **Seal:** Coat of arms of Commonwealth of Massachusetts; Indian points arrow downward, symbolizing peace; star over his right shoulder represents Massachusetts as a state. **Flower:** Mayflower. **Bird:** Chickadee. **Tree:** American elm. **Song:** "Hail Massachusetts." **Nickname:** Bay State.

Governor: Edward J. King. **Annual salary:** $40,000. **Term:** 4 years. **Current term expires:** Jan. 1983. **Voting requirements:** 18 yrs. old & U.S. citizen; resident of state. **U.S. Congressmen:** 12 (1980 reapportionment: 11). **Entered Union:** 1788 (6th state).

Location & boundaries: New England state; bounded on the north by Vermont & New Hampshire; on the east by the Atlantic Ocean; on the south by the Atlantic Ocean, Rhode Island & Connecticut; on the west by New York. **Total area:** 8,257 sq. mi. (ranks 45th). **Extreme length:** 190 mi. **Extreme breadth:** 110 mi. **Coastline:** 192 mi. **Chief rivers:** Connecticut, Merrimack, Charles, Housatonic. **Major lakes:** Assawompset Pond; Quabbin, Wachusett Reservoirs. **No. of counties:** 14.

Population (1980 census): 5,737,037 (ranks 11th). **Pop. increase (1970-80):** 0.8%. **Largest cities:** Boston, Worcester, Springfield. **Pop. density:** 694.8 per sq. mi. (ranks 3rd). **Pop. distribution:** White—5,362,836; Black—221,279; Am. Indian, Eskimo and Aleut—7,743; Asian and Pacific Islander—49,501; Other—95,678; Spanish origin—141,043. **Marriage rate (1978):** 7.4 per 1,000 people. **Divorce rate:** 2.8 per 1,000 people.

State finances (1979): Revenue: $6,824,000,000. **Expenditures:** $6,377,000,000. **State taxes:** $228.88 per capita. **State personal income tax:** Yes. **Public debt (1979):** $938.55 per capita. **Federal aid (1980):** $503.13 per capita. **Personal income (1980):** $9,992.

Sectors of the economy (% of labor force employed in 1970): Manufacturing (29%), Wholesale and retail trade (20%), Government (15%), Educational Services (9%), Services (6%), Construction (5%). **Leading products:** electrical machinery, apparel, leather items, fabricated metals, printing, food. **Agricultural products:** dairy items, poultry, greenhouse & nursery items, vegetables, tobacco. **Fishing:** haddock, flounder, scallops. **Avg. farm (1980):** 125 acres. **Avg. value of farm per acre:** $1,475.

Highway expenditures per capita (1979): $64.10. **Persons per motor vehicle:** 1.50. **Minimum age for driver's license:** 17. **Gasoline tax:** 11.4¢ per gallon. **Diesel tax:** 11.4¢ per gallon. **Motor vehicle deaths (1978):** 15.0 per 100,000 people.

Birthrate (1978): 11.9 per 1,000 people. **Infant mortality rate per 1,000 births (1978):** 11.1. **Physicians per 100,000 pop. (1978):** 255. **Dentists per 100,000 pop. (1978):** 69. **Acceptable hospital beds (1978):** 7.93 per 1,000 people. **State expenditures per capita for health and hospitals (1979):** $90.66.

Education expenditures (1976-77): $451.76 per capita annually. **No. of pupils in public schools (1979):** 1,055,000. **No. of institutions of higher learning (1978-79):** 119. **Public school expenditure per pupil in attendance (1977-78):** $2,458. **Avg. salary of public school teachers (1978-79):** $17,146. **No. full-time teachers (1979):** 67,100. **Educational attainment of adult population (1976):** 12.6 median yrs. of school completed: 2.4% with less than 5 years of education; 16.8% with 4 yrs. of college.

Telephones (1978): 57 per 100 people. **State Chamber of Commerce:** Massachusetts Commonwealth Chamber of Commerce, c/o New Bedford Area Chamber of Commerce; P.O. Box G-827, New Bedford, Massachusetts 02742.

MICHIGAN

Michigan, one of the world's largest producer of automobiles and among the most populous of the states, extends across two peninsulas and consists of two land regions: the Great Lakes Plain that makes up all of the mitten-shaped Lower Peninsula (where 90 percent of the people live) and the eastern portion of the irregularly shaped Upper Peninsula and the Superior Upland that comprise the rest. The state is touched by four of the five Great Lakes (all but Ontario) and has a longer shoreline than any other inland state.

Dividing the peninsulas and linking Lakes Michigan and Huron are the Straits of Mackinac, crossed by one of the world's longest suspension bridges. Largest among the state's approximately 500 islands is the 209-square-mile Isle Royale (a national park) in Lake Superior. Many mountains, forests, rivers, and waterfalls make the state a sportsman's paradise. The somewhat moist climate is marked by well-defined seasons.

Several Indian tribes were living in the Michigan region when the first European, Étienne Brulé of France, arrived (1618). Other Frenchmen, including Marquette, Jolliet, and La Salle, followed, and the first permanent settlement was established (1668) at Sault Sainte Marie. By 1700 there were French missions, fur-trading posts, and forts on both peninsulas; Fort Pontchartrain (founded 1701) was to become the city of Detroit. But the French were more interested in the lucrative pelt trade than in extensive development of the territory; while Mackinac Island became a busy trading center, most of the rest of the region remained sparsely settled and vulnerable to attack by the British, who gained possession in 1763. The Indians in the area, who had lived in peace with the French, detested the British and tried to drive them out, but eventually they joined with them to fight the Americans in the American Revolution and in the War of 1812.

Michigan, initially part of the Northwest Territory and then of Indiana Territory, was made a separate territory in 1805, with Detroit as its capital (succeeded by Lansing in 1847). Statehood was delayed by a boundary dispute with Ohio and Southern opposition to forming another free state. Compromises broke the impasse, as Michigan's admission (1837) was offset by that of slave state Arkansas, while Ohio was given the disputed land in return for awarding to Michigan the Upper Peninsula, which had been a part of the Territory of Wisconsin.

Michigan's development as a state was rapid, and a number of important roads, rail lines, and canals were soon built—including the vital Soo Ship Canal at Sault Sainte Marie (completed 1855), which allows ships to travel between Lakes Huron and Superior; these new routes spurred the state's mining industry. In the political sphere, the Republican party was founded in 1854 at Jackson, and abolitionist sentiment was strong throughout the state which contributed 100,000 troops to the Union cause during the Civil War.

Today Michigan is both a center of tourism and industry. Greenfield Village in Detroit's suburban Dearborn, to which Ford moved some of early America's famous landmarks, including the courthouse where Abraham Lincoln practiced, attracts over a million sightseers annually. Mackinac Island, near the meeting place of Lakes Michigan

MICHIGAN

© Copyright HAMMOND INCORPORATED, Maplewood, N. J.

Longitude West of Greenwich

and Huron, has been a famous resort for 150 years. The spectacular, colorful turning of the Upper Peninsula's forests in fall attract thousands there, and the state has many annual events aimed at attracting others. Summer resorts abound along both the inland and Great Lakes.

The United Automobile, Aerospace and Agricultural Implement Workers of America (UAW), now the nation's third-largest union with over 1.3 million members, got its start in the famed "Sit-Down Strikes" of the 1930s with workers refusing to leave auto plants until their fledgling union was recognized as bargaining agent. UAW international headquarters are in Detroit.

Social reforms, including open housing, have occurred in a number of Michigan communities in recent years and the new constitution created an independent Civil Rights Commission with police powers. A state referendum in 1976 banned the use of throwaway containers for beer and soft drinks.

The recession of 1980-81 was particularly damaging to the state's auto industry, whose grip on the American market had already been shaken by foreign competitors. The bad news was only partially offset in February 1980 when Volkswagen announced plans to establish an assembly plant in the Detroit suburb of Sterling Heights.

Full name: State of Michigan. **Origin of name:** From Michigama, meaning "Great Water." **Inhabitant:** Michiganian. **Capital:** Lansing. **State motto:** Si Quaeris Peninsulam Amoenam, Circumspice (If You Seek a Pleasant Peninsula, Look Around You). **Flag:** State seal on a blue field. **Seal:** Sun rising over water & man in field appear on shield supported by an elk & a moose. **Flower:** Apple blossom. **Bird:** Robin. **Tree:** White pine. **Song:** "Michigan, My Michigan." **Nickname:** Wolverine State.

Governor: William G. Milliken. **Annual salary:** $65,000. **Term:** 4 years. **Current term expires:** Jan. 1983. **Voting requirements:** 18 yrs. old & U.S. citizen; registered resident of state 30 days. **U.S. Congressmen:** 19 (1980 reapportionment: 18). **Entered Union:** 1837 (26th state).

Location & boundaries: Midwestern state: bounded on the north by Lake Superior, the Straits of Mackinac & Lake Huron; on the east by Lakes Huron & St. Clair, Canada & Lake Erie; on the south by Ohio & Indiana; & on the west by Wisconsin & Lake Michigan. **Total area:** 58,218 sq. mi. (ranks 23rd). **Extreme length:** Upper peninsula 334 mi.; lower peninsula 286 mi. **Extreme breadth:** Upper peninsula 215 mi.; lower peninsula 200 mi. **Shoreline:** 2,232 mi. **Chief rivers:** Grand, Kalamazoo, Escanaba, Saginaw. **Major lakes (other than border-forming):** Houghton, Torch, Charlevoix, Burt. **No. of counties:** 83.

Population (1980 census): 9,258,344 (ranks 8th). **Pop. increase (1970-80):** 4.2%. **Largest cities:** Detroit, Grand Rapids, Warren, Flint, Lansing. **Pop. density:** 159.0 per sq. mi. (ranks 12th). **Pop. distribution:** White—7,868,956; Black—1,198,710; **Am. Indian, Eskimo and Aleut**—40,038; **Asian and Pacific Islander**—56,731; Other—93,909; Spanish origin—162,388. **Marriage rate (1978):** 9.6 per 1,000 people. **Divorce rate:** 4.9 per 1,000 people.

State finances (1979). Revenue: $11,449,000,000. **Expenditures:** $10,507,000,000. **State taxes:** $279.26 per capita. **State personal income tax:** Yes. **Public debt (1979):** $272.13 per capita. **Federal aid (1980):** $424.06 per capita. **Personal income (1980):** $9,847.

Sectors of the economy (% of labor force employed in 1970): Manufacturing (36%), Wholesale and retail trade (19%), Government (14%), Educational Services (8%), Services (6%), Construction (5%). **Leading products:** primary & fabricated metals, food, electrical machinery, paper. **Minerals:** iron ore, cement, sand & gravel, copper. **Agricultural products:** cattle, poultry, dairy items, corn, hay, wheat. **Fishing:** whitefish, chubs, lake herring. **Avg. farm (1980):** 167 acres. **Avg. value of farm per acre:** $1089.

Highway expenditures per capita (1979): $93.32. **Persons per motor vehicle:** 1.41. **Minimum age for driver's license:** 16. **Gasoline tax:** 11¢ per gallon. **Diesel tax:** 11¢ per gallon, reduced to 9¢ effective May 1, 1981. **Motor vehicle deaths (1978):** 22.2 per 100,000 people.

Birthrate (1978): 15.2 per 1,000 people. **Infant mortality rate per 1,000 births (1978):** 13.8. **Physicians per 100,000 pop. (1978):** 149. **Dentists per 100,000 pop. (1978):** 52. **Acceptable hospital beds**

(1978): 5.48 per 1,000 people. **State expenditures per capita for health and hospitals (1979):** $83.19.

Education expenditures (1976-77): $554.28 per capita annually. **No. of pupils in public schools (1979):** 1,866,000. **No. of institutions of higher learning (1978-79):** 96. **Public school expenditure per pupil in attendance (1977-78):** $2,307. **Avg. salary of public school teachers (1978-79):** $18,634. **No. full-time teachers (1979):** 96,500. **Educational attainment of adult population (1976):** 12.5 median yrs. of school completed: 1.8% with less than 5 years of education; 12.6% with 4 yrs. of college.

Telephones (1978): 58 per 100 people. **State Chamber of Commerce:** Michigan State Chamber of Commerce, Business and Trade Center, Suite 400, 200 North Washington Square, Lansing, Michigan 48933.

MINNESOTA

Site of the headwaters of the Mississippi, Minnesota is one of the most scenic states in the nation, rich in natural resources and boasting more than 15,000 lakes. Manufacturing, mainly of farm products, has in recent years become the leading industry, while improved techniques and new copper, nickel, and taconite finds signal a resurgence in mining. Tourism is today a major revenue producer for the state, which also ranks high agriculturally, with livestock and corn recently surpassing wheat in importance. Politically, Minnesota has gained a reputation for voter independence, experimentation in local government, and the institution of Scandinavian-type cooperatives.

Duluth has the nation's largest inland harbor and, since the completion of the St. Lawrence Seaway and Power Project (1959), the port has handled an increasingly significant amount of foreign trade. In Minneapolis are the central offices of the University of Minnesota, one of the largest universities in the country, while in Rochester is the famous Mayo Clinic, an international center of medical practice and research. About half of the state's population is centered in the "Twin Cities" of Minneapolis and St. Paul.

Minnesota's topography is marked by rolling prairies, fertile valleys, high bluffs, deep pine woods, and wilderness areas. The two main land regions are the Superior Upland (or, locally, the "arrowhead country"), consisting of a roughly triangular northeastern land segment, and the Central Lowlands, comprising the rest except, in the south, a small projection of the Wisconsin Driftless Area and two small projections of the Dissected Till Plains. The state's continental climate has a relatively low mean temperature, and is subject to wide and often sudden fluctuation.

The timber industry, which flourished from about 1870 to the early 1900s, was vital to the state's early development, while incidentally fostering the well-known legend of Paul Bunyan.

The state's major tourist attractions are Voyageur's National Park and Grand Portage National Monument, both associated with the fur trade of the 1700s; Lumbertown USA at Brainerd; and the lake and winter sports centers of the North Country.

The first inhabitants of the Minnesota region are thought to date from about 20,000 years ago. Norsemen may have visited in the 14th century, but the first Europeans of record to do so were the French fur traders and missionaries, beginning with Radisson and Groseilliers (1659-61) and including La Salle, Marquette and Jolliet, and Daniel Greysolon—Sieur Du Lhut, or Duluth—who claimed (1679) the region for King Louis XIV.

Principal Indian tribes in the region at the time were the Sioux in the west and south and the Ojibwa in the heavily wooded northern section; the

MINNESOTA

two groups, often at war with one another, were generally friendly to the French, who built up a vast pelt-marketing empire but ultimately lost it (1763) to the British.

Serious American development began after the War of 1812, with the powerful American Fur Company leading the way. Eastern Minnesota at this time was still part of the Northwest Territory, while the western region had been acquired (1803) as part of the Louisiana Purchase. A short-lived Spanish claim to the region (dating from 1762) was never effectively enforced. The year 1819 saw the building of Fort St. Anthony (later called Fort Snelling), and in 1832 Henry R. Schoolcraft discovered the source of the Mississippi at Lake Itasca. Six years later, Pierre Parrant settled on the site of present-day St. Paul.

In 1849 the Minnesota region—which in whole or part had been successively a portion of the French, English, and Spanish empires, the Northwest Territory, and seven U.S. territories—was made a territory in its own right. A comprehensive Indian treaty (1851) and statehood (1858) both spurred settlement, which was not deterred by a brief, ill-fated Sioux uprising in 1862.

In the 1890s, the mining of the high-grade iron ore of the Mesabi Ranges became a major industry. As the rich Mesabi mines dwindled after World War II, iron companies began to mine a low-grade ore called taconite, which abounds in Minnesota, and to extract high-grade iron pellets from it. Extraction leaves useless tailings, which contain asbestos and other dangerous substances.

Tailings caused a near-crisis in the city of Silver Bay. In 1975, the Reserve Mining Company, one of Silver Bay's largest employers, was ordered by a Federal court to stop dumping tailings into Lake Superior. At first, the company claimed that it would have to go out of business, thus ruining Silver Bay's economy. Eventually, a compromise allowed the company a "reasonable time" to change. In 1980, the company opened a land dump, linked to its plant by a slurry system, and ended dumping in the lake.

Violence broke out in mid-May 1979 on the Chippewa Indian Reservation at Red Lake because of discontent with the leadership of tribal chairman Roger Jourdain. Two youths were killed and seven buildings and 45 vehicles were destroyed by fire. Five Indians were convicted of conspiracy and assault charges in the incident.

Full name: State of Minnesota. **Origin of name:** From the Sioux meaning "Sky-Tinted Water." **Inhabitant:** Minnesotan. **Capital:** St. Paul. **State motto:** L'Etoile du Nord (The Star of the North). **Flag:** State seal & 19 gold stars on blue field. **Seal:** Indian riding into sunset, farmer plowing field, waterfall, forest. **Flower:** Pink & white lady's-slipper. **Bird:** Common loon. **Tree:** Norway (Red) pine. **Song:** "Hail! Minnesota." **Nickname:** North Star State.

Governor: Albert H. Quie. **Annual salary:** $66,500. **Term:** 4 yrs. **Current term expires:** Jan. 1983. **Voting requirements:** 18 yrs. old & U.S. citizen; registered state resident 20 days. **U.S. Congressmen:** 8. **Entered Union:** 1858 (32nd state).

Location & boundaries: Northern Midwestern state: bounded on the north by Canada; on the east by Lake Superior, Wisconsin & the Mississippi River; on the south by Iowa; & on the west by South Dakota, North Dakota & Red River of the North. **Total area:** 84,068 sq. mi. (ranks 12th). **Extreme length:** 406 mi. **Extreme breadth:** 358 mi. **Coastline:** 180 mi. **Chief rivers:** Mississippi, Red River of the North, Minnesota. **Major lakes:** Superior, Red, Lake of the Woods. **No. of counties:** 87.

Population (1980 census): 4,077,148 (ranks 21st). **Pop. increase (1970-80):** 7.1%. **Largest cities:** Minneapolis, St. Paul, Duluth, Bloomington. **Pop. density:** 48.5 per sq. mi. (ranks 33rd). **Pop. distribution:** White—3,936,948; Black—53,342; Am. Indian, Eskimo and Aleut—35,026; Asian and Pacific Islander—26,533;

Other—25,299; Spanish origin—32,124. **Marriage rate (1978):** 8.3 per 1,000 people. **Divorce rate:** 3.6 per 1,000 people.

State finances (1979). Revenue: $5,316,000,000. **Expenditures:** $4,779,000,000. **State taxes:** $771.86 per capita. **State personal income tax:** Yes. **Public debt (1979):** $461.51 per capita. **Federal aid (1980):** $408.32 per capita. **Personal income (1980):** $9,519.

Sectors of the economy (% of labor force employed in 1970): Wholesale and retail trade (22%), Manufacturing (21%), Government (15%), Educational Services (9%), Services (7%), Construction (6%). **Leading products:** food; electrical & other machinery; printing & publishing; paper items; chemicals; stone, clay & glass items. **Minerals:** iron ore, taconite, sand & gravel, cement, stone. **Agricultural products:** cattle, hogs, dairy items, corn, soybeans. **Fishing:** yellow pike, lake herring, tullibee. **Avg. farm (1980):** 291 acres. **Avg. value of farm per acre:** $1,008.

Highway expenditures per capita (1979): $116.04. **Persons per motor vehicle:** 1.17. **Minimum age for driver's license:** 16. **Gasoline tax:** 13¢ per gallon. **Diesel tax:** 13¢ per gallon. **Motor vehicle deaths (1978):** 24.0 per 100,000 people.

Birthrate (1978): 15.4 per 1,000 people. **Infant mortality rate per 1,000 births (1978):** 12.0. **Physicians per 100,000 pop. (1978):** 185. **Dentists per 100,000 pop. (1978):** 61. **Acceptable hospital beds (1978):** 7.63 per 1,000 people. **State expenditures per capita for health and hospitals (1979):** $67.00.

Education expenditures (1976-77): $545.20 per capita annually. **No. of pupils in public schools (1979):** 788,000. **No. of institutions of higher learning (1978-79):** 65. **Public school expenditure per pupil in attendance (1977-78):** $2,212. **Avg. salary of public school teachers (1978-79):** $16,181. **No. full-time teachers (1979):** 48,600. **Educational attainment of adult population (1976):** 12.5 median yrs. of school completed: 1.1% with less than 5 years of education; 13.3% with 4 yrs. of college.

Telephones (1978): 56 per 100 people. **State Chamber of Commerce:** Minnesota Association of Commerce and Industry, 200 Hanover Bldg., 480 Cedar Street, St. Paul, Minnesota 55101.

MISSISSIPPI

Without renouncing the history that has been both its pride and its handicap, this Deep South state has begun to rework its economic and social structures after a period of transition that began during the Great Depression.

In 1936, wealthy lumberman Hugh White became governor and instituted a "Balance Agriculture with Industry" (BAWI) program which allowed cities to issue bonds and build plants for private industry. By 1965, industrial employment had inched ahead of agricultural employment.

Tourists from outside the state enrich Mississippi's economy by over $700 million yearly as they flock to the beaches of the Gulf Coast winter resort area and other attractions.

The petroleum industry has become a major factor since the discovery of oil in the Tinsley field in 1939. Mississippi is a leading producer of oil and natural gas in the U.S.

The state is made up of two main land regions: the flat and fertile Delta area along the Mississippi River in northwest Mississippi and the rolling hills which cover most other areas, though broken by occasional river valleys. The Bay of St. Louis and Biloxi or Back Bay break the coastline and a chain of small islands lie offshore.

Mississippi was inhabited by the Choctaw, Chickasaw, Natchez and Yazoo Indians before De Soto explored it for Spain in 1540. French explorers La Salle, Iberville and Bienville came later.

The French ceded Mississippi to the British under the treaty of Paris in 1763 but the Spanish claimed it along with West Florida in 1781. Spanish influence virtually ended in 1798 when Mississippi flew the United States flag as a territory of the new republic.

MISSISSIPPI

MILES
0 10 20 30 40 50 60

KILOMETERS
0 10 20 30 40 50 60

⊛ State Capitals
⊙ County Seats

The early settlement of the state was handicapped by conflicting land claims, Indian troubles and the Yazoo Land Fraud in which Georgia, claiming the region, sold lots to speculators. Georgia finally ceded its claim to the Federal Government in 1802 and the Louisiana Purchase in 1803 insured free access to the Mississippi River. Mississippi became a state in 1817.

By the time the Civil War began, Mississippi was among the wealthiest states in the nation. Property assessments totaled $509 million in 1860. By 1880 property assessments had fallen to $110 million. Not until 1920 did assessments reach the pre-Civil War level.

Most black people were effectively disfranchised until the passage of the Federal Voting Rights Act of 1965.

Attacks on segregation brought turbulence. Two persons were killed in rioting at the University of Mississippi; NAACP leader Medgar Evers was shot to death in ambush at his Jackson home in 1963; and three civil rights workers were killed in 1964 near Philadelphia, Miss. However, the state joined the FBI in a massive crackdown on the Ku Klux Klan group behind much of the trouble, and tensions then eased.

Massive public school desegregation came later and Mississippi experienced less trouble than Northern and Eastern states under similar orders. Mississippi experienced some campus unrest as the 1960s closed and two persons were shot to death in a riot at Jackson State College in 1970.

In recent years blacks have made important gains, with an improvement in job opportunities and an increase in numbers elected to public office. The 1979 elections increased the number of blacks in the legislature from four to seventeen.

Mississippi's recent bid for trade with Middle Eastern and South American countries has paid off in massive sales of such products as farm machinery, food products, soybeans and cotton.

The Tennessee-Tombigbee Waterway project, one of a number of such measures cancelled by President Carter as an economy move, was reinstated after Congressional pressure was brought to bear. The project, estimated to cost $1.8 billion, is expected to be a shot in the arm for Mississippi's economy.

Full name: State of Mississippi. **Origin of name:** From the Indian, Maesi, meaning "Large," & Sipu, meaning "River." **Inhabitant:** Mississippian. **Capital:** Jackson. **State motto:** Virtute et Armis (By Valor & Arms). **Flag:** Horizontal red, white & blue bars with Confederate battle flag in upper left. **Seal:** American eagle holds olive branch, representing peace, & three arrows, symbolizing war. **Flower:** Magnolia. **Bird:** Mockingbird. **Tree:** Magnolia. **Song:** "Go, Mississippi." **Nickname:** Magnolia State.

Governor: William F. Winter. **Annual salary:** $53,000. **Term:** 4 years. **Current term expires:** Jan. 1984. **Voting requirements:** 18 yrs. old & U.S. citizen; resident of state and county for 1 year, resident 6 months in election district or municipality. **U.S. Congressmen:** 5. **Entered Union:** 1817 (20th state).

Location & boundaries: Southeastern state bounded on the north by Tennessee; on the east by Alabama; on the south by the Gulf of Mexico & Louisiana; & on the west by the Mississippi River, Louisiana & Arkansas. **Total area:** 47,716 sq. mi. (ranks 32nd). **Extreme length:** 352 mi. **Extreme breadth:** 188 mi. **Coastline:** 44 mi. **Chief rivers:** Mississippi, Yazoo, Pearl, Big Black. **Major lakes:** Grenada, Barnett, Sardis, Enid, Okatibbee Reservoirs. **No. of counties:** 82.

Population (1980 census): 2,520,638 (ranks 31st). **Pop. increase (1970-80):** 13.7%. **Largest cities:** Jackson, Biloxi, Meridian. **Pop. density:** 52.8 per sq. mi. (ranks 31st). **Pop. distribution:** White—615,190; Black—887,206; Am. Indian, Eskimo and Aleut—6,180; Asian and Pacific Islander—7,142; Other—4,650; Spanish origin—24,731. **Marriage rate (1978):** 11.3 per 1,000 people. **Divorce rate:** 5.5 per 1,000 people.

State finances (1979). Revenue: $2,598,000,000. **Expenditures:** $2,367,000,000. **State taxes:** $492.58 per capita. **State personal income tax:** Yes. **Public debt (1979):** $347.11 per capita. **Federal aid (1980):** $467.26 per capita. **Personal income (1980):** $6,508.

Sectors of the economy (% of labor force employed in 1970): Manufacturing (26%), Wholesale and retail trade (18%), Government (18%), Educational Services (9%), Construction (8%), Services (7%). **Leading products:** food, lumber & wood, apparel, chemicals, transportation equipment. **Minerals:** petroleum, natural gas, sand & gravel. **Agricultural products:** cattle, broilers, eggs, cotton lint, soybeans, cottonseed. **Fishing:** menhaden, shrimp, oysters. **Avg. farm (1980):** 322 acres. **Avg. value of farm per acre:** $629.

Highway expenditures per capita (1979): $121.72. **Persons per motor vehicle:** 1.63. **Minimum age for driver's license:** 15. **Gasoline tax:** 9¢ per gallon. **Diesel tax:** 10¢ per gallon. **Motor vehicle deaths (1978):** 32.6 per 100,000 people.

Birthrate (1978): 18.4 per 1,000 people. **Infant mortality rate per 1,000 births (1978):** 18.7. **Physicians per 100,000 pop. (1978):** 109. **Dentists per 100,000 pop. (1978):** 31. **Acceptable hospital beds (1978):** 6.43 per 1,000 people. **State expenditures per capita for health and hospitals (1979):** $65.07.

Education expenditures (1976-77): $378.89 per capita annually. **No. of pupils in public schools (1979):** 482,000. **No. of institutions of higher learning (1978-79):** 46. **Public school expenditure per pupil in attendance (1977-78):** $1,395. **Avg. salary of public school teachers (1978-79):** $11,545. **No. full-time teachers (1979):** 28,200. **Educational attainment of adult population (1976):** 12.1 median yrs. of school completed: 7.9% with less than 5 years of education; 11.5% with 4 yrs. of college.

Telephones (1978): 47 per 100 people. **State Chamber of Commerce:** Mississippi Economic Council, 656 N. State Street, P.O. Box 1849, Jackson, Mississippi 39205.

MISSOURI

Traditional "Gateway to the West," centrally located Missouri owes much of its industrial and agricultural importance to the nation's two largest rivers—the Mississippi and Missouri—which form part of the state's borders while facilitating transportation and enriching its soil. Lead mining, in which the state ranks first nationally, has been important in the region for 200 years, being conducted chiefly in the Viburnum and Bixby areas. Most of the state's manufacturing activity is concentrated in and around St. Louis and Kansas City.

The state is made up of four principal land regions: the Dissected Till Plains, lying north of the Missouri; the Osage Plains in the west; the West Gulf Coastal Plain (known locally as the Mississippi Alluvial Plain), covering the southeastern corner; and the Ozark Plateau, making up most of the southern section and constituting the largest single region. The Dissected Till and Osage Plains are considered subdivisions of the Central Lowlands. Ten major artificial lakes formed by dams in the Ozark region have helped make that area a popular vacationland, contributing greatly to the state's $2 billion annual tourism business. Although two-thirds of the state was once covered by forests, today only half that amount remains, including Mark Twain and Clark National Forests.

The Mound Builders, the earliest known inhabitants of the Missouri region, predated the Osage and Missouri Indians, who were living there when the first European explorers—Frenchmen Marquette and Jolliet—visited (1673). France's claim to the entire Mississippi Valley, including what is now Missouri, was based on La Salle's travels in 1682. In the following years, French fur trading posts were established along the river, and the working of the lead mines was begun. Established about 1735, Ste. Genevieve was the first permanent white settlement.

Having met defeat in the French and Indian Wars, France secretly yielded (1762) to Spain all its

MISSOURI

territory west of the Mississippi; even so, Frenchmen Laclede and Chouteau founded St. Louis two years later. Napoleon regained (1800) possession of the region for France, then sold it three years later as part of the Louisiana Purchase. A year later, in 1804, President Thomas Jefferson sent Meriwether Lewis and William Clark westward up the Missouri River on the famous expedition that tied the United States together as a continental nation. The area was briefly a district of the Territory of Indiana, but was made a separate territory in 1805, comprising at that time all U.S. land west of the Mississippi and north of 33° north latitude and therefore including the future state of Missouri.

The question of admitting Missouri to the Union became bound up, in Congress, with the volatile slavery issue. Bitter controversy was arduously resolved by the Missouri Compromise (1820), which provided for the admission of Missouri (1821) as a slave state and Maine as a free one, while banning slavery in the rest of the Louisiana Purchase north of 36°30'N. Missouri was at this time the nation's western frontier, and fur trading was still its foremost economic pursuit. The state's six northwestern counties were added by the Platte Purchase (1837). An unusual boundary dispute between Missouri and Illinois was settled early in 1970, giving Illinois the site of Old Kaskaskia, the state's original capital, now an island as a result of shifts by the Mississippi River. Illinois received Kaskaskia and Beaver islands, and Missouri, Cottonwoods and Roth islands.

The years preceding the Civil War were marked by growing prosperity in an increasingly tense political climate. The town of Independence became the starting point of the much-traveled Santa Fe and Oregon Trails, while St. Louis prospered as a thriving inland port. St. Joseph was the eastern starting point of the briefly active (1860-61) Pony Express. But bitter Missouri-Kansas border wars over the slavery issue had begun, and although Missouri voted (February 1861) not to secede from the Union, Missourians were sharply divided in their allegiances, supplying both sides with troops.

Missouri today seeks to attract new industry by stressing its central location, good transportation facilities, availability of labor, and relatively low taxes. Tourism has emerged in recent years as one of Missouri's leading businesses.

Missouri's tourist and vacation attractions include the Gateway Arch which is part of the Jefferson National Expansion Memorial in St. Louis, Wilson's Creek National Battlefield near Springfield, the George Washington Carver National Monument near Carthage, the Ozark National Scenic Riverways, Hannibal on the Mississippi of Mark Twain fame, and the Lake of the Ozarks vacation country.

Full name: State of Missouri. **Origin of name:** From name of Sioux tribe. **Inhabitant:** Missourian. **Capital:** Jefferson City. **State motto:** Salus Populi Suprema Lex Esto (Let the Welfare of the People Be the Supreme Law). **Flag:** State seal centered on horizontal red; white & blue bars. **Seal:** Two grizzly bears hold shields of United States & Missouri; 24 stars represent Missouri's entrance into Union. **Flower:** Hawthorn. **Bird:** Bluebird. **Tree:** Flowering dogwood. **Song:** "Missouri Waltz." **Nickname:** Show-Me State.

Governor: Christopher S. Bond. **Annual salary:** $55,000. **Term:** 4 years. **Current term expires:** Jan. 1985. **Voting requirements:** 18 yrs. old & U.S. citizen; registered in state. **U.S. Congressmen:** 10 (1980 reapportionment: 9). **Entered Union:** 1821 (24th state).

Location & boundaries: Southern Midwestern state: bounded on the north by Iowa; on the east by Illinois, Kentucky, Tennessee & the Mississippi River; on the south by Arkansas; & on the west by Oklahoma, Kansas, Nebraska & the Missouri River. **Total area:** 69,686 sq. mi. (ranks 19th). **Extreme length:** 284 mi. **Extreme breadth:** 308 mi. **Chief rivers:** Missouri, Mississippi, Osage. **Major

lakes: Lake of the Ozarks; Stockton, Taneycomo, Clearwater, and Wappapello lakes; Table Rock & Pomme de Terre Reservoirs. **No. of counties:** 114 & the city of St. Louis.

Population (1980 census): 4,917,444 (ranks 15th). **Pop. increase (1970-80):** 5.1%. **Largest cities:** St. Louis, Kansas City, Springfield, Independence. **Pop. density:** 70.5 per sq. mi. (ranks 27th). **Pop. distribution:** White—4,346,267; Black—514,274; **Am. Indian, Eskimo and Aleut**—12,319; **Asian and Pacific Islander**—23,108; **Other**—21,476; **Spanish origin**—51,667. **Marriage rate (1978):** 10.9 per 1,000 people. **Divorce rate:** 5.4 per 1,000 people.

State finances (1979). Revenue: $3,821,000,000. **Expenditures:** $3,337,000,000. **State taxes:** $413.61 per capita. **State personal income tax:** Yes. **Public debt (1979):** $146.21 per capita. **Federal aid (1980):** $345.34 per capita. **Personal income (1980):** $8,846.

Sectors of the economy (% of labor force employed in 1970): Manufacturing (24%), Wholesale and retail trade (22%), Government (15%), Educational Services (8%), Services (7%), Construction (6%). **Leading products:** transportation equipment, food, chemicals, printing & publishing, machinery, fabricated metals. **Minerals:** stone, cement, lead, iron ore. **Agricultural products:** cattle, hogs, dairy items, corn, soybeans, hay. **Avg. farm (1980):** 276 acres. **Avg. value of farm per acre:** $816.

Highway expenditures per capita (1979): $101.05. **Persons per motor vehicle:** 1.48. **Minimum age for driver's license:** 16. **Gasoline tax:** 7¢ per gallon. **Diesel tax:** 7¢ per gallon. **Motor vehicle deaths (1978):** 24.5 per 100,000 people.

Birthrate (1978): 15.0 per 1,000 people. **Infant mortality rate per 1,000 births (1978):** 14.8. **Physicians per 100,000 pop. (1978):** 158. **Dentists per 100,000 pop. (1978):** 47. **Acceptable hospital beds (1978):** 7.20 per 1,000 people. **State expenditures per capita for health and hospitals (1979):** $60.77.

Education expenditures (1976-77): $382.12 per capita annually. **No. of pupils in public schools (1979):** 878,000. **No. of institutions of higher learning (1978-79):** 84. **Public school expenditure per pupil in attendance (1977-78):** $1,657. **Avg. salary of public school teachers (1978-79):** $13,189. **No. full-time teachers (1979):** 55,200. **Educational attainment of adult population (1976):** 12.4 median yrs. of school completed: 2.5% with less than 5 years of education; 11.8% with 4 yrs. of college.

Telephones (1978): 57 per 100 people. **State Chamber of Commerce:** Missouri Chamber of Commerce, P.O. Box 149, Jefferson City, Missouri 65101.

MONTANA

As its Spanish name suggests, Montana is a mountainous region: the Rocky Mountains cover the western two-fifths of the state and the high, gently rolling Great Plains make up the rest. The state is large, ranking fourth nationally in area, but it is sparsely populated. The Rockies' Bitterroot Range, marking the Montana-Idaho boundary, is one of the most rugged and remote areas in the country. Many of the state's mountains are thick with forests below the timber line; fir, pine, and spruce abound. The state is an important producer of Christmas trees for national markets.

Montana's climate is generally cool to cold, and dry. Tourists—mainly hunters, fishermen, and dude ranch patrons—have been coming to the state in growing numbers, attracted by plentiful fish and game and the varied scenery. As an industry, tourism has become increasingly vital in recent years. Attractions include Glacier National Park, 11 national forests, the Lewis and Clark Cavern (one of the country's largest), Big Hole National Battlefield, the Custer Battlefield National Monument, Bighorn Canyon National Recreation Area, the Flathead Lake vacation area, and a number of annual rodeos and Indian ceremonials. Yellowstone National Park, most of which is in Wyoming, has three entrances in Montana.

Arapaho, Blackfoot, Cheyenne, Crow, Atsina, Bannock, Kalispel, Kutenai, and Shoshoni Indians were living in the region before the arrival of

MONTANA

the first Europeans, who were probably fur trappers of the Hudson Bay Company or the Northwest Company. In 1805, Lewis and Clark explored the area on their journeys to and from the Pacific Coast. The American Fur Company, in 1829 and 1846, built two of Montana's earliest non-Indian settlements: Forts Union and Benton.

The major Indian wars (1867-77) included the famous 1876 Battle of Little Bighorn, popularly known as "Custer's Last Stand," in which Cheyennes and Sioux killed General Custer and more than 200 of his men. But the Indians' moment of glory was something of a brief one, for in 1877, when Chief Joseph and his Nez Percé warriors surrendered to Federal troops near the Canadian border, Indian resistance in Montana virtually ended. Today, the state has some 37,000 Indians, almost all of whom live on seven reservations.

The United States obtained most of Montana as part of the Louisiana Purchase (1803). The remaining northwestern section passed into U.S. hands following the 1846 treaty with England. Montana was originally part of the Territory of Idaho, created in 1863; Montana Territory came into being in 1864. Statehood came in 1889.

Much of Montana's early history was bound up with mining, which is still a leading industry: oil, coal, copper, and sand and gravel are important products. The capital of Helena was originally a mining camp called Last Chance Gulch. The Anaconda Company branched out from Butte ("the richest hill on earth") to become a giant conglomerate of its day, with interests in railroading, journalism, banking, and other fields.

Another of Montana's major occupations, ranching, came into its own in 1866 when a cattleman by the name of Nelson Story drove his herd of a thousand longhorn from Texas to Montana, setting an example that many others soon followed. The coming of the railroad in 1883 was another impetus. But the severe winter of 1886-87 spelled disaster; thousands of cattle perished in subzero blizzards. Although the industry eventually recovered, for a long time profit margins were narrow. Ranching is economically important: the state has over three times as many cattle (including calves) and about as many sheep as it has people.

Montana today is attempting to attract new industry while preserving clean air and water. The aims have touched off a clash between environmentalists and the energy companies which are developing reserves of strippable coal.

In May 1980, volcanic ash from the eruption of Mount St. Helens in Washington fell thickly in six counties in western Montana. Streets became impassable, and schools and businesses were closed.

Full name: State of Montana. **Origin of name:** From Spanish word meaning "Mountainous." **Inhabitant:** Montanan. **Capital:** Helena. **State motto:** Oro y Plata (Gold & Silver). **Flag:** State seal on blue field. **Seal:** A plow, pick & shovel rest on soil, symbolizing Montana's agricultural & mineral industries; Great Falls of Missouri River & mountain scenery. **Flower:** Bitterroot. **Bird:** Western meadowlark. **Tree:** Ponderosa pine. **Song:** "Montana." **Nicknames:** Treasure State; the Big Sky Country; Land of the Shining Mountains.

Governor: Thomas L. Judge. **Annual salary:** $40,000. **Term:** 4 years. **Current term expires:** Jan. 1985. **Voting requirements:** 18 yrs. old & U.S. citizen; registered resident of state & county 30 days. **U.S. Congressmen:** 2. **Entered Union:** 1889 (41st state).

Location & boundaries: Rocky Mountain state: bounded on the north by Canada; on the east by North Dakota & South Dakota; on the south by Wyoming & Idaho; and on the west by Idaho. **Total area:** 147,138 sq. mi. (ranks 4th). **Extreme length:** 570 mi. **Extreme breadth:** 315 mi. **Chief rivers:** Missouri, Yellowstone, Kootenai. **Major lakes:** Flathead; Fort Peck & Canyon Ferry Reservoirs. **No. of counties:** 56.

Population (1980 census): 786,690 (ranks 44th). **Pop. increase (1970-80):** 13.3%. **Largest cities:** Billings, Butte-Silver Bow, Great Falls, Missoula. **Pop. density:** 5.3 per sq. mi. (ranks 48th). **Pop. distribution:** White—740,148; Black—1,786; Am. Indian, Eskimo

and Aleut—37,270; Asian and Pacific Islander—2,503; Other—4,983; Spanish origin—9,974. **Marriage rate (1978):** 10.4 per 1,000 people. **Divorce rate:** 6.3 per 1,000 people.

State finances (1979). Revenue: $1,006,000,000. **Expenditures:** $901,000,000. **State taxes:** $509.61 per capita. **State personal income tax:** Yes. **Public debt (1979):** $187.02 per capita. **Federal aid (1980):** $584.34 per capita. **Personal income (1980):** $8,445. •

Sectors of the economy (% of labor force employed in 1970): Wholesale and retail trade (22%), Government (21%), Manufacturing (10%), Educational Services (10%), Services (7%), Construction (6%). **Leading products:** lumber & wood; primary metals; food; petroleum & coal items; printing & publishing; stone, clay & glass items; chemicals. **Minerals:** copper, petroleum, lead & zinc, sand & gravel, phosphate rock, silver, gold. **Agricultural products:** cattle, dairy items, sheep, wheat, hay, barley, flax seed, sugar beets. **Avg. farm (1980):** 2,884 acres. **Avg. value of farm per acre:** $218.

Highway expenditures per capita (1979): $167.10. **Persons per motor vehicle:** .82. **Minimum age for driver's license:** 15. **Gasoline tax:** 9¢ per gallon. **Diesel tax:** 11¢ per gallon. **Motor vehicle deaths (1978):** 34.5 per 100,000 people.

Birthrate (1978): 17.4 per 1,000 people. **Infant mortality rate per 1,000 births (1978):** 11.6. **Physicians per 100,000 pop. (1978):** 131. **Dentists per 100,000 pop. (1978):** 56. **Acceptable hospital beds (1978):** 7.25 per 1,000 people. **State expenditures per capita for health and hospitals (1979):** $64.56.

Education expenditures (1976-77): $575.61 per capita annually. **No. of pupils in public schools (1979):** 160,000. **No. of institutions of higher learning (1978-79):** 13. **Public school expenditure per pupil in attendance (1977-78):** $2,259. **Avg. salary of public school teachers (1978-79):** $14,024. **No. full-time teachers (1979):** 10,200. **Educational attainment of adult population (1976):** 12.6 median yrs. of school completed: 1.2% with less than 5 years of education; 14.2% with 4 yrs. of college.

Telephones (1978): 54 per 100 people. **State Chamber of Commerce:** Montana Chamber of Commerce, 110 Neill Avenue, P.O. Box 1730, Helena, Montana 59601.

NEBRASKA

Nebraska is rich with grass (with more forage varieties than any other state) and grain; agriculture is its mainstay. The grassy Sand Hills make up the state's central region, and rolling farmland, found in the east, rises gradually from 840 feet above sea level to 5,300 feet in the western High Plains region. A portion of the South Dakota Badlands takes up about 1,000 square miles of the northwest corner of the state. The climate of Nebraska is one of extremes: severe winters and sweltering summers.

Nebraska annually harvests large crops of corn, sorghum, oats, wheat, rye, soybeans, alfalfa and dry edible beans. Omaha, with its surrounding area, forms the nation's largest meat-packing center, and it is the second-largest cattle market of both the United States and the world.

The state's numerous rivers and lakes are vitally important to its agricultural and allied processing industries. Many conservation practices, such as dam construction, systematic tree-planting, and irrigation, are widely employed to keep the land productive. Larger farms, more modern equipment, and improved farming techniques have resulted in vastly increased production even with a smaller farm population.

Judging by stone tool and weapon remnants that have been unearthed, the first inhabitants of Nebraska arrived between 10,000 and 25,000 years ago. In the early 1700s, Spanish and French explorers found, among others, the Omaha and Oto Indians living peacefully along the region's rivers. The buffalo-hunting Pawnee, however, battled other tribes—especially the Sioux—but were generally friendly to whites. The Sioux, Arapaho, and Cheyenne Indians constituted the white settlers'

NEBRASKA

MILES
0 10 20   40   60   80

KILOMETERS
0 10 20 40 60 80

★ State Capitals   ⊗ County Seats

© Copyright HAMMOND INCORPORATED, Maplewood, N.J.

principal resistance, waging a losing battle to keep their hunting grounds.

The United States gained possession of the area with the Louisiana Purchase (1803). Pioneers going west along the Oregon Trail, which followed the Platte Valley, stimulated trading and settlement; many early Nebraskans earned a living supplying food, lodging, and fresh mounts. Scotts Bluff National Monument and Chimney Rock National Historic Site are landmarks along the Trail. Statehood came in 1867.

Early times were very hard for settlers. There was bitter, protracted conflict between them and the cattlemen, who wanted the land for their herds. (This struggle was not fully resolved until the 1904 Kinkaid Act gave over the last of the state's open range land to the homesteaders.) And there were harsh blows from nature: blizzards, locust infestations, and droughts. Homestead National Monument near Beatrice commemorates the pioneer spirit of the 19th-century farmers who settled the Great Plains region.

World War I brought prosperity, but hard times returned: depression and drought hit the state simultaneously. Overextended farmers faced foreclosure. Violence was averted by the enactment of a series of farm mortgage moratorium acts; New Deal legislation also helped. In 1937, the Nebraska legislature was reorganized into a "one house" (unicameral) system, under which state senators are elected on a nonpartisan basis.

Border disputes with Iowa have plagued Nebraska ever since the Missouri River was made the dividing line (1867). Through the years, the river's shifting has transferred parcels of land from one state to the other.

Full name: State of Nebraska. **Origin of name:** From Omaha Indian name for the Platte River. **Inhabitant:** Nebraskan. **Capital:** Lincoln. **State motto:** Equality Before the Law. **Flag:** State seal on blue field. **Seal:** Blacksmith represents mechanical arts; settler's cabin, growing corn & shocks of grain stand for agriculture; steamboat & train symbolize transportation. **Flower:** Goldenrod. **Bird:** Western meadowlark. **Tree:** Cottonwood. **Song:** "Beautiful Nebraska." **Nickname:** Cornhusker State.

Governor: Charles Thone. **Annual salary:** $40,000. **Term:** 4 years. **Current term expires:** Jan. 1983. **Voting requirements:** 18 yrs. old & U.S. citizen; state resident and registered voter. **U.S. Congressmen:** 3. **Entered Union:** 1867 (37th state).

Location & boundaries: Midwestern state: bounded on the north by South Dakota; on the east by Iowa, the Missouri River & Missouri; on the south by Kansas; on the southwest by Colorado; & on the west by Wyoming. **Total area:** 77,227 sq. mi. (ranks 15th). **Extreme length:** 415 mi. **Extreme breadth:** 205 mi. **Chief rivers:** Missouri, North Platte, South Platte. **Major lakes:** Lewis & Clark, McConaughy. **No. of counties:** 93.

Population (1980 census): 1,570,006 (ranks 35th). **Pop. increase (1970-80):** 5.7%. **Largest cities:** Omaha, Lincoln, Grand Island. **Pop. density:** 20.3 per sq. mi. (ranks 41st). **Pop. distribution:** White—1,490,569; Black—48,389; Am. Indian, Eskimo and Aleut—9,197; Asian and Pacific Islander—6,996; Other—14,855; Spanish origin—28,020. **Marriage rate (1978):** 8.7 per 1,000 people. **Divorce rate:** 3.9 per 1,000 people.

State finances (1979). Revenue: $1,334,000,000. **Expenditures:** $1,250,000,000. **State taxes:** $471.77 per capita. **State personal income tax:** Yes. **Public debt (1979):** $33.46 per capita. **Federal aid (1980):** $347.64 per capita. **Personal income (1980):** $8,914.

Sectors of the economy (% of labor force employed in 1970): Wholesale and retail trade (22%), Government (16%), Manufacturing (14%), Educational Services (9%), Services (7%), Construction (6%). **Leading products:** food, electrical & other machinery, chemicals, fabricated metal items, printing & publishing, primary metals, transportation equipment. **Agricultural products:** cattle, hogs, dairy items, corn, hay, wheat, sorghums. **Avg. farm (1980):** 759 acres. **Avg. value of farm per acre:** $536.

Highway expenditures per capita (1979): $142.45. **Persons per** motor vehicle: 1.26. **Minimum age for driver's license:** 16. **Gasoline tax:** 13.9¢ per gallon. **Diesel tax:** 13.9¢ per gallon. **Motor vehicle deaths (1978):** 22.3 per 100,000 people.

Birthrate (1978): 16.0 per 1,000 people. **Infant mortality rate per 1,000 births (1978):** 13.0. **Physicians per 100,000 pop. (1978):** 145. **Dentists per 100,000 pop. (1978):** 60. **Acceptable hospital beds (1978):** 7.45 per 1,000 people. **State expenditures per capita for health and hospitals (1979):** $66.44.

Education expenditures (1976-77): $489.37 per capita annually. **No. of pupils in public schools (1979):** 291,000. **No. of institutions of higher learning (1978-79):** 31. **Public school expenditure per pupil in attendance (1977-78):** $1,950. **Avg. salary of public school teachers (1978-79):** $13,113. **No. full-time teachers (1979):** 19,800. **Educational attainment of adult population (1976):** 12.6 median yrs. of school completed: 1.0% with less than 5 years of education; 14.3% with 4 yrs. of college.

Telephones (1978): 59 per 100 people. **State Chamber of Commerce:** Nebraska Association of Commerce & Industry, P.O. Box 81556, 424 Terminal Bldg., Lincoln, Nebraska 68501.

NEVADA

Except for its northeast and southeast corners, Nevada lies entirely within the Great Basin, a broad plateau averaging 5,500 feet in elevation and broken by mountain ranges. The Sierra Nevadas on the California border interrupt moisture-carrying clouds from the Pacific, making Nevada the driest state in the country; its average annual rainfall is only 3.73 inches. Much of the state is uninhabited, sagebrush-covered desert dotted by alkali sinks in which rivers have dried up. Only seven states have fewer inhabitants than Nevada, which in 1980 had but 7.2 persons per square mile. However, the 1980 census revealed that Nevada is the fastest-growing state in the nation.

Nevada's minimal agriculture depends largely on irrigation. Most crops go for livestock feed. Leading income sources have been, first, tourism, then mining—followed by a modest mineral and metals processing industry. In the Reno area, warehousing, aided by a free port law, is growing substantially. Thanks mainly to legalized gambling, spectacular entertainment and lenient divorce laws, tourism today accounts for billions of dollars in revenue. The Las Vegas and Reno metropolitan areas, where nearly four of every five Nevadans live, are the principal tourist attractions. Others include Lake Tahoe on the California-Nevada border, Pyramid Lake, Hoover Dam, Lake Mead National Recreation Area and Death Valley National Monument.

Indians are thought to have inhabited the Nevada region between 10,000 and 20,000 years ago. In more recent times, the Shoshoni, Washoe, Northern Paiute, and other tribes lived there.

In 1775 a Spanish missionary named Francisco Garcés passed through what is now Nevada on his way to the West Coast. In the early 1800s, trappers searched the area for new fur sources. John C. Frémont and Kit Carson explored (1843-45) the Great Basin and Sierra Nevada.

The United States obtained (1848) the region, following the Mexican War, and the first permanent settlement (1851) was a Mormon trading post called Mormon Station (now Genoa). Amid the conflicting pressures of the Civil War, Nevada was made a state (1864), although the territory did not meet the population requirement.

In 1859 the discovery of the Comstock (silver and gold) Lode, near what became Virginia City, brought an influx of both settlers and adventurers. During the next 20 years, the lode yielded more than $300 million of mineral wealth which helped the Union to win the Civil War and was the basis of many American fortunes. Today copper is the ma-

NEVADA

MILES
0 10 20   40   60   80

KILOMETERS
0   20   40   60   80

State Capital ⊛   County Seats ◉

© Copyright HAMMOND INCORPORATED, Maplewood, N. J.

Longitude West of Greenwich

jor ore mined with plants at McGill (Kennecott) and Yerington (Anaconda).

The Federal Government owns 87% of the land in Nevada. The first Federal irrigation project anywhere was the Newlands Irrigation Project, completed in 1907, which helped west central Nevada's agriculture. Another Federal irrigation project—the Southern Nevada Project—was completed in 1971. In the early 1950s, the Federal Government began to test nuclear devices on Federal land in the Nevada desert.

As the 1970s drew to a close, Nevadans became increasingly annoyed by the limitation which Federal ownership of so much land was putting on agriculture, commercial, and residential growth. Moreover, in 1979, reports that nuclear testing may have caused a high rate of cancer in areas near the test site led to a storm of protest. In July 1979, the Nevada legislature declared the state to be owner of 49,000,000 acres of Federal land—apparently in order to facilitate judicial review of Federal policies. Three months later, officials of Nevada and of other Western states met at Reno to discuss common problems.

In 1980, a Federal study advised construction in Nevada of covered mobile launching sites for MX missiles. Many Nevadans complained that the plan would encourage saturation bombing of Nevada in the event of war, and announced their outright opposition to the plan in 1981.

Full name: State of Nevada. **Origin of name:** From Spanish for "Snow-Clad." **Inhabitant:** Nevadan. **Capital:** Carson City. **State motto:** All for Our Country. **Flag:** Blue field with gold & green insignia in upper left; words "Battle Born" recall that Nevada gained statehood during Civil War. **Seal:** Plow & sheaf of wheat represent Nevada's agricultural resources; quartz mill, mine tunnel & carload of ore symbolize mineral wealth of state; 36 stars. **Flower:** Sagebrush. **Animal:** Nelson (Desert) bighorn sheep. **Bird:** Mountain bluebird. **Tree:** Single-leaf piñon. **Song:** "Home Means Nevada." **Nickname:** Silver State.

Governor: Robert F. List. **Annual salary:** $50,000. **Term:** 4 years. **Current term expires:** Jan. 1983. **Voting requirements:** 18 yrs. old & U.S. citizen; state resident 30 days. **U.S. Congressmen:** 1 (1980 reapportionment: 2). **Entered Union:** 1864 (36th state).

Location & boundaries: Rocky Mountain state: bounded on the north by Oregon & Idaho; on the east by Utah & Arizona; & on the south & west by California. **Total area:** 110,540 sq. mi. (ranks 7th). **Extreme length:** 483 mi. **Extreme breadth:** 320 mi. **Chief rivers:** Humboldt, Colorado, Truckee. **Major lakes:** Pyramid, Walker, Tahoe, Mead. **No. of counties:** 17.

Population (1980 census): 799,184 (ranks 43rd). **Pop. increase (1970-80):** 63.5%. **Largest cities:** Las Vegas, Reno, North Las Vegas. **Pop. density:** 7.2 per sq. mi. (ranks 47th). **Pop. distribution:** White—699,377; Black—50,791; Am. Indian, Eskimo and Aleut—13,304; Asian and Pacific Islander—14,109; Other—21,603; Spanish origin—53,786. **Marriage rate (1978):** 172.1 per 1,000 people. **Divorce rate:** 16.8 per 1,000 people.

State finances (1979). Revenue: $1,059,000,000. **Expenditures:** $862,000,000. **State taxes:** $658.95 per capita. **State personal income tax:** No. **Public debt (1979):** $532.85 per capita. **Federal aid (1980):** $402.91 per capita. **Personal income (1980):** $10,458.

Sectors of the economy (% of labor force employed in 1970): Services (22%), Wholesale and retail trade (19%), Government (18%), Construction (8%), Educational Services (6%), Manufacturing (5%). **Leading products:** stone, clay & glass items; chemicals; printing & publishing; food items; lumber; electrical machinery; fabricated metals. **Minerals:** copper, gold, sand & gravel, diatomite. **Agricultural products:** sheep, cattle, hay, alfalfa seed, wheat, dairy items. **Avg. farm (1980):** 4,495 acres. **Avg. value of farm per acre:** $116.

Highway expenditures per capita (1979): $161.30. **Persons per motor vehicle:** 1.38. **Minimum age for driver's license:** 16. **Gasoline tax:** 10.5¢ per gallon. **Diesel tax:** 10.5¢ per gallon. **Motor vehicle deaths (1978):** 46.4 per 100,000 people.

Birthrate (1978): 16.5 per 1,000 people. **Infant mortality rate per 1,000 births (1978):** 12.5. **Physicians per 100,000 pop. (1978):** 138. **Dentists per 100,000 pop. (1978):** 51. **Acceptable hospital beds (1978):** 4.00 per 1,000 people. **State expenditures per capita for health and hospitals (1979):** $55.82.

Education expenditures (1976-77): $463.70 per capita annually. **No. of pupils in public schools (1979):** 143,000. **No. of institutions of higher learning (1978-79):** 6. **Public school expenditure per pupil in attendance (1977-78):** $1,955. **Avg. salary of public school teachers (1978-79):** $16,017. **No. full-time teachers (1979):** 6,500. **Educational attainment of adult population (1976):** 12.6 median yrs. of school completed: 1.2% with less than 5 years of education; 13.1% with 4 yrs. of college.

Telephones (1978): 72 per 100 people. **State Chamber of Commerce:** Nevada Chamber of Commerce Association, P.O. Box 2806, Reno, Nevada 89505.

NEW HAMPSHIRE

New Hampshire is a relatively small but well wooded and scenic state of mountains, lakes, and rapid rivers that provide a good water supply and large hydroelectric-power potential. There are three main land areas: the coastal lowlands covering the southeast corner; the New England Uplands, covering most of the southwest, west central, and south central area; and the White Mountains region in the north, which includes Mount Washington, the Northeast's highest peak (6,288 feet). Near the coast are the rough-hewn Isles of Shoals, three of which belong to New Hampshire. The state's largest harbor is at Portsmouth, near the mouth of the Piscataqua. The climate features cool summers with low humidity and winters marked by heavy snowfall. The ocean tempers the weather along the 17.8 mile Atlantic coastline, shortest of any state bordering an ocean.

About 5,000 Indians were living in the New Hampshire region before the Europeans came. The various tribes coexisted peacefully but often banded together to fight the Iroquois. The first explorers in the area are thought to have been Captain Martin Pring (1603), Samuel de Champlain (1605), and Captain John Smith (1614). Permanent settlement began in 1623, when David Thomson established Little Harbour, now in the town of Rye. Captain John Mason, who had a hand in the founding (1630) of Portsmouth, gave New Hampshire its name. Though the state was once part of Massachusetts, it became a separate royal colony in 1679; the two states had the same governor from 1699 to 1741. New Hampshire established an independent government (1776), one designed to be only temporary but which in fact operated until 1784, when the present constitution was adopted. New Hampshire was the ninth state to ratify the U.S. Constitution (1788), and the one that made that document legal.

Complicated boundary disputes with all its neighbors have marked New Hampshire's history. Royal orders eventually defined the Massachusetts (1741) and New York (1764) boundaries, while the state's northern border was set by the Webster-Ashburton Treaty (1842), which established the international line between the United States and Canada. But not until a 1934 U.S. Supreme Court ruling was the Vermont boundary decided. A border dispute with Maine over 2,400 acres of coastal waters that began in 1974 was resolved in 1976, when the U.S. Supreme Court awarded the bulk of the disputed territory to Maine.

The state is one of the most industrialized in the nation, based on the percentage of its population working in manufacturing. The electronic, chemical, and machinery industries are major employers.

New Hampshire, with its beneficial tax climate, is experiencing an influx of new industrial development, especially in the southern sections along the Massachusetts border. In the absence of a general sales or income tax, state government is financed through the state-operated liquor monopoly, pari-mutuel betting on racing, state taxes on business profits and rooms and meals. Education is funded by the local property tax.

Tourism, meanwhile, has mushroomed into an annual $900-million business. One fifth of the land is in public parklands, including 724,000 acres of the White Mountain National Forest, which extends into Maine. Hiking, boating, and camping are popular, and the state has more than 60 ski lifts. Attractions include Strawbery Banke, a preservation project that has restored about 30 buildings and homes of the original settlement at Portsmouth, N.H., the Lakes Region around Lake Winnipesaukee, the Kancamagus Highway between Lincoln and Conway, Daniel Webster's birthplace near Franklin, the Mount Washington Cog Railway, the first (1869) in North America, and the famous "Old Man of the Mountain" granite head profile at Franconia, the state's official emblem.

New Hampshire today functions as an exceptionally democratic entity, with the state's 222 towns (nicknamed "little republics") using the traditional town meeting to provide a forum for all voters. The state, which for decades had a sometimes disputed reputation as a political bellwether, has been relieved of its position as the first to hold a presidential primary by Puerto Rico, which in 1980 held its first such election.

Nuclear power remains controversial in New Hampshire. In 1976 construction began on a nuclear power plant in the environmentally sensitive seacoast area at Seabrook. Anti-nuclear power forces from all over New England focused on the issue, and in May 1977, a mass occupation of the construction site resulted in the arrest of 1,414 demonstrators by authorities. In October 1979 and again in May 1980, protestors renewed attempts to occupy the site, but their repeated assaults were repelled by state troopers and National Guardsmen armed with nightsticks and high-pressure water hoses. Some injuries were reported.

Full name: State of New Hampshire. **Origin of name:** From the English county of Hampshire. **Inhabitant:** New Hampshirite. **Capital:** Concord. **State motto:** Live Free or Die. **Flag:** State seal on a blue field. **Seal:** A reproduction of Revolutionary War frigate "Raleigh" is surrounded by nine stars in a laurel wreath to symbolize victory. **Flower:** Purple lilac. **Bird:** Purple finch. **Tree:** White birch. **Songs:** "Old New Hampshire" & "New Hampshire, My New Hampshire." **Nickname:** Granite State.

Governor: Hugh J. Gallen. **Annual salary:** $44,520. **Term:** 2 years. **Current term expires:** Jan. 1983. **Voting requirements:** 18 yrs. old & U.S. citizen; registered voter and state resident. **U.S. Congressmen:** 2. **Entered Union:** 1788 (9th state).

Location & boundaries: New England state: bounded on the north by Canada; on the east by Maine & the Atlantic Ocean; on the south by Massachusetts; & on the west by Vermont, Canada & the Connecticut River. **Total area:** 9,304 sq. mi. (ranks 44th). **Extreme length:** 180 mi. **Extreme breadth:** 93 mi. **Coastline:** 17.8 mi. **Chief rivers:** Connecticut, Merrimack, Androscoggin. **Major lake:** Winnipesaukee. **No. of counties:** 10.

Population (1980 census): 920,610 (ranks 42nd). **Pop. increase (1970-80):** 24.8%. **Largest cities:** Manchester, Nashua, Concord. **Pop. density:** 98.9 per sq. mi. (ranks 20th). **Pop. distribution:** White—910,099; Black—3,990; **Am. Indian, Eskimo and Aleut**—1,352; **Asian and Pacific Islander**—2,929; **Other**—2,240; **Spanish origin**—5,587. **Marriage rate (1978):** 10.5 per 1,000 people. **Divorce rate:** 5.4 per 1,000 people.

State finances (1979). Revenue: $840,000,000. **Expenditures:** $784,000,000. **State taxes:** $297.75 per capita. **State personal income tax:** No, except on interest & dividends. **Public debt (1979):**

$832.67 per capita. **Federal aid (1980):** $375.18 per capita. **Personal income (1980):** $8,980.

Sectors of the economy (% of labor force employed in 1970): Manufacturing (36%), Wholesale and retail trade (19%), Government (14%), Educational Services (8%), Construction (7%), Services (6%). **Leading products:** leather items, electrical & other machinery, textile mill items, paper items, food items, printing & publishing. **Agricultural products:** dairy items, eggs, cattle, hay, apples, potatoes. **Avg. farm (1980):** 181 acres. **Avg. value of farm per acre:** $866.

Highway expenditures per capita (1979): $128.09. **Persons per motor vehicle:** 1.40. **Minimum age for driver's license:** 16. **Gasoline tax:** 11¢ per gallon. **Diesel tax:** 11¢ per gallon. **Motor vehicle deaths (1978):** 19.6 per 100,000 people.

Birthrate (1978): 14.3 per 1,000 people. **Infant mortality rate per 1,000 births (1978):** 10.4. **Physicians per 100,000 pop. (1978):** 163. **Dentists per 100,000 pop. (1978):** 53. **Average hospital beds (1978):** 5.43 per 1,000 people. **State expenditures per capita for health and hospitals (1979):** $65.06.

Education expenditures (1976-77): $398.05 per capita annually. **No. of pupils in public schools (1979):** 169,000. **No. of institutions of higher learning (1978-79):** 24. **Public school expenditure per pupil in attendance (1977-78):** $1,654. **Avg. salary of public school teachers (1978-79):** $12,200. **No. full-time teachers (1979):** 10,200. **Educational attainment of adult population (1976):** 12.6 median yrs. of school completed: 1.1% with less than 5 years of education; 15.3% with 4 yrs. of college.

Telephones (1978): 59 per 100 people. **State Chamber of Commerce:** Business and Industry Association of New Hampshire, 23 School Street, Concord, New Hampshire 03301.

NEW JERSEY

New Jersey's importance is disproportionate to its modest size. Strategically located, amid many rich markets, the state has extraordinary transportation facilities and a correspondingly large volume of interstate traffic: railway trackage, highways, tunnels, and bridges abound. The nation's most densely populated state, it is a manufacturing giant with limited but valuable farming and fishing industries.

Many sandy beaches, coupled with a generally mild climate marked by ocean breezes, have made New Jersey popular with vacationers, and tourism is today a major industry. Attractions include such resort areas as Atlantic City and Wildwood, as well as the Thomas A. Edison National Historic Site in West Orange, the Walt Whitman House in Camden, the Garden State Arts Center in Telegraph Hill Park, and several ski areas.

Before the coming of the Europeans, the region was inhabited by Lenni-Lenape (later called Delaware) Indians of the Algonquian group. The area's early colonial history is bound up with that of New York (then New Netherland), of which it was a part. With the passing of power from Dutch to English hands (1664), New Jersey began to emerge as a more distinct entity. Proprietorship of lands between the Hudson and Delaware Rivers was granted by James II to Lord John Berkeley and Sir George Carteret, who then offered territory to settlers in return for sworn allegiance to the king and payment of quitrent (fixed rent). Berkeley eventually sold (1676) his land share to a group of Quakers, who then agreed with Carteret to divide the region into East and West Jersey, the line running southeastward from the Delaware River near the Water Gap to the Atlantic Ocean near Little Egg Harbor. Carteret owned East Jersey—about three-eighths of the total area—until his death (1680), while West Jersey became the nation's first Quaker settlement. Control of both Jerseys eventually reverted to England which governed it

NEW JERSEY

MILES

KILOMETERS

State Capitals ⊕   County Seats ⊙

© Copyright HAMMOND INCORPORATED, Maplewood, N.J.

Longitude West of Greenwich

jointly with New York from 1702 to 1738, when Lewis Morris was made governor of New Jersey alone.

The region remained turbulent for many years. A decade of virtual lawlessness began in 1745, ended only by the advent of the French and Indian War of the mid-1750s, which served to unify New Jerseyans against a common enemy. Because of its location between New York City and Philadelphia, New Jersey was the scene of many important battles of the American Revolution. In 1783 Princeton served briefly as the nation's capital. Statehood dates from 1787.

After the Revolution, many scientific breakthroughs took place in the state, and the country's first model factory town was founded in 1791 at the site of the present Paterson, under the auspices of Alexander Hamilton's Society for the Establishment of Useful Manufactures. (A few years later, Hamilton was killed in Weehawken in a notorious duel with Aaron Burr.)

The state was sharply divided by the Civil War. Most New Jerseyans accepted the ending of slavery, but many businessmen were against the war because of the profitable Southern market. When peace came, the state's population and economy continued their rapid growth, interrupted by the Panic of 1873. Powerful special-interest groups grasped undue political control, bringing a counterwave of reform under Governor Woodrow Wilson, who was elected in 1910. But after Wilson left in 1913 to become president, much of the impetus toward reform in the state withered away.

The institution (1966) of a general sales tax has helped lighten the state's severe financial problems, as has the March 1970 hike in that tax, from three to five percent. One side effect of these measures has been to detract somewhat from the state's traditionally favorable tax climate which, together with streamlined corporation laws, has been a vital weapon in the continuing battle with other states for new industry. New Jersey enacted an income tax in 1976 as a replacement for portions of local property tax burdens, and in December 1977 the tax was made permanent.

Large-scale urban-renewal projects that would eliminate blight while creating jobs are seen as a means of alleviating a major part of the problem. A vast $300-million Hackensack Meadowlands project built on land from ten different north Jersey towns opened in 1976, with the National Football League Giants and the Cosmos professional soccer team as the major long-term tenants and including a racetrack. In 1981 an indoor sports arena was opened, housing the New Jersey Nets basketball team (formerly the New York Nets). Port Jersey, a 707-acre, $160-million industrial center with a 17-berth terminal for containerships has been planned for the New Jersey side of Upper New York Bay, adjoining the U.S. Military Ocean Terminal in Bayonne.

In mid-1977 the courts lifted the ban on drilling East Coast offshore oil leases, and exploration commenced by the end of the year. After six months there had been no announcement of any profitable strikes in the Baltimore Canyon off the New Jersey Coast. Since that time, however, both Texaco Inc. and the U.S. Geological Survey have announced offshore gas finds.

In 1976 New Jersey passed a constitutional amendment authorizing the establishment of gambling casinos in Atlantic City as a means of rejuvenating the ailing resort and rebuilding the tourist industry in general. The first casino opened in May 1978 and has proved successful. Since then additional casinos have opened and others are being constructed.

Full name: State of New Jersey. **Origin of name:** From Channel Island of Jersey. **Inhabitant:** New Jerseyite. **Capital:** Trenton. **State motto:** Liberty & Prosperity. **Flag:** State seal on yellow field. **Seal:** Three plows & goddess Ceres holding a cornucopia represent agriculture; a horse's head lies above sovereign's helmet. **Flower:** Purple violet. **Bird:** Eastern goldfinch. **Tree:** Red oak. **Song:** (unofficial) "New Jersey Loyalty Song." **Nickname:** Garden State.

Governor: Brendan T. Byrne. **Annual salary:** $65,000. **Term:** 4 years. **Current term expires:** Jan. 1982. **Voting requirements:** 18 yrs. old & U.S. citizen; resident of state & county 30 days. **U.S. Congressmen:** 15 (1980 reapportionment: 14). **Entered Union:** 1787 (3rd state).

Location & boundaries: Middle Atlantic state; bounded on the north by New York; on the east by New York, the Hudson River & the Atlantic Ocean; on the south by Delaware Bay; on the southwest by Delaware & the Delaware River; & on the west by Pennsylvania & the Delaware River. **Total area:** 7,836 sq. mi. (ranks 46th). **Extreme length:** 166 mi. **Extreme breadth:** 57 mi. **Coastline:** 130 mi. **Chief rivers:** Raritan, Delaware, Hudson, Passaic. **Major lakes:** Hopatcong, Budd, Culvers. **No. of counties:** 21.

Population (1980 census): 7,364,158 (ranks 9th). **Pop. increase (1970-80):** 2.7%. **Largest cities:** Newark, Jersey City, Paterson, Elizabeth. **Pop. density:** 939.8 per sq. mi. (ranks 1st). **Pop. distribution:** White—6,127,090; Black—924,786; Am. Indian, Eskimo and Aleut—8,394; Asian and Pacific Islander—103,842; Other—200,046; Spanish origin—491,867. **Marriage rate (1978):** 7.2 per 1,000 people. **Divorce rate:** 3.6 per 1,000 people.

State finances (1979). Revenue: $7,881,000,000. **Expenditures:** $7,718,000,000. **State taxes:** $508.63 per capita. **State personal income tax:** Yes. **Public debt (1979):** $734.11 per capita. **Federal aid (1980):** $384.68 per capita. **Personal income (1980):** $10,755.

Sectors of the economy (% of labor force employed in 1970): Manufacturing (32%), Wholesale and retail trade (19%), Government (14%), Services (7%), Educational Services (7%), Construction (5%). **Leading products:** chemicals, machinery, food items, primary & fabricated metals, transportation equipment, apparel. **Agricultural products:** dairy items, cattle, tomatoes, potatoes, corn, hay, asparagus. **Fishing:** clams, flounder, oysters. **Avg. farm (1980):** 129 acres. **Avg. value of farm per acre:** $2,400.

Highway expenditures per capita (1979): $54.17. **Persons per motor vehicle:** 1.70. **Minimum age for driver's license:** 17. **Gasoline tax:** 8¢ per gallon. **Diesel tax:** 8¢ per gallon. **Motor vehicle deaths (1978):** 15.3 per 100,000 people.

Birthrate (1978): 12.8 per 1,000 people. **Infant mortality rate per 1,000 births (1978):** 13.0. **Physicians per 100,000 pop. (1978):** 180. **Dentists per 100,000 pop. (1978):** 64. **Acceptable hospital beds (1978):** 6.00 per 1,000 people. **State expenditures per capita for health and hospitals (1979):** $64.66.

Education expenditures (1976-77): $474.25 per capita annually. **No. of pupils in public schools (1979):** 1,306,000. **No. of institutions of higher learning (1978-79):** 63. **Public school expenditure per pupil in attendance (1977-78):** $2,518. **Avg. salary of public school teachers (1978-79):** $17,125. **No. full-time teachers (1979):** 89,000. **Educational attainment of adult population (1976):** 12.4 median yrs. of school completed; 2.7% with less than 5 years of education; 14.9% with 4 yrs. of college.

Telephones (1978): 65 per 100 people. **State Chamber of Commerce:** New Jersey State Chamber of Commerce, 5 Commerce Street, Newark, New Jersey 07102.

NEW MEXICO

New Mexico is a land of great contrast. It is rich in history yet in the forefront of the Atomic Era—the world's first A-bomb, produced at Los Alamos, was exploded (1945) at Trinity Site near Alamogordo. Three major cultures intermingle—Spanish, Indian, and Anglo-American—and within each is a variety of types and subcultures.

Indians are thought to have lived in this region between 20,000 and 25,000 years ago. In 1980, a total of 104,000 Indians—mainly Navajo, Apache, and Pueblo—were to be found in New Mexico, living much as their ancestors had, despite a few modern trappings. Within the state is the country's

NEW MEXICO

MILES
0 20 40 60 80 100

KILOMETERS
0 20 40 60 80 100

★ State Capital   ⊙ County Seats

Longitude West of Greenwich

© Copyright HAMMOND INCORPORATED, Maplewood, N.J.

largest Indian reservation (more than 16 million acres), which is inhabited by Navajos. At Gallup each August is held the colorful Inter-tribal Indian Ceremonial.

Sharp contrasts also mark the face of the land, a complex blending of deserts, rugged blue-rimmed mesas, and forested mountain regions, with an average mean elevation of 5,700 feet. The generally thin, dry air cools rapidly at night, making for wide daily temperature variations. Because of the great ranges in altitude and rainfall, the state supports six distinct life zones and a correspondingly large variety of plants and animals.

Water is generally scarce in New Mexico, and irrigation difficult. Much of the land, however, is devoted to grazing, sustaining a sizable ranching industry. Cotton lint is the main crop in the irrigated areas. In the dry-farming regions (about two-thirds of the state's farmland), hay and wheat are among the significant outputs. Dry-farmers are gradually shifting to irrigation, as more dams and wells are built. In the river valleys, especially along the Rio Grande, fruits and vegetables are grown.

Francisco Vásquez de Coronado, in search of the fabled "Seven Cities of Cibola," explored (1540-42) the region that became New Mexico, but found no treasure. In 1598 the first Spanish colony was established at the Pueblo of San Juan de Los Caballeros. Santa Fe was founded in 1610 and made provincial capital. Roman Catholic missionaries set up schools in the region. Subjected to harsh treatment and forbidden to worship their gods, the Pueblo Indians revolted in 1680; Spain regained control in 1692. Mexico governed from 1821 until the United States took possession via the 1848 Mexican treaty and the 1853 Gadsden Purchase. Vital to early-day commerce, the Santa Fe Trail between New Mexico and Missouri was opened in 1821; today, east of Santa Fe, the Trail is still in use as U.S. 85.

The surrender (1886) of Geronimo terminated the Apache Wars and marked the virtual end of area Indian troubles. During the 1880s, the mining and ranching industries boomed. New Mexico entered the Union in 1912.

New Mexico is one of the largest energy-producing states in the nation. The state is the leading producer of potash and uranium. It has almost half of the nation's uranium reserves and large deposits of low-sulphur coal and natural gas. Historically, it has been a massive exporter of energy, sending out of the state more than half the electricity it has produced, about three-quarters of the gas generated and almost all of the petroleum pumped in the state.

Since 1945, the state has been a leader in the field of energy research and development. It helps the nation solve its energy needs through research conducted by Los Alamos Scientific Laboratory and Sandia Laboratories in the nuclear, solar and geothermal fields.

The increased demand for domestic energy and the pattern of growth it shares with other states of the sunbelt have brought problems as well as prosperity. School systems are overcrowded and there is a housing shortage in some places. Urban sprawl is spreading around Grants, Albuquerque and Santa Fe, intensifying the contrast between the relatively low economic level of the rural areas and the prosperity of some cities and mining communities. As a result, political power, which has been in the hands of agricultural interests (ranching is still the state's chief industry), is shifting to represent newcomers from out of state and the growing Mexican-American population.

Tourist attractions in New Mexico include the Carlsbad Caverns National Park, Inscription Rock at El Morro National Monument, and the ruins of Fort Union, which in its day was one of the largest

U.S. military outposts on the southwest frontier. Other National Park Service facilities are Bandelier National Monument, Capulin Mountain National Monument, Chaco Canyon National Monument, Gila Cliff Dwellings National Monument, Salinas National Monument, and White Sands National Monument. Santa Fe and Taos attract thousands of visitors every year. At Lincoln are mementos of Billy the Kid, the outlaw who was involved (1878) in the Lincoln County cattle war. And near Aztec are Indian ruins, including a 500-room, E-shaped pueblo dating from A.D. 800-1200.

In February 1980 a prison revolt at the New Mexico state penitentiary left more than 30 inmates dead and about 90 prisoners and guards injured. During the 36-hour siege, convicts turned on one another, torturing and killing suspected informers. The worst U.S. prison riot since that at Attica, New York, nine years before, it focused national attention on the explosive atmosphere in many of the nation's prisons.

Full name: State of New Mexico. **Origin of name:** From the Aztec, Mexitli, meaning "War God." **Inhabitant:** New Mexican. **Capital:** Santa Fe. **State motto:** Crescit Eundo (It Grows As It Goes). **Flag:** Stylized red sun, symbol of Zia pueblo of Indians, on a yellow field. **Seal:** Two eagles represent annexation of New Mexico by the United States, scroll under eagles bears state's motto. **Flower:** Yucca. **Bird:** Roadrunner. **Tree:** Piñon or nut pine. **Gem:** Turquoise. **Vegetable:** Chile and Pinto Beans. **Song:** "O, Fair New Mexico." **Nickname:** Land of Enchantment.

Governor: Bruce King. **Annual salary:** $60,000. **Term:** 4 years. **Current term expires:** Dec. 1982. **Voting requirements:** 18 yrs. old & U.S. citizen; registered state resident 42 days (30 days for Pres. election). **U.S. Congressmen:** 2 (1980 reapportionment: 3). **Entered Union:** 1912 (47th state).

Location & boundaries: Southwestern state: bounded on the north by Colorado; on the east by Oklahoma & Texas; on the south by Texas & Mexico; & on the west by Arizona. **Total area:** 121,666 sq. mi. (ranks 5th). **Extreme length:** 391 mi. **Extreme breadth:** 352 mi. **Chief rivers:** Rio Grande, San Juan, Pecos, Canadian. **Major lakes:** Navajo, Conchas, Cochiti, Elephant Butte Reservoir. **No. of counties:** 32.

Population (1980 census): 1,299,968 (ranks 37th). **Pop. increase (1970-80):** 27.8%. **Largest cities:** Albuquerque, Santa Fe, Las Cruces. **Pop. density:** 10.7 per sq. mi. (ranks 44th). **Pop. distribution:** White—976,465; Black—24,042; Am. Indian, Eskimo and Aleut—104,777; Asian and Pacific Islander—6,816; Other—187,868; Spanish origin—476,089; **Marriage rate (1978):** 13.6 per 1,000 people. **Divorce rate:** 7.9 per 1,000 people.

State finances (1979). Revenue: $1,847,000,000. **Expenditures:** $1,578,000,000. **State taxes:** $681.22 per capita. **State personal income tax:** Yes. **Public debt (1979):** $414.10 per capita. **Federal aid (1980):** $433.55 per capita. **Personal income (1980):** $7,956.

Sectors of the economy (% of labor force employed in 1970): Government (27%), Wholesale and retail trade (21%), Educational Services (12%), Services (11%), Construction (7%), Manufacturing (7%). **Leading products:** food items, petroleum & coal items, electronics, apparel. **Minerals:** coal, lead, zinc, gold, petroleum, silver, natural gas, potassium salts, copper, uranium, molybdenum. **Agricultural products:** cattle, sheep, dairy items, cotton lint, hay, sorghum, grain, poultry. **Avg. farm (1980):** 4,207 acres. **Avg. value of farm per acre:** $112.

Highway expenditures per capita (1979): $175.72. **Persons per motor vehicle:** 1.22. **Minimum age for driver's license:** 15. **Gasoline tax:** 9¢ per gallon. **Diesel tax:** 9¢ per gallon. **Motor vehicle deaths (1978):** 54.5 per 100,000 people.

Birthrate (1978): 19.7 per 1,000 people. **Infant mortality rate per 1,000 births (1978):** 14.1. **Physicians per 100,000 pop. (1978):** 153. **Dentists per 100,000 pop. (1978):** 41. **Acceptable hospital beds (1978):** 5.00 per 1,000 people. **State expenditures per capita for health and hospitals (1979):** $87.65.

Education expenditures (1976-77): $540.21 per capita annually. **No. of pupils in public schools (1979):** 272,000. **No. of institutions of higher learning (1978-79):** 19. **Public school expenditure per pupil in attendance (1977-78):** $1,703. **Avg. salary of public school teachers (1978-79):** $16,720. **No. full-time teachers**

(1979): 14,700. **Educational attainment of adult population (1976):** 12.5 median yrs. of school completed; 5.7% with less than 5 years of education; 15.3% with 4 yrs. of college.

Telephones (1978): 47 per 100 people. **State Chamber of Commerce:** Association of Commerce and Industry of New Mexico, 117 Quincy, N.E., Albuquerque, New Mexico 87108.

NEW YORK

New York is a state of superlatives, ideally located and richly endowed. In many respects, it is a nerve center of the nation, a major marketplace, and a national leader in manufacturing, finance, fashion, art, and communications. Second to California in population, New York is the region that George Washington foresaw as a "seat of empire"—hence its nickname, the Empire State. New York City, the nation's largest city, was the first U.S. capital (1789-90), and Washington was first inaugurated (1789) there.

Roughly triangular in shape, the state has a highly diversified terrain, with many lakes, wooded hills, and fertile valleys. Most of the area south of the Mohawk Valley falls within the province of the Appalachian Plateau, which covers more than half the state and slopes upward from northwest to southeast. New York's land features include the scenic Adirondack Mountains in the north and the Catskill range in the south, as well as imposing Niagara Falls. New York is the only state to border both the Atlantic Ocean and the Great Lakes.

Florentine explorer Giovanni da Verrazano is thought to have discovered New York by entering New York Bay in 1524. In 1609 Henry Hudson, an Englishman in the employ of the Dutch, sailed up the river bearing his name and the same year Samuel de Champlain discovered what is now Lake Champlain. The Dutch West India Company began (1624) settlement of the region, then called New Netherland, at Fort Orange (now Albany). Soon after, Governor Peter Minuit is said to have bought Manhattan Island from the Indians for trinkets worth about $24.

Indian troubles, misgovernment, and other woes hindered the colony's development. As a countermeasure, the Dutch began (1629) the "patroon" (landholder's) system that tended to concentrate economic and governmental power in the hands of a few. Squabbling broke out among the patroons, other settlers, and the home company, and Minuit was recalled (1631) for granting the patroons undue privileges. He then entered the service of Sweden; its colony (New Sweden), along the Delaware River south of Dutch interests, was viewed by the Dutch as a territorial threat. Minuit's successors—Wouter Van Twiller and Willem Kieft—were failures, but Peter Stuyvesant for a time did better. In 1655 he captured New Sweden for the Dutch and reorganized New Amsterdam (now New York City). Stuyvesant was a strict Calvinist whose tactics often provoked resentment.

Meanwhile, English penetration of Long Island and the southeastern part of what is now the mainland state was steadily progressing. In the north and west of the state, Canadian French allied themselves with the Huron Indians, but met with hostility from the Iroquois. Comprised of five tribes confederated about 1570, the Iroquois greatly influenced the struggle for control of the region between France and England that ensued after the Dutch surrender (1664) of the land to the British. New Netherland thus became the colonies New York and New Jersey, granted by King Charles II to his brother, the Duke of York (later James II). The Dutch recaptured New York in 1673, but had to yield it again a year later.

The period was marked by the development of English governmental institutions, amid a welter of conflicts and confrontations. A popular legislative assembly was formed in 1683, after years of struggle by townspeople wanting a meaningful voice in their government; but two years later the assembly was dissolved by James II. In 1686 the king sought to combine New York, New Jersey, and the New England colonies under the vice-regal authority of governor general Edmund Andros, but Andros was very unpopular, and when the king was dethroned in England in 1688, Andros was forced out of power by irate citizens. New York City merchant Jacob Leisler, hoping to foster more democratic government, then seized control, but was soon replaced by a royal governor and executed.

New York played a major role in the French and Indian Wars (1689-1763) in which France was helped by Algonquian Indians, and the Iroquois aided the English. The region also saw much action in the American Revolution and the War of 1812. (Statehood dates from 1788.) With the opening of the Erie Canal (1825), which linked the Hudson and the Great Lakes, the state entered an era of great prosperity, reinforced a few years later by the massive industrial demands of the Civil War. The state contributed more men (nearly 500,000), supplies, and money to the Union cause than any other.

The postwar period was marked by continued industrialization, large-scale immigration, and a corrupt political climate that often led to ineffective reform pressures: it was the notorious era of Boss Tweed and Tammany Hall. The most successful reform efforts were those made between World Wars I and II.

Recent important state developments include a $1 billion state office building complex called the Empire State Plaza in Albany; the Artpark near Niagara Falls, an area devoted to the visual and performing arts, with summer artists-in-residence; and the expansion of the higher education system. The State University of New York is the largest higher education system in the country, with 21 campuses throughout the state and an enrollment of over 225,000.

In 1978, residents of the Love Canal area in Niagara Falls learned they were living on top of a chemical time-bomb. Leakage from toxic wastes dumped 30 years before by the Hooker Chemical Corp., forced 239 families to evacuate the area. In May 1980, the Environmental Protection Agency revealed that 30 percent of Love Canal residents suffered from chromosome damage linked to higher incidences of miscarriages, birth defects and cancer. However, in 1981 New York State health officials reported that cancer rates were no higher among Love Canal residents than among other Niagara Falls residents.

Full name: State of New York. **Origin of name:** In honor of the Duke of York. **Inhabitant:** New Yorker. **Capital:** Albany. **State motto:** Excelsior (Ever Upward). **Flag:** State coat of arms on blue field. **Seal:** Coat of arms surrounded with legend "The Great Seal of State of New York." Coat of arms has figures representing Liberty & Justice, a typical New York river scene & an eagle perched on globe. **Flower:** Rose. **Bird:** Bluebird. **Tree:** Sugar maple. **Gem:** Garnet. **Song:** "I Love New York." **Nickname:** Empire State.

Governor: Hugh L. Carey. **Annual salary:** $85,000. **Term:** 4 years. **Current term expires:** Dec. 1982. **Voting requirements:** 18 yrs. old & U.S. citizen; resident of state and county for 30 days; registered. **U.S. Congressmen:** 39 (1980 reapportionment: 34). **Entered Union:** 1788 (11th state).

Location & boundaries: Middle Atlantic state; bounded on the north by the St. Lawrence River & Canada; on the east by Vermont,

Massachusetts & Connecticut; on the south by the Atlantic Ocean, New Jersey, the Delaware River & Pennsylvania; & on the west by Pennsylvania, Lake Erie, Niagara River, Lake Ontario & Canada. **Total area:** 49,576 sq. mi. (ranks 30th). **Extreme length (exclusive of Long Island):** 20 mi. **Extreme breadth:** 310 mi. **Coastline:** 127 mi. on Atlantic; 371 mi. on Lakes Ontario & Erie. **Chief rivers:** St. Lawrence, Hudson, Mohawk. **Major lakes:** Finger Lakes, Champlain, Erie, Ontario. **No. of counties:** 62.

Population (1980 census): 17,557,288 (ranks 2nd). **Pop. increase (1970-80):** – 3.8%. **Largest cities:** New York, Buffalo, Rochester, Yonkers, Syracuse. **Pop. density:** 354.1 per sq. mi. (ranks 6th). **Pop. distribution: White—**13,961,106; **Black—**2,401,842; **Am. Indian, Eskimo and Aleut—**38,732; **Asian and Pacific Islander—**310,531; **Other—**845,077; **Spanish origin—**1,659,245. **Marriage rate (1978):** 7.7 per 1,000 people. **Divorce rate:** 3.3 per 1,000 people.

State finances (1979). Revenue: $25,181,000,000. **Expenditures:** $22,708,000,000. **State taxes:** $659.21 per capita. **State personal income tax:** Yes. **Public debt (1979):** $1,302.29 per capita. **Federal aid (1980):** $545.03 per capita. **Personal income (1980):** $10,143.

Sectors of the economy (% of labor force employed in 1970): Manufacturing (24%), Wholesale and retail trade (20%), Government (17%), Services (8%), Educational Services (8%), Construction (5%). **Leading products:** printing & publishing, apparel, machinery, instruments, transportation equipment, food items. **Minerals:** cement, stone, sand & gravel, salt. **Agricultural products:** dairy items, poultry, fruit, vegetables. **Fishing:** clams, scallops, flounder. **Avg. farm (1980):** 223 acres. **Avg. value of farm per acre:** $681.

Highway expenditures per capita (1979): $58.66. **Persons per motor vehicle:** 2.13. **Minimum age for driver's license:** 17. **Gasoline tax:** 8¢ per gallon. **Diesel tax:** 10¢ per gallon. **Motor vehicle deaths (1978):** 13.8 per 100,000 people.

Birthrate (1978): 13.2 per 1,000 people. **Infant mortality rate per 1,000 births (1978):** 14.0. **Physicians per 100,000 pop. (1978):** 257. **Dentists per 100,000 pop. (1978):** 72. **Acceptable hospital beds (1978):** 7.65 per 1,000 people. **State expenditures per capita for health and hospitals (1979):** $101.94.

Education expenditures (1976-77): $538.02 per capita annually. **No. of pupils in public schools (1979):** 3,020,000. **No. of institutions of higher learning (1978-79):** 286. **Public school expenditure per pupil in attendance (1977-78):** $2,944. **Avg. salary of public school teachers (1978-79):** $18,980. **No. of full-time teachers (1979):** 187,800. **Educational attainment of adult population (1976):** 12.5 median yrs. of school completed: 3.0% with less than 5 years of education; 16.0% with 4 yrs. of college.

Telephones (1978): 53 per 100 people. **State Chamber of Commerce:** Empire State Chamber of Commerce, Inc., 150 State Street, Albany, New York 12207.

NORTH CAROLINA

One of the 13 Colonies and the Southeast's foremost industrial state, North Carolina presents an unusual amalgam of tradition and progress. It is a leader in both small-farm agriculture and business-applied research, and the nation's major producer of tobacco and tobacco products. The state also ranks high as a producer of textiles, bricks, wood products, and seafood. The first sustained airplane flight, by Orville and Wilbur Wright, took place (1903) near Kitty Hawk. Today, the state boasts of its famous "Research Triangle" at the University of North Carolina, Duke University, and North Carolina State University; the schools use their pooled resources to assist industry.

The state is topographically similar to South Carolina, sharing the same three principal land regions: (from east to west) the Atlantic Coastal Plain, the Piedmont Plateau, and the Blue Ridge Mountains. Mount Mitchell is the highest peak east of the Mississippi. Beyond the state's coastline are the islands, reefs, sheltered sounds, dunes, and capes of the Outer Banks, including Capes Fear

and Hatteras—the latter so treacherous to ships that it is often called the graveyard of the Atlantic. About 60 percent of the state is forested.

The headwaters of the scenic New River in North Carolina were saved from inundation by power company dams in legislation enacted in Congress in 1976 and backed by every major environmental group in the country. The river is considered one of the oldest in the Western Hemisphere.

Much of North Carolina's early history is shared with South Carolina, of which it was a part until 1712. Highlights of this period include Sir Walter Raleigh's unsuccessful attempts (1585, 1587) to establish a colony on Roanoke Island. Although it lasted only about a year, Raleigh's initial settlement was the first English colony in the New World; when all members of his second settlement (1587-?) disappeared, it came to be called the "Lost Colony"; among the missing was Virginia Dare, first child of English parentage born in America.

Among the region's problems were Culpeper's Rebellion (1677), involving colonists angered by the English Navigation Acts; and the Cary Rebellion (1708), brought about by Quakers and other dissenters who refused to support the established Anglican church. In 1705, French Huguenots from Virginia established North Carolina's first permanent settlement at Bath.

Growth in the Carolinas was slow. Swamps and dense forests made land communication difficult, and there were serious Indian troubles, especially during the Tuscarora War (1711-13). Pirates, too, were a hindrance, often menacing the colony's seabound trade; the slaying (1718) of the infamous "Blackbeard" (Edward Teach) in a battle near Ocracoke Island eased the problem. From 1712 to 1729, the proprietors appointed separate governors to administer North and South Carolina. A bitter North Carolina-Virginia boundary dispute was settled in 1728. Dissatisfied with the proprietary system, England eventually made (1729) the region a royal colony, a move that marked a period of progress in which farming and industry expanded as the population rose.

North Carolina contributed troops and materials to help England in its various colonial wars, while a persistent east-west sectionalism began to develop; this rift was caused by sharp differences in geography, politics, economics, and religion. Indian troubles were virtually ended in 1761 by a treaty with the Cherokees, but their final removal from the area did not begin until 1835. In 1768 irate back-country farmers, protesting taxes they considered excessive, organized the short-lived Regulator Movement for reform. The insurgents were eventually suppressed (1771) at Alamance by the provincial militia.

During the American Revolution, there was relatively little fighting on the state's soil, but many North Carolinians saw action elsewhere. In 1779 North Carolina annexed an area of present-day Tennessee settled by the Watauga Association, which lay immediately beyond North Carolina's present border. North Carolina administered the region until 1784, when it ceded its claim to the United States. The "Watauga" settlers then established the independent state of Franklin. Failing to gain official recognition, the new state's territory was again absorbed in 1789 by North Carolina, which later that same year ceded it once more to the Federal government; North Carolina's statehood dates from that year.

From 1815 to 1835, North Carolina languished in backwardness and apathy, and came to be called the "Rip Van Winkle State"; this period was followed until 1860 by one of progress, which saw a

resurgence of political democracy and a lessening of unproductive sectionalism.

Despite the presence of considerable pro-Union and antislavery sentiment, North Carolina joined the Confederacy after the Civil War began. During the conflict, the port of Wilmington became a haven for Confederate blockade-runners. In the postwar period, Reconstruction was followed by the return of white supremacy and a suffrage amendment (1900) that again disenfranchised the Negro.

Among modern North Carolina's most pressing preoccupations is the continued strengthening and diversification of its economy, to curb reliance upon any single factor, such as tobacco. Another task is the peaceable achievement of racial integration. A majority of the rural and small-city school districts in the state are headed toward complete desegregation, but in the larger cities, such as Charlotte, Raleigh, Winston-Salem, and Durham, breaking down the dual systems has been difficult because there are more all-black schools and more rigid residential patterns.

The U.S. Supreme Court, in an historic ruling in the spring of 1971, upheld U.S. District Judge James B. McMillan's ruling that busing was a legitimate tool to use in ending racial segregation. The decision was applied to several school districts and by the fall, few racially identifiable schools remained in the state.

A conflict between extremist groups in Greensboro resulted in the deaths of five persons in November 1979. The slayings occurred at an anti-Ku Klux Klan rally sponsored by the Workers' Viewpoint Organization (WVO), a left-wing group also known as the Communist Workers party, U.S.A. As the protest rally began in a black area of Greensboro, Klansmen and American Nazi party members appeared and taunted the demonstrators. The two groups fought with each other and exchanged gunfire resulting in the deaths. Police arrested 15 Klansmen and American Nazis for allegedly killing five of the anti-Klan group; some were indicted for murder or felonious rioting in December. On November 17, 1980, a trial jury in Greensboro acquitted the six defendants of the charges.

Full name: State of North Carolina. **Origin of name:** In honor of Charles I of England. **Inhabitant:** North Carolinian. **Capital:** Raleigh. **State motto:** Esse Quam Videri (To Be Rather Than to Seem). **Flag:** Gold scrolls & NC (separated by white star) on blue bar; a red & white horizontal bar to right. **Seal:** Liberty holds scroll inscribed "Constitution"; seated figure of plenty; date "May 20, 1775." **Flower:** Dogwood. **Bird:** Cardinal. **Tree:** Pine. **Song:** "The Old North State." **Nickname:** Tar Heel State.

Governor: James B. Hunt, Jr. **Annual salary:** $55,104. **Term:** 4 years. **Current term expires:** Jan. 1985. **Voting requirements:** 18 yrs. old & U.S. citizen; resident of state and district, 30 days. **U.S. Congressmen:** 11. **Entered Union:** 1789 (12th state).

Location & boundaries: South Atlantic state; bounded on the north by Virginia; on the east by the Atlantic Ocean; on the south by South Carolina & Georgia; & on the west by Tennessee. **Total area:** 52,586 sq. mi. (ranks 28th). **Extreme length:** 503 mi. **Extreme breadth:** 187 mi. **Coastline:** 301 mi. **Chief rivers:** Yadkin, Cape Fear, Neuse, Roanoke. **Major lakes:** Fontana, Mattamuskeet, Norman. **No. of counties:** 100.

Population (1980 census): 5,874,429 (ranks 10th). **Pop. increase (1970-80):** 15.5%. **Largest cities:** Charlotte, Greensboro, Raleigh, Winston-Salem. **Pop. density:** 111.7 per sq. mi. (ranks 17th). **Pop. distribution:** White—4,453,010; Black—1,316,050; Am. Indian, Eskimo and Aleut—64,635; Asian and Pacific Islander—21,168; Other—19,566; Spanish origin—56,607. **Marriage rate (1978):** 7.9 per 1,000 people. **Divorce rate:** 4.8 per 1,000 people.

State finances (1979). Revenue: $5,537,000,000. **Expenditures:** $5,249,000,000. **State taxes:** $519.97 per capita. **State personal income tax:** Yes. **Public debt (1979):** $197.53 per capita. **Federal aid (1980):** $328.11 per capita. **Personal income (1980):** $7,852.

Sectors of the economy (% of labor force employed in 1970): Manufacturing (36%), Wholesale and retail trade (18%), Government (13%), Services (8%), Educational Services (7%), Construction (7%). **Leading products:** textile items, tobacco items, furniture & fixtures, food items, electrical machinery, chemicals, apparel. **Agricultural products:** broilers, dairy items, tobacco, corn, soybeans. **Fishing:** shrimp, menhaden, crabs. **Avg. farm (1980):** 126 acres. **Avg. value of farm per acre:** $885.

Highway expenditures per capita (1979): $107.57. **Persons per motor vehicle:** 1.26. **Minimum age for driver's license:** 16. **Gasoline tax:** 12¢ per gallon. **Diesel tax:** 12¢ per gallon. **Motor vehicle deaths (1978):** 23.9 per 100,000 people.

Birthrate (1978): 14.8 per 1,000 people. **Infant mortality rate per 1,000 births (1978):** 16.6. **Physicians per 100,000 pop. (1978):** 150. **Dentists per 100,000 pop. (1978):** 38. **Acceptable hospital beds (1978):** 5.75 per 1,000 people. **State expenditures per capita for health and hospitals (1979):** $80.35.

Education expenditures (1976-77): $437.54 per capita annually. **No. of pupils in public schools (1979):** 1,135,000. **No. of institutions of higher learning (1978-79):** 126. **Public school expenditure per pupil in attendance (1977-78):** $1,507. **Avg. salary of public school teachers (1978-79):** $13,817. **No. full-time teachers (1979):** 58,400. **Educational attainment of adult population (1976):** 12.2 median yrs. of school completed; 6.4% with less than 5 years of education; 11.8% with 4 yrs. of college.

Telephones (1978): 53 per 100 people. **State Chamber of Commerce:** North Carolina Citizens Association, P.O. Box 2508, Insurance Building, Raleigh, North Carolina 27602.

NORTH DAKOTA

North Dakota is the most rural of the states, with more than 90 percent of the land in farms. Agriculture and mining are two of its economic mainstays. Only Kansas produces more wheat, and the state's coal and oil reserves are among the nation's largest. Manufacturing is limited but growing, with food processing leading the way. Tourism is aided by excellent hunting and fishing and such attractions as the Theodore Roosevelt National Park in the Badlands and numerous historic sites including Fort Abercrombie (established 1857), the first U.S. military post in the region. A number of rodeos and fairs take place in the state in the summer and early fall.

Three main regions make up the state: the Red River Valley, comprising a ten-to-forty-mile-wide strip along the eastern border; the Young Drift Plains, just west of this strip; and, covering the state's southwestern half, the Great Plains (also known locally as the Missouri Plateau). The state's continental climate is marked by wide temperature variation, light-to-moderate precipitation, and considerable windiness.

North Dakota's prestatehood history is shared with that of South Dakota. The first Europeans to explore the area were the Sieur de la Vérendrye and sons who visited in 1738, four years before their travels in South Dakota. First settlement attempts were made (1812) at Pembina by Scotch and Irish families. After statehood (1889) separated it from its sister state, North Dakota experienced a spurt in population, growing from about 191,000 in 1890 to more than 577,000 in only 20 years.

The Nonpartisan League was founded in 1915 by farmers who advocated state involvement in the storage and processing of grain to break the power of out-of-state interests, increased funds for rural schools, and tax incentives to improve farms. The legislature which took office in 1919 was controlled by persons elected with the League's support; they enacted the League's educational and tax programs, and established a state-owned bank, a state-owned flour mill, and a state-owned grain elevator.

Work was begun in 1968 on the first stage of an irrigation system to carry water through nearly 2,000 miles of canals to irrigate a million acres of North Dakota soil. The entire project is expected to cost over $500 million. The Lonetree Reservoir and Dam project has come under fire from the Federal Government, the State of Minnesota, and the Canadian government, so work has been halted on the partially completed construction.

The $9 million Omega all-weather navigation system permitting any ship or aircraft with a proper receiver to determine its exact position was completed near Lamoure in 1973. Unique in North America, it is one of eight in the world.

In 1975, legislature was 34th in the nation to ratify the ERA constitutional amendment. Legislature also passed an education reciprocity plan whereby resident students of North Dakota and Minnesota may attend school in either state without paying "out of state" tuition.

The recent energy crisis resulted in the exploitation, chiefly by strip mining, of the coal reserves in the western part of the state, over the objections of environmentalists.

President Reagan approved an important project for North Dakota on August 5, 1981. A $2-billion coal gasification plant is to be built at Beulah in Mercer County. The facility will convert lignite from the extensive deposits nearby into synthetic gas for transmission throughout the nation.

Full name: State of North Dakota. **Origin of name:** From the Sioux meaning "Alliance with Friends." **Inhabitant:** North Dakotan. **Capital:** Bismarck. **State motto:** Liberty & Union, Now & Forever, One & Inseparable. **Flag:** Eagle with American shield on breast, holding sheaf of arrows in left claw & olive branch in right & carrying in beak a banner inscribed "E Pluribus Unum"; above eagle is sunburst enclosing 13 stars, beneath is scroll inscribed "North Dakota"—all on blue field with yellow fringe. **Seal:** Elm tree & setting sun; plow, sheaves of wheat & anvil symbolize agriculture; bow & arrows & Indian hunting a buffalo represent North Dakota's history. **Flower:** Wild prairie rose. **Bird:** Western meadowlark. **Tree:** American elm. **Song:** "North Dakota Hymn." **Nickname:** Flickertail State and The Sioux State.

Governor: Allen I. Olson. **Annual salary:** $47,000. **Term:** 4 years. **Current term expires:** Jan. 1985. **Voting requirements:** 18 yrs. old & U.S. citizen; resident of state and precinct 30 days. **U.S. Congressmen:** 1. **Entered Union:** 1889 (39th state).

Location & boundaries: Northern Midwestern state: bounded on the north by Canada; on the east by Minnesota at the Red River of the North; on the south by South Dakota; & on the west by Montana. **Total area:** 70,664 sq. mi. (ranks 17th). **Extreme length:** 360 mi. **Extreme breadth:** 210 mi. **Chief rivers:** Red River of the North, Missouri, Sheyenne. **Major lakes:** Devils, Sakakawea Reservoir. **No. of counties:** 53.

Population (1980 census): 652,695 (ranks 46th). **Pop. increase (1970-80):** 5.6%. **Largest cities:** Fargo, Bismarck, Grand Forks, Minot. **Pop. density:** 9.2 per sq. mi. (ranks 45th). **Pop. distribution:** White—625,536; Black—2,568; Am. Indian, Eskimo and Aleut—20,157; Asian and Pacific Islander—1,979; Other—2,455; Spanish origin—3,903. **Marriage rate (1978):** 8.7 per 1,000 people. **Divorce rate:** 3.2 per 1,000 people.

State finances (1979). Revenue: $823,000,000. **Expenditures:** $777,000,000. **State taxes:** $494.35 per capita. **State personal income tax:** Yes. **Public debt (1979):** $199.07 per capita. **Federal aid (1980):** $524.90 per capita. **Personal income (1980):** $8,556.

Sectors of the economy (% of labor force employed in 1970): Wholesale and retail trade (23%), Government (19%), Educational Services (11%), Services (7%), Construction (6%), Manufacturing (5%). **Leading products:** food items, printing & publishing, machinery. **Minerals:** petroleum, sand & gravel, natural gas, lignite coal. **Agricultural products:** cattle, dairy items, poultry, potatoes, sugar beets, wheat, barley, hay. **Avg. farm (1980):** 1,042 acres. **Avg. value of farm per acre:** $352.

Highway expenditures per capita (1979): $195.97. **Persons per motor vehicle:** 1.03. **Minimum age for driver's license:** 16. **Gas-**oline tax: 8¢ per gallon. **Diesel tax:** 8¢ per gallon. **Motor vehicle deaths (1978):** 27.9 per 100,000 people.

Birthrate (1978): 17.3 per 1,000 people. **Infant mortality rate per 1,000 births (1978):** 13.5. **Physicians per 100,000 pop. (1978):** 128. **Dentists per 100,000 pop. (1978):** 46. **Acceptable hospital beds (1978):** 8.88 per 1,000 people. **State expenditures per capita for health and hospitals (1979):** $66.44.

Education expenditures (1976-77): $494.22 per capita annually. **No. of pupils in public schools (1979):** 119,000. **No. of institutions of higher learning (1978-79):** 16. **Public school expenditure per pupil in attendance (1977-78):** $1,766. **Avg. salary of public school teachers (1978-79):** $12,344. **No. full-time teachers (1979):** 7,900. **Educational attainment of adult population (1976):** 12.5 median yrs. of school completed: 1.7% with less than 5 years of education; 12.2% with 4 yrs. of college.

Telephones (1978): 56 per 100 people. **State Chamber of Commerce:** Greater North Dakota Association—State Chamber of Commerce, P.O. Box 2467, 107 Roberts Street, Fargo, North Dakota 58108.

OHIO

A leading industrial state and the first to be carved out of the Northwest Territory, Ohio enjoys a variety of important natural resources and a strategic location near many rich markets. Predominantly a producer of iron and steel and their products, the state also ranks high in mining and agriculture (especially livestock). It is among the most populous of states, and only Virginia has produced more U.S. Presidents than Ohio, which claims eight.

Four land regions make up the state: the Appalachian Plateau, making up almost all of the eastern half; the fertile Till Plains, constituting the bulk of the western half; a five-to-50-mile-wide strip of the Great Lakes Plain bordering Lake Erie; and, in the south, an extension of Kentucky's Bluegrass Region forming a small wedge between the plateau and the lowlands. The climate is generally temperate but marked somewhat by extremes and sudden changes. Many dams and reservoirs have been built as a bulwark against disasters such as the floods of 1913 that killed about 500 persons and caused some $150 million in property loss.

Early Amerindian peoples are thought to have lived in the Ohio region between 5,000 and 7,000 years ago, followed by the Adena and Hopewell Mound Builders (c. 800 B.C.—A.D. 1300).

Algonquian and Iroquois Indians were living in the region when the first Europeans arrived. Robert Cavelier, Sieur de La Salle, passed through about 1670, providing a basis for French claims to the region that were sharply contested by the British, who claimed all the territory extending westward from their colonies. Victory in the French and Indian Wars (1689-1763) gave England the upper hand until the American Revolution. Massachusetts, Connecticut, and Virginia land claims in the area were resolved by the Northwest Ordinance (1787). A band of New Englanders led by General Rufus Putnam established (1788) the first permanent white settlement at Marietta. Early settlers were beset by serious Indian troubles that were largely ended after troops under General Anthony Wayne won (1794) the Battle of Fallen Timbers, near present-day Toledo. The Division Act of 1800 created the Indiana Territory out of the western part of the region, then still called the Northwest Territory. In 1803, Ohio entered the Union. A border dispute with the Territory of Michigan gave rise (1835) to the "Toledo War" but, before any actual fighting broke out, Congress awarded the area—about 520 square miles along Lake Erie—to Ohio. At present another land controversy between the two states—over a 200-square-mile area

beneath Lake Erie that is rich in oil and natural gas—remains to be resolved. The state's southern boundary, the Ohio River, has been receding gradually north- and westward for centuries. Fortunately for Ohio, the U.S. Supreme Court ruled in January 1980 that the boundary is to remain fixed at its original position regardless of the river's shifting course.

Ohio was in the forefront of events leading to the Civil War. The abolition movement began at St. Clairsville, and many Ohioans helped slaves escape to Canada via the Underground Railroad. Although there was relatively little actual fighting on its soil, Ohio contributed heavily to the Union cause. In the postwar period the state rapidly emerged as an industrial power while retaining its agricultural status. In the years just prior to the turn of the century, big business became inordinately involved in Ohio politics, causing discontent among the less well-off. Labor troubles developed that culminated in Jacob S. Coxey's march on Washington, D.C. (1894) and a voting shift toward reform candidates. More recent troubles of this nature include major strikes during the mid-1930s, 1949, and 1959.

Tourism, aided by a surge in new highway construction, has developed into a valuable revenue-producer, now bringing in over $3 billion a year. Attractions include numerous state park and recreation areas, prehistoric Indian mounds, and historic sites such as Commodore Perry's Victory and International Peace Memorial at Put-in-Bay on Lake Erie, which commemorates his vital victory there during the War of 1812. Annual events include the All-American Soap Box Derby, held in Akron each summer.

In 1979 Honda Motor Company Ltd. of Japan opened a motorcycle assembly plant (its first in the U.S.) northwest of Columbus. At nearby Marysville, Honda plans to construct an auto assembly complex to employ about 2,000 persons. It is scheduled to open in 1982 or 1983.

Full name: State of Ohio. **Origin of name:** From Iroquois name meaning "Great." **Inhabitant:** Ohioan. **Capital:** Columbus. **State motto:** With God, All Things Are Possible. **Flag:** Pennant-shaped flag; white-bordered red circle & white stars on a blue triangle, with red & white bars. **Seal:** Sheaf of wheat; bundle of arrows; sun rising behind mountains, indicating Ohio was first state west of Allegheny Mountains. **Flower:** Scarlet carnation. **Bird:** Cardinal. **Tree:** Buckeye. **Song:** "Beautiful Ohio." **Nickname:** Buckeye State.

Governor: James A. Rhodes. **Annual salary:** $60,000. **Term:** 4 years. **Current term expires:** Jan. 1983. **Voting requirements:** 18 yrs. as of election day & U.S. citizen; resident of state 30 days. **U.S. Congressmen:** 23 (1980 reapportionment: 21). **Entered Union:** 1803 (17th state).

Location & boundaries: Midwestern state; bounded on the north by Michigan & Lake Erie; on the east by Pennsylvania & West Virginia; on the south by West Virginia, Kentucky & the Ohio River & on the west by Indiana. **Total area:** 41,222 sq. mi. (ranks 35th). **Extreme length:** 230 mi. **Extreme breadth:** 210 mi. **Shoreline:** 312 mi. **Chief rivers:** Ohio, Miami, Muskingum. **Major lakes:** Erie, Grand. **No. of counties:** 88.

Population (1980 census): 10,797,419 (ranks 6th). **Pop. increase (1970-80):** 1.3%. **Largest cities:** Cleveland, Columbus, Cincinnati, Toledo. **Pop. density:** 261.9 per sq. mi. (ranks 8th). **Pop. distribution:** White—9,597,266; Black—1,076,734; Am. Indian, Eskimo and Aleut—12,240; Asian and Pacific Islander—47,813; Other—63,366; Spanish origin—119,880. **Marriage rate (1978):** 9.7 per 1,000 people. **Divorce rate:** 5.5 per 1,000 people.

State finances (1979). Revenue: $11,435,000,000. **Expenditures:** $9,762,000,000. **State taxes:** $430.52 per capita. **State personal income tax:** Yes. **Public debt (1979):** $349.01 per capita. **Federal aid (1980):** $317.97 per capita. **Personal income (1980):** $9,398.

Sectors of the economy (% of labor force employed in 1970): Manufacturing (36%), Wholesale and retail trade (19%), Government (13%), Educational Services (7%), Services (6%), Construction (5%). **Leading products:** transportation equipment, primary & fabricated metals, machinery, rubber & plastic items. **Minerals:** bituminous coal, limestone, sand & gravel, salt, oil. **Agricultural products:** milk, hogs, cattle & calves, corn, soybeans. **Fishing:** yellow perch, catfish, white bass, yellow pike. **Avg. farm (1980):** 169 acres. **Avg. value of farm per acre:** $1,713.

Highway expenditures per capita (1979): $85.24. **Persons per motor vehicle:** 1.44. **Minimum age for driver's license:** 16. **Gasoline tax:** 10.3¢ per gallon. **Diesel tax:** 10.3¢ per gallon. **Motor vehicle deaths (1978):** 19.1 per 100,000 people.

Birthrate (1978): 15.0 per 1,000 people. **Infant mortality rate per 1,000 births (1978):** 13.3. **Physicians per 100,000 pop. (1978):** 156. **Dentists per 100,000 pop. (1978):** 47. **Acceptable hospital beds (1978):** 5.45 per 1,000 people. **State expenditures per capita for health and hospitals (1979):** $71.90.

Education expenditures (1976-77): $454.97 per capita annually. **No. of pupils in public schools (1979):** 2,052,000. **No. of institutions of higher learning (1978-79):** 133. **Public school expenditure per pupil in attendance (1977-78):** $1,704. **Avg. salary of public school teachers (1978-79):** $14,840. **No. full-time teachers (1979):** 113,600. **Educational attainment of adult population (1976):** 12.4 median yrs. of school completed: 1.7% with less than 5 years of education; 11.5% with 4 yrs. of college.

Telephones (1978): 55 per 100 people. **State Chamber of Commerce:** Ohio Chamber of Commerce, Huntington Bank Building, 17 South High Street, 8th Floor, Columbus, Ohio 43215.

OKLAHOMA

Oil-rich Oklahoma, the nation's Indian Territory in the early 19th century, has the largest Indian population of any state (1980). Generally considered an agricultural state, even though the value of its manufacturing and mining output exceeds cash farm revenue, the state earns more from livestock and livestock products (especially cattle) than it does from crops. Manufacturing, although becoming more diverse, is still based largely on the processing of the state's farm and mineral products. Most industry is located in and around Oklahoma City and Tulsa, which also rank among the world's foremost gas and oil centers.

Topographically, the state is largely a rolling plain sloping from northwest to southeast, with a mean altitude of 1,300 feet. About three-fourths of the state, especially the central area, consists of the Osage Plains section of the Central Lowlands. The Great Plains region, making up the northwestern panhandle, slopes from 4,973 feet at Black Mesa in the west (the state's highest point) to about 287 feet in the extreme Southeast. Vast wheat fields and broad grazing lands characterize much of the terrain, punctuated by such features as the Wichita, Arbuckle, Ouachita, and Ozark mountains in the southwest, southcenter, southeast and northeast, respectively. A segment of the West Gulf Coastal Plains covers the extreme southeastern corner of the state. A quarter of the land is forested, but only pine and hardwood in the southeast are commercially significant.

Various bands of buffalo-hunting Indians roamed the Oklahoma region before the coming of the first European, Spanish explorer Coronado, who crossed (1541) what is today the Oklahoma panhandle. All the area except it came under U.S. sovereignty via the Louisiana Purchase (1803), and a year later that part of the purchase north of present-day Louisiana was made the District of Louisiana, governed as part of Indiana Territory. The district became in turn the Territory of Louisiana (1805) and the Missouri Territory (1812).

In 1819, Arkansas Territory, including the present state of Oklahoma, was formed from a part of Missouri Territory. A few years later, the U.S. Government designated part of the region Indian Territory and used it for the forcible resettlement of

OHIO

MILES
0 10 20 30 40 50

KILOMETERS
0 10 20 30 40 50

⊕ State Capital
⊙ County Seats

State Capital
County Seats

⊕ Copyright HAMMOND INCORPORATED, Maplewood, N.J.

Longitude West of Greenwich

the Five Civilized Tribes (Cherokee, Choctaw, Chickasaw, Creek, and Seminole), who had been living in relatively close contact with white men of the southeastern states for more than 100 years. Some of these Indians pursued farming in the traditional Southern mold, even maintaining slaves. When the Civil War erupted, the Indians were caught up in it, fighting on both sides and suffering invasions from both Confederate and Union forces.

After the war, the five tribes were punished collectively for those Indians who had supported the Confederacy; the western part of the Indian Territory was taken from them, and much of it was assigned to other tribes in the country that the government wanted resettled. White encroachments, led by Kansas-bound Texas cattlemen, soon followed despite laws and Indian treaties; a number of cattle trails, including the famed Chisholm Trail, were forged across the state. The first railroad across the region (built 1870-72) brought still more white settlers. The influx was legalized when a large strip of land was opened for settlement on April 22, 1889. Some of the settlers who entered before the proper time were called "sooners," giving rise to Oklahoma's nickname, the Sooner State.

The western section of present-day Oklahoma was made Oklahoma Territory in 1890, and for a time Oklahoma and Indian (the "twin") Territories existed side by side. The Indians wanted separate admission to the Union, as the state of Sequoyah, but in 1907 the territories were merged and admitted as a single state.

Oklahoma's advances in the economic sphere include expanding aerospace facilities in Tulsa, several tire manufacturing plants, one of the world's largest paper mills at Valliant in the southeastern section, and Western Electric, General Motors and Honeywell plants, the FAA center and Wilson & Co., all in Oklahoma City. The state's economy boomed during the seventies and its government finances are in excellent shape.

The Arkansas River navigation project, the largest single domestic project ever undertaken by the Army Corps of Engineers, has made Tulsa a port city via a new channel and system of locks dredged from Tulsa across Arkansas to the Mississippi River. In agriculture, conservation methods have been inaugurated since the Dust Bowl days of the 1930s and, in some areas, irrigation is used to offset frequent droughts. Wheat, hay, cotton and peanuts are the principal crops.

Tourism in recent years has boomed with an increased advertising program, with much of the emphasis put on the state parks, lodges and recreation areas located on the system of large man-made lakes. Lake Texoma and Lake O' the Cherokees are favorites. Other tourist attractions include the Will Rogers Memorial (at Claremore, near his birthplace at Oologah), the Philbrook Art Center (Tulsa), Indian City U.S.A. (near Anadarko) with authentic copies of Indian villages of the early 1800s, Tsa-La-Gi Cherokee Indian village (Tahlequah) where "The Trail of Tears" pageant depicting the Cherokee removal to Oklahoma is performed during the summer, Chickasaw National Recreation Area near Sulphur, and the National Cowboy Hall of Fame and Western Heritage Center (Oklahoma City).

In January 1980 racial violence shook the small farming and lumbering city of Idabell in the southeast corner of the state, leaving two dead.

Full name: State of Oklahoma. **Origin of name:** From Choctaw meaning "Red People." **Inhabitant:** Oklahoman. **Capital:** Oklahoma City. **State motto:** Labor Omnia Vincit (Labor Conquers All Things). **Flag:** Symbols of war & peace on a blue field. **Seal:** Indian & white man shaking hands before justice, representing cooperation of all people of state; large star has symbols of the Five Civilized Tribes from the southeastern states, forced by the government to resettle in

this region. **Flower:** Mistletoe. **Bird:** Scissor-tailed flycatcher. **Tree:** Redbud. **Song:** "Oklahoma!" **Nickname:** Sooner State.

Governor: George Nigh. **Annual salary:** $48,000. **Term:** 4 years. **Current term expires:** Jan. 1983. **Voting requirements:** 18 yrs. old & U.S. citizen; resident of state; registered with County Election Board. **U.S. Congressmen:** 6. **Entered Union:** 1907 (46th state).

Location & boundaries: South Central state; bounded on the north by Colorado & Kansas; on the east by Missouri & Arkansas; on the south by Texas & the Red River; & on the west by Texas & New Mexico. **Total area:** 69,919 sq. mi. (ranks 18th). **Extreme length:** 464 mi. **Extreme breadth:** 230 mi. **Chief rivers:** Red, Arkansas, Cimarron, Canadian. **Major lakes:** Texoma, Eufaula, Oologah Reservoir. **No. of counties:** 77.

Population (1980 census): 3,025,266 (ranks 26th). **Pop. increase (1970-80):** 18.2%. **Largest cities:** Oklahoma City, Tulsa, Lawton, Norman. **Pop. density:** 43.2 per sq. mi. (ranks 34th). **Pop. distribution:** White—2,597,783; Black—204,658; Am. Indian, Eskimo and Aleut—169,464; Asian and Pacific Islander—17,274; Other— 36,087; Spanish origin—57,413. **Marriage rate (1978):** 15.4 per 1,000 people. **Divorce rate:** 7.9 per 1,000 people.

State finances (1979). Revenue: $2,966,000,000. **Expenditures:** $2,733,000,000. **State taxes:** $524.18 per capita. **State personal income tax:** Yes. **Public debt (1979):** $522.46 per capita. **Federal aid (1980):** $349.69 per capita. **Personal income (1980):** $9,081.

Sectors of the economy (% of labor force employed in 1974): Government (20%), Manufacturing (14.4%), Wholesale & retail trade (14.8%), Services (12.7%), Educational Services (9%), Construction (4.2%). **Leading products:** food items; machinery; petroleum and coal items; stone, clay & glass items; transportation equipment; fabricated metals; apparel. **Minerals:** petroleum and coal, natural gas & natural gas liquids, cement. **Agricultural products:** cattle, dairy items, hogs, wheat, hay, sorghum grain. **Avg. farm (1980):** 486 acres. **Avg. value of farm per acre:** $522.

Highway expenditures per capita (1979): $112.33. **Persons per motor vehicle:** 1.10. **Minimum age for driver's license:** 16. **Gasoline tax:** 6.58¢ per gallon. **Diesel tax:** 6.5¢ per gallon. **Motor vehicle deaths (1978):** 31.3 per 100,000 people.

Birthrate (1978): 16.1 per 1,000 people. **Infant mortality rate per 1,000 births (1978):** 14.3. **Physicians per 100,000 pop. (1978):** 127. **Dentists per 100,000 pop. (1978):** 41. **Acceptable hospital beds (1978):** 5.78 per 1,000 people. **State expenditures per capita for health and hospitals (1979):** $54.71.

Education expenditures (1976-77): $417.04 per capita annually. **No. of pupils in public schools (1979):** 576,000. **No. of institutions of higher learning (1978-79):** 43. **Public school expenditure per pupil in attendance (1977-78):** $1,634. **Avg. salary of public school teachers (1978-79):** $12,757. **No. full-time teachers (1979):** 32,800. **Educational attainment of adult population (1976):** 12.4 median yrs. of school completed: 2.9% with less than 5 years of education; 11.7% with 4 yrs. of college.

Telephones (1978): 58 per 100 people. **State Chamber of Commerce:** Oklahoma State Chamber of Commerce, 4020 N. Lincoln Blvd., Oklahoma City, Oklahoma 73105.

OREGON

With more than 30 million acres of trees (nearly half the state's total area), Oregon is the nation's leading lumber state. Its awesome scenery includes mountains, plains, lush valleys, and immense forests. The 400-mile Pacific coast is marked by the thickly forested Coast Range and the Klamath Mountains that parallel it.

There are four other general land areas: the Cascade Mountains, the Willamette Valley between the coastal elevations and the Cascades, the Columbia Plateau, and the Basin and Range Region.

The Cascade Range is a climatic dividing line: there is mild, moist weather in the west, and in the east dry weather that is warmer in summer and colder in winter than the west's.

Except for the section in the southeast known as the Basin and Range Region, the entire area east of the Cascades is called the Columbia Plateau; this

OKLAHOMA

● State Capital   ⊛ County Seats

plateau, comprising two-thirds of the state, was formed thousands of years ago when lava gushed forth from the Earth's crust, which has since been covered by rolling plains, and, along the desolate southern edge, the Harney Desert. It was across these plains that settlers from the East came, along the Oregon Trail.

Portland, 100 miles inland, is reached from the Pacific via the Columbia River, and is one of the West Coast's major ports; the Portland area contains about half of Oregon's total population.

Oregon produces about a fifth of the nation's lumber and a majority of our plywood. Centered in the Willamette Valley, wood processing is the state's leading manufacturing industry.

There is some mining in the state, principally of nickel, gemstones, and construction materials. Agriculture, shipping, fishing (mainly for Chinook and silver salmon), metal and food processing, and tourism are also economically significant. Attractions include Hells Canyon, Mount Hood, and Crater Lake, a brilliantly blue, clear body of water that is the principal feature of the national park bearing its name; the nation's deepest lake (1,932 feet), it is six miles wide and was formed 6,600 years ago when the peak of Mount Mazama, in which the lake is set, collapsed after violent volcanic activity. Another tourist attraction is Kah-Nee-Ta Vacation Resort in the Warm Springs Indian Reservation, which was developed by 2,000 Northwest tribesmen; it offers hot mineral baths, swimming, fishing, and riding.

Chinook, Tillamook, Clackama, and Multnomah Indians were among the Oregon Country's earliest known inhabitants. Spanish seamen, sailing from Mexico to the Philippines, are thought to have been the first Europeans to sight the Oregon coast, in the 1500s and 1600s. Captain Cook, seeking the Northwest Passage to the Atlantic, charted some of the coastline in 1778. The Columbia River was discovered in 1792, and the Lewis and Clark expedition passed through the region in 1805.

The nineteenth century was marked by the conflict of British and American claims to the area that were eventually resolved by treaty in 1846. Two years later, Oregon became a territory, which until 1853 also included present-day Washington. Statehood came in 1859. In 1860 the discovery of gold in what is now Idaho turned Portland into a vital trade center for the Pacific Northwest. Transcontinental rail service came to Oregon in 1883.

In the early part of the 20th century, a series of reform measures were enacted in what came to be known as the Oregon System; this system, designed to make government more responsive to those governed, featured a referendum amendment, a direct primary, and a recall provision. Oregon women were given the vote in 1912.

The state also has developed a broad program for improving the environment and has given its Department of Environmental Quality the power to enforce the regulations. In addition, Oregon has adopted a Scenic Waterways plan for state ownership of land along many rivers in the state as well as a law for public ownership of the ocean beaches. Oregon was a pioneer in outlawing throwaway beverage containers and fluorocarbon aerosol cans. One of the first states to abolish criminal penalties for the possession of small amounts of marijuana, Oregon in 1979 legalized the sale of marijuana for legitimate medical purposes.

The great eruption of Mount St. Helens volcano in neighboring Washington on May 18, 1980, had little effect on Oregon, but the lesser eruption of May 24 sprayed dust and ash over parts of northern Oregon, damaging crops and making roads impassable.

Full name: State of Oregon. **Origin of name:** Probably from Spanish, Orejon, meaning "Big-eared men." **Inhabitant:** Oregonian. **Capital:** Salem. **State motto:** The Union. **Flag:** State seal & lettering in yellow on a blue field. **Seal:** Departing British man-of-war & arriving American merchant ship symbolize end of British influence & rise of American power; sheaf of grain, pickax & plow represent mining & agriculture. **Flower:** Oregon grape. **Bird:** Western meadowlark. **Fish:** Chinook salmon; **Rock:** Thunderegg. **Tree:** Douglas fir. **Song:** "Oregon, My Oregon." **Nickname:** Beaver State.

Governor: Victor G. Atiyeh. **Annual salary:** $55,423. **Term:** 4 years. **Current term expires:** Jan. 1983. **Voting requirements:** 18 yrs. old & U.S. citizen; must be registered and resident. **U.S. Congressmen:** 4 (1980 reapportionment: 5). **Entered Union:** 1859 (33rd state).

Location & boundaries: Pacific state; bounded on the north by the Columbia River & Washington; on the east by Idaho & the Snake River; on the south by Nevada & California; & on the west by the Pacific Ocean. **Total area:** 96,981 sq. mi. (ranks 10th). **Extreme length:** 295 mi. **Extreme breadth:** 395 mi. **Coastline:** 360 mi. **Chief rivers:** Columbia, Snake, Willamette. **Major lakes:** Upper Klamath, Malheur, Crater. **No. of counties:** 36.

Population (1980 census): 2,632,663 (ranks 30th). **Pop. increase (1970-80):** 25.9%. **Largest cities:** Portland, Eugene, Salem. **Pop. density:** 27.1 per sq. mi. (ranks 39th). **Pop. distribution:** White—2,490,192; Black—37,059; Am. Indian, Eskimo and Aleut—27,309; Asian and Pacific Islander—34,767; Other—43,336; Spanish origin—65,833. **Marriage rate (1978):** 8.6 per 1,000 people. **Divorce rate:** 6.9 per 1,000 people.

State finances (1979). Revenue: $3,499,000,000. **Expenditures:** $2,906,000,000. **State Taxes:** $547.88 per capita. **State personal income tax:** Yes. **Public debt (1979):** $1,507.23 per capita. **Federal aid (1980):** $385.58 per capita. **Personal income (1980):** $9,400.

Sectors of the economy (% of labor force employed in 1970): Wholesale and retail trade (22%), Manufacturing (21%), Government (17%), Educational Services (10%), Services (7%), Construction (6%). **Leading products:** lumber & wood items, food items, paper items, machinery, fabricated metals, printing & publishing. **Agricultural products:** wheat, livestock, barley, oats, hops, legumes, potatoes, berries, fruits, nuts, truck crops, dairy and poultry products, sugar beets, corn, green beans and peppermint. **Fishing:** salmon, tuna, bottom fish (sole, rockfish, halibut, cod, etc.) and shellfish. **Avg. farm (1980):** 610 acres. **Avg. value of farm per acre:** $320.

Highway expenditures per capita (1979): $126.06. **Persons per motor vehicle:** 1.22. **Minimum age for driver's license:** 16. **Gasoline tax:** 7¢ per gallon. **Diesel tax:** 7¢ per gallon. **Motor vehicle deaths (1978):** 28.9 per 100,000 people.

Birthrate (1978): 15.9 per 1,000 people. **Infant mortality rate per 1,000 births (1978):** 12.9. **Physicians per 100,000 pop. (1978):** 177. **Dentists per 100,000 pop. (1978):** 69. **Acceptable hospital beds (1978):** 4.40 per 1,000 people. **State expenditures per capita for health and hospitals (1979):** $72.09.

Education expenditures (1976-77): $583.62 per capita annually. **No. of pupils in public schools (1979):** 460,000. **No. of institutions of higher learning (1978-79):** 43. **Public school expenditure per pupil in attendance (1977-78):** $2,404. **Avg. salary of public school teachers (1978-79):** $15,500. **No. of full-time teachers (1979):** 25,700. **Educational attainment of adult population (1978):** 12.7 median yrs. of school completed: 1.1% with less than 5 years of education; 15.4% with 4 yrs. of college.

Telephones (1978): 56 per 100 people. **State Chamber of Commerce:** Associated Oregon Industries, Inc., P.O. Box 12519, 1149 Court Street, N.E., Salem, Oregon 97309.

PENNSYLVANIA

Called the "Keystone State" because of its central location among the 13 Colonies, Pennsylvania is today an important economic center and a rich repository of Americana. The state, which enjoys an abundant water supply, is the nation's fourth most populous, and manufacturing, mining, farming, and tourism are all important to its economy.

Pennsylvania produces nearly all the country's hard coal and a fourth of its steel. Oil is also important, although not so much so as in the 1890s; the first oil well in the world was drilled (1859) near Titusville. Dairy farming flourishes today in the northeast, as does cattle raising in the southwest; throughout the fertile, well-farmed southeast countryside can be seen the highly decorated barns of the Pennsylvania Dutch.

Pittsburgh was the home (1920) of the first radio broadcasting station, and the first electric computer was built (1945) in Philadelphia; these cities, along with Erie, provide the state with three fine ports. Philadelphia is the dominantly large city of the eastern region (as Pittsburgh is of the western).

Roughly rectangular, the state is crossed from west to east by the Erie Lowland, Appalachian Plateau (by far the largest single region), Great Appalachian Valley, Blue Ridge, Piedmont Plateau, New England Uplands, and Atlantic Coastal Plain. Among the many attractions are 495 state park and recreation areas, as well as Valley Forge and Gettysburg Battlefield national shrines, scenes of decisive events in the American Revolution and the Civil War.

The state's early history is shared in large part with neighboring Delaware, which it once contained. Swedes made the first permanent settlement (1643) in the Pennsylvania region at Tinicum Island in the Schuylkill River, but Swedish rule soon gave way (1655) to Dutch. The English supplanted the Dutch in 1664, as King Charles II put the region under the control of his brother James, Duke of York. In 1681, the king granted the region to Quaker William Penn, naming it after Penn's father, an admiral in the Royal Navy to whom the king was indebted. Penn's era, which except for a brief interruption (1692-94) lasted until his death in 1718, was an enlightened and fruitful one.

The so-called Charter of Privileges (1701) gave Pennsylvania the most liberal of colonial governments, and there shortly followed a cultural flowering as well. Benjamin Franklin of Philadelphia published *The Pennsylvania Gazette* (1729-1766) and the *Poor Richard's Almanack* (1732-1757), in addition to pursuing his interest in politics and science. The nation's first magazine, *The American Magazine, or A Monthly View of the Political State of the British Colonies*, was established (1741) in Philadelphia. Penn's notably fair-minded dealings with the Indians, including his famous treaty, kept the region free of the usual frontier bloodshed. But Penn's successors—especially his son Thomas, who took over in 1746—lacked his vision and conciliatory gifts, and troubles with the French and Indians lasted from 1754 until the suppression of Pontiac's Rebellion in 1763. Pennsylvania was involved at various times in boundary disputes with four other colonies: Maryland, Virginia, Connecticut, and New York. The bitterest wrangle was the one with Connecticut over the Wyoming Valley, which gave rise to the Pennamite Wars (1769-71 and 1784). The northwestern "Erie triangle" was bought first from the Indians, and later from the Federal Government, following a 1789 agreement with New York setting the northern border at the 42nd parallel; the parcel was purchased to secure an Erie port for the colony. The establishment of the Mason-Dixon line (1767) settled Pennsylvania's differences with Maryland and Virginia.

After the American Revolution, in which Pennsylvania played a central role, settlement increased in the western region and in the upper Susquehanna Valley. The country's first paved road, the Philadelphia-Lancaster Turnpike, was completed in 1794. In 1811, a Robert Fulton steamboat was launched at Pittsburgh and became the first to traverse the Ohio and Mississippi rivers.

The Schuylkill Canal, one of the nations first long canals (completed 1825), connected Philadelphia and Reading.

The state strongly supported the Union in the Civil War; only New York contributed more troops.

The most widespread flood in the state's history struck in 1972, when Hurricane Agnes, diminished to a tropical storm, remained stationary over the central part of the state for 24 hours. Officials termed it the worst natural disaster in the state's history. In 1975 the Susquehanna again overflowed in the wake of Hurricane Eloise, with damage estimated at over $200 million.

On March 28, 1979, a reactor cooling system at the Three Mile Island nuclear power plant south of Harrisburg malfunctioned in the nation's worst nuclear accident in history. The possibility of a core meltdown or an explosion of the hydrogen gas bubble that had formed in the overheated reactor posed a real threat to nearby residents. Although neither catastrophe occurred, some 144,000 people were evacuated at a cost of $18 million. A 12-member commission appointed by President Carter to investigate the accident issued its report in October 1979: It blamed the plant operator Metropolitan Edison for, among other things, failing to train its personnel adequately to cope with malfunctions. However, the study also concluded that the accident had caused no significant health problems. The Nuclear Regulatory Commission fined Metropolitan Edison $155,000, and only a tie vote on the panel saved the utility company from losing its license. The NRC also cited Babcock & Wilcox, designer of the damaged reactor, for failure to report safety information that may have avoided or lessened the malfunction.

A second accident at Three Mile Island took place in February 1980 when about 1,000 gallons of radioactive water leaked into an auxiliary building. Small amounts of radioactivity were released into the atmosphere and 11 workers were evacuated during the 90-minute crisis, but no health injury was reported.

It is expected to take four years and about $400 million to repair the nuclear facility.

Full name: Commonwealth of Pennsylvania. **Origin of name:** In honor of William Penn, father of the founder. **Inhabitant:** Pennsylvanian. **Capital:** Harrisburg. **State motto:** Virtue, Liberty & Independence. **Flag:** State seal & motto supported by two horses on gold-bordered blue field. **Seal:** Eagle, ship, plow & sheaves of wheat stand for strength, commerce & agricultural abundance; stalk of corn & olive branch represent peace & plenty. **Flower:** Mountain laurel. **Bird:** Ruffed grouse. **Tree:** Hemlock. **Song:** None. **Nickname:** Keystone State.

Governor: Richard L. Thornburgh. **Annual salary:** $66,000. **Term:** 4 years. **Current term expires:** Jan. 1983. **Voting requirements:** 18 yrs. old & U.S. citizen; resident of state (or district) for 60 days. **U.S. Congressmen:** 25 (1980 reapportionment: 23). **Entered Union:** 1787 (2nd state).

Location & boundries: Middle Atlantic state: bounded on the north by New York; on the east by the Delaware River, New York & New Jersey; on the southeast by Delaware & the Delaware River; on the south by Maryland & West Virginia; on the west by West Virginia & Ohio; & on the northwest by Lake Erie. **Total area:** 45,333 sq. mi. (ranks 33rd). **Extreme length:** 307 mi. **Extreme breadth:** 169 mi. **Shoreline:** 51 mi. **Chief rivers:** Delaware, Allegheny, Susquehanna. **Major lakes:** Erie, Wallenpaupack; Pymatuning & Bear Creek Reservoirs. **No. of counties:** 67.

Population (1980 census): 11,866,728 (ranks 4th). **Pop. increase (1970-80):** 0.6%. **Largest cities:** Philadelphia, Pittsburgh, Erie, Allentown. **Pop. density:** 261.7 per sq. mi. (ranks 9th). **Pop. distribution:** White—10,654,325; Black—1,047,609; Am. Indian, Eskimo and Aleut—9,459; Asian and Pacific Islander—64,381; Other—90,954; Spanish origin—154,004. **Marriage rate (1978):** 7.9 per 1,000 people. **Divorce rate:** 3.3 per 1,000 people.

State finances (1979). Revenue: $12,757,000,000. **Expenditures:** $11,575,000,000. **State taxes:** $578.11 per capita. **State personal income tax:** Yes. **Public debt (1979):** $549.66 per capita. **Federal aid (1980):** $380.43 per capita. **Personal income (1980):** $9,294.

PENNSYLVANIA

Sectors of the economy (% of labor force employed in 1970): Manufacturing (34%), Wholesale and retail trade (19%), Government (13%), Educational Services (7%), Services (6%), Construction (5%). **Leading products:** primary and fabricated metals, food items, machinery, chemicals, apparel. **Minerals:** coal, cement, stone, sand & gravel. **Agricultural Products:** dairy items, cattle, hogs, hay, corn, oats, wheat. **Avg. farm (1980):** 148 acres. **Avg. value of farm per acre:** $1,370.

Highway expenditures per capita (1979): $67.05. **Persons per motor vehicle:** 1.72. **Minimum age for driver's license:** 17. **Gasoline tax:** 11¢ per gallon. **Diesel tax:** 11¢ per gallon. **Motor vehicle deaths (1978):** 17.8 per 100,000 people.

Birthrate (1978): 12.9 per 1,000 people. **Infant mortality rate per 1,000 births (1978):** 13.7. **Physicians per 100,000 pop. (1978):** 181. **Dentists per 100,000 pop. (1978):** 54. **Acceptable hospital beds (1978):** 7.29 per 1,000 people. **State expenditures per capita for health and hospitals (1979):** $74.19.

Education expenditures (1976-77): $415.68 per capita annually. **No. of pupils in public schools (1979):** 1,998,000. **No. of institutions of higher learning (1978-79):** 178. **Public school expenditure per pupil in attendance (1977-78):** $2,307. **Avg. salary of public school teachers (1978-79):** $16,000. **No. full-time teachers (1979):** 130,900. **Educational attainment of adult population (1976):** 12.4 median yrs. of school completed: 2.3% with less than 5 years of education; 11.9% with 4 yrs. of college.

Telephones (1978): 61 per 100 people. **State Chamber of Commerce:** Pennsylvania Chamber of Commerce, 222 North Third Street, Harrisburg, Pennsylvania 17101.

RHODE ISLAND

Rhode Island, the nation's smallest state, is not an island, although many small islands are contained within it, including one in Narragansett Bay, Aquidneck Island.

The Bay, which extends inland 28 miles from the Atlantic Ocean, is the predominant feature of the state's eastern section, which comprises about two-thirds of the total area and includes Providence, Pawtucket, and most of Rhode Island's other major cities. The remaining northeastern third of the state is rough, hilly terrain rising east to northwest from 200 to 800 feet above sea level—this section being a part of the New England Uplands, which extend from Maine to Connecticut. Offshore, ten miles south of the mainland, is Block Island, an important navigation landmark. Sixty-seven percent of the state's area is forested, but mostly with "restocked" trees not yet suitable for lumber. Damaging hurricanes occasionally plague the coast.

Once dominated economically by the textile industry, Rhode Island has added many new industries, in a continuing drive toward greater diversification. The Providence area is a major center for the manufacture of jewelry and silverware. Small commercial fishing fleets operate out of several ports.

Explorer Giovanni da Verrazano is thought to have been the first European to visit (1524) the region. Adriaen Block explored there in 1614. In 1636, Roger Williams, looking for a place where "persons distressed for conscience" could go, left Puritan-controlled Massachusetts and founded Providence, the state's first settlement. Two years later Williams organized the country's first Baptist congregation.

Despite harsh, costly combat with the Indians in King Philip's War (1675-76), the region prospered, thanks in large measure to the "triangular trade"—vessels carried rum from Newport to Africa, slaves from there to the West Indies, and molasses from there to Newport, where it was made into rum. Later, Rhode Island renounced slavery, prohibiting (1774) the importation of slaves; it also strongly backed the Union in the Civil War. The economic gap that the passing of the triangular trade left was soon filled by the rapid growth of manufacturing, spurred by Samuel Slater's pioneering in mechanized textile production and by a heavy influx of French Canadian, Italian, Portuguese and Polish immigrants who provided an ample labor pool.

From its beginnings, Rhode Island has been famous for its insistence on political and religious freedom, attracting oppressed and refuge-seeking settlers, and the state's rebellious, iconoclastic character streak soon became evident. In 1769, Newport rebels scuttled the British revenue ship *Liberty* and, three years later, in protest to British trade and navigation laws, a group of Providence men burned the English ship *Gaspee* to the water's edge in Narragansett Bay where it had run aground. The colony was the first of the original 13 to declare independence from England. Rhode Island was the last of the original 13 states to ratify (1790) the Constitution.

Rhode Island also balked at Jefferson's Embargo Act of 1807, and in the War of 1812 it refused to allow its militia to serve outside its borders. Thomas Wilson Dorr and other Rhode Islanders made an abortive revolution in 1842 ("Dorr's Rebellion"), which nonetheless effected a small measure of legislative reform.

In the late 1800s Newport became a fashionable summer home for the very rich, and many palatial mansions were built, some of which are now open for tourists to visit. Today Newport is the country's yachting capital, host to the America's Cup, Newport-Bermuda, and transatlantic races. In 1976, Newport was the first port of welcome for the spectacular fleet of Tall Ships, which sailed from throughout the world to commemorate the bicentennial of the United States. The flotilla assembled was one of the largest ever.

Rhode Island is presently trying to broaden its economic base by expanding its tourist industry. Music festivals and dramas highlight the summer's entertainment possibilities, along with fishing tournaments and regattas.

Newport, with its great mansions and the Touro Synagogue National Historic Site, and the offshore vacation resort of Block Island are major tourist attractions.

Full name: State of Rhode Island & Providence Plantations. **Origin of name:** In honor of the Isle of Rhodes; name chosen by General Court of Colony. **Inhabitant:** Rhode Islander. **Capital:** Providence. **State motto:** Hope. **Flag:** Golden anchor & 12 gold stars on white field. **Seal:** State motto printed above anchor, symbolizing hope; date 1636 was year Roger Williams founded Providence. **Flower:** Violet. **Bird:** Rhode Island red. **Tree:** Red maple. **Song:** "Rhode Island." **Nickname:** Little Rhody.

Governor: John Joseph Garrahy. **Annual salary:** $42,500. **Term:** 2 years. **Current term expires:** Jan. 1983. **Voting requirements:** 18 yrs. old & U.S. citizen; resident of city or town 30 days; positive identification. **U.S. Congressmen:** 2. **Entered Union:** 1790 (13th state).

Location & boundaries: New England state: bounded on the north & east by Massachusetts; on the west by Connecticut; & on the south by New York where Block Island Sound meets Long Island Sound in the Atlantic Ocean. **Total area:** 1,214 sq. mi. (ranks 50th). **Extreme length:** 48 mi. **Extreme breadth:** 37 mi. **Coastline:** 40 mi. **Chief rivers:** Sakonnet, Blackstone, Woonasquatuket, Pawtuxet. **Major lakes:** Worden Pond, Scituate Reservoir. **No. of counties:** 5.

Population (1980 census): 947,154 (ranks 40th). **Pop. increase (1970-80):** − 0.3%. **Largest cities:** Providence, Warwick, Cranston. **Pop. density:** 780.2 per sq. mi. (ranks 2nd). **Pop. distribution:** White—896,692; Black—27,584; Am. Indian, Eskimo and Aleut—2,898; Asian and Pacific Islander—5,303; Other—14,677; Spanish origin—19,707. **Marriage rate (1978):** 7.8 per 1,000 people. **Divorce rate:** 3.7 per 1,000 people.

RHODE ISLAND

State Capital ⊛   Courthouses ⊛

Longitude West of Greenwich

© Copyright HAMMOND INCORPORATED, Maplewood, N.J.

State finances (1979). Revenue: $1,211,000,000. **Expenditures:** $1,171,000,000. **State taxes:** $578.93 per capita. **State personal income tax:** Yes. **Public debt (1979):** $1,267.92 per capita. **Federal aid (1980):** $504.04 per capita. **Personal income (1980):** $9,250.

Sectors of the economy (% of labor force employed in 1970): Manufacturing (35%), Wholesale and retail trade (19%), Government (16%), Educational Services (8%), Services (6%), Construction (5%). **Leading products:** jewelry & silverware, textile items, primary metals, machinery, fabricated metals, electrical equipment, rubber and plastic items. **Avg. farm (1980):** 88 acres. **Avg. value of farm per acre:** $2,304.

Highway expenditures per capita (1979): $46.62. **Persons per motor vehicle:** 1.60. **Minimum age for driver's license:** 16. **Gasoline tax:** 12¢ per gallon. **Diesel tax:** 12¢ per gallon. **Motor vehicle deaths (1978):** 11.6 per 100,000 people.

Birthrate (1978): 12.4 per 1,000 people. **Infant mortality rate per 1,000 births (1978):** 13.6. **Physicians per 100,000 pop. (1978):** 205. **Dentists per 100,000 pop. (1978):** 54. **Acceptable hospital beds (1978):** 7.07 per 1,000 people. **State expenditures per capita for health and hospitals (1979):** $122.79.

Education expenditures (1976-77): $450.70 per capita annually. **No. of pupils in public schools (1979):** 106,000. **No. of institutions of higher learning (1978-79):** 13. **Public school expenditure per pupil in attendance (1977-78):** $2,152. **Average salary of public school teachers (1978-79):** $17,514. **No. full-time teachers (1979):** 10,700. **Educational attainment of adult population (1976):** 12.4 median yrs. of school completed: 3.4% with less than 5 years of education; 14.9% with 4 yrs. of college.

Telephones (1978): 56 per 100 people. **State Chamber of Commerce:** Rhode Island Chamber of Commerce Federation, 206 Smith Street, Providence, Rhode Island 02908.

SOUTH CAROLINA

South Carolina, where the Civil War began, was the first state to secede from the Union. One of the 13 Colonies, it is particularly rich in historic sites, which help draw a growing number of tourists annually. Vivid contrasts often confront the visitor: inlet-dotted swampland gives way to hill country, and estates graced by handsome Georgian homes are set off by poor areas in which shacks are not uncommon. Hilton Head Island and Myrtle Beach are prime vacation spots. A major U.S. Marine Corps training center is located at Parris Island, near Beaufort.

Vast projects such as the Atomic Energy Commission's $1.2-billion Savannah River Plant (near Aiken) underscore South Carolina's transition from a basically agrarian economy to one in which industry plays the leading part. Livestock raising and commercial fishing are also significant.

Two main land regions make up the roughly triangular-shaped state: the "low country," making up two-thirds of the total area and consisting of a part of the Atlantic Coastal Plain rising northwest from the ocean to a fall line running parallel to the coast and bisecting Columbia; and the "up country," consisting of a portion of the Piedmont Plateau and, in the extreme northwest, a small segment of the Blue Ridge Mountains of the Appalachian range. South of the Santee River's mouth are the Sea Islands, a long chain of offshore isles reaching down the rest of the state's length. Water is abundant, and the sharp drops in the land surface make the state rich in hydroelectric-power potential. About two-thirds of the land is forested, contributing to a sizable timber industry.

Giovanni da Verrazano is thought to have been the first to explore (1524) the coast of the region that later became North and South Carolina; an initial Spanish settlement (1526) at Winyah Bay suffered a malaria outbreak and did not endure.

The first English settlement in present-day South Carolina was made (1670) at Albemarle Point on the Ashley River, but poor conditions drove settlers to the site of Charleston (originally Charles Town). There grew the core of a prosperous though ultimately unstable economy based on the slave-supported cultivation of rice and indigo. Although North and South Carolina were officially a single province, they had separate governors until 1691; from that year until 1712, a sole governor was based at Charleston while his deputy governed North Carolina. After 1712, North and South Carolina were governed independently again, and in 1729 they officially became separate royal provinces; the boundary between them was not defined, however, until 1815.

South Carolina, in the years before the American Revolution, progressed economically despite wars with the Spanish and French, and with pirates and Indians; there was a revolt against proprietary rule in 1719, and a slave uprising in 1739. An influx of Germans, Swiss, and Scots-Irish—from abroad and from neighboring states—helped settle the uplands and the lower middle country. Social and economic differences between the small-scale farmers of the up country and the plantation lords of the low country gave rise to regional disputes, culminating in the Regulator Movement for up country reforms. Statehood dates from 1788.

The early part of the 19th century in South Carolina was marked by a decline in agriculture and an increasingly contentious dialogue between the state and the Federal government on the issue of states' rights. South Carolina's Nullification Act (1832) declared a new, higher U.S. tariff act null and void; the immediate issue was resolved (1833) by compromise, but the larger question of the division of power between nation and state remained. A leading national figure of the period was South Carolina's Senator John C. Calhoun, who defended not only the values and rights of his own state, but of the South as a whole. After South Carolina led the way to secession (1860), Confederate artillery fire on Federal troops at Fort Sumter in Charleston Harbor started (April 12, 1861) the Civil War.

During the conflict, there was much fighting along the state's coast, and a Union blockade of Charleston Harbor crippled the economy. In 1865, troops led by General William T. Sherman marched across the state, destroying many plantations and burning Columbia. Reconstruction brought a measure of material recovery, but there was also much waste and political corruption. White supremacy and Negro disenfranchisement soon returned.

The South Carolina legislature in 1977 reinstated the death penalty along the lines of a Georgia measure that has been declared constitutional by the U.S. Supreme Court. It also passed a constitutional amendment that will do much to equalize property taxes in South Carolina.

In 1979 the nation's only commercial nuclear waste disposal facility in operation was at Barnwell, S.C. To prevent the state from becoming a national nuclear dumping ground, Gov. Richard Riley in October ordered a severe reduction in the amount of out-of-state nuclear waste to be processed at Barnwell. In 1981 the Reagan Administration rejected a plan for federal acquisition of the Barnwell plant.

Full name: State of South Dakota. **Origin of name:** From the Sioux meaning "Alliance with Friends." **Inhabitant:** South Dakotan. **Capital:** Pierre. **State motto:** Under God the People Rule. **Flag:** State seal surrounded by gold circle, stylized sun & lettering in yellow on a blue field. **Seal:** Smelter chimney, represents mining; plowman stands for farming; riverboat symbolizes transportation. **Flower:** Pasqueflower. **Bird:** Ringnecked pheasant. **Tree:** Black Hills spruce. **Song:** "Hail, South Dakota." **Nickname:** Coyote State; Sunshine State.

SOUTH CAROLINA

Governor: William J. Janklow. **Annual salary:** $46,750. **Term:** 4 yrs. **Current term expires:** Jan. 1983. **Voting requirements:** 18 yrs. old & U.S. citizen; registered to vote 15 days before election; county resident. **U.S. Congressmen:** 2 (1980 reapportionment: 1). **Entered Union:** 1889 (40th state).

Location & boundaries: Northern Midwestern state: bounded on the north by North Dakota; on the east by Minnesota, Iowa & Big Sioux & Red Rivers; on the south by Nebraska & the Missouri River; & on the west by Wyoming & Montana. **Total area:** 77,047 sq. mi. (ranks 16th). **Extreme length:** 380 mi. **Extreme breadth:** 245 mi. **Chief rivers:** Missouri, James, Cheyenne. **Major lakes:** Lewis & Clark, Big Stone. **No. of counties:** 67.

Population (1980 census): 690,178 (ranks 45th). **Pop. increase (1970-80):** 3.6%. **Largest cities:** Sioux Falls, Rapid City, Aberdeen. **Pop. density:** 8.9 per sq. mi. (ranks 46th). **Pop. distribution:** White—638,955; Black—2,144; Am. Indian, Eskimo and Aleut—45,101; Asian and Pacific Islander—1,728; Other—2,250; Spanish origin—4,028. **Marriage rate (1978):** 15.4 per 1,000 people. **Divorce rate:** 3.5 per 1,000 people.

State finances (1979). Revenue: $656,000,000. **Expenditures:** $642,000,000. **State Taxes:** $356.36 per capita. **State personal income tax:** No. **Public debt (1979):** $841.50 per capita. **Federal aid (1980):** $636.79 per capita. **Personal income (1980):** $7,452.

Sectors of the economy (% of labor force employed in 1970): Wholesale and retail trade (22%), Government (19%), Educational Services (10%), Services (7%), Construction (5%), Manufacturing (4%). **Leading products:** food items; printing & publishing; machinery; stone, clay & glass items; lumber; fabricated metals. **Agricultural products:** cattle, hogs, dairy items, wheat, corn, hay. **Avg. farm (1980):** 1,109 acres. **Avg. value of farm per acre:** $292.

Highway expenditures per capita (1979): $151.34. **Persons per motor vehicle:** 1.84. **Minimum age for driver's license:** 16. **Gasoline tax:** 13¢ per gallon. **Diesel tax:** 13¢ per gallon. **Motor vehicle deaths (1978):** 27.7 per 100,000 people.

Birthrate (1978): 17.7 per 1,000 people. **Infant mortality rate per 1,000 births (1978):** 13.5. **Physicians per 100,000 pop. (1978):** 109. **Dentists per 100,000 pop. (1978):** 42. **Acceptable hospital beds (1978):** 8.26 per 1,000 people. **State expenditures per capita for health and hospitals (1979):** $54.46.

Education expenditures (1976-77): $451.69 per capita annually. **No. of pupils in public schools (1979):** 136,000. **No. of institutions of higher learning (1978-79):** 18. **Public school expenditure per pupil in attendance (1977-78):** $1,516. **Avg. salary of public school teachers (1978-79):** $12,100. **No. full-time teachers (1979 est):** 9,200. **Educational attainment of adult population (1976):** 12.5 median yrs. of school completed: 1.1% with less than 5 years of education; 11.4% with 4 yrs. of college.

Telephones (1978): 54 per 100 people. **State Chamber of Commerce:** Greater South Dakota Chamber of Commerce, P.O. Box 190, Pierre, South Dakota 57501.

SOUTH DAKOTA

South Dakota contains (near Castle Rock) the geographical center of the United States, as well as the largest gold mine in the world, Homestake, at the town of Lead. Rich in Old West lore, with such place names as Belle Fourche, Deadwood, and Wounded Knee, the state is home for 45,000 Indians (mostly Sioux), living on 8,400 square miles of reservations. Within the state's borders is one of the country's most famous landmarks and tourist attractions, Mount Rushmore, in the Black Hills; carved into its granite face, at an altitude of more than a mile, are 60-foot-high busts of Presidents Washington, Jefferson, Lincoln, and Theodore Roosevelt. Badlands National Park contains fantastic pinnacles and canyons in a desert setting.

The state, which has less than five percent forested land, is cut by the Missouri into broadly contrasting, irregularly shaped halves. In the west are the Badlands, the spectacular Black Hills, and the rolling grasslands of the Great Plains, while in the east are the rich farmlands that continue to make agriculture South Dakota's main industry.

There is a heavy emphasis on livestock, including large numbers of cattle, hogs and sheep. Manufacturing consists mainly of meat processing. Sioux Falls is the headquarters of Earth Resource Observation Systems (EROS), the national air and space photography organization.

Early inhabitants were the Mound Builders, dating from about 1200. Living there after 1600 were the Arikara Indians, an advanced agricultural people, eventually forced out by the more warlike Sioux, or Dakota, Indians. South Dakota and southwestern North Dakota were part of the vast territory claimed (1682) for France by Robert Cavelier, Sieur de La Salle, but Frenchmen did not actually visit the region until 1742-43, when the brothers François and Louis Joseph Vérendrye made explorations and planted a lead plate at the site of what is now Pierre. The area was ceded to Spain in 1762, and toward the end of the century it became part of the St. Louis fur-trading empire. Napolean Bonaparte reclaimed (1800) the territory for France, but three years later sold it to the United States, as part of the Louisiana Purchase.

The Lewis and Clark Expedition explored the region which is now the Dakotas in 1804 and 1806. Fort Pierre, the first non-Indian settlement (1817), became a major fur-trading center, and in 1831 the first steamboat on the upper Missouri began operations.

Dakota Territory—comprising both Dakotas and parts of Montana and Wyoming—was created in 1861. In 1868, the Sioux—their way of life disrupted by the decline of the buffalo herds—made a treaty with the U.S., accepting a food subsidy and a reservation which included the Black Hills. But the discovery of gold in the Black Hills caused non-Indian prospectors to pour in. Open war broke out between the Sioux and the prospectors. The Sioux agreed in 1876 to abandon the Black Hills, after the government threatened to cut off their food supply. Rough mining towns grew up, and population soared from about 98,000 (1880) to nearly 350,000 (1890). North and South Dakota were admitted to the Union on November 2, 1889.

The Pine Ridge Indian Reservation was the focus of recurring violence in the early 1970s. Wounded Knee, the site of a massacre of Indians in 1890, was the scene of a 71-day takeover by members of the militant American Indian Movement (AIM) in 1973. There were also numerous incidents on the reservation, including the shooting deaths of two FBI agents in 1975, for each of which a member of AIM was sentenced to life imprisonment in 1977. On June 13, 1979, the U.S. Court of Claims ruled that the removal of the Sioux from the Black Hills in 1876 had violated the tribe's constitutional rights as well as its treaty rights. The Federal Government was ordered to pay the Sioux $17,500,000 for the loss of the Black Hills—and to pay it with interest because of the constitutional violation. The total was estimated to be about $100,000,000—the largest award ever made to a U.S. Indian tribe. The government appealed to the Supreme Court but lost the review on June 30, 1980. Militant Sioux occupied Black Hills campsites on April 4, 1981, near Rapid City.

Full name: State of South Carolina. **Origin of name:** In honor of Charles I of England. **Inhabitant:** South Carolinian. **Captial:** Columbia. **State mottoes:** Animis Opibusque Parati (Prepared in Mind & Resources); Dum Spiro, Spero (While I Breathe, I Hope). **Flag:** White palmetto & crescent on blue field. **Seal:** Palmetto tree, symbolizing successful defense (1776) of fort on Sullivan's Island against British; figure of hope carrying laurel branch across sword-covered beach. **Flower:** Carolina (Yellow) jessamine. **Bird:** Carolina wren. **Tree:** Palmetto. **Song:** "Carolina." **Nickname:** Palmetto State.

Governor: Richard W. Riley. **Annual salary:** $60,000. **Term:** 4 years. **Current term expires:** Jan. 1983. **Voting requirements:** 18

SOUTH DAKOTA

MILES

KILOMETERS

+ Geographical Center of the United States

• State Capital ⊛ County Seats

yrs. old & U.S. citizen; resident of state; registration 30 days before
election. **U.S. Congressmen:** 6. **Entered Union:** 1788 (8th state).

Location & boundaries: South Atlantic state: bounded on the north
& northeast by North Carolina; on the east by the Atlantic Ocean; on
on the south & west by Georgia & the Savannah River. **Total area:**
31,055 sq. mi. (ranks 40th). **Extreme length:** 273 mi. **Extreme
breadth:** 210 mi. **Coastline:** 281 mi. **Chief rivers:** Pee Dee, Santee,
Edisto, Savannah. **Major lakes:** Marion, Moultrie, Murray. **No. of
counties:** 46.

Population (1980 census): 3,119,208 (ranks 24th). **Pop. increase
(1970-80):** 20.4%. **Largest cities:** Columbia, Charleston, North
Charleston, Greenville. **Pop. density:** 100.4 per sq. mi. (ranks 19th).
Pop. distribution: White—2,145,122; Black—948,146; Am. Indian, Eskimo and Aleut—5,758; Asian and Pacific Islander—
11,807; Other—8,375; Spanish origin—33,414. **Marriage rate
(1978):** 18.2 per 1,000 people. **Divorce rate:** 4.1 per 1,000 people.

State finances (1979). Revenue: $3,169,000,000. **Expenditures:**
$3,007,000,000. **State taxes:** $519.43 per capita. **State personal
income tax:** Yes. **Public debt (1979):** $542.33 per capita. **Federal
aid (1980):** $341.56 per capita. **Personal income (1980):** $7,519.

Sectors of the economy (% of labor force employed in 1970):
Manufacturing (36%), Wholesale and retail trade (17%), Government (15%), Services (9%), Educational Services (7%), Construction (7%). **Leading products:** textile items, chemicals, paper
items, food items, machinery, lumber & wood items. **Agricultural
products:** dairy items, cattle, tobacco, soybeans, cotton, peaches,
corn. **Fishing:** shrimp, oysters, crabs. **Avg. farm (1980):** 186 acres.
Avg. value of farm per acre: $629.

Highway expenditures per capita (1979): $86.29. **Persons per
motor vehicle:** 1.54. **Minimum age for driver's license:** 16. **Gasoline tax:** 11¢ per gallon. **Diesel tax:** 11¢ per gallon. **Motor vehicle
deaths (1978):** 30.3 per 100,000 people.

Birthrate (1978): 17.1 per 1,000 people. **Infant mortality rate per
1,000 births (1978):** 18.6. **Physicians per 100,000 pop. (1978):** 134.
Dentists per 100,000 pop. (1978): 35. **Acceptable hospital beds
(1978):** 5.42 per 1,000 people. **State expenditures per capita for
health and hospitals (1979):** $94.48.

Education expenditures (1976-77): $397.92 per capita annually.
No. of pupils in public schools (1979): 609,000. **No. of institutions
of higher learning (1978-79):** 61. **Public school expenditure per
pupil in attendance (1977-78):** $1,515. **Avg. salary of public school
teachers (1978-79):** $12,645. **No. full-time teachers (1979):**
32,800. **Educational attainment of adult population (1976):** 12.2
median yrs. of school completed: 6.9% with less than 5 years of
education; 10.4% with 4 yrs. of college.

Telephones (1978): 51 per 100 people. **State Chamber of Commerce:** South Carolina Chamber of Commerce, 1002 Calhoun St.,
Columbia, South Carolina 29201.

TENNESSEE

Traces of Tennessee's traditionally hardy frontier
spirit remain today in its museums and restored
buildings, as well as in the character and life-style
of many Tennesseans themselves. The first state to
be created out of national territory, Tennessee
came to be called the Volunteer State because of its
readiness to furnish troops in the War of 1812 and
the Mexican War. Its history and culture have been
deeply influenced by its three main land regions—
East, Middle, and West Tennessee.

In East Tennessee, with the heaviest population
outside of the major urban areas in the state, are
the Great Smoky Mountains and the eastern slope
of the Cumberland Mountains, both in the Appalachian range. Middle Tennessee consists of the
fertile Nashville Basin and an elevated plain (the
Highland Rim) and the western slope of the Cum-
berlands, which divide the two sections of the
state, the features being part of the Interior Low
Plateaus. Middle Tennesseans of this gently rolling bluegrass region tend to identify with the Old
South. West Tennessee lies between the western
bend of the Tennessee River and the Mississippi
River and includes a portion of the East Gulf

Coastal Plain and a thin strip of the Mississippi
Alluvial Plain. Here farming predominates. About
half of the state is forested.

Tennessee, once a basically rural region, has become a largely industrial state. Chemicals, textiles, and food and metal products are among the
major manufactures. A Japanese corporation has
announced plans for building a major truck manufacturing facility southeast of Nashville. Massive
hydroelectric installations, developed (beginning
1933) by the Tennessee Valley Authority (TVA),
provide power for Tennessee and six other states.
Mining, lumbering, cotton, tobacco, and livestock
are also vital elements of the state's economy.

Indians similar to the Mound Builders are
thought to have been the early inhabitants of the
Tennessee region. The Chickasaw, Cherokee, and
Shawnee were among the tribes living there when
the first Europeans, led by De Soto, arrived in
1540. De Soto was soon followed by countryman
Juan Pardo, but the Spaniards were seeking gold
and did not settle. A long period of French-British
contention over the land was foreshadowed by the
arrival in the same year (1673) of Marquette and
Jolliet, and Englishmen James Needham and
Gabriel Arthur. In 1682, La Salle and his party
paused in their exploration of the Mississippi Valley and built Fort Prudhomme at the mouth of the
Hatchie River.

Spurred by reports of scouts such as Daniel
Boone, a steady stream of settlers from Virginia
and the Carolinas soon began to enter the region.
French influence waned, and by 1763 the British
were in control, despite strong resistance from the
Cherokees. Between 1772 and 1790 several abortive attempts were made by settlers to establish
self-government and achieve statehood.

In 1790 Congress organized the region into the
"Territory of the United States South of the River
Ohio," commonly called the Southwest Territory.
Tennessee entered the Union in 1796.

Tennessee began life as a state with what Jefferson called the nation's "least imperfect and most
republican" constitution. By 1800, immigration
had swelled the population to 100,000, and the
coming of steam and rail transportation did much
to develop the state's economy. When the Cherokees and the Chickasaws were forced to move west
in the late 1830s, another, smaller wave of immigration ensued. Politically, the new state's dominant figure was Andrew Jackson, who served as a
U.S. representative and senator from Tennessee
before becoming (1829) president.

Although a slaveholding state, Tennessee was at
first pro-Union in the years before the Civil War,
but after Fort Sumter a referendum was held and
two-thirds of the people backed secession (1861).
Tennessee was the last Confederate state to secede,
and the first to be readmitted.

The Reconstruction Era triggered a strong reaction that included the founding (1866) of the Ku
Klux Klan in Pulaski and the adoption (1870) of a
new constitution limiting Negro suffrage via a poll
tax. On the farms, a tenancy system replaced the
plantations, and the state's crippled economy
turned toward increased industrialization for new
life. In 1878, the worst yellow-fever epidemic in
U.S. history hit Memphis, killing thousands.

Among the state's attractions is Great Smoky
Mountains National Park, which it shares with
North Carolina. Parts of five states can be seen
from Lookout Mountain on the Tennessee River
near Chattanooga. The Historic State Capital and
a reproduction of the Parthenon are in Nashville,
the home of the famed "Grand Ole Opry." The new
Opry House and Opryland, U.S.A., a 300-acre
theme park are popular tourist attractions. Liber-

TENNESSEE

tyland, a theme park at Memphis, was opened during the nation's bicentennial. Memphis is also the site of Graceland, Elvis Presley's home.

In 1973, six years after the repeal of the ban on the teaching of the theory of evolution, a new version was enacted. It requires that equal emphasis be given to Genesis in the classroom as well as other theories of man's origin. The original law resulted in the 1925 trial of biology teacher John Scopes in the little town of Dayton, Tenn. The trial pitted Clarence Darrow for the defense against special prosecutor William Jennings Bryan.

The Clinch River nuclear energy project was opposed by President Carter as unnecessary, too expensive and, as a producer of plutonium as a by-product, a substance likely to cause proliferation of atomic weapons technology. Nevertheless, after much controversy, a House committee approved going ahead with the reactor early in 1979. President Reagan's budget for 1982 pledged $222 million for the breeder reactor

Lamar Alexander replaced Governor Ray Blanton on January 17, 1979 (three days before the appointed inauguration day), to stop further convicted criminals from being granted executive clemency. Blanton's clemency grants were in question because of their possible link to a Federal probe of his administration's alleged clemency-for-sale scandal. On April 10, the Tennessee Court of Criminal Appeals upheld 52 grants of clemency allowed by Blanton the day before he left office. Six persons (Blanton not among them) were indicted in connection with the pardon sales. Following conviction by a federal jury on charges of selling state liquor licenses during his administration, Blanton was sentenced to three years in prison and fined $11,000 on August 14, 1981.

Full name: State of Tennessee. **Origin of name:** From Tennese, name of leading Cherokee town. **Inhabitant:** Tennessean. **Capital:** Nashville. **State motto:** Agriculture & Commerce. **Flag:** Three white stars in a white-bordered blue circle on a red field; narrow white & blue stripe at right. **Seal:** Plow, sheaf of wheat & cotton plant represent agriculture; riverboat symbolizes commerce; Roman numerals indicate Tennessee was 16th state to be admitted to Union. **Flower:** Iris. **Bird:** Mockingbird. **Tree:** Tulip poplar. **Song:** "The Tennessee Waltz," "When It's Iris Time in Tennessee," "Tennessee, My Homeland Tennessee," "My Tennessee," & "Oh! Tennessee." **Nickname:** Volunteer State.

Governor: Lamar Alexander. **Annual salary:** $68,226. **Term:** 4 years. **Current term expires:** Jan. 1983. **Voting requirements:** 18 yrs. old & U.S. citizen; resident of state for 20 days. **U.S. Congressmen:** 8 (1980 reapportionment: 9). **Entered Union:** 1796 (16th state).

Location & boundaries: Southeastern state: bounded on the north by Kentucky & Virginia; on the east by North Carolina; on the south by Georgia, Alabama & Mississippi; & on the west by Arkansas, Missouri & the Mississippi River. **Total area:** 42,244 sq. mi. (ranks 34th). **Extreme length:** 432 mi. **Extreme breadth:** 110 mi. **Chief rivers:** Mississippi, Tennessee, Cumberland. **Major lakes:** Watts, Chickamauga, Douglas, Cherokee. **No. of counties:** 95.

Population (1980 census): 4,590,750 (ranks 17th). **Pop. increase (1970-80):** 16.9%. **Largest cities:** Memphis, Nashville, Knoxville, Chattanooga. **Pop. density:** 108.6 per sq. mi. (ranks 18th). **Pop. distribution:** White—3,835,078; Black—725,949; **Am. Indian, Eskimo and Aleut**—5,103; **Asian and Pacific Islander**—13,963; **Other**—10,657; **Spanish origin**—34,081. **Marriage rate (1978):** 13.3 per 1,000 people. **Divorce rate:** 6.6 per 1,000 people.

State finances (1979). Revenue: $3,615,000,000. **Expenditures:** $3,361,000,000. **State taxes:** $420.98 per capita. **State personal income tax:** Yes. **Public debt (1979):** $317.04 per capita. **Federal aid (1980):** $353.69 per capita. **Personal income (1980):** $7,786.

Sectors of the economy (% of labor force employed in 1973): Wholesale and retail trade (16.9%), Government (15.8%), Services (13.9%), Manufacturing (13.8%), Educational Services (7%), Construction (6.1%). **Leading products:** chemicals, food items, electrical equipment, apparel, textile products, primary metals. **Minerals:**

stone, coal, zinc, cement, copper. **Agricultural products:** cattle, soybeans, dairy items, cotton, tobacco. **Avg. farm (1980):** 148 acres. **Avg. value of farm per acre:** $743.

Highway expenditures per capita (1979): $114.30. **Persons per motor vehicle:** 1.48. **Minimum age for driver's license:** 16. **Gasoline tax:** 10¢ per gallon. **Diesel tax:** 12¢ per gallon. **Motor vehicle deaths (1978):** 28.4 per 100,000 people.

Birthrate (1978): 15.4 per 1,000 people. **Infant mortality rate per 1,000 births (1978):** 14.8. **Physicians per 100,000 pop. (1978):** 155. **Dentists per 100,000 pop. (1978):** 47. **Acceptable hospital beds (1978):** 6.75 per 1,000 people. **State expenditures per capita for health and hospitals (1979):** $52.28.

Education expenditures (1976-77): $370.71 per capita annually. **No. of pupils in public schools (1979):** 852,000. **No. of institutions of higher learning (1978-79):** 76. **Public school expenditure per pupil in attendance (1977-78):** $1,487. **Avg. salary of public school teachers (1978-79):** $12,935. **No. full-time teachers (1979):** 45,000. **Educational attainment of adult population (1976):** 12.2 median yrs. of school completed: 6.4% with less than 5 years of education; 10.5% with 4 yrs. of college.

Telephones (1978): 54 per 100 people. **State Chamber of Commerce:** State Chamber Division of the Tennessee Taxpayers Assoc., 1070 Capitol Hill Bldg., Nashville, Tennessee 37219.

TEXAS

Second largest of the states and third most populous, Texas is a fiercely independent land of awesome expanses and great natural resources. It leads the nation in the production of oil, natural gas, cattle, and cotton, and ranks high in fishing and electric power. Texas is also a major agricultural state, as well as a major industrial region. It contains the facilities of 19 of the top 20 U.S. chemical companies, and is the home of the Lyndon B. Johnson Space Center (near Houston) and other space age projects. And while keeping pace technologically, it can also claim a richly varied heritage, having flown the flags of six nations: Spain, France, Mexico, the Republic of Texas, the Confederate States of America, and the United States.

Among the state's many tourist attractions are two national parks, Big Bend with outstanding desert scenery and Guadalupe Mountains with rugged mountain and canyon topography. Padre Island National Seashore stretches for 80 miles along the Gulf shore. Historic sites include the Alamo, San Antonio Missions National Historic Park, Fort Davis National Historic Site, and the Lyndon B. Johnson National Historic Site.

The state consists of four main land regions: the West Gulf Coastal Plain, the largest single area, making up more than two-fifths of the total area and consisting of a 150- to 350-mile-wide strip of land in the east and southeast extending from the Gulf of Mexico to the Balcones Escarpment; the Central Lowland, known locally as the Osage Plains and extending southward to a line running roughly from Fort Worth, through Abilene, to Big Springs and including the southern fringe of the Texas panhandle; the Great Plains, reaching mostly westward (but also north and southward) from the Central Lowland into New Mexico and including the bulk of the panhandle; and the Basin and Range (or Trans-Pecos) Region, making up the westernmost part of the state below New Mexico and including high, rugged, partly arid plains crossed by spurs of the Rocky Mountains; in this region are the Guadalupe Mountains and the state's highest point, Guadalupe Peak (8,749 feet).

Texas has more farmed area than any other state, and about half the land consists of forest, woodland, or brush land. The state's widely varied climate ranges from the warm, damp, subtropical

Gulf Coast and lower Rio Grande Valley to the continental weather of the northern panhandle. Hot, dry weather is typical of the far south as are frequent droughts. Narrow sand bars, enclosing shallow lagoons, lie along the coast and afford some protection against ocean storms and tidal waves. The U.S.-Mexican border, where it follows the Rio Grande has been a continuing problem for the state, because the riverbed shifts occasionally, cutting off land from one or the other country. These shifts have given rise to nearly a century of minor but annoying border disputes. In August 1970, however, Presidents Nixon and Diaz met in Mexico and announced agreement on current disputes and ways to prevent future ones. New, major reservoirs, including giant Amistad Reservoir, built in cooperation with Mexico, will prevent any substantial change in the Rio Grande.

Indians inhabited what is now Texas about 20,000 years before the coming of the Europeans. Spaniards (including Cabeza de Vaca and Francisco Vásquez Coronado) visited the region in the 16th and 17th centuries, settling (1682) at Ysleta (near present-day El Paso). Spain increased its settlement efforts after French explorer Robert Cavelier, Sieur de La Salle, established (1685) a short-lived colony near Matagorda Bay. The first Spanish mission, San Francisco de los Tejas, was founded in 1690 and others soon followed, but generally Spain's efforts to exploit the region's wealth and convert the Indians were not very successful. After the Louisiana Purchase (1803) gave the United States a common border with Texas, Americans began challenging Spanish rule there.

Moses Austin secured (1821) a grant from local authorities permitting him, as an *empresario*, to bring in American settlers; when he died that same year, his son, Stephen F. Austin, established the first permanent Anglo-American settlement at San Felipe de Astin. Often called the "Father of Texas," Austin brought approximately 8,000 colonists to the region. Other *empresarios* brought hundreds more, and during the next 15 years the total approached 30,000. Preoccupied with its birth as an independent republic (1824), Mexico was not effective in curbing what it saw as a growing encroachment on its territory, despite an 1830 law restricting immigration, and the establishment of customs stations and a military force in Texas.

The Anglo-Americans were moved to action when Antonio López de Santa Anna set up (1835) a Mexican dictatorship in Texas; the Texans then proclaimed (1836) a provisional government at Washington-on-the-Brazos and turned command of the revolutionary army over to Sam Houston. Santa Anna and his men quickly gained the upper hand in the struggle, recapturing San Antonio, which had initially fallen to the Texans; the Mexican victory came despite the famous heroic defense of the Alamo by greatly outnumbered Texans (including Davy Crockett and Jim Bowie). After more than 300 Texas prisoners were shot at Goliad, Houston rallied his still relatively small army and, with a surprise attack, won (April 21, 1836) the Battle of San Jacinto, ending the war and bringing to birth the Independent Republic of Texas.

Under its famed Lone Star flag, Texas remained independent for nearly a decade, with Houston serving as president. The country was beset by many grave problems, including Indian and Mexican raids and a money shortage. The issue of annexation by the United States, which most Texans favored, arose early. Slavery, condoned in Texas, made the issue highly controversial: the Southern states favored annexation, while the Northern ones opposed it. Annexation, which came in 1845, precipitated the Mexican War (1846-48).

Settlers, drawn by inexpensive land, came to Texas in great numbers in the pre-Civil War period. Partly because of its slave-holding status but more importantly because of states' rights views, the state sided with the Confederacy, seceding in 1861. Texas saw little action during the war, but contributed 50,000 troops and much matériel to the Southern cause. The state suffered much during the excesses of Reconstruction.

The development of modern Texas was spurred by the growth of the cattle industry, the coming of the railroad, and the discovery, among others before it, of the spectacular Spindletop oil field (1901) near Beaumont. The state's vast petroleum resources spurred the growth of a huge chemical industry. After World War II, Texas became a leader in the aircraft and electronic industries. Texas today, while enjoying great growth, faces serious challenges, such as ways to irrigate with surface water its dry western areas where shrinking underground supplies now help to grow vast crops.

In 1979, inland Texas was damaged by a system of tornados, and the coast by a tropical storm and resulting floods, and by oil spills from a Liberian freighter and from a damaged oil well in Mexican waters.

Texas suffered numerous adverse effects from the summer 1980 heat wave which swept much of the nation. While the mercury climbed beyond 100° in most cities for more than a week, over 100 heat-related deaths were reported, forest fires destroyed thousands of acres, crops wilted in the fields, and milk production was reported down by as much as 20 percent. Dallas suffered 100° days for over a month.

Full name: State of Texas. **Origin of name:** From the Indian meaning "Friends" or "Allies." **Inhabitant:** Texan. **Capital:** Austin. **State motto:** Friendship. **Flag:** Single star on vertical blue bar with a red & a white bar to the right. **Seal:** Single star with branch of oak, representing strength, on left; olive branch, symbolizing peace, to the right. **Flower:** Bluebonnet. **Bird:** Mockingbird. **Tree:** Pecan. **Song:** "Texas, Our Texas." **Nickname:** Lone Star State.

Governor: William P. Clements, Jr. **Annual salary:** $71,400. **Term:** 4 years. **Current term expires:** Jan. 1983. **Voting requirements:** 18 yrs. old & U.S. citizen; registered resident of state 30 days. **U.S. Congressmen:** 24 (1980 reapportionment: 27). **Entered Union:** 1845 (28th state).

Location & boundaries: Southwestern state: bounded on the north by Oklahoma & the Red River; on the northeast by Arkansas; on the east by Louisiana & the Sabine River; on the south by the Gulf of Mexico, the Rio Grande River & Mexico, & on the west by New Mexico. **Total area:** 267,338 sq. mi. (ranks 2nd). **Extreme length:** 801 mi. **Extreme breadth:** 773 mi. **Coastline:** 367 mi. **Chief rivers:** Rio Grande, Red, Pecos, Brazos, Colorado. **Major lakes:** Texoma, Toledo Bend, Amistad, Falcon. **No. of counties:** 254.

Population (1980 census): 14,228,383 (ranks 3rd). **Pop. increase (1970-80):** 27.1%. **Largest cities:** Houston, Dallas, San Antonio, El Paso. **Pop. density:** 53.2 per sq. mi. (ranks 29th). **Pop. distribution:** White—11,197,663; Black—1,710,250; Am. Indian, Eskimo and Aleut—40,074; Asian and Pacific Islander—120,306; Other—1,160,090; Spanish origin—2,985,643. **Marriage rate (1978):** 12.9 per 1,000 people. **Divorce rate:** 6.6 per 1,000 people.

State finances (1979). Revenue: $11,049,000,000. **Expenditures:** $9,665,000,000. **State taxes:** $428.88 per capita. **State personal income tax:** No. **Public debt (1979):** $173.16 per capita. **Federal aid (1980):** $278.40 per capita. **Personal income (1980):** $9,513.

Sectors of the economy (% of labor force employed in 1970): Wholesale and retail trade (22%), Manufacturing (19%), Government (16%), Services (9%), Educational Services (8%), Construction (8%). **Leading products:** chemicals, petroleum & coal items, food items, transportation equipment, machinery, primary & fabricated metals. **Minerals:** petroleum, natural gas & natural gas liquids, cement. **Agricultural products:** cattle, sheep, swine, dairy

TEXAS

MILES

KILOMETERS

State Capital ⊛   County Seats ●

WESTERN PART OF TEXAS
Same scale as main map

HOUSTON

GULF OF MEXICO

© Copyright HAMMOND INCORPORATED, Maplewood, N.J.

Longitude West of Greenwich

items, mohair, sorghum grain, cotton lint, rice, wheat, oats, barley, pecans. **Fishing:** shrimp, oysters, menhaden. **Avg. farm (1980):** 870 acres. **Avg. value of farm per acre:** $411.

Highway expenditures per capita (1979): $93.10. **Persons per motor vehicle:** 1.39. **Minimum age for driver's license:** 16. **Gasoline tax:** 5¢ per gallon. **Diesel tax:** 6.5¢ per gallon. **Motor vehicle deaths (1978):** 30.3 per 100,000 people.

Birthrate (1978): 18.2 per 1,000 people. **Infant mortality rate per 1,000 births (1978):** 14.3. **Physicians per 100,000 pop. (1978):** 158. **Dentists per 100,000 pop. (1978):** 43. **Acceptable hospital beds (1978):** 5.56 per 1,000 people. **State expenditures per capita for health and hospitals (1979):** $56.07.

Education expenditures (1976-77): $436.09 per capita annually. **No. of pupils in public schools (1979):** 2,798,000. **No. of institutions of higher learning (1978-79):** 147. **Public school expenditure per pupil in attendance (1977-78):** $1,947. **Avg. salary of public school teachers (1978-79):** $13,518. **No. full-time teachers (1979):** 161,900. **Educational attainment of adult population (1976):** 12.4 median yrs. of school completed: 6.0% with less than 5 years of education; 13.7% with 4 yrs. of college.

Telephones (1978): 57 per 100 people. **State Chamber of Commerce:** Texas State Chamber of Commerce, 7701 N. Lamar, Suite 302, Austin, Texas 78752.

UTAH

Utah is a rough-hewn, scenically spectacular state consisting of two relatively arid regions (eastern and western), divided by the rain-catching Wasatch Range of the Rocky Mountains. In the west is the Great Basin, which includes the Great Salt Lake (about 75 miles long and 30 miles wide) and the 4,000-square-mile Great Salt Lake Desert. East of the Wasatch Range are the Uinta Mountains (with 11 peaks that rise more than 13,000 feet) and the awesome, many-hued Colorado Plateau. Most of the towns and cities, situated at the base of the mountains, enjoy a pleasant climate with few temperature extremes.

A number of factors—mainly scarcity of water—have limited the state's agricultural growth. Nearly three-quarters of the annual farm revenue comes from livestock and livestock products.

The struggle for better irrigation in Utah began with the early Mormon settlers and still goes on. In 1967 the $325-million Central Utah Project was begun; if completed, it will consist of a vast complex of dams, canals, and aqueducts.

Stimulated by the demands of World War II, manufacturing has become increasingly vital. Leading manufactures include food products; fabricated steel; stone, clay and glass products; missiles; chemicals; and in recent years, electronics equipment. In rural communities, the fabric and apparel industries are active.

In the last ten years, distribution services have become an important part of the Utah economy. Since the state legislature eliminated all taxes on inventories, the state has become an important shipping and receiving point for the entire Western market.

\ Tourism is important, attracting visitors to the Great Salt Lake; Arches, Bryce Canyon, Canyonlands, Capitol Reef and Zion National Parks; Natural Bridges, Cedar Breaks, Dinosaur, Rainbow Bridge and Timpanogos National Monuments; Glen Canyon National Recreation Area, and Golden Spike National Historic Site.

Disfavored by the agrarian Mormons, mining got off to a slow start, but in 1863 huge deposits of copper, silver, and lead were unearthed in Bingham Canyon, which contains the largest open-pit copper mine in the country. The industry came into its own with the coming of the railroad in 1869. Since 1948, significant quantities of oil, natural

gas and uranium have been found. In 1980 an important gas field was opened in the Overthrust Belt near the Wyoming border east of Ogden. Recent discoveries of large oil-shale and tar-sands deposits have raised hopes of further energy development, but uncertainties in the economy and a lagging technology have slowed the exploitation of these resources.

Archaeological findings (1968) in the Great Basin at Hogup Cave, 75 miles northwest of Salt Lake City, show that there was continuous Indian habitation in the area from 6400 B.C. to A.D. 1600. An even older human habitation, Danger Cave near Wendover, was excavated a decade ago and dates to 9000 B.C. Some doubt exists as to whether or not Spanish explorers visited the region in 1540 when they explored the Grand Canyon, but it has been established that in 1776 two Spanish Franciscan friars—Silvestre Velez de Escalante and Francisco Atanasio Dominguez—did explore the area. They recommended colonization, but Spain was apparently not interested. Between 1811 and 1840 British and American fur trappers hunted their prey there.

Permanent occupation of the territory was begun in 1847 by the persecuted Mormons—members of the Church of Jesus Christ of Latter-day Saints—who had emigrated from New York via Missouri, Ohio, and Illinois to Utah in search of "a [secluded] gathering place for Zion." From the time of its founding (1847) Salt Lake City has been the world headquarters of the L.D.S. church.

The Utah region at that time belonged to Mexico, but after the Mexican War (1846-48), it became the property of the United States. At least 70 percent of the state's area is still federally owned and administered, and about ten percent of the people work for Federal agencies.

Two Indian wars were fought: the Walker War (1853-54) and the Black Hawk War (1865-68), involving a number of tribes but principally the Utes, who were eventually placed on a reservation in the Uinta basin.

As early as 1849 Utah asked to be admitted to the Union, but Congress refused—mainly because the Mormon practice of polygamy was frowned upon.

The dismissal of the Mormon leader, Brigham Young, as territorial governor led to the "Utah" or "Mormon" War (1857-58). Federal troops were dispatched to the area, but there was more bad feeling than actual fighting. When the Civil War broke out in 1861, the troops were recalled and peace reigned, although there remained a residue of bitterness between the Mormon stronghold and the "outside" world which time has gradually erased. Utah finally entered the Union in 1896.

Some residents of St. George have filed claims against the Energy Department charging that nuclear blasts which occurred some 25 years ago at the Nevada Testing Site caused cancer deaths among members of their families who lived in the area.

The federal government's planned deployment of the MX missile system in the state has brought vigorous objections from Utahns. Both the Mormon church and U.S. Senator Jake Garn protested the move in 1981.

Full name: State of Utah. **Origin of name:** From the Indian tribe of Utes. **Inhabitant:** Utahn. **Capital:** Salt Lake City. **State motto:** Industry. **Flag:** State seal in a gold circle on blue field. **Seal:** Beehive on shield represents industry; sego lilies surrounding beehive symbolize time when Mormon pioneers ate lily bulbs to avoid starvation. **Flower:** Sego lily. **Bird:** Seagull. **Tree:** Blue spruce. **Song:** "Utah, We Love Thee." **Nickname:** Beehive State.

Governor: Scott M. Matheson. **Annual salary:** $40,000. **Term:** 4 years. **Current term expires:** Dec. 1980. **Voting requirements:** 18

UTAH

MILES
0 10 20 30 40 50 60

KILOMETERS
0 10 20 30 40 50 60

State Capitals ⊛
County Seats ⊙

© Copyright HAMMOND INCORPORATED, Maplewood, N.J.

Longitude West of Greenwich

yrs. old & U.S. citizen; state resident 30 days. **U.S. Congressmen:** 2 (1980 reapportionment: 3). **Entered Union:** 1896 (45th state).

Location & boundaries: Rocky Mountain state: bounded on the north by Idaho; on the northeast by Wyoming; on the east by Colorado; on the south by Arizona; & on the west by Nevada. **Total area:** 84,916 sq. mi. (ranks 11th). **Extreme length:** 345 mi. **Extreme breadth:** 275 mi. **Chief rivers:** Colorado, Green, Sevier. **Major lakes:** Great Salt Lake, Utah, Sevier, Bear Lake. **No. of counties:** 29.

Population (1980 census): 1,461,037 (ranks 36th). **Pop. increase (1970-80):** 37.9%. **Largest cities:** Salt Lake City, Provo, Ogden. **Pop. density:** 17.2 per sq. mi. (ranks 42nd). **Pop. distribution:** White—1,382,550; Black—9,225; Am. Indian, Eskimo and Aleut—19,256; Asian and Pacific Islander—15,076; Other—34,930; Spanish origin—60,302. **Marriage rate (1978):** 12.4 per 1,000 people. **Divorce rate:** 5.4 per 1,000 people.

State finances (1979). Revenue: $1,605,000,000. **Expenditures:** $1,464,000,000. **State taxes:** $508.34 per capita. **State personal income tax:** Yes. **Public debt (1979):** $287.53 per capita. **Federal aid (1980):** $374.73 per capita. **Personal income (1980):** $7,485.

Sectors of the (% of labor force employed in 1970): Government (25%), Wholesale and retail trade (22%), Educational Services (12%), Services (7%), Construction (6%). **Leading products:** food items; stone, clay, & glass items; machinery; printing & publishing; fabricated metals; petroleum & coal items. **Minerals:** copper, petroleum, coal, molybdenum. **Agricultural products:** cattle, dairy items, turkeys, hay, wheat, barley. **Avg. farm (1980):** 1,050 acres. **Avg. value of farm per acre:** $297.

Highway expenditures per capita (1979): $113.86. **Persons per motor vehicle:** 1.45. **Minimum age for driver's license:** 16. **Gasoline tax:** 11¢ per gallon. **Diesel tax:** 11¢ per gallon. **Motor vehicle deaths (1978):** 28.3 per 100,000 people.

Birthrate (1978): 29.5 per 1,000 people. **Infant mortality rate per 1,000 births (1978):** 11.4. **Physicians per 100,000 pop. (1978):** 167. **Dentists per 100,000 pop. (1978):** 65. **Acceptable hospital beds (1978):** 3.49 per 1,000 people. **State expenditures per capita for health and hospitals (1979):** $76.72.

Education expenditures (1976-77): $598.87 per capita annually. **No. of pupils in public schools (1979):** 317,000. **No. of institutions of higher learning (1978-79):** 14. **Public school expenditure per pupil in attendance (1977-78):** $1,644. **Avg. salary of public school teachers (1978-79):** $14,607. **No. full-time teachers (1979):** 13,400. **Educational attainment of adult population (1976):** 12.8 median yrs. of school completed: 0.7% with less than 5 years of education; 17.5% with 4 yrs. of college.

Telephones (1978): 56 per 100 people. **State Chamber of Commerce:** None.

VERMONT

Vermont, the only New England state lacking an ocean coastline, is noted for the independence of thought and action that stem, in part, from this relative insularity; there is much truth to the saying, "Vermonters will do nothing that you tell them to; most anything that you ask them to."

Four main land areas make up the state: the extensively forested Green Mountains, forming a north-south backbone through the center (and inspiring the state's French-rooted name); the White Mountains in the northeast, Lake Champlain and the Champlain Valley in the northwest, and the Taconic Hills in the southwest. Many lakes, ponds, streams, and rivers—including the eastern-border-forming Connecticut River—provide an abundant water supply. Forests cover about 60 percent of the area.

Called a "state in a very natural state" by poet Robert Frost (who lived the latter part of his life near Ripton), Vermont is famous for the rustic charm of its towns and villages, winding roads, covered bridges, and largely unspoiled scenery. In the early 1900s, manufacturing began to replace agriculture in importance through small-scale industralization: only a quarter of the state's land is now devoted to agriculture. Maple sugar and syrup and the finest marble in the United States are among Vermont's better-known products, while an important source of the nation's asbestos is located in the Hyde Park region. Machine tools, electronic equipment, computer components and armaments are the state's leading industrial products.

Four-season tourism has grown enormously in recent years, generating nearly $1 billion in income. Attractions include the Green Mountain National Forest, Shelburne and Bennington museums, a multitude of ski resorts, and many state parks.

French explorer Samuel de Champlain was most likely the first European to visit the region, discovering (1609) the lake now bearing his name. The British established (1724) the first permanent settlement at Fort Dummer (near present-day Brattleboro), and the English assumed control at the end of the French and Indian War (1763). Beginning in the mid-1700s New Hampshire and New York made conflicting claims on the region, and violence erupted when Ethan Allen and his "Green Mountain Boys" resisted New York officers who sought to take possession of the territory.

These differences were soon overshadowed by the American Revolution, in which the Vermonters played an important part, including the capture of Fort Ticonderoga and Crown Point. In 1777, Vermont proclaimed its independence, drawing up the first state constitution that outlawed slavery and established universal manhood suffrage without property qualifications. Land disputes continued, but were finally ended (1791) when Vermont paid New York a $30,000 claims settlement and was admitted to the Union, the first state to be added to the original 13.

The Embargo Act of 1807 and the War of 1812 were unpopular with Vermonters, who relied heavily on trade with Canada. But involvement in the war was unavoidable. Invasion by the British from Canada was averted when Americans, led by Captain Thomas Macdonough, gained a vital naval victory on Lake Champlain in 1814. Two years later, disastrous frosts ruined the state's crops, and thousands of farmers went west; immigration, which had been significant, fell sharply and never regained its former level.

Abolition was popular in the state, which strongly supported Abraham Lincoln in the 1860 presidential election. Vermont's casualties in the Civil War, as a proportion of the male population, were among the heaviest of any Northern state.

Historically a Republican state, Vermont has increasingly become a state in which the two parties are in close balance. The first Democratic governor was elected in 1962 and served until 1968. A second Democrat was elected for two terms beginning in 1972. The Republicans recaptured the governor's chair in 1976, 1978 and 1980, although in 1976 they lost control of the House of Representatives for the first time since the early 19th century. The House seat was regained by the GOP with the 1978 elections. The first Democratic U.S. Senator in the state's history was elected in 1974.

Full name: State of Vermont. **Origin of name:** From the French words meaning "Green Mountain." **Inhabitant:** Vermonter. **Capital:** Montpelier. **State motto:** Freedom & Unity. **Flag:** State seal on a blue field. **Seal:** Pine tree with 14 branches represents 13 original states & Vermont; cow & sheaves of wheat stand for dairying & agriculture; wavy lines at top & bottom symbolize sky & sea. **Flower:** Red clover. **Bird:** Hermit thrush. **Tree:** Sugar maple. **Song:** "Hail, Vermont." **Nickname:** Green Mountain State.

Governor: Richard A. Snelling. **Annual salary:** $44,850. **Term:** 2 years. **Current term expires:** Jan. 1983. **Voting requirements:** 18 yrs. old & U.S. citizen; registered state resident. **U.S. Congressmen:** 1. **Entered Union:** 1791 (14th state).

VERMONT

MILES
0 5 10 15 20 25 30
KILOMETERS
0 5 10 15 20 25 30

State Capitals
County Seats ⊛

© Copyright HAMMOND INCORPORATED, Maplewood, N.J.

Location & boundaries: New England state: bounded on the north by Canada; on the east by New Hampshire & the Connecticut River; on the south by Massachusetts; & on the west by New York & Lake Champlain. **Total area:** 9,609 sq. mi. (ranks 43rd). **Extreme length:** 159 mi. **Extreme breadth:** 86 mi. **Chief rivers:** Connecticut, Winooski, Lamoille. **Major lake:** Champlain. **No. of counties:** 14.

Population (1980 census): 511,456 (ranks 48th). **Pop. increase (1970-80):** 15.0%. **Largest cities:** Burlington, Rutland. **Pop. density:** 53.2 per sq. mi. (ranks 30th). **Pop. distribution:** White— 506,736; Black—1,135; **Am. Indian, Eskimo and Aleut**—984; **Asian and Pacific Islander**—1,355; **Other**—1,246; **Spanish origin**—3,304. **Marriage rate (1978):** 9.9 per 1,000 people. **Divorce rate:** 4.2 per 1,000 people.

State finances (1979). Revenue: $640,000,000. **Expenditures:** $612,000,000. **State taxes:** $542.54 per capita. **State personal income tax:** Yes. **Public debt (1979):** $1,035.74 per capita. **Federal aid (1980):** $694.88 per capita. **Personal income (1980):** $7,839.

Sectors of the economy (% of labor force employed in 1970): Manufacturing (24%), Wholesale and retail trade (18%), Government (15%), Educational Services (11%), Services (8%), Construction (8%). **Leading products:** machinery, food items, computer components, printing, stone items, lumber, wood & paper items, rubber & plastic items. **Agricultural products:** dairy items, cattle, apples, hay, maple items. **Avg. farm (1980):** 276 acres. **Avg. value of farm per acre:** $710.

Highway expenditures per capita (1979): $124.53. **Persons per motor vehicle:** 1.50. **Minimum age for driver's license:** 18. **Gasoline tax:** 11¢ per gallon. **Diesel tax:** None. **Motor vehicle deaths (1978):** 25.9 per 100,000 people.

Birthrate (1978): 14.6 per 1,000 people. **Infant mortality rate per 1,000 births (1978):** 13.6. **Physicians per 100,000 pop. (1978):** 205. **Dentists per 100,000 pop. (1978):** 56. **Acceptable hospital beds (1978):** 5.86 per 1,000 people. **State expenditures per capita for health and hospitals (1979):** $77.58.

Education expenditures (1976-77): $498.80 per capita annually. **No. of pupils in public schools (1979):** 99,000. **No. of institutions of higher learning (1978-79):** 21. **Public school expenditure per pupil in attendance (1977-78):** $1,799. **Avg. salary of public school teachers (1978-79):** $12,331. **No. full-time teachers (1979):** 7,100. **Educational attainment of adult population (1976):** 12.5 median yrs. of school completed: 0.9% with less than 5 years of education; 15.7% with 4 yrs. of college.

Telephones (1978): 52 per 100 people. **State Chamber of Commerce:** Vermont State Chamber of Commerce, P.O. Box 37, Montpelier, Vermont 05602.

VIRGINIA

Virginia, home of the first English settlement in North America (Jamestown, 1607), is a state particularly rich in American history. A Virginian, Richard Henry Lee, introduced (June 7, 1776) the motion for separation of the 13 Colonies from England; Virginian Thomas Jefferson was the main author of the Declaration of Independence; and Virginian George Washington led the way to victory in the American Revolution. Eight U.S. Presidents were Virginians, including four of the first five: Washington (1st), Jefferson (3rd), James Madison (4th), and James Monroe (5th); the latter three, in office 24 consecutive years, made up the so-called "Virginia Dynasty." Famed Chief Justice John Marshall was also a Virginian.

The state, which is named for Elizabeth I ("The Virgin Queen"), has acquired several nicknames including "The Mother of States," because all or part of eight other states were formed from western territory it once claimed: West Virginia, Kentucky, Illinois, Indiana, Michigan, Minnesota, Ohio, and Wisconsin. In the American Revolution, General Charles Cornwallis's surrender (1781) to Washington at Yorktown virtually ended hostilities. During the Civil War, Virginia was the central battleground. Among the major battles fought within it were First and Second Bull Run (Man-

assas), Fredericksburg, Chancellorsville, the Wilderness, Petersburg, and Richmond; Confederate General Robert E. Lee, another Virginian, surrendered at Appomattox (April 9, 1865).

Roughly triangular in shape, the state has four principal land regions (west to east): the Appalachian Plateau, the Great Appalachian Valley (known also locally as the Valley of Virginia, a series of ridges and valleys including the historic Shenandoah Valley), the Piedmont Plateau (the largest single area), and the Atlantic Coastal Plain, also called the Tidewater Region. Prominent local features of the Appalachian range include the Allegheny Mountains along the western border and the Blue Ridge range rising between the Valley and Piedmont sections. Across Chesapeake Bay, making up the lower part of the Delmarva Peninsula, is the state's Eastern Shore. About two-thirds of the land is forested.

Significant agriculture includes fruit, hay, corn, peanuts, and tobacco, the largest crop and a crucial factor in the state's development. Leading manufactures include chemical and tobacco products. Fishing and, to a lesser degree, mining (especially of coal) are considerable, as is tourism. Attractions include the reconstructed colonial town of Williamsburg, Washington's birthplace (Wakefield) and residence (Mount Vernon), Jefferson's Monticello, old Alexandria, Virginia Beach, Shenandoah National Park and the Skyline Drive, Arlington National Cemetery, Cumberland Gap National Historical Park, Assateague Island National Seashore at Chincoteague, and various Civil War battlegrounds.

Indians of three major language groups (Algonquian, Siouan, and Iroquoian) were living in the region when the first British arrived, about 25 years after an unsuccessful settlement by Spanish Jesuits. English settlement proceeded despite great hardship, mainly through the efforts of such men as Captain John Smith and Thomas West, Baron De La Warr, Virginia's first governor. The House of Burgesses, first legislative body in the New World, convened (1619) at Jamestown, and five years later Virginia became England's first royal colony. The importation of Negroes, first as indentured servants and later as slaves, was begun. The production and exportation of tobacco, which was first cultivated (1612) by John Rolfe, spurred the colony's growth, and the plantation became the earliest social unit. Rolfe's marriage (1614) to Pocahontas helped induce a brief period of peace with the Indians, but there were massacres in 1622 and 1644, and not until Lord Dunmore's War (1774) did Indian troubles decrease.

At the time of Sir William Berkeley's governorship (1641-52, 1660-77), the colony was thriving, with freeholders and merchants controlling the government. Hard times came (1660) with the Restoration's Navigation Acts, which stipulated the exclusive use of English ships and ports for the tobacco trade, causing initial transport bottlenecks, price drops, and widespread discontent. This unrest was aggravated by Berkeley's increasingly unpopular practices (including a slacking of vigilance against the Indians), and an abortive revolt (Bacon's Rebellion, 1676) was mounted; when Berkeley harshly overreacted, England recalled him.

Inflamed by such orators as Patrick Henry ("Give me liberty or give me death!"), Virginians in the 18th century traveled a path of inevitable revolt and, after Washington's final military victory had decided the issue, they provided the first Federal leadership. In 1788 Virginia ratified the Constitution and relinquished all its western land claims except Kentucky and West Virginia (Kentucky became an independent state in 1792, as did West

VIRGINIA

WESTERN PART OF
VIRGINIA
Same scale as main map

Virginia in 1863; two counties were added to the latter state in 1866). Virginia seceded from the Union in 1861 and was readmitted in 1870.

A new constitution was drafted (1902) that imposed a poll tax, virtually disenfranchising Blacks, but state and Federal court decisions in the 1960s held the poll tax unconstitutional as a requisite for voting, and a new state constitution approved by voters in 1970 eliminated the tax.

Virginia undertook "massive resistance" to public school desegregation after the Supreme Court's 1954 desegregation ruling, and a few schools were temporarily closed to avoid integration. During the 1960s and 1970s racial tensions have sharply declined. Tension was renewed, however, when federal courts issued orders for massive busing of pupils, climaxed by the decision of a U.S. District Judge ordering the consolidation of the school systems of Richmond and two adjacent, mostly white counties. That order later was overturned.

Full name: Commonwealth of Virginia. **Origin of name:** In honor of Queen Elizabeth of England, the "Virgin Queen." **Inhabitant:** Virginian. **Capital:** Richmond. **State motto:** Sic Semper Tyrannis (Thus Always to Tyrants). **Flag:** State seal on blue field. **Seal:** State motto; standing figure representing virtue, dressed as woman warrior, standing triumphant over figure of tyranny. **Flower:** American Dogwood. **Bird:** Cardinal. **Tree:** American Dogwood. **Song:** "Carry Me Back to Old Virginia." **Nickname:** Old Dominion State.

Governor: John N. Dalton. **Annual salary:** $75,000. **Term:** 4 years. **Current term expires:** Jan. 1982. **Voting requirements:** 18 yrs. old & U.S. citizen; registered in precinct of residence. **U.S. Congressmen:** 10. **Entered Union:** 1788 (10th state).

Location & boundaries: South Atlantic state: bounded on the north by Maryland; on the west by West Virginia & Kentucky; on the south by Tennessee & North Carolina; & on the east by the Atlantic Ocean. **Total area:** 40,817 sq. mi. (ranks 36th). **Extreme length:** 440 mi. **Extreme breadth:** 200 mi. **Coastline:** 342 mi.; 112 mi. along the Atlantic Ocean & 230 mi. along Chesapeake Bay. **Chief rivers:** James, Potomac, Rappahannock. **Major lakes:** Smith Mountain, John H. Kerr Reservoir. **No. of counties:** 95.

Population (1980 census): 5,346,279 (ranks 14th). **Pop. increase (1970-80):** 14.9%. **Largest cities:** Norfolk, Virginia Beach, Richmond. **Pop. density:** 130.9 per sq. mi. (ranks 16th). **Pop. distribution: White**—4,229,734; **Black**—1,008,311; **Am. Indian, Eskimo and Aleut**—9,336; **Asian and Pacific Islander**—66,209; **Other**—32,689; **Spanish origin**—79,873. **Marriage rate (1978):** 11.4 per 1,000 people. **Divorce rate:** 4.4 per 1,000 people.

State finances (1979). Revenue: $5,136,000,000. **Expenditures:** $4,876,000,000. **State taxes:** $493.31 per capita. **State personal income tax:** Yes. **Public debt (1979):** $319.95 per capita. **Federal aid (1980):** $338.16 per capita. **Personal income (1980):** $9,435.

Sectors of the economy (% of labor force employed in 1970): Government (24%), Manufacturing (22%), Wholesale and retail trade (18%), Services (8%), Educational Services (8%), Construction (7%). **Leading products:** chemicals, textile items, apparel, food items, transportation equipment, furniture & fixtures, electrical equipment & supplies. **Minerals:** coal, stone, sand & gravel, lime. **Fishing:** crabs, oysters, menhaden. **Agricultural products:** livestock & livestock items, dairy items, poultry & poultry items, tobacco, corn, hay. **Avg. farm (1980):** 162 acres. **Avg. value of farm per acre:** $942.

Highway expenditures per capita (1979): $159.41. **Persons per motor vehicle:** 1.49. **Minimum age for driver's license:** 16. **Gasoline tax:** 11¢ per gallon. **Diesel tax:** 11¢ per gallon. **Motor vehicle deaths (1978):** 20.6 per 100,000 people.

Birthrate (1978): 14.2 per 1,000 people. **Infant mortality rate per 1,000 births (1978):** 13.8. **Physicians per 100,000 pop. (1978):** 174. **Dentists per 100,000 pop. (1978):** 48. **Acceptable hospital beds (1978):** 6.00 per 1,000 people. **State expenditures per capita for health and hospitals (1979):** $96.30.

Education expenditures (1976-77): $425.10 per capita annually. **No. of pupils in public schools (1979):** 1,030,000. **No. of institutions of higher learning (1978-79):** 71. **Public school expenditure per pupil in attendance (1977-78):** $1,688. **Avg. salary of public school teachers (1978-79):** $13,700. **No. full-time teachers (1979):** 60,900. **Educational attainment of adult population (1976):** 12.4

median yrs. of school completed: 4.6% with less than 5 years of education; 16.4% with 4 yrs. of college.

Telephones (1978): 53 per 100 people. **State Chamber of Commerce:** Virginia State Chamber of Commerce, 611 East Franklin Street, Richmond, Virginia 23219.

WASHINGTON

Washington, traditional gateway to Alaska and the Far East, is a leader in the vital areas of aircraft production, nuclear research, lumbering, and actual and potential waterpower production. It is also a land of rugged beauty that particularly appeals to lovers of the great outdoors.

The Cascade Mountains, running north and south, divide the state in two, the eastern part comprising about three-fifths of the total area. The Olympic Mountains make up the northwest corner of the state, while the Puget Sound Lowland lies between the Olympic Mountains on the west and the Cascades on the east. In the southwest corner is the Coast Range, which extends south into Oregon. East of the Cascades are the Rocky Mountains in the north and the Columbia Plateau in the south.

Most of the state's larger cities, including Seattle and Tacoma, are in the western region along Puget Sound, an unusual 200-mile-long arm of the Pacific Ocean; it varies in width up to 40 miles and harbors more than 300 islands. This area has a milder climate than any other in the country that is as far north. Generally, the weather is drier in the east than in the west, which receives moist Pacific winds and considerable rainfall. Principal irrigated regions are in the Columbia Basin and the valleys of the Walla Walla, Snake, and Yakima rivers. The Lower Granite Dam and Lock System extends navigation on the Columbia and Snake rivers as far inland as Lewiston, Idaho.

Washington is a leading producer of apples, wheat, and hops. Livestock and livestock products make up a third of the total farm revenue, while commercial fishing is significant. Mineral production, including coal and stone, accounted for $251 million in 1978. Aircraft, lumber and food industries dominate the manufacturing sector of the economy.

Today, the state is trying to diversify and stabilize its industry, with less dependency on federal defense contracts. One area of concentration is the brisk tourist trade, which has gained greatly in recent years as more facilities are built to augment the exceptional hunting, fishing, and skiing available. Mount Rainier and Olympic National Parks, and the Grand Coulee Dam National Recreation Area, are among the major attractions. Seattle Center, consisting of structures from the 1962 Century 21 Exposition, includes a monorail and 606-foot "Space Needle." Whitman Mission National Historic Site denotes the place Marcus Whitman founded an Indian mission in 1836; it is also the site of the 1847 Indian massacre in which Whitman and others were killed.

A part of the Oregon country claimed by both Britain and the United States in the 1830s, Washington became U.S. territory by a compromise treaty with Britain in 1846. It became a state in 1889.

The period after World War I was one of discontent and strife in the labor field. There were many disputes, especially between businessmen and the Industrial Workers of the World (IWW); violence erupted at Centralia. During World War II, the state's sizable Japanese-American population suffered discrimination and disruption; over 15,000 people were displaced eastward.

In 1979, Gov. Dixy Lee Ray closed a nuclear

WASHINGTON

● State and Provincial Capitals
● County Seats

by a wildcat strike which began in Logan, spreading to eight other states before it ended. With the announcement of President Carter's energy program in 1977, increased importance was placed on West Virginia's industry, but again production was hampered by a series of wildcat strikes. In a long strike, the United Mine Workers shut down the mines from December 1977 to March 1978. And 5,200 wildcat strikers stayed off the job for 11 days in February and March 1980. The UMW coal strike of 1981 lasted 72 days, with the miners returning to work on June 8.

Full name: State of West Virginia. **Origin of name:** In honor of the "Virgin Queen," Elizabeth I of England. **Inhabitant:** West Virginian. **Capital:** Charleston. **State motto:** Montani Semper Liberi (Mountaineers Are Always Free). **Flag:** State seal on blue-bordered white field. **Seal:** Rock (with date June 20, 1863, when state entered Union) stands between farmer & miner, symbolizing state's industries. **Flower:** Big rhododendron. **Bird:** Cardinal. **Tree:** Sugar maple. **Songs:** "The West Virginia Hills," "This Is My West Virginia," & "West Virginia, My Home Sweet Home." **Nickname:** Mountain State.

Governor: John D. Rockefeller IV. **Annual salary:** $50,000. **Term:** 4 years. **Current term expires:** Jan. 1981. **Voting requirements:** 18 yrs. old & U.S. citizen; resident of state, 60 days, registered, 30 days. **U.S. Congressmen:** 4. **Entered Union:** 1863 (35th state).

Location & boundaries: Southeastern state: bounded on the north by the Ohio River, Pennsylvania, Maryland & the Potomac River; on the east by Maryland & Virginia; on the south by Virginia; & on the west by Kentucky, Ohio & the Ohio River. **Total area:** 24,181 sq. mi. (ranks 41st). **Extreme length:** 265 mi. **Extreme breadth:** 237 mi. **Chief rivers:** Ohio, Potomac, Kanawa. **Major lake:** East Lynn Reservoir. **No. of counties:** 55.

Population (1980 census): 1,949,644 (ranks 34th). **Pop. increase (1970-80):** 11.8%. **Largest cities:** Charleston, Huntington, Wheeling. **Pop. density:** 80.6 per sq. mi. (ranks 25th). **Pop. distribution:** White—1,874,751; Black—65,051; **Am. Indian, Eskimo and Aleut**—1,610; **Asian and Pacific Islander**—5,194; **Other**—3,038; **Spanish origin**—12,707. **Marriage rate (1978):** 9.3 per 1,000 people. **Divorce rate:** 5.2 per 1,000 people.

State finances (1979). Revenue: $2,395,000,000. **Expenditures:** $2,424,000,000. **State taxes:** $612.38 per capita. **State personal income tax:** Yes. **Public debt (1979):** $871.61 per capita. **Federal aid (1980):** $487.01 per capita. **Personal income (1980):** $7,831.

Sectors of the economy (% of labor force employed in 1970): Manufacturing (23%), Wholesale and retail trade (19%), Government (17%), Educational Services (8%), Services (7%), Construction (7%). **Leading products:** chemicals; stone, clay & glass items; primary & fabricated metals; food items; machinery; printing & publishing. **Minerals:** coal, natural gas & natural gas liquids, stone. **Agricultural products:** cattle, dairy items, hay, apples, corn. **Avg. farm (1980):** 214 acres. **Avg. value of farm per acre:** $519.

Highway expenditures per capita (1979): $252.54. **Persons per motor vehicle:** 1.43. **Minimum age for driver's license:** 18. Gas-

WISCONSIN

Although Wisconsin is best known as the leading U.S. dairy state, manufacturing today represents its major economic activity; top products include nonelectrical machinery and the many pulp and paper items that the state's forests make possible. Wisconsin is also the country's largest supplier of beer, with brewers concentrated most heavily in the Milwaukee area. Politically, the state has gained a reputation for progress and reform.

The land itself, rich and diverse, consists of two principal regions: the Superior Upland in the north and the Central Lowlands, covering the lower two-thirds of the state and consisting of the Wisconsin Driftless Area in the west and the Great Lakes Plain in the east. Rolling hills, ridges, and fertile valleys and plains, punctuated by many clear lakes, have made Wisconsin famous for its scenic beauty, and, despite past exploitation, forests still cover almost half the state. By far the largest part of the population lives in the southeastern region. The state's climate is marked by sharply defined seasons that are tempered somewhat by Lakes Superior and Michigan.

Tourist attractions include the Apostle Islands National Lakeshore, the scenic Door Peninsula, and the gorge at Wisconsin Dells.

Frenchman Jean Nicolet was the first European to explore the Wisconsin region, landing (1634) at Green Bay in search of a fur-trading fortune and the legendary "Northwest Passage" to the Orient. At the time, Ottawa, Huron, and other Indians from the east were forcing indigenous Indians (including the Winnebago) westward, and only the Menominees were settled there. The arrival of Nicolet and other Frenchmen soon after established France's claim to the region that was valid until 1763, when the British gained possession.

After the American Revolution, England ceded (1783) the region to the United States, but the British retained actual control until after the War of 1812. A part of the Northwest Territory until 1800, the Wisconsin region became, successively, a part of the territories of Indiana (1800-09), Illinois (1809-18), and Michigan (1818-36). When it was made a separate territory in 1836, Wisconsin included its present area in addition to parts of Iowa, Minnesota, and sections of North and South Dakota east of the Missouri and White Earth Rivers. In 1838, the territory west of the Mississippi was organized as the Territory of Iowa, Wisconsin retaining its present area and a northward extension to Lake of the Woods in what is now Minnesota. A decade later, Wisconsin entered the Union.

Wisconsin's Indian troubles reached a climax in the Black Hawk War (1832), which virtually ended the Indian threat in the area and caused a settlement boom. There followed a substantial influx of immigrants—especially Germans, Irish, English, and Welsh. Liberal leaders, like Carl Schurz, settled in Wisconsin and added to the intellectual development of the state. In 1871, Wisconsin was hit by the great Peshtigo forest fire, the worst natural disaster in its history, which killed more than 1,000 persons and destroyed more than $5 million worth of property. An extensive reforestation program is part of Wisconsin's current far-reaching conservation efforts.

Wisconsin is the home of the three major league sports teams. The Green Bay Packers have won the NFL championship eleven times and the Milwaukee Bucks became the NBA champions in 1971. Major league baseball returned to the state in 1970 when the Seattle club of the American League became the Milwaukee Brewers.

In 1976 Wisconsin became the first of the 1976 primary states to hold an open presidential primary election. The Democratic National Committee decided in 1978 to bar open primaries in this state as well as in Michigan and Montana.

Full name: State of Wisconsin. **Origin of name:** From an Indian name. **Inhabitant:** Wisconsinite. **Capital:** Madison. **State motto:** Forward. **Flag:** State seal on a blue field. **Seal:** A sailor & a miner hold shield with symbols representing Wisconsin's industries; badger is state's nickname; horn of plenty; pyramid of lead. **Flower:** Wood violet. **Bird:** Robin. **Tree:** Sugar maple. **Rock:** Granite. **Mineral:** Galena. **Domestic Animal:** Dairy Cow. **Song:** "On, Wisconsin!" **Nickname:** Badger State.

Governor: Lee Sherman Dreyfus. **Annual salary:** $65,801. **Term:** 4 years. **Current term expires:** Jan. 1983. **Voting requirements:** 18 yrs. old & U.S. citizen; registered 10 days. **U.S. Congressmen:** 9. **Entered Union:** 1848 (30th state).

Location & boundaries: Midwestern state: bounded on the north by Lake Superior & the state of Michigan; on the east by Lake Michigan; on the south by Illinois; & on the west by Iowa, Minnesota, the Mississippi River & the St. Croix River. **Total area:** 56,154 sq. mi. (ranks 26th). **Extreme length:** 315 mi. **Extreme breadth:** 289 mi. **Shoreline:** 785 mi. **Chief rivers:** Mississippi, Wisconsin, St. Croix, Black, Fox. **Major lakes:** Winnebago, Poygan, Mendota, Pentenwell, Castle Rock. **No. of counties:** 72.

Population (1980 census): 4,705,335 (ranks 16th). **Pop. increase (1970-80):** 6.5%. **Largest cities:** Milwaukee, Madison, Green Bay, Racine. **Pop. density:** 83.8 per sq. mi. (ranks 23rd). **Pop. distribution:** White—4,442,598; Black—182,593; Am. Indian, Eskimo and Aleut—29,497; Asian and Pacific Islander—18,165; Other—32,482; Spanish origin—62,981. **Marriage rate (1978):** 8.2 per 1,000 people. **Divorce rate:** 3.4 per 1,000 people.

State finances (1979). Revenue: $6,255,000,000. **Expenditures:** $5,381,000,000. **State taxes:** $690.77 per capita. **State personal income tax:** Yes. **Public debt (1979):** $473.30 per capita. **Federal aid (1980):** $430.02 per capita. **Personal income (1980):** $9,254.

Sectors of the economy (% of labor force employed in 1970): Manufacturing (31%), Wholesale and retail trade (20%), Government (14%), Educational Services (8%), Services (6%), Construction (5%). **Leading products:** machinery, food items, transportation equipment, paper items, primary & fabricated metals. **Agricultural products:** dairy items, cattle, hogs, hay, corn, oats. **Fishing:** whitefish, lake herring, chubs, carp, buffalo. **Avg. farm (1980):** 198 acres. **Avg. value of farm per acre:** $928.

Highway expenditures per capita (1979): $86.64. **Persons per motor vehicle:** 1.46. **Minimum age for driver's license:** 16. **Gasoline tax:** 9¢ per gallon. **Diesel tax:** 9¢ per gallon. **Motor vehicle deaths (1978):** 20.9 per 100,000 pop.

Birthrate (1978): 14.7 per 1,000 people. **Infant mortality rate per 1,000 births (1978):** 11.2. **Physicians per 100,000 pop. (1978):** 150. **Dentists per 100,000 pop. (1978):** 57. **Acceptable hospital beds (1978):** 6.07 per 1,000 people. **State expenditures per capita for health and hospitals (1979):** $65.15.

Education expenditures (1976-77): $536.70 per capita annually. **No. of pupils in public schools (1979):** 865,000. **No. of institutions of higher learning (1978-79):** 62. **Public school expenditure per pupil in attendance (1977-78):** $2,166. **Avg. salary of public school teachers (1978-79):** $15,600. **No. full-time teachers (1979):** 55,400. **Educational attainment of adult population (1976):** 12.5 median yrs. of school completed: 1.4% with less than 5 years of education; 12.7% with 4 yrs. of college.

Telephones (1978): 54 per 100 people. **State Chamber of Commerce:** Wisconsin Association of Manufacturers & Commerce, 111 E. Wisconsin Ave., Room 1600, Milwaukee, Wisconsin 53202.

WYOMING

Wyoming, an awesome, sparsely settled state of alternating plains and mountains, is crossed by the Continental Divide—the junction of the Great Plains and the Rocky Mountains, which slash across the state's rectangle from the northwest corner to the center of the southern boundary.

The plains-mountains dividing line is less marked in the central and northern "intermontane" areas. The horizons are distant, and the land generally high—its average altitude of 6,700 feet is second only to Colorado's. The spectacular Devil's Tower—the country's first national monument—is a volcanic plug in the northeastern plains that stands 865 feet above its 415-foot base and can be seen for many miles.

The face of the land provides a clue to its economy. Short, tough grass covers much of the terrain, 80 percent of which is used for cattle and sheep grazing (Wyoming is second only to Texas in wool production). Recent consolidations have increased the size but decreased the number of farms and ranches within the state. About 20 percent of the farms produce commercial crops; the others are devoted to livestock production.

The growth of agriculture, however, is limited by the state's water supply. Although Wyoming has sufficient precipitation and underground springs to foster crop growth, as late as 1966 only ten percent of these resources were being utilized effectively. The perennial problem is distribution: in some places, where the soil is suitable for farming, the streamflow and precipitation are too light, while many large rivers like the Yellowstone and Tongue run through steep, rocky canyons.

More important to the state than agriculture is mining. In 1975, the assessed valuation on minerals was 48 percent of the entire state valuation. With the rise in oil prices, Wyoming has become one of the most intensively explored states in the Union. The Overthrust Belt near the Utah border shows great promise. Oil and oil products are among Wyoming's leading industries. Other minerals include bentonite, trona, coal, uranium, and iron ore. Wyoming is the second largest uranium producing state. Devastated by the conversion of railroad locomotives to diesel power, coal is making a comeback following formulation of emission standards which make Wyoming's low sulphur coal very much in demand. The state's coal reserves are estimated at 36 billion tons, of which two-thirds is recoverable through strip mining and underground mining methods.

John Colter, a fur-trapper and a member of the Lewis and Clark expedition (1804-06), is the first European known to have entered the state; in 1807 he explored the Yellowstone area and brought back news of its geysers and hot springs.

By 1850, pioneers were "going west" via three famous trails, all of which passed through Wyoming: the California, Mormon (to Utah), and Oregon (to the Pacific Northwest). Meanwhile the Plains Indians, their homeland challenged, grew increasingly hostile, raiding wagon trains and defy-

WYOMING

ing accompanying troops. These troubles climaxed in 1865-66, then tapered off.

The Union Pacific Railroad was built (1867-68) across southern Wyoming, following the coal deposits and bringing in laborers to work the mines. The scant farmland caused many homesteaders to bypass Wyoming, leaving it open for cattlemen, who enjoyed bonanza days from 1865 to 1887.

Rustlers, declining market prices, and the severe winter of 1886-87 in which one-sixth of the herds starved all helped to curtail the cattle industry's dominance. About this time, sheep raising began to increase, leading to conflict between sheepmen and cattlemen over grazing rights.

Today tourism is increasingly vital to Wyoming's economy: over nine million persons—including many sportsmen—visit the state annually. Yellowstone and Grand Teton National Parks are prime attractions. Other National Park Service facilities are Devils Tower and Fossil Butte National Monuments; Bighorn Canyon and Flaming Gorge National Recreation Areas; and Fort Laramie National Historic Site. Wyoming has been decisively thrust into the missile age by Warren AFB (Cheyenne), one of the largest in the nation's ICBM complex.

Full name: State of Wyoming. **Origin of name:** Named after Wyoming Valley, Pennsylvania; Indian word means "Alternating Mountains & Valleys." **Inhabitant:** Wyomingite. **Capital:** Cheyenne. **State motto:** Equal Rights. **Flag:** State seal & buffalo on a red-&-white-bordered blue field. **Seal:** Woman & motto, "Equal Rights," symbolize equal treatment women have had in state; two men represent Wyoming's livestock & mining industries; dates Wyoming became territory & state. **Flower:** Indian paintbrush. **Bird:** Meadowlark. **Tree:** Cottonwood. **Song:** "Wyoming." **Nickname:** Equality State.

Governor: Ed Herschler. **Annual salary:** $55,000. **Term:** 4 years. **Current term expires:** Jan. 1983. **Voting requirements:** 18 yrs. old & U.S. citizen; resident of state & registered to vote before or at primary for general election. **U.S. Congressmen:** 1. **Entered Union:** 1890 (44th state).

Location & boundaries: Rocky Mountain state: bounded on the north by Montana; on the east by South Dakota & Nebraska; on the south by Colorado & Utah; on the west by Utah, Idaho & Montana. **Total area:** 97,914 sq. mi. (ranks 9th). **Extreme length:** 365 mi.

Extreme breadth: 265 mi. **Chief rivers:** North Platte, Bighorn, Green, Snake. **Major lakes:** Yellowstone, Jackson, Flaming Gorge Reservoir. **No. of counties:** 23.

Population (1980 census): 470,816 (ranks 49th). **Pop. increase (1970-80):** 41.6%. **Largest cities:** Casper, Cheyenne, Laramie. **Pop. density:** 4.8 per sq. mi. (ranks 49th). **Pop. distribution:** White—447,716; Black—3,364; Am. Indian, Eskimo and Aleut—7,125; Asian and Pacific Islander—1,969; Other—10,642; Spanish origin—24,499. **Marriage rate (1978):** 14.8 per 1,000 people. **Divorce rate:** 7.4 per 1,000 people.

State finances (1979). Revenue: $789,000,000. **Expenditures:** $633,000,000. **State taxes:** $761.83 per capita. **State personal income tax:** No. **Public debt (1979):** $480.16 per capita. **Federal aid (1980):** $405.25 per capita. **Personal income (1980):** $10,692.

Sectors of the economy (% of labor force employed in 1970): Government (22%), Wholesale and retail trade (20%), Educational Services (11%), Services (9%), Construction (7%), Manufacturing (6%). **Leading products:** petroleum & coal items; food items; stone, clay & glass items; lumber & wood; printing & publishing. **Minerals:** petroleum, natural gas, sodium salts, iron ore, uranium. **Agricultural products:** cattle, sheep, wool, hay, sugarbeets, wheat. **Avg. farm (1980):** 4,875 acres. **Avg. value of farm per acre:** $127.

Highway expenditures per capita (1979): $277.23. **Persons per motor vehicle:** .96. **Minimum age for driver's license:** 16. **Gasoline tax:** 8¢ per gallon. **Diesel tax:** None. **Motor vehicle deaths (1978):** 56.8 per 100,000 people.

Birthrate (1978): 20.4 per 1,000 people. **Infant mortality rate per 1,000 births (1978):** 13.0. **Physicians per 100,000 pop. (1978):** 112. **Dentists per 100,000 pop. (1978):** 51. **Acceptable hospital beds (1978):** 5.30 per 1,000 people. **State expenditures per capita for health and hospitals (1979):** $57.71.

Education expenditures (1976-77): $637.03 per capita annually. **No. of pupils in public schools (1979):** 64,000. **No. of institutions of higher learning (1978-79):** 8. **Public school expenditure per pupil in attendance (1977-78):** $2,454. **Avg. salary of public school teachers (1978-79):** $14,939. **No. full-time teachers (1979):** 6,000. **Educational attainment of adult population (1976):** 12.6 median yrs. of school completed: 1.2% with less than 5 years of education; 14.5% with 4 yrs. of college.

Telephones (1978): 58 per 100 people. **State Chamber of Commerce:** None.

LEADING STATES IN AGRICULTURAL AND MINERAL PRODUCTION

CROPS–1979

Apples	Washington, New York, Michigan
Corn	Iowa, Illinois, Nebraska
Cotton	Texas, California, Mississippi
Grapes	California, Michigan, New York
Lettuce	California, Arizona
Oranges	Florida, California, Arizona
Peaches	California, South Carolina, Georgia
Peanuts	Georgia, Alabama, Texas
Pears	California, Washington, Oregon
Potatoes	Idaho, Washington, Maine
Soybeans	Illinois, Iowa, Missouri
Tobacco	North Carolina, Kentucky, South Carolina
Tomatoes	California, Florida
Wheat	Kansas, North Dakota, Oklahoma

POULTRY–1979

Chickens	Georgia, Arkansas, California
Turkeys	Minnesota, North Carolina, California

LIVESTOCK–1980

Cattle	Texas, Iowa, Nebraska
Hogs	Iowa, Illinois, Indiana, Minnesota
Milk Cows	Wisconsin, New York, California
Sheep	Texas, California, Wyoming

FUELS–1978

Coal	Kentucky, West Virginia, Pennsylvania
Natural Gas	Texas, Louisiana, Oklahoma
Petroleum	Texas, Louisiana, California
Uranium	New Mexico, Wyoming, Texas

METALS–1978

Bauxite	Arkansas, Alabama, Georgia
Copper	Arizona, Utah, New Mexico
Gold	South Dakota, Nevada, Utah
Iron Ore	Minnesota, Michigan, California
Lead	Missouri, Idaho, Colorado
Molybdenum	Colorado, Arizona, Utah
Silver	Idaho, Arizona, Colorado
Tungsten	California, Colorado, Nevada
Vanadium	Colorado, Utah, Idaho
Zinc	Tennessee, Missouri, Idaho

NONMETALS–1978

Phosphate Rock	Florida, Idaho, North Carolina
Potash	New Mexico, Utah, California
Salt	Louisiana, Texas, New York
Sand and Gravel	California, Arkansas, Texas
Stone	Pennsylvania, Texas, Illinois
Sulfur	Texas, Louisiana

REPRESENTATIVE AMERICAN CITIES

ALBUQUERQUE

Location: North-central New Mexico, on upper Rio Grande **County:** Bernalillo **City Area:** 100 sq. miles (259 sq. kilometers) **Altitude:** 5,354 feet (1631.9 meters)
Mayor: David Rusk **Chief Administrative Officer:** Jim Jaramillo
City Population: 331,767 (1980 census) **Metro Area Population:** 454,499 (1980 census)
Daily Newspapers: 2 **No. of Radio Stations:** 22 **No. of TV Stations:** 7
City Chamber of Commerce: Greater Albuquerque Chamber of Commerce, 401 2nd Street, NW, Albuquerque, New Mexico 87102

Albuquerque, seat of Bernalillo County, is the largest city in New Mexico; a fast-growing center of trade, clean industry, and Federal agencies; and a health resort. On a per capita basis, more solar-heated homes stand here than in any other large U.S. city.

The old town of Albuquerque was founded in 1706 and named for the Duke of Alburquerque. After the Mexican War (1846-48), New Mexico was organized as a U.S. territory. Albuquerque was occupied by Confederate forces briefly in 1862. The new Albuquerque was mapped out in 1880 in connection with railroad construction.

After World War II, the city grew rapidly, primarily because of Sandia Laboratory (a nuclear weapons laboratory and the city's largest employer) and Kirtland Air Force Base, a nuclear effects research laboratory and satellite tracking station. Lovelace Foundation for medical research is also located here. Albuquerque now has railroad shops, lumber mills, and food-processing plants. Manufactures include brick and tile, wood products, Indian jewelry, clothing, and business machines. Several national electronic firms have opened facilities recently. New office buildings and hotels are being constructed and a major redevelopment of the downtown area is underway.

Of historic interest is the Old Town Plaza, laid out by Spanish settlers in 1706. Some of the buildings are two centuries old and have recently been restored. The Church of San Felipe de Neri (1706), once used as a fortress against the Indians, is in the Old Town. Other attractions are the University of New Mexico, founded in 1889, with pueblo-style buildings; the Ernie Pyle Memorial Branch Library, former home of the war correspondent; the annual state fair; and the magnificent vistas from the Sandia Peak Aerial Tramway.

ATLANTA

Location: Northwest Georgia, at foot of Blue Ridge Mountains, about 75 miles from northern border **County:** mostly in Fulton, part in DeKalb **City Area:** 136 sq. miles (352 sq. kilometers) **Altitude:** 1,050 feet (319.1 meters)
Mayor: Maynard H. Jackson
City Population: 425,022 (1980 census) **Metro Area Population:** 2,029,618 (1980 census)
Daily Newspapers: 3 **No. of Radio Stations:** 23 **No. of TV Stations:** 8
City Chamber of Commerce: Atlanta Chamber of Commerce, 1300 North Omni International, Atlanta, Georgia 30303

Atlanta, seat of Fulton County and capital and largest city of Georgia, is the leading commercial, industrial, and distribution center of the southeastern United States. It is also a port of entry and cultural center.

The first settler, Hardy Ivy, built a cabin on former Creek Indian land in 1833. The town, founded as Terminus in 1837, was later called Marthasville and in 1845 assumed the name Atlanta. It is said that the name was given it by railroad builder J. E. Thomson for its location at the end of the Western and Atlantic Railroad. It was incorporated as a city in 1847.

An important Confederate communications center during the Civil War, Atlanta fell to General W. T. Sherman on September 2, 1864, and on November 15 was put to the torch and almost completely destroyed. After the war, a new city was constructed and industrialization proceeded rapidly. In 1868 Atlanta became the state capital.

Today there are more than 1,500 manufacturing plants in the area. Products include automobiles, airplanes, chemicals, furniture, steel, paper, fertilizers, soft drinks, and processed foods. Atlanta is a major garment manufacturing center and is the home of the Apparel Mart, opened in 1979 as a showcase for southeastern clothing buyers. It is also a financial center and home of a Federal Reserve district bank. The National Center for Disease Control of the U.S. Public Health Service has its national headquarters here.

A billion-dollar building boom has included major privately financed projects plus several public facilities: a stadium and coliseum are in operation; the $70-million Georgia World Congress convention complex opened in September 1976. The Atlanta Memorial Arts Center, in memory of the 100 members of the Atlanta Art Association killed in a plane crash, opened in 1968. The Metropolitan Atlanta Rapid Transit Authority's $2.1-billion Federally financed subway system started services July 1, 1979. Atlanta's tallest building, the 52-story Georgia-Pacific Tower, will open in 1982.

In recent years Atlanta has developed its international trade, with a dozen foreign banks, 11 consulates and 10 foreign trade bureaus opening, earning the nickname "Paris of the South." Atlanta's new William B. Hartsfield International Airport is the global air hub of the southeast.

Of historic interest are the capitol and state library; the state archives building; the Cyclorama of the Battle of Atlanta; Oakland Cemetery of Civil War dead; Martin Luther King, Jr., National Historic Site; Fort Peachtree; Fort McPherson; and Wren's Nest, the home of Joel Chandler Harris, noted fabulist.

BALTIMORE

Location: In Maryland, 40 miles northeast of Washington, D.C., on the Patapsco River **County:** Baltimore is an independent city **City Area:** 79 sq. miles (205 sq. kilometers) **Altitude:** 20 feet (6.1 meters)
Mayor: William Donald Schaefer
City Population: 786,775 (1980 census) **Metro Area Population:** 2,174,023 (1980 census)
Daily Newspapers: 2 **No. of Radio Stations:** 24 **No. of TV Stations:** 3
City Chamber of Commerce: Greater Baltimore Committee, Inc., Suite 900, Two Hopkins Plaza, Charles Center, Baltimore, Maryland 21201

Baltimore, largest city in Maryland, is an industrial and commercial center and major seaport. Named for Lord Baltimore, first proprietor of Maryland, it was settled in the early 1600s and officially founded in 1729.

The shipbuilding industry grew highly profitable during the Revolution and War of 1812. The famous Baltimore clippers were built in the early 1800s. During the First and Second World Wars, the city was a major shipbuilder and supply port.

Baltimore was the site of the Continental Congress after the British occupation of Philadelphia (1777-78). The city's location, near the eastern terminus of the National Road that eventually ran from Cumberland to St. Louis, helped it develop into a major center of commerce. The opening in 1825 of the Erie Canal, in New York State, diverting trade, led to the chartering of the Baltimore & Ohio Railroad to bolster Baltimore's position.

During the Civil War, Maryland remained in the Union, but many Baltimore residents were pro-Southern and in 1861 some of them attacked Union troops. The city suffered a disastrous fire in 1904 but emerged as a better-planned metropolis.

Of historic interest are the Maryland Historical Society; the Baltimore Cathedral, the 175-year-old U.S. Frigate Constellation; Edgar Allan Poe's grave in Westminster Churchyard, and Ft. McHenry.

Today Baltimore handles the fourth largest volume of foreign trade of any American port. It has attracted diverse industries, including sugar and food processing. Petroleum and chemicals, aircraft, guided missiles, and steel and gypsum products are important industries. Bethlehem Steel Company's Sparrows Point complex, the largest tidewater steel plant in the world, is located here.

Baltimore, which suffers from the deterioration and shrinking population common to all Eastern cities, has attacked these problems vigorously. Through careful planning, long-term renewal efforts have begun to reverse the trend without adding to the city's debt load. A 8.5 mile subway is under construction and a major program of urban redevelopment has reshaped the downtown area. Charles Center, begun twenty years ago, is virtually complete, as is the Civic Center. In the Inner Harbor area, an Academy of Science has been completed, the Convention Center opened in August 1979, the Harborplace Shopping Pavilions opened in July 1980, and the National Aquarium opened in 1981.

To ease traffic jams plaguing the city's harbor tunnel, a $100-million federal grant was approved in 1980 for construction of a second connection, to be named Fort McHenry Tunnel.

BIRMINGHAM

Location: North-central Alabama, in the Jones Valley at the foot of Red Mt. **County:** Jefferson **City Area:** 98.4 sq. miles (254.9 sq. kilometers) **Altitude:** 600 feet (182.3 meters)
Mayor: Richard Arrington
City Population: 284,413 (1980 census) **Metro Area Population:** 847,360 (1980 census)
Daily Newspapers: 2 **No. of Radio Stations:** 17 **No. of TV Stations:** 4
City Chamber of Commerce: Birmingham Area Chamber of Commerce, P.O. Box 10127, Birmingham, Alabama 35202

Birmingham, seat of Jefferson County, is Alabama's principal industrial city and the South's leading iron-and-steel center.

Named after Birmingham, England, the city was founded and incorporated in 1871. A decade earlier the iron ore, coal, and limestone deposits in the region were used by Confederate forces to produce cannonballs and rifles. As railroads expanded and the steel industry developed, Birmingham prospered. A financial panic briefly interrupted its growth in 1900.

Since World War II, the city's economy has undergone diversification. Birmingham, "the Pittsburgh of the South," is now a leader in transportation equipment, construction materials, chemicals, and food processing.

Birmingham experienced a building boom during the 1960s; a $37.5-million civic center includes a coliseum, music hall, theater, and exhibit hall. Development of the University of Alabama in Birmingham is entering its final phase of completion on a 236-acre site adjacent to downtown. The $100-million complex of 40 buildings is expected to outstrip U.S. Steel as the area's biggest employer. By 1990, an estimated 50,000 people will be either an employee, a student, or both.

Of interest is the Arlington Historical Shrine, one of Alabama's few remaining antebellum homes. Overlooking the city on nearby Red Mountain is a giant statue of Vulcan, the largest iron figure ever cast. The Birmingham Museum of Art has recently been enlarged. The city is also the home of the Southern Research Institute, which has a technical staff of 360.

BOSTON

Location: In Massachusetts, on Massachusetts Bay, between Neponset River and the mouths of the Charles and Mystic rivers **County:** Suffolk **City Area:** 49.9 sq. miles (129.2 sq. kilometers) **Altitude:** 27 feet (8.2 meters)
Mayor: Kevin H. White
City Population: 562,994 (1980 census) **Metro Area Population:** 2,763,357 (1980 census)
Daily Newspapers: 3 **No. of Radio Stations:** 23 **No. of TV Stations:** 9
City Chamber of Commerce: Greater Boston Chamber of Commerce, 125 High Street, Boston, Massachusetts 02110

Boston, seat of Suffolk County and capital of Massachusetts, is New England's largest city. It was settled in 1630 by Puritan colonists. It became the center of American Puritanism and a fount of culture and intellect. The Boston Public Latin School, founded in 1635, and Harvard College, founded the following year in nearby Cambridge, were the first American schools.

An important commercial center because of its busy harbor, Boston became a leader in opposing British rule. Among pre-Revolutionary War actions were the Boston Massacre (1770) and the Boston Tea Party (1773). The Battle of Bunker Hill, one of the first of the Revolution, was fought close by in June 1775.

After the war, Boston prospered steadily and became a city in 1822. Prominent families such as the Cabots, Lowells, and Lodges ("the Boston Brahmins") made fortunes in shipping, textiles, and shoes. Because of the cultivated tastes of wealthy Bostonians, the city became known as "the Athens of America." Despite the conservative and wealthy atmosphere, however, it was a center of abolitionism before the Civil War.

A 19th-century flood of immigrants, largely Irish at first, converted Boston into a thriving industrial metropolis. Although it declined during the first half of the 20th century, primarily because industries moved to the South, Boston remained a cultural center and is still the financial and trading center of New England, a leading port, and an important market for fish, seafood, and wool. The electronics industry has helped revived Boston's economy.

Boston is also noted for its hospitals and its universities, among them Northeastern, Boston University and Boston College, as well as Harvard and MIT across the Charles River in Cambridge. In October 1979 the John F. Kennedy Library was dedicated.

History-steeped Boston has many points of interest from colonial and Revolutionary War times, including the Old North Church, Old South Meeting House, Old State House, Paul Revere House, King's Chapel, Boston Common and Faneuil Hall.

Downtown has undergone major redevelopment in recent years, with the building of commercial and residential high-rises, the Government Center and the renovation of Faneuil Hall Marketplace, including Quincy, South and North Markets, the Downtown Crossing Pedestrian shopping mall, and Boston Waterfront Park.

BUFFALO

Location: Western New York, at mouth of Niagara River on Lake Erie **County:** Erie **City Area:** 42.6 sq. miles (110.3 sq. kilometers) **Altitude:** 585 feet (177.8 meters)
Mayor: James D. Griffin
City Population: 357,870 (1980 census) **Metro Area Population:** 1,242,573 (1980 census)
Daily Newspapers: 2 **No. of Radio Stations:** 19 **No. of TV Stations:** 5
City Chamber of Commerce: Buffalo Area Chamber of Commerce, 107 Delaware Ave., Buffalo, New York 14202

Buffalo, seat of Erie County and second largest city in New York State, was named after a local creek, which in turn derived its name from that of an Indian who once lived in the area.

A village was laid out on the site of the present city by Joseph Ellicott for the Holland Land Company in 1803. Almost completely destroyed by fire during the War of 1812, Buffalo grew slowly until the opening of the Erie Canal in 1825 after which it mushroomed. Buffalo was chartered as a city in 1832, became an important transportation center, a major Great Lakes port, and since the opening of the St. Lawrence Seaway, a world port.

The city has had a long association with the Presidency. Millard Fillmore, Buffalo resident, was elected Vice-President in 1848 and two years later became President after the death of Zachary Taylor. Grover Cleveland, mayor of Buffalo in 1881, was elected President in 1884 and 1892. During the 1901 Pan-American Exposition, President McKinley was assassinated in Buffalo.

Industry in the Buffalo area has flourished, largely because of hydroelectric power from Niagara Falls augmented by the Niagara Power Project, one of the largest hydroelectric power projects in the world. Buffalo is the largest grain-milling center in the world. Bethlehem Steel and General Motors are the two largest industrial employers in the area, while the State University at Buffalo is the largest service employer.

Downtown Buffalo has undergone a tremendous facelift in the past ten years. In Oct. 1978, the Buffalo Convention Center was completed, strengthening the Niagara Frontier as a prime locale for conventions. The light rail rapid transit system is underway and will be completed by 1984.

Of interest in the area are nearby Niagara Falls; the Buffalo Museum of Science, Historical Museum, and Zoological Gardens; the Albright-Knox Art Gallery; Botanical Gardens; and Niagara Square.

Buffalo's professional sports teams include the Bills (NFL), Sabres (NHL), Bisons (Eastern-League baseball), and Stallions (indoor soccer).

CHARLESTON

Location: In southeastern part of South Carolina, along coast, on peninsula between Ashley and Cooper Rivers **County:** Charleston **City Area:** 20.6 sq. miles (53.5 sq. kilometers) **Altitude:** sea level **Mayor:** Joseph P. Riley, Jr.
City Population: 69,510 (1980 census) **Metro Area Population:** 430,301 (1980 census)
Daily Newspapers: 2 **No. of Radio Stations:** 11 **No. of TV Stations:** 3
City Chamber of Commerce: Charleston Trident Chamber of Commerce, P.O. Box 975, Charleston, South Carolina 29402

Charleston is a major Atlantic seaport and, as one of America's oldest cities, a leading tourist center. It was originally called Charles Towne in honor of Charles II by the English settlers who first landed in 1670 at Albemarle Point, about 7 miles from modern Charleston. Ten years later they moved to Oyster Point, where the city had been laid out according to the Grande Modell sent from England by the Lords Proprietor. It was incorporated in 1783 as Charleston and became the economic and social center of the region.

By the time of the Revolution, Charleston was the most important city south of Philadelphia. It was a wealthy cultural center to which French Huguenots and other non-English immigrants gave a cosmopolitan touch.

Charleston's role in the Civil War began when the South Carolina ordinance of secession was passed there in December 1860. The city's harbor was also the site of the first hostile act of the war: the firing on Fort Sumter on April 12, 1861. Although under continuous siege from 1863 to 1865, Charleston did not fall to Union forces until February 1865.

Despite the ravages of two wars, disastrous fires, a violent earthquake in 1886, and periodic hurricanes, Charleston has retained many historic buildings and colonial mansions. Of interest are: Fort Sumter, a national monument since 1948; Patriot's Point, a naval museum; the Dock Street Theater, opened in 1735; the original Catfish Row, made famous in Gershwin's *Porgy and Bess*; the Charleston Museum, founded in 1773; the Huguenot Church built in 1680 and rebuilt in 1844, and numerous ante-bellum homes in the peninsula city. Nearby are notable plantation homes and three world famous gardens: Cypress, Magnolia and Middleton. Charles Towne Landing (a park, pavilion, and natural zoo), was established at the time of the city's tricentennial anniversary in 1970.

The city's growing economy is linked to port and transportation expansion and commerce; diversified business, industrial, and education centers; and military installations and facilities maintained by the Army, Navy, Air Force, and the Coast Guard. New construction projects, such as the proposed Charleston Convention Center and a $13-million hotel, will bring in more tourists and more tax revenue, revitalizing the downtown area. However, controversy over the location of the convention center site, on land surrounded by areas under restoration, has held up construction.

Spoleto Festival USA, "the world's most comprehensive art festival," has become an annual event, featuring music, drama, ballet, films, opera, dance and visual arts.

CHICAGO

Location: Northeastern corner of Illinois on shore of Lake Michigan **County:** Cook **City Area:** 228.1 sq. miles (590.8 sq. kilometers) **Altitude:** 578.5 feet (175.8 meters)
Mayor: Jane Byrne
City Population: 3,005,072 (1980 census) **Metro Area Population:** 7,102,328 (1980 census)
Daily Newspapers: 2 **No. of Radio Stations:** 26 **No. of TV Stations:** 9
City Chamber of Commerce: Chicago Association of Commerce and Industry, 130 S. Michigan Ave., Chicago, Illinois 60603

Chicago, seat of Cook County, Illinois, is the largest city between the Eastern seaboard and the Pacific Coast, the most important Great Lakes port, the center of the nation's largest industrial area, and the world's largest railroad terminal. Its O'Hare International Airport is considered the world's busiest.

Father Marquette and Louis Jolliet visited the site of Chicago in 1673, but more than a century elapsed before a trading post was established, by Jean Baptiste Point du Sable. He was succeeded in 1804 by the first permanant non-Indian settler, John Kinzie, who is usually regarded as the "father of Chicago."

The Erie Canal, which was opened in 1825, stimulated growth and helped convert Chicago into a prosperous commercial town. Incorporated as a city in 1837, it developed into a major rail hub and the nation's mid-continent shipping center soon after the arrival of the railroads in the 1840s. By the time of the Civil War, meatpacking had become a leading industry.

In 1871 the city was almost completely destroyed by a great fire. It was quickly rebuilt, and its booming industry attracted immigrants from all over the world. In the 1890s Chicago replaced Philadelphia as the nation's second-largest city. Labor problems led to violent eruptions, such as the Haymarket Riot of 1886 and Pullman strikes in 1894.

Chicago is a leading producer of steel, telephone equipment, appliances, electrical machinery, plastic products, and diesel engines. It boasts a Federal Reserve district bank, the Midwest Stock Exchange, the Chicago Mercantile Exchange, and the Chicago Board of Trade—the world's largest commodity futures market.

The skyscraper was Chicago's contribution to American architecture. The first skyscraper, designed by William Le Baron Jenney, was built here in 1883, and of the world's ten tallest buildings, four are in Chicago. Two of the nation's greatest architects, Louis H. Sullivan and Frank Lloyd Wright, worked in Chicago.

Landmarks of interest in the Chicago area include the Sears Tower, the world's tallest skyscraper; the Chicago Mercantile Exchange, a major international commodity and monetary market; the Merchandise Mart, the largest commercial building in the world; the Art Institute; the Museum of Science and Industry; the Shedd Aquarium; the Adler Planetarium; the Oriental Institute Museum of the University of Chicago; the Lincoln Park and Brookfield Zoos; and the Water Tower, one of the few structures to survive the 1871 fire. In 1974 the Chagall mosaic was unveiled at the First National Bank Plaza; it consists of a colorful wall of glass and stone from all over the world. Since then, monumental outdoor sculpture by such notables as Picasso, Calder, Bertoia, Noguchi, Oldenburg, Moore and Miró have been unveiled in Chicago.

Scheduled for completion in 1989 is the Illinois Center, the nation's largest planned urban development. The Center is situated northeast of the Loop and borders the lakeshore. The daytime working population will total 80,000, some of whom will reside in the Center's high-rise apartment buildings.

CINCINNATI

Location: Southwestern Ohio, on Ohio River **County:** Hamilton **City Area:** 78 sq. miles (202 sq. kilometers) **Altitude:** 550 feet (167.1 meters)
Mayor: David Mann **City Manager:** Sylvester Murray
City Population: 385,457 (1980 census) **Metro Area Population:** 1,401,403 (1980 census)
Daily Newspapers: 2 **No. of Radio Stations:** 25 **No. of TV Stations:** 6
City Chamber of Commerce: Greater Cincinnati Chamber of Commerce, 120 West Fifth Street, Cincinnati, Ohio 45202

Cincinnati, seat of Ohio's Hamilton County, is an industrial, commercial, and cultural center. The first settlers arrived in 1788 and named it Losantiville. In 1790 General Arthur St. Clair, first governor of the Northwest Territory, renamed it Cincinnati for the Society of the Cincinnati, which was formed by Continental Army officers at the end of the American Revolution. Cincinnati was the first seat of the legislature of the Northwest Territory; it was incorporated in 1802 and chartered as a city in 1819.

Completion of the Miami Canal (1827) and the Ohio and Erie Canal in the 1830s increased the growth of Cincinnati and its importance as a shipping center. The city was also a major station on the Underground Railroad.

Cincinnati suffered disastrous floods in 1884 and 1937. The Cincinnati riot (March 28-31, 1884) was the result of a crime wave and corrupt politics. Later the notorious political boss G. B. Cox took control, but a reform movement in the 1920s led to the establishment (1924) of the city-manager type of government.

Located on the Ohio River, Cincinnati is a major manufacturing center and a leading producer of machine tools, soap products, and playing cards. Cosmetics, radar equipment, automobiles, jet engines, and metal goods also are important to the economy. In 1976 the Environmental Protection Agency Laboratory opened here.

Recent additions to the refurbished downtown area are the new Westin Hotel, Atrium One and the First National Bank Center. The architecturally renowned Union Terminal has been given a new lease on life as an urban shopping mall.

Riverfront Stadium, built in 1970, houses the Cincinnati Bengals Football Team and the Cincinnati Reds Baseball Team. The Cincinnati Zoo and the Cincinnati Art Museum are prime attractions of the city.

CLEVELAND

Location: Northeastern Ohio, on Lake Erie at mouth of the Cuyahoga River **County:** Cuyahoga **City Area:** 76 sq. miles (196.8 sq. kilometers) **Altitude:** 680 feet (206.6 meters)
Mayor: George V. Voinovich
City Population: 573,822 (1980 census) **Metro Area Population:** 1,898,720 (1980 census)
Daily Newspapers: 2 **No. of Radio Stations:** 17 **No. of TV Stations:** 5
City Chamber of Commerce: Greater Cleveland Growth Association, 690 Union Commerce Building, Cleveland, Ohio 44115

Cleveland, seat of Cuyahoga County and largest city in Ohio, is a port of entry on Lake Erie. It was laid out in 1796 by General Moses Cleaveland, an ancestor of President Grover Cleveland. Three years later a permanent settlement was established by Lorenzo Carter, and in 1836 Cleveland was chartered as a city.

After the completion of the Ohio and Erie Canal in the 1830s and the arrival of the railroad in 1851, Cleveland became a significant link between the interior of Ohio and eastern markets. Coal from Pennsylvania and iron ore shipped from Minnesota by way of the Great Lakes made the city an important iron and steel producer. It also developed into the main refining area for Pennsylvania oil, and in 1870 John D. Rockefeller began his oil dynasty in Cleveland. Immigrants from all over the world settled in the city to work in the industries. Many of their descendants still live in pleasant suburbs.

Mainstays of the economy today are the manufacture of machine tools and fabricated metal products with iron and steel a close third. Automobile parts, electrical equipment and chemicals are also important.

Cleveland has experienced a decline common to many large northern cities. However, cooperative efforts have produced an almost new downtown skyline, with new commercial and federal and local government buildings. The old flats area along the river has been restored, providing evening entertainment in the many restaurants and pubs.

Of special interest is the Emerald Necklace—a system of parks, trails, and bridle paths looping the city—along with the downtown Convention Center and Municipal Stadium. The East Side's University Circle area is a cultural center housing the Art Museum, Museum of Natural History, Western Reserve Historical Society Museum and Severanall Hall, home of the world-renowned Cleveland Orchestra.

In December 1978, the city failed to pay $14 million worth of promissory notes that had fallen due and thus became the first major U.S. city to default since the Great Depression. To generate additional revenue, voters approved a 50% increase in city income taxes in February 1979. The increase, plus a 20% lay-off of municipal employees, enabled the city to retire $3.5 million of debt and renegotiation of the notes saved Cleveland from bankruptcy.

COLUMBUS

Location: Central Ohio, on Scioto River **County:** Franklin **City Area:** 183.1 sq. miles (474.2 sq. kilometers) **Altitude:** 780 feet (237.0 meters)
Mayor: Tom Moody
City Population: 564,871 (1980 census) **Metro Area Population:** 1,093,293 (1980 census)
Daily Newspapers: 2 **No. of Radio Stations:** 16 **No. of TV Stations:** 4
City Chamber of Commerce: Columbus Area Chamber of Commerce, 50 West Broad Street, P.O. Box 1527, Columbus, Ohio 43216

Columbus, capital of Ohio and seat of Franklin County, is the state's largest city in area. It was laid out to be the capital in 1812, a position it assumed four years later, and chartered as a city in 1834. A feeder canal (1831) to the Ohio and Erie Canal, along with the National Road (1833), spurred development. By the middle of the 19th century the railroad had arrived, making Columbus a commercial and transportation center.

During the Civil War Columbus was an assembly point for recruits and the site of a Union arsenal. A cemetery at Camp Chase, a Civil War prison, contains the graves of 2,260 Confederate soldiers. By the end of the century the city was a leader in the manufacture of buggies, producing about 20,000 a year. In 1913 the Scioto River flooded, causing the death of more than 100 people.

Today about 20 percent of the working population is employed by the federal, state, or municipal government. Because it is the capital of a populous state and the home of a major university (Ohio State), Columbus was the only large northern city to boast of a 1980 census population increase. Industry is also a large employer; among the city's products are coal-mining machinery, concrete mixers, auto parts, paints, shoes, glassware, and refrigerators. Columbus is the headquarters of the Battelle Memorial Institute, an organization engaged in scientific, technological, and economic research.

Several downtown construction projects have generated excitement and confidence about Columbus as a place to work, to shop, and to live. Completion of the Ohio Center (convention center) and the Capitol South recreation, hotel and retail center insure continued growth of the downtown area.

DALLAS

Location: Northeastern Texas on Trinity River, about 75 miles south of Oklahoma border **County:** Dallas **City Area:** 350 sq. miles (906.5 sq. kilometers) **Altitude:** 481 feet (146.2 meters)
Mayor: Jack Evans
City Population: 904,078 (1980 census) **Metro Area Population:** 2,974,878 (1980 census)
Daily Newspapers: 2 **No. of Radio Stations:** 19 **No. of TV Stations:** 7
City Chamber of Commerce: Dallas Chamber of Commerce, 1507 Pacific Avenue, Dallas, Texas 75201

Dallas, seat of Dallas County and second largest city in Texas, is the financial and commercial center of the Southwest.

John Neely Bryan settled here in 1841 and later founded Dallas, probably naming it after George M. Dallas, then Vice President under James K. Polk.

In 1858 followers of the French social philosopher Charles Fourier abandoned their nearby socialist community, La Réunion, and moved to Dallas. Two years later a fire destroyed most of the town, but residents quickly rebuilt it. During the Civil War the Confederate Army had quartermaster, commissary, and administrative headquarters here.

Oil was discovered in eastern Texas in the 1930s, increasing the growth of Dallas, which was the site of the Texas Centennial Exposition in 1936. During and after World War II, population boomed following introduction of first the aircraft and then the electronics industries. Today the city's economy is highly diversified, with a strong manufacturing base and many corporate headquarters of the electronics, oil, gas, finance and insurance industries.

Dallas is the home of the annual Texas state fair, the Cotton Bowl football stadium, the NFL Dallas Cowboys, the Mavericks basketball team, the Tornado soccer team, and shares with Fort Worth the American Baseball

League's Texas Rangers. Dallas hosts annually final matches of the $100,000 World Championship of Tennis, the Byron Nelson Golf Classic, the U.S. Karate National Championships, and the Avon Futures Tennis Finals.

Another advantage which Dallas has created for itself is its role as a tourist/convention center. Its role as a merchandise distribution center helped make it a major buyers' market. Dallas/Fort Worth Airport is one of the world's largest airports.

Dallas is also the cultural center of Texas. Each year the city is host to the Metropolitan Opera and has its own Civic Opera and Symphony as well. There are other community enterprises in the cultural field including the Summer Musicals, the Civic Ballet, the Civic Chorus, the Dallas Theatre Center, and the Bob Hope Theatre.

DENVER

Location: North-central Colorado, on South Platte River **County:** Denver; city and county are coextensive **City Area:** 117 sq. miles (303 sq. kilometers) **Altitude:** 5,280 feet (1604.5 meters)
Mayor: William H. McNichols, Jr.
City Population: 491,396 (1980 census) **Metro Area Population:** 1,619,921 (1980 census)
Daily Newspapers: 2 **No. of Radio Stations:** 21 **No. of TV Stations:** 6
City Chamber of Commerce: Denver Chamber of Commerce, 1301 Welton, Denver, Colorado 80204

Denver, capital and largest city of Colorado, is a major commercial and financial center. It was settled in 1858 after the discovery of placer gold at the junction of the South Platte River and Cherry Creek, and named for James W. Denver, governor of the Kansas Territory, which then included eastern Colorado.

Denver was incorporated in 1861 and became the capital of the Colorado Territory six years later. During the 1870s and 1880s rich lodes of silver, gold, and copper were found in the Rockies, bringing fortune seekers to the area. The city boasted plush opera houses with singers imported from the East, makeshift boarding houses, and noisy saloons, such as the famous Silver Dollar.

By the end of the 19th century, Denver was beginning to develop into a large processing, shipping, and distributing point for an extensive agricultural area, making mining and metalworking less important. A federal mint has been in operation for more than a century. Today the aerospace industry makes a significant contribution to Denver's economy, and food processing is also a major occupation. In addition, the city is the regional center for many federal agencies. The Atomic Energy Commission's Rocky Flats plant is nearby, and the federal Solar Energy Research Institute opened in 1978 in nearby Golden, Colo. Denver is fast becoming a national energy capital, rivalling Houston in importance. The city is the center for the development of the West's energy resources—oil, gas, coal, shale oil, uranium, synthetic fuels and solar energy. As a result, new office construction is booming in Denver.

Military establishments in the area include Lowry Air Force Base; the Air Force Accounting and Finance Center; the army's Rocky Mountain Arsenal; and Fitzsimmons General Hospital. The Air Force Academy is in Colorado Springs, less than 100 miles south of Denver.

Denver, which maintains the largest system of public parks and recreational facilities in the world, is a tourist mecca. Of interest are the Colorado State Historical Museum, the tomb of Buffalo Bill, the Cody Museum, and the $6.1-million Denver Art Museum, a block-square, fortresslike structure set against a distant backdrop of Rocky Mountains, and the Denver Botanic Gardens. Nearby is Red Rocks Park with its famous Easter sunrise service. Denver is the home of the Denver Broncos football team, the Denver Nuggets basketball team and the Colorado Rockies hockey team.

DETROIT

Location: Southeastern Michigan, on Detroit River, between Lakes St. Clair and Erie, 18 miles north of Lake Erie **County:** Wayne **City Area:** 139.6 sq. miles (361.6 sq. kilometers) **Altitude:** 581 feet (176.5 meters)
Mayor: Coleman A. Young
City Population: 1,203,339 (1980 census) **Metro Area Population:** 4,352,762 (1980 census)
Daily Newspapers: 2 **No. of Radio Stations:** 32 **No. of TV Stations:** 8
City Chamber of Commerce: Greater Detroit Chamber of Commerce, 150 Michigan Ave., Detroit, Michigan 48226

Detroit, seat of Wayne County, is the largest city in Michigan and one of the largest in the United States. Antoine de la Mothe Cadillac established a French fort (Pontchartrain) and settlement on the site in 1701.

The settlement took the name Detroit from the French word for "strait," because it was on the water link between Lake Erie and Lake St. Clair. Detroit was ceded to the British in 1763, turned over to the United States in 1796, destroyed by fire in 1805, rebuilt, and occupied by the British for a year during the War of 1812. It became an important commercial center after the opening of the Erie Canal in 1825.

From 1837, when Michigan became a state, until 1847, Detroit was the capital. It was connected by rail to Chicago in 1852 and to New York two years later. The city was a key terminus of the Underground Railroad.

Detroit assumed great importance after the middle of the 19th century because of its shipping, shipbuilding, and manufacturing.

Today, Greater Detroit serves as international headquarters for General Motors, American Motors, Ford and Chrysler. But with the auto industry in a severe slump, the unemployment rate in the "Motor City" soared to nearly twice the national average during the recession of 1980. The Detroit-Pontiac-Flint corridor produces some 25 percent of all the cars and trucks built in the United States. Detroit is linked to Windsor, Ont., by a bridge over and a tunnel under the Detroit River.

The city also is international headquarters for the United Automobile, Aerospace and Agricultural Implement Workers of America (UAW), which has been embroiled in many labor disputes.

Detroit has had two major racial riots. One in 1943 and the other in 1967.

Renaissance Center, a $350-million complex along Detroit's downtown riverfront, the new Joe Louis Arena, and the Senator Philip A. Hart Plaza are three of the new construction projects completed in recent years. The Horace E. Dodge & Son Memorial Fountain, designed by Isamu Noguchi, has become the center of community activity and the permanent home of Detroit's famous international ethnic festivals. The city was host to the 1980 Republican convention.

The Detroit Symphony Orchestra, Detroit Institute of Arts, and the Detroit Zoo are rated among the nation's best. Henry Ford Museum and Greenfield Village, which contains Thomas A. Edison's original laboratories and many early American landmarks, attract more than 1.6 million visitors annually to suburban Dearborn. Belle Isle, a 1,000-acre park in the Detroit River, is a major recreation center, with gardens, a conservatory, children's zoo and aquarium among attractions.

FORT WORTH

Location: Northern Texas, at the junction of the Clear and West forks of the Trinity River about 30 miles west of Dallas **Counties:** Tarrant, Hood, Wise, Parker and Johnson **City Area:** 244 sq. miles (632 sq. kilometers) **Altitude:** 670 feet (203.6 meters)
Mayor: Woodie Woods **City Manager:** Robert Herchert
City Population: 385,141 (1980 census) **Metro Area Population:** 2,974,878 (1980 census)
Daily Newspapers: 3 **No. of Radio Stations:** 26 **No. of TV Stations:** 9
City Chamber of Commerce: Fort Worth Area Chamber of Commerce, 700 Throckmorton, Fort Worth, Texas 76102

Fort Worth, often considered in conjunction with nearby Dallas, is the seat of Tarrant County and a prime cog in the massive North Texas industrial complex, serving as a transportation center, oil-pipeline hub and a major grain and livestock market. It is one of the nation's largest producers of aircraft, an outgrowth of World War II, when aircraft assembly first flourished there.

Settlement of the area began in 1843. Four years later Camp Worth (later Fort Worth) was established by Major Ripley A. Arnold as a frontier outpost to protect settlers against Comanche Indian raids; it was named in honor of Major General William J. Worth, then commander of U.S. troops in Texas, and proved of great use to the Army during the Mexican War.

After the Army departed (1853), the town suffered a brief decline, but soon began to boom. Cowboys driving Longhorn cattle up the Chisholm Trail to the railheads of Kansas would bed their herds outside of Fort Worth and go into town for supplies and relaxation. This brought a heavy influx of merchants and contributed much to the city's growth, which was further spurred by the coming of the railroad in 1876, three years after the city's incorporation. Meat-packing and the milling and shipping of grain were the mainstays of the fledgling town's economy. With the 20th century, came widespread industrialization and a continuing trend toward greater diversification. Besides those mentioned, other of the city's chief industries include brewing, electronics, food processing, and the manufacture of automobiles, containers, furniture, leather goods and machinery.

Despite the bustle of its industry, Fort Worth today retains a distinctive, easy-going Western flavor. It is known all over the world as "Cowtown" or "Where the West Begins," and is committed to retaining its Western heritage. Fort Worth has become increasingly involved in the arts, rivaling Dallas as the state's cultural leader. Its attractions include Casa Mañana, a theater-in-the-round that presents Broadway productions; a renowned museum complex including the Fort Worth Art Museum, the Kimbell Art Museum, the Amon Carter Museum of Western Art, and the Fort Worth Museum of Science and History; the Fort Worth Opera and Symphony; and Trinity Park. In addition, the area boasts the Fort Worth Water Garden Park, the Will Rogers Memorial Complex, and the Tarrant County Convention Center. Fort Worth is host to the Van Cliburn Piano Competition and the Colonial Invitational Golf Tournament and is the home of Six Flags Over Texas. Popular annual events include the Southwestern Exposition, Fat Stock Show and Rodeo.

HONOLULU

Location: In Hawaii, in Pacific Ocean, 2,397 miles southwest of San Francisco **County:** Honolulu **City Area:** 608 sq. miles (574.7 sq. kilometers) **Altitude:** 21 feet (6.4 meters)
Mayor: Eileen R. Anderson **Managing Director:** Andrew I.T. Chang
City Population: 365,048 (1980 census) **Metro Area Population:** 762,874 (1980 census)
Daily Newspapers: 2 **No. of Radio Stations:** 27 **No. of TV Stations:** 5
City Chamber of Commerce: The Chamber of Commerce of Hawaii, Dillingham Building, 735 Bishop Street, Honolulu, Hawaii 96813

Honolulu, capital and principal city of Hawaii, is on the island of Oahu at the crossroads of the Pacific. (The name "Honolulu" is Hawaiian for "sheltered harbor.") Although Honolulu city and county are usually thought of as consisting of Oahu only, Honolulu is technically the most far-reaching city in the nation, with boundaries extending officially 1,381 miles northwest to Kure Island.

Honolulu became the seat of the Kamehameha dynasty, which had succeeded in unifying the Hawaiian Islands in 1810, and in 1845 it was named the permanent capital of the Kingdom of Hawaii. During the 19th century, American and European whalers and sandalwood traders came to Honolulu, and it was occupied successively by Russian, British, and French forces. It developed into an important commercial city after U.S. annexation of Hawaii in 1898.

In the early 20th century, the U.S. Navy established its famous base at Pearl Harbor, now the headquarters of the U.S. Pacific Fleet. Honolulu was bombed during Japan's surprise attack on Pearl Harbor on Dec. 7, 1941, and during World War II became a major staging area for U.S. forces in the Pacific.

The postwar years saw a tourist boom coupled with a diversification of industry. The military, with all branches represented in Hawaii, continued as a mainstay of the economy, but tourism surpassed it as the leading industry. In 1979 alone, 3.9 million visitors came to the islands. However, high air fares and the economic recession on the mainland caused the number of tourists to decline in 1980.

Numerous new high-rise office buildings have changed the skyline and helped revitalize downtown Honolulu. Harbor facilities have been expanded and the Honolulu International Airport has been enlarged.

Structures of interest in the city are Iolani Palace, former home of Hawaii's monarchs and the only royal palace in the U.S.; the state capitol; the Bishop Museum (of Polynesian Ethnology and Natural History); Washington

Place, former private home of Queen Lilioukalani; and the Neal Blaisdell Center, a 22-acre complex of public buildings.

HOUSTON

Location: Southeastern Texas, on Houston Ship Channel, 50 miles from Gulf of Mexico **Counties:** Brazoria, Harris, Fort Bend, Liberty, Montgomery and Waller. **City Area:** 556.3 sq. miles (1440.8 sq. kilometers) **Altitude:** 49 feet (15 meters)
Mayor: Jim McConn
City Population: 1,594,086 (1980 census) **Metro Area Population:** 2,905,350 (1980 census)
Daily Newspapers: 2 **No. of Radio Stations:** 31 **No. of TV Stations:** 6
City Chamber of Commerce: Houston Chamber of Commerce, 1100 Milam, 25th Floor, Houston, Texas 77002

Houston, seat of Harris County, is the leading industrial metropolis not only of Texas but also of the surrounding region. It is the largest city in the Southwest and South, the fifth largest in the nation and the country's third-largest seaport.

Founded in 1836 by J. K. and A. C. Allen, the city was named for General Sam Houston, hero of the Battle of San Jacinto (1836), by which Texas gained independence from Mexico. The city served as capital of the Republic of Texas from 1837 until 1840.

The discovery of oil in Southeast Texas at Spindletop in 1901 and the opening of the man-made Houston Ship Channel in 1914 stimulated the rapid development of the Houston area.

Strategically situated in an area rich in oil, gas, sulfur, salt, lime, timber, industrial soil, seawater and freshwater, the Houston metropolitan area ranks first in the nation in petroleum refining, petrochemical manufacturing, manufacturing and distribution of petroleum equipment and pipeline transmission of oil and gas.

Houston, which became the U.S. center of manned spacecraft activities in the early 1960s, has experienced increasing economic diversification over the past two decades. The city emerged as a corporate center in the 1960s, and since 1970 over 200 major companies have moved their headquarters, subsidiaries or divisions to Houston, capitalizing on the growing nucleus of energy, space and medical technology available in the area.

The Texas Medical Center is a $694-million complex of 24 institutions and organizations on 235 acres in central Houston. More than 80 research firms maintain research facilities in Houston. The number of life, earth, and physical scientists in metropolitan Houston has risen to 11,800, up 104 percent since 1970, while technical engineers have increased 75 percent in the same period, to stand at 31,500.

In addition, the city is growing in prominence in international business. More than 50 foreign banks maintain representative offices in Houston, and 49 nations maintain consular offices there. Houston Intercontinental Airport provides direct service to Europe, the Middle East, South and Central America, the Caribbean, Mexico and Canada.

Bordering the City of Houston on the southeast is the Lyndon B. Johnson Space Center, a $202-million complex for astronaut training, equipment testing, and flight control for the Skylab and Space Shuttle programs.

Houston's Nina Vance Alley Theatre is nationally known, performing repertory works as well as new plays. Elegant Jones Hall for the Performing Arts features the Houston Symphony Society, the Houston Ballet, and the Houston Grand Opera; all tour nationally. The Astrodome, a huge, enclosed and air-conditioned arena, has convertible seating arrangements which allow the presentation of widely varied sports events. The Summit, another sports and entertainment arena, is located in Houston's Greenway Plaza.

Houston is the home of the Houston Astros of the National Baseball League, the Houston Oilers of the American Conference of the National Football League and the Houston Rockets of the National Basketball Association.

Prominent tourist attractions in the area include the Harris County Domed Stadium and Astrohall; Astroworld, a 65-acre family amusement park; the Museum of fine Arts and several other museums; Johnson Space Center; and San Jacinto Battleground, plus the battleship Texas, a veteran of two World Wars.

INDIANAPOLIS

Location: In central Indiana, on White River **County:** Marion **City Area:** 379.4 sq. miles (982.6 sq. kilometers) **Altitude:** 710 feet (215.8 meters)
Mayor: William H. Hudnut, III
City Population: 700,807 (1980 census) **Metro Area Population:** 1,166,929 (1980 census)
Daily Newspapers: 2 **No. of Commercial Radio Stations (AM):** 9
No. of TV Stations: 6
City Chamber of Commerce: Indianapolis Chamber of Commerce, 320 North Meridian Street, Indianapolis, Indiana 46204

Indianapolis, seat of Marion County and capital of Indiana, is the largest city in the state. Its name combines "Indiana" with "polis," the Greek term for "city." It was settled in 1820.

Indianapolis grew slowly until the arrival of the first railroad in 1847. Toward the end of the 19th century the discovery of nearby natural gas, plus the beginning of the automobile industry, helped the city's expansion. On Jan. 1, 1970, the City of Indianapolis merged with surrounding Marion County in the nation's first major city-county consolidation to occur without a popular referendum since modern New York City was formed in 1898. Some autonomy was retained by local units, including eleven school corporations.

Leading products are processed foods, electronics equipment, heavy machinery, and pharmaceuticals. Indianapolis is also an insurance center, with offices of more than 70 firms.

Indianapolis might be called the educational hub of Indiana. It includes the Indiana University Medical School and Center, Butler University, Indiana Central University, Indiana University/Purdue University at Indianapolis (IUPUI), and Marian College.

Urban renewal has made enormous changes in the city's skyline in the last ten years. Indianapolis has kept its famous Soldiers' and Sailors' Monument on Monument Circle, but the city is now dominated by such structures as the Indiana National Bank Tower, Indiana Bell Telephone Building, the Market Square Arena, a new Hyatt Hotel, the new Federal Building, and the Indiana Convention and Exposition Center.

Three of Indianapolis' newest points of interest are: the Museum of Art, the Indiana State Museum, and the Children's Museum, the largest of its kind in the nation. Indianapolis is national headquarters for the American Legion and the home of the Army Finance Center at Fort Harrison. Tourist attractions include the homes of President Benjamin Harrison, James Whitcomb Riley and Booth Tarkington. Eagle Creek Park is the country's largest municipal park.

The city has professional baseball and basketball teams and is the home of the Indianapolis 500 motor speedway track. Indianapolis is also the home of the Amateur Athletic Union and the U.S. Automobile Club.

JACKSONVILLE

Location: Northeastern Florida, on St. Johns River and Atlantic Ocean **County:** Duval **City Area:** 841 sq. miles (2178 sq. kilometers) **Altitude:** 20 feet (6.1 meters)
Mayor: Jake N. Godbold
City Population: 540,898 (1980 census) **Metro Area Population:** 737,519 (1980 census)
Daily Newspapers: 2 **No. of Radio Stations:** 24 **No. of TV Stations:** 6
City Chamber of Commerce: Jacksonville Chamber of Commerce, P.O. Box 329, Jacksonville, Florida 32201

Jacksonville, Florida's most populous city, is the nation's largest in area (841 square miles). A vital seaport with over 80 miles of berthing space and a sizable U.S. Navy installation, the city is a major financial, industrial and transportation center of the Southeast.

Among Jacksonville's chief industries are the manufacturing and/or processing of food products, wood products, computer components, fertilizer, paper, furniture and cigars. It is generally the last port of call for steamships from the North that are bound for the Southern Hemisphere and Far East.

French and Spanish colonization of the Jacksonville region dates from the latter part of the 16th century. Except for a brief period of British rule (1763-1783), Spain managed to maintain tenuous dominion until 1819, when the U.S. bought its claim to the Florida peninsula. Originally known as Cowford (during the English period), the community was eventually renamed for Andrew Jackson, Florida's first territorial governor. It was incorporated in 1832.

Early development of the area was hampered by Florida's two costly wars with the Seminole Indians, and by the Civil War, which brought widespread destruction and periodic occupation by Union forces. Industry's recognition of the city's strategic location and moderate climate spurred recovery in the postwar period, though progress was stalled by a yellow-fever epidemic (1888) and a fire (1901) that destroyed 147 city blocks. Since 1940 the city has expanded greatly, and in 1968 it was consolidated with Duval County. During the 1950s Jacksonville gained the title of "insurance capital of the South."

Jacksonville's nearby beaches, with thousands of guest accommodations, are popular summer attractions, especially for inland Southerners. Other favorites with visitors are the Jacksonville Art Museum and Symphony Orchestra, the Cummer Gallery of Art, the Jacksonville Zoological Park, the Coliseum and the Gator Bowl. Among its historical sites are the Fort Caroline National Monument, site of the state's first French settlement in 1564, and the Delius House, home of the famed British composer.

KANSAS CITY

Location: Western Missouri, on Kansas-Missouri border, on Kansas and Missouri rivers **Counties:** Jackson, Clay, Platte **City Area:** 316 sq. miles (818 sq. kilometers) Altitude: 750 feet (227.9 meters)
Mayor: Richard L. Berkley **City Manager:** Robert A. Kipp
City Population: 448,159 (1980 census) **Metro Area Population:** 1,327,020 (1980 census)
Daily Newspapers: 2 **No. of Commercial Radio Stations (AM):** 14
No. of TV Stations: 5
City Chamber of Commerce: Chamber of Commerce of Greater Kansas City, 600 Ten Main Center, 920 Main Street, Kansas City, Missouri 64105

Kansas City, Missouri's second largest metropolis, is an important industrial, transportation, commercial, and banking center. It is separated from Kansas City, Kansas, by the state line, but both are served by the same railroad terminals and transit and telephone systems.

The area was explored by the French early in the 18th century and toward the end of the century by Daniel Morgan Boone (son of the famous frontiersman), who was probably the first American to set foot in the vicinity. François Chouteau established a trading post in 1826, and a settlement later developed known as Westport Landing. The city was incorporated in 1850 as the Town of Kansas, it became the City of Kansas in 1853, and under a new charter (1889) was named Kansas City. Its name reflects its location on the Kansas (Kaw) River, which in turn honors an Indian tribe.

Kansas City grew into an important trade and transportation hub for pioneers migrating westward over the Oregon and Santa Fe Trails; it was an early center of the nation's cattle business. In 1865 the railroad arrived, and four years later Hannibal Bridge, the first structure to span the Missouri River, was opened.

Today Kansas City is a major market for winter wheat and cattle. Its stockyards are among the nation's busiest. It leads the nation in the manufacture of vending machines, is the country's second largest assembly center for cars and trucks, and is an important warehousing center.

Landmarks of interest include the Liberty Memorial, the Nelson Gallery and Atkins Museum of Fine Arts, Swope Park with its zoo, Country Club Plaza, Crown Center, and the Livestock Yards.

LOS ANGELES

Location: Southwestern California, between Santa Monica and San Pedro bays, near the Pacific coast **County:** Los Angeles **City Area:** 464 sq. miles (1201.8 sq. kilometers) **Altitude:** 275 feet (83.6 meters)
Mayor: Thomas Bradley
City Population: 2,966,731 (1980 census) **Metro Area Population:** 7,477,657 (1980 census)
Daily Newspapers: 2 **No. of Commercial Radio Stations (AM):** 54
No. of TV Stations: 18

City Chamber of Commerce: Los Angeles Area Chamber of Commerce, 404 South Bixel Street, Los Angeles, California 90017

Los Angeles, seat of California's Los Angeles County, is the nation's third-largest city, but its metropolitan area ranks second only to New York in population.

Gaspar de Portolá led an expedition to the site in 1769, and in 1781 El Pueblo de Nuestra Señora la Reina de los Angeles de Porciuncula (The Town of Our Lady the Queen of the Angels of Porciuncula) was founded. The name was later shortened to Los Angeles.

In 1846 during the Mexican War, U.S. military forces took the town. Four years later, Los Angeles was incorporated as a city; that same year California entered the Union. It was soon linked with the Eastern seaboard as railroads arrived: the Southern Pacific in 1876 and the Santa Fe nine years later. Discovery of oil in the 1890s stimulated commercial growth, and the opening of the Panama Canal in 1914 brought further expansion. The motion-picture industry grew up in the early 20th century and more recent years have seen the establishment of television studios.

The Los Angeles area is rich in agricultural resources and well known for its citrus fruit. It ranks third nationally in manufacturing, finance, and trade, and leads the U.S. in production of aircraft and aircraft parts. In addition, Greater Los Angeles is the nation's sportswear center and the world's second largest garment manufacturer. Other important industries are food processing and the production of machinery, chemicals, and electronics equipment. As a port Los Angeles handles the largest cargo tonnage of deep-sea vessels on the Pacific Coast and is a major fishing complex. In 1979, it was reported that 16 industrial corporations with sales exceeding $1 billion were headquartered in the Los Angeles area.

Los Angeles County has the heaviest per-capita concentration of automobiles in the world, and the city is famous for its vast system of freeways radiating from the center of town to outlying areas. Dozens of independent municipalities are incorporated in the county, some completely surrounded by the city. Shore areas include Santa Monica, Manhattan Beach, Hermosa Beach, Redondo Beach, and Long Beach. The industrial section includes Lynwood, Downey, Norwalk, and Torrance.

Los Angeles is the home of a $33.5 million Music Center, the Los Angeles County Museum of Art and the recently constructed Los Angeles Convention Center.

Of interest to the thousands of tourists who flock to the Los Angeles area are Disneyland, at nearby Anaheim, considered the biggest attraction in the West; Mount Wilson Observatory; Mission San Gabriel Arcángel, dedicated in 1771; Santa Catalina Island; the Hollywood Bowl; Griffith Park with its zoo, golf course, and observatory; and Laguna Beach.

Los Angeles will host the 1984 Summer Olympics. The decision by the city to ratify a contract with the International Olympic Committee came after 15 months of conflict between the two over who would bear financial responsibility. Under a compromise incorporated into the agreement, Los Angeles would have no financial liability. The burden would be shared by the U.S. Olympic Committee and a private group.

The city celebrated a year-long bicentennial observance which culminated on September 4, 1981, the 200th anniversary of its founding. Art shows, ballet and plays were be presented under the slogan "L.A.'s the Place."

LOUISVILLE

Location: Northwest Kentucky, at the falls of the Ohio River County: Jefferson City Area: 65.2 sq. miles (168.9 sq. kilometers) Altitude: 477 feet (144.9 meters)
Mayor: William B. Stansbury
City Population: 298,451 (1980 census) Metro Area Population: 906,240 (1980 census)
Daily Newspapers: 2 No. of Radio Stations: 18 No. of TV Stations: 6
City Chamber of Commerce: Louisville Area Chamber of Commerce, 300 West Liberty, Louisville, Kentucky 40202

Louisville, seat of Jefferson County, is the largest city in Kentucky and a major Southern industrial center. The city lies over a mammoth glacial deposit called an "aquifer," which is drawn upon for water.

Laid out in 1773 by General George Rogers Clark and settled six years later, it was named Louisville in 1780 by the Virginia legislature in honor of King Louis XVI of France. Two years later at Louisville, General Clark built Fort Nelson, which served as headquarters for his expeditions to the Northwest. It was then widely known as the "Settlement at the Falls."

Louisville was incorporated as a city in 1828 and grew into an important river port after the opening of the Louisville and Portland Canal in 1830. Arrival of the railroad in 1851 enhanced its position as a transportation center. During the Civil War it was a major Union base, despite the divided loyalties of its citizens.

Today the city has the world's largest electrical appliance and neoprene plants. Other important industries are the manufacture of bourbon whiskey, aluminum products, bathroom fixtures, tobacco processing, auto and truck manufacturing, and meat-packing. The American Printing House for the Blind, the world's largest publisher of Braille books and magazines and talking books, is located in Louisville. More than $300-million in private and public funds have been committed to the redevelopment of the downtown area. A $120-million Galleria office, shopping and apartment complex will open in 1982, as will the $70-million Riverfront development.

Of historic interest are the grave of George Rogers Clark, in Cave Hill Cemetery, and the site of Fort Nelson. The state's tourist attractions include Churchill Downs, scene of the annual Kentucky Derby; the State Fair Grounds; the Louisville Zoological Garden featuring a children's zoo, and the Filson Club, which houses a Kentucky history museum.

MEMPHIS

Location: Southwestern corner of Tennessee, on Mississippi River County: Shelby City Area: 290 sq. miles (651.1 sq. kilometers) Altitude: 275 feet (83.6 meters)
Mayor: Wyeth Chandler Chief Administrative Officer: Wallace Madewell
City Population: 646,356 (1980 census) Metro Area Population: 912,887 (1980 census)
Daily Newspapers: 2 No. of Radio Stations: 24 No. of TV Stations: 4
City Chamber of Commerce: Memphis Area Chamber of Commerce, 555 Beale Street, P.O. Box 224, Memphis, Tennessee 38101

Memphis, seat of Shelby County, is the largest city in Tennessee and a port of entry. It is the commercial center for much of Tennessee, Arkansas, and Mississippi, as well as parts of Missouri and Alabama. It was named after the ancient Egyptian city.

According to tradition, De Soto crossed the Mississippi River in 1540 at the site of this Tennessee city. In 1682 La Salle built Fort Prudhomme overlooking the river, and for almost a century the area was involved in the imperial rivalries of Great Britain, France, and Spain. The United States built Fort Adams in 1797, and in 1819 Memphis was laid out. Thirty years later it was incorporated as a city, having become an important port noted for its gambling casinos and glittering wealth.

The fall of Memphis to Union forces on June 6, 1862, ended the city's early prosperity. After the Civil War, yellow-fever epidemics caused about 25,000 people to flee.

Today Memphis is a major hardwood-lumber center and manufacturer of furniture and flooring. It is also a leading cotton and livestock market and home of the Memphis Cotton Exchange. The city's products include rubber goods, cottonseed oil, textiles, farm machinery, drugs, and livestock feeds. It is headquarters for Plough, Inc., Holiday Inns of America, Inc. and Cook Industries, grain exporters, and the site of Sharp Electronics Corporation, a Japanese microwave and television production plant.

The Tennessee Chute Project has provided Memphis with a dam connecting the mainland to Presidents Island in the Mississippi and has given the city a stillwater harbor with two barge terminals. A 963-acre industrial park is now on the island; across the harbor is the 6,800-acre Frank C. Pidgeon Industrial Park.

Of interest in Memphis is Confederate Park, which contains ramparts used in defense against Union gunboats in 1862, and Beale Street, which was immortalized by jazz composer W.C. Handy. It is the site of Graceland, the mansion and gravesite of Elvis Presley, and two memorials to Rev Martin Luther King, Jr., who was assassinated in the city in 1968. Memphis is the only four-time winner of the Ernest T. Trigg (Cleanest City in the Nation) Award.

MIAMI

Location: Southeastern Florida, on Biscayne Bay **County:** Dade **City Area:** 34 sq. miles (88.1 sq. kilometers) **Altitude:** 25 feet (7.6 meters)
Mayor: Maurice A. Ferre **City Manager:** Howard Gary
City Population: 346,931 (1980 census) **Metro Area Population:** 1,625,979 (1980 census)
Daily Newspapers: 4 **No. of Radio Stations:** 23 **No. of TV Stations:** 7
City Chamber of Commerce: Greater Miami Chamber of Commerce, 391 N.E. 15 St., Miami, Florida 33132

Miami, seat of Florida's Dade County, is an international banking and trade center, and the focal point of a world-famous resort area. The city was founded in 1870 at the site of Fort Dallas, which the United States had built in the 1830s during the war against the Seminoles. "Miami" is an Indian word meaning "big water."

In 1896 the financier Henry M. Flagler extended the Florida East Coast Railroad to Miami, built the Royal Palm Hotel, and dredged the city's harbor. The city was incorporated the same year. By 1910 it was booming.

During the 1920s the Miami region was the scene of wild land speculation in which many fortunes were lost. However, the city continued to grow, despite disastrous hurricanes in 1926 and 1935.

Miami has the largest population of Cuban refugees in the United States—in excess of 500,000. The 1980 boat exodus of thousands of new Cuban refugees strained the resources of Miami's existing first- and second-generation Cuban community. An additional influx of sea-borne refugees from Haiti also taxed public services in the South Florida metropolis.

A major rail, air and shipping point, Miami is considered the principal gateway to Latin America; the Dodge Island passenger terminal is home base for the many cruise ships serving South America and the Caribbean. The Greater Miami Foreign-Trade Zone is the largest of its kind in the U.S.

Although tourism is the leading industry in the area, the city is the nation's third largest garment manufacturing center. Concrete, metal, meat products, and commercial fishing also make substantial contributions to Miami's economy. Miami's booming trade with Latin America and the Caribbean has been spurred by the siting of 13 major overseas banks in the city. The U.S. Environmental Science Services Administration's Oceanographic and Meteorological Laboratories have made Miami a world leader in undersea studies. Construction of the $900-million, 20.5-mile elevated rail system, linking downtown Miami with its suburbs, began in June, 1979.

Greater Miami, which consists of over two dozen independent municipalities, is renowned for its luxurious resort hotels and fine beaches. Recently, many of the visitors have come from Latin America and Europe. Tourist attractions include Bicentennial-New World Center Park, the Museum of Science, the Miami Seaquarium, and Vizcaya, formerly the estate of James Deering and now the Dade County Art Museum. Everglades National Park, a preserve for tropical birds and flora, is nearby. The area has year-round horse racing at Hialeah, Gulfstream and Calder racetracks. Miami is home to the annual Orange Bowl Festival and January 1 football classic, and to the National Football League's Miami Dolphins.

MILWAUKEE

Location: Southeastern Wisconsin, on Lake Michigan **County:** Milwaukee **City Area:** 96.5 sq. miles (249.9 sq. kilometers) **Altitude:** 581 feet (176.6 meters)
Mayor: Henry W. Maier
City Population: 636,212 (1980 census) **Metro Area Population:** 1,397,143 (1980 census)
Daily Newspapers: 2 **No. of Radio Stations:** 26 **No. of TV Stations:** 6
City Chamber of Commerce: Metropolitan Milwaukee Association of Commerce, 756 North Milwaukee Street, Milwaukee, Wisconsin 53202

Milwaukee, seat of Milwaukee County and largest city in Wisconsin, is a leading Great Lakes port and major industrial metropolis.

French missionaries and the French explorer La Salle visited the site in the late 17th century. French Canadian fur traders came to barter with the Indians, and in 1795 the North West Company established a trading post. The first permanent settler, Solomon Juneau, an agent of the American Fur Company, arrived in 1818. His settlement and several neighboring villages merged after 1835 to form Milwaukee, which was incorporated as a city in 1846. Its name is derived from an Indian term interpreted to mean either "gathering place by the waters" or "beautiful land."

The city's excellent harbor, accessible raw materials, and growing population made it a shipping and industrial center, and German immigrants, arriving after 1848, stimulated its political, economic, and social development.

Milwaukee produces more beer than any other city and is the home of three of the four largest breweries. However, machinery manufacturing is the area's largest industry. Milwaukee is also a significant grain market and meat packer.

Of interest in the city are the Greek Orthodox Annunciation Church, designed by Frank Lloyd Wright; the War Memorial Center, on the lakeshore, designed by Eero Saarinen and housing the Milwaukee Art Center; the Milwaukee County Zoo, one of the most modern in the nation; the Mitchell Park Botanical Conservatory, three domed buildings for display of plants under arid, moist and temperate conditions; and the world-famous breweries, which offer tours to the public. A $12-million Performing Arts Center with a large park and fountains is the home of the Milwaukee Symphony Orchestra and the Repertory Theatre. MECCA, the Milwaukee Exposition and Convention Center and Arena, one of Milwaukee's newest buildings, has won national attention because of its artistic design and colors.

Milwaukee has gained recognition from national organizations for cleanliness and beautification for many years and is one of the safest areas in the nation.

MINNEAPOLIS

Location: East-central Minnesota, on both sides of Mississippi River at Falls of St. Anthony **County:** Hennepin **City Area:** 58.8 sq. miles (152.2 sq. kilometers) **Altitude:** 815 feet (247.7 meters)
Mayor: Donald Fraser **Chief Administrative Officer:** David C. Niklaus
City Population: 370,951 (1980 census) **Metro Area Population:** 2,114,256 (1980 census)
Daily Newspapers: 2 **No. of Commercial Radio Stations (AM):** 7 **No. of TV Stations:** 5
City Chamber of Commerce: Greater Minneapolis Chamber of Commerce, 15 South Fifth Street, Minneapolis, Minnesota 55402

Minneapolis, seat of Hennepin County, is the largest city in Minnesota and an important industrial and railroad center. It is contiguous to St. Paul, its twin city and the state capital.

Father Louis Hennepin visited the site in 1680 and gave the Falls of Saint Anthony their name. In 1819 the U.S. government established Fort Snelling, and two years later a sawmill was built at the falls. The village of St. Anthony was soon settled on the east bank of the Mississippi River, while Minneapolis grew up (c. 1847) on the west bank. Minneapolis, from the local Indian "minnea," or water, combined with "polis," Greek for city, was incorporated as a town in 1856 and as a city the following year. In 1872 St. Anthony was annexed.

During the 1890s the lumber business thrived as logs were floated downstream to the sawmills of Minneapolis from the great forests of the north. Minneapolis was also known as the "Flour City of the World" until a change in freight rates after World War I shifted the center of the flour-milling industry to Buffalo.

Today the city is the home of the Minneapolis Grain Exchange, the world's largest cash grain market, and headquarters for a Federal Reserve district bank. Leading industries are electronics, computers, control instruments, food processing, printing and publishing.

Minneapolis and St. Paul constitute the financial and industrial center of a large area rich in natural resources, power, and transportation facilities. The two cities are connected by a massive freeway system that runs through the suburban areas, plus a $300-million Minneapolis Gateway Center in the Loop. A $65-million domed stadium is under construction in the downtown area. The Minneapolis area has 25 industrial parks and a 12-acre river terminal to handle shipping and storage of grain, fertilizer, petroleum products, sand gravel, salt and coal.

The major landmarks in Minneapolis are the 57-story IDS skyscraper and Nicollet Mall. Within the city are 153 parks with 22 lakes; Minnehaha Park with its Stevens House, dating from 1849; the Tyrone Guthrie Theater; the $5.5-million Walker Art Center; the Minneapolis Institute of Arts; and the Minnesota Orchestra's new concert hall.

NASHVILLE

Location: Northcentral Tennessee, on Cumberland River **County:** Davidson **City Area:** 533 sq. miles (1380.5 sq. kilometers) **Altitude:** 500 feet (152.4 meters)
Mayor: Richard H. Fulton
City Population: 455,651 (1980 census) **Metro Area Population:** 850,505 (1980 census)
Daily Newspapers: 2 **No. of Radio Stations:** 22 **No. of TV Stations:** 5
City Chamber of Commerce: Nashville Area Chamber of Commerce, 161 Fourth Avenue, North, Nashville, Tennessee 37219

Nashville, capital of Tennessee and seat of Davidson County, is sometimes called "the Athens of the South" because of its numerous educational institutions and its many buildings of Classical Greek design. The city is an important regional center for finance, industry and transportation, as well as a significant music recording center and the home of the Grand Ole Opry. Principal manufactures include shoes, apparel, books, magazines, chemicals, glass aerostructures, tires and trucks. Nissan Motors of Japan is building a truck plant in Smyrna, southeast of Nashville.

The first settlement on the site of present-day Nashville was made in 1779, with the building of Fort Nashborough, a frontier outpost named for Revolutionary War hero General Francis Nash, who was killed in the Battle of Germantown. The small community grew quickly and in 1784 was incorporated under its present name; it was chartered as a city in 1806.

Nashville's role as a vital trade depot was enhanced in 1796 by the entry of Tennessee into the Union, and in the 1850s by the coming of the railroads. During the Civil War, the city served as a Confederate military headquarters, but fell to Union forces in 1862 and remained under their control despite efforts in 1864 by troops under Confederate General John B. Hood to recapture the city.

Nashville was slow to recover from the effects of war and the period of so-called "carpetbag rule" that followed. In the late 1870s, however, the pace of progress quickened as industry became an increasingly large factor in the city's economy: In the period 1870-1890 the population tripled, from 25,865 to 76,168. After 1900 industry developed more slowly, until the advent of World War II, which acted as a spur to growth.

The city's many attractions include a full-size replica of the Parthenon, in Centennial Park; Andrew Jackson's home, The Hermitage; Tennessee State Museum, containing relics of wars in which Tennesseeans have fought; the Belle Meade Mansion, a plantation home dating from 1853; the Country Music Hall of Fame and Museum; Ryman Auditorium amd Opryland, U.S.A., new home of the Grand Ole Opry and a 110-acre theme park with live entertainment, rides and exhibits.

NEWARK

Location: Northeastern New Jersey, on Passaic River and Newark Bay **County:** Essex **City Area:** 24 sq. miles (62.2 sq. kilometers) **Altitude:** 55 feet (16.7 meters)
Mayor: Kenneth A. Gibson
City Population: 329,248 (1980 census) **Metro Area Population:** 1,965,304 (1980 census)
Daily Newspapers: 1 **No. of Radio Stations:** 2 **No. of TV Stations:** 2
City Chamber of Commerce: Greater Newark Chamber of Commerce, 50 Park Place, Newark, New Jersey 07102

Newark, seat of Essex County and largest city in New Jersey, is an important industrial and commercial center.

It was settled in 1666 by Puritans from Connecticut led by Robert Treat and is said to have been named after the town of Newark, England, although some contend its name was New Ark and had a religious connotation.

During the Revolutionary War, the city was the scene of several skirmishes; General George Washington passed through in 1776 leading his troops south to the Delaware River.

Newark's industrial growth began in the early 19th century. The arrival of railroads and canals in the 1830s stimulated the expansion of shoemaking and tanning and the development of the jewelry, insurance, and shipbuilding industries. After 1880 swarms of immigrants arrived, living in hastily built tenements. In 1915 Port Newark opened; during World War I Newark was the nation's leading shipbuilding city.

Today Newark is the country's third leading insurance center. A significant factor in its economic life is the Port of New York Authority, which operates Port Newark and Newark International Airport. Among the city's products are leather goods, jewelry, malt liquors, plastics, electrical equipment, auto parts, and chemicals.

Of interest in the city are Trinity Cathedral, the Sacred Heart Cathedral (begun in 1898), the First Presbyterian Church (1791); and the old County courthouse (1906), designed by Cass Gilbert.

Newark began to deteriorate economically and politically in the 1930s, a process which continued for 30 years or more. The city suffered the same ills which plagued many of the country's major cities—an exodus of population and business from the central city, with the concommitant drop in revenues, and a high unemployment rate among the remaining population, which is now over 75 percent black and Hispanic. Newark is fighting hard to lure business back to the downtown area and to improve the lot of its underprivileged citizens. Local efforts aided by the receipt of large federal health-care funds have dramatically reduced the death rate over a ten-year period since the mid 60s.

The Prudential and Mutual Benefit life insurance companies have since built new headquarters here, Blue Cross-Blue Shield of New Jersey is also headquartered here, and Public Service Electric and Gas Company, a major utility, has replaced its downtown headquarters with a new $60-million, 27-story corporate complex on an adjacent site. Since then millions of dollars have been spent to rebuild the city. The New Jersey Institute of Technology expanded its facilities. In 1974 New Jersey College of Medicine and Dentistry, Essex County College, Seton Hall and Rutgers University began construction of university facilities. In 1976 construction was completed at Seton Hall Law School, the School of Dentistry, Rutgers University and Essex County College.

NEW ORLEANS

Location: Southeastern Louisiana, on Mississippi River, near Lake Pontchartrain, about 100 miles from Gulf of Mexico **Parish:** Orleans **City Area:** 366 sq. miles (947.9 sq. kilometers) **Altitude:** 5 feet (1.5 meters)
Mayor: Ernest N. Morial **Chief Administrative Officer:** Reynaud Rochon
City Population: 557,482 (1980 census) **Metro Area Population:** 1,186,725 (1980 census)
Daily Newspapers: 1 **No. of Radio Stations:** 20 **No. of TV Stations:** 5
City Chamber of Commerce: Chamber of Commerce of New Orleans and the River Region, P.O. Box 30240, New Orleans, Louisiana 70190

New Orleans, coextensive with Louisiana's Orleans Parish (county), is one of the largest cities in the South, the nation's second largest port, and the third largest port in the world. It was founded in 1718 by the Sieur de Bienville and named for Philippe II, duke of Orleans. Four years later it became the capital of the French colony of Louisiana. In 1762 the city passed to Spain, but remained culturally French.

New Orleans was returned to France in 1800 and in 1803 came under U.S. jurisdiction with the Louisiana Purchase. It developed into a flourishing cotton and slave-trade center, and was an important stopover on the southern routes to the West. After Andrew Jackson's victory over the British at New Orleans (January 8, 1815), the city's prosperity reached great heights, and New Orleans became famous for gaiety and elegance. (Today its colorful Mardi Gras, which is held every February, is one of the country's best-known festivals.)

In 1862 the city fell to Admiral David G. Farragut and did not fully recover from occupation by Union troops under General Benjamin Butler and the subsequent Reconstruction era until the end of World War I. Discovery of oil and the renewed commercial importance of sugar and cotton helped the city regain prosperity.

Today New Orleans is a leading banking and business center of the New South. It has the world's largest sugar refinery and is surrounded, offshore and on, by some of the most productive sources of oil in the nation. Other important industries are aerospace and shipbuilding.

The city's Vieux Carré, the French quarter, which comprised the original settlement, is a popular tourist attraction. Among the points of interest are Royal Street (Rue Royale) and the French Market on Decatur Street. Dixieland jazz was born on Bourbon Street.

Other landmarks include the Hibernia Tower, 33-story International Trade Mart, and the 52-story One Shell Square. The $178-million air-conditioned Superdome, the largest in the world, was dedicated August 3, 1975. The downtown area is being developed with five large-scale multi-use projects, provided for by some $1 billion in investments by private and public sectors. These projects are the Poydras Plaza, the International Rivercenter, the Pan-American Life Insurance Company Headquarters, the Canal Place, and the Piazza D'Italia.

On April 24, 1981, the Bureau of International Expositions in Paris approved New Orleans as the site for the 1984 World's Fair. The exposition will be located along the riverfront and will cost $69 million to construct.

NEW YORK CITY

Location: Southeastern New York, at mouth of Hudson River **Counties:** New York, Bronx, Kings, Queens, and Richmond **City Area:** 320 sq. miles (828.8 sq. kilometers) **Altitude:** 55 feet (16.7 meters) **Mayor:** Edward I. Koch **City Population:** 7,071,030 (1980 census) **Metro Area Population:** 9,119,737 (1980 census) **Daily Newspapers:** 7 **No. of Radio Stations:** 58 **No. of TV Stations:** 9 **City Chamber of Commerce:** New York Chamber of Commerce and Industry, 200 Madison Avenue, New York, New York 10016

New York, the nation's largest city and richest port, is a national leader in business, finance, manufacturing, communications, service industries, fashion, and the arts. It is also one of the world's largest cities, one of the world's leading ports, and headquarters of the United Nations.

As the financial headquarters of the world, New York is the home of some of the world's largest corporations and the New York and American Stock Exchanges.

As a cultural capital and influential arbiter of taste, the city has its renowned theater district and the cultural complex of Lincoln Center for the Performing Arts. It also has innumerable museums, art galleries, and related attractions, as well as scientific collections, libraries, and educational institutions.

Giovanni da Verrazano, a Florentine, was probably the first European to visit (1524) the site of New York. Henry Hudson's explorations (1609) up the river named after him led to the first permanent European settlements. In 1625 the colony of New Netherland was established, with its capital, New Amsterdam, located at the southern tip of Manhattan Island. The following year Peter Minuit of the Dutch West India Company bought the entire island from the Indians for the equivalent of about $24 in trinkets and beads. In 1664 the English seized the city for the Duke of York, for whom it was renamed. Later the Dutch regained control for a brief period (1673-74).

New York was active in the colonial opposition to British rule, and during the first year of the Revolution several battles were fought in the area. In 1776 the British captured the city and controlled it for the rest of the war.

New York, the first capital (1789-90) of the United States under the Constitution, was the site of George Washington's first inauguration. Until 1797 the city was also the capital of New York State.

The opening of the Erie Canal (1825) accelerated the growth of the city, already the nation's largest, and established its dominance over Boston and Philadelphia. The New York and Harlem Railroad was completed in 1832. By 1840 New York was the country's leading port.

During the 19th century, the city expanded northward from the tip of Manhattan, until by 1874 it covered the entire island. That same year saw annexation of parts of

Westchester County that later formed the Bronx. New York assumed its present boundaries in 1898, after annexing Brooklyn, Queens County and Staten Island.

New York's best known attractions include Central Park, the Bronx Zoo and Botanical Gardens, the Aquarium at Coney Island, Hayden Planetarium, the Fifth Avenue shops, the Broadway theatrical district, the United Nations Headquarters, Radio City Music Hall, the Statue of Liberty and the Staten Island ferry, Rockefeller and Lincoln Centers, Madison Square Garden, Yankee and Shea Stadiums, Greenwich Village, Chinatown and the Financial District, the Metropolitan Museum of Art, St. Patrick's Cathedral and the World Trade Center.

New York City was host to the 1980 Democratic Convention on August 11-14, which saw the renomination of Jimmy Carter and Walter Mondale to the presidency and vice-presidency.

During the 1980s work will begin on the massive Westway project, a combined interstate highway and parkland project along the lower Manhattan shoreline of the Hudson River. The project is expected to cost $2.3 billion by completion. The city is also constructing a large convention center on Manhattan's West Side.

NORFOLK

Location: southeastern Virginia, at the mouth of Chesapeake Bay **County:** independent city **City Area:** 54.2 sq. miles (140.4 sq. kilometers) **Altitude:** 10 feet (3 meters) **Mayor:** Vincent J. Thomas **City Manager:** Julian Hirst **City Population:** 266,979 (1980 census) **Metro Area Population:** 806,691 (1980 census) **Daily Newspapers:** 1 **No. of Radio Stations:** 21 **No. of TV Stations:** 6 **City Chamber of Commerce:** Norfolk Chamber of Commerce, 480 Bank Street, Norfolk, Virginia 23510

Norfolk, Virginia's largest city and a world seaport, is adjoined by the city of Portsmouth on the opposite bank of the Elizabeth River and by nearby Newport News, the three communities making up the Port of Hampton Roads, one of the world's finest natural harbors.

Norfolk is the home of the nation's largest naval base, and the Norfolk Naval Shipyard (actually in Portsmouth) has the greatest number of dry docks of any U.S. shipyard. The city is also headquarters for the Fifth Naval District, the Atlantic Fleet, the Second Fleet, and for NATO's Supreme Allied Command, Atlantic (SACLANT). The city's major economic activities include shipping, shipbuilding and repair, meat-packing, fishing and automobile assembly. Among its chief manufactures are lumber and wood products, fertilizer, cement, chemicals, clothing and food products.

Norfolk was established in 1682 by the Virginia colonial government, on the site of an Indian village. It was made a borough in 1736, incorporated as a town in 1805 amd chartered as a city in 1845. It was completely demolished in the American Revolution—first bombarded by British warships anchored in the Elizabeth River, then razed by fleeing Virginians to prevent its use by the British. (Only St. Paul's Church, dating from 1739, survived the flames; it stands today, with a cannonball still embedded in one of its walls.) The city suffered a severe yellow-fever epidemic in 1855, and in 1861, during the Civil War, it was once again bombarded—this time by Union forces. In 1862 it was captured and occupied for the duration. The famous fight between the *Monitor* and the *Merrimack* took place that year in Hampton Roads.

The postwar period saw Norfolk become an increasingly vital international trading center, thanks largely to its development as a major rail terminus. Coal and grain exports have grown dramatically in recent years. Visitors are attracted to the city by the excellent bathing and fishing opportunities it affords, as well as its many historic buildings. Other attractions include the General Douglas MacArthur Memorial, the 114-acre Lafayette Zoological Park, the azalea gardens at Gardens-by-the-Sea, and the Chrysler Museum. The waterfront area is undergoing a major redevelopment, and will contain the headquarters of the Cousteau Society.

OKLAHOMA CITY

Location: Central Oklahoma, on North Canadian River **Counties:** Oklahoma, Canadian, Cleveland and McClain **City Area:** 621 miles (1,608 sq. kilometers) **Altitude:** 1,207 feet (366.8 meters)

Mayor: Patience Latting **City Manager:** James J. Cook
City Population: 403,213 (1980 census) **Metro Area Population:** 834,088 (1980 census)
Daily Newspapers: 3 **No. of Radio Stations:** 24 **No. of TV Stations:** 8
City Chamber of Commerce: Oklahoma City Chamber of Commerce, One Santa Fe Plaza, Oklahoma City, Oklahoma 73102

Oklahoma City, seat of Oklahoma County and state capital, is the largest municipality in Oklahoma. It is also the state's financial, commercial, and industrial center.

The city's origin is one of the most colorful in American history. When the first land run into Indian Territory took place on April 22, 1889, a small Santa Fe Railroad water and coaling station blossomed into a city of 10,000 people between noon and sundown. The name of the city and territory means "red people" and had been proposed by a Choctaw chief in 1866 to designate the area set off for Indians. Oklahoma City was incorporated in 1890 and became the state capital in 1910.

Oil was struck in 1928, and it soon became apparent that rich oil and gas lands lay beneath the city itself. An extensive system of oil wells in the metropolitan area, reaching almost to the governor's mansion, is a large factor in the city's economy.

Oklahoma City is a rapidly growing regional, national and international marketing center. The U.S. Customs Bureau opened an office in 1967 to expedite exports and imports. Industry includes meat packing, including the headquarters of Wilson & Co., electronics components and the production of transportation equipment and oil field supplies. General Motors opened a huge auto assembly plant in 1979. The city is also noted as a convention site.

Oklahoma City has grown into an aeronautical complex with such Federal Aviation Administration facilities as the Aeronautical Center and Civil Aeromedical Institute. Nearby is Tinker Air Force Base with equipment and inventory of over $2 billion.

Of interest are the National Cowboy Hall of Fame and Western Heritage Center, with western art and a recreation of a western scene; the State Historical Society Building and Museum; the zoo; Kirkpatrick Center, with its science, air and space museum; and the State Capitol. The Oklahoma National Stockyards, the nation's largest cattle feeder market, has been designated as a national historical landmark. The National Finals rodeo is held here every December.

OMAHA

Location: East-central Nebraska, on Missouri River **County:** Douglas City **Area:** 87.8 sq. miles (226.5 sq. kilometers) **Altitude:** 1,063 feet (324 meters)
Mayor: Mike Boyle
City Population: 311,681 (1980 census) **Metro Area Population:** 570,399 (1980 census)
Daily Newspapers: 1 **No. of Radio Stations:** 15 **No. of TV Stations:** 6
City Chamber of Commerce: Greater Omaha Chamber of Commerce, Suite 2100, 1620 Dodge, Omaha, Nebraska 68102

Omaha, seat of Douglas County, is the largest city in Nebraska. It is an important cattle market and meatpacking center. It took its name from the Omaha Indians living nearby, who were known as "those who go upstream or against the current."

Omaha's history is associated with the opening of the West beginning with Lewis and Clark's conference with the Indians in 1804. A trading post was set up by Jean Pierre Cabanne in 1825, and the first settlement came in 1846-47, when the Mormons spent the winter there on their way to Utah. The city was officially founded in 1854 after Indians ceded the present Douglas County to the United States. Three years later Omaha was incorporated as a city and was capital of the Nebraska Territory from 1855 to 1867.

As a supply point for westward migration, Omaha grew quickly. The Union Pacific Railroad arrived in 1865, augmenting river traffic and making Omaha, on the west bank of the Missouri, a major transportation and shipping center.

Despite floods, droughts, and a plague of grasshoppers later in the 19th century, the city continued to expand. Today it is an important market for livestock and farm produce and has large meat-packing and food-processing

plants, grain elevators, and stockyards. It also has oil refineries, a large lead smelter, and factories manufacturing farm implements and appliances.

The headquarters of the Strategic Air Command are located here as are the regional headquarters of the Farm Credit Administration and the Reconstruction Finance Corporation. Boys Town, the youth community founded by Father Edward J. Flanagan in 1917, is 11 miles west of the city.

Of interest are Fort Omaha, built in 1868, and the Mormon Cemetery with the Winter Quarters Monument. Riverview Park contains a monument to Friedrich von Schiller and Levi Carter Park has a lake and picnic grounds. The Joslyn Art Museum contains paintings by many of the world's greatest artists.

PHILADELPHIA

Location: Southeastern Pennsylvania, at the junction of the Delaware and Schuylkill rivers, 88 miles from Atlantic Ocean **County:** Philadelphia City **Area:** 129 sq. miles (334.1 sq. kilometers) **Altitude:** 100 feet (30.4 meters)
Mayor: William J. Green **Managing Director:** W. Wilson Goode
City Population: 1,688,210 (1980 census) **Metro Area Population:** 4,716,818 (1980 census)
Daily Newspapers: 4 **No. of Commercial Radio Stations (AM):** 9 **No. of TV Stations:** 7
City Chamber of Commerce: The Greater Philadelphia Chamber of Commerce, Suburban Station Building, 1617 John F. Kennedy Blvd., Philadelphia, Pennsylvania 19103

Philadelphia, coextensive with Philadelphia County, is the largest city in Pennsylvania and the fourth largest in the nation. The site was originally settled by Swedes early in the 17th century. In 1682 William Penn founded a Quaker settlement, naming it Philadelphia from the Greek phrase for "brotherly love."

The city was the largest and wealthiest in the 13 Colonies and served, except during a brief British occupation, as the capital from 1777 to 1788—the period of the adoption of the Articles of Confederation (1778) and the drafting of the United States Constitution (1787). From 1790 to 1800 it was the capital of the United States.

Philadelphia was the site of both Banks of the United States—the first from 1791 to 1811, and the second from 1816 to 1836. It was also an important center of the abolition movement and a major station on the Underground Railroad.

Philadelphia was host to the 1876 Centennial Exposition, commemorating the 100th anniversary of American independence, and the 1926 Sesquicentennial Exposition.

Today its diversified economy includes such industries as printing and publishing, and the manufacture of machinery, chemicals, clothing, carpets, instruments and textiles. It is the largest petroleum refining center on the East Coast and the second largest in the nation. It has the largest freshwater port in the world, with 50 miles of waterfront, and is also a major financial center.

A major renovation of the waterfront, referred to as Penn's Landing, is in progress, and a University City Science Center is being developed. Ground was broken in April 1972 for a $300-million complex called Market Street East, which has transformed Philadelphia's main shopping street from City Hall to Independence Mall into a mall and transportation center. In November 1975 the Chestnut Street Transitway opened to transform the 10 blocks between 8th and 18th streets into a buses-only transitway and a modern shrub-lined pedestrian promenade and shopping mall.

There are numerous historic monuments in the city. Independence Hall, where the Declaration of Independence was signed, is in Independence National Park. Nearby is Congress Hall, seat of Congress from 1790 to 1800; Carpenters' Hall, meeting place for the First Continental Congress; the First and Second U.S. Banks; the Jacob Graff House; old City Hall; and the Merchants' Exchange. Other points of interest are Elfreth's Alley, one of the nation's oldest streets; Christ Church; the Society Hill area; and the Betsy Ross House. Fairmount Park, one of the largest in the world, contains many historic monuments and a famous zoo. Among the city's many outstanding museums are the world-famous Museum of Art, the Franklin Institute Science Museum and the University Museum.

PHOENIX

Location: South-central Arizona on Salt River **County:** Maricopa **City Area:** 325 sq. miles (842 sq. kilometers) **Altitude:** 1,117 feet (340.4 meters)
Mayor: Margaret Hance **City Manager:** Marvin Andrews
City Population: 764,911 (1980 census) **Metro Area Population:** 1,508,030 (1980 census)
Daily Newspapers: 2 **No. of Radio Stations:** 35 **No. of TV Stations:** 7
City Chamber of Commerce: Phoenix Metropolitan Chamber of Commerce, 34 W. Monroe Street, Phoenix, Arizona 85003

Phoenix, seat of Maricopa County and state capital, is the largest city in Arizona and one of the fastest growing in the nation. Because Phoenix grew up on a site that showed traces of an ancient Hohokam Indian settlement, it was named after the mythological bird that rose from its own ashes.

The area was probably visited by the Spanish explorers Cabeza de Vaca in 1536, Marcos de Niza in 1539, and Coronado in 1540. John Y. T. Smith established a hay camp on the Salt River in 1866, and the following year Phoenix was officially founded. It was incorporated as a city in 1881 and replaced Prescott as the territorial capital in 1889, two years after the first railroad arrived. In 1912 Arizona was admitted to the Union, and Phoenix became the state capital.

The completion in 1911 of Roosevelt Dam, part of the first successful large-scale irrigation project in the country, made it possible to grow citrus fruits, dates and other crops in the desert climate. The city has also prospered from rich mineral deposits in the region. Since 1945 electronics, computer, aircraft, furniture, steel, aluminum and chemical manufacturing have become important.

In 1972 the Phoenix Civic Plaza, a $19-million commercial and cultural complex, and the 40-story Valley National Bank Building, Arizona's tallest, were completed.

Abundant sunshine has made Phoenix a health resort and winter vacationland. Of interest in the area are the city's museums; nearby South Mountain Park; and Taliesin West, home of the late Frank Lloyd Wright and now an architectural school directed by Mrs. Wright. An annual rodeo simulates the atmosphere of the Old West each spring.

Phoenix has a mushrooming population—people are moving into this city at a rate of more than 400 a day. Newcomers are discovering that the reasons they moved away—air pollution, traffic congestion, inflation, overburdened utilities and suburban sprawl—are problems that already exist in Phoenix. Major long-range plans for the city are in the beginning stages, with redevelopment and "in-filling" of areas within the inner city being the new direction taken.

As Phoenix has mushroomed in population and development, so it has in athletic stature. Professional sports teams such as the National Basketball Association Phoenix Suns have found a home in the Valley of the Sun and are popular drawing cards.

PITTSBURGH

Location: Southwestern Pennsylvania, at junction where the Allegheny and Monongahela rivers form the Ohio River **County:** Allegheny City **Area:** 55.5 sq. miles (143.8 sq. kilometers) **Altitude:** 745 feet (226.4 meters)
Mayor: Richard S. Caliguiri
City Population: 423,938 (1980 census) **Metro Area Population:** 2,263,894 (1980 census)
Daily Newspapers: 2 **No. of Radio Stations:** 28 **No. of TV Stations:** 6
City Chamber of Commerce: The Greater Pittsburgh Chamber of Commerce, 411 Seventh Avenue, Pittsburgh, Pennsylvania 15219

Pittsburgh, seat of Allegheny County, is the second largest city in Pennsylvania, an important inland port, and one of the world's great steel centers.

It was founded on the site of Shannopin, an Indian settlement that was a fur-trading post in the late 17th century. In the 18th century the French built Fort Duquesne on the site, and after it fell to the British it was renamed Fort Pitt in honor of William Pitt. The fort withstood attack in 1763 during Pontiac's Rebellion, and in the ensuing years a village grew up around it.

When the Northwest Territory opened up, the village became an important trading and shipping center. Anthony Wayne negotiated (1795) with Indian tribes in the area, allowing Pittsburgh to develop in peace. It was incorporated as a city in 1816. Completion of the Pennsylvania Canal in 1837 and rail lines in 1851 further stimulated industrial and commercial development. One of the world's first cable suspension bridges was constructed here in 1847.

In 1936 Pittsburgh suffered the most disastrous flood of its history when the Allegheny and the Monongahela rivers rose 46 feet, inundating much of the business and industrial district, paralyzing the city, and taking 45 lives. Damages amounted to $25 million.

The city is headquarters for some of the country's biggest corporations. Among them are U.S. Steel, Gulf Oil, Rockwell International, Heinz foods, Westinghouse, Alcoa, PPG Industries, and Koppers Co. The reactors for the Nautilus and Skate, the first nuclear submarines, were built here.

Pittsburgh's revolutionary urban-renewal program began when public-spirited citizens formed the Allegheny Conference on Community Development in 1943. Demolition work began in 1950 for the famous Gateway Center and $22-million Civic Auditorium with a retractable dome. The program has been eminently successful in rebuilding the Golden Triangle—the triangular-shaped business district bounded by the Allegheny, Monongahela, and Ohio rivers. It has also been so successful in controlling smoke emitted by the steelmaking and other industrial complexes that Pittsburgh is no longer "Smoky City," a nickname it bore for more than a century. The recent Renaissance II program has been responsible for a surge of massive construction projects. Among them are the $35-million David L. Lawrence Convention Center, opened in 1981; the $150-million PPG Headquarters Building; the Liberty Center office-hotel complex; the Dravo building; and the One Oxford Centre complex.

Pittsburgh has a fine park system. City landmarks include the Carnegie-Mellon University, established by Andrew Carnegie in 1895; the University of Pittsburgh and its Cathedral of Learning, noted for its medical and law schools; the Buhl Planetarium and Institute of Popular Science; and Highland Park, site of the Pittsburgh Zoo and a memorial to Stephen Foster, who was born there. Heinz Hall for the Performing Arts opened in September 1971. It is home for the Pittsburgh Symphony, Pittsburgh Opera, Civic Light Opera, Pittsburgh Ballet and Pittsburgh Youth Symphony.

The bold skyline of Pittsburgh is clearly visible from the top of Mount Washington reached from the south bank of the Monongahela by the "incline," one of two in the city, which acts as a near-verticle tramway up the steep slope.

PORTLAND

Location: Northwestern Oregon, near the junction of the Willamette and Columbia rivers **Counties:** Multnomah and Washington **City Area:** 107 sq. miles (277 sq. kilometers) **Altitude:** 77 feet (23.4 meters)
Mayor: Francis Ivancie
City Population: 366,383 (1980 census) **Metro Area Population:** 1,242,287 (1980 census)
Daily Newspapers: 3 **No. of Radio Stations:** 27 **No. of TV Stations:** 6
City Chamber of Commerce: Portland Chamber of Commerce, 824 S.W. 5th Avenue, Portland, Oregon 97204

Portland, seat of Multnomah County and largest city in Oregon, is a trading, transportation, and manufacturing center, an important deepwater port with shipyards and the world's third-largest floating dry dock.

When it was founded in 1845, a coin was flipped to decide whether it should be named after Boston, Massachusetts or Portland, Maine. Incorporated in 1851, it expanded with the establishment of the salmon industry after the Civil War, the arrival of the railroad (1883), the Alaska gold rush (1897-1900), and the Lewis and Clark Centennial Exposition (1905). A disastrous fire in 1873 destroyed part of the city, but it was rapidly rebuilt. The city made history in 1889 with the first long-distance transmission of electricity; power from a plant on the Willamette Falls at Oregon City was sent over wires to light the streets of Portland. During World War II, Portland emerged as a major shipbuilding port.

Today the city is a major export point for wheat, wool, bauxite and lumber, and the leading manufacturer of specialized lumbering equipment. Also important to the city's economy are the numerous chemical industries. Portland has become a major electronics manufacturing center. It is the home of Tektronics, a major producer of display and signal equipment.

Portland instituted a popularly elected regional government that embraces parts of three counties. The reorganization is the first of its kind in the nation, and calls for a two-tiered government of municipal, county and other local jurisdictions and a regional government.

A $16-million transit mall was completed in the central business district in late 1977. The mall provides partial separation of buses, pedestrians and cars for improved transportation flow and lower pollutant levels in the downtown area. A new transit project is the $161-million light rail route which will extend 15 miles from downtown Portland to a suburb.

Of interest in Portland are the annual rose festival, the Pacific International Livestock Exposition, the Portland Zoo, the Portland Art Museum, and the fine views of various mountains, occasionally including distant Mount Rainier and Mount Jefferson. Mount Tabor, an extinct volcanic crater, is located in Portland.

PROVIDENCE

Location: Northeastern Rhode Island, at the head of the Narragansett Bay, on Providence River **County:** Providence **City Area:** 20 sq. miles (51.8 sq. kilometers) **Altitude:** 80 feet (24.3 meters)
Mayor: Vincent A. Cianci, Jr.
City Population: 156,804 (1980 census) **Metro Area Population:** 919,216 (1980 census)
Daily Newspapers: 2 **No. of Radio Stations:** 7 **No. of TV Stations:** 4
City Chamber of Commerce: Greater Providence Chamber of Commerce, 10 Dorrance Street, Providence, Rhode Island 02903

Providence, seat of Providence County and state capital, is the largest city in Rhode Island and a port of entry. It was founded by Roger Williams in 1636 after he was exiled from Massachusetts. The Narragansett Indians granted him title to the site, which he named in gratitude for "God's merciful providence." Early settlers formed (1638) a "Proprietors Company" cooperative.

The settlement developed slowly during the 17th century and suffered much destruction during King Philip's War (1675-76) when Indians raided it and burned more than a third of its homes. Later, however, Providence developed into an important commercial center, and many families amassed fortunes as ships engaged in the West Indian trade.

Providence served the patriotic cause during the Revolutionary War and signed the Rhode Island Independence Act two months before the signing of the Declaration of Independence. After the War of 1812, Providence became a jewelry and textile manufacturing center. In 1832 the city charter became effective.

In 1842 Thomas Wilson Dorr, a Providence man, led a rebellion that collapsed; however, it was influential in the formation of a more democratic state constitution. In 1900 Providence became Rhode Island's sole capital, having been joint capital with other communities since colonial days.

Today Providence is still noted as a jewelry manufacturing center. Silverware, textiles, machinery, metal products, and rubber goods are also important products.

Among the city's historic structures are the old market building (1773), the Stephen Hopkins House (c. 1755), the John Brown House (1786), and the First Baptist Meetinghouse (1775). Roger Williams Park contains a museum of natural history and a natural amphitheater where concerts are given.

Providence is the home of Brown University, Providence College, Rhode Island College, and Rhode Island School of Design, one of the country's leading art schools.

ROCHESTER

Location: Western New York State, at the mouth of the Genesee River on Lake Ontario, 65 miles east of Buffalo **County:** Monroe **City Area:** 36 sq. miles (93.2 sq. kilometers) **Altitude:** 510 feet (154.9 meters)
Mayor: Thomas P. Ryan, Jr. **City Manager:** Peter Korn
City Population: 241,741 (1980 Census) **Metro Area Population:** 971,879 (1980 census)
Daily Newspapers: 2 **No. of Commercial Radio Stations (AM):** 18 **No. of TV Stations:** 5
City Chamber of Commerce: Rochester Area Chamber of Commerce, Inc., 55 St. Paul Street, Rochester, New York 14604

Rochester, seat of Monroe County, is situated on the falls of the Genesee River, the New York State Barge Canal and Lake Ontario. Known as the home of Eastman Kodak, Bausch & Lomb, R. T. French, and Xerox, the city enjoys an unusually diverse economy; major industries include machinery, optical goods, foundry products, nurseries, food packing and processing, leather goods, printing and publishing. It also has great natural beauty, its many parks and gardens earning for it the nickname, "The Flower City."

The Rochester region was originally the home of the Seneca Indians. In 1789 Ebenezer Allen built a mill at the falls of the Genesee, on land he had been granted on condition he serve the Senecas' needs. But the mill failed, and Allen's land was sold to Colonel Nathaniel Rochester and two friends. In 1811 Colonel Rochester laid out the village and a year later the first white settlement was made; its original name, Rochesterville, was shortened in 1812. The village was incorporated in 1817, the city in 1834.

Blessed with abundant waterpower, and the rich yields of the Genesee Valley, a significant milling industry developed and played a large part in Rochester's early growth. The industry's success was assured by the opening of the Erie Canal to the city in 1823.

Before the Civil War, the city was in the forefront of the anti-slavery movement and a station on the Underground Railroad; it was in Rochester that black abolitionist Frederick Douglass published a newspaper, *The North Star.* The period 1850-1900 saw the decline of milling as the city's chief economic pursuit, and the rise of the nursery trade and a number of technical industries to take its place. In 1916 the city was extended northward, in a strip along the banks of the Genesee, to Lake Ontario.

Among the city's attractions are the Eastman Kodak Company, whose plants are open to tours; the George Eastman House of Photography; the Rochester Museum of Arts and Sciences; the Strassenburgh Planetarium; Eastman Theatre, home of the Rochester Philharmonic and the Susan B. Anthony House, commemorating the women's rights pioneer and former Rochester resident.

SACRAMENTO

Location: North-central California, at the confluence of the Sacramento and American rivers, 90 miles northeast of San Francisco **County:** Sacramento **City Area:** 93.8 sq. miles (242.9 sq. kilometers) **Altitude:** 17 feet (5.2 meters)
Mayor: Phillip Isenberg **City Manager:** Walter Slipe
City Population: 275,741 (1980 census) **Metro Area Population:** 1,014,002 (1980 census)
Daily Newspapers: 2 **No. of Radio Stations:** 16 **No. of TV Stations:** 6
City Chamber of Commerce: Sacramento Metropolitan Chamber of Commerce, P.O. Box 1017, Sacramento, California 95805

Sacramento, capital of California and seat of Sacramento County, is a rare amalgam of industrial strength and natural beauty, and the focal point of the profusely fertile Sacramento Valley. Fruits, vegetables, cattle and dairy products abound, supporting a large food packing and processing industry. Other important resources include oil, natural gas, timber, lead, pottery clay and a plentiful supply of waterpower for generating electricity. In 1963 the city opened deep-water port facilities, with direct access to the Pacific Ocean. The city is also an important missile development and electronics center.

The history of Sacramento is rich in drama and color, dating from its founding in 1839 by John Augustus Sutter, a German-born Swiss citizen who received permission from the Mexican governor to establish a colony for fellow Swiss immigrants. Originally called New Helvetia, it received its present name (from the river which ran beside it) in 1848, when it was laid out as a town.

The following year brought the new community immediate and widespread renown, when gold was discovered (by James W. Marshall) on Sutter's property, triggering the legend-engendering Gold Rush of 1849. Fortune followed fame in swift abundance, as Sacramento became the supply center for prospectors, in an often ruthless seller's market. (Ironically, the Gold Rush brought only impoverishment to Sutter himself, as hordes of prospectors pillaged his property and put him heavily in debt.)

Sacramento was incorporated as a town in 1850 and selected as the state capital four years later. City incorporation came in 1863.

From 1849 to 1862, Sacramento was plagued by a series of disasters, including a serious fire and three devastating floods; yet always the town came back to flourish anew. (Over the years, the development of flood control techniques has greatly aided the city's growth.) A hub of river transport since its inception, Sacramento also became (in 1856) the terminus of California's first railroad and (in 1860) the western terminus of the Pony Express. In 1863 the Central Pacific Railroad began laying track east from Sacramento to meet the westward-reaching Union Pacific, and six years later the link was made, giving the country its first transcontinental rail route.

In 1978, a comprehensive plan was issued to guide public and private efforts in developing and revitalizing the center city. A $30-million redevelopment project is under way in an effort by retailers to move back into the downtown area.

Among Sacramento's many attractions are old Fort Sutter, built by Sutter and now maintained as a museum; the 1860 State Capitol; the old Governor's Mansion; the Crocker Art Gallery; Old Sacramento, a re-creation of the original city, including restaurants, theaters, shops and such museums as the Pony Express Museum and the Railroad Museum.

ST. LOUIS

Location: East-central Missouri, near junction of Mississippi and Missouri rivers **County:** St. Louis is an independent city **City Area:** 61 sq. miles (158 sq. kilometers) **Altitude:** 455 feet (138.3 meters) **Mayor:** Vincent Schoemehl, Jr. **City Population:** 453,085 (1980 census) **Metro Area Population:** 2,355,276 (1980 census) **Daily Newspapers:** 2 **No. of Commercial Radio Stations (AM):** 14 **No. of TV Stations:** 6 **City Chamber of Commerce:** St. Louis Regional Commerce and Growth Association, 10 Broadway, St. Louis, Missouri 63102

St. Louis, the largest city in Missouri and the Mississippi River Valley, is surrounded by, but independent of, St. Louis County.

In 1763 the French fur trader Pierre Laclede chose the site for a trading post and a year later dispatched René Auguste Chouteau to build it. It was named St. Louis after Louis IX, the patron saint of France.

The settlement, which became part of the United States in 1803 with the Louisiana Purchase, was an important point of embarkation for expeditions to the West, such as that of Lewis and Clark in 1804. Incorporated in 1808, it did not expand rapidly until after the War of 1812, when immigrants coming by flatboat began to settle the West. Great Americans associated with the city include Charles Lindbergh, Thomas Hart Benton and Joseph Pulitzer.

Today manufacturing is the most important aspect of the economy. The St. Louis industrial area is the only one in the nation producing six basic metals: iron, lead, zinc, copper, aluminum, and magnesium. The city is also a major center for chemical industries and research. St. Louis has been second only to Detroit in automobile assembly; it has one of the pioneer aerospace manufacturers; and it claims the world's largest brewery, Anheuser-Busch, Inc.

In 1966 St. Louis completed its 50,000-seat Busch Memorial Stadium. The following year the Jefferson National Expansion Memorial, a project of the National Park Service, was dedicated. The city erected the 630-foot stainless steel Gateway Arch, tallest monument in the country, as part of the memorial. The Arch attracts between 4- and 6-million visitors a year.

St. Louis, like many other cities, is seeking to rejuvenate its downtown area. In the Laclede's Landing section on the riverfront, old warehouses are being restored, and new restaurants and nightspots have revived night life in the area. A $25-million Convention Center, completed in 1977, and new hotels are bringing more visitors to the city.

Points of interest in St. Louis include the Old Courthouse, scene of the Dred Scott case; Forest Park; the Mis-

souri Botanical Garden; the Municipal Opera; the McDonnell Planetarium; and the Powell Symphony Hall.

ST. PAUL

Location: Eastern Minnesota, adjacent to Minneapolis at the junction of the Minnesota River with the Mississippi **County:** Ramsey **City Area:** 55.45 sq. miles (143.6 sq. kilometers) **Altitude:** 687 feet (209.4 meters) **Mayor:** George Latimer **City Population:** 270,230 (1980 census) **Metro Area Population:** 2,114,256 (1980 census) **Daily Newspapers:** 2 **No. of Radio Stations (AM):** 18 **No. of TV Stations:** 5 **City Chamber of Commerce:** St. Paul Area Chamber of Commerce, Suite 701, North Central Tower, St. Paul, Minnesota 55101

St. Paul, capital of Minnesota and seat of Ramsey County, is contiguous with Minneapolis, with which it forms the Twin Cities metropolitan area, home for about half the state's population. A port of entry and a major transportation and industrial center, the city is situated on bluffs overlooking the Mississippi, close to the head of navigation. Its diverse economy includes meat packing, printing, publishing, steel fabrication, and the manufacture of automobiles, machinery, petroleum products, aerospace equipment, computers, food products, abrasives and cosmetics.

Permanent white settlement in the area began in 1819 with the establishment of an army post on the Minnesota River, on the site of Mendota, now a St. Paul suburb. The following year, the post was moved across the river, where Josiah Snelling built Fort St. Anthony, later named Fort Snelling. Thanks to its strategic location and a large supply of game, fur-trading flourished at Mendota, as did the trading of food and dry goods. After treaties with the Indians paved the way for settlement, many traders, lumbermen and others came from the East to make the area home.

In 1838 a community was begun on the site of present-day St. Paul, which was originally named Pig's Eye, after one of the settlers, a French-Canadian trader named Pierre "Pig's Eye" Parrant. But it soon came to be called St. Paul, in honor of the church built there in 1841 by Father Lucian Galtier. St. Paul was made the capital of Minnesota Territory in 1849, and was incorporated five years later. It was made the state capital in 1858, when Minnesota was admitted to the Union. With the advent of the railroad and the ready availability of immigrant labor (especially German and Irish), St. Paul's early prosperity was assured.

Among the city's attractions are the Capitol Building, which has the world's largest supported marble dome; the Cathedral of St. Paul; Town Square Park, a unique four level glass enclosed park; Landmark Center; William L. McKnight Omnitheatre; the St. Paul Arts and Science Center; Minnesota Museum of Art; St. Paul Civic Center; and, on the outskirts of the city, Fort Snelling State Park, Como Park Conservatory and Zoo, and Minnesota Zoological Gardens. The major annual events in Saint Paul include the Saint Paul Winter Carnival with ice sculpture contests, dog sled and snowmobile racing and parades and the St. Patrick's Day Parade, one of the largest in the country.

SALT LAKE CITY

Location: North-central Utah, southeast of the Great Salt Lake, at the foot of the Wasatch range **County:** Salt Lake City **Area:** 56 sq. miles (145 sq. kilometers) **Altitude:** 4,260 feet (1294.5 meters) **Mayor:** Ted Wilson **City Population:** 163,033 (1980 census) **Metro Area Population:** 936,255 (1980 census) **Daily Newspapers:** 2 **No. of Radio Stations:** 23 **No. of TV Stations:** 6 **City Chamber of Commerce:** Salt Lake Area Chamber of Commerce, 19 East 200 South, Salt Lake City, Utah 84111

Salt Lake City, seat of Salt Lake County, is Utah's capital, its largest city, and headquarters of the 4 million members of the Mormon faith—the Church of Jesus Christ of Latter-day Saints. It was founded in 1847 by the Mormon leader Brigham Young. Mormon settlers soon transformed the arid region into irrigated farmland.

After 1849 Salt Lake City (called Great Salt Lake City until 1868) was a supply point for California-bound pioneers. A link to the transcontinental railroad in 1870 brought non-Mormons to the city and contributed to its growth. When Utah entered the Union in 1896, Salt Lake City became its capital.

Today the metropolis is an important distribution point for a rich agricultural and mining area, as well as an important air and rail hub. Its industries include printing and publishing, oil refining, copper refining, and the smelting of copper and iron. Electronics manufacturing is increasingly becoming an important industry. Major employers are Hill Air Force Base, 30 miles to the north, local defense industries, and the Kennecott Copper Corp.

The city lies at the foot of the beautiful Wasatch Mountains. The magnificent Utah State Capitol with its copper dome houses noted works of art and many interesting exhibits. The Salt Palace, a $17-million civic auditorium complex, was completed in 1969, since enlarged.

Centrally located Temple Square contains the most important buildings of the Mormon Church—the Mormon Temple, a mammoth granite structure designed under Brigham Young's direction and built between 1853 and 1893; and the Tabernacle, housing one of the world's largest organs.

Now completed is the tallest building in Salt Lake City, a 28-story office building for the Mormon church. A multi-million dollar arts project is the latest phase of the city's building boom. The Bicentennial Arts Center includes a concert hall for the Utah Symphony and a performing arts center. Recently completed is Crossroads Plaza, a downtown shopping mall-hotel complex.

SAN ANTONIO

Location: South-central Texas, on the San Antonio River about 190 miles west of Houston **County:** Bexar **City Area:** 267 sq. miles (692 sq. kilometers) **Altitude:** 701 feet (231.3 meters)
Mayor: Henry Cisneros **City Manager:** Tom Huebner
City Population: 785,410 (1980 census) **Metro Area Population:** 1,071,954 (1980 census)
Daily Newspapers: 2 **No. of Radio Stations:** 24 **No. of TV Stations:** 5
City Chamber of Commerce: Greater San Antonio Chamber of Commerce, 602 East Commerce Street, P.O. Box 1628, San Antonio, Texas 78296

San Antonio, port of entry and seat of Bexar County, has developed into the banking and commerce hub of south central Texas, while retaining its history-rich Spanish-Mexican character, redolent of the days when Indian, Spanish, Mexican, Texan and United States forces all sought dominion there. Only 154 miles from the U.S.-Mexico border at Laredo, it is a bilingual city whose old missions and historic landmarks offer charming contrast to its modern factories, refineries and military installations.

Although the federal government is San Antonio's largest employer, farming, stock-raising, food processing and diversified manufacture are also important to its economy. The city's mild climate and natural beauty have made it a popular winter resort.

The site of San Antonio had been known to the Spanish, and to the Coahuiltecan Indians, long before 1718, when a military expedition led by Martín de Alarcón, Spanish governor of Coahuila and Texas, founded a town and fort there, the Villa (and Presidio) de Béjar. At the same time, missionaries founded the Mission San Antonio de Valero nearby; in 1724 the mission was moved from its original site to where the Alamo stands today.

In 1731 Spanish colonists from the Canary Islands founded San Fernando de Béjar, just west of Alarcón's settlement. By 1791 the three settlements—Villa de Béjar, Mission San Antonio de Valero and San Fernando de Béjar—came to be known as one, San Antonio de Béjar (later, simply, San Antonio).

The settlement grew in prominence and was the principal objective of the Mexican and Texas Revolutions (1821, 1836). In the latter conflict, on March 6, 1836, the famous battle of the Alamo took place, in which all of the nearly 200 defenders (including Davy Crockett) were killed by Mexican forces numbering over 2,400. However, the following month, spurred by the battlecry "Remember the Alamo!," the Texans gained ultimate victory at San Jacinto, and the Texas republic was born; a year later, San Antonio was incorporated.

During the later part of the 19th century, the town became a major cattle center, where herds were assembled and started on overland drives up the Chisholm Trail to the Kansas railheads. San Antonio's prosperity was aided by the advent of the railroad and, later, by the increased military presence there.

Among the city's attractions are the Alamo; La Villita, a reconstructed old Spanish settlement; the historic Governor's Palace and San Fernando Cathedral, both restored; the Arneson River Theater; and the Tower of the Americas, built during HemisFair '68. San Antonio is the home of five major universities and has one of the largest medical centers in the country at the University of Texas (San Antonio campus).

SAN DIEGO

Location: Southern California, on east side of San Diego Bay **County:** San Diego **City Area:** 319.5 sq. miles (810.7 sq. kilometers) **Altitude:** sea level
Mayor: Pete Wilson **City Manager:** Ray Blair
City Population: 875,504 (1980 census) **Metro Area Population:** 1,861,846 (1980 census)
Daily Newspapers: 2 **No. of Commercial Radio Stations (AM):** 11 **No. of TV Stations:** 5
City Chamber of Commerce: San Diego Chamber of Commerce, 110 W. "C" Street, Suite 1600, San Diego, California 92101

San Diego, seat of San Diego County, is a port of entry and the oldest permanent European settlement in California. The city has risen rapidly in size, from fifteenth largest in the country in 1970, and now ranks as the eighth largest in the United States.

Since Juan Rodriguez Cabrillo sailed into its bay in 1542, the area has been under four flags—that of Spain, Mexico, California, and the United States. In 1769 San Diego de Alcalá Mission was established by Junípero Serra, a Franciscan missionary. A settlement grew up and was incorporated (1850) as a city after California became part of the Union.

San Diego's excellent natural harbor has made it an important commercial center and the site of several large U.S. Navy installations. It is the distribution and processing hub for the surrounding farm and dairy region and has a wide variety of manufactures. It is the home of the Atlas missile, an aircraft producer, and it is an important oceanographic and health sciences center. San Diego has a large electronics industry. In the last 12 months 30 new companies have relocated to San Diego because of the availability of land and workers. Its magnificent climate and proximity to Mexico have made tourism a significant part of the economy.

San Diego's Balboa Park contains an art gallery, museums, gardens, a zoo, and some buildings from the Panama-California International Exposition (1915-16) and the California Pacific International Exposition (1935-36). In the Old Town area is a state park containing adobes from the Spanish and Mexican era. The Mission Bay park includes boat landings, water ski, fishing and swimming areas, hotels and Sea World, a huge marine animal amusement park.

A 16-mile trolley line, linking downtown San Diego with the Mexican border at Tijuana, opened in July 1981. The new light rail system is expected to carry 30,000 passengers daily and operates with 14 modern trolley cars built in West Germany.

SAN FRANCISCO

Location: West-central California, on a peninsula between Pacific Ocean and San Francisco Bay **County:** San Francisco **City Area:** 46.3 sq. miles (119.9 sq. kilometers) **Altitude:** 65 feet (19.6 meters)
Mayor: Dianne Feinstein **Chief Administrative Officer:** Roger Boas
City Population: 678,974 (1980 census) **Metro Area Population:** 3,252,721 (1980 census)
Daily Newspapers: 2 **No. of Commercial Radio Stations (AM):** 16 **No. of TV Stations:** 9
City Chamber of Commerce: San Francisco Chamber of Commerce, 465 California Street, San Francisco, California 94104

San Francisco, coextensive with California's San Francisco County, is the financial center of the West and, together with the San Francisco Bay area, the largest port on the Pacific Coast.

In 1579 Sir Francis Drake stopped in the vicinity on his voyage around the world. In 1776 a mission, later known as Mission Dolores, and fort were founded at a site chosen by Juan Bautista de Anza. In 1846, during the Mexican

War, a U.S. naval force under John Montgomery took Yerba Buena, the settlement that had grown up. The following year the community assumed the name of its bay, which, according to tradition, had been named after St. Francis of Assisi by Spanish voyagers in 1595.

In 1848 the California gold rush began and a flood of fortune seekers, adventurers, and settlers brought a period of lawlessness, during which San Francisco's waterfront section became notorious as the Barbary Coast, and vigilantes were organized to restore order. Newcomers from all over the world, including China, gave the city a cosmopolitan air. It was incorporated in 1850 and linked with the East by railroads in 1869.

On April 18, 1906, a disastrous earthquake and fire almost completely destroyed the city; an estimated 700 persons perished.

The opening of the Panama Canal, which stimulated trade, was celebrated by the Panama-Pacific Exposition of 1915. By 1939, the year of the Golden Gate International Exposition, San Francisco had become the leading industrial and commercial center of the Pacific Coast. During the Second World War, the city was the major mainland supply point and port of embarkation for the struggle in the Pacific.

San Francisco is the home of the Pacific Coast Stock Exchange and a Federal Reserve district bank. More than 65 industrial parks lie within a 50-mile radius of the city. Major industries include food processing, shipbuilding, petroleum refining, and the manufacture of metal products and chemicals. The city is also a noted cultural center.

Situated among steep hills, San Francisco is a colorful city of lovely vistas, graceful bridges, ornate mansions, imposing public buildings, and unusual districts. The Golden Gate Bridge (1937) links the city with Marin County to the north. San Francisco's scenic hills now hold apartment complexes and shopping centers, but despite the changes the city maintains its warm personality.

Rejuvenation of the inner city has come from the creation of block and merchant associations and the arrival of new department stores in the downtown area.

San Francisco is famous for its fine restaurants; its cable car system, preserved as a historic landmark; Chinatown—the country's largest—with its Oriental architecture, tearooms, and temples; Telegraph Hill, where in earlier times a signal tower sent word to the city of the arrival of ships and is now crowned with the Coit Memorial Tower; and Nob Hill, once the home of millionaires, is the site of the Cable Car Barn. Also of interest are Fisherman's Wharf, with its fishing fleet and seafood restaurants; the nearby National Maritime Museum and its historic ships; Ghirardelli Square and the Cannery, converted factories housing shops and restaurants; the Cow Hollow district, scene of art, book and specialty shops in an area of Victorian houses; and Golden Gate Park, with its planetarium, museum of natural history, aquarium, and flower gardens. The Cow Palace is the home of political conventions, sports events, and livestock exhibitions. In 1980 San Francisco celebrated the opening of the Louise M. Davies Symphony Hall, a fitting home for the great San Francisco Symphony.

SAN JOSE

Location: Western California, about 40 miles southeast of San Francisco in the Santa Clara Valley **County:** Santa Clara **City Area:** 156.6 sq. miles (405.6 sq. kilometers) **Altitude:** 70 feet (21.3 meters)
Mayor: Janet Gray Hayes **City Manager:** Francis Fox
City Population: 636,550 (1980 census) **Metro Area Population:** 1,295,071 (1980 census)
Daily Newspapers: 2 **No. of Radio Stations:** 15 **No. of TV Stations:** 3
City Chamber of Commerce: San Jose Chamber of Commerce, One Paseo De San Antonio, San Jose, California 95113

San Jose, seat of Santa Clara County, is virtually contiguous with the city of Santa Clara, the two communities together forming the focal point of the "Silicon Valley" area, the nation's leading producer of semi-conductors. Plants producing high technology devices, computers, aerospace equipment and advanced electronic apparatus line the streets and highways of this fast-growing region. San Jose is also the center of the Santa Clara Valley agricultural empire, the World's largest concentration of dried fruit packing and canning.

San Jose (originally the Pueblo de San José de Guadalupe) was founded in 1777 by José Joaquin Moraga, as a Spanish military supply base, and soon also became an ecclesiastical center. After the territory came under U.S. control, San Jose was made (in 1849) California's first capital, although statehood was not officially achieved until 1850, the year San Jose also became the state's first incorporated city. It remained the capital until 1851, when the seat of state government shifted to Vallejo.

In its early years, San Jose served as a supply base for gold prospectors and as a bustling fruit trade depot. The coming of the railroad (in 1864), connecting the community to San Francisco, consolidated its importance as a distribution point for the increasingly bountiful produce of the Santa Clara Valley. This in turn gave rise to the growth of industries to equip the region's farms and service the needs of a growing populace.

Between 1940 and 1960, San Jose's population increased three-fold; from 1960 to 1970, it more than doubled, making San Jose-Santa Clara one of the nation's largest urban areas. The increase between 1970 and 1980 amounted to 36 percent for the city. This rapid growth was seen as a plus by developers, politicians and retailers. However, the growth has led to the decay of the downtown area, air pollution and traffic congestion. A rethinking of San Jose's growth future has come with Mayor Hayes' reelection. Initial efforts at "in-filling" and redevelopment of areas within the city, instead of continued urban sprawl, appears to be successful.

Places of interest in San Jose include the Municipal Rose Garden; Winchester Mystery House; Rosicrucian Egyptian Museum; and nearby, the Lick Observatory (atop Mount Hamilton), Alum Rock Park, a popular 687-acre spa well known for its mineral springs and scenic allure, and Mission Santa Clara de Asis, dating from 1777.

SEATTLE

Location: West-central Washington, on Puget Sound and west shore of Lake Washington **County:** King **City Area:** 92 sq. miles (238 sq. kilometers) **Altitude:** 10 feet (3.0 meters)
Mayor: Charles Royer
City Population: 493,846 (1980 census) **Metro Area Population:** 1,606,765 (1980 census)
Daily Newspapers: 2 **No. of Radio Stations (AM):** 22 **No. of TV Stations:** 5
City Chamber of Commerce: Seattle Chamber of Commerce, 215 Columbia Street, Seattle, Washington 98104

Seattle, seat of King County, is Washington's largest city and the largest in the Pacific Northwest. It is a manufacturing, trade, and transportation center, and a major port of entry. The city is situated on seven hills and is flanked by the majestically beautiful Cascade and Olympic Mountains. Within its limits are four lakes, 48 parks and more than 22 miniparks.

Seattle began as a small lumber settlement in 1851. It was platted two years later and named for a chief of the Duwamish and Suquamish Indians. Incorporated in 1869, it remained a small lumber town until the arrival of the railroad in 1884. Subsequent strikes, anti-Chinese riots, and a great fire in 1889 did not prevent the city from growing rapidly. With the 1897-98 Alaska gold rush, Seattle became a boom town and was the nation's chief link with Alaska. Further growth came with the Alaska-Yukon-Pacific Exposition (1909), the opening of the Panama Canal (1914), and the completion (1917) of a canal and locks making the city both a saltwater and freshwater port. In 1919 the Industrial Workers of the World (IWW) led a general strike in Seattle, long a center of the radical labor movement. A series of various municipal scandals led to the election in 1926 of a reform candidate, Bertha K. Landis, the first woman mayor of a large American city.

World War II made the city a center of aircraft manufacturing and shipbuilding. The Boeing Company is the largest employer in the area. Although the region underwent a severe recession in the early 1970s due to a slackening of the aerospace industry, the area's economy and the aircraft industry are booming again. The construction of the trans-Alaska crude oil pipeline did much to bolster Seattle's economy. Other important industries today are electronics, printing, food processing, lumber, chemical products, metal goods and machinery.

The Seattle downtown area has taken on a new look. Since 1970 almost half of the downtown has been rebuilt. Seattle has become an important cultural center on the

West Coast. It boasts a first-rate Opera House, the Seattle Symphony Orchestra, several active theater companies, and a fine arts museum. Of interest in the city is the Seattle Center, site of the Century 21 Exposition. It is connected to the downtown area by a monorail line and contains the opera house, arena, coliseum, and International Fountain, the world-famous 606-foot Space Needle, and the Pacific Science Center. Also of interest are Pike Place Market, Underground Seattle and the old Pioneer Square district.

Seattle is the home of the Mariners Baseball Team, the Seahawks Football Team, the Supersonics Basketball Team, the Sounders Soccer Team, and the Smashers Volleyball Team.

TAMPA

Location: On the west coast of Florida at the mouth of the Hillsboro River on Tampa Bay. **County:** Hillsborough **City Area:** 84.5 sq. miles (218.9 sq. kilometers) **Altitude:** 15 feet (4.6 meters)
Mayor: Bob Martinez
City Population: 271,523 (1980 census) **Metro Area Population:** 1,569,492 (1980 census)
Daily Newspapers: 2 **No. of Radio Stations:** 9 **No. of TV Stations:** 3
City Chamber of Commerce: Greater Tampa Chamber of Commerce, P.O. Box 420, Tampa, Florida 33601

Tampa, a port of entry and the closest port to the Panama Canal, is located on Tampa Bay, an inlet of the Gulf of Mexico. Once known almost exclusively as a vacation spot and a source of fine cigars, Tampa, which is the seat of Hillsborough County, today has also emerged as one of Florida's most industrialized cities and the trade center of the state's west coast. Its economy ranges from food processing and phosphate shipping to the manufacture of a wide variety of goods, including beer, fertilizer, paint, cement, cigars, fabricated steel, and electronic equipment. Nearby is MacDill Air Force Base, headquarters for the U.S. Readiness Command. Tampa International Airport, which is served by 16 airlines, has been called "the best airport in the world" in the press. The downtown area is undergoing major redevelopment activity.

At least two Spanish explorers, and probably more, visited the site of Tampa in the 16th century: Panfilo de Narváez (1528) and Hernando de Soto (1539). Seminole Indians successfully resisted white men's efforts to settle in the area until 1823, when a contingent of U.S. troops established Fort Brooke there. By 1831 the settlement that had grown up around the fort had come to be known by its former Indian name of Tampa; it was incorporated in 1849. During the Civil War, Tampa was bombarded by gunboats.

Development of Tampa began in earnest in 1885 with the coming of Henry B. Plant's narrow-gauge South Florida Railroad—and his port improvements and tourism promotions. The economy got another boost when the manufacture of cigars was begun (in 1886) at Ybor City, which soon became a part of Tampa proper. Tourism was spurred in 1891 by the completion of the lavish, Moorish-style Tampa Bay Hotel, which today houses the University of Tampa. In 1898, during the Spanish-American War, Tampa served as the embarkation point for Colonel "Teddy" Roosevelt and his "Rough Riders." In the mid-1920s the man-made Davis Islands in Tampa Bay were completed, providing choice sites for hotels, residences and various resort facilities.

Among Tampa's attractions are Ybor city, the city's Latin quarter, famous for its Spanish restaurants and shops, and the Busch Gardens, Florida's second-largest attraction. Tampa Museum, opened in July, 1979, is the city's first major public effort at a permanent art museum. Under construction is the Center for Science and Industry, expected to be completed in 1981. It has already won the Owen Corning Energy Conservation Award for its energy conservation design and for its use of solar panels. The Gasparilla Festival, a one-day event in honor of the alleged pirate José Gaspar, is celebrated in February with a mock invasion of the city.

WASHINGTON, D.C.

Location: Between Virginia and Maryland, on Potomac River **City Area:** 68.2 sq. miles (176.7 sq. kilometers) **Altitude:** 72 feet (21.9 meters)
Mayor: Marion S. Barry, Jr. **City Administrator:** Elijah B. Rogers
City Population: 637,651 (1980 census) **Metro Area Population:** 3,060,240 (1980 census)
Daily Newspapers: 1 **No. of Radio Stations (AM):** 32 **No. of TV Stations:** 8
City Chamber of Commerce: District of Columbia Chamber of Commerce, 1319 F Street, N.W., Suite 904, Washington, D.C. 20004

Washington, D.C., is not only the capital of the United States but an important business and financial center, with over 1,800 professional and trade associations headquartered there. Since 1895, when Georgetown became part of Washington, it has been coextensive with the District of Columbia. Washington's large government work force insures a more recession-proof climate than in other major markets.

The District was established by Congress in 1790-91, and George Washington selected the exact site for the "Federal City," which was designed by Pierre L'Enfant and laid out by Andrew Ellicott. Maryland and Virginia ceded land for the District, and the capital moved there from Philadelphia in 1800. Thomas Jefferson was the first President to be inaugurated in Washington.

During the War of 1812, the city fell to the British, who burned the Capitol, White House, and other public buildings. During the Civil War, the city was threatened by Confederate forces.

1878 marked the end of home rule for the district, with city officials thereafter being appointed by the President. Since 1961, however, when residents were given the right to vote in Presidential elections, Washingtonians have sought to increase local self-government and national political representation. Residents were allowed to elect their own school board in 1968, and full home rule followed in 1975. Under the Nixon Administration, the District of Columbia was granted non-voting representation in Congress, with Walter E. Fauntroy sworn in on April 19, 1971, as Washington's first Representative in nearly 100 years. And in an historic move, Congress voted in 1978 to approve a constitutional amendment giving the District full elected representation in both the House and the Senate. The amendment gives Washington two Senators—expanding the Senate from 100 to 102—and either one or two Representatives, based on the District's 1980 census. The amendment must now be ratified by at least 38 state legislatures by the summer of 1985 for it to become law.

Washington, with its broad tree-shaded thoroughfares and open vistas, has many imposing buildings. The Capitol and White House are the most historic. Other leading tourist attractions are the Washington Monument and Lincoln and Jefferson Memorials. The many additional points of interest in or near the city include the Library of Congress; the National Archives, which houses the Declaration of Independence, the Constitution, and the Bill of Rights; the Supreme Court Building; Constitution Hall; the Smithsonian Institution; the National Gallery of Art; the numerous embassies; the Pentagon; the U.S. Naval Observatory; and Mount Vernon. The fashionable Georgetown area was designated a national monument in 1967.

The Arlington Memorial Bridge across the Potomac River connects Washington with Arlington National Cemetery. Among the city's beautiful parks are West Potomac Park, which includes the Tidal Basin with the famous Japanese cherry trees; East Potomac Park; Rock Creek Park and the adjoining National Zoological Park; and Anacostia Park.

Washington's Metro, the computerized subway system which opened in 1976, is having mixed results. While linking the downtown area with the airport, Capitol Hill and Washington's suburbs, the Metro must accomodate the multitude of passengers with a shortage of cars due to malfunctions.

Public and private redevelopment has given downtown Washington a new face. Currently under way is the joint $500-million public-private PennsylvaniaAvenue Development Plan for combined residential-commercial use, and the $60-million expansion of the Sheraton Park Hotel in northwest Washington. In 1980, construction began on a $99-million convention center north of the Mall that officials hope will one day attract the city's first national political convention.

U.S. OUTLYING AREAS

The areas under United States sovereignty or otherwise associated with some type of American jurisdiction extend through the Caribbean and almost across the Pacific. From east to west, the Virgin Islands of the United States, in the Caribbean, lie 160° from the Palau Islands in the American-administered Trust Territory of the Pacific Islands, nearly halfway around the world. The distance between Point Barrow in northern Alaska, 71.5° north of the equator, and American Samoa in the southwest Pacific, 14° south of the equator, is nearly half of that from pole to pole.

American Samoa—*Status:* Unorganized unincorporated territory. *Population:* 32,395 (1980 census). *Area:* 83 sq. mi. *Seat of government:* Pago Pago (3,058).

American Samoa consists of six small Pacific islands in that part of the Samoan islands lying east of 171°W., plus Swains Island, 250 miles north of Tutuila. It is roughly 2,200 miles southwest of Hawaii and 1,600 miles northeast of the northern tip of New Zealand.

In 1977 American Samoa held its first popular election for governor. The victor, Peter Tali Coleman, a native of the islands, was inaugurated on January 3, 1978. He was reelected on November 4, 1980. There is a legislature, the *Fono,* with limited authority, the House of Representatives being elected by universal suffrage, the Senate by the native chiefs. Samoan society is rigidly stratified, and the chiefs, of whom there are some 600 of varying ranks, have firm, paternalistic control over their followers.

The six islands in the Samoan group came under American hegemony in 1899, when Great Britain and Germany renounced their claims in favor of the United States, and Swains was added in 1925. American Samoa's native inhabitants are U.S. nationals; they are not American citizens but may migrate freely to the United States. In October 1978, President Carter signed into law an act of Congress giving the islands a nonvoting delegate to the U.S. House of Representatives. Fofo I. F. Sunia was elected as the island group's first delegate on November 18, 1980.

Guam—*Status:* Organized unincorporated territory. *Population:* 105,821 (1980 census). *Area:* 212 sq. mi. *Capital:* Agana (881).

This island in the western Pacific is the most southerly of the Marianas, 1,300 miles east of the Philippines and 1,475 miles south of Japan, at 13°27′N. and 144°47′E. Of volcanic origin, it is mountainous in the south, a plateau in the north. The climate is tropical, with moderately heavy rainfall. The indigenes—the Chamorros—make up about half the population. Most of the rest are military or other government transients. English is the official language. About 95 percent of the native Guamanians are Roman Catholics.

U.S. military installations and tourism are the most significant factors in the economy. Guam is the only American territory without excise duties (except for tobacco, liquid fuel, and liquor).

Guam's administration is under the U.S. Department of the Interior. Its people are U.S. citizens (however, they do not vote in national elections but do have a nonvoting delegate in the House of Representatives). The governor and lieutenant governor are elected by the people. There is an elected unicameral legislature. On August 4, 1979, Guam residents rejected a proposed constitution drafted in December 1977 which allowed the island more self-government. Most islanders felt that it did not provide residents with the same rights as other Americans.

Howland, Baker, and Jarvis Islands—*Status:* Unincorporated possession. *Population:* Uninhabited. *Area:* 2.77 sq. mi.

These three small islands are situated in the South Pacific: Howland at 48°N.,176°38′W., Baker at 0°15′N., 176°27′W. and Jarvis at 0°23′S.,160°02′W. Howland and Baker are coral atolls about 35 miles apart and some 2,000 miles southwest of Honolulu. Jarvis lies some 1,500 miles south of Honolulu. They had rich guano deposits that were worked by American interests in the 1850s; however, when that industry faded, the islands had no value until the trans-Pacific aviation era began in the 1930s. In 1934 the United States reasserted its claim to them, based on the fact that they had been mentioned in the Guano Act of 1856.

Johnston Atoll—*Status:* Unincorporated possession. *Population:* 339 (1981 est.). *Area:* .91 sq. mi.

This Pacific atoll lies 715 miles southwest of Honolulu, at 16°45′N. and 169°30′W. It consists of a reef around four islets. Johnston was annexed in 1858 by both the United States and the Kingdom of Hawaii. A quantity of guano was removed during the next 50 years, and for a long time the area was also a bird reservation. It was taken over by the U.S. Navy in 1934.

In 1958 and 1962 it was the site of high-altitude nuclear tests. In 1971 the Defense Department started to move 13,000 tons of nerve and mustard gas stored on Okinawa to igloo-shaped structures on Johnston.

Kingman Reef—*Status:* Unincorporated possession. *Population:* Uninhabited. *Area:* .01 sq. mi.

This bare reef in the Pacific lies 35 miles northwest of Palmyra Island and 1,000 miles south of Honolulu at 6°24′S., 162°22′W. It was annexed by the United States in 1922 and placed under the U.S. Navy in 1934.

Midway Islands—*Status:* Unincorporated possession. *Population:* 526 (1981 est.). *Area:* 1.9 sq. mi.

Midway is near the western end of the Hawaiian chain, 1,200 miles northwest of Honolulu, at 28°12′-17′N. and 177°19′-26′W. It consists of an atoll with two islets.

Made a possession in 1867 and placed under the U.S. Navy in 1903, Midway was the scene of one of the great air/sea battles of World War II. Today it is a naval installation; its chief executive is a naval officer. Midway is noted as a nesting site for seabirds.

Navassa Island—*Status:* Unincorporated possession. *Population:* Uninhabited. *Area:* 2 sq. mi.

Navassa lies in the Caribbean between Jamaica and Haiti, 30 miles west of the latter. It was certified in 1865 as appertaining to the United States under the Guano Act of 1856. A presidential proclamation of 1916 declared it to be under the sole jurisdiction of the United States and reserved it for lighthouse purposes. It is administered by the Coast Guard.

Palmyra Island—*Status:* Unincorporated possession. *Population:* Uninhabited. *Area:* 3.85 sq. mi.

An atoll of more than 50 islets, Palmyra is located in the Pacific 1,000 miles south of Honolulu, at 5°52′N. and 162°06′W. It is covered with dense foliage, coconut trees, and pisonis grandis, a 100-foot-tall balsalike tree.

Claimed by the Kingdom of Hawaii in 1862, the atoll was annexed by the United States with Hawaii in 1898. Excluded from Hawaii's boundaries when the latter became a state in 1959, it was placed under the administration of the U.S. Secretary of the Interior in 1961. In 1979 the U.S. government proposed purchasing the privately-owned island for use as a nuclear waste storage site.

Puerto Rico—*Status:* Commonwealth (Estado Libre Asociado). *Population:* 3,187,570 (1980 census). *Area:* 3,435 sq. mi. *Capital:* San Juan (422,701).

Puerto Rico, 885 miles southeast of the southern coast of Florida, is the easternmost island of the Greater Antilles in the Caribbean. It is separated from the Dominican Republic to the west by the 61 miles of Mona Passage. To the east, St. Thomas in the U.S. Virgin Islands is 34 miles away. Among the offshore islands are Vieques and Culebra to the east, Mona to the west.

The island is crossed by mountain ranges and ringed by a coastal plain that is 15 miles wide at its broadest. The climate is mildly tropical. Rainfall is moderate in the coastal areas, but heavier in the interior mountains.

Many of the people are of mixed African-Spanish descent. (The original Arawak Indians were destroyed in the 16th century.) English and Spanish are the official languages, but Spanish is commonly spoken. Roman Catholicism predominates.

Before World War II, the Puerto Rican economy was based on sugar and such related products as rum. Needlework, mostly piecework produced by women at home, was the second most important activity, and tobacco growing the third. Unemployment was high, poverty widespread; however, after the war a determined drive was begun to foster industrialization on the island.

Under then Governor Rexford Guy Tugwell and the Puerto Rican legislative leader Luis Muñoz Marin, the framework for economic expansion was established. In 1948, "Operation Bootstrap" commenced, giving tax exemptions to new or expanded industry.

By 1971 the program had attracted $2 billion in industrial investments and 2,000 plants. However, while the successor program continued to expand incentives, the federal government froze $13 million in loans to Puerto Rican businesses in 1981.

Today, income from manufacturing is more than three times that from agriculture, although sugar, coffee, tobacco, and rum are still produced and exported. Among the industries attracted by the tax abatement and lower wage scales in Puerto Rico are textiles and apparel, leather and shoes, electronic components, pharmaceuticals, tuna canning, and—increasingly—such heavy industries as metal products and petrochemicals.

In addition, tourist facilities and tourism have greatly expanded. Despite the general economic advance, unemployment continues to be much higher than in the United States. Many Puerto Ricans have been dependent on federal food stamp programs and on CETA jobs; both were cut back in 1981.

Puerto Ricans are U.S. citizens and, if they migrate to this country, vote subject only to local electoral requirements. Puerto Rico does not send members to Congress (although it has a Resident Commissioner in the House of Representatives who may introduce legislation but does not have a vote) and Puerto Rico is not liable to federal taxation.

Beginning in 1948 (as the first elected governor), Luis Muñoz Marin—leader of the Popular Democratic party and the force behind "Operation Bootstrap"—served four terms, retiring in 1964. During this period the main minority faction was the Statehood Republican party, which advocated U.S. statehood for Puerto Rico as opposed to the commonwealth status championed by the Popular Democrats. In a plebiscite held in 1967, the vote was 60.5 percent for continuation of commonwealth status, and 38.9 percent for statehood.

In the 1968 gubernatorial election, however, Luis A. Ferré, long a prominent Statehood Republican, who ran as the candidate of the New Progressive party (which he had helped form during the plebiscite campaign), won with more than 44 percent of the vote. Although Ferré's platform advocated statehood for Puerto Rico, he had made it clear that such a step would depend on a plebiscite "separate from the general elections." In 1972 Ferré was defeated by Rafael Hernández-Colón of the Popular Democratic party, but in 1976 the New Progressives returned to power under Carlos Romero Barcelo. In 1980 Romero-Barcelo narrowly won reelection over Hernandez-Colon. The race was so close that Hernandez-Colon had been declared the apparent winner; a recount tipped the election to the incumbent by a vote of 47.4%-47.2%.

Although advocates of Puerto Rican independence have had little impact at the polls, there has long been such a movement on the island. Perhaps its leading figure was the Harvard-educated Pedro Albizu Campos, who died in 1965, aged 73. A leader of the Nationalist party in Puerto Rico, in 1950 he staged an abortive armed revolt, which included an attempt by some of his followers to assassinate President Truman.

Columbus claimed the island for Spain in 1493 on his second voyage to the New World. Spanish colonization began under Ponce de León in 1508. Occupied by American troops during the Spanish-American War, the island was ceded to the United States by Spain in 1898. Congress provided for its civil government by the Foraker Act of 1900 and granted Puerto Ricans U.S. citizenship in 1917 by an "Organic Act," known as the Jones Act. In 1947 Puerto Rico obtained the right to elect its governor. Commonwealth status in free association with the United States was achieved in 1952. Operating under a constitution much like that of the United States, Puerto Rico has an elected legislature consisting of a Senate and a House of Representatives. In 1977, the Puerto Rican legislature provided for the selection of delegates to the Democratic and Republican conventions by presidential primary. More than 600,000 voters participated in the 1980 election of delegates to the two parties' national conventions.

Migration from Puerto Rico to the mainland has varied with the economic conditions here and on the island. It was very heavy during much of the 1950s, and the 1970 census counted more than 1.8 million persons of Puerto Rican birth in the United States. Substantial numbers of Puerto Ricans have also returned to the island from the United States.

In September 1978, the United Nations Decolonization Committee passed a Cuban-sponsored resolution calling for self-determination for Puerto Rico, recommending that it be included on the UN's list of nongoverning territories as a U.S. colony. In response, committees in both houses of Congress approved resolution in 1979 reaffirming American support of self-determination for the island's people. .

Trust Territory of the Pacific Islands—*Status:* UN Trust Territory. *Population:* 133,732 (1980 census) *Area:* 8,511 sq. mi. including lagoons (707 sq. mi. of land). *Administrative Center:* Saipan, Northern Mariana Islands.

These islands and atolls, generally known as Micronesia, are scattered over an area of more than three million sq. mi. There are more than 3,000 of them, about 100 inhabited. They stretch 2,300 miles from some 500 miles east of the Philippines almost as far east as the international date line, from about 1° to 22°N. and from 130° to 172°E. The islands fall into three major groups—the Carolines (including the Palau Islands), the Marshalls, and the Marianas (excluding Guam). A number of the islands were the scene of bitter fighting during World War II—Peleliu in the Carolines, Saipan in the Marianas, Kwajalein in the Marshalls. Bikini and Enewetak in the Marshalls have been used as nuclear-test sites.

Subsistence agriculture (coconuts, cassava, copra, bananas, yams) and fishing are the main economic activities; copra and fish are the chief exports. Tourism is being developed.

The area is under the jurisdiction of the U.S. Secretary of the Interior; administrative authority is vested in a high commissioner who is appointed by the president. Following the establishment of the new island governments beginning in 1976 (see below), the duties of the high commissioner were limited to carrying out UN Trust Territory policy.

Beginning in 1565 the islands gradually came under tenuous Spanish control. Strong German penetration into the Marshall Islands in the late nineteenth century resulted in the sale of the whole area to Germany by Spain in 1899. Following Germany's defeat in the First World War, they were placed under Japanese mandate. In 1947, following the end of World War II, they entered the UN Trusteeship system under American administration as a "strategic" trust: one in which military bases are permissible.

For many years after assuming its trusteeship, the United States neglected the area, permitting the Japanese-built road system and sanitary facilities to deteriorate. In 1966, the World Health Organization reported that health conditions were bad; the United States has pledged improvements in this field.

In 1969, Secretary of the Interior Hickel visited the islands and promised immediate steps would be taken to increase the territory's self-government and assure that equal wages would be paid to Micronesians and Americans for doing comparable work. At the same time, it was reported that a political status commission, appointed by the Trust Territory-wide Congress of Micronesia in 1967, had recommended that the territory be made a self-governing nation in free association with the United States or, failing that, seek complete independence. An offer by the United States of "Commonwealth status" like that of Puerto Rico was rejected by the Congress of Micronesia in 1970. The Trust Territory's Congress of Micronesia was dissolved in 1978. The United States government signed agreements with the emergent governments of the Marshall Islands, the Federated States of Micronesia and Belau (see below) in October-November 1980. These agreements provided "free association status" with the United States for the new nations, under which the United States would retain military responsibility for the region. The agreements require approval by the U.S. president, Senate and the citizens of the new nations. The new arrangement also requires the approval of the United Nations.

In 1975 the **Northern Mariana Islands** (1980 population: 16,758) voted in favor of future commonwealth status and in 1976 the U.S. Congress approved a plan making the islands a commonwealth associated with the United States. Following a March 1977 referendum approving a new constitution—providing for an elected bicameral legislature and an elected governor— Carlos S. Camacho became the islands' first democratically elected chief executive, and the first native islander to administer the Northern Marianas in over 400 years of foreign domination. The bicameral Legislature consists of a 9-member Senate and a 14-member House of Representatives. The administrative center is on Saipan.

In a July 12, 1978, referendum, four of the six island districts of the Trust Territory—Ponape, Yap, Kosrae and Truk—voted to accept "free association" with the U.S. as the **Federated States of Micronesia (FSM)** (1980 population: 73,755). The new federation officially came into being on May 10, 1979. Such status entails continued American financial support for 15 years, with Washington to retain responsibility for defense; otherwise the islands will become fully self-governing when the United States terminates its UN Trusteeship. Tosiwo Nakayama was elected president on May 11, 1979. The federal Congress consists of a Senate and a House of Representatives. The capital is Kolonia on Ponape.

The **Marshall Islands** (1980 population: 31,042) electorate rejected membership in the FSM in the July 1978 referendum. Under May 1, 1979 constitution, legislation is the function of the 33-member *Nitijela* which meets at the government center on Majuro atoll. The president is Amata Kabua. Bikini and Kwajalein, scene of postwar nuclear tests, are located in the Marshalls.

The Palau group, now the **Republic of Belau** (1980 population: 12,177), also rejected inclusion in the FSM. Under the republican constitution of 1979, the government consists of a president and a bicameral legislature consisting of an 18-member Senate and a 16-member House of Delegates. In elections held on November 4, 1980, Haruo I. Remeliik was elected president and took office on January 1, 1981. The seat of government is on Koror.

Virgin Islands—*Status:* Organized unincorporated territory. *Population:* 95,591 (1980 census). *Area:* 133 sq. mi. *Capital:* Charlotte Amalie (11,756), on St. Thomas.

The Virgin Islands of the United States form the western end of the Lesser Antilles between the Caribbean and the Atlantic, about 34 miles east of Puerto Rico. They comprise nearly 100 islands and cays, but only three islands are significant—St. Thomas (27 sq. mi.), St. Croix (82 sq. mi.), and St. John (19 sq. mi.). The United States bought the Virgin Islands from Denmark for $25 million in 1917.

St. Thomas is mountainous, with many harbors, of which Charlotte Amalie is one of the finest in the Caribbean. The climate is subtropical, moderated by the trade winds. Rainfall is variable and sometimes so light as to cause drought. Seventy percent of the population is black, many of whom are immigrants from other Antillean islands. Of the rest, considerably more than half are from the United States. English is the official language.

Since the phasing out of the peasant-based sugar-cane agriculture, there has been little farming on the islands. Tourism is the major industry, and the area has the greatest number of cruise-ship calls in the world. Oil refining and bauxite processing are important; labor-intensive light industry has been introduced. More than half the island of St. John is occupied by the Virgin Islands National Park.

The U.S. Department of the Interior has jurisdiction over the islands. The governor has been elected since 1970. Juan Luis became governor in January 1978 on the death of Cyril E. King. Virgin Islanders are U.S. citizens, but cannot vote in national elections and have no Congressional representation, except for a non-voting delegate in the House since April 1972. In March 1979 voters rejected a proposed constitution. A new constitution is being submitted to the electorate in the fall of 1981.

Wake Island—*Status:* Possession. *Population:* 150 (1974 est.). *Area:* 2.5 sq. mi. *Administrative Center:* Wake Islet.

Wake lies in the Pacific some 2,000 miles west of Honolulu and 1,500 miles northeast of Guam, at 19°17'N. and 166°35'E. It is an atoll comprising three islets—Wake, Wilkes, and Peale. They are formed of coral built up on the rim of an underwater volcano; the land averages only 12 feet above sea level. Waves driven by 200-knot winds from Typhoon Sarah swept over the three islets in 1967.

The island has an aviation base with a 9,800-foot runway. Responsibility for its civil administration was vested in the U.S. Secretary of the Interior in 1962, but since 1974 has been under the Air Force Department.

Wake Island was annexed in 1899. It was attacked by the Japanese on December 7, 1941, and later that month fell after an heroic defense by the small Marine garrison.

U.S. TERRITORIAL ACQUISITIONS, POSSESSIONS, AND LEASEHOLDS

Year **Acquisition**

—— **Gross Area (888,685 sq. mi.)** Original territory of the first 13 states and their claims, including part of drainage basin of Red River of the North, south of the 49th parallel, sometimes considered part of Louisiana Purchase; completely acquired by independence treaty (1783; ratified, 1784) with Great Britain.

1803 **Gross Area (827,192 sq. mi.)** Louisiana Purchase acquired from France for about $15 million (60 million francs); total payment, including interest: $23,-213,567.73.

1819 **Gross Area (72,003 sq. mi.)** Florida and adjacent areas purchased from Spain for amount not exceeding $5 million; treaty ratified 1821.

1845 **Gross Area (390,144 sq. mi.)** Independent Republic of Texas annexed and admitted as a state.

1846 **Gross Area (285,580 sq. mi.)** Oregon Territory acquired by treaty with Great Britain, terminating joint occupation.

1848 **Gross Area (529,017 sq. mi.)** Mexican Cession acquired out of the Mexican War; the United States paid $15 million.

1853 **Gross Area (29,640 sq. mi.)** Gadsden Purchase negotiated with Mexico for $10 million; treaty ratified 1854.

1858 **Gross Area (.91 sq. mi.)** By terms of the Guano Island Act (1856), stipulating that the United States could take possession of any uninhabited guano island, Johnston and Sand Islands in the Pacific were claimed; they constitute a possession.

1862 **Gross Area (3.85 sq. mi.)** Palmyra Island, 1,000 miles south of Honolulu, annexed by Hawaii but not included in the state; it constitutes a possession.

1863 **Gross Area (1 sq. mi.)** Under the Guano Island Act (1856), the Swan Islands in the Caribbean were claimed by the United States. The U.S. recognized Honduran sovereignty over the islands on September 1, 1972.

1865 **Gross Area (2 sq. mi.)** Under the Guano Island Act (1856), Navassa in the Caribbean was claimed; it constitutes a possession.

1867 **Gross Area (586,412 sq. mi.)** Alaska purchased from Russia for $7.2 million.

Gross Area (1.9 sq. mi) Midway Islands, 1,200 miles NW of Honolulu, annexed; they are a possession.

1898 **Gross Area (6,450 sq. mi.)** Independent Republic of Hawaii annexed.

Gross Area (212 sq. mi.) Guam, in the Western Pacific area, conquered from Spain and formally annexed by peace treaty (ratified, 1899); it constitutes an organized unincorporated territory.

Gross Area (115,707 sq. mi.) Philippines conquered from Spain; peace treaty (ratified, 1899) stipulated payment of $20 million for the islands; the Philippines became independent on July 4, 1946.

Gross Area (3,435 sq. mi.) Puerto Rico conquered from Spain and formally annexed by peace treaty (ratified, 1899); granted commonwealth status by Act of Congress on July 25, 1952.

1899 **Gross Area (2.5 sq. mi.)** Wake Island in Central Pacific claimed; it constitutes a possession.

Year **Acquisition**

1899 **Gross Area (83 sq. mi.)** American Samoa acquired by partition treaty (ratified, 1900) with Great Britain and Germany; it constitutes an unorganized, unincorporated territory.

1903 **Gross Area (647 sq mi.)** Canal Zone leased from Panama (treaty ratified, 1904); United States paid $10 million supplemented by annual amounts of $250,000 (1913-33); $430,000 (1934-55); $1.93 million (1956-1971); $2.095 million (1972); and $2.33 million (1974 to date). Under the terms of the 1977 treaty, the Canal Zone reverted to Panama on October 1, 1979.

Gross Area (30 sq. mi.) Guantanamo leased from Cuba for coaling and naval station.

1914 **Gross Area (4.6 sq. mi.)** Corn Islands leased for 99 years from Nicaragua for payment of $3 million; treaty (ratified, 1916) included perpetual right to construct and maintain a ship canal through Lake Nicaragua. The canal rights and the lease of the islands were terminated on April 25, 1971.

1916 **Gross Area (133 sq. mi.)** Virgin Islands purchased from Denmark for $25 million by treaty (ratified in 1917); they constitute an organized unincorporated territory.

1919 **Gross Area (each less than 0.5 sq. mi.)** By terms of the Guano Island Act (1856), Quita Sueño Bank, Roncador Cay, and Serrana Bank in the Caribbean were claimed; 1928 treaty provided Colombia with fishing rights in adjacent waters. On September 8, 1972, the United States renounced all claims.

1922 **Gross Area (.01 sq. mi.)** Kingman Reef in the South Pacific annexed by Act of Congress; it constitutes a possession.

1925 **Gross Area (1.33 sq. mi.)** Swains Island in the Pacific annexed by Resolution of Congress and incorporated in American Samoa.

1934 **Gross Area (2.77 sq. mi. combined)** U.S. control of Howland, Baker, and Jarvis islands in the South Pacific was reasserted under terms of the Guano Island Act (1856); they are possessions.

1939 **Gross Area (27 sq. mi.)** Canton and Enderbury Islands, 1,660 miles SW of Honolulu, controlled jointly by Britain and the United States. They are to be ceded to Kiribati, when the 1979 draft treaty comes into force.

1947 **Gross Land Area (707 sq. mi.)** Trust Territory of the Pacific Islands, about 3,000 Micronesian islands and atolls including the Caroline, Marshall, and Mariana groups (except Guam) placed under U.S. jurisdiction by UN Trusteeship System.

1952 **Gross Area (848 sq. mi.)** Ryukyu Islands, including Okinawa, under U.S. jurisdiction by peace treaty with Japan; other islands included in treaty but returned to Japan by an agreement, June 26, 1968, are: Volcano Islands, including Iwo Jima (11 sq. mi.), Bonin Islands (40 sq. mi.), Marcus Island (1 sq. mi.), Rosario Island (less than 0.5 sq. mi.), and Parece Vela. All of the remaining territory was formally returned to Japan on May 15, 1972.

1968 **Gross Area (193 acres)** Mexico ceded to the United States the northern half of Cordova Island in the Rio Grande in return for the Chamizal (630 acres) on December 13, 1968, readjusting the border near El Paso, Texas.

ADMISSION DATES OF STATES TO THE UNION

Delaware	Dec. 7, 1787	Louisiana	April 30, 1812	West Virginia	June 20, 1863
Pennsylvania	Dec. 12, 1787	Indiana	Dec. 11, 1816	Nevada	Oct. 31, 1864
New Jersey	Dec. 18, 1787	Mississippi	Dec. 10, 1817	Nebraska	March 1, 1867
Georgia	Jan. 2, 1788	Illinois	Dec. 3, 1818	Colorado	Aug. 1, 1876
Connecticut	Jan. 9, 1788	Alabama	Dec. 14, 1819	North Dakota	Nov. 2, 1889
Massachusetts	Feb. 6, 1788	Maine	March 15, 1820	South Dakota	Nov. 2, 1889
Maryland	April 28, 1788	Missouri	Aug. 10, 1821	Montana	Nov. 8, 1889
South Carolina	May 23, 1788	Arkansas	June 15, 1836	Washington	Nov. 11, 1889
New Hampshire	June 21, 1788	Michigan	Jan. 26, 1837	Idaho	July 3, 1890
Virginia	June 26, 1788	Florida	March 3, 1845	Wyoming	July 10, 1890
New York	July 26, 1788	Texas	Dec. 29, 1845	Utah	Jan. 4, 1896
North Carolina	Nov. 21, 1789	Iowa	Dec. 28, 1846	Oklahoma	Nov. 16, 1907
Rhode Island	May 29, 1790	Wisconsin	May 29, 1848	New Mexico	Jan. 6, 1912
Vermont	March 4, 1791	California	Sept. 9, 1850	Arizona	Feb. 14, 1912
Kentucky	June 1, 1792	Minnesota	May 11, 1858	Alaska	Jan. 3, 1959
Tennessee	June 1, 1796	Oregon	Feb. 14, 1859	Hawaii	Aug. 21, 1959
Ohio	March 1, 1803	Kansas	Jan. 29, 1861		

CANADA

Area: 3,851,809 sq. mi. **Population:** 24,150,000 (Apr. 1, 1981 est.)
Official Name: Canada **Capital:** Ottawa **Nationality:** Canadian **Language:** English and French are both official languages. About 13% of the population is bilingual; 67% speaks English only, 18% French only, and 2% other languages, such as Italian, German and Ukrainian **Religion:** Roman Catholic 46%, United Church 18% and Anglican 12%. The rest is made up of Presbyterian, Lutheran, Baptist, Jewish, etc. **Flag:** A single red maple leaf with eleven points, centered on a white square; flanked by vertical red bars one half the width of the square. **Anthem:** O Canada; God Save the Queen (royal anthem) **Currency:** Canadian Dollar (1.2024 per U.S. $1 as of June 10, 1981)

Location: North America, occupying all of the continent north of the United States except for Alaska and the French islands of St. Pierre and Miquelon, in the Gulf of St. Lawrence. The second largest country in the world, Canada is bordered on the north by the Arctic Ocean; on the east by Baffin Bay, Davis Strait and the Atlantic Ocean; on the south by the United States; and on the west by the Pacific Ocean and Alaska **Features:** The Shield, a rugged area of pre-Cambrian rock, covers most of eastern and central Canada, or roughly half the entire country. To the north is the Arctic Archipelago and to the west of the Shield is a vast prairie region stretching to the Canadian Rockies. Westernmost Canada, which comprises most of British Columbia, is laced with towering mountain ranges **Chief Rivers:** Mackenzie, Yukon, St. Lawrence, Nelson, Columbia, Churchill

Head of State: Queen Elizabeth II, represented by a governor-general, Edward R. Schreyer, born 1936, assumed office 1978 **Head of Government:** Prime Minister Pierre Elliott Trudeau, born 1921, elected Feb. 18, 1980 **Effective Date of Present Constitution:** The British North America Act of 1867 provides Canada with a form of written constitution; however, as in Britain, many of the country's legal and parliamentary practices are based on unwritten conventions **Legislative Body:** Parliament (bicameral), consisting of a Senate and a House of Commons. The Senate is composed of a maximum of 104 members, appointed until age 75 by the governor-general on the advice of the prime minister. The House of Commons has 282 members, elected for 5 years **Local Government:** 10 provinces, governed by a premier and an elected legislature. There are also 2 large northern territories, Yukon and the Northwest Territories. Yukon is governed by a federal government commissioner and a council of 7 elected members. The Northwest Territories are governed by a commissioner and a council of 9, of whom 5 are appointed and 4 elected

Ethnic Composition (1971): 44.6% of the population is of British Isles descent; 28.7% of French origin; German 6.1%; Italian 3.4%; Ukrainian 2.7%; Netherlands 2.0% and others 12.5% **Population Distribution:** 75.5% urban **Density:** 6.5 inhabitants per square mile

Largest Cities (M.A. = Metropolitan Areas as of June 1, 1981): (1976) Toronto, 633,318 (M.A. 2,864,700); Montreal, 1,080,546 (M.A. 2,818,300); Vancouver, 410,188 (M.A. 1,175,200); Ottawa, 304,462 (M.A. 738,600); Winnipeg, 560,874 (M.A. 590,300); Edmonton, 461,361 (M.A. 594,900); Quebec, 177,082 (M.A. 559,100); Hamilton, 312,003 (M.A. 538,600); Calgary, 469,917 (M.A. 522,700); Kitchener, 131,870 (M.A. 288,500); London, 240,392 (M.A. 275,300); Halifax, 117,882 (M.A. 273,200); Windsor, 196,526 (M.A. 245,400); Victoria, 62,551 (M.A. 244,800); Sudbury, 97,604 (M.A. 153,400); Regina, 149,593 (M.A. 163,700)

Per Capita Income: $9,928 (1980) **Gross National Product (GNP):** $288,136 million (1980) **Economic Statistics:** Manufacturing accounts for 21.6% of Gross National Product (chief industries: motor vehicles manufacturers, pulp and paper mills, meat slaughtering and processors, petroleum refining, iron and steel mills, motor vehicles parts and accessories manufacturers, dairy products industry, sawmills and planing mills, miscellaneous machinery and equipment manufacturers, and smelting and refining); about 27.8% is derived from public administration and services; 22.8% from trade and finance; 9.8% from primary industries (agriculture, forestry, fishing, trapping, and mining) **Minerals and Mining:** Crude petroleum, copper, nickel, iron ore, zinc, natural gas, natural gas by-products, sand and gravel, and coal, are exploited in large quantities. Value of mineral production: $32.4 billion (1980) **Labor Force:** 11,026,000 employed (May 1981) with 19.5% employed in manufacturing, 37% in services and public administration, 7.5% in primary industries and 22% in trade and finance **Average industrial earnings:** $339.61 per week. The average monthly wage for agricultural workers is $700.00 with board (Feb. 1981) **Foreign Trade:** Exports, chiefly motor vehicles and parts, crude petroleum, fabricated metals, other machinery and equipment, other fabricated inedible materials, metal ores and concentrates, wheat, totaled $73.8 billion in 1980. Imports, chiefly machinery and equipment, motor vehicles and parts, crude petroleum, food, fabricated metals and other fabricated inedible materials, totaled $68.7 billion **Principal Trade Partners:** United States, Britain, Japan, West Germany, Venezuela, Italy, France, Australia, Netherlands, Saudi Arabia

Vital Statistics: Birthrate, 15.5 per 1,000 of population; death rate, 7.1 (1979) **Life Expectancy:** males 70.2, females 77.5 **Health Statistics:** 7.0 hospital beds per 1,000 inhabitants (1979-80) **Infant Mortality:** 10.9 per 1,000 births (1979) **Education Statistics:** 13,993 primary and secondary schools, with combined enrollment of 4,935,409 **Enrollment in Higher Education:** 645,000 **GDP Expended on all forms of Education:** 8.2%

Transportation: Surfaced roads total 712 938 km; earth roads 171 336; total roads 884 273 **Passenger Cars:** 9,985,146 (1979) **Railway Mileage (in km):** 67 725.0 of first main track; total 94 051.3 **Principal Ports:** Vancouver, Sept Iles, Port Cartier, Montreal, Halifax, Quebec City, Saint John, Hamilton, Baie Comeau, Sarnia **Major Airlines:** Air Canada, the government line, and Canadian Pacific Airlines, a private carrier, operate domestic and international services

Communications: There are both government and privately owned radio and TV stations **No. of Radio Stations:** 737 AM; 470 FM; 10 short wave: 98.6% of homes have radios (excludes car radios) **No. of TV Stations:** 1,100: 97.7% of homes have TVs; 81.2% have color TVs **No. of Telephones:** 15,839,000: 97.2% of homes have telephones **No. of Newspapers:** 127 dailies; daily circulation 5,533,508

Weights and Measures: Old British standards with gradual implementation of the metric system **Travel Requirements:** for entry into Canada, proper identification and valid passport

During his successful campaign to oust the Progressive Conservative government of Prime Minister Joe Clark in 1980, Liberal party leader Pierre Elliott Trudeau pledged that he would be a 'caretaker' prime minister, and not serve out his full five-year term. He declared his goal was to lay the constitutional basis for a strong, united Canadian confederation that he and his party had always envisioned—a "just society" for all Canadians. His campaign broadened traditional Liberal support in Quebec to include the economically hard-pressed Maritime provinces, and the crucial Ontario vote to ensure his return to office.

But Trudeau faces an uphill battle in seeking to bind the nation together. Clark's concessions to the oil and mineral-rich Western provinces was a genuine recognition that the provinces have been economically and politically dominated by the "Eastern" establishment. Clark had promised greater powers to the provinces, and despite his belief in a strong central government, Trudeau cannot ignore the clamor of the ten disparate local governments for more control over their own affairs.

Trudeau's biggest immediate problem remains Quebec. Since 1976, when the separatist *Parti Québécois* won a majority in the provincial assembly, Premier René Lévesque has pursued a policy calculated to make Quebec an independent state. In 1979, Lévesque called for accepting a "sovereign" Quebec within an economic association with Canada, moderating demands for total independence in order to gain acceptance of greater autonomy for the province by the rest of the nation. When Quebec's National Assembly called a referendum on association for 1980, Trudeau came out in support of Quebec Liberal leader Claude Ryan's proposals for more provincial autonomy within the federal system. He attacked the referendum as a ploy by Lévesque and the PQ to gain a yes vote by presenting independence as autonomy. On May 20, 1980, fully 58 percent of those Quebecers who turned out voted *non* to sovereignty-association.

with only 42 percent casting *oui* ballots. These results had been preceeded by a Liberal resurgence in local by-elections, in recent opinion polls showing separatist sentiment waning, and by the December 21, 1979 ruling of Canada's Supreme Court striking down Quebec's Bill 101—making French the official and primary language of that province—as unconstitutional.

Following his impressive victory in Quebec, Trudeau called for a new constitutional conference to spell out the scope of proposed increased territorial powers and self-government for Quebec and the other provinces. The British North American Act of 1867 makes the Canadian charter an act of British Parliament. Despite revisions such as the Citizenship Act of 1977, ending Canadians' status as "British subjects," any change must be approved in London, after unanimous approval by Ottawa and the provinces. Trudeau has long sought patriation—i.e., to bring the constitution solely under Canadian jurisdiction—and remove the amendment procedure from British control.

Trudeau has proposed three main areas of constitutional change: establishment of a federal parliament with real national powers, authorizing provincial assemblies to exert equally valid territorial powers, and codification of a bill of rights, including preservation of language rights for the French-speaking minority. Trudeau met with provincial leaders in September 1980 to consider these proposals. The talks broke down after six days. The leaders of Quebec and Newfoundland objected to the vague wording proposed by Trudeau regarding provincial authority. The Western provinces feared that the proposed bill of rights would make the national courts final arbiters of many local issues and thus erode provincial authority. Unable to work out a solution with provincial leaders, Trudeau promptly announced plans to act unilaterally. He called on parliament to draft a new constitution and pledged to patriate the document with or without the approval of provincial leaders. With a nationwide Gallup Poll, taken in December, showing Canadians overwhelmingly opposed to Trudeau's unilateral action, the prime minister agreed to yield more federal authority to the provinces, but vowed to press for patriation. In April 1981 eight of 10 provincial premiers agreed on their own constitutional plan—one that would permit each province to decide for itself whether or not to accept constitutional amendments. The plan was immediately rejected by the Trudeau government.

In October 1980 the Trudeau government launched a farreaching national energy program designed to make Canada energy self-sufficient by the end of the decade. The plan called for increased Canadianization of oil and natural gas companies operating in the country. By 1990 the government hopes to increase domestic ownership of the oil industry from the present 30% to 50%. To encourage the takeover the government boosted taxes on all oil companies while offering tax incentives for exploration only to companies substantially controlled by Canadian interests. The policy, while popular in Canada, drew charges of discrimination from U.S. and other foreign oil executives, a complaint voiced publicly by President Reagan.

HISTORY: Although the Vikings are believed to have visited Canada about A.D. 1000, the first recorded landing was made by John Cabot in 1497. Cabot, an Italian-born explorer in the service of Henry VII of England, landed near Newfoundland and claimed the area for the English king. In 1534, Jacques Cartier planted a cross on the Gaspé Peninsula and claimed the region for France. The intense rivalry that followed as each country tried to extend its claims was to dominate the history of Canada for more than two centuries

1689-1763: French and Indian Wars, a series of colonial wars in North America that reflect Anglo-French rivalry in Europe, culminate in the loss of French control of Canada and the establishment of British rule

1774: Quebec Act is passed, reversing favored treatment accorded British in Quebec and providing for preservation of French culture; the act is to prove instrumental in maintaining loyalty of Canada to Britain following outbreak of the American Revolution

1791: Constitutional Act divides Lower Canada, now southern Quebec, from Upper Canada, now southern Ontario, and establishes limited self-government

1837-41: Rebellions in the two Canadas and growing movement for responsible government cause British government to reunite the two Canadas

1867: British North America Act establishes Dominion of Canada, a confederation of Nova Scotia, New Brunswick, and Lower and Upper Canada, the latter two becoming the provinces of Quebec and Ontario, respectively. (The other components of present-day Canada are added in subsequent years, the last, Newfoundland, not until 1949.)

1914-18: Canada fights on Allied side in World War I; issue of conscription arouses strong opposition from French Canadians, deepening split between the French- and English-speaking

1931: Statute of Westminster establishes equality of Canadian Parliament with that of Britain

1939-45: Canada plays vital role in World War II and emerges as one of the major nations of the world

1957: Conservatives, led by John Diefenbaker, take office after 22 years of Liberal party rule

1963: Liberals, led by Lester Pearson, return to power

1967: French President Charles de Gaulle, on a visit to Canada, calls for a "free Quebec" during speech in Montreal; his speech prompts a sharp rebuke from the Canadian government, causing the French leader to cut short his Canadian visit

1968: Pearson retires and is succeeded by Pierre Elliott Trudeau, a French Canadian lawyer and former justice minister; new elections are held in which decisive Liberal victory gives Canada its first majority government in six years

1969: Canada opens negotiations with Communist China for the establishment of diplomatic relations between the two countries; Commons passes government-sponsored language bill requiring bilingual federal facilities wherever 10 percent of the people of any district speak French

1970: Government invokes wartime powers after separatist terrorists kidnap British diplomat and Quebec labor minister, who is subsequently slain

1971: Trudeau and Kosygin sign a protocol agreement in Moscow calling for regular, high-level consultations; Communist China and Canada exchange ambassadors

1974: Trudeau reelected with parliamentary majority

1975: Wage and price controls are imposed for three years

1976: The death penalty is abolished throughout Canada. *Parti Québécois* takes the Quebec provincial elections

1977: Bill establishing French as primary language in government and education introduced into Quebec's National Assembly. Berger Commission calls for 10-year halt to construction of natural gas pipeline in Northwest until native land claims settled. Citizenship Act becomes law

1978: Soviet nuclear-powered satellite crashes in northern Canada; radiation threat minimal. Trudeau introduces new federal constitution to supercede 1867 Dominion Act. Government halts all development in northern Yukon, considers measures to protect caribou migration. Four western provinces join Ontario in opposing any future economic association with an independent Quebec

1979: Progressive Conservatives come to power under Joe Clark, ending 11-year term of Prime Minister Trudeau. Task Force on Canadian Unity report calls for recognition of Quebec's right to self-determination and secession, proposes granting province powers to "protect and develop its distinctive character" within the Canadian federation. U.S. and Canada sign pact on disputed Atlantic and Pacific fishing grounds; but "fish war" continues with seizure of U.S. tuna boats and American ban on Canadian tuna imports as treaty is stalled in U.S. Senate. Supreme Court Dec. 13 voids Quebec's French-language Bill 101 as unconstitutional. U.S. and Canada agree to pollution controls along border to prevent "acid rain." Clark government is defeated Dec. 13. Yukon territorial council becomes legislative assembly and appoints a cabinet, in step towards provincial status

1980: Ottawa announces Jan. 29 that Canadian diplomats aided six Americans to escape Tehran after takeover of U.S. Embassy. Joe Clark's Progressive Conservatives are defeated in Feb. 18 general elections; Liberals win majority in parliament, as Pierre Trudeau gains new term as prime minister. Federal report issued March 6 rejects provincial status for Northwest Territories for the immediate future. Voters reject Quebec sovereignty in May 20 referendum. Trudeau and Alberta's Premier Peter Lougheed break off talks July 25 on federal energy policy and price increases for province's oil and natural gas. In September Canada and the U.S. sign a bilateral tax treaty, at the conclusion of eight years of negotiation, resolving such competing claims as the taxation of

ALBERTA

MILES

| 0 | 20 | 40 | 60 | 80 | 100 |

KILOMETERS

| 0 | 20 | 40 | 60 | 80 | 100 |

Provincial Capital ✪

ALBERTA
NORTHERN PART

© C.S. HAMMOND & Co., Maplewood, N.J.

Longitude West of Greenwich

citizens of one country living and earning income in the other. Some 40,000 non-essential federal employees go on strike Sept. 29-Oct. 14 to win a 24.7% pay hike over two years but failing to achieve demands for a cost-of-living escalator clause and a shorter work week.

1981: Joe Clark is renamed Progressive Conservative party leader Feb. 27, but by reduced margin. In March President Reagan visits Trudeau in his first trip outside the U.S. as president; Reagan draws hecklers upset over U.S. policy in El Salvador and failure to resolve acid rain problem; the two leaders sign an agreement renewing for five years the North American Air Defense Command (NORAD). In May Canada agrees to sell the Soviet Union minimum of 25 million metric tons of wheat and feed grains for an estimated $5 billion by 1986; the five-year pact is the longest ever entered into by the two countries. On Sept. 1, federal government and Alberta reach accord on oil prices.

ALBERTA

Area: 255,219 square miles **Population:** 1,838,037 (1976 census); 2,153,200 (April 1, 1981 est.) ranks fourth; population density: 7.5 per sq. mi.; urban, 75.0%; rural 25.0% as of 1976 census **Capital:** Edmonton **Major Cities (Metropolitan Areas as of June 1, 1979):** Edmonton, 594,900; Calgary, 522,700

Ethnic Composition: British Isles, 47%; German, 14%; Ukrainian, 8%; Scandinavian, 6%; French, 6%; Netherlands, 4%; and Native Indian, 3%; other, 12% **Religion:** United Church, 28%; Roman Catholic, 24%; Anglican, 10%; Lutheran, 8%; Presbyterian, 4%; other, 26%

Vital Statistics (per 1,000 population, 1979): birth rate, 18.4; death rate, 6.0; marriage rate, 9.4; divorce rate, 3.3; infant mortality per 1,000 live births, 11.4 (1978)

Location and Geography: Except for the northeast corner and the mountainous fringe on its western border, Alberta is underlain with arable soil, and irrigation has made the semi-arid far south and east productive for agricultural purposes. Most of the province is now very fertile agricultural land

Government: Alberta became a province in 1905 and is represented in the federal government by 21 members in the House of Commons and 6 Senators. The provincial government is unicameral with a Legislative Assembly of 79 members. At present, 73 Progressive Conservatives, 4 members of the Social Credit party, one New Democrat and one Independent in the legislature **Premier:** Honourable Peter Lougheed **Salary and Allowance:** $69,800

Education (1978-79): In Alberta, there are 1,555 primary and secondary schools; 23,207 teachers; and 423,808 grades 1-12 students enrolled. Total full-time winter session students enrolled at 5 universities, 30,542, and 17,872 full-time students enrolled at 18 Alberta community colleges

Net value of production in goods-producing industries (1978 est.): $17,705,185,000. Mining represented 51.5% of this total, construction 24.2%, agriculture 7.7% and manufacturing 14.4%. Value of oil and natural gas production is increasing annually and has made the province Canada's leading producer of mineral products with a value of $16,845,250,000 (1980). In 1980 Alberta produced 87.4% of the crude petroleum, 93.8% of the natural gas and 32% of the coal in the nation **Leading manufacturing industries (1978):** slaughtering and meat processors, petroleum refining, dairy products industries, chemical & chemical products industries, pulp and paper mills **Average industrial earnings (1980):** $341.93 per week **Cash receipts from farming operations (1980):** $3,234,774,000; 39.5% derived from cattle and calves, 18.2% from wheat, 10.3% from rapeseed, 9.1% from barley, and 4.6% from dairy products **Families with incomes over $15,000 (1979):** 81.6% **Per capita personal income (1979):** $9,717

Provincial Finances: Gross general revenue (est., fiscal year 1980-81): $10,530,000,000, gross general expenditures (est., fiscal year 1980-81): $6,548,000,000

Daily newspapers: 9 with a circulation of 455,803 (1978) **Telephones in service (1979):** 1,573,888 **Radio stations (1980):** 110 **Homes with radios (1980):** 98.8% **Homes with TVs (1980):** 96.8%

Hospital beds (1979-80): 15,711 (7.7 beds per 1,000 population) **Residents per physician (Dec. 1980):** 3,406

Motor vehicles (1979-80): 1,530,118 **Residents per motor vehicle (1979):** 1.3 **Motor vehicle deaths (1979):** 698

The first European to explore Alberta was Pierre Boucher, Sieur de Boucherville, in 1751. Boucher was an agent of the English Hudson's Bay Company, but it was not until over forty years later, in 1795, that the Company and its rival, the French Northwest Company, established the first European settlements in the province. Both of the companies set up their trading posts near Edmonton, although trapping activities were concentrated further north.

In 1869 the government of the region was transferred from the Hudson's Bay Company to the newly formed Dominion of Canada, but widespread settlement was delayed until the Canadian Pacific Railroad reached the province in the mid-1880's. After the railroad made eastern markets accessible, settlers—mostly ranchers and farmers—began trickling into the region. They found that although it is far north in latitude, most of the land in Alberta is fertile.

With the development and introduction of earlyripening Marquis wheat in the early part of the 20th century, settlers poured into the west, coming in almost equal numbers from the U.S., the U.K., eastern Canada, and northern Europe. Alberta's population rose from 73,000 in 1901 to 374,000 in 1911. Since then its population has risen steadily, although less spectacularly.

Following World War II, the agricultural nature of the province began to change with the discovery of new oil fields near Leduc in 1947.

Alberta's long term supplies of petroleum are assured by the vast reserves of oil recoverable from Alberta's oil sands. The largest oil sands deposit is found in northeastern Alberta and two plants, Suncor and Syncrude, are currently producing from these deposits. Three additional oil sands plants are in various stages of planning.

Abundant deposits of natural gas are found in Alberta and the province produces approximately 95% of Cananda's pentanes plus propane and butanes. Alberta also has reserves of more than 100 billion tons of high quality coking coal.

Revenues from the sale of petroleum and natural gas enabled the Alberta government to establish the Alberta Heritage Savings Trust Fund in 1976. The Fund was created to invest a portion of the province's non-renewable resource revenue to provide economic and social benefits to Albertans. To protest the federal government's oil price controls, Alberta, which provides Canada with 85% of its domestic oil, cut production by 60,000 barrels, or 6%, on March 1, 1981, and doubled the cutback three months later. The Trudeau government responded by raising taxes on petroleum to help pay for more imported oil. On September 1, the two governments reached a five-year accord on oil prices.

BRITISH COLUMBIA

Area: 366,255 square miles **Population:** 2,466,608 (1976 census); 2,701,900 (April 1, 1981 est.); ranks third in both area & population; population density (1976 census): 7.2 per sq. mi.; urban, 76.9%; rural 23.1% **Capital:** Victoria **Major Cities (Metropolitan Areas as of June 1, 1979):** Vancouver, 1,175,200; Victoria, 224,800

Ethnic Composition: British Isles, 58%; German, 9%; Scandinavian, 5%; French, 4%; Netherlands, 3%; Ukrainian, 3%; Italian, 2%; and Native Indians, 2% **Religion:** United Church, 25%; Roman Catholic, 19%; Anglican, 18%; Lutheran, 6%; Presbyterian, 5%; Baptist, 3%; no religion, 13% **Vital Statistics (per 1,000 population, 1979):** birth rate, 15.0; death rate, 7.5; marriage rate, 8.6; divorce rate, 3.4; infant mortality per 1,000 live births, 12.7 (1978)

Location and Geography: Parallel ranges of mountains and fertile valleys cover all but the northeast corner of the province. There is also a deeply indented Pacific shoreline. Because it is warmed by the Japanese Current, the climate of the coastal region is moderate

Government: British Columbia became a province in 1871 and is represented in the federal government by 28 members in the House of Commons and 6 Senators. The provincial government is unicameral with a Legislative Assembly of 57 members. In May 1979, 31 members of the Social Credit party and 26 members of the New Democratic party were elected to the legislature **Premier:** Honourable William R. Bennett **Salary and allowance:** $68,626

BRITISH COLUMBIA

NORTHERN PART

Provincial and State Capitals

Education: Of the population fifteen years of age and over, 18% have less than Grade 9 education, 63% have a secondary school education and 19% have a post-secondary degree or certification (1976 census). **Total expenditures on education (1979-80):** $1,934,300,000 **Schools:** 1,871 primary and secondary schools, with a combined enrollment of 539,351 **Colleges:** Six degree-granting universities, 20 community colleges with a combined enrollment of 48,095 (1979-80); a total of 1,739 community college teachers and a total of 3,086 university teachers

Value added in goods-producing industries (1978): $11,176,110,000; manufacturing represents 49.7% and construction 22%. Slightly more than half of the manufacturing total comes from wood industries and paper and allied industries. Mining, which accounted for 20% of the province's industry in the 1940's, now accounts for only 10.6% **Leading manufacturing industries (1978):** Pulp and paper mills, sawmills and planing mills, and veneer and plywood mills **Average industrial earnings (1980):** $363.50 per week **Value of fishery products (1980):** $165,069,000 **Cash receipts from farming operations (1980):** $749,120,000, of which 23.1% is derived from dairy products, and 16.3% from poultry and eggs **Families with incomes of $16,000 and over (1979):** 74.9% **Per capita personal income (1979):** $9,821 Unemployment **(1980):** 6.8%

Provincial Finances: Gross general revenue (fiscal year 1980-81): $6,529,000,000; gross general expenditure, $6,385,000,000

Daily Newspapers: 22 **Combined circulation (1978):** 579,465 **Telephones (1979):** 1,802,334 **Homes with radios (1980):** 98.7% **Homes with TVs (1980):** 96.7%

Hospital beds (1979-80): 18,442 (7.1 beds per 1,000 population) **Physicians (Dec. 31, 1980):** 5,265 (510 residents per physician)

Motor vehicles (1979): 1,569,866 **Residents per motor vehicle (1979):** 1.7 **Motor vehicle deaths (1979):** 743

The first European to visit what is now the province of British Columbia was a Spaniard, Juan Perez, who came while on a voyage in search of the Northwest Passage. Two years later Capt. James Cook explored and established the general outline of the northwest coast. Cook stopped only briefly on the coast of Vancouver Island, but while there he obtained several sea-otter pelts from the Indians. When he arrived in Macao, on the south China coast, and traded the pelts, the potential profits of the sea-otter became clear. Soon after Cook published an account of his voyage, a legion of trading ships descended on the coast, setting the stage for a decades-long controversy between Spain and England over which was the rightful claimant to the area.

With the coming of trappers and traders after the 1790's, English control was established, and the merged Northwest and Hudson Bay Companies controlled the region until the middle of the nineteenth century. In 1849 and 1858 Vancouver Island and mainland British Columbia, respectively, were made English colonies. In 1866 the two were united and agreed to become part of the Dominion of Canada in 1871 on condition that a transcontinental railroad be built.

The completion of the railroad in 1885 spurred the development of agriculture, forestry and mining. The economy received a second boost in 1914 when the Panama Canal opened, giving Vancouver direct sea-borne access to European markets.

During the twentieth century the province has continued to grow. The demands of World War II sparked spectacular growth in the forest industries, hydroelectric power, and manufacturing. These additional jobs contributed to a trebling of the population since 1941.

In 1975, the New Democratic party was unseated by the Social Credit party headed by William Bennett. The "Socreds" pledged to repeal the Mineral Royalties Act of the previous administration.

In December 1980 the provincial energy minister asserted that the federal tax on the sale of natural gas produced by provincially-owned plants was unconstitutional and therefore would not be paid.

MANITOBA

Area: 251,000 square miles **Population:** 1,021,506 (1976 census); 1,028,800 (April 1, 1981 est.): ranks fifth; population density 4.8; urban, 69.9%; rural, 30.1% **Capital:** Winnipeg **Largest Cities:** Winnipeg, Metropolitan Area 590,300 (June 1, 1979 est.); Brandon, 34,901 (1976 census)

Ethnic Composition: British Isles, 42%; German, 12%; Ukrainian, 12%; French, 9%; Native Indian, 4%; Polish, 4% and Scandinavian, 4% **Religion:** United Church, 26%; Roman Catholic, 25%; Anglican, 12%; Lutheran, 7%; Mennonite, 6%; Ukrainian Catholic, 6% **Vital Statistics (per 1,000 population, 1979):** birth rate, 15.7; death rate, 8.0; marriage rate, 7.5; divorce rate, 2.09; infant mortality per 1,000 live births, 13.7 (1978)

Location and Geography: Located between Ontario and Saskatchewan, Manitoba is a vast plain which rises gradually to the west and south. On the southern prairie the fertility of the land varies greatly, from the black gumbo of the Red River valley to sandy soil in the southwest and stonier soil between Lakes Winnipeg and Manitoba

Government: Manitoba became a province in 1870 **No. of representatives in Parliament:** 14 members in the House of Commons and 6 Senators **Type of legislature:** Unicameral with a Lieutenant-Governor, Executive Council and a Legislative Assembly of 57 members **Current government:** Standings in the legislature as of June 15, 1981: 32 Progressive Conservatives, 20 New Democrats, 1 Liberal, 3 Progressives, 1 vacant **Premier:** Honourable Sterling Lyon **Salary and allowance:** $53,547

Education (1976 census): 24.4% of the population 15 years of age and over had Grade 8 or less; 51.5% attended high school; 7.2% had some post-secondary education; 9.1% had a post-secondary* certificate or diploma; 8.0% had a university degree **Total education expenditures (1979-80):** $760,600,000 **Schools:** 820 primary and secondary schools (1979-80) with a combined enrollment of 225,441 **Colleges:** Seven degree-granting universities and eight post-secondary non-university institutions with a combined enrollment of 19,405

Value added in goods-producing industries (1978): $3,262,587,000; manufacturing represented 41.0% of this total, construction 21.3%, agriculture 19.8%, and electric power 10.0% **Value of manufacturing shipment (1980):** $4,250,972,000 **Leading manufacturing industries:** slaughtering and meat processing, agricultural implements, dairy products, feed, publishing and printing, and metal stamping and pressing industry **Average industrial earnings (1980):** $283.20 per week **Cash receipts from farming operations (1980):** $1,404,568,000 with 24% from cattle and calves, 24.1% derived from wheat, 8.2% from hogs, 5.7% from barley, 6.7% from rapeseed, 5.3% from dairy products and 6.2% from flaxseed **Per capita personal income (1979):** $8,198 **Unemployment (1980):** 5.5%

Provincial Finances: Estimated gross general revenue (fiscal year 1980-81): $2,269,000,000; estimated gross general expenditure, $2,418,000,000

Daily newspapers: 9 **Total circulation:** 286,001 (1978) **Number of telephones per 100 population (1979):** 66.2 **Homes with radios (1980):** 98.5% **Homes with TVs (1980):** 97.1%

Hospital beds (1979-80): 6,930 (6.7 beds per 1,000 population) **Physicians (Dec. 31, 1980):** 1,878 (population per physician, 547)

Motor Vehicles (1979): 645,552 **Residents per motor vehicle (1979):** 1.6 **Motor vehicle deaths (1979):** 205

Despite the fact that it is known as a "prairie province," only a small southern portion of Manitoba's 251,000 square miles is actually treeless grassland. The remainder ranges from forest land, to lakes, subarctic tundra, and—most surprisingly of all for a "prairie" province—nearly 400 miles of salt-water coast on Hudson Bay. Its name and reputation derives from the fact that only the prairie area south of the infertile Pre-Cambrian shield is suitable for large-scale settlement.

Manitoba is bounded on the south by the U.S., on the west by Saskatchewan, on the north by the Keewatin District, and on the east by Ontario, but it was through its Hudson Bay sea coast that early European explorers, trappers, and settlers first came to the province. The first European to enter the territory was probably Sir Thomas Button in 1612. Nearly 60 years later, in 1670, the Hudson's

MANITOBA

MILES

KILOMETERS

⊗ Provincial Capital

MANITOBA
NORTHERN PART

© C.S. HAMMOND & Co., Maplewood, N.J.

Longitude West of Greenwich

NEW BRUNSWICK

Bay Company began building forts in the area, principally at the mouths of the Nelson and Churchill rivers. Throughout the 18th century the area was affected by the feud between the English Hudson's Bay Company and the French Northwest Company. The feud between the two fur-trading companies continued until 1821 when the rivals amalgamated.

Until the advent of the steamship and railroad in the mid-19th century, white men came to the provinces mostly as trappers and traders. An exception was the historic Red River Settlement (now Winnipeg), which was established in 1812, but it was not until the late 1860's that steam navigation from the north and railroads from the south and east made the area accessible to large numbers of settlers.

In 1870 the province of Manitoba was organized. It was linked by rail to the U.S. in 1878 and with eastern Canada in 1881, and the population, which was a mere 25,000 in 1871, grew to 250,000 in 1901 and 700,000 in 1931.

Like their prairie neighbors in both Canada and the U.S., Manitobans suffered during the 1920s and '30s, but since the hard years of the Great Depression, the growth of mineral, forest, and manufacturing industries, and the return of markets for its agricultural products have helped the province become one of Canada's richest. While it was once solely dependent on agriculture, its economy is now substantially diversified. Manufacturing accounts for over 40 percent of the province's net produced value; agriculture less than 20 percent.

In 1969 the New Democratic party won control after eleven years of Conservative rule. The NDP introduced public automobile insurance, medicare, and other wide-ranging social programs. In 1974, the province agreed to fund 25 percent of a pilot project which would give a guaranteed minimum income to 2,500 residents, the federal government paying the balance.

An upset victory in the October 1977 elections returned the Progressive Conservatives to office after eight years.

NEW BRUNSWICK

Area: 27,633 square miles **Population:** 677,250 (1976 census); 709,600 (Apr. 1, 1981 est.); ranks eighth; population density 24.5 per square mile; urban, 52%; rural, 48% **Capital:** Fredericton **Major cities (1976 census agglomeration) populations:** Fredericton, 45,885; Moncton, 77,571; Saint John Metropolitan Area (June 1, 1979 est.), 118,700

Ethnic Composition: British Isles, 58%; French, 37% **Religion:** Roman Catholic, 52%; Baptist, 14%; United Church, 13%; Anglican, 11% **Vital Statistics (per 1,000 population, 1979):** birth rate, 15.5; death rate, 7.4; marriage rate, 7.6; divorce rate, 1.75; infant mortality per 1,000 live births, 11.8 (1978)

Location and Geography: Nearly rectangular in shape, New Brunswick has an extensive sea coast: on the Bay of Chaleur on the north, the Gulf of St. Lawrence and Northumberland Strait on the east, and the Bay of Fundy on the south. Much of the soil is rocky and unfit for agriculture, but generous rainfall produces prolific forest growth. The Bay of Fundy, which separates New Brunswick and Nova Scotia, has the world's highest tides, and there are proposals to harness these to produce electric power

Government: New Brunswick became a province in 1867 and is represented in the federal government by 10 members in the House of Commons and 10 Senators. The provincial government is unicameral with a Legislative Assembly of 58 members. Present standings in the legislature as of June 1981: 30 Progressive Conservatives and 27 Liberals **Premier:** Honourable Richard Hatfield **Salary and allowance:** $46,023

Education (1972): In the Atlantic Provinces (New Brunswick, Newfoundland, Nova Scotia, and Prince Edward Island) 95% of the population had over Grade IV education; 28.8%, secondary school; and 4.5%, university **Total expenditures on education (1979-80):** $465,400,000 **Schools:** 493 primary and secondary schools (1979-80) with a combined enrollment of 158,066 **Colleges:** Four degree-granting universities with a total enrollment of 10,879.

There are 9 campuses known as New Brunswick Community Colleges with a total enrollment of 1,791 (1979-80)

Value added in goods-producing industries (1978 actual): $1,744,700,000. Manufacturing represented 44.9% of this total, construction 28%, electric power 8%, mining 7.5%, forestry 5.0%, agriculture 3.6% **Leading manufacturing industries (1978):** pulp and paper mills, sawmills and planing mills, and fishery products **Average industrial earnings (1980):** $283.84 per week **Cash receipts from farming operations (1980):** $153,889,000 **Families with incomes over $10,000 (1979):** 74.8% **Per capita personal income (1979):** $6,472 **Unemployment (1980):** 11.1%

Provincial Finances: Estimated gross general revenue (fiscal year 1980-81): $1,609,000,000; estimated gross general expenditure, $1,691,000,000

Daily newspapers (1978): 6 **Circulation:** 145,690 **Telephones per 100 population (1979):** 53.4 **Homes with radios:** 98.5% **Homes with TVs:** 98.5%

Hospital beds (1979-80): 4,260 (6.1 beds per 1,000 population) **Physicians (Dec. 31, 1980):** 786 (population per physician, 902)

Motor vehicles (1979): 356,267 **Residents per motor vehicle (1979):** 2.0 **Motor vehicle deaths (1979):** 258

There was little settlement of New Brunswick during the French period, and for 20 years following the beginning of British rule (1763), the sea coasts and river valleys were largely left to the fur traders. Then "Tories"—"Loyalists" as they are called in New Brunswick—escaping from the rebelling American Colonies southward, settled the area in 1783. At that time the County of Sunbury was split from Nova Scotia and made a separate province named New Brunswick, after the family name of the reigning monarch, George III.

Other immigrations brought Scottish farmers and laborers and immigrants from Great Britain after the Napoleonic wars of the next century. By 1842 the population had swelled to 74,000.

The 600 mile long New Brunswick coast and the softwood forests of the interior encouraged the development of lumbering, shipbuilding, and fisheries and, helped by preferential tariffs and trade agreements with England, the colony was initially prosperous. Its resources were a mixed blessing, however, for they hindered the development of a well balanced economy and political system.

By 1866 declining economic fortunes forced the colony into a not wholly welcome union with the nascent Dominion of Canada. A major railroad link with Montreal was established as a result of a pre-unification agreement, but its promise of economic salvation was dimmed as the coming of the steamship, and the depletion of its forest reserves brought economic ruin to many provincial industries.

Since World War II some success has occurred in developing a more balanced economy. Although still heavily oriented towards extractive industries and their exportation, the province has attempted to develop manufacturing industries for processing the raw materials.

The service sector accounts for 70 percent of provincial employment; nearly one-quarter of the labor force works in the public sector, including military establishments at Oromocto and Chatham.

NEWFOUNDLAND

Area: 156,185 square miles **Population:** 557,725 (1976 census); 584,400 (April 1, 1981 est.); ranks ninth; population density 3.9; urban 58.9%; rural 41.1% **Capital:** St. John's **Major cities:** St. John's Metropolitan Area (June 1, 1979 est.), 147,900; Corner Brook, 25,198 (1976 census)

Ethnic Composition: British Isles, 94%; French, 3% **Religion:** Roman Catholic, 37%; Anglican, 28%; United Church, 19% **Vital Statistics (per 1,000 population, 1979):** birth rate, 17.7; death rate, 5.5; marriage rate, 6.5; divorce rate, .84; infant mortality per 1,000 live births, 12.2

Location and Geography: Newfoundland includes the island of Newfoundland (43,359 square miles) and the coast of Labrador (112,828 square miles) on the mainland. They are separated by the Strait of Belle Isle which is nine and a half miles wide at its narrowest point. The island's surface is low, rolling, and rocky. Its highest point is Lewis Hill (2,672 feet) in the Northern peninsula. The west coast and river valleys are thickly forested

Government: Newfoundland became a province in 1949 and is represented in the federal government by 7 members in the House of Commons and 6 Senators. The provincial government is unicameral with a House of Assembly of 52 members. In June 1979, 33 Progressive Conservatives and 19 Liberals were elected to the house **Premier:** Honourable Brian Peckford **Salary and allowance:** $47,900

Education (1976 census): 34.8% of the population 15 years of age and over had Grade 8 or less; 43.9% attended high school; 6.8% had some post-secondary education; 10.0% had a post-secondary certificate or diploma; 4.5% had a university degree **Total expenditures on education (1979-80):** $411,100,000 **Schools:** 676 primary and secondary schools (1979-80) with a combined enrollment of 150,784 **Colleges:** One degree-granting university and six non-university post-secondary institutions with enrollment of 8,617

Value added in goods-producing industries (1978): $1,413,543,000. Construction represented 22.4% of this total; mining 23.4%, manufacturing 27.9%, electric power 13.9% and fisheries 8.4%. (The development of the huge iron ore deposits in Labrador has boosted Newfoundland to 6th position in the nation's production of minerals. In 1980 production was valued at $1,083,319,000. Iron ore contributed 89% of the total and represented 53.3% of the total Canadian production.) **Value of manufacturing shipments (1980):** $1,044,029,000 **Leading manufacturing industry:** fishery products **Average industrial earnings (1980):** $288.90 per week **Families with incomes over $12,000 (1979):** 67.1% **Per capita personal income (1979):** $5,862 **Unemployment (1980):** 13.5%

Provincial Finances: Estimated gross general revenue (fiscal year 1980-81): $1,505,000,000; estimated gross general expenditure, $336,000,000

Daily newspapers (1978): 3 Circulation: 53,686 **Telephones per 100 population (1979):** 43.8 **Homes with radios (1980):** 97.2% **Homes with TVs:** 97.9%

Hospital beds (1979-80): 3,323 (5.8 beds per 1,000 population) **Physicians (Dec. 31, 1980):** 866 (population per physician, 674)

Motor Vehicles (1979): 197,670 **Residents per motor vehicle (1979):** 2.9 **Motor vehicle deaths (1979):** 106

Newfoundland, which consists of the island of Newfoundland itself and the coast of Labrador, is a land of great natural resources. Huge forests of spruce and pine cover much of the area; the inland wilderness has an abundance of wildlife; great mineral wealth lies hidden beneath the surface; hydroelectric power is abundant; and the Grand Banks, in which it is located, is a fishing ground of legendary richness.

Despite these resources, the history of Newfoundland is largely one of great promise only partially fulfilled. It was discovered by John Cabot in 1497, and Sir Humphrey Gilbert made a formal claim for Britain in 1583, but the island remained a distant outpost visited only by fishing boats until the end of the 18th century. By then a court system and land-based commerce had been established, but by 1850 the population had only increased to 30,000.

Fishing and forestry gave the island limited prosperity through the 1860s and '70s, and fueled by this the small province chose not to join the Canadian nation when it was granted dominion status in 1867. The question of union was taken up again in the 1890s, but by then the province's precarious economic condition made it impossible. It remained independent until February 16, 1934 when, after surveying the province's debts, Britain reestablished direct rule, which was then maintained until Newfoundland was united with Canada in 1949.

Many economists today believe that Newfoundland's continuing economic problems can be solved only by developing resource industries and in-

creasing the volume of local processing and refining, as opposed to the continuing export of raw natural resources. The offshore Hibernia oilfield is considered to be one of the largest in North America.

Provincial elections on June 18, 1979 saw the Progressive Conservatives increase their majority in the 52-member assembly to 33, with the Liberals winning the remaining 19 seats.

NOVA SCOTIA

Area: 20,396.55 square miles **Population:** 828,571 (1976 census); 856,600 (April 1, 1981 est.); ranks seventh; population density 40.6; urban 55.8%; rural 44.2% **Capital:** Halifax **Major city populations:** Halifax Metropolitan Area (June 1, 1979), 273,200; Dartmouth, 65,340 (1976 census)

Ethnic Composition: British Isles, 77%; French, 10%; German, 5% **Religion:** Roman Catholic, 36%; United Church, 21%; Anglican, 17%; Baptist, 13%; Presbyterian, 5% **Vital Statistics (per 1,000 population, 1979):** birth rate, 14.6; death rate, 8.1; marriage rate, 8.2; divorce rate, 2.7; infant mortality per 1,000 live births, 11.9 (1978)

Location and Geography: The province is a 359.6-mile long peninsula. The Atlantic coast is generally rocky; the slopes facing the Bay of Fundy and Gulf of St. Lawrence, sheltered from the Atlantic storms by a series of low ridges that run through the center of the province, consist of fertile plains and river valleys. Cape Breton Island, the northeast portion of the province, is mostly rugged upland and is divided almost in two by the saltwater Bras d'Or Lake, in reality a land-enclosed extension of the sea

Government: Nova Scotia became a province in 1867 and is represented in the federal government by 11 members in the House of Commons and 10 Senators. The provincial government is unicameral with a House of Assembly of 52 members. Presently there are 31 Progressive Conservatives, 17 Liberals and four New Democrats in the house **Premier:** Honourable John M. Buchanan, Q.C. **Salary and Allowance:** $55,400

Education (1976 census): In Nova Scotia 25.3% of the population 15 years of age and over have completed a Grade 8 education; 44.9% have attended high school; 23.9% have taken post-secondary education; and 5.9% have university degrees **Total expenditures on education (1979-80):** $631,600,000 **Schools:** 612 primary and secondary schools with a combined enrollment of 192,000 **Colleges:** 10 degree-granting universities and 14 colleges with a combined enrollment of 20,499 in 1979-80

Value added in goods-producing industries (1978): $2,052,910,000. Manufacturing represents 46.8% of this total; construction, 25.7%; fisheries, 9.5%; and mining, 5.8%. The province vies with British Columbia each year as the nation's leading producer of fish products. These in 1980 had a total value of $214,370,000 (prelim.) **Leading manufacturing industries (1978):** Petroleum refining, fish products industry, pulp and paper mills, dairy products **Average industrial earnings (1980):** $265.95 per week **Cash Receipts from farming operations (1980):** $202,458,000, with 27.6% derived from dairy products, 32.7% from livestock, 16.9% from crops, 18.8% from poultry and eggs **Families with incomes over $10,000 (1979):** 75.9% **Per capita personal income (1979):** $7,088 **Unemployment (1980):** 9.8%

Provincial Finances: Estimated general revenue (fiscal year 1980-81 est.): $1,874,000,000; estimated gross general expenditure, fiscal year 1980-81 est., $2,025,000,000

Daily newspapers (1978): 6 Circulation: 178,473 **Telephones per 100 population (1979):** 55.9 **Homes with radios:** 98.8% **Homes with TVs:** 98.0%

Hospital beds (1979-80 est.): 5,667 (6.7 beds per 1,000 population) **Physicians (Dec. 31, 1980):** 1,588 (population per physician approx. 539)

Motor vehicles (1979): 457,905 **Motor vehicle deaths (1979):** 208

John Cabot is regarded, on the basis of his 1497 visit to Cape Breton Island, as the "discoverer" of Nova Scotia, despite the belief that Norsemen and European fishermen probably visited the island centuries before. Britain's claim to Nova Scotia began with Cabot's visit, but its sovereignty was contested by France until Halifax was firmly established as a naval and military base in 1749, and the Acadians were expelled in 1755. Following the

NEWFOUNDLAND

MILES
0 10 20 40 60 80 100

KILOMETERS
0 10 20 40 60 80 100

Provincial Capital

© C.S. HAMMOND & Co., Maplewood, N.J.

NOVA SCOTIA

MILES

0 10 20 30 40 50 60

KILOMETERS

0 20 40 60

⊛ Provincial Capitals

© C.S. HAMMOND & Co., Maplewood, N.J.

American Revolution, nearly 30,000 "Loyalists" emigrated to Nova Scotia, becoming its first citizens. The province was a founding member of the Canadian confederation.

Population growth, increased trade, and wealth marked the first half of the 19th century. But today Nova Scotia shares many of the problems of its neighboring provinces. Its economy is largely dependent on low-technology industries such as fishing and mining, and though the federal government is attempting to diversify the economy, unemployment and economic disparity between the Maritime Provinces and the rest of Canada remains.

In April 1981 some 3.2 million acres off the coast of Nova Scotia were opened to offshore oil exploration.

A growing vacationland, Nova Scotia has two national parks and nine designated historic parks.

ONTARIO

Area: 412,582 square miles **Population:** 8,264,465 (1976 census); 8,614,200 (April 1, 1981 est.); ranks first; population density, 23.3; urban, 81.2% rural, 18.8% **Capital:** Toronto **Major Cities (1979 metropolitan area population estimates):** Toronto, 2,864,700; Ottawa, 738,600; Hamilton, 538,600; St. Catharines-Niagara Falls, 307,300; London, 275,300; Kitchener, 283,500; Sudbury, 153,400; Thunder Bay, 121,200; Oshawa, 141,300

Ethnic Composition: British Isles, 59%; French, 10%; German, 6%; Italian, 6% **Religion:** Roman Catholic, 33%; United Church, 22%; Anglican, 16%; Presbyterian, 7%; Baptist, 4%; Lutheran, 3% **Vital Statistics (per 1,000 population, 1979):** birth rate, 14.3; death rate, 7.2; marriage rate, 8.0; divorce rate, 2.56; infant mortality per 1,000 live births, 11.3 (1978)

Location and Geography: Located in the center of Canada, Ontario is a geographic and cultural transition between eastern Quebec and the midwestern prairie provinces. It has a freshwater shoreline of 1,700 miles on the Great Lakes and St. Lawrence River and 750 miles of salt-water shorelines on Hudson and James Bays. The northern part is within the Canadian Shield, but nearly 17.5 million acres are arable

Government: Ontario became a province in 1867 and is represented in the federal government by 95 members in the House of Commons and 24 Senators. The provincial government is unicameral with a Legislative Assembly of 125 members. As of March 1981, the standings in the House were: 70 Progressive Conservatives, 34 Liberals, and 21 New Democrats **Premier:** Honourable William G. Davis **Salary and allowance:** $68,400

Education (1976 census): 21.7% of the population 15 years of age and over had Grade 8 or less; 52.3% attended high school; 8.5% had some post-secondary education; 9.1% had a post-secondary certificate or diploma; 8.5% had a university degree **Total expenditures on education (1979-80):** $7,182,500,000 **Schools:** 5,208 primary and secondary schools, with a combined enrollment of 1,942,348 **Colleges:** 21 degree-granting universities and 30 non-university post-secondary institutions with enrollment of 224,817

Value added in goods-producing industries (1978): $38,719,051,000, 37.4% of Canada's total; manufacturing contributed 71.8%; construction, 14.5%; mining, 3.7%; and agriculture, 4.3%. The province is the second-largest producer of mineral products with a total value of $4,660,572,000 in 1980 **Value of manufacturing shipments (1980):** $80,991,160,000, 48.9% of the national total Leading manufacturing industries: motor vehicles and their parts and accessories, iron and steel mills and petroleum refining **Average industrial earnings (1980):** $311.45 per week **Cash receipts from farming operations (1980):** $4,370,039,000, with 27.1% derived from cattle and calves, dairy products 15.9%, hogs 10.8%, tobacco 4.5%, poultry 5.7% and vegetables 4.4% **Families with incomes over $12,000 (1979):** 82.2% **Per capita personal income (1979):** $9,608 **Unemployment (1980):** 6.9%

Provincial finances: Estimated gross general revenue (fiscal year 1980-81): was $17,341,000,000; estimated gross general expenditure, $17,787,000,000

Daily newspapers: 46 English and 1 French **Combined circulation:** 2,283,964 **Telephones per 100 population (1979):** 70.4 **Homes with radios:** 98.5% **Homes with TVs:** 97.7%

Hospital beds (1979-80): 49,322 (5.8 beds per 1,000 population) **Physicians (Dec. 31, 1980):** 16,664 (population per physician, 516)

Motor vehicles (1979): 4,645,706 **Residents per motor vehicle:** 1.8 **Motor vehicle deaths (1978):** 1,653

Ontario was the site of the first European settlement in the interior of North America. In 1639 a combined Jesuit mission, French fort, and Norman town, called Sainte-Marie Among the Hurons, was established on the River Wye, nearly 800 miles from Quebec. The colony lasted for ten years, when it was burned by its founders in the face of attacking Iroquois, who with the Huron Indians were the settlers' chief rivals in the fur trade. Archaeologists and historians have recently restored the outpost on its site 90 miles north of Toronto.

At the time of the founding of Sainte-Marie, Huronia was the most densely populated area of what is now Canada. It was the home of 30,000 Hurons, who controlled the best trade routes and acted as middlemen, trading for furs with more distant tribes and with white settlements on the St. Lawrence River.

In 1774, eleven years after cession to England, the Quebec Act made the area a western extension of Quebec. Loyalist refugees from the American Revolution settled the area around the St. Lawrence, and in 1791 a division was effected, Upper Canada being the future Ontario.

During the War of 1812 the Loyalists defended their lands against the U.S., the town of York suffering invasion and burning by U.S. forces. After the war, emigration by U.S. and British citizens seeking land brought rapid population expansion. The fur trade was slowly replaced with lumbering and wheat production, and by the mid-19th century the economy began to boom as development of railroads and canal systems started a major transportation network. The establishment of the Dominion of Canada in 1867 and of the capital of Ottawa added to the importance of the province.

Today Ontario is the largest province in terms of wealth and population. Its industrial production accounts for nearly 40 percent of the national income and it is the major industrial center of Canada, producing 97 percent of the motor vehicle parts, and over 90 percent of all office and store machinery, motor vehicles and household radios and televisions manufactured domestically. Yet the province's farming, lumber and fishing are still vitally important to the Canadian economy. And its famous lake regions have made Ontario a favorite summer and winter vacationland for Canadians and Americans alike.

For all its wealth, Ontario still suffers from some unemployment. With proposals for independence in Quebec, however, Ontario's position as the center of commerce and industry for Canada has been enhanced by the exodus of businesses from its eastern neighbor.

The provincial elections of March 18, 1981, saw Premier William Davis' Progressive Conservative party increase its control of the government by 12 additional seats in the legislature.

PRINCE EDWARD ISLAND

Area: 2,184 square miles **Population:** 118,229 (1976 census); 124,200 (April 1, 1981 est.); ranks tenth; population density, 54.1; urban, 37.1%; rural, 62.9% **Capital:** Charlottetown (1976 population), 17,063

Ethnic Composition: British Isles, 83%; French 14% **Religion:** Roman Catholic, 46%; United Church, 25%; Presbyterian, 12%; Anglican, 6%; Baptist, 6% **Vital Statistics (per 1,000 population, 1979):** birth rate, 15.7; death rate, 8.3; marriage rate, 7.3; divorce rate, 1.17; infant mortality per 1,000 live births, 7.6

Location and Geography: Separated from the mainland by Northumberland Strait, nine to 25 miles wide, the island is about 120 miles in length and has an average width of 20 miles. The irregular coastline has many large bays and deep inlets and all inland waters are tidal except for one river and one lake. The rich soil is of a distinctive red color; more than half of the area is farmed. There is no mining and forestland is limited to small farm woodlots

Government: Prince Edward Island became a province in 1873 and is represented in the federal government by four members in the

PRINCE EDWARD ISLAND

MILES
0 5 10 15 20

KILOMETERS
0 5 10 15 20

⊛ Provincial Capital

House of Commons and four Senators. The provincial government is unicameral with a Legislative Assembly of 32 members. Current standings in the legislature are: 21 Progressive Conservatives and 11 Liberals **Premier:** Honourable Angus MacLean **Salary and allowance:** $34,000

Education (1976 census): 26.7% of the population 15 years of age and over had grade 8 or less; 51.1% attended high school; 7.8% had some post-secondary education; 8.9% had a post-secondary certificate or diploma; 5.6% had a university degree **Total expenditures on education (1979-80):** $86,300,000 **Schools (1979-80):** 72 primary and secondary schools with a combined enrollment of 27,342. In the same year full-time enrollment in one degree-granting university and two post-secondary non-university institutions was 1,404

Value added in goods-producing industries (1978): $229,980,000. Agriculture represented 22.9% of the total; construction, 33.8%; manufacturing, 27.6%; and fisheries, 10.2% **Leading manufacturing industries:** fish products, dairy products **Average industrial earnings (1980):** $230.03 per week **Cash receipts from farming operations (1980):** $141,507,000, with 31.8% derived from potatoes, 18.6% from cattle and calves, 14.1% from hogs, and 15.3% from dairy products **Per capita personal income (1979):** $6,057 **Unemployment (1980):** 10.8%

Provincial Finances: Estimated gross general revenue (fiscal year 1980-81): $342,000,000; estimated gross general expenditure, $336,000,000

Daily Newspapers: 3 **Combined circulation:** 32,002 **Number of telephones:** 51.5 per 100 population **Homes with radios:** 99% **Homes with TVs:** 99% (1980)

Hospital beds (1979-80): 755 (6.1 beds per 1,000 population) **Physicians (Dec. 31, 1980):** 152 (population per physician, 815)

Motor Vehicles (1979): 68,361 **Residents per motor vehicle:** 1.9 **Motor vehicle deaths (1979):** 29

The great explorer Jacques Cartier, in 1534, was the first European to visit Prince Edward Island. The French called it Ile St. Jean and used the island as a fishery. When the British took over in 1758 most of the nearly 5,000 Acadians living there were deported. The British divided their newly won territory into lots which were granted to persons in Britain, largely Scots, who had a claim on the patronage of the Crown. Few of the new owners fulfilled their obligation to develop their holdings, however, and a century of struggle followed between tenant farmers and nonresident proprietors. It was resolved only after Confederation in 1873 when the Dominion government advanced $800,000 to the provincial government to buy out the landlords and resell the land to tenants. The development of Prince Edward Island was further delayed by its separation from Nova Scotia in 1769 by the British government. Despite the fact that an 1864 meeting in Charlottetown eventually led to the Canadian Confederation, ironically Prince Edward Island itself did not enter the Dominion until 1873.

The province has abundant good soil, and today agriculture remains a principal industry. However, farmers have become overly dependent on potatoes, a crop that generates 32% of total farm income. Silver fox farming originated on the island. From 1910 to 1940 the island was world-famous for the breed, which is now virtually extinct there. Although its isolation from the mainland has made the island increasingly attractive to tourists, it must import its energy needs and thus pays more for electricity and other power sources than any other province. A replica of the house from *Anne of Green Gables*, found in the National Park, is a favorite of travelers. Fort Amherst National Historic Park, at Rocky Point, contains earthworks of the fort built by the British after its capture from the French in 1758.

By the mid-1980s, the Ministry of Veterans Affairs is to be relocated to Charlottetown, thus becoming the first federal ministry to be transferred from Ottawa.

QUEBEC

Area: 594,860 square miles **Population:** 6,234,445 (1976 census); 6,334,700 (April 1, 1981 est.); ranks second; population density, 11.9; urban, 79.1%; rural, 20.9% Capital: Québec **Major cities (June 1, 1979 metropolitan estimates):** Montréal, 2,818,300; Québec, 559,100; Chicoutimi-Jonquière, 130,000 (1976 metropolitan area population): Laval, 246,243; Longueuil, 122,429; Montréal-Nord, 97,250; Sherbrooke, 76,804; Verdun, 68,013; La Salle, 76,713; Ste-Foy, 71,237; Hull, 61,039; St-Laurent, 64,404; Trois Rivières, 52,518; St-Léonard, 78,452

Ethnic Composition: French, 79%; British Isles, 11% **Religion:** Roman Catholic, 87%; United Church, 3%; Anglican, 3% **Vital Statistics (per 1,000 population, 1979):** birth rate, 15.7; death rate, 6.9; marriage rate, 7.4; divorce rate, 2.29; infant mortality per 1,000 live births, 11.9

Location and Geography: The province's northern four-fifths lies in the Canadian Shield, a lake-dotted, partly wooded, rolling plateau. The St. Lawrence Lowlands have climate and soil well suited for general farming. The Appalachian region, south of the St. Lawrence River and including the Gaspé peninsula, is a succession of plateaus and plains, much of it arable and the remainder wooded

Government: Québec became a province in 1867 and is represented in the federal government by 75 members in the House of Commons and 24 Senators. The provincial government is unicameral with a National Assembly of 122 members. As of April 13, 1981, the standings in the legislature were: *Parti Québécois* 80, Liberals 42, **Prime Minister:** Honourable René Lévesque **Salary and allowance:** $76,153

Education (1976 census): 29.5% of the population 15 years of age and over had Grade 8 or less; 48.2% attended high school; 5.3% had some post-secondary education; 10.1% had a post-secondary certificate or diploma; 6.8% had a university degree **Expenditures on Education (1979-80):** $5,957,200,000 **Schools (1979-80):** 2,967 primary and secondary, with a combined enrollment of 1,265,905 **Colleges:** Seven degree-granting universities and 83 post-secondary non-university institutions with a total enrollment of 221,724

Value added in goods-producing industries (1978): $22,272,497,000; manufacturing represented 65.7% of this total and construction, 18.5% **Value of manufactured shipments (1980):** $43,927,066,000, 26.5% of the national total **Leading manufacturing industries (1978):** pulp and paper, petroleum refining, dairy products, smelting and refining **Average industrial earnings (1980):** $315.35 per week **Mineral production (1980 prel. est.):** $2,501,085,000 **Cash Receipts from farming operations (1980):** $2,236,505,000; dairy products contributed 35.4%; hogs, 21.8%; cattle and calves, 11.4%; and poultry, 9.2% Families with incomes over $12,000: 78.8% **Per capita personal income (1979):** $8,341 **Unemployment (1980):** 9.9%

Provincial Finances: Estimated gross general revenue (fiscal year 1980-81): $17,534,000,000; estimated gross general expenditure, $19,044,000,000

Daily newspapers: 10 French language, three English **Combined Circulation:** 1,375,344 **Telephones per 100 population (1979):** 63.1 **Homes with radios:** 99% **Homes with TVs (1980):** 98.6%

Hospital beds (1979-80): 52,601 (8.4 beds per 1,000 population) **Physicians (Dec. 31, 1980):** 12,160 (population per physician, 520)

Motor vehicles (1979): 3,150,580 **Residents per motor vehicle:** 2.0 **Motor vehicle deaths (1979):** 1,718

It was at Quebec that Cartier landed in 1534, proclaiming French sovereignty. In 1608 Champlain established a settlement at the site of Quebec City, and by 1750 65,000 French-Canadian descendants of the original settlers inhabited the land around the St. Lawrence River. When New France, subject of the crown of France, was ceded to Britain in 1763, and the colony officially became the "province of Quebec," it was a land where French law, religion and custom were firmly entrenched. The confusion created by the co-existence of French-Canadian and British rule was somewhat resolved in 1774 by an act guaranteeing maintenance of French civil law and customs, freedom of worship and education, but the problem remains a source of great controversy to this day.

The French nationalist sentiment has become increasingly strident since the late 1950s. French-

QUEBEC

National Capital
Provincial Capitals

© C.S. HAMMOND & CO., Maplewood, N.J.

speaking Canadians have insisted on greater control of their province's industry and commerce, with demands of some that Quebec become a separate nation. In 1974, the legislature gave voice to the separatists' demands and established French as the province's official language.

In 1976 the separatist *Parti Québécois* (PQ) led by René Levesque won a majority in the provincial assembly. Premier Levesque promptly announced his government's intention to seek independence—a goal that thus far has proved elusive. In 1978 French was established as the primary language of government, education and legal record; however, the law subsequently was struck down by the federal Supreme Court. In May 1980 Quebecers, including a majority of the French-speakers, voted down by a 3-2 margin a PQ-sponsored referendum on a "sovereign-association" plan that would have given Quebec greater self-government while maintaining economic ties to the rest of the Canadian federation. With this setback, Levesque called for a new Canadian constitution that would guarantee Quebec's right to self-determination. Still, such a clear defeat stunned PQ leaders and temporarily halted the drive toward independence. But in 1981 separatists prepared to renew the struggle. In an unexpectedly decisive victory in the April general elections, the PQ won 80 of 122 seats and the right to govern for another five years. Convinced that increasing numbers of Quebecers perceived Prime Minister Trudeau's proposed constitutional changes as a threat to provincial rights and thus were beginning to see the value of independence, Premier Levesque in June 1981 urged his party to step up its separatist campaign. The administration also raised the possibility that an independent Quebec might join Canada, the U.S., and Mexico in a North American economic association.

SASKATCHEWAN

Area: 251,633 square miles **Population:** 921,325 (1976 census); 977,400 (April 1, 1981 est.); ranks sixth; population density, 4.2; urban, 55.5%; rural, 44.5% **Capital:** Regina **Major cities (June 1, 1979 population est.):** Regina, 163,700; Saskatoon, 141,600

Ethnic Composition: British Isles, 42%; German, 19%; Ukrainian, 9%; Scandinavian, 6%; French, 6%; and Native Indian, 4% **Religion:** United Church, 30%; Roman Catholic, 28%; Lutheran, 10%; Anglican, 9%; Ukrainian Catholic, 4%; Mennonite, 3% **Vital Statistics (per 1,000 population), 1979:** birth rate, 17.7; death rate, 7.7; marriage rate, 7.6; divorce rate, 1.59; infant mortality per 1,000 live births, 14.3 (1978)

Location and Geography: Situated between Manitoba and Alberta, the southern portion of the province consists of a rolling plain. The northern third begins the Canadian shield

Government: Saskatchewan became a province in 1905 and is represented in the federal government by 14 members in the House of Commons and six Senators. The provincial government is unicameral with a Legislative Assembly of 61 members. Present standings in the legislature: 44 New Democrats and 17 Conservatives **Premier:** Honourable Allan E. Blakeney **Salary and allowance:** $58,669

Education (1976 census): In Saskatchewan, 94% of the population had completed Grade IV; 49.4%, secondary schools and 6.2%, university **Total expenditures on education (1979-80):** $722,000,000 **Schools and students:** 1,062 primary and secondary schools with a combined enrollment of 217,086 **Colleges:** Three degree-granting universities and 3 community colleges, and technical and vocational institutes, with an enrollment of 16,710 (1979-80)

Value added in goods-producing industries (1978 actual): $4,537,325,000; agriculture represented 38.2% of this total, mining 26.8%, construction 18.6%, and manufacturing 12.5% **Value of Mineral Shipments (1980):** $2,290,347,000 **Leading manufacturing industries:** slaughtering and meat processing, agricultural implement industry, sawmills and planing mills, printing and publishing **Average industrial earnings (1980):** $303.71 per week **Cash receipts form farming operations (1980):** $3,149,267,000; with 55.3% derived from wheat, 18.3% from cattle and calves, and 4.4% from barley **Families with incomes over $10,000 (1979):** 78.2% **Per capita personal income (1979):** $8,335 **Unemployment (1980):** 4.4%

Provincial Finances: Estimated gross general revenue (fiscal year 1980-81): $2,670,000,000; estimated gross general expenditure, $2,438,000,000

Daily newspapers: 4 **Combined circulation:** 138,840 **Telephones per 100 population:** 61.5 **Homes with radios (1980):** 99.4% **Homes with TVs (1980):** 97%

Hospital beds (1979-80): 7,873 (8.2 beds per 1,000 population) **Physicians (Dec. 31, 1980):** 1,442 (population per physician, 677)

Motor Vehicles (1979): 682,881 **Residents per motor vehicle (1979):** 1.4 **Motor vehicle deaths (1979):** 272

The first European to reach what is now Saskatchewan and to see the vast buffalo herds that roamed the central plains was Henry Kelsey, an agent of the Hudson's Bay Company. In 1690 he was sent into the Northwest to explore the vast territory and ensure the Company's fur supply by pacifying the Indians. For two centuries fur trading continued, and settlement only began in 1870 with the building of the railroad and the practice of homesteading.

Today the province has Canada's largest area of occupied agricultural land. Yet, after the disasters of the dust bowl of the 1930s, diversification has been a priority and now 65 percent of the province's gross product is from industry, only 35 percent from farming. Petroleum, mining and manufacturing are the major industries; farms are large and highly mechanized.

The 1978 elections affirmed support for the NDP and Premier Blakeney's policy of taking over one-half of the potash mining industry, much of which is owned by United States interests.

SASKATCHEWAN

PRINCIPAL CANADIAN AGRICULTURAL CROPS Source: Statistics Canada

	Area in Acres		Yield per Acre[1]		Total Production[1]	
	1979	1980	1979	1980	1979	1980
			Bushels		Bushels	
Winter wheat	740,000	680,000	42.9	48.0	31,779,000	32,642,000
Spring wheat	22,377,500	23,642,200	23.8	25.4	533,544,000	599,907,000
Durum wheat	2,800,000	3,100,000	23.6	22.7	66,100,000	70,400,000
All wheat	25,917,500	27,422,200	24.4	25.6	631,423,000	702,949,000
Oats for grain	3,806,500	3,742,000	50.7	52.5	193,093,000	196,317,000
Barley for grain	9,199,700	11,303,000	42.2	44.9	388,573,000	507,104,000
Fall rye	760,000	719,000	25.5	23.2	19,632,000	16,654,000
Spring rye	46,000	47,000	22.3	21.1	1,025,000	990,000
All rye	815,000	766,000	25.3	23.0	20,657,000	17,644,000
Mixed grains	1,468,900	1,431,600	55.8	56.4	81,911,000	80,778,000
Flaxseed	2,300,000	1,420,000	14.0	12.9	32,100,000	18,300,000
Rapeseed	8,420,000	5,140,000	17.9	21.5	150,400,000	110,500,000
Corn for grain	2,204,000	2,382,500	89.0	90.3	196,175,000	214,043,000
Buckwheat	154,000	118,500	9.4	10.6	1,445,000	1,259,000
Peas, dry	108,000	122,000	26.4	22.9	2,850,000	2,790,000
Soybeans	700,000	700,000	35.2	37.4	24,652,000	26,204,000
			Cwt			
Beans, dry, white	84,000	95,000	16.2	16.3	1,359,000	1,550,000
			Pounds			
Mustard seed	158,000	244,000	696.0	881.0	110,000,000	215,000,000
Sunflower seed	398,000	338,000	1,206.0	1,083.0	480,000,000	366,000,000
			Tons			
Tame hay	13,640,000	13,534,000	2.14	1.93	229,218,000	26,179,000
Fodder corn	1,198,200	1,187,200	13.44	13.08	16,108,000	15,529,000
Sugar beets	58,714	65,610	16.05	15.14	942,300	993,300

[1]As indicated on or about Nov. 15, 1980.

CANADA: PRINCIPAL TRADE PARTNERS Source: Statistics Canada

	EXPORTS ($000,000 in Canadian dollars)				IMPORTS ($000,000 in Canadian dollars)		
Country	1980*	1979	1978	Country	1980*	1979	1978
United States	46,829	43,439	36,455	United States	48,473	45,420	35,246
Japan	4,364	4,077	3,052	Japan	2,796	2,157	2,268
United Kingdom	3,187	2,589	1,985	Saudi Arabia	2,452	1,242	749
Germany, West	1,640	1,368	782	Venezuela	2,217	1,505	1,283
USSR	1,535	763	567	United Kingdom	1,974	1,929	1,600
Netherlands	1,434	1,082	563	Germany, West	1,455	1,556	1,244
France	995	620	460	France	772	778	684
Belgium/Luxembourg	989	668	475	Italy	610	636	525
Italy	983	729	481	Hong Kong	574	427	332
Brazil	893	422	417	China, Rep. of	558	522	397
China, People's Rep.	870	596	503	Switzerland	522	323	285
Australia	664	557	412	Australia	517	466	350
Venezuela	656	671	686	Sweden	416	383	325
Korea, South	504	364	216	Korea, South	414	463	363
Mexico	483	236	229	South Africa	355	240	149
Cuba	417	257	218	Brazil	348	313	248
Algeria	393	—	—	Mexico	345	208	185
Switzerland	373	—	—	Iraq	281	—	—
India	353	—	—	Netherlands	264	252	227
Poland	346	262	224	Belgium/Luxembourg	251	241	202

* Preliminary, by order of rank.

SALARIES OF SENIOR MEMBERS OF HOUSE OF COMMONS

Position	Sessional Allowance	Expense Allowance	Salary	Motor Vehicle	Total
Prime Minister	$30,600	$13,500	$37,800	$2,000	$83,900
Cabinet Ministers and Leaders of Opposition in the House of Commons	30,600	$13,500	22,600	2,000	68,700
Members of Parliament	30,600	$13,500*	—	—	44,100*

* Certain members for larger northern constituencies have larger expense allowances.

YUKON TERRITORY

MILES

0 25 50 75 100 125

KILOMETERS

0 25 50 75 100 125

Territorial and State Capitals ⊛

© C.S. HAMMOND & Co., Maplewood, N.J.

Longitude West of Greenwich

NORTHWEST TERRITORIES

State and Territorial Capitals

CANADIAN IMPORTS BY LEADING COMMODITIES

SOURCE: Statistics Canada

($000 in Canadian dollars)

	1980*	1979	1978
Motor vehicles and parts	13,478,673	14,122,129	12,170,353
Crude petroleum	6,919,053	4,507,214	3,471,138
Precious metals, including alloys	1,738,651	1,097,810	244,466
Electronic computers	1,652,774	1,102,088	852,664
Other metals in ore, conc., scrap	1,414,098	503,838	208,897
Other telecommunication and rel. equip.	1,085,757	970,485	779,632
Other end products, inedible	957,549	854,840	613,857
Organic chemicals	930,105	895,082	681,954
Aircraft, complete with engines	860,439	679,426	263,395
Coal	811,156	865,021	632,441
Miscellaneous equipment and tools	807,494	768,692	679,084
Other special transactions—trade	763,005	567,508	389,615
Other chemical products	741,425	616,395	512,536
Drilling machinery and drill bits	643,140	—	—
Wheel tractors, new	619,130	655,319	441,696
Aircraft parts, except engines	595,192	—	—
Other measuring, lab. equip. etc.	577,729	—	—
Electronic tubes & semi-conductors	574,642	—	—
Other photographic goods	551,862	479,226	440,063
Machine tools, metalworking	539,538	—	—

*Ranked by value.

CANADIAN EXPORTS BY LEADING COMMODITIES

SOURCE: Statistics Canada

($000 in Canadian dollars)

	1980*	1979	1978
Motor vehicles and parts	10,818,518	10,636,421	11,127,749
Natural gas	8,983,850	2,889,054	2,190,294
Wood pulp and similar pulp	3,870,417	3,084,253	2,180,905
Wheat	3,795,688	2,180,282	1,912,830
Newsprint paper	3,681,857	3,221,678	2,886,235
Lumber, softwood	3,262,927	3,820,586	3,158,220
Crude petroleum	2,899,099	2,404,582	1,572,662
Petroleum and coal products	2,324,316	1,882,655	776,580
Precious metals, including alloys	2,067,529	954,771	567,511
Aluminum, including alloys	1,532,353	917,521	1,140,562
Fertilizers and fertilizer material	1,253,763	987,310	734,933
Iron Ores and concentrates	1,241,282	1,354,086	782,793
Copper and alloys	999,015	—	—
Other end products	971,310	—	—
Other inorganic chemicals	947,287	839,651	653,611
Coal & other crude bitumin substances	933,831	835,217	751,872
Other telecommunication & rel. equip.	931,770	655,349	460,407
Organic chemicals	923,880	704,665	401,529
Nickel and alloys	818,489	—	—
Electricity	773,035	729,234	478,875

*Ranked by value.

CANADA: POPULATION, 1851-1980   SOURCE: Statistics Canada

	1851	1871	1891	1931	1951	1971	1980[3]
Newfoundland	—	—	—	—	361,416	522,104	579,700
Prince Edward Island	62,678[1]	94,021	109,078	88,038	98,429	111,641	124,300
Nova Scotia	276,854	387,800	450,396	512,846	642,584	788,960	852,500
New Brunswick	193,800	285,594	321,263	408,219	515,697	634,557	707,100
Quebec	890,261	1,191,516	1,488,535	2,874,662	4,055,681	6,027,764	6,303,400
Ontario	952,004	1,620,851	2,114,321	3,431,683	4,597,542	7,703,106	8,570,400
Manitoba	—	25,228	152,560	700,139	776,541	988,247	1,028,300
Saskatchewan	—	—	—[2]	921,785	831,728	926,242	969,200
Alberta	—	—	—[2]	731,605	939,501	1,627,874	2,078,500
British Columbia	55,000	36,247	98,173	694,263	1,165,210	2,184,621	2,636,500
Yukon	—	—	—	4,230	9,096	18,388	21,400
Northwest Territory	5,700	48,000	98,967	9,316	16,004	34,807	43,000
Total Canada	2,436,297	3,689,257	4,833,239	10,376,786	14,009,429	21,568,311	23,914,400

[1]1848 figure. [2]Included with the Northwest Territories. [3]Post 1971 census estimate.

LARGEST CANADIAN CITIES   SOURCE: Statistics Canada

	1851	1901	1951	1961	1971	1976
Calgary, Alberta	—	4,091	129,060	249,641	403,343*	469,917
Edmonton, Alberta	—	—	159,631	218,027	438,152	461,361
Halifax, Nova Scotia	20,740	40,832	85,589	92,511	122,035	117,882
Hamilton, Ontario	14,112	52,634	208,321	273,991	309,173	312,003
London, Ontario	—	37,981	95,343	169,569	223,222	240,392
Montreal, Quebec	57,715	267,730	1,021,520	1,191,062	1,214,352	1,080,546
Ottawa, Ontario	—	59,928	202,045	268,206	302,341	304,462
Quebec, Quebec	42,052	68,840	164,016	171,979	187,833*	177,082
Regina, Saskatchewan	—	—	71,319	112,141	139,479*	149,593
Saint John, N.B.	22,745	40,711	50,779	55,153	89,039	85,956
St. John's, Newfoundland	—	—	52,873	63,533	88,414*	86,576
Toronto, Ontario	30,775	208,040	675,754	672,407	712,786	633,318
Vancouver, British Columbia	—	26,133	344,833	384,522	426,298*	410,188
Windsor, Ontario	—	12,153	120,049	114,367	203,300	196,526
Winnipeg, Manitoba	—	42,340	235,710	265,429	504,150*	560,874

*Revised, based on 1976 areas.

WORLD NATIONS

AFGHANISTAN

Area: 250,775 sq. mi. **Population:** 15,540,000 (1979 census)
Official Name: Democratic Republic of Afghanistan **Capital:** Kabul
Nationality: Afghan **Languages:** Pushtu, spoken by the Pathans, and Dari, a Persian dialect spoken by the Tajiks, are official languages **Religion:** About 99% of the population are Moslems, most of whom belong to the Sunni sect **Flag:** Three equal horizontal stripes of black, red and green with the national coat of arms set near the hoist at the intersection of the black and red stripes **Anthem:** N.A. **Currency:** Afghani (44.5 per U.S. $1)

Location: Central Asia. Landlocked Afghanistan is bordered by the USSR on the north, China on the extreme northeast, Pakistan on the east and south, and Iran on the west **Features:** The towering Hindu Kush range and its parallel extensions run through the center of the country from northeast to southwest. Mountains and desert country are interspersed by small, fertile valleys irrigated by snow-fed mountain streams **Chief Rivers:** Helmand, Farah Rud, Hari Rud, Khulm, Amu Darya

Head of State and Government: President Babrak Karmal, born 1929, named head of state, prime minister, Chairman of the Revolutionary Council and General Secretary of the People's Democratic party, following the Soviet-backed coup of December 1979. On June 11, 1981, Karmal relinquished the post of Prime Minister and turned it over to Sultan Ali Kishtmand **Effective Date of Present Constitution:** April 1980 (provisional constitution) **Legislative Body:** Revolutionary Council of 57 members. The Loya Jirgah (Supreme Council) is to be elected under the terms of the provisional constitution of 1980 **Local Government:** 26 provinces, each headed by a governor

Ethnic Composition: The Pathans (Pushtus) make up about half the total population; the rest is made up largely of Tajiks, Uzbeks, Hazara, and Turkmen **Population Distribution:** 15% urban **Density:** 62 inhabitants per sq. mi.

Largest Cities: (1976 estimates) Kabul 603,969, Kandahar 160,684, Herat 115,165; (1973 est.) Baghlan 110,874, Tagab 106,777, Charikar 100,443

Per Capita Income: $207 (1980) **Gross National Product (GNP):** $3.1 billion (1980) **Economic Statistics:** about 53% of GNP comes from agriculture (wheat, corn, fruit, nuts, barley, rice, cotton, sugar beets and cane) and animal husbandry (sheep, cattle, goats); 16% from trade and services; 11% from industry and handicrafts (textiles, cement, flour, sugar, fruit processing, hand-woven carpets); 20% from other activities **Minerals and Mining:** Fields of natural gas in northern Afghanistan are being developed with Soviet assistance. There are large coal deposits; known deposits of iron ore, chromite and beryl are unexploited; lapis lazuli of world-renowned quality is produced. Hydroelectricity is an important source of energy **Labor Force:** 4,600,000 (1970), with 67% in agriculture, and 8% in industry **Foreign Trade:** Exports, chiefly fruit, karakul skins, natural gas, wool and carpets, totaled $322 million in 1979. Imports, mainly textiles, used clothing, petroleum products, tea, tires, thread, sugar and medicine, totaled $420 million **Principal Trade Partners:** USSR, Japan, West Germany, Britain, India, Pakistan, Czechoslovakia

Vital Statistics: Birthrate, 43.2 per 1,000 of pop. (1974); death rate, 21 **Life Expectancy:** 40.3 years **Health Statistics:** 5,879 inhabitants per hospital bed (1976); 28,313 per physician (1974) **Illiteracy:** 90% **Infant Mortality:** 185 per 1,000 births **Primary and Secondary School Enrollment:** 943,326 (1976) **Enrollment in Higher Education:** 12,256 (1975) **GNP Expended on Education:** 1.3% (1974)

Transportation: Paved roads total 1,900 mi. (1975) **Motor Vehicles:** 64,500 (1971) **Passenger Cars:** 38,400 **Railway Mileage:** None **Ports:** None **Major Airlines:** Ariana Afghan Airlines operates international flights **Communications:** Government owned **Radio Transmitters:** 6 **Receivers:** 115,000 (1976) **Television Stations:** 1 **Telephones:** 28,000 (1976) **Newspapers:** 17 dailies, 27 per 1,000 inhabitants (1975)

Weights and Measures: Metric system and local units are used **Travel Requirements:** The U.S. Government advises against travel to Afghanistan (1980)

Divided by tribal loyalties and the country's mountainous terrain, many in Afghanistan live now as their forefathers did: as herdsmen, nomads, and farmers. The cities, especially the capital, Kabul, show tentative signs of modernity, but the gap between the way urban and rural Afghans live and think has long been a major problem in attempts to consolidate the national mosaic.

Afghanistan's modern history has seen tribal rebellions, bloody royal successions and military coups, but no foreign interference ever had resulted in virtually total conquest until the Soviet Union invaded in late December 1979, and quickly became an occupying force—beset, however, by guerrilla resistance in the countryside.

King Mohammed Zahir Shah, who succeeded his assassinated father in 1933 at the age of 19, was a near-prisoner of relatives for years. He did not assume full governmental powers until 1963. Zahir attempted to introduce reforms and presented his people with the first democratic constitution in 1964. Lasting political changes did not take place, however, and a two-year drought in 1971-72 brought an already poor economy to a crisis condition, sealing the fate of the monarchy.

In July 1973 a group of young military officers deposed the king and proclaimed a republic. The leader of the coup, Lt. Gen. Mohammad Daud Khan, a cousin of the king and a former prime minister (1953-1963), became both president and prime minister of the new republic. The constitution of 1964 was put aside and rule by decree instituted. In April 1978 President Daud, members of his family and some 100 police officers and other officials were among an undetermined number who were killed as leftist military elements overthrew the government in two days of fierce fighting in Kabul. The rebels set up a Revolutionary Council to run the country by decree and installed a civilian, Nur Mohammad Taraki, general secretary of the Marxist Khalq Party, as president and prime minister of what became "the Democratic Republic of Aghanistan." On Dec. 5, Taraki signed a 20-year Afghan-USSR friendship treaty in Moscow.

Protesting the Taraki government's atheistic policies, village tribesmen began sporadic attacks on government forces in 1978. Without forming a united front, fervent but poorly armed Moslem bands gained control of an estimated 22 of the country's 28 provinces in 1979. In Herat, Moslems and defecting troops rioted in March and killed hundreds of loyal troops; a government response with helicopter gunships caused an estimated 20,000 deaths in the city. In April, in Kerala in Kunar province, Afghan soldiers and police and Soviet advisors massacred more than 1,000 men and boys.

The Revolutionary Council named Hafizulla Amin as prime minister in March 1979; six months later, in a shootout that took 60 lives at Kabul's People's House, Taraki was apparently slain and Amin became president. But in a Dec. 27 coup backed by Soviet troops, Babrak Karmal, back from exile in Eastern Europe, was installed as head of state, and Amin was executed for "crimes against the people." A 3½-hour battle preceded the takeover of Radio Kabul by the Soviets.

By the start of 1980 the Soviet troops had fanned out to control towns, passes, and key roads throughout the country, but many thousands of Moslem "holy warriors," or *mujahidin*—organized into some 60 guerrilla groups—established effective resistance. In Kabul, a general merchants' strike and student protests were suppressed by force.

By mid-1981, some 100,000 Soviet troops were in Afghanistan, whose gross national product had declined by more than two thirds within one year. Soviet destruction of food supplies caused the *mujahidin* to shift the focus of resistance from rural areas to the towns. They briefly controlled Kandahar, the nation's second-largest city.

HISTORY: Afghanistan has suffered invasions from east and west—by Persians, Greeks, Mongols, and Turks. Among the foreign conquerors was Alexander the Great, in the 4th century B.C. After him came the independent kingdom of Bactria, which lasted until the middle of the 2nd century B.C. Buddhism spread from the east but was superseded by Islam in the 7th century A.D., after which several Moslem kingdoms were set up

11th cent.: Mahmud of Ghazni, an Afghan Moslem, forms kingdom stretching from Caspian Sea to the Ganges River
13th cent.: Genghis Khan and his hordes overrun the country
18th cent.: Persians under Nadir Shah conquer Afghanistan; after Nadir's death in 1747, Ahmad Shah unifies the country for the first time and sets up the Durrani dynasty
1838-42: Attempts by Emir Dost Mohammed to exploit Anglo-Russian rivalry in central Asia and to seize control of British possessions in India lead to first Afghan War, which ends with British withdrawal from Afghanistan
1878-80: Dost Mohammed's son, Shere Ali, turns to Russia for aid, setting off second Afghan War with Britain; Shere Ali is ousted and replaced by Anglophile Abd ur-Rahman
1907: Anglo-Russian agreement guarantees independence of Afghanistan under British influence
1926-29: Afghanistan becomes kingdom, with Amanullah as first king; he attempts to modernize the country but ultra-conservative elements force him to abdicate
1930-33: His successor, Mohammed Nadir Shah, continues reforms until killed; Mohammed Zahir Shah becomes king
1964-65: A new, liberal constitution goes into effect and parliamentary elections are held for the first time
1973: King Mohammed Zahir Shah is overthrown by brother-in-law, General Mohammad Daud Khan; Daud proclaims Afghanistan a republic, declares himself president and prime minister
1974: Daud and Brezhnev sign a joint statement of interest in a collective Asian security system
1975: Daud nationalizes all banks and land reform laws are announced. Increased foreign aid is received
1978: Daud killed as leftist military coup succeeds; Nur Mohammad Taraki becomes president and prime minister. Rural Moslem conservatives begin guerrilla warfare
1979: U.S. Ambassador Adolph Dubs, kidnapped by rebels, is killed in a rescue attempt by government security officers. Hafizullah Amin becomes prime minister in March and advances to president in a coup on Sept. 16, when Taraki reportedly is killed. In a Dec. 27 coup, Babrak Karmal becomes head of state, and Amin is executed. Soviet troops, airlifted into Kabul, win a battle for Radio Kabul, which announces the coup
1980: Soviet troops occupy the country, but the rebels fight on in widespread guerrilla resistance
1981: Nation's economy in ruins. Soviet troop commitment rises to about 100,000

ALBANIA

Area: 11,100 sq. mi. **Population:** 2,591,000 (1979 census)
Official Name: People's Socialist Republic of Albania **Capital:** Tirana **Nationality:** Albanian **Languages:** Albanians are divided into two main language groups: Gheg, north of the river Shkumbi, and Tosk in the south. The official language is based on Tosk. Greek is spoken by the Greek minority in the south **Religion:** 50% Moslem, 20% Orthodox, 10% Roman Catholic. In 1967, however, all religious institutions were closed by the government **Flag:** A red field, with a double-headed black eagle and a gold-edged, five-pointed star above it **Anthem:** Anthem of the Flag **Currency:** Lek (7 per U.S. $1)
Location: Southeast Europe, on the west coast of the Balkan peninsula. Albania is bordered on the north and east by Yugoslavia, on the south by Greece, and on the west by the Adriatic Sea **Features:** About 20% of the country consists of a flat-to-rolling coastal plain. Most of the country, however, consists of hills and mountains, frequently covered with scrub forest **Chief Rivers:** Drin, Mat, Shkumbi, Semun, Vijosë
Political Leader: First Secretary of the Albanian (Communist) Party of Labor: Enver Hoxha, born 1908; in power since 1945 as First Secretary of the Central Committee **Head of State:** Chairman of the Presidium of the People's Assembly: Haxhi Lleshi, born 1913,

reelected by People's Assembly 1978 **Head of Government:** Chairman of the Council of Ministers (premier): Mehmet Shehu, born 1913, reappointed by the People's Assembly in 1978 **Effective Date of Present Constitution:** 1976 **Legislative Body:** People's Assembly (unicameral), consisting of 250 members, elected for 4 years. The People's Assembly is nominally the supreme organ of government, but in practice meets only a few days each year. Real power is vested in the Politburo and Central Committee of the Communist party **Local Government:** 27 districts with locally elected people's councils
Ethnic Composition: The population is homogeneous, with a small Greek minority **Population Distribution:** 34% urban (1971) **Density:** 233 inhabitants per sq. mi.
Largest Cities: (1975 estimates) Tirana 170,000, Durrës 80,000, Vlorë 57,000, Korcë 53,000, Shkodër 49,000
Per Capita Income: $805 (1980) **Gross National Product (GNP):** $2.2 billion (1980) **Economic Statistics:** GNP components are not available. In 1968, however, industrial production accounted for 61.5% of total production in the country; the principal industries are oil refining, chemicals, fertilizers, construction materials, textiles, pig iron, processed minerals, and agricultural products. Agricultural production is chiefly devoted to corn, sugar beets, wheat, cotton, tobacco, and livestock **Minerals and Mining:** Chrome ore, oil, coal, copper, iron, and nickel are exploited and are among Albania's chief exports. Hydroelectric and thermoelectric plants provide the country with full electrification **Labor Force:** In 1972, 343,228 workers were employed in the socialist sector of the economy, with about 30% in industry and 60% in agriculture **Foreign Trade:** Exports, chiefly chrome ores, crude petroleum, bitumen, olives, fruit and tobacco, amounted to $151 million in 1978. Imports, chiefly machinery and equipment, rolled steel and wheat, totaled about $173 million **Principal Trade Partners:** Yugoslavia, Greece, Italy
Vital Statistics: Birthrate, 33.3 per 1,000 of pop.; death rate, 8.1 (1971) **Life Expectancy:** 69 years **Health Statistics:** 164 inhabitants per hospital bed; 159 per physician (1972) **Infant Mortality:** 86.8 per 1,000 births (1965) **Illiteracy:** 25% **Education Statistics:** 1,429 schools with a combined enrollment of 750,000 pupils (1975) **Enrollment in Higher Education:** 28,668 (1971) **GNP Expended on Education:** N.A.
Transportation: There were 800 mi. of paved roads in 1975 **Motor Vehicles:** 10,100 (1967) **Passenger Cars:** 2,600 (1967) **Railway Mileage:** 188 **Ports:** Durrës, Vlorë **Major Airlines:** Albtransport operates international flights **Communications:** Government owned **Radio Transmitters:** 19 **Receivers:** 180,000 (1976) **Television Transmitters:** 1 **Receivers:** 4,500 (1976) **Telephones:** 10,150 (1963) **Newspapers:** 2 dailies, 46 copies per 1,000 inhabitants (1975)
Weights and Measures: Metric system **Travel Requirements:** (1971) Passport, visa obtainable in Paris or Rome

---

Albania's present, like its past, is influenced by its forbidding hills and poor soil. In a land unattractive to migrants, the Albanians have preserved their ancient culture. But the land cannot feed the people; Albania is a food-importing nation. Fearful of strangers, Albania must depend on strangers for its survival.

Since 1946, Albania has been dominated by the Albanian Party of Labor—a party fanatically devoted to Marxist-Leninist ideology. The Party's leaders have rejected calls for de-Stalinization and for détente with the West and have maintained a rigid police state. The government has fallen out, successively, with Yugoslavia, the Soviet Union and China, as these states have moved away from ideological rigidity.

At the beginning of the 20th century, Albania was part of the Ottoman Empire. Serbia took from that Empire much territory inhabited by ethnic Albanians before an alarmed Austria, in 1912, helped the rest of the country to win independence. After World War I, Albania was caught up in the rivalry between Yugoslavia and Italy; the latter annexed Albania in 1939.

Nominally independent under Communist rule in 1946, Albania was virtually a Yugoslav satellite. The two countries joined in aiding Communist guerrillas in Greece. But Albania broke with Yugoslavia in 1947 and ended the Greek adventure, after Yugoslavia broke with the Soviet Union. Territorial claims against Yugoslavia and loyalty to Joseph Stalin led Albania to remain in the Soviet camp, and the Soviet Union took over the task of supplying most of Albania's food.

In 1961, however, Albania's relations with the Soviet Union soured because of Soviet policies of de-Stalinization. Albania turned to Communist China for friendship and food. For practical reasons Albania resumed relations with Yugoslavia in 1970 and with Greece in 1971. Later, China's course became increasingly pragmatic, and Albania criticized the lack of devotion to the Communist cause. After Mao's death in 1976, Albania became hostile to his successors, and in 1978 China ended its assistance to Albania. Because of its continuing anti-Soviet policies, Albania boycotted the 1980 Summer Olympics in Moscow.

HISTORY: Around 300 B.C., the Illyrian kingdom covered much of what is now Albania. Greek colonies were established along the coast, but the hinterland remained independent. In the 6th century A.D., while nominally under Byzantine rule, Albania was invaded by the Slavs and in the 9th century was annexed to Bulgaria. The Turks conquered the country in the 15th century
1912-20: Albania proclaims its independence with the support of Austria-Hungary. During World War I, Albania is occupied by Allied troops but reasserts its independence
1925-28: Ahmed Zogu, chief of the Mat district, seizes power with Yugoslav support. He rules as president until 1928, when he establishes a monarchy and becomes King Zog I
1939: Italy occupies Albania and unites it with Italian crown
1946: Albania becomes a people's republic under the leadership of Enver Hoxha, head of the Communist resistance group during the Italian occupation
1955-60: Backed by the USSR, Albania joins the Warsaw Pact and the United Nations. Relations with the Soviet Union soon cool, however, as Moscow attempts to improve relations with Yugoslavia, behind whose frontiers live more than 750,000 ethnic Albanians; estrangement is sharpened by Albania's support for Peking in Sino-Soviet ideological split
1961: USSR breaks diplomatic relations with Albania
1968: Albania withdraws from Warsaw Pact
1970: Albania signs trade pact with Yugoslavia
1971: Greece and Albania resume full diplomatic relations
1973: Purge of eight officials for anti-party activity
1976: A new constitution is approved by People's Assembly
1978: Chinese aid ended. New agreement with Greece increases trade and opens air route

ALGERIA

Area: 919,591 sq. mi. **Population:** 19,130,000 (1979 est.)

Official Name: Democratic and Popular Republic of Algeria **Capital:** Algiers **Nationality:** Algerian **Languages:** Arabic is the official and principal language. French is also widely spoken and serves as a quasi-official language. Berber dialects are spoken by one-fourth the population **Religion:** 99% Moslem; Islam was declared the state religion in 1976 **Flag:** A red star in a red crescent in center of background of green (left hand of flag) and white (right hand) **Anthem:** We Pledge **Currency:** Algerian dinar (4.25 per U.S. $1)

Location: North Africa. Algeria is bordered on the north by the Mediterranean Sea, on the east by Tunisia and Libya, on the south by Niger and Mali, and on the west by Mauritania, Western Sahara, and Morocco **Features:** Two mountain chains, the Tell Atlas and the Saharan Atlas. The mountains of the Tell Atlas rise from a narrow coastal plain along the Mediterranean and are separated from the Saharan Atlas by a corridor of semiarid plateaus dotted with salt marshes and shallow salt lakes. To the south lies the Sahara itself, broken only by a few oases **Chief River:** Chéliff

Head of State and of Government: President: Chadli Bendjedid, born 1929, elected 1979. He is assisted by Premier Mohamed Ben Ahmed Abdelghani, appointed 1979 **Effective Date of Present Constitution:** 1976 **Legislative Body:** A new National Popular Assembly of 261 members was elected in February 1977 for 5-year terms **Local Government:** 31 departments (wilayas)

Ethnic Composition: The population is of Arabo-Berber stock **Population Distribution:** 52% urban **Density:** 20.8 inhabitants per sq. mi.

Largest Cities: (1978 census) Algiers 1,365,400, Oran 491,900, Constantine 335,100, Annaba 255,900, Blida 160,900

Per Capita Income: $1,483 (1980) **Gross National Product (GNP):** $28 billion (1980) **Economic Statistics:** In 1976, 7% of the GNP came from agriculture (wheat, vineyard, orchards), livestock raising (sheep, cattle, donkeys, mules, horses, pigs, goats) and fishing; 35% from trade and services; and 44% from mining and industry (food processing and beverages, textiles, leather, chemicals, building materials, steel, and engineering) **Minerals and Mining:** Vast deposits of oil and gas, iron ore, phosphates, and coal; small amounts of lead, zinc and copper **Labor Force:** 2.6 million (1975 est.), of which 60% is engaged in agriculture, 12% in industry, and the rest in services **Foreign Trade:** Exports, chiefly petroleum, natural gas, fruit and wine, totaled $8.2 billion in 1979. Imports, mainly textiles, cereals, chemicals, motor vehicles, iron and steel products, sugar, machinery, and electrical apparatus, totaled $8.2 billion **Principal Trade Partners:** United States, France, West Germany, Italy, Japan, Spain, Canada

Vital Statistics: Birthrate, 47.8 per 1,000 of pop. (1975); death rate, 15.4 **Life Expectancy:** 53.3 years (1975) **Health Statistics:** 356 inhabitants per hospital bed, 8,192 per physician (1976) **Infant Mortality:** 70 per 1,000 births **Illiteracy:** 70% **Primary and Secondary School Enrollment:** 3,400,531 (1976) **Enrollment in Higher Education:** 59,100 (1977) **GNP Expended on Education:** 9% (1977)

Transportation: Paved roads total 22,125 mi. (1977) **Motor Vehicles:** 440,800 (1975) **Passenger Cars:** 286,100 **Railway Mileage:** 2,423 **Ports:** Algiers, Oran, Annaba, Bejaia, Arzew **Major Airlines:** Air Algérie operates international and domestic flights **Communications:** Government owned **Radio Transmitters:** 27 **Receivers:** 3,220,000 (1974) **Television Transmitters:** 75 **Receivers:** 525,000 (1976) **Telephones:** 273,000 (1976) **Newspapers:** 4 dailies, 17 copies per 1,000 inhabitants (1975)

Weights and Measures: Metric system **Travel Requirements:** Passport, tourist visa, $3.75, valid for 3 months, 4 photos

Algeria won independence from France in a long struggle organized by a disciplined party—the National Liberation Front (NLF). Independence brought one-party rule, economic dislocation, and a period of military control. The NLF is a party of Islam, socialism, and concern for the aspirations of the Third World in general and of the Arab states in particular. It is strident in its support of those it considers oppressed, and has made Algeria a haven for many kinds of self-proclaimed revolutionaries—including airplane hijackers. Israel is a favorite target of Algerian rhetoric, although not of Algerian military action. Ironically, Algeria's only actual military adventure is that against Morocco—in support of the Polisario movement for Western Saharan independence.

Despite its ideology, Algeria must trade with the capitalist West. Its economy was ruined by the departure of its European inhabitants after independence, and recovery is incomplete. Fortunately, Algeria has oil and gas which the West needs.

France agreed to independence in 1962, after a plebiscite showed a majority to favor "independence in cooperation with France." Benyoussef Ben Khedda, who had headed the NLF's exile government, became Premier. But his power was broken by Ahmed Ben Bella, a firebrand NLF official who had spent most of the struggle in a French jail. Ben Bella established a one-party system that tended toward personal dictatorship. He was deposed in 1965 by Colonel Houari Boumédienne, who established military rule within the NLF framework.

Boumédienne created most of the salient features of the new Algeria. Finding that cooperation with France was working to France's advantage, he ended it in 1971. Then, he increased trade with the United States, although he had broken diplomatic relations with the U.S. in 1967 because of U.S. support for Israel. Discontent of NLF leaders with military rule led to the adoption of a new constitution in 1976 and to ratification by the voters of the NLF's choice of Boumédienne as President. The constitution did not bring democracy, but it broadened the limits within which divergent views were tolerated.

The system of semi-democratic one-party rule was tried and found workable in 1978, when

Boumédienne died after weeks in a coma. As the constitution provided, Rabah Bitat became the interim president, and in 1979 Col. Chadli Bendjedid was elected to the office.

In 1981 Algeria mediated the dispute between the U.S. and Iran over 52 American hostages who had been held in Tehran for 14 months. Algerian Minister Behzat Nabavi negotiated the release of the hostages with U.S. and Iranian diplomats in Algiers. On January 20 the hostages were flown to Algeria on their way to West Germany and their return to the U.S.

HISTORY: In prehistoric times, Algeria was inhabited by a mixture of peoples from whom the Berbers of today are probably descended. About 1200 B.C. the Phoenicians made settlements in the area, and it eventually fell under the control of Carthage. After the destruction of Carthage in 146 B.C., the Romans gradually gained control of the entire North African coast. With the weakening of the Roman Empire, Algeria fell prey to Vandals from Europe and eventually to the Arabs

7th cent.: Algeria, along with the rest of North Africa, falls to Moslem conquerors from Arabia. Islam takes root

11th cent.: Saharan nomads sweep into the country and destroy farms and pastures, forcing the coastal Berbers into seafaring and piracy. The Berbers spread through North Africa and, in the Moorish Conquest, move to the Iberian peninsula to occupy much of Spain

16th cent.: Spain gains a foothold in Algeria and Algerians turn to Turkish corsairs for help in 1518. Turkish rule is established

1830: France sends an expedition to pacify turbulent tribes along the coast and in the interior. French naval forces seize Algiers, depose the bey, and establish French rule

1942: Allies invade North Africa during World War II

1954-61: Discontent with French rule erupts in a widespread rebellion. Rebel leaders form a "provisional government of Algeria" in Cairo, but the fighting continues until the opening of peace talks with the French

1962-63: Algeria becomes an independent republic. Benyoussef Ben Khedda, premier of the provisional government in exile, takes control but is ousted by Vice-Premier Ahmed Ben Bella who later becomes President under one-party constitution

1965: A military revolt led by Colonel Houari Boumédienne overthrows Ben Bella. A revolutionary council assumes power; Ben Bella placed in "comfortable" confinement

1967-68: Algeria declares war on Israel, but no Algerian troops take part in Middle East fighting. Boumédienne fosters closer economic and military ties with USSR

1969: Algeria accuses U.S. State Department and CIA of involvement in a conspiracy to overthrow the government

1971: French oil companies in Algeria partly nationalized; France ends "special relations" with Algeria

1973: The United States arranges to import 1 billion cubic feet of Algerian liquefied natural gas daily for 25 years

1974: Algeria resumes diplomatic relations with U.S. after severance in 1967

1976: Algerian troops clash with Moroccan and Mauritanian forces in Western Sahara. New constitution approved and elections held. Boumédienne elected President

1978: Boumédienne dies

1979: Chadli Bendjedid elected President

1980: Ben Bella is freed after 15 years' imprisonment

ANDORRA

Area: 188 sq. mi. **Population:** 31,000 (1979 est.)

Official Name: Principality of Andorra **Capital:** Andorra la Vella **Nationality:** Andorran **Languages:** Catalan is the official language. French and Spanish are also spoken **Religion:** Roman Catholic **Flag:** Vertical blue, yellow, and red stripes, with the national coat of arms in the center **Anthem:** The Great Charlemagne **Currency:** French franc (5.2 per U.S. $1) and Spanish peseta (89.2 per U.S. $1)

Location: Eastern Pyrenees, between France and Spain **Features:** Drained by the Valira River, Andorra consists of narrow valleys and gorges, bounded by high peaks **Chief Rivers:** Valira

Head of State: Andorra is a co-principality under the joint sovereignty of the president of France and the Spanish bishop of Urgel, each of whom is represented by a viguier, or agent **Head of Government:** Syndic-General Estanislau Sangrà Font, elected 1978 **Legislative Body:** Parliament (unicameral General Council) **Effective Date of Present Constitution:** 1866 Plan of Reform **Local Government:** 7 parishes, each with an elected council

Ethnic Composition: Native Andorrans, who constitute one-third of the population, are of Catalan stock. The rest of the population is primarily Spanish and French **Population Distribution:** 81% urban **Density:** 165 inhabitants per sq. mi. **Largest Towns:** (1977 est.) Andorra la Vella 19,764, Sant Julià 3,510, Encamp 2,268

Per Capita Income: N.A. **Gross National Product (GNP):** N.A. **Economic Statistics:** Tourism is the chief source of income. Cereals, potatoes, livestock raising and tobacco are dominant, while tobacco processing is the chief industry. Timber production and building are also important activities. There is considerable smuggling of merchandise shipped between France and Spain **Minerals and Mining:** Small amounts of iron ore and lead are mined **Labor Force:** 9,500, with about 80% in local industries and 20% in agriculture **Foreign Trade:** Principal exports are timber, cattle and derivatives, and furniture; the chief imports are fuel, perfumes, clothing, radio and television sets. Imports in 1979 totaled $840 million **Principal Trade Partners:** France, Spain

Vital Statistics: Birthrate, 16.5 per 1,000 of pop. (1976); death rate, 5.0 **Life Expectancy:** 70 years **Health Statistics:** N.A. **Infant Mortality:** .16 per 1,000 births **Illiteracy:** negligible **Primary and Secondary School Enrollment:** 5,555 (1975) **Enrollment in Higher Education:** N.A. **GNP Expended on Education:** N.A.

Transportation: Surfaced roads total 77 mi. **Motor Vehicles:** 9,346 (1970) **Passenger Cars:** 8,200 (1969) **Railway Mileage:** None **Ports:** None **Major Airlines:** No air service **Communications:** Privately owned **Radio Stations:** 4 **Licenses:** 6,600 (1976) **Television Stations:** None **Receivers:** 3,000 (1976) **Telephones:** 4,000 (1977) **Newspapers:** One daily established in 1974

Weights and Measures: Metric system **Travel Requirements:** See *France* **International Dialing Code:** 33

Modern tourism, bringing about a million visitors a year, has altered the formerly leisurely pace of life in Andorra. And the pace is destined to quicken even more with easier access to the tiny state in the fastness of the Pyrenees, for France is building a modern highway to Andorra from Toulouse, by way of Foix, on the Ariège River.

Motoring tourists—and automobile traffic in general—are especially important to Andorra, which obtains more than a third of its revenue from gasoline taxes and automobile fines. Tourism as an industry supplements Andorran wool-combing, spinning, tobacco processing, and the manufacture of sandals. Smuggling of goods from France into Spain is also a substantial industry.

What draws tourists is the attraction of towering passes; peaks topped with snow as late as June; a countryside dotted with sheep, goats, and mules; and bargains. Despite the state's need of revenue, there is no income tax.

HISTORY: According to tradition, Charlemagne granted the people of Andorra a charter because of their help in battling the Moors. In 843 Charles the Bald made the Spanish count of Urgel overlord of Andorra. In 1278 the bishop of Urgel was made joint suzerain after contending that Andorra was part of the endowment of his cathedral. The rights of the count eventually passed by inheritance to Henry IV of France and eventually to the presidents of France

1793: French revolutionary government renounces its claims to Andorra

1806: Napoleon restores co-principality at Andorrans' request

1933: Suffrage is granted to all men over the age of 25

1941: Suffrage is restricted to heads of families

1970: Limited women's suffrage granted

1971: New bishop of Urgel installed as the 80th co-prince

1977: Personal income tax voted by the General Council

ANGOLA

Area: 481,351 sq. mi. **Population:** 7,000,000 (1978 est.)

Official Name: People's Republic of Angola **Capital:** Luanda **Nationality:** Angolan **Languages:** Portuguese is the official language. A number of African languages, chiefly of Bantu origin, are commonly spoken **Religion:** Animist 84%, Roman Catholic 12%, Protestant 4% **Flag:** Two equal horizontal stripes of red over black, with yellow five-pointed star, machete, and half a cogwheel in the center **Anthem:** N.A. **Currency:** Kwanza (49.3 per U.S. $1)

Location: West-central Africa. Bounded by the Atlantic Ocean on the west, Namibia on the south, and Zaire and Zambia on the north and east. The exclave of Cabinda lies on the Atlantic coast north of the Congo River mouth **Features:** A narrow coastal strip rises sharply toward an interior plateau, which ranges from 3,000 to 5,000 feet in elevation. A highland area of 6,000 to 7,000 feet lies in the west-central region. Cabinda consists of a low-lying rain forest **Chief Rivers:** Cubango, Cuanza, Cunene, Cuango, Cassai, Cuando, Congo, Cuito

Head of State and of Government: President: José Eduardo dos Santos, born 1942, elected 1979 **Effective Date of Present Constitution:** 1975 **Legislative Body:** National People's Assembly with 206 members **Local Government:** 18 provinces, under appointed commissars

Ethnic Composition: Predominantly indigenous Bantus, with the Ovimbundu constituting 38%, Kimbundu 23%, Bakongo 13%. Only 30,000 Portuguese remained at independence **Population Distribution:** N.A. **Density:** 14.5 inhabitants per sq. mi.

Largest Cities: (1972 est.) Luanda 540,000; (1970 census) Huambo 61,885; Lobito 59,528; Benguela 40,996; Lubango 31,674; Malanje 31,599; Cabinda 21,124

Per Capita Income: $442 (1979) **Gross National Product (GNP):** $2.9 billion (1979) **Economic Statistics:** The economy remains heavily dependent upon agriculture (subsistence and cash crops such as coffee, sisal, cotton, wheat, sugar, and tobacco, with fish and timber of importance). Industry (cement, oil refining, paper, agricultural processing, and metal products) has declined since independence **Minerals and Mining:** Iron ore and diamonds are exploited, and petroleum is being produced in the Cabinda exclave **Labor Force:** Total currently unknown, with an estimated 80% in agriculture, and 10% in industry **Foreign Trade:** Exports, chiefly petroleum, coffee, iron ore, diamonds, cotton, and fish meal, totaled $840 million in 1977. Imports, mainly machinery, textiles, transportation and construction equipment, iron and steel products, rice, and electrical products, totaled $680 million **Principal Trade Partners:** Cuba, USSR, Portugal, United States

Vital Statistics: Birthrate, 47.2 per 1,000 of pop. (1975); death rate, 27 (1974) **Life Expectancy:** 38.5 years **Health Statistics:** 322 inhabitants per hospital bed; 15,404 per physician (1972) **Infant Mortality:** 24.1 per 1,000 births **Illiteracy:** 85% **Education Statistics:** N.A. **Higher Education:** N.A. **GNP Expended on Education:** N.A.

Transportation: Surfaced roads total 8,371 mi. (1974) **Motor Vehicles:** 183,031 (1973) **Passenger Cars:** 127,271 **Railway Mileage:** 1,895 **Ports:** Lobito, Luanda, Moçamades, Cabinda **Major Airlines:** TAAG (Angolan Airlines) **Communications:** Government owned **Radio Transmitters:** 19 (1972) **Receivers:** 116,000 (1976) **Television Transmitters:** 1 **Telephones:** 31,000 (1976) **Newspapers:** 1 daily, 2 copies per 1,000 inhabitants (1975)

Weights and Measures: Metric system **Travel Requirements:** No U.S. representation in Angola. Contact Angola UN Mission in New York for travel information

Fifteen years of rebellion against colonial rule culminated in the granting of Angolan independence by Portugal on November 11, 1975. However, independence did not bring peace to Angola, the largest and most important territory of the former Portuguese overseas empire. Three factions contended for power in this resource-rich country: the Marxist-oriented Popular Movement for the Liberation of Angola (MPLA), the pro-Western National Front for the Liberation of Angola (FNLA), and the pro-Western National Union for the Total Independence of Angola (UNITA). The MPLA, backed by the Soviet Union and Cuba, held the Angolan capital, Luanda, while the pro-Western forces occupied most of the country north and south of the capital.

Initially, following independence, the pro-Western FNLA and UNITA forces scored military successes against the Marxist MPLA in the central area around Luanda. Both sides employed foreign troops in their fight for full control of the nation. Particularly important was the contribution to the MPLA of trained manpower by Cuba and of arms by the USSR. South African armed forces crossed into Angola from Namibia (South-West Africa) to aid the FNLA and UNITA.

In late November of 1975 the military tide turned in favor of the MPLA as a result of the massive Soviet and Cuban assistance. The situation grew increasingly grim for the pro-Western factions on December 19 when the U.S. Senate voted to cut off covert financial aid to the combatants. By mid-February 1976 the MPLA forces had overrun most of Angola. However, UNITA and FNLA continued to wage guerrilla warfare. South African troops withdrew into Namibia but have since continued to launch air and land attacks on SWAPO (South-West African People's Organization) units based in Angola.

The violent conditions of this period resulted in the flight of most of the Portuguese population. The departure of the educationally and technically advanced segment of Angolan society resulted in a drastic decline in the economic life of the country.

The leader of the MPLA, Agostinho Neto, a poet and doctor, became president of independent Angola in November 1975. Faced with massive economic problems, he sought better relations with Western governments, but because of the continued presence of Cuban troops in the country, the United States withheld diplomatic relations.

Although Angola has good agricultural land, food and clothing, as well as other goods, are in short supply. Many small farmers produce only enough for themselves; why raise crops to sell when they can't buy anything with the money? Swelling revenues from oil wells off the shore of Cabinda, however, have made possible increasing imports of food and of machinery and raw materials needed for an industrial revival.

HISTORY: Prior to the coming of the Portuguese in 1483, present-day Angola was part of the African Kingdom of the Kongo. During the 16th century Portugal established trading posts along the coast and exploited Angola as a prime source of the lucrative slave trade. The Dutch captured and held the Angolan port cities for seven years until the Portuguese recaptured them in 1648

1884-85: At Berlin Conference the Portuguese receive "right of occupation" to Angola while losing all claims in central Africa
1910-20: Portugal begins serious colonizing effort in Angola
1926: Portuguese Republic overthrown. Subsequent authoritarian regime of Salazar tightens Portuguese rule over colony
1961: Rebellion against Portugal breaks out, beginning 15-year violent struggle for independence
1962: UN General Assembly votes condemnation of Portuguese administration of colonies
1975: Portugal grants Angolan independence. Rival factions battle for supremacy
1976: Marxist MPLA group wins control of Angola
1978: Cuban troops lead government offensive against pro-Western guerrillas
1979: President Neto dies Sept. 10 and is succeeded by his Minister of Planning, José Eduardo dos Santos, a Soviet-educated petroleum engineer. Government steps up operations against the guerrillas
1980: MPLA launches purge of all anti-Marxist elements. Benguela railway is reopened for first time since 1975, but is still subject to disruptive UNITA attacks
1981: Angola links departure of Cuban force of 20,000 to independence for Namibia. Economic relations with Western countries expand as those with Soviet bloc remain firm

ARGENTINA

Area: 1,068,296 sq. mi. **Population:** 27,862,771 (1980 census)

Official Name: Argentine Republic **Capital:** Buenos Aires **Nationality:** Argentine **Languages:** Spanish is the official and principal language. Italian, French, and German are also frequently heard **Religion:** About 95% of the population belongs to the Roman Catholic Church, which is officially recognized in the Constitution. There are small minorities of Protestants and Jews **Flag:** Horizontal stripes of blue, white, and blue, with the sun on the white stripe **Anthem:** Argentine National Anthem, beginning "Hear, mortals, the sacred cry of Liberty" **Currency:** New Argentine peso (3,165 per U.S. $1)

Location: Southern South America. Argentina is bordered on the north by Bolivia and Paraguay, on the northeast by Brazil and Uruguay, on the east and south by the Atlantic Ocean, and on the west by Chile **Features:** The heartland of Argentina is the rich, temperate plains area known as the Pampas, which fans out from the east-central sector of the country. The north consists of sub-tropical lowlands, while the west is dominated by the Andean Mountains and the south by the Patagonian steppe and the rainy Tierra del Fuego **Chief Rivers:** Paraná, Negro, Salado, Colorado, Chubut

Head of State and Government: President: Lt. Gen. Roberto Edùardo Viola, born 1924, took office on March 29, 1981, following his selection by the military junta on Oct. 3, 1980. The 3-man junta is the supreme ruling body of the state. The president is assisted by a mixed civilian-military cabinet **Effective Date of Present Constitution:** Although the constitution of 1853 is still in effect, its provisions have been made subject to the Statutes of the Revolution, issued after a military coup in 1966 and to other changes following the 1976 coup **Legislative Body:** The National Congress was dissolved in 1976 **Local Government:** 22 provinces, 1 national territory, and 1 federal district, each administered by an appointed governor

Ethnic Composition: 97% of the population is of European origin; persons of Arab descent, Indians and mestizos constitute about 3% **Population Distribution:** 81.1% urban (1975) **Density:** 26 inhabitants per sq. mi.

Largest Cities (M.A. = Metropolitan Area): Buenos Aires (1980 census) 2,908,001 (M.A. 9,749,000—1978 est.); others (1970 census) Córdoba 781,565 (M.A. 790,508), Rosario 750,455 (M.A. 806,942), Lanús 449,824, Lomas de Zamora 410,806, La Plata 391,247 (M.A. 478,666)

Per Capita Income: $2,089 (1980) **Gross National Product (GNP):** $57 billion (1980) **Economic Statistics:** In 1975, 48% of the GNP came from trade and services; 36% from industry (iron and steel, automobiles, machinery, chemicals, cement); 11% from agriculture (meat, hides, grain, fruits); and 8% from mining and construction **Minerals and Mining:** Oil and natural gas supply domestic needs; copper, low-grade iron ore and small amounts of coal, lead, zinc, silver, bismuth, vanadium, beryllium, tantalite, and tungsten are mined **Labor Force:** 9,928,234 in 1975, of which 29% is employed in manufacturing and 15% in agriculture; approximately 2.5 million are organized in unions **Foreign Trade:** Exports, chiefly grains, meat, wool, hides, linseed oil and other agricultural products totaled $7.8 billion in 1979. Imports, mainly machinery and equipment, iron and steel products, chemicals, textiles and fuels, totaled $6.7 billion **Principal Trade Partners:** United States, Brazil, West Germany, Netherlands, Italy, Britain, Japan, USSR

Vital Statistics: Birthrate, 21.8 per 1,000 of pop. (1975); death rate, 8.8 **Life Expectancy:** 68 years **Health Statistics:** 176 inhabitants per hospital bed; 479 per physician (1972) **Infant Mortality:** 59 per 1,000 births (1970) **Illiteracy:** 7% **Primary and Secondary School Enrollment:** 4,945,515 (1977) **Enrollment in Higher Education:** 619,950 **GNP Expended on Education:** 1.6% (1976)

Transportation: Paved roads total 23,000 mi. (1975) **Motor Vehicles:** 3,500,000 (1976) **Passenger Cars:** 2,160,000 (1974) **Railway Mileage:** 25,794 **Ports:** Buenos Aires, Bahía Blanca, La Plata, Rosario **Major Airlines:** Aerollneas Argentinas is the major international and domestic carrier **Communications:** Partly government owned **Radio Transmitters:** 163 (1974) **Receivers:** 26,000,000 (1973) **Television Transmitters:** 82 **Receivers:** 4,500,000 (1974) **Telephones:** 2,400,000 (1976) **Newspapers:** 167 dailies, 179 copies per 1,000 inhabitants (1974)

Weights and Measures: Metric system **Travel Requirements:** Passport and visa required. Check embassy or consulate for specific requirements. No fee **International Dialing Code:** 54

Extending 2,300 miles from north to south and with an Atlantic coastline 1,600 miles long, Argentina is the second-largest country on the South American continent, after Brazil. Its topography and climate are as varied as those of the United States, the terrain ranging from the subtropical lowlands of the north to the towering Andean Mountains in the west and the bleak Patagonian steppe and rainy Tierra del Fuego in the south. More than 60 percent of the country's area is suitable for agriculture, of which about 8 percent is under cultivation and the remainder is pastureland upon which a massive livestock population thrives (there are currently more than two animals for every Argentine man, woman and child). The heartland of Argentina is the rich, temperate plains area known as the Pampas, which fans out for almost 500 miles from Buenos Aires in the east-central sector; here is found some of the richest topsoil in the world.

Politically, the dominant factor of life in Argentina has been turmoil. In the early months of 1976, Argentina was a country on the edge of anarchy, racked by daily kidnappings and bombings. Its treasury, down to its last foreign reserves, was about to default on its overseas debt. Then, on March 24, in a bloodless coup led by the Commander in Chief of the army, Jorge Rafael Videla, the military deposed Isabel Perón, the first woman chief of state in the Americas, from the presidency, her inept government falling along with her.

Mrs. Perón had come into power on the death of her husband, Juan Perón, in July 1974. He had returned to Argentina in June 1973, after 18 years of exile, which had been preceded by an 11-year rule as Argentina's president. He was reelected to the presidency in September of that year, with his wife as vice-president.

After the ouster of Mrs. Perón, Videla was sworn in as president on March 29, 1976. The final executive power was entrusted to a military junta that set two goals: crushing terrorism and reviving the economy. Despite the opposition of President Videla and other moderates there followed a wave of uncontrolled kidnappings and arrests by security forces of the army. In 1981 a report of the United Nations Human Rights Commission stated that Argentina accounted for more than half of 11,000 to 13,000 people reported missing around the world. Amnesty International has placed the number of missing in Argentina as high as 15,000 to 20,000. Adolfo Pérez Esquivel, an Argentine champion of human rights who had formerly been held in jail for more than a year without being charged with any crime, was awarded the Nobel Peace Prize in 1980. He accepted it in the name of the missing persons.

A new "Professional Associations Law," aimed at curbing the political thrust of the trade unions, which were the backbone of Peronist power, took effect Nov. 16, 1979.

In October 1980 the military junta nominated Gen. Roberto Edùardo Viola to succeed President Videla. Viola, a moderate opposed by hardline members of the military, had retired as Commander in Chief of the army in December 1979 to pave the way for this designation. He was sworn in for a three-year term on March 29, 1981, with the understanding that he would share power with the junta pending the restoration of a "republican and representative democracy." Viola said he was committed to follow the political and economic policies that had been initiated under Videla's administration, but he gave no timetable for return to civilian rule. Seven of the 13 members appointed to his cabinet, including the foreign minister, were civilians.

On the economic front the government's program scored some successes, notably in boosting agricultural production, expanding hydroelectric and nuclear power facilities, achieving a very favorable trade balance and a nearly balanced budget, and reducing the inflation rate to less than 100 percent for the first time in years. The government also has contracted with West German and Swiss firms to supply major components for facilities which will give Argentina full control over its nuclear fuel cycle, which generates a growing share of the nation's electric power. However, in 1980-81 some of the country's largest industrial and banking concerns suffered financial collapse as a result of economic dislocations.

HISTORY: The treeless plains of the Pampas were inhabited by fierce nomadic Indian tribes of unknown origin for centuries before 1516, when a band of eight conquistadors led by Juan Díaz de Solís landed on the shores of Río de la Plata. Magellan and Sebastian Cabot soon followed on other voyages of exploration and in 1580 Juan de Garay reached what is now Buenos Aires by way of Paraguay. By the 18th century Buenos Aires had become the capital of a vast Spanish viceroyalty that included Argentina

1810: Argentine revolutionists depose Spanish viceroy and form their own government

1817-19: General José de San Martín crosses the Andes with 5,000 men, defeats Spanish crown forces at Battle of Maipú (1818), and goes on to liberate Chile and Peru. New Argentine constitution sets off civil war between "federalists" and "unitarians," with the latter favoring a central government dominated by Buenos Aires

1829: Juan Manuel de Rosas, the federalist leader, establishes one-man rule

1845-52: Rosas interferes in neighboring countries; aided by Brazil, Uruguay, France and Britain, Justo José de Urquiza overthrows Rosas, who flees to England

1880-81: Long struggle between Buenos Aires and federalist forces ends, with the city becoming a federal district; settlers end Indians' resistance by virtually wiping them out

1916-30: Period of vast immigration and prosperity begins; Hipólito Irigoyen, leader of the Radicals, a bourgeois reform party, is elected president and enacts wide social-reform legislation. He is succeeded in 1922 by another Radical, but returns to power in 1928. Two years later he is overthrown by the military

1943-45: The latest in a string of military coups places Colonel Juan Domingo Perón in a relatively unimportant post as labor secretary. Perón, effecting sweeping social and economic reforms, wins popularity among masses; he is thrown in jail by frightened military men. Released after nine days, Perón asks for election

1946: Perón wins election. A widower, he takes as his second wife Eva Duarte, a radio star, who helps Perón establish trade unions along militant, Fascist lines

1952-55: Eva Perón dies (1952); Perón, unsettled, faces charges of immorality and corruption. After thwarting several coups, he is overthrown and makes his way to Spain

1973: Following a long succession of civilian and military presidents, Perón returns from exile on June 20 and, running on a coalition ticket, is elected president in September

1974: Perón dies and is succeeded by his wife, Isabel Perón

1976: Coup topples Mrs. Perón's government. Argentina is governed by a junta led by Gen. Jorge Rafael Videla

1979: Jacobo Timerman, publisher of *La Opinión* and outspoken critic of the government, is exiled

1980: Argentina defies U.S. call for grain embargo against USSR. Works of art valued at $25 million are stolen on Christmas day from the National Museum in Buenos Aires

1981: Gen. Roberto Eduardo Viola is sworn in as president on March 29. Mrs. Perón is convicted on charges of diverting charity and flood-relief funds to her own account while in office. She is sentenced to eight years in prison and later released on parole. Argentina and the United States move to improve relations

AUSTRALIA

Area: 2,967,909 sq. mi. **Population:** 14,567,000 (1980 est.)

Official Name: Commonwealth of Australia **Capital:** Canberra **Nationality:** Australian **Languages:** English **Religion:** 36% Anglican, 31% Roman Catholic, 10% Methodist, 9% Presbyterian, 2% Baptist, 12% others **Flag:** A blue field, witli the Union Jack in the upper left corner, a large, 7-pointed white star directly beneath, and five smaller white stars in the right half **Anthem:** God Save the Queen **National Song:** Advance Australia Fair **Currency:** Australian dollar (0.87 per U.S. $1)

Location: An island continent between the Indian and Pacific oceans, lying southeast of Asia. It is bounded on the north by the Torres Strait and the Timor Sea, on the east by the Coral and Tasman seas, and on the south and west by the Indian Ocean. The continent and the island of Tasmania, off the eastern part of the south coast, make up the Commonwealth of Australia **Features:** The continent is roughly a low, irregular plateau, with a flat, arid center. The southeastern quarter of the continent is a huge fertile plain covering some 500,000 sq. mi. Relatively low mountains lie close to the east coast **Chief Rivers:** Murray, Darling, Murrumbidgee, Burdekin, Fitzroy, Ord

Head of State: Queen Elizabeth II, represented by a governor-general, Sir Zelman Cowen, born 1919, appointed 1977 **Head of Government:** Prime Minister John Malcolm Fraser, born 1930, took office in 1975 **Effective Date of Present Constitution:** 1900 **Legislative Body:** Federal Parliament (bicameral), consisting of a Senate and House of Representatives. There are 64 Senators, elected for 6-year terms. The House consists of 124 members, elected every 3 years **Local Government:** 6 states, each headed by a governor appointed by the sovereign and with an elected legislature, premier, and a cabinet. There is also one internal territory, one capital territory, and six external territories

Ethnic Composition: The population is mainly of British origin; Aborigines (excluding mixed-bloods) number 40,000 **Population Distribution:** 86% urban **Density:** 4.9 inhabitants per sq. mi.

Largest Cities (Metropolitan Area): (1976 census) Sydney 3,021,300, Melbourne 2,603,000, Brisbane 957,000, Adelaide 900,000, Perth 805,000, Canberra 215,400, Hobart 162,000

Per Capita Income: $9,115 (1980) **Gross Domestic Product (GDP):** $133 billion (1980) **Economic Statistics:** About 30% of GDP comes from industry (steel, automobiles, ships, textiles, chemicals, petroleum refining, electrical equipment). Agriculture and mining, however, are the mainstays of the economy. Australia is the world's foremost wool-growing country, producing almost one-third of the world's wool, and is a leading producer of meats and dairy products. Mining, which accounts for 3% of GDP, plays an important role in the country's export trade **Minerals and Mining:** Australia is a major world producer of coal, iron ore, bauxite, copper, gold, silver, tin, nickel, lead, zinc, manganese, antimony, cobalt, titanium, salt and uranium. A major diamond field is to be exploited. Australian wells provide 50% of the nation's crude oil requirements. About 90% of indigenous oil production is from offshore wells in the Bass Strait, discovered in 1964 and estimated to have reserves of 1,500 million barrels. There have been several natural gas finds; reserves are estimated at 20 trillion cu. ft. of gas **Labor Force:** 6.2 million (1978), of which 22% is employed in manufacturing, 6% in agriculture, and 51% in services **Foreign Trade:** Exports, chiefly wool, wheat, meat, dairy products, iron ore and other minerals, totaled $18.7 billion in 1979. Imports, mainly machinery and transportation equipment, manufactured goods, chemicals, mineral fuels, crude materials, food and beverages, totaled $18.3 billion **Principal Trade Partners:** Japan, United States, Britain, West Germany, New Zealand, Canada, Singapore, France, USSR

Vital Statistics: Birthrate, 15.7 per 1,000 of pop. (1978); death rate, 7.6 **Life Expectancy:** 71 years **Health Statistics:** 80 inhabitants per hospital bed; 600 per physician (1975) **Infant Mortality:** 12.2 per 1,000 births **Illiteracy:** Negligible **Primary and secondary school enrollment:** 2,725,463 (1976) **Enrollment in Higher Education:** 274,738 (1975) **GNP Expended on Education:** 6.3% (1975)

Transportation: Paved roads total 261,170 mi. (1973) **Motor Vehicles:** 6,880,000 (1977) **Passenger Cars:** 5,550,000 **Railway Mileage:** 25,166 **Ports:** Sydney, Melbourne, Newcastle, Port Kembla, Fremantle, Port Hedland, Port Adelaide, Dampier, Brisbane **Major Airlines:** Qantas Airways is the major interna-tional carrier; domestic flights are operated by Trans-Austra-lia Airlines and the privately-owned Ansett Airlines of Australia **Communications:** Both government and privately owned **Radio Transmitters:** 219 **Receivers:** 10,500,000 (1976) **Television Transmitters:** 198 **Receivers:** 4,785,000 (1976) **Telephones:** 6,677,000 (1979) **Newspapers:** 70 dailies, 394 copies per 1,000 inhabitants (1975)

Weights and Measures: British standards are being replaced by the metric system **Travel Requirements:** Passport; visa valid for 48 months or life of passport; no fee **International Dialing Code:** 61

Political and economic pressures of the postwar era, enhanced by the communications revolution of the times, have propelled Australia out of easygoing isolation into an increasing involvement in world and regional affairs.

Australia is one of the foremost donors of foreign aid compared with the national income. Much of this aid goes to Papua New Guinea, which became independent on September 16, 1975. The emergence of new independent island states in the South Pacific has thrust demands for leadership on Australia as the most advanced and affluent power in its geopolitical sphere.

Ties between Australians and the "mother country," Britain, loosened significantly in World War II when it became clear that the hard-pressed British forces were unable to defend Australia against the Japanese onslaught. Americans filled the breach, and from that time on the Australians have looked toward the United States as the guarantor of national security. The new relationship was cemented after the war in the ANZUS (Australia, New Zealand, United States) Treaty of Mutual Security.

Japan has emerged as Australia's foremost customer overseas, taking more than one-fourth of the country's total exports. Japan's late Prime Minister Masayoshi Ohira, in a 1979 visit, expressed hopes for making further deals for long-term supply of raw materials and discussed formation of a Pacific Basin Community.

Assistance to the country's 40,000 full-blood aborigines and 150,000 part-aborigines has been stepped up, but advancement programs have foundered because of administrative problems. Aborigines have been demanding a greater say in their own affairs. In November 1978, the government agreed to grant Northern Territory aborigines a 4.25 percent royalty (estimated $11 million per year) on uranium oxide extracted from a ranger site.

The application of postwar technology to the exploitation of vast mineral resources revolutionized the Australian economy. By the 1970s, Australia had become the leading supplier of lead and zinc, the chief iron ore exporter and furnished 90 percent of the world's rutile and zircon.

At the outset of the 1980s, the country was literally riding a minerals boom as the world sought energy sources other than costly oil. Ranked second (behind the U.S.) in coal exports, Australia was expected to advance to No. 1 in a few years. Uranium, shale, and natural gas exports also were to rise sharply. It was announced in 1980 that a diamond field discovered two years earlier in Western Australia was one of the world's largest and richest, with "pipes" larger than any in South Africa. About 60% of the stones are of gem quality.

Development of underground wealth required massive importation of capital, principally from Japan, Britain and the United States. A major consequence has been a nationalist backlash against the extent of foreign ownership of business, particularly in the mining industry. The government therefore assumed the right to veto foreign takeover bids for Australian companies and to supervise mineral exportation negotiations

Progress in manufacturing was less impressive as Australia entered the 1980's, the heavily protected auto industry being especially troubled. Prime Minister Malcolm Fraser's conservative-leaning coalition government, installed in 1975, emerged from the October 1980 elections with only a bare majority in the House of Representatives

HISTORY: Long before it was first sighted by European explorers in the 17th century, Australia was inhabited by primitive native groups with various languages and customs. In 1770, Captain James Cook explored the east coast of the continent and claimed it for Britain. Within 50 years, the whole of Australia became a British dependency, serving as a penal colony and dumping ground for British criminals and undesirables

1851-59: Gold strikes in Victoria and New South Wales in 1851 attract thousands of new settlers; within two decades the rising population is settled in six self-governing colonies

1901: Constitution providing for federation of colonies is approved by British Parliament; Commonwealth of Australia comes into being

1914-18: Australia fights on Allied side during World War I

1939-45: Australia fights alongside Allies in World War II

1946-48: Immigrants, numbering 2 million by 1965, begin to pour into Australia

1952-54: Australia signs Pacific defense pact (ANZUS) with New Zealand and United States and joins SEATO

1972: The first Labor Party government in 23 years is elected, recognizes the People's Republic of China

1975: The Labor Party government is dismissed. Liberal-Country Party coalition government is elected by a large majority vote. Papua New Guinea is granted independence

1977: Liberal-Country Party government of Prime Minister Malcolm Fraser decisively reelected

1978: One of the world's richest diamond fields is found in Western Australia

1979: January cyclone devastates north Queensland

1980: Liberal-Country Party coalition loses Senate to Labor Party opposition, but retains control of government with reduced majority in the House

1981: Ties to U.S. strengthened with agreement to allow American B-52s to refuel at Darwin

AUSTRIA

Area: 32,375 sq. mi. **Population:** 7,505,000 (1980 est.)
Official Name: Republic of Austria **Capital:** Vienna **Nationality:** Austrian **Languages:** German is the official and principal language. Slovenian, Croatian, and Hungarian are spoken by small minorities **Religion:** 90% Roman Catholic **Flag:** Red, white, and red horizontal stripes, with the national emblem centered on the white stripe **Anthem:** Land of Mountains, Land on the River **Currency:** Schilling (15.7 per U.S. $1)
Location: Central Europe. Landlocked Austria is bordered by West Germany and Czechoslovakia on the north, Hungary on the east, Yugoslavia and Italy on the south, and Switzerland and Liechtenstein on the west **Features:** The country is 70% mountainous, with the Alps and their outliers dominating the west and south. The east and Vienna are located in the Danube basin **Chief Rivers:** Danube, Inn, Mur, Drau, Enns

Head of State: President Rudolf Kirchschlaeger, born 1915, reelected 1980 **Head of Government:** Chancellor Bruno Kreisky, born 1911, took office April 1970, reappointed May 1979 **Effective Date of Present Constitution:** 1920, reinstated 1945 **Legislative Body:** Federal Assembly (bicameral parliament), consisting of the Federal Council (upper house), or *Bundesrat*, with 58 members, and the National Council (lower house), or *Nationalrat*, with 183 members. Members of the Upper House are appointed by provincial diets for 4- to 6-year terms; members of the Lower House are elected for 4 years **Local Government:** 9 provinces, each administered by an elected governor and provincial legislature

Ethnic Composition: Austrians are generally of South Germanic stock, with Slavic admixtures. The only sizeable minority group consists of some 70,000 Slovenes in Carinthia **Population Distribution:** 52% urban **Density:** 232 inhabitants per sq. mi.

Largest Cities: (1976 est.) Vienna 1,592,800, Graz 250,893, Linz 208,000, Salzburg 139,000, Innsbruck 120,355

Per Capita Income: $7,127 (1980) **Gross Domestic Product (GDP):** $53 billion (1980) **Economic Statistics:** About 61% of GDP comes from industry (machinery, iron and steel, food and beverages, electronics, chemicals, textiles, ceramics, stone and glass, and metal goods); 5% from agriculture and forestry **Minerals and Mining:** Iron ore, petroleum, magnesite, lignite, and natural gas **Labor Force:** 2,700,000 (1978), of which 60% is employed in commerce and industry, 14% in agriculture, and 26% in services **Foreign Trade:** Exports, mainly machinery, iron and steel, textiles, chemicals, wood and paper, totaled $15 billion in 1979. Imports, chiefly machinery, transportation equipment, textiles, mineral fuels and chemicals, totaled $20 billion **Principal Trade Partners:** West Germany, Switzerland, Italy, Britain, United States, Sweden, Netherlands, France, USSR, Poland, Yugoslavia

Vital Statistics: Birthrate, 11.3 per 1,000 of pop. (1977); death rate, 12.2 **Life Expectancy:** 73 years **Health Statistics:** 88 inhabitants per hospital bed; 444 per physician (1976) **Infant Mortality:** 16.9 per 1,000 births (1977) **Illiteracy:** Negligible **Primary and Secondary School Enrollment:** 1,263,298 (1976) **Enrollment in Higher Education:** 104,525 (1975) **GNP Expended on Education:** 5.7% (1976)

Transportation: Surfaced roads total 20,357 mi. **Motor Vehicles:** 2,337,400 (1977) **Passenger Cars:** 1,865,300 **Railway Mileage:** 4,081 **Ports:** None **Major Airlines:** Austrian Airlines operates international and domestic flights **Communications:** Government owned **Radio Transmitters:** 399 **Licenses:** 2,185,000 (1976) **Television Transmitters:** 461 **Licenses:** 1,772,000 (1976) **Telephones:** 2,281,000 (1976) **Newspapers:** 30 dailies, 320 copies per 1,000 inhabitants (1975)

Weights and Measures: Metric system **Travel Requirements:** Passport, no visa for 3 months **International Dialing Code:** 43

Once the core of the Hapsburg Empire that covered much of Central and Southern Europe, Austria has been reduced by wars to a relatively small state and, by its geographical position, to a land that is officially neutral between East and West. But its actual sympathies and economic ties lie with the West.

Because Austria was forced by Hitler's 1938 *Anschluss* to become part of the Nazi war machine, the victors of World War II granted it a special state treaty in 1955, which specified the country's official neutrality.

But most of Austria's trade is with Western Europe. After the European Economic Community

(EC) was organized in 1958, Austria sought association with it, despite the objections of the Soviet Union, which argued that association was incompatible with neutrality. Austria joined the European Free Trade Association in 1960, and, over token Soviet opposition, negotiated a special agreement with the EC in 1973.

Internal politics have been influenced by an almost equal division of voting strength between the People's party—which professes Christian values and respect for property—and the Socialist party. From 1945 to 1966, the People's party had a plurality, but not a majority, in the *Nationalrat* and governed in coalition with the Socialists. The two parties made this arrangement because neither trusted the small Freedom party, which held the rest of the seats, and because memories of the chaos of the 1930s caused a desire for stability. This "grand coalition" ended in 1966, when a special election gave the People's party a one-seat majority; the Socialists were offered a coalition, but imposed conditions which the winners thought unreasonable. In 1970 the Socialists won a plurality, but not a majority, and formed a minority government with Bruno Kreisky as chancellor after attempts to reorganize the grand coalition broke down. This government remained in office after winning majorities in the elections of 1971, 1975 and 1979. There is little real difference between the parties, and the economy has remained basically capitalist, but with much state intervention.

Aside from the basic industries, an important source of income in Austria is tourism, as visitors are attracted to Alpine ski slopes and lakes and to city attractions such as the summer festival in Mozart's native city, Salzburg, and the spring festival week in Vienna.

HISTORY: Austria was settled by various tribes in prehistoric times and was subject to numerous invasions long before the Roman conquest around 15 B.C. About A.D. 800 it became a province of Charlemagne's empire and was joined to the Holy Roman Empire two centuries later. German-speaking rulers sponsored migrations, and the German language became predominant. By the end of the 13th century most of Austria was firmly under the rule of the Hapsburgs, who were to build a huge empire in central and southern Europe. By 1815, Austria had also become the leading power in the German Confederation, only to lose that position half a century later
1848: Nationalistic minorities in the Austrian Empire revolt against the monarchy but are subdued by Austrian forces
1866: Austro-Prussian War ends in Austrian defeat and terminates Austrian influence in German Confederation
1867: Hungary gains equal rights with Austria under a dual monarchy
1914-18: On June 28, 1914, a Serbian nationalist assassinates Archduke Francis Ferdinand, triggering World War I; Austria is allied with Germany and other Central Powers and shares in their defeat; Hapsburg monarchy collapses and Austria is proclaimed a republic
1932-34: Engelbert Dollfuss becomes chancellor and opposes *Anschluss* (union) with Germany; the outlawed Nazi party carries out his assassination (1934)
1938: Hitler annexes Austria to Germany
1945: United States, USSR, Britain, and France divide Austria into occupation zones following World War II. People's party wins elections; forms coalition with Socialist party
1955: Occupation forces leave and Austria proclaims permanent neutrality
1966: The conservative People's Party gains absolute majority in parliamentary election, ending 20-year rule of Socialist-conservative coalition
1969: Parliament, by overwhelming majority, ratifies treaty to prevent spread of nuclear weapons. Austria and Italy agree to give major autonomy to the 230,000 German-speaking inhabitants of the Italian province of Alto Adige. Socialists win plurality in Parliment; their leader, Bruno Kreisky, becomes chancellor
1976: 12th Winter Olympics are held in Innsbruck
1979: Socialist Party wins majority in Parliament; Kreisky is sworn in to his 4th term as chancellor

BAHAMAS

Area: 5,382 sq. mi. **Population:** 225,000 (1978 est.)
Official Name: Commonwealth of the Bahamas **Capital:** Nassau **Nationality:** Bahamian **Language:** English **Religion:** There are Baptist, Methodist, Anglican, and Roman Catholic congregations **Flag:** Three horizontal stripes, the upper and lower aquamarine, the middle gold, with a black equilateral triangle on the hoist **Anthem:** March on, Bahamaland **Currency:** Bahamian dollar (1.00 per U.S. $1)

Location: An archipelago located in the northern portion of the West Indies in the Atlantic **Features:** The Bahamas include 700 islands and 2,000 rocks and cays, but less than 30 of the islands are inhabited. The islands are generally low and flat, with many splendid beaches. The climate is pleasantly warm throughout the year

Head of State: Queen Elizabeth II, represented by acting governor-general Gerald C. Cash, born 1917 **Head of Government:** Prime Minister Lynden O. Pindling, reelected 1977 **Effective Date of Present Constitution:** July 1973 **Legislative Body:** A General Assembly consists of a Senate with 16 members and a House of Assembly with 38 elected members **Local Government:** 18 districts, administered by appointed commissioners

Ethnic Composition: 85% Negro; the rest are of British, Canadian, and U.S. descent **Population Distribution:** 57.9% urban **Density:** 42 inhabitants per sq. mi.
Largest Cities: (1970 census) Nassau 105,352, Freeport 15,546

Per Capita Income: $4,000 (1979) **Gross National Product (GNP):** $900 million (1979 est.) **Economic Statistics:** Tourism is the main source of income. **Minerals and Mining:** Salt is extracted from brine by solar radiation; cement and petroleum products are produced **Labor Force:** 101,000 (1979). In 1970,20% were in industry, 7% in agriculture, and the rest in trade and services **Foreign Trade:** Exports, mainly petroleum products, cement, alcoholic beverages, pulpwood, pharmaceuticals, crawfish, and salt extracted from brine by solar radiation totaled about $2.4 billion in 1977. Imports of food, drink, tobacco, crude oil, manufactured articles, and animals totaled $2.1 billion **Principal Trade Partners:** United States, Saudi Arabia, Nigeria, Angola, Libya, Canada, Britain

Vital Statistics: Birthrate, 18.1 per 1,000; death rate, 3.9 per 1,000 **Life Expectancy:** 68.8 years **Infant Mortality:** 29.2 per 1,000 (1975) **Illiteracy:** 7% **Health Statistics:** 140 inhabitants per hospital bed; 2,100 per physician (1976) **Primary and Secondary School Enrollment:** 31,928 (1976) **Enrollment in Higher Education:** 2,160 (1975) **GNP Expended on Education:** 5.4% (1973)

Transportation: Surfaced roads total about 1,000 mi. **Motor Vehicles:** 41,800 (1976) **Passenger Cars:** 36,500 **Railway Mileage:** None **Ports:** Nassau, Freeport **Major Airlines:** Nassau is served by numerous international carriers, and Bahamasair services the Family Islands **Communications:** Government owned **Radio Transmitters:** 6 **Receivers:** 96,000 (1976) **Television Transmitters:** 1 **Telephones:** 58,000 (1976) **Newspapers:** 2 dailies, 152 copies per 1,000 inhabitants (1975)

Weights and Measures: British and metric systems **Travel Requirements:** Passport and visa not required of tourist with onward/return ticket and citizenship identification **Direct Dialing Code:** 809

After three centuries as a British colony, the Bahamas became an independent nation on July 10, 1973. The new country at the same time became an independent member of the British Commonwealth—the 33rd British possession to gain its freedom since World War II. Bahamian Prime Minister Lynden O. Pindling and his ruling Progressive Liberal Party had received a mandate for independence in elections held in September 1972. The party was formed in 1953 by blacks discontented with the policies of the white-dominated government.

In opposition to Pindling's ruling party is the Free National Movement, made up of whites and black PLP dissidents.

Because of the warm climate and beautiful beaches, tourism is the major industry. The islands host over 1,700,000 visitors a year.

A real estate boom drove land prices up so high that in 1979 the government restricted land sales for foreigners. Some $250 million in construction

WORLD FLAGS and MAPS

AFGHANISTAN	ALBANIA	ALGERIA	ANDORRA *
ARGENTINA	AUSTRALIA	AUSTRIA	BAHAMAS
BAHRAIN	BANGLADESH	BARBADOS	BELGIUM
BELIZE	BHUTAN	BOLIVIA	BOTSWANA
BRAZIL	BULGARIA	BURMA	BURUNDI
CAMBODIA (PEOP. REP. KAMPUCHEA)	CAMEROON	CANADA *	CENTRAL AFRICAN REP.
CHAD	CHILE	CHINA (MAINLAND)	CHINA (TAIWAN)
COLOMBIA *	CONGO	COSTA RICA	CUBA
CYPRUS	CZECHOSLOVAKIA	BENIN (DAHOMEY)	DENMARK *

* For flags of ANGOLA, CAPE VERDE, COMOROS, DJIBOUTI and DOMINICA see page 517

DOMINICAN REP. ECUADOR EGYPT EL SALVADOR

EQUATORIAL GUINEA ETHIOPIA FIJI FINLAND

FRANCE GABON GAMBIA EAST GERMANY

WEST GERMANY GHANA GREECE ✱ GUATEMALA

GUINEA ✱ GUYANA HAITI HONDURAS

HUNGARY ICELAND INDIA INDONESIA

IRAN IRAQ IRELAND ISRAEL

ITALY IVORY COAST JAMAICA JAPAN

JORDAN KENYA ✱ NORTH KOREA SOUTH KOREA

✱ For flags of GRENADA, GUINEA-BISSAU and KIRIBATI see page 517

KUWAIT

LAOS

LEBANON

LESOTHO

LIBERIA

LIBYA

LIECHTENSTEIN

LUXEMBOURG

MADAGASCAR

MALAWI

MALAYSIA

MALDIVES

MALI

MALTA

MAURITANIA

MAURITIUS

MEXICO

MONACO

MONGOLIA

MOROCCO *

NAURU

NEPAL

NETHERLANDS

NEW ZEALAND

NICARAGUA

NIGER

NIGERIA

NORWAY

OMAN

PAKISTAN

PANAMA *

PARAGUAY

PERU

PHILIPPINES

POLAND

PORTUGAL

✳ For flags of MOZAMBIQUE and PAPUA NEW GUINEA see page 517

516

QATAR	ZIMBABWE (RHODESIA)	ROMANIA	RWANDA *
SAN MARINO *	SAUDI ARABIA	SENEGAL *	SIERRA LEONE
SINGAPORE *	SOMALIA	SOUTH AFRICA	SPAIN
SRI LANKA (CEYLON)	SUDAN *	SWAZILAND	SWEDEN
SWITZERLAND	SYRIA	TANZANIA	THAILAND
TOGO	TONGA	TRINIDAD & TOBAGO	TUNISIA
TURKEY *	UGANDA	U.S.S.R.	UNITED ARAB EMIRATES
UNITED KINGDOM	UNITED STATES	UPPER VOLTA	URUGUAY
VATICAN CITY	VENEZUELA	VIETNAM	WESTERN SAMOA

* For flags of ST. LUCIA, SÃO TOMÉ E PRÍNCIPE, SEYCHELLES, SOLOMON IS., SURINAME and TUVALU see next page

517

YEMEN (PEOPLES REP.)　　YEMEN ARAB REP.　　YUGOSLAVIA　　ZAIRE

INDEPENDENT NATIONS 1974-1981

ZAMBIA　　GRENADA (1974)　　GUINEA-BISSAU (1974)　　MOZAMBIQUE (1975)

CAPE VERDE (1975)　　COMOROS (1975)　　SÃO TOMÉ E PRÍNCIPE (1975)　　PAPUA NEW GUINEA (1975)

ANGOLA (1975)　　SURINAME (1975)　　SEYCHELLES (1976)　　DJIBOUTI (1977)

SOLOMON ISLANDS (1978)　　TUVALU (1978)　　DOMINICA (1978)　　ST. LUCIA (1979)

KIRIBATI (1979)　　ST. VINCENT & GRENS. (1979)　　ZIMBABWE (1980)　　VANUATU (1980)

BELIZE (1981) flag appears on page 513

TIME ZONES OF THE WORLD

EUROPE

LAMBERT AZIMUTHAL EQUAL-AREA PROJECTION

SCALE OF MILES

100   200   300   400   500   600

SCALE OF KILOMETRES

100 200 300 400 500 600

Capitals of Countries .... ⊛

International Boundaries ....

Internal Boundaries ....

Copyright by C.S. HAMMOND & CO., N.Y.

CAPE VERDE

AFRICA

LAMBERT AZIMUTHAL EQUAL AREA PROJECTION

SCALE OF MILES

SCALE OF KILOMETERS

Capitals of Countries
Other Capitals
Canals
International Boundaries
Mountain Peaks
Elevations in Feet

AFRICA 1939

British
French
Italian
Portuguese
Spanish
Belgian
Mandates

Copyright by C. S. Hammond & Co., N. Y.

523

THE NEAR and MIDDLE EAST

CONIC PROJECTION

SCALE OF MILES

MILES
0   100   200   300   400

KILOMETERS
0   100   200   300   400

Capitals of Countries .... ⊛
International Boundaries _____
Other Boundaries ....

55° Longitude H East of 60° Greenwich J

Copyright by C. S. HAMMOND & Co., N.Y.

SOUTH AMERICA

LAMBERT AZIMUTHAL
EQUAL-AREA PROJECTION

SCALE OF MILES
0   100   200   400   600

SCALE OF KILOMETERS
0   100   200   400   600

Capitals of Countries................ ☆

International Boundaries .... _____

Copyright by C.S. HAMMOND & Co., N.Y.

Religion: About 70% of the population belongs to the Anglican Church. The rest are mainly Methodists, Moravians, and Roman Catholics **Flag:** Vertical bands of blue, gold, and blue, with a black trident centered on the gold band **Anthem:** National Anthem of Barbados, beginning "In plenty and in time of need" **Currency:** Barbadian dollar (2.01 per U.S. $1)

Location: West Indies. The most easterly of the Caribbean islands, Barbados lies immediately east of the Windward Islands and about 270 miles northeast of the mainland of South America **Features:** The island, which is of coral origin, is relatively flat, rising gently from the west coast in a series of terraces to a ridge in the center **Chief Rivers:** None

Head of State: Queen Elizabeth II, represented by a governor-general, Sir Deighton Harcourt Lisle Ward **Head of Government:** Prime Minister John Michael Geoffrey ("Tom") Adams, born 1932, appointed 1976 **Effective Date of Present Constitution:** 1966 **Legislative Body:** Parliament (bicameral), consisting of a House of Assembly and a Senate. The House of Assembly is composed of 24 members, elected for 5 years. The Senate consists of 21 members, 12 of whom are appointed by the governor-general on the advice of the prime minister, 2 on the advice of the leader of the opposition, and 7 appointed by the governor-general to represent various social and economic groups **Local Government:** 11 parishes and the city of Bridgetown

Ethnic Composition: About 80% of the population is of African descent; 4% is white, mainly of British origin **Population Distribution:** 37% urban **Density:** 1,500 inhabitants per sq. mi.

Largest City: (1970 census) Bridgetown 8,868 (Metropolitan Area 97,565)

Per Capita Income: $2,360 (1979) **Gross Domestic Product (GDP):** $644 million (1979) **Economic Statistics:** In 1973 about 42% of GNP was derived from trade and services; 16% from agriculture (sugarcane), fishing and animal husbandry; 11% from industry (sugar, rum, molasses, electronic parts) **Minerals and Mining:** Limestone and coral are quarried for domestic needs; there are small quantities of natural gas **Labor Force:** 97,000 (1973), of which 16% is employed in agriculture and 28% in industry **Foreign Trade:** Exports, chiefly sugar, rum, molasses and clothing, totaled $145 million in 1979. Imports, mainly food, machinery, transportation equipment, chemicals and petroleum products, totaled $424 million **Principal Trade Partners:** Britain, United States, Canada, West Indies, Japan

Vital Statistics: Birthrate, 18.6 per 1,000 of pop. (1976); death rate, 9.2 **Life Expectancy:** 70 years **Health Statistics:** 119 inhabitants per hospital bed; 1,250 per physician (1976) **Infant Mortality:** 28.3 per 1,000 births **Illiteracy:** 2% **Primary and Secondary School Enrollment:** 62,666 (1976) **Enrollment in Higher Education:** 1,417 (1973) **GNP Expended on Education:** 7.5% (1976)

Transportation: Paved roads total 840 mi. **Motor Vehicles:** 28,700 (1976) **Passenger Cars:** 24,700 **Railway Mileage:** None **Ports:** Bridgetown **Major Airlines:** Barbados is served by numerous international airlines **Communications:** Both government and privately owned **Radio Transmitters:** 3 **Receivers:** 130,000 (1976) **Television Transmitters:** 1 **Receivers:** 48,000 (1976) **Telephones:** 44,000 (1976) **Newspapers:** 1 daily, 98 copies per 1,000 inhabitants (1975)

Weights and Measures: Metric system **Travel Requirements:** Passport or proof of citizenship **Direct Dialing Code:** 809

Four centuries ago, the Portuguese sailors who sighted the 21-mile-long strip of coral first noticed its trees, their long branches drooping to the ground, and gave their name, Barbados—the bearded fig tree—to the island. The name is the only sign that Barbados has not always been British, perhaps even more British than Britain.

Nevertheless, since it won independence in 1966, the West Indian country has moved to expand its regional and hemispheric ties. It was admitted to the United Nations immediately after gaining independence and has also joined the Organization of American States and the Inter-American Development Bank.

In recent years the Barbadian economy, once totally dependent on the sugar crop, has been diversified by the development of tourism and light manufacturing, both of which were vigorously promoted by the Barbados Labour Party government of Prime Minister J. M. G. ("Tom") Adams, elected in 1976 and returned to power over Democratic Labour Party opposition in 1981.

After a year of unsuccessful negotiations for a new agreement, the United States announced in 1978 that it would close its naval facility in Barbados after 22 years of operation.

HISTORY: Although both Arawak and Carib Indians had at one time inhabited Barbados, the island was uninhabited when the first white settlers arrived from England in 1627. In less than a decade slaves were brought from Africa to work the sugar plantations, which continue to serve as the mainstay of the island's economy. Slavery was abolished in 1834, but the island's political life continued to be dominated by a small white upper class until well into the 20th century

1954: Sir Grantley Adams, a Negro Barbadian and founder of the Barbados Labour Party, becomes the first prime minister

1966: Barbados achieves full independence

1968-69: Barbados joins Caribbean Free Trade Area and Inter-American Development Bank

1973: Prime ministers of Barbados, Trinidad and Tobago, Guyana, and Jamaica establish CARICOM, a Caribbean common market and community

1976: J.M.G. Adams is appointed prime minister following election victory of his Barbados Labour party

1980: Hurricane Allen (Aug. 11) causes severe damage

BELGIUM

Area: 11,781 sq. mi. **Population:** 9,855,110 (1980 est.)

Official Name: Kingdom of Belgium **Capital:** Brussels **Nationality:** Belgian **Languages:** French, Flemish (Dutch), and German are the official and principal spoken languages. Flemish is spoken by the Flemings (Dutch) in the north and west, and French by the Walloons in the south and east; Brussels is bilingual **Religion:** The population is predominantly Roman Catholic, but there are several Protestant denominations and a Jewish community **Flag:** Vertical stripes of black, yellow, and red **Anthem:** La Brabançonne ("Song of Brabant") **Currency:** Belgian franc (36 per U.S. $1)

Location: Northwest Europe. Belgium is bordered by the Netherlands and the North Sea on the north, by Germany and Luxembourg on the east, and by France on the southwest and west **Features:** Although generally flat, Belgium has increasingly hilly and forested terrain toward the Ardennes region in the southeast **Chief Rivers:** Scheldt, Meuse

Head of State: King Baudouin I, born 1930, ascended the throne 1951 **Head of Government:** Premier Marc Eyskens, appointed 1981 **Effective Date of Present Constitution:** 1831, amended December 1970 **Legislative Body:** Parliament (bicameral), consisting of a Senate and Chamber of Representatives. The Senate, consisting of 182 members elected for 4 years, is partly elected directly and in part chosen by provincial councils and fellow senators. The Chamber, with 212 members, is elected by direct universal suffrage for 4 years **Local Government:** 9 provinces and 589 (1976) communes, with considerable autonomy in local matters. Four regions have been established: Flanders and Wallonia, each with a large degree of autonomy, and Brussels and a German-speaking region with lesser powers

Ethnic Composition: Flemings 58%, French (Walloons) 41%, Germans 1% **Population Distribution:** 94.6% urban **Density:** 837 inhabitants per sq. mi.

Largest Cities: (1971 est.) Brussels 1,071,194, Antwerp 226,570, Ghent 149,265, Liège 147,277, Bruges 117,220

Per Capita Income: $8,619 (1980) **Gross Domestic Product (GDP):** $85 billion (1980) **Economic Statistics:** 30% of the GNP comes from industry (steel, metal manufacturing, nonferrous metal, textile, diamond cutting, chemical, glass); 25% from commerce; 24% from services; 7% from construction; 8% from transport and communications; 4% from agriculture (livestock, sugar beets, hay, potatoes, grain) **Minerals and Mining:** Coal is the only mineral resource of major importance. Iron, lead, zinc, copper, manganese, and phosphates are mined in small quantities **Labor Force:** 4 million (1978), with 47% in services, 30% in industry, 8% in construction, 3% in agriculture and 12% in civil service **Foreign Trade:** Exports, chiefly chemicals, textiles, diamonds, iron and steel products, machinery, automotive vehicles, glass, and nonferrous metals, totaled $53.1 billion in 1979. Imports, mainly grains, ores, petroleum, chemicals, textiles, diamonds, metals and products, machinery, electrical equipment and automotive vehicles, totaled $56.9 billion **Principal Trade Partners:** West Germany, Netherlands, France, Italy, United States, Britain, Switzerland

Vital Statistics: Birthrate, 12.4 per 1,000 of pop. (1977); death rate, 11.4 **Life Expectancy:** 71 years **Health Statistics:** 111 inhabitants per hospital bed; 493 per physician (1976) **Infant Mortality:** 14 per 1,000 births **Illiteracy:** 3% **Primary and Secondary School Enrollment:** 1,773,614 (1976) **Enrollment in Higher Education:** 159,660 (1975) **GNP Expended on Education:** 6.2% (1976)

Transportation: Paved roads total 32,800 mi. **Motor Vehicles:** 3,168,400 (1977) **Passenger Cars:** 2,871,300 **Railway Mileage:** 2,620 **Ports:** Antwerp, Zeebrugge, Ghent, Ostend **Major Airlines:** Sabena airline operates both domestic and international services **Communications:** Government controlled **Radio Transmitters:** 48 **Licenses:** 4,044,000 (1976) **Television Transmitters:** 30 **Licenses:** 2,646,000 (1976) **Telephones:** 2,949,000 (1976) **Newspapers:** 30 dailies, 239 copies per 1,000 inhabitants (1975)

Weights and Measures: Metric system **Travel Requirements:** Passport, no visa for 3 months **International Dialing Code:** 32

The geography of Belgium has brought it misfortune and fortune: the misfortune of having a largely low-lying countryside that served as a route for foreign armies, and the fortune of a location in Western Europe that helps to make the country a key trading and manufacturing center.

In its military misadventures, Belgium was the scene of Caesar's conquest of the Gallic tribes; the site of Napoleon's ultimate defeat, at Waterloo; and the stage for invasion by German armies in both world wars. But conflict also brought Belgium independence; the Belgians revolted against Dutch domination in 1830.

The northern part of the country, in which Belgian basic industry is largely situated, is inhabited by Dutch-speaking Flemings. Most of the rest of Belgium is Walloon country, where French is spoken. Currently the Flemings are dominant, with a majority in both the Senate and Chamber. The bilingual nature of the land has led to much friction.

In 1970, in order to reduce linguistic tensions, the unitary constitution of 1831 was revised to recognize "three cultural communities: French, Dutch, and German." Four linguistic regions—the Flemish and Walloon areas, a small German area along the border of West Germany, and bilingual Brussels—were created. Each has a council with limited authority over education, culture, and the economy. But proposals to increase their authority have been the most divisive issue of the 1970s. In 1980 the coalition government granted more self-governing powers to the Flemish and Walloon areas, but postponed consideration of similar status for Brussels to a later time.

Dependent on trade, Belgium has been a leader in the movement for European integration. It merged its customs with those of Luxembourg in 1921. The Netherlands joined this union to form *Benelux* by an agreement which took full effect in 1950. The Benelux countries joined the European Economic Community in 1958, and their earlier experience has helped to guide the Community. European integration helped to make Belgium prosperous in the 1960s; the Walloon region gained new industries.

In addition to industry, Belgium has gained as the headquarters of major international organizations—NATO, which had run out of its welcome in France, and the European Community, which is headquartered in Brussels.

HISTORY: Belgium, named after ancient Celtic settlers, the Belgae, was conquered by Julius Caesar about 50 B.C. and later formed part of Charlemagne's empire. Ruled by Burgundy in the 15th century, it passed to the Hapsburgs of Austria and then of Spain. In the 16th century, the Low Countries (including modern Belgium, Luxembourg, and the Netherlands) revolted against Spanish rule. But while the northern and predominantly Protestant Netherlands provinces won their independence, Belgium remained under Spanish rule until the 18th century

1713: Belgium is ceded to Austria by the Treaty of Utrecht, which ends the War of the Spanish Succession

1792-97: French armies invade Belgium; country is ceded to France by Treaty of Campo Formio

1815: Belgium is united with the Netherlands by Treaty of Paris

1830-39: Belgians revolt against affiliation with Protestant Netherlands, a provisional government declares Belgium independent; Dutch invade Belgium but are forced by Britain and France to recognize the country's independence. Belgian Parliament chooses Prince Leopold of Saxe-Coburg-Gotha as ruler of the new kingdom

1885-1908: Leopold II becomes absolute monarch of Congo Free State. Belgium reluctantly annexed the area in 1908

1914-18: Germans invade and occupy neutral Belgium

1940-44: Germany again invades Belgium; King Leopold III surrenders unconditionally. Belgian cabinet sets up government-in-exile in London and declares surrender illegal; Belgian underground continues to fight German invaders

1950-51: Belgian electorate votes for return of king, but uprisings against Leopold by Socialists and Liberals force him to abdicate in favor of his son, Baudouin

1960: Belgium grants Congo independence

1968: Cultural-language conflict between Flemish and French-speaking population (Walloons) leads to fall of center-right coalition government; new coalition of Christian Socialists and Socialists is formed

1969: Cultural conflict continues to simmer as Senate studies constitutional reform proposals for regional autonomy

1970: Belgium amends constitution giving autonomous cultural and economic powers to each of the two communities, Flemings and Walloons

1973: Heretofore provisional double presidency (one Fleming, one Walloon) is made permanent part of Socialist party structure

1974: Iran's withdrawal from joint oil refining project adds to Belgium's economic woes and topples Leburton government. Leo Tindemans forms three-party coalition government

1975: Severe inflation and 6 percent unemployment force wage-price measures

1977: Tindemans' coalition government wins April election after cabinet crisis brought on by withdrawal of leftist Walloons

1978: Linguistic tensions trouble coalition. Crisis is resolved in June, but Tindemans resigns in October. Paul Vanden Boeynants becomes caretaker premier, and elections produce no major changes. Belgian Army enters Zaire to rescue victims of violence

1979: Wilfried Martens becomes premier in five-party coalition

1980: Greater authority is given to Flemish and Walloon regions, but not to Brussels

1981: Marc Eyskens is appointed premier

BELIZE

Area: 8,867 sq. mi. **Population:** 144,857 (1980 census)

Official Name: Belize **Capital:** Belmopan **Nationality:** Belizean **Languages:** English is the official language. Most inhabitants speak a Creole dialect of English. Spanish, Carib and Maya are the first languages of certain groups **Religion:** 60% are Roman Catholic; 40% are Protestant **Flag:** A dark blue field upon which is centered a white circle containing the coat of arms **Anthem:** N.A. **Currency:** Belize dollar (2 per U.S. $1)

Location: On the east coast of Central America, bounded on the east by the Bay of Honduras of the Caribbean Sea, on the south and west by Guatemala, and on the northwest by Mexico. It has a swampy coast that rises gradually toward the interior, which is dominated by tropical jungle growth

Head of State: Governor James Hennessy (prior to independence) **Head of Government:** Premier George Price **Effective Date of Present Constitution:** 1981 **Legislative Body:** National Assembly (bicameral), consisting of an 18-member elected House of Representatives and a Senate composed of eight appointed members **Local Government:** 6 districts, with district officers, except for Belize City, which is administered by an elected city council

Ethnic Composition: 51% "Creole" (African and mixed-African descent), 22% Mestizo (Spanish-Maya), 19% Amerindian. There are some people of East Indian, German and Spanish descent **Population Distribution:** N.A. **Density:** 16 inhabitants per sq. mi.

Largest Cities: (1980 census) Belize City 39,887, Orange Walk 8,441, Corozal 6,862, Stann Creek 6,627, Belmopan 2,932

Per Capita Income: $790 (1979) **Gross Domestic Product (GDP):** $120 million (1978) **Economic Statistics:** The economy has traditionally been based on timber and forest products, but these have been superseded by agriculture, particularly sugar, citrus fruit, rice, tobacco, beef and bananas. The fishing industry (lobster, shrimp and conch) is important **Minerals and Mining:** Drilling for oil began in 1977 in offshore and onshore areas **Labor Force:** 34,500, with 39% in agriculture, 20% in services, 14% in manufacturing and 8% in commerce **Foreign Trade:** Exports, chiefly sugar, molasses, citrus fruit, fish, timber and clothing, totaled $80 million in 1978. Imports, mainly food, machinery anmd transport equipment, manufactured goods and fuels, totaled $106 million **Principal Trade Partners:** United States, Britain, Canada, Caribbean countries

Vital Statistics: Birthrate, 38.7 per 1,000 of pop. (1973); death rate, 5.3 (1974) **Life Expectancy:** 60 years **Health Statistics:** 200 inhabitants per hospital bed; 3,500 per physician (1976) **Infant Mortality:** 33.7 per 1,000 births (1972) **Illiteracy:** 7% **Primary and Secondary School Enrollment:** 41,260 (1979) **Enrollment in Higher Education:** 121 (1974) **GNP Expended on Education:** 3.6% (1974)

Transportation: Paved roads total 185 mi. **Motor Vehicles:** 8,800 (1976) **Passenger Cars:** 5,600 **Railway Mileage:** None **Ports:** Belize City, Dangriga **Major Airlines:** Maya Airways provides internal services and Belize Airways provides service to the U.S. and Central America **Communications:** Government owned **Radio Transmitters:** 5 **Receivers:** N.A. **Television Stations:** None **Telephones:** 5,800 **Newspapers:** 4 weeklies

Weights and Measures: Imperial system **Travel Requirements:** Passport and visa not required of tourist with onward/return ticket and citizenship identification **International Dialing Code:** 501

Belize, formerly British Honduras, existed for over a century as a little-known outpost of the globe-encircling British Empire. The colony's chief claim to fame was as an important source of mahogany, the strong cabinet wood prized by furniture makers. Though Belize is only slightly smaller than New Hampshire in area, its isolation and physical drawbacks prevented it from becoming a populous and economically valuable possession of the British crown. Empire builders of the nineteenth century, approaching the shore from the Caribbean Sea, were greeted by a flat and swampy coastal plain and, on landing, suffered from a hot and humid climate, prone to hurricanes. In addition, Britain never possessed clear and uncontested title to the lonesome piece of Central American real estate.

The dispute over ownership of Belize dates back to the seventeenth century, when British log cutters waged intermittent warfare with neighboring Spanish settlers, until the final British victory in 1798. In the nineteenth century, Guatemala pressed its claim to the area as an inheritor of the Spanish claim. It was not until March 11, 1981, that Guatemala and Britain settled the disupte, thus paving the way for the independence of Belize. By that agreement, independence was scheduled to begin for Belize on September 21, 1981, eliminating Britain's last toehold on the American mainland.

Since World War II, the Belizean economy has diversified into new fields. Mahogany and chicle, once the mainstays of the area's livelihood, have declined in relative importance as a result of uncontrolled cutting and of hurricane damage. Sugarcane, citrus fruit, rice, bananas, livestock and fish are now the dominant products of Belize. Tourism holds promise for the future.

The history of Belize in the nineteenth century provided an interesting footnote to the American Civil War. In 1869, refugees from the defeated Confederacy established sugar plantations in the Stann Creek and Toledo districts. A latter-day migration from Anglo-America occurred after World War II, when Mennonite farmers from Canada settled in the interior of Belize.

HISTORY: The Mayan civilization spread into the area of Belize several centuries B.C. and flourished until about A.D. 1000. European contact began in 1502, when Columbus sailed along the coast. The first recorded European settlement was begun by shipwrecked English seamen in 1638. Over the next 150 years, more English settlements were established, although the settlers suffered sporadic attacks by pirates, Indians and neighboring Spanish settlers **1798:** Settlers defeat Spaniards in Battle of St. George's Cay, establishing *defacto* British control **1859:** Britain and Guatemala sign treaty establishing common border. Treaty later declared null and void by Guatemala **1862:** The Crown Colony of British Honduras is established

1964: Internal self-government is attained
1973: British Honduras is renamed Belize
1975: Guatemala threatens invasion. UN General Assembly adopts resolution recognizing Belize's right to self-determination and calls for negotiations between Britain and Guatemala
1977: Britain rushes troops to Belize to counter Guatemalan invasion threats
1981: Britain, Guatemala and Belizean representatives sign pact in London, agreeing to Belizean independence and settlement of Guatemalan claims. Belize becomes independent on Sept. 21

BENIN

Area: 43,483 sq. mi. **Population:** 3,567,000 (1980 est.)

Official Name: People's Republic of Benin **Capital:** Porto Novo **Nationality:** Beninese or Beninois **Languages:** French is the official language; the most common African dialects are Fon, Mina, Yoruba, and Dendi **Religion:** Animists 65%, Moslems 15%, Roman Catholics 14%, Protestants 6% **Flag:** A green flag with a red five-pointed star in the upper left **Anthem:** The New Dawn **Currency:** CFA Franc (263 per U.S. $1)

Location: West Africa. Benin is bordered on the north by Upper Volta and Niger, on the east by Nigeria, on the south by the Bight of Benin, and on the west by Togo **Features:** A 75-mile coastline of sandy beaches and lagoons is unbroken by natural harbors; north of it is a flat area that is the main oil palm region; further inland, a swampy depression is succeeded by hills, plateaus, and the Atakora Mountains, which stretch into Togo **Chief Rivers:** Ouémé, Mono, Couffo

Head of State and of Government: President: Col. Ahmed (Mathieu) Kérékou, born 1933, assumed power in 1972; he also is defense minister **Effective Date of Present Constitution:** August 1977 **Legislative Body:** A 336-member unicameral National Revolutionary Assembly **Local Government:** 6 departments

Ethnic Composition: Of some 42 distinctive African groups the main ones are the Fon, Yoruba, Adja, Bariba, Peul, and Somba. There are also about 5,500 Europeans **Population Distribution:** 13.7% urban (1975) **Density:** 82 inhabitants per sq. mi.

Largest Cities: (1975 est.) Cotonou 178,000, Porto Novo 104,000; (1973 est.) Natatingou 49,000, Abomey 38,000

Per Capita Income: $340 (1980) **Gross National Product (GNP):** $1.1 billion (1980) **Economic Statistics:** In 1978, 33% of GDP came from agriculture (coffee, cotton, peanuts, cassava, fish, yams, corn, oil palm products); 16% from industry (palm oil products, textiles, kenaf, beverages, furniture, ceramics and cement) and mining **Minerals and Mining:** Some low-grade iron ore and limestone deposits are located in the north **Labor Force:** 1.5 million with 85% in agriculture **Foreign Trade:** Exports, chiefly palm kernel oil, cotton, and cocoa beans, totaled $230 million in 1980. Imports, chiefly food products, textiles, machinery, vehicles, and iron and steel products, totaled $435 million **Principal Trade Partners:** France, United States, West Germany, Netherlands, Nigeria, Japan, Britain

Vital Statistics: Birthrate, 49.9 per 1,000 of pop. (1975); death rate, 23 **Life Expectancy:** 41 years **Health Statistics:** 727 inhabitants per hospital bed; 35,555 per physician (1976) **Infant Mortality:** 109.6 per 1,000 births **Illiteracy:** 80% **Primary and Secondary School Enrollment:** 348,723 (1977) **Enrollment in Higher Education:** 2,118 (1975) **GNP Expended on Education:** 7.4% (1976)

Transportation: Paved roads total 446 mi. **Motor Vehicles:** 26,500 (1976) **Passenger Cars:** 17,000 **Railway Mileage:** 360 **Ports:** Cotonou **Major Airlines:** Air Afrique provides intercontinental and regional services **Communications:** State controlled **Radio Transmitters:** 4 (1972) **Receivers:** 150,000 (1976) **Television Stations:** one **Receivers:** 100 (1972) **Telephones:** 8,000 (1974) **Newspapers:** 1 daily, 0.3 copies per 1,000 inhabitants (1975)

Weights and Measures: Metric system **Travel Requirements:** Passport and visa required. Transit visa $3.00 for 24 hours; 1-3 days, $3.00, 2 photos

---

In addition to being one of the smallest, poorest, and most densely populated countries in West Africa, Benin has the unenviable distinction of having had more changes of government than any other newly independent African nation.

Counting the government that was in office when the former French territory won independence in 1960 under the name Dahomey, there were 11 governments between 1960 and 1972. Six of these were installed by military coups. In many cases, governments resigned or were ousted simply because they could not meet a payroll.

In 1970 the government sought to bring a measure of stability to the country by creating a civilian presidential commission which consisted of three former leaders who had served as president or premier in the past. Starting with Hubert Maga, as first president, the chairmanship of the commission was to rotate every two years.

According to schedule Mr. Maga stepped down in May 1972 and was replaced by Justin Ahomadegbe. Five months later, however, the transfer of power by military coup was again the case. On October 26 junior and middle-grade army officers seized power, replacing Ahomadegbe's regime with an 11-man military government headed by then Maj. Mathieu Kérékou.

The Kérékou government represented a clear break from earlier regimes. Persons long in positions of power were swept aside and replaced by a younger generation. A guiding principle of "Marxist-Leninist Scientific Socialism" was proclaimed by President Kérékou and some changes in the political and economic system began to appear. Reports of corruption, incompetence in government and attempted coups followed by wholesale arrests continue to come from Benin, however.

In elections held Nov. 20, 1979, for a National Revolutionary Assembly, more than 80 percent of the electorate voted. The count was overwhelmingly in favor of the single list of candidates of the People's Revolutionary party of Benin (PRPB).

Much of Benin's political instability has been caused by the country's weak economy and dependence on French aid. Producing only a small quantity of palm products, cotton and cocoa beans for export, Benin has been unable to earn enough revenue to meet development requirements.

Benin's imports climbed to an annual level of $435 million in 1980 while exports lagged at $230 million. Membership in the French franc pool is the only thing that makes such a deficit possible.

HISTORY: In the 17th century, the powerful Kingdom of Abomey gained dominance over neighboring kingdoms; it maintained its pre-eminent position until the late 19th century, when it was occupied by the French. Abomey armies, which included an elite corps of women soldiers, warred constantly with Yorubas in the east and raided Ashanti territory to the west. Until well into the 19th century, much of the fighting was stimulated by the slave trade, since prisoners were readily sold to European slavers
1851: French make treaty with King Gezo of Cotonou, where they establish trading post
1892-1904: French crush Abomey rebellion, push inland, and make country part of French West Africa
1958-59: Territory of Dahomey becomes autonomous state within French community; constitution is adopted and in National Assembly elections Hubert Maga becomes premier
1960: Dahomey becomes fully independent, with Maga as president
1963: Maga government is forced to resign in coup led by Col. (later General) Christophe Soglo, army chief of staff, who forms provisional government
1964: Sourou Migan Apithy is elected president
1965: Dissension among government leaders prompts second coup by General Soglo; provisional civilian government is formed and elections are announced, but Soglo again intervenes, proclaims himself president and premier
1967: Soglo government is overthrown by military junta
1968: Military regime returns government to civilian administration headed by Emile-Derlin Zinsou
1972: Dahomey's first peaceful transition of power is aborted by the country's fifth coup since independence. Maj. Mathieu Kérékou assumes power
1975: Rebellion led by Minister of Labor quashed. Dahomey is renamed the People's Republic of Benin by President Kérékou
1977: In January, foreign airborne assault fails to overthrow Kérékou, who claims invasion was French inspired
1979: In November first general elections for a National Revolutionary Assembly are held in accordance with the new constitution
1980: Kérékou, in Libya to sign an agreement for cooperation with that country, is formally converted to Islam and changes his first name to Ahmed

BHUTAN

Area: 18,147 sq. mi. **Population:** 1,240,000 (1978 est.)
Official Name: Kingdom of Bhutan **Capital:** Thimphu **Nationality:** Bhutanese **Languages:** Dzongka, a Tibetan dialect, is the official and principal language; Nepali and tribal dialects are also spoken **Religion:** About 75% are Mahayana Buddhists and many live in Buddhist monasteries; the Nepalese of southern Bhutan (25%) are predominantly Hindu **Flag:** Divided diagonally with saffron to the left and red to the right, with a white dragon outlined in black in the center **Anthem:** National Anthem, beginning "In the sandal-wood ornamented Kingdom of Dragonland" **Currencies:** Ngultrum (8.3 per U.S. $1) and Indian rupee (8.3 per U.S. $1)
Location: Eastern Himalayas of Central Asia. Bhutan is bordered by China (Tibet) on the north and northwest, and by India on the east, west and south **Features:** The undemarcated northern boundary with Tibet stretches along 300 miles of snow-capped peaks that are almost inaccessible. The inner Himalayan region in central Bhutan contains densely populated, fertile valleys; the Duar Plain of southern Bhutan contains dense forests **Chief Rivers:** Manas, Sankosh, Tongsa, Torsa, Raidak
Head of State and of Government: King Jigme Singye Wangchuk, born 1955, ascended the throne 1972. The king governs with the aid of a 5-man council of ministers **Effective Date of Present Constitution:** No formal written constitution **Legislative Body:** Tsongdu (unicameral national assembly), consisting of 150 members, 40 appointed by the king, 10 by the organizations of lamas, and the rest nominated by villages for 3-year terms. Parliamentary government is still rudimentary **Local Government:** 4 regions under appointed governors
Ethnic Composition: Bhutanese, or Bhotias, who are ethnically related to the Tibetans, make up 60% of the population. Nepalese constitute about 25% and the rest consist of various tribal groups, including the Lepcha, an indigenous people, and the Santal, descendants of migrants from India **Population Distribution:** The population is chiefly rural **Density:** 68 inhabitants per sq. mi.
Largest Cities: (1970 est.) Thimphu 50,000, Paro Dzong 35,000, Taga Dzong 18,000, Punakha 12,000, Bumthang 10,000
Per Capita Income: $80 (1979) **Gross National Product (GNP):** $100 million (1979 est.) **Economic Statistics:** The economy is still at a primitive level and many transactions are on a barter basis. The country is self-sufficient in food; the main crops are rice, wheat, and barley, and together with butter from yaks provide a sufficient diet. Large forests provide the potential for lumber and paper-processing plants, and several turbulent rivers furnish a potential source of hydroelectric power. Bhutan's first 5-year development plan was begun in 1961 with the aid of India, the fourth plan covers the years 1976-1981 **Minerals and Mining:** Copper, dolomite, graphite, and coal deposits have been discovered **Labor Force:** Virtually the entire working population is engaged in agriculture and pastoral activities **Foreign Trade:** Almost all external trade is with India, chiefly exports ($1 million) of rice, dolomite and handicrafts, and imports ($1.4 million) of textiles and light equipment
Vital Statistics: Birthrate, 43.6 per 1,000 of pop. (1975); death rate, 20.5 **Life Expectancy:** 43.6 years **Health Statistics:** N.A. **Infant Mortality:** N.A. **Illiteracy:** 95% **Primary and Secondary School Enrollment:** 20,357 (1976) **Enrollment in Higher Education:** Bhutanese students are studying in India, New Zealand, Australia and the U.S. **GNP Expended on Education:** N.A.
Transportation: Paved roads total 250 mi. **Motor Vehicles:** N.A. **Passenger Cars:** N.A. **Railway Mileage:** None **Ports:** None **Major Airlines:** An Indian airline operates flights from Hashimara, West Bengal, to Paro Dzong **Communications:** Teleprinter and postal services link Bhutan with India and the rest of the world **Radio Transmitters:** 1 A.M. station **Receivers:** 6,000 **Television:** None **Telephones:** 1,000 **Newspapers:** A weekly government newspaper is published in 3 languages
Weights and Measures: Traditional and metric standards are used
Travel Requirements: Tourists are admitted only in groups by prearrangement with the Ministry of Tourism, Thimphu. Passport, visa, smallpox and cholera immunizations are required. India requires special passes to enter Bhutan.

Well into the 20th century, the Buddhist kingdom of Bhutan was still living in the 19th, content to be isolated politically from the rest of the world. In 1959 the Chinese takeover of Tibet, Bhutan's northern neighbor, jolted the country into closing its trade routes to Tibet and into building a road to the south.

It took six days then, on the back of a mule, to travel from Bhutan to India. The same trip now, by bus, takes five hours. With the help of foreign, mainly Indian, aid and advisers, similar advances have been made in other sectors in the agrarian kingdom. Where only 2,600 of Bhutan's people had gone even to primary school a decade ago, now 20,000 are studying in schools of all levels. About 500 have studied abroad at universities and returned to Bhutan.

Bhutan's king from 1952 to 1972 was Jigme Dorji Wangchuk, whose name means "fearless thunderbolt master of the cosmic powers." Despite his awesome appellation, the king was surprisingly informal and genuinely loved by his people. To give his rule a popular base, he persuaded the National Assembly to pass a bill (dropped by his successor) empowering it by a two-thirds vote to replace the king with the next in the royal line of succession if the monarch loses the assembly's confidence. After his death, he was succeeded by his son, Jigme Singye Wangchuk.

Bhutan is largely independent and insists that it is not an Indian protectorate, though by a treaty of 1949 it "agrees to be guided by the government of India in regard to external relations." Until 1978, Bhutan was under an agreement to sell its goods only to India. Bhutan has no plans to open its mountain border with China; it has diplomatic missions only at the United Nations, in India and in Bangladesh.

Bhutan's people are thinly spread over a beautiful, mountainous country. Most Bhutanese live as farmers on their own land, bartering for what they need. Since 1974, Bhutanese planners have permitted group tours of rich travelers—a maximum of 200 at a time—who stay in excellent new facilities. In 1979 some 1,500 tourists put $700,000 into Bhutan's economy.

HISTORY: Bhutan's early history is obscure. In the 16th century it was conquered by Tibet and nominally came under a dual spiritual and temporal rule. In the 19th century the southern part of the country was occupied by the British and annexed to India, and Britain began paying Bhutan an annual subsidy. In 1907 Sir Ugyen Wangchuk, a former local governor, established a hereditary monarchy, and in a 1910 treaty Bhutan agreed to British direction of its external affairs

1949: India signs treaty with Bhutan assuming Britain's role in subsidizing kingdom and directing its foreign relations; India returns areas annexed by Britain in 1865

1959: Communist China publishes maps showing parts of Bhutan as Chinese territory; Communist spokesmen claim Bhutan belongs to greater Tibet. Indian government warns that any attack on Bhutan will be regarded as an act of aggression against India

1971: Bhutan is admitted to the United Nations

1973: Bhutan signs agreement with UN under which Bhutan will receive $2.5 million in aid to carry out projects under third five-year plan

1974: King Jigme Singye Wangchuk formally crowned

BOLIVIA

Area: 424,163 sq. mi. **Population:** 5,425,000 (1979 est.)

Official Name: Republic of Bolivia **Capital:** La Paz is the administrative capital, Sucre the legal and judicial capital **Nationality:** Bolivian **Languages:** Spanish, the official language, is spoken by about 55% of the population (but only 36% as a mother tongue). The rest speak a variety of Indian dialects, chiefly Quechua and Aymara **Religion:** The population is about 95% Roman Catholic **Flag:** Red, yellow, and green horizontal stripes, with the national coat of arms on the yellow stripe **Anthem:** National Anthem, beginning "Bolivians, provident destiny" **Currency:** Bolivian peso (24.5 per U.S. $1)

Location: South America. Landlocked Bolivia is bordered on the north and east by Brazil, on the south by Paraguay and Argentina, and on the west by Chile and Peru **Features:** The country is divided into three distinct regions: the Altiplano, a bleak plateau lying between two ranges of the Andes Mountains and one of the world's highest inhabited regions; an intermediate region (yungas) containing the eastern mountain slopes and valleys, and the Amazon-Chaco lowlands (llanos) **Chief Rivers:** Beni, Guaporé-Iténez, Mamoré-Río Grande, Pilcomayo, Paraguay

Head of State and of Government: President: Gen. Celso Torrelio Villa, sworn in Sept. 5, 1981. **Effective Date of Present Constitution:** 1967 (suspended July 1980) **Legislative Body:** Bicameral National Congress (disbanded July 1980) with 27 Senators and 117 Deputies **Local Government:** 9 departments, each headed by an appointed prefect

Ethnic Composition: 65% Amerindian (mainly Quechua and Aymará), 10% of European origin, 25% of mixed origin (Cholo) **Population Distribution:** 38.6% urban (1975) **Density:** 12.8 inhabitants per sq. mi.

Largest Cities: (1976 census) La Paz 635,283, Santa Cruz 254,682, Cochabamba 204,684, Oruro 124,213, Sucre 63,625

Per Capita Income: $692 (1980) **Gross National Product (GNP):** $3.7 billion (1980) **Economic Statistics:** In 1977 about 28% of GNP came from agriculture (sugar, corn, potatoes, wheat, and rice); 10% from manufacturing (food processing, textiles, leather goods, cement, and glass ceramics); 14% from mining; 13% from trade and services; 9% from transportation **Minerals and Mining:** Mining is the most important element of the nation's economy and accounts for the major share of the country's exports. Tin still dominates these exports, which also include lead, zinc, silver, copper, tungsten, bismuth, antimony, gold, petroleum, natural gas, and sulphur **Labor Force:** 2.8 million (1977); 70% in agriculture, 10% in services and utilities, 7% in manufacturing, 3% in mining, 10% other **Foreign Trade:** Exports, chiefly tin, natural gas, petroleum, tungsten, silver, antimony, copper, lead, zinc, sugar, cotton and coffee, totaled $777 million in 1979. Imports, mainly machinery, vehicles, iron and steel, and food staples, totaled $1 billion **Principal Trade Partners:** United States, Argentina, West Germany, Britain, Brazil, Japan, Switzerland, Netherlands

Vital Statistics: Birthrate, 48 per 1,000 of pop. (1976); death rate, 18 **Life Expectancy:** 47 years **Health Statistics:** 526 inhabitants per hospital bed; 2,583 per physician (1975) **Infant Mortality:** 77.3 per 1,000 births **Illiteracy:** 37% **Primary and Secondary School Enrollment:** 1,050,931 (1976) **Enrollment in Higher Education:** 51,585 (1976) **GNP Expended on Education:** 3.2% (1976)

Transportation: Paved roads total 714 mi. **Motor Vehicles:** 59,700 (1977) **Passenger Cars:** 34,300 **Railway Mileage:** 2,400 **Ports:** None **Major Airlines:** Lloyd Aéreo Boliviano (LAB) operates domestic and international services **Communications:** Government controlled **Radio Transmitters:** 140 **Receivers:** 476,000 (1975) **Television Transmitters:** 4 **Receivers:** 100,000 (1976) **Telephones:** 49,000 (1974) **Newspapers:** 14 dailies, 35 copies per 1,000 inhabitants (1975)

Weights and Measures: Metric system; old Spanish units are still used **Travel Requirements:** Passport and tourist visa, 90-day extendable, no fee **International Dialing Code:** 591

Often called the "Tibet of South America," landlocked Bolivia is made up of three distinct topographical regions: a mineral-rich high plateau region, an extensively farmed middle region of semitropical rain forests and somewhat drier valleys, and the sparsely populated Amazon-Chaco lowlands.

Bolivia is among the poorest countries in Latin America, with its Andean Indian peasants and its miners widely separated from the urban minorities of European origin.

Signs of economic and social advance, however, include skyscraper office buildings, modern jet airliner service between La Paz and the tropical lowlands, and the large growth in primary school enrollment.

Bolivia's economy is based on natural gas and petroleum, which make the country self-sufficient in energy, and nonferrous minerals, including tin, of which Bolivia is one of the world's leading producers. The prevailing economic philosophy is nationalist capitalism.

From 1943, when the pro-miner National Revolutionary Movement (MNR) led a revolt against poor working conditions and suppression of strikes, power shifted back and forth between the MNR and rightist military juntas. In August 1971 the regime of Gen. Juan José Torres was overthrown by Col. Hugo Banzer Suárez with support of both the MNR and the rightist Bolivian Socialist Falange. By foiling a series of attempts to unseat him and by establishing (in 1974) an all-military government, Banzer attained a relatively long period of political stability. In 1978, in response to a popular cry for more democratic government, he opened the way for a presidential election. Gen Juan Pereda Asbún, backed by Banzer, received more than half of the popular votes, but the electoral court declared the election void on the grounds of fraud. Pereda then seized power in a coup, but before the year's end he was deposed and Gen. David Padilla Arancibia was named interim president.

Because no candidate received a majority in the election held in July 1979, the National Congress chose Walter Guevara Arze as the first civilian president in 10 years. However, when he was toppled by a coup in November, Lidia Gueiler Tejada, president of the Chamber of Deputies, was selected to serve as interim president until a new election scheduled for June 29, 1980. A former president, Hernán Siles Zuazo, won a plurality in the 1980 election, but not a majority, of votes. Before the National Congress could meet on August 3 to choose a president, a three-man military junta seized power on July 17 and proclaimed Gen. Luis García Meza as president. This coup and reign of terror against political opponents that ensued were condemned by Bolivia's Andean Pact partners, and the United States cut off military and economic aid. However, Argentina, Brazil and a few other countries supported García Meza. Following a series of revolts during July 1981, García Meza was removed from office by a reconstituted junta which assumed full power on August 4.

HISTORY: The Bolivian Altiplano was a center of Indian life long before the days of the Incas, who conquered the region in the 13th century. The Spanish conquest began in the 1530s, and the Indians were soon virtually enslaved to work the rich silver mines of Upper Peru, as Bolivia was then called. Following the occupation of Spain by Napoleon in 1809, Upper Peru became one of the first Spanish colonies to revolt against Spain
1824-26: Revolutionary army under Antonio José de Sucre, chief lieutenant of Simón Bolívar, defeats Spanish forces at Ayacucho. Bolivian independence is proclaimed in 1825
1879-84: Bolivia and Peru fight Chile in War of the Pacific. Chile is victorious and Bolivia is forced to cede province of Atacama, nation's only coastal territory
1903: After bitter conflict, Bolivia cedes large rubber-tree area on Acre River to Brazil
1932-35: Discovery of oil at the foot of the Bolivian Andes precipitates Chaco War with Paraguay, which lays claim to region. More than 100,000 lives are lost on both sides; a defeated Bolivia loses three-quarters of disputed Chaco Boreal area to Paraguay
1943: Economic unrest culminates in widespread strikes by miners; pro-miner Movement of the National Revolution (MNR) stages revolt and takes power
1951-56: Víctor Paz Estenssoro, the MNR candidate, wins presidential election but is prevented from taking office by military junta; he is finally swept into power by a party-led uprising
1964-66: Second administration headed by Paz is overthrown and a military junta installed. Air Force General René Barrientos Ortuño is elected president in 1966
1967: Cuban guerrilla leader Ernesto "Che" Guevara, who had been waging a "liberation" movement in Bolivia, is executed
1969: Barrientos is killed in helicopter crash and is succeeded by Vice-President Luis Adolfo Siles Salinas; Siles is ousted, however, in coup led by General Alfredo Ovando Candia
1970: Ovando regime is overthrown in leftist coup led by General Juan José Torres
1971: Torres is overthrown in rebel uprising; Col. Hugo Banzer Suárez is appointed president
1974: Banzer's government orders price rises to cope with a food shortage; labor strikes and a peasant revolt result
1976: Negotiations are entered into with Chile and Peru concerning their granting Bolivia an outlet to the Pacific Ocean. Juan José Torres is slain in Argentina, resulting in massive strikes and unrest. State takes over all iron ore and manganese deposits
1977: Civilian-military coup attempt fails
1978: Gen. Juan Pereda Asbún seizes presidency in coup following elections but is toppled four months later by Gen. David Padilla Arancibia
1979: When no presidential candidate gains a majority in July elections, congress chooses Walter Guevara Arze to be interim

executive. Guevara is unseated by a coup in November and replaced by Lidia Gueiler Tejada pending new elections in 1980
1980: June election results in plurality, but not majority, for Hernán Siles Zuazo. Before congress can pick a new president, a military junta seizes power and names Gen. García Meza as head of state. Bolivia's output of tin is the lowest since 1965
1981: Nine leftist leaders are slain by security police. Interior Minister Luis Arce Gómez, linked to international cocaine traffic, is dismissed from post. Two civilians are appointed to the cabinet. Following revolts in July, García Meza is deposed by junta which assumes full power. Junta names Gen. Celso Torrelio Villa as president

---

BOTSWANA

Area: 224,764 sq. mi. **Population:** 791,000 (1979 est.)
Official Name: Republic of Botswana **Capital:** Gaborone **Nationality:** Botswana **Languages:** English is the official language; Setswana is the main African language. Various dialects of the Khoisan "click" language are spoken by the Bushmen; Afrikaans is also used **Religion:** About 15% Christian; the rest practice tribal religions **Flag:** A blue field divided by a black horizontal band edged in white **Anthem:** Our Land **Currency:** Pula (0.8 per U.S. $1)

Location: Southern Africa. Landlocked Botswana is bordered by Namibia on the north and west, by Zambia and Zimbabwe on the east, and by South Africa on the southeast and south **Features:** Most of the country is a tableland, with a mean altitude of 3,300 feet. The Kalahari Desert covers much of the southwest; in the northwest the waters of the Okavango River form a great inland delta, known as the Okavango Swamps, which extend over 6,500 sq. mi. **Chief Rivers:** Okavango, Molopo, Shashi, Limpopo

Head of State and of Government: President: Dr. Quett K.J. Masire, born 1925, elected by the National Assembly in July 1980 **Effective Date of Present Constitution:** September 30, 1966 **Legislative Body:** Parliament (unicameral), consisting of a 36-member National Assembly. Of the total membership, 32 are directly elected and 4 chosen by the elected members. The constitution also provides for a House of Chiefs, which plays an advisory role in government affairs **Local Government:** 10 districts and 3 independent towns, governed by local councils

Ethnic Composition: The majority in Botswana are Bantu (Tswana), grouped into 8 main tribes; in addition, there are some 30,000 Bushmen, 5,000 Europeans, and smaller groups of Asians, Hottentots, and those of mixed origin **Population Distribution:** 12.3% urban **Density:** 3.5 inhabitants per sq. mi.

Largest Cities: (1974 est.) Francistown 22,000, Gaborone 21,000, Selebi-Pikwe 20,572 (1975)

Per Capita Income: $337 (1978) **Gross National Product (GNP):** $250 million (1978) **Economic Statistics:** In 1973, 36% of GNP came from animal husbandry (cattle, goats, sheep) and agriculture (corn, sorghum); 17.3% from trade and services; and 16% from industry (meat processing) and mining **Minerals and Mining:** Diamonds, manganese, copper and copper/nickel, and coal are mined **Labor Force:** About 385,000, with most in agriculture **Foreign Trade:** Exports, chiefly diamonds, livestock, hides and skins, copper, nickel, canned meats, beans and sorghum, totaled $383 million in 1979. Imports, chiefly cereals, petroleum products, textiles, sugar, and motor vehicles, totaled $381 million **Principal Trade Partners:** South Africa, Britain, Zambia, United States

Vital Statistics: Birthrate, 45.6 per 1,000 of pop. (1975); estimated death rate, 23 **Life Expectancy:** 45 years **Health Statistics:** 328 inhabitants per hospital bed; 10,476 per physician (1976) **Infant Mortality:** 24.1 **Illiteracy:** 67% **Primary and Secondary School Enrollment:** 141,863 (1976) **Enrollment in Higher Education:** 469 (1975) **GNP Expended on Education:** 9.2% (1975)

Transportation: Paved roads total 500 mi. **Motor Vehicles:** 14,200 (1977) **Passenger Cars:** 3,400 **Railway Mileage:** 450 **Ports:** None **Major Airlines:** Air Botswana operates domestic flights and maintains services to South Africa and Zambia **Communications:** Government owned **Radio Transmitters:** 6 **Receivers:** 6,000 (1976) **Television:** None **Telephones:** 8,000 (1975) **Newspapers:** 1 daily, 20 per 1,000 inhabitants (1975)

Weights and Measures: Metric system **Travel Requirements:** Passport, no visa

---

Since gaining independence in 1966, the former British protectorate of Bechuanaland has seen its previously bleak economic prospects brightened by the discovery of substantial mineral wealth—diamonds, copper, and nickel.

The mineral wealth found in the country's arid northeastern area includes a diamond "pipe" (the core of an ancient volcano) at Orapa, which is one of the largest ever discovered anywhere. Development of the diamonds and other minerals by American and South African companies involves an investment of some $130 million.

With mineral development and new industry, this impoverished African country hopes to gain economic independence that will significantly add to its political independence.

Nearly surrounded by white-ruled areas, Botswana previously had seemed destined to be no more than a cattle ranch for South Africa. As head of a newly independent black African state, Botswana's late president, Sir Seretse Khama, had asserted opposition to South Africa's racist policies, but acknowledged his country's economic dependence on its southern neighbor. Still, Botswana is devoted to strengthening its commercial and psychological ties with Zambia and other independent states of black Africa, while refusing to have diplomatic relations with Pretoria.

Relations between Botswana and white-ruled Zimbabwe Rhodesia became strained as a result of incidents arising out of the guerrilla war between Zimbabwe Rhodesian black nationalists and Zimbabwe Rhodesian security forces. The Botswana deeply resented the infiltration of Zimbabwe Rhodesian security forces into their country. Eventually independence for Zimbabwe in 1980 brought an end to the incursions and opened new opportunities for trade and communications for Botswana.

Sir Seretse, an Oxford-educated lawyer, caused a controversy in his homeland as well as in South Africa by his marriage to an Englishwoman in 1948. However, his popularity gained him victory in the preindependence elections of 1965. He maintained a policy of non-racial democracy for Botswana. Sir Seretse was reelected overwhelmingly for a third term as president Oct. 20, 1979. He died on July 13, 1980, and was succeeded by Dr. Quett K.J. Masire, Vice President and Finance Minister under Sir Seretse.

HISTORY: Little is known of the origins of Botswana's peoples. The early inhabitants, the Bushmen, who now are dying out, have no recorded history. The ancestors of most of the present-day population, the Botswana, probably arrived centuries ago in Bantu migrations from Central or East Africa. In the 19th century, the great chief Khama III loosely united the Botswana against incursions of the neighboring Matabele people and Boer trekkers from the Transvaal. Under British protection, the southern area was made part of the South African Cape Colony, while the northern part, known as Bechuanaland, remained under direct British administration until it became independent Botswana

1909: Constitution of Union (now Republic) of South Africa is drafted, with a provision that Bechuanaland and other British protectorates in southern Africa, Basutoland (now Lesotho) and Swaziland, will some day be included in the union

1920-61: Advisory councils, one representing Africans, the other, Europeans, are established by British Central Authority. Central Authority establishes a Joint Advisory Council with African and European membership, which resolves to form legislative council to assist in governing the territory. A constitution for this purpose is promulgated

1965: New constitution is made effective and general elections are held for new National Assembly; seat of government is moved from Mafeking in South Africa to Gaborone

1966: Bechuanaland becomes independent member of the British Commonwealth and adopts name of Botswana. Sir Seretse Khama, grandson of Chief Khama III and leader of the Botswana Democratic party, is elected president

1973: Botswana severs diplomatic relations with Israel as a result of Middle East war

1975: A five-year treaty is signed with EC

1977: UN Security Council adopts a resolution demanding the cessation of all hostile acts against Botswana by Rhodesia

1979: Khama is reelected president for a third term by a big margin. Drought and hoof-and-mouth disease hurt cattle industry

1980: Sir Seretse dies and is succeeded by Dr. Quett K.J. Masire. Satellite tracking station begins operation at Khale

BRAZIL

Area: 3,286,470 sq. mi. **Population:** 119,024,600 (1980 census) **Official Name:** Federative Republic of Brazil **Capital:** Brasília **Nationality:** Brazilian **Languages:** Portuguese is the official and principal language. In central and southern Brazil, Italian, German, and Japanese immigrants still use their native languages **Religion:** About 93% of the population is Roman Catholic. There are about 8 million Protestants and 150,000 Jews **Flag:** Green, with a yellow diamond enclosing a blue globe containing 23 white stars and a white band inscribed with the words "Ordem e Progresso" (Order and Progress) **Anthem:** Brazilian National Hymn, beginning "From peaceful Ypiranga's banks" **Currency:** Cruzeiro (81 per U.S. $1)

Location: South America. The fifth-largest nation in the world, Brazil is bordered by every country in South America except Chile and Ecuador. It is bounded by French Guiana, Suriname, Guyana, Venezuela, and Colombia on the north, by Peru, Bolivia, and Paraguay on the west, and by Uruguay and Argentina on the south **Features:** The country is divided into four distinct major regions: the northern tropical basin of the Amazon, which flows more than 1,500 miles within the country, bordered on the north by the Guiana Highlands; the semiarid scrub land of the northeast; the agricultural and mineral heartland of the south-central plains, plateaus and highlands; and the narrow coastal belt, fringed by interior mountain ranges, extending from Natal to Porto Alegre **Chief Rivers:** Amazon, São Francisco, Paraná, Uruguay, Paraguay

Head of State and of Government: President João Baptista de Oliveira Figueiredo, born 1918, inaugurated on Mar. 15, 1979, following selection by Electoral College in 1978 for six-year term **Effective Date of Present Constitution:** January 24, 1967, extensively revised in 1969 **Legislative Body:** National Congress (bicameral), composed of the Chamber of Deputies and the Senate **Local Government:** 22 states, each with an indirectly elected governor and legislature, 4 federal territories, and 1 federal district

Ethnic Composition: The primary elements are 60% European, 12% African and a complex mixture (28%) of both **Population Distribution:** 61.2% urban **Density:** 36.2 inhabitants per sq. mi.

Largest Cities: (1975 est.—Metropolitan Areas) São Paulo 7,198,608, Rio de Janeiro 4,857,716, Belo Horizonte 1,557,464, Recife 1,249,821, Salvador 1,237,393, Fortaleza 1,109,839

Per Capita Income: $2,067 (1980) **Gross National Product (GNP):** $251.5 billion (1980) **Economic Statistics:** 38% of GNP comes from industry (food processing, chemicals, textiles, metallurgical products, vehicles and accessories, electrical and communications equipment), mining and construction; 32% from services; 8% from agriculture (rice, corn, coffee, sugarcane, soybeans, livestock, manioc, cotton); 16% from trade, and 6% from transportation and communications **Minerals and Mining:** Large deposits of iron, manganese, and bauxite; nickel, lead, tin, asbestos, chrome ore, gold, tungsten, and copper are also mined but supplies must be augmented by imports. Coal and petroleum production are also supplemented by imports **Labor Force:** Approximately 38,000,000 (1978); of which 38% is employed in agriculture, 24% in industry **Foreign Trade:** Exports, chiefly coffee, soybeans, cotton, iron ore, cane sugar, pine wood, corn, and cocoa beans, totaled $15.1 billion in 1979. Imports, mainly wheat, crude petroleum, machinery, chemicals, metals and heavy equipment, totaled $17.2 billion **Principal Trade Partners:** United States, West Germany, Argentina, Italy, The Netherlands, United Kingdom, France, Japan, Saudi Arabia, Canada, Poland

Vital Statistics: Birthrate, 37.1 per 1,000 of pop. (1975); death rate, 8.8 **Life Expectancy:** 61 years **Health Statistics:** 526 inhabitants per hospital bed; 2,117 per physician (1975) **Infant Mortality:** about 88 per 1,000 births **Illiteracy:** 17% **Primary and Secondary School Enrollment:** 20,968,339 (1974) **Enrollment in Higher Education:** 1,316,640 (1976) **GNP Expended on Education:** 2.3% (1976)

Transportation: Paved roads total 47,000 mi. **Motor Vehicles:** 7,313,500 (1976) **Passenger Cars:** 5,916,300 **Railway Mileage:** 20,447 **Ports:** Santos, Rio de Janeiro, Vitória, Salvador, Rio Grande, Recife, Paranagua, Macapá **Major Airlines:** VARIG and Cruzeiro do Sul operate domestic and international services **Communications:** Government controlled **Radio Transmitters:** 1,100 **Receivers:** 16,980,000 (1975) **Television Transmitters:** 120 **Receivers:** 10,680,000 (1975) **Telephones:** 4,500,000 (1977) **Newspapers:** 280 dailies, 39 per 1,000 inhabitants (1973)

Weights and Measures: Metric system **Travel Requirements:** Passport and visa required. Tourists need onward/return ticket or financial guarantee; $2.00 fee **International Dialing Code:** 55

Long considered the country of the future, Brazil has begun to grow visibly through industrialization within its vast geographical outline. Since 1930 the activist governments of the country, the largest in Latin America and the fifth largest in the world in area, have—despite wide ideological differences—followed roughly similar policies of industrial development and national integration of the huge hinterland and the urban coast. As a result, Brazil is the industrial leader of South America, with by far the largest gross national product.

For all its economic progress, Brazil has had more than its share of political upheaval. It has been by turns a Portuguese colony, an independent empire, a republic, a dictatorship, and, up to 1964, a representative democracy. Since the ousting of a civilian president, João Goulart, in that year, Brazil has had a succession of five army generals as presidents.

Leaving the economy largely under civilian management, the first three military administrations reformed the tax structure, began the reorganization of the state's inefficient bureaucracy, shifted some resources to the country's backward regions, attracted large amounts of U.S. and other foreign investment capital, and whipped up the pace of industrial expansion. The result is often described as Brazil's "economic miracle."

Brazil's economy fared less well under the fourth military administration, in which Ernesto Geisel, a career artillery general, served a five-year term that ended in 1979. The nation's industrial and farm exports were still growing, but these advantages were offset by increased imports, strikes, and the rapidly rising cost of living.

Gen. João Baptista Figueiredo, who had been the chief of intelligence, was sworn in as president on March 15, 1979. He had been elected five months earlier in Brazil's first contested presidential election since the coup that ousted Goulart. The print media—but not television and radio—received full freedom during the campaign.

Figueiredo inherited the economic problems of his predecessor. Almost immediately he had to send troops to restore calm and bring about a settlement of a strike by 180,000 metalworkers in São Paulo. More strikes ensued throughout 1979 and 1980. In February 1981 labor leader Luis Inacio da Silva was tried and convicted under national security laws by a military court for his role in fomenting a long metalworkers strike in 1980 which shut down Brazil's automobile industry.

At the root of the labor discontent has been the cost of living which reached an annual rate of almost 120 percent by early 1981. The rising cost of imported oil, the strikes, financing of the huge national debt, devaluation of the cruzeiro, and loss of much of the coffee crops due to drought and frost, have brought about a precarious economic situation.

On To combat soaring energy costs, the government in 1979 instituted a six-year plan for development of vehicles that run on alcohol which can be produced from Brazil's bountiful sugarcane crop. In the area of nuclear energy, Brazil is buying eight power plants and a uranium reprocessing facility from West Germany.

In his inauguration speech, Figueiredo had announced his "unswerving purpose" of restoring democracy to Brazil in the future. In August 1979, he signed a law granting amnesty to political prisoners and exiles except those held for "acts of terrorism". A Party Reform Bill was passed dissolving the two existing parties but enabling establishment of the Social Democratic Party, which supports the government, and four new opposition parties that would be allowed as long as they were democratic and in accord with the constitution.

HISTORY: In 1500 Pedro Alvares Cabral landed on the Brazilian coast and claimed the land for Portugal. The first Portuguese governor-general of Brazil was appointed in 1549. In 1727 coffee

was introduced in Brazil. In 1808 King John VI, fleeing the Napoleonic invasion of Portugal, arrived in Rio de Janeiro, and in 1815 all Portuguese dominions were designated the United Kingdom of Portugal, Brazil, and the Algarves. The king returned to Portugal in 1821, leaving behind Dom Pedro, his son, as regent

1822: Dom Pedro, later Pedro I, declares Brazil independent of Portugal and assumes title of emperor

1840: Dom Pedro II begins his 40-year rule as emperor

1888: Slavery is abolished and 700,000 slaves are emancipated

1889: The monarchy is toppled by a bloodless revolution and Brazil becomes a republic

1930: Getúlio Vargas comes to power through a revolution and establishes dictatorial rule

1942: Brazil enters WW II and declares war against Axis powers

1945-54: Military coup topples the Vargas dictatorship and restores democracy. In 1951 Vargas again becomes president. Faced with army opposition and threatened with impeachment, he commits suicide in 1954

1956-61: Presidency of Juscelino Kubitschek; capital moved from Rio de Janeiro to Brasília

1964: The elected government of João Goulart is ousted in a military coup led by General Humberto de Alencar Castelo Branco

1974: General Ernesto Geisel "elected" as the fourth successive president from the military

1975: Geisel rejects any return to democratic system of 1954-64

1979: General João Baptista de Oliveira Figueiredo sworn in as president after winning a two-party contest in late 1978

1980: President Figueiredo goes to Buenos Aires to work out agreements for economic cooperation between his country and Argentina. Pope John Paul II is warmly received by Brazilians during his 12-day visit

1981: In Paris, President Figueiredo signs a $388 million trade and credit agreement with France

BULGARIA

Area: 42,823 sq. mi. **Population:** 8,814,000 (1978 est.)

Official Name: People's Republic of Bulgaria **Capital:** Sofia **Nationality:** Bulgarian **Languages:** Bulgarian is the official and principal language; Turkish, Greek, and Armenian are spoken by minority groups **Religion:** Bulgarian Orthodox 85%, Moslem 13%; other denominations are Roman Catholicism, Protestantism, and Judaism. The government is officially atheist **Flag:** Horizontal stripes of white, green, and red, with the state emblem, a lion framed by wheatstalks, located on the white stripe near the hoist **Anthem:** Mila Rodino (Dear Fatherland) national anthem (1964) **Currency:** Lev (0.85 per U.S. $1)

Location: Southeast Europe, on the eastern part of the Balkan peninsula. Bulgaria is bordered on the north by Romania, on the east by the Black Sea, on the south by Turkey and Greece, and on the west by Yugoslavia **Features:** The country is divided into several roughly parallel east/west zones: the Danubian tableland in the north; the Stara Planina (Balkan) Mountains through the central part; and the Thracian Plain and Rhodope Mountains in the south and southwest **Chief Rivers:** Danube, Maritsa, Iskur, Tundzha

Political Leader and Head of State: Todor Zhivkov, born 1911; First Secretary of the Central Committee of the Communist party since 1954, reelected 1981. In 1971 he was elected chairman of the State Council **Head of Government:** Grisha Filipov, appointed 1981, Chairman of the Council of Ministers (premier). The Chairman of the National Assembly is Stanko Todorov **Effective Date of Present Constitution:** May 1971 **Legislative Body:** Parliament (unicameral National Assembly), consisting of 400 members elected for 5 years. Although the National Assembly is nominally the supreme organ of state power, real power is, in fact, wielded by the Politburo and Secretariat of the Communist party **Local Government:** 27 provinces and one city commune, each governed by an elective people's council

Ethnic Composition: 85% of the population consists of ethnic Bulgarians; the only sizable minority is the Turks, who make up about 9%. Macedonians, Armenians, Gypsies, and Greeks constitute smaller ethnic groups **Population Distribution:** 59.4% urban **Density:** 206 inhabitants per sq. mi.

Largest Cities: (1975 census) Sofia 965,355, Plovdiv 305,091, Varna 269,980, Ruse 171,264, Burgas 148,236

Per Capita Income: $3,370 (1980) **Gross National Product (GNP):** $30 billion (1980) **Economic Statistics:** About 43% of GNP comes from industry (food processing, engineering and metallurgy, textiles, chemicals, rubber); 20% from agriculture (wheat, corn, barley, sugar beets); 7% from commerce; and the rest from other activities **Minerals and Mining:** Lead, iron ore, zinc, and copper are produced in substantial quantities. Large coal reserves exist but the coal is of low caloric value **Labor Force:** 4.7 million (1980), of which

26% is employed in industry, and 26% in agriculture **Foreign Trade:** Exports, mainly foodstuffs, machines and equipment and dairy products, fuels, raw materials and minerals, rose oil, totaled $9 billion in 1979. Imports, chiefly machines and equipment, fuels, minerals, raw materials, metals, animal and vegetable products, totaled $8.6 billion **Principal Trade Partners:** USSR, East Germany, Czechoslovakia, West Germany, Poland, Romania, Greece

Vital Statistics: Birthrate 16.1 per 1,000 of pop. (1977); death rate 10.7 **Life Expectancy:** 71 years **Health Statistics:** 115 inhabitants per hospital bed; 453 per physician (1976) **Infant Mortality:** 23.7 per 1,000 births (1977) **Illiteracy:** 5% **Primary and Secondary School Enrollment:** 1,317,659 (1976) **Enrollment in Higher Education:** 128,593 (1975) **GNP Expended on Education:** 5.4% (1976)

Transportation: Surfaced roads total 7,884 mi. **Motor Vehicles:** 39,000 (1967) **Passenger Cars:** 11,400 (1967) **Railway Mileage:** 3,780 **Ports:** Burgas, Varna **Major Airlines:** Bulgarian Airlines-Balkan operates domestic and international services **Communications:** Government controlled **Radio Transmitters:** 32 **Licenses:** 2,750,000 (1976) **Television Transmitters:** 154 **Licenses:** 1,546,000 (1976) **Telephones:** 853,000 (1976) **Newspapers:** 13 dailies, 232 per 1,000 inhabitants (1975)

Weights and Measures: Metric system **Travel Requirements:** Passport and visa required; transit visa, up to 30 hours, $9.00; tourist visa, 30 hours-2 months, $14.00

Long one of the more backward countries of Eastern Europe, Bulgaria has sought to modernize itself under Communist rule along several directions. The country has expanded its industry, often in close coordination with the Soviet Union. Bulgaria and Romania are the only East European countries in which Soviet troops were not stationed.

Bulgaria produces early fruits and vegetables for the rest of the Soviet bloc. The country's Black Sea coast has been developed as a summer resort area.

At the 10th congress of the Bulgarian Communist Party, held in April 1971 and attended by Soviet leader Leonid Brezhnev, a new constitution and a new party program were adopted. The congress reaffirmed the dominance of Todor Zhivkov, the veteran Communist Party boss, and hailed the country's solidarity with the Soviet Union. But in the 1970s the government had to deal with domestic unrest on the part of workers seeking higher pay and better living conditions. In an effort to help the ailing economy, Bulgaria in 1980 permitted foreign companies to establish joint business ventures with Bulgarian companies for the first time.

HISTORY: Bulgaria, part of ancient Thrace and Moesia, was settled by Slavic tribes in the 6th century. In the 7th century the Slavs were conquered by Turkic-speaking Bulgars, who in time fully merged with the Slavs and whose domain continued to expand until the early part of the 11th century, when the Bulgarian state was annexed by the Byzantine Empire. Bulgaria again became a major Balkan power in the 12th and 13th centuries. In the 14th century, however, it was overrun by the Ottoman Turks and remained under their rule for 5 centuries

1876: Bulgarians revolt against Turkish rule but rebellion is crushed by brutal Turkish reprisals

1878: A large Bulgaria is created under Treaty of San Stefano ending Russo-Turkish Wars. However, treaty is revised by Congress of Berlin, making northern Bulgaria a principality under Turkish suzerainty and leaving southern Bulgaria, known as Eastern Rumelia, under direct Turkish rule

1885-1908: Alexander of Battenberg, first prince of Bulgaria, annexes Eastern Rumelia. His successor, Prince Ferdinand of Saxe-Coburg-Gotha, profiting from revolution of Young Turks in 1908, proclaims Bulgaria's independence

1912-13: Bulgaria, allied with Serbia, Greece, and Montenegro, enters first Balkan War against Turkey, which is expelled from all of Europe except the Constantinople area. Bulgarian claims to Macedonia result in second Balkan War, with Bulgaria fighting the armies of Serbia, Romania, Greece, and Turkey; Bulgaria is defeated and loses territory to all its enemies

1915-1918: Bulgaria enters World War I on side of Germany and Austria-Hungary, is defeated and loses territory

1941-44: Bulgaria joins Axis powers in World War II, declaring war on Britain and United States but not on USSR; in 1944 USSR

declares war on Bulgaria and occupies country; Communists seize power with Soviet help

1946-48: Monarchy is abolished and a people's republic established. Industry is nationalized and resistance to collectivization of agriculture is broken

1955: Bulgaria joins Warsaw Pact

1969: Zhivkov regime launches campaign against Western influences in arts and culture and warns against anti-Soviet "revisionist" nationalism

1971: New constitution and new Bulgarian Communist Party program adopted

1976: Bulgaria meets with other Balkan nations for first conference on Balkan cooperation since WW II

1978: Bulgaria extradites suspected West German terrorists. Diplomatic problems arise over steel dumping and assassinations of Bulgarian exiles

---

BURMA

Area: 261,789 sq. mi. **Population:** 32,913,000 (1979 est.) **Official Name:** Socialist Republic of the Union of Burma **Capital:** Rangoon **Nationality:** Burmese **Languages:** Burmese, the official language, is spoken by 80%; the rest speak a variety, including Tamil, Hindi, Chinese, Shan, Karen, Kachin, Chin and Kayah; English is used in business **Religion:** 85% of the people are Buddhists; minority religions are Hinduism, Islam, Christianity, and animism **Flag:** A red field with a blue rectangle in the upper left corner containing a cog wheel and ear of paddy surrounded by 14 white stars **Anthem:** Our Free Homeland **Currency:** Kyat (7.1 per U.S. $1)

Location: Southeast Asia. Burma is bordered on the north and northeast by China, on the east by Laos and Thailand, on the south by the Andaman Sea and the Bay of Bengal, and on the west by Bangladesh and India **Features:** The country is rimmed on the north, east, and west by mountain ranges forming a giant horseshoe. Enclosed within this mountain barrier is a central basin containing most of the country's agricultural land and population. The Salween River, cutting deep gorges through the Shan Plateau and Karenni hills in the east separates the narrow Tenasserim coast from the central basin. A similar narrow coastal strip lies in the west between the Bay of Bengal and the Arakan Yoma mountain range **Chief Rivers:** Irrawaddy, Salween, Sittang, Mekong

Head of State and of Government: President: General U Ne Win, born 1911, chairman of the Council of State, elected president in 1974, reelected 1978 for four years. He is assisted by a Cabinet headed by Prime Minister U Maung Maung Kha, elected 1977 **Effective Date of Present Constitution:** January 1974 **Legislative Body:** Parliament (unicameral People's Assembly) with 464 members elected for 4-year terms **Local Government:** 7 states and 7 divisions. Since March 1974, Peoples Councils have been elected at various local levels

Ethnic Composition: Burmans, ethnically related to the Tibetans, make up about 72% of the population; the Karens (7%), the Shans (6%), the Kachins (2%), and the Chins (2%) are the next largest ethnic groups. Chinese (3%) and Hindus and Pakistanis (6%) constitute the other major ethnic groups **Population Distribution:** 19% urban **Density:** 126 inhabitants per sq. mi.

Largest Cities: (1973 est.) Rangoon 2,055,000; Mandalay 417,000; Moulmein 202,000

Per Capita Income: $186 (1980) **Gross National Product (GNP):** $6.4 billion (1980) **Economic Statistics:** In 1973, 37% of GNP came from agriculture, fishing, and forestry; 11% from industry and mining; and 43% from trade and services **Minerals and Mining:** Burma is rich in minerals, but production is low; petroleum, copper and tin are exploited; small quantities of tungsten, lead, zinc, nickel, cobalt, and precious stones are produced **Labor Force:** 12.2 million, of which 67% is employed in agriculture, and 9% in industry **Foreign Trade:** Exports, chiefly rice, teak and various ores, totaled $414 million in 1979. Imports, mainly textiles, machinery, transport equipment, and foodstuffs, totaled $714 million **Principal Trade Partners:** Singapore, Japan, Indonesia, West Germany, China, Hong Kong, France, Britain, United States

Vital Statistics: Birthrate 39.5 per 1,000 pop. (1975); death rate 15.8 **Life Expectancy:** 53 years **Health Statistics:** 1,125 inhabitants per hospital bed; 5,408 per physician (1976) **Infant Mortality:** 60 per 1,000 births **Illiteracy:** 30% **Education Statistics:** 18,670 primary and secondary schools with a total enrollment of 4,370,987 (1976) **Enrollment in Higher Education:** 56,083 (1975) **GNP Expended on Education:** 1.7% (1976)

Transportation: Surfaced roads total 13,000 mi. **Motor Vehicles:** 79,900 (1977) **Passenger Cars:** 38,600 **Railway Mileage:** 2,040 **Ports:** Rangoon, Sittwe, Bassein, Moulmein, Tavoy, Mergui **Major Airlines:** Burma Airways operates both domestic and international services **Communications:** Government owned **Radio Transmit-**

ters: 5 **Licenses:** 665,000 (1976) **Television:** 1 **Telephones:** 32,000 (1976) **Newspapers:** 7 dailies, 10 copies per 1,000 inhabitants (1975)

Weights and Measures: British weights and measures as well as local units are used **Travel Requirements:** Passport; visa; transit visa, 24 hours, $1.65, 2 photos; tourist visa, one week, $4.85, 3 photos

A neglected adjunct of imperial India until 1937, Burma started its modern nationhood doubly colonialized: by the British and by the Indians, who ran the lower levels of government and, with the Chinese, dominated commerce.

The Japanese occupation of Burma during World War II turned the lush, rich land into a battlefield on which Burmese nationalists first fought the British and then the Japanese, whom they found to be worse oppressors.

The inability of the government to mollify the rebellious hill peoples, the demise of the coalition which had ruled since 1948, and the prevalence of corruption led to the unopposed military take-over of General Ne Win in 1958. He gave Burma two years of comparatively able government and then returned authority to civilians. While U Nu's faction won a convincing victory, the country's troubles proved too powerful for his new government.

In 1962 Ne Win again took over, jailing many politicians and banning all parties but the army's. The 15-man Revolutionary Council began broad nationalization, driving out Indians and generally sealing off Burma. The replacement of Indians and Chinese with Burmese proved politically popular but economically disastrous.

Under a new constitution adopted in 1974, Ne Win was elected president, and in 1978 he was reelected for another four-year term. The 1978 national elections gave the appearance of unity, since all candidates were members of Burma's single party, the Socialist Program party. Burma was beset, however, by internal disunity, underscored by stepped-up guerrilla strife and the flight in early 1978 of some 200,000 Moslems from western Burma into Bangladesh to escape persecution by government forces.

As late as mid-1981, sporadic guerrilla warfare was hampering mining and lumbering activities, but progress in agriculture amd foreign trade was producing an economic upturn. In 1980, Ne Win declared a general amnesty, releasing 5,000 political prisoners and allowing U Nu and 700 other exiles to return home.

HISTORY: A Mongoloid race from Tibet, the Burmese moved southward before the 9th century and settled along the Irrawaddy. In the 11th century, King Anawratha established supremacy over the Irrawaddy delta and introduced Hinayana Buddhism. His kingdom fell to Kublai Khan in 1287, after which it passed to the Shans, who ruled until 1546 as tributaries of China. Following the rise of new Burmese dynasties, Burma was once again unified, only to be annexed piecemeal by Britain in the 19th century

1937: Burma obtains dominionlike status

1942-45: Japan invades Burma during World War II and expels the British from most of the country. U.S., British, and Chinese forces mount a counterattack and expel the Japanese

1948: The Union of Burma is set up as an independent republic. U Nu becomes the first premier

1962: General Ne Win takes over from U Nu

1970: Government troops clash with rebels in northern Burma

1971: Large Karen minority plans new drive against government; Chinese-backed Burmese Communists launch widespread attacks on troop positions in northeast Burma

1974: New constitution adopted by referendum. Ne Win installed as president

1975: Army claims defeat of insurgents. Students riot

1976: Karen rebels and Communist Shan insurgents renew fighting. Military plot to overthrow Ne Win aborted

1978 Ne Win reelected for second four-year term. About 200,000 Moslems flee into Bangladesh

1979: Burma leaves the nonaligned nations movement, saying it was disillusioned by Cuban handling of a summit meeting

1980: Ne Win declares political amnesty, frees 5,000 prisoners. U Nu returns from exile

1981: Ne Win announces that he will resign presidency in November

---

BURUNDI

Area: 10,747 sq. mi. **Population:** 4,021,910 (1979 census)

Official Name: Republic of Burundi **Capital:** Bujumbura **Nationality:** Burundi **Languages:** Kirundi (Rundi), a Bantu tongue, and French are the official languages; Swahili is the trade language **Religion:** 60% are Christians, chiefly Roman Catholic; 2% Moslems and the rest are animists **Flag:** A white saltire (diagonal cross) with green and red quarters, and a white circle in the center bearing 3 red six-pointed stars outlined in green **Anthem:** Dear Burundi, O Sweet Land **Currency:** Burundi franc (90 per U.S. $1)

Location: East-central Africa. Burundi is bordered by Rwanda on the north, Tanzania on the east and south, Lake Tanganyika on the southwest, and Zaire on the northwest **Features:** Most of the country consists of grassy uplands and high plateaus. The Ruzizi River Valley and Lake Tanganyika, both along the western boundary with the Congo, constitute part of the Great Rift Valley **Chief Rivers:** Kagera, Ruvubu, Malagarazi, Ruzizi

Head of State and Government: President: Col. Jean-Baptiste Bagaza, born 1946, seized power in 1976 and appointed president **Effective Date of Present Constitution:** 1974, suspended 1976 **Legislative Body:** None **Local Government:** 8 provinces, each headed by a governor

Ethnic Composition: 85% are Bahutu (Hutu), farmers of Bantu origin; 14% are Tutsi (Watusi, Batutsi), a tall warrior people of Hamitic origin; and 1% Twa (Batwa), aboriginal pygmies **Population Distribution:** 5% urban **Density:** 374 inhabitants per sq. mi.

Largest Cities: (1979 census) Bujumbura 141,000, Gitega 19,500, Bururi 7,800

Per Capita Income: $122 (1978) **Gross National Product (GNP):** $490 million (1978) **Economic Statistics:** In 1977, 58% of GNP was derived from agriculture (coffee, cotton, tea, bananas, sweet potatoes, cassava, millet and sorghum); and 12% from industry (chiefly food processing and textiles) **Minerals and Mining:** Bastnaesite, used for the manufacture of color TV tubes, and small amounts of cassiterite, tungsten, and gold are mined. Important nickel deposits are to be exploited **Labor Force:** 2,000,000 (1976), with 95% in agriculture **Foreign Trade:** Exports, chiefly coffee, cotton, tea, hides, and minerals, totaled $90 million in 1979. Imports, mainly textiles and leather, vehicles, machinery, food products, petroleum, consumer goods, totaled $102 million **Principal Trade Partners:** United States, Belgium, Luxembourg, West Germany, France, Kenya, Tanzania, Britain, Italy

Vital Statistics: Estimated birth rate, 46.8 per 1,000 of pop. (1975); death rate, 20.4 **Life Expectancy:** 41 years **Health Statistics:** 857 inhabitants per hospital bed; 45,432 per physician (1975) **Infant Mortality:** 150 per 1,000 births **Illiteracy:** 90% **Primary and Secondary School Enrollment:** 274,931 (1976) **Enrollment in Higher Education:** 1,002 (I975) **GNP Expended on Education:** 2.2% (1976)

Transportation: Of some 4,800 miles of road only about 190 miles are paved **Motor Vehicles:** 7,300 (1976) **Passenger Cars:** 5,100 **Railway Mileage:** None **Ports:** None **Major Airlines:** Air Burundi provides service to neighboring countries **Communications:** Government owned **Radio Transmitters:** 6 **Receivers:** 105,000 (1976) **Television:** None **Telephones:** 4,000 (1976) **Newspapers:** 2 dailies, 0.3 per 1,000 inhabitants (1974)

Weights and Measures: Metric system **Travel Requirements:** Passport, visa, $11 fee, 3 pictures

---

One of Africa's least-known and poorest countries, Burundi was until independence in 1962 the southern half of the former Belgian trust territory of Ruanda-Urundi. The landlocked country—Bujumbura, the capital, is nearly 1,000 miles by lakerail routes from the nearest seaport, Dar es Salaam, in Tanzania—remains a geophysical, ethnic and economic twin of neighboring Rwanda.

Like Rwanda, Burundi is small, densely populated, heavily eroded, and the home of diverse peoples—the tall Tutsi (better known as Watusi), the traditional ruling minority; the medium-height Hutu, the majority peasant folk; and the dwindling pygmy Twa. However, in contrast to Rwanda where the majority Hutu rule, in Burundi the minority Tutsi caste has control and is reluctant to better the lives of the Hutu masses. As a result, foreign assistance to Burundi is less than half that provided to Rwanda, since donors assume their aid would end up serving the Tutsi elite.

The overthrow of the monarchy and proclamation of a republic in 1966 by a young Tutsi prime minister, Capt. Michel Micombero, opened the way to relative stability and concentration on needed economic development. While there have been gains in fiscal stability, Burundi continues to depend primarily on a small and fluctuating production of coffee.

Discontent among the Hutu has been an obstacle to more rapid development. In 1970 an alleged Hutu plot to massacre the Tutsi and seize power led to executions. In 1972-73 hostilities between the ruling Tutsis and the more numerous Hutus escalated, as Hutu tribesmen entered the country from Tanzania and Rwanda, precipitating fighting in which more than 100,000 were killed.

In November 1976 Burundi's armed forces deposed the president without violence, and a Belgian-trained political scientist, Col. Jean-Baptiste Bagaza, is now in control.

HISTORY: Burundi's earliest inhabitants, the pygmy Twa, were supplanted by the Hutu, a Bantu people, who, in turn, were subjugated in the 15th or 16th century by the Tutsi, a tall, warrior people, coming probably from Ethiopia. Although Burundi was visited briefly by European explorers, it was not until the late 19th century that serious efforts at colonization were attempted
1899: Burundi, along with neighboring Rwanda, is made part of German East Africa
1916: Belgian forces from the Congo defeat Germans, occupy Burundi and Rwanda
1923-61: Burundi and Rwanda become Belgian mandated territory known as Ruanda-Urundi which in 1946 is made United Nations trusteeship. Louis Rwagasore, son of the Tutsi Mwami (king), becomes premier; he is assassinated
1962: Kingdom of Burundi attains full independence under Mwami Mwambutsa IV
1965: Premier Pierre Ngendandumwe assassinated; Dr. Pie Masumbuko becomes acting premier
1966: Premier Michel Micombero deposes King Ntare V, declares himself President of Republic
1972-73: Tutsi-Hutu war results in more than 100,000 deaths
1978: In Oct., outbreak of cholera draws foreign medical teams
1979: Approximately 85 missionaries, mostly Catholic, are expelled in June on grounds of preaching against the government

CAMBODIA

Area: 69,898 sq. mi. **Population:** 5,200,000 (1980 est.-CIA)
Official Name: Democratic Kampuchea (functions in countryside); People's Republic of Kampuchea (pro-Vietnamese, in Phnom Penh) **Capital:** Phnom Penh **Nationality:** Cambodian or Kampuchean **Languages:** Cambodian, or Khmer, is the official and predominant language **Religion:** The vast majority practice Theravada Buddhism **Flag (Democratic Kampuchea):** Red, with a stylized yellow three-towered temple in the middle Flag (People's Republic): Red, with a stylized yellow five-towered temple in the middle **Currency:** Riel

Location: Southeast Asia. Cambodia is bounded by Thailand and Laos on the north, by Vietnam on the southeast, by the Gulf of Thailand on the southwest, and by Thailand on the west **Features:** The country largely consists of a saucer-shaped alluvial plain drained by the Mekong River and shut off by mountains **Chief Rivers:** Mekong, Stung Sen

Head of State (Democratic Kampuchea): Khieu Samphan is Presidium Chairman and Prime Minister **Head of State (People's Republic):** President Heng Samrin, born l93l, is head of the People's Revolutionary Council **Effective Date of Present Constitution:** None **Local Government:** 19 provinces

Ethnic Composition: Cambodians, or Khmer, make up about 87% of the population; Chinese 5%, and Chams (Moslems descended from the people of the ancient kingdom of Champa) make up the rest **Density:** 74 inhabitants per sq. mi.

Largest Cities: Phnom Penh 600,000 (1970 est.); reported to be c. 300,000 in 1980; (1972 est.) Battambang 80,000, Kompong Cham 50,000, Pursat 20,000

Per Capita Income: $114 (1979) **Gross National Product (GNP):** $660 million (1979) **Economic Statistics:** In normal times over-

whelmingly agricultural (rice, rubber, beans, corn), with a little industry (textiles, cement, rubber products) **Minerals and Mining:** Phosphates, gemstones and gold were produced, and there are known quantities of unexploited iron ore, manganese, and phosphates **Foreign Trade:** Rubber and dried fish are known exports, and oil and machinery are imported **Principal Trade Partners:** Vietnam, Laos, Soviet Bloc

Transportation: Paved roads totaled 1,600 mi. in 1975 **Railway Mileage:** 400 (1975) **Port:** Kompong Som **Communications:** Government owned

Weights and Measures: Metric system **Travel Requirements:** No U.S. relations exist, and tourists are not accepted at present

During 22 years of existence as an independent nation, caught in the middle of the East-West political and military struggle in Southeast Asia, Cambodia managed to walk the tightrope of neutrality. Its success was credited to the diplomatic skill of Prince Norodom Sihanouk, who started as a youthful king under the French, abdicated to fill a more active political role as premier, and then became the country's first chief of state.

Sihanouk managed to maintain Cambodia's neutrality even as the Vietnam War intruded increasingly on—and over—the eastern border. Then, in March 1970, while he was out of the country, his government was overthrown in a coup led by Lt. Gen. Lon Nol.

Within a month, Cambodia's small and ill-equipped army was fighting the Vietnamese Communists and Prince Sihanouk was forming a government in exile based in Peking. The war went badly for the Cambodians, who appealed to the world for help against the enemy's sudden consolidation of its enclaves in the east. Late in April there was a response: South Vietnamese and American troops drove across the border to smash the sanctuaries. Many Vietnamese Communists moved west and assumed control of large sections of the country, including the temples at Angkor. Phnom Penh itself was often isolated from the only seaport.

In mid-1973, the United States was hoping to nudge Cambodia's exiled Prince Sihanouk and Khmer insurgent leaders into serious peace talks with members of General Lon Nol's regime. The diplomatic pressure was being brought to bear against a backdrop of urgency caused by the steady advance of Communist troops toward Phnom Penh and the imminent end of U.S. bombing raids in the country. It was at this time that the Pentagon admitted having secretly bombed Communist forces in Cambodia as early as 1969 and supplying false statistics to the U.S. Senate.

The war, with U.S. help, continued through 1974 and into 1975, with Khmer Rouge forces moving ever closer to the capital city of Phnom Penh. The end came swiftly in April 1975, with the departure of President Lon Nol and the evacuation of U.S. civilians and embassy personnel. According to Cambodian estimates, nearly 800,000 people had been killed in the war and 200,000 wounded.

In the following months, refugees who escaped to Thailand reported that hundreds of thousands of people had been forcibly moved from the cities to rural areas. Almost the entire population of Phnom Penh—a city swollen by 2 million refugees—was evacuated and put to work in the rice fields. Refugees spoke of long forced marches, starvation and wholesale killings by the Khmer Rouge.

In January 1976 a new constitution went into effect and the state took a new name: Democratic Kampuchea. Elections were held on March 20 and a People's Representative Assembly of 250 was selected. Prince Sihanouk, who had returned to Phnom Penh in late 1975, announced his resignation as Head of State on April 5 and Khieu Samphan became President of the State Presidium. In September 1977, Pol Pot ended his country's virtual isolation by making a trip to Peking, where he was identified as the Secretary of the Central Committee of the Cambodian Communist Party, Prime Minister and the prime force in making sweeping changes.

Under Pol Pot—he had been Saloth Sar, a schoolteacher, according to Prince Sihanouk—the country's economy and manpower were reshaped drastically. All lands and means of production belonged to the state. Private plots, permitted even in China and the USSR, were forbidden. Wages were paid as food rations, but they were meager, and no money was circulated. The foremost economic activity was the rebuilding of irrigation canals and dikes that had been destroyed in the civil war.

The outside world was ignored, except for China, which sent technical advisers and delivered supplies through Kompong Som, Cambodia's only port. Reports carried to neighboring countries said that the harsh treatment had produced a high death toll—somewhere between 500,000 and 2 million. U.S. President Carter accused Cambodia of being the world's worst violator of human rights.

Enemies for centuries, Cambodia and Vietnam fought frequent border clashes in 1977 and 1978. In December 1978, Vietnamese troops moved steadily across Cambodia with, Hanoi said, the aid of Cambodian insurgents. On Jan. 9, 1979, Phnom Penh fell, and Pol Pot's government was replaced with the Hanoi-backed People's Revolutionary Council of Cambodia. A Cambodian, Heng Samrin took over as president, and he declared that "during the last three years, they [the Khmer Rouge under Pol Pot] killed millions." Entire villages and communes had been slaughtered, he said. On Feb. 18, he signed a treaty of peace and friendship with Vietnam.

Despite the change in governments, the fighting continued. Khmer Rouge loyalists fled into the jungles or mixed with the population, and Pol Pot reportedly was with them. The Khmer Rouge recaptured the port of Kompong Som in January for their first major victory. Soon they were cutting roads and thus denying supplies to Vietnam troops, but they pursued a policy of avoiding big-scale confrontations. Estimates were that Vietnam had 100,000 soldiers in Cambodia, while the Pol Pot forces had 40,000 to 50,000 men and were receiving some aid through Thailand.

Possibly as many as 4 million Cambodians died from 1975 through 1979. Fearing that another 2 million or more might starve because crops had not been planted or were destroyed in the fighting, UNICEF and the International Red Cross took charge of receiving food from 51 nations. Massive tie-ups in ports and warehouses occurred in early 1980, but distribution became more effective toward the end of the year, and, in 1981, a UN study reported that the threat of widespread starvation and malnutrition had receded.

The fighting continued, as several anti-Vietnamese groups other than the Pol Pot forces also became active in the resistance. Early in 1981, the exiled Sihanouk failed in a bid to unite under his own leadership all of the factions opposing the Samrin regime. Later in the year, the new Reagan Administration in Washington expressed qualified U.S. support for a united front.

HISTORY: Modern Cambodia is what remains of the great Khmer Empire, which by the 1200s stretched across Southeast Asia from the South China Sea westward into Burma. By the 1800s the Khmer holdings had been reduced to the present size of Cambodia by the invasions of the Vietnamese and Siamese
1863: French protectorate is established over Cambodia
1887: Cambodia is incorporated in the Union of Indo-China
1945: Japanese invade Cambodia, driving out the Vichy French
1946: French return and grant Cambodia autonomy within the French Union
1953-54: Cambodia achieves full independence; leaves French Union

1970: Prince Sihanouk is ousted in pro-Western coup; U.S. and South Vietnamese troops enter Cambodia in drive against North Vietnamese forces; Cambodians and South Vietnamese continue fighting after withdrawal of U.S. ground troops. Cambodia is declared a republic
1971: United States expands bombing strikes and troop-ferrying missions; South Vietnamese driven from Cambodia
1973: Pentagon admits it conducted 14 months (1969/70) of secret bombings in Cambodia. Bombing halted Aug. 15
1974: Government troops and insurgents continue military operations. Long Boret forms 15-member wartime cabinet to replace the coalition government, which resigned June 13. The U.S. airlifts supplies
1975: U.S. triples its airlift to overcome effect of insurgents' blockade of roads into Phnom Penh and of Mekong River. April 1: Lon Nol leaves country. Government resistance begins to crumble. April 12: U.S. closes Phnom Penh embassy and evacuates staff. April 16: Government surrenders and insurgents enter Phnom Penh. War ends. May 14: U.S. air, sea and ground forces battle Cambodians after seizure of the American merchant ship Mayaguez in the Gulf of Siam. The ship and crew of 39 are freed
1976: New constitution adopted in December goes into effect. Elections held on March 20. April 5: Prince Sihanouk resigns as Head of State
1977: Pol Pot identified as nation's leader
1978: Border clashes with Vietnam and Thailand intensify
1979: Phnom Penh falls, Pol Pot's government ("Democratic Kampuchea") retreats to the countryside, and the Vietnam-backed People's Revolutionary Council takes over, with Heng Samrin as president of the "People's Republic of Kampuchea"
1980: UNICEF and the Red Cross direct a famine-relief effort, but distribution of food apparently is slowed by government inertia. In the "Democratic Kampuchea" government, Khieu Samphan replaces Pol Pot as head of state
1981: Threat of famine eases. Sihanouk attempts to unify anti-Vietnam, anti-Samrin forces

---

CAMEROON

Area: 183,568 sq. mi. **Population:** 8,058,000 (1978 est.)
Official Name: United Republic of Cameroon **Capital:** Yaoundé **Nationality:** Cameroonian **Languages:** French (spoken by 75%) and English (25%) are both official languages; 24 African languages are spoken **Religion:** 33% Christian (mainly in the south); 15% Moslem (mainly in the north); the rest are animists **Flag:** Vertical green, red, and yellow stripes, with a yellow star in the center of the red stripe **Anthem:** O, Cameroon, Cradle of Our Ancestors **Currency:** CFA Franc (263 per U.S. $1)

Location: West-central Africa. Cameroon is bordered by Lake Chad on the north, by Chad and the Central African Republic on the east, by the Congo, Gabon, and Equatorial Guinea on the south, by the Gulf of Guinea on the west, and by Nigeria on the west and northwest **Features:** Of the country's four distinct regions, the south consists of a low coastal plain with equatorial rain forests, the center forms a transitional plateau, the west is an area of mountainous forests, and the north is low rolling savanna **Chief Rivers:** Sanaga, Nyong

Head of State and of Government: President Ahmadou Ahidjo, born 1924, elected 1960, reelected to fifth 5-year term in April 1980, assisted by a cabinet headed by the premier, Paul Biya, appointed 1975 **Effective Date of Present Constitution:** May 1972 **Legislative Body:** National Assembly (unicameral), consisting of 120 members elected by universal suffrage for 5 years **Local Goverment:** 7 provinces with appointed governors

Ethnic Composition: Estimates of the number of tribal groups run as high as 200. The main divisions are the Bantus and semi-Bantus, which include the Beti and Bamiléké; the Sudanese, mainly Kirdis; and the Arab Foulbé. Pygmies inhabit the equatorial forest **Population Distribution:** 25% urban **Density:** 44 inhabitants per sq. mi.
Largest Cities: (1975 estimates) Douala 435,000, Yaoundé 274,000, N'Kongsamba 67,000

Per Capita Income: $600 (1980) **Gross Domestic Product (GDP):** $4.9 billion (1980) **Economic Statistics:** 33% of GDP came from agriculture (coffee, cocoa, bananas, cotton, peanuts, livestock, rubber, palm oil) and 24% from industry (aluminum, paper, chemicals) **Minerals and Mining:** Large deposits of bauxite ore, iron ore, and limestone; traces of mica and phosphates; small deposits of tin and gold. Petroleum and natural gas exploitation is important **Labor Force:** Over 3 million; 75% in agriculture **Foreign Trade:** Exports, chiefly coffee, cocoa beans; aluminum, petroleum, wood, cotton, and rubber, totaled $1.1 billion in 1979. Imports, mainly vehicles and transportation equipment, industrial machinery and other capital goods, consumer goods, food, beverages, and tobacco, totaled

$1.1 billion **Principal Trade Partners:** EC countries (mainly France), United States, Japan, adjacent African nations
Vital Statistics: Birthrate, 40.4 per 1,000 of pop. (1975); death rate, 22 **Life Expectancy:** 41 years **Health Statistics:** 390 inhabitants per hospital bed; 15,820 per physician (1976) **Infant Mortality:** 137 per 1,000 births **Illiteracy:** 82% **Primary and Secondary School Enrollment:** 1,375,548 (1977) **Enrollment in Higher Education:** 7,191 (1975) **GNP Expended on Education:** 4.6% (1976)
Transportation: Paved roads total about 1,338 miles **Motor Vehicles:** 110,700 (1976) **Passenger cars:** 59,500 **Railway Mileage:** 727 **Ports:** Douala, Tiko, Victoria, Kribi **Major Airlines:** Cameroon Airlines operates international and domestic services **Communications:** Government owned **Radio Transmitters:** 8 **Receivers:** 603,000 (1974) **Television:** None **Telephones:** 22,000 (1973) **Newspapers:** 2 dailies, 4 copies per 1,000 inhabitants (1975)
Weights and Measures: Metric system **Travel Requirements:** Passport, visa required beyond 1 month stay, valid up to 3 months, $5 fee, 2 pictures

Cameroon has been one of the main racial crossroads of Africa as a result of Bantu migrations from the east and links to the Sahara caravan trade to the north. Extending nearly 800 miles in length from the Gulf of Guinea to Lake Chad, the country is a cross section of Africa from desert north through central plateau and grasslands to southern rain forest.

Formerly a German colony, Cameroon was divided between France and Britain after World War I, with the French getting about four-fifths of the area. The country was reunited as a federal republic in 1961, after a UN plebiscite had resulted in the addition of the northern part of former British Cameroons to Nigeria.

The two areas, West Cameroon (formerly British) and the larger East Cameroon (formerly French) were governed as constituent states, each with its own legislature. The new constitution which went into effect in May 1972 established a unitary state with a strong executive authority and an elected national assembly.

Cameroon is the only African country in which both French and English are official languages. The Federal University of Cameroon, established in Yaoundé in 1962, is the first in Africa to teach courses in French and English, as well as one of the first to establish a medical school.

Cameroon has been one of Africa's "quiet" countries, in which the single-party government of President Ahmadou Ahidjo has maintained a measure of political and economic stability.

Before Cameroon became an independent republic in 1960, the former French eastern area was torn by a terrorist revolt. Protracted rebel activities in the central part of the country were suppressed in 1970. Despite the diversity of its peoples, cultures, and religions, however, Cameroon has escaped the coups and civil wars that have plagued neighboring countries.

Cameroon's great diversity of tropical produce—timber, cocoa, coffee, rubber, palm oil, cotton, and a wide range of food crops—has been the basis for an economic growth that has been averaging nine percent a year. Although France remains the country's chief partner in trade and investment, British, American, West German, and Japanese interests have been attracted by the favorable economic and investment climate. Petroleum production began in 1978, and by 1980 it amounted to more than three million metric tons.

Education and health services also are increasing and Cameroonians take pride in the fact that 70 percent of the country's children attend school, a high rate for developing Africa.

HISTORY: The country was given its name by 15th century Portuguese explorers. Impressed with the number of shrimp in one of the rivers, they called it Rio dos Camarões (River of Shrimp) and extended the name to the entire region. After being made a German colony in the late 19th century, the country was occupied during World War I by the French and British, who divided it under League of Nations mandates
1946: French and British mandates are converted into United Nations Trusteeships
1959: UN General Assembly votes end of French trusteeship
1960: On Jan. 1, French Cameroon becomes independent Cameroon Republic; draft constitution is approved by referendum; National Assembly names Premier Ahmadou Ahidjo president
1961: In UN-supervised plebiscites, southern part of British Cameroons votes for reunification with Cameroon Republic, northern part for union with Nigeria; federation of East and West Cameroon is established
1966: After unification of major political parties in East and West Cameroon, all opposition parties are dissolved or join in single new party, the Cameroon National Union
1971: Political trials and executions end 10-year guerrilla insurrection
1979: Deposits of good quality light crude oil and natural gas are discovered 50 to 75 miles offshore
1980: President Ahidjo is reelected to his fifth five-year term. Influx of refugees from Chad poses serious food-supply problem for Cameroon government
1981: Five Nigerian soldiers killed in border dispute with Cameroon

CANADA
(See separate Canada section)

CAPE VERDE

Area: 1,557 sq. mi. **Population:** 314,000 (1978 est.)
Official Name: Republic of Cape Verde **Capital:** Praia **Nationality:** Cape Verdean **Languages:** Officially Portuguese, with most speaking a dialect, Crioulo **Religion:** 65% Roman Catholic, and 30% animist **Flag:** Two horizontal stripes, yellow over green, with a red vertical stripe at the hoist, the latter having an emblem of a black star over a yellow seashell, framed by two cornstalks **Anthem:** This Is Our Beloved Country **Currency:** Cape Verdean escudo (38.3 per U.S. $1)
Location: In the Atlantic Ocean, 390 miles west of Dakar, Senegal, off the coast of Africa, centering on 16°N. and 24°W. Ten islands and 5 islets comprise the nation **Features:** Summer climate is extremely hot and there is a lack of potable water. Three of the main islands are flat; the other seven are mountainous, volcanic in origin **Chief Rivers:** No large rivers
Head of State: President Aristides Pereira, named 1975 **Head of Government:** Premier Pedro Pires, appointed 1975 **Effective Date of Constitution:** 1980 **Legislative Body:** National Assembly (unicameral), with 56 members **Local Government:** 24 Electoral Districts
Ethnic Composition: 70% are Creoles (mulattoes) of mixed African and Portuguese descent, 28% are Africans, and 2% Europeans **Population Distribution:** 19.7% urban **Density:** 202 inhabitants per sq. mi.
Largest Cities: (1970 census) Mindelo 28,797, Praia 21,494, Espargos 3,978
Per Capita Income: $180 (1978) **Gross National Product (GNP):** $57 million (1978 est.) **Economic Statistics:** The main economic function of the country is ship and aircraft refueling. The soil is poor and dry, and although some food (corn, beans, coffee, sugar) is grown, much must be imported. Fishing is important **Minerals and Mining:** Salt, pozzolana (used in making cements) **Labor Force:** 84,869 in 1970, with 67% in agriculture, and 5% in industry **Foreign Trade:** Exports, chiefly fish products, bananas, salt, coffee, pozzolana, totaled $11.9 million in 1979. Imports, chiefly corn, wheat, cement, petroleum products, totaled $59 million **Principal Trade Partners:** Portugal, EC, Angola, United States
Vital Statistics: Birthrate, 27.6 per 1,000 of pop. (1975); death rate, 9.4 **Life Expectancy:** 45 years **Health Statistics:** 516 per hospital bed; 7,750 per physician (1977) **Infant Mortality:** 104.9 per 1,000 births (1975) **Illiteracy:** 86% **Primary and Secondary School Enrollment:** 71,790 (1972) **Enrollment in Higher Education:** N.A. **GNP Expended on Education:** 1.5% (1972)
Transportation: Paved roads total 380 mi. **Motor Vehicles:** 4,000 (1977) **Passenger Cars:** 3,100 **Railway Mileage:** None **Ports:** Mindelo, Praia **Major Airlines:** T.A.P. provides international service, and Cape Verde Air Transport domestic service **Communications:** Government owned **Radio Transmitters:** 6 **Receivers:** 36,000 (1976) **Television:** None **Telephones:** 2,000 (1976) **Newspapers:** Three, several times a week
Weights and Measures: Metric system **Travel Requirements:** Passport, visa

Cape Verde became independent on July 5, 1975, ending 515 years of Portuguese rule. In 1460 the Portuguese navigators Diego Gomes and Antonio da Noli discovered Maio and São Tiago Islands, and in 1462 the first settlers landed on São Tiago.

Cape Verde, one of five territories relinquished by Portugal (the others being Guinea-Bissau, Mozambique, São Tomé and Príncipe, and Angola), has strong ties with Guinea-Bissau. Aristedes Pereira and Pedro Pires, heroes of the guerrilla war waged against Portugal in Guinea-Bissau, were named president and premier, respectively in 1975.

The islands have been afflicted with disastrous drought and famine in recent years. Since the mid-1900s, an estimated 300,000 Cape Verdeans have emigrated because of the difficulty in earning a living. Workers' remittances sent home from abroad are estimated at $8 million annually.

HISTORY: The islands were discovered in 1460 by Portuguese navigators in the service of Prince Henry the Navigator. Settlement began two years later. The archipelago was a center for the slave trade with the West African coast

1975: On June 30, the Party for the Independence of Guinea-Bissau and Cape Verde (PAIGC) is the only political group to run candidates for the 56-member Assembly at the first general election

1976: Cape Verde and USSR sign pact granting reciprocal use of each other's ports

1979: UN Food and Agriculture Organization grants $908,000 in emergency food aid to the drought-stricken nation

1980: National Assembly approves a constitution to replace provisional laws. Coup in Guinea-Bissau chills close relations between Cape Verde and that country

CENTRAL AFRICAN REPUBLIC

Area: 236,293 sq. mi. **Population:** 2,370,000 (1978 est.)

Official Name: Central African Republic **Capital:** Bangui **Nationality:** Central African **Languages:** French is the official language; Sangho is the national language **Religion:** 40% Protestant, 28% Roman Catholic, 24% animist, 8% Moslem **Flag:** Horizontal bars of blue, white, green, and yellow, bisected by a vertical red bar. A yellow star appears on the blue band at the upper left **Anthem:** La Renaissance **Currency:** CFA Franc (263 per U.S. $1)

Location: At almost the exact center of the African continent. The landlocked country is bordered by Chad on the north, Sudan on the east, Zaire and Congo on the south, and Cameroon on the west **Features:** The country is a huge, well-watered plateau drained by 2 major river systems **Chief Rivers:** Ouham, Ubangi, Kotto, Lobaye, Sangha

Head of State and of Government: A Military Committee of National Redress, headed by Gen. André Kolingba, took power on Sept. 1, 1981 **Effective Date of Present Constitution:** Feb. 6, 1981; suspended Sept. 1 **Legislative Body:** Parliament (unicameral) with deputies elected for 5 years **Local Government:** 14 prefectures

Ethnic Composition: Of some 80 different ethnic groups, the main ones (66%) are the Banda in the east-central area; the Baya and the Mandjia in the west and in the west-central area; 7% are M'baka **Population Distribution:** 20% urban **Density:** 10 inhabitants per sq. mi.

Largest Cities: (1974 est.) Bangui 301,000, Bouar 48,000, Bangassou 46,000, Bambari 35,000

Per Capita Income: $194 (1978 est.) **Gross National Product:** $370 million (1978 est.) **Economic Statistics:** Agriculture (cotton, coffee, rice, tobacco, rubber, peanuts, palm oil) and livestock (cattle, sheep, goats, pigs, poultry) make up 34% of the GNP; diamond and uranium mining, and small-scale manufacturing (textiles, beer, shoes, bicycles and motor bikes, plastics) 16%; and trade and services 29% **Minerals and Mining:** Diamonds, uranium and gold are exploited. Deposits of iron ore, zinc, copper, and tin exist **Labor Force:** 80% of the population is engaged in farming **Foreign Trade:** Exports, chiefly diamonds, wood, cotton, and coffee, totaled $130 million in 1979. Imports, mainly machinery and equipment, textiles, and petroleum products, totaled $102 million **Principal Trade Partners:** France, other EC countries, United States, Japan, Cameroon, Congo

Vital Statistics: Birthrate, 43.4 per 1,000 of pop. (1975); death rate, 22.5 **Life Expectancy:** 40 years **Health Statistics:** 522 inhabitants per hospital bed; 20,833 per physician (1975) **Infant Mortality:** 190 per 1,000 births **Illiteracy:** 93% **Primary and Secondary School Enrollment:** 245,307 (1975) **Enrollment in Higher Education:** 555 **GNP Expended on Education:** 3.9% (1973)

Transportation: Paved roads total 180 mi. **Motor Vehicles:** 13,000 (1974) **Passenger Cars:** 9,100 **Railway Mileage:** None **Ports:** None **Major Airlines:** Air Centrafrique operates domestic services **Communications:** Government owned **Radio Transmitters:** 6 (1972) **Receivers:** 75,000 (1976) **Television Transmitters:** 1 **Telephones:** 5,000 (1973) **Newspapers:** One, several times a week **Weights and Measures:** Metric system **Travel Requirements:** Passport, visa

Isolation in the heart of Africa constitutes the main problem of the Central African Republic (the Central African Empire from 1976 until 1979), a problem that is compounded by a paucity of resources and a small population.

Most of the former French colony of Ubangi-Shari is a plateau of 2,000-foot elevation, a condition that makes for a relatively temperate climate during the dry season. Stretches of grassy savanna and woodland, in which there is an abundance of wildlife, give the land a magnificent beauty.

With modern techniques, cotton production has increased more than three times to 60,000 metric tons a year and provides a major export. Diamond production and small quantities of coffee and peanuts have also added to exports and income.

While the diamonds may be shipped by air, the other products must be transported at considerable cost by road or river to the nearest ports. Aid from France, the World Bank, and other sources has helped improve roads and create small industry, but clearly a rail link is needed for further crop expansion and development of timber resources.

The recent exploitation of uranium at Bakouma, 540 miles east of Bangui, has brightened economic prospects and, with new exploration indicating deposits of iron ore, manganese, and copper, has heightened the need for a railroad.

On becoming fully independent Aug. 13, 1960, the Central African Republic adopted a parliamentary form of government. David Dacko became president. His cousin, Col. Jean-Bédel Bokassa, a former French army sergeant, led a military coup in 1966 which dissolved the national assembly and established Bokassa as head of the ruling revolutionary council. Ten years later, he proclaimed himself emperor and was crowned in a $22-million ceremony in December 1977. He ruled by imperial decree and sometimes with brutal discipline.

One government decree, that students wear state uniforms, prompted protest demonstrations in the capital in January 1979, resulting in 12 deaths. Amnesty International reported the killing of more than 100 schoolchildren following their arrest for further rioting in April.

Emperor Bokassa was overthrown with French assistance on Sept. 20, 1979, in a bloodless coup led by David Dacko who resumed the presidency he had held from 1960 to 1965. Dacko formed the single-party Central African Democratic Union and was elected to a six-year term as president on March 15, 1981. Demonstrators claimed that the election had been rigged, and Dacko had to declare a state of emergency to stop the rioting. On September 1, Dacko was toppled by a military group headed by Gen. André Kolingba.

HISTORY: For centuries, what is now the Central African Empire was a crossroads for numerous migrations by various groups, mainly of Bantu origin. In the 19th century, French expeditions penetrated the country, which was named Ubangi-Shari after its two main rivers. Early in the 20th century, the country was joined with Chad and became one of the territories of French Equatorial Africa

1946: French constitutional reform confers French citizenship on people of Ubangi-Shari

1958: In a referendum, Ubangi-Shari votes to become an autonomous republic within the French Community. The Central African Republic is proclaimed, with Barthélémy Boganda as president

1959: Boganda, founder of the republic and its mass political party, Social Evolution Movement of Black Africa, is killed in plane crash and succeeded by his cousin, David Dacko

1960-65: Republic becomes a fully independent nation under President Dacko, who dissolves all political parties. He is reelected in an election in which he is the only candidate
1966: Colonel Jean-Bedel Bokassa, chief of staff of the armed forces, overthrows Dacko government, ousts Communist Chinese mission, and establishes rule by revolutionary council
1970: C.A.R. resumes relations with Zaire and Chad
1972: Congress of the sole political party appoints Bokassa president for life
1974: Bokassa promotes himself to Marshal of the Republic. French consulate ordered closed; French journals prohibited
1976: Bokassa escapes assassination attempt in February. He dismisses Domitien and declares his country a parliamentary monarchy with himself as emperor
1979: David Dacko leads a bloodless coup to unseat Bokassa and drive him out of the country
1980: Dacko dismisses two unpopular aides to restore confidence
1981: In Feb. 1 referendum 97% of population approves new constitution. Dacko is elected to a six-year term. Army overthrows Dacko on Sept. 1

CHAD

Area: 495,752 sq. mi. **Population:** 4,309,000 (1978 est.)
Official Name: Republic of Chad **Capital:** N'Djamena **Nationality:** Chadian **Languages:** French is the official language. An Arabic dialect is spoken in northern and central Chad; in the south the main tribal languages are Sara, Massa, and Moudang **Religion:** More than 50% of the population is Moslem, 40% animist, and 5% Christian **Flag:** Vertical stripes of blue, yellow, and red **Anthem:** La Tchadienne, beginning "Chadians, Stand up and Set to Work!"
Currency: CFA Franc (263 per U.S. $1)
Location: North-Central Africa. Landlocked Chad is bordered by Libya on the north, Sudan on the east, the Central African Republic on the south, and by Niger, Nigeria, and Cameroon on the west **Features:** The country is shaped like a shallow basin, rimmed by mountain ranges on the north and east. The northern part of the country is desert, the central part a savanna, and the south tropical, with wooded savanna. Lake Chad on the western border is believed to be the remnant of an inland sea **Chief Rivers:** Shari, Logone
Head of State and of Government: President Goukouni Oueddei, born 1944, assumed power in 1979 **Effective Date of Present Constitution:** 1962; suspended 1975 **Legislative Body:** None **Local Government:** 14 prefectures, under appointed governors
Ethnic Composition: The population is about evenly divided between the northern and eastern people, of predominantly Sudanic origin, and the Nilotic southerners **Population Distribution:** 13.9% urban **Density:** 9 inhabitants per sq. mi.
Largest Cities: (1972 est.) N'Djamena 179,000, Sarh 43,700, Moundou 39,600, Abécher 28,100
Per Capita Income: $86 (1978 est.) **Gross National Product (GNP):** $370 million (1978 est.) **Economic Statistics:** In 1973 about 50% of GNP came from agriculture (cotton, sorghum, rice, sugar, peanuts, gum arabic, livestock) and fishing, 8% from industry and mining, and 23% from trade and services **Minerals and Mining:** Natron, a low-grade salt, is the only exploited mineral. Traces of shale oil, uranium, kaolin, and tungsten have been found in the north. Petroleum has been discovered **Labor Force:** 1.3 million (1970), with about 88% in agriculture **Foreign Trade:** Exports, chiefly cotton and cattle, totaled $102 million in 1978. Imports, mainly mineral products (including petroleum products), foodstuffs and beverages, electrical machinery and parts, textiles, and transportation equipment, totaled $192 million **Principal Trade Partners:** Nigeria, France, Japan, Britain
Vital Statistics: Birthrate, 44 per 1,000 of pop.; death rate, 24 **Life Expectancy:** 43 years **Health Statistics:** 1,140 inhabitants per hospital bed; 44,382 per physician (1974) **Infant Mortality:** 160 per 1,000 births **Illiteracy:** 95% **Primary and Secondary School Enrollment:** 230,462 (1976) **Enrollment in Higher Education:** 547 (1975) **GNP Expended on Education:** 2.4% (1976)
Transportation: Paved roads total 150 mi. **Motor Vehicles:** 12,100 (1973) **Passenger Cars:** 5,800 **Railway Mileage:** None **Ports:** None **Major Airlines:** Air Chad is the domestic carrier; Air Afrique, Air Cameroun, UTA, and Sudan Airways operate services to Chad **Communications:** Government owned **Radio Transmitters:** 6 **Receivers:** 76,000 (1976) **Television Transmitters:** 1 **Telephones:** 5,000 (1975) **Newspapers:** 4 dailies, 0.4 copies per 1,000 inhabitants (1975)
Weights and Measures: Metric system **Travel Requirements:** (1971) Passport, visa, $6.25; 3 photos, round-trip ticket

The remote outpost of former French Equatorial Africa, landlocked Chad suffers from isolation, internal strife, and a loss of arable land.

With its productive area more than 1,000 miles from any seaport, Chad is difficult to reach except by air. There is no railroad and a good part of the network of dirt roads and tracks is impassable during the rainy season.

Since 1968 Arab guerrillas in the northern and eastern part of the country have waged a rebellion against the Bantu-dominated government. Some 3,500 French troops were sent to help the Chadian government quell the revolt, an action that has raised controversy both in France and in Africa. French forces actively fighting the rebels were withdrawn in 1971.

The chief cause of the nomadic northerners' enmity toward the Chadian government was the fact that it had been dominated by southerners—Negroid river peoples whom the Arabs traditionally scorned as slaves. In addition, the northerners, mainly the Toubous, resented the government's tax on their cattle.

The regime of François Tombalbaye, which had been in power since 1962, was toppled by a military coup in 1975. General Félix Malloum, the new Bantu ruler, became the object of a coup attempt himself in February 1979 when the Moslem premier, Hissène Habré, tried to oust him. Malloum fled in March to Nigeria.

For months control passed from one provisional government to another. On Nov. 10 a transitional government of national unity was formed with Goukouni Oueddei as president and Habré as defense minister. The power struggle between these rival Moslem leaders was quieted for only a few months, however. On March 22, 1980, guerrilla forces loyal to the president and the minister fought each other in the streets of N'Djamena, using tanks, artillery and rockets. the number of persons killed, both military and civilian, ran into the hundreds. An estimated 70,000 refugees crossed the Shari River into Cameroon.

All efforts of the Organization of African Unity, France, and the Franco-African conference in Nice in May 1980, failed to bring about a settlement of the civil war. A short-lived cease-fire was arranged in October, but a month later there were reports that Libya's Revolutionary Leader, Col. Muammar el-Qaddafi, had sent armed forces into Chad to support Goukouni Oueddei. Libyan tanks rolled into N'Djamena on Dec. 16, compelling Habré's forces to abandon the city.

In addition to the ravages of political strife, the economy of Chad has been badly injured by prolonged drought. Thousands of persons have died, cattle have perished and former grazing lands have become sandy desert. Production of cotton, the chief export crop, has declined greatly.

HISTORY: Chad is believed to have been a center of ancient cultures before the southward encroachment of the Sahara. The varied ethnic make-up of present-day Chadians is evidence also of a succession of migrations and invasions in past centuries by Bantu southerners, Sudanese Moslems, and Nilotic peoples. Throughout the ages, Chad was the domain of conquerors and warrior slave traders, some of whom held sway until the late 19th century. Among the last of these was Rabah Amoney, a Sudanese ex-slave turned slave merchant and chieftain, whose conquest of the Bornu Kingdom was to lead to French intervention
1897-1900: Traditional rulers, threatened by Rabah's army, seek profection of French, whose forces march across the Sahara from Algeria, defeat Sudanese, and impose own rule
1910: Chad is made one of the four territories of French Equatorial Africa, along with Gabon, the present Congo (Brazzaville), and Ubangi-Shari (now the Central African Empire)
1940: Chad becomes first territory to rally to Free French
1959-60: Chad becomes autonomous member of French Community. On Aug. 11, 1960, complete independence and the Republic of Chad are proclaimed
1962: All opposition parties are banned under new constitution and single-party rule is set up by Chadian Progressive party, led by President François Tombalbaye

1963: State of emergency is declared after abortive coup d'état and arrest of Moslem leaders; constitutional amendments are adopted and new elections are held in an effort to heal the rift between Moslem north and Bantu south
1969: Moslem guerrillas step up attacks on government installations as Arab-Bantu split widens; President Tombalbaye calls in French troops to help quell growing revolt
1973: UN reports Chad is most severely affected of the sub-Saharan countries suffering from drought
1975: President Tombalbaye assassinated (April 13). Military junta headed by Gen. Félix Malloum takes control
1977: Attempted coup against Malloum fails
1979-1980: Malloum is ousted in coup and rival factions battle for control of country; one provisional government follows another in rapid succession; hundreds of persons are killed in streetfighting in the capital in March 1980. Libyan tanks and troops invade Chad to support Goukouni Oueddei's bid for control
1981: Libya announces a "merger" with Chad on Jan. 6. U.S. and French reports of arrival of Soviet military advisors and technicians in Chad are denied by Moscow

---

CHILE

Area: 292,256 sq. mi. **Population:** 11,167,000 (1980 est.)
Official Name: Republic of Chile **Capital:** Santiago **Nationality:** Chilean **Languages:** The official and virtually universal language is Spanish **Religion:** 90% Roman Catholic **Flag:** A white horizontal stripe over a longer red stripe, with a blue square in the upper left corner containing a 5-pointed white star **Anthem:** National Anthem; refrain "Sweet Country, receive the pledge" **Currency:** Chilean peso (39 per U.S. $1)

Location: Southwest coast of South America. Chile is bordered on the north by Peru, on the east by Argentina and Bolivia, on the south by Drake Passage, and on the west by the Pacific Ocean **Features:** The country stretches some 2,650 miles along the Pacific coast and is at no point wider than 250 miles. The north is desert, the central region agricultural, and the south is forest land. The towering Andes dominate most of the eastern frontier **Chief Rivers:** Loa, Maule, Bio-Bio, Valdivia

Head of State and of Government: President: Maj. Gen. Augusto Pinochet Ugarte, born 1915, assumed power September 1973 as head of a 4-man military junta, formally assumed title on March 11, 1981 for 8 years **Effective Date of Present Constitution:** March 1981 **Legislative Body:** Congress (dissolved) **Local Government:** 12 regions, subdivided into 40 provinces, and the metropolitan region of Santiago

Ethnic Composition: About 68% of the population is of Spanish-Indian descent, 30% of European (mainly Spanish) descent, and less than 1% Indian **Population Distribution:** 79% urban **Density:** 38 inhabitants per sq. mi.

Largest Cities: (1978 est.) Santiago 3,691,548, Valparaíso 620,180, Concepción 518,950, Viña del Mar 262,100, Talcahuano 204,100, Antofagasta 157,000, Temuco 156,900

Per Capita Income: $1,880 (1980) **Gross National Product (GNP):** $20 7 billion (1980) **Economic Statistics:** In 1979, 50% of GNP was derived from trade and services; 21% from industry (paper and paper products, iron and steel, petrochemicals, chemicals, and metal products); 11% from mining; and 9% from agriculture (wheat, wine grapes, potatoes, sugar beets, tobacco, fruit), forestry and fishing **Minerals and Mining:** Chile is one of the world's leading copper producers; iron ore is second in importance; natural nitrates, iodine, molybdenum and coal are also exploited **Labor Force:** 3,500,000 (1978), with 28% in agriculture **Foreign Trade:** Exports, mainly copper and copper manufactures, iron ore, pulp and paper, fishmeal, wine, seafood, wool, and fruit, totaled $3.8 billion in 1979. Imports, mainly machinery and equipment, agricultural products, and transport equipment, totaled $4.2 billion **Principal Trade Partners:** United States, Latin American Free Trade Association, EC, Japan

Vital Statistics: Birthrate, 23.9 per 1,000 of pop. (1976); death rate, 7.8 **Life Expectancy:** 67 years **Health Statistics:** 277 inhabitants per hospital bed; 2,177 per physician (1976) **Infant Mortality:** 39.7 per 1,000 births (1978) **Illiteracy:** 8% **Primary and Secondary School Enrollment:** 2,729,375 (1977) **Enrollment in Higher Education:** 149,647 (1975) **GNP Expended on Education:** 3.7% (1975)

Transportation: Paved roads total 5,750 mi. **Motor Vehicles:** 479,100 (1977) **Passenger Cars:** 297,100 **Railway Mileage:** 5,511 **Ports:** Valparaíso, Arica, Antofagasta, Coquimbo, Iquique, Talcahuano **Major Airlines:** LAN-Chile, the government-owned airline, operates domestic and international services **Communications:** Government controlled **Radio Transmitters:** 210 **Receivers:** 3,100,000 (1974) **Television Transmitters:** 56 **Receivers:**

1,700,000 **Telephones:** 514,013 (1978) **Newspapers:** 47 dailies (1975); 94 copies per 1,000 inhabitants (1972)
Weights and Measures: Metric system **Travel Requirements:** Passport, no visa up to 3 months **International Dialing Code:** 56

Chile has long had an outstanding potential—immense natural resources and a relatively sophisticated population—but efforts to match living standards to promise have fallen short. Inflation, once chronic and at runaway rates—it rose 340 percent in 1975, for instance—has been brought down to a manageable 30-40 percent a year, but at the expense of large-scale unemployment and other social problems.

Nature is largely responsible for the economic and social status of Chile, a land dominated by the geological immaturity of the Andes, a mountain range that runs the entire length of the long and narrow country. Relatively "new" and earthquake-prone, the Andes yield the copper and other metals that account for more than half of Chile's foreign-exchange earnings.

Politically, Chile has also been a victim of abrupt change and contrasts. The pride of South American democracies from 1932 until the 1970s, the country since 1973 has seen its military employ coercion at the expense of human rights to remove all vestiges of the Marxist experiment of Salvador Allende Gossens. Allende in 1970 became the first Marxist to be elected president in South America, but on September 11, 1973, one week after the third anniversary of Allende's election, a military junta staged the first successful coup against a civilian government in Chile since 1927. President Allende was reported to have committed suicide. A year later it was learned that the United States had funneled more than $8 million through the CIA to anti-Allende groups.

The current military regime, headed by Chile's president, Gen. Augusto Pinochet Ugarte, is facing world criticism for political repression, torture and news censorship. The regime continues to hold political prisoners, but, under pressure from the U.S. and other democratic nations, the number has been reduced. The junta's aim has been to entrench political power by dictatorial rule, and Pinochet has succeeded in establishing an "authoritarian democracy."

After the UN General Assembly reported that Chile was violating human rights, President Pinochet ordered a national referendum on Jan. 4, 1978, that upheld his government. Despite this support, the government eased up by restoring some autonomy to civil judges and by limiting the president's punitive powers. Also, an amnesty program was set in motion, leading to pardons or voluntary exile for some prisoners.

In 1980, Chile set out to improve its international image, both within and outside Latin America. Diplomatic relations were restored with Great Britain, and a year later the new Reagan Administration in the United States lifted trade sanctions against Chile.

On Sept. 11, 1980, the seventh anniversary of the military coup that overthrew Allende, a national plebiscite was held on a new constitution which would give Pinochet greater powers and an additional eight-year term in office, with an option to serve another term after that. In spite of strong opposition by former President Frei and followers of Allende, Pinochet received two thirds of the votes cast. (Blank ballots were counted as "yes" votes.)

Despite the rising cost of imported fuel, the loss of foreign investment capital and a large foreign debt, Chile has made considerable economic progress since 1973. Gross national product has been increasing at an annual rate of more than 8 percent compared to a drop of 12 percent in 1974. The balance of payments is on the plus side, and inflation and unemployment have been declining. Foreign investors, including such large U.S. companies as Anaconda, Dow Chemical and Exxon, have been returning to Chile. Development of the wood-products industry is helping to alleviate dependence on a one-product (copper) economy.

HISTORY: Prior to the Spanish conquest of Chile in the 16th century, the northern portion of the country was under the rule of the Inca Empire and the south was mainly controlled by the Araucanian Indians, who were to prove fiercely hostile to the Spanish colonists until almost the end of the 19th century. During most of its colonial history, Chile was a captaincy general dependent on the viceroyalty of Peru

1817-18: Argentine revolutionist José de San Martín brings an army over the Andes from Argentina to Chile and, in 1818, defeats Spanish army at Battle of Maipú. Bernardo O'Higgins, who had been chosen supreme director, formally proclaims Chile's independence (Feb. 12)

1879-83: Chile defeats Peru and Bolivia in the War of the Pacific, acquiring the mineral-bearing northern desert region

1891-1925: Internal struggle between executive and legislative branches culminates in overthrow of President José Balmaceda (1891); congressional dictatorship lasts until 1925

1932-38: President Arturo Alessandri, elected for second term, institutes a kind of state capitalism in efforts to wipe out aftermath of 1929 depression; however, he turns to repressive measures and alienates working class

1946-48: Economic dislocations lead to riots and strikes encouraged by aggressive Communist activity

1964-68: Eduardo Frei Montalva is elected president and his Christian Democratic Party wins control of Chamber of Deputies after defeating coalition of Marxist parties. Frei launches reform program

1969: National discontent becomes manifest in congressional elections, when Frei's party retains majority in lower house but loses more than a third of its former seats; right-wing National party scores heavy gains

1970: Salvador Allende Gossens becomes the first Marxist to be elected president of a Latin American country

1971: Government nationalizes all U.S. copper investments

1972: Chile furthers relations with Communist countries

1973: On September 11, Allende government is overthrown by a military junta. Allende dies in coup. State of siege declared

1974: Military junta returns to private ownership 150 companies nationalized by left-wing Allende government. CIA bankrolling of anti-Allende groups is revealed

1978: Referendum shows wide support for Pinochet; opposition charges fraud. Government declares amnesty for political prisoners and exiles and lifts state of siege. Border disputes with neighbors continue; Bolivia breaks diplomatic relations, alleging Chile has hindered negotiations to grant it a corridor to Pacific

1979: Chile refuses to extradite three army officers to U.S. to stand trial on charges of complicity in the 1976 murder in Washington, D.C., of Orlando Letelier, prominent exiled leader of opposition to the Pinochet regime

1980: President Pinochet breaks diplomatic relations with the Philippines (Mar. 24) after Filipino president Ferdinand E. Marcos declines to meet Pinochet on his planned trip to Asia. Voters approve new constitution and 8-year term for Pinochet

1981: Pinochet formally assumes presidency under new constitution on March 11. The border dispute with Argentina is rekindled by arrests of military personnel on both sides as spies

CHINA (PEOPLE'S REPUBLIC)

Area: 3,691,000 sq. mi. **Population:** 953,578,000 (1979 est.)
Official Name: People's Republic of China **Capital:** Peking (Beijing) **Nationality:** Chinese **Languages:** Chinese, spoken with many regional phonetical differences but written with a uniform script, is the principal language. Mandarin, based on the Peking dialect, forms the basis of the new national language being promoted by the government; Shanghai, Cantonese, Fukienese, and Hakka dialects are spoken in the south. Among the national minorities, the Tibetans have their own highly distinctive language and script, while the Uigurs of Xinjiang (Sinkiang) speak a Turkic language **Religion:** Freedom of religion is guaranteed under the constitution. The 3 long-established religions are Confucianism, Buddhism, and Taoism; the average Chinese has practiced a mixture of all 3 faiths. About 5% of the people are Moslems, and there is a very small minority of Christians **Flag:** A red field with a gold star and an arc of

4 smaller stars to the right in the upper left corner **Anthem:** Anthem beginning, "March on, brave people of our nation," set to the music of The March of the Volunteers **Currency:** Yuan (renminbi) (1.75 per U.S. $1)
Location: East Asia. China, the third-largest country in the world after the USSR and Canada, is bounded on the north by Mongolia and the USSR; on the east by the USSR, North Korea, the Yellow Sea, and the East China Sea; on the south by the South China Sea, Vietnam, Laos, Burma, India, Bhutan, and Nepal; and on the west by Afghanistan, Pakistan, and the USSR **Features:** Two-thirds of the country is mountainous or semidesert. The eastern part consists of fertile plains and deltas **Chief Rivers:** Chang Jiang (Yangtze), Huang (Yellow), Amur, Xi (Si)
Head of State: Executive responsibility is vested in a State Council, headed by the premier. Control is exercised by the Standing Committee of the Central Committee's Politburo, within the National People's Congress **Head of Government:** Premier Zhao Ziyang, born 1919, elected by the National People's Congress, Sept. 1980 **Head of Party:** Hu Yaobang, born 1915, Chairman of the Politburo of the Communist party **Effective Date of Present State Constitution:** March 15, 1978 **Legislative Body:** National People's Congress (unicameral), consisting of 3,497 members elected for 5-year terms. The provinces elect 1 deputy for every 800,000 inhabitants; municipalities directly under central authority elect 1 deputy for every 100,000 inhabitants. Ethnic minorities are represented by 381 deputies, the armed forces by 505 deputies, and overseas Chinese by 35 deputies **Local Government:** 21 provinces, 5 autonomous regions, and 3 municipalities directly under central authority. Revolutionary committees and people's congresses are the principal local organs of power
Ethnic Composition: 94% Han Chinese; 6% Chuang, Uigur, Hui, Yi, Tibetan, Miao, Manchu, Mongol, Korean, and numerous lesser minorities **Population Distribution:** 20% urban **Density:** 258 inhabitants per sq. mi.
Largest Cities: (1978 est.) Shanghai 10,980,000, Peking (Beijing) 8,500,000, Tianjin 7,210,000; (1970 est.) Shenyang 2,800,000, Wuhan 2,560,000, Canton 2,500,000, Chongqing 2,400,000, Nanjing 1,750,000, Harbin 1,670,000, Luda 1,650,000
Per Capita Income: $576 (1980) **Gross National Product (GNP):** $592 billion (1979) **Economic Statistics:** Agriculture is still the foundation of the economy. GNP components are not available but official figures disclosed in 1971 indicate that industrial capacity is still comparatively small. The State Statistical Bureau had estimated $409 billion for the gross value of industrial, transport and agricultural production in 1979. Grain output for 1980 was 318 million metric tons; chemical fertilizer, 12 million metric tons; cotton cloth, 13.5 billion meters; petroleum output, more than 106 million metric tons **Minerals and Mining:** Coal, petroleum, iron ore, tin, molybdenum, tungsten, mercury, manganese, antimony **Labor Force:** The working age population is about 476 million, with 75% in agriculture **Foreign Trade:** Exports are estimated at about $15.5 billion for 1980, with imports of about $16.6 billion. Exports are chiefly agricultural and food products, coal, oil products, minerals, and textiles. Imports are mainly wheat, chemical fertilizers, iron and steel, transport equipment, machinery, advanced technology equipment, insecticides, cotton, pulp, consumer goods and rubber **Principal Trade Partners:** Japan, Hong Kong, West Germany, Romania, Singapore, Britain, United States, Malaysia, Canada, France, Australia
Vital Statistics: Birthrate, 26.9 per 1,000 pop. (1975); death rate, 10.3 **Life Expectancy:** 68 years **Illiteracy:** 45%. **Recent Statistics on Health and Infant Mortality:** N.A. **Primary and Secondary School Enrollment:** 203,274,000 (1980) **Enrollment in Higher Education:** 1,144,000 **GNP Expended on Education:** N.A.
Transportation: Surfaced roads total 551,800 mi. **Motor Vehicles:** N.A. **Passenger Cars:** N.A. **Railway Mileage:** 33,688 **Ports:** Shanghai, Tianjin, Luda, Canton **Major Airlines:** The Civil Aviation Administration of China operates domestic flights and international flights abroad **Communications:** Government owned **Radio Transmitters:** 250 **Receivers:** 45,000,000 (1978) **Television Transmitters:** 120 **Receivers:** 1,250,000 (1978) **Telephones:** 5,000,000 (1978) **Newspapers:** 278 (1979)
Weights and Measures: Metric System and local standards **Travel Requirements:** Passport, visa; contact Chinese Embassy, Washington, D.C.

Developments of the early 1970s made the world aware that domestic conditions in the world's most populous country had stabilized; that China had come out of the disorders of the Cultural Revolution and that a new posture had been taken to

CHINA

CONIC PROJECTION

MILES
0   100   200   300   400   500

KILOMETERS
0   100   200   300   400   500

Capitals of Countries.............
Provincial Capitals..................
International Boundaries..........
Provincial Boundaries...............

© Copyright HAMMOND INCORPORATED, Maplewood, N.J.

break out of the diplomatic isolation of the 1950s and 60s.

The Peking regime initiated a fresh approach in foreign affairs in April 1971 by inviting an American table-tennis team, with accompanying journalists, to tour China. This gesture was a surprise even in the context of the new moderation that had become increasingly evident during the year before.

After April 1972 there came a small but steady flow of Americans and other Western nationals, and Peking climaxed their visits in July by arranging to receive President Nixon. The new Peking policy also led to formal diplomatic relations with Japan in 1972 and culminated in the signing of a 10-year treaty of peace and friendship in 1978.

Relations had been established with Canada, Italy, and a number of smaller countries; more Chinese delegations had been sent abroad; more foreign trade agreements had been signed; and Chinese diplomatic missions in foreign countries, which operated without ambassadors during the Cultural Revolution, had been restaffed.

Impressed by Washington's new policy of military pullback in Asia, the Chinese moved to ease relations with the United States. Simultaneously Peking acted to strengthen the home front by slowing the pace of the Cultural Revolution and stabilizing conditions under a reshuffled, pragmatic leadership built with the assent of Communist party Chairman Mao Zedong, around Premier Zhou Enlai.

Thus a situation was created of far-ranging significance for today and the future. Peking's move has shaken loose accustomed world-power alignments and brought about a "big three" constellation susceptible to shifting and jockeying of unpredictable ramifications.

Trade with the United States began in 1972 following the lifting of the American trade embargo, and by 1980 had reached more than $4.3 billion, and is expected to be about $6 billion in 1981. In May 1979, China concluded an agreement on establishing formal commercial relations with the United States, which provided for the lowering of United States tariff restrictions on Chinese imports and the granting of a most-favored nation trade status (approved February 1, 1980).

Following the death of Premier Zhou Enlai on January 8, 1976, the succession of crises intensified. A mounting debate between moderates and radicals culminated in April in the most serious riots since the Cultural Revolution of 1966-69. The Politburo, acting quickly to defuse the potentially explosive situation, dismissed the "moderate" Deng Xiaoping from all his posts, and elevated Hua Guofeng to the premiership.

With the death of Mao Zedong the main task facing Hua Guofeng, Mao's successor, was to resolve the conflict between radical and moderate factions in the party. Late in 1976, he moved decisively against the radicals, known as the "Gang of Four," led by Mao's widow, Jiang Jing, who along with her supporters plus the cohorts of the late Lin Biao were tried in 1980-81 and given sentences ranging from 16 years to suspended death sentences. From late 1976 to mid 1977, in an apparent effort to liberalize Maoist doctrine along pragmatic lines, Deng Xiaoping was brought back into the government as first deputy premier. Together with Chairman Hua and the honorary head of state, Ye Jianying, he became part of China's ruling triumvirate.

Deng's power grew not only with the elevation of his proteges to key party and government positions but also with his plan for the implementation of the "four modernizations"—rapid development of agriculture, industry, defense, and technology. The plan included granting more state aid to poorer areas, the centralization of state planning, the return of private plots to the farmers, a wage increase of 60 percent in the industrial sphere, the upgrading of military hardware and effectiveness, and the advancement of lagging science, technology and education. By 1980, the program was modified to make it more economically viable. Experiments in industrial profit incentives and local accountability proved successful enough for nationwide application. In place of fulfilling arbitrary state quotas, industries were rewarded for quantity, quality and talent, with excess profits after taxes (an innovation) to remain with the industry. Also, workers were given the right to elect and dismiss plant managers. In agriculture, China's largest economic sector, farmers could now both cultivate their private plots, and grow what they could and should. Commune-operated farming changed to household management to help bolster the sagging crop production.

China's chief defense goal is to achieve parity with the United States and the Soviet Union. To do this, the Peking regime has called for the introduction of foreign technology and the purchase of foreign weapons as part of the modernization effort for China's military, considered by Westerners as 20 years behind the Russians.

Relations with the United States improved in 1978 with the announcement of the formal establishment of official diplomatic relations between the two countries, effective on March 1, 1979. At the same time, the announcement included the abrogation of the mutual defense treaty between the United States and the offshore Republic of China and the termination of formal diplomatic relations with Taiwan. By 1981, mutual airline and shipping agreements between the People's Republic and the United States were implemented, further bolstering China's growing tourism and trade.

On February 17, 1979, China invaded Vietnam which after four weeks resulted in no territorial gains, heavy casualties on both sides, and a drain on China's economy.

In 1980 and 1981, inflation, growing unemployment and poor industrial production (particularly coal, chemicals and heavy industrial products bottlenecked by lack of transport and raw materials) reduced the amount of available foreign exchange. Also, heavy borrowing caused the leadership to take a slower course in the modernization program. An austerity plan, announced in February 1981, included reductions in capital construction, in the budget for oil and coal production, and in the importation of foreign equipment. Expensive foreign contracts for large industrial facilities were either cancelled or drastically modified. Oil drilling both on-shore and off-shore with foreign participation continues with less than expected success.

China has changed the policy of self-sufficiency to one of borrowing or obtaining credit from abroad, with US$10 billion in loans from Japan and $17 billion credit from France and Britain. Following admission to the International Monetary Fund and the World Bank in 1980, China's borrowing power will increase and her credit rating will continue to remain good.

In 1980, four members of the party's Politburo, elevated by Mao, were ousted. In the summer, the third annual session of the 5th National People's Congress (NPC) convened to review national problems, to approve recommendations made by the State Council, to vote on a resolution for an amendment to the constitution outlawing criticisms on big character posters, to raise the minimum marriage age to 22 for men and 20 for women, and to approve greater management autonomy for industrial enterprises. The NPC formally elected Zhao Ziyang to replace Hua Guofeng as premier, accepting the resignations of seven vice premiers including Deng Xiaoping, and elected three new vice premiers.

"De-Mao-ification" started in 1980 with the dismissal of key pro-Mao party and government personnel, and the memorialization and posthumous rehabilitation of Liu Shaoqi, who was chief of state before Mao dismissed him in 1969. In early 1981 Hua Guofeng lost his position to Deng Xiaoping as the head of the party's powerful Military Commission. In June 1981, Hua was demoted from the chairmanship of the Politburo to junior vice chairman, while Deng's protege, Hu Yaobang, became the new chairman. Strong criticisms of Mao were publicized in 1981, especially of his concept of party and government administration during his later years, and his promotion of the Cultural Revolution in the late 1960s. Although Deng has gained political backing for his pragmatic approach in strengthening the country, government and party, there have been appearances of dissension in the ranks of those closely allied to the late Mao and his ideology and in the army.

HISTORY: The home of the oldest continuing civilization on earth, China has a recorded history dating back more than 2,000 years before the birth of Christ. By the advent of the Christian era, the Chinese had lived under a succession of dynasties that succeeded in unifying the country and protecting it from the outside world by building the Great Wall. In the end, however, the wall was to prove useless against invaders

1644: Manchu (Ching) dynasty is established, completing the gradual conquest of China by the Manchu peoples of the north

1839-42: Britain provokes Opium War and defeats Chinese; China opens ports and grants extraterritorial rights to British traders, cedes Hong Kong to Britain

1894-95: China and Japan war for control over their co-protectorate of Korea; a defeated China is forced to cede Formosa (Taiwan), Liaotung peninsula, and Pescadores to Japan

1898-1900: Resentment against foreign influence erupts in Boxer Rebellion; revolt is quelled after intervention by European, U.S., and Japanese forces. U.S. Open Door policy, calling for equal treatment for all nations in Chinese ports and respect for China's territorial integrity, wins lip service from European powers

1911-12: Manchu dynasty is overthrown in revolution led by Sun Yat-sen; a republic is established with Sun as president

1917-30: Civil war breaks out between supporters of Sun's Kuomintang Party in the south and the national government and its warlords in the north; Kuomintang army, led by Chiang Kai-shek, sweeps north and defeats warlords. A new civil war breaks out, however, after Chiang breaks alliance formed by Sun with Chinese Communists

1931-39: Japan, taking advantage of turmoil in China, invades Manchuria and sets up puppet government. In 1934, some 100,000 Communist troops led by Mao Zedong, Lin Biao, and Zhou Enlai, begin 6,000-mile "long march" to the north to avoid encirclement by Kuomintang army. Kuomintang and Communists later agree to truce to repel Japanese, but agreement collapses and sporadic fighting resumes

1945-49: U.S. attempts to mediate civil war fail; Communists launch offensive and drive Chiang's forces from mainland to Taiwan; People's Republic of China is proclaimed Oct. 1, 1949

1950: China overruns Tibet; Chinese forces intervene on side of North Korea in Korean War

1960-64: Growing rift between USSR and "hard-line" Chinese leaders unfolds. China explodes its first nuclear bomb

1966-67: Mao Zedong launches "Cultural Revolution" in attempt to reverse trend toward "revisionist" Communism. New policy is marked by widespread purge of leading officials and wave of terrorism by Mao's youthful followers, known as Red Guards. China explodes its first hydrogen bomb

1969: Chinese and Soviet troops exchange fire along borders

1971: People's Republic of China replaces Nationalist China (Taiwan) in the UN. Lin Biao, Mao's designated successor, dies following an abortive coup

1972: Nixon visits China, meets Zhou Enlai and Mao Zedong

1975: China adopts a revised constitution of 30 articles endorsing the doctrines that emerged from the "Great Proletarian Cultural Revolution" of the late 1960s. Ford and Kissinger visit China

1976: Mao Zedong, Zhou Enlai and Zhu De die. Hua Guofeng confirmed premier and chairman of Communist party. Tangshan earthquake kills an estimated 700,000

1977: Deng Xiaoping returns to Politburo

1978: Chairman Hua reappointed

1979: Deng Xiaoping visits the United States and signs scientific and cultural exchange agreement. China invades Vietnam in Febru-

ary. China and the U.S. establish formal diplomatic relations on March 1. The 5th National People's Congress (the highest legislative power) convenes in Peking. Hua Gupfeng visits Western Europe

1980: China admitted to International Monetary Fund and World Bank. Hua Guofeng meets President Carter in Tokyo. U.S. reopens consulates in Shanghai and Canton. National People's Congress convenes and elects Zhao Ziyang as premier to replace Hua Guofeng. Deng Xiaoping and several premiers resign from State Council and are replaced

1981: Sixteen members of the "Gang of Four" and cohorts of Lin Biao tried and sentenced. Central Committee of the Party elects Hu Yaobang chairman of the seven-member Politburo, and Hua Guofeng is demoted to junior vice chairman. Vice Premier Soong Ching-ling (Sun Yat Sen's widow) dies. Premier Zhao Ziyang visits Burma and Thailand. U.S. Secretary of State visits China. Severe drought in North China and floods in Central and South China damage agricultural crops

NATIONALIST CHINA (TAIWAN)

Area: 13,971 sq. mi. **Population:** 17,838,386 (1981 est.)

Official Name: Republic of China **Capital:** Taipei **Nationality:** Chinese **Languages:** Mandarin Chinese is the official language; native Taiwanese speak a variant of the Amoy dialect, although the Hakka dialect is used in northwestern Taiwan; Japanese and English are also widely used by the inhabitants **Religion:** The predominant religion (93%) is a blend of Buddhism, Confucianism and Taoism. 4.5% are Christians **Flag:** A red field with a blue rectangle in the upper left corner containing a 12-pointed white sun **Anthem:** National Anthem of the Republic of China, beginning "Our aim shall be to found a free land" **Currency:** New Taiwan yuan (dollar) (37 per U.S. $1)

Location: The seat of the Republic of China is the island of Taiwan, 90 miles off the southeast coast of the Chinese mainland. In addition to the island proper, Taiwan comprises 14 islands in the Taiwan group and 63 in the Penghu group, known as the Pescadores. The islands of Quemoy and Matsu, just off Fukien province on the China mainland, are also under the control of the Republic of China. Taiwan, also known as Formosa, is bordered on the north by the East China Sea, on the east by the Pacific Ocean, on the south and southwest by the South China Sea, and on the west by the Taiwan (Formosa) Strait **Features:** About two-thirds of the island of Taiwan is composed of rugged foothills and mountain chains. The mountains, towering along the eastern coast, run from northeast to southwest. A flat coastal plain, running from north to south, occupies the western third and supports most of the population **Chief Rivers:** Cho-shui, Tan-shui, Hsia-tan-shui

Head of State: President Chiang Ching-kuo, born 1910, elected 1978 **Head of Government:** Premier Sun Yün-hsüan, born 1913, appointed 1978 **Effective Date of Present Constitution:** 1947 **Legislative Body:** The National Assembly (unicameral); its members (elected 1947) are serving indefinitely. Of the original 3,045 there are now about 1,300. The 5 branches of government are the Legislative, Executive, Control, Examination, and Judicial yuans. The Legislative Yuan is the highest body and now has 410 members; both it and the National Assembly have some parliamentary function, and are dominated by the Nationalist Party (the Kuomintang) under its chairman, the premier **Local Government:** The Provincial Government is under a governor appointed by the national government. There is an elective Provincial Assembly with limited powers

Ethnic Composition: With the exception of about 250,000 aborigines of Indonesian origin, the Taiwanese are descendants of Chinese who migrated from the provinces of Fukien and Kwangtung of mainland China during the past 3 centuries; post-World War II refugees from the mainland constitute about 14% of the population **Population Distribution:** 77% urban (1975) **Density:** 1,277 inhabitants per sq. mi.

Largest Cities: (1981 est.) Taipei 2,238,841; (1979 est.) Kaohsiung 1,002,000, Taichung 549,000, Tainan 525,000, Keelung 343,000

Per Capita Income: $1,826 (1980) **Gross National Product (GNP):** $32.5 billion (1980 est.) **Economic Statistics:** 30% of GNP comes from industry (textiles, electronics, plastics, furniture, other goods), and 12% from agriculture (rice, sweet potatoes, bananas, sugarcane, pineapple, peanuts, and soybeans are the major crops) **Minerals and Mining:** Taiwan is deficient in minerals with the exception of coal. There are reserves of volcanic sulphur and deposits of natural gas and petroleum **Labor Force:** 6.5 million (1980), 39% employed in manufacturing, mining and construction, 35% in commerce and services, 26% in agriculture **Foreign Trade:** Exports, chiefly textiles, chemicals, metals and machinery, plywood, sugar, bananas, and canned mushrooms, totaled $19.8 billion in 1980. Imports, chiefly machinery, chemicals, transportation equipment, soybeans, raw cotton, timber, crude oil, and wheat, totaled $19.7 billion **Principal Trade Partners:** United States, Japan, Hong Kong, West Germany, Australia, Britain, Singapore, Canada, Thailand, Saudi Arabia, South Korea, Kuwait

Vital Statistics: Birthrate, 23 per 1,000 of pop (1980); death rate, 5 **Life Expectancy:** 72 years **Health Statistics:** 580 inhabitants per hospital bed; 1,377 per physician **Infant Mortality:** 14 per 1,000 births **Illiteracy:** 10% **Education Statistics:** 3,269 primary and secondary schools, with combined enrollment of 3,932,000 (1975) **Enrollment in Higher Education:** 282,300 **GNP Expended on Education:** 4.8%

Transportation: Surfaced roads total 5,496 mi. (1974) **Motor Vehicles:** 2,600,000 (1976) **Passenger Cars:** 122,517 (1974) **Railway Mileage:** 2,795 (1978) **Ports:** Kaohsiung, Keelung, Hualien, Taichung, Suao **Major Airlines:** China Airlines operates domestic and international services **Communications:** Both government and privately owned **Radio Stations:** 111 **Receivers:** 3,000,000 **Television Stations:** 3 **Receivers:** 747,444 **Telephones:** 1,689,000 (1979) **Newspapers:** 31 dailies, 80 copies per 1,000 inhabitants

Weights and Measures: Metric system and local units are used **Travel Requirements:** Passport, visa **International Dialing Code:** 886

The government of the Republic of China, defeated on mainland China by the Communists in 1949, established itself on Taiwan, with the goal of regaining power over all of China. That goal, with time, has become more and more remote. In the meantime, with the help of massive American aid, the government has built Taiwan into a prosperous, industrialized island state.

In 1971 a steady stream of countries switched diplomatic recognition from Taiwan to Communist China. With the shift in U.S. policy on China and American support for the seating of Peking in the United Nations, the Nationalist diplomatic position underwent further erosion. Nationalist China was eventually expelled from the UN and replaced by the Communist-led People's Republic of China.

Because of its insistence that it was not only the government of Taiwan, 90 miles off the China mainland, but also the only legal government of all China, the Nationalist regime would not sanction elections that would change the central leadership. But it has held local elections.

The government has been dominated by the Kuomintang, or Nationalist party, and the party in turn was dominated by President Chiang Kai-shek until his death in April 1975. Criticism of government policies and officials is permitted in the press, though the president and his relatives are an exception. Editors practice a form of self-censorship.

Nationalist officials, who like to refer to Taiwan as "Free China," readily concede that the province is still under martial law and freedom is in some respects limited. But they point out that freedom and democracy have to be understood in an Asian context, and declare that, whatever Taiwan's shortcomings, it is infinitely more free and democratic than the People's Republic.

Taiwan, which was devastated when China regained control from Japan after World War II, is flourishing, if overpopulated. The 17.8 million people, the vast majority of whom are native-born Taiwanese, enjoy one of the highest standards of living in Asia. But critics, especially those who advocate an independent Taiwan, say that the current huge military expenditures impede more rapid economic growth. The island developed its economy partly because it has enjoyed U.S. military protection and received U.S. military aid.

In a November 1977 election for local offices, independent candidates scored their largest, if still limited, victory since 1949. Moreover, the unusual fairness of the election was seen as reflecting a decision by the government to allow native Taiwanese a greater share in the political process than did Chiang Kai-shek.

When President Yen Chia-kan (C.K. Yen) retired in March 1978 the National Assembly named Premier Chiang Ching-kuo to succeed him, in an election in which he was the only candidate. The former Economics Minister, Sun Yün-hsüan, was named premier in May.

Formal diplomatic relations between Taiwan and the United States were terminated on March 1, 1979, while cultural, commercial and quasi-official relations continue. The Taiwan-U.S. trade in 1980 amounted to $11.4 billion as compared to $9 billion in 1979. Taiwan's total worldwide trade in 1980 was $39.5 billion, a 28% increase over 1979, and included trade with several communist countries. With the abrogation of the mutual defense treaty with the United States on December 31, 1979, Taiwan has made progress toward self sufficiency both industrially and militarily.

HISTORY: Chinese emigration to Taiwan began in the 7th century. In the 16th century the Portuguese arrived, naming the island Formosa, meaning "beautiful." The Dutch assumed control in 1641 but were driven out in 1662 by Ming dynasty forces fleeing the Manchu takeover in mainland China. In 1683 Taiwan, too, fell to the Manchus. At the end of the Sino-Japanese War of 1894-95 it was ceded to Japan, which held it until the conclusion of World War II, when it was restored to China

1949: The Nationalist government of Chiang Kai-shek and remnants of his army flee to Taiwan, as the Communist forces of Mao Zedong gain control of the Chinese mainland

1950: President Truman orders U.S. Seventh Fleet to patrol the Taiwan Strait, thwarting a planned invasion of Taiwan by Communist China

1955: Following shelling of Nationalist-held offshore islands, the United States pledges to defend Taiwan and the Pescadores

1965: Because of Taiwan's impressive economic growth, U.S. aid is terminated except for surplus-food shipments

1966: Chiang Kai-shek is reelected president for fourth term

1969: Chiang Ching-kuo, elder son of Chiang Kai-shek, is named deputy premier

1971: Nationalist China replaced in UN by Mainland China

1972: Chiang Kai-shek is reelected president for fifth term; Chiang Ching-kuo is named premier

1973: U.S. announces gradual withdrawal of its forces on Taiwan as relations with Communist China improve

1974: U.S. pledges to "safeguard the security of Taiwan"

1975: Generalissimo Chiang Kai-shek, 87, dies of a heart attack in Taipei, April 5, and Yen Chia-kan (C.K. Yen) succeeds him

1978: Yen Chia-kan retires; Chiang Ching-kuo succeeds him in presidency. Taiwan terminates treaty with Japan following the signing of a treaty of friendship between Japan and the People's Republic of China

1979: American and Taiwan embassies are closed on March 1, quasi-official offices are established in each country

1980: Taiwan loses membership in both the International Monetary Fund and the World Bank. Premier Sun Yün-hsüan visits Costa Rica, Panama and the Dominican Republic

1981: The 12th National Congress of the Kuomintang Party meets in its 70th year of existence

---

COLOMBIA

Area: 439,735 sq. mi. **Population:** 27,185,000 (1980 est.)

Official Name: Republic of Colombia **Capital:** Bogotá **Nationality:** Colombian **Languages:** Spanish is the official language and is spoken by all but a few Indian tribes **Religion:** Roman Catholicism is the state religion and that of 95% of the population **Flag:** The top half of the flag is yellow; the bottom half consists of a blue stripe and red stripe of equal widths **Anthem:** National Anthem, beginning "O unwithering glory, immortal joy" **Currency:** Colombian peso (53 per U.S. $1)

Location: Northwest South America. Colombia is bordered on the north by the Caribbean Sea, on the east by Venezuela and Brazil, on the south by Peru and Ecuador, and on the west by the Pacific Ocean and Panama **Features:** Colombia is divided by the Andes Mountains into flat coastal areas, a highland or plateau area, and an eastern plains area **Chief Rivers:** Magdalena, Cauca, Amazon

Head of State and of Government: President Julio César Turbay Ayala, born 1916, took office Aug. 7, 1978 **Effective Date of Present Constitution:** August 1886 **Legislative Body:** Congress (bicameral), consisting of a Senate and a Chamber of Representatives. The Senate has 112 members; the Chamber has 199 members **Local**

Government: 22 departments, the Special District of Bogotá, 3 intendencies, and 5 commissaries, under appointed governors and administrators

Ethnic Composition: 58% Mixed European and Indian descent, 20% European stock, 14% European and African descent, 4% African stock, and 1% Indian **Population Distribution:** 64% urban **Density:** 62 inhabitants per sq. mi.

Largest Cities: (1973 census) Bogotá 2,855,065, Medellin 1,070,924, Cali 898,253, Barranquilla 661,009, Cartagena 292,512, Bucaramanga 291,661, Manizales 199,904

Per Capita Income: $983 (1980) **Gross National Product (GNP):** $26.3 billion (1980) **Economic Statistics:** 32% of GNP comes from agriculture (coffee, rice, cotton, potatoes, bananas, sugar); 17% from trade; 20% from industry (food, beverages, tobacco, textiles, chemicals, metal products and machinery) **Minerals and Mining:** Petroleum, gold, coal, salt, limestone, sand and gravel, platinum and emeralds are exploited **Labor Force:** Wage earners totaled 7,841,742 (1975), with 41% in agriculture, 23% in industry, and 14% in services **Foreign Trade:** Exports, chiefly coffee, crude petroleum, agricultural products, textiles, cattle, and emeralds, totaled $3.4 billion in 1979. Imports, chiefly machinery and electronic equipment, chemicals, transport vehicles, metals and metal products, totaled $4.6 billion **Principal Trade Partners:** United States, West Germany, Japan, Netherlands, Italy, Britain, Sweden, the Andean Group

Vital Statistics: Birthrate, 30 per 1,000 of pop. (1976); death rate, 8.8 **Life Expectancy:** 61 years **Health Statistics:** 530 inhabitants per hospital bed; 1,818 per physician (1975) **Infant Mortality:** 62.8 per 1,000 births **Illiteracy:** 19% **Primary and Secondary School Enrollment:** 5,776,638 (1977) **Enrollment in Higher Education:** 186,635 (1975) **GNP Expended on Education:** 1.9% (1976)

Transportation: Paved roads total 5,092 mi. **Motor Vehicles:** 558,100 (1977) **Passenger Cars:** 453,600 **Railway Mileage:** 2,134 **Ports:** Buenaventura, Sta. Marta, Barranquilla, Cartagena, Tumaco **Major Airlines:** Avianca operates domestic and international services **Communications:** Government and privately owned **Radio Transmitters:** 340 **Receivers:** 2,850,000 (1976) **Television Transmitters:** 3 **Receivers:** 1,700,000 (1976) **Telephones:** 1,769,000 (1976) **Newspapers:** 36 dailies, 69 copies per 1,000 inhabitants (1974)

Weights and Measures: Metric system **Travel Requirements:** Passport, tourist card valid for visits up to 90 days, 2 photos **International Dialing Code:** 57

Colombia, in effect, is a federation of city-states that are reflections of the isolation imposed by the Andes. Traditionally, the economy has been based on coffee on the rocks: Small farmers strive to raise quality coffee beans on the steep and rocky slopes of the Andes. Their crop accounts for the largest part of the nation's legal exports. In recent years, however, the illicit growing and exporting of marijuana and cocaine has risen fast as a major economic activity, estimated at from $1 billion to $2 billion a year even in the face of a government crackdown.

Colombia's social problems are staggering; its population is growing by 2.1 percent a year, despite efforts to expand family-planning programs, and its cities are swelling because of migration from rural areas. (Bogotá's population has doubled in the past 10 years.)

With illiteracy widespread, Colombia has a high unemployment rate and the income distribution of her population is highly skewed in favor of the upper fifth of the population. Access to health services and the quality of health care are even more unequally distributed.

Colombia's people are as varied as its geography. The top hundred or so families are basically European, and American-educated. The bulk of the people are of part-Indian stock, and some are descendants of African slaves. About 18 percent of the population is black or mulatto. There are small groups of nomads who wander the deserts of the northern fringe of the land as well as primitive Amazon Indians in the forests of the south. Indians make up 1 percent of the population.

Politically, Colombia is the largest working democracy in Latin America. Its 27 million people are still awed by *La Violencia*, the bloody period of

anarchy from 1948 to 1958, which cost about 200,000 lives. Its cause is still debated. *La Violencia* gave the Spanish language a new word, *bogotazo*, referring to the sudden eruption of violence in the capital on April 9, 1948, an uprising not clearly linked to a specific cause.

In any event, the civil war led first to the military dictatorship (1953-57) of General Gustavo Rojas Pinilla, then to a return to democracy on the basis of cooperation between the two traditional parties, the Liberals and the Conservatives, who began to rotate the presidency. Colombia permits its notably ineffectual Communist party to operate openly and legally.

With the advent to power of President Misael Pastrana Borrero in August 1970, following an election bitterly contested by General Rojas, Colombia began to achieve substantial progress for the people as a whole. In 1973, however, there were renewed indications that the violence that had marked so much of her history was not yet dead. After a number of bloody guerrilla actions, the government adopted several emergency security measures, including the establishment of special groups within the armed forces to pursue guerrilla bands operating in rural areas.

The 1974 elections offered the first open polls after 16 years of alternate rule by Liberals and Conservatives. Alfonso López Michelsen, the Liberal party candidate, won a constitutional mandate for a four-year term in coalition with the Conservatives. His term was marred somewhat by strikes of workers and students and by attacks and kidnappings by left-wing guerrillas.

The Liberals were again big winners in the 1978 congressional elections, and their candidate, Julio César Turbay Ayala, won the presidency in a close race. He became involved very soon in the twin problems of increased terrorism and rising drug traffic. On January 1, 1979, guerrillas of the M-19 group seized 5,300 weapons from the main Bogotá military arsenal. M-19, the Movement of April 19, got its name from the date in 1970 on which General Rojas was defeated for the presidency. Its original members were radical followers of Rojas. M-19 advocates establishing a socialist state through force of arms. In the wake of the arsenal raid, soldiers arrested several hundred left-wing guerrillas and imprisoned them.

M-19 struck again on February 27, 1980, as a group of masked young men and women shot their way into the Dominican Republic's embassy in Bogotá where a diplomatic reception was being held. They demanded $50 million ransom and release of 311 political prisoners as part of the price for freeing more than 50 hostages, among whom were the Spanish-born U.S. ambassador, Diego C. Asencio, and top-level diplomats of 15 other countries. During two months of negotiations, many of the hostages, including all of the women, were released gradually. The Uruguayan ambassador escaped on March 17, breaking a leg in jumping from a second-story window. For its part, the Colombian government speeded up the trials of political prisoners and acquitted many. On April 27 the siege ended peacefully when the 16 guerrillas settled for an alleged ransom of $2.5 million from unknown sources and safe escort to Cuba.

M-19 claimed success in bringing the world's attention to their allegations of torture and infringement of human rights by the Colombian military. The government won accolades for its painstaking negotiations and for avoiding the use of force to free the hostages.

In March 1981 the government reported that its armed forces had killed 19 guerrillas and captured 74 near the Ecuadoran border, virtually wiping out the M-19 command. The battle followed an M-19 raid on the town of Mocoa. Colombia suspended diplomatic relations with Cuba, which it accused of training and arming the guerrillas.

A three-year development plan, made public in May 1980, calls for investment of $22 billion in transportation, communication, hydroelectric and water-supply facilities. The annnual rate of inflation increased to about 30 percent, but gross national product climbed some 5 percent at constant prices. Coffee exports resulted in record earnings.

The government, meanwhile, was trying to stop another kind of export—illicit drugs. Soldiers swarmed over the Guajira Peninsula, a major point for shipping marijuana to the United States, in late 1978 and in 1979, and the government reported the seizure and burning of more than 100,000 tons of marijuana.

HISTORY: Colombia was inhabited perhaps as early as 5000 B.C. by Indian tribes of whom little is known. Prominent among pre-Colombian cultures was that of the highland Chibchas, a sedentary agricultural people located in the eastern chain of the Andes, in the center of the country. European colonization began about five years after Spanish explorers came to Colombia in 1499. With the founding of Bogotá in 1538, Colombia became the nucleus of New Granada, a vast territory that included parts of Panama, Venezuela, and Ecuador. The struggle for Colombian independence was, as elsewhere in Latin America, precipitated by Napoleon's invasion of Spain in the early 19th century
1810: Revolutionary leaders stage uprising in Bogotá
1819: By defeating Spanish royalist forces, Simón Bolívar secures independence of the new republic of Greater Colombia, which includes the former territory of New Granada
1830: Greater Colombia breaks up and New Granada (now Colombia and Panama) becomes a separate state
1863: New Granada becomes a federal republic, the United States of Colombia
1899: Civil war breaks out between liberal and conservative elements and results in more than 100,000 deaths and virtual economic ruin for the country
1903: Panama proclaims its independence from Colombia
1948-53: Assassination of left-wing liberal leader Jorge Gaitán in 1948 sets off a major revolt, ultimately costing 200,000 lives and leading to the declaration of a state of siege. President Laureano Gómez, an archconservative, takes power in 1950 but is ousted in a coup d'état led by the chief of the armed forces, General Gustavo Rojas Pinilla
1957: Rojas, in turn, is ousted by a military junta, which promises and provides presidential and congressional elections within the year. An amendment to the constitution is approved by plebiscite, providing for 12 years of parity (equal representation) between Liberal and Conservative parties in the 3 branches of government
1970: Departmental and municipal elections result in overwhelming defeat for Rojas and victory for Conservative party
1973: Agrarian reform bill is passed to reduce amount of land held by any person and to expropriate poorly farmed estates
1974: Alfonso López Michelsen elected in landslide Liberal victory
1977: Protests against high prices and continued martial law rule erupt in violence; 13 die, 4,000 arrested
1978: Julio César Turbay Ayala wins presidency
1979: M-19 guerrilla group captures arms from arsenal; hundreds of persons are taken as political prisoners
1980: Diplomats of 16 countries are held hostage for two months by M-19 guerrillas who seize Dominican Republic embassy Feb. 27. Liberal party victorious in March 9 by-elections
1981: Leftists kidnap and kill Chester Bitterman, American linguist and lay missionary, claiming he served the U.S. Central Intelligence Agency

---

COMOROS

Area: 719 sq. mi. **Population:** 290,000 (1978 est.)
Official Name: Federal and Islamic Republic of the Comoros **Capital:** Moroni **Nationality:** Comoran **Languages:** Arabic, French, Swahili **Religion:** Moslem, some Christians **Flag:** A green field with a white crescent in the center, set at an angle and encompassing four five-pointed stars in a line **Anthem:** N.A. **Currency:** CFA Franc (263 per U.S. $1)
Location: The Comoros (12°S., 44E.) lie in the Mozambique Channel of the Indian Ocean 300 miles northwest of Madagascar. There are three main islands: Anjouan, Mohéli and Grand Comoro, and a number of minor ones. The Republic claims nearby Mayotte as part of its territory **Features:** The islands are of volcanic origin and Karthala (elevation 8,399 ft.) on Grand Comoro is still active. The climate is tropical with a hot rainy season from November to April,

becoming more temperate the rest of the year **Chief Rivers:** There are no large rivers
Head of State: President Ahmed Abdallah, born 1919, elected October 1978, following the coup of May 1978 **Head of Government:** Prime Minister Salim Ben Ali, appointed 1978 **Effective Date of Constitution:** 1978 **Legislative Body:** Federal Assembly (unicameral) of 39 members **Local Government:** The 3 islands are organized into 7 regions
Ethnic Composition: The people are largely descendants of Moslem settlers with strains from Africa and Madagascar; there is a small European colony **Population Distribution:** N.A. **Density:** 403 inhabitants per sq. mi.
Largest City: (1974 est.) Moroni 12,000
Per Capita Income: $153 (1976 est.) **Gross Domestic Product (GDP):** $51 million (1976) **Economic Statistics:** A wide variety of crops flourish in the rich volcanic soil: rice, cassava, ambrevade (a pea-family plant), sweet potatoes, citrus fruits, and some European vegetables. The chief commercial crops are vanilla, perfume plants, and copra. Fishing and stock raising are important. In 1976, 40% of GDP came from agriculture, 34% from industry **Minerals and Mining:** There are practically no mineral resources **Labor Force:** 184,000 (1976) with 87% in agriculture **Foreign Trade:** Exports chiefly vanilla, ilang-ilang essence for perfumes, copra, cloves and sisal totaled $12 million in 1979. Imports, primarily rice, vegetables, mineral products, textiles, metals and automobiles, totaled $17 million **Principal Trade Partners:** France, Madagascar, Kenya, Italy, West Germany, Tanzania, United States
Vital Statistics: Birthrate, 46.6 per 1,000 of pop. (1975); death rate, 21.7 **Life Expectancy:** 49 years **Health Statistics:** 458 inhabitants per hospital bed; 13,810 per physician (1972) **Infant Mortality:** 51.7 per 1,000 births **Illiteracy:** 85% **Primary and Secondary School Enrollment:** 26,391 (1973) **Enrollment in Higher Education:** N.A. **GNP Expended on Education:** 8.7% (1971)
Transportation: Paved roads total 183 mi. **Motor Vehicles:** N.A. **Passenger Cars:** N.A. **Railway Mileage:** None **Ports:** Mutsamudu, Moroni, Fomboni, Bambao **Major Airlines:** Air Comores provides domestic service **Communications:** Government controlled **Radio Transmitters:** 3 (1973) **Receivers:** 36,000 (1976) **Television:** None **Telephones:** 2,000 (1976) **Newspapers:** None
Weights and Measures: Metric system **Travel Requirements:** N.A.

After 133 years as, successively, a French colony attached to Madagascar and a French Overseas Territory, three of the four Comoro Islands unilaterally declared independence on July 6, 1975. Still French territory but claimed by the Republic of the Comoros is the fourth island, Mayotte. Ahmed Abdallah was elected president of the new nation. These actions followed a vote in favor of independence in a referendum of December 1974.

In 1975, Ahmed Abdallah was overthrown in a bloodless coup led by Ali Soilih who was selected as president on January 2, 1976. The new nation has been vexed with the problem of the status of the largely Christian island of Mayotte. In 1976, the inhabitants of Mayotte voted to remain within the French Republic and not to join with the other largely Moslem Comoro Islands in independence. An April 12 referendum showed a preference for departmental status within France.

President Ali Soilih was overthrown on May 13, 1978, in a coup led by a French-born mercenary, Bob Denard, and Said Atthoumani, Interior Minister in the former Ahmed Abdallah government of 1975. The new government, headed by Ahmed Abdallah and Mohammed Ahmed, announced the release of political detainees and the restoration of rights and religious freedom. Mohammed Ahmed resigned in October 1978, leaving Ahmed Abdallah in sole command.

HISTORY: The original settlers of the Comoros came from mainland Africa. The first detailed knowledge of the area is undoubtedly due to Arab sailors, although the Phoenicians probably visited the islands much earlier. Two Arab invasions swept over the Comoros, the last coming from the Persian Gulf in the 15th century. In the 16th century the islands were visited by Portuguese, Dutch, French and Malagasy navigators
1843: French seize Mayotte
1886: Anjouan, Grand Comoro and Mohéli come under French protection

1912: The islands join administratively with Madagascar
1946: The Comoros become partially autonomous and receive the status of an Overseas Territory
1961: The islands receive complete internal autonomy
1975: Independence is declared. Comoros is admitted to UN. Government of Ahmed Abdallah overthrown by Ali Soilih
1976: Mayotte votes to remain French
1978: Ali Soilih overthrown in coup. Political-Military Directory under Ahmed Abdallah emerges; voters approve new constitution in Oct. 1 referendum. Ahmed Abdallah elected president
1979: UN General Assembly reaffirms Comoran sovereignty over Mayotte
1980: An increasing number of human-rights violations is reported

CONGO

Area: 132,046 sq. mi. **Population:** 1,459,000 (1978 est.)
Official Name: People's Republic of the Congo **Capital:** Brazzaville **Nationality:** Congolese **Languages:** French is the official language; Lingala and Kikongo are the principal spoken languages **Religion:** 49% animist, 49% Christian (mainly Roman Catholic), and 1% Moslem **Flag:** A red field; in the upper left corner is a yellow 5-pointed star above crossed yellow hammer and hoe, surrounded by green palm branches **Anthem:** The Internationale **Currency:** CFA Franc (263 per U.S. $1)

Location: West-central Africa. The Congo is bordered on the north by Cameroon and the Central African Republic, on the east and south by Zaire, on the southwest by the Angolan exclave of Cabinda and the Atlantic Ocean, and on the west by Gabon and Cameroon **Features:** The country consists of a coastal plain, savanna, highlands, and a plateau. Roughly half the land area is covered by dense equatorial forest, and a quarter of the country covered by marshes **Chief Rivers:** Congo, Ubangi, Sangha, Kouilou-Niari

Head of State and Government: President: Col. Denis Sassou-Nguesso, born 1941, elected July 1979. He is assisted by a Prime Minister, Col. Louis-Sylvain Goma, born 1941, appointed 1979 by the central committee of the Congolese Workers' party (PCT) **Effective Date of Present Constitution:** 1979 **Legislative Body:** Power is in the hands of the sole political party, the Congolese Workers' party (PCT). A National People's Assembly was elected in 1979 **Local Government:** 9 regions and a capital district, under appointed commissioners

Ethnic Composition: The 15 groups and 75 tribes are predominantly Bantu; major ones include the Bakongo, Bateke, M'Boshi, and Sangha. Pygmies number about 5,000. There are about 8,500 Europeans, mostly French **Population Distribution:** 40% urban (1976) **Density:** 11 inhabitants per sq. mi.
Largest Cities: (1974 census) Brazzaville 298,967, Pointe-Noire 141,700

Per Capita Income: $540 (1979) **Gross Domestic Product (GDP):** $805 million (1979) **Economic Statistics:** In 1978 about 19% of GDP was from agriculture (peanuts, palm kernels, coffee, cocoa, bananas, sugarcane, rice, corn, manioc, and sweet potatoes), forestry, and fishing; 10% from industry (forest products, sugar refining, palm and peanut oil, brewing, flour milling) **Minerals and Mining:** Crude petroleum is the major exploited mineral resource. There are high-grade iron-ore reserves, and some zinc, gold, copper, lead, and natural gas are produced. Potash production ended in 1977 **Labor Force:** 600,000, with 80% engaged in subsistence agriculture **Foreign Trade:** Exports, chiefly petroleum, wood, sugar, tobacco, and industrial diamonds, totaled $325 million in 1979. Imports, mainly machinery, electrical equipment, vehicles, textiles, clothing, foods, and chemicals, totaled $339 million **Principal Trade Partners:** France, West Germany, U.S., Italy

Vital Statistics: Birthrate, 45.1 per 1,000 of pop. (1975); death rate, 20.8 **Life Expectancy:** 43.5 years **Health Statistics:** 201 inhabitants per hospital bed (1976); 6,338 per physician (1975) **Infant Mortality:** 180 per 1,000 births **Illiteracy:** 80% **Primary and Secondary School Enrollment:** 421,211 (1975) **Enrollment in Higher Education:** 3,249 **GNP Expended on Education:** 8.2% (1975)

Transportation: Surfaced roads total 345 miles **Motor Vehicles:** 33,000 (1976) **Passenger Cars:** 20,000 **Railway Mileage:** 500 **Ports:** Pointe-Noire **Major Airlines:** Air Congo and Lina Congo operate internal services; Air Afrique, Aeroflot, Air France, KLM, Sabena, and UTA operate international services **Communications:** Government owned **Radio Transmitters:** 10 (1973) **Receivers:** 83,000 (1976) **Television Transmitters:** 1 **Receivers:** 3,300 (1976) **Telephones:** 11,000 (1976) **Newspapers:** 3 dailies, 1 copy per 1,000 inhabitants (1974)

Weights and Measures: Metric system **Travel Requirements:** Passport; visa. Contact Congo UN Mission in New York City

Since gaining independence from France in 1960, Congo has swung sharply from right to left politically and moved ahead very slowly economically.

Despite much leftist rhetoric, Congo's Marxist-Leninist "orientation" remains confusing—perhaps more expedient than orthodox. China and the Soviet Union appear to wield considerable influence over the government and speculation about which of them is in the ascendancy is a popular pastime in Brazzaville.

But it is capitalistic France that continues to be Congo's chief trading partner and source of economic and financial aid. Private French companies control most of the country's commerce and small industry.

President Marien Ngouabi, who came to power in 1968 and set up the ruling Congolese Workers' party (PCT), was assassinated March 18, 1977. Gen. Joachim Yhombi-Opango, who succeeded him, was ousted early in 1979 and replaced by Col. Denis Sassou-Nguesso in a leftist reaction against alleged bourgeois tendencies of the former regime. The new president, in response to a Paris report, acknowledged that more than a thousand Congolese children had been sent to Cuba for training.

Because of the unsettled situation in their country, hundreds of Zairians have sought asylum in the Congo. In 1980 the Brazzaville government denied that it was sheltering rebels planning to invade Zaire. Indeed, it deported many Zairians who were living illegally in the Congo.

HISTORY: When the Portuguese explorer Diego Cão arrived off the mouth of the Congo River in 1482, he found two long-established Bantu empires. To the north lay the Kingdom of Loango and its vassal states, and to the south, the great Mani-Congo stretching into Angola. Four centuries later, Count Pierre Savorgnan de Brazza (for whom Brazzaville is named) established French control over the area north of the river. In 1885, the Congress of Berlin recognized French claims to the region, later renamed Middle Congo
1910: Middle Congo becomes part of French Equatorial Africa
1958: The Congo becomes an autonomous member of French Community
1960: Full independence is proclaimed Aug. 15, and Fulbert Youlou becomes first president of the republic
1963: Youlou is overthrown in a revolt and succeeded by Alphonse Massamba-Débat who founds (in 1964) a Marxist-Leninist party. Chinese mission takes over direction of the economy
1965: Following arrests of American diplomats, United States closes Brazzaville embassy
1968: Capt. Marien Ngouabi, popular northern army officer, leads coup that ousts Massamba-Débat
1970: Ngouabi proclaims a people's republic, the first in Africa
1972: Production in offshore oil fields begins
1977: Ngouabi assassinated March 18. Emile Cardinal Biayenda murdered; Massamba-Débat executed for his role in assassination plot. Col. Joachim Yhombi-Opango, named president April 13 by military junta, abolishes national assembly. U.S. reopens its embassy
1978: Attempted coup to overthrow President Yhombi-Opango fails
1979: Col. Denis Sassou-Nguesso named president by PCT in February, following ouster of Yhombi-Opango who is accused of treason. Official PCT list of National People's Assembly candidates approved in July elections; new constitution also approved
1980: Sharp increases in oil production are predicted

COSTA RICA

Area: 19,652 sq. mi. **Population:** 2,193,000 (1979 est.)
Official Name: Republic of Costa Rica **Capital:** San José **Nationality:** Costa Rican **Languages:** Spanish is the official and predominant language; a Jamaican dialect of English is spoken by many of the country's Negroes, descendants of Jamaican workers who emigrated to Costa Rica in the 19th century **Religion:** Overwhelmingly Roman Catholic **Flag:** A blue stripe at top and bottom, separated by two white stripes from a broad center red stripe bearing the national coat of arms on the lefthand side **Anthem:** National Anthem, beginning "Noble country, thy beautiful banner" **Currency:** Colón (8.57 per U.S. $1)

Location: Central America. Costa Rica is bordered on the north by Nicaragua, on the east by the Caribbean Sea, on the southeast by

Panama, and on the west by the Pacific Ocean **Features:** About two-thirds of the country is covered by forests. There is a fairly wide coastal plain on the eastern side and a narrower plain on the Pacific coast. A volcanic mountain system composed of 3 ranges crosses the country lengthwise **Chief Rivers:** Río Grande, San Carlos

Head of State and of Government: President: Rodrigo Carazo Odio, born 1926, elected 1978 **Effective Date of Present Constitution:** November 1949 **Legislative Body:** Legislative Assembly (unicameral), consisting of 57 members elected by popular vote for 4 years **Local Government:** 7 provinces, each with a governor appointed by the president

Ethnic Composition: The population is predominantly of European (mainly Spanish) descent, with a large mestizo (mixed European and Indian) minority. Negroes of Jamaican origin number about 2% of the population **Population Distribution:** 41% urban **Density:** 112 inhabitants per sq. mi.

Largest Cities: (1973 census) San José 215,441, Alajuela 33,122, Limón 29,621, Puntarenas 26,331, Heredia 22,700, Cartago 21,753

Per Capita Income: $1,431 (1979) **Gross National Product (GNP):** $3.1 billion (1979) **Economic Statistics:** In 1979 about 22% of GNP came from agriculture (coffee, bananas, cocoa, sugarcane, rice, beans, and livestock), forestry, and fishing; 20% from industry (food and beverages, textiles, fertilizers, shoes, furniture) **Minerals and Mining:** Gold and manganese are mined **Labor Force:** 740,000 (1979); 34% in agriculture, 36% in industry and commerce, 25% in services and government **Foreign Trade:** Exports, chiefly coffee, bananas, meat, sugar, cocoa, and fertilizers, totaled $925 million in 1979. Imports, mainly manufactures, machinery and transport equipment, chemicals, foodstuffs, and petroleum, totaled $1.4 billion **Principal Trade Partners:** United States, West Germany, Nicaragua, El Salvador, Guatemala, Japan

Vital Statistics: Birthrate, 29.7 per 1,000 of pop. (1976); death rate, 4.6 **Life Expectancy:** 68 years **Health Statistics:** 261 inhabitants per hospital bed; 1,524 per physician (1975) **Infant Mortality:** 33.6 per 1,000 births **Illiteracy:** 10% **Primary and Secondary School Enrollment:** 481,994 (1976) **Enrollment in Higher Education:** 38,629 (1977) **GNP Expended on Education:** 5.2% (1974)

Transportation: Paved roads total 1,200 mi. **Motor Vehicles:** 107,300 (1976) **Passenger Cars:** 64,900 **Railway Mileage:** 661 **Ports:** Limón, Puntarenas, Golfito **Major Airlines:** LACSA (Costa Rican Airlines) operates domestic and international flights **Communications:** Government controlled **Radio Transmitters:** 65 **Receivers:** 254,774 (1979) **Television Transmitters:** 15 **Receivers:** 155,000 (1976) **Telephones:** 145,000 (1979) **Newspapers:** 6 dailies, 88 copies per 1,000 inhabitants (1975)

Weights and Measures: Metric system and old Spanish weights and measures are used **Travel Requirements:** Passport and visa not required if tourist card obtained prior to departure (valid 30 days, $2.00 fee) **International Dialing Code:** 506

Born in the bloodshed of civil war in 1948, the stable and progressive political institutions of Costa Rica have since provided relative peace and democracy despite severe pressures.

The country's republican form of government, in which presidential power is held in check by a strong Assembly, has been able to renew itself every four years through peaceful and honest elections held under the exclusive authority of a jealously independent electoral board.

The sophistication of Costa Rica's politics goes hand in hand with economic and social levels much higher than the rest of Central America has been able to achieve. Although there are extremes of wealth and poverty here as elsewhere, distribution is generally more equitable.

Even with its orderly process of government, Costa Rica has experienced political problems. In 1966 the country retained the reformist National Liberation party in control of the Assembly while electing as president the candidate of a conservative anti-Liberation coalition, José Joaquín Tréjos Fernández. Legislative and executive branches were at constant loggerheads in a period of financial difficulty requiring decisive action. The voters remedied this in 1970 when they elected the Liberation candidate for president, José Figuéres Ferrer, and his party kept control in the Assembly. In 1974, the National Liberation party retained the presidency with the election of its candidate, Daniel Oduber Quirós.

In the 1978 elections, political power passed peacefully to a new president, Rodrigo Carazo Odio, an economist and businessman, and his coalition Unity party. Carazo continued the government's pro-American stance, and banned the re-entry of Robert Vesco—a fugitive from U.S. charges of embezzlement—when Vesco went to the Bahamas. He defended the left-wing regime established in Nicaragua in 1979 by *Sandinista* guerrillas who attacked from bases in Costa Rica; and he supported the beleaguered civilian government in El Salvador. "We must not repeat Cuba," he has said. "In this polarized world, a country expelled from one side goes automatically to the other."

Costa Rica's stability has been severely tested in the 1980s, both politically and economically. Terrorist bombings in 1981 showed that the country's only security force, the 7,000-member Civil Guard, is inadequate to deal with such a problem. Increased oil imports and declining earnings from coffee exports have contributed to a serious trade deficit, a drop in value of the colón, and inflation edging toward 40% in 1981. Costa Rica has turned to the International Monetary Fund for aid in exchange for adoption of an austerity budget.

The vast Arenal hydroelectric project in Guanacaste province is expected to double the nation's electrical capacity by 1984 and will greatly reduce dependence on imported oil.

HISTORY: Prior to Costa Rica's discovery in 1502 by the Spanish, the country was inhabited by the Guaymi Indians. During the Spanish colonial period, Costa Rica was largely ignored by the mother country because of the paucity of minerals, and administered as part of the captaincy general of Guatemala

1821: Costa Rica obtains independence from Spain, and along with the rest of Central America is annexed to Mexico

1823: Costa Rica and the other Central American countries secede from Mexico and establish the Central American Federation

1838: Costa Rica becomes an independent republic

1856-57: William Walker, an American adventurer, attempts to conquer Costa Rica but is defeated by Central American alliance

1917-19: Revolution breaks out; dictatorship is set up by Frederico Granados

1948-49: President Teodoro Picado annuls elections won by presidential candidate Otilio Ulate. José Figuéres leads civilian uprising, installs own junta, then turns presidency over to Ulate

1963: The volcano Irazú erupts, destroying productive land

1968: The volcano Arenal erupts, bringing new devastation

1970: José Figuéres wins presidential election

1974: Daniel Oduber Quirós is elected president

1976: Trade relations restored with Cuba

1978: Rodrigo Carazo Odio is elected president

1980: Strikes bring wage gains to workers, who claim the increases fail to meet a sharp rise in the cost of living

1981: Government blames terrorist bombings on leftist Salvadoran groups; others claim Costa Rican radicals, having caught Central American revolutionary fever, are responsible. Relations with Cuba are broken

CUBA

Area: 42,827 sq. mi. **Population:** 9,775,000 (1979 est.)

Official Name: Republic of Cuba **Capital:** Havana **Nationality:** Cuban **Languages:** Spanish is the official and universal language **Religion:** Predominantly Roman Catholic before Castro **Flag:** Three horizontal blue stripes separated by two white stripes, with an equilateral red triangle at the left containing a 5-pointed white star **Anthem:** Hymn of Bayamo **Currency:** Cuban peso (0.77 per U.S. $1)

Location: Northern rim of the Caribbean Sea. The largest and most westerly island of the West Indies, Cuba lies at the entrance of the Gulf of Mexico and some 90 miles south of Florida **Features:** About three-fifths of the country consists of flat to gently rolling terrain with many wide and fertile valleys and plains. The rest is mountainous or hilly **Chief Rivers:** Cauto, Sagua la Grande, Zaza, Caonao, San Pedro, Toa

Political Leader, Head of State and of Government: President Fidel Castro Ruz, born 1927, First Secretary of the Central Committee of the Cuban Communist party, and president of the councils of state and of ministers, seized power in 1959 **Effective Date of Present Constitution:** December 1976 **Legislative Body:** National Assembly of People's Power (unicameral), with 481 deputies elected for 5-year terms. Power lies in the Communist party Politburo **Local Govern-**

ment: 14 provinces (including Havana city and the special municipality of Isla de la Juventud (Isle of Pines), with locally elected assemblies

Ethnic Composition: 51% mulatto (mixed European and black), 37% European ancestry, 11% black, 1% Chinese **Population Distribution:** 60.5% urban (1971) **Density:** 228 inhabitants per sq. mi.

Largest Cities: (1976 est.) Havana 1,949,000, Santiago de Cuba 322,000, Camagüey 228,000, Guantánamo 158,000, Holguín 153,000, Santa Clara 150,000

Per Capita Income: $1,407 (1980) **Gross National Product (GNP):** $14 billion (1980) **Economic Statistics:** 10% of GNP is derived from agriculture (sugar, tobacco, cattle, coffee); 41% from industry (mainly sugar refining, cigarettes and cigars, rum, and textiles); and 33% from trade and finance (1974) **Minerals and Mining:** Cuba has the world's largest deposit of nickel; reserves of iron ore, manganese, cobalt, copper, chromite, salt, petroleum, gold, silver **Labor Force:** 2,700,000 (1976), with 39% in transportation and services, 33% in agriculture, and 26% in industry and construction **Foreign Trade:** Exports, chiefly sugar, nickel, tobacco, shrimp, lobster, and beef, were $4.7 billion (1979). Imports, mainly petroleum, equipment and machinery, and food, totaled $5 billion **Principal Trade Partners:** Soviet bloc, Japan, Spain, Canada, West Germany

Vital Statistics: Birthrate, 19.8 per 1,000 of pop. (1976); death rate, 5.6 **Life Expectancy:** 72 years **Health Statistics:** 235 inhabitants per hospital bed; 1,121 per physician (1976) **Infant Mortality:** 23 per 1,000 births (1976) **Illiteracy:** 3.1% **Primary and Secondary School Enrollment:** 2,463,545 (1976) **Enrollment in Higher Education:** 82,688 (1975) **GNP Expended on Education:** 9.9% (1974)

Transportation: Paved roads total 5,470 mi. **Motor Vehicles:** 120,000 (1976) **Passenger Cars:** 80,000 **Railway Mileage:** 9,100 **Ports:** Havana, Matanzas, Nuevitas, Cienfuegos, Santiago de Cuba **Major Airlines:** Cubana de Aviación, the government-owned airline, operates domestic and international flights **Communications:** Government controlled **Radio Transmitters:** 115 (1975) **Receivers:** 2,100,000 (1976) **Television Transmitters:** 19 **Receivers:** 650,000 (1976) **Telephones:** 289,000 (1974) **Newspapers:** 15 dailies (1975), 107 per 1,000 inhabitants

Weights and Measures: Metric system **Travel Requirements:** Passport, visa; tourist visa, $6.00 fee, apply to Czechoslovak Embassy, Washington, D.C. 20009

Cuba, largest of the West Indies and the only Communist-controlled country in the Western Hemisphere, lies only 90 miles south of Key West, Florida. Cuba's capital, Havana, is less than an hour's flight southwest from Miami. The country's largest city and principal port, Havana, was originally important as a well-situated way station between Spain and her colonies in the Western Hemisphere. Eventually, settlers moved inland, devoting themselves mainly to growing sugarcane and tobacco.

Despite the physical proximity of Cuba to the U.S. and the potential trade and other ties, the relationship between the two countries has never developed quite as one might expect. Cuba was the last Latin American nation to gain independence from Spain. The United States actually opposed the first attempt to free Cuba begun by Simón Bolívar. A native-based liberation movement starting in 1868 sputtered out after 10 years of fighting. It was not until 1895 that a revolution led by José Martí successfully challenged Spain. The revolutionaries also won strong sentiments of support in the U.S. After the mysterious sinking of the *Maine*, the U.S. declared war on Spain.

When a freely elected Cuban government took office in 1902, it found it had little to sell except land. Many foreign investors, chiefly Americans, stepped forward and purchased enormous areas and began to rebuild the sugar industry. For years after, Cuba was locked into a one-crop agricultural economy with American ownership of the land, mines and other resources. Income was, and still is, almost totally dependent on the world price of sugar. American interests were protected by the Platt Amendment that allowed U.S. to intervene in Cuban affairs, which it did in 1906-1909 and again in 1912.

Fulgencio Batista, a former army sergeant, dominated the political scene either directly or indirectly from 1934 to 1944 and from 1952 to 1959.

President Batista's regime became repressive and increasingly unpopular, and on July 26, 1953, an armed opposition group led by a young lawyer, Fidel Castro, attacked the Moncada army barracks at Santiago de Cuba. The attack failed and many of those not killed were imprisoned, including Castro. He was released by President Batista under an amnesty in May 1955 and went into exile in Mexico, where he formed his "26th of July Movement." While a number of other groups in Cuba also actively opposed Batista, it was Castro's forces, eventually numbering several thousands, who finally succeeded in forcing Batista to flee the country, on January 1, 1959.

The Castro regime's early promises of agrarian reform to benefit the peasants resulted in state ownership of most of the land and in the organization of state farms. Cuba's business and industrial sectors were nationalized and placed under the direction of the state, which has also effectively abolished all opposition political activity.

A major element of Cuba's foreign policy under Castro has been the "exporting" of revolutionary techniques. To this end, Cuba has supported guerrilla movements in various countries in the Western Hemisphere and elsewhere—notably Africa— by providing weapons, financing, propaganda and, in some cases, advisory personnel. In Cuba itself, on *Isla de la Juventud* (Isle of Youth), formerly the Isle of Pines, more than 10,000 African and Latin American adolescents are receiving standard Cuban education, including Marxist ideology.

A nod toward normalizing U.S.-Cuban relations was made in 1975 by U.S. Secretary of State Henry Kissinger. But the nod became a "no" when Cuba dispatched troops to help Russian-backed forces in Angola's civil war. After Jimmy Carter became president, he first tested the water with some qualified public overtures toward Cuba, and then on March 9, 1977, announced an end to travel restrictions in Cuba. The two countries soon negotiated fishing and maritime rights agreements.

Still, the United States kept a wary eye on Soviet military gifts to Cuba—MiG-23 jet planes in 1978, a non-nuclear submarine in 1979. In August 1979 the Carter Administration affirmed reports that the Soviet Union had a combat brigade of 2,500 to 3,000 men stationed in Cuba. Both Havana and Moscow insisted that Soviet military personnel were there only for training and advisory purposes.

Cuba's economic plight has steadily worsened, so much so that in a December 1979 speech Castro admitted that his country is "sailing on a sea of difficulties." World sugar prices had plunged, and the cane harvest was curbed by a fungus. A blue mold almost totally wiped out the 1979-80 tobacco crop. Many farm workers were becoming slack on the job and production records were being falsified, a government spokesman noted. Shortages of food and other necessities were growing and rationing was strictly enforced. To keep the economy going at all, Cuba had to depend on a subsidy of $8-$10 million a day from the Soviet Union, with which a $45 billion trade agreement for 1981-85 has been signed. Trade pacts were also made with East Germany and Japan in 1980, and in 1981 an accord was reached with Mexico for that country's assistance in oil and natural gas exploration on Cuba's undersea shelf.

In April 1980 more than 10,000 Cubans crashed their way into the Peruvian embassy compound in Havana, seeking safe exit to other countries. Castro eventually acceded, and some 120,000 men, women and children took advantage of the opportunity to escape oppression in their homeland. The vast majority fled to Florida in a flotilla of small boats. A few refugees, dissatisfied with their treatment in the United States, started a wave of airplane hijackings to get back to Havana; some were thwarted by Castro's decision to return them to the United States. Efforts by the U. S. government to get Cuba to take back some 1,800 refugees held in jails as "undesirables" were countered by Castro's threat to release another flood of dissident Cubans in 1981.

HISTORY: Following the discovery of Cuba by Columbus in 1492, the island remained under Spanish rule until almost the end of the 19th century. A revolt against Spain broke out in 1895 and evoked strong sympathy in the United States. After the brief Spanish-American War of 1898, Cuba became an independent republic, though under U.S. protection. With the abrogation of the Platt Amendment in 1934, the U.S. gave up the right to intervene in Cuban affairs, but retained its right to the naval base at Guantánamo
1934-59: Fulgencio Batista y Zaldívar, an army sergeant, overthrows regime and becomes dominant figure in Cuban politics. After ruling through puppet presidents, Batista proclaims new constitution in 1940 and is elected president for four-year term. In 1952 he returns to power through an army coup but his regime is increasingly threatened by rebel uprisings led by Fidel Castro, who finally forces Batista to flee
1960: Castro begins to transform Cuba into socialist state modeled on Soviet pattern and installs Communists in leading government posts. Most U.S.-owned property is nationalized without compensation; United States rescinds Cuban sugar quota
1961: United States severs diplomatic relations with Havana. Castro turns increasingly to Soviet Union for aid and protection, receiving supplies of arms and oil. Cuban exiles in United States, trained and equipped by Central Intelligence Agency, land invasion force at Bay of Pigs in abortive attempt to overthrow Castro
1962: Organization of American States excludes Cuba from membership. Installation of Soviet missiles in Cuba leads to U.S. demand for their removal and to imposition of naval blockade of island to bar further Soviet shipments. Strong U.S. reaction results in Soviet backdown and missiles are withdrawn
1970: Castro concedes that sugar harvest fell far below 10-million-ton goal
1971: Cuba signs economic pact with the Soviet Union
1972: Premier Castro makes his third official visit to Moscow at the end of a two-month world tour of socialist countries
1975: OAS passes resolution to lift the 11 years of formal diplomatic and economic isolation of Cuba
1976: A new constitution is approved by referendum
1978: U.S.-Cuba thaw is stalled, principally on issues of U.S. economic blockade against Cuba, $1.8 billion in claims against Cuba by American companies and individuals, and continued Cuban presence in Africa
1979: As host to the sixth summit conference of Third World nations in the Non-Aligned movement, Castro defends use of Cuban troops to fight for "just causes" in Africa and elsewhere
1980: Castro reorganizes cabinet and personally assumes four portfolios, including defense and interior. Castro releases 33 American prisoners from Cuban jails. Cuba loses bid for membership on UN Security Council
1981: U.S. expels Cuban diplomat charged with trying to persuade American businessmen to circumvent U.S. trade embargo against Cuba. Attempt by 29 Cubans to get safe passage out of country by seizing Ecuadoran embassy fails

---

CYPRUS

Area: 3,572 sq. mi. (including the 99 sq. mi. British-leased Sovereign Base Area) **Population:** 621,000 (1979 est.)

Official Name: Republic of Cyprus **Capital:** Nicosia **Nationality:** Cypriot **Languages:** Greek and Turkish are the official languages. English is widely understood **Religion:** 78% Greek Orthodox, 18% Moslem, 4% Maronite, Armenian and Apostolic Christians **Flag:** An outline map of Cyprus in gold above crossed green olive branches on a white field **Anthem:** None established **Currency:** Cypriot pound (0.41 per U.S. $1)

Location: Middle East. The third largest island in the Mediterranean, Cyprus lies 44 miles south of Turkey, 60 miles west of Syria, and 260 miles east of Rhodes, the nearest part of Greece **Features:** The Troodos Mountains in the southwest and the Kyrenia range along the northern coast dominate the island. The central plain, or Mesaoria, lies between the two mountain ranges **Chief River:** Pedieos (Pedias)

Head of State and of Government: President: Spyros Achilles Kyprianou, born 1932, succeeded August 1977, reelected for full 5-year term 1978 **Effective Date of Present Constitution:** 1960 **Legislative Body:** House of Representatives (unicameral), consisting of

35 Greek Cypriot members, elected for 5 years. Turkish Cypriots declared their independence and established in February 1975 the Turkish Federated State of Cyprus, with a president (Rauf R. Denktash elected in 1976), premier (Mustafa Cagatay, appointed 1978), and a 40-member unicameral Constituent Assembly; a referendum in 1975 approved a constitution **Local Government:** 6 districts

Ethnic Composition: About 78% of the population is of Greek descent, 18% of Turkish origin, and the rest composed of Armenians, Maronites, and other minorities **Population Distribution:** 42.2% urban (1974) **Density:** 174 inhabitants per sq. mi.

Largest Cities: (1973 census) Nicosia 116,125; (1972 estimates) Limassol 61,400, Famagusta 44,200, Larnaca 21,800, Paphos 12,100, Kyrenia 5,200

Per Capita Income: $2,387 (1979) **Gross National Product (GNP):** $1.5 billion (1979) **Economic Statistics:** About 18% of GNP was derived from agriculture and 26% from manufacturing and mining **Minerals and Mining:** Copper is the most important mineral, but the mines are becoming depleted; asbestos is becoming increasingly important. Other minerals are iron pyrites, chromite, umber, and yellow ocher **Labor Force:** 202,700 (1977, Greek area only), with 26% in industry, 23% in agriculture, forestry and fishing, 15% employed overseas or in military, 5% in government **Foreign Trade**—Republic of Cyprus area (Greek): Exports, chiefly fruits and vegetables, wine, cement and clothing, totaled $422 million in 1979. Imports, mainly machinery, manufactures, fuel and food, totaled $1 billion Turkish area: Exports, chiefly fruits and vegetables and pyrites, totaled $40 million in 1979. Imports, chiefly food, fuels and machinery, totaled $108 million **Principal Trade Partners**—Republic of Cyprus area (Greek): Britain, Saudi Arabia, West Germany, France, Japan, Greece, Syria, U.S., Lebanon, Kuwait Turkish area: Turkey, Britain, West Germany, France, Italy

Vital Statistics: Birthrate, 19.6 per 1,000 of pop. (1976); death rate, 9.8 **Life Expectancy:** 73 years **Health Statistics:** 177 inhabitants per hospital bed; 1,092 per physician (Greek area-1977) **Infant Mortality:** 27.2 per 1,000 births **Illiteracy:** 11% **Primary and Secondary School Enrollment:** (Greek area) 104,524 (1977) **Enrollment in Higher Education:** 782 (1976) **GNP Expended on Education:** 4.1% (1976)

Transportation: Paved roads total 2,800 mi. **Motor Vehicles:** 93,100 (1977) **Passenger Cars:** 74,500 **Railway Mileage:** None **Ports:** Famagusta, Limassol, Larnaca, Karavostassi **Major Airlines:** Cyprus Airways (government owned) operates domestic and international flights; there is also a Turkish-Cypriot airline **Communications:** State controlled **Radio Transmitters:** 16 **Licenses:** 200,000 (1976) **Television Transmitters:** 26 **Licenses:** 57,000 (1976) **Telephones:** 77,000 (1976) **Newspapers:** 12 dailies (1975), 107 copies per 1,000 inhabitants (1970)

Weights and Measures: Both British standards and the metric system are used along with local units **Travel Requirements:** Passport, no visa **International Dialing Code:** 357

The picturesque island of Aphrodite, Cyprus has been an independent but strife-torn nation since 1960. Previously, its strategic location had attracted many foreign conquerors, including the Egyptians, Phoenicians, Assyrians, Persians, Romans, Greeks, Turks and British. Today Cyprus is divided into two separate states and its future as a single nation is in doubt.

The island is the homeland of two antagonistic peoples—some half-million ethnic Greeks and slightly more than 120,000 ethnic Turks. The Greek Cypriots have traditionally favored *enosis* (union) with Greece, while the Turkish Cypriots want partition or cantonization of the country. In any case, virtually all Cypriots regard themselves as Greeks or Turks, Christians or Moslems first and as Cypriots second.

More than half the total area of Cyprus is cultivated, a noteworthy accomplishment in the largely arid Middle East. Mineral resources maintain a modest industrial complex. Light manufacturing is growing in the Greek area.

The constitution, in effect after independence in 1960, required that the president be a Greek Cypriot and the vice-president a Turkish Cypriot. Archbishop Makarios III, head of the Greek Orthodox Church on Cyprus became president. The Greek and Turkish communities lived under a form of de facto segregation.

Civil war between the two communities erupted in 1963, and terroristic campaigns became a part of Cypriot life. In 1964, the United Nations sent a peace-keeping force to minimize clashes. Turkish Cypriot leaders withdrew from active participation in the government of Cyprus. In 1967 war between Greece and Turkey over Cyprus was narrowly averted, mainly through the mediation of the United States. Turkey had threatened to invade the island but Greece finally agreed to remove nearly all of the 8,000 troops it had there.

The Cypriot national guard which was dominated by officers from Greece continued to press for union with Greece. In 1971 the EOKA B, a guerrilla movement favoring ties to Greece and led by Gen. George Grivas, stepped up its terrorist activities, which tended to undermine the government of President Makarios, who began his third five-year term in February 1973. (His second term had been extended.)

On July 15, 1974, Greek officers of the Cypriot national guard led a coup which overthrew President Makarios and replaced him with an EOKA B terrorist, Nikos Sampson. Turkey responded by invading Cyprus on July 20, and quickly conquered the northern two-fifths of the island. Most of the Greek Cypriots in the conquered territory fled south, and most of the Turkish Cypriots elsewhere moved north. Sampson's government collapsed.

Amid fears of a wider conflict, the UN ordered a cease-fire. Fighting continued sporadically but order was restored with Glafkos Clerides, president of the Cyprus House of Representatives, as interim president. By the time international pressure effected a real cease-fire on August 16, 200,000 Greek Cypriots were refugees. Makarios returned to power in December 1974.

In February 1975 a Turkish-Cypriot Federated State of Cyprus was created in the occupied area without the approval of Makarios, and in June a Turkish Cypriot referendum established a constitution for the state. Talks to establish a unified form of government continue, but accord at times seems distant. In April 1978 the Cypriot government rejected Turkish proposals for a settlement of the dispute between the island's Greeks and Turks, charging they were aimed at permanently dividing the island into two states. But there was still hope that unity could be restored. In August 1980, the two communities reopened negotiations under UN sponsorship on steps which might lead to the eventual restoration of a unified government for the entire island.

HISTORY: Cyprus, which derives its name from "kypros," the Greek word for copper, was settled first by the Greeks c. 1500 B.C. and passed to the Romans in 58 B.C. Later a part of the Byzantine Empire, the island slumbered until 1191, when Richard I of England conquered Cyprus and it became a base for the Crusaders. In the 16th century, the island was conquered by Turkey. Administration was transferred to Britain in 1878 and in 1928 the island became a Crown Colony

1946: Greece demands union (enosis) with Cyprus

1956: Archbishop Makarios, spiritual and political leader of the Greek Cypriots, is deported by British

1959: Greek-Turkish conferences in Zurich and London reach agreement on independence for Cyprus. Archbishop Makarios returns and is elected president

1960: Independence is officially proclaimed

1963: Violence between Greeks and Turks erupts in Nicosia

1964: Turks withdraw from active participation in government. Threat of war between Greece and Turkey over Cyprus brings United Nations peace-keeping force to island

1968: Makarios announces restoration of freedom of movement for Turkish Cypriots, ending blockade of Turkish sectors

1973: Struggle for enosis erupts into widespread violence

1974: Cypriot National Guard ousts President Makarios. Turkish forces invade Cyprus and gain control of 40 percent of the island. Two-way migration makes occupied territory predominantly Turkish, rest of island predominantly Greek. Makarios returns and resumes the presidency

1975: Turkish Cypriots proclaim their own state in northern Cyprus

1976: Turkish Cypriots elect Rauf Denktash to serve as president of the Turkish Cypriot Zone

1977: Turkish and Greek Cypriot leaders begin talks. Makarios dies. Spyros Kyprianou succeeds him

1978: Deadlock in talks between Cypriot leaders continues

1980: Kyprianou offers economic benefits to Turkish Cypriots

CZECHOSLOVAKIA

Area: 49,373 sq. mi. **Population:** 15,247,000 (1979 est.)

Official Name: Czechoslovak Socialist Republic **Capital:** Prague **Nationality:** Czechoslovak **Languages:** Czech and Slovak are the official and principal languages; Hungarian and German are minority languages **Religion:** About 77% of the population is Roman Catholic; 8% are members of the Czechoslovak Church; and 8% are Protestants. All churches are under close government control **Flag:** A blue triangle on the hoist with its apex toward the center; the rest of the flag consists of a white band on top and a red band on the bottom **Anthem:** Where Is My Home? **Currency:** Koruna (11.5 per U.S. $1)

Location: Central Europe. Landlocked Czechoslovakia is bordered on the north by Poland, on the east by the USSR, on the south by Hungary and Austria, on the west by West Germany, and on the northwest by East Germany **Features:** Bohemia, Moravia, and Slovakia are the country's principal regions. Bohemia, in the west, is a plateau surrounded by mountains; Moravia, in the central region, is somewhat hillier; and Slovakia, in the east, is partly mountainous and partly lowland **Chief Rivers:** Labe, Vltava, Danube, Morava, Váh, Nitra, Hron, Ohre, Hornád

Political Leader and Head of State: President Gustav Husák, born 1913, elected 1975, reelected 1980; general secretary of the Central Committee of the Communist Party **Head of Government:** Premier Lubomir Strougal, born 1924, took office 1970 **Effective Date of Present Constitution:** 1960; the constitution was amended in 1969 to provide for Czech and Slovak local autonomy within a federal state, and again in 1971 and 1975 **Legislative Body:** Federal Assembly (bicameral), consisting of 2 equal chambers, the Chamber of the People and the Chamber of the Nations. The Chamber of the People has 200 members. The Chamber of the Nations consists of 75 representatives from the Czech Republic and 75 from the Slovak Republic. Both houses are elected for 5 years. The Federal Assembly is subordinate to the Central Committee of the Presidium of the Communist Party **Local Government:** The two republics have separate premiers and national councils, subordinate to the Federal Assembly. They are divided into 10 regions and 2 independent cities

Ethnic Composition: Czechs make up about 65% of the population and Slovaks 30%; Hungarians, Germans, Poles, Ukrainians, and Gypsies make up the rest **Population Distribution:** 66.7% urban (1974) **Density:** 309 inhabitants per sq. mi.

Largest Cities: (1976 est.) Prague 1,173,031, Brno 361,561, Bratislava 345,515, Ostrava 302,111, Kosice 179,143, Plzen 157,306

Per Capita Income: $5,542 (1980) **Gross National Product (GNP):** $85 billion (1980) **Economic Statistics:** About 45% of GNP comes from industry (iron and steel, glass, leather products, brewing, and textiles); 12% from agriculture (grains, sugar beets, hops, fruits and vegetables); 8% from construction; 9% from transport and communications; 9% from trade; 5% from housing; 11% from government and other services **Minerals and Mining:** Coal, antimony, magnesite, lignite and uranium **Labor Force:** 8.3 million (1976), with about 37% in industry and construction, and 18% in agriculture **Foreign Trade:** Exports, chiefly machinery, motor vehicles, iron and steel, and chemicals, totaled $13.9 billion in 1979. Imports, mainly machinery, industrial raw materials, food, fuel, and manufactured goods, totaled $14.4 billion **Principal Trade Partners:** USSR, East Germany, Poland, Hungary, Romania, West Germany, Britain, Bulgaria, Switzerland, Austria, Yugoslavia

Vital Statistics: Birthrate, 18.7 per 1,000 of pop. (1977); death rate, 11.5 **Life Expectancy:** 71 years **Health Statistics:** 99 inhabitants per hospital bed; 404 per physician (1976) **Infant Mortality:** 19.6 per 1,000 births (1977) **Illiteracy:** Negligible **Primary and Secondary School Enrollment:** 2,210,915 (1976) **Enrollment in Higher Education:** 155,059 (1975) **GNP Expended on Education:** 4.5% (1976)

Transportation: Paved roads total 37,350 mi. **Motor Vehicles:** 2,117,500 (1977) **Passenger Cars:** 1,827,700 **Railway Mileage:** 8,228 **Ports:** None **Major Airlines:** Czechoslovak Airlines operates domestic and international services **Communications:** State owned **Radio Transmitters:** 123 **Licenses:** 3,928,000 (1976) **Television Transmitters:** 788 **Licenses:** 3,793,000 (1976) **Telephones:** 2,743,000 (1976) **Newspapers:** 29 dailies, 300 copies per 1,000 inhabitants (1975)

Weights and Measures: Metric system **Travel Requirements:** Passport, visa, 2 pictures, $8 fee

The problem of Czechoslovakia today is trying to mold a socialist state of Marxist-Leninist traditions as determined by its Russian guardians while satisfying a native desire for the freedom and openness of a Western democracy.

The Communist party seized power in 1948, and established one of the world's least free societies. In the 1960s, with a new constitution, a cautious liberalizing movement emerged. A flowering of Czechoslovak artistry in films, the theater and other arts began. When the economy stagnated, Slovak Communists found a chance to replace hard-liner Antonin Novotny with Alexander Dubcek as first secretary of the Communist Party in January 1968.

Under Dubcek the trend toward freedom accelerated. Press censorship was reduced and grievances were aired, thus adding to the pressure for reforms while at the same time arousing the fears of Soviet leaders. The radical experiment to establish "socialism with a human face" ended abruptly on August 20, 1968. Armored units of the Warsaw Pact countries, led by Soviet tanks, entered Czechoslovakia at night to ensure the restoration of a more orthodox brand of Communism.

The dramatic incursion was characterized by its initiators as necessary to thwart a "threatened counterrevolution" by "imperialist forces." It was seen by Western observers—and most Czechs—as a final desperate move by Leonid I. Brezhnev, the Soviet Communist party chief, to curtail Dubcek's essay in socialist democracy.

Dubcek was forced in succeeding days to sign a protocol in Moscow accepting the military "assistance." He was formally replaced in April 1969 by Gustav Husák, who has since moved resolutely to restore the former system of state control in Czechoslovakia.

The aftermath of Dubcek's "Prague Spring" has been characterized by a reversal of his reforms; a broad purge of liberal economists, writers, educators and artists; and a "cleansing" of party ranks as well as the removal of the former leader himself from public life.

Dubcek's error had been to move too quickly, too prominently, and certainly too radically to shed the restrictions and repressions of the earlier Stalinist period of postwar Communist rule.

The new Czech party chief, Husák, has spent the intervening years walking a line between hardliners in the party, who want to carry the anti-Dubcek purges beyond the stages of ousters and restrictions to arrests and trials, and the many Czechs—revisionists, in party terminology—who watch now with sullen hostility to the withering of a brief, bright flowering of intellectual freedom.

As politically adroit as Dubcek was unsophisticated, Husák removed 400,000 members from the Czech Communist party—one-fifth of the national membership—but only a few have been tried for "anti-State" activities. Many leading educators, commentators, economists, and other leaders who supported Dubcek left the country.

In recent years a slight easing can be detected. Husák has given a second chance to lesser participants in the reform movement and hard-liners were unable to dominate the Communist party congress in April 1975. But the government has harassed dissidents who spread the ideas of the 1968 "Prague Spring." Dissident attacks on Husak's "normalization" have been leaked to the West, where they have hindered Czech officials seeking trade contacts. In 1981 the Czech government took a hard line against the successful reform movement in neighboring Poland, apparently fearing that the Polish ideas might spread to Czechoslovakia.

HISTORY: In the 6th and 7th centuries, Slavic migrants absorbed Celtic, Germanic, and other cultures. The Czechs, in Bohemia and Moravia, and the Slovaks, in Slovakia, were united in the Great Moravian Empire in the ninth century, a period that also saw the introduction of Christianity. After the empire's collapse in the 10th century, the Slovaks were incorporated into the Kingdom of Hungary and the Czechs established the Kingdom of Bohemia. The 14th century, with its Hussite Revolution, marked the beginning of religious wars in the Czech lands that were to continue through the Reformation and Counter-Reformation. During the decline of the Kingdom of Bohemia, the Czechs came under foreign dynasties, ending up, along with the Slovaks, in the Austro-Hungarian Empire

1918: Following the defeat of Austria-Hungary in World War I, Czechoslovakia, incorporating the Czech lands and Slovakia, is proclaimed an independent republic with nationalist leader Thomas Masaryk its first president

1935: Masaryk dies. Eduard Beneš elected president

1938: Britain, France, Germany, and Italy, without having invited Czechoslovakia to the negotiating table, sign the Munich Pact, a capitulation to German demands for the Sudetenland, the border region of Bohemia inhabited by a large German minority. President Eduard Beneš resigns and goes into exile

1939-46: German troops occupy Czechoslovakia during World War II. The country is liberated by Soviet and U.S. forces. Beneš returns and resumes presidency

1948: Communists seize power; Beneš resigns; Foreign Minister Jan Masaryk, son of Thomas Masaryk, plunges to death from a window. Though officially termed a suicide, he is believed to have been murdered by the Communists

1955: Czechoslovakia joins the Warsaw Pact, the Soviet-bloc military organization

1968: Alexander Dubcek, a progressive, becomes first secretary of the Czechoslovak Communist party, replacing Antonin Novotny. The Soviet Union, alarmed by liberalization measures in Czechoslovakia, invades the country

1969: Gustav Husák replaces Dubcek as leader of the Czechoslovak Communist party and rescinds liberalization; Dubcek is ousted from ruling Presidium in purge of party progressives

1970: Dubcek is expelled from the Communist party and removed from his post as ambassador to Turkey

1973: First direct consular agreement between Communist Czechoslovakia and the United States is signed

1974: U.S. and Czechoslovakia reach preliminary agreement on settlement of postwar financial counterclaims

1975: Husák is elected president by Federal Assembly

1977: Czech dissidents publish manifesto (Charter 77) protesting the suppression of human rights; detention of signers follows

1978: Subdued public protests and destruction of statue mark 10th anniversary of invasion

1979: Charter 77 group falters, elects new leaders

DENMARK

Area: 16,629 sq. mi. **Population:** 5,125,000 (1980 est.)

Official Name: Kingdom of Denmark **Capital:** Copenhagen **Nationality:** Danish **Languages:** Danish is the official and universal language **Religion:** About 96% of the people belong to the established Lutheran Church **Flag:** A white cross on a red field **Anthem:** There is a Lovely Land **Currency:** Danish krone (7.0 per U.S. $1)

Location: Northwest Europe. Denmark is bordered on the north by the Skagerrak; on the east by the Kattegat, Öresund, and the Baltic Sea; on the south by West Germany; and on the west by the North Sea **Features:** Low-lying elevation, with flat or rolling landscape **Chief Rivers:** Stora, Skjern, Varde, Gudena

Head of State: Queen Margrethe II, born 1940, ascended the throne 1972 **Head of Government:** Premier Anker Joergensen, born 1922, appointed 1972 and 1975, reappointed 1979 **Effective Date of Present Constitution:** 1953 **Legislative Body:** Parliament (unicameral Folketing), with 179 members, including 2 each from Greenland and the Faeroe Islands, elected on the basis of proportional representation for 4 years **Local Government:** 14 counties and two urban communes, with elected chief administrative officers and councils

Ethnic Composition: Except for foreign "guest workers" the population is almost entirely Scandinavian **Population Distribution:** 80% urban **Density:** 308 inhabitants per sq. mi.

Largest Cities (M.A. = Metropolitan Area) (1976 est.): Copenhagen 699,300 (M.A. 1,327,940), Aarhus 246,111, Odense 167,911, Aalborg 154,605

Per Capita Income: $9,868 (1980) **Gross Domestic Product (GDP):** $50.7 billion (1980) **Economic Statistics:** About 35% of GDP (1978) comes from manufacturing (food processing, machinery, chemicals), crafts, building and construction; 8% from agriculture (dairy and poultry farming, cattle raising, hog breeding, grain and root crops), forestry and fisheries **Minerals and Mining:** Oil and gas produced from North Sea wells **Labor Force:** 2,625,223 (1979); 25% in manufacturing, 15% in trade, 9% in agriculture, 8% in construction **Foreign Trade:** Exports, chiefly machinery and equipment, textiles and agricultural commodities, totaled $14.6 billion in 1979. Imports, mainly machinery and fittings, fuels, chemicals, iron and steel, totaled $18.5 billion **Principal Trade Partners:** Sweden, West Germany, Britain, United States, Norway, Netherlands

Vital Statistics: Birthrate, 12.2 per 1,000 of pop. (1977); death rate, 9.9 **Life Expectancy:** 73 years **Health Statistics:** 103 inhabitants per hospital bed; 624 per physician (1972) **Infant Mortality:** 8.9 per 1,000 (1977) **Illiteracy:** Negligible **Primary and Secondary School Enrollment:** 854,442 (1976) **Enrollment in Higher Education:** 110,271 (1975) **GNP Expended on Education:** 8.3% (1975)

Transportation: Roads total 40,000 mi. **Motor Vehicles:** 1,655,200 (1977) **Passenger Cars:** 1,381,300 **Railway Mileage:** 1,609 **Ports:** Copenhagen, Aalborg, Aarhus, Esbjerg **Major Airlines:** Scandinavian Airlines System (SAS) operates domestic and international services. Danair operates domestic routes **Communications:** Government owned **Radio Transmitters:** 19 **Licenses:** 1,851,000 (1976) **Television Transmitters:** 34 **Licenses:** 1,637,000 (1976) **Telephones:** 2,734,000 (1977) **Newspapers:** 49 dailies, 341 copies per 1,000 inhabitants (1974)

Weights and Measures: Metric system **Travel Requirements:** Passport, no visa for 3 months **International Dialing Code:** 45

Denmark, located strategically at the mouth of the Baltic Sea, consists of the Jutland Peninsula (projecting north from West Germany) and about 500 islands, of which 100 are inhabited. It is one of the smallest countries in the world if only its low-lying islands and the Jutland Peninsula are considered. However, the kingdom also embraces the Faeroe Islands and the island of Greenland, both of which now enjoy great autonomy.

Occupied during World War II by the Nazis, Denmark did not return in the postwar era to the policy of neutrality that it had followed through World War I. Instead it became a charter member of the North Atlantic Treaty Organization in 1949 and joined with the West Germans in forming a joint Baltic command within the alliance in 1961. But the Danes, like the Norwegians, have limited their NATO membership by declaring that neither foreign troops nor nuclear weapons may be stationed on their territory in peacetime.

Small-scale production of oil from wells on the Danish share of the North Sea continental shelf began in 1972, and surface mining of iron ore began in Greenland on a limited scale in 1973. But so far Denmark's natural resources remain largely limited to its rich farmland, and the nation relies heavily upon imports.

Through membership in the British-led European Free Trade Association (EFTA), Denmark and its neighbors—Norway, Sweden and Finland—created what amounted to a Nordic common market in 1960. Most of this was retained when Denmark, along with Britain and Ireland, opted out of EFTA to join the European Communities (European Community, European Coal and Steel Community and European Atomic Energy Community) on January 1, 1973.

The political process is firmly democratic. But no election since 1945 has given any party a majority in the *Folketing*. The Social Democratic party is the largest and usually leads the governing coalition, but decision-making is slow and marked by compromise. Efforts to reduce unemployment and to promote needed exports also require the help of unions and businesses, which are reluctant to help unstable coalitions and which resent the country's high taxes. A two-year austerity program, involving strict wage controls, took effect in 1977 after strikes thwarted it for eight months.

HISTORY: During the Viking age the Danes figured importantly in the Norse raids on Western Europe. Denmark became at once an Atlantic and a Baltic power and warred with the English, with German princes, and with Norwegian and Swedish kings. Den-

mark's period of expansion lasted until about 1600 and was followed by a losing struggle against Swedish and German rivals
1643-60: Wars with Sweden determine eastern borders
1815: Denmark, having sided with France in the Napoleonic Wars, is among the losers and is forced by Sweden to cede Norway
1864: War with Prussia and Austria ends with the loss of Schleswig-Holstein, a third of Denmark's territory, to Prussia
1914-18: Denmark remains neutral in World War I
1920: Denmark's present southern border is established as northern Schleswig is recovered in a plebiscite
1940-45: Nazi troops invade Denmark and occupy country until its liberation by British forces in May 1945
1949: Denmark joins in forming NATO
1960: Denmark joins European Free Trade Association
1968: Social Democrats, Denmark's largest party, are ousted in general elections after 15 years in office
1972: King Frederik IX dies; is succeeded on the throne by Queen Margrethe II, Denmark's first reigning queen in six centuries
1973: Denmark joins the EC
1978: Social Democratic Prime Minister Anker Joergensen forms minority coalition with Liberals and others
1979: Greenland is granted autonomy. Liberals quit government, forcing elections in which Social Democrats increase plurality in parliament; Joergensen forms new coalition

---

DJIBOUTI

Area: 8,880 sq. mi. **Population:** 250,000 (1978 est.)

Official Name: Republic of Djibouti **Capital:** Djibouti **Nationality:** Djibouti **Languages:** French is the official language; Somali (Issa) and Afar are spoken by their communities; Arabic **Religion:** 94% Moslem, 6% Christian **Flag:** Horizontal stripes of light blue over green, with a red star on a white triangle at the hoist **Anthem:** N.A. **Currency:** Djibouti franc (178 per U.S. $1)

Location: Northeastern Africa, around the Gulf of Tadjoura at the western end of the Gulf of Aden, near the southern entrance to the Red Sea. Bordered on the north, west and southwest by Ethiopia, and on the southeast by Somalia **Features:** An arid rocky coastal plain (with salt and freshwater pans) fringed by foothills of the Ethiopian ranges, and an interior plateau in the north and west **Chief Rivers:** None

Head of State: President Hassan Gouled Aptidon, born 1916, assumed office June 1977, reelected June 1981 **Head of Government:** Premier Barkat Gourad Hamadou, appointed October 1978 **Effective Date of Present Constitution:** Not yet drafted **Legislative Body:** Parliament (unicameral Assembly), with 65 members (33 Issas, 30 Afars, 2 Arabs) elected for 5 years **Local Government:** 5 districts

Ethnic Composition: Somalis (chiefly Issas), Afars (including seasonal nomads), French, Arabs, Italians, Greeks, Sudanese and Indians **Population Distribution:** c. 65% urban **Density:** 28 inhabitants per sq. mi.

Largest City: (1977 est.) Djibouti 130,000

Per Capita Income: $1,727 (1978 est.) **Gross National Product (GNP):** $190 million (1978 est.) **Economic Statistics:** Derivation from GNP not available. Nomadic herding (goats, cattle, sheep, camels, donkeys) is the chief occupation in the hinterland. In the capital, shipbuilding, repair and servicing, construction, and the production of liquid gas and foodstuffs (bottling) are the chief activities **Minerals and Mining:** No production other than salt panning **Labor Force:** N.A. **Foreign Trade:** Exports (transit from Ethiopia), chiefly hides and skins, sugar, and Ethiopian coffee, totaled $5 million in 1976. Imports, chiefly machinery, fuels, steel products, chemicals, foods, and grain, totaled $72 million **Principal Trade Partners:** France, Ethiopia, Japan

Vital Statistics: Birthrate, 42 per 1,000 of pop. (1970); death rate, 7.6 **Life Expectancy:** N.A. **Health Statistics:** 107 inhabitants per hospital bed; 1,964 per physician (1976) **Infant Mortality:** N.A. **Illiteracy:** 95% **Primary and Secondary School Enrollment:** 11,758 (1975) **Enrollment in Higher Education:** N.A. **GNP Expended on Education:** 4.9% (1971)

Transportation: Surfaced roads total 162 mi. **Motor Vehicles:** 15,100 (1977) **Passenger Cars:** 11,800 **Railway Mileage:** 60 **Port:** Djibouti **Major Airlines:** Air France and five other lines provide international service; Air Djibouti, which also flies to Ethiopia, Yemen, Southern Yemen and Somalia, provides domestic service **Communications:** Government controlled **Radio Transmitters:** 4 (1974) **Receivers:** 15,000 (1976) **Television Transmitters:** 1 **Receivers:** 3,500 (1976) **Telephones:** 4,000 **Newspapers:** 1 weekly, 34 copies per 1,000 inhabitants (1975)

Weights and Measures: Metric system **Travel Requirements:** Passport, visa; contact French embassy or Consulate for requirements

On June 27, 1977, the last remnant of France's once-vast empire on the African continent achieved independence as the Republic of Djibouti.

During its first 83 years of existence, the dependency was known as French Somaliland, but in 1967 this small coastal area was renamed the French Territory of Afars and Issas, in recognition of the two major ethnic groups comprising the population. The Republic of Djibouti takes its name from its capital city, a Red Sea port with a majority of the nation's population.

Economic prospects for the Republic of Djibouti are not auspicious, as the barren tract, smaller in area than New Hampshire, lacks resources. The sole economic reason for the existence of the Republic is the commercial activity at the port of Djibouti, which is the terminus of the 486-mile railway from Addis Ababa, Ethiopia. The line carries half of Ethiopia's exports along its single track, and Djibouti is the transshipment point to the outer world for this trade. Out beyond the urban environment of the capital, the meager population subsists through nomadic herding.

The indigenous population is divided between the Afars, or Danakils, and the Issas, a branch of the Somali ethnic family. Though the two groups had disagreed in the past about the timing of independence, a majority of voters approved an independence proposal on May 8, 1977. France, by agreement, continues to maintain a military force in Djibouti.

In March 1978, Ethiopian forces, aided by 1,000 Soviet advisors, and 11,000 Cuban troops, ended the eight-month Ogaden war by driving the Somalis from the region. Although Kenya and Ethiopia in late 1980 urged Somalia to renounce its territorial claims to parts of Djibouti and of their own countries, the Somalian government has refused. Meanwhile, thousands of Somali refugees have flooded Djibouti, straining the fledgling nation's economy and finances. The government showed its concern over the fighting in Yemen by welcoming U.S. warships to its port in March 1979.

HISTORY: French interest in the area began in the 1840s, culminating in the signing of friendship treaties with the local sultans. The purchase of the anchorage at Obock signaled the beginning of French occupation. The opening of the Suez Canal in 1869 and growing Anglo-French competition for territorial spoils in Africa caused France to expand its toehold to include all of the shores of the Gulf of Tadjoura
1884-85: The protectorate of French Somaliland is established
1896: The administrative capital is moved from Obock to Djibouti
1897-1917: The Franco-Ethiopian railway is built from Djibouti to Addis Ababa
1958: French Somaliland becomes an Overseas Territory of the French community
1967: In a referendum on independence, 60 percent of the voters choose to continue the ties with France. The area is renamed the French Territory of Afars and Issas
1977: Following a majority vote for independence, the independent Republic of Djibouti is proclaimed. Premier Ahmed Dini resigns after renewal of tensions between Afars and Issas
1978: Abdallay Mohamed Kamil appointed premier in February. In October, he is followed in office by Barkat Gourad Hamadou

---

DOMINICA

Area: 291 sq. mi. **Population:** 81,000 (1978 est.)
Official Name: Commonwealth of Dominica **Capital:** Roseau **Nationality:** Dominican **Languages:** English is the official language and is everywhere understood, but a patois, based on French and containing many African elements, is widely spoken **Religion:** Mainly Roman Catholic; some Anglicans and Methodists **Flag:** A dark green field quartered by three equal vertical and horizontal stripes of yellow, white and black. In the center a large red disk bears a parrot surrounded by a circle of ten five-pointed stars **Anthem:** Isle of Beauty, Isle of Splendour **Currency:** Dominican dollar (2.7 per U.S. $1)
Location: The island, located in the Windward Islands of the West Indies, lies between the French islands of Guadeloupe to the north

and Martinique to the south. It is 20 miles long and 16 miles wide with a thickly forested mountainous terrain
Head of State: President Aurelius Marie, born 1903, appointed 1980
Head of Government: Prime Minister: Mary Eugenia Charles, born 1919, appointed July 1980 **Effective Date of Present Constitution:** November 3, 1978 **Legislative Body:** House of Assembly (unicameral) with 21 elected representatives and 9 appointed senators
Local Government: 2 town councils and 25 village councils
Ethnic Composition: Nearly all of the population is of African or mixed African-European origin. There is a small Carib Indian community **Density:** 278 inhabitants per sq. mi.
Largest Cities: (1976 est.) Roseau 16,800, Portsmouth 3,500
Per Capita Income: $430 (1979) **Gross National Product (GNP):** $34 million (1979) **Economic Statistics:** The economy is primarily agricultural, with bananas dominant. Citrus fruit and coconut production are also important. Industry and tourism are to be developed **Minerals and Mining:** None **Labor Force:** 25,150 (1976), primarily employed in agriculture **Foreign Trade:** Exports, chiefly bananas, grapefruit, lime juice, essential oils and coconuts, totaled $8 million in 1979. Imports, chiefly foods, machinery and consumer goods, totaled $24 million **Principal Trade Partners:** Britain, United States, Canada, Caribbean nations
Vital Statistics: Birthrate, 21.8 per 1,000 of pop. (1977); death rate, 6.7 **Life Expectancy:** N.A. **Health Statistics:** 234 inhabitants per hospital bed (1973): 5,385 per physician (1973) **Infant Mortality:** 24.1 per 1,000 births (1977) **Illiteracy:** 20% Primary and Secondary School Enrollment: 24,106 (1976) **Enrollment in Higher Education:** N.A. **GNP Expended on Education:** N.A.
Transportation: Surfaced (paved) roads total 300 mi. **Motor Vehicles:** 4,000 (1975) **Passenger Cars:** N.A. **Railway Mileage:** None **Port:** Roseau **Major Airlines:** LIAT, Air Martinique and Air Guadeloupe provide service to neighboring islands **Communications:** Government and privately owned **Radio Transmitters:** 2 **Receivers:** N.A. **Television Transmitters:** 1 **Receivers:** N.A. **Telephones:** 4,000 (1976) **Newspapers:** 2 weeklies
Weights and Measures: British and metric systems **Travel Requirements:** N.A. **Direct Dialing Code:** 809

The northernmost of the Windward Islands, Dominica has a pleasant climate and a great natural beauty that make it a haven for the sightseer, but its sparse, rocky soil makes life difficult for its predominantly black population, one of the poorest in the Caribbean.

One of the country's most urgent priorities since gaining independence in 1978 is the balanced development of the island's economy. Unemployment is chronic, over 20 percent, and agriculture is the mainstay of most islanders, with one crop—bananas—representing almost 80 percent of exports. Yet barely one third of the arable land is cultivated, mainly because of the mountainous and heavily wooded terrain. Foreign aid has become increasingly important, with Britain being Dominica's chief benefactor since independence.

Since achieving nationhood, Dominica has tottered on the brink of civil turmoil, with islanders divided between two political factions; the social-democratic Dominica Labor party (DLP), which had pressed for independence by termination of the association with the United Kingdom, and the more conservative Dominica Freedom party (DFP), which had opposed independence except by referendum.

On May 29, 1979, amid charges of governmental corruption, police fired on a crowd of 15,000 demonstrators in Roseau, sparking a general strike and the resignation of DLP Prime Minister Patrick R. John, who was replaced by James Oliver Seraphine. In August, Hurricane David killed 42, made 65,000 homeless, and destroyed the banana and grapefruit crops.

The DFP won a landslide victory in July 1980 elections, and its leader, Mary Eugenia Charles, became the first woman prime minister of a Caribbean nation. Charles launched a development program that included business incentives to spur an economy in which unemployment had reached 30 percent. She achieved only modest results by late 1981.

In March 1981, an anti-government plot involving high-ranking military officers was aborted. And, in a bizarre incident a month later, 10 American and Canadian mercenaries were arrested by U.S. authorities near New Orleans as they were about to set sail for Dominica to spearhead another coup attempt. They were reportedly financed by an underworld figure and right-wing extremist groups in the U.S.

HISTORY: The warlike Carib Indians are thought to have migrated north from South America to the West Indies in the 1300s, capturing the islands from the more peaceful Arawaks. Columbus first sighted the island on a Sunday in 1493 (by tradition) and named it Dominica after the Latin for that day of the week. Permanent European occupation did not occur until the mid-eighteenth century, when the French established settlements along the coast. Since that time the island has changed hands three times: captured by the British in 1759, retaken by the French in 1778, and restored to Britain by the Treaty of Paris in 1783. With the abolition of the slave trade in 1834, restricted local government developed under British colonial administration

1871: Dominica and other British islands to the north are formed into a federation of the Leeward Islands

1940: Dominica transferred to jurisdiction of Windward Islands group, under same government as Grenada, St. Vincent and St. Lucia

1958: Dominica joins Federation of the West Indies; remains member until its dissolution in 1962

1960: Windward Islands Group dissolved; direct rule by Britain reestablished

1967: Dominica becomes self-governing member of the West Indies Associated States within British Commonwealth

1970: DLP led by Premier Edward O. LeBlanc wins first general election under Associated status

1974: Legislature approves emergency powers to combat "Dread" Black Power terrorist movement; Dominica joins Caribbean Community and Common Market (CARICOM)

1975: DLP under Patrick R. John, who succeeds LeBlanc, retains power in March 24 elections against opposition DFP

1978: Dominica becomes fully independent November 3

1979: Antigovernment demonstrations in Roseau May 29 fired on by police, sparking general strike that forces Prime Minister John to resign. Hurricane David makes 65,000 homeless

1980: DFP wins landslide election victory. Its leader, Mary Eugenia Charles, becomes prime minister

1981: Coup attempt by military officers thwarted in March; rightist mercenaries who planned to lead a revolt in Dominica arrested in U.S. in April

---

DOMINICAN REPUBLIC

Area: 18,816 sq. mi. **Population:** 5,431,000 (1980 est.)

Official Name: Dominican Republic **Capital:** Santo Domingo **Nationality:** Dominican **Languages:** Spanish is the official and universal language **Religion:** About 95% of the people are Roman Catholic, the state religion **Flag:** Four rectangular sections divided by a white cross bearing the national coat of arms in the center; the upper left and lower right sections are dark blue and the other two sections are red **Anthem:** National Anthem, beginning "Brave men of Quisqueya" **Currency:** Dominican peso (1 per U.S. $1)

Location: West Indies, occupying the eastern two-thirds of the Island of Hispaniola. The Dominican Republic is bounded on the north by the Atlantic Ocean; on the east by the Mona Passage, which separates the country from Puerto Rico; on the south by the Caribbean Sea; and on the west by Haiti **Features:** The country is crossed by four east-west mountain ranges, the principal one being the Cordillera Central, which runs across the middle of the country. In the upper central part of the country lies the Cibao valley, often known as the nation's "food basket" **Chief Rivers:** Yaque del Norte, Jaina, Ozama, Yaque del Sur

Head of State and of Government: President Antonio Guzmán Fernández, born 1911, took office Aug. 1978 for a 4-year term **Effective Date of Present Constitution:** November 28, 1966 **Legislative Body:** National Congress (bicameral), consisting of a 27-member Senate and a 91-member Chamber of Deputies, with members of both houses elected every 4 years by popular vote **Local Government:** 26 provinces and 1 national district, each headed by a governor appointed by the president

Ethnic Composition: 73% mulatto, 16% of European (chiefly Spanish) origin, 11% Negro **Population Distribution:** 46.8% urban (1976) **Density:** 289 inhabitants per sq. mi.

Largest Cities: (1970 census—Metropolitan Areas) Santo Domingo 802,619, Santiago 173,975, San Cristóbal 69,875, La Vega 64,370

Per Capita Income: $1,066 (1980) **Gross National Product (GNP):** $6.1 billion (1980) **Economic Statistics:** In 1977 about 21% of GNP came from agriculture (sugar, coffee, cocoa, rice, cotton, tobacco, bananas); 35% from trade and services; 19% from manufacturing (sugar refining, processing of other food products, beverages, tobacco, chemicals) **Minerals and Mining:** Bauxite, nickel, gold, silver and some iron ore are exploited **Labor Force:** 1.5 million (1979), with 55% in agriculture **Foreign Trade:** Exports, chiefly sugar, coffee, chocolate, tobacco, bauxite, gold, silver and nickel, totaled $871 million in 1979. Imports, mainly wheat, petroleum, automobiles, tractors, and pharmaceutical products, totaled $1.1 billion **Principal Trade Partners:** United States, Netherlands, West Germany, Venezuela, Japan, Morocco, Spain, Switzerland

Vital Statistics: Birthrate, 45.8 per 1,000 of pop. (1975); death rate, 11 **Life Expectancy:** 61 years **Health Statistics:** 351 inhabitants per hospital bed; 1,866 per physician (1973) **Infant Mortality:** 43.5 per 1,000 births (1975) **Illiteracy:** 33% **Primary and Secondary School Enrollment:** 984,039 (1973) **Enrollment in Higher Education:** 41,352 (1974) **GNP Expended on Education:** 2.6% (1973)

Transportation: Paved roads total 3,500 mi. **Motor Vehicles:** 116,700 (1976) **Passenger Cars:** 77,300 **Railway Mileage:** 1,000 **Ports:** Santo Domingo, Haina, Barahona, Puerto Plata, La Romana, San Pedro de Macorís **Major Airlines:** Dominicana, the national airline, provides internal and international services **Communications:** Partly government controlled **Radio Transmitters:** 146 **Receivers:** 200,000 (1976) **Television Transmitters:** 7 **Receivers:** 160,000 (1976) **Telephones:** 160,000 (1979) **Newspapers:** 10 dailies, 42 copies per 1,000 inhabitants (1975)

Weights and Measures: Metric system **Travel Requirements:** Passport, visa, tourist card valid for 60 days, $6.00 fee **Direct Dialing Code:** 809

With the possible exception of Cuba, the Dominican Republic has been the most disrupted Latin American country of this century. Its proximity—physically, historically, and economically—to the United States has produced two armed interventions ordered by Washington since 1916. In the years between 1930 and 1961, the country, which occupies the eastern two-thirds of the island of Hispaniola, lived under the oppression of Generalissimo Rafael Leonidas Trujillo Molina.

Since 1966 the Dominican Republic has enjoyed a measure of stability, thanks to improved economic planning and agrarian reform. With massive assistance from the United States and from international lending agencies, the country continues to be one of the most dynamic and stable nations in Latin America.

In May 1978, after 12 years in office, President Joaquín Balaguer was defeated in his bid for a fourth straight four-year term by Antonio Guzmán of the opposition Dominican Revolutionary party (a centrist movement despite its misleadingly radical name). Balaguer's generals attempted to halt the ballot count, but pressure from U.S. and other American nations' leaders compelled them to acknowledge an overwhelming defeat.

In his first state-of-the-nation speech, made in 1979, President Guzmán announced that agricultural development would be stressed in an effort to overcome a stagnant economy. And in its first venture into the Eurodollar market, the Dominican Republic signed a $185-million loan agreement with a group of international banks. In 1980, Guzmán's own party took him to task for not implementing its policies before the 1982 elections. The economy worsened and many strikes occurred. Taxes and prices of electricity and gasoline were raised. Sugar production in 1980 declined as a result of two 1979 hurricanes, heavy rain, cane rust and labor problems.

HISTORY: The eastern part of the island of Hispaniola was known in pre-Columbian times as Quisqueya and was first settled by Carib and Arawak Indians. The island was discovered by Columbus in 1492 and soon became the springboard for Spanish conquest of the Caribbean. The western third of Hispaniola (Haiti) was ceded to

France in 1697, and in 1795 France acquired the eastern part, known as Santo Domingo. The French were expelled from the eastern region in 1809 and in 1814 it reverted to Spain
1821: Dominicans proclaim their independence and attempt to unite with the Republic of Gran Colombia, founded by Bolívar
1822: Dominicans are conquered by Haiti and the whole island of Hispaniola falls under oppressive Haitian rule
1844: Dominicans revolt against Haiti and regain independence; a republic is established under Pedro Santana
1861-69: Widespread revolts and continued attacks from Haiti lead Santana to place country under Spanish rule, but popular opposition forces Spain to withdraw (1865). Opposition leader Buenaventura Báez, who succeeds Santana, negotiates treaty calling for annexation of country to the United States; U.S. Senate, however, refuses to ratify it
1905-24: United States takes over administration of Dominican customs to forestall intervention by foreign powers seeking to collect their debts; following mounting disorders, the republic is brought under U.S. military rule from 1916 until 1924
1930-61: Republic is ruled by dictator Rafael Leonidas Trujillo Molina, who is assassinated in 1961
1962-63: Juan Bosch, a leader of the democratic left, is elected president in republic's first free elections since 1924; after only seven months in office Bosch is overthrown by the military
1965: Civilian triumvirate installed by leaders of the 1963 coup is overthrown, precipitating civil war between left-wing forces seeking to restore Bosch and right-wing and military elements; U.S. troops intervene against pro-Bosch forces but fail to halt civil war, which ends after mediation by the OAS
1966: Joaquín Balaguer defeats Bosch for the presidency
1970: Balaguer is reelected president in a disputed election
1974-75: Balaguer is reelected to third consecutive term. Anti-government violence and political uncertainty plague the country
1976: King Juan Carlos and Queen Sofía of Spain visit, the first ruling Spanish monarchs ever to set foot in Latin America
1978: Antonio Guzmán is elected president
1979: Two hurricanes leave 1,300 dead, 500 missing and 100,000 homeless. Rosario Dominica gold mines are nationalized
1980: Diplomats are held hostage for two months in Dominican embassy in Bogota, Colombia. Gulf and Western Industries agrees to undertake economic aid and social development of republic's sugarcane region in settlement of dispute with Santo Domingo government
1981: President Guzman announces that he will not seek reelection in 1982

ECUADOR

Area: 109,483 sq. mi. **Population:** 8,354,000 (1980 est.)

Official Name: Republic of Ecuador **Capital:** Quito **Nationality:** Ecuadorean **Languages:** Spanish, the official language, is spoken by about 93% of the population, and Quechua by 7% **Religion:** Overwhelmingly Roman Catholic **Flag:** Half the width of the flag is yellow and the remaining half consists of blue and red bands; in the center is the national coat of arms **Anthem:** Hail, O Fatherland **Currency:** Sucre (25 per U.S. $1)

Location: South America. Crossed by the Equator, from which the country gets its name, Ecuador is bordered on the north by Colombia, on the east and south by Peru, and on the west by the Pacific Ocean. The Galápagos Islands, some 600 miles west of the mainland, are part of the national territory **Features:** About a fourth of the country consists of a coastal plain, and another fourth of the Sierra, or highlands, lying between two chains of the Andes Mountains. The Oriente, or eastern jungle, covers the remaining half of the country **Chief Rivers:** Guayas, Esmeraldas

Head of State and of Government: President Oswaldo Hurtado Larrea, born 1939, assumed office on death of President Roldós on May 24, 1981 **Effective Date of Present Constitution:** August 10, 1979 **Legislative Body:** Congress (unicameral) with 12 national and 57 provincial deputies **Local Government:** 20 provinces, each headed by an appointed governor

Ethnic Composition: 40% Indian, 40% mestizo, 10% of European (chiefly Spanish) origin, 5% African, 5% Oriental and other **Population Distribution:** 42.4% urban (1977) **Density:** 76 inhabitants per sq. mi.

Largest Cities: (1978 est.) Guayaquil 1,022,010, Quito 742,858, Cuenca 128,788, (1974 census) Ambato 77,052, Machala 68,379

Per Capita Income: $1,052 (1980) **Gross National Product (GNP):** $8.4 billion (1980). **Economic Statistics:** In 1979 about 20% of GNP was derived from agriculture (bananas, coffee, cocoa, rice, sugar, cotton, grains, fruits and vegetables), forestry, and fishing; 28% from manufacturing (textiles, food processing, petroleum refining, cement) and petroleum; and 14% from trade and hotels **Minerals**

and Mining: Petroleum is the primary mineral product. There are large deposits of calcium carbonate and copper; small quantities of gold are mined **Labor Force:** 2,500,000 (1978), of which 55% is employed in agriculture **Foreign Trade:** Exports, chiefly bananas, petroleum, coffee, cocoa, sugar and fish products, totaled $2 billion in 1979. Imports, mainly machinery, transportation equipment, chemicals, and paper products, totaled $1.3 billion **Principal Trade Partners:** United States, West Germany, Japan, Panama, Italy, Colombia, Chile

Vital Statistics: Birthrate, 41.8 per 1,000 of pop. (1975); death rate, 9.5 **Life Expectancy:** 57 years **Health Statistics:** 495 inhabitants per hospital bed; 2,017 per physician (1973) **Infant Mortality:** 65.8 per 1,000 births **Illiteracy:** 43% **Primary and Secondary School Enrollment:** 1,709,717 (1976) **Enrollment in Higher Education:** 170,173 **GNP Expended on Education:** 3.3% (1971)

Transportation: Paved roads total 2,050 mi. **Motor Vehicles:** 128,500 (1975) **Passenger Cars:** 51,300 **Railway Mileage:** 697 **Ports:** Guayaquil, Puerto Bolívar, Manta, Bahía de Caráquez, Salinas, Esmeraldas **Major Airlines:** Ecuatoriana de Aviación operates internal and international flights **Communications:** Government and privately owned **Radio Transmitters:** 288 **Receivers:** 1,700,000 (1970) **Television Transmitters:** 17 **Receivers:** 300,000 (1976) **Telephones:** 220,000 **Newspapers:** 29 dailies, 49 copies per 1,000 inhabitants (1975)

Weights and Measures: Metric system; Spanish measures are also used **Travel Requirements:** Passport, migratory control card, valid for 90 days, tourist visa valid for 180 days, no fee **International Dialing Code:** 593

Despite incredibly rich mineral and agricultural resources, Ecuador remains one of the least developed countries in South America—the result of sharp racial, geographic, and political differences.

Two fifths of Ecuador's population is Indian—people held in low esteem by those of mixed blood, African heritage, and the small ruling élite of European background. Although many of the Indians retain their languages and customs, they have been stripped of the rest of their culture by four centuries of European domination.

Aside from the Indians in the Andean highlands and the Amazonian tribes in the east, most of the rest of Ecuador's people live along the western littoral that borders the Pacific Ocean. Mainly of mixed African/Indian/European background, the coastal people have a tropical culture that differs markedly from the highlanders.

In a further division, Ecuador is dominated by the mutual dislike of two "city-states"—Quito, the capital, and Guayaquil, the industrial port.

Some 9,300 feet above sea level in the Andes, long considered the most beautiful city in South America and certainly the cleanest, Quito is a conservative, gracious administrative center. Its residents look with distaste on the boisterous, tropical people of Guayaquil, who, for their part, resent their tax payments to the capital. Despite their industry and commercial aggressiveness, they say, the appalling slums of their city reflect the indifference of Quito.

Since petroleum exports started in 1972, there has been a spurt in overall economic development. The oil, which is pumped out of the Amazon jungles by Texaco and by the government oil company, CEPE, is Ecuador's No. 1 export. Intensive exploration in 1980 raised reserves to over three billion barrels. The country is now accustomed to trade and balance-of-payment surpluses, and its inflaton rate—running at 15% to 20% in 1980—is moderate by South American standards.

In 1978 and 1979 the country held its first free national elections since the military seized power in 1972. First, in a referendum on Jan. 15, 1978, the voters chose a new constitution over a revision of the 1945 constitution. Then, on July 16, Jaime Roldós Aguilera, a law professor and a member of the Concentration of Popular Forces (CFP), led the first-round balloting for president. The military, wary because Roldós was a protégé of populist leader Assad Bucaram, delayed the final election for six months, but Roldós won handily in a two-party contest on April 29, 1979. A struggle developed between Roldós and his former chief, Bucaram, the CFP leader in congress. However, Roldós had popular support, and his candidate, Raúl Baca Carbo, was elected leader of congress in August 1980.

President Roldós, his wife and three military leaders were killed in an airplane crash May 24, 1981. Vice President Hurtado Larrea assumed the presidency.

HISTORY: Ecuador was ruled by the Incas until their empire fell to the Spanish conquistadors in 1533. Spanish rule, which lasted until the early 19th century, was marked by ruthless exploitation of the native Indians and bloody rivalry among the Spaniards

1822: Ecuador is freed from Spanish rule after Spanish forces are defeated at Battle of Pichincha; country becomes part of Greater Colombia, a confederation consisting of the present territories of Ecuador, Colombia, Panama, and Venezuela, constituted under the leadership of Simón Bolívar

1830-45: Federation is dissolved in 1830; Republic of Ecuador is proclaimed, with Juan José Flores as first president; his conservative dictatorial rule arouses liberal opposition

1861-75: Gabriel García Morena rules as virtual dictator; he consolidates country after years of domestic strife and carries out major economic and social reforms, but his strong conservatism results in bitter strife that culminates in his assassination

1895-1912: Liberals dominate Ecuador's politics; separation of church and state is clearly defined, and basic personal freedoms are established

1913-44: Liberals continue to dominate political scene, but rival factions, supported by military juntas, bring about rapid changes in government

1948-52: Galo Plazo Lasso becomes president; his regime is marked by unprecedented political freedom

1961: President José María Velasco Ibarra is forced into exile; Vice-President Julio Arosemena Monroy succeeds as president

1963: Arosemena is ousted in military coup; a four-man military junta, headed by R. Adm. Ramon Castro Jijon, takes over. Junta dissolves Congress, decrees martial law, suspends the constitution, and bans Communist party

1968-69: In the first election held in seven years, Velasco Ibarra is elected president for fifth time as Ecuador experiences widespread economic and social unrest. Within eight months after taking office, president loses support of Liberal party

1970: President Velasco assumes dictatorial powers

1971: U.S. imposes financial sanctions on Ecuador following seizure of U.S. tuna boats

1972: Brig. Gen. Guillermo Rodriguez Lara replaces Velasco Ibarra in bloodless military coup. Lara declares a "nationalist, military, and revolutionary government"

1975: Seizure of American fishing boats continues. Gen. Raúl González Alvear leads unsuccessful revolt against Lara

1976: President Lara is overthrown in a bloodless coup led by armed forces commanders, who form a military junta

1977: Ecuadorean government buys the local assets of Gulf Oil Corp. of the U.S., giving the government a 62.5 percent share in Ecuador's petroleum operations

1978: Elections held to choose new president; Jaime Roldós Aguilera is leader in first round; wins run-off in April 1979

1981: U.S. tuna boat *Rosa D.*, accused of operating in Ecuadoran waters, is held for payment of $1.2 million fine. Ecuador fails in armed attempt to set up a military base in region of Peru it claims. President Roldós dies in airplane crash

EGYPT

Area: 386,659 sq. mi. **Population:** 41,572,000 (1979 est.)

Official Name: Arab Republic of Egypt **Capital:** Cairo **Nationality:** Egyptian **Languages:** Arabic is the official and national language **Religion:** About 90% of the population is Sunni Moslem and Islam is the state religion; about 7% belongs to the Coptic Church (perhaps as high as 18%) **Flag:** Red, white, and black horizontal stripes with a golden hawk and Arabic inscription on the white stripe **Anthem:** National Anthem, beginning "The Time Has Come to Reach for Our Arms" **Currency:** Egyptian pound (0.70 per U.S. $1)

Location: Northeast Africa. Egypt is bordered on the north by the Mediterranean Sea; on the east by Israel and the Red Sea; on the south by the Sudan; and on the west by Libya **Features:** About 95% of the country is desert, with only the Nile Valley and delta, and a few oases, under cultivation **Chief River:** Nile

* **Head of State and of Government:** President Anwar el-Sadat, born 1918, reelected for 6 years in 1976. He assumed the post of premier in May 1980 **Effective Date of Present Constitution:** 1971 **Legislative Body:** People's Assembly (unicameral), consisting of 392 members **Local Government:** 26 governorates headed by governors appointed by the president

Ethnic Composition: The homogeneous population is mainly Hamitic **Population Distribution:** 44% urban **Density:** 108 inhabitants per sq. mi.; inhabitable areas 3,000

Largest Cities: (1976 census) Cairo 5,084,463, Alexandria 2,318,655, Giza 1,246,713, El Mahalla el Kubra 292,853

Per Capita Income: $573 (1980) **Gross National Product (GNP):** $24 billion (1980) **Economic Statistics:** 30% of GNP comes from agriculture (cotton, wheat, corn, rice); 22% from industry (food processing, textiles, petroleum and petroleum products, iron and steel manufactures, chemicals) and mining; 25% from services; 19% from trade and finance **Minerals and Mining:** Petroleum is the chief mineral resource; others are phosphate, iron ore, tin, uranium, manganese, and limestone **Labor Force:** 13,400,000, of which 44% is in agriculture, and 13% in industry **Foreign Trade:** Exports, chiefly cotton and cotton goods, rice, crude oil, and oil products, totaled $2.7 billion in 1979. Imports, mainly wheat, petroleum, industrial machinery, vehicle parts, and edible oils, totaled $6.3 billion **Principal Trade Partners:** EC countries, United States, Japan

Vital Statistics: Birthrate, 37.7 per 1,000 of pop. (1977); death rate, 11.8 **Life Expectancy:** 54 years **Health Statistics:** 479 inhabitants per hospital bed (1976); 1,516 per physician (1973) **Infant Mortality:** 101.3 per 1,000 births **Illiteracy:** 56% **Primary and Secondary School Enrollment:** 6,228,827 (1975) **Enrollment in Higher Education:** 455,097 **GNP Expended on Education:** 5.4% (1976)

Transportation: Paved roads total 7,640 mi. **Motor Vehicles:** 347,200 (1977) **Passenger Cars:** 283,200 **Railway Mileage:** 3,000 **Ports:** Alexandria, Port Said, Suez, Mersa Matruh, Safaga **Major Airlines:** Egypt Air operates internal and international services **Communications:** Government owned **Radio Transmitters:** 43 (1973) **Receivers:** 5,250,000 (1976) **Television Transmitters:** 28 (1977) **Receivers:** 1,300,000 (1977) **Telephones:** 503,000 (1974) **Newspapers:** 14 dailies, 21 copies per 1,000 inhabitants (1974)

Weights and Measures: Metric system is official but various local units are also used **Travel Requirements:** Passport, visa good for stay up to 3 months, $2.80 contribution to Abu Simbel fund

For Egypt, recent years have brought one pressing challenge after another: adjustments to the death of President Gamal Abdel Nasser, fateful decisions on war or peace with Israel, conspiracies against President Anwar el-Sadat, friendship with the United States at the expense of Soviet-Egyptian amity, and relentless economic problems.

Added to these challenges are the realities of Egypt's difficulties as the most populous country in the Arab world and the second most populous on the African continent, with 99 percent of its people compressed into 3.5 percent of its area.

President Sadat, who had been a leading figure in the 1952 revolution led by Nasser against King Farouk, quickly emerged as an unexpectedly strong president in the "collective leadership" that succeeded Nasser. He won support by curbing arbitrary police procedures and surveillance, calling for a society based on "the sovereignty of law," and outlining a program for accelerated economic development.

Egypt's economic problems are extensive and resistant to ready solutions. There are few natural resources, limited cultivable land and investment funds; in addition, bureaucracies are swollen with unproductive workers. Unemployment and inflation are rising, and illiteracy is 56%. The increasing number of university-trained graduates have little prospect for professional advancement.

To present a more progressive image while dealing with these economic difficulties, Sadat has implemented limited political reforms, including an upgrading of the People's Assembly. In late 1976, he announced that he would allow the formation of independent political parties, which had been banned since 1953, when the Arab Socialist Union was made the only legal political organization. Three parties were subsequently formed, but in 1978, new restrictions on them were enacted.

The peace treaty with Israel, signed in 1979, calls for Israel's phased withdrawal from Sinai within three years. By the end of 1979, Israel had returned most of the Sinai territory, including oil fields and Mt. Sinai itself, to Egypt. The treaty binds Egypt to sell oil to Israel, and other trade with Israel, plus increased U.S. aid and reduced military needs, have helped Egypt economically. But other Arab nations have tried to isolate Egypt and have suspended her from the Arab League and other Arab organizations. Yet Sadat got over-whelming domestic support for the treaty.

The treaty was the result of 14 months of difficult negotiations, which began in 1977, when President Sadat visited Israel and Israeli Prime Minister Menachem Begin returned the visit. After this dramatic opening, Palestinian raids on Israel, Israeli strikes at Palestinians in southern Lebanon, and arguments about the future of Palestinian territory slowed the negotiations. United States officials, including President Jimmy Carter, helped at crucial times to prevent a rupture.

On Feb. 26, 1980, Egypt exchanged ambassadors with Israel as another step toward normalization of relations. But the countries were deadlocked on the issue of granting Palestinian autonomy in the Gaza Strip and on the West Bank of the Jordan. In early 1981, Sadat reportedly refused to resume negotiations with Israel until after new elections were held in that country.

HISTORY: The history of Egypt dates back about 5,000 years. The country was united into a single kingdom about 3200 B.C. and was ruled by a succession of dynasties down to the time of Alexander the Great, who conquered Egypt in 332 B.C. Less than three centuries later, the country was under Roman rule. In 616, Egypt was conquered by the Persians before being invaded by the Arabs, who introduced Islam

1517: Egypt becomes part of the Ottoman Empire

1798: Napoleon conquers Egypt

1801-5: British and Turkish troops drive out the French; Mohammed Ali, an Albanian soldier, is appointed Egyptian pasha

1869: The Suez Canal is completed

1914: Egypt becomes a British protectorate

1936: Britain agrees to withdraw eventually from all of Egypt, except the Suez Canal Zone

1940-42: British forces use Egypt as a base to fight Italy and Germany in World War II

1948-49: Egypt plays major role in war between Arab states and the newly established state of Israel, but suffers humiliating defeats; war ends with an armistice

1952: King Farouk is deposed in army coup

1953-54: A republic is proclaimed, with Gen. Mohammed Naguib as president; Naguib is forced out of office and replaced by Col. Gamal Abdel Nasser

1956: Nasser nationalizes Suez Canal. Israel, barred from the canal, invades the Gaza Strip and the Sinai peninsula; England and France attack Egypt. Forces of all three invading countries are forced to withdraw under pressure from the United States, the USSR and the United Nations

1958: Egypt and Syria form the United Arab Republic (U.A.R.)

1961: Syrian army revolts and proclaims Syria's withdrawal from U.A.R.

1962: Egypt sends troops to Yemen to aid a republican revolution

1967: In the Six-Day War with Israel, Egypt loses the entire Sinai peninsula and the Gaza Strip, which are occupied by Israeli armies; Egypt withdraws its troops from Yemen

1968: Widespread student riots break out in protest against Nasser regime, which is accused of police-state rule. Egyptian and Israeli troops engage in repeated artillery duels along Suez Canal

1970: Egypt agrees to U.S.-sponsored truce with Israel as step toward peace talks; talks are stalled after Israel charges truce is being violated by the installation of Soviet-built missiles in the Suez Canal zone. Nasser dies of heart attack and is succeeded by Vice-President Anwar el-Sadat

1971: Sadat allows cease-fire with Israel to lapse but defers warfare. Conspiracy against Sadat erupts; six cabinet members, Vice-President Aly Sabry, and dozens of others are arrested. New constitution approved by national referendum

1972: Dr. Aziz Sidky replaces Dr. Mahmoud Fawzi as premier. President Sadat orders the departure of all Soviet military advisors (about 10,000)

1973: Sadat forces Sidky to resign, assumes premiership; Egypt launches attack across the Suez Canal, beginning fourth Arab-Israeli War. The Arabs attack on Yom Kippur, the holiest day of the year for Jews. It takes several days for the Israelis to mobilize, but they soon outmaneuver the Arab armies. Iraq, Tunisia, Morocco, and other Arab countries send troops to aid Egypt and Syria. Egypt and Israel negotiate ceasefire

1974: President Sadat changes the date of Egypt's national holiday from July 23 to October 6 to commemorate the onset of the Yom Kippur War; Sadat relinquishes the office of premier and appoints Abdul Aziz Hegazy in his place

1975: Premier Hegazy resigns and is replaced by Mamdouh Salem. The Suez Canal, closed since Dec. 1967, reopens. With the assistance of U.S. Secretary of State Kissinger, Egypt and Israel agree on removal of troops in the Sinai Peninsula. American Congress approves of U.S. civilian presence in Sinai to supervise electronic early warning stations

1976: Egyptian parliament approves of President Sadat's proposal to end 15-year Treaty of Friendship and Cooperation with the USSR. Saudi Arabia, Kuwait, Qatar and the United Arab Emirates establish the Gulf Authority for Egyptian Development with a capital of $2 billion. Sadat is elected to a second six-year term

1977: Egyptian and Libyan forces clash along desert border. President Sadat launches peace initiative; he and Israeli Premier Begin trade historic visits

1978: Peace talks bog down as Israeli troops enter southern Lebanon following Palestinian terror raid in Israel. Diplomatic relations with Cyprus severed after Cypriot troops kill 15 Egyptian commandos who were storming jet at Larnaca Airport in which Palestinian terrorists held 16 hostages. Egypt to get 50 F-5E fighter-bombers from the U.S. National referendum gives Sadat mandate to carry out proposals for curtailing political dissent, "to protect the home front and social peace"

1979: Egypt and Israel sign peace treaty, calling for phased Israeli withdrawal from Sinai within three years. Arab states suspend Egypt from several Arab organizations. Referendum in Egypt approves treaty. Sadat dissolves parliament; his National Democratic party wins overwhelming victory in June election

1980: Two thirds of Sinai territory is returned to Egypt as Israel completes 2nd phase of withdrawal; countries exchange ambassadors; negotiations continue on Palestinian issue. Sadat assumes premiership; voters approve constitutional amendment permitting Sadat more than two 6-year terms as president (ending in 1982)

* Sadat assassinated on Oct. 6. Hosni Mubarak succeeds to presidency

EL SALVADOR

Area: 8,260 sq. mi. **Population:** 4,485,000 (1979 est.)

Official Name: Republic of El Salvador **Capital:** San Salvador **Nationality:** Salvadorean **Languages:** Spanish is the official and predominant language; a small number of Indians still speak Nahuatl **Religion:** Overwhelmingly Roman Catholic **Flag:** Blue, white, and blue horizontal stripes, with the national coat of arms centered on the white stripe **Anthem:** National Anthem, beginning "We proudly hail thee, motherland" **Currency:** Salvadorean colón (2.5 per U.S. $1)

Location: Central America. El Salvador is bordered on the north, northeast, and east by Honduras, on the south and southwest by the Pacific Ocean, and on the west and northwest by Guatemala **Features:** Mountain ranges running east to west divide the country into a narrow Pacific coastal belt on the south; a subtropical central region of valleys and plateaus, where most of the population lives; and a mountainous northern region **Chief Rivers:** Lempa, Grande de San Miguel

Head of State and of Government: President José Napoleón Duarte Fuentes, born 1925, sworn in Dec. 13, 1980. He is a member of the 4-man ruling junta **Effective Date of Present Constitution:** 1962. A new constitution is planned for 1982 **Legislative Body:** The unicameral National Assembly was dissolved in 1979. Legislative elections are planned for 1982 **Local Government:** 14 departments, each headed by an appointed governor

Ethnic Composition: 89% mestizo (of mixed European—mainly Spanish—and Indian descent); the rest consists of small minorities of European and of Indian ancestry **Population Distribution:** 41.9% urban (1975) **Density:** 543 inhabitants per sq. mi.

Largest Cities: (1973 est.) San Salvador 368,000; (1971 census) Santa Ana 96,306, San Miguel 59,304

Per Capita Income: $751 (1979) **Gross National Product (GNP):** $3.3 billion (1979) **Economic Statistics:** In 1973 about 27% of GNP was from agriculture (coffee, cotton, sugar, rice, livestock); and 19% from industry (food processing, textiles, shoes, chemicals) **Minerals and Mining:** Substantial deposits of quartz, diatomaceous earth, kaolin, gypsum, limestone, and pumice **Labor Force:** 1,500,000 with 57% in agriculture and 14% in industry

Foreign Trade: Exports, chiefly coffee, cotton, shrimp, sugar, cottonseed cakes, and cotton fabric, totaled $1.1 billion in 1979. Imports, mainly transport equipment, chemical products, fuels and lubricants, raw materials, industrial machinery, and consumer goods, totaled $1 billion **Principal Trade Partners:** United States, Latin America, Japan, EC countries

Vital Statistics: Birthrate, 41.7 per 1,000 of pop. (1977); death rate, 7.8 **Life Expectancy:** 64 years **Health Statistics:** 597 inhabitants per hospital bed; 3,745 per physician (1976) **Infant Mortality:** 59.5 per 1,000 births (1977) **Illiteracy:** 60% **Primary and Secondary School Enrollment:** 887,872 (1977) **Enrollment in Higher Education:** 28,281 **GNP Expended on Education:** 3.3% (1975)

Transportation: Paved roads total 930 mi. **Motor Vehicles:** 61,000 (1974) **Passenger Cars:** 41,000 **Railway Mileage:** 400 **Ports:** La Unión (Cutuco), Acajutla, La Libertad **Major Airlines:** TACA operates internal and international flights **Communications:** Partly government controlled **Radio Transmitters:** 65 **Receivers:** 1,400,000 (1976) **Television Transmitters:** 5 **Receivers:** 136,000 (1976) **Telephones:** 70,000 **Newspapers:** 12 dailies, 51 copies per 1,000 inhabitants (1974)

Weights and Measures: Metric system **Travel Requirements:** Proof of citizenship for issuance of tourist card on arrival, valid 90 days **International Dialing Code:** 503

As the most densely populated country on the entire American mainland, El Salvador has long aroused suspicions of expansionism among its neighbors, particularly Honduras, which has had up to 600,000 immigrant Salvadoreans among its populace. The constant pressure of too many people for El Salvador's diminutive land area has led to frequent border clashes with Honduras and, in July 1969, to a four-day war. In late 1976, an agreement was signed between the two countries providing for mediation by a third country in this recurrent, and often violent, dispute. A draft treaty was signed in 1980.

After the disputed election of Gen. Carlos Humberto Romero as president in 1977, a wave of bombings, kidnappings and murders by leftists and extreme rightists ensued. With the situation worsening, Col. Jaime Abdul Gutiérez and Col. Adolfo Arnoldo Majano Ramos deposed Romero Oct. 15, 1979, and formed a *junta* with three moderate civilians. In a move to keep the nation's predominantly poor peasants from joining the leftist-led revolutionary forces, the junta initiated a program in 1980 to split up the larger sharecropped plantations— or *latifundistas*—owned by about 300 families. By 1981 more than 200,000 families owned the land they tilled. Agrarian reform was seen by the right-wing oligarchy as a leftist move to give political power to the peasants. In January 1981 the head of the agricultural reform program and two American advisers were shot to death.

Following the slaying of three American nuns and a lay worker, attributed to government security personnel, the United States cut off military aid to El Salvador in December 1980. It was soon resumed, however, after the junta named the moderate Christian Democratic party leader, José Napoleón Duarte, to the presidency on Dec. 13. In January 1981 the guerrillas launched a "final offensive" with materiel and advisory assistance from Cuba and other communist countries brought in chiefly through Nicaragua. U.S. aid, including more military advisers, was increased by the new Reagan administration. The offensive bogged down, but guerrilla activity continued.

HISTORY: El Salvador was the home of the Pipil Indians before the arrival of Pedro de Alvarado, who conquered the country for Spain in the 1520s. Until its independence in the 19th century, El Salvador was administered as part of the captaincy general of Guatemala

1821: El Salvador and the other Central American countries gain independence from Spain and are annexed to Mexico

1824-39: Central American countries withdraw from Mexico and establish the Central American Federation

1841-56: El Salvador's independence is decreed in January 1841; a republic is formally proclaimed in 1856

1931-44: Gen. Maximiliano Hernández Martínez seizes power

1945-61: Nation is wracked by political instability as governments rise and fall in numerous coups d'état; in 1961 a civilian-military directorate is formed

1962-67: A new constitution is promulgated and Lt. Col. Adalberto Rivera is elected president; during his term nation's currency is stabilized, an income tax is introduced, pro-labor laws are passed. In 1967 Col. Fidel Sánchez Hernández is elected president

1968: Government's National Conciliation party suffers setback as reform-minded Christian Democrats score gains in legislative and municipal elections

1969: El Salvador wages brief war with Honduras

1977: Violent unrest grips the country after Gen. Carlos Humberto Romero wins the presidency amid charges of fraud

1978: Scores die as widespread unrest continues

1979: Two colonels oust Romero, deport him with his aides, and form a governing junta along with three civilians

1980: Archbishop Oscar Romero, outspoken champion of peace and human rights, assassinated Mar. 24. José Napoleón Duarte sworn in as president, Dec. 13. Col. Majano ousted from junta

1981: Violent deaths continue at rate of about 1,000 per month. In March, President Duarte announces appointment of an electoral commission to prepare for election of a constitutional assembly in 1982. Security forces kill 30 unarmed civilians in Soyopango, Apr. 7

EQUATORIAL GUINEA

Area: 10,831 sq. mi. **Population:** 346,000 (1978 est.)

Official Name: Republic of Equatorial Guinea **Capital:** Malabo **Nationality:** Equatorial Guinean **Languages:** Spanish is the official language. On the mainland Fang is spoken, while the principal local language on Bioko island is Bubi **Religion:** About 80% of the population is Roman Catholic, the rest chiefly animists, with a small number of Moslems **Flag:** Green, white, and red horizontal stripes, with a blue triangle joining them at the staff side; in the center is the national coat of arms **Anthem:** National Anthem, beginning "Let's walk through the jungle of our immense happiness" **Currency:** ekuele (66.1 per U.S. $1)

Location: West Africa. Equatorial Guinea consists of 2 areas: the mainland—Río Muni (Mbini), bordered by Cameroon on the north, Gabon on the east and south, and the Atlantic Ocean on the west; and Bioko (Fernando Po), consisting of the main island of that name, Pagalu, and other small islands **Features:** There are 2 large volcanic formations on the main island, separated by a valley which crosses the island from east to west at its narrowest point. Río Muni consists of a coastal plain, and a series of valleys separated by low hills and spurs of the Crystal Mountains **Chief Rivers:** Benito, Muni, Campo

Head of State and of Government: President: Lt. Col. Teodoro Obiang Nguema Mbasogo. He is head of the Supreme Military Council **Effective Date of Present Constitution:** July 1973 **Legislative Body:** Power is in the hands of the Supreme Military Council **Local Government:** 2 provinces

Ethnic Composition: On Bioko the aboriginal Bubis are the major ethnic group; others include the descendants of liberated slaves. In Río Muni the main tribes are the Fang, Kombe, and Bujeba **Population Distribution:** 15% urban **Density:** 40 inhabitants per sq. mi.

Largest Cities: (1973 est.) Malabo 60,000, Bata 30,000

Per Capita Income: $312 (1978) **Gross National Product (GNP):** $100 million (1978) **Economic Statistics:** Production is predominantly agricultural, although forestry and fishing are also important. High-grade cocoa, coffee, bananas, and palm oil are the main crops. There is little industry **Minerals and Mining:** Geological surveys have raised hopes for the eventual discovery of petroleum; uranium deposits have been found and there are indications of iron ore **Labor Force:** More than 95% of the working population is engaged in agriculture **Foreign Trade:** Exports, chiefly cocoa, wood, and coffee, totaled $36 million in 1976. Imports, principally foodstuffs, building materials, petroleum products, textiles, motor vehicles, and pharmaceutical products, totaled $12 million **Principal Trade Partners:** Spain, United States, Britain, West Germany, France

Vital Statistics: Birthrate, 36.8 per 1,000 of pop. (1975); death rate 19.7 **Life Expectancy:** 43.5 years **Health Statistics:** 171 inhabitants per hospital bed (1967); 62,000 per physician (1975) **Infant Mortality:** 53.2 per 1,000 births **Illiteracy:** 80% **Primary and Secondary School Enrollment:** 40,500 (1975) **Enrollment in Higher Education:** N.A. **GNP Expended on Education:** N.A.

Transportation: Surfaced roads total 200 mi. **Motor Vehicles:** about 1,000 **Passenger Cars:** N.A. **Railway Mileage:** None **Ports:** Malabo, Bata **Major Airlines:** Iberia Airlines provides an international service **Communications:** State controlled **Radio Transmitters:** 2 **Receivers:** 80,000 (1976) **Television:** None **Telephones:** 2,000 **Newspapers:** 1 daily, 3 copies per 1,000 inhabitants **Weights and Measures:** Metric system **Travel Requirements:** Passport, visa

---

One of the smallest of Africa's nations, Equatorial Guinea gained independence from Spain in 1968. For 11 years the country experienced repressive rule by President Masie Nguema Biyogo Negue Ndong, along with economic deterioration.

While severing all ties with Spain and taking a sharply anti-Western stance, President Masie welcomed new links with the Soviet Union, Communist China and North Korea.

The island people of Bioko, until recently more prosperous, include the native Bubis; Fernandinos, descendants of freed African slaves; Nigerians, who have been contract laborers on cocoa plantations; and a number of Europeans. The poorer, majority mainland people, the Fangs, looked to independence and the leadership of President Masie, a Fang, to improve their lot, a hope as yet unmaterialized.

Europeans, mainly Spanish and Portuguese, who ran the high-quality cocoa plantations, coffee and lumber production, and other businesses, numbered 7,000 in 1968. But with increasing physical terrorism by government and a youth movement, the *Juventud*, only a few hundred Europeans remain in the country. Thousands of citizens were reportedly killed by the Masie regime, and more thousands fled to other countries.

President Masie was overthrown in a bloodless coup on August 3, 1979, and executed following a public trial. Masie was replaced by a Supreme Military Council led by his nephew, Lt. Col. Teodoro Nguema Mbasogo. Relations were resumed late in 1979 with Spain, which agreed to provide military, economic and technical aid. Despite this and additional help from France and the United States, hopes for economic development remained slim. The government is seeking to establish its territorial waters so it can arrange search concessions with foreign oil companies.

HISTORY: Equatorial Guinea's island province of Fernando Po was discovered in the late 15th century by the Portuguese explorer Fernão do Po. It was ceded to Spain, along with mainland trading rights, in 1778. In the early 19th century, the island port of Santa Isabel was leased for a time to the British, who made it a naval base and refuge for freed slaves. Not until the 20th century did Spain actively begin administering and developing the colony, known as Spanish Guinea
1958-60: Spain makes colony a Spanish province, grants inhabitants Spanish citizenship and representation in *Cortés*
1963-64: Colony is renamed Equatorial Guinea; limited self-government is instituted
1968: After numerous appeals to United Nations and long negotiations, Equatorial Guinea becomes an independent republic
1969: Rivalry between the continental and island portions results in serious riots. President Masie assumes dictatorial powers, purges opposition leaders
1979: President Masie is deposed in coup
1980: Soviet fishing fleet withdraws after treaty lapses. Former Spanish residents are invited to return if they offer investment plans

---

ETHIOPIA

Area: 471,776 sq. mi. **Population:** 30,421,000 (1979 est.)
Official Name: Ethiopia **Capital:** Addis Ababa **Nationality:** Ethiopian **Languages:** Amharic is the official and predominant language; English is frequently used. Arabic is spoken by about one-third of the population; other spoken languages are Gallinya, Tigrinya, Ge'ez, and Italian **Religion:** About 40% of the population belongs to the established Ethiopian Orthodox (Coptic Christian) Church; 40% is Moslem and the rest animist **Flag:** Green, yellow, and red hori-

zontal stripes **Anthem:** National Anthem, beginning "Let Ethiopia be joyous!" **Currency:** Birr (2.07 per U.S. $1)
Location: Eastern Africa. Ethiopia is bordered on the north by the Sudan and the Red Sea, on the east by Djibouti and Somalia, on the south by Kenya, and on the west by the Sudan **Features:** The center of the country consists of a high, partly mountainous plateau cut by numerous rivers and split diagonally by the Rift Valley. The terrain gradually slopes to lowlands in the west and to a plains region in the southeast **Chief Rivers:** Shibeli, Abbai (Blue Nile), Ganale Dorya, Awash, Omo
Head of State and of Government: Lt. Col. Mengistu Haile-Mariam, born 1937?, named chairman of the Provisional Military Administrative Council (*Dergue*) in 1977 **Effective Date of Present Constitution:** 1955 (suspended) **Legislative Body:** The bicameral National Assembly was dissolved in 1974. All decisions are made by the *Dergue* **Local Government:** 14 provinces
Ethnic Composition: The Amharas and the Tigreans are of Semitic origin and make up 37% of the population; the Gallas, a Hamitic people, account for 40%. There are also numerous mixed, Negroid, and other groups, including the Falashas, or so-called "Black Jews," Sidamas, Somalis, and Yemenite Arabs, as well as some 30,000 Europeans, chiefly Italians **Population Distribution:** 12.4% urban (1975) **Density:** 64 inhabitants per sq. mi.
Largest Cities: (1978 est.) Addis Ababa 1,196,300, Asmara 393,800; (1975 est.) Dire Dawa 80,890, Dessye 57,420, Harar 56,360
Per Capita Income: $118 (1980) **Gross National Product (GNP):** $3.8 billion (1980) **Economic Statistics:** About 52% of GNP comes from agriculture (coffee, cotton, corn, sugar, wheat, sorghum, oilseeds, pulses) and livestock raising; 5% from industry (textiles, food processing, building materials, printing, leather, chemicals) **Minerals and Mining:** Limited output of gold, platinum, salt, iron, and manganese ore. Deposits of potash, copper, nickel, and asbestos have been discovered **Labor Force:** 11,300,000 (1971), with some 86% engaged in subsistence agriculture **Foreign Trade:** Exports, chiefly coffee, hides and skins, oilseeds, and pulses, totaled $348 million in 1979. Imports, mainly machinery and transport equipment, textiles, yarns and fabrics, foodstuffs, building materials, and petroleum products, totaled $585 million **Principal Trade Partners:** United States, Yugoslavia, West Germany, Saudi Arabia, Italy, Japan, Britain, Djibouti
Vital Statistics: Birthrate, 49.4 per 1,000 of pop. (1975); death rate, 25.8 **Life Expectancy:** 38 years **Health Statistics:** 3,277 inhabitants per hospital bed; 93,966 per physician (1976) **Infant Mortality:** 84.2 per 1,000 births **Illiteracy:** 95% **Primary and Secondary School Enrollment:** 1,150,194 (1974) **Enrollment in Higher Education:** 6,474 **GNP Expended on Education:** 2.3% (1975)
Transportation: Paved roads total about 2,000 mi. **Motor Vehicles:** 65,600 (1976) **Passenger Cars:** 52,500 **Railway Mileage:** 680 **Ports:** Massawa, Assab; a substantial portion of Ethiopia's trade moves through Djibouti **Major Airlines:** Ethiopian Airlines, the government line, operates domestic and international services **Communications:** State controlled **Radio Transmitters:** 8 (1975) **Receivers:** 210,000 (1976) **Television Transmitters:** 8 (1975) **Receivers:** 21,000 (1976) **Telephones:** 73,000 (1976) **Newspapers:** 8 dailies, 2.5 copies per 1,000 inhabitants (1975)
Weights and Measures: Metric system is official but traditional units are also used **Travel Requirements:** Passport, visa; check with Ethiopian embassy or consulates for requirements

---

The 44-year reign of Emperor Haile Selassie ended September 12, 1974, when a group of army officers completed a process which months before had begun to strip the emperor of most of his powers. This Provisional Military Administrative Council (PMAC) or *Dergue* removed him and installed his son, Asfa Wossen, 57, as a figurehead king. And in March 1975 a proclamation ended the monarchy, annulling the Crown Prince's appointment.

Since he became emperor in 1930, the Lion of Judah had promoted economic innovation and political reform, but progress was slow. Strong resistance came from farmers, aristocratic landowners and the Coptic Church, which owns about a third of all land in a country where agriculture is a livelihood for 86 percent of the population.

Civilian rioting and strikes protesting soaring prices, unemployment, and the government's mismanagement of relief efforts dealing with the country's drought and famine undermined Selassie's power. What finally led to his downfall was the cover-up of the 1973 famine, which caused the deaths of over 100,000 peasants.

In February 1974 an army mutiny forced Selassie's cabinet to resign. Selassie sought to maintain control of the country by naming a new premier, Endalkachew Makonnen, installing a new cabinet, and raising army wages. Meanwhile, Ethiopia remained under military control.

In March, Selassie agreed to call a constitutional convention that could lead to a replacement of his absolute monarchy by a more democratic form of government. Finally, in September, came the coup which ousted him. He died in 1975.

A turning point for the ruling PMAC came in November 1974 when its members voted to execute 60 Ethiopians, including their chairman, Lt. Gen. Aman Michael Andom. These executions solidified the powers of Maj. Mengistu Haile-Mariam, the First Deputy Chairman, and Lt. Col. Atnafu Abate, the Second Deputy Chairman, while the chairman of the Military Council, Brig. Gen. Teferi Bante, remained a figurehead. In February 1977 Bante and six other members of the *Dergue* were killed in a shootout.

With Lt. Col. Mengistu now in control of one of the most brutal and arbitrary regimes in power today, Ethiopia's secretive council has turned into a one-man dictatorship. Among the problems Mengistu faces are the implementation of the land reform program ending 2,000 years of feudalism, domestic dissidence (especially that of the Ethiopian People's Revolutionary party) and the consolidation of the "Socialist revolution."

Under his rule the government is taking a harder and more violent path in dealing with its enemies, both in and outside the country. Among the regime's enemies in arms are three different forces of Eritrean guerrillas fighting for the past 17 years for independence of the northernmost province, containing Ethiopia's entire 540-mile Red Sea coastline; a right-wing army of exiles loyal to the era of Haile Selassie that has made gains in the provinces of Gojjam and Gondar; Somali irrendentists along the Somali frontier; and guerrillas who control one-third of Tigre province.

In March 1978 Ethiopian forces, aided by some 16,000 Cuban troops and 1,500 Soviet military advisors, captured the last major towns in the Ogaden region after an eight-month campaign. An estimated one million Somalis had fled to Somalia by early 1980, but at least 20,000 guerrillas continued the fight and claimed to control 70 percent of the countryside. Ethiopia launched two full-scale offensives, again with Cuban and Soviet help, against Eritrean rebels in 1978 and 1979; but with limited success.

The Ethiopian Orthodox Christian church, a dominant force under Haile Selassie, is struggling against government attempts to control or crush it. In March 1979, Mengistu launched a full-scale crackdown on the country's 12 million Christians, forcing some to register with the government and others to renounce their faith. Some reportedly were executed for refusing to cooperate.

Friction developed between Ethiopia's Marxist government and the United States in 1980. In July, the Ethiopian government asked for the recall of the American ambassador, and in September, Lt. Col. Mengistu criticized the U.S. for attempting to acquire military bases in Somalia.

HISTORY: Long isolated from outside influences, Ethiopia developed a culture still suggestive of biblical times. Among its proudest traditions is that of the descent of Ethiopian emperors from King Solomon and the Queen of Sheba, who according to legend was the Ethiopian Queen Makeda of Aksum. Christianity was introduced by Coptic missionaries in the 4th century A.D. Over the centuries, repeated incursions by Arabs and constant feuding by feudal lords disrupted the empire, and it was not until the reign of Menelik II (1889-1913) that it was consolidated. In 1896, Menelik

defeated an invading Italian army, but the invaders later took over Eritrea

1916: Menelik's grandson, Lij Yasu, suspected of Moslem leanings, is deposed; Menelik's daughter, Judith, is installed as empress, with her cousin, Ras Tafari Makonnen, as regent and heir

1930-31: Following death of the empress in 1930, Ras Tafari becomes emperor, taking the name Haile Selassie, meaning "Power of the Trinity"; he proclaims the first constitution

1935-36: Italians occupy Ethiopia; emperor flees the country and appeals vainly to the League of Nations for protection

1941: Following Italian defeat in World War II East African campaign, Haile Selassie, with Ethiopian and British forces, returns in triumph to Addis Ababa

1942: Emperor begins modernization and reforms

1952: United Nations approves federation of Eritrea, former Italian colony, with Ethiopia

1955: Revised constitution provides for popularly elected Chamber of Deputies and first elections are held

1960: Military coup involving crown prince is crushed

1974: Army mutiny and general strikes cause Selassie to appoint new cabinet and premier and promise reforms; Haile Selassie's rule ended. Lt. Gen. Aman Michael Andom is appointed premier and chairman of the military government (Sept.). Andom shot to death. Brig. Gen. Teferi Bante emerges as figurehead controlled by Maj. Mengistu Haile-Mariam and Lt. Col. Atnafu Abate

1975: Fighting erupts between Eritrean rebels and government troops in Asmara, provincial capital of Eritrea. Selassie dies

1977: Bante is killed. Mengistu becomes chief of state and commander in chief of armed forces

1978 Eight-month Ogaden War ends as Cuban- and Soviet-aided Ethiopian forces drive Somalis from region. Ethiopia launches major offensive against Eritrean rebels, again with Cuban and Soviet help. A million-and-a-half Ethiopians are reportedly starving in nation's worst famine since 1973. In November Ethiopia and the Soviet Union sign a 20-year friendship pact

1979: Ethiopia abandons second full-scale offensive in Eritrea

1980: Government moves Ethiopians into Eritrea to displace Eritrean civilians; rebels hold Nakfa and countryside. U.S. ambassador recalled at Ethiopia's request

---

FIJI

Area: 7,055 sq. mi. **Population:** 618,979 (1979 est.)

Official Name: Fiji **Capital:** Suva **Languages:** English is the official language; Fijian, Hindi **Religion:** Almost all indigenous Fijians are Christians, mainly Methodist. The Indian population is mostly Hindu **Flag:** A light blue field with the Union Jack in the upper left and the shield of the Fiji coat of arms in the fly **Anthem:** God Bless Fiji **Currency:** Fijian dollar (0.83 per U.S. $1)

Location: Southwest Pacific. Fiji consists of about 320 islands, grouped around the Koro Sea, about 1,100 miles north of New Zealand. The largest of the islands, Viti Levu (18°S., 178°E.), constitutes more than half the land area and is the seat of the capital. The island of Rotuma, about 240 miles north of Vanua Levu, is part of the Fijian group **Features:** The larger islands are of volcanic origin, mountainous, and surrounded by coral reefs. The windward sides of the islands are covered with dense tropical forests; the leeward sides contain grassy plains **Chief Rivers:** Rewa, Dreketi, Sigatoka, Navua, Mba

Head of State: Queen Elizabeth II, represented by a governor-general, Ratu Sir George Cakobau, born 1912, took office 1973 **Head of Government:** Prime Minister: Ratu Sir Kamisese Mara, born 1920, appointed Chief Minister in 1967, assumed the office of prime minister in 1970, and reappointed in 1977 **Effective Date of Present Constitution:** October 1970 **Legislative Body:** Parliament (bicameral), consisting of the Senate and the House of Representatives. The Senate has 22 members, appointed for 6 years. The House of Representatives has 52 members elected on a communal basis for 5 years **Local Government:** 4 administrative divisions, each headed by a government-appointed commissioner; 10 urban areas have elected councils

Ethnic Composition: 50% of the population is descended from Indian laborers who came to Fiji in the late 19th century; the indigenous Fijians, who number 45%, are Melanesians, but with a considerable admixture of Polynesian blood. 2% are Europeans and part Europeans, 2% Rotumans and other Pacific islanders, and 1% Chinese **Population Distribution:** 37% urban **Density:** 88 inhabitants per sq. mi.

Largest Cities: (1979 est.) Suva 66,018, Lautoka 26,595, Nadi 7,099, Vatukoula 6,807, Ba 6,529, Nausori 6,610, Labasa 5,062

Per Capita Income: $1,300 (1979) **Gross National Product (GNP):** $811 million (1979) **Economic Statistics:** In 1973 about 27% of GNP was from agriculture (sugar, coconuts, rice, bananas, ginger); 16% from industry (sugar milling, coconut oil) and mining; and 41% from trade and services **Minerals and Mining:** Gold is mined and exported, although production has declined in recent years **Labor Force:** 176,000 (1979), with about 44% in agriculture, 16% in industry **Foreign Trade:** Exports, chiefly sugar, coconut oil, fish, gold, molasses, and lumber, totaled $258 million in 1979. Imports, mainly machinery, fuels, clothing, cotton fabrics, and food, totaled $471 million **Principal Trade Partners:** Australia, Japan, Britain, New Zealand, United States, Canada, Singapore

Vital Statistics: Birthrate, 28.6 per 1,000 of pop. (1976); death rate, 4.4 **Life Expectancy:** 70 years **Health Statistics:** 320 inhabitants per hospital bed; 1,763 per physician (1976) **Infant Mortality:** 9.1 per 1,000 births (1977) **Illiteracy:** 15% **Primary and Secondary School Enrollment:** 162,563 (1980) **Enrollment in Higher Education:** 1,810 (1975) **GNP Expended on Education:** 5.1% (1976)

Transportation: All-weather roads total 746 mi. **Motor Vehicles:** 43,037 (1979) **Passenger Cars:** 19,087 **Railway Mileage:** 400 miles of narrow-gauge track **Ports:** Suva, Lautoka, Levuka **Major Airlines:** Fiji Air operates domestic services **Communications:** State owned **Radio Transmitters:** 11 **Receivers:** 300,000 (1976) **Television:** None **Telephones:** 31,000 (1976) **Newspapers:** 2 dailies, 35 copies per 1,000 inhabitants (1975)

Weights and Measures: Metric system **Travel Requirements:** Passport and onward/return ticket required. Visa issued on arrival for 4 months stay **International Dialing Code:** 679

In 1874, when Fiji was the haunt of cannibals, its chiefs ceded the islands to Queen Victoria. Ninety-six years to the day later, on October 10, 1970, Britain granted Fiji independence. With independence, domestic problems have risen to the surface, such as differences between mainly urban-dwelling Indians, who make up half of the population, and the indigenous Melanesians, who number about a tenth less than the Indians, but who own over 80 percent of the land.

Political equanimity is kept by an arrangement in which each group elects an equal number of members of government, the balance of power being held by representatives of the minority of voters who are neither Indian nor Melanesian.

Since 1975, political harmony has been threatened because of the formation of splinter groups from both major parties. This imbalance was exemplified in the 1976 elections in which Prime Minister Sir Kamisese Mara resigned after his ruling Alliance party suffered defeat in the general election. The defeat meant political turmoil for Fijians, with no party able to gain an overall majority in the House of Representatives. As a result of this impasse, the governor-general reappointed Mara prime minister. A measure of stability was regained in September 1977 when the Alliance party, led by Mara, won by a landslide in the general elections. The victory was seen as vindicating Mara's determination to preserve Fiji's multiracial society.

Today, Fiji is more than a tourist haven. In education, Fiji draws islanders to its University of the South Pacific, its medical school, and even its Protestant theological school. It is a leading voice of the South Pacific in the United Nations. In commerce, Fiji is a transshipment point for trade to the Pacific islands. Exports include sugar, coconut products, and gold.

HISTORY: Vanua Levu, Taveuni and some smaller islands in the northeast of the Fiji archipelago were discovered by the Dutch navigator Tasman in 1643. Other islands in the group were discovered in the following century by Captain James Cook and other British explorers, but it was not until 1804 that the first European settlement was established, at Levuka. Missionaries soon followed and succeeded in abolishing cannibalism and in converting Cakobau, the most influential of the native chiefs, to Christianity
1874: Britain annexes the islands at the request of the tribal chiefs
1879: Importation begins of indentured Indian laborers for work on the sugar plantations
1900: Plan by European settlers for federation with New Zealand is rejected

1904: Europeans win elective representation in a 10-man Legislative Council, whose one Indian member and two Fijian members are nominated by governor
1929: Indians win right to elective representation in council
1963: Legislative Council is reconstituted, giving Fijians elective representation
1965: New constitution is introduced, providing for greater self-government
1970: Fiji wins independence and joins the UN
1972: First general elections since independence are held
1977: Alliance party wins by landslide in general elections
1978: Fiji contributes 500-man contingent to the United Nations Interim Force in Lebanon (UNIFIL) peacekeeping force
1979: Two Fijian soldiers of the UNIFIL peacekeeping force are killed Feb. 3 in clashes with Palestinian guerrillas. Cyclone Meli devastates part of Fiji archipelago (March 27); 52 are killed, thousands left homeless. Fiji provides 1,300-man contingent for peacekeeping force in Zimbabwe-Rhodesia
1980: Angry demonstrators cause Chilean dictator Pinochet to cut short his visit to the Islands. Fiji obtains apology from China for holding missile tests in Pacific without prior consultation

FINLAND

Area: 130,128 sq. mi. **Population:** 4,778,000 (1980 est.)

Official Name: Republic of Finland **Capital:** Helsinki **Nationality:** Finnish **Languages:** Finnish, the dominant tongue, and Swedish, spoken by 6.5% of the population, are both official languages. Lappish is spoken by a small minority **Religion:** More than 92% of the population belongs to the established Evangelical Lutheran Church; less than 8% belongs to the Orthodox Church of Finland and the so-called free churches **Flag:** An extended blue cross on a white field with the national coat of arms centered on the cross **Anthem:** Our Land **Currency:** Markka (4.2 per U.S. $1)

Location: Northern Europe. Finland is bordered by Norway on the north, by the USSR on the east, by the Gulf of Finland and the Baltic Sea on the south, and by the Gulf of Bothnia and Sweden on the west. A third of Finland's total length lies north of the Arctic Circle **Features:** Finland is a land of 60,000 lakes, nearly all of them in the southern half of the country. About 70% of the land area is covered with forests; swamps, many of them wooded, cover about 30%. The generally low-lying coastal belt rises slightly to a forested plateau. The far north is marked by low, mountainous terrain **Chief Rivers:** Kemijoki, Oulujoki, Muoniojoki-Torniojoki

Head of State: President Urho Kaleva Kekkonen, born 1900, in office since 1956, reelected (to fifth term) in 1978 **Head of Government:** Premier Mauno Koivisto, born 1923, appointed May 1979 **Effective Date of Present Constitution:** 1919 **Legislative Body:** Parliament (unicameral *Edhuskunta*), consisting of 200 members elected by direct universal suffrage for 4-year terms **Local Government:** 12 provinces, (including autonomous Ahvenanmaa—the Aland Islands), each headed by a governor. Urban and rural communes have elected councils

Ethnic Composition: Finnish-speaking Finns make up 93.2% of the population and Swedish-speaking Finns 6.6%. Lapps number about 3,000 and "Kazan Turks" 1,000 **Population Distribution:** 59% urban **Density:** 37 inhabitants per sq. mi.

Largest Cities: (1976 est.) Helsinki 493,324, Tampere 166,179, Turku 164,520, Espoo 123,954, Vantaa 122,301

Per Capita Income: $7,004 (1980) **Gross Domestic Product (GDP):** $33.4 billion (1980) **Economic Statistics:** 31% of GDP comes from industry (metals, engineering, foodstuffs, paper and paper products, furniture, textiles, chemicals); 9% from agriculture (oats, barley, wheat, rye), fishing and forestry; 14% from commerce and finance **Minerals and Mining:** Copper, nickel, iron, zinc, vanadium, silver and lead are mined in substantial quantities **Labor Force:** 2.2 million (1977), with 14% in agriculture and forestry, 34% in industry and construction, and 38% in trade and services **Foreign Trade:** Exports, chiefly paper products, machinery, transport equipment, chemicals, textiles, dairy products totaled $11.1 billion in 1979. Imports, mainly raw materials for industry, fuels and lubricants, machinery, automobiles, aircraft, foodstuffs, and textiles, totaled $11.3 billion **Principal Trade Partners:** Britain, Sweden, USSR, West Germany, United States

Vital Statistics: Birthrate, 13.9 per 1,000 of pop. (1977); death rate, 9.4 **Life Expectancy:** 72 years **Health Statistics:** 66 inhabitants per hospital bed; 703 per physician (1975) **Infant Mortality:** 12 per 1,000 births (1977) **Illiteracy:** Negligible **Primary and Secondary School Enrollment:** 869,894 (1976) **Enrollment in Higher Education:** 77,206 (1975) **GNP Expended on Education:** 7.1% (1976)

Transportation: Paved roads total 19,300 mi. **Motor Vehicles:** 1,220,400 (1977) **Passenger Cars:** 1,075,400 **Railway Mileage:**

3,752 **Ports:** Helsinki, Turku, Naantali, Hamina, Hanko, Kemi, Oulu, Pori, Kotka, Sköldvik **Major Airlines:** Finnair operates domestic and international flights **Communications:** Government owned **Radio Transmitters:** 101 **Licenses:** 2,199,575 (1976) **Television Transmitters:** 83 **Licenses:** 1,779,469 (1976) **Telephones:** 1,936,000 (1976) **Newspapers:** 57 dailies, 537 copies per 1,000 inhabitants (1976)

Weights and Measures: Metric system **Travel Requirements:** Passport; no visa for 3 months **International Dialing Code:** 358

With a self-assurance that has grown over the last decade, neutral Finland, which borders the Soviet Union, has been playing a role in international affairs unthinkable a decade ago.

It has served a two-year term (1969-70) on the UN Security Council, where small powers, in taking their turn in the chair, find themselves presiding at times over big-power disputes. Ministers of 35 nations, including the United States and Canada, met in Helsinki in June 1973 to lay groundwork for a European détente. The Conference on Security and Cooperation in Europe (CSCE), held in August 1975 in Helsinki, dealt with the inviolability of frontiers, economic cooperation, and freer movement of people and ideas. The conference was regarded by Finland as an assurance of its independence from the Soviet Union.

To the Finns, these actions are among a series of initiatives that would have been out of the question at the beginning of the 1960s, a period of uneasy relations with the neighboring Soviets.

At the time, a major Finnish political organization, the Social Democratic party, was being kept out of government to avoid repercussions in Moscow. But the Social Democrats returned to cabinet posts in 1966 and were part of the coalition government that achieved the signing of the Free Trade Agreement with the European Community (EC). President Kekkonen's third six-year term was lengthened by parliamentary decision after the major parties failed to find a candidate who could run Finland's sensitive foreign policy—especially Finland's relations to the Soviet Union—as well as Kekkonen, at the helm since 1956.

The Free Trade Agreement with the EC came after 13 months of hesitation and often bitter political debate in which Finland's relations with the Soviet Union played a significant part.

In January 1978, in the first presidential election in a decade, President Kekkonen was reelected to his fifth consecutive term. In May 1979, Kekkonen appointed Mauno Koivisto premier of a new centrist coalition government, which was formed without the leftist Liberal party.

HISTORY: The earliest known inhabitants of Finland were the Lapps. By the 8th century A.D., however, they had been pushed northward by the Finns, coming from the south and southeast. In the 12th century Finland was Christianized by the Swedes and in the 16th century became a grand duchy under the Swedish crown. Russia acquired the province of Vyborg in 1721 and was ceded the rest of the duchy in 1809. Although Finland enjoyed considerable autonomy under Russian rule, Finnish nationalism developed into a powerful movement

1899-1906: Tsar Nicholas II begins strong Russification program, evoking stiff Finnish resistance. Russian governor-general is assassinated and a general strike breaks out. Finns win concessions, set up a unicameral diet and introduce universal suffrage

1917-20: Following the Bolshevik seizure of power in the Russian Revolution, Finnish diet proclaims Finland's independence. Civil war breaks out between Russian sympathizers (Reds) and Finnish nationalists (Whites), led by Marshal Carl Gustav Mannerheim and aided by German troops. Whites are victorious and after a brief regency under Mannerheim a republic is set up. The Soviet Union recognizes Finland

1939-40: Soviet Union, which has been given a free hand in Finland under Moscow's nonaggression pact with Nazi Germany, demands demilitarization of Finnish fortifications on Karelian Isthmus north of Leningrad, use of a naval base in Finland, and the cession of islands in Gulf of Finland. Finns refuse to bow to

demands and Soviet troops attack. Despite strong resistance by Finnish troops, led by Mannerheim, Finland is defeated and is forced to cede one-tenth of its territory to USSR

1941-45: Finland is caught up in war between the Soviet Union and Nazi Germany, the Finns fighting what they regard as the Continuation War against the Russians and not as allies of Germany. Full-scale Soviet offensive results in Finnish defeat in 1944. Armistice terms oblige Finns to expel German troops; resulting warfare leads to further devastation of Finland

1947: Under peace treaty signed in Paris, Finland cedes more territory to USSR and agrees to pay heavy indemnity

1955-61: Finland joins Nordic Council, and becomes associate member of European Free Trade Association; continues policy of neutrality and cooperation with Soviet Union

1973: Finland signs Free Trade Agreement with the EC. President Kekkonen's term extended by four years

1975: Finland hosts concluding session of the Conference on Security and Cooperation in Europe (CSCE)

1976: Finland hit by first police strike in postwar Europe

1977: Kalevi Sorsa succeeds Martti Miettunen as premier

1978: President Kekkonen reelected to fifth straight term

1979: Mauno Koivisto succeeds Sorsa as premier

FRANCE

Area: 210,038 sq. mi. **Population:** 53,478,000 (1979 est.)

Official Name: French Republic **Capital:** Paris **Nationality:** French **Languages:** French is the official and predominant language. Other languages spoken include Breton (akin to Welsh) in Brittany; a German dialect in Alsace and Lorraine; Flemish in northeastern France; Spanish, Catalan, and Basque in the southwest; and Italian in the southeast and on the island of Corsica **Religion:** Chiefly Roman Catholic, 4% Moslem (mostly immigrants from North Africa), 2% Protestant, 1% Jewish **Flag:** A tricolor of blue, white, and red vertical stripes **Anthem:** La Marseillaise **Currency:** Franc (5.2 per U.S. $1)

Location: Western Europe. France is bounded on the north by the English Channel and the Strait of Dover; on the northeast by the North Sea, Belgium and Luxembourg; on the east by Germany, Switzerland, and Italy; on the southeast by the Mediterranean Sea; on the south by Andorra and Spain; and on the west by the Atlantic Ocean **Features:** About two thirds of the country consists of flat or gently rolling terrain, and the remaining third is mountainous. A broad plain covers most of northern and western France, from the Belgian border in the northeast to Bayonne in the southwest. The lowland plains area is bounded on the south by the Pyrenees; on the southeast by the mountainous Massif Central; and on the east by the Alps, Jura, and Vosges mountains **Chief Rivers:** Seine, Loire, Garonne, Rhône, Rhine

Head of State: President François Mitterrand, born 1916, elected 1981 for 7 years **Head of Government:** Premier Pierre Mauroy, born 1928, appointed 1981 **Effective Date of Present Constitution:** 1958 **Legislative Body:** Parliament (bicameral), with a National Assembly and the Senate. The National Assembly, elected by direct universal suffrage for 5 years, is composed of 491 deputies. The Senate is composed of 315 members, elected indirectly for 9 years by an electoral college made up of National Assembly members, the General Departmental Councils, and the delegates of the Municipal Councils. The National Assembly can be dissolved by the president with the advice of the premier **Local Government:** Metropolitan France is divided into 96 departments, each headed by a prefect appointed by the central government and each under the authority of an elected General Council. The departments are divided into cantons and communes, with each commune electing its own municipal council and designated mayor. There are also 21 economic regions

Ethnic Composition: The French are a mixture of the 3 basic European stocks: Nordic, Alpine, and Mediterranean. The largest foreign-born groups are North Africans, Italians, Portuguese, Spaniards, Czechoslovaks, Poles, and Yugoslavs **Population Distribution:** 71% urban **Density:** 255 inhabitants per sq. mi.

Largest Cities: (1975 census) Paris 2,291,554 (Metropolitan Area 9,878,524), Marseille 901,421, Lyon 454,265, Toulouse 371,143, Nice 331,002, Nantes 252,537, Strasbourg 251,520, Bordeaux 220,830, Saint-Étienne 218,289, LeHavre 216,917, Rennes 194,094, Toulon 180,508, Reims 177,320, Lille 171,010, Grenoble 165,431, Brest 163,940

Per Capita Income: $9,479 (1980) **Gross Domestic Product (GDP):** $508 billion (1980) **Economic Statistics:** About 38% of GDP comes from industry (metalworking, machinery, chemicals, transport equipment, food and beverages, textiles, clothing) and construction; 57% from trade and services; 5% from agriculture and fishing (wheat, barley, potatoes, beet sugar, apples, wine, fish, beef cattle, and pigs) **Minerals and Mining:** The country is an important producer of iron ore, potash, bauxite, coal, natural gas, sulphur, and building raw materials. It also has deposits of zinc, lead, pyrites, phosphates, and uranium **Labor Force:** 20.5 million, with 47% in trade and services, 38% in manufacturing and construction, 10% in agriculture, fishing, and forestry **Foreign Trade:** Exports, chiefly machinery, chemicals, textiles, automobiles, steel, grain, and aircraft, totaled $98 billion in 1979. Imports, mainly machinery, foodstuffs, petroleum, chemicals, steel, nonferrous metals, and transportation equipment, totaled $107 billion **Principal Trade Partners:** West Germany, Belgium, Luxembourg, Italy, United States, Switzerland, Britain, Netherlands, Algeria, Japan, Saudi Arabia, USSR

Vital Statistics: Birthrate, 14.0 per 1,000 of pop. (1977); death rate, 10.1 **Life Expectancy:** 72 years **Health Statistics:** 97 inhabitants per hospital bed, 678 per physician (1976) **Infant Mortality:** 11.4 per 1,000 births **Illiteracy:** Negligible **Primary and Secondary School Enrollment:** 9,511,719 (1976) **Enrollment in Higher Education:** 1,038,576 (1975) **GNP Expended on Education:** 5.8% (1976)

Transportation: Surfaced roads total 520,000 mi. **Motor Vehicles:** 19,340,000 (1977) **Passenger Cars:** 16,700,000 **Railway Mileage:** 26,380 **Ports:** Marseille, Le Havre, Dunkirk, Nantes, St-Nazaire, Rouen, Bordeaux, Brest, Nice **Major Airlines:** Air France and UTA operate international flights; Air-Inter operates domestic flights **Communications:** Government owned **Radio Transmitters:** 290 **Licenses:** 26,000,000 (1976) **Television Transmitters:** 3,001 (1974) **Licenses:** 14,197,000 (1975) **Telephones:** 15,554,000 (1976) **Newspapers:** 98 dailies, 214 copies per 1,000 inhabitants (1975)

Weights and Measures: Metric system **Travel Requirements:** Passport; no visa for 3 months **International Dialing Code:** 33

For a country with a reputation for being ungovernable, France has moved and is continuing to move through a difficult period of transition, politically, economically, and socially, with an uncharacteristic amount of smoothness.

That there is some unrest and dissatisfaction is attested to by strikes, demonstrations, manifestations of violence, and angry meetings. But these fits of temper surge up and die down quickly, and the appearance of crisis they create is quickly dissipated.

Despite some dire predictions, France has moved out of the Gaullist era into more prosaic leadership with the institutions that General de Gaulle had bequeathed intact. A people that history books describe as undisciplined and individualistic appear to accept strong executive power as a fact of political life, particularly when it concentrates as it now does on domestic problems and eschews to a large extent the kind of global diplomacy practiced by de Gaulle.

The main goal of de Gaulle's successor, Georges Pompidou, was to eliminate France's industrial backwardness and move her into the forefront of advanced technical nations. The rich, varied soil of France that produces the food and wines that have contributed to the French art of living have also produced a powerful, conservative rural society that over the centuries has dominated the country.

The shift to an urban, industrialized society is one of the great central facts of contemporary France. As people move from farm to city and enter into radically different ways of life and work, tensions are created. They are aggravated by the failure of the cities to accommodate ever increasing populations with adequate housing and transport. More and more, once sleepy provincial centers are starting to take on the bustle, noise, and discomfort of Paris.

More than just the rural population is in transition. Shopkeepers and artisans who flourished in a slow-moving, small-scale economy are finding themselves squeezed out of the market by the demand for more efficient and cheaper ways of making and distributing goods and services. Workers in small inefficient plants or in traditional industries that are dying out are finding themselves having to adjust to new lines of work in new places.

Students and educational authorities are trying to make their schools relevant to a new kind of society that places a premium on technical proficiency and accords declining prestige to the contemplative man of letters.

All these are long-range problems that are more or less painful to resolve and create tensions that sometimes may cause explosions. In May 1968, students and workers exploded together, bringing the government of General de Gaulle and the whole regime into peril. Although de Gaulle weathered the storm, it was the beginning of the end for him; the following year he was defeated in a referendum and was forced into lonely and somewhat bitter retirement. When he died in November 1970, there was a great national and international outpouring of sentiment for him.

The events of May 1968 left a decided impact. The franc was no longer sacrosanct and monetary policies henceforth were more closely coordinated with those of France's European partners. The upheaval has led to a style of government that places great importance on discussion and participation in decisions. At the same time, the memory of the 1968 disorders made most Frenchmen very law-and-order conscious. How to protect civil liberties while putting down the disorders that continue to crop up has become a major subject of debate.

Another great theme of debate is how to loosen the power of one of the most highly centralized countries in the world without destroying national unity. The move is on to satisfy municipal and regional desires for more of a say over personal futures, but the habit of deciding everything in Paris is deep-rooted and hard to change.

Abroad, France, no longer a colonial power, has paid the greatest attention to the movement toward western European unity. Under Pompidou, European unity, long blocked by his predecessor's refusal to accept Britain as a European partner, began again to show movement. The successful negotiation with Britain for entry into the Common Market was due largely to Pompidou.

In April 1974 Pompidou died at the age of 62. On May 19, Finance Minister Valéry Giscard d'Estaing was elected president by a narrow margin. During his seven-year term as president, Giscard d'Estaing displayed an informal style and a willingness to attack France's problems. In foreign affairs, he pursued independent policies which often conflicted with those of the United States. Domestically, his administration at first kept the annual inflation rate under 10 percent, reduced unemployment, and cut France's international payments deficit. In March 1978, his center-right coalition won a formidable 291-to-200 majority of seats in the National Assembly.

In the second round of presidential elections on May 10, 1981, Giscard lost to the candidate of the united left, François Mitterrand, the Socialist Party's leader who won about 52 percent of the popular vote. The bitter political campaign had featured an American-style televised debate between the two candidates, neither of whom appeared to have won the confrontation decisively. Giscard charged that Mitterrand could not govern without the support of the Communists, and Mitterrand said his program to nationalize industry was needed to deal with France's real economic problems.

Following the elections, prices on the Paris Stock Exchange and the value of the French franc fell sharply. The stock market soon recovered after Mitterrand promised that his economic changes would be gradual. Mitterrand's Socialists won an absolute majority in the National Assembly in the June parliamentary elections.

HISTORY: The land of France was inhabited in ancient times by the Gauls, who, by 51 B.C., had been subdued by the Romans. The Latin language predominated by the 5th century A.D., when Roman power collapsed, and the Franks from Germany made the land part of a large domain. Charlemagne ruled from 768 to 814 and extended the domain, but it was divided in 838—"Francia," with its Latin-based language, going to Charles the Bald. The kings lost power to local nobles in the 10th century, but recovered it slowly in later centuries

1337: The Hundred Years War breaks out, actually a series of short wars and truces between France and England, whose kings lay claim to the French throne

1429-53: Joan of Arc successfully leads French armies in lifting the siege of Orléans but is burned at the stake in 1431 after falling into English hands; English are finally driven out

1643-1715: Louis XIV gains military and political primacy for France in continental Europe, creates a great overseas empire, and establishes an absolute monarchy with a highly centralized government; his reign marks the golden age of French culture

1789-94: The French Revolution sweeps away Old Regime. A National Convention is formed, the monarchy abolished, Louis XVI executed, and a republic proclaimed. The Reign of Terror sets in, leading to arrest and execution of a huge number of royalists and members of minority political blocs. France's neighbors form an alliance to suppress the Revolution

1799-1804: Napoleon Bonaparte becomes first consul under the Consulate, a tripartite executive body; he restores domestic stability and defeats Austrian-British coalition

1804-14: Napoleon proclaims himself emperor, leads French armies in a series of unequaled victories against the other powers of Europe. His attempt to conquer Russia, however, results in a decisive defeat for France and the formation of an armed European coalition which forces his abdication

1815: Napoleon escapes from exile on Elba, rallies a French army, and is decisively defeated at Waterloo

1848: Revolution overthrows Bourbon monarchy, restored after Napoleon; the Second Republic is formed

1852: Louis Napoleon, Bonaparte's nephew, engineers coup d'état and overthrows republic; as Napoleon III, he establishes the Second Empire

1870-71: France defeated in Franco-Prussian War; Second Empire collapses and the Third Republic is formed

1914-18: France plays a major role in World War I against the Austro-German coalition. Nation shares in Allied victory but its economy is devastated by the war

1939: France joins Britain in declaring war on Germany following Nazi invasion of Poland

1940: France suffers ignominious defeat by Germany. Marshal Henri Pétain forms government at Vichy and sues for peace; Germans occupy half of France. Gen. Charles de Gaulle escapes to London, forms a wartime government and the Free French army

1944: Paris is liberated by Allied armies. De Gaulle's provisional exile government is officially recognized by the Allies

1945-46: De Gaulle is unanimously elected provisional president of the Fourth Republic but resigns after leftists withdraw support

1958-61: De Gaulle is recalled to power as the Fourth Republic is threatened with collapse because of the Algerian conflict. He engineers a new constitution vesting strong powers in the executive and establishing the Fifth Republic; despite considerable opposition, he negotiates Algerian independence

1966: De Gaulle withdraws French forces from NATO

1968: Student-worker uprisings paralyze France and threaten to topple Gaullist regime, but de Gaulle weathers the storm; his Gaullist party wins smashing victory in parliamentary election

1969: President de Gaulle resigns after the defeat of a referendum for constitutional reform; Gaullist candidate Georges Pompidou is elected president; he devalues the franc

1970: President Pompidou initiates broad reforms designed to benefit blue-collar workers

1974: Pompidou dies; Giscard d'Estaing is elected president. Laws on voting age of 18 and legalized abortion are passed

1975: Giscard d'Estaing visits Algeria; first such trip by French head of state since Algerian independence

1976: Political parties of the left win a majority in nationwide local elections in March. Premier Jacques Chirac resigns, reconstitutes Gaullist party into the Assembly for the Republic. Raymond Barre, nonpartisan technocrat, becomes premier

1977: Socialists and Communists gain in municipal elections; Chirac elected mayor of Paris

1978: Center-right candidates win large majority in legislative elections, repulsing strong leftist challenge. France reportedly explodes neutron bomb at South Pacific test base

1981: Socialist Party leader François Mitterrand elected president, defeating Giscard; in parliamentary elections, Socialists gain absolute majority. Pierre Mauroy is named premier

GABON

Area: 103,346 sq. mi. **Population:** 538,000 (1978 est.)

Official Name: Gabonese Republic **Capital:** Libreville **Nationality:** Gabonese **Languages:** French is the official language; Fang is spoken in the north and a variety of Bantu tongues in the rest of the country **Religion:** About 46% of the population is Christian, mainly Roman Catholic; there are about 3,000 Moslems and the rest are animists **Flag:** Green, yellow, and blue horizontal stripes **Anthem:** Harmony **Currency:** CFA Franc (263 per U.S. $1)

Location: West-central Africa. Gabon is bordered on the north by Equatorial Guinea and by Cameroon, on the east and south by the Congo, and on the west by the Atlantic Ocean **Features:** About 85% of the entire country is covered by dense equatorial rain forest. The coastal plain is deeply indented in the north, while inland there are plateaus and mountains through which rivers have carved deep valleys and channels **Chief Rivers:** Ogooué, Ngounié, Abanga

Head of State and of Government: President: El Hadj Omar (Albert-Bernard) Bongo, born 1935; succeeded 1967; reelected 1979. He is assisted a prime minister, Léon Mébiame, appointed 1975 **Effective Date of Present Constitution:** 1961 **Legislative Body:** National Assembly (unicameral), consisting of 93 members **Local Government:** 9 regions divided into 36 prefectures, and 8 urban communes, with appointed officials

Ethnic Composition: Almost all Gabonese are of Bantu origin. The Fang are the largest of the country's tribes, followed by the Eshira, Bapounou, Bateke, and Okandé **Population Distribution:** 32% urban **Density:** 5.2 inhabitants per sq. mi.

Largest Cities: (1973 est.) Libreville 57,000, Port-Gentil 35,000, Franceville 5,000

Per Capita Income: $4,186 (1980) **Gross National Product (GNP):** $2.5 billion (1980) **Economic Statistics:** In 1973 about 18% of GNP was from agriculture (cocoa, coffee, palm oil, rice, cassava, bananas, yams, corn, and peanuts) and forestry; 14% from manufacturing and construction; (largely timber and mineral processing); 30% from mining; 22% from trade and services **Minerals and Mining:** Very rich deposits of manganese and iron ore; uranium and gold are also produced; there are known deposits of lead, zinc, phosphate, and diamonds. Rich offshore oil and natural gas deposits are being developed **Labor Force:** About 280,000, of which 58% are engaged in agriculture **Foreign Trade:** Exports, wood, petroleum, uranium, manganese and coffee, totaled $1.8 billion in 1979. Imports, chiefly machinery, foods, transportation equipment, metal products, tobacco, refined petroleum products, and industrial chemicals, totaled $615 million **Principal Trade Partners:** France, United States, West Germany, Netherlands, Britain, Japan, Argentina, Brazil

Vital Statistics: Birthrate, 32.2 per 1,000 of pop. (1975); death rate, 22.2 **Life Expectancy:** 39 years **Health Statistics:** 132 inhabitants per hospital bed; 5,208 per physician (1975) **Infant Mortality:** 83 per 1,000 births **Illiteracy:** 70% **Primary and Secondary School Enrollment:** 153,858 (1976) **Enrollment in Higher Education:** 1,014 (1975) **GNP Expended on Education:** 4.5% (1976)

Transportation: Paved roads total 400 mi. **Motor Vehicles:** 17,400 (1974) **Passenger Cars:** 10,100 **Railway Mileage:** 184 miles; the 400-mile Transgabon line is under construction **Ports:** Libreville, Port-Gentil **Major Airlines:** Air Gabon provides international and domestic services **Communications:** Government owned **Radio Transmitters:** 10 **Receivers:** 93,000 (1976) **Television Transmitters:** 8 **Receivers:** 8,500 (1976) **Telephones:** 11,000 (1976) **Newspapers:** 1 daily, 1 copy per 1,000 inhabitants (1975)

Weights and Measures: Metric system **Travel Requirements:** Passport, visa, $10 fee

As the smallest territory of French Equatorial Africa, jungle-matted Gabon was noted chiefly as a source of tropical hardwoods and as the unhealthy land where for 53 years the famous medical missionary, the late Dr. Albert Schweitzer, operated a hospital at Lambaréné.

Most of Gabon is still a humid tangle of trees and creepers, but the increasing number of roads slicing through the jungle attest to the dramatic change that has made the country potentially one of the richest in Africa.

Not long after gaining independence from France in 1960, Gabon was found to possess some of the world's largest deposits of manganese, iron ore, and uranium.

Development of these resources is proceeding impressively, and the airline passenger approaching Libreville, the capital and chief port, may see evidence of new wealth also in the offshore oil rigs glinting above the gray Atlantic.

While tropical woods, particularly those from which the best plywood is made, are still a major export, the rising production of minerals has given Gabon a continuing trade surplus and the highest per capita annual income in black Africa.

Meanwhile, on the economic scene, because of the attractions of newfound mineral wealth, French participation in Gabon's development has grown even greater than it was in the colonial period. In February 1974 the two nations agreed that a detachment of French troops would remain in Gabon, which was to stay within the French zone.

Frenchmen run the new enterprises, the schools, banks, shops, and most businesses, and six French advisors serve in the President's office. President Bongo is actively seeking trade ties and investment from the United States, Britain, and West Germany in an effort to reduce French domination.

By 1976, relations with France had grown increasingly cool, with verbal attacks by President Bongo against "savage capitalism" and "exploitation" of Gabon's natural resources, becoming more frequent. However, Gabon still participates in the annual French-African summit. In 1980, joint Franco-Gabonese military maneuvers were held, and Bongo paid an official visit to France.

HISTORY: In the 15th century, Portuguese voyagers became the first Europeans to explore the coastal area of Gabon. However, because of dense jungles and impenetrable highlands the country remained relatively undisturbed by Europeans until the mid-19th century, when the French began making treaties with coastal chieftains and penetrating the interior. In 1890 Gabon formally became part of the French Congo and in 1910 was made a separate colony as part of French Equatorial Africa

1913: Dr. Albert Schweitzer, Alsatian-born physician, theologian, and musicologist, establishes medical mission at Lambaréné

1958-59: Republic of Gabon is established as autonomous member of the French Community; Léon M'Ba, leader of Gabonese Democratic party, becomes premier of provisional government

1960: Republic proclaims full independence

1961-63: Two main parties agree on joint list of candidates for election, in which M'Ba becomes president; factional disputes disrupt coalition and new elections are called

1964: When election decrees bar opposition candidates, Gabonese Army overthrows M'Ba government, but it is promptly restored by French military intervention; in subsequent elections in which opposition participates, M'Ba forces win 31 seats, compared with 16 for the opposition

1967: President M'Ba dies and is succeeded by Vice-President Albert-Bernard Bongo

1968: President Bongo declares Gabon a one-party state and forms new Gabonese Democratic party open to all citizens

1971: A new $500-million four-year plan is begun to further develop timber and mineral resources

1973: Bongo is elected to a seven-year term as president

1975: Léon Mébiame is named premier. Treaty is signed with EC. Gabon is admitted to full membership in OPEC

1976: Gabon becomes world's largest exporter of manganese

1979: Nation's financial status improves under stabilization plan. President Bongo is re-elected to a third term

1980: Candidates of Bongo's party win overwhelmingly in legislative elections

THE GAMBIA

Area: 4,127 sq. mi. **Population:** 601,000 (1980 est.)

Official Name: Republic of The Gambia **Capital:** Banjul **Nationality:** Gambian **Languages:** English is the official language; Malinke and Wolof are the main spoken languages **Religion:** Approximately 85% of the population is Moslem; about 14% Christian; and the rest animist **Flag:** Red, blue, and green horizontal stripes, with the center blue stripe edged in white **Anthem:** For the Gambia, Our Homeland **Currency:** Dalasi (1.9 per U.S. $1)

Location: West Africa. The Gambia is a narrow strip 7-20 miles wide on either side of the Gambia River, extending eastward 200 miles

from the Atlantic, and surrounded by Senegal on the land sides **Features:** Coastal mangrove swamps and salt water flats graduate to sand hills and inland plateaus **Chief River:** Gambia

Head of State and of Government: President: Alhaji Sir Dawda Kairaba Jawara, born 1924; prime minister since 1962, he became president in April 1970, and was reelected in 1977 **Effective Date of Present Constitution:** 1970 **Legislative Body:** House of Representatives (unicameral); 35 members elected by universal suffrage for a 5-year term, and 8 special members **Local Government:** Banjul, and 6 administrative divisions

Ethnic Composition: The principal groups are the Mandingo (38%), Fula (16%), Wolof (14%), Jola (9%), and Serahuli (8%) **Population Distribution:** 16% urban **Density:** 146 inhabitants per sq. mi.

Largest Cities: (1978 est.) Banjul 45,604; (1973 census) Sarekunda 16,637

Per Capita Income: $280 (1979) **Gross National Product (GNP):** $161 million (1979) **Economic Statistics:** 58% of GNP is from agriculture (chiefly peanuts), 26% from trade and services **Minerals and Mining:** No known resources of value apart from laterite and stone **Labor Force:** 165,000, about 85% being engaged in agriculture **Foreign Trade:** Exports, mainly peanuts, fish and palm kernels, totaled $57 million (1979). Imports, chiefly food, textiles and clothing, oil, machine and transport equipment, totaled $96 million **Principal Trade Partners:** Britain, Netherlands, France, United States, Japan, West African countries

Vital Statistics: Birthrate, 43.3 per 1,000 of pop. (1975); death rate, 24.1 **Life Expectancy:** 33 years **Health Statistics:** 771 inhabitants per hospital bed; 13,500 per physician (1976) **Infant Mortality:** 82.6 per 1,000 births **Illiteracy:** 90% **Primary and Secondary School Enrollment:** 32,969 (1976) **Enrollment in Higher Education:** 947 (1971) **GNP Expended on Education:** 4.4% (1976)

Transportation: Paved roads total 197 mi. **Motor Vehicles:** 6,092 (1973) **Passenger Cars:** 3,000 **Railway Mileage:** None **Ports:** Banjul **Major Airlines:** Gambia Airways provides service **Communications:** Partly government owned **Radio Stations:** 4 **Receivers:** 61,000 (1976) **Television:** None **Telephones:** 3,000 (1976) **Newspapers:** 1 newspaper published 3 times a week

Weights and Measures: British Imperial system is used; transfer to metric system started in 1976 **Travel Requirements:** Passport, transit visa $1.25, other visas $5.00

The Gambia, Africa's smallest country, has been gaining increasing self-reliance through the unlikely combination of peanut production, Scandinavian tourists, and careful fiscal management. Attention has been focused on The Gambia because of the 1976 bestseller by Alex Haley, *Roots*, which chronicles the story of Haley's ancestors from tribal life in The Gambia to slavery in America.

Formerly Britain's oldest African colony, The Gambia became independent in 1965 and proclaimed itself a republic in 1970. It added "The" to its official name to avoid confusion with Zambia, another African country.

Except for a short Atlantic coast, the country is enclosed within Senegal. A sandy strip of land, it stretches some 200 miles in length along either side of the Gambia River and varies in width from seven to 30 miles. The broad mouth of the Gambia River is one of West Africa's finest harbors and the site of the capital, Banjul. Mandingoes, a handsome, friendly people, form the main element of the population.

Peanuts, planted on most of the available land, account for 95 percent of exports, but, in recent years, tourism has become a welcome and fast-growing addition to the economy, luring 25,000 Scandinavians a year. Old hotels have been enlarged and new ones built to meet growing demand. With tourist organizations in other countries now showing interest in The Gambia, prospects are bright for a continuance of the boom and creation of more jobs and revenue. With Soviet, Chinese and British aid, The Gambia is beginning fishery development and irrigation projects.

While President Jawara was visiting London for the wedding of Prince Charles and Lady Diana Spencer, leftist rebels seized the capital on July 30,

1981. The coup attempt was promptly broken through the intervention of troops from neighboring Senegal, called on for help by Jawara.

HISTORY: Along with neighboring Senegal, The Gambia was inhabited in past ages by peoples associated with the great empires of Ghana, Mali, and Songhay. Reached by Portuguese navigators in the 15th century, in 1588 the territory became, through purchase, the first British colony in Africa. After prolonged struggle, the British and French fixed the borders of Senegal and Gambia; in 1888 the latter became a crown colony

1965: The Gambia becomes a fully independent member of the British Commonwealth; a referendum to make the country a republic fails to receive necessary two-thirds majority

1966: Elections give Prime Minister Sir Dawda Jawara's People's Progressive party an increased majority

1967-69: Britain loans The Gambia over $10 million

1970: The Gambia becomes a republic

1979: Jawara forms special court to handle charges of corruption

1980: Economy is hurt by drought and by rising prices of imported oil. Libya-backed coup attempt is forestalled with aid of Senegalese troops

1981: Leftist coup is crushed with aid of Senegalese troops

EAST GERMANY

Area: 41,768 sq. mi. **Population:** 16,745,000 (1979 est.)

Official Name: German Democratic Republic **Capital:** East Berlin **Nationality:** German **Languages:** German is the official and universal language **Religion:** 53% Protestant, 8% Roman Catholic, 39% no affiliation. Although the constitution provides for religious freedom, all churches are closely regulated by the state **Flag:** Black, red, and gold horizontal stripes, with the national emblem in the center **Anthem:** Arisen from the Ruins **Currency:** GDR mark (2.2 per U.S. $1)

Location: North-central Europe. East Germany is bordered on the north by the Baltic Sea, on the east by Poland, on the southeast by Czechoslovakia, and on the southwest and west by the Federal Republic of Germany **Features:** In the north are the lakes and low hills typical of the Baltic Sea country; the center is partly mountainous and in addition consists of a sandy arid section and a fertile plain. The heavily forested southern region consists of the Mittelgebirge, and the extension of the North German lowlands **Chief Rivers:** Elbe, Oder, Saale, Havel, Spree, Neisse

Political Leader and Head of State: Erich Honecker, born 1912, secretary general of the Central Committee of the Socialist Unity Party, since 1971, and chairman of the State Council, since 1976 **Head of Government:** Willi Stoph, born 1914, appointed October 1976 chairman of the Council of Ministers (premier) **Effective Date of Present Constitution:** 1968, amended 1974 **Legislative Body:** Volkskammer (unicameral) consisting of 500 members, elected by universal suffrage for 5-year terms; final decisions are made by the party's Politburo **Local Government:** 15 administrative districts named after their respective chief towns. All urban and rural divisions have locally elected bodies

Ethnic Composition: The population is ethnically homogeneous. The only minority is a Slavic group called the Sorbs which makes up about 0.2% of the population **Population Distribution:** 75.5% urban **Density:** 401 inhabitants per sq. mi.

Largest Cities: (1977 est.) East Berlin 1,111,398, Leipzig 565,178, Dresden 511,223, Karl-Marx-Stadt (Chemnitz) 309,457, Magdeburg 280,570, Halle 233,049, Rostock 219,035, Erfurt 206,293, Potsdam 123,210, Zwickau 122,334

Per Capita Income: $5,945 (1980) **Gross National Product (GNP):** $99.6 billion (1980) **Economic Statistics:** About 54% of GNP comes from industry, and 20% from agriculture. The chief industries are iron and steel, chemicals, fertilizers, machinery, transport equipment, synthetic rubber and fibers, drugs, plastics, and vehicles. The chief crops are barley, oats, potatoes, rye, sugar beets, and wheat **Minerals and Mining:** The arbitrary division of Germany left the East with few natural resources. Its only major resources are lignite, potash and uranium **Labor Force:** 8,900,000, with 39% in industry, 21% in services, 10% in commerce, 9% in agriculture **Foreign Trade:** Exports, chiefly machinery, railway rolling stock, chemicals, fertilizers and pesticides, fuel oil, construction materials, ships, motor vehicles, clothing and textiles, were estimated at $17.3 billion in 1979. Imports, mainly mineral ores, coal, rolled steel, fertilizer, tires, crude oil, wood, cotton and wool, paper pulp, foodstuffs, forage and feeds, and raw skins, were estimated at $19.2 billion **Principal Trade Partners:** USSR, Czechoslovakia, Poland, Hungary, France, Britain, West Germany, Bulgaria, Netherlands, Sweden

Vital Statistics: Birthrate, 13.3 per 1,000 of pop. (1977); death rate, 13.4 **Life Expectancy:** 72 years **Health Statistics:** 93 inhabitants per hospital bed; 523 per physician (1976) **Infant Mortality:** 13.1 per 1,000 births (1977) **Illiteracy:** Negligible **Primary and Secondary School Enrollment:** 3,014,086 (1976) **Enrollment in Higher Education:** 386,000 (1975) **GNP Expended on Education:** 5.6% (1974)

Transportation: Surfaced roads total 29,538 mi., with 1,000 mi. of superhighways **Motor Vehicles:** 2,806,700 (1977) **Passenger Cars:** 2,236,700 **Railway Mileage:** 8,823 **Ports:** Rostock, Wismar, Stralsund, Sassnitz **Major Airlines:** Interflug operates domestic and international services **Communications:** State controlled **Radio Transmitters:** 66 **Licenses:** 6,167,000 (1976) **Television Transmitters:** 461 **Licenses:** 5,180,000 (1976) **Telephones:** 2,751,000 (1976) **Newspapers:** 40 dailies, 472 copies per 1,000 inhabitants (1975)

Weights and Measures: Metric system **Travel Requirements:** Passport; visa obtainable at border or at East German embassy; visa entitlement certificate **International Dialing Code:** 37

The German Democratic Republic is mainly the work of one man, Walter Ulbricht, a ruthless and fanatical leader. Without his dedication and his seemingly tireless efforts from 1945 to 1971, his ruling Communist party and state apparatus, East Germany would undoubtedly have remained in a kind of Central European limbo.

Throughout the 1960s his prestige and power increased dramatically. In this period East Germany grew to be the 10th largest industrial power in the world and the country with the best living standard in the Communist world. Working to his advantage was the desire for security and comfort of the East Germans and their willingness to persevere under adverse conditions.

A major threat to Ulbricht's rule was posed by the reform program of the new Czechoslovak Communist leadership in 1968. The reform aims proclaimed in Prague by Alexander Dubcek were viewed in East Berlin as an elemental danger to the more or less orthodox, militant Marxism/ Leninism practiced by the Ulbricht team. The East German leader recommended suppression; his advice was followed by the Soviet leaders who ordered the August 21, 1968, invasion of Czechoslovakia. Ulbricht was at his zenith in the wake of this move, and it seemed, for a while, that he was setting the tone of Russian foreign policy in Central Europe until his dismissal in 1971 as First Party Secretary for bypassing the Central Committee, over-emphasizing large-scale development projects and obstructing Soviet aims for an accommodation with West Germany.

Ulbricht's successor, Erich Honecker, negotiated agreements of recognition with West Germany in 1974. When workers in neighboring Poland challenged their Communist rulers in 1980-81, Honecker at first echoed Ulbricht's view that democratic unions endangered Communist rule, and East Germany took part in Warsaw Pact military exercises in Poland during early 1981. But at the East German Communist Party Congress in April, Honecker softened his hard-line attitude by supporting the Polish government's actions in dealing with the crisis. Honecker undoubtedly feared that the Polish liberalization might spread to East Germany. He also reversed the Communist government's positon that Germany's division into two states was necessarily permanent.

HISTORY: The Germans made their first major appearance in recorded history when they came into contact with the Romans in the 1st century B.C. By the 5th century A.D. various Germanic tribes had overrun the Roman Empire. After the division of Charlemagne's possessions in 843, the kingdom of the Eastern Franks emerged as the nucleus of Germany, but for most of Germany's history political unification was to prove beyond reach. In 1517 Martin Luther precipitated the Protestant Reformation and Germany was torn by religious strife until the end of the Thirty Years' War (1618-48). In the 18th century Prussia began to emerge as an important power and in the next century successfully challenged Austria for domination of Germany

1815: Congress of Vienna perpetuates the political divisions of Germany and provides for a German Confederation

1862: Bismarck becomes chancellor of Prussia; his goal is to create a unified Germany dominated by Prussia and excluding Austria

1866: Prussia is victorious in the Austro-Prussian War

1870-71: Prussia defeats France in the Franco-Prussian War, enabling Bismarck to achieve his goal of a unified Germany under Prussia; in 1871 William I of Prussia is proclaimed German Emperor

1914-19: Germany is ranged against Allied Powers in World War I and suffers crushing defeat; German Empire collapses and newly formed Weimar Republic is forced to accept harsh terms of Versailles Treaty

1933-36: Hitler is appointed chancellor in 1933 and assumes dictatorial powers; Germany is transformed into a brutal police state; anti-Semitism becomes official policy, culminating eventually in the extermination of six million European Jews; intensive rearmament begins

1938: Hitler annexes Austria and later takes over the Sudetenland from Czechoslovakia

1939-45: Hitler seizes the rest of Czechoslovakia in March 1939; six months later Nazi forces invade Poland, triggering World War II; Nazi forces overrun Western Europe and in 1941 invade the Soviet Union; by 1945, however, Germany is totally defeated, its cities in ruins, and its territory under U.S., Soviet, British, and French occupation; Hitler commits suicide

1945-48: East Germany and part of Berlin come under Soviet occupation and are brought under the control of the Communist-dominated Socialist Unity party. A separate East German state is established under Soviet auspices as a result of the failure of the USSR and the Western occupying powers to agree on a uniform policy for all of Germany

1948-49: Soviet opposition to the plans of the three other Allies for Germany's future results in breakdown of joint Four Power rule; Russians attempt to blockade Berlin, whereupon Western Allies mount gigantic airlift to bring food to West Berliners; in October 1949, following the creation of the Federal Republic of Germany, Russians set up the German Democratic Republic

1953: Anti-Communist revolt in East Germany is crushed by Soviet forces

1955: Soviet Union signs treaty declaring East Germany a sovereign state

1961: Wall is erected around non-Soviet sectors of Berlin to prevent flight of East Germans to the west via West Berlin

1968: East German leader Walter Ulbricht meets with other East European leaders and calls for concerted action to halt liberalization in Czechoslovakia; within months, East German troops join in Soviet-led invasion of Czechoslovakia

1971: Ulbricht resigns as head of Socialist Unity party, is succeeded by Erich Honecker of the party's Central Committee

1972: Traffic Treaty, is signed with West Germany, providing for access to West Berlin

1973: East and West Germany ratify a treaty calling for closer relations. Later in the year, both join the UN. Ulbricht dies

1974: U.S. establishes diplomatic relations with East Germany in September. The two Germanys exchange representatives

1978: Agreement reached with West Germany on construction of new highway to West Berlin and other transit matters. Diplomatic problems arise over status of East Berlin

1979: Soviets begin token withdrawal of 20,000 troops

WEST GERMANY

Area: 95,704 sq. mi. **Population:** 61,517,000 (1980 est.)

Official Name: Federal Republic of Germany **Capital:** Bonn **Nationality:** German **Languages:** German is the official and universal language **Religion:** 49% Protestant, 45% Roman Catholic **Flag:** Black, red, and gold horizontal stripes **Anthem:** The official national anthem consists of the third verse of the old Deutschlandlied, beginning "Unity and Justice and Freedom" **Currency:** Deutsche Mark (2.2 per U.S. $1)

Location: North-central Europe. West Germany is bordered by Denmark and the North Sea on the north, by East Germany and Czechoslovakia on the east, by Austria and Switzerland on the south, and by France, Luxembourg, Belgium, and the Netherlands on the west **Features:** The country is generally flat in the north and hilly in the central and western areas, rising to more than 4,000 feet in the Black Forest and to more than twice that height in the Bavarian Alps **Chief Rivers:** Rhine, Danube, Ems, Weser, Elbe, Main, Mosel, Neckar, Isar

Head of State: President Karl Carstens, born 1914, elected 1979 for 5 years **Head of Government:** Chancellor Helmut Schmidt, born

1918, appointed 1974, elected 1976 **Effective Date of Present Constitution:** May 23, 1949 **Legislative Body:** Parliament (bicameral), consisting of the *Bundestag* and *Bundesrat*. The *Bundestag* has 497 elected members and 22 nonvoting members representing West Berlin, chosen for a term of 4 years. The *Bundesrat* has 41 members appointed by the state governments and 4 consultative members appointed by the West Berlin Senate **Local Government:** 10 states (*Länder*), each with its own legislative and ministerial government. West Berlin, though not legally a component state of West Germany, is closely integrated into the government's political and administrative system

Ethnic Composition: With the exception of a small Danish population in Schleswig-Holstein, the population is German **Population Distribution:** 86% urban **Density:** 643 inhabitants per sq. mi.

Largest Cities: (1976 est.) Berlin (West) 1,984,837, Hamburg 1,717,383, Munich 1,314,865, Cologne 1,013,771, Essen 677,568, Düsseldorf 664,336, Frankfurt-am-Main 636,157, Dortmund 630,609, Stuttgart 600,421

Per Capita Income: $10,509 (1980) **Gross Domestic Product (GDP):** $642 billion (1980) **Economic Statistics:** About 54.6% of GDP is derived from manufacturing (food industry, chemicals, iron and steel, electrical engineering, machinery); 18.5% is from trade, transportation and communications; 13.5% is from agriculture (rye, wheat, oats, barley, potatoes), forestry and fishing **Minerals and Mining:** Coal is the most important mineral resource. There are also substantial deposits of iron ore (mostly low grade), lead and zinc, potash, salt, fluorspar, barites, pyrites, graphites, and basalt. Some natural gas is produced **Labor Force:** 27 million, with 37% in services, 36% in industry, and 6% in agriculture **Foreign Trade:** Exports, chiefly mechanical engineering products, motor vehicles, chemicals, electrical engineering products, and iron and steel, totaled $172 billion in 1979. Imports, mainly foodstuffs, crude oil, nonferrous metals and semifinished products, chemical products, iron and steel, textiles, totaled $160 billion **Principal Trade Partners:** United States, Canada, France, Netherlands, Great Britain, Belgium, Italy, Japan, Switzerland, Austria, Sweden

Vital Statistics: Birthrate, 9.5 per 1,000 of pop. (1977); death rate, 11.5 **Life Expectancy:** 71 years **Health Statistics:** 84 inhabitants per hospital bed, 503 per physician (1976) **Infant Mortality:** 15.5 per 1,000 births **Illiteracy:** Negligible **Primary and Secondary School Enrollment:** 10,262 047 (1976) **Enrollment in Higher Education:** 836,002 (1975) **GNP Expended on Education:** 5.2% (1975)

Transportation: Surfaced roads total 104,487 mi., with 4,200 mi. of superhighways **Motor Vehicles:** 21,410,100 (1977) **Passenger Cars:** 20,020,200 **Railway Mileage:** 19,876 **Ports:** Hamburg, Wilhelmshaven, Bremen, Kiel, Emden, Lübeck **Major Airlines:** Lufthansa operates domestic and international services **Communications:** Partly government controlled **Radio Transmitters:** 346 **Licenses:** 20,909,000 (1975) **Television Transmitters:** 1,153 **Licenses:** 19,226,000 (1975) **Telephones:** 22,800,000 (1977) **Newspapers:** 320 dailies, 289 copies per 1,000 inhabitants (1974)

Weights and Measures: Metric system **Travel Requirements:** Passport, no visa for 90 days **International Dialing Code:** 49

The Federal Republic of Germany was created in 1949 in the British, French, and U.S. occupation zones of Germany, as a vehicle for solving the German problem. Located in the center of Europe and in the center of big-power politics, Germany was divided for centuries; in eight decades as a unified nation, it twice frightened the world. At first resentful of their division into two after 1949, the Germans gradually became accustomed to it.

The Christian Democratic Union/Christian Social Union (CDU/CSU) has been the largest party in every West German *Bundestag*, but has had a majority in only one. Konrad Adenauer, CDU/CSU Chancellor from 1949 to 1963, aligned West Germany with NATO, and presided over an "economic miracle" in which the country recovered from the ravages of war and absorbed millions of ethnic German immigrants from East Germany and Eastern Europe. The free-enterprise policies of Adenauer's Minister of Economics, Ludwig Erhard, were credited with the country's surprising growth, but West Germany was aided by having inherited most of prewar Germany's iron ore, coal, and hydropower, and—after 1958—by membership in the European Community.

The Social Democratic party of Germany (SPD) has been the second-largest in every *Bundestag*;

the Free Democratic party (FDP) has held the balance of power between the CDU/CSU and the SPD since 1961. The FDP went into coalition with the CDU/CSU in 1961, forced the aging Adenauer to retire in favor of Ludwig Erhard in 1963, and brought down Erhard by withdrawing from the coalition in 1966. Kurt Kiesinger then became leader of the CDU/CSU, formed a "grand coalition" with the SPD, and served as chancellor until 1969.

Originally a socialist party, the SPD has become a party of moderate reform within capitalism. Willy Brandt, former Mayor of West Berlin, was its leader in 1969, when it took power in coalition with the FDP. He concentrated on foreign policy, and shocked many Germans by abandoning talk of reunification and by recognizing the East German regime. He also improved relations with other Communist countries and worked to strengthen and expand the EC. Forced to resign because of an espionage scandal in 1974, he was succeeded by Helmut Schmidt, also a Social Democrat. Two successive SPD chancellors have done little to modify their predecesors' free-enterprise policies, and West Germany has remained an economic giant. Growth is slower than in the heady years of the economic miracle, but inflation and unemployment are lower than elsewhere. Prosperity has not eliminated discontent. Terrorist activity has been severe, especially in 1977. In 1978, a controversial new law increased the authority of the police.

In 1981, Chancellor Schmidt sharply attacked the Soviet Union for having invaded Afghanistan and warned Communist leaders not to suppress the workers' movement in Poland. He supported NATO's future deployment of new missiles in Europe but urged that the U.S. first try to negotiate arms reductions with the USSR.

HISTORY: The history of West Germany is bound up with that of Germany as a whole until the years immediately following World War II (*See* East Germany *for pre-WW II chronology*)

1948-49: Western Allies mount massive airlift to Berlin, thwarting Soviet attempt to blockade city; West German constituent assembly adopts provisional constitution for the Federal Republic of Germany; Konrad Adenauer is elected chancellor; East Germany, under Soviet occupation, is set up as a Communist state named the German Democratic Republic

1961: East German government erects Berlin Wall in effort to halt flight of East Germans to the west via West Berlin

1963: Adenauer retires and is succeeded by Ludwig Erhard

1968: Country is rocked by student demonstrations following attempted slaying of left-wing student leader in West Berlin

1966: Kurt Kiesinger becomes chancellor

1969: Willy Brandt becomes chancellor

1970: A nonaggression treaty, recognizing present European borders, is signed with Soviet Union

1972: Nonaggression pact with Soviet Union and Poland ratified. U.S., USSR, Britain, and France sign Final Quadripartite Protocol in Berlin, putting into effect earlier agreements on civilian travel in and around Berlin

1974: Chancellor Willy Brandt resigns over a spy scandal involving a member of his staff. Helmut Schmidt succeeds him. Legal age of majority is lowered from 21 to 18. Two German states recognize each other

1975: Economy is slowed by inflation and high unemployment

1976: Treaty with Poland to allow ethnic Germans to emigrate is ratified. Ruling coalition of Social Democrats and Free Democrats wins close victory in nationwide parliamentary elections

1978: Controversial anti-terrorist laws enacted

1979: Karl Carstens is elected president by the Federal Convention (the *Bundestag* plus members of the *Länder* parliaments)

1980: Signs agreement with East Germany to improve road, rail, and canal links between the two countries

GHANA

Area: 92,099 sq. mi. **Population:** 11,450,000 (1980 est.)

Official Name: Republic of Ghana **Capital:** Accra **Nationality:** Ghanaian **Languages:** English is the official and commercial language; of some 50 tribal languages and dialects spoken, the chief ones are Twi, Fanti, Ga, Ewe, Hausa, Dagbani, and Akan **Religion:** About 43% Christian, 12% Moslem, and the rest animist **Flag:** Red,

gold, and green horizontal stripes, with a 5-pointed black star centered on the gold stripe **Anthem:** National Anthem, beginning "Lift high the flag of Ghana" **Currency:** Cedi (2.75 per U.S. $1)

Location: West Africa. Ghana is bordered on the north by Upper Volta, on the east by Togo, on the south by the Gulf of Guinea, and on the west by the Ivory Coast **Features:** Half of Ghana is less than 500 feet above sea level. The coastline is largely a low sandy shore, backed by plains and intersected by rivers. Northward is a belt of tropical rain forest, broken by densely forested hills and rivers. The far north is a region covered by savanna and grassland plains **Chief Rivers:** Volta, Pra, Tano

Head of State and of Government: President Hilla Limann, born 1934, elected 1979 **Effective Date of Present Constitution:** 1979 **Legislative Body:** National Parliament with 140 members **Local Government:** 9 regions divided into districts; each region is administered by a regional commissioner

Ethnic Composition: Ghanaians are chiefly of black Sudanese stock, the principal groups being the Akan, living mostly along the coast, and the Ashanti, in the forest areas immediately to the north; the Guans, living on the plains of the Volta River; the Ga- and Ewe-speaking peoples of the south and southeast; and the Moshi-Dagomba-speaking tribes of the north **Population Distribution:** 31% urban **Density:** 124 inhabitants per sq. mi.

Largest Cities (M.A. = Metropolitan Area): (1970 census) Accra 564,194 (M.A. 738,498); Kumasi 260,286 (M.A. 345,117); Sekondi-Takoradi 91,874 (M.A. 160,868); Tema 60,767

Per Capita Income: $501 (1980) **Gross National Product (GNP):** $6 billion (1980) **Economic Statistics:** In 1975 about 45% of GNP was from agriculture (cocoa, of which Ghana is the world's leading producer, livestock, fish); 15% from manufacturing and mining; and 40% from trade and services. Industry consists of aluminum smelting and the processing of cocoa, kola nuts, coffee, coconuts, oil palms, and rubber **Minerals and Mining:** Gold is the most important mineral exploited, followed by diamonds. There are large reserves of manganese and bauxite; other minerals include low-grade deposits of iron ore, and deposits of beryl, ilmenite, nickel, graphite, and chromite **Labor Force:** 3.4 million, of which 57% is employed in agriculture, forestry, and fishing, 15.5% in industry and mining, and 27.5% in trade and services **Foreign Trade:** Exports, chiefly cocoa, cocoa butter, manganese, gold, diamonds, timber and aluminum, totaled $1.1 billion in 1979. Imports, mainly machinery and transport equipment, cereals, alumina, petroleum, and textiles, totaled $803 million **Principal Trade Partners:** Britain, United States, Netherlands, West Germany, Switzerland

Vital Statistics: Birthrate, 47 per 1,000 of pop. (1976); death rate, 22 **Life Expectancy:** 52 years **Health Statistics:** 648 inhabitants per hospital bed; 10,310 per physician (1976) **Infant Mortality:** 59 per 1,000 births **Illiteracy:** 70% **Primary and Secondary School Enrollment:** 1,790,270 (1976) **Enrollment in Higher Education:** 9,079 (1975) **GNP Expended on Education:** 4.2% (1976)

Transportation: Paved roads total 3,780 mi. **Motor Vehicles:** 121,700 (1977) **Passenger Cars:** 72,400 **Railway Mileage:** 600 **Ports:** Tema, Takoradi **Major Airlines:** Ghana Airways operates internal and international services **Communications:** Government controlled **Radio Transmitters:** 10 **Receivers:** 10,080,000 (1976) **Television Transmitters:** 4 **Receivers:** 35,000 (1976) **Telephones:** 62,000 (1976) **Newspapers:** 4 dailies, 51 copies per 1,000 inhabitants (1975)

Weights and Measures: Metric system **Travel Requirements:** Passport, visa, valid up to 14 days, $2.25 fee, 3 photos

The first of Britain's African possessions to gain freedom in the postwar decolonization era, Ghana has gone from a democratic parliamentary system, through dictatorship, rule by a military junta, a return to democracy, back to military rule for a short period, and, at present, democratic rule.

During this time, the country also experienced overly ambitious industrialization and near bankruptcy as a result of the extravagances of Kwame Nkrumah, its first leader. Nkrumah was deposed in 1966, and died in exile in 1972.

Ghana, however, possesses a potentially strong economy; major resources range through cocoa, timber, manganese, gold, and electric power. Her people are capable and progressive.

As the Gold Coast, the country had moved steadily toward self-government prior to independence in 1957 and with its new name of Ghana—that of an ancient African empire—was otherwise well prepared for complete sovereignty.

Ghana has many educators, lawyers, doctors, economists, and a well-trained civil service. Development programs are concentrating on diversification of agriculture, an increase of arable land, and the improvement of rural communities. The prime objective is to reduce Ghana's dependency on cocoa exports by increasing exports and self-sufficiency in other products.

From 1966 until 1970, and again beginning with a coup in 1972, Ghana was ruled by military leaders. In 1977 students and professionals rose up in an "intellectuals" revolt, accusing the military government of repression, corruption and fiscal mismanagement. Gen. Ignatius Kutu Acheampong, head of state since 1972, resigned on July 5, 1978, and was succeeded by Lt. Gen. Fred W. K. Akuffo. On Jan. 1, 1979, following a declared state of emergency brought on by workers' and civil servants' strikes, the government legalized political activity for the first time in seven years.

On June 4, 1979, Akuffo's government was overthrown in a coup staged by junior army officers. Fight Lieut. Jerry Rawlings took control. Akuffo and two other former heads-of-state were executed in spite of an appeal for mercy from UN Secretary-General Kurt Waldheim.

Hilla Limann, conservative leader of the People's National Party, was victorious in a run-off following the 1979 elections and took office as president on Sept. 24. Although his party had a slim majority in parliament, Limann found it difficult to get support for his programs.

Progress has been slow in dealing with Ghana's economic problems—lagging production, shortage of staple foods, depressed prices for cocoa and rising costs of imported petroleum products. Transportation has been particularly hard hit by a strike at Ghana Airways in 1980 and by a shortage of replacement parts for the railroad and motor vehicles. The Limann government knows that if it doesn't solve Ghana's problems soon, another military coup may occur.

HISTORY: Ghana was dominated by independent black kingdoms in precolonial times. Following the arrival of the Portuguese in the 15th century, the coastal region soon became known as the Gold Coast because of the rich trade in gold. The gold trade later gave way to the slave trade, which was eventually abolished by the British in the 19th century. In 1874, Britain established the colony of the Gold Coast and in 1901 annexed the neighboring Ashanti kingdom. In the same year a region to the north, known as the Northern Territories, became a British protectorate
1922: Part of neighboring Togoland, a former German colony, is mandated to Britain by League of Nations and administered as part of the Gold Coast
1942-46: Africans are admitted into the government of the Gold Coast, but native agitation for independence mounts under the leadership of United Gold Coast Convention party; party leaders Joseph B. Danquah and Kwame Nkrumah are imprisoned
1949: Nkrumah, following his release, breaks with Danquah and forms his own party, the Convention People's party, and leads campaign of civil disobedience against the British
1951-52: Britain grants new constitution and elections are held; Nkrumah becomes prime minister
1957: The state of Ghana, comprising the Gold Coast and British Togoland, obtains independence, becoming the first black African colony to do so. Joins the UN
1960: Ghana becomes a republic within the British Commonwealth; Nkrumah becomes both chief of state and head of government, and is given the power to rule without parliament whenever he deems it necessary
1962-64: Nkrumah establishes one-party rule; several attempts on his life lead to arrests of numerous leaders in his own Convention People's party and of opposition leader Joseph Danquah, who dies in prison
1966: Nkrumah is deposed by a military coup; a National Liberation Council, headed by Lt. Gen. Joseph A. Ankrah, is set up to rule the country
1969: Ankrah resigns after admitting he received money for political purposes and is succeeded by Gen. Akwasi Afrifa. Civilian government is restored under new constitution
1970: Three-man presidential commission headed by Afrifa is dissolved; former Chief Justice Edward Akufo-Addo is elected president by electoral college

1972: Col. Ignatius Kutu Acheampong leads military coup against the Busia Government and assumes power as head of state; offices of president and prime minister abolished and constitution withdrawn. Kwame Nkrumah dies and his body is returned from Guinea for burial in Ghana
1978: Acheampong is replaced as head of state by Lt. Gen. Fred W.K. Akuffo
1979: Akuffo is overthrown on June 4, and is replaced by an Armed Forces Revolutionary Council, headed by Flight Lieut. Jerry Rawlings. Hilla Limann is elected president and takes office Sept. 24
1980: Pope John Paul II visits Ghana. Pact is made with Romania for building an agro-industrial complex at Brong-Ahafo. Ghana objects to activities of Libya's embassy staff and breaks relations with Tripoli

---

GREECE

Area: 50,944 sq. mi. **Population:** 9,440,000 (1979 est.)

Official Name: Hellenic Republic **Capital:** Athens **Nationality:** Greek **Languages:** Modern Greek; Turkish and Albanian are minority languages **Religion:** 97% of the population belongs to the Greek Orthodox Church; 2% are Moslems **Flag:** Nine equal horizontal stripes of blue and white with a white cross on a blue field in the upper left corner **Anthem:** Hymn of Liberty **Currency:** Drachma (53.7 per U.S. $1)

Location: Southeast Europe, occupying the southern part of the Balkan peninsula and more than 3,000 offshore islands. The Greek mainland is bordered on the north by Bulgaria, Yugoslavia, and Albania; on the east by Turkey and the Aegean Sea; on the south by the Mediterranean Sea; and on the west by the Ionian Sea **Features:** The country is predominantly mountainous, with much of the land dry and rocky **Chief Rivers:** Aliakmon, Peneus, Vardar, Achelous, Nestos, Alpheus, Struma

Head of State: President Constantine Karamanlis, born 1907, elected May 1980 **Head of Government:** Premier George Rallis, born 1918, appointed May 1980 **Effective Date of Present Constitution:** June 1975 **Legislative Body:** Parliament (unicameral), consisting of 300 deputies **Local Government:** 51 prefectures, each headed by an appointed prefect and the autonomous Mt. Athos district

Ethnic Composition: About 96% of the population is Greek. Minorities include Turks (1%), Slavs, Vlachs, Albanians and Bulgarians **Population Distribution:** 64.8% urban **Density:** 185 inhabitants per sq. mi.

Largest Cities (M.A. = Metropolitan Area): (1971 census) Athens 867,023 (M.A. 2,566,775), Salonika 345,799 (M.A. 482,361), Piraeus 187,362, Patras 111,607 (M.A. 112,228)

Per Capita Income: $3,089 (1980) **Gross Domestic Product (GDP):** $29.3 billion (1980) **Economic Statistics:** Agriculture accounted for about 17% of the GDP in 1975 (the principal crops are wheat, tobacco, currants, grapes, olives, citrus fruits, and cotton); the industrial sector contributed about 31% (major industries include textiles; aluminum, nickel and chemical refineries; food processing; mining); services accounted for 50% **Minerals and Mining:** Lignite, bauxite, iron ore, petroleum, chromite, barite and magnesite are exploited **Labor Force:** 3,400,000 (1978), with 38% in agriculture, 30% in services, and 19% in industry **Foreign Trade:** Exports, mainly tobacco, currants, cotton, unprocessed aluminum, iron, nickel, and citrus fruits, totaled $3.9 billion (1979). Imports, chiefly machinery, iron and steel, crude oil, meat, passenger cars and trucks, totaled $9.6 billion **Principal Trade Partners:** West Germany, Italy, United States, France, Japan, Saudi Arabia, Britain, Libya, Netherlands

Vital Statistics: Birthrate, 15.4 per 1,000 of pop. (1977); death rate, 8.2 **Life Expectancy:** 71 years **Health Statistics:** 156 inhabitants per hospital bed; 475 per physician (1976) **Infant Mortality:** 20 per 1,000 births (1977) **Illiteracy:** 10% **Primary and Secondary School Enrollment:** 1,615,286 (1975) **Enrollment in Higher Education:** 111,435 (1975) **GNP Expended on Education:** 1.8% (1974)

Transportation: Paved roads total 10,000 mi. **Motor Vehicles:** 894,900 (1977) **Passenger Cars:** 618,800 **Railway Mileage:** 1,580 mi. **Ports:** Piraeus, Salonika, Iraklion, Patras, Eleusis, Volos **Major Airlines:** Olympic Airways operates domestic and international services **Communications:** Government controlled **Radio Transmitters:** 61 **Receivers:** 2,750,000 (1976) **Television Transmitters:** 120 **Receivers:** 1,165,000 (1976) **Telephones:** 2,180,000 (1975) **Newspapers:** 106 dailies, 107 copies per 1,000 inhabitants (1975)

Weights and Measures: Metric system **Travel Requirements:** Passport, no visa for 2 months **International Dialing Code:** 30

The Hellenes (Greeks) inhabit a mountainous peninsula and its neighboring rocky islands. Agriculture is difficult—and so is administration. Trade and navigation—fostered by excellent harbors—have been vital for thousands of years. Individualism and loyalty to locality are strong.

The ancient Greeks had no national unity, but they were leaders in art, literature, and philosophy; and some of their city-states were the world's first democracies.

Conquered by Macedonia, then by Rome, then by the Ottoman Empire, Greece achieved independence and unity in struggles against the last in the 19th and 20th centuries. Disputes with Turkey concerning land and—more recently—territorial waters are still troublesome. Political stability within Greece has been rare.

Greece was occupied by Germany in World War II and needed considerable assistance from the United States to quell a Commmunist guerrilla movement in the war's aftermath. Greece entered NATO, despite the misgivings of many Greeks about U.S. influence, and Turkish membership, in the alliance. Later, the troubles in Cyprus aggravated ill-feelings toward Turkey.

Governed by short-lived coalition governments from 1946 until 1952, Greece achieved stability under Premier Alexander Papagos in 1952. He died in 1955, and Constantine Karamanlis succeeded him, serving until 1963, when he went into exile after a squabble with King Paul. George Papandreou formed a stable government in 1964, but anti-NATO elements in his past worried many. King Constantine II fired him in 1965, and political unrest followed until the army seized power in 1967.

Col. George Papadopoulous emerged as strong man and premier. He abolished the monarchy and made himself president in 1973, only to be deposed by military colleagues. Gen. Demetrios Ioannides ran the government from behind the scenes until 1974, when he sponsored the ill-fated coup against President Makarios of Cyprus. His fellow-officers deposed him and invited Constantine Karamanlis to resume the premiership.

Karamanlis held an election, which his own New Democracy party won handily. He loosened Greece's connection with NATO and objected to the decision of the United States to end the arms embargo against Turkey. Despite his party's reduced mandate after special elections in 1977, Karamanlis took bold initiatives in foreign affairs. He negotiated a trade treaty with Albania in 1978 that opened the outside world for the strict Albanian Communist regime. In 1979 his government signed an even more important treaty making Greece the 10th full member of the European Community, as of Jan. 1, 1981. Earlier, Greece had rejoined NATO's military wing, from which it had withdrawn in 1974 to protest the Turkish invasion of Cyprus.

After serving six years as premier, Karamanlis was elected president of Greece by the parliament to succeed Konstantinos Tsatsos on May 5, 1980. The new president pledged to stay out of party politics and to represent the entire nation. The former foreign minister, George John Rallis, was elected premier by caucus of the New Democracy party.

HISTORY: Ancient Greece, a small land fragmented into frequently warring city-states, attained its golden age in the Athens of the 5th century B.C. In the following century it fell to the forces of Philip of Macedon, whose son, Alexander the Great, spread Hellenistic civilization widely. In the 2nd century B.C., Greece became a territory of the Roman Empire and eventually was incorporated into the Byzantine Empire. Turkish conquests, completed in the 15th century, made Greece part of the Ottoman Empire

1821-30: Greeks wage war of independence against Turks, who gain help of Egypt; following intervention by Britain, France, and Russia, Greece wins autonomy and finally independence

1832-63: European powers choose Prince Otto of Bavaria to be king of a fully independent Greece; he is deposed in 1862. The following year a Danish prince is chosen as monarch, becoming King George I of the Hellenes

1912-22: Greece takes part in the Balkan Wars of 1912-13 and increases its territory. Outbreak of World War I leads to split between pro-Allied government and neutralist King Constantine I; king abdicates in 1917; Greece joins Allied side and gains additional territory in the postwar settlements; Greece invades Asia Minor and is defeated by Turks

1923: Hostility to dynasty forces George II to leave Greece

1924-35: Greece is proclaimed a republic; after more than a decade of political strife, a plebiscite restores the monarchy

1936-41: John Metaxas becomes premier and institutes a dictatorship that lasts through Italy's World War II invasion of Greece, begun in 1940, and continues up to his death in 1941

1941-50: Germany invades in 1941 and Greece is occupied by Axis forces. With the expulsion of the last of the German troops in 1944, rivalry between Greek Communist and royalist guerrillas erupts into civil war. Under the Truman Doctrine, announced in 1947, the United States sends advisers to the Greek Army and provides $300 million in economic and military aid; Communist forces are finally defeated in 1950

1967: Military junta seizes power. King Constantine II and the royal family flee to Rome after an abortive countercoup; Col. George Papadopoulos becomes premier

1973: Papadopoulos decrees end to monarchy, appoints himself head of new "Hellenic Republic." He is toppled by a bloodless coup. Gen. Phaedon Gizikis becomes president with Dimitrios Ioannides as military dictator; elections are postponed indefinitely

1974: Ioannides sponsors coup in Cyprus. Turkish army invades Cyprus. Military junta leaders turn government over to civilians, ending seven years of military rule. Former Premier Constantine Karamanlis returns from self-imposed exile in Paris and is sworn in as premier by President Gizikis. Britain, Turkey, and Greece, meeting in Geneva, impose new cease-fire on Cyprus. Soon after, when Geneva peace talks break down, Turkish forces resume their advance on Cyprus. Greece withdraws its armed forces from NATO. First free elections in more than a decade result in decisive victory for Premier Karamanlis. In national referendum voters reject monarchy in favor of a republic

1975: Parliament adopts a new constitution and elects Konstantinos Tsatsos as president. Trial of the principal organizers of the 1967 coup results in their death sentences being commuted by cabinet to life imprisonment

1977: Karamanlis's New Democracy party loses 41 seats in parliamentary election, Panhellenic Socialist Movement gains 77 seats

1978: Greek leaders deplore U.S. ending its arms embargo against Turkey. New law makes terrorism a capital offense

1980: Karamanlis becomes president; George John Rallis is selected as premier. Greece rejoins NATO's military wing

1981: Greece becomes full member of European Community (it had previously been an associate member)

GRENADA

Area: 133 sq. mi. **Population:** 110,000 (1979 est.)

Official Name: Grenada **Capital:** St. George's **Nationality:** Grenadian **Languages:** English, with a rarely used Franco-African patois **Religion:** Roman Catholicism, Protestantism **Flag:** A diagonally divided field, yellow at top and bottom and green at sides, with red border on all sides, bearing along top and bottom three yellow stars each; in center a yellow star on a red disk; in center a green triangle with a nutmeg with yellow shell and brown fruit **Anthem:** Hail Grenada **Currency:** East Caribbean dollar (2.70 per U.S. $1)

Location: The southernmost of the Windward Islands in the West Indies. Includes the southern Grenadines, the largest of which is Carriacou **Features:** Volcanic in origin, the islands are chiefly mountainous **Chief Rivers:** There are no large rivers

Head of State: Queen Elizabeth II, represented by a governor-general, Sir Paul Scoon **Head of Government:** Prime Minister Maurice Bishop, born 1944, seized power in 1979 **Effective Date of Present Constitution:** 1967, suspended 1979 **Legislative Body:** Rule is by a 14-member People's Revolutionary Government (PRG) **Local Government:** 7 parishes

Ethnic Composition: Largely of mixed descent, with strains of white settlers, Africans brought in as slaves, and Carib Indians **Population Distribution:** N.A. **Density:** 827 inhabitants per sq. mi.

Largest Cities: (1970 census) St. George's 6,313, Gouyave 2,498, Grenville 1,723, Victoria 1,673

Per Capita Income: $660 (1979 est.) **Gross Domestic Product (GDP):** $71 million (1979 est.) **Economic Statistics:** The economy is agricultural, with sugar, coconuts, nutmeg, cocoa, and bananas the chief exports. Yams, rice, breadfruit, and corn are grown for food. Tourism is important **Minerals and Mining:** Offshore exploration for gas and oil in progress **Labor Force:** 36,000, of which 40% are employed in agriculture, forestry and fishing **Foreign Trade:** Exports, chiefly cocoa, nutmeg and bananas, totaled $22 million (1979). Imports totaled $45 million **Principal Trade Partners:** Britain, West Germany, United States, Canada, Caribbean countries, Netherlands

Vital Statistics: Birthrate, 27.4 per 1,000 of pop. (1975); death rate, 5.9 **Life Expectancy:** 63 years **Health Statistics:** 144 inhabitants per hospital bed; 4,000 per physician (1974) **Infant Mortality:** 23.5 per 1,000 births **Illiteracy:** 24% **Education Statistics:** 71 primary and secondary schools with a combined enrollment of 34,863 (1971) **Enrollment in Higher Education:** c. 100 (1974) **GNP Expended on Education:** 9.4% (1975)

Transportation: Surfaced roads total 375 mi. **Motor Vehicles:** 3,900 (1971) **Passenger Cars:** 3,800 **Railway Mileage:** None **Ports:** St. George's, Grenville, Hillsborough **Major Airlines:** LIAT **Communications:** Government owned **Radio Transmitters:** 5 **Receivers:** 22,000 (1976) **Television:** None **Telephones:** 5,000 (1976) **Newspapers:** N.A.

Weights and Measures: British and metric systems **Travel Requirements:** Passport or proof of citizenship **Direct Dialing Code:** 809

Formerly a dependency of the United Kingdom and later a member of the British-controlled Federation of the West Indies, Grenada became an internally self-governing state on March 3, 1967. The United Kingdom retained responsibility for defense and external affairs. On February 7, 1974, Grenada became independent within the British Commonwealth of Nations, with a parliamentary system of government based on Great Britain's.

Grenada, known as the "Isle of Spice," is famous for its nutmeg, cocoa and cinnamon. Tourism is another mainstay of the island's economy.

Politically, Grenada has been the scene of widespread unrest since independence. The controversy centered on Prime Minister Eric Gairy's rule, considered by many Grenadians to be dictatorial. Rioting broke out in 1973 and 1974, and a secret police squad retaliated by employing strong-arm tactics. Subsequently, tourism declined and many Grenadians fled. In late 1976 Gairy was narrowly reelected with rural support.

In a coup marked by the killing of two policemen, Maurice Bishop, a London-educated lawyer, and the socialistic New Jewel Movement seized the government on March 13, 1979. Bishop then became prime minister, and a 14-member People's Revolutionary Government took office. The constitution was suspended, but Grenada remained within the British Commonwealth. Bishop invited Cuban instructors to train his new People's Revolutionary Army and made a deal for Cuban workers to build a jet airport near St. George's. In 1981, some 300 islanders (more than one of every 350) were reportedly being held as political prisoners. Land reform had been launched, with state farms created out of some of Grenada's private holdings, and cooperative farming was being vigorously encouraged.

HISTORY: The original inhabitants of the islands were Arawak Indians who were expelled by the warlike Caribs shortly before the visit of Columbus in 1498. An abortive English settlement in 1609 was followed by French settlement and control from 1650 to 1762. Britain controlled the islands for over 200 years, except for five years of French rule (1779-83) during the American Revolution
1833: Slavery is abolished
1967: Grenada assumes Associated State status
1974: Independence is attained. Grenada is admitted to UN
1975: Treaty is signed with EC
1979: The New Jewel (for Joint Endeavor for Welfare, Education and Liberation) Movement seizes the government, and Maurice Bishop becomes prime minister. Grenada joins the "nonaligned" nations in a summit meeting in Cuba
1980: Bombing assassination attempt against the life of Bishop fails

---

GUATEMALA

Area: 42,042 sq. mi. **Population:** 7,046,000 (1979 est.)

Official Name: Republic of Guatemala **Capital:** Guatemala **Nationality:** Guatemalan **Languages:** Spanish is the official and predominant language; 20 varieties of the Maya-Quiché Indian dialects are spoken in the countryside **Religion:** Overwhelmingly Roman Catholic **Flag:** Blue, white, and blue vertical bands, with the national coat of arms in the center **Anthem:** National Anthem, beginning "Blessed Guatemala" **Currency:** Quetzal (1 per U.S. $1)

Location: Central America. Guatemala is bordered on the north by Mexico, on the east by Belize and the Caribbean, on the southeast by Honduras and El Salvador, on the southwest by the Pacific Ocean, and on the west by Mexico **Features:** The central highland region constitutes about one-fifth of the country's land surface. The Pacific plain is a narrow belt between mountains and ocean, while the Caribbean lowlands consist of fertile river valleys. The northern part of the country is dominated by the lowland forest of Petén **Chief Rivers:** Motagua, Usumacinta, Polochic, Samalá

Head of State and of Government: President: Gen. Fernando Romeo Lucas García, born 1924, elected 1978 **Effective Date of Present Constitution:** 1966 **Legislative Body:** National Congress (unicameral), consisting of 61 deputies elected for 4 years **Local Government:** 22 departments, administered by governors appointed by the president, and a central district, the capital city

Ethnic Composition: Pure-blooded descendants of the Maya Indians make up almost 50% of the population; the rest is largely of mixed Spanish and Indian descent **Population Distribution:** 36% urban **Density:** 168 inhabitants per sq. mi.

Largest Cities: (1973 census) Guatemala 700,538, Tiquisate 67,555, Quezaltenango 65,526, Escuintla 64,851

Per Capita Income: $1,067 (1980) **Gross National Product (GNP):** $7.5 billion (1980) **Economic Statistics:** In 1973 about 28% of GNP came from agriculture (coffee, cotton, sugar cane, bananas, corn, beans, rice, wheat); 16% is derived from industry (foodstuffs, tobacco, textiles, furniture, paper and paper products, leather goods, chemical products, tires, machinery and metal products); and 44% from trade and services **Minerals and Mining:** Zinc, silver, lead, nickel, petroleum and limestone are exploited **Labor Force:** 1,895,168 (1975), of which 58% is employed in agriculture, 24% in trade and services and 18% in industry **Foreign Trade:** Exports, chiefly coffee, bananas, cotton, sugar and meat, totaled $1.2 billion in 1979. Imports, mainly industrial machinery, textiles, chemicals and pharmaceutical products, and construction materials, totaled $1.5 billion **Principal Trade Partners:** United States, Central American countries, West Germany, Japan, Venezuela

Vital Statistics: Birthrate, 42.6 per 1,000 of pop. (1976); death rate, 9.3 (1976) **Life Expectancy:** 52 years **Health Statistics:** 457 inhabitants per hospital bed; 4,338 per physician (1973) **Infant Mortality:** 77 per 1,000 births (1976) **Illiteracy:** 70% **Primary and Secondary School Enrollment:** 749,450 (1975) **Enrollment in Higher Education:** 25,978 (1976) **GNP Expended on Education:** 1.7% (1976)

Transportation: Paved roads total 1,700 mi. **Motor Vehicles:** 132,800 (1976) **Passenger Cars:** 82,700 **Railway Mileage:** 588 **Ports:** Pto. Barrios, Sto. Tomás de Castilla, San José, Champerico **Major Airlines:** AVIATECA operates domestic and international services **Communications:** Partly government controlled **Radio Transmitters:** 95 **Receivers:** 265,000 (1976) **Television Transmitters:** 12 **Receivers:** 120,000 **Telephones:** 53,000 (1974) **Newspapers:** 11 dailies, 39 copies per 1,000 inhabitants (1972)

Weights and Measures: Metric system and local units **Travel Requirements:** Proof of citizenship; tourist card good for stay up to 6 months but usable only within 6 months of issue; $1 fee **International Dialing Code:** 502

Assassinations and kidnappings by extremists of both the left and right continue to plague Guatemala, the largest and potentially the wealthiest of the Central American republics.

In effect, there are two Guatemalas—one Spanish and one Indian. The Indians, concentrated in the picturesque central highlands, speak little Spanish and cling to peasant ways that originated with their Mayan ancestors well before the Spanish conquest. Constituting almost half the population, they account for the low economic and social standards of the country as a whole. They have been caught in the middle of the conflict, and some have been joining guerrilla groups.

The educational deficit alone is staggering. Illiteracy still hovers at over 60 percent, and about half the children of school age get little or no schooling despite some progress in school construction. The problem is complicated by the necessity of teaching in Indian languages before transferring to Spanish, and by the government's failure to provide funds.

Guatemala's wealth has traditionally been land-based. Coffee and cotton, the major products, are picked by the Indian population at low wages. In recent years, wider industrial opportunities have been provided by the Central American Common Market. Tires, clothing, foodstuffs, and pharmaceuticals have helped to diversify the economy although many of the industries are little more than assembly operations employing few workers. Oil reserves were discovered in 1976, and in 1980 Petromaya began to export modest amounts.

Since the election to the presidency in 1978 of Gen. Romeo Lucas Garcia, Guatemala has been virtually in a state of civil war. On one side is a coalition of guerrillas, Social Democratic politicians, unions, professors, students and Indian peasants. On the other side is the army, whose frequent brutal attacks on suspected rebel leaders have been abetted by right-wing "death squads." Assassinations, kidnappings, and other violent acts have been commonplace.

HISTORY: The Mayas, one of the most advanced of the Indian tribes, flourished in Guatemala for centuries before the arrival of the Spanish conquistadors. In the 12th century, however, Mayan civilization began to decline and its downfall was completed by the Spanish conquest in the 16th century. Under Spanish rule Guatemala was the seat of a captaincy general

1821: Guatemala is granted independence from Spain and with the other Central American countries is annexed to Mexico

1823-1825: Central American nations secede from Mexico and establish United Provinces of Central America

1839-1944: Guatemala becomes an independent republic and for more than a century is governed by the military

1951-57: Col. Jacobo Arbenz Guzmán, a leftist-leaning president, institutes social and agrarian reforms and expropriates holdings of foreign plantation owners, including United Fruit Co. Communist influence in Arbenz regime leads to strained relations with United States. With U.S. support, Col. Carlos Castillo Armas overthrows Arbenz in 1954 and returns expropriated land; Castillo Armas is assassinated in 1957

1958-63: Country is thrown into political turmoil and ruled by military juntas. State of siege is declared in 1963 to deal with growing terrorism and sabotage by extremists of right and left

1965-68: A new constitution takes effect in 1965; free elections are held the following year and Julio César Méndez Montenegro, candidate of moderately leftist Revolutionary party, becomes president. He suspends constitutional guarantees in January 1968 following terrorist slayings of two U.S. military officials. In August, U.S. Ambassador John Mein is killed

1970: Carlos Arana Osorio, leading a right-wing coalition, wins presidential election. Terrorists kidnap several foreign diplomats, kill West German Ambassador. State of siege imposed

1974: Alleged vote fraud installs Gen. Kjell Laugerud García as president; violence ensues

1975: Britain agrees to resume talks with Guatemala on future of Belize (British Honduras). Guatemala has claimed sovereignty over the British dependency for more than 100 years

1976: Severe damage and 22,500 deaths caused by earthquakes

1978: Gen. Romeo Lucas García, government-backed moderate conservative, is elected president in runoff vote in Congress

1980: Indian peasants seize Spanish embassy in Guatemala City to protest government strong-arm measures; police storm building and 39 persons die in ensuing fire. Left-wing groups unify as Patriotic Liberation Front. Vice-President Francisco Villegrán Kramer resigns, protesting his government's violations of human rights

1981: During Holy Week 152 persons die in acts of political violence. Guatemala signs treaty with Britain settling century-old Belize dispute

GUINEA

Area: 94,925 sq. mi. **Population:** 4,890,000 (1979 est.)

Official Name: People's Revolutionary Republic of Guinea **Capital:** Conakry **Nationality:** Guinean **Languages:** French is the official language; the languages of 8 ethnic groups are recognized as national languages. The two main languages are Peul (Fulani) and Mandé **Religion:** About 75% Moslem, 24% animist, less than 1% Christian **Flag:** Red, yellow, and green vertical stripes **Anthem:** Liberty **Currency:** Syli (20.6 per U.S. $1)

Location: West Africa. Guinea is bordered by Senegal and Mali on the north, the Ivory Coast on the east, Liberia and Sierra Leone on the south, the Atlantic Ocean on the west, and Guinea-Bissau on the northwest **Features:** The country consists of a low-lying coastal area, a pastoral plateau, a forest region along the Liberian border, and a dry area in the north **Chief Rivers:** Niger, Bafing, Konkouré, Koliba, Milo

Head of State: President Ahmed Sékou Touré born 1922; in power since 1958, reelected 1975 for 7 years; he is secretary-general of the country's only party **Head of Government:** Premier: Dr. Lansana Béavogui took office April 1972 **Effective Date of Present Constitution:** November 12, 1958 **Legislative Body:** National Assembly (unicameral), consisting of 210 members elected for 5 years. All members belong to the Democratic party of Guinea **Local Government:** 35 administrative regions

Ethnic Composition: Of about 18 tribes in the country the most important are the Peuls (Fulani), Malinké (Mandingo), and Soussou **Population Distribution:** 9% urban **Density:** 52 inhabitants per sq. mi.

Largest City: (1973 est.) Conakry 198,000

Per Capita Income: $178 (1978) **Gross National Product (GNP):** $850 million (1978) **Economic Statistics:** About 40% of GNP is from agriculture (coffee, palm products, corn, millet, pineapples, bananas, rice, cassava), forestry, and fishing; 20% from mining, 14% from manufacturing (textiles, truck assembly, sawmilling, canning, paints, soap, cigarettes, plastics, furniture) **Minerals and Mining:** Bauxite and iron ore deposits are among the richest in the world; other minerals are diamonds and gold **Labor Force:** About 85% of the working population is engaged in plantation and subsistence agriculture. About 136,000 are wage earners (1976), mostly in public service **Foreign Trade:** Exports, chiefly alumina, pineapples, coffee, palm kernels, bananas, and iron ore, totaled $334 million in 1978. Imports, cotton textiles, rice, vehicles, cement, machinery, petroleum products, and sugar, totaled $272 million **Principal Trade Partners:** United States, France, West Germany, Spain, Italy, Romania, Canada, USSR, Britain

Vital Statistics: Birthrate, 47 per 1,000 of pop. (1975); death rate, 23 **Life Expectancy:** 41 years **Health Statistics:** 588 inhabitants per hospital bed; 15,100 per physician (1976) **Infant Mortality:** 172 per 1,000 births **Illiteracy:** 90% **Education Statistics:** 2,287 primary and secondary schools, with combined enrollment of 241,033 (1971) **Enrollment in Higher Education:** 2,874 (1972) **GNP Expended on Education:** 5.9% (1972)

Transportation: Paved roads total 3,000 mi. **Motor Vehicles:** 21,000 (1972) **Passenger Cars:** 10,200 **Railway Mileage:** 500 **Ports:** Conakry, Kassa, Benty, Kamsar **Major Airlines:** Air Guinée is the local carrier; 7 other lines provide international service **Communications:** State owned **Radio Transmitters:** 5 **Receivers:** 120,000 (1976) **Television Transmitters:** 1 **Telephones:** 10,000 (1974) **Newspapers:** 1 daily, 1 copy per 1,000 inhabitants (1975)

Weights and Measures: Metric system **Travel Requirements:** Passport, visa, valid 3 months, $5 fee, 3 pictures

Committed by its militant leader, Ahmed Sékou Touré, in 1958 to "poverty in freedom rather than riches in slavery," Guinea has followed a tortuous course that has assured poverty but little freedom.

In 1958 Guinea was the only French colony to vote *non* to General de Gaulle's proposed community of semiautonomous nations still closely linked to France. Although, for France's former colonies, the community was to be a step toward eventual sovereignty, accompanied by aid and trade, Guinea opted for independence.

Hostility between France and Guinea persisted for the next two decades and ended officially only with a state visit by French President Valéry Giscard d'Estaing in December 1978.

Until recently, Guinea's huge mineral resources and great hydroelectric potential had been neglected. In addition to iron ore, gold, and diamonds, Guinea possesses bauxite deposits estimated to be a third of the world's total. An international consortium of aluminum companies, in which the Guinean government holds 49 percent interest, is now operating a big bauxite mining complex at Boké in northern Guinea. Production at more than nine million tons a year is expected to earn Guinea $500 million over a 20-year period.

In late 1970, Touré's long rule was shaken by the landing at Conakry of a small, seaborne guerrilla force, which Touré charged was an invasion by Portuguese mercenaries and Guinean renegades, backed by Portugal and launched from neighboring Portuguese Guinea. Denied by Portugal, the charge was supported by a UN commission.

HISTORY: Guinea possesses a rich ethnic and cultural heritage derived from the empires of Ghana, Mali, and Songhai, which ranged from the western Sudan to the West African coast between the 10th and 15th centuries. In the 15th century, the Portuguese, followed by the Dutch, English, and French, opened the country to European contacts and trade. Following the establishment of a protectorate by France in 1849, French penetration inland met with strong resistance from Fulani and Malinké chieftains. Resistance was finally crushed with the defeat in 1898 of the popular hero and chieftain Samory Touré, from whom President Sékou Touré is said to be descended

1958: Guinea, the only French West African territory to vote against membership in the French Community, becomes an independent republic; Sékou Touré, an acknowledged Marxist although rejecting Marxism as inapplicable to Africa, becomes president and his Democratic party of Guinea becomes the only political party; France abruptly withdraws all aid

1959-61: Guinea turns to the Soviet bloc and Communist China for assistance, and promotes African unity by forming short-lived union with Ghana and Mali

1965: Guinea suspends relations with France after charging that France encouraged a plot to overthrow Touré government

1966: Touré grants asylum to deposed Ghanaian President Nkrumah and names him honorary co-president of Guinea; new Ghanaian government breaks relations with Guinea

1970: Dispute with Portugal develops over charges of rebel infiltration from Guinea to Portuguese Guinea. Post of prime minister is created and the government is reorganized. Dr. Louis Lansana Béavogui becomes prime minister

1975: Relations restored with France. Touré elected for third term

1976: Discovery of a series of assassination plots on the life of President Touré announced by his administration

1978: Guinea and Senegal restore diplomatic relations; French President Giscard d'Estaing visits

1979: In move to improve human-rights situation, several hundred political prisoners are freed. Touré visits United States

1980: Touré escapes assassination attempt May 14. Dispute arises with neighboring Guinea-Bissau over boundaries of possibly oil-bearing ocean floor

GUINEA-BISSAU

Area: 13,948 sq. mi. **Population:** 777,214 (1979 census)

Official Name: Republic of Guinea-Bissau **Capital:** Bissau **Nationality:** Guinean **Languages:** Portuguese and Crioulo, a creole lingua franca **Religion:** 66% animist, 30% Moslem, 4% Christian **Flag:** A black star on a red vertical stripe at the hoist and equal horizontal stripes in the fly of gold over light green **Anthem:** Long Live the Glorious Country **Currency:** Guinea-Bissau escudo (36.7 per U.S. $1)

Location: On the west coast of Africa, bounded by the Atlantic Ocean on the west, Senegal on the north, and Guinea on the east and south **Features:** A low-lying coastal plain with savanna, swamps, and rain forest. Large sections are frequently covered by tidal waters. There are 18 main offshore islands, including the Bijagós Archipelago **Chief Rivers:** Cacheu, Mansoa, Geba, Grande de Buba, Corubal

Head of State and Goverment: President of the Council of the Revolution, Gen. João Bernardo Vieira, born 1939, assumed power in coup of Nov. 14, 1980 **Effective Date of Constitution:** New constitution pending **Legislative Body:** All power resides with the 9-member Council of the Revolution **Local Government:** 12 administrative regions

Ethnic Composition: Except for small groups of Portuguese and mulattos the people are mostly indigenous (Balanta, Fulani, Mandyako, Malinké, and Pepel) **Population Distribution:** N.A. **Density:** 56 inhabitants per sq. mi.

Largest Cities: (1979 census) Bissau 109,486

Per Capita Income: $280 (1978) **Gross Domestic Product (GDP):** $174 million (1978) **Economic Statistics:** Agriculture probably accounts for well over 50% of the GDP. About 70% of the agricultural production is consumed locally **Minerals and Mining:** No commercial mining exists. There are potentially large deposits of bauxite **Labor Force:** 410,000; 94% are employed in agriculture **Foreign Trade:** Exports, chiefly peanuts, coconuts, frozen shrimp and fish, wood, totaled $11 million in 1978. Imports, chiefly textiles, vehicles, rice, consumer goods, fuel totaled approximately $50 million **Principal Trade Partners:** Portugal, Angola, Spain, West Germany, Sweden, Britain, U.S., Cape Verde

Vital Statistics: Birthrate, 40.1 per 1,000 of pop. (1975); death rate 25.1 **Life Expectancy:** 34 years **Health Statistics:** 481 inhabitants per hospital bed; 7,571 per physician (1976) **Infant Mortality:** 47.1 per 1,000 births **Illiteracy:** 95% **Primary and Secondary School Enrollment:** 86,756 (1976) **Enrollment in Higher Education:** N.A. **GNP Expended on Education:** 1.2% (1972)

Transportation: Paved roads total 265 mi. **Motor Vehicles:** 5,124 **Passenger Cars:** 3,268 **Railway Mileage:** None **Ports:** Bissau, Bolama **Major Airlines:** TAP **Communications:** Government owned **Radio Transmitters:** 2 **Licenses:** 11,000 (1976) **Television:** None **Telephones:** 3,000 (1973) **Newspapers:** 1 daily, 11 copies per 1,000 inhabitants (1975)

Weights and Measures: Metric system **Travel Requirements:** Passport, visa

---

Poor, diseased and subject to forced labor, Africans of Portuguese Guinea developed a national liberation movement in the early 1960s. By 1970 rebels claimed control of two-thirds of the country. The movement was led by the African Party for the Independence of Guinea and Cape Verde (PAIGC), whose basic tenet of doctrine was the "unity" of Guinea-Bissau and Cape Verde Islands, and was headed by Amilcar and Luis Cabral. The PAIGC proclaimed independence in 1973, but Portugal rejected the claim. However, the 1974 coup in Portugal ultimately resulted in an agreement granting independence for Guinea-Bissau on September 24 of that year, making Guinea-Bissau the first Portuguese African territory to achieve independence. Luis de Almeida Cabral became president, Amilcar Cabral having been killed in 1973.

Guinea-Bissau is currently struggling with all the problems that face developing nations, especially in the areas of education, health care, road development and electrification.

HISTORY: The Portuguese, sailing for Prince Henry the Navigator, reached the area in 1446. Slave trading was important in the 17th and 18th centuries

1879: Portuguese Guinea is separated from the administrative control of the Cape Verde Islands

1962: Revolt against Portuguese rule begins

1974: Portuguese Guinea attains independence as Guinea-Bissau

1978: Premier Francisco Mendes dies in auto crash

1980: Dispute with Guinea arises over limits of possible offshore oilfields. Cabral government is overthrown Nov. 14 in coup led by Premier João Bernardo Vieira, who opposes union with Cape Verde

GUYANA

Area: 83,000 sq. mi. **Population:** 820,000 (1978 est.)

Official Name: Cooperative Republic of Guyana **Capital:** Georgetown **Nationality:** Guyanese **Languages:** English is the official language; other spoken languages include various East Indian dialects, Chinese, Portuguese, and a patois used by those of African origin **Religion:** About 57% Christian (chiefly Anglican), 33% Hindu, 9% Moslem **Flag:** A green field with a black-edged red triangular pennant superimposed on a white-edged yellow triangular pennant **Anthem:** Dear land of Guayana **Currency:** Guyana dollar (2.55 per U.S. $1)

Location: Northeast coast of South America. Guyana is bordered on the north by the Atlantic Ocean, on the east by Suriname, on the south and southwest by Brazil, and on the northwest by Venezuela **Features:** The country is divided into a low-lying coastal region, a heavily forested interior, and a region of mountains and savannas in the south and west **Chief Rivers:** Essequibo, Courantyne, Berbice, Mazaruni, Cuyuni, Demerara

Head of State and Government: Executive President Linden Forbes Sampson Burnham, born 1923, took office Oct. 6, 1980. He is assisted by a prime minister, Ptolemy Alexander Reid, who is also First Vice President **Effective Date of Present Constitution:** Oct. 6, 1980 **Legislative Body:** National Assembly (unicameral), consisting of 53 members elected by proportional-representation for 5 years and 12 members elected by local councils **Local Government:** 10 regions

Ethnic Composition: About 51% of the population is of East Indian descent; 31% African and African mixed; 6% indigenous Amerindians, and small groups of Portuguese and Chinese **Population Distribution:** 40% urban **Density:** 9.9 inhabitants per sq. mi.

Largest Cities (M.A. = Metropolitan Area): (1976 est.) Georgetown 72,049 (M.A. 187,056); (1971 est.) Linden 23,956; New Amsterdam 17,782; Corriverton 10,502; Rosehall 5,018

Per Capita Income: $660 (1979) **Gross National Product (GNP):** $548 million (1979) **Economic Statistics:** In 1973 about 20% of GNP came from agriculture (sugar, rice, corn, coconuts, coffee); 12% from manufacturing (cigarettes, matches, margarine, edible oils, beverages, sugar milling, aluminum smelting, wood and pulp); 18% from mining; and 22% from trade and services **Minerals and Mining:** Bauxite is the principal mineral. Diamonds and gold are also mined **Labor Force:** 242,000 (1975), with 31% in industry and mining and 29% in agriculture **Foreign Trade:** Exports, chiefly bauxite and aluminum, sugar, rice, timber, shrimp, gold, and diamonds, totaled $291 million in 1979. Imports, mainly foodstuffs, manufactured goods, machinery, petroleum products, beverages, and tobacco, totaled $318 million **Principal Trade Partners:** Britain, United States, Commonwealth Caribbean countries, Canada, Japan

Vital Statistics: Birthrate 26.6 per 1,000 of pop. (1976); death rate, 7.1 **Life Expectancy:** 67 years **Health Statistics:** 199 inhabitants per hospital bed; 3,249 per physician (1975) **Infant Mortality:** 40 per 1,000 births **Illiteracy:** 13% **Primary and Secondary School Enrollment:** 213,679 (1976) **Enrollment in Higher Education:** 2,307 (1973) **GNP Expended on Education:** 7.0% (1976)

Transportation: Paved roads total 480 mi. **Motor Vehicles:** 41,400 (1977) **Passenger Cars:** 28,400 **Railway Mileage:** 68 **Port:** Georgetown **Major Airlines:** Guyana Airways Corp. operates domestic passenger and international cargo flights **Communications:** Government and privately owned **Radio Transmitters:** 8 **Receivers:** 275,000 (1976) **Television:** None **Telephones:** 23,000 (1976) **Newspapers:** 3 dailies, 155 copies per 1,000 inhabitants (1974)

Weights and Measures: British standards. The metric system is being introduced **Travel Requirements:** Passport; no visa for 30 days; onward ticket **International Dialing Code:** 592

Aptly termed the "land of the waters" by the indigenous Amerindians, Guyana, along most of its coastline, is below sea level. The land along the Atlantic, where most people of the South American country live, is made habitable by the 300-year-old seawalls and drainage system built by the Dutch.

Until the early 19th century, under the British, various colonization plans failed before the lucrative sugar industry was introduced. The British imported African slaves, indentured Portuguese and East Indians, and Chinese. These waves of immigration have determined Guyana's racial composition and the experience of slavery and indentured servitude has molded the country's political and social life.

Guyana has unresolved boundary disputes with two of its neighbors, Venezuela and Suriname. Venezuela claims the area west of the Essequibo River, more than half the size of Guyana as now constituted, while the dispute with Suriname relates to which interior river—the Courantyne or the New River—is the Guyana/Suriname border.

Gaining independence from Britain in 1966, Guyana set out on an autonomous line of development as a "cooperative republic" in 1970. In the words of its prime minister, Forbes Burnham, it planned to "pursue relentlessly the policy of owning and controlling our natural resources." Burnham has established the only Marxist government in South America.

In early 1975, Guyana nationalized the important bauxite mining industry by taking over Reynolds Metal Co. operations. By mid-1976, after sugar production had also been nationalized, some 80 percent of the nation's goods and services were in government hands. Succeeding years saw a steady deterioration of the economy, and in 1981 it was estimated that the republic had experienced its first year of negative economic growth in 1980.

In the meantime, Burnham's government became increasingly authoritarian. By 1979, it was estimated that as much as one sixth of the national budget was devoted to the maintenance of the military forces and various paramilitary organizations loyal to the prime minister.

Toward the end of 1980, Burnham promulgated a new constitution which concentrated power in the office of the president, to which post he was then elected by the parliament. In December parliamentary elections, denounced by the opposition as fraudulent, his People's National Congress party (PNC) captured 41 of 53 seats, defeating another leftist faction, the People's Progressive party (PPP), led by Burnham's long-time political rival, former Prime Minister Cheddi B. Jagan.

A mass-murder suicide on an appalling scale at Jonestown, a community set up in the jungle by the San Francisco-based People's Temple, turned world attention to Guyana in November 1978. The bizarre tragedy began with the murders of U.S. Representative Leo J. Ryan of California, who had flown to Guyana to investigate reports that cult members were being held against their will, and four members of his party. The five were killed at the Port Kaituma airport on November 18, just after visiting Jonestown and getting word that 20 Temple members wanted to defect. After news of the murders was radioed to Jonestown, the Rev. Jim Jones, self-proclaimed messiah, led the whole community in a previously rehearsed suicide plan. It was carried out mainly by mixing a flavored drink with cyanide, but there was also some gunfire. The U.S. military removed 913 bodies of Temple members by air to Dover (Del.) Air Force Base. As many as 26 Guyanese children may have been among the victims. Nearly all of the other dead, including Jones, were from the U.S.

HISTORY: Little is known of the history of Guyana before the arrival of Europeans. When European explorers came to Guyana in the late 1500s and early 1600s, they found Arawak, Carib, and Warrau Indians living in the area. In the late 17th century the country was settled by the Dutch and in the following century alternated between Dutch and British rule. By 1815, British rule was firmly established

1831: Three colonies of Berbice, Essequibo, and Demerara are united into the colony of British Guiana

1837: Slaves are emancipated

1928: British Guiana gains limited representative government

1953-57: A new constitution is adopted providing for a bicameral legislature and ministerial responsibility. Elections are held, People's Progressive party (PPP), led by Cheddi Jagan and generally supported by East Indians, captures 18 of the 24 elective seats. Six months after the election, the British suspend the constitution, charging Communist subversion of the British Guiana government; interim regime takes over

1961: Colony is granted full internal self-government, a new constitution is introduced; the PPP wins 20 of the 35 seats in the Legislative Assembly, Jagan is named prime minister

1962-64: Rivalry between PPP and People's National Congress (PNC), supported by the Negroes, leads to violence

1964: Two parties, PNC and the United Force, form a coalition government, with PNC leader Forbes Burnham as prime minister. Communal rioting re-erupts, a state of emergency is declared, and British troops are brought in to restore order

1966: Guyana becomes an independent state within the British Commonwealth and joins the UN

1968: Burnham's PNC wins general election

1970: Guyana is proclaimed a republic

1973: Guyana, Barbados, Jamaica, and Trinidad-Tobago establish the Caribbean Community and Common Market (CARICOM)

1976: People's Progressive party (PPP), led by Dr. Cheddi Jagan, ends its three-year boycott of the National Assembly

1978: More than 900 die in murder-suicide tragedy of the People's Temple cult in Jonestown

1980: New constitution adopted, vesting executive power in the president; Burnham assumes presidency. Amid charges of fraud, PNC overwhelms PPP in general election

HAITI

Area: 10,683 sq. mi. **Population:** 4,919,000 (1979 est.)
Official Name: Republic of Haiti **Capital:** Port-au-Prince **Nationality:** Haitian **Languages:** French is the official language but is spoken by only about 10% of the population; Creole, a mixture of 17th century French, African dialects, and English, Spanish, and Indian words, is spoken by 90% **Religion:** Most of the population professes Roman Catholicism, the state religion; voodoo is widely practiced, especially in the rural areas **Flag:** Black and red vertical halves with the national coat-of-arms in the center **Anthem:** Song of Dessalines **Currency:** Gourde (5 per U.S. $1)
Location: West Indies, occupying the western third of the island of Hispaniola in the Caribbean Sea. Haiti's only land border is with the Dominican Republic, on the east **Features:** About two-thirds of the country is mountainous terrain unsuitable for cultivation **Chief Rivers:** Artibonite, Guayamouc
Head of State and of Government: President Jean-Claude Duvalier, born 1951; elected president in February 1971, he assumed the title "President for Life" on the death of his father, François Duvalier, in April 1971 **Effective Date of Present Constitution:** June 1964, amended in 1971 **Legislative Body:** Legislative Chamber (unicameral), consisting of 58 deputies, elected for 6 years but with little power **Local Government:** 5 departments, each headed by an appointed prefect
Ethnic Composition: Over 90% of the population is of African descent, nearly 10% is mulatto **Population Distribution:** 23.7% urban **Density:** 460 inhabitants per sq. mi.
Largest Cities: (1978 est.) Port-au-Prince 493,932, (1971 census) Cap-Haïtien 46,217, Pétionville 35,257, Gonaives 29,261
Per Capita Income: $269 (1979) **Gross National Product (GNP):** $1.3 billion (1979) **Economic Statistics:** 44.7% of GNP comes from agriculture (coffee, sugar, sisal, cotton); 37% from services, of which 21.8% is derived from tourism; 14.4% from manufacturing (processing of coffee, sugarcane, sisal, and edible oils; textiles, soap, cement); 3.9% from mining **Minerals and Mining:** Bauxite and copper are mined; deposits of gold, silver, antimony, tin, sulphur, coal, nickel, and gypsum are undeveloped **Labor Force:** 3,004,544 (1975), with 80% self-employed in agriculture **Foreign Trade:** Exports, mainly coffee, sugar, bauxite, essential oils; baseballs and softballs, sisal, shellfish, and fruits, totaled $184 million in 1980. Imports, mainly wheat, fish, fats and oils, paper, cotton fabrics, vehicles, petroleum, machinery, electrical equipment, and raw materials, totaled $233 million **Principal Trade Partners:** United States, EC economies, Japan, Curaçao, Canada
Vital Statistics: Birthrate, 35.8 per 1,000 of pop. (1975); death rate, 16.3 **Life Expectancy:** 50 years **Health Statistics:** 1,037 inhabitants per hospital bed (1976); 8,505 per physician (1973) **Infant Mortality:** 200 per 1,000 births **Illiteracy:** 85% **Primary and Secondary School Enrollment:** 566,499 (1976) **Enrollment in Higher Education:** 3,309 **GNP Expended on Education:** 0.9% (1976)
Transportation: Paved roads total 400 mi. **Motor Vehicles:** 21,100 (1976) **Passenger Cars:** 18,700 **Railway Mileage:** 50 **Ports:** Port-au-Prince, Miragoâne, Les Cayes **Major Airlines:** Haiti Air Inter operates internal services **Communications:** Partly government controlled **Radio Transmitters:** 72 **Receivers:** 95,000 (1976) **Television Transmitters:** 1 **Receivers:** 14,000 (1976) **Telephones:** 18,000 (1976) **Newspapers:** 7 dailies, 20 copies per 1,000 inhabitants (1975)
Weights and Measures: Metric system **Travel Requirements:** Proof of citizenship; tourist card valid for 30 days; no fee **International Dialing Code:** 509

Fourteen years of implacable dictatorship, with little economic or social progress for compensation, ended for Haiti in 1971 with the death of Dr. François Duvalier at the age of 64. Under the harsh rule of his police state, the country had become an anachronism in the Western Hemisphere after having been in the vanguard to win freedom from foreign rule.

Haiti's politics and economy are primitive. The country is nominally a republic with a president, but Dr. Duvalier—"Papa Doc"—was all-powerful. For most of Haiti's independent life, the country

was dominated by a cultured and literate, generally mulatto, minority.

Illiteracy persists at nearly 85 percent, and most people lead subsistence lives on little plots of land amid luxuriant and colorful vegetation set against stark, eroded mountains. Roman Catholicism is the dominant religion, but it is mixed with voodoo, a religion of fetish and incantation rooted in the Haitians' African past. Manifestations of Duvalier rule include a force called the *Tontons Macoute*, or Bogeymen, a bulwark of the regime feared for its arbitrary dealings with ordinary people.

All in all, Papa Doc left a staggering legacy to his successor as "President for Life," his son Jean-Claude. When "Baby Doc" assumed power in April 1971, at the age of 19, there were few who assumed he could last long. But so far he has been successful in walking a political tightrope between the "old dinosaurs" of his father's era, who seek to hold the status quo, and the younger technocrats and businessmen who, while not desiring a dramatic change in the form of government, do seek a modernization of Haitian life. The young Duvalier has also had to contend with the political power wielded by his mother, Simone Duvalier. However, his marriage to Michele Bennett in 1979, which is said to have cost the country $5 million, is expected to reduce this influence.

Duvalier has acted in some instances to ease repression in an apparent attempt to gain favor with other countries. Nevertheless, in 1980 he revised his cabinet to strengthen his rule. In November of the same year 200 human-rights activists, journalists and other opponents of the regime were arrested; 9 were allowed to go into exile in the United States. Duvalier asserted that he supports human rights and democracy, but on his own terms.

He has acted to ease repression somewhat, in an apparent attempt to gain favor with the Carter Administration, which was critical of Haiti's bleak human rights record. The government said that it released the last political prisoners in 1977, and it invited the Red Cross and the Inter-American Commission on Human Rights to inspect its jails. On the other hand, there are reliable reports that conditions are improved solely for such visits and that inhumane conditions prevail again soon afterward.

The country has few resources with which to solve its staggering economic and social problems and has been characterized as an "environmental disaster." The destruction of the forests for charcoal has triggered massive soil erosion, reducing the amount of arable land. Exports remain largely confined to primary products such as sugar, coffee, essential oils, sisal, and some minerals. Over 150 U.S. companies now have plants in Haiti, and Haitian-controlled companies assemble imported U.S. components. Another major resource is tourism.

HISTORY: Haiti was largely ignored by Spain following the discovery of the island of Hispaniola by Columbus in 1492. While most Spanish colonists settled on the eastern part of the island, Haiti became a base for English and French pirates and was eventually ceded to France in the late 17th century. French colonists began to settle in the area, developing a plantation economy based on sugar and worked by black slaves. Following the outbreak of the French Revolution, the slaves rebelled and murdered most of their former masters

1793: A French army sent to crush the rebellion is defeated by guerrilla bands led by Toussaint L'Ouverture, a former slave
1801-03: Toussaint occupies the entire island of Hispaniola, abolishes slavery, and introduces a constitution; his rule ends when he is captured by a French force sent by Napoleon
1804-11: Jean Jacques Dessalines, another black general, continues the struggle against the French and defeats their army; he assumes title of emperor but is soon assassinated; nation becomes split into a northern kingdom ruled by Henri Christophe, a black, and a southern republic governed by a mulatto, Alexandre Pétion

1820-44: Haiti is reunited by Jean Pierre Boyer, who also brings Santo Domingo, in the eastern part of the island, under Haitian control; Boyer overthrown; nation regains independence

1849-59: Haiti is ruled by a former president and self-declared emperor, Faustin Élie Soulouque, a black; he is dethroned in a revolution led by a mulatto, Nicholas Fabre Geffrard

1905-34: United States takes Haiti's customs into receivership in 1905; in 1915, United States takes full control of country; occupation, which lasts for 19 years, results in many material improvements but arouses hostility throughout Latin America

1957-64: François Duvalier, a black middle-class physician, is elected president; with the help of a secret police force known as Tontons Macoute, he establishes dictatorship; in 1964 Duvalier has himself declared president for life

1968: Haitian exiles attempt to invade the country but fail

1969: The Organization of American States charges Duvalier government with terrorism

1970: Haitian Coast Guard vessels shell presidential palace in abortive coup

1971: François Duvalier dies after 14-year rule; his son, Jean-Claude, succeeds him

1977: Severe drought brings hundreds of thousands to brink of starvation and causes major shortages of electricity

1980: Thousands of Haitians flee in small boats from economic and social conditions in their homeland. Over 100 are forcibly removed the Bahamas and taken home. In August, hurricane Allen destroys most of the coffee crop

---

HONDURAS

Area: 43,277 sq. mi. **Population:** 3,691,000 (1980 est.)

Official Name: Republic of Honduras **Capital:** Tegucigalpa **Nationality:** Honduran **Languages:** Spanish is the official and predominant language; English is spoken along the north coast and on the Bay Islands **Religion:** Overwhelmingly Roman Catholic **Flag:** Two blue horizontal stripes separated by a white stripe bearing a cluster of five blue stars **Anthem:** National Anthem, beginning "Thy flag is a heavenly light" **Currency:** Lempira (2 per U.S. $1)

Location: Central America. Honduras is bordered on the north by the Caribbean Sea; on the southeast by Nicaragua; on the southwest by El Salvador and the Pacific Ocean; and on the west by Guatemala **Features:** Except for the Caribbean and Pacific coastal plains, the country is generally mountainous **Chief Rivers:** Guayape, Patuca, Aguán, Ulúa

Head of State and of Government: President: Gen. Policarpo Paz García, born 1932, designated as "provisional president" by the Constituent Assembly (July 20, 1980) **Effective Date of Present Constitution:** A new constitution is being prepared **Legislative Body:** A 71-member Constituent Assembly is fashioning a new constitution and election laws **Local Government:** 18 departments, each with a governor appointed by the president

Ethnic Composition: About 90% of the population is mestizo (of mixed European and Indian origin); Indians, Negroes, and Caucasians constitute small minorities **Population Distribution:** 31% urban **Density:** 85 inhabitants per sq. mi.

Largest Cities: (1976 est.) Tegucigalpa 316,500, San Pedro Sula 213,600, Choluteca 51,700, La Ceiba 49,900

Per Capita Income: $596 (1979) **Gross National Product (GNP):** $1.4 billion (1979) **Economic Statistics:** About 32% of GNP comes from agriculture (bananas, coffee, lumber, corn, meat, cotton), forestry and fishing; about 17% from industry (light consumer goods; processing of sugar, fruit juices, vegetable oils; meat packing); and 14% from trade **Minerals and Mining:** Gold, silver, lead, zinc, cadmium, mercury, and lime are extracted; other minerals are antimony, iron, copper, tin, coal, limestone, marble, and pitchblende. Petroleum exploration is under way **Labor Force:** 816,000 (1976), with some 66% in agriculture, 17% in trade and services, 8% in manufacturing and mining **Foreign Trade:** Exports, chiefly bananas, coffee, lumber, silver, meat, shellfish, cotton and tobacco, totaled $843 million in 1979. Imports, mainly transportation equipment, machinery, chemicals, fertilizer, petroleum products, and consumer durables, totaled $1 billion **Principal Trade Partners:** United States, West Germany, Japan, Venezuela, Nicaragua, Guatemala

Vital Statistics: Birthrate, 47 per 1,000 of pop. (1976); death rate, 12 **Life Expectancy:** 56 years **Health Statistics:** 598 inhabitants per hospital bed; 2,992 per physician (1975) **Infant Mortality:** 31 per 1,000 births (1976) **Illiteracy:** 43% **Primary and Secondary School Enrollment:** 546,096 (1976) **Enrollment in Higher Education:** 15,499 **GNP Expended on Education:** 3.2% (1974)

Transportation: Paved roads total 1,060 mi. **Motor Vehicles:** 50,700 (1976) **Passenger Cars:** 20,500 **Railway Mileage:** 350

Ports: Puerto Cortés, Tela, La Ceiba, Amapala, Trujillo **Major Airlines:** SAHSA and TAN operate domestic and international services **Communications:** Partly government controlled **Radio Transmitters:** 151 **Receivers:** 161,000 (1976) **Television Transmitters:** 5 **Receivers:** 48,000 (1976) **Telephones:** 19,000 (1976) **Newspapers:** 8 dailies (1975), 44 copies per 1,000 inhabitants

Weights and Measures: Metric system, but local units are also used **Travel Requirements:** Passport, visa, no fee **International Dialing Code:** 504

The weak link in the Central American Common Market, Honduras is the archetype of a Central American banana republic, with a slow economic growth rate and 66 percent of the population involved in agriculture. It is a small country, constantly struggling to keep up with its neighbors and always falling further behind; its politics are frequently subject to military intervention; its economy is tied to the whims and fortunes of the big foreign banana exporters.

Economically, Honduras seems to have little hope of catching up to its neighbors. Its few resources have been squandered by administrative incompetence and inexperience. Hopes for new growth are in part pinned on development of timbering in a 3-million-acre forest in northern Honduras.

In foreign affairs, Honduras' principal problem has been its relations with neighboring El Salvador and Nicaragua. Rioting at a soccer match between the teams of Honduras and El Salvador in 1969 led to a war which lasted only four days when the OAS intervened. In October 1980 the two countries finally signed a treaty ending the state of war and setting up procedures for settling their boundary dispute. However, there is evidence that Cuba has been using Honduras as a staging area for Salvadoran guerrillas attacking the government of their homeland. In 1981 Nicaragua charged that Honduran army support for anti-Sandinista guerrilla forces operating from Honduras caused a series of clashes. Troops of both nations massed on the border.

In January 1978 President Juan Melgar announced he would convene a Constitutional Assembly to "reform" the constitution. In August he was overthrown by a three-member military junta, headed by Gen. Policarpo Paz García, which promised free elections by 1980. On April 20, 1980, the Liberal party surprisingly defeated the National party, backed by the military, in close elections for the constituent assembly which was to write a new constitution and return Honduras to civilian rule. However, the Liberals did not win a clear majority.

HISTORY: Honduras was a center of Mayan civilization centuries before the arrival of Columbus in 1502. Following attempts by rival Spanish factions in Central America to gain control of it, Honduras was made part of the captaincy general of Guatemala

1821: Honduras declares independence from Spain and, along with the other Central American countries, is annexed to Mexico

1825: Honduras secedes from Mexico and becomes part of the Central American Federation

1838: Honduras becomes an independent republic in 1838

1933-49: Tiburcio Carias Andino rules as dictator

1957-63: Ramón Villeda Morales is elected first Liberal president in 25 years; he is overthrown by a military coup led by Oswaldo López Arellano, who takes over government

1965: Honduras returns to democratic rule when Constituent Assembly elects López president and adopts a new constitution

1969: Honduras invaded by El Salvador in "Soccer War"

1970: Honduras and El Salvador agree to set up demilitarized zone

1971: Honduras holds first direct election of a president since 1932; National party candidate Ramón Ernesto Cruz wins. U.S. recognizes Honduran sovereignty over long-disputed Swan Islands

1972: Bloodless coup puts Gen. López Arellano back in power

1974: Hurricane Fifi strikes, killing about 9,000

1975: Pres. López Arellano overthrown in bloodless coup after reports that he accepted $1.25 million bribe from United Brands. Juan Alberto Melgar Castro, Commander in Chief of armed forces, becomes president

1978: Melgar overthrown by three-member military junta
1980: Liberal party gains plurality in Constituent Assembly which names Gen. Paz Garcí, the junta head, as provisional president
1981: Border clashes occur as Nicaragua accuses Honduras of giving support to Nicaraguan guerrillas

HUNGARY

Area: 35,919 sq. mi. **Population:** 10,709,536 (1980 census)

Official Name: Hungarian People's Republic **Capital:** Budapest **Nationality:** Hungarian **Languages:** Hungarian (Magyar) is the official and universal language **Religion:** 68% Roman Catholic, 20% Calvinist, 5% Lutheran, 7% other (Unitarian, Jewish, etc.) **Flag:** Red, white, and green horizontal stripes **Anthem:** God bless the Hungarians **Currency:** Forint (29.5 per U.S. $1)

Location: East-central Europe. Landlocked Hungary is bordered on the north by Czechoslovakia, on the northeast by the USSR, on the east by Romania, on the south by Yugoslavia, and on the west by Austria **Features:** Most of the country is a flat plain, with the exception of low mountain ranges in the north-central and northeastern portions and to the north and south of Lake Balaton in the west **Chief Rivers:** Danube, Tisza, Drava, Rába

Political Leader: First Secretary of the Hungarian Socialist Workers' (Communist) party: János Kádár, born 1912, took over in 1956 **Head of State:** The Presidential Council is collectively the head of state, usually represented by its president, Pál Losonczi, born 1919, appointed 1967 **Head of Government:** Premier György Lázár, appointed 1975 **Effective Date of Present Constitution:** 1949, amended 1972 **Legislative Body:** National Assembly (unicameral) consisting of 352 members elected for 5 years **Local Government:** 19 counties (each divided into districts with locally elected councils); 4 autonomous cities and the capital, all with county status

Ethnic Composition: Hungarians (Magyars) make up 97% of the population; minority groups include Germans, Slovaks, Gypsies, Serbs, Croats, and Romanians **Population Distribution:** 50.6% urban **Density:** 298 inhabitants per sq. mi.

Largest Cities: (1980 census) Budapest 2,060,170, Miskolc 206,727, Debrecen 192,484, Szeged 171,342, Pécs 168,788, Gyor 123,618

Per Capita Income: $3,665 (1980) **Gross National Product (GNP):** $39 billion (1980) **Economic Statistics:** About 38.5% of GNP is derived from industry (mining, chemical refining, metallurgy, food processing); 18.6% from agriculture (corn, wheat, sugar beets, vegetables, wine grapes); 12% from trade; 11% from services **Minerals and Mining:** Coal, bauxite, iron ore, and lignite are mined **Labor Force:** 5,230,000 (1979), of which 33% is employed in industry and construction, and 20% in agriculture **Foreign Trade:** Exports, chiefly transport equipment, medicine, machinery and shoes, totaled $11 billion in 1979. Imports, mainly crude oil, raw cotton, passenger cars, trucks, and rolled steel, totaled $12 billion **Principal Trade Partners:** USSR, W. Germany, E. Germany, Czechoslovakia, Poland, Italy, Austria

Vital Statistics: Birthrate, 16.7 per 1,000 of pop. (1977); death rate, 12.4 **Life Expectancy:** 70 years **Health Statistics:** 114 inhabitants per hospital bed; 439 per physician (1974) **Infant Mortality:** 26.2 per 1,000 births **Illiteracy:** 2% **Primary and Secondary School Enrollment:** 1,438,785 (1976) **Enrollment in Higher Education:** 107,555 (1975) **GNP Expended on Education:** 4.6% (1976)

Transportation: Surfaced roads total 15,107 mi. **Motor Vehicles:** 973,600 (1977) **Passenger Cars:** 744,700 **Railway Mileage:** 5,293 **Ports:** None **Major Airlines:** Malev, the state-owned airline, operates domestic and international services **Communications:** Government owned **Radio Transmitters:** 37 **Licenses:** 2,538,000 (1975) **Television Transmitters:** 22 **Licenses:** 2,495,000 (1976)* **Telephones:** 1,076,000 (1976) **Newspapers:** 27 dailies, 233 copies per 1,000 inhabitants (1975)

Weights and Measures: Metric system **Travel Requirements:** Passport, visa valid for 30 days, fee $6, 2 photos

"Socialism with gaiety" is the way a top Hungarian has described his country's political formula to an American audience. The slogan is not far from the Czechoslovakian idea of "Socialism with a human face"—a concept that brought the violent downfall of Alexander Dubcek and his reformist government in 1968. However, the implementation of the formula in Hungary is so cautious, moderate, and delicate that no analogy with Czechoslovakia is appropriate.

In the midst of ideological regimentation, the breakdown of which brought Warsaw Pact troops into Prague, there is gaiety in Hungary. Political cabarets in Budapest pull few punches in criticizing bureaucratic ineptness and stuffiness. A television forum in which listeners quiz political leaders on their performance and promises brings sharp questions out into public discussion. Music, dancing, and plentiful good food add esthetic grace notes to the sense of gradual political progress.

The country is no longer traumatized by the uprising that Russian tanks crushed in 1956 and that caused some 200,000 Hungarians to flee to the West. The regime of János Kádár, imposed to fight the liberal ideas of the 1956 revolt, has proved far more progressive than was first thought possible. A surprising degree of dissent is allowed, though there are definite if generally unexpressed limits. Hungary remains, after all, a Communist state, basically faithful to the party line.

Thus, when it was necessary for someone to attack Romania for flirting with Communist China, a Hungarian editor was detailed to fire the first critical salvo. Similarly, the economic liberalization has been only partially mirrored in an effort to develop local political autonomy in small towns and not reflected at all in the repressive policies toward the Catholic Church.

What has emerged in Hungary, however, is a consumer-oriented economy that is the envy of all its neighbors. Hungarians have refined their New Economic Model since its introduction in 1968 to boost exports and imports.

The economy, however, is not without its problems. The high degree of centralization in Budapest sometimes results in mismanagement and inefficiencies, and in return for supplying oil needs in excess of rigid, outdated quotas, the Soviet Union requires agricultural surpluses that might otherwise earn valuable hard currency in the West. In April 1978, the regime adopted a two-year program of phasing out most price controls, subsidies for consumer goods, and heavy producer taxes. In 1979, Kádár called for greater productivity to increase workers' incomes and to combat inflation. But Hungary's industrial growth slowed to a standstill in 1980, while agricultural production increased only slightly.

HISTORY: The Magyars migrated from beyond the Urals about the end of the 9th century A.D., conquered most of present-day Hungary, and established a dynasty that lasted more than four centuries. Pre-Magyar inhabitants had included Celts, Germans, Huns, Slavs, and Avars. In the last years of the 10th century, the Magyars embraced Christianity and made alliances with the Holy Roman Empire. Following a disastrous defeat by the Turks in 1526, a faction of Hungarian nobles elected Ferdinand I of Austria as king of Hungary, laying the foundations of Hapsburg rule
1686: Budapest is liberated from the Turks, who cede most of Hungary proper and Transylvania to Austria
1713: Hungarian Diet accepts Pragmatic Sanction aimed at guaranteeing the integrity of the Hapsburg possessions, thereby binding Hungary to Austria
1848-49: Hungarian revolt against Austrian rule is suppressed by Austrian and Russian armies
1867: Austro-Hungarian monarchy is established, giving Hungary nearly equal status with Austria
1918-19: Monarchy collapses in the aftermath of World War I defeat. A Hungarian republic is proclaimed but is soon supplanted by a Communist regime headed by Bela Kun; Romanian troops invade Hungary and help to suppress leftist government
1920: Under Treaty of Trianon, Hungary is deprived of three-fourths of its territory and over one-third of its population; country becomes a kingdom without a king, under the regency of Admiral Nicholas Horthy
1938-40: Aided by Italy and Germany, Hungary recovers lands lost to Czechoslovakia and Romania. In 1940 Hungary joins Axis powers and enters World War II
1944: Soviet troops occupy Hungary; a provisional government is set up and declares war against Germany
1947: Communists win 22 percent of vote in general elections
1948-49: Hungarian Communists seize power with Soviet support; in 1949 Hungary is proclaimed a People's Republic

1955: Hungary joins the UN

1956: Popular anti-Communist uprising breaks out in Budapest and spreads to rest of the country; a new coalition government under Imre Nagy declares Hungary neutral and withdraws country from Warsaw Pact; János Kádár sets up counter-government and calls for Soviet support; Soviet troops and tanks suppress revolution, causing nearly 200,000 Hungarians to flee the country

1958: Imre Nagy and some of his ministers are executed. János Kádár resigns as premier and is succeeded by Ferenc Münnich

1961: Kádár resumes premiership

1965: Gyula Kallai becomes premier; Kádár remains First Secretary of ruling Hungarian Socialist Workers' party

1967: Hungary signs a new 20-year friendship and mutual assistance pact with Soviet Union, replacing one signed in 1948. Jeno Fock succeeds Gyula Kallai as premier

1968: Hungarian troops march with Soviet troops when Soviets invade Czechoslovakia

1971: Government holds first general elections in which voters could choose between nonofficial and official candidates. Newcomers unseat eight incumbents in parliament

1975: György Lázár becomes premier

1978: Crown of St. Stephen, 1,000-year-old traditional symbol of Hungary's nationhood, is returned by U.S. after having been held in protective custody since the end of World War II. Government announces measures to phase out most subsidies for consumer goods and end heavy producer taxes

1979: 12th Communist Party Congress reduces Politburo to 13 members, including young associates of Kádár

---

ICELAND

Area: 39,768 sq. mi. **Population:** 224,000 (1978 est.)

Official Name: Republic of Iceland **Capital:** Reykjavík **Nationality:** Icelandic **Languages:** Icelandic is the official and universal language **Religion:** 95% of the population belongs to the state church, the Evangelical Lutheran Church **Flag:** A red cross edged in white on a field of blue **Anthem:** Our Country's God **Currency:** Króna (6.7 per U.S. $1)

Location: North Atlantic. A large island extending about 300 miles from east to west and about 190 miles from north to south, Iceland is the westernmost state of Europe, lying 600 miles west of Norway. The Arctic Circle runs through the small island of Grímsey off Iceland's northern coast **Features:** Almost three fourths of the country's land area, which is of recent volcanic origin, consists of glaciers, lakes, a mountainous lava desert, and other wasteland, with the remainder used for cultivation or grazing. Most of the inhabited areas are on the coast, particularly, in the southwest **Chief Rivers:** Thjórsá, Jökulsa, Ólfusá-Hvítá, Skjálfandafljót

Head of State: President: Mrs. Vigdís Finnbogadóttir, born 1930, elected June 1980 **Head of Government:** Premier Gunnar Thoroddsen, born 1910, appointed February 1980 **Effective Date of Present Constitution:** 1874, amended 1903 and 1944 **Legislative Body:** Parliament (Althing), composed of 60 members elected for 4 years. After elections it becomes bicameral, dividing itself into 2 chambers with equal powers, one of 20 members and the other of 40 members. The 2 houses meet together **Local Government:** 16 counties, each with a council, and 14 urban municipalities

Ethnic Composition: The population is homogeneous **Population Distribution:** 87.1% urban **Density:** 5.6 inhabitants per sq. mi.

Largest Cities: (1977 est.) Reykjavík 83,887; (1973 est.) Kópavogur 11,639, Akureyri 11,484, Hafnarfjördhur 10,926

Per Capita Income: $7,018 (1980) **Gross Domestic Product (GDP):** $1.6 billion (1980) **Economic Statistics:** About 14% of GDP comes from fishing and fish processing; 18% from industry other than fish processing (manufacture of electric motors, fertilizer, chemicals, cement, clothing, furniture, books); 7% from agriculture (sheep raising, dairy products, hay, potatoes); 32% from services; 15% from construction **Minerals and Mining:** Diatomite, peat, lignite, perlite; hydroelectric power **Labor Force:** 100,000 (1977), of which 42% is employed in fishing, fish processing, and other industries; 11% in agriculture; 46% in trade and services **Foreign Trade:** Exports, chiefly fish and fish products (about 75% of the total), aluminum ingots, and agricultural products, totaled $791 million in 1979. Imports, mainly machinery, textiles, petroleum products, metals and metal products, ships, and food grains, totaled $825 million **Principal Trade Partners:** United States, West Germany, Britain, USSR, Norway, Denmark, Portugal, Sweden

Vital Statistics: Birthrate, 18 per 1,000 of pop. (1977); death rate, 6.5 **Life Expectancy:** 75 years **Health Statistics:** 64 inhabitants per hospital bed; 550 per physician (1974) **Infant Mortality:** 9.5 per 1,000 births **Illiteracy:** Negligible **Primary and Secondary School Enrollment:** 52,271 (1975) **Enrollment in Higher Education:** 2,970 (1975) **GNP Expended on Education:** 4.2% (1975)

Transportation: Paved roads total 120 miles; there are over 6,000 miles of gravel road **Motor Vehicles:** 78,000 (1977) **Passenger Cars:** 70,100 **Railway Mileage:** None **Ports:** Reykjavík, Akureyri **Major Airlines:** Icelandair operates domestic and international services **Communications:** Government owned **Radio Transmitters:** 29 **Licenses:** 64,000 (1976) **Television Transmitters:** 80 **Licenses:** 53,000 (1976) **Telephones:** 91,000 (1976) **Newspapers:** 5 dailies, 431 copies per 1,000 inhabitants (1975)

Weights and Measures: Metric system **Travel Requirements:** Passport, no visa for 3 months

Out in the North Atlantic, closer to Greenland than to Western Europe, lies the rugged, largely desolate island of volcanic origin called Iceland, with 224,000 fiercely individualistic inhabitants who have a tradition of preserving their heritage. Their language, for example, has remained virtually unchanged since the 12th century.

Although Iceland has no armed forces, it joined in the cold-war days of 1949 in forming the North Atlantic Treaty Organization. As its contribution, it granted NATO the right to maintain a base, manned by Americans, at Keflavík, 30 miles outside of Reykjavík, the capital. A leftist coalition formed in 1971 announced plans to phase out the installation, but in 1974 a coalition of the former governing and opposition parties agreed to allow the base to remain.

The government extended the fishing limits in 1972 from 12 miles offshore to 50, and in 1975 from 50 to 200 miles. With fish and fish products accounting for 14 percent of the country's gross domestic product and 75 percent of its total exports, the moves were a logical progression of a conservation drive begun in 1958 when Iceland extended its fishing limits from four miles to 12.

Foreign reaction to these extensions has been far more serious than in 1958. In 1973 and 1975-76, Britain, which gets 45 percent of its fish from the waters off Iceland, sent heavily armed frigates into the disputed waters, touching off a "cod war" between the two countries, with shots being fired, boats rammed and nets cut.

In 1976 the two countries reached a diplomatic settlement and British ships were removed. In conjunction with this agreement, important tariff concessions by the European Community (EC) for fish products became effective for Iceland. The EC's adoption of a common 200-mile fishing limit imposed new problems, as it excludes Icelandic vessels from rich waters to which they had previously had access.

Parliamentary elections were called December 1979 after the Social Democrats withdrew from the coalition government. A political crisis ensued when no party won a sizable plurality in the new parliament. After the major parties failed to form a new government, Gunnar Thoroddsen deserted his own conservative Independence party and formed a new coalition government with the People's Alliance and Progressive party in February 1980. To control spiraling inflation, the Thoroddsen government froze prices as of Jan. 1, 1981. At the same time, it announced currency reforms making one new krona equal to 100 old kronas.

Vigdís Finnbogadóttir, manager of the Reykjavík Theater Company, became the world's first popularly elected female head of state by winning the June 1980 presidential election.

HISTORY: The first permanent settler of Iceland was Ingolfur Arnason of Norway, who arrived with his family around 870. Others of Norwegian origin followed, some bringing with them Irish and Scottish wives and slaves. In 930 a commonwealth was established and a general assembly, the Althing, instituted. Christianity was introduced in the year 1000. Iceland came under the Norwegian crown in the 13th century, but in 1380 both Iceland and Norway passed under the Danish crown. The former was destined to remain linked to Denmark until the 20th century

1918: Iceland is declared a sovereign state in union with Denmark

1940-41: British troops occupy Iceland following Germany's World War II occupation of Denmark; U.S. forces take over Iceland's defense in 1941

1944: Icelanders vote to terminate union with Denmark; Iceland is proclaimed a republic

1949: Iceland joins in forming NATO

1958-61: Fishing limits are extended from four miles to 12; so-called "cod war" begins, with Britain challenging the Icelandic pronouncement by sending in trawlers backed by warships; in 1961 Britain finally agrees to the 12-mile limit

1970: Iceland becomes member of European Free Trade Association. Premier Bjarni Benediktsson perishes in fire; Justice Minister Johann Hafstein is designated his successor

1971: Government defeated in elections. Hafstein resigns. New leftwing coalition government announces it will close the American-manned NATO base at Keflavlk

1972-73: Fishing limits are extended from 12 miles to 50, touching off new "cod war" with Britain; West Germany joins Britain in protesting extension

1973: Iceland signs agreement with Britain giving limited fishing rights within the new zone

1974: Iceland signs agreement with U.S. allowing U.S. to maintain NATO base at Keflavlk

1975: Fishing limits extended from 50 to 200 miles

1976: British and Icelandic foreign ministers sign an interim pact to end the "cod war" between the two countries and restore diplomatic relations which had been severed. British frigates, sent into fishing zone in November '75 to protect British trawlers from harassment by Icelandic patrol boats, withdraw. Dr. Kristján Eldjárn is unopposed for third four-year term as president

1978: Strike by government workers temporarily isolates nation by cutting international flights, mail and telephone links

1980: New center-left coalition govenment is formed under Premier Gunnar Thoroddsen. Vigdls Finnbogadóttir is elected president

---

INDIA

Area: 1,269,339 sq. mi. **Population:** 683,810,051 (1980 census)

Official Name: Republic of India **Capital:** New Delhi **Nationality:** Indian **Languages:** Hindi is the official language; English is an associate language. In addition to Hindi, the constitution recognizes 14 national languages, although as many as 1,652 languages and dialects are spoken in the country. Hindi, however, is spoken by 38% of the population. Telugu 9%, Bengali 8%, Marathi 8%, Tamil 7%, Urdu 6%, Gujarati 5%, Kanarese 4%, Punjabi 3%, Oriya 3%, Malayalam 3% **Religion:** 84% Hindu, 10% Moslem, 3% Christian, 2% Sikh, 1% Buddhist, Jain and others **Flag:** Saffron, white, and green horizontal stripes, with the 24-spoke Wheel of Asoka (chakra) in blue on the white stripe **Anthem:** Morning Song of India **Currency:** Rupee (8.3 per U.S. $1)

Location: Southern Asia, occupying most of the Indian sub-continent. India is bordered on the north by Afghanistan, China, Nepal, and Bhutan; on the east by Bangladesh, Burma, and the Bay of Bengal; on the south by the Indian Ocean's Gulf of Mannar and Palk Strait, which separate India from Sri Lanka; on the west by the Arabian Sea; and on the northwest by Pakistan **Features:** The country consists of three major topographical areas: the Himalaya mountains extending along the whole of the northern border; the Indo-Gangetic Plain, a fertile and heavily populated region; and the southern peninsula, including the Deccan Plateau, which is of moderate elevation and less densely populated **Chief Rivers:** Ganges, Brahmaputra, Godavari, Kistna (Krishna), Narbada, Mahanadi

Head of State: President Neelam Sanjiva Reddy, born 1913, elected July 1977 **Head of Government:** Prime Minister: Mrs. Indira Gandhi, born 1917, appointed Jan. 1980. She held the same office from 1966 to 1977 **Effective Date of Present Constitution:** 1950 **Legislative Body:** Parliament (bicameral), consisting of the Lok Sabha (House of the People) and the Rajya Sabha (Council of States). The Lok Sabha has 542 members, elected by universal suffrage for 6 years. The Rajya Sabha has 244 members, 13 of whom are appointed by the president and the rest elected for 6 year terms by the state and territorial legislatures **Local Government:** 22 states and 9 union territories, each with an appointed governor and with its own elected legislature

Ethnic Composition: Two major strains predominate: the Indo-Aryan (72%) in the north and the Dravidian (25%) in the south. There is also an aboriginal population in the central part, and some Mongoloid peoples in the north **Population Distribution:** 21% urban **Density:** 539 inhabitants per sq. mi.

Largest Cities: (1971 census) Bombay 5,970,575, Delhi 3,287,883, Calcutta 3,148,746 (with suburbs 7,031,382), Madras 2,469,449, Hyderabad 1,607,396, Ahmadabad 1,585,544, Bangalore 1,540,741, Kanpur 1,154,388

Per Capita Income: $202 (1980) **Gross National Product (GNP):** $137 billion (1980) **Economic Statistics:** About 43% of GNP comes from agriculture (rice, wheat, tea, jute, pulses, cotton, sugar, peanuts); 23% from mining and manufacturing (iron and steel, textiles, chemicals, cement, industrial machinery and equipment); 16% from commerce, transportation, and communications **Minerals and Mining:** Coal and iron are the country's main mineral assets; mica, manganese, and bauxite are also abundant. Iron ore reserves are estimated at about one fourth of the world's total; oil supplies less than half of the nation's refinery requirements **Labor Force:** 240 million (1976), of which 72% is engaged in agriculture, 11% in industry, and 17% in trade and services **Foreign Trade:** Exports, chiefly cotton and jute textiles, tea, sugar, coffee, metallic ores, and iron and steel manufactures, totaled $8.5 billion in 1979. Imports, mainly petroleum, food grains, nonelectrical machinery and fertilizer, totaled $11.5 billion **Principal Trade Partners:** United States, Japan, Britain, USSR, Iran, West Germany

Vital Statistics: Birthrate, 36 per 1,000 of pop. (1980); death rate, 14.8 **Life Expectancy:** 51 years **Health Statistics:** 1,465 inhabitants per hospital bed; 3,961 per physician (1973) **Infant Mortality:** 130 per 1,000 births (1974) **Illiteracy:** 64% **Primary and Secondary School Enrollment:** 93,310,864 (1976) **Enrollment in Higher Education:** 3,198,550 **GNP Expended on Education:** 2.7% (1975)

Transportation: Surfaced roads totaled about 370,000 mi. **Motor Vehicles:** 1,495,800 (1977) **Passenger Cars:** 805,400 **Railway Mileage:** 38,614 **Ports:** Calcutta, Bombay, Madras, Mormugao, Cochin, Kandla, Visakhapatnam, Paradeep, Mangalore, Tuticorin **Major Airlines:** Indian Airlines Corporation is the domestic carrier and Air India the international line **Communications:** Government controlled **Radio Transmitters:** 174 **Licenses:** 14,848,000 (1976) **Television Transmitters:** 18 **Licenses:** 280,000 (1976) **Telephones:** 2,096,000 (1976) **Newspapers:** 835 dailies, 16 copies per 1,000 inhabitants (1975)

Weights and Measures: Metric system and local units are used **Travel Requirements:** Passport, no visa required for stay up to 30 days

---

Successive invasions and a long period of subjugation under alien rule have made India what it is today—a land of diverse, often conflicting cultures, religions, and people that is held in unity by a complicated yet resilient political system. The British, who were the masters of the subcontinent for a century and a half, brought its disparate regions under one administration. To overcome the myriad languages and dialects, they made English the communication medium of the elite, the tiny minority that still dominates the government, industry, education, and art.

Indian leaders, as fruit of their long fight for freedom, inherited a truncated land after the carving out of Pakistan as a homeland for Moslems; they have been struggling with the overwhelming problems of the subcontinent ever since.

The country's successive five-year plans, while laying the foundation for a prosperous industrial nation at some future date, have not so far produced any substantial improvement in the average Indian's quality of life. All the benefits of the large development expenses over the last 25 years have been neutralized by a runaway population increase—now almost 2.5 percent a year—that has pushed more and more people below the poverty line. Unemployment has risen sharply. Pressure is increasing on living space, schools, and hospitals. Despite recent record food crops and a rise in industrial output, the population increase, on which only a marginal dent has been made by a costly birth-control program, has resulted in deteriorating living conditions for most Indians.

The social structure, ever in conflict, throws up many obstacles to progress. The Hindus, who make up 84 percent of the population, are divided into countless subcastes. The downtrodden untouchables, who constitute one seventh of the population, have begun asserting their rights. Clashes with upper-caste Hindus have become frequent and often violent.

The Moslem minority, 10 percent of the population, has remained suspect in the eyes of the majority ever since the creation of Pakistan. They live in constant insecurity and threat from militant Hindus. Bloody riots between Hindus and Moslems erupt periodically. The smaller minorities, the Sikhs, Buddhists, Jains, Parsis, and Christians, live in relative security, but the chances of their assimilation into the Hindu-dominated national life are remote.

In 1975 India went through the most important political crisis in its years as a republic when in April the government declared a state of emergency, arrested political leaders opposed to Prime Minister Indira Gandhi, began press censorship and suspended protection of fundamental rights. This repressive action was precipitated by Gandhi's conviction on charges of corrupt practices in the 1971 general election.

In July 1975 Mrs. Gandhi's power was restored when new laws approved by parliament permitted her to rule by proclamation, barred the courts from reviewing her actions and changed the election law retroactively to remove any criminal offenses. In December Gandhi's Congress party delayed general elections, due in March 1976, and extended the state of emergency for six months.

In January 1977 Mrs. Gandhi announced the elections that had been postponed would be held in March; press censorship was subsequently lifted. In what was hailed as a victory for Indian democracy, Morarji R. Desai, 81, and his Janata party defeated Mrs. Gandhi and her 30-year-old son, Sanjay, in the election. It was the first defeat suffered by the ruling Congress party in the 30 years of India's independence. The new government immediately revoked the emergency rule legislation and released the political prisoners who had been jailed without charges. And since Desai himself was one of the thousands of political prisoners detained during Mrs. Gandhi's 19-month "emergency rule" period, it came as no surprise when the new government launched a series of civil and criminal investigations into her alleged abuses of power.

In February 1978, a month after leaving the Congress party to form a splinter group, Mrs. Gandhi reemerged as a major force in Indian politics when her Congress-I (for Indira) party entered a series of state elections and won decisively in two. Her comeback may have contributed to a split in the ruling Janata party in April. In November, Gandhi herself won a parliamentary seat.

However, Mrs. Gandhi found herself fighting for political survival a month later when the Lok Sabha, the lower house of parliament, expelled her on charges of contempt of the house and breach of privilege for her actions while as prime minister. In addition, the government set up special courts that would keep her tied up in litigation. In February 1979 her son, Sanjay, was convicted of the theft and burning of a film (during the "emergency rule" period) that ridiculed his mother's conduct in office. Sentenced to prison, he was freed on bail pending appeal.

Desai meanwhile grappled with an increase in crime, caste violence, chronic power shortages, labor unrest, and soaring inflation. Food grain production was a bright spot, rising high enough to meet all of the country's needs. In general, however, Desai's government turned India away from large-scale industrialism and toward a "cottage industry" system.

On July 15, 1979, Prime Minister Desai resigned following growing defections from and splits within his Janata party. He was succeeded by Chaudhury Charan Singh, who himself resigned on August 20 when Mrs. Gandhi withdrew support from his coalition. He was reappointed as a caretaker premier pending general elections in January 1980.

Mrs. Gandhi regained the premiership as the Congress-I party swept to a huge victory in those elections, winning 351 seats out of 542 in the lower house. Her son Sanjay also won a seat, and the Supreme Court subsequently acquitted him in the film case. Widely regarded as his mother's most likely political heir, Sanjay was at the peak of his career when he died in a plane crash in June 1980.

Endeavoring to reestablish strong central rule and resume India's industrialization, Indira Gandhi used her new power to considerable effect. Her party took control of nearly all of the 22 state governments by mid-1980, steadily increased its membership in the Lok Sabha, and in May 1981 overwhelmingly defeated the first no-confidence motion brought against the leadership by the splintered opposition.

Even so, India's problems multiplied. Crime increased alarmingly, as did ethnic violence, particularly against immigrants from Bangladesh in the northeast. In 1981, the decennial census revealed that the population was growing far more rapidly than had been supposed, and the prime minister resumed the vigorous promotion of birth control, a policy whose unpopularity had contributed to her defeat in 1977. In foreign policy, Mrs. Gandhi condemned both the Soviet occupation of Afghanistan, and the U.S. plan—announced in 1981—to give greater aid to Pakistan for military and nuclear development.

HISTORY: The Indus Valley was the site of a flourishing civilization from the 3rd millennium to about 1500 B.C., when the region was conquered by the Aryans who, over the next 2,000 years, developed a Brahmanic civilization and introduced a caste system. In 327-325 B.C., Alexander the Great invaded northwest India, only to be driven out, and in the following century most of the subcontinent was united under Asoka the Great, who established Buddhism as the state religion. After his death, however, Buddhism declined in India as Hinduism experienced a resurgence

4th cent.: Hindu kingdoms are established

8th cent.: Islam is introduced into Sind by Arab invaders

1498-1510: European contact with India, begun with the arrival of Portuguese explorer Vasco da Gama, is followed by Portuguese conquest of Goa and spurs rivalry among European powers for trade with subcontinent

1526-1707: India is ruled by Mogul dynasty; a large Moslem population grows up and a new culture evolves, developing a characteristic Indo-Islamic style in art and architecture, as evidenced by the Taj Mahal

1746-63: India is turned into a battleground for the forces of France and Britain as each tries to carve out colonial domains; with the 1763 Treaty of Paris, British supremacy is assured

1857-58: Sepoy Rebellion by native soldiers in the employ of British East India Company is brutally suppressed; company is dissolved and India is placed under the direct rule of the British Crown

1919: Mohandas K. Gandhi, later known as the Mahatma or "greatsouled," organizes the first of many passive resistance campaigns against British rule; he is imprisoned

1942-45: Indian National Congress, largely Hindu-supported, splits with Moslem League, which favors creation of Pakistan as a separate Moslem state, over support for Britain during World War II; Congress is outlawed, while League, which supports Britain, gains strength

1947: Subcontinent is partitioned into the independent nations of India and Pakistan; Jawaharlal Nehru becomes India's first prime minister; bloody riots break out between Hindus and Moslems and millions flee in crisscross migration to new states; India and Pakistan fight over Kashmir

1948: Gandhi is assassinated by Hindu fanatic who blames him for partition; Kashmir fighting ends with UN cease-fire

1950: India becomes republic within Commonwealth of Nations

1954: India signs nonaggression pact with Communist China

1956: Constitutional amendment redrawing state boundaries along linguistic lines put into effect

1962: Chinese Communist troops occupy Ladakh region of Kashmir

1964: Nehru dies and is succeeded by Lal Bahadur Shastri

1965-66: India and Pakistan fight three-week war in 1965 over Kashmir; hostilities end in a truce, followed by accord signed in 1966 at Tashkent, in the Soviet Union. Indian Prime Minister Lal Bahadur Shastri dies at Tashkent and is succeeded by Mrs. Indira Gandhi, daughter of the former prime minister, Jawaharlal Nehru

1969: Death of President Zakir Husain touches off power struggle in governing Congress party as Mrs. Gandhi and old guard party bosses clash over choice of successor; party splits following election of V.V. Giri, the candidate backed by Mrs. Gandhi, as president; bulk of party members remain with her New Congress party but she loses majority strength in parliament, forcing her to rely on Communists and independents for crucial votes

1970: Supreme Court rules bank nationalization law unconstitutional; prime minister counters court's action by issuing new ordinance nationalizing the banks. Mrs. Gandhi dissolves lower house of parliament and orders new elections

1971: Mrs. Gandhi's party is landslide victor in the elections held in March, winning two-thirds of the parliamentary seats. Civil war breaks out in Pakistan. Millions of East Pakistani refugees flee to India. India supports East Pakistan in fight against West Pakistan, and latter is soon defeated. East Pakistan becomes Bangladesh

1972: At Simla Conference India and Pakistan agree to observe "lines of control" in Kashmir

1973: At Delhi Conference India and Pakistan agree to repatriation of 93,000 Pakistani POWs held since their 1971 war

1974: World Health Organization estimates 30,000 have died in northern India in worst smallpox epidemic of the century. Sikkim becomes an associated state of India. Worst famine since 1943 in West Bengal, Assam, and Bihar

1975: Prime Minister Gandhi is convicted on charges of illegal activities in connection with her election. She suspends civil liberties and orders arrest of hundreds of political opponents. Gandhi's powers are restored by parliament and the Supreme Court

1976: Suspension of civil liberties continues throughout the year. India and Pakistan formally establish diplomatic ties

1977: Morarji R. Desai elected prime minister. President Fakhruddin Ali Ahmed dies; he is succeeded by Neelam Sanjiva Reddy. Government launches probes into alleged abuses of power by Mrs. Gandhi during her "emergency rule" period. India acts to improve relations with neighbors and U.S. while stressing friendship with Soviet Union

1978: High-level talks between India and Pakistan begin; disputed state of Kashmir tops agenda. Mrs. Gandhi's newly formed Congress-I party wins two important state elections. Elected to parliament, she is expelled; special courts are set up to try her for actions taken when prime minister

1979: The Soviet Union and India sign agreements covering trade and technological and scientific cooperation for 10 to 15 years, calling for Indian rice to be traded for Soviet oil. Desai government curtails some large-scale industry and encourages "cottage industries" to help rural poor. Desai resigns in June, and is succeeded by Chaudhury Charan Singh in July. Singh resigns in August

1980: Indira Gandhi's Congress-I party wins by landslide in January elections, and she becomes prime minister for second time. Student movement to expel illegal immigrants (Bangladeshi) in Assam State spreads through northeast India and leads to shutting of colleges and reduced oil production. Congress-I party wins eight of nine state elections in May. Mrs. Gandhi's son, Sanjay, dies in crash of his light plane in June 1980.

1981: U.S. plan to increase aid to Pakistan for military and nuclear development denounced by Prime Minister Gandhi. Census reveals that, if current trend continues, India's population will double by the year 2000. In worst railroad disaster, June 6, an overcrowded train plunges off bridge in Bihar; death toll may have exceeded 1,000

INDONESIA

Area: 788,430 sq. mi. **Population:** 147,400,000 (1980 census)

Official Name: Republic of Indonesia **Capital:** Jakarta **Nationality:** Indonesian **Languages:** Bahasa Indonesia, a form of Malay developed as a product of Indonesia's nationalist movement, is the official language; English is the second language and is compulsory in secondary schools **Religion:** 90% Moslem, 5% Christian, 3% Hindu (Bali has retained its Buddhist/Hindu heritage) **Flag:** A red horizontal stripe above a white stripe **Anthem:** Great Indonesia **Currency:** Rupiah (629 per U.S. $1)

Location: Southeast Asia, in the Malay archipelago. Indonesia consists of six large and 13,662 lesser islands, which form an arc between Asia and Australia. The principal group of islands is the Greater Sunda Islands, which include Java, Bali, Sumatra, Borneo (Kalimantan), and Celebes (Sulawesi). The country shares land borders with Malaysia, Brunei, and Papua New Guinea **Features:** The large islands have a central mountain range rising from fairly extensive lowlands and coastal plains. Many islands throughout the archipelago are dotted with volcanoes, both active and dormant **Chief Rivers:** Kapuas, Digul, Barito, Mahakam, Kajan, Hari, Mamberamo, Idenburg

Head of State and of Government: President: Gen. Suharto (Soeharto), born 1921, reelected 1978 **Effective Date of Present**

Constitution: 1945 **Legislative Body:** Peoples' Consultative Assembly, consisting of 920 members, within it a 460-member (360 elected and 100 nominated by the president) House of Representatives (Parliament) **Local Government:** 27 provinces, each with an appointed governor and an elected legislature

Ethnic Composition: Malayans and Papuans constitute the main ethnic groups, each with numerous subdivisions. Chinese make up the largest nonindigenous group **Population Distribution:** 18.2% urban **Density:** 187 inhabitants per sq. mi.

Largest Cities: (1973 est.) Jakarta 5,000,000, Surabaya 2,000,000, Bandung 2,000,000, Medan 1,000,000, Yogyakarta 500,000; (1971 census) Semarang 646,590, Palembang 582,961

Per Capita Income: $417 (1980) **Gross National Product (GNP):** $63.1 billion (1980) **Economic Statistics:** About 31% of GNP comes from agriculture (rubber, copra, tea, coffee, tobacco, sugar, palm oil, rice), 15% from manufacturing (chiefly processing of agricultural and mineral products and light manufactures), forestry and fishing, 18% from mining **Minerals and Mining:** The country is one of the world's leading producers of tin and rubber and is the leading oil producer in the Far East. Other minerals are bauxite, nickel, copper, natural gas, and coal **Labor Force:** 55,000,000, of which some 64% is in agriculture and 7% in industry **Foreign Trade:** Exports, chiefly petroleum and petroleum products (52%), tin ore, copper, nickel, copra, coffee, and tobacco, totaled $15.6 billion in 1979. Imports, mainly textiles, machinery, transportation equipment, rice, fertilizer, and chemicals, totaled $7.2 billion **Principal Trade Partners:** Japan, United States, West Germany, Netherlands, Singapore, Taiwan, Trinidad & Tobago

Vital Statistics: Birthrate, 35.9 per 1,000 of pop. (1980); death rate, 12.5 **Life Expectancy:** 48 years **Health Statistics:** 1,625 inhabitants per hospital bed; 16,390 per physician (1975) **Infant Mortality:** 126 per 1,000 births **Illiteracy:** 38% **Primary and Secondary School Enrollment:** 22,613,072 (1976) **Enrollment in Higher Education:** 278,200 (1975) **GNP Expended on Education:** 1.4% (1976)

Transportation: Paved roads total c. 16,500 mi. **Motor Vehicles:** 806,400 (1977) **Passenger Cars:** 479,300 **Railway Mileage:** 4,874 **Ports:** Jakarta, Surabaya, Semarang, Palembang, Belawan, Dumai, Balikpapan, Samarinda **Major Airlines:** Garuda Airways and Merapti Nusantara operate domestic and international services **Communications:** Government controlled **Radio Transmitters:** 588 **Licenses:** 5,100,000 (1976) **Television Transmitters:** 29 **Licenses:** 325,000 (1976) **Telephones:** 314,000 (1976) **Newspapers:** 172 dailies (1975), 10 copies per 1,000 inhabitants

Weights and Measures: Metric system **Travel Requirements:** Passport, tourist visa (to 30 days, $2.80 fee), 2 photos **International Dialing Code:** 62

Indonesia, with 13,662 tropical islands (992 of them inhabited), strung like a necklace along the equator, is one of the world's most beautiful nations. It is green and fertile, but until recently political upheavals guaranteed its backward, impoverished status among nations.

Ruled by Dutch colonialists for about 300 years, Indonesia declared its independence on August 17, 1945, following Japanese occupation during World War II. Four years of fighting and negotiation followed and its sovereignty was recognized in 1949.

The colonial economic and administrative machinery decayed under President Sukarno, who concentrated on building a national identity and pride among a conglomeration of races and religions scattered throughout the islands. He also sought to cast Indonesia in the role of leader of the "third world" while slowly moving closer to Communist China for support.

It was the gradual growth of the ideology of Communism that eventually led to Sukarno's downfall and plunged Indonesia not only into political and economic chaos but also into one of the worst bloodbaths in history.

On the night of September 30, 1965, the Communists and other leftists attempted a coup that was put down by anti-Communist military units under General Suharto. In an ensuing purge of Communists, more than 300,000 Indonesians were slaughtered. Political prisoners were held for years, but the government, pressured by Amnesty International and others, released many thousands annually for several years, beginning in 1977.

President Sukarno was gradually eased out of power and General Suharto became president, running the country under the tight rein of the military. The Communist party was banned.

President Suharto found Indonesia in financial ruin and deeply in debt to other nations for money Sukarno had borrowed to spend on military equipment and prestige projects such as public buildings and monuments. Under the new regime capital was lured into the country with tempting interest rates and guarantees.

Indonesia faces enormous problems, and tremendous overcrowding of the island of Java, where an estimated 80 million people live, tops the list. Efforts to move people to underpopulated outer island regions have largely failed. Despite development of roads, electrification, hospitals and schools, much of the outer island area still remains a wilderness.

However, a vast natural treasure of oil, minerals and forests is beginning to be harvested, to the benefit of both Indonesia and the foreign investors who have poured in the money and technical skills to exploit it. Currently, Indonesia is East Asia's main oil exporter and a member of the Organization of Petroleum Exporting Countries (OPEC). Its estimated foreign trade surplus of $13 billion in 1980 was due mainly to its $21 billion in oil and gas exports.

After a parliamentry election in 1977, President Suharto was unanimously reelected by the Congress to a third five-year term in March 1978. Adam Malik was elected vice-president and a new cabinet with increased military representation was installed. A five-year plan was announced for 1979-83, stressing development of small-scale industries and non-petroleum exports to ease the nation's massive and persistent unemployment. In 1980, after he was publicly castigated in a petition signed by 50 prominent political figures, Suharto moved to restict the rights of his most strident opponents. These included the Moslem Unitary Development party, representing conservative Islamic elements, and a variety of activist student groups in Indonesia's major universities and high schools.

Ideological, political, and economic factors all contributed to Indonesia's growing hostility toward Vietnam as the decade of the 1980's began. In June 1981, a major Indonesian military airfield was opened in the Natuna Islands in the South China Sea, dominating an oil-rich area claimed by both nations.

HISTORY: The complex racial mixture found in Indonesia today is the result of two waves of invasions from Asia and the Pacific. Early in the Christian era the country came under the influence of Indian civilization and of Hinduism and Buddhism. In the 16th century, however, both of these were replaced by Islam as the dominant religion. In the 17th century, the Dutch emerged as the dominant power in Indonesia, maintaining their rule almost uninterruptedly until World War II, when the islands were occupied by Japan

1945-49: Nationalist leaders Sukarno and Mohammad Hatta proclaim Indonesia an independent republic following Japanese defeat in World War II. Attempts to reestablish Dutch rule evoke nationalist resistance; agreement is finally reached for creation of the United States of Indonesia, linked to Netherlands

1950-54: United States of Indonesia is dissolved; Republic of Indonesia is proclaimed, with Sukarno as president. Netherlands-Indonesian Union is dissolved

1959-60: Sukarno combines premiership with office of president and adopts authoritarian system of "guided democracy"; following disagreement with Hatta, who resigns as vice-president, Sukarno dissolves parliament and bans political parties

1962: Dutch withdraw from West Irian, on island of New Guinea, under agreement with United Nations, on condition that territory's people be permitted to decide their own political future

1965-66: Indonesia withdraws from UN; Sukarno adopts policy of collaboration with Communist China, which the Indonesian Communist party (PKI) supports in Sino-Soviet split. An attempted Communist coup is suppressed by army and is followed by anti-Communist riots in which more than 300,000 Indonesians are killed; General Suharto emerges as new strong man

1967-68: Sukarno is stripped of power and Suharto named acting president. Abandonment of pro-Peking stance is followed by riots directed against Indonesia's economically important Chinese minority; Suharto is formally elected president by People's Consultative Congress

1969: Government quells uprising by Papuan natives in West Irian; despite widespread native opposition, Indonesia annexes territory with the approval of tribal leaders

1971: July parliamentary elections are first to be held since 1955. The government party wins a majority of House seats

1973: Suharto reelected to second five-year term

1975-76: Portuguese Timor is incorporated into Indonesia, becoming its 27th province

1977: Ruling Golkar party wins elections. Government releases 10,000 political prisoners

1978: Weeks of student protests precede presidential election; hundreds arrested, some campuses occupied; Suharto is reelected to third five-year term by Indonesian Congress. Government says it freed another 10,000 political prisoners

1979: A volcanic eruption on Mount Sinila, in central Java, kills 175 persons and injures 1,000. Food and medicine are rushed to the province of East Timor, where more than 100,000 persons suffer from famine and disease

1980: After he is denounced in a joint statement by 50 prominent politicians, Suharto places restrictions on free expression of criticism in the press

1981: In nation's worst maritime disaster, as many as 580 perish when an inter-island passenger ship catches fire and sinks in Java Sea on Jan.27

IRAN

Area: 636,293 sq. mi. **Population:** 35,504,000 (1978 est.)

Official Name: Islamic Republic of Iran **Capital:** Tehran **Nationality:** Iranian **Languages:** Persian, or Farsi, an Aryan language of the Indo-European group and written Arabic characters, is the official and dominant language. Kurdish, various forms of Turkic, and Arabic are among the other languages spoken **Religion:** About 98% of the population is Moslem, with 90% belonging to the Shi'a sect of Islam and the rest to the Sunni sect. Minority religious groups include Jews, the persecuted Baha'is, Zoroastrians, and Christian Armenians and Assyrians **Flag:** Three unequal horizontal stripes of green, white and red with the red stylized word "Allah" in the center of the white stripe. The words "Allahu Akbar" are written eleven times in Kufic script on the inside edges of the green and red stripes **Anthem:** N.A. **Currency:** Iranian rial (76.8 per U.S. $1)

Location: Southwest Asia. Iran is bordered on the north by the USSR and the Caspian Sea, on the east by Afghanistan and Pakistan, on the south by the Persian Gulf, and on the west by Iraq and Turkey **Features:** The country is largely a semiarid plateau, with high mountain ranges and much barren desert. The Caspian coastal region is semitropical and fertile; the area around the Persian Gulf is extremely hot and dry **Chief Rivers:** Karun, Safid, Karkheh, Zayandeh, Dez

Religious Leader: Ayatollah Ruhollah Khomeini, born 1900?, is the *faghi* (religious leader) for life, according to the new constitution. The executive, legislative and judicial branches of the government are under the authority of the *faghi* **Head of State:** An interim presidency exercises power following the death of President Rajai on Aug. 30, 1981 **Head of Government:** Acting Prime Minister: Ayatollah Mohammad Mahdavi-Kani, appointed Sept. 1,1981 **Effective Date of Present Constitution:** December 3, 1979 (approved by electorate in special referendum) **Legislative Body:** *Majlis* or Parliament (unicameral), consisting of 270 members popularly elected for a four-year term **Local Government:** 23 provinces

Ethnic Composition: Iranians (Persians) make up about 60% of the population. In addition, there are approximately 5 million Azerbaijanis, over 4 million Kurds, 2 million Arabs, 1 million Turkomans, 1 million Baluchis, 500,000 Qashqais, and smaller numbers of Lurs and Bakhtiaris **Population Distribution:** 46.8% urban **Density:** 56 inhabitants per sq. mi.

Largest Cities: (1976 census) Tehran 4,496,159, Isfahan 671,825, Meshed 670,180, Tabriz 598,576, Shiraz 416,408, Ahwaz 329,006, Abadan 296,081, Kermanshah 290,861

Per Capita Income: $1,128 (1980) **Gross National Product (GNP):** $43.7 billion (1980) **Economic Statistics:** About 25% of GNP comes from agriculture (wheat, cotton, barley, rice, fresh and dried fruits and vegetables, pulses, oilseeds, sugar beets), forestry, and fishing; 27% from oil; 17% from industry (textiles, food processing, building materials, rubber tires and mining); 5% from construction; and 21% from trade and services **Minerals and Mining:** Oil (Iran has 10% of the world's known oil resources), iron ore, chromite, natural gas, copper, lead, zinc, coal, gypsum, gold, manganese, and salt

Labor Force: 12,000,000 (1979) of which 33% is engaged in agriculture and 21% in industry **Foreign Trade:** Exports, mainly oil, carpets, cotton, and fruits, totaled $19.8 billion in 1979. Imports, chiefly machinery, iron and steel, chemicals and drugs, totaled $8.7 billion **Principal Trade Partners:** Japan, West Germany, Britain, Italy, Spain, France, Netherlands

Vital Statistics: Birthrate, 41.7 per 1,000 of pop (1976); death rate, 13 **Life Expectancy:** 54 years **Health Statistics:** 650 inhabitants per hospital bed; 2,696 per physician (1975) **Infant Mortality:** 100 per 1,000 births (1977) **Illiteracy:** 63% **Primary and Secondary School Enrollment:** 7,125,466 (1976) **Enrollment in Higher Education:** 154,215 **GNP Expended on Education:** 5.4% (1976)

Transportation: Paved roads total 11,620 mi. (1976) **Motor Vehicles:** 1,136,700 (1977) **Passenger Cars:** 932,700 **Railway Mileage:** 3,700 **Ports:** Khorramshahr, Bandar Khomeini (Bandar Shahpur), Bushire, Bandar Abbas, Kharg, Abadan, Enzeli **Major Airlines:** Iran National Airlines operates internal and international services **Communications:** Government controlled **Radio Transmitters:** 64 **Receivers:** 6,500,000 (1976) **Television Transmitters:** 157 **Receivers:** 1,720,000 (1976) **Telephones:** 1,000,000 (1977) **Newspapers:** 20 dailies, 15 copies per 1,000 inhabitants (1974)

Weights and Measures: Metric system **Travel Requirements:** The U.S. government has banned all travel to Iran by American citizens, except for newsmen **International Dialing Code:** 98

Iran's revolution of 1979, a popular uprising of civilians, overthrew Shah Mohammed Reza Pahlavi and opened the way for creation of the Islamic Republic of Iran. Shock waves surged through the world with the exit of the Shah, long regarded as an ally of the U.S., a strong opponent of the spread of communism in the Middle East, and a key figure in assuring the flow of petroleum so vital to the Western world. Terrorism intensified the turmoil later, on Nov. 4, 1979, when young militants seized the U.S. embassy compound in Tehran and vowed to hold the American diplomatic personnel as hostages until the Shah was returned to Iran for trial. A 79-year-old religious leader, Ruhollah Khomeini, successor to the Shah in power, gave his blessing to the capture, and more than 14 months passed before the captives were released. Unemployment and inflation climbed steeply after the revolution. Oil exports, which in 1980 dropped to a fraction of those during the Shah's reign, declined further in 1981 as the result of a war with neighboring Iraq.

Iran is a country about two and one-half times larger than Texas. Prone to earthquakes, the country has arable portions that are divided from one another by mountain ranges and deserts. Its most important ethnic group are the Farsi (Persians, whence the traditional name of the country—Persia), but over a third of the population are of other ethnic groups, most of them Indo-European, as are the Farsi. Its oil industry, founded in 1908, is the backbone of the national economy. The wells, although they are beginning to run out, still have enormous potential.

Seat of ancient empires, Iran was conquered by Moslem Arabs in the 7th century A.D. Over centuries, most Iranians became Moslems, but kept their Indo-European languages. In the 15th century, Iran adhered to the Shi'a movement, turning away from Arab leadership.

Shah Reza Pahlavi, an army colonel, who seized power in a military coup in 1921, was favorable to the army and to the promotion of Western ways. Britain and the USSR ousted him in 1941 because he looked to Nazi Germany as a counterweight to British and Soviet influence.

His son and successor, Mohammed Reza Pahlavi, ruled as a figurehead until 1953, when, with the help of the army and Western governments, he ousted Prime Minister Mossadegh. The Shah was identified with foreign influence, and he became more and more dictatorial. The Shah launched a "revolution from the throne" in 1961, and carried out plans to modernize the country, improve public health, and raise the status of women and the poor.

Moreover, he offended the mullahs by disregarding their interpretations of the Koran and by seizing mosque property. SAVAK, his secret police, dealt harshly with those considered to be enemies of progress. Wealth increasingly concentrated in the cities, and city ways became offensive to country people.

When Britain withdrew its soldiers from the Persian Gulf region in 1970, the Shah gave military assistance to neighboring countries. U.S. strategists considered his army crucial to the stability of the region. The army supported him, and the United States gave him aid. The mosques became the centers of opposition to the Shah. In 1978, riots broke out in the name of Khomeini, an exiled mullah who bore the holy title *Ayatollah*.

In 1979, the Shah left Iran, after appointing Shahpur Bakhtiar, a Mossadegh partisan, prime minister. Khomeini, still in exile, mocked the government and appointed a Council of the Islamic Revolution. He returned to Iran and designated Mehdi Bazargan, another Mossadegh partisan, prime minister. There were violent demonstrations on behalf of Bazargan. The armed forces at first supported Bakhtiar, but later became neutral, and Bakhtiar's government collapsed.

Khomeini, Bazargan, and the Council of the Islamic Revolution became power centers—not always in cooperation with each other. Mullahs and *ad hoc* militia units took most of the local authority. But the new order ran into multiple troubles. The Kurds, who had joined in overthrowing the Shah, pursued guerrilla tactics against the Islamic regime. Also opposing it were such ethnic minorities as the Azerbaijanis and the Baluchis and, at various times, certain elements within Iran's badly splintered Marxist movement.

Sixteen days after the embassy seizure, the militants released five white women and eight black men—although all had been denounced initially as "spies." Still held were 50 in the embassy and three in the Foreign Ministry. When Bazargan and his government resigned in protest, Khomeini strengthened the role of the clergy by making the Revolutionary Council the government.

In January 1980, after the adoption of a new constitution, Abolhassan Bani-Sadr, an economist and a critic of the hostage seizure, was elected president, but in parliamentary voting in March and May, the fundamentalist Islamic Republican party, led by the Ayatollah Mohammad Beheshti, won control of the legislature and installed a Moslem "hard-liner," Mohammad Ali Rajai, as prime minister. An unequal power struggle between Bani-Sadr and the fundamentalists continued until June 22, 1981, when Iran's supreme authority, the reclusive Ayatollah Khomeini, stripped the president of his office. Bani-Sadr went into exile in Paris following an order for his arrest. Ayatollah Beheshti was killed on June 28 with 71 others when a bomb exploded at a meeting of the fundamentalist group. In the election of July 24, Prime Minister Ali Mohammad Ali Rajai was elected to the presidency. On August 30, Rajai and newly-appointed Prime Minister Bahonar were killed in a bomb explosion.

In the hostage crisis, the U.S. had retaliated in November 1979 by cutting off oil imports from Iran and freezing Iranian assets in U.S. banks. On April 24, 1980, an attempt by American airborne force to rescue the hostages was halted, before combat, when three helicopters developed mechanical troubles on an Iranian salt desert. Despite the death of the Shah in Cairo in July, negotiations dragged on until January 1981, when, due in part to mediation by Algeria, agreement was reached. The major U.S. concession was the release of frozen Iranian assets. The 52 remaining hostages left Iran on January 20, the day that U.S. President Carter left office.

IRAN and IRAQ
CONIC PROJECTION
MILES
KILOMETRES
Capitals of Countries ⊛
International Boundaries -----
Ruins ∴
Elevations in Feet

Skirmishes between Iran and Iraq over a disputed boundary alignment escalated into a full-scale war in late September 1980. Iraqi troops drove deep into Iran's Khuzistan province and heavily damaged the oil refinery at Abadan. Iranian planes struck at Iraqi targets, including the capital city of Baghdad. Fighting diminished before the end of the year, but broke out sporadically during 1981, with neither country gaining a decisive advantage. With ideological and political differences complicating the search for a settlement, attempts by other Moslem nations to mediate an end to the conflict failed.

HISTORY: An agricultural civilization existed in Iran as far back as 4000 B.C. The Aryans arrived about 2000 B.C. and split into two main groups, the Medes and the Persians. About 550 B.C., Cyrus the Great founded the Persian Empire, which later fell to successive invaders. The Arabs conquered the country and introduced Islam in the 7th century A.D.; they were in turn replaced by the Turks and Mongols. Internal order was restored by the Safavid dynasty, which ruled from 1499 to 1736

1736-47: Nadir Shah establishes Afshar dynasty; he invades India in 1738 and brings back great riches; a despotic ruler, he is assassinated in 1747

1794: Aga Mohammad Khan established Kajar dynasty

19th cent.: Iran loses vast territories to Afghanistan and Russia

1901: Discovery of oil intensifies the rivalry between Britain and Russia over Iran

1907: Britain and Russia divide Iran into spheres of influence

1921-25: Reza Khan, an army officer, stages coup d'état, overthrows Kajar dynasty, and establishes military dictatorship; he is elected shah and founds Pahlavi dynasty

1941: British and Soviet forces occupy Iran to counter German threat; Reza Shah abdicates and is succeeded by his son, Mohammad Reza Pahlavi

1946: Soviet troops are withdrawn from Iran

1951-53: Premier Mossadegh, a militant nationalist, forces parliament to nationalize oil industry, which collapses after Britain imposes a blockade. Shah, who opposes Mossadegh, flees the country but returns after Mossadegh is ousted

1961-62: Shah launches "revolution from the throne," calling for the end of serfdom, for land distribution, and electoral reform; he personally distributes crown land to peasants

1963: Women gain vote

1971: U.S. and Britain underwrite a $1-billion defense program for Iran as prelude to British withdrawal from the Persian Gulf

1972: Earthquake leaves over 5,000 dead

1975: Shah dissolves two-party system. U.S. and Iran sign $15 billion economic pact for non-oil trade

1978: Ultraconservative Moslems, leftist extremists and others join in widespread riots. Theater fire kills 380 in port city of Abadan; government blames extremists

1979: Shah appoints Shahpur Bakhtiar, former Mossadegh partisan, prime minister, and leaves country. Exiled Ayatollah Ruhollah Khomeini condemns government and returns to Iran, designating Mehdi Bazargan as prime minister. Mass uprising sweeps out Bakhtiar government. Ethnic minorities revolt against government for local autonomy. Bazargan government holds referendum which results in 98% majority for "Islamic republic." Young militants seize the U.S. embassy compound, vowing to hold the hostages until the Shah is returned to Iran for trial. The U.S. freezes an estimated $12 billion in Iranian assets. The World Court orders that the hostages be freed. New constitution is approved in a special referendum

1980: Abolhassan Bani-Sadr is elected president, a position subservient to a *faghi* (religious leader), the leading theologian of Iran, Khomeini. U.S. puts embargo on American exports to Iran (April). Eight U.S. soldiers die in collision of plane and helicopter on Iranian desert on April 24 after U.S. military mission to rescue hostages is aborted due to aircraft malfunctions. Clergy-dominated Islamic Republican party wins control of the *Majilis* (parliament) in May voting; Mohammad Ali Rajai becomes premier. One of 53 U.S. hostages released for medical reasons. Shah dies in Egypt on July 27. Iraqi invasion of Iran (Sept. 22) begins an all-out war; Abadan refinery damaged; Iran's planes bomb Baghdad

1981: Hostage crisis resolved with help of Algerian mediators; Iranian assets in U.S. unfrozen; 52 hostages flown out of Iran on U.S. Inauguration Day, Jan. 20. Moslem nations fail to persuade Iran and Iraq to end hostilities. Over 3,000 die in June 11 earthquake in Kerman province. Bani-Sadr is ousted as president on June 22. Ayatollah Mohammad Beheshti and 71 other anti-Bani-Sadr politicians are killed June 28 bomb explosion. Premier Rajai is elected president on July 24 Rajai and newly-appointed Premier Bahonar are killed in bomb blast Aug. 30

IRAQ

Area: 172,476 sq. mi. **Population:** 12,767,000 (1979 est.)

Official Name: Republic of Iraq **Capital:** Baghdad **Nationality:** Iraqi **Languages:** Arabic is the official and dominant language; Kurdish is spoken in the northeast **Religion:** About 90% of the population is Moslem, almost evenly divided between the Shi'a sect and the Sunni sect; about 8% is Christian **Flag:** Red, white, and black horizontal stripes, with three five-pointed green stars on the white stripe **Anthem:** Anthem of the Republic, no words **Currency:** Iraqi dinar (.29 per U.S. $1)

Location: Southwest Asia. Iraq is bordered on the north by Turkey, on the east by Iran, on the southeast by Kuwait and the Persian Gulf, on the southwest by Saudi Arabia, and on the west by Jordan and Syria **Features:** The country consists of a mountain region in the northeast, a rugged and sparsely wooded area with some good pastures; the vast Syrian Desert, contiguous with the Arabian desert; and a fertile lowland region between the mountains and the desert, watered by the Euphrates and Tigris rivers **Chief Rivers:** Tigris, Euphrates

Head of State and of Government: President: Gen. Saddam Hussein, born 1937, took office on July 16, 1979. He is chairman of the Revolutionary Command Council **Effective Date of Present Constitution:** A provisional constitution was issued in 1968; a National Charter was drafted in 1971 as a basis for a permanent constitution **Legislative Body:** National Assembly (unicameral) of 250 members **Local Government:** 18 provinces, each headed by a governor

Ethnic Composition: Arabs constitute about 71% of the population; Kurds constitute an estimated 18% **Population Distribution:** 66% urban **Density:** 74 inhabitants per sq. mi.

Largest Cities: (1970 estimates) Baghdad 1,028,083, Mosul 333,177, Basra 286,955

Per Capita Income: $2,666 (1980) **Gross National Product (GNP):** $35.6 billion (1980) **Economic Statistics:** In 1976, 8% of GNP was from agriculture (dates, wheat, barley, rice, cotton, wool, hides, and skins); 16% from industry, excluding the petroleum industry (foodstuffs, water and power services, bricks and cement, beverages, cigarettes and textiles); 26% from trade and services; and 50% from oil industry **Minerals and Mining:** Petroleum, sulphur, phosphate, natural gas, and salt are exploited **Labor Force:** 3,200,000, of which 53% is employed in agriculture, 17% in industry, 11% in services **Foreign Trade:** Exports, chiefly petroleum (98% of total), agricultural products, livestock, and cement, totaled $22 billion in 1979. Imports, mainly industrial machinery, iron and steel, automobiles, tea, sugar, clothing, and pharmaceutical products, totaled $11 billion **Principal Trade Partners:** EC countries, USSR, Japan, UAE, Brazil, United States, Lebanon, Kuwait, Yugoslavia

Vital Statistics: Birthrate, 48.1 per 1,000 of pop. (1975); death rate, 14.6 **Life Expectancy:** 62 years **Health Statistics:** 491 inhabitants per hospital bed; 2,555 per physician (1976) **Infant Mortality:** 27.5 per 1,000 births **Illiteracy:** 49% **Primary and Secondary School Enrollment:** 2,552,347 (1976) **Enrollment in Higher Education:** 86,111 (1975) **GNP Expended on Education:** 4.3% (1976)

Transportation: Paved roads total 4,000 mi. **Motor Vehicles:** 224,900 (1977) **Passenger Cars:** 150,400 **Railway Mileage:** 1,462 **Ports:** Basra, Umm Qasr, Fao, Az Zubair **Major Airlines:** Iraqi Airways operates domestic and international services **Communications:** Government controlled **Radio Transmitters:** 12 **Receivers:** 1,252,000 (1975) **Television Transmitters:** 7 **Receivers:** 425,000 (1976) **Telephones:** 320,000 (1976) **Newspapers:** 7 dailies (1975), 22 copies per 1,000 inhabitants (1974)

Weights and Measures: Metric system **Travel Requirements:** Passport, visa, valid 3 months, 1 photo **International Dialing Code:** 964

Iraq, the site of the ancient Sumerian, Babylonian, and other civilizations, was among the first Arab countries to free itself from Western European domination, joining the League of Nations in 1932, at the termination of British-mandate rule.

In 1958, after the monarchy was overthrown in a bloody military coup, Iraq became a republic. Ten years later, in the fourth coup in a decade, Maj. Gen. Ahmed Hassan al-Bakr came to power as the head of a military junta. Thirteen days later, he deposed his two partners in the junta and proclaimed himself president. But his ill health resulted in the rise to prominence of Saddam Hussein, Deputy Chairman of the Revolutionary

Command Council. On July 16, 1979, Bakr resigned and Saddam Hussein became president.

It is generally accepted that the country is ruled today by the inner core of the Ba'ath party, an ultranationalistic, left-wing, Pan-Arab group, a rival faction of which controls Syria. The Iraqi inner core consists of young intellectual zealots, who rarely appear in public, leaving such functions to the president. The ruling Ba'ath party controls the Revolutionary Command Council, which is the nation's highest authority.

Although the Iraqi authorities have tended to isolate themselves even from the rest of the Arab world, there have been some recent indications that they are beginning to make an effort to enhance their reputation abroad.

The mainstay of Iraq's economy is oil. The revenue it receives through its petroleum exports pays for the bulk of the national expenditure. The oil revenues have been handled sensibly by Iraqi officials and not squandered on prestige projects as in other Middle Eastern lands. There has been a gradual improvement in living standards.

The militant Kurdish minority in the north has long been a problem to Iraqi officials. The Kurds, a nomadic non-Arab people, have traditionally been hostile to rule from Baghdad, and in recent years they engaged the Iraqi army in guerrilla warfare.

Closely related to the issue of the Kurds, who have ethnic ties to the Persians, is Iraq's conflict with Iran over navigation rights in the Shatt al Arab, the estuary formed by the confluence of the Tigris and Euphrates that forms part of a mutual border. In 1975 Iran and Iraq signed a reconciliation agreement, with Iraq abandoning its claim to the estuary and with Iran ending its support of the Kurdish rebellion, which shortly collapsed. On Sept. 17, 1980, Iraq cancelled the 1975 agreement about the estuary, and Iraqi armed forces invaded Iran's oil-rich Khuzistan province on September 23, heavily damaging the major oil refinery at Abadan. Iranian planes bombed the Iraqi refineries at Mosul and Basra, as well as numerous other targets.

After the initial Iraqi thrust in the full-scale war, President Hussein proposed a cease-fire that was rejected by Iran. The war soon settled down to a stalemate highlighted by the exaggerated claims and counter-claims of both sides. A peace plan offered in early 1981 by the 42-nation Islamic Conference called for an Iraqi withdrawal from Iranian territory. Hussein objected to the plan, however, and said that a settlement must cede the Shatt al Arab to Iraq. Afterwards, Iraq resumed limited probing actions by its ground forces and sporadic bombing attacks by aircraft and missiles in Khuzistan province.

Iraq concluded an agreement with France in 1975 to construct a nuclear reactor station near Baghdad and, by June 1981, the reactor was close to completion. On June 7, Israeli warplanes bombed the facility completely destroying the nuclear installation. An official Israeli statement declared that the purpose of the plant was to produce atomic bombs for use against Israel. The United Nations Security Council condemned Israel for the air attack on June 19.

HISTORY: About 3000 B.C. the Sumerians, already long established in the region, founded city-states in southern Mesopotamia. Among the civilizations that flourished there later were the Akkadian, Babylonian, and Assyrian. After about 500 B.C., Persia, and later Macedonia, dominated the area. In the 7th century A.D., Mesopotamia was overrun by the Arabs, who established their capital at Baghdad. Mongol invasions followed in the 12th and 15th centuries, and in the 16th century the region fell to the Ottoman Turks, under whose rule it remained until World War I
1920: Iraq is made a British mandate under the League of Nations
1932: An independent Iraq is admitted to the League
1941: A pro-Axis government, briefly in power, collapses under British military attack

1948-49: Iraq sends its forces into Palestine during Arab/Israeli War. The war ends with an armistice
1958: Army coup led by Brig. Gen. Abdul Karim Kassem overthrows monarchy and proclaims a republic; King Faisal and Crown Prince Abdul Illah, the king's uncle, are slain
1961: Civil war flares as Kurdish tribesmen rebel
1963: A Ba'athist military coup, headed by Col. Abdul Salem Aref, ousts regime of Kassem, who is executed
1964: Cease-fire is arranged between army and Kurdish rebels, but fighting soon resumes
1966: Abdul Salem Aref is killed in helicopter crash; he is succeeded by his brother Abdul Rahman Aref
1967: Following Arab defeat in Six-Day War with Israel, Aref forms a new government under Lt. Gen. Tahir Yahya
1968: Bloodless coup overthrows Aref and Yahya; Revolutionary Command Council takes control under Gen. Hassan al-Bakr
1969: Iraq executes about 40 Iraqis, many of them Jews, convicted of spying for Israel, the United States, and Iran
1970: Periodic war with Kurds is ended by granting of a degree of autonomy. Dispute with Iran over Persian Gulf area grows
1971: Iraq, in support of Palestinian militants, closes its border with Jordan. U.S. Embassy properties in Iraq are seized
1973: Coup attempt led by Col. Nazem Kazzar, Iraqi security chief, fails; Kazzar and 35 followers are executed
1974: Kurds declare war on Iraq
1975: Agreement with Iran, which had supported Kurds. Iraqi troops complete the takeover of former Kurdish strongholds
1977: President Bakr's power base is widened as Revolutionary Command Council is increased from 5 to 22 members
1979: Iraq helps to settle dispute between North Yemen and South Yemen, and hosts conference of Arab ministers protesting Israel-Egypt peace treaty. Bakr resigns on July 16, turning the presidency over to Saddam Hussein
1980: Iraq cancels 1975 agreement ceding Shatt al Arab estuary to Iran; Iraqi forces drive deep into Iran's Khuzistan province and Iraqi planes bomb Abadan oil refinery; Iran bombs Iraqi refineries at Mosul and Basra; war develops into stalemate
1981: Hussein objects to peace plan proposed by other Moslem nations; sporadic fighting continues in Khuzistan. Israeli warplanes destroy French-built nuclear reactor near Baghdad (June 7)

IRELAND

Area: 27,136 sq. mi. **Population:** 3,364,881 (1979 census)
Official Name: Ireland **Capital:** Dublin **Nationality:** Irish **Languages:** Irish (Gaelic) and English are the official languages; English, however, is the language in common use **Religion:** About 94% of the population is Roman Catholic, about 5% Protestant Episcopal **Flag:** Green, white, and orange vertical stripes **Anthem:** The Soldier's Song **Currency:** Irish Pound (0.6 per U.S. $1)

Location: The republic of Ireland is situated on the second largest of the British Isles, occupying all of the island of Ireland with the exception of Northern Ireland (part of the United Kingdom) with which the republic has its only land border. It is bounded on the east by the Irish Sea, on the southeast by St. George's Channel, and on the west by the Atlantic Ocean **Features:** The country is shaped like a basin, with high coasts sloping inland to low-lying plains **Chief Rivers:** Shannon, Liffey, Suir, Boyne, Blackwater, Erne, Barrow

Head of State: President: Dr. Patrick John Hillery, born 1923, inaugurated 1976 **Head of Government:** Prime Minister Garret Michael Desmond FitzGerald, born 1926, appointed June 1981 **Effective Date of Present Constitution:** December 29, 1937 **Legislative Body:** Parliament (bicameral *Oireachtas*) consisting of the Senate (*Seaned*) and the House of Representatives (*Dáil*). The Senate is composed of 60 members, of whom 11 are nominated by the prime minister, 6 elected by the National University of Ireland and the University of Dublin, and 43 from 5 panels of candidates established on a vocational basis. The *Dáil* has 148 elected members. The maximum term of office is 5 years in both houses **Local Government:** 26 administrative counties and 4 county boroughs, each with popularly elected councils

Ethnic Composition: The population is mainly Irish, with an Anglo-Irish minority **Population Distribution:** 52.2% urban **Density:** 124 inhabitants per sq. mi.

Largest Cities: (1979 census) Dublin 543,563, Cork 138,092, Limerick 60,769, Dún Laoghaire 54,217, Galway 36,824

Per Capita Income: $3,770 (1980) **Gross Domestic Product (GDP):** $12.4 billion (1980) **Economic Statistics:** In 1977 about 17% of GDP came from agriculture (cattle, dairy products, barley, wheat, oats, potatoes, sugar beets); 33% from industry (food processing, metal and engineering products, beverages, tobacco, textiles, chemicals, clothing, and footwear) **Minerals and Mining:** Rich deposits of lead, zinc, copper, iron ore, natural gas, and silver. Offshore oil resources are being investigated **Labor Force:** 1,133,000 (1978), of which 26% is employed in agriculture and fishing, 19% in industry **Foreign Trade:** Exports, chiefly meat, livestock, textiles, machinery and transportation equipment, dairy products, and metal ores, totaled $7 billion in 1979. Imports, mainly machinery and transportation equipment, chemicals, grains and other foodstuffs, textiles, metals and metal products, and petroleum, totaled $9.9 billion **Principal Trade Partners:** Britain, United States, West Germany, France, Netherlands, Japan, Italy

Vital Statistics: Birthrate, 21.4 per 1,000 of pop. (1977); death rate, 10.5 **Life Expectancy:** 72 years **Health Statistics:** 94 inhabitants per hospital bed; 831 per physician (1976) **Infant Mortality:** 15.7 per 1,000 births **Illiteracy:** Negligible **Primary and Secondary School Enrollment:** 547,824 (1977) **Enrollment in Higher Education:** 34,615 (1976) **GNP Expended on Education:** 6.2% (1976)

Transportation: Surfaced roads total 54,324 mi. **Motor Vehicles:** 645,900 (1977) **Passenger Cars:** 577,600 **Railway Mileage:** 1,334 **Ports:** Dublin, Cork, Limerick, Waterford, Rosslare, New Ross **Major Airlines:** Aer Lingus operates domestic and international services **Communications:** Government controlled **Radio Transmitters:** 18 **Licenses:** 949,000 (1976) **Television Transmitters:** 28 **Receivers:** 655,000 (1976) **Telephones:** 480,000 (1976) **Newspapers:** 7 dailies, 222 copies per 1,000 inhabitants (1975)

Weights and Measures: British standards and the metric system are used **Travel Requirements:** Passport, no visa for 90 days **International Dialing Code:** 353

After 30 years of something of an economic miracle in which Ireland turned from an agrarian to an industrial society, a little of the power has gone out of Ireland's boom. A period of relatively slow growth, high inflation and unemployment, and problems with its balance of payments has confronted the government with warnings of trouble. Even so, Ireland has come a long way.

Over a half a century ago, when the 26 counties constituting the republic became an independent state, the economy was unbalanced and in indifferent shape. More than 90 percent of exports were agricultural and went to one market—Britain. Beyond a few established businesses—breweries, distilleries, and bakeries—there was no industry. As a result, the drain upon the nation's young through emigration—first to the United States, and later to Britain—was excessive.

Ireland has been greatly aided by foreigners—both as tourists and as developers. Canadians were given mining rights and their exploration and development have shown that Ireland has rich deposits of zinc, lead, copper, and silver. Additionally, Germans helped harness the Shannon River and gave Ireland its first big hydroelectric generators. Beet sugar production was begun, and for many years Ireland has been self-sufficient in sugar supplies. And promising reserves of oil and gas have recently been discovered off the Irish coast in the Irish Sea. In 1977 foreign investment in Ireland amounted to $1 billion.

Ireland, although committed to upholding the rights of private property and private enterprise, has governmental industries. The national transport company, the airline, the sugar company, the tourist board, the peat board, the radio and television service, and the electricity supply board are all owned by the state and administered by semi-governmental bodies. In January 1973, Ireland's economic prospects were brightened somewhat by its entry into the European Common Market.

Economic progress, however, has not erased the age-old "Irish Question," which again came to the fore with the 1969 outbreak of violence between Catholics and Protestants in Northern Ireland. Sporadic street violence has continued since that time. A series of bombings and bank and post-office raids, coupled with the 1976 assassination of British ambassador Christopher Ewart-Biggs by I.R.A. members, unleashed a chain of events which disrupted the government. An Emergency Powers Bill and a Criminal Law Bill, giving police broad powers in dealing with extremist groups was passed; President Cearbhall O'Dálaigh resigned over the laws and was succeeded as president by Patrick J. Hillery.

Prime Minister Jack Lynch resigned the post after two years in office on Dec. 5, 1979, after his Fianna Fáil party lost some local elections. The party chose Charles Haughey to replace him. Following the June 1981 elections to the *Dáil*, Garret FitzGerald was chosen as Prime Minister in a coalition deal between his Fine Gael party and the Labour party.

Unemployment increased to a record 12 percent of the Irish workforce by the end of 1980, and the government announced a $3.2 billion investment program intended to provide 10,000 new jobs.

HISTORY: Celtic tribes from Gaul or Iberian Galicia conquered Ireland about the 4th century B.C. and established a Gaelic civilization. By the 3rd century A.D., five Gaelic kingdoms had been established and gradually became Christianized. Until the 8th century arrival of the Vikings, Ireland remained free from foreign invasion, escaping even the Roman conquest that befell neighboring Britain. In the end, however, beginning with the 12th-century Anglo-Norman conquest, that neighbor was to prove the most troublesome invader of all

1542: Henry VIII of England assumes the title of King of Ireland

1649: Oliver Cromwell confiscates nine-tenths of Irish land and distributes it among English Protestant settlers

1801: United Kingdom of Great Britain and Ireland is formed

1846-54: About one million Irish die of starvation as a result of famine, brought on by recurring potato blight; more than 1.5 million Irish emigrate, mostly to the United States

1916-20: Easter Rebellion against British rule breaks out in 1916 under leadership of Sinn Fein, a nationalist movement; rebellion is crushed and its leaders executed

1921-22: Irish Free State is set up as a British dominion; six northern counties of Ulster remain in United Kingdom. Sinn Fein splits into conservative and republican groups, the latter headed by Eamon de Valera and opposed to division of Ireland; civil war breaks out but conservative elements prevail

1931: Equality with Britain is affirmed by Statute of Westminster

1932: De Valera becomes prime minister

1937: New Constitution makes British monarch ceremonial head of Ireland for external purposes only

1939-45: Ireland remains neutral during World War II, but many Irish volunteer for service with British forces

1949: Ireland declares itself a republic, withdraws from British Commonwealth, and maintains jurisdictional claims over Northern Ireland

1951-59: De Valera becomes prime minister, following victory by Fianna Fáil in parliamentary elections; De Valera resigns his post as prime minister to take over presidency

1966: De Valera is reelected president for seven-year term; Jack Lynch becomes prime minister

1969: Lynch's Fianna Fáil party wins overall majority in parliament in general elections; government sends troops to northern border as Catholics battle Protestants in Ulster

1973: Erskine Childers succeeds De Valera as president. Liam Cosgrave is elected prime minister

1974: Cearbhall O'Dálaigh becomes fifth president on death of Childers

1975: Severe drought conditions imperil crops

1976: British ambassador to Ireland, Christopher Ewart-Biggs, is killed in Dublin by a land mine explosion. O'Dálaigh resigns presidency; Dr. Patrick J. Hillery becomes president

1977: Jack Lynch's Fianna Fáil Party wins election, making him new prime minister

1979: Prime Minister Lynch resigns and Charles Haughey becomes prime minister. Pope John Paul II visits Ireland

1981: Garret FitzGerald becomes prime minister following *Dáil* elections

---

ISRAEL

Area: 7,847 sq. mi. **Population:** 3,878,000 (1980 est.)

Official Name: State of Israel **Capital:** Jerusalem; Tel Aviv is the diplomatic capital **Nationality:** Israeli **Languages:** Hebrew is the official and dominant language; Arabic is spoken by about 15% of the population; English is the most commonly used foreign language **Religion:** Judaism is the predominant religion; the Arab minority is largely Moslem and the Christian Arabs chiefly Greek Catholic and Greek Orthodox **Flag:** A white field with a blue six-pointed Star of David bordered above and below by blue horizontal stripes **Anthem:** The Hope **Currency:** Shekel (8.9 per U.S. $1)

Location: Middle East, at the eastern end of the Mediterranean. Israel is bordered on the north by Lebanon, on the east by Syria and Jordan, on the south by Egypt, and on the west by the Mediterranean Sea **Features:** The Negev Desert in the south constitutes about 50% of the country. The rest of the country consists of a narrow coastal plain in the center and a hilly region to the north **Chief Rivers:** Jordan, Kishon

Head of State: President Yitzhak Navon, born in 1921, elected by parliament in 1978 for a 5-year term **Head of Government:** Prime Minister Menachem Begin, born 1913, assumed office June 1977 **Effective Date of Present Constitution:** There is no written constitution; the structure of government is defined by fundamental laws **Legislative Body:** Parliament (unicameral *Knesset*) consisting of 120 members elected by universal suffrage for 4 years **Local Government:** 6 districts, headed by appointed commissioners

Ethnic Composition: Jews constitute about 85% of the population, with the rest mainly Arabs **Population Distribution:** 86% urban **Density:** 494 inhabitants per sq. mi.

Largest Cities: (1977 est.) Jerusalem 376,000, Tel Aviv 343,300, Haifa 227,800, Bat Yam 124,100, Holon 121,200

Per Capita Income: $5,052 (1980) **Gross National Product (GNP):** $19 billion (1980) **Economic Statistics:** 7% of GNP comes from agriculture (citrus fruits, eggs, vegetables); 29% from manufacturing (food processing, metals and machinery, textiles, chemicals, and petroleum products), mining, and quarrying; 20% from commerce and finance; 19% from services **Minerals and Mining:** Potash, phosphate, bromine, phosphate rock, copper, iron, ceramic clays and glass sand, and gypsum are exploited **Labor Force:** 1,252,000, of which 24% is employed in industry, 36% in services, 12% in commerce, 6% in agriculture **Foreign Trade:** Exports, chiefly polished diamonds, citrus fruits, textiles, clothes, food products, chemicals, fertilizers, and mining products, totaled $4.7 billion in 1979. Imports, chiefly rough diamonds, machinery, transport equipment, nonmetallic mineral manufactures, food and live animals, raw materials, and chemicals, totaled $8 billion **Principal Trade Partners:** United States, Britain, West Germany, Netherlands, Belgium, France, Switzerland, Hong Kong, Japan, Italy

Vital Statistics: Birthrate, 26.1 per 1,000 of pop. (1977); death rate, 6.8 **Life Expectancy:** 72 years **Health Statistics:** 178 inhabitants per hospital bed; 351 per physician (1976) **Infant Mortality:** 20.1 per 1,000 births **Illiteracy:** 10% **Primary and Secondary School Enrollment:** 705,488 (1975) **Enrollment in Higher Education:** 75,338 (1974) **GNP Expended on Education:** 6.8% (1975)

Transportation: Paved roads total 3,350 mi. **Motor Vehicles:** 420,300 (1977) **Passenger Cars:** 312,700 **Railway Mileage:** 476 **Ports:** Haifa, Ashdod, Eilat **Major Airlines:** El Al Israel Airlines, the government airline, handles foreign travel, while Arkia, its subsidiary, handles domestic travel **Communications:** State controlled **Radio Transmitters:** 39 **Receivers:** 655,000 (1976) **Television Transmitters:** 28 **Receivers:** 475,000 (1976) **Telephones:** 888,000 (1976) **Newspapers:** 23 dailies, 208 copies per 1,000 inhabitants (1975)

Weights and Measures: Metric system **Travel Requirements:** Passport, no visa for 3 months **International Dialing Code:** 972

The proclamation of Israel as a nation in 1947 established after an absence of many centuries a Hebrew state in a land regarded by Jews as their homeland. The ancient kingdoms of Israel and Judah had been conquered repeatedly through several centuries, and the Jews had scattered through many lands. Following the Moslem conquest of the 7th century A.D., Arab culture had become predominant. The 19th-century Zionist movement for restoration of the Jewish homeland promoted Jewish migration to the land—then the Ottoman province of Palestine. Palestine was occupied during World War I by Britain, which governed it as a mandate of the League of Nations from 1919 to 1946, and of the United Nations from 1946 to 1948. Jewish immigration continued, especially after the Nazi persecutions; by 1947, the Jews were in the majority in much of Palestine.

The UN moved to divide Palestine into an Arab and a Jewish state, over the objections of the Palestine Arabs, who rejected the proposal to organize a state. Israel declared its independence on May 14, 1948, and was attacked by five Arab nations. An uneasy truce in 1949 gave Israel almost 50 percent more territory than originally granted; Jordan (then Transjordan) annexed the rest.

Arab-Israeli hostilities continued to seethe under the surface until they erupted in war on October 29, 1956, when Israel staged a "preemptive attack" on Egypt's Sinai during the Suez Canal crisis. A UN cease-fire ended the fighting on November 6 and Israel withdrew its forces.

During the Six Day War of 1967, Israel made large-scale territorial gains in the Gaza Strip, Sinai Peninsula, Old Jerusalem, the Golan Heights, and Jordan's West Bank. The memory of these gains set the stage for the war of 1973-74, when Egyptian, Syrian, and Iraqi forces attacked on October 6. The Arab forces first made large gains, but these were considerably reduced by the time a truce ended the fighting on November 7.

Despite the truce, sporadic fighting continued between Israel and Syrian troops, until U.S. Secretary of State Henry Kissinger arranged a cease-fire on May 31, 1974.

Border agreements with Syria and Egypt which included UN buffer zones were a stabilizing factor in those areas, but in November 1974 there was increased Israeli concern for the future of the West Bank of the Jordan River when the UN General Assembly voted that Palestinians should be entitled to return to their land and property, and granted the Palestine Liberation Organization (PLO) permanent observer status.

In 1975 Kissinger completed negotiations for a second Egyptian-Israeli disengagement agreement setting out details of the new military position in the Sinai Peninsula and the extent of Israeli withdrawal to the eastern entrances of the Giddi and Mitla passes and from the Abu Rudays and Ras Sudar oil fields, which had been supplying 55 percent of Israel's oil needs. By February 1976 the final phase of the troop disengagement agreement was implemented. Meanwhile, many Israelis had settled in the occupied territory, claiming that all of the historic homeland was their land.

In 1977, the Labor Alignment, which had been the largest bloc in every previous legislature, suffered scandal and internal discord. The Likud party won the ensuing election and with two religious groups formed a coalition government more favorable to private enterprise and to Jewish religious tradition. Menachem Begin became prime minister.

Despite Begin's reputation as a hard-liner, President Anwar el-Sadat of Egypt visited Israel in 1977 as an initiative to peace. Begin returned the visit, and negotiations for peace opened. Despite disagreement over Jewish settlements Israel had established in the occupied territory, Begin and Sadat, with the help of U.S. President Jimmy Carter's diplomacy, signed a peace treaty in March 1979. Israel agreed to withdraw from occupied Sinai within three years, and from the oil fields there within a year, and agreed to take steps toward Palestinian self-government. The treaty also obligated Egypt to sell oil to Israel. By early 1980, Israel had withdrawn from two thirds of the Sinai, and the two countries opened their borders to each other and exchanged ambassadors.

The deadline of May 26, 1980, for resolving the Palestinian autonomy issue for the West Bank and Gaza was missed, and talks were suspended. Israel continued to establish settlements on the West Bank despite Egypt's protests and Arab terrorism. In March the United States aroused a furor in Israel by voting for an Arab resolution in the UN Security Council condemning the Israeli resettlement policy, although the vote was later disavowed by President Carter.

Israeli-Arab relations were exacerbated in April 1981 when Israeli jets shot down two Syrian military helicopters in Lebanon. Syria responded by deploying Soviet-made missiles in that country, and Israeli aircraft bombed PLO bases there through July. In retaliation, Palestinian gunners fired rockets at northern Israeli towns. On July 17, Israeli jets struck at PLO headquarters in Beirut, killing 300 persons and wounding 800 others, mostly Lebanese civilians. Israel and the PLO agreed to a cease-fire on July 24.

The Israeli bombing of a nearly-completed Iraqi nuclear reactor station near Baghdad on June 7 also resulted in increased Arab-Israeli tensions, and in a UN Security Council condemnation of Israel. The official Israeli announcement of the air attack stated that the real purpose of the nuclear facility was to produce atomic bombs for use against Israel.

Poor in soil and minerals, beset by inflation, high taxes, and an enormous military budget, Israel nevertheless attracts many Jewish immigrants by promising a them a new life. Tourists are also attracted to historical sites and to places sacred to Christianity, as well as to Judaism.

HISTORY: In biblical times Israel (then Canaan and later Palestine) was the home of scattered Hebrew tribes. By about 1000 B.C. a Hebrew kingdom was firmly established at Jerusalem, under King David. After the reign of Solomon, the kingdom split into two states, Israel and Judah, which were respectively destroyed by Assyria and Babylonia. Palestine later fell to the Greeks and finally to the Romans. In the 7th century, the region was conquered by the Moslems. Later, it was an Ottoman province. During World War I, it came under British control. Modern Israel marks the culmination of the Zionist movement for the reconstitution of a Jewish state

1947: United Nations adopts Palestine partition plan to divide Palestine into two states, one Jewish and one Arab

1948: Israel is proclaimed a nation and British withdraw from Palestine. Armies of surrounding Arab states attack Israel

1949: Fighting ends with Israel in possession of almost 50 percent more territory than originally granted. Armistice agreements, but no peace treaties, are signed with Arab countries

1956: Israeli forces invade Egypt and occupy Sinai Peninsula and Gaza Strip

1957: Under American and Soviet pressure, Israel completes withdrawal to old borders. United States guarantees Israeli passage into Red Sea through previously blockaded Strait of Tiran

1964: Palestine Liberation Organization is formed

1967: Egyptians reimpose blockade. Israel attacks in Sinai and then into Jordan and Syria. At end of Six-Day War, Israelis occupy all of Sinai Peninsula, Gaza, and east bank of Suez Canal, the Gaza Strip, all of west bank of Jordan, and Golan Heights of Syria

1969: Prime Minister Levi Eshkol dies and is succeeded by Mrs. Golda Meir of the Israel Labor party. Arab guerrilla activity continues; Labor Alignment is returned to power

1972: Terrorist activity by PLO guerrillas and sympathizers increases, extending to a random massacre at Lod Airport and the kidnapping and death of Israeli athletes at the Olympic games in Munich. Israel carries out retaliatory raids on guerrilla settlements in Lebanon

1973: David Ben-Gurion, first prime minister and principal founder of the state of Israel, dies

1973-74: Fourth Arab-Israeli war breaks out when Egyptian, Syrian, and Iraqi forces launch surprise attack on October 6, 1973, Yom Kippur, the holiest day of the year for Jews. In January, Israel and Egypt agree on disengagement of forces. Fighting with Syria continues through May 1974

1975: Sporadic raids and bombing incidents, are carried out chiefly by the PLO, followed by Israeli reprisals on PLO camps in Syria; tension makes settlement of Arab-Israeli differences difficult

1976: Israeli airborne commandos rescue 103 hostages held at Uganda's Entebbe Airport by pro-Palestinian hijackers of an Air France airliner

1977: Israeli troops cross into Southern Lebanon and fight with Palestinians in the first direct clash between the two sides in more than two years. Likud party is victorious in general elections; Menachem Begin becomes prime minister. Begin confers with President Carter in Washington. Austerity moves, defense spending cuts, and Israeli pound devaluation are announced. President Sadat's Mideast "peace initiative" spurs round of talks

1978: PLO terror attack, worst in Israel's history, leaves 37 dead and 82 wounded; Israeli forces retaliate by invading southern Lebanon and occupy area for three months

1979: Peace treaty with Egypt signed. Treaty requires Israel to withdraw from Egypt within three years, from remaining oil fields within one year; and requires Egypt to sell oil to Israel

1980: Israeli forces complete withdrawal from Sinai oil fields; government opens borders to Egypt and exchanges ambassadors. Israeli-Egyptian talks on Palestinian autonomy are suspended. A Knesset bill reaffirms all of Jerusalem as the Israeli capital

1981: Relations with Syria worsen after Syrian forces in Lebanon deploy anti-aircraft missiles. Israeli aircraft destroy Iraqi nuclear reactor near Baghdad. Lebanon-based PLO units fire rockets at Israeli towns. Israeli planes bomb Palestinian targets, including PLO headquarters in Beirut; killing 300 and wounding 800, mostly Lebanese civilians. Cease-fire truce arranged on July 24. Begin's Likud party wins election on June 30 by narrrow one-seat parliamentary victory

ITALY

Area: 116,303 sq. mi. **Population:** 57,030,000 (1980 est.)

Official Name: Italian Republic **Capital:** Rome **Nationality:** Italian **Languages:** Italian is the official and predominant language; German, French, Friulian, Slovene, Ladin, Albanian, and Greek are spoken by minorities **Religion:** Roman Catholicism is the religion of about 99% of the population **Flag:** Green, white, and red vertical stripes **Anthem:** Hymn of Mameli **Currency:** Italian lira (1102 per U.S. $1)

Location: Southern Europe. Italy has common land frontiers in the west with France, and in the north with Switzerland, Austria, and Yugoslavia. Its boot-shaped peninsular coastline is bordered by three branches of the Mediterranean: the Tyrrhenian Sea on the west, the Ionian Sea on the south, and the Adriatic Sea on the east. Major offshore islands are Sicily and Sardinia **Features:** The country is rugged and mountainous, except for the Po Valley area in the north, the heel of "the boot" in the south, and small coastal areas **Chief Rivers:** Po, Tiber, Arno, Adige

Head of State: President Alessandro Pertini, born 1896, elected in 1978 by Electoral Assembly (Parliament plus 58 regional representatives) **Head of Government:** Premier Giovanni Spadolini, born 1925, appointed 1981 **Effective date of Present Constitution:** January 1, 1948 **Legislative Body:** Parliament (bicameral), consisting of the Senate and the Chamber of Deputies. The Senate is composed of 322 members elected for 5 years. The Chamber of Deputies has 630 members elected for 5 years **Local Government:** 94 provinces, each headed by a prefect appointed by the central government. These are grouped into 20 regions, with limited governing powers.

Ethnic Composition: The population is virtually homogeneous, with small minority groups of Germans, Friulians, Slovenes, Albanians, Ladins and French **Population Distribution:** 48% urban **Density:** 490 inhabitants per sq. mi.

Largest Cities: (1977 est.) Rome 2,897,505, Milan 1,706,268, Naples 1,225,227, Turin 1,181,567, Genoa 795,027, Palermo 679,493, Bologna 481,120, Florence 464,020

Per Capita Income: $5,300 (1980) **Gross Domestic Product (GDP):** $303 billion (1980) **Economic Statistics:** 43% of GDP comes from industry (automobiles, oil refining, textiles, machinery, chemicals, food processing); 7% from agriculture (wheat, rice, grapes, olives, fruit and vegetables) **Minerals and Mining:** Italy is a leading producer of mercury, but is poor in most other minerals. Iron ore, petroleum, natural gas, lignite, pyrites, and sulphur are produced in small quantities **Labor Force:** 20.1 million, with some 43% in industry and 15% in agriculture **Foreign Trade:** Exports, chiefly industrial machinery, office machines, motor vehicles, textiles, and footwear, totaled $72 billion in 1979. Imports, mainly crude oil, minerals, machinery iron and steel, totaled $78 billion **Principal Trade Partners:** EC and EFTA countries, Latin America, United States, Libya, Saudi Arabia, Iraq, USSR

Vital Statistics: Birthrate, 13.2 per 1,000 of pop. (1977); death rate, 9.6 **Life Expectancy:** 70 years **Health Statistics:** 95 inhabitants per hospital bed; 502 per physician (1973) **Infant Mortality:** 17.6 per 1,000 births **Illiteracy:** 5% **Primary and Secondary School Enrollment:** 9,799,953 (1976) **Enrollment in Higher Education:** 976,712 **GNP Expended on Education:** 5.0% (1975)

Transportation: Surfaced roads total 179,241 mi., including 3,600 mi. of superhighways **Motor Vehicles:** 17,607,300 (1977) **Passenger Cars:** 16,371,200 **Railway Mileage:** 12,624 **Ports:** Genoa, Augusta, Venice, Naples, Trieste, Taranto, La Spezia **Major Airlines:** Alitalia, a government airline, conducts international flights while Itavia and ATI are domestic **Communications:** Partly government controlled **Radio Transmitters:** 1,964 **Licenses:** 13,024,000 (1976) **Television Transmitters:** 1,199 **Licenses:** 12,377,000 (1976) **Telephones:** 15,246,000 (1976) **Newspapers:** 78 dailies, 113 copies per 1,000 inhabitants (1974)

Weights and Measures: Metric system **Travel Requirements:** Passport, no visa for 3 months **International Dialing Code:** 39

Italy—one of the younger of Europe's nation-states, home of one of its oldest civilizations—is a society undergoing profound political, economic, and cultural transformations.

Unified politically only a century ago, Italians still seek a common sense of nationhood that will bridge their vast regional differences and rivalries. The Brenner Pass, in the Alps, and Cape Correnti, on the southern tip of Sicily, lie 750 miles apart, but the distance between them is far greater in terms of the environment, culture, traditions, and temperaments of their peoples.

The northerner is the heir to the Renaissance and *risorgimento*: vigorous, forward-looking, in the mainstream of European life, living in a temperate climate on land endowed with the lion's share of Italy's slender resources.

The southerner, on the other hand, has been less favored both by nature and by history. His land is poor, his climate marked by extremes, his political and cultural tradition still rooted in the aftermath of a feudalism that long resisted the liberating winds of the Renaissance, the French Revolution, and 19th-century liberalism.

The task of molding and governing a postwar republican Italy that will reconcile these vastly divergent interests and enlist equally the loyalties of the Milan industrialist, Roman aristocrat or shopkeeper, and Calabrian peasant has fallen on shifting coalitions of the democratic parties of the center and moderate left.

Until June 1981, the Christian Democratic party had been the largest in every parliament—and had supplied every premier—since 1946. But it never had a majority, and had to negotiate agreements for coalition with other parties. Italy's 40th government since World War II, a four-party coalition formed by Christian Democratic President Arnaldo Forlani in October 1980, fell in May 1981 because of a scandal. Public revelations about *Propaganda Due*, a secretive Masonic lodge which may have been involved in criminal activities, disclosed that its 953 members included 3 cabinet ministers, 43 members of Parliament, and 38 generals and admirals. The cabinet members involved were forced to resign, bringing down the Forlani government. On June 28, Giovanni Spadolini, leader of the small Republican party, was sworn in as premier.

The Communist party of Italy (PCI) became the second-largest in parliament by professing dedication to democracy and to national independence and by governing a number of cities with scrupulous honesty. But participation in the Cabinet eluded it because the Christian Democrats and others feared both the PCI's motives and the difficulties that a government with Communist ministers would face with the United States.

Italy has been troubled by acts of political terrorism, the most spectacular being the kidnap and murder of former Premier Aldo Moro in 1978, and the bombing of the Bologna railroad station in August 1980, which killed 81 people.

HISTORY: About 500 B.C. Rome began its rise to power, supplanting the earlier Etruscan civilization. The Roman Empire fell in the 5th century A.D. and thereafter the Italian peninsula was largely politically fragmented until modern times. After the great cultural and intellectual flowering of the Renaissance, which reached its height in the late 15th century, much of Italy, divided into kingdoms, principalities, duchies, city-republics, and the Papal States, fell increasingly under foreign sway

1815: Following collapse of Napoleonic Empire, former states of Italian peninsula are reconstituted—some under Austrian rule

1848-49: Movement for the unification of Italy, known as the *risorgimento*, leads to revolts, but these are suppressed after initial successes

1859: Kingdom of Sardinia, aided by France, defeats Austrians at Solferino

1860-70: The Italian unification movement, whose most notable figures were Giuseppe Garibaldi, Giuseppe Mazzini, and Camillo di Cavour, moves ahead as various Italian states vote for union with Sardinia; following conquest of Kingdom of Two Sicilies by Garibaldi, that kingdom also votes for union with Sardinia, and in 1861 the Kingdom of Italy is proclaimed under Victor Emmanuel II. With the seizure of the papal possessions, Italian unification is completed by 1870

1915-18: Italy engages in World War I on side of Allies after initially declaring neutrality; country suffers heavy losses

1922: Benito Mussolini comes to power in wake of severe depression and establishes a fascist dictatorship

1935-36: Italy conquers Ethiopia

1940-43: Italy enters World War II as ally of Nazi Germany; Italian defeats in Greece and North Africa, and the Allied invasion of Sicily, help topple Mussolini's regime. New government is set up and an armistice signed with the Allies

1945: Mussolini is executed by Italian partisans

1946: Italy becomes a republic after voters decide by plebiscite to abolish the monarchy

1947: Peace treaty is ratified; Italy loses Fiume, Zara, Pula, and Istria to Yugoslavia and the Dodecanese Islands to Greece; its African colonies are placed under UN supervision

1949: Italy becomes a founding member of NATO

1966: Floods in northern and central Italy destroy or damage many art treasures, especially in Florence

1974: Premier Aldo Moro forms Christian-Democratic/Republican minority government

1975: Voting age is lowered to 18. The 1954 partition of Trieste territory becomes official

1976: Death toll from earthquake in Friuli reaches 1,200. Aldo Moro's government falls and new elections held. Italian Communist party makes major gains but Christian Democrats retain slight edge. Giulio Andreotti is sworn in as premier

1977: Italy and Yugoslavia ratify agreement ending World War II border dispute over area south of Trieste, with Italy ceding territory to Yugoslavia. Public protest and extremist violence erupts over Italy's economic crisis

1978: Government resigns as wave of violence continues; Communists withdraw tacit support and demand cabinet seats in emergency coalition. President Giovanni Leone reappoints Premier Andreotti to form new government, nation's 40th since World War II. Red Brigades kidnap former Premier Aldo Moro on same day Andreotti presents new government to parliament; Communists given direct role (short of cabinet-level) for first time since 1947. Red Brigades demand release of 13 leftist prisoners for Moro's life; government refuses to negotiate, as huge manhunt is mounted; government decree enhances power of police; Moro found dead; public reaction against Red Brigades noted. Abortion is legalized. President Leone resigns in face of corruption charges and is replaced by Alessandro Pertini. Trial of Red Brigades members ends (29 are sentenced up to 15 years in prison; 16 are acquitted)

1979: Communists withdraw from coalition after their demand for cabinet seats is rebuffed. Andreotti resigns; parliament is dissolved; Communists lose seats in elections for new parliament

1980: Christian Democrat leader Arnaldo Forlani forms new four-party coalition government. Bombing of Bologna railroad station by right-wing terrorists kills 81 people

1981: Forlani government falls after scandal involves three cabinet members; Republican party leader, Giovanni Spadolini, forms new coalition government

---

IVORY COAST

Area: 127,520 sq. mi. **Population:** 7,920,000 (1979 est.) **Official Name:** Republic of the Ivory Coast **Capital:** Abidjan **Nationality:** Ivorian **Languages:** French is the official and commercial language, but the most common African language is Dioula **Religion:** 66% animist, 22% Moslem, 12% Roman Catholic **Flag:** Orange, white, and green vertical stripes **Anthem:** L'Abidjanaise, beginning "Greetings, O land of hope" **Currency:** CFA Franc (263 per U.S. $1)

Location: West Africa. Ivory Coast is bordered on the north by Mali and Upper Volta, on the east by Ghana, on the south by the Gulf of Guinea, and on the west by Liberia and Guinea **Features:** From the coast, a rain forest extends over about 40% of the country. The remainder is wooded and grassy savanna, with a mountainous area in the northwest **Chief Rivers:** Bandama, Sassandra, Komoé, Nzi, Cavally

Head of State and of Government: President Félix Houphouët-Boigny, born 1905, reelected October 1980 for fifth 5-year term **Effective Date of Present Constitution:** 1960 **Legislative Body:** National Assembly (unicameral), consisting of 147 members elected for 5 years. All members belong to the Democratic Party of the Ivory Coast, the nation's only party **Local Government:** 24 administrative departments, each headed by an elected council, and 2 autonomous municipalities

Ethnic Composition: About 60 groups, the largest being the Mande (26%), Akan (25%), Krou (18%), Sénoufo (13%), Lagoon people (7%) **Population Distribution:** 32.4% urban **Density:** 62 inhabitants per sq. mi.

Largest Cities: (1977 est.—Metropolitan Area) Abidjan 950,000; (1974 est.) Bouaké 140,000

Per Capita Income: $932 (1980) **Gross National Product (GNP):** $7.5 billion (1980) **Economic Statistics:** In 1976 about 31% of GNP came from agriculture (coffee, palm oil, cocoa, cotton, bananas, pineapples, rice, coconuts, sugar, rubber, yams, cassava, corn, millet, sorghum, livestock, tropical woods), 15% from industry (tuna-packing, sawmilling, agricultural processing, textiles, clothing, auto, truck and bus assembly, oil refining) **Minerals and Mining:** Small quantities of diamonds and manganese have been produced and exploitation of petroleum, natural gas, iron ore, oil, nickel and gold is under way **Labor Force:** 2,600,000 (1970), with 78% in agriculture and 14% in industry and trade. Only 356,000 are wage earners **Foreign Trade:** Exports, chiefly coffee, wood, cocoa, palm oil, cotton, bananas, and pineapples, totaled $2.8 billion in 1979. Imports, mainly machinery, transport equipment, electrical equipment, and petroleum products, totaled $2.2 billion **Principal Trade Partners:** France, Netherlands, West Germany, Italy, Japan, United States, Spain, Britain

Vital Statistics: Birthrate, 45.6 per 1,000 of pop. (1975); death rate, 20.6 **Life Expectancy:** 43 years **Health Statistics:** 589 inhabitants per hospital bed; 15,234 per physician (1975) **Infant Mortality:** 138 per 1,000 births **Illiteracy:** 75% **Primary and Secondary School Enrollment:** 792,189 (1975) **Enrollment in Higher Education:** 8,701 (1976) **GNP Expended on Education:** 7.4% (1975)

Transportation: Surfaced roads total 1,500 mi. **Motor Vehicles:** 128,400 (1976) **Passenger Cars:** 84,900 **Railway Mileage:** 408 **Ports:** Abidjan, Sassandra, San Pedro **Major Airlines:** State-owned Air Ivoire is the domestic carrier; Air Afrique, a multinational airline, provides the main regional service **Communications:** Government owned **Radio Transmitters:** 17 **Receivers:** 600,000 (1976) **Television Transmitters:** 10 **Receivers:** 257,000 (1976) **Telephones:** 70,000 (1976) **Newspapers:** 1 daily, 7 copies per 1,000 inhabitants (1975)

Weights and Measures: Metric system **Travel Requirements:** Passport; visa; onward ticket **International Dialing Code:** 225

The Ivory Coast, the richest and most economically self-sufficient state in former French West Africa, lies on the south side of the African bulge and is slightly larger than New Mexico. The southern boundary is a 340-mile coastline on the Gulf of Guinea, characterized by heavy surf and a lack of natural harbors. Early European voyagers were discouraged by this coastline and the dense tropical forest, as well as by the scant gold to be found.

Shortly after the former French colony became independent in 1960, officials of the International Monetary Fund advised Ivorian leaders to coordinate fiscal and developmental planning, encourage competitive private enterprise, and create a favorable investment climate—advice Ivorians followed with huge success.

Ivorian President Félix Houphouët-Boigny, who continues to head the government, set up incentives for foreign investors. Himself an experienced administrator in French government service, he brought in top French economic planners to minutely map development.

Helped by high earnings from coffee and cocoa, the Ivory Coast concentrated initially on diversifying agriculture. Systematically, large new plantations of rubber, palm oil, pineapples, sugarcane, rice, and cotton were established. Proven petroleum reserves have been found that could make Ivory Coast self-sufficient for fuel. In 1980, recognizing that its dense tropical forests are being depleted, Ivory Coast began a reforestation project with World Bank assistance.

Since 1960 the Ivorian gross national product has grown by more than 11 percent a year, and the per capita income is among the highest in black Africa. Projects are under way to spread the prosperity of Abidjan, the capital, to other parts of the country. The new port of San Pedro, designed to open up the little-developed southwestern area, has been completed and iron-ore deposits in the northwest are being readied for development.

Although the French still maintain a strong economic position, they have had to share it with increasing numbers of German, Dutch, British, American, Italian, and Israeli enterprises.

Despite the impressive progress, along with increases of public housing, education, and health facilities, there remains an urgent need for raising rural living standards and creating employment.

HISTORY: Although evidence of a neolithic culture has been found in the Ivory Coast, little is known of the country's past before the first contacts by Portuguese and French in the 16th century. The Baoulés and the Agnis, both related to the Ashantis of Ghana, did not arrive until the 18th century, and most of the other tribal groups have their main centers in neighboring countries. The French began to establish control over the area in the 19th century and succeeded in colonizing it after much local resistance

1893: Ivory Coast is organized as a French protectorate

1898: Anti-French resistance collapses with the defeat of Almamy Samory, the Malinké warrior chief

1946-57: Félix Houphouët-Boigny founds African Democratic Rally, the first all-African political party; he is elected to the French National Assembly and wins far-reaching freedoms for France's African territories

1947: Upper Volta is detached from the Ivory Coast

1958: Ivory Coast becomes an autonomous republic within the French Community

1960: Ivory Coast achieves full independence; Houphouët-Boigny is elected president

1963: More than 80 persons, including government ministers and Guinean nationals, are convicted of plotting to stage a coup and assassinate the president

1967: Ivory Coast and Guinea exchange prisoners in effort to smooth relations

1970: President Houphouët-Boigny is elected to third term

1974: Proposals for dialogue between black African nations and South Africa lead to talks between South African Premier John Vorster and President Houphouët-Boigny

1975: President Houphouët-Boigny reelected without opposition for another five-year term

1979: Asylum is granted to Bokassa I, deposed ruler of Central African Empire

1980: President Houphouët-Boigny is reelected without opposition for a fifth five-year term. In the first National Assembly elections since 1960, 80% of the deputies are new. Oil begins to flow from offshore wells

1981: Ivory Coast receives $626 million in loans from International Monetary Fund to aid stabilization

---

JAMAICA

Area: 4,244 sq. mi. **Population:** 2,161,000 (1979 est.)

Official Name: Jamaica **Capital:** Kingston **Nationality:** Jamaican **Languages:** English is the official and dominant language; a Jamaican Creole, a mixture of archaic English and African, is also used **Religion:** 75% Protestant, 5% Roman Catholic, 20% other religions or no affiliation **Flag:** A gold diagonal cross, or saltire, divides the flag into four triangles; the top and bottom triangles are green and the remaining two are black **Anthem:** National Anthem, beginning "Eternal Father bless our land" **Currency:** Jamaican dollar (1.78 per U.S. $1)

Location: West Indies. The island of Jamaica lies in the Caribbean Sea, about 90 miles south of Cuba and 100 miles west of Haiti **Features:** Mountains cover about 80% of the island; lowlands stretch across the western end and a narrow plain covers the south **Chief Rivers:** Black, Minho, Cobre

Head of State: Queen Elizabeth II, represented by a governor-general, Florizel Glasspole, appointed June 1973 **Head of Government:** Prime Minister Edward Philip George Seaga, born 1930, appointed Nov. 1, 1980 **Effective Date of Present Constitution:** 1962 **Legislative Body:** Parliament (bicameral), consisting of the Senate and the House of Representatives. The Senate is composed of 21 members, 13 of whom are appointed by the governor-general on the advice of the prime minister and the rest on the advice of the leader of the opposition. The 60-member House of Representatives is elected for 5-year terms **Local Government:** 14 parishes, 12 of which are administered by elected councils. Kingston and St. Andrew are jointly governed by a corporation

Ethnic Composition: About 95% of the population is of African and mixed descent; other racial and nationality groups are Chinese, East Indian, Syrian, and European **Population Distribution:** 41% urban **Density:** 509 inhabitants per sq. mi.

Largest Cities: (1975 est.) Kingston 600,000 (metro area), Montego Bay 50,000, Spanish Town 50,000, May Pen 26,074 (1970)

Per Capita Income: $1,602 (1980) **Gross National Product (GNP):** $3.6 billion (1980) **Economic Statistics:** About 15% of GNP comes from manufacturing (sugar processing, rum, beer, clothing, furniture); 14% from wholesale and retail trade; 11% from agriculture (sugar, bananas, cocoa, coffee, citrus fruits, copra), forestry and fishing; 11% from construction; and 10% from mining and refining **Minerals and Mining:** Jamaica is one of the world's largest producers of bauxite; other minerals of commercial significance are gypsum, silica, marble, and limestone **Labor Force:** 859,500 (1975), with 31% in agriculture, forestry, fishing and mining; 26% in public administration and commerce; 19% in manufacturing and construction; 4% in transport and communication; and 20% in other services **Foreign Trade:** Exports, chiefly bauxite, alumina, sugar, rum, molasses, and bananas, totaled $798 million in 1979. Imports, mainly fuel, foodstuffs, manufactured goods, machinery and transportation equipment, totaled $1 billion **Principal Trade Partners:** United States, Britain, Canada, Venezuela, Caribbean countries

Vital Statistics: Birthrate, 30 per 1,000 of pop. (1976); death rate, 7 **Life Expectancy:** 69 years **Health Statistics:** 257 inhabitants per hospital bed; 3,509 per physician (1974) **Infant Mortality:** 20 per 1,000 births (1976) **Illiteracy:** 18% **Primary and Secondary School Enrollment:** 593,366 **Enrollment in Higher Education:** 9,039 **GNP Expended on Education:** 6.9% (1976)

Transportation: Paved roads total about 4,700 mi. **Motor Vehicles:** 151,591 (1974) **Passenger Cars:** 109,628 **Railway Mileage:** 205 **Ports:** Kingston, Portland Bight **Major Airlines:** Air Jamaica operates international service; Trans-Jamaican Air Service provides domestic flights **Communications:** Government owned **Radio Transmitters:** 21 **Receivers:** 555,000 (1976) **Television Transmitters:** 13 **Receivers:** 111,000 (1976) **Telephones:** 109,000 (1976) **Newspapers:** 3 dailies, 91 copies per 1,000 inhabitants (1976)

Weights and Measures: Metric and British standards are used **Travel Requirements:** Proof of U.S. citizenship; return ticket **Direct Dialing Code:** 809

Like other Caribbean countries, Jamaica is trying to deal with an economy and a society in difficult transition. From slave days, Jamaica's mountains and lush fields, under British ownership, produced sugar, coffee, bananas, and spices. While these are still the economic mainstays, the island is striving now for more balance.

Industry and tourism are the watchwords, and investment in both in the last decade has been considerable. The sugar industry remains the island's single biggest employer, but, agriculture overall has fallen behind industry in its contribution to the gross national product.

Disaffection with agriculture—particularly with the sugar industry, an activity associated with slave exploitation—has caused an influx into Kingston in search of industrial and service jobs. Industry and tourism have not kept pace with the demand, and the result has been a jobless rate often exceeding 30 percent and heavy emigration to the U.S. and Britain.

Prime Minister Michael Manley won a huge mandate for his program of democratic socialism in 1976, after which the government purchased eight of the island's 12 sugar estates and acquired several other businesses. But the economy went into a steep decline. Bauxite, sugar, cement and banana production fell dramatically and, by 1980, neither private banks nor the International Monetary Fund were willing to make further loans in the absence of austerity measures that Manley remained unwilling to adopt. Serious international payments problems developed as Jamaica's oil import costs came to rival its total export sales.

In the elections of October 1980, which were preceded by a summer of violence in which scores died, the economic crisis proved decisive and Manley's party was defeated by a faction led by Edward P.G. Seaga.

Quickly adopting more moderate, pragmatic policies, Prime Minister Seaga managed to restore some confidence in the economy. By mid-1981, the IMF had approved a $650 million loan and Seaga had launched a program to restore bauxite production and other export industries.

HISTORY: Jamaica was inhabited by Arawak Indians when Columbus discovered the island in 1494. It was settled by the Spaniards early in the 16th century and remained under Spanish rule until 1655, when it was captured by the English. By the 18th century most of the Arawaks had died off, but a huge population of black slaves grew up around the island's sugar plantations. With the abolition of slavery in 1833, the plantation economy suffered a severe blow, resulting in long-lasting poverty and social unrest

1865-66: Uprising by blacks leads to imposition of martial law; British parliament establishes a crown colony government

1944: Britain grants the island a new constitution based on adult suffrage and a wide measure of self-government

1953: Island is granted full internal autonomy

1958-62: Jamaica joins West Indies Federation in 1958 along with nine other British possessions in the Caribbean; three years later, however, the island withdraws. In August 1962, Jamaica wins full independence, with Sir Alexander Bustamente, the island's labor leader, as prime minister

1967: Hugh Shearer becomes prime minister following sudden death of Sir Donald Sangster, leader of Jamaica Labor party

1968: Jamaica joins Caribbean Free Trade Association

1972: Jamaica Labor party is defeated in general election by People's National party; Michael Manley becomes prime minister

1974: The Suppression of Crime Act passed unanimously by the legislature. Its purpose is to reduce the rash of murders and other violent crimes on Jamaica. It provides for secret trials, no bail, and, for convicted offenders, indeterminate prison sentences

1975: Jamaica signs treaty with EC and reaches agreements with foreign companies mining bauxite on the island whereby the government would purchase controlling shares of stock

1976: Martial law is declared in Kingston because of violence among warring extremist factions of Prime Minister Manley's People's National party (PNP) and the opposition Jamaica Labor party (JLP). PNP wins overwhelming victory

1978: Government launches five-year economic program based on land reform

1979: Tourism drops after seven die in gasoline-price riots

1980: Foreign-exchange shortage develops in wake of economic slowdown and refusal of banks to extend further credit. Many killed in pre-election violence. A moderate, Edward Seaga, becomes prime minister after JLP outpolls PNP in October. At least 144 elderly women die in nursing home fire in Kingston

1981: Nearly $1 billion in loans pledged by banks and International Monetary Fund to help the island's economy

---

JAPAN

Area: 145,730 sq. mi. **Population:** 117,057,485 (1980 census)

Official Name: Japan **Capital:** Tokyo **Nationality:** Japanese **Languages:** Japanese is the official and universal language **Religion:** Buddhism and Shintoism are the chief religions; virtually all Japanese practice one or the other and most subscribe to both **Flag:** A red sun on a white field **Anthem:** The Reign of Our Emperor **Currency:** Yen (215 per U.S. $1)

Location: Japan is an archipelago forming a 2,360-mile-long arc off the east coast of Asia, between the Sea of Japan and the Pacific Ocean proper. It consists of four main islands: Hokkaido, Honshu, Shikoku, and Kyushu, and more than 3,000 smaller islands **Features:** 72% of the country is covered by hills and mountains, many of them active or dormant volcanoes. Because of the country's unstable geological position beside the Pacific deeps, numerous earthquakes are felt throughout the islands **Chief Rivers:** Tone, Shinano, Ishikari, Kitakami

Head of State: Emperor Hirohito, born 1901, ascended the throne 1926 **Head of Government:** Prime Minister Zenko Suzuki, born 1911, appointed Aug. 1980 **Effective Date of Present Constitution:** May 3, 1947 **Legislative Body:** Parliament, or Diet (bicameral), consisting of the House of Representatives and the House of Councillors. The House of Representatives has 511 members elected for 4 years. The House of Councillors has 252 members elected for 6 years **Local Government:** 43 prefectures, each with an elected governor and local assembly, 2 urban prefectures, 1 metropolitan prefecture, and 1 territory

Ethnic Composition: The Japanese are a Mongoloid people, closely related to the other groups of east Asia, although there is evidence of admixture with Malayan and Caucasoid strains. Over 700,000 Koreans constitute the only important minority group; about 15,000 Ainu in Hokkaido, physically similar to Caucasians, are rapidly being assimilated **Population Distribution:** 76% urban **Density:** 803 inhabitants per sq. mi.

Largest Cities: (1975 census) Tokyo 8,646,520, Osaka 2,778,987, Yokohama 2,621,771, Nagoya 2,079,740, Kyoto 1,461,059, Kobe 1,360,605, Sapporo 1,240,613, Kitakyushu 1,058,058, Kawasaki 1,014,951

Per Capita Income: $8,426 (1980) **Gross Domestic Product (GDP):** $986 billion (1980) **Economic Statistics:** 36.8% of GDP comes from industry (transportation equipment, electrical machinery, iron and steel, ships, chemicals), 8.1% from agriculture (rice, vegetables, fruit, wheat, barley, fish, and potatoes), 23.1% from trade, 11.1% from services **Minerals and Mining:** Coal is plentiful, but only about 25% can be used for industrial purposes. There are small amounts of zinc, limestone, lead, and sulphur **Labor Force:** 55,300,000 (1979) with 34% employed in industry, 11% in agriculture, and 48% in trade and services **Foreign Trade:** Exports, chiefly iron and steel, textiles, electronic equipment, motor vehicles, ships, totaled $101 billion in 1979. Imports, chiefly mineral fuels, metal ores and scrap, machinery and equipment, and foodstuffs, totaled $94 billion **Principal Trade Partners:** United States, Australia, Canada, Iran, South Korea, West Germany, Kuwait, Britain, Saudi Arabia, Indonesia, China

Vital Statistics: Birthrate, 15.5 per 1,000 of pop. (1977); death rate, 6.1 **Life Expectancy:** 74 years **Health Statistics:** 95 inhabitants per hospital bed; 845 per physician (1976) **Infant Mortality:** 8.9 per 1,000 live births **Illiteracy:** Negligible **Primary and Secondary School Enrollment:** 20,069,305 pupils (1977) **Enrollment in Higher Education:** 2,354,841 **GNP Expended on Education:** 5.5% (1975)

t**Transportation:** Paved roads 243,212 mi. **Motor Vehicles:** 31,379,000 (1977) **Passenger Cars:** 19,826,000 **Railway Mileage:** 17,966 mi. **Ports:** Yokohama, Kobe, Tokyo, Nagoya, Osaka, Chiba, Kawasaki, Hakodate **Major Airlines:** Japan Air Lines, partly government owned and partly privately financed, operates international and domestic flights **Communications:** Government and privately owned **Radio Transmitters:** 944 **Receivers:** 59,650,000 (1976) **Television Transmitters:** 6,117 **Receivers:** 26,545,000 (1975) **Telephones:** 50,600,000 **Newspapers:** 180 dailies, 526 copies per 1,000 inhabitants (1974)

Weights and Measures: Metric system **Travel Requirements:** Passport, visa, valid 60 days **International Dialing Code:** 81

Japan, having soared from crushing defeat in World War II to a position among the world's leading industrial nations, is today building for itself an international role commensurate with its economic power, while attempting at the same time to resolve the great social problems caused by swift industrialization.

Crowded into a small island territory off the Asian mainland and isolated from the world by their own choice for centuries prior to 1854, the Japanese created a distinctive society and culture. There has been a large measure of modernization and Westernization, but traditional customs, social practices, and business procedures still are deep-rooted.

Close government/business ties and encouragement for export industries enabled Japan to build a huge international trade throughout the 1970s, while curbs on imports and foreign investments continued to afford protection for domestic industry. Eventually, the trade gap between Japan and the U.S. widened so greatly that relations between the two countries became acrimonious. As protectionist sentiment rose in the U.S., the Japanese voluntarily cut down on their shipments of TV sets and automobiles, removed some restraints on importing foreign goods, and sent buying missions to the U.S. In 1980, the U.S. lifted quotas on imports of Japanese color TV sets and, in 1981, Japan agreed to further limit auto exports, forestalling threatened protective action by the U.S. Congress.

By the start of the 1980s, the Japanese clearly had moved beyond the roles of traders and merchants engaged in export and had also become worldwide investors, producing Japanese goods overseas. In 1980, for example, Honda and Nissan announced plans to build cars in the U.S.; a deal was made with Rolls-Royce to build jet engines in Britain and Japan; and Japanese heavy industry companies joined with Australia's state of Victoria in plans to build a coal liquefaction plant. The country's Ministry of International Trade and Industry (MITI) provides a cohesive business-government approach—sometimes called "Japan Inc."—that has proved effective in economic expansion. The approach includes official subsidy and direction, such as "administrative guidances" in concentrating computer research efforts.

With only one brief interruption, Japan has been ruled by conservatives during the postwar years under the "no-war" 1946 constitution, which was imposed by American occupation authorities. The constitution provided the framework for democratic development and made the emperor, who had served as the nationalistic symbol for prewar militarism, a largely ceremonial chief of state.

Support for the ruling Liberal Democratic party (LDP), which derived much of its strength in rural areas, has gradually declined as a result of the migration, within two decades, of more than one-third of Japan's population from the countryside to the cities. The 1976 Lockheed scandal, involving LDP members accused of accepting bribes from the U.S.-based Lockheed Aircraft Corporation in exchange for lucrative sales contracts, also damaged the party's standing. The 1979 McDonnell Douglas and Grumman scandal, also arising from aircraft sales, again turned the spotlight on the activities of the trading companies and Japanese politicians. The LDP entered the 1980 elections fearing that it would win with such small margins that it would have to share power in a coalition. Instead, it won handily—thanks, in part, to a sympathy vote when Prime Minister Masayoshi Ohira died during the campaign. In July, Zenko Suzuki was chosen prime minister. He proved himself an able and persuasive spokesman for Japan during a tour of Southeast Asia and visits to Canada and the U.S. in 1981.

Pollution of air and water have reached near-crisis proportions. Despite depletion of the rural population, farmland remains fragmented and an outdated subsidy system has caused huge overproduction of rice. A critical housing shortage persists, transport systems are overburdened, the educational structure is in need of broad reform, and social welfare systems are on a modest scale.

In recent years American troops and bases in Japan have been substantially reduced and, though still sheltered under the American nuclear umbrella, Japan has assumed a larger role in its own military defense. Dependent on Mideast oil for much of its energy, it has also been building nuclear power plants. Both of these developments have aroused much opposition in the only nation ever to have been a victim of nuclear bombing. Massive demonstrations against the government occurred in 1981 in response to accidents in a nuclear plant and the revelation that U.S. naval vessels bearing nuclear weapons had regularly put in at Japanese ports. Anti-U.S. sentiment was also aroused by an April incident in which an American nuclear submarine accidentally rammed and sank a Japanese freighter and failed to assist in a search for survivors.

Although in 1972 Japan restored diplomatic ties with China, the peace treaty was not ratified until October 1978, because special care had to be exercised to avoid offending another giant neighbor and traditional enemy, the USSR.

HISTORY: Legend attributes the founding of the Japanese empire to Jimmu, a lineal descendant of the sun goddess and ancestor of the present imperial dynasty, in 660 B.C. Reliable records of Japanese history, however, date back only to about 400 A.D. From the 6th to 8th century, Japan came under the strong cultural influence of China and Buddhism was introduced. The development of a feudal system weakened the already diminished power of the emperors, who were to remain in obscurity for 700 years

1192: Yoritomo, leader of the feudal family of Minamato, takes the title of shogun (military governor) and sets up dictatorship

1542: First European contact is established with the arrival of Portuguese sailors

1637: Tokugawa shogunate bans all intercourse with the outside world, with the exception of Dutch traders in Nagasaki

1854: Commodore Matthew C. Perry, a U.S. naval officer, forces the opening of Japanese trade with the West

1867-68: Shogunate collapses and power is restored to Emperor Mutsuhito; Meiji Restoration, so called after emperor's reign name, is followed by formation of a pro-Western government which proceeds to modernize Japan

1894-95: Japan defeats China in Sino-Japanese War and annexes Formosa, the Pescadores, and Liaotung peninsula

1904-05: Russian power is smashed by Japanese in Russo-Japanese War

1910: Japan annexes Korea

1931: Japan seizes Manchuria from China and sets up puppet state of Manchukuo

1937: Japan invades China's northern provinces; Chinese resistance leads to full-scale though undeclared war

1940: Japan signs military alliance with Germany and Italy

1941-45: Surprise Japanese attack on Pearl Harbor in December 1941 triggers U.S. entry into World War II; successive Japanese victories give Japan control over vast territories stretching from India to the Aleutians; in late 1942, however, tide begins to turn and Japan loses ground to Allies; with the dropping of U.S. atomic bombs on Hiroshima and Nagasaki, Japan is forced to surrender and is occupied by U.S. forces

1946-47: The occupation, under direction of General Douglas MacArthur, initiates series of reforms aimed at democratization and demilitarization of Japan; a new constitution is adopted and emperor publicly disclaims his divinity

1954: Japan and United States sign military assistance pact

1960: Antigovernment riots and protests against military pacts force cancellation of visit by U.S. President Eisenhower

1964: Eisaku Sato becomes prime minister

1969: Japan steps up demand for the return of Okinawa, occupied by U.S. forces since World War II

1970: Japan renews security pact with United States

1971: Agreement is reached on reversion of Okinawa from U.S. to Japanese rule; Emperor Hirohito becomes first reigning monarch to leave Japan, visiting seven countries in Europe

1972: Okinawa is returned to Japan; Japan opens diplomatic relations with China. Eisaku Sato resigns as prime minister and is succeeded by Kakuei Tanaka

1974: Tanaka resigns as a result of accusations that he used his political office to amass a personal fortune. Takeo Miki becomes prime minister

1975: Emperor Hirohito makes first visit to U.S. by a reigning Japanese monarch

1976: Revelations emerge concerning $12.6 million in alleged payoffs by Lockheed Aircraft Corp. (U.S.) to secure Japanese aircraft contracts. Tanaka is arrested. Miki resigns after his party (LDP) suffers setback in elections. LDP leader, Takeo Fukuda, is elected prime minister by House of Representatives

1977: Prime Minister Fukuda shuffles cabinet in effort to better deal with Japan's mounting trade surplus and strained economic relations with industrial nations; he calls it the "gravest situation" since World War II

1978: New Tokyo International Airport opens under heavy guard as protesters try to disrupt flights. Earthquake near Tokyo is worst in 14 years; 21 died, 350 injured. On October 23, four decades after Japan invaded China, the two countries exchange ratifications of a peace treaty. Masayoshi Ohira defeats Fukuda in a party election and becomes prime minister on Dec. 7

1979: Ohira visits U.S. President Carter and they jointly pledge to seek "over the next several years a more harmonious pattern of international trade and payments." The LDP wins a September election but lacks a majority until independents lend support.

1980: Japan and the U.S. sign an agreement for joint research on high-risk, high-technology problems. A no-confidence vote topples the Ohira government in May. Ohira dies on June 12—10 days before the next parliamentary elections, in which he is a candidate—but the LDP wins by strong majorities and Zenko Suzuki becomes prime minister

1981: Pope visits Japan in February. U.S. submarine accidentally sinks Japanese freighter in East China Sea in April. Suzuki visits U.S. in May, gives President Reagan a pledge that Japan will

reduce export of autos to U.S. and will increase military spending. Furor over closer U.S.-Japanese military cooperation leads to resignation of foreign minister and Japanese withdrawal from joint naval exercises

---

JORDAN

Area: 34,990 sq. mi. (excluding West Bank) **Population:** 2,152,273 (1979 census)

Official Name: Hashemite Kingdom of Jordan **Capital:** Amman **Nationality:** Jordanian **Languages:** Arabic is the official and universal language **Religion:** 95% Sunni Moslem, 5% Christian **Flag:** Horizontal black, white, and green stripes, with a seven-pointed white star on a red triangle at the staff **Anthem:** The Royal Salute **Currency:** Jordanian dinar (0.33 per U.S. $1)

Location: Southwest Asia. Jordan is bordered by Syria on the north, Iraq on the northeast, Saudi Arabia on the east and south, and Israel on the west **Features:** About four fifths of the country consists of desert. The Jordan River valley divides the land into the small, rocky West Bank (controlled by Israel) and the large East Bank, the latter forming a dry plateau that slopes to flat terrain in the northeast **Chief Rivers:** Jordan, Yarmuk

Head of State: King Hussein Ibn Talal, born 1935, proclaimed king 1952 **Head of Government:** Prime Minister Abdul Hamid Sharaf, born 1939, appointed December 1979 **Effective Date of Present Constitution:** 1952, amended 1974 and 1976 **Legislative Body:** National Assembly (bicameral) consists of a 60-seat House of Representatives (dissolved by the King in 1976) and a Senate of 30 members, appointed by the King. A National Consultative Council, with advisory functions, was established in 1978 **Local Government:** 8 governorates, each headed by an appointed governor; 3 are in the Israeli-occupied West Bank

Ethnic Composition: Virtually 100% Arab **Population Distribution:** 44% urban **Density:** 61.5 inhabitants per sq. mi.

Largest Cities: (1977 est.) Amman 711,850, Zarqa 263,400, Irbid 136,770

Per Capita Income: $1,112 (1980) **Gross National Product (GNP):** $2.6 billion (1980) **Economic Statistics:** About 10% of GNP comes from agriculture (wheat, citrus fruits, olives, grapes, melons, vegetables, barley), 25% from industry (phosphate mining, cement, beverages, tobacco, soap, oil refining, tanning, vegetable oils), and 65% from trade and services **Minerals and Mining:** Exploited minerals include phosphates, potash, copper, and marble; manganese, iron, sulphur and oil deposits also exist **Labor Force:** 638,000, with 20% in agriculture, 20% in industry, and 60% in trade and services **Foreign Trade:** Exports, chiefly fruits and vegetables, phosphates, cement, and marble, totaled $410 million in 1979. Imports, mainly foodstuffs, machinery, vehicles, petroleum, and textiles, totaled $2 billion **Principal Trade Partners:** EC countries, United States, Lebanon, Iraq, Kuwait, Saudi Arabia, Japan, Syria, Romania

Vital Statistics: Birthrate, 41.0 per 1,000 of pop. (1977); death rate, 14.7 **Life Expectancy:** 52 years **Health Statistics:** 937 inhabitants per hospital bed; 2,438 per physician (1974) **Infant Mortality:** 21.6 per 1,000 births **Illiteracy:** 38% **Primary and Secondary School Enrollment:** 588,101 (1976) **Enrollment in Higher Education:** 9,302 **GNP Expended on Education:** 3.5% (1976)

Transportation: Paved roads total 3,440 mi. **Motor Vehicles:** 78,000 (1977) **Passenger Cars:** 57,000 **Railway Mileage:** 500 **Port:** Aqaba **Major Airlines:** Royal Jordanian Airlines (ALIA) operates international services **Communications:** Government owned **Radio Transmitters:** 7 **Receivers:** 531,000 (1976) **Television Transmitters:** 3 **Receivers:** 125,000 (1976) **Telephones:** 44,000 (1976) **Newspapers:** 4 dailies, 18 copies per 1,000 inhabitants (1975)

Weights and Measures: Metric system **Travel Requirements:** Passport, visa valid for 4 years for multiple entry, no fee

---

The Hashemite Kingdom of Jordan is a largely uninhabited desert, about the size of Indiana. In 1921, after centuries of Turkish rule, the area now comprising Jordan and Israel was awarded to the United Kingdom by the League of Nations as the Mandates for Palestine and Transjordan. In 1922, Britain divided the administration of the Mandate and established Abdullah, grandfather of the present King Hussein, as ruler of a semi-autonomous Amirate of Transjordan in the area east of the

Jordan River. The western portion (Palestine) remained under the administration of a British High Commissioner.

Britain granted the eastern territory full independence in 1946, with Abdullah as king. When Arab Palestinians and Jews fought each other and the British for the control of Palestine, Britain asked the UN to help settle the conflict. The UN suggested that Palestine be divided into two states, one Jewish and one Arab.

In the fighting which broke out upon the proclamation of Israeli statehood in 1948, the Transjordan Arab Legion occupied most of the West Bank territories allotted to the Arab Palestinians in the United Nations partition plan, including East Jerusalem, and the Jews established the state of Israel, in large measure on the land given to them in the UN plan. Transjordan became the Hashemite Kingdom of Jordan in 1949.

The present ruler, Hussein Ibn Talal, became king in 1952. In 1967, during the Six-Day War, Israel occupied the West Bank territories.

The problems of the Middle East—particularly, resolution of Arab-Israeli issues—dominate Jordan's foreign policy. The current Mideast peace negotiations, with respect to Jordan, revolve around the ultimate disposition of the Israeli-occupied West Bank and Arab Jerusalem and the issue of the roles for Jordan and the Palestinian Liberation Organization (PLO) in the negotiations. Within Jordan, there is friction between the Palestinian refugees and the Bedouins—the principal ethnic group of unoccupied Jordan.

Following the decision of the Rabat summit conference of Arab heads of state in October 1974 to recognize the PLO's right to represent all Palestinians, King Hussein gave the PLO and its leader, Yassir Arafat, the responsibility for the West Bank. Hussein's foreign policy—long pro-Western—has become increasingly favorable to Arab aspirations—largely because of increasing foreign aid from Arab oil states to his resource-poor kingdom. In 1980, Hussein refused again to commit Jordan to joining the peace negotiations under the Israeli-Egyptian 1979 peace treaty, which had promised Palestinian autonomy in the West Bank.

Jordan, which had taken Iraq's side in the Iraqi-Iranian war of 1980-81, severed relations with Iran in February 1981, shortly after Iran had cut its ties with Jordan.

HISTORY: The present territory of Jordan was the biblical home of the Moabites, the Ammonites, the Edomites, and some Hebrew tribes. It was conquered in 64 B.C. by Rome, in the 7th century A.D. by Moslem Arabs (from whom it derived its now-prevailing language and religion), in the 16th century by the Ottoman Empire, and in 1916 by Britain

1916: Sykes-Picot Agreement between France and Britain divides Ottoman holdings, with Transjordan (the present East Bank) in British sphere of influence
1921: British recognize Abdullah as ruler of Transjordan and Hashemite dynasty is founded
1928: Britain recognizes Transjordan as independent but retains suzerainty in the form of military and financial control
1946: Kingdom of Transjordan is proclaimed
1948: British mandate ends, fighting breaks out with new state of Israel
1949: Transjordan and Israel sign armistice, with Transjordan in control of West Bank and part of Jerusalem. Transjordan adopts name of Hashemite Kingdom of Jordan
1950: Arab Palestine (West Bank) is formally annexed by Jordan
1951: King Abdullah is assassinated in Jerusalem. His son, Talal, becomes king
1952: Talal is declared insane and ousted; his son, Hussein, becomes king
1967: King Hussein and President Nasser of Egypt sign mutual defense pact. Jordan is drawn into Six-Day War with Israel, which occupies all of Jerusalem and all of West Bank
1968-69: Israel attacks Arab guerrilla bases on East Bank
1970: Guerrillas hijack four Western airliners to Jordan and hold crews and passengers hostage; all are later released. Civil war breaks out between guerrillas and Jordanian forces

1971: Jordanian army's July offensive virtually eliminates all guerrilla bases. Syria severs relations with Jordan. Prime Minister Wasfi Al Tal is assassinated in Cairo
1973: Jordan joins in war against Israel
1974: Arab leaders at a summit conference recognize the Palestine Liberation Organization as the sole representative of the Palestinian people; King Hussein concurs
1975: Syria and Jordan establish a joint military command
1976: Syria and Jordan co-ordinate their foreign diplomatic representation in countries where either one maintains a mission. King Hussein reconvenes parliament, with representatives of the West Bank in attendance, after having dissolved it in 1974 to decrease Palestinian participation in Jordanian politics. Prime Minister Zaid al-Rifai resigns and King Hussein asks Mudar Badran, chief of the cabinet, to form a new government
1977: Queen Alia is killed in helicopter crash
1978: King Hussein marries Elizabeth Halaby, 26-year-old American and proclaims her Jordan's new queen
1980: Hussein visits Washington, D.C., for talks with President Carter; refuses to join Israeli-Egyptian peace negotiations
1981: Jordan cuts ties with Iran after supporting Iraq in its war with Iran

---

KENYA

Area: 224,960 sq. mi. **Population:** 15,322,000 (1979 census)

Official Name: Republic of Kenya **Capital:** Nairobi **Nationality:** Kenyan **Languages:** Swahili and English are used officially; of more than 30 languages, Kikuyu and Luo are the most used **Religion:** 56% are Christian, 36% animist, 7% Moslem, 1% Hindu **Flag:** Horizontal stripes of black, red, and green, with the center red stripe bordered in white; a shield with black and white markings, and crossed spears behind, appears in the center of the flag **Anthem:** National Anthem, beginning "O, God of all Creation" **Currency:** Kenya shilling (8.3 per U.S. $1)

Location: East Africa. Kenya is bordered on the north by Sudan and Ethiopia, on the east by Somalia and the Indian Ocean, on the south by Tanzania, and on the west by Uganda **Features:** The Great Rift Valley in the center and west is girded by rugged plateaus and mountains. To the east are dry bush land and a marshy coastal plain. In the north the land turns to scrub and desert. Kenya has numerous lakes, including a portion of Lake Victoria **Chief Rivers:** Tana, Athi-Galana, Suam-Turkwel, Keiro

Head of State and of Government: President Daniel arap Moi, born 1924, took office in 1978, elected 1979 **Effective Date of Present Constitution:** 1963, revised 1969 **Legislative Body:** National Assembly (unicameral), consisting of 158 members elected for up to 5 years and 12 members nominated by the president **Local Government:** 7 provinces and the Nairobi area

Ethnic Composition: 30-40 groups fall into four main linguistic divisions: the Bantu, who constitute the majority, Nilo-Hamitics, Nilotics, and Hamitics. The largest tribes are the Kikuyu, Luhya, Luo, Kamba, Kisii and Meru. There are some 200,000 non-Africans, including Arabs, Europeans, and Hindu and Moslem Indians **Population Distribution:** 10% urban **Density:** 68 inhabitants per sq. mi.

Largest Cities: (1978 est.) Nairobi 818,000, Mombasa 391,000, (1976 est.) Nakuru 66,000, Kisumu 46,000

Per Capita Income: $288 (1980) **Gross National Product (GNP):** $4.6 billion (1980) **Economic Statistics:** About 20% of GNP comes from manufacturing (chiefly agricultural processing, oil refining, and small-scale consumer goods), mining and quarrying; 18% from trade, transportation and communications; 27% from services and about 31% from agriculture (coffee, tea, pyrethrum, sisal, livestock, meat and dairy products, wool, hides, corn, wheat, millet, and cassava), forestry, and fishing **Minerals and Mining:** Small quantities of soda ash, fluorspar, limestone, salt, copper, gold, and silver are produced **Labor Force:** 5,400,000 (1971), 86% in agriculture and 13% in industry **Foreign Trade:** Exports, chiefly coffee, tea, sisal, pyrethrum extract and flowers, meat and meat preparations, totaled $589 million in 1979. Imports, mainly machinery, transport equipment, manufactured goods, lubricants, and chemicals, totaled $1 billion **Principal Trade Partners:** EC countries, United States, Japan, Saudi Arabia, Iran, Zambia, India, Sweden, Uganda

Vital Statistics: Birthrate, 48 per 1,000 of pop.; (1976) death rate, 14 **Life Expectancy:** 51 years **Health Statistics:** 759 inhabitants per hospital bed; 16,292 per physician (1973) **Infant Mortality:** 51.4 per 1,000 births **Illiteracy:** 70% **Primary and Secondary School Enrollment:** 3,183,673 (1976) **Enrollment in Higher Education:** 11,351 (1974) **GNP Expended on Education:** 5.7% (1974)

Transportation: Paved roads total 3,300 mi. **Motor Vehicles:** 198,000 (1977) **Passenger Cars:** 114,100 **Railway Mileage:** 1,500

Port: Mombasa **Major Airlines:** Kenya Airways operates domestic and international services **Communications:** Government controlled **Radio Transmitters:** 18 **Receivers:** 514,000 (1976) **Television Transmitters:** 5 **Receivers:** 50,000 (1976) **Telephones:** 144,000 **Newspapers:** 3 dailies, 10 copies per 1,000 inhabitants (1975)

Weights and Measures: Metric system **Travel Requirements:** Passport, visa, valid 6 months, $3.15 fee **International Dialing Code:** 254

Kenya is one of Africa's best-known countries; the land of the safari, gameparks, and the lure of the green hills Ernest Hemingway made famous. Tourism has grown spectacularly, with annual earnings rivaling those from coffee export.

The Asian population is being rapidly reduced under a phased program of canceling government permits for Asians to carry on businesses. The influence of Europeans is also declining.

Kenya has made considerable progress in industry and in agriculture, particularly in the success of African farmers settled on the former large British holdings in the old "White Highlands." But these gains have been offset by high population growth, unemployment, and drought. A slump in world demand for coffee and tea produced a severe trade deficit in 1978 that continued into 1981. Kenya is energy-poor, and 60 percent of its foreign exchange goes for oil. Wood is a major fuel. However, hydroelectric power is being developed on the Tana River.

In leading the former British colony to independence in 1963, President Jomo Kenyatta stressed the need for unity with the slogan of *Harambee!* (Swahili for "Let us all pull together"). Kenyatta, affectionately known as *Mzee* ("the Old One"), was able to hold Kenya together, but not without strain. The Kenyatta government's strength was tested in 1975 when a wave of political unrest was touched off by the murder of Josiah Kariuki, a popular member of parliament and critic of Kenyatta. An investigation committee implicated police officials and top aides of Kenyatta.

Although all Assembly members belong to Kenya's only party, the Kenya African National Union (KANU), dissident members formed an opposition group, which resulted in a KANU leadership decree that any Assembly member not following the party position would be expelled.

In August 1978, Kenyatta died peacefully in his sleep. Daniel arap Moi, 54, became president.

HISTORY: Kenya's coast was a familiar area to mariners of past eras, including Phoenicians, Egyptians, and Greeks. Arab coastal colonies were established as early as the 8th century and in the 15th century Portuguese joined in the thriving spice and slave trade. Britain gained a foothold in the 19th century and in 1895 established a protectorate over the area, then known as British East Africa. With the influx of British and South African settlers, Kenya continued to be dominated by the white population

1944: Africans win token political representation with the appointment of the first black member of the Legislative Council

1952-59: Mau Mau rebellion, led by secret terrorist organization comprising mainly Kikuyu tribesmen, results in brutal slayings of whites and Africans serving whites, and equally brutal retaliation by white community; Africans are granted larger, but still minority, representation in Legislative Council

1960-61: Britain agrees to new elections for Legislative Council, in which Africans win majority

1961-62: Jomo Kenyatta, imprisoned as alleged Mau Mau leader, is released; he enters Legislative Council as leader of the Kenya African National Union (KANU), backed largely by the Kikuyu and Luo tribes, and forces cooperation with the governing Kenya African Democratic Union (KADU), which is chiefly supported by the smaller tribal units

1963: Kenyatta leads KANU to overwhelming election victory; Kenya gains independence, with Kenyatta as prime minister

1964: Kenya becomes a republic within the British Commonwealth, under the presidency of Kenyatta; KADU voluntarily dissolves itself and Kenya becomes a one-party state

1966: Vice-President Oginga Odinga, an early Kenyatta follower and Luo tribal leader, resigns, charging KANU government with being "capitalistic"; he forms new opposition party, the Kenya People's Union

1969: Economics Minister Tom Mboya, a Luo, is slain by a Kikuyu; slaying sparks antigovernment demonstrations and arrest of Oginga Odinga. KPU party is dissolved

1971: Opposition leader Oginga Odinga is released from detention

1974: Kenyatta orders all unauthorized noncitizen traders to leave. Swahili declared official language. Severe drought affects 70 percent of country

1977: Tanzania closes 500-mile border with Kenya indefinitely. This action follows Kenya's withdrawal from participation in East African Airways, which forced the airline to close. Government bans all game hunting in an effort to save wildlife from extinction. Kenya claims Somali troops cross border. The two nations set up border commission to prevent recurrence

1978: Kenyatta dies. Daniel arap Moi becomes president

1979: Kenya launches 5-year development plan to eliminate poverty, disease and illiteracy, and to reduce unemployment. Moi retains office in November elections

1980: Moi travels widely seeking foreign aid for Kenya's trade-balance problem and food relief for northwest drought area. Thousands of Ugandans in exile are forcibly repatriated. The United States is given port rights in Mombasa

1981: Raids on bandit strongholds in Northeast Frontier District bring charges of police harrassment of Somali tribes

KIRIBATI

Area: 264 sq. mi. **Population:** 56,213 (1978 census)

Official Name: Republic of Kiribati **Capital:** Bairiki, on Tarawa **Nationality:** Kiribati **Languages:** I-Kiribati (Gilbertese) and English **Religion:** Evenly divided between Protestant and Roman Catholic **Flag:** Bottom half consists of six wavy, horizontal white stripes over navy blue; top half is red with a flying yellow frigate bird over a yellow sun, displaying nine straight and eight wavy yellow rays **Anthem:** Stand Up Kiribati **Currency:** Australian dollar (0.87 per U.S. $1)

Location: The island nation extends widely over the western Pacific, from 5°N to 11°S and 169°E to 150°W, and is scattered over two million sq. mi. of ocean. It includes 33 islands and atolls in the Gilbert, Phoenix and Line groups, plus Banaba (Ocean Island). All but Banaba have coral-ringed lagoons circling the tops of submerged mountains

Head of State and of Government: President Ieremia Tabai, born 1950, assumed office, July 12, 1979. The governor general is Reginald James Wallace **Effective Date of Present Constitution:** July 12, 1979 **Legislative Body:** a unicameral House of Assembly (*Maneaba ni Maungatabu*) of 35 elected members, one nominated representative of Banaba and the attorney general **Local Government:** 23 election districts

Ethnic Composition: Predominantly Micronesian with some Polynesians, mixed Micronesian-Polynesian, and Europeans **Population Distribution:** 30 % urban **Density:** 213 inhabitants per sq. mi.

Largest City: Bairiki 1,300

Per Capita Income: $630 (1979) **Gross Domestic Product (GDP):** $36 million (1979) **Economic Statistics:** The economy is based largely on the export of copra. The brine shrimp industry on Christmas Island grows shrimps and shrimp eggs for fish farms throughout the world. There is a soft drink factory, a biscuit factory and a boatbuilding concern **Minerals and Mining:** Phosphate mining on Banaba (Ocean Island) is due to end in 1980 **Labor Force:** 15,921 (1973) **Foreign Trade:** Exports, chiefly phosphate rock and copra, totaled $21.2 million in 1978. Imports totaled $18.4 million **Principal Trade Partners:** Britain, Australia

Vital Statistics: Birthrate, 22.3 per 1,000 of pop. (1971); death rate, 6.5 **Life Expectancy:** 58 years **Health Statistics:** 201 inhabitants per hospital bed (1977); 2,692 per physician (1975) **Infant Mortality:** 48.9 per 1,000 births (1971) **Illiteracy:** under 10% **Primary and Secondary School Enrollment:** 14,511 (1977) **Enrollment in Higher Education:** N.A. **GNP Expended on Education:** N.A.

Transportation: Motorable roads total 300 mi. **Motor Vehicles:** N.A. **Passenger Cars:** N.A. **Railway Mileage:** None **Ports:** Tarawa, Canton Island **Major Airlines:** Air Tunguru provides domestic service. Air Nauru and Air Pacific provide international service **Communications:** Government owned **Radio Transmitters:** 1 **Receivers:** 8,200 (1975) **Television Transmitters:** None **Telephones:** 866 **Newspapers:** 4 non-dailies, 89 copies per 1,000 inhabitants (1974)

Weights and Measures: British and metric **Travel Requirements:** not available

In November 1943, U.S. Marines landed on Tarawa, the central island in the far-flung Gilbert chain, and fought one of the bloodiest battles of the Second World War, defeating Japanese garrison of 5,000. Although time seemed to have forgotten these peaceful islands since, the realities of the modern world have caught up to this newly independent nation—one of the world's poorest—of 33 coral atolls stretched across two million square miles of the South Pacific, at the crossroads of the equator and the international date line.

Independence came to the former Gilbert Islands on July 12, 1979, after 87 years of British rule. One of the most pressing problems facing Kiribati (pronounced "Kiribass") is economic; 99 percent of its annual income was derived from phosphate mining controlled by a joint Australian-New Zealand authority on Banaba. The phosphate deposit was exhausted in 1980, but machinery was maintained pending a redevelopment survey. Diversification is thus the main priority facing the new government on Tarawa. Agriculture is limited by poor soil, although the export of copra—derived from the native coconut palms—has been a source of revenue. There are plans to develop local industries—mainly fruit canning and handicrafts—as well as to exploit the potentially rich fishing grounds within Kiribati's 200-mile offshore boundaries. British pledges of aid and unrestricted access to Australian and New Zealand markets hold some promise for future economic development.

Although fourteen of the islands in the Phoenix and Line groups have long been claimed by both Britain and the United States—including Kanton (Canton), Enderbury and Christmas Islands—the U.S. has agreed to relinquish Canton and Enderbury in 1980, and will cede the rest to Kiribati by treaty in the near future.

But the birth pangs of the new nation have caused other political problems the new government must face. The former residents of Banaba (Ocean Island), who were relocated following World War II after mining had despoiled their island, have fought for 10 years to reassert their claims to their traditional homes, and continue to oppose being part of an independent Kiribati. Kiribati, while assuring the islanders of their continued rights on Banaba, has refused so far to agree to Banaban demands for separation.

HISTORY: The main wave of Micronesian settlement of the area is thought to have originated from Samoa around the thirteenth century. Although Spanish navigators are credited with sighting some of the islands in 1537 and 1606, true European discovery of the area came only much later, with the first white settlement dating from the 1830s. Missionaries visited the islands in 1857, and by the 1860s a flourishing trade in coconut oil and copra had been established. Between 1850 and 1875 the islands were raided by "blackbirders" for slave labor in South America, Fiji, Tahiti, Hawaii and Australia. To stamp out this activity, the British established the High Commmision for the Western Pacific over the area in 1877
1888-89: Britain annexes Christmas, Fanning and Washington Islands
1892: Britain establishes protectorate over Gilberts and neighboring Ellice Islands
1915: Protectorate reorganized as Gilbert and Ellice Islands Colony, extended to include Ocean Island (Banaba) and the Northern Line Islands by 1919
1937: Phoenix Islands incorporated into the colony
1939: Britain and U.S. sign treaty providing for joint control of Kanton (Canton) and Enderbury
1941-45: Japanese seize Tarawa and Ocean Island (Banaba) from British at outset of World War II. U.S. forces land on Tarawa November 1943, defeating Japanese occupation force. Australian forces liberate Ocean Island (Banaba) in 1945
1945-47: Banabans, dispersed during conflict, are resettled on Rabi, in Fiji Islands
1972: Gilbert and Ellice Islands, removed from jurisdiction of Western Pacific Commission, are placed under a British governor
1975: Ellice Islands separate from Gilberts, becoming Tuvalu (independent in 1978)

1978: London conference, Nov.21-Dec. 7, sets constitutional framework for independence; Banaba representatives bolt meeting after Gilbertese officials reject demands for separation
1979: Gilberts become independent nation of Kiribati, July 12
1980: Phosphate on Banaba runs out, mining stops. Kiribati is host to a forum which draws up South Pacific Regional Trade and Cooperation Agreement

NORTH KOREA

Area: 46,540 sq. mi. **Population:** 17,072,000 (1978 est.)
Official Name: Democratic People's Republic of Korea **Capital:** Pyongyang **Nationality:** Korean **Languages:** Korean is the official and universal language **Religion:** The traditional religions are Buddhism, Confucianism, Shamanism, and Ch'ondokyo, which combines elements of Buddhism and Christianity; the practice of religion has been discouraged by the government **Flag:** A broad center red stripe bordered on top and bottom by a thin white stripe and a broader blue stripe: left of center is a white disc containing a five-pointed red star **Anthem:** National Anthem, beginning "Morning sun, shine over the rivers and mountains" **Currency:** Won (1.79 per U.S. $1)
Location: North Korea occupies the northern portion of a peninsula in northeast Asia projecting southeast from Manchuria. It is bordered on the north by China, on the extreme northeast by the USSR, on the east by the Sea of Japan, on the south by South Korea, and on the west by the Yellow Sea and Korea Bay **Features:** A land of mountains, North Korea contains thousands of peaks, leaving less than one fifth of the total area as cultivable **Chief Rivers:** Tumen, Yalu, Ch'ongch'on, Taedong, Yesong
Head of State and Political Leader: President: Marshal Kim Il Sung, born 1912, reelected 1977. The premier is Li Jong Ok **Effective Date of Present Constitution:** 1972 **Legislative Body:** Supreme People's Assembly (unicameral), consisting of 579 members elected by universal suffrage for 4 years. Power is in the hands of the Central People's Committee of the Korean Workers' (Communist) party **Local Government:** 9 provinces
Ethnic Composition: North Koreans, like the South Koreans, are believed to be of Tungusic stock, ethnically related to the Mongols with some Chinese mixture. There are no ethnic minorities **Population Distribution:** 38.1% urban **Density:** 367 inhabitants per sq. mi.
Largest Cities: (1972 est.) Pyongyang 1,500,000, Hamhung 484,000, Chongjin 306,000, Sinuiju 300,000, Wonsan 275,000
Per Capita Income: $824 (1980) **Gross National Product (GNP):** $15.9 billion (1980) **Economic Statistics:** About 70% of GNP comes from industry and mining (coal, iron ore, steel, machinery, textiles); 15% from agriculture (rice, corn, barley, wheat, cotton) **Minerals and Mining:** Large deposits of coal, iron ore, lead, zinc, molybdenum, gold, graphite, and tungsten **Labor Force:** 6.1 million, with 48% in agriculture **Foreign Trade:** Exports, mainly ferrous and nonferrous metals, minerals, chemicals, fuel and oil, machinery and equipment, totaled $1.3 billion in 1979. Imports, chiefly machinery and equipment, fuels, chemicals, and textiles, totaled $1.3 billion **Principal Trade Partners:** USSR, China and other Communist countries, Japan
Vital Statistics: Birthrate, 35.7 per 1,000 of pop. (1975); death rate, 9.4 **Life Expectancy:** 61 years **Health Statistics:** 333 inhabitants per hospital bed; 909 per physician **Infant Mortality:** N.A. **Illiteracy:** 10% **Primary School Enrollment:** 2,561,674 (1976) **Enrollment in Higher Education:** 214,000 (1973)
Transportation: Total road mileage is c. 12,600 **Motor Vehicles:** 60,000 (1971) **Railway Mileage:** 2,950 **Ports:** Chongjin, Hamhung, Nampo, Wonsan, Unggi **Major Airlines:** Civil Aviation Administration operates both international and domestic flights **Communications:** State controlled **Radio Transmitters:** 19 **Receivers:** 800,000 (1971) **Television Transmitters:** 1 **Receivers:** 50,000 (1973) **Telephones:** N.A. **Newspapers:** 11 dailies
Weights and Measures: Metric system **Travel Requirements:** N.A.

To the West, North Korea is one of the most isolated and least-known Communist countries. Contacts even between North and South Koreans are almost nonexistent since North and South are still in a technical state of war; the demilitarized zone across the peninsula, set up by the armistice in 1953, is probably the world's most tightly closed border.

The division of Korea along the 38th parallel at the end of World War II left the North with almost all the country's mineral resources and a major share of the industries developed by the Japanese in the former colony. The three-year Korean War devastated much of the industry, but planning, regimentation, and utilization of a trained labor force brought great strides in production by the early 1960s.

The highly authoritarian, military-dominated government of Marshal Kim Il Sung has sought to steer an independent course between the Soviet Union and China, while remaining antagonistic toward United States "imperialism" and what it calls the "puppet" South Korean regime.

Premier Kim, previously a guerrilla against the Japanese, arrived in Pyongyang with Soviet troops in October 1945 as a leader in the émigré forces trained by the Russians to take over in Korea. He established his dominance as premier when the Democratic People's Republic of Korea was set up in September 1948.

North Korea's military forces were strengthened rapidly as Soviet troops were withdrawn, and in June 1950 a North Korean military attack came close to seizing the entire peninsula before United Nations forces, led by American troops, gained the initiative.

The end of the war was followed by collectivization of agriculture; industry in the North had already been nationalized. Economic progress has been notable, educational facilities have been expanded, and extreme poverty has been sharply reduced.

However, life in the North is highly regimented. Consumer goods are scarce, the vast housing projects are drab, travel is tightly controlled and freedom of expression is restricted.

In a June 1973 dispatch, Kim was quoted as saying: "We hold that the North and the South should not enter the United Nations separately but as one state under a confederation." Since that time, he has reiterated his wish for a unified Korea under Communist rule.

Tension between the two countries increased after the finding in November 1974 of tunnels under the demilitarized zone emerging into South Korea. The victories of the Communists in South Vietnam and Cambodia and a visit to China by Kim, allegedly to seek Chinese support for military pressure on South Korea, had a negative effect on relations between the two Koreas. A new era was in prospect after the 1977 announcement by the U.S. that it planned the gradual withdrawal of all American ground forces from the demilitarized zone over the next five years.

When South Korea proposed, on Jan. 19, 1979, that fresh talks be held in an effort to prevent war and to unify the two countries, North Korea answered, only six days-later, that a "new start" would be a good idea. Delegations began talks almost at once, but quickly bogged down in procedural disputes, as they did again in early 1980, when they met at the behest of UN Secretary General Kurt Waldheim. In 1981, with U.S. plans to reduce troop levels apparently abandoned, South Korean requests for talks were rejected.

In October 1980, Kim Il Sung's son , Kim Jong Il, was named the second ranking member of the powerful Communist party Secretariat, making him his father's potential political heir.

HISTORY: Korean history goes back into a legendary past, with one of the earliest legends centering around Kitze, or Kija, a scholar credited with the introduction of Chinese culture into the Korean peninsula in the 12th century B.C. Chinese influence remained strong until well after the emergence of separate Korean kingdoms in the early centuries of the Christian era, and it was with Chinese help that one of these, the kingdom of Silla, conquered its rivals in the 7th century A.D. and unified the peninsula. In the 10th century

Silla fell to the Koryo dynasty of Kaesong, under whose rule Confucianism gradually replaced Buddhism as the dominant religion
1231-60: Mongols occupy Korea
1392: Yi Sung-ke, a Korean general, seizes Korean throne
1592: Yi dynasty, aided by China, repels invasion by Japanese
1637: Korea is made a vassal of Manchu China, beginning a period of isolation from the rest of the world and giving Korea the name of "hermit kingdom"
1876-82: Korean ports are opened to Japanese, U.S. and European trade after Japan compels Korea to agree to commercial treaty
1894-1905: Japanese victories in Sino-Japanese and Russo-Japanese wars end in complete control of Korea by Japan
1910: Japan formally annexes Korea
1919: Nationalist leader Syngman Rhee sets up Korean government-in-exile in Shanghai
1945: Soviet and U.S. forces occupy Korea after Japan's defeat in World War II; they establish the 38th parallel as the dividing line between their occupation zones, with the Russians in the north and the Americans in the south
1948: Division of the peninsula is formalized with the establishment of the two separate regimes of North Korea and South Korea; Democratic People's Republic of North Korea is set up in 1948 under Premier Kim Il Sung, a Moscow-trained military man; Soviet forces evacuate North Korea
1950-53: North Korea invades South Korea in 1950; in response to UN request, the U.S. and 15 other member nations send troops to aid South Korea; after initial retreats, UN forces stage counteroffensive and drive North Koreans deep into North Korea; in October 1950 Chinese Communists join North Koreans in successful counterattack; fighting continues until a cease-fire is reached in 1953, leaving Korea divided as before
1954-61: Kim Il Sung pushes ambitious program of industrialization; North Korea is economically integrated with Soviet Union and Communist China; military aid treaties are signed with both
1968: North Korea seizes U.S. intelligence ship Pueblo, charging vessel violated North Korean territorial waters; crew is released after 11 months when U.S. signs a statement, which it labels false, admitting the Pueblo's intrusion
1970: Kim government proposes a federated Korea, conditional upon U.S. withdrawal from the south
1975: North Korea becomes first Communist country to not meet payment of Western debts
1976: North Korean soldiers kill two U.S. Army officers at Panmunjom
1977: Travel restrictions for U.S. citizens to North Korea are lifted
1978: Working-level talks between North and South Korea break down. Communist Chinese Premier Hua visits, describes North Korea as "sole legitimate sovereign Korean state" and calls for complete withdrawal of U.S. forces from Korea. North Korea denounces "slow" pace of U.S. troop pullout, calls for direct talks with U.S. on reunification of Korea
1979: In response to a South Korean suggestion, North Korea enters into unification talks, which soon collapse. Table tennis players from 70 contries participate in world tournament in Pyongyang. Kim Il Sung, now president, denounces U.S. report that Korea's army is the world's fifth largest. UN Secreatary General Kurt Waldheim visits both Koreas
1980: North and south Korean delegations meet again at Waldheim's request, but fail to make progress. President Kim's son, Kim Jong Il, is given number two post in party Secretariat
1981: President Kim rejects repeated bids by South Korea's new leader, Chun Doo Hwan, for a face-to-face meeting

---

SOUTH KOREA

Area: 38,175 sq. mi. **Population:** 37,448,836 (1980 census)
Official Name: Republic of Korea **Capital:** Seoul **Nationality:** Korean **Languages:** Korean is the official and universal language **Religion:** The traditional religions are Buddhism, Confucianism, Shamanism, and Ch'ondokyo, which combines elements of Buddhism and Christianity. However, accurate figures of the numbers of their adherents are not available. There are at least 4 million Christians, chiefly Protestant **Flag:** A divided circle of red (top) and blue (bottom) centered on a white field. A black bar design appears in each corner of the flag **Anthem:** National Anthem, beginning "Until the Eastern Sea is drained" **Currency:** Won (679 per U.S. $1)

Location: South Korea occupies the southern portion of a peninsula in northeast Asia projecting southeast from Manchuria. It is bounded on the north by North Korea, on the east by the Sea of Japan, on the south by the Korea Strait, and on the west by the Yellow Sea **Features:** The country is largely mountainous, with the limited arable land in the lowlands and river valleys of the south and southwest **Chief Rivers:** Somjin, Kum, Naktong, Han, Pukhan

Head of State and of Government: President Chun Doo Hwan, born 1931, elected by the National Conference for Unification Aug. 27, 1980, and sworn in for 7 years under new constitution, March 3, 1981, following election of Feb. 25. He is assisted by a Prime Minister, Nam Duck Woo **Effective Date of Present Constitution:** Oct. 27, 1980 **Legislative Body:** National Assembly (unicameral), consisting of 276 members partly elected for 4 years **Local Government:** 9 provinces and 2 specially administered cities

Ethnic Composition: The Korean population is one of the most homogeneous in the world. The primary stock is believed to be Tungusic, related to the Mongols with some Chinese mixture **Population Distribution:** 60% urban **Density:** 981 inhabitants per sq. mi.

Largest Cities: (1977 est.) Seoul 7,500,000; (1975 census) Pusan 2,454,051; Taegu 1,311,078, Inchon 799,982, Kwangju 607,058

Per Capita Income: $1,067 (1980) **Gross National Product (GNP):** $42 billion (1980) **Economic Statistics:** 30% of GNP comes from manufacturing (textiles, chemicals, food processing, clay, glass and stone products, transportation equipment) and mining; 21% from agriculture (rice, barley, soybeans, potatoes, wheat, millet, livestock raising), forestry and fishing **Minerals and Mining:** South Korea has less than 30% of the peninsula's estimated reserves of gold, silver, tungsten, molybdenum, and graphite, and about 10% of its coal and iron ore. It produces anthracite coal, tungsten, iron ore, lead, amorphous graphite, fluorite, kaolite, and talc **Labor Force:** 14.2 million (1979), with 36% in agriculture and forestry; 24% in manufacturing and mining **Foreign Trade:** Exports, chiefly clothing and textiles, plywood, ships, iron and steel products, cars, marine products, raw silk, and electronic products, totaled $15 billion in 1979. Imports, mainly fuel, nonelectric machinery, transportation equipment, food grains, electric machinery, textiles yarns and fabrics, totaled $20.3 billion **Principal Trade Partners:** United States, Japan, Saudi Arabia, Kuwait, West Germany

Vital Statistics: Birthrate, 28.8 per 1,000 of pop. (1975); death rate 8.9 **Life Expectancy:** 68 years **Health Statistics:** 1,310 inhabitants per hospital bed; 2,128 per physician (1976) **Infant Mortality:** 38 per 1,000 births **Illiteracy:** 6.8% **Primary and Secondary School Enrollment:** 9,060,787 (1977) **Enrollment in Higher Education:** 325,460 (1976) **GNP Expended on Education:** 4.1% (1974)

Transportation: Paved roads total 8,400 mi. **Motor Vehicles:** 270,500 (1977) **Passenger Cars:** 125,600 **Railway Mileage:** 3,594 **Ports:** Pusan, Inchon, Pohang, Masan, Mokpo, Gunsan, Mukho **Major Airlines:** Korean Airlines operates domestic and international services **Communications:** Government and privately owned **Radio Transmitters:** 94 **Receivers:** 12,300,000 (1978) **Television Transmitters:** 59 **Receivers:** 5,135,496 (1978) **Telephones:** 2,000,000 **Newspapers:** 36 dailies, 173 copies per 1,000 inhabitants (1975)

Weights and Measures: Metric system and old Korean units are used **Travel Requirements:** Passport, tourist visa valid for initial period of 2 months, no fee; 1 photo; affidavit of support **International Dialing Code:** 82

The Korean peninsula has often been described as a dagger pointed from the Asian heartland toward Japan, and its strategic position made it several times a battleground for more powerful neighbors. Long a "hermit kingdom" with a strong indigenous culture, Korea was annexed by the Japanese in 1910. Until the end of World War II it was ruled by a repressive colonial regime and exploited for its mineral resources, living space, and markets.

Considerable dislocation occurred when the primarily agricultural and densely populated South was separated from the industrial North in 1945 and put under United States occupation. After unsuccessful attempts to arrange nationwide elections under United Nations supervision, voting was held in 1948 in the South only and the government of the Republic of Korea was established under the presidency of Syngman Rhee.

The Korean War caused more than 800,000 military and civilian casualties in South Korea and approximately $3 billion worth of property damage. For a decade thereafter the huge U.S. aid effort, coupled with international assistance, was directed toward providing food and shelter, repairing war damage, and laying the groundwork for eventual economic development. During the 1970s, the South Korean economy flourished, and the nation became an important industrial power. By 1981, however, the price of this rapid expansion was

being felt in increased labor trouble and inflation. Negative economic growth had occurred in 1980 and the annual cost of servicing a huge foreign debt soared past the $4-billion mark.

President Rhee won reelection in 1952 and 1956, but as he grew more despotic and ruthless, police repression and official corruption aroused wide protests. Finally, rigging of elections in 1960 set off student demonstrations that overthrew Dr. Rhee. The subsequent government of Dr. John M. Chang proved ineffective and a military coup in May 1961 brought to power a junta led by Park Chung Hee, then a major general. General Park retired from the army, won the presidency in a national election in 1963, and was reelected in 1967 and 1972. In 1978 his presidency was extended for six years; no other name was on the ballot as the electoral college, the National Conference for Unification, elected him, 2,577 to 0. At the time of voting, all opposition leaders were under house arrest in Seoul.

Threatened by North Korean military power, Park maintained close ties with the U.S. to ensure military assistance, but relations became frayed, especially after the banning of all political dissent from 1975 on. In 1979, in the wake of nationwide student unrest, Park and six of his bodyguards were slain by Kim Jae Kyu, chief of the Korean Central Intelligence Agency, and several aides. Kim and four accomplices were hanged in May 1980.

Park's prime minister, Choi Kyu Hah, became president in December 1979, but real power soon passed to Chun Doo Hwan, a paratroop general who was put in charge of a "special security" committee to cope with spreading insurrections. On May 27, 1980, Chun's forces recaptured the city of Kwangjun, which had been held by rebellious students for ten days. Taking over the presidency in August, Chun promulgated a new constitution which established a less powerful legislature and an electoral-college system for the indirect selection of a president. The constitution was overwhelmingly approved in an October referendum and, in early 1981, a pro-Chun electoral college and National Assembly were elected.

President Chun relaxed security measures before visiting newly inaugurated U.S. President Ronald Reagan in February 1981 and securing his pledge of increased military and economic assistance.

HISTORY: The history of South Korea is bound up with that of Korea as a whole up until 1948 when the government of the Republic of Korea was established under the presidency of Syngman Rhee

1950-53: Korean War, brought on by North Korea's invasion of South Korea, rages for three years as U.S. troops and forces of 15 other nations, responding to a request for help by the United Nations, try to repel the invaders; the conflict, broadened in 1951 with the entry of Communist China on the side of North Korea, ends with the establishment of a cease-fire and the continued division of the peninsula at the 38th parallel

1960: Rhee is elected for fourth term as president but is accused of rigging the elections; after widespread rioting he is forced from office and goes into exile

1961: South Korean armed forces overthrow government; Gen. Park Chung Hee takes power

1963-67: Park is elected president in 1963 and is reelected in 1967 amid charges by his opponents that elections were rigged

1969: South Korean voters approve a constitutional amendment that allows president to seek a third consecutive term

1970: United States agrees to bolster South Korean army after announcing U.S. troop cuts in South Korea

1972: Following secret talks, governments of North and South Korea announce agreement in principle on unification. Park institutes constitutional changes that increase his power

1973: Opposition leader Kim Dae-Jung is kidnapped in Japan, resulting in widespread demonstrations. Brought back to Korea, he is placed under house arrest and later released

1975: Assassination attempt on President Park fails but wife is victim. North Korea rejects a South Korean proposal to renew talks on unification

1978: Economy continues on uptrend. Strained relations between South Korea and U.S. worsen over planned pullout of American ground forces (as withdrawal begins); U.S. bugging of South Korean executive mansion is alleged, and influence-buying scandal comes to light, in which South Korean businessman Tongsun Park and former ambassador Kim Dong Jo allegedly paid U.S. Congressmen for continued American economic and military aid; Kim Dong Jo resigns post as national security adviser. Park, unopposed, is reelected for another six-year presidential term

1979: Park asks North Korea for talks "any time, any place" to reunify the countries; delegations meet but bog down on procedural questions. U.S. President Carter visits Seoul in June, prompting government's release of many political dissidents. Student demonstrations sweep the cities in October. President Park and his chief bodyguard are killed on October 26 by Kim Jae Kyu, director of the Korean Central Intelligence Agency. Premier Choi Kyu Hah is elected president in December

1980: Student protests against martial law start in Seoul in May and spread to other cities. Rebel students seize Kwangju and hold it for 10 days, until paratroopers win back the city in a 3:30 A.M. assault on May 27. The death toll is 200 to 300. A paratroop officer, Lt. Gen. Chun Doo Hwan, as top security chief, takes charge of government and is elected president in August. His proposed new constitution is approved by more than 90 percent of voters in October. Economy slows as inflation tops 25 percent. U.S. troop withdrawals suspended

1981: Martial law, in force since October 1979, is ended in January, and Chun commutes death sentence against opposition leader Kim Dae Jung before flying to U.S. to meet President Ronald Reagan. Electoral college, chosen in February, names Chun to full presidential term. His newly created Democratic Justice party sweeps Assembly elections in March. Chun renews Park's call for meeting of North and South Korean presidents

---

KUWAIT

Area: 7,780 sq. mi. **Population:** 1,355,827 (1980 census)

Official Name: State of Kuwait **Capital:** Kuwait **Nationality:** Kuwaiti **Languages:** Arabic is the official and universal language; English is widely spoken **Religion:** About 99% Moslem, chiefly of the Sunni sect; and 1% of other or no affiliation **Flag:** Green, white, and red horizontal stripes with a black trapezoid at the staff **Anthem:** National Anthem (no words) **Currency:** Kuwaiti dinar (.27 per U.S. $1)

Location: Northeast corner of the Arabian Peninsula. Kuwait is bordered on the north and west by Iraq, on the east by the Persian Gulf, and on the south by Saudi Arabia **Features:** The country is mainly flat desert, with a few oases **Chief Rivers:** There are no rivers

Head of State and Government: Emir: Sheikh Jabir al-Ahmad al-Jabir as-Sabah, born 1928, acceded 1977. The emir is assisted by a council of ministers headed by a prime minister, Sheikh Saad al-Abdullah al-Salim as-Sabah, appointed 1978 **Effective Date of Present Constitution:** 1962 **Legislative Body:** National Assembly (unicameral), with 50 elected members **Local Government:** 3 governorates

Ethnic Composition: The population is about 85% Arab but only 48% are native-born. Non-Kuwaitis include Palestinians, Iraqis, Iranians, Egyptians, Indians, Syrians, Lebanese, and others **Population Distribution:** 99% urban **Density:** 174 inhabitants per sq. mi.

Largest City: (1980 census) Kuwait 181,774

Per Capita Income: $12,920 (1980) **Gross National Product (GNP):** $18 billion (1980) **Economic Statistics:** The economy is based almost entirely on oil, which accounts for about 70% of GNP. About 15% comes from trade and services; the remainder from nonoil industries (chemical fertilizers, building materials, fishing) **Minerals and Mining:** Kuwait possesses nearly one fifth of the world's oil reserves. Large amounts of natural gas are produced from the oil fields **Labor Force:** 360,000, with 70% held by non-Kuwaitis. 40% of the labor force is employed by the government, 34% are in industry (less than 5% in the heavily automated oil industry), and 1% in agriculture **Foreign Trade:** Exports, 96% crude oil and petroleum products, totaled $17.6 billion in 1979. Imports, chiefly foodstuffs, building materials, automobiles, industrial equipment and electrical products, totaled $5.7 billion **Principal Trade Partners:** Japan, United States, Britain, West Germany, Italy, Korea, Netherlands, Saudi Arabia

Vital Statistics: Birthrate, 43.3 per 1,000 of pop. (1976); death rate, 4.4 **Life Expectancy:** 69 years **Health Statistics:** 240 inhabitants per hospital bed; 883 per physician (1976) **Infant Mortality:** 34.3 per 1,000 births **Illiteracy:** 20% **Primary and Secondary School Enrollment:** 215,451 (1976) **Enrollment in Higher Education:** 9,934 **GNP Expended on Education:** 2.8% (1976)

Transportation: Paved roads total 1,400 mi. **Motor Vehicles:** 380,900 (1977) **Passenger Cars:** 285,800 **Railway Mileage:** None **Ports:** Mina al-Ahmadi, Shuwaikh, Shuaibah, Mina Abdullah **Major**

Airlines: Kuwait Airways, government owned, operates international flights **Communications:** Government owned **Radio Transmitters:** 8 **Receivers:** 502,000 (1976) **Television Transmitters:** 7 **Receivers:** 375,000 (1978) **Telephones:** 153,000 **Newspapers:** 8 dailies, 86 copies per 1,000 inhabitants (1976)

Weights and Measures: Metric system **Travel Requirements:** Passport, transit visa, valid 2 days, $1.00; entry visa, valid 1 month, 1 entry, $4.00, 2 photos **International Dialing Code:** 965

Tiny, torrid Kuwait, an opulent strip of desert at the northwestern end of the Persian Gulf, enjoys one of the world's highest standards of living. In 1980 it ranked second among all nations in per capita gross national product with $12,920 GNP per person.

Since 1967 Kuwait has helped to subsidize the national economies of Egypt and of Jordan, both of which were defeated in the war with Israel. It must import all of its food but exports enough oil to pay for the people's basic needs.

As a capitalistic welfare state, where poverty is virtually unknown, it provides lavish public services that include: free universal medical service, free education through the university level (including free food and clothing for students), free telephone service, subsidized housing for which only token rentals are paid, and subsidies for those wishing to start business enterprises.

Kuwait has a higher proportion of the latest American cars than any country outside the United States, and the cars are driven over wide, well-surfaced roads. It has more than twice as many air-conditioning units as people, and there is said to be a millionaire for every 230 citizens.

As late as the 1940s, before large-scale oil exports began, Kuwait was little more than a feudal wilderness. It was a primitive, forbidding land, where the temperature would often reach 125 degrees in the shade.

Abd Allah al-Salim as-Sabah, who was emir when the oil boom began, developed the growth program. Following his death in 1965, his policies were continued by his successor, Sheikh Sabah al-Salim as-Sabah. On December 31, 1977, Sheikh Sabah died and his cousin, Sheikh Jabir al-Ahmad al-Jabir as-Sabah, became emir.

The Kuwaitis themselves are a minority of the population of their own country, and they make up only 30 percent of the work force. Of those Kuwaitis who are employed, 70 percent are on the government payroll. Non-Kuwaitis (mainly Palestinians, Saudis, Egyptians, Iraqis, Pakistanis, Indians, and Americans), share in the welfare services, but do not own property or vote.

Kuwaiti society generally consists of five layers, with the members of the ruling family at the top, followed by the old Kuwaiti merchant families. Then come the former Bedouins now living in luxurious urban surroundings, the Arabs from other countries who have been granted Kuwaiti citizenship, and, last, the foreigners.

Many foreigners feel unappreciated by the Kuwaitis, and members of a large Palestinian underground have tried to force the government to take a stronger position than it has against Israel. The activities of this underground were cited by the government in explaining its decision to dissolve the National Assembly in 1976. The assembly was reconvened in 1981 after pro-government conservatives won a majority of its 50 seats.

A British protectorate from 1897 to 1961, Kuwait received informal military protection from the Shah of Iran after 1970. After the Shah fell in 1979, Britain's Queen Elizabeth and Foreign Secretary David Owen visited Kuwait to indicate continuing commitment.

Despite the connection with Britain, Kuwait is very much involved in the Arab bloc. It sent soldiers to fight in the Yom Kippur War against Israel in 1973. The Kuwaiti government joined other Arab states in breaking relations with Cairo after Egypt made peace with Israel in 1979. Kuwait has raised its oil prices along with other Arab oil-producing nations, and in 1980 it cut back crude oil production to maintain high prices.

HISTORY: Kuwait was settled by Arab tribes in the early 18th century. The present dynasty was established in 1756 by Sheikh Sabah Abdul Rahim. Nominally an Ottoman province, Kuwait asked for British protection in 1897, when the ruling sheikh feared that the Turks wanted to make their authority effective

1899: In return for British protection, Kuwait undertakes not to cede or lease any of its territory without Britain's approval

1914-22: Britain declares Kuwait independent of Turkey and under British protection. British troops help repel invasion by Saudi Arabia; Saudis and Kuwait set up neutral zone in which they share sovereignty

1934: Kuwait's ruler grants a concession to Kuwait Oil Company, a joint American-British enterprise, to drill for oil

1961: Britain recognizes Kuwait as an independent state and pledges protection against foreign aggression; Iraq claims Kuwait as a province; British troops prevent Iraqi invasion

1967: During Arab-Israeli war, Kuwait declares support for the Arab cause and contributes large subsidies to Egypt and Jordan

1969: Government shows increasing alarm over growing Soviet inroads in Persian Gulf area; proposal for the formation of a federation of nine neighboring sheikhdoms raises fear that many will succumb to revolutionary movements

1973: Kuwait's forces fight along Suez Canal during Yom Kippur War. Along with other oil-producing nations, Kuwait announces huge increase in oil prices

1975: Government announces it intends to acquire 100 percent ownership of domestic oil operations

1980: Kuwait reduces oil output to 1.5 million bbls. daily

1981: National Assembly reconvenes after 5-year hiatus; pro-government candidates win majority of seats

LAOS

Area: 91,428 sq. mi. **Population:** 3,546,000 (1978 est.)

Official Name: Lao People's Democratic Republic **Capital:** Vientiane **Nationality:** Laotian **Languages:** Lao, a tonal language of the Thai group, is the official and dominant language; French serves as the second language **Religion:** Theravada Buddhism is the official and predominant religion (90%); the country's mountain tribes are principally animist **Flag:** Two narrow red bands either side of a wide blue band, with a white disc in the middle **Anthem:** N.A. **Currency:** Kip (16 per U.S. $1)

Location: Southeast Asia. Landlocked Laos is bordered on the north by China, on the east by Vietnam, on the south by Cambodia, on the west by Thailand, and on the northwest by Burma **Features:** Northern Laos is laced with jungle-covered mountains and plateaus cut by narrow valleys. Lower Laos is marked by arid limestone terraces, sparsely forested and descending westward to the Mekong River Valley **Chief Rivers:** Mekong, Nam Hou

Head of State: President Souphanouvong, born 1902, named in 1975 **Head of Government:** Premier: Kaysone Phoumvihan, born 1920, appointed 1975; he is also secretary general of the party **Effective Date of Present Constitution:** none, at present **Legislative Body:** An appointed 45-member People's Supreme Assembly. The government is actually controlled by the Central Committee of the Lao People's Revolutionary (Communist) Party under its secretary general **Local Government:** 13 provinces

Ethnic Composition: More than half of the people are ethnic Lao, descendants of the Thai, a people who migrated from southwestern China in the 13th century. Mountain tribes of Sino-Tibetan and Thai strains are found in the north; many of these tribes, as well as others of Malay background, inhabit central and south Laos **Population Distribution:** 15% urban **Density:** 39 inhabitants per sq. mi.

Largest Cities: (1970 est.) Vientiane 150,000, Savannakhet 39,000, Pakse 37,200, Luang Prabang 25,000, Khammouane 13,000

Per Capita Income: $86 (1979) **Gross National Product (GNP):** $310 million (1979) **Economic Statistics:** Components of GNP are not available. The economy of the country, the least developed of the nations of the Indochinese peninsula, is 85% agricultural. Major crops are rice, corn, coffee, cotton, tea, and tobacco. Industry is limited to light consumer goods, with some cottage and family-type production. Lumber, cigarettes, alcohol, and cement are produced in small plants **Minerals and Mining:** Tin is the major mineral resource; surveys indicate deposits of iron ore, gold, copper, and manganese **Labor Force:** About 90% of the population is engaged in agriculture **Foreign Trade:** Exports, chiefly wood, tin, coffee, and resins, totaled $15 million in 1979. Imports, mainly foods, petroleum products, and transportation equipment, totaled $80 million **Principal Trade Partners:** Thailand, Japan, Malaysia, Singapore, Vietnam

Vital Statistics: Birthrate, 44.6 per 1,000 of pop. (1975); death rate, 22.8 **Life Expectancy:** 35 years **Health Statistics:** 401 inhabitants per hospital bed (1975); 21,667 per physician (1976) **Infant Mortality:** N.A. **Illiteracy:** 88% **Primary and Secondary School Enrollment:** 346,649 (1976) **Enrollment in Higher Education:** 828 (1974) **GNP Expended on Education:** N.A.

Transportation: Paved roads total about 800 mi. **Motor Vehicles:** 16,600 (1974) **Passenger Cars:** 14,100 **Railway Mileage:** None **Ports:** None **Major Airlines:** Air Lao operates domestic and international flights **Communications:** Government owned **Radio Transmitters:** 9 **Licenses:** 200,000 (1976) **Television:** None **Telephones:** 5,000 (1973) **Newspapers:** 8 dailies (1975)

Weights and Measures: Metric system **Travel Requirements:** Passport, visa; check Laotian embassy for requirements

---

The old Kingdom of Laos, which formed part of French Indochina, was little known to the outside world until the Vietnam War made its strategic location significant. The largest segment of French Indochina, it was also the most remote and the least developed. French rule did little to turn the ethnic groups into a united Laotian nation.

Most of the people live in the western quarter of the nation, where they practice subsistence agriculture. Widely scattered hill tribes inhabit the rest of the country, which is mountainous and jungle-covered. Laos lacks modern industrial facilities and technological resources. The country has few significant exports.

The development of Laos has been impeded both by warfare and by the country's physical features. The absence of a network of roads makes communication between the Mekong Valley towns and the rest of the country difficult. The North Vietnamese supply trails into South Vietnam ran through Laos, and these had been the target of intense bombing by U.S. planes. The land war itself spilled over from Vietnam into Laos in 1971, when the South Vietnamese launched a drive into eastern Laos with the stated intention of cutting off the Ho Chi Minh Trail.

The fighting was not confined to the southeast. A civil war was waged, with varying intensity, elsewhere in the country, with the United States supporting the Laotian government forces and the North Vietnamese helping the pro-Communist Pathet Lao.

On February 21, 1973, the war officially ended, as the Pathet Lao and the government signed a cease-fire agreement. By the end of July, a political settlement was reached, whereby the two Laotian parties agreed on the sharing of ministries, the creation of two deputy premierships, and the formation of a political consultative council. On the military side, the parties agreed to the neutralization of the two capitals, Vientiane and Luang Prabang, and the division of the country into two zones.

In April 1974, a third coalition government of neutralists, rightists and pro-Communist Pathet Lao was established and in May and June Thai and U.S. forces withdrew, ending their 10 years of military involvement.

By December of 1975, as an indirect result of the South Vietnamese collapse, a relatively low-key Pathet Lao takeover of Laos was completed with the abolition of both the 600-year-old monarchy and the coalition government and the establishment of a People's Democratic Republic. Prince Souphanouvong, titular leader of the Pathet Lao, was named president and Kaysone Phoumvihan, head of the Marxist-Leninist Laos People's party, was appointed premier.

The tide of refugees flowing out of Vietnamese-dominated Laos has drained the country of most of its professional and commercial elite. The refugees are estimated variously at 130,000 to 250,000, imposing a heavy burden on neighboring Thailand. An additional 40,000 Laotians, many of them officials or military officers of earlier governments, are possibly being detained in "political re-education" centers. By 1981, the economy was in further trouble due to a mid-1980 Thai ban on trade with Laos, Thailand having been a major source of industrial goods and food.

U.S. involvement in Laos was briefly revived in 1981 when a U.S.-sponsored patrol was sent into the country in a vain attempt to find Americans "missing in action" in the Vietnam War.

HISTORY: The Lao began moving south from China in the 13th century, gradually settling in the territory of the Khmer Empire. After centuries of warfare among the small feudal states of the region, the ruler of Luang Prabang state united most of what is now Laos and Northeast Thailand in the Kingdom of Lan Xang (Kingdom of the Million Elephants). The kingdom split into 2 states in 1707; after constant quarreling they were overrun by neighboring armies. By the early 1800s the Thai had won ascendancy and retained this hold until the French moved in and established a protectorate in 1893

1945-46: Japanese invade Lao region of French Indochina. French return and reestablish control

1949: Laos becomes independent state within French Union

1950: Pathet Lao, a Communist nationalist movement, is founded by Prince Souphanouvong

1953: Government battles Pathet Lao and Viet Minh, Vietnamese Communist forces

1954: Under terms of Geneva Conference agreement ending Indochina war, Laos becomes fully independent and Pathet Lao is permitted to occupy country's two northern provinces

1960: Neutralist-Pathet Lao coalition breaks down. Tug-of-war between Moscow-backed neutralists, American-backed rightists, and Pathet Lao erupts. Rightist Gen. Phoumi Nosavan drives neutralists from Vientiane; Premier Souvanna Phouma, the neutralist leader, flees to Cambodia

1962: U.S. troops move into northeast Thailand to discourage Pathet Lao drive on Vientiane. Three factions reach accord on coalition, and second Geneva Conference agrees on Laotian neutrality. Prince Souvanna Phouma returns as premier

1963: Pathet Lao abandons its role in the government as neutralist and leftist forces renew fighting

1965: Right-wing faction seizes government, banishing Gen. Phoumi Nosavan and reinstating Souvanna Phouma as premier. Neutralist-led government agrees to U.S. flights over Laos and to bombing of Ho Chi Minh Trail

1967: The premier, Prince Souvanna Phouma, states that Laos has been invaded by more than 40,000 North Vietnamese troops

1969: U.S. planes bomb Ho Chi Minh Trail and other North Vietnamese infiltration routes through Laos

1971: South Vietnamese troops supported by U.S. planes and artillery invade Laos in a drive against North Vietnamese supply lines; invasion ends after the retreat of South Vietnamese

1973: War in Laos ends as government, Pathet Lao sign cease-fire in February and agree on political settlement in July

1974: King Savang Vatthana dissolves Vientiane government and installs new coalition cabinet under Prince Souvanna Phouma, who remains premier

1975: National Assembly is dissolved by Pathet Lao. Prince Souphanouvong becomes president

1977: Rebels mount attacks against government throughout Laos. Vietnam and Laos sign a 25-year agreement for military and economic cooperation

1978: Laos faces flood and drought-caused food shortages and likelihood of famine in many areas. Rebel attacks continue; government is helped by Vietnamese troops. U.S. promises Laos $5 million worth of rice to help ease food shortages

1979: The 1977 Vietnam-Laos pact is alluded to indirectly in the 1979 Vietnam-Cambodia pact, which says that the three countries "must unite with one another in political, military, diplomatic, and other affairs." Soon Laos contributes 1,000 soldiers to the Vietnamese operations in Cambodia

1980: Thailand officially bans trade with Laos

1981: U.S. Central Intelligence Agency sponsors an expeditionary force of Laotian mercenaries which fails to discover evidence that U.S. military personnel "missing in action" are being detained in Laotian prison camps

LEBANON

Area: 4,015 sq. mi. **Population:** 3,012,000 (1978 est.)
Official Name: Republic of Lebanon **Capital:** Beirut **Nationality:** Lebanese **Languages:** Arabic is the official and dominant language; French and English are also widely used **Religion:** 62% Moslem (Sunni and Shi'ite) and 37% Christian (Maronite, Greek Orthodox, Armenian, Greek and Roman Catholic). There are also about 90,000 Druzes and 7,000 Jews **Flag:** A broad white horizontal stripe between narrower red stripes; in the center is a green cedar tree with a brown trunk **Anthem:** National Anthem, beginning "All of us" **Currency:** Lebanese pound (3.9 per U.S. $1)

Location: Southwest Asia. Lebanon is bordered on the north and east by Syria, on the south by Israel, and on the west by the Mediterranean Sea **Features:** The country consists of a narrow costal plain behind which are the high Lebanese Mountains. Farther east are the fertile Beqaa Valley and finally the Anti-Lebanon Mountains extending to the Syrian frontier **Chief Rivers:** Litani, Hasbani

Head of State: President Elias Sarkis, born 1924, assumed office in September 1976. By convention, the president is a Maronite **Head of Government:** Premier Shafiq Wazzan, appointed Oct. 22, 1980. By convention, the premier is a Sunni Moslem **Effective Date of Present Constitution:** 1926 **Legislative Body:** Parliament (unicameral National Assembly), consisting of 99 members elected for 4 years. By convention, the speaker is a Shi'ite Moslem **Local Government:** 5 provinces

Ethnic Composition: 93% Arab, 6% Armenian, and 1% others **Population Distribution:** 60% urban **Density:** 750 inhabitants per sq. mi.

Largest Cities: (1972 est.) Beirut 1,000,000, Tripoli 200,000

Per Capita Income: $975 (1979) **Gross National Product (GNP):** $1.4 billion (1979) **Economic Statistics:** In 1973 about 55% of GNP came from trade and services; 9% from agriculture (citrus fruits, vegetables, tobacco, livestock production); 21% from industry (food processing, textiles, cement, oil refining) **Minerals and Mining:** Small amounts of bitumen, iron ore, lime, and salt **Labor Force:** 1,000,000, with about 49% in agriculture; and 11% in industry **Foreign Trade:** Exports, chiefly fruits, vegetables, and textiles, totaled $705 million in 1979. Imports, mainly aircraft, motor vehicles, cigarettes, household appliances, wheat and corn, totaled $2.2 billion **Principal Trade Partners:** Saudi Arabia, Kuwait, Jordan, United States, West Germany, France, Britain

Vital Statistics: Birthrate 39.8 per 1,000 of pop. (1975); death rate, 9.9 **Life Expectancy:** 63 years **Health Statistics:** 260 inhabitants per hospital bed; 1,330 per physician (1973) **Infant Mortality:** 82 per 1,000 births **Illiteracy:** 14% **Primary and Secondary School Enrollment:** 672,434 (1972) **Enrollment of Higher Education:** 44,296 (1971) **GNP Expended on Education:** 3.0% (1973)

Transportation: Paved roads total 3,775 mi. **Motor Vehicles:** 243,600 (1974) **Passenger Cars:** 220,200 **Railway Mileage:** 250 **Ports:** Beirut, Tripoli, Sidon **Major Airlines:** Middle East Airlines operates international services **Communications:** Government and privately owned **Radio Transmitters:** 6 **Receivers:** 1,600,000 (1976) **Television Transmitters:** 8 **Receivers:** 425,000 (1976) **Telephones:** 222,000 (1975) **Newspapers:** 33 dailies (1975), 92 copies per 1,000 inhabitants

Weights and Measures: Metric system **Travel Requirements:** Passport, 6-month visa valid for 2 entries, $5 fee

Lebanon is situated on the eastern shore of the Mediterranean and has an area slightly smaller than that of Connecticut. Its chief topographic features are a narrow coastal plain behind which are the Lebanese Mountains, then the fertile Beqaa Valley, and finally the Anti-Lebanon Mountains extending to the Syrian border. An estimated 64 percent of the land is desert, waste, or urban; 27 percent farmland; and nine percent forest.

Traditionally a part of Greater Syria, which in turn was a sector of the Ottoman Empire, Lebanon became a separate entity after World War I to satisfy its Christian inhabitants. It was administered by France from 1920 to 1941, when it was declared independent by the Free French. With few natural resources besides a good location, Lebanon became a center of commerce and banking. For a time, general prosperity and a desire to keep peace discouraged challenges to the privileged position of the Christians. Uneasy political stability prevailed. So did laissez-faire capitalism and personal freedom; the government governed as little as possible to avoid offending anybody.

In the 1970s, however, Palestinian guerrillas established bases in Lebanon and began raids on Israel, prompting Israeli retaliation. Bitter disputes resulted between the Moslems, who tended to sympathize with the Palestinian cause, and the Christians, who had less sympathy for it. Open war broke out in the spring of 1975, with armed Christian bands on one side, Palestinians and Lebanese Moslem and Druse bands on the other. Israel armed the Christians, but their opponents came close to winning, and Syria sent in army units to protect the Christians and deny Israel a pretext for intervening. Later, under the nominal command of the Arab League, the Syrians actually became a disturbing element, clashing with the Christians, whom they were supposed to protect.

The worst fighting ended in 1976, but Lebanon remained functionally divided along communal lines and unable to repair the damage of the war or to return to its former commercial and banking activities. Most of the soldiers in its army had joined warring bands, but the government retained its ability to collect taxes—and paid soldiers for fighting each other. The legislature elected Elias Sarkis, a Christian respected by Moslems, as president, and he appointed a Moslem, Selim al-Hoss, premier; their conciliatory efforts failed.

In 1978, Israel occupied much of southern Lebanon but shortly withdrew to permit a UN peace-keeping force to establish a buffer zone there. Low-level fighting has continued throughout the country, however, with Christians pitted against Syrian soldiers, Moslems, Druzes, and other Christians. Palestinian terrorists have raided Israel from bases in Lebanon, and Israeli forces have raided Palestinian bases there. From 1975 to 1980, an estimated 42,000 people have been killed.

In 1981, Israel intervened in the air war between Lebanese and Christian militias, and Syria responded by installing surface-to-air missiles. Israeli planes bombed Palestinian bases and, in retaliation, PLO gunners fired rockets at northern Israeli towns. On July 17, Israeli jets struck at PLO headquarters in Beirut, killing 300 and wounding 800, mostly Lebanese civilians. Israel and the PLO agreed to a cease-fire on July 24.

HISTORY: In ancient times, Hittite and Aramaean kingdoms occupied the area. The Lebanese coast later became the base for the sea-trading Phoenicians, but their cities soon fell prey to the Assyrians, Persians, and Greeks. Along with neighboring Syria, Lebanon was then brought under Roman rule and afterwards became part of the Byzantine Empire. Even after the spread of Islam by the Arabs, who invaded Lebanon in the 7th century, the country long remained largely Christian

1516-17: Lebanon and Syria are absorbed into the Ottoman Empire, but Lebanon retains considerable autonomy

1841-64: Massacres of Maronite Christians by Druzes cause European governments to force Ottoman sultans to agree to a pro-Christian government for the area and to the establishment of autonomous province of Mount Lebanon

1918: Anglo-French force occupies Lebanon following collapse of Ottoman Empire in World War I

1920: Lebanon, along with Syria, becomes a French mandate

1941-45: Lebanon, under Free French occupation, is declared independent in 1941; however, French retain actual control of country until 1945

1958: Opposition to pro-Western policies of President Camille Chamoun erupts in rebellion; at Chamoun's request, U.S. troops are ordered to Lebanon by President Eisenhower; troops are withdrawn after formation of new Lebanese government

1968: Israeli commandos raid Beirut airport, destroying 13 civil aircraft; Israel claims raid was in retaliation for an earlier attack on Israeli airliner in Athens, carried out by two Arab terrorists from Beirut; Lebanon disclaims responsibility for commandos operating against Israel from Lebanese territory

1970: Suleiman Franjieh is elected president by legislature; Saeb Salaam succeeds Rashid Karami as premier

1972: Israel raids guerrilla bases in Lebanon in retaliation for the killing of Israeli athletes at the Munich Olympics

1973: Israeli commando raid on Beirut in which three guerrilla leaders are slain forces resignation of Premier Saeb Salaam and sparks two weeks of fighting in Beirut between guerrillas and Lebanese army; new Premier Takieddin Solh negotiates uneasy truce, but guerrilla activity and Israeli reprisals continue before and after Arab-Israeli war in October

1974: Border clashes between Israeli forces and Palestinian guerrillas based in Lebanon continue

1975-76: Some 60,000 die in 19-month civil war between Christians and Moslems; army disintegrates; economy nears collapse. Syria invades; Arab summit arranges cease-fire and establishes Arab League peacekeeping forces—consisting mostly of Syrians who are already there. Elias Sarkis becomes president; he appoints Selim al-Hoss premier

1977: Moslem leader Kamal Jumblat is assassinated

1978: Israelis, avenging a PLO terror raid, invade southern Lebanon, attacking PLO bases there; about 200,000 Lebanese and 65,000 Palestinian refugees flee to the north; most return as Israelis pull out three months later. UN peacekeeping forces form buffer zone between Israelis and PLO guerrillas. Conflict develops in southern border zone between central government, attempting to reassert its authority, and Israeli-backed Christian militia units. Israeli planes raid Palestinian camps in retaliation for terrorist attack on airline bus in London

1979: Continued fighting on all fronts. Premier al-Hoss forms new Moslem-Christian coalition government

1980: Israeli forces occupy Lebanon's southern border region for five days, in retaliation for Palestinian terrorist raid. Takieddin Solh succeeds al-Hoss as premier for a short time, and is followed by Shafiq Wazzan in office

1981: Syria installs missiles in Lebanon and shoots down Israeli jets; heavy fighting between Syrian troops and Christian forces. Israeli aircraft attack PLO bases and Palestinians fire rockets at northern Israeli towns. Israeli airplane raid on PLO headquarters in Beirut kills 300 and wounds 800, mostly Lebanese civilians. Cease-fire truce agreed to by Israel and PLO on July 24.

LESOTHO

Area: 11,720 sq. mi. **Population:** 1,279,000 (1978 est.)

Official Name: Kingdom of Lesotho **Capital:** Maseru **Nationality:** Basotho **Languages:** Sesotho, the language of the Sotho people, and English are the official languages **Religion:** About 70% Christian, chiefly Roman Catholic, the rest being mostly animist **Flag:** Green and red vertical stripes to the left of a blue field bearing a white conical Sotho hat **Anthem:** National Anthem, beginning "Lesotho, the country of our fathers" **Currency:** Loti (0.82 per U.S. $1)

Location: An enclave within the east-central part of the Republic of South Africa, Lesotho is bordered on the west and north by the Orange Free State Province, on the east by the Province of Natal, and on the south by Cape Province and Transkei **Features:** About a fourth of the western sector is lowland terrain; the rest of the country is mountainous **Chief Rivers:** Orange, Caledon

Head of State: King Moshoeshoe II, born 1938; formerly Paramount Chief, he became king in 1966 **Head of Government:** Prime Minister, Dr. Leabua Jonathan, born 1914, appointed 1965; he also acts as defense and internal security minister **Effective Date of Present Constitution:** 1966, suspended 1970 **Legislative Body:** Parliament (bicameral), suspended 1970. An interim National Assembly with limited powers was formed in 1973, the members being nominated by the government **Local Government:** 9 districts, with appointed administrators

Ethnic Composition: The population is almost entirely Bantu, with 85% Sotho and 15% Nguni. There are less than 1% South Africans, Asians and mixed **Population Distribution:** 6% urban **Density:** 109 inhabitants per sq. mi.

Largest City: (1978 est.) Maseru 71,500

Per Capita Income: $160 (1978) **Gross National Product (GNP):** $210 million (1978) **Economic Statistics:** In 1976 about 40% of GNP came from agriculture (corn, sorghum, wheat, beans, peas, livestock), 10% from industry (printing, carpet weaving, brewing, candlemaking, tire retreading) and mining **Minerals and Mining:** Few known mineral deposits except for diamonds **Labor Force:** 87% of population engaged in subsistence agriculture. 150,000 to 200,000 work six months to many years as wage earners in South Africa **Foreign Trade:** Exports, mainly diamonds, wool, mohair, and livestock, totaled $34.8 million in 1978. Imports, chiefly foodstuffs, textiles, clothing, transportation equipment, and chemicals, totaled $262 million **Principal Trade Partner:** South Africa

Vital Statistics: Birthrate, 39 per 1,000 of pop. (1975); death rate, 19.7 **Life Expectancy:** 46 years **Health Statistics:** 552 inhabitants per hospital bed; 20,570 per physician (1976) **Infant Mortality:** 114.4 per 1,000 births **Illiteracy:** 60% **Primary and Secondary School Enrollment:** 239,943 (1976) **Enrollment in Higher Education:** 577 (1974) **GNP Expended on Education:** 3.7% (1973)

Transportation: Improved roads total 625 mi. **Motor Vehicles:** 7,800 (1975) **Passenger Cars:** 4,600 **Railway Mileage:** One mile of track links Maseru with South Africa **Ports:** None **Major Airlines:** Government-owned Lesotho Airways operates domestic and international services **Communications:** Government owned **Radio Transmitters:** 3 **Licenses:** 23,000 (1976) **Television:** None **Telephones:** 4,000 (1974) **Newspapers:** Several weeklies

Weights and Measures: Metric system **Travel Requirements:** Passport, visa valid for 20 days

An enclave in the southeastern area of South Africa, Lesotho, the former British protectorate of Basutoland, is an island of black African nationalism in a sea of apartheid. The small mountainous kingdom is the remnant of a larger realm, the refuge to which the Basotho were driven by tribal wars and Boer incursions.

In 1818, Moshesh I, a tribal chief from the north, succeeded in uniting the Basotho people. He ruled from about 1820 to 1870 and consolidated various tribes that had been scattered earlier by Zulu and Matabele warriors. During his reign, a series of wars with the Orange Free State (1856-68) resulted in the loss of a large area to the Free State, now known as the "Conquered Territory." Moshesh appealed to the British for help, and in 1868 the country was annexed by Britain.

For a considerable time thereafter the energies of the British administrators were absorbed largely in the task of settling intertribal disputes and in maintaining the position of the Paramount Chief as a symbol of national unity. From 1884 to 1959 legislative and executive authority was vested in a British High Commissioner.

Badly eroded and subject to droughts, the country produces mohair, wool, and hides from livestock. There are only about 1,000 square miles of cultivable land and many food supplies must be imported. Although there has been an increase of revenue under a revised customs union with South Africa, much of Lesotho's income is derived from the wages of Basotho men who work as contract laborers in South African gold and coal mines. Unemployment is a major problem within Lesotho itself.

There has been some development of light industry, tourism, and an increase of diamond mining, but Lesotho has little prospect of ending its economic dependence on South Africa. To a large extent, Lesotho is little more than one of the *bantustans*, or separate African homelands, that have been created in South Africa itself.

With the attainment of political independence in 1966, the traditional ruler, King Moshoeshoe II, tried to reassert royal authority, but after being forced into exile by the prime minister, Chief Leabua Jonathan, agreed to accept a titular, symbolic position.

Although professing to abhor apartheid, Chief Jonathan has advocated what he calls a realistic "bread-and-butter good-neighbor policy." But despite extreme poverty, Lesotho has achieved considerable progress in education—it has one of the highest literacy rates in Africa—and many Basotho, who are well educated and highly politicized, resent South Africa's racist regime.

When in early 1970, Jonathan appeared to have lost the country's first national elections, he declared the results invalid, jailed his leading opponents, and seized control. Although threatened with withdrawal of British aid, the plump, disarmingly jolly Jonathan ruled by decree until 1973.

Chief Jonathan has welcomed back the king from exile, talked of political reconciliation, and successfully suppressed several outbreaks of rebellion, including one in 1974 in which 20 rebels were killed in a plot allegedly hatched by the opposition Congress party.

HISTORY: Decimated by Zulu and Matabele raids in the early 19th century, the Basotho were later fused into a new nation in the mountains of Basutoland (Lesotho) by Moshesh (Moshoeshoe) I. The king soon had to contend with Boers in the neighboring Orange Free State and sought the protection of the British Cape Colony. Annexation by the colony in 1868, however, led to more fighting, and in 1884 Basutoland again was made a British protectorate. In 1909 a British act of Parliament, establishing the Union of South Africa, stipulated that Basutoland, as well as Bechuanaland (Botswana) and Swaziland, would not be transferred to their more powerful neighbor without prior consent of the inhabitants

1910: A consultative Basutoland Council, made up of Basotho chiefs and leaders, is established by the British

1959-60: A constitution is promulgated and a more representative legislative body, the Basutoland National Council, is set up

1961: South Africa's apartheid policies cause Britain to reaffirm that Basutoland and other protectorates will not be handed over to South African rule

1966: Basutoland gains independence as Lesotho

1967: Held under house arrest after attempting to assert absolute authority, King Moshoeshoe II accedes to Prime Minister Leabua Jonathan's demands that he reign as constitutional monarch

1970: Prime Minister Jonathan seizes control, suspends constitution, declares a state of emergency (ended in 1973); imprisons his opponent, Ntsu Mokhehle, following disputed election

1975: Miners recruited from Lesotho strike gold mine in South Africa to protest a Lesotho law requiring miners to remit 60 percent of their pay and deposit it in Lesotho banks

1979: Bombings attributed to outlawed Congress party cause great damage and loss of life; Jonathan converts paramilitary police unit into regular army to suppress violence

1980: New currency, the loti, is introduced, backed by the South African rand

1981: West Germany is building a communications satellite station in Lesotho

LIBERIA

Area: 43,000 sq. mi. **Population:** 1,742,000 (1978 est.)

Official Name: Republic of Liberia **Capital:** Monrovia **Nationality:** Liberian **Languages:** English, the official and commerical language, is spoken by about 20% of the population; some 28 African dialects are also spoken **Religion:** 75% animist, 10% Christian, 15% Moslem **Flag:** Eleven red and white horizontal stripes, with a five-pointed white star on a blue field in the upper left corner **Anthem:** National Anthem, beginning "All hail, Liberia, hail!" **Currency:** U.S. (Liberian) dollar

Location: West Africa. Liberia is bordered on the northeast by Guinea, on the east by the Ivory Coast, on the south and west by the Atlantic Ocean, and on the north by Sierra Leone **Features:** The country is flat, with the exception of some hills in the region of Monrovia, the Bomi Hills, and the Guinea Highlands. About 40% of the country is covered by tropical woodlands **Chief Rivers:** Mano, Lofa, St. Paul, St. John, Cestos

Head of State and of Government: Master Sgt. Samuel Kanyon Doe, born 1951, took power following the coup of April 12, 1980. He is Chairman of the People's Redemption Council, the highest body of the new government **Effective Date of Present Constitution:** 1847; suspended Apr. 1980 **Legislative Body:** Executive and legislative power is held by the People's Redemption Council with 18 members and 10 co-members (June 1981) **Local Government:** 9 counties, headed by appointed superintendents

Ethnic Composition: More than 97% of the population is made up of indigenous Africans belonging to about 16 tribal groups. About 2.5% of the population are Americo-Liberian descendants of 19th century emancipated black American slaves **Population Distribution:** 28% urban **Density:** 41 inhabitants per sq. mi.

Largest Cities: (1976 est.) Monrovia 204,000, Harbel 60,000, Buchanan 25,000, Yekepa 16,000, Harper 14,000

Per Capita Income: $670 (1979) **Gross National Product (GNP):** $937 million (1979) **Economic Statistics:** About 33% of GNP comes from mining; 17% from agriculture (rubber, cassava, rice, bananas, plantains), forestry, and fishing; and 11% from wholesale and retail trade **Minerals and Mining:** Liberia is a major producer of high-grade iron ore. Diamonds are of importance, and there are unexploited reserves of manganese, gold, columbite, tantalite, and bauxite **Labor Force:** 510,000, with 72% in agriculture, and only 31% in the monetary economy, chiefly on rubber plantations, in government, construction, and mining **Foreign Trade:** Exports, chiefly iron ore, rubber, and diamonds, totaled $525 million in 1979. Imports, mainly manufactured goods, machinery, transportation equipment, fuel, and food, totaled $505 million **Principal Trade Partners:** United States, West Germany, Belgium, Italy

Vital Statistics: Birthrate, 49.8 per 1,000 of pop. (1971); death rate, 20.9 **Life Expectancy:** 46 years **Health Statistics:** 652 inhabitants per hospital bed; 11,761 per physician (1973) **Infant Mortality:** 159.2 per 1,000 births **Illiteracy:** 76% **Primary and Secondary School Enrollment:** 191,972 (1975) **Enrollment in Higher Education:** 2,404 (1975) **GNP Expended on Education:** 2.4% (1975)

Transportation: Paved roads total 500 mi. **Motor Vehicles:** 22,100 (1974) **Passenger Cars:** 12,100 **Railway Mileage:** 310 **Ports:** Monrovia, Buchanan, Greenville, Harper **Major Airlines:** Air Liberia operates internal services **Communications:** Partly government owned **Radio Transmitters:** 15 **Receivers:** 265,000 (1976) **Television Transmitters:** 4 **Receivers:** 18,800 (1974) **Telephones:** 7,500 (1974) **Newspapers:** 3 dailies, 8 copies per 1,000 inhabitants

Weights and Measures: U.S. standards are used **Travel Requirements:** Passport, visa valid for 90 days, $2 fee, 3 pictures **International Dialing Code:** 231

A green, rainy land settled in the 1820s by freed slaves from the United States, Liberia is Africa's oldest independent republic. As more and more blacks were being liberated early in the 19th century, some Americans became uneasy about their numbers. In 1816 the American Colonization Society was chartered by Congress to promote a "back-to-Africa" movement. The society purchased land from African chiefs in a region that had been largely depopulated by the slave trade, and the first group of an eventual 15,000 settlers established their colony at the present site of Monrovia.

Although it was a neglected stepchild, Liberia modeled its constitution, institutions and flag after those of the United States. It established itself as a sovereign nation in 1847, a status which the United States did not recognize until 1862, long after European powers had done so.

Lacking money and technology, as well as outside interest, the early Liberians were unable to progress beyond a simple rural economy. Contemporary Liberians often say, "We missed out on the benefits of colonialism." However, in the 1920s the Firestone Tire and Rubber Company started to develop a rubber industry which today employs about half of Liberia's wage earners. During World War II, American money and manpower poured in to give the country the big Robertsfield Airport, a new seaport at Monrovia, and the first network of modern roads. There followed the iron-ore boom of the 1950s with huge investments by foreign mining companies.

The making of Liberia into a modern country, with a viable economy and position of leadership in African affairs, has been almost entirely the work of the late William V.S. Tubman, Liberia's president from 1944 until his death in 1971.

A forceful and sometimes autocratic leader, Mr. Tubman spurred economic development through industry and iron-ore mining at a time when Liberia seemed to be lagging behind newer African nations.

Tubman was succeeded as president in 1971 by Vice-President William R. Tolbert, Jr., son of a former South Carolina slave who had prospered as a farmer in Liberia. Tolbert launched a program of widespread reform, but dissatisfaction increased with his autocratic rule and with continued control of the government and economy by the 2½% minority of descendants of American slaves. In April 1979, when police and soldiers opened fire on student-led demonstrators protesting an increase in the price of rice, 74 persons were killed and hundreds injured.

Tolbert's unpopular repressive measures led to his downfall. On April 12, 1980, he was killed in a coup of non-commissioned officers led by 28-year-old Master Sgt. Samuel K. Doe. Twenty-seven of Tolbert's aides were summarily executed. Liberia was left governed by a poorly educated and inexperienced regime.

HISTORY: Before being colonized early in the 19th century by freed black slaves from the United States, Liberia was known as the Grain Coast for its production of grains of melegueta pepper. The indigenous peoples, among them Kru, Gola, Mandingo, and Vai, are believed to derive from ancient black nations of sub-Saharan regions farther north. During the several centuries of the slave trade, the country was steadily drained of population

1816: American Colonization Society is founded to send freed slaves to Western Africa
1822: First group of settlers arrives from United States and establishes colony on Providence Island, at present site of Monrovia, purchased by American Colonization Society
1824: Name "Liberia" is adopted and chief settlement is named Monrovia in honor of U.S. President James Monroe
1847: Joseph Jenkins Roberts, governor of the Liberian Commonwealth, a Virginia-born freeman of part-black ancestry, proclaims Republic of Liberia and becomes first president
1850-1920: Territory is lost to neighboring British, French colonies; economy and finances deteriorate, but government rejects proposal for international receivership
1923-26: Firestone Tire and Rubber Company assists government financially and begins development of rubber
1943: True Whig party candidate William V.S. Tubman becomes president; begins programs of social unification to speed assimilation of indigenous population into the rest of the community, and policy of "open door" for foreign investment
1955: Opposition Reformation and Independent True Whig parties are charged with plot to overthrow government by force and are banned; True Whig party becomes dominant
1967: President Tubman is reelected to sixth successive term
1971: Tubman dies and is succeeded by Vice-President Tolbert
1975: Tolbert is elected for an eight-year term as president
1979: Police and army fire on demonstrators against food-price increases in April, killing 74
1980: Tolbert is killed in coup April 12 by enlisted men of army; Master Sgt. Samuel K. Doe becomes head of state
1981: U.S. military and economic aid bolsters Doe government. Doe appoints a commission to draft a constitution

LIBYA

Area: 679,358 sq. mi. **Population:** 2,856,000 (1979 est.)

Official Name: Socialist People's Libyan Arab Jamahiriya **Capital:** Tripoli **Nationality:** Libyan **Languages:** Arabic is the official and dominant language; English and Italian are also used **Religion:** 97% Sunni Moslem **Flag:** A plain green field **Anthem:** Almighty God **Currency:** Libyan dinar (.30 per U.S. $1)

Location: North Africa. Libya is bordered on the north by the Mediterranean Sea, on the east by Egypt, on the southeast by the Sudan, on the south by Chad and Niger, on the west by Algeria, and on the northwest by Tunisia **Features:** About 90% of the terrain consists of barren, rock-strewn plains and deserts, with three elevated regions in the northwest, northeast and extreme south **Chief Rivers:** There are no permanent rivers

Head of State: Colonel Muammar Qaddafi, born 1943; seized power in 1969; elected Revolutionary Leader (Head of State) in 1977. He also is defense minister **Head of Government:** Muhammad al-Zarruq Rajab is Secretary General of the General Secretariat of the General People's Congress, appointed 1981. Jadallah Azzuz al Talhi is secretary of the General People's Committee, appointed 1979 **Effective Date of Present Constitution:** The political structure is guided by the principles announced at the General People's Congress in March 1977 **Legislative Body:** General People's Congress (unicameral), closely controlled by the central government **Local Government:** 10 governorates, each under an appointed governor

Ethnic Composition: The population is chiefly a racial mixture of Arabs and Berbers **Population Distribution:** 30% urban **Density:** 4 inhabitants per sq. mi.

Largest Cities: (1973 census) Tripoli 281,497, Benghazi 131,970, Zawia 52,327, Misurata 45,146, Sabratha 30,817, Tarhuna 23,338

Per Capita Income: $7,357 (1980) **Gross National Product (GNP):** $22 billion (1980) **Economic Statistics:** In 1975 about 52% of GNP came from oil, 3% from agriculture (wheat, barley, tomatoes, dates, citrus fruits, olives, livestock); and 13% from manufacturing (food processing, textiles, soaps, detergents, paper bags and wrapping paper) **Minerals and Mining:** Libya is one of the world's largest oil producers. Other minerals are gypsum, natural gas, marble, iron ore, and potassium **Labor Force:** 900,000 (1977) of which 350,000 are resident foreigners **Foreign Trade:** Exports, consisting almost exclusively of crude oil, totaled $15 billion in 1979. Imports, mainly oil drilling equipment and machinery, iron and steel pipes, tubes, and fittings, manufactured goods, and food products, totaled $7.9 billion **Principal Trade Partners:** West Germany, Britain, Italy, United States, France, Japan

Vital Statistics: Birthrate, 45 per 1,000 of pop. (1975); death rate, 14.7 **Life Expectancy;** 53 years **Health Statistics:** 200 inhabitants per hospital bed; 938 per physician (1976) **Infant Mortality:** N.A. **Illiteracy:** 64% **Primary and Secondary School Enrollment:** 790,569 (1976) **Enrollment in Higher Education:** 11,997 **GNP Expended on Education:** 5.2% (1975)

Transportation: Paved roads total 4,800 mi. **Motor Vehicles:** 394,400 (1975) **Passenger Cars:** 263,100 **Railway Mileage:** none **Ports:** Tripoli, Benghazi, El Brega, Ras Lanuf, Zueitina, Syrte, El Hariga, Derna, Tobruk **Major Airlines:** Libyan Arab Airways operates domestic and international services **Communications:** Government-owned **Radio Transmitters:** 12 **Licenses:** 110,000 (1976) **Television Transmitters:** 2 **Licenses:** 10,000 (1975) **Telephones:** 45,000 (1975) **Newspapers:** 2 dailies, 17 copies per 1,000 inhabitants (1975)

Weights and Measures: Metric system **Travel Requirements:** Passport (with Arabic translation), visa valid for 3 months; $7 fee, 2 pictures **International Dialing Code:** 218

Consisting mostly of arid desert, the land that is now Libya was a bone of contention among empires for thousands of years. Its most influential conquerors were the Moslem Arabs of the seventh century A.D.; they gave Libya the language and the religion that now prevail. Its most recent conqueror was Italy. After losing World War II, Italy was forced to grant independence to Libya in 1951. Idris, a Moslem chieftain, became king. But, with no natural resources except a location that was strategic in the Cold War, Libya was heavily dependent on the United States, which gave considerable assistance in return for the use of Wheelus Air Force Base.

With the discovery of oil in 1959, Libya, with less than 3 million people, became potentially a power in its own right. King Idris used the oil revenue to build schools, hospitals, highways, and low-cost housing.

But Libya did not achieve its real international potential until after the overthrow of King Idris by the army in 1969. A Revolutionary Command Council of military officers, headed by Col. Muammar Qaddafi, took control of the nation. Desert-born, with little understanding of the non-Moslem world, Qaddafi made Libya a bastion of strict Moslem traditionalism. He outlawed liquor, imposed a strict dress code for women, and made amputation the standard penalty for theft. A bitter enemy of big powers, he closed Wheelus Air Force Base, published manifestos condemning both the U.S. and USSR, and helped Malta to force the closing of British bases. A strident foe of Israel, he joined other Arab militant leaders in denouncing Egypt for making a separate peace with Israel in 1979. Qaddafi tried to intervene surreptitiously in Uganda to keep President Idi Amin Dada in power; after Amin's overthrow, he gave him asylum in Libya. In November, Uganda released the last of 56 Libyan soldiers captured during its civil war. On December 2, a mob in Tripoli attacked and damaged the U.S. embassy. The United States closed the embassy in May 1980.

Qaddafi moved in 1980 to silence his opponents and warned Libyan exiles to return or "be liquidated." After four anti-Qaddafi exiles were killed in London and Rome, the United States, in May, expelled four Libyan diplomats charged with threatening Libyan students in America. A year later, the U.S. closed the Libyan mission in Wash-

ington, D.C., saying Qaddafi's "support for international terrorism" was unacceptable. Relations between the two countries worsened in August 1981 when U.S. Navy jets shot down two attacking Libyan fighter planes over the Gulf of Sidra.

HISTORY: In ancient times, Libya was successively ruled by Carthage, Rome, and the Vandals. The Arabs conquered the country in the 7th century A.D. In the Middle Ages, Egypt and Tunisia vied for control of the country, and in the early 16th century Spain and the Knights of Malta replaced the African rivals in dominating Libya. The Ottoman Empire seized control in 1551, although Libya's local pashas continued to enjoy autonomy

1830: Turks reassert control over Libya

1911-33: Italy occupies Libya following Turco-Italian War (1911-12) and engages in long series of wars of pacification against the Sanusi, a Moslem religious brotherhood

1943-49: Libya is conquered by Allied forces in World War II; Tripolitania and Cyrenaica are placed under British administration and the Fezzan under French administration

1951: Kingdom of Libya gains formal independence, with Idris I, leader of the Sanusi brotherhood, as the country's first king

1954: United States is granted military air base in Libya

1959-61: Oil is discovered in Tripolitania and Cyrenaica in 1959

1967: Libya charges United States with helping Israel in Six-Day War, calls on U.S. to liquidate Wheelus Air Force Base

1969: Monarchy is overthrown by a military junta composed of young nationalist army officers. Colonel Qaddafi, their leader, becomes prime minister in 1970

1970: Junta takes over Wheelus Air Force Base, buys Mirage jets from France, and renegotiates contracts with Western oil companies to gain greater share of oil revenues

1973: Qaddafi introduces the "cultural revolution," an attempt to govern Libya according to the tenets of Islam. Establishes "people's committees" to carry out the revolution

1974: Qaddafi relinquishes political and administrative functions; announces he will concentrate on ideology and organization. Premier Abdul Salam Jalloud assumes Qaddafi's former duties

1975: Creation of 618-member General National Congress is decreed to implement theories of Colonel Qaddafi

1976: Relations with Egypt deteriorate when Libyan soldiers are arrested in Cairo in connection with a plot to kidnap Maj. Omar Meheishi, a dissident member of the Revolutionary Command Council who fled Libya in 1975 after an attempted coup against Colonel Qaddafi. In retaliation Egyptians are expelled from Libya

1977: Libyan and Egyptian troops and aircraft battle along border

1979: Libya secretly sends soldiers to Uganda to defend government of President Idi Amin Dada against Tanzanian attack; grants asylum to Amin. Tripoli mob damages U.S. embassy

1980: Qaddafi orders Libyan exiles to return to Libya; four of his political opponents are murdered in Europe; U.S. closes embassy in Tripoli. In Washington it is revealed that Billy Carter acted as an agent for Libya and received a loan from the Libyan government. Qaddafi and Syrian President Assad sign merger agreement proclaiming Libya and Syria a single state (unimplemented as of July 1981). Libyan troops invade Chad to support President Goukouni

1981: Qaddafi announces a "merger" of Chad with Libya. U.S. expels Libyan mission from Washington because of Libya's support for international terrorists. Libyan planes shot down by U.S. jets over Gulf of Sidra (Aug. 19)

LIECHTENSTEIN

Area: 61 sq. mi. **Population:** 25,220 (1980 census)

Official Name: Principality of Liechtenstein **Capital:** Vaduz **Nationality:** Liechtensteiner **Languages:** German is the official language; Alemannic, a dialect, is spoken by most **Religion:** Roman Catholicism is the official religion and claims about 92% of the population **Flag:** Blue and red horizontal stripes, with a golden crown near the staff end of the blue stripe **Anthem:** National Anthem, beginning "Above on the German Rhine" **Currency:** Swiss franc (2.02 per U.S. $1)

Location: Western Europe. Liechtenstein, situated in the Rhine River Valley, is bordered by Austria on the east and by Switzerland on the south and west **Features:** One third of the area is level land bordering the right bank of the Rhine, and an upland and mountainous area occupies the remainder **Chief Rivers:** Rhine, Samina

Head of State: Prince Franz Josef II, born 1906, ascended the throne 1938 **Head of Government:** Prime Minister: Hans Brunhart, born 1945, chairman of the 5-man Collegial Board, appointed April 1978 **Effective Date of Present Constitution:** 1921 **Legislative Body:** Parliament (unicameral Landtag), consisting of 15 members, elected for 4 years by male suffrage **Local Government:** 11 communes, with limited powers of self-government

Ethnic Composition: The population is of Germanic descent; one third is alien, mostly Swiss, Italian, Austrian and German **Population Distribution:** Predominantly rural **Density:** 413 inhabitants per sq. mi.

Largest Towns: (1980 census) Vaduz 4,614, Schaan 4,552

Per Capita Income: $11,330 (1979) **Gross National Product (GNP):** $340 million (1979) **Economic Statistics:** Some 40% of the land is used for raising crops (corn and other cereals), potatoes, garden produce, fruits), but the main source of income from land use is raising beef and dairy cattle. Industry is mainly devoted to the small-scale production of precision manufactures (calculating machines, optical lenses, high vacuum pumps), false teeth and textiles. Between 20,000 and 30,000 foreign firms maintain nominal headquarters in Vaduz, because of liberal tax incentives. Tourism and the sale of stamps are also important sources of income **Minerals and Mining:** Except for some quarrying, there is no mining **Labor Force:** 11,368 (5,078 foreign workers) with 54% in industry, trade and construction, 42% in services and 4% in agriculture, forestry and hunting **Foreign Trade:** Exports are chiefly special machinery and tools, artificial teeth, textiles, cnemicals, and food. Liechtenstein has a customs union with Switzerland and there are no records of foreign trade totals **Principal Trade Partners:** EFTA and Common Market countries

Vital Statistics: Birthrate, 12.5 per 1,000 of pop. (1977); death rate, 6.1 **Life Expectancy:** 65 years **Health Statistics:** Hospital facilities exist in nearby Switzerland; 1,633 inhabitants per physician (1971) **Infant Mortality:** 6.5 per 1,000 births **Illiteracy:** Negligible **Primary and Secondary School Enrollment:** 4,445 pupils (1972) **Enrollment in Higher Education:** 243 **GNP Expended on Education:** N.A.

Transportation: Good paved roads serve the principality **Motor Vehicles:** 11,000 (1976) **Passenger Cars:** 10,000 **Railway Mileage:** 11.5 **Ports:** None **Major Airlines:** None **Communications:** Served by Switzerland **Radio Stations:** None **Licenses:** 5,000 (1976) **Television Stations:** None **Licenses:** 4,500 (1976) **Telephones:** 16,000 (1976) **Newspapers:** 1 daily, 286 copies per 1,000 inhabitants

Weights and Measures: Metric system **Travel Requirements:** Passport, no visa for 3 months **International Dialing Code:** 41

Since 1923 the tiny principality of Liechtenstein, wedged between Austria and Switzerland, has had a customs union with Switzerland, and that country also provides Liechtenstein's currency, administers its postal, telegraph, and telephone services, and handles Liechtenstein's international affairs. In World War II, Liechtenstein, like Switzerland, was a neutral.

Though bucolic, with lush green valleys and houses with red-tile roofs, the state has mainly an industrial economy. Only four percent of the population is engaged in agricultural pursuits.

Liechtenstein has become industrialized in the last quarter of a century; it contains Europe's biggest producer of false teeth and dental supplies, and is noted for such precision products as thin optic coatings and electronic microscopy. The industrialization has brought an influx of Swiss, Austrian, and German workers.

The principality is a tax haven for corporations and holding companies. Additional sources of income are tourism and the sale of postage stamps. Though Liechtenstein has neither a broadcasting station nor an airport, it is the repository of art valued at somewhere near $150 million, the holdings of Liechtenstein's monarch.

In 1978, Liechtenstein joined the Council of Europe, although other nations represented in the Council objected to the principality's voting laws; alone in Europe, Liechtenstein does not allow women to vote for members of its national legislature. Women may vote in local elections in Vaduz.

HISTORY: The principality of Liechtenstein was created in 1719 as a fief of the Holy Roman Empire by uniting the barony of Schellenberg and the county of Vaduz, both of which had been purchased from the counts of Hohenem by the Austrian family of Liechtenstein. During the Napoleonic Wars, the principality was invaded by the French. In 1815, after Napoleon's downfall, Liechtenstein joined the newly formed Germanic Confederation

1866: Germanic Confederation is dissolved after Prussia's victory over Austria in the Seven Weeks' War, thus ending Liechtenstein's ties to other German states

1868: Liechtenstein, which had furnished Austria with 80 soldiers during the war with Prussia, disbands its military force and adopts policy of permanent neutrality

1919-24: Switzerland assumes control of Liechtenstein's external affairs and forms customs union with principality

1938: Prince Franz I is succeeded by his great-nephew, who, as Franz Josef II, becomes the first ruler to make Liechtenstein his permanent home

1945-65: Having avoided involvement in World War II, Liechtenstein enjoys rapid economic growth, developing into a center of tourism, trade, and small-scale manufacturing

1970: Traditional minority Patriotic Union wins one-vote majority in *Landtag*, ending 42-year leadership of coalition government by Progressive Citizens party

1973: Electorate again denies women the franchise

1974: Progressive Citizens party regains majority in parliament

1978: Hans Brunhart of Fatherland Union party is appointed prime minister; government is virtually paralyzed for two months as outgoing prime minister balks at relinquishing post of foreign minister, in addition to prime ministership; president rules former prime minister and his successor may share foreign ministership

---

LUXEMBOURG

Area: 999 sq. mi. **Population:** 363,000 (1979 est.)

Official Name: Grand Duchy of Luxembourg **Capital:** Luxembourg **Nationality:** Luxembourgian **Languages:** French is the official language. German is used in local newspapers. Letzeburgisch is everyday language **Religion:** 97% Roman Catholic; 3% Protestant and Jewish **Flag:** A tricolor of red, white, and blue horizontal stripes **Anthem:** Our Homeland **Currency:** Luxembourg franc (36 per U.S. $1)

Location: Western Europe. Landlocked Luxembourg is bordered on the north and west by Belgium, on the east by the Federal Republic of Germany, and on the south by France **Features:** The northern part of the country contains the rugged uplands of the Ardennes plateau, while the south consists of undulating terrain with broad valleys **Chief Rivers:** Alzette, Süre, Moselle, Our

Head of State: Grand Duke Jean, born 1921, ascended the throne 1964 **Head of Government:** Premier Pierre Werner, appointed 1979 **Effective Date of Present Constitution:** 1868 **Legislative Body:** Parliament (bicameral), consisting of a Chamber of Deputies of 59 members, elected for 5 years, and a Council of State appointed by the Grand Duke **Local Government:** 12 cantons grouped into 3 districts

Ethnic Composition: Luxembourgers are ethnically a mixture of French and German. Throughout the 20th century, a considerable number of immigrants from Italy and other Mediterranean countries have settled in Luxembourg **Population Distribution:** 68% urban **Density:** 363 inhabitants per sq. mi.

Largest Cities: (1974 est.) Luxembourg 78,403; (1970 census) Esch/Alzette 27,574, Differdange 17,964, Dudelange 14,615

Per Capita Income: $8,972 (1980) **Gross Domestic Product (GDP):** $3.2 billion (1980) **Economic Statistics:** About 41% of GDP comes from industry (steel, chemicals, auto parts, rubber, synthetic fibers), 3% from agriculture (livestock, dairy products, wine) **Minerals and Mining:** Vast deposits of iron ore are mined; slate is also quarried in commercial quantities **Labor Force:** 147,300 (33% aliens) of which 48% is in services, 46% in industry, 6% in agriculture (grapes, livestock) **Foreign Trade:** Exports, chiefly steel, chemical products, plastic fibers, rubber and textiles, totaled $2.9 billion in 1979. Imports, mainly coal and iron ore, machinery, transportation equipment, and food, totaled $3.1 billion **Principal Trade Partners:** EC countries

Vital Statistics: Birthrate, 11.4 per 1,000 of pop. (1977); death rate, 11.5 **Life Expectancy:** 73 years **Health Statistics:** 85 inhabitants per hospital bed; 900 per physician (1976) **Infant Mortality:** 10.6 per 1,000 births (1977) **Illiteracy:** 2% **Primary and Secondary School Enrollment:** 53,423 (1976) **Enrollment in Higher Education:** 446 **GNP Expended on Education:** 5.2% (1973)

Transportation: Surfaced roads total 3,085 mi. **Motor Vehicles:** 152,200 (1977) **Passenger Cars:** 141,400 **Railway Mileage:** 168 **Ports:** None **Major Airlines:** LUXAIR operates regular services to Western Europe; Icelandair maintains a regular service to the United States **Communications:** Privately owned **Radio Transmitters:** 7 **Licenses:** 205,000 (1976) **Television Transmitters:** 4 **Licenses:** 105,000 (1976) **Telephones:** 158,000 (1976) **Newspapers:** 7 dailies, 560 copies per 1,000 inhabitants (1975)

Weights and Measures: Metric system **Travel Requirements:** Passport, no visa for less than 3 months **International Dialing Code:** 352

The Grand Duchy of Luxembourg, covering an area of 999 square miles, and with a population of over 360,000, is the equal of Sweden in the production of iron and steel. Centered at Esch-sur-Alzette, Luxembourg's iron and steel industry uses iron ore mined in the area for about half of its needs and imports the remainder, as well as coal. The duchy's steel mills, among the largest and oldest in Europe, were hard hit by the worldwide reduced demand for steel in 1979-80. But Luxembourg has many other manufacturing industries, of which the principal ones are chemicals and automotive parts. American capital was the source of much of this diversification, with investments coming also from Luxembourg's Common Market partners.

Agriculture is of the small-scale, mixed-farming type, and livestock breeding is important. Among Luxembourg's exports are dairy products, pigs, and roses, and its vineyards in the Moselle Valley produce fine white wines. Trilingual Luxembourgers, speaking their own patois plus French and German, call the southern part of the grand duchy *Bon Pays* or *Gutland*—in English, the "Good Land"— because of its agricultural qualities.

Most industry is concentrated in the extreme south, and, all-in-all, Luxembourg offers the tourist picturesque scenery, good food and drink, an excellent road system, and, for the hiker, extensive paths between old villages.

On the darker side is the fact that the duchy has twice been overrun in this century by German troops, with liberation coming both times with the arrival of American forces. At Hamm, outside Luxembourg City, more than 5,000 American soldiers, including General George S. Patton, Jr., lie buried.

Since the war Luxembourg has abandoned neutrality. In 1949 it became a charter member of the North Atlantic Treaty Organization and has since been one of the leading promoters of closer European cooperation. It was a pioneer in the kind of economic cooperation now exemplified by the European Community, having formed, in 1921, a customs union with Belgium; the union became *Benelux* when the Netherlands joined in 1948.

HISTORY: The county of Luxembourg, including the present Belgian province of Luxembourg, emerged in the 10th century and rose to prominence in 1308, when its ruler was elected Holy Roman Emperor. Raised to a duchy in 1354, Luxembourg passed to the Hapsburgs in 1482. During the next three centuries, the duchy's history was bound up with the southern Netherlands, which passed from Spanish to Austrian rule in 1714. France occupied the duchy during the French Revolutionary Wars and formally annexed it in 1797
1815: Congress of Vienna makes Luxembourg a grand duchy, in personal union with the Kingdom of the Netherlands
1839: Belgium, having won its independence from the Netherlands, annexes the present Belgian province of Luxembourg; it constituted the major part of the grand duchy
1867: Luxembourg is declared an independent, neutral state in personal union with the Netherlands by the Treaty of London
1890: William III of the Netherlands dies and is succeeded on the Dutch throne by his daughter Wilhelmina; however, Luxembourg passes to Duke Adolf of Nassau, who becomes grand duke
1914-18: Luxembourg, its neutrality violated by Germany, is occupied by German forces during World War I
1940: German forces invade grand duchy in World War II; ducal family and cabinet flee to London
1944: Luxembourg is liberated by Allied forces
1949: Grand duchy formally abandons its perpetual neutrality and joins North Atlantic Treaty Organization
1964: Grand Duchess Charlotte abdicates in favor of son Jean
1968-69: Christian Socialist/Socialist coalition government of Premier Pierre Werner falls in October 1968 after government refuses to agree to demands by Socialist trade union leaders for higher wages and greater welfare benefits; following new elections, Werner forms a new government of Christian Socialists and Socialists and is reappointed premier in 1969

1972: Voting age is lowered from 21 to 18
1974: Premier Werner's government falls, ending 55 years of unbroken control by Christian Socialists. Democrat Gaston Thorn becomes premier, leading a coalition of socialists and liberals
1979: Christian Democrats regain control of parliament following new elections; Pierre Werner replaces Thorn as premier and forms Christian Democrat-Liberal coalition

MADAGASCAR

Area: 226,657 sq. mi. **Population:** 8,289,000 (1978 est.)
Official Name: Democratic Republic of Madagascar **Capital:** Antananarivo **Nationality:** Malagasy **Languages:** Malagasy and French are the official languages; Hova and other dialects are also widely spoken **Religion:** About 55% animist, 40% Christian, and 5% Moslem **Flag:** A white vertical band at the staff and 2 horizontal bands, the upper red, the lower green **Anthem:** O, Our Beloved Fatherland **Currency:** Malagasy franc (263 per U.S. $1)

Location: Indian Ocean. The 4th-largest island in the world—after Greenland, New Guinea, and Borneo—Madagascar is situated some 250 miles off the east coast of Africa, from which it is separated by the Mozambique Channel **Features:** The terrain consists of a central belt of eroded highlands extending from the northeast to the southwest, sloping steeply eastward to a narrow, swampy coast and passing gradually to more extensive lowlands in the west. An inland plateau rises to 9,450 feet **Chief Rivers:** Mangoro, Ikopa, Onilahy, Tsiribihina, Mangoky, Sofia

Head of State and of Government: President: Cmdr. Didier Ratsiraka, born 1936, assumed power in a coup in June 1975 as head of Supreme Revolutionary Council, and elected president in December 1975; he is aided by a cabinet headed by the premier, Desire Rakotoarijaona, appointed August 1977 **Effective Date of Present Constitution:** 1975 **Legislative Body:** National Popular Assembly (unicameral) consisting of 137 members, elected for five years **Local Government:** 6 provinces

Ethnic Composition: The population is of Malayan-Indonesian origin, with an admixture of Arab and African strains; of 18 major groups, the most numerous are the Merina (Hova), Betsileo, Betsimisaraka, Sakalava and Tsimihety **Population Distribution:** 14% urban **Density:** 37 inhabitants per sq. mi.

Largest Cities: (1975 census) Antananarivo 451,808, Toamasina (Tamatave) 77,395, Fianarantsoa 68,054, Majunga 65,864, Toliary (Tuléar) 45,676, Antsiranana (Diégo-Suarez) 40,443

Per Capita Income: $300 (1979) **Gross National Product (GNP):** $2.5 billion (1979) **Economic Statistics:** In 1978 about 40% of the GNP came from agriculture (rice, coffee, tobacco, cloves, cocoa, vanilla, livestock), 17% from industry (including oil refining) and mining **Minerals and Mining:** Graphite, mica, gold, and industrial beryl are mined, but are not extensive. Offshore oil deposits are to be exploited **Labor Force:** 3.4 million, of which 90% is in agriculture **Foreign Trade:** Exports, chiefly coffee, vanilla, sugar, rice, cloves, and raffia, totaled $412 million in 1979. Imports, mainly transportation machinery, crude oil, textiles, chemicals, pharmaceuticals, machinery, and electrical appliances, totaled $673 million **Principal Trade Partners:** France, United States, West Germany, Japan, Italy, United Arab Emirates, Spain

Vital Statistics: Birthrate, 46.0 per 1,000 of pop. (1966); death rate 25.0 **Life Expectancy:** 46 years **Health Statistics:** 417 inhabitants per hospital bed; 10,337 per physician (1976) **Infant Mortality:** 53.2 per 1,000 births (1972) **Illiteracy:** 55% **Primary and Secondary School Enrollment:** 1,264,849 (1975) **Enrollment in Higher Education:** 8,385 (1975) **GNP Expended on Education:** 3.1% (1975)

Transportation: Paved roads total 2,800 mi. **Motor Vehicles:** 109,700 (1977) **Passenger Cars:** 57,400 **Railway Mileage:** 549 **Ports:** Toamasina (Tamatave), Majunga, Nossi-Be, Antsiranana (Diégo-Suarez), Toliary (Tuléar) **Major Airlines:** Air Madagascar operates domestic and international services **Communications:** Government controlled **Radio Transmitters:** 16 **Receivers:** 609,000 (1975) **Television Transmitters:** 4 **Receivers:** 8,000 (1976) **Telephones:** 32,000 (1976) **Newspapers:** 9 dailies, 9 copies per 1,000 inhabitants (1974)

Weights and Measures: Metric system **Travel Requirements:** Passport, visa valid for stay up to 1 month, $6.76 fee, 4 photos

Madagascar, known as the Malagasy Republic until 1976, is "the land at the end of the earth," a blend of Shangri-la and Lost World. Although near Africa—250 miles off the continent's southeast coast—Madagascar and its people, the Malagasy, appear to be more a part of southeast Asia. The island was settled, according to folklore, more than 2,000 years ago by people who drifted across the Indian Ocean from the Malay-Indonesia area. Their descendants speak a language considered to be of Malayan-Polynesian origin and, while some show admixtures of African and Arab settlers, most have an Indochinese physique.

While unknown to much of the world, Madagascar was prized as a naval base in the contest of the British and French imperialism. Triumph by the French brought an overthrow of the Malagasy monarchy, but not submission.

Despite their placid appearance, the Malagasy rose in a bloody and unsuccessful revolt against French rule in 1947. When, in 1960, the island became a fully sovereign republic under President Philibert Tsiranana, the Malagasy regarded the event as a return to self-rule rather than a granting of independence from a colonial power.

With self-rule, Madagascar has faced problems of resolving internal conflicts, mainly between the traditionally dominant Merina, or plateau people, and the *côtiers*, or coastal peoples. President Tsiranana was a *côtier* and former professor who sought to promote both national unity and the development of a sluggish agricultural economy.

Tsiranana favored continued close ties with France and, despite Madagascar's membership in the Organization of African Unity and his own condemnation of apartheid, he welcomed investment and economic aid from South Africa. That policy changed in 1972.

The economy is overwhelmingly agricultural, largely of a subsistence type. Rice is the main crop. New development efforts have been concentrated in mining, with occasional investments made in light manufacturing.

A major change in Madagascar's political life came in 1972 when President Tsiranana was removed from office. Student riots had begun to plague his administration, and a formal referendum was held which transferred power to a new military government headed by Premier Gabriel Ramanantsoa, a moderate leftist.

In February 1975, Ramanantsoa turned over full power to Col. Richard Ratsimandrava after 12 days of political crisis. After six days, Ratsimandrava was assassinated by paramilitary policemen.

The National Military Guidance Committee governed the country until June 15 when it invested Cmdr. Didier Ratsiraka as head of state and dissolved itself. In a referendum, Ratsiraka's presidency and a new constitution were approved by 95 percent of the voters. The nation was to be known henceforth as the Democratic Republic of Madagascar. The military, in control since 1972, has sought to nationalize important segments of the economy.

HISTORY: Despite Madagascar's proximity to Africa, Malagasy tradition and language support the belief that the first waves of migration came from the Sunda Islands (present-day Indonesia), starting a century or two before the Christian era. About A.D. 900, Arab settlers and Africans, brought by slave traders, were added to the population. Beginning in the 16th century, Portuguese, French, and English contested with rival Malagasy kingdoms for dominance of the island

1885-1905: France invades Madagascar and establishes a limited protectorate. Local resistance continues for many years

1942-43: British occupy Vichy-ruled Madagascar to prevent seizure by Japanese; Free French take over

1947: Armed revolt by Malagasy nationalists breaks out in opposition to "French Union" self-rule; lasts nearly a year before French suppress it; death toll is put as high as 80,000

1958: After reforms in 1956 paving way for independence, Madagascar votes "yes" in referendum creating Malagasy Republic within the French Community

1959: Philibert Tsiranana, a former teacher and founder of the Social Democratic party, is elected first president of the republic

1960: Madagascar is proclaimed a sovereign, independent nation

1965: President Tsiranana is reelected by smashing majority

1972: Executive powers are transferred to Gen. Ramanantsoa as premier of a military government

1975: Ramanantsoa turns over power to Col. Richard Ratsimandrava, who is assassinated after six days. A military committee invests Cmdr. Didier Ratsiraka as head of state. Nation renamed Democratic Republic of Madagascar

1978: Madagascar lays claim to four Indian Ocean islands administered by French Réunion

1979: Contract made with China to build a 1,200-kw. hydroelectric plant 60 miles from Antananarivo

1980: Oil is discovered. Madagascar arranges for major arms purchases from Soviet Union and signs cultural cooperation agreement with Cuba

---

MALAWI

Area: 45,747 sq. mi. **Population:** 5,817,000 (1979 est.)

Official Name: Republic of Malawi **Capital:** Lilongwe **Nationality:** Malawian **Languages:** English is the official language and Chichewa is the national language. Among the other various Bantu languages are Nyanja, Tumbuka, Yao, Tonga, and Ngoni **Religion:** About 35% of the people are Christians, 12% Moslems, and the rest animists **Flag:** 3 horizontal stripes of black, red, and green with a red rising sun on the black stripe **Anthem:** National Anthem, beginning "O God, bless our land of Malawi" **Currency:** Malawian kwacha (.87 per U.S. $1)

Location: East Africa. Landlocked Malawi is bordered on the north and northeast by Tanzania, on the southeast and southwest by Mozambique, and on the northwest by Zambia **Features:** The Great Rift Valley traverses the country from north to south, its deep trough containing the 360-mile-long Lake Nyasa (Malawi). West of the valley, the land rises to form high plateaus between 3,000 and 4,000 feet above sea level, while in the north the Nyika uplands rise to 8,500 feet. South of Lake Nyasa are the Shire Highlands, which rise to steep mountains ranging up to 10,000 feet **Chief Rivers:** Shire, Bua, Rukuru

Head of State and of Government: President: Dr. Hastings Kamuzu Banda, born 1906, elected by National Assembly in 1966, made president for life by constitutional amendment in November 1970; he also holds 4 cabinet posts **Effective Date of Present Constitution:** July 1966 **Legislative Body:** National Assembly (unicameral); 87 members for 5-year terms **Local Government:** 3 regions, divided into 24 districts. Each region has an appointed regional minister

Ethnic Composition: The people are almost all descended from Bantu tribes that arrived between the 16th and 19th centuries. They include the Chewa and the Nyanja, descendants of the Maravi, who emigrated from present-day Zaire; the Yao; the Tumbuka; the Lonwe; and the Sena **Population Distribution:** 10% urban **Density:** 127 inhabitants per sq. mi.

Largest Cities: (1977 census) Blantyre 222,153, Lilongwe 102,924, Zomba 21,000

Per Capita Income: $150 (1979) **Gross Domestic Product (GDP):** $871 million (1979) **Economic Statistics:** In 1973 over 50% of the GDP was derived from agriculture (tea, tung nuts and oil, sugarcane, tobacco), 13% from industry, and 19% from trade and services **Minerals and Mining:** Production is limited to quarrying constructional stone and limestone; however there are unexploited deposits of bauxite and coal **Labor Force:** 1,500,000, with 85% in subsistence agriculture **Foreign Trade:** Exports, chiefly tobacco, tea, sugar, peanuts, corn, and cotton, totaled $233 million in 1979. Imports, mainly textiles, motor vehicles, petroleum products, medical and pharmaceutical goods, and food products, totaled $314 million **Principal Trade Partners:** Britain, South Africa, Netherlands, United States, Japan, West Germany

Vital Statistics: Birthrate, 50.5 per 1,000 of pop. (1974); death rate, 26 **Life Expectancy:** 42 years **Health Statistics:** 576 inhabitants per hospital bed; 48,462 per physician (1977) **Infant Mortality:** 142.1 per 1,000 births **Illiteracy:** 85% **Primary and Secondary School Enrollment:** 680,089 (1976) **Enrollment in Higher Education:** 1,148 (1975) **GNP Expended on Education:** 2.0% (1975)

Transportation: Paved roads total 1,474 mi. **Motor Vehicles:** 20,800 1976 **Passenger Cars:** 10,200 **Railway Mileage:** 420 **Ports:** None **Major Airlines:** Air Malawi, Ltd. operates domestic and international services **Communications:** Government controlled **Radio Transmitters:** 15 **Receivers:** 130,000 (1976) **Television:** None **Telephones:** 21,000 (1976) **Newspapers:** 1 daily, 1.8 copies per 1,000 inhabitants (1975)

Weights and Measures: Metric and British standards **Travel Requirements:** Passport, no visa required for stay up to 1 year

Malawi is among Africa's most picturesque yet poorest countries. It is distinguished also in being one of the few independent black African countries to establish official relations with South Africa and in having a despotic president, Dr. H. Kamuzu Banda, who banned the miniskirt, set rules on the length of men's shorts, and, in 1978, banned foreign journalists from the country indefinitely for what he considered unfair, false reporting of recent elections.

Soaring mountains and the long inland sea of Lake Nyasa have won the country the title of "Switzerland of Africa." But the resemblance ends with the scenery. Malawi's economy has been gaining with increased production of tea and tobacco and industrial investment from South Africa, but with a dense population and a very low per capita income, the country is still far from economic takeoff.

Dr. Banda, an associate and admirer of Ghana's erstwhile ruler, Kwame Nkrumah, has been president of Malawi since the former British protectorate became independent in 1964. In 1970 he had himself made president for life.

While maintaining that he is as much opposed to South Africa's racial policies as any black African leader, Dr. Banda has cited Malawi's need and landlocked position in southern Africa as necessitating close economic ties with her white-ruled neighbor. "I would do business with the Devil himself to help Malawian development," he has said. Employment of more than 20,000 Malawian workers in South Africa brings in needed foreign exchange.

Tourism has become an important business for Malawi. Many hotels, however, have recently reported a drop in bookings as a result of Dr. Banda's rulings about dress, which were aimed at tourists.

Pressures for "Africanization" of property and jobs have been aimed at European landowners and Asian traders. As many as 200,000 Asians have had their businesses "Africanized."

The building of a new capital at Lilongwe, a pet project of Dr. Banda's, was aided by South African loans. Most of the $60-million cost of the new capital is being underwritten by South Africa.

In addition to increasing industry, plans are progressing for bauxite mining and construction of a large aluminum plant. Dr. Banda has said that Malawi either will become economically viable in the next 5 to 10 years or will cease to exist as a truly independent state.

HISTORY: Little is known about the history of Malawi, formerly Nyasaland, prior to the arrival of the Scottish missionary and explorer David Livingstone in 1859. His revulsion at the Arab slave trade moved him to promote establishment of Scottish missions and business groups to develop legitimate commerce as a substitute for the trade in human beings. Britain, in fighting the slave trade and also seeking to prevent encroachment by the Portuguese and Germans, gradually gained control of Nyasaland and set up a protectorate in 1891

1953: Nyasaland, despite strong Nyasa opposition, is joined to new Central African Federation, including also Northern and Southern Rhodesia

1959: Dr. Hastings Kamuzu Banda, leader of Nyasaland African Congress, and more than 1,000 of his followers, are imprisoned, charged with plotting massacre of white officials; after they were absolved they set up Malawi Congress party

1960-61: Britain grants Nyasaland constitution assuring African majority in Legislative Council; Malawi party wins overwhelming victory in council election

1963: Nyasaland secedes from Central African Federation, which is dissolved; Banda becomes prime minister under new constitution

1964-65: Nyasaland becomes independent Malawi

1966: Malawi becomes a republic within British Commonwealth, with Banda as president

1969: Malawi, at meeting of East and Central African States, refuses to join in manifesto criticizing white-dominated governments of Rhodesia and South Africa

1970: Prime Minister John Vorster of South Africa makes official visit to Malawi, the first such visit by a South African leader to a black African state

1971: President Banda visits South Africa, continuing close relations between Malawi and South Africa

1975: Official transfer to new capital at Lilongwe takes place on January 1. Jehovah's Witnesses movement protests alleged persecution of 30,000 members by government

1977: President Banda dismisses his entire cabinet

1980: Government imposes import controls to offset rising oil prices

MALAYSIA

Area: 128,308 sq. mi. **Population:** 13,435,588 (1980 census) **Official Name:** Malaysia **Capital:** Kuala Lumpur **Nationality:** Malaysian **Languages:** Malay (Bahasa Malaysia) is the official language; English, Tamil, and a variety of native, Chinese, and Indian dialects are also spoken **Religion:** Chiefly Moslem, and Islam is the state religion; in Sabah and Sarawak there are many animists. Most of the Chinese follow Buddhism, Confucianism, and Taoism. Of the Indian community, about 70% are Hindu, 20% Moslem, 5% Christian, and 2% Sikh **Flag:** Fourteen red and white stripes with blue field in upper left corner containing crescent and star in yellow **Anthem:** Our Country **Currency:** ringgit (2.3 per U.S. $1)

Location: Southeast Asia. Malaysia consists of West Malaysia (Malaya), and East Malaysia (Sabah and Sarawak). West Malaysia, on the Malay Peninsula, is bordered on the east by the South China Sea, on the south by the Strait of Johore, on the west by the Strait of Malacca and the Andaman Sea, and on the north by Thailand. Sarawak and Sabah, on the northwestern coast of the island of Borneo, are bordered by Brunei, and by the Indonesian province of Kalimantan on the southeast; on the west, north, and east are the South China, Sulu, and Celebes seas **Features:** Some 80% of the total land area of the country is forested. The Malay Peninsula consists of a spinal mountain range running roughly north and south and flanked by coastal plains. In Sabah and Sarawak, coastal plains rise to mountainous interiors **Chief Rivers:** Perak and Pahang in Malaya; Rajang in Sarawak, Kinabatangan in Sabah

Head of State: Paramount Ruler: Tuanku Haji Ahmad Shah Al-Mustain Billah Ibni Al-Marhum Sultan Abu Bakar Ri'ayatuddin Al-Mu'adzam Shah, shah of Pahang, born 1930, elected April 1979 by the Conference of Rulers for a 5-year term **Head of Government:** Prime Minister: Dr. Mahathir bin Mohamad, took office July 16, 1981 **Effective Date of Present Constitution:** 1957 **Legislative Body:** Parliament (bicameral), consisting of a Senate (Dewan Negara) and a House of Representatives (Dewan Rakyat). The Senate is composed of 58 members, 32 appointed by the Paramount Ruler and 26 elected by state assemblies, for 6-year terms. The House of Representatives consists of 154 members, 114 from West Malaysia, 24 from Sarawak, and 16 from Sabah, all elected for a 5-year term **Local Government:** 13 states, headed by titular rulers and governors. Effective power is in the hands of the chief ministers, selected from the state assemblies

Ethnic Composition: Malayans constitute about 45% of the population, Chinese 36%, non-Malay indigenous peoples 8%, and Indians and Pakistanis 9.1% **Population Distribution:** 29% urban **Density:** 105 inhabitants per sq. mi.

Largest Cities: (1980 census) Kuala Lumpur 937,875; (1970 census) George Town (Penang) 269,247, Ipoh 247,969

Per Capita Income: $1,355 (1980) **Gross National Product (GNP):** $19 billion (1980) **Economic Statistics:** In 1978, 30% of GNP was derived from agriculture (rubber, timber, rice, palm oil, coconut oil, fruits, sago, tea, and pepper); 16% from manufacturing (oil and sugar refining, steel plants, fertilizers, and many smaller import-substitute industries); and 6% from mining (tin, oil, iron) **Minerals and Mining:** Tin, oil and iron ore are the chief minerals. Petroleum from offshore wells is of growing importance in Sarawak and Sabah **Labor Force:** About 4,800,000 (1978 est.), with approximately 50% engaged in agriculture and fishing, and 14% in industry **Foreign Trade:** Exports, chiefly rubber, tin, petroleum, palm oil and forest products, totaled $11 billion in 1979. Imports, mainly foodstuffs, industrial machinery, transportation equipment, metals, electrical equipment, and petroleum products, totaled $7.9 billion **Principal Trade Partners:** Britain, Singapore, Japan, United States, Australia, China, West Germany, Thailand

Vital Statistics: Birthrate, 30.9 per 1,000 of pop. (1977); death rate, 6.1 **Life Expectancy:** 68 years **Health Statistics:** 347 inhabitants per hospital bed; 8,319 per physician (1974) **Infant Mortality:** 30.7 per 1,000 births **Illiteracy:** 39% **Primary and Secondary School Enroll-**

ment: 2,462,682 (1977) **Enrollment in Higher Education:** 39,658 **GNP Expended on Education:** 5.1% (1971)

Transportation: Paved roads total 10,480 mi. **Motor Vehicles:** 658,200 (1977) **Passenger Cars:** 491,200 **Railway Mileage:** 1,132 **Ports:** Pinang, Port Dickson, Klang, Malacca, Kuching, Miri, Sandakan, Tawau, Kota Kinabalu **Major Airlines:** Malaysian Airline System operates international and domestic flights **Communications:** Government owned **Radio Transmitters:** 92 **Receivers:** 1,450,000 (1976) **Television Transmitters:** 38 **Receivers:** 555,000 (1976) **Telephones:** 320,000 (1976) **Newspapers:** 31 dailies, 87 copies per 1,000 inhabitants (1975)

Weights and Measures: British standards are used; metric conversion scheduled for 1976-1982 **Travel Requirements:** Passport, no visa for 3 months **International Dialing Code:** 60

For more than a century Malaya, with its rich deposits of tin and its ideal climate for growing rubber trees, has been prosperous and sought after. With the addition in 1963 of Sarawak and Sabah, the former British colonies on the island of Borneo, the new Federation of Malaysia now contains one of the largest undeveloped areas in Asia.

The long center spine of Malaya and vast sections of Sarawak and Sabah are covered solidly with towering rain forests and low mountain ranges. Only the coastal areas and the occasional valleys are open and settled. Malaya, economically balanced and commercially progressive, continues to clear new tracts of jungle land for planting for rubber and coconut palm oil. But the efforts to enlarge the slender bands of modern development in Sarawak and Sabah have barely crept along since British colonial rule over these remote territories ended.

Although Malaysia enjoys a healthy balance of trade and its people have the highest per capita income in Southeast Asia after Singapore's, the economy suffers from overspecialization. Two commodities, rubber and tin, account for an important part of the export trade. Both are vulnerable to price swings in world markets. In addition, synthetic rubber has been gaining favor while readily exploitable tin reserves are dwindling. On the plus side the new oil fields in Sabah are now producing; they now account for almost a fifth of Malaysia's exports. The Malaysian Industrial Development Authority has used the "hard sell" since the early 1970s, and the country has attracted 600 multinational companies, most of them with plants in 60 widely dispersed industrial estates. Penang has become an electronics center, and Johore has received many companies that left Singapore.

Malaysia, which was actively anti-Communist, has since 1970 modified her foreign policy in favor of peaceful coexistence. In 1974, Prime Minister Abdul Razak visited Peking and established full diplomatic relations with Communist China.

The level of living in Malaysia's cities and small towns is the highest in Southeast Asia and there are no pressures on the land from the population. Malaya has been notably successful in completing a series of five-year development plans. Similar, though less ambitious, plans have been prepared for East Malaysia. The British, whose business firms reaped impressive profits from Malaya, left behind in that region an excellent civil service, comparatively good medical facilities, and a soundly administered school system that has been markedly successful in the cities and towns where most of the ethnic Chinese and Indians are concentrated.

But amid the prosperity of Malaysia there runs a continuing struggle between the Moslem Malays, who consider themselves the indigenous owners of Malaya, and the ethnic Chinese. The Chinese own 90 percent of the federation's commercial outlets, occupy the majority of the positions in medical, legal, and engineering circles, and possess an energy and drive that the graceful, deliberate, and

highly religious Malays do not admire. Since Malaya first became independent in 1957 there has been a subsurface fear among the Malays that the ethnic Chinese may take control by winning a majority in the elected parliament.

The Malays, who now dominate the government, are also in conflict with the native groups in Sarawak and Sabah, with whom they are neither religiously nor culturally allied.

The bloody race riots of 1969 led to a 21-month suspension of parliament and rule by decree. Though parliament reconvened in February 1971, full democracy did not return. A constitutional amendment to outlaw discussion of sensitive issues likely to inflame race hatred was adopted. The 48-member National Unity Council became the sole body permitted to question the government's racial and linguistic policies.

A heavy tide of refugees from Vietnam, known as the "boat people" because of their arrival from across the South China Sea, caused political turbulence in Malaysia in 1978 and 1979. They were mostly Chinese and therefore were viewed by the Malays as a threat to the country's delicate political and social balance. The government had about 70,000 such refugees in makeshift camps in 1979, a number that gradually shrank thereafter as they were resettled in the U.S. and other countries. In 1981, the government began to adopt restrictive measures to deal with new social pressures created by a massive influx of Indonesian unskilled laborers into developing areas of Malaysia.

HISTORY: By the beginning of the 13th century the coasts of Malaya, Sarawak, and Sabah, which now are joined in the Federation of Malaysia, were dotted with small trading ports where the natives, most of them of ethnic Malay stock, fished and produced spices. The lure of this spice trade brought the Portuguese, Dutch, and British merchant adventurers. As their trade grew, they found it profitable to take control of the ports to protect their enterprises from the natives and from the other European merchants. In 1511 the Portuguese occupied Malacca, on the west coast of Malaya, and in 1592 the British East India Company appeared at Penang

1867: British establish the Straits Settlements—Penang, Malacca, Singapore—as a crown colony

1888: British declare North Borneo (Sabah), Sarawak, and Brunei British protectorates

1941: Japanese invade Malaya in World War II, eventually driving the British and Dutch from the East Indies

1946: After Japanese surrender, British form Union of Malaya by uniting Penang and Malacca with the nine Malay states; Singapore, Sabah, and Sarawak become crown colonies

1948: Union of Malaya is succeeded by Federation of Malaya; Communist insurrection by ethnic Chinese breaks out, and government declares state of emergency

1957: Malaya becomes independent and member of British Commonwealth

1960: Emergency is ended with defeat of Communist guerrillas

1962-63: Britain and Malaya agree on formation of new Federation of Malaysia that is to include Malaya, Sarawak, Sabah, the tiny Sultanate of Brunei, and Singapore. Brunei decides at last minute to remain outside federation; Malaysia is officially created and joins Commonwealth

1965: After months of dispute over status of ethnic Chinese and Malays, stimulated by Malay fear of Chinese dominance, Singapore secedes from federation

1966: After three years of sporadic guerrilla war and threats of invasion from Indonesia, which had opposed the creation of the federation, Malaysia and Indonesia agree to peace

1969: Tension and rioting between Chinese and Malays in capital leads to suspension of the constitution and formation of a state-of-emergency ruling council

1970: Prime Minister Abdul Rahman, the founder and leader of Malaysia, resigns and is succeeded by Abdul Razak

1971: State of emergency, in effect for 21 months, is ended on February 19 and parliamentary government restored

1974: Prime Minister Razak's National Front Coalition wins an overwhelming election victory

1975: Prosperity of early 1970s ends and government faces an ailing economy, student unrest and guerrilla war by the Communists

1976: Razak dies on January 14, Deputy Prime Minister Datuk Hussein bin Onn takes office. Government tightens security measures in drive on Communist insurgents. Ethnic Chinese professionals flee to avoid racial discrimination

1978: Hussein calls early elections and wins large majority. Number of refugee "boat people" who crossed South China Sea from Vietnam passes 50,000 mark by year's end. Hussein resigns and is replaced by Dr. Mahathir bin Mohamad as prime minister

1979: On Jan. 5, Prime Minister Hussein announces that the government will accept no more refugees. On March 3, a Vietnamese boat is turned back by naval gunfire; eventually it capsizes and 104 persons drown. Tens of thousands of Philippine Moslems flee to the state of Sabah (northeastern Borneo). The elected figurehead king, Sultan Yahya Petra, died; Sultan Ahmad Shah, shah of Pahang, is elected for a five-year term

1980: Peasants riot against government in the state of Kedah. Incidents in which Thais are killed disrupts cooperation with Thailand to suppress Communist guerillas at the border

1981: Visiting Japanese Prime Minister Suzuki announces grants in aid for Malaysian economic development. Government moves to control growing immigration of Indonesian workers

MALDIVES

Area: 115 sq. mi. **Population:** 143,046 (1978 est.)

Official Name: Republic of Maldives **Capital:** Male **Nationality:** Maldivian **Languages:** Divehi, a dialect of Sinhalese, is the official and universal language; Arabic is also spoken **Religion:** Virtually all Maldivians are Sunni Moslems and Islam is the state religion **Flag:** A green rectangle with a white crescent superimposed on a red field **Anthem:** National Anthem **Currency:** Maldivian rupee (7.6 per U.S. $1)

Location: Indian Ocean. The Maldive Islands are a 500-mile-long archipelago of some 2,000 coral islands, 400 miles southwest of Sri Lanka. Male, the capital, is located at 4° 10' N., 73°30'W. **Features:** The Maldives rest on a submarine ridge, believed to be of volcanic origin. They are grouped into 19 atolls, or rings of coral islands, each ring encircling a lagoon. Most of the islands are covered with coconut palms **Chief Rivers:** None

Head of State and of Government: President: Maumoon Abdul Gayoom, born 1939, elected in 1978 **Effective Date of Present Constitution:** 1964, amended 1968, 1970, 1972, 1975 **Legislative Body:** Majlis (unicameral), 48 members, of whom 8 are appointed by the president and 40 are popularly elected for a 5-year term **Local Government:** Each of the 19 atolls has an elected committee with a head man (Verin) appointed by the government

Ethnic Composition: The people are of mixed Indian, Sinhalese, and Arabic descent **Population Distribution:** 12% urban **Density:** 1,244 inhabitants per sq. mi. (215 islands are inhabited)

Largest City: (1978 census) Male 29,555

Per Capita Income: $190 (1978) **Gross National Product (GNP):** $27 million (1978) **Economic Statistics:** The economy has a narrow base, being almost totally dependent on fisheries for its export earnings. Fishing is the basic industry, the catch consisting mainly of bonito and tuna. Cooked and smoked, they are known as Maldive fish and are used as a condiment. The second-largest commercial industry is copra and coconut oil production. A cottage industry based on coir yarn weaving provides work for many of the women in the islands. Tourism is growing **Minerals and Mining:** There are no mineral resources **Labor Force:** 50% of the population is engaged in fishing **Foreign Trade:** Exports, chiefly fish, coconuts, copra, coir, cowrie shell, tortoise shell, and local handicraft products, totaled $4.6 million in 1979. Imports, mainly rice, flour, kerosene, oil, sugar, textiles, and drugs, totaled $22 million **Principal Trade Partners:** Japan, Sri Lanka, Singapore, Britain

Vital Statistics: Birthrate, 40.5 per 1,000 of pop. (1977); death rate, 11.8 **Health Statistics:** 3,500 inhabitants per hospital bed; 15,555 per physician (1977) **Infant Mortality:** 118.8 per 1,000 births **Illiteracy:** very high **Primary and Secondary School Enrollment:** 3,549 (1977) **GNP Expended on Education:** 3% (1970)

Transportation: N.A. **Motor Vehicles:** 97 (1969) **Passenger Cars:** 20 (1969) **Railway Mileage:** None **Port:** Male **Major Airlines:** Maldive International Airlines connects Male with India and Sri Lanka **Communications:** Government controlled **Radio Transmitters:** 5 **Licenses:** 3,500 (1976) **Television Transmitters:** 1 **Telephones:** 227 (1969) **Newspapers:** 2 dailies, 182 copies per 1,000 inhabitants

Weights and Measures: Local units are used **Travel Requirements:** Passport, no visa required

The 2,000 islands that comprise the Maldives in the Indian Ocean consist of atolls, none of which are more than 20 feet in elevation. The islands are mostly protected by reefs, which have been the

scene of numerous shipwrecks. The total land area is a third that of New York City. The 143,046 Maldivians inhabit only 215 of the islands.

Coconut palms cover the larger islands, on which breadfruit, figs, millet, and edible nuts are grown. Widespread in the hot and humid Maldive climate, malaria has been fought by the World Health Organization.

The Maldivian people live at a more or less subsistence level, and their basic economy is of the one-crop type—what is known as "Maldive fish." This is bonito, caught in local waters, cut up, boiled, smoked, and dried until it resembles hardwood. It is considered a delicacy in Sri Lanka and India, where it is whittled into fragments, cooked with onions and spices, and served as a condiment.

The staple foods of the Maldives are fish and rice. The rice has to be imported along with a host of other necessities, such as salt, sugar, kerosene, oil, and textiles.

There is no income tax, and the bulk of internal revenue is derived from customs duties, the rental of uninhabited islands, the licensing of boats and vehicles, and sale of postage stamps. Tourism is booming, reaching a total of 30,000 visitors annually, most of them West Germans traveling in tour groups that promise sun-and-swim vacations at soft, white beaches.

According to native legend, it was a Sinhalese prince who was the first sultan, having stayed on to rule after becoming becalmed in the Maldives with his royal bride. The country, with one brief exception in 1953, was a sultanate for eight centuries before adopting a republican form of government in 1968.

The role of the Maldives in international affairs has thus far been a limited one, but in 1974 the Maldives and India issued a joint communiqué expressing "full support for the concept of the Indian Ocean as a zone of peace, free from great power rivalries, tensions and military escalations." To stay clear of big-power involvement, the Maldives declined, in 1977, a Soviet offer to move into the Gan Island air base—the site of an 8,700-foot runway—that the British had abandoned two years earlier. But in 1980 a new Maldivian regime signed a cultural agreement with the USSR. Whatever the Soviet's intentions, the Maldives government appeared bent on widening contacts with the outside world, as evidenced by its opening of diplomatic relations with Saudi Arabia in 1981. India and Japan aid the fishing industry through canneries and boat-bulding in the Maldives.

HISTORY: Sighted and described by Ibn Batuta in the 14th century, the Maldive Islands were occupied by the Portuguese from 1518 until the 17th century, when they came under the protection of the Dutch, then in control of Ceylon. The Maldives retained a similar status under the British, who expelled the Dutch from Ceylon during the occupation of the Netherlands by French Revolutionary forces

1887: British protection of the Maldives is formally recorded in an exchange of letters between the sultan and the governor of Ceylon

1948: After Ceylon achieves full independence, new agreement provides that British will control Maldivian foreign affairs but not interfere internally

1953: Sultanate is abolished and Maldives become a republic; efforts at reform by the new president arouse opposition from conservative elements; National Assembly votes to restore the sultanate

1957: An agreement allowing Britain to reactivate an air base on Gan Island stirs wide opposition

1960: Government makes "free gift" to Britain of Gan Island until 1986 in return for British help in quelling a rebellion in the three southernmost atolls

1965: Maldives achieve full independence

1968: Republican form of government is adopted; Ibrahim Nasir is elected president

1975: Premier Ahmed Zaki deposed for attempted coup and exiled in March. British withdraw from base on Gan

1977: USSR proposal to use the old air base is declined

1978: President Nasir goes into exile under unclear circumstances. He is succeeded by Maumoon Abdul Gayoom

1979: About 20 officials of the Nasir government are tried and sentenced. The usual punishment is banishment to a remote island for three or four years
1980: The USSR and the Maldives sign a cultural agreement

MALI

Area: 464,873 sq. mi. **Population:** 6,290,000 (1978 est.)
Official Name: Republic of Mali **Capital:** Bamako **Nationality:** Malian **Languages:** French is the official language and is the language of instruction in the nation's schools. The chief native languages are Bambara, Malinké, and Dyula **Religion:** About 90% Moslem, 9% animist, 1% Christian **Flag:** 3 vertical stripes of green, yellow, and red **Anthem:** National Anthem, beginning "At thy call, O Mali" **Currency:** Mali franc (525 per U.S. $1)
Location: West Africa. Landlocked Mali is bordered on the north by Algeria, on the east by Niger, on the south by Upper Volta, Ivory Coast, and Guinea, and on the west by Senegal and Mauritania **Features:** The country is mainly flat and dry, varying from the desolate Sahara in the north to pasture and croplands in the center and savanna scrub land in the south. The flatness of the landscape is broken in places by striking sandstone mountains and plateaus **Chief Rivers:** Niger, Senegal
Head of State and of Government: President: Gen. Moussa Traoré, born 1936; seized power in 1968, elected June 1979 **Effective Date of Present Constitution:** Approved by referendum June 2, 1974, effective June 1979 **Legislative Body:** National Assembly (unicameral) of 82 members, elected for 4-year terms **Local Government:** 6 regions, each headed by an appointed governor
Ethnic Composition: Of some 23 ethnic groups, about 50% are Mandé, 17% Peul (Fulani), 12% Voltaic, 6% Songhai, and 5% Tuareg and Moor **Population Distribution:** 17% urban **Density:** 14 inhabitants per sq. mi.
Largest Cities: (1976 census) Bamako 404,022, Ségou 64,890, Mopti 53,885, Sikasso 47,030, Kayes 44,736, Gao 30,714
Per Capita Income: $130 (1978) **Gross Domestic Product (GDP):** $839 million (1978) **Economic Statistics:** In 1977 about 45% of GDP was from agriculture (millet, sorghum, rice, cotton), livestock-raising, and fishing; 19% was derived from industry (textiles, cement, fruit processing) **Minerals and Mining:** Unexploited deposits of bauxite, uranium, oil, copper, manganese, and iron. Phosphates, salt and a small amount of gold are mined **Labor Force:** 2,800,000 with about 90% engaged in agriculture and livestock-raising **Foreign Trade:** Exports, mainly cotton, livestock, peanuts, and fish, totaled $117 million in 1979. Imports, chiefly vehicles and parts, cotton cloth, iron and steel, and petroleum products, totaled $263 million **Principal Trade Partners:** France, West Germany, Ivory Coast, Senegal, Britain, China, USSR, United States
Vital Statistics: Birthrate, 44.8 per 1,000 of pop. (1975); death rate, 24.9 **Life Expectancy:** 38 years **Health Statistics:** 1,426 inhabitants per hospital bed; 58,400 per physician (1976) **Infant Mortality:** 187 per 1,000 births **Illiteracy:** 95% **Primary and Secondary School Enrollment:** 307,858 (1975) **Enrollment in Higher Education:** 2,936 **GNP Expended on Education:** 4.7% (1975)
Transportation: Paved roads total 1,050 mi. **Motor Vehicles:** 24,200 (1976) **Passenger Cars:** 15,000 **Railway Mileage:** 401 **Ports:** None **Major Airlines:** Air Mali operates both domestic and international services **Communications:** Government owned **Radio Transmitters:** 14 **Receivers:** 82,000 (1976) **Television:** None **Telephones:** 5,000 (1971) **Newspapers:** 1 daily, 0.5 copies per 1,000 inhabitants (1972)
Weights and Measures: Metric system **Travel Requirements:** Passport, visa valid 1 week, $8 fee, 2 photos

---

Once the center of a succession of mighty African empires, present-day Mali lives in the shadow of past glories. The old empires gained power and wealth from conquest and the caravan trade in slaves, gold, and salt. But with the decay of this trade and the imposition of French colonial rule, the country reverted to a meager agricultural and pastoral economy.

Now independent, modern Mali, while hoping for the discovery of oil or other minerals, struggles to improve a limited production of cotton, livestock, and food crops.

Mali's most famous city—the fabled Timbuktu—is a symbol of lost prosperity and also of the efforts to regain some of that prosperity. This golden city

of the 14th-century Songhai empire, built at the edge of the Sahara on the bend of the Niger, is today a dusty town of 20,000 inhabitants. Malian officials have discovered that the old lure of Timbuktu has lost none of its appeal for tourists.

The majority of Malians, on the other hand, are more concerned with regaining a healthy economy and restoration of traditional freedom of enterprise.

Under former President Modibo Keita, Mali was set "irreversibly" on a path of socialism mainly of the Maoist variety. Large numbers of Communist Chinese were brought in to manage the economy, state enterprises were created and a program of farm collectivization started.

Keita acquired all power and even began wearing Mao tunics in place of the traditional boubou. The people were increasingly terrorized by the president's private militia, which also became a threat to the regular army.

The "irreversible" Keita socialism was reversed in 1968 with a bloodless coup by a group of young army officers. Although aware of growing opposition, the former president took no measures to prevent the military revolt and seemed to accept his ouster fatalistically.

Under the new government, the Military Committee of National Liberation, headed by Lt. Moussa Traoré, farm collectivization was abolished and a start made, with French help, on converting state enterprises into mixed-economy enterprises. While ties were retained with China and Russia the government adopted incentives for private foreign investment.

The ending of farm collectives has brought a marked increase in crop production, and in Bamako and other cities, private business and availability of goods have increased substantially. An American company is exploring for oil and a West German company for uranium. Financial aid has come also from France, the United States, and West Germany, as well as from the Soviet Union and East European countries.

Ten years of military government ended in June 1979 with elections under the new constitution. President Traoré, the only presidential candidate, retained the office for another five years. All 82 elected members of the National Assembly belonged to the only political party, the Democratic Union of the Malian People.

HISTORY: Modern Mali was a major part of past Sudanic empires—Ghana, Malinké (Mali), and Songhai—that flourished from the 8th through the 16th century. Ancient Mali reached its zenith about 1325 with the conquest of Gao and Timbuktu, the fabulous Saharan center of trade and learning. Following destruction of the Songhai empire by Moroccan invaders, the country came under the shifting rule of local chieftains. Two of these, Al-Haji Umar, a Tukulor, and Samory Touré, the Mandingo warrior hero and slave trader, waged fierce resistance against the incursions of French forces during the 19th century. With the defeat of Samory in 1898, French control was effectively extended over the country, which became known as French Sudan
1946: Sudanese Territorial Assembly is established with limited internal authority
1957: Territorial Assembly is given increased powers
1958: Sudan votes in constitutional referendum to become autonomous republic within the French Community
1959: Sudan and Senegal form union as the Federation of Mali
1960: Federation collapses as result of political and economic differences; Sudan proclaims itself the independent Republic of Mali with Modibo Keita as president
1964: President Keita and his Sudanese Union are reelected
1968: Army officers overthrow Keita government in bloodless coup; set up military junta with Lt. Moussa Traoré as president
1969-74: Severe drought and famine take heavy toll in human life and livestock; refugees flock to the cities
1974: Referendum approves the new constitution calling for elections of president and National Assembly by universal suffrage
1978: Malian defense minister, foreign minister and two others are accused of treason. They are convicted in 1979
1979: Traoré, the only candidate, is reelected to presidency in June; civilians outnumber military in new government

1980: Student violence, strikes, drought and bad government management of public enterprises disrupt Mali's economy and political stability

MALTA

Area: 122 sq. mi. **Population:** 343,970 (1979 est.)

Official Name: Republic of Malta **Capital:** Valletta **Nationality:** Maltese **Languages:** Maltese, a Semitic tongue, and English are the official languages. Maltese is the principal spoken language but Italian is also widely spoken **Religion:** Roman Catholicism is the official religion and about 98% of the population is Catholic **Flag:** Two vertical stripes of white and red with a George Cross edged in red in the upper left corner **Anthem:** To This Sweet Land **Currency:** Maltese pound (0.39 per U.S. $1)

Location: Mediterranean Sea, about 58 miles south of Sicily and 180 miles from the coast of North Africa. Malta is comprised of 2 main islands, Malta and Gozo, and several smaller ones **Features:** The country consists of a series of low hills, with terraced fields on the slopes **Chief Rivers:** The country has no rivers

Head of State: President: Dr. Anton Buttigieg, born 1912, elected December 1976 **Head of Government:** Prime Minister Dominic Mintoff, born 1916, appointed June 1971; he is also foreign affairs and interior minister **Effective Date of Present Constitution:** 1964, revised 1974 **Legislative Body:** House of Representatives (unicameral), consisting of 65 members elected for 5-year terms **Local Government:** There is no formally organized local government

Ethnic Composition: Chiefly of Carthaginian and Phoenician stock, later mixed with Arabs, Italians, and British **Population Distribution:** 94% urban **Density:** 2,819 inhabitants per sq. mi.

Largest Cities: (1979 est.) Sliema 20,095, Valletta 14,042

Per Capita Income: $2,331 (1979) **Gross National Product (GNP):** $831 million (1979) **Economic Statistics:** Tourism, ship repair and light manufacturing are the bases of the economy **Minerals and Mining:** There are no mineral resources except for salt and stone **Labor Force:** 119,554 (1977) of which 26% is employed in industry, 6% in agriculture and fishing, and most of the rest in trade and services **Foreign Trade:** Exports, chiefly textiles, potatoes, flowers and seed, totaled $425 million in 1979. Imports, mainly machinery, chemicals, meat, mineral fuels and lubricants, and motor vehicles, totaled $759 million **Principal Trade Partners:** Britain, EC countries, Libya

Vital Statistics: Birthrate, 18.5 per 1,000 of pop. (1979); death rate, 9.4 **Life Expectancy:** 71 years **Health Statistics:** 96 inhabitants per hospital bed; 864 per physician (1971) **Infant Mortality:** 15.6 per 1,000 births **Illiteracy:** 17% **Primary and Secondary School Enrollment:** 61,148 (1976) **Enrollment in Higher Education:** 2,158 **GNP Expended on Education:** 4% (1976)

Transportation: Surfaced roads total 760 mi. **Motor Vehicles:** 73,200 (1977) **Passenger Cars:** 60,700 **Railway Mileage:** None **Ports:** Valletta **Major Airlines:** Air Malta operates flights to Europe and Africa **Communications:** Both government and privately owned **Radio Transmitters:** 2 **Licenses:** 63,000 (1976) **Television Transmitters:** 1 **Licenses:** 63,000 (1976) **Telephones:** 55,000 (1976) **Newspapers:** 6 dailies (1975)

Weights and Measures: Metric and English standards are used **Travel Requirements:** Passport, visa for stay exceeding 3 months

Over the centuries, the islands of Malta have been occupied by powers that sought control of the Mediterranean. And while under such occupations, the strategically placed islands have suffered much from attackers: in 1565, held by the Knights Hospitalers, a Turkish siege was defied; in World War II, Malta, as the "unsinkable aircraft carrier," withstood merciless Axis aerial bombardment, earning Britain's George Cross for heroism.

Independent from Britain since 1964, a republic since 1974, Malta has asserted some control over its own destiny. In 1971, Dominic Mintoff returned to power as Labor party prime minister following the defeat of the coalition of Giorgio Borg Olivier, the pro-Catholic prime minister. Mintoff took a neutral position between the Soviet and Western blocs. He forced Britain to renegotiate its lease on Maltese military facilities providing for increased rent to be paid to Malta and fixed an expiration date of April 1, 1979. Britain withdrew on schedule,

and Malta was free of foreign soldiers for the first time in centuries.

Mintoff promoted light industry, notably textiles and plastics, and cultivated relations with the Arab states. Libya especially has been a good customer for the new industries—and a good provider of foreign aid. However, in 1980 a dispute developed with Libya over offshore oil rights.

HISTORY: The strategic importance of Malta was recognized as far back as the time of the Phoenicians, whose occupation of the island was followed by invasions by the Greeks, Carthaginians, Romans, Byzantines, and Arabs. Malta was seized by the Normans in 1091. In 1530 it was given by Holy Roman Emperor Charles V to the Knights Hospitalers, who became known as the Knights of Malta and who in 1565 successfully withstood a siege by the Turks. The Knights continued to hold the island until 1798, when it was surrendered to Napoleon

1800: The French are ousted from the island by Britain, with the aid of a revolt by the Maltese
1814: Treaty of Paris confirms British possession
1921: Malta is granted limited self-government
1939-45: Malta sustains heavy bombing by Germans and Italians during World War II; entire population is awarded the George Cross in 1942
1964: Malta becomes independent
1969: Last British warships leave Malta
1972: Malta signs new financial and defense agreements with Britain and NATO, replacing the 1964 agreements
1974: Malta becomes a republic. Sir Anthony Mamo sworn in as first president
1976: Dr. Anton Buttigieg is elected president
1977: China promises continued economic and technical aid
1979: British lease of military bases ends; last British soldiers leave
1980: Giorgio Borg Olivier, former prime minister (1966-71), dies Oct. 29

MAURITANIA

Area: 397,954 sq. mi. **Population:** 1,544,000 (1978 est.)

Official Name: Islamic Republic of Mauritania **Capital:** Nouakchott **Nationality:** Mauritanian **Languages:** Arabic is the language most spoken, and with French is the official one; Wolof and Tukolor are also spoken in the South **Religion:** The population is almost entirely Moslem, and Islam is the state religion **Anthem:** National Anthem (no words) **Currency:** Ouguiya (47.6 per U.S. $1)

Location: West Africa. Mauritania is bordered on the north by Morocco, Algeria and the contested Western Sahara area, on the east and southeast by Mali, on the southwest by Senegal, and on the west by the Atlantic Ocean **Features:** The country on the whole is fairly flat. The Sahara zone in the north consists of shifting dunes and gravel plains, while the south is more fertile and suitable for cultivation **Chief River:** Senegal

Head of State and of Government: President: Lt. Col. Mohamed Khouna Ould Haidalla, born 1939, assumed presidency on Jan. 4, 1980. He is chairman of the Military Committee for National Salvation. The MCNS is assisted by a prime minister, Col. Maaouya Ould Sidi Ahmed Taya. **Effective Date of Present Constitution:** 1961, suspended 1978. A new constitution has been prepared and is to be submitted to popular vote **Legislative Body:** Mauritania is now governed by a Military Committee for National Salvation **Local Government:** 12 regions and one district (Nouakchott)

Ethnic Composition: Divided into three groups: 40% Arab-Berber-Negroid, 30% Arab-Berber (Moors), 30% Negroid **Population Distribution:** 23% urban, **Density:** 3.9 inhabitants per sq. mi.

Largest Cities: (1976 census) Nouakchott 134,986, Nouadhibou 21,961, Kaédi 20,848, Zouérate 17,474, Rosso 16,466

Per Capita Income: $400 (1979) **Gross Domestic Product (GDP):** $619 million (1979) **Economic Statistics:** In 1977 about 22% of the GDP was derived from agriculture (livestock, millet, corn, rice, sweet potatoes, peanuts, beans, gum arabic); 21% from industry, mining, and fish processing **Minerals and Mining:** Mauritania is second only to Liberia in West African iron-ore production. There are large deposits of gypsum **Labor Force:** 420,00 (1975), of which 90% is in agriculture **Foreign Trade:** Exports, chiefly iron ore, livestock, fish, dates, and gum arabic, totaled $153 million in 1979. Imports, mainly machinery, vehicles, electrical equipment, petroleum products, cement, tires, and tea, totaled $299 million **Principal Trade Partners:** France, Italy, Britain, West Germany, Senegal, Japan, Spain, United States

Vital Statistics: Birthrate, 44.8 per 1,000 of pop. (1975); death rate, 24.9 **Life Expectancy:** 39 years **Health Statistics:** 2,328 inhabitants per hospital bed; 15,172 per physician (1975) **Infant Mortality:** 187 per 1,000 births **Illiteracy:** 88% **Primary and Secondary School Enrollment:** 83,029 (1977) **Enrollment in Higher Education:** c. 1,000 study abroad **GNP Expended on Education:** 4.3% (1972)

Transportation: Paved roads total 370 mi. **Motor Vehicles:** 11,800 (1974) **Passenger Cars:** 4,400 (1972) **Railway Mileage:** 450 **Ports:** Nouadhibou, Nouakchott **Major Airlines:** Air-Mauritanie operates domestic and international services **Communications:** Government controlled **Radio Transmitters:** 4 **Receivers:** 95,000 (1976) **Television Transmitters:** 1 **Telephones:** 1,300 est. (1969) **Newspapers:** 1 daily, 0.2 per 1,000 inhabitants (1972)

Weights and Measures: Metric system **Travel Requirements:** Passport, visa valid for 3 months, $10 fee, 3 photos

Mauritania is a borderland between Moorish/Arab North Africa and black West Africa. Although cast in the mold of a modern state and with membership in the Organization of African Unity, the former West African territory continues to be divided by racial distinctions dating from the medieval migrations of light-skinned Arabs and Berbers, who forced the darker-skinned natives into the southern region and enslaved many of them. French rule, established by 1920, favored the blacks, who were more inclined than the Arabs to take advantage of European education.

President Moktar Ould Daddah, the country's leader from 1960 to 1978, steered an enlightened and adroit course racially and politically. While promoting more education for the Moorish/Arab majority, President Moktar sought to gain foreign aid from both Western and Eastern sources. In July 1978 the president was overthrown in a bloodless coup led by military officers. Col. Mustapha Ould Salek was named president. In June 1979 Salek resigned and was succeeded by Col. Ahmed Louly. Louly, in turn, was replaced by Lt. Col. Haidalla in 1980.

Although France continues to provide most of the country's aid and development funds, Communist China recently has played a major role in such projects as rice-growing, irrigation, and cement manufacture and in drilling numerous wells to tap ground water.

Mauritania's main source of wealth has been rich deposits of iron ore, which have been developed since independence by French interests. These have provided substantial earnings that have made it possible for the government to embark on the improvement of social services and of agriculture, on which more than 80 percent of Mauritanians depend.

Meanwhile, in addition to French and Chinese aid, Mauritanian development is being aided by countries such as the United States, Yugoslavia, and Spain.

Mauritanian gains in territory from the southern part of former Spanish Sahara were offset by the disruption to the nation's economy caused by raids of the *Polisario Front,* a Saharan liberation guerrilla group based in Algeria. But, after the seizure of power by the army in 1978, the *Polisario* proclaimed a unilateral cease-fire. The military government informally decided to respect the truce, and fighting fell to a sporadic level. On August 5, 1979, Mauritania signed a peace agreement with the *Polisario* under which it renounced all claim to its portion of the contested Western Sahara area. Morocco promptly occupied the region. Mauritania then resumed diplomatic relations with Algeria, ending a three-year break.

HISTORY: Mauritania's original inhabitants, a Sudanic black people, were enslaved or driven southward by the 11th-century Berber invasion that destroyed the empire of Ghana to the east. The Berbers in turn were conquered in the 16th century by Arab invaders, the Beni Hassan. Trade with Europeans, opened by the Portuguese in the 15th century, attracted the Dutch, English, and French. Throughout the 19th century, the French gradually extended control over the country, and established a protectorate in 1903. Mauritania was made a French colony in 1920

1946-56: Internal self-rule gradually increases along with Mauritanian representation in French parliament and Assembly of the French Union

1958: In referendum, Mauritania votes to become autonomous republic within new French Community

1960: Mauritania wins full independence, with Moktar Ould Daddah continuing as prime minister

1961: With adoption of presidential system, Daddah, the only candidate, is elected president; new People's party becomes the sole political organization

1963-66: Completion of iron-ore mining project by French-led consortium and development of extensive copper deposits give strong boost to nation's economy

1973-74: Drought causes widespread famine

1975: Agreement is signed among Spain, Morocco and Mauritania providing for withdrawal of the Spanish presence from Western Sahara. Daddah is reelected president

1976: Morocco and Mauritania partition Western Sahara, giving Mauritania the southern third. The proclamation of an independent republic by the *Polisario Front,* the Saharan liberation movement, is ignored. *Polisario* guerrillas raid Nouackchott

1977: *Polisario* units raid iron-mining center at Zouérate

1978: Group of Western and Arab banks lends Mauritania $360 million for exploitation of iron ore mines. President Moktar Ould Daddah is overthrown in a bloodless coup by military officers, led by Col. Mustapha Ould Salek, who becomes president. *Polisario* proclaims cease-fire

1979: Premier Ahmed Oul Bouicf and 10 other Mauritanian delegates to the Economic Community of West African States die in air crash. He is succeeded by Lt. Col. Mohamed Khouna Ould Haidalla. President Salek resigns. Lt. Col. Mohamed Mahmoud Ould Ahmed Louly is chosen by the MCNS to replace him

1980: President Louly resigns; Prime Minister Haidalla becomes president

1981: Attempted military coup, backed by Morocco, fails as rebel leaders are killed or captured by government soldiers

MAURITIUS

Area: 790 sq. mi. **Population:** 941,000 (1979 est.)

Official Name: Mauritius **Capital:** Port Louis **Nationality:** Mauritian **Languages:** English is the official language, but a Creole patois, basically French, is spoken by 52% of the people; Chinese, Hindi, Urdu, and French are also spoken **Religion:** About 51% Hindu, 33% Christian (chiefly Roman Catholic), and 16% Moslem **Flag:** Four horizontal stripes of red, blue, yellow, and green **Anthem:** Motherland **Currency:** Mauritian rupee (8.3 per U.S. $1)

Location: Indian Ocean. Mauritius (20°S.,57°30'E.) lies about 500 miles east of Madagascar. Dependencies include Rodrigues and distant smaller islands **Features:** The island is volcanic in origin and almost entirely surrounded by coral reefs. The land rises to a central plateau, surrounded by mountains believed to be the rim of an ancient volcano **Chief Rivers:** Grand, Rempart, Poste

Head of State: Queen Elizabeth II, represented by a governor-general, Sir Dayendranath Burrenchobay **Head of Government:** Prime Minister: Sir Seewoosagur Ramgoolam, born 1900; reappointed 1976 **Effective Date of Present Constitution:** 1968 **Legislative Body:** Parliament (unicameral Legislative Assembly), 70 members with 5-year terms, 62 of whom are elected **Local Government:** 9 administrative districts, with local councils

Ethnic Composition: Indo-Mauritians (67%), Creoles (28%), Sino-Mauritians (3%), and Franco-Mauritians (2%) **Population Distribution:** 44% urban **Density:** 1,191 inhabitants per sq. mi.

Largest Cities: (1977 est.) Port Louis 141,022; (1975 est.) Beau Bassin/Rose Hill 81,353, Curepipe 53,068, Quatre Bornes 52,134

Per Capita Income: $817 (1978 est.) **Gross National Product (GNP):** $730 million (1978 est.) **Economic Statistics:** 22% of the GNP comes from agriculture (sugar, tea, ginger, tobacco, vegetables, bananas, peanuts) and 17% from industry (sugar processing, rum, beer) and construction **Minerals and Mining:** There are no known mineral deposits **Labor Force:** 175,000, with 50% in agriculture and 6% in industry **Foreign Trade:** Exports, sugar and sugar products, tea, clothing, and molasses, totaled $331 million in 1979. Imports, chiefly foodstuffs, manufactured goods, machinery and transportation equipment, fuel, chemicals and fertilizers, totaled $423 million **Principal Trade Partners:** Britain, France, South Africa, Japan, Bahrain, United States, West Germany, Belgium

MEXICO

CONIC PROJECTION

SCALE OF MILES
0   100   200   300

SCALE OF KILOMETERS
0 100 200 300

National Capitals......⊛   State Capitals......⊛

© Copyright HAMMOND INCORPORATED, Maplewood, N.J.

States Indicated by Numbers:

1 Tlaxcala   6 Querétaro
2 Morelos   7 Guanajuato
3 Distrito Federal 8 Aguascalientes
4 México   9 Nayarit
5 Hidalgo   10 Colima

Longitude West 102° of Greenwich

Vital Statistics: Birthrate, 41.4 per 1,000 of pop. (1977); death rate, 7.0 **Life Expectancy:** 67 years **Health Statistics:** 271 inhabitants per hospital bed; 2,900 per physician (1976) **Infant Mortality:** 40 per 1,000 births **Illiteracy:** 39% **Primary and Secondary School Enrollment:** 208,272 (1976) **Enrollment in Higher Education:** 1,096 (1975) **GNP Expended on Education:** 4.5% (1976)

Transportation: Paved roads total 1,020 mi. **Motor Vehicles:** 37,300 (1977) **Passenger Cars:** 24,300 **Railway Mileage:** None **Ports:** Port Louis **Major Airlines:** Air Mauritius provides international service **Communications:** Government controlled **Radio Transmitters:** 3 **Licenses:** 200,000 (1976) **Television Transmitters:** 4 **Licenses:** 41,000 (1976) **Telephones:** 27,000 (1976) **Newspapers:** 12 dailies, 91 copies per 1,000 inhabitants (1975)

Weights and Measures: Metric system **Travel Requirements:** Passport, visa, no charge except postage

---

Encircled by coral reefs and the blue-green Indian Ocean, Mauritius looks like the perfect model of a placid tropical island. The former British crown colony, lying nearly 1,500 miles east of southern Africa—its closest proximity to any continent—is renowned as the source of rare postage stamps and as the last refuge of the extinct dodo bird.

The remote volcanic island is also a microcosm of the present-day problems of less-developed countries: overpopulation, racial conflict, and dependence on a single crop, sugar. With no solutions in sight, it seems only a matter of time before the combined pressures of these problems bring an eruption. Indeed, a ban on 12 unions was imposed by the government in 1971 and only lifted in 1974, following lengthy negotiations between dockworkers and government officials.

Within the island's 790 square miles, there are, in addition to a large Indian-Hindu majority, major groups of Africans, Europeans (mainly French), and Creoles (an Afro-French mixture), and a small element of Chinese. Despite efforts of a coalition government headed by Prime Minister Sir Seewoosagur Ramgoolam to promote harmony, racial rivalries are intense. Violent racial rioting and also labor unrest preceded and accompanied Mauritius' independence in 1968.

Since elimination of malaria recently, the island's population is growing by 1.5 percent a year and birth control is opposed equally by Hindu, Catholic, and Moslem groups.

Some 90 percent of cultivated land is planted with sugarcane, but production is often drastically reduced by cyclones, as it was in 1979. Faced with depressed sugar prices, Mauritius merged some of the largest estates in 1980 to raise cattle for beef and milk.

At the same time, the Mauritian government has found itself in a dilemma in being opposed to white minority rule in South Africa even though South Africa is one of Mauritius' main trading partners. South Africa itself has shown interest in aiding Mauritius in return for a less anti-Pretoria stand and, in view of the island's problems, Mauritian officials appear inclined to accept.

It has been a rule of thumb on Mauritius that one ton of sugar exports was needed for each inhabitant. But sugar production is unlikely to exceed 700,000 tons a year, although population is now climbing toward the one million mark.

HISTORY: Originally uninhabited, Mauritius was first settled and named by the Dutch in the 17th century. The island was abandoned early in the 18th century, after which it was claimed by the French, who renamed it Ile-de-France and laid the foundations of a slave-owning plantation economy based on sugar. In 1814, the island was ceded to Britain and reverted to its original name. Slavery was abolished in 1834, and the planters began importing indentured Indians. Although they soon came to form a majority, the Indians long remained politically powerless because of a restricted franchise based on property qualifications

1948: Franchise is broadened by new constitution; in new elections, Indians win majority in legislative council, overthrowing dominance of Franco-Mauritians but causing other minority groups to fear Indian domination

1961: Constitutional conference in London paves way toward full self-government, but talks are marred by disputes between Hindu-dominated majority Labour party and minority parties

1967: Mauritius becomes self-governing; Labour party leader Seewoosagur Ramgoolam is appointed prime minister; island is wracked by racial and labor unrest

1968: Mauritius wins independence amid Creole-Moslem rioting

1970: Government begins drafting plans for crop diversification, light industry, and tourism

1975: Cyclone Gervaise leaves 90,000 homeless and destroys 30 percent of sugar harvest

1979: General strike in support of sugar workers paralyzes economy. Cyclone Claudette makes 4,000 homeless

1980: Organization of African Unity supports Mauritius' claim to Diego Garcia Island which United States uses as a naval base, but Britain rejects it

---

MEXICO

Area: 761,600 sq. mi. **Population:** 67,395,826 (1980 census)

Official Name: United Mexican States **Capital:** Mexico City **Nationality:** Mexican **Languages:** Spanish is the official and predominant language; 7% speak only Indian dialects **Religion:** 97% Roman Catholic; there are some 600,000 Protestants and 100,000 Jews **Flag:** Green, white, and red vertical stripes with the national emblem in the center **Anthem:** National Anthem, beginning "Mexicans, to the call of war" **Currency:** Mexican peso (24 per U.S. $1)

Location: North America. Mexico is bordered on the north by the United States, on the east by the Gulf of Mexico, on the south by Belize and Guatemala, and on the west by the Pacific Ocean **Features:** The country consists of a large central plateau, flanked by the eastern and western coastal ranges of the Sierra Madre. From a low desert plain in the north, the plateau rises to 8,000 feet near Mexico City **Chief Rivers:** Rio Bravo (Rio Grande), Lerma, Santiago, Usumacinta, Grijalva, Balsas, Pánuco

Head of State and of Government: President José López Portillo y Pacheco, born 1920, elected 1976 for 6-year term **Effective Date of Present Constitution:** 1917 **Legislative Body:** Congress (bicameral), consisting of the Senate and the Chamber of Deputies. The Senate is composed of 64 members elected for 6-year terms. The Chamber of Deputies has 400 members elected for 3 years **Local Government:** 31 states, 1 federal district. Each state has its own governor and popularly elected legislature

Ethnic Composition: About 60% of the population are mestizos of mixed Indian and Spanish descent. 30% are pure Indian, while 9% are of Spanish or other European ancestry **Population Distribution:** 64% urban **Density:** 88 inhabitants per sq. mi.

Largest Cities: (1980 census) Mexico City 9,377,300; (1975 est.) Guadalajara 1,560,805, Monterey 1,049,957, Ciudad Juárez 520,539, León 496,598, Puebla 482,155, Tijuana 386,852, Acapulco 352,673

Per Capita Income: $2,045 (1980) **Gross National Product (GNP):** $138 billion (1980) **Economic Statistics:** In 1977 about 12% of GNP came from agriculture (farming, livestock), forestry, and fishing, 37% from industry (cars, machinery, construction, petrochemicals, steel, cement) and mining (including oil) **Minerals and Mining:** Mexico is the world's largest producer of silver and a major producer of oil, gas, gold, sulfur, lead, and zinc. Coal, tin, antimony, mercury, copper, and iron are also mined **Labor Force:** 20 million (1980), 42% in agriculture and 18% in industry **Foreign Trade:** Exports, chiefly petroleum, gas, cotton, sugar, fruits, vegetables, coffee, sulfur, and shrimp, totaled $15.3 billion in 1980. Imports, mainly industrial machinery, motor vehicles and parts, chemicals, communications and transportation equipment, and electric power equipment, totaled $18.5 billion **Principal Trade Partners:** United States, West Germany, Britain, Japan, France, Spain, Canada

Vital Statistics: Birthrate, 34.6 per 1,000 of pop. (1976); death rate, 6.8 **Life Expectancy:** 65 years **Health Statistics:** 530 inhabitants per hospital bed; 1,385 per physician (1972) **Infant Mortality:** 54.7 per 1,000 births (1976) **Illiteracy:** 17% **Primary and Secondary School Enrollment:** 15,389,642 (1976) **Enrollment in Higher Education:** 539,372 (1976) **GNP Expended on Education:** 4.3% (1976)

Transportation: Paved roads total 42,727 mi. **Motor Vehicles:** 3,759,600 (1977) **Passenger Cars:** 2,682,000 **Railway Mileage:** 15,600 **Ports:** Veracruz, Tampico, Coatzacoalcos, Guaymas, Salina Cruz, Mazatlán, Manzanillo **Major Airlines:** Aeroméxico, the government-owned line and Mexicana, a privately owned line, operate both international and domestic flights **Communications:** Partly government controlled **Radio Transmitters:** 668 **Receivers:** 17,514,000 (1974) **Television Transmitters:** 150 **Receivers:** 4,885,000 **Telephones:** 3,309,000 (1976) **Newspapers:** 256 dailies (1975), 116 copies per 1,000 inhabitants (1975)

Weights and Measures: Metric system **Travel Requirements:** Tourist card, valid for stay up to 6 months; no charge **Direct Dialing Code:** Mexico City 905; Northwest Mexico 903

Mexico experienced the world's first social and political revolution of the 20th century, but to this day it still suffers seriously from economic underdevelopment. The bloody struggle that began in 1910 and cost over a million lives gave Mexico stable institutions and a strong constitution, yet most of the revolution's high-sounding principles have yet to be implemented. Glittering long-term hopes for economic advancement were raised, however, with major oil discoveries in 1972 and afterward.

Today this third-largest of Latin American republics, and the most populous Spanish-speaking country in the world, enjoys a large measure of political solidity, under a system of government that falls somewhere between dictatorship and democracy. But the benefits of an economic "miracle" have reached only a small part of Mexico's 67 million inhabitants, and the country's large peasant population is only marginally better off now than in 1910. The unemployed and underemployed exceed 50 percent of the work force.

In politics, as in other fields, the contrasts between theory and practice in Mexico are vast. Under the republican form of government, contending parties are permitted, and six of them participated in the 1979 elections. In reality, however, Mexican politics is dominated by one amorphous party—the Revolutionary Institutional party (PRI)—which has provided every president since its creation in 1929.

During his six-year term, the president is an immensely powerful figure, but it is the party that reflects a wide spectrum of national opinion and eventually dictates the limits within which he can move. All significant support for and opposition to a president's policies come from within the ruling party. However, because the constitution forbids immediate reelection for members of the Senate and Chamber of Deputies, many talented politicians are attracted to the bureaucracy instead. Congress traditionally has been regarded as little more than a rubber stamp that ratifies executive decisions.

Although the PRI is technically structured around the three pillars of the peasant, worker, and popular movements, business interests have gained increasing control over the party and government in the past 20 years, giving weight to the saying that "in Mexico business is government and government is business." The economic boom that gave political strength to the business sector also spawned a host of conservative politicians.

The Roman Catholic Church has carried little political weight in Mexico, unlike most Latin American countries, since the revolution, although most people are nominally Catholic and there was a tremendous outburst of enthusiasm when Pope John Paul II visited the country in 1979. The constitution defends religious freedom, and in practice there is considerable tolerance of different creeds.

Mexico's economy, which had been growing at a remarkable average of 6.5 percent annually for the past 20 years, reversed that trend beginning in 1973 with an accelerating inflation rate. In an effort to stimulate exports, investments, and job creation, the government devalued the peso in 1976 for the first time in 22 years. The extremely high unemployment rate also increased the number of Mexicans crossing the border to the U.S. illegally to search for work.

Despite a fundamental agrarian reform following the revolution, which gave most peasants their own small plots of land and established a system of farm cooperatives, the shortage of irrigation, credit, and marketing facilities has kept most peasants living at subsistence level.

Mexico's considerable social and economic problems are made more acute by the country's population growth rate, presently close to 3 percent per year. Improved health facilities have brought down the death rate dramatically since World War II, but successive governments have strongly opposed an official family planning program.

In foreign policy, Mexico has long followed a policy of nonintervention, which led it to maintain diplomatic relations with Cuba when all other members of the Organization of American States broke their ties in 1964.

Because of proximity and close economic ties, the United States has considerable influence in Mexican politics. This reality sometimes leads Mexico to take strongly nationalist stands, although differences between the countries are usually settled amicably.

Mexico has been in the oil business since the beginning of the century when foreign companies began to produce "black gold" there. By 1918 Mexico was second only to the United States in output. After the government nationalized the petroleum industry in 1938, production declined, then recovered slowly. In 1972, before new discoveries of oil in the Reforma area of Chiapas and Tabasco, Mexico's known petroleum reserves were put at 2.5 billion barrels. Since then, with new findings of oil and natural gas in the Gulf and Pacific coastal regions and offshore in the Gulf of Campeche, proven reserves have grown by leaps and bounds. In 1981 they were put at nearly 70 billion barrels. Moreover, potential reserves were estimated at as much as 250 billion barrels, more than those of Saudi Arabia.

By reason of its oil wealth and large labor pool, Mexico was being acclaimed by economists at the outset of the 1980s as one of a handful of less-developed countries likely to gain rapidly in economic power and worldwide political influence.

HISTORY: Before the Spanish conquest of Mexico in 1519, Indian civilizations had flourished there for centuries, with that of the Mayas dating as far back as about 1500 B.C. With the conquest of the Aztecs by Hernán Cortéz, Indian culture was modified and the Indians themselves reduced to peonage on the land and in the mines. Corruption in the Spanish administration helped fan growing discontent among the Creoles, Mexican-born descendants of the Spaniards, leaving the country ripe for the revolutionary ideals spread by the French Revolution

1810: Miguel Hidalgo y Costilla, a Creole priest, begins the fight for independence; armies spring up under various leaders

1821: Mexico is granted independence; anarchy, corruption, and political rivalry are rife

1836-45: Texas, under domination of U.S. settlers, secedes from Mexico and declares its independence

1846-48: Annexation brings on Mexican War with the United States; Mexico is defeated, signs Treaty of Guadalupe Hidalgo ceding vast block of territory to the United States

1857-61: Benito Juárez, reform-minded minister of justice and later president, introduces liberal constitution transferring power from Creoles to mestizos and secularizing church lands; conservative opposition leads to War of the Reform (1858-61), which ends in victory for liberals

1864-67: France establishes puppet empire under Austrian-born Emperor Maximilian; Juárez leads popular resistance; empire collapses

1876-1909: Porfirio Díaz leads successful revolt and establishes ruthless dictatorship; he reforms Mexico's finances, but despite nation's growing prosperity vast numbers of people are reduced to virtual slavery when their communal lands are apportioned to large estate owners; almost three-quarters of Mexico's mineral resources become by purchase the property of foreign interests

1910-17: Francisco I. Madero organizes rebellion and forces Díaz to resign; Mexico is thrown into ferment of revolt culminating in rise of leaders such as Venustiano Carranza, Francisco (Pancho) Villa, and Emiliano Zapata. Villa breaks with Carranza, who has U.S. support, and Villa's irregulars raid New Mexico (1916); U.S. Gen. John J. Pershing leads punitive expedition into Mexico in pursuit of Villa. Carranza frames liberal constitution of 1917 nationalizing mineral resources and restoring lands to Indians

1934-40: President Lázaro Cárdenas undertakes extensive land reform and expropriates foreign-owned companies
1968: Army and police clash with students protesting alleged government repression and violation of constitutional rights
1970: Luis Echeverría Alvarez is elected president
1973: Mexican terrorists kidnap diplomatically and politically prominent people and ransom them for the release of political prisoners and for money to support their cause
1974: Mexico signs agreement for commercial co-operation with European Community, the first Latin American nation to do so
1976: José López Portillo is elected president
1977: President López Portillo visits U.S., stressing Mexico's independent stance, yet seeking cooperation. U.S. and Mexico sign first formal trade agreement since 1942
1978: Government legalizes Communist party for first time in 40 years. Government continues campaign of spraying marijuana fields with toxic chemical known as "paraquat." President López Portillo, visiting Japan, makes arrangements to sell oil there and concludes agreements by which Japanese banks will finance oil-related projects
1979: Pope John Paul II comes to Mexico to open third meeting of Latin American Episcopal Conference in Puebla. Government announces a plan to spur productivity and overcome bottlenecks in transportation of goods. On June 3, a flaming gusher erupts at offshore Ixtoc I well, creating oil slick in Gulf of Mexico which fouls fishing grounds and beaches as far north as Texas. In July 1 congressional elections, PRI wins 296 of 300 seats in Chamber of Deputies; 100 new seats are apportioned among minority parties. Agreement is reached to sell natural gas to U.S. at price above U.S. domestic price. Crude oil output reaches 1.9 billion barrels a day of which U.S. buys about 70%
1980: Government introduces a 10% value added tax (VAT) to increase revenues. Mexican ban on fishing within 200 miles of coast by American boats leads to "tuna war." López Portillo visits France, West Germany, Sweden and Canada to negotiate oil deals, joint investments in Mexican enterprises and exchange of scientific and technical knowledge. Natural gas begins to flow into U.S. at an initial rate of 300,000 cu. ft. per day. Ixtoc I well is at last fully capped after worst spill in history. Mexico and Venezuela reach accord on plan to meet oil needs of Caribbean and Central American countries. Severe drought forces Mexico to import 9 million metric tons of food. Current-account payments deficit reaches $6.6 billion, highest in nation's history. Inflation rate climbs to 30%
1981: Mexico moves to modernize its armed forces, especially in the air, in a bid to strengthen its power in the Caribbean basin. Although disapproving of repression, López Portillo backs Sandinist regime in Nicaragua and stays neutral toward government in Guatemala; however, he criticizes U.S. support for El Salvador's civilian-military junta. Significant quantities of natural gas are struck in the Gulf of California. A reduction of $4 per barrel in Mexico's price for oil on June 2, in the face of a world oversupply, provokes a political storm which leads to resignation of the head of Petróleos Mexicanos; there is a price hike of $2 July 1. Investment in Mexico by foreign companies, attracted by oil boom, increases. López Portillo goes to Washington in June to discuss critical issues with Ronald Reagan; the two presidents establish warm rapport despite some conflicting views

MONACO

Area: 0.708 sq. mi. (453 acres) **Population:** 25,000 (1978 est.)
Official Name: Principality of Monaco **Capital:** Monaco **Nationality:** Monacan or Monégasque **Languages:** French is the official language; the principal spoken languages are French, Monégasque, English and Italian **Religion:** 95% Roman Catholic, the official religion **Flag:** Red over white horizontal stripes **Anthem:** Monacan Hymn, beginning "Principality of Monaco, my fatherland" **Currency:** French franc (5.2 per U.S. $1)

Location: A coastal enclave within the Alpes-Maritimes department of southeastern France, bordering the Mediterranean Sea **Features:** The principality consists of 3 main areas: La Condamine, the business district around the port; Monte Carlo, the site of the famous casino, which is at a higher elevation; and Monaco, the capital, known also as the Rock because of its situation on a high promontory extending into the sea **Chief Rivers:** There are no rivers

Head of State: Prince Rainier III, born 1923, succeeded to the throne in 1949 **Head of Government:** Minister of State André Saint-Mleux (by law a French citizen), appointed 1972. He is assisted by a 3-man Council of Government **Effective Date of Present Constitution:** 1911, revised December 1962 **Legislative Body:** National Council (unicameral), consisting of 18 members elected for 5 years **Local Government:** 1 commune (with 4 quarters), under a mayor and a 15-member elected council

Ethnic Composition: The native Monacans are a minority (19%); 58% are French, and 17% Italian **Population Distribution:** 100% urban

Largest Cities: (1968 census) La Condamine 11,438, Monte Carlo 9,948; (1972 est.) Monaco 1,685

Per Capita Income: N.A. **Gross National Product (GNP):** N.A. **Economic Statistics:** About 55% of the income is derived from tourism, 30% from local industry, and 4% from the casino. The substantial part of the tourist revenue is derived from the government controlled Société Anonyme des Bains de Mer, which operates the gambling casino at Monte Carlo as well as hotels and motion picture theaters. Many foreign companies have established their headquarters in Monaco because of the low taxation **Minerals and Mining:** There are no minerals **Labor Force:** Most of the working population is employed by SBM; and some are employed by the small handicraft industry and by service establishments **Foreign Trade:** N.A. **Principal Trade Partner:** France

Vital Statistics: Birthrate 7.5 per 1,000 of pop. (1977); death rate, 10.6 **Life Expectancy:** 75 years **Health Statistics:** 75 inhabitants per hospital bed; 500 per physician (1976) **Infant Mortality:** 9.3 per 1,000 births (1970) **Illiteracy:** Negligible **Primary and Secondary School Enrollment:** 4,227 (1973) **Enrollment in Higher Education:** N.A. **GNP Expended on Education:** N.A.

Transportation: City streets **Motor Vehicles:** N.A. **Passenger Cars:** N.A. **Railway Mileage:** 0.6 **Port:** La Condamine **Major Airlines:** None **Communications:** Both government and privately owned **Radio Transmitters:** 6 **Receivers:** 7,500 (1976) **Television Transmitters:** 3 **Receivers:** 16,000 (1976) **Telephones:** 24,000 (1976) **Newspapers:** The Journal de Monaco, an official weekly, is the only local newspaper

Weights and Measures: Metric system **Travel Requirements:** Passport, no visa for 3 months **International Dialing Code:** 33

Monaco has been a principality of three towns covering an area about half the size of New York's Central Park, but Monaco is growing and expanding into the sea. A land-filling program added more than 20 percent to Monaco's area, to a total of 453 acres, or about 0.7 square miles.

Still, the microscopic principality is a state, the second smallest independent state in the world, after the Vatican City. Crammed into its small size are Riviera weather, scenery to match, the gambling paradise of Monte Carlo's casino, a reigning Prince Rainier with a movie-queen wife (Grace Kelly), the world-famous Oceanographic Museum (under the direction of France's Jacques Cousteau), and the daily changing of the Caribinier Guard at Palace Square.

Of course, as a long-time vacation resort, Monaco is filled with noted hotels. To keep pace with modernization of the principality, existing hotels are being modernized and new ones built, all with government help.

Monaco has a customs union and interchangeable currency with France, whose consent, by a treaty of 1918, is required for accession to the throne of the principality. The birth of Princess Grace's son in 1958 assured a male ruler to follow Prince Rainier.

Without this royal line, Monaco would come under French protection, making the Monégasques, now free of income taxes, subject to French levies. Tax freedom for Monaco-based companies was curtailed by a 1963 fiscal convention with France, under which concerns in Monaco doing more than 25 percent of their business elsewhere must pay taxes. The convention also applies French income taxes to French citizens who moved to Monaco after mid-October 1957.

HISTORY: Monaco was occupied by the Phoenicians from the 10th to the 5th century B.C. and then by the Greeks. During the early Christian era it was dominated by Rome until occupied by the barbarians and Saracens. In 1191, the Genoese took possession of Monaco; the Grimaldi family took control in 1297. The male line died out in 1731, but the French Goyon-Matignon family, which succeeded by marriage, assumed the name Grimaldi, still used by the ruling prince
1793: Monaco is annexed to France

1815: Monaco is placed under the protection of the Kingdom of Sardinia

1861: Monaco becomes a French protectorate

1918: Principality signs treaty with France, stipulating that succession to the throne of Monaco must be French approved

1949: Prince Rainier III succeeds his father, Prince Louis II, as ruler

1956: Prince Rainier marries American movie star, Grace Kelly

1963: "Tax war" with France ends in signing of new fiscal convention under which Monégasques and others remain free of direct taxation, but French citizens who had taken up residence in Monaco after October 13, 1957, have to pay income taxes, and companies doing more than a quarter of their business outside Monaco are made subject to a levy

1967: Prince Rainier wrests control of Société des Bains de Mer (SBM) from Greek shipping magnate Aristotle Onassis, principal stockholder and director of the company, which through its control of the Monte Carlo casino and the principality's hotels, was accused of impeding Monaco's tourist development

1978: Princess Caroline, daughter of Prince Rainier and Princess Grace, marries Philippe Junot, French investment banker. They divorce in 1980

MONGOLIA

Area: 606,163 sq. mi. **Population:** 1,594,800 (1979 census)
Official Name: Mongolian People's Republic **Capital:** Ulaanbaatar **Nationality:** Mongol **Languages:** Khalkha Mongolian, one of the large dialect groups of the Mongolian branch of the Altaic language family, is the official and dominant spoken language (90%). About 7% of the population speak Turkic languages **Religion:** Lamaistic Buddhism is the predominant religion (95%), but religious activity is discouraged by the Communist regime; Moslem 4% **Flag:** Vertical stripes of red, blue, and red with a yellow star and traditional symbols on the left **Anthem:** Our Free Revolutionary Land **Currency:** Tughrik (3.05 per U.S. $1)

Location: North Central Asia. Landlocked Mongolia is bordered on the north by the USSR, and on the east, south, and west by China **Features:** The country is essentially a huge steppe plateau with an average elevation of 4,000 feet. It is fringed by forested mountains in the north, while the south includes much of the Gobi Desert **Chief Rivers:** Selenge, Kerulen, Orhon, Dzavhan

Political Leader, Head of State and of Government: Yumjaagiyn Tsedenbal, born 1916; first secretary of the Mongolian People's Revolutionary (Communist) party since 1958; chairman of the presidium of the Hural since June 1974. He is assisted by Jambyn Batmonh, chairman of the Council of Ministers since 1974 **Effective Date of Present Constitution:** July 1960 **Legislative Body:** People's Great Hural (unicameral), 354 members elected for a 4-year term by universal suffrage; actual power lies with the Politburo of the Party's Central Committee **Local Government:** 18 provinces and 2 independent cities

Ethnic Composition: Khalkha Mongols make up about 76% of the population, Oirat Mongols and Buryat Mongols 13%, and Kazakhs, a Turkic-speaking people about 2%. Russians, Chinese, Khotan Turks, and Tuvinians form smaller minorities **Population Distribution:** 48% urban **Density:** 2.6 inhabitants per sq. mi.

Largest Cities: (1977 est.) Ulaanbaatar 345,000, Darhan 32,900; (1969 census) Choybalsan 20,500, Nalayn 14,100

Per Capita Income: $782 (1980) **Gross National Product (GNP):** $1.3 billion (1980) **Economic Statistics:** In 1976, 25% of GNP was derived from industry, related to the processing of livestock products, 21% was from animal husbandry (sheep, goats, camels, cattle, and horses) and some field crops. Coal, copper, and molybdenum are the chief mining industries **Minerals and Mining:** Coal, copper, fluorspar and molybdenum **Labor Force:** Most work in state farms and collectives. Agriculture employs 55%, industry 11%, and services 10% **Foreign Trade:** Exports are chiefly cattle, coal, copper, molybdenum, wool, raw hides, and butter and meat products. Imports are mainly consumer goods, machinery, equipment, and industrial raw materials **Principal Trade Partners:** USSR (85%), Czechoslovakia, East Germany, Hungary, Poland, Romania

Vital Statistics: Birthrate, 37.1 per 1,000 of pop. (1976); death rate, 9.9 **Life Expectancy:** 64 years **Health Statistics:** 94 inhabitants per hospital bed; 493 per physician (1977) **Infant Mortality:** N.A. **Illiteracy:** 20% **Primary and Secondary School Enrollment:** 341,500 (1976) **Enrollment in Higher Education:** 9,861 (1975) **GNP Expended on Education:** N.A.

Transportation: Surfaced roads total 992 mi. **Motor Vehicles:** 24,000 **Passenger Cars:** N.A. **Railway Mileage:** 940 **Ports:** None **Major Airlines:** Air Mongol flies internally and to the Soviet Union **Communications:** Government owned **Radio Transmitters:** 90 **Receivers:** 124,000 (1976) **Television Stations:** 1 **Receivers:** 33,800

(1976) **Telephones:** 38,000 (1976) **Newspapers:** 1 daily, 78 copies per 1,000 inhabitants (1975)
Weights and Measures: Metric system **Travel Requirements:** Passport, visa (obtainable in London, Paris, or Moscow)

One of the most thinly populated countries in the world, Mongolia is three times as large as France, but most of its territory is desert and semiarid rangeland. Mongolia's importance in international politics is less a matter of its size than of its position: wedged directly between Communist China and the Soviet Union, and long a cause for friction between them.

All of Mongolia was considered part of China for centuries. A Mongol movement to gain independence at the turn of the century, supported by the tsarist Russian government, resulted in "autonomy" for Outer Mongolia. However, in 1919, after the tsarist government itself was overthrown by the 1917 revolution, the Chinese sent troops into Mongolia and canceled its autonomy. The Chinese troops were expelled in the early 1920s by White Russian forces, which in turn were defeated by the Soviet Red Army. Outer Mongolia was then established as the second socialist state in the world and the first Soviet satellite.

Lavish Soviet aid has enabled Mongolia to make impressive economic advances. The economy still relies heavily on its livestock base—the country's most important resource—but collective farms for stockbreeding have been established and there are a few nomadic herdsmen left. Industrial production has increased sharply.

The help given by the Soviet Union has not gone unnoticed in China. In a 1973 speech before the UN General Assembly, Chinese Deputy Foreign Minister Chiao Kuan-hua challenged the Soviet Union to remove its troops from Mongolia. China's problem is that there are more Mongols in China—in Inner Mongolia—than there are in the Mongolian Republic, and fears that Mongol nationalism might result in efforts to detach further segments of Chinese territory are apparently real. Possibly to guard against a Mongol nationalist movement in China, Peking in 1970 assigned large segments of Inner Mongolia to neighboring provinces, since rescinded.

In 1968 and 1969 there were small flare-ups along the 2,500-mile Chinese/Mongolian border, and the Mongols charged that the Chinese had sought to subvert their government and install a pro-Peking regime.

A nation of pivotal importance, Mongolia seems to have no alternative but to try to maneuver between Moscow and Peking while striving to maintain its independence.

HISTORY: The Mongols, loosely organized nomadic tribes living in Mongolia, China, and Siberia, were united in the 13th century under the leadership of Genghis Khan, who established a far-flung Eurasian empire. After his death, the empire was divided and eventually disintegrated, and a cleavage developed between the southern, or inner, Mongols, ruled by the Chinese and the northern, or outer, Mongols. In 1691 the northern Mongols accepted Chinese authority and remained under their rule until the 20th century

1911: Mongol princes proclaim Outer Mongolia an independent monarchy following the overthrow of China's Manchu dynasty; the throne is given to Bogdo Gegen, the Living Buddha of Urga

1915: Outer Mongolia signs treaty with republican China and tsarist Russia accepting autonomous status under Chinese authority; Russia gains control over Mongolia's foreign affairs

1919-21: Attempts by China to reassert sovereignty over Outer Mongolia following the Russian Revolution are defeated; Russian forces expel Chinese, and Outer Mongolia again proclaims its independence

1924: Mongolian People's Republic is proclaimed following the death of the Living Buddha; Communist rule is inaugurated with Soviet help

1950: Communist China and USSR sign treaty guaranteeing Mongolia's independence

1962: Mongolia and Communist China sign treaty fixing their 2,500-mile border. Premier Tsedenbal backs Soviet policy on peaceful coexistence, challenged by Peking

1963: Mongolia establishes diplomatic relations with Britain in the first such pact with a Western power. Mongolia asks Communist China to withdraw laborers sent by Peking to work on Mongolian construction projects

1964: Pro-Peking sympathizers are purged from Mongolian Communist party

1966-67: Relations between Mongolia and Communist China become strained. Soviet troops are stationed on Mongolia border

1969: Soviet and Communist Chinese troops clash at the Ussuri River, and tension rises on the Chinese-Mongolian frontier. Yumjaagiyn Tsedenbal reelected premier

1970: Soviet-Mongolian five-year economic plan drafted. Border troubles with Communist China continue

1976: Tsendenbal reelected first secretary for the fifth time

1978: The government introduces restrictions to stop the flow of rural people to the cities

1981: Severe two-year drought eases; Soviet aid mitigates effect of heavy livestock losses. Mongolian astronaut is member of two-man team in Soviet space launch

MOROCCO

Area: 172,413 sq. mi. **Population:** 20,242,000 (1980 est.)

Official Name: Kingdom of Morocco **Capital:** Rabat **Nationality:** Moroccan **Languages:** Arabic, the official language, is spoken by about 65%; Berber dialects are spoken by about 35%. French is also widely used **Religion:** The majority of Moroccans are Sunni Moslems and Islam is the state religion; there are small minorities of Christians and Jews **Flag:** A red field with a green 5-pointed star in the center **Anthem:** National Anthem (no words) **Currency:** Moroccan dirham (5 per U.S. $1)

Location: Northwest Africa. Morocco is bordered on the north by the Mediterranean Sea, on the east by Algeria, on the south, with the contested Western Sahara area interposed, by Mauritania, and on the west by the Atlantic Ocean **Features:** The center is occupied by the dry, rocky Atlas Mountains, which slope downward to narrow fertile coastal plains along the Mediterranean and the Atlantic. The south is occupied by the Sahara **Chief Rivers:** Oum-er-Rbia, Dra, Moulouya, Sous, Sebou

Head of State: King Hassan II, born 1929, ascended the throne 1961 **Head of Government:** Prime Minister Maati Bouabid, appointed March 1979 **Effective Date of Present Constitution:** March 1972 **Legislative Body:** Parliament (unicameral Chamber of Representatives), with 264 members elected for 4 years **Local Government:** 31 provinces and 2 urban prefectures, headed by governors

Ethnic Composition: The majority of Moroccans are of Arab descent; about 35% are of Berber origin **Population Distribution:** 38% urban **Density:** 117 inhabitants per sq. mi.

Largest Cities: (1973 est.—Metropolitan Areas) Casablanca 1,753,400, Rabat 596,600, Marrakech 436,300, Fez 426,000, Meknès 403,000, Oujda 394,400, Kénitra 341,600, Tetuan 308,700, Safi 214,600, Tangier 208,000, Agadir 189,000

Per Capita Income: $605 (1980) **Gross National Product (GNP):** $12.7 billion (1980) **Economic Statistics:** 22% of the GNP is derived from agriculture (wheat, barley, fruits, corn, sugar, livestock), forestry and fishing; 21% from commerce; 16% from transportation and services; 12% from industry (food processing and canning, sugar refining, milling, tobacco production); and 4% from mining **Minerals and Mining:** Leading minerals are phosphates, iron ore, coal, manganese, fluorite, cobalt, lead, zinc, copper **Labor Force:** 4.5 million in 1977, with 51% in agriculture, 20% in industry, and 29% in services **Foreign Trade:** Exports, chiefly vegetables, citrus fruit, phosphates, wine, and canned fish, totaled $1.9 billion in 1979. Imports, mainly wheat, sugar, fuel, industrial machinery and equipment, cotton and synthetic textile yarn, iron and steel products, are estimated at $3.7 billion **Principal Trade Partners:** EC countries, United States, USSR, Spain

Vital Statistics: Birthrate, 46.2 per 1,000 of pop. (1975); death rate, 15.7 **Life Expectancy:** 54 years **Health Statistics:** 739 inhabitants per hospital bed; 11,143 per physician (1976) **Infant Mortality:** 117 per 1,000 births **Illiteracy:** 79% **Primary and Secondary School Enrollment:** 2,196,800 (1976) **Enrollment in Higher Education:** 45,322 (1975) **GNP Expended on Education:** 6% (1976)

Transportation: Paved roads total 15,300 mi. **Motor Vehicles:** 493,100 (1976) **Passenger Cars:** 347,400 **Railway Mileage:** 1,105 **Ports:** Casablanca, Safi, Kénitra, Mohammedia, Agadir, Essaouira **Major Airlines:** Royal Air Maroc operates both domestically and internationally **Communications:** Government controlled **Radio Transmitters:** 33 **Receivers:** 1,500,000 (1976) **Television Transmitters:** 27 **Receivers:** 522,000 (1976) **Telephones:** 204,000 (1976) **Newspapers:** 9 dailies; 21 copies per 1,000 inhabitants (1975)

Weights and Measures: Metric system **Travel Requirements:** Passport, no visa for 3 months

Geographically, Morocco is the westernmost Arab country, the only one with a border on the Atlantic coast of North Africa. It stands almost as close to the United States as to the eastern end of the Arab world, and at one point—the Strait of Gibraltar—it is literally within sight of Europe.

Politically, too, Morocco shows Western tendencies. Although nominally a member of the Arab League, it remains outside the main thrust of Arab politics, commerce, and culture. In recent years, it has made great efforts to cultivate the friendship of the United States and Western Europe, with which it seems to have closer interests than with the militant Arab countries to its east.

Since independence from France in 1956, Morocco has been a monarchy with a liberal-sounding constitution, but King Hassan II has been as absolute as any ruler in the world.

Dissolving the National Assembly in 1965, the king instituted a "state of exception" that gave him virtually unlimited power. In 1970, by national referendum, a new constitution provided a modified form of parliamentary government; the 1972 constitution further limited the king's powers to challenge legislative decisions. He retains the power to declare a state of emergency.

The nation's chief problems are its rapidly expanding population—the growth rate is three percent a year—and the inability of its economy to keep pace. Since independence, investment has been mostly in agriculture, dams, and irrigation projects.

Although there has been some economic progress, considerably more is still needed. It is estimated that 40 percent of the youth between 20 and 30 are unemployed. Unemployment has forced workers to emigrate to western Europe to find jobs. The money they have returned to their families in Morocco has provided a valuable addition to the Moroccan balance of payments. Tourism has increased greatly in recent years.

A Marxist party exists in the country, but most Moroccan intellectuals, like their Algerian neighbors, have their own ideas about socialism and are not particularly attracted by either the Soviet or Chinese brand. The main support for the king—who is also the country's religious leader—comes from the rural areas.

By Arab-world standards, Morocco has a large middle class, imbued with both Arab and French culture, whose high standard of living coexists with the feudal rural society. In addition, it has the largest remaining French community—numbering some 100,000—in North Africa. The coexistence of the Arab and French cultures, however, adds to the frustration of many young intellectuals, who are increasingly demanding the Arabization of their country.

In March 1973 King Hassan reacted to steadily mounting pressures for an economic shake-up by decreeing the nationalization of farmlands in foreign hands and the elimination of foreign ownership of businesses.

In 1974 opposition to Spain's plans to grant self-rule to the Spanish Sahara, which Morocco claimed, united all Moroccan political elements behind the monarchy for the first time since the early 1960s. By November 1975 Spain agreed to partition Spanish Sahara. Despite Algeria's opposition to the partition, the northern two-thirds, including rich phosphate deposits at Bu Craa, went to Morocco and the southern third to Mauritania, and in December Moroccan officials proclaimed the annexation of Western Sahara as Moroccan troops marched into its capital.

Because Morocco did not recognize the proclamation of the *Polisario Front*, the Saharan liberation movement, and Algeria did, Morocco cut its ties with Algeria. The *Polisario* guerrillas observed a tacit cease-fire with Mauritania, which in 1979 gave up its claim to the southern portion of Western Sahara, which Morocco then occupied. In June 1981, King Hassan offered to hold a "controlled referendum" in the Western Sahara. Pending a solution of the dispute, U.S. military aid to Morocco was made conditional in 1980. In March 1981, however, the new administration of President Ronald Reagan announced that the U.S. would sell army tanks to Morocco without any conditions attached.

In 1979, Ahmed Osman resigned as premier, and King Hassan appointed Maati Bouabid, a former labor leader, to succeed him. In May 1981, Bouabid raised prices for basic foodstuffs to improve the nation's balance of payments. Ensuing riots resulted in the death of 100 protesters.

HISTORY: In ancient times, Morocco was part of the empire of Carthage. Under the Romans it was formed into the province of Mauritania and later experienced successive invasions until conquered by the Arabs c. A.D. 683. Morocco became an independent kingdom in 788, but by the 10th century had broken up into several tribal states. The country was ultimately united under the Almoravids, a Berber Moslem dynasty that established a kingdom stretching from Senegal to Spain

15th cent.: Portugal and Spain capture all Moroccan ports

17th cent.: Morocco recaptures many European strongholds

1906: Algeciras Conference grants France special privileges in Morocco

1912: Morocco becomes a protectorate; under a French-Spanish agreement the country is divided administratively into French Morocco, Spanish Morocco, and a Southern Protectorate of Morocco, administered as part of the Spanish Sahara, and the international zone of Tangier

1953: Faced with growing movement for independence, French depose Sultan Sidi Mohammed ben Youssef and exile him to Madagascar

1955: French permit sultan to return

1956-57: Morocco gains freedom in 1956; Tangier is restored. In 1957 Sidi Mohammed ben Youssef becomes King Mohammed V

1961-62: King Mohammed dies and is succeeded by his son, Hassan II. In 1962 a draft constitution presented by Hassan is approved by referendum

1965: Hassan declares state of emergency and assumes executive and legislative power

1970: New constitution is adopted ending king's absolutist rule

1971: Hassan survives attempted coup by rebellious army officers and cadets; king charges Libya with inciting the rebellion

1972: Hassan survives second attempted coup within 13 months. Defense Minister Oufkir, who had exercised wide civil and military powers after the 1971 attempt, found dead after leading counterattack on rebels. He is charged by Hassan with organizing the attempted takeover

1974: Massive deposit of oil shale discovered in Middle Atlas Mountains. King Hassan presses Spain to return Spanish Sahara territory to Morocco

1975: Some 200,000 unarmed Moroccans who moved over the border in the "Green March" into Spanish Sahara "to regain the Sahara peacefully," are called back by Hassan

1976: Morocco and Mauritania divide the disputed Western Sahara. Relations are severed with Algeria because of Algeria's support of *Polisario* guerrillas

1977: Moroccan troops are sent to Zaire to help repel invaders of Shaba province

1978: Moroccan government sends troops to Shaba Province in Zaire following invasion there by Katangan rebels. Railway workers and civil servants strike for higher pay

1979: Maati Bouabid succeeds Ahmed Osman as premier. Morocco occupies southern third of Western Sahara, after Mauritania renounces claim to area

1981: U.S. resumes unconditional aid to Morocco after holding up tank shipments because of dispute over Western Sahara. Hassan offers to hold "controlled referendum" in area. About 100 are killed in food price rise protest riots

MOZAMBIQUE

Area: 303,769 sq. mi: **Population:** 12,130,000 (1980 census)

Official Name: People's Republic of Mozambique **Capital:** Maputo **Nationality:** Mozambican **Languages:** Bantu languages; Portuguese is the official language **Religion:** 66% animist, 22% Christian, 11% Moslem **Flag:** Four diagonal wedges of green, red, black and yellow separated by narrow white wedges, the national emblem of a white cogwheel with red star, white book, black silhouettes of hoe and rifle is at the upper left **Anthem:** N.A. **Currency:** Metical (35 per U.S. $1)

Location: On the east coast of Africa, bounded by the Mozambique Channel on the east, Swaziland on the south, South Africa on the south and west, Zimbabwe on the west, Zambia and Malawi on the northwest, and Tanzania on the north **Features:** Lowlands along the 1,700-mile-long coast rise to an 8,000-ft. plateau, with mountains to the north. The northern coastal plain is hot and humid, but is cooler to the south and inland **Chief Rivers:** Ruvuma, Lurio, Zambezi, Save, Limpopo

Head of State and of Government: President Samora Moisés Machel, born 1933, installed June 1975. He is head of the Frelimo party **Effective Date of Present Constitution:** 1975 **Legislative Body:** People's Assembly of 210 members **Local Government:** 10 provinces

Ethnic Composition: The people are mostly of Bantu stock, with a minority (perhaps 10,000) Europeans (mostly Portuguese) **Population Distribution:** 8% urban **Density:** 40 inhabitants per sq. mi.

Largest Cities: (1980 census) Maputo 755,300; (1970 census) Beira 46,293, Nampula 23,072, Quelimane 10,522

Per Capita Income: $200 (1979) **Gross National Product (GNP):** $2.4 billion (1979) **Economic Statistics:** In 1975 the service sector (including transportation and tourism) accounted for 30% of the GNP; agriculture, 40%; and industry 20% **Minerals and Mining:** Copper, coal, beryl, columbite, fluorite, bauxite and tantalite **Labor Force:** 600,000 wage earners, with 80% of the population in subsistence agriculture **Foreign Trade:** Exports, chiefly cashew nuts, cotton and cotton products, sugar, copra, sisal fiber, tea and vegetable oils, amounted to $284 million in 1978. Imports, chiefly machinery, transportation equipment, metals and metal products, petroleum and wheat, reached $597 million **Principal Trade Partners:** South Africa, Britain, Portugal, West Germany, United States

Vital Statistics: Birthrate, 43 per 1,000 of pop. (1975); death rate, 20 **Life Expectancy:** 43.5 years **Health Statistics:** 772 inhabitants per hospital bed; 16,392 per physician (1972) **Infant Mortality:** 92.5 per 1,000 births **Illiteracy:** 88% **Primary and Secondary School Enrollment:** 632,647 (1972) **Enrollment in Higher Education:** 906 (1976) **GNP Expended on Education:** 1.1% (1972)

Transportation: Paved roads total 2,686 mi. **Motor Vehicles:** 110,800 (1972) **Passenger Cars:** 89,300 **Railway Mileage:** 2,135 miles **Ports:** Maputo, Beira, Nacala, Pemba, Quelimane **Major Airlines:** LAM provides domestic and international service **Communications:** Government controlled **Radio Transmitters:** 49 **Licenses:** 225,000 (1976) **Television Transmitters:** None **Telephones:** 52,000 (1976) **Newspapers:** 5 dailies, 9 copies per 1,000 inhabitants (1975)

Weights and Measures: Metric system **Travel Requirements:** Apply to Permanent Mission of the People's Republic of Mozambique, New York 10017

Portuguese rule left an inheritance of poverty and disease for much of Mozambique's population. Forced labor was widespread, political rights and education limited. Ten years of pre-independence guerrilla war, the flight of skilled whites and the imposition of doctrinaire socialism have also taken their toll.

Nationalist forces aiming at independence began guerrilla warfare in 1964, starting in the north. The chief rebel movement was the Front for the Liberation of Mozambique (FRELIMO) which had been working for independence since 1962.

Clashes between the Portuguese army and insurgents increased in early 1974. In September after the military overthrew the home government in Portugal, FRELIMO and the Portuguese High Commissioner signed an agreement under which Mozambique would be ruled by a joint transitional government until full independence.

On June 25, 1975, Mozambique achieved full independence after 500 years of colonial rule, becoming the 45th African state to do so. Samora Moisés Machel, the first president, pledged to transform the country into the "first truly Marxist state in Africa." FRELIMO became the country's sole political party in the new state and the nucleus for the new People's Republic of Mozambique government. Since then the government has been establishing its authority and Marxist-oriented philosophy at all levels of society and planning a post-colonial economy. Among the goals of the FRELIMO program is the eradication of tribalism, regionalism, and racism.

At first Mozambique's future looked relatively bright in comparison to Portugal's other African territories, but most of the 220,000 whites fled, leaving the country almost without skilled and professional workers. All land was nationalized and food production declined by 75 percent in some areas while production of major cash crops was off by half. Many factories have been abandoned and the government now offers incentives for Portuguese managers to stay on. The major income remaining is foreign exchange earned by Mozambique miners in South Africa.

In March 1976 Machel closed the border with Rhodesia (now Zimbabwe) and increased its efforts to train black guerrillas and help them infiltrate the white-ruled nation. The border closing was costly as it shut off Mozambique's major source of food. With the end of the war and independence for Zimbabwe, the border was reopened in January 1980.

HISTORY: Bantu peoples entered Mozambique after 1000 A.D. from Central Africa. Arab traders touched on the coast prior to the coming of the Portuguese under Vasco da Gama in 1498. The Portuguese developed trading posts and a thriving slave trade during the following centuries. Mozambique's colonial boundaries were fixed by the end of the 19th century
1951: Portugal establishes Mozambique as an Overseas Province
1964: Independence forces begin guerrilla warfare
1974: FRELIMO (Mozambique Liberation Front) and Portugal agree to joint rule prior to independence
1975: Mozambique achieves independence
1976: Mozambique closes border with Rhodesia and declares a state of war. Intermittent border clashes occur
1977: Border clashes continue. Black refugees from Rhodesia fill camps in Mozambique
1978: Virtually all foreign and local banks are nationalized
1979: Government closing of 15 Catholic missions strains relations with the Church. National Resistance Movement, based in Zimbabwe-Rhodesia, commits acts of sabotage aimed at overthrow of Machel. Mozambique rejects Soviet request for naval base
1980: Though still committed to Marxism, Machel seeks economic aid from capitalist West; announces plan to encourage private enterprise and promises incentives for former white businessmen who return to Mozambique. New currency, the metical, replaces the escudo
1981: U.S. food aid is suspended after expulsion of American diplomats and arrest of other U.S. citizens accused of espionage

NAMIBIA

(See Territories and Dependencies section)

NAURU

Area: 7.7 sq. mi. **Population:** 7,100 (1978 est.)
Official Name: Republic of Nauru **Capital:** Yaren (district) **Nationality:** Nauruan **Languages:** Nauruan and English **Religion:** Christian, mainly Protestant **Flag:** A blue field halved by a horizontal gold bar, with a white star at the lower left **Anthem:** N.A. **Currency:** Australian dollar (0.87 per U.S. $1)
Location: Central Pacific, 0°30'S.,166°55'E. The island of Nauru lies just south of the equator, about 1,300 miles northeast of Australia **Features:** The island is completely surrounded by a coral reef. A narrow, fertile coastal strip lying between a sandy beach and coral cliffs is the most populated part of the island. The interior consists of a barren plateau containing extensive phosphate deposits, Nauru's major economic resource **Chief Rivers:** No rivers
Head of State and Government: President Hammer De Roburt, born 1922, took office in 1978 **Effective Date of Present Constitu-**

tion: 1968 **Legislative Body:** Parliament (unicameral Legislative Assembly), consisting of 18 members elected by universal suffrage for 3 years **Local Government:** The island is divided into 14 districts
Ethnic Composition: The Nauruans are believed to be a mixture of Polynesian, Micronesian, and Melanesian, with Polynesian predominating. Other Pacific Islanders number about 1,800, Chinese 1,100, and Europeans 500 **Population Distribution:** Virtually the entire population is concentrated in settlements along the coast **Density:** 922 inhabitants per sq. mi.
Per Capita Income: $21,400 (1977) **Gross National Product (GNP):** $155 million (1977) **Economic Statistics:** Nauru's economy is built around the phosphate industry, which enables the islanders to enjoy one of the highest per capita incomes in the world. Although some food products are grown on the island, the inhabitants are largely dependent on imports of food supplies and all manufactured goods **Labor Force:** Nauruans, as a rule, do not engage in manual labor, and the phosphate industry is largely dependent on outside labor. About 60% of Nauruans are employed in the civil service **Foreign Trade:** Exports, consisting entirely of phosphates, totaled $50 million in 1977. Imports, chiefly food, consumer goods, machinery and fuel, totaled $32 million **Principal Trade Partners:** Australia, New Zealand, Britain, Japan, South Korea
Vital Statistics: Birthrate, 19.8 per 1,000 of pop. (1976); death rate, 8.3 **Life Expectancy:** 53 years **Health Statistics:** 34 inhabitants per hospital bed; 700 per physician (1971) **Infant Mortality:** 19 per 1,000 births **Illiteracy:** Negligible **Primary and Secondary School Enrollment:** 1,973 (1975) **Enrollment in Higher Education:** 92 studying abroad (1975) **GNP Expended on Education:** 2.8% (1970)
Transportation: Paved roads total 13 mi. **Motor Vehicles:** Over 1,000 **Railway Mileage:** A three-mile railway links the phosphate workings with the coast **Ports:** None. Barges transport cargo to offshore ships **Major Airlines:** Air Nauru operates flights to Pacific and Asian cities **Communications:** Government owned **Radio Transmitters:** 1 **Receivers:** 3,600 (1976) **Television:** None **Telephones:** 1,500 **Newspapers:** 1 fortnightly
Weights and Measures: British standards are used **Travel Requirements:** Applications for permission to enter Nauru must be made in writing to the Secretary of Justice in Nauru or to the Nauruan representative in Melbourne, Australia

The barren central plateau of Nauru, the tiny Pacific island, which is the smallest independent republic in the world, consists of large phosphate deposits, the result of centuries of bird droppings, that provide Nauru with a good source of income: the phosphate, much prized as fertilizer, is the island's main natural resource and only export.

This unique export helps to give the people of Nauru one of the highest per capita incomes in the world, as well as shops filled with luxury goods, free medical care, good housing, good schools, no taxes, and jobs for all.

Only 12 miles in circumference and three-and-a-half-miles wide, Nauru was named Pleasant Island by the captain of a British whaling ship who discovered it in 1798. Early contacts with Europeans brought guns and disease, and a consequent ravaging of the population. The people of Nauru now are more concerned with depletion of the phosphate deposits. Totaling 45 million tons, the deposits are expected to be exhausted in the 1990s.

Intense debate over the nation's course once the phosphate has been depleted led to a rare period of political instability. In April 1978 President Dowiyogo, reelected the preceding November, resigned; his plan to raise a $22-million development loan overseas had been opposed by parliament. He was succeeded by Lagumot Harris, who himself resigned a month later after a money bill of his met a similar fate. Harris was succeeded by Hammer de Roburt, the man who led Nauru to independence in 1968.

HISTORY: Nauru, discovered by a British whaling team in 1798, was long known as Pleasant Island. In 1888 it was annexed by Germany and henceforth known by its native name. Phosphate was discovered on the island in the late 1890s and exploitation begun in 1901. With the outbreak of World War I, Australian forces occupied the island. After the war, Nauru was administered by Australia under a League of Nations mandate, which also named Britain and New Zealand as cotrustees

1942-45: Nauru is occupied by Japanese forces; 1,200 islanders are deported to Truk as forced labor

1947: Island is placed under United Nations Trusteeship, with Australia acting as administrator on behalf of the Australian, New Zealand, and British governments

1964: In anticipation of the exhaustion of Nauru's phosphate deposits, expected in about 30 years, Australia proposes that inhabitants be resettled on Curtis Island, off the Queensland coast; islanders reject proposal, choosing to remain on Nauru

1968: Nauru becomes independent republic; islanders reject proposals that Australia handle their defense and external affairs. Hammer De Roburt is elected president

1970: Nauru assumes management of its phosphate industry

1976: Bernard Dowiyogo is elected president

1977-78: Debate over nation's future leads to period of instability. President Dowiyogo resigns; Lagumot Harris succeeds him. Harris resigns; Hammer de Roburt succeeds Harris

---

NEPAL

Area: 54,663 sq. mi. **Population:** 13,713,000 (1979 est.)

Official Name: Kingdom of Nepal **Capital:** Kathmandu **Nationality:** Nepalese **Languages:** Nepali, the official language, is the first language of roughly 50% of the population and is spoken by another 30%; Tibeto-Burman languages (chiefly Newari), Indo-Aryan dialects, and English are also spoken **Religion:** Hinduism, the official religion, is the dominant faith (90%); Mahayana Buddhism is the dominant religion in the sparsely inhabited north, and both faiths are followed by many people of the central region **Flag:** Two red right-angled triangles bordered in blue at the hoist; the upper with a white moon crescent, the lower with a white sun **Anthem:** National Anthem, beginning "May glory crown our illustrious sovereign" **Currency:** Nepalese rupee (12 per U.S. $1)

Location: Central Asia. Landlocked Nepal is bordered on the north by China (Tibet), and on the east, south and west by India **Features:** The country is mountainous, with dense swampy jungles. Across the south lies the 20-mile-wide Terai, a region of plain and swamp. Most of the country, a band across the center, is broken by sharp mountain ranges and traversed by high, fertile valleys. Along the northern border lies the high Himalaya, with 8 of the world's 12 highest peaks, including Mount Everest, whose 29,028-ft. elevation is the highest in the world **Chief Rivers:** Kali, Karnali, Gandak, Kosi

Head of State: King Birendra Bir Bikram Shah Dev, born 1945, acceded to the throne January 1972 **Head of Government:** Prime Minister: Surya Bahadur Thapa, born 1928, appointed June 1979 **Effective Date of Present Constitution:** December 1962 **Legislative Body:** Parliament (unicameral National *Panchayat*), with 135 members, of which 112 are representatives from zonal assemblies and class groups, and 23 are nominees of the king. The king has absolute veto power over parliamentary bills **Local Government:** 14 zones, each headed by an appointed commissioner, and 75 districts, each with a district assembly and 11-member executive committee known as the district *panchayat*. The latter, in turn, form a zonal assembly

Ethnic Composition: The Nepalese are descendants of 3 major migrations from India and Tibet. In addition to the Brahmans and Chetris whose ancestors came from India, the numerous tribes, called castes, include the Gurungs and Magars in the west; Tamangs and Newars in the center; Bhotias in the north; Rais, Limbus, and Sherpas in the east; and Tharus in the south **Population Distribution:** 5% urban **Density:** 251 inhabitants per sq. mi.

Largest Cities: (1971 census) Kathmandu 150,402, Lalitpur 59,049, Biratnagar 45,100, Bhaktapur 40,112

Per Capita Income: $111 (1979) **Gross National Product (GNP):** $1.6 billion (1979) **Economic Statistics:** In 1973 about 65% of GNP was from agriculture (paddy rice, maize, wheat, millet, jute) and forestry; 12% from mining and manufacturing (jute, textiles, yarns, cigarettes, vegetable oil crushing); and 17.3% from trade and services **Minerals and Mining:** Coal is mined. There are unexploited deposits of iron ore, copper, mica, lead, zinc, cobalt, nickel, and talc **Labor Force:** 4,852,524 (1971), 94% of which is in agriculture and 2% in industry **Foreign Trade:** Exports, chiefly rice, jute and jute products, ghee, oilseeds, timber, and herbs, totaled $51 million in 1979. Imports, mainly textiles, foodstuffs, petroleum products, machinery and equipment, vehicles and parts, totaled $159 million **Principal Trade Partners:** India, Japan, United States

Vital Statistics: Birthrate, 42.9 per 1,000 of pop. (1975); death rate, 20.3 **Life Expectancy:** 40 years **Health Statistics:** 6,630 inhabitants per hospital bed; 36,450 per physician (1974) **Infant Mortality:** 152 per 1,000 births **Illiteracy:** 80% **Primary and Secondary School Enrollment:** 1,031,797 (1977) **Enrollment in Higher Education:** 23,504 **GNP Expended on Education:** 1.5% (1975)

Transportation: Paved roads total 1,088 mi. **Motor Vehicles:** 12,646 (1970) **Passenger Cars:** 7,281 **Railway Mileage:** 40 **Ports:** None **Major Airlines:** Royal Nepal Airlines operates domestic and international services **Communications:** Government owned **Radio Transmitters:** 5 **Receivers:** 150,000 (1976) **Television:** None **Telephones:** 9,162 (1974) **Newspapers:** 29 dailies (1975), 3 copies per 1,000 inhabitants (1974)

Weights and Measures: Metric system and local standards **Travel Requirements:** Passport, visa valid for 30-day stay, $5 fee, 1 photo

---

Beguiled by the slightly touristic, but not untrue, face that Nepal presents to the outside world, mountaineers, tourists, and hippies have flocked there and found what they sought: a peaceful Himalayan kingdom, backward but pleasant, a land of green valleys and towering mountains (including the world's highest, 29,028-ft. Mt. Everest, shared with Tibet), all presided over by the world's only Hindu king, thought by his people to be an incarnation of the god Vishnu.

The other side of Nepal's character is harsher, but no less true. Nepal is a primitive, divided, stratified society caught between two powerful and jealous neighbors, China and India, and unsettled by the pressures of modernization. With its history marked by bitter political feuding, Nepal is in a difficult position to shape the modernity its leaders want.

In recent years Nepal has halted Indian interference in its internal affairs and has established close relations with China.

Rising taxes, high prices, and shortages have contributed to recent unrest. In 1979, what began as student demands for academic changes turned into a broad call for parliamentary democracy joined by peasants, laborers, and the middle class. About 20 persons died in riots in several towns. In national elections in May 1980, voters settled the issue by casting 54% of their ballots for a streamlined version of the existing system of indirect representation, called *panchayat*, in which King Birenda retained virtually absolute power. Having failed to restore the system of political parties that existed before 1960, pro-democratic forces boycotted the 1981 elections.

HISTORY: Nepal, the world's only Hindu kingdom, has a long historical continuity, although little is known about the country before the 15th century. The modern kingdom of Nepal was established in the 18th century by the ruler of Gurkha, a small principality west of Kathmandu. His descendants introduced Hinduism as the state religion and established most of the present boundaries

1790-93: Gurkhas invade Tibet. A large Chinese army forces the Gurkhas to come to terms. Seeking assistance against the Chinese, the Gurkhas sign treaty with the British in India

1814-16: Series of frontier incidents leads to war between the British and Nepal. Nepal surrenders much of its territory and permits a British residency to be set up at Kathmandu

1846: Jung Bahadur Rana seizes the government and reduces the king to a figurehead

1951: An end is made to more than a century of rule by a succession of hereditary prime ministers from a noble family, the Ranas, during which the royal family played little part in governing. King Tribhuvana assumes power with Indian help, promises elections to a constituent assembly to formulate new constitution

1955: King Tribhuvana dies and is succeeded by Crown Prince Mahendra. Nepal joins UN

1959: King Mahendra declares Nepal a constitutional monarchy. In the country's first election, the Nepali Congress party wins an absolute majority

1960: King Mahendra dismisses the cabinet, dissolves parliament, bans political parties, and assumes powers of government; many political leaders are arrested

1962: New constitution is promulgated, introducing *panchayat* system of government from the village to the national level

1963: King Mahendra forms an advisory state council

1972: King Mahendra dies and is succeeded by his son, Crown Prince Birendra Bir Bikram Shah Dev

1974: Nepal and China sign trade pact

1975: King Birendra, who received part of his education at Harvard, is formally crowned. Prime Minister Nagendra Prasad Rijal is

replaced by Dr. Tulsi Giri. Heavily armed Khampa refugees from Tibet are driven from the Himalayan passes by Nepalese troops
1977: Prime Minister Tulsi Giri resigns; Kirti Nidhi Bista, who has held the post three times in eight years, succeeds him
1978: King Birendra slightly eases his stern control of Nepalese life
1979: Students, joined by other dissidents, stage violent demonstrations to demand that the monarchy be liberalized. B.P. Koirala, former prime minister who leads efforts for constitutional reform, is charged with sedition. Prime Minister Bista resigns; Surya Bahadur Thapa is appointed in his place
1980: Voters reject a parliamentary democracy and instead approve a modified version of partyless government, leaving King Birenda almost unlimited power. Earthquake kills thousands
1981: China's Premier Zhao Ziyang visits Nepal

THE NETHERLANDS

Area: 15,892 sq. mi. **Population:** 14,192,000 (1980 est.)
Official Name: Kingdom of the Netherlands **Capital:** Amsterdam, but the seat of government is at The Hague **Nationality:** Netherlands or Dutch **Languages:** Hollands, or Dutch, is the official and predominant language; Frisian is spoken in the northern province of Friesland **Religion:** About 40.4% Roman Catholic, 32.9% Protestant, and 23.6% no religion **Flag:** Red, white, and blue horizontal stripes **Anthem:** Wilhelmus van Nassouwen (William of Nassau) **Currency:** Guilder (florin) (2.5 per U.S. $1)
Location: Northwest Europe. The Netherlands is bounded on the west and north by the North Sea, on the east by West Germany, and on the south by Belgium **Features:** The country is low and flat except for some hills in the southeast. About one-third of the land area is below sea level, and more than one-fifth reclaimed from the sea and protected by dikes **Chief Rivers:** Maas, IJssel, Waal, Lek
Head of State: Queen Beatrix, born 1938, invested April 30, 1980 **Head of Government:** Premier Andries A.M. van Agt, born 1931, appointed 1977 **Effective Date of Present Constitution:** 1814; frequently revised **Legislative Body:** The States General (bicameral), consisting of the First Chamber, or upper house, and the Second Chamber, or lower house. The First Chamber consists of 75 members chosen by the 11 provincial legislatures for 6 years The Second Chamber has 150 members elected directly for 4 years **Local Government:** 11 provinces, with elected provincial executive councils and appointed commissioners, and the IJsselmeer polders
Ethnic Composition: 99% Dutch, 1% Indonesian and other **Population Distribution:** 77% urban **Density:** 893 inhabitants per sq. mi.
Largest Cities: (1977 est.) Amsterdam 733,593, Rotterdam 595,662, The Hague 467,997, Utrecht 243,001, Eindhoven 192,361, Haarlem 162,032, Groningen 161,181, Tilburg 150,449
Per Capita Income: $7,048 (1980) **Gross Domestic Product (GDP):** $99 billion (1980) **Economic Statistics:** About 42.3% of GDP comes from industry (capital and consumer goods, food processing, chemicals, textiles), mining, construction, and utilities; 17.8% from commerce, banking, and finance; 6.5% from agriculture; and the rest from other activities **Minerals and Mining:** Large reserves of natural gas are exploited along with some salt, and crude oil **Labor Force:** 4,800,000 (1978), of which 35% is employed in industry, 7% in agriculture, 58% in services **Foreign Trade:** Exports, mainly meats, flower bulbs, petroleum products, natural gas, chemicals, textiles, machinery, and electrical equipment, totaled $64 billion in 1979. Imports, chiefly grains, petroleum, chemicals, textiles, iron and steel products, machinery and electrical equipment, and motor vehicles, totaled $67 billion **Principal Trade Partners:** EC countries, United States, Saudi Arabia
Vital Statistics: Birthrate, 12.5 per 1,000 of pop. (1977); death rate, 7.9 **Life Expectancy:** 72 years **Health Statistics:** 99 inhabitants per hospital bed; 601 per physician (1976) **Infant Mortality:** 9.5 per 1,000 births **Illiteracy:** Negligible **Primary and Secondary School Enrollment:** 2,779,065 (1976) **Enrollment in Higher Education:** 288,026 (1975) **GNP Expended on Education:** 8.7% (1975)
Transportation: Surfaced roads total 53,470 mi. **Motor Vehicles:** 4,206,000 (1977) **Passenger Cars:** 3,851,000 **Railway Mileage:** 1,760 **Ports:** Rotterdam, Amsterdam, IJmuiden, Terneuzen, Vlissingen, Delfzijl **Major Airlines:** K.L.M. (Royal Dutch Airlines) operates domestic and international flights **Communications:** Government owned **Radio Transmitters:** 30 **Licenses:** 3,997,000 (1976) **Television Transmitters:** 21 **Licenses:** 3,774,000 (1976) **Telephones:** 5,412,000 (1976) **Newspapers:** 93 dailies, 311 copies per 1,000 inhabitants (1973)
Weights and Measures: Metric System **Travel Requirements:** Passport, no visa up to 90 days **International Dialing Code:** 31

The Netherlands is just that, as much of the country lies below sea level. To a large extent it is manmade and is still being made. In 1932 a barrier dam closed the North Sea mouth of the Zuyder Zee, creating a vast freshwater lake, the IJsselmeer, out of which the hard-working Dutch have been carving habitable tracts, which by 1980 had increased the Netherlands' arable land by a tenth. Spurred by a destructive storm in 1953, the country began to erect dams to create lakes and keep the sea out of southern estuaries.

This age-old battle against the depredations of the sea and the Rhine, Maas, and Scheldt rivers mirrors the centuries-old struggle of the Dutch against encroachment by man, from the conquest by Julius Caesar's legions in 55 B.C. to German occupation in World War II.

Aside from enlarging the country and bringing it freedom, the unity of purpose in the Netherlands' struggles has produced a people able to get along harmoniously and tolerant of other cultures, as shown in the integration of more than 300,000 nonwhite colonials from the former far-flung overseas empire. However the recent seizures of hostages by South Moluccan terrorists has led to a deterioration in relations between the Moluccans and the Dutch. The South Moluccans had emigrated to the Netherlands in the late 1940s when their islands became part of Indonesia.

Binding the loyalty of its citizens to the state is the four-centuries-old House of Orange, now headed by Queen Beatrix, who succeeded her mother, Juliana, when she abdicated on her 71st birthday, April 30, 1980. Though political parties are organized on religious and ideological principles, recent cabinets have been coalitions. A constitutional democracy, the Netherlands reflects rule by Burgundian kings five centuries ago, Dutch republicanism, and modern liberalism.

Ultimate power lies with parliament, which presides over jammed cities that blend charming old architecture with the new, and a countryside filled with canals, broad rivers, and tidy farms, few of which are larger than 50 acres. In fact, though the Netherlands is popularly believed to be an agricultural land, national income depends more on commerce and industry than on farming.

HISTORY: At the time of the conquest of the Lowland areas by Julius Caesar in 55 B.C., the region was settled by Celtic and Germanic tribes. The dominant tribes were the Saxons and Frisians. In the 3rd century A.D. the West Franks (Salic Franks) invaded the Low Countries and gradually conquered the region. Following the breakup of Charlemagne's empire in the 9th century, the Lowlands were parceled up into numerous duchies and counties. In the 16th century, the area passed to Charles V of the House of Hapsburg and then to his son, Philip II of Spain
1568-81: Dutch wage war of independence against Spain under leadership of William the Silent, Prince of Orange, who unites the seven northern provinces; Spanish garrisons are expelled and United Provinces declare their independence
17th cent.: Treaty of Westphalia (1648), ending the Thirty Years War, recognizes independence of United Provinces. Meanwhile, Dutch build vast overseas empire and by 1700 the Netherlands is the world's leading maritime and commercial power
18th cent.: Dutch power begins to decline after 1715. In 1794, French revolutionary forces invade Netherlands; the following year French set up the Batavian Republic
1815: Congress of Vienna establishes Kingdom of Netherlands composed of Belgium and Holland
1830: Belgium revolts and gains independence
1914-39: Netherlands pursues policy of neutrality
1940-45: During World War II German forces overrun the Netherlands and subject country to ruthless occupation
1948: Queen Wilhelmina abdicates and is succeeded by her daughter, Juliana
1949: Netherlands grants Indonesia independence after four years of bitter strife
1954: The colonies of Surinam and Netherlands Antilles are incorporated into the Kingdom of the Netherlands
1957: Netherlands joins Common Market (EC)

1962-63: Netherlands turns western New Guinea (West Irian) over to the United Nations, which places it under Indonesian jurisdiction pending a referendum

1975: Independence is granted to Surinam (now Suriname) after 300 years of Dutch rule

1976: South Moluccan terrorists, who in support of the independence of South Molucca from Indonesia had in December 1975 hijacked a train and laid siege to the Indonesian consulate, are convicted and sentenced

1977: Prime Minister den Uyl's Labor party captures a plurality in parliament in May elections. South Moluccan terrorists hold 100 children hostage in a school and 50 others hostage in a train in an effort to force the Dutch government to help them in their independence struggle. The siege is ended by a Dutch military team staging a raid in which six terrorists and two hostages are killed. Christian Democrat Andreas van Agt becomes prime minister of new center-right coalition government

1978: In Assen, South Moluccan terrorists seize hostages for fourth time since 1975, in attempt to force granting of various demands; the three captors kill one of the 72 hostages, though one is killed in crossfire; terrorists arrested

1979: Parliament rejects U.S. proposal to deploy medium-range nuclear missiles in Europe

1980: Queen Juliana, 71, abdicates throne in favor of her daughter, Beatrix, 42

1981: Prime Minister van Agt's center-right coalition loses its majority by just one seat in parliamentary elections

NEW ZEALAND

Area: 103,736 sq. mi. **Population:** 3,164,000 (1980 est.)

Official Name: New Zealand **Capital:** Wellington **Nationality:** New Zealand **Languages:** English is the official and predominant language; Maori, a Malayo-Polynesian language, is also spoken, but for the Maoris English is the first language **Religion:** 34% Anglican, 22% Presbyterian, 15% Roman Catholic, 7% Methodist, 22% other denominations or non-affiliated **Flag:** A blue field, with the British Union Jack in the upper left and four stars of the Southern Cross in red edged in white on the right **Anthem:** God Save the Queen; National Song: God Defend New Zealand **Currency:** New Zealand dollar (1.1 per U.S. $1)

Location: South Pacific, about 1,200 miles southeast of Australia. New Zealand consists of two principal islands, North Island and South Island, separated by Cook Strait; Stewart Island lies off the southern tip of South Island; the Chatham Islands are about 400 miles east of South Island **Features:** North Island contains 72% of the country's population. The northern part of the island has rolling hills and low mountains; the southern half rises from fertile coastal plains to volcanic mountain peaks in the center. South Island is narrow and contains 28% of the population. The Southern Alps extend the entire length of the island and include New Zealand's highest peak, Mount Cook, with an elevation of 12,349 feet. Stewart Island is covered with rugged, forested peaks that rise more than 3,000 feet **Chief Rivers:** Waikato, Clutha, Taieri, Clarence, Oreti, Rangitikei, Wanganui, Waitaki, Mataura

Head of State: Queen Elizabeth II, represented by a governor-general, Sir David Beattie, appointed Oct. 1980 **Head of Government:** Prime Minister Robert D. Muldoon, born 1921, reelected November 1978 **Effective Date of Present Constitution:** No written constitution **Legislative Body:** Parliament (unicameral House of Representatives), with 92 members elected by universal suffrage for 3 years **Local Government:** 239 local authority areas

Ethnic Composition: About 92% of the population is of European descent; Maoris number 8% **Population Distribution:** 77.4% urban **Density:** 31 inhabitants per sq. mi.

Largest Cities (Urban Areas): (1976 census) Auckland 742,786, Wellington 327,414, Christchurch 295,296, Dunedin 113,222, Lower Hutt Valley 97,194, Hamilton 94,777, Palmerston North 63,873

Per Capita Income: $6,227 (1980) **Gross Domestic Product (GDP):** $19.5 billion (1980) **Economic Statistics:** Agriculture, forestry and fishing account for 14.2% of the GDP, industry and mining 34.8%, and services 51.2%. The chief industries are food processing (meat and dairy products), transport equipment, textiles, cement, oil refining, and fertilizers. Wool, meat, and dairy products form the bulk of agricultural output **Minerals and Mining:** Iron sands, natural gas, coal, gold, and industrial minerals such as aggregate, limestone, pumice, serpentine, clays, and bentonite **Labor Force:** 1,316,000, of which 33% is engaged in industry and 13% in agriculture **Foreign Trade:** Exports, chiefly meat, dairy products, and wool, amounted to $4.6 billion in 1979. Imports, mainly machinery and related equipment, fuel, and industrial raw materials, totaled $4.5 billion **Principal Trade Partners:** Britain, Australia, United States, Japan, Canada, West Germany

Vital Statistics: Birthrate, 17.8 per 1,000 of pop. (1976); death rate, 8.2 **Life Expectancy:** 72 years **Health Statistics:** 97 inhabitants per hospital bed; 772 per physician (1977) **Infant Mortality:** 13.9 per 1,000 births (1976) **Illiteracy:** Negligible **Primary and Secondary School Enrollment:** 755,303 (1976) **Enrollment in Higher Education:** 74,929 **GNP Expended on Education:** 5.5% (1976)

Transportation: Paved roads total 29,000 mi. **Motor Vehicles:** 1,427,100 (1976) **Passenger Cars:** 1,205,400 **Railway Mileage:** 2,987 **Ports:** Auckland, Wellington, Lyttelton, Whangarei, Tauranga, Dunedin, Napier, Nelson **Major Airlines:** Air New Zealand operates domestic and international services **Communications:** Both government and privately owned **Radio Transmitters:** 64 **Receivers:** 2,715,000 (1976) **Television Transmitters:** 144 **Receivers:** 813,000 (1976) **Telephones:** 1,610,000 (1976) **Newspapers:** 39 dailies, 376 copies per 1,000 inhabitants (1975)

Weights and Measures: Metric system **Travel Requirements:** Passport, no visa for 30 days, onward ticket **International Dialing Code:** 64

Blessed with an equable climate that lets grass grow green the year around, New Zealand is renowned for butter, race horses, and lush scenery. The New Zealand dairy industry is said to be the most efficient anywhere, and the export of dairy products is the largest in the world despite the country's small size and population.

The reorganization of overseas markets for pastoral products resulting from the formation of the European Community (Common Market), particularly the prospective phasing out of special trading advantages in Britain for New Zealand butter and cheese, accelerated the postwar trend toward economic diversification. Many dairy farmers have turned successfully to raising meat animals, especially sheep, with government encouragement. In recent years New Zealand has been developing rich new outlets for its farm products in Asia and the Middle East. In 1979, Iran became the country's second-largest customer for lamb (after England), and Iraq also signed a big lamb contract.

Geothermal wells, hydropower, natural gas, and coal abound. New Zealand has no oil, but its Maui natural gas field, discovered in 1969, will be used to make gasoline in the first commercial application of a process developed by Mobil Oil Co. A plant to be built near New Plymouth will use gas provided by Maui Development Ltd., which is a partnership made up of the New Zealand government, Todd Petroleum Mining, Shell Oil (N.Z.), and British Petroleum. The diverse economy includes steel and aluminum production and varied forest products.

With the appearance of new independent states in the South Pacific, New Zealand began providing needed guidance and assistance to the fledgling nations. The first conference of the island heads of government, attended also by high-ranking representatives of Australia and New Zealand, was held in Wellington in August 1971 at the joint request of all the new states—Fiji, Western Samoa, Tonga, Nauru, and the Cook Islands, a self-governing dependency of New Zealand.

The island peoples are attracted to New Zealand by a variety of factors, including the high quality of education available to islanders and the easy interracial relationships. (Eight percent of the New Zealand population are Maoris, a branch of the Polynesian race; Auckland is said to be the biggest Polynesian city in the world, with more than 70,000 Maoris, Cook Islanders, Samoans, Tongans and others in the population.)

Like their Australian neighbors, the New Zealanders are overwhelmingly of British stock. Many of the hardworking pioneer white settlers came from Scotland, some to escape religious conflicts.

With a small population heavily endowed with skills, New Zealand enjoys one of the highest standards of living in the world. Government welfare programs provide "womb-to-tomb" security.

The New Zealanders have shared with the Australians a growing consciousness since World War

II of belonging to the Pacific and Asian region. New Zealand has joined with Australia and Britain in a five-power pact for the defense of Singapore and Malaysia, and is a partner in the ANZUS (Australia, New Zealand, United States) Treaty of Mutual Security, the keystone of national defense.

The year 1975 saw the replacement of Wallace Rowling's Labour government by Robert Muldoon and the National party after a period of economic uncertainty. Prime Minister Muldoon's party won reelection in 1978, but by a much smaller majority, and by 1981 had suffered further erosion of support due to increased unemployment and government spending and a record inflation, spurred by the previous year's 25 percent rise in food prices.

HISTORY: The first European to discover New Zealand was the Dutch explorer Abel Tasman, who sighted the islands in 1642 but was prevented from landing by hostile Maori natives. The British explorer Captain James Cook visited the islands in 1769, and by the end of the century British whaling settlements were established along the coast. It was not until the 19th century, however, that large-scale British immigration began

1840: By the Treaty of Waitangi, Maoris surrender sovereignty to Britain in exchange for guarantees that they would be allowed to remain in possession of their lands; British New Zealand Company begins first organized attempt to colonize islands with British settlers

1845-48: Maoris, angered by Britain's failure to honor land guarantees, rebel against British rule until uprisings are suppressed by military force

1860-70: Maori Wars against Britain are resumed; Maoris are again defeated by superior British force after 10 years of fighting; immigrant population continues to rise, spurred by discovery of gold in 1861

1907: New Zealand wins dominion status

1914-18: New Zealand fights on Allied side in World War I

1939-45: New Zealand fights on Allied side again in World War II

1945: New Zealand becomes a founding member of the UN

1951: United States, New Zealand, and Australia sign ANZUS treaty binding three nations in mutual defense alliance

1960: National party defeats ruling Labour party in general election; Keith J. Holyoake becomes prime minister

1972: Norman E. Kirk becomes prime minister when Labour party wins

1973: New Zealand and Australia unsuccessfully attempt to block French nuclear testing in the Pacific

1974: Wallace Rowling succeeds after Kirk's death

1975: Rowling is defeated by Robert Muldoon of National party

1978: Muldoon reelected with reduced majority

1979: A sightseeing flight over the South Pole costs 257 lives when an Air New Zealand DC-10 hits a mountain

1980: To reduce the country's dependence on imported oil, the government and Mobil Oil Co. plan a $500-million plant to convert natural gas into methanol and then into gasoline. Attempt by members of his own party to oust Muldoon fails

1981: A June meeting of ANZUS group in Wellington, New Zealand, seeks to mitigate harshness of U.S. anti-Vietnam policy on grounds that it will make Vietnam more dependent on USSR

NICARAGUA

Area: 50,193 sq. mi. **Population:** 2,481,000 (1979 est.)

Official Name: Republic of Nicaragua **Capital:** Managua **Nationality:** Nicaraguan **Languages:** Spanish is the official and universal language; some English is spoken on the east coast **Religion:** 95% Roman Catholic **Flag:** Horizontal stripes of blue, white, blue with the national coat of arms in the center **Anthem:** Hail Nicaragua **Currency:** Córdoba (10.0 per U.S. $1)

Location: Central America. Nicaragua, the largest of the Central American republics, is bounded on the north by Honduras, on the east by the Caribbean Sea, on the south by Costa Rica, and on the west by the Pacific Ocean **Features:** The western part of the country consists of a coastal plain, gradually rising toward rugged mountains. Beyond these mountains lies the interior, a sparsely populated wilderness of timbered plains and rolling hills cut by rivers. The eastern coastal plain extends about 50 miles inland and is partly swampland **Chief Rivers:** Grande de Matagalpa, Escondido, Coco, San Juan

Head of State and of Government: The country is governed by a 3-member junta: Sergio Ramírez Mercado, Daniel Ortega Saavedra, and Rafael Cordoba Rivas **Effective Date of Present Constitution:**

April 1974, abrogated 1979 **Legislative Body:** A 47-member Council of State acts as a legislative body **Local Government:** 16 departments

Ethnic Composition: 70% of the population is mestizo (of mixed European and Indian ancestry), 17% of European ancestry, 9% Negro, and 4% Indian **Population Distribution:** 50% urban **Density:** 49 inhabitants per sq. mi.

Largest Cities: (1976 est.) Managua 437,666, León 73,757, Granada 50,094, Masaya 40,907, Chinandega 38,646

Per Capita Income: $732 (1979) **Gross National Product (GNP):** $1.8 billion (1979) **Economic Statistics:** In 1973 about 40% of GNP came from trade and services, 26% from agriculture (cotton, coffee, cattle), forestry and fishing; 10% from industry (chemicals, insecticides, food processing, textiles), and mining **Minerals and Mining:** Copper, gold, silver, tungsten, gypsum, and precious stones **Labor Force:** 728,419 (1977), of which 43% is in agriculture, 15% in manufacturing and 13% in commerce **Foreign Trade:** Exports, mainly cotton, cottonseed, coffee, meat, gold, sesame, and wood, totaled $567 million in 1979. Imports, mainly machinery, transportation equipment, manufacturing products, chemical products, and raw materials for industry, totaled $371 million **Principal Trade Partners:** Central American countries, United States, Japan, West Germany

Vital Statistics: Birthrate, 48.3 per 1,000 of pop. (1975); death rate, 13.9 **Life Expectancy:** 54 years **Health Statistics:** 474 inhabitants per hospital bed; 1,592 per physician (1976) **Infant Mortality:** 37 per 1,000 births **Illiteracy:** 48% **Primary and Secondary School Enrollment:** 741,477 (1975) **Enrollment in Higher Education:** 17,184 **GNP Expended on Education:** 2.5% (1974)

Transportation: Paved roads total 975 mi. **Motor Vehicles:** 52,000 (1973) **Passenger Cars:** 32,000 **Railway Mileage:** 235 **Ports:** Corinto, San Juan del Sur **Major Airlines:** Lineas Aéreas de Nicaragua (LANICA) operates domestic and international flights **Communications:** Partly government controlled **Radio Transmitters:** 85 **Receivers:** 126,000 (1974) **Television Transmitters:** 2 **Receivers:** 90,000 (1976) **Telephones:** 55,000 (1976) **Newspapers:** 7 dailies, 26 copies per 1,000 inhabitants (1975)

Weights and Measures: Metric system **Travel Requirements:** Passport, visa, valid for 30 days, one photo, no fee **International Dialing Code:** 505

A civil war that cost an estimated 30,000 lives brought an end in 1979 to the Somoza family's political and economic rule of Nicaragua after more than four decades. President Gen. Anastasio ("Tacho") Somoza Debayle, who had made a Managua bunker his home and command post for almost two years, fled by helicopter and airplane to the United States on July 17. In August he went into exile in Paraguay, where he was assassinated on Sept. 16, 1980. The Sandinist National Liberation Front (FSLN), winner over the National Guard that the Somozas had headed since 1933, named a five-member junta as the provisional government.

On the victory day, July 19, cheering Managua crowds toppled the statue of Tacho Somoza's father, Gen. Anastasio Somoza García, founder of the family dynasty. The elder Somoza had taken command of the National Guard in 1933, just after the U.S. Marines ended intermittent intervention that had begun in 1912. It was allegedly Somoza's guardsmen who, in 1934, assassinated Gen. Augusto César Sandino, the revolutionary hero from whom the Sandinists took their name. The elder Somoza seized the presidency on Jan. 1, 1937, and held virtually complete control of Nicaragua—the largest country in Central America—until his assassination in 1956. A son, Luis, president of the senate, was named president immediately; Luis' brother, Anastasio, a West Point graduate, became president in a 1967 election in which charges of fraud and intimidation arose.

The assassination of Pedro Joaquín Chamorro, publisher of *La Prensa* and a longtime critic of Somoza, in downtown Managua in January 1978 was widely attributed to the Somoza regime. Massive unrest and violence followed, culminating in the seizure of the National Palace by the FSLN seven months later. That action won release of 58 political prisoners and safe conduct out of the country. But the National Guard largely succeeded in putting the lid back on the violence until the Sandinists launched a successful revolution from the Costa Rican border on May 29, 1979.

The junta that took over the reins of government in 1979, and also the 15-member cabinet which it appointed, included conservative businessmen and other non-Sandinisists. The United States recognized the new regime and sent badly needed food aid. In 1980, the new government began to lean more and more to the left. Banks and the mining industry were nationalized, and the government assumed control of coffee, cotton and seafood exports. It also imposed severe austerity measures as part of its reconstruction program. It has inherited the large foreign debt contracted by the Somoza regime, and is faced with heavy unemployment and inflation.

Originally, the Sandinist junta disclaimed helping the leftist guerrillas who have been trying to seize power in El Salvador. Gradually, however, evidence came forth that, under pressure from Cuba, Nicaragua was becoming a staging area and supply base for the Salvadoran rebels. In April 1981 the United States suspended all aid to Nicaragua. With this aid cut off, Nicaragua looked elsewhere and obtained moral and material help from Mexico, a $100 million loan from Libya and 30,000 tons of wheat from the Soviet bloc. Nicaragua also looked to western European and Arab countries for assistance.

HISTORY: Various Indian tribes inhabited Nicaragua before the arrival of the Spanish conquistador Gil Gonzálalez de Ávila in 1552. During the Spanish colonial period, Nicaragua was administered as part the captaincy general of Guatemala

1821: Nicaragua wins independence from Spain and along with the other countries of Central America becomes annexed to Mexico

1825-38: Nicaragua secedes from Mexico and joins Central American Federation. In 1838 the federation is dissolved, and Nicaragua becomes an independent republic

1856-57: U.S. soldier of fortune William Walker seizes presidency but is ousted by alliance of Central American states

1912-33: Prolonged political turmoil between Liberals and Conservatives leads Provisional President Adolfo Díaz to ask for intervention of U.S. Marines to maintain order. In 1916 the Bryan-Chamorro Treaty is ratified, giving United States an option on route for a canal, but Liberals continue guerrilla warfare in protest against American intervention. U.S. Marines, withdrawn in 1925, again occupy country from 1926 to 1933

1934: Gen. Augusto César Sandino, who had defied efforts of U.S. Marines to catch him and who later had won concessions from the government, is assassinated, apparently by members of Gen. Anastasio Somoza's National Guard

1936-57: General Somoza seizes power; until his death by an assassin's bullet in 1956 he rules country as virtual private estate. His son, Luis, finishes his father's term and is reelected

1967: Anastasio Somoza Debayle, brother of Luis and head of armed forces, is elected president

1972: On December 23, earthquakes destroy much of Managua, killing an estimated 10,000, injuring about 15,000 and leaving half the city's population homeless

1974: Somoza is reelected for second presidential term, after resigning in 1972 because of election provisions but retaining full power in the interim as commander of the armed forces

1978: Widespread civil unrest follows assassination of publisher Pedro Joaquín Chamorro, longtime Somoza foe. National Palace seized by leftist guerrillas, who hold members of congress hostage until they win release of 58 political prisoners and safe conduct out of country. Guerrillas gain broad support in efforts to oust Somoza, who vows to serve out term. Even the National Federation of the Chambers of Commerce joins a general strike in August, and the guerrillas capture several towns. However, in heavy fighting, the National Guard recaptures the places

1979: On May 29, Sandinist rebels launch a five-pronged attack from Costa Rican border. They quickly take León and other towns, and control the *barrios* of Managua. President Somoza flees the country on July 17

1980: Nicaraguan leaders sign accord with Soviet Union to increase trade and obtain technical aid. Junta puts off elections until 1985, claiming need for 5-year reconstruction period. Non-Sandinists

walk out of Nov. 12 meeting of advisory Council of State, claiming political repression

1981: Head of Nicaraguan Human Rights Commission is arrested for openly criticizing regime. Junta membership is reduced to three—two Sandinists and one Conservative. Nicaraguan exiles are reported to be training in Florida for action against the Sandinist regime. Nicaragua closes border after series of clashes with Honduran troops; accuses Honduras of aiding anti-Sandinist rebels

NIGER

Area: 489,189 sq. mi. **Population:** 5,098,427 (1977 census)

Official Name: Republic of Niger **Capital:** Niamey **Nationality:** Nigerien **Languages:** French is the official language; the principal African languages are Fulani, Tamashek, Djerma, Songhai, and Hausa, used primarily in trade **Religion:** The population is predominantly Moslem **Flag:** Horizontal stripes of orange, white, and green with an orange disc in the center **Anthem:** La Nigérienne **Currency:** CFA Franc (263 per U.S. $1)

Location: West-central Africa. Landlocked Niger is bordered on the north by Algeria and Libya, on the east by Chad, on the south by Nigeria and Benin, on the southwest by Upper Volta, and on the west by Mali **Features:** Four fifths of the country (north) is arid desert, and the remainder (south) is mostly savanna **Chief River:** Niger

Head of State and of Government: President of the Supreme Military Council: Lt. Col. Seyni Kountché, born 1931, assumed power in 1974 **Effective Date of Present Constitution:** 1960, suspended 1974 **Legislative Body:** All powers are in the hands of the Council **Local Government:** 7 departments under appointed prefects, divided into 32 districts

Ethnic Composition: Hausa make up almost 50% of the population and Djerma-Songhai 23%, the rest are nomadic and seminomadic Peuls, or Fulani (15%), Tuaregs (12%), Toubous, and others **Population Distribution:** 8% urban **Density:** 10 inhabitants per sq. mi.

Largest Cities: (1977 census) Niamey 225,314, Zinder 58,436, Maradi 45,852, Tahoua 31,265

Per Capita Income: $127 (1978) **Gross National Product (GNP):** $640 million (1978) **Economic Statistics:** In 1973 over 50% of GNP was derived from agriculture (peanuts, cotton, tobacco, millet, sorghum, beans, rice, livestock), 27% from trade and services and 12% from manufacturing (textiles, peanut oil, oxygen-acetylene) and mining **Minerals and Mining:** Niger's uranium deposits are mined in the Arlit and Akouta regions. Two more are to open by 1985. Tin, coal, and phosphates are also mined **Labor Force:** 1,900,000 (1970), with about 90% in agriculture and stockraising **Foreign Trade:** Exports, mainly peanuts, uranium and livestock, totaled $494 million in 1979. Imports, chiefly fuels, machinery, motor vehicles and parts, food and clothing, totaled $555 million **Principal Trade Partners:** France, Nigeria, West Germany, Ivory Coast, Japan, United States

Vital Statistics: Birthrate, 52.2 per 1,000 of pop. (1975); death rate, 25.5 **Life Expectancy:** 39 years **Health Statistics:** 1,200 inhabitants per hospital bed; 47,300 per physician (1974) **Infant Mortality:** 162 per 1,000 births **Illiteracy:** 94% **Primary and Secondary School Enrollment:** 177,613 (1976) **Enrollment in Higher Education:** 541 (1975) **GNP Expended on Education:** 3.2% (1976)

Transportation: Paved roads total 1,176 mi. **Motor Vehicles:** 21,700 (1976) **Passenger Cars:** 9,900 **Railway Mileage:** None **Ports:** None **Major Airlines:** Air-Niger operates domestic and international flights **Communications:** Government owned **Radio Transmitters:** 13 **Receivers:** 150,000 (1971) **Television Transmitters:** 1 **Receivers:** N. A. **Telephones:** 8,000 (1976) **Newspapers:** 2 dailies, 0.5 copy per 1,000 inhabitants (1974)

Weights and Measures: Metric system **Travel Requirements:** Passport, visa valid for 7 days, no fee; for stay up to 3 months, $6.25 fee; 2 photos, onward ticket or guarantee from a bank

Niger has been called "a land where the harvest is won with the soul's scythe." For most of this neglected hinterland of former French West Africa is rocky desert, broken by bleak mountains. The productive southern area, watered in part by the Niger River, is semiarid and subject to droughts and floods.

While rich uranium deposits are being developed in the northern desert area and there is hope for discovery of oil and exploitation of other minerals, Niger still must depend on cattle and on limited export and food crops, chiefly peanuts, cotton, and grains. A hostile climate and need for irrigation are obstacles to increased production.

Lack of transportation is Niger's most serious problem. The landlocked country has no railroad and the rapids-strewn Niger River, a potentially low-cost route to the seacoast, has yet to be made navigable. The nearest seaport, Cotonou, in Benin, is 600 miles from Niamey, Niger's capital, and it is often noted that it takes more than two gallons of gasoline to import a single gallon.

Internal roads and links to neighboring countries, however, are gradually being built with French, American, World Bank, and United Nations aid. Canada, through new ties with French-speaking African countries, has recently become a major aid source for Niger.

A $60-million uranium project at Arlit, which began production in 1971, is a joint Nigerien/French/German/Italian undertaking. A second uranium project, organized in 1974 under a company started by the Nigerien government, the French Atomic Energy Commission, and a Japanese company, is developing deposits in the Akouta district. Additional uranium deposits were discovered in 1979 and 1980.

Like the other nations of the West African Sahel, Niger suffered greatly during the drought and famine of 1968-74. In 1973 cattle were dying; in 1974 people were dying. An estimated two million were starving in the Tuareg tribe alone. By October 1974, the drought ended, but massive international relief efforts were required to prevent starvation.

Hamani Diori, Niger's president from the time the country gained independence from France in 1960 until 1974, sought to promote national development and to unify Niger's traditionally hostile nomadic and settled farming peoples. He emphasized government stability; gradual improvement of agriculture, health, and education; and economic aid from numerous sources.

However, in 1974 when Diori was unable to stop his people's starvation resulting from the drought in the Sahel, he was overthrown by Lt. Col. Seyni Kountché who formed a 12-member military government with himself as president. Kountché dissolved the National Assembly, suspended the constitution and banned all political groups.

HISTORY: The region around Niger was probably known to Egyptians before the beginning of recorded history. Through the next 1,000 years it was a battleground for Arabs; Berbers; Toubous; the Ghana, Mali, Songhai, and Bornu empires; the Hausa states; and the Djermas, Fulanis, and Tuaregs. The first European explorers arrived in the late 18th century and were soon followed by French forces pushing forward still another empire

1901-22: French build chain of forts, crush Tuareg resistance, and establish colony of Niger

1946: French set up local advisory assembly, grant people of Niger French citizenship

1958: Niger becomes an autonomous republic within the French Community

1960: Complete independence is declared and Niger joins the UN

1964-65: Terrorist attacks and attempts to assassinate President Hamani Diori are quelled by government forces

1968-74: Drought and famine strike the Sahel

1974: Army Chief of Staff Lt. Col. Seyni Kountché ousts Diori, and declares himself head of state. Drought ends

1979: Rich uranium deposits discovered near Agadez in the Sahara

1980: Kountché frees former President Hamani Diori from custody. Drop in uranium price hurts Niger's economy

1981: Niger fears takeover by Libya following latter's occupation of Chad, but continues sale of uranium to Libya

---

NIGERIA

Area: 379,628 sq. mi. **Population:** 84,500,000 (1978 est.)
Official Name: Federal Republic of Nigeria **Capital:** Lagos **Nationality:** Nigerian **Languages:** English is the official and business language. Among the 250 African languages and dialects, the most

widely spoken are Hausa, Yoruba, Ibo, and Edo. Sizable minorities speak Fulani, Kanuri, Ijaw, Ibibio, and Tiv **Religion:** Northern Nigeria is largely Moslem, while the south and west have been strongly influenced by Christianity. About 47% of the population are Moslem, 34% Christian and 19% animist **Flag:** Vertical stripes of green, white, green **Anthem:** National Anthem, beginning "Nigeria, we hail thee" **Currency:** Naira (.57 per U.S. $1)

Location: West Africa. Nigeria is bounded on the northwest and north by Niger, on the northeast by Lake Chad, on the east by Cameroon, on the south by the Gulf of Guinea, and on the west by Benin **Features:** The coastal area consists of a belt of mangrove swamps intersected by delta branches of the Niger and innumerable smaller rivers and creeks. Inland, a belt of tropical rain forest extends up to 100 miles over gradually rising country. The country then rises to a plateau, which reaches an elevation of over 6,000 feet in the east. In the north, the savanna approaches the southern part of the Sahara **Chief Rivers:** Niger, Benue, Sokoto, Yobe, Gana, Kaduna, Cross, Gongola, Ogun

Head of State and of Government: President Alhaji Shehu Shagari, born 1925, elected Aug. 1979, took office Oct. 1 **Effective Date of Present Constitution:** 1979 **Legislative Body:** National Assembly (bicameral) consisting of a Senate and a House of Representatives. The Senate is composed of 95 members with each of the 19 states sending 5 members. The House of Representatives has 449 members. Both branches are directly elected and their maximum terms are 4 years **Local Government:** 19 states and a federal capital territory

Ethnic Composition: Of the country's 250 tribal groups, the dominant ones are the Yoruba (15%) in the west, the Ibo (16%) in the east, and the Hausa (19%) and Fulani (10%) in the north. Other large groups are the Edo (900,000) in the west, the Ibibio (about 1 million) and the Ijaw (900,000) in the east, and the Kanuri (2.9 million), Nupe (500,000), and Tiv (1.5 million) in the north **Population Distribution:** 23% urban **Density:** 223 inhabitants per sq. mi.

Largest Cities: (1975 est.) Lagos 1,060,848, Ibadan 847,000, Ogbomosho 432,000, Kano 399,000, Oshogbo 282,000, Ilorin 282,000, Abeokuta 253,000, Port Harcourt 242,000

Per Capita Income: $704 (1980) **Gross Domestic Product (GDP):** $54 billion (1980) **Economic Statistics:** More than 33% of GDP comes from oil and mining, an estimated 23% from agriculture (cocoa, peanuts, African oil palm products, rubber and cotton), and 10% from manufacturing (mainly food processing, oil refining, cotton textiles and cement) **Minerals and Mining:** Nigeria is sub-Saharan Africa's largest oil producer; other minerals are tin, coal, and limestone. Large natural gas deposits are being developed **Labor Force:** 30 million of which 64% are in agriculture, forestry and fishing, and 10% in industry **Foreign Trade:** Exports, crude petroleum (95%), cocoa, peanuts, palm nuts, rubber, tin and raw cotton, totaled $18 billion in 1979. Imports, chiefly machinery, transport equipment, industrial raw materials, manufactured goods, chemicals and food, amounted to $11 billion **Principal Trade Partners:** Britain, United States, West Germany, Japan, Netherlands, France

Vital Statistics: Birthrate, 49.3 per 1,000 of pop. (1975); death rate, 22.7 **Life Expectancy:** 50 years **Health Statistics:** 1,378 inhabitants per hospital bed; 19,000 per physician (1976) **Infant Mortality:** 150 per 1,000 births **Illiteracy:** 65% **Primary and Secondary School Enrollment:** 5,458,160 (1973) **Enrollment in Higher Education:** 32,971 (1975) **GDP Expended on Education:** 2.6% (1975)

Transportation: Paved roads total 15,650 mi. **Motor Vehicles:** 255,000 (1975) **Passenger Cars:** 150,000 **Railway Mileage:** 2,178 **Ports:** Lagos, Port Harcourt, Bonny, Burutu **Major Airlines:** Nigeria Airways operates international and domestic services **Communications:** Government controlled **Radio Transmitters:** 46 **Licenses:** 5,100,000 (1976) **Television Transmitters:** 10 **Licenses:** 121,000 (1976) **Telephones:** 121,000 (1976) **Newspapers:** 12 dailies, 9 copies per 1,000 inhabitants (1974)

Weights and Measures: Metric system **Travel Requirements:** Passport, visa valid 3 months from date of issue, $2.30 fee **International Dialing Code:** 234

Nigeria, a country of extraordinary potential—oil, agricultural diversity, talented political leaders, a population that embraces fully a fifth of the black people in Africa—is also a country with extraordinary problems of instability. One of the underlying reasons for that instability is the nation's great ethnic diversity.

Nigeria's major tribal divisions consist of the seminomadic Hausa-Fulani of the north, the urbanized Yorubas in the west, and in the east, the industrious Ibos. Under British rule, the three regions, together with Lagos, the administrative center, were amalgamated into one vast colonial possession.

As Britain prepared Nigeria for self-government after World War II, it was recognized that the country could achieve its great economic potential only if it remained intact. Nigerian leaders and British authorities were confident, however, that old animosities could be submerged. In 1960 Britain granted full independence and in 1963 Nigeria became a republic.

The largely Moslem north dominated the new government. Distrust soon fanned tribal rivalries into open conflict after incidents of corruption, nepotism, and rigged elections. Ibos grew increasingly resentful as they saw excessive shares of the oil revenues from their region go to northern projects.

Early in 1966, a coup led by young Ibo army officers was accompanied by the murder of many Northern and Western officials, including Prime Minister Sir Abubakar Tafawa Balewa. Gen. Johnson Aguiyi-Ironsi, an Ibo who promised a government free of corruption and tribalism, was installed as president.

However, in a countercoup led by northern officers in July 1966, Ironsi was murdered. He was replaced by Lt. Col. (later Maj. Gen.) Yakubu Gowon, who, as a Christian and member of a minor tribe, was regarded as a neutralist in the tribal conflicts.

Late in 1966 thousands of Ibos working in the north were massacred. Thousands more fled back to their homeland and Gowon's efforts for new political cooperation were frustrated by Ibo fear and distrust. Ibo leader Lt. Col. Odumegwu Ojukwu unsuccessfully sought autonomy for the Eastern Region, then, in May 1967, proclaimed a Republic of Biafra.

In the ensuing conflict Biafran forces were at first victorious, but with growing federal strength, the rebel state was gradually reduced to a small area. As the war dragged on, starvation ravaged the East—a densely populated, food-deficient region. Despite relief efforts by many groups, Biafran resistance collapsed in January 1970, and Ojukwu fled to the Ivory Coast. The struggle took an estimated one million lives. In the years since there has been a gradual reintegration of Ibos into the national economy.

The Biafra trouble was scarcely over when prolonged drought desiccated the Sahel region in northern Nigeria. Cattle died by the thousands, farm lands suffered and fishing industry on Lake Chad collapsed as the lake shrank in size. The area is recovering, but many problems remain.

In October 1974 General Gowon announced that a previously scheduled return to civilian government (1976) had been canceled because of dispute over the 1973 census and the violent sectional political ambitions that were emerging. This announcement led to student demonstrations. Labor unrest increased over pay demands.

On July 29, 1975, Gowon was deposed in a bloodless coup; Brig. Gen. Murtala Rufai Mohammed was named head of state. In February 1976 Brig. Gen. Mohammed was assassinated by a group of "young revolutionaries" who later failed to gain control of the government. The nation's ruling Supreme Military Council named Lt. Gen. Olusegun Obasanjo as head of state.

A total of 37 persons were executed for their alleged involvement in the abortive coup and assassination. Nigeria's request that Great Britain extradite former Head of State Gowon, so that he could defend himself against accusations of involvement in the attempted coup, was denied.

Political activity, banned since 1966, was restored in September 1978. Four parties sprang up

to compete for the right to form the long-promised civilian government. In August 1979 Alhaji Shehu Shagari was declared the winner of the election balloting for president, held under Nigeria's new constitution. The military surrendered control to a civilian government on Oct. 1.

Oil, first discovered in 1958, has made Nigeria the wealthiest black African nation. Oil exports account for more than 90 percent of the nation's foreign-exchange earnings and provide most of its government revenues. Nigeria is the second largest source of oil for the United States.

In spite of the country's big oil revenues, the Shagari government has had to deal with major problems of unemployment, inflation, crime, piracy, and shortages of rice and other foods. In 1981 a "Green Revolution" was initiated with the acquisition of 35,000 acres of land in each state to be used for grain production. Shagari has also sought to strenghen the federal relationship between his government and the states. Nevertheless, the two ruling coalition parties split on the issue of dividing federal revenues with state and local governments.

Nigeria has pushed for closer trading ties with its West African neighbors. The government is also seeking greater "Nigerianization" of foreign-owned-and-run enterprises to give Nigerians a greater share of the wealth. Although militant on anti-colonial issues involving the white-ruled nations of Africa, Nigeria maintains a moderate foreign policy.

HISTORY: Nigeria's earliest known culture, Nok, flourished around 700-200 B.C. During the 12th century, Nigeria's next great culture grew up around Ife, a sacred Yoruba city. In medieval times, northern Nigeria had contact with the large kingdoms of the western Sudan and by the end of the 14th century A.D. Islam was firmly established in the north. Between the 15th and 17th centuries, the Portuguese and British engaged in commerce and slave trading
1861-1914: Britain annex Lagos (1861); gradually establish administrative control over Nigeria
1947-54: Successive steps are taken to allow participation in the government by Africans in preparation for self-government
1960: Nigeria becomes an independent federal state within the British Commonwealth
1963: Nigeria becomes a federal republic within the Commonwealth
1966: Government is ousted by a military coup and a military government is established under Gen. Johnson Aguiyi-Ironsi (an Ibo from the Eastern Region); Ironsi is murdered when another military coup is staged by anti-Ibo elements in the army; a federal military government is set up under Lt. Col. (later Maj. Gen.) Yakubu Gowon. Thousands of Ibos are massacred and more than a million are driven from the north
1967: Military government announces the creation of 12 ethnically based states to replace the previous four regions. The Eastern Region, under the leadership of Lt. Col. Odumegwu Ojukwu, secedes from the Federation of Nigeria and proclaims itself the independent Republic of Biafra. Federal troops invade Biafra
1968-69: Mass starvation threatens millions in Biafra as a result of the federal government's blockade of the region
1970: Surrender of Biafran forces brings end to 30-month civil war; federal government chief, Gen. Yakubu Gowon, pledges protection and political rights to former Biafrans
1972: Many small foreign-owned businesses are "Nigerianized"
1975: General Gowon is deposed in a bloodless coup. Brig. Gen. Murtala Rufai Mohammed is named head of state
1976: Mohammed assassinated in unsuccessful coup. Lt. Gen. Olusegun Obasanjo is named head of state. Nigeria discards British Parliament as a model for its upcoming 1979 civilian government and looks instead to presidential system of the U.S.
1978: Twelve-year-old ban on political activity lifted
1979: Alhaji Shehu Shagari is elected president under new constitution. Daily oil output reaches 2.5 million barrels
1980: Inquiry exonerates previous regime's Petroleum Commission on charges of misappropriating funds. Attacks by fanatical Islamic sects on "corrupted" believers around Kano lead to clashes with army and police; death toll is as high as 10,000
1981: Two-day strike, which closes factories and ports, ends with government pledges of higher minimum wages and improved benefits for workers. Nigeria cuts its price of oil by $2.50 per barrel. Nigerian troops clash with Cameroon forces along border

NORWAY

Area: 125,053 sq. mi. **Population:** 4,092,000 (1980 est.)

Official Name: Kingdom of Norway **Capital:** Oslo **Nationality:** Norwegian **Languages:** Norwegian is the official and predominant language; Lappish and Finnish are spoken in the north **Religion:** The state church, the Evangelical Lutheran Church, includes 94% of the population **Flag:** An extended white bordered blue cross on a red field **Anthem:** Yes, We Love This Land of Ours **Currency:** Norwegian krone (5.6 per U.S. $1)

Location: Northern Europe, occupying the smaller, western part of the Scandinavian peninsula. Norway has common land frontiers in the east with Sweden, Finland, and the Soviet Union. It is bounded on the north by the Arctic Ocean, on the west by the Norwegian Sea, and on the south by the Skagerrak, an arm of the North Sea **Features:** The country has a 2,125-mile coastline, deeply indented by numerous fjords. From the coast, the land rises to high plateaus and mountain ranges, the highest of which, Glittertind, reaches 8,110 feet. The highlands are cut by fertile valleys and rapid rivers and are dotted with lakes. Forests cover roughly one-fourth of the country, which also has numerous glaciers. Jostedalsbreen, in the southwest, is the largest ice field in Europe **Chief Rivers:** Glomma, Lagen

Head of State: King Olav V, born 1903, acceded to the throne in 1957 **Head of Government:** Premier Gro Harlem Brundtland, born 1939, appointed 1981 **Effective Date of Present Constitution:** 1814 **Legislative Body:** *Storting* (bicameral parliament) consisting of 155 members elected by universal suffrage for a 4-year term. When assembled, parliament divides itself by election into 2 chambers, one of 39 members, the other of 116. Bills are introduced in the larger chamber and, when passed, are sent to the smaller one. If the chambers disagree, a joint session is held in which the fate of the bill is decided by a two-thirds majority **Local Government:** 19 counties and the city county of Oslo, each with a council and a governor

Ethnic Composition: Norwegians are mainly of Nordic origin; there has been some mixture with the Finns and Lapps, especially in the north, where some 20,000 Lapps still live **Population Distribution:** 57% urban **Density:** 33 inhabitants per sq. mi.

Largest Cities: (1976 est.) Oslo 462,732, Bergen 213,434, Trondheim 134,910, Stavanger 86,639, Kristiansand 59,488

Per Capita Income: $9,887 (1980) **Gross Domestic Product (GDP):** $40 billion (1980) **Economic Statistics:** 6% of GDP comes from agriculture (dairy farming, beef, pork, eggs and poultry), including animal husbandry, forestry, fishing and whaling; 20% from industry (transport equipment, shipbuilding, metal products, food manufactures, chemicals and chemical products, printing and publishing, paper and paper products, electrical and other machinery, nonmetallic mineral products); 19% from trade and finance **Minerals and Mining:** Offshore oil and natural gas, limestone, pyrites, ilmenite, iron ore, coal, molybdenite, copper, zinc, lead **Labor Force:** 1,800,000, of which 29% is employed in services, 25% in industry, and 11% in agriculture **Foreign Trade:** Exports, chiefly petroleum, ships, nonferrous metals, paper and paperboard, paper pulp, iron and steel, totaled $13.5 billion in 1979. Imports, mainly industrial machinery, petroleum and petroleum products, iron and steel, and textiles, amounted to $13.7 billion **Principal Trade Partners:** Britain, West Germany, Sweden, Denmark, United States, Japan, Netherlands, Liberia, France

Vital Statistics: Birthrate, 12.5 per 1,000 of pop. (1977); death rate, 9.7 **Life Expectancy:** 75 years **Health Statistics:** 68 inhabitants per hospital bed; 567 per physician (1976) **Infant Mortality:** 10.5 per 1,000 births **Illiteracy:** Negligible **Primary and Secondary School Enrollment:** 726,011 (1976) **Enrollment in Higher Education:** 66,628 **GNP Expended on Education:** 7.7% (1976)

Transportation: Paved roads total 22,976 mi. **Motor Vehicles:** 1,268,500 (1977) **Passenger Cars:** 1,106,600 **Railway Mileage:** 2,645 **Ports:** Oslo, Narvik, Bergen, Stavanger, Tonsberg, Porsgrunn, Trondheim, Tromso **Major Airlines:** Scandinavian Airlines System (SAS), a consortium owned by the governments of Norway, Denmark, and Sweden, operates domestic and international services **Communications:** Government owned **Radio Transmitters:** 357 **Radio Licenses:** 1,288,000 (1976) **Television Transmitters:** 870 **Licenses:** 1,087,000 (1976) **Telephones:** 1,476,000 (1976) **Newspapers:** 80 dailies, 412 copies per 1,000 inhabitants (1975)

Weights and Measures: Metric system **Travel Requirements:** Passport, no visa for 3 months **International Dialing Code:** 47

Lying atop Western Europe with nearly half its 1,100-mile length north of the Arctic Circle, Norway—a rugged land of mountains, forests, glaciers, and a coastline deeply cut by fjords—is the most

sparsely populated country on the Continent. It has, however, one of the highest living standards in Europe and, like the other Nordic lands, a far-reaching social welfare system.

Norway helped to form NATO in 1949, following its experience during World War II as a country invaded and occupied by the Germans. In doing so, it departed from the strict neutrality that it had observed since 1814, when it was forced during brief hostilities to enter with Sweden into a dual monarchy. Like Denmark, Norway, which, with Denmark, Sweden, and Finland, is a member of the Nordic Council, limits its membership in NATO by stipulating that neither foreign troops nor nuclear weapons may be stationed on its soil. The only Western European country that shares a frontier with the Soviet Union, Norway has a small garrison guarding that border, which is 122 miles long, in the far northeast.

The Norwegians were charter members of the British-led European Free Trade Association, organized in 1960, and for a time sought entry to the European Community (the Common Market). But in a national referendum held September 24-25, 1972, the Norwegian electorate decisively rejected such entry. However, the government negotiated a free trade agreement with the EC to gain advantages for Norway's major exports, particularly fish, aluminum, paper, and steel.

Rich in hydroelectric power, Norway has developed into an industrial nation that produces more than a fifth of its gross national product through manufacturing. All but about nine percent of Norwegian enterprises are privately owned. Small and medium-size plants predominate, with about 70 percent employing fewer than 10 persons.

Along with its promise of considerable riches, the 1968 discovery of huge oil and gas deposits on the continental shelf of the North Sea has brought Norway some major economic problems as well. After borrowing heavily to finance development, the government has found reserves to be smaller than first thought, and production costs higher. In April 1977 a spectacular oil well blowout cost $111 million in lost revenues and has delayed development of the Statfjord fields, where the nation expects to get most of its future oil. In March 1980, a tragic accident claimed the lives of 123 workers when a floating platform at Norway's Ekofisk offshore oil field capsized during a storm. Output of oil and natural gas amounted to only about two thirds of the projected 25 million tons in 1977, while the nation's balance of payments showed a record $5.3 billion deficit. As a result, the government devalued the krone by eight percent, froze prices and tightened credit. Further austerity measures are likely.

HISTORY: The history of Norway before the age of the Vikings is indistinct from that of the rest of Scandinavia. Norse Vikings emerge as an identifiable group in the 8th century, when the Anglo-Saxon Chronicle records their arrival in Britain. Norway itself, split into kingdoms and earldoms, was united in the 11th century and reached its peak in the 13th century, holding sway over Iceland and Greenland. Briefly united with Sweden in 1319, Norway formally joined with Denmark and Sweden in the Union of Kalmar in 1397, which lasted until the end of the Napoleonic Wars, although Sweden seceded in the 16th century

1814: Denmark, having sided with France in the Napoleonic Wars, is among the losers and is forced to cede Norway to Sweden. The Norwegians react by adopting a constitution of their own and choose a Danish prince to be king of Norway, but a Swedish army forces Norway to agree to a dual monarchy with Sweden

1905: Union with Sweden is dissolved and Norway becomes independent. Prince Charles of Denmark is elected king of Norway and ascends throne as Haakon VII

1914-18: Norway remains neutral during World War I, but its merchant fleet suffers heavy losses

1940-45: Nazi Germany attacks Norway and quickly occupies most of country despite strong Norwegian resistance. King Haakon and his cabinet leave the country and set up a government in exile in London. In occupied Norway, meanwhile, a puppet government is established under Norwegian Nazi leader Vidkun Quisling; despite his attempts to promote collaboration with Germans, the Norwegians continue to defy invaders. Norway is liberated in May 1945

1945: Norway becomes founding member of the UN. Trygve Lie elected first UN Secretary-General

1957: King Haakon dies and is succeeded by son, Olav V

1965: Labor party, which has been dominant for 30 years, is swept out of office in general elections; Per Borten, leader of Center party, forms non-socialist coalition government, which remains in power till 1971

1968: Huge oil and gas deposits are discovered in Norwegian sector of North Sea

1972: Voting in a national referendum, the Norwegian electorate rejects entry to the European Community (Common Market), toppling Labor government of Premier Bratteli, in power since 1971 and a strong advocate of EC entry; Lars Korvald of the Christian People's party forms a minority coalition government

1973: In general elections the Labor party obtains 35.29 percent of popular vote as the largest single group and returns to power with a minority government headed by Premier Trygve Bratteli

1974: Norway and the Soviet Union open negotiations to define the disputed boundary of the potentially oil-rich continental shelf of the Barents Sea

1975: The *Storting* (parliament) passes a tax law providing for a large surtax on North Sea oil production by oil companies, which will bring the government $1 billion a year

1976: Odvar Nordli becomes premier

1978: Further austerity measures proposed as Norway's foreign debt nears $19 billion. Work proceeds on nation's third major oil find, the Statfjord field (discovered in 1974)

1980: Floating platform at Ekofisk oil field collapses, killing 123 workers, most of whom are Norwegians

1981: Gro Harlem Brundtland becomes Norway's first woman premier, succeeding Nordli as head of Labor government

---

OMAN

Area: 120,000 sq. mi. **Population:** 839,000 (1978 est.)

Official Name: Sultanate of Oman **Capital:** Muscat **Nationality:** Omani **Languages:** Arabic is the official and predominant language; Hindi, Baluchi, English, Farsi, and Urdu are spoken by the minorities **Religion:** 50% are Ibadi Moslems and about 25% Sunni Moslems. Islam is the official religion **Flag:** Horizontal white, red, and green bands, with a vertical red band at the hoist, a white symbol of crossed swords in the upper left **Anthem:** National Anthem, beginning "God save our sultan" **Currency:** Omani rial (0.35 per U.S. $1)

Location: Southeast Arabia. Bounded on the north and northwest by the Gulf of Oman and the United Arab Emirates, on the east and south by the Arabian Sea, and on the west by Southern Yemen and Saudi Arabia **Features:** The coastline extends for about 1,000 miles, with fertile coastal plain (the Batina), a range of barren hills, and a plateau and desert area with an average height of 1,000 feet. Also included are the detached tip of the Musandam Peninsula, and offshore the Kuria Muria and Masira islands **Chief Rivers:** There are no permanent rivers

Head of State and of Government: Sultan Qabus ibn Said al Bu Said, born 1940, seized power in July 1970. The sultan is an absolute monarch and also premier **Constitution and Legislative Body:** None **Local Government:** 37 regions, one province and the capital area, ruled by appointed governors

Ethnic Composition: The population is almost evenly divided between those of South and North Arabian stock. Minorities (60,000) of Iranians, Pakistanis, Indians, and East Africans **Population Distribution:** 10% urban **Density:** 7 inhabitants per sq. mi.

Largest Cities: (1974 estimate) Matrah 20,000, Salala 10,000, Nizwa 10,000, Muscat 7,000

Per Capita Income: $5,434 (1979) **Gross National Product (GNP):** $3 billion (1979) **Economic Statistics:** About 74% from industry (oil providing 70% of the total GNP, fishing, date-drying) and 2% of GNP is derived from agriculture (dates, bananas, onions, limes, tobacco, oranges, coconuts, melons, grapes, wheat, livestock) **Minerals and Mining:** Oil is the country's chief mineral resource, and there are deposits of natural gas, asbestos, marble, chrome and copper **Labor Force:** 250,000 of which 36% are non-Omani **Foreign Trade:** Exports, oil (95%), dates, fish, and limes, totaled $2.3 billion in 1979. Imports, chiefly foods, machinery, manufactured goods, materials, and clothing, totaled $1.4 billion **Principal Trade Partners:** India, Pakistan, Australia, UAE, Britain, Japan, United States, West Germany

Vital Statistics: Birthrate, 50 per 1,000 of pop. (1974); death rate, 19 **Life Expectancy:** 47 years **Health Statistics:** 658 inhabitants per

hospital bed; 1,975 per physician (1976) **Infant Mortality:** 145 per 1,000 births **Illiteracy:** 75% **Primary and Secondary School Enrollment:** 65,000 (1976) **GNP Expended on Education:** 7.4% (1975)

Transportation: Paved roads total 1,094 mi. **Motor Vehicles:** 8,168 **Railway Mileage:** None **Ports:** Muscat (Port Qabus), Matrah, Mina al Fahal, Rasyut **Major Airlines:** Gulf Air provides international service **Communications:** Government controlled **Radio Transmitters:** 4 **Receivers:** 1,000 **Television Transmitters:** 2 **Receivers:** 55,000 **Telephones:** 9,000 (1976) **Newspapers:** 1 daily

Weights and Measures: Metric system **Travel Requirements:** Passport; business visa, $9.00 fee, valid 7 days, 2 photos, letter from applicant's company and from sponsor in Oman

---

In 1970, Sultan Qabus ibn Said al Bu Said changed the name of Muscat and Oman to simply Oman, but he has not been able to change the fact that Oman is, in a sense, several countries. He belongs to the dynasty of the port city of Muscat, the dynasty which survived the long-standing rivalry among port cities and foreign conquerors for control of the coast. And whoever has controlled the coast has also tried to control the nomads of the desert interior—part of which is traditionally known as Oman. Despite Sultan Qabus's attempt to give a single name to his dominion, Oman is more a dynastic conglomeration than a nation. It has no definite boundaries; control of the interior is weak; and the port cities have little loyalty to the dynasty, and less to an entity called "Oman."

For over a century, the dynasty has relied on British assistance, and many of the high-ranking officers in the army are on loan from Britian. During most of the 1970s, Sultan Qabus could also borrow entire army units from the shah of Iran. The shah's overthrow in 1979 increased Oman's strategic importance in the Middle East to the West. In 1980, Oman agreed to allow the United States to use some ports and air bases in return for U.S. military and economic aid, estimated at $100 million in 1980-81.

Sultan Qabus, who had been educated in Britain, came to power in 1970 by overthrowing his father, Said ibn Taimur, who had been sultan since 1932. The older man had tried to keep his domain together by fear and by preventing change; he had forbidden nomads to enter the cities and city people to enter the interior, outlawed the cultivation of new land, and required his personal approval to build a new house or to repair an old one. Long an exporter of dates and camels, Muscat and Oman began to export oil in 1967. Although not a member of the Organization of Petroleum Exporting Countries (OPEC), Oman has followed its lead in raising oil prices. At the end of 1979, Oman increased the price for a barrel of crude oil by $4.00 to $28.20, about the average OPEC price.

An open revolt against the government which began in Dhofar in 1969 was put down by Sultan Qabus with the assistance of Iraq, Jordan, Iran, and Britain by 1975. However, in 1979 he risked isolation from the Arab world by endorsing the peace treaty between Egypt and Israel. While wishing to become the constitutional monarch of a democratic country, the sultan has indicated that Oman is not yet ready for democracy.

HISTORY: Muscat and Oman was converted to Islam in the 7th century, during the lifetime of Mohammed. In 1508, the Portuguese conquered the the coastal region. In the 17th century, they were driven out by the Turks, who were themselves expelled in 1741 by Ahmed Ibn Said of Yemen, founder of the present ruling family. In the early 19th century, Muscat and Oman was the most powerful state in Arabia, controlling Zanzibar, much of the Persian coast, and part of present-day West Pakistan, but during this period Muscat lost control of Oman—the interior region

1856-61: Rival heirs dispute succession to throne on death of Said ibn Sultan in 1856; dispute is settled through British mediation under an arrangement in 1861 calling for separation of Zanzibar from Muscat

1913-20: Tribes in interior of Oman rebel against sultan of Muscat, who controls only the cities of Muscat and Matrah, and elect Imam spiritual head of country; Imam is murdered in 1920, and sultan signs treaty with his successor calling for internal tribal autonomy and mutual nonaggression

1951: Traditional association with Britain is confirmed by new treaty of friendship, commerce, and navigation

1954-57: Imam dies in 1954; his successor breaks 1920 treaty and is driven from his capital; Muscat regains control of Oman

1958: Port of Gwadar in Baluchistan is sold to Pakistan

1965-66: UN General Assembly adopts resolution in 1965 calling for elimination of British presence in Muscat and Oman

1969: Leftist rebels in Dhofar province engage in guerrilla warfare in effort to overthrow sultan

1970: Sultan Said ibn Taimur is overthrown by son, Qabus ibn Said, who promises to establish modern government, end country's isolation, and use oil revenues for the good of the people

1975: Victory over rebels in Dhofar province is declared by sultan

1977: Britain closes its military base on the Omani island of Masira

1980: Oman and United States sign agreement to permit U.S. access to country's ports and airfields in exchange for American military and economic aid

---

PAKISTAN

Area: 342,750 sq. mi. **Population:** 83,700,000 (1981 census)
Official Name: Islamic Republic of Pakistan **Capital:** Islamabad
Nationality: Pakistani **Languages:** Urdu (spoken by only 7%) is the official language, but English is also widely used in government and commerce; Punjabi (64%), Sindhi (12%), Pushtu, Brahui, and Baluchi are regional languages **Religion:** Islam is the state religion and is practiced by 97% of the population; the rest are Hindus, Christians, Buddhists, or of no religious affiliation **Flag:** Green with a white vertical stripe at the hoist and a white crescent and a 5-pointed star in the center **Anthem:** National Anthem, beginning "Blessed be the sacred land" **Currency:** Pakistani rupee (9.9 per U.S. $1)

Location: South Asia. It extends c. 1,000 miles from the sea north to the mountain wall of the Hindu Kush and the towering peaks of the Karakoram. It adjoins Iran and Afghanistan on the west and northwest, China on the northeast, India on the east, and the Arabian Sea on the south **Features:** A barren plain stretches along the foothills of the mountains; in the center is the fertile Indus plain **Chief Rivers:** Indus, Sutlej, Chenab, Ravi

Head of State and of Government: President: Gen. Mohammad Zia-ul-Haq, born 1924, assumed office in 1978. He is also Chief Martial Law Administrator, an office he has occupied since the coup of July 1977 **Effective Date of Present Constitution:** 1973, amended 1976, temporarily suspended 1977 **Legislative Body:** Parliament (bicameral), with a National Assembly and a Senate, dissolved 1977; rule is by President Zia and a council of military chiefs. A "Federal Council" is planned **Local Government:** 4 provinces and a federal capital territory plus tribal areas

Ethnic Composition: The population of Pakistan is made up chiefly of Punjabi, Sindhi, Pathan, and Baluchi. Several small tribes live in the mountainous areas **Population Distribution:** 26% urban **Density:** 244 inhabitants per sq. mi.

Largest Cities: (1972 census) Karachi 3,498,634, Lahore 2,165,372, Lyallpur 822,263, Hyderabad 628,310, Rawalpindi 615,392, Multan 542,195, Gujranwala 360,419; (1974 est.) Islamabad 250,000

Per Capita Income: $239 (1980) **Gross National Product (GNP):** $21 billion (1980) **Economic Statistics:** In 1977 about 33% of GNP came from agriculture (wheat, cotton, rice); 16% from manufacturing (textiles, food processing, chemicals, cement, paper, metal manufacturing) and mining; 15% from trade; and 6% from construction **Minerals and Mining:** There are large reserves of natural gas, coal, copper, and some crude oil **Labor Force:** 24 million, with 54% in agriculture **Foreign Trade:** Exports, chiefly cotton, cotton products, leather goods, rugs, fish and rice, amounted to $1.8 billion in 1979. Imports, mainly machinery, transportation equipment, iron and steel, animal and vegetable oils and fats, petroleum and products, chemicals, tea and food grains, amounted to $4.5 billion **Principal Trade Partners:** United States, Japan, Kuwait, Britain, Hong Kong, West Germany

Vital Statistics: Birthrate, 40.5 per 1,000 of pop. (1976); death rate, 12 **Life Expectancy:** 51 years **Health Statistics:** 1,871 inhabitants per hospital bed; 4,049 per physician (1973) **Infant Mortality:** 115 per 1,000 births (1976) **Illiteracy:** 76% **Primary and Secondary School Enrollment:** 7,325,303 (1975) **Enrollment in Higher Education:** 114,913 (1974) **GNP Expended on Education:** 2.1% (1976)

Transportation: Surfaced roads total 16,000 mi. **Motor Vehicles:** 287,800 (1975) **Passenger Cars:** 196,100 **Railway Mileage:** 5,475

Ports: Karachi, Port Qasim **Major Airlines:** Pakistan International Airlines, operates domestic and international services **Communications:** Partly government owned **Radio Transmitters:** 27 **Licenses:** 1,200,000 (1976) **Television Transmitters:** 16 **Receivers:** 350,000 (1976) **Telephones:** 240,000 (1975) **Newspapers:** 102 dailies (1975), 18 copies per 1,000 inhabitants

Weights and Measures: Metric system **Travel Requirements:** Passport, visa not required for stay up to 30 days

---

Throughout its relatively short history, Pakistan has been shot through with powerfully divisive forces. When the Indian subcontinent was granted independence from Britain in 1947, it was decided that a national homeland for Moslems should be created as a nation separate from predominantly Hindu India. For centuries there had been periodic bloodbaths resulting from communal rioting between Hindus and Moslems, and an independent Pakistan was seen as the solution.

Unfortunately, Indian Moslems were concentrated in two widely separated parts. The first consisted of all or part of four provinces now known as Pakistan, which borders Afghanistan, Iran, India, and China. The second and more populous part was carved from the old state of Bengal and is now Bangladesh, bordering India and Burma.

The gulf between the two wings of Pakistan was reflected in and intensified by the 1970 election, the first since independence. Of the 313 seats that were to be filled in the new National Assembly, 167 were won by the Awami League—a Bengali nationalist party, all the strength of which was in Bangladesh. The runner-up was the Pakistan People's party with 88 seats, all for West Pakistan. There was no major national party to bridge the two wings, and virtually the only cement holding them together was a common religion.

On March 1, 1971, at the urging of the Pakistan People's party, Gen. Yahya Khan announced that the convening of the National Assembly would be postponed pending further discussions of major constitutional issues. Leaders of the Awami League claimed they were being cheated.

Widespread rioting in Bangladesh ensued, and strikes crippled the cities. Bengali extremists murdered substantial numbers of non-Bengalis.

On March 25, President Yahya Khan ordered the national army into Bangladesh to crush the separatist movement. The East Bengal Regiment of the army promptly defected to join Bangladesh armed forces, and key bridges, railroads, and communications were blown up or damaged.

An occupation army remained in Bangladesh and had to contend with hostility from the province, sniping and sabotage from Bangladesh guerrillas, and a vast economic drain on the nation as a whole. Millions of refugees fled and hundreds of civilians were killed in the conflict.

In the ensuing months tension between India and Pakistan increased, and on December 4 Indian troops entered the Bengali province. On December 16 the Pakistani armed forces there surrendered to the Indian and Bangladesh command.

This defeat, and the secession of Bangladesh, for which the Pakistani public had been unprepared, led to the resignation of President Yahya Khan and the succession of Zulfikar Ali Bhutto, leader of the People's party, as the first civilian president. Bhutto negotiated the release of 90,000 prisoners and, as a spellbinding orator, set out to restore national pride. He put in train a series of reforms in education, politics, and social life and announced that the state would assume control, but not ownership, of ten basic industries.

In July 1977, following four months of political violence in which at least 350 people were killed, the Pakistani army seized power in a bloodless coup. The Army Chief of Staff, Gen. Mohammad Zia-ul-Haq, then became chief martial law administrator. The initial violence was touched off by alleged election fraud by the ruling People's party.

In March 1978, Bhutto, the most popular civilian politician in Pakistan's history, was convicted of a 1974 political murder and sentenced to hang. Denying his guilt, he appealed to the nation's Supreme Court, but lost, 4-3. Despite clemency pleas from many world leaders, he was hanged in April 1979. Later that year, Zia postponed scheduled national elections, placed opposition leaders under detention for several months, silenced newspaper criticism, and virtually banned political activity.

The U.S. cut off economic aid in 1979 after accusing Pakistan of secret efforts to build nuclear weapons by importing various pieces and materials from Europe and the U.S. After the USSR invasion of Afghanistan put 80,000 Soviet troops at Pakistan's border, the U.S., in early 1980, offered a modest aid package that Zia scornfully refused, but in 1981, a more militantly anti-Soviet U.S. administration negotiated a five-year, $3 billion military and economic aid plan which included a provision for the sale to Pakistan of American F-16 fighter planes, which Zia had eagerly sought. During that year, relations with India became more hostile as the two nations traded charges about each others' nuclear and conventional armament plans.

By late 1981, with as many as two million refugees from Afghanistan straining its resources, Pakistan's economy had seriously worsened and, despite continued suppression of political dissent, resistance to Zia's junta government appeared to be growing.

HISTORY: In the 8th century Moslems from Arabia introduced Islam to the lower reaches of what is now Pakistan. Two centuries later, Moslem warriors swept from the northwest down through the Khyber Pass and conquered the upper reaches of Pakistan, converting millions of the inhabitants to Islam. Moslem power and culture on the Indian subcontinent reached their zenith under the Mogul empire (1526-1857). Despite cultural interchange with the Hindus, the Moslem community continued to maintain its distinct identity under British rule, which lasted until the middle of the 20th century

1906-40: The Moslem League is founded as a separate political organization. Led by Mohammad Ali Jinnah, it demands the establishment of a Moslem state in India

1947: Pakistan is set up as a separate British dominion, with Jinnah as governor-general and Liaqat Ali Khan as prime minister. Establishment of the new state is followed by widespread communal strife between Moslems and Hindus, costing more than a million lives and uprooting millions of Hindus and Moslems

1948-49: Pakistan and India are involved in an undeclared war over the state of Jammu and Kashmir (a state whose predominantly Moslem population is ruled by a Hindu prince who signs Kashmir over to India). A cease-fire is arranged, and the state partitioned by a temporary demarcation line

1951-56: Liaqat Ali Khan is assassinated (1951), ushering in a period of political instability and tension between East and West Pakistan. A new constitution is adopted, and Pakistan becomes a republic within the British Commonwealth with Gen. Iskander Mirza as president

1958-62: Following continued turmoil in both parts of the country, Mirza abrogates the constitution, dismisses the cabinet, and hands over power to the army under Gen. Ayub Khan. Ayub takes over the presidency, dismisses the prime minister, and rules by decree. The new president proclaims new constitution

1965: Ayub Khan is elected president. Pakistan and India fight a brief war over the Rann of Kutch and Kashmir

1969: Ayub resigns in the face of widespread political unrest. Martial law is proclaimed under Gen. Agha Mohammad Yahya Khan, who takes over as president

1970: Yahya Khan proclaims Pakistan an Islamic federal state

1971: Civil war breaks out between Bengali and federal forces and Bengalis are defeated; in December brief war between India and Pakistan results in defeat of Pakistan and the secession of the Bengali province, now Bangladesh. Yahya Khan resigns and Zulfikar Ali Bhutto becomes president

1972: Pakistan and India sign Simla agreement to stabilize relations

1973: New constitution is adopted. Fazal Elahi Chaudhry is elected president by the National Assembly. Former President Bhutto becomes prime minister with no loss of power

1974: Civil rights restored. Pakistan recognizes Bangladesh

1975: Assassination of Provincial Minister Sherpao leads to opposition Awami party being declared illegal. U.S. lifts 10-year ban on sale of arms to Pakistan

1976: India and Pakistan agree to resume diplomatic relations

1977: Pakistani army under Gen. Mohammad Zia-ul-Haq seizes power in a bloodless coup, ending the Bhutto regime. Elections, promised for October, are canceled; political activity is banned; martial-law rule is extended indefinitely

1978: Bhutto is convicted of a 1974 murder and sentenced to die; denying charge, he appeals to Supreme Court, which later rules against him. General Zia assumes the presidency

1979: On April 4, Bhutto, still declaring his innocence, is hanged. Days of rioting follow. U.S. cuts off economic aid, contending that Pakistan is secretly trying to build nuclear weapons with equipment and materials purchased abroad. On Oct. 16, Zia indefinitely postpones national elections scheduled for Nov. 17. He dissolves all political parties, detains opposition leaders, expands jurisdiction of military courts, shuts down critical newspapers. On Nov. 21, a mob, inflamed by false reports from Iran, sets fire to U.S. embassy in Islamabad; Pakistani army rescues embassy personnel after unexplained six-hour delay

1980: Soviet invasion of Afghanistan sends hoards of Afghans across border, where they are held in Pakistani internment camps. Offered $400 million over two years by the U.S. to improve defenses against the Soviets, Zia scoffs at it as "peanuts"

1981: In March, Zia releases 54 prisoners, capitulating to skyjackers who commandeered a Pakistani airliner carrying more than 100 passengers and flew it to Syria. New Reagan Administration in U.S. reverses Carter policy, offering a $3 billion, five-year military and economic aid package, including sale of F-16 fighter aircraft. Some estimates put number of Afghan refugees in Pakistan at more than two million. Relations with India worsen as a result of U.S. military aid offer and mutual suspicions about Indian and Pakistani plans to develop nuclear arsenals; several border clashes occur. Martial law remains in effect

---

PANAMA

Area: 29,762 sq. mi. **Population:** 1,830,175 (1980 census)

Official Name: Republic of Panama **Capital:** Panama **Nationality:** Panamanian **Languages:** Spanish is the official and predominant language; English is widely used in the capital and Colón; and small minorities of Italians, French, Greeks, East Indians, and indigenous Cuna Indians retain their national languages **Religion:** 93% Roman Catholic, 6% Protestant **Flag:** Divided into 4 rectangles: the lower left is blue; the upper right red; the upper left white with a blue star in the center; the lower right white with a red star in the middle **Anthem:** Istmeño Hymn **Currency:** Balboa (1 per U.S. $1)

Location: Latin America, occupying the southern end of the Isthmus of Panama, which forms the land connection between the North and South American continents. Panama is bounded on the north by the Caribbean Sea, on the east by Colombia, on the south by the Gulf of Panama and the Pacific Ocean, and on the west by Costa Rica **Features:** The country is largely mountainous and hilly, with 2 mountain ranges forming the backbone of the isthmus. Lowlands lie along both coastlines; the Atlantic side and eastern Panama are covered almost entirely by tropical rain forests. The Panama Canal bisects the country **Chief Rivers:** Tuira, Bayano, Santa Maria, Chepo, Indio

Head of State and of Government: President Aristides Royo, born 1940, elected 1978 for 6 years **Effective Date of Present Constitution:** October 11, 1972 **Legislative Body:** A National Assembly of Community Representatives, with 505 members elected for 6 years; a 56-member National Legislative Council performs legislative functions when the Assembly is not in session **Local Government:** 9 provinces, each headed by an appointed governor, and one intendency

Ethnic Composition: The population is 70% mestizo, 14% Antilleans (immigrants from the West Indies and their descendants), 10% white and 6% Indian **Population Distribution:** 53.7% urban **Density:** 61 inhabitants per sq. mi.

Largest Cities: (1980 census) Panama 388,638, San Miguelito 157,063, Colón 59,832, David 50,621

Per Capita Income: $1,680 (1980) **Gross National Product (GNP):** $3.2 billion (1980) **Economic Statistics:** In 1973 about 18% came from agriculture (rice, sugar, and bananas); 18% from trade; and 16% from industry (food processing, textiles, clothing, shoes, cement, pharmaceuticals, oil refining, sugar refining) **Minerals and Mining:** There are many minerals that remain unexploited because of poor quality; however, major copper and molybdenum deposits are to be exploited **Labor Force:** 543,000 (1978), of which 45% was engaged in services and commerce, 29% in agriculture, 10% in manufacturing, and 4% in canal activities **Foreign Trade:** Exports, chiefly bananas, shrimp, sugar and petroleum derivatives, totaled $334 million in 1979. Imports, mainly machinery, vehicles and parts, petroleum and food totaled $1.1 billion **Principal Trade Partners:** United States, Saudi Arabia, Ecuador, Venezuela

Vital Statistics: Birthrate, 29.5 per 1,000 of pop. (1977); death rate, 7.1 (1975) **Life Expectancy:** 59 years **Health Statistics:** 284 inhabitants per hospital bed; 1,335 per physician (1977) **Infant Mortality:** 28.5 per 1,000 births **Illiteracy:** 18% **Primary and Secondary School Enrollment:** 502,932 (1977) **Enrollment in Higher Education:** 32,063 (1976) **GNP Expended on Education:** 4.9% (1976)

Transportation: Paved roads total 1,700 mi. **Motor Vehicles:** 103,900 (1975) **Passenger Cars:** 83,800 **Railway Mileage:** 225 **Ports:** Colón, Cristobal, Balboa, Bocas del Toro, Puerto Armuelles **Major Airlines:** Air Panama and Compañía Panameña de Aviación operate international and domestic services **Communications:** Partly government controlled **Radio Transmitters:** 120 **Receivers:** 270,000 (1976) **Television Transmitters:** 13 **Receivers:** 186,000 (1976) **Telephones:** 155,000 (1976) **Newspapers:** 6 dailies, 79 copies per 1,000 inhabitants (1975)

Weights and Measures: Metric system **Travel Requirements:** Passport, visa or 30-day tourist card obtainable from airline, $2 fee **International Dialing Code:** 507

Panama, the narrow serpentine isthmus connecting North and South America, is a largely mountainous country, bisected by a 51-mile-long Panama Canal. Since Nov. 1, 1979, Panama has been building up its financial and commercial status through possession of the land, dry docks, ports, and railroads of the former Canal Zone. (The waterway itself is scheduled to be controlled until Dec. 31, 1999, by the U.S.-operated Canal Commission, in which Panama is a junior partner.) As the home of 85 international banks, and well situtated for the distribution or transshipment of goods, Panama is rapidly becoming the business center of Central America.

Within the country, access roads are sparse, a handicap that the government, with outside help, has been trying to remedy. The eastern half of the country, down to the Colombian border, consists largely of impenetrable jungle inhabited by a few primitive Indian tribes.

On June 16, 1978, in Panama City, President Carter and Panamanian head of state Brig. Gen. Omar Torrijos Herrera took part in ceremonies formally concluding the two new Panama Canal treaties, thus bringing to fruition 13 years of often difficult negotiations. Basically, one treaty covers control of the canal while the other establishes its future neutrality. Under the accords, Panama will obtain full control of the canal in the year 2000, the U.S. will pay Panama $10 million annually in toll revenues (plus added amounts dependent on traffic), and the U.S. has the right to intervene unilaterally in Panama if the canal's operation is ever threatened after the year 2000.

In the final phase of the canal talks, both leaders absorbed considerable criticism from countrymen who felt too much was being given to the other nation. Carter narrowly averted a serious political setback in April 1978 when the U.S. Senate ratified, with but one vote to spare, the second of the two treaties. In order to gain ratification, the Administration accepted reservations favorable to the U.S. but politically embarrassing for Torrijos, who nonetheless accepted them.

The Panama Canal dominates life in the central region, and it has played an overriding role in the nation's politics. Its transfer to Panamanian control, however, has failed to bring about the economic revival the people anticipated. Unemployment and inflation have increased, and strikes and riots have been recurring.

In 1979 facilities were opened on the Pacific coast for transferring Alaskan oil from supertankers to smaller craft to go through the canal for reloading on big ships at the other end.

HISTORY: Little is known about the Indians inhabiting Panama before the arrival of the Spanish explorer Rodrigo de Bastidas in 1502. The region soon fell under the control of Balboa, who in 1513 made his famous crossing of the isthmus and discovered the Pacific. Under Spanish occupation the isthmus became the route by which Inca treasures were shipped to Spain. But Panama was to lose most of its importance in the carrying trade with the collapse of the Spanish Empire

1821: Panama breaks away from Spain and becomes part of Colombia

1848-49: California gold rush enhances importance of Panama as westward-bound U.S. settlers use isthmus as bridge between Atlantic and Pacific; crossings stimulate interest in a canal

1881-89: French company headed by Ferdinand de Lesseps begins work on a canal in 1881; disease among workers and financial problems drive company into bankruptcy within the decade

1903: Panamanians revolt when Colombian senate refuses to ratify Hay-Herrán Treaty granting United States right to build a canal across Panamanian isthmus; United States prevents Colombia from quelling rebellion and Panamanians declare their independence; new republic grants United States exclusive control of a canal zone in perpetuity and permits United States to intervene to protect Panamanian independence

1914: Panama Canal is opened

1939: Canal treaty is amended, eliminating U.S. right to intervene in Panamanian affairs

1964: Riots break out in Canal Zone as Panamanians protest U.S. failure to abide by agreement calling for simultaneous display of Panamanian and American flags

1967: United States and Panama negotiate new treaties under which United States would give up sovereignty over canal to U.S.-Panamanian authority and provide military defense for canal, and under which construction of a new canal might be undertaken; treaties, however, remain unratified

1968: National Assembly impeaches President Marco Aurelio Robles for having violated constitution by backing government candidate in presidential election; Assembly's decision is voided by Supreme Court. Following a dispute over the outcome of the election, opposition candidate Arnulfo Arias is declared president but is overthrown on October 1, 11 days after taking office, in coup led by National Guard; National Assembly is dissolved and constitutional guarantees suspended; Col. José M. Pinilla is sworn in as provisional president

1969: Brig. Gen. Omar Torrijos Herrera, one of the principal leaders of the 1968 coup, emerges as nation's strong man

1972: Torrijos acquires full civil and military powers

1975: Government moves toward nationalization of banana industry. U.S. and Panama sign a preliminary agreement to end U.S. jurisdiction over the Panama Canal and Zone

1977: President Carter and General Torrijos sign two new Panama Canal treaties in Washington, providing for transfer of canal to Panama by the year 2000 and establishing its future neutrality. Panamanians approve treaties in referendum

1978: U.S. Senate barely ratifies second of two treaties; last-minute reservations favorable to U.S. prove a political embarrassment to Torrijos but he finally accepts them; Carter visits Panama for formal conclusion of pacts. Aristides Royo, a lawyer and former education minister who helped negotiate the canal treaties, is elected president by the National Assembly. Torrijos continues as commander of National Guard

1979: Canal Zone is transferred to Panama on Oct. 1

1980: Panama turns down Iran's request for extradition of deposed Shah who had gained asylum there Dec. 15, 1979. Shah departs for Cairo Mar. 23

1981: Petroterminal de Panama awards a contract for constructing a 78-mile pipeline across western Panama; it would save time and cost of shipping Alaskan oil to Gulf and Atlantic ports. Gen. Torrijos is killed in plane crash

---

PAPUA NEW GUINEA

Area: 183,540 sq. mi. **Population:** 3,006,799 (1980 census) Official Name: Papua New Guinea **Capital:** Port Moresby **Nationality:** Papua New Guinean **Languages:** Melanesian Pidgin and Hiri (Police) Motu serve as linguas franca, but are not universal; English is the official language; about 750 localized Papuan languages are spoken **Religion:** About 1,400,000 profess Christianity, with half a million Roman Catholics and the rest Protestants; the rest practice animistic forms of worship **Flag:** Divided diagonally from upper left to lower right; the upper section is red with a gold bird of paradise, and the lower section is black with the five principal stars of the Southern Cross in white **Anthem:** O Arise All You Sons **Currency:** Kina (.67 per U.S. $1)

Location: Southwest Pacific. About 100 miles northeast of Australia, it occupies the eastern half of the island of New Guinea and is bordered on the west by Indonesia. 15% of the area is on islands to the north and east: the Bismarck Archipelago, the northwestern Solomons, and the smaller Trobriand, Woodlark, D'Entrecasteaux and Louisiade groups **Features:** A high mountain ridge bisecting the New Guinea portion rises to about 15,000 feet, graduating north and south to broad upland valleys, plains, and along much of the coast vast swamps. The larger islands are mountainous, some with active volcanoes **Chief Rivers:** Fly, Sepik, Markham, Ramu

Head of State: Queen Elizabeth II, represented by a governor-general, Sir Tore Lokoloko, born 1930, appointed March 1977 **Head of Government:** Prime Minister: Sir Julius Chan, born 1939, appointed March 1980; he is assisted by a National Executive Council **Effective Date of Present Constitution:** 1975 **Legislative Body:** Parliament (unicameral), with 109 members elected for 5 years **Local Government:** 19 provinces and a national capital district

Ethnic Composition: The indigenous population is composed of two major groups, Papuans in the interior and on the south coast of New Guinea, and Melanesians on the north and east coastal areas, and on the islands; minorities include Chinese, Europeans, and Polynesians **Population Distribution:** 13% urban **Density:** 16 inhabitants per sq. mi.

Largest Cities: (1980 census) Port Moresby 122,761, Lae 61,682, Madang 21,332, Wewak 19,554, Goroka 18,797

Per Capita Income: $650 (1979) **Gross National Product (GNP):** $2.1 billion (1979) **Economic Statistics:** About 39% of GNP is derived from manufacturing (meat packing, lumbering, fish and tobacco processing, light industries) and mining and 22% from agriculture (coffee, cocoa, rubber, copra, tea, palm products, timber, livestock) and fishing **Minerals and Mining:** Copper, gold, and silver are exploited, and a search for oil and gas has been started **Labor Force:** 352,500, with 53% in agriculture, 20% in government, 17% in industry and commerce, and 10% in services **Foreign Trade:** Exports, chiefly copper, copra, palm oil, coffee, cocoa, rubber, tea, plywood, tuna, and gold, totaled $960 million in 1979. Imports, mainly foods, machinery, and manufactured goods, chemicals, and petroleum products, totaled $936 million **Principal Trade Partners:** Australia, Japan, United States, West Germany, Singapore

Vital Statistics: Birthrate, 40.6 per 1,000 of pop. (1975); death rate, 17.1 **Life Expectancy:** 49 years **Health Statistics:** 169 inhabitants per hospital bed; 11,327 per physician (1973) **Infant Mortality:** 10.2 per 1,000 births **Illiteracy:** 67% **Primary and Secondary School Enrollment:** 295,503 (1977) **Enrollment in Higher Education:** 9,667 **GNP Expended on Education:** 6.8% (1971)

Transportation: Paved roads total 400 mi. **Motor Vehicles:** 36,900 (1976) **Passenger Cars:** 17,700 **Railway Mileage:** None **Ports:** Kieta, Rabaul, Lae, Port Moresby, Madang **Major Airlines:** Air Niugini maintains domestic and international services; domestic flights are handled by Talair **Communications:** Government owned **Radio Transmitters:** 31 **Receivers:** 100,000 (1976) **Television:** None **Telephones:** 38,000 (1976) **Newspapers:** 2 dailies, 7 copies per 1,000 inhabitants (1974)

Weights and Measures: Metric system **Travel Requirements:** Passport, visa **International Dialing Code:** 675

Papua New Guinea is one of the more recent additions to the world family of nations. The people of this Pacific island country until recent years lived in a near-Stone Age culture. For many of the dark-skinned Melanesian and Papuan indigenous population, the modern world of the 20th century did not exist until the area became the battleground for opposing Japanese and Allied forces.

The native population, one of the most heterogeneous in the Pacific, includes, besides Melanesians and Papuans, a number of Chinese, Australian and Polynesian peoples. These ethnic groups are divided by language, custom and tradition. The land itself is divisive, with physical isolation, difficult terrain and heavy vegetation reinforcing the pattern of diversity. Contact with the outside world was a hit-or-miss proposition for the long colonial period. Today for many of its people the main way of life is still subsistence farming based on taro, yams and bananas.

Commercial agriculture is largely in the hands of foreign investors who have developed plantations for coffee, copra, rubber and tea. Timber is a more recent cash crop that is being developed and has a great potential. Recently, copper from the mines of Bougainville has become the chief export.

Despite the great potential for self-sufficiency, Papua New Guinea is dependent on food imports. With a growing urban population and a poor road network, rice and other staples have to be imported. It also continues to rely heavily on Australia and New Zealand for financial aid.

Since independence, continuing border problems with the neighboring Indonesian province of Irian Jaya (West New Guinea) due to an off-and-on guerrilla war waged by separatists of the Free West Papua Movement has strained relations between the two nations. Refugees that crossed the border to flee the fighting—and reported Indonesian reprisals—have added to the economic burden on Port Moresby. In 1978, the government cracked down on the guerrillas' highland sanctuaries, and in October captured West Papuan leader Jacob Prai. Indonesia and Papua New Guinea began talks in 1979 to set permanent boundaries in the western highlands area—one of the most rugged and inaccessible in the world.

HISTORY: Little is known about the prehistory of Papua New Guinea but it is now established that man was in the New Guinea highlands at least by 8000 B.C. and perhaps as early as 50,000 B.C. The area was settled by Asian peoples by way of Indonesia. The first Europeans to sight New Guinea were probably Portuguese and Spanish navigators in the early 16th century
1828: Dutch take possession of West New Guinea; occasional contact is made with eastern regions
1870s: German firm began to develop copra trade to meet European demand for coconut oil
1884: The British establish protectorate over southern littoral (Papua) after concern in Australia over German encroachment
1906: British New Guinea turned over to Australia
1914: Australian troops occupy German New Guinea
1920: Australia assumes League of Nations mandate over Territory of New Guinea
1941: Japanese invade New Guinea
1942-43: American and Australian forces halt Japanese advance on Port Moresby and regain control of New Guinea and adjacent islands in a series of hard-fought campaigns
1947: Australian rule is reconfirmed by United Nations
1949: Australian territory of Papua and UN trust territory of New Guinea joined under single international trusteeship
1950-60: Native local government councils are established
1951: Legislative Council is established but with limited indigenous participation
1964: House of Assembly replaces Legislative Council
1973: Self-government established in December with Michael Somare as Chief Minister. Australia retains control of defense and foreign relations
1975: Full independence is achieved on September 16
1976: Agreement is reached with Bougainville secessionist leaders after eruption of violence
1977: Prime Minister Michael Somare's Pangu Pati coalition is returned to power in general elections for parliament
1978: Government, proclaiming 200-mile offshore economic zone, takes control of coastal fishing and seabed resources. Papua New Guinea and Australia sign (Dec. 18) treaty settling 6-year boundary dispute with Queensland over Torres Strait
1980: Somare loses vote of confidence in March and is succeeded by Sir Julius Chan as prime minister

PARAGUAY

Area: 157,047 sq. mi. **Population:** 2,973,000 (1979 est.)

Official Name: Republic of Paraguay **Capital:** Asunción **Nationality:** Paraguayan **Languages:** Spanish, the official language spoken by 75%, and Guaraní, spoken by 90%, are the national languages **Religion:** Roman Catholicism is the state religion and embraces about 97% of the population; there are Mennonite colonies in the Chaco **Flag:** Horizontal stripes of red, white, and blue; the national coat of arms in the center of the obverse and the treasury seal in the center of the reverse **Anthem:** National Anthem, beginning "Once the land of America" **Currency:** Guaraní (126 per U.S. $1)

Location: Southern South America. Landlocked Paraguay is bordered on the northeast and east by Brazil, on the south by Argentina, and on the west and north by Bolivia **Features:** The country is divided by the Paraguay River into 2 disparate regions. The eastern part consists of rolling terrain, with wooded hills, tropical forests, and fertile grasslands. To the west is the Chaco, a low plain covered with marshes and dense scrub forests **Chief Rivers:** Paraguay, Pilcomayo, Paraná, Verde

Head of State and of Government: President: Gen. Alfredo Stroessner, born 1912, originally elected in 1954; in 1978 reelected to sixth term of office **Effective Date of Present Constitution:** 1967 **Legislative Body:** Congress (bicameral), consisting of the Senate and the Chamber of Deputies. The Senate is composed of 30 members and the Chamber of Deputies has 60 members, with members of both houses elected for 5 years. Two thirds of the seats in each house are allocated to the majority party and the remaining third proportionately divided among the minority parties **Local Government:** 19 departments, each headed by a governor appointed by the president, and a federal district

Ethnic Composition: About 95% of the population is of mixed Spanish and Indian (Guaraní) descent. Italians, Germans, and Japanese constitute small minorities **Population Distribution:** 40% urban **Density:** 19 inhabitants per sq. mi.

Largest Cities: (1972 census) Asunción 392,753, Fernando de la Mora 36,834, Lambaré 31,656, Encarnación 23,343, Pedro Juan Caballero 21,033

Per Capita Income: $843 (1979) **Gross National Product (GNP):** $2.7 billion (1979) **Economic Statistics:** 39% of the GNP comes from agriculture (livestock, lumber, bananas, rice, coconuts, cocoa); 20% from manufacturing (meat packing, refining of quebracho and cotton, sugar, wood, vegetable oils); and 41% from services **Minerals and Mining:** No important deposits of minerals exist, but hydroelectric potential is immense **Labor Force:** 1 million, with 49% in agriculture, 28% in industry and commerce, 19% in services and 4% in government **Foreign Trade:** Exports, chiefly cotton, soybeans, meat products, quebracho extract, vegetable oils, and essential oils, totaled $305 million in 1979. Imports, mainly foodstuffs, machinery and motors, transportation equipment, nonferrous metals and manufactures, and iron and its products, totaled $432 million **Principal Trade Partners:** United States, Argentina, EC countries, Brazil, Switzerland, Japan

Vital Statistics: Birthrate, 39.8 per 1,000 of pop. (1975); death rate, 8.9 **Life Expectancy:** 62 years **Health Statistics:** 694 inhabitants per hospital bed; 1,189 per physician (1975) **Infant Mortality:** 38.6 per 1,000 births (1971) **Illiteracy:** 26% **Primary and Secondary School Enrollment:** 527,668 (1975) **Enrollment in Higher Education:** 12,212 (1973) **GNP Expended on Education:** 1.4% (1974)

Transportation: Paved roads total 680 mi. **Motor Vehicles:** 30,000 (1971) **Passenger Cars:** 16,000 **Railway Mileage:** 296 **Ports:** Asunción and Concepción on the Paraguay River **Major Airlines:** Lineas Aéreas Paraguayas (LAP) provides international and domestic service **Communications:** Government and privately owned **Radio Transmitters:** 42 **Receivers:** 180,000 (1976) **Television Transmitters:** 2 **Receivers:** 55,000 (1976) **Telephones:** 40,000 (1976) **Newspapers:** 5 dailies, 40 copies per 1,000 inhabitants (1973)

Weights and Measures: Metric system **Travel Requirements:** Passport, no visa for 3 months **International Dialing Code:** 595

Wars have shaped Paraguay's progress to an uncommon degree; the most disastrous was the War against the Triple Alliance—Uruguay, Argentina, and Brazil—in which hundreds of thousands of Paraguayans were killed. The six-year conflict ended in 1870. In the Chaco War, which was fought from 1932 to 1935 in the desert lands with Bolivia, Paraguay lost additional men.

World War II brought a period of prosperity, as the prices of beef, hides, and quebracho wood extract (used in tanning leather) rose sharply. But the war had a more lasting effect on Paraguay's economy. The universal shortages of imported goods and the introduction of cargo aircraft in South America combined to produce a still-flourishing, highly lucrative contraband trade.

The last major civil war was in 1947, in which Gen. Alfredo Stroessner rose to power. He assumed command in 1954 and has been president since then, making Paraguay Latin America's most durable dictatorship. Until recently, political dissidents suffered repression in anonymity because Paraguay is a small country out of the spotlight of world attention. However, U.S. President Carter's emphasis on human rights brought increased attention to these violations.

Relations with the U.S. were strained in 1976 when Domingo Laino, a leader of the Authentic

Radical Liberal party, was arrested upon his return home after denouncing Paraguayan human rights' practices before the Organization of American States. Reports of curtailed rights persist, and in 1979 the Inter-American Association for Democracy and Freedom asserted that the Stroessner government retains power by use of torture. Alcibiades González Valle, head of the Newswriters' Union, was imprisoned in June 1980 for his article deploring the denial of due process to a man held in jail for seven years without formal charges.

The employment picture has been brightened as work progresses on a gigantic Brazilian-Paraguayan hydroelectric project on the Paraná River. Paraguay and Argentina plan to build another complex farther downstream on the Paraná.

HISTORY: The several Indian tribes that inhabited eastern Paraguay before the advent of Europeans were known collectively as Guaraní because of their common language. While not as advanced as the Incas or the Mayas, the Guaraní were farmers and lived in large thatched houses, thus presenting a strong contrast to the nomadic tribes of the Chaco and the Amazon Valley. With the coming of the Spaniards in the 16th century, Paraguay at first dominated the La Plata region but by the 18th century was reduced to an outpost of the viceroyalty, which had become centered on Buenos Aires

1811-13: Paraguay gains its independence from Spain and rejects the leadership of Buenos Aires

1865-70: Paraguay is disastrously defeated in a war against Argentina, Brazil, and Uruguay, losing 55,000 square miles of territory and more than half its population

1932-35: Unsettled boundary dispute leads to Chaco War between Paraguay and Bolivia; Paraguay wins but is economically ruined

1940-48: President Higinio Morínigo, leader of the Colorado party, establishes a period of dictatorial stability, but civil war breaks out when rival forces rise against him. Rebels are defeated, but the Colorados split into two rival groups; the group opposing Morínigo forces him to leave the country

1954: Gen. Alfredo Stroessner engineers a successful coup and is elected president without opposition

1958: Stroessner, unopposed, is reelected to the presidency for five years; all 60 congressmen elected are members of Stroessner's Colorado party

1959-60: Government troops crush rebel uprisings

1964: A "colonels' plot," allegedly organized by exiled officers in Argentina to overthrow Stroessner's government, is crushed

1967: A new constitution is adopted providing for redistribution of congressional seats

1968: Stroessner is reelected for his fourth term of office; for the first time since 1954, opposition parties are permitted to take part in elections, but Stroessner's Colorado party wins majority in both chambers

1969-70: Catholic Church throws down sharp challenge to Stroessner regime, calling on president to undertake reforms

1973: General Stroessner is reelected with 84 percent of the popular vote. Paraguay and Brazil agree to construct a huge hydroelectric complex on the Paraná River

1974: Reports of new antigovernment plots lead to stricter controls and political imprisonments

1975: U.S. oil companies continue explorations in the Chaco region under pacts strongly criticized as unfavorable to Paraguayan interests

1977: Three Communist Party leaders and 11 other political prisoners, jailed since General Stroessner's takeover in 1954, are released, in apparent response to U.S. pressure

1978: Stroessner is reelected to sixth term

1980: Exiled Nicaraguan dictator Anastasio Somoza is assassinated in Asunción Sept. 17; Paraguay breaks relations with Sandinist government, holding it responsible

PERU

Area: 496,222 sq. mi. **Population:** 17,795,000 (1980 est.)

Official Name: Republic of Peru **Capital:** Lima **Nationality:** Peruvian **Languages:** Spanish and Quechua are official languages, many Indians speaking only the latter or Aymara **Religion:** More than 90% of the population is Roman Catholic **Flag:** Vertical bands of red, white, and red with the national coat of arms in the center **Anthem:** National Anthem, beginning "We are free, let us always be so" **Currency:** Sol (405 per U.S. $1)

Location: West coast of South America. Peru is bordered on the north by Ecuador and Colombia, on the east by Brazil and Bolivia,

on the south by Chile, and on the west by the Pacific Ocean
Features: The country is divided into a narrow coastal desert; the high sierra, the zone of the great Andean cordilleras; and the eastern lowlands (montaña), with uncharted hills, forests, and tropical jungles **Chief Rivers:** Amazon, Ucayali-Apurímac, Marañón-Huallaga

Head of State and of Government: President Fernando Belaúnde Terry, born 1912, elected May 1980, took office July 1980. He is assisted by a cabinet headed by Prime Minister Manuel Ulloa Elías
Effective Date of Present Constitution: July 28, 1980 **Legislative Body:** Congress (bicameral), consisting of a Senate of 60 members elected on a regional basis for 5 years plus the former presidents of constitutional govenments as life senators, and a Chamber of Deputies of 180 members elected for 5 years **Local Government:** 24 departments and the constitutional province of Callao

Ethnic Composition: 46% Indian, 38% mestizo, 15% white **Population Distribution:** 63% urban **Density:** 36 inhabitants per sq. mi.

Largest Cities: (1972 census) (M.A. = Metropolitan Area) Lima 2,981,292 (M.A. 4,000,000), Arequipa 304,653, Callao 296,220, Chimbote 159,045, Chiclayo 148,932

Per Capita Income: $1,200 (1980) **Gross National Product (GNP):** $21 billion (1980) **Economic Statistics:** 24% of the GNP is derived from manufacturing (textiles, foodstuffs, iron and steel, ships, metal products and chemicals, automobile assembly) and 12% from agriculture (cotton, sugar, rice, coffee), fisheries, and forestry **Minerals and Mining:** Copper, silver, lead, zinc, iron, petroleum, natural gas, bismuth, molybdenum, gold, and tungsten **Labor Force:** 5.3 million (1978), with 42% engaged in agriculture, 20% in services, and 13% in industry **Foreign Trade:** Exports, mainly copper, fishmeal, silver, iron, petroleum, sugar, cotton, and coffee, totaled $3.5 billion in 1979. Imports, chiefly capital goods, industrial raw materials, and intermediate goods, totaled $2.1 billion **Principal Trade Partners:** United States, Japan, West Germany, Britain, Ecuador, Argentina, Chile, Netherlands

Vital Statistics: Birthrate, 41 per 1,000 of pop. (1975); death rate, 11.9 **Life Expectancy:** 58 years **Health Statistics:** 463 inhabitants per hospital bed; 1,556 per physician (1975) **Infant Mortality:** 58.2 per 1,000 births (1972) **Illiteracy:** 39% **Primary and Secondary School Enrollment:** 3,988,753 (1977) **Enrollment in Higher Education:** 233,420 (1977) **GNP Expended on Education:** 3.6% (1976)

Transportation: Paved roads total 3,350 mi. **Motor Vehicles:** 466,600 (1977) **Passenger Cars:** 300,400 **Railway Mileage:** 1,335 **Ports:** Callao, Talara, Chimbote, Matarani, Ilo, Paita, Pisco **Major Airlines:** Compañía de Aviación Faucett and Aeroperú fly internationally and domestically **Communications:** Government controlled **Radio Transmitters:** 279 **Receivers:** 2,068,000 (1976) **Television Transmitters:** 63 **Receivers:** 600,000 (1976) **Telephones:** 389,000 (1976) **Newspapers:** 35 dailies (1975), 118 copies per 1,000 inhabitants (1974)

Weights and Measures: Metric system **Travel Requirements:** Passport, 90-day tourist card obtainable at port of entry, $10 fee **International Dialing Code:** 51

Peru's economy and social structure were long controlled by a few rich families and foreign mining interests. The aristocrats have always been reluctant to see to the business of government themselves, and consequently the army and, occasionally, popular governments have filled the gap. Racial strains between the major groups—Indian, mestizo, and white—have further complicated politics.

Inflation and crippling political infighting led, on October 3, 1968, to a coup by a military junta, which named Gen. Juan Velasco Alvarado as president. Despite broad social and economic reforms—including land reform and redistributions, a half share in business profits for the workers in Peruvian companies, and nationalization of large industries and public utilities—no protest was heard when Velasco was deposed by Gen. Francisco Morales Bermúdez in August 1975. By that time a faltering economy with rampant unemployment and a rise in the cost of living had offset any benefits gained from the socioeconomic changes.

Morales' government suffered from internal unrest, however, when it imposed an unpopular austerity program in its efforts to cope with an immense foreign debt. Its rule was marked by repression of extremist political publications and ex-

pulsions of leftist military officers and labor leaders. Nevertheless, a Constituent Assembly elected in 1978 drew up a new constitution in the following year. Fernando Belaúnde Terry, Peru's last civilian president, was reelected to that office in the May 1980 elections and embarked on a course to revive the economy. There were substantial increases in 1980 in industrial activity, exports and gross national product. However, inflation rose to a rate of more than 60 percent.

HISTORY: At the time of the Spanish Conquest, Peru was the heartland of the great Inca Empire extending from northern Ecuador to central Chile. In 1532 the empire, which had recently undergone a civil war, fell to Spaniards led by Francisco Pizarro. In the colonial era the Indians of Peru were reduced to a serfdom from which the majority still have not fully emerged. In 1824 Spain's colonial rule came to an end with the defeat of Spanish forces by the revolutionary armies led by José de San Martín and Simón Bolívar

1863-79: Attempts by Spain to regain its former colonies lead to an intermittent war of small naval engagements; in a treaty signed in 1879 Spain finally recognizes the independence of Peru

1879-84: Peru and Bolivia fight unsuccessful War of the Pacific with Chile; Peru is forced to cede the nitrate province of Tarapacá to Chile and to allow Chilean occupation of Tacna and Arica

1924: Víctor Raúl Haya de la Torre founds APRA (Alianza Popular Revolucionaria Americana), dedicated to radical economic and social reforms to improve the lot of the lower classes, especially the Indians, and nationalization of foreign enterprises

1929: A controversy over Tacna and Arica dating back to the War of the Pacific is resolved through U.S. mediation; Arica is awarded to Chile and Tacna is returned to Peru

1945-48: APRA, though barred from putting up candidates, helps elect José Luis Bustamante to the presidency; he is deposed by a military junta led by General Manuel Odría

1956: Ex-President Manuel Prado is elected president with APRA support and legalizes the party

1962: Haya de la Torre wins slim plurality in disputed presidential elections; attempts to form a coalition government fail and army seizes power

1963-68: Military junta permits new elections and Fernando Belaúnde Terry, a moderate, becomes president; his government confronts rising opposition from legislature and a deteriorating economy; in 1968 Belaúnde is overthrown by a military junta headed by Gen. Juan Velasco Alvarado, which nationalizes U.S.-owned oil property

1970: An earthquake hits northern Peru, killing 50,000

1971: Government takes over U.S. copper concession

1972: Government seizes U.S. potash and phosphate concessions

1974: Major newspapers are expropriated and transferred to community guilds by the military regime

1975: Government action against striking civil employees results in widespread rioting in Lima, where hundreds are arrested as army quells demonstrations. Velasco overthrown by Morales

1976: Government declares a state of emergency after students and workers riot to protest a new set of austerity measures and call for a return to elected civilian government. Entire cabinet resigns after Prime Minister Fernandez Maldonado quits following an army crisis. Morales replaces resigning leftists with moderates. Huge foreign debt is accumulated

1977: Trans-Andean oil pipeline begins operation. Peru, in grave cash squeeze, is told by international banking community to enact austerity measures as condition for further credit

1978: Peru's foreign debt is put at $5.5 billion; annual inflation rate reaches 80 percent; unemployment and recession deepen. Government launches austerity program. APRA wins largest bloc of Constituent Assembly seats in Peru's first nationwide election since 1963; the Assembly has the task of rewriting the constitution and leading the nation to civilian government by 1980

1979: New constitution is signed by APRA founder Haya de la Torre in July, shortly before he dies; it gains limited approval by Morales. Inflation rate is reduced to 40%, but a comparable drop in real wages leads to a general strike, which soon collapses

1980: Fernando Belaúnde Terry is elected president. Seven newspapers confiscated by the military government are returned to their owners

1981: Government's announcement in January of wage increases, but greater rises in prices of fuel and foods, leads to strike by General Confederation of Peruvian Workers and some acts of terrorism. President Belaúnde acts Jan. 29 to oust an encampment set up by Ecuadorean troops eight miles inside Peru in the Cordillera del Condor

PHILIPPINES

Area: 115,707 sq. mi. **Population:** 47,914,017 (1980 prelim. census)

Official Name: Republic of the Philippines **Capital:** Manila **Nationality:** Filipino **Languages:** Pilipino (the national language based on Tagalog), English and Spanish are the official languages; almost 90 Philippine languages and dialects are spoken **Religion:** 74% Roman Catholic, 9% Protestant, 7% Moslem, and the rest of other or no affiliation **Flag:** Top half blue, bottom, red, with a white triangle at the hoist containing a gold star in each corner and a golden sun in the center **Anthem:** National Anthem *(Pambansang Awit)*, beginning "Land of the morning, child of the sun returning" **Currency:** Philippine peso (piso) (7.82 per U.S. $1)

Location: Southeast Asia. The Philippines is an archipelago of 7,107 islands stretching about 1,100 miles along the southeastern rim of Asia, with the northern islands about 330 miles from China and the southwestern tip about 30 miles from Malaysia **Features:** 11 islands account for 94% of the total land area and population. Most of the larger islands are mountainous, and are also characterized by extensive coastal plains, wide valleys, volcanoes, mineral and hot springs **Chief Rivers:** Cagayan, Agno, Pampanga, Agusan, Cotabato

Head of State and of Government: President Ferdinand E. Marcos, born 1917, elected 1965, reelected 1981. He is assisted by a prime minister, César Virata, appointed April 1981 **Effective Date of Present Constitution:** 1973 **Legislative Body:** Interim National Assembly of 187 members **Local Government:** 13 regions, comprised of 73 provinces

Ethnic Composition: The dominant racial stock of the Philippines is Malay, with an admixture of Indonesian and Chinese strains. Chinese, Americans, and Spaniards constitute the largest alien minorities **Population Distribution:** 32% urban **Density:** 414 inhabitants per sq. mi.

Largest Cities: (1980 census) Manila 1,626,249, Quezon City 1,165,990, Davao 611,311, Cebu 489,208, Caloocan 471,289, Zamboanga 344,275

Per Capita Income: $589 (1980) **Gross National Product (GNP):** $29 billion (1980) **Economic Statistics:** 39% of the GNP is derived from services, 29% from agriculture (including rice cultivation, sugar, copra, abaca, logs, coconuts); 24% from industry (mining, textiles, and other durable items manufacture) **Minerals and Mining:** There are deposits of iron ore, copper, gold, manganese, chromite, nickel, zinc, coal, and molybdenum. Oil production is beginning **Labor Force:** 17,500,000, with 47% in agriculture, forestry, and fishing; about 12% are in industry **Foreign Trade:** Exports, mainly copra, logs and lumber, sugar, coconut oil, copper concentrates, abaca, and canned pineapple, totaled $4.6 billion in 1979. Imports, chiefly nonelectrical machinery, transportation equipment, mineral fuel and lubricants, base metals, cereals, electric machinery, and textiles, totaled $6.1 billion **Principal Trade Partners:** United States, Japan, EEC, Saudi Arabia

Vital Statistics: Birthrate, 43.8 per 1,000 of pop. (1975); death rate, 10.5 **Life Expectancy:** 58 years **Health Statistics:** 639 inhabitants per hospital bed (1973); 3,154 per physician (1975) **Infant Mortality:** 58.9 per 1,000 births (1974) **Illiteracy:** 17% Primary and Secondary School Enrollment: 10,210,725 (1976) **Enrollment in Higher Education:** 764,725 GNP Expended on Education: 1.4% (1976)

Transportation: Paved roads total 12,500 mi. **Motor Vehicles:** 667,200 (1976) **Passenger Cars:** 386,200 **Railway Mileage:** 1,200 **Ports:** Cebu, Manila, Zamboanga, Iloilo, Davao, Batangas **Major Airlines:** Philippine Air Lines operates domestic and international flights **Communications:** Partly government controlled **Radio Transmitters:** 333 **Receivers:** 1,875,000 (1976) **Television Transmitters:** 24 **Receivers:** 800,000 (1976) **Telephones:** 542,000 (1976) **Newspapers:** **15 dailies, 18 copies per 1,000 inhabitants (1975)**

Weights and Measures: Metric system **Travel Requirements:** Passport, no visa for 21 days, onward ticket **International Dialing Code:** 63

The Philippines, an island nation of plentiful resources, has been unable thus far to realize its rich potential for development. Independence, gained in 1946, has failed to produce effective democratic government. A high rate of population growth has eaten up much of the slow increase in gross na-

tional product, while the gap between the ruling rich and the restless poor remains wide.

Among the bright spots have been the dramatic advance in food production and the modest growth of industry, particularly electronics companies, which swarmed to Manila in 1978 and 1979. Aided by new agricultural technology, the Philippines progressed from being a major rice importer to self-sufficiency in the staple. The birth rate is one of the highest in the world, and the country needs 500,000 new jobs a year, more than it has been able to provide. Thus, malnutrition remains widespread.

Three hundred years of Spanish rule made the Filipinos, a people of basic Malayan stock, the only Roman Catholic nation in Asia, and left a deep Latin imprint. The subsequent 48-year administration of the extensive archipelago by the United States helped impose a Western educational and political structure, but surging nationalism has recently led the people to try to cast off their long dependence on the United States.

Philippine elections have never been free of violence and corruption, and Ferdinand E. Marcos' decisive victory in the November 1969 race was accompanied by widespread charges of fraud, vote-buying, and intimidation, as well as by huge spending. Marcos, assaulted by a mob in 1970 as he was leaving the Congress building, blamed Communism for the climate of violence, while acknowledging that the discontent could be resolved only by creating more jobs, removing social inequities, reforming the machinery of government and developing a constructive nationalism.

In September 1972, Marcos tightened his grip on the reins of power by imposing martial law. In January 1973, he proclaimed the ratification of a new constitution changing the Philippines from a presidential to a parliamentary form of government. Yet he also extended martial law.

Miffed by U.S. criticism of reported human rights violations, Marcos called a national election for April 1978 (the first in six years) to choose members of an interim parliament that is to legislate until martial law is lifted and a regular parliament is formed. (Before permitting the vote, Marcos guaranteed himself a seat in the new assembly, along with the offices of president and prime minister.)

Marcos' strategy, however, backfired badly, as his brief cautious relaxation of restrictions on political activity just prior to the election led to an outburst of antigovernment sentiment, punctuated by public demonstrations against his authoritarian rule. (His main rival, former Senator Benigno Aquino, had to campaign from prison, where he faced a death sentence on a questionable murder conviction.) Though the election results—widely considered fraudulent—showed Aquino to have done poorly, massive anti-Marcos rallies and the arrests of hundreds of protesting workers, students and nuns, demonstrated the existence of widespread opposition to the president. Among the more persistent charges against the regime was that it condoned and fostered corruption in the military. The Marcos government also had to deal with a long-standing Moslem insurrection in the southern Philippines and continuing guerrilla activity in Luzon and the central islands by the Communist New Peoples' Army.

In a new move to consolidate his power, Marcos lifted martial law in January 1981 and, in April, mounted a plebiscite by which he won approval of another constitutional change—the introduction of a six-year presidential term, with no limit on the number of terms that a president might serve. Marcos was elected to the office again in June in a contest boycotted by major opposition leaders on grounds that his control of the nation's election machinery made an effective campaign against him impossible.

HISTORY: For centuries after the birth of Christ the Philippine archipelago was an area of trade and settlement for Southeast Asian people of Malay stock. The area came into the sphere of European influence when it was discovered in 1521 by Magellan. By 1571 the Spanish had assumed control over the Philippines (named for Philip II of Spain) and for next 300 years ruled the islands as a colony

1898: Control of Philippines is ceded to the United States following Spanish-American War

1899: Guerrilla war breaks out against the Americans, ending with complete pacification of islands by 1905

1934: United States passes Philippine independence law providing for a 10-year period for final transfer of sovereignty

1941: Japanese attack Philippines without warning

1945: All of Philippines are freed of Japanese troops

1946: On July 4 the Republic of the Philippines is proclaimed. Independence is followed by widespread unrest and violence by Communist-led Huk guerrillas

1947: Under a 99-year treaty (amended, 1959), Philippines grants U.S. use of 23 strategically vital military bases

1954: Huk rebellion is largely put down

1970: Leftist students stage antigovernment demonstrations; Manila is crippled by general strike

1971: Urban disturbances and guerrilla violence continue. President Marcos accuses Communists of inciting rebellion

1972: Marcos imposes martial law

1973: New constitution goes into effect. Marcos assumes indefinite rule; extends martial law; receives endorsement by electorate, voting in national referendum. Conflict triggered by Moslem insurgency grows

1977: Voters reject a plan calling for a provisional government in the southwestern portion of the Philippines. Talks are deadlocked over the demands of the Moro National Liberation Front for control of the proposed autonomous region

1978: With an eye on U.S. and world opinion, Marcos briefly lifts ban (imposed in 1972) on political activity, prior to election of "interim" national assembly. Election results, allegedly fraudulent, show big win for Marcos' New Society Movement. Propaganda value is mitigated by demonstrations and mass arrests

1979: The total of Moslems fleeing the southern Philippines for Sabah, a nearby Malaysian state, passes the 100,000 mark. A treaty gives the U.S. "unhampered use" of Clark Air Force Base and the Subic Bay naval facility, over which the Filipino flag is raised for the first time; the U.S. agrees to give $500 million in military and economic aid over five years

1981: Martial law lifted in January. Pope John Paul II visits Manila in February. In April plebiscite, Marcos gains approval of change to a six-year presidential term, without limitation on the number of times a candidate may serve. He is elected to a six-year term in June in an election boycotted by opposition political leaders. U.S. Vice President George Bush, in Manila, promises Reagan administration support

---

POLAND

Area: 120,725 sq. mi. **Population:** 35,734,000 (1980 est.)

Official Name: Polish People's Republic **Capital:** Warsaw **Nationality:** Polish **Languages:** Polish is the official and universal language **Religion:** About 95% of the population is Roman Catholic; the rest are Eastern Orthodox, Protestant, Jewish, and of other or no affiliation **Flag:** Horizontal bands of white over red **Anthem:** National Anthem, beginning "Poland still is ours forever" **Currency:** Zloty (33 per U.S. $1)

Location: Eastern Europe. Poland is bounded on the north by the Baltic Sea, on the east by the Soviet Union, on the south by Czechoslovakia, and on the west by East Germany **Features:** The country consists mainly of lowlands, except the mountains on its southern border **Chief Rivers:** Vistula, Oder, Bug, Warta, Narew, San

Political Leader: First Secretary of the Central Committee of the United Workers' Party: Stanislaw Kania, born 1927, elected Sept. 6, 1980, reelected July 17, 1981 **Head of State:** Chairman of the Council of State: Henryk Jablonski, born 1909, reelected 1976 **Head of Government:** Chairman of the Council of Ministers (Premier): Wojciech Jaruzelski, born 1923, appointed Feb. 9, 1981 **Effective Date of Present Constitution:** July 1952 **Legislative Body:** Parliament (unicameral Sejm), with 460 members elected for 4 years. The Sejm is virtually a rubber stamp for the endorsement of party programs **Local Government:** 49 provinces and 3 city provinces, each with a local people's council

Ethnic Composition: The population is virtually homogeneous (98% Polish), with Ukrainians and Byelorussians constituting tiny minorities **Population Distribution:** 58% urban **Density:** 296 inhabitants per sq. mi.

Largest Cities: (1979 est.) Warsaw 1,572,200, Lodz 832,400, Cracow 704,900, Wroclaw 608,400, Poznan 544,000, Gdańsk 448,200, Szczecin 387,800, Katowice 352,500

Per Capita Income: $3,513 (1980) **Gross National Product (GNP):** $125 billion (1980) **Economic Statistics:** 65.9% of the GNP is derived from industry (mining, steel, ships, machine manufacture, chemicals, power production, and foodstuffs); 9.1% is derived from commerce, and 8.9% from agriculture (wheat, rye, potatoes, oats, barley, sugar beets) **Minerals and Mining:** There are large deposits of coal, lignite, sulphur, copper ore, salt, vanadium, titanium, natural gas and zinc **Labor Force:** 19,300,000, with 31% in agriculture and forestry, 25% in industry **Foreign Trade:** Exports, chiefly copper, sulphur, coal, ships, textiles, steel, cement, chemicals, and foodstuffs, totaled $16.8 billion (1979). Imports, mainly oil, iron ore, fertilizers, wheat, and leather footwear, totaled $18.1 billion **Principal Trade Partners:** USSR, East Germany, Czechoslovakia, West Germany, Britain, United States, Iran, Italy, France, Romania, Austria

Vital Statistics: Birthrate, 19 per 1,000 of pop. (1977); death rate, 9.0 **Life Expectancy:** 71 years **Health Statistics:** 129 inhabitants per hospital bed; 615 per physician (1976) **Infant Mortality:** 24 per 1,000 births (1977) **Illiteracy:** negligible **Primary and Secondary School Enrollment:** 5,627,132 (1976) **Enrollment in Higher Education:** 575,499 (1975) **GNP Expended on Education:** 6% (1976)

Transportation: Paved roads total 40,000 mi. **Motor Vehicles:** 2,116,300 (1977) **Passenger Cars:** 1,547,300 **Railway Mileage:** 16,683 **Ports:** Gdańsk, Gdynia, Szczecin **Major Airlines:** Polish Airlines LOT operates both domestically and internationally **Communications:** Government controlled **Radio Transmitters:** 51 **Licenses:** 8,230,000 (1976) **Television Transmitters:** 69 **Licenses:** 6,822,000 (1976) **Telephones:** 2,753,000 (1976) **Newspapers:** 44 dailies, 248 copies per 1,000 inhabitants (1975)

Weights and Measures: Metric system **Travel Requirements:** Passport, visa (2 photos, $10 fee) for 90 days

---

Four times in Poland's postwar history workers' revolts have set the nation on new economic and political courses. The first was in 1956, when factory employees in Poznan took to the streets to demand food. A political convulsion followed, bringing Wladyslaw Gomulka to power as first secretary of the Polish United Workers (Communist) party and ending much of the repression of the Stalinist period. Fourteen years later, in December 1970, port workers in Gdańsk marched in protest and set in motion the riots that led to Gomulka's downfall. His replacement, Edward Gierek, charted new policies in an effort to repair the errors of Gomulka's autocratic rule and improve the living conditions of the average Polish citizen. The June 1976 riots over food-price increases were a warning to Gierek's regime of what had happened twice before. The fourth great upheaval occurred in July and August 1980, when thousands of workers went on strike in Gdańsk and othr Baltic cities. The strike caused a major shakeup in the government.

Gierek, with his premier, Piotr Jaroszewicz, a trained economist, recharted Poland's five-year economic plan for 1971-75, emphasizing consumer industries and raising wages significantly. Following the 1976 riots, a system of compulsory deliveries for farmers was replaced by long-term contract deliveries, and planning has been even more consumer-oriented. Gierek also opened the state-controlled press to a limited measure of meaningful debate. Poland has expanded business and political relations with the West.

Gierek sought to resume normal relations with the Roman Catholic Church. In 1979, the Polish-born Pope John Paul II visited Poland—according to the government as sovereign of the Vatican City-State on the occasion of the 35th anniversary of the Communist regime. But the Pope ostensibly paid tribute to the 900th anniversary of the murder of

Saint Stanislaw, whose festival the government had refused to allow him to attend, and praised the saint as an opponent of oppressive government. Stefan Cardinal Wyszynski, Roman Catholic primate of Poland for 32 years, died at the age of 79 on May 28, 1981.

The national crisis of 1980 which began with wildcat strikes by workers protesting price hikes of meat in Gdańsk and other industrial cities in July, grew to involve about 800,000 strikers by mid-August, and resulted in Gierek's resignation in early September. The new government formed by Stanislaw Kania recognized the independent Solidarity workers' union of about 10 million members and agreed to most of their economic demands. Lech Walesa, the strike leader at the Lenin shipyards in Gdańsk who emerged as the workers' spokesman, tried to give the government time to institute political reforms, but sporadic strikes continued into 1981. In May the government finally recognized the independent farmers' union, Rural Solidarity.

The Soviet Union condemned the strike leaders as counter-revolutionaries who endangered the Communist system, but apart from sending in Soviet troops to hold army maneuvers on Polish soil at critical times, it refrained from military intervention. To ease Poland's staggering foreign debt, the U.S. and 14 other Western nations rescheduled Poland's debt repayments of about $2.5 billion.

Party chief Kania, a moderate, began to meet Solidarity's demands that abuses by privileged party officials be stopped and the union be given access to the media. He assured the special congress of the Communist Party which met in July that the party would continue its socialist "renewal,"'or democratic reforms. Despite the recent political upheaval, however, Poland remained a Soviet-bloc state.

HISTORY: The recorded history of Poland dates from the 10th century, when Slavic tribes in the region united and their conversion to Christianity began. The medieval era was one of incessant wars, culminating in the defeat of the Teutonic Knights by Poland and Lithuania, united under the Jagiello dynasty. After the last Jagiello king died in 1572, Polish power began a gradual decline as a result of internal weaknesses and external conflicts. Beginning in 1772, and despite the national uprising of 1794 led by Thaddeus Kosciusko, successive partitions eliminated Poland as a sovereign state, a condition that persisted until the close of World War I

1918-21: Independent Polish republic is proclaimed; Versailles Treaty gives Poland access to Baltic Sea through Polish Corridor, free city of Danzig is set up; attempts by Allies to award Poland's eastern provinces to Russia lead to war between the 2 countries in 1920; Poles, aided by French, defeat Russians and win most of territorial claims in 1921 Treaty of Riga

1926-35: General Joseph Pilsudski, former chief of state, governs as virtual dictator after overthrowing democratic government; at his death in 1935, he is succeeded by Edward Smigly-Rydz

1939-45: Germany and Soviet Union, allied in nonaggression pact, invade Poland in September 1939, and the country is once again partitioned; all Poland comes under Nazi rule after Germany attacks USSR in 1941; about six million Poles, half of them Jews, are exterminated by Nazis, and 2.5 million more are deported to Germany as slave labor; Soviet troops reenter Poland in 1944; in August, Poles stage Warsaw uprising, which is crushed by Germans while Soviet forces remain inactive outside city; Germans are expelled in 1945

1947: Soviet-dominated government claims huge majority in the officially controlled elections of 1947; Communist regime proceeds to Sovietize country

1956: Workers and students in Poznan stage mass demonstration against Communist rule and Soviet control; Wladyslaw Gomulka becomes leader of the Polish United Workers' (Communist) party; Stefan Cardinal Wyszynski, under arrest since 1953, is released

1968: Poland joins Soviet Union and other Warsaw Pact members in invasion of Czechoslovakia. At home a campaign against "Zionists" and "revisionists" is waged

1970: Agreement is reached with West Germany on diplomatic relations, including acceptance of Oder-Neisse line as border between Germany and Poland. Economic unrest leads to ouster of Gomulka, who is succeeded by Edward Gierek

1973: Rapprochement with the Vatican
1974: Land reform law reorganizes small farms into larger units in exchange for increased social benefits
1975: Administrative reform changes the three-level system of local government into a two-level system, increasing Gierek's power. Gierek is named first secretary for a second five-year term
1976: Workers stage violent demonstrations and strikes to protest proposed drastic increases in food prices
1979: Polish-born Pope John Paul II draws huge crowds during visit to Poland
1980: Edward Babiuch replaces Piotr Jaroszewicz as premier. At 8th Communist Party Congress, Gierek admits economy is in bad shape, says economic recovery in 1980s will be slow. Workers in Gdańsk and other cities protest meat price hikes with work stoppages. Strike spreads until 800,000 workers are on strike. Józef Pińkowski supplants Babiuch as premier; other party leaders dismissed in major change. Government gives in to the strikers' demand for independent trade unions. Gierek resigns; he is succeeded by Stanislaw Kania as party leader
1981: Wojciech Jaruzelski succeeds Pińkowski as premier. Government recognizes independent national farmers' union, Rural Solidarity. Communist First Secretary Kania, on reelection, assures special party congress that democratic reforms will continue. Nation experiences severe food shortages

---

PORTUGAL

Area: 35,549 sq. mi. **Population:** 9,866,000 (1979 est.)

Official Name: Portuguese Republic **Capital:** Lisbon **Nationality:** Portuguese **Languages:** Portuguese is the official and universal language **Religion:** 97% Roman Catholic **Flag:** Green and red vertical stripes, the red covering two-thirds of the flag; at the dividing line is the national coat of arms encircled in gold **Anthem:** The Portuguese **Currency:** Escudo (59.2 per U.S. $1)

Location: Western Europe, occupying the western portion of the Iberian peninsula. Portugal is bounded on the north and east by Spain and on the south and west by the Atlantic Ocean **Features:** The Tagus River divides the country into 2 distinct regions, the north being mountainous and the south consisting of rolling plains **Chief Rivers:** Tagus, Douro, Guadiana, Sado, Mondego

Head of State: President: Gen. António dos Santos Ramalho Eanes, born 1935, elected 1976, reelected 1980 **Head of Government:** Premier Francisco Pinto Balsemão, born 1937, took office Jan. 10, 1981 **Effective Date of Present Constitution:** April 1976 **Legislative Body:** Parliament (unicameral Assembly), with 250 members elected for 4 years. An all-military Revolutionary Council reviews Assembly laws as to their constitutionality **Local Government:** 22 districts (including locally autonomous Madeira and the Azores), each with an appointed governor and district assembly

Ethnic Composition: The people are a homogeneous mixture of ethnic strains, including Celtic, Arab, Berber, Roman, Germanic, and Iberian **Population Distribution:** 37% urban **Density:** 278 inhabitants per sq. mi.

Largest Cities: (1975 est.) Lisbon 829,900, Oporto 335,700; (1973 est.) Amadora 65,870, Coimbra 55,985, Barreiro 53,690

Per Capita Income: $2,009 (1980) **Gross Domestic Product (GDP):** $20 billion (1980) **Economic Statistics:** 43% of the GDP is derived from mining, manufacturing, and construction (electronics, textiles, wines, cork, food processing, ship-building, and ship repair) 18% from agriculture (grains, fruits, vegetables, wines); 14% from commerce and finance; and 25% from services **Minerals and Mining:** Wolfram, cassiterite, beryl, copper pyrites, and iron ore **Labor Force:** 4.1 million (1979), with 35% in industry, 34% in services, and 31% in agriculture **Foreign Trade:** Exports, chiefly cork, sardines, wines, textiles, minerals, machinery, and diamonds, totaled $3.4 million in 1979. Imports, mainly machinery and industrial equipment, petroleum products, optical instruments, cotton, steel, wheat, and corn, amounted to $6.5 billion **Principal Trade Partners:** West Germany, United States, Britain, France, Italy, Spain, Sweden, Iraq

Vital Statistics: Birthrate, 19.2 per 1,000 of pop. (1976); death rate, 10.5 **Life Expectancy:** 69 years **Health Statistics:** 187 inhabitants per hospital bed; 817 per physician (1976) **Infant Mortality:** 39 per 1,000 births (1975) **Illiteracy:** 29% **Primary and Secondary School Enrollment:** 1,676,378 (1975) **Enrollment in Higher Education:** 79,702 **GNP Expended on Education:** 3.7% (1975)

Transportation: Paved roads total 24,800 mi. **Motor Vehicles:** 1,322,000 (1976) **Passenger Cars:** 1,034,000 **Railway Mileage:** 2,214 **Ports:** Lisbon, Leixões, Setúbal, Funchal, Douro **Major Airlines:** Transportes Aéreos Portugueses (TAP) flies internationally **Communications:** Government owned **Radio Transmitters:** 180 **Licenses:** 1,525,000 (1976) **Television Transmitters:** 42 **Licenses:**

723,000 (1976) **Telephones:** 1,119,000 (1976) **Newspapers:** 30 dailies, 70 copies per 1,000 inhabitants (1975) **Weights and Measures:** Metric system **Travel Requirements:** Passport, no visa for 60 days **International Dialing Code:** 351

Portugal is the poorest country in Western Europe. Most of its people still make their living from the soil, but there is a bitter division between the hilly north, with its small independent farmers, and the more level south, where landless peasants lived for centuries in fear of the owners of huge estates. Portugal's experiment in democratic socialism, which began in 1976, has been complicated by the nation's relative lack of experience with democracy. António de Oliveira Salazar, who was premier from 1932 to 1968, governed as a harsh dictator, and his successor, Marcello Caetano, made few meaningful changes. After Portugal's African territories had revolted against Portuguese rule in the 1960s, Caetano was overthrown in 1974 by the Armed Forces Movement (MFA), a coalition of soldiers who were tired of the struggle in Africa and sympathetic to socialism. The MFA government granted independence to the African territories.

A National Assembly was elected in April 1975. "Rightist" parties had been outlawed, but the Social Democratic Center became the voices of those favoring a role for private enterprise. The Socialist party won a plurality in the Assembly, but the MFA remained in control of the government.

Despite continued unrest, a new constitution was adopted in 1976; it is distinctly socialist, and is democratic in all its essentials, although it reserves some power for the military-dominated Revolutionary Council. Gen. António dos Santos Ramalho Eanes was elected president; the National Assembly became an effective legislature; most restrictions on freedom of expression ended; and peace returned to the country.

The weak economy and continued arguments over the return to private ownership of farms illegally seized in 1974 have troubled the fledgling democracy. Mário Soares was premier in a minority socialist government from July 1976 to December 1977. In January 1978, he formed a majority coalition with the Social Democratic Center—actually the most non-socialist of the major parties. President Eanes dismissed him in July after the coalition broke down, and appointed a government of technocrats who were not members of the Assembly. Soares complained that a government drawn from outside the Assembly was unconstitutional, and the Assembly rejected the technocratic government. After a second government of technocrats, with Carlos Alberto Mota Pinto as premier, took office, Soares and the socialists joined the Communists in forcing Mota Pinto to resign in June 1979.

In the elections of Dec. 2, 1979, the moderate Democratic Alliance won 45 percent of the popular vote and formed a new government with Francisco Sá Carneiro as premier. He managed to curb government spending and to reduce inflation slightly, and his coalition made impressive gains in parliamentary elections on Oct. 5, 1980, at the expense of the Communists. But Sá Carneiro died in a plane crash on December 4; he was succeeded as premier by Francisco Pinto Balsemáo on Jan. 9, 1981.

HISTORY: Lusitania, the western part of the Iberian peninsula, was conquered by Julius Caesar and Augustus. The Visigoths gained control over most of the region in the 5th century A.D. and maintained their rule until the coming of the Moors three centuries later. Portugal was established as an independent state by 1185 and was consolidated after the final expulsion of the Moors in 1249. Its independence, however, remained threatened by Castile until 1385, when the Castilians were defeated in battle
15th cent.: Prince Henry the Navigator captures Ceuta, on northwest African coast, in 1415; under his aegis, Portuguese naviga-

tors undertake series of voyages that result in rediscovery of Madeira Islands and penetration of Africa; Vasco da Gama becomes first European to sail to India (1497-99)
1500-20: Pedro Cabral reaches coast of Brazil in 1500 and claims land for Portugal
1580-1640: Philip II of Spain seizes Portuguese throne, beginning Portugal's 60-year period of "Spanish Captivity"; Portuguese revolt against Spanish rule and regain independence under John of Braganza, who becomes king
1807: Napoleon's forces march on Portugal
1822: Brazil declares its independence
1910: Manuel II is deposed; Portugal is declared a republic
1932: António de Oliveira Salazar, former finance minister, becomes premier after a long period of civil unrest and political instability; he institutes dictatorial rule
1961: India annexes Portuguese enclave of Goa; Portuguese crush insurrection in Angola, in southwest Africa
1968: Marcello Caetano becomes premier
1974: Liberal reforms initiated following bloodless coup which toppled Caetano and installed António de Spínola as president. He is succeeded later the same year by Francisco da Costa Gomes. Violent clashes occur between revolutionary and rightist forces
1975: In April, the first free elections in almost half a century give an Assembly majority to moderates and centrists. Azevedo replaces Gonçalves as premier
1976: New constitution is enacted. António dos Santos Ramalho Eanes is elected president and appoints Mário Soares premier
1977-78: International Monetary Fund issues stringent conditions as price to Portugal for $750-million loan; ensuing austerity measures lead to collapse of government. Soares forms new government of Socialists and conservatives, which also collapses; President Eanes dismisses him. Carlos Alberto Mota Pinto becomes premier in government of technocrats
1979: Mota Pinto submits government's resignation; Democratic Alliance wins plurality in parliamentary elections
1980: New cabinet is headed by Premier Francisco Sá Carneiro, who is killed in plane crash in December. President Eanes is reelected to a second four-year term
1981: Francisco Pinta Balsemáo becomes premier (Jan. 10); he resigns on Aug. 10, but is redesignated as premier on Aug. 25

QATAR

Area: 4,247 sq. mi. **Population:** 250,000 (1979 est.)
Official Name: State of Qatar **Capital:** Doha **Nationality:** Qatari **Language:** Arabic is the official and dominant language; English and Farsi are spoken by some **Religion:** 98% of Qataris are Sunni Moslems of the Wahabi sect. **Flag:** Maroon with white serrated border near the hoist **Anthem:** National Anthem (no words) **Currency:** Qatari riyal (3.64 per U.S. $1)
Location: Southwest Asia. Qatar forms a 100-mile long peninsula stretching north into the Persian Gulf. It borders Saudi Arabia and the United Arab Emirates on the south **Features:** A low, hot, dry plain, consisting of nearly flat limestone with loose sand and gravel on top **Rivers:** None
Head of State and of Government: Emir: Khalifa ibn Hamad al-Thani, born 1932, assumed power in 1972. He is advised by an appointed Council of Ministers which he heads as prime minister **Effective Date of Present Constitution:** 1970; not fully implemented **Legislative Body:** A 30-member advisory council
Ethnic Composition: Arabs (38%), Pakistanis (29%), Iranians (15%). The population is almost 80% non-native **Population Distribution:** 71% urban **Density:** 59 inhabitants per sq. mi.
Largest Cities: Doha 150,000, (1979 est.); Umm Said 5,500
Per Capita Income: $31,838 (1980) **Gross National Product (GNP):** $5.5 billion (1980) **Economic Statistics:** Qatar's national income derives almost wholly from oil recovery; the chemical industry is growing **Minerals and Mining:** Oil is the chief resource; natural gas deposits are being developed; limestone and clay are also mined **Labor Force:** 100,000 (90% non-Qatari) with about 70% in industry, service and commerce, 20% in government and 10% in agriculture **Foreign Trade:** Exports totaled $4 billion in 1979, 93% from oil. Imports, chiefly consumer goods and industrial equipment, totaled $1.5 billion **Principal Trade Partners:** EC countries, United States, Japan
Vital Statistics: Birthrate, 50 per 1,000 of pop. (1974); death rate, 19 **Life Expectancy:** 47 years **Health Statistics:** 96 inhabitants per hospital bed; 938 per physician (1974) **Infant Mortality:** 42 per 1,000 births (1972) **Illiteracy:** 75% **Primary and Secondary School Enrollment:** 38,000 (1980) **Enrollment in Higher Education:** 910 **GNP Expended on Education:** 2.0% (1975)

Transportation: Paved roads total 275 mi. **Motor Vehicles:** N.A. **Railway Mileage:** None **Ports:** Doha, Umm Said **Major Airlines:** Gulf Air serves Doha **Communications:** Government owned **Radio Transmitters:** 6 **Receivers:** 40,000 (1976) **Television Transmitters:** 3 **Receivers:** 30,000 (1976) **Telephones:** 29,400 (1978) **Newspapers:** 2 dailies

Weights and Measures: Metric system **Travel Requirements:** Passport, visa, valid 6 months, 2 photos

---

Oil production, begun shortly after World War II and now valued at roughly $3.8 billion a year, is the country's economic base. With oil proceeds, roads have been built, a sea-distilled water supply established, an educational program instituted, and free medical services introduced. Steps toward diversification have included the exploitation of the Gulf's fishery potential, the production of cement from local raw materials, encouragement of investment in domestic projects, investigation of the mechanics of natural gas recovery, transportation, marketing and usage, and the introduction of domestic refining. Qatar has developed a steel and petrochemical industry.

After Britain declared it would withdraw its military forces from the Persian Gulf area by the end of 1971, Qatar declared its independence on September 1, 1971. The ruler of Qatar, Emir Ahmad ibn Ali ben Abdullah al-Thani, was deposed in a bloodless coup by his cousin, Emir Khalifa ibn Hamad al-Thani, on February 22, 1972.

Qatar is a member of the Organization of Petroleum Exporting Countries (OPEC), and the government has gone along with the organization's anti-Israeli policies. Qatar severed diplomatic relations with Egypt in 1979 in concert with other Arab countries after the Egyptian-Israeli peace treaty was signed. It has increased oil prices periodically to the OPEC base price of $32 per barrel of crude oil as of June 1980.

HISTORY: For a long time Qatar was under Persian rule, and paid a bounty to the governor of Bushire for the right to fish for pearls. In the 19th century it became independent of Persia under Thani, the founder of the al-Thani dynasty
1871-1913: Qatar is occupied by Ottoman Turks
1916: Qatar comes under British protection
1971: Qatar declares its independence
1973: Qatar announces embargo on oil to U.S.
1977: Government completes nationalization of all oil operations
1979: Qatar cuts diplomatic ties with Egypt after Egyptian-Israeli peace treaty

---

ROMANIA

Area: 91,699 sq. mi. **Population:** 22,048,305 (1979 est.)
Official Name: Socialist Republic of Romania **Capital:** Bucharest
Nationality: Romanian **Languages:** Romanian is the official and dominant language. Hungarian, German, Ukrainian, and Yiddish are minority languages **Religion:** About 80% of the population nominally belongs to the Romanian Orthodox Church, and about 9% to the Roman Catholic Church. The rest are mainly Protestant, Jewish, and Moslem **Flag:** Blue, yellow, and red vertical stripes with the national coat of arms in the center **Anthem:** The Tricolored Song **Currency:** Leu (4.47 per U.S. $1)
Location: Southeastern Europe. Romania is bounded on the northeast by the Soviet Union, on the east by the Black Sea, on the south by Bulgaria, on the southwest by Yugoslavia, and on the west by Hungary **Features:** The Carpathian Mountains and Transylvanian Alps form a semi-circle through the center of the country, separating the plains in the east and south from the Transylvanian plateau in the northwest **Chief Rivers:** Danube, Prut, Siret, Olt, Ialomita, Jiu, Mures

Political Leader and Head of State: President Nicolae Ceausescu, born 1918, elected 1974, reelected 1975; since 1965, Secretary-General of the Central Committee of the Romanian Communist Party, and since 1967 president of the State Council; the primary legislative body **Head of Government:** Prime Minister Ilie Verdet,

born 1924, appointed 1979 **Effective Date of Present Constitution:** August 1965 **Legislative Body:** Grand National Assembly (unicameral), consisting of 349 members elected for 5 years; it actually performs little legislative work **Local Government:** 39 counties with people's councils elected for 5 years, and Bucharest municipality

Ethnic Composition: 88% of the population is of Romanian stock, tracing its ancestry back to the Latin settlers of the Roman Empire. Hungarians (8%) are the leading ethnic minority, with smaller numbers of Germans, Ukrainians, Serbo-Croats, Jews, and Turks **Population Distribution:** 49% urban **Density:** 240 inhabitants per sq. mi.

Largest Cities: (1979 est.) Bucharest 1,832,015, Brasov 299,172, Timisoara 281,320, Constanta 279,308, Cluj 274,095, Iasi 262,493, Galati 252,884, Craiova 220,893

Per Capita Income: $4,017 (1980) **Gross National Product (GNP):** $89 billion (1980) **Economic Statistics:** In 1978 industry accounted for 57% of the national income, while agriculture accounted for 15% **Minerals and Mining:** Large deposits of petroleum, natural gas, copper, lead, zinc, bauxite, manganese, bismuth, mercury, silver, iron ore, and coal **Labor Force:** 12 million (1979) with 36% in agriculture and 26% in industry **Foreign Trade:** Exports, mainly oilfield equipment, farm and other machinery, furniture and textiles totaled $11 billion in 1979. Imports, chiefly machinery and equipment, iron ores, coke, fuel, and electric motors, totaled $10 billion **Principal Trade Partners:** West Germany, USSR, Czechoslovakia, Italy, Britain, France, East Germany, Poland, China, United States, Iran, Libya

Vital Statistics: Birthrate, 19.6 per 1,000 of pop. (1977); death rate, 9.6 **Life Expectancy:** 70 years **Health Statistics:** 108 inhabitants per hospital bed; 750 per physician (1976) **Infant Mortality:** 31.2 per 1,000 births (1977) **Illiteracy:** negligible **Primary and Secondary School Enrollment:** 4,110,930 (1975) **Enrollment in Higher Education:** 381,321 (1976) **GNP Expended on Education:** N.A.

Transportation: Paved roads total 17,680 mi. **Motor Vehicles:** 45,100 (1970) **Railway Mileage:** 6,910 **Ports:** Constanta, Galati, Braila **Major Airlines:** Tarom flies internationally and domestically **Communications:** Government owned **Radio Transmitters:** 62 **Licenses:** 3,104,000 (1976) **Television Transmitters:** 194 **Licenses:** 2,963,000 (1976) **Telephones:** 1,076,000 (1974) **Newspapers:** 20 dailies, 129 copies per 1,000 inhabitants (1974)

Weights and Measures: Metric system **Travel Requirements:** Passport, visa, valid 60 days **International Dialing Code:** 40

For centuries a rural, backward country, Romania has the largest oil fields (now declining) of any country in Eastern Europe. Building on oil wealth, the Romanians have invested in modern chemical, steel, machinery, and related industries. Close economic ties have been fostered with Western Europe as well as with the Soviet bloc.

Although it remains a member of the Warsaw Pact alliance and of the Communist Council for Mutual Economic Assistance, Romania has successfully asserted its right to conduct its own foreign affairs. Alone among the Eastern European countries, Romania was outspoken in criticizing the Russian invasion of Afghanistan in 1979.

Not wanting to be merely a supplier of raw materials and agricultural products to the more developed Communist countries, Romania has persistently refused to subordinate its desire for rapid economic development to Soviet plans for complete integration of Eastern European and Soviet economies. The nation's industrial production increased by about 8.5% in 1980—the largest gain among Eastern European countries. But Romania's trade debt to the West totaled about $8 billion by the end of 1980, mainly because of a decline in exports and a rise in the cost of imports.

The heart of Romanian tactics aimed at resisting Moscow's pressure is a balancing act. Its essence is the matching of moves that irritate Moscow with moves that are pleasing. For instance, President Nicolae Ceausescu was the first East European leader to establish (1967) diplomatic relations with West Germany and the first leader of a Communist country in a quarter century to be visited by a U.S. president (Nixon in 1969).

More recently, this balancing act has become noticeable in Ceausescu's handling of political dissidents. In 1978 the government freed a group of political dissidents as part of an amnesty program in celebration of Romania's 100th anniversary of independence from Turkey. However, Ceausescu continues to keep a tight rein on the dissidents.

Ceausescu in 1974 strengthened his position as undisputed leader by naming himself president, installing a colorless loyalist, Manea Manescu, as premier, and abolishing the nine-member presidium, the top ruling body of the Communist party. He replaced the presidium with a twenty-three-member Executive Committee which is packed with loyalists. In 1979 President Ceausescu appointed Ilie Verdet as premier, and in 1980 he named his wife, Elena Ceausescu, first deputy premier.

HISTORY: Ancient Dacia, comprising most of present-day Romania, was part of the Roman Empire until the 3rd century A.D. After the Romans legions withdrew, the region was overrun by Goths, Huns, Avars, Slavs, and Mongols. The withdrawal of the Mongols in the 13th century was followed by the establishment of the principalities of Walachia and Moldavia, which soon fell under Turkish rule. Both were to remain in the Ottoman Empire until well into the 19th century

1828-29: Walachia and Moldavia are occupied by Russia in Russo-Turkish War; although technically remaining part of the Ottoman Empire, they actually become Russian protectorates

1859-66: Alexander John Cuza is elected prince of Walachia and Moldavia, which are officially united as Romania in 1861; 5 years later, Cuza is deposed and is succeeded by Carol I of the house of Hohenzollern-Sigmaringen

1878: Congress of Berlin grants Romania full independence

1916-19: Romania fights on Allied side in World War I; overrun by Austro-German forces, it is forced to accept a harsh peace treaty, which is later annulled by the Allied victory; Romania seizes Bessarabia from Russia, Bukovina from Austria, and Transylvania from Hungary

1938: King Carol II establishes Fascist dictatorship

1940-45: Under German pressure, Romania returns territories taken from Russia and Hungary; King Carol is overthrown by Marshal Ion Antonescu, aided by Iron Guard, a militaristic Fascist group; in 1941, Romania enters World War II on Axis side; following the invasion of Soviet troops in 1944, Antonescu is overthrown and Romania switches to Allied side; a Communist-led government is set up in 1945

1964: Showing increasing independence of the Soviet Union, Romanian Communist party asserts the right of each Communist party to form its own political program without interference

1968: Romania supports liberalization program in Czechoslovakia and refuses to join in invasion of Czechoslovakia by Soviet and other Warsaw Pact forces

1971: After declining to do so a year earlier, Romania joins the Soviet bloc's new international investment bank

1974: Communist Party Central Committee approves constitutional change establishing the office of President, which is assumed by Ceausescu. Manea Manescu becomes premier

1975: U.S. Congress passes resolution granting Romania most-favored-nation trade status

1977: Earthquake kills at least 1,500. Ceausescu asks for eight more years of austerity and sacrifice to raise Romania to ranks of developed nations

1979: Government established regional councils to supervise agriculture. Ilie Verdet becomes premier

---

RWANDA

Area: 10,169 sq. mi. **Population:** 4,819,317 (1978 census)

Official Name: Republic of Rwanda **Capital:** Kigali **Nationality:** Rwandan **Languages:** Kinyarwanda (the national language) and French are the official languages; Kiswahili is spoken in the commercial centers **Religion:** More than 55% of the population is Christian, chiefly Roman Catholic; the rest are animist and Moslem **Flag:** Vertical stripes of red, yellow, and green with a black "R" in the center **Anthem:** Our Rwanda **Currency:** Rwanda franc (92.8 per U.S. $1)

Location: Central Africa. Landlocked Rwanda is bordered on the north by Uganda, on the east by Tanzania, on the south by Burundi, and on the west by Zaire **Features:** Known as the "Land of a Thousand Hills," the country consists largely of grassy uplands and hills, which roll down southeastward from the chain of volcanoes in the northwest **Chief Rivers:** Kagera, Nyabarongo, Akanyaru

Head of State and Government: President: Maj. Gen. Juvénal Habyarimana seized power in a bloodless coup July 1973 **Effective Date of Present Constitution:** Dec. 17, 1978 **Legislative Body:** National Development Council (unicameral) of 50 members **Local Government:** 10 prefectures, administered by appointed prefects

Ethnic Composition: 89% Hutu, a Bantu farming people; 10% Tutsi, a pastoral people of Hamitic origin; 1% Twa pygmies **Population Distribution:** 5% urban **Density:** 474 inhabitants per sq. mi.

Largest Cities: (1978 census) Kigali 117,749, Butare 21,691

Per Capita Income: $210 (1979) **Gross Domestic Product (GDP):** $959 million (1979) **Economic Statistics:** 60% of the GDP is derived from agriculture (bananas, coffee, pyrethrum, tea, cotton, manioc, corn, spices, sweet potatoes); 18% from mining (cassiterite, columbo-tantalite, wolfram, amblygonite, beryl), 16% from commerce, and 6% from construction and manufacturing **Minerals and Mining:** Cassiterite is the most abundant mineral, although columbo-tantalite, wolfram, amblygonite, and beryl are also mined. There are unexploited deposits of bismuth, phosphates, monazite, magnatite, and natural gas **Labor Force:** 1,940,000 (1970), with 95% engaged in small handicrafts or agriculture, and less than 5% in industry. Wage earners numbered 70,000 in 1973 **Foreign Trade:** Exports, mainly Arabica coffee, cassiterite, tea, and wolfram, totaled $203 million in 1979. Imports, chiefly textiles, iron, petroleum, and vehicles, totaled $155 million **Principal Trade Partners:** Belgium, France, United States, Britain, Japan, Kenya, Iran, West Germany

Vital Statistics: Birthrate, 50 per 1,000 of pop. (1975); death rate, 23.6 **Life Expectancy:** 44 years **Health Statistics:** 510 inhabitants per hospital bed; 42,900 per physician (1976) **Infant Mortality:** 132.9 per 1,000 births **Illiteracy:** 75% **Primary and Secondary School Enrollment:** 446,720 (1976) **Enrollment in Higher Education:** 1,108 (1975) **GNP Expended on Education:** 2.6% (1976)

Transportation: Paved roads total 200 mi. **Motor Vehicles:** 11,300 (1975) **Passenger Cars:** 6,500 **Railway Mileage:** None **Ports:** None **Major Airlines:** Air Rwanda operates international flights **Communications:** Government controlled **Radio Transmitters:** 4 **Receivers:** 70,000 (1976) **Television:** None **Telephones:** 3,000 (1975) **Newspapers:** 1 daily, .04 copies per 1,000 inhabitants (1975)

Weights and Measures: Metric system **Travel Requirements:** Passport, visa for stay up to 3 months, $10 fee, 4 photos

---

Rwanda, formerly part of the Belgian UN trust territory of Ruanda-Urundi, is Africa's most densely populated country. Over four and a half million people live in an area slightly smaller than the state of Maryland. Small and landlocked, it lies atop the mountainous western slope of the Great Rift Valley known as "the Roof of Africa." Through centuries of migratory settlement and population increase, the clearing of land for food production, together with overgrazing of cattle, has made Rwanda one of tropical Africa's most eroded areas. Its people contend with drought as well as poor soil in raising their crops of beans, bananas, sorghum, cassava, corn, and potatoes.

Despite erosion, Rwanda possesses scenic grandeur and great touristic potential, especially around Lake Kivu, considered by many the most beautiful of African lakes. However, the serene-looking highlands have known dark tragedy. In 1959-60, the Hutu people, the short stocky peasants who made up 85 percent of the population, rose up in bloody revolt against the Tutsi (or Watusi), the tall aristocratic people who kept the Hutu in feudal bondage for centuries. Thousands of Tutsi were killed or fled into neighboring countries. Neither willing nor able to stem the tide of Hutu unrest, the Belgian administration gave support to the Hutu on the eve of independence. In 1961 the Tutsi king, Mwami Kigeri V, was deposed and a republic declared, causing more than 160,000 Tutsi to flee to Burundi. Many returned later but in 1963-64 an armed invasion by Tutsi refugees set off another massacre of the tall people and put an apparent end to their minority caste domination.

Since independence, the government has concentrated on food production and the building of internal roads and road links into neighboring coastal countries. More than a fourth of national expenditures are for education and there has been some progress in light industry, but the major problems—population pressures, malnutrition, and poverty—remain largely unsolved.

In July 1973 Rwanda's manifold problems were compounded further as the government of President Grégoire Kayibanda was overthrown in a bloodless military coup, after months of tribal unrest between the governing Hutu majority and the Tutsi minority. The leader of the coup, Maj. Gen. Juvénal Habyarimana assumed the presidency.

HISTORY: Rwanda, along with neighboring Burundi, originally was inhabited by the pygmy Twa people, and later occupied by Bantu Hutus from the Congo basin. By the 15th century, the Tutsi, or Watusi, a tall, cattle-keeping people believed to have originated in Ethiopia, had arrived in both countries and imposed a feudal overlordship on the more numerous Hutus. European explorers reached the area in the 19th century, and in 1885 the region was taken over by Germany. It was made a Belgian League of Nations mandate after World War I and remained under Belgian control after World War II. With the growth of African nationalism, Hutu leaders in Rwanda began seeking independence and emancipation from Tutsi domination
1955-58: Tutsi extremists, viewing Belgian political reforms as threat, repress Hutu movement and murder several Hutu leaders
1959: Bloody Hutu revolt overthrows Tutsi monarchy; Tutsis suffer heavy casualties and 120,000 of them flee to Burundi and other neighboring countries
1960: Leaders of Hutu Emancipation Movement (PARMEHUTU) establish provisional government
1961: Belgium recognizes PARMEHUTU regime, but United Nations, hoping to preserve ethnic-economic union of Rwanda and Burundi, rules it unlawful and orders elections; PARMEHUTU scores overwhelming victory
1962: UN resolution ends Belgian trusteeship and grants Rwanda full independence
1963: Abortive Tutsi invasion from Burundi results in massacre of 12,000 Tutsi in Rwanda and renewed Tutsi exodus
1970: Rwanda signs friendship pact with Belgium; work is begun on road link to Kampala, Uganda
1973: President Grégoire Kayibanda overthrown in bloodless military coup; Maj. Gen. Juvénal Habyarimana takes over
1974: Death sentences of ex-President Kayibanda and seven other government officials commuted to life imprisonment
1976: Ugandan oil blockade brings economic hardship
1978: Habyarimana is elected to a 5-year term as president
1980: France gives Rwanda 14.6 million francs for its protein food development program and for modernization of Rehenger hospital

---

SAINT LUCIA

Area: 238 sq. mi. **Population:** 115,783 (1980 census)
Official Name: Saint Lucia **Capital:** Castries **Nationality:** Saint Lucian **Languages:** English is the official language; a French patois containing many African elements is widely spoken **Religion:** Chiefly Roman Catholic (90%) with several Protestant churches represented **Flag:** A blue field containing a white-bordered black triangle covered at the bottom by a yellow triangle **Anthem:** N.A. **Currency:** East Caribbean dollar ($2.70 per U.S. $1)
Location: St. Lucia, the second largest of the Windward Islands, lies south of Martinique and northeast of St. Vincent in the Eastern Caribbean **Features:** The island is of volcanic origin and mountainous, with magnificent scenery; there is a good harbor at Castries. The climate is tropical and humid, with heavy rainfall in the summer
Head of State: Queen Elizabeth II through Acting Governor-General Boswell Williams **Head of Government:** Prime Minister Winston Cenac, appointed 1981 **Effective Date of Present Constitution:** Feb. 22, 1979 **Legislative Body:** Parliament (bicameral) consisting of a House of Assembly with 17 elected members and a Senate of 11 members, of whom 6 are appointed on the advice of the prime minister, 3 by the Opposition, and two by the governor-general. The Parliament has a five-year term **Local Government:** 16 parishes
Ethnic Composition: Chiefly African or of mixed origin **Population Distribution:** N.A. **Density:** 486 inhabitants per sq. mi.
Largest City: (1980 census) Castries 42,770
Per Capita Income: $690 (1979) **Gross Domestic Product (GDP):** $83 million (1979) **Economic Statistics:** The economy is primarily

agricultural, with tourism and industry gaining in importance. The chief crops are bananas, coconuts, cocoa, citrus fruits, sugar, spices; there is some timber production and commercial fishing. Industrial development is increasing rapidly. An oil refining and transshipment facility and an industrial free port zone are under construction **Labor Force:** 45,000 (1979), with 40% engaged in agriculture **Foreign Trade:** Exports, including bananas and a growing amount of manufactured goods, totaled $28 million in 1979. Imports, including manufactured goods, machinery, food, fuel and clothing, totaled $78 million **Principal Trade Partners:** Britain, Commonwealth and CARICOM countries, United States
Vital Statistics: Birthrate, 31.5 per 1,000 of pop. (1979); death rate, 7.2 **Life Expectancy:** 57 years **Health Statistics:** 202 inhabitants per hospital bed; 4,231 per physician (1975) **Infant Mortality:** 19.2 per 1,000 births (1977) **Illiteracy:** 20% Primary and Secondary School **Enrollment:** 25,386 (1976) **Enrollment in Higher Education:** N.A. **GDP Expended on Education:** N.A.
Transportation: Paved roads total 280 mi. **Motor Vehicles:** 5,500 (1975) **Passenger Cars:** 3,700 **Railway Mileage:** None **Port:** Castries **Major Airlines:** St. Lucia Airways and major international airlines **Communications:** Government and privately owned **Radio Transmitters:** 3 **Receivers:** 82,000 (1975) **Television Transmitters:** 1 **Receivers:** 1,700 (1974) **Telephones:** 7,000 (1976) **Newspapers:** 3: 1 twice weekly, 1 weekly, 1 fortnightly; 78 copies per 1,000 inhabitants
Weights and Measures: Metric and British systems are used **Travel Requirements:** Passport and/or return ticket **Direct Dialing Code:** 809

A former British possession in the Windward Islands, Saint Lucia is an island nation characterized by its African heritage, French accent, British political system and all the social and economic burdens attendant on many newly independent mini-states. Independence was attained on February 22, 1979.

Traditionally tied to agriculture for its livelihood, the island had embarked on the path of new industrial and commercial development. The largest single project is a combined oil transshipment terminal and free trade zone being developed by American oil interests. The manufacturing sector has been expanded, accounting for nearly half of the island's exports. The island's even climate and great beauty has made tourism a major industry, especially since the construction of a modern jetport near Castries in 1975. Traditional cash crops (bananas, cocoa, coconuts) have been bolstered under a development plan supported by the World Bank and the International Monetary Fund.

Yet, although St. Lucia's future appears bright in comparison with some of its neighbors, it shares many of their problems. Dependence on imports of finished goods has been largely responsible for continuing balance of payments deficits, and high unemployment (25% or more) remains a major problem.

A landslide victory for the opposition Labor party in the July 2, 1979, general elections turned Prime Minister Compton and his United Workers party out of power after 15 years. A moderate, Compton had sought close cooperation with the Caribbean Economic Community (CARICOM). Former judge Allan Louisy became the new prime minister but was unable to cope with St. Lucia's virulent brand of confrontation politics, which featured constant disruptive strikes by civil servants and others, as well as bitter infighting between some half dozen charismatic political leaders. When Louisy's colleague, Foreign Minister George Odlum, formed a new party early in 1981, Louisy resigned in favor of Attorney General Winston Cenac.

HISTORY: Little is known of the island's early history, but successive waves of Amerindian migration are thought to have populated the island in the 1300s. By the time of the first European landing, in the 16th century, the island was inhabited by the war-like Caribs. Initially a Spanish possession, the first attempts at settlement were made by the English, in 1605 and 1638-40; both succumbed to the Caribs. Subsequent French settlement proved more successful. Britain and France fought for control of the island over the next 150 years, with the last British occupation—in June, 1803—finally accepted by France in the Treaty of Paris in 1814. A plantation economy flourished, based on slavery; by 1834, when slavery was abolished in all British possessions, the island's African population numbered over 13,000.

1838: St. Lucia, administered as a separate colony, is merged with the government of the Windward Islands
1958: St. Lucia joins Federation of the West Indies; remains member until its dissolution in 1962
1959: St. Lucia separated from Windward group, becomes dependency under direct British administration
1962-65: Discussions ensue between St. Lucia and other smaller British territories on federation with Barbados, without success
1967: St. Lucia becomes self-governing member of the West Indies Associated States May 3
1974: Elections return United Workers party government to power; Prime Minister John G.N. Compton promises full independence
1977: July 24-27 constitutional conference in London agrees on framework for independence
1979: Independence attained Feb. 22; Labor party boycotts ceremony, as striking teachers and civil servants threaten the new nation's stability. Labor party scores upset victory over Compton's UWP in July. Allan Louisy becomes prime minister
1980: Banana industry devastated by Hurricane Allen, Aug. 4
1981: Louisy resigns, but refuses to call new election, after his party rival, George Odlum, forms a third faction (the Progressive Labor party). Attorney General Winston Cenac becomes Labor party prime minister in April

SAINT VINCENT AND THE GRENADINES

Area: 150 sq. mi. **Population:** 104,000 (1978 est.)
Official Name: Saint Vincent and the Grenadines **Capital:** Kingstown **Nationality:** Saint Vincentian **Languages:** English, with some French patois spoken **Religion:** Methodist, Anglican and Roman Catholic **Flag:** Five unequal vertical stripes of blue, white, yellow, white and green with a breadfruit leaf, scroll, sprig of cotton and coat of arms centered on the yellow stripe **Anthem:** National Anthem, beginning "St. Vincent! Land So Beautiful" **Currency:** East Caribbean dollar (2.70 per U.S. $1)
Location: Eastern Caribbean. The islands are situated south of St. Lucia and north of Carriacou Island, a part of Grenada **Features:** The island of St. Vincent, 18 miles long and 11 miles wide, is volcanic in origin with a mountain ridge running its length and rising in the north to Soufrière volcano. The climate is tropical with heavy summer rains. The Grenadines portion consists of the islands of Bequia, Canouan, Mayreau, Mustique, Prince, Palm, Petite St. Vincent and Union, among others
Head of State: Queen Elizabeth II, represented by a governor-general, Sir Sydney Douglas Gun-Munro **Head of Government:** Prime Minister Robert Milton Cato, born 1915, appointed Dec. 1979 **Effective Date of Present Constitution:** Oct. 27, 1979 **Legislative Body:** House of Assembly (unicameral) with 13 elected representatives and 6 senators (4 appointed on the advice of the prime minister and 2 on the advice of the opposition leader). The normal term is 5 years **Local Government:** 5 parishes plus the Grenadines
Ethnic Composition: Mainly of African or mixed origin **Population Distribution:** N.A. **Density:** 693 inhabitants per sq. mi.
Largest City: (1978 est.) Kingstown 25,000

Per Capita Income: $380 (1979) **Gross National Product (GNP):** $43 million (1979) **Economic Statistics:** About 20% of GNP is from agriculture (bananas, arrowroot, coconuts, nutmeg, mace, sugar, vegetables). St. Vincent is the world's largest producer of arrowroot. 9% of GNP is from industry (agricultural and food processing, furniture, clothing, sugar refining, flour). Tourism is important **Minerals and Mining:** None **Labor Force:** 61,000 (1979) **Foreign Trade:** Exports, chiefly bananas, arrowroot, copra and mace, totaled $15 million in 1979. Imports, mainly fuel, fertilizer, transportation equipment and textiles, totaled $50 million **Principal Trade Partners:** Britain, Trinidad and Tobago, Barbados, Canada, United States
Vital Statistics: Birthrate, 35 per 1,000 of pop. (1979); death rate, 7.1 **Life Expectancy:** N.A. **Health Statistics:** 170 inhabitants per hospital bed (1972) **Infant Mortality:** 38 per 1,000 births (1979) **Illiteracy:** 5% **Primary and Secondary School Enrollment:** 26,938 (1975) **Enrollment in Higher Education:** N.A. GNP Expended on Education: N.A.
Transportation: Paved roads total 185 mi. **Motor Vehicles:** 4,300 (1976) **Passenger Cars:** 3,500 **Railway Mileage:** None **Port:** Kings-

town **Major Airlines:** LIAT and Caribbean Airways provide service **Communications:** Privately owned **Radio Transmitters:** 2 **Receivers:** N.A. **Television Transmitters:** None **Telephones:** 5,000 (1977) **Newspapers:** 1 weekly
Weights and Measures: British system **Travel Requirements:** N.A. **Direct Dialing Code:** 809

On October 27, 1979, Saint Vincent and its dependent islands, the Grenadines, gained independence after 10 years as a British Associated State. But along with its newly independent neighbors in the Caribbean, St. Vincent faces acute social and economic growing pains in the 1980's.

Dependent on tourism and agriculture for their livelihood, the residents of this tiny nation in the Lesser Antilles average an annual per capita income of $380. Unemployment is estimated at 20 percent of the labor force, and the annual growth rate in the population is 2%, which threatens to put an even greater strain on the country's resources.

Despite these inherent problems, the island prospered in the 1970s, with gross domestic product growing 14 percent between 1976 and 1978. Its favorable climate encouraged good harvests and a booming tourist industry, matched by a modest growth in the manufacturing sector aided by government investment. But the eruption of the long-dormant volcano, Soufrière, on April 13, 1979, proved a heavy blow to the island's fragile economy. Although no one was injured—unlike the last major eruption in 1902, in which 2,000 died—the volcano spewed clouds of ash and smoke over the northern half of St. Vincent, forcing evacuation of 20,000 local residents. The eruption also gravely damaged the banana crop, which received another devastating blow from Hurricane Allen on Aug. 4, 1980.

General elections held December 5 of 1979 saw Milton Cato and his moderately socialist Saint Vincent Labour party returned to power. The SVLP won 11 of the 13 seats in the House of Assembly, with the others going to the centrist New Democrats; the conservative People's Political party failed to gain a seat. A brief rebellion by would-be secessionists on Union and Palm islands on Dec. 7 was quelled by police on the following day, although a state of emergency imposed when the revolt began was not lifted until May 1980.

By 1981, the government had launched a campaign to diversify the economy and, in that year, sugar production was revived, but the island was also experiencing severe labor troubles as several unions struck sporadically, interrupting water delivery, police work, and other services. Proposed legislation that would have given government greater power to impose "public order" had to be diluted in the face of a threat of a general strike by workers in both the public and private sectors.

HISTORY: The earliest known inhabitants of the island were the Arawak Indians, soon supplanted by the warlike Caribs, who migrated from South America to people most of the Lesser Antilles from 1300 to 1600. Christopher Columbus was the first European to see the island, landing there on January 22, 1498 (Saint Vincent Day). Claimed by the British since 1627, a dispute ensued with France for control of the island, ending only with its formal ceding to Britain in the Treaty of Versailles in 1783. After an abortive uprising by the Caribs in 1795-96, most of the native population was deported to the island of Rattan in the Bay of Honduras, with the island thereafter peopled mainly by African slaves and their descendants
1833: St. Vincent is included in the Government of the Windward Islands, remaining a part of that colony until its dissolution in 1960, when it becomes a separately administered territory
1902: Volcano of Soufrière erupts, killing over 2,000 people
1958: St. Vincent participates in Federation of West Indies until its dissolution in 1962
1962-65: St. Vincent joins in discussions on federation of the Windward Island territories—including Grenada and St. Lucia—with Barbados; talks prove fruitless

1969: St. Vincent becomes an internally self-governing Associated State, with Britain controlling defense and foreign relations
1974: Milton Cato and St. Vincent Labour party swept into power in Dec. 9 elections, with support of Ebenezer Joshua's People's Progressive party; Cato becomes chief minister
1978: Constitutional talks are held in London Sept. 18-21
1979: Soufrière erupts April 13; 20,000 inhabitants are evacuated, crops destroyed and tourism disrupted. St. Vincent and the Grenadines gain their independence from Britain Oct. 27. Dec. 5 general elections to the House of Assembly result in victory for Milton Cato and the SVLP, which wins 11 of 13 seats
1980: St. Vincent continues ongoing discussions with St. Lucia and Barbados on forming a common coast guard. Hurricane Allen causes extensive damage and crop losses, Aug. 4
1981: Widespread strikes disrupt the economy. The sugar industry is revived, after a 20-year hiatus, with the opening of a grinding plant bought from Trinidad and Tobago

SAN MARINO

Area: 23.4 sq. mi. **Population:** 21,000 (1978 est.)
Official Name: Most Serene Republic of San Marino **Capital:** San Marino **Nationality:** Sanmarinese **Language:** Italian is the official and universal language **Religion:** Roman Catholicism **Flag:** Horizontal bands of white and blue with the national coat of arms in the center **Anthem:** National Anthem, beginning "Honor to you, O ancient Republic" **Currency:** Italian lira (1102 per U.S. $1)

Location: Landlocked San Marino is situated in the Apennines, southwest of Rimini, Italy **Features:** The town of San Marino is situated on the slopes of Mount Titano, and much of the republic is coextensive with the mountain, which has three pinnacles **Chief Rivers:** San Marino, Fumicello

Head of State and of Government: 2 Captains Regent, elected by the Council for six-month terms, assisted by a Congress of State (cabinet) **Effective Date of Present Constitution:** October 1600 **Legislative Body:** Great and General Council (unicameral), with 60 members elected every 5 years **Local Government:** 9 parishes (*castelli*), headed by Captains of the Castle and elected committees

Ethnic Composition: The Sanmarinese are of Italian origin. A small number of aliens reside in the republic **Population Distribution:** 92% urban **Density:** 897 inhabitants per sq. mi.

Largest Town: (1977 census) San Marino 4,628

Per Capita Income: N.A. **Gross National Product (GNP):** N.A. **Economic Statistics:** The principal occupations are farming, manufacturing, and animal husbandry. Main agricultural products are wheat, cheese and wine, while chief industrial goods are textiles, cement, paper, leather, and furs. Tourism (3 million a year) and the sale of postage stamps are major sources of income **Minerals and Mining:** Building stones are quarried for export **Labor Force:** 4,300 mostly employed in the agricultural sector. The rest work for manufacturing and service industries **Foreign Trade:** Exports consist of wine, woolens, furniture, ceramics, and postage stamps. Manufactured goods of all kinds make up the main imports. Because of a customs union with Italy, no record is kept of foreign payment transactions

Vital Statistics: Birthrate, 14.8 per 1,000 of pop. (1977); death rate, 6.9 **Life Expectancy:** 72 years **Health Statistics:** Public health institutions include a hospital, a dispensary, and a laboratory of hygiene; 750 inhabitants per physician **Infant Mortality:** 14.8 per 1,000 births **Illiteracy:** Negligible **Primary and Secondary School Enrollment:** 2,884 (1976) **Enrollment in Higher Education:** N.A. **GNP Expended on Education:** N.A.

Transportation: Streets and roads total more than 60 miles **Motor Vehicles:** 9,584 **Passenger Cars:** 4,724 **Railway Mileage:** 20 miles of electric funicular railway **Ports:** None **Radio Transmitters:** No radio or TV transmitters **Radio Licenses:** 6,000 (1976) **Television Licenses:** 4,000 (1976) **Telephones:** 6,000 (1976) **Newspapers:** No dailies, but an edition of *Il Resto Del Carlino* of Bologna gives special attention to San Marino news; there are 3 fortnightlies

Weights and Measures: Metric system **Travel Requirements:** Passport, no visa **International Dialing Code:** 39

The Apennine slopes shelter a tiny country with a legendary beginning and an existence almost as fabled. Its founder is said to be Marinus, a Christian stonecutter from Dalmatia seeking refuge from persecution in the fourth century. The republic, named San Marino after the canonized Saint Marinus, is the world's smallest and oldest,

having remained independent for some 1,600 years. It lived on after the collapse of the Roman Empire and survived such upheavals as an interdiction by the pope in the Middle Ages, occupation by troops of Giulio Cardinal Alberoni in 1739-40, the conquests of Napoleon, and the unification of Italy in the late 19th century.

San Marino's knack for survival carried it through the Mussolini era and World War II. In 1943 it rid itself of the Fascistlike regime of the Mussolini period, and from 1945 to the autumn of 1957 was ruled by a coalition of Communists and left-wing Socialists. After the defection of six members of the ruling group, an anti-Communist coalition gained control and went on to win subsequent elections. In 1973 that coalition resigned over economic policy disputes. The Christian Democrats formed a new coalition cabinet with Socialists and a splinter party. A coalition of Christian Democrats and Socialists governed from 1976 to 1977; in 1978, a coalition of Communists and Socialists formed a government. No major changes in government policy were made.

San Marino, situated on three-peaked Mount Titano, derives approximately 80 percent of its gross national product from tourism and the sale of postage stamps to collectors. The tourists, numbering about 3 million annually, are afforded a magnificent view of Rimini and the Adriatic Sea from three old fortresses and may visit stately buildings, churches, and museums.

HISTORY: According to tradition, San Marino was founded in the 4th century A.D. by Marinus, a Christian stonecutter from Dalmatia who was later canonized. Reputedly the world's oldest republic, it is the last of the Italian peninsula's once-numerous city-states
1631: Pope Urban VIII recognizes the independent status of San Marino
1739-40: San Marino is occupied by a military force under a papal legate, Giulio Cardinal Alberoni, who attempts to establish sovereignty over republic; occupation is terminated by Pope Clement II
1862: San Marino and Italy form a customs union
1939-44: San Marino, although officially neutral in World War II, is occupied by the German army and is the scene of heavy fighting during Allied advance into northern Italy
1945: Communist and left-wing Socialist coalition wins majority of seats in elections for the Grand Council
1957: Defection of six Council members leads to fall of coalition; anti-Communist councillors form new government
1973: Coalition government resigns; new cabinet is formed with Socialists and Christian Democrats; women are given expanded legal rights
1974: General elections are held and coalition of Christian Democrats and Socialists remains in power. New cabinet is formed. Three women win seats in the Council
1975: Socialists withdraw from the two-party coalition, leaving the Christian Democrats without an absolute parliamentary majority
1976: New coalition of Socialists and Christian Democrats is formed
1977: Socialist-Christian Democrat coalition collapses; Communists fail to form new government
1978: Communists form new government after Christian Democrats, winners of a plurality in May elections, fail to do so
1981: First woman Captain-Regent, Maria Lea Pedini, takes office

SAO TOME and PRINCIPE

Area: 372 sq. mi. **Population:** 83,000 (1978 est.)
Official Name: Democratic Republic of São Tomé and Principe **Capital:** São Tomé **Nationality:** São Tomean **Languages:** Portuguese is the main language, and a local creole is also spoken **Religion:** Roman Catholicism is the predominant religion: **Flag:** Three equal horizontal stripes of green, yellow and green with a red triangle at the hoist and two black stars on the yellow stripe **Anthem:** Total Independence **Currency:** Dobra (37.8 per U.S. $1)

Location: These two islands are in the Gulf of Guinea, about 125 miles off the west coast of Africa **Features:** Hilly, wooded interiors and flat coastal plains **Chief Rivers:** Grande, Abade

Head of State and of Government: President Manuel Pinto da Costa, elected 1975 **Effective Date of Constitution:** 1975 **Legislative Body:** Popular Assembly (unicameral), with members elected for 4 years. Control is in the hands of the MLSTP party, headed by the president **Local Government:** 2 island provinces

Ethnic Composition: The native population is mostly African, with some Portuguese admixture **Population Distribution:** N.A. **Density:** 223 inhabitants per sq. mi.

Largest Cities: (1970 census) São Tomé 7,681; Santo António 1,618 **Per Capita Income:** $260 (1977) **Gross Domestic Product (GDP):** $19.7 million (1977) **Economic Statistics:** Most of the population is engaged in the growing of plantation agricultural products and fishing **Minerals and Mining:** None **Labor Force:** 40,000, with 62% in agriculture (coffee, cocoa, coconuts, bananas), 7% in industry (beverages, copra, palm oil and fish processing) and commerce **Foreign Trade:** Exports, mostly palm products, coffee, cocoa and fruit, totaled $23 million (1977). Imports totaled $14 million **Principal Trade Partners:** Portugal, Netherlands

Vital Statistics: Birthrate, 45 per 1,000 of pop. (1972); death rate, 11.2 **Life Expectancy:** N.A. **Health Statistics:** 160 inhabitants per hospital bed; 6,666 per physician (1976) **Infant Mortality:** 64.3 per 1,000 births (1973) **Illiteracy:** 90% **Primary and Secondary School Enrollment:** 17,329 (1976) **Enrollment in Higher Education:** N.A. **GDP Expended on Education:** 2.2% (1972)

Transportation: All roads total 179 mi. **Motor Vehicles:** 2,000 (1973) **Passenger Cars:** 1,600 **Railway Mileage:** None **Ports:** São Tomé (on São Tomé) and Santo António (on Príncipe) **Major Airlines:** Transportes Aereos de São Tomé **Communications:** Government owned **Radio Transmitters:** 4 **Licenses:** 20,000 (1976) **Television:** None **Telephones:** 900 **Newspapers:** 2 weeklies

Weights and Measures: Metric system **Travel Requirements:** Passport, visa

---

One of Africa's smallest countries, São Tomé and Príncipe is part of an extinct volcanic mountain range. The islands' economy is based on cocoa, with copra and coffee also important. A steep drop in the world price of cocoa has greatly affected the country's financial outlook. The crops are grown on company-owned plantations worked by labor imported from Mozambique and Angola. This temporary labor force outnumbers the permanent population, which largely refuses to work on the plantations, where conditions have been much criticized. Most of the 1,000 white settlers, who ran the plantations, and the Cape Verdeans, who served as foremen, left the islands after independence was declared. Malnutrition is a major health problem.

São Tomé and Príncipe, which lie 150 miles west of Gabon in the Gulf of Guinea, became independent on July 12, 1975, after 500 years of Portuguese rule, the fourth and smallest of Portugal's African territories to emerge from colonial status. Manuel Pinto da Costa was proclaimed first president.

HISTORY: São Tomé and Príncipe were discovered in 1471 by the Portuguese, who began to settle convicts and exiled Jews on the islands and to establish sugar plantations using slaves from the African mainland
1951: The islands are designated a Portuguese Overseas Province
1975: São Tomé and Príncipe becomes independent
1979: Prime Minister Miguel Trovoada, accused of attempting a coup, is arrested
1980: President Pinto da Costa assumes duties of the prime minister; looks to Cuba and other socialist countries for aid

---

SAUDI ARABIA

Area: 829,995 sq. mi. **Population:** 7,866,000 (1978 est.)
Official Name: Kingdom of Saudi Arabia **Capital:** Riyadh (Jidda serves as the administrative center, and Taif is the summer capital)
Nationality: Saudi Arabian **Languages:** Arabic is the official and universal language **Religion:** The overwhelming majority of the population is Sunni Moslem, and Islam is the state religion **Flag:** Green, with a white sword below the Arabic inscription "There is no god but God, and Mohammed is His Prophet" **Anthem:** Royal Anthem of Saudi Arabia, a short instrumental selection **Currency:** Saudi riyal (3.36 per U.S. $1)
Location: Arabian peninsula in Southwest Asia, Saudi Arabia is bounded on the north by Jordan, Iraq, and Kuwait; on the east by the Persian Gulf, Qatar, the United Arab Emirates, and Oman; on the

south by Yemen and Southern Yemen, and on the west by the Red Sea **Features:** Nine-tenths of the country is covered by a barren plateau, including the Rub al-Khali and Al-Nafud desert regions. In the west, the Hejaz mountains border the narrow coastal plain along the Red Sea; to the east of the central plateau is the low-lying coastal region along the Persian Gulf **Chief Rivers:** There are no permanent rivers

Head of State and of Government: King Khalid ibn Abdul-Aziz Al Saud, born 1912, succeeded to the throne in March 1975. He named himself premier and his brother, Crown Prince Fahd ibn Abdel Aziz Al Saud, first deputy premier **Effective Date of Present Constitution:** None. Authority is based on Islamic law (Shari'a) and on Bedouin tradition **Legislative Body:** None. The appointed Council of Ministers performs some legislative functions **Local Government:** 18 provinces, 6 major and 12 minor, each with an appointed governor

Ethnic Composition: The population is largely homogeneous, descended from indigenous Arab tribes, with some admixture of Africans, Turks, Iranians, Indians, and Indonesians. At present about 30% are expatriates **Population Distribution:** 28% urban **Density:** 9.5 inhabitants per sq. mi.

Largest Cities: (1974 census) Riyadh 666,840, Jidda 561,104, Mecca 366,801, Taif 204,857, Medina 198,186, Dammam 127,844 **Per Capita Income:** $12,521 (1980) **Gross National Product (GNP):** $84 billion (1980) **Economic Statistics:** 62% of GNP is derived from industry, (oil refining, electrical goods, fertilizers, cement, iron and steel) and mining (80% in oil); 15% from trade and services; and 4% from agriculture (dates, grain, vegetables, livestock) **Minerals and Mining:** Saudi Arabia is the world's third-largest producer of oil. Other abundant minerals are natural gas, gypsum, copper, salt, manganese, silver, gold, sulphur, and lead **Labor Force:** About 2.7 million (one-half foreign), with 44% in commerce, services and government, 28% in agriculture, 21% in construction, 4% in industry and 3% in oil **Foreign Trade:** Exports, 99% petroleum and petroleum products, totaled $58 billion in 1979. Imports, principally motor vehicles, cereals, and power generating machinery, totaled $28 billion **Principal Trade Partners:** United States, West Germany, Japan, Italy, Netherlands

Vital Statistics: Birthrate, 49.5 per 1,000 of pop. (1975); death rate, 20.2 **Life Expectancy:** 45 years **Health Statistics:** 840 inhabitants per hospital bed; 2,200 per physician (1976) **Infant Mortality:** over 110 per 1,000 births (1976) **Illiteracy:** 70% **Primary and Secondary School Enrollment:** 908,905 (1975) **Enrollment in Higher Education:** 26,437 (1975) **GNP Expended on Education:** 10% (1977)

Transportation: Paved roads total 11,800 mi. **Motor Vehicles:** 112,000 (1974) **Passenger Cars:** 59,400 **Railway Mileage:** 357 **Ports:** Jidda, Dammam, Yenbo, Ras Tanura, Jubail **Major Airlines:** Saudia operates both domestic and international flights **Communications:** Government controlled **Radio Transmitters:** 20 **Receivers:** 260,000 (1976) **Television Transmitters:** 12 **Receivers:** 130,000 (1976) **Telephones:** 200,000 **Newspapers:** 11 dailies, 11 copies per 1,000 inhabitants (1974)

Weights and Measures: Metric system **Travel Requirements:** Passport, transit visa valid 72 hours, no charge, onward ticket. No tourist visas issued **International Dialing Code:** 966

The world's 587 million adherents of Islam regard Saudi Arabia with a special reverence because it contains Mecca, the holiest of holy sites. The birthplace of the Prophet Mohammed, Mecca is the direction to which these Moslems turn as they bow in prayer five times each day. It is the destination of some half million people a year from all parts of the world who follow the Koranic exhortation of making the pilgrimage, or *Haj*, during one's lifetime. Closed to non-Moslems, the city contains the Great Mosque, or *Haram*, and the *Kaaba*, with its sacred Black Stone.

The ruler of Saudi Arabia is considered the custodian of the holy sites and the chief defender of Islam. In addition, the present ruler, King Khalid, is the secular head of one of the world's leading oil-exporting countries and, consequently, one of its richest men, although his realm consists mostly of vast expanses of trackless desert. The combination of these functions has long given the Saudi king a strong voice in the Arab world.

Saudi Arabia has been also a country in which the deep Arab tradition of hospitality conflicts with an equally strong xenophobic tendency. It is a country where distrust of Western "imperialism" and American support for Zionism is often overshadowed by dependence on American technology and a fear of Communism.

The assassination of King Faisal by a nephew in 1975 caused reverberations throughout the Middle East. Faisal's brother, Crown Prince Khalid, succeeded him as king and named himself premier and Crown Prince Fahd first deputy premier. The new leaders are less concerned with fierce anti-Communism and are slightly more moderate on the Arab-Israel dispute.

Saudi Arabia has used its tremendous financial power to exert diplomatic pressure and has assumed a major role as a mediator in Middle Eastern affairs. Saudi Arabia has exercised a moderating influence on other Arab nations in raising oil prices in recent years.

The Saudi position in regard to the United States is ambivalent. On the one hand, the government maintains close ties with Washington as the leader of the non-Communist world and admires American know-how; but Saudi Arabia does not hesitate to pressure the United States to stop supporting Israel. In practice, the chief link between Saudi Arabia and the United States is their oil relationship. Saudi Arabia has the largest known oil reserves in the world (180 billion barrels), and the United States has been the world's leading consumer, by far, of Saudi Arabian oil, now being produced at the rate of about 9.5 million barrels a day. Soon after oil was discovered in the Saudi deserts in the 1930s, King Ibn Saud, Khalid's father, granted oil primary exploitation rights to the Standard Oil Company of California. The concession was subsequently transferred to the Arabian American Oil Company, known as Aramco, a conglomerate of several oil companies. Still 40 percent owned by four American oil companies, Aramco is the world's largest oil-producing company.

Aside from Islam, Aramco is perhaps the dominant force in Saudi Arabia. The Saudis have made some attempts to diversify the economy by encouraging agricultural and industrial development, but even the new projects involve Aramco because the company is often the final contractor. It has become almost an administrative arm of the Saudi government; it builds and runs schools and housing, constructs and maintains roads, and manages other important projects.

Before his assassination, King Faisal drafted a far-reaching and comprehensive plan calling for $142 billion in investment and affecting all areas of development. Cities are being transformed with modern buildings; new highway systems are complete, even with rush-hour traffic jams; and two major new industrial centers are being built: at Jubail in the midst of Saudi Arabia's Gulf Coast oil fields and at Yanbu, the Red Sea port for Medina. A $15-20 billion gas-gathering system—a project larger than the trans-Alaska pipeline—is being built by an Arabian-American company. Other projects are giant desalination plants and a new airport the size of Manhattan Island to serve Jidda.

Although much of Saudi Arabia's oil revenue goes either to these projects or to the armed forces, some of it is now being spent for social welfare. Free medical service has been made available to all citizens, and elementary, secondary, and higher education is also free, although not compulsory. By contrast, the religious tenets of Islam, which form the common law of the land, are enforced with fundamentalist zeal.

On November 20, 1979, the Grand Mosque in Mecca, which is Islam's holiest shrine, was seized by a band of some 500 Islamic militants, whose leader claimed to be the *Mahdi*, or messiah of the Shiite Moslems. Saudi soldiers retook the mosque by December 4, but some 300 militants and 60 soldiers were killed. Another 63 raiders were ex-

ecuted in early 1980. The Saudi government unofficially declared that the seizure had been led by religious fanatics but was supported by certain international leftist forces.

The Saudi government's official complaint to the U.S. about the 1980 showing of a controversial film, *Death of a Princess*, did not prevent the film from being televised by American Public Broadcasting stations. But U.S.-Saudi relations took a turn for the better in 1981 when the U.S. announced that it would sell Saudi Arabia five new electronic surveillance aircraft called AWACS (Advanced Warning and Command Systems). However, the proposed sale was condemned by Israel and met with opposition in the U.S. Senate, resulting in postponement of the actual sale until Congress acted on the matter.

HISTORY: Arabia has been inhabited for thousands of years by nomadic Semitic tribes. Followers of Mohammed, who was born in Mecca in the 6th century A.D., conquered most of the area between Persia on the east and Spain on the west, but Arabia itself declined in importance. As a political unit, Saudi Arabia is of relatively recent origin, dating from the 18th century, when the Saud family, adherents of the puritanical Wahabi movement, gained control over most of the Arabian peninsula

19th cent.: Wahabi movement is crushed (1811) by Egyptian expedition led by Mohammed Ali; movement revives temporarily, only to be defeated by Rashid dynasty, which gains control of central Arabia and expels Saud family

1902-32: Ibn Saud, the exiled Wahabi leader, conquers the Nejd, Hasa, and Hejaz regions and forms the kingdom of Saudi Arabia

1936: Oil is discovered near the Persian Gulf

1953: Ibn Saud dies and is succeeded by his eldest son, Saud

1962: Saud sends aid to royalist troops in Yemen after pro-Nasser rebels depose Imam. Relations with Egypt are cut

1964: Saud is deposed and succeeded by Crown Prince Faisal, who introduces sweeping government reorganization and abolishes slavery. Relations with Egypt are restored

1967-68: Saudi Arabian troops are sent to Jordan during six-day Arab-Israeli war but take no part in fighting. King Faisal halts aid to Yemeni royalists in return for withdrawal of Egyptian troops; however, aid is temporarily resumed to counteract support for republicans by Soviet Union, Syria, and Southern Yemen

1969: Hundreds are arrested as government acts to head off attempt at coup d'état

1970: Resumption of ties to Yemen is marked by financial aid from Saudi Arabia

1973: The Yom Kippur War prompts King Faisal to cut exports of oil to the U.S. by 10 percent in order to compel the U.S. to demand a cease-fire and Israeli withdrawal from Arab territory

1975: King Faisal is assassinated by his nephew, Prince Faisal ibn Musad Abdel Aziz, 31; his brother, Crown Prince Khalid ibn Abdul-Aziz al Saud, 62, succeeds him

1976: Saudis hold down OPEC price increases to 5 percent

1978: Saudi Arabia buys 60 F-15 jet fighter-planes from U.S.

1979: Moslem militants seize and hold Grand Mosque in Mecca for two weeks before Saudi soldiers retake the holy shrine

1980: Saudi Arabian jetliner burns at Riyadh airport killing 301

SENEGAL

Area: 76,124 sq. mi. **Population:** 5,381,000 (1978 est.)

Official Name: Republic of Senegal **Capital:** Dakar **Nationality:** Senegalese **Languages:** French is the official language; among the spoken African languages, Wolof is used by nearly 50%, and Peul (Fulani), Mende, Diola and Mandingo are other main languages **Religion:** More than 80% of the population are Moslems; about 5% are Christians, and the rest animists **Flag:** Vertical stripes of green, yellow, and red with a green star in the center **Anthem:** National Anthem, beginning "Pluck your koras, strike the balafons" **Currency:** CFA Franc (263 per U.S. $1)

Location: West Africa. Senegal is bounded on the north by Mauritania, on the east by Mali, on the south by Guinea and Guinea-Bissau, and on the west by the Atlantic Ocean. The nation of The Gambia is an enclave within Senegal **Features:** The country is a transitional zone between the Sahara and the equatorial jungle with semidesert in the north, and open savanna in the center and south **Chief Rivers:** Senegal, Saloum, Gambia, Casamance

Head of State: President Abdou Diouf, born 1935, took office Jan. 1, 1981 **Head of Government:** Premier Habib Thiam, born 1933, appointed Jan. 2, 1981 **Effective Date of Present Constitution:** March

3, 1963 **Legislative Body:** National Assembly (unicameral), consisting of 100 members elected for 5 years **Local Government:** 8 regions, each headed by an appointed governor

Ethnic Composition: The largest ethnic group, the Wolof, makes up about 36% of the population. Other important groups are the Peul (Fulani), with 17.5%; the Serere, with 16.5%; the Tukulor, with 9%; Diola, with 9%; and the Mandingo, with 6.5%. A small non-African population, largely French, is concentrated in Dakar **Population Distribution:** 35% urban **Density:** 71 inhabitants per sq. mi.

Largest Cities: (1976 census) Dakar 798,792, Thiès 117,353, Kaolack 106,899, St-Louis 88,404, Ziguinchor 72,726, Rufisque 66,995, Diourbel 50,618, Mbour 37,663, Louga 35,063

Per Capita Income: $359 (1979) **Gross National Product (GNP):** $2 billion (1978) **Economic Statistics:** In 1978 about 38% of GNP was derived from trade and finance; 30% from agriculture and fishing (peanuts, accounting for about half of total production; fish; millet; sorghum; rice; cassava; potatoes; livestock); 20% from manufacturing (peanut oil mills, cement, food processing, textiles, leather, shoes, chemicals, and phosphate mining) **Minerals and Mining:** Calcium and aluminum phosphates, limestone, titanium, salt, and ilmenite are being worked **Labor Force:** Of 1,732,000, 80% are engaged in agriculture **Foreign Trade:** Exports, chiefly peanuts, phosphates, and canned fish, totaled $627 million in 1979. Imports, mainly food, textiles, machinery, chemical and petroleum products, totaled $1 billion **Principal Trade Partners:** France, United States, Britain, Netherlands

Vital Statistics: Birthrate, 47.6 per 1,000 of pop. (1975); death rate, 23.9 **Life Expectancy:** 44 years **Health Statistics:** 853 inhabitants per hospital bed; 17,066 per physician (1976) **Infant Mortality:** 62.7 per 1,000 births (1972) **Illiteracy:** 90% **Primary and Secondary School Enrollment:** 373,534 (1975) **Enrollment in Higher Education:** 8,213 (1975) **GNP Expended on Education:** 3.0% (1976)

Transportation: Paved roads total 1,840 mi. **Motor Vehicles:** 69,800 (1974) **Passenger Cars:** 44,800 **Railway Mileage:** 642 **Ports:** Dakar, Kaolack, Ziguinchor, Saint-Louis **Major Airlines:** Air Senegal **Communications:** Government controlled **Radio Transmitters:** 14 **Receivers:** 290,000 (1976) **Television Transmitters:** 2 **Receivers:** 35,000 (1974) **Telephones:** 39,000 (1976) **Newspapers:** 2 dailies (1975), 7 copies per 1,000 inhabitants (1974)

Weights and Measures: Metric system **Travel Requirements:** Passport, visa, valid 3 months, 2 photos, $4.75 fee **International Dialing Code:** 221

Ever since it gained independence, discouraging economic reverses have beset Senegal, the former administrative and commercial center of the defunct French West African empire. In colonial times, the French federation, with a population of 20 million, was the market for industry and business based on the great port of Dakar, the Senegalese capital.

With the grant of independence to French African possessions, Senegal was forced to rely on its own meager resources and limited aid. The country has experienced increasing economic difficulty. Peanuts, introduced by the French more than a century ago, are the main cash crop. In the past they have accounted for nearly 80 percent of exports and provided the main income for more than 90 percent of Senegalese. But with the end of French subsidies, lower prices and droughts, production has fallen sharply. Despite government appeals, growing numbers of farmers have stopped planting peanuts.

American and other foreign assistance is gradually increasing production of rice, millet, sorghum, sugar, and livestock, but the effort is offset by the rapid fall in export earnings, rising debt, the cost of imported oil, and tightened budgets.

Compounding these problems have been the continuing severe drought and famine plaguing not just Senegal but other countries of the sub-Sahara. An estimated 100,000 people died in 1973 and millions more were starving in the sub-Sahara region. Relief efforts were hampered by poor transportation and communications facilities.

President Léopold Senghor, Senegal's leader before and for two decades since independence, showed considerable skill in maintaining stability despite his many problems. A longtime Francophile and also a poet of note, Senghor in 1974 renegotiated all of the accords reached with France in 1960. Terms of the revised accords included partial withdrawal of French troops and the transfer of a military base at Dakar to Senegal. Relations with Arab countries have become closer, although in 1980 Senegal broke off relations with Libya, accusing that Arab country of interfering in Senegal's affairs. In 1973 relations with Israel were ended, and in 1976 Senegal sponsored a UN Commission on Human Rights resolution accusing Israel of war crimes in the occupied Arab territories.

In the 1970s the aging Senghor brought younger men and union leaders into his government. His choice as new premier was Abdou Diouf, an industrious and capable administrator. When Senghor retired on Dec. 31, 1980, Diouf succeeded him on the following day.

Diouf came into office Jan. 1, 1981, advocating a moderate program for legitimizing all political parties, recognizing human rights, and dealing with very rapid population growth through a campaign of family planning.

HISTORY: Senegal was largely dominated by the Moslem Tukuler tribe until 1893, when the Tukuler dynasty was overthrown by the French. European settlement, however, had begun as early as the 15th century, when the Portuguese settled along the Senegalese coastline. The French established a foothold in the area in the 17th century and by the 19th century Senegal was the center of French West Africa. In 1946, along with other parts of French West Africa, Senegal became part of the French Union

1958: Senegal becomes an autonomous republic within the French Community. Léopold-Sédar Senghor elected president

1959-60: Senegal is joined with the Sudanese Republic in the short-lived Mali Federation, which is dissolved after strong political differences develop between the two states

1963: Senghor, unopposed, is reelected president

1964: All opposition parties are banned, except for small African Reunion party

1968: Senghor is reelected and an unopposed list of 80 candidates of his party, the Senegalese Progressive Union, is elected to National Assembly. Widespread strikes by students and workers break out in protest against government austerity measures

1969: Senghor declares state of emergency to deal with unrest

1970: Senegal denies use of its roads as supply route for Portuguese Guinea rebels. Constitution revised; Abdou Diouf is chosen to be premier

1973: Severe drought affects crop production

1974: New political party, Senegalese Democratic party, formed

1976: At a conference of the Organization of African Unity and the Arab League in Dakar, President Senghor calls for a union of the two groups and for the establishment of an Arab-African arbitration and conciliation court

1978: Senghor is reelected in first multiparty election in 12 years. Senegal secures $26-million loan from International Monetary Fund to offset economic effects of drought

1979: Work begins on $550-million three-nation Senegal River irrigation and hydroelectric project

1980: Led by the Parti Démocratique Sénégalaise, 1,000 members of opposition parties demonstrate in Dakar. Senegal breaks relations with Libya June 28. President Senghor retires Dec. 31

1981: Abdou Diouf is sworn in as president Jan. 1 to complete Senghor's 5-year term which expires in 1983

SEYCHELLES

Area: 171 sq. mi. **Population:** 63,000 (1979 est.)

Official Name: Republic of Seychelles **Capital:** Victoria **Nationality:** Seychellois **Languages:** Creole is spoken by 94% of the population; English and French are official **Religion:** 91% Roman Catholic, 8% Anglican **Flag:** A field of red over green separated by a wavy white band **Anthem:** National Anthem, beginning "Seychellois both staunch and true" **Currency:** Seychellois rupee (6.7 per U.S. $1)

Location: Indian Ocean. The republic lies about 1,000 miles east of Kenya, just south of the Equator **Features:** An archipelago of about 90 islands, it is divided almost equally between a Granitic Group and a Coralline Group. Mahé (4°45′S., 55°30′E.), the mountainous main island, comprises just over half of the total area, and contains most of the population **Chief Rivers:** None

Head of State and of Government: President France Albert René, born 1934, assumed office in coup in June 1977, elected 1979

Effective Date of Present Constitution: March 26, 1979 **Legislative Body:** National Assembly (unicameral) consists of 25 members. The Seychelles People's Progressive Front is the only party **Local Government:** 8 districts, one including all outlying island groups

Ethnic Composition: Most are descendants of 18th century French settlers and their African slaves, with a later mixture of other Europeans and Asians; there is a small minority of Indians and Chinese **Population Distribution:** 37% urban **Density:** 368 inhabitants per sq. mi.

Largest City: (1977 census) Victoria 15,559

Per Capita Income: $1,470 (1977) **Gross Domestic Product (GDP):** $89 million (1977) **Economic Statistics:** Percentages of GDP not available. Plantation agriculture (coconuts, vanilla, cinnamon, patchouli, fibers) and fishing at a subsistence level engage most of the population. Tourism is the chief income-making industry, and there is processing of coconuts and vanilla **Minerals and Mining:** None **Labor Force:** 19,827 in 1971; 55% of the wage earners are engaged in tourism and agricultural processing, and 27% in plantation agriculture **Foreign Trade:** Exports, chiefly copra, coconut oil, cinnamon bark, dried fish, vanilla oil, and patchouli, totaled $13 million (1978). Imports, mainly foods, manufactured goods, textiles, machinery, and petroleum products, totaled $51 million **Principal Trade Partners:** Pakistan, Britain, Kenya, Mauritius, South Africa

Vital Statistics: Birthrate, 25.9 per 1,000 of pop. (1977); death rate, 7.7 **Life Expectancy:** 65 years **Health Statistics:** 200 inhabitants per hospital bed; 2,857 per physician (1975) **Infant Mortality:** 43.2 per 1,000 births (1977) **Illiteracy:** 20% **Primary and Secondary School Enrollment:** 12,986 (1976) **Enrollment in Higher Education:** 142 (1976) **GDP Expended on Education:** 6.2% (1972)

Transportation: Paved roads total 90 mi. **Motor Vehicles:** 3,900 (1977) **Passenger Cars:** 3,000 **Railway Mileage:** None **Port:** Victoria **Major Airlines:** Air Mahé operates domestic flights **Communications:** Partly government owned **Radio Transmitters:** 2 **Receivers:** 17,000 (1976) **Television:** None **Telephones:** 4,600 **Newspapers:** 2 dailies, 60 copies per 1,000 inhabitants (1975)

Weights and Measures: British system is used **Travel Requirements:** Passport, no visa, onward ticket

---

This 90-island archipelago is a beautiful tropical paradise largely isolated from the rest of the world. The climate is equable and healthful, although quite humid, since the islands are small and subject to marine influences. Temperatures on the main island of Mahé vary from 75° to 85°F, and high winds are rarely encountered, as this "lotus land" lies outside the cyclone belt. The fortunate natural environment once caused an early visitor to declare seriously that the Seychelles archipelago was the original Garden of Eden.

Although the new republic is promoting agriculture, its principal hopes lie in tourism. The opening of the islands' first commercial airport in 1971 has increased the number of tourists attracted by the beautiful beaches, impressive scenery and fine climate. The government has made considerable effort to assure that the expansion of tourism neither disrupts the islands' cultural life nor spoils the natural beauty. Hotels and condominiums are well spaced so not to "wall off" the beaches. Whale-watching is promoted as a tourist attraction.

Under the stimulus of development and tourism, the Seychelles has virtually obtained full employment for its work force. But even paradise must pay a price, and in the Seychelles, like elsewhere, progress has brought inflation.

Under the nation's first president, James Mancham, the Seychelles remained neutral in foreign affairs, with a pro-Western outlook. The only intrusion of big-power presence is the hosting of an American satellite tracking station on Mahé.

In 1977 Mancham was overthrown by leftist rebels thought to have been supplied with Chinese and Soviet weapons from Tanzania. Mancham's ouster was attributed to his playboy lifestyle, his frequent absences from the country, and his proposal to postpone the 1979 elections. Former Prime Minister France Albert René subsequently became president and vowed some form of socialism

for the country, as well as an emphasis on housing, agriculture, fishing and tourism.

HISTORY: Although the islands appeared on Portuguese charts as early as 1505 and may have been visited by Arabs much earlier, the Seychelles remained unclaimed and uninhabited until 1742. In that year the French governor of Mauritius, Mahé de Labourdonnais, sent an expedition to the islands. However, the full settlement of the archipelago did not take place until 1794. As a result of French defeat in the Napoleonic Wars, the Seychelles passed to the British in 1814 and became a dependency of Mauritius
1903: The Seychelles become a separate crown colony
1970: Limited internal self-government is granted
1976: Independence is proclaimed on June 29
1977: President Mancham overthrown in leftist coup. Former Prime Minister France Albert René assumes presidency
1979: René reelected to 5-year term under new one-party constitution. Attempted coup in November fails
1980: India agrees to help Seychelles to develop fisheries

SIERRA LEONE

Area: 27,925 sq. mi. **Population:** 3,470,000 (1978 est.)

Official Name: Republic of Sierra Leone **Capital:** Freetown **Nationality:** Sierra Leonean **Languages:** English is the official language. Mende and Temne are widely spoken, but the most commonly spoken language is Krio, a form of pidgin English **Religion:** 70% are animists, 25% Moslems, and 5% Christians **Flag:** Horizontal stripes of green, white, and blue **Anthem:** National Anthem, beginning "High we exalt thee, realm of the free" **Currency:** Leone (1.14 per U.S. $1)

Location: West Africa. Sierra Leone is bounded on the north and east by Guinea, on the southeast by Liberia, and on the west by the Atlantic Ocean **Features:** The country consists of a coastal plain of mangrove swamps that gradually gives way to wooded hills and upland plateaus in the interior, with mountains near the eastern border **Chief Rivers:** Rokel, Sewa, Moa, Jong, Little and Great Scarcies, Sherbro

Head of State and of Government: President Siaka P. Stevens, born 1905, elected April 1971, reelected 1976 for 5 years, sworn in for 7-year term in 1978 under new constitution **Effective Date of Present Constitution:** 1978 **Legislative Body:** Parliament (unicameral House of Representatives), with 104 members; 85 are elected by universal suffrage, 12 indirectly elected paramount chiefs, and 7 appointed by the president, all for 5 years. The All-People's Congress is the sole officially recognized party **Local Government:** 3 provinces governed by a minister with cabinet rank, and the Western (Freetown) area, under a council

Ethnic Composition: 18 tribal groups, with the Mende and Temne each making up about 30% of the population; others include the Limba, Loko, Kono, Sherbro, Vai, Gallina, Susu, Kissi, Mandingo, and Peul (Fulani). Less than 2% are Creoles, descendants of freed slaves, mostly from the Americas **Population Distribution:** 18% urban **Density:** 124 inhabitants per sq. mi.

Largest Cities: (1974 census) Freetown 274,000, Bo 42,216

Per Capita Income: $222 (1978) **Gross National Product (GNP):** $710 million (1978) **Economic Statistics:** 31% of the GNP is derived from agriculture (palm kernels, cocoa, coffee, rice, piassava, ginger, cola nuts); 26% from trade and services; 19% from extractive industries (diamonds, rutile, bauxite); and 6% from manufacturing (soap, flour, mineral water, furniture) **Minerals and Mining:** Chiefly diamonds, iron ore, bauxite and the world's largest deposits of rutile **Labor Force:** 1.5 million, with 80% engaged in agriculture **Foreign Trade:** Exports, diamonds, palm kernels, bauxite, rutile, coffee, and cocoa, totaled $230 million in 1979. Imports, chiefly manufactured goods, fuel, machinery and transportation equipment, and food, totaled $308 million **Principal Trade Partners:** Britain, Japan, United States, EC countries, China, Nigeria

Vital Statistics: Birthrate, 44.7 per 1,000 of pop. (1975); death rate, 20.7 **Life Expectancy:** 44 years **Health Statistics:** 927 inhabitants per hospital bed; 17,114 per physician (1972) **Infant Mortality:** 136.3 per 1,000 births **Illiteracy:** 90% **Primary and Secondary School Enrollment:** 256,388 (1975) **Enrollment in Higher Education:** 1,642 **GNP Expended on Education:** 3.1% (1976)

Transportation: Paved roads total 760 mi. **Motor Vehicles:** 25,200 (1976) **Passenger Cars:** 18,900 **Railway Mileage:** 52 **Ports:** Freetown, Bonthe, Pepel **Major Airlines:** Sierra Leone Airways, government owned, operates domestic flights **Communications:** Government owned **Radio Transmitters:** 3 **Receivers:** 62,000 (1975) **Television Transmitters:** 2 **Receivers:** 8,500 **Telephones:** 15,000 (1976) **Newspapers:** 1 daily, 10 copies per 1,000 inhabitants (1975)

Weights and Measures: Metric system **Travel Requirements:** Passport, visa valid for 1 month, $6.50 fee, 3 photos

One of the oldest and most progressive of Britain's former West African colonies, Sierra Leone got off to a favorable start on independence in 1961 with stable government and promising economic development. But since then the small nation, which depends mainly on the production of diamonds, coffee and cocoa, has experienced increasingly violent political upheaval.

In addition to the tendency of some officials to seek personal fortunes at public expense, Sierra Leone has been plagued by coups, states of emergency and, in March 1971, an attempted assassination of the country's present leader, President Siaka Stevens. In the process, economic improvements—particularly in agriculture—have been repeatedly disrupted and new development programs delayed.

Serious trouble began with elections in 1967. Then opposition leader, Stevens appeared to have won by a narrow margin over the bumptious Sir Albert Margai, whose government had been marked by corruption. But almost as soon as Stevens had been sworn in as prime minister, a group of army officers ousted him in a coup. The junta said it had acted to prevent a civil war between the Mende, the largest tribal group, and the rival Temne, a main source of Stevens' strength.

Rule by the military group proved unpopular, and in 1968 it was ousted by a counter-coup led by noncommissioned officers and police. This group promptly restored Stevens to the premiership and the country settled down to legally elected government. Two years later, however, opposition to Stevens' party resumed, with clashes that led to the declaration of a state of emergency.

Then in March 1971 Brig. Gen. John Bangura, the army commander, led an attempted coup and assassination plot. The coup fizzled when other army officers arrested Bangura and proclaimed their loyalty to the Stevens government. Another state of emergency was declared and, under a new mutual defense pact by Stevens and Guinean President Sékou Touré, 200 Guinean troops were flown into Freetown to bolster local troops. Bangura and three followers were executed.

On April 19, 1971, Stevens proclaimed a republic and two days later he was sworn in as president. His power was reconfirmed by elections in 1973 and 1976. In 1978 Stevens pushed through legislation introducing a new constitution which extended the presidential term of office to seven years, abolished the office of prime minister and made the All-People's Congress the only legal party.

On the economic scene, Sierra Leone has taken strides toward the development of the production of bauxite, which amounted to over 700,000 metric tons in 1978. Another resource, rutile, a mineral used in paint manufacture, is being developed under a U.S. investment agreement. Sierra Leone's deposits are among the world's largest.

HISTORY: Sierra Leone was originally divided into numerous kingdoms or chiefdoms. The Portuguese explorer Pedro da Cintra visited the coastal area in 1460 and named the mountainous peninsula at the mouth of the Rokel River Serra Lyoa (Lion Mountain), later corrupted to Sierra Leone. Until the 18th century, the region was an important source of slaves. In 1787, a group of abolitionists founded Freetown to resettle freed slaves from Britain, and in 1808 the settlement became a crown colony. In 1896, the interior was made a British protectorate.
1924: New constitution is introduced permitting nomination of protectorate chiefs to legislative council but fails to satisfy nationalist aspirations
1943: Africans are admitted to the executive council
1951: New constitution is introduced, providing a framework for decolonization

1957-58: Elected House of Representatives replaces legislative council; Dr. Milton Margai, whose Sierra Leone People's party wins a majority of seats, becomes prime minister
1961: Sierra Leone becomes an independent Commonwealth state
1964: Prime Minister Milton Margai dies; his brother, Finance Minister Albert Margai, is asked by governor-general to form new government
1967: Siaka Stevens, leader of the opposition All People's Congress, is appointed prime minister after hotly contested election but is ousted by army chief; group of young army officers stage bloodless coup and a National Reformation Council composed of army and police officers is set up; constitution is suspended
1968: Military coup is staged by noncommissioned officers and police; House of Representatives is reconvened and asks Stevens to resume premiership
1969: Sierra Leone People's party loses strength in House of Representatives following by-elections; party leaders charge that losses were due to government intimidation of voters
1971: An attempted coup led by Brig. Gen. John Bangura, the army commander, is crushed; Prime Minister Stevens calls in troops from Guinea to help suppress dissident elements. Sierra Leone is declared a republic
1973: A plot to overthrow the government is uncovered. Sierra Leone increases its military capacity. The All People's Congress wins election, taking 84 of 97 parliamentary seats
1976: President Stevens is elected for second five-year term
1977: Students demand that Stevens resign, but APC wins elections decisively amid charges of vote fraud
1978: New constitution increases presidential term to seven years and makes APC sole recognized party
1979: Rising prices and shortage of rice cause discontent
1980: Public outcry against U.S. firm's proposal to dump chemical wastes in Sierra Leone leads Stevens to reject it. Organization of African Unity meets in Freetown, elects Stevens chairman for 1980-81. Agreement is reached with a European mining company to revive iron mines abandoned in 1975. Strong effort is launched to improve agricultural production

---

SINGAPORE

Area: 233 sq. mi. **Population:** 2,413,945 (1980 census)

Official Name: Republic of Singapore **Capital:** Singapore **Nationality:** Singaporean **Languages:** Malay, the national language, and English, Chinese, and Tamil are all official languages **Religion:** The majority of the ethnic Chinese are Buddhists, Taoists, or Confucianists; the Malays and Pakistanis are Moslems; and the Indians mainly Hindus. The Europeans and Eurasians are almost all Christians **Flag:** Horizontal stripes of red and white with a white crescent and 5 white stars in the upper left-hand corner **Anthem:** Forward Singapore **Currency:** Singapore dollar (2.12 per U.S. $1)

Location: Southeast Asia. The island of Singapore lies south of the Malay peninsula, separated by the Strait of Johore. A three-quarter-mile-long causeway connects the island with Malaysia; 54 small islets lie offshore **Features:** Except for a central plateau, most of the island is low lying and originally consisted of swamp and jungle. Downtown Singapore occupies land that for the most part was reclaimed from the sea **Chief Rivers:** Sungei Seletar, Singapore

Head of State: Acting President: Dr. Yeoh Ghim Seng, took office following death of President Sheares, May 1981 **Head of Government:** Prime Minister Lee Kuan Yew, born 1923, appointed 1965, reelected 1976 **Effective Date of Present Constitution:** 1959 (pre-independence) **Legislative Body:** Parliament (unicameral), consisting of 69 members elected by adult suffrage for 5 years

Ethnic Composition: About 77% of the population is ethnically Chinese, 15% Malays, and 6% Indians and Pakistanis. The rest are largely Europeans and Eurasians **Population Distribution:** 100% urban **Density:** 10,360 inhabitants per sq. mi.

Largest City: (1980 census) Singapore 2,413,945

Per Capita Income: $4,580 (1980) **Gross National Product (GNP):** $11 billion (1980) **Economic Statistics:** In 1973 about 56% of GNP came from trade and services (including banks, financial institutions, transportation and communications); 21% from manufacturing; and 3% from agriculture and fishing **Minerals and Mining:** None **Labor Force:** 919,000, with 27% in industry and 24% in commerce **Foreign Trade:** Exports, mainly crude rubber, petroleum products, electrical machinery, electronics, textiles, timber and coffee, totaled $17.6 billion in 1979. Imports, chiefly rubber, petroleum products, machinery, vehicles, and woven fabrics other than cotton, totaled $19 billion **Principal Trade Partners:** Malaysia, United States, Japan, Saudi Arabia, Britain, China, Hong Kong, Australia, West Germany

Vital Statistics: Birthrate, 16.6 per 1,000 of pop. (1977); death rate, 5.3 **Life Expectancy:** 69 years **Health Statistics:** 265 inhabitants per hospital bed; 1,341 per physician (1976) **Infant Mortality:** 12.4 per 1,000 births **Illiteracy:** 16% **Primary and Secondary School Enrollment:** 506,008 (1976) **Enrollment in Higher Education:** 22,607 (1975) **GNP Expended on Education:** 2.7% (1976)

Transportation: Paved roads total 1,286 mi. **Motor Vehicles:** 197,000 (1977) **Passenger Cars:** 142,100 **Railway Mileage:** 24 **Port:** Singapore **Major Airlines:** Singapore Airlines operates international flights **Communications:** Government controlled **Radio Transmitters:** 17 **Licenses:** 356,000 (1976) **Television Transmitters:** 2 **Licenses:** 294,000 **Telephones:** 329,000 (1976) **Newspapers:** 10 dailies, 201 copies per 1,000 inhabitants (1974)

Weights and Measures: Metric system; British, Chinese, and local standards are used **Travel Requirements:** Passport, no visa **International Dialing Code:** 65

Since 1819, when Singapore was created out of a mangrove swamp by Sir Stamford Raffles, the visionary agent of the British East India Company, it has served as East Asia's major transshipping point, as the wholesaler for other countries' products, as the bastion of the British Empire, and, more recently, as the area's leading processor of other countries' raw materials.

Blessed with one of the few natural harbors in the region, Singapore grew to become the largest port in Southeast Asia and the fourth largest in the world. Through this port have flowed rubber and tin from Malaysia and Indonesia to the markets of Europe and the United States.

The expanding rubber and tin industries early this century spurred immigration, mainly from southern China. In fact, up to 1957, Singapore's population consisted predominantly of noncitizen aliens. Today, Singapore is the only nation in the world with a population made up primarily of overseas Chinese, although immigration has now been slowed to a minimum. Malays, Indians, and Pakistanis are the other dominant ethnic groups.

Singapore has continued to thrive and maintains the highest per capita income in Southeast Asia, as well as virtually full employment. The Jurong area, a sprawling section of the island devoted to industrial development, today pulses with the processing of many types of raw materials and the manufacturing of finished goods. In 1977 it was announced that a consortium of Japanese companies plans to build an $800-million petrochemical complex which will be half owned by the Singapore government, on one of Singapore's offshore islands. At the outset of the 1980s, Singapore appeared to be veering away from labor-intensive industry, with large and inexpensive work forces, and toward capital-intensive industry. The ministry of trade and industry said that, for the decade, it expected an 8 percent real growth rate and diversification into computers, medical equipment, optical equipment, and machine tools.

Business travel and tourism have increased sharply, raising the number of Singapore's visitors from less than one million in 1973 to nearly three million in 1980. July 1, 1981, saw the opening of what was to be, at its completion in 1984, Asia's largest airport. Situated about 20 miles from downtown Singapore, the facility was designed to handle up to 10 million passengers per year.

Since 1959, when Singapore was granted internal self-government, the People's Action party, headed by Lee Kuan Yew, has controlled the island's affairs. In recent years the government has been accused of authoritarianism and repression. In 1974 drastic penalties were decreed for armed robbers, gun runners, and traffickers in illegal immigrants. The Internal Security Act provides for detention without trial for those accused of pro-Communist activities. In 1977 a new campaign was begun to repress dissent—a series of arrests of prominent critics of government policies, who sub-

sequently were pressured into signing confessions and appearing on television to recant.

In 1975 Foreign Minister S. Rajaratnam responded to Peking's more moderate attitude by leading Singapore's first goodwill mission to China where he met with the late Premier Zhou Enlai. In 1976 Prime Minister Lee was one of the last foreign officials to be allowed to meet with Chairman Mao Zedong. With a population that is overwhelmingly of Chinese ancestry, many of whom retain warm feelings for their ancestral land, Singapore cannot afford to antagonize Peking, but neither does it want to be a Chinese satellite.

HISTORY: For centuries the island of Singapore was little more than a mangrove swamp occupied by Malay fishermen who owed allegiance to the Sultan of Johore. In 1819, Sir Stamford Raffles of the British East India Company, who saw in Singapore potential for a great trading port, founded a trading post on the island

1824: Sultan of Johore cedes Singapore to the British East India Company

1826: Singapore becomes part of the British Straits Settlements

1942: Supposedly impregnable fortress of Singapore is captured by the Japanese in World War II

1946: Singapore becomes a separate British crown colony

1959: Singapore becomes a self-governing colony

1963: Federation of Malaysia is formed and Singapore joins Malaya, Sarawak, and Sabah in new nation

1965: Singapore withdraws from Malaysia federation

1971: Singapore, Malaysia, Britain, Australia, and New Zealand sign accord on joint defense of Singapore and Malaysia

1976: Prime Minister Lee's ruling People's Action party, in its fifth straight election victory, wins all 69 seats in parliament

1978: Amnesty International alleges serious human rights violations in Singapore, including detention without trial of at least 70

1979: As one of five countries making up the Association of Southeast Asian Nations (ASEAN), Singapore joins in a decision June 30 to accept no more Vietnamese refugees

1980: PAP candidates again win all parliamentary seats in December elections, getting 75% of popular vote

1981: President Sheares dies. Changi Airport, Asia's largest, opens in July

SOLOMON ISLANDS

Area: 11,500 sq. mi. **Population:** 221,000 (1979 est.)

Official Name: Solomon Islands **Capital:** Honiara **Nationality:** Solomon Islander **Language:** English is the official language; Melanesian Pidgin is the universal lingua franca. A variety of Melanesian tongues are spoken throughout most of the islands. On Vella Lavella, Savo and the Russell Islands the dominant languages are of the Papuan family. Polynesian languages, closely related to Maori, are spoken on the outlying islands of Ontong Java, Rennell and Tikopia **Religion:** 33% Anglican, 17% Roman Catholic, 17% South Sea Evangelical Church. The remainder of the inhabitants are members of the United Church and the Christian Fellowship Church, except for 5%, who are animists **Flag:** A blue triangle with five white stars in the upper left and a plain green triangle in the lower right separated by a diagonal yellow stripe **Anthem:** God Save Our Solomons **Currency:** Solomon Islands dollar (.83 per U.S. $1)

Location: Southwest Pacific Ocean. About 1000 miles northeast of Australia, the islands form a scattered archipelago stretching 900 miles in a southeasterly direction from Papua New Guinea. The six major islands are Choiseul, New Georgia, Santa Isabel, Guadalcanal, Malaita and San Cristobal **Features:** The large islands have a mountainous spine which on one side drops steeply to sea level and on the other drops through a series of foothills to the coast. The highest peaks are found on Guadalcanal, which possesses the only extensive coastal plains in the Solomons. The weather varies from warm to hot and is humid, with annual rainfall exceeding 100 inches **Chief Rivers:** There are many short rivers on the larger islands

Head of State: Queen Elizabeth II, represented by a governor-general, Baddeley Devesi, born 1941, sworn in July 1978 **Head of Government:** Prime Minister Peter Kenilorea, born 1943, sworn in July 1978 **Effective Date of Present Constitution:** July 1978 **Legislative Body:** National Parliament (unicameral) consisting of 38 members elected for 4 years **Local Government:** At present 4 districts; provinces are to be established

Ethnic Composition: Melanesians 93%, Polynesians 4%, Gilbertese 1%, European stock 1% **Population Distribution:** 9% urban **Density:** 19 inhabitants per sq. mi.

Largest City: (1976 census) Honiara 14,942

Per Capita Income: $320 (1977) **Gross Domestic Product (GDP):** $71 million (1977) **Economic Statistics:** Copra and rice are the only important cash crops. Fisheries contribute to the economy, and the timber industry is being developed **Minerals and Mining:** Copper, bauxite and nickel deposits are being developed **Labor Force:** 14,184 (1974) **Foreign Trade:** Exports, chiefly fish, timber, and copra, amounted to $41 million in 1977. Imports, mainly machinery, transport equipment, food and fuels totaled $32.5 million **Principal Trade Partners:** Australia, Japan, Britain

Vital Statistics: Birthrate, 41 per 1,000 of pop. (1970); death rate, 11 **Life Expectancy:** 51 years **Health Statistics:** 120 inhabitants per hospital bed; 5,135 per physician (1975) **Infant Mortality:** 68 per 1,000 births **Illiteracy:** 40% **Primary and Secondary School Enrollment:** 29,243 (1976) **Enrollment in Higher Education:** 160 (1976) **GDP Expended on Education:** 3.7% (1972)

Transportation: All weather roads total 800 miles **Motor Vehicles:** 1,796 (1972) **Passenger Cars:** 727 **Railway Mileage:** None **Ports:** Honiara, Gizo, Yandina **Major Airlines:** Solomon Islands Airways operates domestic and international flights **Communications:** Government owned **Radio Transmitters:** 3 **Radio Receivers:** 11,000 (1976) **Television Transmitters:** None **Television Receivers:** None **Telephones:** 1,726 Newspapers: 2 weeklies

Weights and Measures: Imperial weights and measures are still in use, but the metric system has been adopted as the future standard **Travel Requirements:** Passport, no visa

For a short period during World II the Solomon Islands were a focus of world attention as Japan and the United States engaged in land, air and sea battles for the control of the South Pacific. Guadalcanal, New Georgia, "the Slot," and Iron Bottom Sound—scenes of major clashes in 1942 and 1943—are all within the confines of the newly independent Solomon Islands.

Following hostilities, the islands returned to the peaceful obscurity of being a remote British protectorate unbothered by the tides of history. However, the worldwide retreat of colonialism during the 1960s resulted in a growing interest in eventual independence for the Solomons on the part of both the British and the islanders. Finally, on July 7, 1978, the Duke of Gloucester, representing Queen Elizabeth II, handed over power to the government of the new nation.

The most pressing problem facing the Solomon Islands is the maintenance of unity among the diverse and geographically separated peoples of the island chain. The commercially developed western islands have demanded more autonomy, and the non-Melanesian minority fears the neglect of its needs by the central government.

One of the main objectives of the government is to diversify the economy. In the past, production has been limited to copra planting, timber cutting and fishing. It is hoped that plans for the introduction of beef cattle and the growing of rice and oil palm will be implemented. Another source of future economic growth would be the successful exploitation of the islands' mineral ores.

HISTORY: Ancestors of the present Melanesian inhabitants entered the area from the Malay Archipelago some time between 1000 and 500 B.C. Polynesians came to the islands much later, from Uvea in the Wallis group, northeast of Fiji. The Spaniards reached Santa Isabel in the Solomons in 1568. During the 19th century missionaries and coconut traders made contact with the Solomon Islanders, and many of the inhabitants were recruited, sometimes forcibly, for labor in Fiji, Australia and New Caledonia

1893-98: Britain establishes a protectorate over the Solomons
1899: Germany transfers Santa Isabel, Choiseul, the Shortlands and Ontong Java to Britain
1942-43: Japanese invade the Solomons. American counteroffensive recaptures Guadalcanal; fighting continues on the islands until Allied forces move on to Bougainville
1946-52: Opposition to British rule is carried on by "Marching Rule" movement, a nativist cargo-cult
1960: Legislative Council established
1976: The Solomons become a self-governing dependency
1977: Constitutional conference is held in London to plan for independence
1978: Full independence is achieved on July 7

1979: Government opens talks with Papua New Guinea on boundary dispute in North Solomons island group
1980: Two-thirds of legislators lose seats in first general election since independence, but Prime Minister Peter Kenilorea retains his post

SOMALIA

Area: 246,200 **Population:** 3,443,000 (1978 est.)

Official Name: Somali Democratic Republic **Capital:** Mogadishu **Nationality:** Somali **Languages:** Somali is the official language; Arabic, English, and Italian are still used extensively **Religion:** 99% are Sunni Moslems and Islam is the state religion **Flag:** Blue field with a 5-pointed white star in the center **Anthem:** Long Live Somalia **Currency:** Somali shilling (Somalo) (12.46 per U.S. $1)

Location: East Africa. Somalia is bounded on the north by the Gulf of Aden and Djibouti, on the southeast by the Indian Ocean, and on the west by Kenya and Ethiopia **Features:** Much of the country is arid or semiarid. The northern region is mountainous; the southern part is mostly desert, but with a large fertile area crossed by two large rivers flowing from Ethiopia **Chief Rivers:** Juba, Shebelli

Head of State and of Government: President: Maj. Gen. Mohamed Siad Barré, born 1919, chairman of the Supreme Revolutionary Council and secretary general of the Somali Socialist Revolutionary Party (SRSP), assumed power in 1969, elected 1980 **Effective Date of Present Constitution:** Sept. 23, 1979 **Legislative Body:** People's Assembly (unicameral) of 171 members, elected for 5 years. The SRSP is the only legal party **Local Government:** 15 regions

Ethnic Composition: The Hamitic population is mainly Somali. Other sizable ethnic groups include some 35,000 Arabs, 1,000 Indians and Pakistanis, and about 2,000 Italians **Population Distribution:** 9% urban **Density:** 14 inhabitants per sq. mi. **Largest City:** (1975 census) Mogadishu 371,000

Per Capita Income: $70 (1978) **Gross National Product (GNP):** $260 million (1978) **Economic Statistics:** Industry accounts for only about 8% of the GNP with the rest from livestock (cattle, camels, sheep, goats), the mainstay of the Somali economy; banana growing; wild animal hides such as Somali leopard skins; spices, fishing, and some minerals **Minerals and Mining:** Commercial production is confined to salt, charcoal, limestone, and meerschaum; uranium, iron ore and certain rare earths are currently being explored **Labor Force:** 1,100,000 (1970). Livestock production employs about 60% of the total; and agriculture 20% **Foreign Trade:** Exports, chiefly livestock, bananas, hides, meat and tuna, totaled $112 million in 1978. Imports, mainly manufactured goods, fuel, cereals, food preparations, transportation equipment, and chemicals, totaled $234 million **Principal Trade Partners:** Italy, Britain, United States, Saudi Arabia, USSR, Kuwait, Guatemala, Yugoslavia

Vital Statistics: Birthrate, 47.2 per 1,000 of pop. (1975); death rate, 21.7 **Life Expectancy:** 41 years **Health Statistics:** 569 inhabitants per hospital bed; 15,544 per physician (1972) **Infant Mortality:** 177 per 1,000 births **Illiteracy:** 80% **Primary and Secondary School Enrollment:** 241,419 (1976) **Enrollment in Higher Education:** 2,100 (1976) **GNP Expended on Education:** 4.8% (1976)

Transportation: Paved roads total 1,340 mi. **Motor Vehicles:** 16,000 (1972) **Passenger Cars:** 8,000 **Railway Mileage:** None **Ports:** Mogadishu, Berbera, Merka, Kismayu **Major Airlines:** Somali Airlines operates domestically and internationally **Communications:** Government owned **Radio Transmitters:** 5 **Receivers:** 69,000 (1976) **Television:** None **Telephones:** 6,000 (1971) Newspapers: 1 daily, 1 copy per 1,000 inhabitants (1973)

Weights and Measures: Metric system **Travel Requirements:** Passport, visa valid 3 months, $14 fee, 4 photos, onward ticket

Major power changes in the strategically located Horn of Africa have spotlighted Somalia, an arid East African country at the juncture of the Indian Ocean and the Gulf of Aden, as a link important to both the Middle East and Africa. A union of the former Italian and British Somalilands, Somalia became independent in 1960, but efforts at transforming its seminomadic society into a modern state have made scarcely any headway.

Somalis, a lean, handsome, fiercely proud people, have an oral history going back 2,000 years. Because of disputes among scholars, the Somali language had no written form until, in 1972, President Siad announced a system would be developed using the Roman alphabet.

Western and Communist aid has added some modern facilities—an American-built seaport and a Russian-built slaughterhouse—but the Somali economy remains largely a low-yield herding/farming system.

The current regime of Major General Mohamed Siad Barré, who overthrew the government of Premier Mohammed Ibrahim Egal in 1969, until recently had been marked by close ties with the Soviet Union and vociferous anti-Westernism. In exchange for military aid, Somalia provided the Soviets with a missile storage base. Angered by the Soviet buildup in Ethiopia, Somalia's arch-foe, Siad Barré expelled the Soviets from Somalia in mid-1977, and the Somali army invaded Ogaden, an area of Ethiopia claimed by Somalia, to help the Somali rebels operating in the region. But the Ethiopian forces, aided by some 11,000 Cuban troops and 1,000 Soviet military advisors, drove the Somali troops from Ogaden by early 1978. Ethiopia has stated that there can be no lasting peace in the area until Somalia renounces its territorial claims on Ogaden, Djibouti and northern Kenya, and pays for damages caused in the war. Meanwhile, two "western Somali" liberation groups continue to fight on, guerrilla-style.

As a result of the eight-month Ogaden War, Somalia was burdened by the influx of about 1,300,000 refugees who fled from the region. Most of the food supplied to the refugees has been provided by the U.S. In August 1980, Somalia agreed to give the U.S. access to military ports and airfields in the country in return for military aid, and Somalia reportedly promised not to invade the Ogaden region again.

HISTORY: Although arid and desolate in many areas, Somalia was known as the Land of Punt (God's Land) in ancient Egyptian writings. It was reputedly the source of the biblical frankincense and myrrh, and was probably also the breeding ground of the locusts that invaded Egypt in the time of Joseph. Over the centuries the Somalis, a blend of Asian and African peoples, formed a confederation of closely knit clans in which Arab trading enclaves and sultanates evolved. Later, the nation was divided into British and Italian possessions, and, with union of these in 1960, it began a new era as the Somali Republic

19th cent.: British and Italians, through treaties with sultans and mutual agreements, divide country, with British occupying northwestern portion, Italians, the east and south

1901-20: Mohammed bin Abdallah Hasan, the "Mad Mullah," wages holy war against British

1936: Italian Somaliland is merged with Eritrea and Ethiopia as "Italian East Africa," following Ethiopian defeat in Italo-Ethiopian War of 1935-36

1940-41: Italians occupy British Somaliland during World War II; they are ousted by British, who take over Italian Somaliland

1947-50: Italy renounces colonial rights and is given 10-year UN trusteeship to prepare former possession for independence

1960: British and Italian Somaliland are united as Somali Republic

1961-64: Droughts and floods deplete crops, livestock; food shipments by United States and other countries avert famine

1969: President Abdirashid Ali Shermarke is slain by an assassin; army, with police backing, seizes power

1975: 120,000 Somali nomads are airlifted by Soviet planes from drought-stricken areas of north to southern regions

1977: Kenya and Somalia pledge maintenance of peace along border, following Kenya's charge of a Somali invasion

1978: Eight-month Ogaden war ends in March as Cuban- and Soviet-aided Ethiopian forces drive Somalis from region. Somalia reports that army officers "influenced by foreign powers" attempted coup which failed; thwarted rebels are said to have killed 20 people and injured 34. Ethiopian jets bomb Somali towns and villages while Somali guerrillas recapture major military base in southern part of Ogaden region

1979: Somalia criticizes U.S. for failure to deliver $15 million in weapons as promised. New constitution adopted

1980: People's Assembly, meeting for first time in ten years, reconfirms Siad Barré as president for new six-year term. Somalia gets food from U.S. and other countries for Ogaden refugees. U.S. and Somalia sign agreement granting U.S. use of Somali naval and air bases in exchange for arms aid

SOUTH AFRICA

Area: 472,359 sq. mi. (inc. Bophuthatswana, Transkei and Venda) **Population:** 23,771,970 (1980 census) (excluding Bophuthatswana, Transkei and Venda)

Official Name: Republic of South Africa **Capitals:** Cape Town (legislative), Pretoria (administrative), and Bloemfontein (judicial) **Nationality:** South African **Languages:** English and Afrikaans are the official languages. Of the white population, 63% speak Afrikaans and 37% speak English. In the *Bantustans*, the individual African languages are official. Indians, who constitute the bulk of the Asian minority, speak Tamil, Hindi, Gujarati, and Telugu **Religion:** Most of the population is Christian, chiefly Protestant. About 50% of the Africans in the *Bantustans* are animists. Most of the Asians are Hindus and Moslems **Flag:** Horizontal stripes of orange, white, and blue with small replicas of the Union Jack, the Boer flag of the Orange Free State, and old Transvaal Vierkleur banner in the center **Anthem:** Die Stem (The Voice of South Africa) **Currency:** Rand (0.82 per U.S. $1)

Location: Southern tip of the African continent, between the South Atlantic Ocean on the west and the Indian Ocean on the east. South Africa is landbound on the north and northeast by Namibia, Botswana, Zimbabwe, Swaziland, and Mozambique. Independent Lesotho lies entirely within the borders of South Africa. Walvis Bay, on the Namibian coast, is an exclave of the Cape Province **Features:** On the west, south, and east is a narrow coastal belt of lowlands extending into an extensive interior plateau **Chief Rivers:** Orange, Limpopo

Head of State: President Marais Viljoen, born 1915, elected 1979 **Head of Government:** Prime Minister Pieter W. Botha, born 1916, appointed 1978 **Effective Date of Present Constitution:** May 1961 **Legislative Body:** House of Assembly (unicameral) with 165 members elected by white voters, 8 additional members chosen by the House and 4 others nominated by the President **Local Government:** 4 provinces, each with an appointed administrator and an elected provincial council. Ten self-governing *Bantustans* have been created since 1963, three of which, Transkei, Bophuthatswana and Venda have been granted independence

Ethnic Composition: (excl. "independent Bantustans"): Blacks (Bantus) constitute 67% of the population, whites (largely of Dutch and British descent) 19%, coloureds (mixed Bushmen, Hottentot and white descent) 11%, and Asians 3% **Population Distribution:** 48% urban

Largest Cities: (1970 census) (M.A. = Metropolitan Area) Johannesburg 654,232 (M.A. 1,417,818), Cape Town 697,514 (M.A. 833,731), Durban 736,852 (M.A. 975,494), Soweto 602,043, Pretoria 545,450 (M.A. 573,283), Port Elizabeth 392,231 (M.A. 413,961), Germiston 221,972 (M.A. 293,257)

Per Capita Income: $1,690 (1980) **Gross National Product (GNP):** $48 billion (1980) **Economic Statistics:** About 27% of GNP is derived from manufacturing (textiles, iron and steel, chemicals, fertilizer, automobile assembly, metalworking, electrical and non-electrical machinery and equipment, mining machinery); 21% from mining (gold, platinum, coal, diamonds, antimony, iron ore, copper, uranium, manganese, chrome, asbestos); 8% from agriculture (sugar, tobacco, wool, corn, fruit, dairy products, wheat, fish) **Minerals and Mining:** Extensive mineral deposits, including gold, platinum, coal, diamonds, vanadium, antimony, iron ore, copper, uranium, manganese, chrome, asbestos **Labor Force:** 9,532,000 (1976), with 22.8% in industry, 23.4% in services, and 9.6% in agriculture **Foreign Trade:** Exports, chiefly diamonds, wool, fruit, copper, iron and steel, and gold, amounted to $18 billion in 1979 (excluding gold bullion). Imports, mainly industrial machinery and equipment, transportation equipment, and precision instruments, totaled $9 billion **Principal Trade Partners:** Britain, West Germany, Japan, United States

Vital Statistics: Birthrate, 42.9 per 1,000 of pop. (1975); death rate, 15.5 **Life Expectancy:** 52 years **Health Statistics:** 152 inhabitants per hospital bed; 2,016 per physician (1973) **Infant Mortality:** 59 per 1,000 births (1974) **Illiteracy:** Negligible (white); 50% (others) **Primary and Secondary School Enrollment:** 4,653,452 (1972) **Enrollment in Higher Education:** 98,577 **GNP Expended on Education:** N.A.

Transportation: Paved roads total 50,000 mi. **Motor Vehicles:** 2,984,700 (1977) **Passenger Cars:** 2,163,500 **Railway Mileage:** 13,950 **Ports:** Durban, East London, Port Elizabeth, Cape Town, Richards Bay, Saldanha Bay **Major Airlines:** South African Airways, the government-owned airline, operates international and domestic flights **Communications:** Government controlled **Radio Transmitters:** 177 **Radio Receivers:** 2,500,000 (1976) **Television Transmitters:** 34 **Licenses:** 719,000 (1977) **Telephones:** 2,300,000 **Newspapers:** 22 dailies, 70 copies per 1,000 inhabitants (1975)

Weights and Measures: Metric system **Travel Requirements:** Passport, visa valid for 1 year **International Dialing Code:** 27

BOPHUTHATSWANA

Area: 15,570 sq. mi. **Population:** 1,200,000 **Density:** 77 inhabitants per sq. mi. **Official Name:** Republic of Bophuthatswana **Capital:** Mmabatho **Flag:** An orange diagonal stripe across a blue field with a white disk bearing a black leopard head in the upper hoist **Head of State and of Government:** President and Prime Minister: Chief Lucas Mangope, born 1923, elected December 1977 **Legislative Body:** Legislative Assembly (unicameral), with 99 members of which 48 are elected, 48 appointed by the 12 regional authorities, and 3 appointed by the president **Largest Cities:** (1970 census) Garankuwa 45,631, Mabopane 22,559, Mafikeng 6,515

TRANSKEI

Area: 16,910 sq. mi. **Population:** 2,000,000 **Density:** 118 inhabitants per sq. mi. **Official Name:** Republic of Transkei **Capital:** Umtata **Flag:** Ochre, white, and green horizontal stripes **Head of State:** President: Kaiser Daliwonga Matanzima, born 1915, took office 1979 **Head of Government:** Prime Minister: George Matanzima, born 1919, appointed 1979 **Legislative Body:** National Assembly (unicameral), with 150 members, composed of 75 elected, 70 nominated chiefs, and 5 paramount chiefs, all serving 5-year terms **Largest Cities:** (1974 est.) Umtata 28,100, Butterworth (Gcuma) 24,000

VENDA

Area: 2,510 sq. mi. **Population:** 449,000 **Density:** 179 inhabitants per sq. mi. **Official Name:** Republic of Venda **Capital:** Thohoyandou **Flag:** Three equal horizontal stripes of green, yellow and brown with a vertical blue stripe at the hoist. A brown "V" is centered on the yellow stripe **Head of State and of Government:** Chief Patrick R. Mphephu **Legislative Body:** National Assembly (unicameral), with 84 members of which 42 are elected and 42 are chiefs or their nominees **Largest Centers:** Thohoyandou, Sibasa, Makwarela

CISKEI

A fourth area, Ciskei, is to be granted independence on Dec. 4, 1981

South Africa is a land of great physical beauty and harsh social contrasts. Its rugged coastlines, steep escarpments, sweeping plateaus, and magnificent mountains afford unparalleled vistas. The setting of Cape Town, the country's oldest city, is among the most beautiful in the world. The modern skyscrapers of Johannesburg tower above the rolling countryside of the plateau *highveld.* The 19th century buildings that dominate the center of the administrative capital, Pretoria, form reminders of the period of conflict between Boer and Briton and the emergence of the Union of South Africa, predecessor of the present Republic.

Contrasted against the wealthy suburbs, modern highways, beach resorts and golf courses lie the bleak, much poorer African townships that house the urban labor reservoirs, the crowded workers' quarters near the mines, the traditional but often deteriorated African villages in the Bantu homelands. Rich South Africa is white South Africa; poorer South Africa tends to be the domain of the black, colored, and to a lesser extent the Asian communities. All *nationwide* statistics relating to the Republic should be considered in this context.

Although racial segregation as a way of life had characterized South Africa for many decades, a turning point came in 1948 when D. F. Malan's National party defeated the United party led by J. C. Smuts. Apartheid now became official state policy, and even the slightest trend toward racial integration was reversed. Public facilities became

rigorously segregated, the major universities were restricted to whites, and numerous other steps were taken to eliminate racial contact in daily life. More significantly, however, the Nationalist government also embarked on a program of racial-territorial separation for the country as a whole, with the ultimate aim of the creation of a set of autonomous African states within South Africa's borders. Initially these areas were called *Bantustans,* and the first such territory to be awarded a degree of self-government was the Transkei in 1963. Transkei was declared to be an independent "homeland" in 1976. Two more such black homelands have since been granted independence, Bophuthatswana in 1977 and Venda in 1979. The homeland plan involves land exchanges, population movements, and numerous hardships for many of the people affected. Other nations have withheld recognition of the independence of these homelands which receive most of their income from South Africa.

South Africa's policies of separate development have been the target of sharp criticism throughout the world, and especially in black Africa. Demands have been voiced for boycotts on trade, business, and sports contests with the Republic. In South Africa itself, leaders of the African Homelands also have begun to put pressure on the government for greater sovereignty than the *Bantustan* plan had first envisaged, and for better conditions for Africans still residing and working in "white" South Africa. The response has been comparatively slight. Some concessions have been made in areas of job opportunity for blacks, equalization of salaries, acceptance of some interracial sports events and in ending discrimination in the use of restrooms and elevators. However, the legacy of apartheid and the straightjacket of separate development continue to dominate life in the Republic.

In 1979 a major political scandal rocked Pretoria, forcing John Vorster to resign the ceremonial post of president. An official investigation alleged that Vorster, while prime minister, had approved, and later tried to cover up, a propaganda program under which some $90 million in secret funds were funneled to friendly politicians and other leaders in Europe and the U.S. Pieter W. Botha, who became prime minister in 1978, was absolved of complicity and attempted to set his government on a reform course of relaxation in apartheid rules and more skilled jobs for blacks. Marais Viljoen, former president of the senate, became the republic's president in June 1979.

HISTORY: When European settlers first arrived, there were several distinct native groups occupying different parts of the territory, including the Bushmen, nomadic hunters of the western desert upland country, and the Hottentots, a pastoral people who occupied the southern and eastern coastal areas. At the same time, Bantu people were moving toward the Cape of Good Hope, having already occupied territories in the north and east
1488: Portuguese led by Bartholomew Diaz arrive at Cape
1652: First Dutch settlers establish Cape Colony
1814: Britain gains formal possession of the Cape Colony as a result of the Napoleonic Wars. Dutch begin eastward movement
1835-36: In a migration known as the Great Trek, the Boers (descendants of the Dutch settlers) leave Cape Colony for the north in protest against British rule
1899-1902: Boer War breaks out with Britain. By the Treaty of Vereeniging, the Boers acknowledge British sovereignty over Transvaal and the Orange Free State
1910: Union of South Africa is constituted under the terms of the South African Act passed by the British Parliament
1926-47: Ruling whites initiate separatist policies
1948: Afrikaner National Party, led by D. F. Malan, defeats J. C. Smuts' governing United Party and apartheid is introduced as official state policy
1959: Promotion of Bantu Self-Government Act is passed, providing for eight self-governing African states
1960: Seventy-two blacks are killed in protest demonstration against forced carrying of identity passes in Sharpeville

1961: South Africa becomes a republic and formally withdraws from British Commonwealth

1963: The first partially self-governing *Bantustan* (Bantu "homeland"), the Transkei, is established

1966: Prime Minister Hendrik Verwoerd is assassinated and is succeeded by Balthazar J. Vorster

1969: UN Security Council condemns South Africa for its refusal to permit the UN to take control of South-West Africa following the termination of a League of Nations mandate

1971: World Court rules that South Africa's administration of South-West Africa is illegal

1976: Forced use of Afrikaans language in black schools precipitates rioting in Soweto, leaving 380 dead. Transkei homeland granted independence in October

1977: Black political activist Stephen Biko dies under suspicious circumstances while in police custody. UN Security Council unanimously orders worldwide mandatory embargo on arms supplies to South Africa because of its racial policies. Government scores overwhelming victory in general elections. Bophuthatswana granted independence

1978: Transkei breaks diplomatic relations with South Africa. South African forces enter Angola in "limited military operation" against guerrillas of SWAPO (South-West African People's Organization); action is condemned by UN Security Council. Prime Minister Vorster resigns and is named president. Pieter W. Botha is appointed prime minister

1979: Vorster resigns amid scandal, is succeeded by Marais Viljoen. Botha, exonerated, shuffles cabinet, removes hard-line minister of justice, proposes new approach to race relations. His program to provide more skilled jobs for blacks prompts wildcat strike by mine workers. Venda is granted independence. White-dominated Namibian National Assembly is organized and given legislative powers

1980: Wave of unrest occurs in Cape Town area and elsewhere over inadequacy of nonwhite education. Blacks in Soweto riot against rent increases. Two synthetic fuel plants near Johannesburg are bombed. Economic growth rate of 7.5% per year is stimulated largely by higher gold prices, but is hampered by shortage of skilled labor. Except in mining, black workers are increasingly accepted in skilled occupations and to membership in trade unions. South Africa accuses UN of being too prejudiced to supervise free elections in South-West Africa. Botha visits Taiwan to strengthen ties. Ciskei votes overwhelmingly in favor of independent homeland status. Parliament is enlarged by 12 seats of which 11 go to the ruling National Party

1981: A UN-sponsored conference in Geneva on a cease-fire in South-West Africa fails as South Africa refuses to deal with SWAPO delegation. An Advisory President's Council of hand-picked whites, coloureds and Asiatics—but excluding blacks—is inaugurated on Feb. 3, replacing the Senate dissolved at close of 1980. South Africa fails in effort to reclaim its UN General Assembly seat. General Assembly votes 114-0 for sanctions against South Africa for its failure to settle Namibian question; sanctions are later vetoed in Security Council. South African forces continue raids on SWAPO units training in Angola. National Party wins heavily in parliamentary elections open only to whites. South Africa seeks self-sufficiency in enriched uranium by rushing completion of new plant near Pretoria

---

SPAIN

Area: 195,988 sq. mi. **Population:** 37,430,000 (1980 est.)

Official Name: Spanish State **Capital:** Madrid **Nationality:** Spanish **Languages:** Spanish is the official and predominant language; Catalan, Galician, Valencian, and Basque are regional languages recognized for legal purposes **Religion:** The population is overwhelmingly Roman Catholic **Flag:** Horizontal stripes of red **Anthem:** Royal March **Currency:** Peseta (89.2 per U.S. $1)

Location: Southwest Europe, occupying most of the Iberian peninsula. Spain is bounded on the north by the Bay of Biscay, on the northeast by France and Andorra, on the east and south by the Mediterranean Sea, and on the west by Portugal and the Atlantic Ocean **Features:** Most of the country consists of a high plateau divided by mountains and broad depressions. The landmass rises sharply from the sea, leaving a narrow coastal plain except in the Andalusian lowlands in the south **Chief Rivers:** Ebro, Guadalquivir, Duero, Tajo, Guadiana, Miño

Head of State: King Juan Carlos I (de Borbón), born 1938, proclaimed king in 1975 **Head of Government:** Premier Leopoldo Calvo Sotelo y Bustelo, born 1926, sworn in Feb. 26, 1981 **Effective Date of Present Constitution:** December 29, 1978 **Legislative Body:** *Cortes* (bicameral), with an elected 350-member Chamber of Deputies, and a Senate with 208 members, all for 4 years **Local Govern-**ment: 50 provinces, each headed by an appointed governor and a provincial council, and the 2 African presidios of Ceuta and Melilla. Catalonia and the Basque country have received regional autonomy

Ethnic Composition: The Castilians of central Spain, the Basques in the north, the Catalans in the northeast, the Galicians in the northwest, the Valencians in the east, and the Andalusians in the south represent separate cultural groups **Population Distribution:** 49% urban **Density:** 191 inhabitants per sq. mi.

Largest Cities: (1975 est.) Madrid 3,520,320, Barcelona 1,809,722, Valencia 713,026, Seville 588,784, Saragossa 542,317, Bilbao 457,655, Málaga 402,978

Per Capita Income: $3,022 (1980) **Gross Domestic Product (GDP):** $115 billion (1980) **Economic Statistics:** About 53% of GDP is derived from trade and services; 37% from mining, manufacturing, construction, energy; and 10% from agriculture (cereals, fruits, vegetables, olive oil). Tourism is of great importance **Minerals and Mining:** Coal, iron, mercury, pyrites, zinc, copper and potash are produced **Labor Force:** 13,300,000 (1978), with 40% in services, 36% in industry and construction, and 20% in agriculture **Foreign Trade:** Exports, mainly footwear, textiles and clothing, steel products, transportation equipment, machinery, chemicals, and furniture, totaled $18 billion in 1979. Imports, chiefly feed grains, machinery, transportation and electrical equipment, fuels, metals, chemicals, and tobacco, totaled $25 billion **Principal Trade Partners:** United States, West Germany, France, Britain, Saudi Arabia, Iran, Netherlands, Italy

Vital Statistics: Birthrate, 18 per 1,000 of pop. (1977); death rate, 7.7 **Life Expectancy:** 72 years **Health Statistics:** 190 inhabitants per hospital bed; 647 per physician (1975) **Infant Mortality:** 10.7 per 1,000 births (1976) **Illiteracy:** 3% **Primary and Secondary School Enrollment:** 6,812,755 (1976) **Enrollment in Higher Education:** 540,238 (1975) **GNP Expended on Education:** 1.7% (1974)

Transportation: Surfaced roads total 86,665 mi. **Motor Vehicles:** 7,102,600 (1977) **Passenger Cars:** 5,944,900 **Railway Mileage:** 10,824 **Ports:** Barcelona, Bilbao, Valencia, Cartagena, Sta. Cruz de Tenerife, Gijón, Huelva, Algeciras, Cádiz, Vigo **Major Airlines:** Iberia operates domestic and international flights, Aviaco operates domestic flights **Communications:** Government controlled **Radio Transmitters:** 430 **Receivers:** 9,300,000 (1976) **Television Transmitters:** 791 **Receivers:** 6,640,000 (1976) **Telephones:** 9,530,000 **Newspapers:** 115 dailies, 48 copies per 1,000 inhabitants (1975)

Weights and Measures: Metric system **Travel Requirements:** Passport, no visa for 6 months **International Dialing Code:** 34

Since the death of the dictatorial head of state, Francisco Franco, on November 20, 1975, Spain has moved steadily toward democracy. Two days after the passing of *El Caudillo*, the 500-year-old monarchy was restored with the proclamation of Juan Carlos de Borbón as king of Spain.

In 1977, in the first free election in 41 years, Premier Adolfo Suárez González and his Democratic Center Union, a center-right grouping, captured 34 percent of the popular vote, with the Socialists coming in a close second with 28 percent. Suárez, a former Franco supporter, has held the premiership since his appointment by the King in 1976. The pardoning of more than half of the country's 1,600 political prisoners, the granting of the right of assembly, a loosening of press controls and legalization of the Communist party have all occurred since the new monarch promised "profound improvements" at his swearing-in ceremony on November 22, 1975. A new bicameral parliament was instituted in place of the appointed parliament left by Franco.

However, the problem of the "nations within the Spanish nation" still remains; Basque and Catalan separatism and Galician and Valencian regionalism present difficulties. Some concessions have been made to the aspirations to cultural freedom of the non-Castilian peoples, but many more will be required before the ethnic sensibilities of these ethnic groups will be satisfied.

In its economic life, Spain has progressed far from the devastation left by the 1936-1939 civil war. A good part of the prosperity results from the popularity of Spain as a tourist haven for other Europeans and for North Americans. The beauty of the Iberian seaside, plus its easy accessibility from Western Europe and relative inexpensiveness, have turned sleepy fishing villages into thriving vacation resorts.

Burgeoning industry, flourishing foreign trade and an ever-increasing middle class are all signs pointing to the fact that Spain has become a prosperous, 20th-century nation. Though there are still wide areas of poverty, the better life is noticeable in the cities—such as Madrid, Barcelona and Seville—and the wealthier provinces—such as Castile and Catalonia. The deteriorating economy resulted in a high unemployment rate of 11% and an inflation rate of 15 percent in 1980, however.

A new constitution adopted in 1978 limited the king to an essentially ceremonial role, guaranteed human rights, and provided for the establishment of autonomous provinces in the Basque country and Catalonia. King Juan Carlos' firm actions foiled a military coup led by three right-wing generals on Feb. 23-24, 1981, when rebel civil guards seized Parliament and held the legislators captive for 18 hours. The king went on television to denounce the rebellion and ordered all military commanders to obey their top leaders; when they did, the rebellion collapsed and the rebels surrendered.

HISTORY: About 1000 B.C. the Iberian peninsula was invaded by Celtic tribes from the north, and two centuries later Phoenicians and Greeks began to establish colonies along the Spanish coast. The Carthaginians conquered most of the peninsula in the 3rd century B.C., but were forced out by the Romans, during whose rule political unity was established and Christianity introduced. Early in the 5th century, Spain was overrun by the Germanic Vandals and Visigoths. After forcing the Vandals to emigrate to Africa, the Visigoths were themselves conquered by the Moors

711-18: Roderick, the last of the Visigothic kings, is defeated in battle by the Moors, who gain control over virtually the entire peninsula. Asturias, the only remnant of Visigothic Spain, becomes the focus of the Christian reconquest

1492: King Ferdinand of Aragon and his wife, Queen Isabella of Castile, complete the reconquest of Spain by capturing Granada, the last remaining Moorish stronghold. The Catholic rulers order the expulsion of the Jews. Columbus wins the monarchs' support for his voyages and discovers America, where a vast Spanish empire is soon to be established

1588: Defeat of the Spanish Armada by England hastens the demise of Spanish power

1808-14: Napoleon's armies invade Spain and his brother Joseph is placed on the Spanish throne. The French are finally driven out by Spanish resistance fighters and British troops led by Wellington. Wars of independence break out in Spanish America, leading to the disruption of the empire

1898: Spanish-American War destroys remaining empire

1931-36: Alfonso XIII is deposed and a republic established. Economic and political unrest culminate in an army revolt against the republic, under the leadership of General Francisco Franco. The revolt precipitates the Spanish Civil War

1936-39: The war rages for two and a half years, with the Loyalists (Republicans), aided by the Soviet Union and foreign volunteers, gradually defeated by Franco's forces, aided by Nazi Germany and Fascist Italy. The Loyalist government flees to France, and Franco sets up a dictatorship, with the Fascist Falange as the only legal party

1942-47: Franco reestablishes the *Cortes* but on Fascist lines without genuine popular representation. The Law of Succession is promulgated, declaring Spain a kingdom and setting up a regency council, with Franco as head of state

1966-68: A new constitution curbing the political power of the National Movement and its political organ, the Falange, is approved by referendum. The position of president of government (premier) is created. However, dissatisfaction with the regime makes itself felt in strikes and university unrest, which lead to severe police repression

1969: Franco designates Prince Juan Carlos de Borbón y Borbón to be chief of state and king upon Franco's death or incapacitation

1970-71: Military court sentences six Basque separatists to death; Franco commutes sentences following world outcry

1973: Spain establishes full diplomatic relations with East Germany and Communist China; Premier Carrero Blanco is assassinated; Carlos Arias Navarro becomes premier

1975: U.S. use of Spanish bases is renewed. Franco dies. Prince Juan Carlos becomes head of state as King Juan Carlos I

1976: Spain withdraws from Western Sahara, last remnant of this once-vast colonial empire. Carlos Arias Navarro resigns premiership. He is replaced by Adolfo Suárez González

1977: Communist party is legalized and declared eligible for participation in national elections. Premier Suárez' Democratic Center Union emerges victorious in first free elections in 41 years. Government devalues peseta by 22 percent as economy continues slump. Catalonians and Basques granted self-rule

1978: Basques legally celebrate their national day for first time since civil war. Communist party, holding its ninth congress (first since 1932), drops "Leninist" label despite strong Soviet advice against doing so. Suárez government suffers setback as Senate by-elections show victory for opposition Socialists and big surge by Communists. Government grants provisional autonomy to Balearic Islands and two other regions. New constitution limits king's role and contains detailed bill of rights

1979: Democratic Center Union wins plurality in new elections; Suárez is reappointed premier

1980: Basque country and Catalonia become autonomous regions

1981: Suárez resigns as premier; Leopoldo Calvo Sotelo replaces him. Attempted military coup by a few rebellious army officers fails when most military commanders remain loyal to King Juan Carlos and refuse to join rebellion

SRI LANKA

Area: 25,332 sq. mi. **Population:** 14,859,295 (1981 census)
Official Name: Democratic Socialist Republic of Sri Lanka **Capital:** Colombo **Nationality:** Sri Lankan **Languages:** Sinhala is the official language; both Sinhala and Tamil are national languages. English is used widely **Religion:** 64% Hinayana Buddhist, 20% Hindu, 9% Christian (mainly Roman Catholic), 6% Moslem, 1% other **Flag:** Narrow green and orange vertical stripes on the left side, with a yellow lion carrying a sword in one upraised paw against a red background occupying the rest of the flag. The entire flag is bordered in yellow, with a vertical yellow band separating the orange and green stripes from the red background of the rest of the flag **Anthem:** Hail, Hail, Motherland **Currency:** Sri Lanka rupee (18.4 per U.S. $1)

Location: Island in the Indian Ocean, off the southeastern tip of India. Sri Lanka is bounded on the north by the Palk Strait, on the east by the Bay of Bengal, on the south by the Indian Ocean, and on the west by the Gulf of Mannar **Features:** A low-lying plain makes up the northern half of the island and continues around the southern coast. The south-central part is mountainous **Chief Rivers:** Mahaweli, Ganga, Kelani, Walawe, Kalu, Gal

Head of State and of Government: President Junius Richard Jayewardene, born 1906, sworn in 1978 for a 6-year term. He is assisted by a prime minister, Ranasinghe Premadasa, born 1924, appointed 1978 **Effective Date of Present Constitution:** September 7, 1978 **Legislative Body:** Parliament (unicameral), with 196 members for 6-year terms **Local Government:** 22 districts, each headed by a governor

Ethnic Composition: 72% Sinhalese and 20% Tamil. (11% of the Tamil population are "Sri Lanka Tamils," citizens whose ancestors have lived in Sri Lanka for many generations and who have full voting rights. The 9% "Indian Tamils" came from south India in the 19th century) **Population Distribution:** 22.4% urban **Density:** 587 inhabitants per sq. mi.

Largest Cities: (1974 est.) Colombo 592,000, Dehiwala-Mount Lavinia 162,000, Jaffna 114,000, Moratuwa 100,000; (1971 census) Kandy 93,602, Kotte 93,042, Galle 72,720

Per Capita Income: $324 (1980) **Gross National Product (GNP):** $4.8 billion (1980) **Economic Statistics:** In 1973 about 34% of GNP was from agriculture (tea, rice, rubber, pineapples, coconuts), forestry, and fishing; 33% from trade and services; and 13% from industry (foodstuffs, tobacco products, chemicals, garments, leather and footwear, cement, paper and paperboard, tires and tubes, metal products) and mining **Minerals and Mining:** Graphite mining is the principal mineral industry; there are also gemstones, mineral sands and limestone **Labor Force:** 4 million, with 53% in agriculture, and 15% in industry **Foreign Trade:** Exports, chiefly tea, rubber, gems, graphite, and coconut products, totaled $1 billion in 1979. Imports, mainly rice and other food products, textiles, machinery and transport equipment and petroleum, totaled $1.4 billion **Principal Trade Partners:** Britain, China, United States, Japan, India, West Germany, Pakistan, Saudi Arabia

Vital Statistics: Birthrate, 26.5 per 1,000 of pop. (1976); death rate, 9 **Life Expectancy:** 68 years **Health Statistics:** 334 inhabitants per hospital bed; 4,007 per physician (1976) **Infant Mortality:** 43 per 1,000 births **Illiteracy:** 18% **Primary and Secondary School Enrollment:** 2,462,141 (1977) **Enrollment in Higher Education:** 14,568 (1974) **GNP Expended on Education:** 3.1% (1976)

Transportation: Paved roads total 15,000 miles **Motor Vehicles:** 143,000 (1976) **Passenger Cars:** 93,800 **Railway Mileage:** 1,016 **Ports:** Colombo, Trincomalee, Galle **Major Airlines:** Air Lanka operates domestic and international services **Communications: Government controlled Radio Transmitters:** 24 **Receivers:** 800,000 (1976) **Television Transmitters:** 1 **Telephones:** 72,000 (1975) **Newspapers:** 18 dailies (1975), 42 copies per 1,000 inhabitants (1971)

Weights and Measures: Metric system **Travel Requirements:** Passport, no visa for 30 days, onward ticket **International Dialing Code:** 94

Isolated from global and regional rivalries at independence in 1948, Sri Lanka, formerly known as Ceylon, was without an enemy and appeared to be assured of peace and prosperity. But parliamentary democracy has been a forum for radical communal nationalism that has divided the Sinhalese Buddhist majority and the large Tamil minority and often brought the country near civil war. A positive action was the program to settle the "Indian Tamils" question through the naturalization of some and the repatriation to India of others. However, the Tamils have continued to press for a separate state.

In April 1971 ultraleftist students plunged the country into a full-scale guerrilla war before they faded into the jungled countryside. The movement was believed to have been born in 1964 when youth wings of the various Communist party factions split from adult leaders, accusing them of being both corrupt and irrelevant to the needs of Sri Lanka's peasantry. The revolutionary movement had an obvious attraction to the many students who were the sons of peasants and who had taken advantage of free college education only to find no jobs available upon graduation. The 1971 uprising led to the declaration of a state of emergency that did not end until February 1977.

Mrs. Sirimavo Bandaranaike, the prime minister from 1960-65 and again from 1970-77, was defeated in the general elections of 1977 by Junius Jayewardene's United National party. Nepotism, abuses of power, and corruption, in addition to the poor economic situation, were the major issues in the campaign. In 1976 there had been severe student and labor unrest.

Under the Jayewardene government, Sri Lanka made a dramatically swift turn away from socialism and toward capitalism. The tea plantations, for instance, had been allowed to run down after being seized by the government in the early 1970s; under Jayewardene, private managers were put in charge of money-losing state corporations, particularly in efforts to boost the major exports—tea, rubber, and coconut. Foreign investment increased sharply, aided by tax holidays and other incentives, as well as what Sri Lankans said was worker productivity second only to Singapore in Asian industry. The price of the new policies was an escalation of inflation, particularly affecting food, consumer goods, and some services previously subsidized by the government. The 1980's began with a newly united labor movement calling an unsuccessful general strike to protest official wage restraints and the growing inequality of income distribution.

HISTORY: The earliest inhabitants of Sri Lanka (formerly Ceylon) have left few traces. The Sinhalese, who form the bulk of the present population, came to the island from northern India in the 6th century B.C. They founded their capital at Anuradhapura, which became a major religious center following the conversion of Sri Lanka to Buddhism in the 3rd century B.C. Invasions from south India, notably by the Tamils, forced the Sinhalese into the southwest of the island. In the 12th century A.D., Arab traders appeared in Ceylon. The island's coastal areas were occupied by the Portuguese in the 16th century. By the middle of the 17th century, their possessions had been taken over by the Dutch

1795: The Dutch possessions are taken over by Britain
1802: The Crown Colony of Ceylon is established
1815: All of the island of Ceylon is brought under British rule
1948: Sri Lanka becomes independent, with dominion status in the British Commonwealth

1956-59: S.W.R.D. Bandaranaike becomes prime minister, heading a leftist coalition. His term is marked by bloody riots between Sinhalese and Tamils, and ends with his assassination
1960-65: New elections bring another leftist coalition to power, with Mrs. Sirimavo Bandaranaike, wife of the slain leader, as the world's first woman prime minister. Her government adopts a neutralist policy and nationalizes a number of Western oil companies. A dispute with the United States and Britain results
1965-66: Elections result in the victory of the pro-Western United National party, led by Dudley Senanayake. His government agrees to compensation for the expropriated oil companies, and the United States agrees to resume economic aid to Sri Lanka, cut off at the time the companies were nationalized
1968: Sri Lanka becomes first of the developing nations to achieve the goal of a 5 percent rise in per capita income
1970: Mrs. Bandaranaike returns to power
1971: Revolutionary students, seeking to replace the government with one more militantly socialist, lead an uprising that results in the death of thousands of rebels and civilians
1972: Ceylon becomes a republic within the Commonwealth and is renamed Sri Lanka under a new constitution; William Gopallawa is appointed the republic's first president by Mrs. Bandaranaike; National Assembly approves land reform plan
1977: Sirimavo Bandaranaike's Freedom party is defeated in general elections; Junius Richard Jayewardene becomes prime minister following his United National party's victory. Sri Lanka amends constitution to give nation French-style presidential governing system which dilutes power of elected assembly, reduces prime minister and cabinet to figureheads and concentrates power in hands of a president popularly elected every six years
1978: Prime Minister Jayewardene is sworn in as president
1979: Foreign investment, encouraged by President Jayewardene's politics, rises to an annual rate of $40 million, 13 times greater than in the last year of the previous government. Tamil extremist group stages a series of killings
1980: Trade unions combine to oppose presidential policies. A general strike in July is effectively suppressed by government. Mrs. Bandaranaike is expelled from parliament for "abuses of power" before 1977
1981: Foreign investment continues to rise, as does inflation. Religious group reports that 35,000 workers are still barred from jobs due to participation in 1980 strike. Emergency rule imposed in north after new Tamil unrest

---

SUDAN

Area: 967,494 sq. mi. **Population:** 18,691,000 (1980 est.)

Official Name: Democratic Republic of the Sudan **Capital:** Khartoum **Nationality:** Sudanese **Languages:** Arabic, the official language, is the native tongue of about 51% of the population; the Negroes of southern Sudan speak about 32 different languages, with English the chief commercial language **Religion:** The religion of the 12 northern provinces is Islam, whose adherents include about 70% of the population; most of the southern tribes are animist (25%). There are also some small Christian communities (5%) **Flag:** Horizontal stripes of red, white, and black, with a green triangle at the hoist **Anthem:** Soldiers of God **Currency:** Sudanese pound (.50 per U.S. $1)

Location: Northeast Africa. Sudan, the largest country in Africa is bounded on the north by Egypt, on the east by the Red Sea and Ethiopia, on the south by Kenya, Uganda, and Zaire, and on the west by the Central African Republic, Chad, and Libya **Features:** An immense plateau sprawls over 3 distinct natural regions, ranging from the Libyan and Sahara deserts and plateaus in the north to grassy plains in the center to a great swamp and tropical savanna in the south **Chief Rivers:** Nile (the Blue Nile and White Nile join at Khartoum)

Head of State and of Government: President: Gen. Jaafar Muhammad al-Nimeiry, born 1929, seized power in 1969, became the first elected president in 1971 and was reelected in 1977. He is also prime minister (since 1977) **Effective Date of Present Constitution:** 1973 **Legislative Body:** People's Assembly (unicameral), with 304 members (274 popularly elected) belonging to the Sudanese Socialist Union party **Local Government:** 18 provinces, headed by appointed commissioners and councils; the 6 provinces of the Southern Region have a joint semiautonomous government

Ethnic Composition: The population of the 12 northern provinces is comprised mainly of Moslem Arabs and Nubians, who together constitute more than two thirds of the population; in the south are Nilotic, Sudanic and black tribes **Population Distribution:** 20% urban **Density:** 19 inhabitants per sq. mi.

Largest Cities: (1975 est.) Khartoum 321,666, Omdurman 305,308, Khartoum North 161,278, Port Sudan 123,000

Per Capita Income: $346 (1980) **Gross National Product (GNP):** $6.5 billion (1980) **Economic Statistics:** In 1978, 40% of GNP was from agriculture (long-staple cotton, peanuts, sugarcane, gum arabic, livestock), and 24% from industry (food and vegetable oil processing) **Minerals and Mining:** Small-scale production of iron ore, chromite, manganese ore, petroleum, slate, gold, and gypsum; deposits of asbestos, slate and tin exist **Labor Force:** 8.6 million (1979), with 85% in agriculture **Foreign Trade:** Exports, mainly cotton, gum arabic, sesame, peanuts, oil cake and meal, and sheep and goats, totaled $840 million in 1979. Imports, chiefly cotton textiles, motor vehicles and parts, electrical and nonelectrical machinery, base metals and manufactures, chemicals and petroleum products, totaled $1.1 billion **Principal Trade Partners:** Britain, India, Japan, France, China, West Germany, Italy, United States, Egypt

Vital Statistics: Birthrate, 47.8 per 1,000 of pop. (1975); death rate, 17.5 **Life Expectancy:** 50 years **Health Statistics:** 932 inhabitants per hospital bed; 9,488 per physician **Infant Mortality:** 93.6 per 1,000 births **Illiteracy:** 85% **Primary and Secondary School Enrollment:** 1,544,553 (1976) **Enrollment in Higher Education:** 21,342 (1975) **GNP Expended on Education:** 5.5% (1974)

Transportation: Paved roads total 375 mi. **Motor Vehicles:** 50,400 (1972) **Passenger Cars:** 29,200 **Railway Mileage:** 3,400 **Ports:** Port Sudan, Suakin **Major Airlines:** Sudan Airways operates domestically and internationally **Communications:** Government owned **Radio Transmitters:** 7 **Licenses:** 1,300,000 (1973) **Television Transmitters:** 2 **Receivers:** 100,000 (1975) **Telephones:** 60,000 (1976) **Newspapers:** 4 dailies, 8 copies per 1,000 inhabitants (1975)

Weights and Measures: Metric system **Travel Requirements:** Passport, visa valid 3 months, $13.13 fee, 3 photos

The Sudan is Africa's largest country, almost one-third the size of the continental United States, but only a small part of its area, ranging from barren desert to tropical rain forest, is productive. Forty percent of the potentially arable land in the Arab world lies within its boundaries, but only 10 percent of this is under cultivation. Long-staple cotton, the chief export, is grown mainly in the irrigated triangle of land known as the Gezira Plain. This fertile area, just below the confluence of the White and Blue Niles at Khartoum, the capital, and other irrigated areas are a major source also of food and fodder crops.

Crops are raised also in the central rainlands, but production is uncertain because of droughts. Waters of the White Nile backing up into northern Sudan behind Egypt's Aswan Dam will eventually fill the need for additional irrigation.

Of all the African nations only Benin has had a greater number of coups and countercoups. Only Nigeria and Zaire have fought civil wars as cruel as the 17-year conflict, during which 500,000 died, between the Sudan's majority-status Arabs in the north and the minority Christian and pagan blacks in the south. Maj. Gen. Jaafar al-Nimeiry, who himself had seized power in a coup in May 1969, negotiated an end to the war in 1972 by granting regional autonomy to the south.

Nimeiry has survived numerous assassination attempts and two coups that were uncovered before they were begun. Three that were attempted did not succeed, including the revolt led by dissident army elements in July 1976. In this most recent attempt the rebels were defeated by loyal soldiers after having managed to travel 1,000 miles across the desert undetected. Accusing Libya of being behind the uprising, the Sudanese government severed diplomatic relations with the Libyans.

In foreign affairs, the Sudan is a member of the UN, the Arab League, and the Organization of African Unity. The nation participated on the Arab side in the Yom Kippur War. Relations with the U.S. had been troubled by the Arab-Israeli War, but in 1981 the Sudan offered air and naval facilities to the U.S., which in turn tripled the amount of its military aid for the Sudan to about $100 million in fiscal year 1982. During March the Sudan and Egypt resumed diplomatic ties after a year's disruption, mainly because of their mutual fear of Libya's recent hostility towards both countries.

In 1979, the Sudan was one of only three Arab states to endorse Egypt's peace treaty with Israel.

HISTORY: Nubia, the northern half of Sudan, was colonized by Egypt centuries before the Christian era. In the 6th century A.D., the Nubians embraced Coptic Christianity, but in the 15th century were converted to Islam by conquering Arabs. Although the Arabs extended their conquests to the south, it was not until 1821 that all of Sudan was unified by Egypt

1881-85: Sudanese, led by the Mahdi, a Moslem religious fanatic, revolt against Egyptian rule and win control over most of Sudan

1898-99: Anglo-Egyptian army defeats Mahdi's followers; Sudan is proclaimed an Anglo-Egyptian condominium under a governor-general; however, Britain dominates the administration

1924: Egyptian troops mutiny in the Sudan; the British governor-general is murdered; the British expel the Egyptians from the Sudan and assume its rule

1936: Status of Sudan is affirmed by Anglo-Egyptian treaty

1948: In Sudan's first elections, Independence Front, favoring an independent republic, wins large majority over National Front, which favors union with Egypt

1953: Britain and Egypt conclude an agreement providing for Sudanese self-government

1956: Sudan is proclaimed an independent republic

1958: Gen. Ibrahim Abboud seizes power in military coup, dissolves parliament, nullifies constitution, and promises reforms

1964-65: Abboud resigns following popular rioting against his regime and a civilian government is set up; elections are held for a constituent assembly to draft new constitution; Mohammed Ahmed Mahgoub becomes prime minister of a coalition government; black Sudanese rebels in southern provinces launch widespread attacks against government forces

1968: Constituent assembly is dissolved and new elections are held; new assembly elects a supreme council, with Ismail al-Azhari as president

1969: A military coup led by Col. (now Gen.) Jaafar al-Nimeiry overthrows supreme council, annuls provisional constitution, and establishes revolutionary council

1971: Nimeiry is briefly toppled by Communist-backed rebel officers but regains power in countercoup and is elected president

1973: Sudan adopts a new constitution. Oil discovered in Red Sea

1976: Diplomatic relations with Libya are severed following Libyan support of an abortive coup against Nimeiry

1977: U.S. agrees to sell 12 F-5 jet fighters to Sudan

1978: Government and opposition announce reconciliation, formally ending nine years of intermittent conflict

SURINAME

Area: 60,239 sq. mi. **Population:** 374,000 (1978 est.)

Official Name: Republic of Suriname **Capital:** Paramaribo **Nationality:** Surinamese **Languages:** Dutch is the official language; English is also widely used. The majority speak a Creole lingua franca called Sranang Tongo, or Taki Taki **Religion:** 26% Hindu, 26% Moslem, 24% Protestant, and 23% Roman Catholic **Flag:** A wide horizontal red band with a centered golden yellow star, separated by narrow white stripes from green stripes top and bottom **Anthem:** Elevating Our Glorious Land **Currency:** Suriname guilder (florin) (1.785 per U.S. $1)

Location: Northeast coast of South America. It is bordered on the north by the Atlantic Ocean, on the east by French Guiana, on the south by Brazil, and on the west by Guyana **Features:** The three chief zones are the coastal belt (partly protected by dikes), the central zones of forests and savannas, and the southern hill zone, comprising 75% of the area, and rising to over 4,000 feet **Chief Rivers:** Suriname, Saramacca, Coppename, Nickerie, Tapanahoni, Marowijne (Maroni), Corantijn (Courantyne)

Head of State and of Government: Henk R. Chin A Sen, installed as prime minister by a National Military Council following coup of Feb. 25, 1980. He was named president following a second coup by the same group on Aug. 14, 1980 **Effective Date of Present Constitution:** November 1975, suspended Aug. 1980 **Legislative Body:** Parliament was abolished in 1980 **Local Government:** 9 districts, under appointed commissioners

Ethnic Composition: 37% Hindustanis (descendants of Indian laborers), 31% Creoles (of African descent), 17% Javanese, 11% Bush Negroes (descendants of escaped African slaves), 3% Amerindians (of Carib and Arawak stock), and minorities of 7,000 Chinese and 7,000 Europeans (chiefly Dutch) and Lebanese. More than 100,000 Surinamese Hindustani are currently living in the Netherlands **Population Distribution:** N.A. **Density:** 6.2 inhabitants per sq. mi.

Largest Cities: (1974 est.) Paramaribo 150,000; (1964 census) Nieuw-Nickerie 7,400, Meerzorg 5,000, Marienburg 3,500, Moengo 2,100

Per Capita Income: $1,721 (1979) **Gross National Product (GNP):** $685 million (1979) **Economic Statistics:** About 36% of the GNP is derived from the bauxite industry. Most of the balance comes from agriculture (rice, coffee, sugar, citrus fruits, coconuts, corn, cocoa, tobacco), fishing and shrimping, and lumbering. Industry, other than the processing of alumina and aluminum from bauxite, is confined to sawmilling, rice and sugar milling, and the production of rum and cement **Minerals and Mining:** Suriname is a major source of bauxite; gold is also mined commercially **Labor Force:** 118,000; in 1974, 29% of the workers were engaged in agriculture and 15% in industry **Foreign Trade:** Exports, more than 80% of which was bauxite ore, alumina and aluminum, the rest being citrus fruits, bananas, shrimp, rice, and plywood, totaled $440 million in 1979. Imports, mainly machinery, manufactured goods, textiles, vehicles, petroleum products, iron and steel, and foods, totaled $420 million **Principal Trade Partners:** United States, Netherlands, Norway, Venezuela, Japan, Trinidad and Tobago

Vital Statistics: Birthrate, 40.9 per 1,000 of pop.; death rate, 7.2 **Life Expectancy:** 66 years **Health Statistics:** 184 inhabitants per hospital bed; 2,030 per physician (1975) **Infant Mortality:** 30.4 per 1,000 births **Illiteracy:** 20% **Primary and Secondary School Enrollment:** 120,224 (1976) **Enrollment in Higher Education:** 2,138 **GNP Expended on Education:** 4.7%

Transportation: Paved roads total about 300 mi. **Motor Vehicles:** 39,000 (1976) **Passenger Cars:** 28,800 **Railway Mileage:** 100 **Ports:** Paramaribo, Nieuw-Nickerie, Albina **Major Airlines:** Suriname Airways handles domestic and international flights **Communications:** Government and privately owned **Radio Transmitters:** 7 **Receivers:** 112,000 (1976) **Television Transmitters:** 6 **Receivers:** 38,000 (1976) **Telephones:** 21,000 **Newspapers:** 7 dailies (1975), 52 copies per 1,000 inhabitants (1974)

Weights and Measures: Metric system **Travel Requirements:** Passport, no visa, onward ticket **International Dialing Code:** 597

On attaining independence in 1975, Suriname immediately faced a major problem stemming from its multiracial composition—37 percent Hindustani, 31 percent Creole of African descent, 17 percent Javanese, 11 percent Bush Negro. Owing to Hindustani fears of the Creole-dominated government, over 100,000 Surinamers emigrated to the Netherlands prior to independence, thus stripping the emerging nation of a third of its human resources. The emigrants were predominantly well-educated middle- and upper-class entrepreneurs, managers and technicians. The Surinamese government has appealed for the émigrés to return home to help in the development of the resource-rich former colony. To assist in this development the Netherlands has promised to grant Suriname $1.5 billion in aid over the next decade. It has been suggested that the Dutch generosity is based on a desire to improve economic conditions in Suriname enough so that the refugees will return to their tropical homeland and leave poor-paying jobs and welfare rolls in Amsterdam. Another problem is the migration from the countryside to the city, with the result that Suriname may have to import food rather than export it.

Suriname is rich in minerals, forests and potential water power. The country's bauxite deposits are believed to be among the richest in the world. The mining, processing, and exporting of this resource (and since 1965 of alumina and aluminum) constitute the backbone of the economy. Sites of the two major deposits—Moengo and Paranam—are accessible to navigable rivers emptying into the Atlantic. Food processing and lumbering account for other important industries. Alcoa, at a cost of $150 million, has built a dam for the production of hydroelectric energy on the Suriname River.

A government headed by Premier Henck Arron took power in the 1973 elections, when the National Party Coalition, composed mostly of Creoles, unseated the United Reformed Party, led by Jaggernath Lachmon and composed mainly of Hindustanis and Javanese. The Arron government was toppled in February 1980 by a sergeants' coup that appeared to be outside party lines; the army had just been denied the right to form a labor union to seek higher pay and better working conditions. Henk Chin A Sen was chosen to head a civilian government supervised by the newly formed National Military Council. In August 1980 the military installed Chin in the presidency as well.

HISTORY: Christopher Columbus sighted the coast of the area in 1498, but the first successful settlement was not established until 1651 by the British. The colony prospered on a plantation economy based on slave labor imported from Africa. Notable among the emigrants from other New World colonies were Jews from Brazil, who in 1665 erected the first synagogue in the Western Hemisphere. The Netherlands acquired Suriname from Britain in exchange for Dutch rights in Nieuw Amsterdam (Manhattan Island, New York). In the 18th and early 19th centuries the colony, as a result of wars and treaties, was shuffled among England, France and the Netherlands
1815: Netherlands finally regains Suriname at Vienna Congress
1863: Slavery is abolished. Importation of Hindustani, Javanese and Chinese contract laborers follows
1954: Suriname is granted internal autonomy
1973: Creole-dominated National Party Coalition (NPK) wins elections. NPK leader Henck Arron becomes premier
1975: Suriname gains independence
1978: National Party Coalition reelected by landslide in nation's first elections since independence
1980: The army is denied the right to form a labor union. On February 25, a sergeants' coup, staged at the cost of six lives and the burning of a police station, ousts the Arron government. Henk Chin A Sen becomes head of a military-supervised civilian government. In May, 300 mercenaries, led by a former Surinamese soldier, invade Suriname from French Guiana, but all are captured and their leader executed. In August, Chin is made president by the military
1981: Second attempt to overthrow the military government fails in April. Harsh security measures are introduced

---

SWAZILAND

Area: 6,705 sq. mi. **Population:** 530,000 (1979 est.)

Official Name: Kingdom of Swaziland **Capital:** Mbabane **Nationality:** Swazi **Languages:** The official languages are English and si-Swati; Zulu is used by a minority **Religion:** About 43% are animists, with about 500 Moslems; the rest of the population is Christian **Flag:** Horizontal stripes of blue, yellow, red, yellow, and blue with a traditional Swazi shield, spears and staff in black and white in the center **Anthem:** National Anthem, beginning "O God, Bestower of the blessings of the Swazi" **Currency:** Lilangeni (0.82 per U.S. $1)

Location: Southern Africa. Swaziland is almost entirely surrounded by South Africa, except for a 70-mile-long border with Mozambique on the east **Features:** The country consists of three well-defined regions known locally as the high, middle, and low velds, all roughly of equal breadth. The humid *highveld* in the west is mountainous; a plateau lies in the center, and to the east is a subtropical low plain **Chief Rivers:** Komati, Umbuluzi, Great Usutu, Mkonda

Head of State: King Sobhuza II, born 1899; Ngwenyama (the Lion), head of the Swazi nation since 1921, made head of state in 1968 **Head of Government:** Prime Minister: Prince Mabandla Dlamini, appointed Nov. 1979 **Effective Date of Present Constitution:** October 13, 1978 **Legislative Body:** Parliament, or *Liblandla*, (bicameral) consists of a 20-member Senate, and a 50-member House of Assembly; 10 of each are appointed by the king, the rest are chosen by an electoral college. There are no political parties, and the function of parliament is restricted to advising the king and debating proposals **Local Government:** 4 districts

Ethnic Composition: The African population is predominantly Swazi, with a Zulu minority; both belong to the Bantu group. About 2% are white **Population Distribution:** 15% urban **Density:** 79 inhabitants per sq. mi.

Largest Cities: (1976 census) Manzini 28,837, Mbabane 23,109

Per Capita Income: $634 (1978) **Gross National Product (GNP):** $340 million (1978) **Economic Statistics:** The main activity is subsistence agriculture (maize and such commercial crops as sugar, timber, citrus fruits, cotton, rice, and pineapples), which accounts for about 29% of GNP. Mining and manufacturing (machinery, beverages, chemicals, apparel, metal products, processed agricultural products) contribute about 37% of GNP **Minerals and Mining:** Deposits of iron ore, asbestos, and coal are exploited; kaolin, barites, gold, and pyrophyllite are exploited on a smaller scale **Labor Force:** 120,000 (1978), with 60,000 engaged in subsistence agriculture and 18,114 employed in South African mines **Foreign Trade:** Exports, chiefly iron ore, sugar, wood pulp and other forest products, and asbestos, totaled $207 million in 1978. Imports, mainly manufactured goods, machinery and transport equipment, fuel, food and beverages, and tobacco, totaled $270 million **Principal Trade Partners:** South Africa, Britain, Japan

Vital Statistics: Birthrate, 49 per 1,000 of pop. (1975); death rate, 21.8 **Life Expectancy:** 44 years **Health Statistics:** 294 inhabitants per hospital bed; 10,000 per physician (1976) **Infant Mortality:** N.A. **Illiteracy:** 75% **Primary and Secondary School Enrollment:** 111,071 (1976) **Enrollment in Higher Education:** 1,150 (1976) **GNP Expended on Education:** 5% (1975)

Transportation: Paved roads total 241 mi. **Motor Vehicles:** 15,000 (1976) **Passenger Cars:** 7,900 **Railway Mileage:** 192 **Ports:** None **Major Airlines:** Royal Swazi National Airways operates international flights **Communications:** Government and private **Radio Transmitters:** 7 **Receivers:** 60,000 (1976) **Television Transmitters:** 1 **Telephones:** 9,000 **Newspapers:** 1 daily, 111 copies per 1,000 inhabitants (1974)

Weights and Measures: Metric system **Travel Requirements:** Passport, no visa

---

The smallest of three former British protectorates in southern Africa to attain independence, Swaziland is the home of a gentle Bantu people. For the Swazis, British protection was not merely a colonialist device. It saved them from Zulu and Boer invasions and was also the shield against absorption into South Africa's apartheid system when the black African nation of Swaziland became independent in 1968.

Along with the other former protectorates, Botswana and Lesotho, Swaziland is geographically and economically linked to South Africa, but all three nations have asserted a determination to preserve political independence. Although all are members of the South African Customs and Monetary Area, in 1974 Swaziland issued its own currency, and political and economic tensions with South Africa have increased.

Despite its small size and landlocked situation between South Africa's *highveld* and the Mozambique border, Swaziland possesses exceptional potential for economic independence. In addition to major resources of iron ore, asbestos, and coal, the country produces sugar, rice, tobacco, cotton, citrus fruits, and other crops. It also has a wood-pulp industry based on a rapidly growing forest of pine and eucalyptus. Japan has become a major customer for iron ore, and rice production has been increased with the help of Nationalist China.

Most of the country's industries are still owned by British and South African interests, but Swazis are buying back foreign-owned property, especially farmland. In order to lessen economic dependence on South Africa, in 1980 Swaziland reached an understanding with Mozambique for cooperation, including use of Mozambique's port of Maputo. Operation of the gambling casino of the Royal Swazi Hotel, near Mbabane, is an attraction for tourists and a major source of revenue for the country.

In 1973 King Sobhuza discarded Swaziland's five-year-old constitution and, in 1977, replaced the nation's parliamentary system with an assembly of tribal leaders. The electoral process was restored in October 1978, under a new constitution, as Swazis voted for members of an electoral college, which in turn, was to name 40 members of the 50-man National Assembly and 10 of the nation's 20 senators. The remaining legislators were to be appointed by King Sobhuza.

HISTORY: The Swazis settled in present-day Swaziland in 1820 after being expelled by the Zulus from the land north of the Pongola River. Continued harassment by the Zulus led them to seek aid from the British, who succeeded in establishing friendly relations between the two tribes. The country's independence was guaranteed by the British and Transvaal governments in 1881 and 1884, and was followed by the establishment in 1890 of a provisional government representative of the Swazi and the two guarantors

1902-7: The Transvaal's rights in Swaziland pass to Britain following the Boer War; after a period of administration by the British governor of the Transvaal, Swaziland becomes a high commission territory ruled by a British commissioner

1921: Sobhuza II becomes Ngwenyama, head of the Swazi nation, after 20-year regency of his mother

1949: Opposition to South Africa's apartheid policy causes Britain to reject request that Swaziland, along with Basutoland (now Lesotho) and Bechuanaland (now Botswana), be transferred to South African control

1967: Swaziland wins self-government under a new constitution with Sobhuza as king

1968: Swaziland becomes independent state and a UN member

1969: Swaziland, disappointed by aid offered by Britain, moves to expand trade with African neighbors to boost national revenue

1973: Sobhuza repeals constitution; assumes supreme power

1976: Colonel Maphevu Dlamini becomes prime minister

1977: King Sobhuza abolishes the parliamentary system and replaces it with an assembly based on tribal leadership

1978: Voters create electoral college under new constitution. New railroad to South African coast completed

1979: Prime Minister Dlamini dies and is replaced by Prince Mabandla Dlamini

1980: Economy suffers from drought and inflation

SWEDEN

Area: 173,665 sq. mi. **Population:** 8,320,000 (1980 est.)

Official Name: Kingdom of Sweden **Capital:** Stockholm **Nationality:** Swedish **Languages:** Swedish, the official language, is spoken by the vast majority; in the north there are Lapp- and Finnish-speaking minorities **Religion:** About 94% of the population is Lutheran, the state religion **Flag:** An extended yellow cross on a field of blue **Anthem:** Thou Ancient, Thou Freeborn **Currency:** Swedish Krona (4.8 per U.S. $1)

Location: Northern Europe, occupying the eastern part of the Scandinavian Peninsula. It is bordered on the northeast by Finland, on the east and south by the Gulf of Bothnia and the Baltic Sea, on the southwest by the Öresund, Kattegat, and Skagerrak, and on the west by Norway **Features:** The land is gently rolling in the south and mountainous in the north. About half the country is wooded, and lakes cover some 9% of the area **Chief Rivers:** Göta-Klar, Lule, Ume, Angerman, Dal

Head of State: King Carl XVI Gustaf, born 1946, succeeded 1973 **Head of Government:** Prime Minister Thorbjörn Fälldin, born 1926, assumed office Oct. 12, 1979 **Effective Date of Present Constitution:** January 1975 **Legislative Body:** Parliament (unicameral). The *Riksdag* consists of 349 members elected for 3-year terms **Local Government:** 24 counties, with appointed governors and elected councils

Ethnic Composition: The population is largely homogeneous, with a Lapp minority of 17,000. There are 425,000 immigrants, mainly from other Nordic countries, Greece, Yugoslavia, and Turkey **Population Distribution:** 83% urban **Density:** 48 inhabitants per sq. mi. **Largest Cities:** (M.A. = Metropolitan Area) (1977 est.) Stockholm 658,743 (M.A. 1,374,897), Göteborg 440,221 (M.A. 693,562), Malmö 238,567 (M.A. 453,914), Uppsala 141,234, Norrköping 120,669, Västeras 118,131

Per Capita Income: $11,111 (1980) **Gross Domestic Product (GDP):** $92 billion (1980) **Economic Statistics:** About 59% of the GDP is derived from trade and services; 36% from manufacturing, construction and mining and 5% from agriculture (chiefly oats, wheat, rye, barley, potatoes, and dairy produce) **Minerals and Mining:** High grade iron ore is the primary mineral but there are also smaller deposits of gold, silver, lead, copper, zinc, pyrites, tungsten, manganese, granite, quartz, and marble **Labor Force:** 4.2 million (1978), with 37% in mining, manufacturing and construction; 31% in public service; 22% in trade and transportation; 6% in agriculture **Foreign Trade:** Exports, chiefly lumber, pulp and paper, ships, iron ore, machinery, and base metals totaled $27.5 billion in 1979. Imports, mainly machinery, chemicals and fuel products, and base metals, totaled $28.6 billion **Principal Trade Partners:** EC countries, United States, Canada, Norway, Finland, USSR, Saudi Arabia

Vital Statistics: Birthrate, 11.6 per 1,000 of pop. (1977); death rate, 10.7 **Life Expectancy:** 74 years **Health Statistics:** 66 inhabitants per hospital bed; 580 per physician (1975) **Infant Mortality:** 8.0 per 1,000 births (1977) **Illiteracy:** Negligible **Primary and Secondary School Enrollment:** 1,229,611 (1976) **Enrollment in Higher Education:** 162,640, (1975) **GNP Expended on Education:** 7.7% (1976)

Transportation: Surfaced roads total 17,514 mi. (1973) **Motor Vehicles:** 3,045,400 (1976) **Passenger Cars:** 2,881,000 **Railway Mileage:** 7,538 **Ports:** Göteborg, Stockholm, Malmö, Helsingborg, Trelleborg, Gävle, Luleå, Sundsvall, Norrköping **Major Airlines:** Scandinavian Airlines System (SAS), owned jointly by Sweden, Norway and Denmark, operates internationally; AB Linjeflyg, the Swedish affiliate of SAS, operates domestically **Communications:** Government controlled **Radio Transmitters:** 282 **Licenses:** 3,203,000 (1976) **Television Transmitters:** 358 **Licenses:** 2,988,000 (1976) **Telephones:** 5,673,000 (1976) **Newspapers:** 135 dailies, 572 copies per 1,000 inhabitants (1975)

Weights and Measures: Metric system **Travel Requirements:** Passport, no visa for 3 months **International Dialing Code:** 46

Once upon a time Sweden was world-renowned for its idyllic stability; for life without hunger, war, or other material distress; for an overall reasonableness in settling its affairs. Intruding on the Swedish idyll in the last few years, however, have been such extraordinary developments as strikes by workers in defiance of union leaders now considered part of the Establishment, a new militance among organized salaried employees in the face of heavy taxes and an increasingly steep cost of living. However, Swedish unemployment is still among the world's lowest, and Swedish per capita income is among the highest.

Although Sweden is often described abroad as a socialist state, it is not so in the Marxist sense. According to Swedish authorities, theirs is a pragmatic socialism dedicated to assuring material security for all and establishing state-owned enterprises only in areas that private enterprise cannot or will not enter. Roughly 90 percent of Swedish industry is privately owned. A little more than 5 percent is in public hands, and the remaining enterprises are cooperatives.

The high cost of social welfare, for which roughly one third of the budget is earmarked, is met from the high taxes and from contributions to compulsory insurance plans. Among the principal features of the social welfare state are a national health insurance, a pension system, free prenatal care and child delivery, annual allowances to the mother until a child reaches 16, free tuition at Swedish universities, home-furnishing loans for newlyweds, and rent rebates for large families.

Under a national policy of full employment, the state operates a job service, moves unemployed persons to areas where work is available and offers retraining to those who lose jobs through automation or disability. Despite recent labor troubles, Sweden's union-management relations, compared with those of most other highly industrialized countries, have on the whole been placid since the 1930s. In general, labor's demands have been tempered by the need to compete in world markets; exports account for roughly one fourth of the GNP.

Figuring largely in Sweden's economic and social achievements is its policy of neutrality, under which it has managed to avoid war for close to 160 years. But Sweden's neutrality, the Swedes insist, is an avoidance of alliances, not a neutrality of opinion. This policy, they say, is not abridged by strong stands taken on conflicts far from their shores, notably denunciations by government ministers of U.S. involvement in Vietnam and the military takeover in Chile.

The welfare programs were developed by the Social Democratic party, which dominated Swedish politics from 1936 until 1976. A majority of voters, reacting to high taxes and an unimaginative bureaucracy, then voted into power a coalition of three nonsocialist parties, with Thorbjörn Fälldin as prime minister. The coalition broke down in 1978 and was replaced by a minority Liberal government under Ola Ullsten. In the 1979 parliamentary elections, the Social Democrats failed by only one seat of regaining power as the three non-

socialist parties won 175 seats in the *Riksdag*. Fälldin again became prime minister.

Sweden's first nationwide strike in 70 years involved nearly one million workers for ten days in May 1980, before the unions agreed to a 6.8 percent wage increase.

After Conservatives withdrew from the three-party governing coalition in 1981, due to disagreements over a tax package, Prime Minister Fälldin formed a minority government of Liberals and Centrists. The new government survived a vote of confidence because the Conservatives merely abstained and did not vote against it.

HISTORY: The earliest known reference to the Swedes is by the Roman historian Tacitus, who wrote in A.D. 98 that the Suiones (of the Lake Mälaren area) had a mighty fleet and a host of warriors, and were ruled by an absolute king. By the 6th century they had conquered their southern neighbors, the Götar, and merged with them. During the Viking period (9th—12th centuries), Swedes extended their influence across Russia to the Black Sea and joined with Danes and Norwegians in raids and voyages to Western Europe and the British Isles

829: Christianity is introduced by a Frankish monk, St. Anskar

1150-60: Erik IX stamps out paganism among the Swedes and undertakes a crusade against the Finnish heathens, adding Finland to the Kingdom of Sweden

1319: Sweden and Norway are united under Norway's Magnus VII

1397: Denmark, Sweden, and Norway are united under Denmark's Queen Margrethe to combat the superiority of the German mercantile organization, the Hanse

1523-60: Gustav Eriksson, elected king as Gustavus I, establishes Vasa dynasty, ends the union with Denmark and Norway, cuts ties to the Roman Catholic Church, and establishes a Lutheran state church

1611-32: Gustavus II establishes Sweden as a great European power, expanding the kingdom in wars with Russia and Poland and in the Thirty Years War against the Hapsburgs

1648: Peace of Westphalia gives Sweden German territory and makes Swedish kings princes of the Holy Roman Empire

1700-21: Charles XII launches a brilliant defensive campaign against Russia, Poland, and Denmark in the Northern War, but a series of victories is followed by a disastrous invasion of Russia, capped by the capitulation of the Swedish Army at Poltava (1709). After further defeats, Sweden declines as a major European power, having been forced to give up most of its continental conquests and possessions

1805-09: Sweden joins the Allies against Napoleon, loses its German territories to France and Finland to Russia. Gustavus IV is overthrown; constitutional monarchy is established

1813-14: Entering its last major war, Sweden again joins the Allies against Napoleon, with Swedish forces led by the former French Marshal Jean Bernadotte, the chosen successor to the Swedish throne. He compels Denmark to cede Norway to Sweden

1818: Bernadotte ascends throne as Charles XIV; he steers Sweden toward a policy of neutrality

1905: Union with Norway is terminated peacefully

1917: Parliamentary form of government is established

1920: Sweden's first Social Democratic government is formed

1959: Sweden joins European Free Trade Association

1973: Carl XVI Gustaf succeeds to the throne upon the death of his grandfather, Gustaf VI Adolf

1975: A new constitution comes into effect which restricts the function of the king to a ceremonial role and approves the unicameral parliament in effect since 1971

1976: King Carl XVI Gustaf marries Sylvia Sommerlath. Swedish parliament adopts a law giving employees of certain companies the right to place two worker-delegates on the board of directors. Nonsocialist bloc (Center, Liberal and Moderate Unity parties) wins election; Thorbjörn Fälldin becomes prime minister

1977: Swedish cradle-to-grave "welfare state" palls as economy continues slumping badly, with many once-profitable exports reaching uncompetitive price levels due to high labor costs and sated world markets. Three of nation's largest shipbuilders are nationalized and merged. Three devaluations of krona improve its monetary position; investments, GNP decline

1978: *Riksdag* abrogates *Salic Law*, thus allowing female succession to the throne; second parliamentary vote needed to make this part of constitution. Liberal and Moderate Unity parties reject plans of Fälldin's Center party to stop building nuclear power plants. Fälldin resigns. Ola Ullsten becomes prime minister in minority Liberal government

1979: Nonsocialist bloc wins parliamentary elections by one seat over Social Democrats; Fälldin again becomes prime minister

1981: Fälldin forms two-party minority government after Conservatives withdraw from his government coalition

---

SWITZERLAND

Area: 15,943 sq. mi. **Population:** 6,329,000 (1980 census)

Official Name: Swiss Confederation **Capital:** Bern **Nationality:** Swiss **Languages:** German (65%), French (18%), Italian (12%), and Romansch, a Romance language spoken in eastern Switzerland (1%) are official languages. Many Swiss speak more than one language **Religion:** About 48% Protestant, 49% Roman Catholic, 0.3% Jewish **Flag:** A square red field with a white cross in the center **Anthem:** Swiss Psalm **Currency:** Swiss franc (2.03 per U.S. $1)

Location: Central Europe. Switzerland is bounded on the north by Germany, on the east by Austria and Liechtenstein, on the south by Italy, and on the west by France **Features:** About 60% of the country is covered by the great Alpine mountain chain running through the south. The Jura Mountains in the west make up about 10% of the land. The rest is a plateau between the two mountain ranges **Chief Rivers:** Rhine, Rhône, Aare, Inn

Head of State and of Government: Executive authority is vested in the Federal Council, composed of 7 councilors elected for 4 years by the Federal Assembly; each year a president and vice-president are elected. The council, whose members head the 7 federal departments, is the directing power in the nation. President (for 1981): Kurt Furgler **Effective Date of Present Constitution:** 1848, amended 1874 **Legislative Body:** Federal Assembly (bicameral), consisting of the Council of States, with 46 members and either 3 or 4 year terms, and the National Council, with 200 members elected directly for 4 years **Local Government:** 26 cantons, with elected unicameral legislatures, divided into communes

Ethnic Composition: Traditionally 4 ethnic groups: German, French, Italian, and Romansch, with 932,743 resident foreigners (1978) **Population Distribution:** 58% urban **Density:** 397 inhabitants per sq. mi.

Largest Cities: (1978 est.) Zürich 379,600, Basel 185,300, Geneva 150,100, Bern 145,500, Lausanne 132,400

Per Capita Income: $10,245 (1980) **Gross Domestic Product (GDP):** $65 billion (1980) **Economic Statistics:** 47% of GDP is derived from industry (machinery, chemicals, watches); 46% from commerce and services; and 7% from agriculture (dairy products, grains, fruit and vegetables, and wine-growing) **Minerals and Mining:** None; rich in forests and waterpower **Labor Force:** 2,800,000. About 21% are foreigners. Of the total, some 48% are in trade and services, 44% in industry, and 8% in agriculture and forestry **Foreign Trade:** Exports, chiefly machinery, watches, chemicals, and textiles, totaled $27 billion in 1979. Imports, mainly chemicals, crude oil, clothing, machines, and motor vehicles, totaled $29 billion **Principal Trade Partners:** West Germany, France, United States, Italy, Britain, Austria

Vital Statistics: Birthrate, 11.5 per 1,000 of pop. (1977); death rate, 8.8 per 1,000 **Life Expectancy:** 75 years **Health Statistics:** 87 inhabitants per hospital bed; 524 per physician (1976) **Infant Mortality:** 10.7 per 1,000 births (1977) **Illiteracy:** Negligible **Primary and Secondary School Enrollment:** 946,048 (1977) **Enrollment in Higher Education:** 64,720 (1975) **GNP Expended on Education:** 5.2% (1976)

Transportation: Paved roads total 38,600 mi. **Motor Vehicles:** 2,086,800 (1977) **Passenger Cars:** 1,932,800 **Railway Mileage:** 3,168 **Ports:** None **Major Airlines:** Swissair operates domestic and international flights **Communications:** Government controlled **Radio Transmitters:** 211 **Licenses:** 2,108,000 (1976) **Television Transmitters:** 583 **Licenses:** 1,809,000 (1976) **Telephones:** 4,016,000 (1976) **Newspapers:** 95 dailies, 402 copies per 1,000 inhabitants (1975)

Weights and Measures: Metric system **Travel Requirements:** Passport, no visa for 3 months **International Dailing Code:** 41

If pacifists want proof of their contentions, they can point to Switzerland, the country that has not sent its troops into foreign wars since 1815. Switzerland has low unemployment amid growing joblessness in much of the rest of the world, and it ranks among the world's wealthiest countries. But, like other countries, it has been plagued by growing inflation rates during the past few years, and federal budgets recently ceased to be balanced.

The Swiss guard their neutrality with a modern army. Switzerland's neutrality was guaranteed by the Congress of Vienna in 1815; dedication to neutrality has even kept Switzerland out of the United Nations. However, Switzerland is a member of several special agencies of the UN and has a permanent observer at the UN. A member of the Council of Europe, Switzerland in 1972 was one of five members of the European Free Trade Association that signed a free-trade agreement with the EEC.

In part, the Swiss have been able to remain neutral because of the rugged Alps, which cover half the country and are uninviting as a battleground. At the same time, the country, which lacks actual mineral resources, has in its terrain and geographical location features that act as natural resources, and which are in fact the bases of the country's prosperity.

Snow-clad Alpine peaks from whose rushing streams hydroelectric power has been widely developed also constitute a winter vacation mecca, and the central European location of their country has enabled the hardworking Swiss to make it a center for trade, shipping, freight-forwarding, banking, and insurance. And more than a third of Swiss exports consists of machinery, precision instruments, and watches.

The Swiss spirit of tolerance is more recent than the policy of neutrality; religious disputes produced a civil war as late as 1847—a revolt of Catholic rural cantons against the increasing influence of the Protestant cities over the federal government. But division along ethnic lines of French-, German-, and Italian-speaking peoples has been avoided by giving the cantons much power and keeping the federal government tightly reined. Taxes, for example, cannot be increased without a constitutional amendment, which requires a national referendum.

Hard-fought issues are usually absent, because Switzerland has been governed for decades by a coalition of major parties. One of the hardest-fought issues was resolved when the male electorate voted in 1971 to enfranchise Swiss women in federal elections, ending Swiss political backwardness and reversing a decision of 12 years before. The national trend of reaching decisions by consensus has produced a well-ordered country where even strikes are almost unknown, and there are no drastic extremes of wealth and poverty.

In 1979, after long discussion, the French-speaking communes of the Canton of Bern were organized into a new canton—Jura.

The staid Swiss were startled by the sudden rioting of 8,000 young people in Zurich in May 1980. They were protesting the city's refusal to provide an "alternative culture" center for youths. After the city government supplied a site for the center but then closed it down because of problems, about 4,000 demonstrators rioted again in March 1981.

HISTORY: The Helvetii, a Celtic tribe, were the first known inhabitants of Switzerland. The land was conquered by the Romans in 58 B.C. and remained a Roman province for approximately 300 years. In the 5th century, it was overrun by the Alemanni and the Burgundii, and then passed to the Franks. After being split between Swabia and Transjurane Burgundy in the 9th century, it was united under the Holy Roman Empire in 1033

1291: Forest cantons of Schwyz, Uri, and Unterwalden form defensive league in face of growing encroachments by House of Hapsburg

1315: League defeats Austrian armies at Morgarten Pass

1386-88: Joined by five other cantons, the league decisively defeats Austrians, insuring existence of the confederation

1499: Swiss gain virtual independence from Holy Roman Emperor Maximilian I

1519: Ulrich Zwingli, vicar of Zurich Cathedral, attacks practices of Roman Catholic Church; his lectures on New Testament mark beginning of Protestant Reformation in Switzerland

1541: John Calvin introduces Protestantism into Geneva and establishes a theocratic state

1648: Switzerland's formal independence is recognized in the Peace of Westphalia, which ended the Thirty Years War

1798-1803: French Revolution results in creation of Helvetic Republic, which is governed as a French appendage

1815: Perpetual neutrality is guaranteed by Vienna Congress
1914-18: Swiss remain neutral in World War I
1939-45: Swiss maintain neutrality during World War II
1959: Women's suffrage, in federal elections, although advocated by federal council and assembly, is rejected in referendum
1971: Constitutional amendment gives Swiss women the vote in federal elections and the right to hold federal office
1974: A plebiscite in the French-speaking Jura region of the largely German-speaking canton of Bern results in a narrow majority favoring a separate Jura canton
1978: Acting to stem rise of Swiss franc and protect its export industry and tourism business, government decides to ban further foreign capital investment
1979: Canton of Jura established
1981: Voters approve constitutional amendment guaranteeing equal rights to women

SYRIA

Area: 71,722 sq. mi. **Population:** 8,979,000 (1980 est.)
Official Name: Syrian Arab Republic **Capital:** Damascus **Nationality:** Syrian **Languages:** Arabic is the official and predominant language; French and English are also used, and Armenian and Kurdish are spoken by minorities **Religion:** 74% Sunni Moslem, 16% other Moslem, and 10% Christian **Flag:** Three equal horizontal stripes of red, white and black with two five-pointed green stars symmetrically aligned on the white stripe **Anthem:** National Anthem, beginning "Defenders of the homeland, salute" **Currency:** Syrian pound (3.925 per U.S. $1)

Location: Southwest Asia. Syria is bounded on the north by Turkey, on the east by Iraq, on the south by Jordan and Israel, and on the west by Lebanon and the Mediterranean Sea **Features:** The country consists of a narrow coastal plain, east of which is a highland region that is continued to the south by the Lebanon and Anti-Lebanon Mountains. Fertile plains form the central region, with the Syrian Desert to the southeast. North of the desert region lies the fertile Euphrates River Valley **Chief Rivers:** Euphrates, Orontes

Head of State and of Government: President: Lt. Gen. Hafez al-Assad, born 1928, reelected in 1978 for a 7 years. He is assisted by Prime Minister Abdul Rauf al-Kasm, appointed Jan. 1980 **Effective Date of Present Constitution:** 1973 **Legislative Body:** People's Council (unicameral), consisting of 195 elected members **Local Government:** 13 provinces and the municipality of Damascus

Ethnic Composition: 90% are Arabs; minorities include Circassians, Armenians, Turks, and Kurds **Population Distribution:** 48% urban **Density:** 125 inhabitants per sq. mi.

Largest Cities: (1978 est.) Damascus 1,142,000, Aleppo 878,000, Homs 306,000, Latakia 204,000, Hama 180,000

Per Capita Income: $988 (1980) **Gross National Product (GNP):** $8.6 billion (1980) **Economic Statistics:** 36% of the GNP is derived from services; 26% from industry (petroleum refining, textiles, cement, glass, apparel, soap, food processing); 19% from commerce; and 18% from agriculture (wheat, barley, cotton) **Minerals and Mining:** Oil, natural gas, phosphates, asphalt, gypsum and rock salt **Labor Force:** 1.8 million; 32% engaged in agriculture and 26% in industry **Foreign Trade:** Exports, chiefly petroleum (70% of total) and raw cotton, totaled $1.7 billion in 1979. Imports, mainly textiles, machinery, petroleum products, vehicles, and foodstuffs, totaled $3.6 billion **Principal Trade Partners:** EC countries, USSR, Arab countries, United States, Romania

Vital Statistics: Birthrate, 45.4 per 1,000 of pop. (1975); death rate, 14.8 **Life Expectancy:** 57 years **Health Statistics:** 956 inhabitants per hospital bed; 2,529 per physician (1977) **Infant Mortality:** 15.3 per 1,000 births (1976) **Illiteracy:** 47% **Primary and Secondary School Enrollment:** 1,828,339 (1976) **Enrollment in Higher Education:** 73,660 **GNP Expended on Education:** 5.8% (1975)

Transportation: Paved roads total 7,484 mi. **Motor Vehicles:** 118,700 (1976) **Passenger Cars:** 62,800 **Railway Mileage:** 958 **Ports:** Latakia, Baniyas, Tartus **Major Airlines:** Syrian Arab Airlines operates domestically and internationally **Communications:** Government owned **Radio Transmitters:** 13 **Receivers:** 2,500,000 (1972) **Television Transmitters:** 21 **Receivers:** 230,000 (1976) **Telephones:** 193,000 **Newspapers:** 6 dailies (1975), 9 copies per 1,000 inhabitants

Weights and Measures: Metric system and local units are used **Travel Requirements:** Check with Syrian embassy, Washington, D.C.

Once the center of one of the most ancient civilizations on earth, Syria today seeks a leadership role

in the Arab world. As an ardent champion of the Palestinian Liberation Organization, Syria has trained and armed guerrillas at bases within the country.

Syria merged with Egypt in 1958, but seceded in 1961. In the 1970s, it established a joint command and diplomatic coordination with Jordan. In 1979, President Hafez al-Assad of Syria and President Ahmed Hassan al-Bakr of Iraq formed a joint political command. They also agreed to merge their two Ba'ath socialist countries, but took no immediate steps to implement the agreement. Relations between Syria and Iraq have been marred by squabbles about ideological points and national goals. Each expelled the other's diplomats in August 1980.

President Assad is a military man who took power in a coup in 1970 and has brought stablility to Syria. Assad's Ba'ath (Socialist) party is predominant. The press and radio are directly controlled by the state.

Before World War I, Syria was part of the Ottoman Empire and loosely included all of what is now Lebanon, Israel, and Jordan, as well as Syria itself. Even today some people speak wistfully of a "Greater Syria." Between the two world wars, the country was under French mandate; it became independent in 1946.

The Syrian people are considered among the most sophisticated in the Arab world, because for centuries the country has been a passageway between the Mediterranean world and the Far East.

In recent years Syria has aligned itself closely with the Soviet Union. Its armed forces are equipped by Moscow, and there are believed to be upward of 1,000 Soviet military and civilian advisors in the country. However, Syrian intervention in Lebanon has placed a strain on Soviet relations because Russia has been a supporter of the Palestinians in Lebanon and the use of Soviet weapons by Syria against them has embarrassed Moscow. President Assad tried to patch up the differences in his spring 1977 trip to Moscow. In spite of the Soviet presence, the left-wing military rulers have outlawed the Syrian Communist party.

Israeli soldiers have occupied part of southwestern Syria since 1967. A demilitarized zone, patrolled by a multinational force under United Nations command, has been established between the Israeli and Syrian forces. The Israeli-occupied area is of strategic importance, and many Israelis want their government to annex it. Syria has little to gain from negotiations with Israel and opposes Egypt's negotiations.

Most recently Syria has been concerned with the civil war in Lebanon, having historically regarded Lebanon as part of "Greater Syria" and not wanting a radical state on its western frontier. In the final phase of the 19-month conflict, Syrian troops and tanks intervened against Palestinian-led forces when it appeared they might win, install a radical state, and incite war with Israel. Since 1978 Syrian-dominated peace-keeping forces have battled Lebanese troops and right-wing militia in and around Beirut. After Israeli jet aircraft had shot down two Syrian helicopters in Lebanon, Syrian forces installed surface-to-air missiles and shot down Israeli planes in Lebanese air space in May 1981. Israel threatened to remove the missiles by force, but Syria declared it would not withdraw the missiles because they were "defensive weapons." The U.S. and the Arab League tried to mediate this latest Middle Eastern crisis.

Recent clashes between the minority Moslem Alawite sect and the extremist Moslem Brotherhood of the majority Sunnis have threatened the Alawite-dominated government. In 1979, 60 Syrian army cadets, mostly Alawites, were killed in an attack by the brotherhood's militants on an academy in Aleppo, and other such attacks occurred. In March 1980, following antigovernment riots in Aleppo and Hama, a general strike by merchants and professional people demanded democratic freedoms, release of political prisoners, and free elections for a new parliament. The government promised to consider the strikers' demands.

HISTORY: Ancient Syria was the home of Amorites, Aramaeans, Phoenicians, and Hebrews. After a succession of invaders that included Assyrians, Babylonians, Egyptians, Hittites, and Persians, the country was unified under Alexander the Great in 331 B.C. It later fell under Roman rule, becoming part of the Byzantine Empire when the Roman Empire was divided between East and West. In the 7th century, the country was conquered by the Arabs and became the center of a vast Islamic domain

11th cent: Seljuk Turks invade Syria from Asia Minor

12th cent: Crusaders gain control over Syrian coastal areas (1189-92) and fight the Moslems led by Saladin

1516-1918: Syria is conquered by the Ottoman Empire, remains largely stagnant during four centuries of Turkish rule

1920: Syria is made a French mandate

1941-46: Free French and British forces occupy Syria during World War II; French proclaim an independent Syrian republic but complete independence is not achieved until 1944. All foreign troops are withdrawn in 1946

1958-61: Egypt and Syria form United Arab Republic under presidency of Egypt's President Nasser; attempts to integrate the two economies, nationalization of Syrian industry, and domination of Syrian army posts by Egyptian officers cause widespread discontent, culminating in military coup and restoration of Syrian independence

1963-66: Series of military coups results in succession of governments, although left-wing Ba'ath party continues to dominate political scene. In 1966, a new coup leads to installation of Nureddin al-Attassi as president

1967: Syria shares in Arab defeat in Six-Day War with Israel, whose forces occupy Golan Heights in southwestern Syria

1968-71: Struggle between factions of Ba'ath party led by President Attassi and those of Gen. Hafez al-Assad ends with Assad's seizing power in 1970 and being elected president in 1971

1971: Syria breaks off relations with Jordan after border clash

1973: Syria settles her differences with Jordan, joins other Arab nations in a full-scale war against Israel and adopts a new constitution

1975: King Hussein of Jordan and President Assad announce that their countries will establish a Permanent Joint High Commission to coordinate political, economic, and cultural policies

1976: Syria sends troops into Lebanon during the civil war there

1977: Syria rejects Egyptian proposals for preliminary meeting to prepare for Geneva Middle-East peace talks involving Israel; it takes part in so-called "refusal summit" with Iraq, Algeria, Libya, Southern Yemen and the PLO; events constitute virtual rupture between Syria and Egypt

1978: Syrians and Lebanese Christians battle in Beirut area in heaviest fighting there since Lebanese civil war. Assad, first Syrian president to serve full seven-year term since nation gained independence in 1946, runs unopposed and is reelected in "yes-or-no" referendum; overwhelming "yes" vote seen as indicating broad support for his opposition to peace initiatives of Egyptian President Sadat. Cost of Syria's 30,000-man presence in Lebanon is put at $3 million a day; death toll includes 600-700 Syrian troops

1979: Syrian and Israeli warplanes clash in Lebanese air space. Military Moslem Brotherhood attacks Alawite miniority in Aleppo

1980: President Hassad purges 14 members of Ba'ath Socialist party from cabinet, including Premier Halabi; forms new 37-member cabinet with Abdul Rauf al-Kasm as premier. Syria and Iraq expel each other's diplomats. Assad and Libyan leader Qaddafi sign merger agreement proclaiming Syria and Libya a single state. (not implemented as of August 1981)

1981: Syrian forces in Lebanon employ "defensive" missiles to shoot down Israeli jet aircraft; Israel threatens to remove them by force. Government troops gun down over 150 Moslem Brotherhood terrorists in Hama

---

TANZANIA

Area: 363,708 sq. mi. **Population:** 17,982,000 (1979 est.)

Official Name: United Republic of Tanzania **Capital:** Dar es Salaam (future capital by 1990—Dodoma) **Nationality:** Tanzanian **Languages:** English and Swahili, the national language, are official languages. Some 120 dialects, mostly Bantu, are also spoken **Religion:** 35% Moslem, 35% Christian, and the rest animist **Flag:** A green triangle in the upper left and a blue one in the lower right, separated by a diagonal black band edged in yellow **Anthem:** Na-

tional Anthem, set to new words of hymn "God Bless Africa" **Currency:** Tanzanian shilling (8.23 per U.S. $1)

Location: East Africa, comprising the former republics of Tanganyika and Zanzibar. Mainland Tanzania (Tanganyika) is bounded on the north by Lake Victoria, Kenya and Uganda, on the east by the Indian Ocean, on the south by Mozambique, Malawi, and Zambia, and on the west by Rwanda, Burundi, and Zaire. The island of Zanzibar lies some 20 miles to the east of Tanganyika's coastline, in the Indian Ocean **Features:** Tanganyika consists of a low-lying eastern coastal area, a high plateau in the west-central region, and scattered mountainous zones. Zanzibar is a low-lying island of coral limestone **Chief Rivers:** Pangani, Wami, Rufiji, Malagarasi, Ruvuma

Head of State and of Government: President Julius Kambarage Nyerere, born 1922, took office 1962 (Tanganyika), reelected 1980, head of the Revolutionary Party. He is assisted by the first vice-president (chairman of the Zanzibar Revolutionary Council), Sheikh Aboud Jumbe, born 1920, and by a prime minister, Cleopa David Msuya, appointed 1980 **Effective Date of Present Constitution:** April 1977 **Legislative Body:** National Assembly (unicameral), with 239 members, of whom 111 are elected for 5 years and the rest appointed **Local Government:** 25 regions, including 20 on the mainland and 5 in Zanzibar, each administered by an appointed commissioner

Ethnic Composition: About 99% of the population are Africans who belong to some 130 different tribes, mostly Bantu. Only the Sukuma numbers over a million members. European, Arab, and Indo-Pakistani minorities total about 150,000 **Population Distribution:** 7% urban **Density:** 49 inhabitants per sq. mi.

Largest Cities: (1978 census) Dar es Salaam 757,346, Zanzibar 110,669, Mwanza 110,611, Tanga 103,409, Mbeya 76,606

Per Capita Income: $197 (1980) **Gross National Product (GNP):** $3.5 billion (1980) **Economic Statistics:** In 1977, 51% of GNP was from agriculture (sisal, cotton, coffee, oilseeds, nuts, tea, tobacco, sugar, livestock; Zanzibar is the world's largest producer of cloves); 12% from trade and services; and 9% from manufacturing and mining **Minerals and Mining:** Diamonds and gold are the most important minerals being exploited, in addition to salt, mica sheets, gem stones and tin concentrates. Coal and iron deposits are to be exploited **Labor Force:** 5,600,000 (1970), with 90% engaged in subsistence agriculture. The monetary-sector employment in 1977: 457,000 workers **Foreign Trade:** Exports, chiefly cotton, coffee, diamonds, sisal, petroleum products, cloves, and cashew nuts, totaled $574 million in 1977. Imports, mainly machinery and transportation equipment, manufactured goods, fuel, and textiles, totaled $784 million **Principal Trade Partners:** Britain, China, United States, West Germany, Zambia, India

Vital Statistics: Birthrate, 47 per 1,000 of pop. (1967); death rate, 22 **Life Expectancy:** 44 years **Health Statistics:** 619 inhabitants per hospital bed; 18,480 per physician (1975) **Infant Mortality:** 152 per 1,000 births **Illiteracy:** 39% **Primary and Secondary School Enrollment:** 2,024,179 (1976) **Enrollment in Higher Education:** 3,064 **GNP Expended on Education:** 4.4% (1976)

Transportation: Paved roads total 2,228 mi. **Motor Vehicles:** 90,000 (1977) **Passenger Cars:** 43,600 **Railway Mileage:** 2,788 **Ports:** Dar es Salaam, Tanga, Mtwara, Lindi **Major Airlines:** Air Tanzania flies domestically and internationally **Communications:** Government owned **Radio Transmitters:** 10 **Receivers:** 300,000 (1976) **Television Transmitters:** 1 **Receivers:** 4,000 (1970) **Telephones:** 75,000 (1976) **Newspapers:** 3 dailies, 5 copies per 1,000 inhabitants (1974)

Weights and Measures: Metric system **Travel Requirements:** Passport, visa, $3.15 fee, 1 photo, onward ticket

---

Tanzania, a union of Tanganyika and Zanzibar, is the site of some of the oldest and newest forms of human society. Its link to man's past was established in 1959 at Olduvai Gorge in the northern part of what was then Tanganyika. There Dr. Louis S. B. Leakey, the British-born anthropologist, unearthed one of the oldest human fossils ever found, the skull of *Homo zinjanthropus*. Its age was estimated to be more than 1.5 million years.

Now, over a decade after independence from Britain, Tanzania is the testing ground for a form of African Socialism—*ujamaa*—as conceived by President Julius K. Nyerere. *Ujamaa*, which means familyhood in Swahili, refers to kibbutz-like rural developments whose members join in communal farming and general improvement on a basis of "love, sharing, and work." On a broader scale, it means a joint effort by which all Tanzanians may gain an equal share of the nation's resources. In 1973 the ruling party, the Tanganyika African National Union (TANU), decided that all peasants had to join *ujamaa* villages, making the movement no longer voluntary.

The Nyerere government has progressively nationalized private business, banks, and privately owned buildings and homes. The economy depends largely on agriculture—coffee, tea, cotton, sisal and other crops—and between rising population and the vagaries of African weather, there has been little gain on a per-capita share basis.

The government, while striving for self-reliance, has not scorned foreign aid. U.S. funds are providing new highways, but the main new project is the Tanzam Railway, which was built with money, equipment, and labor provided by Communist China, and was handed over to Tanzania and Zambia by China in July 1976 after six years of construction. Although Tanzania had seemed to favor the Chinese, Soviet President Podgorny's 1977 visit to Tanzania was warmly received because of the Zimbabwe nationalist cause, which was actively supported by both countries.

In November 1978 Tanzanian forces invaded neighboring Uganda after Idi Amin had occupied more than 700 square miles of Tanzanian soil. Within five months Tanzanians and Ugandan rebels captured Kampala and drove the Ugandan dictator into exile. The war cost Tanzania more than $500 million, crippling its internal economy. The last Tanzanian troops were withdrawn by mid-1981, leaving only a police force of 1,000.

HISTORY: Archaeological discoveries indicate that man inhabited Tanzania more than one million years ago. However, little is known about the early history of the area. Zanzibar, colonized by the Arabs in the 8th century, controlled the East African coastal region until the early 16th century, when both the island and the coast came under Portuguese rule. Arab rule was reestablished in the 17th century by the sultans of Muscat, under whom a large trade in ivory and slaves was established

1861: Zanzibar, under British pressure, is separated from control of Sultan of Muscat and becomes an independent sultanate

1885: Germany establishes a protectorate over the mainland region, which becomes known as German East Africa

1920: As a result of Germany's defeat in World War I, German East Africa is mandated to Britain; territory's name is changed to Tanganyika and German settlers are expelled

1946: Tanganyika becomes a trust territory

1961: Tanganyika wins independence; Julius K. Nyerere, head of Tanganyika African National Union (TANU) party, becomes prime minister

1962: Tanganyika becomes independent republic within Commonwealth; Nyerere is named as republic's first president

1963: Zanzibar achieves independence within the Commonwealth

1964: Afro-Shirazi party, representing the African majority in Zanzibar, overthrows Arab minority government and forces sultan to flee; Zanzibar becomes a republic, with Sheik Abeid Amani Karume as president. Tanganyika and Zanzibar agree to form United Republic of Tanzania, with Nyerere as president and Karume as first vice-president

1965-69: Tanzania becomes one-party state, with TANU constituting the one party in Tanganyika and the Afro-Shirazi party in Zanzibar, and both sharing power on national level. In 1967 government announces plans for socialist development and embarks on widespread nationalization in industry and agriculture

1971: Refusal of Tanzania to recognize Uganda government of General Idi Amin leads to bitter dispute and border clashes

1972: Sheik Abeid Amani Karume, Chairman of the Revolutionary Council which governed Zanzibar, assassinated. General Amin charges Tanzania with invading Uganda and threatens retaliation

1975: Kenya reopens Tanzanian border saying that outbreak of cholera was under control. Nyerere is elected to a fourth term

1976: Tanzania is a training ground for Zimbabwe (Rhodesia) guerrillas. Tanzam Railway is completed

1977: Tanzania closes its border with Kenya after Kenya withdraws from jointly-operated East African Airways in order to form separate Kenya Airlines. The Tanganyika African National Union and the Afro-Shirazi party of Zanzibar merge into one party called the Revolutionary party, headed by President Nyerere

1978: Government takes steps to combat cholera epidemic, which it reports has killed more than 400 persons. War with Uganda

erupts as Idi Amin's troops occupy 710 square miles of northwestern Tanzania before being driven back

1979: Idi Amin is ousted

1980: Zanzibar elects its own National Assembly under a separate constitution. Nyerere, unopposed, is reelected president of Tanzania, but more than half of the members of the National Assembly lose seats in response to government failure to solve nation's economic problems

1981: Nyerere begins year of "struggle against economic saboteurs" by firing two top officers of state-run Tanzania Investment Bank. Last of 10,000 Tanzanian troops leave Uganda in June

THAILAND

Area: 198,455 sq. mi. **Population:** 46,445,000 (1980 est.)

Official Name: Kingdom of Thailand **Capital:** Bangkok **Nationality:** Thai **Languages:** Thai is the official language and is spoken by most of the population; minority languages are Chinese, Malay, Khmer, and Lao **Religion:** Hinayana Buddhism is the religion of 95.5% of the population; Islam (4%), Confucianism and Christianity are minority religions **Flag:** Horizontal stripes of red, white, blue (double width), white, red **Anthem:** National Anthem, beginning "Thailand is the place for all Thais" **Currency:** Baht (23 per U.S. $1)

Location: Southeast Asia. Thailand is bounded on the north and east by Laos, on the east by Cambodia, on the south by Malaysia, and on the west and north by Burma. It extends down the Malay Peninsula between the Andaman Sea and the Gulf of Thailand **Features:** The core of the country is the central plain, with flat alluvial lands watered by a network of canals and irrigation projects. The north consists of parallel north-south mountain ranges and narrow, fertile valleys, while the region east of the central plain, the Khorat Plateau, is relatively barren. North-south mountain ranges also dominate peninsular Thailand **Chief Rivers:** Chao Phraya, Mekong, Nan, Ping, Mun, Pa Sak, Mae Klong

Head of State: King Bhumibol Adulyadej (Phumiphol Aduldet), born 1927, succeeded 1946 **Head of Government:** Prime Minister: Gen. Prem Tinsulanonda, born 1920, appointed March 1980 **Effective Date of Present Constitution:** December 1978 **Legislative Body:** Parliament (bicameral), consisting of 225-member Senate, appointed on the recommendation of the prime minister, and a popularly elected 301-member House of Representatives **Local Government:** 72 provinces, under appointed governors

Ethnic Composition: 75% Thai, 14% Chinese, 11% minorities (Malays, northern hill tribes, Khmer, Lao) **Population Distribution:** 25% urban **Density:** 234 inhabitants per sq. mi.

Largest Cities: (1975 est.) Bangkok 4,178,000; (1970 census) Thonburi 628,015, Chiengmai 83,729, Nakhon Ratchasima 66,071

Per Capita Income: $601 (1980) **Gross National Product (GNP):** $28.5 billion (1980) **Economic Statistics:** 33% of 1974 GNP was derived from industry (mining and quarrying, manufacturing, construction, transportation and communications); 28% from agriculture; 25% from commerce and finance (wholesale and retail trade, banking, insurance, real estate, ownership of dwellings); 10% from services **Minerals and Mining:** Major offshore natural gas fields are being exploited. Sizable tin, tungsten and lignite deposits. Other minerals are manganese, molybdenum, antimony and gem stones **Labor Force:** 16,243,000 (1975); 67% agriculture and forestry, 10% industry **Foreign Trade:** Exports, chiefly tapioca, rubber, rice, maize, tin, sugar, brought in $5.3 billion in 1979. Imports, mainly machinery, spare parts, fuel, iron, steel, automobiles, electrical equipment, totaled $7.2 billion **Principal Trade Partners:** United States, Japan, Malaysia, Hong Kong, Singapore, West Germany, Britain, Netherlands, Saudi Arabia

Vital Statistics: Birthrate, 35 per 1,000 of pop. (1976); death rate, 10 **Life Expectancy:** 61 years **Health Statistics:** 808 inhabitants per hospital bed (1974); 8,374 per physician (1975) **Infant Mortality:** 25 per 1,000 births (1976) **Illiteracy:** 18% **Primary and Secondary School Enrollment:** 8,069,829 (1976) **Enrollment in Higher Education:** 130,965 (1975) **GNP Expended on Education:** 4.1% (1976)

Transportation: Paved roads total 12,150 mi. (1975) **Motor Vehicles:** 532,800 (1975) **Passenger Cars:** 266,100 **Railway Mileage:** 2,380 **Ports:** Bangkok, Sattahip **Major Airlines:** Thai Airways, domestic and international (gov't owned) **Communications:** Government controlled **Radio Transmitters:** 217 **Receivers:** 5,500,000 (1976) **Television Transmitters:** 48 **Receivers:** 761,000 (1976) **Telephones:** 334,000 (1976) **Newspapers:** 56 dailies, 24 copies per 1,000 inhabitants (1975)

Weights and Measures: Metric system **Travel Requirements:** Passport, no visa for 15 days **International Dialing Code:** 66

One of the largest countries in Southeast Asia, Thailand is favored with superb rice land, vast stands of teak, and a guaranteed rainfall that insures agricultural abundance. Thailand is the only Southeast Asian nation that has never been colonized: the word *thai* itself means free, and the Thai people are proud of this heritage.

For generations they have successfully resisted pressure not only of China to the north but also of Cambodia to the east. The Thais, the vast majority of whom are Buddhists, have lived for centuries under the cohesive influence of their line of kings.

A constitutional monarchy replaced the absolute rule of the kings in 1932, but parliamentary democracy was placed in abeyance in 1958, when a military junta seized control of the government in a bloodless coup. Since that time, a series of successful coups has occurred—the most recent being a bloodless coup in October 1977 led by Defense Minister Sa-ngad Chaloryu, a former admiral that said he was deposing Premier Thanin Kraivchien's civilian government because it was taking too long to restore democracy.

Thailand's military commander, Gen. Kriangsak Chamanan, was named to replace Thanin as premier. Kriangsak stayed in power as a result of the elections of April 1979. None of the 36 political groupings won a majority in the 301-seat lower house; he appointed all 225 senators as called for by the constitution, and then the members of the two houses, meeting jointly, reelected him premier. But his government fell on February 19, 1980, after permitting, withdrawing, and reimposing big price rises in electricity and petroleum, and drawing criticism for rising crime and labor unrest. He was succeeded, on March 3, by Gen. Prem Tinsulanonda, whose government was beset by internal divisions that required frequent reshuffling of the cabinet. Prem did, however, survive the so-called "April Fool coup" of April 1981, when a dissident general's attempt to oust him was thwarted, largely because of the extraordinary intervention of the king, who is traditionally "above" partisanship.

Thailand continues to be beset by insurgent activities in the south, north and northeastern provinces, involving groups as diverse as the Thai Communists, the Thai-Muslim separatists and a group of Meo mountain tribesmen.

With an economy that is based on agriculture and is rising 7 percent annually even when inflation is taken into account, Thailand is prospering. The tapioca root, exported to Europe as an animal feed, became the nation's top agricultural moneyearner in 1978, surpassing rice. Rubber and tin remain important, and light industry is growing.

An influx of Indochinese refugees into Thailand's "rice bowl" threatens to overwhelm the country's economy. Once Cambodia had been a buffer against Vietnam, but the Vietnamese takeover of that nation put Cambodia on the front lines in 1979. An initial wave of 80,000 Cambodians crossed the border into Thailand to escape hunger and death; the Thais at first responded by forcibly returning 45,000 of them. But then Thailand gave international officials assurance that it would let refugees stay in camps "for a short and specified period" while other countries arranged resettlement. Occasionally in later years it revived the threat to refuse entry to further refugees, but it was still accepting them in late 1981. By then it was playing host to an estimated 250,000 Cambodians—a figure exclusive of 130,000 refugees from the 1975 Communist takeover of Indochina.

HISTORY: In the 11th century the Thai people, living in Yunnan Province of what is now China, began moving southward under pressure from the expanding Chinese. They settled in the valleys of the Chao Phraya and Mekong Rivers and formed political states, many of which were under the rule of King Rama Kamhaeng. In the 15th century they were united with other Thais around Chiang Mai,

in the northeast, and with the northern Malays in the south. By the 18th century trade had been established with Europe and Thailand began to consolidate as a nation

1833: Trade agreement is signed with the United States

1917: Siam (as Thailand was then called) declares war on Germany and sends expeditionary force to Europe

1932: Coup d'état by army officers establishes constitutional government to replace absolute monarchy

1941: Japanese troops enter Thailand, which is forced to sign alliance

1946: King Ananda Mahidol is found shot to death and is succeeded on throne by his younger brother, Bhumibol Adulyadej

1947: Coup by military officers forces change in government

1957-58: In another bloodless coup, government is replaced by a short-lived military junta. This is followed by another shift of power when Field Marshal Sarit Thanarat seizes control

1962: U.S. military unit is sent to northeast Thailand as Lao Communists threaten to sweep to Mekong River

1963: Sarit dies and is replaced by Marshal Thanom Kittikachorn

1971: On November 17, Thanom's government takes absolute power in bloodless coup

1973: U.S. congressional order ends U.S. bombing flights from Thai bases. Antigovernment protests organized by students result in violence. Thanom's government resigns and university rector Sanya Thammasak is named premier

1974: Exiled former premier Thanom Kittikachorn returns and is expelled. Agreement reached for U.S. to withdraw two of its six remaining air bases by the end of 1974. Air America, funded by CIA, ceases operations in Thailand

1975: Kukrit Pramoj becomes premier

1976: Seni Pramoj becomes premier. All operations are ended at U.S. installations and military personnel are withdrawn

1977: Thai and Cambodian troops fight along the border. Thai military leadership takes power under Gen. Kriangsak Chamanan; 23-member Revolutionary Council is established; new government proclaims interim constitution promising elections by 1979; parliament is dissolved; King appoints 360-member national legislature with heavy military representation

1978: Amnesty International, estimating there are possibly up to 1,000 political prisoners in Thailand, calls for their release. Thailand and Cambodia agree to try to end bloody border fighting and to exchange ambassadors

1979: Some 80,000 refugees flee to Thailand in the wake of Vietnam's invasion of Cambodia and its establishment of a client regime there. Some 45,000 are forced back across the border. By midyear, Thailand agrees to let Cambodians enter UN transit camps, pending resettlement abroad

1980: Kriangsak, facing a no-confidence vote over economic policies, quits as premier; Gen. Prem Tinsulanonda, formerly defense minister and army chief, succeeds him. Vietnamese troops attack Cambodian refugees in two camps inside Thailand for two days in June to show displeasure over shipping of some armed Cambodian refugees back to their own country. Flow of refugees into Cambodia rises

1981: Attempted coup, led by a general, fails in April when the king departs from tradition of political neutrality to openly support Premier Prem; the conspirators are later pardoned. Some 250,000 Cambodians remain in Thai border encampments. Thailand leads other members of Association of Southeast Asian Nations (Philippines, Singapore, Indonesia, and Malaysia) in passing an ASEAN resolution in June condemning Vietnam for its role in Cambodia and urging its withdrawal

---

TOGO

Area: 21,853 sq. mi. **Population:** 2,472,000 (1979 est.)

Official Name: Togolese Republic **Capital:** Lomé **Nationality:** Togolese **Languages:** French is the official language; the dominant indigenous languages are Ewe, Twi, and Hausa. In all, more than 44 different languages are spoken **Religion:** 75% animist, 20% Christian (mostly Roman Catholics), 5% Moslem **Flag:** Five alternating horizontal stripes of green (3) and yellow (2), with a white star on a red square in the upper left **Anthem:** National Anthem, beginning "Hail to thee, land of our forefathers" **Currency:** CFA Franc (263 per U.S. $1)

Location: West Africa. Togo is bounded on the north by Upper Volta, on the east by Benin, on the south by the Gulf of Guinea, and on the west by Ghana **Features:** The country is cut in two from the northeast to the southwest by the Chaine du Togo hills. To the north is a large savanna, with a plain in the east and south **Chief Rivers:** Oti, Mono, Haho, Anié

Head of State and of Government: President: General Gnassingbé Eyadéma, born 1937, seized power in 1967, elected 1979 **Effective**

Date of Present Constitution: Dec. 30, 1979 **Legislative Body:** National Assembly (unicameral), with 67 members elected for 5 years. The Assembly of the Togolese People (RPT) is the only party **Local Government:** 4 regions, headed by appointed inspectors

Ethnic Composition: Of the nation's 18 major ethnic groups, the dominant ones are the Ewe and Mina in the south and the Kabyé in the north **Population Distribution:** 15% urban **Density:** 113 inhabitants per sq. mi.

Largest Cities: (1970 census) Lomé 148,443, Sokodé 30,271

Per Capita Income: $380 (1979) **Gross Domestic Product (GDP):** $960 million (1980) **Economic Statistics:** In 1973, 44% of GDP was from agriculture (coffee, cocoa, yams, cassava, corn, millet, sorghum, rice); 20% from trade and services; 18% from mining (phosphates) and manufacturing (food processing, cement, a brewery, textile mills) **Minerals and Mining:** Phosphates are abundant; there are iron ore and limestone deposits **Labor Force:** 730,000, with 78% in agriculture and 22% in industry. There are 30,000 wage earners **Foreign Trade:** Exports, mainly phosphates, cocoa, coffee, palm nuts, and cotton, totaled $290 million in 1979. Imports, chiefly cotton textiles, machinery, motor vehicles, tobacco, and petroleum products, totaled $448 million **Principal Trade Partners:** France, Japan, Britain, West Germany, United States, Netherlands

Vital Statistics: Birthrate, 50.6 per 1,000 of pop. (1975); death rate, 23.3 **Life Expectancy:** 40 years **Health Statistics:** 684 inhabitants per hospital bed; 23,500 per physician (1977) **Infant Mortality:** 127 per 1,000 births **Illiteracy:** 84% **Primary and Secondary School Enrollment:** 476,755 (1976) **Enrollment in Higher Education:** 2,353 (1975) **GNP Expended on Education:** 6.7% (1976)

Transportation: Paved roads total 764 mi. **Motor Vehicles:** 20,000 (1974) **Passenger Cars:** 13,000 **Railway Mileage:** 274 **Ports:** Lomé, Kpémé **Major Airlines:** Air Afrique maintains international services **Communications:** Government owned **Radio Transmitters:** 5 **Receivers:** 52,000 (1976) **Television Transmitters:** 3 **Telephones:** 10,000 (1976) **Newspapers:** 1 daily, 6 copies per 1,000 inhabitants (1975)

Weights and Measures: Metric system **Travel Requirements:** Passport, visa for a 3 months maximum, $2.39 fee for stay up to 15 days, $3.58 fee for stay up to 30 days, 3 photos

---

One of West Africa's smallest countries, Togo has had a disproportionate amount of trouble since it attained independence from France in 1960. The country's first president, Sylvanus Olympio, was assassinated. He was succeeded by his brother-in-law, the late Nicolas Grunitzky, the son of a Polish father and a Togolese mother.

The Grunitzky government became increasingly insecure, and on January 13, 1967 Grunitzky was ousted by then Lt. Col. Étienne Eyadéma (now Gen. Gnassingbé Eyadéma). Eyadéma admitted that he was responsible for the killing of President Olympio in the 1963 coup.

Eyadéma has maintained firm control over the country. With political stability, the nation's economy—based on phosphates, cocoa, and coffee—has shown steady progress. The government also hopes to exploit the country's large limestone deposits. Largely because of improving economic conditions, an attempted coup in August 1970 was taken with relative calm by the Togolese. Nevertheless, President Eyadéma charged that a French mining company had plotted to kill him by causing the crash of an airplane in which he was a passenger in 1974. Two weeks earlier, Eyadéma had announced a 15 percent increase in the government's controlling interest in the mining company. Shortly after making the charges, the Eyadéma government took over the mining facilities.

Liberal trade policies have strengthened an otherwise feeble Togolese economy. Following independence, Togo was the only former French African colony not to give preferential tariff treatment to French goods. As a result, imports from all countries enter Togo at the same relatively low rates. Togo's famous marketing women have consequently benefited from the lower prices granted by the competition in imports.

Although officially nonaligned, Togo has sought closer identification with the Third World, but

maintains close ties with Western nations. France remains Togo's principal trading partner.

HISTORY: The Ewes, who now constitute the population of southern Togo, moved into the region from the Niger River Valley between the 12th and 14th centuries. Portuguese explorers and traders visited the coast of Togo in the 15th and 16th centuries. During the next two centuries, the coastal region was a major raiding ground for European traders in search of slaves, gaining Togo the name "Coast of Slaves." In 1884, Germany set up a small protectorate on the coast and later expanded inland

1914: Togoland is occupied by the French in the east and by the British in the west after the outbreak of World War I

1922: League of Nations confirms a French mandate in eastern Togoland and a British mandate in western Togoland

1946: United Nations changes the mandates to trusteeships

1956: British Togoland votes to join the Gold Coast; as the result of a plebiscite among the French-ruled Togolese, French Togoland is made an autonomous republic within the French Union, but the UN Trusteeship Council rejects this procedure

1958: In a UN-supervised election, the Committee for Togolese Unity party (CTU), wins control of Togo's legislature; its leader, Sylvanus Olympio, becomes premier

1960: French Togoland becomes the independent Republic of Togo, with Sylvanus Olympio as president

1963: Olympio, a southerner, is assassinated by a group of northern noncommissioned army officers; Nicolas Grunitzky, leader of the Togolese Party for Progress, is named president

1967: Army chief of staff Lt. Col. Étienne Eyadéma overthrows the Grunitzky government, names himself president, and institutes direct military rule; the constitution is suspended, the National Assembly dissolved, and all political activity prohibited

1968: Eyadéma announces indefinite postponement of a promised referendum for a new constitution and return to civilian rule

1969: After carefully staged demonstrations demanding that he remain as president, Eyadéma announces he has "acceded to the popular will"

1970-77: Government thwarts three plots to overthrow Eyadéma

1979: Regime convicts 13 of conspiracies, including two sons of Sylvanus Olympio living in exile. Eyadéma is reelected to another seven-year term under new constitution which creates a parliament to replace the one he dissolved in 1967

1980: Eyadéma celebrates proclamation of Third Togolese Republic Jan. 13 by freeing 34 political prisoners and 200 criminals. Forty of his opponents briefly occupy embassy in Paris

---

TONGA

Area: 270 sq. mi. **Population:** 94,000 (1978 est.)

Official Name: Kingdom of Tonga **Capital:** Nuku'alofa **Nationality:** Tongan **Languages:** Tongan and English **Religion:** Christian, with 60% belonging to sects of the Wesleyan (Methodist) faith, and 20% to the Latter Day Saints (Mormons) **Flag:** A red field with a white rectangle in the upper left containing a red cross **Anthem:** National Anthem, beginning "O Almighty God above" **Currency:** Pa'anga (.83 per U.S. $1)

Location: Southwest Pacific Ocean. An archipelago of 150 islands (45 inhabited), covering 100,000 sq. mi. of sea (24°-15°S.,173°-180°W.), about 400 miles east of Fiji **Features:** There are 3 principal groups. Divided by a north-south line, the eastern chain (including the main island of Tongatapu) is low-lying coralline. The western chain (Ha'apai and Vava'u groups) is volcanic

Head of State and of Government: King Taufa'ahau Tupou IV, born 1918, ascended the throne in 1965. He is also president of the appointed Privy Council (cabinet) which includes the prime minister, Prince Fatafehi Tu'ipelehake, born 1922, appointed 1965 **Effective Date of Present Constitution:** 1875, revised 1970 **Legislative Body:** Parliament (unicameral Legislative Assembly), with 23 members, with the 7 cabinet ministers, 7 nobles elected by the 33 hereditary nobles, 7 elected by adult suffrage for 3 years, and the ex-officio governors of Ha'apai and Vava'u **Local Government:** 3 island districts, under appointed governors

Ethnic Composition: The Tongans are Polynesians, and make up 98% of the population, which also includes small groups of other Pacific islanders, Europeans and mixed **Population Distribution:** 60% is on Tongatapu **Density:** 348 inhabitants per sq. mi.

Largest Cities: (1976 census) Nuku'alofa 18,356

Per Capita Income: $370 (1976) **Gross National Product (GNP):** $34 million (1976) **Economic Statistics:** The economy is based on agriculture, (sweet potatoes, yams, taro, tapioca, cassava, corn, coconuts, bananas, vanilla, pineapples, melons, fish, citrus fruits, livestock) and manufacturing (coconut and agricultural processing and canning, coir, tobacco, handicrafts, plastic products) **Minerals**

and Mining: None Labor Force: 9,300 in agriculture, 9,000 in services and government, 400 in industry and commerce (1976) Foreign Trade: Exports, chiefly copra, vanilla and bananas, totaled $5.6 million in 1978. Imports, mainly food, fuels and textiles, totaled $12.4 million Principal Trade Partners: Australia, New Zealand, Britain, Japan, Fiji, Netherlands

Vital Statistics: Birthrate 13.0 per 1,000 of pop.; death rate, 1.9 Life Expectancy: 56 years Health Statistics: 300 inhabitants per hospital bed; 3,000 per physician (1976) Infant Mortality: 20.5 per 1,000 births (1976) Illiteracy: Negligible Primary and Secondary School Enrollment: 30,825 (1976) Enrollment in Higher Education: 15 (1976), with 116 studying abroad (1974) GNP Expended on Education: 4.4% (1973)

Transportation: Surfaced roads total 121 mi. Motor Vehicles: 1,400 (1974) Passenger Cars: 1,000 Railway Mileage: None Ports: Nuku'alofa, Neiafu, Pangai Major Airlines: Air Pacific and Polynesian Airlines operate international services; South Pacific Islands Airways operates domestically Communications: Government owned Radio Transmitters: 2 Receivers: 15,000 (1976) Television: None Telephones: 1,090 (1974) Newspapers: 1 weekly, 49 copies per 1,000 inhabitants (1974)

Weights and Measures: British standards are used, but the metric system is being introduced Travel Requirements: Passport, no visa for 30 days, onward ticket

---

Though comprising 150 coral and volcanic islands, the Pacific kingdom of Tonga is considered to be one of the world's tiniest countries. For 70 years, it was a British protectorate, becoming an independent nation in the British Commonwealth in 1970. With independence, Tonga has moved to broaden the base of its economy, which has been based on the export of copra, bananas and coconuts.

There are two long-range hopes for broadening the economy. One is oil, the existence of which was discovered through seepage into water wells. An agreement with an international consortium provides that the country will get half the profits from possible oil production.

The other hope is to make Tonga a vacation paradise, with the kingdom looking for further economic development stemming from earnings from planned tourist hotels. Present air service to Tonga is only by small regional airlines that fly from Samoa and Fiji. The drive to independence from Britain was spurred by reported British reluctance to encourage the building of a jetport. In 1976 the Soviets agreed to upgrade the airport and Tonga's dockyard in return for the establishment of fisheries. Japan also expressed interest in Tonga through the signing of an agreement on hotel and fisheries development.

However, King Taufa'ahau Tupou IV has cautioned his countrymen, who wear ta'ovalas, or woven mats, around their waists, against basing their future on income from tourism, warning that "if too much tourism happens, we will become like Hawaii, where there are no more Hawaiians."

HISTORY: Tonga was at one time ruled by a line of sacred kings, one of whom eventually divested himself on his executive powers and delegated them to a temporal king. The system of dual kingship had become firmly established by the 17th century, when the first European contact was made by Dutch navigators. The peaceful conditions on the islands so impressed the 18th-century explorer Captain James Cook that he christened one of them the Friendly Island, a name later applied to the whole group. Within a few years of his departure, however, the islands were rent by civil war

1845-93: Taufa'ahau, a leading chief, rules over Tonga as King George Tupou I after suppressing civil war. He makes treaties with France, Germany, the United States and Britain, all of which recognize his sovereignty, and introduces parliamentary government and a system under which every male taxpayer is entitled to eight and one-quarter acres of suitable farmland

1900: Tonga becomes a British protectorate

1918-65: Reign of Queen Salote, granddaughter of George Tupou I, sees the elimination of illiteracy and of Tonga's national debt

1970: Tonga gains independence from Britain

1978: Tonga's Bank of the South Pacific declared bankrupt after its president Jack Meier flees, defaulting on $600,000 contract to develop airport to handle jumbo jets

1979: King Taufa'ahau Tupou IV negotiates with Libyan strong man Col. Muammar Qaddafi for a $3-million loan to finish airport

1980: Tonga's economy suffers from drop in copra prices, but gains from new trade pact with Australia and New Zealand

---

TRINIDAD AND TOBAGO

Area: 1,980 sq. mi. Population: 1,133,000 (1978 est.)

Official Name: Republic of Trinidad and Tobago Capital: Port-of-Spain Nationality: Trinidadian, Tobagonian Languages: English is the official and predominant language; Hindi and other Indian languages are also spoken Religion: About 71% Christian, chiefly Roman Catholic and Anglican; 23% Hindu; 6% Moslem Flag: Red with a black diagonal stripe bordered in white running from upper left to lower right Anthem: National Anthem, beginning "Forged from the love of liberty" Currency: Trinidad/Tobago dollar (2.4 per U.S. $1)

Location: West Indies. Trinidad and Tobago are the most southerly of the Lesser Antilles. They lie 7 miles northeast of the Venezuelan coast and are separated from each other by a 19-mile channel Features: Three relatively low mountain ranges cross Trinidad from east to west. The land between the northern and central ranges is flat and well watered; south of the central range it is undulating. On Tobago, a main ridge of volcanic origin runs down the center of the island Chief Rivers: Ortoire, Caroni, Oropuche

Head of State: President Ellis Emmanuel Innocent Clarke, born 1917, elected by Parliament 1976 Head of Government: Prime Minister: George M. Chambers, born 1929, appointed March 1981 Effective Date of Present Constitution: August 1976 Legislative Body: Parliament (bicameral), consisting of a Senate with 31 appointed members, and a House of Representatives with 36 members elected for 5 years Local Government: 8 counties, governed by elected councils. Tobago has an elected House of Assembly

Ethnic Composition: 43% of Trinidad's population is black, 40% East Indian, 14% of mixed ancestry, 2% Chinese, and 1% European. Tobago's population is largely black Population Distribution: 49% urban Density: 572 inhabitants per sq. mi.

Largest Cities: (1970 census) Port-of-Spain 62,680 (Metropolitan Area 250,000), San Fernando 36,879, Arima 11,636

Per Capita Income: $3,283 (1979) Gross National Product (GNP): $3.7 billion (1979) Economic Statistics: Trinidad is a major producer of crude oil and is also a major supplier of natural asphalt. Chief crops are sugar, fruits, bananas, coconuts, cocoa, and rice. Industries are oil refining and the manufacture of sugar, chemicals, fertilizers, molasses, rum, fruit juices, and cotton textiles. Tourism is important Minerals and Mining: Petroleum, lignite, asphalt, coal, gypsum, iron, clay, and natural gas Labor Force: 395,800 (1978), with 50% in manufacturing and construction, 19% in commerce and transportation and 13% in agriculture Foreign Trade: Exports, mainly mineral fuels, lubricants and related products, sugar, chemicals, fertilizers, fruits and vegetables, and coffee totaled $2.5 billion in 1979. Imports, chiefly petroleum for refining machinery and transportation equipment, foodstuffs, manufactured goods by material, and chemicals, totaled $1.9 billion Principal Trade Partners: United States, Britain, Saudi Arabia, Indonesia, Caribbean countries, Canada, Japan

Vital Statistics: Birthrate, 25.3 per 1,000 of pop. (1976); death rate 6.9 Life Expectancy: 66 years Health Statistics: 224 inhabitants per hospital bed; 1,964 per physician (1975) Infant Mortality: 27.2 per 1,000 births (1977) Illiteracy: 5% Primary and Secondary School Enrollment: 183,238 (1975) Enrollment in Higher Education 2,962 (1974) GNP Expended on Education: 4.1% (1973)

Transportation: Paved roads total 2,480 mi. Motor Vehicles 149,700 (1977) Passenger Cars: 117,700 Railway Mileage: None Ports: Port-of-Spain, Pte-à-Pierre, Point Lisas Major Airlines: British West Indian Airways (BWIA) operates internationally Communications: Partly government controlled Radio Transmitters: Receivers: 270,000 (1976) Television Transmitters: 3 Receivers 110,000 (1976) Telephones: 70,000 (1976) Newspapers: 3 dailies 92 copies per 1,000 inhabitants (1975)

Weights and Measures: British standards are used; the metric system is being introduced Travel Requirements: Passport, tourist card valid for 60 days

---

Trinidad's petroleum-fed industry has long bee the most advanced in the former British West In dies. Offshore oil and gas finds have also contri uted to the economy and have helped to mak Trinidad a major oil exporter in the Wester Hemisphere.

The economic problems are those of any developing country—lack of investment capital, shortage of jobs and lack of skilled personnel to fill those that are available, a small market for the products of light industry, and lack of administrative and technical capability below the top echelons of business and government. However, the democratic legislative and judicial structure inherited from the British has given the nation stability.

Trinidad's main problem is the lack of jobs, with the unemployment rate hovering around 15 percent and mainly affecting the islands' blacks—43 percent of the population. A development program with large investment incentives for foreign capital and high import duties to protect local products have kept joblessness from rising much higher, and a family planning program has substantially reduced the rate of population growth—once the highest in the Caribbean area.

These policies were the work of the island's long-dominant political party, the People's National Movement (PNM), created and led by one of the West Indies' most impressive statesmen, Eric Eustace Williams, Trinidad's first prime minister, who served from 1962 until his death in March 1981. Potential problems for the PNM after Williams' death included the continuing racial orientation of the nation's politics—with the PNM commanding the loyalty of most blacks and the Democratic Labor party supported by the less numerous East Indians—and the apparently growing sentiment for independence on the smaller island of Tobago, which had been politically associated with Trinidad since the late 1800's.

HISTORY: Trinidad and Tobago were discovered by Columbus in 1498 but were long ignored by the Spaniards because of the lack of precious metals in the islands. Spanish colonists began to establish plantations on Trinidad in the 17th century, importing African slaves to work them. The British captured the island in 1797 and in 1802 it was formally ceded to Britain. Tobago changed hands repeatedly during the 17th and 18th centuries, and in 1814 passed under the British crown

1834: Slavery is abolished in Trinidad

1845: Trinidad begins to import contract workers from India to replace the former slaves

1889: Trinidad and Tobago are amalgamated into a single colony

1958: Trinidad and Tobago joins the West Indies Federation

1962: Federation is dissolved; Trinidad and Tobago becomes independent

1970: Government restores order after island is rocked by black power demonstrations and mutiny in armed forces

1971: Elections result in complete victory for the People's National Movement under Prime Minister Dr. Eric Williams

1975: Strikes paralyze oil and sugar industries, causing worst government crisis since black power unrest in 1970

1976: Trinidad and Tobago becomes a republic, ending a 179-year link with the British monarchy. Governor General Sir Ellis Clarke becomes the first president. People's National Movement retains majority in Parliament following the general elections

1978: The nation's reserves of dry natural gas are put at 12 trillion cu. ft., and drilling continues

1980: Tobago gets its first island legislature since independence; voters there give a majority of seats to the secessionist Democratic Action Congress party

1981: Prime Minister Eric Williams dies on March 29. President Clarke names George M. Chambers, minister of Agriculture, Industry, and Commerce, as Williams' successor. PNM rule is consolidated in May, when two of Chambers' rivals with-in the party withdraw their candidacies

TUNISIA

Area: 63,170 sq. mi. **Population:** 6,367,000 (1979 est.)

Official Name: Republic of Tunisia **Capital:** Tunis **Nationality:** Tunisian **Languages:** Arabic is the official language, but French is widely used **Religion:** 98% are Moslems, and Islam is the official religion **Flag:** A red field with a white disc containing a red crescent and star in the center **Anthem:** National Anthem, beginning "Immortal and precious the blood we have shed" **Currency:** Tunisian dinar (0.49 per U.S. $1)

Location: North Africa: Tunisia is bounded on the north and east by the Mediterranean Sea, on the south by Libya, and on the west by Algeria **Features:** The country consists of a wooded and fertile region in the north, a central region comprising the coastal plains, and a southern region bordering the Sahara **Chief River:** Medjerda

Head of State and of Government: President Habib Bourguiba, born 1903, named president for life in 1975. He is assisted by a premier, Mohamed Mzali, appointed 1980 **Effective Date of Present Constitution:** 1959 **Legislative Body:** National Assembly (unicameral), consisting of 112 members elected by universal suffrage for 5 years **Local Government:** 18 governorates

Ethnic Composition: The population is largely Arab, with a Berber minority; Europeans number about 50,000 **Population Distribution:** 49% urban **Density:** 101 inhabitants per sq. mi.

Largest Cities: (1975 census—Metropolitan Areas) Tunis 873,515, Sfax 256,739, Bizerte 109,879, Sousse 102,097, Kairouan 67,589

Per Capita Income: $1,207 (1980) **Gross National Product (GNP):** $7.8 billion (1980) **Economic Statistics:** 30% of the GNP is derived from services; 28% from industry including mining; 23% from commerce and finance; 19% from agriculture **Minerals and Mining:** There are large phosphate deposits and smaller amounts of oil, natural gas, lead, zinc **Labor Force:** 1,400,000, with 58% in agriculture, 23% in services and 19% in industry **Foreign Trade:** Exports, chiefly petroleum, phosphates, olive oil, wine, and cork, totaled $1.8 billion in 1979. Imports, mainly foodstuffs, industrial raw materials, machinery and equipment, and transportation equipment, totaled $2.8 billion **Principal Trade Partners:** EC countries, United States, Greece, Libya

Vital Statistics: Birthrate, 36.4 per 1,000 of pop. (1976); death rate, 13.8 **Life Expectancy:** 55 years **Health Statistics:** 428 inhabitants per hospital bed; 4,675 per physician (1976) **Infant Mortality:** 52.1 per 1,000 live births (1974) **Illiteracy:** 45% **Primary and Secondary School Enrollment:** 1,222,776 (1977) **Enrollment in Higher Education:** 23,137 (1976) **GNP Expended on Education:** 4.9% (1975)

Transportation: Paved roads total 6,663 mi. **Motor Vehicles:** 169,800 (1975) **Passenger Cars:** 102,600 **Railway Mileage:** 1,256 **Ports:** Tunis, Sousse, Sfax, Bizerte, Skhirra **Major Airlines:** Tunis Air, a government-owned line, operates domestically and internationally **Communications:** Government owned **Radio Transmitters:** 8 **Receivers:** 280,000 (1975) **Television Transmitters:** 11 **Receivers:** 208,000 (1976) **Telephones:** 135,000 (1976) **Newspapers:** 4 dailies, 33 copies per 1,000 inhabitants (1975)

Weights and Measures: Metric system **Travel Requirements:** Passport, no visa for 4 months **International Dialing Code:** 216

Wedged in between Algeria and Libya—two larger and more militant neighbors—Tunisia has traditionally been one of the most stable and moderate Arab countries.

No Arab country has been more closely identified with one individual than Tunisia with Habib Bourguiba, its only president since the establishment of the republic in 1957. Bourguiba has long been one of the most magnetic and controversial figures in the Arab world. A professed "pragmatic idealist," he has befriended both the West and the Soviet Union and has not hesitated to quarrel publicly over the Arab struggle against Israel. His dovish views on that subject have infuriated many Arab leaders. However, Tunisia gained some prestige in the Arab world after the 1970 Jordanian civil war, which was mediated by an inter-Arab conciliation mission headed by Bourguiba's personal envoy. Moreover, Tunisia has condemned the peace treaty between Egypt and Israel.

The only Arab President outside of Lebanon without a military background, Bourguiba is a French-educated lawyer. He brought to Tunisia a benevolent despotism that has been comparatively free of corruption, and he has permitted relative individual freedom.

As part of a program to modernize the country, special attention was placed on the status of women, who enjoy few rights in much of the Arab world. Polygamy was outlawed; the marriageable age for girls was raised from 15 to 17; and divorce was made a matter of court discretion, rather than that of the husband.

The increase in Tunisia's literacy rate in the last decade was among the most rapid in the world, although some 45 percent of the population has had no schooling. In fact, Tunisia is turning out more educated people than the economy can absorb and they have trouble in finding suitable jobs.

Economically, Tunisia is a significant producer of phosphates, oil, textiles and olives. The government has actively promoted foreign investment in all of these areas, although France remains Tunisia's principal trade partner. Since a 1976 trade agreement with the European Community, the first such pact signed with an Arab country, it is expected that large-scale investment will increase greatly.

Relations have deteriorated between Tunisia and neighboring Libya since a failed merger attempt in 1974, attributed to Tunisia's more moderate Arab-Israeli stance. A further erosion of relations occurred after a 1976 assassination plot against Bourguiba by Libyan commandos was uncovered. Subsequently, Tunisian workers were expelled from Libya, and diplomats were withdrawn from both countries. Relations have been restored.

Tunisia today is a nation poised, not always peacefully, on the brink of change. Many Tunisians contend that although a single party system was tolerable during the early years of nationhood, the time has come for full freedom of political expression. They are also concerned that a struggle for power could destroy Tunisian stability. In January 1978, Tunisia was rocked by an outbreak of anti-government violence when a general strike by the nation's powerful labor union escalated into a direct challenge to Bourguiba's leadership. Rioting in Tunis and other cities left at least 100 dead and about 450 injured. The government blamed the disorders on "extremists" who were supported by Libya's leftist leaders. In 1980 an attack on Gafsa by Tunisian expatriated workers resulted in 41 deaths, and the Tunisian government again held Libya responsible for the attack. Tunisia's anti-Libyan policy was supported by the United States, which in June 1981 allocated a huge increase in its military aid to Tunisia, from $15 million annually to $95 million during the 1982 fiscal year.

HISTORY: Tunisia was settled by seafaring Phoenicians as far back as the 12th century B.C. In the 6th century B.C. the city of Carthage was founded near modern Tunis and became the center of a powerful city-state that lasted until 146 B.C., when it was destroyed by Rome. A new city of Carthage, built by Julius Caesar, was conquered by the Vandals in the 5th century A.D. and was later recovered for the Byzantine Empire. The Arabs conquered the region in the 7th century and during the Middle Ages transformed it into a major center of Arab power

1574: Turks add Tunisia to Ottoman Empire, but under its Turkish governors (beys) country enjoys virtual independence
1705: Hussein dynasty of hereditary beys is established
1881: Tunisia becomes a French protectorate
1934: Habib Bourguiba founds Neo-Destour (New Constitution) Party, which becomes spearhead of independence movement
1942-43: Tunisia becomes the site of World War II campaigns
1956: Tunisia wins independence
1957: Bey Sidi Lamine is deposed; Tunisia is proclaimed a republic; Bourguiba is elected as president
1963: France evacuates naval base at Bizerte
1968: Tunisia, at meeting of Arab League in Cairo, accuses Egypt of having provoked Six-Day War with Israel in 1967 and calls for Arab recognition of Israel; charges provoke uproar and Tunisian delegation walks out of meeting
1973: Tunisia sends token force to aid Arabs in Yom Kippur War
1974: Merger is proposed between Libya and Tunisia to form single nation, but the plan fails to materialize
1975: Bourguiba is named president for life
1976: Relations with Libya are strained by Libyan plot against Tunisian leaders
1977: Tunisian police arrest alleged Libyan agents suspected of plotting to assassinate Premier Hédi Nouira
1978: At least 100 die as general strike leads to worst antigovernment violence since nation gained independence
1980: Tunisia blames Libya for attack on Gafsa by Tunisia expatriated workers. Mohamed Mzali succeeds ailing Nouira as premier

TURKEY

Area: 300,946 sq. mi. **Population:** 45,217,556 (1980 census) **Official Name:** Republic of Turkey **Capital:** Ankara **Nationality:** Turkish **Languages:** Turkish is the official language and is spoken by 90% of the population; Kurdish (7%) and Arabic are spoken by the leading minorities **Religion:** 98% Sunni Moslem; the rest are Christians and Jews **Flag:** A white star and crescent on a red field **Anthem:** March of Independence **Currency:** Turkish lira (99 per U.S. $1)

Location: Asia Minor and Southeast Europe. Asiatic Turkey (Asia Minor) occupies 97% of the total area. Turkey is bounded on the north by the Black Sea, on the northeast by the USSR, on the east by Iran, on the south by Iraq, Syria, and the Mediterranean Sea, on the west by the Aegean Sea, and on the northwest by Greece and Bulgaria **Features:** European Turkey (Eastern Thrace) is separated from Asia Minor by the Dardanelles, the Sea of Marmara, and the Bosporus. The European part consists of rolling agricultural land. Asiatic Turkey has fertile coastal strips and is occupied in the center by the semiarid Anatolian plateau, surrounded by hills and mountains **Chief Rivers:** Kizilirmak, Yesilirmak, Seyhan, Menderes, Tigris (Dicle), Euphrates (Firat), Sakarya

Head of State: Following the coup of Sept. 12, 1980, the country is governed by a five-man National Security Council headed by Gen Kenan Evren, born 1918, assisted by a prime minister, Adm. Bulent Ulusu **Effective Date of Present Constitution:** October 1961, abolished Sept. 1980. A new constitution is to be prepared **Legislative Body:** Parliament (bicameral Grand National Assembly), with a National Assembly and a Senate of the Republic. The National Assembly has 450 members elected by popular vote for 4 years. The Senate consists of 150 elected members for 6 year terms, 19 lifetime members, 15 members appointed by the president, and former presidents **Local Government:** 67 provinces, under governors

Ethnic Composition: Turks constitute 90% of the population; ethnic minorities include 7% Kurds and small groups of Greeks, Armenians, and Jews **Population Distribution:** 45% urban **Density:** 150 inhabitants per sq. mi.

Largest Cities (M.A. = Metropolitan Area): (1975 est.) Istanbul 2,534,839 (M.A. 3,864,493), Ankara 1,698,542 (M.A. 2,572,562), Izmir 636,078 (M.A. 1,660,529), Adana 467,122 (M.A. 1,234,735), Bursa 346,084 (M.A. 960,035)

Per Capita Income: $865 (1980) **Gross Domestic Product (GDP):** $39.5 billion (1980) **Economic Statistics:** About 27% of the GDP is derived from agriculture (cereals, tobacco, grapes, fruits, and cotton) and animal husbandry and 21% from industry (steel, iron, sugar and cotton refining, tires, textiles, fertilizers) **Minerals and Mining:** Exploited minerals include copper, chrome (about 8% of the world's production), boracite, mercury, iron, manganese, coal, oil, natural gas **Labor Force:** 17,000,000 (1979), with 60% in agriculture, and 15% in industry **Foreign Trade:** Exports, mainly tobacco, cotton, hazelnuts, raisins, chrome, and citrus fruits, totaled $2.3 billion in 1979. Imports, chiefly machinery and transportation equipment, petroleum products, iron, steel and related products, fertilizers, and plastics, totaled $5.1 billion **Principal Trade Partners:** West Germany, France, Iraq, United States, Britain, Switzerland, Italy, U.S.S.R.

Vital Statistics: Birthrate, 39.6 per 1,000 of pop. (1967); death rate, 14.6 **Life Expectancy:** 57 years **Health Statistics:** 456 inhabitants per hospital bed; 1,804 per physician (1975) **Infant Mortality:** 145 per 1,000 births (1970) **Illiteracy:** 38% **Primary and Secondary School Enrollment:** 5,689,506 (1974) **Enrollment in Higher Education:** 322,965 (1975) **GNP Expended on Education:** 4.6% (1976)

Transportation: Paved roads total 13,000 mi. **Motor Vehicles:** 702,300 (1976) **Passenger Cars:** 471,500 **Railway Mileage:** 5,700 **Ports:** Istanbul, Izmir, Mersin, Samsun, Iskenderun, Izmit, Trabzon **Major Airlines:** Turkish Airlines, government owned, operates domestically and internationally **Communications:** Government owned **Radio Transmitters:** 21 **Licenses:** 4,228,000 (1976) **Television Transmitters:** 38 **Receivers:** 1,769,000 (1976) **Telephones:** 1,131,000 (1976) **Newspapers:** 450 dailies

Weights and Measures: Metric system **Travel Requirements:** Passport, no visa for 3 months **International Dialing Code:** 90

Modern Turkey is the product of its first president, Mustafa Kemal, later surnamed Kemal Atatürk, or Father of the Turks. He was a dictator who believed that he had to be ruthless in bringing his country into the 20th century. Before his death in 1938, Atatürk cut as many ties with the past as possible. He had the Turkish alphabet transcribed from Arabic to Latin characters, outlawed the wearing in public of the traditional fez for men and the veil for women, and secularized the theocratic Moslem state of the former sultans. Islam is still a strong force among Turks, however; more people from Turkey make the holy pilgrimage to Mecca than from any other Moslem country.

Turkey is still plagued by a wide disparity between life in its more affluent cities and its backward rural areas in Asia Minor. There has been a rapid migration to the cities, causing crowding and a demand for goods and services on the part of the peasant who will wait no longer for the benefits of modernization to reach him.

The country's economy is still largely based on agriculture, but the government has been pushing industrial expansion at a rapid pace, causing a strain resulting in high inflation, a foreign exchange crisis marked by declining foreign reserves, and a huge balance-of-payments deficit.

Turkey, which under the sultans ruled virtually the entire Arab world, is the only Moslem country to maintain formal diplomatic relations with Israel. Its chief concern in foreign policy—other than the presence of the Soviet Union as a neighbor—is a recurring conflict with Greece over the nearby island republic of Cyprus. Turkey has maintained troops on the island since 1974 to protect the Turkish Cypriot community. Despite strong U.S. pressure Turkey's occupation of the northern part of the island continues.

In parliamentary by-elections of October 1979, public discontent with the worsening economy and with escalating street violence led to formation of a new government headed by Suleyman Demirel, leader of the conservative Justice party. But increasing terrorism by both rightist and leftist extremists continued to threaten Turkey's fragile democracy. The violent incidents included the murders of a U.S. soldier and three Americans working in Turkey by a left-wing terrorist group in an Istanbul suburb in December 1979. In July 1980, such prominent Turks as a former premier, Nihat Erim, and a labor leader, Kemal Turkler, were assassinated. It was estimated that more than 5,000 persons had been killed by the end of 1980.

Amid public demands that the army take over the country in the crisis, as it had done during past national emergencies, Turkish military leaders seized power in a bloodless coup on Sept. 12, 1980. The new government was headed by a five-man National Security Council, chaired by Gen. Kenan Evren. It immediately abolished the constitution, placed Demirel and other political leaders in protective custody, and arrested thousands of suspected terrorists, of whom eight had been executed by mid-1981.

The military council assumed unlimited powers and banned activities of all political parties. Bulent Ecevit resigned as leader of the Republican People's party to protest the ban. The government announced in June 1981 that a constituent assembly to prepare a new constitution retoring democratic rule would include the National Security Council of five members and 160 advisory members. But it did not say when the assembly would convene.

HISTORY: Asiatic Turkey is one of the oldest inhabited regions on earth and for centuries served as a battleground for foreign conquerors. It was the site of the ancient states of Hatti, Urartu, Phrygia, Troy, Lydia, and Armenia. In the 7th century B.C., the Greeks founded the city of Byzantium on the site of present-day Istanbul. It was captured by the Romans in A.D. 196 and later rebuilt as Constantinople by the Christian Emperor Constantine. The Ottoman Empire was founded in 1299 by Turkish tribes from Central Asia on the remnants of the Byzantine and the Seljuk Turkish empires in Asia Minor. With its collapse in 1918, modern Turkey was born. The Turks had absorbed most of the major ethnic groups; the major exception were the Armenians, who were virtually exterminated by Ottoman attacks in the early 20th century

1920-23: Allied powers strip Ottoman Empire of its vast possessions, reducing it to a small state; Sultan Mohammed VI accepts Allied terms, but Turkish nationalists rally under Mustafa Kemal, later known as Kemal Atatürk, and organize resistance. Sultan is deposed and Turkey is declared a republic, with Atatürk as president

1924-38: A constitution is promulgated, providing for parliamentary government, but Atatürk rules as virtual dictator. He introduces sweeping reforms to westernize Turkey, which undergoes an unparalleled revolutionary transformation

1950-59: Celal Bayar, leader of the Democratic party, becomes president, with Adnan Menderes as premier. Turkey joins NATO in 1952. In 1955, Turkey and Iraq sign a mutual defense agreement, the Baghdad Pact. Marshall Plan aid leads to expansion of Turkish economy, but rapid industrialization results in economic crisis, forcing government to adopt restrictive measures to deal with discontent. Menderes is returned to office in 1957 elections; political controls tightened

1960: Army junta, led by General Cemal Gursel, stages coup, bans Democratic party, and puts Menderes, Bayar, and hundreds of other Democratic party members on trial for having violated the constitution. Most receive long prison sentences, but Menderes and several others are hanged

1961-62: A new constitution providing for a bicameral legislature and a strong executive is approved by referendum. Gursel is elected president and Ismet Inonu becomes premier. An attempted coup by army elements is crushed and many officers purged. Government amnesties most of imprisoned supporters of Menderes but keeps Bayar and a number of others in jail

1964: Relations between Turkey and Greece, long embroiled in dispute over Cyprus, become further strained as heavy fighting breaks out between Greek and Turkish Cypriots

1965: Suleyman Demirel, leader of Justice party, becomes premier following general elections

1966: Gursel falls ill; national assembly chooses General Cevdet Sunay, army chief of staff, to succeed him

1971: Following prolonged political and economic unrest, armed forces commanders demand resignation of Demirel government; Nihat Erim is named premier

1973: Bulent Ecevit elected premier. Retired Admiral Fahri Korutürk elected president

1974: Cypriot National Guard, under Greek officers, overthrows Cyprus President Archbishop Makarios. Turkish troops invade Cyprus and fight Greek Cypriots. Cease-fire arranged by UN representatives. Ecevit's coalition government collapses; interim government formed

1975: Citing "lack of progress" in Cyprus peace negotiations, U.S. Congress votes to cut off all military aid to Turkey. Turkey responds by seizing all American installations except the NATO base at Adana. Former Prime Minister Suleyman Demirel forms new coalition government

1977: Ecevit's Republican People's party wins close to a majority of parliamentary seats in the general elections. Ecevit resigns the premiership 10 days later after his center-left government loses its first vote of confidence in parliament. Prime Minister Suleyman Demirel forms new government but his coalition soon dissolves. Economy continues serious decline

1978: Ecevit named premier. Turkey and Soviet Union sign nonaggression, trade and cultural pacts. U.S. Congress votes to allow President Carter to end embargo on arms sales to Turkey and provide substantial military aid. U.S. military bases reopen

1979: Ecevit's party loses local by-elections; Demirel forms new coalition government. Martial law extends to 19 provinces

1980: Political violence escalates, prominent leaders are assassinated. Military leaders, headed by Gen. Kenan Evren, seize power on Sept. 12 and assume unlimited powers; new cabinet appointed with Bülent Ulusu as premier

1981: Terrorism is reduced drastically under martial law, but violent acts continue sporadically; Gen. Evren announces that a new constitution restoring democratic rule will be prepared by a constituent assembly

---

TUVALU

Area: 9.78 sq. mi. **Population:** 7,349 (1979 census)

Official Name: Tuvalu **Capital:** Fongafale, on Funafuti **Nationality:** Tuvaluan **Languages:** Tuvaluan and English **Religion:** Christian, mostly Protestant **Flag:** A light blue field with the Union Jack in the upper left corner and nine yellow five-pointed stars in the right half **Anthem:** N.A. **Currency:** Australian dollar (0.87 per U.S. $1)

Location: Tuvalu is comprised of nine low-lying coral atolls, eight of which are inhabited; the islands form a chain approximately 360 miles long in the southwest Pacific Ocean (5°30′-11°S.,

176°-180°E.). Tuvalu's nearest neighbors are Fiji and Kiribati **Features:** The islands have a tropical climate and are mostly covered with coconut palms

Head of State: Queen Elizabeth II through a governor-general, Sir Fiatau Penitala Teo, born 1912 **Head of Government:** Prime Minister Toalipi Lauti, born 1932, took office October 1, 1978 **Effective Date of Present Constitution:** October 1, 1978 **Legislative Body:** Unicameral Parliament, consisting of 12 members elected by universal suffrage **Local Government:** Island councils for the eight inhabited islands

Ethnic Composition: Almost entirely Polynesian **Population Distribution:** Non-urban **Density:** 751 inhabitants per sq. mi.

Largest center: (1973 census) Fongafale 871

Per Capita Income: $180 (1975) **Gross National Product (GNP):** 1.2 million (1975) **Economic Statistics:** A large part of personal income in Tuvalu is derived from cash remittances from Tuvaluan men working as seamen and in the phosphate industries of Nauru and Banaba (Ocean Island) in Kiribati. Other income is derived from copra, the chief cash crop, the sale of postage stamps and coins, and handicrafts. Fishing is on a subsistence basis. Other agricultural crops are pulaka (taro), pandanus fruit, bananas and pawpaws **Minerals and Mining:** None **Labor Force:** N.A. **Foreign Trade:** Exports of copra totaled $67,000 in 1977. Copra exports usually average 120 tons per year. Imports, chiefly food and fuel, totaled $1.4 million **Principal Trade Partners:** Australia, Britain

Vital Statistics: Birthrate, N.A; death rate, N.A. **Life Expectancy:** N.A. **Health Statistics:** 42 inhabitants per hospital bed (1978) **Infant Mortality:** N.A. **Illiteracy:** Over 50% **Primary and Secondary School Enrollment:** 1,788 (1976) **GNP Expended on Education:** N.A.

Transportation: Gravel roads total 5 mi. **Motor Vehicles:** About 12 cars on Funafuti **Railway Mileage:** None **Port:** Funafuti **Major Airlines:** Air Pacific provides service to Fiji and Kiribati. See Bee Air operates domestic inter-island service with one 5-passenger seaplane **Communications:** Government owned **Radio Transmitters:** 1 **Receivers:** 4,000 **Television:** None **Telephones:** 300 **Newspapers:** 1 fortnightly

Weights and Measures: N.A. **Travel Requirements:** N.A.

On October 1, 1978, the nine atolls of the Ellice Islands (Tuvalu's name before 1975) became the independent nation of Tuvalu (Polynesian for "cluster of eight islands," after the eight inhabited atolls). The main post-independence aim of Tuvalu's people is for greater economic self-sufficiency. This goal, however, is not readily forthcoming. The climate makes these "paradise islands" beautiful to see; but the thin, alkaline soil makes them ill-suited for agriculture. The islands are dotted with coconut palms, and copra is the main export. Handicrafts and subsistence fishing are the chief occupations. The chief source of revenue is from remittances from overseas Tuvaluans, working as seamen or as phosphate workers on nearby Nauru and Banaba (Ocean Island). With the end of phosphate production on Banaba in 1980, the economic impact of returning workers has exacerbated an already serious situation.

Future development will probably center on the potentially rich fishing grounds to be found in Tuvalu's lagoons and ocean waters. The South Pacific Commission plans to open a tuna canning plant, and fisheries and other industrial projects may be forthcoming. Foreign aid will also be important in further development. Great Britain has been the islands' chief benefactor and has built up the new nation's administrative infrastructure, but independence is expected to attract aid and possible investment from Australia, New Zealand, the United States and Japan.

HISTORY: Tuvaluans consider Samoa as their ancestral home, with which they share a common Polynesian language and culture. Fishermen are thought to have drifted westward from the central Pacific and populated the islands, which were periodically raided by Micronesians from Tonga and the Gilberts. The Spaniard Mendaña is thought to have sighted Nui in 1568 and Niulakita in 1595. Permanent contact with Westerners came in the late 18th and early 19th centuries; the first European settlers were from the London Missionary Society, who arrived in 1865 and soon converted the islanders to Protestantism. During the "blackbirders" slave trade from 1850 to 1875, the islands' population was reduced from 20,000 to about 3,000

1856: Guano Act of U.S. Congress establishes American claims to Funafuti, Nukefetau, Nukulaelae and Niulakita atolls

1877: Britain establishes the High Commission for the Western Pacific to stamp out "blackbird" raiders

1892: Britain proclaims a protectorate over Ellice Islands and neighboring Gilberts

1915: Protectorate reorganized as Gilbert and Ellice Islands Colony

1973: Britain appoints commissioner to study growing Polynesian demands for autonomy of the Ellice Islands

1974: August-September referendum, observed by UN, shows overwhelming support for separation from Gilbert Islands

1975: The islands are established as a separate dependency under British administration under the name *Tuvalu*

1978: Independence is declared October 1

1979: Prime Minister Toalipi Lauti signs Friendship Treaty with the United States; pact recognizes U.S. renunciation of claims over disputed islands and provides for continued consultations on security and marine reserves

1980: Tuvalu reaches agreements with Japan and South Korea on fisheries in nearby seas. Chinese tests of intercontinental ballistic missiles near Tuvalu are protested. Tuvalu signs agreement for better access to Australian and New Zealand markets. Overseas press reports indicate that, in 1968, Lauti handed over $640,000 in government funds to a California businessman for investment in west Texas real estate

---

UGANDA

Area: 91,076 sq. mi. **Population:** 12,630,076 (1980 census)

Official Name: Republic of Uganda **Capital:** Kampala **Nationality:** Ugandan **Languages:** English is the official language and Swahili the national language; of the many local languages the most important is Luganda **Religion:** About half the population is Christian, 10% Moslem, and the rest animists **Flag:** 6 alternate horizontal stripes of black, yellow, and red, with the national emblem, a crested crane, in a white circle in the center **Anthem:** National Anthem, beginning "O Uganda! May God uphold thee" **Currency:** Ugandan shilling (7.7 per U.S. $1)

Location: East Africa. Landlocked Uganda is bordered on the north by Sudan, on the east by Kenya, on the south by Tanzania, Lake Victoria, and Rwanda, and on the west by Zaire **Features:** Most of the country consists of a plateau about 4,000 feet above sea level. About 18% of the total area consists of swamps and open water, including Lakes Victoria, George, Albert (Mobutu Sese Seko), Edward, and Kyoga. Thick forest covers parts of the south; the north is largely savanna with some semidesert areas in the northeast **Chief Rivers:** Victoria Nile, Albert Nile, Katonga

Head of State and of Government: President Milton Obote, born 1925, sworn in on Dec. 15, 1980. He is assisted by Prime Minister Erifasi Otema Allimadi, appointed Dec. 18, 1980 **Effective Date of Present Constitution:** 1967 **Legislative Body:** National Assembly (unicameral) of 126 elected members **Local Government:** 10 provinces, divided into 33 districts

Ethnic Composition: About 98% of the population is African. The largest tribes include the Baganda, Iteso, Banyankore, and Basoga. Asians, mainly of Indian extraction, now number fewer than 500, and Europeans less than 3,500 **Population Distribution:** 7% urban **Density:** 139 inhabitants per sq. mi.

Largest Cities: (1980 census) Kampala 478,895; (1969 census) Jinja 52,509, Mbale 23,544, Entebbe 21,096

Per Capita Income: $256 (1980) **Gross National Product (GNP):** $3.5 billion (1980) **Economic Statistics:** 52.7% of the GNP is derived from agriculture (coffee, cotton, tea, tobacco); 18.7% from commerce and finance; 15.7% from services; and 12.9% from industry (the manufacture of food products and textiles, cigarettes, brewing, enamel hollow ware, cement, wooden boxes, and soap) **Minerals and Mining:** There are substantial deposits of copper and smaller amounts of wolfram, beryl, and cassiterite **Labor Force:** 353,768 salaried workers (1974). 90% of the population is in agriculture, 4% in industry **Foreign Trade:** Exports, mainly coffee, copper, cotton, tea and feeds, totaled $376 million in 1978. Imports, chiefly machinery and transportation equipment, cotton and synthetic fabrics and petroleum products, totaled $308 million **Principal Trade Partners:** Britain, Kenya, United States, West Germany, Japan, Italy, Netherlands, Tanzania

Vital Statistics: Birthrate, 45.2 per 1,000 of pop. (1975); death rate, 15.9 **Life Expectancy:** 49 years **Health Statistics:** 636 inhabitants per hospital bed; 24,700 per physician (1975) **Infant Mortality:** 160 per 1,000 births **Illiteracy:** 65% **Primary and Secondary School**

Enrollment: 1,103,906 (1976) **Enrollment in Higher Education:** 5,474 (1975) **GNP Expended on Education:** 3.0% (1975)
Transportation: Paved roads total 1,200 mi. **Motor Vehicles:** 35,900 (1975) **Passenger Cars:** 27,000 **Railway Mileage:** 756 **Ports:** None **Major Airlines:** Uganda Airlines operates both domestically and internationally **Communications:** Government owned **Radio Transmitters:** 8 **Receivers:** 250,000 (1976) **Television Transmitters:** 9 **Licenses:** 71,000 (1976) **Telephones:** 46,000 (1976) **Newspapers:** 1 daily, 5 copies per 1,000 inhabitants (1974)
Weights and Measures: Metric system **Travel Requirements:** Passport, visa, $3.15 fee, 1 photo

---

From the lushly green shores of Lake Victoria to the snow-capped Mountains of the Moon on its western border, Uganda's natural beauty is the fulfillment of a tourist's dream. Until recently elephant herds, great flocks of birds and other wildlife, vivid flowers, neat tea plantations, and farmlands rich in coffee and cotton delighted the visitor and gave support to the country's claim to being "the pearl of East Africa."

But Uganda changed drastically under the harsh regime of Field Marshal Idi Amin Dada. The eight-year reign of terror claimed the lives of possibly as many as 300,000 Ugandans. An estimated 250,000 fled to neighboring Kenya, and many more lived in exile in Britain.

Hopes were bright at the outset of Ugandan independence from British rule in 1962, with Milton Obote, leader of the Uganda People's Congress (UPC), as prime minister. The country became a republic in 1963 and elected as president Mutesa II, the revered *Kabaka* (king) of Buganda, largest of the four old kingdoms. In 1966, Obote, a rival Lango tribesman, forced the *Kabaka* into exile. Under a new constitution adopted in 1967, the kingdoms were abolished; Obote became president.

But in January 1971, Obote was ousted in a coup led by the Ugandan army commander, Maj. Gen. Idi Amin. Amin then declared himself president for life, abolished parliament and purged the judiciary and the civil service. During the next eight years he forced some 50,000 Asians to leave the country and had several thousand Acholi and Lango tribesmen killed. Many other persons died in the purge directed mainly at Christians. As a result of the regime's inefficiency and lavish spending, Uganda's economy deteriorated badly.

Amin committed a fatal mistake in October 1978 when he sent troops into Tanzania and occupied more than 700 square miles of foreign soil. Tanzania quickly counterattacked, carried the war into Uganda the next month, and in April 1979 captured Kampala, whose residents greeted the invaders as liberators. Amin eluded capture and gained asylum in Libya.

Virtually the entire world welcomed Amin's ouster, but Uganda was left in a state of upheaval. Yussufu Lule, the man chosen to succeed Amin, lasted barely two months before political wrangling forced his resignation. He was replaced by Godfrey Binaisa, a longtime defender of human rights. In May 1980 a six-man military commission headed by Paulo Muwanga displaced Binaisa and held power until national elections were held in December. Despite charges of fraud and opposition from the Buganda whose king, the *Kabaka*, Obote had forced into exile, the Uganda People's Congress won 68 of the 126 seats in Parliament and Milton Obote became president for a 5-year term.

With many problems, including famine and violence in the drought-stricken northwest region and uncontrolled rampaging by ill-disciplined soldiers, the withdrawal of the last Tanzanian peacekeeping forces in June 1981 left Obote's hold on Uganda shakier than ever.

HISTORY: Until the latter part of the 19th century, Uganda experienced a series of migrations extending over hundreds of years. As a

result, a number of major chiefdoms grew up, the most powerful of which were the chiefdom of Bunyoro-Kitara and the rival state of Buganda. Britain established a protectorate over Buganda in 1894 and subsequently extended the protectorate to the rest of Uganda. However, the stubborn independence of Buganda's rulers, which continued well into the 20th century, hampered the development of national unity

1953: Kabaka (king) Mutesa II of Buganda is deposed and exiled to London when he refuses to help put down riots by local chiefs
1955: British restore Mutesa but stipulate he is to reign as constitutional monarch and that Buganda will participate in the central government of Uganda
1962: Uganda gains independence with a federal constitution that gives Buganda large measure of autonomy; Milton Obote becomes prime minister
1963: Post of governor-general is abolished; Mutesa is elected president by parliament
1966: Obote removes Mutesa, suspends constitution, abolishes federal system, and assumes full powers of government
1967: Uganda adopts republican constitution with a presidential form of government headed by Obote; traditional kingdoms are abolished
1971: Obote is ousted in coup led by Maj. Gen. Idi Amin, who assumes presidency; refusal of Tanzania to recognize his government results in minor warfare between the two countries
1972: Amin orders the expulsion of the estimated 50,000 Asians in Uganda holding British passports
1973: U.S. severs ties with Uganda after repeated threats against U.S. Embassy officials and the detention of 100 American Peace Corps volunteers
1976: Israeli commandos rescue skyjacked hostages being held at Entebbe airport, crippling Amin's Soviet-equipped air force
1977: Anglican Archbishop Janani Luwum and two of Amin's cabinet ministers are arrested and murdered; the government claims the three were killed in an automobile accident after attempting to escape. Thirty-three Commonwealth nations, including 13 African nations, condemn Amin's regime for its repression. Twelve Ugandans are convicted of plotting a coup and are shot. Thirteen die in new anti-Christian purge; many arrested
1978: Ugandan forces invade Tanzania; general war ensues
1979: Ugandan rebels join Tanzanian forces in advance on Kampala, which falls on April 12 amid wild rejoicing and looting. Amin flees north and eventually to asylum in Libya. Yussufu Lule becomes provisional president; he is replaced in June by Godfrey Binaisa
1980: Six-man Military Commission headed by Paulo Muwanga ousts Binaisa, May 11. Rebel forces loyal to Idi Amin invade Uganda from Zaire and Sudan, but are repulsed. Uganda People's Congress wins majority of seats in Dec. 9-10 elections; Milton Obote is inaugurated president Dec. 15 for 5-year term
1981: Leaders of Kenya, Tanzania and Zambia meet with Obote in Kampala Jan. 17 to discuss regional cooperation. Tanzania withdraws last of its peace-keeping force in June

---

UNION OF SOVIET SOCIALIST REPUBLICS (SOVIET UNION)

Area: 8,649,490 sq. mi. **Population:** 262,400,000 (1979 census) **Population of Union Republics:** (1979 census) Russian S.F.S.R. 137,551,000, Ukraine 49,755,000, Uzbek 15,391,000, Kazakh 14,681,000, Byelorussia 9,560,000, Azerbaidzhan 6,028,000, Georgia 5,015,000, Moldavia 3,947,000, Tadzhik 3,801,000, Kirgiz 3,529,000, Lithuania 3,398,000, Armenia 3,031,000, Turkmen 2,759,000, Latvia 2,521,000, Estonia 1,466,000
Official Name: Union of Soviet Socialist Republics **Capital:** Moscow **Nationality:** Soviet **Languages:** Russian, the official language, is the native tongue of about 60% of the population and is spoken as a second language by less than half of the rest; other languages are Ukrainian, Byelorussian, Lithuanian, Latvian, Estonian, Moldavian, Yiddish, Georgian, Armenian, Uzbek, Tatar, Kazakh, Azerbaijani, and over 100 other languages and dialects **Religion:** Atheism, officially propagated by the government, is followed by about 70% of the population; there are also 18% Russian Orthodox, 9% Moslems, and small groups of Roman Catholics, Protestants, Jews, and Buddhists **Flag:** Red field with a golden hammer and sickle (representing the industrial and farm workers) under a golden star in the upper-left corner **Anthem:** Hymn of the Soviet Union **Currency:** Ruble (0.72 per U.S. $1)
Location: Northern Eurasia, from the Baltic Sea to the Pacific, with the Arctic Ocean on the north. The largest country in the world, the USSR is bordered on the northwest by Norway and Finland; on the west by Poland, Czechoslovakia, Hungary, and Romania; on the south by Turkey, Iran, and Afghanistan, and on the southeast by China, Mongolia, and North Korea **Features:** In the west, from the Pripet Marshes near the Polish frontier to the Ural Mountains, the

UNION OF SOVIET SOCIALIST REPUBLICS
(European Part)
CONIC PROJECTION

MILES

0 50 100   200   300

KILOMETRES

0   100   200   300

⊛ National Capitals
⊚ Capitals of Union Republics
– – – International boundaries
–·–·– Union Republic boundaries
≈≈≈≈ Canals

The government of the United States does not recognize the incorporation of Estonia, Latvia and Lithuania into the Soviet Union.

Post-war territorial changes shown on this map do not necessarily represent the final status of such boundaries. Only after the signing of peace treaties can changes be considered official and definite.

Copyright by C.S. HAMMOND & Co., N.Y.

Longitude 40° East of Greenwich 45°

land consists of a broad plain broken by occasional low hills and crossed by numerous rivers. Between the Black and Caspian seas lie the Caucasus Mountains. East of the Ural Mountains, which mark the traditional division between European and Asiatic Russia, are the Aral Sea, vast Siberian lowlands, steppes, and deserts of Central Asia. Beyond are the vast Siberian highlands and mountain ranges of the Soviet Far East. The highest ranges lie along the Chinese and Mongolian borders **Chief Rivers:** In Europe, the Dnieper, Dniester, Don, Volga; in Asia, the Ob, Yenisey, Lena, Amur, Kolyma, Amu Darya, Syr Darya

Political Leader and Head of State: Chairman of the Presidium of the Supreme Soviet (President) and General Secretary of the Central Committee of the Communist Party: Marshal Leonid Ilyich Brezhnev, born 1906, appointed general secretary in 1964 and president in 1977 **Head of Government:** Chairman of the Council of Ministers (Premier): Nikolai Aleksandrovich Tikhonov, born 1905, appointed 1980 **Effective Date of Present Constitution:** 1977 **Legislative Body:** Supreme Soviet (bicameral), consisting of the Soviet (Council) of the Union and the Soviet of Nationalities. The Soviet of the Union has 750 members elected on the basis of population; the Soviet of Nationalities has 750 elected on the basis of territorial units. Elections are called for every 5 years. Formal power is vested in the Presidium of the Supreme Soviet, which also appoints the Council of Ministers. Under Communist party direction, the council supervises all of the work of the government **Local Government:** 15 republics, each with its own Supreme Soviet and Council of Ministers, the latter headed by a premier. Ethnic divisions within the republics include 20 autonomous republics, 8 autonomous regions, and 10 national districts

Ethnic Composition: Russians constitute 53% of the population, Ukrainians 17%, Byelorussians 4%, Uzbeks 4%, and more than 150 other nationalities **Population Distribution:** 62% urban **Density:** 30 inhabitants per sq. mi.

Largest Cities: (1979 census) Moscow 8,011,000, Leningrad 4,588,000, Kiev 2,144,000; Tashkent 1,780,000, Baku·1,550,000, Khar'kov 1,444,000, Gor'kiy 1,344,000, Novosibirsk 1,312,000, Minsk 1,276,000, Kuybyshev 1,216,000, Sverdlovsk 1,211,000, Dnepropetrovsk 1,066,000, Tbilisi 1,066,000, Odessa 1,046,000

Per Capita Income: $4,820 (1980) **Gross National Product (GNP):** $1,281 billion (1980) **Economic Statistics:** 77.5% of the GNP is derived from industry (main industries include oil, steel, electricity, cement, pig iron, foodstuffs, textiles, and other heavy industry); 16.5% from agriculture (2 million square miles of arable land provide wheat, rye, corn, oats, potatoes, sugarbeets, linseed, sunflower seed, cotton, and flax; main livestock are cattle, sheep, and pigs) **Minerals and Mining:** Vast deposits of coal, iron, petroleum, natural gas, copper, nickel, bauxite, zinc, lead, gold, manganese, platinum, and tin **Labor Force:** Of 99,600,000 workers in 1974, there were 10,000,000 engaged in agricultural labor, 40,000,000 in industry and construction, 11,000,000 in transportation and communications, 13,000,000 in education, social security, and public health, and 25,000,000 in other sectors of the economy **Foreign Trade:** Exports, mainly machinery, iron and steel, crude oil, foodstuffs, lumber and paper products, and textiles, amounted to $65 billion in 1979. Imports, chiefly machinery, foodstuffs, and consumer goods, totaled $58 billion **Principal Trade Partners:** East Germany, Czechoslovakia, Poland, Hungary, Bulgaria, Romania, Cuba, Japan, West Germany, Finland, United States, Italy, France, Yugoslavia, Britain

Vital Statistics: Birthrate, 18.1 per 1,000 of pop. (1976); death rate, 9.6 **Life Expectancy:** 70 years **Health Statistics:** 83 inhabitants per hospital bed; 299 per physician (1976) **Infant Mortality:** 27.7 per 1,000 births (1974) **Illiteracy:** Negligible **Primary and Secondary School Enrollment:** 45,283,000 (1976) **Enrollment in Higher Education:** 4,853,958 **GNP Expended on Education:** 7.5% (1976)

Transportation: Paved roads total 230,000 mi. **Motor Vehicles:** 4,950,000 (1967) **Passenger Cars:** 1,100,000 **Railway Mileage:** 87,680 **Ports:** Main transfer ports on the Volga-Don system are Astrakhan, Rostov, Moscow, Perm; main transfer ports: Volgograd, Saratov, Kuybyshev, Kazan, Gorky, Yaroslavl; seaports: Leningrad, Odessa, Kaliningrad, Murmansk, Archangel, Riga, Vladivostok, Nakhodka **Major Airlines:** Aeroflot operates all international and domestic flights **Communications:** Government controlled **Radio Transmitters:** 3,034 **Receivers:** 122,477,000 (1975) **Television Transmitters:** 1,749 **Receivers:** 55,181,000 (1975) **Telephones:** 18,000,000 (1976) **Newspapers:** 691 dailies, 347 copies per 1,000 inhabitants (1975)

Weights and Measures: Metric system **Travel Requirements:** Passport, visa, valid 3 months, 3 photos. Make arrangements through travel agency that has a contract with Intourist **International Dialing Code:** 7

The Soviet Union, the world's largest country and one of the leading superpowers, has in recent years been experiencing alternating success and setbacks. Its policy of détente, the peaceful co-existence with non-Communist nations, has raised more ideological dilemmas than its original supporters could have imagined.

Leonid Brezhnev, General Secretary of the Communist party, the only political body in the Soviet Union, has now been in power longer than any of his predecessors since Stalin. Brezhnev's active role in the 25th Congress of the Communist Party of the Soviet Union dispelled rumors of possible illness or lack of support in the Soviet power structure. The Congress, which met in February-March 1976, endorsed the leadership of Secretary Brezhnev. In June 1977 Brezhnev was elected Chairman of the Presidium of the USSR and thus became the first leader in Soviet history to hold both the chief party and state posts.

In the five-year plan for 1976-80 the party leaders had to lower their targets for economic growth. In effect this was an admission of failure of the previous five-year plan to reach anticipated goals. For the new 1981-85 plan, heavy industry continued to receive strong emphasis at the expense of consumer goods. There again was a retrenchment in the expansion of agriculture. Recent harvest failures have plagued Soviet planners hoping to achieve self-sufficiency in food needs.

Foreign trade, once a small part of the Russian economy, is now of great importance. Commerce with the West has reached an unprecedented level. Trade with the United States was over $2.8 billion in 1978 compared to $200 million in 1971. Purchases of much needed wheat in the United States and Canada have had substantial impact on world prices. Other Western nations, Japan, Britain, West Germany, have become involved with the USSR in trade pacts and long-range projects that require large investments in plant technology and resource development. The Soviets have been funding their trade deficits with the Western nations by selling gold or taking long-term loans.

The USSR built up its armed forces in the 1960s and 1970s, and sought influence in the Middle East and Africa. It transported Cuban soldiers to help pro-Soviet governments in Angola, Ethiopia, and Southern Yemen defeat domestic and foreign enemies. Enmity between China and the USSR continues to divide the Communist world, but the Soviets have maintained the solidarity of most East European Communist nations.

In late December 1979, the Soviet Army invaded Afghanistan to shore up its tottering Communist puppet regime. This was the first time the Soviets had used military force against a neutral country. Brezhnev declared the invasion was directed against "aggressive external forces of reaction" which were threatening Afghanistan, but the military move outraged the West and alarmed neutral countries. The U.S. government banned sales of grain and of high technology systems to the USSR, halted its efforts to have SALT II (strategic arms limitation treaty) ratified by the Senate, and boycotted the 1980 Summer Olympic Games in Moscow. The USSR poured an estimated 90,000 soldiers into Afghanistan, but Soviet forces met with stiff opposition from Afghan guerrillas in the mountainous areas and reportedly suffered heavy casualties. Brezhnev said the troops would be withdrawn when the political situation there was stabilized, and the government tried to persuade its people that the invasion was necessary.

Soviet leaders denounced the workers' revolt in Poland in mid-1980 and threatened military intervention if Communist rule were endangered.

Shortly after the new U.S. administration of President Ronald Reagan took office in 1981, Soviet spokesmen detected an anti-Soviet tone and began to denounce the U.S. for reviving the old Cold War. But their rhetoric cooled somewhat when President Reagan lifted the embargo on grain sales to the USSR in April.

HISTORY: About the 5th century A.D. the Russian steppes began to be peopled by the Slavs. By the 9th century, despite repeated invasions by other tribes, the Slavs constituted the majority of Russia's inhabitants

862-79: Rurik, a Scandinavian chieftain, establishes the first Russian city-state, at Novgorod. His successor, Oleg, expands his territory in 879 and makes Kiev his capital

1237-40: Mongol (Tatar) hordes overrun Russia, initiating two centuries of the "Tatar Yoke"

1547: Ivan IV (the Terrible), Prince of Moscow, is crowned tsar

1712: Peter the Great transfers capital from Moscow to St. Petersburg (now Leningrad)

1812: Napoleon invades Russia and occupies Moscow. Returning westward, he loses almost his entire army in the Russian snows

1861: Alexander II liberates the serfs

1914: Russia enters World War I

1917: Military setbacks lead to overthrow of Tsar Nicholas II. Succeeding Provisional Government is ousted by Bolsheviks, led by Lenin, who ends war by surrendering much territory

1922: Four Communist-ruled states—all formerly parts of Tsar's domain—form Union of Soviet Socialist Republics

1924-38: Lenin dies (1924). After a power struggle with Leon Trotsky, Stalin emerges as dictator. He institutes the forcible collectivization of agriculture, liquidating more than five million peasant families. In a great purge of his opponents, thousands of leading officials are executed

1941-45: Germany invades the USSR. After years of bitter warfare on Soviet soil, the Nazi armies are crushed. USSR regains most land surrendered in 1917 and dominates Eastern Europe

1953-56: Stalin dies (1953), causing another Kremlin power struggle. Nikita Khrushchev assumes leadership, denounces Stalin's "personality cult," and begins "de-Stalinization." Soviet forces invade Hungary and suppress anti-Communist revolution

1957: USSR launches world's first artificial satellite (Sputnik)

1961: Sino-Soviet split emerges over Khrushchev's policies of de-Stalinization and "peaceful coexistence" with the West

1962: USSR secretly installs missiles in Cuba; withdraws them after U.S. Navy quarantines island

1968: Soviet troops invade Czechoslovakia in move to halt liberalization of country's Communist regime

1974: Novelist Alexander Solzhenitsyn is arrested and deported for his criticisms of Soviet political repression

1976: Leadership of Brezhnev is reaffirmed at 25th Communist Party Congress. New five-year plan calls for lowered economic goals

1979: Brezhnev and U.S. President Jimmy Carter sign treaty to limit strategic arms (SALT II). Soviet army invades Afghanistan to save tottering Communist regime

1980: Estimated 90,000 Soviet troops meet bitter resistance by Afghan rebels. UN condemns Soviet invasion; U.S. halts grain sales to USSR and refuses to ratify SALT treaty to protest Soviet military move; 1980 Olympic Games held in Moscow despite boycott by U.S. and some other Western nations. Kosygin resigns as premier due to ill health (he dies Dec. 18); Nikolai A. Tikhonov is appointed premier

1981: U.S. lifts boycott on Soviet grain sales. Soviet leaders caution Polish Communists not to go too far in meeting workers' demands for democratic reforms, such as independent unions

---

UNITED ARAB EMIRATES

Area: 32,278 sq. mi. **Population:** 1,040,275 (1980 census)

Official Name: United Arab Emirates **Capital:** Abu Dhabi **Nationality:** Emiran **Languages:** Arabic is the official language; English is widely used **Religion:** 90% Sunni Moslem **Flag:** Equal green, white, and black horizontal stripes, with a red vertical stripe at the hoist **Anthem:** The National Anthem **Currency:** UAE Dirham (3.7 per U.S. $1)

Location: Southwest Asia on the Persian Gulf. The federation of seven emirates is bounded by Oman, Saudi Arabia, Qatar, and the Persian Gulf **Features:** A flat, barren island-dotted coastal plain gives way to extensive sand dunes in the interior. At the eastern end are the western Hajar Mountains

Head of State: President: Sheikh Zaid ibn Sultan al-Nahayan of Abu Dhabi, born 1918, reelected 1976, assisted by a Vice President, Sheikh Rashid ibn Said al-Maktum of Dubai, born 1914, elected 1971, and a Supreme Council of the 7 rulers **Head of Government:**

Premier: Sheikh Rashid ibn Said al-Maktum of Dubai, appointed 1979 **Effective Date of Present Constitution:** 1971 interim constitution amended 1976, and extended through 1981 **Legislative Body:** Federal National Council (unicameral), of 40 members in proportion to emirate population, appointed by the seven emirs **Local Government:** Each of the seven emirates (Abu Dhabi, Ajman, Dubai, Fujairah, Ras al-Khaimah, Sharjah, Umm al-Qaiwain) is self-governing, under a sheikh

Ethnic Composition: Arabs (42%), Iranians, Pakistanis, and Indians (50%); only about 25% are native-born **Population Distribution:** 90% urban **Density:** 32 inhabitants per sq. mi.

Largest Cities: (1979 est.) Abu Dhabi 347,000; (1972 est.) Dubai 60,000, Sharjah 25,000, Ras al-Khaimah 10,000, Ajman 4,000

Per Capita Income: $10,600 (1980) **Gross National Product (GNP):** $9.6 billion (1980) **Economic Statistics:** Oil production in 1978 was 1.8 million barrels per day, with Abu Dhabi producing 80%. Aside from the area's rich oil and natural gas deposits, the economy includes herding, date growing, fishing, and trading **Minerals and Mining:** There are rich oil and natural gas deposits, notably in Abu Dhabi, and copper, gypsum, and limestone exist **Labor Force:** 490,000 (1978), of which 87% is foreign **Foreign Trade:** Exports, 95% oil, totaled $14 billion in 1979. Imports, chiefly machinery, foods, and consumer goods, totaled $6.5 billion **Principal Trade Partners:** EC countries, United States, Japan, India

Vital Statistics: Birthrate, 50 per 1,000 of pop. (1974); death rate, 18 **Life Expectancy:** 60 years **Health Statistics:** 342 inhabitants per hospital bed; 230 per physician (1977) **Infant Mortality:** 65 per 1,000 births (1974) **Primary and Secondary School Enrollment:** 90,000 (1977) **Enrollment in Higher Education:** 2,100 (1976) **GNP Expended on Education:** 9.1% (1976)

Transportation: Paved roads total 500 mi. **Motor Vehicles:** 15,000 (1978) **Railway Mileage:** None **Ports:** Dubai, Abu Dhabi, Ruwais **Major Airlines:** Gulf Air **Communications:** Government controlled **Radio Transmitters:** 12 **Receivers:** 55,000 (1976) **Television Transmitters:** 9 **Receivers:** 26,065 **Telephones:** 95,000 **Newspapers:** 3 dailies

Weights and Measures: Metric, British and local standards **Travel Requirements:** Passport, visa, valid 3 months, $2.75 fee, 1 month stay, sponsorship required **International Dialing Code:** 971

The United Arab Emirates consists of seven emirates on the eastern Arabian Peninsula, extending from the southern base of the Qatar Peninsula to Fujairah on the Gulf of Oman. From west to east, they are Abu Dhabi, Dubai, Sharjah, Ajman, Umm al-Qaiwain, Ras al-Khaimah, and Fujairah. Before independence, the area was sometimes referred to as Trucial Oman, the Trucial Coast, or the Trucial Sheikdoms. Boundaries are vague and in many places disputed. The sheikdoms are largely desert, hot and dry.

The main economic link among the emirates is the desire to share in the vast oil wealth of one of them, Abu Dhabi, at least until reserves are found in their own areas, as has happened in Dubai.

British influence in the area was formalized by treaty with the principal sheiks of the coast as early as 1820. The Exclusive Agreement of 1892 provided for British control of foreign agreements and affairs. The agreement terminated, however, following the withdrawal of British troops. Independence was declared on December 2, 1971. The pending withdrawal, coupled with the possibility of border claims by Iran and Saudi Arabia, had led to a proposal for federation with Qatar and Bahrain. But in August 1971, Bahrain announced it would go it alone and Qatar followed suit.

The UAE supported the Arab states in their war against Israel in 1973, and ended diplomatic relations with Egypt after Egypt made peace with Israel in 1979.

HISTORY: European and Arab pirates roamed the Trucial Coast area from the 17th to the 19th centuries, hence the former label "Pirate Coast." Successful British expeditions against the pirates led to further campaigns against their headquarters at Ras al-Khaimah and other harbors along the southwest coast in 1819. In 1820 the sheiks signed a General Treaty of Peace with Britain

1853: Coastal sheiks sign treaty with the United Kingdom agreeing to a "perpetual maritime truce"

1892: UK and the Trucial States establish closer bonds in another treaty, similar to those entered into by the British and other Persian Gulf principalities

1955: UK effectively intervenes on the side of Abu Dhabi in the latter's dispute with Saudi Arabia over the Buraimi Oasis, resulting in control of the Oasis being shared between Abu Dhabi and the Sultanate of Oman

1958-60: Vast oil reserves are discovered in Abu Dhabi

1971: British protective treaty with the Trucial Sheikdoms ends. They become fully independent as the United Arab Emirates. Oil is discovered in Dubai

1975: UAE joins OPEC as its third largest contributor

1976: Supreme Defense Council unites the UAE's armed forces. Dubai officials announce plans for a $765-million port, a new airport and an oil refinery at Jebel Ali

1978: Dubai pulls forces from federal army and puts them on alert in dispute with Abu Dhabi over appointment of UAE armed forces commander

UNITED KINGDOM

Area: 94,399 sq. mi. **Population:** 55,883,100 (1979 est.)
Official Name: United Kingdom of Great Britain and Northern Ireland **Capital:** London **Nationality:** British **Languages:** English is the official and predominant language; Gaelic is spoken in parts of Scotland, while Welsh is the first language in western Wales and enjoys equal validity with English as an official language in Wales **Religion:** Although the Church of England and the Church of Scotland are established churches, there is complete religious freedom. About half the population belongs to the Church of England (Protestant Episcopal) and to its nonestablished branches in Scotland, Wales, and Northern Ireland. The Church of Scotland (Presbyterian) has about 1.3 million members. The other major Christian denominations are Roman Catholic (6 million); Methodist (900,000); Baptist (300,000); and Congregationalist (200,000). There are several hundred thousand Moslems, 410,000 Jews, and several thousand Buddhists **Flag:** Known as the Union Jack, the flag is a superimposition of the red cross of St. George of England, the white cross of St. Andrew of Scotland, and the red cross of St. Patrick of Ireland, all on a blue background **Anthem:** God Save the Queen **Currency:** Pound sterling (.47 per U.S. $1)
Location: Off the northwest coast of Europe. The island of Great Britain, containing England, Scotland, and Wales, is bordered by the Atlantic Ocean on the north and west, and is separated from the European continent by the North Sea, the Strait of Dover, and the English Channel on the east and south. The Irish Sea and the North Channel separate Great Britain from Ireland, the northern area of which constitutes Northern Ireland, bordered on the south by the Republic of Ireland **Features:** England is divided into hill districts in the north, west, and southwest, and the undulating downs and low-lying plains in the east and southeast. In the extreme north, the Cheviot Hills, running from east to west, separate England from Scotland. The Pennine Chain extends southward from the Cheviots into the Midlands, a plains region with low, rolling hills and valleys. Scotland has three natural topographic divisions: the Southern Uplands; the Central Lowlands; and the Northern Highlands, which contain the highest point in the British Isles. Wales is generally mountainous. Northern Ireland contains many plateaus and hills **Chief Rivers:** Severn, Thames, Trent, Aire, Great Ouse, Wye, Tay, Nene, Clyde, Spey, Tweed, Tyne
Head of State: Queen Elizabeth II, born 1926, ascended the throne 1952 **Head of Government:** Prime Minister Margaret Thatcher, born 1925, appointed May 4, 1979 **Effective Date of Present Constitution:** The British Constitution is formed partly by statute, partly by common law, and partly by "traditional rights" known as conventions. The rules of the constitution have never been codified, and can be adapted to changing conditions at any time by Act of Parliament or by the general acceptance of a new convention **Legislative Body:** Parliament (bicameral), consisting of the House of Lords and the House of Commons. The House of Commons, which is the ultimate authority for lawmaking, consists of 635 members elected by universal suffrage for a maximum term of 5 years. The House of Lords, which also functions as the highest court in the land, consists of some 1,200 members, including hereditary and life peers and peeresses, law lords appointed for life to carry out the judicial duties of the house, and the 2 archbishops and 24 senior bishops of the Church of England. The House of Lords has the power to delay, but not prevent, legislation **Local Government:** England is divided into 39 counties, 6 metropolitan counties, Greater London, and the Isles of Scilly; Wales is divided into 8 counties. Scotland is divided into 9 regions and 3 island areas. Northern Ireland is divided into 26 districts. Each local authority division throughout the United Kingdom is administered by its own

elected council. In Northern Ireland the shape of the new institutions which will replace the former parliament had not been completely decided, although a 78-seat assembly and an executive or provincial cabinet which shares power between Roman Catholics and Protestants had been formed. A Constitutional Convention begun in 1975 was dissolved in 1976, having failed to agree on a system of government. Direct rule, first initiated in 1974, was therefore renewed. Northern Ireland continues to be represented in the U.K. House of Commons

Ethnic Composition: The contemporary Briton is descended from varied racial stocks that settled in the British Isles before the 12th century. Under the Normans, descendants of Scandinavian Vikings, pre-Celtic, Celtic, Roman, Anglo-Saxon, and Norse influences were blended into the Briton. The population includes some 1.9 million immigrant Pakistanis, Indians, West Indians and their British-born children **Population Distribution:** 78% urban **Density:** 592 inhabitants per sq. mi.
Largest Cities: (1976 est.) London 7,028,200, Birmingham 1,058,800, Glasgow 816,265, Leeds 744,500, Sheffield 558,000, Liverpool 539,700, Manchester 490,000, Bradford 458,900, Edinburgh 445,000, Bristol 416,300, Belfast 350,000
Per Capita Income: $5,340 (1980) **Gross Domestic Product (GDP):** $298 billion (1980) **Economic Statistics:** About 32% of the GDP comes from manufacturing (iron and steel, engineering [vehicles and aircraft], textiles, chemicals, food products, and consumer goods); 12% from mining and quarrying (coal, petroleum, natural gas, iron ore, limestone, tin, gravel), construction, and public utilities; 9% from transportation and communications; 42% from trade and services; and 3% from agriculture **Minerals and Mining:** There are significant amounts of coal, small deposits of iron, limestone, tin, gravel and oilshale. There are large quantities of natural gas and oil in the North Sea **Labor Force:** 26.1 million (1977), with 28% in manufacturing and 2% in agriculture **Foreign Trade:** Exports, mainly manufactured goods including engineering products, motor vehicles, nonelectric and electric machinery, petroleum and nonmetallic mineral manufactures, totaled $92 billion in 1979. Imports, chiefly petroleum and petroleum products, machinery, nonferrous metals, meat and meat preparations, fruit and vegetables, amounted to $105 billion **Principal Trade Partners:** United States, West Germany, South Africa, Ireland, Canada, France, Netherlands, Switzerland

Vital Statistics: Birthrate, 11.8 per 1,000 of pop. (1977); death rate, 11.7 **Life Expectancy:** 72 years **Health Statistics:** 117 inhabitants per hospital bed; 761 per physician (1974) **Infant Mortality:** 14 per 1,000 births (1977) **Illiteracy:** Negligible **Primary and Secondary School Enrollment:** 10,801,957 (1974) **Enrollment in Higher Education:** 703,645 **GNP Expended on Education:** 6.2% (1974)
Transportation: Paved roads total 208,151 mi. **Motor Vehicles:** 16,460,000 (1976) **Passenger Cars:** 14,562,400 **Railway Mileage:** 11,467 **Ports:** London, Liverpool, Glasgow, Southampton, Belfast, Cardiff, Milford Haven, Manchester, Bristol, Hull, Swansea, Edinbugh, Newcastle **Major Airlines:** British Airways flies both domestically and internationally. There are many other independent air transport operations **Communications:** Government and privately owned **Radio Transmitters:** 364 **Receivers:** 39,500,000 (1976) **Television Transmitters:** 596 **Licenses:** 17,729,000 (1976) **Telephones:** 22,012,000 (1976) **Newspapers:** 111 dailies, 388 copies per 1,000 inhabitants (1975)
Weights and Measures: Metric system **Travel Requirements:** Passport, no visa **International Dialing Code:** 44

The basic problem for Great Britain has been that ever since losing an empire it has been unable to find a new role. When Britain dismantled the Empire, beginning in 1947, it also lost its captive markets and sources of supply. Britain was forced to compete in a changed world market with the disadvantages of aging industrial plants, war-depleted natural resources and an agricultural base that produced only half of the nation's food needs. In the postwar rebuilding, it did not do as well as its competitors, especially West Germany, France and Japan. Even the traditional British luxury goods—autos, liquor, and clothing, faced strong competition.

In economic terms Britain has suffered from slow growth, poor foreign trade results, low investment, weak currency, high inflation—in sum, a sluggish economy. No government has been able to arrest this decline. Entry into the Common Market in 1973 was supposed to revitalize the economy.

It has not. Europe sells more to Britain than it buys. Trade balances improved only slightly.

But the economic picture is not all grim. The trickle of North Sea oil which began to flow from the British sector in 1974 has now grown to half a million barrels a day. By 1980 Britain was practically self-sufficient in oil and also able to earn enough in exports to put the country in the black for the first time since World War II.

Although Britain has lost most of its 19th- and early 20th-century empire, troubles from former colonies as well as parts of the United Kingdom persisted, most notably in Northern Ireland, Zimbabwe (Rhodesia), Belize, Scotland, and Wales. The violent troubles in Northern Ireland, where some 14,000 troops are stationed, have resisted solution ever since the rioting between Protestant and Catholic communities broke out in Belfast and Londonderry in 1969. Sporadic acts of violence by Irish Republican Army guerrillas continued to occur there and in Britain into the 1980's. In 1981 an IRA prisoner in Belfast named Bobby Sands, who demanded that IRA inmates be treated as political prisoners, died as the result of his 66-day, protesting hunger strike. Although riots ensued in Belfast after his death and nine other IRA prisoners died from similar hunger strikes by mid-August, the British government refused to meet the strikers' demands.

The Labour party, originally an outgrowth of the trade-union movement, has promoted social programs and nationalization of industry. It won a plurality, but not a majority, in the House of Commons in 1974 by promising a deal with the trade unions to end crippling strikes. Harold Wilson became prime minister in a Labour government and made the promised "social compact" with the unions. He retired in 1976 and was succeeded by a close ally, James Callaghan.

The Labour government fell in 1979 when it lost a no-confidence vote in Parliament on the issue of Scottish autonomy. The Conservatives won the ensuing elections in May with a solid majority and installed Margaret Roberts Thatcher, an outspoken free enterpriser, as the country's first woman prime minister. Mrs. Thatcher promised to set Britain on a different economic course by trying to establish a market-oriented, capital-owning economy that would free private business from extreme government regulation so that it might create new wealth. The economy worsened, however; the nation's unemployment rate of 11.1 percent in June 1981 was the highest in 50 years, while inflation ran at an annual rate of 11.7 percent.

Rioting by youths against the police occurred in London, Liverpool, and nearly 30 other towns and cities during July 1981. The trouble was regarded as protests against authority and high unemployment. In response, the Thatcher government introduced sterner police-control methods and youth-employment legislation.

Despite these woes, Britons were cheered by the gorgeous spectacle of the royal wedding of 32-year-old Charles, Prince of Wales, and 20-year-old Lady Diana Spencer on July 29, 1981.

HISTORY: The first known settlers of Britain were the Celts, who invaded the island from northern Europe before the 6th century B.C. A brief invasion by Julius Caesar in 55 B.C. paved the way for a long Roman occupation that began in the 1st century A.D. and lasted until the early 5th century. As the Roman army withdrew, waves of Anglo-Saxons and Jutes invaded Britain, forcing the Celts to retreat westward and into Brittany. The newcomers gradually established kingdoms of their own but were in turn invaded by the Danes, one of whom, Canute, became king of a united England in 1016

1066: William the Conqueror leads Norman army in the last successful invasion of England

1215: King John signs Magna Carta; the most important document of the British constitution, it establishes supremacy of law over the king and lays the foundation for parliamentary government

1337-1453: Hundred Years War rages as English kings seek to enforce claims to French territory; England is ultimately defeated and ceases to be a continental power

1455-85: Houses of York and Lancaster contend for English throne in Wars of the Roses, which end in victory for Henry Tudor, the Lancastrian claimant, and establishment of Tudor dynasty

1534: Breach with Rome, precipitated by pope's refusal to grant Henry VIII a divorce, is completed by Act of Supremacy declaring king head of the Church of England

1558-1603: Reign of Elizabeth I sees the rise of England as a leading European power, strengthened by the defeat of the Spanish Armada in 1588, and the flowering of the Renaissance in English literature; queen is succeeded by James VI of Scotland who, as James I of England, rules over both kingdoms

1642-49: Civil war rends England as Charles I and parliament struggle for power; war ends in defeat and execution of the king and establishment of a commonwealth dominated by Oliver Cromwell

1660: Monarchy is restored under Charles II

18th cent.: Britain undergoes marked transformation with development of parliamentary government and beginning of the Industrial Revolution; overseas, a huge empire is gained in Canada and India and another lost with the American Revolution, followed by war with Napoleonic France

1815: Duke of Wellington's army defeats Napoleon at Waterloo

1832: Enactment of Reform Bill extends franchise to middle class

1837-1901: Reign of Queen Victoria witnesses Britain's rise to world leadership in commerce and industry; reign closes with Britain industrially outstripped by United States and Germany, and fighting Boer War in South Africa

1902: Boers are defeated and accept British sovereignty

1914-18: Britain plays leading role in World War I, sharing in Allied victory over Germany but drained of wealth

1921: Southern Ireland is separated from United Kingdom

1924: Ramsay MacDonald forms Britain's first Labour Cabinet

1939-45: Britain again fights Germany in World War II; standing virtually alone after fall of France in 1940, British, under leadership of Winston Churchill, withstand intensive German bombing and defeat Luftwaffe in Battle of Britain; war ends with Britain again victorious but economically weakened; Labour party, under Clement Attlee, is swept into power

1956: Britain, under Conservative government of Anthony Eden, joins France and Israel in invasion of Egypt following nationalization of Suez Canal

1964: Labour party, led by Harold Wilson, is returned to power

1969: Troops are rushed to Northern Ireland after bloody riots break out between Protestants and Roman Catholics

1970: Wilson is defeated by Conservative leader Edward Heath

1971: Common Market approves Britain's bid for admission. New violence flares in Ulster

1973: Participation in Common Market (EC) begins

1974: Harold Wilson becomes prime minister in minority Labour government, negotiates "social compact" with unions for labor peace

1975: Voters in referendum approve the government's recommendation to remain in EC under new terms

1976: Wilson resigns. He is succeeded by James Callaghan

1979: Unions call winter-time strikes despite social compact. Ambiguous results of autonomy referendum in Scotland lead to a parliamentary vote of no confidence in Callaghan. Conservatives win majority in new House; their leader, Margaret Thatcher, becomes Britain's first woman prime minister. Thatcher government sets new economic course by freeing economy of wage, price, and foreign exchange controls

1981: David Owen and 11 other dissident Labour MP's form new Social Democratic party to oppose what they called Labour's leftward drift. Hunger strikes by IRA prisoners in Belfast result in ten deaths by mid-August and sporadic rioting in Northern Ireland. Rioting by youths in 30 British towns and cities, protesting police authority and lack of jobs. Charles, Prince of Wales, weds Lady Diana Spencer in London's St. Paul's Cathedral

---

UNITED STATES

Area: 3,615,123 sq. mi. **Population:** 226,504,825 (1980 census)

Official Name: United States of America **Capital:** Washington, D.C. **Nationality:** American or United States **Languages:** English is the official and predominant language. Spanish is the preferred language of about 4 million, Italian of 400,000, French and Chinese of 300,000 each, and German, Greek, Japanese, Filipino, and Korean of 100,000 each. Other minority languages include Polish, Yiddish, Russian, and American Indian tongues **Religion:** About two-thirds of the population is Protestant, one-fourth Roman Catholic, 3% Jewish, and the rest of other or no affiliation **Flag:** Popularly known as the "Stars and Stripes" or "Old Glory," the flag consists of 13 horizontal, alternate red and white stripes, and a union of 50 five-pointed white stars arranged in alternate rows of 6 and of 5 on a blue field in the upper left corner **Anthem:** The Star-Spangled Banner

Location: The United States proper (excluding Hawaii and Alaska) stretches across North America from the Atlantic Ocean on the east to the Pacific Ocean on the west, from Canada on the north to Mexico and the Gulf of Mexico on the south **Features:** The United States proper (excluding Hawaii and Alaska) consists of the Atlantic coastal plain, the Appalachian highlands, a vast interior plains region, the Rocky Mountains belt, the intermontane basin and plateaus west of the Rockies, and the mountains and valleys of the Pacific borderland. Another division, part of the Laurentian Plain of Canada, dips into the United States in the Great Lakes region. Alaska's main physical divisions are the Pacific mountain system, the Central Plateau, the Arctic mountain system, and the Arctic Slope. Hawaii consists of a 1,610-mile-long chain of 122 islands, which represent mountain peaks of volcanic origin largely submerged in the Pacific **Chief Rivers:** Mississippi, Missouri, Rio Grande, Yukon, Arkansas, Colorado, Ohio-Allegheny, Red, Columbia, Snake, Pecos, Canadian

Head of State and of Government: President Ronald W. Reagan, born 1911, took office 1981 **Effective Date of Constitution:** March 4, 1789 **Legislative Body:** Congress (bicameral), consisting of the Senate and the House of Representatives. The Senate consists of 100 members—2 from each state—chosen by popular vote for a 6-year term; a third of its membership is renewed every 2 years. The House of Representatives has 435 members elected by popular vote every 2 years; each state is entitled to at least one Representative, with the total number determined periodically according to population **Local Government:** 50 states, each with a popularly elected governor and legislature. Below the state level, local self-government is usually conducted through municipalities, townships, and counties

Ethnic Composition: The nation's ethnic diversity is chiefly due to large-scale immigration, most of which took place before 1920. Whites comprise about 83.2% of the population, Blacks 11.7%, and other races the remaining 5.1% **Population Distribution:** 74% urban **Density:** 62.7 inhabitants per sq. mi.

Largest Cities: (1980 Census; M.A. = Metropolitan Area) New York 7,071,030 (M.A. 9,119,737), Chicago 3,005,072 (M.A. 7,102,328), Los Angeles 2,966,763 (M.A. 7,477,657), Philadelphia 1,688,210 (M.A. 4,716,818), Houston 1,594,086 (M.A. 2,905,350), Detroit 1,203,339 (M.A. 4,352,762), Dallas 904,078 (M.A. 2,974,878), San Diego 875,504 (M.A. 1,861,846), Baltimore 786,775 (M.A. 2,174,023), San Antonio 785,410 (M.A. 1,071,954), Phoenix 764,911 (M.A. 1,508,030), Indianapolis 700,807 (M.A. 1,166,929), San Francisco 678,974 (M.A. 3,252,721)

Per Capita Income: $11,596 (1980) **Gross National Product (GNP):** $2,626.5 billion (1980) **Economic Statistics:** About 24% of the GNP is derived from manufacturing; 17% from wholesale and retail trade; 14% from finance, insurance, and real estate; 13% from services; 12% from government and government enterprises; 3% from agriculture, forestry, and fisheries; 5% from construction; 7% from transportation and communications; 2% from electric, gas, and sanitary services; and 3% from mining **Minerals and Mining:** The United States produces a great variety of minerals and consumes more than any other nation in the world. It is the world's leading producer of coal, copper, lead, natural gas, and molybdenum. Though no longer the leading producer, the United States ranks among the top group in petroleum and iron ore, zinc, sulfur, vanadium, cadmium, uranium, phosphate rock, bauxite, gypsum, aluminum, nitrates, magnesium, potash, titanium, tungsten, feldspar and barite are among the other major minerals produced, and the nation is also rich in waterpower **Labor Force:** 106,821,000 (1980) **Foreign Trade:** Exports, chiefly machinery and transport equipment, food and live animals, crude materials (soybeans, textile fibers, ores and metal scrap), chemicals and other manufactured goods (metals and manufactures, scientific instruments, textiles, rubber, and paper) totaled $220.7 billion in 1980. Imports, mainly machinery and transport equipment, other manufactured goods (metals and manufactures, textiles, iron and steel-mill products, and nonferrous base metals), food and live animals, crude materials, and mineral fuels, totaled $240.8 billion **Principal Trade Partners:** Canada, Japan, Britain, West Germany, Saudi Arabia, Netherlands, Mexico, Nigeria, Italy, France, Venezuela, Brazil, Belgium, China, South Korea, Libya, Algeria

Vital Statistics: Birthrate, 15.8 per 1,000 of pop. (1979); death rate, 8.7 **Life Expectancy:** 74 years **Health Statistics:** 130 inhabitants per hospital bed; 621 per physician (1976) **Infant Mortality:** 13.8 per 1,000 births (1978) **Illiteracy:** Negligible **Primary and Secondary School Enrollment:** 46,000,000 (1979) **Enrollment in Higher Education:** 10,000,000 **GNP Expended on Education:** 6.7% (1979)

Transportation: Surfaced roads total 3,885,000 mi. (1978) **Motor Vehicles:** 154,412,000 (1979) **Passenger Cars:** 120,485,000 **Railway Mileage:** 178,000 (1978) **Ports:** New York, Philadelphia, Portland, Baltimore, Boston, Houston, Norfolk, Tampa, San Francisco, New Orleans, Los Angeles, Corpus Christi, Baton Rouge, Beaumont **Major Airlines:** Major international and domestic carriers are American Airlines, Braniff Airways, Eastern Airlines, Trans World Airlines, Pan American World Airways, Continental Air Lines, Delta Airlines, Northwest Orient Airlines, and United Air Lines **Communications:** Privately owned **Radio Transmitters:** 7,307 (1976) **Receivers:** 402,000,000 (1975) **Television Transmitters:** 3,853 (1974) **Receivers:** 121,100,000 (1975) **Telephones:** 169,027,000 (1978) **Newspapers:** 1,763 dailies (1978)

Weights and Measures: Avoirdupois units of weight and linear measures. Metric system gradually being introduced

---

For articles and statistics on the separate states, see *The Fifty States;* for important national events, see *'80/'81 Month-By-Month Chronology*

UPPER VOLTA

Area: 105,869 sq. mi. **Population:** 6,554,000 (1978 est.)

Official Name: Republic of Upper Volta **Capital:** Ouagadougou **Nationality:** Upper Voltan **Languages:** The official language is French. Mossi is the main African language, others being Samo, Gourounsi, and Lobi, which belong to the Niger-Congo family of languages **Religion:** The majority of the population are animists. There are over 1 million Moslems, 130,000 Roman Catholics, and 9,000 Protestants **Flag:** Horizontal stripes of black, white, and red **Anthem:** The Volta **Currency:** CFA Franc (263 per U.S. $1)

Location: West Africa. Landlocked Upper Volta is bordered on the west and north by Mali, on the east by Niger, and on the south by Benin, Togo, Ghana, and Ivory Coast **Features:** The country consists for the most part of a vast plateau, slightly inclined toward the south and notched by valleys and formed by the three main rivers, with some savanna and semidesert **Chief Rivers:** Black, White, and Red Voltas, and their main tributaries

Head of State and of Government: Col. Sayé Zerbo, born 1932, president of the Military Committee of Reform for National Progress, which took power following the coup of Nov. 25, 1980. He is also premier **Effective Date of Present Constitution:** 1977, suspended 1980 **Legislative Body:** Power resides with the Military Committee of Reform for National Progress **Local Government:** 10 departments

Ethnic Composition: The two main ethnic groups are the Voltaic people and the Mande (Mandingos). Among the Voltaic; 65% are Mossi and 5% Bobo; the Samo are the most numerous of the Mande group **Population Distribution:** 11% urban **Density:** 62 inhabitants per sq. mi.

Largest Cities: (1975 census) Ouagadougou 172,661, Bobo-Dioulasso 115,063, Koudougou 36,838, Ouahigouya 25,690, Banfora 12,358

Per Capita Income $130 (1979) **Gross National Product (GNP):** $869 million (1979) **Economic Statistics:** In 1976 about 67% of GNP was from agriculture (sorghum, millet, cotton, sesame, maize, rice, livestock products, peanuts); 6% from industry (textiles, bicycle assembly, maintenance and repairing of vehicles) **Minerals and Mining:** Manganese deposits are to be exploited; deposits of copper, gold, bauxite, and limestone exist **Labor Force:** 2,700,000 in 1976, with 87% engaged in subsistence agriculture **Foreign Trade:** Exports, chiefly livestock, cotton, and peanuts, totaled $128 million in 1978. Imports, mainly textiles, petroleum products, motor vehicles and parts, fruits and vegetables, and machinery, totaled $292 million **Principal Trade Partners:** EEC countries, Ivory Coast, Ghana

Vital Statistics: Birthrate, 48.5 per 1,000 of pop. (1975); death rate, 25.8 **Life Expectancy:** 38 years **Health Statistics:** 1,174 inhabitants per hospital bed; 59,595 per physician (1974) **Infant Mortality:** 260 per 1,000 births **Illiteracy:** 90% **Primary and Secondary School Enrollment:** 167,330 (1976) **Enrollment in Higher Education:** 1,067 (1975) **GNP Expended on Education:** 2.9% (1973)

Transportation: Paved roads total 535 mi. **Motor Vehicles:** 19,600 (1975) **Passenger Cars:** 9,500 **Railway Mileage:** 341 **Ports:** None **Major Airlines:** Air Afrique provides international services; Air Volta flies domestically **Communications:** Government owned **Radio Transmitters:** 5 **Receivers:** 105,000 (1976) **Television Transmitters:** 1 **Receivers:** 6,000 (1974) **Telephones:** 6,000 (1975) **Newspapers:** 3 dailies, 0.3 copies per 1,000 inhabitants (1975)

Weights and Measures: Metric system **Travel Requirements:** Passport, visa valid for 3 months, $2 fee, 2 photos

---

Upper Volta's name derives simply from the fact that its central region is watered by the upper tributaries of the Volta River, which flows southward through Ghana. Most of the country is a plateau where woodland and pasture contrast with a dry northern area seared by the desert wind.

Once the center of the ancient Mossi empire that provided a shield against Moslem conquest of the coastal regions, Upper Volta today is a land of hardworking farmers and cattle-raisers. Poor soil and variable rains, however, make the task of raising food and export crops, chiefly peanuts and cotton, a recurrent struggle. The nation's landlocked situation adds a further handicap.

Since independence from France in 1960, the country has faced the familiar trials of new African nations. Its first president, Maurice Yaméogo, proved an inept financial administrator. In 1966, with the country in virtual bankruptcy, his government was ousted by a military regime headed by army chief Lt. Col. Sangoulé Lamizana.

Elections were held in 1970, establishing a civilian parliament, but in 1974 Lamizana created a new cabinet composed largely of military officers. In 1976 another change occurred, when after two months of strife between the government and the unions, President Lamizana dismissed the military government and formed a new, largely civilian government. In May 1978, Lamizana was elected to the office he had assumed.

Meanwhile Upper Volta has received new aid from France, the Common Market, and the World Bank for further improvement of agriculture and transportation. At the same time, an even greater boost for the country's development is expected from the manganese deposits at Tambao.

Offsetting these pluses in the early 1970s was the long siege of severe drought and famine that plagued Upper Volta and five other nations of the sub-Sahara (Chad, Mali, Mauritania, Niger, and Senegal); at least 150,000 persons were estimated to have died of starvation. Steps were taken in 1977 to deal with this problem through the adoption of a regional agricultural development program aimed at creating food self-sufficiency within 20 years. Nevertheless, drought continued to plague Upper Volta's cattle and cash crop industries.

On Nov. 25, 1980, following a two-month teachers' strike supported by the opposition, a Military Committee of Reform for National Progress, headed by Col. Sayé Zerbo, overthrew Lamizana and assumed control.

HISTORY: Upper Volta occupies the site of the former Mossi empire and its early history is mostly that of the Mossi people. According to legend, they entered the region as a warrior group between the 11th and 13th centuries and established three independent kingdoms, the most powerful of which was Ouagadougou. Between the 14th and 19th centuries, the Mossi engaged in recurrent wars with the neighboring empires of Mali and Songhai, and after severe defeats their power declined

1896: French subjugate territory and establish a protectorate
1904: Present-day Upper Volta is incorporated into a French colony called Upper Senegal and Niger
1919: Upper Volta is established as a separate French colony
1932: Upper Volta is divided among the colonies of French Sudan, Niger, and the Ivory Coast; is reunited in 1947
1958: Upper Volta becomes a self-governing state, called the Voltaic Republic, within the French Community
1959: Republic's name is changed to Upper Volta; in a general election, the pro-French African Democratic Rally wins a majority of seats in the national assembly and party's leader Maurice Yaméogo is elected premier
1960: Upper Volta becomes an independent republic; with Maurice Yaméogo as president
1966: Army chief of staff Lt. Col. Sangoulé Lamizana seizes control of the government, dismisses President Yaméogo and declares himself chief of state

1970-71: Elections and adoption of a new constitution mark return to constitutional rule the following year
1974: Lamizana suspends constitution, abolishes office of prime minister, and dissolves legislature
1976: President Lamizana dismisses military government and forms a new, largely civilian cabinet
1977: Government lifts three-and-one-half-year ban on political parties. Upper Voltans vote in favor of draft constitution aimed at restoring civilian rule after twelve years of military rule
1978: Military rule ends as Lamizana is elected president
1979: National Assembly institutes a three-party system
1980: Lamizana is ousted in a bloodless coup led by Col. Sayé Zerbo

---

URURGUAY

Area: 68,536 sq. mi. **Population:** 2,899,000 (1980 est.)
Official Name: Oriental Republic of Uruguay **Capital:** Montevideo **Nationality:** Uruguayan **Languages:** Spanish is the official and universal language **Religion:** 66% Roman Catholic, 2% Protestant, 2% Jewish, 30% other **Flag:** Four blue stripes and 5 white stripes, with a golden sun on a white field in the upper left corner **Anthem:** National Anthem, beginning "Easterners our country or death" **Currency:** Uruguayan peso (10 per U.S. $1)

Location: Southeast coast of South America. Uruguay is bounded on the north and northeast by Brazil, on the east by the Atlantic Ocean, on the south by the Rio de la Plata estuary, and on the west by Argentina **Features:** The country consists of rolling, grassy plains and low hills. There are scattered forest areas along the banks of the numerous streams, which provide natural irrigation for the soil **Chief Rivers:** Uruguay, Negro, Rio de la Plata, Cuareim, Yaguarón

Head of State and of Government: President: Gen. Gregorio Alvarez, designated Aug. 1, 1981, for 3 ½-year term **Effective Date of Present Constitution:** 1967, partially suspended 1973 **Legislative Body:** Congress dissolved 1973; a 25-member Council of State governs at present **Local Government:** 19 departments

Ethnic Composition: About 85% of the population is of European origin, mainly Spanish and Italian, with 10% mestizo, and 5% mulatto or black **Population Distribution:** 83% urban **Density:** 42 inhabitants per sq. mi.
Largest Cities: (1975 census) Montevideo 1,173,254, Salto 72,948, Paysandu 62,412, Las Piedras 53,983

Per Capita Income: $1,704 (1980) **Gross National Product (GNP):** $5 billion (1980) **Economic Statistics:** In 1979, 29% of GNP from manufacturing (meat packing, shoes, leather, textiles, construction and building materials, beverages, chemicals); 15% of GNP was from agriculture (livestock products, beef, wool, wheat, corn, rice) **Minerals and Mining:** Marble, building stone, gravel, and iron ore **Labor Force:** 1,174,376 (1975), with 34% in industry; 8% in agriculture; 40% in trade and services; 5% in construction; and 6% in transportation and communications **Foreign Trade:** Exports, chiefly wool, meat, and hides, totaled $788 million in 1979. Imports, mainly raw materials, fuels and lubricants, machinery and parts, automotive vehicles and parts, construction materials, and foodstuffs, totaled $1.2 billion **Principal Trade Partners:** Brazil, United States, West Germany, Iraq, Nigeria, Argentina, Netherlands

Vital Statistics: Birthrate, 20.9 per 1,000 of pop. (1976); death rate, 10.2 **Life Expectancy:** 71 years **Health Statistics:** 235 inhabitants per hospital bed; 700 per physician (1976) **Infant Mortality:** 45.9 per 1,000 births (1976) **Illiteracy:** 9% **Primary and Secondary School Enrollment:** 453,781 (1977) **Enrollment in Higher Education:** 32,627 (1975) **GNP Expended on Education:** 3.6% (1970)

Transportation: Paved roads total 4,100 mi. **Motor Vehicles:** 231,300 (1976) **Passenger Cars:** 127,100 **Railway Mileage:** 1,736 **Ports:** Montevideo **Major Airlines:** Primeras LIneas Uruguayas de Navegación Aérea (PLUNA) operates domestically and internationally **Communications:** Government and privately controlled **Radio Transmitters:** 101 **Receivers:** 1,600,000 (1976) **Television Transmitters:** 27 **Receivers:** 355,000 (1976) **Telephones:** 258,000 (1976) **Newspapers:** 30 dailies, 140 copies per 1,000 inhabitants (1974)

Weights and Measures: Metric system **Travel Requirements:** Passport, no visa for 3 months

---

The Oriental Republic of Uruguay takes its name from the fact that it is situated on the east bank of the Uruguay River. Uruguay, the second smallest country in South America, is characterized by a high literacy rate and a large urban middle class.

Economic reverses and political repression have seriously affected Uruguayans in the last decade. Although politically stable since 1903, Uruguay began to experience problems in the late 1960s with a series of student riots, general strikes, and the rise of urban terrorism. A series of repressive government measures followed, then a 1973 coup against the presidency of Juan Bordaberry. The military group responsible for the coup retained Bordaberry as president and began tightening its already firm grip on the country. Stability was not enhanced by Bordaberry's government, and dissidents were eliminated through a campaign of arrests, torture and murder. By 1976 the military had ousted Bordaberry in a peaceful putsch because he planned to set up a corporate state structure with the participation of the armed forces written into law. The military preferred a gradual return to representative democracy. Bordaberry was replaced by Aparicio Méndez, who was named president by the conservative Council of the Nation.

Things were not always so sorrowful for Uruguay. Not long ago it could boast one of the highest per capita incomes in the hemisphere and a widely desired currency. The country was envied for its advanced laws, six-hour work day, retirement of workers at age 50 or 55, and incredibly rich soil. But the utopian social system, based on a growing population, became overburdened and began to fall behind in its payments. A 1963 census showed that the population had not grown, that, in fact, well-educated Uruguayans had been leaving for other lands in large numbers.

The economy has been marked by high inflation and, until recently, a high balance of payments deficit. In an effort to deal with the situation, the government has issued a series of mini-devaluations of the peso.

The political situation looked no brighter under Méndez. Upon taking office he immediately issued a decree suspending the political rights of the leaders of existing parties for 15 years. It has been reported that Uruguay, with a population of less than three million, has the highest proportion of political prisoners to total population. In 1978, the regime conceded that 2,511 persons accused of "crimes against state security" had served jail sentences and been released in the preceding six years. In May 1981 human rights leaders asserted that more than 1,200 political prisoners were still being held.

On August 1, 1981, the ruling military group's Council of the Nation selected a retired army commander-in-chief, Gregorio Alvarez, to serve as president for a 3 ½-year term.

HISTORY: The eastern side of the Uruguay and La Plata rivers was occupied by warlike and seminomadic Indians, the Charrúa, until late in the colonial period when Europeans began to settle the area. The first settlers were the Spanish, who established a colony at Soriano in 1624. They were followed by the Portuguese, who were driven out in the 18th century by the Spanish, under whom Uruguay became part of a viceroyalty centered in Argentina. During the Napoleonic Wars, Uruguay was briefly occupied by the British, and the spread of revolutionary ideas during this period soon swept the country into the general Latin American fight for independence
1810-14: A war of independence, led by José Gervasio Artigas, begins; Uruguay, with aid from Argentina, ends Spanish rule
1820-28: Uruguay is occupied by Brazil. In 1825, a group of patriots known as the Thirty-Three Immortals declare Uruguay an independent republic; country throws off Brazilian rule and, in 1828, Uruguay is established as an independent buffer state between Brazil and Argentina
1865-70: Argentina, Brazil, and Uruguay unite in a victorious war against Paraguay
1911-15: President José Batlle y Ordóñez introduces wide range of social and economic reforms
1919-51: Fearful of the development of a dictatorship, nation adopts new constitution restricting president's power and vesting broad powers in Council of Administration; resulting conflict leads to restoration of strong executive powers to president in 1934. In

1951, office of president is abolished and executive power vested in nine-member national council
1958: The conservative Blancos (National party) win general elections, displacing liberal Colorado party which had governed for more than 90 years
1966: Presidential form of government is restored in referendum; Colorados regain majority in general elections
1967-68: President Oscar D. Gestido dies and is succeeded by Vice-President Jorge Pacheco Areco; general strikes and student riots become widespread
1969: Pacheco decrees a limited state of siege in June following a new wave of disabling strikes
1971: Juan M. Bordaberry is elected president
1973: President Bordaberry's military-dominated civilian government suspends constitutional rule, replaces congress with a council of state, and curbs opposition press
1976: Bordaberry is ousted. Aparicio Méndez is named president
1977: U.S. moves to reduce aid to Uruguay because of human rights violations; Uruguay then rejects aid linked to human rights, claiming it is an internal matter
1978: OAS panel charges Uruguay with wholesale violations of human rights
1979: Elimination of duties on imported fertilizers and farm machinery leads to increased productivity of farmlands and herds
1980: Nov. 30 plebiscite overwhelmingly rejects draft constitution which would give armed forces a permanent share of power
1981: Foreign minister resigns in dispute with military rulers over their orders to dismiss certain civilian officials. Gen. Gregorio Alvarez is named president. Salto Grande hydroelectric complex nears completion

---

VANUATU

Area: 5,700 sq. mi. **Population:** 112,596 (1979 census)
Official Name: Republic of Vanuatu **Capital:** Vila **Nationality:** Vanuatuan **Languages:** Bislama, a pidgin dialect, is the national language. English, French and Bislama are official languages. There are many Melanesian languages throughout the islands **Religion:** Mostly Christian (Presbyterian, Roman Catholic, Anglican); some animists **Flag:** Two equal horizontal stripes of red over green with a black triangle at the hoist containing two crossed yellow mele leaves surrounded by a yellow hog tusk. The triangle is framed on two sides by borders of yellow and black which extend into a triple horizontal stripe of black-yellow-black running to the fly end of the flag **Anthem:** N.A. **Currency:** Vatu
Location: The Y-shaped chain of islands, located in the southwestern Pacific between 13°08′ and 20°12′S., and 166°33′ and 169°49′E., are 600 miles west of Fiji and 250 miles northeast of New Caledonia **Features:** The main islands are Espiritu Santo (the largest), Malekula, Epi, Pentecost and Efate. They are of coral and volcanic origin with active volcanoes on Ambryn, Lopevi and Tanna. Most islands are covered with dense forests
Head of State: President Ati George Sokomanu, born 1938, elected June 1980 **Head of Government:** Prime Minister: Rev. Walter Lini, born 1943, appointed July 1980 **Effective Date of Present Constitution:** July 1980 **Legislative Body:** Representative Assembly (unicameral) with 39 members **Local Government:** 4 regions
Ethnic Composition: The population is 92% indigenous Melanesian. There are 5,000 French, 460 British and 1,500 Commonwealth citizens **Population Distribution:** 23% urban **Density:** 20 inhabitants per sq. mi.
Largest Cities: (1979 census) Vila 14,797, Luganville 4,935
Per Capita Income: N.A. **Gross National Product (GNP):** N.A. **Economic Statistics:** Copra is the principal product, and cocoa and coffee are also grown. Yams, taro, manioc and bananas are produced for local consumption and there are a large number of cattle. Fishing is important, and tourism is growing **Minerals and Mining:** Manganese deposits are exploited **Labor Force:** The native population is mainly engaged in peasant farming **Foreign Trade:** Exports, chiefly copra, fish, prepared meats, and manganese, totaled $32 million in 1977. Imports, chiefly food, fuel, textiles and machinery, totaled $40 million **Principal Trade Partners:** Australia, France, United States, Japan
Vital Statistics: Birthrate, 45 per 1,000 of pop. (1966); death rate, 20 **Life Expectancy:** N.A. **Health Statistics:** 102 inhabitants per hospital bed; 3,200 per physician (1975) **Infant Mortality:** N.A. **Illiteracy:** 85% **Primary and Secondary School Enrollment:** 23,840 (1977) **Enrollment in Higher Education:** N.A. **GNP Expended on Higher Education:** N.A.
Transportation: Surfaced roads total 160 mi. **Motor Vehicles:** 3,400 (1974) **Passenger Cars:** 2,600 **Railway Mileage:** None **Ports:** Vila, Luganville **Major Airlines:** Air Melanesiae provides domestic serv-

ice **Communications:** Government and privately owned **Radio Transmitters:** 2 **Receivers:** 15,000 (1976) **Television:** None **Telephones:** 2,400 **Newspapers:** 2 (fortnightly) **Weights and Measures:** Metric system **Travel Requirements:** N.A.

A South-Sea islands paradise in so many ways—its main island of Espiritu Santo was the locale for James Michener's *Tales of the South Pacific*—the island nation of Vanuatu faced independence beset by internal divisions and outright rebellion that threatened to tear it apart at the seams.

This small Pacific archipelago situated west of the international date line—formerly known as the New Hebrides, and ruled since 1906 as a joint British-French Condominium—gained its independence July 30, 1980. Though its tropical climate makes it a potential haven for tourism, Vanuatu remains one of the more primitive and underdeveloped areas in the Pacific, with an economy dependent on subsistence agriculture and many tribal Melanesians still practicing various "cargo cult" religions.

In December 1978, a majority coalition government was formed to draft a new constitution and prepare the islands for independence. Father Gerard Lemyang—a French-educated Roman Catholic priest and moderate political leader—became chief minister and formed a Government of National Unity (GNU), with the pro-independence Vanuaaku Party (VP) sharing half the cabinet posts, and its leader, Rev. Walter Lini—an Anglican priest and nationalist spokesman—becoming deputy chief minister.

The constitution adopted in September 1979 provided for elections prior to independence, which was set for May-July 1980. It guaranteed French language rights, established a council of tribal chiefs to preserve traditional Melanesian customs, and set up regional assemblies for Santo and Tanna, in an attempt to mollify separatist sentiment there.

The VP won the November 14 elections to the Representative Assembly, beating the New Hebrides Federal party—a coalition including Lemyang, the Santo-based Na-Griamel separatists and pro French groups—by two-to-one, with Lini becoming chief minister. The VP also won a majority in the two regional assemblies on Santo and Tanna, causing outbreaks of violence from separatist gangs claiming election fraud.

But on May 25 of 1980, Jimmy (Moli) Stevens and several hundred followers armed with bows and arrows—and backed up by 50 or more French-speaking planters armed with shotguns—stormed government offices in Luganville, took the British District Commissioner hostage, and declared Santo the independent nation of Vemarana. Stevens, a mixed-race plantation owner and hereditary tribal chief who founded the Na-Griamel movement in the 1960s, was seeking autonomy for Santo under French tutelage, and was supported by many French-speaking residents who feared the VP would nationalize their big plantations following independence.

The insurrection died down when a joint 300-man Anglo-French military force arrived to restore order July 24, after clashes between insurgents and local police resulted in one rebel killed. But these troops were withdrawn soon after independence was declared, as rebel violence increased. Now prime minister of an independent state, Lini called on the United Nations for aid in maintaining Vanuatu's territorial integrity. Support came from other independent Pacific states, with Papua New Guinea sending 400 troops to replace the Anglo-French peacekeeping force. Authorities later arrested some 40 rebels on Santo August 19, including several French citizens. By

the end of the month all resistance was crushed and Stevens was under arrest. In November he was sentenced to 14 years in prison.

HISTORY: Little is known of the pre-history of the archipelago, though Melanesian settlement is thought to pre-date 400 B.C. The Spanish explorer de Quiros was the first European to sight the islands (1606). The islands were later visited by Bougainville in 1768 and by Captain Cook—who discovered, charted and named most of the southern islands—in 1774. Missionaries came to the islands in the 1820s, and were followed by settlers from Britain and France. The islands suffered during the 1860s from raids by "blackbirders" recruiting forced labor to work in Australia and Fiji

1887: Disputes between French and English-speaking settlers over control of the islands—and their possible annexation by either Australia or French New Caledonia—lead Britain and France to set up Joint Naval Commission to protect their subjects in the archipelago

1902: Resident Commissioners representing Britain and France are appointed to administer islands

1906: Anglo-French Condominium is established, with dual administration for British and French citizens, the terms of which are set officially in the Anglo-French Protocol of 1914

1940-45: French residency in Vila is one of first overseas departments to support Gen. de Gaulle's Free French government against Vichy. Islands become a major base for the Allied offensive in the South Pacific. John Frum "cargo cult" develops as anti-colonial movement among tribal people on Tanna Island; but near-rebellion is avoided with jailing of main leaders

1957: Advisory Council, partly elected and partly appointed by the Resident Commissioners, is established

1974: Nationalist agitation wins elected Representative Assembly, replacing Advisory Council; Luganville and Vila are granted municipal assemblies in move toward increased self-government

1975: August municipal elections in Vila and Luganville are won by pro-French and autonomist parties, but pro-independence Nationalist party wins majority in the Representative Assembly. Jimmy (Moli) Stevens, leader of the Na-Griamel movement on Santo, calls for unilateral independence for that island, demanding British withdrawal from the New Hebrides

1977: Pro-French "moderates" win uncontested Assembly elections in November; pro-independence Vanuaaku party, led by Rev. Walter Lini, boycotts elections and later forms "People's Provisional Government." George Kalsakau of Natatok party becomes chief minister

1978: French Secretary of State for Overseas Departments and Territories Paul Dijoud calls for coalition government to end political crisis and move toward independence. Gerard Lemyang becomes chief minister and forms Government of National Unity

1979: New constitution is adopted, mandating pre-independence elections and regional legislatures for Espiritu Santo and Tanna. VP wins Nov. 14 elections, gaining 26 seats in the Assembly, with New Hebrides Federal party winning the other 13; Lini becomes chief minister. Violence flares as VP also wins majority in Santo and Tanna assemblies, but order is soon restored

1980: Jimmy Stevens stages revolt on Espiritu Santo May 25, proclaiming the island independent state of Vemarana; rebellion is joined by separatists on Tanna, but Anglo-French military force temporarily restores order July 24. At George Sokomanu is chosen president by electoral college. New Hebrides becomes the independent nation of Vanuatu July 30; Walter Lini becomes nation's first prime minister. Secession continues as Lini calls for UN aid; Papua New Guinea sends strong detachment Aug. 18 to replace Anglo-French force. All resistance is crushed. Stevens is arrested, tried and sentenced to 14 years in prison; 110 French citizens are deported

1981: Government workers stage 4-day strike

VATICAN CITY

Area: 0.17 sq. mi. (108.7 acres) **Population:** 728 (1978 est.)

Official Name: State of the Vatican City **Nationality:** The Papacy has a citizenship of its own, which is granted to those residing in the Vatican because of their work or rank **Languages:** Italian is the official language of the state; Latin is the official language of the Holy See, the administrative and legislative body for the Roman Catholic Church, and is used for most papal encyclicals and other formal pronouncements **Flag:** Yellow and white vertical bands, with the crossed keys of St. Peter under the triple papal tiara on the white band **Anthem:** Pontifical March (no words) **Currency:** Italian lira (1102 per U.S. $1)

Location: Located in Rome, Vatican City is roughly a triangular area lying near the west bank of the Tiber River and to the west of Castel

Sant' Angelo. On the west and south it is bounded by the Leonine Wall. The Vatican area comprises St. Peter's Square; St. Peter's Basilica, the largest Christian church in the world; a quadrangular area north of the square, containing the museums, library, and administrative buildings, and Belvedere Park; the Vatican Palace; and the Papal Gardens. Outside the Vatican City itself, extraterritoriality (but not sovereignty) is exercised over 12 churches and palaces in and near Rome, including St. John Lateran, St. Mary Major, and St. Paul Without the Walls Basilicas, and the papal villa at Castel Gandolfo

Government: Vatican City is the center of the worldwide organization of the Roman Catholic Church and the seat of the Pope, who is the absolute sovereign of the tiny state. The Supreme Pontiff is John Paul II (Karol Wojtyla), born 1920, elected Pope on October 16, 1978. He is assisted as temporal ruler by the Pontifical Commission, consisting of the cardinals, and the Administration of the Patrimony of the Apostolic See. Both of these organizations are presided over by a secretary of state (premier), at present held by Archbishop Agostino Casaroli, born 1914, appointed 1979. Religious affairs are governed under the Pope's direction by a number of ecclesiastical bodies collectively known as the Roman Curia. The Pope rules from his election until death, at which time a successor is chosen by the College of Cardinals

Ethnic Composition: While the citizenry of the Vatican includes cardinals and other clergymen from all over the world, most of the inhabitants are Italian. The 75 members of the Swiss Guard are a notable exception

Economic Statistics: Vatican City does not engage in the economically productive activity common to other states. It is almost entirely dependent for income on the receipt of charitable contributions, the sale of Vatican stamps and tourist mementos, fees for admission to Vatican museums, and the sale of Vatican publications

Illiteracy: None **Enrollment in Higher Education:** 7,758 (1975)

Transportation: Vatican City is easily reached by the public transportation system of Rome. It has its own railroad station **Communications:** State controlled Radio Vatican, with 17 transmitters. There is no television **Newspapers:** 1 daily, the semiofficial l'Osservatore Romano

Weights and Measures: Metric system **International Dialing Code:** 39

For a long time after the unification of Italy in 1870, which stripped the popes of most of their temporal possessions, the status of the Vatican, the chief papal residence, was uncertain. Then, by the 1929 Lateran Treaty with Italy, the independent enclave of Vatican City came into being. In the treaty, the pontificate formally renounced all claims to the former Papal States.

Vatican City stands on the spot where Caligula constructed a circus and Nero had gardens. The ruler of Vatican City, the Pope, bears the title of Bishop of Rome, Vicar of Jesus Christ, Successor of the Prince of Apostles, Supreme Pontiff of the Universal Church, Patriarch of the West, Archbishop and Metropolitan of the Roman Province, and Sovereign of the State of the Vatican City. Currently he is Pope John Paul II. His .17-square-mile realm includes St. Peter's basilica, the largest church in Christendom; St. Peter's square, a roughly circular plaza set off by Bernini's colonnade; and the pontifical palaces, or the Vatican proper, with magnificent chapels, museums, archives, a library, and a new hall for mass papal audiences.

Among the chapels are the Sistine, the ceiling and one wall of which are decorated with paintings by Michelangelo. The museums, galleries, and various interiors contain works by such masters as Raphael, Leonardo da Vinci, Fra Angelico, Titian, and Correggio, priceless sculpture that includes the Apollo Belvedere and Laocoön, and Egyptian, Etruscan, and other collections. The library, with its enormous wealth of books and manuscripts, is one of the world's great research institutions, and the archives house original material on such matters as the trial of Galileo and the request for annulment of the marriage of Henry VIII to Catherine of Aragon. Among other things, Vatican City also has gardens, courts, and quiet streets; its

own daily newspaper and postal, telegraph, and broadcasting facilities; its own "armed forces," the colorfully garbed Swiss Guards; and its own railroad station, used almost exclusively as a freight terminal. Outside its confines but nonetheless enjoying extraterritoriality are a number of churches, palaces, and other structures in Rome and the papal villa at nearby Castel Gandolfo.

Vatican City is administered by a commission of cardinals, and a papal decree of 1968 established a body of 21 lay experts to advise them. A simultaneous decree reorganized the papal court, renaming it the papal household, abolishing hereditary offices, and putting an end to various picturesque anachronisms.

HISTORY: The State of the Vatican City and other places over which the Vatican retains control are the remnants of the old Papal States. For almost 1,000 years the papacy held vast temporal possessions, including large areas of Italy, and, until the French Revolution, parts of southern France. During the unification of the Italian peninsula in the 19th century, virtually all these possessions were absorbed by the House of Savoy, leaving only Rome and surrounding territory, protected by a French garrison, still under papal control
1870: French garrison withdraws and Rome is annexed by the Kingdom of Italy; Pope Pius IX refuses to recognize the loss of temporal power and initiates what becomes more than a half-century of self-imposed "imprisonment" of Popes
1929: Lateran Treaty is signed, by which Italy recognizes the sovereignty and independence of the new Vatican City state
1947: Italian Republic reaffirms Italy's adherence to Lateran Treaty
1962: Pope John XXIII convenes Second Vatican Council to promote Christian unity
1963: Archbishop Giovanni Montini of Milan is elected pope on death of John XXIII and reigns as Paul VI
1965: Pope Paul VI makes a historic journey to speak before the UN in New York "for the cause of peace in the world"
1978: Pope Paul VI dies on August 6 at age 80; Albino Cardinal Luciani, Patriarch of Venice, is elected new pontiff, John Paul I, but he dies on September 28. Karol Cardinal Wojtyla, Archbishop of Krakow, Poland, succeeds as Pope John Paul II on October 16
1979: Pope John Paul II visits Mexico, Poland, Ireland, and U.S.
1980: The Pope visits Africa, France and Brazil
1981: Pope John Paul II is shot by a deranged Turkish terrorist May 13, but recovers from abdominal wounds and resumes duties

---

VENEZUELA

Area: 352,143 sq. mi. **Population:** 13,913,000 (1980 est.)

Official Name: Republic of Venezuela **Capital:** Caracas **Nationality:** Venezuelan **Languages:** Spanish is the official and universal language **Religion:** 96% Roman Catholic **Flag:** Horizontal stripes of yellow, blue, and red with an arc of 7 white stars in the center and the national coat of arms in the upper left **Anthem:** National Anthem, beginning "Glory to the brave people" **Currency:** Bolivar (4.3 per U.S. $1)

Location: North coast of South America. Venezuela is bounded on the north by the Caribbean Sea, on the east by Guyana, on the south by Brazil, and on the west by Colombia **Features:** The main regions are the Andes Mountains and outliers in the northwest; the northern coastal zone, the plains, or llanos, stretching from the mountains south and east to the Orinoco River; and the Guayana Highlands south and east of the Orinoco, consisting of high plateaus and rolling plains **Chief Rivers:** Orinoco, Caroní, Caura, Apure

Head of State and of Government: President Luis Herrera Campins, born 1925, inaugurated March 1979 for 5 years **Effective Date of Present Constitution:** January 1961 **Legislative Body:** Congress (bicameral), consisting of the Senate, with 47 members and the 199-man Chamber of Deputies, both elected by adult suffrage for 5-year terms **Local Government:** 20 states, 2 federal territories, a federal district, and the 72 islands of the federal dependencies. The governors of each are appointed by the president, and each, except the dependencies, has its own elected legislature

Ethnic Composition: About 70% of the population is mestizo (of mixed Indian and European ancestry), 17% of European (mainly Spanish) origin, 7% black, 1% Indian, and the rest mulattos of mixed Indian and black ancestry **Population Distribution:** 75% urban **Density:** 40 inhabitants per sq. mi.

Largest Cities: (1976 est.) Caracas 2,576,000, Maracaibo 792,000, Valencia 439,000, Barquisimeto 430,000, Maracay 301,000, Barcelona 242,000

Per Capita Income: $3,398 (1980) **Gross National Product (GNP):** $51 billion (1980) **Economic Statistics:** 45% of GNP is derived from industry (including oil refining, textiles, building materials, clothing, shoes, food, steel, and chemicals), and 20% from agriculture **Minerals and Mining:** There are large deposits of oil, natural gas, bauxite, iron ore, salt, and smaller amounts of coal, gold, and diamonds **Labor Force:** 4.1 million (1977); 35% were in services, 15% in industry, and 10% in agriculture **Foreign Trade:** Exports, chiefly petroleum (95%) and products, and iron ore, totaled about $14 billion in 1979. Imports, mainly vehicles, iron and steel, wheat, mining and construction equipment, machinery and chemicals, totaled $10 billion **Principal Trade Partners:** United States, Canada, West Germany, Japan, Britain, Netherlands Antilles, Spain

Vital Statistics: Birthrate, 33.5 per 1,000 of pop.; death rate, 6.0 **Life Expectancy:** 67 years **Health Statistics:** 342 inhabitants per hospital bed; 870 per physician (1976) **Infant Mortality:** 40.4 per 1,000 births (1977) **Illiteracy:** 13% **Primary and Secondary School Enrollment:** 2,835,284 (1976) **Enrollment in Higher Education:** 247,518 **GNP Expended on Education:** 7% (1976)

Transportation: Paved roads total 14,800 mi. **Motor Vehicles:** 1,324,515 (1975) **Passenger Cars:** 955,151 **Railway Mileage:** 232 **Ports:** La Guaira, Maracaibo, Puerto Cabello, Puerto La Cruz, Puerto Ordaz **Major Airlines:** VIASA, a government-owned airline, flies internationally; Avensa, privately owned, and LAV, government owned, fly domestically **Communications:** Government and privately controlled **Radio Transmitters:** 265 **Receivers:** 5,034,000 (1976) **Television Transmitters:** 48 **Receivers:** 1,431,000 (1976) **Telephones:** 847,000 **Newspapers:** 49 dailies, 93 copies per 1,000 inhabitants (1975)

Weights and Measures: Metric system **Travel Requirements:** Passport, tourist card valid 45 days, visa valid 1 year **International Dialing Code:** 58

Venezuela's prosperity has been based for years on petroleum, and this richest, most dynamic and most "American" country in Latin America is one of the world's largest petroleum exporters. In 1975-76 Venezuela nationalized the huge holdings of foreign petroleum and iron-ore mining companies, but did so peacefully, and the firms have been compensated. A government holding company, PETROVEN, controls and regulates the industry. In view of the world oversupply of oil, production was cut 10 percent in 1981 to about 2 million barrels per day, of which almost 90 percent is exported, half of that to the United States. Venezuela's proven reserves amount to about 18 billion barrels. No new fields have been discovered since 1958.

Along with the steady rise in oil prices since 1973, the government has been pumping revenue into construction and industrial development. Rapid industrialization has created an urban people, alleviating the problem of land hunger, but decreasing agricultural production. Severe food shortages began to develop in 1977.

Venezuela has shown willingness to share part of its oil income with poorer nations of the Caribbean region. However, the reward for this generosity includes suspicion that Venezuela has imperialistic motives and is acting in "Yanqui" interests.

Venezuela's political stability—its last dictatorship was overthrown in 1958—was further demonstrated in 1978 when a new president was elected in what was basically a two-party race. Luis Herrera Campins, the candidate of the Social Christians, the "out" party, defeated Luis Piñerúa Ordaz, of the Democratic Action party. In a six-party contest, the two top parties polled 85% of the vote. In his inaugural speech in 1979, Herrera declared he had inherited "a mortgaged country." He promised to halt runaway public spending, and corruption, and give private business more flexibility in its operations.

Basic industries, such as steel and power, are owned and subsidized by the state. Venezuela's best hope for an industrial base to take the place of oil's proved reserves, which will last only through

the year 2000, lies in Guayana, a region containing natural reserves of iron ore, sufficient for 75 years of production at current levels, and the hydroelectric potential of the Caroní River. Enough bauxite has been found to make the aluminum industry self-sufficient. The nation's oil riches are being used in a $12-billion industrialization program, in which the U.S. accounts for slightly more than half the foreign participation. However, a Spanish-Canadian group received the contracts for a national railroad grid, and the French for the $250-million Caracas subway.

HISTORY: Prior to the Spanish conquest in the 16th century, Venezuela was inhabited by 2 dominant Indian tribes—the Arawaks, who lived in agricultural communities, and the warlike Caribs. Charles I of Spain granted the Welsers, a German banking firm, the right to explore and colonize Venezuela but rescinded the right in 1546, after which the colony reverted to the Spanish crown

1811: Venezuela, under the leadership of Francisco de Miranda, declares its independence from Spain, but royalist forces maintain control

1812-21: Simón Bolívar leads a bloody war of independence against Spain, sets up Greater Colombia, encompassing the present territories of Venezuela, Colombia, Panama, and Ecuador, and is named president

1830-1900: Venezuela breaks away from Greater Colombia and becomes an independent republic; during the remainder of the century the nation is wracked by internal strife as dictator succeeds dictator. In 1895, Venezuela loses territory to British Guiana after a heated boundary dispute with Britain

1908-35: Gen. Juan Vicente Gómez becomes dictator; a tyrannical ruler, he succeeds in lifting the country to solvency by allotting oil concessions to foreign companies

1937-38: Gen. Eleázar López Contreras, Gómez' successor as president, exiles opposition political and labor leaders, declaring a moratorium on political and labor activities; he inaugurates a broad program of social and economic development

1945: A revolution breaks out and a liberal government headed by President Rómulo Betancourt takes power; he declares universal suffrage, and institutes social reforms

1947-48: A new constitution is adopted, providing for election of the president by direct popular vote. Rómulo Gallegos, of the Democratic Action party, is elected president but is ousted in 1948 by a military junta led by Colonels Marcos Pérez Jiménez and Carlos Delgado Chalbaud

1953-59: Pérez Jiménez takes power; he is overthrown in 1958 during a revolt supported by liberal elements of the armed forces. After brief interim government by a civilian-military junta, Betancourt is elected president

1962: Venezuela adopts new constitution limiting president to five-year term. Communists launch terrorist campaign to oust Betancourt because of his support for U.S. blockade of Cuba

1963-67: Raúl Leoni, leader of the liberal Democratic Action party, is elected president on a platform pledging economic and social reform; he suspends constitutional guarantees in drive against Castro-supported terrorists

1968: Rafael Caldera, the Social Christian candidate, is elected president; Democratic Action party retains control of Congress

1970: Venezuela and Guyana declare 12-year moratorium on border dispute

1973: Caldera government quadruples petroleum reference prices. Venezuela joins the Andean Pact, formed by Bolivia, Chile, Colombia, Ecuador and Peru. Carlos Andrés Pérez of Democratic Action party is elected president

1976: Oil industry is nationalized

1977: President Pérez announces a series of austerity measures aimed at controlling inflation and cutting government spending. Pérez visits President Carter; commonality of aims voiced

1978: Presidents Pérez and Carter sign agreements on maritime boundaries between Venezuela and U.S. and curbing flow of illicit drugs. Luis Herrera Campins of Social Christian party wins presidential election on Dec. 6

1979: Herrera is inaugurated on March 12. A U.S. businessman, William F. Niehous, is freed after being held prisoner 41 months by guerrillas. Foreign debt rises from $7.4 to $12.2 billion

1980: Venezuela reaches agreement with Mexico on plan to supply oil and loans to nine countries of the Caribbean region. Aid to Bolivia is cut off following a military coup there. Relations with Cuba are strained by acquittal of four men accused of bombing a Cuban passenger plane in 1976

1981: PETROVEN cuts its price for best grade of residual fuel by $7 in June. Buildup of armed forces reported

VIETNAM

Area: 128,405 sq. mi. **Population:** 52,741,766 (1979 census) **Official Name:** Socialist Republic of Vietnam **Capital:** Hanoi **Nationality:** Vietnamese **Languages:** Vietnamese, spoken by the majority, is the official language; minorities speak Chinese, French, Khmer, Cham, and Montagnard (mountain tribal) languages **Religion:** The majority of the people nominally practice Buddhism and animism, although many combine these with elements of Taoism, Confucianism, and Christianity. However, organized religious activities have been discouraged in the North **Flag:** A yellow five-pointed star centered on a red field **Anthem:** Tien Quan Ca (Hymn of the Marching Army) **Currency:** Dong (2.18 per U.S. $1)

Location: Southeast Asia, occupying the eastern part of the Indochinese peninsula. It is bordered by China on the north, by the South China Sea on the east and south, and by Laos and Cambodia on the west **Features:** The jungle-covered hills in the north and northwest rise southeastward into the Annamese Cordillera and its outlying plateaus. East of the mountains are fertile coastal lowlands, with the deltas of the Mekong and Red rivers being the largest and most densely populated **Chief Rivers:** Red, Black, Lo, Ca, Mekong, Ba, Dong Nai

Political Leader: Le Duan, Secretary General of the Communist Party, born 1908, appointed 1960 **Head of State:** Truong Chinh, appointed July 4, 1981, is chairman of the Council of State, a collective presidency **Head of Government:** Premier Pham Van Dong, born 1906, elected 1976 **Effective Date of Present Constitution:** Dec. 1980 **Legislative Body:** National Assembly (unicameral), with 492 members. The chief executive and legislative organ of government is the Communist party's 17-man Politburo, the core of the 133-member Central Committee headed by Le Duan **Local Government:** 36 provinces, 3 city provinces, and one special area

Ethnic Composition: Vietnamese constitute about 85% of the population; Montagnards of both Malayo-Polynesian and Mon-Khmer ethnic groups make up about 8%, and the rest include Chinese, Khmer, and Cham minorities **Population Distribution:** 19% urban **Density:** 411 inhabitants per sq. mi.

Largest Cities: (1979 census) Ho Chi Minh City (Saigon) 3,419,978, Hanoi 2,570,905, Haiphong 1,279,067

Per Capita Income: $113 (1980) **Gross National Product (GNP):** $6 billion (1980) **Economic Statistics:** Basically agricultural (rice, sugarcane, tea, maize, manioc, coffee, fish, rubber), rice, the staple food, still has to be imported. Light industry is confined to food processing, textiles, glass, paper, machinery, cement and, in the North, steel **Minerals and Mining:** Coal, iron ore, apatite, phosphates, chromite, tin, salt, granite, and limestone **Labor Force:** About 15 million with 70% in agriculture and 8% in industry **Foreign Trade:** Exports ($300 million, 1978) consist mainly of coal, rubber, ores, wood, tea, spices, and coffee. Imports ($900 million, 1978) include rice, heavy machinery, transportation equipment, vehicles, chemicals, and fuels **Principal Trade Partners:** USSR, Eastern Europe, Japan

Vital Statistics: Birthrate, 41.5 per 1,000 of pop. (1975); death rate, 20.5 **Life Expectancy:** 44 years **Health Statistics:** About 750 per hospital bed; 11,000 per physician **Infant Mortality:** North—N.A.; South—36.7 per 1,000 births **Illiteracy:** About 25% **Primary and Secondary School Enrollment:** 10,923,436 (1976) **Enrollment in Higher Education:** 100,027 **GNP Expended on Education:** N.A.

Transportation: Paved roads total 3,400 mi. **Motor Vehicles:** N.A. **Railway Mileage:** 1,718 **Ports:** Ho Chi Minh City, Haiphong, Da Nang, Qui Nhon, Cam Ranh, Ben Thuy, Hong Gai, Nha Trang **Major Airlines:** Air Vietnam **Communications:** Government controlled **Radio Transmitters:** North—3; South—27 **Receivers:** North—1,000,000 (1974); South—1,550,000 (1973) **Television Transmitters:** North—1; South—6 **Receivers:** North—N.A.; South—500,000 **Telephones:** North—N.A.; South—46,509 **Newspapers:** North—6 dailies

Weights and Measures: Metric system **Travel Requirements:** Traveler should consult U.S. Department of State

---

A unified Vietnam, from the China border to the Gulf of Siam, came into being on July 2, 1976. The formal reunification after 22 years of division came 16 months after the collapse and surrender of the South Vietnamese government in Saigon to its North Vietnamese conquerors. After 30 years of struggle against foreign powers and the regimes they fostered, revolutionary forces of Vietnam realized the goal of the late Ho Chi Minh. The Communists, with more than a little help from their friends, had all of Vietnam under one flag and one government. In the years since the fall of the Saigon Government the problems of peace have proved as hard to solve as those of war.

The split into North Vietnam and South Vietnam that marked the end of French presence and the beginnings of American involvement occurred in 1954. As a colonial war ended, a period of insurgency and war began. It was to last over two decades and leave a legacy of bomb craters, street rubble, bullet-pocked buildings, abandoned rice fields and patches of defoliated forest—in addition to the thousands of lost, maimed and dislocated Vietnamese people.

The long war that could not be won came to a close for U.S. troops in 1973. A peace accord that could not be enforced lasted only 20 months after the American withdrawal. The end to the tragic war came with unbelievable swiftness in April of 1975 as the Communist forces swept the coastal cities and took Saigon almost unopposed. The cost to the United States for its misadventure in Indochina was 57,000 lives and $150 billion.

For Vietnam, the process of rebuilding a shattered economy and restructuring society in the South left little time for looks backward. In the South a provisional government took over from the military and began the task of dealing with three million unemployed urban residents and reshaping the economy to fit a different ideology.

To achieve self-sufficiency in food the new unified government resettled millions of refugees from the cities into rural areas so they could resume food production. It is said that nearly 700,000 were moved from Saigon to work abandoned rice fields or develop new agricultural areas, and the population of Da Nang was reduced by half. For many, life in the "new economic zones" is tough, with former clerks, unaccustomed to manual labor, trying to coax crops from marginal lands.

The transfer of people also involves Northerners. Tens of thousands of civil servants, teachers and tax collectors have been moved to the South to provide a dependable cadre at lower echelons. Plans call for the eventual movement of millions from densely populated rural places in the North to the more agriculturally productive South.

To restore trade and industry the unified government has shown surprising flexibility and respect for private business. Factories that had not been abandoned by their owners were allowed to continue operating. However, inflation in Saigon (now called Ho Chi Minh City) has pushed up food prices while salaries have been cut.

Vietnam found itself involved in two wars in 1979, piling up further troubles for its wrecked economy and internal tumult—the latter attested to by an outflow of hundreds of thousands of refugees. The fighting in Cambodia seemingly ended on Jan. 7, when Vietnamese troops captured the enemy capital, Phnom Penh, but it turned into a guerrilla war, with Pol Pot's rebels controlling the countryside and the Vietnamese troops dominant around Phnom Penh. Then on Feb. 17, the Chinese, saying they wanted to "teach a lesson" to Vietnamese who allegedly crossed their border in hundreds of incidents, invaded northern Vietnam. The Chinese fought for four weeks, advanced no more than 20 miles, and then departed, calling their punitive invasion a victory. Vietnam's defenders obviously put up a strong fight, because months later China conceded that its own army suffered 20,000 killed and wounded. (China placed Vietnam's casulaties at 50,000.) The fighting did cause Vietnam to remove some veteran troops from Cambodia, China's ally, but Vietnam quickly sent great numbers of less-experienced troops to Cambodia.

The warfare and economic distress have made the Soviet Union a closer ally of the Vietnamese, who have a 2,000-year history of animosity toward the Chinese. Vietnam and the USSR signed a 25-year treaty of friendship and cooperation in 1978. By 1981, the Soviets were reported to be contributing about $1 billion a year to a Vietnamese economy beset by declining exports, a 100% annual rate of inflation, and a shortage of rice—a situation that had been aggravated by some of the century's worst floods in late 1978 and mid-1980.

HISTORY: The Vietnamese are believed to have originated in North China, from where they were slowly driven southward by the Han Chinese. By the 3rd century B.C., the Vietnamese had become settled in the Red River Delta in northern Vietnam. China annexed the region in the 2nd century B.C. and ruled it until 938 A.D., when independence was reestablished by Ngo Quyen. The new state gradually expanded, occupying much of Cambodia and southern Vietnam

1858: French and Spanish forces intervene in Vietnam's southern region of Cochin China to halt persecution of native Catholics

1862-67: Vietnam is forced to yield Cochin China to the French

1884: France establishes a protectorate over Annam, in central Vietnam, and over Tonkin, in the north

1887: Cambodia, Cochin China, Annam, and Tonkin are incorporated into the Indo-Chinese Union

1940-45: Vietnam is occupied by Japanese forces during World War II; with defeat impending, Japan grants Vietnam independence under a puppet government headed by Bao Dai, emperor of Annam; following Japan's surrender to the Allies, Communist Viet Minh guerrillas, under leadership of Ho Chi Minh, set up Democratic Republic of Vietnam

1946-54: Viet Minh wages war against the French for eight years, culminating in the defeat of French forces at Dien Bien Phu; armistice is signed under a series of agreements concluded at Geneva, providing for the partition of Vietnam along the 17th parallel, with the north going to the government of Ho Chi Minh and the south placed under the control of Saigon. The agreements provided for the joining of North and South Vietnam into one country by holding elections in 1956. These were never held

NORTH VIETNAM

1955: Ho Chi Minh visits Communist China and USSR and signs aid agreements with both

1956: Peasant revolts break out in opposition to government's land collectivization program, but are crushed by troops

1959: North Vietnam, working through Viet Cong guerrillas, instigates campaign of terror and subversion in South Vietnam in attempt to annex state and unify Vietnam under Communist rule

1964-65: U.S. planes bomb North Vietnamese military targets following attacks on U.S. warships in Gulf of Tonkin in 1964; sustained U.S. air attacks are begun in 1965 to stem flow of equipment and North Vietnamese troops into the south

1968: United States orders halt to all bombing north of 20th parallel; move leads to an agreement between Hanoi and Washington to open peace talks in Paris

1969: Ho Chi Minh dies

1971: North Vietnamese troops drive South Vietnamese forces from Laos after the latter fail to cut Ho Chi Minh Trail

1973: Peace agreement signed in Paris officially ends Vietnam War, though fighting continues on a diminished scale

1974-75: Fighting escalates as both North and South repeatedly violate the cease-fire agreement. A stepped-up Communist offensive in early 1975 results in the abandonment by Saigon forces of the Central Highlands. The last resistance from the Saigon government ends on April 30 as Viet Cong and North Vietnamese troops enter Saigon

SOUTH VIETNAM

1955: Bao Dai is deposed and a republic established under the presidency of former Prime Minister Ngo Dinh Diem; a U.S. military advisory group is set up in South Vietnam

1959-63: South Vietnamese Communist guerrillas, known as Viet Cong, wage war against Diem government; harsh security measures introduced by Saigon regime incur wide resentment; Buddhist monks immolate themselves to protest what they charge is persecution by Diem. After violent demonstrations the government is overthrown and Diem is murdered

1965: New military regime is formed, with Gen. Nguyen Van Thieu as chief of state and Air Vice Marshal Nguyen Cao Ky as premier; U.S. planes begin systematic bombing of North Vietnam, while in the south U.S. troop strength mounts to 200,000 men

1967: In South Vietnam's first national elections, Nguyen Van Thieu becomes president and Nguyen Cao Ky vice-president

1968: President Johnson announces a halt of U.S. bombings over most of North Vietnam; peace talks between United States and North Vietnam open in Paris

1970: South Vietnamese and U.S. troops invade Cambodia in drive against Viet Cong and North Vietnamese forces; Saigon troops continue operations after U.S. withdrawal

1971: South Vietnamese forces attempting to cut Ho Chi Minh Trail in Laos are driven out by North Vietnamese. Enemy steps up attacks in South Vietnam on eve of elections. Thieu runs unopposed for president and is reelected

1973: Paris peace agreement formally ends Vietnam War in January, but fighting continues on reduced level. The first prisoner exchanges worked out at the conference table begin

1974: Fighting intensifies in the central highlands near the Cambodian border; the Saigon government suspends its participation with the Viet Cong in Paris reconciliation talks

1975: North Vietnamese and Viet Cong forces step up their offensive in the South, seizing major cities. President Ford orders U.S. naval ships to help evacuate refugees. President Thieu resigns but the Viet Cong refuse to negotiate with the new South Vietnamese leadership. Communist troops enter and occupy Saigon. War ends as the South Vietnamese government unconditionally surrenders to the Viet Cong on April 29, 1975. Provisional Revolutionary Government takes control on June 6

UNIFIED VIETNAM

1976: First countrywide assembly elections are held April 25. North and South are officially reunited July 2. Rail link between Hanoi and Saigon reopened

1977: Security Council approves Vietnam membership in the UN. Border fighting flares up between Vietnam and Cambodia. Vietnamese face serious food problem, with rice shortage estimated at 18% of need. Talks with U.S. on establishing relations recess after making little progress; behind impasse is Hanoi's insistence that promise of U.S. aid be made before ties are established

1978: Government introduces new national currency, cracks down on black-marketeers. Vietnamese-Cambodian border war intensifies. Refugees reportedly leaving Vietnam at highest rate since end of war in 1975. President Carter approves interim refugee policy permitting admission of Vietnamese "boat people" refused asylum elsewhere. In July, Vietnam is admitted to Soviet bloc's economic and trade group; in November, Vietnam and the Soviet Union sign a 25-year friendship treaty. China blames Vietnam in first shooting incident along their mutual border, ends aid to Vietnam and closes Vietnamese consulates in southern China. Government inducts over 350,000 into armed forces "to defend country's territorial integrity against foreign aggressors" and to work at construction sites. The worst floods in 35 years destroy 500,000 homes and almost three million tons of rice. In December, Vietnamese troops advance into Cambodia

1979: Vietnamese troops, together with Cambodian rebels, capture Phnom Penh on Jan. 7. But the deposed Cambodian premier, Pol Pot, escapes, and some 130,000 Vietnamese are tied down in Cambodia fighting guerrillas. On Feb. 7, China invades Vietnam with 100,000 troops that penetrate 15 or 20 miles in four weeks. The main fighting is at Lang Son, which is evacuated. The Chinese depart, with both sides claiming victory. By midyear, the number of ethnic Chinese fleeing Vietnam is estimated at 300,000 in a 12-month span

1980: More than 200,000 Vietnamese soldiers remain in Cambodia, and 50,000 are still stationed in Laos. At home, at least 20,000 former Vietnamese bureaucrats, military and professional men, and others are confined to "re-education camps." Vietnamese troops stage two-day June attack on refugee camps in Thailand. Mid-year monsoon rains make three million homeless. A new constitution is announced

1981: Exodus of "boat people" increases again early in the year. China reports sporadic Vietnamese forays across its border, claims 150 Vietnamese died in a May clash

---

WESTERN SAMOA

Area: 1,133 sq. mi. **Population:** 156,000 (1980 est.)

Official Name: Independent State of Western Samoa **Capital:** Apia **Nationality:** Western Samoan **Languages:** Samoan, the predominant Polynesian language, and English are official **Religion:** The population is almost entirely Christian, with 50% Congregationalist, 20% Methodist, and 20% Roman Catholic **Flag:** A red field with a blue rectangle in the upper left corner bearing 5 white stars representing the Southern Cross **Anthem:** The Flag of Freedom **Currency:** Tala (0.94 per U.S. $1)

Location: South Pacific, forming part of an island group lying midway between Honolulu and Sydney, Australia. Western Samoa (14°S., 172°W.) consists of the islands of Savai'i and Upolu and seven smaller islands of which only Manono and Apolima are inhabited **Features:** The islands are formed mainly of volcanic rock, with coral reefs surrounding much of the coasts. Rugged mountain ranges form the core of the two main islands, and there are many dormant volcanoes and lava fields **Chief Rivers:** There are no large rivers

Head of State: Chief Malietoa Tanumafili II, born 1913, appointed in 1962; future holders of the office will be elected by the Legislative Assembly for 5-year terms **Head of Government:** Prime Minister Taisi Tupuola Efi, born 1948, reappointed 1979 **Effective Date of Present Constitution:** January 1962 **Legislative Body:** Legislative Assembly (unicameral), consisting of 47 members, 45 of whom are Samoans elected by family chiefs (*matai*), and 2 are elected by universal suffrage, all for 3-year terms **Local Government:** 24 legislative districts (*faipule*), grouped into 12 political districts. Local government is carried out by the village councils (*fono*)

Ethnic Composition: Samoans, who form the second-largest branch of the Polynesian race, constitute 88% of the population. Euronesians (of mixed Polynesian and European ancestry) make up 10%, and the rest consists of Europeans (700) and other Pacific Islanders **Population Distribution:** 21% urban **Density:** 138 inhabitants per sq. mi.

Largest City: (1976 census) Apia 32,099

Per Capita Income: $450 (1978) **Gross National Product (GNP):** $70 million (1978) **Economic Statistics:** There are no detailed GNP statistics available; however, industries include handicrafts, foods, fruit processing, clothing, soap, and furniture; and agricultural products include taro, timber, fish, coconuts, cocoa, bananas, and pineapples **Minerals and Mining:** None **Labor Force:** 38,200, with 90% in agriculture and fishing **Foreign Trade:** Exports, mainly copra, cocoa, bananas, timber, and taro, totaled $11 million in 1978. Imports, chiefly clothing and textiles, flour, canned fish and meat, motor vehicles, tobacco, sugar, and timber totaled $53 million **Principal Trade Partners:** New Zealand, Australia, Britain, West Germany, United States, Japan

Vital Statistics: Birthrate, 21.4 per 1,000 of pop. (1977); death rate, 3.4 **Life Expectancy:** 67 years **Health Statistics:** 214 inhabitants per hospital bed; 2,884 per physician (1977) **Infant Mortality:** 17.8 per 1,000 births (1977) **Illiteracy:** 10% **Primary and Secondary School Enrollment:** 51,025 (1977) **Enrollment in Higher Education:** 180 **GNP Expended on Education:** 3% (1977)

Transportation: Paved roads total 230 mi. **Motor Vehicles:** 3,200 (1976) **Passenger Cars:** 1,300 **Railway Mileage:** None **Ports:** Apia, Asau **Major Airlines:** Polynesian Airlines operates international and domestic flights **Communications:** Government controlled **Radio Transmitters:** 2 **Receivers:** 50,000 (1973) **Television Transmitters:** None; received from American Samoa **Receivers:** 1,800 **Telephones:** 3,800 **Newspapers:** 2 several times a week, 103 copies per 1,000 inhabitants

Weights and Measures: British standards are used **Travel Requirements:** Passport, no visa for stay up to 30 days

---

Western Samoa became, on January 1, 1962, the first fully independent Polynesian state. Until then, the country, along with Eastern Samoa, had been under foreign control or tutelage since the turn of the century. In 1899 the Samoan islands were apportioned between Germany, which got Western Samoa as a protectorate, and the United States, which obtained, and still holds, the eastern part as American Samoa. Western Samoa was held from 1914 to 1962 by New Zealand, which, after ousting the Germans in World War I, obtained a League of Nations mandate and then a UN trusteeship. Although independent, Western Samoa still has New Zealand handling its foreign relations.

Western Samoa is a nation in transition, struggling to preserve its traditional ways while grappling with a backward economy. The most striking of those ways, perhaps, is the social system, based on *aigas*, or extended family groups, which are headed by *matais*, or chiefs. The *matais* direct the use of *aiga* assets. Supported by most Western Samoans, the system is a conservative force that many observers feel hampers the country, but the government, now headed by younger men, points to the possibility of change.

Western Samoa's economy is predominantly agricultural but efforts are underway to develop its fishing industry and increase tourism.

HISTORY: Archaeological evidence indicates that Samoa may have been settled as far back as 1000 B.C., but little is known with certainty of its early history. The first Europeans to visit Samoa were the Dutch in 1722. Throughout the 19th century, the islands became pawns in a struggle for control by the United States, Germany, and Britain. After a brief attempt at tripartite control of Samoa, a treaty was signed in 1899 assigning Eastern Samoa to the United States and Western Samoa to Germany

1914-20: New Zealand occupies Western Samoa following outbreak of World War I and is later awarded mandate over islands by League of Nations

1927-36: Samoans and European settlers wage campaign of civil disobedience in opposition to the administration; campaign develops into movement for independence

1946: Western Samoa becomes United Nations trusteeship under continued supervision of New Zealand

1962: Western Samoa becomes independent, with Chief Tupua Tamasese Meaole and Chief Malietoa Tanumafili II as joint heads of state

1963: Tupua Tamasese Meaole dies, leaving Western Samoa with a single head of state

1970: Tamasese Lealofi IV is named prime minister as head of reform-minded government of younger men

1973: Fiame Mata'afa Mulinuu is elected prime minister

1975: Treaty is signed with EC. Mata'afa dies and is replaced by Tamasese Lealofi IV

1976: Taisi Tupuola Efi becomes prime minister

1979: Prime Minister Tupuola Efi barely retains post in 24-23 vote of the parliament following February 28 *matai* elections; criticized for seeking too rapid a rate of economic growth

1980: Government tightens controls on imports and overseas payments to offset loss of foreign exchange. Visiting Japanese mission is greeted by public demonstrations against dumping of nuclear wastes in the Pacific

---

YEMEN (YEMEN ARAB REPUBLIC)

Area: 77,220 sq. mi. **Population:** 7,080,000 (1978 est.)

Official Name: Yemen Arab Republic **Capital:** San'a **Nationality:** Yemeni **Languages:** Arabic is the official and universal language **Religion:** Islam is the state religion, with the population almost equally divided between the Zaidi Shi'ite and Shafai Sunnite sects **Flag:** Horizontal stripes of red, white, and black with a green star in the center **Anthem:** National Anthem, beginning "Peace to the land" **Currency:** Yemeni rial (4.56 per U.S. $1)

Location: Southwest Arabia. Yemen is bounded on the north and east by Saudi Arabia, on the south by Southern Yemen, and on the west by the Red Sea **Features:** The country consists of a semidesert coastal plain (the Tihama) along the Red Sea and a mountainous area in the interior which receives abundant rainfall **Chief Rivers:** There are no permanent rivers

Head of State: President: Col. Ali Abdullah Saleh, born 1942, elected July 1978 **Head of Government:** Premier Abdel Karim Iryani, appointed Oct. 15, 1980 **Effective Date of Present Constitution:** 1971, suspended 1974 **Legislative Body:** Constituent People's Assembly of 159 members **Local Government:** 10 governorates under appointed emirs, divided into 40 districts

Ethnic Composition: The population is predominantly Arab. 10% are Afro-Arabs, residing in the Tihama **Population Distribution:** 11% urban **Density:** 92 inhabitants per sq. mi.

Largest Cities: (1975 census) San'a 134,588, Hodeida 80,314, Ta'izz 78,642, Dhamar 19,467, Ibb 19,066, Al Beida 5,975

Per Capita Income: $543 (1979) **Gross National Product (GNP):** $2.8 billion (1979) **Economic Statistics:** About 50% of GNP comes from agriculture (cotton, Mocha coffee, livestock, cereals, vegetables, fruit). There is some light industry (textiles, food products) **Minerals and Mining:** The only industrial mining enterprise is the extraction of salt. There are traces of copper, coal, sulfur, gypsum and quartz **Labor Force:** 800,000; 70% of the population is engaged in agriculture and animal husbandry, and 13% in trade. Many work abroad **Foreign Trade:** Exports, mainly cotton, coffee, hides and skins, salt, and qat, totaled $2.1 million in 1979. Imports, chiefly textiles, machinery, fuels, foods, totaled $1.4 billion **Principal Trade Partners:** Southern Yemen, Saudi Arabia, Australia, EC countries, India, Japan

Vital Statistics: Birthrate, 49.6 per 1,000 of pop. (1975); death rate 20.6 **Life Expectancy:** 38 years **Health Statistics:** 1,443 inhabitants per hospital bed (1974); 17,175 per physician (1976) **Infant Mortality:** N.A. **Illiteracy:** 85% **Primary and Secondary School Enrollment:** 279,541 (1975) **Enrollment in Higher Education:** 2,408 **GNP Expended on Education:** 0.6% (1974)

Transportation: Paved roads total 300 mi. **Motor Vehicles:** 44,500 (1975) **Passenger Cars:** 14,000 **Railway Mileage:** None **Ports:** Hodeida, Mocha **Major Airlines:** Yemen Airways, government owned, operates domestic and international flights **Communica-**

tions: Government controlled **Radio Transmitters: 4 Receivers:** 90,000 (1976) **Television Transmitters: 2 Receivers:** N.A. **Telephones:** 5,000 (1975) **Newspapers:** 6 dailies, 10 copies per 1,000 inhabitants (1970)

Weights and Measures: Local units are used **Travel Requirements:** Passport, visa valid 3 months, $2 fee

---

Yemen is a land whose interior contains gauntly beautiful mountains and green, cultivated fields— a rarity in the Arabian peninsula—and whose crucially important location between the Gulf of Aden and the Red Sea, athwart the Arabian oil route to the West, has brought it a disproportionate degree of world attention.

Yemen remains a country that is difficult to govern, where tribal loyalties are stronger than national considerations. Those tendencies have been aggravated by a civil war (1962-1969), and by memories of ancient times when Yemen and Southern Yemen had common ties. The civil war began in 1962 as a revolt against Mohammed al-Badr, heir to a dynasty of Imams (religious rulers) who had become arbitrary and capricious. The rebels established a republic with Egyptian backing; the Imam continued resistance from the hills, with an army of tribesmen and mercenaries supported by Saudi Arabia. Egypt sent almost a third of its army to help the republic. Egypt and Saudi Arabia agreed to end their intervention in 1967, and the Imam's forces were defeated by those of the republic in 1969. But the republic was, and remained, unstable, plagued by coups and counter-coups.

In a 48-hour period in June 1978, the Presidents of both Yemen and Southern Yemen were killed. The violence began in Sa'na just as Yemen's President Ahmed Hussein al-Ghashmi, a close ally of Saudi Arabia, was about to consider Southern Yemen's proposals for a merger of the Yemens. Yemen, blaming Soviet-backed Southern Yemen for the killing, severed their relations. Two days later, Southern Yemen President Salem Rubaye Ali, a moderate Marxist, lost a power struggle with the ultraleftist general secretary of the country's National Liberation Front party, Abdul Fattah Ismail, whom Western and Arab observers suspect may have been behind Ghashmi's murder. Ghashmi was succeed by Ali Abdullah Saleh, and tensions with Southern Yemen continued to build. Southern Yemeni soldiers—with Soviet, Cuban, and East German help—invaded Yemen in February 1979. Saudi Arabia and the United States rushed arms to Yemen, and U.S. ships showed the flag in nearby waters. In March, the League of Arab States arranged a cease-fire; and a special force, under the League's command, was established to patrol the border. President Saleh and President Ismail met in Kuwait and drew up a plan to merge their two countries, but Ismail's resignation as president of South Yemen in early 1980 left the plan in abeyance.

HISTORY: Yemen formed part of what was known as Arabia Felix in classical times and was the site of a series of rich mercantile kingdoms. One of these was Sheba, or Saba, which flourished from about 750 to 115 B.C. The Sabaeans were superseded by the Himyarites, under whom Judaism and Christianity took root. Himyarite rule was ended in 525 by an invading force of Christian Ethiopians, who in turn were driven out by the Persians in 575

7th cent.: Islam is introduced

9th cent.: Yemen comes under the control of the Rassite dynasty, religious leaders, called imams, of the Zaydi sect, who lay the foundations of a theocratic political structure lasting to 1962

1517-1918: Ottoman Empire exercises nominal sovereignty

1948: Imam Yahya is assassinated; his son, Crown Prince Ahmad, defeats forces of new government and succeeds as imam

1958: Yemen and United Arab Republic (union of Egypt and Syria) form confederation called United Arab States

1961: Following Syria's withdrawal from UAR, President Nasser dissolves the association with Yemen, denouncing Imam Ahmad as a reactionary

1962: Ahmad dies and is succeeded by Crown Prince Mohammad al-Badr, who favors a neutralist foreign policy; he is overthrown by pro-Nasser army officers who proclaim a republic under the leadership of Col. Abdullah al-Salal; civil war breaks out between republican and royalist forces, who win the respective backing of Egypt and Saudi Arabia

1963: Egypt sends 40,000 troops to Yemen to assist republicans

1967: Egypt withdraws troops from Yemen; riots in San'a force al-Salal to form new government free of Egyptian influence; he is deposed, however, while on a visit to Moscow and a new republican government is set up; royalist forces move on San'a

1968: Republicans, aided by Soviet-built aircraft, regain initiative; royalists retreat, reorganize their forces and in an effort to widen their political base fill top posts with officials not related to the imam, who is deprived of all political power

1969: Republican government asserts that civil war has ended; Lt. Gen. Hassan al-Amri resigns as prime minister; a new cabinet is formed and Abdullah al-Karshumi becomes prime minister

1970: Amicable settlement is reached between republicans and royalists; Moshen al-Aini is named premier

1972: Yemen and Southern Yemen end hostilities after series of border clashes; they agree to future merger. Aini is replaced by Abdullah al-Hagri

1973: Border clashes resume between the two Yemens

1974: Hagri is replaced by Hassan Makki. Army ousts government in bloodless coup and establishes military junta headed by Col. Ibrahim al-Hamdi. Aini forms new government

1975: Premier Aini is replaced by Abd al-Aziz Ad al-Ghani

1977: Col. Ibrahim al-Hamdi is assassinated; new military rulers impose martial law, as Maj. Ahmed Hussein al-Ghashmi assumes leadership of government

1978: Constituent assembly formally elects Ghashmi president. Ghashmi is assassinated; Yemen blames Southern Yemen, severs relations. Ghashmi's murder is factor in overthrow two days later of Southern Yemen's President Rubaye Ali by colleagues in pro-Soviet National Front. Constituent People's Assembly elects Col. Ali Abdullah Saleh president

1979: Southern Yemen invades Yemen, which gets aid from United States and Saudi Arabia. Cease-fire agreement places Yemen-Southern Yemen border under patrol commanded by League of Arab States. Presidents Saleh and Ismail agree to merger plan

SOUTHERN YEMEN

Area: 111,101 sq. mi. **Population:** 1,853,000 (1978 est.)

Official Name: People's Democratic Republic of Yemen **Capital:** Aden **Nationality:** Southern Yemenite or Yemeni **Languages:** Arabic is the official language; Mahri is spoken in the east, and English is also widely understood **Religion:** 98% of the population are Sunni Moslems of the Shafai sect **Flag:** Horizontal stripes of red, white, and black with a red star on a blue triangle at the hoist **Anthem:** National Anthem (no words) **Currency:** Yemeni dinar (0.35 per U.S. $1)

Location: Southern part of the Arabian peninsula. Southern Yemen is bounded on the north by Saudi Arabia, on the east by Oman, on the south by the Gulf of Aden, and on the northwest by Yemen **Features:** A narrow, sandy plain along the coast gives way to mountainous terrain, interspersed with deep valleys. The land retains its mountainous character until it reaches the interior sands. Offshore islands include Socotra, Perim, and Kamaran **Chief Rivers:** There are no permanent rivers

Head of State and of Government: Chairman of the Presidium of the Supreme People's Council (President) and Prime Minister: Ali Nasir Mohammed, born 1938, appointed prime minister 1971, became head of state April 1980 **Effective Date of Present Constitution:** December 1, 1970 **Legislative Body:** Supreme People's Council (unicameral) of 111 elected members **Local Government:** 6 governorates under appointed governors

Ethnic Composition: The population is mainly Arab; Indians, Pakistanis, and Somalis constitute small minorities **Population Distribution:** 33% urban **Density:** 17 inhabitants per sq. mi.

Largest Cities: (1977 est.) Aden 285,373; (1972 est.) Mukalla 45,000, Seiyun 20,000

Per Capita Income: $402 (1979) **Gross National Product (GNP):** $716 million (1979) **Economic Statistics:** The subsistence economy is based on agriculture (sorghum, millet, wheat) and fishing, though some cotton is grown for export. Aden, a leading oil bunkering port, is slowly recovering with the reopening of the Suez Canal. There is an oil refinery, and some light industry **Minerals and Mining:** Salt **Labor Force:** 395,568 (1977), with 62% in subsistence agriculture, and 18% in industry, with 72% of the latter in oil refining **Foreign Trade:** Exports, mainly petroleum products, raw cotton, hides and skins, and fuel oil, totaled $187 million in 1975. Imports, chiefly rice, wheat flour, tea, cotton and rayon piece goods, and petroleum products, totaled $312 million **Principal Trade Partners:** Kuwait, Britain, Japan, Yemen, India, Iraq

Vital Statistics: Birthrate, 49.6 per 1,000 of pop. (1975); death rate, 20.6 **Life Expectancy:** 45 years **Health Statistics:** 648 inhabitants per hospital bed; 8,750 per physician (1976) **Infant Mortality:** 79.9 per 1,000 births **Illiteracy:** 72% **Primary and Secondary School Enrollment:** 236,162 (1974) **Enrollment in Higher Education:** 934 **GNP Expended on Education:** 3.9% (1976)

Transportation: Paved roads total 200 mi. **Motor Vehicles:** 22,400 (1976) **Passenger Cars:** 11,900. **Railway Mileage:** None **Port:** Aden **Major Airlines:** Democratic Yemen Airlines, government owned **Communications:** Government controlled **Radio Transmitters:** 4 **Receivers:** 100,000 (1976) **Television Transmitters:** 5 **Receivers:** 32,000 (1976) **Telephones:** 10,000 (1973) **Newspapers:** 3 dailies, 1 copy per 1,000 inhabitants (1973)

Weights and Measures: British standards are generally used in Aden; local measures are used in the rest of the country **Travel Requirements:** Traveler should consult U.S. Department of State for travel information

---

One of the poorest member of the Arab League, Southern Yemen comprises the former colony of Aden, at the southwestern corner of the Arabian peninsula, and a forbidding hinterland with poorly defined borders. Under British rule, the country was known as "Aden," and later as the "Federation of South Arabia." It declared independence in 1967 as "People's Republic of Southern Yemen." In 1970, the official name was changed to the "People's Democratic Republic of Yemen." Hopes for union with the neighboring "Yemen Arab Republic" exist in both states, but each wants union on its own terms.

With its oppressively hot climate and barren terrain, Southern Yemen has few natural resources and little industry, and relied heavily on foreign aid for its 1974-79 five-year development plan. About 62 percent of the population is engaged in primitive agriculture.

The departure of the British in 1967 and the closing of their naval base at Aden has further scarred the country's economy. Aden, once a flourishing port, now gripped by poverty, has not experienced the revitalization which was expected after the reopening of the Suez Canal in 1975.

In a two-day period in June 1978, as Yemen and Southern Yemen were about to work out details of a proposed merger, both Yemeni presidents were killed—the first in an unsolved assassination plot and the latter before a firing squad following a military coup led by Abdul Fattah Ismail, staunchly pro-Soviet general secretary of the country's National Liberation Front party. Assisted by the Soviet Union, East Germany, and Cuba, Southern Yemen invaded the Yemen Arab Republic in February 1979. Saudi Arabia and the United States supplied arms to the YAR. In March, both countries agreed to a resolution of the League of Arab States, under which their armies withdrew from the border, and soldiers under the League's command were stationed between them. The two Yemens agreed on a plan to merge their countries. But Ismail resigned as president in April 1980 and was replaced by the premier, Ali Nasir Mohammed, who reportedly opposed unification.

HISTORY: Southern Yemen formed part of the Minaean, Sabaean, and Himyarite kingdoms that flourished between 1200 B.C. and the 6th century A.D. The Himyarites were conquered in 525 by Christian Ethiopians, who were driven out by the Persians in 575. Islam was introduced in the 7th century and by the 9th century the highland regions of Southern Yemen had fallen under the rule of the Islamic religious leaders, or imams, of Yemen. The coastal area recognized the primacy of the Baghdad Caliphate and later fell under Egyptian and Turkish rule

19th cent.: Britain gains control of Aden and concludes treaties with southern Yemeni sheikhs to protect them from overland attack from Turkey

1914: Anglo-Turkish convention establishes demarcation line separating British-controlled Southern Yemen from Turkish-occupied Yemen

1959: Six of the states of Southern Yemen form Federation of Arab Emirates of the South, later renamed Federation of South Arabia

1963-66: Aden joins federation; revolt, led by National Liberation Front (NLF), breaks out against British rule; Britain promises to grant southern Yemen independence by 1968 but NLF refuses to negotiate; joined by other groups, it forms Front for the Liberation of Occupied South Yemen (FLOSY) but soon breaks away from new group

1967: NLF defeats FLOSY. Britain withdraws from Southern Yemen

1969: Qahtan al-Shaabi, Southern Yemen's first president, resigns and is replaced by a five-man Presidential Council

1970: Al-Shaabi is ousted from NLF

1971: Ali Nasir Mohammed al-Hassani is appointed prime minister, succeeding Mohammed Ali Haithem

1972: Southern Yemen and Yemen sign truce after brief border fighting; agreement provides for future merger

1973: Border clashes resume between the two Yemens

1974: U.S. charges Soviet military buildup in Red Sea-Indian Ocean area involves use of Aden as submarine base

1975: Perim Island, which controls southern entrance to Red Sea, is leased to Egypt, as agent for the Arab League, in return for financial aid. Discussion on unity with Yemen is revived

1976: A cease-fire between Southern Yemen and Oman, where Southern Yemen had supported left-wing rebel forces, comes into force

1978: Yemen blames Southern Yemen for assassination of Yemen president; two days later ultraleftist Abdul Fattah Ismail ousts President Salem Rubaye Ali, who is immediately tried and shot; five-man council headed by Prime Minister al-Hassani takes over government. Ismail is elected president

1979: Southern Yemen invades Yemen, withdraws after both sides agree to station between them a multinational patrol under command of League of Arab States. President Ismail and President Ali Abdullah Saleh of Yemen agree on merger plan

1980: Ismail resigns; succeeded by Ali Nasir Mohammed

YUGOSLAVIA

Area: 98,766 sq. mi. **Population:** 22,441,000 (1980 est.)

Official Name: Socialist Federal Republic of Yugoslavia **Capital:** Belgrade **Nationality:** Yugoslavia is officially made up of 6 "nations": Serbs, Croats, Slovenes, Macedonians, Montenegrins and Moslems. "Moslem" does not mean religion but nationality. Officially there exists no Yugoslav nation **Languages:** All "national" languages are official, with Serbo-Croatian serving as a lingua franca **Religion:** About 34% of the population belong to the Orthodox Church; 24% are Roman Catholics and 8% Moslems; 34% are of other or no affiliation **Flag:** Horizontal stripes of blue, white, and red with a red star edged in gold in the center **Anthem:** Fellow Slavs **Currency:** Yugoslav dinar (33 per U.S. $1)

Location: Southeast Europe. Yugoslavia, on the Balkan Peninsula, is bounded on the north by Austria and Hungary, on the east by Romania and Bulgaria, on the south by Greece and Albania, and on the west by the Adriatic Sea and Italy **Features:** The northern and eastern part consists of lowland hills and plains, with a few mountain ranges. The remaining two-thirds of the country is mountainous, culminating in the Dinaric Alps **Chief Rivers:** Danube, including its tributaries (Drava, Sava, Morava, Tisza), and Vardar

Head of State: President Sergej Kraigher, born 1914, succeeded to leadership of the 8-man collective presidency on May 15, 1981, for one-year term **Political Leader:** Lazar Mojsov, selected Oct. 1980 for a one-year term as Chairman of the Presidium of the Central Committee of the League of Communists of Yugoslavia **Head of Government:** Premier: Veselin Djuranović, born 1926, appointed president of 29-member Federal Executive Council in 1977 **Effective Date of Present Constitution:** February 1974 **Legislative Body:** Federal Assembly (bicameral), with a Federal Council of 220 proportionately elected delegates, and a Council of Republics and Provinces with 58 delegates **Local Government:** 6 republics and 2 autonomous provinces (within Serbia), each with its own locally elected executive council and assembly

Ethnic Composition: Serbs (40%), Croats (22%), Slovenes (8%), Bosnian Moslems (8%), Macedonians (6%), Albanians (6%), Montenegrins (2%), Hungarians (2%), Turks (1%) **Population Distribution:** 39% urban **Density:** 227 inhabitants per sq. mi.

Largest Cities: (Metropolitan Areas) (1976 est.) Belgrade 1,319,000; (1974 est.) Zagreb 700,000, Skopje 440,000, Sarajevo 400,000, Ljubljana 300,000; (1971 census) Novi Sad 216,358

Per Capita Income: $3,232 (1980) **Gross National Product (GNP):** $72 billion (1980) **Economic Statistics:** About 37% of the GNP is derived from mining and manufacturing (metals, woodworking, chemicals, textiles, food processing); 12% from agriculture (corn, wheat, fruits including wine grapes, sugar beets, tobacco, livestock, timber). Tourism is also an important source of revenue **Minerals and Mining:** Coal, copper, iron ore, lead, zinc, petroleum, bauxite, natural gas **Labor Force:** 8,900,000 (1979), with 32% in agriculture and 24% in industry **Foreign Trade:** Exports, chiefly fresh meat, ships, machinery, clothing, and hardwood, totaled $6.8 billion in 1979. Imports, mainly machinery and transport equipment, iron and steel, fuel raw materials, and chemicals, totaled $14 billion **Principal Trade Partners:** USSR, West Germany, Italy, United States, France, Poland, Iraq

Vital Statistics: Birthrate, 17.7 per 1,000 of pop. (1977); death rate, 8.4 **Life Expectancy:** 68 years **Health Statistics:** 167 inhabitants per hospital bed; 792 per physician (1975) **Infant Mortality:** 35.2 per 1,000 births (1977) **Illiteracy:** 15% **Primary and Secondary School Enrollment:** 3,772,937 (1976) **Enrollment in Higher Education:** 394,992 (1975) **GNP Expended on Education:** 5.4% (1976)

Transportation: Paved roads total 31,023 mi. **Motor Vehicles:** 2,123,100 (1977) **Passenger Cars:** 1,923,900 **Railway Mileage:** 6,190 **Ports:** Rijeka, Split, Dubrovnik, Kotor; on the Danube River: Novi Sad, Belgrade **Major Airlines:** Yugoslav Airlines operates domestically and internationally **Communications:** Government owned **Radio Transmitters:** 487 **Licenses:** 4,526,000 (1976) **Television Transmitters:** 430 **Licenses:** 3,463,000 (1976) **Telephones:** 1,431,000 (1976) **Newspapers:** 26 dailies (1975), 80 copies per 1,000 inhabitants (1976)

Weights and Measures: Metric system **Travel Requirements:** Passport, visa valid up to 1 year, no fee **International Dialing Code:** 38

A perennial subject of debate among orthodox Communists has been whether Yugoslavia is really Communist. The Yugoslavs insist they are. Others insist that they are not and that Yugoslavia's brand of political ideology is more Titoism than Communism. The question is now being asked after President Josip Broz Tito died in 1980: Can Titoism survive in Yugoslavia without Tito?

The Communist party of Yugoslavia was renamed the League of Communists of Yugoslavia in 1952. It has remained the dominant political force. But some scope for political activity is provided by the less disciplined Socialist Alliance of Working People of Yugoslavia, to which all League members and about half of the other adults belong. There are few state or collective farms; agriculture is dominated by private small holdings. Most businesses are managed by councils elected by the workers, and workers have been known to strike against their own councils. The worker-managed businesses compete vigorously against each other, and they are allowed to advertise. Individuals may own businesses with no more than five employees, and occupational licensure is almost unknown. More than half of Yugoslavia's trade is with non-Communist countries, and many Yugoslavs work in Western Europe, entering and leaving Yugoslavia across an open frontier. The press is not strictly controlled, and foreign publications are available to those who can read them.

The political system features a parliament with genuine independent power and a decentralization of authority among the nationality sub-republics. Yugoslavia is made up of many different peoples—notably the Serbs, Croats, Slovenes, and Macedonians—and their rivalry has not been diminished by the attempt to give each group a sense of political and cultural independence.

In 1974, Marshal Tito had himself proclaimed president for life and confirmed plans for Communist collective leadership of Yugoslavia after his death. In January 1980, Tito fell ill and had his leg amputated due to poor blood circulation. He grew steadily worse and died on May 4, at the age of 87. His funeral in Belgrade was attended by the heads of state or delegates from 115 nations.

As Tito lay dying, leadership of the Yugoslav presidency and Communist party began to rotate among the leaders of the country's six republics and two autonomous provinces. The goal was to avert ethnic rivalries for power while preserving Yugoslavia's independence and structure of a workers' state.

After 1948, when Yugoslavia was expelled from the world Communist movement, Marshal Tito moved closer to and received much aid from the United States, Britain, and France. After the reconciliation with the Soviet Union in 1955, Yugoslavia tended to follow the Soviet line on many world issues. Nevertheless, it sought a measure of independence in foreign policy by rallying African and Asian countries into a bloc of non-aligned nations. Yugoslavia's relations with the Soviet Union grew cool following the Russian invasion of Czechoslovakia in 1968, and again in 1979 after the Soviet invasion of Afghanistan.

HISTORY: In ancient times, what is now Yugoslavia was inhabited chiefly by Illyrian peoples who came under Roman rule in the 1st century B.C. In the 6th century A.D., Slavic immigrants settled in the country; their languages and cultures gradually became dominant. Most of the Yugoslav (Southern Slav) peoples were conquered by the Ottoman Empire in the 14th and 15th centuries. The House of Hapsburg pushed back the Turkish tide, and, by 1878, ruled Croatia, Slovenia, and Bosnia-Hercegovina. Montenegro had maintained a precarious independence, and Serbia had become independent in the 19th century, and had assumed the leadership of the movement for a Pan-Slav state

1914-15: Serbia and Montenegro are overrun by Central Powers in World War I, precipitated by assassination of Archduke Francis Ferdinand at Sarajevo, in Bosnia, by a Serbian nationalist

1918: Kingdom of Serbs, Croats, and Slovenes is proclaimed under the rule of King Peter I of Serbia

1929: Alexander I, Peter's successor, establishes dictatorship following moves toward separatism by Croatia; country's name is changed to Yugoslavia

1934: Alexander is assassinated in Marseilles by Croat terrorist; his son succeeds as Peter II under the regency of Prince Paul, Alexander's cousin

1941: Yugoslavia signs Berlin-Rome-Tokyo Pact; Prince Paul and his pro-German government are ousted in bloodless coup; new government signs nonaggression pact with USSR; Germany and Italy, joined by Hungary and Bulgaria, invade Yugoslavia, which collapses a week later

1943: Civil war breaks out between Chetniks, a Serbian resistance force headed by Draja Mikhailovich, and Communist partisans led by Josip Broz Tito

1944: Tito's forces expel Germans

1945: Monarchy is abolished and the People's Republic of Yugoslavia is proclaimed under Tito's leadership

1946: Tito launches vigorous program of socialization; political opposition is crushed and Mikhailovich executed; Roman Catholic Church comes under government attack, culminating in arrest and imprisonment of Archbishop Aloysius Stepinac

1948: Yugoslavia is expelled from Cominform after Tito resists Soviet attempts to control his regime; Tito begins to develop "national communism" and turns to West for aid

1960: Yugoslavia moves toward closer relations with Moscow

1968: Soviet-led invasion of Czechoslovakia draws warning from Yugoslav Communists that Yugoslavia will defend its independence

1972: Tito introduces presidency of Yugoslavia, a collective body designed to rule the country after he dies

1973: Tito purges Serbian and Slovenian Communist party leaders accused of "liberalism;" new constitution calls for collective presidency of Yugoslavia

1976: Tito attends European Communist party meeting, ending Yugoslav boycott of such Communist conferences since 1957

1977: U.S. agrees to expand military ties with Yugoslavia. Government frees dissident author Mihajlo Mihajlov in amnesty affecting 723 prisoners

1978: Tito visits U.S. China's Hua Guofeng visits Yugoslavia

1980: Tito dies at the age of 87 after long illness. Vice President Lazar Kolisevski heads collective presidency, which is to rotate annually among Communist leaders of the republics and autonomous provinces; Cvijetin Mijatović takes office as president for one-year term on May 15

1981: Albanian nationalist students demanding autonomy for Kosovo province clash with police at Pristina University, which then is closed by authorities. Sergej Kraigher takes his one-year turn as president of the republic

ZAIRE

Area: 918,962 sq. mi. **Population:** 27,869,000 (1979 est.)

Official Name: Republic of Zaire **Capital:** Kinshasa **Nationality:** Zairian **Languages:** French is the official and only common language; about 700 languages and dialects are spoken, the four serving as linguas franca being Lingala, Kingwana, Kikongo, and Tshiluba **Religion:** About 60% Christian (75% Roman Catholic); most of the remaining population practices traditional religions, especially animism **Flag:** A green field with yellow disc, in which a brown hand holds a red and brown torch **Anthem:** Song of Independence **Currency:** Zaire (3.7 per U.S. $1)

Location: South-central Africa. The Republic of Zaire is bordered on the west and north by the Congo, the Central African Republic, and Sudan; on the east by Uganda, Rwanda, Burundi, and Tanzania; and on the south by Angola and Zambia. Its only outlet to the ocean is a narrow strip of land on the north bank of the Congo (Zaire) estuary on the Atlantic **Features:** The huge Congo Basin, a low-lying, basin-shaped plateau sloping toward the west, is covered by tropical rain forest. Surrounding it are mountainous terraces on the west, plateaus merging into savannas to the south and southeast, and dense grasslands toward the northwest. High mountains lie to the east **Chief Rivers:** The Congo (Zaire) and its many tributaries, including the Ubangi, Aruwimi, Lindi, Lualaba, Lomami, Lomela, Momboyo, Kasai, Kwango, and Kwilu

Head of State and of Government: President: Lt. Gen. Mobutu Sese Seko, born 1930; seized power in a coup in 1965, reelected 1977 for a second seven-year term. He is assisted by the first state commissioner (premier), Joseph Nsigna (Singa Udjuu), appointed Apr. 1981 **Effective Date of Present Constitution:** Feb. 1978 **Legislative Body:** National Legislative Council (unicameral), with 268 members, elected for 5 years. Actual power resides with the president, as head of the Political Bureau of the Popular Revolutionary Movement (MPR) **Local Government:** 8 regions and Kinshasa

Ethnic Composition: There are some 200 tribal groups, which can be divided into 3 main categories: the Negroes (Bantu [80%], Sudanese, and Nilotics); the Hamites; and the Pygmies **Population Distribution:** 30% urban **Density:** 30 inhabitants per sq. mi.

Largest Cities: (1974 est.) Kinshasa 2,008,352, Kananga 601,239, Lubumbashi 403,623, Mbuji-Mayi 336,654, Kisangani 310,705, Bukavu 181,774, Kikwit 150,253, Matadi 143,598

Per Capita Income: $142 (1980) **Gross National Product (GNP):** $4.1 billion (1980) **Economic Statistics:** About 17% of GNP comes from industry (food processing, consumer durables, and construction materials); 15% from public administration; 15% from commerce and transportation; 15% from subsistence production; 13% from agriculture (coffee, rubber, and palm oil); 7% from mining **Minerals and Mining:** The country is the world's largest producer of industrial diamonds and cobalt; copper provides one-half of export earnings. Other important minerals include bauxite, gold, cassiterite, manganese, oil, and zinc **Labor Force:** 8.3 million, with about 75% in agriculture **Foreign Trade:** Exports, chiefly copper, cobalt, zinc, diamonds, coffee, palm oil and rubber totaled $1.3 billion in 1978. Imports, mainly machinery, transportation equipment, textiles, fuel, and foodstuffs, totaled $597 million **Principal Trade Partners:** Belgium, United States, Italy, France, West Germany, Britain, Japan

Vital Statistics: Birthrate, 45.2 per 1,000 of pop. (1975); death rate, 20.5 **Life Expectancy:** 44 years **Health Statistics:** 327 inhabitants per hospital bed; 28,802 per physician (1973) **Infant Mortality:** 104 per 1,000 births **Illiteracy:** 70% **Primary and Secondary School Enrollment:** 3,875,143 (1974) **Enrollment in Higher Education:** 21,021 (1974) **GNP Expended on Education:** 4.2% (1970)

Transportation: Paved roads total about 1,650 mi. **Motor Vehicles:** 161,200 (1974) **Passenger Cars:** 84,800 **Railway Mileage:** 3,593 (1970) **Ports:** Matadi, Banana, Boma **Major Airlines:** Air Zaire provides domestic and international services **Communications:** Partly government owned **Radio Transmitters:** 22 **Receivers:** 2,448,000 (1974) **Television Transmitters:** 3 **Receivers:** 7,000 (1976) **Telephones:** 48,000 (1976) **Newspapers:** 11 dailies, 9 copies per 1,000 inhabitants (1974)

Weights and Measures: Metric system **Travel Requirements:** Passport, visa valid 1 to 3 months, $4 fee, 1 photo

Torn by bloody strife through more than half of its first decade of independence, Zaire's early name of Congo had been almost a synonym for disorder. For 85 years the big African country—its area equal to that of the United States east of the Mississippi—was the possession of Belgium. While Belgian administration checked tribal enmities, colonial mo-

nopolies reaped the wealth of ivory, gold, copper, and other minerals. Plantations used labor under conditions little different from slavery.

Although the colonial regime grew less harsh in the 20th century, with missionary schools and better economic treatment for Zairians (Congolese), Belgium administrators did little to prepare for self-government.

In 1960, spurred by rebellion in Zaire and the wave of decolonization elsewhere in Africa, the Belgian government reluctantly acceded to the independence demands of Zaire leaders headed by Joseph Kasavubu and Patrice Lumumba. The calm, conservative Kasavubu, who became the first president, and other leaders favored a loose federation, while the passionate, radical Lumumba, who became premier, wanted a strong central government. And with the formal grant of independence on June 30, 1960, the issue remained basically unresolved.

Peaceful independence lasted only five days. On July 5 the army mutinied, public authority broke down and on July 10 Belgian troops intervened to protect Belgian nationals caught in a wave of terror. On July 11 Moise Tshombe, governor of Katanga, declared his mineral-rich province an independent country.

With a UN force backing up the national army, there began the long struggle to quell the Katangan secession. The Katangan forces, with a hard core of white mercenaries—les affreux ("the frightful ones")—put up a stiff resistance and it was not until mid-1963 that Tshombe was defeated and forced into exile.

Meanwhile, breakaway governments arose in South Kasai and in Kivu Province. Following a quarrel between Kasavubu and Lumumba, the national army commander, Col. Joseph D. Mobutu, a tough, Israeli-trained paratrooper, took over the government on September 5, 1960 and expelled Soviet and Communist-bloc diplomats and technicians.

The following November, the deposed Lumumba was captured while trying to flee to Kivu Province. Lumumba was taken to Katanga and assassinated in February 1961, becoming a martyr for third-world radicals. That same month Mobutu returned the reins of government to Kasavubu and four groups then contended for power. The country was not unified until 1963.

In 1964 when Zaire seemed to be pulling itself together, Kasavubu, in a gesture of national reconciliation, recalled Tshombe from exile and made him premier. There followed renewed rebellion by former Lumumba followers. The rebels, however, were soon defeated in an attack by Belgian paratroopers brought in by U.S. planes.

But neither Tshombe nor his successor could end the country's malaise of disunity. (Tshombe went into exile and died in Algeria in 1969.) Mobutu, now a general, seized power in November 1965. He reduced provincial authority and began building a strong central government to unify the country's hundred tribes. In a campaign for "African authenticity," in 1971 he changed the name of his country to Zaire.

Mobutu Sese Seko—as the president renamed himself—proved to be an effective salesman in promoting foreign investment to develop his nation's industries. However, by 1975, his mismanaged fiscal policies had resulted in an economic crisis which has persisted: an extremely high rate of inflation, unemployment of more than half of the urban work force, a declining standard of living, and a foreign debt approaching $5 billion.

An important factor in Zaire's economic dislocation is the concentration of most of its mineral wealth in the southern province of Shaba (formerly Katanga). From there the most practical route for shipment abroad is the railroad through Angola to the Atlantic port of Benguela. Mobutu at first backed the guerrilla forces opposed to the Popular Movement for the Liberation of Angola, but after the Movement's victory in 1976 he threw his support to this regime which was backed by Cuba and the Soviet Union. Zaire was then dealt a double blow. The Angolan guerrillas sabotaged the Benguela railroad and have kept it closed. Moreover, the leftist government of Angola has aided Katangan rebels in two invasions of Shaba—in 1977 and 1978—from Angola. With military help from Belgium and other countries, Zairean forces were able to repulse both attacks.

HISTORY: Pygmy tribes are believed to be among the earliest inhabitants of Zaire. Bantus from eastern Africa and Nilotes from the Nile region later entered the area. The Bantus established several kingdoms, including Bahuba, Baluba, and the Congo. When Portuguese explorers arrived at the mouth of the Zaire (Congo) River in the 15th century, the kingdom of the Congo included what is now Zaire and Angola

1879-84: Henry Stanley explores Zaire on behalf of Belgian king
1885: Leopold II sets up the Congo Free State and becomes its absolute monarch
1908: Congo Free State becomes Belgian Congo
1960: Colony is granted independence; within a week Congolese Army mutinies and Belgian troops intervene to protect Belgian nationals. Premier Moise Tshombe of Katanga, the Congo's richest region, proclaims his province an independent country; Albert Kalonji proclaims the independence of part of Kasai Province. At the request of the central government, UN troops are sent to the Congo to maintain order. Intense rivalry breaks out between Joseph Kasavubu, the head of state, and his premier, Patrice Lumumba; Col. Joseph Mobutu, commander of the Congo Army, seizes control of the government
1961: Mobutu returns reins of government to Kasavubu. Lumumba is killed under mysterious circumstances and his death plunges the Congo into further strife
1962-63: Heavy fighting takes place between UN troops and Katanga forces; secession of Katanga is ended
1964: Tshombe, who had gone into exile, is invited to return and is sworn in as Congo's new premier
1965: Tshombe is dismissed and goes into exile. Mobutu again stages military coup and overthrows Kasavubu government
1967: Mobutu announces new constitution providing for a federal system of government, with strong president and unicameral legislature. Central government takes over assets of Union Minière, the rich Belgian copper mining company in Katanga
1969: Kasavubu dies in March; Tshombe, captive in Algeria, in June
1970: Mobutu elected president for a new 7-year term
1971: The name of the republic is changed to Zaire
1973: Many foreign-owned firms are nationalized
1974-75: World price of copper falls, earnings are cut
1976: Angolan war disrupts export of Zaire copper. Mobutu establishes relations with Agostinho Neto's victorious Marxist government in Angola after backing losing pro-Western faction
1977: Shaba Province invaded by former Katangan soldiers; Moroccan troops, and French, Belgian and U.S. aid end threat. Mobutu wins new seven-year term as president
1978: About 4,000 Angolan-based Katangan rebels capture towns in Shaba; France and Belgium drop in paratroopers to rout rebels. Zaire and Angola agree to establish full ties and reopen rail line from Kolwezi to Angolan coast
1979: A $150-million conditional credit from International Monetary Fund improves recovery effort. Mpinga Kasenda is removed as prime minister on corruption charges and replaced by Boboliko Lokonga. Drought causes severe food shortages. Mobutu seeks to improve relations with neighbor states and Soviet bloc while keeping friendship with West
1980: Widespread discontent results from country's continuing economic problems. Zaire fails to meet strict conditions for second part of IMF loan. Consultation group of 9 industrial powers, IMF, World Bank and EEC decides in May to recommend more aid for Zaire. Nguza Karl-I-Bond named premier
1981: Joseph Nsigna, a planter and cattleman from the central Bandundu region, succeeds Nguzu as premier in April. Zaire announces intent to market its diamonds independently of De Beers Consolidated Mines Ltd., which controls about 85% of the world supply of uncut diamonds

---

ZAMBIA

Area: 290,586 sq. mi. **Population:** 5,679,808 (1980 census)
Official Name: Republic of Zambia **Capital:** Lusaka **Nationality:** Zambian **Languages:** The official language is English. Some 70

different Bantu languages and dialects are spoken, but 5 main languages are recognized for educational and administrative purposes: Nyanja, Bemba, Lozi, Luvale, and Tonga **Religion:** Most of the African population follow traditional religions. Christians number about 900,000, and the small Asian community practices Islam and Hinduism **Flag:** A green field with a swatch in the lower right corner of red, black, and orange vertical stripes topped by an orange flying eagle **Anthem:** National Anthem, beginning "Stand and sing of Zambia, proud and free" **Currency:** Zambian kwacha (.82 per U.S. $1)

Location: South-central Africa. Landlocked Zambia is bordered on the north by Zaire, on the east by Tanzania and Malawi, on the southeast by Mozambique, on the south by Zimbabwe, Botswana, and Namibia, and on the west by Angola **Features:** Most of the land mass is a high plateau lying between 3,500 and 4,000 feet above sea level. In the northeast the Muchinga Mountains exceed 7,000 feet in height. Elevations below 2,000 feet are encountered in the valleys of the major river systems. There are 3 large natural lakes: Bangweulu, Mweru, and Tanganyika, all in the northeast **Chief Rivers:** Zambezi, Luangwa, Chambeshi, Kafue, Luapula

Political Leader and Head of State: President: Dr. Kenneth David Kaunda, born 1924, head of the United National Independence party, reelected 1978 **Head of Government:** Prime Minister Nalumino Mundia, appointed Feb. 1981 **Effective Date of Present Constitution:** Aug. 1973 **Legislative Body:** National Assembly (unicameral), consisting of 125 members elected for 5 years, and 10 appointed members **Local Government:** 9 provinces, each administered by a cabinet member

Ethnic Composition: Over 98% of the population are Africans belonging chiefly to various Bantu-speaking tribes. There are approximately 40,000 Europeans and Asians **Population Distribution:** 43% urban **Density:** 20 inhabitants per sq. mi.

Largest Cities: (1980 census) Lusaka 538,469, Kitwe 314,794, Ndola 282,439, Mufulira 149,778, Chingola 145,869, Kabwe 143,635, Luanshya 132,164, Livingstone 71,987

Per Capita Income: $455 (1980) **Gross National Product (GNP):** $2.7 billion (1980) **Economic Statistics:** Quarrying and mining account for 50% of the GNP. Agriculture (tobacco, corn, peanuts, cotton) accounts for 11%; indigenous manufacturing (food processing, textile, furniture and construction materials) for 8% **Minerals and Mining:** Zambia is a ranking producer of copper; cobalt, lead, zinc, and unexploited deposits of iron are also abundant **Labor Force:** 402,000 wage earners (1977); 23% in government, 15% in mining, 10% in manufacturing, 9% in agriculture, 9% in commerce and 6% in transportation **Foreign Trade:** Exports, mainly refined copper, lead, zinc, cobalt, and unmanufactured tobacco, totaled $1.4 billion in 1979. Imports, chiefly machinery and transportation equipment, petroleum products, manufactured articles, chemicals, and food totaled $748 million **Principal Trade Partners:** Britain, Japan, West Germany, United States, South Africa, China

Vital Statistics: Birthrate, 51.5 per 1,000 of pop. (1975); death rate, 20.3 **Life Expectancy:** 47 years **Health Statistics:** 250 inhabitants per hospital bed (1975); 8,159 per physician (1971) **Infant Mortality:** 160 per 1,000 births **Illiteracy:** 72% **Primary and Secondary School Enrollment:** 945,441 (1975) **Enrollment in Higher Education:** 8,403 (1975) **GNP Expended on Education:** 6.7% (1976)

Transportation: Paved roads total 3,410 mi. **Motor Vehicles:** 171,900 (1976) **Passenger Cars:** 93,500 **Railway Mileage:** 1,360 **Ports:** None **Major Airlines:** Zambia Airways operates domestically and internationally **Communications:** Government owned **Radio Transmitters:** 22 **Receivers:** 110,000 (1976) **Television Transmitters:** 4 **Receivers:** 25,000 (1976) **Telephones:** 55,000 (1976) **Newspapers:** 2 dailies, 22 copies per 1,000 inhabitants (1975)

Weights and Measures: Metric system **Travel Requirements:** Passport, visa, $3.50 fee

---

The land above the Zambezi River, Zambia was called a "rich pauper" when, as the former British protectorate of Northern Rhodesia, it adopted a new name and became independent in 1964. The designation was based on the fact that while the country produced great wealth in copper, most Zambians gained barely enough to eat from their meager agricultural economy. Since then President Kenneth D. Kaunda has taken forceful measures to end the paradox. By 1975 Zambia assumed full control of its copper industry.

The government has faced a costly adjustment in trade and transportation in line with black Africa's boycott of Rhodesia (now Zimbabwe). Zambian copper, which formerly had gone out through Rhodesia, was rerouted through Tanzania. The Tanzam railroad, built to link Zambian copper mines with Indian Ocean ports, was completed in 1976.

Kaunda has committed Zambia to a form of socialism which he calls "humanism," designed to satisfy all Zambians' requirements through even distribution of the nation's wealth.

In December 1972 a bill went into effect making the governing United National Independence party (UNIP) Zambia's only legal political party. At the same time, President Kaunda ordered UNIP officials owning businesses to convert them into producers' cooperatives or relinquish their managing directorships.

After Kaunda allowed Patriotic Front guerrilla fighters from Rhodesia to establish bases in Zambia, those bases became subject to repeated air and ground attacks. Many Zambian civilians were killed, Lusaka's new rail link to Indian Ocean ports was broken, and the country's economy suffered severely. Since the struggle in Zimbabwe ended in 1979, efforts to revive the Zambian economy have been handicapped by continuing low prices for copper, chronic strikes by the miners, and general social unrest. In a bid to make peace with the unions, Kaunda in 1981 had expelled union officials readmitted to UNIP, and he appointed Nalumino Mundia, a man experienced in labor relations, as prime minister.

HISTORY: The history of the territory constituting present-day Zambia before the coming of the white man is sparse. The first European to penetrate into the region was the Scottish missionary David Livingstone, who made extensive explorations of the area between 1851 and 1873. In 1891, the British South Africa Co., which was developing the local copper resources, took over administration of the territory, naming it Northern Rhodesia

1924: British South Africa Co. is relieved of the administration of Northern Rhodesia

1930-44: Discovery of large copper deposits brings rush of Europeans to Northern Rhodesia

1953-63: Northern Rhodesia is part of the Federation of Rhodesia and Nyasaland

1964: Northern Rhodesia becomes independent republic of Zambia; Kenneth Kaunda, leader of the ruling United National Independence party, becomes the nation's first president

1967: Zambia accepts offer by Communist China to finance 1,000-mile railroad linking Lusaka with Dar es Salaam

1968: Kaunda is reelected president

1969: Kaunda announces measures for government takeover of country's $1.2-billion copper industry from foreign owners

1973: New constitution is enacted to coincide with new one-party system of government. Kaunda is reelected for third term

1976: Angolan MPLA government recognized and Rhodesian guerrillas aided; Tanzam Railway is completed

1978: Zambia undertakes austerity measures to meet International Monetary Fund terms for $390-million loan needed to bolster ailing economy. Rhodesia raids guerrilla camps in Zambia. Kaunda is reelected president without opposition

1980: Leaders of 9 nations meet in Lusaka to develop a regional economic plan aimed at less dependence on white-ruled South Africa. Government nationalizes petroleum supplies held by 5 international companies and launches a 10-year plan to increase food production. Industrial strikes are banned. China promises aid to repair railroad damaged in Zimbabwe struggle. Kaunda announces failure of an attempt in October to overthrow him; claims South Africa supported plot

1981: Government tightens restrictions on use of foreign exchange funds, and, in May, obtains a $944 million loan from IMF to aid Zambia's economic development. Zambia expels 2 U.S. diplomats June 23, charging that they are C.I.A. agents

---

ZIMBABWE

Area: 150,803 sq. mi. **Population:** 7,360,000 (1980 est.)

Official Name: Republic of Zimbabwe **Capital:** Salisbury (Harare) **Nationality:** Zimbabwean **Languages:** English, the official language, is spoken by the white population and a great number of Africans; the chief Bantu languages are Shona and Ndebele **Religion:** Over 50% practice a combination of animism and Christianity. There are also 24% Christians (mainly Anglicans) and some Moslems **Flag:** 7 equal horizontal stripes of green, yellow, red,

black, red, yellow and green separated by a narrow black border from a white triangle at the hoist. The triangle contains a representation of the Great Zimbabwe bird superimposed on a red five-pointed star **Anthem:** Rise, O Voices of Zimbabwe **Currency:** Zimbabwe dollar (0.63 per U.S. $1)

Location: South-Central Africa. Landlocked Zimbabwe is bordered on the north by Zambia, on the east by Mozambique, on the south by the Republic of South Africa, and on the west by Botswana **Features:** Most of the country is a high, rolling plateau between 3,000 and 5,000 feet above sea level. The land is largely South African veld, or grassland, with scattered shrubs or trees **Chief Rivers:** Zambezi, Limpopo, Sabi, Gwaai, Shangani

Head of State: President: Rev. Canaan Banana, born 1935, took office April 18, 1980, for 6-year term **Head of Government:** Prime Minister Robert Gabriel Mugabe, born 1924, sworn in April 18, 1980 **Effective Date of Present Constitution:** April 18, 1980 **Legislative Body:** Parliament (bicameral), consists of (1) a House of Assembly with 100 members elected for 5 years from 80 black voters' roll constituencies and 20 white roll constituencies, (2) a 40-member Senate for 5 years consisting of 14 Senators elected by the 80 black members of the Assembly, 10 Senators chosen by the 20 white members of the Assembly, 10 Senators elected by traditional chiefs, and 6 appointed by the President **Local Government:** 7 provinces under appointed commissioners

Ethnic Composition: 95.2% are indigenous Bantus, principally Mashona and Matabele; 4.3% are of European descent, chiefly British **Population Distribution:** 20% urban **Density:** 49 inhabitants per sq. mi.

Largest Cities: (1977 est.—Metropolitan Areas) Salisbury (Harare) 601,000, Bulawayo 359,000, Gwelo 68,000, Umtali 61,000, Que Que 54,000, Wankie 33,000, Gatooma 32,000

Per Capita Income: $509 (1980) **Gross National Product (GNP):** $3.8 billion (1980) **Economic Statistics:** In 1973 about 36% of GNP was derived from trade and services; 25% from manufacturing (metals and metal products, food processing, textiles, clothing and footwear, beverages, tobacco, chemicals); 17% from agriculture (Oriental tobacco, stock-raising, maize, groundnuts, cotton); and 6% from mineral wealth **Minerals and Mining:** There are deposits of asbestos, chrome ore, coal, copper, gold, iron ore, limestone, lithium, nickel, phosphate rock, and tin **Labor Force:** 991,600 (1978) **Foreign Trade:** Exports, mainly tobacco, asbestos, copper, apparel, meats, chrome, and sugar, totaled $919 million in 1978. Imports, chiefly machinery and transportation equipment, textiles, petroleum products, iron and steel products, fertilizers, and foodstuffs, totaled $677 million **Principal Trade Partner:** South Africa (pre-1980)

Vital Statistics: Birthrate, 47.9 per 1,000 of pop. (1975); death rate, 14.4 **Life Expectancy:** 52 years **Health Statistics:** 316 inhabitants per hospital bed; 5,700 per physician (1973) **Infant Mortality:** 17 per 1,000 births **Illiteracy:** 61% **Primary and Secondary School Enrollment:** 963,671 (1976) **Enrollment in Higher Education:** 1,076 (1972) **GNP Expended on Education:** 3.6% (1973)

Transportation: Paved roads total 5,007 mi. **Motor Vehicles:** 250,000 (1974 **Passenger Cars:** 180,000 **Railway Mileage:** 2,133 **Ports:** None **Major Airlines:** Air Zimbabwe operates domestic and international flights **Communications:** Government and privately controlled **Radio Transmitters:** 22 **Receivers:** 255,000 (1976) **Television Transmitters:** 5 **Receivers:** 72,000 (1976) **Telephones:** 190,000 (1976) **Newspapers:** 3 dailies, 18 copies per 1,000 inhabitants (1975)

Weights and Measures: British standards are being replaced by the metric system

---

At midnight April 17, 1980, with Britain's Prince Charles presiding and representatives of a hundred other countries looking on, the Union Jack was lowered for the last time in Salisbury and the striped flag of Zimbabwe went up in its place. The last but one (South Africa) of white-dominated, black-majority states of Africa had been recognized by the world as an independent country. Robert Mugabe, whose Zimbabwe African National Union party had won in free elections, was installed as prime minister. Soldiers of the former Rhodesian army, black and white, paraded side by side with guerrillas against whom they had so recently fought.

Lord Soames, the British governor who had ruled the country since the 1979 cease-fire, said, "This has been nothing less than a series of miracles." As it indeed had been. When, in 1964, Britain granted independence to Northern Rhodesia (now Zambia) and Nyasaland (Malawi), it denied such status to Southern Rhodesia until a government representative of the black majority as well as the whites was assured. A year later, Ian Smith, the white prime minister, unilaterally declared Rhodesia to be independent. Britain said the government was illegal, and the United Nations refused to recognize it.

With Smith's proclamation of a State of Rhodesia in March 1970, following a referendum the previous year in which white Rhodesians formally renounced their last British tie, loyalty to the Crown, there was an eventual withdrawal of all diplomatic missions except that of South Africa.

Despite diplomatic isolation, a total British trade blockade, UN economic sanctions, and its landlocked position in southern Africa, Rhodesia did manage to survive as an economic outcast.

Inspired by successful moves to black rule in the countries surrounding Rhodesia on three sides, nationalists organized the Patriotic Front to try to topple the Smith government by means of guerrilla warfare. Leading the estimated 12,000 guerrillas were Joshua Nkomo, patriarchal figure of Zimbabwe nationalism and Soviet-backed leader of the wing based in Zambia, and Robert Mugabe, whose Chinese-trained forces operated from bases in Mozambique and Tanzania.

Smith steadfastly refused to support equal voting rights as a step toward black rule. He relented only when escalating guerrilla warfare left him no alternative and not before safeguards had been built into an agreement to protect white interests. Finally, he gave in to a plan worked out with moderate black leaders for a black-majority government in which the white minority would retain much of the power. In May 1979, the name of the country was changed to Zimbabwe Rhodesia. Methodist Bishop Abel Muzorewa, who became the country's first black prime minister, faced insurmountable problems, notably the opposition of Patriotic Front leaders who regarded him as a puppet of white Rhodesians.

Bowing to the pressures, Muzorewa agreed late in 1979 to step down pending supervised elections in which all factions, including those of the Patriotic Front, could be represented. An uneasy truce with the guerrilla forces followed as Lord Soames became the interim governor. But after many threatened boycotts, the elections were held Feb. 27-29, 1980. The Zimbabwe African National Union (ZANU) won 57 of the 80 seats allotted to blacks in a 100-member House of Assembly, and Robert Mugabe, the revolutionary most feared by the white Rhodesians, became prime minister. "There is a place for everybody in this country," he said, seeking to reassure the whites and also the blacks who had supported Nkomo and Muzorewa.

Mugabe included two prominent whites in his broad-based cabinet and offered the presidency to his rival, Nkomo, who refused the figurehead post but accepted appointment as Minister of Home Affairs. Mugabe also encouraged white civil servants to remain, promising them security in their positions and prospects for promotion.

Since the coming of independence, some whites, and blacks as well, have been murdered. There have been several armed clashes between members of the rival independence factions. Whites have left the country at an average rate of over 1,200 per month. However, the bloodbath, wholesale exodus of whites, confiscation of property and near-anarchy predicted for Zimbabwe by many pundits have failed to materialize. The change from white rule to black has been remarkably peaceful. Some of Mugabe's followers complain that he is moving too slowly toward socialism and black supremacy.

HISTORY: The remains of Stone Age culture dating back 500,000 years have been found in Zimbabwe and it is thought that the Bushmen, who still survive, mostly in the Kalahari Desert of Botswana, are the last descendants of these original inhabitants. The first Bantu are thought to have reached Zimbabwe between the 5th and 10th centuries A.D., though southward migrations continued long after. The first Europeans to visit the region were 16th-century Portuguese explorers

1889-97: Cecil Rhodes forms the British South Africa Company; assisted by British troops, the company conquers the Mashona and Matabele; European colonists follow

1923: Southern Rhodesia becomes a self-governing colony within the British Commonwealth

1953: Britain establishes the Federation of Rhodesia and Nyasaland, linking Northern Rhodesia (now Zambia), Southern Rhodesia, and Nyasaland (now Malawi); the Federation remains dominated by the European settlers

1964: Federation of Rhodesia and Nyasaland is dissolved. Britain grants the two northern territories independence under African majority rule, but refuses independence to Southern Rhodesia unless representative government is assured

1965: Prime Minister Ian Smith unilaterally declares Rhodesia's independence from Britain and promulgates a new constitution. Britain declares the Smith government an illegal, rebel regime

1966: UN Security Council calls on all member states to break off economic relations with Rhodesia; only Portugal and South Africa refuse to impose an embargo

1968: Smith government executes five black Africans convicted of murder, despite commutation of death sentences by Queen Elizabeth; act is viewed as most serious act of defiance against Britain by break-away Rhodesian regime

1969: Government publishes proposed constitution designed to perpetuate white minority rule. In a referendum in which 81,583 whites as against 6,634 blacks are eligible to vote, the Smith regime wins a mandate to place the proposed constitution before the Legislative Assembly and to proclaim Rhodesia a republic and cut formal remaining ties to British Crown

1970: Rhodesia proclaims a republic, severing ties with Britain; neither Britain nor the United Nations grant recognition

1974: Government suppression of black nationalists resumed as terrorism against white minority continues

1975: New 90-mile railway link with South Africa is opened

1976: John Wrathall is sworn in as Rhodesia's second president. Mozambique closes its 800-mile border with Rhodesia

1978: On March 3, Prime Minister Smith and three moderate nationalist leaders agree on plan for black-majority rule; while containing many guarantees for whites. Guerrilla leaders denounce pact as "sellout." Bush war turns bloodier

1979: Blacks, voting in national elections for first time, elect Bishop Abel Muzorewa as first black prime minister. Zimbabwe Rhodesia is born May 31. Guerrilla war continues until Muzorewa agrees to turn over rule to a British governor pending all-party elections in 1980

1980: Robert Mugabe's Zimbabwe African National Union is victorious in elections; Canaan Banana, a Methodist minister, is chosen as president. Britain turns over reins of government of the new Republic of Zimbabwe to Mugabe, as prime minister, April 17. Major Western powers offer financial and technical assistance. Zimbabwe severs diplomatic, but not trade, ties with South Africa. Cabinet Minister Edgar Z. Tekere, indicted on charge of murdering a white farmer, is acquitted after a long trial

1981: Tekere is dismissed from cabinet; Nkomo accepts a ministry without portfolio related to defense and public-service affairs. Zimbabwe establishes diplomatic relations with Soviet Union, but requires latter to cut its long-held ties with Nkomo faction. Conference of 31 nations and 26 international agencies pledges $1.8 billion in aid to Zimbabwe. Salisbury is to be renamed Harare

TERRITORIES AND DEPENDENCIES

Anguilla—*Status:* British Dependency. *Population:* 6,600 (1977 est.). *Area:* 35 sq. mi. *Capital:* The Valley (760).

The island of Anguilla lies in the northern part of the Leeward group of the Lesser Antilles, in the eastern Caribbean. Anguilla is approximately 65 miles N.N.W. of St. Christopher and 9 miles from its neighbor, St. Martin.

Anguilla is a flat, coralline island with its highest point at 213 feet above sea level. The island is covered with low scrub and fringed with white coral-sand beaches. Apart from sheep and goats, Anguilla's main product is salt. The majority of the population are African or of mixed descent, with a small white minority.

Anguilla unilaterally seceded from the associated state of St. Christopher-Nevis-Anguilla when it was formed in 1967. Britain took control of the island in 1969 after landing an "invasion" force, and in 1971 began direct administration of the island. On February 10, 1976, Anguilla was established as a self-governing British dependency with a new constitution, but it remained a legal part of the associated state. The charter created a seven-member Legislative Assembly and a chief minister, and gave the British Commissioner authority over defense, police and civil service, and foreign affairs. On December 16, 1980, Anguilla received full legal separation from St. Christopher-Nevis. The chief minister, Ronald Webster, was reelected in 1981. British engineers have installed a telephone system and improved the roads. In the early 1980s, more hotels were built to support a bid for additional tourist business.

Antigua—*Status*: British Associated State. *Population*: 74,000 (1978 est.). *Area*: 171 sq. mi. *Capital*: St. John's (25,000).

Antigua, with its dependency of Barbuda and the small uninhabited island of Redonda, is in the Leeward Islands of the West Indies at the eastern edge of the Caribbean, 250 miles southeast of Puerto Rico. Its topography is rolling; its climate is tropical and subject to drought. Most of the people are of Negro-white descent. English is the formal language, but a patois is commonly spoken.

Primarily agricultural, Antigua produces cotton and sugar. Bananas, citrus fruits, yams, and rice are also grown. Tourism is increasingly important.

There is a Crown-appointed governor, a premier, and a parliament consisting of an elected House of Representatives and an appointed Senate. Antigua's government is ruled by Prime Minister Vere Bird's Labour party, which was returned to power in April 1980. Antigua was scheduled for independence in late 1981, but there were difficulties due to secession sentiment on Barbuda, where, early that year, voters elected separatist candidates to all local posts.

Ashmore and Cartier Islands—*Status*: Australian External Territory. *Population*: Uninhabited. *Area*: 1.9 sq. mi.

These islands lie in the Indian Ocean, about 300 miles north of Broome in northwestern Australia (12°S.,123°E.). They are administered by the Northern Territory.

Australian Antarctic Territory—*Status*: External Territory of Australia. *Population*: Uninhabited. *Area*: 2,362,875 sq. mi. (of which 29,251 sq. mi. are ice shelf).

Australia claims all Antarctic islands and territories south of 60°S and between 45° and 160°E, except for French-claimed Adélie Land. (The United States does not recognize any Antarctic claims south of 60°S.)

Bermuda—*Status*: British Colony. *Population*: 158,000 (1978 est.). *Area*: 21 sq. mi. *Capital*: Hamilton (3,000).

The colony is in the western Atlantic (32°20'N.,64°40'W.), less than 600 miles east of Cape Hatteras, North Carolina. There are some 150 small islands, about 20 of which are inhabited. The main islands are close together, connected by bridges, and collectively called Bermuda. The islands are rocky, with lush vegetation. The climate, moderated by the Gulf Stream, is warm and pleasant. About two-thirds of the people are African or of mixed descent, the rest mostly British in origin. They are predominantly Protestant.

Tourism, largely from the United States, accounts for 70 percent of the economy. Also important is the provision of goods to British and American servicemen stationed on the islands. Almost all food is imported.

In 1968 a new constitution put most executive powers in the hands of the premier, who is the head of the majority party in the elected House of Assembly of the bicameral legislature (the oldest among British possessions). The Crown-appointed governor retains direct responsibility for external affairs, defense and internal security.

On March 10, 1973, the governor, Sir Richard Sharples, and his aide-de-camp were assassinated. The execution of their two convicted assassins, both black, in 1977 sparked rioting, with great property loss and lasting damage to tourism. The industry was disrupted again in May 1981 by a runaway strike that shut down hotel operations and other services. It was attributed in part to frustration over Bermuda's high cost of living and the continuing political domination of the conservative United Bermuda party.

Bouvet Island (Bouvetøya)—*Status*: Norwegian Dependency. *Population*: Uninhabited. *Area*: 23 sq. mi.

Situated between the extreme tip of South Africa and the Antarctic coast, Bouvet is in the South Atlantic Ocean at 54°26'S and 3°24'E. It is volcanic in origin and almost completely ice-covered. There are fur seals and seals of other varieties, penguins, and petrels.

British Antarctic Territory—*Status*: British Colony. *Population*: Uninhabited, except for personnel at scientific stations. *Area*: 600,000 sq. mi. *Administrative Center*: Stanley, Falkland Islands.

The territory, created in 1962, extends below 60°S. from 20° to 80°W. and includes the South Orkney Islands, the South Shetland Islands, and the Antarctic Peninsula. Argentina claims the area and occupied one of the South Shetlands in 1976, resulting in a British protest.

British Indian Ocean Territory—*Status*: British Colony. *Population*: Unknown since removal of original inhabitants in 1971. *Area*: 29 sq. mi. (land). *Administration Center*: London (U.K.).

The territory, made a separate colony in 1965, includes only the Chagos Archipelago at 7°20'S and 72°25'E, formerly a dependency of Mauritius; Diego Garcia (11 sq. mi.) is the largest island. The climate is tropical, with heavy rainfall.

The territory is administered from London by a commissioner. Diego Garcia is the site of a major U.S. air and naval base. Mauritius has reinstated its claim to Diego Garcia.

British Virgin Islands—*Status*: British Crown Colony. *Population*: 12,000 (1978 est.). *Area*: 59 sq. mi. *Capital*: Road Town (3,500) on Tortola.

These are in the eastern Caribbean, east of the U.S. Virgin Islands. They include 36 islands, 16 of which are inhabited, plus numerous rocks and *cays*. Tortola, Virgin Gorda, Anegada, and Jost Van Dyke are the largest islands. The climate is subtropical and pleasant; rainfall is light. Almost all the people are of African descent.

Cattle raising, farming, and fishing are the main activities. The shortage of water is a major problem. Tourism is an increasing factor in the economy.

The colony is governed by a Crown-appointed governor assisted by an appointed executive council and a chief minister. There is a partly elected legislative council.

Brunei—*Status*: British Protected State. *Population*: 213,000 (1979 est.). *Area*: 2,226 sq. mi. *Capital*: Bandar Seri Begawan, formerly Brunei Town (50,000).

This sultanate is on the north coast of Borneo, being two enclaves within the Malaysian state of Sarawak, washed by the South China Sea. The climate is tropical and humid, the rainfall heavy. The population is more than half Malay and is largely Moslem. Chinese are the second-largest element, and there are Dayak groups.

Oil and natural gas are the major factors in Brunei's economy, making it the richest state in Southeast Asia. Rice, cassava and bananas are grown.

Britain is responsible for Brunei's defense and foreign relations. A Crown-appointed high commissioner conducts relations between the two states. There is a council of ministers, presided over by the sultan. In 1967, after 17 years of rule, the Sultan, unwilling to bow to British demands for more representative government, abdicated and was succeeded by his son. In 1970, the new ruler dissolved the partly elected legislative council in favor of an entirely appointive body. Under a 1971 agreement with Britain, Brunei is fully self-governing in internal affairs. In 1979 it was announced in London that Brunei is to become independent on January 1, 1984.

Cayman Islands—*Status*: British Crown Colony. *Population*: 16,677 (1979 census). *Area*: 100 sq. mi. *Capital*: George Town (7,617) on Grand Cayman.

Consisting mainly of three islands—Grand Cayman, Little Cayman, and Cayman Brac—this colony is in the Caribbean about 175 miles west of Jamaica. Grand Cayman is flat and rockbound, protected by coral reefs. The climate is tropical, hot and humid. About one-half of the people are of mixed Negro-white descent, about a third of European, and the rest of African ancestry.

Seafaring, commerce, and banking are the principal occupations. Tourism is important. Scuba divers are attracted to the Caymans—considered one of the world's best diving destinations—by the clear waters, wrecks, shallow reefs, walls, and caves.

There is a Crown-appointed governor, a partly elected legislative assembly and an executive council.

Ceuta and Melilla—*Status*: Under Spanish sovereignty. *Population*: Ceuta, 67,187; Melilla, 65,271 (1970 census). *Area*: Ceuta, 7.5 sq. mi.; Melilla, 4.8 sq. mi.

These two enclaves are on the Mediterranean coast of Morocco. Ceuta is opposite Gibraltar; Melilla, some 200 miles farther east, is on a rocky promontory. A good deal of fish are caught and exported from both towns. Ceuta, with a splendid climate, is increasingly visited by tourists. In 1975 Morocco laid formal claim.

Channel Islands—*Status*: British Crown Bailiwicks. *Population*: 130,000 (1978 est.). *Area*: 74 sq. mi.

These islands lie 80 miles south of the English coast, off the northwest coast of France. They consist of Jersey, Guernsey, and the latter's dependencies of Alderney, Brechou, Sark, Herm, Jethou, and Lihou. Ecrehou Rocks and Les Minquiers are dependencies of Jersey. The land is low and undulating and the climate mild with about 40 inches of annual rainfall. The people are mainly of Norman descent, with some of Breton ancestry. French is the official language of Jersey, English of Guernsey; in some country districts of Jersey and Guernsey and throughout Sark, a Norman-French dialect is spoken. English, however, is commonly used throughout the islands.

The main occupations are agriculture, dairying, and tourism. Agriculture is highly specialized, with Guernsey being noted for its hothouse tomatoes and cut flowers, Jersey for new potatoes and open-grown tomatoes. The farms of Jersey and Guernsey are, typically, tiny fields, the result of centuries of subdivision among heirs.

The Crown appoints the chief executives of Jersey and Guernsey, both of whom have the titles of lieutenant-governor and commander-in-chief. Jersey's partly elected legislature is called the States of Jersey, and St. Helier is the administrative center. The legislative body of Guernsey, partially elected, is the States of Deliberation. St. Peter Port is Guernsey's administrative center. Alderney and Sark have local legislative bodies subordinate to that of Guernsey. St. Anne is the administrative center of Alderney, Creux that of Sark. The head of Sark is *Le Seigneur de Sercq*.

Chilean Antarctica—*Status*: Chilean Dependency. *Population*: No permanent inhabitants. *Area*: 482,502 sq. mi.

Chile claims the Antarctic (or O'Higgins) Peninsula in the Antarctic, lying between 59° and 67°W. Parts of the area are also claimed by Great Britain and Argentina.

Christmas Island—*Status*: Australian External Territory. *Population*: 3,184 (1980). *Area*: 52 sq. mi. *Administrative Center*: Flying Fish Cove (1,300).

The island is in the Indian Ocean (10°30′S.,105°40′E.) some 1,630 miles northwest of Perth, Australia, and 225 miles south of the island of Java. It is hilly and rather barren. The climate is warm and dry. Over half the people are Chinese, with some Malayans and fewer Europeans.

Phosphate extraction, undertaken by the governments of Australia and New Zealand, is the island's only economic activity. Most of the deposits are expected to be exhausted at the end of this century.

Clipperton Island—*Status*: French Dependency. *Population*: Uninhabited. *Area*: 2 sq. mi.

This atoll is in the eastern Pacific (10°17′N.,109°13′W.), 700 miles southwest of Mexico. Formerly part of French Polynesia, it was placed in 1979 under the direct control of the French government in Paris.

Cocos (Keeling) Islands—*Status*: Australian External Territory. *Population*: 487 (1980). *Area*: 5.4 sq. mi. *Administrative Center*: West Island (193).

The territory, two separate atolls with 27 small coral islands, is in the Indian Ocean about 1,725 miles northwest of Perth, Australia, at 12°05′S and 96°53′E. The principal islands are West, Home, Direction, South, and Horsburgh. The climate is pleasant, with moderate rainfall. Three-quarters of the people are Cocos Islanders living on Home Island; the rest are of European descent, most of whom live on West Island, and Asians. Coconuts are the principal product.

Though the islands were placed under Australian authority in 1955, it was not until July 1978 that the Australian government purchased the Cocos from their owner, John Clunies Ross. His family had been granted title to the islands in 1886.

Cook Islands—*Status*: New Zealand Dependency. *Population*: 18,200 (1979 est.). *Area*: 91 sq. mi. *Administrative Center*: Avarua (4,429) on Rarotonga.

Situated in the South Pacific some 2,000 miles northeast of New Zealand, between 8° and 23°S and 156° and 167°W, the islands are in two groups—the Northern, with seven islands or atolls, and the Lower or Southern Group, with eight. The Northern islands are low and barren; the Lower ones, which are more elevated and fertile, support the greater part of the population. The climate is warm and humid, and the islands sometimes experience hurricanes. The people are Polynesian Christians, similar in language and traditions to the New Zealand Maori.

The economy is basically agricultural, with citrus fruits and juices, copra, and tomatoes, among other produce, being exported. Manufactured wearing apparel is also exported. The sale of postage stamps to collectors throughout the world is an important source of revenue.

The Cooks attained internal self-government in 1965, with New Zealand responsible for external affairs and defense. There is a prime minister and cabinet, and an elected legislative assembly.

Coral Sea Islands Territory—*Status*: Australian External Territory. *Population*: 3 (1979 est.). *Area*: 8.5 sq. mi.

These islands, spread over 400,000 square miles, are situated east of Queensland, Australia, between the Great Barrier Reef and the 157°10′E meridian. One of the islands in the Willis Group has a meteorological station. The land consists mainly of scattered reefs and sand cays, many little more than sandbanks.

The Coral Sea Islands became an Australian External Territory on August 14, 1969, after having been acquired by acts of sovereignty over a number of years. The Australian Minister for Home Affairs is responsible for matters affecting the Territory.

Easter Island—*Status*: Chilean Dependency. *Population*: 1,598 (1970 census). *Area*: 63 sq. mi. *Settlement*: Hanga Roa (900).

Easter Island (*Rapa Nui* in Polynesian) lies in the Pacific Ocean some 2,300 miles west of Chile at 27°08′S. and 109°23′W. It is volcanic in origin, rising sharply from the sea. The climate is subtropical: warm, somewhat humid, and there is moderate rainfall. The island has no streams or lakes, and rainwater collects in the extinct volcanoes. The people, who are believed to be Polynesian in origin, speak Spanish. Easter Island is noted for its monolithic, stylized heads carved of volcanic rock.

Sheep raising is the most important activity. Despite the scarcity of fresh water, certain crops, including corn, wheat, taro, and tropical fruits, are grown. The island is administered as part of metropolitan Chile.

Faeroe Islands—*Status*: Integral part of the Danish Kingdom. *Population*: 44,000 (1980 est.). *Area*: 540 sq. mi. *Capital*: Tórshavn (11,618) on Streymoy.

These islands are in the Atlantic Ocean, north of Scotland, between 61°26′ and 62°24′N and 6°15′ and 7°41′W. Among the larger of the 18 islands (17 are inhabited) are Streymoy, Eysturoy and Váagar. They contain many lakes and peat bogs. The climate is mild, rainy, and foggy. The economy is based on fishing and sheep raising. Root vegetables, potatoes, and barley are grown. Norse-descended, the inhabitants speak an old Norse dialect; Danish, however, is the official language. Most of the people are Lutherans.

A self-governing community within the Danish kingdom with a Crown commissioner, the Faeroes have their own elected parliament (*Lögting*) which chooses an administrative body (*Landsstyri*). The Faeroes send two representatives to the Danish parliament.

Falkland Islands—*Status*: British Crown Colony. *Population*: 1,812 (1980 census). *Area*: 6,198 sq. mi. *Capital*: Stanley (1,079) on East Falkland.

Located in the South Atlantic some 500 miles northeast of Cape Horn, this group's major islands are East Falkland and West Falkland (4,618 sq. mi.), South Georgia (1,450 sq. mi.), and South Sandwich Islands (130 sq. mi.). East and West Falkland, which contain most of the population, consist largely of hilly moorland. The climate is cool and rainy, with persistently strong winds. The people are mostly of British origin.

Sheep farming is the main occupation, wool the main export. Offshore oil deposits are believed to exist.

The colony is administered by a Crown-appointed governor, assisted by partly elected councils. Argentina claims sovereignty over the islands, and refers to them as *Las Malvinas*. British and Argentine diplomats held discussions over the future sovereignty of the islands during the last four years.

French Guiana—*Status*: French Overseas Department. *Population*: 64,000 (1980 est.). *Area*: 35,135 sq. mi. *Capital*: Cayenne (29,405).

Situated on the northeast coast of South America, French Guiana is bounded by the Atlantic Ocean on the north, by Brazil on the east and south, and by Suriname on the west. Its coastline is 200 miles long, and Devil's Island (no longer used as a prison) is among its offshore islands. Extending almost 250 miles into the continent, French Guiana is divided into a low, swampy coastal area that ranges from 10 to 30 miles in width, and a plateau forming a series of low, steep hills inland. Most of the country is covered by rain forest. The climate is tropical, tempered by trade winds, and there is heavy rainfall from December to July. Ninety percent of the people live in the coastal areas; these are mostly a Negro-white mixture. In the interior are small groups of Indians (Carib, Arawak, Tupi-Guarani) and descendants of escaped African slaves.

Forestry, including wood-veneer production, is a major element in the economy. Gold is mined, and bauxite and tantalite deposits are to be exploited. Arable land is scarce and limited to the coastal areas, where manioc, yams, sugarcane, and bananas are grown. The main source of income is French investment and contributions toward operating expenses and welfare. France's space center at Kourou was the site of an 11-nation European vehicle launching project in the early 1980s.

Guiana is administered by a Paris-appointed prefect, assisted by an elected general council. It elects a deputy and a senator to the French Parliament.

French Polynesia—*Status*: French Overseas Territory. *Population*: 137,382 (1977 census). *Area*: 1,544 sq. mi. *Capital*: Papeete (51,987) on Tahiti.

These widely scattered islands in the south central Pacific lie between 7° and 27°S. and 134° and 155°W. The territory includes island groups totaling 118 islands and atolls. The Society Islands (named after the Royal Society by their British discoverers) are the most important group and include Tahiti and Moorea; they contain about 70 percent of the Territory's population. Other groups are the Marquesas Islands, the Tuamotu Archipelago, the Gambier Islands, and the Tubuai or Austral Islands. All of these except the Tuamotus are volcanic in origin and mountainous, with fast-flowing streams, and are often circled by coral reefs and lagoons. The climate is hot and humid, tempered by steady winds. The people are predominantly Polynesians, with some Asians and a smaller number of Europeans, principally French. More than 60 percent of the people are Protestants.

The economy is based on agriculture. The main crops are copra, vanilla, and coffee. All common tropical plants and most European vegetables are grown. There has been extensive building in the islands to provide facilities for French nuclear tests, the first of which was held in 1966 on Mururoa Atoll, 800 miles southeast of Tahiti. In August 1968 the French exploded their first H-bomb nearby, at Fangataufa Atoll. In 1971 and 1973, French nuclear test activity in the Mururoa Atoll area met with worldwide protest. French nuclear testing has since continued. Vocal adherents of autonomy increased their representation in the assembly in 1976, and again in 1977.

The Territory is administered by a Paris-appointed high commissioner, aided by a government council, with an elected territorial assembly, and elects two deputies and a senator to the French Parliament.

French Southern and Antarctic Territories—Status: French Overseas Territory. *Population*: 183 (1975). *Area*: 202,916 sq. mi. *Administrative Center:* Port-aux-Français (94) on Kerguélen.

These territories comprise a number of islands in the far southern Indian Ocean and Adélie Land on the Antarctic continent. The latter, with an area of 200,000 sq. mi., lies between 136° and 142°E. The Kerguélen Islands are between 48° and 50°S. and 68° and 70°E. The principal island, Kerguélen, has an area of 2,510 sq. mi. and is mostly mountainous. The Crozet Islands at 46°S. and between 50° and 52°E. are also mountainous, cold, windy, and inhospitable. Saint Paul Island is at 38°S. and 77°E. and its center is occupied by a large crater with volcanic hot springs. Amsterdam Island is at 37°S. and 70°E., and maintains a hospital.

The Territory, on which various research stations have been established, is under the authority of a high administrator assisted by a consultative council in Paris.

Gibraltar—Status: British Colony. *Population*: 29,760 (1979 est.). *Area*: 2.28 sq. mi. *Administrative Center:* Gibraltar.

Gibraltar is a tiny peninsula jutting into the western Mediterranean from Spain. It rises from a sandy plain to the 1,400-foot Rock, a cave-riddled, fortified limestone mass. The climate is temperate. The people are mostly of Genoese, Portuguese and Maltese descent. The language of the home is generally Spanish, with English the language of instruction in school. Most of the civilian population are Roman Catholics.

The colony has no natural resources other than its strategic position at the mouth of the Mediterranean, and is dependent on its naval and military bases, transshipments, dockyards, and tourist traffic.

Gibraltar is administered by a governor (also the commander of the fortress) appointed by the Crown, with the advice of the Gibraltar Council, the elected members of which compose a council of ministers presided over by a chief minister. There is also a partly elected House of Assembly.

Gibraltar was ceded in 1713 to Great Britain by Spain in the Treaty of Utrecht. Since 1964, Spain has been seeking its return, applying such pressures as the restriction of transit to and from the mainland. In 1967, the people of Gibraltar voted overwhelmingly to retain the British connection. At the end of 1968, the UN General Assembly's Trusteeship Committee called on Britain to surrender control to Spain. Talks have been held between Britain and Spain on the Gibraltar question since 1972.

Greenland (Kalátdlit-Nunât)—Status: Semiautonomous state of the Danish Kingdom. *Population*: 49,773 (1980 est.). *Area*: 840,000 sq. mi. *Capital*: Nûk (Godthab) (9,561).

Greenland, the largest island in the world, lies northeast of Canada between the Arctic Ocean on the north and the Atlantic Ocean on the south. Its ice-free areas—the coastal strips plus the coastal islands—cover 132,000 sq. mi. The rest of Greenland is sheathed in ice at places 11,000 feet thick. The climate is arctic, with considerable variation in temperature between localities. The population, predominantly Eskimo, with some Europeans, lives mostly on the west coast. Danish and Greenlandic are the official languages. The principal occupations are fishing and hunting.

Home rule was established on May 1, 1979, with Denmark retaining control of defense and foreign affairs, and retaining mineral rights. A prime minister, the leader of the majority party in the 21-member parliament (*Landsting*) and four secretaries preside over the government (*Landsstyre*). Greenland sends two elected members to the Danish Parliament.

Guadeloupe—Status: French Overseas Department. *Population*: 319,000 (1980 est.). *Area*: 687 sq. mi. *Capital*: Basse-Terre (16,000) on the island of that name.

Guadeloupe lies in the Leeward Islands of the West Indies. In addition to Guadeloupe proper (584 sq. mi.), which a narrow channel divides into two islands, Basse-Terre and Grande-Terre, there are the nearby dependencies of Marie-Galante, La Désirade, Îles des Saintes, and Isle de la Petite Terre. About 135 miles to the northwest are the dependencies of Saint Barthélemy and the French portion of Saint Martin.

Basse-Terre has a 4,000-foot active volcano, La Soufrière. Grande-Terre is low and encircled by coral reefs; it has the largest town in the department, Point-à-Pitre, twice the size of the capital. The climate is tropical, moderated by trade winds. Basse-Terre's mountains receive heavy rainfall, which feeds numerous streams. The people are blacks and, especially on the dependencies, descendants of Normans and Bretons who settled there in the 17th century, or a racial mixture.

The main crops are sugar and bananas, with cotton, sisal, coffee, vegetables and tropical fruits also grown. Fishing and rum production are significant activities.

Guadeloupe is administered by a Paris-appointed prefect and an elected general council; it elects three deputies and two senators to the French Parliament.

There were serious riots in Guadeloupe in 1967, reportedly sparked by an organization advocating independence. Although support for secession seems slight, another "liberation" group became active in 1980, staging a series of bombings, including one overseas, in the city of Paris, in early 1981.

Heard and McDonald Islands—Status: Australian External Territory. *Population*: Uninhabited. *Area*: 113 sq. mi.

These islands lie in the south Indian Ocean, 2,575 miles southwest of Perth, Australia, at 53°S.,73°E. Heard Island is mountainous, the McDonald Islands, small and rocky.

Hong Kong—Status: British Colony. *Population*: 4,900,000 (1979 est.). *Area*: 403 sq. mi. *Capital*: Victoria (658,042) on the island of Hong Kong.

The colony is on the southern coast of China about 80 miles southeast of Canton, and surrounded by the Chinese province of Guangdong. It includes Hong Kong proper, an island of about 30 sq. mi., many other islands, and Kowloon and the New Territories on the mainland. The New Territories (370 sq. mi., including a number of small islands) are held under a 99-year lease from China, which expires in 1997. Most of the area is either swampy or rocky and hilly. The climate is subtropical, with hot, humid summers and heavy rainfall, but can be chilly January to April.

The population density of Hong Kong is very high, as more than 80 percent of the people live in the urban area. An overwhelming number of them are Chinese, including more than a million refugees. (English and Chinese are both official languages.)

Hong Kong is a major center for shipping, banking, commerce and industry, situated as it is at a crossroad of world trade. Light industries, particularly machinery, textiles and clothing, are important. Tourism is important and growing. Agriculture and fishing are intensively practiced, but much food must be imported, mostly from China. A large part of the water supply must also be brought in from China. A tunnel now links Hong Kong Island with the mainland.

Hong Kong is administered by a Crown-appointd governor, advised by executive and legislative councils. Communist China officially claims Hong Kong.

Isle of Man—Status: British Crown Fiefdom. *Population*: 63,000 (1978 est.). *Area*: 227 sq. mi. *Capital*: Douglas (20,262).

Situated in the Irish Sea, the Isle of Man is about 35 miles from Northern Ireland and the northwest coast of England. The central mass consists of treeless hills, extending in the north and south to low-lying agricultural land. The climate is pleasant, with mild winters and cool summers. Wesleyan Methodists predominate, but there are Roman Catholics and Anglicans.

By far the most important factor in the economy is the tourist trade. The major export is kippered herring, processed from fish landed by a Scottish fleet. Oats are the main crop, and there is sheep raising and dairying.

The Isle is administered under its own laws (Acts of Parliament do not apply unless they specifically so note). The ruling body is the Court of Tynwald, composed of the Crown-appointed governor, a legislative council, and the elected House of Keys.

Jan Mayen—Status: Norwegian Dependency. *Population*: Uninhabited. *Area*: 143 sq. mi.

This island 300 miles north-northeast of Iceland at 71°N.,8°30'W. is bleak and desolate. The Norwegian government operates radio, meteorological, and navigational stations and an airstrip. Norway and Iceland are negotiating a settlement to their dispute over the offshore area around Jan Mayen.

Juan Fernández—Status: Chilean Dependency. *Population*: 540. *Area*: 70 sq. mi. (the two main islands). *Administrative Center:* Juan Bautista, on Robinson Crusoe Island.

This island group is in the Pacific some 360 miles west of Chile. Volcanic in origin, rugged and wooded, it was discovered in 1572 by Juan Fernández, a Spanish explorer. The two main islands, about 100 miles apart from east to west, are Robinson Crusoe (33°45'S.,79°W.) and Alejandro Selkirk (33°45'S.,80°45'W.). Lobster fishing is the main occupation.

Daniel Defoe's *Robinson Crusoe* is generally acknowledged to have been inspired by Alexander Selkirk's stay on Robinson Crusoe Island (1704-09).

Macau—Status: Portuguese Administered Territory *Population*: 271,000 (1978 est.). *Area*: 6.2 sq. mi. *Capital*: Macau (226,880).

Macau or Macao (*Ao-men* in Chinese) is situated on a small peninsula of the south coast of China. It lies at the mouth of the Pearl (Canton) River and 40 miles west of Hong Kong; the territory also includes two small islands. Macau proper is almost entirely urban, the islands forested. The climate is hot and humid, but sea breezes make the temperatures tolerable. Only about one percent of the population is Portuguese, the rest is Chinese.

Macau is almost completely dependent on imported food, mostly from China. Fishing, commerce, and, in recent years, light industry—textiles, clothing and electronics—are important. There is a brisk tourist trade, some attracted by Macau's gambling houses—which accounted for one-third of total government income in 1977.

The territory is administered by a Lisbon-appointed governor, a council, which serves as a cabinet, and a partially elected 18-member legislative assembly. China still officially claims dominion over Macau, although the Peking government has not pressed the issue.

Martinique—Status: French Overseas Department. *Population*: 308,000 (1980 est.). *Area*: 425 sq. mi. *Capital*: Fort-de-France (98,561).

This island is in the West Indies some 130 miles south of Guadeloupe. It is largely mountainous, and its two highest peaks are active volcanoes. In 1902, Mount Pelée erupted and destroyed the city of St-Pierre. The climate is tropical, tempered by the trade winds. The people are descendants of blacks, Europeans, and Carib Indians.

Martinique's economy is agricultural, with sugarcane, pineapples and bananas being the principal crops. Rum is distilled, and there is livestock raising and fishing. Tourism is increasing. The economy is heavily dependent on direct and indirect French subsidies, and substantial emigration to France has not solved the island's stubborn unemployment problem. Efforts have been made for some time to broaden and diversify Martinique's economic base. Yet demand for Martinique's major export crops is leveling off at a time when the number of young persons coming into the labor market is increasing as a result of a high birthrate since the 1940s. Martinique's international Airport is its principal transport link with the world, but the island is also visited by numerous oceangoing vessels and cruise ships.

Administration is in the hands of a Paris-appointed prefect with the aid of an elected general council of 36 members. Martinique elects three deputies and two senators to the French Parliament.

Strike violence in 1980 was blamed on Cuba; France flew in 225 elite police to assist in putting it down. Later France and Cuba concluded an economic agreement, and Cuba's Castro denied that he had intervened in Martinique. In late 1980 and early 1981 there were a few terrorist acts by separatists in Fort-de-France.

Mayotte—*Status:* French Territorial Collectivity. *Population:* 47,300 (1978 census). *Area:* 144 sq. mi. *Capital:* Dzaoudzi.

The easternmost of the Comoro Islands in the Indian Ocean (13°S.,45°E.), Mayotte is a volcanic island surrounded by coral reefs and islets, with a tropical climate. The population is of African, Arab, and Malagasy origin, and the majority are Moslems. French, Arabic, and Swahili are spoken. Most of the people are engaged in the production of such agricultural products as vanilla, sisal, sugarcane, essential oils, and rum.

An Arab dynasty from Shiraz reigned from the 16th century to 1843, when a French colony was established. It was attached first to Réunion and later to Madagascar as a part of the Comoro Islands territory. When a future Comoro Islands referendum was first announced in 1974, Mayotte was the only island to vote against it, and after the unilateral declaration of independence in 1975, Mayotte refused to be considered a part of the new republic. In 1976 an island referendum resulted in 99.41 percent voting to remain French, and two months later the status as a French Territorial Collectivity was approved. The island sends one deputy to the French Parliament.

Montserrat—*Status:* British Crown Colony. *Population:* 12,073 (1980 census). *Area:* 40 sq. mi. *Capital:* Plymouth (1,623).

Situated in the Leeward Islands of the West Indies, Montserrat is 260 miles southeast of Puerto Rico and north of Guadeloupe. In 1493, on his second voyage, Christopher Columbus reached the island and gave it its present name, after the mountaintop monastery in Spain. It has elevations of more than 3,000 feet, and the climate is tropical and humid. The people are mostly of Negro-white descent. English is the formal language and everywhere understood, but a patois is commonly spoken. As a result of an Irish settlement in the 1630s, many people on the island speak with a brogue.

The island is agricultural; cattle, fruit and vegetables being the main exports. Cotton and bananas are also exported and yams, rice, breadfruit, and corn are raised for food. Tourism is of increasing economic importance.

There is a Crown-appointed governor, an executive council and a partly elected legislative council. In 1967, Montserrat elected to remain a British colony.

Namibia—*Status:* In dispute; administered by South Africa. *Population:* 1,000,000 (1979 est.). *Area:* 317,827 sq. mi. *Capital:* Windhoek (61,369).

Namibia (formerly South-West Africa) is bounded by Angola on the north, by Zambia on the northeast, by Botswana on the east, by South Africa on the east and south, and by the Atlantic Ocean on the west. The Namib Desert, stretching for 1,000 miles along the coast, is uninhabited except for three towns, including the South African enclave of Walvis Bay (434 sq. mi.), and the diamond workings at the mouth of the Orange River in the south. The Kalahari Desert of sand and limestone is on the east. The Caprivi Strip, 20 to 60 miles wide and some 300 miles long, extends from the northeast corner of the country and separates Botswana from Angola. The greater part of the country consists of a plateau, averaging 3,600 feet, with scattered mountains. The climate is generally hot and dry. There are only a few rivers and water must generally be obtained from boreholes. The people are largely African of various tribal groups, including Ovambo, Damara, Herero, Nama, and Bushmen. Whites are a minority of about 15 percent, mostly of South African and German descent. There is a smaller number of mixed descent, including the Rehoboth Bastards, of Nama-white ancestry. In general, the whites live in the Police Zone in the south, the native population in homelands in the north. Official languages are Afrikaans and English, but German is widely used, as are tribal languages.

Parts of the nonwhite population follow the traditional animist religions, although many Africans have been converted

to Christianity. Missionary activity, which began in the 1800s, encompasses several denominations, including Lutheran, Roman Catholic, Methodist, Anglican, and Dutch Reformed.

Diamonds are Namibia's most valuable economic product, and copper, zinc, lead, uranium, cadmium, and manganese are also mined. Sheep, cattle, and goats are raised, and the production of karakul sheep pelts is increasingly important. The annual haul of fish has reached over three-quarters of a million tons.

South-West Africa had been mandated to South African administration by the League of Nations. When the UN Trusteeship System was established in 1945, South Africa refused to place South-West Africa under it (it was the only such case), claiming that the UN was not the legal successor to the League. In 1966 the UN General Assembly declared that the mandate was terminated; in 1967 it established a council to administer the area until independence; and in 1968 it proclaimed that the area be renamed Namibia. South Africa, however, declaring that the removal of the mandate was an "illegal act" because the UN charter makes no provision for such a move, announced its intention to continue administration, and has done so even after a 1971 ruling against its position by the International Court of Justice.

In January 1976, the UN Security Council voted to invoke mandatory sanctions against South Africa if it failed to accept a UN-supervised election leading to independence. In August the South African government announced plans for a multiracial Namibian government to bring about independence by December 31, 1978. Inasmuch as the South African proposal did not mention a specific date for elections, both the UN and the powerful guerrilla group, the South-West Africa People's Organization (SWAPO) rejected the plan. At a conference in the Turnhalle in Windhoek in August 1976, South Africa announced that it intended to set up an interim government. Sanctions against South Africa for not withdrawing were vetoed in the UN. In 1977 the United States, Britain, France, Canada and West Germany began diplomatic efforts to arrive at an independence plan acceptable to both South Africa and SWAPO. South Africa agreed to the Western plan in April, but SWAPO withheld its consent after a South African raid on its bases in Angola. Further efforts were made by the Western powers, and SWAPO's agreement was secured in July with the help of five black-ruled "front-line" states. Under the plan, all South African troops would be withdrawn except for 1,500 men who would be restricted to camps near the Angolan border. A United Nations force of 5,000 men would be sent into the territory to insure a free election, after which the territory would become independent. In the period leading up to the election, the territory would be administered jointly by a South African administrator and a UN representative. A dispute has arisen between South Africa and SWAPO over the Walvis Bay enclave, the future status of which was not determined in the Western powers' plan.

Negotiations between the UN and South Africa continued throughout 1978, 1979, 1980 and into 1981 without resolution of their differences regarding Namibian independence, originally scheduled for Dec. 31, 1978. A South African-sponsored election in Namibia in early Dec. 1978 elected a 50-member constituent assembly, with the Democratic Turnhalle Alliance winning 41 seats. SWAPO did not vote, and the UN Security Council declared the election null and void. The assembly met on May 21, with limited legislative powers, while South Africa retained ultimate powers over the territory. In May 1980 South Africa announced its willingness to cooperate in implementing the 1977 peace plan, but demanded assurances that the UN would not favor SWAPO.

Netherlands Antilles—*Status:* Autonomous Part of the Kingdom of the Netherlands. *Population:* 246,000 (1978 est.). *Area:* 390 sq. mi. *Capital:* Willemstad (95,000) on Curaçao.

The Netherlands Antilles, in the Caribbean, consists of two groups of three islands each: Curaçao, Aruba, and Bonaire, 15 to 38 miles off the northern coast of Venezuela; and Saba, St. Eustatius, and St. Maarten, which shares an island with the French St. Martin, more than 500 miles to the northeast. Curaçao and Aruba are by far the most populous and important. On these two islands, Dutch, English, Spanish, and Papiamento (a mixture of the three) are spoken.

The Leewards are semiarid and flat; the Windwards are mountainous, with enough rainfall for flourishing vegetation. The climate is warm and humid. The people are largely blacks, or Carib Indians, or either of these mixed with white strains. Dutch is the official language, and English is current in the Windwards. Papiamento is common. Catholicism predominates on the Leeward Islands, Protestantism on the Windward.

Curaçao and Aruba, with a higher per capita income than the Netherlands, owe their prosperity to oil refineries, which process crude oil from Venezuela. The refineries also stimulate other industries and commerce on the two islands. After oil refining, tourism is their most important economic factor. On Curaçao and Aruba little farming is possible because the land is so rocky. Most food is imported. On the other islands, small-scale agriculture and fishing are pursued.

In an effort to lessen dependence on the petroleum industry, the government has been attempting to attract new industries by offering tax holidays and customs exceptions to firms locating there and by creating free zones on Curaçao and Aruba.

Fully autonomous in internal affairs, the Netherlands Antilles are constitutionally equal with the Netherlands. There is a governor, who represents the sovereign, and a council of ministers—headed by a prime minister—which is responsible to an elected legislature (Staten). Aruba, Curaçao, Bonaire, and the Windward group each have autonomy in local affairs.

In 1974, Juancho Evertaz, premier of the Netherlands Antilles, met with the Dutch premier at The Hague to discuss the future status of the islands. It was decided that they would wait at least until 1980 to achieve independent status (since postponed into the mid-1980s). In 1977, Aruba held its own referendum, with 57 percent voting for separate independence. In 1979, a strike by police and firemen led the government of Premier Silvios Rosendal to resign. The New Antilles Movement, a coalition of trade unions, won the subsequent elections, both in the local council in Curaçao and throughout the islands, and its head, Don Martina, became the premier.

New Caledonia—Status: French Overseas Territory. Population: 137,000 (1979 est.). Area: 7,335 sq. mi. Capital: Nouméa (74,335).

This group of about 25 islands in the South Pacific is situated about 750 miles east of Australia. The territory takes its name from the main island, New Caledonia or Grande-Terre (22°S.,166°E.), which is 6,530 square miles in area and mountainous. The territory includes the dependencies of Île des Pins, Loyalty Islands, Île Huon, Îles Belep, Îles Chesterfield, and Île Walpole. The British explorer, James Cook, was the first European to visit New Caledonia (1774). Other Europeans followed. In 1853, France took over control and, eleven years later, turned it into a prison colony. The climate is mildly tropical, tempered by the trade winds. About half the people are Australo-Melanesian indigenes. Most of the rest are of French descent or are Polynesians.

Agriculture and mining are the basic economic activities. Coffee and copra are the commercial crops, while root plants, wheat, corn, fruits, and vegetables are also grown, but food must be imported. Nickel is mined on a large scale, and iron and chrome are also exploited.

Administration is in the hands of a Paris-appointed High Commissioner. In 1979 a new Territorial Assembly of 36 elected members was established. Independence cannot come before 1989. Two deputies and a senator are elected to the French Parliament.

Niue—Status: New Zealand Self-governing Territory. Population: 4,000 (1979 est.). Area: 100 sq. mi. Administrative Center: Alofi (957).

Niue is in the South Pacific some 1,340 miles northeast of New Zealand (19°S.,170°W.); although geographically associated with the Cook Islands, its distance and cultural differences have led to separate administration. Niue is a coral island with fertile but sparse soil. The climate is hot and the islands suffer from hurricanes. The people are of Polynesian stock, speaking Samoan.

There is a prime minister and cabinet, and an elected island assembly. Niue became self-governing in 1974.

Norfolk Island—Status: Australian External Territory. Population: 2,180 (1979 est.). Area: 13.3 sq. mi. Administrative Center: Kingston.

The island lies in the South Pacific 930 miles northeast of Sydney, Australia (29°S.,168°E.). Many of its inhabitants are descendants of H.M.S. Bounty mutineers, who were moved here in 1856 when they became too numerous for Pitcairn Island. Fruits and bean seed are grown and tourism is important. There is an Australian-appointed administrator and an elected Legislative Assembly.

Peter I Island—Status: Norwegian Dependency. Population: Uninhabited. Area: 96 sq. mi.

An Antarctic island, it is southwest of the South Shetland Islands, at 68°47′S and 90°35′W. It is of volcanic origin and almost entirely ice-covered.

Pitcairn Islands—Status: British Colony. Population: 63 (1980 est.). Area: 18 sq. mi. Administrative Center: Adamstown.

The colony is in the South Pacific, 4,000 miles southwest of the Panama Canal and 3,200 miles northeast of New Zealand. There are four islands: Pitcairn (1.75 sq. mi.), Henderson, Ducie, and Oeno, of which only Pitcairn (25°05′S.,130°05′W.) is inhabited. The climate is warm throughout the year. The people are descendants of H.M.S. Bounty mutineers and Polynesian women from Tahiti. The inhabitants were resettled on Norfolk Island in 1856 when their numbers grew too large for Pitcairn, but several families of them returned soon after.

Subsistence agriculture and fishing are the main occupations. Some fruits, vegetables, and handicrafts are sold to passing ships.

The colony is administered by the British High Commissioner in New Zealand with the assistance of a partly elected island council, presided over by an island magistrate.

Queen Maud Land—Status: Norwegian Dependency. Population: Uninhabited.

The portion of Antarctica between 20°W and 45°E, it is claimed by Norway.

Réunion—Status: French Overseas Department. Population: 491,000 (1980 est.). Area: 969 sq. mi. Capital: Saint-Denis (103,513).

An island in the Indian Ocean (21°S.,55°30′E.), it is about 400 miles east of Madagascar. Réunion is of volcanic origin and mountainous, the highest peak—Piton des Neiges—rising to more than 10,000 feet. One of its volcanoes is still active. There are many torrential rivers. The climate is essentially tropical, but varies greatly with altitude and exposure to the trade winds. Rainfall is heavy, and there are severe tropical storms. The people are of Malabar Indian, African, Malay, Vietnamese, Chinese, and French descent; the last make up about 20 percent of the population. Ninety-four percent of the population is Roman Catholic.

The cultivation of sugarcane is the main economic activity. Essential oils from geranium and vetiver plants are also important. Corn, potatoes and beans are grown for consumption, but food must be imported.

Réunion is administered by a Paris-appointed prefect and an elected general council; the island elects three deputies and two senators to the French Parliament.

Ross Dependency—Status: New Zealand Territory. Population: No permanent inhabitants. Area: 290,000 sq. mi. (of which 130,000 sq. mi. are ice shelf).

New Zealand claims that portion of Antarctica south of 60°S between 160°E and 150°W.

There are research and exploration activities in the area, and whaling in its territorial waters.

Saint Christopher-Nevis—Status: British Associated State. Population: 44,404 (1980 census). Area: 120 sq. mi. Capital: Basseterre (14,725) on St. Christopher.

In the Leeward Islands of the West Indies, it includes St. Christopher (commonly called St. Kitts; 68 sq. mi.), Nevis (50 sq. mi.), and Sombrero (2 sq. mi.). The climate of the islands is tropical and humid. The people are largely of mixed black-white descent. English is the formal language, but a patois is commonly spoken.

Sugar, molasses, and cotton are the chief exports. Yams, rice, breadfruit, and corn are grown for food. Tourism is increasingly important.

There is a Crown-appointed governor, a prime minister, and a partially elected house of assembly. In 1975 separatist delegates from Nevis won their assembly seats. Although Anguilla became a self-governing British colony in 1976, the rupture was formally approved only after a five-year delay. In talks in London in late 1979, it was decided that St. Kitts-Nevis should proceed toward independence in 1980, but independence was still pending in 1981. It was agreed in London that a post-independence referendum would determine whether Nevis wants to stay within the state.

Saint Helena—Status: British Colony. Population: 6,400 (1977 est.). Area: 162 sq. mi. Capital: Jamestown (1,601).

The island of Saint Helena (47 sq. mi.) is in the southeastern Atlantic about 1,200 miles from Africa, at 16°S. and 5°21′W. Its dependencies—Tristan da Cunha (38 sq. mi.) and Ascension (34 sq. mi.)—are about 1,500 miles south-southwest and 750 miles northwest, respectively. Near Tristan da Cunha are the uninhabited islands of Gough, Nightingale, and Inaccessible. St. Helena is rocky, with a pleasant climate due to the trade winds. It was the place of Napoleon's exile from 1815 until his death in 1821. Tristan da Cunha suffered a volcanic eruption in 1961, and the tiny population of 248 was resettled in England. They suffered from respiratory diseases in that climate, however, and returned to their island in 1963 (1980 pop.—320). The people of the colony are of mixed origin, and their language is English.

St. Helena grows flax, fodder, and vegetables. Potatoes are the staple subsistence crop on Tristan da Cunha. Ascension is an important cable and missile tracking station.

The colony is administered by a Crown-appointed governor, assisted by an executive council and a partly elected legislative council.

Saint Kitts-Nevis: See Saint Christopher-Nevis.

Saint Pierre and Miquelon—Status: French Overseas Department. Population: 5,900 (1977 est.). Area: 93.5 sq. mi. Capital: Saint Pierre (5,232) on St. Pierre.

This archipelago lies some 15 miles south of Newfoundland in the North Atlantic. There are three main islands, Saint Pierre, Miquelon, and Langlade, the latter two connected by a low isthmus. Although volcanic in origin, the islands are low-lying. The climate is cool to cold, with seasons of strong winds and heavy fogs; there is a good deal of rain and snow. The people are mostly descendants of Breton, Norman, and Basque settlers.

The chief occupation is cod fishing, together with fish freezing and fish meal production.

The department is administered by a Paris-appointed prefect. There is an elected general council, and a deputy and a senator are elected to the French Parliament.

Sala y Gómez Island—Status: Chilean Dependency. Population: Uninhabited. Area: .05 sq. mi.

In the Pacific Ocean at 26°28′S.,105°28′W., some 2,100 miles west of Chile and 250 miles east of Easter Island, Sala y Gómez, an arid island of volcanic origin, is administered by Valparaíso Province.

San Ambrosio Island and San Felix Island—*Status*: Chilean Dependencies. *Population*: Uninhabited. *Area*: 1.29 sq. mi.

These two small islands—some 12 miles apart—are in the Pacific Ocean at 26°20'S.,80°W., about 600 miles west of Chile. They were discovered by the Spanish navigator, Juan Fernández, in 1574, and are administered by Atacama Province.

Svalbard—*Status*: Norwegian Dependency. *Population*: 3,431 (1975 est.). *Area*: 23,957 sq. mi. *Administrative Center*: Longyearbyen.

Svalbard is the name of an island territory in the Arctic Ocean between 74° and 81°N and 10° and 35°E. By far the most important of these islands is the Spitsbergen group, the largest of which are Spitsbergen, North East Land, Edge Island, and Barents Island. The islands are bleak and rugged, largely covered with ice running to the sea in glaciers. The climate is moderated, however, by winds from the Atlantic, and the Gulf Stream keeps open water for six months of the year. About two-thirds of the people are Russians who live in mining camps, the rest are Norwegians. Coal is the principal product.

Tokelau—*Status*: New Zealand Territory. *Population*: 1,625 (1977 est.). *Area*: 3.95 sq. mi. *Administrative Center*: Fenuafala (649) on Fakaofo.

These islands are in the South Pacific at 9°S.,172°W., 2,100 miles northeast of New Zealand, 300 miles north of Samoa. Geographically the group consists of four atolls—Atafu, Nukunono, Fakaofo, and Swains—but the last belongs to American Samoa. The people are of Polynesian origin. Their language, now dying, resembles Samoan, the official language.

Subsistence farming and copra production for export are the main occupations. Revenue is also derived from the sale of postage stamps.

The islands are administrated by the New Zealand Minister for Foreign Affairs.

Turks and Caicos Islands—*Status*: British Colony. *Population*: 7,436 (1980 census). *Area*: 166 sq. mi. *Capital*: Cockburn Town (2,287), on Grand Turk.

Geographically part of the Bahamas, of which they form the southeastern groups, the Turks and Caicos lie in the Atlantic Ocean some 575 miles southeast of Florida. Of the 30 or so small islands, only six are inhabited, among them Grand Turk, Grand Caicos, and Salt Cay. The climate is hot, dry, and subject to hurricanes. The people are almost all of African descent.

Fishing and salt production are economic staples.

The administration of the islands is under a Crown-appointed governor and a partly elected state legislature.

Wallis and Futuna—*Status*: French Overseas Territory. *Population*: 9,192 (1976 census). *Area*: 106 sq. mi. *Capital*: Mata Utu (566) on Wallis.

These small island groups are in the South Pacific, Wallis (13°18'S.,176°10'W.) and its surrounding uninhabited islands being about 250 miles west of Samoa, while Futuna (14°19'S.,178°05'W.) and the uninhabited Alofi island are 120 miles to the southwest. The islands are of volcanic origin. The climate is tropical, mitigated by sea breezes, with seasonal hurricanes. The people are mostly Polynesians. The principal crop is copra.

The territory is administered by a Paris-appointed administrator. A territorial assembly is elected, as are a deputy and a senator to the French Parliament.

ANTARCTICA

SCALE ON MERIDIANS

MILES
0 200 400 600 800 1000

KILOMETRES
0 200 400 600 800 1000

DIPLOMATIC AFFAIRS

ROSTER OF THE UNITED NATIONS: 1981 (155 Members as of September 15)

Member Nation	Date of Admission		Member Nation	Date of Admission		Member Nation	Date of Admission	
Afghanistan	19 Nov.	1946	Ghana	8 Mar.	1957	Papua New Guinea	10 Oct.	1975
Albania	14 Dec.	1955	Greece	25 Oct.	1945	Paraguay	24 Oct.	1945
Algeria	8 Oct.	1962	Grenada	17 Sept.	1974	Peru	31 Oct.	1945
Angola	1 Dec.	1976	Guatemala	21 Nov.	1945	Philippines	24 Oct.	1945
Argentina	24 Oct.	1945	Guinea	12 Dec.	1958	Poland	24 Oct.	1945
Australia	1 Nov.	1945	Guinea-Bissau	17 Sept.	1974	Portugal	14 Dec.	1955
Austria	14 Dec.	1955	Guyana	20 Sept.	1966	Qatar	21 Sept.	1971
Bahamas	18 Sept.	1973	Haiti	24 Oct.	1945	Romania	14 Dec.	1955
Bahrain	21 Sept.	1971	Honduras	17 Dec.	1945	Rwanda	18 Sept.	1962
Bangladesh	17 Sept.	1974	Hungary	14 Dec.	1955	Saint Lucia	18 Sept.	1979
Barbados	9 Dec.	1966	Iceland	19 Nov.	1946	Saint Vincent and The		
Belgium	27 Dec.	1945	India	30 Oct.	1945	Grenadines	16 Sept.	1980
Belize	25 Sept.	1981	Indonesia	28 Sept.	1950	São Tomé and Príncipe	16 Sept.	1965
Benin	20 Sept.	1960	Iran	24 Oct.	1945	Saudi Arabia	24 Oct.	1945
Bhutan	21 Sept.	1971	Iraq	21 Dec.	1945	Senegal	28 Sept.	1960
Bolivia	14 Nov.	1945	Ireland	14 Dec.	1955	Seychelles	21 Sept.	1976
Botswana	17 Oct.	1966	Israel	11 May	1949	Sierra Leone	27 Sept.	1961
Brazil	24 Oct.	1945	Italy	14 Dec.	1955	Singapore	21 Sept.	1965
Bulgaria	14 Dec.	1955	Ivory Coast	20 Sept.	1960	Solomon Islands	19 Sept.	1978
Burma	19 Apr.	1948	Jamaica	18 Sept.	1962	Somalia	20 Sept.	1960
Burundi	18 Sept.	1962	Japan	18 Dec.	1956	South Africa	7 Nov.	1945
Byelorussian SSR	24 Oct.	1945	Jordan	14 Dec.	1955	Spain	14 Dec.	1955
Cambodia (Kampuchea)	14 Dec.	1955	Kenya	16 Dec.	1963	Sri Lanka	14 Dec.	1955
Cameroon	20 Sept.	1960	Kuwait	14 May	1963	Sudan	12 Nov.	1956
Canada	9 Nov.	1945	Laos	14 Dec.	1955	Suriname	4 Dec.	1975
Cape Verde	16 Sept.	1975	Lebanon	24 Oct.	1945	Swaziland	24 Sept.	1968
Central African Republic	20 Sept.	1960	Lesotho	17 Oct.	1966	Sweden	19 Nov.	1946
Chad	20 Sept.	1960	Liberia	2 Nov.	1945	Syria	24 Oct.	1945
Chile	24 Oct.	1945	Libya	14 Dec.	1955	Tanzania	14 Dec.	1961
China	24 Oct.	1945	Luxembourg	24 Oct.	1945	Thailand	16 Dec.	1946
Colombia	5 Nov.	1945	Madagascar	20 Sept.	1960	Togo	20 Sept.	1960
Comoros	12 Nov.	1975	Malawi	1 Dec.	1964	Trinidad and Tobago	18 Sept.	1962
Congo	20 Sept.	1960	Malaysia	17 Sept.	1957	Tunisia	12 Nov.	1956
Costa Rica	2 Nov.	1945	Maldives	21 Sept.	1965	Turkey	24 Oct.	1945
Cuba	24 Oct.	1945	Mali	28 Sept.	1960	Uganda	25 Oct.	1962
Cyprus	20 Sept.	1960	Malta	1 Dec.	1964	Ukrainian SSR	24 Oct.	1945
Czechoslovakia	24 Oct.	1945	Mauritania	27 Oct.	1961	USSR	24 Oct.	1945
Denmark	24 Oct.	1945	Mauritius	24 Apr.	1968	United Arab Emirates	9 Dec.	1971
Djibouti	20 Sept.	1977	Mexico	7 Nov.	1945	United Kingdom	24 Oct.	1945
Dominica	18 Dec.	1978	Mongolia	27 Oct.	1961	United States	24 Oct.	1945
Dominican Republic	24 Oct.	1945	Morocco	12 Nov.	1956	Upper Volta	20 Sept.	1960
Ecuador	21 Dec.	1945	Mozambique	16 Sept.	1975	Uruguay	18 Dec.	1945
Egypt	24 Oct.	1945	Nepal	14 Dec.	1955	Vanuatu	15 Sept.	1981
El Salvador	24 Oct.	1945	Netherlands	10 Dec.	1945	Venezuela	15 Nov.	1945
Equatorial Guinea	12 Nov.	1968	New Zealand	24 Oct.	1945	Vietnam	20 Sept.	1977
Ethiopia	13 Nov.	1945	Nicaragua	24 Oct.	1945	Western Samoa	15 Dec.	1976
Fiji	13 Oct.	1970	Niger	20 Sept.	1960	Yemen	30 Sept.	1947
Finland	14 Dec.	1955	Nigeria	7 Oct.	1960	Yemen (Southern Yemen)	14 Dec.	1967
France	24 Oct.	1945	Norway	27 Nov.	1945	Yugoslavia	20 Oct.	1945
Gabon	20 Sept.	1960	Oman	7 Oct.	1971	Zaïre	20 Sept.	1960
Gambia	21 Sept.	1965	Pakistan	30 Sept.	1947	Zambia	1 Dec.	1964
Germany (Dem. Rep.)	18 Sept.	1973	Panama	13 Sept.	1945	Zimbabwe	25 Aug.	1980
Germany (Fed. Rep.)	18 Sept.	1973						

PRINCIPAL ORGANS OF THE UNITED NATIONS

There are six principal organs of the UN: the General Assembly, the Security Council, the Economic and Social Council, the Trusteeship Council, the International Court of Justice, and the Secretariat. The official languages in all these organs, other than the International Court of Justice, are Chinese, English, French, Russian, and Spanish. Working languages are English and French, with the addition of Russian, Spanish and Chinese in the General Assembly and the Security Council and Spanish in the Economic and Social Council. Arabic is an official and working language in the General Assembly. The official languages in the International Court of Justice are English and French.

General Assembly

The UN's main deliberative body, the General Assembly, consists of all member states, each of which has one vote. Any question may be discussed that is within the scope of the UN Charter or relates to the functions of any organ provided for in the Charter, as well as any questions on international peace and security that are brought up by a member, by the Security Council, or by a nonmember, if that state accepts in advance obligations of pacific settlement. The General Assembly may make recommendations to member states or to the Security Council with one exception: it may not make recommendations on any dispute under consideration by the Security Council unless the Council so requests.

Regular sessions of the Assembly convene once a year, commencing on the third Tuesday in September. There is provision for special and emergency special sessions. Voting is by simple majority of those present and voting, except on questions adjudged important, when a two-thirds majority is required. The Assembly controls the finances of the UN; it also elects the 10 nonpermanent members of the Security Council, all the members of the Economic and Social Council, and—with, but independently of, the Security Council—the International Court of Justice. On Security Council recommendations, the Secretary-General is appointed by the General Assembly.

The assembly elects its president and 17 vice-presidents for each session and adopts its own rules of procedure. It distributes most agenda items among its seven main committees (see list below). There is also a General Committee that organizes the work of each session, a Credentials Committee, an Advisory Committee on Administrative and Budgetary Questions, and a Committee on Contributions, which recommends the scale of members' payments to the UN. They may establish ad hoc and subsidiary bodies such as the Conference on Trade and Development (UNCTAD).

General Assembly Main Committee Chairmen, 34th Session:

First Committee (Political and Security) — Niaz Ahmed Naik (Pakistan)

Special Political Committee — Leonardo Mathias (Portugal)

Second Committee (Economic and Financial) — Abelhadi Sbihi (Morocco)

Third Committee (Social, Humanitarian and Cultural) — Ivan Garvalov (Bulgaria)

Fourth Committee (Decolonization) — Noel G. Sinclair (Guyana)

Fifth Committee (Administrative and Budgetary) — Enrique Buj-Flores (Mexico)

Sixth Committee (Legal) — Abdul G. Koroma (Sierra Leone)

Assembly Actions of the 35th Session:
The opening session of the UN General Assembly took place on September 16, 1980. Rudiger von Wechmar of West Germany was elected president of the assembly. Saint Vincent and the Grenadines was admitted as the UN's 154th member at that opening session.

SOUTHERN AFRICA — South Africa tried on March 2, 1981, to regain its General Assembly seat denied it since 1974 and was promptly ejected by a vote of 112 to 22. On March 6, 1981, the Assembly voted a resolution requesting the Security Council to impose sanctions against South Africa for its failure to settle the war in Namibia.

MIDDLE EAST — The Assembly approved several resolutions in December 1980 which condemned Israel for the Camp David accords, the annexation of East Jerusalem and its occupation of Arab lands. A plan by Moslem states seeking the ouster of Israel from the General Assembly was dropped at least for the present time. The Assembly approved a resolution on Dec. 16, 1980, calling for a PLO-backed independent Palestinian state.

CAMBODIA — The Assembly voted on Oct. 13, 1980, to defeat a motion to unseat the representatives of the deposed Cambodian government of former Premier Pol Pot. The Assembly supported a resolution for an international conference in mid-1981 to seek an end to the conflict in Cambodia.

OTHER MATTERS — Cuba was defeated in October 1980 in her bid for a seat on the Security Council for the second year in a row. The Assembly renewed its appeal to the Soviet Union to withdraw its troops from Afghanistan.

Security Council

There are 15 members on the Security Council, five of them permanent—The People's Republic of China, France, the USSR, the United Kingdom, and the United States—and 10 elected by the General Assembly for two-year terms and ineligible for immediate reelection. As of August 1980 the ten nonpermanent members were: Bangladesh, Germany (Dem. Rep.), Jamaica, Mexico, Niger, Norway, Philippines, Portugal, Tanzania and Zambia.

The council bears primary responsibility under the UN Charter for the maintenance of international peace and security. It may investigate any situation bearing the seeds of international friction. These may be brought to its attention by any UN member, by any nonmember accepting in advance the obligations of pacific settlement, by the General Assembly, or by the Secretary-General.

Having determined the existence of a threat to peace, the council may make recommendations, or may call on members to take such measures as economic sanctions or other steps short of armed force. Should these be inadequate, the council may take military action against an aggressor; all members agree under the charter to make available to the council, in accordance with agreements to be negotiated, armed forces necessary for maintaining international peace. The council also has responsibility for plans to regulate armaments.

On matters other than procedural, council decisions need an affirmative vote of nine, including all permanent members (hence the veto; abstentions do not in practice constitute a veto). On procedural matters, an affirmative vote of any nine members suffices. A UN member not on the council may take part in council discussion when it is considered that its interests are especially affected. The council presidency is held by members in monthly rotation in English alphabetical order. There is a *Committee of Experts* to advise the council on procedural and technical matters, a *Committee on Admission of New Members*, and a *Military Staff Committee*, which is composed of the chiefs of staff of the permanent members or their representatives, to advise on military matters.

Security Council Actions Fall 1980 — Fall 1981:

MIDDLE EAST — The Security Council extended the peacekeeping forces in Cyprus, Lebanon and Golan Heights for six-month periods. A resolution asking for a cease-fire in the Iraq-Iran war was accepted by Iraq but rejected by Iran in October 1980. On June 19, 1981, the Council condemned

Israel for its June 7 air attack on Iraq's nuclear reactor near Baghdad.

SOUTHERN AFRICA — The UN-sponsored conference in Namibia in January 1981 ended in failure as South Africa refused to confer with the South-West Africa People's Organization. South Africa had previously agreed to a March 1981 cease-fire in the disputed territory of Namibia if a pre-cease-fire meeting of all the participants was held. A Security Council resolution to impose economic and political sanctions against South Africa was blocked by the U.S., Great Britain and France on April 30, 1981.

Economic and Social Council

The council makes studies and recommendations to the General Assembly on international social, economic, cultural, educational, health, and related matters. It negotiates agreements with the specialized agencies, defining their relationship with the UN, and coordinates their activities by means of consultation and recommendation.

It is composed of 54 members, 18 of whom are elected each year by the General Assembly to a three-year term. Each member has one vote, and a simple majority rules. The council works through committees, commissions, and various other subsidiary bodies. Its functional commissions include: the *Statistical Commission*, the *Population Commission*, the *Commission for Social Development*, the *Commission on Human Rights*, the *Commission on the Status of Women*, the *Commission on Narcotic Drugs* and the *Commission on Transnational Corporations*. There are also regional commissions for Europe, Asia and the Far East, Latin America, and Africa. There are a number of other related bodies, including the executive board of the children's fund (UNICEF) and the International Narcotics Control Board.

For list of members, see page 717: Membership of Principal United Nations Organizations.

Recent Developments: Resolutions in 1979 sessions dealt with human rights, advancement of women, crime prevention and racial discrimination.

Trusteeship Council

The council bears prime responsibility for supervision of territories placed under the UN Trusteeship System. It consists of member states administering trust territories and permanent members of the Security Council not administering territories. The present administering state is the United States (Trust Territory of the Pacific Islands). The nonadministering members are the People's Republic of China, France, the United Kingdom, and the USSR.

Voting is by simple majority. The Trusteeship Council meets once a year, usually in June.

Recent Developments: The Trusteeship Council moved ahead with its plans for a 1981 plebiscite under UN supervision on the future status of the Trust Territory of the Pacific Islands.

International Court of Justice

The principal judicial organ of the UN functions in accordance with its statute, which is an integral part of the UN Charter and is based on the Statute of the Permanent Court of International Justice of the League of Nations. The court is open to all UN members, plus nonmembers who become party to the statute (at present Switzerland, Liechtenstein, and San Marino), as well as other states fulfilling certain conditions. It is not open to private individuals. The court has jurisdiction over all cases that the parties refer to it and over all matters specifically provided for in the charter or in treaties or conventions in force, including treaties that refer to the Permanent Court of International Justice. In the event of a dispute as to whether the court has jurisdiction, it decides the issue itself.

The court is composed of 15 judges of different nationalities, who are elected independently by the General Assembly and the Security Council (election in the latter does not permit the veto). Terms are for nine years. All questions are decided by a majority of judges present, nine constituting a quorum. In case of a tie, the president of the court (elected by the court for a three-year term) casts the deciding vote. The court sits at The Hague, Netherlands.

Secretariat

The UN's administrative spine is composed of the Secretary-General, who is appointed by the General Assembly on the recommendation of the Security Council, and "such staff as the organization may require." As chief administrative officer, the Secretary-General acts in his capacity at all meetings of the General Assembly, the Security Council, the Economic and Social Council, and the Trusteeship Council. He makes an annual report to the General Assembly and appoints the Secretariat staff. The Secretary-General is also empowered to bring before the Security Council any matter that in his opinion threatens the maintenance of international peace.

The structure of the Secretariat includes the Offices of the Secretary-General (the Executive Office of the Secretary-General, the Director-General for Development and International Economic Cooperation, the Offices of the Under-Secretaries for Special Political Affairs, the Office for Special Political Questions, the Office of Legal Affairs, the Office of the Controller, and the Department of Administration and Management), the Department of Political and Security Council Affairs, the Department of Economic and Social Affairs, the Department of Trusteeship and Non-Self-Governing Territories, the Department of Public Information, the Department of Conference Services, the Office of General Services, and the UN Office in Geneva. There are also separate staffs serving subsidiary organs established by the General Assembly or the Economic and Social Council, including: the children's fund (UNICEF), the development program (UNDP), the office of the high commissioner for refugees (UNHCR), the relief and works agency for Palestine refugees (UNRWA), the institute for training and research (UNITAR), the industrial development organization (UNIDO) and trade and development (UNCTAD).

SPECIALIZED AGENCIES AND OTHER BODIES OF THE UNITED NATIONS

Specialized agencies are intergovernmental organizations linked to the UN by special agreement, working in partnership with it in social, scientific, and technical fields. The specialized agencies proper report annually to the Economic and Social Council. Although usually listed with them, the IAEA and GATT agencies are not, strictly speaking, specialized agencies. The former is an intergovernmental agency "established under the aegis of the UN" and reports to the General Assembly and, as appropriate, to the Security Council and the Economic and Social Council. The latter cooperates with the UN at the secretariat and intergovernmental levels.

Food and Agriculture Organization of the United Nations (FAO) *Function:* To help countries increase food production and improve distribution, to coordinate the Freedom from Hunger Campaign, and to help administer the World Food Program. *Members:* 147 countries. *Headquarters:* Rome. *Chief Officer:* Director-General Edouard Saouma (Lebanon).

General Agreement of Tariffs and Trade (GATT) *Function:* To establish and administer the code for orderly conduct of international trade; to assist governments to reduce customs tariffs and abolish other trade barriers; and to operate, jointly with the UN Conference on Trade and Development, the International Trade Center providing export promotion assistance for developing countries. (GATT rules govern as estimated 80 percent of international trade.) *Members:* 85 participating nations. *Headquarters:* Geneva. *Chief Officer:* Director-General Arthur Dunkel (Switzerland). *Recent Developments:* In the annual report of GATT for 1980 the volume of international trade increased only 1% in 1980 compared to 6% in 1979.

Inter-Governmental Maritime Consultative Organization (IMCO) *Function:* To promote cooperation on téchnical matters affecting shipping, to encourage the highest standards of maritime safety and efficient navigation, to convene international conferences on shipping, and to draft international maritime conventions. *Members:* 121 countries plus one associate. *Headquarters:* London. *Chief Officer:* Secretary-General C.P. Srivastava (India). *Recent Developments:* The ninth session of the UN Law of the Sea Conference approved in 1980 a draft treaty that has taken some six years of deliberations. The draft treaty calls for a system of exploitation of mineral deposits of the sea bed which will benefit private companies who do the mining and the world community, chiefly have-not nations. It gives maritime countries exclusive mineral, oil and fishing rights out to 200 miles, reaffirms right of free passage on the high seas and in world straits, and calls for protection of the seas from pollution. Further progress on Draft Law of the Sea was delayed in the tenth session of March 1981 when the U.S. dismissed its head delegate and asked for time to complete a full review of the draft accord.

International Atomic Energy Agency (IAEA) *Function:* To promote the use of nuclear energy for peaceful purposes; to assist in nuclear research, development, and applications; and to apply safeguards against diversion of nuclear materials to military use. *Members:* 110 countries. *Headquarters:* Vienna. *Chief Officer:* Director-General Sigvard Eklund (Sweden).

International Bank for Reconstruction and Development (World Bank; IBRD) *Function:* To further members' economic development by loans (all loans made to or guaranteed by government) and technical advice. *Members:* 139 countries. *Headquarters:* Washington, DC *Chief Officer:* President Alden W. Clausen (United States).

International Civil Aviation Organization (ICAO) *Function:* To promote safety of international civil aviation, to provide statistical and economic information for governments and airlines, to work to reduce the red tape of customs formalities, and to help developing countries benefit from air transport. *Members:* 148 countries. *Headquarters:* Montreal. *Chief Officer:* Secretary-General Yves Lambert (France).

International Development Association (IDA) *Function:* To further economic development of members by providing finance on terms bearing less heavily on balance of payments than conventional loans. (Its credits have been for 50-year terms, interest free.) *Members:* 125 countries. *Headquarters:* Washington, DC (IDA is an affiliate of IBRD and has the same officers and staff.)

International Finance Corporation (IFC) *Function:* To assist less developed member countries by providing risk capital, without government guarantee, for the growth of productive private enterprise. *Members:* 118 countries. *Headquarters:* Washington, DC *Chief Officer:* Alden W. Clausen (United States). (IFC is an affiliate of IBRD.)

International Fund for Agricultural Development (IFAD) *Function:* To grant loans to promote agricultural improvement in developing countries. *Members:* 133 countries. *Headquarters:* Rome. *President:* Abdelmuhsin al-Sudeary (Saudi Arabia).

International Labour Organization (ILO) *Function:* To bring together government, labor, and management on pressing international labor and manpower problems; to provide governments with technical assistance, and to develop world labor standards. *Members:* 145 countries. *Headquarters:* Geneva. *Chief Officer:* Director-General Francis Blanchard (France). *Recent Developments:* The U.S. rejoined the ILO on February 18, 1980. It had withdrawn its membership in 1977 in protest that the agency had become politicized. In March 1981 the ILO rebuked the Soviet Union for its harsh treatment of workers who had sought to organize independent trade unions.

International Monetary Fund (IMF) *Function:* To promote international monetary cooperation and stabilization of currencies, to facilitate expansion of international trade, and to help members meet temporary difficulties in foreign payments. *Members:* 141 countries. *Headquarters:* Washington, DC *Chief Officer:* Managing Director Jacques de Larosière (France). *Recent Developments:* The IMF revised the calculation of Special Drawing Rights (SDR's) beginning Jan. 1, 1981, from a basis of 16 leading currencies to a basket of 5 currencies (U.S., West Germany, United Kingdom, France and Japan).

International Telecommunications Union (ITU) *Function:* To promote international cooperation in radio, telegraph, telephone, and space radio communications; to be instrumental in allocating radio frequencies, and to work to establish the owest possible charges for telecommunications. *Members:* 155 countries. *Headquarters:* Geneva. *Chief Officer:* Secretary-General Mohammed Mili (Tunisia). *Recent Developments:* The second World Administration Radio Conference was held September 1979 (the last conference was in 1959). The U.S. proposed the expansion of the number of possible transmission frequencies and development of geosynchronous orbiting communications satellites. The proposals were opposed by third world representatives who anticipated added domination by developed countries.

United Nations Children's Fund (UNICEF) *Function:* Established in 1946 to carry out post-war relief in Europe but now mainly concerned with the welfare of children in developing countries. *Headquarters:* New York. *Chief Officer:* Executive Director James P. Grant (United States). *Recent Developments:* Relief to the starving children in Cambodia and other areas of Southeast Asia was of prime concern.

United Nations Development Programme (UNDP) *Function:* To help developing countries increase the wealth-producing capabilities of their natural and human resources by providing experts or training of the local people. *Headquarters:* New York. *Chief Officer:* Administrator F. Bradford Morse (United States).

United Nations Educational, Scientific and Cultural Organization (UNESCO) *Function:* To broaden the base of education in the world, to bring the benefits of science to all countries, and to encourage cultural exchange and appreciation. *Members:* 56 countries. *Headquarters:* Paris. *Chief Officer:* Director-General Amadou M'Bow (Senegal). *Recent Developments:* At the Belgrade conference of October 1980 a resolution was passed calling for a new order" in world information. Western nations viewed mention of overseeing journalistic conduct as potential curbs on the freedom of the press. Third World countries viewed "new order" as a way of reducing wholly negative coverage by the Western press and as a chance to promote "developmental strategies."

United Nations Environment Programme (UNEP) *Function:* Established in 1972 to provide machinery for international cooperation in matters relating to the human environment. *Members:* 58 countries on the Governing Council. *Headquarters:* Nairobi. *Chief Officer:* Executive Director Mostafa K. Tolba (Egypt). *Recent Developments:* UNEP sponsored a pollution pact signed May 17, 1980, by most of the countries bordering the Mediterranean Sea.

United Nations Fund for Population Activities (UNFPA) *Function:* Created in 1967 to promote population programs and in extending systematic and sustained population assistance to developing countries and help them in dealing with their population problems. *Headquarters:* New York. *Chief Officer:* Rafael M. Salas (Philippines).

United Nations High Commissioner for Refugees (UNHCR) *Function:* Set up in 1950, the office of the High Commissioner on Refugees aims chiefly to provide international protection for refugees and seek permanent solution to their problems through voluntary repatriation, migration to other countries or local integration. UNHCR also undertakes special humanitarian tasks. *Headquarters:* Geneva. *High Commissioner:* Poul Hartling (Denmark). *Recent Developments:* A United Nations conference of African refugee problems was held in April 1981. A pledge of $563 million in aid was made for 1981-1982. The agency reported a resurgence of refugees fleeing Vietnam in early 1981.

United Nations Industrial Development Organization (UNIDO) *Function:* To encourage and extend assistance to developing countries for development, expansion and modernization of industry; to achieve full utilization of locally available natural and human resources; to provide a forum for consultation and negotiations among developing countries and between developing and industrialized countries. Administers UN Industrial Development Fund. *Headquarters:* Vienna. *Chief Officer:* Executive Director Dr. Abd-El Rahman Khane (Algeria). *Recent Developments:* Operates as an executing agency of the UN Development Programme (UNDP) until final ratification of autonomous specialized agency status.

Universal Postal Union (UPU) *Function:* To assure the organization and improvement of the various postal services and to promote, in the sphere, the development of international cooperation. *Members:* 162. *Headquarters:* Bern. *Chief Officer:* Director-General Mohamed I. Sobhi (Egypt).

World Health Organization (WHO) *Function:* To direct and coordinate international health work, to help governments in public health programs, to set international drug and vaccine standards, and to promote medical research. *Members:* 156 countries. *Headquarters:* Geneva. *Chief Officer:* Director-General Dr. Halfdan Mahler (Denmark). *Recent Developments:* At the May 20, 1981, meeting of WHO in Geneva, a code to curtail the use of infant formulas was passed. U.S. cast the sole dissenting vote.

World Intellectual Property Organization (WIPO) *Function:* To promote and protect intellectual property, such as trademarks, industrial designs, literary and artistic works, throughout the world through new international treaties and harmonization of national legislation. *Members:* 95. *Headquarters:* Geneva. *Chief Officer:* Director-General Arpad Bogsch (United States).

World Meteorological Organization (WMO) *Function:* To promote international meteorological cooperation, especially in the establishment of a worldwide network of meteorological stations and rapid exchange of weather data, to promote standardization and publication of observations, and to further meteorological applications. *Members:* 154. *Headquarters:* Geneva. *Secretary-General:* Aksel Wiin-Nielson (Denmark).

UN SECRETARIES-GENERAL

Lie, Trygve Halvdan (1896-1968), Secretary-General from 1946 to 1953. Born in Oslo, Norway, the son of a carpenter, Lie earned a law degree from Oslo University in 1919 and later served as legal adviser to the Norwegian Trade Unions Federation. From 1935 to 1946 he held various Cabinet ministries, including justice, the department of shipping and supply, and foreign affairs. In the last capacity, he led the Norwegian delegation to the 1945 UN conference in San Francisco, where he headed the commission that drafted the security-council provisions of the Charter.

The rugged Norwegian was elected the first Secretary-General of the UN as a compromise candidate acceptable to both East and West. He immediately asserted himself and established the independence of the Secretary-General's office.

His strong stand on East-West issues alienated, at different times, both the United States and the Soviet Union. By endorsing UN membership for Communist China, he angered the Americans; his stand, however, against North Korean aggression so infuriated the Russians that they refused to deal with him during the remainder of his term. Lie's resignation in 1953 was partly due to Soviet ostracism, but was also brought on by McCarthy-era claims of subversives in the Secretariat.

Hammarskjöld, Dag Hjalmar Agne Carl (1905-1961), Secretary-General from 1953 to 1961. He was born in Jonkoping, Sweden, of an aristocratic family; his father, an eminent jurist, was Sweden's Prime Minister during World War I. Hammarskjöld earned a law degree from Uppsala University in 1930 and a Ph.D. in political economy from the University of Stockholm in 1934.

In 1949 he entered the foreign ministry, where he established his reputation as an international monetary expert. He became vice-chairman of Sweden's UN delegation in 1952 and was its chairman the following year, when he was elected Secretary-General. Hammarskjöld greatly extended the scope and influence of his office. His personal missions in the cause of peace began with his visit to Peking in 1955 to secure the release of captured American fliers and ended with his 1961 Congo mission on which he died in a plane crash near Ndola, Northern Rhodesia.

He created the international peace-keeping force sent to the Middle East after the 1956 Suez crisis. Hammarskjöld's most controversial action was his insistence, against strong Soviet opposition, on maintaining the UN peace force in the Congo. All these efforts won him the Nobel Peace Prize, awarded posthumously in 1961. Publicly, the bachelor Hammarskjöld was a cool, realistic diplomat, but his diary, published as Markings in 1964, revealed a profoundly mystical man.

U Thant (1909-1974), Secretary-General from 1961 to 1971. Born in Pantanaw, Burma, the son of a prosperous landowner, Thant graduated from the National High School in Pantanaw and attended University College in Rangoon. He taught English and modern history at his old high school where in 1931 he became headmaster. For many years he was also an active writer on politics.

He became a member of the Burmese UN delegation in 1952 and its chairman five years later. In 1959 he was chosen vice-president of the General Assembly. After Hammarskjöld's death in 1961, Thant, known as a moderate and neutralist, was elected acting Secretary-General, and a year later he was unanimously elected to office for a full five-year term, retroactive to 1961. Thant was widely praised for his role in calming international tensions during the 1962 Cuban missile crisis, for his part in healing the secessionist Katanga breach in the Congo, and for his handling of the 1964 UN financial crisis, when France and the Communist bloc refused to pay their share of peace-keeping operations.

On the other hand, he was criticized for precipitous speed in complying with Cairo's request in 1967 that the UN emergency force be withdrawn from the Sinai peninsula. It was also remarked that while he was an outspoken critic of American policy in Vietnam, he demonstrated marked restraint toward the 1968 Soviet invasion of Czechoslovakia. In 1971 he announced his December resignation.

Waldheim, Kurt (1918), Secretary-General since January 1972. Born in Lower Austria, the son of a teacher, Waldheim earned a law degree from the University of Vienna in 1944 and joined the Austrian foreign service the following year. He headed the ministry's personnel department for four years, then in 1955, when Austria was admitted to the UN, was appointed Austria's permanent observer at the UN. Since then he has been a member of Austria's delegation at all General Assembly sessions, while also active in other high-ranking foreign ministry appointments. After four years as head of the Austrian mission in Canada he returned to Vienna in 1960, directing the political affairs section there in 1962-1964. He was Austria's UN ambassador from 1964; he left his UN duties early in 1968 to become foreign minister, returning in 1970 to the UN. In April 1971, he contested unsuccessfully in Austria's presidential election.

After election as secretary-general, Waldheim, whose repute is that of a diplomat in the classic mold rather than an "activist," told the UN that he viewed admission of the divided countries as a move toward the goal of UN universality.

Waldheim was reelected for a second five-year term in December 1976. In the difficult Middle East negotiations Waldheim has often met with the national leaders involved and used his office to keep peace talks alive. He created somewhat of a political stir in Middle East affairs by publicly supporting the proposal to create a Palistinian state. Waldheim's special trip to Iran to seek release of the U.S. hostages did not achieve its goal.

UNITED STATES REPRESENTATIVES AND DELEGATES TO THE UNITED NATIONS: 36th Session

(As of September 15, 1981)

Jeane J. Kirkpatrick (Ambassador Extraordinary and Plenipotentiary) — Permanent United States Representative to the United Nations and Chairman of the Delegation to the General Assembly[°]

Kenneth L. Adelman (Ambassador) — Deputy Representative to the United Nations

Representative Andy Ireland—U.S. Delegate to the General Assembly

Representative Benjamin A. Gilman—U.S. Delegate to the General Assembly

John Sherman Cooper—U.S. Delegate to the General Assembly

Bruce Caputo—Alternate U.S. Representative to the General Assembly

George Christopher—Alternate U.S. Representative to the General Assembly

Charles M. Lichenstein—Alternate Representative for Special Political Affairs

William C. Sherman—Deputy Representative to the Security Council

Jose S. Sorzano—Representative to the Economic and Social Council

Dr. Ruth Morgenthau—Representative to the Commission for Social Development of the Economic and Social Council

Michael Novak—Representative to the Commission on Human Rights of the Economic and Social Council

Nancy C. Reynolds—Representative to the Commission on the Status of Women of the Economic and Social Council

[°] The Secretary of State, Alexander M. Haig, Jr., serves as *ex officio* Chairman when present at a session.

MEMBERSHIP OF PRINCIPAL UNITED NATIONS ORGANIZATIONS

SECURITY COUNCIL

Fifteen members: the 5 permanent members and 10 members are elected for two-year terms by the General Assembly.

Permanent members:	China	France	USSR	United Kingdom	United States
Elected members:					
Until December 1981:	Germany (Dem. Rep.)	Mexico	Niger	Philippines	Tanzania
Until December 1982:	Ireland	Japan	Panama	Spain	Uganda

ECONOMIC AND SOCIAL COUNCIL

54 members: elected for 3-year terms by the General Assembly.

Algeria	Burundi	Ethiopia	Ireland	Nicaragua	Thailand
Argentina	Byelorussian SSR	Fiji	Italy	Nigeria	Turkey
Australia	Cameroon	France	Jordan	Norway	USSR
Bahamas	Canada	Germany (Dem. Rep.)	Kenya	Pakistan	United Kingdom
Bangladesh	Chile	Germany (Fed. Rep.)	Libya	Peru	United States
Barbados	China	Ghana	Malawi	Poland	Venezuela
Belgium	Cyprus	India	Mexico	Senegal	Yugoslavia
Brazil	Denmark	Indonesia	Morocco	Spain	Zaire
Bulgaria	Ecuador	Iraq	Nepal	Sudan	Zambia

TRUSTEESHIP COUNCIL

5 members: one (*) an administering state, and four nonadministering permanent members of the Security Council.

China	France	USSR	United Kingdom	United States*

INTERNATIONAL COURT OF JUSTICE

15 members, elected by the General Assembly for 9-year terms that end on 5 February of the year indicated. Judges are listed in order of precedence.

Sir Humphrey Waldock,* (UK, 1982) president for 3 years
Isaac Forster (Senegal, 1982)
André Gros (France, 1982)
Manfred Lachs (Poland, 1985)
Platon D. Morozov (USSR, 1988)

Nagendra Singh (India, 1982)
José Maria Ruda (Argentina, 1982)
Taslim Olawale Elias (Nigeria, 1985)
Hermann Mosler (Germany, Fed. Rep., 1985)
Shigeru Oda (Japan, 1985)

Abdullah Fikri El-Khani (Syria, 1985)
Roberto Ago (Italy, 1988)
Stephen M. Schwebel (U.S., 1988)
Abdullah Ali El-Erian (Egypt, 1988)
José Sette Câmara (Brazil, 1988)

[°] Died August 17, 1981.

HEADS OF MISSIONS TO THE UNITED NATIONS (as of September 1, 1981)

Country	Permanent Representative	Country	Permanent Representative	Country	Permanent Representative
Afghanistan	vacant	Germany		Paraguay	Luis Gonzales Arias
Albania	Abdi Baleta	(Fed. Rep.)	Guenter van Well	Peru	Juan José Calle
Algeria	Mohamed Bedjaoui	Ghana	James Victor Gbeho		y Calle
Angola	Elisio de Figueiredo	Greece	Nicolas Katapodis	Philippines	Alejandro D. Yango
Argentina	Juan Carlos M. Beltramino	Grenada	Caldwell Taylor	Poland	vacant
Australia	H.D. Anderson	Guatemala	Eduardo Castillo Arriola	Portugal	vacant
Austria	Thomas Klestil	Guinea	Djebel Coumbassa	Qatar	Jasim Yousif Jamal
Bahamas	Davidson L. Hepburn	Guinea-Bissau	vacant	Romania	Teodor Marinescu
Bahrain	Salman Mohamed Al-Saffar	Guyana	Noel G. Sinclair	Rwanda	Juvenal Renzaho
Bangladesh	Khwaja Mohammed Kaiser	Haiti	Fritz Cineas	Saint Lucia	Barry B.L. Auguste
Barbados	Ronald G. Mapp	Honduras	Mario Carías	Saint Vincent & The	
Belgium	André Ernemann	Hungary	Pál Rácz	Grenadines	Joel G. Toney
Benin	Thomas Setondji Boya	Iceland	Tómas A. Tómasson	São Tomé &	
Bhutan	Om Pradhan	India	Natarajan Krishnan	Príncipe	vacant
Bolivia	Fernand Ortiz Sanz	Indonesia	Abdullah Kamil	Saudi Arabia	vacant
Botswana	Legwaila Joseph Legwaila	Iran	vacant	Senegal	Massamba Sarré
Brazil	Sérgio Corréa da Costa	Iraq	Salah Omar Al-Ali	Seychelles	vacant
Bulgaria	Boris Tsvetkov	Ireland	Noel Dorr	Sierra Leone	vacant
Burma	vacant	Israel	Yehuda Z. Blum	Singapore	T.T.B. Koh
Burundi	Artémon Simbananiye	Italy	Umberto La Rocca	Solomon Islands	vacant
Byelorussian		Ivory Coast	vacant (4 places)	Somalia	Ahmed Mohamed Adan
SSR	Anatoly Nikitich Sheldov	Jamaica	Egerton Richardson	South Africa	Jacobus Adriaan Eksteen
Cambodia		Japan	Masahiro Nisibori	Spain	Don Jaime de Piniés
(Kampuchea)	M. Thiounn Prasith	Jordan	Hazem Nuseibeh	Sri Lanka	Ignatius Benedict Fonseka
Cameroon	Ferdinand Léopold Oyono	Kenya	Charles Gatere Maina	Sudan	Abdel-Rahman Abdalla
Canada	Gérard Pelletier	Kuwait	Abdalla Yaccoub Bishara	Suriname	Inderdew Sewrajsing
Cape Verde	Amaro Alexandre da Luz	Laos	Vithaya Sourinho	Swaziland	Norman M. Malinga
Central African		Lebanon	Ghassan Tuéni	Sweden	Anders I. Thunborg
Republic	Simon Pierre Kibanda	Lesotho	vacant	Syria	Dia Allah El-Fattal
Chad	vacant	Liberia	Abeodu Bowen Jones	Tanzania	Paul Milyango Rupia
Chile	vacant (4 places)	Libya	vacant	Thailand	Birabhongse Kasemsri
China	Ling Qing	Luxembourg	Paul Peters	Togo	Biyemi Kekeh
Colombia	Indalecio Lievano	Madagascar	Blaise Rabetafika	Trinidad &	
Comoros	vacant	Malawi	N. T. Mizere	Tobago	Frank Owen Abdulah
Congo	Nicolas Mondjo	Malaysia	Datuk Zainal Abidin	Tunisia	Taieb Slim
Costa Rica	Rodolfo Piza Escalante	Maldives	Ahmed Zaki	Turkey	A. Coşkun Kirca
Cuba	Raúl Roa-Kouri	Mali	Seydou Traore	Uganda	Olara Otunnu
Cyprus	Andreas V. Mavrommatis	Malta	Victor J. Gauci	Ukrainian SSR	Vladimir Alekseyevich
Czechoslovakia	Ilja Hulinský	Mauritania	Mohamed Said Ould Hamody		Kravets
Denmark	Wilhelm Ulrichsen	Mauritius	Radha Krishna Ramphul	USSR	Oleg Aleksandrovich
Djibouti	Saleh Haji Farah Dirir	Mexico	Porfirio Muñoz Ledo		Troyanovsky
Dominica	vacant	Mongolia	Buyzntyn Dashtseren	United Arab	
Dom. Rep.	Enriquillo A. Del Rosario	Morocco	Mehdi Mrani Zentar	Emirates	Fahim Sultan Al-Qasimi
Ecuador	Migual A. Albornoz	Mozambique	José Carlos Lobo	United Kingdom	Anthony Parsons
Egypt	Ahmed Esmat Abdel Meguid	Nepal	Uddhav Deo Bhatt	United States	Jeane J. Kirkpatrick
El Salvador	Mauricio Rosales-Rivera	Netherlands	Hugo Scheltema	Upper Volta	Aïssé Mensah
Equatorial		New Zealand	Harold Huyton Francis	Uruguay	vacant
Guinea	Carmelo Nvono-Nca	Nicaragua	Javier Chamorra Mora	Venezuela	Alberto Martini Urdaneta
Ethiopia	Mohamed Hamid Ibrahim	Niger	Idé Oumarou	Vietnam	Ha Van Lau
Fiji	Filipe Nagera Bole	Nigeria	Alhaji Y. Maitama-Sule	Western Samoa	Maiava Iulai Toma
Finland	Ilkka Olavi Pastinen	Norway	Ole Aalgaard	Yemen	Mohsin Ahmed Alaini
France	Jacques Leprette	Oman	Mahmoud Aboul-Nasr	Yemen (Southern)	Abdalla Saleh Ashtal
Gabon	Jean Davin	Pakistan	Niaz A. Naik	Yugoslavia	Miljan Komatina
Gambia	Ousman Ahmadou Sallah	Panama	Carlos Ozores Typaldos	Zaire	Kamanda wa Kamanda
Germany		Papua		Zambia	Paul J.F. Lusaka
(Dem. Rep.)	Peter Florin	New Guinea	Ilinome Tarua	Zimbabwe	Elieck Mashingaidze

UN GENERAL ASSEMBLY PRESIDENTS

Session	Year	President	Session	Year	President
1st	1946	Paul Henri Spaak	19th	1964-65	Alex Quaison-Sackey
2nd	1947	Oswaldo Aranha	20th	1965	Amintore Fanfani
3rd	1948-49	Herbert V. Evatt	21st	1966	Abdul Rahman Pazhwak
4th	1949	Carlos P. Romulo	22nd	1967-68	Corneliu Manescu
5th	1950-51	Nasrollah Entezam	23rd	1968	Emilio Arenales
6th	1951-52	Luis Padilla Nervo	24th	1969	Miss Angie Brooks
7th	1952-53	Lester B. Pearson	25th	1970	Edvard Isak Hambro
8th	1953-54	Mrs. Vijaya Lakshmi Pandit	26th	1971	Adam Malik
9th	1954	Eelco N. van Kleffends	27th	1972	Stanislaw Trepczynski
10th	1955	José Maza	28th	1973	Leopoldo Benites
11th	1956-57	Prince Wan Waithayakon	29th	1974	Abdelaziz Bouteflika
12th	1957	Sir Leslie Munro	30th	1975	Gaston Thorn
13th	1958-59	Charles Malik	31st	1976	Hamilton Shirley Amerasinghe
14th	1959	Victor Andrés Belaúnde	32nd	1977	Lazar Mojsov
15th	1960-61	Frederick H. Boland	33rd	1978	Indalecio Lievano Aguirre
16th	1961-62	Mongi Slim	34th	1979	Salim Ahmed Salim
17th	1962	Muhammad Zafrulla Khan	35th	1980	Rudiger von Wechmar
18th	1963	Carlos Sosa Rodriguez	36th	1981	Ismat Kittani

REPRESENTATIVE INTERNATIONAL ORGANIZATIONS

Afro-Mauritian Common Organization (OCAM) *Formed:* 1965 *Members:* 10 African countries *Headquarters:* Bangui, Central African Empire *Secretary-General:* Sidney Moufia *Purpose:* To promote economic, technical, and cultural development of member French-speaking states within the framework of the OAU. *Recent Developments:* On September 7, 1976, Gabon withdrew from the Organization, and on February 9, 1977, Seychelles became a member.

Andean Group *Formed:* 1969 *Members:* Bolivia, Colombia, Ecuador, Peru and Venezuela *Headquarters:* Lima, Peru *Director-General:* Alberto Zelado Castedo *Purpose:* Regional association with the aim of closer economic and political cooperation among member countries. Venezuela joined in 1973. The Andean Reserve Fund (1977) and Andean Development Corporation (1968) are funding and planning arms for the Andean Group. *Recent Developments:* In December 1980, Bolivia dropped active participation in the Andean Group after the Group condemned the 1980 military take-over in Bolivia.

ANZUS Council *Formed:* 1951 *Members:* Australia, New Zealand, and the United States *Headquarters:* Canberra, Australia *Purpose:* This loose military alliance is pledged to respond to aggression against any of its members. *Recent Developments:* In its June 1981 conference, the Council agreed on the need for an early political solution to the Cambodian-Vietnam conflict and for a stronger response to the increasing Soviet military presence in the South Pacific area.

Arab League (AL) *Formed:* 1945 *Members:* Algeria, Bahrain, Djibouti, Egypt, Iraq, Jordan, Kuwait, Lebanon, Libya, Mauritania, Morocco, Oman, Qatar, Saudi Arabia, Somalia, Sudan, Syria, Tunisia, United Arab Emirates, Yemen, Southern Yemen, and the PLO government. *Headquarters:* Tunis *Secretary-General:* Chedli Klibi (Tunisia) *Purpose:* To strengthen member ties and further promote Arab aspirations. *Recent Developments:* All 20 members of the League have severed economic and political ties with Egypt because of the peace treaty signed with Israel.

Association of Southeast Asian Nations (ASEAN) *Formed:* 1967 *Members:* Indonesia, Malaysia, the Philippines, Singapore and Thailand *Headquarters:* Jakarta, Indonesia *Secretary-General:* Narcisco G. Reyes (Philippines) *Purpose:* To promote economic progress and political stability in Southeast Asia; it seeks to lower trade tariffs for intraregional trade, encourage exchange programs and sharing of scientific knowledge. *Recent Developments:* At the June 1981 meeting of foreign ministers ASEAN supported the planned UN conference on the Cambodian conflict.

Benelux Economic Union *Formed:* 1958 *Members:* Belgium, Luxembourg, and the Netherlands *Headquarters:* Brussels *Secretary-General:* Egbert Kruijtbosch (Netherlands) *Purpose:* To achieve complete economic union of its members (as a subdivision of the EC).

Caribbean Community and Common Market (CARICOM) *Formed:* 1973 *Members:* Antigua, Barbados, Belize, Dominica, Grenada, Guyana, Jamaica, Montserrat, St. Kitts-Nevis-Anguilla, St. Lucia, St. Vincent & the Grenadines, and Trinidad and Tobago *Headquarters:* Georgetown, Guyana *Secretary-General:* Kurleigh D. King (Barbados) *Purpose:* To promote unity in the Caribbean through economic integration, a common external tariff and coordination of development plans.

Central African Economic and Customs Union (UDEAC) *Formed:* 1966 *Members:* Cameroon, Central African Republic, Congo, Gabon; Chad has had observer status since 1975 *Headquarters:* Bangui, Central African Republic *Secretary-General:* Vincent Efon (Cameroon) *Purpose:* To promote the gradual establishment of a Central African Common Market and see to the general improvement of living standards of the peoples of member states.

Central American Common Market (CACM) *Formed:* 1960 *Members:* Costa Rica, El Salvador, Guatemala, Honduras and Nicaragua. (Honduras withdrew from active membership in 1970) *Headquarters:* Guatemala City, Guatemala *Secretary-General:* Raúl Sierra Franco *Purpose:* To establish a free trade area and a customs union with joint planning for social and economic development of the region.

Colombo Plan for Cooperative Development in Asia and the Pacific *Formed:* 1950 *Members:* 26 countries *Headquarters:* Colombo, Sri Lanka *President:* Young Kyo Yoon (Rep. of Korea) *Purpose:* To aid developing countries through bilateral member agreements for the provision of capital, technical experts and training, and equipment.

Commonwealth, The (formerly British Commonwealth) *Formed:* 1931 *Members:* 44 *Headquarters:* London *Secretary-General:* Shridath Ramphal (Guyana) *Purpose:* A voluntary association of independent states and their dependencies who meet and consult a regular basis to foster Commonwealth links and achieve a more equitable world society. All Commonwealth countries accept Queen Elizabeth II as the symbolic head of the association.

Council for Mutual Economic Assistance (COMECON) *Formed:* 1949 *Members:* Bulgaria, Cuba, Czechoslovakia, East Germany, Hungary, Mongolia, Poland, Romania, the Soviet Union and Vietnam; Associate Member: Yugoslavia *Headquarters:* Moscow *Secretary:* N.V. Faddeyev (Soviet Union) *Purpose:* To coordinate and integrate members' economies, under USSR leadership. *Recent Developments:* On April 24, 1981, the Soviet Union announced that it would not be responsible for Poland's financial obligations to Western creditors.

Council of Europe *Formed:* 1949 *Members:* 21 countries, mostly in Western Europe but also includes Greece and Turkey *Headquarters:* Strasbourg, France *Secretary-General:* Franz Karasek (Austria) *Purpose:* To protect human rights, bring European countries closer together, and voice the views of the European public on the main political and economic questions of the day.

Eastern European Mutual Assistance Treaty (Warsaw Pact) *Formed:* 1955 *Members:* Bulgaria, Czechoslovakia, East Germany, Hungary, Poland, Romania, and the Soviet Union *Headquarters:* Moscow *Supreme Military Commander:* Marshal Viktor G. Kulikov (Soviet Union) *Purpose:* This major European military alliance is the Soviet bloc's equivalent of the North Atlantic Treaty Organization, and its forces, like NATO's, are composed of military elements from member countries.

Economic Community of West African States (ECOWAS) *Formed:* 1975 *Members:* 16 West African states *Headquarters:* Lagos, Nigeria *Executive Secretary:* Aboubacar Diaby-Quattara (Ivory Coast) *Purpose:* Promoting trade, cooperation and self-reliance in West Africa.

European Atomic Energy Community (Euratom) *Formed:* 1958 *Members:* Belgium, France, West Germany, Greece, Italy, Luxembourg, the Netherlands, Denmark, Ireland, and Britain *Headquarters:* Brussels *Purpose:* To promote the common development of nuclear energy for peaceful purposes.

European Coal and Steel Community (ECSC) *Formed:* 1952 *Members:* Belgium, France, West Germany, Greece, Italy, Luxembourg, Britain, Ireland, Denmark and the Netherlands *Headquarters:* Luxembourg *Purposes:* To maintain a common market for coal, iron, ore, and steel, and harmonize external tariffs; to abolish discriminatory pricing systems and transport-rates among members, while safe-guarding continuity of employment.

European Community (EC, the Common Market) *Formed:* 1958 *Members:* Belgium, France, West Germany, Greece, Italy, Luxembourg, the Netherlands, Britain, Denmark, and Ireland. *Headquarters:* Brussels *President:* Roy Jenkins (Britain) *Purpose:* To abolish all internal tariffs and other trade barriers and to align external tariffs, so that there can be free movement of goods, persons, services, and capital within the EC. *Recent Developments:* Greece became the 10th member of EC on January 1, 1981. EC national leaders met in March 1981 but were unable to resolve controversial issues on fishing rights, steel industry subsidies and EC-supported farm prices. Steel production curbs went into effect for members on July 1, 1981.

European Free Trade Association (EFTA) *Formed:* 1960 *Members:* Austria, Iceland, Norway, Portugal, Sweden, and Switzerland; Associate Member: Finland *Headquarters:* Geneva *Secretary-General:* Charles Müller (Switzerland) *Purpose:* To maintain the elimination of internal tariffs on industrial goods (achieved at the end of 1966) and negotiate bilateral agreements on agricultural products. *Recent Developments:* Once called the Outer Seven, EFTA has aimed at a lesser degree of economic integration than the European Community. A customs union with the EC came into force July 1, 1977.

International Committee of the Red Cross (ICRC) *Formed:* 1863 *Members:* 25 Swiss citizens *Headquarters:* Geneva *President:* Alexandre Hay (Switzerland) *Purpose:* To organize care for the victims of war and enforce the various Conventions on wartime practices. The ICRC constitutes, with the League of Red Cross Societies, the International Red Cross. The League of Red Cross Societies, founded in 1929, has member societies in 126 countries.

International Criminal Police Organization (Interpol) *Formed:* 1956 *Members:* Official police bodies in 122 countries *Headquarters:* Paris (St. Cloud) *Secretary-General:* A.A. Bossard (France) *Purpose:* To ensure maximum cooperation between police authorities, with the strict exclusion of political, military, religious, and racial matters. As successor to the International Criminal Police Commission, established in 1923, Interpol acts as a clearinghouse for information on international criminal activities.

International Energy Agency (IEA) *Formed:* 1974 *Members:* 21 countries including most Western European nations with Greece and Turkey plus the U.S., Canada and Japan *Headquarters:* Paris *Chief Officer:* Chairman Niels Ersboll (Denmark) *Purpose:* To develop cooperation among major oil importing nations and to strengthen the security and stability of world energy markets. *Recent Developments:* Member nations showed a decline of 7.5% in oil consumption in 1980 and agreed in December 1980 to 10% cut in oil imports for the first quarter of 1981.

Latin American Free Trade Association (LAFTA) *Formed:* 1960 *Members:* Argentina, Bolivia, Brazil, Chile, Columbia, Ecuador, Mexico, Paraguay, Peru, Uruguay, and Venezuela *Headquarters:* Montevideo, Uruguay *Executive Secretary:* Daniel Mesa Bernal (Colombia) *Purpose:* To work toward the establishment of a Latin American common market.

Nordic Council *Formed:* 1953 *Members:* Denmark, Finland, Iceland, Norway, and Sweden *Headquarters:* Stockholm *Secretary of the Presidium:* Gudmund Saxrud (Norway) *Purpose:* To arrange cooperation among members in cultural, legal, social, and economic matters.

North Atlantic Treaty Organization (NATO) *Formed:* 1949 *Members:* Belgium, Canada, Denmark, France, West Germany, Great Britian, Greece, Iceland, Italy, Luxembourg, the Netherlands, Norway, Portugal, Turkey, and the United States *Headquarters:* Brussels *Secretary-General:* Dr. Joseph Luns (Netherlands) *Supreme Commander:* Gen. Bernard Rogers (U.S.) *Purpose:* This major Western military alliance, with prime responsibility for opposing Communist forces in Europe, is composed of elements from the armed forces of member nations. *Recent Developments:* NATO has committed itself to a modernization of its nuclear forces. Greece rejoined NATO's military wing October 20, 1980. NATO ministers meeting in Rome on May 4-5, 1981, criticized the Soviet Union's military activities and linked improved East-West relations to less aggressive Soviet behavior. NATO allies have agreed to deployment of cruise missiles but seeking to ease the nuclear arms race have encouraged renewed Soviet-American arms limitation talks.

Organization for Economic Cooperation and Development (OECD) *Formed:* 1961 *Members:* 24 countries, mostly in Western Europe, but also U.S., Australia, New Zealand and Japan *Headquarters:* Paris *Secretary-General:* Emile van Lennep (Netherlands) *Purpose:* To achieve economic growth and full employment and to further world economic development. As successor to the Organization for European Economic Cooperation (OEEC) that was established in 1948 to oversee Marshall Plan reconstruction, OECD has a broadened scope, having established an extensive aid program to developing countries.

Organization of African Unity (OAU) *Formed:* 1963 *Members:* All 50 independent African countries, except the white-dominated states and territories of the south. *Headquarters:* Addis Ababa, Ethiopia

Secretary-General: Edem Kodjo (Togo) *Purpose:* To promote African solidarity, coordinate policies, defend member sovereignty, and eliminate colonialism in Africa. *Recent Developments:* Attempts by the OAU in 1980 to end the civil strife in Chad were unsuccessful. The OAU leadership was later split on the issue of the intervention of Libyan troops in Chad. At the June 1981 meeting of OAU ministers and heads of state, Morocco announced an offer for a cease-fire in the guerrilla war in Western Sahara and a referendum on Moroccan rule there.

Organization of American States (OAS) *Formed:* 1948 *Members:* 28 American countries *Headquarters:* Washington, D.C. *Secretary-General:* Alejandro Orfila (Argentina) *Purpose:* To promote the solidarity and defend the sovereignty of members and provide through the Pan American Union—the OAS central organ and secretariat—social, political, economic, and technical services. *Recent Developments:* The tenth General Assembly November 1980 took up the controversial issue of human rights violations in several countries, especially Argentina. A mild resolution was passed which did not name specific nations. Self-determination for Belize was approved.

Organization of Petroleum Exporting Countries (OPEC) *Formed:* 1960 *Members:* Algeria, Ecuador, Gabon, Indonesia, Iran, Iraq, Kuwait, Libya, Nigeria, Qatar, Saudi Arabia, United Arab Emirates and Venezuela *Headquarters:* Vienna *Secretary-General:* René G. Ortiz (Ecuador) *Purpose:* To coordinate policies and establish prices regarding petroleum exported to consumer nations. *Recent Developments:* OPEC members failed to reach agreement on pricing and marketing policies in the fall of 1980. The Iraq-Iran war and Saudi Arabian unwillingness to cooperate with other OPEC nations upset any plans for uniform goals. The May 25-26, 1981 meeting of OPEC nations decided to freeze prices in the face of the present glut of oil stocks.

West African Economic Community (CEAO) *Formed:* 1973 *Members:* Ivory Coast, Mali, Mauritania, Niger, Senegal and Upper Volta (*Observers:* Benin and Togo) *Headquarters:* Ouagadougou, Upper Volta *Secretary-General:* Moussa N'gom (Senegal) *Purpose:* To establish an economic and customs union for West African states.

World Council of Churches (WCC) *Formed:* 1948 *Members:* 313 churches in over 90 countries, including most major Protestant and Eastern Orthodox denominations *Headquarters:* Geneva *General Secretary:* Dr. Philip A. Potter (West Indies) *Purpose:* To promote cooperation and unity among the churches of the world. It is active in missionary work, aid to refugees, the sick and under-privileged and in helping promote education and the cause of world peace.

U.S. CONTRIBUTIONS TO INTERNATIONAL ORGANIZATIONS

SOURCE: U.S. Department of State

FISCAL YEAR 1980 (In Millions of Dollars)

Organization	Estimated Amount	Organization	Estimated Amount
United Nations and Specialized Agencies:		**Special Voluntary Programs:**	
United Nations	$149.54	Consultative Group on International Agricultural Research	29.00
Food and Agricultural Organization	28.63	Intergovernmental Committee for European Migration	138.27
International Atomic Energy Agency	4.64	International Atomic Energy Agency—	
International Civil Aviation Organizations	2.00	Operational Program	12.00[1]
Joint Financing Program	2.00	Organization of American States—Special	
International Telecommunications Union	2.76	Development Assistance Fund	6.60
UNESCO	33.44	Organization of American States—Special Multilateral Fund (Education and Science)	6.50
World Health Organization	50.36	Organization of American States—Special	
World Meteorological Organization	4.51	Projects	2.00
Others (7 programs, less than $1 million)	1.23	Pan American Health Organization—	
		Special Voluntary Program	4.12
United Nations Peacekeeping Forces:		United Nations Capital Development Fund	2.00
United Nations Emergency Force (UNEF/UNDOF/UNIFIL)	50.81	United Nations Children Fund	34.60
United Nations Force in Cyprus	9.00	United Nations Decade for Women	1.00
		United Nations Development Program	126.05
Inter-American Organizations		United Nations Educational and Training	
Organization of American States	35.94	Program for South Africa	1.00
Inter-American Institute of Agricultural Sciences	7.97	United Nations Environment Fund	10.00
Pan American Health Organization	25.16	UN/FAO World Food Program	97.00
Inter-American Tropical Tuna Commission	1.88	United Nations Fund for Drug Abuse Control	1.12
Other (4 programs, less than $1 million)	0.44	United Nations Fund for Population Activities	32.00
		United Nations High Commissioner for Refugees	73.14
Regional Organizations:		Special Resettlement and Relief Programs	50.31
NATO Civilian Headquarters	14.85	United Nations Relief and Works Agency	55.20
Organization for Economic Cooperation and Development	20.22	West African Rice Development Association	1.00
Others (3 programs, less than $1 million)	1.05	World Health Organization—Special Programs	8.72
		World Meteorological Organization—	
Other International Organizations:		Voluntary Assistance Program	2.00
Customs Cooperation Council	1.68	Others (8 programs less than $1 million)	2.55
General Agreement on Tariffs and Trade	3.52		
Intergovernmental Committee for European Migration	4.12		
International Institute for Cotton	1.97		
Others (30 programs, less than $1 million)	4.14	**Total U.S. Contributions**	**$1,177.41**

[1] Includes cash, commodities and services and $5.1 million for Safeguards Program

U.S. FOREIGN ECONOMIC ASSISTANCE

SOURCE: Program Data Services Division, Bureau for Program and Policy Coordination, Agency for International Development

The table below gives total U.S. foreign economic aid under the Foreign Assistance Act of 1961 and related precedent legislation—loans and grants—since 1946 and foreign aid data for fiscal year 1980. Included also is other foreign economic assistance provided by the U.S. (contributions to multilateral development banks, Food for Peace, Peace Corps, and International Narcotics Control).

The Agency for International Development (AID) has been the administering agency for foreign economic assistance under the Foreign Assistance Act since November 4, 1961. Agencies dealing with economic assistance programs prior to that date have been, successively: the Economic Cooperation Administration (Apr. 3, 1948-Oct. 31, 1951); the Mutual Security Agency (Nov. 1, 1951-July 31, 1953); the Foreign Operations Administration (Aug. 1, 1953-June 30, 1955); the International Cooperation Administration (July 1, 1955-Nov. 3, 1961); and the Development Loan Fund (Aug. 14, 1957-Nov. 3, 1961).

The latter two agencies operated concurrently for approximately four years until their functions were combined under the provisions of the Foreign Assistance Act of 1961.

Region and Country	Total 1946-1980 (Millions)	Fiscal Year 1980 (Millions)
GRAND TOTAL	$141,635.0	$7,573.0
Near East and South Asia	**36,669.0**	**2,801.9**
Afghanistan	536.8	—
Bahrain	2.4	—
Bangladesh	1,503.2	157.3
Bhutan	0.8	0.8
Cyprus	149.3	15.2
Egypt	6,373.2	1,166.4
Greece	1,910.2	—
India	10,122.2	221.5
Iran	765.6	—
Iraq	45.5	—
Israel	5,585.8	786.0
Jordan	1,423.0	72.7
Lebanon	184.1	0.5
Nepal	258.7	20.6
Oman	7.8	5.6
Pakistan	4,970.9	58.6
Saudi Arabia	31.8	—
Sri Lanka	505.2	60.3
Syria	586.0	1.1
Turkey	2,983.9	198.1
Yemen Arab Republic	122.7	13.3
Yemen, People's Democratic Rep.	4.5	—
Central Treaty Organization	39.6	—
Regional	556.0	24.0
Latin America	**12,326.6**	**498.6**
Argentina	199.3	—
Bahamas	0.3	—
Barbados	3.3	0.2
Belize	10.3	0.8
Bolivia	807.2	30.1
Brazil	2,426.4	2.4
Chile	1,171.8	10.2
Colombia	1,362.1	23.2
Costa Rica	265.0	16.0
Cuba	4.0	—
Dominican Republic	645.5	55.8
Ecuador	320.0	11.9
El Salvador	261.9	58.4
Guatemala	451.1	13.0
Guyana	126.8	4.9
Haiti	273.2	27.1
Honduras	324.0	53.1
Jamaica	191.5	14.6
Mexico	327.0	7.4
Nicaragua	337.4	38.7
Panama	424.6	2.0
Paraguay	181.5	3.7
Peru	660.8	53.3
Suriname	5.8	—
Trinidad & Tobago	40.9	0.3
Uruguay	159.5	—
Venezuela	201.2	—
Other West Indies— Eastern Caribbean Regional	182.1	47.7
Regional Office Central America & Panama-ROCAP	285.1	4.2
Regional	677.1	19.5
East Asia	**27,079.2**	**406.4**
Burma	108.3	6.8
Cambodia	889.3	38.3
China	0.5	0.5
Hong Kong	43.8	—
Indochina[a]	825.6	—
Indonesia	2,752.4	196.4
Japan	2,711.1	—
Korea	5,982.8	30.9
Laos	902.6	—
Malaysia	88.5	2.6
Philippines	2,102.3	83.3
Ryukyu Islands (U.S.)	413.7	—
Singapore	2.8	—
Taiwan	2,206.9	—
Thailand	742.2	29.6
Vietnam	6,945.5	—
Regional	356.5	-17.8
Africa	**8,221.2**	**799.1**
Algeria	203.3	—
Angola	8.9	6.2
Benin	48.4	3.7

Region and Country	Total 1946-1980 (Millions)	Fiscal Year 1980 (Millions)
Botswana	$ 118.9	$ 19.3
Burundi	24.8	6.5
Cameroon	81.5	9.4
Cape Verde	37.4	5.8
Central African Republic	15.8	1.5
Chad	65.2	3.8
Comoros	0.3	0.3
Congo, People's Republic of	10.4	1.0
Djibouti, Democratic Republic of	4.7	1.9
Entente States	38.3	—
Ethiopia	387.6	15.0
Gabon	12.4	1.0
Gambia, The	22.6	7.3
Ghana	390.0	27.7
Guinea	161.1	11.4
Guinea-Bissau	15.0	2.1
Ivory Coast	46.7	1.6
Kenya	284.7	53.9
Lesotho	78.9	18.8
Liberia	309.0	23.4
Libya	212.5	—
Madagascar	21.2	—
Malawi	64.2	5.9
Mali, Republic of	145.7	17.5
Mauritania	61.3	11.7
Mauritius	23.5	3.5
Morocco	1,006.4	27.1
Mozambique	62.0	18.9
Niger	119.6	12.9
Nigeria	406.5	—
Rwanda	29.7	4.1
São Tomé and Príncipe	0.6	0.1
Senegal	151.8	27.2
Seychelles	3.1	1.0
Sierra Leone	82.0	7.1
Somali Republic	199.3	67.3
South Africa	1.3	—
Sudan	96.4	263.1
Swaziland	43.6	9.0
Tanzania	271.4	25.2
Togo	50.1	5.9
Tunisia	894.9	29.0
Uganda	53.5	6.1
Upper Volta	138.7	22.9
Zaire	628.4	25.9
Zambia	182.5	46.4
Zimbabwe	29.9	22.4
Portuguese Territories	3.4	—
Central & West Africa Regional	114.5	21.6
East Africa Regional	33.3	—
Southern Africa Regional	90.9	8.1
Regional	466.7	53.6
Europe	**28,542.9**	**88.0**
Albania	20.4	—
Austria	1,135.2	—
Belgium	592.3	—
Czechoslovakia	193.0	—
Denmark	281.9	—
Finland	56.8	—
France	3,918.1	—
Germany, East	0.8	—
Germany, West	4,041.1	—
West Berlin	131.9	—
Hungary	32.7	—
Iceland	82.2	—
Ireland	146.5	—
Italy	3,338.8	3.0
Malta	83.9	—
Netherlands	1,027.6	—
Norway	301.8	—
Poland	539.3	—
Portugal	841.1	78.0
Romania	22.4	—
Spain	1,054.7	7.0
Sweden	109.0	—
United Kingdom	7,672.1	—
USSR	186.4	—
Yugoslavia	2,109.1	—
Regional	624.0	—
Oceania	**886.6**	**10.2**
Canada	17.5	—
Interregional	**25,894.1**	**2,969.9**

*Less than $50,000.—No economic assistance. [a]Prior to division into Vietnam, Cambodia, and Laos in 1955.

SELECTED FOREIGN EMBASSIES AND AMBASSADORS

SOURCE: Department of State (as of September 1, 1981)

Algeria: 2118 Kalorama Rd. NW, 20008
Amb: Redha Malek

Argentina: 1600 New Hampshire Ave. NW, 20009
Amb: Jorge A. Aja Espil

Australia: 1601 Massachusetts Ave. NW, 20036
Amb: Nicholas F. Parkinson

Austria: 2343 Massachusetts Ave. NW, 20008
Amb: Karl H. Schober

Bahamas: Suite 865, 600 New Hamphshire Ave. NW, 20037
Amb: Reginald L. Wood

Bangladesh: 3421 Massachusetts Ave. NW, 20007
Amb: Tabarak Husain

Belgium: 3330 Garfield St. NW, 20008
Amb: J. Raoul Schoumaker

Bolivia: 3014 Massachusetts Ave. NW, 20008

Brazil: 3006 Massachusetts Ave. NW, 20008
Amb: Antonio F.A. da Silveira

Bulgaria: 2100 16th St. NW, 20009
Amb: Stoyan I. Zhulev

Canada: 1746 Massachusetts Ave. NW, 20036
Amb: Peter M. Towe

Chad: 1901 Spruce Dr. NW, 20012
Chargé: Mahamat Ali Adoum

Chile: 1732 Massachusetts Ave. NW, 20036
Amb: Jose Miguel Barros

China (P.R.C.): 2300 Connecticut Ave. NW, 20008 Amb: Chai Zemin

Colombia: 2118 Leroy Pl. NW, 20008
Amb: Jorge Mario Eastman

Costa Rica: 2112 S St. NW, 20008
Amb: Jose R. Echeverria

Cyprus: 2211 R St. NW, 20008
Amb: Andrew J. Jacovides

Czechoslovakia: 3900 Linnean Ave. NW, 20008
Amb: Dr. Jaromlr Johanes

Denmark: 3200 Whitehaven St. NW, 20008
Amb: Otto R. Borch

Dominican Republic: 1715 22nd St. NW, 20008
Amb: Rafael Molina Morillo*

Ecuador: 2535 15th St. NW, 20009
Amb: Ricardo Crespo-Zaldumbide

Egypt: 2310 Decatur Pl. NW, 20008
Amb: Dr. Ashraf A. Ghorbal

El Salvador: 2308 California St. NW, 20008
Chargé: Roberto Jimenez Ortiz

Ethiopia: 2134 Kalorama Rd. NW, 20008
Chargé: Tesfaye Demeke

*Appointed

Finland: 3216 New Mexico Ave. NW, 20016
Amb: Jaakko Iloniemi

France: 2535 Belmont Rd. NW, 20008
Amb: Francois de Laboulaye

Germany (Federal Rep.): 4645 Reservoir Rd. NW, 20007
Amb: Peter Hermes

German Democratic Rep.: 1717 Massachusetts Ave. NW, 20036
Amb: Dr. Horst Grunert

Ghana: 2460 16th St. NW, 20009
Amb: Dr. Joseph K. Baffour-Senkyire

Greece: 2221 Massachusetts Ave. NW, 20008
Amb: John A. Tzounis

Guatemala: 2220 R St. NW, 20008
Amb: Gen. Felipe D. Monterroso

Guinea: 2112 Leroy Pl. NW, 20008
Amb: Mamadi Lamine Conde

Guyana: 2490 Tracy Pl. NW, 20008
Amb: Laurence E. Mann

Haiti: 2311 Massachusetts Ave. NW, 20008
Chargé: Miss Josette Philippeaux

Honduras: Suite 100, 4301 Connecticut Ave. NW, 20008
Amb: Col. Federico A. Poujol

Hungary: 3910 Shoemaker St. NW, 20008
Amb: Ferenc Esztergalyos

India: 2107 Massachusetts Ave. NW, 20008
Amb: K. R. Narayanan

Indonesia: 2020 Massachusetts Ave. NW, 20036
Amb: D. Ashari

Ireland: 2234 Massachusetts Ave. NW, 20008
Amb: Sean Donlon

Israel: 3514 International Dr. NW, 20008
Amb: Ephraim Evron

Italy: 1601 Fuller St. NW, 20009
Amb: Paolo Pansa Cedronio

Jamaica: Suite 355, 1850 K St. NW, 20006
Amb: Keith Johnson

Japan: 2520 Massachusetts Ave. NW, 20008
Amb: Yoshio Okawara

Jordan: 2319 Wyoming Ave. NW, 20008
Amb: Al-Sharif Fawaz Sharif

Kenya: 2249 R St. NW, 20008
Amb: John P. Mbogua

Korea: 2370 Massachusetts Ave. NW, 20008
Amb: Yong Shik Kim

Laos: 2222 S St. NW, 20008
Chargé: Khamtan Ratanavong

Lebanon: 2560 28th St. NW, 20008
Amb: Khalil Itani

Liberia: 5201 16th St. NW, 20011
Amb: Dr. Joseph S. Guannu

Luxembourg: 2200 Massachusetts Ave. NW, 20008
Amb: Adrien Meisch

Malawi: Bristol House, 1400 20th St. NW, 20036
Amb: Nelson T. Mizere

Malaysia: 2401 Massachusetts Ave. NW, 20008
Amb: Zain Azraai

Malta: 2017 Connecticut Ave. NW, 20008
Chargé: Emanuel C. Farrugia

Mexico: 2829 16th St. NW, 20009
Amb: Hugo B. Margain

Morocco: 1601 21st St. NW, 20009
Amb: Ali Bengelloun

Nepal: 2131 Leroy Pl. NW, 20008
Amb.: Bekh Bahadur Thapa

Netherlands: 4200 Linnean Ave. NW, 20008
Amb: Dr. Jan Hendrik Lubbers

New Zealand: 37 Observatory Cir. NW, 20008
Amb: Thomas F. Gill

Nicaragua: 1627 New Hampshire Ave. NW, 20009
Amb: Arturo J. Cruz*

Nigeria: 2201 M St. NW, 20037
Amb: Olujimi Jolaoso

Norway: 2720 34th St. NW, 20008
Amb: Knut Hedemann

Pakistan: 2315 Massachusetts Ave. NW, 20008
Amb: Lt. Gen. Ejaz Azim*

Panama: 2862 McGill Terr. NW, 20008
Amb: Juan Jose Amado

Paraguay: 2400 Massachusetts Ave. NW, 20008
Amb: Mario López Escobar

Peru: 1700 Massachusetts Ave. NW, 20036
Amb: Fernando Schwalb

Philippines: 1617 Massachusetts Ave. NW, 20036
Amb: Eduardo Z. Romualdez

Poland: 2640 16th St. NW, 20009
Amb: Romauld Spasowski

Portugal: 2125 Kalorama Rd. NW, 20008
Chargé: Pedro Ribeiro de Menezes

Romania: 1607 23rd St. NW, 20008
Amb: Nicolae Ionescu

Saudi Arabia: 1520 18th St. NW, 20036
Amb: Sheikh Faisal Alhegelan

Senegal: 2112 Wyoming Ave. NW, 20008
Amb: André Coulbary

Singapore: 1824 R St. NW, 20009
Amb: Punch Coomaraswamy

South Africa: 3051 Massachusetts Ave. NW, 20008
Amb: Donald B. Sole

Spain: 2700 15th St. NW, 20009
Amb: José Llado

Sri Lanka: 2148 Wyoming Ave. NW, 20008
Amb: Ernest Corea*

Sudan: Suite 400, 600 New Hampshire Ave. NW, 20037
Amb: Omer Salih Eissa

Sweden: Suite 1200, 600 New Hampshire Ave. NW, 20037
Amb: Count Wilhelm Wachtmeister

Switzerland: 2900 Cathedral Ave. NW, 20008
Amb: Anton Hegner

Syria: 2215 Wyoming Ave. NW, 20008
Chargé: Abdul Hassib Istwani

Tanzania: 2139 R St. NW, 20008
Amb: Paul Bomani

Thailand: 2300 Kalorama Rd. NW, 20008
Amb: Prok Amaranand

Trinidad and Tobago: 1708 Massachusetts Ave. NW, 20036 Amb: Victor C. McIntyre

Tunisia: 2408 Massachusetts Ave. NW, 20008
Amb: Ali Hedda

Turkey: 1606 23rd St. NW, 20008
Amb: Sukru Elekdag

Union of Soviet Socialist Republics: 1125 16th St. NW, 20036
Amb: Anatoliy F. Dobrynin

United Kingdom: 3100 Massachusetts Ave. NW, 20008
Amb: Sir Nicholas Henderson

Upper Volta: 2340 Massachusetts Ave. NW, 20008
Amb: Télesphore Yaguibou

Uruguay: 1918 F St. NW, 20006
Amb: Jorge Pacheco Areco

Venezuela: 2445 Massachusetts Ave. NW, 20008
Amb: Marcial Perez-Chiriboga

Yugoslavia: 2410 California St. NW, 20008
Amb: Budimir Loncar

Zaire: 1800 New Hampshire Ave. NW, 20008
Amb: Kasongo Mutuale

Zambia: 2419 Massachusetts Ave. NW, 20008
Amb: Putteho M. Ngonda

Zimbabwe: 2852 McGill Ter. NW, 20008
Amb: Dr. Elleck K. Mashingaidze

ACTION

As of July 1, 1971, a number of federal volunteer service programs—the Peace Corps and its domestic equivalent, VISTA, most prominent among them—were merged into a single agency, called ACTION. It is headed by Thomas Weir Pauken, former White House staff assistant.

The components of the organization and their volunteer strengths estimated in fiscal year 1981 are:

The Peace Corps is an independent agency within ACTION with 5,994 volunteers serving full-time in 64 developing countries. Its estimated fiscal year 1981 budget is $99.9 million.

Volunteers in Service to America (VISTA), with 3,982 volunteers at work full-time in programs throughout the United States. Its fiscal 1981 budget is $30 million.

The Retired Senior Volunteer Program (RSVP), which provides volunteer opportunities for elderly persons. It has 274,700 volunteers and a budget of $26 million.

Two other volunteer programs provide stipends to low-income senior citizens who devote 20 hours each week to institutionalized children or to the homebound elderly. With an estimated FY 1981 budget of $47 million, ACTION supports 17,610 volunteers in the Foster Grand-parent Program. Approximately 3,820 elderly men and women serve as Senior Companions, a program that has an FY 1981 budget of $10 million.

ACTION's Urban Crime Prevention Program has 9 grantees with 86 project organizations, 88 full-time volunteers and 4,300 part-time volunteers. Its 1981 budget is $3.5 million.

Fixed Income Consumer Counseling has 15 projects, 4,500 volunteers, and a current budget of $381,000.

AMERICAN DIPLOMATS ABROAD

SOURCE: U.S. Department of State (as of September 1, 1981)   *Chargé d'Affaires.   **Ambassador-nominated.   ***Named.

Country	Chief of Mission
Afghanistan	Hawthorne Q. Mills*
Algeria	Michael H. Newlin**
Argentina	Harry W. Shlaudeman
Australia	Robert D. Nesen
Austria	Theodore E. Cummings
Bahamas	Andrew F. Antippas*
Bahrain	Peter A. Sutherland
Bangladesh	Jane A. Coon
Barbados	Virgil P. Randolph III*
Belgium	Charles H. Price II
Benin	James R. Bullington*
Bolivia	Alexander F. Watson*
Botswana	Horace G. Dawson, Jr.
Brazil	Robert M. Sayre
Bulgaria	Jack R. Perry
Burma	Patricia M. Byrne
Burundi	Frances D. Cook
Cameroon	Hume A. Horan
Canada	Paul H. Robinson, Jr.
Cape Verde	Peter deVos
Central African Republic	Arthur H. Woodruff
Chile	George W. Landau
China (People's Rep.)	Arthur W. Hummel, Jr.
Colombia	Thomas D. Boyatt
Comoros	Fernando E. Rondon
Congo	Arlene Render*
Costa Rica	Francis J. McNeil
Cyprus	Galen L. Stone
Czechoslovakia	Jack F. Matlock, Jr.**
Denmark	John L. Loeb, Jr.
Djibouti	Jerrold M. North
Dominica	Virgil P. Randolph III*
Dominican Rep.	Robert L. Yost
Ecuador	Raymond E. Gonzalez
Egypt	Alfred L. Atherton, Jr.
El Salvador	Deane R. Hinton
Equatorial Guinea	Hume A. Horan
Ethiopia	Owen W. Roberts*
Fiji	William Bodde, Jr.
Finland	Keith F. Nyborg
France	Evan G. Galbraith***
Gabon	Arthur T. Tienken
The Gambia	Larry G. Piper
German Democratic Rep.	Herbert S. Okun
Germany, Fed. Rep. of	Arthur F. Burns
Ghana	Thomas W. M. Smith
Greece	Monteagle Stearns
Grenada	Virgil P. Randolph III*
Guatemala	Frederic L. Chapin
Guinea	Allen C. Davis
Guinea-Bissau	Peter deVos
Guyana	George B. Roberts, Jr.

Country	Chief of Mission
Haiti	Ernest H. Preeg
Honduras	Jack R. Binns
Hungary	Harry E. Bergold, Jr.
Iceland	Marshall Brement
India	Harry G. Barns**
Indonesia	Edward E. Masters
Ireland	Peter Murphy***
Israel	Samuel W. Lewis
Italy	Maxwell M. Rabb
Ivory Coast	Nancy V. Rawls
Jamaica	Loren E. Lawrence
Japan	Michael J. Mansfield
Jordan	Richard N. Viets
Kenya	William C. Harrop
Kiribati	William Bodde, Jr.
Korea	Richard L. Walker
Kuwait	Francois M. Dickman
Laos	Leo J. Moser*
Lebanon	Robert S. Dillon
Lesotho	John R. Clingerman
Liberia	William L. Swing
Luxembourg	John E. Dolibois**
Madagascar	Fernando E. Rondon
Malawi	John A. Burroughs, Jr.
Malaysia	Ronald D. Palmer
Maldives	Donald R. Toussaint
Mali	Parker W. Borg
Malta	Frank Wardlaw*
Mauritania	Stanley N. Schrager*
Mauritius	Robert C. F. Gordon
Mexico	John A. Gavin
Morocco	Joseph V. Reed, Jr.***
Mozambique	William H. Twaddell*
Nauru	Robert D. Nesen
Nepal	Carleton S. Coon
Netherlands	William J. Dyess
New Zealand	H. Monroe Browne
Nicaragua	Roger Gamble*
Niger	James K. Bishop
Nigeria	Stephen Low
Norway	Richard Barkley*
Oman	John R. Countryman
Pakistan	Ronald I. Spiers**
Panama	Ambler H. Moss, Jr.
Papua New Guinea	M. Virginia Schafer**
Paraguay	Lyle F. Lane
Peru	Frank V. Ortiz**
Philippines	James D. Rosenthal*
Poland	Francis J. Meehan
Portugal	Richard J. Bloomfield
Qatar	Charles E. Marthinsen
Romania	David B. Funderburk**
Rwanda	Harry R. Melone
Saint Lucia	Virgil P. Randolph III*

Country	Chief of Mission
St. Vin. & Grens.	Virgil P. Randolph III**
São Tomé & Principe	Arthur T. Tienken
Saudi Arabia	Richard W. Murphy**
Senegal	Charles W. Bray III
Seychelles	William C. Harrop
Sierra Leone	Theresa A. Healy
Singapore	Harry E. T. Thayer
Solomon Isls.	M. Virginia Schafer**
Somalia	Donald K. Petterson
South Africa	William B. Edmundson
Spain	Terence A. Todman
Sri Lanka	Donald R. Toussaint
Sudan	C. William Kontos
Suriname	John P. Crowley, Jr.
Swaziland	Richard C. Matheron
Sweden	William C. Hamilton*
Switzerland	Richard D. Vine
Syria	Robert P. Paganelli**
Tanzania	David J. Fischer*
Thailand	Morton I. Abramowitz
Togo	Marilyn P. Johnson
Tonga	Willaim Bodde, Jr.
Trinidad and Tobago	Irving G. Cheslaw
Tunisia	Stephen Warren Bosworth
Turkey	Robert Strausz-Hupé
Tuvalu	William Bodde, Jr.
Uganda	Gorden R. Beyer
U.S.S.R.	Arthur A. Hartman**
United Arab Emirates	William D. Wolle
United Kingdom	John J. Louis, Jr.
Upper Volta	Julius W. Walker, Jr.
Uruguay	N. Shaw Smith
Venezuela	William H. Luers
Western Samoa	H. Monroe Browne
Yemen	David E. Zweifel
Yugoslavia	David Anderson
Zaire	Robert B. Oakley
Zambia	Frank G. Wisner II
Zimbabwe	Robert V. Keeley
Special Missions:	
United Nations	Jeane J. Kirkpatrick
U.N. (European Office)	Gerald B. Helman
U.N.E.S.C.O.	Vacant
O.A.S.	J. William Middendorf II
T.O.	W. Tapley Bennett, Jr.
O.E.C.D.	Abraham Katz
I.A.E.A.	Richard T. Kennedy
U.S.E.C.	Vacant
I.C.A.O.	John E. Downs
Ambassadors at Large	Daniel J. Terra

BRITISH PRIME MINISTERS

Monarch and Prime Minister	Party	Served
George I, 1714–27		
Robert Walpole	Whig	1721–1727
George II, 1727–60		
Robert Walpole, Earl of Orford	Whig	1727–1742
Spencer Compton, Earl of Wilmington	Whig	1742–1743
Henry Pelham	Whig	1743–1754
Thomas Pelham-Holles,[1] Duke of Newcastle	Whig	1754–1756
William Cavendish, Duke of Devonshire	Whig	1756–1757
Thomas Pelham-Holles, Duke of Newcastle	Whig	1757–1760
George III, 1760–1820		
Thomas Pelham-Holles, Duke of Newcastle	Whig	1760–1762
John Stuart, Earl of Bute	Tory	1762–1763
George Grenville	Whig	1763–1765
Charles Watson-Wentworth, Marquis of Rockingham	Whig	1765–1766
William Pitt, Earl of Chatham	Coalition	1766–1767
Augustus Henry Fitzroy, Duke of Grafton	Whig	1767–1770
Frederick North, Lord North	Tory	1770–1782
Charles Watson-Wentworth, Marquis of Rockingham	Whig	1782
William Petty, Earl of Shelburne	Whig	1782–1783
William Henry Cavendish Bentinck, Duke of Portland	Coalition	1783
William Pitt (the Younger)	Tory	1783–1801
Henry Addington	Tory	1801–1804
William Pitt (the Younger)	Tory	1804–1806
William Wyndham Grenville,[2] Lord Grenville	Whig	1806–1807
William Henry Cavendish Bentinck, Duke of Portland	Tory	1807–1809
Spencer Perceval (assassinated)	Tory	1809–1812
Robert Banks Jenkinson, Earl of Liverpool	Tory	1812–1820
George IV, 1820–30		
Robert Banks Jenkinson, Earl of Liverpool	Tory	1820–1827
George Canning	Tory	1827
Frederick John Robinson, Viscount Goderich	Tory	1827–1828
Arthur Wellesley, Duke of Wellington	Tory	1828–1830
William IV, 1830–37		
Charles Grey, Earl Grey	Whig	1830–1834
William Lamb, Viscount Melbourne	Whig	1834
Sir Robert Peel	Tory	1834–1835
William Lamb, Viscount Melbourne	Whig	1835–1837
Victoria, 1837–1901		
William Lamb, Viscount Melbourne	Whig	1837–1841
Sir Robert Peel	Tory	1841–1846
John Russell,[3] Lord Russell	Whig	1846–1852
Edward George Geoffrey Smith Stanley, Earl of Derby	Tory	1852
George Hamilton Gordon, Earl of Aberdeen	Peelite[4]	1852–1855

Monarch and Prime Minister	Party	Served
Victoria, 1837–1901		
Henry John Temple, Viscount Palmerston	Liberal	1855–1858
Edward George Geoffrey Smith Stanley, Earl of Derby	Tory	1858–1859
Henry John Temple, Viscount Palmerston	Liberal	1859–1865
John Russell, Earl Russell	Liberal	1865–1866
Edward George Geoffrey Smith Stanley, Earl of Derby	Conservative	1866–1868
Benjamin Disraeli	Conservative	1868
William Ewart Gladstone	Liberal	1868–1874
Benjamin Disraeli, Earl of Beaconsfield	Conservative	1874–1880
William Ewart Gladstone	Liberal	1880–1885
Robert Arthur Talbot Gascoyne-Cecil, Marquis of Salisbury	Conservative	1885–1886
William Ewart Gladstone	Liberal	1886
Robert Arthur Talbot Gascoyne-Cecil, Marquis of Salisbury	Conservative	1886–1892
William Ewart Gladstone	Liberal	1892–1894
Archibald Philip Primrose, Earl of Rosebery	Liberal	1894–1895
Robert Arthur Talbot Gascoyne-Cecil, Marquis of Salisbury	Conservative	1895–1901
Edward VII, 1901–1910		
Robert Arthur Talbot Gascoyne-Cecil, Marquis of Salisbury	Conservative	1901–1902
Arthur James Balfour	Conservative	1902–1905
Sir Henry Campbell-Bannerman	Liberal	1905–1908
Herbert Henry Asquith	Liberal	1908–1910
George V, 1910–36		
Herbert Henry Asquith	Liberal	1910–1915
Herbert Henry Asquith	Coalition	1915–1916
David Lloyd George	Coalition	1916–1922
Andrew Bonar Law	Conservative	1922–1923
Stanley Baldwin	Conservative	1923–1924
James Ramsay MacDonald	Labour	1924
Stanley Baldwin	Conservative	1924–1929
James Ramsay MacDonald	Labour	1929–1931
James Ramsay MacDonald	Coalition	1931–1935
Stanley Baldwin	Coalition	1935–1936
Edward VIII, 1936 (abdicated)		
George VI, 1936–52		
Stanley Baldwin, Earl Baldwin of Bewdley	Coalition	1936–1937
(Arthur) Neville Chamberlain	Coalition	1937–1940
Winston Leonard Spencer Churchill	Coalition	1940–1945
Winston Leonard Spencer Churchill	Conservative	1945
Clement Richard Attlee	Labour	1945–1951
Winston Leonard Spencer Churchill	Conservative	1951–1952
Elizabeth II, 1952–		
Sir Winston Leonard Spencer Churchill	Conservative	1952–1955
Sir (Robert) Anthony Eden	Conservative	1955–1957
(Maurice) Harold Macmillan	Conservative	1957–1963
Sir Alec Douglas-Home	Conservative	1963–1964
(James) Harold Wilson	Labour	1964–1970
Edward Heath	Conservative	1970–1974
Harold Wilson	Labour	1974–1976
James Callaghan	Labour	1976–1979
Margaret Thatcher	Conservative	1979–

[1] Brother of Henry Pelham. [2] Son of George Grenville. [3] Lord Russell, later Earl Russell, sat in the House of Commons in his first ministry and in the House of Lords in his second. [4] On the sudden death of Sir Robert Peel in 1850, the Earl of Aberdeen became the leader of the Peelites, a coalition that supported the corn law and public reform policies of Sir Robert Peel.

THE COMMONWEALTH (September 21, 1981)

Formed in 1931, the Commonwealth is now a free association of 45 sovereign states and their dependencies.

State (date of entry)	Location	Administrative Center	Area (sq. mi.)	Population
UNITED KINGDOM* (12/31/31)	Europe	London	94,399	55,883,100
Brunei	Borneo	Bandar Seri Begawan	2,226	213,000
Dependencies				
Anguilla	West Indies	The Valley	35	6,600
Bermuda	Atlantic Ocean	Hamilton	21	58,000
British Antarctic Terr.	Antarctica	—	600,000	uninhabited
British Indian Ocean Terr.	Indian Ocean	Stanley, Falkland Islands		
British Virgin Islands	West Indies	London, U.K.	29	unknown
Cayman Islands	West Indies	Road Town	59	12,000
Falkland Islands	Atlantic Ocean	George Town	100	16,677
Gibraltar	Europe	Stanley	6,198	1,812
Gibraltar	Europe	Gibraltar	2.28	29,760
Hong Kong	Asia	Victoria	403	4,900,000
Montserrat	West Indies	Plymouth	40	12,073
Pitcairn Islands	Oceania	Adamstown	18	63
St. Helena	Atlantic Ocean	Jamestown	162	6,400
Turks and Caicos Islands	West Indies	Cockburn Town (on Grand Turk)	166	7,436
West Indies Associated States				
Antigua	West Indies	St. John's	171	74,000
St. Christopher-Nevis	West Indies	Basseterre	120	44,404
AUSTRALIA (12/31/31)	Oceania	Canberra	2,967,909	14,567,000
Dependencies				
Ashmore & Cartier Islands	Indian Ocean	—	1.9	uninhabited
Australian Antarctic Terr.	Antarctica	—	2,362,875	uninhabited
Christmas Island	Indian Ocean	Flying Fish Cove	52	3,184
Cocos Islands	Indian Ocean	West Island	5.4	487
Coral Sea Islands	Oceania	—	8.5	3
Heard and McDonald Islands	Indian Ocean	—	113	uninhabited
Norfolk Island	Oceania	Kingston	13.3	2,180
NEW ZEALAND (12/31/31)	Oceania	Wellington	103,736	3,164,000
Dependencies				
Cook Islands	Oceania	Avarua	91	18,200
Niue	Oceania	Alofi	100	4,000
Ross Dependency	Antarctica	—	290,000	uninhabited
Tokelau Islands	Oceania	Fenuafala	3.95	1,625
BAHAMAS (7/10/73)	Atlantic Ocean	Nassau	5,382	225,000
BANGLADESH (4/18/72)	Asia	Dacca	55,126	87,657,000
BARBADOS (11/30/66)	West Indies	Bridgetown	166	249,000
BELIZE (9/21/81)	Central America	Belmopan	8,867	144,857
BOTSWANA (9/30/66)	Africa	Gaborone	224,764	791,000
CANADA (12/31/31)	North America	Ottawa	3,851,809	24,150,000
CYPRUS (3/13/61)	Mediterranean	Nicosia	3,572	621,000
DOMINICA (11/3/78)	West Indies	Roseau	291	81,000
FIJI (10/10/70)	Oceania	Suva	7,055	618,979
GAMBIA, THE (2/18/65)	Africa	Banjul	4,127	601,000
GHANA (3/6/57)	Africa	Accra	92,099	11,450,000
GRENADA (2/7/74)	West Indies	St. George's	133	110,000
GUYANA (5/26/66)	South America	Georgetown	83,000	820,000
INDIA (8/15/47)	Asia	New Delhi	1,269,339	683,810,051
JAMAICA (8/6/62)	West Indies	Kingston	4,244	2,161,000
KENYA (12/12/63)	Africa	Nairobi	224,960	15,322,000
KIRIBATI (7/12/79)	Oceania	Bairiki (on Tarawa)	354	56,213
LESOTHO (10/4/66)	Africa	Maseru	11,720	1,279,000
MALAWI (7/6/64)	Africa	Lilongwe	45,747	5,817,000
MALAYSIA (9/16/63)	Asia	Kuala Lumpur	128,308	13,435,588
MALTA (9/21/64)	Mediterranean	Valletta	122	343,970
MAURITIUS (3/12/68)	Indian Ocean	Port Louis	790	941,000
NAURU (1/31/68)‡	Oceania	Yaren district	7.7	7,100
NIGERIA (10/1/60)	Africa	Lagos	379,628	84,500,000
PAPUA NEW GUINEA (9/16/75)	Oceania	Port Moresby	183,540	3,006,799
SAINT LUCIA (2/22/79)	West Indies	Castries	238	115,783
SAINT VINCENT & THE GRENADINES (10/27/79)	West Indies	Kingstown	150	104,000
SEYCHELLES (6/28/76)	Indian Ocean	Victoria	171	63,000
SIERRA LEONE (4/27/61)	Africa	Freetown	27,295	3,200,000
SINGAPORE (10/16/65)	Asia	Singapore	233	2,413,945
SOLOMON ISLANDS (7/7/78)	Oceania	Honiara	11,500	221,000
SRI LANKA (2/4/48)	Asia	Colombo	25,332	14,859,295
SWAZILAND (9/6/68)	Africa	Mbabane	6,705	530,000
TANZANIA (4/26/64)	Africa	Dar es Salaam	363,708	17,982,000
TONGA (6/4/70)	Oceania	Nuku'alofa	270	94,000
TRINIDAD AND TOBAGO (8/31/62)	West Indies	Port-of-Spain	1,980	1,133,000
TUVALU (10/1/78)‡	Oceania	Fongafale	9.78	7,349
UGANDA (10/9/62)	Africa	Kampala	91,076	12,630,076
VANUATU (7/30/80)	Oceania	Vila	5,700	112,596
WESTERN SAMOA (8/28/70)	South Pacific	Apia	1,133	154,000
ZAMBIA (10/24/64)	Africa	Lusaka	290,586	5,679,808
ZIMBABWE (4/18/80)	Africa	Salisbury(Harare)	150,803	7,360,000

*As crown fiefdoms, the Isle of Man (227 sq. mi.; 63,000 pop.) and the Channel Islands (74 sq. mi.; 130,000 pop.) are included in the Commonwealth.
‡Special member

WORLD COMMUNIST PARTY STRENGTH

Source: Richard F. Staar (ed.), *1981 Yearbook on International Communist Affairs*. Hoover Institution Press, Stanford, CA 94305 © 1981

Country or Area	Communist Party Membership	Percent of vote; seats in legislature	Status	Sino-Soviet Dispute
Afghanistan	50,000	No elections scheduled	In power	Pro-Soviet
Albania	101,500	99.9 (1978); all 250 seats	In power	Neutral
Algeria	400-500	— (1976)	Proscribed	Pro-Soviet
Argentina	70,000	No elections scheduled	Proscribed	Pro-Soviet
Australia	2,000	— (1980); no seats	Legal	Split (3)
Austria	25,000	0.96 (1979); no seats	Legal	Pro-Soviet
Bangladesh	2,500	— (1979); 1 of 300 seats	Legal	Split (11)
Belgium	9,000	3.3 (1978); 4 of 212 seats	Legal	Pro-Soviet
Berlin, West	7,500	1.1 (1979); no seats	Legal	Pro-Soviet
Bolivia	3,500	— (1980); elections voided	Proscribed	Split (7)
Brazil	10,000	— (1978); 5 seats	Proscribed	Split (4)
Bulgaria	821,600	99.9 (1976); 272 of 400 seats	In power	Pro-Soviet
Burma	3,000	— (1978)	Proscribed	Pro-Chinese
Cambodia	Unknown	Elections "forthcoming"	In power	Pro-Soviet
Canada	2,000	0.1 (1980); no seats	Legal	Split (3)
Chile	20,000	Elections promised	Proscribed	Split (4)
China	38,000,000	Indirect elections	In power	—
Colombia	11,000	1.9 (1978); 3 of 311 seats	Legal	Split (2)
Costa Rica	3,200	2.7 (1978); 3 of 57 seats	Legal	Pro-Soviet
Cuba	434,000	91.7 (1976); 441 of 481 seats	In power	Pro-Soviet
Cyprus	12,000	30.0 (1976); 9 of 35 Greek Cypriot seats	Legal	Pro-Soviet
Czechoslovakia	1,532,000	99.7 (1976); all 350 seats	In power	Pro-Soviet
Denmark	7,750	1.9 (1979); no seats	Legal	Pro-Soviet
Dominican Republic	1,650	— (1978); no seats	Legal	Split (13)
Ecuador	2,000	3.2 (1979); 1 of 69 seats	Legal	Split (2)
Egypt	500	— (1979)	Proscribed	Pro-Soviet
El Salvador	800	— (1976)	Legal	Pro-Soviet
Finland	45-48,000	17.9 (1979); 35 of 200 seats	Legal	Pro-Soviet
France	600,000	20.6 (1978); 44 of 491 seats (1981 election)	Legal	Pro-Soviet
Germany, East	2,130,671	99.9 (1976); 127 of 500 seats	In power	Pro-Soviet
Germany, West	40,000	0.2 (1980); no seats	Legal	Pro-Soviet
Greece	27,500	9.3 (1977); 12 of 300 seats	Legal	Split (3)
Guadeloupe	3,000	— (1979); 7 of 36 seats	Legal	Pro-Soviet
Guatemala	750	— (1974)	Proscribed	Pro-Soviet
Guyana	100	20.4 (1980); 12 of 65 seats	Legal	Pro-Soviet
Haiti	350	— (1973)	Proscribed	Pro-Soviet
Honduras	1,500	— (1980)	Proscribed	Split (2)
Hong Kong	2,000	City council	Legal	Pro-Chinese
Hungary	811,833	99.3 (1980); all 352 seats	In power	Pro-Soviet
Iceland	2,200	19.7 (1979); 11 of 60 seats	Legal	Split (3)
India	100,000	9.0 (1980); 35 of 244 seats	Legal	Neutral
Indonesia	1,000	— (1977)	Proscribed	Split (2)
Iran	1,500	— (1980); no seats	Legal	Pro-Soviet
Iraq	2,000	— (1980); no seats	Allowed	Pro-Soviet
Ireland	600	— (1977); no seats	Legal	Pro-Soviet
Israel	1,500	4.6 (1977); 5 of 120 seats	Legal	Pro-Soviet
Italy	1,814,740	30.4 (1979); 201 of 630 seats	Legal	Pro-Soviet
Jamaica	400	— (1980); no seats	Allowed	Pro-Soviet
Japan	440,000	10.4 (1980); 29 of 511 seats	Legal	Neutral
Jordan	500	No elections since 1967	Proscribed	Pro-Soviet
Korea, North	2,000,000	100.0 (1977); all 579 seats	In power	Neutral
Laos	15,000	No elections scheduled	In power	Pro-Soviet
Lebanon	2,500	— (1972); no seats	Legal	Pro-Soviet
Lesotho	Negligible	—	Proscribed	Pro-Soviet
Luxembourg	600	4.8 (1979); 2 of 59 seats	Legal	Pro-Soviet
Malaysia	3,425	— (1978)	Proscribed	Split (2)
Malta	100	— (1976); no seats	Legal	Pro-Soviet
Martinique	1,000	— (1979); 3 of 36 seats	Legal	Pro-Soviet
Mexico	100,000	5.4 (1979); 18 of 300 seats	Legal	Pro-Soviet
Mongolia	67,000	99.9 (1979); all 354 seats	In power	Pro-Soviet
Morocco	3,000	— (1977); 1 seat	Allowed	Pro-Soviet
Nepal	6,500	— (1959)	Proscribed	Split (3)
Netherlands	13,000	1.7 (1977); 2 of 150 seats	Legal	Pro-Soviet
New Zealand	400	0.2 (1978); no seats	Legal	Split (5)
Nicaragua	1,200	— (1974)	Uncertain	Split (4)
Nigeria	Unknown	— (1976)	Proscribed	Pro-Soviet
Norway	2,500	5.2 (1977); 2 of 155 seats	Legal	Neutral
Pakistan	Few hundred	— (1979); elections postponed	Proscribed	Split (2)
Panama	550	— (1972); no seats	Allowed	Pro-Soviet
Paraguay	3,500	— (1973)	Proscribed	Split (5)
Peru	3,200	2.8 (1980); 10 of 60 seats	Legal	Split (7)
Philippines	3-4,000	— (1978)	Proscribed	Split (2)
Poland	3,040,000	99.5 (1980); 261 of 460 seats	In power	Pro-Soviet
Portugal	164,713	16.7 (1980); 41 of 250 seats	Legal	Pro-Soviet
Puerto Rico	125	5.7 (1976); no seats	Legal	Pro-Soviet

Country or Area	Communist Party Membership	Percent of vote; seats in legislature	Status	Sino-Soviet Dispute
Réunion	2,000	32.8 (1978); none in Paris	Legal	Independent
Romania	3,003,164	98.5 (1980); all 369 seats	In power	Neutral
San Marino	300	21.1 (1978); 16 of 60 seats	Legal	Pro-Soviet
Saudi Arabia	Negligible	No elections scheduled	Proscribed	Pro-Soviet
Senegal	2,000	0.32 (1978); no seats	Legal	Pro-Soviet
Singapore	350	— (1976)	Proscribed	Pro-Chinese
South Africa	Unknown	— (1977)	Proscribed	Pro-Soviet
Spain	140,000	10.5 (1979); 23 of 350 seats	Legal	Neutral
Sri Lanka	6,000	1.9 (1977); no seats	Legal	Split (6)
Sudan	1,500	— (1980)	Proscribed	Pro-Soviet
Sweden	17,000	5.6 (1979); 20 of 349 seats	Legal	Neutral
Switzerland	5,000	1.5 (1979); 3 of 200 seats	Legal	Pro-Soviet
Syria	5,000	— (1977); 6 of 195 seats	Allowed	Pro-Soviet
Thailand	1,200	— (1979)	Proscribed	Pro-Chinese
Tunisia	100	— (1974)	Proscribed	Pro-Soviet
Turkey	Negligible	— (1977)	Proscribed	Pro-Soviet
USSR	17,193,376	99.9 (1979); all 1,500 seats CPSU-approved	In power	—
United Kingdom	20,599	0.5 (1979); no seats	Legal	Neutral
United States	15-20,000	0.2 (1976); no seats	Legal	Pro-Soviet
Uruguay	7,500	Elections promised by 1981	Proscribed	Pro-Soviet
Venezuela	4,500	9.0 (1978); 22 of 195 seats	Legal	Split (4)
Vietnam	1,533,000	99.0 (1976); all 492 seats	In power	Pro-Soviet
Yugoslavia	2,006,000	— (1978); all 308 seats	In power	Neutral

SOVIET LEADERS: 1981 SOURCE: U.S. Department of State

Brezhnev, Leonid I.
General Secretary, Soviet Communist party; b. 1906

POLITBURO
FULL MEMBERS

Brezhnev, Leonid I.
Chairman of the Presidium of the Supreme Soviet (President of the Soviet Union)

Suslov, Mikhail A.
A secretary, Soviet Communist party (ideology, foreign affairs); b. 1902

Kirilenko, Andrei P.
A secretary, Soviet Communist party (party affairs, industry); b. 1906

Pelshe, Arvid Y.
Chairman, Party Control Commission; b. 1899

Grishin, Viktor V.
First Secretary, Moscow city party organization; b. 1914

Kunayev, Dinmukhamed A.
First Secretary, Kazakhstan Communist party; b. 1912

Shcherbitsky, Vladimir V.
First Secretary, Ukrainian Communist party; b. 1918

Andropov, Yuriy V.
KGB chief; b. 1914

Gromyko, Andrei A.
Minister of Foreign Affairs; b. 1909

Romanov, Grigory V.
First Secretary, Leningrad Oblast Party Committee; b. 1923

Ustinov, Dmitry F.
Minister of Defense; b. 1908

Chernenko, Konstantin U.
Head, General Department, Soviet Communist party Central Committee; b. 1911

Tikhonov, Nikolai A.
Premier; b. 1905

Gorbachev, Mikhail S.
Secretary of CPSU Central Committee (agriculture); b. 1931

CANDIDATE MEMBERS

Demichev, Pyotr N.
Minister of Culture; b. 1918

Masherov, Pyotr M.
First Secretary, Byelorussian Communist party; b. 1918

Solomentsev, Mikhail S.
Chairman of RSFSR Council of Ministers; b. 1913

Rashidov, Sharaf R.
First Secretary, Uzbek Communist party; b. 1917

Ponomaryov, Boris N.
A secretary (relations with nonruling parties); b. 1905

Aliyev, Geidar A.
First Secretary, Azerbaidzhan Communist party; b. 1923

Kuznetsov, Vasily V.
First Deputy Chairman, Presidium of the USSR Supreme Soviet; b. 1901

Shevardnadze, Eduard A.
Georgian Republic First Secretary; b. 1928

COMMUNIST PARTY SECRETARIAT
Brezhnev, Leonid I.; Suslov, Mikhail A.; Kirilenko, Andrei P.; Chernenko, Konstantin U.; Gorbachev, M.S.

Ponomaryov, B. N.
(candidate member of Politburo)

Dolgikh, Vladimir I.
A secretary (heavy industry); b. 1924

Rusakov, Konstantin V.
A secretary (relations with ruling Communist parties); b. 1909

Kapitonov, Ivan V.
Head, Organizational Party Work Department, Soviet Communist Party Central Committee; b. 1915

Zimyanin, Mikhail V.
A secretary (culture, propaganda); b. 1914

RULERS OF CHINA: 1981 SOURCE: Donald W. Klein, Department of Political Science, Tufts University

POLITBURO—FULL MEMBERS

*Hu Yaobang (Chairman), b. 1915
*Ye Jiangying (Vice-Chairman), b. 1898
*Deng Xiaoping (Vice-Chairman), b. 1904
*Zhao Ziyang (Vice-Chairman), b. 1919
*Li Xiannian (Vice-Chairman), b. 1907
*Chen Yun (Vice-Chairman), b.c. 1900
Hua Guofeng (Vice-Chairman), b.c. 1920
Chen Yonggui, b.c. 1913
Deng Yingchao (Mrs. Zhou Enlai), b. 1903
Fang Yi, b. 1916
Geng Biao, b. 1909
Li Desheng, b. 1912
Liu Bocheng, b. 1892
Ni Zhifu

Nie Rongzhen, b. 1899
Peng Chong, b. 1915
Ulanhu, b. 1906
Wang Zhen, b. 1909
Wei Quoqing, b.c. 1914
Xu Shiyou, b.c. 1906
Xu Xiangqian, b. 1902
Yu Qiuli, b. 1914
Zhang Tingfa

STATE COUNCIL
Zhao Ziyang (Premier)
Bo Yibo (V.P.), b. 1907
Chen Muhua (V.P.)
Fang Yi (V.P.)
Geng Biao (V.P.)
Gu Mu, (V.P.), b. 1914
Huang Hua (V.P.) b.c. 1913
Ji Pengfei (V.P.)
Kang Shien (V.P.)
Wang Li (V.P.), b. 1916
Yang Jingren (V.P.), b.c. 1918
Yao Yilin (V.P.), b. 1917
Zhang Aiping (V.P.), b.c. 1910

SECRETARIAT OF THE CHINESE COMMUNIST PARTY CENTRAL COMMITTEE
Hu Yaobang (General Secretary)
Fang Yi
Gu Mu
Hu Qiaomu, b. 1912
Hu Yaobang
Peng Chong
Song Renqiong, b. 1909
Wan Li
Wang Renzhong
Xi Chongxun, b. 1913
Yang Dezhi, b. 1910
Yao Yilin
Yu Qiuli

MILITARY AFFAIRS COMMITTEE
(of the Chinese Communist Party)
Deng Xiaoping (Chairman)
Geng Biao (Secretary-General)
Liu Bocheng (V.C.)
Nie Rongzhen (V.C.)
Xu Xiangqian (V.C.)
Ye Jiangying (V.C.)

MILITARY AFFAIRS

U.S. WARS AND CASUALTIES SOURCE: U.S. Department of Defense

Data prior to World War I are based, in many cases, on incomplete records. Casualty data are confined to dead and wounded personnel and therefore exclude personnel captured or missing in action who were subsequently returned to military control.

War	Branch of Service†	Number Serving	CASUALTIES Battle Deaths	Other Deaths	Not Mortal Wounds
Revolutionary War	Total	184,000–250,000	4,435	—	6,188
(1775–1783)	Army	(estimated)	4,044	—	6,004
	Navy	—	342	—	114
	Marines	—	49	—	70
War of 1812	Total	286,730	2,260	—	4,505
(1812–1815)	Army	—	1,950	—	4,000
	Navy	—	265	—	439
	Marines	—	45	—	66
Mexican War	Total	78,718	1,733	11,550	4,152
(1846–1848)	Army	—	1,721	—	4,102
	Navy	—	1	—	3
	Marines	—	11	—	47
Civil War	Total	2,213,363	140,414	224,097	281,881
(Union Forces only)*	Army	2,128,948	138,154	221,374	280,040
(1861–1865)	Navy }	84,415	2,112	2,411	1,710
	Marines }		148	312	131
Spanish-American War	Total	306,760	385	2,061	1,662
(1898)	Army	280,564	369	2,061	1,594
	Navy	22,875	10	0	47
	Marines	3,321	6	0	21
World War I	Total	4,734,991	53,402	63,114	204,002
(6 April 1917–	Army	4,057,101	50,510	55,868	193,663
11 November 1918)	Navy	599,051	431	6,856	819
	Marines	78,839	2,461	390	9,520
World War II	Total	16,112,566	291,557	113,842	670,846
(7 December 1941–	Army	11,260,000	234,874	83,400	565,861
31 December 1946)††	Navy	4,183,466	36,950	25,664	37,778
	Marines	669,100	19,733	4,778	67,207
Korean War	Total	5,720,000	33,629	20,617	103,284
(25 June 1950–	Army	2,834,000	27,704	9,429	77,596
27 July 1953)	Navy	1,177,000	458	4,043	1,576
	Marines	424,000	4,267	1,261	23,744
	Air Force	1,285,000	1,200	5,884	368
Vietnam War	Total	3,300,000	47,752	10,390	303,706
(1961—7 May 1975)					

* Authoritative statistics for the Confederate Forces are not available. Estimates of the number who served range from 600,000 to 1,500,000. Based upon incomplete information, 133,821 Confederates died (74,524 in battle and 59,297 otherwise). In addition, an estimated 26,000–31,000 Confederate personnel died in Union prisons. † U.S. Coast Guard data are excluded. †† World War II hostilities declared terminated on December 31, 1946, by Presidential Proclamation.

U.S. VETERANS SOURCE: Veterans Administration

Veterans in civil life, end of month—

Total, September 1980	30,118,000
War Veterans—Total	26,065,000
Vietnam Era—Total	9,015,000
And service in Korean Conflict	552,000
No service in Korean Conflict	8,463,000
Korean Conflict—Total (includes line 4)	5,826,000
And service in WW II	1,167,000
No service in WW II	4,659,000
World War II (includes line 7)	12,422,000
World War I	521,000
Spanish-American War	147
Service between Korean Conflict (Jan. 31, 1955) and Vietnam (Aug. 5, 1964)	3,050,000

U.S. DEFENSE EXPENDITURES SOURCE: U.S. Office of Management and Budget

Fiscal Year	National defense[1] $ Billion	GNP $ Billion	Defense as % of GNP	Fiscal Year	National defense[1] $ Billion	GNP $ Billion	Defense as % of GNP
1960	45.2	497.3	9.1	1972	76.6	1,110.5	6.9
1961	46.6	508.3	9.2	1973	74.5	1,237.5	6.0
1962	50.4	546.9	9.2	1974	77.8	1,359.2	5.7
1963	51.5	576.3	8.9	1975	85.6	1,457.3	5.9
1964	52.7	616.2	8.6	1976	89.4	1,621.0	5.5
1965	48.6	657.1	7.4	TQ[2]	22.3	—	—
1966	55.9	721.1	7.8	1977	97.5	1,843.3	5.3
1967	69.1	774.4	8.9	1978	105.2	2,060.4	5.1
1968	79.4	829.9	9.6	1979	117.7	2,369.0	5.0
1969	79.4	903.7	8.8	1980	145.8	2,626.0	5.6
1970	78.6	959.0	8.2	1981 est.[3]	179.9	2,951.0	6.1
1971	75.8	1,019.3	7.4	1982 est.[3]	225.7	3,296.0	6.8

[1] Includes budget outlays for military activities of the Department of Defense, military assistance, atomic energy defense activities, and defense-related activities of civilian agencies. [2] See footnote 2, page 184. [3] Based on estimates of the 1982 Budget of the Mid-Session Review in July 1981.

NATIONAL GUARD 1980

SOURCE: National Guard Bureau, U.S. Departments of the Army and the Air Force

State or Area	Units*	Personnel*
TOTAL	5,352	79,843
Alabama	222	21,831
Alaska	107	3,099
Arizona	82	6,251
Arkansas	119	11,196
California	241	20,884
Colorado	55	4,532
Connecticut	63	6,691
Delaware	34	2,849
Dist. of Columbia	32	3,557
Florida	96	10,555
Georgia	126	13,638
Hawaii	59	5,278
Idaho	48	3,567
Illinois	130	11,162
Indiana	130	14,631
Iowa	100	7,338
Kansas	104	6,962
Kentucky	71	7,631
Louisiana	112	9,069
Maine	46	4,622
Maryland	83	7,339
Massachusetts	136	14,235
Michigan	128	13,060
Minnesota	120	10,242
Mississippi	155	14,319
Missouri	124	10,570
Montana	45	3,155
Nebraska	54	5,173
Nevada	31	1,920
New Hampshire	40	2,862
New Jersey	138	14,265
New Mexico	51	4,549
New York	237	20,787
North Carolina	151	12,877
North Dakota	47	4,580
Ohio	188	18,877
Oklahoma	134	9,418
Pennsylvania	203	19,778
Puerto Rico	77	10,688
Rhode Island	47	4,434
South Carolina	119	12,337
South Dakota	68	4,698
Tennessee	156	15,658
Texas	226	18,725
Utah	64	5,476
Vermont	45	3,603
Virginia	35	7,801
Virgin Islands	82	796
Washington	82	7,061
West Virginia	65	5,003
Wisconsin	117	10,215
Wyoming	44	2,434

*Army National Guard and Air National Guard.

U.S. MILITARY PAY SCALES BY GRADE: PER MONTH (Aug.) 1981

Effective Oct. 1, 1980, military pay was increased by 11.7 percent. Subject to final approval, pay increases between 4.8 and 14.3 percent should become effective Oct. 1, 1981.

Pay Grade	2 years or less	Over 2	Over 3	Over 4	Over 6	Over 8	Over 10	Over 12	Over 14	Over 16	Over 18	Over 20	Over 22	Over 26
Commissioned Officers														
O-10[1]	$3,529.80	$3,654.00	$3,654.00	$3,654.00	$3,654.00	$3,794.10	$3,794.10	$4,084.80	$4,084.80	$4,377.00*	$4,377.00*	$4,669.80*	$4,669.80*	$4,961.10*
O-9	3,128.40	3,210.60	3,278.70	3,278.70	3,278.70	3,362.40	3,362.40	3,501.90	3,501.90	3,794.10	3,794.10	4,084.80	4,084.80	4,337.00*
O-8	2,833.50	2,914.40	2,987.70	2,987.70	2,987.70	3,210.60	3,210.60	3,362.40	3,362.40	3,501.90	3,654.00	3,794.10	3,946.20	3,946.20
O-7	2,354.40	2,514.60	2,514.60	2,514.60	2,627.10	2,627.10	2,779.80	2,779.80	2,918.40	3,210.60	3,431.10	3,431.10	3,431.10	3,431.10
O-6	1,745.10	1,917.60	2,042.70	2,042.70	2,042.70	2,042.70	2,042.70	2,042.70	2,112.00	2,446.50	2,571.60	2,627.10	2,779.80	3,014.70
O-5	1,395.90	1,639.20	1,752.30	1,752.30	1,752.30	1,833.90	1,833.90	1,902.30	2,029.50	2,181.60	2,307.00	2,376.60	2,459.70	2,459.70
O-4	1,176.60	1,432.20	1,528.20	1,528.20	1,556.10	1,625.40	1,736.10	1,833.90	1,917.60	2,001.30	2,057.10	2,057.10	2,057.10	2,057.10
O-3	1,093.50	1,222.20	1,306.50	1,445.70	1,514.70	1,569.60	1,653.90	1,736.10	1,778.70	1,778.70	1,778.70	1,778.70	1,778.70	1,778.70
O-2[2]	953.10	1,041.30	1,250.70	1,293.00	1,319.70	1,319.70	1,319.70	1,319.70	1,319.70	1,319.70	1,319.70	1,319.70	1,319.70	1,319.70
O-1[2]	827.40	861.30	1,041.30	1,041.30	1,041.30	1,041.30	1,041.30	1,041.30	1,041.30	1,041.30	1,041.30	1,041.30	1,041.30	1,041.30
Commissioned Officers with over 4 years active service as enlisted members														
O-3	0.	0.	0.	1,445.70	1,514.70	1,569.60	1,653.90	1,736.10	1,805.70	1,805.70	1,805.70	1,805.70	1,805.70	1,805.70
O-2	0.	0.	0.	1,293.00	1,319.70	1,361.70	1,432.20	1,487.40	1,528.20	1,528.20	1,528.20	1,528.20	1,528.20	1,528.20
O-1	0.	0.	0.	1,041.30	1,112.10	1,153.20	1,194.90	1,236.60	1,293.00	1,293.00	1,293.00	1,293.00	1,293.00	1,293.00
Warrant Officers														
W-4	1,113.90	1,194.90	1,194.90	1,222.20	1,278.00	1,334.40	1,390.20	1,487.40	1,556.10	1,611.30	1,653.90	1,707.90	1,765.20	1,902.30
W-3	1,012.50	1,098.30	1,098.30	1,112.10	1,125.30	1,207.50	1,278.00	1,319.70	1,361.70	1,402.50	1,445.70	1,501.50	1,556.10	1,611.30
W-2	886.30	959.10	959.10	987.00	1,041.30	1,098.30	1,139.70	1,181.40	1,222.20	1,265.10	1,306.50	1,347.90	1,402.50	1,402.50
W-1	738.90	847.20	847.20	917.70	959.10	1,000.50	1,041.30	1,084.20	1,125.30	1,166.70	1,207.50	1,250.70	1,250.70	1,250.70
Enlisted Members														
E-9[3]	0.	0.	0.	0.	0.	0.	1,265.40	1,294.20	1,323.60	1,354.20	1,384.20	1,411.20	1,485.60	1,629.60
E-8	0.	0.	0.	0.	0.	1,061.70	1,091.40	1,120.50	1,149.90	1,179.90	1,207.20	1,236.90	1,309.50	1,455.60
E-7	741.30	800.10	829.80	858.60	888.30	916.20	945.60	975.00	1,019.10	1,047.90	1,077.60	1,091.40	1,164.90	1,309.60
E-6	640.20	698.10	727.20	757.80	786.00	814.80	844.60	888.30	916.20	945.60	960.00	960.00	960.00	960.00
E-5	562.20	611.70	641.40	669.30	713.10	742.20	771.90	800.10	814.80	814.80	814.80	814.80	814.80	814.80
E-4	540.30	570.30	603.90	651.00	676.80	676.80	676.80	676.80	676.80	676.80	676.80	676.80	676.80	676.80
E-3	519.60	548.10	570.30	592.80	592.80	592.80	592.80	592.80	592.80	592.80	592.80	592.80	592.80	592.80
E-2	500.10	500.10	500.10	500.10	500.10	500.10	500.10	500.10	500.10	500.10	500.10	500.10	500.10	500.10
E-1	448.80	448.80	448.80	448.80	448.80	448.80	448.80	448.80	448.80	448.80	448.80	448.80	448.80	448.80

[1]While serving as Chairman of the Joint Chiefs of Staff of the Army, Chief of Naval Operations, Chief of Staff of the Air Force, or Commandant of the Marine Corps, basic pay for this grade is $5,473.80 regardless of cumulative years of service. [2]Does not apply to commissioned officers who have been credited with over 4 years active service as enlisted members. [3]Highest Enlisted Rank, while serving as Sergeant Major of the Army, Master Chief Petty Officer of the Navy, Chief Master Sergeant of the Air Force, or Sergeant Major of the Marine Corps, basic pay for this grade is $1,980.90 regardless of cumulative years of service.

*Basic pay is limited to $4,466.40 by Level V of the Executive Schedule.

U.S. MILITARY PAY GRADES

SOURCE: U.S. Department of Defense

COMMISSIONED OFFICERS

Pay Grade	Army	Navy	Marines	Air Force
O-1	Second Lieutenant	Ensign	Second Lieutenant	Second Lieutenant
O-2	First Lieutenant	Lieutenant Junior Grade	First Lieutenant	First Lieutenant
O-3	Captain	Lieutenant	Captain	Captain
O-4	Major	Lieutenant Commander	Major	Major
O-5	Lieutenant Colonel	Commander	Lieutenant Colonel	Lieutenant Colonel
O-6	Colonel	Captain	Colonel	Colonel
O-7	Brigadier General	Rear Admiral (lower half)	Brigadier General	Brigadier General
O-8	Major General	Rear Admiral (upper half)	Major General	Major General
O-9	Lieutenant General	Vice Admiral	Lieutenant General	Lieutenant General
O-10	General	Admiral	General	General

WARRANT OFFICERS (All Services)

W-1	Warrant Officer	W-3	Chief Warrant Officer
W-2	Chief Warrant Officer	W-4	Chief Warrant Officer

ENLISTED PERSONNEL

Pay Grade	Army	Navy	Marines	Air Force
E-1	Private	Seaman Recruit	Private	Airman Basic
E-2	Private	Seaman Apprentice	Private First Class	Airman
E-3	Private First Class	Seaman	Lance Corporal	Airman First Class
E-4	Corporal Specialist 4	Petty Officer, Third Class	Corporal	Sergeant Senior Airman
E-5	Sergeant Specialist 5	Petty Officer, Second Class	Sergeant	Staff Sergeant
E-6	Staff Sergeant Specialist 6	Petty Officer, First Class	Staff Sergeant	Technical Sergeant
E-7	Sergeant First Class Specialist 7 Platoon Sergeant	Chief Petty Officer	Gunnery Sergeant	Master Sergeant
E-8	First Sergeant Master Sergeant	Senior Chief Petty Officer	First Sergeant Master Sergeant	Senior Master Sergeant
E-9	Command Sergeant Major Sergeant Major	Master Chief Petty Officer	Sergeant Major Master Gunnery Sergeant	Chief Master Sergeant

AMERICAN MILITARY CEMETERIES ON FOREIGN SOIL

SOURCE: The American Battle Monuments Commission

The American Battle Monuments Commission, an agency of the U. S. Government, is responsible to the people of the United States for the construction and permanent maintenance of military cemeteries and memorials on foreign soil, as well as for certain memorials on American soil. Monuments are located in Au- denarde, Belgium; Bellicourt, Aisne, France; Brest, Finistere, France; Cantigny, Somme, France; Chateau-Thierry, France; Gibraltar; Kemmel, Ypres, Belgium; Montfaucon, Meuse, France; Sommepy, Marne, France; Tours, France; Indre-et-Loire, France; and Pointe du Hoc, Calvados, France.

Cemetery	Location	Size (acres)	Burials Known	Burials Unknown	Missing Commemorated
Aisne-Marne	Belleau (Aisne), France	282.5	2,039	249	1,060
Ardennes	Neupre (Neuville-en-Condroz), Belgium	90.5	4,534	786	462
Brittany	St. James, France	27.5	4,313	97	497
Brookwood	Surrey, England	4.5	427	41	563
Cambridge	Cambridge, England	30.5	3,787	24	5,126
Corozal	Panama City, Panama	16	4,218	000	000
Epinal	Epinal, France	46	5,186	69	424
Flanders Field	Waregem, Belgium	6	347	21	43
Florence	Florence, Italy	70	4,189	213	1,409
Henri-Chapelle	Henri-Chapelle, Belgium	57	7,895	94	450
Lorraine	St. Avold, France	114	10,338	151	444
Luxembourg	Luxembourg City, Luxembourg	50.6	4,975	101	370
Manila	Fort Bonifacio, Philippines	152	13,462	3,744	36,279
Meuse-Argonne	Romagne, France	130.5	13,760	486	954
Mexico City	Mexico City, Mexico	1	813	750	000
Netherlands	Margraten, Holland	65.5	8,195	106	1,722
Normandy	St. Laurent, France	172.3	9,079	307	1,557
North Africa	Carthage, Tunisia	27	2,601	240	3,724
Oise-Aisne	Fere-en-Tardenois, France	36.5	5,415	597	241
Rhone	Draguignan, France	12	799	62	293
St. Mihiel	Thiaucourt, France	40.3	4,036	117	284
Sicily-Rome	Nettuno, Italy	75	7,372	490	3,094
Somme	Bony, France	14.3	1,707	137	333
Suresnes	Seine, France	7.5	1,535	30	974

THE JOINT CHIEFS OF STAFF
SOURCE: Office of the Assistant Secretary of Defense

Chairman	From	To
Gen. Omar N. Bradley, USA	Aug. 16, 1949	Aug. 14, 1953
Adm. Arthur W. Radford, USN	Aug. 15, 1953	Aug. 14, 1957
Gen. Nathan F. Twining, USAF	Aug. 15, 1957	Sept. 30, 1960
Gen. Lyman L. Lemnitzer, USA	Oct. 1, 1960	Sept. 30, 1962
Gen. Maxwell D. Taylor, USA	Oct. 1, 1962	July 3, 1964
Gen. Earle G. Wheeler, USA	July 3, 1964	July 2, 1970
Adm. Thomas H. Moorer, USN	July 2, 1970	June 30, 1974
Gen. George S. Brown, USAF	July 1, 1974	June 30, 1978
Gen. David C. Jones, USAF	July 1, 1978	To Date

Chief of Staff, U.S. Army

Gen. of the Army	From	To
Dwight D. Eisenhower	Nov. 19, 1945	Feb. 7, 1948
Gen. Omar N. Bradley	Feb. 17, 1948	Aug. 15, 1949
Gen. J. Lawton Collins	Aug. 16, 1949	Aug. 14, 1953
Gen. Matthew B. Ridgway	Aug. 15, 1953	June 30, 1955
Gen. Maxwell D. Taylor	June 30, 1955	June 30, 1959
Gen. Lyman L. Lemnitzer	July 1, 1959	Sept. 30, 1960
Gen. George H. Decker	Sept. 30, 1960	Sept. 30, 1962
Gen. Earle G. Wheeler	Oct. 1, 1962	July 3, 1964
Gen. Harold K. Johnson	July 3, 1964	July 3, 1968
Gen. William C. Westmoreland	July 3, 1968	July 1, 1972
Gen. Creighton W. Abrams	Oct. 16, 1972	Sept. 1974
Gen. Fred C. Weyand	Oct. 7, 1974	Oct. 1, 1976
Gen. Bernard W. Rogers	Oct. 1, 1976	July 1, 1979
Gen. Edward C. Meyer	July 1, 1979	To Date

Chief of Naval Operations

	From	To
Fleet Adm. Chester W. Nimitz	Dec. 5, 1945	Dec. 15, 1947
Adm. Louis E. Denfeld	Dec. 15, 1947	Nov. 2, 1949
Adm. Forrest P. Sherman	Nov. 2, 1949	July 22, 1951

Chief of Naval Operations (Cont.)

	From	To
Adm. William M. Fechteler	Aug. 16, 1951	Aug. 17, 1953
Adm. Robert B. Carney	Aug. 17, 1953	Aug. 16, 1955
Adm. Arleigh A. Burke	Aug. 17, 1955	Aug. 1, 1961
Adm. George W. Anderson	Aug. 1, 1961	July 31, 1963
Adm. David L. McDonald	Aug. 1, 1963	July 31, 1967
Adm. Thomas H. Moorer	Aug. 1, 1967	July 1, 1970
Adm. Elmo R. Zumwalt	July 1, 1970	June 30, 1974
Adm. James L. Holloway 3rd	July 1, 1974	June 30, 1978
Adm. Thomas C. Hayward	July 1, 1978	To Date

Chief of Staff, U.S. Air Force

Gen. Carl Spaatz	From	To
Gen. Carl Spaatz	Sept. 26, 1947	April 29, 1948
Gen. Hoyt S. Vandenberg	April 30, 1948	June 29, 1953
Gen. Nathan F. Twining	June 30, 1953	June 30, 1957
Gen. Thomas D. White	July 1, 1957	June 30, 1961
Gen. Curtis E. LeMay	June 30, 1961	Jan. 31, 1965
Gen. John P. McConnell	Feb. 1, 1965	Aug. 1, 1969
Gen. John D. Ryan	Aug. 1, 1969	July 31, 1973
Gen. George S. Brown	Aug. 1, 1973	June 30, 1974
Gen. David C. Jones	July 1, 1974	June 30, 1978
Gen. Lew Allen	July 1, 1978	To Date

Commandant, U.S. Marine Corps

	From	To
Gen. Lemuel C. Shepherd	Dec. 21, 1951	Dec. 31, 1955
Gen. Randolph McC. Pate	Jan. 1, 1956	Dec. 31, 1959
Gen. David M. Shoup	Jan. 1, 1960	Dec. 31, 1963
Gen. Wallace M. Greene, Jr.	Jan. 1, 1964	Dec. 31, 1967
Gen. Leonard F. Chapman, Jr.	Jan. 1, 1968	Dec. 31, 1971
Gen. Robert E. Cushman, Jr.	Jan. 1, 1972	July 1, 1975
Gen. Louis H. Wilson	July 1, 1975	July 1, 1979
Gen. Robert H. Barrow	July 1, 1979	To Date

U.S. CASUALTIES IN VIETNAM
SOURCE: U.S. Department of Defense

47,752 U.S. military personnel were killed during the period 1961-1976 (June). Hospitalized wounded totaled 153,329. Casualties were highest during 1968, the year of the Tet offensive, with 14,589 killed and 46,796 wounded. Total casualties: 360,706.

TOTAL COST ESTIMATES OF AMERICAN WARS, BY RANK

SOURCE: James L. Clayton, University of Utah. (Data in millions of dollars)

	Original Incremental Cost[1] Constant Dollars (1967)	Current dollars	Cost to Oct. 1, 1979[2]	SERVICE-CONNECTED VETERANS' BENEFITS Total Cost Under Present Programs	INTEREST PAYMENTS ON WAR LOANS % of Original Incremental Costs	Total Cost to 1980[3]	Estimated Current Cost (1980)
World War II	546,490	288,000	57,565	UKN	69	200,000	545,565
Vietnam Conflict	106,526	111,000	9,330	UKN	3	3,000	123,330
Korean Conflict	67,925	54,000	9,564	UKN	14	7,500	71,064
World War I	57,650	26,000	13,383	UKN	43	11,000	50,383
Civil War (Union only)	6,957	3,200[4]	3,289	3,300	60	1,200	7,689
Spanish-American War	1,600	400	2,096	2,500	15	60	2,556
American Revolution	UKN	100	28	28	20	20	148
War of 1812	182	93	20	20	15	14	127
Mexican War	270	73	26	26	14	10	109

[1]Except for Korean and Vietnam conflicts, original incremental costs are outlays for national security during war years minus avg. annual outlay for preceding five years. Vietnam conflict estimate is from Dept. of Defense and represents incremental costs from 1965-79. Korean conflict estimate uses running avg. of national security outlays from 1948-50 as a base, and then includes additional outlays over this base for 1951-52 and one-half increase for 1953 (because outlays for the Cold War increased at the same time outlays for Korean conflict declined). [2]For World War I and later wars, benefits are actual service-connected figures from 1979 Annual Report of the Veterans Admin. For earlier wars, service-connected veterans' benefits are estimated at 40% of total, the approximate ratio of service-connected to total benefits since World War I. [3]Interest costs use same formula as in footnote 1. Interest costs for wars since 1940 are rough approximations. [4]Data from Goldin and Lewis, "The Economic Cost of the American Civil War," *Journal of Economic History*, June 1975. Expenditures by Confederate Govt. are estimated by this study at $1.0 billion. UKN=Unknown.

VETERANS BENEFITS

SOURCE: Veterans Administration

Benefits: In order to qualify for most benefits, veterans must have been separated from the Armed Forces under conditions other than dishonorable.

Compensation for Service-Connected Disability: Veterans disabled by injury or disease incurred or aggravated during active service in the line of duty may be entitled to monthly payments ranging from $54, for a 10 percent disability, to $1,016 for total disability. Loss of, or loss of use of, certain limbs and organs entitles the disabled veteran to additional compensation, up to a maximum monthly payment of $2,898. Certain veterans who are at least 30 percent disabled are entitled to additional allowances for dependents.

Pension: Wartime veterans, including those of Mexican Border Service, World Wars I and II, the Korean conflict, and the Vietnam era who served 90 days or more, or—if less than 90 days—were discharged for a service-connected disability, and who are permanently and totally disabled for reasons not traceable to service, may be eligible for pension benefits. A veteran 65 years of age or older is considered totally and permanently disabled. Pension payment amounts depend upon other income. Veterans with dependents may be entitled to higher amounts.

Medical Care: Complete care in VA hospitals, other federal hospitals, and in some cases, private hospitals is authorized under a priority system for otherwise qualified veterans who require treatment of service-connected disabilities, have compensable disabilities but require treatment of nonservice-connected disabilities, and/or have no service-connected disabilities but require medical treatment (subject to financial need and availability of facilities). Other benefits authorized when certain conditions are met include domiciliary care; outpatient medical and dental treatment in VA field stations or, in some cases, by approved private physicians; fitting and training with prosthetic appliances; medical examinations; aid for the blind; and vocational rehabilitation.

Educational Assistance—G.I. Bill: Veterans who served on active duty for more than 180 continuous days, any part of which occurred after Jan. 31, 1955, but before Jan. 1, 1977, and who (a) were released under conditions other than dishonorable, (b) were discharged for a service-connected disability or (c) continue on active duty are eligible for educational assistance for a period of 1.5 months for each month served, up to 45 months. The full 45-month entitlement is earned after 18 months' service.

War orphans and surviving spouses are eligible for similar education benefits, and education benefits are also available to spouses and children of veterans who are permanently and totally disabled as the result of military service.

Educational institutions may include approved public and private secondary schools, junior or senior colleges, and vocational, scientific, or correspondence schools. Farm cooperative, on-the-job, and flight training are included. Eligibility ends ten years after release from active duty, but not later than Dec. 31, 1989.

Basic monthly payments to veterans enrolled in school courses: full time, no dependents, $342; one dependent, $407; two dependents, $464; and $29 for each additional.

A veteran who must complete elementary or high school training to qualify for higher education may receive this training without a charge against his basic entitlement.

Contributory Plan: Those who initially entered the service on or after Jan. 1, 1977, may participate by contributing $25 to $100 from their military pay, with a maximum contribution of $2,700. The VA then matches contributions at the rate of $2 for every $1 made by the participant. Payments from the fund may be received for school or training purposes for the number of months they contributed, or for 36 months, whichever is less.

Home Loans: The VA is authorized to guarantee home loans made to eligible veterans by private lenders. Such loans may be for the purpose of purchasing a conventionally constructed home or mobile home (with or without a lot), refinancing an existing home mortgage, purchasing a condominium unit, or buying a farm home. Loans may also be guaranteed for home improvement purposes, including the installation of a solar heating and/or cooling system or other weatherization improvements.

Eligibility requirements vary based on the period of service. For World War II, Korean Conflict and Vietnam veterans, active duty of at least 90 days' duration (unless discharged earlier for service-connected disability) and a discharge or separation under other than dishonorable conditions are required. Post-World War II, Post-Korean and Post-Vietnam veterans must have 181 days of active duty (unless discharged earlier for service-connected disability) and a discharge or

separation under other than dishonorable conditions.

Service personnel who have served at least 181 continuous days in active duty status, though not discharged, are eligible while their service continues without a break.

Unmarried surviving spouses of veterans, including service personnel, who served during a period which occurred between September 16, 1940 and the present and who died as a result of service-connected disabilities are eligible for home loan purposes. Spouses of service personnel on active duty who are officially listed as missing in action or prisoners of war and have been in such status for more than 90 days are also eligible for home loan benefits. Spouses of POWs/MIAs are, however, limited to one loan.

Loan guaranty benefits are available to all eligible veterans and service personnel until used.

The VA may guarantee the lender against loss for up to 60 percent of the loan amount or $27,500, whichever is less, on all types of home loans, except for mobile home loans, for which the maximum guaranty is 50 percent of the loan amount, or $20,000, whichever is less.

There are no established loan maximums. However, no loan may exceed the property value established by VA.

Veterans who used their entitlement before October 1, 1978, may have additional entitlement available for GI home loan purposes. Veterans' maximum home loan entitlement was raised from $4,000 to $7,500 in 1950, to $12,500 in 1968, to $17,500 in 1974, to $25,000 in 1978, and to $27,500 in 1980. The amount of such additional entitlement is the difference between $25,000 and the amount used on prior home loans.

Certain veterans may meet the requirements for having used GI entitlement restored. A veteran may qualify for restoration if VA has been relieved of liability on the GI loan which normally is accomplished by the loan being paid in full and if the property has been disposed of; or if an immediate veteran-transferee agrees to substitute his or her entitlement for that of the original veteran-borrower and meets all other requirements for substitution of entitlement.

Insurance: Members of the uniformed services including Ready Reservists, Army and Air National Guards, ROTC members, Reservists eligible for assignment to Retired Reserves who have not received their first increment of retired pay or reached their 61st birthday, whichever is earlier; and the full-time duty cadet or midshipman at a service academy are eligible for Servicemen's Group Life Insurance. Maximum coverage is for $20,000 and premiums are deducted from service pay, except Retired Reservists, who must pay direct. Coverage continues for 120 days after discharge, within which period veterans can apply for automatic conversion of SGLI to a non-renewable 5-year term policy under Veterans Group Life Insurance which may be converted at the end of the 5-year period to an individual policy with a commercial company. For a member totally disabled the 120-day period is extended to one year or to the end of total disability, whichever is earlier.

Dependency and Indemnity Compensation (DIC): Payments are authorized for widows, widowers, unmarried children under 18, helpless children, children between 18 and 23 who are attending an approved school, and certain parents of a serviceman or veteran who died on or after January 1, 1957, from a disease or injury incurred or aggravated in the line of duty while on active duty, active or inactive duty for training, or from a disability otherwise compensable under VA-administered laws.

Employment Preference and Reemployment Rights: Veterans are entitled to certain preference over nonveterans in obtaining federal civil service jobs, in referral to training programs and job openings by state employment offices, and in restoration to a former job in private employment or with the federal government. The Department of Labor has jurisdiction over veteran employment.

Burial: A payment of up to $300 is authorized for the person incurring burial expenses for a wartime veteran, or for a peacetime veteran who was receiving compensation or was discharged or retired for disability incurred in the line of duty. Up to $1,100 will be payable when death is due to service-connected causes.

Burial is allowed in a national cemetery (except Arlington, Va.) for veterans whose last period of service terminated honorably, and for reservists who die while performing active-duty training. The benefit applies to the deceased person's spouse, minor children, and certain unmarried adult children. Effective August 1, 1973, an interment allowance not exceeding $150, in addition to the $300 basic burial allowance, is payable when burial is in other than a national cemetery.

U.S. MILITARY AID: PROGRAM DELIVERIES: FISCAL YEARS 1950-1980

SOURCE: Department of Defense (figures in thousands of dollars)

	1950-80		1950-80		1950-80
Worldwide	55,566,305	Honduras	9,740	Pakistan	324,615
Argentina	178,234	Iceland	543	Panama	4,978
Australia	1,493,815	India	75,786	Paraguay	745
Austria	104,857	Indochina	8,542	Peru	152,498
Bahrain	1,639	Indonesia	147,806	Philippines	141,215
Belgium	619,146	Iran	9,928,886	Portugal	15,484
Bolivia	2,036	Iraq	13,152	Qatar	21
Brazil	264,288	Ireland	679	Saudi Arabia	11,312,495
Brunei	10	Israel	6,278,536	Senegal	6
Burma	3,938	Italy	754,763	Singapore	149,889
Cameroon	3,167	Jamaica	155	South Africa	3,149
Canada	1,403,280	Japan	554,009	Spain	722,076
Chile	177,119	Jordan	735,957	Sri Lanka	4
China (Taiwan)	1,230,727	Kenya	60,249	Sudan	61,638
Colombia	33,400	Korea, South	1,545,850	Suriname	1
Costa Rica	1,472	Kuwait	529,912	Sweden	70,507
Cuba	4,510	Lebanon	45,238	Switzerland	566,682
Denmark	396,504	Liberia	4,442	Syria	1
Dominican Republic	2,287	Libya	29,594	Thailand	472,647
Ecuador	45,767	Luxembourg	3,102	Trinidad & Tobago	85
Egypt	457,498	Malaysia	65,128	Tunisia	60,435
El Salvador	4,344	Mali	154	Turkey	688,074
Ethiopia	87,177	Mexico	21,212	United Arab Emirates	2,989
Fiji	86	Morocco	375,005	United Kingdom	2,477,835
Finland	24	Nepal	73	Uruguay	18,344
France	378,053	Netherlands	720,499	Venezuela	236,446
Gabon	2,239	New Zealand	133,621	Vietnam	1,167
Germany, West	6,349,934	Nicaragua	5,222	Yemen	201,224
Ghana	394	Niger	8	Yugoslavia	14,591
Greece	1,349,277	Nigeria	29,591	Zaire	58,328
Guatemala	30,020	Norway	566,168	International Organizations	528,284
Haiti	1,288	Oman	9,700		

NUCLEAR ARMAMENTS: UNITED STATES AND SOVIET UNION

SOURCE: International Institute for Strategic Studies, London

United States

	Type[a]	Max. range (miles)[b]	Estimated Warhead yield[c]	Number deployed July 81
LAND-BASED MISSILES				
ICBM	Titan II	9,000	9 MT	52
	Minuteman II	7,000	1-2 MT	450
	Minuteman III	8,000	3 × 165 KT	550
SRBM	Pershing	450	KT-range	108[g]
	Lance	70	KT-range	36[g]
SEA-LAUNCHED MISSILES				
SLBM	Polaris A3	2,860	3 × 200 KT	80
	Poseidon C3	2,860	10 × 50 KT	432
	Trident C4	4,600	8 × 100 KT	64
AIR-LAUNCHED MISSILES				
ALCM	SRAM	35-100	KT range	1,250

Soviet Union

	Type[a] [d]	Max. range (miles)[b]	Estimated Warhead yield[c]	Number deployed July 81
LAND-BASED MISSILES				
ICBM	SS-11 Sego	6,500	1-2 MT[e]	580
	SS-13 Savage	6,200	1 MT	60
	SS-17	6,200	5 MT[e]	150
	SS-18	5,700 +	18-50 MT[e]	308
	SS-19	6,300 +	5 MT[e]	300
M/IRBM	SS-4 Sandal	1,200	1 MT	340
	SS-5 Skean	2,500	1 MT	40
	SS-20	3-4,500	50 KT-1.5 MT	230
SRBM	SS-1b Scud A	90	KT range	⎫
	SS-1c Scud B	100-190	KT range	⎪
	FROG 7	10-45	KT range	⎪
	SS-12 Scaleboard	300-550	MT range	⎬ 950 +
	SS-21	40-75	f	⎪
	SS-22	330-600	f	⎪
	SS-23	120-220	f	⎭
GLCM	SS-C-1b Sepal	280	100[h]	
SEA-LAUNCHED MISSILES				
SLBM	SS-N-5 Serb	700	1-2 MT	57
	SS-N-6 Sawfly	1,500 +	1-2 MT[e]	453
	SS-N-8	4,900	1-2 MT	291
	SS-NX-17	3,100	1 MT[e]	12
	SS-N-18	5,000	1-2 MT	176
SLCM	SS-N-3 Shaddock	280	KT range	324
	SS-N-7 Siren	30	KT range	138
	SS-N-9	175	KT range	130
	SS-N-12	600-2,300	f	56
	SS-N-19	f	f	40
AIR-LAUNCHED MISSILES				
ALCM	AS-2 Kipper	125	KT range	f
	AS-3 Kangaroo	370	MT range	70[f]
	AS-4 Kitchen	190	KT range	135[h]
	AS-6 Kingfish	160	KT range	65[h]

HISTORICAL CHANGES FOR STRENGTH, 1971-1981 (MID-YEARS)

		1971	1972	1973	1974	1975	1976	1977	1978	1979	1980	1981
USA	ICBM	1,054	1,054	1,054	1,054	1,054	1,054	1,054	1,054	1,054	1,054	1,052
	SLBM	656	656	656	656	656	656	656	656	656	656	576
	Long-range bombers [i]	360	390	397	397	397	387	373	366	365	338	316
USSR	ICBM	1,527	1,527	1,575	1,618	1,527	1,477-	1,350	1,400	1,398	1,398	1,398
	SLBM	448	500	628	720	784	845	909	1,028	1,028	1,028	989
	Long-range bombers	140	140	140	140	135	135	135	135	156	156	150

[a] ICBM = inter-continental ballistic missile (range over 4,000 miles); M/IRBM = medium/intermediate-range ballistic missile (500-4,000 miles); SRBM = short-range ballistic missile (under 500 miles); LRCM = long-range cruise missile (over 350 miles); SLBM = submarine-launched ballistic missile; SLCM = submarine-launched cruise missile; ALCM = air-launched cruise missile; GLCM = ground launched cruise missile. [b] Operational range depends upon payload carried; figures are given in statute miles. [c] MT = megaton = millions tons of TNT equivalent (MT range = 1 MT or over); KT = kiloton = thousands tons of TNT equivalent (KT range = less than 1 MT); 3 × , 10 × = 3 warheads, 10 warheads. [d] Numerical designation of Soviet missiles are of U.S. origin; names are of NATO origin. [e] Also exists in multiple warhead mode with lesser yield per warhead. [f] Information not available. [g] Figures for systems in Europe only. [h] Estimate. [i] Reserves not included.

WARPLANES: UNITED STATES AND THE SOVIET UNION

| | | United States | | | | | Soviet Union | | | |
AIRCRAFT	Type	Max. range (statute miles)	Max. speed (Mach no.)	Max. weapons load (lb.)	Number deployed (July 1981)	Type	Max. range (statute miles)	Max. speed (Mach no.)	Max. weapons load (lb.)	Number deployed (July 1981)
Long-range	B-52 D	6,000	0.95	60,000	}	Tu-95 Bear	8,000	0.78	40,000	105
bombers	B-52 G	7,500	0.95	70,000	} 400	Mya-4 Bison	7,000	0.87	20,000	45
	B-52 H	10,000	0.95	70,000	}	Tu-22M/-26				
						Backfire	5,000	2.5	17,500	135
Medium-range						Tu-16 Badger	4,000	0.8	20,000	580
bombers	FB-111A	3,000	2.5	37,500	60	Tu-22 Blinder	1,400	1.5	12,000	165
						Su-7 Fitter A	900	1.7	5,500	165
Strike aircraft						MiG-21 Fishbed				
(incl. short-	F-4 C/D/E	1,400	2.4	16,000	}	J/K/L/N	700	2.2	2,000	750
range					} 360	Mig-27 Flogger D	900	1.7	7,500	500
bombers):	F-111 E/F	2,925	2.2-2.5	28,000	}	Su-19/-24 Fencer	1,000	2.3	8,000	480
land-based						Su-17/-20 Fitter				
Strike aircraft:						C/D	1,100	1.6	11,000	740
carrier-	F-4 J/N	1,400	2.2	16,000	}					
based	A-6 E	2,000	0.9	18,000	} 348k					
	A-7 E	1,750	0.9	20,000	}					

WARPLANES: NATO AND WARSAW PACT COUNTRIES

| | | NATO | | | | | Warsaw Pact | | | | |
AIRCRAFT[a]	Type[c]	Oper-ated by[d]	Max. range[e] (statute miles)	Max. speed (Mach no.)[f]	Max. weapons load (lb)	No. de-ployed (July 1981)	Type[g]	Oper-ated by[d]	Max. range[e] (statute miles)	Max. speed (Mach no.)[f]	Max. weapons load (lb)	No. de-ployed (July 1981)
Medium-range bombers	Vulcan B2[b]	BR	4,000	0.95	21,000	48						
Strike air-craft (incl.	F-104	h	1,500	2.2	4,000	318[j]	Su-7 Fitter A[i]	CZ, PO	900	1.7	5,500	115
short-range bombers)	F-4	{ BR / GE, GR }	1,400	2.4	16,000	180[i]	Su-20 Fitter C[i]	PO	1,100	1.6	4,000	35
	Buccaneer	BR	2,300	0.95	12,000	60[j]						
	Mirage IVA	FR	2,000	2.2	16,000	33[j]						
	Mirage III E	FR	1,500	1.8	19,000	30[j]						
	Jaguar	{ BR } / FR	1,000	1.4	10,000	80[j]						
	Super Etendard	FR	900	1.0	16,000	36[j]						

[a] All aircraft listed are dual-capable and many would be more likely to carry conventional than nuclear weapons. [b] Medium-range bomber = maximum range 3,500-6,000 miles, primarily designed for bombing missions. [c] Vulcan and Buccaneer are of British origin; F-104 and F-4 are of American origin; Mirage is of French origin; Jaguar is Anglo-French. [d] BR = Britain, FR = France, CZ = Czechoslovakia; HU = Hungary, PO = Poland, GE = West Germany, GR = Greece. [e] Theoretical maximum range, with internal fuel only, at optimum altitude and speed. Ranges for strike aircraft assume no weapons load. Especially in the case of strike aircraft, therefore, range falls sharply for flights at lower altitudes, at higher speed or with full weapons load (e.g. combat radius of F-104, at operational height and speed, with typical weapons load, is approximately 420 miles). [f] Mach 1 (M = 1.0) = speed of sound. [g] Warsaw Pact aircraft of Soviet origin; names (e.g. Fitter) of NATO origin. [h] The dual-capable F-104 is operated by Belgium, West Germany, Greece, Italy, the Netherlands and Turkey. The warheads for all of these aircraft are held in American custody. [i] Nuclear warheads for these dual-capable aircraft are held in Soviet custody. [j] Uncertain as to how many of these nuclear-capable aircraft actually have a nuclear role. [k] Estimate.

ACTIVE U.S. MILITARY FORCES Source: U.S. Office of Management and Budget

Description	Actual Sept. 30 1980	Estimated Sept. 30 1981	Estimated Sept. 30 1982
Military personnel (in thousands):			
End strength:			
Army	777	775	786
Navy	527	540	555
Marine Corps	189	191	192
Air Force	558	569	587
Total, Department of Defense	2,050	2,075	2,120
Average strength:			
Army	766	771	774
Navy	525	535	546
Marine Corps	184	188	190
Air Force	558	565	575
Total, Department of Defense	2,033	2,059	2,089
General purpose forces:			
Land forces:			
Army divisions	16	16	16
Marine Corps divisions	3	3	3
Tactical air forces:			
Air Force wings	26	26	26
Navy attack wings	12	12	12
Marine Corps wings	3	3	3
Naval forces:			
Attack and multipurpose carriers	13	12	13
Nuclear attack submarines	74	83[1]	92[1]
Other warships	183	194	204
Amphibious assault ships	63	59	60

[1] Includes ex-Polaris ships operating as attack submarines.

BLACKS IN U.S. ARMED FORCES
Source: U.S. Department of Defense (as of September 30, 1980)

	Officers		Enlisted		TOTAL	
ARMY	7,931	(7.5%)	245,416	(33.4%)	253,347	(30.1%)
NAVY	1,798	(2.6%)	56,894	(11.7%)	58,692	(10.5%)
AIR FORCE	5,434	(5.1%)	82,826	(16.3%)	88,260	(14.4%)
MARINE CORPS	729	(3.9%)	39,565	(22.4%)	40,294	(20.6%)
TOTAL	15,892	(5.3%)	424,701	(22.3%)	440,593	(20.0%)

THE MILITARY-INDUSTRIAL COMPLEX Source: U.S. Department of Defense

Companies doing more than $200,000,000 worth of business with the Department of Defense during the 1980 fiscal year, in thousands of dollars.

Rank	Company Name	1980 Contracts	% of Total	Rank	Company Name	1980 Contracts	% of Total
1.	General Dynamics Corp.	$3,517,906	4.58	31.	Singer Co.	$435,426	0.57
2.	McDonnell Douglas Corp.	3,246,557	4.23	32.	Texas Instruments Inc.	431,428	0.56
3.	United Technologies Corp.	3,108,901	4.05	33.	Teledyne Inc.	396,237	0.52
4.	Boeing Co.	2,385,459	3.11	34.	Ford Motor Co.	395,777	0.52
5.	General Electric Co.	2,202,042	2.87	35.	Todd Shipyards Corp.	394,298	0.51
6.	Lockheed Corp.	2,037,044	2.65	36.	Congoleum Corp.	377,879	0.49
7.	Hughes Aircraft Co.	1,819,058	2.37	37.	International Tel. & Tel. Corp.	335,107	0.44
8.	Raytheon Co.	1,745,107	2.27	38.	Amerada Hess Corp.	331,699	0.43
9.	Tenneco Inc.	1,524,414	1.98	39.	Bendix Corp.	322,485	0.42
10.	Grumman Corp.	1,322,023	1.72	40.	General Tire & Rubber Co.	317,893	0.41
11.	Northrop Corp.	1,227,339	1.60	41.	General Tel. & Elec. Corp.	309,970	0.40
12.	Motor Oil Hellas	1,058,646	1.38	42.	Avco Corp.	286,665	0.37
13.	Chrysler Corp.	970,881	1.26	43.	Atlantic Richfield Co.	285,673	0.37
14.	Rockwell International Corp.	969,234	1.26	44.	Harsco Corp.	280,256	0.36
15.	Westinghouse Electric Corp.	932,053	1.21	45.	Mobil Corp.	276,244	0.36
16.	Sperry Corp.	844,977	1.10	46.	Sam Whan Corp.	266,340	0.35
17.	FMC Corp.	834,640	1.09	47.	Goodyear Tire & Rubber Co.	264,156	0.34
18.	Martin Marietta Corp.	808,681	1.05	48.	North American Philips Corp.	260,518	0.34
19.	Honeywell Inc.	687,018	0.89	49.	Coastal Corp.	250,432	0.33
20.	Litton Industries, Inc.	652,383	0.85	50.	Gould Inc.	244,184	0.32
21.	American Tel. & Tel. Co.	597,074	0.78	51.	Sun Co. Inc.	230,065	0.30
22.	RCA Corp.	588,935	0.77	52.	Royal Dutch Shell Group	225,090	0.29
23.	Textron Inc.	578,738	0.75	53.	AGIP SPA	223,660	0.29
24.	Fairchild Industries, Inc.	559,277	0.73	54.	Texaco Inc.	221,123	0.29
25.	LTV Corp.	510,902	0.67	55.	Hercules, Inc.	220,302	0.29
26.	General Motors Corp.	508,803	0.66	56.	Hanil Dev Co. Ltd. &		
27.	TRW Inc.	508,084	0.66		Al Mabani JV	217,558	0.28
28.	IBM Co.	496,953	0.65	57.	Standard Oil of Indiana	202,129	0.26
29.	Exxon Corp.	479,637	0.62	58.	Reynolds (RJ) Ind. Inc.	202,003	0.26
30.	Standard Oil Co. of Calif.	474,954	0.62				

ARMED FORCES OF THE WORLD: 1979
Source: U.S. Arms Control and Disarmament Agency (in thousands)

Country	Active-duty Military Personnel	Country	Active-duty Military Personnel	Country	Active-duty Military Personnel	Country	Active-duty Military Personnel
Afghanistan	40	Equatorial Guinea	2	Laos	55	Senegal	8
Albania	53	Ethiopia	250	Liberia	7	Singapore	60
Algeria	89	Finland	36	Libya	53	Somalia	54
Angola	47	France	522	Madagascar	20	South Africa	70
Argentina	155	German Dem. Rep.	228	Malawi	5	Spain	349
Australia	71	Germany, Fed. Rep.	470	Malaysia	66	Sri Lanka	15
Austria	40	Ghana	15	Mali	5	Sudan	65
Bangladesh	72	Greece	182	Malta	6	Sweden	68
Belgium	88	Guatemala	14	Mauritania	7.5	Switzerland	23
Bolivia	20	Guinea	18	Mexico	145	Syria	250
Brazil	450	Guinea-Bissau	6	Mongolia	36	Tanzania	53
Bulgaria	164	Guyana	7	Morocco	98	Thailand	230
Burma	174	Haiti	7	Mozambique	24	Togo	4
Burundi	8	Honduras	13.5	Nepal	22	Tunisia	24
Cambodia	N.A.	Hungary	110	Netherlands	101	Turkey	583
Cameroon	11	India	1,104	New Zealand	12.7	Uganda	6
Canada	80	Indonesia	242	Nicaragua	N.A.	USSR	4,800
Chad	N.A.	Iran	415	Nigeria	164	United Arab Emirates	25
Chile	111	Iraq	212	Norway	36	United Kingdom	320
China,People's Rep.	4,500	Ireland	14	Oman	19	UNITED STATES	2,024
China, Rep. of	475	Israel	165	Pakistan	439	Upper Volta	4
Colombia	60	Italy	366	Panama	8	Uruguay	28
Congo	16	Ivory Coast	6	Paraguay	15	Venezuela	55
Cuba	210	Japan	241	Peru	125	Vietnam	750
Cyprus	15	Jordan	67	Philippines	113	Yemen Arab Rep.	36
Czechoslovakia	211	Kenya	13	Poland	425	Yemen, P.D.R.	20
Denmark	34	Korea, Dem. People's		Portugal	64	Yugoslavia	260
Dominican Republic	19	Rep.	678	Qatar	5	Zaire	23
Ecuador	35	Korea, Rep. of	600	Romania	218	Zambia	20
Egypt	395	Kuwait	11	Saudi Arabia	50	Zimbabwe	22
El Salvador	10.5						

EDUCATION: FACTS/FIGURES

EXPENDITURES FOR PUBLIC ELEMENTARY AND SECONDARY SCHOOL EDUCATION

Source: National Center for Education Statistics

School year	Total	Total per pupil	School year	Total	Total per pupil
1929/1930	$ 2,316,790,000	$108	1963/1964	$21,324,993,000	$ 559
1939/1940	2,344,049,000	106	1965/1966	26,248,026,000	654
1949/1950	5,837,643,000	259	1967/1968	32,977,182,000	786
1953/1954	9,092,449,000	351	1969/1970	40,683,428,000	955
1955/1956	10,955,047,000	388	1971/1972	48,050,283,000	1,128
1957/1958	13,569,163,000	449	1973/1974	56,970,355,000	1,364
1959/1960	15,613,255,000	472	1975/1976	70,600,573,000	1,697
1961/1962	18,373,339,000	530	1977/1978	80,844,366,000	2,002
			1978/1979	86,711,615,000	2,210
¹ Estimated.			1979/1980¹	94,300,000,000	2,450

HIGH SCHOOL GRADUATES Source: National Center for Education Statistics

School year	Population 17 years old	High school graduates Total	Boys	Girls	School year	Population 17 years old	High school graduates Total	Boys	Girls
1889/1890	1,259,177	43,731	18,549	25,182	1965/1966	3,515,000	2,632,000	1,308,000	1,324,000
1899/1900	1,489,146	94,883	38,075	56,808	1966/1967	3,518,000	2,679,000	1,331,000	1,348,000
1909/1910	1,786,240	156,429	63,676	92,753	1967/1968	3,521,000	2,702,000	1,341,000	1,361,000
1919/1920	1,855,173	311,266	123,684	187,582	1968/1969	3,622,000	2,839,000	1,408,000	1,431,000
1929/1930	2,295,822	666,904	300,376	366,528	1969/1970	3,825,343	2,896,000	1,433,000	1,463,000
1939/1940	2,403,074	1,221,475	578,718	642,757	1970/1971	3,859,000	3,036,000	1,506,000	1,530,000
1949/1950	2,034,450	1,199,700	570,700	629,000	1971/1972	3,957,000	3,006,000	1,490,000	1,516,000
1951/1952	2,040,800	1,196,500	569,200	627,300	1972/1973	4,024,000	3,037,000	1,501,000	1,536,000
1953/1954	2,128,600	1,276,100	612,500	663,600	1973/1974	4,096,000	3,080,000	1,515,000	1,565,000
1955/1956	2,270,000	1,414,800	679,500	735,300	1974/1975	4,210,000	3,140,000	1,541,000	1,599,000
1957/1958	2,324,000	1,505,900	725,500	780,400	1975/1976	4,215,000	3,155,000	1,554,000	1,601,000
1959/1960	2,862,005	1,864,000	898,000	966,000	1976/1977	4,206,000	3,161,000	1,550,000	1,611,000
1961/1962	2,768,000	1,925,000	941,000	984,000	1977/1978	4,208,000	3,147,000	1,541,000	1,606,000
1963/1964	3,001,000	2,290,000	1,121,000	1,169,000	1978/1979	4,238,000	3,134,000	1,532,000	1,602,000
					1979/1980¹	4,162,000	3,100,000	1,520,000	1,580,000

¹ Estimated.

COLLEGE AND UNIVERSITY GRADUATES Source: National Center for Education Statistics

School year	All degrees	Degrees conferred Bachelor's and First Professional	Master's	Doctor's	School year	All degrees	Degrees conferred Bachelor's and First Professional	Master's	Doctor's
1869/1870	9,372	9,371	0	1	1965/1966	709,832	551,040	140,555	18,237
1889/1890	16,703	15,539	1,015	149	1966/1967	768,871	590,548	157,706	20,617
1899/1900	29,375	27,410	1,583	382	1967/1968	866,548	666,710	176,749	23,089
1909/1910	39,755	37,199	2,113	443	1968/1969	984,129	764,185	193,756	26,188
1919/1920	53,516	48,622	4,279	615	1969/1970	1,065,391	827,234	208,291	29,866
1929/1930	139,752	122,484	14,969	2,299	1970/1971	1,140,292	877,676	230,509	32,107
1939/1940	216,521	186,500	26,731	3,290	1971/1972	1,215,680	930,684	251,633	33,363
1949/1950	496,661	432,058	58,183	6,420	1972/1973	1,270,528	972,380	263,371	34,777
1953/1954	356,608	290,825	56,788	8,995	1973/1974	1,310,441	999,592	277,033	33,816
1955/1956	376,973	308,812	59,258	8,903	1974/1975	1,305,382	978,849	292,450	34,083
1957/1958	436,979	362,554	65,487	8,938	1975/1976	1,334,230	988,395	311,771	34,064
1959/1960	476,704	392,440	74,435	9,829	1976/1977	1,334,304	983,908	317,164	33,232
1961/1962	514,323	417,846	84,855	11,622	1977/1978	1,331,536	987,785	311,620	32,131
1963/1964	614,194	498,654	101,050	14,490	1978/1979	1,324,047	990,238	301,079	32,730
					1979/1980¹	1,365,000	1,017,000	315,000	33,000

¹ Estimated.

EDUCATION AND INCOME Source: U.S. Bureau of the Census (based on 1979 data)

Income Levels	Percent of Male Income Recipients*	School Years Completed**	Income Levels	Percent of Male Income Recipients*	School Years Completed**	Income Levels	Percent of Male Income Recipients*	School Years Completed**
$1 to $1,999 or less	3.3	11.7	$7,000 to $8,499	5.8	12.1	$20,000 to $24,999	13.4	12.8
$2,000 to $2,999	3.1	8.6	$8,500 to $9,999	5.2	12.3	$25,000 to $29,999	7.4	13.5
$3,000 to $3,999	3.7	9.3	$10,000 to $12,499	10.5	12.4	$30,000 to $34,999	3.7	15.5
$4,000 to $4,999	3.8	10.2	$12,500 to $14,999	8.2	12.6	$35,000 to $49,999	4.2	16.2
$5,000 to $5,999	3.9	11.4	$15,000 to $17,499	9.6	12.7	$50,000 to $74,999	1.8	16.6
$6,000 to $6,999	3.6	11.4	$17,500 to $19,999	7.8	12.8	$75,000 and over	0.9	17.0

* Males 25 years old and over. ** Median

LEVEL OF EDUCATION: WHITE AND BLACK ADULTS Source: U.S. Bureau of the Census

Race and Sex	Persons 25 years old or older (1,000)	YEARS OF SCHOOL COMPLETED 1980 (percent distribution)							Median School Years Completed
		Elementary School			High School		College		
		Less than 5 years	5–7 years	8 years	1–3 years	4 years	1–3 years	4 years or more	
Total, all races, March 1980	127,882	3.3	5.9	8.2	13.9	36.9	14.8	17.1	12.5
Male	60,257	3.6	5.9	8.1	13.1	32.8	15.6	20.9	12.6
Female	67,624	3.1	5.9	8.2	14.6	40.5	14.2	13.6	12.5
White	112,900	2.6	5.3	8.3	18.1	37.7	15.1	17.9	12.5
Male	53,557	2.7	5.4	8.3	12.5	33.2	15.8	22.2	12.6
Female	59,343	2.5	5.2	8.4	13.7	41.7	14.5	14.0	12.5
Black	12,613	9.2	11.0	7.2	21.2	30.9	12.5	7.9	12.0
Male	5,586	11.5	10.6	7.1	19.7	30.0	13.4	7.6	12.0
Female	7,027	7.4	11.4	7.3	22.5	31.6	11.8	8.1	12.0

ESTIMATED U.S. EDUCATIONAL EXPENDITURES

Source: National Center for Education Statistics (amounts in billions of dollars)

Source of funds, by level of institution and type of control	1969-70		1975-76		1978-79		1980-81	
	Amount	Percent	Amount	Percent	Amount	Percent	Amount	Percent
All levels:	(Billions)		(Billions)		(Billions)		(Billions)	
Total public and nonpublic	$70.4	100.0	$121.6	100.0	$152.1	100.0	$181.3	100.0
Federal	7.5	10.7	12.8	10.5	16.1	10.6	19.2	10.6
State	22.2	31.5	44.4	36.5	56.4	37.1	68.8	37.9
Local	22.6	32.1	34.6	28.5	40.1	26.4	46.6	25.7
All other	18.1	25.7	29.8	24.5	39.5	26.0	46.7	25.8
Elementary and secondary schools:*								
Total public and nonpublic	45.7	100.0	78.9	100.0	98.0	100.0	116.3	100.0
Federal	3.4	7.4	6.3	8.0	8.5	8.7	10.1	8.7
State	15.8	34.6	31.6	40.1	39.8	40.6	48.5	41.7
Local	21.7	47.5	32.9	41.7	38.5	39.3	44.6	38.3
All other	4.8	10.5	8.1	10.3	11.2	11.4	13.1	11.3
Total public	41.0	100.0	70.9	100.0	87.1	100.0	103.5	100.0
Federal	3.4	8.2	6.3	8.9	8.5	9.8	10.1	9.8
State	15.8	38.6	31.6	44.6	39.8	45.7	48.5	46.9
Local	21.7	52.9	32.9	46.4	38.5	44.2	44.6	43.1
All other	.1	.3	.1	.1	.3	.3	.3	.3
Total nonpublic	4.7	100.0	8.0	100.0	10.9	100.0	12.8	100.0
Federal	—	—	—	—	—	—	—	—
State	—	—	—	—	—	—	—	—
Local	—	—	—	—	—	—	—	—
All other	4.7	100.0	8.0	100.0	10.9	100.0	12.8	100.0
Institutions of higher education:								
Total public and nonpublic	24.7	100.0	42.7	100.0	54.2	100.0	65.0	100.0
Federal	4.1	16.6	6.5	15.2	7.6	14.0	9.1	14.0
State	6.4	25.9	12.8	30.0	16.6	30.7	20.3	31.2
Local	.9	3.6	1.7	4.0	1.6	3.0	2.0	3.1
All other	13.3	53.9	21.7	50.8	28.3	52.3	33.6	51.7
Total public	15.8	100.0	29.1	100.0	36.4	100.0	43.9	100.0
Federal	2.4	14.9	4.0	13.8	4.4	12.1	5.3	12.0
State	6.3	39.7	12.5	43.0	16.3	45.0	20.0	45.6
Local	.8	5.1	1.6	5.4	1.5	4.1	1.9	4.3
All other	6.3	40.3	11.0	37.8	14.1	38.8	16.7	38.1
Total nonpublic	8.9	100.0	13.6	100.0	17.8	100.0	21.1	100.0
Federal	1.7	18.8	2.5	18.1	3.2	18.0	3.8	17.8
State	.1	1.6	.3	2.3	.3	1.7	.3	1.5
Local	.1	.7	.1	.8	.1	.6	.1	.7
All other	7.0	78.9	10.7	78.8	14.2	79.7	16.9	80.0

* In addition to regular schools, these figures include other elementary and secondary schools, such as residential schools for exceptional children, Federal schools for Indians, federally operated elementary and secondary schools on posts, and subcollegiate departments of colleges.

ELEMENTARY AND SECONDARY SCHOOLS Source: National Center for Education Statistics

In the school year 1978-79, there were approximately 16,000 public school systems in the United States that included about 62,900 public elementary schools and 25,300 public secondary schools. As the accompanying table indicates, the number of school districts and public elementary schools has been declining, with a more rapid drop in the number of districts. However, since WWII, the number of pupils per school has risen substantially. In addition to the public schools, there are about 16,100 nonpublic elementary schools and 5,800 nonpublic secondary schools in the country.

School Year	Districts	PUBLIC SCHOOLS Elementary	PUBLIC SCHOOLS Secondary	NONPUBLIC SCHOOLS* Elementary	NONPUBLIC SCHOOLS* Secondary
1945–46	101,382	160,227	24,314	9,863	3,294
1949–50	83,718	128,225	24,542	10,375	3,331
1955–56	54,859	104,427	26,046	12,372	3,887
1959–60	40,520	91,853	25,784	13,574	4,061
1965–66	26,983	73,216	26,597	15,340	4,606
1970–71	17,995	65,800	25,352	14,372	3,770
1972–73	16,960	64,945	25,922	NA	NA
1973–74	16,730	65,070	25,906	NA	NA
1974–75	16,570	63,619[1]	25,697[1]	NA	NA
1975–76	16,376	63,242[1]	25,330[1]	NA	NA
1976–77	16,271	62,644[1]	25,378[1]	16,385	5,904
1978–79	16,014	62,900 (est.)	25,300 (est.)	16,097	5,766

* Data for most years are partly estimated.
[1] Excludes special education schools for the handicapped (not reported by level).

EDUCATION AND INCOME Source: U.S. Bureau of the Census

MEDIAN INCOME OF FULL-TIME YEAR-ROUND WORKERS, 25 YEARS OLD AND OVER, BY EDUCATIONAL ATTAINMENT

		Median Income, 1979 Male	Median Income, 1979 Female
Elementary:	Total	$ 12,370	$ 7,613
	Less than 8 years	10,993	7,414
	8 years	14,454	7,788
High school:	Total	17,348	10,192
	1 to 3 years	15,198	8,555
	4 years	18,100	10,513
College:	1 or more years	21,626	13,268
	5 or more years	25,860	16,693

MEDIAN INCOME OF MEN 25 YEARS OLD AND OVER, BY EDUCATIONAL ATTAINMENT

		Median Income, 1979 Black	Median Income, 1979 White	Median Income, 1979 All Races
Elementary:	Total	$ 4,949	$ 7,220	$ 6,824
	Less than 8 years	4,560	6,335	5,903
	8 years	6,226	8,260	8,085
High school:	Total	10,441	14,767	14,183
	1 to 3 years	8,855	11,420	11,000
	4 years	11,467	15,924	15,522
College:	1 or more years	14,784	19,774	19,380
	5 or more years	19,468	23,507	23,261

U.S. PUBLIC LIBRARIES—1978 (with over one million volumes)

U.S. Department of Health, Education, and Welfare, National Center for Education Statistics.

Library	Number of Volumes*	Library	Number of Volumes*
New York Public Library	8,275,240	Miami-Dade County Library	1,426,519
Chicago Public Library	6,214,748	St. Louis County Library	1,419,587
Los Angeles Public Library	5,236,538	Public Library of Newark	1,385,496
Boston Public Library	4,236,364	St. Louis Public Library	1,364,175
Cleveland Public Library	3,535,967	Memphis & Shelby County Library	1,358,026
Queens Borough Public Library (N.Y.)	3,506,309	Montgomery County Library (Md.)	1,313,061
Brooklyn Public Library	3,452,709	Dayton & Montgomery County Pub. Lib. (Ohio)	1,302,269
Cincinnati-Hamilton County Public Library	3,318,683	Indianapolis-Mario County Library	1,285,152
Free Library of Philadelphia	3,040,254	Toledo-Lucas County Library	1,255,038
Buffalo & Erie County Library System	3,010,577	Baltimore County Public Library	1,220,679
Providence (R.I.) Library	2,861,937	Library Association of Portland	1,191,870
Detroit Public Library	2,405,694	Kansas City Public Library	1,186,484
Enoch Pratt Free Library (Baltimore)	2,375,721	Fairfax County Library (Va.)	1,180,190
Milwaukee Public Library	2,353,672	Prince Georges County Library (Md.)	1,169,173
Carnegie Library of Pittsburgh	2,039,904	Columbus Public Library	1,164,423
Houston Public Library	1,974,451	King County Library (Wash.)	1,127,393
Public Library of Washington, D.C.	1,930,341	Phoenix Public Library	1,088,095
Dallas Public Library	1,816,019	Mid-Continent Public Library (Mo.)	1,077,405
Cuyahoga County Public Library (Ohio)	1,804,431	Atlanta Public Library	1,033,507
Denver Public Library	1,709,563	Orange County Public Library (Calif.)	1,029,148
San Francisco Public Library	1,642,683	Louisville Free Public Library	1,013,217
Public Library of Fort Wayne & Allen County (Ind.)	1,512,285	Hennepin County Library (Minn.)	1,011,029
Seattle Public Library	1,493,712	Birmingham-Jefferson County Library	1,001,615
Minneapolis Public Library	1,454,462		

* Book stock and serials

INDEX OF U.S. COLLEGES AND UNIVERSITIES: 1979-80

This list includes all regionally accredited four-year colleges and universities in the United States that grant baccalaureate degrees. Highly specialized institutions such as schools of mortuary science, optometry, and pharmacy are not included, nor are such professional colleges as law, medicine, or theology, which generally offer only post-baccalaureate work.

Institutions are listed in standard letter-by-letter alphabetical order. For example, University of Michigan will be found under U, not M; Marshall University comes before Mars Hill College.

The explanation of the data contained in each column is as follows. Column 1: **Est** shows the founding date of the institution. Column 2: **Type/Control** shows the student body makeup (C = coed, M = primarily men, W = primarily women) and the institutional control (Ind

= independent, Pub = public, Cath = Catholic, Jewish, LDS = Latter-Day Saints, Prot = Protestant). Column 3: **UG Enroll** shows undergraduate enrollment as of fall 1979. Column 4: **% State Res** shows the percentage of the fall 1979 undergraduate enrollment that were state residents. Column 5: **Grad** shows whether graduate-level work is offered. Column 6: **Fac size** shows the number of total faculty teaching graduate and undergraduate programs as of fall 1979. Column 7: **Cmps** shows the campus setting (R = rural, S = suburban, T = college town, U = urban). Column 8: **ROTC** shows which ROTC branch has a program on campus (A = Army, N = Navy, AF = Air Force). Column 9: **Tuition** shows tuition per credit or per year for all students at private colleges or for in-state students at public colleges; X indicates campus room and board not available.

An asterisk appears where no information is available.

Name and Location	Est	Type/ Control	UG Enroll	% of State Res	Grad	Fac Size	Cmps	ROTC	Tuition
Abilene Christian University, Abilene, TX 79699	1906	C/Prot	3800	65%	G	175	S	A	$2160
Abilene Christian University at Dallas, Garland, TX 75041	1971	C/Prot	600	80%	G	40	S		1584x
Academy of the New Church, Bryn Athyn, PA 19009	1876	C/Ind	149	42%		36	S		1005
Adams State College, Alamosa, CO 81102	1921	C/Pub	1679	87%	G	107	T		490
Adelphi University, Garden City, NY 11530	1896	C/Ind	5517	90%	G	800	S		3510
Adrian College, Adrian, MI 49221	1859	C/Ind	946	84%		95	T		3760
Agnes Scott College, Decatur, GA 30030	1889	W/Ind	544	50%		85	S		3900
Alabama A&M University, Normal, AL 35762	1875	C/Pub	3615	85%	G	500	S	A	530
Alabama Christian College, Montgomery, AL 36109	1942	C/Prot	1119	69%		93	S		1800
Alabama State University, Montgomery, AL 36101	1874	C/Pub	3653	86%	G	242	U	AF	525
Alaska Pacific University, Anchorage, AK 99504	1957	C/Prot	106	95%	G	38	U		2250
Albany State College, Albany, GA 31705	1903	C/Pub	4962	90%		128	U	A	699
Albertus Magnus College, New Haven, CT 06511	1925	W/Cath	561	82%		55	S		3600
Albion College, Albion, MI 49224	1835	C/Prot	1800	85%		119	T		4180
Albright College, Reading, PA 19604	1856	C/Prot	1275	60%		125	S		4180
Alcorn State University, Lorman, MS 39096	1871	C/Pub	2500	92%	G	150	R	A	744
Alderson-Broaddus College, Philippi, WV 26416	1871	C/Ind	878	43%		112	R		2835
Alfred University, Alfred, NY 14802	1836	C/Ind	1765	75%	G	176	R		4900
Alice Lloyd College, Pippa Passes, KY 41844	1923	C/Ind	231	93%		20	R		2000
Allegheny College, Meadville, PA 16335	1815	C/Prot	1850	50%	G	152	T		4300
Allentown Coll of St Francis de Sales, Center Valley, PA 18034	1965	C/Cath	600	70%		58	R		3530
Allen University, Columbia, SC 29204	1870	C/Prot	419	*		41	S		1800
Alliance College, Cambridge Springs, PA 16403	1912	C/Ind	251	53%		24	R		2200
Alma College, Alma, MI 48801	1886	C/Prot	1210	74%		99	T		4144
Alvernia College, Reading, PA 19607	1958	C/Cath	750	60%		80	S		1850
Alverno College, Milwaukee, WI 53215	1936	W/Cath	1340	95%		107	U		2950
Ambassador College, Pasadena, CA 91123	1947	C/Ind	331	18%	G	36	U		1350
American Baptist College, Nashville, TN 37207	1924	M/Prot	125	20%		16	S		920
American Conservatory of Music, Chicago, IL 60603	1886	C/Ind	311	90%	G	188	U		2400x
American International College, Springfield, MA 01109	1885	C/Ind	1463	60%	G	115	S		3060
American Technological University, Killeen, TX 76541	1973	C/Pub	401	*	G	29	S		1488
American University, Washington, DC 20016	1893	C/Ind	5717	27%	G	1173	S		4620
Amherst College, Amherst, MA 01002	1821	C/Ind	1541	18%		170	T		6250
Anderson College, Anderson, IN 46011	1917	C/Prot	1858	40%	G	132	S		3200
Andrews University, Berrien Springs, MI 49104	1874	C/Ind	2087	38%	G	272	T		3975
Angelo State University, San Angelo, TX 76909	1928	C/Pub	5292	95%	G	201	T	AF	344
Anna Maria College, Paxton, MA 01612	1946	C/Cath	580	75%	G	63	S		2950
Antioch College, Yellow Springs, OH 45387	1852	C/Ind	989	12%		83	T		5500
Antioch U-Maryland at Columbia, Columbia, MD 21044	1852	C/Ind	*	90%		*	*		*x
Appalachian Bible Institute, Bradley, WV 25818	1950	C/Ind	230	14%		20	T		1825
Appalachian State University, Boone, NC 28608	1899	C/Pub	8277	93%	G	554	T	A	620
Aquinas College, Grand Rapids, MI 49506	1886	C/Ind	1907	89%	G	122	S		3555
Arizona State University, Tempe, AZ 85281	1885	C/Pub	27,570	66%	G	1267	S	A,AF	600
Arkansas Baptist College, Little Rock, AR 72202	1884	C/Ind	534	*		*	*		*
Arkansas College, Batesville, AR 72501	1872	C/Prot	496	65%		52	T		1100
Arkansas State University, State University, AR 72467	1909	C/Pub	6641	88%	G	339	T	A	600
Arkansas Tech University, Russellville, AR 72801	1909	C/Pub	2846	85%	G	150	T	A	600
Armstrong College, Berkeley, CA 94704	1918	C/Ind	362	50%	G	48	U		2052x
Armstrong State College, Savannah, GA 31406	1935	C/Pub	2854	95%	G	160	S	A,N	627x
Art Center College of Design, Pasadena, CA 91103	1930	C/Ind	1057	50%	G	173	S		3250x
Asbury College, Wilmore, KY 40390	1890	C/Ind	1273	12%		101	T		2689
Ashland College, Ashland, OH 44805	1878	C/Prot	1901	75%	G	149	T		4205
Assumption College, Worcester, MA 01609	1904	C/Cath	1400	50%	G	151	S		3300
Athens State College, Athens, AL 35611	1822	C/Pub	1204	90%		70	T		675
Atlanta Christian College, East Point, GA 30344	1937	C/Ind	207	56%		17	S		1184
Atlanta College of Art, Atlanta, GA 30309	1928	C/Ind	260	40%		35	U		2950
Atlantic-Christian College, Wilson, NC 27893	1902	C/Prot	1650	80%		112	S		2200
Atlantic Union College, South Lancaster, MA 01561	1882	C/Ind	640	38%		98	T		4048
Auburn University, Auburn, AL 36849	1856	C/Pub	16,336	68%	G	1123	T	A,N,AF	720
Auburn University at Montgomery, Montgomery, AL 36109	1856	C/Pub	3627	100%	G	350	U	A	555
Augsburg College, Minneapolis, MN 55454	1869	C/Ind	1625	88%		140	U	AF	3550
Augusta College, Augusta, GA 30904	1925	C/Pub	3378	90%	G	173	U	A	534x
Augustana College, Rock Island, IL 61201	1860	C/Prot	2220	80%	G	179	U		3540
Augustana College, Sioux Falls, SD 57102	1860	C/Prot	1874	55%	G	188	U		3650
Aurora College, Aurora, IL 60507	1893	C/Prot	1058	90%		99	S		3300
Austin College, Sherman, TX 75090	1849	C/Prot	1069	90%	G	107	S		3000
Austin Peay State University, Clarksville, TN 37040	1927	C/Pub	4407	88%	G	245	T	A	546
Averett College, Danville, VA 24541	1859	C/Prot	1077	78%	G	54	S		1525x
Avila College, Kansas City, MO 64145	1916	C/Cath	1980	31%	G	199	S		2550
Azusa Pacific College, Azusa, CA 91702	1899	C/Ind	1230	85%	G	128	S		3632
Babson College, Babson Park, MA 02157	1919	C/Ind	1335	75%	G	124	S		4512
Baker University, Baldwin City, KS 66006	1858	C/Prot	872	55%	G	89	T		2600

Name and Location	Est	Type/ Control	UG Enroll	% of State Res	Grad	Fac Size	Cmps	ROTC	Tuition
Baldwin-Wallace College, Berea, OH 44017	1845	C/Prot	2656	80%	G	169	S		$4131
Ball State University, Muncie, IN 47306	1918	C/Pub	15,205	93%	G	963	S	A	975
Baltimore Hebrew College, Baltimore, MD 21215	1919	C/Ind	95	96%	G	17	S		1200x
Baptist Bible College of Pennsylvania, Clarks Summit, PA 18411	1932	C/Prot	780	8%		45	S		2176
Baptist College at Charleston, Charleston, SC 29411	1965	C/Prot	2420	85%		92	S	AF	2616
Barat College, Lake Forest, IL 60045	1858	W/Cath	737	88%		82	S		3650
Barber-Scotia College, Concord, NC 28025	1867	C/Prot	435	61%		38	T		1829
Bard College, Annandale, NY 12504	1860	C/Ind	700	43%		95	R		5440
Barnard College, New York, NY 10027	1889	W/Ind	2441	45%		225	U		5940
Barrington College, Barrington, RI 02806	1900	C/Ind	456	26%		47	S		3450
Barry College, Miami Shores, FL 33161	1940	C/Cath	1249	79%	G	171	S		2900
Bartlesville Wesleyan College, Bartlesville, OK 74003	1959	C/Prot	662	51%		53	S		2200
Bates College, Lewiston, ME 04240	1864	C/Ind	1450	11%		130	T		5720
Bayamon Central University, Bayamon, PR 00619	1961	C/Prot	2615	100%		66	U		600x
Baylor University, Waco, TX 76706	1845	C/Prot	8551	60%	G	476	U	AF	2100
Beacon College, Washington, DC 20009	1971	C/Ind	43	*	G	143	U		1950x
Beaver College, Glenside, PA 19038	1853	C/Prot	994	69%	G	130	S		4300
Belhaven College, Jackson, MS 39202	1883	C/Prot	886	85%		58	S		2215
Bellarmine College, Louisville, KY 40205	1950	C/Cath	1820	85%	G	96	S		2250
Bellevue College, Bellevue, NE 68005	1966	C/Ind	2272	99%		77	U		1050x
Belmont Abbey College, Belmont, NC 28012	1876	C/Prot	777	37%		57	S		2700
Belmont College, Nashville, TN 37203	1951	C/Prot	1483	75%		131	U		2050
Beloit College, Beloit, WI 53511	1846	C/Ind	1019	17%		120	T		5070
Bemidji State University, Bemidji, MN 56601	1919	C/Pub	4014	93%	G	247	R	A	585
Benedict College, Columbia, SC 29204	1870	C/Ind	1584	90%		107	U	A	2200
Benedictine College, Atchison, KS 66002	1971	C/Cath	1045	60%		75	T		2800
Bennett College, Greensboro, NC 27420	1873	W/Prot	645	35%		56	U		1950
Bennington College, Bennington, VT 05201	1932	C/Ind	655	1%	G	80	R		7380
Bentley College, Waltham, MA 02154	1917	C/Ind	4950	60%	G	190	S		3970
Berea College, Berea, KY 40403	1855	C/Ind	1438	38%		127	T		91
Berklee College of Music, Boston, MA 02215	1945	C/Ind	2583	20%		218	U		2880
Berkshire Christian College, Lenox, MA 01240	1897	C/Prot	136	33%		21	T*		2200
Bernard M Baruch College, See City U of NY, Baruch College									
Berry College, Mount Berry, GA 30149	1902	C/Ind	1385	60%		98	S		2400
Bethany Bible College, Santa Cruz, CA 95066	1919	C/Prot	598	60%		33	R		1900
Bethany College, Lindsborg, KS 67465	1881	C/Prot	827	73%		67	T		2434
Bethany College, Bethany, WV 26032	1840	C/Prot	900	16%		77	R		3835
Bethany Nazarene College, Bethany, OK 73008	1899	C/Prot	1277	30%	G	85	S		1860
Bethel College, Mishawaka, IN 46544	1947	C/Prot	464	97%		37	U		2573
Bethel College, North Newton, KS 67117	1887	C/Prot	638	63%		63	T		2685
Bethel College, St Paul, MN 55112	1871	C/Prot	1989	59%		184	S		3400
Bethel College, McKenzie, TN 38201	1842	C/Prot	360	80%		36	T		1800
Bethune-Cookman College, Daytona Beach, FL 32015	1904	C/Prot	1736	84%		110	U		2425
Biola College, La Mirada, CA 90639	1908	C/Prot	2384	73%	G	170	S		3216
Birmingham-Southern College, Birmingham, AL 35204	1856	C/Prot	1402	75%		71	U	AF	2550
Biscayne College, Miami, FL 33054	1962	C/Cath	2109	65%	G	150	S		3050
Bishop College, Dallas, TX 75241	1881	C/Prot	926	38%		61	S	A	2100
Blackburn College, Carlinville, IL 62626	1837	C/Prot	531	85%		48	T		2250
Black Hills State College, Spearfish, SD 57783	1883	C/Pub	2056	91%	G	98	T	A	592
Bloomfield College, Bloomfield, NJ 07003	1868	C/Prot	2268	99%		141	S		3450
Bloomsburg State College, Bloomsburg, PA 17815	1839	C/Pub	5803	94%	G	325	T		1110
Bluefield College, Bluefield, VA 24605	1922	C/Prot	391	68%		29	S		1565
Bluefield State College, Bluefield, WV 24701	1895	C/Pub	2747	8%		100	U		380x
Blue Mountain College, Blue Mountain, MS 38610	1873	C/Prot	340	82%		32	T		1440
Bluffton College, Bluffton, OH 45817	1899	C/Prot	660	90%		56	T		3429
Boise State University, Boise, ID 83725	1932	C/Pub	8825	95%	G	457	U	A	475
Borromeo College of Ohio, Wickliffe, OH 44092	1953	M/Cath	80	90%		25	S		2375
Boston College, Chestnut Hill, MA 02167	1863	C/Cath	10,185	52%	G	674	S	AF	4530
Boston Conservatory of Music, Boston, MA 02215	1867	C/Ind	481	*	G	108	U		3400
Boston State College, Boston, MA 02115	1852	C/Pub	5241	90%	G	536	U		600x
Boston University, Boston, MA 02215	1869	C/Ind	11,279	25%	G	2449	U		5515
Bowdoin College, Brunswick, ME 04011	1794	C/Ind	1340	11%		115	T		5800
Bowie State College, Bowie, MD 20715	1865	C/Pub	2049	85%	G	159	S	A	655
Bowling Green State University, Bowling Green, OH 43403	1910	C/Pub	14,868	95%	G	791	T	A,AF	918
Bradford College, Bradford, MA 01830	1803	C/Ind	341	31%		41	S		4500
Bradley University, Peoria, IL 61625	1897	C/Ind	4780	78%	G	377	S	A	3626
Brandeis University, Waltham, MA 02154	1948	C/Ind	2798	22%	G	403	S		5835
Brenau College, Gainesville, GA 30501	1878	C/Ind	686	75%	G	78	T		2450
Brescia College, Owensboro, KY 42301	1950	C/Cath	832	91%		75	U		2100
Briar Cliff College, Sioux City, IA 51104	1930	C/Cath	1258	93%		70	U		2760
Bridgeport Engineering Institute, Bridgeport, CT 06606	1924	C/Ind	630	95%		80	S		1480x
Bridgewater College, Bridgewater, VA 22812	1880	C/Prot	914	71%		78	T		2670
Bridgewater State College, Bridgewater, MA 02324	1840	C/Pub	4358	96%	G	272	S		600
Brigham Young University, Provo, UT 84602	1875	C/Prot	24,107	31%	G	1315	S	A,AF	970
Brigham Young U-Hawaii Cmps, Laie, Oahu, HI 96762	1955	C/Prot	1053	34%		65	T	A	550x
Brooklyn College, See City U of NY, Brooklyn College									
Brooks Institute, Santa Barbara, CA 93108	1945	C/Ind	785	30%	G	32	U		3750x
Brown University, Providence, RI 02912	1764	C/Ind	5487	7%	G	527	U		6140
Bryan College, Dayton, TN 37321	1930	C/Prot	645	12%		45	R		2250
Bryant College, Smithfield, RI 02917	1863	C/Ind	2731	24%	G	145	S		3000
Bryn Mawr College, Bryn Mawr, PA 19010	1885	W/Ind	1026	12%	G	216	S		5950
Bucknell University, Lewisburg, PA 17837	1846	C/Ind	3084	35%	G	252	T	A	5500
Buena Vista College, Storm Lake, IA 50588	1891	C/Prot	899	94%		58	T		3710
Butler University, Indianapolis, IN 46208	1855	C/Ind	2516	75%	G	249	S		3400
Cabrini College, Radnor, PA 19087	1957	C/Cath	515	75%		58	S		3060
Caldwell College, Caldwell, NJ 07006	1939	W/Cath	723	85%		78	S		2700
California Baptist College, Riverside, CA 92504	1950	C/Prot	746	78%		58	S		2550
California College of Arts and Crafts, Oakland, CA 94618	1907	C/Ind	906	60%	G	145	U		3130

Name and Location	Est	Type/ Control	UG Enroll	% of State Res	Grad	Fac Size	Cmps	ROTC	Tuition
California Institute of Technology, Pasadena, CA 91125	1891	C/Ind	817	45%	G	339	S	A,AF	$5229
California Institute of the Arts, Valencia, CA 91355	1961	C/Ind	543	54%	G	139	S		4500
California Lutheran College, Thousand Oaks, CA 91360	1959	C/Prot	1435	87%	G	256	S	A,AF	3500
California Maritime Academy, Vallejo, CA 94590	1929	M/Pub	485	85%		30	U		645
California Polytechnic State U, San Luis Obispo, CA 93407	1901	C/Pub	14,669	98%	G	*	T	A	324
California State College, California, PA 15419	1852	C/Pub	975	98%	G	305	T	A	1100
Calif State College, Bakersfield, Bakersfield, CA 93309	1970	C/Pub	2272	85%	G	200	R		180
Calif State College, San Bernardino, San Bernardino, CA 92407	1962	C/Pub	2752	93%	G	272	S		258
Calif State College, Stanislaus, Turlock, CA 95380	1957	C/Pub	2474	93%	G	227	T		212
California State Polytechnic U, Pomona, Pomona, CA 91768	1938	C/Pub	12,879	88%	G	813	S		180
Calif State U, Chico, Chico, CA 95929	1887	C/Pub	11,390	97%	G	704	T	A	225
Calif State U, Dominquez Hills, Carson, CA 90747	1960	C/Pub	6121	35%	G	307	U		189x
Calif State U, Fresno, Fresno, CA 93740	1911	C/Pub	11,954	90%	G	937	U	AF	240
Calif State U, Fullerton, Fullerton, CA 92634	1957	C/Pub	17,153	97%	G	1272	S		228x
Calif State U, Hayward, Hayward, CA 94542	1957	C/Pub	7970	98%	G	550	U		210x
Calif State U, Long Beach, Long Beach, CA 90840	1949	C/Pub	24,143	90%	G	1600	U		218
Calif State U, Los Angeles, Los Angeles, CA 90032	1947	C/Pub	15,420	95%	G	1200	U		200x
Calif State U, Northridge, Northridge, CA 91330	1958	C/Pub	22,302	98%	G	*	S		200x
Calif State U, Sacramento, Sacramento, CA 95819	1947	C/Pub	16,191	95%	G	1000	U	A,AF	200
Calumet College, Whiting, IN 46394	1951	C/Cath	1460	68%		75	U		1500x
Calvary Bible College, Kansas City, MO 64111	1932	C/Prot	454	33%	G	38	U		1600
Calvin College, Grand Rapids, MI 49506	1876	C/Prot	3900	57%	G	240	S		3000
Camden College of Arts and Sciences, See Rutgers University, Camden College of Arts and Sciences									
Cameron University, Lawton, OK 73501	1927	C/Pub	4712	99%		172	U	A	453
Campbellsville College, Campbellsville, KY 42718	1906	C/Prot	674	76%		60	T		2150
Campbell University, Buies Creek, NC 27506	1887	C/Prot	1790	75%	G	120	T	A	3020
Canisius College, Buffalo, NY 14208	1870	C/Cath	2422	95%	G	344	U	A	3050
Capital University, Columbus, OH 43209	1850	C/Prot	1825	87%	G	189	S	AF	4280
Capitol Institute of Technology, Kensington, MD 20795	1964	C/Ind	525	75%		26	S		2160x
Cardinal Glennon College, St Louis, MO 63119	1898	M/Cath	94	73%		29	S		1825
Cardinal Stritch College, Milwaukee, WI 53217	1937	C/Ind	597	65%	G	116	S	A	2900
Caribbean University College, Bayamon, PR 00619	1969	C/Ind	1600	100%		53	U		1350x
Carleton College, Northfield, MN 55057	1866	C/Ind	1850	25%		168	T		4855
Carlow College, Pittsburgh, PA 15213	1929	W/Cath	792	91%		81	U		3630
Carnegie-Mellon University, Pittsburgh, PA 15213	1900	C/Ind	3880	45%	G	552	U	A,AF	4700
Carroll College, Waukesha, WI 53186	1846	C/Prot	1168	77%		106	S		3760
Carroll College of Montana, Helena, MT 59601	1909	C/Cath	1342	74%		111	T		2160
Carson-Newman College, Jefferson City, TN 37760	1851	C/Prot	1649	52%		113	T	A	2200
Carthage College, Kenosha, WI 53141	1847	C/Prot	1134	45%	G	113	S		3650
Case Western Reserve University, Cleveland, OH 44106	1826	C/Ind	3158	60%	G	1465	U		4800
Castleton State College, Castleton, VT 05735	1787	C/Pub	1758	65%	G	123	R		970
Catawba College, Salisbury, NC 28144	1851	C/Prot	1000	50%		72	S		2850
Cathedral Coll of Immac Conception, Douglaston, NY 11362	1914	M/Cath	147	98%		30	U		2600
Catholic University of America, Washington, DC 20064	1887	C/Cath	2700	*	G	500	S		4250
Catholic University of Puerto Rico, Ponce, PR 00731	1948	C/Cath	8749	95%	G	534	U		*x
Cedar Crest College, Allentown, PA 18104	1867	W/Prot	1013	65%		81	S		4000
Cedarville College, Cedarville, OH 45314	1887	C/Prot	1185	50%		70	T		2376
Centenary College, Hackettstown, NJ 07840	1867	W/Ind	705	60%		67	T		3450
Centenary College of Louisiana, Shreveport, LA 71104	1825	C/Prot	808	63%	G	80	U	A	2400
Ctr for Creative Studies-Coll of Art & Design, Detroit, MI 48202	1926	C/Ind	756	92%		99	U		3200x
Central Baptist College, Conway, AR 72032	1952	C/Prot	231	60%		18	T		480
Central Bible College, Springfield, MO 65802	1922	C/Prot	1115	14%		60	S		1400
Central Connecticut State College, New Britain, CT 06050	1849	C/Pub	9886	97%	G	646	S		390
Central Methodist College, Fayette, MO 65248	1854	C/Prot	667	88%		62	R		3200
Central Michigan University, Mount Pleasant, MI 48858	1892	C/Pub	14,556	98%	G	855	T	A	1787
Central Missouri State University, Warrensburg, MO 64093	1871	C/Pub	8319	95%	G	530	T	A	465
Central New England College, Worcester, MA 01608	1905	C/Ind	*	60%		92	U		2400
Central State University, Wilberforce, OH 45384	1887	C/Pub	2380	75%		171	S		650
Central State University, Edmond, OK 73034	1890	C/Pub	8518	95%	G	430	S	A	413
Central University of Iowa, Pella, IA 50219	1853	C/Prot	1545	68%		90	T		3650
Central Washington University, Ellensburg, WA 98926	1890	C/Pub	5858	97%	G	332	T	AF	618
Central Wesleyan College, Central, SC 29630	1906	C/Prot	413	60%		30	T		2920
Centre College of Kentucky, Danville, KY 40422	1819	C/Ind	760	55%		64	T		3900
Chadron State College, Chadron, NE 69337	1911	C/Pub	1554	85%	G	104	T		570
Chaminade University of Honolulu, Honolulu, HI 96816	1955	C/Cath	1059	68%	G	162	S	A,AF	1900
Chapman College, Orange, CA 92666	1861	C/Prot	1259	70%	G	167	S		3790
Chatham College, Pittsburgh, PA 15232	1869	W/Ind	615	60%		86	U		4425
Chestnut Hill College, Philadelphia, PA 19118	1871	W/Cath	650	73%	G	102	U		2650
Cheyney State College, Cheyney, PA 19319	1837	C/Pub	2300	82%	G	198	R	A	1060
Chicago Conservatory College, Chicago, IL 60605	1932	C/Ind	121	98%	G	100	U		1550
Chicago State University, Chicago, IL 60628	1867	C/Pub	5165	99%	G	359	U		522x
Christian Brothers College, Memphis, TN 38104	1871	C/Cath	1330	79%		114	U		2690
Christopher Newport College, Newport News, VA 23606	1971	C/Pub	3918	90%		201	U	A	780x
Cincinnati Bible College, Cincinnati, OH 45204	1924	C/Prot	522	55%	G	40	U		1232
Circleville Bible College, Circleville, OH 43113	1948	C/Prot	226	65%		18	T		1392
Citadel, Charleston, SC 29409	1842	M/Pub	2378	65%	G	148	U	A,N,AF	125
City College, See City U of NY, City College									
City U of NY, Baruch College, New York, NY 10010	1968	C/Pub	12,425	95%	G	850	U		925x
City U of NY, Brooklyn College, Brooklyn, NY 11210	1930	C/Pub	14,651	98%	G	1318	U		925x
City U of NY, City College, New York, NY 10031	1847	C/Pub	11,510	96%	G	1183	U		925x
City U of NY, College of Staten Island, Staten Island, NY 10301	1955	C/Pub	10,500	99%	G	379	U		925x
City U of NY, Herbert H Lehman Coll, Bronx, NY 10468	1931	C/Pub	9076	99%	G	820	U		925x
City U of NY, Hunter College, New York, NY 10021	1870	C/Pub	14,872	98%	G	1234	U		925x
CUNY, JJ Col of Crim Justice, New York, NY 10019	1964	C/Pub	5223	97%	G	418	U	A	925x
City U of NY, Medgar Evers College, Brooklyn, NY 11225	1969	C/Pub	2894	97%		150	U		1425x
City U of NY, Queens College, Flushing, NY 11367	1937	C/Pub	13,000	99%	G	1400	U		925x
City U of NY, York College, Jamaica, NY 11451	1967	C/Pub	3889	95%		200	U		925x

Name and Location	Est	Type/Control	UG Enroll	% of State Res	Grad	Fac Size	Cmps	ROTC	Tuition
Claflin College, Orangeburg, SC 29115	1869	C/Prot	866	88%		65	T	A	$1850
Claremont Men's College, Claremont, CA 91711	1946	C/Ind	849	60%		99	S	A	5502
Clarion State College, Clarion, PA 16214	1867	C/Pub	4900	85%	G	360	T	A	1150
Clark College, Atlanta, GA 30314	1869	C/Prot	2031	60%		142	U		2080
Clarke College, Dubuque, IA 52001	1843	W/Cath	606	75%	G	72	S		3100
Clarkson College, Potsdam, NY 13676	1896	C/Ind	3304	84%	G	219	T	A	4400
Clark University, Worcester, MA 01610	1887	C/Ind	1810	25%	G	194	U		5400
Cleary College, Ypsilanti, MI 48197	1883	C/Ind	453	95%		46	U		2205x
Clemson University, Clemson, SC 29631	1889	C/Pub	9240	79%	Q	671	T	A,AF	150
Cleveland College of Jewish Studies, Beachwood, OH 44122	1963	C/Jewish	84	100%	G	16	S		460x
Cleveland Institute of Art, Cleveland, OH 44106	1882	C/Ind	546	74%		71	U		3180
Cleveland Institute of Music, Cleveland, OH 44106	1920	C/Ind	179	25%	G	142	U		4450
Cleveland State University, Cleveland, OH 44115	1964	C/Pub	12,396	98%	G	700	U	A	984
Clinch Valley College of the U of Va, Wise, VA 24293	1954	C/Pub	942	91%		66	T		750
Coe College, Cedar Rapids, IA 52402	1851	C/Prot	1320	62%		104	U		3890
Cogswell College, San Francisco, CA 94108	1887	C/Ind	425	100%		54	U		2400x
Coker College, Hartsville, SC 29550	1908	C/Ind	321	88%		43	T		3030
Colby College, Waterville, ME 04901	1813	C/Ind	1677	18%		132	T		5390
Colby-Sawyer College, New London, NH 03257	1837	W/Ind	700	14%		69	T		4443
Colegio Cesar Chavez, Mount Angel, OR 97362	1882	C/Ind	81	*		*	*		*
Colgate University, Hamilton, NY 13346	1819	C/Ind	2600	50%	G	184	T		5400
College for Human Services, New York, NY 10014	1964	C/Ind	100	*		13	U		5016x
College Misericordia, Dallas, PA 18612	1924	W/Cath	1043	80%	G	97	S		2630
College of Charleston, Charleston, SC 29401	1770	C/Pub	4137	95%	G	220	U		850
College of Great Falls, Great Falls, MT 59405	1932	C/Cath	1200	80%		82	S		2550
College of Idaho, Caldwell, ID 83605	1891	C/Prot	482	52%	G	72	T		3465
College of Insurance, New York, NY 10038	1962	C/Ind	1825	45%	G	131	U		1700x
Coll of Mount St Joseph on-the-Ohio, Mt St Joseph, OH 45051	1920	W/Cath	1311	88%	G	122	S		2912
College of Mount Saint Vincent, Riverdale, NY 10471	1847	W/Ind	1308	90%		99	S		3200
College of New Rochelle, New Rochelle, NY 10801	1904	W/Ind	3669	75%	G	398	S		3150
College of Notre Dame, Belmont, CA 94002	1868	C/Cath	910	64%	G	114	S		3200
College of Notre Dame of Maryland, Baltimore, MD 21210	1896	W/Cath	540	75%		71	S		3150
College of Our Lady of the Elms, Chicopee, MA 01013	1928	W/Cath	425	65%		61	S		3000
Col.ege of Saint Benedict, Saint Joseph, MN 56374	1913	W/Cath	1620	88%		129	R		3350
College of St Catherine, St Paul, MN 55105	1905	W/Cath	2004	75%		120	U		3260
College of Saint Elizabeth, Convent Station, NJ 07961	1899	W/Cath	581	85%		83	S		3000
College of St Francis, Joliet, IL 60435	1925	C/Cath	745	90%	G	56	S		2870
College of St Joseph the Provider, Rutland, VT 05701	1954	C/Cath	212	70%	G	44	S		2825
College of Saint Mary, Omaha, NE 68124	1923	W/Cath	592	77%		78	U		3072
College of Saint Rose, Albany, NY 12203	1920	C/Ind	1627	95%	G	194	U		2850
College of Saint Scholastica, Duluth, MN 55811	1906	C/Cath	1082	72%	G	126	U		3219
College of Saint Teresa, Winona, MN 55987	1907	W/Cath	791	97%		100	T		3489
College of Saint Thomas, St Paul, MN 55105	1885	C/Cath	3183	89%	G	265	U	AF	3080
College of Santa Fe, Santa Fe, NM 87501	1947	C/Cath	1203	80%		90	U		2700
College of Staten Island, See City U of NY, College of Staten Island									
College of the Atlantic, Bar Harbor, ME 04609	1969	C/Ind	170	15%		25	T		3800
Coll of the Ctr for Early Education, Los Angeles, CA 90048	1939	C/Ind	7	100%		10	U		1932x
College of the Holy Cross, Worcester, MA 01610	1843	C/Cath	2500	47%	G	200	S	N,AF	4600
College of the Ozarks, Clarksville, AR 72830	1834	C/Prot	543	57%		40	T	A	1050
College of the Southwest, Hobbs, NM 88240	1956	C/Ind	156	87%		27	S		845
College of the Virgin Islands, St Thomas, VI 00801	1962	C/Pub	1784	70%	G	108	S		344x
College of William and Mary, Williamsburg, VA 23185	1693	C/Pub	4449	70%	G	454	T	A	1076
College of Wooster, Wooster, OH 44691	1866	C/Prot	1760	48%		155	T		5285
Colorado College, Colorado Springs, CO 80903	1874	C/Ind	1940	33%	G	205	U		4700
Colorado School of Mines, Golden, CO 80401	1874	C/Pub	2166	70%	G	195	T	A	1100
Colorado State University, Fort Collins, CO 80523	1870	C/Pub	15,346	75%	G	1158	T	A,AF	605
Colorado Women's College, Denver, CO 80220	1888	W/Ind	500	40%		44	U	A,AF	4350
Columbia Bible College, Columbia, SC 29203	1923	C/Ind	539	30%	G	32	S		2150
Columbia Christian College, Portland, OR 97220	1956	C/Prot	325	34%		33	U		2301
Columbia College, Chicago, IL 60605	1890	C/Ind	3200	90%		295	U		1350x
Columbia College, Columbia, MO 65201	1851	C/Ind	843	45%		72	T		3100
Columbia College, New York, NY 10027	1887	M/Ind	2800	*		560	U		5850
Columbia College, Columbia, SC 29203	1854	W/Prot	1103	90%		77	S		2800
Columbia Union College, Takoma Park, MD 20012	1904	C/Prot	956	40%		91	S		2990
Columbia University, See Barnard College and Columbia College, NY									
Columbus College, Columbus, GA 31907	1958	C/Pub	4070	88%	G	266	S	A	459x
Combs College of Music, Philadelphia, PA 19119	1885	C/Ind	91	70%	G	38	U		3420
Conception Seminary College, Conception, MO 64433	1891	M/Cath	94	43%		25	R		1450
Concord College, Athens, WV 24712	1872	C/Pub	2081	80%		97	T		368
Concordia College, River Forest, IL 60305	1864	C/Prot	984	55%	G	114	S		2400
Concordia College, Ann Arbor, MI 48105	1962	C/Prot	560	50%		52	T		2088
Concordia College, Moorhead, MN 56560	1891	C/Prot	2607	66%	G	191	S	A,AF	3635
Concordia College, St Paul, MN 55104	1893	C/Prot	664	60%		68	U		2790
Concordia College, Bronxville, NY 10708	1881	C/Prot	430	65%		56	S		2475
Concordia College, Portland, OR 97211	1905	C/Prot	313	40%		38	U		2400
Concordia Lutheran College, Austin, TX 78705	1926	C/Prot	334	87%		21	U	A	1750
Concordia Teachers College, Seward, NE 68434	1894	C/Prot	1137	25%	G	100	T	A	2500
Connecticut College, New London, CT 06320	1911	C/Ind	1627	25%	G	188	S		5900
Conservatory of Music, San Juan, PR 00936	1959	C/Pub	262	97%		38	U		*x
Converse College, Spartanburg, SC 29301	1889	W/Ind	732	40%	G	85	U		3650
Cook College, See Rutgers University, Cook College									
Cooper Union for Adv of Sci & Art, New York, NY 10003	1859	C/Ind	881	78%	G	132	U		300x
Coppin State College, Baltimore, MD 21216	1900	C/Pub	2638	97%	G	141	U		620x
Cornell College, Mount Vernon, IA 52314	1853	C/Prot	898	30%		104	T		4220
Cornell University, Ithaca, NY 14853	1865	C/Ind	11,945	55%	G	1848	T	A,N,AF	5860
Cornish Institute, Seattle, WA 98102	1914	C/Ind	422	84%		115	U		2700x
Corpus Christi State University, Corpus Christi, TX 78412	1925	C/Pub	1631	99%	G	144	U	A	100
Covenant College, Lookout Mountain, GA 37350	1955	C/Prot	494	15%		38	S		3380

Name and Location	Est	Type/ Control	UG Enroll	% of State Res	Grad	Fac Size	Cmps	ROTC	Tuition
Cranbrook Academy of Art, Bloomfield Hills, MI 48013	1932	C/Ind	5	20%	G	9	S		$ *x
Creighton University, Omaha, NE 68178	1878	C/Cath	3520	38%	G	881	U	A	3300
Culver-Stockton College, Canton, MO 63435	1853	C/Ind	443	56%		46	T		2980
Cumberland College, Williamsburg, KY 40769	1889	C/Prot	2000	62%		107	T	A	1848
Curry College, Milton, MA 02186	1879	C/Ind	831	58%		69	S		4400
C W Post Center of Long Island U, Greenvale, NY 11548	1954	C/Ind	7229	93%	G	635	S		3380
Daemen College, Amherst, NY 14226	1947	C/Ind	1317	95%		120	S		3250
Dakota State College, Madison, SD 57042	1881	C/Pub	895	94%		61	T		555
Dakota Wesleyan University, Mitchell, SD 57301	1885	C/Prot	521	72%		56	T		2340
Dallas Baptist College, Dallas, TX 75211	1898	C/Prot	1008	85%		66	U	A	2100
Dallas Bible College, Dallas, TX 75228	1940	C/Ind	225	51%		20	U		1840
Dana College, Blair, NE 68008	1884	C/Ind	527	40%		45	T		3000
Daniel Hale Williams University, Chicago, IL 60644	1974	C/Ind	2195	*		*	*		2400
Daniel Payne College, Birmingham, AL 35214	1889	C/Prot	*	93%		*	U		*x
Daniel Webster College, Nashua, NH 03060	1965	C/Ind	500	25%		32	S	AF	3350
Dartmouth College, Hanover, NH 03755	1769	C/Ind	3200	6%	G	671	T		6075
David Lipscomb College, Nashville, TN 37203	1891	C/Prot	2293	51%		120	S		1920
Davidson College, Davidson, NC 28036	1837	C/Prot	1352	30%		115	T	A	4100
Davis and Elkins College, Elkins, WV 26241	1904	C/Prot	1098	25%		86	T		3600
Defiance College, Defiance, OH 43512	1850	C/Prot	800	82%		70	T		3520
Delaware State College, Dover, DE 19901	1891	C/Pub	2153	62%		144	R		515
Delaware Valley Coll of Science & Agr, Doylestown, PA 18901	1896	C/Ind	1428	65%		90	R		2457
Delta State University, Cleveland, MS 38733	1925	C/Pub	2521	97%	G	167	T	A	720
Denison University, Granville, OH 43023	1831	C/Ind	2080	26%		182	T		4880
DePaul University, Chicago, IL 60604	1898	C/Cath	8101	90%	G	671	U	A	3120
DePauw University, Greencastle, IN 46135	1837	C/Prot	2251	48%	G	185	T	A	4658
Detroit Bible College, Farmington Hills, MI 48018	1945	C/Ind	345	98%		20	S		1962
Detroit Institute of Technology, Detroit, MI 48201	1891	C/Ind	800	84%		59	U		2402x
DeVry Institute of Technology, Phoenix, AZ 85016	1967	C/Ind	2562	22%		*	U		2425x
DeVry Institute of Technology, Atlanta, GA 30341	1969	C/Ind	1019	18%		19	U		2425x
DeVry Institute of Technology, Chicago, IL 60618	1931	C/Ind	2497	84%		44	U		2425x
DeVry Institute of Technology, Dallas, TX 75235	1969	C/Ind	832	61%		30	U		2425x
Dickinson College, Carlisle, PA 17013	1773	C/Prot	1650	40%		125	T	A	4885
Dickinson State College, Dickinson, ND 58601	1918	C/Pub	1062	90%		*	T		477
Dillard University, New Orleans, LA 70122	1869	C/Prot	1217	60%		90	U	A,AF	2100
Divine Word College, Epworth, IA 52045	1912	M/Cath	92	21%		22	R		2600
Doane College, Crete, NE 68333	1858	C/Prot	689	76%		62	T	A	2995
Dr Martin Luther College, New Ulm, MN 56073	1884	C/Ind	849	15%		72	T		940
Dominican College, Orangeburg, NY 10962	1952	C/Ind	1230	74%		69	S	A	2100x
Dominican College of San Rafael, San Rafael, CA 94901	1890	C/Cath	451	81%	G	102	S		3300
Dominican School of Philos and Theol, Berkeley, CA 94709	1932	C/Cath	21	50%	G	18	U		1210x
Don Bosco College, Newton, NJ 07860	1928	M/Cath	83	30%		25	R		2600
Dordt College, Sioux Center, IA 51250	1955	C/Prot	1218	28%		75	R		2600
Douglass College, See Rutgers University, Douglass College									
Dowling College, Oakdale, NY 11769	1959	C/Ind	1500	98%	G	197	S		3350
Drake University, Des Moines, IA 50311	1881	C/Ind	4871	40%	G	340	S	AF	4060
Drew University, Madison, NJ 07940	1866	C/Prot	1510	50%	G	189	S		4700
Drexel University, Philadelphia, PA 19104	1891	C/Ind	6577	65%	G	292	U	A	3585
Drury College, Springfield, MO 65802	1873	C/Prot	1087	65%	G	104	U		2855
Duke University, Durham, NC 27710	1838	C/Ind	5700	16%	G	1256	S	N,AF	4740
Duns Scotus College, Southfield, MI 48075	1930	C/Cath	55	0%	G	13	S		1500
Duquesne University, Pittsburgh, PA 15219	1878	C/Cath	4530	85%	G	427	U	A	3510
Durham College, Durham, NC 27707	1947	C/Ind	275	40%		18	U		1580
Dyke College, Cleveland, OH 44114	1848	C/Ind	1375	98%		65	U		1800x
D'Youville College, Buffalo, NY 14201	1908	C/Ind	1550	98%		112	U		3100
Earlham College, Richmond, IN 47374	1847	C/Prot	1015	20%	G	103	S		4912
East Carolina University, Greenville, NC 27834	1907	C/Pub	10,824	89%	G	619	R	AF	310
East Central Oklahoma State U, Ada, OK 74820	1909	C/Pub	3517	91%	G	*	S	A	400
Eastern College, St Davids, PA 19087	1932	C/Prot	708	68%		71	S		3550
Eastern Connecticut State College, Willimantic, CT 06226	1889	C/Pub	2200	95%	G	200	T		390
Eastern Illinois University, Charleston, IL 61920	1895	C/Pub	8858	98%	G	494	T		606
Eastern Kentucky University, Richmond, KY 40475	1906	C/Pub	11,366	84%	G	784	T	A	580
Eastern Mennonite College, Harrisonburg, VA 22801	1917	C/Prot	1056	29%		64	T		3360
Eastern Michigan University, Ypsilanti, MI 48197	1849	C/Pub	14,502	96%	G	795	T	A	780
Eastern Montana College, Billings, MT 59101	1927	C/Pub	3103	95%	G	175	U		519
Eastern Nazarene College, Quincy, MA 02170	1918	C/Prot	771	32%	G	66	S		2520
Eastern New Mexico U, Portales Campus, Portales, NM 88130	1934	C/Pub	3100	85%	G	170	T	A	619
Eastern Oregon State College, La Grande, OR 97850	1929	C/Pub	1490	80%	G	100	T		930
Eastern Washington University, Cheney, WA 99004	1890	C/Pub	6069	95%	G	390	T	A	618
East Stroudsburg State College, East Stroudsburg, PA 18301	1893	C/Pub	3568	81%	G	269	T	A	1100
East Tennessee State University, Johnson City, TN 37601	1911	C/Pub	8487	86%	G	527	U	A	570
East Texas Baptist College, Marshall, TX 75670	1912	C/Prot	878	87%		90	S		1350
East Texas State University, Commerce, TX 75428	1889	C/Pub	5402	95%	G	456	T	AF	436
Eckerd College, St Petersburg, FL 33733	1958	C/Ind	1060	32%		79	S		4435
Edgecliff College, Cincinnati, OH 45206	1935	C/Cath	951	75%		98	U		2176
Edgewood College, Madison, WI 53711	1927	C/Cath	587	75%		60	U		2850
Edinboro State College, Edinboro, PA 16444	1857	C/Pub	4556	92%	G	396	T	A	1100
Edward Waters College, Jacksonville, FL 32209	1866	C/Ind	660	90%		43	U		1800
Eisenhower College of Rochester Inst of Tech, Seneca Falls, NY 13148	1965	C/Ind	550	70%		61	T		3879
Elizabeth City State University, Elizabeth City, NC 27909	1891	C/Pub	1600	90%		130	T		540
Elizabethtown College, Elizabethtown, PA 17022	1899	C/Prot	1466	68%		128	T		3825
Elmhurst College, Elmhurst, IL 60126	1871	C/Prot	3317	94%		129	S		3450
Elmira College, Elmira, NY 14901	1855	C/Ind	1913	52%	G	170	U		4100
Elon College, Elon College, NC 27244	1889	C/Prot	2501	64%		138	T	A	2230
Embry-Riddle Aeronautical University, Daytona Beach, FL 32014	1926	C/Ind	7115	10%	G	242	U	A,N,AF	2400
Emerson College, Boston, MA 02116	1880	C/Ind	1476	45%	G	134	U		4360
Emmanuel College, Boston, MA 02115	1919	W/Cath	542	65%	G	103	U		3920

Name and Location	Est	Type/ Control	UG Enroll	% of State Res	Grad	Fac Size	Cmps	ROTC	Tuition
Emory and Henry College, Emory, VA 24327	1836	C/Prot	825	78%		61	R		$2250
Emory University, Atlanta, GA 30322	1836	C/Ind	3041	25%	G	1305	S		4605
Emporia State University, Emporia, KS 66801	1863	C/Pub	4473	94%	G	283	T	A	600
Erskine College, Due West, SC 29639	1839	C/Prot	653	65%	G	60	T		2950
Eureka College, Eureka, IL 61530	1855	C/Prot	463	88%		37	T		3375
Evangel College, Springfield, MO 65802	1955	C/Prot	1612	21%		90	T	A	1940
Evergreen State College, Olympia, WA 98505	1967	C/Pub	2554	76%	G	155	S		456
Fairfield University, Fairfield, CT 06430	1942	C/Cath	2772	50%	G	326	S		3900
Fairleigh Dickinson U, Florham—Madison Cmps, Madison, NJ 07940	1958	C/Ind	3354	80%	G	303	S		3552
Fairleigh Dickinson U, Rutherford Campus, Rutherford, NJ 07070	1942	C/Ind	2787	85%	G	369	S		3552
Fairleigh Dickinson U, Teaneck-Hackensack Cmps, Teaneck, NJ 07666	1954	C/Ind	5532	85%	G	788	S		3552
Fairmont State College, Fairmont, WV 26554	1865	C/Pub	4848	94%		254	T	A,AF	360
Faith Baptist Bible College, Ankeny, IA 50021	1921	C/Prot	530	42%		28	T		1800
Fashion Institute of Technology, New York, NY 10001	1944	C/Pub	3468	71%		700	U		900
Fayetteville State University, Fayetteville, NC 28301	1877	C/Pub	2283	87%		160	U	AF	270
Felician College, Lodi, NJ 07644	1942	W/Cath	457	99%		77	T		2100x
Ferris State College, Big Rapids, MI 49307	1884	C/Pub	10,486	96%		673	T		891
Ferrum College, Ferrum, VA 24088	1913	C/Prot	1546	85%		81	R		2040
Findlay College, Findlay, OH 45840	1882	C/Prot	926	80%		100	S		3596
Fisk University, Nashville, TN 37203	1866	C/Ind	1063	10%	G	92	U		5985
Fitchburg State College, Fitchburg, MA 01420	1894	C/Pub	3719	97%	G	231	U	A	600
Flagler College, St Augustine, FL 32084	1968	C/Ind	745	40%		57	T		2200
Florida A&M University, Tallahassee, FL 32307	1887	C/Pub	5223	88%	G	527	T	A,N	675
Florida Atlantic University, Boca Raton, FL 33431	1961	C/Pub	5036	92%	G	317	S		780
Florida Institute of Technology, Melbourne, FL 32901	1958	C/Ind	2626	20%	G	332	S	A	3024
Florida International University, Miami, FL 33199	1965	C/Pub	6280	81%	G	630	U		750x
Florida Memorial College, Miami, FL 33054	1879	C/Prot	794	59%		88	U	A	2840
Florida Southern College, Lakeland, FL 33802	1885	C/Prot	1735	67%		135	T	A	2430
Florida State University, Tallahassee, FL 32306	1857	C/Pub	15,765	90%	G	1180	U	A,AF	735
Fontbonne College, St Louis, MO 63105	1917	C/Cath	757	90%	G	91	S		3200
Fordham University, Bronx, NY 10458	1841	C/Cath	7675	86%	G	930	U	A	3750
Fordham University at Lincoln Center, New York, NY 10023	1841	C/Cath	3042	90%	G	898	U	A	3296x
Fort Hays State University, Hays, KS 67601	1902	C/Pub	4050	92%	G	323	T	A	637
Fort Lauderdale College, Ft Lauderdale, FL 33301	1940	C/Ind	1087	85%		40	U		1225x
Fort Lewis College, Durango, CO 81301	1911	C/Pub	3028	70%		143	T		483
Fort Valley State College, Fort Valley, GA 31030	1895	C/Pub	1778	84%	G	156	T	A	729
Fort Wayne Bible College, Fort Wayne, IN 46807	1904	C/Prot	510	50%		56	S		2160
Fort Wright College, Spokane, WA 99204	1907	C/Cath	368	78%	G	59	S		3240
Framingham State College, Framingham, MA 01701	1839	C/Pub	3125	97%	G	170	S		600
Francis Marion College, Florence, SC 29501	1970	C/Pub	2392	99%	G	123	R	A	200
Franklin and Marshall College, Lancaster, PA 17604	1787	C/Ind	2094	30%		154	T		4950
Franklin College of Indiana, Franklin, IN 46131	1834	C/Ind	653	90%		51	T		3820
Franklin Pierce College, Rindge, NH 03461	1962	C/Ind	904	10%		57	R		4025
Franklin University, Columbus, OH 43215	1902	C/Ind	4214	100%		201	U		1470x
Freed-Hardeman College, Henderson, TN 38340	1869	C/Prot	1428	39%		82	T		2030
Free Will Baptist Bible College, Nashville, TN 37205	1942	C/Ind	528	16%		27	U		1440
Fresno Pacific College, Fresno, CA 93702	1944	C/Prot	450	84%	G	63	S		2955
Friends Bible College, Haviland, KS 67059	1917	C/Prot	167	37%		15	T		2600
Friends University, Wichita, KS 67213	1898	C/Prot	908	92%		79	S		2870
Friends World College, Huntington, NY 11743	1965	C/Ind	150	35%		23	S		3350
Frostburg State College, Frostburg, MD 21533	1898	C/Pub	3200	93%	G	185	T	A	620
Furman University, Greenville, SC 29613	1826	C/Prot	2698	47%	G	157	S	A	3008
Gallaudet College, Washington, DC 20002	1856	C/Ind	1063	*		200	U		618
Gannon University, Erie, PA 16541	1944	C/Cath	3200	89%	G	231	U	A	2400
Gardner-Webb College, Boiling Springs, NC 28017	1905	C/Prot	1354	10%	G	88	T		2650
General Motors Institute, Flint, MI 48502	1919	C/Ind	2241	42%		148	U		1200
Geneva College, Beaver Falls, PA 15010	1848	C/Prot	1500	64%		91	S		3230
George Fox College, Newberg, OR 97132	1891	C/Prot	734	70%		71	T		3600
George Mason University, Fairfax, VA 22030	1957	C/Pub	8984	89%	G	697	S		888
Georgetown College, Georgetown, KY 40324	1829	C/Prot	1031	57%	G	84	T		2640
Georgetown University, Washington, DC 20057	1789	C/Cath	5612	7%	G	1434	S	A	4970
George Washington University, Washington, DC 20052	1821	C/Ind	6123	20%	G	1512	U	A	3400
George Williams College, Downers Grove, IL 60515	1890	C/Ind	686	88%	G	128	S		3534
Georgia College, Milledgeville, GA 31061	1889	C/Pub	2810	95%	G	179	T		645
Georgia Institute of Technology, Atlanta, GA 30332	1885	C/Pub	9429	55%	G	770	U	A,N,AF	585
Georgian Court College, Lakewood, NJ 08701	1908	W/Cath	730	80%	G	110	S		2500
Georgia Southern College, Statesboro, GA 30458	1906	C/Pub	5735	91%	G	355	T	A	534
Georgia Southwestern College, Americus, GA 31709	1908	C/Pub	1784	97%	G	131	T		564
Georgia State University, Atlanta, GA 30303	1913	C/Pub	13,389	89%	G	968	U	A	585x
Gettysburg College, Gettysburg, PA 17325	1832	C/Prot	1900	30%		187	T	A	4720
Glassboro State College, Glassboro, NJ 08028	1923	C/Pub	9800	97%	G	534	T		903
Glenville State College, Glenville, WV 26351	1872	C/Pub	1845	92%		96	T		220
Goddard College, Plainfield, VT 05667	1938	C/Ind	1050	5%		55	R		5100x
Golden Gate University, San Francisco, CA 94105	1901	C/Ind	2847	80%	G	852	U		1740x
Gonzaga University, Spokane, WA 99258	1887	C/Cath	1937	45%	G	261	U	A	3490
Gordon College, Wenham, MA 01984	1889	C/Prot	1000	25%		64	S		3825
Goshen College, Goshen, IN 46526	1894	C/Prot	1209	37%		76	T		3325
Goucher College, Towson, MD 21204	1885	W/Ind	1000	39%	G	133	S		4650
Governors State University, Park Forest South, IL 60466	1969	C/Pub	1630	98%	G	309	S		558x
Grace Bible College, Grand Rapids, MI 49509	1945	C/Ind	210	25%		18	S		1220
Grace College, Winona Lake, IN 46590	1948	C/Prot	804	99%		44	T		2752
Grace College of the Bible, Omaha, NE 68108	1943	C/Ind	458	43%		33	U		1950
Graceland College, Lamoni, IA 50140	1895	C/Prot	1345	26%		101	T		3245
Grambling State University, Grambling, LA 71245	1901	C/Pub	3293	79%	G	200	T	AF	544
Grand Canyon College, Phoenix, AZ 85017	1949	C/Prot	1143	82%		67	S		1952
Grand Rapids Baptist College, Grand Rapids, MI 49505	1941	C/Prot	935	47%	G	76	S		2320
Grand Valley State Colleges, Allendale, MI 49401	1960	C/Pub	6170	97%	G	325	R		877

Name and Location	Est	Type/ Control	UG Enroll	% of State Res	Grad	Fac Size	Cmps	ROTC	Tuition
Grand View College, Des Moines, IA 50316	1896	C/Prot	1186	90%		84	U		$2390
Gratz College, Philadelphia, PA 19141	1895	C/Ind	142	95%	G	24	U		275x
Green Mountain College, Poultney, VT 05764	1834	C/Ind	475	10%		56	T		3700
Greensboro College, Greensboro, NC 27420	1838	C/Prot	664	60%		50	S		2500
Greenville College, Greenville, IL 62246	1892	C/Prot	879	62%		60	T		3168
Grinnell College, Grinnell, IA 50112	1846	C/Ind	1258	14%		117	T		5140
Grove City College, Grove City, PA 16127	1876	C/Prot	2211	72%		119	T	AF	°x
Guilford College, Greensboro, NC 27410	1837	C/Prot	1105	40%		107	S		3225
Gulf Coast Bible College, Houston, TX 77008	1953	C/Prot	341	98%		21	U		1890
Gustavus Adolphus College, St Peter, MN 56082	1862	C/Prot	2278	70%		255	T		4100
Gwynedd-Mercy College, Gwynedd Valley, PA 19437	1948	W/Cath	1573	90%		126	S		2600
Hamilton College, Clinton, NY 13323	1812	C/Ind	1600	50%		146	R		6150
Hamline University, St Paul, MN 55104	1854	C/Prot	1189	80%	G	170	U		4150
Hampden-Sydney College, Hampden-Sydney, VA 23943	1776	M/Ind	720	70%		58	R		4200
Hampshire College, Amherst, MA 01002	1965	C/Ind	1200	11%		101	R		6350
Hampton Institute, Hampton, VA 23668	1868	C/Ind	2700	39%	G	238	U	A	2290
Hannibal-LaGrange College, Hannibal, MO 63401	1858	C/Prot	450	60%		35	T		2000
Hanover College, Hanover, IN 47243	1827	C/Prot	1000	50%		73	R		2740
Harding University, Searcy, AR 72143	1924	C/Prot	2979	28%	G	154	T		2175
Hardin-Simmons University, Abilene, TX 79601	1891	C/Prot	1645	93%	G	121	U	A	1650
Harris-Stowe State College, St Louis, MO 63103	1857	C/Pub	1102	100%		66	U		350x
Hartwick College, Oneonta, NY 13820	1928	C/Ind	1418	52%		106	T		4900
Harvard and Radcliffe Colleges, Cambridge, MA 02138	1636	C/Ind	6557	21%	G	1579	U		5300
Harvard University, See Harvard and Radcliffe Colleges									
Harvey Mudd College, Claremont, CA 91711	1955	C/Ind	489	60%	G	63	S	A	5510
Hastings College, Hastings, NE 68901	1882	C/Prot	780	80%		66	T		2850
Haverford College, Haverford, PA 19041	1833	C/Ind	985	19%		97	S		5480
Hawaii Loa College, Kaneohe, HI 96744	1965	C/Ind	327	40%		29	S		2000
Hawaii Pacific College, Honolulu, HI 96813	1965	C/Ind	1463	70%		62	U		1700x
Hebrew College, Brookline, MA 02146	1921	C/Jewish	112	90%	G	7	U		600x
Hebrew Union Coll, Jewish Inst of Rel, New York, NY 10023	1948	C/Jewish	44	°		°	U		3300x
Heed University, Hollywood, FL 33020	1970	C/Ind	°	°	G	°	°		
Heidelberg College, Tiffin, OH 44883	1850	C/Prot	790	75%		92	T		4300
Hellenic College, Brookline, MA 02146	1937	C/Cath	78	5%		37	S		2200
Henderson State University, Arkadelphia, AR 71923	1890	C/Pub	2611	95%	G	180	T	A	600
Hendrix College, Conway, AR 72032	1876	C/Prot	980	85%		63	T		2400
Herbert H Lehman College, See City U of NY, Herbert H Lehman College									
High Point College, High Point, NC 27262	1924	C/Prot	1228	62%		61	S	A	2300
Hillsdale College, Hillsdale, MI 49242	1844	C/Ind	1025	48%		73	T		4140
Hillsdale Free Will Baptist College, Moore, OK 73160	1964	C/Prot	150	59%		20	S		2800
Hiram College, Hiram, OH 44234	1850	C/Prot	1150	66%		80	R		4487
Hobart College, Geneva, NY 14456	1822	M/Ind	1050	50%		121	U		5500
Hofstra University, Hempstead, NY 11550	1935	C/Ind	7049	80%	G	660	S	A	3400
Hollins College, Roanoke, VA 24020	1842	W/Ind	854	32%	G	91	S		4650
Holy Apostles College, Cromwell, CT 06416	1957	M/Cath	72	25%	G	20	S		1600
Holy Family College, Fremont, CA 94538	1946	W/Cath	143	°		98	U		1232
Holy Family College, Philadelphia, PA 19114	1954	W/Cath	1162	99%		112	S		2150x
Holy Names College, Oakland, CA 94619	1868	C/Cath	415	8%	G	101	U		3300
Holy Redeemer College, Waterford, WI 53185	1965	M/Cath	55	15%		22	R		1575
Hood College, Frederick, MD 21701	1893	W/Ind	1145	53%	G	154	S		4060
Hope College, Holland, MI 49423	1851	C/Prot	2371	67%		168	S		3920
Houghton College, Houghton, NY 14744	1883	C/Prot	1209	60%		80	R		3200
Houston Baptist University, Houston, TX 77074	1960	C/Prot	1757	88%	G	131	S		2475
Howard Payne University, Brownwood, TX 76801	1889	C/Prot	1173	95%		87	T		1650
Howard University, Washington, DC 20059	1867	C/Ind	7107	31%	G	1911	U	A,AF	1750
Humboldt State University, Arcata, CA 95521	1913	C/Pub	6677	98%	G	485	T		210
Hunter College, See City U of NY, Hunter College									
Huntingdon College, Montgomery, AL 36106	1854	C/Prot	693	70%		51	S	A,AF	2250
Huntington College, Huntington, IN 46750	1897	C/Prot	544	80%	G	60	T		3180
Huron College, Huron, SD 57350	1883	C/Prot	318	79%		41	T		2700
Husson College, Bangor, ME 04401	1898	C/Ind	812	65%	G	35	S		3350
Huston-Tillotson College, Austin, TX 78702	1875	C/Prot	634	56%		48	U		1400
Idaho State University, Pocatello, ID 83201	1901	C/Pub	5569	95%	G	505	T	A	460
Illinois Benedictine College, Lisle, IL 60532	1887	C/Cath	1669	98%	G	124	S		3200
Illinois College, Jacksonville, IL 62650	1829	C/Ind	760	88%		60	T		2550
Illinois Institute of Technology, Chicago, IL 60616	1892	C/Ind	4002	76%	G	692	U	N,AF	4290
Illinois State University, Normal, IL 61761	1857	C/Pub	17,605	98%	G	1091	T	A	596
Illinois Wesleyan University, Bloomington, IL 61701	1850	C/Ind	1638	94%		157	T		4380
Immaculata College, Immaculata, PA 19345	1920	W/Cath	581	90%		77	S		2500
Incarnate Word College, San Antonio, TX 78209	1881	C/Cath	1278	87%	G	108	U		2560
Indiana Central University, Indianapolis, IN 46227	1902	C/Prot	2892	96%	G	190	S		3200
Indiana Institute of Technology, Fort Wayne, IN 46803	1930	C/Ind	430	30%		41	U	A	1890
Indiana State University, Terre Haute, IN 47809	1865	C/Pub	9738	83%	G	728	U	A	1007
Indiana State University at Evansville, Evansville, IN 47712	1965	C/Pub	2863	95%		186	S		822x
Indiana University, Bloomington, IN 47405	1820	C/Pub	22,816	80%	G	1486	T		930
Indiana University at Kokomo, Kokomo, IN 46901	1945	C/Pub	1950	98%		145	U		900x
Indiana University at South Bend, South Bend, IN 46615	1922	C/Pub	4303	97%	G	330	U	A,N,AF	678x
Indiana University Northwest, Gary, IN 46408	1959	C/Pub	3364	99%	G	279	U		780x
Indiana University of Pennsylvania, Indiana, PA 15705	1871	C/Pub	10,866	97%	G	664	T	A	1100
Indiana U-Purdue U at Fort Wayne, Fort Wayne, IN 46805	1917	C/Pub	7781	97%	G	495	U	A	790x
Indiana U-Purdue U at Indianapolis, Indianapolis, IN 46202	1969	C/Pub	12,889	95%	G	2150	U	A	870
Indiana University Southeast, New Albany, IN 47150	1941	C/Pub	3868	97%	G	200	S	AF	780x
Inter Amer U of PR, San German Cmps, San German, PR 00753	1912	C/Ind	6188	100%	G	247	T		1290
Inter American U of PR, Hato Rey, PR 00919	1966	C/Prot	5908	°	G	270	U	A,N,AF	60cx
International College, Los Angeles, CA 90024	1970	C/Ind	60	85%	G	88	U		2600x
Inupiat University of the Arctic, Barrow, AK 99723	1975	C/Ind	33	100%	G	12	R		°x
Iona College, New Rochelle, NY 10801	1940	C/Ind	3683	90%	G	246	S		3280

Name and Location	Est	Type/ Control	UG Enroll	% of State Res	Grad	Fac Size	Cmps	ROTC	Tuition
Iowa State University, Ames, IA 50011	1858	C/Pub	18,558	79%	G	1992	T	A,N,AF	$816
Iowa Wesleyan College, Mount Pleasant, IA 52641	1842	C/Prot	730	72%		55	T		3560
Ithaca College, Ithaca, NY 14850	1892	C/Ind	4520	48%	G	442	T		4584
Jackson College, See Tufts University									
Jackson State University, Jackson, MS 39217	1877	C/Pub	6013	92%	G	375	U	A	750
Jacksonville State University, Jacksonville, AL 36265	1882	C/Pub	6208	80%	G	340	T	A	600
Jacksonville University, Jacksonville, FL 32211	1934	C/Ind	2141	51%	G	170	S	N	3000
James Madison University, Harrisonburg, VA 22807	1908	C/Pub	7198	81%	G	482	T	A	1026
Jamestown College, Jamestown, ND 58401	1883	C/Prot	540	55%		47	T		3235
Jarvis Christian College, Hawkins, TX 75765	1912	C/Prot	622	48%	G	55	R		1125
Jersey City State College, Jersey City, NJ 07305	1927	C/Pub	7700	95%	G	469	U		690
Jewish Theol Seminary of America, New York, NY 10027	1886	C/Jewish	158	26%	G	108	U		570
John Brown University, Siloam Springs, AR 72761	1919	C/Ind	742	25%		56	R		2100
John Carroll University, University Heights, OH 44118	1886	C/Cath	3133	60%	G	238	S	A	3300
John F Kennedy University, Orinda, CA 94563	1964	C/Ind	135	100%	G	199	S		1800x
John Jay College of Criminal Justice, See City U of NY, John Jay College of Criminal Justice									
Johns Hopkins University, Baltimore, MD 21218	1876	C/Ind	2156	32%	G	382	U	A	5075
Johnson and Wales College, Providence, RI 02903	1914	C/Ind	3000	20%		104	U		2985
Johnson Bible College, Knoxville, TN 37920	1893	C/Prot	396	29%		29	R		920
Johnson C Smith University, Charlotte, NC 28216	1867	C/Prot	1473	37%		85	U	A	1840
Johnson State College, Johnson, VT 05656	1828	C/Pub	904	72%	G	73	R		1070
Johnston College of the U of Redlands, Redlands, CA 92373	1969	C/Prot	1124	67%	G	173	T	A	5000
John Wesley College, Owosso, MI 48867	1909	C/Prot	80	60%		12	T		3000
Jones College, Jacksonville, FL 32211	1918	C/Ind	1088	92%		32	S		900x
Jones College, Orlando, FL 32803	1918	C/Ind	1350	96%		38	U		1093.50x
Judson Baptist College, Tha Dalles, OR 97058	1956	C/Prot	219	64%		28	T		2850
Judson College, Marion, AL 36756	1838	W/Prot	355	85%		42	R		1940
Judson College, Elgin, IL 60120	1963	C/Prot	486	60%		40	U		2640
Juilliard School, New York, NY 10023	1905	C/Ind	1000	40%	G	*	U		3500x
Juniata College, Huntingdon, PA 16652	1876	C/Ind	1250	73%		92	T		4065
Kalamazoo College, Kalamazoo, MI 49007	1833	C/Prot	1440	70%		91	S		4794
Kansas City Art Institute, Kansas City, MO 64111	1885	C/Ind	590	30%		54	U		4200
Kansas Newman College, Wichita, KS 67213	1933	C/Cath	660	91%		65	S		2400
Kansas State University, Manhattan, KS 66506	1863	C/Pub	14,525	85%	G	3000	T	A,AF	746
Kansas Wesleyan, Salina, KS 67401	1886	C/Prot	470	83%		41	S		2700
Kean College of New Jersey, Union, NJ 07083	1855	C/Pub	11,110	96%	G	716	S		690
Kearney State College, Kearney, NE 68847	1903	C/Pub	5865	*	G	300	T	A	570
Keene State College, Keene, NH 03431	1909	C/Pub	2700	65%	G	232	T		800
Kendall College, Evanston, IL 60201	1934	C/Prot	416	97%		34	S		3200
Kennesaw College, Marietta, GA 30061	1966	C/Pub	4132	95%		151	S	A	459x
Kent State University, Kent, OH 44242	1910	C/Pub	12,786	93%	G	774	T	A,AF	794
Kentucky Christian College, Grayson, KY 41143	1919	C/Prot	441	23%		27	R		1088
Kentucky State University, Frankfort, KY 40601	1886	C/Pub	2167	74%	G	165	S	A,AF	480
Kentucky Wesleyan College, Owensboro, KY 42301	1858	C/Prot	852	87%		73	S		2520
Kenyon College, Gambier, OH 43022	1824	C/Ind	1445	28%		120	R		5190
Keuka College, Keuka Park, NY 14478	1890	W/Ind	566	85%		49	R		4500
King College, Bristol, TN 37620	1867	C/Prot	238	36%		42	S		2925
King's College, Briarcliff Manor, NY 10510	1938	C/Ind	853	41%		70	S		3410
King's College, Wilkes-Barre, PA 18711	1946	C/Cath	1717	74%		126	U		3150
Knox College, Galesburg, IL 61401	1837	C/Ind	1042	80%		86	T	A	4850
Knoxville College, Knoxville, TN 37921	1875	C/Prot	699	21%		52	U	A,AF	2400
Kutztown State College, Kutztown, PA 19530	1866	C/Pub	4728	90%	G	303	T	A	1100
Ladycliff College, Highland Falls, NY 10928	1933	W/Ind	501	70%		78	T		3045x
Lafayette College, Easton, PA 18042	1826	C/Prot	2071	30%		167	S	A	5225
La Grange College, La Grange, GA 30240	1831	C/Prot	847	90%	G	51	T		1845
Lake Erie College, Painesville, OH 44077	1859	W/Ind	400	50%	G	90	S		4160
Lake Forest College, Lake Forest, IL 60045	1857	C/Ind	1067	41%		93	S		5240
Lake Land College, Mattoon, IL 61938	1966	C/Pub	3517	99%		285	R		1488x
Lakeland College, Sheboygan, WI 53081	1862	C/Prot	609	72%		47	R		3220
Lake Superior State College, Sault Ste Marie, MI 49783	1946	C/Pub	2309	90%		136	T	A	930
Lamar University, Beaumont, TX 77710	1923	C/Pub	12,213	91%	G	659	U	AF	150
Lambuth College, Jackson, TN 38301	1843	C/Prot	807	84%		72	U		2300
Lancaster Bible College, Lancaster, PA 17601	1933	C/Ind	437	82%		23	S		2220
Lander College, Greenwood, SC 29646	1872	C/Pub	1696	96%		109	T	A	850
Lane College, Jackson, TN 38301	1882	C/Prot	673	58%		47	U		1780
Langston University, Langston, OK 73050	1897	C/Pub	1087	60%		71	T		403
Laredo State University, Laredo, TX 78040	1969	C/Pub	458	95%	G	39	U		100x
La Roche College, Pittsburgh, PA 15237	1963	C/Cath	1122	*	G	103	S		2450
La Salle College, Philadelphia, PA 19141	1863	C/Cath	6318	80%	G	289	U	A	3320
Lawrence Institute of Technology, Southfield, MI 48075	1932	C/Ind	4991	90%		239	S		1530
Lawrence University, Appleton, WI 54911	1847	C/Ind	1156	45%		108	T		5256
Lebanon Valley College, Annville, PA 17003	1866	C/Prot	938	60%		90	T		4080
Lee College, Cleveland, TN 37311	1918	C/Prot	1442	30%		70	U		1800
Lehigh University, Bethlehem, PA 18015	1865	C/Ind	4400	43%	G	397	S	A,AF	5130
Le Moyne College, Syracuse, NY 13214	1946	C/Cath	1947	80%		136	S		3450
LeMoyne-Owen College, Memphis, TN 38126	1870	C/Ind	990	95%		62	U		2400x
Lenoir-Rhyne College, Hickory, NC 28601	1891	C/Prot	1291	70%	G	111	S		3000
Lesley College, Cambridge, MA 02138	1909	W/Ind	815	58%	G	334	U		4200
LeTourneau College, Longview, TX 75601	1946	M/Ind	962	15%		57	S		2650
Lewis and Clark College, Portland, OR 97219	1867	C/Ind	1887	42%	G	139	S		4498
Lewis-Clark State College, Lewiston, ID 83501	1893	C/Pub	1454	80%		100	T		400
Lewis University, Romeoville, IL 60441	1930	C/Cath	2437	99%	G	200	S		3360
Liberty Baptist College, Lynchburg, VA 24505	1971	C/Prot	2537	14%		130	S		1400
Limestone College, Gaffney, SC 29340	1845	C/Ind	1124	85%		77	T		3170
Lincoln Memorial University, Harrogate, TN 37752	1897	C/Ind	1067	60%		53	R		2100
Lincoln University, San Francisco, CA 94118	1919	C/Ind	216	0%	G	*	U		1750x
Lincoln University, Jefferson City, MO 65101	1866	C/Pub	2085	69%	G	189	T	A	400

Name and Location	Est	Type/ Control	UG Enroll	% of State Res	Grad	Fac Size	Cmps	ROTC	Tuition
Lincoln University, Lincoln University, PA 19352	1854	C/Pub	1062	10%	G	88	T		$1430
Lindenwood Colleges, St Charles, MO 63301	1827	C/Prot	1403	21%	G	146	T		3400
Linfield College, McMinnville, OR 97128	1849	C/Ind	1072	50%	G	104	T		3940
Livingston College, See Rutgers University, Livingston College									
Livingstone College, Salisbury, NC 28144	1879	C/Prot	921	57%		55	T		1400
Livingston University, Livingston, AL 35470	1835	C/Pub	1055	86%	G	75	T		495
Lock Haven State College, Lock Haven, PA 17745	1870	C/Pub	2416	87%		168	T	A	1100
Loma Linda University, Loma Linda, CA 92354	1905	C/Prot	3108	58%	G	931	T		4125
Loma Linda University, La Sierra Cmps, Riverside, CA 92515	1922	C/Prot	2212	78%	G	174	S		4125
Long Island U, Brooklyn Center, Brooklyn, NY 11201	1926	C/Ind	4365	90%	G	481	U		3200
Long Island University, C W Post Center, See CW Post Center of Long Island U									
Long Island U, Southampton College, Southampton, NY 11968	1963	C/Ind	1298	70%	G	142	R		3720
Longwood College, Farmville, VA 23901	1839	C/Pub	2300	92%	G	158	T	A	1200
Loras College, Dubuque, IA 52001	1839	C/Cath	1700	60%	G	125	U		3050
Loretto Heights College, Denver, CO 80236	1918	C/Ind	850	65%		94	S		3900
Los Angeles Baptist College, Newhall, CA 91322	1927	C/Prot	393	75%		53	T		2700
Louisiana College, Pineville, LA 71360	1906	C/Prot	1314	90%		92	T	A	1088
Louisiana State U and A&M College, Baton Rouge, LA 70803	1860	C/Pub	21,504	88%	G	1187	S	A,AF	522
Louisiana State U in Shreveport, Shreveport, LA 71115	1965	C/Pub	3103	98%	G	146	S	A	480x
Louisiana Tech University, Ruston, LA 71272	1894	C/Pub	8476	85%	G	417	T	AF	651
Loyola College, Baltimore, MD 21210	1852	C/Cath	2111	75%	G	302	S	A	2775
Loyola Marymount University, Los Angeles, CA 90045	1911	C/Cath	3459	92%	G	298	S	AF	4020
Loyola University, New Orleans, LA 70118	1912	C/Cath	3216	75%	G	303	S	A	2500
Loyola University of Chicago, Chicago, IL 60611	1870	C/Cath	8593	95%	G	1370	U	A	3100
Lubbock Christian College, Lubbock, TX 79407	1957	C/Prot	1128	66%		97	S		2400
Lutheran Bible Institute of Seattle, Issaquah, WA 98027	1944	C/Prot	260	50%		18	R		1678
Luther College, Decorah, IA 52101	1861	C/Prot	1999	56%		148	T		4250
Lycoming College, Williamsport, PA 17701	1812	C/Prot	1159	58%		75	S		3720
Lynchburg College, Lynchburg, VA 24501	1903	C/Prot	1852	51%	G	148	S		3100
Lyndon State College, Lyndonville, VT 05851	1911	C/Pub	1037	48%	G	99	R		970
Macalester College, St Paul, MN 55105	1874	C/Prot	1763	35%		149	U		4725
MacMurray College, Jacksonville, IL 62650	1846	C/Prot	686	90%		67	T		3550
Madonna College, Livonia, MI 48150	1947	C/Ind	3011	98%		132	S		1500
Maharishi International University, Fairfield, IA 52556	1971	C/Ind	582	5%	G	55	T		3060
Maine Maritime Academy, Castine, ME 04421	1941	M/Pub	643	70%		60	T		1610
Malone College, Canton, OH 44709	1892	C/Prot	772	89%		50	S	N	3180
Manchester College, North Manchester, IN 46962	1889	C/Prot	1226	80%		98	T		3010
Manhattan College, Bronx, NY 10471	1853	C/Ind	4090	82%	G	329	S	AF	3200
Manhattan School of Music, New York, NY 10027	1917	C/Ind	427	55%	G	158	U		3350x
Manhattanville College, Purchase, NY 10577	1841	C/Ind	858	50%	G	168	S		4880
Mankato State University, Mankato, MN 56001	1867	C/Pub	9048	88%	G	640	U	A	586
Mannes College of Music, New York, NY 10021	1916	C/Ind	195	40%		110	U		3200x
Mansfield State College, Mansfield, PA 16933	1857	C/Pub	2501	90%	G	205	T		1100
Marian College, Indianapolis, IN 46222	1851	C/Cath	748	86%		77	S		2640
Marian College of Fond du Lac, Fond du Lac, WI 54935	1936	W/Cath	499	87%		60	T	A	2300
Marietta College, Marietta, OH 45750	1835	C/Ind	1488	45%	G	117	T		4500
Marion College, Marion, IN 46952	1920	C/Prot	1088	67%	G	78	S		2880
Marist College, Poughkeepsie, NY 12601	1949	C/Ind	1850	80%	G	120	S		3120
Marlboro College, Marlboro, VT 05344	1947	C/Ind	232	10%		35	R		4970
Marquette University, Milwaukee, WI 53233	1881	C/Cath	8818	54%	G	898	U	A,N	362c
Marshall University, Huntington, WV 25701	1837	C/Pub	8948	88%	G	514	U	A	196
Mars Hill College, Mars Hill, NC 28754	1856	C/Prot	1958	71%		127	T		2455
Mary Baldwin College, Staunton, VA 24401	1842	W/Prot	700	48%	G	62	T		3900
Mary College, Bismarck, ND 58501	1955	C/Cath	917	92%		76	R		2090
Marycrest College, Davenport, IA 52804	1939	C/Cath	708	54%	G	106	S		3225
Marygrove College, Detroit, MI 48221	1910	C/Cath	752	98%	G	56	U		3100
Maryland Institute College of Art, Baltimore, MD 21217	1826	C/Ind	780	55%	G	90	U		3750x
Marylhurst Education Center, Marylhurst, OR 97036	1893	C/Ind	526	97%		120	S		2100x
Marymount College, Tarrytown, NY 10591	1922	W/Cath	931	51%		132	S		3830
Marymount College of Kansas, Salina, KS 67401	1922	C/Cath	787	87%		70	T		2400
Marymount College of Virginia, Arlington, VA 22207	1950	W/Cath	852	34%	G	123	S		3100
Marymount Manhattan College, New York, NY 10021	1937	W/Ind	2252	94%		210	U		2790
Maryville College, Maryville, TN 37801	1819	C/Ind	634	45%		60	T	A	2803
Maryville College - Saint Louis, St Louis, Maryville College-Saint Louis 63141	1827	C/Cath	1355	82%	G	100	S		3230
Mary Washington College, Fredericksburg, VA 22401	1908	C/Pub	2471	78%	G	149	T		788
Marywood College, Scranton, PA 18509	1915	W/Cath	2100	55%	G	190	S		2250
Mason Gross School of the Arts, See Rutgers University, Mason Gross School of the Arts									
Massachusetts College of Art, Boston, MA 02215	1873	C/Pub	1050	85%	U	100	U		600x
Massachusetts Institute of Technology, Cambridge, MA 02139	1861	C/Ind	4232	17%	G	1700	U	A,N,AF	5300
Massachusetts Maritime Academy, Buzzards Bay, MA 02532	1891	M/Pub	850	85%		53	T		600
Mayville State College, Mayville, ND 58257	1889	C/Pub	746	80%		65	T		589
McKendree College, Lebanon, IL 62254	1828	C/Prot	805	81%		83	S		3200
McMurry College, Abilene, TX 79605	1923	C/Ind	1450	89%		84	S		2000
McNeese State University, Lake Charles, LA 70609	1939	C/Pub	4435	94%	G	302	S	A	452
McPherson College, McPherson, KS 67460	1887	C/Prot	493	56%		42	R		2660
Medaille College, Buffalo, NY 14214	1875	C/Ind	700	99%	G	64	U		2659x
Medgar Evers College, See City U of NY, Medgar Evers College									
Memphis Academy of Arts, Memphis, TN 38112	1936	C/Ind	217	62%		27	U		1900x
Memphis State University, Memphis, TN 38152	1912	C/Pub	15,770	93%	G	932	U	AF	556
Menlo College, Menlo Park, CA 94025	1927	C/Ind	681	56%		50	S		4530
Mercer University, Macon, GA 31207	1833	C/Prot	2070	50%	G	150	U	A	3117
Mercer University in Atlanta, Atlanta, GA 30341	1968	C/Prot	1177	95%	G	95	S		2250x
Mercy College, Dobbs Ferry, NY 10522	1951	C/Ind	10,500	92%		560	T		1950x
Mercy College of Detroit, Detroit, MI 48219	1941	C/Cath	2454	95%	G	236	U		2580
Mercyhurst College, Erie, PA 16501	1926	C/Ind	1300	79%	G	127	S	A	2975

Name and Location	Est	Type/Control	UG Enroll	% of State Res	Grad	Fac Size	Cmps	ROTC	Tuition
Meredith College, Raleigh, NC 27611	1891	W/Prot	1427	85%		120	U		$2500
Merrimack College, North Andover, MA 01845	1947	C/Cath	2196	74%		141	S		3700
Mesa College, Grand Junction, CO 81501	1925	C/Pub	4259	95%		155	T	A	494
Messiah College, Grantham, PA 17027	1909	C/Prot	1149	60%		108	T		3200
Methodist College, Fayetteville, NC 28301	1956	C/Prot	762	70%		57	S	A	2400
Metropolitan State College, Denver, CO 80204	1965	C/Pub	13,350	95%		584	U		262x
Metropolitan State University, St Paul, MN 55101	1971	C/Pub	1993	98%		372	U		750x
Miami Christian College, Miami, FL 33167	1949	C/Ind	190	81%		21	U		1900
Miami University, Oxford, OH 45056	1809	C/Pub	12,828	88%	G	800	T	N,AF	890
Michigan State University, East Lansing, MI 48824	1855	C/Pub	36,372	86%	G	2628	T	A,AF	1103
Michigan Technological University, Houghton, MI 49931	1885	C/Pub	7341	85%	G	508	T	A,AF	1059
Mid-America Nazarene College, Olathe, KS 66061	1966	C/Prot	1292	46%		78	S		1908
Middlebury College, Middlebury, VT 05753	1800	C/Ind	1870	7%	G	161	R		2400x
Middle Tennessee State University, Murfreesboro, TN 37132	1911	C/Pub	9144	95%	G	450	T	A	472
Midland Lutheran College, Fremont, NE 68025	1883	C/Prot	757	70%		65	T		3200
Midway College, Midway, KY 40347	1847	W/Ind	310	88%		57	T		2100
Midwest College of Engineering, Lombard, IL 60148	1967	C/Ind	179	95%	G	52	S		3600x
Midwestern State University, Wichita Falls, TX 76308	1922	C/Pub	3884	90%	G	195	S	A	120
Miles College, Birmingham, AL 35208	1907	C/Prot	1152			94	R	AF	2000
Millersville State College, Millersville, PA 17551	1854	C/Pub	5216	96%	G	360	T	A	1100
Milligan College, Milligan College, TN 37682	1866	C/Prot	772	27%		57	S		2072
Millikin University, Decatur, IL 62522	1901	C/Ind	1358	93%		121	S		3925
Millsaps College, Jackson, MS 39210	1890	C/Prot	972	74%	G	80	U		3000
Mills College, Oakland, CA 94613	1852	W/Ind	822	60%	G	104	U		4800
Milton College, Milton, WI 53563	1844	C/Ind	320	75%		38	R	A	3300
Milwaukee School of Engineering, Milwaukee, WI 53201	1903	M/Ind	1393	70%		80	U	A	3600
Minneapolis College of Art and Design, Minneapolis, MN 55404	1886	C/Ind	591	50%		60	U		3400
Minnesota Bible College, Rochester, MN 55901	1913	C/Prot	128	55%		13	U		1425
Minot State College, Minot, ND 58701	1913	C/Pub	2303	92%	G	138	T		568
Mississippi College, Clinton, MS 39058	1826	C/Ind	1871	90%	G	179	T		1920
Mississippi Industrial College, Holly Springs, MS 38635	1905	C/Prot	265	*					
Miss State University, Mississippi State, MS 39762	1878	C/Pub	9752	95%	G	802	T	A,AF	870
Mississippi University for Women, Columbus, MS 39701	1884	W/Pub	1970	75%	G	184	T		674
Mississippi Valley State University, Itta Bena, MS 38941	1946	C/Pub	2675	88%	G	175	T	A,AF	607
Missouri Baptist College, St Louis, MO 63141	1968	C/Prot	434	98%		37	S		1900
Missouri Institute of Technology, Kansas City, MO 64114	1931	C/Ind	740	40%		18	U		2425x
Missouri Southern State College, Joplin, MO 64801	1937	C/Pub	3790	95%		206	T	A	440
Missouri Valley College, Marshall, MO 65340	1889	C/Prot	376	62%		38	T		2644
Missouri Western State College, St Joseph, MO 64507	1915	C/Pub	3777	93%		175	S	A	470
Mobile College, Mobile, AL 36613	1961	C/Prot	1074	91%		66	S	A	1760
Molloy College, Rockville Centre, NY 11570	1955	W/Cath	1533	100%		176	S		3050x
Monmouth College, Monmouth, IL 61462	1853	C/Prot	700	86%		76	T	A	3675
Monmouth College, West Long Branch, NJ 07764	1933	C/Ind	2900	90%	G	214	S	A	3830
Montana Coll of Mineral Sci & Tech, Butte, MT 59701	1893	C/Pub	1283	80%	G	80	R		461
Montana State University, Bozeman, MT 59717	1893	C/Pub	9156	84%	G	743	T	A,AF	333
Montclair State College, Upper Montclair, NJ 07043	1908	C/Pub	11,695	95%	G	779	S		736
Monterey Institute of International Studies, Monterey, CA 93940	1955	C/Ind	92	61%	G	71	U		4590x
Moody Bible Institute, Chicago, IL 60610	1886	C/Ind	1363	25%		94	U		100
Moore College of Art, Philadelphia, PA 19103	1844	W/Ind	508	56%		84	U		3700
Moorhead State University, Moorhead, MN 56560	1885	C/Pub	6414	67%	G	320	S		700
Moravian College, Bethlehem, PA 18018	1742	C/Ind	1342	56%		118	T		3900
Morehead State University, Morehead, KY 40351	1922	C/Pub	5429	80%	G	306	U		270
Morehouse College, Atlanta, GA 30314	1867	M/Ind	1754	30%		141	U	A	2350
Morgan State University, Baltimore, MD 21239	1867	C/Pub	4779	63%	G	452	U	A	595
Morningside College, Sioux City, IA 51106	1894	C/Ind	1520	75%	G	105	S		3550
Morris Brown College, Atlanta, GA 30314	1881	C/Pub	1530	*		150	T	AF	2050
Morris College, Sumter, SC 29150	1908	C/Prot	727	95%		48	*		2025
Mount Angel Seminary, St Benedict, OR 97373	1887	M/Cath	41	70%	G	31	R		1650
Mount Holyoke College, South Hadley, MA 01075	1837	W/Ind	1850	20%	G	206	T		5430
Mount Marty College, Yankton, SD 57078	1936	C/Cath	590	46%		63	R		2500
Mount Mary College, Milwaukee, WI 53222	1913	W/Cath	1126	91%		124	S		2550
Mount Mercy College, Cedar Rapids, IA 52402	1928	C/Cath	1042	90%		74	U		3115
Mount Saint Mary College, Newburgh, NY 12550	1930	C/Ind	1046	80%		80	U		2700
Mount St Mary's College, Los Angeles, CA 90049	1925	W/Cath	944	86%	G	127	U		3450
Mount Saint Mary's College, Emmitsburg, MD 21727	1808	C/Cath	1400	38%	G	83	R		3200
Mount Senario College, Ladysmith, WI 54848	1962	C/Ind	474	80%		54	T		3260
Mount Union College, Alliance, OH 44601	1846	C/Prot	1020	82%		95	S		3825
Mount Vernon College, Washington, DC 20007	1875	W/Ind	462	14%		60	U		3700
Mount Vernon Nazarene College, Mt Vernon, OH 43050	1968	C/Prot	1005	75%		65	T		2200
Muhlenberg College, Allentown, PA 18104	1848	C/Prot	1530	35%		117	S		4575
Multnomah School of the Bible, Portland, OR 97220	1936	C/Ind	619	30%	G	43	U		2410
Mundelein College, Chicago, IL 60660	1929	W/Ind	1400	88%	G	145	U		3390
Murray State University, Murray, KY 42071	1922	C/Pub	6023	80%	G	381	T	A	480
Museum Art School, Portland, OR 97205	1909	C/Ind	175	60%		45	U		2650x
Muskingum College, New Concord, OH 43762	1837	C/Prot	883	80%		77	R		4337
Nasson College, Springvale, ME 04083	1912	C/Ind	643	16%		53	T	A	3490
Nathaniel Hawthorne College, Antrim, NH 03440	1962	C/Ind	500	5%		50	R	AF	3060
National College of Business, Rapid City, SD 57701	1941	C/Ind	1083	62%		55	U	A	2775
National College of Education, Evanston, IL 60201	1886	C/Ind	532	65%	G	118	S	N	4225
National Coll of Education, Urban Cmps, Chicago, IL 60603	1886	C/Ind	257	100%	G	50	U		3425x
National University, San Diego, CA 92106	1971	C/Ind	2687	*	G	391	U		3480x
Nazareth College, Nazareth, MI 49074	1924	C/Cath	540	97%		61	T	A	700
Nazareth College of Rochester, Rochester, NY 14610	1924	C/Ind	1678	92%	G	180	S		3400
Nebraska Wesleyan University, Lincoln, NE 68504	1887	C/Prot	1160	84%		100	S		3050
Newark College of Arts and Sciences. See Rutgers University, Newark College of Arts and Sciences									
Newberry College, Newberry, SC 29108	1856	C/Prot	883	75%		76	T		3265
New College of California, San Francisco, CA 94110	1971	C/Ind	200	40%	G	20	U		2700x

Name and Location	Est	Type/Control	UG Enroll	% of State Res	Grad	Fac Size	Cmps	ROTC	Tuition
New College of the University of South Florida, See University of South Florida, New College									
Newcomb College, See Tulane University, Newcomb College									
New England College, Henniker, NH 03242	1946	C/Ind	1249	15%		108	T		$4680
New England Conservatory of Music, Boston, MA 02115	1867	C/Ind	508	35%	G	165	U		4700
New Hampshire College, Manchester, NH 03104	1932	C/Ind	1475	30%	G	69	S		4234
New Jersey Institute of Technology, Newark, NJ 07102	1881	C/Pub	4531	95%	G	387	U	AF	832
New Mexico Highlands University, Las Vegas, NM 87701	1893	C/Pub	1680	85%	G	115	T		424
New Mexico Inst of Mining & Tech, Socorro, NM 87801	1889	C/Pub	904	86%	G	100	T		365
New Mexico State University, Las Cruces, NM 88003	1888	C/Pub	10,469	91%	G	800	S	A,AF	708
Newport College-Salve Regina, Newport, RI 02840	1934	C/Cath	1522	51%	G	152	T		3300
New School for Social Research, New York, NY 10011	1919	C/Ind	238	67%	G	125	U		3700
New School of Music, Philadelphia, PA 19103	1943	C/Ind	81	45%		46	U		3000x
NY Inst of Tech, Metropolitan Ctr, New York, NY 10023	1831	C/Ind	2387	59%	G	202	U		2816x
New York Inst of Tech, Old Westbury, Old Westbury, NY 11568	1910	C/Ind	10,443	95%	G	631	S		2816x
New York University, New York, NY 10006	1831	C/Ind	12,685	80%	G	5422	U		5062
Niagara University, Niagara University, NY 14109	1856	C/Cath	3328	88%	G	254	S	A	3300
Nicholls State University, Thibodaux, LA 70301	1948	C/Pub	5652	97%	G	233	T	A	530
Nichols College, Dudley, MA 01570	1815	C/Ind	776	50%	G	41	T		3490
Norfolk State University, Norfolk, VA 23504	1935	C/Pub	6550	80%	G	425	U	A	740
North Adams State College, North Adams, MA 01247	1894	C/Pub	2350	90%	G	190	T		600
North Carolina A&T State University, Greensboro, NC 27411	1891	C/Pub	4863	76%	G	347	T	A,AF	620
North Carolina Central University, Durham, NC 27707	1910	C/Pub	3922	90%	G	329	U	AF	310
North Carolina School of the Arts, Winston-Salem, NC 27107	1963	C/Pub	453	45%		105	U		568
N Carolina State U at Raleigh, Raleigh, NC 27650	1862	C/Pub	15,539	87%	G	1352	S	A,AF	364
North Carolina Wesleyan College, Rocky Mount, NC 27801	1956	C/Prot	743	74%		53	S		2760
North Central Bible College, Minneapolis, MN 55404	1930	C/Prot	587	*		*	*		*
North Central College, Naperville, IL 60540	1861	C/Prot	1111	96%		81	S		3729
North Dakota State University, Fargo, ND 58102	1890	C/Pub	6882	71%	G	570	U	A,AF	633
Northeastern Bible College, Essex Fells, NJ 07021	1950	C/Prot	337	74%		33	S		2592
Northeastern Illinois University, Chicago, IL 60625	1961	C/Pub	7752	99%	G	448	U	AF	558x
Northeastern Oklahoma State U, Tahlequah, OK 74464	1846	C/Pub	4323	96%	G	220	T	A	372
Northeastern University, Boston, MA 02115	1898	C/Ind	19,275	65%	G	2517	U	A,AF	3675
Northeast Louisiana University, Monroe, LA 71209	1931	C/Pub	8108	92%	G	400	U	A	450
Northeast Missouri State University, Kirksville, MO 63501	1867	C/Pub	5380	75%	G	312	T	A	340
Northern Arizona University, Flagstaff, AZ 86011	1899	C/Pub	*	75%	G	553	T	AF	600
Northern Illinois University, DeKalb, IL 60115	1895	C/Pub	17,411	99%	G	1268	T	A	548
Northern Kentucky University, Highland Heights, KY 41076	1968	C/Pub	6567	90%	G	408	S	A	540x
Northern Michigan University, Marquette, MI 49855	1899	C/Pub	7524	94%	G	396	U	A	1040
Northern Montana College, Havre, MT 59501	1929	C/Pub	1114	90%	G	81	T		453
Northern State College, Aberdeen, SD 57401	1901	C/Pub	2320	97%	G	110	T		592
North Georgia College, Dahlonega, GA 30533	1873	C/Pub	1609	95%	G	120	T	A	1815
Northland College, Ashland, WI 54806	1892	C/Prot	622	35%		46	T		3290
North Park College, Chicago, IL 60625	1891	C/Prot	1284	40%		98	U		3465
Northrop University, Inglewood, CA 90306	1942	C/Ind	1705	25%	G	43	S		2952
North Texas State University, Denton, TX 76203	1890	C/Pub	12,308	83%	G	1165	T	AF	420
Northwest Bible College, Minot, ND 58701	1934	C/Prot	150	32%		12	T		1275
Northwest Christian College, Eugene, OR 97401	1895	C/Prot	382	35%		23	U	A	2520
NW Coll of the Assemblies of God, Kirkland, WA 98033	1934	C/Prot	787	55%		46	S		1590
Northwestern College, Orange City, IA 51041	1882	C/Prot	861	65%		64	R		3220
Northwestern College, Roseville, MN 55113	1902	C/Prot	706	65%		60	S		3000
Northwestern Oklahoma State U, Alva, OK 73717	1897	C/Pub	1721	92%	G	71	T	A	400
Northwestern State University of Louisiana, Natchitoches, LA 71457	1884	C/Pub	4653	*	G	225	T	A	550
Northwestern University, Evanston, IL 60201	1851	C/Ind	6800	30%	G	1686	S	N	5985
Northwest Missouri State University, Maryville, MO 64468	1905	C/Pub	3860	65%	G	245	T		490
Northwest Nazarene College, Nampa, ID 83651	1913	C/Prot	1284	30%	G	82	T	A	2520
Northwood Institute-Midland Campus, Midland, MI 48640	1959	C/Ind	1770	50%		62	S		2640
Norwich University, Northfield, VT 05663	1819	M/Ind	1448	8%	G	166	R	A,AF	3190x
Notre Dame College, Manchester, NH 03104	1950	W/Cath	581	1%		69	S		2500
Notre Dame College of Ohio, Cleveland, OH 44121	1922	W/Cath	604	86%		57	S		2375
Nova University, Ft Lauderdale, FL 33314	1964	C/Ind	638	100%	G	403	S		2900x
Nyack College, Nyack, NY 10960	1882	C/Prot	602	50%	G	65	S		2768
Oakland City College, Oakland City, IN 47660	1885	C/Prot	545	71%		39	T		2403
Oakland University, Rochester, MI 48063	1957	C/Pub	9331	99%	G	527	S		872
Oakwood College, Huntsville, AL 35806	1896	C/Prot	1266	16%		92	R		3300
Oberlin College, Oberlin, OH 44074	1833	C/Ind	2724	14%	G	226	T		4725
Oblate College, Washington, DC 20017	1916	M/Cath	15	20%	G	15	U		1230x
Occidental College, Los Angeles, CA 90041	1887	C/Ind	1602	60%	G	157	U		5349
Oglethorpe University, Atlanta, GA 30319	1835	C/Ind	1030	51%	G	49	S		3100
Ohio Dominican College, Columbus, OH 43219	1911	C/Cath	849	84%		67	S	AF	3280
Ohio Institute of Technology, Columbus, OH 43219	1952	C/Ind	2327	40%		75	U		2425x
Ohio Northern University, Ada, OH 45810	1871	C/Prot	2174	80%		183	T		3651
Ohio State University, Columbus, OH 43210	1870	C/Pub	40,715	94%	G	3161	U	A,N,AF	1005
Ohio State University, Lima, OH 45804	1961	C/Pub	777	99%		56	T		960x
Ohio State University, Mansfield, OH 44906	1958	C/Pub	1081	99%		59	T		960x
Ohio University, Athens, OH 45701	1804	C/Pub	11,870	80%	G	826	T	A,AF	1071
Ohio University, Lancaster, OH 43130	1968	C/Pub	1450	97%	G	136	S	A	900x
Ohio Wesleyan University, Delaware, OH 43015	1841	C/Prot	2250	33%		180	T		4875
Oklahoma Baptist University, Shawnee, OK 74801	1909	C/Prot	1531	69%		127	T		1800
Oklahoma Christian College, Oklahoma City, OK 73111	1949	C/Prot	1522	44%		73	S		1570
Oklahoma City University, Oklahoma City, OK 73106	1904	C/Prot	1496	95%	G	171	U		1070
Oklahoma Panhandle State U, Goodwell, OK 73939	1909	C/Pub	1041	80%		60	R	A	422
Oklahoma State University, Stillwater, OK 74074	1890	C/Pub	18,714	90%	G	1041	T	A,AF	495
Old Dominion University, Norfolk, VA 23508	1930	C/Pub	10,768	86%	G	824	U	A	816
Olivet College, Olivet, MI 49076	1844	C/Prot	629	96%	G	51	T		3990
Olivet Nazarene College, Kankakee, IL 60901	1907	C/Prot	1905	40%	G	110	S		2448
Open Bible College, Des Moines, IA 50321	1930	C/Prot	117	70%		12	U		1600
Oral Roberts University, Tulsa, OK 74171	1963	C/Ind	3880	19%	G	300	S		2950

Name and Location	Est	Type/Control	UG Enroll	% of State Res	Grad	Fac Size	Cmps	ROTC	Tuition
Oregon College of Education, Monmouth, OR 97361	1856	C/Pub	2290	66%	G	200	T	AF	$921
Oregon Institute of Technology, Klamath Falls, OR 97601	1947	C/Pub	2195	87%		207	T		955
Oregon State University, Corvallis, OR 97331	1868	C/Pub	14,312	86%	G	1071	T	A,N,AF	924
Otis Art Inst of Parsons Sch of Design, Los Angeles, CA 90057	1918	C/Ind	143	6%	G	29	U		2900x
Ottawa University, Ottawa, KS 66067	1865	C/Prot	555	50%		47	T		2600
Otterbein College, Westerville, OH 43081	1847	C/Prot	1687	85%		110	S	•	4428
Ouachita Baptist University, Arkadelphia, AR 71923	1885	C/Prot	1438	81%	G	102	T	A	1910
Our Lady of Angeles College, Aston, PA 19014	1965	C/Cath	703	83%		65	S		2175x
Our Lady of Holy Cross College, New Orleans, LA 70114	1916	C/Cath	783	100%		93	S		1540x
Our Lady of the Lake U of San Antonio, San Antonio, TX 78285	1896	C/Cath	1150	90%	G	130	S		2400
Pace University, New York, NY 10038	1906	C/Ind	6143	91%	G	647	U		3264
Pace U, College of White Plains, White Plains, NY 10603	1923	C/Ind	1200	86%		90	S		3500
Pace U—Pleasantville/Briarcliff, Pleasantville, NY 10570	1963	C/Ind	4214	84%	G	536	S		3060
Pacific Christian College, Fullerton, CA 92631	1928	C/Prot	315	83%	G	42	U		2230
Pacific Lutheran University, Tacoma, WA 98447	1890	C/Prot	2878	72%	G	263	S		4064
Pacific Oaks College, Pasadena, CA 91105	1945	C/Ind	55	60%	G	31	U		2880x
Pacific Union College, Angwin, CA 94508	1882	C/Prot	2108	79%		162	R		4125
Pacific University, Forest Grove, OR 97116	1849	C/Ind	889	35%	G	106	T		4300
Paine College, Augusta, GA 30901	1882	C/Prot	828	82%		57	U		2175
Palm Beach Atlantic College, West Palm Beach, FL 33401	1968	C/Prot	580	76%		62	U		1700
Pan American University, Edinburg, TX 78539	1927	C/Pub	8351	95%	G	428	R	A	120
Park College, Parkville, MO 64152	1875	C/Prot	460	50%		40	S		2910
Parks Coll of St Louis Univ, Cahokia, IL 62206	1927	C/Cath	958	45%		56	S	AF	2560
Parsons School of Design, New York, NY 10011	1896	C/Ind	1400	27%	G	235	U		3980
Patten Bible College, Oakland, CA 94601	1944	C/Ind	125	95%		16	U		1638
Paul Quinn College, Waco, TX 76703	1872	C/Prot	421	71%		34	U	AF	1800
Peabody Cons of Johns Hopkins U, Baltimore, MD 21202	1857	C/Ind	260	35%	G	104	U		4575
Pembroke State University, Pembroke, NC 28372	1887	C/Pub	2102	97%	G	130	R		500
Penna State U-Behrend College, Erie, PA 16563	1926	C/Pub	1810	96%	G	102	S	A	1281
Penna State U-Capitol Campus, Middletown, PA 17057	1966	C/Pub	1604	97%	G	137	S		1440
Penna State U-Univ Park Campus, University Park, PA 16802	1855	C/Pub	27,131	91%	G	1640	T	A,N,AF	1485
Pepperdine University, Los Angeles, CA 90044	1937	C/Prot	532	•	G	184	U		3420x
Pepperdine University, Malibu, CA 90265	1937	C/Ind	2099	68%	G	136	S		5406
Peru State College, Peru, NE 68421	1867	C/Pub	718	75%		52	R		570
Pfeiffer College, Misenheimer, NC 28109	1885	C/Prot	844	70%		83	R		2345
Philadelphia College of Art, Philadelphia, PA 19104	1876	C/Ind	1131	57%	G	170	U		4500
Philadelphia College of Bible, Langhorne, PA 19047	1913	C/Ind	525	49%		45	S		2350
Philadelphia Coll of Textiles & Sci, Philadelphia, PA 19144	1884	C/Ind	1784	80%	G	168	S		3200
Phila College of the Performing Arts, Philadelphia, PA 19102	1870	C/Ind	355	69%	G	135	U		3800x
Philander Smith College, Little Rock, AR 72203	1877	C/Prot	600	75%		61	U		1413
Phillips University, Enid, OK 73701	1906	C/Prot	947	30%	G	121	T		2100
Piedmont Bible College, Winston-Salem, NC 27101	1947	C/Prot	470	48%		31	U		1570
Piedmont College, Demorest, GA 30535	1897	C/Prot	406	90%		26	R	A	1485
Pikeville College, Pikeville, KY 41501	1889	C/Prot	615	78%		52	T		2150
Pine Manor College, Chestnut Hill, MA 02167	1911	W/Ind	494	17%		48	S		4900
Pittsburg State University, Pittsburg, KS 66762	1903	C/Pub	3846	84%	G	324	T	A	440
Pitzer College, Claremont, CA 91711	1963	C/Ind	708	45%		103	S		5460
Plymouth State College, Plymouth, NH 03264	1871	C/Pub	2700	70%	G	150	T	A,AF	800
Point Loma College, San Diego, CA 92106	1902	C/Prot	1511	89%	G	84	U	AF	3120
Point Park College, Pittsburgh, PA 15222	1960	C/Ind	2072	77%		147	U		3500
Polytechnic Institute of New York, Brooklyn, NY 11201	1854	C/Ind	2455	90%	G	348	U	A	3850x
Pomona College, Claremont, CA 91711	1887	C/Ind	1362	58%		144	S		5320
Pontifical College Josephinum, Columbus, OH 43085	1888	M/Cath	80	56%	G	45	U		2063
Portland School of Art, Portland, ME 04101	1882	C/Ind	230	49%		24	U		2980x
Portland State University, Portland, OR 97207	1946	C/Pub	12,061	89%	G	824	U		693x
Post College, Waterbury, CT 06708	1890	C/Ind	1527	80%		86	S		3000
Prairie View A&M University, Prairie View, TX 77445	1876	C/Pub	3848	83%	G	305	T	A,N	144
Pratt Institute, Brooklyn, NY 11205	1887	C/Ind	3294	58%	G	490	U		4400
Presbyterian College, Clinton, SC 29325	1880	C/Prot	925	67%	G	67	T	A	3060
Princeton University, Princeton, NJ 08544	1746	C/Ind	4447	20%	G	777	S	A	6300
Principia College, Elsah, IL 62028	1910	C/Ind	866	11%	G	82	R		4426
Providence College, Providence, RI 02918	1917	C/Cath	3500	27%	G	235	U	A	3342
Purdue University, West Lafayette, IN 47907	1869	C/Pub	26,407	75%	G	3748	S	A,N,AF	1008
Purdue University-Calumet, Hammond, IN 46323	1951	C/Pub	5783	87%	G	377	U		960x
Purdue University-North Central Cmps, Westville, IN 46391	1967	C/Pub	1884	99%		•	R		883x
Queens College, See City U of NY, Queens College									
Queens College, Charlotte, NC 28274	1857	W/Prot	640	64%	G	70	S		3396
Quincy College, Quincy, IL 62301	1859	C/Cath	1715	83%	G	87	S		3200
Quinnipiac College, Hamden, CT 06518	1929	C/Ind	2936	50%	G	313	S		3800
Radcliffe College, See Harvard and Radcliffe Colleges									
Radford University, Radford, VA 24142	1913	C/Pub	4600	90%	G	290	R	A	945
Ramapo College of New Jersey, Mahwah, NJ 07430	1969	C/Pub	4318	96%		195	S		700
Randolph-Macon College, Ashland, VA 23005	1830	C/Prot	959	64%		72	T		3870
Randolph-Macon Woman's College, Lynchburg, VA 24503	1891	W/Prot	760	38%		83	S		4500
Reed College, Portland, OR 97202	1911	C/Ind	1139	20%	G	117	S		5560
Reformed Bible College, Grand Rapids, MI 49506	1940	C/Prot	230	50%		18	U		1800
Regis College, Denver, CO 80221	1877	C/Cath	1100	45%	G	95	S		3910
Regis College, Weston, MA 02193	1927	W/Cath	1099	80%	G	83	S		3395
Rensselaer Polytechnic Institute, Troy, NY 12181	1824	C/Ind	4155	43%	G	345	S	A,N,AF	5400
Rhode Island College, Providence, RI 02908	1854	C/Pub	6093	90%	G	393	S		625
Rhode Island School of Design, Providence, RI 02903	1877	C/Ind	1395	10%	G	159	U		5200
Rice University, Houston, TX 77001	1891	C/Ind	2430	60%	G	476	S	A,N	2900
Rider College, Lawrenceville, NJ 08648	1865	C/Ind	4984	76%	G	314	S	A	3250
Ringling School of Art, Sarasota, FL 33580	1931	C/Ind	465	30%		25	S		2000
Rio Grande Coll/Community Coll, Rio Grande, OH 45674	1876	C/Ind	1144	75%		66	R		2230
Ripon College, Ripon, WI 54971	1851	C/Ind	928	32%		91	T	A	4690
Rivier College, Nashua, NH 03060	1933	W/Cath	1083	43%	G	115	S		2750

Name and Location	Est	Type/ Control	UG Enroll	% of State Res	Grad	Fac Size	Cmps	ROTC	Tuition
Roanoke College, Salem, VA 24153	1842	C/Prot	1344	50%		86	T		$3500
Robert Morris College, Coraopolis, PA 15108	1921	C/Ind	4368	95%	G	179	S		2180
Roberts Wesleyan College, Rochester, NY 14624	1866	C/Prot	645	74%		89	S		3286
Rochester Institute of Technology, Rochester, NY 14623	1829	C/Ind	2108	60%	G	1125	S	A	3879
Rockford College, Rockford, IL 61101	1847	C/Ind	1600	75%	G	57	S		3490
Rockhurst College, Kansas City, MO 64110	1910	C/Cath	1315	73%	G	111	U		3000
Rockmont College, Denver, CO 80226	1914	C/Ind	311	61%		25	S		2312
Rocky Mountain College, Billings, MT 59102	1878	C/Prot	503	25%		56	S		2490
Roger Williams College, Bristol, RI 02809	1948	C/Ind	2000	15%		211	T		3460
Rollins College, Winter Park, FL 32789	1885	C/Ind	1350	30%	G	97	T		4350
Roosevelt University, Chicago, IL 60605	1945	C/Ind	4152	90%	G	505	U	-	3105
Rosary College, River Forest, IL 60305	1848	C/Cath	924	94%	G	136	S		3400
Rose-Hulman Institute of Technology, Terre Haute, IN 47803	1874	M/Ind	1221	61%	G	101	T	A	3600
Rosemont College, Rosemont, PA 19010	1921	W/Cath	585	40%		75	S		3800
Russell Sage College, Troy, NY 12180	1916	W/Ind	1400	62%	G	130	U		4100
Rust College, Holly Springs, MS 38635	1866	C/Prot	734	76%		40	R	A	2125
Rutgers U, Camden Coll of Arts and Sciences, Camden, NJ 08102	1950	C/Pub	3220	98%		167	U		940x
Rutgers University, College of Engineering, New Brunswick, NJ 08903	1864	C/Pub	2307	91%		98	S	A,AF	940
Rutgers University, College of Nursing, Newark, NJ 07102	1956	W/Pub	564	98%		47	U		940
Rutgers University, Cook College, New Brunswick, NJ 08903	1973	C/Pub	2943	90%		144	S	A,AF	940
Rutgers University, Douglass College, New Brunswick, NJ 08903	1918	W/Pub	3718	95%		266	S	A,AF	940
Rutgers U, Livingston College, New Brunswick, NJ 08903	1969	C/Pub	3717	90%		242	S	A,AF	940
Rutgers U, Mason Gross School of the Arts, New Brunswick, NJ 08903	1976	C/Pub	*	100%	G	16	S	A,AF	940
Rutgers U, Newark Coll of Arts and Sciences, Newark, NJ 07102	1892	C/Pub	4085	98%	•	254	U		940x
Rutgers University, Rutgers College, New Brunswick, NJ 08903	1766	C/Pub	8389	92%		578	S	A,AF	940
Sacred Heart College, Belmont, NC 28012	1892	W/Cath	475	76%		45	T	A	2354
Sacred Heart Seminary, Detroit, MI 48206	1919	M/Cath	50	100%		23	U		1150x
Sacred Heart University, Bridgeport, CT 06606	1963	C/Cath	1180	99%	· G	168	S		2600x
Saginaw Valley State College, University Center, MI 48710	1963	C/Pub	3275	99%	G	213	S		840x
St Alphonsus College, Suffield, CT 06078	1963	M/Cath	55	92%		23	S		2700
St Ambrose College, Davenport, IA 52803	1882	C/Cath	1818	70%	G	126	U		3300
St Andrews Presbyterian College, Laurinburg, NC 28352	1958	C/Prot	601	52%		60	T		2850
St Anselm's College, Manchester, NH 03102	1889	C/Cath	1923	99%		145	S	A,AF	3600
Saint Augustine's College, Raleigh, NC 27611	1867	C/Prot	1709	61%		81	U	A	1550
St Bonaventure University, St Bonaventure, NY 14778	1854	C/Cath	2333	79%	G	181	R	A	3150
St Charles Borromeo Seminary, Philadelphia, PA 19151	1832	M/Cath	70	90%	G	*	S		1820x
St Cloud State University, St Cloud, MN 56301	1869	C/Pub	9970	98%	G	692	U	A	547
St Edward's University, Austin, TX 78704	1881	C/Cath	1893	80%	G	101	U		2428
Saint Francis College, Fort Wayne, IN 46808	1890	C/Cath	872	75%	G	85	S	A	2176
St Francis College, Brooklyn, NY 11201	1858	C/Cath	3356	97%		203	U	-	2480
Saint Francis College, Loretto, PA 15940	1847	C/Cath	1226	56%	G	89	R		2976
Saint Francis de Sales College, Milwaukee, WI 53207	1856	M/Cath	55	84%		24	S		1400
St Hyacinth College and Seminary, Granby, MA 01033	1927	M/Cath	51	30%		24	T		900
St John Fisher College, Rochester, NY 14618	1948	C/Ind	3007	53%		139	S		3753
St John's College, Camarillo, CA 93010	1927	M/Cath	112	95%		22	U		1750x
St John's College, Annapolis, MD 21404	1696	C/Ind	350	20%		56	T		5400
St John's College, Santa Fe, NM 87501	1964	C/Ind	270	5%	G	35	T		5400
Saint John's University, Collegeville, MN 56321	1857	M/Cath	1860	74%	G	146	R	A	3475
St John's University, Jamaica, NY 11439	1870	C/Cath	11,194	92%	G	824	U	A	2900x
St John Vianney College Seminary, Miami, FL 33165	1959	M/Cath	70	65%		22	U		2075x
Saint Joseph College, West Hartford, CT 06117	1932	W/Cath	771	74%	G	108	S		3100
Saint Joseph's College, Rensselaer, IN 47978	1889	C/Cath	1030	46%	G	75	T		2950
St Joseph's College, North Windham, ME 04062	1915	C/Cath	500	44%		54	R		2800
St Joseph's College, Brooklyn, NY 11205	1916	C/Ind	388	98%		70	U		2400x
St Joseph's Coll, Suffolk Campus, Patchogue, NY 11772	1916	C/Cath	500	100%		54	S		2400x
Saint Joseph Seminary College, St Benedict, LA 70457	1891	M/Cath	110	85%		30	T		1650
Saint Joseph's University, Philadelphia, PA 19131	1851	C/Cath	2220	70%	G	173	U	AF	3250
St Lawrence University, Canton, NY 13617	1856	C/Ind	2440	49%	G	175	T	A	4995
Saint Leo College, Saint Leo, FL 33574	1889	C/Cath	1053	50%		64	R	A	2670
Saint Louis Conservatory of Music, St Louis, MO 63130	1974	C/Ind	68	52%	G	44	U		3000x
Saint Louis University, St Louis, MO 63103	1818	C/Cath	6863	60%	G	2237	U	AF	3700
Saint Martin's College, Olympia, WA 98503	1895	C/Cath	515	77%		60	S		3422
Saint Mary College, Leavenworth, KS 66048	1923	W/Cath	798	74%		73	T		2400
Saint Mary of the Plains College, Dodge City, KS 67801	1952	C/Cath	616	60%		46	R		2550
Saint Mary-of-the-Woods College, St Mary-of-the-Woods, IN 47876	1846	W/Cath	625	44%		77	T		3145
Saint Mary's College, Notre Dame, IN 46556	1844	W/Cath	1817	16%		164	S		3950
Saint Mary's College, Orchard Lake, MI 48034	1885	C/Cath	225	85%		40	S		1800
Saint Mary's College, Winona, MN 55987	1912	C/Cath	1250	30%	G	95	T		3379
Saint Mary's College of California, Moraga, CA 94575	1863	C/Cath	1545	80%	G	137	S		3922
St Mary's College of Maryland, St Mary's City, MD 20686	1839	C/Pub	1318	93%		91	R		675
St Mary's Dominican College, New Orleans, LA 70118	1860	W/Cath	805	83%		77	U		2900
St Mary's of the Barrens Sem Coll, Perryville, MO 63775	1818	M/Cath	56	*		15	T		2500
St Mary's University of San Antonio, San Antonio, TX 78284	1852	C/Cath	2236	77%	G	221	S	A	2496
Saint Meinrad College, St Meinrad, IN 47577	1861	M/Cath	210	20%		40	R		1956
Saint Michael's College, Winooski, VT 05404	1904	C/Cath	1575	12%	G	101	S	AF	3660
St Norbert College, De Pere, WI 54178	1898	C/Cath	1642	45%		105	S	A	3425
St Olaf College, Northfield, MN 55057	1874	C/Cath	2971	60%		250	T		3925
St Patrick's College, Mountain View, CA 94042	1898	M/Cath	52	84%		22	S		1800
St Paul Bible College, Bible College, MN 55375	1916	C/Prot	656	54%		42	R		1792
Saint Paul's College, Lawrenceville, VA 23868	1888	C/Prot	615	73%		41	T	A	2040
Saint Peter's College, Englewood Cliffs, NJ 07632	1975	C/Ind	*	*	G	*	S		2574
Saint Peter's College, Jersey City, NJ 07306	1872	C/Cath	2790	95%		315	U	A	3069x
St Thomas Aquinas College, Sparkill, NY 10976	1958	C/Ind	1300	80%		67	S		2375
Saint Vincent College, Latrobe, PA 15650	1846	M/Cath	896	86%		93	R		3410
Saint Xavier College, Chicago, IL 60655	1847	C/Cath	1900	96%	G	160	U	AF	3200

Name and Location	Est	Type/ Control	UG Enroll	% of State Res	Grad	Fac Size	Cmps	ROTC	Tuition
Salem College, Winston-Salem, NC 27108	1772	W/Prot	530	53%		66	U		$3400
Salem College, Salem, WV 26426	1888	C/Ind	1241	25%	G	92	R		2960
Salem State College, Salem, MA 01970	1854	C/Pub	5580	98%	G	297	S		600
Salisbury State College, Salisbury, MD 21801	1925	C/Pub	3644	86%	G	238	T	A	824
Samford University, Birmingham, AL 35209	1841	C/Prot	2860	67%	G	267	S	AF	2464
Sam Houston State University, Huntsville, TX 77340	1879	C/Pub	9326	96%	G	372	T	A	386
San Diego State University, San Diego, CA 92182	1897	C/Pub	24,787	96%	G	1935	U	A,AF	200
San Francisco Art Institute, San Francisco, CA 94133	1871	C/Ind	625	26%	G	63	U		3900x
San Francisco Conservatory of Music, San Francisco, CA 94122	1917	C/Ind	150	60%	G	*	U		4100x
San Francisco State University, San Francisco, CA 94132	1899	C/Pub	11,210	97%	G	1728	U	AF	284
Sangamon State University, Springfield, IL 62708	1969	C/Pub	1768	98%	G	211	R		596
San Jose Bible College, San Jose, CA 95108	1939	C/Prot	238	70%		21	U		1680
San Jose State University, San Jose, CA 95192	1857	C/Pub	21,426	90%	G	1685	U	A,AF	224
Sarah Lawrence College, Bronxville, NY 10708	1926	C/Ind	814	48%	G	126	S		6200
Savannah State College, Savannah, GA 31404	1890	C/Pub	2140	75%	G	150	U	N	608
School for International Training, Brattleboro, VT 05301	1962	C/Ind	48	2%	G	23	T		3968
School of the Art Inst of Chicago, Chicago, IL 60603	1866	C/Ind	934	75%	G	110	U		3180x
School of the Museum of Fine Arts, Boston, MA 02115	1948	C/Ind	*	*	G	*	U		3005
School of the Ozarks, Point Lookout, MO 65726	1906	C/Ind	1200	70%		82	T		2400
School of the Worcester Art Museum, Worcester, MA 01608	1898	C/Ind	112	95%		14	U		2575x
Scripps College, Claremont, CA 91711	1926	W/Ind	560	61%		68	S		5176
Seattle Pacific University, Seattle, WA 98119	1891	C/Prot	2185	64%	G	161	U		3525
Seattle University, Seattle, WA 98122	1891	C/Cath	2705	47%	G	276	U	A	3555
Seaver College, See Pepperdine University, Malibu									
Seton Hall University, South Orange, NJ 07079	1856	C/Cath	6555	90%	G	496	S	A	3270
Seton Hill College, Greensburg, PA 15601	1882	W/Cath	917	84%		97	T		3200
Shaw College at Detroit, Detroit, MI 48202	1936	C/Ind	603	99%		48	U		2700x
Shaw University, Raleigh, NC 27611	1865	C/Prot	1263	50%		83	U		1900
Sheldon Jackson College, Sitka, AK 99835	1878	C/Ind	170	85%		23	T		2500
Shenandoah Coll & Conserv of Music, Winchester, VA 22601	1875	C/Prot	875	55%	G	128	T		2700
Shepherd College, Shepherdstown, WV 25443	1871	C/Pub	2862	60%		136	T		370
Sherwood Music School, Chicago, IL 60605	1895	C/Ind	35	80%		24	U		2100x
Shimer College, Waukegan, IL 60085	1853	C/Ind	70	50%		14	U		3300
Shippensburg State College, Shippensburg, PA 17257	1871	C/Pub	4628	94%	G	304	T		1100
Shorter College, Rome, GA 30161	1873	C/Prot	840	78%		55	U		2150
Siena College, Loudonville, NY 12211	1938	C/Cath	3054	94%		180	S	A	3150
Siena Heights College, Adrian, MI 49221	1919	C/Cath	1039	87%	G	97	T		2520
Sierra Nevada College, Incline Village, NV 89450	1969	C/Ind	225	52%		30	R		2300x
Silver Lake College, Manitowoc, WI 54220	1869	C/Cath	320	98%		49	T		2900
Simmons College, Boston, MA 02115	1899	W/Ind	1797	51%	G	289	U		4928
Simon's Rock of Bard College, Great Barrington, MA 01230	1964	C/Ind	212	20%		34	T		5265
Simpson College, San Francisco, CA 94134	1921	C/Prot	220	60%	G	30	U		2000
Simpson College, Indianola, IA 50125	1860	C/Prot	850	75%		68	S		3985
Sinte Gleska College, Rosebud, SD 57570	1970	C/Pub	373	97%		110	R		396x
Sioux Falls College, Sioux Falls, SD 57101	1883	C/Prot	770	44%	G	52	U		2650
Skidmore College, Saratoga Springs, NY 12866	1922	C/Ind	2082	38%		185	T		5580
Slippery Rock State College, Slippery Rock, PA 16057	1889	C/Pub	5042	80%	G	350	R	AF	1100
Smith College, Northampton, MA 01063	1871	W/Ind	2651	23%	G	328	T		5900
Sonoma State University, Rohnert Park, CA 94928	1960	C/Pub	3982	97%	G	360	R		194
Southampton College, See Long Island U, Southampton College									
South Carolina State College, Orangeburg, SC 29117	1896	C/Pub	3201	97%	G	250	T	A	150
South Dakota School of Mines & Tech, Rapid City, SD 57701	1885	C/Pub	1552	80%	G	109	U	A	763
South Dakota State University, Brookings, SD 57007	1881	C/Pub	5992	88%	G	348	R	A,AF	624
Southeastern Baptist College, Laurel, MS 39440	1955	C/Prot	58	75%		12	U		720
Southeastern Bible College, Birmingham, AL 35205	1935	C/Ind	243	50%	G	26	U		1120
Southeastern College of the Assemblies of God, Lakeland, FL 33801	1935	C/Prot	1232	29%		50	S	A	1344
Southeastern Louisiana University, Hammond, LA 70402	1925	C/Pub	6346	95%	G	294	T	A	618
Southeastern Massachusetts University, North Dartmouth, MA 02747	1895	C/Pub	5063	96%	G	352	S		664
Southeastern Oklahoma State U, Durant, OK 74701	1909	C/Pub	3972	85%	G	180	T		448
Southeastern University, Washington, DC 20024	1879	C/Ind	650	66%	G	150	U		30
Southeast Missouri State University, Cape Girardeau, MO 63701	1873	C/Pub	7893	95%	G	432	T	AF	360
Southern Arkansas University, Magnolia, AR 71753	1909	C/Pub	1825	75%	G	112	T	A	600
Southern California College, Costa Mesa, CA 92626	1920	C/Prot	670	80%		62	S		2290
Southern Connecticut State College, New Haven, CT 06515	1893	C/Pub	6620	94%	G	639	U		768
Southern Illinois U at Carbondale, Carbondale, IL 62901	1869	C/Pub	18,836	89%	G	3304	R	A,AF	622
Southern Illinois U at Edwardsville, Edwardsville, IL 62026	1958	C/Pub	7895	90%	G	614	R	AF	615
Southern Methodist University, Dallas, TX 75275	1911	C/Prot	5802	45%	G	589	S		3840
Southern Missionary College, Collegedale, TN 37315	1892	C/Prot	2033	24%		130	T		3390
Southern Oregon State College, Ashland, OR 97520	1926	C/Pub	4177	90%	G	240	T		300
Southern Technical Institute, Marietta, GA 30060	1948	C/Pub	2380	85%		120	S	A	508.50
Southern U and A&M Coll, Baton Rouge, LA 70813	1880	C/Pub	7231	81%	G	486	S	A,N	450
Southern University in New Orleans, New Orleans, LA 70126	1959	C/Pub	2700	99%		111	U		494x
Southern Utah State College, Cedar City, UT 84720	1897	C/Pub	2048	81%		113	T		462
Southern Vermont College, Bennington, VT 05201	1926	C/Ind	364	39%		32	T		2550
Southwest Baptist College, Bolivar, MO 65613	1878	C/Prot	1383	75%		92	T		2250
Southwestern Assemblies of God Coll, Waxahachie, TX 75165	1927	C/Prot	809	44%		31	T		960
Southwestern at Memphis, Memphis, TN 38112	1848	C/Prot	1024	49%		104	U		4000
Southwestern Baptist Bible College, Phoenix, AZ 85032	1960	C/Prot	215	60%		21	S		1600
Southwestern College, Winfield, KS 67156	1885	C/Prot	656	74%		44	T		2400
Southwestern Oklahoma State U, Weatherford, OK 73096	1903	C/Pub	4143	87%	G	226	T	A	500
Southwestern Union College, Keene, TX 76059	1893	C/Prot	717	59%		70	T		3648
Southwestern University, Georgetown, TX 78626	1840	C/Pub	1001	92%		77	T		2500
Southwest Missouri State University, Springfield, MO 65802	1906	C/Pub	12,624	96%	G	640	S	A	420
Southwest State University, Marshall, MN 56258	1963	C/Pub	2040	79%		105	R		650
Southwest Texas State University, San Marcos, TX 78666	1899	C/Pub	14,018	98%	G	668	T	AF	120
Spalding College, Louisville, KY 40203	1920	C/Ind	664	88%	G	96	U		2400
Spelman College, Atlanta, GA 30314	1881	W/Ind	1257	29%		122	U		2350
Spertus College of Judaica, Chicago, IL 60605	1925	C/Jewish	337	95%		23	U		2700x

Name and Location	Est	Type/Control	UG Enroll	% of State Res	Grad	Fac Size	Cmps	ROTC	Tuition
Spring Arbor College, Spring Arbor, MI 49283	1873	C/Prot	847	87%		70	R		$3600
Springfield College, Springfield, MA 01109	1885	C/Ind	2146	38%	G	175	S		3360
Spring Garden College, Chestnut Hill, PA 19118	1851	C/Ind	1103	70%		80	S		3156x
Spring Hill College, Mobile, AL 36608	1830	C/Cath	904	32%		80	S	A	3300
Stanford University, Stanford, CA 94305	1891	C/Ind	6638	52%	G	1205	S		6285
State U of NY at Albany, Albany, NY 12222	1844	C/Pub	10,730	99%	G	840	S		900
State U of NY at Binghamton, Binghamton, NY 13901	1950	C/Pub	8100	97%	G	556	S		925
State U of NY at Buffalo, Buffalo, NY 14260	1846	C/Pub	16,960	95%	G	1917	S		900
State U of NY at Stony Brook, Stony Brook, NY 11794	1957	C/Pub	11,000	99%	G	1000	S		900
State U of NY at Stony Brook Health Sci Ctr, Stony Brook, NY 11794	1970	C/Pub	•	•	G	•	•		850
State U of NY College at Brockport, Brockport, NY 14420	1867	C/Pub	8201	99%	G	560	T		900
State U of NY College at Buffalo, Buffalo, NY 14222	1871	C/Pub	9291	98%	G	556	U		900
State U of NY College at Cortland, Cortland, NY 13045	1868	C/Pub	5274	98%	G	338	T		900
State U of NY College at Fredonia, Fredonia, NY 14063	1867	C/Pub	4776	97%	G	252	T	A	900
State U of NY College at Geneseo, Geneseo, NY 14454	1867	C/Pub	4886	99%	G	316	T		900
State U of NY College at New Paltz, New Paltz, NY 12561	1885	C/Pub	4980	95%	G	350	R		900
State U of NY College at Old Westbury, Old Westbury, NY 11568	1968	C/Pub	2854	96%		141	S		900
State U of NY College at Oneonta, Oneonta, NY 13820	1889	C/Pub	5702	98%	G	373	T		900
State U of NY College at Oswego, Oswego, NY 13126	1861	C/Pub	6500	90%	G	390	T	A	900
State U of NY College at Plattsburgh, Plattsburgh, NY 12901	1889	C/Pub	5183	98%	G	345	T		900
State U of NY College at Potsdam, Potsdam, NY 13676	1816	C/Pub	3927	98%	G	316	T		900
State U of NY College at Purchase, Purchase, NY 10577	1972	C/Pub	2100	75%		189	S		900
State U of NY Coll of Envr Sci & For, Syracuse, NY 13210	1911	C/Pub	1284	85%	G	125	U		900
SUNY College of Tech at Utica/Rome, Utica, NY 13502	1966	C/Pub	2600	98%	G	181	U		900x
State U of NY Health Science Ctr at Buffalo, Buffalo, NY 14214	1846	C/Pub	•	•	G	•	•		809
State U of NY Maritime College, Bronx, NY 10465	1874	C/Pub	970	80%	G	70	S	N	900
Steed College, Johnson City, TN 37601	1940	C/Ind	1150	85%		35	S		1440x
Stephen F Austin State University, Nacogdoches, TX 75961	1923	C/Pub	9200	97%	G	450	T	A	120
Stephens College, Columbia, MO 65215	1833	W/Ind	1402	23%		148	T		3800
Sterling College, Sterling, KS 67579	1887	C/Prot	534	45%		50	T		2770
Stern College for Women, New York, NY 10033	1886	W/Ind	523	34%		347	U		3550
Stetson University, Deland, FL 32720	1883	C/Ind	1950	60%	G	138	S	A	3345
Stevens Institute of Technology, Hoboken, NJ 07030	1870	C/Ind	1476	68%	G	230	U	AF	4800
Stillman College, Tuscaloosa, AL 35401	1876	C/Prot	645	69%		42	T	A	2972
Stockton State College, Pomona, NJ 08240	1971	C/Pub	4699	95%		213	R		736
Stonehill College, North Easton, MA 02356	1948	C/Cath	1687	60%		111	R	A	3725
Strayer College, Washington, DC 20005	1904	C/Ind	1807	55%		102	U		2160x
Suffolk University, Boston, MA 02114	1906	C/Ind	1954	98%	G	277	U		2900x
Sul Ross State University, Alpine, TX 79830	1917	C/Pub	1574	•	G	79	T		128
Susquehanna University, Selinsgrove, PA 17870	1858	C/Prot	1478	46%		126	T		4066
Swain School of Design, New Bedford, MA 02740	1881	C/Ind	167	71%		17	S		3150x
Swarthmore College, Swarthmore, PA 19081	1864	C/Ind	1280	25%		145	S		5400
Sweet Briar College, Sweet Briar, VA 24595	1901	W/Ind	685	19%		84	R		5200
Syracuse University, Syracuse, NY 13210	1870	C/Ind	11,044	50%	G	1233	U	A,AF	4950
Syracuse University, Utica College, Utica, NY 13502	1946	C/Ind	1312	84%		161	S		3940
Tabor College, Hillsboro, KS 67063	1908	C/Prot	434	58%		55	T		2416
Talladega College, Talladega, AL 35160	1867	C/Ind	647	50%		56	T		1740x
Tampa College, Tampa, FL 33607	1890	C/Ind	1413	90%		65	U		1620x
Tarkio College, Tarkio, MO 64491	1883	C/Prot	585	35%		35	R		2825
Tarleton State University, Stephenville, TX 76402	1899	C/Pub	2631	74%	G	156	T	A	128
Taylor University, Upland, IN 46989	1846	C/Ind	1540	30%		97	R		3618
Temple University, Philadelphia, PA 19122	1884	C/Pub	17,444	91%	G	2527	U	A	1810
Temple University, Ambler Campus, Ambler, PA 19002	1958	C/Pub	2455	95%		206	S	A	2086
Temple U Health Sciences Ctr, Philadelphia, PA 19140	1884	C/Pub	•	•		•	U		1300
Tennessee State University, Nashville, TN 37203	1909	C/Pub	8438	75%	G	517	U	AF	504
Tennessee Technological University, Cookeville, TN 38501	1915	C/Pub	5912	94%	G	376	T	A	483
Tennessee Wesleyan College, Athens, TN 37303	1857	C/Prot	453	78%		38	T		2160
Texas A&I University at Kingsville, Kingsville, TX 78363	1925	C/Pub	5004	90%	G	253	T	A	363
Texas A&M University, College Station, TX 77843	1876	C/Pub	25,947	89%	G	1879	T	A,N,AF	120
Texas Christian University, Fort Worth, TX 76129	1873	C/Prot	4493	70%	G	420	S	A,AF	3200
Texas College, Tyler, TX 75701	1894	C/Prot	531	57%		49	U	A	1800
Texas Lutheran College, Seguin, TX 78155	1891	C/Prot	1029	81%		77	T	A	2410
Texas Southern University, Houston, TX 77004	1947	C/Pub	7010	73%	G	499	U		120
Texas Tech University, Lubbock, TX 79409	1923	C/Pub	19,444	85%	G	864	U	A	120
Texas Wesleyan College, Fort Worth, TX 76105	1891	C/Prot	1555	91%	G	124	U		2300
Texas Woman's University, Denton, TX 76204	1901	W/Pub	4146	84%	G	554	T	AF	120
Thiel College, Greenville, PA 16125	1866	C/Prot	1042	77%		81	T		3793
Thomas College, Waterville, ME 04901	1894	C/Ind	962	72%		45	T		3560
Thomas Jefferson University, Philadelphia, PA 19107	1969	C/Ind	482	70%		55	U		4400
Thomas More College, Fort Mitchell, KY 41017	1921	C/Cath	1270	65%		130	S		2304
Tiffin University, Tiffin, OH 44883	1918	C/Ind	395	97%		20	T		1980
Tift College, Forsyth, GA 31029	1849	W/Prot	489	70%		43	T		1599
Toccoa Falls College, Toccoa Falls, GA 30577	1907	C/Ind	582	19%		38	T		1900
Tougaloo College, Tougaloo, MS 39174	1869	C/Prot	1031	73%		86	S	A	1930
Touro College, New York, NY 10036	1971	C/Ind	1957	85%		253	U		3105
Towson State University, Baltimore, MD 21204	1866	C/Pub	13,499	96%	G	926	U		620
Transylvania University, Lexington, KY 40508	1780	C/Ind	810	75%		84	U		4000
Trenton State College, Trenton, NJ 08625	1855	C/Pub	7500	97%	G	500	S		690
Trevecca Nazarene College, Nashville, TN 37210	1901	C/Prot	1225	65%		75	U		2265
Trinity Christian College, Palos Heights, IL 60463	1959	C/Prot	383	85%		53	S		2950
Trinity College, Hartford, CT 06106	1823	C/Ind	1840	22%		167	U		5350
Trinity College, Washington, DC 20017	1897	W/Cath	600	6%	G	103	S		4050
Trinity College, Deerfield, IL 60015	1897	C/Prot	780	64%		64	S		3410
Trinity College, Burlington, VT 05401	1925	W/Cath	648	75%		52	T		3150
Trinity University, San Antonio, TX 78284	1869	C/Prot	2554	72%	G	290	U	A	3000
Tri-State University, Angola, IN 46703	1884	C/Ind	1298	39%		80	T		3015
Troy State University, Troy, AL 36081	1887	C/Pub	5394	95%	G	579	T	AF	630
Troy State U at Fort Rucker/Dothan, Dothan, AL 36301	1962	C/Pub	926	100%	G	71	U		630x

Name and Location	Est	Type/ Control	UG Enroll	% of State Res	Grad	Fac Size	Cmps	ROTC	Tuition
Troy State U at Montgomery, Montgomery, AL 36104	1965	C/Pub	1700	100%		154	U	AF	$630x
Tufts University, Medford, MA 02155	1852	C/Ind	4576	33%	G	448	S		5850
Tulane University, New Orleans, LA 70118	1834	C/Ind	5000	22%	G	804	U	A,N,AF	4500
Tulane University, Newcomb College, New Orleans, LA 70118	1886	W/Ind	1629	26%		133	U	A,N,AF	3940
Tusculum College, Greeneville, TN 37743	1794	C/Prot	378	36%		32	U		2700
Tuskegee Institute, Tuskegee, AL 36088	1881	C/Ind	2978	36%	G	289	T	A,AF	2000
Union College, Barbourville, KY 40906	1879	C/Ind	660	72%	G	46	T	A	2700
Union College, Lincoln, NE 68506	1891	C/Ind	909	25%		100	S		3454
Union College, Schenectady, NY 12308	1795	C/Ind	2062	71%	G	183	S		5520
Union for Experimenting Colleges and Universities, Cincinnati, OH 45201	1964	C/Ind	196	100%	G	37	U		2800x
Union University, Jackson, TN 38301	1825	C/Prot	1217	85%		76	T		1900
United States Air Force Academy, USAF Academy, CO 80840	1954	C/Pub	4400	5%		550	R		0x
United States Coast Guard Academy, New London, CT 06320	1876	C/Pub	831	7%		120	S		0x
U S International U, San Diego Campus, San Diego, CA 92131	1952	C/Ind	1565	52%	G	166	S		3690
United States Merchant Marine Academy, Kings Point, NY 10024	1936	C/Pub	1100	23%		80	S		0x
United States Military Academy, West Point, NY 10996	1802	C/Pub	4400	12%		639	T		0x
United States Naval Academy, Annapolis, MD 21402	1845	M/Pub	4300	2%		540	T		0x
United Wesleyan College, Allentown, PA 18103	1921	C/Prot	206	49%		19	U		2150
Unity College, Unity, ME 04988	1966	C/Ind	427	18%		40	R		3450
University of Akron, Akron, OH 44304	1870	C/Pub	19,090	98%	G	1875	U	A,AF	790
University of Alabama, University, AL 35486	1831	C/Pub	13,776	82%	G	952	T	A,AF	770
University of Alabama in Birmingham, Birmingham, AL 35294	1966	C/Pub	9794	94%	G	1472	U	A	891
University of Alabama in Huntsville, Huntsville, AL 35899	1950	C/Pub	4114	95%	G	294	S	A	768
University of Alaska, Anchorage, Anchorage, AK 99504	1970	C/Pub	3009	93%	G	174	U		177x
University of Alaska, Fairbanks, Fairbanks, AK 99701	1915	C/Pub	3153	80%	G	395	T	A	410
University of Alaska, Juneau, Juneau, AK 99803	1972	C/Pub	1700	98%	G	117	T		410
University of Albuquerque, Albuquerque, NM 87140	1920	C/Cath	2084	70%		148	S	N,AF	2640
University of Arizona, Tucson, AZ 85721	1885	C/Pub	24,155	74%	G	1689	U	A,AF	600
University of Arkansas, Fayetteville, AR 72701	1871	C/Pub	12,645	85%	G	750	T	A,AF	600
University of Arkansas at Little Rock, Little Rock, AR 72204	1927	C/Pub	8982	96%	G	450	U		600
University of Arkansas at Monticello, Monticello, AR 71655	1909	C/Pub	1800	89%		101	T		600
University of Arkansas at Pine Bluff, Pine Bluff, AR 71601	1873	C/Pub	2999	90%		174	U	A	600
University of Baltimore, Baltimore, MD 21201	1925	C/Pub	3087	94%	G	253	U		800x
University of Bridgeport, Bridgeport, CT 06602	1927	C/Ind	4837	69%	G	528	U	A	4500
University of California, Berkeley, Berkeley, CA 94720	1868	C/Pub	19,850	95%	G	3163	U	A,N,AF	730
University of California, Davis, Davis, CA 95616	1906	C/Pub	12,974	88%	G	1409	T	A	713
University of California, Irvine, Irvine, CA 92664	1960	C/Pub	7689	96%	G	731	S		768
University of California, Los Angeles, Los Angeles, CA 90024	1919	C/Pub	21,082	93%	G	2800	U	A,N,AF	759
University of California, Riverside, Riverside, CA 92521	1954	C/Pub	3199	97%	G	456	S	A	774
University of California, San Diego, La Jolla, CA 92093	1959	C/Pub	8818	90%	G	820	S		741x
U of Calif, Santa Barbara, Santa Barbara, CA 93106	1891	C/Pub	12,623	92%	G	890	S	A	860
University of California, Santa Cruz, Santa Cruz, CA 95064	1965	C/Pub	5695	90%	G	500	T		831
University of Central Arkansas, Conway, AR 72032	1907	C/Pub	4921	96%	G	311	T	A	600
University of Central Florida, Orlando, FL 32816	1963	C/Pub	9929	94%	G	455	S	A,AF	675
University of Charleston, Charleston, WV 25304	1888	C/Ind	1507	78%		101	U		2050
University of Chicago, Chicago, IL 60637	1890	C/Ind	2670	36%	G	1040	U		5100
University of Cincinnati, Cincinnati, OH 45221	1819	C/Pub	32,836	86%	G	2215	U	A,AF	1005
U of Cincinnati Ohio Coll of App Sci, Cincinnati, OH 45210	1870	C/Pub	818	*		*	U		780
U of Colorado at Boulder, Boulder, CO 80309	1876	C/Pub	17,965	66%	G	1162	S	A,N,AF	762
U of Colorado at Colorado Sprgs, Colorado Springs, CO 80907	1965	C/Pub	3263	90%	G	215	S	A	526x
U of Colorado at Denver, Denver, CO 80220	1912	C/Pub	5371	91%	G	507	U	A	522x
University of Connecticut, Stamford, CT 06903	1969	C/Pub	*	*	G	*	*		540
University of Connecticut, Storrs, CT 06268	1881	C/Pub	15,131	90%	G	1600	R	A,AF	1068
University of Dallas, Irving, TX 75061	1956	C/Cath	1111	49%	G	132	S		2730
University of Dayton, Dayton, OH 45469	1850	C/Cath	6158	59%	G	619	S	A	2874
University of Delaware, Newark, DE 19711	1743	C/Pub	13,525	52%	G	1025	T	A	940
University of Denver, Denver, CO 80208	1864	C/Ind	4522	39%	G	487	S		4530
University of Detroit, Detroit, MI 48221	1877	C/Cath	6005	80%	G	551	U	A	3840
University of Dubuque, Dubuque, IA 52001	1852	C/Prot	1034	60%		75	S	A	3100
University of Evansville, Evansville, IN 47702	1854	C/Prot	4206	75%	G	278	S		3249
University of Florida, Gainesville, FL 32611	1853	C/Pub	25,989	93%	G	2802	S	A,N,AF	450
University of Georgia, Athens, GA 30602	1785	C/Pub	17,730	82%	G	1916	T	A,AF	708
University of Guam, Agana, GU 96910	1952	C/Pub	2912	90%	G	236	R	A	360
University of Hartford, West Hartford, CT 06117	1877	C/Ind	7012	70%	G	707	S		4050
U of Hawaii at Hilo, Hilo, HI 96720	1970	C/Pub	2976	87%		212	T		150
University of Hawaii at Manoa, Honolulu, HI 96822	1907	C/Pub	15,173	87%	G	1581	U	A,AF	450
University of Houston, Houston, TX 77004	1927	C/Pub	21,665	87%	G	1863	U	A,N	354
U of Houston at Clear Lake City, Houston, TX 77058	1971	C/Pub	2036	93%	G	226	S		96x
U of Houston, Downtown Campus, Houston, TX 77002	1974	C/Pub	4612	87%		200	U		120x
University of Houston, Victoria Campus, Victoria, TX 77901	1973	C/Pub	300	99%	G	58	U		100x
University of Idaho, Moscow, ID 83843	1889	C/Pub	6662	83%	G	532	T	A,N	474
U of Illinois at Chicago Circle, Chicago, IL 60680	1946	C/Pub	17,036	*	G	1233	U	A	681x
U of Illinois at Urbana-Champaign, Urbana, IL 61801	1868	C/Pub	26,127	97%	G	2771	U	A,N,AF	682
University of Iowa, Iowa City, IA 52242	1847	C/Pub	15,449	79%	G	1555	T	A,AF	830
University of Judaism, Los Angeles, CA 90024	1947	C/Jewish	108	80%	G	50	U		2000x
University of Kansas, Lawrence, KS 66045	1865	C/Pub	16,898	74%	G	1027	T	A,N,AF	720
University of Kentucky, Lexington, KY 40506	1865	C/Pub	17,694	89%	G	1900	U	A,AF	682
University of La Verne, La Verne, CA 91750	1891	C/Ind	1557	98%	G	184	T		3900
University of Louisville, Louisville, KY 40208	1798	C/Pub	13,931	92%	G	2173	U	AF	670
University of Lowell, Lowell, MA 01854	1894	C/Pub	6866	93%	G	842	U	AF	700
University of Maine at Farmington, Farmington, ME 04938	1863	C/Pub	1590	85%		100	T	A	960
University of Maine at Fort Kent, Fort Kent, ME 04743	1878	C/Pub	325	63%		26	T		930
University of Maine at Machias, Machias, ME 04654	1909	C/Pub	698	80%		42	T		770
University of Maine at Orono, Orono, ME 04469	1865	C/Pub	10,566	77%	G	694	T	A	1080
University of Maine at Presque Isle, Presque Isle, ME 04769	1902	C/Pub	1027	88%		86	R		770
University of Mary Hardin-Baylor, Belton, TX 76513	1845	C/Prot	1050	81%		74	S	AF	*x
U of Maryland at College Park, College Park, MD 20742	1859	C/Pub	29,835	81%	G	2018	S	AF	884

Name and Location	Est	Type/Control	UG Enroll	% of State Res	Grad	Fac Size	Cmps	ROTC	Tuition
University of Maryland, Baltimore, Baltimore, MD 21201	1807	C/Pub	1341	94%	G	1092	U		$705
U of Maryland Baltimore County, Catonsville, MD 21228	1966	C/Pub	5000	96%	G	330	S		1165
U of Maryland Eastern Shore, Princess Anne, MD 21853	1886	C/Pub	1069	63%	G	89	R		500
U of Massachusetts at Amherst, Amherst, MA 01003	1863	C/Pub	18,481	88%	G	1465	T	A,AF	750
U of Massachusetts at Boston, Boston, MA 02125	1965	C/Pub	7848	96%	G	594	U		750x
University of Miami, Coral Gables, FL 33124	1925	C/Ind	10,325	45%	G	1398	U	A,AF	4340
University of Michigan, Ann Arbor, MI 48109	1817	C/Pub	22,057	78%	G	2828	T	A,N,AF	1297
University of Michigan—Dearborn, Dearborn, MI 48128	1959	C/Pub	5913	99%	G	311	U		964
University of Michigan—Flint, Flint, MI 48503	1956	C/Pub	4054	99%	G	194	U		882x
University of Minnesota, Duluth, Duluth, MN 55812	1948	C/Pub	6507	87%	G	426	U	AF	918
U of Minnesota, Minneapolis-St Paul, Minneapolis, MN 55455	1851	C/Pub	31,404	88%	G	4419	U	A,N,AF	1135
University of Minnesota, Morris, Morris, MN 56267	1959	C/Pub	1450	95%		132	T		930
University of Mississippi, University, MS 38677	1844	C/Pub	7865	74%	G	574	T	A,N,AF	807
University of Missouri -Columbia, Columbia, MO 65211	1839	C/Pub	17,497	89%	G	1610	T	A,N,AF	822
University of Missouri -Kansas City, Kansas City, MO 64111	1933	C/Pub	6453	88%	G	1448	U		856
University of Missouri -Rolla, Rolla, MO 65401	1870	C/Pub	5117	84%	G	325	T	A	898
University of Missouri -St Louis, St Louis, MO 63121	1963	C/Pub	9409	98%	G	432	U		774x
University of Montana, Missoula, MT 59812	1893	C/Pub	6972	72%	G	447	T	A	625
University of Montevallo, Montevallo, AL 35115	1896	C/Pub	2526	90%	G	175	T		644
University of Nebraska-Lincoln, Lincoln, NE 68588	1869	C/Pub	19,903	93%	G	1259	U	A,N,AF	720
University of Nebraska at Omaha, Omaha, NE 68182	1968	C/Pub	12,815	94%	G	548	U	AF	860x
University of Nevada, Las Vegas, NV 89154	1957	C/Pub	6223	80%	G	380	U	A	720
University of Nevada, Reno, NV 89557	1874	C/Pub	5890	83%	G	398	U	A	368
University of New England, Biddeford, ME 04005	1939	C/Cath	406	18%	G	47	T		3600
University of New Hampshire, Durham, NH 03824	1866	C/Pub	8887	65%	G	625	T	A,AF	1150
University of New Haven, West Haven, CT 06516	1920	C/Ind	2399	75%	G	475	U		3496
University of New Mexico, Albuquerque, NM 87131	1889	C/Pub	17,980	92%	G	1265	U	N,AF	666
University of New Orleans, New Orleans, LA 70122	1958	C/Pub	12,452	96%	G	529	U	A,AF	524
University of North Alabama, Florence, AL 35630	1872	C/Pub	4592	88%	G	241	U	A	680
U of North Carolina at Asheville, Asheville, NC 28804	1927	C/Pub	1446	95%		106	S		270
U of North Carolina at Chapel Hill, Chapel Hill, NC 27514	1795	C/Pub	14,661	87%	G	1745	T	N,AF	364
U of North Carolina at Charlotte, Charlotte, NC 28223	1946	C/Pub	7703	91%	G	628	U		310
U of North Carolina at Greensboro, Greensboro, NC 27412	1891	C/Pub	7082	88%	G	637	U		364
U of North Carolina at Wilmington, Wilmington, NC 28401	1947	C/Pub	4132	94%	G	250	S		270
University of North Dakota, Grand Forks, ND 58201	1883	C/Pub	7729	80%	G	*	R		660
University of Northern Colorado, Greeley, CO 80639	1889	C/Pub	8500	80%	G	680	T	AF	606
University of Northern Iowa, Cedar Falls, IA 50613	1876	C/Pub	9169	97%	G	637	T		774
University of North Florida, Jacksonville, FL 32216	1965	C/Pub	3671	99%	G	155	S	A	742x
University of Notre Dame, Notre Dame, IN 46556	1842	C/Cath	6900	8%	G	798	U	A,N,AF	4700
University of Oklahoma, Norman, OK 73019	1890	C/Pub	16,252	85%	G	756	U	A,N,AF	488
University of Oregon, Eugene, OR 97403	1876	C/Pub	12,534	76%	G	1287	U	A	900
U of Oregon Health Sciences Center, Portland, OR 97201	1932	C/Pub	*		G	*	U		570
University of Pennsylvania, Philadelphia, PA 19104	1740	C/Ind	8730	28%	G	2500	U	A,N	6000
University of Pittsburgh, Pittsburgh, PA 15261	1787	C/Pub	17,815	95%	G	2267	U	A,AF	1590
University of Pittsburgh at Bradford, Bradford, PA 16701	1963	C/Pub	1100	93%		45	R	A,AF	1450
University of Pittsburgh at Johnstown, Johnstown, PA 15904	1927	C/Pub	3000	90%		161	S		1690
University of Portland, Portland, OR 97203	1901	C/Cath	2165	40%	G	175	U	AF	3300
U of PR, Cayey University Coll, Cayey, PR 00633	1966	C/Pub	2695	100%		139	U	A	170x
U of PR, Mayaguez, Mayaguez, PR 00708	1911	C/Pub	8081	98%	G	553	U	A,AF	120x
U of PR, Medical Science Cmps, San Juan, PR 00905	1950	C/Pub	*		G	*	*		*
U of PR, Rio Piedras, Rio Piedras, PR 00931	1903	C/Pub	20,819	*	G	1102	U	A,AF	200x
University of Puget Sound, Tacoma, WA 98416	1888	C/Prot	2744	52%	G	206	U	AF	4280
University of Redlands, Redlands, CA 92373	1909	C/Ind	1124	69%	G	174	T		5000
University of Rhode Island, Kingston, RI 02881	1892	C/Pub	9280	70%	G	830	T	A	3100
University of Richmond, University of Richmond, VA 23173	1830	C/Prot	2583	50%	G	318	S	A	4100
University of Rochester, Rochester, NY 14627	1850	C/Ind	4288	58%	G	1684	S	N	5300
University of St Thomas, Houston, TX 77006	1946	C/Cath	1637	90%	G	126	U		2250
University of San Diego, San Diego, CA 92110	1949	C/Cath	2636	65%	G	263	U		4050
University of San Francisco, San Francisco, CA 94117	1855	C/Cath	3272	63%	G	434	U	A	1925
University of Santa Clara, Santa Clara, CA 95053	1851	C/Cath	3600	78%	G	387	S	A	3990
U of Science and Arts of Oklahoma, Chickasha, OK 73018	1908	C/Pub	1289	90%		80	T		417
University of Scranton, Scranton, PA 18510	1888	C/Cath	3542	69%	G	227	U	A	2784
University of South Alabama, Mobile, AL 36688	1963	C/Pub	5996	75%	G	394	S	A	930
U of S Carolina at Columbia, Columbia, SC 29208	1801	C/Pub	18,636	84%	G	1456	U	N,AF	890
U of S Carolina at Spartanburg, Spartanburg, SC 29303	1967	C/Pub	2424	99%		176	U		710x
U of S Carolina, Coastal Carolina Coll, Conway, SC 29526	1959	C/Pub	1888	93%		136	R		710x
University of South Dakota, Vermillion, SD 57069	1862	C/Pub	4419	82%	G	399	T	A	624
University of South Dakota at Springfield, Springfield, SD 57062	1881	C/Pub	828	83%		64	T	A	686
University of Southern California, Los Angeles, CA 90007	1880	C/Ind	15,404	73%	G	2554	U	N,AF	5310
University of Southern Colorado, Pueblo, CO 81001	1933	C/Pub	4500	88%	G	230	S	A	720
U of Southern Maine, Gorham, ME 04038	1878	C/Pub	5084	89%	G	326	S	A	950
University of Southern Mississippi, Hattiesburg, MS 39401	1910	C/Pub	9560	88%	G	563	T	A,AF	776
U of South Florida, St Petersburg, FL 33701	1956	C/Pub	1700	94%	G	75	S		800
U of South Florida, Tampa, FL 33620	1956	C/Pub	17,214	91%	G	1059	S		690
University of South Florida, New College, Sarasota, FL 33580	1960	C/Pub	508	50%		*	S		800
University of Southwestern Louisiana, Lafayette, LA 70504	1898	C/Pub	12,070	87%	G	600	U	AF	543
University of Steubenville, Steubenville, OH 43952	1946	C/Cath	900	45%		65	T		2860
University of Tampa, Tampa, FL 33606	1931	C/Ind	1845	25%	G	142	U	A	3716
U of Tennessee at Chattanooga, Chattanooga, TN 37403	1886	C/Pub	6050	88%	G	288	U	A	546
U of Tennessee at Knoxville, Knoxville, TN 37916	1794	C/Pub	22,592	88%	G	1650	U	A,AF	483
U of Tennessee at Martin, Martin, TN 38238	1927	C/Pub	4686	92%	G	231	T	A	600
University of Texas at Arlington, Arlington, TX 76019	1895	C/Pub	16,322	87%	G	885	S	A	120
University of Texas at Austin, Austin, TX 78712	1876	C/Pub	34,617	75%	G	2000	S	A,N,AF	520
U of Texas at El Paso, El Paso, TX 79968	1913	C/Pub	13,907	90%	G	665	U	A	360
U of Texas at San Antonio, San Antonio, TX 78285	1969	C/Pub	7689	98%	G	383	U	A	375x
University of Texas at Tyler, Tyler, TX 75701	1972	C/Pub	1242	98%	G	120	U		120x
U of Texas of the Permian Basin, Odessa, TX 79762	1970	C/Pub	887	95%	G	92	U		300
U of the District of Columbia, Washington, DC 20004	1966	C/Pub	14,434	91%	G	905	U	AF	165x

Name and Location	Est	Type/ Control	UG Enroll	% of State Res	Grad	Fac Size	Cmps	ROTC	Tuition
University of the Pacific, Stockton, CA 95211	1851	C/Ind	3654	70%	G	355	S		$5682
U of the Sacred Heart, Santurce, PR 00914	1935	C/Cath	6425	97%		275	U		1400
University of the South, Sewanee, TN 37375	1857	C/Prot	1000	22%	G	116	R		4480
University of Toledo, Toledo, OH 43606	1872	C/Pub	14,505	95%	G	1195	S	A	783
University of Tulsa, Tulsa, OK 74104	1894	C/Ind	4592	70%	G	409	U		2380
University of Utah, Salt Lake City, UT 84112	1850	C/Pub	17,446	86%	G	3564	U	A,N,AF	642
University of Vermont, Burlington, VT 05401	1791	C/Pub	7670	50%	G	990	S	A	1500
University of Virginia, Charlottesville, VA 22903	1819	C/Pub	10,838	64%	G	1579	S	A,N,AF	555
University of Washington, Seattle, WA 98195	1861	C/Pub	28,187	92%	G	2178	U	A,N,AF	687
University of West Florida, Pensacola, FL 32504	1963	C/Pub	4295	97%	G	342	S		743
University of West Los Angeles, Culver City, CA 90230	1966	C/Ind	45	95%		15	S		1755x
U of Wisconsin-Eau Claire, Eau Claire, WI 54701	1916	C/Pub	10,111	90%	G	516	U		830
U of Wisconsin-Green Bay, Green Bay, WI 54302	1968	C/Pub	3541	85%	G	166	U	A	810
U of Wisconsin-La Crosse, La Crosse, WI 54601	1909	C/Pub	7926	91%	G	777	U	A	955
U of Wisconsin-Madison, Madison, WI 53706	1849	C/Pub	26,428	82%	G	3400	U	A,N,AF	877
U of Wisconsin-Milwaukee, Milwaukee, WI 53201	1956	C/Pub	20,610	96%	G	1687	U	A	972
U of Wisconsin-Oshkosh, Oshkosh, WI 54901	1871	C/Pub	8500	97%	G	675	S	A	885
U of Wisconsin-Parkside, Kenosha, WI 53140	1965	C/Pub	5292	97%	G	280	S		865x
U of Wisconsin-Platteville, Platteville, WI 53818	1866	C/Pub	4510	89%	G	244	T	A	721
U of Wisconsin-River Falls, River Falls, WI 54022	1874	C/Pub	4733	61%	G	279	R		700
U of Wisconsin-Stevens Point, Stevens Point, WI 54481	1894	C/Pub	8363	91%	G	550	T	A	732
U of Wisconsin-Stout, Menomonie, WI 54751	1893	C/Pub	6528	70%	G	434	T		677
U of Wisconsin-Superior, Superior, WI 54880	1893	C/Pub	1706	71%	G	145	U	AF	885
U of Wisconsin-Whitewater, Whitewater, WI 53190	1868	C/Pub	7793	91%	G	626	T	A	920
University of Wyoming, Laramie, WY 82071	1886	C/Pub	7332	69%	G	868	T	A,AF	592
Upper Iowa University, Fayette, IA 52142	1850	C/Ind	580	70%		60	T	A	3250
Upsala College, East Orange, NJ 07019	1893	C/Prot	1801	85%	U	117	U		3794
Urbana College, Urbana, OH 43078	1850	C/Ind	750	95%		153	T		2631
Ursinus College, Collegeville, PA 19426	1869	C/Prot	1040	66%		91	T		4000
Ursuline College, Pepper Pike, OH 44124	1871	W/Cath	840	95%		70	S		2570
Utah State University, Logan, UT 84322	1888	C/Pub	7996	65%	G	1250	T	A	552
Utica College, See Syracuse University, Utica College									
Valdosta State College, Valdosta, GA 31601	1906	C/Pub	3903	87%	G	245	S	AF	579
Valley City State College, Valley City, ND 58072	1890	C/Pub	1145	93%		64	T	A	472
Valparaiso University, Valparaiso, IN 46383	1859	C/Prot	3678	29%	G	360	T		3600
Vanderbilt University, Nashville, TN 37212	1873	C/Ind	5860	21%	G	2021	U	A,N	4700
Vandercook College of Music, Chicago, IL 60616	1928	C/Ind	92	75%	G	19	U		2760
Vassar College, Poughkeepsie, NY 12601	1861	C/Ind	2295	41%	G	228	S		4525
Vennard College, University Park, IA 52595	1910	C/Ind	211	20%		19	T		1502
Vermont College, Montpelier, VT 05602	1834	W/Ind	447	50%		45	T	A,AF	*x
Vermont Institute of Community Involvement, South Burlington, VT 05401	1972	C/Ind	91	*		*	*		2127
Villa Maria College, Erie, PA 16505	1925	W/Cath	616	93%		76	S	A	3000
Villanova University, Villanova, PA 19085	1842	C/Cath	6000	44%	G	439	S	N	3900
Virginia Commonwealth University, Richmond, VA 23284	1838	C/Pub	10,407	93%	G	1727	U	A	820
Virginia Intermont College, Bristol, VA 24201	1884	C/Prot	631	38%		56	U		2750
Virginia Military Institute, Lexington, VA 24450	1839	M/Pub	1310	53%		98	T	A,N,AF	720
Virginia Polytechnic Inst & State U, Blacksburg, VA 24061	1872	C/Pub	17,847	80%	G	1743	T	A,AF	885
Virginia State College, Petersburg, VA 23803	1882	C/Pub	3998	78%	G	254	S	A	979
Virginia Union University, Richmond, VA 23220	1865	C/Ind	1112	58%	G	129	S		3610
Virginia Wesleyan College, Norfolk, VA 23502	1963	C/Prot	775	70%		55	S		3175
Viterbo College, La Crosse, WI 54601	1890	C/Cath	1012	80%		116	U		2970
Voorhees College, Denmark, SC 29042	1897	C/Prot	708	81%		49	T	A	2118
Wabash College, Crawfordsville, IN 47933	1832	M/Ind	803	80%		77	T		4100
Wadhams Hall Seminary-College, Ogdensburg, NY 13669	1924	M/Cath	63	87%		21	R		2000
Wagner College, Staten Island, NY 10301	1883	C/Prot	1947	80%	G	216	S		3828
Wake Forest University, Winston-Salem, NC 27109	1834	C/Prot	3160	47%	G	242	S	A	3600
Walla Walla College, College Place, WA 99324	1892	C/Prot	1813	40%	G	163	T		4125
Walsh College, North Canton, OH 44720	1958	C/Cath	690	90%		60	S		3000
Walsh Coll of Acc & Bus Admin, Troy, MI 48084	1922	C/Ind	1250	100%	G	75	S		1272x
Warner Pacific College, Portland, OR 97215	1937	C/Prot	409	49%	G	42	U	AF	2925
Warner Southern College, Lake Wales, FL 33853	1964	C/Prot	264	30%		39	S		2220
Warren Wilson College, Swannanoa, NC 28778	1893	C/Prot	527	30%		75	R		3000
Wartburg College, Waverly, IA 50677	1852	C/Prot	1086	65%		86	T		3500
Washburn University of Topeka, Topeka, KS 66621	1865	C/Pub	5049	97%	G	260	U	AF	720
Washington and Jefferson College, Washington, PA 15301	1781	C/Ind	1053	*		97	T	A	4508
Washington and Lee University, Lexington, VA 24450	1749	M/Ind	1364	25%		175	T	A	4050
Washington Bible College, Lanham, MD 20801	1938	C/Ind	506	45%	G	38	S		2016
Washington College, Chestertown, MD 21620	1782	C/Ind	783	44%	G	68	T		3350
Washington International College, Washington, DC 20005	1970	C/Ind	234	90%		*	U		2100x
Washington State University, Pullman, WA 99163	1892	C/Pub	13,751	84%	G	1064	R	A,AF	686
Washington University, St Louis, MO 63130	1853	C/Ind	5631	23%	G	2277	S	A,AF	5350
Wayland Baptist College, Plainview, TX 79072	1908	C/Prot	1268	87%	G	67	T		1700
Waynesburg College, Waynesburg, PA 15370	1849	C/Prot	820	70%		68	T	A	3700
Wayne State College, Wayne, NE 68787	1910	C/Pub	2143	85%	G	119	T		456
Wayne State University, Detroit, MI 48202	1868	C/Pub	23,883	99%	G	2200	U	A	1238
Webb Institute of Naval Architecture, Glen Cove, NY 11542	1889	M/Ind	78	39%		16	S		0
Weber State College, Ogden, UT 84408	1889	C/Pub	9568	93%	G	476	U	A,AF	588
Webster College, St Louis, MO 63119	1915	C/Ind	950	70%	G	621	S		3350
Wellesley College, Wellesley, MA 02181	1870	W/Ind	2147	26%		290	S		5400
Wells College, Aurora, NY 13026	1868	W/Ind	529	35%		54	T		5150
Wentworth Institute of Technology, Boston, MA 02115	1904	M/Ind	2300	75%		117	U		3050
Wesleyan College, Macon, GA 31297	1836	W/Prot	500	50%		61	S		3270
Wesleyan University, Middletown, CT 06457	1831	C/Ind	2400	20%	G	269	T		5600
Wesley College, Dover, DE 19901	1873	C/Prot	1345	95%		77	T		3500
Westbrook College, Portland, ME 04103	1831	C/Ind	500	58%		80	S		3825
West Chester State College, West Chester, PA 19380	1871	C/Pub	7016	89%	G	495	T	A	1100
West Coast University, Los Angeles, CA 90020	1909	C/Ind	734	80%	G	250	*		2820x

Name and Location	Est	Type/Control	UG Enroll	% of State Res	Grad	Fac Size	Cmps	ROTC	Tuition
Western Baptist College, Salem, OR 97302	1936	C/Prot	394	33%		28	T		$2790
Western Bible College, Morrison, CO 80465	1948	C/Ind	214	64%		14	S		1920
Western Carolina University, Cullowhee, NC 28723	1889	C/Pub	5350	91%	G	363	R	A	648
Western Connecticut State College, Danbury, CT 06810	1903	C/Pub	2732	90%	G	220	U		540
Western Illinois University, Macomb, IL 61455	1889	C/Pub	10,514	98%	G	741	T	A	606
Western Kentucky University, Bowling Green, KY 42101	1906	C/Pub	8984	84%	G	757	T	A	580
Western Maryland College, Westminster, MD 21157	1868	C/Ind	1359	70%	G	150	T	A	3875
Western Michigan University, Kalamazoo, MI 49008	1903	C/Pub	17,070	91%	G	1043	S	A	892
Western Montana College, Dillon, MT 59725	1893	C/Pub	679	90%	G	45	R	A	474
Western New England College, Springfield, MA 01119	1919	C/Ind	2634	64%	G	285	S	A	2850
Western New Mexico University, Silver City, NM 88061	1893	C/Pub	1463	91%	G	75	T		220
Western State College of Colorado, Gunnison, CO 81230	1911	C/Pub	2843	80%	·	165	R		500
Western States Chiropractic College, Portland, OR 97230	1907	C/Ind	431	*		*	U		0
Western Washington University, Bellingham, WA 98225	1893	C/Pub	8598	87%	G	498	T		618
Westfield State College, Westfield, MA 01085	1838	C/Pub	2862	97%	G	180	S		600
West Georgia College, Carrollton, GA 30118	1933	C/Pub	3808	96%	G	281	T	A	612
West Liberty State College, West Liberty, WV 26074	1837	C/Pub	2679	65%		162	R		390
Westmar College, Le Mars, IA 51031	1890	C/Pub	646	76%		50	T		3170
Westminster Choir College, Princeton, NJ 08540	1926	C/Ind	376	36%	G	65	T		4100
Westminster College, Fulton, MO 65251	1851	C/Ind	664	45%		57	T	A	3700
Westminster College, New Wilmington, PA 16142	1852	C/Prot	1540	72%	G	140	T		3620
Westminster College, Salt Lake City, UT 84105	1875	C/Ind	1129	65%	G	105	S	A,N,AF	2850
Westmont College, Santa Barbara, CA 93108	1940	C/Prot	1021	75%		93	S	A	4250
West Texas State University, Canyon, TX 79016	1909	C/Pub	5259	93%	G	363	T	A	382
West Virginia Institute of Technology, Montgomery, WV 25136	1895	C/Pub	3005	80%		185	T	A	372
West Virginia State College, Institute, WV 25112	1891	C/Pub	3905	90%	G	210	S	A	50
West Virginia University, Morgantown, WV 26506	1867	C/Pub	14,479	59%	G	2071	T	A,AF	80
West Virginia Wesleyan College, Buckhannon, WV 26201	1890	C/Prot	1780	32%	G	128	T		2950
Wheaton College, Wheaton, IL 60187	1860	C/Prot	2044	25%	G	184	S	A	3534
Wheaton College, Norton, MA 02766	1834	W/Ind	1227	33%		125	T		6100
Wheeling College, Wheeling, WV 26003	1954	C/Cath	1031	40%	G	72	S		3240
Wheelock College, Boston, MA 02215	1888	W/Ind	600	41%	G	93	U		4240
Whitman College, Walla Walla, WA 99362	1859	C/Ind	1110	51%		90	T		4510
Whittier College, Whittier, CA 90608	1901	C/Ind	1340	62%	G	105	S		4200
Whitworth College, Spokane, WA 99251	1890	C/Prot	1533	46%	G	144	S		3950
Wichita State University, Wichita, KS 67208	1895	C/Pub	12,700	93%	G	588	U	A	558
Widener University, Chester, PA 19013	1821	C/Ind	1954	75%	G	131	S	A	3760
Wilberforce University, Wilberforce, OH 45384	1856	C/Prot	1112	31%		66	R	A	2360
Wiley College, Marshall, TX 75670	1873	C/Prot	603	52%		47	T		2220
Wilkes College, Wilkes-Barre, PA 18703	1933	C/Ind	2050	80%	G	152	U	AF	3750
Willamette University, Salem, OR 97301	1842	C/Prot	1281	49%	G	153	T		4110
William Carey College, Hattiesburg, MS 39401	1906	C/Prot	1460	65%	G	110	T		1800
William Jewell College, Liberty, MO 64068	1849	C/Prot	1410	70%		127	S		2720
William Paterson College of New Jersey, Wayne, NJ 07470	1855	C/Pub	10,732	97%	G	601	S	AF	850
William Penn College, Oskaloosa, IA 52577	1873	C/Prot	617	65%		52	T		3890
Williams College, Williamstown, MA 01267	1793	C/Ind	1987	17%	G	209	T		5950
William Smith College, Geneva, NY 14456	1906	W/Ind	700	50%		126	T		5500
William Woods College, Fulton, MO 65251	1870	W/Ind	1000	39%		94	T		*x
Wilmington College, New Castle, DE 19720	1967	C/Ind	683	63%	G	67	S	A	1920x
Wilmington College, Wilmington, OH 45177	1870	C/Prot	750	65%		75	R		3105
Wilson College, Chambersburg, PA 17201	1869	W/Prot	221	37%		50	T		4050
Wingate College, Wingate, NC 28174	1895	C/Prot	1501	88%		73	T		1570
Winona State University, Winona, MN 55987	1858	C/Pub	4000	75%	G	240	T	A	585
Winston-Salem State University, Winston-Salem, NC 27102	1892	C/Pub	2224	91%		145	U	A	270
Winthrop College, Rock Hill, SC 29733	1886	C/Pub	3913	89%	G	261	U	A	903
Wisconsin Conservatory of Music, Milwaukee, WI 53202	1899	C/Ind	160	90%	G	54	U		2900x
Wittenberg University, Springfield, OH 45501	1845	C/Prot	2270	60%	G	174	S		4494
Wofford College, Spartanburg, SC 29301	1854	C/Prot	1078	74%		73	U	A	3275
Woodbury University, Los Angeles, CA 90017	1884	C/Ind	1243	35%	G	67	U		3100x
Worcester Polytechnic Institute, Worcester, MA 01609	1865	C/Ind	2388	49%	G	224	U	A,AF	4950
Worcester State College, Worcester, MA 01602	1874	C/Pub	3125	98%	G	204	U		600
World College West, San Rafael, CA 94902	1971	C/Ind	51	60%		36	S		2700
World University, Hato Rey, PR 00917	1965	C/Ind	4187	96%	G	194	U		1700
Wright State University, Dayton, OH 45435	1967	C/Pub	11,218	97%	G	885	S	A	1005
Wright State University, Piqua Center, Piqua, OH 45356	1968	C/Pub	*	*		28	T		816x
Xavier University, Cincinnati, OH 45207	1831	C/Cath	3144	80%	G	280	S	A	2990
Xavier University of Louisiana, New Orleans, LA 70125	1915	C/Cath	1797	80%	G	161	U	A	2350
Yale University, New Haven, CT 06520	1701	C/Ind	5170	11%	G	2005	U		5550
Yankton College, Yankton, SD 57078	1881	C/Prot	289	38%		44	T	A	2820
Yeshiva College, New York, NY 10033	1886	M/Ind	809	54%		253	U		3550
Yeshiva University, See Stern College for Women and Yeshiva College									
York College, See City U of NY, York College									
York College of Pennsylvania, York, PA 17405	1941	C/Ind	3536	74%	G	195	S	A	2248
Youngstown State University, Youngstown, OH 44555	1908	C/Pub	13,736	91%	G	799	U	A	915

LARGE U.S. UNIVERSITY LIBRARIES Source: Digest of Education Statistics, 1980

University	Number of Volumes	University	Number of Volumes
Harvard University	9,913,992	Ohio State University, Main Campus	3,446,729
Yale University	7,246,195	Princeton University	3,172,238
University of Illinois (Urbana Campus)	5,759,666	Duke University	3,022,839
University of California at Berkeley	5,597,154	University of Pennsylvania	2,889,788
University of Michigan, Ann Arbor	5,135,952	Northwestern University	2,714,938
Indiana University at Bloomington	5,029,534	New York University	2,700,201
Columbia University (Main Division)	4,924,469	Michigan State University	2,523,553
Stanford University	4,577,827	University of N. Carolina at Chapel Hill	2,487,122
University of Texas at Austin	4,406,113	University of Pittsburgh, Main Campus	2,375,542
Cornell University	4,207,146	University of Virginia, Main Campus	2,351,842
University of Chicago	4,182,938	Johns Hopkins University	2,287,058
University of California, L.A.	4,109,146	University of Iowa	2,216,970
University of Washington	3,788,788	University of Arizona	2,184,023
University of Minnesota, Minn.-St. Paul	3,702,599	Rutgers University	2,166,200
University of Wisconsin, Madison	3,475,184	Pennsylvania State University, Main Campus	2,092,139

THE REFERENCE SHELF

This list of reference books constitutes the nucleus of a reference shelf for small private, public, and organizational libraries.

Acronyms, Initialisms & Abbreviations Dictionary: Vol. 1; Vol. 2: New Acronyms, Initialisms, and Abbreviations, 1979 & 1980; Vol. 3: Reverse Acronyms, Initialisms, and Abbreviations Dictionary, Ed. Ellen T. Crowley (Gale Research Co., Vol. 1, 7th ed., 1980; Vol. 2, 6th ed., 1979; Vol. 3, 6th ed., 1978).

American Authors, 1600-1900, Ed. Stanley J. Kunitz and Howard Haycraft (H. W. Wilson, 1938).

American Heritage Dictionary of the English Language, Ed. William Morris (Houghton Mifflin Co., 1976).

American Men and Women of Science: The Physical and Biological Sciences, Ed. The Jaques Cattell Press, 14th ed., 7 vols. plus index vol. (R. R. Bowker Co., 1979).

American Men and Women of Science: The Social and Behavioral Sciences, Ed. The Jaques Cattell Press, 13th ed., 2 vols. (R. R. Bowker Co., 1978).

American Negro Reference Book, Ed. John P. Davis (Prentice-Hall, Inc., 1966).

American Universities and Colleges, Ed. W. Todd Furniss, 11th ed. (American Council on Education, 1973).

The Amy Vanderbilt Complete Book of Etiquette, rev. & expanded by Letitia Baldridge (Doubleday and Co., Inc., 1978).

Baby and Child Care, Benjamin Spock, new rev. ed. (Hawthorn Books, 1976).

Baker's Biographical Dictionary of Musicians, Theodore Baker, ed. Nicolas Slonimsky, 6th ed. (Schirmer Books, 1978).

Biographical Directory of the American Congress, 1774-1961, U.S. Congress (Government Printing Office, 1961).

Biographical Encyclopaedia and Who's Who of the American Theatre, Ed. Walter Rigdon (James H. Heineman Inc., Publishers, 1966).

Biography Index: A Cumulative Index to Biographical Materials in Books and Magazines, annual (H. W. Wilson, 1946).

Black's Law Dictionary, Henry C. Black, Ed. Joseph R. Nolan & Michael J. Connolly, 5th ed. (West Publishing Co., 1979).

The Book of the States, biennial, Ed. Paul Albright (The Council of State Governments, 1936).

Books in Print, annual, 2 vols. (R. R. Bowker Co., 1948).

Careful Writer: A Modern Guide to English Usage, Theodore M. Bernstein (Atheneum Pubs., 1965).

Chases' Calendar of Annual Events, annual, William D. Chase (Apple Tree Press, Inc., 1957; rev. ed., 1979).

Columbia Encyclopedia, Ed. William H. Harris and Judith S. Levy, 4th ed. (Columbia University Press, 1975).

Columbia-Lippincott Gazetteer of the World, Ed. Leon E. Seltzer (Columbia University Press, 1952).

Commercial Atlas and Marketing Guide, annual (Rand McNally & Co., 1870).

Concise Dictionary of American Biography, 3rd ed. (Charles Scribner's Sons, 1978).

Congress and the Nation, vol. 1, 1945-1964; vol. 2, 1965-1968, vol. 3, 1969-1972, vol. 4, 1972-1976 (Congressional Quarterly, Inc., 1965; 1969; 1973; 1977).

Congressional Directory, annual (Government Printing Office, 1935).

Contemporary Authors, semiannual, Ed. Frances C. Locher & Ann Evory, 96 vols. to date, vol 1-44 rev. ed.(Gale Research Co., 1962).

Current Biography Yearbook, annual (H. W. Wilson, 1946).

Demographic Yearbook, annual, Ed.United Nations Statistical Office (International Publications Service, 1949).

Dictionary of American Biography, Ed. American Council of Learned Societies, 16 vols. and supplements (Charles Scribner's Sons, 1927-80).

Dictionary of American History, Michael Martin & Leonard Gelber, Ed. Leo Lieberman, rev. & enlarged ed. (Littlefield, Adams, & Co., 1978).

Dictionary of Modern English Usage, Henry W. Fowler, 2nd ed., rev. by Sir Ernest Gowers (Oxford University Press, Inc., 1965).

Dictionary of Music and Musicians, George Grove, Ed. Eric Blom, 5th ed., 10 vols. (St. Martin's Press, Inc., 1954; supplement, 1961).

Dictionary of National Biography, George Smith, Ed. Leslie Stephen & Sir Sidney Lee, 22 vols. including 1st supplement, 7 supplements total, 7th suppl. Ed. E.T. Williams & Helen M. Palmer (Oxford University Press, Inc.; 22 vols. reprinted, 1938); abridged: **Concise Dictionary of National Biography,** 2 vols. (Oxford University Press, Inc., vol. 1, 1953; vol. 2, 1961).

Dictionary of Quotations, Bergen Evans (Delacorte Press, 1968).

Dictionary of the Social Sciences, Hugo F. Reading (Routledge & Kegan Paul, LTD, 1977).

Dictionary of Universal Biography, Albert M. Hyamson, 2nd rev. ed. (Routledge & Kegan Paul, LTD, 1976).

Directory of American Scholars, Ed. The Jaques Cattell Press, 7th ed., 4 vols. (R. R. Bowker, 1978).

Documents of American History, Ed. A. Commager, 9th ed., 2 vols. (Prentice-Hall, Inc., 1974).

Dorland's Illustrated Medical Dictionary, 25th ed. (W. B. Saunders Co., 1974).

Editor & Publisher International Yearbook, annual (Editor & Publisher, 1920).

Encyclopaedia Britannica, Latest ed. 1980, 30 vols. (Encyclopaedia Britannica, 1768).

Encyclopedia Americana, 30 vols. (Grolier Educational Corporation, 1981).

Encyclopedia of American Facts and Dates, Ed. Gorton Carruth et al., 7th rev. ed. (Thomas Y. Crowell Co., 1979).

Encyclopedia of American History, Ed. Richard B. Morris & Jeffrey B. Morris, 5th ed. (Harper & Row Publishers, Inc., 1976).

Encyclopedia of Associations, Ed. Denise Akey, 15th ed., 3 vols. (Gale Research Co., 1980).

Encyclopedia of Biological Sciences, Peter Gray, 2nd ed. (Van Nostrand Reinhold Co., 1970).

Encyclopedia of Chemistry, Ed. Clifford A. Hampel and Gessner G. Hawley, 3rd ed. (Van Nostrand Reinhold Co., 1973).

Encyclopedia of Philosophy, Ed. Paul Edwards, 4 vols. (The Free Press, 1973).

Encyclopedia of Physics, Ed. Robert M. Besancon, 2nd ed. (Van Nostrand Reinhold Co., 1974).

Encyclopedia of Sports, Frank G. Menke, 6th rev. ed. (A. S. Barnes & Co., Inc., 1978).

Encyclopedia of World Art, 15 vols. (McGraw-Hill Book Co., 1959-68).

Encyclopedia of World History, Ed. William L. Langer, 5th ed. (Houghton Mifflin Co., 1972).

Europa Year Book, annual 2 vols. (International Publications Service, 1959).

European Authors, 1000-1900, Ed. Stanley J. Kunitz and Vineta Colby (H. W. Wilson, 1967).

Facts about the Presidents, Joseph N. Kane, 3rd ed. (H. W. Wilson, 1974).

Facts on File, annual (Facts on File, Inc., 1940).

Familiar Quotations, John Bartlett, 15th ed., rev. and enl. (Citadel Press, 1971).

Famous First Facts, Joseph N. Kane, 3rd ed. (H. W. Wilson, 1964).

Foundation Directory, biannual, 8th ed. (The Foundation Center, 1981).

Future: A Guide to Information Sources, The, (World Future Society, 1977).

Granger's Index to Poetry, Edith Granger, Ed. William J. Smith, 6th ed. (Columbia University Press, 1973).

Guide to Reference Books, Ed. Eugene P. Sheehy, 9th ed. (American Library Association, 1976; 1st suppl., 1980).

Guinness Book of World Records, Ed. Norris McWhirter, rev. ed. (Sterling Publishing, Inc., 1980).

Hammond Medallion World Atlas (Hammond Inc., 1979).

Harper Bible Dictionary, Madeleine S. and John L. Miller, 8th ed. (Harper & Row Publishers, Inc., 1973).

Harper Encyclopedia of Science, Ed. James R. Newman, rev. ed. (Harper & Row Publishers, Inc., 1967).

Harvard Guide to American History, Ed. F. Freidel and R.K. Showman, rev. ed., 2 vols. (Harvard University Press, 1974).

Historical Statistics of the United States: 1790 to 1970, 2 vols. (University of Alabama Press, vol. 1, 1973; vol. 2, 1976).

Home Book of Quotations, Ed. Burton Stevenson, rev. ed. (Dodd, Mead & Co., 1967).

Home Book of Verse, Ed. Burton E. Stevenson, 10th ed., 2 vols. (Holt, Rinehart & Winston, 1953).

International Encyclopedia of the Social Sciences, Ed. David E. Sills, 17 vols. (Macmillan Publishing Co., Inc., 1968).

International Who's Who, annual (International Publications Service, 1935).

Keesing's Contemporary Archives, weekly (Keesing's, London, 1931).

Lincoln Library, see New Lincoln Library Encyclopedia

Literary Market Place, annual (R. R. Bowker Co., 1940)

McGraw-Hill Encyclopedia of Science and Technology, McGraw-Hill, 4th ed., 15 vols. (McGraw-Hill Book Co., 1977).

Macmillan Book of Proverbs, Ed. Burton Stevenson (Macmillan Publishing Co., Inc., 1965).

Manual of Style, Staff of the University of Chicago Press, rev. 12th ed. (University of Chicago Press, 1969).

Masterpieces of World Literature in Digest Form, Ed. Frank N. Magill, 4 vols. (Harper & Row Publishers, Inc., 1952-69).

Monthly Catalog of United States Government Publications, monthly (Government Printing Office, 1895).

Municipal Year Book, Ed. International City Management Association (National Association of Counties, 1979).

National Geographic Atlas of the World, Melville B. Grovenor, 4th ed. (National Geographic Society, 1975).

Negro Almanac, Harry A. Ploski and Warren Marr, rev. ed. (Bellwether Publishing Co., 1971).

New Catholic Encyclopedia, Editorial Staff at Catholic University of America, 17 vols. (McGraw-Hill Book Co., 1967).

New Century Cyclopedia of Names, ed. Clarence L. Barnhart and William D. Halsey, 3 vols. (Prentice-Hall, Inc., 1954).

New Emily Post's Etiquette, Emily Post, rev. by Elizabeth L. Post, 12th rev. ed. (Funk & Wagnalls Co., 1975).

New Encyclopedia of the Opera, David Ewen (Hill and Wang, Inc., 1971).

New Lincoln Library Encyclopedia, Ed by William H. Seibert, 40th ed., 3 vols. (Frontier Press Co., 1980).

New York Times Index, semimonthly and cumulated annually (The New York Times, 1851).

Oxford Classical Dictionary, Ed. N. G. Hammond and H. H. Scullard, 2nd ed. (Oxford University Press Inc., 1970).

Oxford Companion to American History, Thomas H. Johnson (Oxford University Press, Inc., 1966).

Oxford Companion to American Literature, James D. Hart, 4th ed. (Oxford University Press, Inc., 1965).

Oxford Companion to Classical Literature, Ed. Paul Harvey, 2nd ed. (Oxford University Press, Inc., 1937).

Oxford Companion to English Literature, Ed. Paul Harvey and Dorothy Eagle, 4th ed. (Oxford University Press, Inc., 1967).

Oxford Companion to Film, Ed. Liz-Anne Bawden (Oxford University Press, Inc., 1976).

Oxford Companion to the Theatre, Phyllis Hartnoll, 3rd ed. (Oxford University Press, Inc., 1967)

Oxford Dictionary of Quotations, 3rd ed. (Oxford University Press, Inc., 1979).

Oxford English Dictionary, Ed. James A. Murray et al., 13 vols. (Oxford University Press, Inc., 1933).

Peterson's Annual Guides to Graduate and Undergraduate Study, Ed. Karen C. Hegener, 14th ed., 6 vols. (Peterson's Guides Inc., 1979).

Political Handbook of the World: 1980, Ed. Arthur S. Banks, 6th ed. (McGraw-Hill Book Co., 1980).

Random House Dictionary of the English Language, Ed. Jess Stein (Random House, Inc., 1966).

Reader's Adviser, 12th ed., 3 vols. (R. R. Bowker Co., 1974-1977).

Reader's Encyclopedia, Ed. William R. Benet, 2nd ed. (Thomas Y. Crowell Co., 1965).

Reader's Guide to Periodical Literature, annual, 38 vols. (H. W. Wilson, 1900-79).

Roget's International Thesaurus, Peter M. Roget, 4th ed. (Thomas Y. Crowell Co., 1977).

Shepherd's Historical Atlas, William R. Shepherd, 9th rev. ed. (Barnes & Noble Books, 1976).

Statesman's Year-Book, annual, Ed. John Paxton (St. Martin's Press, Inc., 1864).

Statistical Abstract of the United States, annual (Government Printing Office, 1878).

Statistical Yearbook, annual (United Nations, 1949).

Stedman's Medical Dictionary, Thomas L. Stedman, 23rd ed. (The William & Wilkins Co., 1976).

Times Atlas of the World, comprehensive ed., London Times (Times Books, 1975).

Times Atlas of World History, Ed. Geoffrey Barraclough (London Times/Hammond Inc., 1979).

Timetables of History, Bernard Grun (Simon & Schuster, Inc., 1979).

Twentieth Century Authors, Ed. Stanley J. Kunitz and Howard Haycraft (H. W. Wilson, 1942; 1st supplement, 1955).

Ulrich's International Periodicals Directory, 18th ed. (R. R. Bowker Co., 1979).

United States Government Organization Manual, annual (Government Printing Office, 1935).

Universal Jewish Encyclopedia and Readers Guide, Ed. Isaac Landman, 11 vols. (Ktav Publishing House, Inc., 1944).

Van Nostrand's International Encyclopedia of Chemical Science (Van Nostrand Reinhold Co., 1964).

Van Nostrand's Scientific Encyclopedia, Ed. Douglas M. Considine, 5th ed. (Van Nostrand Reinhold Co., 1976).

Webster's New Geographical Dictionary, Merriam-Webster Editorial Staff, rev. ed. (G. & C. Merriam Co., 1977).

Webster's Third New International Dictionary of the English Language, unabridged, Ed. Merriam Co. (G. & C. Merriam Co., 1980).

What's What: A Visual Glossary of the Physical World, Ed. David Fisher and Reginald Bragonier, Jr. (Hammond Inc., 1981).

Who Was Who, 6 vols. (St. Martin's Press, Inc., 1897-1961).

Who Was Who in America, 7 vols. (Marquis Who's Who, Inc., 1897-1976).

Who Was Who in America, Historical Volume, 1607-1896 (Marquis Who's Who, Inc., 1963).

Who's Who, annual (St. Martin's Press, Inc., 1849).

Who's Who in America, biennial (Marquis Who's Who, Inc., 1899).

Who's Who in American Politics, 1978-1980, Ed. The Jaques Cattell Press, 7th ed. (R. R. Bowker Co., 1979).

Who's Who of American Women, 1979-1980, 11th ed. (Marquis Who's Who, Inc., 1979).

Worldmark Encyclopedia of the Nations, Ed. Moshe Y. Sachs, 5th ed., 5 vols. (John Wiley & Sons, Inc., 1976).

World of Learning, annual, 2 vols. (International Publications Service, 1947).

World Who's Who in Science, Ed. Allen G. Debus (Marquis Who's Who, Inc., 1968).

Yearbook of International Organizations, annual, Ed. Union of International Associations (International Publications Service, 1948).

Yearbook of the United Nations, annual (International Publications Service, 1946/47).

COMMUNICATIONS/LANGUAGE

CURRENT WORDS AND PHRASES

The following list of words and phrases consists of terms and meanings that have only recently made an appearance in English or of terms that have had some restricted usage over a period of time but are now acquiring widespread usage. Many of these words have passed the test of time and have already entered the dictionaries. Some will prove to be fleeting, and will remain only as a curious reminder of some passing vogue. The list was prepared by the staff of Laurence Urdang Inc.

ABSCAM acronym for **Arab Scam**, an undercover operation conducted by the U.S. Department of Justice in which federal agents, posing as wealthy Arabs or their representatives, enticed government officials with offers of money in exchange for their favorable influence in a variety of schemes.

acid rain natural rainfall containing high concentrations of sulfuric and nitric acids, resulting from the ejection into the atmosphere of sulfur dioxide from the industrial burning of high-sulfur fuels and of nitrogen oxide from auto exhaust emissions. These compounds mix with water vapor and fall to earth as rain, often many miles from their source, raising the acid content of lakes and rivers to a level that is lethal to fish and other marine life. Compare **acid smog.**

acid smog smog containing high concentrations of sulfur and nitrogen oxides which, when combined with the moisture in the air, produce sulfuric and nitric acids. Acid smog differs from acid rain in that it does not fall to the ground as precipitation but is deposited in a more or less dry state, damaging structural materials, plastics and rubber, and plant life. Also called **acid dust.** Compare **acid rain.**

Agent Orange a herbicide used as a defoliant in the Vietnam War, held by some to cause birth defects and cancer.

Airbus a trade name for a wide-bodied airplane used chiefly as a domestic passenger carrier.

almost-developed country one of the more populous Third-World nations capable of supplying the workers for labor-intensive manufacturing developed by technologically advanced nations. Abbreviation: **ADC.**

appropriate technology technology that is focused on such ecological practices as conservation of natural resources, protection of the environment, and other activities characterized by low cost, use of local materials, low maintenance, etc.

angel dust Slang. phencyclidine, an addictive, halucinatory, narcotic drug. Also called **PCP.**

Ayatollah an honorary Islamic title, equivalent to "Your holiness," bestowed on a select few teachers with recognized followings. [Literally, 'reflection of God.']

bioclock n. Informal. biological clock.

biological clock the normal circadian rhythm of waking and sleeping within a given time zone as reflected by the habits of an individual.

bird n. Slang. any satellite.

blood reinfusion. See **reinfusion.** Also, Informal. **blood doping.**

brown goods Informal. scotch and bourbon. Compare **white goods.**

chop shop Slang. a place where stolen cars are stripped of their parts, which are then sold as replacements in the repair of other cars.

chronopharmacology n. the study of how the effectiveness of drugs is influenced by the time of the day, month, or year when they are administered.

chronotherapy n. a form of therapy in which the time during which a patient sleeps and remains awake is gradually shifted to adjust for jet-lag, a change in work shift, etc.

closet n. used attributively. secret; clandestine: a closet homosexual; a closet novelist.

CPR abbreviation of **cardiopulmonary resuscitation.** A method for administering first aid to a victim of a heart attack, esp. as taught to laymen.

devastator bullet a bullet with a slug that explodes upon impact.

dimethyl sulfoxide a pharmaceutical being tested as a broad-spectrum analgesic. Abbreviation: **DMSO.**

DMSO abbreviation for **dimethyl sulfoxide.**

downlink n. Informal. an earth station for receiving signals from a geostationary satellite. Compare **uplink.**

eco-fiction [short for ecological fiction] a fictional work in which a main theme is the participation of the characters in ecological activities, as the preservation of natural resources, protection of the environment, etc.

Electronic Mail Service a proposed system for the rapid transmittal of mail in which businesses transmit a letter or document electronically to specially equipped post offices near the intended destination; the message is then transcribed onto paper, placed in an envelope, and delivered to the addressee along with the regular mail.

endorphin n. one of a group of chemicals, naturally produced in the human body and present in the brain, that act as pain suppressors.

enterprise zone a blighted area of a city selected for rehabilitation in order to create jobs and business investment, esp. in economically depressed sections of the country.

eyeflick n. an instant; a twinkling of an eye.

folio show a theatrical production made up of a variety of sources and not having a plot or book.

footprint n. Informal. an area on the surface of the earth where the signal from a geostationary satellite can be received.

freebase n. a highly concentrated white lump of cocaine, prepared by boiling off the liquid from a solution of drug in an alkaline.—vb. to prepare or use cocaine in this form.

gasohol a mixture of 10% alcohol and 90% unleaded gasoline, slightly more expensive than premium unleaded gasoline, said to increase mileage per gallon of cars by 5%, used to reduce consumption of gasoline in internal combustion engines.

geostationary adj. (of an artificial satellite) orbiting around the earth at such velocity that it remains fixed at the zenith over a particular point on the equator of the earth.

GPM abbreviation for **graduated payment mortgage.** Also Informal. **Jeep.**

gridlock a deadlock in which the streets of a city become so congested with cars that it becomes impossible for traffic to move in any direction.

HBO abbreviation for **Home Box Office,** a subsidiary of Time, Inc. that broadcasts television programs over a channel that is scrambled for all viewers except subscribers with cable TV who pay an extra fee.

hearing dog a dog trained to alert its deaf master to a sound like that of an alarm, telephone, doorbell, etc.

Heimlich maneuver a technique for preventing someone from choking on food by applying pressure at specific places on the body.

Home Box Office. See **HBO.**

HVR abbreviation for **home video recorder,** a device by which television programs can be recorded on videotape for playback at another time. Also called **VCR.**

in-kind tax the payment of the tax on one's property by exchange of services.

innumerate *adj.* incapable of dealing with or understanding arithmetic, numerical relationships, etc. [Origin: modeled on *illiterate*.]

ion deposition imaging a technique for reproducing digitized images from a projection cartridge onto a dielectric drum that transfers character images in a dot matrix on a surface. A toner, which adheres only to the sensitized areas, is then fused to the surface under pressure. Compare **laser xerography.**

Jeep. See **GPM.**

laser xerography a technique in which images are projected on a light-sensitive drum and then onto paper to create an electrostatic field. Toner of opposite charge, when sprinkled on the paper, clings to the charged image areas, which are fixed under heat or pressure or both. Compare **ion deposition imaging.**

laxman *n. Informal.* a member of a lacrosse team.

mcte abbreviation for **million tons of coal equivalent** (used as a measure of saving of fossil fuels).

meltdown 1. physical disintegration of the core of a nuclear reactor 2. *Figurative.* any internal disintegration, as of the directorship of a company, etc.

MFT abbreviation for **made for television.** See **vidpic.**

microsurgery *n.* a combination of surgical techniques used in the reattachment of severed limbs and other body parts. See also **replantation.**

MIS abbreviation for **manager of information services.**

mole *Informal.* an espionage agent who has infiltrated the spy network of another country.

Moral Majority an ultra-conservative, U.S. political organization made up of traditionally nonpolitical, fundamentalist Christians, led by the evangelist, Rev. Jerry Falwell. Its program, which is based on scripture and stands for God, country, and home, supports voluntary prayer in schools, free enterprise, and a strong America and opposes abortion, ERA, gay rights, drugs, pornography, Salt II, and reduction in defense spending.

mortgage out *Informal.* to take out a second mortgage on one's home in order to acquire equity in cash that can be spent for a child's education, investment in a business, etc.

mutagenicity *n.* the ability of a substance, esp. a chemical, to create genetic change and, consequently, to act as a carcinogenic.

narrowcast *vb.* to broadcast special-interest television programs, esp. via subscriber cable, to children, Spanish Americans, sports enthusiasts, etc.

ob/gyn (pronounced oh-bee, gee-why-en) the fields of *obstetrics* and *gynecology*, considered as a unit for some applications, as in clinical treatment.

Pinyin a system for transcribing Chinese into the Roman alphabet, in official use in China for communication with other countries and recently adopted by the United Nations, the U.S. Board on Geographic Names, and many Western newspapers, magazines, etc. It is considered a more accurate transcription of the sounds of Chinese than the Wade-Giles system, developed in the mid-19th century, which it replaces.

piperack *n. used attributively.* unadorned; produced with a low budget; lacking in decorative amenities: *piperack news broadcasts.* [Originally applied to stores equipped with "plain piperacks" instead of expensive fixtures for displaying men's clothing sold at reduced prices.]

preppy *n.* 1. a student at a preparatory school. 2. noting a fashion, esp. in clothing but to some extent in behavior as well, whose devotees exhibit an affection for traditional garb.

ragtop *n. Slang.* a convertible car with a cloth top that can be folded down.

Raku *n.* a technique for firing and glazing pottery, developed by and named for a 16th-century Japanese family.

rehab *n.* a rehabilitated building.—*vb.* to rehabilitate (a building).—**rehabber,** *n.*

reinfusion *n.* a technique of withdrawing some of an athlete's blood and reinfusing it into the body at a later date to improve athletic performance. Also called **blood reinfusion,** *Informal.* **blood doping.**

replantation *n.* the reattachment of severed limbs and other body parts by microsurgical techniques.

seismic gap an area of seismic inactivity around which earthquakes of high magnitude have taken place within 30 years.

shield law a law, within a state of the U.S., intended to protect the confidentiality of the notes and sources of a journalist.

shopping-bag lady a female derelict who carries all her worldly possessions about in one or more paper shopping bags.

slimnastics a system of calisthenics for those who wish to lose weight. [from *slim* and *gymnastics*.]

smart *adj.* (of an electronically controlled device) capable of simulating human judgments to a greater or lesser degree.

snurf *vb.* to balance oneself on a four-foot by seven-inch board while coasting down a snow-covered slope.

soft not involved in or directly to those functions of a business requiring expenditure unavoidable in producing a profit, as public relations, public affairs, and advertising staffs.

SPF abbreviation for **sun protection factor,** a numerical scale from 2 to 23 indicating the extent to which a substance can provide protection from the sun. A factor of 2 means twice as long as with no protection; a factor of 23 signifies a complete blockage.

Sunbelt a section of the United States in the southerly part, including Virginia, North Carolina, South Carolina, Georgia, Florida, Alabama, Louisiana, Tennessee, Mississippi, Arkansas, Oklahoma, Texas, New Mexico, Arizona, and southern California.

sun protection factor. See **SPF.**

sunrise law legislation that requires a governmental agency to describe in advance its goals for every new program and to provide for periodic reviews to determine whether those goals have been accomplished.

sunset law legislation that requires a governmental agency to justify its existence periodically.

superstation *n.* a local television station that transmits its signal to a geostationary satellite whence it can be received by receiving stations situated wthin the footprint of the satellite. See also **footprint.**

taggant *n.* a substance added to commercially produced chemical explosives in order to enable its identification as to source, date of manufacture, etc.

taphonomy *n.* the study of fossils, sediments, and other paleontological evidence in an effort to reconstruct the natural history and ecology of the past. — **taphonomist,** *n.*

text-fiche *n.* the publication of a book with an accompanying microfiche on which illustrative matter is,reproduced for use as an adjunct to the text.

t-f abbreviation for **text-fiche.**

THC abbreviation for **tetrahydrocannabinol.**

tofu a high-protein, cholesterol-free food made by solidifying soy milk. Also called **bean curd, soy cheese.**

Universal Product Code a pattern of lines and numbers by which information about a product may be encoded for automatic scanning by a device at the checkout counter in a supermarket that records its price for charging the consumer as well as for its stock numbers, inventory, etc.

uplink *n. Informal.* an earth station for transmitting signals to a geostationary satellite. Compare **downlink.**

VCR abbreviation for **video cassette recorder.** Also called **HVR.**

videocassette recorder *n.* an HVR for recording a television program on a tape cassette.

videodisc *n.* a disc on which a visual scene has been recorded electronically for playback by a suitable device.

videotex, videotext *n.* a display of alphanumeric information on a television screen. Also called **viewdata.**

white goods *Informal.* gin and vodka. Compare **brown goods.**

workfare *n.* a system under which able-bodied recipients of welfare stipends are required to work to qualify for payments.

MOST COMMON AMERICAN SURNAMES

Source: U.S. Social Security Administration

This tabulation is based on the surnames that appear most frequently in social security records for the period of 1936 to 1973.

Rank	Surname	No. of Persons	Rank	Surname	No. of Persons	Rank	Surname	No. of Persons
1	Smith	2,382,509	21	Walker	486,498	41	Campbell	361,958
2	Johnson	1,807,263	22	Robins(on)	484,991	42	Gonzalex(ez)	360,994
3	Williams(on)	1,568,939	23	Peters(on)	479,249	43	Carter	349,950
4	Brown	1,362,910	24	Hall	471,479	44	Garcia	346,175
5	Jones	1,331,205	25	Allen	458,375	45	Evans	343,897
6	Miller	1,131,861	26	Young	455,416	46	Turner	329,752
7	Davis	1,047,848	27	Morris(on)	455,179	47	Stewart	329,581
8	Martin(ez), (son)	1,046,297	28	King	434,791	48	Collin(s)	324,680
9	Anders(on)	825,648	29	Wright	431,157	49	Parker	322,482
10	Wilson	787,825	30	Nelson	421-638	50	Edward	317,197
11	Harris(on)	754,083	31	Rodriguez	416,178	51	Murphy	311,337
12	Taylor	696,046	32	Hill	414,646	52	Cook	298,396
13	Moore	693,304	33	Baker	442,676	53	Rogers	298,288
14	Thomas	688,054	34	Richards(on)	409,262	54	Griffin, Griffith	291,862
15	White	636,185	35	Lee	409,068	55	Christian(son),	
16	Thompson	635,426	36	Scott	408,439		Christopher	281,525
17	Jackson	630,003	37	Green	406,989	56	Morgan	273,267
18	Clark	549,107	38	Adams	406,841	57	Cooper	269,560
19	Robert(s), (son)	524,688	39	Mitchell	371,434	58	Reed	267,589
20	Lewis	495,026	40	Phillips	362,013	59	Bell	267,026

MAJOR WORLD LANGUAGES

Source: Kenneth Katzner, author, The Languages of the World.

Language	Speakers*	Chief Location	Language	Speakers*	Chief Location	Language	Speakers*	Chief Location
Chinese	900	China	Nepali	10	Nepal	Lithuanian	2.5	USSR (Lithuania)
English	325	U.S., U.K., Canada, Ireland, Australia, New Zealand	Sinhalese	10	Sri Lanka	Moldavian	2.5	USSR (Moldavia)
			Fulani	10	West Africa	Turkmen	2.5	USSR (Turkmen SSR), Iran
			Assamese	9	India (Assam)			
Spanish	225	Spain, Latin America	Sindhi	9	Pakistan, India	Karen	2.5	Burma
Russian	200	USSR	Amharic	9	Ethiopia	Lao	2.5	Laos
Hindi	200	India	Swedish	8	Sweden	Buginese	2.5	Indonesia (Celebes)
Bengali	135	Bangladesh, India	Bulgarian	8	Bulgaria	Tigrinya	2.5	Ethiopia
Portuguese	130	Portugal, Brazil	Madurese	8	Indonesia (Java, Madura)	Tswana	2.5	South Africa, Botswana
Arabic	130	Middle East, North Africa				Makua	2.5	Mozambique
Japanese	115	Japan	Ibo	8	Nigeria	Kirgiz	2	USSR (Kirgiz SSR)
German	100	Germany, Austria, Switzerland	Galla	8	Ethiopia	Gilaki	2	Iran
			Belorussian	7	USSR (Belorussia)	Bhili	2	India
Indonesian	100	Indonesia	Kazakh	7	USSR (Kazakhstan)	Achinese	2	Indonesia (Sumatra)
French	75	France, Belgium, Switzerland, Canada	Berber	7	Morocco, Algeria	Balinese	2	Indonesia (Bali)
			Malagasy	7	Malagasy Republic	Bikol	2	Philippines (Luzon)
Punjabi	65	India (Punjab), Pakistan	Quechua	7	Peru, Bolivia	Kikuyu	2	Kenya
			Catalan	6	Spain, France, Andorra	Malinke	2	West Africa
Italian	60	Italy				Kanuri	2	Nigeria
Korean	55	Korea	Uighur	6	China, USSR	Guarani	2	Paraguay
Telugu	50	India (Andhra Pradesh)	Malay	6	Malaysia, Singapore	Slovenian	1.5	Yugoslavia
			Danish	5	Denmark	Latvian	1.5	USSR (Latvia)
Marathi	45	India (Maharashtra)	Finnish	5	Finland	Chuvash	1.5	USSR (Chuvash ASSR)
Tamil	45	India (Tamil Nadu) Sri Lanka	Flemish	5	Belgium	Mazanderani	1.5	Iran
			Tatar	5	USSR (Tatar ASSR)	Baluchi	1.5	Pakistan, Iran
Javanese	45	Indonesia (Java)	Kurdish	5	Iraq, Iran, Turkey, Syria, USSR	Gondi	1.5	Central India
Turkish	40	Turkey	Yi (Lolo)	5	China	Puyi	1.5	China
Urdu	40	Pakistan, India	Khmer	5	Cambodia	Shan	1.5	Burma
Vietnamese	40	Vietnam	Somali	5	Somalia, Ethiopia	Batak	1.5	Indonesia (Sumatra)
Polish	35	Poland	Ruanda	5	Rwanda, Zaire	Wolof	1.5	Senegal
Ukrainian	35	USSR (Ukraine)	Zulu	5	South Africa	Bambara	1.5	Mali
Thai	35	Thailand	Xhosa	5	South Africa	Ewe	1.5	Ghana, Togo
Persian	25	Iran, Afghanistan	Yiddish	4	U.S., USSR, Israel	Fang	1.5	Cameroon, Gabon
Gujarati	25	India (Gujarat)	Norwegian	4	Norway	Dinka	1.5	Sudan
Kanarese	25	India (Karnataka)	Slovak	4	Czechoslovakia	Lingala	1.5	Zaire, Congo
Malayalam	25	India (Kerala)	Armenian	4	USSR (Armenia)	Bemba	1.5	Zambia
Burmese	25	Burma	Mongolian	4	Mongolia, China	Tsonga	1.5	Mozambique
Tagalog	25	Philippines	Tibetan	4	Tibet	Aymara	1.5	Bolivia, Peru
Romanian	20	Romania	Miao	4	China	Breton	1	France (Brittany)
Bihari	20	India (Bihar)	Twi	4	Ghana	Macedonian	1	Yugoslavia
Oriya	20	India (Orissa)	Sidamo	4	Ethiopia	Estonian	1	USSR (Estonia)
Hausa	20	Nigeria, Niger	Rundi	4	Burundi	Mordvin	1	USSR (Mordovian ASSR)
Serbo-Croatian	15	Yugoslavia	Shona	4	Rhodesia			
			Nyanja	4	Malawi, Zambia	Bashkir	1	USSR (Bashkir ASSR)
Pushtu	15	Afghanistan, Pakistan	Sotho	4	South Africa, Lesotho	Tulu	1	India (Karnataka)
			Afrikaans	4	South Africa	Kurukh		
Rajasthani	15	India (Rajasthan)	Albanian	3	Albania	(Oraon)	1	Eastern India
Swahili	15	East Africa	Georgian	3	USSR (Georgia)	Tung	1	China
Dutch	13	Netherlands	Tadzhik	3	USSR (Tadzhikistan)	Yao	1	China
Sundanese	13	Indonesia (Java)	Hebrew	3	Israel	Mende	1	Sierra Leone
Hungarian	12	Hungary, Romania	Kashmiri	3	Kashmir	Fon	1	Benin
Uzbek	12	USSR (Uzbekistan)	Santali	3	Eastern India	Tiv	1	Nigeria
Chuang	12	China	Minangkabau	3	Indonesia (Sumatra)	Ibibio	1	Nigeria
Visayan	12	Philippines	Ilocano	3	Philippines (Luzon)	Luo	1	Kenya
Yoruba	12	Nigeria	Mossi	3	Upper Volta	Kamba	1	Kenya
Czech	10	Czechoslovakia	Ganda	3	Uganda	Sukuma	1	Tanzania
Greek	10	Greece	Luba	3	Zaire	Swazi	1	Swaziland, South Africa
Azerbaijani	10	USSR (Azerbaijan), Iran	Kongo	3	Zaire, Congo, Angola			
			Mbundu	3	Angola	Nahuatl	1	Mexico
			Mayan	3	Mexico, Guatemala			

* In millions of speakers.

LEADING AMERICAN MAGAZINES SOURCE:Magazine Publishers Association, Inc.

Based on average circulations per issue, 1st six months of 1980

Rank	Magazine*	Circulation	Rank	Magazine*	Circulation
1	TV Guide	18,870,730	26	Southern Living	1,812,834
2	Reader's Digest	18,193,255	27	Outdoor Life	1,714,138
3	National Geographic	10,560,885	28	Popular Mechanics	1,695,733
4	Better Homes & Gardens	8,057,386	29	V.F.W. Magazine	1,686,754
5	Woman's Day	7,574,478	30	Today's Education	1,674,413
6	Family Circle	7,366,482	31	Mechanix Illustrated	1,669,808
7	McCall's	6,256,183	32	Elks Magazine	1,648,809
8	Playboy	5,746,536	33	Hustler	1,641,080
9	Ladies' Home Journal	5,403,015	34	Globe	1,572,476
10	Good Housekeeping	5,138,948	35	Workbasket	1,561,727
11	National Enquirer	5,013,475	36	Boys' Life	1,537,601
12	Penthouse	4,502,810	37	Parents Magazine	1,489,507
13	Time	4,451,816	38	Changing Times	1,482,863
14	Redbook	4,234,141	39	Seventeen	1,455,561
15	Star, The	3,380,779	40	Life	1,410,273
16	Newsweek	2,952,515	41	Sunset	1,405,685
17	Cosmopolitan	2,812,507	42	True Story	1,369,634
18	American Legion	2,591,644	43	Farm Journal	1,276,443
19	Sports Illustrated	2,343,380	44	Nation's Business	1,272,173
20	People Weekly	2,308,635	45	Ebony	1,270,143
21	U.S. News & World Report	2,085,229	46	New Woman	1,253,868
22	Field & Stream	2,019,102	47	Sport	1,204,086
23	Popular Science	1,913,879	48	Psychology Today	1,171,362
24	Smithsonian	1,890,466	49	Bon Appetit	1,155,303
25	Glamour	1,846,691	50	1,001 Decorating Ideas	1,104,698

*Includes general and farm magazine members of the Audit Bureau of Circulations. Groups and comics not included.

U.S. ADVERTISING VOLUME SOURCE: Reprinted with permission from the January 5, 1981 issue of Advertising Age. Copyright 1981 by Crain Communications Inc.

Medium	1979 Millions	1979 % of total	1980 Millions	1980 % of total	% change
Newspapers					
Total	$14,493	29.3	$15,615	28.5	+ 7.7
National	2,085	4.2	2,335	4.3	+12.0
Local	12,408	25.1	13,280	24.2	+ 7.0
Magazines					
Total	2,932	5.9	3,225	5.9	+10.0
Weeklies	1,327	2.7	1,440	2.6	+ 8.5
Women's	730	1.5	795	1.5	+ 9.0
Monthlies	875	1.7	990	1.8	+13.0
Farm publications	120	0.3	135	0.3	+12.0
Television					
Total	10,154	20.5	11,330	20.7	+11.6
Network	4,599	9.3	5,105	9.3	+11.0
Spot	2,873	5.8	3,260	6.0	+13.5
Local	2,682	5.4	2,965	5.4	+10.5
Radio					
Total	3,277	6.6	3,690	6.7	+12.6
Network	161	0.3	185	0.3	+15.0
Spot	659	1.3	750	1.4	+14.0
Local	2,457	5.0	2,755	5.0	+12.0
Direct mail	6,653	13.4	7,655	14.0	+15.0
Business publications	1,575	3.2	1,695	3.1	+ 7.5
Outdoor					
Total	540	1.1	610	1.1	+12.8
National	355	0.7	400	0.7	+13.0
Local	185	0.4	210	0.4	+12.5
Miscellaneous					
Total	9,776	19.7	10,795	19.7	+10.5
National	5,063	10.2	5,690	10.4	+12.4
Local	4,713	9.5	5,105	9.3	+ 8.3
Total					
National	27,075	54.7	30,435	55.6	+12.4
Local	22,445	45.3	24,315	44.4	+ 8.3
U.S. Grand Total	49,520	100.0	54,750	100.0	+10.6

LARGEST U.S. SUNDAY NEWSPAPERS

Source: Audit Bureau of Circulations

Newspaper	Circulation*	Newspaper	Circulation*	Newspaper	Circulation*
New York News	1,995,702	Houston Chronicle	453,036	Washington Star	294,086
New York Times	1,479,263	St. Louis Post-Dispatch	436,298	Cincinnati Enquirer	293,710
Los Angeles Times	1,271,603	Portland Oregonian	420,688	Hartford Courant	290,167
Chicago Tribune	1,150,540	Houston Post	419,308	Memphis Commercial Appeal	281,978
Philadelphia Inquirer	851,376	Phoenix Republic†	411,156	Omaha World-Herald	281,041
Washington Post	845,176	Kansas City Star	404,424	Orange Co. (Calif.) Register	272,369
Detroit News	819,992	Des Moines Register	391,421	San Jose Mercury-News	269,351
Boston Globe	741,614	Baltimore Sun	375,644	Buffalo Courier Express	263,584
Detroit Free Press	737,119	Indianapolis Star†	363,201	Fort Worth Star-Telegram	256,660
Chicago Sun-Times	715,892	Denver Post	357,157	St. Paul Pioneer Press	251,320
San Francisco Examiner and		Seattle Times	344,724	Orlando Sentinel Star	248,282
Chronicle	665,887	Columbus Dispatch	343,721	Charlotte Observer	246,327
Pittsburgh Press	637,435	San Diego Union†	329,820	Boston Herald American	246,298
Minneapolis Tribune	587,255	Louisville Courier Journal	327,565	Tampa Tribune	246,271
Newark Star-Ledger†	585,174	New Orleans Times-Picayune/		Nashville Tennessean	244,204
Long Island Newsday	573,726	States-Item†	323,731	Sacramento Bee	238,854
Miami Herald	545,898	Denver Rocky Mountain News	306,627	Providence (R.I.) Journal	233,813
Milwaukee Journal	519,365	Oklahoma City		Rochester Democrat &	
Atlanta Journal & Const.	499,341	Sunday Oklahoman	304,552	Chronicle	233,343
Cleveland Plain Dealer	468,541	St. Petersburg Times	304,039	Syracuse Herald-American	233,220
Philadelphia Bulletin	466,409	Los Angeles Herald Examiner	303,724	Tulsa World†	222,755

*Averages for 6 months ending March 31, 1981. †Average for 3 months.

LARGEST U.S. DAILIES[1]

Source: Audit Bureau of Circulations

Newspaper	Circulation*	Newspaper	Circulation*	Newspaper	Circulation*
New York News	1,491,556	Milwaukee Journal	318,203	Omaha World-Herald[2]	229,044
Los Angeles Times	1,026,092	Cleveland Press	302,410	Indianapolis Star†	220,292
New York Times	930,546	Kansas City Times	297,406	Atlanta Constitution	215,684
Chicago Tribune	790,475	Denver Rocky Mountain News	288,410	Sacramento Bee	214,021
New York Post	732,158	Los Angeles Herald-Examiner	285,099	Hartford Courant	212,032
Chicago Sun-Times	661,531	New Orleans Times-Picayune/		Des Moines Register	210,465
Washington Post	618,111	States-Item‡	281,546	Boston Herald American	209,128
Detroit News	617,879	Denver Post	276,389	Orlando Sentinel Star	207,621
Detroit Free Press	613,311	Phoenix Republic†	272,173	San Diego Union‡	207,171
San Francisco Chronicle	515,453	Buffalo Evening News	268,928	Jacksonville Journal	203,251
Long Island Newsday	503,336	Pittsburgh Press	268,490	Columbus Dispatch	202,209
Boston Globe	502,920	Seattle Times	261,432	Tampa Tribune	198,489
Miami Herald	444,860	St. Louis Globe-Democrat	256,226	Cincinnati Enquirer	194,469
Philadelphia Inquirer	428,862	Kansas City Star	253,064	Oklahoma City	
Philadelphia Bulletin	412,268	Portland Oregonian	247,811	Daily Oklahoman	194,119
Cleveland Plain Dealer	406,444	St. Louis Post-Dispatch	244,599	Louisville Courier Journal	186,348
Newark Star-Ledger‡	403,798	St. Petersburg Times	244,226	Seattle Post-Intelligencer	185,962
Houston Chronicle	367,782	Orange Co. (Calif.) Register	238,757	Fort Lauderdale News	180,332
Baltimore Sun[2]	348,459	Philadelphia Daily News	232,190	Milwaukee Sentinel	173,264
Houston Post	347,921	Minneapolis Tribune	231,759	Birmingham News	167,321
Washington Star	322,827	Fort Worth Star-Telegram[2]	229,474	San Francisco Examiner	154,099

[1]Does not include Wall Street Journal, 1,948,121 circulation (National Edition). [2]Combined morning and evening editions.
*Averages for 6 months ending March 31, 1981. ‡Average for 3 months.

WORLD'S LARGEST DAILY NEWSPAPERS

Country and Newspaper	Daily Circulation	Country and Newspaper	Daily Circulation
JAPAN		CHINA, con't.	
Yomiurii Shimbun (A.M. P.M. ed.)	13,300,000	Renmin Ribao (People's Daily)	c. 6-7,000,000
Asahi Shimbun (A.M. P.M. ed.)	12,200,000	UNITED KINGDOM	
Mainichi Shimbun (A.M. P.M. ed.)	7,348,299	London Daily Sun[1]	3,741,373
USSR		London Daily Mirror[1]	3,598,676
Pravda	11,000,000	London Daily Express[1]	2,194,174
Izvestia	c. 8-8,500,000	UNITED STATES	
CHINA		New York News	1,491,556
Cankao Xiaoxi (Reference News)	c. 9-10,000,000	Los Angeles Times	1,026,092

[1]U.K. Audit Bureau of Circulation, Ltd.

LEADING TV ADVERTISERS

Source: Television Bureau of Advertising, Inc.

Company	Total TV Expenditure (1980)	Company	Total TV Expenditure (1980)	Company	Total TV Expenditure (1980)
Procter & Gamble Co.	$486,310,200	Warner-Lambert Phar. Co.	$84,490,200	Heublein, Inc.	$47,481,800
General Foods Corp.	278,406,400	Pillsbury Co.	83,418,500	Revlon, Inc.	46,989,800
American Home		Dart & Kraft, Inc.	78,622,900	Wm. Wrigley Jr. Co.	46,126,100
Products Corp.	157,281,500	Kellogg Co.	76,901,600	Internat'l Telephone &	
Ford Motor Co.	153,848,000	Chrysler Corp.	75,695,100	Telegraph Corp.	45,173,500
Pepsico, Inc.	144,462,600	The Gillette Co.	71,302,600	Norton Simon, Inc.	45,014,700
General Motors Corp.	140,380,500	Mars, Inc.	64,035,000	General Electric Co.	40,620,500
General Mills, Inc.	136,855,300	Consolidated Foods Corp.	63,326,200	Warner Comm. Inc.	40,532,800
Bristol Myers Co.	124,868,900	Sterling Drug, Inc.	61,678,000	Schering-Plough Corp.	40,360,600
McDonalds Corp.	120,213,100	Richardson Merrell, Inc.	61,625,300	Jos. Schlitz Brew. Co.	40,305,700
Philip Morris, Inc.	118,971,500	Colgate Palmolive Co.	61,534,200	Bayer A.G.	39,704,000
Lever Brothers Co.	108,880,000	Nestfood, Inc.	58,816,800	Mobil Corp.	39,481,200
American Telephone &		Quaker Oats Co.	57,205,300	H.J. Heinz Co.	39,137,600
Telegraph Co.	105,702,300	Chesebrough Ponds, Inc.	55,134,100	Morton-Norwich Pdts. Inc.	38,228,700
Coca Cola Co.	101,952,600	Toyota Motors		Eastman Kodak Co.	37,999,400
Sears, Roebuck & Co.	101,603,200	Distributors, Inc.	53,309,700	Time Inc.	36,251,400
Johnson & Johnson	95,240,700	Nabisco, Inc.	50,915,000	Union Carbide Corp.	36,677,500
Ralston Purina Co.	92,002,400	Esmark, Inc.	49,918,800	Gulf & Western	
Anheuser-Busch		Beecham Group, Ltd.	48,817,400	Industries Inc.	35,180,500
Companies, Inc.	86,955,600	The Clorox Co.	48,485,600	Greyhound Corp.	32,811,100

FORMS OF ADDRESS

Personage	Address	Social Correspondence	Salutation of Informal Letter*	Salutation of Formal Letter*
The President	The President The White House	The President and Mrs. Taylor	Dear Mr. President: or (if preferred) My dear Mr. President:[1]	Mr. President: or Sir:
The Vice-President	The Vice-President United States Senate	The Vice-President and Mrs. Taylor	Dear Mr. Vice-President: or (if preferred) My dear Mr. Vice-President:	Sir:
Chief Justice of the United States	The Chief Justice The Supreme Court	The Chief Justice and Mrs. Taylor	Dear Mr. Chief Justice: or (if preferred) My dear Mr. Chief Justice:	Sir:
Associate Justice, Supreme Court	Mr. Justice Taylor The Supreme Court	Mr. Justice Taylor and Mrs. Taylor	Dear Mr. Justice: or (if preferred) My dear Mr. Justice:	Sir:
Cabinet Member[2]	The Honorable Stephen Taylor Secretary of the Treasury (or applicable Cabinet-level department)	The Honorable The Secretary of the Treasury and Mrs. Taylor	Dear Mr. Secretary: or (if preferred) My dear Mr. Secretary:	Sir:
United States Senator[3]	The Honorable Stephen Taylor United States Senate	The Honorable Stephen Taylor and Mrs. Taylor (Dear Senator and Mrs. Taylor:) or (for a married woman senator) Mr. and Mrs. Stephen Taylor	Dear Senator Taylor: or (if preferred) My dear Senator:	Sir: or Madam:
Member, House of Representatives	The Honorable Stephen Taylor House of Representatives	The Honorable Stephen Taylor and Mrs. Taylor or (for a married woman member) Mr. and Mrs. Stephen Taylor	Dear Mr. [Mrs.] Taylor: or (if preferred) My dear Mr. [Mrs.] Taylor:	Sir: or Madam:
American Ambassador	The Honorable Stephen Taylor American Ambassador London	The Honorable The American Ambassador[4] and Mrs. Taylor (Dear Mr. Ambassador and Mrs. Taylor:) or (for a married woman ambassador) Mr. and Mrs. Stephen Taylor	Dear Mr. [Madam] Ambassador: or (if preferred) My dear Mr. [Madam] Ambassador:	Sir: or Madam:
American Chargé d'Affaires ad interim[5]	Stephen Taylor, Esquire[6] American Chargée d'Affaires ad interim (or other title)	Mr. and Mrs. Stephen Taylor	Dear Mr. Taylor: or (if preferred) My dear Mr. Taylor:	Sir:
Foreign Ambassador	His Excellency Dr.[7] Juan Luis Ortega Ambassador of Mexico	His Excellency The Ambassador of Mexico and Mrs. Ortega	Dear. Mr. [Madam] Ambassador: or (if preferred) My dear Mr. [Madam] Ambassador:	Excellency:
Secretary-General, United Nations	His Excellency Juan Luis Ortega Secretary-General of the United Nations	The Secretary-General of the United Nations and Mrs. Ortega	Dear Mr. Secretary-General: or (if preferred) My dear Mr. Secretary-General:	Sir:
Governor of a State	The Honorable Stephen Taylor Governor of Idaho or His Excellency[8] Stephen Taylor Governor of the Commonwealth of Massachusetts	The Governor of Idaho and Mrs. Taylor	Dear Governor Taylor: or (if preferred) My dear Governor:	Sir:
Mayor of a Large City	The Honorable Stephen Taylor Mayor of Baltimore	The Honorable Stephen Taylor and Mrs. Taylor	Dear Mayor Taylor: or Dear Mr. Mayor:	Sir:
Mayor of a Town	Stephen Taylor, Esquire Mayor of Newtown	The Mayor of Newtown and Mrs. Taylor	Dear Mr. Taylor:	Sir:

*"Sincerely" or "Sincerely yours" is the acceptable mode of ending both informal and formal letters to distinguished personages. [1] In the United States, "My dear Mr. President:" or "My dear Mrs. Taylor:" is a more formal salutation than "Dear Mr. President:"; however, in Great Britain, the reverse is true. [2] All but two Cabinet members use the title "Secretary": The Attorney General and the Postmaster General. Their full titles are used (e.g., on envelope: The Attorney General). [3] State senators and representatives are referred to and addressed the same way as U.S. Senators and Representatives. [4] For an American ambassador on home leave, the proper form of social address on an envelope is: "The Honorable Stephen Taylor and Mrs. Taylor," plus home address. [5] "Chargé d'affaires ad interim" is the official title given to the individual who assumes responsibility for an embassy during an ambassador's absence or change of ambassadors. [6] "Esquire" is never used, if the individual is addressed by another title, even "Mr." [7] "His Excellency" is followed by the individual's personal title, if he has one (e.g., Dr., Prince, Baron). [8] "His Excellency" is acceptable for addressing the governors of the four Commonwealths: Massachusetts, Virginia, Kentucky, and Pennsylvania; however, the State Department prefers to address all U.S. governors as "The Honorable."

U.S. POSTAL INFORMATION AND REGULATIONS*   Source: U.S. Postal Service

First-Class Mail includes letters, postal cards, postcards, all matter wholly or partly in writing (except authorized additions to second-, third-, and fourth-class mail), as well as matter closed against inspection.

Kind of mail	Rate
All first-class mail weighing 12 oz. or less, except postal cards and postcards	18¢ 1st oz. & 17¢ each additional oz.
Single postal cards and postcards	12¢ each
Double postal cards and postcards (reply portion of double postcard does not have to bear postage when originally mailed)	24¢ (12¢ each portion)
Business reply mail:	same as above (for each category)
With Advance Deposit Account:	5¢ surcharge
Without Advance Deposit Account:	18¢ surcharge

Second-Class Mail includes all newspapers, magazines, and other periodicals marked as second-class mail. Within the county, the bulk rate is 3.2¢ per pound or 1.6¢ per piece. Outside the county, the non-advertising portion is charged at a rate of 10.6¢ per pound, while the advertising portion is charged at a rate of from 14.2¢ to 34.8¢ per pound.

Charges for copies mailed by public vary with the level of presorting. Consult local postmaster. For special rates available to nonprofit organizations, publishers, and news agents, consult local postmaster.

Third-Class Mail is mailable matter that is not sent or required to be mailed as first-class mail, not entered as second-class mail, and weighs less than 16 oz. Single-piece rate: 18¢ 0 to 1 oz., additional 17¢ per oz. or fraction through 4 oz., additional 1¢ 4 to 6 oz., additional 22¢ per 2 oz. or fraction through 14 oz., additional 23¢ 14 to under 16 oz. Bulk rates reflect the level of presort.

Circulars and printed matter are considered third-class mail. Certain loose enclosures relating exclusively to the book or catalogue that they accompany may be enclosed and mailed at the third-class bulk rate. Third-class mail must be prepared so that it can be easily examined. For special bulk rates for nonprofit organizations, consult local postmaster. Note: If matter and mailing qualify both for bulk third-class and fourth-class (in everything except weight), and bulk third-class rate is higher, fourth-class rate may apply without adding additional weight.

Special Fourth-Class Rate. A single-piece rate of 63¢ up to 1 pound or fraction, and 23¢ for each additional pound or fraction through 7 lbs., 14¢ per lb. thereafter, is provided for the following: bound books with no advertising; 16 mm films; printed music; book mss, magazine articles, and music; sound recordings; and certain other matter. The maximum size is 84″ combined length and girth. The identification statement: Special Fourth Class Rate—Books (or other appropriate notation) must be placed conspicuously.

Fourth-Class (Parcel Post) Mail includes merchandise, printed matter, mailable live animals, and all other matter not included in first-, second-, or third-class mail. Parcels weighing 1 pound or more are mailable as fourth-class mail. Rates are determined by a variety of factors. Mail sent within Bulk Mail Center (BMC) or Auxiliary Service Facility (ASF) areas are charged at a lower rate than intra BMC/ASF mail. In addition, size and weight requirements vary for different classes of post office, and surcharges are applied to nonmachinable and overweight mail. Your local post office can advise you on the best methods to mail parcels of all types and sizes and on the rates which will apply. For faster delivery of parcels over long distances, use first-class zone-rated (priority) mail or express mail.

Library Rate. A special library rate applies to certain items that are conspicuously marked Library Rate and show nonprofit associations or organizations in the address or return address. The postage rate is 21¢ for the first pound, 8¢ for each additional pound through 7 pounds, and 5¢ per pound thereafter.

Priority Mail (heavy pieces) is carried by air and the fastest connecting surface carriers. It is given the most expeditious handling in dispatch and delivery. Priority mail may weigh over 12 oz., but not more than 70 lbs. Rates depend upon the zone of destination as well as weight, with a minimum charge for parcels under 15 lbs. which measure 84″ but no more than 100″ in length plus girth.

Size Standards for Domestic Mail. Min. size: .007″ thick; all mail ¼″ or less thick must be rectangular, with min. height 3½″, and min. length 5″. (Note: Mail more than ¼″ thick can be mailed even if height and length are smaller than specified above.) First-class mail or single-piece rate third-class mail which is 1 oz. or less is considered nonstandard mail under the following conditions: exceeds 11½″x6″x¼″, or length divided by height does not fall between 1.3 and 2.5 inclusive. Nonstandard mail is subject to a 9¢ surcharge.

SPECIAL HANDLING

Third and fourth-class mail only. Special handling fees (fees in addition to postage):

Weight	Fee
10 lbs. or less	$0.75
More than 10 lbs.	1.30

SPECIAL DELIVERY

Special delivery fees (fees in addition to postage):

Class of Mail	2 lbs. and under	10 lbs. and less, but over 2 lbs.	Over 10 lbs.
First class and priority	$2.10	$2.35	$3.00
All other classes	2.35	3.00	3.40

MONEY ORDERS

Amount of money order	Amount of fee Domestic
$ 0.01 to $ 25	$0.75
$25.01 to $ 50	1.10
$50.01 to $500	1.55

INSURANCE

Fees (in addition to postage):

Liability	Fee
$ 0.01 to $ 20	$0.45
$ 20.01 to $ 50	0.85
$ 50.01 to $100	1.25
$100.01 to $150	1.70
$150.01 to $200	2.05
$200.01 to $300	3.45
$300.01 to $400	4.70

Insurance is optional for registered mail.

C.O.D. MAIL

Consult postmaster for fees and conditions of mailing.

CERTIFIED MAIL

Fee (in addition to postage) $0.75

REGISTRY

Registry fees (in addition to postage):

Declared actual value	For articles without postal insurance coverage	For articles with postal insurance coverage
$ 0.00 to $ 100	$3.25	$3.30
$ 100.01 to $ 500	3.55	3.60
$ 500.01 to $1,000	3.85	3.90
$1,000.01 to $2,000	4.10	4.20

For higher values and their fees, consult local postmaster.

RESTRICTED DELIVERY

Delivery only to addressee (or person authorized by addressee).
Fee for insured (over $20), certified, registered, or COD mail ... $1.00

RETURN RECEIPTS

For insured (over $20), certified, registered, or COD mail.
Requested at the time of mailing:

Showing to whom and when delivered	$0.60
Showing to whom, when and address where delivered	0.70

Requested after mailing:

Showing to whom and when delivered	3.75

INTERNATIONAL POSTAL CHARGES

LETTERS AND LETTER PACKAGES:

    Surface Mail: Canada and Mexico, 18¢ for the first oz. or fraction, 17¢ per additional oz. or fraction through 12 oz., $2.42 (tot.) over 12 oz. to 1 lb., $2.93 (tot.) over 1 to 1½ lbs., 50¢ every ½ lb. thereafter through 3½ lbs., 51¢ for the next ½ lb.; all other countries, 30¢ for the first oz. or fraction, 17¢ per additional oz. or fraction through 8 oz., $2.76 (tot.) 8 oz. to 16 oz., $3.78 (tot.) over 1 to 1½ lbs., $4.80 (tot.) over 1½ to 2 lbs., $5.55 (tot.) over 2 to 2½ lbs., $6.30 (tot.) over 2½ to 3 lbs., $7.05 (tot.) over 3 to 3½ lbs., $7.80 (tot.) over 3½ to 4 lbs. **Airmail:** Canada and Mexico, see surface rates (mail at these rates are considered first-class in U.S. and airmail in Can. and Mex.); Colombia, Venezuela, Central America, and selected islands, 35¢ per ½ oz. through 2 oz., 30¢ per additional ½ oz. through 8 oz., 30¢ per additional oz. or fraction thereafter; all other countries, 40¢ per ½ oz. through 2 oz., 35¢ per additional ½ oz. through 32 oz., 35¢ per additional oz. over 32 oz. **Aerogrammes:** To all countries, 30¢ each. Weight limit: 4 lbs., except to Canada, 60 lbs.

POSTCARDS:

    Surface Mail: To Canada and Mexico, 12¢, to all other countries, 19¢. **Airmail:** to Canada and Mexico, 12¢; to all other countries, 28¢.

*As of late July 1981, a possible rate increase was being considered.

PARCEL POST ZONE RATES*

Weight 1 lb. and not exceeding	Local	Zones 1 & 2 Up to 150 mi.	3 150 to 300 mi.	4 300 to 600 mi.	5 600 to 1,000 mi.	6 1,000 to 1,400 mi.	7 1,400 to 1,800 mi.	8 Over 1,800 mi.
2	$1.52	$1.55	$1.61	$1.70	$1.83	$1.99	$2.15	$2.48
3	1.58	1.63	1.73	1.86	2.06	2.30	2.55	3.05
4	1.65	1.71	1.84	2.02	2.29	2.61	2.94	3.60
5	1.71	1.79	1.96	2.18	2.52	2.92	3.32	4.07
6	1.78	1.87	2.07	2.33	2.74	3.14	3.64	4.54
7	1.84	1.95	2.18	2.49	2.89	3.38	3.95	5.02
8	1.91	2.03	2.30	2.64	3.06	3.63	4.27	5.55
9	1.97	2.11	2.41	2.75	3.25	3.93	4.63	6.08
10	2.04	2.19	2.52	2.87	3.46	4.22	5.00	6.62
11	2.10	2.28	2.60	3.00	3.68	4.51	5.38	7.15
12	2.17	2.36	2.66	3.10	3.89	4.80	5.75	7.69
13	2.21	2.41	2.72	3.19	4.02	4.96	5.95	7.97
14	2.26	2.46	2.78	3.28	4.13	5.12	6.14	8.24
15	2.31	2.51	2.83	3.36	4.25	5.26	6.32	8.48
16	2.35	2.56	2.89	3.44	4.35	5.40	6.49	8.72
17	2.40	2.59	2.94	3.51	4.45	5.53	6.65	8.94
18	2.44	2.64	2.99	3.59	4.55	5.65	6.80	9.15
19	2.48	2.68	3.04	3.66	4.64	5.77	6.94	9.35
20	2.52	2.72	3.10	3.73	4.73	5.89	7.09	9.55
21	2.56	2.76	3.14	3.79	4.82	6.00	7.22	9.73
22	2.60	2.81	3.20	3.86	4.90	6.10	7.35	9.91
23	2.64	2.84	3.26	3.92	4.99	6.21	7.48	10.08
24	2.68	2.93	3.36	4.02	5.07	6.31	7.60	10.24
25	2.72	3.00	3.47	4.15	5.14	6.40	7.75	10.40
26	2.76	3.04	3.56	4.27	5.27	6.58	8.02	10.56
27	2.79	3.08	3.65	4.40	5.44	6.79	8.28	10.71
28	2.83	3.13	3.70	4.47	5.59	7.00	8.53	10.85
29	2.87	3.17	3.75	4.53	5.76	7.17	8.64	10.99
30	2.90	3.21	3.80	4.59	5.84	7.27	8.75	11.13
31	2.97	3.25	3.85	4.65	5.91	7.36	8.86	11.29
32	3.01	3.30	3.90	4.71	5.98	7.44	8.96	11.41
33	3.05	3.34	3.95	4.76	6.05	7.53	9.06	11.53
34	3.08	3.38	4.00	4.82	6.12	7.61	9.16	11.76
35	3.12	3.42	4.04	4.88	6.19	7.69	9.26	12.07
36	3.16	3.44	4.08	4.93	6.25	7.78	9.36	11.88
37	3.20	3.50	4.14	4.98	6.32	7.86	9.45	12.20
38	3.23	3.54	4.18	5.04	6.39	7.93	9.54	12.51
39	3.27	3.58	4.23	5.09	6.45	8.01	9.63	12.82
40	3.31	3.62	4.27	5.14	6.51	8.09	9.72	13.08
41	3.34	3.66	4.32	5.19	6.58	8.16	9.81	13.20
42	3.38	3.70	4.36	5.24	6.64	8.24	9.90	13.31
43	3.42	3.74	4.40	5.29	6.70	8.31	9.98	13.42
44	3.46	3.78	4.45	5.34	6.76	8.38	10.14	13.53
45	3.49	3.81	4.49	5.39	6.82	8.45	10.36	13.64
46	3.53	3.85	4.53	5.44	6.88	8.52	10.58	13.74
47	3.56	3.89	4.58	5.49	6.94	8.66	10.80	13.85
48	3.60	3.93	4.62	5.54	6.99	8.83	11.02	13.95
49	3.64	3.97	4.66	5.59	7.05	9.01	11.24	14.05
50	3.67	4.01	4.71	5.64	7.13	9.18	11.46	14.15
51	3.71	4.04	4.75	5.69	7.27	9.36	11.68	14.25
52	3.74	4.08	4.79	5.79	7.40	9.53	11.90	14.35
53	3.78	4.12	4.83	5.90	7.54	9.71	12.12	14.44
54	3.82	4.16	4.87	6.00	7.67	9.88	12.34	14.54
55	3.85	4.19	4.94	6.11	7.81	10.06	12.56	14.76
56	3.89	4.23	5.02	6.21	7.94	10.23	12.78	15.02
57	3.92	4.27	5.11	6.32	8.08	10.41	13.00	15.28
58	3.96	4.32	5.19	6.42	8.21	10.58	13.22	15.54
59	3.99	4.39	5.28	6.53	8.35	10.76	13.44	15.80
60	4.03	4.46	5.36	6.63	8.48	10.93	13.66	16.06
61	4.06	4.53	5.45	6.74	8.62	11.11	13.88	16.32
62	4.10	4.60	5.53	6.84	8.75	11.28	14.10	16.58
63	4.13	4.67	5.62	6.95	8.89	11.46	14.32	16.84
64	4.17	4.74	5.70	7.05	9.02	11.63	14.54	17.10
65	4.20	4.81	5.79	7.16	9.16	11.81	14.76	17.36
66	4.24	4.88	5.87	7.26	9.29	11.98	14.98	17.62
67	4.27	4.95	5.96	7.37	9.43	12.16	15.20	17.88
68	4.31	5.02	6.04	7.47	9.56	12.33	15.42	18.14
69	4.34	5.09	6.13	7.58	9.70	12.51	15.64	18.40
70	4.38	5.16	6.21	7.68	9.83	12.68	15.86	18.66

* Rates shown apply to mail sent between BMC areas only. Consult post office for weight and size limits. Parcels mailed within BMC areas are eligible for a discount from the rates shown in this table. Nonmachinable Surcharge: Parcels mailed to Zip Code destinations outside the BMC area are subject to a surcharge if they are nonmachinable or if they are over-weight.

U.S. TOWNS AND CITIES: ZIP CODES AND 1980 POPULATIONS

The following is a list of larger places in the United States, according to advanced final population counts of the 1980 U. S. Census. The ZIP code listed for each place is the five-digit national coding system that identifies each postal delivery area and is designated to expedite mail delivery. An asterisk indicates that there is more than one ZIP code for the town or city and that the code number applies to general delivery. To determine the exact ZIP code for a particular area within a place marked by an asterisk, consult the National Zip Code Directory or your nearest post office.

LOCATION	POPULATION	ZIP
ALABAMA		
Albertville	12,039	35950
Alexander City	13,807	35010
Andalusia	10,415	36420
Anniston	29,523	36201*
Athens	14,558	35611
Atmore	8,789	36503
Attalla	7,737	35954
Auburn	28,471	36830
Bay Minette	7,455	36507
Bessemer	31,729	35020
Birmingham	284,413	35203*
Brewton	6,680	36426
Chickasaw	7,402	36611
Cullman	13,084	35055
Decatur	42,002	35601*
Demopolis	7,678	36732
Dothan	48,750	36303*
Enterprise	18,033	36330
Eufaula	12,097	36027
Fairfield	13,040	35064
Florence	37,029	35630*
Fort Payne	11,485	35967
Gadsden	47,565	35901*
Gardendale	7,928	35071
Greenville	7,807	36037
Guntersville	7,041	35976
Hartselle	8,858	35640
Homewood	21,271	35209
Hoover	15,064	35216
Hueytown	13,309	35020
Huntsville	142,513	35804*
Jacksonville	9,735	36265
Jasper	11,894	35501
Lanett	6,897	36863
Leeds	8,638	35094
Midfield	6,536	35228
Mobile	200,452	36601*
Montgomery	178,157	36104*
Mountain Brook	17,400	35223
Muscle Shoals	8,911	35660
Northport	14,291	35476
Opelika	21,896	36801
Opp	7,204	36467
Oxford	8,939	36201
Ozark	13,188	36360
Phenix City	26,928	36867
Prattville	18,647	36067
Prichard	39,541	36610
Russellville	8,195	35653
Saraland	9,833	36571
Scottsboro	14,758	35768
Selma	26,684	36701
Sheffield	11,903	35660
Sylacauga	12,708	35150
Talladega	19,128	35160
Tarrant City	8,148	35217
Troy	12,587	36081
Tuscaloosa	75,143	35401*
Tuscumbia	9,137	35674
Tuskegee	12,716	36083
Vestavia Hills	15,733	35216
ALASKA		
Anchorage	173,017	99510*
Fairbanks	22,645	99701
Juneau	19,528	99801
Ketchikan	7,198	99901
Skagway	7,803	99840
ARIZONA		
Apache Junction	9,935	85220
Avondale	8,134	85323
Bisbee	7,154	85603
Casa Grande	14,971	85222
Chandler	29,673	85224
Douglas	13,058	85607
Flagstaff	34,641	86001
Glendale	96,988	85301*
Globe	6,708	85501

LOCATION	POPULATION	ZIP
Kingman	9,257	86401
Lake Havasu City	15,737	86403
Mesa	152,453	85201*
Nogales	15,683	85621
Paradise Valley	10,832	85253
Peoria	12,251	85345
Phoenix	764,911	85026*
Prescott	20,055	86301
Scottsdale	88,364	85251*
Sierra Vista	25,968	85635
Tempe	106,743	85282*
Tucson	330,537	85702*
Winslow	7,921	86047
Yuma	42,433	85364
ARKANSAS		
Arkadelphia	10,005	71923
Batesville	8,263	72501
Benton	17,437	72015
Bentonville	8,756	72712
Blytheville	24,314	72315
Camden	15,356	71701
Conway	20,375	72032
El Dorado	26,685	71730
Fayetteville	36,604	72701
Forrest City	13,803	72335
Fort Smith	71,384	72901*
Harrison	9,567	72601*
Helena	9,598	72342
Hope	10,290	71801
Hot Springs	35,166	71901
Jacksonville	27,589	72076
Jonesboro	31,530	72401
Little Rock	158,461	72201*
Magnolia	11,909	71753
Malvern	10,163	72104
Monticello	8,259	71655
Morrilton	7,355	72110
Newport	8,339	72112
North Little Rock	64,419	72114*
Osceola	8,881	72370
Paragould	15,214	72450
Pine Bluff	56,576	71601*
Rogers	17,429	72756
Russellville	14,000	72801
Searcy	13,612	72143
Sherwood	10,586	72116
Springdale	23,458	72764
Stuttgart	10,941	72160
Texarkana	21,459	75502
Van Buren	12,020	72956
Warren	7,646	71671
West Helena	11,367	72390
West Memphis	28,138	72301
Wynne	7,805	72396
CALIFORNIA		
Alameda	63,852	94501
Albany	15,130	94706
Alhambra	64,615	91802*
Altadena	—	91001
Anaheim	221,847	92803*
Anderson	7,381	96007
Antioch	43,559	94509
Apple Valley	—	92307
Aptos	—	95003
Arcadia	45,994	91006
Arcata	12,338	95521
Arroyo Grande	11,290	93420
Artesia	14,301	90701
Arvin	6,863	93203
Atascadero	15,930	93422
Atherton	7,797	94025
Atwater	17,530	95301
Auburn	7,540	95603
Azusa	29,380	91702
Bakersfield	105,611	93302*
Baldwin Park	50,554	91706
Banning	14,020	92220
Barstow	17,690	92311
Beaumont	6,818	92223
Bell	25,450	90201

LOCATION	POPULATION	ZIP
Bellflower	53,441	90706
Bell Gardens	34,117	90201
Belmont	24,505	94002
Benicia	15,376	94510
Berkeley	103,328	94701*
Beverly Hills	32,367	90213*
Bloomington	—	92316
Blythe	6,805	92225
Brawley	14,946	92227
Brea	27,913	92621
Broderick	—	95605
Buena Park	64,165	90622*
Burbank	84,625	91505*
Burlingame	26,173	94010
Calexico	14,412	92231
Camarillo	37,732	93010
Campbell	27,067	95008
Capitola	9,095	95010
Carlsbad	35,490	92008
Carmichael	—	95608
Carpinteria	10,835	93013
Carson	81,221	90745
Castro Valley	—	94546
Ceres	13,281	95307
Cerritos	52,756	90701
Chico	26,601	95926
Chino	40,165	91710
Chula Vista	83,927	92010*
Citrus Heights	—	95610
Claremont	30,950	91711
Clovis	33,021	93612
Coachella	9,129	92236
Coalinga	6,593	93210
Colton	27,419	92324
Commerce	10,509	90040
Compton	81,286	90220*
Concord	103,251	94520*
Corcoran	6,454	93212
Corona	37,791	91720
Coronado	16,859	92118
Corte Madera	8,074	94925
Costa Mesa	82,291	92626*
Covina	33,751	91722*
Cucamonga (Rancho Cucamonga)	55,250	91730
Cudahy	17,984	90201
Culver City	38,139	90230
Cupertino	25,770	95014
Cypress	40,391	90630
Daly City	78,519	94015*
Davis	36,640	95616
Delano	16,491	93215
Dinuba	9,907	93618
Dixon	7,541	95620
Downey	82,602	90241*
Duarte	16,766	91010
Dublin	—	94566
El Cajon	73,892	92020*
El Centro	23,996	92243
El Cerrito	22,731	94530
El Monte	79,494	91734*
El Segundo	13,752	90245
El Toro	—	92630
Escondido	62,480	92025*
Eureka	24,153	95501
Fairfax	7,391	94930
Fairfield	58,099	94533
Fair Oaks	—	95628
Fall Brooks	—	92028
Fillmore	9,602	93015
Folsom	11,003	95630
Fontana	37,109	92335
Fortuna	7,591	95540
Foster City	23,287	94404
Fountain Valley	55,080	92708
Fremont	131,945	94538*
Fresno	218,202	93706*
Fullerton	102,034	92631*
Gardena	45,165	90247*
Garden Grove	123,351	92640*
Gilroy	21,641	95020
Glendale	139,060	91209*
Glendora	38,654	91740

*General Delivery—for all towns so marked there is more than one zip code.

LOCATION	POPULATION	ZIP
Grand Terrace	8,498	92324
Grass Valley......	6,697	95945
Grover City	8,827	93433
Half Moon Bay....	7,282	94019
Hanford	20,958	93230
Hawaiian Gardens .	10,548	90716
Hawthorne........	56,447	90250
Hayward..........	94,167	94544*
Healdsburg........	7,217	95448
Hemet	23,211	92343
Hermosa Beach ...	18,070	90254
Highland	—	92346
Hillsborough	10,451	94010
Hollister	11,488	95023
Huntington Beach .	170,505	92647*
Huntington Park ..	46,223	90255
Imperial Beach....	22,689	92032
Indio	21,611	92201
Inglewood	94,245	90306*
Irvine............	62,134	92713
La Canada-Flintridge	20,153	91011
Lafayette	20,879	94549
Laguna Beach	17,860	92652*
La Habra	45,232	9063l
Lakeside	—	92040
Lakewood	74,654	90714*
La Mesa	50,342	92041
La Mirada	40,986	90638
Lamont	—	93241
Lancaster........	48,027	93534
La Palmas	15,663	90620
La Puente	30,882	91747*
Larkspur	11,064	94939
La Verne	23,508	91750
Lawndale........	23,460	90260
Lemon Grove	20,780	92045
Lemoore	8,832	93245
Lindsay	6,924	93243
Live Oak........	—	95073
Livermore	48,349	94550
Lodi	35,221	95240
Loma Linda	10,694	92354
Lomita	17,191	90717
Lompoc.........	26,267	93436
Long Beach	361,334	90801*
Los Alamitos	11,529	90720
Los Altos	25,769	94022
Los Altos Hills...	7,421	94022
Los Angeles......	2,966,763	90053*
Los Banos	10,341	93635
Los Gatos	26,593	95030
Lynwood	48,548	90262
Madera	21,732	93637
Manhattan Beach.	31,542	90266
Manteca........	24,925	95336
Marina	20,647	93933
Martinez........	22,582	94553
Marysville	9,898	95901
Maywood	21,810	90270
Menlo Park	25,673	94025
Merced	36,499	95340
Millbrae.........	20,058	94030
Mill Valley	12,967	94941
Milpitas	37,820	95035
Mira Loma.......	—	91752
Modesto	106,105	95350*
Monrovia	30,531	91016
Montclair	22,628	91763
Montebello.......	52,929	90640
Monterey	27,558	93940
Monterey Park ...	54,338	91754
Moraga	15,014	94556
Morgan Hill	17,060	95037
Morro Bay	9,064	93442
Mountain View...	58,655	94042*
Napa	50,879	94558
National City	48,772	92050
Newark.........	32,126	94560
Newport Beach ..	63,475	92660*
Norco..........	21,126	91760
North Highlands ..	—	95660
Norwalk........	85,232	90650
Novato	43,916	94947
Oakdale	8,474	95361
Oakland	339,288	94617*
Oceanside	76,698	92054
Ojai	6,816	93023
Olivehurst.......	—	95961
Ontario.........	88,820	91761*
Orange..........	91,788	92667*
Orangevale.......	—	95662
Orinda	—	94563
Oroville	8,683	95965
Oxnard..........	108,195	93030
Pacifica	36,866	94044
Pacific Grove	15,755	93950
Palmdale	12,277	93550
Palm Desert......	11,801	92260
Palm Springs	32,271	92262
Palo Alto	55,225	94302*
Palos Verdes Estates........	14,376	90274
Paradise........	22,571	95969
Paramount.......	36,407	90723
Pasadena	119,374	91109*
Paso Robles	9,163	93446
Perris	6,740	92370
Petaluma	33,834	94952
Pico Rivera	53,459	90660
Piedmont........	10,498	94611
Pinole	14,253	94564
Pittsburg	33,034	94565
Placentia	35,041	92670
Placerville	6,739	95667
Pleasant Hill.....	25,124	94523
Pleasanton......	35,160	94566
Pomona	92,742	91766*
Porterville	19,707	93257
Port Hueneme	17,803	93041
Poway	—	92064
Rancho Cordova ..	—	95670
Rancho Cucamonga	55,250	91730
Rancho Mirage ..	6,281	92270
Rancho Palos Verdes	35,227	90274
Red Bluff	9,490	96080
Redding..........	41,995	96001
Redlands	43,619	92373
Redondo Beach ..	57,102	90277*
Redwood City	54,965	94063*
Reedley	11,071	93654
Rialto	35,615	92376
Richmond	74,676	94802*
Ridgecrest	15,929	93555
Rio Linda.......	—	95673
Riverside	170,876	92502*
Rocklin	7,344	95677
Rohnert Park	22,965	94928
Rolling Hills Estates........	9,412	90274
Rosemead	42,604	91770
Roseville	24,347	95678
Sacramento	275,741	95814*
Salinas.........	80,479	93901*
San Anselmo	11,927	94960
San Bernardino ...	118,057	92403*
San Bruno	35,417	94066
San Buenaventura (Ventura)	74,474	93001*
San Carlos	24,710	94070
San Clemente	27,325	92672
San Diego	875,504	92101*
San Dimas	24,014	91773
San Fernando ...	17,731	91340*
San Francisco ...	678,974	94101*
San Gabriel	30,072	91776*
Sanger	12,558	93657
San Jacinto	7,098	92383
San Jose	636,550	95113*
San Juan Capistrano	18,959	92691*
San Leandro	63,952	94577*
San Lorenzo	—	94580
San Luis Obispo ..	34,252	93401
San Marcos	17,479	92069
San Marino	13,307	91108
San Mateo	77,561	94402*
San Pablo	19,750	94806
San Rafael	44,700	94902*
Santa Ana	203,713	92711*
Santa Barbara ...	74,542	93102*
Santa Clara	87,746	95050*
Santa Cruz	41,483	95060*
Santa Fe Springs .	14,559	90670
Santa Maria	39,685	93454
Santa Monica ...	88,314	90406*
Santa Paula	20,552	93060
Santa Rosa	83,205	95402*
Santee	—	92071
Saratoga	29,261	95070
Sausalito	7,090	94965
Scotts Valley	6,891	95066
Seal Beach.......	25,975	90740
Seaside	36,567	93955
Selma	10,942	93662
Shafter	7,010	93263
Sierra Madre	10,837	91024
Simi Valley.......	77,500	93065*
Sonoma	6,054	95476
South El Monte ..	16,623	91733
South Gate	66,784	90280
South Lake Tahoe	20,681	95705
South Pasadena...	22,681	91030
South San Francisco	49,393	94080
Spring Valley	—	92077*
Stanton	21,144	90680
Stockton	149,779	95202*
Suisun City	11,087	94585
Sunnymead	—	92388
Sunnyvale	106,618	94088*
Susanville	6,520	96130
Temple City	28,972	91780
Thousand Oaks ..	77,797	91360*
Tiburon	6,685	94920
Torrance	131,497	90510*
Tracy	18,428	95376
Tulare	22,475	93274
Turlock.........	26,291	95380
Tustin	32,073	92680
Ukiah	12,035	95482
Union City	39,406	94587
Upland	47,647	91786
Vacaville	43,367	95688
Vallejo	80,188	94590
Ventura (San Buenaventura) .	74,474	93001*
Victorville	14,220	92392
Villa Park	7,137	92667
Visalia	49,729	93277
Vista	35,834	92083
Walnut	9,978	91789
Walnut Creek	53,643	94596*
Wasco	9,613	93280
Watsonville	23,543	95076
West Covina	80,094	91793*
Westminster	71,133	92683
West Sacramento .	—	95691
Whittier	68,872	90605*
Woodland	30,235	95695
Yorba Linda	28,254	92686
Yuba City	18,736	95991
Yucaipa	—	92399

COLORADO

LOCATION	POPULATION	ZIP
Alamosa.........	6,830	81101
Arvada	84,576	80001*
Aurora	158,588	80010*
Boulder	76,685	80302*
Brighton........	12,773	80601
Broomfield......	20,730	80020
Canon City	13,037	81212
Colorado Springs..	215,150	80901*
Commerce City ..	16,234	80022
Cortez	7,095	81321
Craig	8,133	81625
Denver	491,396	80201*
Durango........	11,426	81301
Englewood	30,021	80110*
Federal Heights ..	7,846	80221
Fort Collins	64,632	80521
Fort Morgan	8,768	80701
Fountain........	8,324	80817
Golden	12,237	80401
Grand Junction ..	28,144	81501
Greeley.........	53,006	80631
Gunnison.......	5,785	81230
Lafayette	8,985	80026
La Junta	8,338	81050
Lakewood	112,848	80215
Lamar	7,713	81052
Littleton........	28,631	80120*
Longmont	42,942	80501
Loveland	30,244	80537
Montrose	8,722	81401
North Glenn	29,847	80233
Pueblo.........	101,686	81002*
Sterling	11,385	80751
Thornton	40,343	80229
Trinidad........	9,663	81082
Westminster	50,211	80030
Wheat Ridge	30,293	80033

LOCATION	POPULATION	ZIP	LOCATION	POPULATION	ZIP	LOCATION	POPULATION	ZIP
			Waterbury	103,266	06720*	Lauderhill	37,271	33313
CONNECTICUT			Waterford	17,843	06385	Leesburg	13,191	32748
			Watertown	19,489	06795	Lighthouse Point	11,488	33064
Ansonia	19,039	06401	West Hartford	61,301	06107	Live Oak	6,732	32060
Avon	11,201	06001	West Haven	53,184	06516	Longwood	10,029	32750
Berlin	15,121	06037	Weston	8,284	06880	Lynn Haven	6,239	32444
Bethel	16,004	06801	Westport	25,290	06880	Maitland	8,763	32751
Bloomfield	18,608	06002	Wethersfield	26,013	06109	Margate	36,044	33063
Branford	23,363	06405	Willimantic	14,652	06226	Marianna	7,074	32446
Bridgeport	142,546	06601*	Wilton	15,351	06897	Melbourne	46,536	32901
Bristol	57,370	06010	Winchester	10,841	06094	Miami	346,931	33101*
Brookfield	12,872	06804	Windham	21,062	06280	Miami Beach	96,298	33139
Canton	7,635	06019	Windsor	25,204	06095	Miami Shores	9,244	33153
Cheshire	21,788	06410	Windsor Locks	12,190	06096	Miami Springs	12,350	33166
Clinton	11,195	06413	Winsted	—	06098	Milton	7,206	32570
Colchester	7,761	06415	Wolcott	13,008	06716	Miramar	32,813	33023
Coventry	8,895	06238	Woodbridge	7,761	06515	Naples	17,581	33940*
Cromwell	10,265	06416				New Port Richey	11,196	33552*
Danbury	60,470	06810	**DELAWARE**			New Smyrna Bch.	13,557	32069
Darien	18,892	06820				Niceville	8,543	32578
Derby	12,346	06418	Dover	23,512	19901	North Lauderdale	18,479	33314
East Hampton	8,572	06424	Eismere	6,493	19804	North Miami	42,566	33161
East Hartford	52,563	06108	Milford	5,356	19963	North Miami Bch.	36,481	33160
East Haven	25,028	06512	Newark	25,247	19702*	North Palm Bch.	11,344	33403
East Lyme	13,870	06333	Seaford	5,256	19973	Oakland Park	21,939	33334
East Windsor	8,925	06088	Wilmington	70,195	19899*	Ocala	37,170	32670*
Ellington	9,711	06029				Ocobe	7,803	32761
Enfield	42,695	06082	**DISTRICT OF COLUMBIA**			Opa-Locka	14,460	33054
Fairfield	54,849	06430				Orange Park	8,766	32073
Farmington	16,407	06032	Washington	637,651	20013*	Orlando	128,394	32802*
Glastonbury	24,327	06033				Ormond Beach	21,378	32074
Granby	7,956	06035	**FLORIDA**			Pahokee	6,346	33476
Greenwich	59,578	06830				Palatka	10,175	32077
Griswold	8,967	06351	Altamonte Springs	22,028	32701	Palm Bay	18,560	32905
Groton	41,062	06340	Apopka	6,019	32703	Palm Beach	9,729	33480
Guilford	17,375	06437	Arcadia	6,002	33821	Palm Beach		
Hamden	51,071	06514	Atlantic Beach	7,847	32233	Gardens	14,407	33403
Hartford	136,392	06101*	Auburndale	6,501	33823	Palmetto	8,637	33561
Killingly	14,519	06241	Avon Park	8,026	33825	Palm Springs	8,166	33460
Ledyard	13,735	06339	Bartow	14,780	33830	Panama City	33,346	32401*
Litchfield	7,605	06759	Belle Glade	16,535	33430	Pembroke Pines	35,776	33024
Madison	14,031	06443	Boca Raton	49,505	33432*	Pensacola	57,619	32502*
Manchester	49,761	06040	Boynton Beach	35,624	33435*	Perry	8,254	32347
Mansfield	20,634	06250	Bradenton	30,170	33506*	Pinellas Park	32,811	33565
Meriden	57,118	06450	Callaway	7,154	32401	Plantation	48,501	33317
Middletown	39,040	06457	Cape Coral	32,103	33904	Plant City	19,270	33566
Milford	49,101	06460	Casselberry	15,247	32707	Pompano Beach	52,618	33060*
Monroe	14,010	06468	Clearwater	85,450	33515*	Port Charlotte	—	33952
Montville	16,455	06353	Cocoa	16,096	32922	Port Orange	18,756	32019
Naugatuck	26,456	06770	Cocoa Beach	10,926	32931	Port St. Lucie	14,690	33452
New Britain	73,840	06050*	Coconut Creek	6,288	33060	Punta Gorda	6,797	33950*
New Canaan	17,931	06840	Cooper City	10,140	33328	Quincy	8,591	32351
New Fairfield	11,260	06810	Coral Gables	43,241	33134	Riviera Beach	26,596	33404
New Haven	126,109	06510*	Coral Springs	37,349	33065	Rockledge	11,877	32955
Newington	28,841	06111	Crestview	7,617	32536	Safety Harbor	6,461	33572
New London	28,842	06320	Dania	11,811	33004	St. Augustine	11,985	32084
New Milford	19,420	06776	Davie	20,877	33314	St. Cloud	7,840	32769
Newtown	19,107	06470	Daytona Beach	54,176	32015*	St. Petersburg	236,893	33733*
North Branford	11,554	06471	Deerfield Beach	39,193	33441	St. Petersburg		
North Haven	22,080	06473	De Land	15,354	32720	Bch.	9,354	33736
Norwalk	77,767	06856*	Delray Beach	34,325	33444*	Sanford	23,176	32771
Norwich	38,074	06360	Dunedin	30,203	33528	Sarasota	48,868	33578*
Old Saybrook	9,287	06475	Edgewater	6,726	32632	Satellite Beach	9,163	32901
Orange	13,237	06477	Eustis	9,453	32726	Sebring	8,736	33870
Plainfield	12,774	06374	Fernandina Beach	7,224	32034	South Daytona	9,608	32021
Plainville	16,401	06062	Florida City	6,174	33034	South Miami	10,884	33143
Plymouth	10,732	06782	Fort Lauderdale	153,256	33310*	Springfield	7,220	32401
Portland	8,383	06480	Fort Myers	36,638	33902*	Stuart	9,467	33495
Prospect	6,807	06712	Fort Pierce	33,802	33450*	Sunrise	39,681	33313
Putnam	8,580	06260	Fort Walton Beach	20,829	32548	Sweetwater	8,251	33144
Redding	7,272	06875	Gainesville	81,371	32601*	Tallahassee	81,548	32301*
Ridgefield	20,120	06877	Greenacres City	8,843	33460	Tamarac	29,142	33321
Rocky Hill	14,559	06067	Gulfport	11,180	33737	Tampa	271,523	33602*
Seymour	13,434	06483	Haines City	10,799	33844	Tarpon Springs	13,251	33589*
Shelton	31,314	06484	Hallandale	36,517	33009	Temple Terrace	11,097	33617
Simsbury	21,161	06070	Hialeah	145,254	33010*	Titusville	31,910	32780
Somers	8,473	06071	Holly Hill	9,953	32017	Treasure Island	6,316	33740
Southbury	14,156	06488	Hollywood	117,188	33022*	Valparaiso	6,142	32580
Southington	36,879	06489	Homestead	20,668	33030*	Venice	12,153	33595*
South Windsor	17,198	06074	Jacksonville	540,898	32201*	Vero Beach	16,176	32960
Stafford	9,268	06075	Jacksonville Bch.	15,462	32250	West Palm Beach	62,530	33401*
Stamford	102,453	06904*	Jupiter	9,868	33458	Wilton Manors	12,742	33305
Stonington	16,220	06378	Key West	24,292	33040	Winter Garden	6,789	32787
Stratford	50,541	06497	Kissimmee	15,487	32741	Winter Haven	21,119	33880
Suffield	9,294	06078	Lake City	9,257	32055	Winter Park	22,314	32789*
Thomaston	6,276	06787	Lakeland	47,406	33802*	Winter Springs	10,475	32708
Thompson	8,141	06277	Lake Park	6,909	33403			
Tolland	9,694	06084	Lake Wales	8,466	33853	**GEORGIA**		
Torrington	30,987	06790	Lake Worth	27,048	33460*			
Trumbull	32,989	06611	Lantana	8,048	33462	Albany	73,934	31706*
Vernon	27,974	06066	Largo	58,977	33540*	Americus	16,120	31709
Wallingford	37,274	06492	Lauderdale Lakes	25,426	33313	Athens	42,549	30601*

LOCATION	POPULATION	ZIP
Atlanta	425,022	30301*
Augusta	47,532	30903*
Bainbridge	10,553	31717
Brunswick	17,605	31520
Cairo	8,777	31728
Carrollton	14,078	30117
Cartersville	9,508	30120
Cedartown	8,619	30125
Chamblee	7,137	30341
College Park	24,632	30337
Columbus	169,441	31902*
Cordele	10,914	31015
Covington	10,586	30209
Dalton	20,743	30720
Decatur	18,404	30030*
Doraville	7,414	30340
Douglas	10,980	31533
Dublin	16,083	31021
East Point	37,486	30344
Elberton	5,686	30635
Fitzgerald	10,187	31750
Forest Park	18,782	30050
Fort Valley	9,000	31030
Gainesville	15,280	30501
Griffin	20,728	30223
Hapeville	6,166	30354
Hinesville	11,309	31313
Jesup	9,418	31545
La Grange	24,204	30240
Macon	116,860	31201*
Marietta	30,805	30060*
Milledgeville	12,176	31061
Monroe	8,854	30655
Moultrie	15,708	31768
Newnan	11,449	30263*
Perry	9,453	31069
Rome	29,654	30161
Roswell	23,337	30075*
Savannah	141,634	31402*
Smyrna	20,312	30080
Statesboro	14,866	30458
Swainsboro	7,602	30401
Thomaston	9,682	30286
Thomasville	18,463	31792
Thomson	7,001	30824
Tifton	13,749	31794
Toccoa	9,104	30577
Valdosta	37,596	31601
Vidalia	10,393	30474
Warner Robins	39,893	31093
Waycross	19,371	31501
Winder	6,705	30680

GUAM

LOCATION	POPULATION	ZIP
Tamuning	—	96911

HAWAII

LOCATION	POPULATION	ZIP
Aiea	—	96701
Ewa Beach	—	96706
Hilo	—	96720
Honolulu	365,048	96819*
Kahului	—	96732
Kailua Kona	—	96734
Kaneohe	—	96744
Lahaina	—	96761
Lihue	—	96766
Mokapu	—	96734
Nanakuli	—	96792
Pearl City	—	96782
Schofield Barracks	—	96786
Wahiawa	—	96786
Wailuku	—	96793
Waipahu	—	96797

IDAHO

LOCATION	POPULATION	ZIP
Blackfoot	10,065	83221
Boise	102,451	83701*
Burley	8,761	83318
Caldwell	17,699	83605
Chubbock	7,052	83201
Coeur d'Alene	20,054	83814
Idaho Falls	39,590	83401
Lewiston	27,986	83501
Moscow	16,513	83843
Mountain Home	7,540	83647
Nampa	25,112	83651
Pocatello	46,340	83201
Rexburg	11,559	83440
Twin Falls	26,209	83301

ILLINOIS

LOCATION	POPULATION	ZIP
Addison	28,836	60101
Alsip	17,134	60658
Alton	34,171	62002
Arlington Hts.	66,116	60004*
Aurora	81,293	60507*
Barrington	9,029	60010
Bartlett	13,254	60103
Batavia	12,574	60510
Beardstown	6,338	62618
Belleville	42,150	62220*
Bellwood	19,811	60104
Belvidere	15,176	61008
Bensenville	16,124	60106
Benton	7,778	62812
Berwyn	46,849	60402
Bethalto	8,630	62010
Bloomingdale	12,659	60108
Bloomington	44,189	61701
Blue Island	21,855	60406
Bolingbrook	37,261	60439
Bourbonnais	13,280	60914
Bradley	11,008	60915
Bridgeview	14,155	60455
Broadview	8,618	60153
Brookfield	19,395	60513
Buffalo Grove	22,230	60090
Burbank	28,462	60459
Cahokia	18,904	62206
Calumet City	39,673	60409
Calumet Park	8,788	60643
Canton	14,626	61520
Carbondale	27,194	62901
Carol Stream	15,472	60187
Carpentersville	23,272	60110
Centralia	15,126	62801
Centreville	9,747	62206
Champaign	58,133	61820
Charleston	19,355	61920
Chicago	3,005,072	60607*
Chicago Heights	37,026	60411
Chicago Ridge	13,473	60415
Cicero	61,232	60650
Clarendon Hills	6,857	60514
Clinton	8,014	61727
Collinsville	19,613	62234
Country Club Hills	14,676	60477
Crest Hill	9,252	60431
Crestwood	10,712	60445
Creve Coeur	6,851	61611
Crystal Lake	18,590	60014
Danville	38,985	61832
Darien	14,968	60559
Decatur	94,081	62521*
Deerfield	17,430	60015
De Kalb	33,099	60115
Des Plaines	53,568	60016*
Dixon	15,659	61021
Dolton	24,766	60419
Downers Grove	39,274	60515
Du Quoin	6,594	62832
East Alton	7,123	62024
East Moline	20,907	61244
East Peoria	22,385	61611
East St. Louis	55,200	62201*
Edwardsville	12,460	62025
Effingham	11,270	62401
Elgin	63,798	60120
Elk Grove Village	28,907	60007
Elmhurst	44,251	60126
Elmwood Park	24,016	60635
Evanston	73,706	60204*
Evergreen Park	22,260	60642
Fairview Heights	12,414	62232
Flossmoor	8,423	60422
Forest Park	15,177	60130
Franklin Park	17,507	60131
Freeport	26,406	61032
Galesburg	35,305	61401
Geneva	9,881	60134
Glencoe	9,200	60022
Glendale Heights	23,163	60108
Glen Ellyn	23,649	60137
Glenview	30,842	60025
Glenwood	10,538	60425
Granite City	36,815	62040
Hanover Park	28,850	60103
Harrisburg	9,322	62946
Harvey	35,810	60426
Harwood Heights	8,228	60656
Hazel Crest	13,973	60429
Herrin	10,040	62948
Hickory Hills	13,778	60457
Highland Park	30,611	60035
Hillside	8,279	60162
Hinsdale	16,726	60521
Hoffman Estates	38,258	60195
Homewood	19,724	60430
Hoopeston	6,411	60942
Jacksonville	20,284	62650
Jerseyville	7,506	62052
Joliet	77,956	60431*
Justice	10,552	60458
Kankakee	30,141	60901
Kewanee	14,508	61443
La Grange	15,681	60525
La Grange Park	13,359	60525
Lake Forest	15,245	60045
Lansing	29,039	60438
La Salle	10,347	61301
Libertyville	16,520	60048
Lincoln	16,327	62656
Lincolnwood	11,921	60645
Lisle	13,625	60532
Litchfield	7,204	62056
Lockport	9,017	60441
Lombard	37,295	60148
Loves Park	13,192	61111
Lyons	9,925	60534
Macomb	19,632	61455
Marion	14,031	62959
Markham	15,172	60426
Matteson	10,223	60443
Mattoon	19,787	61938
Maywood	27,998	60153
McHenry	10,908	60050
Melrose Park	20,735	60160*
Mendota	7,134	61342
Metropolis	7,171	62960
Midlothian	14,274	60445
Moline	45,709	61265
Monmouth	10,706	61462
Morris	8,833	60450
Morton	14,178	61550
Morton Grove	23,747	60053
Mount Carmel	8,908	62863
Mount Prospect	52,634	60056
Mount Vernon	16,995	62864
Mundelein	17,053	60060
Murphysboro	9,866	62966
Naperville	42,330	60540
Niles	30,363	60648
Normal	35,672	61761
Norridge	16,483	60656
Northbrook	30,735	60062
North Chicago	38,774	60064
Northlake	12,166	60164
North Riverside	6,764	60546
Oak Forest	26,096	60452
Oak Lawn	60,590	60454*
Oak Park	54,887	60303*
O'Fallon	10,217	62269
Olney	9,026	62450
Orland Park	23,045	60462
Ottawa	18,166	61350
Palatine	32,166	60067
Palos Heights	11,096	60463
Palos Hills	16,654	60465
Paris	9,885	61944
Park Forest	26,222	60466
Park Ridge	38,704	60068
Pekin	33,967	61554
Peoria	124,160	61601*
Peoria Heights	7,453	61614
Peru	10,886	61354
Pontiac	11,227	61764
Princeton	7,342	61356
Prospect Heights	11,808	60070
Quincy	42,352	62301
Rantoul	20,161	61866
Richton Park	9,403	60471
Riverdale	13,233	60627
River Forest	12,392	60305
River Grove	10,368	60171
Riverside	9,236	60546
Robbins	8,119	60472
Robinson	7,285	62454
Rochelle	8,982	61068
Rock Falls	10,624	61071
Rockford	139,712	61125*
Rock Island	47,036	61201
Rolling Meadows	20,167	60008
Romeoville	15,519	60441

LOCATION	POPULATION	ZIP	LOCATION	POPULATION	ZIP	LOCATION	POPULATION	ZIP
Roselle	16,948	60172*	Mishawaka	40,224	46544	Coffeyville	15,185	67337
Round Lake Beach	12,921	60073	Mount Vernon	7,656	47620	Concordia	6,847	66901
St. Charles	17,492	60174	Muncie	77,216	47302*	Derby	9,786	67037
Sauk Village	10,906	60411	Munster	20,671	46321	Dodge City	18,001	67801
Schaumburg	52,319	60194	New Albany	37,103	47150	El Dorado	10,510	67042
Schiller Park	11,458	60176	New Castle	20,056	47362	Empria	25,287	66801
Skokie	60,278	60076*	Noblesville	12,056	46060	Fort Scott	8,893	66701
South Holland	24,977	60473	Peru	13,764	46970	Garden City	18,256	67846
Springfield	99,637	62708*	Plainfield	9,191	46168	Great Bend	16,608	67530
Steger	9,269	60475	Plymouth	7,693	46563	Hays	16,301	67601
Sterling	16,273	61081	Portage	27,409	46368	Haysville	8,006	67060
Streamwood	23,456	60103	Portland	7,074	47371	Hutchinson	40,284	67501
Streator	14,769	61364	Princeton	8,976	47670	Independence	10,598	67301
Summit	10,110	60501	Richmond	41,349	47374	Iola	6,938	66749
Sycamore	9,219	60178	Rushville	6,113	46173	Junction City	19,305	66441
Taylorville	11,386	62568	Schererville	13,209	46375	Kansas City	161,087	66110*
Tinley Park	26,171	60477	Seymour	15,050	47274	Lawrence	52,738	66044
Urbana	35,978	61801	Shelbyville	14,989	46176	Leavenworth	33,656	66048
Vernon Hills	9,827	60061	South Bend	109,727	46624*	Leawood	13,360	66206
Villa Park	23,185	60181	Speedway	12,641	46224	Lenexa	18,639	66215
Washington	10,364	61571	Tell City	8,704	47586	Liberal	14,911	67901
Washington Park	8,223	62204	Terre Haute	61,125	47808*	Manhattan	32,644	66502
Waukegan	67,653	60085	Valparaiso	22,247	46383	McPherson	11,753	67460
Westchester	17,730	60153	Vincennes	20,857	47591	Merriam	10,794	66203
West Chicago	12,550	60185	Wabash	12,985	46992	Mission	8,643	66205
Western Springs	12,876	60558	Warsaw	10,647	46580	Newton	16,332	67114
West Frankfort	9,437	62896	Washington	11,325	47501	Olathe	37,258	66061
Westmont	16,718	60559	West Lafayette	21,247	47906	Ottawa	11,016	66067
Wheaton	43,043	60187				Overland Park	81,784	66204
Wheeling	23,266	60090	**IOWA**			Parsons	12,898	67357
Wilmette	28,229	60091				Pittsburg	18,770	66762
Winnetka	12,772	60093	Ames	45,775	50010	Prairie Village	24,657	66208
Wood Dale	11,251	60191	Ankeny	15,429	50021	Pratt	6,885	67124
Woodridge	22,322	60517	Atlantic	7,789	50022	Roeland Park	7,962	66205
Wood River	12,449	62095	Bettendorf	27,381	52722	Salina	41,843	67401
Woodstock	11,725	60098	Boone	12,602	50036	Shawnee	29,653	66202*
Worth	11,592	60482	Burlington	29,529	52601	Topeka	115,266	66601*
Zion	17,861	60099	Carroll	9,705	51401	Wellington	8,212	67152
			Cedar Falls	36,322	50613	Wichita	279,272	67202*
INDIANA			Cedar Rapids	110,243	52401*	Winfield	10,736	67156
			Centerville	6,558	52544			
Anderson	64,695	46011*	Charles City	8,778	50616	**KENTUCKY**		
Auburn	8,122	46706	Cherokee	7,004	51012			
Bedford	14,410	47421	Clear Lake	7,458	50428	Ashland	27,064	41101
Beech Grove	13,196	46107	Clinton	32,828	52732	Bellevue	7,678	41073
Bloomington	51,646	47401	Coralville	7,687	52241	Berea	8,226	40403
Bluffton	8,705	46714	Council Bluffs	56,449	51501	Bowling Green	40,450	42718
Brazil	7,852	47834	Creston	8,429	50801	Campbellsville	8,715	42718
Carmel	18,272	46032	Davenport	103,264	52802*	Corbin	8,075	40701
Cedar Lake	8,754	46303	Decorah	7,991	52101	Covington	49,013	41011*
Clarksville	15,164	47130	Denison	6,675	51442	Danville	12,942	40422
Columbus	30,292	47201	Des Moines	191,003	50318*	Dayton	6,979	41074
Connersville	17,023	47331	Dubuque	62,321	52001	Edgewood	7,230	41017
Crawfordsville	13,325	47933	Estherville	7,518	51334	Elizabethtown	15,380	42701
Crown Point	16,455	46307	Fairfield	9,428	52556	Elsmere	7,203	41018
Decatur	8,649	46733	Fort Dodge	29,423	50501	Erlanger	14,433	41018
Dyer	9,555	46311	Fort Madison	13,520	52627	Flatwoods	8,354	41139
East Chicago	39,786	46312	Grinnell	8,868	50112	Florence	15,586	41042
Elkhart	41,305	46514	Indianola	10,843	50125	Fort Mitchell	7,297	41017
Elwood	10,867	46036	Iowa City	50,508	52240	Fort Thomas	16,012	41075
Evansville	130,496	47708*	Iowa Falls	6,174	50126	Frankfort	25,973	40601
Fort Wayne	172,196	46802*	Keokuk	13,536	52632	Franklin	7,738	42134
Frankfort	15,168	46041	Knoxville	8,143	50138	Georgetown	10,972	40324
Franklin	11,563	46131	Le Mars	8,276	51031	Glasgow	12,958	42141
Gary	151,953	46401*	Marion	19,474	52302	Harrodsburg	7,265	40330
Goshen	19,665	46526	Marshalltown	26,938	50158	Henderson	24,834	42420
Greencastle	8,403	46135	Mason City	30,144	50401	Hopkinsville	27,318	42240
Greenfield	11,439	46140	Mount Pleasant	7,322	52641	Independence	7,998	41051
Greensburg	9,254	47240	Muscatine	23,467	52761	Jeffersontown	15,795	40299
Greenwood	19,327	46142	Newton	15,292	50208	Lebanon	6,590	40033
Griffith	17,026	46319	Oelwein	7,564	50662	Lexington	204,165	40507*
Hammond	93,714	46320*	Oskaloosa	10,629	52577	Louisville	298,451	40202*
Hartford City	7,622	47348	Ottumwa	27,381	52501	Madisonville	16,979	42431
Highland	25,935	46322	Pella	8,349	50219	Mayfield	10,705	42066
Hobart	22,987	46342	Perry	7,053	50220	Maysville	7,983	41056
Huntington	16,202	46750	Red Oak	6,810	51566	Middlesborough	12,251	40965
Indianapolis	700,807	46204*	Sioux City	82,003	51101*	Morehead	7,789	40351
Jasper	9,097	47546	Spencer	11,726	51301	Murray	14,248	42071
Jeffersonville	21,220	47130	Storm Lake	8,814	50588	Newport	21,587	41071*
Kendallville	7,299	46755	Urbandale	17,869	50322	Nicholasville	10,400	40356
Kokomo	47,808	46901	Waterloo	75,985	50701*	Owensboro	54,450	42301
Lafayette	43,011	47902*	Waverly	8,444	50677	Paducah	29,315	42001
Lake Station	14,294	46405	Webster City	8,572	50595	Paris	7,935	40361
LaPorte	21,796	46350	West Des Moines	21,894	50265	Princeton	7,073	42445
Lawrence	25,591	46226				Radcliff	14,519	40160
Lebanon	11,456	46052	**KANSAS**			Richmond	21,705	40475
Logansport	17,899	46947				Russellville	7,520	42276
Madison	12,472	47250	Abilene	6,572	67410	St. Matthews	13,354	40207
Marion	35,874	46952	Arkansas City	13,201	67005	Shively	16,819	40216
Martinsville	11,311	46151	Atchison	11,407	66002	Somerset	10,649	42501
Merrillville	27,677	46410	Augusta	6,968	67010	Versailles	6,427	40383
Michigan City	36,850	46360	Chanute	10,506	66720	Winchester	15,216	40391

LOCATION	POPULATION	ZIP
LOUISIANA		
Abbeville	12,391	70510
Alexandria	51,565	71301
Baker	12,865	70714
Bastrop	15,527	71220
Baton Rouge	219,486	70821*
Bogalusa	16,976	70427
Bossier City	49,969	71111*
Cooper Road	—	71107
Covington	7,892	70433
Crowley	16,036	70526
Denham Springs	8,412	70726
De Ridder	11,057	70634
Donaldsonville	7,901	70346
Eunice	12,749	70535
Franklin	9,584	70538
Gonzales	7,287	70737
Gretna	20,615	70053
Hammond	15,043	70401
Harahan	11,384	70123
Harvey	—	70058
Houma	32,602	70360
Jeanerette	6,511	70544
Jennings	12,401	70546
Kenner	66,382	70062
Lafayette	81,961	70501*
Lake Charles	75,051	70601*
Lake Providence	6,361	71254
Leesville	9,054	71446
Mansfield	6,485	71052
Marrero	—	70072
Metairie	—	70001*
Minden	15,074	71055
Monroe	57,597	71201*
Morgan City	16,114	70380
Natchitoches	16,664	71457
New Iberia	32,766	70560
New Orleans	557,482	70140*
Oakdale	7,155	71463
Opelousas	18,903	70570
Pineville	12,034	71360
Plaquemine	7,521	70764
Rayne	9,066	70578
Reserve	—	70084
Ruston	20,585	71270
St. Martinsville	7,965	70582
Scotlandville	—	70807
Shreveport	205,815	71102*
Slidell	26,718	70458
Springhill	6,516	71075
Sulphur	19,709	70663
Tallulah	10,392	71282
Thibodaux	15,810	70301
Ville Platte	9,201	70586
West Monroe	14,993	71291
Westwego	12,663	70094
Winnfield	7,311	71483
Zachary	7,297	70791
MAINE		
Auburn	23,128	04210
Augusta	21,819	04330
Bangor	31,643	04401
Bath	10,246	04530
Biddeford	19,638	04005
Brewer	9,017	04412
Brunswick	17,366	04011
Cape Elizabeth	7,838	04107
Caribou	9,916	04736
Falmouth	6,853	04105
Gardiner	6,485	04345
Gorham	10,101	04038
Houlton	6,766	04730
Kittery	9,314	03904
Lewiston	40,481	04240
Limestone	8,719	04750
Lisbon	8,769	04250
Millinocket	7,567	04462
Old Town	8,422	04468
Orono	10,578	04473
Portland	61,572	04101*
Presque Isle	11,172	04769
Rockland	7,919	04841
Rumford	8,240	04276
Saco	12,921	04072
Sanford	18,020	04073
Scarborough	11,347	04074
Skowhegan	8,098	04976
South Portland	22,712	04106

LOCATION	POPULATION	ZIP
Waterville	17,779	04901
Westbrook	14,976	04092
Windham	11,282	04082
Winslow	8,057	04901
MARYLAND		
Aberdeen	11,533	21001
Annapolis	31,740	21401*
Arbutus	—	21227
Aspen Hill	—	20906
Baltimore	786,775	21233*
Bel Aire	7,814	21014
Beltsville	—	20705
Bethesda	—	20014*
Bladensburg	7,691	20710
Bowie	33,695	20715
Brooklyn	—	21225
Cambridge	11,703	21613
Camp Springs	—	20743
Catonsville	—	21228
Cheverly	5,751	20785
Chevy Chase	—	20815
Chillum	—	20783
Colesville	—	20904
College Park	23,614	20740
Columbia	—	21045*
Cumberland	25,933	21502
Defense Heights	—	20710
District Heights	6,799	20747
Dundalk	—	21222
Easton	7,536	21601
Edgewood	—	21040
Elkton	6,468	21921
Ellicott City	24,274	21043
Essex	—	21221
Ferndale	—	21061
Forestville	—	20028
Frederick	27,557	21701
Frostburg	7,715	21532
Gaithersburg	26,424	20760
Glen Burnie	—	21061
Greenbelt	16,000	20770
Hagerstown	34,132	21740
Havre de Grace	8,763	21078
Hillcrest Heights	—	20031
Hyattsville	12,709	20781*
Joppatowne	—	21085
Kemp Mill	—	20902
Kentland	—	20785
Langley Park	—	20787
Lanham-Seabrook	—	20801
Lansdowne	—	21227
Laurel	12,103	20810*
Lexington Park	—	20653
Linthicum	—	21090
Lutherville	—	21093
Middle River	—	21220
Mount Rainier	7,361	20822
New Carrollton	12,632	20784
Overlea	—	21201
Owings Mills	—	21117
Oxon Hill	—	20745
Parkville	—	21234
Pikesville	—	21208
Pumphrey	—	21090
Randallstown	—	21133
Randolph	—	20852
Reisterstown	—	21136
Riviera Beach	—	21061
Rockville	43,811	20850*
Rosedale	—	21237
Salisbury	16,429	21801
Seat Pleasant	5,217	20027
Severna Park	—	21146
Silver Spring	—	20907*
Suitland	—	20746
Takoma Park	16,231	20912
Towson	—	21204
Waldorf	—	20601
Westminster	8,808	21157
Wheaton	—	20902
White Oak	—	20904
Woodlawn	—	21207
MASSACHUSETTS		
Abington	13,517	02351
Acton	17,544	01720
Acushnet	8,704	02743
Adams	10,381	01220
Agawam	26,271	01001

LOCATION	POPULATION	ZIP
Amesbury	13,971	01913
Amherst	33,229	01002
Andover	26,370	01810
Arlington	48,219	02174
Ashland	9,165	01721
Athol	10,634	01331
Attleboro	34,196	02703
Auburn	14,845	01501
Ayer	6,993	01432*
Barnstable	30,898	02630
Bedford	13,067	01730
Belchertown	8,339	01007
Bellingham	14,300	02019
Belmont	26,100	02178
Beverly	37,655	01915
Billerica	36,727	01821
Blackstone	6,570	01504
Boston	562,994	02109*
Bourne	13,874	02532
Braintree	36,337	02184
Bridgewater	17,202	02324
Brockton	95,172	02403*
Brookline	55,062	02146
Burlington	23,486	01803
Cambridge	95,322	02138
Canton	18,182	02021
Carver	6,988	02330
Chelmsford	31,174	01824
Chelsea	25,431	02150
Chicopee	55,112	01021*
Clinton	12,771	01510
Cohasset	7,174	02025
Concord	16,293	01742
Dalton	6,797	01226
Danvers	24,100	01923
Dartmouth	23,966	02714
Dedham	25,298	02026
Dennis	12,360	02638
Dracut	21,249	01826
Dudley	8,717	01570
Duxbury	11,807	02332
East Bridgewater	9,945	02333
Easthampton	15,580	01027
East Longmeadow	12,905	01028
Easton	16,623	02334
Everett	37,195	02149
Fairhaven	15,759	02719
Fall River	92,574	02722*
Falmouth	23,640	02540*
Fitchburg	39,580	01420
Foxboro	14,148	02035
Framingham	65,113	01701
Franklin	18,217	02038
Gardner	17,900	01440
Gloucester	27,768	01930
Grafton	11,238	01519
Great Barrington	7,405	01230
Greenfield	18,436	01301
Hamilton	6,960	01936
Hanover	11,358	02339
Hanson	8,617	02341
Harvard	12,170	01451
Harwich	8,971	02645
Haverhill	46,865	01830
Hingham	20,339	02043
Holbrook	11,140	02343
Holden	13,336	01520
Holliston	12,622	01746
Holyoke	44,678	01040
Hudson	16,408	01749
Hull	9,714	02045
Hyannis	—	02601
Ipswich	11,158	01938
Lawrence	63,175	01842*
Lee	6,247	01238
Leicester	9,446	01524
Lenox	6,523	01240
Leominster	34,508	01453
Lexington	29,479	02173
Lincoln	7,098	01773
Littleton	6,970	01460
Longmeadow	16,301	01106
Lowell	92,418	01853*
Ludlow	18,150	01056
Lunenburg	8,405	01462
Lynn	78,471	01901*
Lynnfield	11,267	01940
Malden	53,386	02148
Mansfield	13,453	02048
Marblehead	20,126	01945
Marlborough	30,617	01752
Marshfield	20,916	02050

LOCATION	POPULATION	ZIP
Maynard	9,590	01754
Medfield	10,220	02052
Medford	58,076	02155
Medway	8,447	02053
Melrose	30,055	02176
Methuen	36,701	01844
Middleboro	16,404	02346
Milford	23,390	01757
Millbury	11,800	01527
Millis	6,908	02054
Milton	25,860	02186
Monson	7,315	01057
Montague	8,011	01351
Natick	29,461	01760
Needham	27,901	02192
New Bedford	98,478	02740*
Newburyport	15,900	01950
Newton	83,622	02158
North Adams	18,063	01247
Northampton	29,286	01060
North Andover	20,129	01845
North Attleboro	21,095	02760*
North Reading	11,455	01864
Norton	12,690	02766
Norwell	9,182	02061
Norwood	29,711	02062
Orange	6,844	01364
Oxford	11,680	01540
Palmer	11,389	01069
Peabody	45,976	01960
Pembroke	13,487	02359
Pepperell	8,061	01463
Pittsfield	51,974	01201
Plymouth	35,913	02360
Quincy	84,743	02169
Randolph	28,218	02368
Raynham	9,085	02767
Reading	22,678	01867
Rehoboth	7,570	02769
Revere	42,423	02151
Rockland	15,695	02370
Rockport	6,345	01966
Salem	38,220	01970
Sandwich	8,727	02563
Saugus	24,746	01906
Scituate	17,317	02066
Seekonk	12,269	02771
Sharon	13,601	02067
Shrewsbury	22,674	01545
Somerset	18,813	02725
Somerville	77,372	02143
Southbridge	16,665	01550
South Hadley	16,399	01075
Southwick	7,382	01077
Spencer	10,774	01562
Springfield	152,319	01101*
Stoneham	21,424	02180
Stoughton	27,710	02072
Sudbury	14,027	01776
Swampscott	13,837	01907
Swansea	15,461	02777
Taunton	45,001	02780
Tewksbury	24,635	01876
Townsend	7,201	01469
Uxbridge	8,374	01569
Wakefield	24,895	01880
Walpole	18,859	02081
Waltham	58,200	02154
Ware	8,953	01082
Wareham	18,457	02571
Watertown	34,384	02172
Wayland	12,170	01778
Webster	14,480	01570
Wellesley	27,209	02181
Westboro	13,619	01581
West Bridgewater	6,359	02379
Westfield	36,465	01085
Westford	13,434	01886
Weston	11,169	02193
Westport	13,763	02790
West Springfield	27,042	01089
Westwood	13,212	02090
Weymouth	55,601	02188
Whitman	13,534	02382
Wilbraham	12,053	01095
Williamstown	8,741	01267
Wilmington	17,471	01887
Winchendon	7,019	01475
Winchester	20,701	01890
Winthrop	19,294	02152
Woburn	36,626	01801
Worcester	161,799	01613*

LOCATION	POPULATION	ZIP
Wrentham	7,580	02093
Yarmouth	18,449	02675

MICHIGAN

LOCATION	POPULATION	ZIP
Adrian	21,186	49221
Albion	11,059	49224
Allen Park	34,196	48101
Alma	9,652	48801
Alpena	12,214	49707
Ann Arbor	107,316	48106*
Battle Creek	35,724	49016*
Bay City	41,593	48706
Benton Harbor	14,707	49022
Berkley	18,637	48072
Beverly Hills	11,598	48010
Big Rapids	14,361	49307
Birmingham	21,689	48012*
Burton	29,976	42503
Cadillac	10,199	49601
Center Line	9,293	48015
Charlotte	8,251	48813
Clawson	15,103	48017
Coldwater	9,461	49036
Dearborn	90,660	48120*
Dearborn Heights	67,706	48127
Detroit	1,203,339	48226*
Dowagiac	6,307	49047
East Detroit	38,280	48021
East Grand Rapids	10,914	49506
East Lansing	48,309	48823
Ecorse	14,447	48229
Escanaba	14,355	49829
Farmington	11,022	48018*
Farmington Hills	58,056	48024
Fenton	8,098	48430
Ferndale	26,227	48220
Flat Rock	6,853	48134
Flint	159,611	48502*
Flushing	8,624	48433
Fraser	14,560	48026
Garden City	35,640	48135
Grand Blanc	6,848	48439
Grand Haven	11,763	49417
Grand Ledge	6,920	48837
Grand Rapids	181,843	49501*
Grandville	12,412	49418
Greenville	8,019	48838
Grosse Pointe	5,901	48236
Grosse Pte. Farms	10,551	48236
Grosse Pte. Pk.	13,639	48236
Grosse Pte. Woods	18,886	48236
Hamtramck	21,300	48212
Harper Woods	16,361	48225
Hastings	6,418	49058
Hazel Park	20,914	48030
Highland Park	27,909	48203
Hillsdale	7,432	49242
Holland	26,281	49423
Houghton	7,512	49931
Howell	6,976	48843
Huntington Woods	6,937	48070
Inkster	35,190	48141
Ionia	5,920	48846
Iron Mountain	8,341	49801
Ironwood	7,741	49938
Ishpeming	7,538	49849
Jackson	39,739	49201*
Kalamazoo	79,722	49003*
Kentwood	30,438	49508
Lansing	130,414	48924*
Lapeer	6,225	48446
Lincoln Park	45,105	48146
Livonia	104,814	48150
Ludington	8,937	49431
Madison Heights	35,375	48071
Manistee	7,566	49660
Marquette	23,288	49855
Marshall	7,201	49068
Melvindale	12,322	48122
Menominee	10,099	49858
Midland	37,250	48640
Monroe	23,531	48161
Mount Clemens	18,806	48043*
Mount Pleasant	23,746	48858
Muskegon	40,823	49440*
Muskegon Heights	14,611	49444
Niles	13,115	49120
Norton Shores	22,025	49441
Novi	22,525	48050
Oak Park	31,537	48237
Owosso	16,455	48867

LOCATION	POPULATION	ZIP
Petoskey	6,097	49770
Plymouth	9,986	48171*
Pontiac	76,715	48056
Portage	38,157	49081
Port Huron	33,981	48060
River Rouge	12,912	48218
Riverview	14,569	48192
Rochester	7,203	48063
Romulus	24,857	48174
Roseville	54,311	48066
Royal Oak	70,893	48067*
Saginaw	77,508	48605*
St. Clair Shores	76,210	48083*
St. Johns	7,376	48879
St. Joseph	9,622	49085
Saline	6,483	48176
Sault Ste. Marie	14,448	49783
Southfield	75,568	48034*
Southgate	32,058	48195
South Haven	5,943	49090
Sterling Heights	108,999	48077
Sturgis	9,468	49091
Taylor	77,568	48180
Tecumseh	7,320	49286
Three Rivers	7,015	49093
Traverse City	15,516	49684
Trenton	22,762	48183
Troy	67,102	48084*
Walker	15,088	49504
Warren	161,134	48089*
Wayne	21,159	48184
Westland	84,603	48185
Wixom	6,705	48096
Woodhaven	10,902	48183
Wyandotte	34,006	48192
Wyoming	59,616	49509
Ypsilanti	24,031	48197

MINNESOTA

LOCATION	POPULATION	ZIP
Albert Lea	19,190	56007
Alexandria	7,608	56308
Andover	9,387	55303
Anoka	15,634	55303
Apple Valley	21,818	55124
Arden Hills	8,012	55112
Austin	23,020	55912
Bemidji	10,949	56601
Blaine	28,558	55433
Bloomington	81,831	55420
Brainerd	11,489	56401
Brooklyn Center	31,230	55429
Brooklyn Park	43,332	55444
Burnsville	35,674	55378
Champlin	9,006	55316
Chaska	8,346	55318
Cloquet	11,142	55720
Columbia Heights	20,029	55421
Coon Rapids	35,826	55433
Cottage Grove	18,994	55016
Crookston	8,628	56716
Crystal	25,543	55428
Detroit Lakes	7,106	56501
Duluth	92,811	55806*
Eagan	20,532	55121
East Grand Forks	8,537	56721
Eden Prairie	16,263	55344
Edina	46,073	55424
Fairmont	11,506	56031
Faribault	16,241	55021
Fergus Falls	12,519	56537
Fridley	30,228	55432
Golden Valley	22,775	55427
Grand Rapids	7,934	55744
Ham Lake	7,832	55303
Hastings	12,827	55033
Hibbing	21,193	55746
Hopkins	15,336	55343
Hutchinson	9,244	55350
Inver Grove Hts.	17,171	55075
Lakeville	14,790	55044
Little Canada	7,102	55110
Little Falls	7,250	56345
Mankato	28,651	56001
Maple Grove	20,525	55369
Maplewood	26,990	55109
Marshall	11,161	56258
Mendota Heights	7,288	55118
Minneapolis	370,951	55401*
Minnetonka	38,683	55343
Moorhead	29,998	56560
Mound	9,280	55364

LOCATION	POPULATION	ZIP
Mounds View	12,593	55112
New Brighton	23,269	55112
New Hope	23,087	55428
New Ulm	13,755	56073
Northfield	12,562	55057
North Mankato	9,145	56001
North St. Paul	11,921	55109
Oakdale	12,123	55109
Orono	6,845	55323
Owatonna	18,632	55060
Plymouth	31,615	55441
Prior Lake	7,284	55372
Ramsey	10,093	55303
Red Wing	13,736	55066
Richfield	37,851	55423
Robbinsdale	14,422	55422
Rochester	57,855	55901
Roseville	35,820	55113
St. Anthony	7,981	55418
St. Cloud	42,566	56301
St. Louis Park	42,931	55426
St. Paul	270,230	55101*
St. Peter	9,056	56082
Shakopee	9,941	55379
Shoreview	17,300	55112
South St. Paul	21,235	55075
Spring Lake Pk.	6,477	55432
Stillwater	12,290	55082
Thief River Falls	9,105	56701
Virginia	11,056	55792
Waseca	8,219	56093
West St. Paul	18,527	55118
White Bear Lake	22,538	55110
Willmar	15,895	56201
Winona	25,075	55987
Woodbury	10,297	55119
Worthington	10,243	56187

MISSISSIPPI

LOCATION	POPULATION	ZIP
Aberdeen	7,184	39730
Amory	7,307	38821
Bay St. Louis	7,891	39520
Biloxi	49,311	39530*
Brandon	9,626	39042
Brookhaven	10,800	39601
Canton	11,116	39046
Clarksdale	21,137	38614
Cleveland	14,524	38732
Clinton	14,660	39056
Columbia	7,733	39429
Columbus	27,383	39701
Corinth	13,839	38834
Greenville	40,613	38701
Greenwood	20,115	38930
Grenada	12,641	38901
Gulfport	39,676	39501*
Hattiesburg	40,829	39401
Holly Springs	7,285	38635
Indianola	8,221	38751
Jackson	202,895	39205*
Kosciusko	7,415	39090
Laurel	21,897	39440
Long Beach	7,987	39560
Louisville	7,323	39339
McComb	12,331	39648
Meridian	46,577	39301
Moss Point	18,998	39563
Natchez	22,015	39120
New Albany	7,072	38652
Ocean Springs	14,504	39564
Oxford	9,882	38655
Pascagoula	29,318	39567
Pearl	20,778	39208
Petal	8,476	39465
Picayune	10,361	39466
Starkville	15,169	39759
Tupelo	23,905	38801
Vicksburg	25,434	39180
West Point	8,811	39773
Yazoo City	12,426	39194

MISSOURI

LOCATION	POPULATION	ZIP
Arnold	19,141	63010
Ballwin	12,750	63011
Bellefontaine Neighbors	12,082	63137
Belton	12,708	64012
Berkeley	16,146	63134
Blue Springs	25,927	64015
Boonville	6,959	65233

LOCATION	POPULATION	ZIP
Brentwood	8,209	63144
Bridgeton	18,445	63044
Cape Girardeau	34,361	63701
Carthage	11,104	64836
Caruthersville	7,958	63830
Chillicothe	9,089	64601
Clayton	14,219	63105
Clinton	8,366	64735
Columbia	62,061	65201
Crestwood	12,815	63126
Creve Coeur	12,694	63141
Des Peres	8,254	63131
Dexter	7,043	63841
Excelsior Springs	10,424	64024
Farmington	8,270	63640
Ferguson	24,740	63135
Festus	7,574	63028
Florissant	55,372	63033*
Fulton	11,046	65251
Gladstone	24,990	64118
Grandview	24,502	64030
Hannibal	18,811	63401
Hazelwood	12,935	63042*
Independence	111,806	64050*
Jackson	7,827	63755
Jefferson City	33,619	65101
Jennings	17,026	63136
Joplin	38,893	64801
Kansas City	448,159	64108*
Kennett	10,145	63857
Kirksville	17,167	63501
Kirkwood	27,987	63122
Ladue	9,376	64758
Lebanon	9,507	65536
Lee's Summit	28,741	64063
Liberty	16,251	64068
Maplewood	10,960	63143
Marshall	12,781	65340
Maryville	9,558	64468
Mexico	12,276	65265
Moberly	13,418	65270
Neosho	9,493	64850
Nevada	9,044	64772
O'Fallon	8,654	63366
Olivette	8,039	63124
Overland	19,620	63114
Perryville	7,343	63775
Pine Lawn	6,662	63120
Poplar Bluff	17,139	63901
Raytown	31,759	64133
Richmond Hts.	11,516	63117
Rolla	13,303	65401
St. Ann	15,523	63074
St. Charles	37,379	63301
St. John	7,854	63114
St. Joseph	76,691	64501*
St. Louis	453,085	63166*
St. Peters	15,700	63376
Sedalia	20,927	65301
Sikeston	17,431	63801
Springfield	133,116	65801*
• Trenton	6,811	64683
University City	42,738	63130
Warrensburg	13,807	64093
Washington	9,251	63090
Webb City	7,309	64870
Webster Groves	23,097	63119
West Plains	7,741	65775

MONTANA

LOCATION	POPULATION	ZIP
Anaconda	12,518	59711
Billings	66,798	59101*
Bozeman	21,645	59715
Butte	37,205	59701
Great Falls	56,725	59401*
Havre	10,891	59501
Helena	23,938	59601
Kalispell	10,648	59901
Lewistown	7,104	59457
Livingston	6,994	59047
Miles City	9,602	59301
Missoula	33,388	59801

NEBRASKA

LOCATION	POPULATION	ZIP
Alliance	9,869	69301
Beatrice	12,891	68310
Bellevue	21,813	68005
Columbus	17,328	68601
Fremont	23,979	68025
Gering	7,760	69341

LOCATION	POPULATION	ZIP
Grand Island	33,180	68801
Hastings	23,045	68901
Kearney	21,158	68847
La Vista	9,588	68128
Lexington	6,898	68850
Lincoln	171,932	68501*
McCook	8,404	69001
Nebraska City	7,127	68410
Norfolk	19,449	68701
North Platte	24,479	69101
Omaha	311,681	68108*
Scottsbluff	14,156	69361
South Sioux City	9,339	68776
York	7,723	68467

NEVADA

LOCATION	POPULATION	ZIP
Boulder City	9,590	89005
Carson City	32,022	89701
East Las Vegas	—	89112
Elko	8,758	89801
Henderson	24,363	89015
Las Vegas	164,674	89114*
North Las Vegas	42,739	89030
Paradise Valley	—	89119
Reno	100,756	89501*
Sparks	40,780	89431

NEW HAMPSHIRE

LOCATION	POPULATION	ZIP
Berlin	13,084	03570
Claremont	14,557	03743
Concord	30,400	03301
Derry	18,875	03038
Dover	22,377	03820
Durham	10,652	03824
Exeter	11,024	03833
Franklin	7,901	03235
Goffstown	11,315	03045
Hampton	10,493	03842
Hanover	9,119	03755
Hudson	14,022	03051
Keene	21,449	03431
Laconia	15,575	03246
Lebanon	11,134	03766
Manchester	90,936	03101*
Merrimack	15,406	03054
Milford	8,685	03055
Nashua	67,865	03060
Portsmouth	26,254	03801
Rochester	21,560	03867
Salem	24,124	03079
Somersworth	10,350	03878

NEW JERSEY

LOCATION	POPULATION	ZIP
Absecon	6,859	08201
Asbury Park	17,015	07712
Atlantic City	40,199	08401*
Audubon	9,533	08106
Barnegat	8,702	08005
Barrington	7,418	08007
Bayonne	65,047	07002
Beachwood	7,687	08722
Belleville	35,367	07109
Bellmawr	13,721	08031
Belmar	6,771	07719
Bergenfield	25,568	07621
Berkeley Hts.	12,549	07922
Bernardsville	6,715	07924
Bloomfield	47,792	07003
Bloomingdale	7,867	07403
Bogota	8,344	07603
Boonton	8,620	07005
Bound Brook	9,710	08805
Brick	53,629	08723
Bridgeton	18,795	08302
Bridgewater	29,175	08807
Brigantine	8,318	08203
Burlington	10,246	08016
Butler	7,616	07405
Caldwell	7,624	07006
Camden	84,910	08101*
Carteret	20,598	07008
Cedar Grove	12,600	07009
Chatham	8,537	07928
Cherry Hill	68,785	08034*
Cinnaminson	16,072	08077
Clark	16,699	07066
Cliffside Park	21,464	07010
Clifton	74,388	07015*
Closter	8,164	07624

LOCATION	POPULATION	ZIP	LOCATION	POPULATION	ZIP	LOCATION	POPULATION	ZIP
Collingswood	15,838	08108	Millville	24,815	08332	Union Beach	6,354	07735
Colts Neck	7,888	07722	Montclair	38,321	07042*	Union City	55,593	07087
Cranford	24,573	07016	Montvale	7,318	07645	Upper Saddle		
Cresskill	7,609	07626	Montville	14,290	07045	River	7,958	07458
Delran	14,811	08075	Moorestown	15,596	08057	Ventnor City	11,704	08406
Denville	14,380	07834	Morris Twp.	18,486	07961	Vernon	16,302	07462
Deptford	23,473	08096	Morristown	16,614	07960	Verona	14,166	07044
Dover . . . . »	14,681	07801	Mountainside	7,118	07092	Vineland	53,753	08360
Dumont	18,334	07628	Mount Holly	10,818	08060	Waldwick	10,802	07463
Dunellen	6,593	08812	Mount Laurel	17,614	08054	Wall	18,952	07719
East Brunswick . . .	37,711	08816	Mount Olive	18,748	07828	Wallington	10,741	07057
East Hanover	9,319	07936	Neptune	28,366	07753	Wanaque	10,025	07465
East Orange	77,025	07019*	Newark	329,248	07101*	Warren	9,805	07060
East Rutherford . . .	7,849	07073	New Brunswick . . .	41,442	08901*	Wayne	46,474	07470
Eatontown	12,703	07724	New Milford	16,876	07646	Weehawken	13,168	07087
Edgewater Park . . .	9,273	08010	New Providence . . .	12,426	07974	West Caldwell	11,407	07006
Edison	70,193	08817	Newton	7,748	07860	West Deptford	18,002	08066
Elizabeth	106,201	07207*	North Arlington . . .	16,587	07032	Westfield	30,447	07091*
Elmwood Park	18,377	07407	North Bergen	47,019	07047	West Long Branch. .	7,380	07764
Emerson	7,793	07630	North Brunswick . .	22,220	08902	West Milford	22,750	07480
Englewood	23,701	07631*	Northfield	7,795	08225	West New York	39,194	07093
Evesham Twp.	21,659	08053	North Haledon	8,177	07508	West Orange	39,510	07052
Ewing Twp.	34,842	08618	North Plainfield . . .	19,108	07060	West Paterson	11,293	07424
Fairfield	7,987	07006	Nutley	28,998	07110	Westwood	10,714	07675
Fair Lawn	32,229	07410	Oakland	13,443	07436	Willingboro	39,912	08046
Fairview	10,519	07022	Ocean City	13,949	08226	Woodbridge	90,074	07095
Fanwood	7,767	07023	Old Bridge	51,515	08857	Woodbury	10,353	08096
Florham Park	9,359	07932	Oradell	8,658	07649	Wood-Ridge.	7,929	07075
Fort Lee	32,449	07024	Orange	31,136	07050*	Wyckoff	15,500	07481
Franklin Lakes	8,769	07417	Palisades Park	13,732	07650			
Freehold	10,020	07728	Palmyra	7,085	08065	**NEW MEXICO**		
Garfield	26,803	07026	Paramus	26,474	07652			
Glassboro	14,574	08028	Park Ridge.	8,515	07656	Alamogordo	24,024	88310
Glen Ridge	7,855	07028	Parsippany-Troy			Albuquerque	331,767	87101*
Glen Rock	11,497	07452	Hills	49,868	07054	Artesia	10,385	88210
Gloucester City . . .	13,121	08030	Passaic	52,463	07055	Carlsbad	25,496	88220
Guttenberg	7,340	07093	Paterson	137,970	07510*	Clovis	31,194	88101
Hackensack	36,039	07601*	Paulsboro	6,944	08066	Deming	9,964	88030
Hackettstown	8,850	07840	Pennsauken	33,775	08110	Espanola	6,803	87532
Haddonfield	12,337	08033	Pennsville	13,848	08070	Farmington	30,729	87401
Haddon Heights. . .	8,361	08035	Pequannock	13,776	07440	Gallup	18,161	87301
Haledon	6,607	07508	Perth Amboy	38,951	08861*	Grants	11,451	87020
Hamilton Twp.	82,801	08619	Phillipsburg	16,647	08865	Hobbs	28,794	88240
Hammonton	12,298	08037	Pine Hill	8,684	08021	Las Cruces	45,086	88001
Hanover	11,846	07981	Piscataway	42,223	08854	Las Vegas	14,322	87701
Harrison	12,242	07029	Pitman	9,744	08071	Los Alamos	—	87544
Hasbrouck Hts. . . .	12,166	07604	Plainfield	45,555	07061*	Lovington	9,727	88260
Hawthorne	18,200	07507	Pleasantville	13,435	08232	Portales	9,940	88130
Hazlet	23,013	07730	Point Pleasant	17,747	08742	Raton	8,225	87740
Highland Park	13,396	08904	Pompton Lakes	10,660	07442	Roswell	39,676	88201
Hillsdale	10,495	07642	Princeton	12,035	08540	Santa Fe.	48,899	87501
Hillside Twp.	21,440	07205	Rahway	26,723	07065*	Silver City	9,887	88061
Hoboken	42,460	07030	Ramsey	12,899	07446	Socorro	7,576	87801
Holmdel	8,447	07733	Randolph	17,828	07869	Tucumcari	6,765	88401
Hopatcong	15,531	07843	Readington	10,855	08870			
Howell	25,065	07731	Red Bank	12,031	07701	**NEW YORK**		
Irvington	61,493	07111	Ridgefield	10,294	07657			
Jackson	25,644	08527	Ridgefield Park . . .	12,738	07660	Albany	101,727	12201*
Jersey City.	223,532	07303*	Ridgewood	25,205	07451*	Alden Town	10,093	14004
Keansburg	10,613	07734	Ringwood	12,625	07456	Amherst Town	108,706	14226
Kearny	35,735	07032	River Edge	11,111	07661	Amityville	9,076	11701
Kenilworth	8,221	07033	Riverside	7,941	08075	Amsterdam	21,872	12010
Keyport	7,413	07735	River Vale	9,489	07675	Auburn	32,548	13021
Kinnelon	7,770	07405	Rockaway	6,852	07866	Babylon	12,388	11702*
Lakewood	38,464	08701	Roselle	20,641	07203	Baldwin	—	11510
Leonia	8,027	07605	Roselle Park	13,377	07204	Baldwinsville	6,446	13027
Lincoln Park	8,806	07035	Rumson	7,623	07760	Batavia	16,703	14020
Linden	37,836	07036	Runnemede	9,461	08078	Bay Shore	—	11706
Lindenwold	18,196	08021	Rutherford	19,068	07070*	Bayville	7,034	11709
Little Falls	11,496	07424	Saddle Brook	14,084	07662	Beacon	12,937	12508
Little Ferry	9,399	07643	Salem	6,959	08079	Bedford Town	15,137	10506
Livingston	28,040	07039	Sayreville	29,969	08872	Bellmore	—	11710
Lodi	23,956	07644	Scotch Plains.	20,774	07076	Bethpage	—	11714
Long Branch	29,819	07740	Secaucus	13,719	07094	Binghamton	55,860	13902*
Lyndhurst	20,326	07071	Somers Point	10,330	08244	Brentwood	—	11717
Madison.	15,357	07940	Somerville	11,973	08876	Briarcliff Manor . . .	7,115	10510
Mahwah	12,127	07430	South Amboy	8,322	08879	Brighton Town	35,776	14610
Mantua . . . . »	9,193	08051	South Orange	15,864	07079	Brockport	9,776	14420
Manville	11,278	08835	South Plainfield . . .	20,521	07080	Bronx Borough	1,169,115	10401*
Maple Shade	20,525	08052	South River	14,361	08882	Bronxville	6,267	10708
Maplewood	22,950	07040	Sparta	13,333	07871	Brooklyn Borough . .	2,230,936	11201*
Margate City	9,179	08402	Spotswood	7,840	08884	Buffalo	357,870	14240*
Marlboro	17,560	07746	Springfield	13,955	07081	Camillus Town	24,333	13031
Matawan	8,837	07747	Stratford	8,005	08084	Canandaigua	10,419	14424
Maywood	9,895	07607	Summit	21,071	07901	Canton	7,055	13617
Medford	17,471	08055	Teaneck	39,007	07666	Carmel Town	27,948	10512
Metuchen	13,762	08840	Tenafly	13,552	07670	Central Islip	—	11722
Middlesex	13,480	08846	Tinton Falls	7,740	07724	Cheektowaga Town	109,442	14225
Middletown	62,574	07748	Toms River	—	08753	Chili Town	23,676	14428
Midland Park	7,381	07432	Totowa	11,448	07512	Cicero Town	23,689	13039
Millburn Twp.	19,543	07041	Trenton	92,124	08608*	Clarence Town	18,146	14031
Milltown	7,136	08850	Union	50,184	07083	Clifton Park Town .	23,989	12065

LOCATION	POPULATION	ZIP	LOCATION	POPULATION	ZIP	LOCATION	POPULATION	ZIP
Cohoes	18,144	12047	Loudonville	—	12211	Schenectady	67,972	12305*
Colonie	8,869	12212	Lynbrook	20,431	11563	Scotia	7,280	12302
Colonie Town	74,593	12212	Lysander Town	13,897	13094	Seaford	—	11783
Commack	—	11725	Malone	7,668	12953	Selden	—	11784
Copiague	—	11726	Malverne	9,262	11565	Seneca Falls	7,466	13148
Corning	12,953	14830	Mamaroneck	17,616	10543	Setauket	—	11733
Cortland	20,138	13045	Manhattan			Shirley	—	11967
Croton-on-Hudson	6,889	10520	Borough	1,427,533	10001*	Solvay	7,140	13209
Deer Park	—	11729	Manhasset	—	11030	South Farmingdale	—	11735
Depew	19,819	14043	Manlius	28,489	13104	Southport	—	14904
De Witt Town	26,868	13214	Massapequa	—	11758	Spring Valley	20,537	10977
Dix Hills	—	11746	Massapequa Pk.	19,779	11762	Staten Island		
Dobbs Ferry	10,053	10522	Massena	12,851	13662	Borough	352,121	10301*
Dryden Town	12,156	13053	Mattydale	—	13211	Stony Brook	—	11790
Dunkirk	15,310	14048	Medina	6,392	14103	Stony Point Town	12,838	10980
East Aurora	6,803	14052	Melville	—	11747	Suffern	10,794	10901
Eastchester Town	32,648	10709	Merrick	—	11566	Syosset	—	11791
East Greenbush			Middletown	21,454	10940	Syracuse	170,105	13201*
Town	12,913	12061	Mineola	20,757	11501	Tappan	—	10983
East Hampton			Monroe Town	14,948	10950	Tarrytown	10,648	10591
Town	14,029	11937	Monsey	—	10952	Thornwood	—	10594
East Hills	7,160	11576	Montgomery Town	16,576	12549	Tonawanda	18,693	14150
East Meadow	—	11554	Monticello	6,306	12701	Troy	56,638	12180*
East Northport	—	11731	Mount Kisco	8,025	10549	Tuckahoe	6,076	10707
East Rochester	7,596	14445	Mount Vernon	66,713	10551*	Uniondale	—	11553
East Rockaway	10,917	11518	Nanuet	—	10954	Utica	75,632	13503*
Elmira	35,327	14902*	Nesconset	—	11767	Valley Stream	35,769	11580*
Elmont	—	11003	Newark	10,017	14513	Vernon Valley	—	11768
Elwood	—	11731	Newburgh	23,438	12550	Vestal	—	13850
Endicott	14,457	13760	New City	—	10956	Wantagh	—	11793
Fallsburg Town	9,862	12733	New Hartford Town	21,286	13413	Warwick	20,976	10990
Farmingdale	7,946	11735	New Hyde Park	9,801	11040	Watertown	27,861	13601
Floral Park	16,805	11002*	New Paltz Town	10,183	12561	Watervliet	11,354	12189
Franklin Square	—	11010	New Rochelle	70,794	10802*	Webster Town	28,925	14580
Fredonia	11,126	14063	New Windsor Town	19,534	12550	West Babylon	—	11704
Freeport	38,272	11520	New York City	7,071,030	10001*	Westbury	13,871	11590
Fulton	13,312	13069	Niagara Falls	71,384	14302*	West Haverstraw	9,181	10993
Garden City	22,927	11530	North Babylon	—	11703	West Hempstead	—	11552
Gates Town	29,756	14624	North Bellmore	—	11710	West Islip	—	11795
Geddes Town	18,528	13209	North Massapequa	—	11758	West Sayville	—	11796
Geneseo	6,746	14454	North Merrick	—	11566	West Seneca Town	51,210	14224
Geneva	15,133	14456	North New Hyde			White Plains	46,999	10602*
Glen Cove	24,618	11542	Pk.	—	11040	Williston Park	8,216	11596
Glens Falls	15,897	12801	Northport	7,651	11768	Woodmere	—	11598
Gloversville	17,836	12078	North Syracuse	7,970	13212	Wyandanch	—	11798
Grand Island Town	18,474	14217	North Tarrytown	7,994	10591	Yonkers	195,351	10701*
Great Neck	9,168	11022*	North Tonawanda	35,760	14120	Yorktown Heights	—	10598
Greece Town	81,367	14616	Norwich	8,082	13815			
Greenburgh Town	82,881	10591	Nyack	6,428	10960	**NORTH CAROLINA**		
Greenlawn	—	11740	Oakdale	—	11769			
Guilderland Town	26,515	12084	Oceanside	—	11572	Albemarle	15,110	28001
Hamburg	10,582	14075	Ogdensburg	12,375	13669	Asheboro	15,252	27203
Harrison	23,046	10528	Old Bethpage	—	11804	Asheville	53,281	28801*
Hartsdale	—	10530	Olean	18,207	14760	Boone	10,191	28607
Hastings-on-			Oneida	10,810	13421	Burlington	37,266	27215
Hudson	8,573	10706	Oneonta	14,933	13820	Carrboro	7,517	27510
Hauppauge	—	11787	Orangetown Town	48,612	10960	Cary	21,612	27511
Haverstraw	8,800	10927	Ossining	20,196	10562	Chapel Hill	32,421	27514
Hempstead	40,404	11551*	Oswego	19,793	13126	Charlotte	314,447	28202*
Henrietta Town	36,134	14467	Oyster Bay	—	11771	Clinton	7,552	28328
Herkimer	8,383	13350	Patchogue	11,291	11772	Concord	16,942	28025
Hewlett	—	11557	Pearl River	—	10965	Dunn	8,962	28334
Hicksville	—	11802*	Peekskill	18,236	10566	Durham	100,831	27701*
Hornell	10,234	14843	Pelham	6,848	10803	Eden	15,672	27288
Horseheads	7,348	14845	Penfield Town	27,201	14526	Elizabeth City	13,784	27909
Hudson	7,986	12534	Plainview	—	11803	Fayetteville	59,507	28302*
Hudson Falls	7,419	12839	Plattsburgh	21,057	12901	Forest City	7,688	28043
Huntington	—	11743	Pleasantville	6,749	10570	Garner	9,556	27529
Huntington Sta.	—	11746	Port Chester	23,565	10573	Gastonia	47,333	28052
Hyde Park Town	20,768	12538	Port Jefferson	6,731	11777	Goldsboro	31,871	27530
Ilion	9,190	13357	Port Jervis	8,699	12771*	Graham	8,415	27253
Inwood	—	11696	Port Washington	—	11050	Greensboro	155,642	27420*
Irondequoit Town	57,648	14617	Potsdam	10,635	13676	Greenville	35,740	27834
Islip	—	11751	Poughkeepsie	29,757	12601*	Havelock	17,718	28532
Ithaca	28,632	14850	Queens Borough	1,891,325	11101*	Henderson	13,522	27536
Jamestown	35,775	14701	Rensselaer	9,047	12144	Hendersonville	6,862	28739
Jericho	—	11753	Riverhead Town	20,243	11901	Hickory	20,757	28601
Johnson City	17,126	13790	Rochester	241,741	14603*	High Point	64,107	27260*
Johnstown	19,360	12095	Rockville Centre	25,405	11570	Jacksonville	17,056	28540
Kenmore	18,474	14217	Rome	43,826	13440	Kannapolis	—	28081
Kingston	24,481	12401	Ronkonkoma	—	11779	Kernersville	6,802	27284
Lackawanna	22,701	14218	Roosevelt	—	11575	Kings Mountain	9,080	28086
Lake Grove	9,692	11755	Roslyn Heights	—	11577	Kinston	25,234	28501
Lancaster	13,056	14086	Rotterdam Town	29,451	12303	Laurinburg	11,480	28352
Larchmont	6,308	10538	Rye	15,083	10580	Lenoir	13,748	28645
Latham	—	12110	St. James	—	11780	Lexington	15,711	27292
Levittown	—	11756	Salamanca	6,890	14779	Lumberton	18,340	28358
Lewiston Town	16,219	14092	Salina Town	37,400	13208	Mint Hill	9,830	28212
Liberty Town	9,879	12754	Saranac Lake	5,578	12983	Monroe	12,639	28110
Lindenhurst	26,919	11757	Saratoga Springs	23,906	12866	Mooresville	8,575	28115
Lockport	24,844	14094	Sayville	—	11782	Morganton	13,763	28655
Long Beach	34,073	11561	Scarsdale	17,650	10583	Mount Airy	6,862	27030

LOCATION	POPULATION	ZIP
New Bern	14,557	28560
Newton	7,624	28658
Oxford	7,580	27565
Raleigh	149,771	27611*
Reidsville	12,492	27320
Roanoke Rapids	14,702	27870
Rockingham	8,300	28379
Rocky Mount	41,283	27801
Roxboro	7,532	27573
Salisbury	22,677	28144
Sanford	14,773	27330
Shelby	15,310	28150
Smithfield	7,288	27577
Southern Pines	8,620	28387
Spring Lake	6,273	28390
Statesville	18,622	28677
Tarboro	8,634	27886
Thomasville	14,144	27360
Washington	8,418	27889
Waynesville	6,765	28786
Wilmington	44,000	28402*
Wilson	34,424	27893
Winston-Salem	131,885	27102*

NORTH DAKOTA

LOCATION	POPULATION	ZIP
Bismarck	44,485	58501
Devils Lake	7,442	58301
Dickinson	15,924	58601
Fargo	61,308	58102
Grand Forks	43,765	58201
Jamestown	16,280	58401
Mandan	15,513	58554
Minot	32,843	58701
Valley City	7,774	58072
Wahpeton	9,064	58075
West Fargo	10,099	58078
Williston	13,336	58801

OHIO

LOCATION	POPULATION	ZIP
Akron	237,177	44309*
Alliance	24,315	44601
Amherst	10,638	44001
Ashland	20,326	44805
Ashtabula	13,449	44004
Athens	19,743	45701
Aurora	8,177	44202
Austintown	—	44515
Avon	7,241	44011
Avon Lake	13,222	44012
Barberton	29,751	44203
Bay Village	17,846	44140
Beachwood	9,983	44122
Beavercreek	31,589	45401
Bedford	15,056	44146
Bedford Heights	13,214	44146
Bellaire	8,241	43906
Bellefontaine	11,888	43311
Bellevue	8,187	44811
Belpre	7,193	45714
Berea	19,567	44017
Bexley	13,405	43209
Blacklick	—	43004
Blue Ash	9,506	45242
Bowling Green	25,728	43402
Brecksville	10,132	44141
Broadview Heights	10,920	44141
Brooklyn	12,342	44144
Brook Park	26,195	44142
Brunswick	27,689	44212
Bryan	7,879	43506
Bucyrus	13,433	44820
Cambridge	13,573	43725
Campbell	11,619	44405
Canton	94,730	44711*
Celina	9,137	45822
Centerville	18,000	45459
Cheviot	9,888	45211
Chillicothe	23,420	45601
Cincinnati	385,457	45202*
Circleville	11,700	43113
Cleveland	573,822	44101*
Cleveland Heights	56,438	44118
Columbus	564,871	43216*
Conneaut	13,835	44030
Coshocton	13,405	43812
Cuyahoga Falls	43,710	44222*
Dayton	203,588	45401*
Deer Park	6,745	45236
Defiance	16,810	43512
Delaware	18,780	43015

LOCATION	POPULATION	ZIP
Delphos	7,314	45833
Dover	11,526	44622
East Cleveland	36,957	44112
Eastlake	22,104	44094
East Liverpool	16,687	43920
Eaton	6,839	45320
Elyria	57,504	44035*
Englewood	11,329	45322
Euclid	59,999	44117
Fairborn	29,702	45324
Fairfield	30,777	45014
Fairview Park	19,311	44126
Findlay	35,594	45840
Forest Park	18,675	45405
Fostoria	15,743	44830
Franklin	10,711	45005
Fremont	17,834	43420
Gahanna	18,001	43230
Galion	12,391	44833
Garfield Heights	33,380	44125
Geneva	6,655	44041
Girard	12,517	44420
Grandview Heights	7,420	43212
Greenville	12,999	45331
Grove City	16,793	43123
Hamilton	63,189	45012*
Heath	6,969	43055
Hilliard	8,008	43026
Hillsboro	6,356	45133
Hubbard	9,245	44425
Huber Heights	—	45424
Huron	7,123	44839
Independence	8,165	44131
Ironton	14,290	45638
Jackson	6,675	45640
Kent	26,164	44240
Kenton	8,605	43326
Kettering	61,186	45429
Lakewood	61,963	44107
Lancaster	34,953	43130
Lebanon	9,636	45036
Lima	47,381	45801*
Logan	6,557	43138
London	6,958	43140
Lorain	75,416	44052*
Louisville	7,873	44641
Loveland	9,106	45140
Lyndhurst	18,092	44124
Macedonia	6,571	44056
Madeira	9,341	45243
Mansfield	53,927	44901*
Maple Heights	29,735	44137
Marietta	16,467	45750
Marion	37,040	43302
Martins Ferry	9,331	43935
Mason	8,692	45040
Massillon	30,557	44646
Maumee	15,747	43537
Mayfield Heights	21,550	44124
Medina	15,268	44256
Mentor	42,065	44060
Mentor-on-the-Lake	7,919	44060
Miamisburg	15,304	45342
Middleburg Hts.	16,218	44017
Middletown	43,719	45042
Mount Healthy	7,562	45231
Mount Vernon	14,380	43050
Napoleon	8,614	43545
Newark	41,200	43055
New Carlisle	6,498	45344
New Philadelphia	16,883	44663
Niles	23,088	44446
North Canton	14,228	44720
North College Hill	10,990	45239
North Olmsted	36,486	44070
Northridge	—	45414
North Ridgeville	21,522	44035
North Royalton	17,671	44133
Norton	12,242	44203
Norwalk	14,358	44857
Norwood	26,342	45212
Oakwood	9,372	45419
Oberlin	8,660	44074
Oregon	18,675	43616
Orrville	7,511	44667
Oxford	17,655	45056
Painesville	16,391	44077
Parma	92,548	44129
Parma Heights	23,112	44130
Perrysburg	10,215	43551
Piqua	20,480	45356
Port Clinton	7,223	43452

LOCATION	POPULATION	ZIP
Portsmouth	25,943	45662
Ravenna	11,987	44266
Reading	12,879	45215
Reynoldsburg	20,661	43068
Richmond Hts.	10,095	44143
Rittman	6,063	44270
Rocky River	21,084	44116
St. Marys	8,414	45885
Salem	12,869	44460
Sandusky	31,360	44870
Seven Hills	13,650	44131
Shaker Heights	32,487	44120
Sharonville	10,108	45241
Sheffield Lake	10,484	44054
Shelby	9,645	44875
Sidney	17,657	45365
Solon	14,341	44139
South Euclid	25,713	44121
Springdale	10,111	45246
Springfield	72,563	45501*
Steubenville	26,400	43952
Stow	25,303	44224
Streetsboro	9,055	44240
Strongsville	28,577	44136
Struthers	13,624	44471
Sylvania	15,527	43560
Tallmadge	15,269	44278
Tiffin	19,549	44883
Toledo	354,635	43601*
Toronto	6,934	43964
Trenton	6,401	45067
Trotwood	7,802	45426
Troy	19,086	45373
Twinsburg	7,632	44087
University Hts.	15,401	44118
Upper Arlington	35,648	43221
Urbana	10,762	43078
Vandalia	13,161	45377
Van Wert	11,035	45891
Vermilion	11,012	44089
Wadsworth	15,166	44281
Wapakoneta	8,402	45895
Warren	56,629	44482*
Warrensville Hts.	16,565	44128
Washington	12,682	43160
West Carrollton	13,148	45449
Westerville	23,414	43081
Westlake	19,483	44145
Whitehall	21,299	43213
Wickliffe	16,790	44092
Willoughby	19,329	44094
Willoughby Hills	8,612	44094
Willowick	17,834	44094
Wilmington	10,431	45177
Wooster	19,289	44691
Worthington	15,016	43085
Wyoming	8,282	45215
Xenia	24,653	45385
Youngstown	115,436	44501*
Zanesville	28,655	43701

OKLAHOMA

LOCATION	POPULATION	ZIP
Ada	15,902	74820
Altus	23,101	73521
Alva	6,416	73717
Anadarko	6,378	73005
Ardmore	23,689	73401
Bartlesville	34,568	74003
Bethany	22,130	73008
Bixby	6,969	74008
Blackwell	8,400	74631
Broken Arrow	35,761	74012
Chickasha	15,828	73018
Choctaw	7,520	73020
Claremore	12,085	74017
Clinton	8,796	73601
Cushing	7,720	74023
Del City	28,424	73115
Duncan	22,517	73533
Durant	11,972	74701
Edmond	34,637	73034
Elk City	9,579	73644
El Reno	15,486	73036
Enid	50,363	73701
Guthrie	10,312	73044
Guymon	8,492	73942
Henryetta	6,432	74437
Hugo	7,172	74743
Idabel	7,622	74745
Lawton	80,054	73501*
McAlester	17,255	74501

LOCATION	POPULATION	ZIP
Miami	14,237	74354
Midwest City	49,559	73110
Moore	35,063	73160
Muskogee	40,011	74401
Mustang	7,496	73064
Norman	68,020	73069*
Oklahoma City	403,213	73125*
Okmulgee	16,263	74447
Ponca City	26,238	74601
Poteau	7,089	74953
Pryor	8,483	74361
Sallisaw	6,403	74955
Sand Springs	13,246	74063
Sapulpa	15,853	74066
Seminole	8,590	74868
Shawnee	26,506	74801
Stillwater	38,268	74074
Tahlequah	9,708	74464
The Village	11,049	73120
Tulsa	360,919	74101*
Vinita	6,740	74301
Warr Acres	9,940	73132
Weatherford	9,640	73096
Woodward	13,610	73801
Yukon	17,112	73099

OREGON

LOCATION	POPULATION	ZIP
Albany	26,546	97321
Ashland	14,943	97520
Astoria	9,998	97103
Baker	9,471	97814
Beaverton	30,582	97005
Bend	17,263	97701
Canby	7,659	97013
Central Point	6,357	97502
Coos Bay	14,424	97420
Corvallis	40,960	97330
Cottage Grove	7,148	97424
Dallas	8,530	97338
Eugene	105,624	97401*
Forest Grove	11,499	97116
Gladstone	9,500	97027
Grants Pass	14,997	97526
Gresham	33,005	97030
Hermiston	9,408	97838
Hillsboro	27,664	97123
Klamath Falls	16,661	97601
La Grande	11,354	97850
Lake Oswego	22,868	97034
Lebanon	10,413	97355
McMinnville	14,080	97128
Medford	39,603	97501
Milwaukie	17,931	97222
Newberg	10,394	97132
Newport	7,519	97365
North Bend	9,779	97459
Ontario	8,814	97914
Oregon City	14,673	97045
Pendleton	14,521	97801
Portland	366,383	97208*
Redmond	6,452	97756
Roseburg	16,644	97470
St. Helens	7,064	97051
Salem	89,233	97301*
Springfield	41,621	97477
Sweet Home	6,921	97386
The Dalles	10,820	97058
Tigard	14,286	97223
Tualatin	7,348	97062
West Linn	12,956	97068
Woodburn	11,196	97071

PENNSYLVANIA

LOCATION	POPULATION	ZIP
Abington Twp.	59,084	19001
Aliquippa	17,094	15001
Allentown	103,758	18105*
Altoona	57,078	16603*
Ambler	6,628	19002
Ambridge	9,575	15003
Arnold	6,853	15068
Avalon	6,240	15202
Bala-Cynwyd	—	19004
Baldwin	24,598	15208
Beaver Falls	12,525	15010
Bellefonte	6,300	16823
Bellevue	10,128	15202
Berwick	12,189	18603
Bethel Park	34,755	15102
Bethlehem	70,419	18015*
Blakely	7,438	18447

LOCATION	POPULATION	ZIP
Bloomsburg	11,717	17815
Bradford	11,211	16701
Brentwood	11,907	15227
Bridgeville	6,154	15017
Bristol	10,867	19007
Brookhaven	7,912	19015
Butler	17,026	16001
Camp Hill	8,422	17011
Canonsburg	10,459	15317
Carbondale	11,255	18407
Carlisle	18,314	17013
Carnegie	10,099	15106
Castle Shannon	10,164	15234
Chambersburg	16,174	17201
Chester	45,794	19013*
Clairton	12,188	15025
Clarion	6,664	16214
Clearfield	7,580	16830
Clifton Heights	7,320	19018
Coatesville	10,698	19320*
Collingdale	9,539	19023
Columbia	10,466	17512
Connellsville	10,319	15425
Conshohocken	8,475	19428
Coraopolis	7,308	15108
Corry	7,149	16407
Crafton	7,623	15205
Darby	11,513	19023
Dickson City	6,699	18519
Donora	7,524	15033
Dormont	11,275	15216
Downingtown	7,650	19335
Doylestown	8,717	18901
Du Bois	9,290	15801
Dunmore	16,781	18512
Duquesne	10,094	15110
Easton	26,027	18042
East Stroudsburg	8,039	18301
Economy	9,538	15005
Elizabethtown	8,233	17022
Ellwood City	9,998	16117
Emmaus	11,001	18049
Ephrata	11,095	17522
Erie	119,123	16501*
Farrell	8,645	16121
Folcroft	8,231	19032
Forest Hills	8,198	15221
Franklin	8,146	16323
Gettysburg	7,194	17325
Glassport	6,242	15045
Glenolden	7,633	19036
Glenside	—	19038
Greensburg	17,558	15601
Greenville	7,730	16125
Grove City	8,162	16127
Hanover	14,890	17331
Harrisburg	53,264	17105*
Hatboro	7,579	19040
Hazleton	27,318	18201
Hellertown	6,025	18055
Hershey	—	17033
Huntingdon	7,042	16652
Indiana	16,051	15701
Jeannette	13,106	15644
Jefferson	8,643	15344
Johnstown	35,496	15901*
Kingston	15,681	18704
Lancaster	54,725	17604*
Lansdale	16,526	19446
Lansdowne	11,891	19050
Latrobe	10,799	15650
Lebanon	25,711	17042
Lewistown	9,830	17044
Lititz	7,590	17543
Lock Haven	9,617	17745
Lower Burrell	13,200	15068
Mahanoy City	6,167	17948
McKeesport	31,012	15134*
McKees Rocks	8,742	15136
Meadville	15,544	16335
Mechanicsburg	9,487	17055
Media	6,119	19063*
Middletown	10,122	17057
Millersville	7,668	17551
Milton	6,730	17847
Monaca	7,661	15061
Monessen	11,928	15062
Monroeville	30,977	15146
Morrisville	9,845	19067
Mount Carmel	8,190	17851
Munhall	14,532	15120

LOCATION	POPULATION	ZIP
Murrysville	16,036	15668
Nanticoke	13,044	18634
New Brighton	7,364	15066
New Castle	33,621	16101*
New Cumberland	8,051	17070
New Kensington	17,660	15068
Norristown	34,684	19401*
Northampton	8,240	18067
North Braddock	8,711	15104
Norwood	6,647	19074
Oakmont	7,039	15139
Oil City	13,881	16301
Old Forge	9,304	18518
Palmyra	7,228	17078
Philadelphia	1,688,210	19104*
Phoenixville	14,165	19460
Pittsburgh	423,938	15230*
Pittston	9,930	18640*
Pleasant Hills	9,676	15236
Plum	25,390	15239
Plymouth	7,605	18651
Pottstown	22,729	19464
Pottsville	18,195	17901
Prospect Park	6,593	19076
Punxsutawney	7,479	15767
Quakertown	8,867	18951
Reading	78,686	19603*
Ridley Park	7,889	19078
Roslyn	—	19001
St. Marys	6,417	15857
Sayre	6,951	18840
Scranton	88,117	18501*
Shamokin	10,357	17872
Sharon	19,057	16146
Sharon Hill	6,221	19079
Shenandoah	7,589	17976
Somerset	6,474	15501
Souderton	6,657	18964
South Williamsport	6,581	17701
State College	36,130	16801
Steelton	6,484	17113
Sunbury	12,292	17801
Swissvale	11,345	15218
Tamaqua	8,843	18252
Tarentum	6,419	15084
Taylor	7,246	18517
Titusville	6,884	16354
Turtle Creek	6,959	15145
Tyrone	6,346	16686
Uniontown	14,510	15401
Vandergrift	6,823	15690
Warren	12,146	16365
Washington	18,363	15301
Waynesboro	9,726	17268
West Chester	17,435	19380
West Mifflin	26,279	15122
Westmont	6,113	15905
West View	7,648	15229
Whitehall	15,206	15234
White Oak	9,480	15131
Wilkes-Barre	51,551	18703*
Wilkinsburg	23,669	15221
Williamsport	33,401	17701
Willow Grove	—	19090
Wilson	7,564	15025
Wyomissing	6,551	19610
Yeadon	11,727	19050
York	44,619	17405*

PUERTO RICO

LOCATION	POPULATION	ZIP
Aguadilla	20,879	00603
Aibonito	9,369	00609
Arecibo	48,586	00612
Arroyo	8,486	00615
Bayamón	184,854	00619
Cabo Rojo	10,254	00623
Caguas	87,218	00625
Canovanas	7,263	00629
Carolina	147,100	00630
Cataño	26,318	00632
Cayey	23,315	00633
Coamo	12,834	00640
Comerio	5,751	00642
Dorado	10,204	00646
Fajardo	26,845	00648
Guánica	9,627	00653
Guayama	21,044	00654
Guaynabo	65,091	00657
Gurabo	7,646	00658
Hormigueros	11,991	00660
Humacao	19,135	00661

LOCATION	POPULATION	ZIP
Isabela	12,097	00662
Juana Díaz	10,496	00665
Juncos	7,898	00666
Levittown	—	00632
Manatí	17,254	00701
Mayagüez	82,703	00708
Ponce	161,260	00731
Río Grande	12,068	00745
Sabana Grande	7,368	00747
Salinas	6,240	00751
San Germán	13,093	00753
San Juan	422,701	00936*
San Lorenzo	8,886	00754
San Sebastián	10,792	00755
Santa Isabel	6,965	00757
Trujillo Alto	41,097	00760
Utuado	11,049	00761
Vega Alta	10,584	00762
Vega Baja	18,020	00763
Yabucoa	6,782	00767
Yauco	14,598	00768

RHODE ISLAND

LOCATION	POPULATION	ZIP
Barrington	16,174	02806
Bristol	20,128	02809
Burrillville	13,164	02830
Central Falls	16,995	02863
Coventry	27,065	02816
Cranston	71,992	02910
Cumberland	27,069	02864
East Greenwich	10,211	02818
East Providence	50,980	02914
Johnston	24,907	02919
Lincoln	16,949	02865
Middletown	17,216	02840
Narragansett	12,088	02882
Newport	29,259	02840
North Kingstown	21,938	02852
North Providence	29,188	02908
North Smithfield	9,972	02876
Pawtucket	71,204	02860*
Portsmouth	14,257	02871
Providence	156,804	02940*
Scituate	8,405	02857
Smithfield	16,886	02917
South Kingstown	20,414	02879
Tiverton	13,526	02878
Wakefield	—	02880*
Warren	10,640	02885
Warwick	87,123	02887*
Westerly	18,580	02891
West Warwick	27,026	02893
Woonsocket	45,914	02895

SOUTH CAROLINA

LOCATION	POPULATION	ZIP
Aiken	14,978	29801
Anderson	27,313	29621*
Beaufort	8,634	29902
Bennettsville	8,774	29512
Berea	—	29611
Camden	7,462	29020
Cayce	11,701	29169
Charleston	69,510	29401*
Chester	6,820	29706
Clemson	8,118	29631
Clinton	8,596	29325
Columbia	99,296	29201*
Conway	10,240	29526
Darlington	7,989	29532
Dillon	7,042	29536
Easley	14,264	29640
Florence	30,062	29501
Forest Acres	6,033	29206
Gaffney	13,453	29340
Georgetown	10,144	29440
Goose Creek	17,811	29445
Greenville	58,242	29602*
Greenwood	21,613	29646
Greer	10,525	29651
Hanahan	13,224	29410
Hartsville	7,631	29550
Lancaster	9,603	29720
Laurens	10,587	29360
Marion	7,700	29571
Mauldin	8,245	29662
Mount Pleasant	13,838	29464
Myrtle Beach	18,758	29577
Newberry	9,866	29108
North Augusta	13,593	29841
North Charleston	65,630	29406

LOCATION	POPULATION	ZIP
Orangeburg	14,933	29115
Rock Hill	35,344	29730
St. Andrews	—	29407
Seneca	7,436	29678
Simpsonville	9,037	29681
Spartanburg	43,968	29301*
Summerville	6,368	29483
Sumter	24,890	29150
Taylors	—	29687
Union	10,523	29379
Walterboro	6,036	29488
West Columbia	10,409	29169
York	6,412	29745

SOUTH DAKOTA

LOCATION	POPULATION	ZIP
Aberdeen	25,956	57401
Brookings	14,951	57006
Huron	13,000	57350
Madison	6,210	57042
Mitchell	13,916	57301
Pierre	11,973	57501
Rapid City	46,492	57701
Sioux Falls	81,343	57101*
Vermillion	9,582	57069
Watertown	15,649	57201
Yankton	12,011	57078

TENNESSEE

LOCATION	POPULATION	ZIP
Alcoa	6,870	37701
Athens	12,080	37303
Bartlett	17,170	38134
Bolivar	6,597	38008
Brentwood	9,431	37027
Bristol	23,986	37620
Brownsville	9,307	38012
Chattanooga	169,565	37401*
Clarksville	54,777	37040
Cleveland	26,415	37311
Collierville	7,839	38017
Columbia	25,767	38401
Cookeville	20,350	38501
Crossville	6,394	38555
Dickson	7,040	37055
Dyersburg	15,856	38024
East Ridge	21,236	37412
Elizabethton	12,431	37643
Fayetteville	7,559	37334
Franklin	12,407	37064
Gallatin	17,191	37066
Germantown	20,459	38138
Goodlettsville	8,327	37072
Greeneville	14,097	37743
Harriman	8,303	37748
Hendersonville	26,561	37075
Humboldt	10,209	38343
Jackson	49,131	38301
Johnson City	39,753	37601
Kingsport	32,027	37662*
Knoxville	183,139	37901*
La Follette	8,176	37766
Lawrenceburg	10,175	38464
Lebanon	11,872	37087
Lewisburg	8,760	37091
McMinnville	10,683	37110
Manchester	7,250	37355
Martin	8,898	38237
Maryville	17,480	37801
Memphis	646,356	38101*
Milan	8,083	38358
Millington	20,236	38053
Morristown	19,683	37814
Murfreesboro	32,845	37130
Nashville	455,651	37202*
Newport	7,580	37821
Oak Ridge	27,662	37830
Paris	10,728	38242
Pulaski	7,184	38478
Red Bank	3,297	37415
Ripley	6,366	38063
Savannah	6,992	38372
Shelbyville	13,530	37160
Smyrna	8,839	37167
Soddy-Daisy	8,388	37319
Springfield	10,814	37172
Tullahoma	15,800	37388
Union City	10,436	38261

TEXAS

LOCATION	POPULATION	ZIP
Abilene	98,315	79604*

LOCATION	POPULATION	ZIP
Alice	20,961	78332
Allen	8,314	75002
Alvin	16,515	77511
Amarillo	149,230	79105*
Andrews	11,061	79714
Angleton	13,929	77515
Aransas Pass	7,173	78336
Arlington	160,123	76010*
Athens	10,197	75751
Austin	345,496	78767*
Balch Springs	13,746	75180
Bay City	17,837	77414
Baytown	56,923	77520*
Beaumont	118,102	77704*
Bedford	20,821	76021
Beeville	14,574	78102
Bellaire	14,950	77401
Bellmead	7,569	76704
Belton	10,660	76513
Benbrook	13,579	76126
Big Spring	24,804	79720
Bonham	7,338	75418
Borger	15,837	79007
Breckenridge	6,921	76024
Brenham	10,966	77833
Bridge City	7,667	77611
Brownfield	10,387	79316
Brownsville	84,997	78520*
Brownwood	19,203	76801
Bryan	44,337	77801
Burkburnett	10,668	76354
Burleson	11,734	76028
Canyon	10,724	79015
Carrizo Springs	6,886	78834
Carrollton	40,591	75006*
Cedar Hill	6,849	75104
Cleburne	19,218	76031
Clute	9,577	77531
College Station	37,272	77840
Colleyville	6,700	76034
Commerce	8,136	75428
Conroe	18,034	77301*
Copperas Cove	19,469	76522
Corpus Christi	231,999	78408*
Corsicana	21,712	75110
Crockett	7,405	75835
Crystal City	8,334	78839
Cuero	7,124	77954
Dalhart	6,854	79022
Dallas	904,078	75221*
Deer Park	22,648	77536
Del Rio	30,034	78840
Denison	23,884	75020
Denton	48,063	76201
De Soto	15,538	75115
Dickinson	7,505	77539
Donna	9,952	78537
Dumas	12,194	79029
Duncanville	27,781	75116*
Eagle Pass	21,407	78852
Edinburg	24,075	78539
El Campo	10,462	77437
El Paso	425,259	79940*
Ennis	12,110	75119
Euless	24,002	76039
Farmers Branch	24,863	75234
Forest Hill	11,684	76119
Fort Stockton	8,688	79735
Fort Worth	385,141	76101*
Freeport	13,444	77541
Gainesville	14,081	76240
Galena Park	9,879	77547
Galveston	61,902	77550*
Garland	138,857	75040*
Georgetown	9,468	78626
Gonzales	7,152	78629
Graham	9,055	76046
Grand Prairie	71,462	75050*
Grapevine	11,801	76051
Greenville	22,161	75401
Groves	17,090	77619
Haltom City	29,014	76117
Harker Heights	7,345	76541
Harlingen	43,543	78550
Henderson	11,473	75652
Hereford	15,853	79045
Highland Park	8,909	75205
Hillsboro	7,397	76645
Houston	1,594,086	77052*
Humble	6,729	77338*
Huntsville	23,936	77340
Hurst	31,420	76053

LOCATION	POPULATION	ZIP
Irving	109,943	75061*
Jacinto City	8,953	77029
Jacksonville	12,264	75766
Jasper	6,959	75951
Kermit	8,015	79745
Kerrville	15,276	78028
Kilgore	10,968	75662
Killeen	46,296	76541
Kingsville	28,808	78363
Lake Jackson	19,102	77566
La Marque	15,372	77568
Lamesa	11,790	79331
Lancaster	14,807	75146*
La Porte	14,062	77571
Laredo	91,449	78040*
League City	16,578	77573
Leon Valley	8,951	78238
Levelland	13,809	79336
Lewisville	24,273	75067*
Liberty	7,945	77575
Littlefield	7,409	79339
Live Oak	8,183	78233
Lockhart	7,953	78644
Longview	62,762	75601*
Lubbock	173,979	79408*
Lufkin	28,562	75901
Mansfield	8,092	76063
Marlin	7,099	76661
Marshall	24,921	75670
McAllen	67,042	78501
McKinney	16,249	75069
Mercedes	11,851	78570
Mesquite	67,053	75149*
Mexia	7,094	76667
Midland	70,525	79701*
Mineral Wells	14,468	76067
Mission	22,589	78572
Missouri City	24,533	77459*
Monahans	8,397	79756
Mount Pleasant	11,003	75455
Nacogdoches	27,149	75961
Nederland	16,855	77627
New Braunfels	22,402	78130
North Richland Hills	30,592	76118
Odessa	90,027	79760*
Orange	23,628	77630
Palestine	15,948	75801
Pampa	21,396	79065
Paris	25,498	75460
Pasadena	112,560	77501*
Pearland	13,248	77581
Pearsall	7,383	78061
Pecos	12,855	79772
Perryton	7,991	79070
Pharr	21,381	78577
Plainview	22,187	79072
Plano	72,331	75074*
Port Arthur	61,195	77640
Portland	12,023	78374
Port Lavaca	10,911	77979
Port Neches	13,944	77651
Raymondville	9,493	78580
Richardson	72,496	75080*
Richland Hills	7,977	76118
Richmond	9,692	77469
River Oaks	6,890	77019
Robstown	12,100	78380
Rosenberg	17,995	77471
Round Rock	11,812	78664
Rowlett	7,522	75088
San Angelo	73,240	76901*
San Antonio	785,410	78205*
San Benito	17,988	78586
San Juan	7,608	78589
San Marcos	23,420	78666
Schertz	7,262	78154
Seagoville	7,304	75159
Seguin	17,854	78155
Sherman	30,413	75090
Silsbee	7,684	77656
Slaton	6,804	79364
Snyder	12,705	79549
South Houston	13,293	77587
Stephenville	11,881	76401
Sugar Land	8,826	77478*
Sulphur Springs	12,804	75482
Sweetwater	12,242	79556
Taylor	10,619	76574
Temple	42,483	76501
Terrell	13,225	75160
Texarkana	31,271	75501*

LOCATION	POPULATION	ZIP
Texas City	41,403	77590
The Colony	11,586	75067
Tyler	70,508	75701*
Universal City	10,720	78148
University Park	22,254	75205
Uvalde	14,178	78801
Vernon	12,695	76384
Victoria	50,695	77901
Vidor	12,117	77662
Waco	101,261	76703*
Watauga	10,284	76148
Waxahachie	14,624	75165
Weatherford	12,049	76086
Weslaco	19,331	78596
West University Pl.	12,010	77005
Wharton	9,033	77488
White Settlement	13,508	76108
Wichita Falls	94,201	76307*
Woodway	7,091	76710

UTAH

American Fork	12,417	84003
Bountiful	32,877	84010
Brigham City	15,596	84302
Cedar City	10,972	84720
Centerville	8,069	84014
Clearfield	17,982	84015
Kaysville	9,811	84037
Layton	22,862	84041
Lehi	6,848	84043
Logan	26,844	84321
Midvale	10,144	84047
Murray	25,750	84107
North Ogden	9,309	84404
Ogden	64,407	84401*
Orem	52,399	84057
Payson	8,246	84651
Pleasant Grove	10,669	84062
Price	9,086	84501
Provo	73,907	84601
Riverton	7,293	84065
Roy	19,694	84067
St. George	11,350	84770
Salt Lake City	163,033	84101*
Sandy	51,022	84070
South Jordan	7,492	84065
South Ogden	11,366	84403
South Salt Lake	10,561	84115
Spanish Fork	9,825	84660
Springville	12,101	84663
Tooele	14,335	84074
Vernal	6,600	84078
Washington Terr.	8,212	84403
West Jordan	26,794	84084

VERMONT

Barre	9,824	05641
Bennington	15,815	05201
Brattleboro	11,886	05301
Burlington	37,712	05401
Colchester	12,629	05446
Essex	14,392	05451
Essex Junction	7,033	05452
Hartford	7,963	05047
Middlebury	7,574	05753
Montpelier	8,241	05602
Rutland	18,436	05701
St. Albans	7,308	05478
St. Johnsbury	7,938	05819
South Burlington	10,679	05401
Springfield	10,190	05156
Winooski	6,318	05404

VIRGINIA

Alexandria	103,217	22313*
Annandale	—	22003
Arlington	152,599	22210*
Bailey's Crossroads	—	22041
Blacksburg	30,638	24060
Bon Air	—	23235
Bristol	19,042	24201
Buena Vista	6,717	24416
Charlottesville	45,010	22906*
Chesapeake	114,226	23320*
Christiansburg	10,345	24073
Colonial Heights	16,509	23834
Covington	9,063	24426
Culpeper	6,621	22701
Danville	45,642	24541

LOCATION	POPULATION	ZIP
Fairfax	19,390	22030
Falls Church	9,515	22046
Franklin	7,308	23851
Fredericksburg	15,322	22401
Front Royal	11,126	22630
Galax	6,524	24333
Hampton	122,617	23369*
Harrisonburg	19,671	22801
Herndon	11,449	22070*
Highland Springs	—	23075
Hopewell	23,397	23860
Lake Barcroft	—	22041
Lakeside	—	23228
Leesburg	8,357	22075
Lexington	7,292	24450
Lynchburg	66,743	24505*
Manassas	15,438	22110
Manassas Park	6,524	22110
Marion	7,029	24354
Martinsville	18,149	24112*
McLean	—	22101*
Newport News	144,903	23607*
Norfolk	266,979	23501*
Petersburg	41,055	23803
Poquoson	8,726	23662
Portsmouth	104,577	23705*
Pulaski	10,106	24301
Radford	13,225	24141
Richmond	219,214	23232*
Roanoke	100,427	24001*
Salem	23,958	24153
South Boston	7,093	24592
Springfield	—	22150*
Staunton	21,857	24401
Suffolk	47,621	23432*
Vienna	15,469	22180
Vinton	8,027	24179
Virginia Beach	262,199	23458*
Waynesboro	15,329	22980
Williamsburg	9,870	23185
Winchester	20,217	22601
Woodbridge	—	22191*
Wytheville	7,135	24382

VIRGIN ISLANDS

Charlotte Amalie	11,670	00801

WASHINGTON

Aberdeen	18,739	98520
Anacortes	9,013	98221
Auburn	26,417	98002
Bellevue	73,903	98009*
Bellingham	45,794	98225
Bothell	7,943	98011
Bremerton	36,208	98310
Centralia	10,809	98531
Cheney	7,630	99004
Clarkston	6,903	99403
Des Moines	7,378	98188
Edmonds	27,526	98020
Ellensburg	11,752	98926
Everett	54,413	98201*
Hoquiam	9,719	98550
Kelso	11,129	98626
Kennewick	34,397	99336
Kent	23,152	98031
Kirkland	18,779	98033
Lacey	13,940	98503
Longview	31,052	98632
Lynnwood	21,937	98036
Mercer Island	21,522	98040
Moses Lake	10,629	98837
Mountlake Terr.	16,534	98043
Mount Vernon	13,009	98273
Oak Harbor	12,271	98277
Olympia	27,447	98501*
Opportunity	—	99214
Parkland	—	98444
Pasco	17,944	99301
Port Angeles	17,311	98362
Pullman	23,579	99163
Puyallup	18,251	98371
Redmond	23,318	98052
Renton	30,612	98055
Richland	33,578	99352
Seattle	493,846	98101*
Shelton	7,629	98584
Spokane	171,300	99210*
Sunnyside	9,225	98944
Tacoma	158,501	98402*

LOCATION	POPULATION	ZIP	LOCATION	POPULATION	ZIP	LOCATION	POPULATION	ZIP
Toppenish	6,517	98948	Brown Deer	12,921	53209	Platteville	9,580	53818
Tumwater	6,705	98501	Burlington	8,385	53105	Portage	7,896	53901
University Place	—	98416	Cedarburg	9,005	53012	Port Washington	8,612	53074
Vancouver	42,834	98660*	Chippewa Falls	11,845	54729	Racine	85,725	53401*
Walla Walla	25,618	99362	Cudahy	19,547	53110	Rhinelander	7,873	54501
Wenatchee	17,257	98801	De Pere	14,892	54115	Rice Lake	7,691	54868
Yakima	49,826	98901*	Eau Claire	51,509	54701	Ripon	7,111	54971
			Elm Grove	6,735	53122	River Falls	9,036	54022
WEST VIRGINIA			Fond du Lac	35,863	54935	St. Francis	10,066	53207
			Fort Atkinson	9,785	53538	Shawano	7,013	54166
Beckley	20,492	25801	Fox Point	7,649	53117	Sheboygan	48,085	53081
Bluefield	16,060	24701	Franklin	16,871	53132	Shorewood	14,327	53211
Bridgeport	6,604	26330	Germantown	10,729	53022	South Milwaukee	21,069	53172
Buckhannon	6,820	26201	Glendale	13,882	53209	Sparta	6,934	54656
Charleston	63,968	25301	Grafton	8,381	53024	Stevens Point	22,970	54481
Clarksburg	22,371	26301	Green Bay	87,899	54305*	Stoughton	7,589	53589
Dunbar	9,285	25064	Greendale	16,928	53129	Sturgeon Bay	8,847	54235
Elkins	8,536	26241	Greenfield	31,467	53220	Sun Prairie	12,931	53590
Fairmont	23,863	26554	Hales Corners	7,110	53130	Superior	29,571	54880
Grafton	6,845	26354	Hartford	7,046	53027	Tomah	7,204	54660
Huntington	63,684	25701*	Howard	8,240	54303	Two Rivers	13,354	54241
Keyser	6,569	26726	Janesville	51,071	53545	Watertown	18,113	53094
Martinsburg	13,063	25401	Kaukauna	11,310	54130	Waukesha	50,319	53186
Morgantown	27,605	26505	Kenosha	77,685	53141*	Waupun	8,132	53963
Moundsville	12,419	26041	La Crosse	48,347	54601	Wausau	32,426	54401
New Martinsville	7,109	26155	Little Chute	7,907	54140	Wauwatosa	51,308	53226
Nitro	8,074	25143	Madison	170,616	53703*	West Allis	63,982	53214
Oak Hill	7,120	25901	Manitowoc	32,547	54220	West Bend	21,484	53095
Parkersburg	39,967	26101	Marinette	11,965	54143	Whitefish Bay	14,930	53217
Princeton	7,493	24740	Marshfield	18,290	54449	Whitewater	11,520	53190
St. Albans	12,402	25177	Menasha	14,728	54952	Wisconsin Rapids	17,995	54494
South Charleston	15,968	25303	Menomonee	12,769	54751			
Vienna	11,618	26105	Menomonee Falls	27,845	53051	**WYOMING**		
Weirton	24,736	26062	Mequon	16,193	53092			
Weston	6,250	26452	Merrill	9,578	54452	Casper	51,016	82601
Wheeling	43,070	26003	Middleton	11,779	53562	Cheyenne	47,283	82001
			Milwaukee	636,212	53201*	Cody	6,790	82414
WISCONSIN			Monona	8,809	53716	Evanston	6,421	82930
			Monroe	10,027	53566	Gillette	12,134	82716
Antigo	8,653	54409	Muskego	15,277	53150	Green River	12,807	82935
Appleton	59,032	54911	Neenah	23,272	54956	Lander	9,126	82520
Ashland	9,115	54806	New Berlin	30,529	53151	Laramie	24,410	82070
Ashwaubenon	14,486	54304	New London	6,210	54961	Rawlins	11,547	82301
Baraboo	8,081	53913	Oak Creek	16,932	53154	Riverton	9,588	82501
Beaver Dam	14,149	53916	Oconomowoc	9,909	53066	Rock Springs	19,458	82901
Beloit	35,207	53511	Onalaska	9,249	54650	Sheridan	15,146	82801
Brookfield	34,035	53005	Oshkosh	49,678	54901	Worland	6,391	82401

BIRTHSTONES
SOURCE: Jewelry Industry Council

January	Garnet
February	Amethyst
March	Aquamarine, bloodstone
April	Diamond
May	Emerald
June	Pearl, alexandrite, moonstone
July	Ruby, star ruby
August	Peridot, sardonyx
September	Sapphire, star sapphire
October	Opal, tourmaline
November	Topaz
December	Turquoise, zircon

FLOWERS OF THE MONTH
SOURCE: Society of American Florists, Alexandria, Va. in conjunction with *Red Book* Magazine 1977

January	Carnation
February	Violet
March	Daffodil
April	Sweet Pea
May	Lily of the Valley
June	Rose
July	Larkspur (Delphinium)
August	Gladiolus
September	Aster
October	Calendula (Pot Marigold)
November	Chrysanthemum
December	Narcissus

WEDDING ANNIVERSARY GIFTS

Anniversary	Traditional	Modern	Anniversary	Traditional	Modern
1	Paper/Plastics	Clocks	12	Silk or nylon/Linen	Pearl or colored gem
2	Cotton/Calico/Straw	China	13	Lace	Textiles/Furs
3	Leather or leatherlike items	Crystal or glass	14	Ivory/Agate	Gold jewelry
4	Fruit/Flowers/Books; also Linen/Silk or synthetic silks	Electrical appliance	15	Crystal or glass	Watch
			20	China/Occasional furniture	Platinum
5	Wood/Decorative home	Silverware accessories			
6	Candy or sugar/Iron	Wood	25	Silver	Silver
7	Wool/Copper, brass, or bronze	Desk set/Pen and pencil set	30	Pearl/Personal gifts	Diamond
8	Bronze/Pottery/Rubber; also Electrical applicances	Linens/Lace	35	Coral/Jade	Jade
			40	Ruby/Garnet	Ruby
9	Pottery/Willow/China, glass or crystal	Leather	45	Sapphire	Sapphire
			50	Gold	Gold
			55	Emerald/Turquoise	Emerald
10	Tin or aluminum	Diamond jewelry	60	Diamond/Gold	Diamond/Gold
11	Steel	Fashion jewelry or accessories	75	Diamond/Gold	Diamond/Gold

HISTORY: ANCIENT/MODERN

PRESENT MONARCHS AND DYNASTIES

AFRICA

Lesotho—**Dynasty:** Before independence, the people of Lesotho accepted authority of the "Paramount Chief" of the House of Moshesh. With independence (October 1966), Moshoeshoe II of the Moshesh became head of state. **Monarch:** Moshoeshoe II ascended the throne in October 1966. In "voluntary exile" Feb.-Dec. 1970 **Born:** May 2, 1938 **Married:** Tabitha' Masentle Lerotholi Mojela **Children:** Two sons, one daughter **Heir:** Crown Prince David Letsie (b. 1963) **Religion:** Christian

Morocco—**Dynasty:** The Alaouite dynasty (Filali) has ruled Morocco since the 17th century. The country has been ruled by constitutional kings since independence (1956), and in 1957 King Mohammed V changed his title from "His Sherifian Majesty, the Sultan" to "His Majesty, the King of Morocco." **Monarch:** King Hassan II, son of Mohammed V, ascended the throne on March 3, 1961, following the death of his father on February 26, 1961. **Born:** July 9, 1929 **Married:** Lalla Latifa **Children:** Two sons and three daughters **Heir:** Crown Prince Sidi Mohammed (born 1963). **Religion:** Moslem (Sunni)

Swaziland—**Dynasty:** Descended from Sobhuza I, the present king succeeded as Ngwenyama (or lion) of the Swazi nation, after a 20-year regency of the Queen Mother, in 1921. The country gained independence on September 6, 1968. **Monarch:** King Sobhuza II was chosen to succeed his father upon the latter's death in December 1899, was installed as king of the Swazi nation in 1921, and was recognized as the country's king in 1967. He is the world's longest-reigning monarch. **Born:** 1899 **Married:** approximately 70 wives **Children:** over 100 **Heir:** By custom, the heir to the throne is not chosen until after the death of the monarch. **Religion:** Christian

ARABIA

Bahrain—**Dynasty:** The Emir of Bahrain, head of the powerful Bedouin Al Khalifa family, is the tenth of his family to rule in Bahrain. Succession is by primogeniture. **Monarch:** Sheikh Isa ibn Salman al Khalifa became ruler on the death of his father in 1961, and the first Emir of Bahrain on August 14, 1971, the date of Bahrain's independence. **Children:** Hamad, others **Heir:** Sheikh Hamad ibn Isa al Khalifa, defense minister, and the Emir's oldest son **Religion:** Moslem (Sunni)

Jordan—**Dynasty:** Hashemite cooperation with the British in World War I resulted in Abdullah Ibn Hussein's rule of British mandated Transjordan. By a 1946 treaty with Great Britain, Abdullah became the first king of the independent Hashemite Kingdom of Jordan. Assassinated in 1951, Abdullah was succeeded by his son, Talal, father of the present king. **Monarch:** King Hussein I (ibn Talal) ascended the throne on May 2, 1953, following the deposition of his sickly father, Talal, on August 11, 1952. **Born:** November 14, 1935 **Married:** Princess Dina Abdel Hamid April 1955; divorced, 1957); Antoinette (Toni) Avril Gardiner (Muna al Hussein) (May 1961; divorced, 1972); Alia Toukan (1972; died 1977); Elizabeth Halaby (Nur al Hussein) (June 1978) **Children:** Five sons (Abdullah, born 1962; Faisal, born 1963; Ali, born 1976; Hamzah, born 1980; Hashem, born 1981) and four daughters (Alia, born 1956; Zein, born 1968; Ayeshia, born 1968; Haya, born 1974). Abir, an adopted daughter, was born in 1972. **Heir:** Prince Hassan, younger brother of the king **Religion:** Moslem (Sunni)

Kuwait—**Dynasty:** The Emir of Kuwait is the thirteenth ruler of the Al Sabah royal family. The nominated successor of the Emir must be approved by the National Assembly; succession usually alternates between the two branches of the royal family. **Monarch:** Sheikh Jabir al-Ahmad al-Jabir as-Sabah of the al-Jabir branch became Emir on the death of his cousin on Dec. 31, 1977. **Married:** one wife **Children:** several **Heir:** Crown Prince Sheikh Saad

Oman—**Dynasty:** The al Bu Said dynasty dates from 1741 when its founder, Ahmed Ibn Said, expelled the Turks from Muscat and Oman. **Monarch:** Sultan Qabus ibn Said al Bu Said ascended the throne in July 1970 after overthrowing his father, Said bin Taimur (1910-72), who had reigned since 1932. **Born:** November 18, 1940 **Married:** Kamilla (1976; reportedly divorced, 1980) **Heir:** no heir apparent has been designated **Religion:** Moslem (Ibadi)

Qatar—**Dynasty:** In the 19th century, the ruling Khalifa family deposed and forced to move to Bahrain, were succeeded by the Al Thani family. The present Emir, Khalifa ibn Hamad al-Thani, is the sixth ruler. In 1972 Khalifa assumed full power. Succession is designated by family consensus. **Monarch:** Sheikh Khalifa ibn Hamad al-Thani, Emir of Qatar, assumed power Feb. 22, 1972. **Born:** 1937 **Children:** Two sons—Hamad and Abd al Aziz, others **Heir:** no heir apparent has been designated **Religion:** Moslem (Wahhabi)

Saudi Arabia—**Dynasty:** The kingdoms of Nejd and Hejaz and their dependencies became the Kingdom of Saudi Arabia in 1932, under King Abdul-Aziz Ibn Abdur-Rahman Al-Faisal Al Saud. His son, King Saud, ruled from 1953 to 1964, when he was deposed, and succeeded by a brother, Faisal ibn Abdul-Aziz. **Monarch:** King Khalid ibn Abdul-Aziz Al Saud ascended the throne following the assassination of Faisal on March 25, 1975, by a nephew. **Born:** 1912 **Married:** one wife **Children:** five **Heir:** Prince Fahd ibn Abdul-Aziz, a younger brother **Religion:** Moslem (Sunni-Wahhabi sect)

ASIA

Bhutan—**Dynasty:** The present hereditary dynasty of Bhutan was founded in 1907 by Ugyen Dorji Wangchuk, a provincial governor, following the abolition of a dual system of government by spiritual and temporal rulers. The present king, installed in July 1972 after the death of his father, Jigme Dorji Wangchuk, is his great-grandson. **Monarch:** King Jigme Singhi Wangchuk (formally crowned on June 2, 1974) **Born:** 1955 **Children:** None **Heir:** To be selected from the royal family by the National Assembly **Religion:** Buddhist (Mahayana)

Japan—**Dynasty:** The Meiji Restoration (1867) placed Emperor Mutsuhito and his male descendants in command of a unified Japan. During the postwar American occupation of Japan, the Emperor, a grandson of Mutsuhito, renounced any claims to divinity, becoming a symbolic ruler. **Monarch:** Emperor Hirohito ascended the throne on the death of his father, Yoshihito, on December 25, 1926; he was enthroned on November 10, 1928. **Born:** April 29, 1901 **Married:** Princess Nagako (1924) **Children:** Seven; two sons (Akihito, born 1933; Masahito, born 1935) and three daughters (Kazuko, born 1929; Atsuko, born 1931; Takako, born 1939) survive **Heir:** Crown Prince Akihito **Religion:** Shinto

Nepal—**Dynasty:** The Shah family has ruled the kingdom of Nepal since the middle of the 18th century; however, a hereditary prime minister from the Rana family held actual power from 1846 to 1951. The last prime minister resigned in November 1951, and King Tribhuvan assumed full control. **Monarch:** Maharajadhiraja Birendra Bir Bikram Shah Dev succeeded to the throne in January 1972 (crowned in 1975) at the death of his father, Mahendra Bir Bikram Shah Dev **Born:** 1946 **Married:** Aishwarya Rajya Lakshmi Shah Devi **Children:** Two sons, one daughter **Heir:** Crown Prince Dependra Bir Bikram Shah Dev (b. 1971) **Religion:** Hindu

Thailand—**Dynasty:** The present ruling family of Thailand began with Rama I in 1782. His great-grandson, Chulalongkorn, King Rama V, was responsible for accelerating the modernization of Thailand; his nephew is the current monarch. **Monarch:** King Bhumibol Adulyadej, or Phumiphol Aduldet (Rama IX) succeeded to the throne

after the death of his elder brother, King Ananda Ma-
hidol, on June 9, 1946; he was crowned on May 5, 1950
Born: December 5, 1927 **Married:** Princess Sirikit Kit-
tiyakara (1950) **Children:** One son (Prince Vajiralongkorn,
born 1952), and three daughters (Ubol Ratana, born 1951;
Sirindhorn, born 1955; Chulabhorn, born 1957) **Heir:**
Crown Prince Vajiralongkorn **Religion:** Buddhist
(Hinayana)

EUROPE

Belgium—**Dynasty:** The ruling family of Belgium is of the
Saxe-Coburg-Gotha line. After Belgian separation from
the Netherlands (1830), Leopold, prince of Saxe-Coburg-
Gotha, was elected hereditary King of the Belgians on
June 4, 1831, as King Leopold I; he was enthroned on
July 21, 1831. **Monarch:** King Baudouin I (Albert Charles
Leopold Axel Marie Gustave) succeeded to the throne on
July 17, 1951, on the abdication of his father, Leopold III,
on the previous day. **Born:** September 7, 1930 **Married:**
Fabiola de Mora y Aragón (1960) **Children:** None **Heir:** Al-
bert, Prince of Liège, brother of the king (born 1934) **Re-
ligion:** Roman Catholic

Denmark—**Dynasty:** The House of Glücksburg has ruled
Denmark since King Frederik VII of the House of Oldenburg died childless in November 1863. By a treaty (1852),
King Frederik VII designated as heir Prince Christian X
of Schleswig-Holstein-Sonderburg-Glücksburg, who be-
came King Christian IX on Frederik's death. **Monarch:**
Queen Margrethe II succeeded to the throne on the death
of her father, King Frederik IX, on January 14, 1972.
Born: April 16, 1940 **Married:** Count Henri de Laborde de
Monpezat, now Prince Henrik of Denmark (1967) **Children:** Two sons: Frederik André Henrik Christian, born
1968; Joachim Holger Waldemar Christian, born 1969
Heir: Crown Prince Frederik **Religion:** Evangelical
Lutheran

Liechtenstein—**Dynasty:** The ruling House of Liechtenstein is descended from Huc von Liechtenstein, who be-
came hereditary ruler of the country in January 1719.
Royal Ruler: Prince Franz Josef II succeeded at the death
of his great-uncle, Prince Franz de Paula, on July 25,
1938. **Born:** August 16, 1906 **Married:** Countess Georgine
von Wilczek (1943) **Children:** Four sons, one daughter:
Prince Johannes Adam Ferdinand Alois Josef Maria
Marko d'Aviano Pius (b. 1945), Prince Philipp Erasmus
Alois Ferdinand Maria Sebaldus (b. 1946), Prince
Nikolaus Ferdinand Maria Josef Raphael (b. 1947),
Prince Franz-Josef Wenzel George Maria (b. 1962), and
Princess Nora Elisabeth Maria Anunta Josefine
Georgine Omnès Sancti (b. 1950) **Heir:** Crown Prince
Johannes (Hans) Adam **Religion:** Roman Catholic

Luxembourg—**Dynasty:** Made a Grand Duchy in 1815, the
country has been ruled by the Nassau family, the elder
line of the House of Nassau, since 1890. According to the
succession agreement, Adolphe, Duke of Nassau, succeeded at the death of King William III of the Netherlands. The Grand Duchy is today ruled by the great-
grandson of Adolphe. **Royal Ruler:** Grand Duke Jean suc-
ceeded to the throne on the abdication of his mother, the
Grand Duchess Charlotte, on November 12, 1964. **Born:**
January 5, 1921 **Married:** Princess Josephine-Charlotte of
Belgium, daughter of King Leopold III (1953) **Children:**
Three sons and two daughters: Prince Henri Albert
Gabriel Félix Marie Guillaume (b. 1955), Prince Jean
Félix Marie Guillaume (b. 1957), Prince Guillaume Marie
Louis Christian (b. 1963), Princess Marie Astrid
Charlotte Leopolding Wilhelmine Ingeborg Antonia
Lilane Alberta Elisabeth Anne (b. 1954), and Princess
Margaretha Antonia Maria Félicité (b. 1957) **Heir:** Prince
Henri **Religion:** Roman Catholic

Monaco—**Dynasty:** The House of Grimaldi has controlled
the principality of Monaco since 1297. **Royal Ruler:** Prince
Rainier III (Louis Henri Maxence Bertrand) succeeded
his grandfather, Prince Louis II, at his death on May 9,
1949. **Born:** May 31, 1923 **Married:** Grace Patricia Kelly of
Philadelphia (1956) **Children:** One son and two daughters:
Prince Albert Alexandre Louis Pierre (b. 1958), Princess
Caroline Louise Marguerite (b. 1957), and Princess Stép-
hanie Marie Elisabeth (b. 1965) **Heir:** Prince Albert **Religion:** Roman Catholic

Netherlands—**Dynasty:** The Congress of Vienna, which
settled the Napoleonic Wars, created the hereditary
kingdom of the Netherlands under King William I in

March 1815. The present sovereign is the sixth monarch
of the dynasty. **Monarch:** Queen Beatrix Wilhelmina
Armgard succeeded her mother, Queen Juliana, at the
latter's abdication on April 30, 1980; she was invested on
April 30, 1980. **Born:** January 31, 1938 **Married:** Prince
Claus von Amsberg (1966) **Children:** Three sons: Prince
Willem-Alexander Claus George Ferdinand (b. 1967),
Johan Frisco Bernhard Christiaan David (b. 1968), Con-
stantijn Christof Frederik Aschwin (b. 1969) **Heir:** Crown
Prince Willem-Alexander **Religion:** Dutch Reformed
Church

Norway—**Dynasty:** Norway was ruled by the kings of Denmark and Sweden from 1319 until its separation (1905),
when Prince Carl of Denmark was elected King Haakon
VII of an independent Norway. Married to Queen Maud,
daughter of Edward VII of England, King Haakon VII
was followed by his son, the present ruler. **Monarch:** King
Olav V, succeeded to the throne on the death of his father,
King Haakon VII, on September 21, 1957. **Born:** July 2,
1903 **Married:** Princess Märtha, daughter of Prince Carl of
Sweden (1929; d. 1954) **Children:** One son and two daughters: Prince Harald (b. 1937), Princess Ragnhild Alexandra (b. 1930), and Princess Astrid Maud Ingeborg (b.
1932) **Heir:** Crown Prince Harald **Religion:** Evangelical
Lutheran

Spain—**Dynasty:** The 1947 law of succession recreated the
Spanish Kingdom under the tutelage of Generalissimo
Franco, who would select a successor from the royal fam-
ily. The Bourbon dynasty had ruled from 1700-1808,
1814-1869, and again after 1875 until the abdication of
Alfonso XIII in April 1931. In 1969 Franco named Juan
Carlos, grandson of Alfonso, as heir, and after being ap-
proved by the Cortes he was entitled Prince of Spain on
July 23, 1969. He was proclaimed king on November 22,
1975, following the death of Franco. **Monarch:** Juan Carlos
I de BorboJAn y Borbón **Born:** January 5, 1938 **Married:**
Princess Sofía of Greece (1962) **Children:** One son and two
daughters: Prince of Asturias Felipe Juan Pablo Alfonso
de Borbón y Sonderburg-Gluckberg (b. 1968), Princess
Elena, Princess Cristina **Heir:** Prince Felipe **Religion:** Roman Catholic

Sweden—**Dynasty:** Jean-Baptiste-Jules Bernadotte was
elected (1810) Prince Royal of Sweden and adopted by
childless King Carl XIII. He ascended to the throne of
Norway and Sweden in 1818 as King Carl XIV Johan. His
descendant King Oscar II renounced the throne of Norway in 1905; however, the House of Bernadotte still reigns over Sweden. **Monarch:** King Carl XVI Gustav,
succeeded to the throne on the death of his grandfather,
King Gustav VI Adolf on September 16, 1973. King Carl's
father died in 1947. **Born:** April 30, 1946 **Married:** Silvia
Renate Sommerlath (1976) **Children:** Crown Princess Victoria Ingrid Alice Desiree (b. 1977), Prince Carl Philip
Edmund Bertil (b. 1979) **Heir:** Crown Princess Victoria
Ingrid Alice Desiree **Religion:** Lutheran

United Kingdom—**Dynasty:** The House of Windsor, a
branch of the Saxe-Coburg and Brunswick-Lüneburg
line, dates from the accession of King George V in 1910.
Although of German heritage, George V abandoned the
German name Wettin and adopted the surname Windsor
during World War I. He was succeeded by his sons Edward VIII (the Duke of Windsor) and George VI, father of
the present monarch. **Monarch:** Queen Elizabeth II succeeded her father, George VI, at his death on February 6
1952. **Born:** April 21, 1926 **Married:** Philip Mountbatten
(Duke of Edinburgh, Earl of Merioneth, Baron Greenwich, and Prince of Great Britain), the son of Prince Andrew of Greece and Denmark (1947) **Children:** Three sons
and one daughter: Prince Charles Philip Arthur George
(Prince of Wales and Duke of Cornwall) (b. 1948), Prince
Andrew Albert Christian Edward (b. 1960), Prince Edward Antony Richard Louis (b. 1964), and Princess Anne
Elizabeth Alice Louise (b. 1950) **Heir:** Prince Charles **Religion:** Anglican

OCEANIA

Tonga—**Dynasty:** Tonga was unified by Taufa'ahau Tupou
(George I) in 1845. The kingdom is currently ruled by his
descendants. **Monarch:** King Taufa'ahau Tupou IV succeeded to the throne at the death of his mother, Queen
Salote, in December 1965; he was crowned on April 7
1967 **Born:** July 4, 1918 **Married:** Princess Halaevalu
Mata'aho 'Ahome'e (1947) **Children:** four **Heir:** Crown
Prince Tupou To'a (Toufa'ahau Manumatuongo Tukuaho
(b. 1948) **Religion:** Christian

SELECTED PAST RULERS AND DYNASTIES

BRITISH RULERS

Victorious over his neighbors, Egbert of Wessex (d. 839) consolidated what was to become the first English kingdom. The British monarchy, although altered by Danish (1016) and Norman (1066) conquest, civil wars, and Cromwell's Commonwealth and weakened by constitutional restraints, still prevails.

Saxons and Danes	Reign Dates
Egbert	802–839
Ethelwulf	839–858
Ethelbald	858–860
Ethelbert	860–c. 866
Ethelred	c. 866–871
Alfred the Great	871–c. 899
Edward the Elder	c. 899–924
Athelstan	924–939
Edmund I	939–946
Edred	946–955
Edwy	955–959
Edgar	959–975
Edward the Martyr	975–978
Ethelred II	978–1016
Edmund Ironside	1016
Canute the Dane	1016–1035
Harold I	1035–1040
Hardicanute	1040–1042
Edward the Confessor	1042–1066
Harold II	1066

Norman	
William I (the Conqueror)	1066–1087
William II	1087–1100

	Reign Dates
Henry I	1100–1135
Stephen	1135–1154

Plantagenet	
Henry II	1154–1189
Richard I (Lion-Heart)	1189–1199
John	1199–1216
Henry III	1216–1272
Edward I	1272–1307
Edward II	1307–1327
Edward III	1327–1377
Richard II	1377–1399

Lancaster	
Henry IV (Bolingbroke)	1399–1413
Henry V	1413–1422
Henry VI	1422–1461
	1470–1471

York	
Edward IV	1461–1470
	1471–1483
Edward V	1483
Richard III	1483–1485

Tudor	
Henry VII	1485–1509
Henry VIII	1509–1547
Edward VI	1547–1553
Lady Jane Grey (nine days)	1553
Mary I	1553–1558
Elizabeth I	1558–1603

	Reign Dates
Stuart	
James I (VI of Scotland)	1603–1625
Charles I	1625–1649
Commonwealth	
Oliver Cromwell	1653–1658
Richard Cromwell	1658–1659
Military Rule	1659–1660
Stuart Restoration	
Charles II	1660–1685
James II	1685–1688
Interregnum	1688–1689
Orange	
William III	1689–1702
and Mary II	1689–1694
Stuart	
Anne	1702–1714
Hanover	
George I	1714–1727
George II	1727–1760
George III	1760–1820
George IV	1820–1830
William IV	1830–1837
Victoria	1837–1901
Saxe-Coburg	
Edward VII	1901–1910
Windsor (Wettin until 1917)	
George V	1910–1936
Edward VIII (325 days)	1936
George VI	1936–1952

CHINESE DYNASTIES

Hsia (legendary)	c. 1994 B.C.–c. 1523 B.C.
Shang	c. 1523 B.C.–c. 1027 B.C.
Chou	c. 1027 B.C.–256 B.C.
Western Chou	c. 1027 B.C.–771 B.C.
Eastern Chou	
Spring and Autumn Period	722 B.C.–481 B.C.
Warring States Period	403 B.C.–221 B.C.
Chin	221 B.C.–206 B.C.
Western Han	206 B.C.–9 A.D.
Hsin	9 A.D.–23 A.D.
Eastern Han	25–220

The Three Kingdoms	220–280
Shu	221–263
Wei	220–265
Wu	222–280
Western Tsin	266–316
Eastern Tsin	317–420
Southern and Northern Dynasties	420–581
Liu Sung	420–479
Southern Ch'i	479–502
Liang	502–557
Ch'en	557–589
Northern Wei and four minor dynasties	386–535

Sui	589–618
Tang	618–907
Five Dynasties	907–960
Later Liang	907–923
Later Tang	923–936
Later Chin	936–947
Later Han	947–951
Later Chou	951–960
Northern Sung	960–1127
Liao	916–1125
Southern Sung	1127–1279
Chin	1115–1234
Yuan	1271–1368
Ming	1368–1644
Ching (Manchu)	1644–1911

FRENCH RULERS

After the death (511) of Clovis I, the Merovingian founder of the Frankish monarchy, his kingdom was divided into Austrasia, Neustria, and Burgundy. These kingdoms were frequently at war. Dagobert I was the last active Merovingian ruler, and his descendants, called the idle kings, were completely subject to their mayors of the palace, the Carolingians, who became the actual rulers of France when Pepin the Short deposed (752) the last Merovingian king.

Carolingians	
*Pepin the Short	751–768
*Charlemagne (with Carloman up to 771)	768–814
*Louis I the Pious	814–840
Charles II the Bald	840–877
Louis II the Stammerer	877–879
Louis III and Carloman	879–882
Carloman	882–884
Charles the Fat, regent	884–887
Eudes (Capetian family)	888–898
Charles III the Simple	893–922
Robert I (Capetian)	922–923
Raoul of Burgundy	923–936
Louis IV d'Outremer	936–954
Lothaire	954–986
Louis V	986–987

Capetians	
Hugh Capet	987–996
Robert II	996–1031
Henry I	1031–1060
Philip I	1060–1108
Louis VI	1108–1137
Louis VII	1137–1180
Philip II (Augustus)	1180–1223
Louis VIII	1223–1226
Louis IX (Saint)	1226–1270
Philip III	1270–1285
Philip IV	1285–1314
Louis X	1314–1316
John I (the Posthumous)	1316–1317
Philip V	1317–1321
Charles IV	1321–1328

Valois	
Philip VI	1328–1350
John II	1350–1364
Charles V	1364–1380
Charles VI	1380–1422
Charles VII	1422–1461
Louis XI	1461–1483
Charles VIII	1483–1498

Valois-Orléans	
Louis XII	1498–1515

Valois-Angoulême	
Francis I	1515–1547

Henry II	1547–1559
Francis II	1559–1560
Charles IX	1560–1574
Henry III	1574–1589

Bourbons	
Henry IV	1589–1610
Louis XIII	1610–1643
Louis XIV	1643–1715
Louis XV	1715–1774
Louis XVI	1774–1793
Louis XVII (titular)	1793–1795

First Republic	1792–1804
First Empire	
Napoleon I (Bonaparte)	1804–1814
Bourbon Restoration	
Louis XVIII	1814–1824
First Empire (100 days)	1815
Bourbons	
Charles X	1824–1830
Bourbon-Orleans	
Louis Philippe	1830–1848
Second Republic	
(Louis) Napoleon III	1848–1851
Second Empire	
(Louis) Napoleon III	1852–1870

* King of the Franks.

GERMAN AND PRUSSIAN RULERS

House of Hohenzollern, Kings of Prussia

Frederick I	1701–1713
Frederick William I	1713–1740

King of Prussia and Emperor of Germany.

Frederick II (the Great)	1740–1786
Frederick William II	1786–1797
Frederick William III	1797–1840
Frederick William IV	1840–1861

William I (German emperor after 1871)	1861–1888
*Frederick III	1888
*William II	1888–1918

ITALIAN RULERS

Guided by Camillo di Cavour, the House of Savoy undertook to liberate and unify the Italian peninsula, a movement known as the Risorgimento. Italy became a kingdom in 1861 and a republic in 1946.

House of Savoy

Emmanuel Philibert	1553–1580

Charles Emmanuel I	1580–1630
Victor Amadeus I	1630–1637
Charles Emmanuel II	1637–1675
Victor Amadeus II	1675–1730
Charles Emmanuel III	1730–1773
Victor Amadeus III	1773–1796
Charles Emmanuel IV	1796–1802
Victor Emmanuel I	1802–1821
Charles Felix	1821–1831

House of Savoy-Carignano

Charles Albert	1831–1849

Kings of Italy

Victor Emmanuel II (king after 1861)	1849–1878
Humbert I	1878–1900
Victor Emmanuel III	1900–1946
Humbert II	1946

ROMAN EMPERORS

Successor to Julius Caesar, Octavian (also known as Augustus), became the first Roman emperor in 27 B.C. His rule began a long period (200 years) of peace, called the Pax Romana. Stretching westward to the British Isles and eastward to the Caucasus, the vast Roman Empire was permanently divided into West and East Empires after the death (395) of Theodosius the Great. The Western Roman Empire came to an end in 476, when the German Odoacer deposed Romulus Augustulus. The Eastern Empire, with its capital at Constantinople, was gradually supplanted by the Byzantine Empire.

Emperor

Augustus	27 B.C.–14 A.D.
Tiberius	14–37
Caligula	37–41
Claudius	41–54
Nero	54–68
Galba	68–69
Otho	69
Vitellius	69
Vespasian	69–79
Titus	79–81
Domitian	81–96
Nerva	96–98
Trajan	98–117
Hadrian	117–138
Antoninus Pius	138–161
Marcus Aurelius	161–180
Commodus	180–192
Pertinax	193
Didius Julianus	193
Septimius Severus	193–211
Caracalla	211–217
Macrinus	217–218
Elagabalus (Heliogabalus)	218–222
Alexander Severus	222–235
Maximinus	235–238
Gordian I	238
Gordian II	238
Pupienus	238

Balbinus	238
Gordian III	238–244
Philip the Arab	244–249
Decius	249–251
Hostilianus	251
Gallus	251–253
Volusianus	c. 251–253
Valerian	253–260
Gallienus	253–268
Claudius II	268–270
Aurelian	270–275
Tacitus	275–276
Florianus	276
Probus	276–282
Carus	282–283
Carinus	283–285
Numerianus	283–284
Diocletian	284–305
Maximian	286–305
Constantius	305–306
Galerius	305–310
Maxentius	306–312
Constantine I the Great	306–337
Licinius	308–324
Constantine II	337–340
Constans	337–350
Constantius II	337–361
Magnentius	350–353
Julian the Apostate	361–363

Jovian	363–364
Valentinian I	364–375
Valens	364–378
Gratian	375–383
Valentinian II	375–392
Magnus Maximus	383–388
Eugenius	392–394
Theodosius I the Great	379–395

Emperors in the East

Arcadius	395–408
Theodosius II	408–450
Marcian	450–457
Leo I	457–474
Leo II	474

Emperors in the West

Honorius	395–423
Constantius III	421
Valentinian III	425–455
Petronius Maximus	455
Avitus	455–456
Majorian	457–461
Libius Severus	461–465
Anthemius	467–472
Olybrius	472
Glycerius	473
Julius Nepos	474–475
Romulus Augustulus	475–476

RUSSIAN RULERS

Grand Dukes of Moscow

Ivan I, Prince of Moscow	1328–1341
Ivan II, Ivanovich	1353–1359
Dmitry Donskoi	1359–1389
Vasily I Dmitrievich	1389–1425
Vasily II	1425–1462
Ivan III Vasilyevich	1462–1505
Vasily III Ivanovich	1505–1533
Ivan IV (the Terrible), tsar of Russia from 1547	1533–1584
Fyodor Ivanovich	1584–1598

Boris Godunov	1598–1605
Fyodor II	1605
False Dmitry I	1605–1606
Vasily Shuisky	1606–1610
Interregnum	1610–1613

House of Romanov

Tsar Mikhail	1613–1645
Tsar Alexei Mikhailovich	1645–1676
Fyodor Alexeyevich	1676–1682
Peter I, the Great (with Ivan V until 1689)	1682–1725
Catherine I	1725–1727

Peter II	1727–1730
Anna Ivanovna	1730–1740
Ivan VI	1740–1741
Elizabeth	1741–1761
Peter III	1761–1762
Catherine II (the Great)	1762–1796
Paul I	1796–1801
Alexander I	1801–1825
Nicholas I	1825–1855
Alexander II	1855–1881
Alexander III	1881–1894
Nicholas II	1894–1917

SPANISH RULERS

Spain was unified by the marriage of Ferdinand of Aragon and Isabella of Castile. Alfonso XIII was exiled in 1931, when Spain became a republic. The country came under the rule of Gen. Francisco Franco in 1939. The grandson of Alfonso XIII was proclaimed king, as Juan Carlos I, on the death of Franco in 1975.

Houses of Aragon and Castile

Ferdinand II of Aragon and Isabella of Castile	1474–1504
Ferdinand II and Philip I	1504–1506
Ferdinand II and Charles I	1506–1516

Spanish Hapsburgs

Charles I (V of Holy Roman Empire)	1516–1556
Philip II	1556–1598
Philip III	1598–1621
Philip IV	1621–1665
Charles II	1665–1700

Spanish Bourbons

Philip V	1700–1724
Louis I	1724
Philip V	1724–1746
Ferdinand VI	1746–1759
Charles III	1759–1788
Charles IV	1788–1808

French King of Spain

Joseph Bonaparte	1808–1813

Bourbon Restoration

Ferdinand VII	1814–1833
Isabella II	1833–1868

Provisional Government | 1868–1870

House of Savoy

Amadeo I	1870–1873

First Spanish Republic | 1873–1874

Bourbon Restoration

Alfonso XII	1875–1885
Alfonso XIII	1886–1931

FAMILY HISTORY IS FOR EVERYONE

Harriet Stryker Rodda, certified genealogist, lecturer and teacher; author of family histories and professional articles, including How to Climb Your Family Tree.

Everyone in America is descended from immigrant stock, no matter what the ethnic or cultural background. Even the "native American Indians" were immigrants. They just happened to arrive before the European sailors and settlers.

With the Bicentennial celebrations mostly behind us, we are facing the coming of our Tricentennial in the year 2076. By then, each of us could be an ancestor who could be a missing link to our descendants. Far too many people in this country are bemoaning the fact that they cannot complete their connections with their ancestral families because their folks left no records or they neglected to listen when stories were being told.

Families in the United States are the backbone of the nation, although they are not as stereotyped as they once were. No matter what the ethnic or cultural background, the family unit is still the core of our young, 202-year-old America. *Newsweek* declared in May 1978 "there is an underlying stability of family life that often goes unnoticed. Ninety-eight percent of all American children are raised in families, and last year 79 percent of those were living with their parents." These are the children, plus many more, who by 2076 will be asking "Who am I?", "Where did my family come from?", "When did they get here?", "How did they live?", "Why are we as we are?"

These very same questions are being asked today. The answers are not to be found easily for some, because the fore-parents left no private and often few public records of themselves. For the majority, however, most of the facts they need to answer the who, where, when, why and how are available. They can be found and the family history preserved to be passed along for years to come. "But how do I start?" is the first question.

Start with yourself. You are to be author of your family history. Your autobiography will not only inform others of the facts and facets of your life, but more importantly will reveal to you the debt you owe your family. It will show you what you would like to know about those earlier members of the family. *Who, when, where, how* and *why* will be your guides as you record yourself and your times. Add pictures to illustrate, and dig out the certificates of your birth, education, honors, marriage or anything else that will add documentation to your record. Even if you never go on to compile a family history, this autobiography may be of inestimable assistance to someone else who will take up the task where you left off.

Contact all older living members of your family. With tape recorder or pencil and notebook, get all the information on the family members they can supply. It will amaze you how much they know and how they will have contacts with relatives you have never heard of. Don't overlook the stories or traditions they may relate to you. There is a core of truth in most of them. Try not to antagonize, but tell them of your deep interest in preparing and preserving the family's history.

Check their possession of family or Bible records; ask about certificates, passports, naturalization records, pictures, letters, heirloom furniture or other items. You may want some of these, but don't be greedy. Take pictures of whatever you can and copy whatever you find in their records. But leave the original with the owner unless it is freely given to you.

Record your in-family findings. How you do this is for you to decide, but make the final record easily understandable by anyone who sees it. It should contain the time and place and from whom you received the statements so that later you won't have to wonder who told you that and where you heard it. For every statement you use in your final record, you should have some documentation to prove it. Birth, marriage, divorce, death and land ownership records are the basic public records that should be found to support your story.

Visit a good genealogical library and use their catalogs to determine whether someone in the past has written a family history or genealogy to which your family can relate. Read the local and general histories for a better understanding of where and how your people lived. See the vital records collected for researchers like you: church records, newspaper items, census records, maps, cemetery records, diaries, account books, and many, many more, including the work of genealogists whose notes on your family may have been deposited for safekeeping. Get acquainted with the publications of genealogical societies, especially those that publish genealogical records. Begin to took at some of the books on the shelves with a critical eye. Decide which of their features you like and what you would not want in your final record. Are they readable, interesting in form and format, well documented and illustrated; do they feel good in the hand; does the type of binding let them lie open readily for reading and research? Make note of those that please you so that you can refer to them when you are ready to prepare your final history.

Despite the wealth of recorded information to be found in the form of tax rolls, military records, probate, land, court and census records, not to mention church and cemetery records and the cemeteries themselves, with their informative gravestones, this information is not always easy to obtain. Help is available. Along the way you will have become acquainted with the many "how-to" books written by people who want to share their knowledge with you. You will hear and read of genealogical seminars, lectures and conferences at every level from the local historical society to the large university and the Federal Archives. Take advantage of as much of this as you can, for you will meet a vast number of people who are learning as you are, who are as eager to accomplish as you will be, and who are happy to share their knowledge with you.

Today, family history is recognized for its value in establishing a keen sense of identity. Such simple projects in elementary schools as collecting information about parents and grandparents are known to help children establish a sense of personal worth and dignity. Genealogy is no longer considered a snob hobby. It has come of age. Good hunting! Become an honored ancestor!

OUTLINE OF WORLD HISTORY

This capsule presentation of the history of the world covers the period from 4000 B.C. through 1980.

4000 B.C.—3000 B.C.

EUROPE
4000 B.C. Farmers living along **Danube River** in villages designed stone replicas of deities.

NEAR AND MIDDLE EAST
4000 B.C. Ubadians, who were settled in southern Mesopotamia, developed towns in the Tigris-Euphrates plain, laying foundation for future civilization of **Ur.** Semitic nomads from Syria and the Arabian peninsula invaded area and intermingled with Urbaidians.

3500 B.C. Sumerians, possibly from Asia, settled along the Euphrates and developed a civilization that flourished.

FAR EAST
4000 B.C. Farmers lived in villages in northern **China.**

AMERICAS
4000 B.C. Indians in North and South America, descendants of people who migrated from Asia over the Bering Strait many centuries earlier, obtained food by hunting and cultivating corn. The remains of extinct animals, such as the mastodon, as well as arrowheads and spear points found in caves at **Folsom** and **Clovis,** New Mexico, attest to the antiquity of Indians in the Americas.

AFRICA
4000 B.C. An early Negro civilization thrived in the Sahara. The Tassili rock paintings in southeast Algeria, which date from about 6000 B.C., portray an organized society of hunters and herders who had horses and cattle.

c. 3200 B.C. Upper and Lower Egypt were united by the legendary **Menes,** the first Pharaoh, who built his capital at Memphis.

3000 B.C.—2000 B.C.

EUROPE
2700–2000 B.C. Early **Helladic** culture existed on Greek mainland, and **Cycladic** culture in the Aegean islands; both noted for primitive figurines.

2500–1200 B.C. Barbarian **Celts,** who overran western Europe, rode horses, carried iron weapons, and were ruled by **Druids,** a priestly class.

2500–1100 B.C. Megalithic culture of western Europe was noted for its huge stone ceremonial constructions, such as **dolmens,** or chamber tombs, and **menhirs,** or monumental stone slabs, sometimes arranged in circles, as at **Stonehenge** in England; remains also exist at **Carnac,** Brittany.

NEAR AND MIDDLE EAST
c. 3000 B.C. Kish, near modern Baghdad, became leading Sumerian city in the reign of King Etana.

c. 2800 B.C. Meskiaggasher founded dynasty in **Erech,** which began to rival Kish.

2686–2181 B.C. Old Kingdom of Egypt: Egyptian art and architecture developed; great pyramid for Pharaoh Khufu, one of the Seven Wonders of the Ancient World, was completed (c. 2600 B.C.) at Gizeh.

c. 2650 B.C. Gilgamesh, hero of Sumerian legends, reigned as king of Erech.

2500 B.C. King Lugalannemundu of Adab briefly united Sumerian city-states; following his death, city-states fought each other for 200 years.

c. 2450 B.C. King Eannatum made the Sumerian city-state of Lagash supreme.

c. 2325 B.C. Sargon the Great ruled over vast empire in Mesopotamia and built capital at Agade in Akkad that had beautiful temples and palace.

c. 2300 B.C. Ebla flourishes in Syria.

2200 B.C. Gutians, barbarians from Iran, conquered Sumeria and destroyed Agade.

2133–1786 B.C. Middle Kingdom of Egypt: Egypt expanded territory southward and engaged in extensive foreign trade.

2100 B.C. Ur-Nammu founded last Sumerian dynasty and promulgated law code, the oldest in existence.

FAR EAST
3000–1500 B.C. Indus valley civilization of northern India: a sophisticated culture thrived and cities of Harappa and Mohenjo-Daro were built with courtyard houses and modern drainage systems.

c. 2205–c. 1766 B.C. Hsia dynasty of China: first historic Chinese dynasty thrived; horses were domesticated and rice and millet were cultivated.

AMERICAS
2500 B.C. Indians began to make pottery.

2000 B.C.—1500 B.C.

EUROPE
c. 2000–1700 B.C. Mycenaeans, Greek-speaking people, settled in Greece, established flourishing civilization, and traded with Crete.

c. 1900–1400 B.C. Stonehenge, a massive stone complex used for religious purposes, was erected on Salisbury Plain, England.

c. 1700–c. 1500 B.C. Minoan culture on Crete reached its zenith; magnificent Minoan palaces built at Knossos and Phaistos showed evidence of advanced engineering skills.

c. 1500 B.C. Linear B script existed in Crete, evidence of Mycenaean influence.

NEAR AND MIDDLE EAST
2000 B.C. Elamites destroyed Ur, marking end of Sumerian dominance in Mesopotamia.

c. 2000–c. 1900 B.C. Abraham, founder of **Judaism,** is said to have lived.

2000–1700 B.C. Hebrews lived as nomadic shepherds in Canaan.

1786–1567 B.C. Egypt ruled by **Hyksos** kings, who probably came from Canaan, introduced horse-drawn chariots.

1750–c. 1708 B.C. Hammurabi ruled Babylonia, brought most of Mesopotamia and Assyria under his control, and introduced his law code.

c. 1600 B.C. Babylonian dynasty destroyed by Hittites from Anatolia and Syria.

1567–1085 B.C. New Kingdom in Egypt: Hyksos kings ousted and Egyptian power and civilization reached its height.

FAR EAST
1523–1027 B.C. Shang dynasty ruled China, developing a high civilization characterized by specialized classes, writing, a medium of exchange, and ancestor worship.

AMERICAS
2000 B.C. By this time, Indians had permanent village settlements and were cultivating manioc, squash, maize, and beans and domesticating dogs.

1500 B.C.—1000 B.C.

EUROPE
1400 B.C. Mycenaeans gained supremacy of the Mediterranean, and Mycenae, in northern Peloponnesus, became major ancient city following collapse of Knossus.

c. 1200 B.C. Trojan Wars: Greece conquered Troy in Asia Minor.
Dorian barbarians from the north began to invade Greece, initiating Dark Ages of Greek history.

1150–1000 B.C. Greeks settled on Ionian coast of Asia Minor.

NEAR AND MIDDLE EAST
c. 1500 B.C. Mitanni kingdom of Hurrians (known as Horites in Old Testament) ruled much of Mesopotamia and Assyria.

1468 B.C. Battle of Megiddo: Egyptians, under Thutmose III, conquered Syria and part of Mesopotamia.

1292–1225 B.C. Ramses II ruled Egypt and completed temples at Karnak, Thebes, Luxor, and Abu-Simbel. Moses led Hebrews out of Egypt.

1250 B.C. Phoenicians flourished on coasts of Syria and Lebanon, establishing great city-states of **Tyre** and **Sidon** and beginning to colonize Mediterranean coast.

c. 1250 B.C. Hebrews entered Canaan.

1020–1004 B.C. Saul became the first king of the Hebrews.

FAR EAST

1500–500 B.C. Barbarian **Aryans**, Sanskrit-speaking people from central Asia, invaded India and destroyed Indus valley civilization; early *Vedas*, sacred Hindu texts, were composed.

1027–256 B.C. Chou dynasty of China superseded Shang dynasty and represented the Classical Age of China with the *Five Classics*, and teachings of **Confucius**, **Lao-tze**, and **Mencius**.

AMERICAS

c. 1250 B.C. Olmecs began to settle at San Lorenzo, Mexico, and developed civilization with widespread influence that was famous for gigantic sculptured heads (sometimes weighing over 20 tons) and austere figurines; ceremonial center was established at **La Venta** (fl. 800–c. 400 B.C.) for jaguar cult; Stele C found at Tres Zapotes has date equivalent to 31 B.C. carved in Mayan calendric system.

AFRICA

1200 B.C. Negroes in Nigeria developed **Nok** culture, which became advanced civilization, noted for expressive terra-cotta sculpture, but died out c. 200 B.C.

1000 B.C.—700 B.C.

EUROPE

1000 B.C. Teutonic tribes settled northern Europe.

Latin tribes began to settle in Italy.

900–400 B.C. Etruscan people, who had probably migrated from Lydia in Asia Minor, established a high civilization in Italy and became maritime power.

850–600 B.C. Homeric Greece: Greeks established colonies in Italy and along Mediterranean; the *Iliad* and the *Odyssey* were probably composed by **Homer**, **Hesiod** wrote poetry, and music developed.

776 B.C. Olympic games initiated.

753 B.C. Traditional date for founding of **Rome** by **Romulus** and **Remus**.

750 B.C. Romans seized Sabine women at public spectacle, taking them as wives.

747 B.C. Rome taken by Sabines, who united with Romans as one people.

736–630 B.C. Sparta became powerful on Greek mainland.

NEAR AND MIDDLE EAST

1000–774 B.C. Phoenicians dominated the seas, perhaps sailing to Cornwall, England, for tin and probably sailing down west coast of Africa.

910–606 B.C. Assyrian Empire controlled Mesopotamia.

774–625 B.C. Phoenicia came under Assyrian rule.

747–728 B.C. Tiglath-Pilser III, king of Assyria, subdued Aramaean tribes in Babylonia, conquered Urartu (Armenia), and established control over Syria.

721–705 B.C. Sargon II, king of Assyria, completed conquest of Israel, exiling most Israelites.

705–681 B.C. Sennacherib, king of Assyria, destroyed Babylon and built magnificent palace at Nineveh.

AMERICAS

c. 1000 B.C. Chavin culture in northern Peru began to flourish; elaborate stone ceremonial center with painted relief sculpture was erected at Chavin de Huantar for jaguar cult; and gold ornaments and ceramics were designed; this culture declined after 200 B.C.

AFRICA

c. 800–586 B.C. Carthage, founded in North Africa by Phoenicians, became a wealthy commercial center.

c. 750 B.C. Kushites settled in Sudan and developed high civilization, erecting palaces and pyramids; extensive archaeological remains of ironworks at Meroë; Kushites used elephants and traded as far as Rome and India; their last king died in 320 A.D.

700 B.C.—500 B.C.

EUROPE

c. 700 B.C. Temple to Hera erected at **Olympia**.

Spartans, after a series of wars, annexed eastern part of Messenia.

Celts began to invade Spain and France.

c. 660 B.C. Byzantium founded by Megara.

c. 621 B.C. Draco codified harsh Athenian law.

600–300 B.C. Teutonic tribes invaded western Europe: the **Alemanni** settled on the upper Rhine, the **Franks** and **Saxons** between the Weser and the Elbe, and the **Thuringians** south of the Saxons.

594 B.C. Solon introduced constitutional and social reforms into Athens, establishing limited democracy.

c. 580 B.C. Thales, first Western philosopher, flourished.

566 B.C. First Roman census taken.

c. 560–510 B.C. Athens ruled by **tyrants** after Pisistratus seized power.

560 B.C. Croesus, wealthy king of Lydia, conquered Ionian cities and was defeated (546 B.C.) by Cyrus the Great.

c. 550 B.C. Temple of **Artemis** (Diana) erected at Ephesus.

c. 534–510 B.C. Reign of **Tarquinius Superbus**, Etruscan ruler; Etruscan supremacy ended soon after his death.

509 B.C. Traditional date for founding of the Roman Republic.

The **Temple of Jupiter**, on the Roman Capitol, was dedicated.

NEAR AND MIDDLE EAST

681–668 B.C. Esarhaddon, king of Assyria, reigned; at its peak Assyrian Empire extended from Iran to Egypt.

625–539 B.C. Chaldean Empire of Mesopotamia.

612 B.C. Nineveh, Assyrian capital, fell to Medes, Chaldeans, and Scythians.

606 B.C. Battle of Carchemish ended Assyrian Empire.

c. 605–562 B.C. Reign of **Nebuchadnezzar II**, king of Babylonia; Babylon, with its hanging gardens (one of Seven Wonders of Ancient World), was greatest city of its time during his reign; massive palaces, "Tower of Babel," and a temple to the god Marduk were also constructed.

586 B.C. Nebuchadnezzar took **Jerusalem**, destroying the temple of Solomon and carrying inhabitants back to Babylonia.

c. 550 B.C. Persian Empire, founded by Cyrus the Great, included vast areas of the Near and Middle East; Persian art and architecture flourished, and Zoroastrian religion spread.

538 B.C. Cyrus the Great conquered Babylon and returned Hebrews to Jerusalem.

525–404 B.C. Persians conquered and ruled Egypt.

521–486 B.C. Darius I (the Great), king of Persia, extended and strengthened the empire, warred with Greece, and unified Persian power in the East.

FAR EAST

c. 563–483 B.C. Gautama Buddha preached in India.

c. 551–479 B.C. Confucius taught in China.

AFRICA

c. 631 B.C. Greeks founded North African city of **Cyrene**, which became important commercial center.

500 B.C.—400 B.C.

EUROPE

500–449 B.C. Greek-Persian Wars were fought, caused by commercial rivalry between Athens and Persia; Athens became leading city-state of Greece.

500 B.C. Classical Greek civilization (drama, philosophy, and the arts) developed and flourished, declining after 300 B.C.

498 B.C. Earliest extant poem of **Pindar** was written.

490 B.C. Battle of **Marathon**: 30,000 Persians, who were sent by Darius I, landed at Marathon to march on Athens and were turned back by Athenian infantrymen under **Miltiades**.

460 B.C. Athens warred against **Peloponnesian cities**, which were allied with Sparta.

457–429 B.C. Age of **Pericles** or Golden Age of Athens: philosophy, sculpture, and painting flourished; Parthenon was built (447–432 B.C.) on the Acropolis.

c. 451 B.C. The Twelve Tablets: **Roman law** codified for the first time.

c. 435 B.C. Phidias completed his statue of Zeus (one of Seven Wonders of Ancient World) for temple of Olympia.

431–404 B.C. Peloponnesian War developed, growing out of Spartan-Athenian rivalry; Athens destroyed (430).

c. 411 Thucydides wrote *The Peloponnesian War*.

404–371 B.C. Sparta was leading Greek power.

NEAR AND MIDDLE EAST

490 B.C. First Persian expedition to Greece under Darius I was turned back at Marathon.

480–479 B.C. Second Persian expedition to Greece under Xerxes I was turned back at Plataea.

AMERICAS

c. 500 B.C. Zapotecs established ceremonial center at Monte Albán, Mexico, which showed Olmec influence.

AFRICA

c. 500 B.C. Kingdom of Axum in Ethiopia came into existence; palaces, temples, and carved stone obelisks were built and trade took place with Near East and India; this kingdom declined c. 700 A.D.

400 B.C.—300 B.C.

EUROPE

400–270 B.C. Rome conquered Italy, subduing Etruscans, Samnites, and Greek colonists.

399 B.C. Socrates was condemned to death and made to drink hemlock.

390 B.C. Rome sacked by Gauls.

c. 387 B.C. Plato founded his Academy in Athens, which is considered the first university of the Western world.

359–336 B.C. Philip II of Macedon conquered Thrace, Thebes, and Athens, and attempted to unite Greece during his reign; Demosthenes, greatest Greek orator, warned Athenians of Macedonian aims.

336–323 B.C. Reign of Alexander the Great of Macedon (son of Philip II), first of the great European conquerors; Alexander extended empire to include Egypt and the Near East and invaded India.

335 B.C. Aristotle founded a school in the Lyceum at Athens known as Peripatetic from his practice of lecturing in a covered portico (peripatos).

323 B.C. Hellenistic Age began, during which Greek influence spread throughout Mediterranean; this age ended in 31 B.C.

NEAR AND MIDDLE EAST

c. 352 B.C. Mausoleum at Halicarnassus in Asia Minor (one of Seven Wonders of Ancient World) was erected in memory of Mausolus of Caria.

334–330 B.C. Alexander the Great conquered Asia Minor, Phoenicia, Palestine, Egypt, and Persia and founded Alexandria.

323 B.C.–30 A.D. Ptolemies, a Greek dynasty, ruled Egypt.

FAR EAST

327–326 B.C. Alexander the Great and his Greek troops entered India, withdrawing after troops revolted.

325–298 B.C. Reign of Chandragupta Maurya, who founded Maurya dynasty and united India.

AFRICA

350 B.C. Meroë, Kushite capital, fell to Ethiopians and was abandoned.

300 B.C.—200 B.C.

EUROPE

300 B.C. City of Rome became a major power in Mediterranean world.

292–280 B.C. Colossus of Rhodes (one of Seven Wonders of Ancient World), a bronze statue, probably more than 100 feet tall, of the sun god, Helios, was constructed on promontory overlooking harbor.

282–272 B.C. Pyrrhus, king of Epirus, fought Romans and caused its ruin.

264–241 B.C. First Punic War: Carthage warred against Roman occupation of Sicily.

227 B.C. Rome annexed Sardinia and Corsica.

218–201 B.C. Second Punic War: Hannibal, the Carthaginian leader, crossed the Alps and invaded Italy; victorious Romans gained Spanish provinces and Carthaginian war fleet.

NEAR AND MIDDLE EAST

300 B.C. Alexandria, Egypt, became intellectual center of Hellenistic world until its influence ended in 50 B.C.

c. 280 B.C. Under Ptolemy II, a lighthouse (one of Seven Wonders of Ancient World) was constructed on Pharos, Alexandria.

250 B.C. Parthian Empire, which succeeded Persian Empire, ended in 226 A.D.

FAR EAST

269–232 B.C. Emperor Asoka the Great ruled India, making Buddhism state religion.

221–207 B.C. Ch'in dynasty of China: country was unified for first time, and construction of Great Wall was initiated.

202 B.C. Han dynasty of China established: during long peaceful rule, Chinese realized great artistic achievements, expanded territory, and introduced Buddhism; this dynasty collapsed in 220 A.D.

200 B.C.—100 B.C.

EUROPE

192–189 B.C. During Syrian War between Rome and Seleucid kingdom, Romans acquired territory in Asia Minor.

c. 150 B.C. Polybius completed six books of his Universal History, a political analysis of the rise of Rome.

149–146 B.C. Third Punic War.

146 B.C. Macedonia became a Roman province.

121 B.C. Rome conquered southeastern Gaul, modern Provence.

NEAR AND MIDDLE EAST

192–189 B.C. Syrian War between Rome and Seleucids: Antiochus III forced to give up Asia Minor.

167 B.C. Hebrew Maccabees revolted against Antiochus IV, king of Syria, who had tried to Hellenize Palestine.

FAR EAST

c. 200 B.C. Mahabharata, Sanskrit epic poem, began to be composed and was completed c. 200 A.D.

AFRICA

149–146 B.C. Third Punic War: Carthage destroyed by Romans, who established Roman province of Africa.

100 B.C.—A.D. 1

EUROPE

73–71 B.C. Spartacus led slave revolt in southern Italy; Pompey crushed revolt and crucified 6,000 slaves.

63 B.C. Cicero, greatest Roman orator, exposed Catiline's plot to seize consulship by force.

60–53 B.C. First Triumvirate: Julius Caesar, Pompey, and Marcus Licinius Crassus ruled Rome.

58–49 B.C. Gallic Wars: Caesar's campaigns brought Gaul under Roman rule.

48 B.C. Caesar met Cleopatra in Egypt.

46–44 B.C. Caesar ruled Rome, which included Gaul, Italy, part of Illyria, Macedonia, Greece, Asia Minor, Egypt, and part of North Africa.

44 B.C. Caesar stabbed to death in the Senate on Ides of March.

43–31 B.C. Second Triumvirate: Marc Antony, Lepidus, and Octavian, Caesar's grandnephew, ruled Rome.

c. 35 B.C. Roman poets Vergil and Horace flourished.

31 B.C. Octavian defeated Antony and Cleopatra at Actium, assuming title Augustus and becoming first Roman emperor; Augustus made Egypt a Roman province.

27 B.C. Roman Empire established.

14 B.C. Pax Romana: Roman Empire began 200 years of peace, which ended in 192 A.D.

NEAR AND MIDDLE EAST

74–63 B.C. Third Mithridatic War between King Mithridates VI of Pontus and Rome, which resulted in further Roman conquests in Near East.

48 B.C. Cleopatra, daughter of Ptolemy XI of Egypt, with the aid of Julius Caesar, became Queen of Egypt (47–30 B.C.).

37 B.C. Rome began to rule Palestine; this rule ended in 395 A.D.

36 B.C. Queen Cleopatra married Marc Antony.

30 B.C. Egypt annexed by Roman Empire, following the suicides of Antony and Cleopatra.

6 or 4 B.C. Jesus born in Bethlehem.

AMERICAS

100 B.C. Paracus culture, an offshoot of Chavin civilization in Peru, flourished.

A.D. 1—A.D. 100

EUROPE

1 Christian era began.
Gothic kingdom on the lower Vistula (Poland) developed.

5–40 Cymbeline reigned in Britain.

9 Arminius defeated Roman commander Varus at the Battle of Teutoburg Forest, ending Roman attempts to conquer Germany.

37 Caligula made emperor of Rome by army; his cruel regime ended (41) with his assassination.

41–54 Reign of Roman Emperor **Claudius I,** who disenfranchised many non-Italians, annexed Mauretania, expelled Jews from Rome, and initiated Roman rule of Britain.

43 Romans ruled **Britain** until 407.

54–69 Reign of Emperor **Nero,** last of Julio-Claudian line of Roman emperors; he blamed Christians for fire that almost destroyed (64) Rome and rebuilt city magnificently; Roman persecution of Christians was begun, which may have caused death of St. Peter and St. Paul; Nero committed suicide.

61–62 Boadicea, British queen of Iceni (Norfolk), led revolt against Romans at Fort Londinium; defeated, she took poison.

65 Seneca, philosopher and adviser to Nero, committed suicide after he was accused of conspiracy.

69–79 Reign of Emperor **Vespasian,** who founded Flavian dynasty and erected the **Colosseum** and **Forum** in Rome.

79 Mount **Vesuvius** erupted, destroying Pompeii and Herculaneum.

81–96 Reign of Emperor **Domitian,** son of Vespasian, was characterized by persecution of Christians; Domitian erected **Arch of Titus** to memorialize his brother's conquest of Jerusalem.

96–180 Reign of "the Five Good Emperors" of Rome: Nerva, Trajan, Hadrian, Antonius Pius, and Marcus Aurelius; the empire was enlarged and great public works undertaken.

c. 98 Tacitus, Roman historian, completed *Germania.*

NEAR AND MIDDLE EAST

c. 28 St. John the Baptist began preaching.

c. 30 Jesus crucified in Jerusalem.

c. 42–60 St. Paul, one of the apostles, conducted missionary work in Asia Minor and Greece and wrote his *Epistles.*

66 Jews revolted against Roman rule in Palestine; Titus suppressed rebellion and destroyed (70) Jerusalem.

FAR EAST

9 Emperor **Wang Mang** usurped Chinese throne, initiating agrarian reforms.

25 Han dynasty held Chinese throne until 220; Buddhism was introduced during reign of Emperor **Ming-ti** (58–76), and cultural ties with India were increased.

60 Kushan kings of Grandhara began to rule in West Pakistan, establishing an empire that extended from central Asia to India; a famous school of Buddhist sculpture was organized.

100—200

EUROPE

100 For the next 375 years, Goths, Vandals, and Huns raided Roman Empire.

117 Roman Empire reached its greatest extent after Emperor **Trajan** subdued Dacia (Rumania), Armenia, and Upper Mesopotamia; Trajan's Column was erected in Rome to honor his conquests.

117–138 Reign of Emperor **Hadrian;** he standardized Roman law throughout the empire, and constructed a 73-mile-long wall named after him in Britain.

130 Pantheon built at Rome and consecrated as Christian church in 609.

160–180 Marcus Aurelius, Stoic philosopher and author of *Meditations,* ruled Roman Empire and was forced to wage numerous wars.

192–284 Roman Empire ruled by army, "Barracks Emperors."

196 Barbarians overran northern Britain.

NEAR AND MIDDLE EAST

132–135 Bar Kokba led Jewish revolt; defeated by Romans, Jews were barred from Jerusalem and further dispersed.

FAR EAST

100 Traditional date for beginning of Japanese state.

c. 100 Funan Empire established in Cambodia.

Champa kingdom founded in South Vietnam and parts of Cambodia.

c. 132 Indo-Scythians destroyed last traces of Hellenic rule in northern India.

c. 150 Kanishka reigned in India.

AMERICAS

100 Teotihuacán civilization, one of America's most splendid early civilizations, developed in central Mexico; Pyramid of the Sun was as tall as 20-story building, Temple of Quetzalcoátl erected to Feather Serpent deity, and agricultural techniques advanced enough to support large urban population around huge pyramid complex; influence ceased when city fell c. 700 to Chichimecs.

200—300

EUROPE

205 British revolt against Romans was suppressed in 211.

211–217 Reign of Emperor Caracalla, who constructed in Rome Baths named for him.

220–238 Goths invaded Balkans, Asia Minor, and eastern Roman Empire.

c. 240 Franks first appeared in Europe.

c. 252 Franks, Goths, and Alemanni broke through borders of Roman Empire.

268 Goths sacked Athens, Corinth, and Sparta.

270–275 Emperor Aurelian consolidated empire by retreating to Danubian borders, recovered Gaul, and overthrew Queen Zenobia of Palmyra (Syria).

276 Great wall around Rome erected against barbarian attacks.

284–305 Reign of Emperor Diocletian, who divided empire into western part (Italy and Africa), which was governed from Milan by Maximian; Diocletian ruled eastern part (Near and Middle East and Egypt) from Nicomedia (now Izmit, Turkey).

NEAR AND MIDDLE EAST

200–230 Clement and Origen, Christian theologians, taught in Alexandria.

226–240 Ardashir I (or Artaxerxes) overthrew Parthian Empire; founded Neo-Persian Empire under Sassanid dynasty.

232 Sassanian-Roman War established Sassanians as major Eastern power.

c. 242 Mani, founder of Manichaeism, began to preach in Persia; he was martyred c. 276.

260 Persians under Shapur I captured Roman Emperor Valerian and Roman territory in Near and Middle East.

268 Zenobia, queen of Palmyra, conquered Syria, Mesopotamia, and parts of Egypt; Zenobia was overthrown (273) by Roman Emperor Aurelian.

FAR EAST

205–225 Reign of Fan Shih-man in Cambodia extended empire to lower Mekong River.

220 Han dynasty came to an end; China was divided and invaded for next three centuries.

265 Western Tsin (Ch'in) dynasty began, uniting China until White Huns began to invade in 317.

300—400

EUROPE

303 Diocletian harshly persecuted Christians.

306–337 Reign of Constantine I, first Christian emperor.

313 Edict of Milan recognized Christianity as a legal religion in Roman Empire.

325 First ecumenical council, which was convened by Constantine at Nicaea, voted against Arianism.

330 Constantine made Constantinople (now Istanbul) new capital of Roman Empire.

337 Romans fought series of wars with Persians, which ended (363) with loss of parts of Armenia and Mesopotamia.

c. 340 Monasticism developed in the West.

341 Wulfila began Christianizing Visigoths and resettling them (c. 348) in Balkans.

c. 350 Huns, central Asian nomads, began to invade Europe, forcing Goths westward.

360–367 Picts, Irish, and Saxons invaded Britain.

361–363 Reign of Julian the Apostate, who tried unsuccessfully to revive paganism.

363 Emperor Jovian restored Christianity.

379–395 Theodosius, Roman emperor, resettled Goths in empire, many of whom became soldiers.

383–407 Roman legions evacuated Britain.

390 Massacre of 7,000 following anti-Roman rebellion at Thessalonica; Theodosius did public penance before Bishop Ambrose of Milan.

395 Alaric, former head of Visigothic troops under Theodosius, became king of Visigoths and pillaged Balkans and Greece.

Roman Empire permanently partitioned.

NEAR AND MIDDLE EAST

310–379 Reign of **Shapur II** of Persia, who recovered Armenia from Romans.

337 Persians fought series of wars with **Romans**, securing (363) territory in Armenia and Mesopotamia.

378 Battle of **Adrianople: Roman** defeat left Greece unprotected from barbarians.

381 First Council of Constantinople, **second ecumenical council** convened, formalized Nicene Creed, and outlawed paganism.

387 Armenia partitioned between Rome and Persia.

399–420 Reign of **Yazdegerd I** of Persia; Christianity was tolerated initially, but later persecutions were begun in Armenia and Persia.

FAR EAST

c. 300 Funan (**Cambodia**) ruled by an Indian Brahman, who introduced Hindu customs, Indian legal code, and alphabet of central India.

317 **China** was divided into Northern and Southern dynasties; reunited in 590. Eastern Tsin dynasty ruled southern China, and capital at Nanking was established.

c. 320–c. 380 Reign of **Chandragupta I**, who established Gupta Empire that ruled India until c. 544; his reign marked the Golden Age of Hindu art and literature.

386 **Northern Wei** dynasty gained control of northern China, ruled until 495.

AMERICAS

300 **Mayan civilization** in southern Mexico entered its Classical Age during which its influence spread into **Guatemala** and **Honduras;** Mayans, ruled by priests, had advanced arts and science: calendar, hieroglyphic writing, and major works of stone architecture; this civilization collapsed in 900.

AFRICA

300 Kingdom of **Ghana** developed in western Sudan.

320–350 Christianity introduced into kingdom of **Axum.**

400—500

EUROPE

400 Eastern Roman Empire superseded by **Byzantine Empire.**

400–450 Europe overrun by **Goths.**

402 Roman capital moved to **Ravenna.**

408–450 Reign of **Theodosius II**, Byzantine emperor, who systematized (438) Roman laws (*Codex Theodosianus*) and made separation of Eastern and Western sections of empire official.

410 **Alaric** and Visigoths sacked Rome.

413–426 St. Augustine wrote *The City of God.*

432 St. Patrick began missionary work among the Irish.

445–453 **Attila**, king of the Huns, ruled from Hungary over Russia, Poland, and Germany, extorting concessions from Theodosius II and ravaging Balkans.

449 **Angles, Saxons,** and **Jutes** began conquest of Britain.

451 Attila, defeated at Châlons in Champagne, then invaded northern Italy, but allegedly was stopped by Pope **Leo I.**

455–475 Rome ruled by series of puppet emperors; **Ricimer,** Suebi general from central Germany, was virtual ruler of western empire until 472.

466–484 Reign of **Euric**, who established kingdom in Spain, bringing Visigothic power to its peak.

476 **Odoacer**, Ostrogoth chieftain, deposed **Romulus Augustulus**, last Roman emperor of the West; Odoacer was recognized as head of western empire by Zeno, Byzantine emperor.

481–511 Reign of **Clovis I**, king of the Franks and founder of **Merovingian** dynasty, who defeated (486) Romans at Soissons, ending Roman rule in Gaul, and was converted (496) to Christianity.

493 **Theodoric the Great**, king of Ostrogoths, seized Ravenna, assassinated Odoacer, and established Ostrogothic kingdom in Italy.

NEAR AND MIDDLE EAST

428 Persians began to rule **Armenia;** their control ceased in 633.

491 **Armenian Church** separated from Byzantine and Roman churches.

FAR EAST

420 **Liu Sung** dynasty came to power in southern China and ruled until 479.

c. 450 Buddhism established in Burma.

465 By this time, **White Huns** had almost destroyed **Gupta** empire in India.

479 **Chi** dynasty began to rule southern China; its rule ceased in 502.

AFRICA

429 **Vandal** kingdom established in Africa by **Gaiseric,** who took his people out of Spain.

439 Gaiseric made **Carthage** Vandal capital.

476 Gaiseric concluded **treaty** with **Zeno,** who recognized Vandal rule over Roman Africa, Sicily, Sardinia, Corsica, and Balearic Islands.

500—600

EUROPE

500 Golden age of **Irish monastic** scholarship began, which died out c. 800.

506 **Alaric II,** king of Visigoths, issued *Lex Romana Visigothorum,* law code.

527–565 Reign of **Justinian,** Byzantine emperor, who was strongly influenced by his wife **Theodora;** Justinian issued *Corpus Juris Civilis* (also known as the **Justinian Code**), a comprehensive code of Roman law; erected public works; and recovered Africa from Vandals and Italy from Ostrogoths.

529 Benedict of Nursia founded Monte Cassino in Subiaco, Italy, first **Benedictine monastery.**

532–537 Cathedral of **Hagia Sophia** erected in Constantinople.

c. 537 Traditional date of **King Arthur's death** at the Battle of Camlan.

c. 560–616 Reign of **Ethelbert,** king of Kent, who received St. Augustine and was converted to Christianity; Ethelbert made Kent supreme in Britain and drew up first code of English laws.

563 **St. Columba,** an Irish missionary to Scotland, founded church and converted king of the Picts.

567 **Frankish kingdom** divided into Austrasia, Neustria, and Burgundy.

568 **Lombards,** ancient German tribe, invaded northern Italy and established a kingdom that lasted over 200 years.

584 **Slavs** in Balkan peninsula overran Greece and began to menace Byzantine Empire.

c. 585 **Avars,** conquering nomads from steppes of central Asia, reached Danube.

590–604 Papacy of **St. Gregory I** (the Great) laid basis for later papal claims to temporal authority and independence and codified church music; the Gregorian chant is named for him.

597 **St. Augustine,** a Roman monk, sent by Pope Gregory to convert English, founded a church at **Canterbury,** becoming (601) first Archbishop of Canterbury.

NEAR AND MIDDLE EAST

c. 500 Arabs invaded Palestine.

525 Yemen conquered by Abyssinians.

531–579 Reign of **Khosru I** (or Chosroes) of Persia marked political and cultural prime of Persia; Khosru fought Byzantines and overthrew Abyssinian control of Yemen.

c. 550 Migration of **Turks** began, which broke up (565) White Hun settlements in Western Turkestan.

570 **Mohammed,** prophet of Islam, born.

590–628 Reign of **Khosru II** of Persia, who conquered Jerusalem, Damascus, and Egypt and restored Persian boundaries to those at time of Darius I.

FAR EAST

c. 550 **Khmers** from Chen-la state to north began to overrun Funan and made **Cambodia** (about equal to Cambodia and Laos) dominant in Southeast Asia until c. 1400.

Japanese began to adopt **Chinese culture,** using Chinese script and introducing Buddhism.

590 **Sui** dynasty began to rule China; Great Wall of China was reconstructed as defense against Turks and Mongols, five million people were employed to construct complex water transport system, and **civil service examination** was introduced; this dynasty ended in 618.

600—700

EUROPE

610–641 Reign of **Heraclius,** Byzantine emperor, who recovered lands lost to Persia and then lost them to Moslem Arabs at end of his reign.

613–629 Reign of **Clotair (Lothair) II**, Merovingian king, who reunited Frankish realm and appointed **Pepin of Landen** and **Arnulf**, bishop of Metz, (ancestors of the Carolingians) to govern Austrasia.

617 **Northumbria** became dominant kingdom in Britain.

655 **Saracens**, Arab Moslems, destroyed Byzantine fleet.

664 Saracens began series of attacks on **Constantinople**.

c. 670 **Caedmon**, English poet, wrote early English version of *Old Testament*.

679 First **Bulgarian Empire** founded by **Khan Asparuhk**.

685–695 First part of reign of **Justinian II**, Byzantine emperor, who was defeated by Arabs at Sevastopol and later deposed and exiled to Crimea.

687 **Pepin of Héristal** became ruler of all Frankish kingdoms, except Aquitaine.

NEAR AND MIDDLE EAST

c. 610 **Mohammed** began his mission as prophet of Islam.

622 Traditional date of the **Hegira**, Mohammed's flight from Mecca to Medina, that marked beginning of **Moslem Era**.

630 **Moslems** conquered **Mecca**, which became spiritual center of Islam.

633 Islam began conquests by taking **Syria** and **Iraq**.

639 Moslems began to conquer **Egypt**.

640 Persia taken by Moslems.

651–652 First edition of the *Koran* issued.

661 Moawiya founded **Omayyad dynasty** (caliphs of Damascus), which held caliphate until 750.

FAR EAST

c. 606–647 Reign of **King Harsha**, ruler of Kanauj in northern India, which enjoyed **Hindu renaissance** of literature, arts, and theology; Harsha received Chinese pilgrim Hsuan-Tsang.

618 **T'ang dynasty** founded in China, which annexed Korea and led successful campaigns in Mongolia, Nepal, Tibet, and Turkestan; it marked the **Golden Age of medieval China** with notable advances in astronomy and mathematics, first historical encyclopedia (801), and the development of art of printing, painting, and poetry; this dynasty ended in 906.

664 Saracens attacked Afghanistan and India.

670 **Silla** kingdom established in **Korea**; Chinese helped Koreans unite peninsula, instituting a period of prosperity and artistic achievement that lasted until 935.

AMERICAS

600 **Tiahuanaco** became a major ceremonial center near Lake Titicaca; Tiahuanacans established first unified empire that included most of **Peru**; their rule ended c. 1000.

AFRICA

698 Carthage fell to **Saracens**, ending Byzantine rule in North Africa.

700—800

EUROPE

700–730 *Beowulf*, oldest extant English epic, was composed.

711 **Tarik**, Berber leader of Moslems, invaded Spain, initiating **Moorish rule** in Spain, which lasted until 1492.

715–741 Reign of **Charles Martel**, son of Pepin of Héristal and grandfather of · Charlemagne; as Frankish ruler, he defeated (732) Saracens at battle of Tours, halting their advance into Europe.

c. 732 **St. Bede** (the Venerable Bede) wrote his *Ecclesiastical History of the English Nation*.

751–768 **Pepin the Short**, first Carolingian king of the Franks and son of Charles Martel, defended Rome from Lombards.

756 Papal states began when Pepin granted lands around Ravenna to pope.

Omayyad dynasty of Córdoba came to power in Moslem Spain and was to rule until 1031.

768–814 Reign of **Charlemagne** (son of Pepin the Short), who subdued Saxony, annexed Lombardy and Bavaria, and was crowned (800) emperor of the West by Pope Leo III at Rome; Charlemagne created Palace School at his capital, Aix-la-Chapelle, which helped preserve classical and early Christian scholarship.

NEAR AND MIDDLE EAST

749 Caliph Abul Abbas overthrew Omayyads and founded **Abbasid dynasty**, which ruled until 1258.

762 Baghdad founded by Caliph Al-Mansur.

786–809 Reign of **Caliph Harun al-Rashid**, during which Baghdad became major Islamic city; this glorious period is reflected in *The Thousands and One Nights*.

FAR EAST

712 **Moslem Arabs** devastated most of northwestern India.

Kojiki [= records of ancient matters], sacred book of the Shinto, was completed.

794 **Heian period** of Japan began; during this era, Japanese began to develop their own culture and established capital at Kyoto; this period ended 1185.

AMERICAS

700 **Chichimec** nomads from northern Mexico invaded Teotihuacán civilization.

Mayan temples built at **Tikal**, in jungles of Guatemala.

AFRICA

700 **Moslem Arabs** conquered northern **Africa**, which became base for invasions of Europe.

Kingdom of Ghana developed as first of Sudanese empires and became wealthy trading center, extending from Timbuktu to the Atlantic.

800—900

EUROPE

c. 800 **Cynewulf**, Old English religious poet, wrote *Fates of the Apostles*.

802 The **Vikings** raided British Isles and by 880 had permanent settlements in Ireland and England.

803–814 Reign of **Khan Krum**, Bulgarian ruler, who captured Sofia from Byzantines and besieged Constantinople.

813–820 Reign of **Leo V**, the Armenian, who ruled Byzantium and revived iconoclasm; he defeated Bulgars and concluded 30-year truce.

827–880 Moslems invaded Sicily, Palermo, Messina, Rome, and Malta.

835 Vikings began to raid **Continent**.

843 Treaty of **Verdun**: the Carolingian kingdom was divided into three separate states: the future **France**, **Italy**, and **Germany** with Charles the Bald, Emperor Lothair, and Louis the German as rulers of the respective territories.

847–c. 877 **John Scotus Erigena** headed court school at Paris for Charles the Bald and wrote translations and original philosophical works.

c. 850 **Feudalism** developed in western Europe.

858 **Photius** became patriarch of Constantinople, and a schism between eastern and western churches developed during his reign.

860–869 **St. Cyril** and **St. Methodius** performed missionary work among Slavs living near Black Sea and later in Moravia; Cyril developed early **Slavic alphabet**.

862 **Rurik**, a Varangian (Viking), settled Novgorod, Russia; house of Rurik ruled Grand Duchy of Moscow and later all Russia until 1598.

865 **Boris I**, ruler of Bulgaria, introduced Christianity of the Greek rite.

871–899 Reign of **Alfred the Great**, king of England, who made a treaty establishing Danish territory in England and began overseeing compilation of *Anglo-Saxon Chronicle*.

882 Oleg, Rurik's nephew, made Kiev capital of Russia.

893–927 Reign of **Simeon I** (Tsar of the Bulgars and autocrat of the Greeks), who drove Magyars into Hungary and conquered most of Serbia; Bulgarian Empire flourished during his reign, which is considered the Golden Age of **Church Slavonic literature**.

c. 895 **Árpád**, chief of Magyars, led his people into Hungary.

c. 899 Medical school in **Salerno** had been established, which merged Greek, Jewish, Arabic, and Latin influences.

FAR EAST

800 **Feudalism** developed in Japan.

889 Golden Age of **Khmer** civilization, which ruled modern Cambodia, Laos, Thailand, and South Vietnam, from capital at Angkor; the temple complex constructed at **Angkor Wat** is one of the largest religious centers in the world; this civilization declined after 1434.

AFRICA

800 Arabs colonized **Madagascar** and **Zanzibar**, making expeditions into African interior for slaves for the next 200 years.
Rulers of **Kanem** developed kingdom near caravan routes of eastern Sudan.

900—1000

EUROPE

900 Danish kingdom founded by **Gorm**.

904 Saracens sacked Salonika.

906 Magyars began invading Germany, and were defeated (955) at Augsburg.

911 Rollo, Norse chieftain, received in fief the future duchy of **Normandy** from King Charles III; he was baptized (912), and his descendants included William the Conqueror.

912—960 Omayyad rule in **Spain** at its zenith under Abdu-r-Rahman III; **Córdoba** became intellectual center of Europe.

919—936 Reign of **Henry I**, the Fowler, who was considered the founder of German realm and recovered Lorraine for Germany.

962 Holy Roman Empire founded after Otto I, German king, united Italy and Germany; it lasted until Francis II renounced the imperial title in 1806.

976—1025 Reign of **Basil II** (Bulgar slayer), Byzantine emperor, who annexed Syria and Bulgaria, bringing empire to greatest size since the time of Justinian I.

c. 980—1015 Reign of **Vladimir I** (Saint Vladimir), duke of Kiev, who made Christianity of the Greek rite the Russian religion.

c. 985 Eric the Red established a Viking colony in **Greenland**.

987 Hugh Capet became king of **France**, beginning of the Capetian line that ruled France until 1328.

992—1025 Reign of **Boleslaus I** (the Brave), founder of the Polish kingdom, who brought most of the western Slavs under his rule.

997—1038 Reign of **Stephen I** (Saint Stephen), called the Apostle of Hungary, first king of Hungary.

NEAR AND MIDDLE EAST

969 Fatimite caliph established in Egypt; Fatimites, who captured Palestine, parts of Syria, and west Arabia, ruled until 1171.

996 Hakin, sixth Fatimite caliph, persecutor of Jews and Christians and self-proclaimed (1020) reincarnation of God, a claim still maintained by Druses in Syria and Lebanon; Fatimite power declined rapidly after Hakin's assassination in 1021.

999 Sultan Mahmud of Ghazni founded Ghaznevid dynasty, which ruled Afghanistan until c. 1155; he annexed Punjab, India; forced conversions to Islam; destroyed Hindu temples; and built a mosque, the Celestial Bride, at Ghazni, his capital.

FAR EAST

907 Khitan Mongols began to rule northern China, holding sway until 1123. Kingdom of the Five Dynasties and Ten States in China: chaos existed in China until 960.

935 Koryo kingdom established in Korea, in which literature was cultivated and Confucianism replaced Buddhism; this kingdom ended in 1392.

960 Sung dynasty established in China; scholarly works were composed, and drama and picaresque novel flourished; gunpowder was used for first time, and trade was carried on with India and Persia; the dynasty ruled until 1279.

986 Ghaznevids from Afghanistan began to rule Punjab, remaining there until 1001.

AMERICAS

900 Toltec civilization developed in **Mexico**; capital was established (c. 950) at Tula, and warrior gods were worshiped; the Toltec Indians conquered most of Mexico, before influence died out c. 1200.

AFRICA

c. 912—1043 Fatimite dynasty dominated most of northwestern Africa and the Near East; fleets raided Mediterranean, capturing Malta, Sardinia, Corsica, and Balearics.

c. 990 Great Zimbabwe civilization, probably developed by Bantu people, flourished in **Southern Rhodesia**; huge stone buildings were constructed in about the 15th century; this civilization ended c. 1750.

1000—1100

EUROPE

1000 End of the world expected throughout Christendom.

c. 1000—1010 Early edition of *Chanson de Roland* probably composed, but not transcribed for many years.

1002 Massacre of St. Brice: Danes in England were murdered and, in retaliation, raided England regularly until 1014.

1014 Knut (Canute) II, king of Denmark, became (1017) king of England and later of Norway; his kingdom was divided after his death in 1035.

1019—1054 Reign of Yaroslav, duke of Kiev; he drew up Russian law code, encouraged learning, erected Cathedral of Sancta Sophia and monastery of Lavra, and consolidated power and prestige of Kiev.

1024 Franconian house began to rule Germany; great imperial age ended in 1125.

1039—1056 Henry III, king of Germany and Holy Roman Emperor (1046–1056); with authority over Hungary, Poland, and Bohemia, his empire was at its height.

1040 Macbeth became king of Scotland after murdering his predecessor, Duncan; Macbeth was killed (1057) by Malcolm, who became king until 1093.
Attempts were made to implement Truce of God in France, which would have prohibited war during certain seasons and times of the day.

1042—1066 Reign of Edward the Confessor, king of England; he began (c. 1050) construction of Westminster Abbey.

1054 Reciprocal excommunication of Roman and Greek Churches announced; it was repealed in 1965.

1063 Construction was begun on Cathedral at Pisa, an example of Romanesque style of architecture that flourished in 11th and 12th centuries.

1065—1109 Alfonso VI of Leon, king of Castile, reconquered Moorish lands, beginning with capture of Toledo in 1085.

1066 William, duke of Normandy, defeated Saxons under King Harold at the Battle of Hastings, ending Saxon rule in England; known as William I (the Conqueror) of England, he ordered (1086) all landed property surveyed for tax purposes and recorded in Domesday Book.

c. 1071 Saint Mark's Church in Venice was rebuilt in Byzantine style.

c. 1078 The White Tower, later named the Tower of London, was constructed.

1081 The Cid (Rodrigo Diaz) fought Moors and Spaniards; he founded and ruled Valencia until 1099.

1086 Almoravides, Berber Moslems from Morocco, took over control of Islam in Spain.

c. 1088 University of Bologna founded.

1093 St. Anselm, founder of Scholasticism, became Archbishop of Canterbury.

1095 First Crusade proclaimed by Pope Urban II, who urged battle cry to be *Deus vult* [God wills it]; he established (1099) Latin Kingdom of Jerusalem in Syria and Palestine that endured until 1291.

1097 Construction began on the Houses of Parliament.

NEAR AND MIDDLE EAST

c. 1000 Avicenna, Arabian philosopher and physician, wrote *Canon of Medicine*.

1055 Seljuk Turks conquered Baghdad.

1063—1072 Alp Arslan, ruler of Seljuks, conquered much of Near East and Asia Minor; he defeated Byzantine army at Manzikert, Armenia.

1072—1092 Reign of Malik Shah (son of Arslan), who was protector of Omar Khayyam, Persian poet and author of the *Rubáiyát*.

1096 The First Crusade began, and Crusaders captured Nicaea, Antioch, and Jerusalem, where they massacred the Moslems; Crusaders established (1099) Latin Kingdom of Jerusalem in Syria and Palestine, which endured until 1291.

FAR EAST

c. 1020 *The Tale of Genji*, said to be the world's first novel, written by Lady Murasaki Shikibu in Japan.

1044 King Anawratha made Pagan, Burma, the capital of his dynasty; it became known as the "city of a thousand temples."

AMERICAS

c. 1000 Lief Ericsson allegedly discovered part of North American coast and called it **Vinland**.

Chichén Itzá, ancient Mayan city in north-central Yucatán, became **Toltec** city and was occupied until 1194.

Mixtec people, who developed high culture in Oaxaca valley of Mexico, practised picture writing.

AFRICA

c. **1000 Kano,** city in northern Nigeria, began to flourish; it became leading Moslem sultanate of **Hausa States,** which were vassals of **Bornu** after 1400.

1054 Almoravides, Moslem Berber tribes, began Islamic conquest of **West Africa;** they sacked Kumbi, capital of Ghana, in 1076.

1100—1200

EUROPE

1100–1135 Reign of **Henry I** of England; he gained control of Normandy; his attempts to have his daughter **Matilda** succeed him caused long civil strife.

1108–1137 Reign of **Louis VI** (the Fat) of France, who battled with Henry I and checked German invasion.

1113–1125 Reign of **Vladimir Monomakh,** grand duke of Kiev; state grew in power during his reign.

1118 Order of **Knights Templar** founded.

1120–1220 Aristotelian philosophy introduced into the West, especially through writings of **Averroës,** Spanish-Arabian philosopher, and **Maimonides,** Hebrew scholar.

1122–1152 Suger, abbot of Saint-Denis, was leading French statesman under Louis VI and Louis VII.

1128–1185 Reign of **Alfonso I Henriques** of Portugal; Portugal received (1144) papal consent to be independent kingdom.

1134–1150 Western facade of **Chartres Cathedral** was built.

c. **1135 Geoffrey of Monmouth** completed *History of the Kings of Britain,* major source of Arthurian legends.

1147 Second Crusade preached by St. Bernard of Clairvaux after Turks captured (1144) Edessa; it was led by Conrad III of Germany and Louis VII of France.

c. **1150 University of Paris** came into being; Peter Abelard is usually regarded as its founder.

1152 Frederick I (Barbarossa), became king of Germany, and was crowned (1155) Holy Roman Emperor; he acquired land in Italy, Germany, and Poland and was drowned (1190) in Asia Minor during Third Crusade.

Louis VII annulled his marriage to Eleanor of Aquitaine; Henry (Plantagenet) married Eleanor.

1154–1189 Reign of **Henry II** (Plantagenet) of England; he appointed **Thomas à Becket** his chancellor and centralized royal administration.

1154–1213 Georgian power reached its peak in Russia, a period known as **Golden Age of Georgian literature.**

1159 John of Salisbury dedicated *Policraticus,* his treatise on government, to Thomas à Becket.

Peter Lombard, bishop of Paris, began his theological text, *Sentences.*

1162 Becket became Archbishop of Canterbury; he opposed Henry's restrictions on ecclesiastical jurisdiction, but was formally reconciled after long quarrel in 1170, only to be murdered five months later by Norman knights.

1163–1235 Cathedral of **Notre Dame** constructed in Paris.

c. **1168 Oxford University** founded.

1176 Construction of **London Bridge** was begun, and completed in 1209.

Lombard League of northern Italian states defeated Barbarossa at **Legnano,** representing the first major defeat of feudal cavalry by infantry.

c. **1180 Chrestien de Troyes** composed the first literary works of Arthurian legend.

1182 Jews banished from **France,** but returned in 1189.

c. **1187** *Igor's Campaign,* first notable work of **Russian** literature, was based on true account of Prince Igor's defeat and release by Cumans.

1189–1193 Third Crusade led by Barbarossa, Richard I of England, and Philip II of France.

1189–1199 Reign of **Richard I** (the Lionhearted), king of England; returning from Crusades, he was captured by Leopold of Austria; after release two years later, he warred against Philip II.

1190–1199 Teutonic Knights, a German military religious order, was founded.

1191 The *Nibelungenlied* first appeared.

NEAR AND MIDDLE EAST

1144 Zengi, Turkish conqueror of Syria, seized **Edessa.**

1145–1174 Reign of **Nureddin,** Zengi's son and Sultan of **Syria;** he ousted Crusaders from northern Syria, made (1154) **Damascus** his capital, and conquered (1171) **Egypt.**

1147–1149 Second Crusade.

1157 Seljuk Empire fell to **Khorezm shah.**

1169–1193 Reign of **Saladin,** sultan of Egypt; he conquered Syria and Aleppo, defeated (1187) Christians at battle of **Hattin** (near Tiberias) and took Jerusalem, and signed treaty with **Richard the Lionhearted** that allowed Christians small strip of land along Jerusalem coast.

FAR EAST

1149 Rulers of **Ghor** took over **Ghazni** in Afghanistan, which became headquarters for campaigns into India; subjugation of Upper India was completed in 1203.

1186 Kamakura era began in Japan, establishing rule of military warriors; **Yoritomo,** first shogun, set up centralized feudal system; China and Korea were raided; Zen Buddhism was promoted; this era ended in 1333.

c. **1190 Temujin** consolidated Mongol tribes in central Asia; he assumed (1206) title **Jenghiz Khan** and led Mongol hordes in conquests of eastern Europe and western Asia.

AFRICA

c. **1174 Almohades,** fierce Berber Moslems, succeeded Almoravides in Morocco and conquered other parts of North Africa, ruling area until 1550.

1200—1300

EUROPE

1202–1204 The Fourth Crusade, was led by Venetian doge, **Enrico Dandolo;** Constantinople was captured and a Latin empire established.

1204 Philip II of France took English lands north of the Loire and established **France** as a leading European power.

1209 Franciscan order founded by **Saint Francis of Assisi.**

1211 Construction began on **Rheims Cathedral.**

1215 Magna Carta, signed by **King John,** became basis of modern English constitution with its principle that the king is subject to law.

1217–1221 Fifth Crusade led by **Pelasius,** papal legate, was directed against Moslems in Egypt and failed.

1218 Amiens Cathedral begun.

1223 Mongols invaded Russia.

1226–1270 Reign of **Louis IX** (Saint Louis), a period known as **Golden Age of medieval France.**

1226–1283 Teutonic Knights subjugated Prussia and achieved commercial power.

1227 Gothic **Cathedral of Toledo,** Spain, began to be constructed.

1228–1229 Sixth Crusade; led by Frederick II, it resulted in Sultan of Egypt signing treaty that restored Jerusalem, Nazareth, and Bethlehem to Christians.

c. **1230 Salamanca University** founded in Spain.

c. **1231 Cambridge University** founded.

1233 The Inquisition was established when Pope Gregory IX gave Dominicans authority to investigate Albigensian heresy in southern France.

1236–1263 Reign of **Alexander Nevsky** in Russia, under whom country was united; he defeated (1242) Teutonic Knights at Lake Peipus, and Mongols named him **Grand Prince of Russia.**

1237–1242 Batu Khan led Mongol invasions, taking Moscow and most of Russia, Hungary, and Poland, and invading Germany; his empire was known as the **Golden Horde** because of brilliant tents.

1238 Kingdom of Granada became last refuge of the Moors until their expulsion from Spain in 1492.

1248–1254 Seventh Crusade; King Louis IX of France was its leader.

1270 Eighth Crusade; Tunis was attacked, and Louis IX died from plague.

1271 Marco Polo left Venice for China and other parts of the Far East; he returned in 1292 and informed Europeans of Oriental splendors.

1273 Rudolph I founded **Hapsburg** dynasty, which ruled Austria until 1918.

St. Thomas Aquinas completed *Summa Theologica*.

1272–1307 Reign of Edward I of England; he systematized laws and institutions and called (1295) his "**Model Parliament**," which represented all classes.

1285–1314 Reign of Philip IV (the Fair); he made France an absolute monarchy and called (1302) the first meeting of the **Estates-General** (clergy, nobility, and townsmen) to rally against Pope Boniface VIII's claims of papal supremacy.

1290 Jews were expelled from **England;** they returned c. 1650.

NEAR AND MIDDLE EAST

1202–1204 Fourth Crusade: Crusaders took Constantinople, sacked Byzantine territories, and established a Latin Empire.

1217–1221 Fifth Crusade; Crusaders failed in Egypt.

1218–1224 Mongols from central Asia conquered Turkestan, Afghanistan, and Persia.

1228–1229 Sixth Crusade; Sultan of Egypt signed a treaty with Crusaders allowing free access to Jerusalem.

1245–1253 Mesopotamia and Armenia ravaged by **Mongols.**

1248–1253 Seventh Crusade; Crusaders massacred in Egypt.

1250 Mamelukes, former slave-soldiers, began to rule Egypt and checked Mongol advances; their rule ended in 1517.

1258 Baghdad fell to **Hulagu Khan,** grandson of Jenghiz, who devastated surrounding lands.

1270 Eighth Crusade; Crusaders attacked **Tunis** and were turned back.

1288 Osman I, leader of Ottoman Turks, founded **Ottoman dynasty,** which endured until 1918.

FAR EAST

1206 Delhi Sultanate began, the first Moslem kingdom of India; Sultan Iltutmish (1210–1235) erected famous minaret, **Qutb Minar;** this dynasty ended in 1398.

1220–1227 Jenghiz Khan established his capital at **Karakorum** controlling most of Ch'in Empire of northern China; he conquered Turkestan, Afghanistan, Persia, and southern Russia.

1221–1241 Ogotai Khan, son of Jenghiz, captured Ghazni, Afghanistan.

1260 Yüan, Mongolian dynasty of China, founded by Kublai Khan, grandson of Jenghiz; Kublai's attempts to conquer Japan, Southeast Asia, and Indonesia failed; Marco Polo and other westerners visited capital at Peiping; during dynasty an advanced postal system and extensive network of roads and canals were created; gunpowder and printing were introduced into Europe from China at this time; this dynasty ended in 1368.

AMERICAS

1200 The **Incas** began to build empire centered at Cuzco, Peru, and established central control over local rulers; eventually empire extended from Quito, Ecuador, to Rio Maule, Chile, with population c. seven million people, who were linked by messenger system and common language; Incan civilization was noted for political organization and luxurious cities; stonework in Machu Picchu, fortress city in Andes, shows skillful engineering techniques; empire destroyed by Francisco Pizarro in 1533.

Aztecs entered the valley of Mexico, establishing powerful political and cultural civilization and capital (c. 1325) at **Tenochtitlán** (now **Mexico City**); Aztecs were noted for developed social organization and religion demanding human sacrifice; in 1519 their population numbered about five million; **Hernán Cortés** destroyed empire in 1521.

AFRICA

1200 Mali Empire developed in western Sudan, absorbing **Ghana** and neighboring lands; King **Mansa Musa's** pilgrimage (1324) to Mecca brought attention to empire's great wealth; **Timbuktu** grew into center of learning and culture; **Songhai** began to control region c. 1500.

1300—1400

EUROPE

1300 The **Renaissance** began, signaling end of Middle Ages and beginning of modern Europe; greatest cultural developments in European history occurred during next 300 years.

1305 "**Babylonian Captivity**" began; chaos in Italy forced Pope Clement V to desert (1309) Rome for Avignon, France, which was the papal seat until 1377.

c. 1306 Giotto completed Arena Chapel frescoes in Padua.

1321 Death of Dante following completion of *Divine Comedy.*

1325–1341 Reign of Ivan I (Money Bag), grand prince of Moscow and vassal of Mongols; Russian Orthodox Church became centered in Moscow during his reign.

1326 Ottoman Turks began invading eastern Europe.

1327–1377 Reign of Edward III of England, during which Parliament divided into two houses, later called **Lords** and **Commons.**

1337 Hundred Years War, which began after Edward III claimed French crown, ended in 1453; English defeated, but French devastated by famine, plague, and marauders who terrorized countryside.

1341 Petrarch, Italian humanist, crowned poet laureate at Rome.

1346–1355 Reign of Stephen Dushan over Serbs, Greeks, Bulgars, and Albanians; his rule marked height of Serbian power.

1347–1352 Black Death, an epidemic of plague that began (1334) in Constantinople, struck Europe; within 20 years, it killed up to three quarters of population of Europe and Asia.

1353 Giovanni Boccaccio completed the *Decameron.*

1358 French army suppressed the *Jacquerie,* a peasant revolt protesting war taxation.

1362 William Langland wrote *Piers the Plowman.*

1370 Hanseatic League, mercantile association of German towns, signed a treaty with Denmark giving League a virtual trade monopoly in Scandinavia.

1378 Great Western Schism: Rome and France began fight for control of papacy that lasted until 1417.

1379 After Parliament imposed poll tax, **Wat Tyler** led peasant revolt in England.

1382 John Wycliffe directed translation of the **Vulgate Bible** into English.

1386 Heidelberg University founded by Rupert I, Elector of Palatinate.

Lithuania and Poland united under Jagiello dynasty; Golden Age of Polish culture and power began; this dynasty came to an end in 1572.

1387 Chaucer began to compose his *Canterbury Tales.*

1389 Turks defeated Serbs at **Kossovo,** and Serbia became vassal state of Turks.

1391 Ottoman Turk began conquering Byzantine lands.

1399 House of Lancaster began reign in England that lasted until 1461.

NEAR AND MIDDLE EAST

1334 Epidemic of plague, **Black Death,** began in Constantinople, spreading throughout Europe and Asia and causing extremely large number of fatalities.

1354 Ottoman Turks expanded their empire and established capital at Adrianople; by end of century, Ottomans controlled most of Balkans and Byzantine possessions in Asia Minor.

1356–1363 Sultan Hassan mosque was constructed in Cairo.

1392 Baghdad sacked by **Tamerlane,** Mongol conqueror.

FAR EAST

1336 Ashikaga family began to dominate **Japan,** holding sway until 1558; Ashikaga period of warfare among feudal nobles was also a time of extraordinary economic and commercial growth.

1350 Thais from southern China established kingdom in modern **Thailand.**

1353 Lao kingdom of Lan Xang (Land of a Million Elephants) established by branch of Thais in **Laos.**

1368 Ming dynasty began to rule China after driving out Mongols; empire at its height extended from Burma to Korea; European settlements made at Macao and Canton; finest **Chinese porcelain** dates from this period, which ended in 1644.

1369–1405 Reign of **Tamerlane** (or Timur), Mongol leader and conqueror of Persia, Mesopotamia, and western India; Tamerlane ravaged Georgia and captured Angora from Ottomans.

1392 Yi dynasty began to rule **Korea** and established capital at Seoul; this dynasty ended in 1919.

AFRICA

1300 **Kingdom of Ife** flourished in Nigeria; Ife, a holy city noted for its fine **bronze sculpture**, probably died out c. 1500.

1350 **Kingdom of Benin** developed in **Nigeria**; within a century, Benin became famous commercial center and seat of royal court; bronze plaques on king's palace depict civilization of hunters, traders, and warriors; trade was established with Portugal c. 1486; Benin had disintegrated by 1897.

1400—1500

EUROPE

1409 **Leipzig University** founded by German émigrés from Prague.

1415 **Henry V** of England defeated French in Battle of **Agincourt**, making England first among European powers.

1415–1460 Reign of **Prince Henry the Navigator** of Portugal, who promoted explorations along the coast of Africa.

c. 1417 **Donatello** completed his statue of *St. George and the Dragon*.

1419–1436 **Hussite** religious wars that broke out following martyrdom of **John Huss** were fought in Bohemia.

c. 1427 **Thomas à Kempis**, German monk, wrote *The Imitation of Christ*.

1429 **Joan of Arc** liberated Orléans; she was burned at the stake in Rouen in 1431.

1432 **Jan van Eyck** completed his altarpiece with panels portraying the *Annunciation* and *Adoration of the Lamb*.

1434 **Medicis** began their domination of **Florence**, which lasted until 1494 and made Florence center of Italian Renaissance.

1450 **Fra Angelico** completed the *Annunciation*.

Vatican Library founded by Pope Nicholas V.

1453 **Constantinople** was lost to Turks, ending 1,000-year-old Byzantine Empire.

Hundred Years War came to an end, and English territory on Continent was limited to Calais.

1455–1485 **Wars of the Roses:** English Houses of Lancaster and York fought for throne.

1456 **John Hunyadi**, Hungarian ruler, defeated Turks at Belgrade, preventing their conquest of Hungary for 70 years.

c. 1456 Printing of **Mazarin Bible** was completed in Mainz, Germany; it is considered earliest book printed from movable type and attributed to **Gutenberg**.

1458–1490 Reign of **Matthias Corvinus** of Hungary (son of John Hunyadi), who took (1485) Vienna and made Hungary most important state of central Europe.

1461–1483 Reign of **Louis XI**, who made France a nation by annexing Burgundy, Provence, Maine, and Anjou.

1462–1505 Reign of **Ivan III (the Great)**, first national sovereign of Russia; he subjugated Novgorod and almost all Russian principalities under Moscow's rule and repudiated "Tartar Yoke"; Ivan also adopted Byzantine court ceremonials and constructed great **Kremlin palaces** and cathedrals in Moscow.

1463 Turks and **Venetians** began major war, in which Venetians were defeated (1479) and had to pay Turks for trading privileges.

1466 **Teutonic Knights** ceded Pomerania and West Prussia to Poland.

1469 King **Ferdinand** of Aragon married Queen **Isabella I** of Castile, initiating unification of Spain.

1473 The **Sistine Chapel** in the Vatican was built under Pope Sixtus IV.

1478 Ferdinand and Isabella instituted the **Spanish Inquisition**.

1481 **Botticelli** began his Biblical frescoes in the Sistine Chapel.

1485 **Henry VII** of England founded the **House of Tudor**, increased power of the **Star Chamber**, developed English navy, sponsored explorations to New World, and ended feudalism by outlawing private armies.

1488 **Bartolomeu Dias** was the first European to round the Cape of Good Hope, thus opening sea route to India.

1490 **Verrocchio's equestrian monument** of *condottiere* Colleoni was cast.

1492 Ferdinand and Isabella conquered Moorish kingdom of **Granada**, expelled Jews who refused to accept Catholicism, and financed **Christopher Columbus** on his first voyage to America.

1494 Treaty of **Tordesillas**: Spain and Portugal divided the New World.

Italian Wars among Italian states and Spain began when Charles VIII of France invaded Italy; after 1559 Spain dominated Italy.

1497 **Portugal** expelled Jews who refused Catholic conversion.

1497–1498 **John Cabot** explored North American coast south of Labrador.

1497–1499 **Vasco da Gama** sailed from Lisbon to India.

1498 **Savonarola**, Dominican monk who preached against corruption in Florence, was burned at the stake.

Leonardo da Vinci, painter, engineer, and scientist, completed the *Last Supper* in Milan.

1499 **Swiss independence** acknowledged by Emperor Maximilian I.

NEAR AND MIDDLE EAST

1451–1481 Reign of **Mohammed II**, Ottoman sultan; he completed conquest of Byzantine Empire by taking (1453) **Constantinople** and making it his capital; conquering most of Balkans and several Venetian possessions in Aegean islands, he was stopped (1478) at Belgrade by John Hunyadi and in Albania by Scanderbeg.

FAR EAST

1412–1443 Reign of **Ahmad Shah**, king of Gujarat (India), who founded city of **Ahmedabad**; Gujarat became an independent, prosperous sultanate.

1495–1530 Reign of **Baber** (or Babar), remote descendant of Tamerlane; Baber founded **Mogul Empire** of India, captured (1504) Kabul and established a kingdom in Afghanistan, and conquered most of northern India.

1498 Portuguese explorer **Vasco da Gama** landed at Calicut, India.

AMERICAS

1492–1504 **Christopher Columbus** made four voyages to America; landed on Canary Islands, Bahamas, Cuba, Hispaniola, Jamaica, Virgin Islands, Trinidad, and Honduras.

1497 **John Cabot** arrived in North America; explored coast south of Labrador.

AFRICA

1400 **Baluba Kingdom** of the **Congo** first emerged and eventually controlled Katanga and Kivu provinces.

1415 Portuguese began to explore **West Africa**, gradually building up profitable trade.

1482 **Diego Cão**, Portuguese explorer, discovered mouth of **Congo River**.

1488 **Bartolomeu Dias**, Portuguese explorer, rounded **Cape of Good Hope**.

1491 **Vasco da Gama** rounded the Cape and sailed up East African coast en route to Asia.

1500—1600

1502 **Cesare Borgia**, son of Pope Alexander VI, completed conquest of neighboring states and added them to the Papal domain.

1503 **Leonardo da Vinci** began painting the *Mona Lisa*.

Alexander I, king of Poland and grand duke of Lithuania, ceded left bank of Dnieper to Ivan the Great.

1508 **Michelangelo** began to paint ceiling of **Sistine Chapel**.

1509 **Erasmus**, Dutch humanist, published *The Praise of Folly*.

1509–1547 Reign of **Henry VIII** of England; his first wife was Katharine of Aragon (m. 1509, div. 1533), mother of Mary I; second wife, Anne Boleyn (m. 1533, beheaded 1536), mother of Elizabeth I; third wife, **Jane Seymour** (m. 1536, d. 1537), mother of Edward VI; fourth wife, **Anne of Cleves** (m. 1540, div. 1540); fifth wife, **Katharine Howard** (m. 1540, beheaded 1542); sixth wife, **Katharine Parr** (m. 1543); Henry waged war against France and Scotland.

1513 Macchiavelli wrote *The Prince*.
Raphael painted the *Sistine Madonna*.

1515–47 Francis I ruled France; he fought Italian Wars and captured Milan at Battle of Marignano.

1515 Henry VIII appointed **Thomas Wolsey** cardinal and lord chancellor.

1516 Sir Thomas More, English statesman, wrote *Utopia*.

1517 Martin Luther began **Protestant Reformation** by posting his 95 theses against the sale of indulgences on door of Wittenberg Palace Church.

1518 Titian completed his altarpiece *Assumption of the Virgin*.

1519 Ulrich Zwingli began Reformation in **Switzerland**.

1519–1522 Ferdinand Magellan circumnavigated the globe.

1519–1556 Charles V, Holy Roman Emperor, ruled Spanish lands in Europe and America, as well as Hapsburg lands in central Europe; he sacked (1527) Rome and captured Pope Clement VII.

1520 Luther was declared a heretic by Pope Leo X and formally excommunicated (1521) by **Edict of Worms**.

1523–1560 Reign of **Gustavus I** (Vasa) of Sweden; he ended (1537) trade monopoly of Hanseatic League and promoted Reformation.

1524–1525 Peasants' War in Germany: revolt by south German peasants that was inspired by Lutheran religious ideas; however, Luther sided with princes.

1532 Rabelais wrote *Gargantua and Pantagruel*.

1533–1584 Reign of **Ivan IV** (the Terrible), first tsar of Russia; his conflicts with **boyars**, the powerful nobles who controlled regency, resulted in reign of terror; Ivan seized part of Livonia from Poles and concluded peace among Russia, Sweden, and Poland after much warfare.

1534 St. Ignatius Loyola founded Jesuit order, which became chief force in Roman Catholic Counter-Reformation.
Act of Supremacy: English Parliament made Henry VIII head of Church of England, initiating **English Reformation.**

1535 Sir Thomas More, former lord chancellor of England, was beheaded for refusing to subscribe to Act of Supremacy.

1536 Menno Simons, Dutch religious reformer, began preaching **Anabaptist** doctrines.
Hans Holbein, the younger, of Germany became court painter to Henry VIII.

1541–1564 John Calvin headed a theocratic state at Geneva.

1543 Nicholas Copernicus published his **astronomy** discoveries.

1545 Council of Trent was convened by Pope Paul III; it made internal reforms in Roman Catholic Church.

1553–1558 Reign of Mary Tudor (Bloody Mary) of England, who restored Catholicism and persecuted Protestants; she lost (1558) Calais, last English stronghold on Continent, to the French.

1555 Peace of Augsburg signed, which allowed German princes to choose Catholicism or Lutheranism, but not Calvinism, as religion of their states; Lutheranism prevailed in north; Catholicism, in south.

1556–1598 Reign of Philip II of Spain, during which Hapsburg power reached its zenith and **Golden Age of Spanish art** and literature was initiated.

1558–1603 Reign of Elizabeth I of England, who established (1563) **Church of England** and increased English power; **Elizabethan Age** was marked by great flowering of literature.

1559 Pope Paul IV established the **Index of Forbidden Books.**

1559–1567 Reign of Mary Stuart, Queen of Scots, who abdicated in favor of her son, James VI (later James I of England); she was imprisoned by Elizabeth I because of her claims to English throne.

1562 French began harsh persecution of **Huguenots,** French Protestants; Catherine de' Medici ordered (1572) **St. Bartholomew's Day Massacre**; religious wars ended in 1598.

1566 Netherlands, led by William the Silent of Orange, revolted against Spanish domination and gained independence in 1581.

1571 Battle of Lepanto: Ottoman Turks defeated in naval battle with Austrian and Holy League forces, the greatest naval battle since Actium.

1580 Montaigne began composing *Essays*.

1582 Gregorian calendar introduced.
Douay version of New Testament published.

1587 John Knox, founder of Presbyterianism in Scotland, wrote *History of the Reformation in Scotland*.

1588 Spanish Armada defeated by English fleet under Sir Francis Drake.

c. 1589 Christopher Marlowe produced *Dr. Faustus*.

1589 Henry IV founded House of Bourbon; this dynasty ruled France until 1792.

1591–1613 William Shakespeare composed his plays and poems.

1597–1625 Francis Bacon wrote his *Essays*.

1598 Henry IV of France issued the **Edict of Nantes,** which granted religious toleration to Huguenots.
Boris Godunov became tsar of Russia and ruled until 1605.

NEAR AND MIDDLE EAST

1501 Safavid dynasty began rule of Iran that lasted until 1736.

1512–1520 Reign of Selim I, Ottoman sultan; he defeated Mamelukes in Syria and Egypt and assumed succession to Moslem Caliphate.

1520–1566 Reign of Suleiman I (the Magnificent), Ottoman sultan; he captured Belgrade, Rhodes, and Hungary during rule, which was marked by greatest flowering of **Turkish literature, art, and architecture.**

1571 Turks seized Cyprus and then suffered their first major defeat from Austrian and Holy League forces at Lepanto, the greatest naval battle since Actium.

1587–1628 Reign of Abbas I, shah of Iran, who erected palace and mosque at Isfahan.

FAR EAST

1510 Portuguese conquered **Goa, India.**

1526 Mogul Empire that was to endure until 1857 founded in India by **Baber.**

1549–1552 St. Francis Xavier introduced Christianity into Japan.

1557 Portuguese settled in Macao and began trade with China.

1560–1605 Reign of Akbar the Great (grandson of Baber), who enlarged domain and founded (1569) city of Fathpur Sikri, noted for Mogul architecture, especially **Jami Masjid** (the Great Mosque); Akbar also encouraged Persian arts and received European traders.

1568–1582 Nobunaga, who ruled Japan as military dictator, destroyed Buddhism as political force.

1571 Spanish founded Manila and began to colonize Philippines.

1582 Hideyoshi became military dictator of Japan; he initiated unification of country and unsuccessfully invaded Korea.

1590 Portuguese landed in Taiwan, calling it **Formosa.**

1595 Dutch began to colonize **East Indies.**

AMERICAS

1500 Cabral claimed **Brazil** for Portugal.

1501–1502 Amerigo Vespucci explored the coast of Brazil.

1511 Spanish took **Cuba** and **Puerto Rico,** founding San Juan and settling Jamaica.

1513 Ponce de Leon discovered **Florida.**
Balboa discovered the **Pacific.**

1519 Hernán Cortés of Spain landed in Mexico; Aztecs thought Cortés was Quetzalcoatl, their god who was supposed to appear at that period; Cortés, who met Montezuma II and later imprisoned him, captured (1521) Tenochtitlán and began harsh rule of Mexico.

1523–1524 Alvarado took **Guatemala** and Salvador for Spain.

1524 Verrazano explored the New England coast.

1530 Portuguese colonized Brazil.

1531–1535 Francisco Pizarro subjugated Inca Empire of Peru, executing Atahuallpa and installing Manco Capac as puppet ruler; Spanish founded (1535) Lima, which became capital of viceroyalty of Peru.

1534–1541 Jacques Cartier explored St. Lawrence River, stopping at sites of Quebec and Montreal.

1539–1542 De Soto made an expedition through Florida to the Mississippi.

1540–1542 Coronado explored the Southwest, reaching as far as Kansas.

1551 National University of Mexico founded.
University of San Marcos founded in Lima, Peru.

1565 St. Augustine, Florida, oldest permanent settlement in the United States, was founded.
Portuguese settled Rio de Janeiro.

1576–1577 Martin Frobisher searched for Northwest Passage.

1579 Sir Francis Drake claimed New Albion (California) for England.

1580 Buenos Aires, Argentina, founded by Juan de Garay for Spain.

AFRICA

1503–1507 Leo Africanus, Spanish Moslem of Morocco, explored Sudan; he issued (1526) book describing Mali and Songhai kingdoms.

1508 Portuguese began to colonize Mozambique.

1513 Songhai Empire conquered Hausa States.

1520 Portuguese visited Ethiopian court.

1529 Somali war in Ethiopia began; Moslems tried to conquer Ethiopia but were defeated (1543) when Portuguese aided Somalis.

1562 Sir John Hawkins of England began slave trade between Africa and the Americas.

1590 Moroccan invasions destroyed Songhai Empire.

1600—1700

EUROPE

1603 James VI of Scotland became James I of England, founding house of Stuart, which ruled England until 1688.

1605 Guy Fawkes executed for "Gunpowder Plot" to blow up Parliament.

1607 Jonson completed *Volpone*.

1609 Kepler published *Astronomia Nova*, laws of orbits of planets.

1609–1631 Newspapers were started on the Continent: *Avisa Relation oder Zeitung* (1609) in Germany; the *Nieuwe Tijdingen* (1616), Antwerp; the *Gazette*, later the *Gazette de France* (1631), Paris.

1609–1610 Douay version of Old Testament published.

1611 King James version of the Bible compiled by leading English scholars.

1613 Michael Romanov, tsar of Russia, founded Romanov dynasty, which ruled until 1917.

1614 The Estates General met for last time until the French Revolution.

1615 Cervantes published *Don Quixote*.

1618 Thirty Years War, final great religious war, broke out in Prague; this conflict between Catholic and Protestant Europe devastated Germany.

1624 Cardinal de Richelieu became chief minister of Louis XIII; he consolidated royal authority, strengthened army, built navy, and founded (1635) French Academy.

1625 Grotius published *De Jure Belli ac Pacis*, pioneer work in international law.

1625–1649 Reign of Charles I of England, who was involved with conflicts over supremacy of king or parliament and summoned (1640–1641) the Long Parliament, which abolished the courts of High Commission and the Star Chamber; Charles was beheaded for treason.

1628 William Harvey discovered principle of blood circulation.
Petition of Right signed by Charles I; it prohibited arbitrary imprisonment, martial law, forced loans, and billeting of soldiers and sailors.

1632 Galileo published his work confirming Copernican theory of astronomy.

1640 Puritan revolution in England began; monarchists fought civil war that ended in 1649 against those who wanted republic.

1643–1715 Reign of Louis XIV (the Sun King) of France, during which royal absolutism reached a new peak; Louis allegedly said, "*L'état c'est moi*"; French art and culture flourished and Versailles palace was constructed.

1644 Milton wrote *Areopagitica*.

1645–1664 Venetian-Turkish wars caused further decline of Ottoman power.

1648 Peace of Westphalia, which ended Thirty Years War, recognized independence of Netherlands and of Swiss cantons and sovereignty of German states.

1649 King Charles I beheaded, and England had commonwealth form of government under Oliver Cromwell until 1660.

1651 Hobbes published *Leviathan*.

1652 England began series of wars with French and Dutch that lasted until 1678 over supremacy of the seas.

1659 Spanish power in Europe ended with Peace of Pyrennes.

1660 Monarchy restored by Charles II of England; Cavalier Parliament enacted repressive measures against Puritans.

1665 Great Plague hit London; the following year fire virtually destroyed city.

1675 Sir Christopher Wren began St. Paul's Cathedral, London.

1682–1725 Reign of Peter the Great of Russia; he tried to "Westernize" Russia and established schools and a newspaper.

1683 Turkish siege of Vienna repulsed.

1684 Newton published his theories of motion and gravitation.

1685 Edict of Nantes revoked by Louis XIV; Protestants fled abroad.

1688 "Glorious Revolution" occurred in England; this bloodless revolution against James II ended when William of Orange and Mary, his British wife, accepted crown.
France began war against Grand Alliance of European powers that resulted in decline of French power.

1689 William and Mary began to rule England and signed Bill of Rights, limiting royal power; their rule ended in 1702.

1699 Peace of Karlowitz: Turkey ceded some of her conquered territories to Austria, Poland, and Venice.

NEAR AND MIDDLE EAST

1638 Turks won back Baghdad from Persians.

1656 Mohammed Kuprili became grand vizier to Mohammed IV and helped Ottoman empire regain some former power.

1699 Peace of Karlowitz: Turkey ceded Hungary, Croatia, and Slavonia to Austria; Podolia and Ukraine to Poland; and the Peloponnesus to Venice.

FAR EAST

1600 William Adams, an Englishman, arrived in Japan and imparted some technology to Japanese.
British East India Company chartered for trade in India.

1603 Ieyasu Tokugawa came to power in Japan, and his dynasty ruled until 1867; it centralized feudalism, encouraged trade, and established capital at Tokyo; Kabuki theater was developed.

1611 British began to send envoys to Mogul Empire and later established settlements at Surat and factories in Bengal and Madras.

1615 Dutch seized Moluccas (Spice Islands) from Portuguese.

1616 Manchu Tartars from Manchuria began to invade China.

1619 Dutch founded Batavia, Java.

1627 Japan began to exclude foreigners, allowing one Dutch trading post to remain.

1628–1658 Reign of Shah Jehan, ruler of Mogul Empire; he erected Taj Mahal, one of the most beautiful buildings in the world.

1636 Dutch occupied Ceylon.

1641–1662 Dutch controlled Formosa.

1644 Ch'ing dynasty in China was founded by Manchus and ruled until 1912; Korea became vassal state known as the "Hermit Kingdom" because of its isolation.

1661–1722 Reign of K'ang Hsi, Chinese emperor who consolidated empire and issued edict of toleration after Jesuit missionaries appeared.

1668 Bombay became headquarters of East India Company.

1674 Mahratta State in west central India founded by Sivaji.

1675–1708 Guru Govind Singh ruled Sikhs and built up their military power.

AMERICAS

1607 English founded Jame town, tueir first permanent settlement in America; John Smith became leader.

1608 Champlain founded Quebec.
Jesuit state in Paraguay founded.

1620 Pilgrims arrived at Plymouth, Massachusetts.

1630 Massachusetts Bay colony established by Puritans.

1671 Danes took St. Thomas.
British settled Barbados, and Leeward and Windward Islands.

1673 Jacques Marquette and Louis Joliet explored the Mississippi.

1682 After La Salle descended Mississippi River to its mouth, French began to rule colonial empire in North America that extended from Quebec to New Orleans.

AFRICA

1642 French established base on Madagascar.

c. 1650 Slave trade from Gold Coast thrived until early 19th century.

1652 Dutch founded Capetown; Jan van Riebeeck led settlers.

1680 Germans began to colonize West Africa.

1684 English lost Tangier to Morocco.

1687 Arguin, Guinea, established as Brandenburgian colony.

c. 1695 Osei Tutu founded Ashanti kingdom in western Africa and established capital at Kumasi; Ashanti, noted for high-quality gold work, grew wealthy from slave trade.

OCEANIA

1601 Australia began to be visited by Portuguese, Spanish, and Dutch.

1642 Abel Tasman, Dutch navigator, discovered New Zealand and Tasmania, which was named Van Diemen's Land.

1688 William Dampier of England landed on northwest coast of Australia.

1700—1800

EUROPE

1700 Great Northern War began: Russia, Poland, and Denmark fought Sweden for supremacy in the Baltic; when war ended in 1721, Russia emerged as a major European power with "window" on the Baltic.
Philip V became first Bourbon king of Spain.

1701 Act of Settlement, which was passed by English parliament, provided that crown would pass to house of Hanover; king could not be Roman Catholic.
Hohenzollerns came to power in Prussia and Germany, ruling until 1918.
War of the Spanish Succession began; Treaty of Utrecht (1713) separated thrones of France and Spain and marked rise of British and decline of French.

1705 Moscow University founded by Peter the Great.

1707 Great Britain formed by union of England and Scotland.

1711 Joseph Addison and Richard Steele began publishing the Spectator in England.

1713–1740 Reign of Frederick William I, king of Prussia, who became known as the soldier king because he strengthened Prussian army.

1714 George I began the Hanoverian rule of England; house of Hanover was succeeded (1840) by house of Wettin when Queen Victoria married.

1715 The Age of Enlightenment began; also known as the Age of Reason; Europe experienced a rich period of philosophy that died out after 1789.
Louis XV began to rule France, but wars and financial policy weakened government.

1733 War of Polish Succession began: Russia and Austria defeated Spain and placed Augustus III on Polish throne two years later.

1738 John Wesley, founder of Methodism, began preaching in England.

1740 War of the Austrian Succession: a general European war broke out after Maria Theresa became Hapsburg ruler; it ended in 1748.

1740–1786 Reign of Frederick the Great, king of Prussia, who expanded territory and made Prussia leading European military power.

1747 Denis Diderot and other writers began editing the Encyclopédie.

1748 Montesquieu published Spirit of the Laws.

c. 1750 Industrial Revolution had begun in England; factory system, economic specialization, and urbanization changed social structure during next century.

1755 An earthquake devastated Lisbon, killing 30,000.

1756 Seven Years War began between England and France over colonial possessions in America and India; it ended in 1763; France lost Canada and India, England became world's major colonial power.

1758 Voltaire completed Candide.

1760 George III began his 60-year reign in England.

1762 Jean Jacques Rousseau completed Social Contract.

1762–1796 Reign of Catherine II (the Great) of Russia, who promoted education, the arts, and social reforms.

1768 Major Russo-Turkish Wars: Russia and Turkey waged a series of wars for over a century; in 1878 Turkey was finally ousted from Crimea and much of Slavic Europe.

1769 James Watt, Scottish inventor, patented his steam engine.

1772–1795 Poland was partitioned among Russia, Austria, and Prussia.

1773–1774 Pugachev led rebellion of Russian peasants and Cossacks, causing Catherine II to institute tighter control over serfs.

1774 Louis XVI and Marie Antoinette became king and queen of France.

1776 Adam Smith published The Wealth of Nations.
Edward Gibbon began The Decline and Fall of the Roman Empire.

1785 The Times of London was founded by John Walter.

1789 The French Revolution began when Paris mob stormed the Bastille; third estate drafted (1791) new constitution; Louis XVI and Marie Antoinette beheaded (1793).

1790 Edmund Burke wrote Reflections on the French Revolution.

1791 Thomas Paine wrote The Rights of Man, directed against critics of French Revolution.

1798 Robert Malthus published Essay on the Principle of Population.

1799 Napoleon Bonaparte staged a coup d'état in France; his conquests made France the most powerful country in Europe; Code Napoléon reformed legal system; Napoleon was exiled in 1815.

NEAR AND MIDDLE EAST

1736 Nadir Shah established Afshar dynasty in Persia; considered last of the great Asian conquerors, he conquered Afghanistan, sacked Delhi, and defeated Turks.

1768 Turkey and Russia began a century of wars, causing Turkey to lose Crimea and much of Slavic Europe to Russia.

1794 Kajar dynasty of Persia founded by Aga Mohammed; it remained in power until 1925.

1798 Napoleon Bonaparte attempted to occupy Egypt but was driven out (1801) by British and Turkish forces.

FAR EAST

1735–1796 Reign of Emperor Ch'ien Lung, during which Chinese empire reached its greatest territorial extent; Christian missionaries were persecuted.

1739 Nadir Shah of Persia sacked Delhi and conquered Punjab.

1757 Defeat of Nawab of Bengal by Robert Clive marked beginning of British Empire in India.

1758 Burma became an independent state with capital at Rangoon.

1782 Rama I founded Chakri dynasty in Thailand and established capital at Bangkok; this dynasty rules today.

1786 British East India Company leased the island of Penang in Malaya, first step in British domination of Malay Peninsula.

1798 Ceylon became British territory.

AMERICAS

1721 Revolts in Paraguay initiated a series of wars in Latin America for independence from Spain.

1754 French and Indian Wars started in North America; British general, James Wolfe, defeated (1759) French under Montcalm on the Plains of Abraham, Quebec, Canada, ending the wars; British dominated Canada thereafter.

1775 American Revolution began with battle of **Lexington** and **Concord**; it ended with British surrender at Yorktown in 1783.
1776 Declaration of Independence signed in Philadelphia.
1788 U.S. Constitution ratified.
1789 George Washington became first U.S. President.
1791 Canada Act: Canada was divided into Upper Canada (chiefly English) and Lower Canada (predominantly French).

AFRICA
1787 British abolitionists established colony at **Freetown,** which became center for British settlement of **Sierra Leone.**
1795–1796 Mungo Park, British explorer, explored Niger River.
1799 By this time Portuguese, French, Spanish, Danes, Dutch, and Swedes all held **trading posts** along West African coast and engaged in **slave trade.**

OCEANIA
1770 Captain James Cook claimed Cape York Peninsula, Australia, for Great Britain.
1777 Cook visited **Tasmania.**
1788 British established a penal colony in Sydney, Australia.

1800—1900

EUROPE
1800 Socialism developed in Europe in reaction to deplorable industrial conditions.
1801 United Kingdom was formed by union of Great Britain and Ireland.
1802 John Dalton introduced **atomic theory** into chemistry.
First **factory law** was introduced in England; it pertained to **child labor.**
1804 Napoleon I became emperor of France.
1806 Holy Roman Empire came to an end when Francis II renounced the imperial title.
1812 Napoleon invaded Russia, a disastrous campaign.
1814–1815 Congress of Vienna: Metternich of Austria, **Talleyrand** of France, **Alexander I** of Russia, **Frederick William I** of Prussia, and **Castlereagh** of England tried to restore European balance of power; the congress reestablished monarchies and organized German Confederation, which was dominated by Austria.
1815 Napoleon I returned from Elba and was later defeated by British and Prussian armies at **Waterloo.**
1821 Greeks began war with **Turkey,** achieving independence in 1830.
1830 July Revolution in France forced abdication of King Charles X; Louis Philippe became constitutional monarch.
1831 Russians suppressed **Polish insurrection,** marking beginning of "Russification" of Poland.
1837–1901 Reign of Queen Victoria of England, who married (1840) her cousin **Prince Albert** of Saxe-Coburg; English enjoyed era of prosperity due to industrial and colonial expansion.
1838 Chartist movement began, marking first attempt of British working classes to attain power.
1845 Friedrich Engels wrote *Situation of the Working Classes in England.*
Potato blight began in Ireland, which resulted by 1851 in death of about one million people from starvation and disease.
1848 Marx and **Engels** issued *Communist Manifesto.*
Revolutions broke out in France, Germany, Austria, Hungary, Bohemia, and Italy.
1848–1916 Reign of Francis Joseph, Emperor of Austria, who became (1867) ruler of **Austro-Hungarian Empire.**
1852–1870 Reign of Napoleon III, emperor of the Second French Empire.
1854–1856 Crimean War: Britain and France ended Russian domination of southeastern Europe.
1855–1881 Reign of Alexander II, tsar of Russia; he attempted to modernize government, emancipated (1861) **serfs,** and ceded (1867) Alaska to the United States; **Russian literature** began its most creative period.
1856 Bessemer invented process of converting iron into steel.

1859 De Lesseps began **Suez Canal,** which opened in 1869.
Darwin published *Origin of the Species.*
1859–1870 Risorgimento in Italy: a nationalist movement led by middle classes and nobility for political unification; its leaders included **Mazzini, Cavour,** and **Giuseppe Garibaldi.**
1861 Kingdom of Italy proclaimed, and Victor Emmanuel II of Sardinia became king.
Rumania formed by unification of Moldavia and Walachia.
1862 Otto von Bismarck became premier and chancellor of Germany and created German Empire.
1864 First International organized in London under leadership of **Karl Marx.**
1866 First permanent transatlantic cable laid by Cyrus Field.
Austro-Prussian War: Bismarck expelled Austrians from German Confederation; and established North German Confederation; Austria lost Venetia to Italy. **Nobel** invented **dynamite.**
1867 Marx published first volume of *Das Kapital.*
Austro-Hungarian Empire founded: under pressure from Hungarian nationalists, Francis Joseph created dual monarchy; this empire collapsed in 1918.
1868–1894 British statesmen **Benjamin Disraeli,** an imperialist and Tory leader, and **William Gladstone,** an anti-imperialist and Liberal party leader, vied for control of prime ministry.
1870 Dogma of papal infallibility declared by Vatican Council.
Vladimir Lenin (V. I. Ulyanov), founder of modern Communism, was born.
1870–1871 Franco-Prussian War: Germans, directed by von Moltke, invaded and defeated France; French deposed Napoleon III and established **Third Republic** of France, which endured until 1940.
Italy incorporated **Papal States,** completing unification of the country.
1871 German Empire proclaimed at Versailles with William I as Emperor; north and south Germany became united into single *Reich.*
Paris Commune formed when Parisians refused to surrender to new regime; national troops suppressed revolutionaries.
1875 Charles Stewart Parnell, Irish nationalist leader, was elected to Parliament and began movement for Irish independence.
1878 Congress of Berlin: much of Ottoman Empire divided among Russia, Britain, and Austro-Hungarian Empire.
1881 Alexander II of Russia assassinated by member of revolutionary group called **People's Will.**
1882 Triple Alliance formed by Germany, Austria-Hungary, and Italy.
1885 Louis Pasteur used vaccine to prevent rabies in young boy.
1894–1906 Dreyfus Affair: Capt. Alfred Dreyfus, French Jewish military officer, was unjustly convicted of treason by a court-martial, sentenced to Devils Island, but eventually exonerated; his case divided France between left and right factions, causing (1905) separation of church and state.
1894–1917 Reign of Nicholas II, last tsar of Russia.
1895 Roentgen discovered **X rays.**
Marconi sent message over **wireless.**
1898 Zeppelin invented motor-driven **airship** and made first trial flight two years later.
The Curies discovered radium.
1899 First Peace Conference at The Hague established a permanent court of arbitration.

NEAR AND MIDDLE EAST
1811–1849 Reign of Mohammed Ali in Egypt extended Egyptian territory to Persian Gulf.
1854–1856 Crimean War: Britain and France backed Turkey in war with Russia that forced Russian concessions and guaranteed integrity of Ottoman Empire.
1859–1869 Suez Canal was built by **De Lesseps.**
c. 1870 Turkish government permitted European **Jews** to settle in Palestine.
1878 Congress of Berlin: Turks lost Cyprus to British, part of Asian lands to Russians, and Bosnia-Hercegovina to Austrians.

1888 European powers declared **neutrality of Suez Canal**; free passage was guaranteed to merchant and war vessels.

1892 British took over **Trucial Oman**, a region of eastern Arabia, and denied local sheiks treaty-making powers.

1894–1896 Sultan Abdu-l-Hamid II initiated extermination plan against Armenians; persecutions and massacres were resumed in 1915.

1896 Young Turks, a new national force, developed in Turkey, leading (1908) revolt against Sultan.

FAR EAST

1819 Sir T. Stamford Raffles secured transfer of Singapore to British East India Company.

1839–1842 **Opium War**: British provoked war with China and acquired commercial concessions and Hong Kong.

1848 **Taiping Rebellion** began in China, further weakening Ch'ing dynasty; with aid of Western powers, it was suppressed in 1865.

1853 **Commodore Perry**, an American, landed in isolationist Japan; the following year Japanese agreed to trade with West.

1857–1858 **Sepoy Rebellion**, or Great Mutiny: Indian soldiers revolted against British, representing first serious revolt of Indians against foreign rule.

1868 Emperor **Meiji Mutsuhito** began to rule Japan; he modernized country by abolishing feudalism, promoting foreign trade, and initiating industrialization and military conscription; Meiji period ended in 1912.

1887 France joined Vietnam and Cambodia as Indo-China; Laos was added to union in 1893.

1888 Britain completed annexation of Burma, making it a dependency of India.

1889 Meiji Mutsuhito issued modern **constitution** for Japan.

1894–1895 **Sino-Japanese War**: Japan became an imperial power by defeating Chinese in Korea and acquiring Formosa (Taiwan) and the Pescadores.

1898 Spain ceded Philippines to the United States.

1899 Western powers forced **Open Door** policy upon China by which equal trade rights for all nations were guaranteed.

AMERICAS

1801–1803 **Toussaint L'Ouverture**, martyred Haitian patriot, liberated **Santo Domingo** from the French and governed the island, thwarting Napoleon's colonial ambitions.

1803 United States purchased **Louisiana Territory** from France.

1806 **Henri Christophe**, Haitian revolutionary, elected president of Haitian republic.

1810 **Mexico** began to fight for independence from Spain.

1811 Paraguay achieved independence.

1811–1813 **Venezuela**, led by Francisco de Miranda, gained independence.

1812–1814 **War of 1812**: United States and Great Britain fought over neutrality of the seas and impressment of sailors; struggle strengthened American nationalist feelings.

1816 Argentina won independence.

1818 Chile gained independence under José de San Martín.

1818–1823 **Bernardo O'Higgins**, Chilean revolutionist, ruled Chile.

1819–1830 **Simón Bolívar**, the Liberator and greatest Latin American hero, defeated Spanish forces at Boyacá and was elected President of Greater Colombia (modern Colombia, Venezuela, Ecuador, and Panama).

1821 Mexicans achieved independence.

1822 Independence was won in Brazil and **Peru**.

1823 **Monroe Doctrine**: President James Monroe declared that the United States would neither interfere in European affairs nor tolerate European interference in American hemisphere.

1825 Bolivia became independent, the last Latin American country to win freedom from Spain.

1841 Act of Union joined Upper and Lower Canada.

1844 Samuel Morse transmitted message over **telegraph** from Washington to Baltimore.

1846 The **Mexican war** between United States (and Texas) and Mexico began; Treaty of Guadalupe Hidalgo established (1848) Rio Grande as Mexican-U.S. boundary and made New Mexico and California U.S. territory and Texas a possession.

1848 Gold discovered in **California**.

1861 **Civil War** (that ended in 1865) began in the United States.

1863 The **Emancipation Proclamation** ended slavery in the rebel states.

1864 **Maximilian**, Austrian archduke, became emperor of Mexico; he and his wife Carlotta retained power with aid of French troops; their rule was overthrown (1867) by Benito Juárez, an Indian, who became Mexican national hero.

1865 War of the **Triple Alliance** began: Paraguay fought against Argentina, Brazil, and Uruguay; it ended (1870) with devastation of Paraguay.

1867 **British North America Act**: Canada became a confederation.

United States purchased **Alaska** from Russia.

1868 Cubans fought **Ten Years War** for independence, being defeated by Spanish in 1878.

1876 **Porfirio Diaz** seized presidency of Mexico and ruled ruthlessly; he encouraged foreign capital, made Mexico prosperous but kept peasants in virtual bondage; deposed by Madero revolution in 1911.

1879–1884 **War of the Pacific**: Chile fought against Bolivia and Peru, securing territory from both countries; Bolivia lost sea access.

1889 Republic of Brazil established.

1895 Cuban poet, **José Martí**, led revolt against Spain.

1898 **Spanish-American War**: after U.S. battleship *Maine* was sunk in Havana harbor, the United States declared war on Spain and by Treaty of Paris (1898) acquired Puerto Rico, Guam, and the Philippines; the war dissolved Spanish control in Latin America.

1899 **Cuba** became an independent republic under U.S. protection.

AFRICA

1806 Britain annexed **Cape Province** in South Africa.

1807 Britain outlawed **slave trade** with France, Spain, and Portugal following suit.

1808 **Sierra Leone** became a British crown colony and administered Gambia.

1822 **Liberia** founded as haven for freed American slaves; it was declared an independent republic in 1847.

1830 French troops began conquest of Algeria.

1835 **Boers** began to leave Cape Province; the "Great Trek" established republics of Transvaal, Natal, and Orange Free State.

1841 Dr. **David Livingstone** began three decades of explorations in central Africa; he discovered (1855) Victoria Falls and his reports created interest in the "Dark Continent" and its natural resources.

1843 British annexed **Natal** after short war with Boers; it was made crown colony in 1856.

1848 British annexed **Orange Free State**.

1867–1871 **Diamonds** were discovered in South Africa, inciting diamond rush; Kimberley became center of diamond industry.

1874–1889 Henry Morton **Stanley** explored **Congo** River.

1876 **Leopold II**, with Stanley's aid, set up organization to exploit Congo; he founded (1885) **Congo Free State**, ruling as supreme monarch until 1908.

1878 Cetewayo led **Zulu** revolt against British that was defeated (1879) at Ulundi.

1880 **Brazzaville** founded in Congo by French.

1881 **Tunis** became French protectorate.

1884–1885 Germans proclaimed protectorates over **Tanganyika, Togoland, Cameroons, and South-West Africa**.

1886 **Gold** discovered in Witwatersrand in southern Transvaal.

1888 **Cecil Rhodes**, British diamond tycoon, gained monopoly of Kimberley diamond production; Rhodes became (1890) virtual dictator of Cape Province but resigned (1897) and thereafter developed Rhodesia.

1889 **Menelik II** of Ethiopia unwittingly signed Treaty of Uccialli that made Ethiopia an Italian protectorate; Italians invaded after he repudiated treaty; Menelik crushed (1896) Italians at Aduwa.

1891 British annexed Nyasaland and fought Arab slave traders.

1896 British, after a series of wars, defeated Ashanti kingdom and annexed it in 1901.

1899–1902 Boer War: British defeated Boers in South Africa and formed (1910) Union of South Africa.

OCEANIA

1803 British took possession of Tasmania, establishing a penal colony there.

1840 Treaty of Waitangi guaranteed Maoris in New Zealand that they would retain their land for surrendering sovereignty to British crown.

1900—1980

EUROPE

1903 Social Democrats held second party congress in London and split into Mensheviks and Bolsheviks, the nascent Communist party.

1904 France and England signed the Entente Cordiale, which became (1907) the Triple Entente when Russia joined.

1905 Einstein formulated theory of relativity.

1906 Britain launched the *Dreadnought*, first large battleship, signaling start of world naval buildup.

1908 Brief Balkan crisis erupted after Austria announced annexation of Bosnia and Hercegovina.

1910–1936 Reign of George V, king of Great Britain and Northern Ireland and emperor of India, was marked by Home Rule for Ireland (1914) and World War I.

1911 Italy declared war on Turkey and acquired Tripoli.

1912 First Balkan War began between Balkan countries and Turkey; a second broke out when Bulgaria attacked Serbia and Greece.

1913 European nations increased preparations for war.

1914 Assassination of Archduke Francis Ferdinand of Austria in Sarajevo by Gavrilo Princip, a member of Serbian terrorist society, sparked World War I; Triple Entente of France, Britain, and Russia and their allies Japan, Belgium, Serbia, and Montenegro fought Central Powers of Germany, Austria-Hungary, and Turkey; Italy, Portugal, Rumania, and the United States later sided with Triple Entente, which with its allies achieved victory in 1918, when an armistice was signed. At least 10,000,000 died during war.

1915 Cunard ship *Lusitania* sunk off the coast of Ireland after attack by German submarine; 1,198 were lost.

1916 President Wilson submitted his peace proposals to warring nations.

Gregory Rasputin, a hedonistic mystic who influenced Russian royal family, was murdered.

1917 Bolshevik Revolution broke out in Russia; Alexander Kerensky, a Menshevik, headed provisional government but was overthrown by Bolshevik leader, Vladimir Lenin.

Balfour Declaration: Great Britain announced that Palestine should become home for Jews.

1918 Treaty of Brest-Litovsk: Russians signed peace treaty with Germans, losing Poland, the Ukraine, and border areas inhabited by non-Russians.

Kaiser Wilhelm abdicated, and Germans adopted Weimar Constitution the following year.

Austro-Hungarian Empire ended, and Austria became a republic, while Poland and Hungary proclaimed their independence.

Czechoslovakia became independent; Thomas Masaryk served as president and Eduard Beneš as foreign minister.

"Kingdom of the Serbs, Croats, and Slovenes" was proclaimed under the regency of Peter I of Serbia; its name was changed to Yugoslavia (land of southern Slavs) in 1929.

Civil War began in Russia between Reds and Whites that was complicated by Allied interventions; by end of war in 1920, Russia had been devastated.

1919 Treaty of Versailles ending World War I was negotiated by Woodrow Wilson (United States), Georges Clemenceau (France), David Lloyd George (England), and Vittorio Orlando (Italy).

1920 League of Nations was established in Geneva; the United States refused to join.

Northern and Southern Ireland separated; Southern Ireland became (1921) Irish Free State with dominion status.

1922 Russia became the Union of Soviet Socialist Republics, the first Communist state in the world.

Benito Mussolini, founder of Fascism, became premier of Italy, gradually creating dictatorship.

Major powers agreed to limit size of navies at Washington Disarmament Conference.

1923 Adolf Hitler, leader of National Socialist (Nazi) Party, led unsuccessful "Beer Hall Putsch" in Munich; during imprisonment he wrote *Mein Kampf*.

1924 A power struggle began in Russia after Lenin's death; ultimately Joseph Stalin was victorious and became dictator.

1928 Stalin initiated Five Year Plan for rapid industrialization and collectivized farms; peasants who refused collectivization were either sent to Siberia to perform forced labor or killed; measures caused "liquidation" of more than five million peasants.

Kellogg-Briand Pact outlawing war was signed by the United States and 62 other nations in Paris.

1929 Lateran Treaties created independent state of Vatican City in Rome.

1930 Worldwide economic depression developed, pushing many countries into bankruptcy; this disaster encouraged rise of extremist movements.

1931 British Commonwealth of Nations established.

Spain became a republic.

1932 Antonio Salazar became prime minister of Portugal, ruling (1936–1968) as dictator.

1933 The democratic Weimar Republic fell in Germany.

Hitler's Nazi party won majority in *Reichstag* and the government granted him dictatorial powers; Hitler built up war economy and began to rearm Germany; he withdrew from the League of Nations and set up concentration camps, where, in the years that followed, over six million people (mainly Jews and Poles) died.

1935 Nuremberg Laws deprived Jews of citizenship, barred them from certain professions, and prohibited marriage between Germans and Jews.

Ethiopia, in League of Nations, brought charges against Italy; League economic sanctions against Italy did not prevent annexation (1936) of Ethiopia.

1936 Hitler repudiated Locarno Pact and sent troops into Rhineland.

Rome-Berlin-Tokyo Axis formed.

Spanish Civil War began: Republicans were backed by Communist Russia, while Nazi Germany and Fascist Italy supported Falangists; liberals from many countries fought to save republic; Falangist forces, headed by General Francisco Franco, were victorious by 1939.

Stalin began liquidation of his enemies with series of purge trials that lasted until 1939.

George VI became king of England after Edward VIII abdicated.

1938 Germany annexed Austria.

Munich Pact: French and British, led by Neville Chamberlain, appeased Hitler and allowed Germany to occupy Sudetenland; Germans took remainder of Czechoslovakia in 1939.

1939 Germany signed nonaggression pact with Soviet Union.

Germans invaded Poland, beginning World War II.

Russian troops invaded Poland, which was partitioned between Soviet Union and Germany.

Russians took Lithuania, Latvia, and Estonia.

Russians invaded Finland, defeating her the following year.

League of Nations performed its final act by expelling Soviet Union for invading Finland.

World War II broke out and developed into global conflict between Axis and Allies.

1940 Marshal Henri Pétain became head of French government and concluded peace treaty with Germany; Pétain set up government for unoccupied France in Vichy, which collaborated with Germans.

1940–1945 Winston Churchill was prime minister of England; his inspiring leadership helped British during dark days of war.

1941 Germany and Italy declared war on the United States on Dec. 11.

1942 Vidkun Quisling appointed by Germans to head puppet government in Norway; he was executed for collaboration in 1945.

1943 Mussolini's regime collapsed; **Marshal Pietro Badoglio** became prime minister, and Italy surrendered unconditionally to Allies and declared war on Germany.
President Roosevelt and **Prime Minister Churchill** held conferences at Casablanca, Cairo, and Teheran to coordinate war plans.
German defeat by Russian forces at **Stalingrad** (now Volgograd) marked turning point of war on the Eastern front.

1944 **D-Day:** Allied troops, commanded by **General Dwight D. Eisenhower,** invaded Fortress Europa at Normandy, France.
German generals staged unsuccessful attempt on Hitler's life.
U.S. and French troops liberated **Paris.**
General Charles de Gaulle established provisional government in France.

1945 **Yalta (Crimea) Conference:** Roosevelt, Churchill, and Stalin made postwar plans for German occupation and agreed to form a United Nations.
Josip Broz Tito, partisan leader, became head of Yugoslavia.
Mussolini captured and executed by Italian partisans.
Hitler died in Berlin, reportedly a suicide.
Germany surrendered unconditionally to Allies; **Allied Control Council** set up to rule Germany and **Berlin,** both of which were divided among four powers. **President Truman, Churchill,** and Stalin met at **Potsdam,** Germany, to discuss control of Germany.
Clement Attlee, Labour party leader, became prime minister of England.
International War Crimes Tribunal began in **Nuremberg;** Nazi military and civilian leaders were tried for war crimes.

1946 **United Nations General Assembly** held its first session, in London; **Trygve Lie** of Norway became first secretary-general, holding office until 1951.
Civil war erupted in Greece between Communists and rightist government forces; Bulgaria, Albania, and Yugoslavia aided Communist guerrillas; conflict, which ended in 1949 with royalists retaining power, brought increased Western-Soviet hostility.

1946–1947 Bulgaria and Rumania proclaimed people's republics.

1947 **Cominform** was established in response to **Marshall Plan** when Communist leaders from nine countries met in Poland; it was dissolved in 1956.

1948 Communists came to power in **Hungary** and **Czechoslovakia;** Czech President Beneš resigned, and Foreign Minister Jan Masaryk was found dead.
Yugoslavia withdrew from Cominform, proclaiming its independence of Soviet influence.
European Recovery Plan (the Marshall Plan) went into effect; ERP ended in 1951.
Berlin Blockade: Soviets barred road and rail travel between Berlin and West Germany; West airlifted supplies until ban was lifted in 1949.

1949 **North Atlantic Treaty Organization** set up by the United States, Canada, and 10 European countries for collective self-defense.
Soviet Union exploded atomic bomb, ending U.S. monopoly
Germany divided into West Germany (Federal Republic of Germany) and **East Germany** (German Democratic Republic).

1952 Reign of **Queen Elizabeth II** of England began.

1953 Joseph Stalin died; **Georgi Malenkov** became Soviet premier; **Nikita S. Khrushchev** elected first secretary of the Soviet Communist party's Central Committee.
Russians exploded their first **hydrogen bomb.**
Workers in **East Germany** staged riots that were suppressed by Soviet troops.

1954 Geneva settlement divided Vietnam into North and South Vietnam and recognized independence of Cambodia and Laos.

1955 **Warsaw Pact:** mutual defense treaty signed by Soviet Union, Albania, Czechoslovakia, Bulgaria, Hungary, Poland, Rumania, and East Germany.

1956 Premier Khrushchev denounced Stalin at 20th Communist Party Congress in Moscow, ushering in a period of de-Stalinization in Soviet Union and Eastern Europe. Workers rioted in Poznan, Poland.
Hungarian rebellion against Communist regime ruthlessly put down by Soviet troops and tanks.

1957 **Common Market:** European Economic Community established by Belgium, Netherlands, Luxembourg, West Germany, France, and Italy; its ultimate aim was political union.
Sputnik: Soviet Union launched world's first artificial earth satellite, initiating Space Age.

1958 Nuclear test ban negotiations began in Geneva between Western and Soviet blocs.
De Gaulle elected president of France.
Russians provoked Berlin crisis that was limited to diplomatic confrontation.

1960 Cyprus gained independence with **Archbishop Makarios** as president.
European Free Trade Association established by "Outer Seven": Austria, United Kingdom, Denmark, Norway, Portugal, Sweden, and Switzerland; Finland joined in 1961.
American U-2 plane, on photoreconnaissance mission, was shot down over Russian territory; United States agreed to suspend flights.

1961 **Berlin Wall:** East Germans erected wall between East and West Berlin, causing war scare.
Yuri A. Gagarin, Russian astronaut, was first man to orbit earth.

1963 Pope John XXIII died; **Giovanni Battista Cardinal Montini** elected as **Pope Paul VI.**
The United States, Soviet Union, and Great Britain signed treaty banning nuclear tests above ground and under water.
Fighting broke out between Greek and Turkish Cypriots; UN force is still on island to maintain order.

1964 Soviet Presidium ousted Khrushchev and made **Aleksei N. Kosygin** premier and **Leonid I. Brezhnev** first secretary of Communist party.

1966 **De Gaulle** requested **NATO** troop removal from France.

1967 Military staged coup d'état in Greece, installing dictatorship and driving **King Constantine II** into exile.
Britain devalued the pound and instituted austerity program.

1968 International monetary crises developed because of faltering British pound and French franc, but both currencies were held.
Soviet troops invaded **Czechoslovakia;** President Ludvík Svoboda and Alexander Dubcek allowed to retain posts, but Czechs had to accept Soviet troop occupation for indefinite time.
Peace talks opened in Paris between representatives of Hanoi, National Liberation Front, Saigon, and Washington to discuss **Vietnam** cease-fire.

1969 **Charles de Gaulle** resigned as president of France and was replaced by Georges Pompidou.

1970 **West Germany** and **USSR** signed a nonaggression pact.
Conservative leader **Edward Heath** became prime minister in England.
Violent food price riots in **Poland** led to Wladyslav Gomulka's resignation. He was replaced by Edward Gierek as the first secretary of the Communist party.
Charles De Gaulle died.

1972 **Great Britain, Ireland,** and **Denmark** joined the EEC.
Arab commandos disrupt the XXth Olympic games at Munich by taking 13 Israeli athletes hostage. The terrorists and hostages were later killed.
Terrorism rocked Northern Ireland in continued Protestant-Catholic conflict.

1973 **East** and **West Germany** established diplomatic relations, formally acknowledging their separation.
Greece formally abolished the monarchy.
Western Europe was plunged into an energy crisis when the Arabs embargoed oil shipments to Europe, the U.S., and Japan.

1975 Western Europe experiences severe inflation and unemployment.

In Helsinki, Western and Eastern leaders signed pact at Conference on Security and Cooperation.

Francisco Franco dies; Juan Carlos is proclaimed Spanish king.

1978 Pope Paul VI died; Albino Cardinal Luciani elected as Pope John Paul I, but lives only 34 days. Karol Cardinal Wojtyla of Poland elected Pope John Paul II.

1980 Tito of Yugoslavia dies.

Polish workers granted right to form unions following nationwide strikes; Stanislaw Konia replaced Gierek as party chief.

MIDDLE EAST

1900 Ibn Saud began to conquer Arabia, which became (1932) kingdom of Saudi Arabia.

1901 Persians discovered petroleum, causing increased rivalry in the area between Russia and England.

1914 British declared Egypt a protectorate, which it remained until 1922.

1915–1918 Turks slaughtered over one million Armenians.

1916 British Colonel T. E. Lawrence (Lawrence of Arabia) led Arab military campaigns against Turks, hoping for independent Arab states.

1919 Kemal Ataturk organized Turkish Nationalist party and began to form army; he was elected (1923) president of newly founded Turkish republic and began "Westernization" of country, abolishing (1923) caliphate and ruling until 1938.

1920 Syria and Lebanon became French mandates; their independence was recognized when they were admitted to United Nations in 1945.

Palestine, including Jordan, became British mandate; three-way struggle among Jews, Arabs, and British developed, lasting until 1948.

1921 Reza Shah Pahlavi, who staged coup d'etat in Persia, eventually ruled as dictator; changed (1935) name of country to Iran; abdicated in 1941.

1936 Farouk became king of Egypt.

1941 Mohammed Reza Shah Pahlevi became shah of Iran.

1945 The Arab League, an association of Arab states, was formed for economic unity and as opposition to establishment of Jewish state in Palestine.

1946 Iran protested to UN Security Council the presence of Russian troops in Azerbaijan province; this incident, which ended the following year, was the first crisis of the Cold War.

Kingdom of Jordan proclaimed.

1948 State of Israel achieved independence after bitter struggle; David Ben-Gurion first prime minister.

1948–1949 Arab-Israeli war ended in defeat of Arab League forces.

1951–1953 Iran oil industry nationalized by Prime Minister Mohammed Mossadegh.

1952 Gamal Abdel Nasser led army coup against King Farouk; Nasser was elected (1956) president of Egypt and promoted Arab unity.

1956 Suez Crisis: when Nasser nationalized Suez Canal, Israel, Britain, and France attacked Egypt but withdrew after UN Emergency Task-Force entered conflict.

1958 United Arab Republic formed by unification of Egypt and Syria; Syria withdraws in 1961.

Lebanon accused U.A.R. of intervention; President Eisenhower dispatched troops to area.

Iraqi monarchy overthrown in bloody coup led by General Kassem.

British paratroopers landed in Jordan to prevent pro-Nasser take-over.

1960 U.A.R., with Russian aid, began construction of a new Aswan Dam.

1961 Kuwait achieved independence.

1962 Kurdish tribes in northern Iraq rebelled, demanding independent state. Revolt is crushed in 1975.

Adolf Eichmann, chief administrator of Nazi program for exterminating Jews, was tried and executed by Israel.

Yemen monarchy overthrown; civil war broke out between republicans, who were supported by Egyptians, and royalists, backed by Saudi Arabia.

1963 British controlled Federation of South Arabia formed by union of Aden and Aden Federation; area achieved independence in 1968 as Southern Yemen.

1967 Arab-Israeli war: six-day conflict broke out after Nasser closed Gulf of Aqaba to Israeli ships; Israelis defeated Arabs; Sinai and Jerusalem occupied.

1968 President Abdul Rahman Arif of Iraq was ousted in bloodless coup led by former premier Ahmed Hassan al-Bakr, who later assumed premiership.

1970 Nasser died in Cairo; succeeded by Anwar Sadat. Civil war broke out between Jordanian army and Palestinian guerrilla groups.

1973 Large-scale fighting once again broke out between Israel and the Arab nations. The war ended in an inconclusive cease-fire.

The Arabs embargoed the shipment of oil to the U.S., Europe, and Japan, and boosted prices.

1974 The organization of petroleum exporting countries (OPEC) ended its oil embargo.

1975 Civil war raged in Lebanon between Christians and Moslems. Israel and Egypt signed Sinai disengagement pact. Suez Canal reopened.

1979 Israel and Egypt signed peace treaty calling for phased Israeli withdrawal from Sinai. Islamic Republic of Iran was proclaimed under the leadership of the Ayatollah Khomeini following the departure of the Shah and subsequent revolution. Militants seized U.S. Embassy in Tehran and held personnel hostage. Soviet troops occupied Afghanistan.

1980 Iraq invaded southwestern Iran.

FAR EAST

1904–1905 Russo-Japanese War: Russia's fleet was destroyed, and Japan's victory gained her recognition as world power.

1907 Mohandas Gandhi organized his first campaign of civil disobedience in Africa; he returned (1915) to India and supported England during World War I, hoping to attain Indian independence.

1910 Japan annexed Korea.

1911 Chinese Revolution: Sun Yat-sen forced Manchu emperor to abdicate and served briefly as president of Chinese Republic.

1917 War developed in China between Kuomintang, Sun Yat-sen's party of the Republic, and "war lords" of the national government in the North; Kuomintang established capital in Canton.

1919 Amritsar Massacre: hundreds of Indian nationalists were fired upon and killed by British.

1921 Chinese Communist party founded and became allied (1923) with Kuomintang.

1926 Chiang Kai-shek led Nationalist army in capture of Hankow, Shanghai, and Nanking; he drove (1927) Chinese Communists from Shanghai, initiating long civil war between Kuomintang forces and Communists.

1927 Mao Tse-tung, one of the founders of the Chinese Communist party, led peasant uprising in Hunan province.

1931 Japanese invaded Manchuria and set up Manchukuo, a puppet state.

Mao Tse-tung elected chairman of Soviet Republic of China.

1934–1935 Mao Tse-tung led Red Army on Long March (6,000 miles) from Kiangsi province north to new headquarters at Yenan.

1937 Burma became independent of India.

Japanese invaded northern China and fought war that continued until 1945.

Gandhi's long fasts forced some Indian states to grant democratic reforms.

1940 Japanese established puppet government in Nanking and signed military alliance with Germany and Italy.

1941 Japan bombed Pearl Harbor, captured Singapore, Philippines, and other areas of the Pacific, initiating World War II in the Pacific and drawing United States into war.

1945 United States dropped atomic bombs on Hiroshima and Nagasaki, marking the beginning of the Nuclear Age; as a result, Japan surrendered, ending World War II.

Korea was divided into Russian and American occupation zones; partition was formalized in 1948 when country became North Korea (Democratic People's Republic of Korea) and South Korea (Republic of Korea), which were separated by 38th parallel.

Vietnamese nationalists began demands for independence from France; war broke out; Ho Chi Minh, founder of Communist party in Vietnam, led Viet Minh forces.

Indonesian nationalists led by Sukarno began to fight Dutch for independence.

1946 Philippines granted independence by the United States.

1947 India and Pakistan became separate independent dominions; Jawaharlal Nehru became prime minister of Hindu state of India and Mahomed Ali Jinnah, governor general of Moslem state of Pakistan; bloody rioting broke out after partition, causing the death of millions of Hindus and Moslems.

1948 Gandhi assassinated by Hindu fanatic.

Communists began guerrilla warfare in Malaya that lasted over a decade.

1949 Chinese People's Republic headed by Mao Tse-tung established government at Peking, after defeating Chiang Kai-shek, whose Nationalist government was forced to Taiwan (Formosa).

1950 Sukarno elected president of the Republic of Indonesia.

Korean war broke out when North Koreans invaded South Korea; United Nations force under U.S. command intervened.

Chinese Communists invaded Tibet and sent troops to aid North Koreans.

1951 Armistice talks began at Panmunjon to end Korean war.

1954 Battle of Dienbienphu: Crushing French defeat ended her control in Indo-China; Vietnam divided at 17th parallel, with Ho Chi Minh as president of North Vietnam; Cambodia and Laos became independent.

1955 A U.S. military advisory group took over training of South Vietnamese army.

Premier Ngo Dinh Diem became president of South Vietnam.

1957 Federation of Malaya gained independence.

1959 Communist Chinese suppressed uprising in Tibet.

Communist Pathet Lao forces began civil war in Laos; a temporary cease-fire was secured (1961) in Geneva. China and India begun a series of border wars.

1961 India forcibly annexed Portuguese Goa, Damão, and Diu.

United States sent guerrilla warfare specialists to train South Vietnamese soldiers.

1962 Neutralist government set up in Laos under Prince Souvanna Phouma, but Pathet Lao continued sporadic fighting in North.

1963 Federation of Malaysia created by union of Federation of Malaya, Singapore, Sarawak, and North Borneo; the union suffered infiltration by Indonesian guerrillas until 1966; Singapore seceded (1965) and became independent.

Diem regime in South Vietnam overthrown; government changed hands frequently until military regime of Nguyen Cao Ky took over in 1965.

1964 China exploded her first atomic bomb.

France recognized Communist China.

Nehru died in India and was succeeded by Lal Bahadur Shastri.

1965 United States began bombing North Vietnam.

After an abortive Communist coup in Indonesia, the army slaughtered at least 100,000 Communists; Indonesia withdrew from United Nations.

India and Pakistan fought over Kashmir.

1966 Communist China initiated "cultural revolution" aimed at ideological conformity of party leaders.

Sukarno forced to yield power to Suharto, who outlawed Communist party.

Indira Gandhi, Nehru's daughter, became prime minister of India after Shastri's death.

1967 Communist China exploded first hydrogen bomb.

South Vietnam: first national election; Nguyen Van Thieu president and Nguyen Cao Ky vice-president.

1968 North Korea seized *Pueblo*, U.S. Navy intelligence ship, holding its officers and crew for 11 months.

Peace talks for Vietnam cease-fire began in Paris. President Johnson ordered halt to bombing of North Vietnam.

1969 Soviet and Chinese forces fought on the Manchurian border over a disputed island in the Ussuri River.

1970 Prince Sihanouk was deposed as chief of state in Cambodia. He was replaced by Gen. Lon Nol.

U.S. and South Vietnamese troops invaded Cambodia.

1971 Communist China admitted to U.N.; Nationalist Chinese (Taiwan) ousted.

East Pakistan became independent state of Bangladesh after bloody civil war.

1972 President Nixon visits Peking and Moscow.

1973 U.S. and South Vietnamese signed cease-fire agreement with North Vietnamese and Vietcong. Fighting continued through Indochina.

1975 The thirty year Indochina war ended with the military collapse of U.S.-backed South Vietnam and Cambodia.

1976 Communist Chinese leader Mao Tse-tung dies.

1978-79 Vietnam invaded Cambodia and drove Pol Pot regime from Phnom Penh.

1979 U.S. extended dipolmatic representation to the People's Republic of China (Communists) and broke relations with Taiwan.

China invaded Vietnam; withdrew after one month.

AMERICAS

1901 President William McKinley assassinated by anarchist; Theodore Roosevelt became President and held office until 1909.

1903 Panama, with U.S. assistance, revolted against Colombia and gained independence.

Orville and Wilbur Wright made their first airplane flight near Kitty Hawk, North Carolina.

1910 Francisco Madero led Mexican Revolution against President Diaz; after Madero's assassination, Francisco (Pancho) Villa, Emiliano Zapata, and Venustiano Carranza continued revolution; Mexico's constitution was enacted 1917.

1914 Panama Canal opened.

1916-1924 U.S. troops occupied Dominican Republic.

1917 United States entered World War I on side of Allies.

1929 Stock Market crash in the United States initiated the Great Depression; during height of depression, 12 million people were unemployed.

1932-1935 Chaco War: Bolivia and Paraguay fought exhausting war over disputed Chaco plain.

1933 President Franklin D. Roosevelt was inaugurated; he enacted New Deal legislation aimed at improving social and economic conditions in the U.S.

1938 Mexico nationalized foreign oil companies.

1941-1945 United States in World War II: after Japanese bombed Pearl Harbor, December 7, 1941, the United States declared war; Nazi Germany and Fascist Italy declared war on the United States; war was terminated after defeat of German army and surrender of Japanese after atomic bombing of Hiroshima and Nagasaki.

1942 Enrico Fermi achieved first self-sustaining nuclear chain reaction.

1944 Bretton Woods (New Hampshire) Conference established the International Bank for Reconstruction and the International Monetary Fund.

Dumbarton Oaks, Washington, D.C., Conference: the United States, Great Britain, and Soviet Union laid plans for an international organization.

1945 Roosevelt died and was succeeded by Harry S Truman.

United Nations Charter signed at San Francisco.

United States made first atom bomb test at Los Alamos, New Mexico, warned Japan of her complete destruction unless she surrendered, and dropped atomic bombs on Hiroshima and Nagasaki.

1946 Juan Perón elected president of Argentina; he established totalitarian regime and an ultranationalistic program that ultimately ruined economy, and was deposed (1955) by military coup.
Churchill gave "iron curtain" speech at Fulton, Missouri, warning of Soviet expansionism.

1948 Truman won upset Presidential victory; he initiated overseas military and economic aid to contain Communism and became leader in NATO formation.
Organization of American States (OAS) founded for hemispheric unity and mutual defense.

1949 U.S. Senate ratified NATO treaty, establishing collective self-defense among Western powers.

1950 United States in UN Security Council charged North Korea with invading South Korea and initiated military intervention against aggressors with General MacArthur as UN Commander.

1952 Fulgencio Batista seized power in Cuba.
United States exploded its first hydrogen bomb.

1954 General Alfredo Stroessner staged coup in Paraguay; in spite of opposition, he remains in power.
Brown v. Board of Education: U.S. Supreme Court outlawed racial segregation in public schools, initiating civil rights movement.

1957 François Duvalier elected president of Haiti; his harsh rule included reign of terror.

1958 Explorer I: United States successfully launched her first artificial satellite.

1959 Fidel Castro came to power in Cuba; he gradually linked country with Soviet bloc and proclaimed (1961) loyalty to Communism.

1960 John F. Kennedy elected U.S. President.

1961 United States severed relations with Cuba.
Bay of Pigs: U.S.-trained Cuban exiles' invasion of Cuba ended disastrously.
Charter of the Alliance for Progress signed in Punta del Este, Uruguay; it was aimed at increasing economic and social development in Latin America with U.S. aid.

1962 The United States and Soviet Union appeared on the brink of war when Soviet missiles were discovered on Cuba; President Kennedy forced Khrushchev to have them dismantled.
John H. Glenn was first American to orbit earth.

1963 President Kennedy assassinated in Dallas, Texas, November 22; Lyndon Baines Johnson sworn in as President and defeated Barry M. Goldwater in 1964.

1964 Panamanians staged anti-U.S. riots.

1965 U.S. marines landed in Dominican Republic.
President Johnson signed Medicare and war on poverty legislation.
Race riots ravaged Los Angeles suburb of Watts.

1966 Guyana became independent.

1967 Race riots wasted Newark, Detroit, and other cities.

1968 Frank Borman, William A. Anders, and James A. Lovell, Jr., were first men to orbit the moon.
Dr. Martin Luther King, Jr. and Senator Robert Kennedy were assassinated in the United States.
Richard M. Nixon won U.S. Presidential contest.
Military coup deposed Peruvian President Fernando Belaúnde Terry.
Pierre Elliott Trudeau succeeded to Canadian premiership.

1969 U.S. astronaut Neil A. Armstrong became first man to walk on the Moon.

1970 U.S. student protests against the Viet Nam war resulted in the killing of four students by National Guard at Kent State, Ohio, and of two students by police at Jackson State, Miss.
Trudeau invoked the War Measures Act in Canada after the murder of Quebec Labor Minister Pierre Laporte by the Quebec Liberation Front.
Salvador Allende was elected president of Chile and Luis Echeverria Alvarez of Mexico.

1971 Wage-price freeze enacted by Nixon administration.

1972 Governor Wallace seriously injured in attempted assassination while campaigning in Maryland.
Watergate burglars apprehended in Democratic National Headquarters; "Watergate" begins.
Richard M. Nixon reelected president.

1973 Spiro T. Agnew resigned from the vice-presidency; Gerald R. Ford named to replace Agnew. "Watergate" dominates American political scene.
Salvador Allende Gossens, Marxist President of Chile, overthrown and reportedly committed suicide.
Juan Perón returned from exile to become Argentine president.

1974 Juan Peron died in Buenos Aires; His wife, Vice-President Isabel Peron assumes the presidency.
Richard M. Nixon resigned from the presidency; Gerald R. Ford succeeds to the office.

1975 Surinam and Grenada attained independence.
U.S. suffered severe economic recession.

1976 Argentine military junta deposed Mrs. Peron.
Jose Lopez Portillo elected to Mexican presidency.
Jimmy Carter elected U.S. President.

1979 Somoza regime was toppled in Nicaragua by Sandinista rebels following 18-month civil war. Canal Zone was ceded to Panama by the U.S.

1980 Ronald Reagan elected U.S. President.

AFRICA

1906 Algeçiras Conference recognized predominance of French and Spanish interests in Morocco but also assured protection of German interests.

1908 Belgium annexed Congo Free State, calling it Belgian Congo.

1910 Union of South Africa formed from former British colonies of Cape of Good Hope and Natal, Orange Free State, and Transvaal.

1911 Germans sent gunboat *Panther* to Morocco as show of force.

1912 African partition among European powers was completed; only Ethiopia and Liberia remained independent.

1914 World War I in Africa: British and French troops occupied German colonies of Togoland and the Cameroons.

1920 Former German colonies became League mandates under Great Britain (Tanganyika, parts of Togoland and Cameroons), Belgium (Ruanda-Urundi), France (parts of Togoland and Cameroons), and Union of South Africa (South-West Africa).
Most of Kenya became British crown colony.
Abd-el-Krim, leader of Riff tribes of Morocco, began fight against Spanish and French rule in Africa; early successes followed by his defeat and deportation (1926) by combined Franco-Spanish troops.

1923 Rhodesia was divided into Southern and Northern Rhodesia and placed under British rule.

1930 Emperor Haile Selassie ascended Ethiopian throne.

1935 Italy invaded Ethiopia, causing Haile Selassie to flee country; League of Nations issued economic sanctions to no avail.

1946 India broke diplomatic relations with Union of South Africa because of her treatment of Indian minority.

1948 Apartheid: D. F. Malan made apartheid in Union of South Africa a political issue; the policy was aimed at perpetuating supremacy of white minority.

1951 Rising African nationalism achieved first victory with independence of Libya.

1952 Mau Mau, secret terrorist organization in Kenya, began bloody campaign to oust white settlers; British declared state of emergency that lasted until 1960.

1954 Algerian nationalists formed National Liberation Front and began terrorist campaign against French; war ended with Algeria gaining independence in 1962.

1956 Tunisia gained independence from France with Habib Bourguiba as premier.

1960 Immediately after Republic of the Congo achieved independence, civil war broke out; political struggle within central government developed between Patrice Lumumba, premier, and Joseph Kasavubu, head of state; UN peace-keeping force entered dispute; when Lumumba was seized by army and murdered (1961), Moise Tshombe became premier.
African nationalism reached peak of success when 16 nations gained freedom and African nations made up one third of UN membership.

1961 Dag Hammarskjöld, UN secretary-general, killed in plane crash on mission to Congo.
Union of South Africa became a republic; later left British Commonwealth.

1963 Jomo Kenyatta became Kenya's first premier.

1964 Tanzania formed by unification of Tanganyika and Zanzibar; Julius K. Nyerere became first president.
Nyasaland became independent state of Malawi; Northern Rhodesia gained independence as Zambia.

1965 Mohammed Ben Bella, Algerian premier, overthrown by Col. Houari Boumédiene.
Rhodesia unilaterally declared independence from Great Britain.
President Kasavubu dismissed Tshombe and his government; General Mobutu, commander of Congolese National army, seized power.

1966 Kwame Nkrumah's government in Ghana toppled by military coup; Nkrumah went into exile.
United Nations terminated South Africa's mandate over South-West Africa and proclaimed UN administration over country.

1967 Congolese troops engaged rebel forces in Kisangani and Bukavu. Tshombe died (1969) in Algeria.
Republic of Biafra proclaimed when eastern province of Nigeria seceded; Nigerian government sent troops and blockaded province, causing widespread famine throughout 1968/69.

1969 Pope Paul VI became the first pope to visit Africa when he flew to Kampala, Uganda to attend an African episcopal symposium meeting.
Portugal utilized 40% of her national budget and 120,000 troops to quell rebels in territories of Angola, Mozambique, and Portuguese Guinea.

1970 Surrender of secessionist Biafra on January 12 ended the 31-month civil war in Nigeria.

1971 Republic of the Congo renamed Zaire.

1973 A drought-induced famine cripples much of western Africa.

1975 Mozambique, Cape Verde, São Tomé and Príncipe, and Angola gained independence, ending centuries-old Portuguese colonial empire.

1976 Proponents of black majority rule wage guerrilla war against white regime in Rhodesia.

1977 Ethiopia and Somalia made war over disputed Ogaden region.

1978 Belgian and French paratroopers repelled Angola-based rebel invasion of Shaba province of Zaire.

1979 Amin regime was overthrown in Uganda following invasion by Tanzania.

1980 Black majority took power in Rhodesia with establishment of Republic of Zimbabwe.

OCEANIA

1901 Commonwealth of Australia formed by unification of Australia and Tasmania.

1907 New Zealand attained dominion status.

1959 Hawaii became a U.S. state.

1962 Western Samoa obtained independence.

1968 Nauru became an independent republic.

1970 Fiji and Tonga gained independence.

1975 Papua New Guinea achieved independence.

1978 Solomon Islands and Tuvalu gained independence.

1979 Kiribati became independent.

1980 Vanuatu gained independence.

ARCTIC AND ANTARCTICA

1908-1909 E. H. Shackleton's expedition to Antarctica failed to reach South Pole.

1909 Robert E. Peary discovered North Pole.

1911 Roald Amundsen reached South Pole.

1926 Richard E. Byrd flew over North Pole.

1928 Byrd established Little America, in Antarctica.

1955-1958 Edmund Hillary and Vivian Fuchs from Great Britain led overland crossing of Antarctica.

1957-1958 During the International Geophysical Year, many nations participated in studies of Antarctica and the Arctic.

1958 Nautilus, U.S. nuclear submarine, was first ship to cross North Pole under ice pack.

1959-1960 Treaty accepted by 12 nations, including the United States, reserved Antarctica for scientific research and recognized no existing national claims to territory in area.

1967 Peter J. Barrett and geologists from New Zealand discovered bone fragment and plant fossils embedded beneath icy surface of Antarctica indicating that Antarctica formerly had warmer climate.

1968-1969 First overland crossing of the North Pole by foot and dog sled. Royal Geographic Society of Britain's 3,600-mile expedition, encompassing more than 15 months, reached Pole in April 1969.

SEVEN WONDERS OF THE ANCIENT WORLD

The Great Pyramid of Khufu (or Cheops)—the world's largest pyramid located at Gizeh near Cairo. Built of limestone blocks, it originally stood 756 feet square, 482 feet high and covered 13 acres.

The Hanging Gardens of Bablyon—luxurious gardens which added to the glamorous atmosphere of Mesopotamia's most important ancient city.

The Mausoleum at Halicarnassus—a magnificent sepulcher in Asia Minor constructed of white marble richly decorated with sculpture and erected (c. 352 B.C.) in memory of Mausolus of Caria.

The Artemision at Ephesus—great temple built (c. 550 B.C.) as a center of worship for the nature-goddess Artemis.

The Colossus of Rhodes—large bronze statue (height about 100 feet) of the sun god Helios situated in the harbor of Rhodes and thought to be built by Chares of Rhodes between 292 and 280 B.C.

The Olympian Zeus by Phidias—built for the temple of Olympia (c. 435 B.C.); it consisted of a majestic bearded figure wearing a mantle and seated upon a huge ornamented throne.

The Pharos at Alexandria—celebrated lighthouse (estimated height: 200-600 feet) built by Ptolemy II (c. 280 B.C.) on the peninsula of Pharos.

WORLD BIOGRAPHY

Abd-el-Krim, c. 1882-1963, Moroccan Rif leader and national hero.

Abdullah, 1882-1951, assassinated first Hashemite king of Jordan.

Abrams, Creighton W., Jr., 1914-1974, American general in Vietnam.

Abruzzi, Duca degli (Luigi Amedeo), 1873-1933, Italian explorer of the Arctic (1899-1900).

Acheson, Dean G., 1893-1971, U.S. Secretary of State (1949-52) who helped to establish NATO.

Adams, Samuel, 1722-1803, American patriot, signer of Declaration of Independence, and firebrand of Boston Tea Party.

Addams, Jane, 1860-1935, American social worker and co-founder of Hull House.

Adenauer, Konrad, 1876-1967, German statesman, postwar chancellor, and architect of West German recovery.

Aga Khan III, 1877-1957, fabulously wealthy Moslem leader and statesman.

Agnelli, Giovanni, 1921- , Italian industrialist and chairman of FIAT.

Agrippina the Younger, A.D. c. 16-59, Nero's mother, who contrived his accession to the throne.

Aguinaldo, Emilio, c. 1869-1964, Filipino revolutionary against Spain and the United States.

Akbar, 1542-1605, greatest Mogul emperor of India.

Alanbrooke, Viscount (Alan F. Brooke), 1883-1963, British general, W.W. II chief of imperial general staff.

Alaric I, c. 370-410, Visigothic ruler who devastated southern Europe.

Albert, Prince, 1819-61, German-born consort of Victoria of England.

Albuquerque, Afonso de, 1453-1515, Portuguese admiral and founder of Portuguese empire in the East.

Alcibiades, c. 450-404 B.C., Athenian statesman and general in Peloponnesian War.

Alexander (III) the Great, 356–323 B.C., king of Macedon, Greek conqueror, and one of the greatest generals of all time.

Alexius I (Alexius Comnenus), 1048–1118, emperor who restored Byzantine military and political power.

Allen, Ethan, 1738–89, American Revolutionary hero, leader of Green Mountain Boys.

Allende (Gossens), Salvador, 1908–73, President of Chile (1970–73); advocated democratic socialism.

Altgeld, John P., 1847–1902, German-born American political leader and social reformer.

Amin Dada, Idi, 1925– , Ugandan president (1971–79).

Amundsen, Roald, 1872–1928, Norwegian polar explorer, first to reach the South Pole (December 14, 1911).

Andrada e Silva, José Bonifácio de, 1763–1838, Brazilian statesman, chief founder of independent Brazil.

Andrassy, Julius (Count), 1823–90, Hungarian statesman and first constitutional premier (1867–71).

Andreotti, Giulio, 1919– , Italian premier (1972-73, 1976–79).

Andropov, Yuri V., 1914– , head of Soviet secret police, ambassador to Hungary during 1956 uprising.

Anthony, Susan B., 1820–1906, American reformer and suffragette leader.

Antonescu, Ion, 1882–1946, Rumanian dictator (1940–44), executed as a war criminal.

Antony, Mark, c. 83-80 B.C., Roman politician and soldier who allied himself with Cleopatra and defied Rome.

Arafat, Yasir, 1929– , leader of the Palestine Liberation Organization.

Armstrong, Neil, 1930– , American astronaut; first person to set foot on the moon (1969).

Arnold, Benedict, 1741–1801, American Revolutionary general and traitor.

Asoka, ?–232 B.C., first great Indian emperor; spreader of Buddhism.

al-Assad, Hafez, 1928– , Syrian president (1971–).

Astor, John Jacob, 1763–1848, American merchant and fur trader, the richest man in America at his death.

Astor, Lady (Nancy W.), 1879–1964, American-born British political leader, first woman member of Parliament.

Astor, William W. (Viscount), 1848–1919, Anglo-American financier and philanthropist.

Atahualpa, d. 1533, Inca (ruling chief) of Peru, executed by Pizarro.

Ataturk, Kemal (b. Mustafa Kemal), 1881–1938, father of modern Turkey and president (1923–1938).

Attila, d. 453, Hun leader, conqueror of eastern Europe.

Attucks, Crispus, c. 1723–70, American Negro patriot killed by British in Boston Massacre.

Augustus (Octavius), 63 B.C.–14 A.D., first Roman emperor; he defeated Antony and returned Rome from military dictatorship to constitutional rule.

Aurangzeb, 1618–1707, Mogul Indian emperor who brought his empire to its greatest expanse.

Auriol, Vincent, 1884–1966, first president (1947–54) of French Fourth Republic.

Austin, Stephen F., 1793–1836, American leader of colonization in Texas.

Ayub Khan, Mohammad, 1907-74, Pakistani military leader who became (1958) president and resigned (1969).

Babar, c. 1482-1530, founder of Mogul empire in India.

Babeuf, François N., 1760–97, executed French revolutionary, philosophical forerunner of Marx.

Badoglio, Pietro, 1871–1956, Italian field marshal in Ethiopia, premier after fall of Mussolini.

Bakunin, Mikhail, 1814–76, militant Russian anarchist, expelled from First International by Marxists.

Balboa, Vasco Núñez de, c. 1475–1519, beheaded Spanish conquistador, discoverer of Pacific Ocean.

Bancroft, George, 1800–91, American statesman and historian, founder of U.S. Naval Academy.

Bani-Sadr, Abolhassan, 1933– , Iranian president (1980–81).

Banneker, Benjamin, 1731–1806, American Negro colonial astronomer, mathematician, and inventor.

Barton, Clara, 1821–1912, American humanitarian, organizer of the American Red Cross.

Baruch, Bernard M., 1870–1965, American financier and government economic adviser.

Batista y Zaldívar, Fulgencio, 1901-73, Cuban dictator (president 1940-44, 1952-59), overthrown by Castro.

Batu Khan, d. 1255, Mongol leader of Golden Horde.

Beauregard, Pierre G. T., 1818–93, American Confederate general.

Beaverbrook, Lord (William Maxwell Aitken), 1879–1964, Canadian-born British statesman and publisher.

Begin, Menachem, 1913– , Israeli prime minister.

Belisarius, c. 505-565, Byzantine general under Justinian.

Bellinghausen, Fabian von, 1778–1852, Russian admiral and discoverer (1819–21) of Antarctica.

Ben Bella, Ahmed, 1918– , Algerian revolutionary, elected (1962) premier and deposed (1965) by Boumédienne.

Beneš, Eduard, 1884–1948, Czechoslovak president.

Ben-Gurion, David, 1886–1973, Israeli statesman, first prime minister (beginning in 1948).

Benjamin of Tudela, d. 1173, Jewish traveler and author of an itinerary of his trip (1159–73) to China.

Bennett, James Gordon, Jr., 1841-1918, American publisher who financed Stanley's trip to find Livingstone.

Bentinck, Lord William C., 1774–1839, British statesman, appointed (1833) first governor-general of British India.

Beria, Lavrenti P., 1899–1953, executed Soviet secret police chief under Stalin.

Bering, Vitus J., 1681–1741, Russian-backed Danish discoverer (1728) of Bering Strait.

Bernadotte, Count (Folke), 1895–1948, Swedish internationalist, UN mediator in Palestine until assassinated.

Betancourt, Romulo, 1908–81, progressive Venezuelan president (1945-48, 1959-64).

Bevan, Aneurin, 1897–1960, British political leader, developer of England's socialized medicine system.

Bevin, Ernest, 1881–1951, British labor leader and Labour government foreign minister (1945–51).

Bhave, Acharya Vinoba, 1895– , foremost Indian advocate of nonviolent (Gandhian) social revolution.

Bhutto, Zulfikar Ali, 1928–79, Pakistani president (1971-73) and prime minister (1973–77). Overthrown (1977) and executed in 1979.

Biddle, Francis B., 1886–1968, American jurist, U.S. Attorney General (1941–45).

Bismarck, Otto von, 1815–98, German statesman who unified Germany under Prussian leadership.

Blackstone, Sir William, 1723–80, English jurist, first professor of English law at Oxford University.

Bloomer, Amelia J., 1818–94, American reformer, devoted to women's rights.

Blücher, Gebhard L. von, 1742–1819, Prussian field marshal who helped Wellington defeat Napoleon at Waterloo.

Blum, Léon, 1872–1950, French Socialist statesman, Popular Front organizer, and writer.

Boleyn, Anne, c. 1507–36, beheaded second wife of Henry VIII of England, mother of Elizabeth I.

Bolívar, Simón, 1783–1830, South American revolutionary who liberated much of the continent from Spanish rule.

Bonaparte, Joseph, 1768–1844, eldest brother of Napoleon I, ineffective king of Naples and Spain.

Bonaparte, Napoleon see Napoleon Bonaparte.

Booth, John Wilkes, 1838–65, egomaniacal American actor, assassin of Abraham Lincoln.

Booth, William, 1829–1912, English religious leader, founder and first general of Salvation Army.

Borgia, Caesar, c. 1475–1507, Italian Renaissance ecclesiastic and statesman; brother of Lucretia Borgia.

Borgia, Lucretia, 1480–1519, famous figure of Italian Renaissance, daughter of Pope Alexander VI.

Bormann, Martin L., 1900–1945, German Nazi leader.

Bosch, Juan, 1909– , progressive Dominican leader.

Botha, Louis, 1862–1919, Boer soldier and first prime minister (1910–19) of Union of South Africa.

Bougainville, Louis Antoine de, 1729–1811, French navigator, leader of scientific expeditions in South Pacific.

Boumédiene, Houari, 1927–78, Algerian revolutionary, deposed (1965) Ben Bella.

Bourguiba, Habib, 1903– , Tunisian independence leader and first premier (subsequently president).

Braddock, Edward, 1695–1755, British general in French and Indian Wars.

Bradley, Omar N., 1893–1981, U.S. Army WW II general, later chairman of joint chiefs of staff.

Braille, Louis C., 1809–52, French inventor of Braille system of printing and writing for the blind.

Brandt, Willy, 1913– , West German chancellor (1969-74), leader of Social Democratic party.

Brauchitsch, Walther von, 1881–1948, German WW II general.

Brezhnev, Leonid I., 1906– , Soviet Communist party leader, successor to Khrushchev; Chairman of the Presidium of the Supreme Soviet (1977–).

Brian Boru, c. 940–1014, Irish king who broke Norse power in Ireland.

Briand, Aristide, 1862–1932, French statesman, chief architect of antiwar Kellogg-Briand Pact (1928).

Brown, John, 1800–59, hanged American abolitionist whose raid at Harpers Ferry stunned North and South.

Bryan, William Jennings, 1860–1925, American political leader, greatest orator of his day.

Brzezinski, Zbigniew, 1928– , foreign affairs adviser to President Carter (1977–81).

Bulganin, Nikolai A., 1895–1975, Soviet Communist leader and premier (1955–58).

Bullitt, William C., 1891–1967, American diplomat, first American ambassador to USSR (1933–36).

Bunche, Ralph J., 1904–1971, American Negro government official and UN mediator.

Bundy, McGeorge, 1919– , American professor, Presidential adviser, and Ford Foundation head.

Bunker, Ellsworth, 1894– , American business executive and diplomat.

Burghley, William Cecil (Baron), 1520–98, English statesman, influential adviser to Elizabeth I for 40 years.

Burgoyne, John, 1722–92, British statesman and general in American Revolution.

Burke, Edmund, 1729–97, English political writer and statesman, proponent of conservatism.

Burnside, Ambrose E., 1824–81, American Union general.

Burton, Sir Richard F., 1821–90, English writer, orientalist, and discoverer (1858) of Lake Tanganyika.

Byrd, Richard E., 1888–1957, American admiral and polar explorer, first to fly over the North Pole (1926).

Caesar, Julius, c. 102–44 B.C., Roman statesman and general who enlarged and pacified Rome's provinces.

Cagliostro, Alessandro (Giuseppe Balsamo), 1743–95, Italian adventurer.

Callaghan, James, 1912– , Labour prime minister of Great Britain (1976–79).

Calles, Plutarco E., 1877–1945, Mexican Revolutionary statesman and president (1924–28).

Calvo Sotelo (y Bustelo), Leopoldo, 1926– , Spanish premier (1981–).

Campesino, El (Valentín Gonzáles), c. 1909– , Spanish Republican soldier in the civil war (1936–39).

Canaris, Wilhelm, 1887–1945, German WW II admiral and intelligence chief who opposed Hitler.

Cárdenas, Lázaro, 1895–1970, Mexican president (1934–40) and revolutionary general.

Cardigan, Earl of (James T. Brudenell), 1797–1868, British Crimean War general who led disastrous cavalry attack at Balaklava, immortalized in Tennyson's "The Charge of the Light Brigade."

Carnegie, Andrew, 1835–1919, Scottish-American iron and steel tycoon and philanthropist.

Carnot, Lazare, 1753–1823, French revolutionary general.

Carpini, Giovanni de Piano, c. 1180–1252, Italian monk who produced a full record of Mongol life from missionary experiences in Central Asia.

Carranza, Venustiano, 1859–1920, Mexican revolutionary leader who arranged Zapata's assassination.

Casanova de Seingalt, Giovanni G., 1725-98, Venetian adventurer and author.

Castelo Branco, Humberto, 1900–67, Brazilian revolutionary president.

Castiglione, Baldassare (Conte), 1478–1529, Italian Renaissance statesman and author.

Castlereagh, Robert S. (Viscount), 1769–1822, Irish-born British foreign secretary, and organizer of successful coalition against Napoleon I.

Castro, Fidel, 1927– , Cuban Communist premier who wrested power from Fulgencio Batista in 1959.

Catherine de' Medici, 1519–89, queen of France who helped to plan (1572) French Protestant massacre on Saint Bartholomew's Day.

Catherine II, 1729–96, forceful German-born empress and tsarina of Russia, also known as Catherine the Great.

Cato the Elder (Cato the Censor), 234–149 B.C., Roman statesman and moralist.

Cavell, Edith, 1865–1915, English nurse executed by Germans during WW I.

Cavour, Camillo Benso (conte di), 1810–61, Italian statesman, leader in unifying Italy under house of Savoy.

Ceausescu, Nicolae, 1918– , Romanian head of state.

Chamberlain, (A.) Neville, 1869–1940, British prime minister who signed (1938) Munich Pact with Hitler.

Chang Tso-lin, 1873–1928, Chinese general, warlord of Manchuria.

Charcot, Jean B., 1867–1936, French neurologist and explorer in the Antarctic.

Charlemagne, 742–814, king of the Franks, (768–814) and Emperor of the West (800–814).

Chase, Salmon P., 1808–73, American abolitionist, statesman, and Secretary of the Treasury under Lincoln.

Cheops (or Khufu), fl. c. 2680 B.C., king of Egypt, builder of great pyramid at Gizeh.

Chiang Kai-shek, 1887–1975, Chinese Nationalist leader whose government was driven (1950) from mainland China to island of Taiwan.

Chiang Kai-shek, Madame (Soong Mei-ling), 1896– , politically active wife of the Chinese Nationalist leader.

Ch'ien Lung (Hung-li), 1711–99, fourth emperor of Ching dynasty who greatly extended borders of China.

Chou En-lai see Zhou Enlai.

Christophe, Henri, 1767–1820, Haitian revolutionary and self-proclaimed king (Henri I).

Churchill, Sir Winston L. S., 1874–1965, British prime minister, soldier, author, and war leader.

Ciano, Galeazzo, 1903–44, Italian Fascist foreign minister who helped create Rome-Berlin Axis, executed by Mussolini—his father-in-law.

Cid, El, d. c. 1099, Spanish national hero, whose real name was Rodrigo (or Ruy) Díaz de Vivar.

Clarendon, Earl of (Edward Hyde), 1609–74, English statesman, historian, and adviser to Charles II.

Clark, Charles Joseph 1939– , Conservative prime minister of Canada (1979–80).

Clay, Henry, 1777–1852, American statesman, author of Compromise of 1850.

Clemenceau, Georges, 1841–1929, French statesman (the "Tiger"), twice premier (1906–09, 1917–20).

Cleopatra, 69–30 B.C., Ptolemaic queen of Egypt, one of the great romantic figures of all time.

Clinton, De Witt, 1769–1828, American statesman, Presidential nominee (1812), sponsor of Erie Canal.

Cobden, Richard, 1804–65, British statesman, advocate (after 1849) of peace and international conferences.

Coen, Jan P., 1587–1629, Dutch colonial governor, founder of Dutch East Indian empire.

Coke, Sir Edward, 1552–1634, one of the most eminent English jurists in history.

Colbert, Jean B., 1619–83, French statesman under Louis XIV, successful practitioner of mercantilism.

Columbus, Christopher, 1451–1506, Italian-born discoverer of America for Spain (1492).

Constantine I (the Great), ?–337, first Christian Roman emperor (306–337).

Constantine V (Constantine Copronymus), 718–775, iconoclastic Byzantine emperor (741–775).

Constantine VI, b. c. 770, Byzantine emperor (780–797), blinded by Irene, his mother and successor.

Constantine XI (Constantine Palaeologus), d. 1453, last Byzantine emperor (1449–53).

Cook, James (Captain), 1728–79, English explorer along coasts of Australia and New Zealand.

Cooper, Peter, 1791–1883, American inventor, industrialist, and philanthropist.

Corday, Charlotte, 1768–93, aristocratic French Revolution sympathizer who assassinated Jean Paul Marat.

Cornwallis, Charles (Marquess), 1738–1805, English general in American Revolution.

Cortés, Hernán, 1485–1547, Spanish conquistador in Mexico who toppled Aztec empire of Montezuma.

Cossiga, Francesco, 1928– , Italian premier (1979–80).

Coty, René, 1882–1962, last president of French Fourth Republic.

Cox, James M., 1870–1957, American political leader, U.S. Presidential candidate (1920), and journalist.

Cranmer, Thomas, 1489–1556, English churchman, adviser to Henry VIII.

Croesus, d. c. 547 B.C., king of Lydia; his name has become synonym for wealth.

Cromwell, Oliver, 1599–1658, English general and statesman, lord protector of England (1653–58).

Cuauhtémoc, d. c. 1525, Aztec emperor executed by Cortés.

Cunard, Sir Samuel, 1787–1865, Canadian pioneer of regular transatlantic steam navigation (Cunard Line).

Curtis, Cyrus H. K., 1850–1933, American publisher and philanthropist.

Curzon, George H. (Marquess), 1859–1925, British statesman and viceroy of India.

Cyrano de Bergerac, Savinien, 1619–55, French poet and duelist romanticized by Edmond Rostand's drama.

Cyrus (the Great), ?–529 B.C., founder of the ancient Persian Empire.

Dalai Lama, 1935– , theocratic ruler of Tibet, ousted (1959) by Chinese invasion of his country.

Danton, Georges J., 1759–94, French statesman and a leading figure of French Revolution.

Darius I (the Great), d. 486 B.C., king of Persia (521–486 B.C.) who consolidated Persian power in the East.

Darlan, Jean F., 1881–1942, assassinated French admiral, vice-premier of Vichy government.

Darnley, Lord (Henry S.), 1545–67, claimant to English throne, second husband of Mary Queen of Scots.

Davis, Angela, 1944– , university lecturer and black political activist.

Davis, Jefferson, 1808–89, American statesman, president of Southern Confederacy.

Davitt, Michael, 1846–1906, Irish revolutionary and land reformer.

Dayan, Moshe, 1915– , Israeli statesman, soldier, and hero of 1967 June War.

Debs, Eugene V., 1855–1926, American Socialist leader, Presidential candidate (1900, 1904, 1908, 1912, 1920).

De Gasperi, Alcide, 1881–1954, Italian premier (1945–53), organizer of Christian Democratic party.

de Gaulle, Charles, 1890–1970, French general and controversial nationalist president (1959–69).

Deng Xiaoping, 1904– , Chinese Communist Politburo vice-chairman (1977–).

Desai, Morarji, 1895– , Indian prime minister (1977–79).

De Soto, Hernando, c. 1500–42, Spanish conquistador and explorer in what is now United States.

Dessalines, Jean J., c. 1758–1806, emperor of Haiti, born a slave.

De Valera, Eamon, 1882–1975, long-time Irish prime minister and president.

Dewey, George, 1837–1917, American admiral, hero of battle of Manila.

Dewey, Thomas E., 1902–71, governor of New York (1942–54), Republican Presidential candidate (1944, 1948).

Dias, Bartolomeu, d. 1500, Portuguese navigator, first European to round (1488) the Cape of Good Hope.

Díaz, Porfirio, 1830–1915, Mexican president (1876–1911), whose ruthless rule fostered revolution.

Díaz Ordaz, Gustavo, 1911-79, progressive Mexican president (1964-70) and lawyer.

Diefenbaker, John G., 1895–1979, Conservative prime minister of Canada (1957-63).

Diem, Ngo Dinh, 1901–63, assassinated South Vietnamese president.

Dimitrov, Georgi, 1882–1949, Bulgarian Communist premier (1946–49), acquitted of Reichstag fire.

Dirksen, Everett M., 1896–1969, U.S. Senator (Ill., first elected 1950) and Republican minority leader.

Disraeli, Benjamin (Earl of Beaconsfield), 1804–81, British prime minister (1868, 1874–80), founder of the Conservative party.

Dix, Dorothea L., 1802–87, American social reformer, champion of specialized treatment for the mentally ill.

Djilas, Milovan, 1911– , Yugoslavian political leader and intellectual, frequently imprisoned by Tito.

Dobrynin, Anatoly F., 1919– , Soviet ambassador to U.S.

Dollfuss, Engelbert, 1892–1934, Austrian chancellor assassinated by Austrian Nazis.

Douglas, Stephen A., 1813–61, American statesman who opposed (1860) Lincoln for Presidency.

Douglass, Frederick, c. 1817–95, American Negro abolitionist leader.

Drake, Sir Francis, c. 1540–96, first Englishman to circumnavigate the earth (1577–80).

Dreyfus, Alfred, 1859–1935, French soldier whose treason trial (and ultimate exoneration) was a *cause célèbre.*

Du Barry, Madame (Jeanne B.), 1743–93, mistress of Louis XV of France, guillotined during French Revolution.

Dubcek, Alexander, 1921– , liberal Czechoslovak Communist party secretary during 1968 Soviet invasion.

Du Bois, William E. B., 1868–1963, American Negro editor, author, exponent of equality for the Negro.

Duclos, Jacques, 1896–1975, French Communist leader.

Dulles, Allen W., 1893–1969, U.S. public official, director of CIA (1953–61).

Dulles, John Foster, 1888–1959, U.S. Secretary of State (1953–59), strong anti-Communist.

Duvalier, François, 1907–71, Haitian dictator.

Dzerzhinsky, Felix E., 1877–1926, Russian Bolshevik politician, organizer of Soviet secret police.

Earhart, Amelia, 1898–1937, pioneering American aviatrix who disappeared on a round-the-world flight.

Eban, Abba, 1915– , Israeli diplomat and statesman.

Ebert, Friedrich, 1871–1925, first president (1919–25) of the German republic.

Echeverría Álvarez, Luis, 1922– , President of Mexico (1970–76).

Eden, Sir Anthony (Earl of Avon), 1897–1977, British statesman, Conservative prime minister (1955–57).

Edinburgh, Duke of (Philip Mountbatten), 1921– , consort of Elizabeth II of Great Britain.

Eichmann, Adolf, 1906–62, German Nazi official executed by Israel for crimes against the Jewish people and humanity.

Elizabeth I, 1533–1603, queen of England during the great age of British expansion and exploration.

Ellsworth, Lincoln, 1880–1951, American explorer, the first man to fly over Antarctic (1935).

Emin Pasha (Eduard Schnitzer), 1840–92, German physician, colonial administrator, and explorer of Sudan.

Emmet, Robert, 1778–1803, executed Irish patriot.

Engels, Friedrich, 1820–95, German Socialist, co-founder with Karl Marx of modern Communism.

Enver Pasha, 1881–1922, Turkish general and political leader.

Erlander, Tage F., 1901– , Swedish Social Democratic premier (1946–69).

Ervin, Samuel J., Jr., 1896– , U.S. Senator from North Carolina (1954-1974).

Eshkol, Levi, 1895–1969, Israeli prime minister (1963-69)

Essex, Earl of (Robert Devereux), 1567–1601, favorite of Elizabeth I of England who signed his death warrant.

Fanfani, Amintore, 1908– , Italian statesman and premier (1958-59, 1960-63).

Farouk I, 1920–65, king of Egypt (1936–52), forced to abdicate (1952) by military coup.

Fawkes, Guy, 1570–1606, English Roman Catholic conspirator involved in scheme to blow up Parliament.

Fish, Hamilton, 1808–93, American statesman, one of the ablest of U.S. Secretaries of State.

Foch, Ferdinand, 1851–1929, French marshal, commander (1918) of British, French, and American armies.

Ford, Henry, 1863–1947, American industrialist, pioneer automobile manufacturer.

Forrestal, James V., 1892–1949, U.S. Secretary of the Navy (1944–47), first Secretary of Defense (1947–49).

Fox, Charles J., 1749–1806, British statesman, orator, and liberal reformer.

Francis (Franz) Ferdinand, 1863–1914, Austrian archduke whose assassination precipitated WW I.

Franco, Francisco, 1892–1975, leader of rebel forces in Spanish Civil War (1936–39) and dictator of Spain (1937–75).

Frank, Anne, 1929–45, Dutch Jewish girl killed by the Nazis; her diary made her posthumously famous.

Franklin, Benjamin, 1706–90, outstanding American statesman, also printer, scientist, and writer.

Fraser, John Malcolm, 1930– , Australian prime minister (1975–).

Frederick II (the Great), 1712–86, king of Prussia (1740–86) and military genius.

Frederick William, 1620–88, "Great Elector" of Brandenburg, who laid the base of the state of Prussia.

Frémont, John C., 1813–90, American explorer, soldier, and politician, a controversial figure of history.

Frobenius, Leo, 1873–1938, German archaeologist and authority on prehistoric African art and culture.

Fugger, Jacob (Jacob the Rich), 1459–1525, German merchant prince.

Fukuda, Takeo, 1905– , Japanese premier (1976–78).

Fulbright, J. William, 1905– , U.S. Senator (Ark., 1945-75) chairman of Senate Foreign Relations Committee (1959–75).

Gage, Thomas, 1721–87, English general in America whose orders led to battles of Lexington and Concord.

Gallatin, Albert, 1761–1849, American statesman and financier.

Gama, Vasco da, c. 1469–1524, Portuguese navigator, first European to journey to India by sea (1497–99).

Gambetta, Léon, 1838–82, French republican statesman.

Gamelin, Maurice G., 1872–1958, French general, leader of Allied forces at WW II's outbreak.

Gandhi, Indira, 1917– , Indian prime minister (1966–77, 1980–), daughter of Nehru, and first woman ever elected to head the government of a major power.

Gandhi, Mohandas K., 1869–1948, Indian ascetic who advocated nonviolent resistance to secure independence of India from Great Britain.

Garibaldi, Giuseppe, 1807–82, Italian patriot and soldier who fought for Italy's unification.

Garrison, William Lloyd, 1805–79, American abolitionist and social reformer.

Garvey, Marcus, 1887–1940, American Negro nationalist leader.

Genghis Khan see Jenghiz Khan.

Giap, Vo Nguyen, 1912– , North Vietnamese statesman and victor at Dienbienphu in 1954.

Giscard d'Estaing, Valéry, 1926– , French president (1974–81).

Gladstone, William Ewart, 1809–98, British Liberal prime minister (1868–74, 1880–85, 1886, 1892–94).

Gneisenau, August (Graf Neithardt von), 1760–1831, Prussian field marshal in Napoleonic Wars.

Godfrey of Bouillon, c. 1058–1100, crusader, ruler of Jerusalem.

Godunov, Boris, c. 1551–1605, Russian tsar, advisor to Ivan the Terrible.

Goebbels, Paul J., 1897–1945, German Nazi propagandist, master of mass psychology.

Goering, Hermann W., 1893–1946, German Nazi leader, early supporter of Hitler, and head of Luftwaffe.

Goldwater, Barry M., 1909– , U.S. Senator (Ariz.), unsuccessful Republican Presidential candidate (1964).

Gompers, Samuel, 1850–1924, American labor leader, founder and president of AFL.

Gomulka, Wladyslav, 1905– , Polish Communist Party leader.

Gordon, Charles G. (Chinese Gordon), 1833–85, British soldier and administrator killed by Moslems at Khartoum.

Gottwald, Klement, 1896–1953, Czechoslovak Communist leader, who ushered Communism into his country.

Gowon, Yakubu, 1934– , Nigerian head of state who opposed the unsuccessful secession of the late 1960s.

Grasso, Ella T., 1919–81, first woman to be elected governor in her own right (Conn. 1974–80).

Greeley, Horace, 1811–72, American newspaper publisher and Presidential candidate (1872).

Grenville, Sir Richard, c. 1542–91, English naval hero against Spanish.

Grey, Lady Jane, 1537–54, queen of England for nine days, succeeded by Mary I.

Gromyko, Andrei A., 1909– , Soviet foreign minister and ambassador.

Grotius, Hugo, 1583–1645, Dutch jurist and humanist, considered the founder of international law.

Guevara, Che (Ernesto), 1928–67, Argentine-born Cuban guerrilla leader killed in Bolivia.

Gwyn, Nell (Eleanor), 1650–87, English actress, mistress of Charles II.

Haig, Alexander Meigs, Jr., 1924– , U.S. Army General; Chief of Staff of the White House (1973–74); Secretary of State (1981–).

Haile Selassie, 1892–1975, emperor of Ethiopia (1930–74).

Hale, Nathan, 1755–76, American Revolutionary patriot, hanged by the British without trial as a spy.

Halsey, William F., 1882–1959, American WW II admiral in Pacific.

Hamilton, Alexander, 1755–1804, American Federalist statesman, first Secretary of the Treasury.

Hammurabi, fl. 1792–1750 B.C., king of Babylonia; his code of laws is one of the greatest of ancient codes.

Hannibal, 247–c. 182 B.C., Carthaginian general, great military opponent of Rome (Second Punic War).

Harriman, W. Averell, 1891– , American diplomat, U.S. representative (1968) at Vietnam peace talks.

Harun-al-Rashid, c. 764–809, famous caliph of Baghdad under whom the Abbasid empire reached its apogee.

Hastings, Warren, 1732–1818, controversial first governor-general of British India.

Hawkins, Sir John, 1532–95, Elizabethan sea dog, knighted for his actions in defeat of Spanish Armada.

Hay, John, 1838–1905, American author and statesman, who formulated the Open Door policy toward China.

Haya de la Torre, Victor Raúl, 1895–1979, Peruvian leader, advocate of Latin-American nationalist revolutions.

Hearst, William Randolph, 1863–1951, American journalist and publisher, innovator in mass-appeal newspapers.

Heath, Edward R. G., 1916– , British Conservative prime minister (1970–74).

Henry, Patrick, 1736–99, American orator and patriot, who worked to have Bill of Rights added to the Constitution.

Henry the Navigator, 1394–1460, Portuguese geographer and prince, who was the patron of the great age of Portuguese exploration.

Herodotus, c. 484–c. 425 B.C., Greek historian and traveler considered the father of history.

Herzl, Theodor, 1860–1904, Hungarian writer, founder of modern Zionism.

Hess, Rudolf, 1894– , erratic German Nazi leader, imprisoned (1946) for life as a war criminal.

Heydrich, Reinhard, 1904–42, German Nazi police official ("the Hangman") whose assassination by Czech patriots led to Lidice massacre.

Heyerdahl, Thor, 1914– , Norwegian explorer-ethnologist, substantiated the diffusionist theory of anthropology with his trans-pacific raft journeys.

Hidalgo y Costilla, Miguel, 1753–1811, executed Mexican national hero and priest.

Hillary, Sir Edmund P., 1919– , New Zealand mountain climber; first to reach summit of Mt. Everest (1953).

Hillel, fl. 30 B.C.–10 A.D., Jewish scholar; many of Christ's teachings resemble Hillel's sayings.

Hillman, Sidney, 1887–1946, Lithuanian-born American labor leader.

Himmler, Heinrich, 1900–45, terroristic Nazi chief of SS and Gestapo.

Hindenburg, Paul von, 1847–1934, German president (1925–34) who appointed Hitler as chancellor.

Hitler, Adolf, 1889–1945, founder of German Nazism and infamous tyrant who precipitated WW II.

Ho Chi Minh, c. 1890–1969, Vietnamese Communist leader and national hero; first president of North Vietnam.

Hoover, J. Edgar, 1895–1972, American administrator, director of FBI (1924–72).

Horthy de Nagybanya, Nicholas, 1868–1957, Hungarian admiral and political leader.

Houphouët-Boigny, Félix, 1905– , president of Ivory Coast, leader of former French Africa.

Houston, Samuel, 1793–1863, American frontier hero and Texan statesman.

Howe, Julia Ward, 1819–1910, American social reformer and writer of "The Battle Hymn of the Republic."

Howe, Richard (Earl), 1726–99, admiral and commander (1776–78) of British fleet in American Revolution.

Howe, William (Viscount), 1729–1814, English general in American Revolution.

Hoxha, Enver 1908– , Albanian Communist leader.

Hua Guofeng (Kuo-feng), 1921– , Chinese Communist premier (1976–80) and Politburo chairman (1976–81).

Hull, Cordell, 1871–1955, U.S. Secretary of State (1933–44), recipient (1945) Nobel Peace Prize.

Hunyadi, John, c. 1385–1456, Hungarian national hero, resistance leader against Turks.

Hu Yaobang, 1915– , Chinese Communist Politburo chairman (1981–).

Ibn Saud, c. 1880-1953, founder (1932) and first king of Saudi Arabia.

Ikhnaton, d. c. 1354 B.C., pharaoh of Egypt who established perhaps the world's first monotheistic religion.

Iqbal, Mohammad, 1873–1938, Moslem leader, national hero of Pakistan.

Irene, 752–803, repressive Byzantine empress who had her son blinded.

Isabella I, 1451–1504, queen of Spain who supported the 1492 New World voyage of Columbus.

Jabotinsky, Vladimir, 1880–1940, Russian-born Zionist leader.

Jackson, Stonewall (Thomas J.), 1824–63, American Confederate general.

Jaurès, Jean, 1859–1914, assassinated French Socialist leader and historian.

Jenghiz (also Genghis) Khan, c. 1167–1227, brilliant Mongol conqueror, ruler of a vast Asian empire.

Jinnah, Mohammad Ali, 1876–1948, founder and first governor-general of Pakistan (1947–48).

Joan of Arc, c. 1412–31, French saint and national heroine, burned at the stake for heresy.

Joffre, Joseph J. C., 1852–1931, French WW I marshal.

John III (John Sobieski), 1620-96, king of Poland, champion of Christian Europe against Turks.

Jones, John Paul, 1747–92, Scottish-born American naval hero of American Revolution.

Jordan, Vernon E., Jr., 1935– , civil rights leader and executive director of the National Urban League.

Josephine, 1763–1814, empress of the French (1804–09), first wife of Napoleon I.

Juárez, Benito, 1806–72, Mexican Indian president, revered by Mexicans as great political figure.

Juin, Alphonse, 1888–1967, French soldier and marshal.

Justinian I, 483–565, Byzantine emperor (527–65) whose accomplishment was codification of Roman law.

Kadar, Janos, 1912– , Hungarian Communist premier who sided with Soviets in 1956 Hungarian revolt.

Kamenev, Lev B., 1883–1936, Soviet Communist leader executed during 1936 Moscow purges.

Karamanlis, Constantine, 1907– , twice Greek premier, president of Greece (1980–).

Kasavubu, Joseph, c. 1910–69, first president of the Congo.

Kaunda, Kenneth, 1924– , Zambian president, proponent of Gandhian principles.

Kefauver, (C.) Estes, 1903–63, U.S. Senator (Tenn., 1949–63), supporter of civil rights legislation.

Kekkonen, Urho K., 1900– , Finnish president (beginning 1956).

Kennedy, Edward M., 1932– , U. S. Senator (Mass., (1962–), brother of John and Robert Kennedy.

Kennedy, Robert F., 1925–68, assassinated U.S. Senator (N.Y., 1965–68), brother of slain President John F. Kennedy under whom he was U.S. Attorney General.

Kenyatta, Jomo, c. 1893–1978, first Kenyan president, an early African nationalist leader.

Kerensky, Aleksandr F., 1881–1970, exiled Russian revolutionary premier (1917), overthrown by Bolsheviks.

Keynes, John Maynard, 1883–1946, influential English economist and monetary authority.

Khomeini, Ayatollah Ruhollah, 1900– , Moslem religious leader who led Iranian Revolution of 1979.

Khrushchev, Nikita S., 1894–1971, Soviet Communist leader, deposed (1964) as premier.

Kidd, Captain (William), c. 1645–1701, British privateer hanged for murder and piracy.

Kiesinger, Kurt G., 1904– , West German chancellor (1966–69), advocate of reconciliation with Eastern Europe.

Kim Il Sung, 1912– , first premier of Communist North Korea.

King, Martin Luther, Jr., 1929–68, assassinated American Negro rights leader and Nobel Prize winner.

King, (W. L.) Mackenzie, 1874–1950, liberal Canadian prime minister (1921–30, 1935–48).

Kissinger, Henry A., 1923– , chief foreign affairs adviser to President Nixon, and leading authority on international relations and national defense policy. U.S. Secretary of State (1973-77).

Kitchener, Horatio H. (Earl), 1850–1916, British field marshal during the imperial era.

Kittikachorn, Thanom, 1911– , Thai premier and minister of defense (1963–73).

Knox, Henry, 1750–1806, American patriot and Revolutionary general, U.S. Secretary of War (1785–94).

Konev, Ivan S., 1897-1973, Soviet WW II field marshal, commander (1955–60) of Warsaw Pact military forces.

Konoye, Prince Fumimaro, 1891–1945, Japanese premier who allied Japan with Axis.

Koo, (V. K.) Wellington, 1887– , Chinese statesman elected (1957) to International Court of Justice at The Hague.

Kornilov, Lavr G., 1870–1918, Russian anti-Bolshevik general.

Kosciusko, Thaddeus, 1746–1817, Polish general who fought for patriot cause in American Revolution.

Kossuth, Louis, 1802–94, exiled Hungarian revolutionary leader.

Kosygin, Aleksey N., 1904–80, Soviet Communist premier, successor to Khrushchev.

Kropotkin, Prince (Peter), 1842–1921, Russian anarchist who championed peasantry but opposed Bolshevism.

Kruger, S. J. Paulus (Paul Kruger), 1825–1904, South African pioneer, soldier, farmer, and statesman.

Krupp, Alfred, 1812–87, German armaments magnate known as the "Cannon King."

Krupp, Alfred (von Bohlen und Halbach), 1907–67, German industrialist and imprisoned war criminal.

Kublai Khan, c. 1215–94, Mongol emperor, founder of Yüan dynasty in China.

Kun, Bela, 1886–c. 1939, Hungarian Communist dictator.

Kutuzov, Mikhail I., 1745–1813, Russian field marshal, victor over Napoleon I.

Ky, Nguyen Cao, 1930– , South Vietnamese general and political leader.

Lafayette, Marquis de, 1757–1834, French statesman and general who served in American Revolution.

La Follette, Robert M., 1855–1925, U.S. Senator (Wis., 1906–25), Progressive Party Presidential candidate (1924).

LaFontaine, Sir Louis H., 1807–64, distinguished French-Canadian statesman.

LaGuardia, Fiorello H., 1882–1947, U.S. Congressman (1916, 1923–33) and reform mayor of New York City (1934–45), affectionately known as the "Little Flower."

Laing, Alexander G., 1793–1826, Scottish soldier and explorer who was murdered by Arabs near Timbuktu.

Langton, Stephen, c. 1155–1228, English archbishop who acted with barons to obtain Magna Carta's signing.

Largo Caballero, Francisco, 1869–1946, Spanish Socialist leader and premier (1936–37).

Laski, Harold J., 1893–1950, English political scientist, economist, author, and lecturer.

Lassalle, Ferdinand, 1825–64, a founder of German Socialist movement, killed in a duel over a love affair.

Lattre de Tassigny, Jean de, 1889–1952, French general who fought in Indo-China.

Laval, Pierre, 1883–1945, executed French politician and foreign minister of Vichy government.

Lawrence, Thomas E. (Lawrence of Arabia), 1888–1935, British scholar and Middle East soldier-adventurer.

Leahy, William D., 1875–1959, American diplomat and WW II admiral.

Leclerc, Jacques P. (comte de Hauteclocque), 1902–47, French WW II general who later served in Indo-China.

Lee, Henry, 1756–1818, American cavalry leader in the Revolution; known as Light-Horse Harry Lee.

Lee, Robert E., 1807–70, brilliant American Confederate commander in chief.

Lee Kuan Yew, 1923– , Singaporean Socialist prime minister.

Lehman, Herbert H., 1878–1963, liberal U.S. Senator (N.Y.), opponent of Senator Joseph R. McCarthy.

Lemnitzer, Lyman L., 1899– , American general, NATO commander (1963-1969).

Lenin, Vladimir I., 1870–1924, Russian revolutionary statesman, founder of Bolshevism and U.S.S.R.

Leo Africanus, c. 1465–1550, Moorish traveler in Africa and the Near East.

Lesseps, Ferdinand (Vicomte de), 1805–94, French diplomat and engineer who conceived idea of Suez Canal.

Lewis, John L., 1880–1969, important American labor spokesman, head of UMW and CIO.

Liaquat Ali Khan, 1895–1951, assassinated Moslem leader and first prime minister (1947–51) of Pakistan.

Liebknecht, Karl, 1871–1919, murdered German Communist leader.

Lindbergh, Charles A., 1902–74, American aviator, who made first solo transatlantic flight.

Lin Piao, 1907–1971, Chinese Communist leader and political heir to Mao.

Litvinov, Maxim M., 1876–1951, Soviet statesman, proponent of Soviet cooperation with Western powers.

Liu Shao-ch'i, c. 1898-1974, Chinese Communist leader who fell from grace in "cultural revolution" (1966-67).

Livingston, Edward, 1764–1836, American jurist and statesman, U.S. Secretary of State under Andrew Jackson.

Livingston, Robert R., 1746–1813, American Revolutionary political leader who negotiated Louisiana Purchase.

Livingstone, David, 1813–73, Scottish medical missionary, abolitionist, and African explorer.

Lodge, Henry Cabot, 1850–1924, conservative U.S. Senator (Mass., 1893–1924).

Lodge, Henry Cabot, Jr., 1902– , U.S. Senator, ambassador, and Vietnam peace negotiator.

Long, Huey P., 1893–1935, assassinated American political demagogue in Louisiana.

López Portillo, José, 1920– , Mexican president (1976–).

Low, Sir David, 1891–1963, British cartoonist, famous for caricatures.

Lübke, Heinrich, 1894–1972, West German administrator and president.

Luce, Henry R., 1898–1967, American publisher, founder of Time, Inc.

Luckner, Felix, Graf von, 1881-1966, German WW I naval commander, nicknamed "the Sea Devil."

Lumumba, Patrice E., 1925–61, murdered first prime minister (1960) of Republic of the Congo.

Luthuli, Albert J., 1898–1967, South African Zulu leader and Nobel Prize winner.

Luxemburg, Rosa, c. 1870–1919, Polish-born German Communist leader, murdered while being taken to prison.

MacArthur, Douglas, 1880–1964, distinguished American general in WW II, recalled (1951) from Korea for insubordination.

Maccabee, Judas, d. c. 161 B.C., Jewish military leader who opposed foreign rule in Judea.

McCarthy, Eugene J., 1916– , U.S. Senator (Minn.) who became nationally prominent for his opposition to American participation in Vietnam war.

McCarthy, Joseph R., 1908–57, U.S. Senator (Wis.) known for his charges of Communism in government.

McClellan, George B., 1826–85, American Union general.

McCormick, Robert R., 1880–1955, American publisher (Chicago Tribune), famous for his isolationist views.

McGill, James, 1744–1813, Scottish-born Canadian fur trader and university founder.

Machado, Gerardo, 1871–1939, repressive Cuban president (1925–33).

Machiavelli, Niccolò, 1469–1527, Florentine diplomat and political philosopher, an outstanding Renaissance figure.

Macmillan, M. Harold, 1894– , conservative British prime minister (1957–63).

McNamara, Robert S., 1916– , U.S. Secretary of Defense under Presidents Kennedy and Johnson.

Madero, Francisco I., 1873–1913, assassinated Mexican revolutionist and president (1911–13).

Magellan, Ferdinand, c. 1480–1521, Portuguese leader of first expedition to circumnavigate the earth (1519-22).

Magsaysay, Ramón, 1907–57, president of the Philippines (1953–57) who campaigned against the Huk rebels.

Mahan, Alfred T., 1840–1914, American naval officer and historian.

Mahdi, title claimed by Mohammed Ahmed, 1844–85, Moslem religious leader in Anglo-Egyptian Sudan.

Mahmud of Ghazni, c. 971–1030, Afghan emperor and conqueror.

Makarios III, 1913–77, Cypriot Greek Orthodox archbishop, first president (elected 1960) of Cyprus.

Malan, Daniel F., 1874–1959, Afrikaner prime minister of South Africa.

Malcolm X (b. Malcolm Little), 1925–65, assassinated American Negro separatist leader.

Malenkov, Georgi M., 1902– , Soviet Communist successor to Stalin (1953–55), expelled (1964) from party.

Malinovsky, Rodion Y., 1898–1967, Soviet marshal and minister of defense.

Malraux, André, 1901–76, French man of letters and political figure, minister of culture under de Gaulle.

Mannerheim, Baron Carl G. E., 1867–1951, Finnish field marshal, later president (1944–46).

Mansur, d. 775, Abbasid caliph (754–775), founder of Baghdad.

Mao Zedong (Tse-tung), 1893–1976, founder of Communist China, leader of radical wing of international Communism.

Marat, Jean Paul, 1743–93, French revolutionary stabbed to death in his bath by Charlotte Corday.

Marcos, Ferdinand E., 1917– , Filipino president.

Maria Theresa, 1717–80, popular Hapsburg empress, queen of Bohemia and Hungary.

Marie Antoinette, 1755–93, guillotined queen of France, wife of Louis XVI.

Marion, Francis ("the Swamp Fox"), c. 1732–95, American guerrilla leader in the Revolution.

Marlborough, Duke of (John Churchill), 1650–1722, English general and statesman.

Marti, José, 1853–95, Cuban poet and patriot, leader of Cuban struggle for independence.

Marx, Karl H., 1818–83, German philosopher, proponent of modern Communism, author of *Das Kapital.*

Masaryk, Jan, 1886–1948, Czechoslovak statesman whose "suicide" mysteriously followed Communist coup.

Masaryk, Thomas G., 1850–1937, Czechoslovak statesman, founder and president (1918–35) of Czechoslovakia.

Massey, Vincent, 1887–1967, Canadian diplomat and governor-general.

Mata Hari (Margaretha G. Zelle), 1876–1917, Dutch dancer executed by the French as a WW I German spy.

Matteotti, Giacomo, 1885–1924, murdered Italian Socialist leader, opponent of Mussolini.

Matthias Corvinus, c. 1443–90, king of Hungary (1458–90) and of Bohemia (1478–90), crusader against Turks.

Mawson, Sir Douglas, 1882–1958, English-born Australian geologist who charted Antarctic coast.

Maximilian, 1832–67, Austrian archduke and emperor of Mexico (1864–67), executed by the forces of Juarez.

Mazarin, Jules, 1602–61, French statesman and Roman Catholic cardinal.

Mazzini, Giuseppe, 1805–72, Italian patriot and revolutionary who figured in Italy's unification.

Mboya, Tom (Thomas J.), 1930–69, Kenyan political leader, instrumental in securing independence for his country.

Medici, Cosimo de', 1389–1464, Florentine merchant prince and first Medici ruler of Florence.

Medici, Lorenzo de' (Lorenzo the Magnificent), 1449–92, Florentine statesman, Renaissance patron of the arts.

Meir, Golda, 1898–1978, Israeli prime minister (1969–74).

Mendès-France, Pierre, 1907– , French premier (1954–55), who opposed Charles de Gaulle's return to power.

Menelik II, 1844–1913, emperor of Ethiopia after 1899, who expanded and modernized his country.

Mengistu Haile Mariam, 1937?– , Ethiopian head of state.

Metaxas, John, 1871–1941, Greek general and dictator.

Metternich, Clemens W. N. L., Fürst von, 1773–1859, Austrian foreign minister and arbiter of Europe.

Mikhailovich, Draja (Dragoljub), c. 1893–1946, executed Yugoslav soldier, foe of Tito.

Miki, Takeo, 1907– , Japanese prime minister (1974–76).

Mikoyan, Anastas I., 1895–1978, Soviet Communist leader.

Mindszenty, Cardinal (Jozsef), 1892–1975, Hungarian Roman Catholic prelate who sought asylum in U.S. legation after Hungarian uprising (1956).

Minuit, Peter, c. 1580–1638, director general (1626–31) of New Netherland, who purchased Manhattan for $24.

Mirabeau, Honoré G. R., comte de, 1749–91, French revolutionary who favored a strong constitutional monarchy.

Mitchell, Billy (William), 1879–1936, American general, demoted for criticism of U.S. military leaders.

Mitterrand, François, 1916– , French president (1981–).

Mobuto Sese Seko, 1930– , Zairean president who deposed (1960) Patrice Lumumba.

Mohammad Reza Pahlavi, 1919–80, shah of Iran (1941–1979).

Mohammed V, 1910–61, sultan of Morocco (1927–53), first king (1957–61) of independent Morocco.

Moi, Daniel arap, 1924– , Kenyan president (1978–).

Molotov, Vyacheslav M., 1890– , Soviet Communist leader whose political fortunes waned in post-Stalin era.

Moltke, Helmuth J. L., Graf von, 1800–91, Prussian field marshal, victor in Franco-Prussian War.

Mongkut (Rama IV), 1804–68, king of Siam, a main character in 1944 book, *Anna and the King of Siam.*

Monnet, Jean, 1888–1979, French political economist who conceived idea of the Common Market.

Montcalm, Louis de (Marquis de Saint-Véran), 1712–59, French general in French and Indian Wars, killed at Quebec.

Montezuma, c. 1480–1520, murdered Aztec emperor who defied Cortés.

Montgomery, Bernard L. (1st Viscount Montgomery of Alamein), 1887–1976, British WW II field marshal.

More, Sir Thomas, 1478–1535, English author (*Utopia*) and statesman, celebrated as a Roman Catholic martyr.

Morelos y Pavón, José M., 1765–1815, executed Mexican leader in revolution against Spain.

Morgan, Daniel, 1736–1802, American Revolutionary general, victor in the Carolina campaign.

Morgan, Sir Henry, c. 1635–88, English buccaneer, later acting governor of Jamaica.

Morgan, J. P. (John Pierpont), 1837–1913, American banker who built his family's fortunes into a financial colossus.

Morgenthau, Henry, Jr., 1891–1967, U.S. Secretary of the Treasury (1934–45).

Morris, Gouverneur, 1752–1816, American Revolutionary statesman who advocated centralized government.

Morris, Robert, 1734–1806, "financier of the American Revolution," signer of Declaration of Independence.

Mossadegh, Mohammed, 1880–1967, deposed and imprisoned Iranian premier (1951–53) who attempted to nationalize Iran's British-controlled oil industry.

Mountbatten, Lord Louis, 1900–79, British WW II admiral who commanded in both the Atlantic and Pacific.

Muñoz Marin, Luis, 1898–1980, long-time governor of Puerto Rico, supporter of its commonwealth status.

Mussolini, Benito ("Il Duce"), 1883–1945, Italian dictator 1922–45), founder of Fascism, ally of Adolf Hitler.

Mutsuhito (Meiji), 1852–1912, Japanese emperor (1867–1912) during whose reign feudalism came to an end.

Nadir Shah, 1688–1747, shah of Iran, perhaps the last great Asiatic conqueror.

Nagy, Imre, c. 1895–1958, Hungarian Communist premier (1953–55), executed after the 1956 uprising.

Nansen, Fridtjof, 1861–1930, Norwegian arctic explorer, statesman, and Nobel Peace Prize winner (1922).

Napoleon Bonaparte (Napoleon I), 1769–1821, Corsican-born emperor of the French (1804–15).

Napoleon III (Louis Napoleon Bonaparte), 1808–73, emperor of the French (nephew of Napoleon I).

Nasser, Gamal Abdel, 1918–70, Egyptian leader of Arab unification, became (1956) first president of Egypt.

Nebuchadnezzar, d. 562 B.C., king of Babylonia and destroyer of Jerusalem (586 B.C.).

Necker, Jacques, 1732–1804, Swiss-born French financier and statesman, father of Madame de Staël.

Negrin, Juan, 1891–1956, Spanish Socialist premier (1937–39), who fled from his country after the civil war.

Nehru, Jawaharlal, 1889–1964, first prime minister of India, guided country during early years of independence.

Nelson, Lord (Horatio), 1758–1805, English admiral in Napoleonic Wars, killed during victory at Trafalgar.

Nenni, Pietro, 1891–1980, Italian Socialist leader.

Ne Win, 1911– , Burmese general and president, leader of 1962 coup against U Nu.

Newman, Cardinal (John Henry), 1801–90, English prelate, a founder (1833) of Oxford Movement.

Ney, Michel, 1769–1815, executed marshal of France, commander at Waterloo.

Nightingale, Florence, 1820–1910, English nurse in Crimean War, founder of modern nursing.

Nimeiry, Jaafar Muhammad al, 1929– , Sudanese president (1971–).

Nimitz, Chester W., 1885–1966, American admiral who headed Pacific naval forces throughout WW II.

Nkrumah, Kwame, 1909–1972, former dictatorial prime minister of Ghana, deposed in 1966.

Nobel, Alfred B., 1833–96, Swedish inventor of dynamite who established annual philanthropic prizes.

Nobile, Umberto, 1885–1978, Italian aeronautical engineer, arctic explorer, and pilot.

Norris, George W., 1861–1944, U.S. Senator (Neb.).

Nostradamus (Michel de Nostredame), 1503–66, French astrologer and physician.

Novotny, Antonin, 1904–1975, Czechoslovak leader eight months before 1968 Soviet invasion.

Nu, U, 1907– , Burmese Socialist premier overthrown in 1962 coup.

Nyerere, Julius K., 1922– , African statesman in Tanganyika, elected (1962) first president of Tanzania.

Oates, Titus, 1649–1705, English fabricator of Popish Plot (1678).

Obote, Milton, 1925?– , Ugandan president.

Obregón, Alvaro, 1880–1928, assassinated Mexican revolutionary general and president (1920–24).

Ochs, Adolph S., 1858–1935, American publisher of *The New York Times.*

O'Connell, Daniel (the Liberator), 1775–1847, Irish political leader whose nationalism affected Ireland's history.

O'Connor, Thomas P. (Tay Pay), 1848–1929, Irish journalist and nationalist who aided cause of Irish Home Rule.

O'Higgins, Bernardo, 1778–1842, Chilean revolutionary and dictator (1817–23) who died in exile in Peru.

Ohira, Masayoshi, 1910–80, Japanese premier (1978–80).

Ojukwu, C. Odumegwu, 1933– , leader of Biafra's unsuccessful war of secession in the late 1960s.

Oppenheimer, J. Robert, 1904–67, American physicist who led research effort culminating in atom bomb.

Orlando, Vittorio Emanuele, 1860–1952, Italian jurist and premier (1917–19), one of the "Big Four" at WW I Paris Peace Conference.

Osman I, 1259–1326, founder of Ottoman dynasty who inaugurated a policy of religious toleration.

Oswald, Lee Harvey, 1939–63, President John F. Kennedy's assassin; murdered in Dallas jail by Jack Ruby.

Owen, Robert, 1771–1858, British social reformer, socialist, and cooperative-movement pioneer.

Paderewski, Ignace J., 1860–1941, Polish statesman, composer, and popular classical pianist.

Paley, William S., 1901– , American radio and television executive.

Palmer Nathaniel B., 1799–1877, American sea captain, ship designer and Antarctic explorer.

Pandit, Madame (Vijaya L.), 1900– , Indian diplomat and president of UN General Assembly (1953–54).

Pankhurst, Emmeline (née Goulden), 1858–1928, revered English woman suffragist.

Papadopoulos, George, 1919– , Greek premier, seized power in April 1967 and was overthrown in Nov. 1973.

Papandreou, George, 1888–1968, Greek premier, opponent of King Constantine and military junta.

Papen, Franz von, 1879–1969, German chancellor, diplomat under Hitler, acquitted by Nuremberg tribunal.

Park Chung Hee, 1917–79, South Korean president (1963–79).

Park, Mungo, 1771–1806, Scottish explorer of Niger River and western Africa.

Parnell, Charles S., 1846–91, magnetic Irish nationalist leader, "uncrowned king of Ireland."

La Pasionaria (Dolores Ibarruri), 1895– , Spanish revolutionist and a founder of Spain's Communist party.

Patiño, Simón I., 1868–1947, Bolivian tin king, reputed to have been one of world's wealthiest men.

Patterson, Joseph M., 1879–1946, American publisher of first successful U.S. tabloid, *Daily News.*

Patton, George S., Jr., 1885–1945, brilliant but controversial American WW II general ("Old Blood and Guts").

Paulus, Friedrich, 1890-1957, German field marshal who surrendered (1943) to Russians at Stalingrad.

Peabody, George, 1852-1938, American banker and philanthropist who fought for Negro education.

Pearson, Lester B., 1897–1972, Liberal prime minister of Canada (1963–68).

Peary, Robert E., 1856–1920, American rear admiral and first man to reach the North Pole (April 6, 1909).

Peel, Sir Robert, 1788–1850, British reformist statesman, organizer of London police force.

Pérez Jiménez, Marcos, 1914– , Venezuelan dictator and army officer.

Pericles, c. 495–429 B.C., democratic Athenian statesman, great patron of the arts.

Perkins, Frances, 1882–1965, U.S. Secretary of Labor during New Deal era, first woman cabinet member.

Perón, Juan D., 1895-1974, Argentine general and dictator (President 1946-55; 1973-74).

Perry, Oliver H., 1785–1819, American naval hero (Battle of Lake Erie) in War of 1812.

Pershing, John J. (Jack), 1860–1948, American WW I general, AEF commander in chief.

Pétain, Henri P., 1856–1951, French marshal, head of Vichy France (1940–42).

Peter I (the Great), 1672–1725, Russian czar (1682–1725), who westernized his country and made it a great power.

Pham Van Dong, 1906– , Vietnamese premier, a founder of the Vietminh.

Philby, Harold St. J. B., 1885–1960, British explorer, author and adviser to King Ibn Saud of Saudi Arabia.

Philip II, 382–336 B.C., father of Alexander the Great.

Pilsudski, Joseph, 1867–1935, Polish general and authoritarian premier (1926–28, 1930–35).

Pizarro, Francisco, c. 1476–1541, rapacious Spanish conquistador, conqueror of Peru.

Podgorny, Nikolai V., 1903– , Chairman of the Presidium of the Supreme Soviet (1965–77).

Poincaré, Raymond, 1860–1934, French president (1913–20) and advocate of harsh punishment for Germany after WW I.

Polo, Marco, c. 1254–c. 1324, Venetian traveler, favorite of Mongol Emperor Kublai Khan, and author of remarkably accurate Asian travelogue.

Pol Pot, 1928– , Communist leader in Cambodia whose regime is believed to be responsible for 2 million deaths in Cambodia after April 1975.

Pompadour, Madame, 1721–64, French mistress of Louis XV and his confidante until her death.

Pompey (the Great), 106–48 B.C., assassinated Roman general and statesman, rival of Caesar.

Pompidou, Georges J. R., 1911–74, French president (1969–1974).

Potemkin, Grigori A., 1739–91, eccentric Russian field marshal, a favorite of Catherine the Great.

Primo de Rivera, José A., 1903–36, Spanish founder of fascist Falange, executed by Loyalists after outbreak of Spanish Civil War.

Primo de Rivera, Miguel, 1870–1930, Spanish general and dictator (1923–30), father of José Primo de Rivera.

Princip, Gavrilo, 1895–1918, Serbian political agitator and hero, assassin (1914) of Archduke Francis Ferdinand.

Przhevalsky, Nikolai M., 1839–88, Russian geographer and explorer in central Asia and the Russian Far East.

Pugachev, Emelyan I., d. 1775, beheaded Russian leader who posed as Peter III in peasant rebellion (1773–75).

Pulaski, Casimir, c. 1748–79, Polish military commander in American Revolution, mortally wounded at Savannah.

Pulitzer, Joseph, 1847–1911, Hungarian-born publisher who established annual prizes for American letters.

Pu Yi, Henry, 1906–67, last emperor (1908–12) of China, later emperor of Japanese puppet state of Manchukuo.

el-Qaddafi, Muammar, 1938– , Libyan head of state since 1969.

Quezon, Manuel L., 1878–1944, first president of Philippines (1935–44), led it to independence.

Quisling, Vidkun, 1887–1945, executed Norwegian Fascist leader who helped Germany conquer his country.

Radek, Karl, 1885–1939?, Russian Communist leader and journalist, purged by Stalin.

Raeder, Erich, 1876–1960, German WW II admiral who disagreed with Hitler on strategy.

Raffles, Sir Thomas S. B., 1781–1826, British East Indian administrator, founder of Singapore.

Raglan, Lord (Fitzroy J. H. Somerset), 1788–1855, British general in Napoleonic and Crimean wars.

Rahman, Tunku Abdul, Prince, 1903-1973, first prime minister of Malaya (1957-1970).

Randolph, Edmund, 1753–1813, first U.S. Attorney General (1789–94), figure at Constitutional Convention (1787).

Rasmussen, Knud J. V., 1879–1933, Danish explorer of Greenland and the Arctic.

Rasputin, Grigori Y., 1872–1916, Russian libertine monk, a notorious influence on Nicholas II's court.

Rathenau, Walter, 1867–1922, assassinated German industrialist, idealistic social theorist, and statesman.

Rayburn, Sam (Samuel T.), 1882–1961, U.S. Congressman (Tex.), long-time Democratic House speaker.

Récamier, Madame (Juliette), 1777–1849, French beauty who presided over a salon of notables.

Reid, Ogden M., 1882–1947, American newspaper publisher.

Revere, Paul, 1735–1818, American Revolutionary patriot immortalized by Longfellow's poem.

Reza Shah Pahlavi, 1877–1944, shah of Iran (1925-41) who gained independence for his country.

Rhee, Syngman, 1875–1965, authoritarian president (1948–60) of Republic of (South) Korea.

Rhodes, Cecil J., 1853–1902, British statesman and business magnate in South Africa who set up Rhodes scholarship; Rhodesia (now Zimbabwe) was named for him.

Ribbentrop, Joachim von, 1893–1946, Anglophobic Nazi foreign minister (1938–45).

Ricci, Matteo, 1552–1610, Italian missionary and geographer in China, a favorite at the Chinese court.

Richelieu, Cardinal (Armand J.), duc de, 1585–1642, French prelate and statesman, founder of French Academy.

Riis, Jacob A., 1849–1914, Danish-American social reformer and journalist.

Rizal, José, 1861–96, Filipino patriot, author, poet, physician; his martyrdom inspired anti-Spanish revolt.

Robert I (Robert the Bruce), 1274–1329, king of Scotland who freed his country from England's grip.

Robert Guiscard, c. 1015–85, Norman conqueror of southern Italy.

Robespierre, Maximilien M. I., 1758–94, guillotined French revolutionary associated with the Reign of Terror.

Rob Roy (Robert MacGregor), 1671–1734, Scottish outlaw who figures in Scott's novel *Rob Roy.*

Rochambeau, Count (Jean B.), 1725–1807, French marshal in American Revolution.

Rockefeller, John D., 1839–1937, American oil tycoon and philanthropist, a founder of University of Chicago.

Rockefeller, Nelson A., 1908–79, governor of New York (1959–73), Vice-President of U.S. (1974–1977).

Rodino, Peter W., 1909– , chairman of the House Judiciary Committee which considered the impeachment of President Nixon in 1974.

Rokossovsky, Konstantin, 1896–1968, Soviet marshal, symbol of Russian influence in Poland (1949–56).

Rommel, Erwin, 1891–1944, German field marshal in Africa ("the Desert Fox") and France (1940–44).

Romulo, Carlos P., 1900– , Filipino statesman, president of UN General Assembly (1949).

Ronne Finn, 1899–1980, Norwegian-born American explorer and geographer.

Root, Elihu, 1845–1937, U.S. Secretary of State (1905–09), an architect of League of Nations; Nobel Peace Prize winner (1912).

Rosecrans, William S., 1818–98, American Union general.

Ross, James C., 1800–62, British rear admiral and polar explorer.

Rothschild, Guy, Baron de, 1909– , descendant of the prominent French banking family and head of the Banque Rothschild.

Rothschild, Meyer A., 1743–1812, German founder (in Frankfurt) of international banking house of Rothschild.

Rundstedt, Karl R. G. von, 1875–1953, German WW II field marshal and supreme commander in West (1942–45).

Rusk, (D.) Dean, 1909– , U.S. Secretary of State under Presidents Kennedy and Johnson.

Sadat, Anwar, 1918–81, Egyptian president (1970-81).

Sage, Russell, 1816–1906, American tycoon whose widow established (1907) Russell Sage Foundation.

Saladin, c. 1137–93, Moslem warrior and sultan of Egypt, major opponent of Crusaders.

Salazar, Antonio de Oliveira, 1889–1970, long-time Portuguese dictator (beginning in 1932).

Salomon, Haym, 1740–85, American Revolutionary patriot and financier.

Sandracottus (Greek for Chandragupta), fl. c. 321–c. 298 B.C., Indian emperor, founder of the Maurya dynasty.

Sanger, Margaret, 1879–1966, American founder of the birth-control movement.

San Martín, José de, 1778–1850, South American revolutionary, protector of Peru (1821–22).

Santa Anna, Antonio L. de, 1794–1876, Mexican general at Alamo and in Mexican War, several times president.

Santander, Francisco de Paula, 1792–1840, Colombian revolutionary and political leader.

Sarnoff, David, 1891–1971; Russian-born American pioneer in radio and television.

Savonarola, Girolamo, 1452–98, executed Florentine religious reformer.

Saxe, Comte de (Maurice), 1696–1750, French marshal, one of the greatest generals of his era.

Scanderbeg (George Castriota), c. 1404–68, Albanian national hero who led his people against Turks.

Schacht, Hjalmar H. G., 1877–1970, German president of Reichsbank (1923–30, 1933–39), acquitted by Nuremberg tribunal.

Schlieffen, Alfred, Graf von, 1833–1913, German field marshal whose battle strategy was reflected in WWI.

Schliemann, Heinrich, 1822–90, German archaeologist, discovered ruins of Troy.

Schmidt, Helmut, 1918– , West German chancellor since 1974.

Schuman, Robert, 1886–1963, French premier (1947–48) who worked to promote a European community.

Schurz, Carl, 1829–1906, German-born U.S. Secretary of the Interior (1877–81), newspaper editor, and author.

Schuschnigg, Kurt von, 1897–1977, Austrian chancellor (1934–38) imprisoned by Nazis until 1945.

Scipio Africanus Major, c. 234–183 B.C., Roman general, victor over Hannibal in Punic Wars.

Scott, Dred, c. 1795–1858, American slave and central figure in law case argued (1856–57) before U.S. Supreme Court.

Scott, Robert F., 1868–1912, British naval officer and antarctic explorer.

Scott, Winfield, 1786–1866, American army commander (1841–61), and Mexican War hero.

Scripps, Edward W., 1854–1926, American newspaper publisher.

Senghor, Léopold S., 1906– , African statesman and poet, first president of independent Senegal.

Sennacherib, d. 681 B.C., king of Assyria (705–681 B.C.) and conqueror who was murdered by his sons.

Seward, William H., 1801–72, U.S. Secretary of State, purchaser (1867) of Alaska ("Seward's folly").

Sforza, Ludovico, c. 1451–1508, duke of Milan (1494–99), Renaissance prince, patron of Leonardo da Vinci.

Shackleton, Sir Ernest H., 1874–1922, Irish-born British explorer whose antarctic expedition (1907–09) crossed within 100 miles of the South Pole.

Shaftesbury, Earl of (Anthony A. Cooper), 1801–85, leading English social reformer who advocated government action to reduce misery caused by Industrial Revolution.

Sharett, Moshe, 1894–1965, Israeli prime minister (1953–55), Ben-Gurion's closest associate in promoting an independent Jewish state.

Shastri, Shri L. B., 1904–66, prime minister of India (1964–66), disciple of Gandhi.

Shays, Daniel, c. 1747–1825, American Revolutionary soldier, leader of Shays's Rebellion (1786–87) of financially depressed small farmers in Massachusetts.

Sheridan, Philip H., 1831–88, American Union general, observer with Prussian army in Franco-Prussian War.

Sherman, William Tecumseh, 1820–91, American Union general who practiced war of attrition in the South.

Smith, Ian Douglas, 1919– , Rhodesian prime minister (1964–79).

Smith, John, c. 1580–1631, English adventurer and colonial leader; Pocahontas probably saved his life.

Smith, Walter Bedell, 1895–1961, U.S. WW II general, ambassador to USSR (1946–49), CIA head (1950–53).

Smuts, Jan C., 1870–1950, South African prime minister twice, WW II field marshal, and a UN organizer.

Snorri Sturluson, 1178–1241, Icelandic chieftain and historian, leading light in medieval Norse literature.

Somoza, Anastasio, 1896–1956, assassinated dictator of Nicaragua (1937–47, 1950–56).

Soong, T. V., 1894–1971, Harvard-educated Chinese statesman.

Sorge, Richard, 1895–1944, executed German spy for USSR in Japan.

Souphanouvong, Prince, 1902– , Laotian politician, leader of leftist Pathet Lao forces. President since 1975.

Souvanna Phouma, Prince, 1901– , Laotian neutralist prime minister (1962–75).

Spaak, Paul Henri, 1899–1972, Belgian statesman and Socialist leader, first president of UN general assembly (1946), and secretary-general of NATO (1957–61).

Spartacus, d. 71 B.C., Thracian gladiator and leader of Italian slave revolt, killed in battle.

Speke, John H., 1827–64, English explorer in Africa and discoverer (1858) of Lake Victoria.

Springer, Axel C., 1912– , powerful German publisher.

De Staël, Germaine, 1766–1817, French-Swiss writer and intellectual leader.

Stalin, Joseph V. (b. J. V. Dzhugashvili), 1879–1953, Russian Communist dictator.

Stambuliski, Alexander, 1879–1923, murdered Bulgarian premier (1919–23) and agrarian reformer.

Stanley, Sir Henry M., 1841–1904, Anglo-American adventurer, journalist, and empire builder, who was commissioned (1871) by the *New York Herald* to find David Livingstone in Africa.

Stanton, Edwin M., 1814–69, U.S. Secretary of War under Presidents Lincoln and Andrew Johnson.

Stavisky, Serge A., 1886–1934, French swindler, chief figure in scandal that rocked France (1934).

Stefansson, Vilhjalmur, 1879–1962, Canadian-born Icelandic ethnologist and arctic explorer.

Stepinac, Cardinal (Aloysius), 1898–1960, Yugoslav Roman Catholic prelate convicted (1946) by Tito government of Nazi collaboration but released (1951).

Steuben, Baron von (Friedrich W.), 1730–94, Prussian general in American Revolution.

Stevens, Thaddeus, 1792–1868, U.S. Congressman (Pa., 1849–53, 1859–68) active during Civil War and Reconstruction, devoted to Negro betterment.

Stevenson, Adlai E., 1900–65, eloquent American lawyer, Presidential candidate (1952, 1956), and U.S. ambassador to UN (1961–65).

Stimson, Henry L., 1867–1950, U.S. Secretary of War (1911–13, 1940–45) and Secretary of State (1929–33).

Stolypin, Piotr A., 1862–1911, Russian premier and minister of interior (1906–11).

Stowe, Harriet Beecher, 1811–96, American humanitarian whose novel *Uncle Tom's Cabin* was a factor in bringing about the Civil War.

Strabo, b. c. 63 B.C., Greek geographer, historian, and traveler.

Stresemann, Gustav, 1878–1929, German foreign minister dedicated to regaining world friendship for post-WW I Germany, and sharer of 1926 Nobel Peace Prize.

Stroessner, Alfredo, 1912– , repressive Paraguayan general and president.

Stuart, Charles Edward, 1720–88, claimant (Bonnie Prince Charlie) to English throne.

Stuyvesant, Peter, c. 1610–72, autocratic Dutch director general of New Netherland (beginning 1647).

Suárez González, Adolfo, 1932– , Spanish premier (1976-81).

Sucre, Antonio J. de, 1795–1830, South American revolutionary and military commander, associate of Bolívar.

Suharto, 1921– , Indonesian general and chief executive who overthrew (1965) Sukarno.

Sukarno, 1902–70, independence leader and dictatorial first president of republic of Indonesia (1945–66).

Sukhe-Bator, 1893–1923, Mongolian political leader who helped set up Mongolian People's Revolutionary party.

Suleiman I (the Magnificent), 1494–1566, Ottoman sultan under whom Ottoman Empire reached its height.

Sulla, Lucius C., 138–78 B.C., notorious Roman general and dictator.

Sully, Maximilien de B., duc de, 1560–1641, French statesman and closest adviser to Henry IV of France.

Sun Yat-sen, 1866–1925, Chinese revolutionary founder of the Chinese republic and of the Kuomintang.

Suslov, Mikhail A., 1902– , Soviet ideologist.

Suvarov, Aleksandr V., 1729–1800, revered Russian marshal in French Revolutionary Wars (1798–99).

Svoboda, Ludvík, 1895–1979, Communist president of Czechoslovakia during 1968 Soviet invasion.

Taft, Robert A., 1889–1953, conservative U.S. Senator who helped write Taft-Hartley Labor Act.

Talleyrand, Charles M. de, 1754–1838, French statesman and diplomat.

Tamerlane, c. 1336–1405, cruel Mongol conqueror of Asia, subject of a play by Christopher Marlowe.

Tanaka, Kakuei, 1918– , self-made businessman and premier of Japan (1972–74).

Tasman, Abel Janszoon, c. 1603–59, Dutch explorer who discovered (1642) Tasmania.

Teng Hsiao-ping see Deng Xiaoping.

Tetzel, Johann, c. 1465–1519, German Roman Catholic preacher who was attacked by Martin Luther.

Thatcher, Margaret, 1925– , British Conservative prime minister (1979–).

Themistocles, c. 525–c. 460 B.C., Athenian statesman and naval commander.

Theodora, d. 548, Byzantine empress, joint ruler with her husband, Justinian I.

Thiers, Adolphe, 1797–1877, French statesman, journalist, and historian of the Revolution and Bonaparte.

Thieu, Nguyen Van, 1923– , South Vietnamese president (1967–75), instrumental in 1963 overthrow of Diem.

Thomas, Norman M., 1884–1968, American Socialist leader, lecturer, and writer; frequent Socialist Party Presidential candidate after 1928.

Thomas à Becket, Saint, c. 1118–70, martyred English archbishop (Canterbury).

Thomson, Roy H., (1st Baron Thomson of Fleet), 1894–1976, Canadian-born British publisher.

Thorez, Maurice, 1900–64, French Communist leader, vice premier (1946–47).

Thurmond, (J.) Strom, 1902– , conservative U.S. Senator (S.C.), States' Rights Presidential candidate (1948).

Tilden, Samuel J., 1814–86, Democratic Presidential candidate (1876 against Rutherford B. Hayes).

Tirpitz, Alfred von, 1849–1930, German WW I admiral, advocate of unrestricted submarine warfare.

Tito, Josip B. (b. Josip Broz), 1892–1980, unorthodox Yugoslav Communist leader (1945–80).

Togliatti, Palmiro, 1893–1964, Italian Communist leader and party founder in his country.

Togo, Heihachiro, Count, 1847–1934, Japanese admiral and naval hero of Russo-Japanese War.

Tojo, Hideki, 1884–1948, Japanese general and prime minister (1941–44), executed by Allies as a war criminal.

Torquemada, Tomás de, 1420–98, severe Spanish Dominican who headed Spanish Inquisition.

Touré, Sékou, 1922– , African left-wing political leader, first president of Republic of Guinea.

Toussaint L'Ouverture, François D., c. 1744–1803, Haitian patriot and martyr who thwarted French colonial aims.

Trotsky, Leon, 1879–1940, exiled Soviet revolutionary and a principal founder of USSR.

Trudeau, Pierre E., 1919– , French-Canadian Liberal prime minister (1968–79, 1980–) and lawyer.

Trujillo Molina, Rafael L., 1891–1961, murdered president (1930–38, 1942–60) of Dominican Republic.

Trung Trac, fl. 39–43 A.D., Vietnamese national heroine who led a revolt against China.

Tshombe, Moise K., 1919–69, Congolese political leader of Katanga, which he proclaimed (1960) independent.

Tubman, Harriet, c. 1820–1913, slave-born American abolitionist and Underground Railroad "conductor."

Tubman, William V. S., 1895–1971, long-time Liberian president.

Tukhachevsky, Mikhail N., 1893–1937, Soviet marshal who helped to modernize and mechanize Red Army.

Tupac Amaru, c. 1742–81, Indian national hero of Peru, executed leader of antigovernment rebellion (1780).

Turner, Nat, 1800–31, executed American leader of slave rebellion (1831, Southampton Co., Va.).

Tutankhamen, fl. c. 1350 B.C., Egyptian pharaoh whose tomb revealed new knowledge of XVIII dynasty life.

Tweed, Boss (William M.), 1823–78, American politician and Tammany leader, who defrauded New York City.

Tyler, Wat, d. 1381, English leader of great peasant rebellion (1381) over labor conditions.

Tz'u Hsi, 1834–1908, dowager empress of China who encouraged Boxer Rebellion (1898–1900).

Ulbricht, Walter, 1893–1973, Communist who became (1960) East German head of state.

Vance, Cyrus R., 1917– , American lawyer, government official, and Secretary of State (1977–80).

Vanderbilt, Commodore (Cornelius), 1794–1877, American railroad magnate, founder of Vanderbilt University.

Vargas, Getúlio D., 1883–1954, Brazilian statesman and president (1930–45, 1951–54).

Venizelos, Eleutherios, 1864–1936, Cretan-born Greek statesman and reformer.

Verwoerd, Hendrik F., 1901–66, assassinated South African prime minister (1958–66), proponent of apartheid.

Victoria, 1819–1901, longest reigning English monarch in history (64 years), who ruled during the height of the British Empire's prestige.

Videla, Jorge Rafael, 1925– , Argentine general and president (1976–81).

Villa, Pancho (b. Doroteo Arango), c. 1877–1923, assassinated Mexican bandit and revolutionary.

Viola, Roberto Eduardo, 1924– , Argentine general and president (1981–).

Visconti, Gian C., c. 1351–1402, Italian duke of Milan who reformed and centralized the government.

Vishinsky, Andrei Y., 1883–1954, Soviet jurist and diplomat, foreign minister (1949–53) of USSR.

Volstead, Andrew J., 1860–1947, American legislator, author (1919) of Volstead (alcohol prohibition) Act.

Voroshilov, Kliment Y., 1881–1969, Soviet general and statesman, close associate of Stalin.

Vorster, Balthazar J., 1915– , South African prime minister (1966–78) and lawyer.

Wainwright, Jonathan M., 1883–1953, American general who in World War II defended Bataan and Corregidor.

Waldheim, Kurt, 1918– , Austrian career diplomat and Secretary General of the United Nations (1972–).

Walesa, Lech, 1943?– , Polish labor leader.

Wallace, George C., 1919– , American conservative politician, third party Presidential candidate (1968).

Washington, Booker T., 1856–1915, Black American educator, organizer (1881) of Tuskegee Institute; author.

Wavell, Archibald P. (Earl), 1883–1950, British field marshal and viceroy of India (1943–47).

Webb, Beatrice (née Potter), 1858–1943, English Socialist economist; she and her husband, Sidney J. Webb (1859–1947), were leading figures in Fabian Society and building British Labour party.

Webster, Daniel, 1782–1852, American statesman, a leading political figure, noted orator, and Whig luminary.

Weizmann, Chaim, 1874–1952, Russian-born scientist, Zionist leader, and first president of Israel (1948–52).

Welles, Sumner, 1892–1961, American diplomat and statesman, specialist in Latin American affairs.

Westmoreland, William C., 1914– , American general in Vietnam.

White, William A., 1868–1944, American author and editor (1895–1944) of Emporia (Kans.) *Gazette.*

Wilkes, Charles, 1798–1877, American naval officer and discoverer of area in Antarctic named Wilkes Land.

William I (the Conqueror), 1027?–1087, Norman duke and English king (1066–87), conquered England in 1066.

Willkie, Wendell L., 1892–1944, American industrialist and Republican Presidential candidate (1940).

Wilson, J. Harold, 1916– , Labour prime minister (1964–1970, 1974–76), of Great Britain.

Wingate, Orde C., 1903–44, British WW II general, who demonstrated effectiveness of guerrilla warfare.

Wolfe, James, 1727–59, British victor against French in battle of Quebec (Plains of Abraham).

Wollstonecraft, Mary, 1759–97, English feminist whose writings inspired the American women's rights movement.

Wolsey, Cardinal (Thomas), c. 1473–1530, English prelate and favorite of Henry VIII.

Wrangel, Baron Ferdinand von, 1796–1870, Russian naval officer, arctic explorer, governor of Russian Alaska.

Wyszynski, Cardinal (Stefan), 1901–81, Polish prelate often in conflict with Gomulka government.

Xenophon, c. 430 B.C.–c. 355 B.C., Greek historian who led retreat of "Ten Thousand" Greek mercenaries from Persia (401 B.C.).

Yamamoto, Isoroku, 1884–1943, Japanese admiral who masterminded (1941) attack on Pearl Harbor.

Yamani, Ahmed Zaki, 1930– , Saudi Arabian oil minister; leading figure in Arab and OPEC oil activities.

Yamashita, Tomoyuki, 1888–1946, Japanese general defeated (1945) by General MacArthur's invasion of Philippines, hanged in Manila as a war criminal.

Yoshida, Shigeru, 1878–1967, Japanese Liberal prime minister (1946–54).

Yüan Shih-kai, 1859–1916, dictatorial president of China (1912–16) who declared (1916) himself emperor.

Zaharoff, Sir Basil (b. Basileios Zacharias), 1850–1936, Turkish-born British financier and munitions manufacturer.

Zapata, Emiliano, c. 1879–1919, Mexican revolutionary.

Zenger, John Peter, 1697–1746, German-American journalist whose libel trial acquittal furthered press freedom.

Zhdanov, Andrei A., 1896–1948, murdered Soviet Communist leader who fostered extreme nationalism.

Zhou Enlai, 1898–1976, Chinese Communist premier and foreign minister (1949–76).

Zhukov, Georgi K., 1896–1974, Soviet marshal who defeated Germans at Stalingrad and occupied Berlin.

Zinoviev, Grigori E., 1883–1936, Russian Communist leader executed by Stalin after the first spectacular purge trial.

SCIENTISTS AND MATHEMATICIANS

Ampère, André Marie, 1775–1836, French physicist, discovered, 1820, the left-hand and right-hand rules of the magnetic field about a current-carrying wire.

***Archimedes,** c. 287–212 B.C., Greek mathematician.

Aston, Francis William, 1877–1945, English chemist and physicist, developed, 1919, the mass spectrograph.

Avogadro, Amedeo, 1776–1856, Italian physicist, put forth a hypothesis in which equal volumes of all gasses at the same temperature and pressure contain the same number of molecules.

Becquerel, Antoine Henri, 1852–1908, French physicist.

Bernoulli, Daniel, 1700–82, Dutch-Swiss mathematician, 1738, advanced the kinetic theory of gases and fluids.

Berzelius, Jons Jakob, 1779–1848, Swedish chemist, introduced chemical symbols and chemical radical theory.

Bethe, Hans Albrecht, 1906– , German-born American physicist, proposed, 1938, the nuclear mechanism by which stars obtain their energy.

***Bohr, Niels,** 1885–1962, Danish physicist.

Brahe, Tycho, 1546–1601, Danish astronomer.

Carnap, Rudolf, 1891–1970, German-born American philosopher of science, founded logical positivism.

Cavendish, Henry, 1731–1810, English chemist and physicist, discovered, 1766, hydrogen; devised, 1798, a gravitational method for weighing the Earth.

Charles, Jacques Alexandre César, 1746–1823, French physicist, discovered, 1787, the law governing the expansion and contraction of gases with changes in temperature.

Cockcroft, John Douglas, 1897–1967, English nuclear physicist, with E. T. S. Walton, constructed (c. 1932), the first atomic particle accelerator.

Compton, Arthur Holly, 1892–1962, American physicist, discovered, 1923, that X-rays scattered by diffraction in crystals have their wavelengths lengthened, the Compton effect; discovered, c. 1930, that cosmic rays consist of particles.

***Copernicus (Mikolaj Kopernik),** 1473–1543, Polish astronomer.

Coulomb, Charles Augustin de, 1736–1806, French engineer and physicist, established the law describing the attraction and repulsion of electric charges.

***Crick, Francis H. C.,** 1916– , English biophysicist.

Ctesibius, 2d century B.C., Greek engineer, invented the water clock, force pump, and air as motive force.

Curie, Marie, 1867–1934, and **Pierre,** 1859–1906, French chemists, isolated, 1898, the first radioactive element —radium.

***Darwin, Charles,** 1809–1882, English naturalist.

Davy, Humphry, 1778–1829, English chemist, established the electrical nature of chemical affinity.

***Descartes, René,** 1596–1650, French mathematician.

Dewar, James, 1842–1923, British chemist and physicist, liquified, 1898, and solidified, 1899, hydrogen.

Dirac, Paul Adrien Maurice, 1902– , English physicist, in 1920s, unified relativity and quantum theories, and unified wave mechanics and special relativity; proposed, 1930–31, antiparticles.

Dubos, René, 1901– , French microbiologist and environmentalist in America.

Edison, Thomas Alva, 1847–1931, prolific American inventor. Discovered "Edison effect."

***Einstein, Albert,** 1879–1955, American physicist (born Germany).

Euler, Leonhard, 1707–83, Swiss mathematician and physicist, produced work in astronomy, mechanics, hydrodynamics, and optics; founded higher mathematics.

Fahrenheit, Gabriel Daniel, 1686–1736, German physicist, developed temperature scale that bears his name.

***Faraday, Michael,** 1791–1867, English chemist, physicist.

Fermat, Pierre de, 1601–65, French mathematician, discovered analytic geometry; founded modern theory of numbers and the calculus of probabilities.

Fermi, Enrico, 1901–54, Italian-born American physicist.

Fischer, Emil, 1852–1919, German chemist, especially noted for his work on structure of sugars.

Fourier, Jean Baptiste Joseph, 1768–1830, French mathematician, discovered, c. 1822, the theorem governing periodic oscillation.

Franklin, Benjamin, 1706–90, American statesman and scientist, discovered, 1752, the electrical nature of lightning; proposed the one-fluid theory of electricity.

Gabor, Dennis, 1900–79, Hungarian-born British physicist known for the development of holography.

***Galileo Galilei,** 1564–1642, Italian scientist.

***Gauss, Karl F.,** 1777–1855, German mathematician.

Gay-Lussac, Joseph Louis, 1778–1850, French chemist, discovered, 1809, the law of combining volumes.

Gibbs, Josiah Willard, 1839–1903, American physicist, founded, 1876–78, chemical thermodynamics.

Grzimek, Bernhard, 1909– , Polish zoologist and wildlife conservationist.

Guericke, Otto von, 1602–86, German physicist and engineer, invented the first vacuum pump and used it, (c. 1650) to demonstrate atmospheric pressure.

Haber, Fritz, 1868–1934, German chemist, developed, 1900–1911, a process for "fixing" atmospheric nitrogen in chemical compounds.

Hall, James, 1761–1832, British geologist and chemist, founded, c. 1797, experimental geology, geochemistry.

Halley, Edmund, 1656–1742, English astronomer, calculated orbits of many comets.

***Heisenberg, Werner Karl,** 1901–1976, German physicist.

Helmont, Jan Baptista Van, 1577–1644, Flemish physician and alchemist, initiated quantitative biochemistry.

Hero of Alexandria, c. 1st century, Greek engineer, invented principle of the steam engine; extended Archimedes' principle of the lever.

***Hertz, Heinrich,** 1857–94, German physicist.

Herzberg, Gerhard, 1904– , Canadian physicist known for his work on electronic structure and molecular geometry.

Hilbert, David, 1862–1943, German mathematician, formulated, 1899, the first set of axioms for geometry.

Hubble, Edwin Powell, 1889–1953, American astronomer, discovered, 1929, the universal recession of galaxies.

Humboldt, Friedrich Wilhelm Heinrich Alexander von, 1769–1859, established, c. 1830–1859, geophysics.

Janssen (or Jansen), Zacharias, 1580–c. 1638, Dutch optician, invented, c. 1590, the microscope.

Jensen, Arthur Robert, 1923– , educational psychologist. His view is that intelligence is primarily inherited.

Kamerlingh Onnes, Heike, 1853–1926, Dutch physicist, established, 1882, cryogenics.

Kapitza, Peter, 1894– , Soviet physicist, research contributed to Soviet space achievements.

Kelvin, Lord (William Thompson), 1826–1907, British physicist, made advances in thermodynamics and thermometry.

***Kepler, Johannes,** 1571–1630, German astronomer.

Khorana, Har Gobind, 1922– , Indian organic chemist, synthesized functioning gene, 1976.

Landau, Lev Davidovich, 1908–68, Russian physicist, developed mathematical theory explaining behavior of superfluid helium at temperatures near absolute zero.

LaPlace, Pierre Simon, 1749–1827, French astronomer and mathematician, put forth, 1796, the nebular hypothesis of the origin of the solar system.

***Lavoisier, Antoine,** 1743–94, French chemist.

Lawrence, Ernest Orlando, 1901–58, American physicist, constructed, 1930, the first cyclotron.

Leakey, Louis, 1903-72, **Mary,** 1913- , and **Richard,** 1944- , Anglo-Kenyan anthropologists, discovered important fossil remains of early hominids.

Lee, Tsung-Dao, 1926– , Chinese-born American physicist, with Yang refuted the law of parity.

Leeuwenhoek, Anton van, 1632–1723, Dutch microscopist and the father of microbiology.

***Leibniz, Gottfried,** 1646–1716, German mathematician, philosopher.

Levene, Phoebus Aaron Theodore, 1869–1940, Russian-born American chemist, discovered, 1909, the nucleic acids RNA and, 20 years later, DNA.

Lévi-Strauss, Claude, 1908– , French anthropologist, leader of the structuralist school of ethnology.

Liebig, Justus von, 1803–73, German chemist, established, c. 1831, quantitative organic chemical analysis.

Lowell, Percival, 1855–1916, American astronomer, 1930, discovered Pluto.

Mach, Ernst, 1838–1916, Austrian physicist, psychologist, and philosopher of science, influential in the development of logical positivism.

Marshak, Robert E., 1916– , American nuclear physicist who helped to develop the first atomic bomb.

***Maxwell, James C.,** 1831–79, English physicist.

***Mendel, Gregor Johann,** 1822–84, Austrian founder of genetics.

Mead, Margaret, 1901–78, American anthropologist noted for her studies in primitive and contemporary cultures.

---

* See listing in "Landmarks of Science," pp. 338-339.

°Mendeleyev, Dmitri Ivanovich, 1834–1907, Russian chemist.

Michelson, Albert Abraham, 1852–1931, German-born American physicist, developed the interferometer, which measured, 1881 and 1887, the velocity of light and proved the nonexistence of ether in space.

Mohorovicic, Andrija, 1857–1936, Croatian geophysicist, discovered, 1909, the ("Moho") discontinuity that marks the bottom of the Earth's crust.

Mössbauer, Rudolf Ludwig, 1929–   , German-born American physicist, discovered, 1958, the recoilless emission and absorption of gamma rays by atoms in crystals.

°Napier, John, 1550–1617, Scottish mathematician.

°Newton, Isaac, 1642–1727, English mathematician.

Ochoa, Severo, 1905–   , Spanish-born American biochemist, synthesized, 1955, ribonucleic acid (RNA).

Ostwald, Wilhelm, 1853–1932, German chemist, was chief founder, beginning in 1887, of physical chemistry.

Pascal, Blaise, 1623–62, French scientist, mathematician, and religious philosopher, founded the modern theory of probability and the law of hydrostatic pressure (Pascal's law).

Pauling, Linus Carl, 1901–   , American chemist, developed, 1939, the theory of the chemical bond.

°Planck, Max, 1858–1947, German physicist.

Priestley, Joseph, 1733–1804, English theologian and scientist, discovered, 1774, oxygen.

Raman, Chandrasekhara Vankata, 1888–1970, Indian physicist, discovered, 1928, the change in wavelength and frequency of monochromatic light passing through a transparent medium.

Riemann, Georg F. B., 1826–66, German mathematician, developed non-Euclidian system of geometry representing elliptic space.

°Rutherford, Lord (Ernest), 1871–1937, British physicist, born in New Zealand.

°Schroedinger, Erwin, 1887–1961, Austrian physicist.

Seaborg, Glenn T., 1912–   , American chemist, led, 1941–c. 1951, the group that discovered the transuranium elements americium, curium, berkelium, californium, einsteinium, fermium, plutonium, mendelevium and nobelium.

Stanley, Wendell Meredith, 1904–71, American biochemist, crystallized, 1935, the tobacco mosaic virus, thus demonstrating that matter may have both living and nonliving forms.

Steno, Nicolaus (Niels Stensen), 1638–86, Danish anatomist and Catholic prelate, recognized the nature of fossils.

Szilard, Leo, 1898–1964, Hungarian-born American physicist, proved, 1939, with Walter Zinn, the possibility of self-sustaining nuclear fission; worked, 1942, with Enrico Fermi, on development of first nuclear reaction.

Tsvett (or Tswett), Mikhail Semenovich, 1872–1919, Italian-born Russian botanist, discovered, 1906, chromatography.

Urey, Harold Clayton, 1893–1981, American chemist, discovered, 1931, heavy hydrogen (deuterium).

Volta, Alessandro, 1745–1827, Italian physicist, invented the first electric cell and electric battery.

Von Neumann, John, 1903–57, Hungarian-born American mathematician, was a founder of the mathematical theory of games and contributed to computer theory.

Walton, Ernest Thomas Sinton, 1903–   , Irish physicist, constructed, 1929, the first atomic particle accelerator.

°Watson, James Dewey, 1928–   , American biochemist.

Wegener, Alfred Lothar, 1880–1930, German meteorologist and geophysicist, postulated theory of continental drift.

Wiener, Norbert, 1894–1964, American mathematician, contributed to development of computers; founded cybernetics.

Wigner, Eugene Paul, 1902–   , Hungarian-born American physicist, accomplished pioneering work in nuclear structure.

°Wilkins, Maurice H. F., 1916–   , British biophysicist.

Yang, Chen Ning, 1922–   , Chinese-born American physicist. See Lee.

Yukawa, Hideki, 1907–81, Japanese physicist who predicted the existence of mesons.

PHILOSOPHERS, THEOLOGIANS, AND RELIGIONISTS

Abelard, Peter (1079–1142), French philosopher.

Abravanel, Isaac (1437–1508), Jewish theologian.

Adler, Felix (1851–1933), German-American Ethical Culture movement founder.

Alexander of Hales (d. 1245), English scholastic philosopher.

Ambrose, Saint (c. 340–397), bishop of Milan.

Anaxagoras (c. 500–c. 428 B.C.), Greek philosopher.

Anaximander (c. 611–c. 547 B.C.), Greek philosopher.

Anaximenes (6th cent. B.C.), Greek philosopher.

Anselm, Saint (c. 1033–1109), Italian founder of scholasticism.

Anthony, Saint (c. 251–c. 350), Egyptian father of Christian monasticism.

Antisthenes (c. 444 B.C.–after 371 B.C.), Greek philosopher.

Aristotle (384–322 B.C.), Greek philosopher.

Arius (c. 256–336), Libyan theologian.

Arminius, Jacobus (1560–1609), Dutch Reformed theologian.

Augustine, Saint (354–430), North African Doctor of the Church.

Averroës (1126–98), Spanish-Arabian philosopher.

Avicenna (980–1037), Arabian philosopher.

Ayer, Alfred Jules (1910–   ), British philosopher.

Baal-Shem-Tov (1700–60), Jewish founder of modern Hasidism.

Bacon, Francis (1561–1626), English philosopher.

Bacon, Roger (c. 1214–c. 1294), English philosopher.

Balthasar, Hans Urs von (1905–   ), German theologian.

Barth, Karl (1886–1968), Swiss Protestant theologian.

Bentham, Jeremy (1748–1832), English philosopher, founder of utilitarianism.

Berdyaev, Nicholas (1874–1948), Russian philosopher.

Berengar of Tours (c. 1000–c. 1088), French theologian.

Bergson, Henri (1859–1941), French philosopher.

Berkeley, George (1685–1753), Anglo-Irish philosopher.

Bernard of Clairvaux, Saint (c. 1090–1153), French mystic.

Bernard of Cluny (fl. 1150), Anglo-French monk.

Bernardine of Siena, Saint (1380–1444), Italian preacher.

Biddle, John (1615–62), English founder of Unitarianism.

Boehme, Jakob (1575–1624), German religious mystic.

Boethius (c. 475–525), Roman philosopher.

Bonaventure, Saint (1221–74), Italian scholastic theologian.

Bonhoeffer, Dietrich (1906–45), German theologian.

Brunner, Emil (1889–1966), Swiss Protestant theologian.

Bruno, Giordano (1548–1600), Italian philosopher.

Buber, Martin (1878–1965), German-Israeli philosopher.

Büchner, Ludwig (1824–99), German philosopher.

Bultmann, Rudolf (1884–1976), German existentialist theologian.

Cabrini, Mother Francesca (1850–1917), Italian-born American nun and first American saint.

Calvin, John (1509–64), French Protestant theologian.

Carnap, Rudolf (1891–1970), German-American philosopher.

Cassirer, Ernst (1874–1945), German philosopher.

Comte, Auguste (1798–1857), French positivist philosopher.

Cranmer, Thomas (1489–1556), English churchman.

Croce, Benedetto (1866–1952), Italian philosopher.

Democritus (c. 460–c. 370 B.C.), Greek philosopher.

Descartes, René (1596–1650), French philosopher.

Dewey, John (1859–1952), American philosopher.

Diderot, Denis (1713–84), French philosopher.

Diogenes (c. 412–323 B.C.), Greek Cynic philosopher.

Duns Scotus, John (c. 1266–1308), Scottish theologian.

Eckhart, Meister (c. 1260–c. 1328), German theologian.

Edwards, Jonathan (1703–58), American theologian.

Emerson, Ralph Waldo (1803–82), American transcendentalist.

Empedocles (c. 495–c. 435 B.C.), Greek philosopher.

Engels, Friedrich (1820–95), German social philosopher.

Enrique Tarancón, Vicente Cardinal (1907–   ), Spanish religious reformer.

Epictetus (c. 50–c. 138), Phrygian Stoic philosopher.

Epicurus (341–270 B.C.), Greek philosopher.

Erigena, John Scotus (c. 810–c. 877), Irish philosopher.

Fichte, Johann G. (1762–1814), German philosopher.

Fox, George (1624–91), English founder of Society of Friends.

George, Henry (1839–97), American economic theorist.

Ghazali, al (c. 1058–1111), Islamic philosopher.

Gilson, Etienne (1884–1978), French philosopher.

Gorton, Samuel (c. 1592–1677), Anglo-American religious founder.

Graham, Billy (1918–   ), American evangelist.

Groote, Gerard (1340–84), Dutch ecclesiastical reformer.

Guardini, Romano (1885–1968), Italian-born German Catholic theologian.

Hegel, Georg W. F. (1770–1831), German philosopher.

Heidegger, Martin (1889–1976), German philosopher.

* See listing in "Landmarks of Science"

Heraclitus (c. 535–c. 475 B.C.), Greek philosopher.
Hobbes, Thomas (1588–1679), English philosopher.
Hooker, Richard (c. 1554–1600), English theologian.
Hume, David (1711–76), Scottish philosopher.
Hus, Jan (c. 1369–1415), Czech religious reformer.
Husserl, Edmund (1859–1938), German philosopher, founder of phenomenology.
Huxley, Thomas H. (1825–95), English agnostic philosopher.
Ignatius of Loyola, Saint (1491–1556), Spanish founder of the Jesuits.
James, William (1842–1910), American philosopher.
Jansen, Cornelis (1585–1638), Dutch Roman Catholic theologian.
Jaspers, Karl (1883–1969), German philosopher and psychopathologist.
John of the Cross, Saint (1542–91), Spanish mystic.
Kant, Immanuel (1724–1804), German metaphysical philosopher.
Kierkegaard, Soren (1813–55), Danish philosopher.
Knox, John (c. 1514–72), Scottish founder of Presbyterianism.
Küng, Hans (1928–   ), Swiss Roman Catholic theologian.
Laing, R. D. (1927–   ), Scottish existentialist psychoanalyst, writer, and social critic.
Law, William (1686–1761), English churchman and mystic.
Leibniz, Gottfried W., Baron von (1646–1716), German philosopher.
Locke, John (1632–1704), English philosopher.
Lombard, Peter (c. 1100–c. 1160).Italian theologian.
Lonergan, Bernard J. F. (1904–   ), Canadian theologian and Thomist philosopher.
Lucretius (c. 99–c. 55 B.C.), Roman philosopher-poet.
Luther, Martin (1483–1546), German Protestant leader.
Mahesh Yogi, Maharishi (1911?–   ), Hindu guru.
Maimonides (1135–1204), Spanish-Jewish philosopher.
Malthus, Thomas R. (1766–1834), English economic and social philosopher.
Marcel, Gabriel (1889–1973), French philosopher.
Marcus Aurelius (121–180), Stoic philosopher.
Marias, Julián (1914–   ), Spanish philosopher.
Maritain Jacques (1882–1973), French Neo-Thomist philosopher.
Marx, Karl (1818–83), German social philosopher.
Mather, Cotton (1663–1728), American Puritan minister.
Mather, Increase (1639–1723), American Puritan minister.
May, Rollo (1909–   ), American humanistic psychoanalyst-philosopher.
Melanchthon, Philip (1497–1560), German theologian.
Mencius (c. 371–c. 288 B.C.), Chinese sage.
Mill, John Stuart (1806–73), English philosopher and economist.
Molina, Luis (1535–1600), Spanish Jesuit theologian.
Moore, George E. (1873–1958), English philosopher.
Murray, John (1741–1815), English founder of American Universalist denomination.
Nestorius (d. c. 451), Byzantine theologian.
Newman, John Henry, Cardinal (1801–90), English philosopher.
Nicholas of Cusa (c. 1401–46), German humanist.
Niebuhr, H. Richard (1894–1962), American theologian.
Niebuhr, Reinhold (1892–1971), American theologian.
Nietzsche, Friedrich W. (1844–1900), German philosopher.
Origen (c. 185–c. 254), Egyptian Christian philosopher.
Parmenides (b. c. 514 B.C.), Greek philosopher.
Pascal, Blaise (1623–62), French philosopher and mathematician.
Peirce, Charles S. (1839–1914), American philosopher.

Philo (c. 20 B.C.–A.D. c. 50), Alexandrian Jewish philosopher.
Plato (c. 427–c. 347 B.C.), Greek philosopher.
Plotinus (c. 205–270), Egyptian Neoplatonist philosopher.
Protagoras (c. 480–c. 410 B.C.), Greek Sophist.
Rapp, George (1757–1847), German-American Harmony Society founder.
Rousseau, Jean Jacques (1712–78), French philosopher.
Royce, Josiah (1855–1916), American philosopher.
Russell, Bertrand (1872–1970), British philosopher and mathematician.
Santayana, George (1863–1952), American philosopher.
Savonarola, Girolamo (1452–98), Italian religious reformer.
Schelling, Friedrich W. J. von (1775–1854), German philosopher.
Schopenhauer, Arthur (1788–1860), German philosopher.
Schweitzer, Albert (1875–1965), Alsatian philosopher and theologian.
Seneca (c. 3 B.C.–A.D. 65), Roman philosopher.
Seton, Elizabeth Ann Bayley (1774–1821), 1st U.S.-born canonized saint.
Shaftesbury, Anthony Ashley Cooper, 3d earl of (1671–1713), English philosopher.
Smith, Adam (1723–90), Scottish economist and philosopher.
Socrates (469–399 B.C.), Greek philosopher.
Spencer, Herbert (1820–1903), English philosopher of evolution.
Spinoza, Baruch (1632–77), Dutch philosopher.
Suso, Heinrich (c. 1295–1366), German mystic.
Suzuki, Daisetz Teitaro (1870–1966), Japanese Buddhist scholar.
Swedenborg, Emanuel (1688–1772), Swedish theologian and mystic.
Taylor, Jeremy (1613–67), English theologian.
Teilhard de Chardin, Pierre (1881–1955), French Jesuit scientist-theologian.
Thales (c. 636–c. 546 B.C.), Greek philosopher.
Theresa, Saint (1515–82), Spanish mystic.
Thomas Aquinas, Saint (1225–74), Italian philosopher and Doctor of the Church.
Tillich, Paul (1886–1965), German-born American theologian.
Tyndale, William (c. 1494–1536), English Bible translator.
Ussher, James (1581–1656), Irish prelate and scholar.
Veblen, Thorstein (1857–1929), American economic and social philosopher.
Vico, Giovanni B. (1668–1744), Italian philosopher and historian.
Watts, Isaac (1674–1748), English clergyman and hymn writer.
Wesley, John (1703–91), English founder of Methodism.
Whitehead, Alfred North (1861–1947), English philosopher and mathematician.
William of Occam (d. c. 1349), English philosopher.
Williams, Roger (c. 1603–83), Anglo-American clergyman.
Winebrenner, John (1797–1860), American founder of Churches of God in North America.
Wise, Stephen (1874–1949), American reform rabbi and Zionist leader.
Wittgenstein, Ludwig (1889–1951), Austrian philosopher.
Woodbridge, Frederick J. E. (1867–1940), American philosopher.
Wyclif, John (c. 1328–84), English reformer.
Zeno of Citium (c. 334–c. 262 B.C.), Greek philosopher, founder of Stoicism.
Zoroaster (628–551 B.C.), Persian prophet.
Zwingli, Huldreich (1484–1531), Swiss Protestant reformer.

MEN OF MEDICINE AND PHYSIOLOGY

Abulcasis, or Abu Khasim, fl. 11th century, Arabian physician, author of the *Tasrif* (collection), a detailed account of surgery and medicine of his day.
Addison, Thomas, 1793–1860, English physician, discoverer of the malady of the suprarenal cortex, known as Addison's disease.
Allbutt, Thomas Clifford, 1836–1925, English physician, invented, 1866, the clinical thermometer.
Avicenna, or Ibn Sina, A.D. 980–1037, Arabian physician and philosopher, wrote the *Canon of Medicine*, most famous textbook of medicine until the 17th century.
Baer, Karl Ernst von, 1792–1876, Estonian biologist, founded, 1827–37, embryology.
Banting, Frederick G., 1891–1941, Canadian physician, with Charles Best, discovered, 1921, the use of insulin in diabetic therapy.

Barnard, Christiaan N., 1923–   , South African surgeon, performed, 1967, first transplant of a human heart.
Beaumont, William, 1785–1853, American physician, first to describe, 1822, the process of digestion.
Behring, Emil Adolf von, 1854–1917, German bacteriologist noted for work on diphtheria antitoxin.
Berger, Johannes (Hans), 1873–1941, German neurologist, invented, 1929, the electroencephalograph.
Bernard, Claude, 1813–78, French physiologist, considered founder of experimental medicine.
Best, Charles Herbert, 1899–1978, Canadian physiologist, with Frederick Banting discovered, 1921, the use of insulin in diabetic therapy.
Bichat, Marie François Xavier, 1771–1802, French physician, founded, 1800, histology, the study of living tissues.

Blalock, Alfred, 1899–1964, American surgeon, with Helen B. Taussig introduced, 1944, corrective heart surgery enabling survival of "blue babies."

Braun, Heinrich Friedrich Wilhelm, 1862–1934, German surgeon, introduced, 1905, procaine (Novocain) into clinical use.

Bright, Richard, 1789–1858, English physician, first to describe, 1827, the kidney disease known as Bright's disease.

Canano, Giovanni Battista, 1515–79, Italian anatomist, first to describe, c. 1547, venous valves.

Carrel, Alexis, 1873–1944, French-American surgeon, developed methods for transplanting blood vessels; invented, with Charles A. Lindbergh, a mechanical heart.

Cohn, Ferdinand Julius, 1828–98, German botanist, founded, c. 1872, science of bacteriology.

Cooley, Denton A., 1920–   , American surgeon, pioneer in cardiovascular surgery.

De Bakey, Michael Ellis, 1908–   , American surgeon, developed artificial heart.

De Forest, Lee, 1873–1961, American inventor, invented, 1907, the electrical high-frequency surgical knife.

Dick, George F., 1881–1967, and **Gladys H. Dick,** isolated, 1923, the scarlet fever toxin.

Domagk, Gerhard, 1895–1964, German chemist, used, c. 1932, the first sulfa drug (prontosil) in therapy.

Eberth, Karl Joseph, 1835–1926, German pathologist, discovered, 1880, the typhoid bacillus.

Edelman, Gerald M., 1929–   , American biochemist, deciphered, 1969, the structure of gamma globulin.

Ehrlich, Paul, 1854–1915, German bacteriologist and pathologist, developed, 1897, the differential blood count; established, 1892–94, serology and immunology; established, 1909, chemotherapy.

Eijkman, Christiaan, 1858–1930, Dutch bacteriologist, proved, 1896, that beriberi is a deficiency disease, thus leading to discovery of the first vitamin.

Einthoven, Willem, 1860–1927, Dutch physiologist, invented, 1903, the electrocardiograph.

Ermengem, Émile P. M. van, 1851–1932, Belgian bacteriologist, discovered, 1897, the food-poisoning bacillus.

Fabricius, Hieronymus, or Geronimo Fabrizio, 1537–1619, Italian anatomist, discovered, 1603, venous valves.

Fauchard, Pierre, 1678–1761, French dentist, founder of modern dentistry; described pyorrhea.

Finlay, Carlos Juan, 1833–1915, Cuban physician, first to suggest mosquitoes might be carriers of yellow fever.

Fleming, Alexander, 1881–1955, Scottish bacteriologist, discovered, 1928, penicillin.

Fleming, Lady Amalia, 1909–   , British bacteriologist, physician, civil libertarian.

Flourens, Marie J. P., 1794–1867, French physiologist, distinguished the three main parts of the brain.

Freud, Sigmund, 1856–1939, Austrian psychiatrist, founded, c. 1895, psychoanalysis.

Funk, Casimir, 1884–1967, Polish-American biochemist, discovered, 1912, the first vitamin.

Gaffky, Georg T. A., 1850–1918, German bacteriologist, proved, 1884, that *Bacillus typhosus,* discovered by Eberth, is cause of typhoid fever.

Galen, Claudius, c. A.D. 130–c. 200, Greco-Roman physician, systematized medical knowledge of his day; made first scientific dissections.

Goldberger, Joseph, 1874–1929, American public health physician, discovered, 1915, the cure for pellagra.

Golgi, Camillo, 1844–1926, Italian physician, established, 1870–1909, the science of neuroanatomy.

Good, Robert, 1922–   , American pediatrician; pioneer in fields of immunology and cancer research.

Gross, Robert E., 1905–   , performed, 1938, first surgery for congenital heart disease.

Hales, Stephen, 1677–1761, English physiologist and clergyman, first to demonstrate, c. 1705, blood pressure.

Haller, Albrecht von, 1708–77, Swiss physiologist and anatomist, established physiology as a branch of science.

Harvey, William, 1578–1657, English physician, discovered, 1628, the circulation of the blood.

Helmholtz, Hermann Ludwig Ferdinand von, 1821–94, German physicist and physiologist, invented, 1851, the modern type of ophthalmoscope.

Hench, Philip S., 1896–1965, American physician, introduced, 1949, the use of ACTH in the treatment of disease.

Herophilus, fl. 300 B.C., Egyptian-Greek physician and anatomist, distinguished sensory and motor nerves.

Hippocrates of Cos, c. B.C. 460–c. 370, Greek physician, "Father of Medicine," took medicine from the realm of superstition to that of disciplined observation.

Holmes, Oliver Wendell, 1809–94, American physician and author, recognized, 1843, contagious nature of puerperal fever and advocated antiseptic techniques.

Hunter, John, 1728–93, Scottish surgeon, raised surgery from a technical treatment mode to a branch of scientific medicine.

Ivanovski, Dmitri Iosifovich, 1864–1920, Russian botanist, discovered, 1892, filterable viruses, thus establishing virology.

Janssen, Zacharias, fl. late 16th–early 17th cent., Dutch spectacle maker, invented, c. 1590, the microscope.

Jenner, Edward, 1749–1823, English physician, introduced, 1796, the technique of vaccination against disease.

Kitasato, Shibasaburo, 1852–1931, Japanese bacteriologist, discovered, 1894, the bubonic plague bacillus.

Klebs, Edwin T. A., 1834–1913, German-American bacteriologist, discovered, 1875, pneumococcus, the bacillus causative of lobar pneumonia; discovered, 1883–84, the diphtheria causative bacillus.

Koch, Robert, 1843–1910, German bacteriologist, set forth criteria for establishing the etiology of a disease; introduced, 1877, staining of bacteria with aniline dyes; established, 1882, the identity of the tuberculosis causative cholera.

Laënnec, René T. H., 1781–1826, French physician, invented, 1816, the stethoscope.

Landsteiner, Karl, 1868–1943, Austrian-American pathologist, established, 1900, the basis for blood grouping; isolated, 1908, the poliomyelitis virus; discovered, 1940, the Rh factor.

Lister, Joseph, 1827–1912, English surgeon, introduced, 1865, antisepsis into surgical procedure.

Löffler, Friedrich A. J., 1852–1915, German pathologist, discovered, 1883–84, the diphtheria causative bacillus.

Long, Crawford Williamson, 1815–78, American surgeon, introduced, 1842, the use of ether in surgery.

Magnus-Levy, Adolf, 1865–1955, German physiologist, developed, 1893, the method for measuring the basal metabolic rate.

Malpighi, Marcello, 1628–94, Italian anatomist, discovered, 1661, that capillaries are vein-artery junctions.

Mesmer, Friedrich (or Franz) Anton, c. 1733–1815, Austrian physician, introduced, c. 1778, the use of hypnotism.

Metchnikoff, Élie, 1845–1916, Russian biologist, introduced theory of phagocytosis, i.e., the defensive nature of blood cells.

Minot, George Richards, 1885–1950, American physician, discovered, 1926, the liver extract treatment for anemia.

Morgan, Thomas Hunt, 1886–1945, American geneticist, discovered and demonstrated, c. 1907, the role of chromosomes in heredity.

Nitze, Max, 1848–1906, German surgeon and urologist, constructed, 1877, first cystoscope, with the aid of an instrument maker named Leiter.

Paracelsus (Theophrastus Bombastus von Hohenheim), c. 1493–1541, Swiss chemist, alchemist, and physician, established, 1526, chemotherapy.

Paré, Ambroise, 1510 or 1517–90, French surgeon, introduced modern surgery, including the tying-off of arteries to control bleeding.

Pasteur, Louis, 1822–95, French chemist and bacteriologist, discovered (1880–1885) methods for inoculation and vaccination against anthrax, rabies, and chicken cholera.

Perthes, Georg Clemens, 1869–1927, German surgeon, noted, 1903, effects of X rays on cancerous growths.

Piaget, Jean, 1896–1980, Swiss psychologist, explored cognitive growth in the child.

Plenciz, Marcus Antonius von, 1705–1786, Viennese physician, published, 1762, the germ theory of disease.

Pylarino, James, or Giacomo, 1659–1715, Italian physician, inoculated, 1701, three Turkish children with smallpox exudate in first attempt at immunization.

Reed, Walter, 1851–1902, American surgeon, studied the etiology of yellow fever and reported, 1901, that the disease was caused by a filterable virus transmitted by the mosquito.

Rhazes, or Rasis, c. A.D. 860–c. 925, Persian physician, first to differentiate, c. 910, measles and smallpox.

Roentgen, Wilhelm Conrad, 1845–1923, German physicist, discovered, 1895, X rays.

Roux, Pierre Paul Émile, 1853–1933, French physician and bacteriologist, with A. E. J. Yersin, demonstrated, 1888, that the diphtheria bacillus produces a toxin.

Rush, Benjamin, c. 1745–1813, American physician, established, 1786, first free dispensary in U.S.

Sabin, Albert Bruce, 1906–   , Russian-American bacteriologist, 1957, produced an oral vaccine for poliomyelitis.

Sakel, Manfred J., 1900–1957, Austro-American psychiatrist, introduced, 1929, insulin shock treatment.

Salk, Jonas Edward, 1914– , American virologist, introduced, 1954, hypodermic vaccine for poliomyelitis.

Sanctorius, 1561–1636, Italian physician, described, c. 1626, the first use of the clinical thermometer in the diagnosis of disease.

Schick, Bela, 1877–1967, Hungarian-American pediatrician, developed, 1913, a test for determining susceptibility to diphtheria.

Schleiden, Matthias Jakob, 1804–1881, German botanist, founded, 1838, cytology.

Schwann, Theodor, 1810–1882, German anatomist, founder, 1839, of cell theory as applied to animals.

Selye, Hans, 1907– , Canadian endocrinologist, explored stress and disease relationship.

Semmelweis, Ignaz P., 1818–65, Hungarian physician, obstetrician, independently identified, c. 1850, puerperal (childbed) fever as an infectious disease.

Servetus, Michael, 1511–1553, Spanish physician and theologian, described, 1546, pulmonary circulation.

Sherrington, Charles Scott, 1857–1952, English physiologist, established, 1906–1940, neurophysiology.

Spallanzani, Lazzaro, 1729–99, Italian naturalist, performed, 1768, experiments that led to the discrediting of the doctrine of spontaneous generation.

Steptoe, Patrick C., 1913– , British gynecologist, performed laboratory-conceived human birth (1978).

Swammerdam, Jan, 1637–80, Dutch naturalist, discovered, 1658, red blood cells.

Takamine, Jokichi, 1854–1922, Japanese chemist working in U.S., isolated, 1901, crystalline epinephrine (adrenalin), the first hormone known in pure form.

Taussig, Helen Brooke, 1898– , American physician, with Alfred Blalock, introduced, 1944, corrective heart surgery enabling survival of "blue babies."

Vesalius, Andreas, 1514–64, Flemish anatomist, published, 1543, first anatomical text based entirely on observation.

Virchow, Rudolf L. K., 1821–1902, German pathologist, founder, c. 1855, of cellular pathology.

Waksman, Selman Abraham, 1888–1973, Russian-American bacteriologist, discovered, 1943, streptomycin and its use in tuberculosis therapy.

Wassermann, August von, 1866–1925, German bacteriologist, developed, 1906, specific test for syphilis.

Wells, Horace, 1815–48, American dentist, first to use, 1844, nitrous oxide as an anesthetic in surgery.

Wiley, Harvey Washington, 1844–1930, American chemist, led fight for U.S. Pure Food Law of 1906.

Wundt, Wilhelm Max, 1832–1920, German psychologist, established, 1878, the first laboratory for experimental psychology, bringing mind into the realm of science.

Yersin, Alexandre Émile John, 1863–1943, French bacteriologist, discovered, 1888, the diphtheria toxin; discovered, 1894, *Pasteurella pestis*, the bubonic plague causative bacillus.

NOTABLES OF ART AND ARCHITECTURE

Aalto, Alvar (1898–1976), Finnish architect and designer.

Agam, Yaacov (1928–), Israel artist.

Agostino di Duccio (1418–1498), Florentine sculptor.

Albers, Josef (1888–1976), German-American painter.

Alberti, Leone B. (1404–72), Italian architect and painter.

Alma-Tadema, Sir Lawrence (1836–1912), English painter.

Angelico, Fra (c. 1400–55), Florentine painter.

Antonello da Messina (c. 1430–79), Italian painter.

Apelles (fl. 330 B.C.), Greek painter.

Apollodorus (fl. 430–400 B.C.), Athenian painter.

Archipenko, Alexander (1887–1964), Ukrainian-American sculptor.

Arp, Jean (1887–1966), French sculptor and painter.

Asplund, Erik Gunnar (1885–1940), Swedish architect.

Audubon, John J. (d. 1851), American artist.

Avery, Milton (1893–1965), American painter.

Bacon, Francis (1910–), English painter.

Baldovinetti, Alessio, (c. 1425–99), Florentine painter.

Barlach, Ernst (1870–1938), German sculptor.

Barthé, Richmond (1901–), American sculptor.

Bartolomeo, Fra (1475–1517), Italian painter.

Baskin, Leonard (1922–), American sculptor.

Baziotes, William (1912–63), American painter.

Bearden, Romare (1914–), American realistic painter.

Beardsley, Aubrey (1872–98), English illustrator.

Beckmann, Max (1884–1950), German painter.

Bellini, Giovanni (c. 1430–1516), Venetian painter.

Bellows, George W. (1882–1925), American painter.

Benjamin, Asher (1773–1845), American architect.

Benton, Thomas Hart (1889–1975), American painter.

Berlage, Hendrik P. (1856–1934), Dutch architect.

Bernini, Giovanni Lorenzo (1598–1680), Italian architect.

Bertola, Harry (1915–78), American sculptor and designer.

Beuys, Joseph (1921–), German artist.

Bierstadt, Albert (1830–1902), American Western painter.

Bingham, George Caleb (1811–79), American genre painter.

Boccioni, Umberto (1882–1916), Italian futurist painter.

Böcklin, Arnold (1827–1901), Swiss painter.

Bonheur, Rosa (1822–99), French painter.

Bonnard, Pierre (1867–1947), French painter.

Borromini, Francesco (1559–1677), Italian architect.

Bosch, Hieronymus (c. 1450–1516), Flemish painter.

Botero, Fernando (1932–), Colombian painter.

Botticelli, Sandro (c. 1444–1510), Florentine painter.

Boucher, François (1703–70), French painter.

Boudin, Eugène L. (1824–98), French painter.

Bouts, Dierick (c. 1420–75), Dutch painter.

Brady, Mathew B. (c. 1823–96), American photographer.

Bramante, Donato (1444–1514), Italian architect.

Brancusi, Constantin (1876–1957), Rumanian sculptor.

Braque, Georges (1882–1963), French painter.

Breuer, Marcel (1902–81), Hungarian-born American architect and designer.

Bronzino, Il (1503–72), Florentine mannerist painter.

Brouwer, Adriaen (c. 1606–38), Flemish painter.

Breugel Pieter, the elder (c. 1525–69), Flemish painter.

Brunelleschi, Filippo (1377–1446), Florentine architect.

Bulfinch, Charles (1763–1844), American architect.

Burchfield, Charles E. (1893–1967), American painter.

Burne-Jones, Sir Edward (1833–98), English painter.

Calder, Alexander (1898–1976), American sculptor.

Canaletto (1697–1768), Venetian painter.

Candela, Felix (1910–), Mexican architect.

Caravaggio, Michelangelo M. da (1573–1610), Italian painter.

Carracci, Annibale (1560–1609), Bolognese painter.

Carracci, Lodovico (1555–1619), Bolognese painter.

Cartier-Bresson, Henri (1908–), French photographer.

Cassatt, Mary (1845–1926), American painter.

Castagno, Andrea del (c. 1423–57), Florentine painter.

Catlin, George (1796–1872), American painter.

Cellini, Benvenuto (1500–71), Italian sculptor and metalsmith.

Cézanne, Paul (1839–1906), French painter.

Chagall, Marc (1889–), Russian painter.

Chardin, Jean Baptiste (1699–1779), French painter.

Chippendale, Thomas (1718–79), English cabinetmaker.

Chirico, Giorgio de (1888–1978), Italian painter.

Christo (1935–), Bulgarian-born American artist.

Cimabue, Giovanni (d. c. 1302), Florentine painter.

Claude Lorrain (1600–82), French landscape painter.

Cole, Thomas (1801–48), English-born American painter.

Constable, John (1776–1837), English painter.

Copley, John Singleton (1738–1815), American painter.

Cornelius, Peter von (1783–1867), German painter.

Corot, Jean B. C. (1796–1875), French landscape painter.

Correggio, Antonio (1494–1534), Italian painter.

Costa, Lucio (1902–), Brazilian architect.

Courbet, Gustave (1819–77), French painter.

Cox, Kenyon (1856–1919), American painter and critic.

Cranach, Lucas, the elder (1472–1553), German painter.

Currier, Nathaniel (1813–88), American printmaker.

Curry, John S. (1897–1946), American painter.

Dali, Salvador (1904–), Spanish surrealist painter.

Daubigny, Charles F. (1817–78), French landscape painter.

Daumier, Honoré (1808–79), French painter.

David, Gerard (c. 1460–1523), Flemish painter.

David, Jacques L. (1748–1825), French painter.

Davis, Stuart (1894–1964), American painter.

Decamps, Alexandre G. (1803–60), French painter.

Degas, Edgar (1834–1917), French painter and sculptor.

de Kooning, Willem (1904–), Dutch-born American painter.

Delacroix, Ferdinand V. E. (1798–1863), French painter.

Delaunay, Robert (1885–1941), French painter.

Della Robbia, Luca (c. 1400–82), Florentine sculptor.

Demuth, Charles (1883–1935), American watercolorist.

Derain, André (1880–1954), French painter.

Dine, Jim (1935–), American neosurrealist artist.

Dix, Otto (1891–1969), German painter and draughtsman.

Doesburg, Theo van (1883–1931), Dutch painter.

Donatello (c. 1386–1466), Italian sculptor.
Dongen, Kees van (1877–1968), Dutch painter.
Dou, Gerard (1613–75), Dutch painter.
Dubuffet, Jean (1901–), French painter.
Duccio di Buoninsegna (fl. 1278–1319), Italian painter.
Duchamp, Marcel (1887–1968), French painter.
Dufy, Raoul (1877–1953), French painter and illustrator.
Dürer, Albecht (1471–1528), German painter and engraver.
Eakins, Thomas (1844–1916), American painter.
Eiffel, Alexandre G. (1832–1923), French engineer.
Elisofon, Eliot (1911–73), American photographer.
Ensor, James (1860–1949), Belgian painter and etcher.
Epstein, Sir Jacob (1880–1959), American-born English sculptor.
Ernst, Max (1891–1976), German painter.
Evergood, Philip (1901–1973), American painter.
Eyck, Hubert van (c. 1370–1426), Flemish painter.
Eyck, Jan van (c. 1390–1441), Flemish painter.
Fabritius, Carel (1622–54), Dutch painter.
Feininger, Lyonel (1871–1956), American painter and illustrator.
Flagg, Ernest (1857–1947), American architect.
Flandrin, Hippolyte J. (1809–64), French painter.
Fouquet, Jean (c. 1420–1480), French painter.
Fragonard, Jean-Honoré (1732–1806), French painter.
Frasconi, Antonio (1919–), South American-born woodcut artist in U.S.
Friesz, Othon (1879–1949), French painter.
Fuller, George (1822–84), American painter.
Fuller, (Richard) Buckminster (1895–), American architect and engineer.
Fuseli, Henry (1741–1825), Anglo-Swiss painter and draughtsman.
Gabo, Naum (1890–1977), Russian sculptor and architect.
Gainsborough, Thomas (1727–88), English painter.
Gaudi i Cornet, Antonio (1852–1926), Spanish architect.
Gauguin, Paul (1848–1903), French painter.
Gentile da Fabriano (c. 1370–1427), Italian painter.
Gentileschi, Orazio (c. 1562–1647), Tuscan painter.
Gérard, François P. S., Baron (1770–1837), French painter.
Géricault, Jean Louis A. T. (1791–1824), French painter.
Gérôme, Jean Léon (1824–1904), French painter.
Ghiberti, Lorenzo (c. 1378–1455), Florentine sculptor.
Ghirlandaio, Domenico (1449–94), Florentine painter.
Giacometti, Alberto (1901–66), Swiss sculptor and painter.
Gilbert, Cass (1859–1934), American architect.
Giordano, Luca (1632–1705), Italian painter.
Giorgio, Francesco di (1439–1502), Italian architect, painter, and sculptor.
Giorgione (c. 1478–1510), Venetian painter.
Giotto (c. 1266–c. 1337), Florentine painter.
Giovanni di Paulo (c. 1403–83), Italian painter.
Glackens, William J. (1870–1938), American painter.
Gleizes, Albert L. (1881–1953), French cubist painter.
Goes, Hugo van der (d. 1482), Flemish painter.
Gogh, Vincent van (1853–90), Dutch postimpressionist painter.
Gorky, Arshile (1904–48), Armenian-born American painter.
Goya y Lucientes, Francisco José de (1746–1828), Spanish painter and etcher.
Goyen, Jan van (1596–1656), Dutch landscape painter.
Greco, El (c. 1541–1614), Cretan painter in Spain.
Greuze, Jean Baptiste (1725–1805), French painter.
Gris, Juan (1887–1927), Spanish cubist painter.
Grooms, Red (1937–), American painter.
Gropius, Walter (1883–1969), German-American architect.
Gropper, Wiliam (1897–1977), American painter and cartoonist.
Grosz, George (1893–1959), German-American caricaturist and painter.
Grunewald, Mathias (c. 1475–1528), German painter.
Guardi, Francesco (1712–93), Venetian painter.
Guston, Philip (1913–1980), Canadian-born American painter.
Hals, Franz (c. 1580–1666), Dutch portrait painter.
Hartley, Marsden (1877–1943), American painter.
Harunobu, Suzuki (1725–70), Japanese color-print artist.
Hassam, Childe (1859–1935), American painter and etcher.
Hennebique, François (1842–1921), French architect.
Henri, Robert (1865–1929), American painter.
Hicks, Edward (1780–1849), American painter.
Hilliard, Nicholas (1537–1619), English miniaturist.
Hobbema, Meindert (1638–1709), Dutch landscape painter.
Hockney, David (1937–), English painter.
Hodler, Ferdinand (1853–1918), Swiss painter.
Hofmann, Hans (1880–1966), German-American painter.

Hogarth, William (1697–1764), English painter, satirist, and engraver.
Hokusai, Katsushika (1760–1849), Japanese wood engraver.
Holbein, Hans, the younger (c. 1497–1543), German-Swiss painter.
Homer, Winslow (1836–1910), American painter.
Hooch, Pieter de (c. 1629–after 1677), Dutch painter.
Hopper, Edward (1882–1967), American painter.
Houdon, Jean A. (1741–1828), French neoclassic sculptor.
Indiana, Robert (1928–), American pop artist.
Ingrès, Jean A. D. (1780–1867), French painter.
Inman, Henry (1801–46), American painter.
Inness, George (1825–1894), American landscape painter.
Ives, James Merritt (1824–95), American printmaker.
Jackson, William H. (1843–1942), American artist and pioneer photographer.
Jacobsen, Arne (1902–1971), Danish architect.
Jenney, William Le Baron (1832–1907), American architect.
John, Augustus Edwin (1879–1961), British painter.
Johns, Jasper (1930–), American pop artist.
Johnson, Philip C. (1906–), American architect.
Jones, Inigo (1573–1652), English architect.
Jordaens, Jacob (1593–1678), Flemish baroque painter.
Kandinsky, Wassily (1866–1944), Russian abstract painter.
Kano Motonobu (c. 1476–1559), Japanese artist.
Kaufmann, Angelica (1741–1807), Swiss painter and etcher.
Kepes, György (1906–), Hungarian-born artist.
Kirchner, Ernst L. (1880–1938), German painter and graphic artist.
Kiyonaga (1752–1815), Japanese woodcut designer.
Klee, Paul (1879–1940), Swiss painter and graphic artist.
Klimt, Gustav (1862–1918), Austrian painter.
Kokoschka, Oskar (1886–1980), Austrian expressionist painter.
Kollwitz, Käthe S. (1867–1945), German graphic artist and sculptor.
Kuhn, Walt (1880–1949), American painter.
Kuniyoshi, Yasuo (c. 1892–1953), Japanese-born American painter.
Kupka, Frank (1871–1957), Czech painter and illustrator.
Lachaise, Gaston (1882–1935), French-born American sculptor.
La Farge, John (1835–1910), American painter.
Lancret, Nicolas (1690–1743), French rococo painter.
Landseer, Sir Edwin H. (1802–73), English animal painter.
La Tour, Georges de (1593–1652), French painter.
Lawrence, Jacob (1917–), American painter.
Lawrence, Sir Thomas (1769–1830), English portrait painter.
Le Corbusier (1887–1965), Swiss-born French architect.
Ledoux, Claude N. (1736–1806), French architect.
Léger, Fernand (1881–1955), French painter.
Lehmbruck, Wilhelm (1881–1919), German sculptor.
L'Enfant, Pierre C. (1754–1825), French-American architect and engineer.
Leonardo da Vinci (1452–1519), Italian painter, sculptor, and architect.
Lescaze, William (1896–1969), Swiss-born American architect.
Leutze, Emanuel (1816–68), German-American painter.
Levine, Jack (1915–), American painter.
Lichtenstein, Roy (1923–), American pop artist.
Lipchitz, Jacques (1891–1973), Lithuanian-born French sculptor.
Lippi, Fra Filippo (c. 1406–69), Italian painter.
Lippo, Filippino (c. 1457–1504), Italian painter.
Lippold, Richard (1915–), American sculptor and engineer.
Lochner, Stephan (d. 1451), German religious painter.
Lombardo, Pietro (c. 1435–1515), Venetian architect.
Lorenzetti, Ambrogio (d. c. 1348), Sienese painter.
Lucas van Leyden (1494–1533), Dutch painter and engraver.
Luini, Bernardino (c. 1480–1532), Italian painter.
Luks, George B. (1867–1933), American painter.
Lysippus (4th cent. B.C.), Greek sculptor.
Mabuse, Jan de (c. 1478–c. 1533), Flemish painter.
Macke, August (1887–1914), German painter.
McKim, Charles F. (1847–1909), American architect.
Magritte, René (1898–1967), Belgian surrealist painter.
Maillol, Aristide (1861–1944), French sculptor and painter.
Manet, Edouard (1832–83), French painter.
Mansart, François (1598–1666), French architect.
Mansart, Jules H. (1646–1708), French architect.
Mantegna, Andrea (1431–1506), Italian painter of the Paduan school.
Marc, Franz (1880–1916), German painter.
Marisol (1930–), Venezuelan-American sculptor.

Marsh, Reginald (1898–1954), French-born American painter.
Martini, Simone (c. 1283–1344), Sienese painter.
Masaccio (1401–c. 1428), Florentine painter.
Massys, Quentin (c. 1466–1530), Flemish painter.
Matisse, Henri (1869–1954), French painter and sculptor.
Maurer, Alfred H. (1868–1932), American painter.
Meissonier, Jean L. E. (1815–91), French military painter.
Memling, Hans (c. 1430–94), German-born Flemish painter.
Mendelsohn, Eric (1887–1953), German architect.
Mestrovic, Ivan (1883–1962), Yugoslav sculptor.
Michelangelo Buonarroti (1475–1564), Italian sculptor, painter, and architect.
Mies van der Rohe, Ludwig (1886–1969), German-American architect.
Millais, Sir John E. (1829–96), English painter.
Millet, Jean F. (1814–75), French painter.
Miró, Joan (1893–   ), Spanish surrealist painter.
Modigliani, Amadeo (1884–1920), Italian painter.
Mondrian, Piet (1872–1944), Dutch painter.
Monet, Claude (1840–1926), French impressionist painter.
Moore, Henry (1898–   ), English sculptor.
Moreau, Gustave (1826–98), French painter.
Morisot, Berthe (1841–95), French impressionist painter.
Moronobu, Hishikawa (c. 1618–c. 1694), Japanese painter.
Morris, William (1834–96), English artist, printer, and poet.
Morse, Samuel F. B. (1791–1872), American artist and inventor.
Moses, Grandma (Anna Mary R. Moses) (1860–1961), American primitive painter.
Motherwell, Robert (1915–   ), American painter.
Munch, Edvard (1863–1944), Norwegian painter.
Murillo, Bartholomé E. (c. 1617–82), Spanish painter.
Muybridge, Eadweard (1830–1904), English photographer.
Myron (5th cent. B.C.), Greek sculptor.
Nash, John (1752–1835), English architect.
Nash, Paul (1889–1946), English painter and wood engraver.
Neel, Alice (1900–   ), American painter.
Nervi, Pier Luigi (1891–1979), Italian architect.
Neutra, Richard (1892–1970), American architect.
Nevelson, Louise (1900–   ), Russian-born American sculptor.
Nicholson, Ben (1894–   ), English abstract painter.
Niemeyer, Oscar (1907–   ), Brazilian architect.
Noguchi, Isamu (1904–   ), American sculptor.
Noland, Kenneth (1924–   ), American color-field painter.
Nolde, Emil (1867–1956), German expressionist painter.
O'Keeffe, Georgia (1887–   ), American painter.
Oldenburg, Claes (1929–   ), Swedish-born American pop artist.
Olmsted, Frederick L. (1822–1903), American landscape architect.
Orley, Bernard van (c. 1491–1542), Flemish painter.
Orozco, José C. (1883–1949), Mexican mural painter.
Ostade, Adriaen van (1610–85), Dutch genre painter.
Palladio, Andrea (1508–80), Italian architect.
Parks, Gordon (1912–   ), American photographer.
Parmigiano (1503–40), Italian mannerist painter.
Parrhasius (fl. c. 400 B.C.), Greek painter.
Parrish, Maxfield (1870–1966), American illustrator.
Patinir, Joachim de (d. 1524), Flemish landscape and religious painter.
Paxton, Sir Joseph (1803–65), English architect.
Peale, Charles Willson (1741–1827), American painter.
Peale, James (1749–1831), American portrait painter.
Peale, Raphaelle (1774–1825), American portrait painter.
Peale, Rembrandt (1778–1860), American portrait painter.
Pearlstein, Philip (1924–   ), American realist painter.
Pechstein, Max (1881–1955), German expressionist painter.
Pei, I(eoh) M(ing) (1917–   ), Chinese-born American architect.
Perrault, Claude (1613–88), French architect.
Perugino (c. 1445–c. 1523), Umbrian painter.
Pevsner, Antoine (1886–1962), Russian sculptor and painter.
Phidias (c. 500–c. 432 B.C.), Greek sculptor.
Phyfe, Duncan (c. 1768–1854), Scottish-born cabinetmaker.
Picasso, Pablo (1881–1973), Spanish painter and sculptor in France.
Piero della Francesca (c. 1420–92), Italian painter.
Piero di Cosimo (1462–1521), Florentine painter.
Pinturicchio (c. 1454–1513), Umbrian painter.
Piranesi, Giovanni B. (1720–78), Italian architect.
Pisanello (c. 1395–c. 1455), Italian medalist and painter.
Pisano, Andrea (c. 1290–c. 1348), Italian sculptor.
Pisano, Giovanni (c. 1250–after 1314), Italian architect.

Pisano, Nicola (c. 1220–between 1278 and 1287), Italian sculptor.
Pissarro, Camille (1830–1903), French impressionist painter.
Pollaiuolo, Antonio (c. 1429–98), Florentine goldsmith, painter, sculptor, and engraver.
Pollock, Jackson (1912–56), American painter.
Polyclitus the elder (fl. c. 450–c. 420 B.C.), Greek sculptor.
Polygnotus (fl. c. 460–447 B.C.), Greek painter.
Poussin, Nicolas (1594–1665), French painter.
Praxiteles (fl. c. 370–c. 330 B.C.), Greek sculptor.
Prendergast, Maurice B. (1859–1924), American painter.
Primaticcio, Francesco (1504–70), Italian painter.
Prud'hon, Pierre Paul (1758–1823), French painter.
Puvis de Chavannes, Pierre (1824–98), French mural painter.
Pyle, Howard (1853–1911), American painter, illustrator and writer.
Quercia, Jacopo della (c. 1374–1438), Italian sculptor.
Raeburn, Sir Henry (1756–1823), Scottish portrait painter.
Raphael Santi (1483–1520), Italian Renaissance painter.
Rauschenberg, Robert (1925–   ), American pop artist.
Ray, Man (1890–1976), American painter and photographer.
Redon, Odilon (1840–1916), French painter.
Reinhardt, Ad (1913–67), American painter.
Rembrandt Harmenszoon van Rijn (1606–69), Dutch painter and etcher.
Remington, Frederic (1861–1909), American painter and sculptor.
Renoir, Pierre A. (1841–1919), French impressionist painter.
Reynolds, Sir Joshua (1723–92), English portrait painter.
Ribera, Jusepe (c. 1590–1652), Spanish baroque painter.
Rivera, Diego (1886–1957), Mexican muralist.
Rivers, Larry (1923–   ), American pop artist.
Rodin, Auguste (1840–1917), French sculptor.
Romney, George (1734–1802), English portrait painter.
Rosa, Salvator (1615–73), Italian baroque painter.
Rosenquist, James (1933–   ), American pop artist.
Roszak, Theodore (1907–81), American sculptor.
Rothko, Mark (1903–70), Russian-born American abstract expressionist painter.
Rouault, Georges (1871–1958), French painter.
Rousseau, Henri (1844–1910), French primitive painter.
Rubens, Peter Paul (1577–1640), Flemish painter.
Rudolph, Paul (1918–   ), American architect.
Ruisdael, Jacob van (c. 1628–82), Dutch painter and etcher.
Ryder, Albert P. (1847–1917), American painter.
Saarinen, Eero (1910–61), Finnish-American architect.
Saarinen, Eliel (1873–1950), Finnish-American architect.
Saint-Gaudens, Augustus (1848–1907), Irish-born American sculptor.
Samaras, Lucas (1936–   ), Greek collage artist.
Sargent, John Singer (1856–1925), American painter.
Sarto, Andrea del (1486–1531), Florentine painter.
Sassetta (c. 1400–1450), Sienese painter.
Schongauer, Martin (1430–1491), German engraver and painter.
Scopas (fl. 4th cent. B.C.), Greek sculptor.
Scorel, Jan van (1495–1562), Dutch painter.
Segal, George (1924–   ), American sculptor.
Seurat, Georges (1859–91), French neoimpressionist painter.
Shahn, Ben (1898–1969), American painter and graphic artist.
Signac, Paul (1863–1935), French neoimpressionist painter.
Signorelli, Luca (c. 1441–1523), Italian painter of the Umbrian school.
Siqueiros, David A. (1898–1974), Mexican muralist.
Sisley, Alfred (1839–99), French landscape painter.
Sloan, John (1871–1951), American painter and etcher.
Sloane, Eric (1910–   ), American landscape painter.
Sluter, Claus (d. 1406), Flemish sculptor.
Smith, David (1906–65), American sculptor.
Soleri, Paolo (1919–   ), Italian architect.
Soutine, Chaim (1894–1943), Russian-born French painter.
Steen, Jan (1626–79), Dutch genre painter.
Steichen, Edward (1879–1973), Luxembourg-born American photographer.
Stella, Joseph (1877–1946), Italian-born American painter.
Stieglitz, Alfred (1864–1946), American photographer.
Still, Clyfford (1904–   ), American painter.
Stone, Edward Durell (1902–78), American architect.
Stoss, Veit (c. 1445–1533), German sculptor.
Stuart, Gilbert (1755–1828), American portrait painter.
Stuart, James (1713–88), English architect and painter.
Sullivan, Louis Henry (1856–1924), American architect.

Sutherland, Graham (1903–80), English painter.
Tamayo, Rufino (1899–   ), Mexican painter.
Tange, Kenzo (1913–   ), Japanese architect.
Tanguy, Yves (1900–55), French surrealist painter.
Tchelitchew, Pavel (1898–1957), Russian-American painter.
Teniers, David, the younger (1610–90), Flemish genre painter.
Ter Borch, Gerard (1617–81), Dutch painter.
Terbrugghen, Hendrick (1588–1629), Dutch painter.
Thoma, Hans (1839–1924), German painter and lithographer.
Thorvaldsen, Albert B. (1770–1844), Danish sculptor.
Tiepolo, Giovanni B. (1696–1770), Venetian painter.
Tiffany, Louis C. (1848–1933), American artist and decorative designer.
Tinguely, Jean (1925–   ), Swiss sculptor.
Tintoretto (1518–94), Venetian painter.
Titian (c. 1490–1576), Venetian painter.
Toulouse-Lautrec, Henri de (1864–1901), French painter and lithographer.
Trumbull, John (1756–1843), American painter.
Tura, Cosmé (c. 1430–95), Italian painter.
Turner, Joseph M. W. (1775–1851), English landscape painter.
Uccello, Paolo (c. 1396–1475), Florentine painter.
Utamaro, Kitagawa (1753–1806), Japanese color-print artist.
Utrillo, Maurice (1883–1955), French painter.
Utzon, Joern (1918–   ), Danish architect.
Van Dyck, Sir Anthony (1599–1641), Flemish portrait painter.
Vasari, Giorgio (1511–74), Italian architect, painter, and writer.

Vaux, Calvert (1824–95), English-born American landscape architect.
Velázquez, Diego R. de S. y (1599–1660), Spanish painter.
Velde, Henri van de (1863–1957), Belgian designer and architect.
Vermeer, Jan (1632–75), Dutch genre and landscape painter.
Veronese, Paolo (1528–88), Italian painter.
Verrocchio, Andrea del (1435–88), Florentine sculptor.
Vigée-Lebrun, Elisabeth (1755–1842), French painter.
Vignola, Giacomo da (1507–73), Italian architect.
Viollet-le-Duc, Eugène E. (1814–79), French architect.
Vlaminck, Maurice de (1876–1958), French painter.
Vos, Cornelis de (1584–1651), Flemish painter.
Vuillard, Edouard (1868–1940), French painter.
Warhol, Andy (1927?–   ), American pop artist.
Watteau, Antoine (1684–1721), French painter.
Wedgwood, Josiah (1730–95), English potter.
Wesselmann, Tom (1931–   ), American pop artist.
West, Benjamin (1738–1820), American historical painter.
Westermann, H. C. (1922–   ), American pop sculptor.
Weyden, Roger van der (c. 1400–64), Flemish painter.
Whistler, James A. McN. (1834–1903), American painter and etcher.
White, Stanford (c. 1853–1906), American architect.
Witz, Conrad (fl. c. 1434–c. 1447), German painter.
Wood, Grant (1891–1942), American painter.
Wren, Sir Christopher (1632–1723), English architect.
Wright, Frank Lloyd (1869–1959), American architect.
Wyeth, Andrew N. (1917–   ), American painter.
Wyeth, Newell Convers (1882–1945), American painter and illustrator.
Zorach, William (1887–1966), Lithuanian-born American sculptor.

NOVELISTS, DRAMATISTS, POETS, AND OTHER WRITERS

Adams, Henry (1838–1918), American biographer, historian, and novelist.
Addison, Joseph (1672–1719), English essayist and poet.
Aeschylus (525–456 B.C.), Athenian tragedian.
Aesop (c. 620–c. 560 B.C.), Greek fabulist.
Agee, James (1909–55), American essayist and journalist.
Agnon (b. Czaczkes), Shmuel Y. (1888–1970), Polish-born Israeli novelist.
Aiken, Conrad (1889–1973), American novelist and poet.
Alarcón, Pedro Antonio de (1833–91), Spanish novelist.
Albee, Edward (1928–   ), American dramatist.
Alcott, Louisa May (1832–88), American novelist.
Aldington, Richard (1892–1962), English poet and novelist.
Aleichem, Sholom (Solomon Rabinowitz) (1859–1916), Russian-born Yiddish writer.
Algren, Nelson (1909–81), American novelist.
Amado, Jorge (1912–   ), Brazilian novelist.
Ambler, Eric (1909–   ), English suspense novelist.
Amis, Kingsley (1922–   ), English novelist.
Andersen, Hans Christian (1805–75), Danish poet and fairy tale writer.
Anderson, Maxwell (1888–1959), American dramatist.
Anderson, Robert (1917–   ), American dramatist.
Anderson, Sherwood (1876–1941), American novelist.
Andreyev, Leonid (1871–1919), Russian writer.
Andric, Ivo (1892–1975), Yugoslav novelist.
Angelou, Maya (1928–   ), American writer.
Anouilh, Jean (1910–   ), French dramatist.
Apollinaire, Guillaume (1880–1918), French poet.
Apuleius, Lucius (fl. 2d cent. A.D.), Latin romance writer.
Aragon, Louis (1897–   ), French novelist and poet.
Arden, John (1930–   ), English dramatist.
Ariosto, Ludovico (1474–1533), Italian epic and lyric poet.
Aristophanes (c. 448–after 388 B.C.), Athenian comic poet.
Arnold, Matthew (1822–88), English poet and critic.
Arrabel (Terán), Fernando (1932–   ), Spanish dramatist.
Asch, Sholem (1880–1957), Polish-born Yiddish novelist.
Auchincloss, Louis (1917–   ), American novelist.
Auden, W(ystan) H(ugh) (1907–73), Anglo-American poet.
Austen, Jane (1775–1817), English novelist.
Ayckbourn, Alan (1939–   ), English playwright.
Azuela, Mariano (1873–1952), Mexican novelist.
Bacon, Francis (1561–1626), English essayist.
Bagnold, Enid (1889–1981), English dramatist and novelist.
Baldwin, James (1924–   ), American novelist and essayist.
Balzac, Honoré de (1799–1850), French novelist.
Barrie, Sir James M. (1860–1937), British playwright.
Barth, John (1930–   ), American novelist.
Baudelaire, Charles (1821–67), French poet and critic.

Beaumarchais, Pierre A. C. de (1732–99), French dramatist.
Beaumont, Francis (c. 1584–1616), English dramatist.
Beauvoir, Simone de (1908–   ), French novelist and essayist.
Beckett, Samuel (1906–   ), Irish-French dramatist.
Bede (c. 673–735 A.D.), Old English historian.
Beerbohm, Sir Max (1872–1956), English parodist.
Behan, Brendan (1923–64), Irish dramatist.
Behn, Aphra (1640–89), English novelist and dramatist.
Behrman, S. N. (1893–1973), American playwright.
Belloc, Hilaire (1870–1953), British poet, essayist, satirist, and historian.
Bellow, Saul (1915–   ), Canadian-American novelist.
Benchley, Robert (1889–1945), American humorist.
Benét, Stephen Vincent (1898–1943), American poet, novelist, and short story writer.
Bennett, Arnold (1867–1931), English novelist.
Bernstein, Carl (1944–   ), American journalist and author.
Berryman, John (1914–72), American poet.
Betjeman, John (1906–   ), English poet.
Betti, Ugo (1892–1953), Italian poet and dramatist.
Bierce, Ambrose (1842–1914?), American short story writer and journalist.
Bishop, Elizabeth (1911–79), American poet.
Bjornson, Bjornstjerne (1832–1910), Norwegian novelist.
Blackmur, R(ichard) P. (1904–65), American critic and poet.
Blake, William (1757–1827), English poet.
Blasco-Ibáñez, Vicente (1867–1928), Spanish novelist.
Boccaccio, Giovanni (1313–75), Italian poet and storyteller.
Bodenheim, Maxwell (1893–1954), American poet.
Bogan, Louise (1897–1970), American poet.
Boileau-Despréaux, Nicolas (1636–1711), French literary critic and poet.
Böll, Heinrich (1917–   ), German novelist.
Bolt, Robert (1924–   ), English dramatist.
Borges, Jorge Luis (1899–   ), Argentine poet.
Boswell, James (1740–95), Scottish biographer and diarist.
Bowen, Elizabeth (1899–1973), Anglo-Irish novelist.
Bowles, Paul (1910–   ), American novelist.
Boyle, Kay (1903–   ), American novelist.
Bradbury, Ray (1920–   ), American science fiction writer.
Braine, John (1922–   ), English novelist.
Brecht, Bertolt (1898–1956), German dramatist and poet.
Breton, André (1896–1966), French surrealist writer.
Bridges, Robert (1844–1930), English poet.
Brontë, Charlotte (1816–55), English novelist.
Brontë, Emily (1818–48), English novelist.
Brooke, Rupert (1887–1915), English poet.
Brooks, Van Wyck (1886–1963), American critic.

Brophy, Brigid (1929–　), English novelist and critic.
Brown, John Mason (1900–69), American critic and biographer.
Browne, Sir Thomas (1605–82), English author and physician.
Browning, Elizabeth Barrett (1806–61), English poet.
Browning, Robert (1812–89), English poet.
Bryant, William Cullen (1794–1878), American poet.
Buchan, John (1875–1940), British novelist and historian.
Bullins, Ed (1935–　), American dramatist.
Bunin, Ivan (1870–1953), Russian novelist.
Bunyan, John (1628–88), English allegorist.
Burgess, Anthony (1917–　), English novelist and critic.
Burns, Robert (1759–96), Scottish poet.
Burroughs, Edgar Rice (1875–1950), American novelist.
Burroughs, William (1914–　), American novelist.
Butler, Samuel (1835–1902), English novelist and essayist.
Byron, Lord (George Gordon) (1788–1824), English poet.
Cabell, James Branch (1879–1958), American novelist.
Caedmon (fl. 670 A.D.), Old English poet.
Calderón de la Barca, Pedro (1600–81), Spanish dramatist.
Calisher, Hortense (1911–　), American novelist.
Callimachus (fl. c. 265 B.C.), Greek poet and critic.
Camoes, Luis de (1524?–80), Portuguese poet.
Camus, Albert (1913–60), French essayist, novelist, and dramatist.
Capek, Karel (1890–1938), Czech playwright.
Capote, Truman (1924–　), American novelist.
Carew, Thomas (c. 1595–c. 1639), English poet.
Carlino, Lewis John (1932–　), American dramatist.
Carlyle, Thomas (1795–1881), Anglo-Scottish essayist, critic, translator, and historian.
Carroll, Lewis (Charles Lutwidge Dodgson) (1832–98), English novelist.
Cary, Joyce (1888–1957), English novelist.
Cassill, R(onald) V(erlin) (1919–　), American novelist, short story writer, and essayist.
Castiglione, Baldassare (1478–1529), Italian social critic.
Cather, Willa (1876–1947), American novelist.
Catton, Bruce (1899–1978), American historian.
Catullus, Caius Valerius (c. 84 B.C.–c. 54 B.C.), Roman poet.
Céline, Louis Ferdinand (1894–1961), French novelist.
Cervantes Saavedra, Miguel de (1547–1616), Spanish novelist.
Chandler, Raymond (1888–1959), American detective story writer.
Chateaubriand, François R. (1768–1848), French novelist.
Chaucer, Geoffrey (c. 1340–1400), English poet.
Chayefsky, Paddy (1923–81), American dramatist.
Cheever, John (1912–　), American novelist and short story writer.
Chekhov, Anton (1860–1904), Russian dramatist.
Chesterton, G(ilbert) K(eith) (1874–1936), English novelist, poet, biographer, and essayist.
Christie, Agatha (1891–1976), English mystery writer.
Ciardi, John (1916–　), American poet and critic.
Cicero, Marcus Tullius (106–43 B.C.), Roman essayist.
Claudel, Paul (1868–1955), French poet and dramatist.
Cocteau, Jean (1889?–1963). French novelist and filmmaker.
Coleridge, Samuel Taylor (1772–1834), English poet.
Colette (Sidonie Gabrielle Collette) (1873–1954), French novelist.
Collins, Wilkie (1824–89), English novelist.
Collins, William (1721–59), English poet.
Colum, Padraic (1881–1972), Irish-American poet, dramatist, and novelist.
Compton-Burnett, Ivy (1892–1969), English novelist.
Congreve, William (1670–1729), English dramatist.
Connolly, Cyril (1903–74), English critic and editor.
Conrad, Joseph (1857–1924), Polish-born English novelist.
Cooper, James Fenimore (1789–1851), American novelist.
Corneille, Pierre (1606–84), French dramatist.
Coward, Sir Noël (1899–1973), English dramatist, composer, lyricist, and autobiographer.
Cowley, Abraham (1618–67), English poet.
Cowper, William (1731–1800), English poet.
Cozzens, James Gould (1903–78), American novelist.
Crabbe, George (1754–1832), English poet.
Crane, Hart (1899–1932), American poet.
Crane, Stephen (1871–1900), American novelist.
Crashaw, Richard (c. 1612–49), English poet.
cummings, e. e. (1894–1962), American poet.
Cunha, Euclides da (1866–1909), Brazilian writer.
Cynewulf (fl. c. early 9th cent.), Old English poet.
D'Annunzio, Gabriele (1863–1938), Italian poet.

Dante (Alighieri) (1265–1321), Italian poet.
Daudet, Alphonse (1840–97), French novelist, poet, and short story writer.
Day Lewis, C(ecil) (1904–72), Anglo-Irish poet.
Defoe, Daniel (c. 1660–1731), English novelist.
Delaney, Shelagh (1939–　), English dramatist.
De la Mare, Walter (1873–1956), English novelist and poet.
De la Roche, Mazo (1885–1961), Canadian novelist.
Demosthenes (c. 384–322 B.C.), Greek orator.
De Quincey, Thomas (1785–1859), English essayist.
De Vries, Peter (1910–　), American novelist.
Dickens, Charles (1812–70), English novelist.
Dickey, James (1923–　), American poet and critic.
Dickinson, Emily (1830–86), American poet.
Diderot, Denis (1713–84), French encyclopedist, novelist, dramatist, satirist, and critic.
Didion, Joan (1934–　), American novelist.
Dinesen, Isak (Karen Blixen) (1885–1962), Danish writer.
Donleavy, J(ames) P(atrick) (1926–　), American-born, Irish novelist.
Donne, John (1572–1631), English poet and essayist.
Doolittle, Hilda ("H.D.") (1886–1961), American poet.
Dos Passos, John (1896–1970), American novelist.
Dostoyevsky, Feodor (1821–81), Russian novelist.
Doyle, Sir Arthur Conan (1859–1930), English detective story and romance writer.
Drabble, Margaret (1939–　), British writer.
Dreiser, Theodore (1871–1945), American novelist.
Drexler, Rosalyn (1926–　), American dramatist.
Dryden, John (1631–1700), English poet and dramatist.
Dumas, Alexandre (fils) (1824–95), French dramatist.
Dumas, Alexandre (père) (1802–70), French novelist and dramatist.
Duras, Marguerite (1914–　), French novelist.
Durrell, Lawrence (1912–　), British novelist and poet.
Durrenmatt, Friedrich (1921–　), Swiss dramatist.
Eberhart, Richard (1904–　), American poet.
Ehrenburg, Ilya (1891–1967), Russian novelist.
Eliot, George (Mary Ann Evans) (1819–80), English novelist.
Eliot, T(homas) S(tearns) (1888–1965), American-born British poet, dramatist, and critic.
Ellison, Ralph (1914–　), American novelist.
Elytis, Odysseus (1911–　), Greek poet.
Emerson, Ralph Waldo (1803–82), American essayist and poet.
Erasmus, Desiderius (c. 1466–1536), Dutch humanist.
Euripides (c. 480–406 B.C.), Greek tragic poet.
Farrell, James T. (1904–79), American novelist.
Faulkner, William (1897–1962), American novelist.
Feuchtwanger, Lion (1884–1958), German novelist.
Fielding, Henry (1707–54), English novelist.
FitzGerald, Edward (1809–83), English translator.
Fitzgerald, F. Scott (1896–1940), American novelist.
Flaubert, Gustave (1821–80), French novelist.
Fleming, Ian (1908–64), English secret agent novelist.
Fletcher, John (1579–1625), English dramatist.
Ford, Ford Madox (Ford Madox Hueffer) (1873–1939), English poet, novelist, critic, and essayist.
Ford, John (1586–c. 1640), English dramatist.
Forster, E(dward) M(organ) (1879–1970), English novelist.
Foster, Paul (1931–　), American dramatist.
France, Anatole (Jacques Anatole Thibault) (1844–1924), French novelist and satirist.
Friedman, Bruce Jay (1930–　), American novelist.
Friel, Brian (1929–　), Irish dramatist.
Frisch, Max (1911–　), Swiss dramatist.
Froissart, Jean (c. 1337–1410?), French chronicler.
Frost, Robert (1874–1963), American poet.
Fry, Christopher (1907–　), English dramatist.
Fuentes, Carlos (1928–　), Mexican short story writer.
Galsworthy, John (1867–1933), English novelist.
Garcia Lorca, Federico (1898–1936), Spanish poet.
García Márquez, Gabriel José (1928–　), Colombian writer.
Gardner, Erle Stanley (1889–1970), American detective story writer.
Garland, Hamlin (1860–1940), American novelist.
Gaskell, Elizabeth (1810–65), English novelist and biographer.
Gay, John (1685–1732), English playwright and poet.
Gelber, Jack (1932–　), American dramatist.
Genet, Jean (1910–　), French novelist and dramatist.
George, Stefan (1868–1933), German poet.
Ghelderode, Michel de (1898–1962), Belgian dramatist.
Gibbon, Edward (1737–94), English historian.
Gide, André (1869–1951), French novelist.
Gilroy, Frank D. (1925–　), American dramatist.

Ginsberg, Allen (1926–), American poet.
Giraudoux, Jean (1882–1944), French dramatist.
Gissing, George (1857–1903), English novelist.
Glasgow, Ellen (1873–1945), American novelist.
Godwin, William (1756–1836), English novelist and political philosopher.
Goethe, Johann Wolfgang von (1749–1832), German novelist.
Gogol, Nikolai (1809–52), Russian novelist.
Golding, William (1911–), English novelist.
Goldman, James (1927–), American dramatist.
Goldoni, Carlo (1707–93), Italian dramatist.
Goldsmith, Oliver (1730?–74), English essayist and dramatist.
Goodman, Paul (1911–1972), American writer and pacifist.
Gordimer, Nadine (1923–), South African novelist.
Gorey, Edward (1925–), American writer and artist.
Gorki, Maxim (Aleksey Maximovich Pyeshkov) (1868–1936), Russian novelist, dramatist, and short story writer.
Grass, Günter (1927–), German novelist.
Graves, Robert (1895–), English poet and novelist.
Gray, Thomas (1716–71), English poet.
Greene, Graham (1904–), English novelist.
Gregory, Lady Augusta (1859–1932), Irish dramatist.
Grimm, Jakob (1785–1863), German folklorist.
Grimm, Wilhelm (1786–1859), German folklorist.
Hafiz (Shams-ud-Din-Mohammed) (d. 1389?), Persian poet.
Haley, Alex (1921–), American historian.
Hammett, Dashiell (1894–1961), American novelist.
Hamsun, Knut (1859–1952), Norwegian novelist.
Hansberry, Lorraine (1930–65), American dramatist.
Hardy, Thomas (1840–1928), English novelist.
Harris, Joel Chandler (1848–1908), American short story writer.
Harte, Bret (1836–1902), American short story writer.
Hauptmann, Gerhart (1862–1946), German dramatist, novelist, and poet.
Hawthorne, Nathaniel (1804–64), American novelist.
Hazlitt, William (1778–1830), English essayist.
Hecht, Ben (1894–1964), American journalist and author.
Heine, Heinrich (1797–1856), German poet.
Heller, Joseph (1923–), American novelist.
Hellman, Lillian (1905–), American dramatist and author.
Hemingway, Ernest (1899–1961), American novelist.
Henry, O. (William Sydney Porter) (1862–1910), American short story writer.
Herbert, George (1593–1633), English poet.
Herder, Johann G. von (1744–1803), German poet.
Herodotus (c. 484–c. 425 B.C.), Greek historian.
Herrick, Robert (1591–1674), English poet.
Hersey, John (1914–), American novelist and journalist.
Hesiod (fl. c. 8th cent. B.C.), Greek poet.
Hesse, Hermann (1877–1962), German novelist.
Heyward, DuBose (1885–1940), American novelist.
Heywood, Thomas (1574?–1641), English dramatist.
Hochhuth, Rolf (1931–), German dramatist.
Hoffmann, E(rnst) T(heodor) A(madeus) (1776–1822), German novelist and short story writer.
Hölderlin, Johann C. F. (1770–1843), German poet.
Homer (before 700 B.C.), Greek epic poet.
Hopkins, Gerard Manley (1844–89), English poet.
Horace (65 B.C.–8 B.C.), Latin poet.
Horovitz, Israel (1939–), American dramatist.
Housman, A. E. (1859–1936), English poet.
Howard, Sidney (1891–1939), American dramatist.
Howe, Irving (1920–), American historian and critic.
Hughes, Langston (1902–67), American poet.
Hugo, Victor (1802–85), French novelist.
Huxley, Aldous (1894–1963), English novelist and essayist.
Huxtable, Ada Louise (1921–), American journalist and architecture critic.
Ibsen, Henrik (1828–1906), Norwegian dramatist.
Inge, William (1913–73), American dramatist.
Ionesco, Eugène (1912–), French dramatist.
Irving, John (1942–), American novelist.
Irving, Washington (1783–1859), American short story writer, historian, and biographer.
Isherwood, Christopher (1904–), Anglo-American novelist and dramatist.
Jackson, Shirley (1919–65), American novelist.
James, Henry (1843–1916), American novelist.
James, P(hyllis) D(orothy) (1920–), English mystery writer.
Jarrell, Randall (1914–65), American poet and novelist.
Jeffers, Robinson (1887–1962), American poet.

Jellicoe, Ann (1927–), English dramatist and director.
Jewett, Sarah Orne (1849–1909), American novelist.
Johnson, Samuel (1709–84), English critic, essayist, lexicographer, poet, and biographer.
Jones, James (1921–77), American novelist.
Jones, LeRoi (Imamu Baraka) (1934–), American dramatist.
Jonson, Ben (1572–1637), English dramatist and poet.
Joyce, James (1882–1941), Irish novelist.
Juvenal (1st–2d cent. A.D.), Roman satirical poet.
Kafka, Franz (1883–1924), German novelist.
Kawabata, Yasunari (1899–1972) Japanese novelist.
Kazantzakis, Nikos (c. 1883–1957), Greek novelist.
Keats, John (1795–1821), English poet.
Keller, Gottfried (1819–90), Swiss novelist.
Kempton, J. Murray (1918–), American journalist.
Kennedy, Adrienne (1932–), American dramatist.
Kerouac, Jack (1922–69), American novelist.
Kesey, Ken (1935–), American novelist.
Kingsley, Charles (1819–75), English novelist.
Kingsley, Sidney (1906–), American playwright.
Kipling, Rudyard (1865–1936), British poet and novelist.
Kleist, Heinrich von (1777–1811), German dramatic poet.
Knowles, John (1926–), American novelist.
Koestler, Arthur (1905–), Hungarian-born English novelist and essayist.
Kopit, Arthur (1937–), American dramatist.
Kyd, Thomas (1558–94), English dramatist.
La Fontaine, Jean de (1621–95), French fabulist and poet.
Lagerkvist, Pär (1891–1974), Swedish novelist.
Lagerlof, Selma (1858–1940), Swedish novelist.
Lamartine, Alphonse (1790–1869), French poet.
Lamb, Charles (1775–1834), English essayist.
Langland, William (c. 1332–c. 1440), English poet.
Lanier, Sidney (1842–81), American poet.
Lardner, Ring (1885–1933), American short story writer.
La Rochefoucauld, François, duc de (1613–80), French classical writer, maximist, and epigrammatist.
Lash, Joseph (1909–), American biographer.
Lawrence, D(avid) H(erbert) (1885–1930), English novelist.
Laxness, Halldor (1902–), Icelandic novelist.
Lear, Edward (1812–88), English humorist.
Leavis, F(rank) R(aymond) (1895–1978), English critic.
Le Carré, John (David J. M. Cornwell) (1931–), English spy novelist.
Lee, Robert E. (1918–), American playwright.
Leopardi, Giacomo (1798–1837), Italian poet.
Lermontov, Mikhail Y. (1814–41), Russian novelist.
Lessing, Doris (1919–), English novelist.
Lessing, Gotthold E. (1729–81), German dramatist.
Lewis, C(live) S(taples) (1898–1963), Anglo-Irish critic, spiritual writer, and novelist.
Lewis, Sinclair (1885–1951), American novelist.
Lewis, Wyndham (1886–1957), English novelist.
Lind, Jakov (1927–), Anglo-Austrian novelist.
Lindsay, Vachel (1879–1931), American poet.
Livy (59 B.C.–17 A.D.), Roman historian.
London, Jack (1876–1916), American novelist.
Longfellow, Henry Wadsworth (1807–82), American poet.
Lope de Vega Carpio, Félix (1562–1635), Spanish poet.
Lord, Walter (1917–), American historical novelist.
Lovelace, Richard (1618–57?), English poet.
Lowell, Amy (1874–1925), American poet and critic.
Lowell, James Russell (1819–91), American poet.
Lowell, Robert (1917–77), American poet and translator.
Lucian (c. 125–after 180), Greek satirist.
Lucretius (c. 99–c. 55 B.C.), Roman poet.
Macaulay, Thomas Babington (1800–59), English historian, essayist, and critic.
McCarthy, Mary (1912–), American novelist and literary critic.
McCullers, Carson (1917–67), American novelist.
Machiavelli, Niccolò (1469–1527), Italian political essayist.
MacLeish, Archibald (1892–), American poet.
McNally, Terrence (1939–), American dramatist.
Maeterlinck, Maurice (1862–1949), Belgian dramatist.
Mailer, Norman (1923–), American novelist and essayist.
Malamud, Bernard (1914–), American novelist.
Mallarmé, Stéphane (1842–98), French poet.
Malory, Sir Thomas (d. 1471), English Arthurian romance writer.
Malraux, André (1901–76), French man of letters.
Mann, Heinrich (1871–1950), German novelist.
Mann, Thomas (1875–1955), German novelist.
Mansfield, Katherine (1888–1923), British short story writer.
Manzoni, Alessandro (1785–1873), Italian novelist.

Marcus, Frank (1928–), English dramatist.
Marlowe, Christopher (1564–93), English dramatist.
Marquand, John P. (1893–1960), American novelist.
Marsh, Ngaio (1899–), New Zealand detective story writer.
Martial (c. 40–c. 104 A.D.), Roman epigrammatic poet.
Marvell, Andrew (1621–78), English poet.
Masefield, John (1878–1967), English poet.
Masters, Edgar Lee (1869–1950), American poet and biographer.
Maugham, W(illiam) Somerset (1874–1965), English novelist.
Maupassant, Guy de (1850–93), French novelist and short story writer.
Mauriac, François (1885–1970), French novelist.
Maurois, André (1885–1967), French biographer.
Melville, Herman (1819–91), American novelist.
Menander (c. 342 B.C.–c. 291 B.C.), Greek dramatist.
Mencken, H(enry) L(ouis) (1880–1956), American satirist, editor, critic, and philologist.
Meredith, George (1828–1909), English novelist and poet.
Mérimée, Prosper (1803–70), French novelist, dramatist, and poet.
Merrill, James (1926–), American poet.
Michener, James (1907–), American novelist.
Millay, Edna St. Vincent (1892–1950), American poet.
Miller, Arthur (1915–), American dramatist.
Miller, Henry (1891–1980), American novelist.
Milne, A(lan) A(lexander) (1882–1956), English poet, dramatist, and children's author.
Milton, John (1608–74), English poet.
Mistral, Frédéric (1830–1914), French Provençal poet.
Mistral, Gabriela (1889–1957), Chilean poet.
Molière, Jean Baptiste (Jean Baptiste Poquelin) (1622–73), French dramatist.
Molnar, Ferenc (1878–1952), Hungarian dramatist.
Montaigne, Michel Eyquem de (1533–92), French essayist.
Moore, George (1852–1933), Irish novelist.
Moore, Marianne (1887–1972), American poet.
Moore, Thomas (1779–1852), Irish poet.
Moravia, Alberto (1907–), Italian novelist.
More, Sir Thomas (1478–1535), English humanist.
Morison, Samuel Eliot (1887–1976), American historian.
Morley, Christopher (1890–1957), American novelist.
Morris, William (1834–96), English poet.
Murdoch, Iris (1919–), British novelist.
Musset, Alfred de (1810–57), French dramatist and poet.
Nabokov, Vladimir (1899–1977), Russian-American novelist.
Naipaul, V.S. (1932–), West Indian novelist.
Neruda, Pablo (1904–73), Chilean poet.
Nerval, Gérard de (Gérard Labrunie) (1808–55), French poet, translator, and short story writer.
Nevins, Allan (1890–1971), American historian.
Norris, Frank (1870–1902), American novelist.
Novalis (Friedrich von Hardenberg) (1772–1801), German poet.
Oates, Joyce Carol (1938–), American novelist.
O'Casey, Sean (1884–1964), Irish dramatist.
O'Connor, Flannery (1925–64), American novelist and short story writer.
O'Connor, Frank (Michael O'Donovan) (1903–66), Irish short story writer.
Odets, Clifford (1906–63), American dramatist.
O'Faoláin, Seán (1900–), Irish novelist.
O'Flaherty, Liam (1897–), Irish novelist.
O'Hara, John (1905–70), American novelist.
Omar Khayyam (fl. 11th cent.), Persian poet.
O'Neill, Eugene (1888–1953), American dramatist.
Orwell, George (Eric Blair) (1903–50), British novelist and essayist.
Osborne, John (1929–), English dramatist.
Ovid (43 B.C.–18 A.D.), Latin poet.
Parker, Dorothy (1893–1967), American poet, short story writer, satirist, and critic.
Pasternak, Boris (1890–1960), Russian poet and novelist.
Pater, Walter (1839–94), English essayist and critic.
Paton, Alan (1903–), South African novelist.
Pavese, Cesare (1908–50), Italian novelist.
Peacock, Thomas Love (1785–1866), English novelist.
Pepys, Samuel (1633–1703), English diarist.
Perelman, S(idney) J(oseph) (1904–79), American humorist.
Perse, St. John (Alexis St. Léger) (1887–1975), French poet.
Petrarch (1304–74), Italian poet and humanist.
Petronius (d. c. 66 A.D.), Roman satirist.
Peyrefitte, Roger (1907–), French novelist.
Pindar (c. 518–438 B.C.), Greek lyric poet.
Pinero, Sir Arthur Wing (1855–1934), English dramatist.

Pinter, Harold (1930–), English dramatist.
Pirandello, Luigi (1867–1936), Italian dramatist.
Plath, Sylvia (1932–63), American poet and novelist.
Plautus (c. 254 B.C.–184 B.C.), Roman comic poet.
Plutarch (c. 46–c. 120 A.D.), Greek biographer.
Poe, Edgar Allan (1809–49), American poet, short story writer, and critic.
Pope, Alexander (1688–1744), English poet.
Porter, Katherine Anne (1890–1980), American short story writer and novelist.
Pound, Ezra (1885–1972), American poet and critic.
Powell, Anthony (1905–), English novelist.
Priestley, J(ohn) B(oynton) (1894–), English novelist, dramatist, and critic.
Pritchett, V(ictor) S(awdon) (1900–), English novelist and critic.
Proust, Marcel (1871–1922), French novelist.
Purdy, James (1923–), American novelist.
Pushkin, Aleksandr (1799–1837), Russian poet.
Queneau, Raymond (1903–), French novelist.
Quintilian (c. 35–95 A.D.), Roman rhetorician.
Rabe, David (1940–), American playwright.
Rabelais, François (c. 1490–1553), French satirist.
Racine, Jean (1639–99), French dramatist.
Ransom, John Crowe (1888–1974), American poet and critic.
Rattigan, Terence (1911–77), English dramatist.
Remarque, Erich Maria (1897–1970), German-American novelist.
Reston, James (1909–), Scottish-American journalist.
Rexroth, Kenneth (1905–), American poet and critic.
Rice, Elmer (1892–1967), American dramatist.
Richards, I. A. (1893–1979), British poet and critic.
Richardson, Jack (1935–), American dramatist.
Richardson, Samuel (1689–1761), English novelist.
Richler, Mordecai (1931–), Canadian novelist.
Richter, Conrad (1890–1968), American novelist.
Rilke, Rainer Maria (1875–1920), German poet.
Rimbaud, Arthur (1854–91), French poet.
Robinson, Edwin Arlington (1869–1935), American poet.
Roethke, Theodore (1908–63), American poet.
Rolland, Romain (1866–1944), French novelist.
Rolvaag, O(le) E(dvart) (1876–1931), Norwegian-American novelist.
Romains, Jules (1885–1972), French novelist.
Ronsard, Pierre de (c. 1524–85), French poet.
Rossetti, Christina (1830–94), English poet.
Rossetti, Dante G. (1828–82), English poet and translator.
Rostand, Edmond (1868–1918), French dramatist and poet.
Roth, Phillip (1933–), American novelist.
Ruskin, John (1819–1900), English critic and essayist.
Russell, George ("A.E.") (1867–1935), Irish poet.
Sachs, Nelly (1891–1970), German-born Swedish poet.
Sagan, Françoise (1935–), French novelist.
Sainte-Beuve, Charles A. (1804–69), French critic.
Saint-Exupéry, Antoine de (1900–44), French writer.
Saki (Hector H. Munro) (1870–1916), English short story writer.
Salinger, J(erome) D(avid) (1919–), American novelist.
Sand, George (Amandine A. L. Dupin, baronne Dudevant) (1804–76), French novelist.
Sandburg, Carl (1878–1967), American poet.
Santayana, George (1863–1952), American philosopher, poet, and essayist.
Sappho (fl. early 6th cent. B.C.), Greek lyric poet.
Saroyan, William (1908–81), American novelist, dramatist, and short story writer.
Sartre, Jean Paul (1905–80), French philosopher, novelist, and dramatist.
Sayers, Dorothy L. (1893–1957), English novelist.
Schiller, Friedrich von (1759–1805), German dramatist.
Schisgal, Murray (1926–), American dramatist.
Schlegel, Friedrich von (1772–1829), German philosopher, critic, and writer.
Schnitzler, Arthur (1862–1931), Austrian dramatist and novelist.
Schwartz, Delmore (1913–66), American poet.
Scott, Sir Walter (1771–1832), Scottish novelist.
Seferis, George (1900–71), Greek poet.
Seneca, Lucius Annaeus (c. 3 B.C.–65 A.D.), Roman dramatist and philosopher.
Shakespeare, William (1564–1616), English dramatist and poet.
Shange, Ntozake (1948–), American dramatist and poet.
Shapiro, Karl (1913–), American poet, critic, and editor.
Shaw, George Bernard (1856–1950), Irish dramatist.

Shaw, Irwin (1913–), American novelist.
Sheed, Wilfrid (1930–), American novelist and critic.
Shelley, Mary Wollstonecraft (1797–1851), English novelist.
Shelley, Percy Bysshe (1792–1822), English poet.
Shepard, Sam (1943–), American playwright.
Sheridan, Richard Brinsley, (1751–1816), Irish-born dramatist.
Sherwood, Robert E. (1896–1955), American dramatist.
Sholokhov, Mikhail (1905–), Russian novelist.
Sidney, Sir Philip (1554–86), English poet and essayist.
Sienkiewicz, Henryk (1846–1916), Polish novelist.
Sillanpää, Frans E. (1888–1964), Finnish novelist.
Silone, Ignazio (1900–78), Italian novelist.
Simenon, Georges (1903–), Franco-Belgian novelist.
Simon, Neil (1927–), American playwright.
Sinclair, Upton (1878–1968), American novelist.
Singer, Isaac Bashevis (1904–), Polish-born Yiddish American novelist and short story writer.
Sitwell, Dame Edith (1887–1964), English poet and critic.
Sitwell, Sir Osbert (1892–1969), English poet and essayist.
Sitwell, Sacheverell (1897–), English poet and essayist.
Smollett, Tobias (1721–71), Scottish-born novelist.
Snow, C(harles) P(ercy) (1905–80), English critic and novelist.
Solzhenitsyn, Aleksandr I. (1918–), Russian novelist.
Sontag, Susan (1933–), American critic and novelist.
Sophocles (c. 496–406 B.C.), Greek tragic poet.
Southey, Robert (1774–1843), English poet.
Spark, Muriel (1918–), Scottish novelist, short story writer, poet, and biographer.
Spender, Stephen (1909–), English poet.
Spengler, Oswald (1880–1936), German historian.
Spenser, Edmund (1552?–99), English poet.
Spigelgass, Leonard (1908–), American playwright.
Steegmuller, Francis (1906–), American biographer.
Steele, Sir Richard (1672–1729), English essayist.
Stein, Gertrude (1874–1946), American poet, novelist, critic, and autobiographer.
Steinbeck, John (1902–68), American novelist.
Stendhal (Marie Henri Beyle) (1783–1842), French novelist.
Sterne, Laurence (1713–68), English novelist.
Stevens, Wallace (1879–1955), American poet.
Stevenson, Robert Louis (1850–94), Scottish novelist.
Stoker, Bram (1847–1912), Irish-born novelist.
Stone, I. F. (1907–), American journalist and editor.
Stoppard, Tom (1937–), English dramatist.
Strindberg, August (1849–1912), Swedish dramatist.
Styron, William (1925–), American novelist.
Sudermann, Hermann (1857–1928), German dramatist.
Swados, Harvey (1920–1972), American novelist, short story writer, and essayist.
Swift, Jonathan (1667–1745), English satirist, poet, and essayist.
Swinburne, Algernon Charles (1837–1909), English poet.
Symonds, John Addington (1840–93), English cultural historian, critic, and translator.
Symons, Arthur (1865–1945), English poet and critic.
Synge, John Millington (1871–1909), Irish dramatist and poet.
Tacitus (c. 55–c. 117 A.D.), Roman historian.
Tagore, Sir Rabindranath (1861–1941), Indian poet, novelist, and essayist.
Taine, Hippolyte (1828–93), French critic and historian.
Tarkington, Booth (1869–1946), American novelist.
Tasso, Torquato (1544–95), Italian poet.
Tate, Allen (1899–1979), American poet and critic.
Taylor, Samuel (1912–), American playwright.
Teichmann, Howard (1916–), American dramatist.
Tennyson, Alfred (1809–92), English poet.
Thackeray, William Makepeace (1811–63), English novelist.
Theocritus (fl. c. 270 B.C.), Greek poet.
Thomas, Dylan (1914–53), Anglo-Welsh poet.
Thompson, Francis (1859–1907), English poet.
Thoreau, Henry David (1817–62), American essayist.

Thucydides (c. 460–c. 400 B.C.), Greek historian.
Thurber, James (1894–1961), American humorist.
Tolkien, J(ohn) R(onald) R(euel) (1892–1973), English novelist and critic.
Tolstoy, Leo (1828–1910), Russian novelist.
Toynbee, Arnold (1889–1975), English historian.
Traven, B. (Traven Torsvan) (1890–1969), American expatriate novelist.
Trollope, Anthony (1815–82), English novelist.
Trumbo, Dalton (1905–76), American screenwriter.
Turgenev, Ivan (1818–83), Russian novelist.
Tutuola, Amos (1920–), Nigerian writer.
Twain, Mark (Samuel L. Clemens) (1835–1910), American novelist and humorist.
Undset, Sigrid (1882–1949), Norwegian novelist.
Updike, John (1932–), American novelist and poet.
Valéry, Paul (1871–1945), French poet and critic.
van Itallie, Jean-Claude (1936–), Belgian-born American dramatist.
Van Doren, Mark (1894–1972), American poet and critic.
Vergil (70–19 B.C.), Roman poet.
Verne, Jules (1828–1905), French novelist.
Vidal, Gore (1925–), American novelist and critic.
Vigny, Alfred de (1797–1863), French dramatist.
Villon, François (1431–c. 1463), French poet.
Voltaire, François M. A. de (1694–1778), French novelist, dramatist, critic, and poet.
Vonnegut, Kurt, Jr. (1922–), American novelist.
Wain, John (1925–), English poet and novelist.
Waller, Edmund (1606–87), English poet.
Walpole, Horace (1717–97), English man of letters.
Walton, Izaak (1593–1683), English essayist.
Ward, Douglas Turner (1930–), American dramatist.
Warren, Robert Penn (1905–), American novelist, poet, and critic.
Wassermann, Jakob (1873–1934), Austrian novelist.
Waugh, Evelyn (1903–66), English novelist and satirist.
Webster, John (c. 1580–c. 1625), English dramatist.
Webster, Noah (1758–1843), American lexicographer.
Weidman, Jerome (1913–), American novelist.
Weiss, Peter (1916–), German-born Swedish dramatist.
Wells, H(erbert) G(eorge) (1866–1946), English novelist, essayist, and historian.
Werfel, Franz (1890–1945), Austrian novelist.
Wescott, Glenway (1901–), American novelist and critic.
Wesker, Arnold (1932–), English novelist.
West, Nathanael (Nathan Weinstein) (1903–40), American novelist.
Wharton, Edith (1862–1937), American novelist.
White, E(lwyn) B(rooks) (1899–), American essayist.
White, Patrick (1912–), Australian novelist.
Whitman, Walt (1819–92), American poet.
Whittier, John Greenleaf (1807–92), American poet.
Wilbur, Richard (1921–), American poet.
Wilde, Oscar (1854–1900), Irish dramatist.
Wilder, Thornton (1897–1975), American novelist and dramatist.
Williams, Tennessee (1914–), American dramatist.
Williams, William Carlos (1883–1963), American poet.
Wilson, Edmund (1895–1972), American writer and literary critic.
Wolfe, Thomas (1900–38), American novelist.
Woodward, Robert (1943–), American journalist.
Woolf, Virginia (1882–1941), English novelist.
Wordsworth, William (1770–1850), English poet and critic.
Wright, Richard (1908–60), American novelist.
Wyatt, Sir Thomas (1503–42), English poet.
Wylie, Elinor (1885–1928), American poet and novelist.
Xenophon (c. 430–c. 355 B.C.), Greek historian.
Yeats, William Butler (1865–1939), Irish poet.
Yevtushenko, Yevgeny (1933–), Russian poet.
Zola, Émile (1840–1902), French novelist.
Zweig, Stefan (1881–1942), Austrian novelist, poet, and biographer.

NOTABLES OF THE MUSICAL WORLD

Abbado, Claudio (1933–), Italian conductor.
Addinsell, Richard (1904–77), English film composer.
Adler, Kurt (1905–), American opera director.
Ailey, Alvin, Jr. (1931–), American choreographer.
Albanese, Licia (1913–), Italian-American soprano.
Albéniz, Isaac (1860–1909), Spanish pianist and composer.
Amara, Lucine (1927–), American soprano.
Amram, David (1930–), American composer.
Anderson, Marian (1902–), American contralto.

Ansermet, Ernest (1883–1969), Swiss conductor.
Antheil, George (1900–59), American composer.
Antonio (1921–), Spanish dancer.
Arnold, Malcolm (1921–), English composer.
Arpino, Gerald (1928–), American choreographer.
Arrau, Claudio (1903–), Chilean pianist.
Ashton, Sir Frederick (1906–), English choreographer.
Auber, Daniel F. E. (1782–1871), French operatic composer.

Auer, Leopold (1845–1930), Hungarian violinist-teacher.
Auric, Georges (1899–), French composer.
Babbitt, Milton (1916–), American composer.
Babin, Victor (1908–), Russian-American pianist.
Bach, Carl P. E. (1714–88), German composer.
Bach, Johann C. (1735–82), German composer.
Bach, Johann Sebastian (1685–1750), German composer.
Bach, Wilhelm F. (1710–84), German composer.
Bachauer, Gina (1913–76), Greek pianist.
Bachaus, Wilhelm (1884–1969), German pianist.
Badura-Skoda, Paul (1927–), Austrian pianist.
Baker, Janet (1933–), British mezzo-soprano.
Balanchine, George (1904–), American choreographer.
Balfe, Michael (1808–70), Irish operatic composer.
Barber, Samuel (1910–81), American composer.
Barbirolli, Sir John (1899–1970), English conductor.
Barenboim, Daniel (1942–), Israeli pianist and conductor.
Bartók, Béla (1881–1945), Hungarian composer.
Baryshnikov, Mikhail (1948–), Russian ballet dancer.
Bastianini, Ettore (1923–67), Italian operatic baritone.
Beecham, Sir Thomas (1879–1961), English conductor.
Beethoven, Ludwig van (1770–1827), German composer.
Bellini, Vincenzo (1801–35), Italian operatic composer.
Bennett, Robert Russell (1894–1981), American composer.
Berg, Alban (1885–1935), Austrian composer.
Berganza, Teresa (1935–), Spanish mezzo-soprano.
Berlin, Irving (1888–), American popular composer.
Berlioz, Hector (1803–69), French composer.
Berman, Lazar (1930–), Russian pianist.
Bernstein, Leonard (1918–), American composer, conductor, and pianist.
Bettis, Valerie (1920–), American choreographer.
Biggs, E. Power (1906–77), English-American organist.
Bing, Rudolf (1902–), Austrian-English operatic manager.
Bizet, Georges (1838–75), French composer.
Björling, Jussi (1911–60), Swedish tenor.
Bliss, Sir Arthur (1891–1975), English composer.
Blitzstein, Marc (1905–64), American composer.
Bloch, Ernest (1880–1959), Swiss-American composer.
Boccherini, Luigi (1743–1805), Italian composer.
Boehm, Karl (1894–1981), German conductor.
Boito, Arrigo (1842–1918), Italian composer and librettist.
Bonynge, Richard (1930–), Australian conductor.
Borkh, Inge (1921–), German soprano.
Borodin, Aleksandr (1833–87), Russian composer.
Boulanger, Nadia (1887–1979), French pianist.
Boulez, Pierre (1925–), French composer and conductor.
Boult, Sir Adrian (1889–), English conductor.
Brahms, Johannes (1833–97), German composer.
Brailowsky, Alexander (1896–1976), Russian pianist.
Bream, Julian (1933–), English guitarist and lutenist.
Britten, Benjamin (1913–76), English composer.
Browning, John (1933–), American pianist.
Bruch, Max (1838–1920), German composer.
Bruckner, Anton (1824–96), Austrian composer.
Bülow, Hans von (1830–94), German pianist and conductor.
Bumbry, Grace (1937–), American mezzo-soprano.
Buxtehude, Dietrich (1637–1707), Swedish composer.
Cage, John (1912–), American composer.
Caldwell, Sarah (1928–), American opera conductor.
Callas, Maria (1923–77), Greek-American soprano.
Carreras, José (1946–), Spanish operatic tenor.
Caruso, Enrico (1873–1921), Italian operatic tenor.
Casadesus, Robert (1899–72), French pianist.
Casals, Pablo (1876–1973), Spanish cellist and conductor.
Chabrier, Alexis E. (1841–94), French composer.
Chaliapin, Feodor (1873–1938), Russian operatic bass.
Charpentier, Gustave (1860–1956), French composer.
Chausson, Ernest (1855–99), French composer.
Chávez, Carlos (1899–1978), Mexican composer.
Cherubini, Luigi (1760–1842), Italian composer.
Chopin, Frédéric (1810–49), Polish composer.
Christoff, Boris (1919–), Bulgarian bass.
Cimarosa, Domenico (1749–1801), Italian composer.
Cleva, Fausto (1902–), Italian-American conductor.
Cliburn, Van (1934–), American pianist.
Clifford, John (1947–), American dancer.
Copland, Aaron (1900–), American composer.
Corelli, Arcangelo (1653–1713), Italian composer.
Corelli, Franco (1924–), Italian dramatic tenor.
Couperin, François (1668–1733), French composer.
Crespin, Régine (1927–), French dramatic soprano.
Creston, Paul (1906–), American composer.
Cunningham, Merce (1922?–), American choreographer.
Curtin, Phyllis (c. 1930–), American operatic soprano.
Dallapiccola, Luigi (1904–75), Italian pianist and composer.

D'Amboise, Jacques (1934–), American ballet dancer.
Damrosch, Leopold (1832–85), German conductor.
Damrosch, Walter (1862–1950), German-American conductor and composer.
Danilova, Alexandra (1906–), Russian ballerina.
Debussy, Claude (1862–1918), French composer.
De Lavallade, Carmen (1931–), American dancer.
Délibes, Léo (1836–91), French composer.
Delius, Frederick (1862–1934), English composer.
Della Casa, Lisa (1921–), Swiss lyric soprano.
Dello Joio, Norman (1913–), American composer.
Del Mar, Norman (1919–), English conductor.
De Mille, Agnes (1908–), American choreographer.
Del Monaco, Mario (1915–), Italian dramatic tenor.
De los Angeles, Victoria (1923–), Spanish lyric soprano.
Diaghilev, Sergei (1872–1929), Russian ballet impresario.
Di Stefano, Giuseppe (1921–), Italian lyric tenor.
Dittersdorf, Karl D. von (1739–99), Austrian composer.
Dobbs, Mattiwilda (1925–), American coloratura soprano.
Dohnanyi, Ernst von (1877–1960), Hungarian composer.
Dolin, Anton (1904–), English ballet choreographer.
Domingo, Placido (1941–), Spanish opera tenor.
Donizetti, Gaetano (1797–1848), Italian composer.
Dorati, Antal (1906–), Hungarian-American conductor.
Druckman, Jacob (1928–), American composer.
Dukas, Paul (1865–1935), French composer.
Duncan, Isadora (1878–1927), American dancer.
Dunham, Katherine (1910–), American choreographer.
Dvorak, Antonin (1841–1904), Czech composer.
Eglevsky, André (1917–77), Russian-born American dancer.
Elgar, Sir Edward (1857–1934), English composer.
Ellington, Duke (1899–1974), American composer.
Elman, Mischa (1891–1967), Russian-American violinist.
Enesco, Georges (1881–1955), Rumanian composer.
Entremont, Philippe (1934–), French pianist and conductor.
Falla, Manuel de (1876–1946), Spanish composer.
Farrar, Geraldine (1882–1967), American operatic soprano.
Farrell, Eileen (1920–), American dramatic soprano.
Farrell, Suzanne (1945–), American ballerina.
Fauré, Gabriel (1845–1924), French composer.
Feuermann, Emanuel (1902–42), Polish-American cellist.
Fiedler, Arthur (1894–1979), American conductor.
Fischer-Dieskau, Dietrich (1925–), German baritone.
Flagstad, Kirsten (1895–1962), Norwegian soprano.
Flotow, Friedrich von (1812–83), German operatic composer.
Fokine, Michel (1880–1942), Russian-American dancer.
Fonteyn, Dame Margot (1919–), English ballerina.
Foss, Lukas (1922–), German-born American composer.
Foster, Stephen (1826–64), American song writer.
Francescatti, Zino (1905–), French violinist.
Franck, César (1822–90), Belgian-French composer.
Frescobaldi, Girolamo (1583–1643), Italian composer.
Friml, Rudolf (1879–1972), Czech-American composer.
Furtwängler, Wilhelm (1886–1954), German conductor.
Gades, Antonio (1936–), Spanish dancer.
Galli-Curci, Amelita (1882–1963), Italian-American soprano.
Galway, James (1939–), Irish flutist.
Garden, Mary (1877–1967), Scottish-American soprano.
Gatti-Casazza, Giulio (1869–1940), Italian opera manager.
Gedda, Nicolai (1925–), Swedish operatic tenor.
Gershwin, George (1898–1937), American composer.
Gieseking, Walter (1895–1956), German pianist.
Gigli, Beniamino (1890–1957), Italian tenor.
Gilbert, Sir William S. (1836–1911), English librettist.
Gilels, Emil (1916–), Russian pianist.
Ginastera, Alberto (1916–), Argentinian composer.
Glazunov, Aleksandr (1865–1936), Russian composer.
Glière, Reinhold (1875–1956), Russian composer.
Glinka, Mikhail (1804–57), Russian composer.
Gluck, Christoph W. von (1714–87), German composer.
Gobbi, Tito (1915–), Italian operatic baritone.
Godowsky, Leopold (1870–1938), Polish pianist.
Goldmark, Karl (1830–1915), Hungarian composer.
Goldovsky, Boris (1908–), Russian-American conductor.
Golschmann, Vladimir (1893–1972), French-American conductor.
Goossens, Sir Eugene (1893–1962), English conductor.
Gould, Glenn (1932–), Canadian pianist.
Gould, Morton (1913–), American conductor.
Gounod, Charles (1818–93), French composer.
Graham, Martha (1893?–), American choreographer.
Grainger, Percy (1882–1961), Australian-American pianist and composer.
Greco, Jose (1918–), Italian-born American dancer.
Gretchaninov, Aleksandr (1864–1956), Russian composer.

Grieg, Edvard (1843–1907), Norwegian composer.
Grofé, Ferde (1892–1972), American composer.
Gueden, Hilde (1917–), Austrian operatic lyric soprano.
Halévy, Jacques (1799–1862), French operatic composer.
Hammerstein, Oscar, II (1895–1960), American lyricist.
Handel, George Frederick (1685–1759), German composer.
Hanson, Howard (1896–1981), American composer.
Harris, Roy (1898–1979), American composer.
Hart, Lorenz (1895–1943), American lyricist.
Haydée, Marcia (1937–), Brazilian ballerina.
Haydn, Franz Joseph (1732–1809), Austrian composer.
Heifetz, Jascha (1901–), Russian-American violinist.
Henze, Hans Werner (1926–), German composer.
Herbert, Victor (1859–1924), Irish-American musician.
Hess, Dame Myra (1890–1965), English pianist.
Hindemith, Paul (1895–1963), German-American composer.
Hines, Jerome (1921–), American operatic bass.
Hofmann, Joseph (1876–1957), Polish-American pianist.
Holst, Gustav (1874–1934), English composer.
Honegger, Arthur (1892–1955), Swiss-French composer.
Horne, Marilyn (1934–), American mezzo-soprano.
Horowitz, Vladimir (1904–), Russian-American pianist.
Humperdinck, Engelbert (1854–1921), German composer.
Humphrey, Doris (1895–1958), American choreographer.
Hurok, Sol (1888–1974), Russian-American impresario.
Ibert, Jacques (1890–1962), French composer.
Indy, Vincent d' (1851–1931), French composer.
Ippolitov-Ivanov, Mikhail (1859–1935), Russian composer.
Istomin, Eugene (1925–), American pianist.
Iturbi, José (1895–1980), Spanish-American pianist.
Ives, Charles (1874–1954), American composer.
Jamison, Judith (1944–), American dancer.
Jeritza, Maria (1887–), Austrian-American soprano.
Joffrey, Robert (1930–), American ballet director.
Kabalevsky, Dmitri (1904–), Russian composer.
Karajan, Herbert von (1908–), Austrian conductor.
Kempff, Wilhelm (1895–), German pianist.
Kern, Jerome (1885–1945), American popular composer.
Khachaturian, Aram (1903–1978), Russian composer.
Kidd, Michael (1919–), American choreographer.
Kiepura, Jan (1902–66), Polish tenor.
Kipnis, Alexander (1891–1978), Russian-American bass.
Kleiber, Erich (1890–1956), Austrian conductor.
Klemperer, Otto (1885–1973), German conductor.
Kodály, Zoltán (1882–1967), Hungarian composer.
Kogan, Leonid (1924–), Russian violinist.
Kondrashin, Kyril (1914–81), Russian conductor.
Kostelanetz, André (1901–80), Russian-American conductor.
Koussevitzky, Serge (1874–1951), Russian-American conductor.
Kreisler, Fritz (1875–1962), Austrian-American violinist.
Krips, Josef (1902–1974), Austrian conductor.
Kubelik, Rafael (1914–), Czech conductor and composer.
Kunz, Erich (1909–), Austrian singer.
Lalo, Edouard (1823–92), French composer.
Lambert, Constant (1905–51), English composer.
Landowska, Wanda (1877–1959), Polish-French harpsichordist and pianist.
Lehár, Franz (1870–1948), Hungarian composer.
Lehmann, Lilli (1848–1929), German operatic soprano.
Lehmann, Lotte (1888–1976), German-American soprano.
Leinsdorf, Erich (1912–), Austrian-American conductor.
Leoncavallo, Ruggiero (1858–1919), Italian composer.
Lerner, Alan Jay (1918–), American lyricist.
Lewis, Henry (1932–), American conductor.
Lhevinne, Joseph (1874–1944), Russian-American pianist.
Lhevinne, Rosina (1880–1976), Russian-American pianist.
Limón, José (1908–72), Mexican-American choreographer.
Lind, Jenny (1820–87), Swedish soprano.
Liszt, Franz (1811–86), Hungarian composer.
Loewe, Frederick (1904–), American composer.
London, George (1920–), Canadian bass baritone.
Lorengar, Pilar (1931?–), Spanish lyric soprano.
Loring, Eugene (1914–), American choreographer.
Lully, Jean B. (1632–87), French operatic composer.
Lympany, Moura (1916–), English pianist.
Maazel, Lorin (1930–), American conductor.
McBride, Patricia (1942–), American ballerina.
McCormack, John (1884–1945), Irish-American tenor.
McCracken, James (1926–), American dramatic tenor.
MacDowell, Edward (1861–1908), American composer.
Mahler, Gustav (1860–1911), Austrian composer.
Makarova, Natalia (1940–), Russian ballerina.
Markevich, Igor (1912–), Russian-Swiss conductor.
Markova, Dame Alicia (1910–), English ballerina.
Martinelli, Giovanni (1885–1969), Italian-American tenor.

Martinon, Jean (1910–76), French conductor and composer.
Mascagni, Pietro (1863–1945), Italian operatic composer.
Massenet, Jules (1842–1912), French operatic composer.
Massine, Léonide (1896–1979), Russian-American choreographer.
Mehta, Zubin (1936–), Indian conductor.
Melba, Dame Nellie (c. 1859–1931), Australian soprano.
Melchior, Lauritz (1890–1973), Danish heroic tenor.
Mendelssohn, Felix (1809–47), German composer.
Mengelberg, Josef W. (1871–1951), Dutch conductor.
Mennin, Peter (1923–), American composer.
Menotti, Gian-Carlo (1911–), Italian-American composer.
Menuhin, Yehudi (1916–), American violinist.
Merrill, Robert (1919–), American operatic baritone.
Merriman, Nan (1920–), American mezzo-soprano.
Meyerbeer, Giacomo (1791–1864), German composer.
Milanov, Zinka (1906–), Yugoslavian operatic soprano.
Milhaud, Darius (1892–1974), French composer.
Milstein, Nathan (1904–), Russian violinist.
Mitchell, Arthur (1934–), American ballet dancer.
Mitropoulos, Dimitri (1896–1960), Greek-American conductor.
Moffo, Anna (c. 1935–), American soprano.
Moiseiwitsch, Benno (1890–1963), Russian-English pianist.
Moiseyev, Igor (1906–), Russian choreographer.
Monteux, Pierre (1875–1964), French-American conductor.
Monteverdi, Claudio (1567–1643), Italian composer.
Moore, Douglas (1893–1969), American operatic composer.
Moore, Grace (1901–47), American soprano.
Morini, Erica (c. 1905–), Austrian-American violinist.
Moussorgsky, Modest (1839–81), Russian composer.
Mozart, Wolfgang Amadeus (1756–91), Austrian composer.
Münch, Charles (1891–1968), French conductor.
Münchinger, Karl (1915–), German conductor.
Munsel, Patrice (1925–), American operatic soprano.
Muti, Riccardo (1941–), Italian conductor.
Muzio, Claudia (1889–1936), Italian operatic soprano.
Neway, Patricia (c. 1923–), American soprano.
Nicolai, Otto (1810–49), German composer.
Nielsen, Carl (1865–1931), Danish composer.
Nijinsky, Vaslav (1890–1950), Russian ballet dancer.
Nikolais, Alwin (1912–), American dancer.
Nilsson, Birgit (1918–), Swedish dramatic soprano.
Novaes, Guiomar (1895–1979), Brazilian pianist.
Nureyev, Rudolf (1938–), Russian ballet dancer.
Offenbach, Jacques (1819–80), French composer.
Oistrakh, David (1908–74), Russian violinist.
Olivero, Magda (1913–), Italian operatic soprano.
Orff, Carl (1895–), German composer.
Ormandy, Eugene (1899–), Hungarian-born American conductor.
Ozawa, Seiji (1935–), Japanese conductor.
Paderewski, Ignace J. (1860–1941), Polish pianist and composer.
Paganini, Niccolò (1782–1840), Italian violinist.
Palestrina, Giovanni P. da (c. 1525–94), Italian composer.
Pavarotti, Luciano (1935–), Italian opera singer.
Pavlova, Anna (c. 1882–1931), Russian ballerina.
Peerce, Jan (1904–), American tenor.
Pergolesi, Giovanni B. (1710–36), Italian composer.
Peters, Roberta (1930–), American coloratura soprano.
Petit, Roland (1924–), French choreographer and dancer.
Piatigorsky, Gregor (1903–76), Ukrainian-American cellist.
Pinza, Ezio (1892–1957), Italian-American basso.
Piston, Walter (1894–1976), American composer.
Pizzetti, Ildebrando (1880–1968), Italian composer.
Plisetskaya, Maya (1925–), Russian ballerina.
Pollini, Maurizio (1942–), Italian pianist.
Ponchielli, Amilcare (1834–86), Italian composer.
Pons, Lily (1904–76), French-American coloratura soprano.
Ponselle, Rosa (1897–1981), American operatic soprano.
Porter, Cole (1893–1964), American composer and lyricist.
Poulenc, Francis (1899–1963), French composer.
Previn, André (1929–), German-American conductor.
Price, Leontyne (1927–), American dramatic soprano.
Primrose, William (1904–), Scottish-American violist.
Prokofiev, Sergei (1891–1953), Russian composer.
Puccini, Giacomo (1858–1924), Italian operatic composer.
Purcell, Henry (1659–95), English composer and organist.
Queler, Eve (1936–), American conductor.
Rabin, Michael (1936–1972), American violinist.
Rachmaninoff, Sergei (1873–1943), Russian composer.
Ramey, Samuel (1942–), American basso.
Ravel, Maurice (1875–1937), French composer.
Reiner, Fritz (1888–1963), Hungarian-American conductor.
Reisenberg, Nadia (1905–), Russian-American pianist.
Resnik, Regina (1924–), American mezzo-soprano.

Respighi, Ottorino (1879–1936), Italian composer.
Reszke, Edouard de (1853–1917), Polish bass.
Reszke, Jan de (1850–1925), Polish tenor.
Ricci, Ruggiero (1918–), American violinist.
Richter, Sviatoslav (1914–), Russian pianist.
Rimsky-Korsakov, Nikolai (1844–1908), Russian composer.
Robbins, Jerome (1918–), American choreographer.
Robeson, Paul (1898–1976), American bass.
Rodgers, Richard (1902–79), American popular composer.
Rodzinski, Artur (1894–1958), Polish-American conductor.
Romberg, Sigmund (1887–1951), Hungarian-American operetta composer.
Rorem, Ned (1923–), American composer.
Rose, Leonard (1918–), American cellist.
Rosenthal, Moriz (1862–1946), Polish pianist.
Rossini, Gioacchino (1792–1868), Italian composer.
Rostropovitch, Mstislav (1927–), Russian cellist.
Roussel, Albert (1869–1937), French composer.
Rózsa, Miklos (1907–), Hungarian-American composer.
Rubinstein, Anton (1829–94), Russian pianist and composer.
Rubinstein, Artur (1886–), Polish-American pianist.
Rysanek, Leonie (1926–), Austrian dramatic soprano.
St. Denis, Ruth (1877?–1968), American dancer.
Saint-Saëns, Camille (1835–1921), French composer.
Sargent, Sir Malcolm (1895–1967), English conductor.
Satie, Erik (1866–1925), French composer.
Scarlatti, Alessandro (c. 1660–1725), Italian composer.
Scarlatti, Domenico (1685–1757), Italian composer.
Scherman, Thomas (1917–79), American conductor.
Schipa, Tito (1889–1965), Italian operatic tenor.
Schippers, Thomas (1930–77), American conductor.
Schmidt-Isserstedt, Hans (1900–1973), German conductor.
Schnabel, Artur (1882–1951), Austrian-American pianist.
Schneider, Alexander (1908–), Russian-American violinist.
Schoenberg, Arnold (1874–1951), Austrian composer.
Schubert, Franz (1797–1828), Austrian composer.
Schuller, Gunther (1925–), American composer.
Schuman, William (1910–), American composer.
Schumann, Clara (1819–96), German pianist and composer.
Schumann, Elisabeth (1885–1952), German soprano.
Schumann, Robert (1810–56), German composer.
Schumann-Heink, Ernestine (1861–1936), Austrian-American contralto.
Schwarzkopf, Elisabeth (1915–), German lyric soprano.
Scotti, Antonio (1866–1936), Italian operatic baritone.
Scotto, Renata (1936–), Italian soprano.
Scriabin, Aleksandr (1872–1915), Russian composer.
Seefried, Irmgard (1919–), German soprano.
Segovia, Andrés (1893–), Spanish guitarist.
Serkin, Rudolph (1903–), Czech-born American pianist.
Sessions, Roger (1896–), American composer.
Shaw, Robert (1916–), American choral conductor.
Shawn, Ted (1891–1972), American dancer.
Shostakovich, Dmitri (1906–1975), Russian composer.
Sibelius, Jean (1865–1957), Finnish composer.
Siepi, Cesare (1923–), Italian operatic bass.
Sills, Beverly (1929–), American coloratura soprano.
Slezak, Leo (1873–1946), Czech tenor.
Smallens, Alexander (1899–1972), Russian-born American conductor.
Smetana, Bedřich (1824–84), Czech composer.
Solomon (1902–), English pianist.
Solti, Georg (1912–), Hungarian conductor.
Somes, Michael (1917–), English ballet dancer.
Sousa, John Philip (1854–1932), American bandmaster and composer.
Sowerby, Leo (1895–1968), American organist.
Spivakovsky, Tossy (1907–), Russian-American violinist.
Steber, Eleanor (1916–), American operatic soprano.
Steinberg, William (1899–1978), German conductor.
Steiner, Max (1888?–1971), Austrian-American composer.
Stern, Isaac (1920–), Russian-born American violinist.
Stevens, Risë (1913–), American mezzo-soprano.
Stich-Randall, Teresa (c. 1928–), American soprano.

Stokowski, Leopold (1882–1977), English-born American conductor.
Stratas, Teresa (1938–), Canadian soprano.
Straus, Oscar (1870–1954), Austrian operetta composer.
Strauss, Johann (1804–49), Austrian composer.
Strauss, Johann, Jr. (1825–99), Austrian composer.
Strauss, Richard (1864–1949), German composer.
Stravinsky, Igor (1882–1971), Russian composer.
Sullivan, Sir Arthur (1842–1900), English composer.
Sutherland, Joan (1926–), Australian soprano.
Swarthout, Gladys (1904–69), American mezzo-soprano.
Szell, Georg (1897–1970), Hungarian-born American conductor.
Szigeti, Joseph (1892–1973), Hungarian violinist.
Tagliavini, Ferruccio (1913–), Italian lyric tenor.
Tallchief, Maria (1925–), American ballerina.
Tauber, Richard (1892–1948), Austrian tenor.
Taylor, Deems (1885–1966), American music critic.
Taylor, Paul (1930–), American choreographer.
Tchaikovsky, Piotr Ilich (1840–93), Russian composer.
Tebaldi, Renata (1922–), Italian lyric soprano.
Te Kanawa, Kiri (1946–), New Zealand mezzo-soprano.
Telemann, Georg P. (1681–1767), German composer.
Tetley, Glen (1926–), American choreographer.
Tetrazzini, Luisa (1871–1940), Italian coloratura soprano.
Tharp, Twyla (1941–), American choreographer.
Thebom, Blanche (1918–), American mezzo-soprano.
Theodorakis, Mikis (1925–), Greek composer.
Thomas, Ambroise (1811–96), French operatic composer.
Thomas, John Charles (1891–1960), American baritone.
Thomson, Virgil (1896–), American composer and critic.
Tibbett, Lawrence (1896–1960), American baritone.
Toscanini, Arturo (1867–1957), Italian conductor.
Tourel, Jennie (1910–73), Canadian operatic soprano.
Traubel, Helen (1899–1972), American soprano.
Troyanos, Tatiana (1938–), American mezzo-soprano.
Tucker, Richard (c. 1914–75), American dramatic tenor.
Tudor, Antony (1909–), English choreographer.
Tureck, Rosalyn (1914–), American pianist.
Ulanova, Galina (1910–), Russian ballerina.
Varèse, Edgard (1885–1965), French-American composer.
Varnay, Astrid (1918–), Swedish dramatic soprano.
Vaughan Williams, Ralph (1872–1958), English composer.
Verdi, Giuseppe (1813–1901), Italian composer.
Verrett, Shirley (c. 1933–), American mezzo-soprano.
Vickers, Jon (1926–), Canadian operatic tenor.
Villa-Lobos, Heitor (1887–1959), Brazilian composer.
Villella, Edward (1936–), American ballet dancer.
Vishnevskaya, Galina (1926–), Russian soprano.
Vivaldi, Antonio (c. 1675–1741), Italian composer.
von Stade, Frederica (1945–), American mezzo-soprano.
Wagner, Richard (1813–83), German composer.
Walter, Bruno (1876–1962), German-American conductor.
Walton, Sir William (1902–), English composer.
Warren, Leonard (1911–60), American baritone.
Watts, André (1946–), American pianist.
Weber, Carl M. von (1786–1826), German composer.
Webern, Anton von (1883–1945), Austrian composer.
Weidman, Charles (1901–75), American choreographer.
Weill, Kurt (1900–50), German-American composer.
Weingartner, Felix (1863–1942), Austrian conductor.
Weissenberg, Alexis (1929–), French pianist.
Welitsch, Ljuba (1913–), Bulgarian soprano.
Whiteman, Paul (1890–1967), American jazz conductor.
Wilde, Patricia (1928–), Canadian ballerina.
Wilder, Alec (1907–80), American popular composer.
Wolf, Hugo (1860–1903), Austrian composer of lieder.
Wolf-Ferrari, Ermanno (1876–1948), German-Italian operatic composer.
Wunderlich, Fritz (1930–66), German lyric tenor.
Wuorinen, Charles (1938–), American composer.
Youmans, Vincent (1898–1946), American composer.
Youskevitch, Igor (1912–), Russian ballet dancer.
Zimbalist, Efrem (1889–), Russian-American violinist.
Zukerman, Pinchas (1948–), Israeli-American violinist.

FILM DIRECTORS

FRANCE

Allégret, Yves (1907–): The Proud and the Beautiful, Oasis, Germinal.

Becker, Jacques (1906–60): Casque d'Or, Montparnasse 19, The Hole.

Bresson, Robert (1901–): Les Dames du Bois de Boulogne, Pickpocket, The Trial of Joan of Arc.

Camus, Marcel (1912–): Black Orpheus, Le Chant du Monde.

Carné, Marcel (1909–): Quai des Brumes, Les Enfants du Paradis, Terrain Vague.

Cayatte, André (1909–): Avant de Déluge, Le Passage du Rhin, La Vie Conjugale, La Raison d'état.

Chabrol, Claude (1930–): Les Cousins, A Double Tour, Landru, Une Partie de plaisir, Violette Nozière.

Christian-Jaque (1904–): La Chartreuse de Parme, Fanfan la Tulipe.

Clair, René (1898–1981): Sous les Toits de Paris, À Nous la Liberté, And Then There Were None.

Clément, René (1913–): Forbidden Games, Gervaise, Is Paris Burning?

Clouzot, Henri-Georges (1907–77): The Wages of Fear, Diabolique, La Vérité.

Cocteau, Jean (1889–1963): The Blood of a Poet, Beauty and the Beast, Orpheus.

De Broca, Philippe (1933–):Cartouche, That Man from Rio, King of Hearts.

Delannoy, Jean (1908–): La Symphonie Pastorale, La Princesse de Clèves.

Demy, Jacques (1931–): Lola, The Umbrellas of Cherbourg.

Duvivier, Julien (1896–1967): Poil de Carotte, Un Carnet de Bal, The Little World of Don Camillo.

Godard, Jean-Luc (1930–): Breathless, La Chinoise, Weekend.

Guitry, Sacha (1885–1957): La Poison, Désiré, Assassins et Voleurs.

Malle, Louis (1932–): Les Amants; Viva Maria!; Le Voleur; Lacombe, Lucien; Pretty Baby; Atlantic City.

Marker, Chris (1921–): Cuba Si!, Joli Mai.

Melville, Jean-Pierre (1917–73): Les Enfants Terribles, Le Doulos.

Ophuls, Max (1902–57): La Ronde, Madame De, Lola Montès.

Pagnol, Marcel (1895–1974): César, Angèle, Topaze.

Renoir, Jean (1894–1979): The Crime of M. Lange, La Grande Illusion, The Diary of a Chambermaid.

Resnais, Alain (1922–): Hiroshima, Mon Amour; Last Year at Marienbad; La Guerre Est Finie; Providence, Mon Oncle d'Amérique.

Tati, Jacques (1908–): Jour de Fête, Mr. Hulot's Holiday, Mon Oncle, Traffic.

Truffaut, François (1932–): The 400 Blows, Stolen Kisses, Bed and Board, Jules et Jim, The Wild Child, Day for Night, The Story of Adele H., Small Change, Last Metro.

Vadim, Roger (1928–): And God Created Woman, Les Liaisons Dangereuses, Barbarella.

Varda, Agnes (1928–): Cléo from 5 to 7, Le Bonheur.

Vigo, Jean (1905–34): Zéro de Conduite, L'Atalante.

GERMANY

Fassbinder, Rainer W. (1946–): Fox and His Friends, Mother Küsters Goes to Heaven, The Marriage of Maria Braun, Berlin-Alexanderplatz, Lili Marleen.

Harlan, Veit (1899–1964): Kreutzer Sonata, Jew Süss.

Herzog, Werner (1942–): Aguirre: the Wrath of God, The Mystery of Kaspar Hauser, Stroszek, Woyzeck.

Käutner, Helmut (1908–): The Captain from Kopenick, The Wonderful Years, The Redhead.

Murnau, Friedrich W. (1899–1931): Nosferatu, Faust, Sunrise.

Pabst, Georg W. (1885–1967): The Joyless Street, Kameradschaft, The Threepenny Opera.

Riefenstahl, Leni (1902–): Triumph of the Will, Olympiad 1936.

GREAT BRITAIN

Anderson, Michael (1920–): The Naked Edge, The Quiller Memorandum.

Asquith, Anthony (1902–68): The Importance of Being Earnest, The Net, The Yellow Rolls-Royce.

Clayton, Jack (1921–): Room at the Top, The Innocents, The Great Gatsby.

Cornelius, Henry (1913–58): Passport to Pimlico; Genevieve; I Am a Camera.

Crichton, Charles (1910–): The Lavender Hill Mob, Battle of the Sexes, The Third Secret.

Hamer, Robert (1911–63): Kind Hearts and Coronets, The Scapegoat, School for Scoundrels.

Lean, David (1908–): Great Expectations, The Bridge on the River Kwai, Lawrence of Arabia, Dr. Zhivago, Ryan's Daughter.

Lester, Richard (1932–): A Hard Day's Night, Help!

Mackendrick, Alexander (1912–): The Man in the White Suit, The Ladykillers, The Sweet Smell of Success.

Olivier, Sir Laurence (1907–): Henry V, Hamlet, Richard III, Othello.

Powell, Michael (1905–): One of Our Aircraft Is Missing, The Red Shoes, Tales of Hoffmann.

Reed, Sir Carol (1906–76): Odd Man Out, The Third Man, Oliver!

Reisz, Karel (1926–): Saturday Night and Sunday Morning, Morgan, Isadora, The Gambler, French Lieutenant's Woman.

Richardson, Tony (1928–): Look Back in Anger, The Entertainer, A Taste of Honey, Tom Jones.

Schlesinger, John (1926–): A Kind of Loving, Billy Liar, Darling, Midnight Cowboy, Sunday, Bloody Sunday.

ITALY

Antonioni, Michelangelo (1912–): L'Avventura, La Notte, Red Desert, Blow-Up, Zabriskie Point.

Camerini, Mario (1895–): I Promessi Sposi, Wife for a Night.

Comencini, Luigi (1916–): The Mill on the Po; Bread, Love, and Dreams; Mariti in Citta.

De Santis, Giuseppe (1917–): Bitter Rice, Rome Eleven O'Clock, Anna.

De Sica, Vittorio (1902–74): The Bicycle Thief, Umberto D, Two Women.

Fellini, Federico (1920–): La Strada, Nights of Cabiria, La Dolce Vita, 8½, Fellini Satyricon, Amarcord.

Germi, Pietro (1914–74): Divorce, Italian Style; Seduced and Abandoned.

Monicelli, Mario (1915–): The Organizer, Casanova 70.

Pasolini, Pier Paolo (1922–75): Accattone, Mamma Roma, The Gospel According to St. Matthew, Salo.

Pontecorvo, Gillo (1919–): Kapo, The Battle of Algiers.

Rossellini, Roberto (1906–77): Open City, Stromboli, Il Generale Della Rovere, The Rise of Louis XIV.

Visconti, Luchino (1906–76): Rocco and His Brothers, The Leopard, The Stranger, The Damned, Death in Venice, The Innocent.

Wertmuller, Lina (1929–): Swept Away, All Screwed Up, Seven Beauties.

Zampa, Luigi (1905–): City on Trial, The Woman of Rome.

Zeffirelli, Franco (1922–): The Taming of the Shrew, Romeo and Juliet, The Champ.

SWEDEN

Bergman, Ingmar (1918–): The Seventh Seal, Wild Strawberries, Virgin Spring, Persona, The Passion of Anna, The Magic Flute, Face to Face, Cries and Whispers.

Sjöberg, Alf (1903–): Miss Julie, Barabbas, The Judge.

Sjöström, Victor (1879–1960): He Who Gets Slapped, The Scarlet Letter.

Stiller, Mauritz (1883–1928): The Story of Gösta Berling, Hotel Imperial, The Street of Sin.

UNITED STATES

Allen, Woody, (1935–), Annie Hall, Interiors, Manhattan.

Altman, Robert (1925–): M°A°S°H, Nashville, Buffalo Bill and the Indians, 3 Women, A Wedding, Popeye.

Bogdanovich, Peter (1939–): Targets, The Last Picture Show, What's Up Doc?, Saint Jack.

Brooks, Richard (1912–): The Brothers Karamazov, Cat on a Hot Tin Roof, In Cold Blood, Looking for Mr. Goodbar.

Capra, Frank (1897–): It Happened One Night, You Can't Take It with You, A Hole in the Head.

Cassavetes, John (1929–): Shadows, A Child Is Waiting, Faces.

Chaplin, Charles (1889–1977): The Gold Rush, City Lights, Modern Times, The Great Dictator, Limelight.

Coppola, Francis Ford (1939–): The Godfather I & II, The Conversation, Apocalypse Now.

Cukor, George (1899–): Dinner at Eight, Camille, The Women, A Star Is Born, My Fair Lady.

Curtiz, Michael (1888–1962): Casablanca, Mildred Pierce.

Dassin, Jules (1911–): The Naked City, Rififi, He Who Must Die, Never on Sunday.

De Mille, Cecil B. (1881–1959): The King of Kings, Samson and Delilah, The Greatest Show on Earth.

Donen, Stanley (1924–): Seven Brides for Seven Brothers, Funny Face, Charade, Two for the Road.

Flaherty, Robert (1884–1951): Nanook of the North, Moana, Louisiana Story.

Fleischer, Richard (1916–): 20,000 Leagues under the Sea, Compulsion, The Boston Strangler.

Fleming, Victor (1883–1949): Captains Courageous, The Wizard of Oz, Gone with the Wind.

Ford, John (1895–1973): *Stagecoach, The Grapes of Wrath, The Quiet Man, Mogambo.*

Frankenheimer, John (1930–): *Birdman of Alcatraz, The Manchurian Candidate, Grand Prix, Black Sunday.*

Goulding, Edmund (1891–1959): *Grand Hotel, The Razor's Edge, Nightmare Alley.*

Griffith, D. W. (1875–1948): *The Birth of a Nation, Intolerance, Orphans of the Storm.*

Hawks, Howard (1896–1977): *Scarface, Twentieth Century, Bringing Up Baby, The Big Sleep.*

Hitchcock, Alfred (1899–1980): *The 39 Steps, Strangers on a Train, Rear Window, North by Northwest, Family Plot.*

Huston, John (1906–): *The Maltese Falcon, The Treasure of the Sierra Madre, The African Queen.*

Kazan, Elia (1909–): *A Streetcar Named Desire, Viva Zapata!, On the Waterfront, East of Eden.*

King, Henry (1891–): *Stella Dallas, State Fair, The Gunfighter.*

Kramer, Stanley (1913–): *Inherit the Wind, Judgment at Nuremberg, Guess Who's Coming to Dinner?*

Kubrick, Stanley (1928–): *Paths of Glory, Lolita, Dr. Strangelove, 2001, Clockwork Orange, Barry Lyndon.*

Le Roy, Mervyn (1900–): *I Am a Fugitive from a Chain Gang, Quo Vadis, Gypsy.*

Lubitsch, Ernst (1892–1947): *The Love Parade, Design for Living, Angel, Ninotchka.*

Lucas, George (1944–): *American Graffiti, Star Wars.*

Lumet, Sidney (1924–): *Long Day's Journey into Night, The Pawnbroker, The Seagull, Murder on the Orient Express, Network, Equus, The Wiz.*

McCarey, Leo (1898–1969): *The Awful Truth, Going My Way, An Affair to Remember.*

Mankiewicz, Joseph L. (1909–): *All About Eve, Julius Caesar, Suddenly Last Summer, Cleopatra.*

Milestone, Lewis (1895–1980): *All Quiet on the Western Front, Of Mice and Men, A Walk in the Sun.*

Nichols, Mike (1931–): *Who's Afraid of Virginia Woolf?, The Graduate, Catch 22, Carnal Knowledge.*

Peckinpah, Sam (1925–): *The Wild Bunch, Straw Dogs, Junior Bonner.*

Penn, Arthur (1922–): *The Miracle Worker, Mickey One, Bonnie and Clyde, Alice's Restaurant.*

Perry, Frank (1930–): *David and Lisa, Diary of a Mad Housewife, Last Summer, Mommie Dearest.*

Preminger, Otto (1906–): *Laura, The Moon Is Blue, The Man with the Golden Arm, Anatomy of a Murder.*

Ray, Nicholas (1911–79): *Knock on Any Door, Rebel without a Cause, Johnny Guitar, In a Lonely Place.*

Ritt, Martin (1920–): *Edge of the City; The Long, Hot Summer; Hud; The Brotherhood; Sounder; The Front, Norma Rae.*

Rossen, Robert (1908–66): *Body and Soul, All the King's Men, The Hustler.*

Scorsese, Martin (1942–): *Mean Streets, Alice Doesn't Live Here Anymore, Taxi Driver, New York, New York, The Last Waltz, Raging Bull.*

Silverstein, Elliot (1927–): *Cat Ballou, The Happening, A Man Called Horse.*

Siodmak, Robert (1900–73): *The Spiral Staircase, The Dark Mirror, The Killers.*

Spielberg, Steven (1947–): *The Sugarland Express, Jaws, Close Encounters of the Third Kind, 1941, Raiders of the Lost Ark.*

Sternberg, Josef von (1894–1969): *The Blue Angel, Morocco, Shanghai Express.*

Stevens, George (1904–75): *A Place in the Sun, Shane, Giant, The Diary of Anne Frank.*

Stroheim, Erich von (1885–1957): *Merry Go Round, Greed, The Merry Widow.*

Sturges, Preston (1898–1959): *The Great McGinty, Sullivan's Travels, Hail the Conquering Hero.*

Vidor, King (1894–): *The Big Parade, Northwest Passage, Duel in the Sun, War and Peace.*

Walsh, Raoul (1892–1980): *Thief of Bagdad, They Drive by Night, The Naked and the Dead.*

Warhol, Andy (1927?–): *Chelsea Girls, Lonesome Cowboys, Blue Movie.*

Welles, Orson (1915–): *Citizen Kane, The Magnificent Ambersons, Touch of Evil, The Trial.*

Wellman, William (1896–1975): *Nothing Sacred, The Story of G. I. Joe, The High and the Mighty.*

Wilder, Billy (1906–): *The Lost Weekend, Sunset Boulevard, Stalag 17, Some Like It Hot.*

Wood, Sam (1883–1949): *A Night at the Opera; A Day at the Races; Goodbye, Mr. Chips; Our Town.*

Wyler, William (1902–81): *Wuthering Heights, Mrs. Miniver, The Best Years of Our Lives, Ben Hur.*

Zinnemann, Fred (1907–): *High Noon, From Here to Eternity, The Nun's Story, A Man for All Seasons.*

USSR

Alexandrov, Grigori (1903–): *Jazz Comedy, Circus, Volga Volga.*

Bondarchuk, Sergei (1922–): *Destiny of a Man, War and Peace, The Steppe.*

Chukrai, Grigori (1921–): *The Forty-First, Ballad of a Soldier, Clear Sky.*

Donskoi, Mark (1897–1981):*The Maxim Gorki Trilogy, The Rainbow.*

Dovzhenko, Alexander (1894–1956): *Arsenal, Earth, Life in Blossom.*

Eisenstein, Sergei (1898–1948): *Potemkin, Alexander Nevsky, Ivan the Terrible.*

Gerasimov, Sergei (1906–): *Young Guard, And Quiet Flows the Don.*

Kalatosow, Mikhail (1903–1973): *The First Echelon, The Cranes Are Flying.*

Pudovkin, Vsevolod (1893–1953): *Mother, Storm over Asia, The Deserter.*

Pyryev, Ivan (1901–68): *The Wealthy Bride, The Idiot.*

Romm, Mikhail (1901–71): *Boule de Suif, Nine Days of One Year.*

OTHER COUNTRIES

Buñuel, Luis (1900–), Spain: *Evil Eden, Nazarin, Viridiana, Belle de Jour, Las Olvidados, Tristana, The Discrete Charm of the Bourgeoisie.*

Cacoyannis, Michael (1922–), Greece: *Stella, Electra, Zorba the Greek.*

Cavalcanti, Alberto (1897–), Brazil: *Dead of Night, Champagne Charlie, Monster.*

Costa-Gavras, Henri (1933–), Greece: *Z, The Confession, Claire de Femme.*

Dreyer, Carl Theodore (1889–1968), Denmark: *Joan of Arc, Vampyr, Day of Wrath, Gertrud.*

Fábri, Zoltán (1917–), Hungary: *Professor Hannibal, Twenty Hours, Late Season.*

Ford, Alexander (1908–), Poland: *The Young Chopin, Kings of the Teutonic Order.*

Forman, Milos (1932–), Czechoslovakia: *Loves of a Blonde, The Fireman's Ball, One Flew Over the Cuckoo's Nest, Hair.*

Ivens, Joris (1898–), Netherlands: *Zuyderzee, Spanish Earth.*

Jancso, Miklos (c. 1922–), Hungary: *The Round Up, The Red and the White.*

Kadar, Jan (1918–79), Czechoslovakia: *The Shop on Main Street, The Angel Levine, Adrift, Lies My Father Told Me.*

Kinugasa, Teinosuke (1898–), Japan: *Gate of Hell, The White Heron.*

Kurosawa, Akira (1910–), Japan: *Rashomon, Seven Samurai, Ikiru, The Lower Depths, Kagemushu.*

Lang, Fritz (1890–1976), Austria: *Metropolis, M, The 1,000 Eyes of Dr. Mabuse.*

Lindtberg, Leopold (1902–), Switzerland: *The Last Chance, Four in a Jeep, The Village.*

McLaren, Norman (1914–), Canada: *Blinkity-Blank; Dots, Loops.*

Menzel, Jiri (1938–), Czechoslovakia: *Closely Watched Trains, Capricious Summer, Those Wonderful Movie Cranks.*

Mizoguchi, Kenji (1898–1956), Japan: *Ugetsu, The Princess Yang, Street of Shame.*

Nemec, Jan (1936–), Czechoslovakia: *Diamonds of the Night, A Report on the Party and the Guests, The Martyrs of Love.*

Polanski, Roman (1933–), Poland: *Knife in the Water, Repulsion, Rosemary's Baby, Chinatown, The Tenant.*

Ray, Satyajit (1921–), India: *The Apu Trilogy, The Music Room, Devi, The Chess Players.*

Saura, Carlos (1932–), Spain: *The Hunt, Cousin Angelica, Cria!*

Teshigahara, Hiroshi (1927–), Japan: *Pitfall, Woman in the Dunes.*

Torre-Nilsson, Leopoldo (1924–78), Argentina: *The House of the Angel, The Hand in the Trap, Summer Skin.*

Wajda, Andrzej (1926–), Poland: *Kanal, Ashes and Diamonds, Fury is a Woman, Man of Iron.*

Weir, Peter (1944–), Australia: *Picnic at Hanging Rock, The Last Wave, Gallipoli.*

CELEBRITIES: PAST AND PRESENT

The Almanac celebrity list includes well-known personalities of stage, screen, radio, and television, as well as notables of other popular worlds. Entries indicate the celebrity's birthplace.

Aaron, Hank Mobile, Ala., 1934
Abbott, George Forestville, N.Y. 1887
Abel, Walter St. Paul, Minn., 1898
Abdul-Jabbar, Kareem New York, 1947
Ace, Goodman Kansas City, Mo., 1899
Acuff, Roy Maynardsville, Tenn., 1907
Adams, Don New York City, 1927
Adams, Edie Kingston, Pa., 1929
Adams, Joey New York City, 1911
Adams, Julie Waterloo, Iowa, 1928
Addams, Charles Westfield, N. J., 1912
Addams, Dawn Felixstowe, Eng., 1930
Adjani, Isabelle Paris, 1956
Adler, Larry Baltimore, 1914
Adler, Luther New York City, 1903
Adler, Stella New York City, 1902
Alberghetti, Anna Maria Pesaro, Italy, 1936
Albert, Eddie Rock Island, Ill., 1908
Albert, Edward Los Angeles, 1951
Albertson, Jack Malden, Mass., 1910
Albright, Lola Akron, O., 1925
Alda, Alan New York City, 1936
Alda, Robert New York City, 1914
Alexander, Ben Goldfield, Nev., 1911-69
Alexander, Jane Boston, 1939
Allen, Fred Boston, 1894-1956
Allen, Gracie San Francisco, 1906-64
Allen, Mel Birmingham, Ala., 1913
Allen, Steve New York City, 1921
Allen, Woody New York City, 1935
Allison, Fran La Porte City, Iowa, 1924?
Allyson, June New York City, 1923
Alpert, Herb Los Angeles, 1935
Ameche, Don Kenosha, Wis., 1908
Ames, Ed Boston, 1929
Ames, Leon Portland, Ind., 1903
Ames, Nancy Washington, D. C., 1937
Amory, Cleveland Nahant, Mass., 1917
Amsterdam, Morey Chicago, 1912
Anderson, Judith Adelaide, Austral., 1898
Anderson, Michael, Jr. London, 1943
Andersson, Bibi Stockholm, 1935
Andersson, Harriet Stockholm, 1932
Andress, Ursula, Berne, Switz., 1936
Andretti, Mario Trieste, 1940
Andrews, Dana Collins, Miss., 1912
Andrews, Julie Walton-on-Thames, Eng., 1935
Andrews, La Verne Minneapolis, 1915-67
Andrews, Maxine Minneapolis, 1918
Andrews, Patty Minneapolis, 1920
Angeli, Pier Sardinia, 1932-71
Anka, Paul Ottawa, Can., 1941
Annabella La Varenne-St. Hilaire, Fr., 1910
Ann-Margret Valsjobyn, Sweden, 1941
Arbuckle, "Fatty" Smith Center, Kans., 1887-1933
Arcaro, Eddie Newport, Ky., 1916
Arden, Elizabeth Ontario, 1891-1966
Arden, Eve Mill Valley, Cal., 1912
Arkin, Alan New York City, 1934
Armstrong, Louis New Orleans, 1900-71
Arnaz, Desi Santiago, Cuba, 1917
Arness, James Minneapolis, 1923
Arno, Peter New York, 1904-68
Arnold, Eddy Henderson, Tenn., 1918
Arnold, Edward New York, 1890-1956
Arquette, Cliff Toledo, O., 1905-74
Arthur, Beatrice New York, 1926
Arthur, Jean New York City, 1908
Ashcroft, Peggy London, 1907
Ashe, Arthur Richmond, Va., 1943
Ashley, Elizabeth Ocala, Fla., 1940
Asner, Edward Kansas City, Kans., 1929
Astaire, Adele Omaha, Neb. 1898-1981
Astaire, Fred Omaha, Neb., 1899
Astor, Mary Quincy, Ill., 1906
Atkins, Chet Luttrell, Tenn., 1924
Attenborough, Richard Cambridge, Eng., 1923
Aumont, Jean-Pierre Paris, 1913
Austin, Tracy Redondo Beach, Cal., 1962
Autry, Gene Tioga, Tex., 1907
Avalon, Frankie Philadelphia, 1940
Avedon, Richard New York City, 1923

Ayres, Lew Minneapolis, 1908
Aznavour, Charles Paris, 1924
Bacall, Lauren New York City, 1924
Baccaloni, Salvatore Rome, 1900-69
Bacharach, Burt Kansas City, Mo., 1929
Backus, Jim Cleveland, 1913
Baer, Max Omaha, 1909-59
Baez, Joan New York City, 1941
Bailey, Mildred Washington, 1903-51
Bailey, Pearl Newport News, Va., 1918
Bainter, Fay Los Angeles, 1893-1963
Baird, Bil Grand Island, Neb., 1904
Baker, Carroll Johnstown, Pa., 1935
Baker, Diane Hollywood, Cal., 1940?
Baker, Josephine St. Louis, 1906-75
Baker, Kenny Monrovia, Cal., 1912
Balenciaga, Cristobal Guetaria, Sp., 1895-1972
Ball, Lucille Jamestown, N. Y., 1911
Ballard, Kaye Cleveland, 1926
Balmain, Pierre St.-Jean-de-Maurienne, Fr., 1914
Balsam, Martin New York City, 1919
Bancroft, Anne New York City, 1931
Bankhead, Tallulah Huntsville, Ala., 1903-68
Bara, Theda Cincinnati, 1890-1955
Barber, Red Columbus, Miss., 1908
Bardot, Brigitte Paris, 1934
Barnes, Binnie London, 1906
Barrault, Jean-Louis Vesinet, Fr., 1910
Barrie, Wendy London, 1913-78
Barry, Gene New York City, 1921
Barrymore, Diana New York, 1922-60
Barrymore, Ethel Phila., 1879-1959
Barrymore, John Phila., 1882-1942
Barrymore, John Blyth Beverly Hills, Cal., 1932
Barrymore, Lionel Phila. 1878-1954
Barthelmess, Richard New York, 1895-1963
Bartholomew, Freddie London, 1924
Bartok, Eva Budapest, 1926
Basehart, Richard Zanesville, O., 1914
Basie, Count Red Bank, N. J., 1904
Bassey, Shirley Cardiff, Wales, 1937
Bates, Alan Allestree, Eng., 1934
Baxter, Anne Michigan City, Ind., 1923
Baxter, Warner Columbus, O., 1893-1951
Bean, Orson Burlington, Vt., 1928
Beaton, Cecil London, 1904-80
Beatty, Clyde Bainbridge, O., 1905-65
Beatty, Warren Richmond, Va., 1938
Bechet, Sidney New Orleans, 1897-1959
Bee Gees see Gibb
Beene, Geoffrey Haynesville, La., 1927
Beery, Noah Kansas City, Mo., 1883-1946
Beery, Noah, Jr., New York City, 1916
Beery, Wallace Kansas City, Mo., 1886-1949
Begley, Ed Hartford, Conn., 1901-70
Belafonte, Harry New York City, 1927
Belasco, David San Francisco, 1854-1931
Bel Geddes, Barbara New York, 1922
Bellamy, Ralph Chicago, 1904
Belmondo, Jean-Paul Neuilly-sur-Seine, Fr., 1933
Belushi, John Chicago, 1949
Benatar, Pat Brooklyn, 1953
Benchley, Robert Worcester, Mass., 1889-1945
Bendix, William New York, 1906-64
Benjamin, Richard New York City, 1939
Bennett, Constance New York, 1914-65
Bennett, Joan Palisades, N. J., 1910
Bennett, Michael Buffalo, 1943
Bennett, Richard Indiana, 1873-1944
Bennett, Tony New York City, 1926
Benny, Jack Waukegan, Ill. 1894-1974
Benzell, Mimi Bridgeport, Conn., 1924-70
Berg, Gertrude New York, 1900-66
Bergen, Candice Beverly Hills, Cal., 1946
Bergen, Edgar Chicago, 1903-78

Bergen, Polly Knoxville, Tenn., 1930
Bergerac, Jacques Biarritz, Fr., 1927
Bergman, Ingrid Stockholm, 1917
Bergner, Elisabeth Vienna, 1900
Berkeley, Busby Los Angeles, 1895-1976
Berle, Milton New York City, 1908
Berlin, Irving Russia, 1888
Berman, Pandro S. Pittsburgh, 1905
Berman, Shelley Chicago, 1926
Bernardi, Herschel New York City, 1923
Bernhardt, Sarah Paris, 1844-1923
Bernie, Ben Bayonne, N.J., 1893-1943
Berra, Yogi St. Louis, 1925
Bickford, Charles Cambridge, Mass., 1889-1967
Bikel, Theodore Vienna, 1924
Birney, David Washington, 1940
Bishop, Joey New York City, 1918
Bisset, Jacqueline Weybridge, Eng., 1944
Black, Karen Park Ridge, Ill., 1942
Blackman, Honor London, 1929
Blackmer, Sidney Salisbury, N. C., 1898-1973
Blaine, Vivian Newark, N. J., 1924
Blair, Janet Altoona, Pa., 1921
Blair, Linda Westport, Conn., 1959
Blake, Eubie Baltimore, 1883
Blake, Robert Nutley, N.J., 1938
Blakeley, Ronee Idaho, 1946
Blass, Bill Fort Wayne, Ind., 1922
Blocker, Dan Bowie Co., Tex., 1929-72
Blondell, Joan New York City, 1912-79
Bloom, Claire London, 1931
Blue, Ben Montreal, 1901-75
Blyth, Ann New York City, 1928
Bogarde, Dirk London, 1921
Bogart, Humphrey New York, 1899-1957
Boland, Mary Phila., 1885-1965
Bolger, Ray Dorchester, Mass., 1904
Bombeck, Erma Dayton, Ohio, 1927
Bond, Ward Denver, 1904-60
Bono, Sonny Detroit, 1940
Boone, Pat Jacksonville, Fla., 1934
Boone, Richard Los Angeles, 1917-81
Booth, Shirley New York City, 1909
Borg, Björn Södertalje, Sweden, 1956
Borge, Victor Copenhagen, 1909
Borgnine, Ernest Hamden, Conn., 1917
Bosley, Tom Chicago, 1927
Bourke-White, Margaret New York City, 1906-71
Bow, Clara New York, 1905-65
Bowes, "Major" San Francisco, 1874-1946
Bowie, David Brixton, Eng., 1947
Bowman, Lee Cincinnati, 1914-79
Boyd, Stephen Belfast, Northern Ireland, 1928-77
Boyd, William Cambridge, O., 1898-1972
Boyer, Charles Figeac Lot, Fr., 1899-1978
Bracken, Eddie New York City, 1920
Bradshaw, Terry Shreveport, La., 1948
Brady, Alice New York City, 1892-1939
Brady, Scott New York City, 1924
Brand, Neville Kewanee, Ill., 1921
Brando, Marlon Omaha, Neb., 1924
Brasselle, Keefe Lorain, O., 1923
Brazzi, Rossano Bologna, Italy, 1916
Brel, Jacques Brussels, 1929-78
Brennan, Walter Lynn, Mass., 1894-1974
Brenner, David Philadelphia, 1945
Brent, George Dublin, 1904-79
Brewer, Teresa Toledo, O., 1931
Brice, Fanny New York, 1891-1951
Bridges, Beau Los Angeles, 1941
Bridges, Lloyd San Leandro, Cal., 1913
Brinkley, David Wilmington, N. C., 1920
Brisson, Frederick Copenhagen, 1917
Britt, Mai Lidingo, Swed., 1936
Brock, Lou El Dorado, Ark., 1939
Broderick, Helen Phila., 1890-1959
Brokaw, Tom Webster, S.D., 1940
Bronson, Charles, Ehrenfeld, Pa., 1922
Brooks, Mel New York City, 1926
Brothers, Joyce New York City, 1928

Broun, Heywood New York, 1888-1939
Broun, Heywood Hale New York, 1918
Brown, Helen Gurley Portland, Me., 1922
Brown, James Augusta, Ga., 1930?
Brown, Jim Manhasset, N. Y., 1936
Brown, Joe E. Holgate, O., 1892-1973
Brown, Vanessa Vienna, 1928
Brubeck, Dave Concord, Cal., 1920
Bruce, Carol Great Neck, N. Y., 1919
Bruce, Nigel Mexico, 1895-1953
Bruce, Virginia Minneapolis, 1910
Bryant, Anita Barnsdall, Okla., 1940
Brynner, Yul Sakhalin, 1917
Buchanan, Edgar Humansville, Mo., 1903-79
Buchanan, Jack Scotland, 1891-1957
Buchholz, Horst Berlin, 1933
Buchwald, Art Mount Vernon, N. Y., 1925
Buckley, William F. New York City, 1925
Bujold, Genevieve Montreal, 1942
Burke, Billie Washington, D.C., 1884-1970
Burnett, Carol Dallas, 1934
Burns, George New York City, 1896
Burr, Raymond New Westminster, Can., 1917
Burrows, Abe New York City, 1910
Burstyn, Ellen Detroit, Mich., 1932
Burton, Richard Pontrhydyfen, Wales, 1925
Busch, August A., Jr. St. Louis, 1899
Bushman, Francis X. Norfolk, 1883-1966
Butterworth, Charles South Bend, Ind., 1897-1946
Buttons, Red New York City, 1919
Buzzi, Ruth Westerly, R. I., 1936
Byington, Spring, Colorado Springs, 1893-1971
Byrd, Charlie Chuckatuck, Va., 1925
Caan, James New York City, 1939
Caen, Herb Sacramento, Cal., 1916
Caesar, Irving New York City, 1895
Caesar, Sid Yonkers, N. Y., 1922
Cagney, James New York City, 1904
Cahn, Sammy New York City, 1913
Caine, Michael London, 1933
Caldwell, Zoë Melbourne, Austral., 1933
Calhern, Louis New York, 1895-1956
Calhoun, Rory Los Angeles, 1923
Callan, Michael Philadelphia, 1935
Calloway, Cab Rochester, N. Y., 1907
Cambridge, Godfrey New York, 1933-76
Cameron, Rod Calgary, Can., 1912
Campbell, Glen near Delight, Ark., 1938
Cannon, Dyan Tacoma, Wash., 1938?
Canova, Judy Jacksonville, Fla., 1916
Cantinflas Mexico City, 1911
Cantor, Eddie New York, 1892-1964
Cantrell, Lana Sydney, Austral., 1944
Capp, Al New Haven, Conn., 1909-79
Capucine Toulon, Fr., 1935?
Cardin, Pierre near Venice, 1922
Cardinale, Claudia Tunis, 1940
Carew, Rod Gatun, C.Z., 1945
Carey, Macdonald Sioux City, Iowa, 1913
Carlin, George New York City, 1938
Carlisle, Kitty New Orleans, 1914
Carmichael, Hoagy Bloomington, Ind., 1899
Carmines, Al Hampton, Va., 1937
Carne, Judy Northampton, Eng., 1939
Carney, Art Mt. Vernon, N. Y., 1918
Carnovsky, Morris St. Louis, 1897
Caron, Leslie Paris, 1931
Carr, Vikki El Paso, Tex., 1942
Carradine, David Los Angeles, 1936
Carradine, John New York City, 1906
Carrillo, Leo Los Angeles, 1881-1961
Carroll, Diahann New York City, 1935
Carroll, Leo G. Weedon, Eng., 1892-1972
Carroll, Madeleine West Bromwich, Eng., 1906
Carroll, Nancy New York, 1906-65
Carroll, Pat Shreveport, La., 1927
Carson, Jack Carman, Can., 1910-63
Carson, Johnny Corning, Iowa, 1925
Carter, Billy Plains, Ga., 1937
Carter, Jack New York City, 1923
Cash, Johnny Kingsland, Ark., 1932
Cass, Peggy Boston, 1925

Cassavetes, John New York, 1929
Cassidy, Shaun Los Angeles, 1958
Cassini, Oleg Paris, 1913
Castle, Irene New Rochelle, N.Y., 1893-1969
Cauthen, Steve Covington, Ky., 1960
Cavett, Dick Gibbon, Neb., 1936
Cerf, Bennett New York City, 1898-1971
Chakiris, George Norwood, O., 1933
Chamberlain, Richard Beverly Hills, Cal., 1935
Chamberlain, Wilt Philadelphia, 1936
Champion, Gower Geneva, Ill., 1920-80
Champion, Marge Hollywood, Cal., 1925
Chancellor, John Chicago, 1927
Chandler, Jeff New York, 1918-61
Chanel, "Coco" Issoire, Fr., 1883-1971
Chaney, Lon Colorado Springs, 1883-1930
Chaney, Lon, Jr. Oklahoma City, 1915-73
Channing, Carol Seattle, 1921
Chaplin, Charles London, 1889-1977
Chaplin, Geraldine Santa Monica, Cal., 1944
Chaplin, Sydney Los Angeles, 1926
Charisse, Cyd Amarillo, Tex., 1923
Charles, Ray Albany, Ga., 1932
Chase, Chevy New York City, 1943
Chase, Ilka New York City, 1905-78
Chatterton, Ruth New York, 1893-1961
Cher El Centro, Cal., 1946
Chevalier, Maurice Paris, 1888-1972
Child, Julia Pasadena, Cal., 1912
Christian, Linda Tampico, Mexico, 1923
Christie, Julie Chukua, India, 1941
Christopher, Jordan Akron, O., 1941
Cilento, Diane Brisbane, Austral., 1933
Claire, Ina Washington, D. C., 1895
Clapton, Eric Ripley, Eng., 1945
Clark, Bobby Springfield, O., 1888-1960
Clark, Dane New York City, 1915
Clark, Dick Mt. Vernon, N. Y., 1929
Clark, Fred Lincoln, Cal., 1914-68
Clark, Petula Ewell, Eng., 1932
Clark, Roy Meherrin, Va., 1933
Clayburgh, Jill New York City, 1944
Clift, Montgomery Omaha, 1920-66
Clooney, Rosemary Maysville, Ky., 1928
Cobb, Irvin S. Paducah, Ky., 1876-1944
Cobb, Lee J. New York City, 1911-76
Coburn, Charles Macon, Ga., 1877-1961
Coburn, James Laurel, Neb., 1928
Coca, Imogene Philadelphia, 1908
Coco, James New York City, 1929
Coe, Sebastian London, 1956
Cohan, George M. Providence, R.I., 1878-1942
Cohen, Myron Grodno, Poland, 1902
Colbert, Claudette Paris, 1905
Colby, Anita Washington, D. C., 1914
Cole, Nat "King" Montgomery, Ala., 1919-65
Cole, Natalie Los Angeles, 1950
Coleman, Ornette Fort Worth, Tex., 1930
Collingwood, Charles Three Rivers, Mich., 1917
Collins, Dorothy Windsor, Can., 1926
Collins, Joan London, 1933
Collins, Judy Seattle, 1939
Colman, Ronald Richmond, Eng., 1891-1959
Colonna, Jerry Boston, 1905
Comaneci, Nadia Onesti, Romania, 1961
Comden, Betty New York City, 1919
Como, Perry Canonsburg, Pa., 1913
Condon, Eddie Goodland, Ind., 1905-73
Conklin, Peggy Dobbs Ferry, N. Y., 1912
Connelly, Marc McKeesport, Pa. 1890-1980
Connery, Sean Edinburgh, 1930
Connolly, Walter Cincinnati, 1887-1940
Connors, Chuck New York City, 1921
Connors, Jimmy St. Louis, 1952
Connors, Mike Fresno, Cal., 1925
Conrad, William Louisville, Ky., 1920
Conried, Hans Baltimore, 1917
Conte, Richard New York City 1914-75
Conway, Tim Willoughby, Ohio, 1933

Conway, Tom Russia, 1904-67
Coogan, Jackie Los Angeles, 1914
Cook, Joe Chicago, 1890-1959
Cooke, Alistair Manchester, Eng., 1908
Coolidge, Rita Nashville, 1944
Cooney, Joan Ganz Phoenix, 1929
Cooper, Alice Detroit, 1948
Cooper, Gary Helena, Mont., 1901-61
Cooper, Gladys Lewisham, Eng., 1888-1971
Cooper, Jackie Los Angeles, 1922
Coote, Robert London, 1909
Corey, Wendell Dracut, Mass., 1914-68
Corio, Ann Hartford, Conn., 1914?
Cornell, Katharine Berlin, 1898-1974
Cosby, Bill Philadelphia, 1937
Cosell, Howard Winston-Salem, N.C., 1920
Costello, Lou Paterson, N.J., 1906-59
Cotten, Joseph Petersburg, Va., 1905
Courrèges, André Pau, Fr., 1923
Courtenay, Tom Hull, Eng., 1937
Cousins, Norman Union Hill, N. J., 1912
Cousteau, Jacques Yves St. André-de-Cubzac, Fr., 1910
Cox, Wally Detroit, 1924-73
Crabbe, Buster Oakland, Cal., 1909
Crain, Jeanne Barstow, Cal., 1925
Craven, Frank Boston, 1878-1948
Crawford, Broderick Philadelphia, 1911
Crawford, Joan San Antonio, 1908-77
Cregar, Laird Phila., 1916-44
Crenna, Richard Los Angeles, 1927
Croce, Jim Philadelphia, Pa., 1943-73
Cronkite, Walter St. Joseph, Mo., 1916
Cronyn, Hume London, Can., 1911
Crosby, Bing Tacoma, Wash., 1904-77
Crosby, Bob Spokane, Wash., 1913
Crosby, David Los Angeles, 1941
Crouse, Russel Findlay, O., 1893-1966
Csonka, Larry Stow, O., 1946
Cugat, Xavier Barcelona, 1900
Cukor, George New York City, 1899
Cullen, Bill Pittsburgh, 1920
Culp, Robert Berkeley, Cal., 1930
Cummings, Robert Joplin, Mo., 1910
Curtis, Tony New York City, 1925
Dahl, Arlene Minneapolis, 1927
Dailey, Dan New York City, 1915-78
Dale, Jim Rothwell, Eng., 1935
Daly, John Johannesburg, 1914
Damone, Vic New York City, 1928
Dana, Bill Quincy, Mass., 1924
Dandridge, Dorothy Cleveland, 1924-65
Daniels, Bebe Dallas, 1901-71
Daniels, Billy Jacksonville, Fla., 1914?
Danner, Blythe Philadelphia, 1944
Danton, Ray New York City, 1931
Darcel, Denise Paris, 1925
Darin, Bobby New York City, 1936-73
Darnell, Linda Dallas, 1921-65
Darren, James Philadelphia, 1936
Darrieux, Danielle Bordeaux, Fr., 1917
Darwell, Jane Palmyra, Mo., 1880-1967
da Silva, Howard Cleveland, 1909
Dauphin, Claude Corbeil, Fr., 1903-78
Davenport, Harry New York 1866-1949
Davenport, Nigel Cambridge, Eng., 1928
Davidson, John Pittsburgh, Pa., 1941
Davies, Marion New York, 1897-1961
Davis, Bette Lowell, Mass., 1908
Davis, Joan St. Paul, Minn., 1908-61
Davis, Mac Lubbock, Tex., 1942
Davis, Miles Alton, Ill., 1927
Davis, Ossie Cogdell, Ga., 1921
Davis, Sammy, Jr. New York City, 1925
Day, Dennis New York City, 1917
Day, Doris Cincinnati, 1924
Day, Laraine Roosevelt, Utah, 1920
Dean, Dizzy Lucas, Ark., 1911-74
Dean, James Fairmount, Ind., 1931-55
DeCamp, Rosemary Prescott, Ariz., 1914
De Carlo, Yvonne Vancouver, Can., 1924
Dee, Frances Los Angeles, 1907
Dee, Ruby Cleveland, 1923?
Dee, Sandra Bayonne, N. J., 1942
De Fore, Don Cedar Rapids, Iowa, 1916
De Haven, Gloria Los Angeles, 1925
de Havilland, Olivia Tokyo, 1916
Dekker, Albert New York, 1905-68
De Laurentiis, Dino Torre Annunziata, Italy, 1919

Delon, Alain Scéaux, Fr., 1935
Del Rio, Dolores Durango, Mex., 1905
DeLuise, Dom Brooklyn, N.Y., 1933
Demarest, William St. Paul, 1892
De Mille, Cecil B. Ashfield, Mass., 1881-1959
Dempsey, Jack Manassa, Colo., 1895-1974
Deneuve, Catherine Paris, 1943
De Niro, Robert New York City, 1943
Dennis, Sandy Hastings, Neb., 1937
Denny, Reginald Richmond, Eng., 1891-1967
Denver, John Roswell, N.M., 1943
Derek, Bo Long Beach, Cal., 1956
Dern, Bruce Chicago, 1936
Desmond, Johnny Detroit, 1921
Devine, Andy Flagstaff, Ariz., 1905-77
Dewhurst, Colleen Montreal, 1926
de Wilde, Brandon New York, 1942-72
De Wolfe, Billy Wollaston, Mass. 1907-74
Diamond, Neil Brooklyn, N.Y., 1941
Dickinson, Angie Kulm, N.D., 1932
Dietrich, Marlene Berlin, 1904
Dietz, Howard New York City, 1896
Diller, Phyllis Lima, O., 1917
Dillman, Bradford San Francisco, 1930
Di Maggio, Joe San Francisco, 1914
Dior, Christian Granville, Fr., 1905-57
Disney, Walt Chicago, 1901-66
Dixon, Jeane Medford, Wis., 1918
Dolly, Jenny Hungary, 1892-1941
Dolly, Rosie Hungary, 1892-1970
Donahue, Phil Cleveland, 1935
Donahue, Troy New York City, 1937
Donat, Robert Manchester, Eng., 1905-59
Donlevy, Brian Portadown, Ire., 1899-1972
Donovan (Leitch) Glasgow, 1946
Dors, Diana Swindon, Eng., 1931
Dorsey, Jimmy Mahonoy Plane, Pa., 1904-57
Dorsey, Tommy Mahonoy Plane, Pa., 1905-56
Douglas, Kirk Amsterdam, N. Y., 1918?
Douglas, Melvyn Macon, Ga., 1901-81
Douglas, Michael New Brunswick, N.J., 1944
Douglas, Mike Chicago, 1925
Douglas, Paul Phila., 1907-59
Downs, Hugh Akron, O., 1921
Drake, Alfred New York City, 1914
Drake, Betsy Paris, 1923
Draper, Paul Florence, Italy, 1909
Draper, Ruth New York, 1884-1956
Dressler, Marie Canada, 1869-1933
Dreyfuss, Richard New York City, 1947
Dru, Joanne Logan, W. Va., 1923
Duchin, Eddy Boston, 1909-51
Duchin, Peter New York City, 1937
Duff, Howard Bremerton, Wash., 1917
Duke, Doris New York City, 1912
Duke, Patty New York City, 1946
Dullea, Keir Cleveland, 1939
Dunaway, Faye Tallahassee, Fla., 1941
Duncan, Sandy Henderson, Tex., 1946
Dunn, James New York, 1906-67
Dunne, Irene Louisville, Ky., 1904
Dunnock, Mildred Baltimore, 1906
Durante, Jimmy New York, 1893-1980
Durbin, Deanna Winnipeg, Can., 1922
Durocher, Leo West Springfield, Mass., 1906
Duryea, Dan White Plains, N.Y., 1907-68
Duse, Eleanora Italy, 1858-1924
Duvall, Robert San Diego, Cal., 1931
Dylan, Bob Duluth, Minn., 1941
Eagels, Jeanne Kansas City, Mo., 1894-1929
Eastwood, Clint San Francisco, 1933
Ebsen, Buddy Orlando, Fla., 1908
Eddy, Nelson Providence, R.I., 1901-67
Eden, Barbara San Francisco, 1936
Edwards, Ralph Merino, Colo., 1913
Edwards, Vince New York City, 1928
Egan, Richard San Francisco, 1923
Eggar, Samantha London, 1940
Ekberg, Anita Malmö, Swed., 1931
Eldridge, Florence New York City, 1901
Elliot, Cass Arlington, Va., 1943?-74

Elliott, Bob Boston, 1923
Elliott, Maxine Rockland, Me., 1868-1940
Emerson, Faye Elizabeth, N. J., 1917
Erickson, Leif Alameda, Cal., 1914
Erving, Julius Roosevelt, N.Y., 1950
Erwin, Stuart Squaw Valley, Cal., 1903-67
Esposito, Phil Sault Ste. Marie, Ont., 1942
Evans, Bergen Franklin, O., 1904-78
Evans, Dale Uvalde, Tex., 1912
Evans, Madge New York City, 1909-81
Evans, Maurice Dorchester, Eng., 1901
Evert-Lloyd, Chris Fort Lauderdale, Fla., 1954
Ewell, Tom Owensboro, Ky., 1909
Fabray, Nanette San Diego, Cal., 1920
Fadiman, Clifton New York City, 1904
Fairbanks, Douglas Denver, 1883-1939
Fairbanks, Douglas, Jr. New York, 1909
Faith, Percy Toronto, 1908-76
Falk, Peter New York City, 1927
Farber, Barry Baltimore, 1930
Farrell, Glenda Enid, Okla., 1904-71
Farrow, Mia Los Angeles, 1945
Faulk, John Henry Austin, Tex., 1913
Fawcett, Farrah Corpus Christi, Tex., 1947
Fay, Frank San Francisco, 1897-1961
Faye, Alice New York City, 1915
Feiffer, Jules New York City, 1929
Feldman, Marty London, 1933
Feldon, Barbara Pittsburgh, 1939
Feliciano, Jose Larez, P. R., 1945
Feller, Bob Van Meter, Iowa, 1918
Ferguson, Maynard Verdun, Can., 1928
Fernandel Marseilles, 1903-71
Ferrer, José Santurce, P. R., 1912
Ferrer, Mel Elberon, N. J., 1917
Field, Betty Boston, 1918-73
Field, Sally Pasadena, Cal., 1946
Fields, Dorothy Allenhurst, N. J., 1905
Fields, Gracie Rochdale, Eng., 1898-1979
Fields, Totie Hartford, Conn., 1931-78
Fields, W. C. Phila., 1879-1946
Finch, Peter London, 1916-77
Finney, Albert Salford, Eng., 1936
Fischer, Bobby Chicago, 1943
Fisher, Carrie Beverly Hills, 1956
Fisher, Eddie Philadelphia, 1928
Fitzgerald, Barry Dublin, 1888-1961
Fitzgerald, Ella Newport News, Va., 1918
Fitzgerald, Geraldine Dublin, 1914
Flack, Roberta Black Mountain, N. C., 1940
Fleming, Rhonda Los Angeles, 1923
Fletcher, Louise Birmingham, Ala., 1934
Flynn, Errol Tasmania, 1909-59
Foch, Nina Leyden, Neth., 1924
Fonda, Henry Grand Island, Neb., 1905
Fonda, Jane New York City, 1937
Fonda, Peter New York City, 1939
Fontaine, Frank Haverhill, Mass., 1920-78
Fontaine, Joan Tokyo, 1917
Fontanne, Lynn Woodford, Eng., 1887?
Ford, Glenn Quebec, 1916
Ford, Tennessee Ernie Bristol, Tenn., 1919
Forsythe, John Penns Grove, N. J., 1918
Fosse, Bob Chicago, 1927
Foster, Jodie Los Angeles, 1962
Foxx, Redd St. Louis, 1922
Foy, Eddie, Jr. New Rochelle, N.Y., 1910
Frampton, Peter Beckenham, Eng., 1950
Franciosa, Anthony New York City, 1928
Francis, Arlene Boston, 1908
Francis, Connie Newark, N. J., 1938
Francis, Kay Oklahoma City, 1905-68
Franklin, Aretha Memphis, Tenn., 1942
Frazier, Walt Atlanta, 1945
Freberg, Stan Pasadena, Cal., 1926
Freed, Arthur Charleston, S. C., 1894
Friedan, Betty Peoria, Ill., 1921
Friendly, Fred W. New York City, 1915
Fröbe, Gert Planitz, Ger., 1913
Froman, Jane St. Louis, 1908-80
Frost, David Tenterden, Eng., 1939
Funt, Allen New York City, 1914
Furness, Betty New York City, 1916

Gabel, Martin Philadelphia, 1912
Gable, Clark Cadiz, O., 1901-60
Gabor, Eva Budapest, 1926?
Gabor, Zsa Zsa Budapest, 1923?
Gallico, Paul New York City, 1897-1976
Gam, Rita Pittsburgh, 1928
Garagiola, Joe St. Louis, 1926
Garbo, Greta Stockholm, 1906
Gardiner, Reginald Wimbledon, Eng., 1903-80
Gardner, Ava Smithfield, N. C., 1922
Garfield, John New York, 1913-52
Garfunkel, Arthur New York City, 1941
Gargan, William New York City, 1905-79
Garland, Judy Grand Rapids, Minn., 1922-69
Garner, Erroll Pittsburgh, 1921-77
Garner, James Norman, Okla., 1928
Garner, Peggy Ann Canton, O., 1932
Garroway, Dave Schenectady, N.Y., 1913
Garson, Greer County Down, Northern Ireland, 1908
Gassman, Vittorio Genoa, Italy, 1922
Gavin, John Los Angeles, 1928
Gayle, Crystal Paintsville, Ky., 1951
Gaxton, William San Francisco, 1893-1963
Gaynor, Janet Philadelphia, 1906
Gaynor, Mitzi Chicago, 1931
Gazzara, Ben New York City, 1930
Geer, Will Frankfort, Ind., 1902-78
Gehrig, Lou New York City, 1903-41
Gentry, Bobbie Chickasaw Co., Miss., 1944
George, Gladys Patten, Me., 1904-54
George, Grace New York, 1879-1961
Gere, Richard Philadelphia, 1950
Gernreich, Rudi Vienna, 1922
Gershwin, George New York, 1898-1937
Gershwin, Ira New York City, 1896
Gerulaitis, Vitas Brooklyn, 1954
Getz, Stan Philadelphia, 1927
Ghostley, Alice Eve, Mo., 1926
Giannini, Giancarlo La Spezia, Italy, 1942
Gibb, Andy Manchester Eng., 1958
Gibb, Barry Manchester, Eng., 1946
Gibb, Maurice Manchester, Eng., 1949
Gibb, Robin Manchester, Eng., 1949
Gibbs, Georgia Worcester, Mass., 1923?
Gielgud, John London, 1904
Gilbert, Billy Louisville, Ky., 1894-1971
Gilbert, John Logan, Utah, 1895-1936
Gilford, Jack New York City, 1913?
Gillespie, Dizzy Cheraw, N. C., 1917
Gingold, Hermione London, 1897
Gish, Dorothy Massillon, O., 1898-1968
Gish, Lillian Springfield, O., 1899
Givenchy, Hubert Beauvais, Fr., 1927
Gleason, Jackie New York City, 1916
Gleason, James New York, 1886-1959
Gobel, George Chicago, 1920
Goddard, Paulette Great Neck, N. Y., 1911
Godfrey, Arthur New York City, 1903
Goldberg, Rube San Francisco, 1883-1970
Golden, Harry New York City, 1902
Goldwyn, Samuel Warsaw, 1882-1974
Gonzales, Pancho Los Angeles, 1928
Goodman, Benny Chicago, 1909
Goodman, Dody Columbus, O., 1929
Goodson, Mark Sacramento, Cal., 1915
Goolagong, Evonne Barellan, Australia, 1951
Gordon, Ruth Wollaston, Mass., 1896
Goren, Charles Philadelphia, 1901
Goring, Marius Isle of Wight, 1912
Gormé, Eydie New York City, 1932
Gould, Chester Pawnee, Okla., 1900
Gould, Elliott New York City, 1939
Goulding, Ray Lowell, Mass., 1922
Goulet, Robert Lawrence, Mass., 1933
Grable, Betty St. Louis, 1916-73
Graham, Sheilah London, 1905?
Graham, Virginia Chicago, 1912
Grahame, Gloria Los Angeles, 1929
Granger, Farley San José, Cal., 1925
Granger, Stewart London, 1913
Grant, Cary Bristol, Eng., 1904
Grant, Lee New York City, 1927
Gray, Barry Red Lion, N. J., 1916

Gray, Dolores Chicago, 1930
Grayson, Kathryn Winston-Salem, N.C., 1923
Graziano, Rocky New York City, 1922
Greco, Buddy Philadelphia, 1926
Green, Adolph New York City, 1915
Green, Johnny New York City, 1908
Green, Martyn London, 1899-1975
Greene, Lorne Ottawa, 1915
Greene, Richard Plymouth, Eng., 1918
Greenstreet, Sydney Sandwich, Eng., 1879-1954
Greenwood, Joan London, 1921
Greer, Jane Washington, D. C., 1924
Gregory, Dick St. Louis, 1932
Grey, Joel Cleveland, 1932
Griffin, Merv San Mateo, Cal., 1925
Griffith, Andy Mt. Airy, N. C., 1926
Griffith, Hugh Anglesey, Wales, 1912-80
Grimes, Tammy Lynn, Mass., 1934
Grizzard, George Roanoke Rapids, N. C., 1928
Guardino, Harry New York City, 1925
Guidry, Ron Lafayette, La., 1950
Guinness, Alec London, 1914
Gunn, Moses St. Louis, 1930?
Guthrie, Arlo New York City, 1947
Guthrie, Tyrone Tunbridge Wells, Eng., 1900-71
Guthrie, Woody Okemah, Okla., 1912-67
Gwenn, Edmund London, 1875-1959
Hackett, Buddy New York City, 1924
Hackman, Gene Danville, Ill., 1931
Hagen, Uta Göttingen, Ger., 1919
Hagman, Larry Weatherford, Tex., 1931
Hailey, Arthur Luton, Eng., 1920
Hale, Barbara De Kalb, Ill., 1922
Haley, Jack Boston, 1901-79
Hall, Gus Virginia, Minn., 1910
Hall, Juanita Keyport, N.J., 1901-68
Hall, Monty Winnipeg, Canada, 1923
Halston (Roy Halston Frowick) Des Moines, 1932
Hamill, Dorothy Riverside, Conn., 1956
Hamilton, George Memphis, Tenn., 1939
Hamilton, Margaret Cleveland, 1902
Hamlisch, Marvin New York, 1944
Hampden, Walter New York, 1879-1955
Hampton, Lionel Louisville, Ky., 1913
Handy, W. C. Florence, Ala., 1873-1958
Harburg, E. Y. New York City, 1896-1981
Harding, Ann San Antonio, 1902-81
Hardwicke, Cedric Lye, Eng., 1893-1964
Hardy, Oliver Atlanta, 1892-1957
Harlow, Jean Kansas City, Mo., 1911-37
Harmon, Tom Rensselaer, Ind., 1919
Harper, Valerie Suffern, N.Y., 1940
Harrington, Michael St. Louis, 1928
Harris, Barbara Evanston, Ill., 1935
Harris, Emmylou Birmingham, Ala., 1949
Harris, Jed Vienna, 1900-79
Harris, Julie Grosse Pointe, Mich., 1925
Harris, Phil Linton, Ind., 1906
Harris, Richard Limerick, Ireland, 1933
Harris, Rosemary Ashby, Eng., 1930
Harrison, George Liverpool, Eng., 1943
Harrison, Noel London, 1936
Harrison, Rex Huyton, Eng., 1908
Harry, Deborah Hawthorne, N.J., 1945
Hartford, Huntington New York, 1911
Hartman, David Pawtucket, R.I., 1935
Hartman, Elizabeth Youngstown, O., 1941
Hartman, Paul San Francisco, 1910-73
Harvey, Laurence Yonishkis, Lith., 1928-73
Hasso, Signe Stockholm, 1910
Haver, June Rock Island, Ill., 1926
Havoc, June Vancouver, Can., 1916
Hawkins, Jack London, 1910-73
Hawn, Goldie Washington, D. C., 1945
Haworth, Jill Sussex, Eng., 1945
Hayakawa, Sessue Chiba Prov., Japan, 1890-1973
Hayden, Melissa Toronto, 1928
Hayden, Sterling Montclair, N.J., 1916
Hayden, Tom Royal Oak, Mich., 1940
Hayes, "Gabby" Wellsville, N.Y., 1885-1969

Hayes, Helen Washington, D. C., 1900
Hayes, Isaac Covington, Ten., 1942
Hayes, Peter Lind San Francisco, 1915
Haymes, Dick Argentina, 1918-80
Hayward, Susan New York City, 1919-75
Hayworth, Rita New York City, 1919
Head, Edith Los Angeles, 1907
Healy, Mary New Orleans, 1918
Heatherton, Joey Rockville Centre, N. Y., 1944
Heckart, Eileen Columbus, O., 1919
Heflin, Van Waters, Okla., 1919-71
Hefner, Hugh Chicago, 1926
Heiden, Eric Madison, Wis., 1958
Hemingway, Margaux, Portland, Ore., 1955
Hemmings, David Surrey, Eng., 1941
Henderson, Florence Dale, Ind., 1934
Henderson, Skitch Halstad, Minn., 1918
Hendrix, Jimi Seattle, 1943-70
Henie, Sonja Oslo, 1913-69
Henning, Doug Ft. Garry, Can., 1947
Henreid, Paul Trieste, 1908
Henson, Jim Greenville, Miss., 1936
Hentoff, Nat Boston, 1925
Hepburn, Audrey Brussels, 1929
Hepburn, Katharine Hartford, 1909
Herman, Woody Milwaukee, 1913
Hersholt, Jean Copenhagen, 1886-1956
Heston, Charlton Evanston, Ill., 1923
Hickman, Darryl Los Angeles, 1931
Hickman, Dwayne Los Angeles, 1934
Hildegarde Adell, Wis., 1906
Hill, Arthur Melfort, Can., 1922
Hiller, Wendy Bramhall, Eng., 1912
Hines, Earl Fatha Duquesne, Pa., 1905
Hingle, Pat Denver, 1924
Hirsch, Judd New York, 1935
Hirschfeld, Al St. Louis, 1903
Hirt, Al New Orleans, 1922
Hodiak, John Pittsburgh, 1914-55
Hoffman, Dustin Los Angeles, 1937
Holbrook, Hal Cleveland, 1925
Holden, William O'Fallon, Ill., 1918
Holder, Geoffrey Port-of-Spain, 1930
Holiday, Billie Baltimore, 1915-59
Holliday, Judy New York, 1921-65
Holloway, Stanley London, 1890
Holm, Celeste New York City, 1919
Holman, Libby Cincinnati, 1906-71
Holmes, Larry Cuthbert, Ga., 1949
Holt, Jack Winchester, Va., 1888-1951
Homeier, Skip Chicago, 1930
Homolka, Oscar Vienna, 1903-78
Hope, Bob Eltham, Eng., 1903
Hopkins, Anthony Port Talbot, Wales, 1937
Hopkins, Miriam Bainbridge, Ga., 1902-72
Hopper, Dennis Dodge City, Kans., 1936
Hopper, De Wolfe New York City, 1858-1935
Hopper, Hedda Hollidaysburg, Pa., 1890-1966
Horne, Lena New York City, 1917
Hornung, Paul Louisville, Ky., 1935
Horton, Edward Everett New York, 1886-1970
Houdini, Harry Budapest, 1874-1926
Howard, Joe New York, 1867-1961
Howard, Leslie London, 1893-1943
Howard, Ron Duncan, Okla., 1954
Howard, Trevor Cliftonville, Eng., 1916
Howe, Gordie Floral, Sask., 1928
Howe, James Wong China, 1899-1976
Howes, Sally Ann London, 1934
Hudson, Rock Winnetka, Ill., 1925
Hughes, Howard Houston, Tex., 1905-76
Hull, Bobby Pt. Anne, Ont., 1939
Humperdinck, Engelbert Madras, India, 1940
Hunt, Marsha Chicago, 1917
Hunter, Alberta Memphis, 1895
Hunter, Jeffrey New Orleans, 1925-69
Hunter, Kim Detroit, 1922
Hunter, Tab New York City, 1931
Huntley, Chet Cardwell, Mont., 1911-74
Hussey, Ruth Providence, R. I., 1917
Huston, Walter Toronto, 1884-1950
Hutton, Barbara New York City, 1912-79
Hutton, Betty Battle Creek, Mich., 1921
Hutton, Lauren Tampa, Fla., 1948?
Hyde-White, Wilfrid Bourton-on-the-water, Eng., 1903

Ian, Janice New York City, 1951
Ireland, John Victoria, Can., 1916
Ives, Burl Hunt City, Ill., 1909
Jackson, Anne Millvale, Pa., 1926
Jackson, Glenda Birkenhead, Eng., 1940
Jackson, Gordon Glasgow, 1923
Jackson, Jesse Greenville, N.C., 1941
Jackson, Kate Birmingham, Ala., 1949
Jackson, Mahalia New Orleans, 1911-72
Jackson, Michael Gary, Ind., 1958
Jackson, Reggie Philadelphia, 1946
Jacobi, Derek Leytonstone, Eng., 1938
Jacobi, Lou Toronto, 1913
Jaffe, Sam New York City, 1893
Jaggar, Dean Lima, O., 1903
Jagger, Mick Dartford, Eng., 1944
Jamal, Ahmad Pittsburgh, 1930
James, Dennis Jersey City, N. J., 1917
James, Harry Albany, Ga., 1916
James, Joni Chicago, 1930
Janis, Elsie Columbus, O., 1889-1956
Jannings, Emil Switzerland, 1884?-1950
Janssen, David Naponee, Neb., 1930-80
Jeanmaire, Zizi Paris, 1924
Jeffreys, Anne Goldsboro, N. C., 1928
Jenkins, Allen New York City, 1900-74
Jenkins, Gordon Webster Groves, Mo., 1910
Jenner, Bruce Mt. Kisco, N.Y., 1949
Jennings, Waylon Littlefield, Tex., 1937
Jens, Salome Milwaukee, 1935
Jessel, George New York, 1898-1981
Joel, Billy New York City, 1949
John, Elton Middlesex, Eng., 1947
Johns, Glynis Pretoria, South Africa, 1923
Johnson, Van Newport, R. I., 1916
Jolson, Al Russia, 1880?-1950
Jones, Allan Scranton, Pa., 1908
Jones, Carolyn Amarillo, Tex., 1933
Jones, Dean Morgan Co., Ala., 1936
Jones, Jack Hollywood, Cal., 1938
Jones, James Earl Tate Co., Miss., 1931
Jones, Jennifer Tulsa, Okla., 1919
Jones, Shirley Smithton, Pa., 1934
Jones, "Spike" Long Beach, Cal., 1911-64
Jones, Tom Pontypridd, Wales, 1940
Jong, Erica New York City, 1942
Joplin, Janis Port Arthur, Tex., 1943-70
Jory, Victor Dawson City, Can., 1903
Jourdan, Louis Marseilles, 1920
Jurado, Katy Guadalajara, Mexico, 1927
Jurgens, Curt Munich, 1915
Kael, Pauline Petaluma, Calif., 1919
Kahn, Madeline Boston, 1942
Kaminska, Ida Odessa, Russ., 1899-1980
Kanin, Garson Rochester, N. Y., 1912
Kaplan, Gabe New York City, 1946
Karloff, Boris London, 1887-1969
Karpov, Anatoly Zlatoust, U.S.S.R., 1951
Karsh, Yousuf Mardin, Armenia, 1908
Kasznar, Kurt Vienna, 1913-79
Kaye, Danny New York City, 1913
Kaye, Sammy Lakewood, O., 1913
Kazan, Elia Constantinople, 1909
Kazan, Lainie New York City, 1940
Keach, Stacy Savannah, Ga., 1941
Keaton, Buster Piqua, Kans., 1895-1966
Keaton, Diane Los Angeles, Cal., 1946
Keel, Howard Gillespie, Ill., 1919
Keeler, Ruby Halifax, Nova Scotia, 1910
Keeshan, Bob Lynbrook, N.Y., 1927
Keith, Brian Bayonne, N. J., 1921
Keller, Helen Tuscumbia, Ala., 1880-1968
Kellerman, Sally Long Beach, Cal., 1938
Kelly, Gene Pittsburgh, 1912
Kelly, Grace Philadelphia, 1929
Kelly, Nancy Lowell, Mass., 1921
Kelly, Patsy Brooklyn, N. Y., 1910-81
Kennedy, Arthur Worcester, Mass., 1914
Kennedy, George New York City, 1925
Kenneth, Mr. (Batelle) Syracuse, 1927
Kenton, Stan Wichita, Kans., 1912-79
Kern, Jerome New York, 1885-1945
Kerr, Deborah Helensburgh, Scot., 1921
Kerr, Jean Scranton, Pa., 1923
Kerr, John New York City, 1931

Kibbee, Guy El Paso, Tex., 1882-1956
Kilbride, Percy San Francisco, 1888-1964
Kiley, Richard Chicago, 1922
Kilgallen, Dorothy Chicago, 1913-65
Killy, Jean-Claude St.-Cloud, Fr.,1943
King, Alan New York City, 1927
King, Billie Jean Long Beach, Cal.,1943
King, Carole New York City, 1941
King, Dennis Coventry, Eng., 1897-1971
Kirk, Lisa Brownsville, Pa., 1925
Kirsten, Dorothy Montclair, N.J., 1919
Kitt, Eartha North, S.C., 1928
Klein, Calvin New York City, 1942
Klein, Robert New York City, 1942
Klemperer, Werner Cologne, Ger., 1920
Klugman, Jack Philadelphia, 1922
Knievel, Evel Butte, Mont., 1938
Knight, Gladys Atlanta, 1944
Knotts, Don Morgantown, W. Va., 1924
Knox, Alexander Strathroy, Can., 1907
Korbut, Olga Grodno, Russia, 1956
Korman, Harvey Chicago, 1927
Koufax, Sandy New York City, 1935
Kovacs, Ernie Trenton, N.J., 1919-62
Kramer, Jack Las Vegas, Nev., 1921
Kramer, Stanley New York City, 1913
Kristofferson, Kris Brownsville, Tex., 1936
Krupa, Gene Chicago, 1909-73
Kuralt, Charles Wilmington, N.C., 1934
Kwan, Nancy Hong Kong, 1939
Ladd, Alan Hot Springs, Ark., 1913-64
Ladd, Cheryl Huron, S. Dak., 1951
Lahr, Bert New York, 1895-1967
Laine, Frankie Chicago, 1913
Lake, Veronica Lake Placid, N.Y., 1919-73
Lamarr, Hedy Vienna, 1915
Lamas, Fernando, Buenos Aires, 1920
Lamour, Dorothy New Orleans, 1914
Lancaster, Burt New York City, 1913
Lanchester, Elsa Lewisham, Eng., 1902
Landau, Martin New York City, 1925?
Landers, Ann Sioux City, Iowa, 1918
Landi, Elissa Venice, 1904-48
Landis, Carole Fairchild, Wis., 1919-48
Landon, Michael New York City, 1937
Lane, Abbe New York City, 1935
Langdon, Harry Council Bluffs, Iowa, 1884-1944
Lange, Hope Redding Ridge, Conn., 1933
Langella, Frank Bayonne, N. J.,.1940
Langford, Frances Lakeland, Fla., 1914?
Langtry, Lily Jersey, Eng., 1852-1929
Lansbury, Angela London, 1925
Lanza, Mario Philadelphia, 1921-59
La Rosa, Julius New York City, 1930
Lasser, Louise New York, 1941
Lauder, Harry Scotland, 1870-1950
Laughton, Charles Scarborough, Eng., 1899-1962
Laurel, Stan Ulverson, Eng., 1890-1965
Laurie, Piper Detroit, 1932
Lawford, Peter London, 1923
Lawrence, Carol Melrose Park, Ill., 1934
Lawrence, Gertrude London, 1898-1952
Lawrence, Steve Brooklyn, 1935
Lawrence, Vicki Los Angeles, 1949
Leachman, Cloris Des Moines, 1926
Lear, Norman New Haven, 1922
Learned, Michael Washington, 1939
Lederer, Francis Prague, 1906
Lee, Brenda Atlanta, 1944
Lee, Christopher London, 1922
Lee, Gypsy Rose Seattle, 1914-70
Lee, Peggy Jamestown, N. D., 1920
Le Gallienne, Eva London, 1899
Legrand, Michel Paris, 1932
Lehrer, Tom New York City, 1928
Leigh, Janet Merced, Cal., 1927
Leigh, Vivien India, 1913-67
Leighton, Margaret Barnt Green, Eng., 1922-76
Lembeck, Harvey New York City, 1923
Lemmon, Jack Boston, 1925
Lennon, John Liverpool, Eng., 1940-80
Lenya, Lotte Vienna, 1900
Leonard, Sheldon New York City, 1907

Leonard, Sugar Ray Wilmington, N.C., 1956
Leslie, Joan Detroit, 1925
Letterman, David Indianapolis, 1947
Levant, Oscar Pittsburgh, 1906-72
Levene, Sam Russia, 1905-80
Levenson, Sam New York City, 1911-80
Lewis, Jerry Newark, N. J., 1926
Lewis, Joe E. New York City, 1902?-71
Lewis, Ramsey Chicago, 1935
Lewis, Robert Q. New York City, 1921
Lewis, Shari New York City, 1934
Lewis, Ted Circleville, O., 1891-1971
Liberace West Allis, Wis., 1919
Lightfoot, Gordon Orillia, Can., 1938
Lillie, Beatrice Toronto, 1898
Linden, Hal New York, 1931
Lindfors, Viveca Uppsala, Swed., 1920
Lindsay, Howard Saratoga, N.Y., 1889-1968
Lindsay, Margaret Dubuque, Iowa, 1910-81
Linkletter, Art Moose Jaw, Can., 1912
Lippmann, Walter New York, 1889-1974
Lisi, Virna Ancona, Italy, 1937
Little, Rich Ottawa, Can., 1938
Littlewood, Joan London, 1916
Livingstone, Mary Seattle, 1909
Lloyd, Harold Burchard, Neb., 1893-1971
Lockhart, Gene London, Can., 1891-1957
Lockhart, June New York City, 1925
Lockwood, Margaret Karachi, Pakistan, 1916
Loesser, Frank New York, 1910-69
Logan, Ella Glasgow, 1913-69
Loggins, Kenny Everett, Wash., 1948
Lollobrigida, Gina Subiaco, Italy, 1928
Lom, Herbert Prague, 1917
Lombard, Carole Fort Wayne, Ind., 1908-42
Lombardi, Vince New York, 1913-70
Lombardo, Guy London, Can., 1902-77
London, Julie Santa Rosa, Cal., 1926
Loos, Anita Sissons, Cal., 1888-1981
Lopez, Nancy Torrence, Cal., 1957
Lopez, Trini Dallas, 1937
Lopez, Vincent New York, 1895-1975
Lord, Jack New York City, 1930
Loren, Sophia Rome, 1934
Lorre, Peter Hungary, 1904-64
Louis, Joe near Lafayette, Ala., 1914-81
Louise, Anita New York, 1917-70
Louise, Tina New York City, 1937
Lovejoy, Frank New York, 1912-62
Lowe, Edmund San Jose, Cal., 1892-1971
Loy, Myrna Helena, Mont., 1905
Lubitsch, Ernst Berlin, 1892-1947
Luce, Clare Boothe New York City, 1903
Lugosi, Bela Lugos, Hung., 1888-1956
Lukas, Paul Budapest, 1894-1971
Lulu Glasgow, 1948
Lumet, Sidney Philadelphia, 1924
Lund, John Rochester, N. Y., 1913
Lundigan, William Syracuse, 1914-75
Lunt, Alfred Milwaukee, 1892-1977
Lupino, Ida London, 1918
Lynde, Paul Mt. Vernon, O., 1926
Lynley, Carol New York City, 1942
Lynn, Diana Los Angeles, 1926-71
Lynn, Loretta Butcher Hollow, Ky., 1935
Lyon, Sue Davenport, Iowa, 1946
Lyons, Leonard New York City, 1906-76
MacArthur, James Los Angeles, 1937
McCallum, David Scotland, 1933
McCambridge, Mercedes Joliet, Ill., 1918
McCarey, Leo Los Angeles, 1898-1969
McCartney, Paul Allerton, Eng., 1942
McClure, Doug Glendale, Cal., 1938
McCormick, Myron Albany, Ind., 1907-62
McCrea, Joel Los Angeles, 1905
McDaniel, Hattie Wichita, 1895-1952
MacDonald, Jeanette Phila., 1906-65
McDowell, Malcolm Leeds, Eng., 1943
McDowell, Roddy London, 1928
McEnroe, John Wiesbaden, Ger., 1959
McGavin, Darren San Joaquin Valley, Cal., 1922

McGraw, Ali Westchester Co., N. Y., 1939
McGuire, Dorothy Omaha, Neb. 1919
McHugh, Frank Homestead, Pa. 1898-1981
McKenna, Siobhan Belfast, 1922
MacKenzie, Gisele Winnipeg, Can., 1927
McKuen, Rod Oakland, Calif. 1933
McLaglen, Victor Tunbridge Wells, Eng., 1886-1959
MacLaine, Shirley Richmond, Va., 1934
MacLane, Barton Columbia, S.C., 1902-68
McLean, Don New Rochelle, N.Y., 1945
McLuhan, Marshall Edmonton, Can., 1911-80
MacMahon, Aline McKeesport, Pa., 1899
McMahon, Ed Detroit, 1923
MacMurray, Fred Kankakee, Ill., 1908
McNair, Barbara Chicago, 1937?
MacNeil, Robert Montreal, 1931
McNichol, Kristy Los Angeles, 1962
McQueen, Butterfly Tampa, Fla., 1911
McQueen, Steve Indianapolis, 1930-80
MacRae, Gordon East Orange, N. J., 1921
MacRae, Sheila London, 1923?
Madison, Guy Bakersfield, Cal., 1922
Magnani, Anna Rome, 1908-73
Maharis, George New York City, 1928
Main, Marjorie Acton, Ind., 1890-1975
Mainbocher Chicago, 1890-1976
Makeba, Miriam Prospect Township, South Africa, 1932
Malbin, Elaine New York City, 1932
Malden, Karl Chicago, 1914
Malina, Judith Kiel, Ger., 1926
Malone, Dorothy Chicago, 1930
Mamoulian, Rouben Tiflis, Russ., 1897
Manchester, Melissa New York, 1951
Mancini, Henry Cleveland, 1924
Mangano, Silvana Rome, 1930
Mangione, Chuck Rochester, N.Y., 1940
Manilow, Barry New York City, 1946
Mann, Herbie New York City, 1930
Mannes, Marya New York City, 1904
Mansfield, Jayne Bryn Mawr, Pa., 1933-67
Mantle, Mickey Spavinaw, Okla., 1931
Mantovani, Annunzio Venice, 1905-80
Marceau, Marcel Strasbourg, Fr., 1923
March, Fredric Racine, Wis., 1897-1975
March, Hal San Francisco, 1920-70
Marciano, Rocky Boston, 1924-69
Margo Mexico City, 1920
Marlowe, Hugh Philadelphia, 1911
Marsh, Jean London, 1934
Marshall, E. G. Owatonna, Minn., 1910
Marshall, Herbert London, 1890-1966
Marshall, Penny New York City, 1942
Martin, Dean Steubenville, O., 1917
Martin, Dick Battle Creek, Mich., 1927
Martin, Mary Weatherford, Tex., 1913
Martin, Steve Waco, Tex., 1945
Mervin, Lee New York City, 1924
Marx, Chico New York, 1891-1961
Marx, Groucho New York, 1895-1977
Marx, Harpo New York, 1893-1964
Masina, Giulietta Bologna, Italy, 1925?
Mason, Jackie Sheboygan, Wis., 1931
Mason, James Huddersfield, Eng., 1909
Mason, Marsha St. Louis, 1942
Mason, Pamela Westgate, Eng., 1918
Massey, Raymond Toronto, 1896
Mastroianni, Marcello Fontana Liri, Italy, 1924
Mathis, Johnny San Francisco, 1935
Matthau, Walter New York City, 1920
Mature, Victor Louisville, Ky., 1916
Mauldin, Bill Mountain Park, N. M., 1921
Maxwell, Elsa Keokuk, Iowa, 1883-1963
Maxwell, Marilyn Clarinda, Iowa, 1922-72
May, Elaine Philadelphia, 1932
Mayehoff, Eddie Baltimore, 1914
Mayer, Louis B. Minsk, Russ., 1885-1957
Mayo, Virginia St. Louis, 1928
Mays, Willie Westfield, Ala., 1931
Meadows, Audrey Wuchang, China, 1922?

Meadows, Jayne Wuchang, China, 1920?
Medford, Kay New York City, 1920-80
Meek, Donald Glasgow, 1880-1946
Meeker, Ralph Minneapolis, 1920
Melton, James Moultrie, Ga., 1904-61
Mendes, Sergio Niteroi, Brazil, 1941?
Menjou, Adolphe Pittsburgh, 1890-1963
Menken, Helen New York, 1902-66
Mercer, Johnny Savannah, Ga., 1909-76
Mercouri, Melina Athens, 1925
Meredith, Burgess Cleveland, 1908
Merkel, Una Covington, Ky., 1903
Merman, Ethel New York City, 1909
Merrick, David St. Louis, 1912
Merrill, Dina New York City, 1925
Merrill, Gary Hartford, Conn., 1915
Mesta, Perle Sturgis, Mich., 1891-1975
Middleton, Ray Chicago, 1907
Midler, Bette Honolulu, 1945(?)
Mielziner, Jo Paris, 1901-76
Mifune, Toshiro Tsingtao, China, 1920
Miles, Sarah Ingatestone, Eng., 1941
Miles, Vera Boise City, Okla., 1929
Milland, Ray Neath, Wales, 1908
Miller, Ann Chireno, Tex., 1923
Miller, Glenn Clarinda, Iowa, 1909-44
Miller, Marilyn Findlay, O., 1898-1936
Miller, Mitch Rochester, N.Y., 1911
Miller, Roger Erick, Okla., 1936
Millett, Kate St. Paul, 1934
Mills, Hayley London, 1946
Mills, John Felixstowe, Eng., 1908
Mills, Juliet London, 1941
Mimieux, Yvette Los Angeles, 1939
Mineo, Sal New York City, 1939-76
Mingus, Charlie Nogales, Ariz., 1922-79
Minnelli, Liza Los Angeles, 1946
Minnelli, Vincente Chicago, 1913
Minnesota Fats New York City, 1903?
Miranda, Carmen Portugal, 1917-55
Mitchell, Cameron Dallastown, Pa., 1918
Mitchell, Joni Ft. MacLeod, Can., 1943
Mitchell, Thomas Elizabeth, N.J., 1892-1962
Mitchum, Robert Bridgeport, Ct., 1917
Mix, Tom El Paso, Tex., 1880-1940
Monk, Thelonius Rocky Mount, N. C., 1918
Monroe, Marilyn Los Angeles, 1926-62
Monroe, Vaughan Akron, O., 1912-73
Montalban, Ricardo Mexico City, 1920
Montand, Yves Monsummano, Italy, 1921
Montgomery, Elizabeth Hollywood, Cal., 1933
Montgomery, Robert Beacon, N.Y. 1904-81
Moore, Constance Sioux City, Iowa, 1922
Moore, Dudley Dagenham, Eng., 1935
Moore, Garry Baltimore, 1915
Moore, Grace Del Rio, Tenn., 1901-47
Moore, Mary Tyler New York City, 1937
Moore, Melba New York City, 1945
Moore, Terry Los Angeles, 1929
Moore, Victor Hammonton, N.J., 1876-1962
Moorehead, Agnes Clinton, Mass., 1906-74
Moreau, Jeanne Paris, 1928
Moreno, Rita Humacao, P. R., 1931
Morgan, Frank New York, 1890-1949
Morgan, Helen Danville, Ill., 1900-41
Morgan, Henry New York City, 1915
Morgan, Jane Newton, Mass., 1924
Morgan, Ralph New York, 1883-1956
Mori, Hanae Shimane, Japan, 1926
Moriarty, Michael Detroit, 1941
Morison, Patricia New York City, 1915
Morley, Robert Somley, Eng., 1908
Morris, Chester New York, 1919-70
Morris, Wayne Los Angeles, 1914-59
Morse, Robert Newton, Mass., 1931
Morton, "Jelly Roll" New Orleans, 1885-1941
Mostel, Zero New York City, 1915-77
Mowbray, Alan London, 1897-1969
Mudd, Roger Washington, 1928
Muhammad Ali (Cassius Clay) Louisville, Ky., 1942
Mulhare, Edward County Cork, Ire., 1928
Mull, Martin Chicago, 1943
Muni, Paul Lemberg, Pol., 1895-1967

Murphy, Audie Kingston, Tex., 1924-71
Murray, Anne Springhill, Can., 1946
Murray, Arthur New York City, 1895
Murray, Don Hollywood, Cal., 1929
Murray, Jan New York City, 1917
Murray, Kathryn Jersey City, N. J., 1906
Murray, Ken New York City, 1903
Murray, Mae Portsmouth, Va., 1885-1965
Murrow, Edward R. Greensboro, N.C., 1908-65
Musial, Stan Donora, Pa., 1920
Myerson, Bess New York City, 1924
Nabors, Jim Sylacauga, Ala., 1932?
Nader, Ralph Winsted, Conn., 1934
Nagel, Conrad Keokuk, Iowa, 1897-1970
Naish, J. Carrol New York City, 1900-73
Naldi, Nita New York, 1899-1961
Namath, Joe Beaver Falls, Pa., 1943
Nash, Graham Blackpool, Eng., 1942
Nash, Ogden Rye, N.Y., 1902-71
Natwick, Mildred Baltimore, 1908
Nazimova, Alla Yalta, Russ., 1879-1945
Neagle, Anna London, 1904
Neal, Patricia Packard, Ky., 1926
Neff, Hildegarde Ulm, Ger., 1925
Nelson, Barry Oakland, Cal., 1920
Nelson, Harriet Des Moines, 1912?
Nelson, Ozzie Jersey City, 1907-75
Nelson, Rick Teaneck, N.J. 1940
Nelson, Willie Abbott, Tex., 1933
Nero, Peter New York City, 1934
Newhart, Bob Chicago, 1929
Newley, Anthony London, 1931
Newman, Edwin New York, 1919
Newman, Paul Cleveland, 1925
Newman, Phyllis Jersey City, N. J., 1935
Newman, Randy Los Angeles, 1943
Newmar, Julie Los Angeles, 1935
Newton, Wayne Roanoke, Va., 1944
Newton-John, Olivia Cambridge, Eng., 1948
Nichols, Mike Berlin, 1931
Nicholson, Jack Neptune, N.J., 1937
Nicklaus, Jack Columbus, Ohio 1940
Nimoy, Leonard Boston, 1932
Niven, David Kirriemuir, Scot., 1910
Nizer, Louis London, 1902
Nolte, Nick Omaha, 1942
Normand, Mabel Boston, 1894-1930
North, Sheree Los Angeles, 1933
Novak, Kim Chicago, 1933
Novarro, Ramon Durango, Mex., 1899-1968
Novello, Ivor Cardiff, Wales, 1893-1951
Nugent, Elliot Dover, O., 1896-1980
Nuyen, France Marseilles, 1939
Nyad, Diana New York City, 1949
Oakie, Jack Sedalia, Mo., 1903-78
Oberon, Merle Hobart, Tasmania, 1911-79
O'Brian, Hugh Rochester, N.Y., 1930
O'Brien, Edmond New York City, 1915
O'Brien, Margaret San Diego, 1937
O'Brien, Pat Milwaukee, 1899
O'Connell, Arthur New York, 1908-81
O'Connor, Carroll New York City, 1924
O'Connor, Donald Chicago, 1925
O'Connor, Una Belfast, 1881-1959
O'Day, Anita Chicago, 1920
O'Hara, Jill Warren, Pa., 1947
O'Hara, Maureen Milltown, Ire., 1921
O'Herlihy, Dan Wexford, Ire., 1919
O'Keefe, Dennis Fort Madison, Iowa, 1910-68
Oland, Warner Umea, Swed., 1880-1938
Oliver, Edna May Malden, Mass., 1883-1942
Olivier, Laurence Dorking, Eng., 1907
Onassis, Aristotle Smyrna, Turkey, 1906-75
Onassis, Christina New York City, 1950
O'Neal, Patrick Ocala, Fla., 1927
O'Neal, Ryan Los Angeles, 1941
O'Neal, Tatum Los Angeles, 1963
Ono, Yoko Tokyo, 1933
Opatoshu, David New York City, 1918
Orbach, Jerry New York City, 1935
Orbison, Roy Texas, 1936
Orlando, Tony New York City, 1944
Osmond, Donny, Ogden, Utah, 1957
Osmond, Marie Ogden, Utah, 1959

O'Sullivan, Maureen Boyle, Ire., 1911
O'Toole, Peter Connemarra, Ire., 1932
Ouspenskaya, Maria Russia, 1876-1949
Owens, Buck Sherman, Tex., 1929
Owens, Jesse Decatur, Ala., 1913-80
Paar, Jack Canton, O., 1918
Pacino, Al New York City, 1940
Page, Geraldine Kirksville, Mo., 1924
Page, Patti Claremore, Okla., 1927
Paige, Janis Tacoma, Wash., 1922
Paige, "Satchel" Mobile, Ala., 1906?
Palance, Jack Lattimore Mines, Pa., 1920
Paley, William S. Chicago, 1901
Pallette, Eugene Winfield, Kans., 1889-1943
Palmer, Arnold Latrobe, Pa., 1929
Palmer, Betsy East Chicago, Ind., 1929
Palmer, Lilli Posen, Poland, 1914
Papas, Irene Chiliomodion, Gr., 1926
Papp, Joseph New York City, 1921
Parker, Eleanor Cedarville, O., 1922
Parker, Fess Fort Worth, Tex., 1927
Parker, Suzy San Antonio, Tex., 1933
Parks, Bert Atlanta, 1915
Parsons, Estelle Lynn, Mass., 1927
Parton, Dolly nr. Sevierville, Tenn., 1946
Pauley, Jane Indianapolis, 1950
Paulsen, Pat South Bend, Wash., 1930?
Paxinou, Katina Piraeus, Gr., 1900
Payne, John Roanoke, Va., 1912
Peale, Norman Vincent Bowersville, Ohio, 1898
Pearl, Minnie Centerville, Tenn., 1912
Peck, Gregory La Jolla, Cal., 1916
Pelé Três Coracoes, Brazil, 1941
Pendleton, Nat Davenport, Iowa, 1899-1967
Peppard, George Detroit, 1932
Perkins, Anthony New York City, 1932
Perrine, Valerie Galveston, Tex., 1943
Persoff, Nehemiah Jerusalem, 1920
Peters, Bernadette New York City, 1948
Peters, Jean Canton, O., 1926
Peterson, Oscar Montreal, 1925
Piaf, Edith Paris, 1912-63
Piazza, Ben Little Rock, Ark., 1934
Piazza, Marguerite New Orleans, 1926
Pickens, Slim Kingsberg, Cal., 1919
Pickford, Mary Toronto, 1893-1979
Picon, Molly New York City, 1898
Pidgeon, Walter East St. John, Can., 1897
Pleasance, Donald Worksop, Eng., 1921
Pleshette, Suzanne New York City, 1937
Plimpton, George New York City, 1927
Plowright, Joan Scunthorpe, Eng., 1929
Plummer, Christopher Toronto, 1929
Poitier, Sidney Miami, Fla., 1924
Pollard, Michael J. Passaic, N. J., 1939
Ponti, Carlo Milan, 1913
Portman, Eric Halifax, Eng., 1903-69
Porter, Cole Peru, Ind., 1893-1964
Poston, Tom Columbus, O., 1927
Powell, Dick Mountain View, Ark., 1904-63
Powell, Eleanor Springfield, Mass., 1912
Powell, Jane Portland, Ore., 1929
Powell, William Pittsburgh, 1892
Power, Tyrone Cincinnati, 1913-58
Powers, Stefanie Hollywood, Cal., 1942
Prentiss, Paula San Antonio, Tex., 1939
Presley, Elvis Tupelo, Miss., 1935-77
Preston, Robert Newton, Mass., 1918
Price, Leontyne Laurel, Miss., 1927
Price, Vincent St. Louis, 1911
Primus, Pearl Trinidad, B.W.I., 1919
Prince, Harold New York City, 1928
Prinze, Freddie New York City, 1954-77
Provine, Dorothy Deadwood, S. D., 1937
Prowse, Juliet Bombay, 1936
Pryor, Richard Peoria, Ill., 1940
Pucci, Emilio Naples, 1914
Purdom, Edmund London, 1926
Quant, Mary London, 1934
Quayle, Anthony Ainsdale, Eng., 1913
Quinn, Anthony Chihuahua, Mex., 1915
Quintero, José Panama, 1924
Radner, Gilda Detroit, 1946
Radziwill, Lee New York City, 1933
Raft, George, New York, 1895-1980

Raines, Ella Snoqualmie Falls, Wash., 1921
Rains, Claude London, 1889-1967
Raitt, Bonnie Los Angeles, 1950
Raitt, John Santa Ana, Cal., 1917
Rambeau, Marjorie San Francisco, 1889-1970
Rand, Sally Hickory, Mo., 1904?-79
Randall, Tony Tulsa, Okla., 1920
Rathbone, Basil South Africa, 1892-1967
Rather, Dan Wharton, Tex., 1931
Ratoff, Gregory Russia, 1893-1961
Rawls, Lou Chicago, 1935
Ray, Aldo Pen Argyl, Pa., 1926
Ray, Johnny Dallas, Ore., 1927
Raye, Martha Butte, Mont., 1916
Raymond, Gene New York City, 1908
Reagan, Ronald, Tampico, Ill., 1911
Reasoner, Harry Dakota City, Iowa, 1923
Reddy, Helen Melbourne, Australia, 1941
Redford, Robert Santa Monica, Cal., 1937
Redgrave, Lynn London, 1943
Redgrave, Michael Bristol, Eng., 1908
Redgrave, Vanessa London, 1937
Reed, Donna Iowa, 1921
Reed, Rex Fort Worth, 1940?
Reese, Della Detroit, 1932
Reeves, Steve Glasgow, Mont., 1926
Régine Etterbeck, Belgium, 1929
Reiner, Carl New York City, 1922
Reiner, Rob Beverly Hills, Calif., 1947
Reinhardt, Max Austria, 1873-1943
Remick, Lee Quincy, Mass., 1935
Rennie, Michael Bradford, Eng., 1909-71
Rey, Fernando La Coruña, Spain, 1917
Reynolds, Burt Waycross, Ga., 1936
Reynolds, Debbie El Paso, Tex., 1932
Rich, Buddy New York City, 1917
Rich, Charlie Forrest City, Ark., 1932
Rich, Irene Buffalo, N. Y., 1897
Richardson, Ralph Cheltenham, Eng., 1902
Rickles, Don New York City, 1926
Riddle, Nelson Hackensack, N. J., 1921
Rigg, Diana Doncaster, Eng., 1938
Ritchard, Cyril Sydney, Austral., 1897-1977
Ritter, John Burbank, Cal., 1948
Ritter, Tex Murvaul, Tex., 1907-74
Ritter, Thelma New York, 1905-69
Rivera, Chita Washington, D. C., 1933
Rivers, Joan New York City, 1937?
Roach, Hal Elmira, N. Y., 1892
Robards, Jason, Jr. Chicago, 1922
Robbins, Harold New York City, 1916
Robertson, Cliff La Jolla, Cal., 1925
Robertson, Dale Oklahoma City, 1923
Robeson, Paul, Princeton, N.J., 1898-1976
Robinson, "Bojangles" Richmond, Va., 1878-1949
Robinson, Edward G. Bucharest, 1893-1973
Robinson, Jackie Cairo, Ga., 1919-72
Robinson, Smokey Detroit, 1940
Robinson, Sugar Ray Detroit, 1921
Robson, Flora South Shields, Eng., 1902
Rockwell, Norman New York City, 1894-1978
Rogers, Buddy Olathe, Kans., 1904
Rogers, Ginger Independence, Mo., 1911
Rogers, Kenny Houston, 1939?
Rogers, Roy Cincinnati, 1912
Rogers, Will Ool.gah, Okla., 1879-1935
Roland, Gilbert Juarez, Mexico, 1905
Roman, Ruth Boston, 1924
Rome, Harold Hartford, Conn. 1908
Romero, Cesar New York City, 1907
Ronstadt, Linda Tucson, Ariz., 1946
Rooney, Mickey New York City, 1920
Rooney, Pat New York, 1880-1962
Rose, Billy New York, 1899-1966
Rose, David London, 1910
Rose, Pete Cincinnati, 1942
Ross, Diana Detroit, 1944
Ross, Katharine Hollywood, Cal., 1943
Ross, Lanny Seattle, 1906
Roth, Lillian Boston, 1910-80
Rowan, Dan Okla., 1926
Rowlands, Gena Cambria, Wis., 1936
Rozelle, Pete South Gate, Cal., 1914

Ruggles, Charles Los Angeles, 1892-1970
Rule, Janice Norwood, O., 1931
Runyon, Damon Manhattan, Kans., 1884-1946
Rush, Barbara Denver, 1929
Russell, Jane Lake Bemidji, Minn., 1921
Russell, Kurt Springfield, Mass., 1951
Russell, Lillian Clinton, Iowa, 1861-1922
Russell, Mark Buffalo, 1932
Russell, Nipsey Atlanta, 1924?
Russell, "Pee Wee" St. Louis, 1906-69
Russell, Rosalind Waterbury, Conn., 1911-76
Ruth, "Babe" Baltimore, 1895-1948
Rutherford, Ann Toronto, 1924
Rutherford, Margaret London, 1892-1972
Ryan, Peggy Long Beach, Cal., 1924
Ryan, Robert Chicago, 1913-73
Rydell, Bobby Philadelphia, 1942
Sabu Mysore, India, 1924-63
Safer, Morley Toronto, 1931
Sahl, Mort Montreal, 1927
Saint, Eva Marie Newark, N. J., 1929
St. John, Jill Los Angeles, 1940
Saint Laurent, Yves Oran, Algeria, 1936
Saint-Subber, Arnold Washington, D. C., 1918
Sainte-Marie, Buffy Saskatchewan, 1942
Sakall, "Cuddles" Budapest, 1884-1955
Sales, Soupy Wake Forest, N. C., 1926?
Sanders, George St. Petersburg, Russ., 1906-72
Sanders, Col. Harland Henryville, Ind., 1890-1980
Sarnoff, Dorothy New York City, 1919
Sarrazin, Michael Quebec, Can., 1940
Sassoon, Vidal London, 1928
Savalas, Telly Garden City, N. Y., 1924
Sayer, Leo Sussex, Eng., 1948
Schary, Dore Newark, N.J., 1905-80
Scheider, Roy Orange, N.J., 1935
Schell, Maria Vienna, 1926
Schell, Maximilian Vienna, 1930
Schildkraut, Joseph Vienna, 1895-1964
Schiff, Dorothy New York, 1903
Schneider, Romy Vienna, 1938
Schulz, Charles Minneapolis, 1922
Schwarzenegger, Arnold Graz, Austria, 1947
Scofield, Paul King's Norton, Eng., 1922
Scott, George C. Wise, Va., 1927
Scott, Hazel Port of Spain, Trin., 1920
Scott, Lisbeth Scranton, Pa., 1922
Scott, Martha Jamesport, Mo., 1914
Scott, Randolph Orange Co., Va., 1903
Scott, Zachary, Austin, Tex., 1914-65
Scourby, Alexander New York City, 1913
Scruggs, Earl Flint Hill, N.C., 1924-79
Searle, Ronald Cambridge, Eng., 1920
Seaver, Tom Fresno, Cal., 1944
Seberg, Jean Marshalltown, Iowa, 1938-79
Sedaka, Neil Brooklyn, 1939
Seeger, Pete New York City, 1919
Segal, George New York City, 1934
Sellers, Peter Southsea, Eng., 1925-80
Selznick, David O. Pittsburgh, 1902-65
Sennett, Mack Danville, Can., 1880-1960
Serban, Andrei Bucharest, 1943
Sevareid, Eric Velva, N. D., 1912
Seymour, Dan Chicago, 1915
Shankar, Ravi Benares, India, 1920
Sharif, Omar Cairo, 1933
Shatner, William Montreal, 1931
Shaw, Artie New York City, 1910
Shaw, Robert Westhoughton, Eng., 1927-78
Shawn, Dick Buffalo, N. Y., 1929?
Shearer, Moira Dunfermline, Scot., 1926
Shearer, Norma Montreal, 1905
Shearing, George London, 1919
Sheen, Martin Dayton, Ohio, 1940
Shepherd, Jean Chicago, 1923
Sheridan, Ann Denton, Tex., 1916?-67
Sherman, Allan Chicago, 1924-73
Shields, Brooke New York City, 1965
Shire, Talia Long Island, N.Y., 1947
Shoemaker, Willie El Paso, 1931
Shore, Dinah Winchester, Tenn., 1917

Short, Bobby Danville, Ill., 1936
Shrimpton, Jean High Wycombe, Eng., 1942
Shriner, Herb Toledo, O., 1918-70
Shubert, Lee Syracuse, N.Y., 1875-1953
Shumlin, Herman Atwood, Colo., 1898-1979
Sidney, Sylvia New York City, 1910
Signoret, Simone Wiesbaden, Ger., 1921
Silverman, Fred New York City, 1937
Silvers, Phil New York City, 1911
Sim, Alastair Edinburgh, 1900-76
Simmons, Jean London, 1929
Simon, Carly, New York City, 1945
Simon, Paul Queens, N.Y., 1941
Simon, Simone Marseilles, 1914
Simpson, Adele New York City, 1903
Simpson, O. J., San Francisco, 1947
Sinatra, Frank Hoboken, N. J., 1915
Sinatra, Nancy Jersey City, N. J., 1940
Sissle, Noble Indianapolis, 1889-1975
Skelton, Red Vincennes, Ind., 1913
Skinner, Cornelia Otis Chicago, 1901-79
Skinner, Otis Cambridge, Mass., 1858-1943
Skulnik, Menasha Warsaw, 1898-1970
Slezak, Walter Vienna, 1902
Slick, Grace Chicago, 1939
Smith, Alexis Penticton, Can., 1921
Smith, Bessie Chattanooga, 1894-1937
Smith, C. Aubrey London, 1863-1948
Smith, Howard K. Ferriday, La., 1914
Smith, Kate Greenville, Va., 1909
Smith, Maggie Ilford, Eng., 1934
Smith, Roger South Gate, Cal., 1932
Smothers, Dick New York City, 1938
Smothers, Tommy New York City, 1937
Snodgress, Carrie Park Ridge, Ill., 1945
Snowdon, Lord (Antony Armstrong-Jones) London, 1930
Snyder, Tom Milwaukee, 1936
Somers, Suzanne San Bruno, Cal., 1946
Sommer, Elke Berlin, 1941
Sondergaard, Gale Litchfield, Minn., 1907
Sondheim, Stephen New York City, 1930
Sothern, Ann Valley City, N. D., 1909
Spacek, Sissy Quitman, Tex., 1949
Sparks, Ned Guelph, Can., 1884-1957
Spassky, Boris V. Leningrad, 1937
Spewack, Bella Bucharest, 1899
Spitalney, Phil Russia, 1890-1970
Spitz, Mark Modesto, Calif., 1950
Spivak, Lawrence E. New York City, 1900
Spock, Benjamin N. Haven, Ct., 1903
Springsteen, Bruce Freehold, N. J., 1949
Stack, Robert Los Angeles, 1919
Stafford, Jo Coalinga, Cal., 1918
Stallone, Sylvester New York City, 1946
Stamp, Terence London, 1940
Stang, Arnold Chelsea, Mass., 1925
Stanislavsky, Konstantin Moscow, 1863-1938
Stanley, Kim Tularosa, N. M., 1925
Stanwyck, Barbara New York City, 1907
Stapleton, Jean New York City, 1923
Stapleton, Maureen Troy, N. Y., 1925?
Starr, Ringo Dingle, Eng., 1940
Staubach, Roger Cincinnati, 1942
Steele, Tommy London, 1936
Steiger, Rod Westhampton, N. Y., 1925
Stein, Jules C. South Bend, Ind., 1896-1981
Steinberg, Saul Rumania, 1914
Steinem, Gloria Toledo, O., 1936
Stengel, Casey Kansas City, Mo., 1891-1975
Sterling, Jan New York City, 1923
Sternberg, Josef von Vienna, 1894-1969
Stevens, Connie New York City, 1938
Stevens, Kaye Pittsburgh, 1935
Stevens, Mark Cleveland, 1922
Stevens, Stella Yazoo City, Miss., 1938
Stevenson, McLean Bloomington, Ill., 1929
Stewart, James Indiana, Pa., 1908
Stewart, Rod London, 1945
Stickney, Dorothy Dickinson, N. D., 1900
Stigwood, Robert Adelaide, Australia, 1934
Stills, Stephen Dallas, 1945
Stockwell, Dean Hollywood, Cal., 1936
Stone, Ezra New Bedford, Mass., 1917

Stone, Lewis Worcester, Mass., 1879-1953
Straight, Beatrice Long Island, N.Y., 1918
Strasberg, Lee Austria-Hungary, 1901
Strasberg, Susan New York City, 1938
Streep, Meryl Summit, N.J., 1949
Streisand, Barbra New York City, 1942
Stritch, Elaine Detroit, 1925
Stroheim, Erich von Vienna, 1885-1957
Struthers, Sally Portland, Ore., 1948
Sturges, Preston Chicago, 1898-1959
Styne, Jule London, 1905
Sullavan, Margaret Norfolk, 1911-60
Sullivan, Barry New York City, 1912
Sullivan, Ed New York City, 1902-74
Sullivan, Francis L. London, 1903-56
Summer, Donna Boston, 1948
Susann, Jacqueline Philadelphia, 1923-74
Susskind, David Brookline, Mass., 1920
Sutherland, Donald St. John, Can., 1934
Suzuki, Pat Cressy, Cal., 1931
Swanson, Gloria Chicago, 1899
Swarthout, Gladys Deepwater, Mo., 1904-69
Syms, Sylvia London, 1934
Talbot, Lyle Pittsburgh, 1902
Talmadge, Norma Jersey City, N.J., 1897-1957
Tamblyn, Russ Los Angeles, 1934
Tamiroff, Akim Baku, Russ., 1901-72
Tandy, Jessica London, 1909
Tanguay, Eva Marbleton, Can., 1878-1947
Tarkenton, Fran Richmond, 1940
Taurog, Norman Chicago, 1899-1981
Taylor, Elizabeth London, 1932
Taylor, James Boston, 1948
Taylor, June Chicago, 1918
Taylor, Laurette New York, 1884-1946
Taylor, Robert Filley, Neb., 1911-69
Taylor, Rod Sydney, Austral., 1930
Teagarden, Jack Vernon, Tex., 1905-64
Temple, Shirley Santa Monica, Cal., 1928
Templeton, Alec Cardiff, Wales, 1910-63
Ter-Arutunian, Rouben Tiflis, Russ., 1920
Terry, Ellen Coventry, Eng., 1848-1936
Terry-Thomas London, 1911
Thalberg, Irving New York, 1899-1939
Thaxter, Phyllis Portland, Me., 1921
Thomas, Danny Deerfield, Mich., 1914
Thomas, John Charles Meyersdale, Pa., 1892-1960
Thomas, Lowell Woodington, O., 1892-1981
Thomas, Marlo Detroit, 1937
Thomas, Richard New York City, 1951
Thompson, Sada Des Moines, 1929
Thorndike, Sybil Gainsborough, Eng., 1882-1976
Thorpe, Jim Prague, Okla., 1888-1953
Thulin, Ingrid Sollefta, Sweden, 1929
Tierney, Gene New York City, 1920
Tiffin, Pamela Oklahoma City, 1942
Tilden, William Phila., 1893-1953
Tillis, Mel Tampa, 1932
Tillstrom, Burr Chicago, 1917
Tiny Tim (Herbert Khaury) New York City, 1923?
Tiomkin, Dmitri Russia, 1894-1979
Todd, Ann Hartford, Eng., 1910
Todd, Mike Minneapolis, 1907-58
Todd, Richard Dublin, 1919
Toler, Sidney Warrensburg, Mo., 1874-1947
Tomlin, Lily Detroit, 1936
Tone, Franchot Niagara Falls, N.Y., 1905-68
Toomey, Regis Pittsburgh, 1902
Torme, Mel Chicago, 1925
Torn, Rip Temple, Tex., 1931
Tracy, Spencer Milwaukee, 1900-67
Travers, Mary Louisville, Ky., 1936
Travolta, John Englewood, N.J., 1954
Treacher, Arthur Brighton, Eng., 1894-1975
Trevor, Claire New York City, 1909
Trigère, Pauline Paris, 1912
Truex, Ernest Kansas City, 1889-1973
Tryon, Tom Hartford, Conn., 1926

Tucker, Forrest Plainfield, Ind., 1919
Tucker, Sophie Russia, 1888-1966
Tufts, Sonny Boston, 1911-70
Tunney, Gene New York City, 1897-1978
Turner, Lana Wallace, Ida., 1921
Turner, Ted Cincinnati, 1938
Turpin, Ben New Orleans, 1874-1940
Tushingham, Rita Liverpool, Eng., 1942
Twelvetrees, Helen New York, 1908-58
Twiggy (Leslie Hornby) London, 1949
Uggams, Leslie New York City, 1943
Ullmann, Liv Tokyo, 1939
Ulric, Lenore Milwaukee, 1894-1970
Unitas, John Pittsburgh, 1933
Uris, Leon Baltimore, 1924
Ustinov, Peter London, 1921
Vaccaro, Brenda New York City, 1939
Valenti, Jack Houston, 1921
Valentino, Rudolf, Castellaneta, Italy, 1895-1926
Vallee, Rudy Island Pond, Vt., 1901
Valli, Alida Pola, Italy, 1921
Valli, Frankie Newark, N.J., 1937
Vallone, Raf Tropea, Italy, 1918
Van Buren, Abigail Sioux City, Iowa, 1919
Vance, Vivian Cherryvale, Kan., 1911-79
Van Cleef, Lee Somerville, N. J., 1925
Vanderbilt, Alfred G. London, 1912
Vanderbilt, Amy Staten Island, N. Y., 1908-74
Vanderbilt, Gloria New York City, 1924
Van Doren, Mamie Rowena, S. D., 1933
Van Dyke, Dick West Plains, Mo., 1925
Van Fleet, Jo Oakland, Cal., 1922
Van Heusen, Jimmie Syracuse, N. Y., 1913
Van Vooren, Monique Brussels, 1933
Vaughan, Sarah Newark, N. J., 1924
Vaughn, Robert New York City, 1932
Veidt, Conrad Berlin, 1893-1943
Velez, Lupe Mexico, 1908-44
Vera-Ellen Cincinnati, O., 1926-81
Verdon, Gwen Culver City, Cal., 1925
Vereen, Ben Miami, 1946
Vernon, Jackie New York City, 1928
Vinton, Bobby Canonsburg, Pa., 1935
Vitti, Monica Rome, 1933
Voight, Jon Yonkers, N. Y., 1938
Von Furstenberg, Betsy Neiheim-Heusen, Ger., 1932
Von Fürstenberg, Diane Brussels, Belg., 1946
Von Sydow, Max Lund, Sweden, 1929
Wagner, Lindsay Los Angeles, 1949
Wagner, Robert Detroit, 1930
Walker, Clint Hartford, Ill., 1927
Walker, Nancy Philadelphia, 1922
Walker, Robert Salt Lake City, 1919-51
Wallace, DeWitt St. Paul, Minn., 1889-1981
Wallace, Irving Chicago, 1916
Wallace, Mike Brookline, Mass., 1918
Wallach, Eli New York City, 1915
Waller, "Fats" New York, 1904-43
Wallis, Hal B. Chicago, 1899
Walters, Barbara Boston, 1931
Wanger, Walter San Francisco, 1894-1968
Warden, Jack Newark, N. J., 1920
Warfield, William West Helena, Ark., 1920
Waring, Fred Tyrone, Pa., 1900
Warner, Jack L. London, Can., 1892-1978
Warwicke, Dionne Orange, N. J., 1941
Washington, Dinah Tuscaloosa, Ala., 1924-64
Waters, Ethel Chester, Pa., 1900-77
Waters, Muddy Rolling Fork, Miss., 1915
Wayne, David Traverse City, Mich., 1914
Wayne, John Winterset, Iowa, 1907-79
Weaver, Dennis Joplin, Mo., 1925
Weaver, Fritz Pittsburgh, 1926
Webb, Clifton Indianapolis, 1891-1966
Webb, Jack Santa Monica, Cal., 1920
Weissmuller, Johnny Windber, Pa., 1904
Welch, Raquel La Jolla, Cal., 1942
Weld, Tuesday New York City, 1943
Welk, Lawrence Strasburg, N. D., 1903
Welles, Orson Kenosha, Wis., 1915
Werner, Oskar Vienna, 1922

West, Adam Walla Walla, Wash., 19387
West, Mae New York City, 1893-1980
Wheeler, Bert Paterson N.J., 1895-1968
White, Barry Galveston, 1944
White, Josh Greenville, S.C., 1908-69
White, Pearl Greenridge, Mo., 1889-1938
Whiting, Margaret Detroit, 1924
Whitmore, James White Plains, N. Y., 1921
Whitty, Dame May Liverpool, 1865-1948
Widmark, Richard Sunrise, Minn., 1914
Wilde, Cornel New York City, 1918
Wilder, Gene Milwaukee, 1935
Wilding, Michael Westcliff, Eng., 1912-79
William, Warren Aitkin, Minn., 1895-1948
Williams, Andy Wall Lake, Iowa, 1930
Williams, Cindy Van Nuys, Cal., 1948
Williams, Emlyn Glanrafon, Wales, 1905
Williams, Esther Inglewood, Cal., 1923
Williams, Hank Georgiana, Ala., 1923-53
Williams, Joe Cordele, Ga., 1918
Williams, Paul Omaha, 1944?
Williams, Robin Chicago, 1952
Williams, Roger Omaha, Neb., 1926
Williams, Ted San Diego, 1918
Williamson, Nicol Hamilton, Scot., 1938
Wills, Chill Seagoville, Tex., 1903-78
Wilson, Meredith Mason City, Iowa, 1902
Wilson, Don Lincoln, Neb., 1900
Wilson, Earl Rockford, O., 1907
Wilson, Flip Jersey City, N. J., 1933
Wilson, Julie Omaha, Neb., 1925
Wilson, Marie Anaheim, Cal., 1917-72
Wilson, Nancy Chillicothe, O., 1937
Winchell, Paul New York City, 1923
Winchell, Walter New York, 1897-1972
Windsor, Duchess of (Wallis Warfield Simpson) Blue Ridge Summit, Pa., 1896
Windsor, Duke of Richmond Park, Eng., 1894-1972
Winkler, Henry New York City, 1947
Winninger, Charles Athens, Wis., 1884-1969
Winters, Jonathan Dayton, O., 1925
Winters, Shelley St. Louis, Ill., 1923
Withers, Jane Atlanta, 1926
Wolfit, Donald Newark-on-Trent, Eng., 1902-68
Wonder, Stevie Detroit, 1951
Wong, Anna May Los Angeles, 1907-61
Wood, Natalie San Francisco, 1939
Wood, Peggy New York City, 1892-1978
Woodward, Joanne Thomasville, Ga., 1930
Woollcott, Alexander Phalanx, N.J., 1887-1963
Woolley, Monty New York, 1888-1962
Worth, Irene Nebraska, 1916
Wray, Fay Alberta, Can., 1907
Wright, Martha Seattle, 1926
Wright, Teresa New York City, 1918
Wyatt, Jane Campgaw, N. J., 1912
Wyman, Jane St. Joseph, Mo., 1914
Wynette, Tammy Tupelo, Miss., 1942
Wynn, Ed Philadelphia, 1886-1966
Wynn, Keenan New York City, 1916
Wynter, Dana London, 1930?
Yarborough, Glenn Milwaukee, 1930
Yarrow, Peter New York City, 1938
York, Dick Fort Wayne, Ind., 1928
York, Michael Fulmer, Eng., 1942
York, Susannah London, 1942
Young, Gig St. Cloud, Minn., 1917-78
Young, Loretta Salt Lake City, 1913
Young, Neil Toronto, 1945
Young, Robert Chicago, 1907
Young, Roland Chicago, 1887-1953
Young, Sheila Birmingham, Mich., 1950
Young, Victor Chicago, 1900-56
Youngman, Henny London, 1906?
Yurka, Blanche St. Paul, 1887-1974
Zanuck, Darryl F. Wahoo, Neb., 1902-79
Zeffirelli, Franco Florence, Italy, 1923
Ziegfeld, Florenz Chicago, 1869-1932
Zimbalist, Efrem, Jr. New York, 1923
Zimbalist, Efrem Rostov, Russ., 1889-
Zolotow, Maurice New York City, 1913
Zorina, Vera Berlin, 1917

ARTS: POPULAR/CLASSICAL

ALL-TIME MOVIE MONEYMAKERS

SOURCE: *Variety*

The following list includes all feature films that have grossed $22 million or more domestically (U.S. and Canada), as of Jan. 14, 1981. The film title is followed by the name of the director, producer, production company, and release year.

Film	Gross
Star Wars (G. Lucas; G. Kurtz; 20th; 1977).	$175,685,000
Jaws (S. Spielberg; Zanuck/Brown; Universal; 1975).	133,435,000
The Empire Strikes Back (I. Kershner; G. Lucas/ G. Kurtz; 20th; 1980).	120,000,000
Grease (R. Kleiser; R. Stigwood/A. Carr; Par; 1978).	96,300,000
The Exorcist (W. Friedkin; W.P. Blatty; WB; 1973).	88,500,000
The Godfather (F.F. Coppola; A. Ruddy; Par; 1972).	86,275,000
Superman (R. Donner; P. Spengler; WB; 1978).	82,500,000
The Sound of Music (R. Wise; 20th; 1965).	79,748,000
The Sting (G.R. Hill; T. Bill, M. & J. Phillips; Univ; 1973).	78,963,000
Close Encounters of the Third Kind (S. Spielberg; J. & M. Phillips; Col; 1977).	77,000,000
Gone With The Wind (V. Fleming; D. Selznick; MGM-UA; 1939).	76,700,000
Saturday Night Fever (J. Badham; R. Stigwood; Par; 1977).	74,100,000
National Lampoon's Animal House (J. Landis; M. Simmons/I. Reitman; Univ; 1978).	74,000,000
Smokey and the Bandit (H. Needham; M. Engelberg; Univ; 1977).	61,055,000
Kramer vs. Kramer (R. Benton; S. Jaffe; Col; 1979).	60,528,000
One Flew Over The Cuckoo's Nest (M. Forman; S. Zaentz/M. Douglas; UA; 1975).	59,000,000
Star Trek (R. Wise; G. Roddenberry; Par; 1979).	56,000,000
American Graffiti (G. Lucas; F.F. Coppola; Univ; 1973).	55,886,000
Jaws II (J. Szwarc; Zanuck/Brown; Univ; 1978).	55,608,000
Rocky (J. Avildsen; Chartoff/Winkler; UA; 1976).	54,000,000
Every Which Way But Loose (J. Fargo; R. Daley; WB; 1978).	51,800,000
Love Story (A. Hiller; H. Minsky; Par; 1970).	50,000,000
Towering Inferno (J. Guillermin; I. Allen; 20th; 1975).	50,000,000
Heaven Can Wait (W. Beatty; Par; 1978).	49,400,000
The Graduate (M. Nichols; L. Turman; Avco Embassy; 1968).	49,078,000
Doctor Zhivago (D. Lean; C. Ponti; MGM-UA; 1965).	46,550,000
Butch Cassidy and the Sundance Kid (G.R. Hill; J. Foreman; 20th; 1969).	46,039,000
Airport (G. Seaton; R. Hunter; Univ; 1970).	45,300,000
Blazing Saddles (M. Brooks; M. Hertzberg; WB; 1974).	45,200,000
Mary Poppins (R. Stevenson; W. Disney; BV; 1964).	45,000,000
Rocky II (S. Stallone; UA; 1979).	43,049,274
The Ten Commandments (C.B. DeMille; Par; 1956).	43,000,000
The Jerk (C. Reiner; D. V. Picker/W. E. McEuen; Univ; 1979).	43,000,000
The Poseidon Adventure (R. Neame; I. Allen; 20th; 1972).	42,000,000
Goodbye Girl (H. Ross; R. Stark; MGM-WB; 1977).	41,700,000
Fiddler on the Roof (N. Jewison; UA; 1971).	40,498,669
Alien (R. Scott; G. Carroll/D. Giler/W. Hill; 20th; 1979).	39,847,000
Young Frankenstein (M. Brooks; M. Gruskoff; 20th; 1975).	38,823,000
Airplane (J. Abrahams/D. Zucker/J. Zucker; H. W. Koch/J. Davidson; Par; 1980).	38,000,000
Smokey and the Bandit II (H. Needham; H. Moonjean; Univ; 1980).	37,600,000
A Star is Born (F. Pierson; J. Peters; WB; 1976).	37,100,000
King Kong (J. Guillermin; D. DeLaurentiis; Par; 1976).	36,915,000
Apocalypse Now (F.F. Coppola; UA; 1979).	36,846,471
MASH (R. Altman; I. Preminger; 20th; 1970).	36,720,000
Ben-Hur (W. Wyler; S. Zimbalist; MGM-UA; 1959).	36,650,000
Earthquake (M. Robson; Univ; 1974).	36,250,000
Coal Miner's Daughter (M. Apted; B. Larson; Univ; 1980).	36,000,000
Amityville Horror (S. Rosenberg; R. Saland/E. Geisinger; AIP; 1979).	35,000,000
Hooper (H. Needham; B. Reynolds/L. Gordon; WB; 1978).	34,900,000

Film	Gross
Moonraker (L. Gilbert; A. Broccoli; UA; 1979).	33,934,074
Private Benjamin (H. Zieff; N. Meyers/C. Shya/ H. Miller; WB; 1980).	33,500,000
Billy Jack (T. Frank; M. Solti; WB; 1971).	32,500,000
The Muppet Movie (J. Frawley; J. Henson; AFD; 1979).	32,000,000
Oh, God! (C. Reiner; J. Weintraub; WB; 1977).	31,440,000
The Deep (P. Yates; P. Guber; Col; 1977).	31,300,000
The Blues Brothers (J. Landis; R. K. Weiss; Univ; 1980).	31,000,000
The Electric Horseman (S. Pollack; Col; 1979).	30,917,000
Godfather, Part II (F.F. Coppola; Coppola/Frederickson/Roos; Par; 1974).	30,673,000
The Deer Hunter (M. Cimino; B. Spikings/M. Deeley/M. Cimino; Univ; 1978).	30,425,000
The Shining (S. Kubrick; WB; 1980).	30,200,000
Silver Streak (A. Hiller; E.K. Milkis/T.L. Miller; 20th; 1976).	30,018,000
All The President's Men (A. Pakula; W. Coblenz; WB; 1976).	30,000,000
California Suite (H. Ross; R. Stark; Col; 1978).	29,200,000
The Omen (R. Donner; H. Bernhard; 20th; 1976).	28,544,000
Thunderball (T. Young; Eon; UA; 1965).	28,530,000
The Blue Lagoon (R. Kleiser; Col; 1980).	28,456,000
Up In Smoke (L. Adler; Adler/Lombardo; Par; 1978).	28,300,000
Patton (F. Schaffner; F. McCarthy; 20th; 1970).	28,100,000
What's Up Doc? (P. Bogdanovich; WB; 1972).	28,000,000
Foul Play (C. Higgins; Miller/Milkis; Par; 1978).	27,500,000
The Jungle Book (W. Reitherman; W. Disney; BV; 1967).	27,300,000
Snow White (animated; W. Disney; RKO/BV; 1937).	26,750,000
Funny Girl (W. Wyler; R. Stark; Col; 1968).	26,325,000
The French Connection (W. Friedkin; P. D'Antoni/ Schine-Moore; 20th; 1971).	26,315,000
Main Event (H. Zieff; J. Peters/B. Streisand; WB; 1979).	26,300,000
The China Syndrome (J. Bridges; M. Douglas; Col; 1979).	26,073,700
Cleopatra (J. Mankiewicz; W. Wanger; 20th; 1963).	26,000,000
Airport 1975 (J. Smight; W. Fry; Univ; 1974).	25,805,000
Guess Who's Coming To Dinner? (S. Kramer; Col; 1968).	25,500,000
The Way We Were (S. Pollack; R. Stark; Col; 1973).	25,000,000
Revenge of the Pink Panther (B. Edwards; UA; 1978).	25,000,000
10 (B. Edwards; B. Edwards/T. Adams; Orion; 1979).	25,000,000
Black Hole (G. Nelson; R. Miller; BV; 1979).	25,000,000
The Lady and the Tramp (animated; W. Disney; BV; 1955).	24,900,000
The Bad News Bears (M. Ritchie; S. Jaffe; Par; 1976).	24,888,000
2001: A Space Odyssey (S. Kubrick; MGM-UA; 1968).	24,100,000
Trial of Billy Jack (F. Laughlin; D. Cramer; T-L/ WB; 1974).	24,000,000
The Enforcer (J. Fargo; R. Daley; WB; 1976).	24,000,000
In Search of Noah's Ark (J.L. Conway; C.E. Sellier, Jr.; Sunn; 1977).	23,770,000
1941 (S. Spielberg; B. Feitshans; Univ; 1979).	23,400,000
The Love Bug (R. Stevenson; W. Walsh; BV; 1969).	23,150,000
Around the World in 80 Days (M. Anderson; M. Todd; UA; 1956).	23,120,000
The Longest Yard (R. Aldrich; A. Ruddy; Par; 1974).	23,017,000
Goldfinger (G. Hamilton; Eon; UA; 1964).	22,860,000
Semi-Tough (M. Ritchie; D. Merrick; UA; 1977).	22,807,962
101 Dalmatians (animated; W. Disney; BV; 1961).	22,750,000
Bonnie and Clyde (A. Penn; W. Beatty; WB; 1967).	22,700,000
Urban Cowboy (J. Bridges; R. Evans/I. Azoff; Par; 1980).	22,700,000
Deliverance (J. Boorman; WB; 1972).	22,500,000
Papillon (F. Schaffner; R. Dorfmann; AA; 1973).	22,500,000
Dog Day Afternoon (S. Lumet; M. Bregman/M. Elfand; WB; 1975).	22,500,000
Midway (J. Smight; W. Mirisch; Univ; 1976).	22,329,000
Shampoo (H. Ashby; W. Beatty; Col; 1975).	22,000,000
Murder By Death (R. Moore; R. Stark; Col; 1976).	22,000,000
The Spy Who Loved Me (L. Gilbert; A. Broccoli; UA; 1977).	22,000,000

LONGEST BROADWAY RUNS

SOURCE: *Variety*

Play	Perfor-mances	Play	Perfor-mances	Play	Perfor-mances
Grease.	3,388	How To Succeed in Business		Damn Yankees.	1,019
Fiddler on the Roof.	3,242	without Really Trying.	1,417	Never Too Late.	1,007
Life with Father.	3,224	Hellazapoppin.	1,404	Any Wednesday.	984
Tobacco Road.	3,182	Ain't Misbehavin'*.	1,383	A Funny Thing Happened on	
Hello, Dolly!.	2,844	The Music Man.	1,375	the Way to the Forum.	964
My Fair Lady.	2,717	Funny Girl.	1,348	The Odd Couple.	964
A Chorus Line*.	2,405	The Best Little Whorehouse		Kiss and Tell.	962
Man of La Mancha.	2,329	in Texas*.	1,336	Anna Lucasta.	957
Abie's Irish Rose.	2,327	Mummenschanz.	1,316	The Moon is Blue.	924
Oklahoma!.	2,212	Angel Street.	1,295	Bells Are Ringing.	924
Oh! Calcutta!*.	2,070	Lightnin'.	1,291	Beatlemania.	914
Pippin.	1,944	Promises, Promises.	1,281	Luv.	902
South Pacific.	1,925	The King and I.	1,246	Can-Can.	895
Magic Show.	1,920	Cactus Flower.	1,234	Carousel.	890
Annie*.	1,820	Sleuth.	1,222	Hats Off to Ice.	890
Gemini*.	1,781	1776.	1,217	Fanny.	888
Harvey.	1,775	Equus.	1,209	Follow the Girls.	882
Hair.	1,742	Guys and Dolls.	1,200	The Bat.	878
The Wiz.	1,661	Cabaret.	1,166	Camelot.	873
Born Yesterday.	1,642	Mister Roberts.	1,157	My Sister Eileen.	866
Mary, Mary.	1,572	Annie Get Your Gun.	1,147	White Cargo.	864
The Voice of the Turtle.	1,557	The Seven Year Itch.	1,141	No, No, Nanette.	861
Barefoot in the Park.	1,532	Butterflies Are Free.	1,128	Song of Norway.	860
Mame.	1,503	Pins and Needles.	1,108	A Streetcar Named Desire.	855
Deathtrap*.	1,456	Plaza Suite.	1,097	Comedy in Music.	849
Arsenic and Old Lace.	1,444	Kiss Me Kate.	1,071	You Can't Take It with You.	837
Same Time, Next Year.	1,444	Don't Bother Me I Can't Cope.	1,065	La Plume de Ma Tante.	835
The Sound of Music.	1,443	Pajama Game.	1,063	Three Men on a Horse.	835
Dancin'*.	1,431	The Teahouse of the August Moon.	1,027	The Subject Was Roses.	832

*As of August 30, 1981. Figures reflect consecutive performances.

MAJOR WORLD DANCE GROUPS

SOURCE: The Dance Collection, Library & Museum of the Performing Arts, Lincoln Center, New York

Dates in parentheses indicate the founding year.

AMSTERDAM: **The Dutch National Ballet** (1961); *Director:* Rudi van Dantzig.

BOSTON: **Boston Ballet** (1964); *Director:* E. Virginia Williams.

BRUSSELS: **Ballet of the 20th Century** (1960); *Artistic Director:* Maurice Bejart.

COPENHAGEN: **Royal Danish Ballet** (1771); *Director:* Henning Kronstam.

GLASGOW: **Scottish Ballet** (1969); *Director:* Peter Darrell.

THE HAGUE: **Nederlands Dans Theater** (1959); *Artistic Director:* Jiri Kylián.

HAMBURG: **Hamburg State Opera Ballet** (c. 1959); *Artistic Director:* John Neumeier.

HAVANA: **Ballet Nacional de Cuba** (1948); *Director:* Alicia Alonso.

HOUSTON: **Houston Ballet** (1968); *Artistic Director:* Ben Stevenson.

LENINGRAD: **Kirov Ballet** (1738); *Director:* Oleg Vinogradov.

LONDON:

Festival Ballet (1950); *Director:* John Field.

Royal Ballet, Covent Garden (formerly **Sadler's Wells Ballet**) (1931); *Director:* Norman Morrice.

Ballet Rambert (1926); *Directors:* Dame Marie Rambert, John Chesworth.

London Contemporary Dance Theatre (1967); *Director:* Robert Cohan.

MELBOURNE: **Australian Ballet** (1962); *Artistic Director:* Marilyn Jones.

MOSCOW: **Bolshoi Ballet** (c. 1776); *Artistic Director:* Yuri Grigorovich.

NEW YORK CITY:

Nikolais Dance Theatre (1948); *Director:* Alwin Nikolais.

American Ballet Theatre (1940); *Director:* Mikhail Baryshnikov.

Alvin Ailey American Dance Theatre (1958); *Director:* Alvin Ailey.

The Joffrey Ballet (1954); *Artistic Director:* Robert Joffrey.

The Dance Theatre of Harlem (1968); *Directors:* Arthur Mitchell and Karel Shook.

The Feld Ballet (1974); *Director:* Eliot Feld.

Martha Graham Dance Company (1927); *Director:* Martha Graham.

Merce Cunningham Dance Group (1952); *Director:* Merce Cunningham.

New York City Ballet (1948); *Dance Masters:* George Balanchine, Jerome Robbins, John Taras.

Paul Taylor Dance Company (1954); *Director:* Paul Taylor.

Twyla Tharp Dance Foundation (1965); *Artistic Director:* Twyla Tharp.

PARIS: **Paris Opera Ballet** (1671); *Director:* Rosella Hightower.

PHILADELPHIA: **Pennsylvania Ballet** (1963); *Director:* Barbara Weisberger; *Artistic Director:* Benjamin Harkarvy.

PITTSBURGH: **Pittsburgh Ballet Theatre** (1970); *Artistic Director:* Patrick Frantz.

SAN FRANCISCO: **San Francisco Ballet** (1933); *Directors:* Lew Christensen and Michael Smuin.

STOCKHOLM: **Royal Swedish Ballet** (1773); *Artistic Director:* Gunilla Roempke.

STUTTGART: **Stuttgart Ballet** (c. 1759); *Director:* Marcia Haydée.

TORONTO: **National Ballet of Canada** (1951); *Artistic Director:* Alexander Grant.

WASHINGTON (CONN.): **Pilobolus Dance Theatre** (1971); *Manager:* Susan Mandler.

WASHINGTON (D.C.): **Washington Ballet** (1962); *Director:* Mary Day.

WINNIPEG: **Royal Winnipeg Ballet** (1938); *Artistic Director:* Arnold Spohr.

POPULAR DISCOGRAPHY

Note: Numeral and hyphen preceding record label indicate multi-disc album, the numeral indicating the number of discs

STANDARD POP

Herb Alpert—Rise/A&M 3714; Paul Anka—His Best/U. Artists LA922-H; Burt Bacharach—Greatest Hits/A&M 3661; Tony Bennett—Tony/Harmony KH 32171; Glen Campbell—Wichita Lineman/Capitol SM 103; Captain & Tennille—Love Will Keep Us Together/A&M SP4552; Carpenters—Singles/A&M 3601; Nat "King" Cole—Best/Capitol SKAO-2944; Ray Conniff—Harmony/Columbia KC-32553; Bing Crosby—Feels Good/London 679; Christopher Cross—Warner Bros. 3383; John Denver—Greatest Hits/Victor CPL1-0374; Neil Diamond—The Jazz Singer/Capitol SWAV-12120; José Feliciano—Fireworks/RCA LSP 4370; Four Seasons—2nd Vault of Golden Hits/Philips PHS 600-221; Bobbie Gentry—Fancy/Capitol ST-428; Tom Jones—Greatest Hits/Paramount XPAS 71062; Peggy Lee/Arc. Folk. 294; Henry Mancini—Pure Gold/RCA AYL1-3667; Barry Manilow—Greatest Hits/2-Arista 8601; Mantovani—Greatest Hits, Vol. 1/London XPS 906; Johnny Mathis—All-Time Greatest Hits/2-Columbia Pg 31345; Mabel Mercer (w. Bobby Short)—At Town Hall/2-Atlantic S-604; Olivia Newton-John—Totally Hot/MCA 3067; Tony Orlando & Dawn—Prime Time/Bell 1317; Donny & Marie Osmond—Winning Combination/Polydor I-6127; Pointer Sisters—That's a Plenty/Blue Thumb 48; Diana Ross—Diana/Motown 8-936; Frank Sinatra—Trilogy/3-Reprise SFS-2300; Kate Smith—At Carnegie Hall/Camden CAS-2587; Barbra Streisand—Guilty/Columbia FC-36750; Dionne Warwick—Dionne/Arista 4230; Andy Williams—Solitaire/Columbia KC-32383; Nancy Wilson—Best/Capitol SKAO-2947.

ROCK 'N' ROLL

ABBA—Greatest Hits Vol. 2/Atlantic 16009; Beach Boys—Good Vibrations/Reprise 2223; Beatles—Rubber Soul/Apple ST 2442; Bee Gees—Greatest Hits/2-RSO 4200; Pat Benatar—Crimes of Passion/Chrysalis 1275; Blondie—Autoamerican/Chrysalis 1290; Boston—Epic PE 34188; David Bowie—Space Oddity/RCA LSP-4813; Cars—Candy-O/Elektra 507; Cheap Trick—Dream Police/Epic FE-35773; Chicago—Hot Streets/Columbia FC-35512; Alice Cooper—Welcome to My Nightmare/Atlantic SD 18130; Cream—Best of/Atco SD 33-291; Crosby, Stills, Nash & Young—Déjà Vu/Atlantic SD 7200; Doors—Elektra 74007; Eagles—The Long Run/Asylum 5E-508; Earth, Wind & Fire—Best of, Vol. 1/Columbia FC-35647; Fleetwood Mac—Tusk/2-Warner Bros. 2HS-3350; Jimi Hendrix—Are You Experienced?/Reprise S-6261; Jefferson Starship—Red Octopus/Grunt BFL1-0999; Jethro Tull—War Child/Chrysalis 1067; Billy Joel—Glass Houses/Columbia FC-36384; Elton John—Greatest Hits/MCA 2128; Carole King—Tapestry/Ode 77009; Kiss—Alive/Casablanca NBLP 7020; John Lennon & Yoko Ono—Double Fantasy/Geffen GHS-2001; Meat Loaf—Bat Out of Hell/Epic PE-34974; Bette Midler—The Rose/Atlantic 16010; Steve Miller—Greatest Hits 1974-78/Capitol S00-11872; Mothers of Invention—We're Only in it for the Money/Verve 65045; Randy Newman—Little Criminals/Warner Bros. 3079; Gary Numan—Telekon/Atco 38-117; Pink Floyd—The Wall/2-Columbia PC2-36183; Police—Zenyatta Mondatta/A&M 4831; Elvis Presley—Elvis/RCA APL1-0283; Suzi Quatro—If You Knew Suzi/RSO 3044; Queen—The Game/Elektra 513; Gerry Rafferty—City to City/U. Artists LA840-H; Rolling Stones—Some Girls/Roll. Stones Rec. 39108; Santana—Abraxas/Columbia SK-30130; Sex Pistols—Never Mind the Bollocks/Warner Bros. K-3147; Simon & Garfunkel—Bridge Over Troubled Water/Columbia KCS-9914; Southside Johnny & The Asbury Jukes—Hearts of Stone/Epic JE-35488; Bruce Springsteen—The River/2-Columbia PC2-36854; Rod Stewart—Greatest Hits/Warner Bros. HS-3373; Donna Summer—On the Radio, Greatest Hits Vol. 1 & 2/2-Casablanca NBLP2-7191; T. Rex/Reprise 6440; The Who—Who Are You?/MCA 3050; Wings—Greatest/Capitol S00-11905; Neil Young & Crazy Horse—Rust Never Sleeps/Warner Bros. HS 2295; Warren Zevon—Excitable Boy/Asylum 118.

FOLK AND FOLK-ROCK

Hoyt Axton—Free Sailin'/MCA 2319; Joan Baez—Blessed Are/2-Vanguard VSD 6570/1; Jackson Browne—For Everyman/Asylum 5067; Leonard Cohen—Songs of/Columbia CS 9533; Judy Collins—Whales & Nightingales/Elektra 75010; Jim Croce—Photographs & Memories/ABC 835; Bob Dylan—Blonde on Blonde/2-Columbia C2S-841, Jack Elliott/Vanguard 79151; Kinky Friedman—Sold American/Vanguard 79333; Bob Gibson—Where I'm Bound/Elektra 7239; Steve Goodman—Somebody Else's Troubles/Buddah 5121; Arlo Guthrie—Washington County/Reprise 6411; Woody Guthrie—Dust Bowl Ballads/Folkways 5212; Tim Hardin—I/Verve Folk. FTS 3004; Fred Holstein—Chicago & Other Ports/Philo PH 1030; Ian & Sylvia—Best/2-Columbia

CG-32516; Michael Johnson—Dialogue/EMI SW-17010; Bonnie Koloc—Close-Up/Epic PE-34184; Leo Kottke—Balance/Chrysalis 1234; Leadbelly—Huddie Ledbetter/Fantasy 24715; Gordon Lightfoot—Gord's Gold/2-Reprise 2RS 2237; Melanie—Candles in the Rain/Buddah BDS-5060; Joni Mitchell—Court & Spark/Elek. Asylum 7E 1001; Maria Muldaur—Sweet Harmony/Reprise MS 2235; Harry Nilsson—Nilsson Schmilsson/RCA LSP-4515; Jim Post—Slow to 20/Fantasy 9408; John Prine—Bruised Orange/Asylum 139; Linda Ronstadt—Greatest Hits/Asylum 1092; Rotary Connection—Peace/Cadet-Concept LPS 318; Leon Russell—Will o' the Wisp/Shelter SR 2138; Buffy Sainte-Marie—It's My Way!/Vanguard VSD 79142; Skymonters (w. Hamid Hamilton Camp)/Elektra 75073; Cat Stevens—Foreigner/A&M 4391; James Taylor—Mud Slide Slim/Warner Bros. BS-2561.

RHYTHM AND BLUES, SOUL, GOSPEL

Big Bill Broonzy—Blues/Encore 22017; James Brown—Jam 1980s/Polydor 6140(6); Ray Charles—Genius Sings the Blues/Atlantic SD 8052; Sam Cooke—You Send Me/Camden ACS1 0445; Bo Diddley—Greatest/Checker 8034; Fats Domino—Very Best/U. Artists LA 233-G; Sleepy John Estes—Broke & Hungry/Delmark 608; Roberta Flack—Killing Me Softly/Atlantic 7271; Aretha Franklin—With Everything I Feel in Me/Atlantic SD 18116; B.B. King—Best/ABC 724; Gladys Knight & the Pips—Knight Time/Soul 741; Taj Mahal—Mo Roots/Columbia KC 33051; Curtis Mayfield—Curtis in Chicago/Curtom 8018; Mighty Clouds of Joy—It's Time/Dunwich 50177; Teddy Pendergrass—T.P./Phila. Int'l FZ-36745; Wilson Pickett—Greatest Hits/2-Atlantic 2-501; Lou Rawls—Sit Down & Talk to Me/Philadelphia Intl. JZ-36304; Otis Redding—Tell the Truth/Atco SD 33-333; Smokey Robinson & Miracles—1957-72/2-Tamla 320; Sly & Family Stone—Fresh/Epic KE-32134; Bessie Smith—Empty Bed Blues/Columbia G 30450; Sweet Inspirations—Sweet Sweet Soul/Atlantic SD 8253; Temptations—Greatest Hits, Vol. 2/Gordy 5 954; Muddy Waters—Live/Chess 50012; Stevie Wonder—Hotter Than July/Tamla 8-373.

JAZZ

Amanda Ambrose—Amanda/Dunwich 668; George Benson—Give Me the Night/Qwest-Warner Bros. HS3453; Dave Brubeck—Greatest Hits/Columbia CS-9284; John Coltrane—My Favorite Things/Atlantic 1361; Miles Davis—Kind of Blue/Columbia PC 8163; Ella Fitzgerald—Best/Reprise S 6354; Erroll Garner—Misty/Mercury 60662; Stan Getz (w. Charlie Byrd)—Jazz Samba/Verve 68432; Dizzy Gillespie—Groovin' High/Savoy 12020; Benny Goodman—1938 Carnegie Hall Jazz Concert/2-Columbia OSL-160; Woody Herman—Woody/Cadet 845; Earl Hines—Tea for Two/Black Lion BL-112; Billie Holiday—Lady Day/Columbia CL-637; Scott Joplin—Ragtime, Vol. 3/Biograph 1010Q; Roland Kirk—Gifts & Messages/Mercury S 90939; Chuck Mangione—Chase the Clouds Away/A&M 4518; Charles Mingus—Mingus Dynasty/Columbia CL 1440; Wes Montgomery—Best/Verve 68714; Jelly Roll Morton—King of New Orleans Jazz/Victor LPM 1649; Oliver Nelson—Blues & the Abstract Truth/Impulse A-5; Charlie Parker—Complete Savoy Sessions/5-Savoy 5500; Joe Pass—Virtuoso/Pablo 2810708; Oscar Peterson—Newport Years/Verve 8828; Django Reinhardt—Djangology/Victor LPM 2319; Judy Roberts—Inner City 1078; Sonny Rollins (w. Max Roach)—Freedom Suite/2-Milestone 47007; Art Tatum—Essential/Verve 68433; Sarah Vaughan—Golden Hits/Mercury 60645; Fats Waller—One Never Knows, Do One?/Victor LPM 1503; Lester Young—Essential/Verve 68398.

COUNTRY AND WESTERN

Bill Anderson—Bill/MCA 320; Lynn Anderson—Greatest Hits/Columbia KC 31641; Eddy Arnold—Best, Vol. 3/RCA LSP 4844; Chet Atkins—Mr. Atkins, Guitar Picker/Camden CASX 2464(e); Jimmy Buffett—Changes in Latitudes, Changes in Attitudes/ABC 990; Johnny Cash—Silver/Columbia JC-36086; Charlie Daniels—Full Moon/Epic FE-36571; Jimmy Dean—Favorite Son/Harmony 11270; Flatt & Scruggs—Greatest Hits/Columbia CS 9370; Crystal Gayle—Classic Crystal/U. Artists LOO 982; Merle Haggard—190Proof/MCA 3089; Wanda Jackson—Country Keepsakes/Capitol ST 11161; Waylon Jennings—Greatest Hits/RCA AHL 1-1378; Loretta Lynn—Greatest Hits, Vol. 2/MCA 420; Jody Miller—Country Girl/Epic KE-33349; Willie Nelson—Stardust/Columbia JC-35305; Oak Ridge Boys—Greatest Hits/MCA 5150; Dolly Parton—9 to 5 and Odd Jobs/RCA AHL1-3852; Charley Pride—Pride of America/Victor APL1-0757; Kenny Rogers—Greatest Hits/U. Artists LOO-1072; Carl Smith—Country on My Mind/Columbia CS-9688; Statler Bros.—Best/Mercury 1037; Hank Williams—Greatest Hits/2-MGM S-4755; Bob Wills—Anthology/Columbia KG 32416; Tammy Wynette—My Man/Epic KE 31717.

CLASSICAL DISCOGRAPHY

OPERA

Beethoven—Fidelio: Klemperer/3-Angel S-3625; **Bellini**—Norma: Serafin/3-Angel S-3615; **Berg**—Wozzeck: Böhm/2-DGG 2707023; **Bizet**—Carmen: Troyanos, Solti, London Phil./3-London 13115; **Debussy**—Pelléas et Mélisande: Ansermet/London 1379; **Donizetti**—Lucia di Lammermoor: Pritchard/London 25702; **Flotow**—Martha (highlights): Berlin Mun. Op./Angel S-36236; **Gilbert & Sullivan**—Pirates of Penzance: D'Oyly Carte Op. Co./2-London 1277; **Gluck**—Orfeo ed Euridice: Fasano/3-RCA LSC-6169; **Gounod**—Faust: Cluytens/4-Angel S-3622; **Leoncavallo**—Pagliacci: Gobbi/2-Angel S-3618; **Mascagni**—Cavalleria Rusticana: Serafin/3-London 1330; **Massenet**—Manon: Rudel/4-ABC ATS-20007; **Mozart**—Marriage of Figaro: Fricsay/3-DG 2728004; Don Giovanni: Klemperer/4-Angel S-3700; The Magic Flute: Böhm/3-DG-2709017; **Moussorgsky**—Boris Godunov: Cluytens/4-Angel S-3633; **Puccini**—La Bohème: Serafin/2-London 1208; Tosca: Karajan/2-London 1284; Madama Butterfly: Serafin/3-Angel S-3604; **Rossini**—The Barber of Seville: Leinsdorf/4-RCA 6143; **Schoenberg**—Moses and Aaron: Gielen/2-Philips 6700084; R. **Strauss**—Der Rosenkavalier: Solti/4-London 1435; **Verdi**—Aida: Leinsdorf/3-RCA LSC-6198; Falstaff: Karajan/3-Angel S-3552; La Forza del Destino: Previtali/3-London 13122; Otello: Karajan/3-London 1324; Rigoletto: Solti/2-Angel S-3718; La Traviata: Previtali/3-RCA LSC-6154; **Wagner**—Gotterdämmerung: Solti/6-London 1604.

SYMPHONY

Beethoven—Complete Symphonies, 1-9: Karajan/8-DG 2721001; **Berlioz**—Symphonie Fantastique: Munch/RCA LSC-2608; **Bizet**—Symphony No. 1: Ansermet/London 6208; **Brahms**—Complete Symphonies 1-4: Szell/3-Columbia D3S-758; **Bruckner**—No. 4: Klemperer/Angel S-36245; No. 9: Mehta/London 6462; **Copland**—Symphony No. 3: Bernstein/Columbia MS-6954; **Dvořák**—Nos. 7-9: Szell/3-Columbia D3S-814; **Franck**—Symphony in D minor: Monteux/RCA LSC-2514; **Haydn**—Nos. 93-104: Dorati/3-London STS 15319-15324; **Mahler**—No. 1: Giulini/DG 2707097; No. 4: Reiner/RCA 2364; No. 9: Walter/2-Odyssey Y2-30308; **Mendelssohn**—Nos. 4-5: Munch/RCA LSC-2221; **Mozart**—Nos. 25,29: Marriner/Argo ZRG-706; Nos. 32, 35, 38: Boehm/DG 138112; Nos. 40,41: Klemperer/Angel S-36183; **Nielsen**—No. 5: Bernstein/Columbia MS-6414; **Prokofiev**—Classical Symphony, Lt. Kijé and "Three Oranges" Suites: Ormandy/Columbia MS-6545; **Saint-Saëns**—No. 3: Munch/RCA LSC-2341; **Schubert**—Nos. 5,8: Walter/Columbia MS-6218; No. 9: Szell/Angel S-36044; **Schumann**—Complete Symphonies, 1-4: Bernstein/3-Columbia D3S-725; **Shostakovich**—No. 2: Ormandy/Columbia MS-6124; **Sibelius**—No. 5: Bernstein/Columbia MS-6749; **Stravinsky**—Symphony in Three Movements: Ansermet/London MS-6190; **Tchaikovsky**—No. 6: Monteux/RCA 2369; No. 6: Ormandy/Columbia MS-6160; **Vaughan Williams**—No. 5: Barbirolli/Angel S-35952.

ORCHESTRAL AND CHORAL

Bach—Brandenburg Concertos: Harnoncourt/Telefunken S-9459/60; Cantatas 56 & 169: Saar Ch. Orch./Nonesuch 71142; Suites for Orchestra: Casals/2-Columbia M2S-755; **Bartók**—Concerto for Orchestra: Ormandy/Columbia MS-6626; Hungarian Sketches: Reiner/RCA VICS 1620; Music for Strings, Percussion and Celesta: Boulez/Cþlumbia MS-7206; **Beethoven**—Overtures: Karajan/2-DG 2707046; **Copland**—Appalachian Spring; El Salon Mexico: Bernstein/Columbia MS-6355; Billy the Kid; Rodeo: Bernstein/Columbia MS-6175; **Debussy**—La Mer; Nocturnes: Giulini/Angel S-35977; Images pour Orchestre: Boulez/Columbia MS-7362; **Dvořák**—Slavonic Dances: Szell/Columbia MS-7208; **Elgar**—Enigma Variations; Cockaigne Overture: Barbirolli/Angel S-36120; **Falla**—Three Cornered Hat & La Vida Breve Dances: Reiner/RCA 2230; **Gershwin**—An American in Paris; Rhapsody in Blue: Bernstein/Columbia MS-6091 Op. 6: Leppard/Mercury 9124; Water Music and Royal Fireworks Suites: Szell/London 6236; **Hindemith**—Symphonic Metamorphoses of Themes by Weber; Mathis der Maler: Ormandy/Columbia MS-6562; **Kodály**—Háry János Suite; Dances from Galánta: Kertész/London 6417; **Liszt**—A Faust Symphony; Les Preludes: Bernstein/2-Columbia MG-699; **Mendelssohn**—A Midsummer Night's Dream: Klemperer/Angel S-3588l; **Mozart**—Eine Kleine Nachtmusik; Serenade No. 9: Szell/Columbia MS-7273; **Moussorgsky-Ravel**—Pictures at an Exhibition: Ansermet/London 6177; **Orff**—Carmina Burana: Thomas & Cleveland Orch. Chorus & Boys' Choir/Columbia M-33172; **Ravel**—Daphnis et Chloe: Ansermet/London 6456; La Valse; Menuet Antique; Ma Mère l'Oye: Boulez/Columbia M-32838Q; **Respighi**—The Pines of Rome; The Fountains of Rome: Reiner/RCA LSC-2436; **Rimsky-Korsakov**—Scheherazade: Rostropovich/Angel S-37061(Q); **Rossini**—Overtures: Toscanini/Victrola 1274; **Smetana**—Moldau; Bartered Bride Dances: Szell/Odyssey Y-30049; J. **Strauss**—Waltzes: Ormandy/Columbia MS-6217; R. **Strauss**—Also Sprach Zarathustra; Don Juan & Till Eulenspiegel: Solti/London 6978; **Stravinsky**—The

Firebird: Stokowski/London 21026; Le Sacre du Printemps: Bernstein/Columbia MS-6010; **Tchaikovsky**—The Nutcracker: Ansermet/London 2203; Romeo and Juliet; Francesca da Rimini: Munch/RCA VICS-1197; The Sleeping Beauty: Previn/3-Angel SX 3812(Q).

SOLOS WITH ORCHESTRA

Bach—Clavier Concertos Nos. 1,2: Kirkpatrick/DG ARC 198013; Violin Concertos Nos. 1, 2; Concerto for 2 Violins: David and Igor Oistrakh/DG 138820; **Bartók**—Piano Concertos Nos. 2,3: Anda/DG 138111; **Beethoven**—Piano Concertos Nos. 1-5: Ashkenazy/4-London 2404; Violin Concerto: Stern/Columbia MS-6093; **Berg**—Violin Concerto: Grumiaux/Philips 900194; **Berlioz**—Harold in Italy: Menuhin/Angel S-36123; **Brahms**—Piano Concerto No. 2: Dichter/Philips 9500414; Violin Concerto: Heifetz/RCA LSC-1903; Double Concerto: Oistrakh-Rostropovich/Angel S-36032; **Bruch**—Violin Concerto No. l: Stern/Columbia MS-7003; **Chopin**—Piano Concertos Nos. 1,2; Andante: Rubinstein/2-RCA VCS-7091; **Dvořák**—Cello Concerto: Starker/Mercury 90303; **Grieg**—Piano Concerto: Rubinstein/RCA LSC-2566; **Lalo**—Symphonie Espagnole; **Liszt**—Piano Concertos Nos. 1,2: Richter/Philips 835474; **Mendelssohn**—Violin Concerto: Francescatti/Columbia MS-6758; **Mozart**—Horn Concertos Nos. 1-4; Rondo K.371: Civil/Philips 6500325; Piano Concertos Nos. 25,27: Gulda/DG 2530642; Violin Concertos Nos. 3,4: Francescatti/Columbia MS-6063; **Paganini**—Violin Concertos Nos. 1,2: Gitlis/Turn. 34203; **Poulenc**—Organ Concerto: Duruflé (w. Gloria: Carteri)/Angel S-35953; **Prokofiev**—Piano Concertos Nos. 3,4: Browning/RCA 3019; **Rachmaninoff**—Piano Concerto No. 2: Ashkenazy/London 6390; **Saint-Saëns**—Cello Concertos Nos. 1,2, etc.: Walevska/Philips 6500459; **Schumann**—Cello Concerto: Rostropovich/DG 138674; Piano Concerto: Rubinstein/RCA LSC-2997; **Sibelius**—Violin Concerto: Heifetz/RCA LSC-2435; **Tchaikovsky**—Piano Concerto No. l: Cliburn/RCA LSC-2252; Violin Concerto: Zuckerman/Columbia MS-7313; **Vivaldi**—Concerti for Cello & Orchestra: Waleyska/Philips 9500144; The Four Seasons: Virtuosi di Roma/Angel S-35877.

CHAMBER MUSIC

Bartók—Quartets Nos. 1-6: Juilliard Quartet/3-Columbia D3S-717; **Beethoven**—Quartets (complete): Amadeus Quartet/4-DG 2721006; "Archduke" Trio: Stern-Rose-Istomin/Columbia MS-6819; Violin & Piano Sonatas (complete): Francescatti-Casadesus/4-Columbia D4S-724; **Berg**—Lyric Suite: RCA/Juilliard Quartet/RCA 2531; **Brahms**—Quintet Op. 34: Previn, Yale Quartet/Angel S-36928; Trio Op. 40: Tuckwell-Perlman-Ashkenazy/London 6628; Violin Sonatas: Szeryng, Rubinstein/2-RCA LSC-2619/20; **Debussy, Ravel**—Quartets: Juilliard Quartet/Columbia M-30650; **Dvořák**—Quartets Nos. 2,6; Janácek Quartet/London 6394; Piano Quintet: Curzon/Vienna Phil. Quartet/London 6357; **Haydn**—Quartets Op. 76, Nos. 2,5: Hungarian Quartet/Turnabout 34012; Quartets Op. 77, Nos. 1,2: Amadeus Quartet/DG 138980; **Hindemith**—Kleine Kammermusik: Boston Symphony Players/RCA 3166; **Mendelssohn**—Octet: Laredo, et al/Columbia MS-6848; **Mozart**—Quartets Nos. 14-19: Italiano/3-Philips S-C 71AX301; Piano Quartets: Horszowski, Budapest/Columbia MS-6683; Quintets K. 515,516: Primrose, Griller/Vanguard S-158; Quintet, K. 581, Trio K. 498: De Peyer, Melos Ensemble/Angel S-36241; **Schubert**—Octet: Melos Ensemble/Angel S-36529; Quartets Nos. 12,14: Amadeus Quartet/DG 138048; "Trout" Quintet: Marlboro Players/Vanguard 71145; **Schumann**—Piano Quintet: Serkin, Budapest/2-Columbia M2S-734; **Stravinsky**—L'Histoire du Soldat: Cocteau, Markevitch/Philips 90044.

SOLO INSTRUMENTAL

Bach—Goldberg Variations: Leonhardt/Vanguard S-175; Well-tempered Clavier, Bk. 1: Kirkpatrick/2-DG ARC 2708006; Sonatas and Partitas for Violin: Grumiaux/3-Philips 835198/200; Organ Music: Walcha/DG 198305; **Beethoven**—Piano Sonatas 8,14,23: Kempff/DG 139300; 17,21: Brendel/Turnabout 34394; 28,31: Serkin/Columbia M 31239; 30,32: Backhaus/London CS-6246; **Chopin**—Ballades: Rubinstein/RCA LSC-2370; Mazurkas: Novaes/Vox 57920; Nocturnes: Rubinstein/RCA LSC-7050; Scherzos: Rubinstein/RCA LSC-2368; Sonatas Nos. 2,3: Rubinstein/RCA 3194; **Debussy**—Piano Music (complete): W. Haas/5-Philips S-012; **Liszt**—Sonata in B minor; Piano Music: Curzon/London 6371; **Mendelssohn**—Songs without Words: Novaes/Turnabout 34245; **Mozart**—Piano Sonatas (complete). Eschenbach/7-DG 2720031; **Rachmaninoff**—Preludes, etc.: Weissenberg/RCA 7069; **Ravel**—Piano Music (complete): Simon/3-Vox SVBX-5473; **Scarlatti**—Sonatas: Kirkpatrick/DG ARC-2533072; **Schubert**—Sonata in A; Wanderer Fantasy: Richter/Angel S-36150; Sonata in D; Impromptus: Curzon/London 6416; Sonata in A, Op. Posth.: Serkin/Columbia MS-6849; **Schumann**—Carnaval; Fantasia, Op. 17: Arrau/Philips 802746; **Scriabin**—Piano Sonatas 3,4,5,9: Ashkenazy/London 6920.

LEADING OPERA COMPANIES SOURCE: Central Opera Service

WORLD OPERA COMPANIES (exclusive of U.S.)

AMSTERDAM: **Nederlandse Operastichting;** *Manager:* J.H. de Roo

BARCELONA: **Gran Teatro del Liceo;** *General Director:* Juan A. Pamias

BAYREUTH: **Bayreuther Festspiele;** *Director:* Wolfgang Wagner

BELGRADE: **Srpsko Narodno Pozoriste;** *Director:* D. Djurdjevic

BERLIN: (West) **Deutsche Oper;** *Artistic Director:* Jesus Lopez-Lobos. (East) **Deutsche Staatsoper;** *General Director:* Hans Pischner. (East) **Deutsche Oper;** *Director:* Harry Kupfer

BRUSSELS: **Théâtre Royal de la Monnaie;** *Director:* Gérard Martier

BUCHAREST: **Romanian Opera;** *Director:* Petre Codreanu.

BUDAPEST: **Magyar Allami Operahaz & Erkel Theater (Hungarian State Opera);** *Director:* Andras Mikaly

BUENOS AIRES: **Teatro Colon**

COLOGNE: **Bühnen der Stadt Köln;** *Director:* Michael Hampe; *Music Director:* John Pritchard

COPENHAGEN: **Det kongelige Teater;** *Manager:* Niels Moeller

DRESDEN: **Staatsoper Dresden;** *Director:* Horst Seeger

DUSSELDORF/DUISBURG: **Deutsche Oper am Rhein;** *Director:* Hiroshi Wakasugi

EDINBURGH: **Edinburgh Festival;** *Director:* John Drummond

EDMONTON: **Edmonton Opera Association;** *Artistic Director:* Irving Guttman

FLORENCE: **Teatro Comunale & Maggio Fiorentino;** *Music Director:* Riccardo Muti

FRANKFURT: **Stadtische Buhnen;** *Director:* Michael Gielen

GENEVA: **Grand Theatre de l'Opera;** *General Director:* Hugues Gall

GLASGOW: **Scottish Opera;** *General Director:* Vacant

GLYNDEBOURNE: **Festival Opera;** *Chairman:* George W. Christie

HAMBURG: **Staatsoper;** *Dir. & Chief conductor:* Christoph von Dohnányi

HELSINKI: **Finnish National Opera;** *General Manager:* J. Raiskinen

LEIPZIG: **Staedtische Theater;** *Director Opera:* Karl Kayser

LENINGRAD: **Kirov Opera & Ballet Theatre;** *Director:* Yuri Temirkanov

LONDON: **D'Oyly Carte Ltd.;** *Musical Director:* Royston Nash. **Royal Opera, Covent Garden;** *General Administrator:* John Tooley. **English National Opera Ltd.;** *Managing Director:* Lord Harewood

MARSEILLE: **Opera Municipal;** *Director:* R. Giovaninetti

MILAN: **Teatro alla Scala;** *Music Director:* Francisco Siciliani

MONTE CARLO: **L'Opera de Monte-Carlo;** *Director:* Guy Grinda

MOSCOW: **Bolshoi Theatre of the USSR;** *Director:* Giorgy Ivanov

MUNICH: **Bayerische Staatsoper;** *Director:* August Everding. **Theater am Gartnerplatz;** *Director:* Kurt Pscherer

NAPLES: **Teatro San Carlo;** *Acting General Manager:* Adriano Falvo

OSLO: **Den Norske Opera (The Norwegian Opera);** *Director:* Aase Nordmo-Loevberg

OTTAWA: **Ottawa Festival Opera;** *General Director:* Donald MacSween

PARIS: **Theatre National de l'Opera;** *Administrator:* Bernard Lefort

PRAGUE: **National Theatre & Smetana Theatre & Tyl Theatre;** *Director:* Jiri Pauer

RIO DE JANEIRO: **Opera Estaveldo Teatro Municipal;** *Director:* Edmundo Barreto Pintos

ROME: **Teatro dell'Opera;** *Gen. Mgr.:* Roman Vlad

SALZBURG: **Salzburg Festival;** *Director:* Dr. Otto Seril. **Easter Festival;** *Director:* Herbert von Karajan

SOFIA: **Bulgarian National Opera;** *Director:* Dimitar Petkov

STOCKHOLM: **Kungliga Teatern;** *General Manager:* Folke Abenius

STRASBOURG: **L'Opera du Rhin;** *Artistic Director:* Alain Lombard

TUTTGART: **Wurttembergisches Staatstheater;** *Music Director:* Dennis Russell Davies

SYDNEY: **Australian Opera;** *General Manager:* Patrick Veitch

TEL AVIV: **Israel National Opera;** *Director:* Simha Evan Zohar

TORONTO: **Canadian Opera Company;** *General Director:* Lotfi Mansouri

VANCOUVER: **Vancouver Opera Association;** *General Manager:* Hamilton McClymont

VENICE: **Teatro La Fenice;** *General Manager:* Italo Gomez

VERONA: **Arena di Verona;** *Artistic Director:* Luciano Chailly

VIENNA: **Staatsoper;** *Director:* Egon Seefehlner; *Director Designate:* Lorin Maazel. **Volksoper;** *Director:* Karl Doench

WARSAW: **Teatr Wielki (Grand Theatre Warsaw);** *Artistic Director:* Antoni Wicherek

ZURICH: **Opernhaus Zurich;** *General Manager:* Klaus Helmut Drese

AMERICAN OPERA COMPANIES

BALTIMORE: **Baltimore Opera Company;** *General Manager:* Jay Holbrook

BOSTON: **Opera Company of Boston;** *Artistic Director:* Sarah Caldwell

CENTRAL CITY: **Central City Opera House Association;** *Artistic Director:* Robert Darling

CHARLESTON: **Spoleto Festival USA;** *General Manager:* James Kearney

CHARLOTTE: **Charlotte Opera Association;** *General Director:* Richard Marshall

CHICAGO: **Lyric Opera of Chicago;** *General Manager:* Ardis Krainick. **Chicago Opera Theatre;** *Artistic Director:* Alan Stone

CINCINNATI: **Cincinnati Opera Association;** *General Manager:* James de Blasis

CLEVELAND: **Cleveland Opera;** *Artistic Director:* David Bamberger

DALLAS: **Dallas Civic Opera;** *General Manager:* Plato Karayanis

DAYTON/TOLEDO: **Dayton/Toledo Opera Associations;** *General Director:* Lester Freedman

DETROIT: **Michigan Opera Theater;** *General Director:* David Di Chiera

DISTRICT OF COLUMBIA: **Washington Opera, Inc.;** *Executive Director:* Martin Feinstein

FORT WORTH: **Fort Worth Opera Association;** *General Manager:* Rudolf Kruger

GLENS FALLS: **Lake George Opera Company;** *General Director:* Paulette Haupt-Nolen

HARTFORD: **Connecticut Opera Association, Inc.;** *General Manager:* George Osborne

HONOLULU: **Hawaii Opera Theatre;** *General Manager:* Alice Taylor

HOUSTON: **Houston Grand Opera Association;** *General Director:* R. David Gockley

KANSAS CITY (MO.): **Lyric Opera of Kansas City;** *General Manager.* Russell Patterson

LOUISVILLE: **Kentucky Opera Association;** *Artistic Director:* Thomson Smillie

MEMPHIS: **Opera Memphis;** *General Director:* Anne Randolph

MIAMI: **Greater Miami Opera Association;** *General Manager:* Robert Herman

MILWAUKEE: **Florentine Opera Company;** *General Manager:* John Gage. **Skylight Opera;** *Managing Director:* Colin Cabot

NEW ORLEANS: **New Orleans Opera;** *General Director:* Arthur Cosenza

NEW YORK: **Metropolitan Opera Association;** *General Manager:* Anthony A. Bliss. **New York City Opera;** *General Director:* Beverly Sills

NEWARK: **New Jersey State Opera;** *Artistic Director:* Alfredo Silipigni

NORFOLK: **Virginia Opera Association;** *Artistic Director:* Peter Mark

OMAHA: **Opera/Omaha;** *General Manager:* Norman Kaderlan

PHILADELPHIA: **Opera Company of Philadelphia;** *Acting General Manager:* Margaret Everitt

PITTSBURGH: **Pittsburgh Opera Company;** *Manager:* Vincent Artz

PORTLAND (ORE.): **Portland Opera Association;** *General Director:* Stefan Minde

PROVIDENCE: **Artists Internationale;** *Executive Director:* Dorothy McKenzie

ST. LOUIS: **Opera Theater of St. Louis;** *General Manager:* Richard Gaddes

ST. PAUL: **Minnesota Opera Company;** *General Manager:* Charles Fullmer

SAN DIEGO: **San Diego Opera Association;** *Artistic Director:* Tito Copobianco

SAN FRANCISCO: **San Francisco Opera Association;** *General Director:* Kurt Herbert Adler; *General Director Designate:* Terry McEwen. **Western Opera Theatre;** *Manager:* Earl Jay Schub

SANTA FE: **Santa Fe Opera;** *General Director:* John O. Crosby

SEATTLE: **Seattle Opera Association, Inc.;** *General Director:* Glynn Ross

TUCSON: **Arizona Opera Company;** *General Director:* James Sullivan

TULSA: **Tulsa Opera Company;** *General Manager:* Edward Purrington

MAJOR SYMPHONY ORCHESTRAS OF THE UNITED STATES AND CANADA

1980-81 Season

SOURCE: American Symphony Orchestra League

Atlanta Symphony Orchestra
1280 Peachtree Street, NE, Atlanta, Georgia 30309
Mus. Dir.: Robert Shaw
Gen. Mgr.: Stephen Sell

Baltimore Symphony Orchestra
1313 St. Paul St., Baltimore, MD 21202
Mus. Dir.: Sergiu Comissiona
Gen. Mgr.: Joseph Leavitt

Boston Symphony Orchestra
301 Massachusetts Ave.,
Boston, Massachusetts 02115
Mus. Dir.: Seiji Ozawa
Exec. Dir.: Thomas W. Morris

Buffalo Philharmonic Orchestra
26 Richmond Avenue, Buffalo, New York 14222
Mus. Dir.: Julius Rudel
Co-Mgrs.: Michael Bielski & Ruth Spero

Chicago Symphony Orchestra
220 South Michigan Avenue, Chicago, Illinois 60604
Mus. Dir.: Sir Georg Solti
Exec. V. Pres. & Gen. Mgr.: John S. Edwards

Cincinnati Symphony Orchestra
1241 Elm Street, Cincinnati, Ohio 45210
Mus. Dir.: Michael Gielen
Gen. Mgr.: Steven I. Monder
Manager: Judith Arron

Cleveland Orchestra
11011 Euclid Avenue, Cleveland, Ohio 44106
Mus. Dir.: Lorin Maazel
Gen. Mgr.: Kenneth Haas

Dallas Symphony Orchestra
P.O. Box 26207, Dallas, Texas 75226
Mus. Dir.: Eduardo Mata
Mng. Dir.: Leonard D. Stone

Denver Symphony Orchestra
1245 Champa Street, Denver, Colorado 80204
Mus. Dir.: Gaetano Delogu
Exec. Dir.: Carlos Wilson

Detroit Symphony Orchestra
20 Auditorium Drive, Detroit, Michigan 48226
Mus. Dir.: Antal Dorati
Exec. Dir.: Ralph O. Guthrie

Honolulu Symphony Orchestra
1000 Bishop Street, Suite 901
Honolulu, Hawaii 96813
Mus. Dir.: Donald Johanos
Act. Exec. Dir.: Robert Sandla

Houston Symphony Orchestra
615 Louisiana Street, Houston, TX 77002
Prin. Guest Cond.: Erich Bergel
Exec. Dir.: Michael J. Woolcock

Indianapolis Symphony Orchestra
P.O. Box 88207, Indianapolis, IN 46208
Mus. Dir.: John Nelson
Gen. Mgr.: Fred H. Kumb, Jr.

Kansas City Philharmonic Orchestra
200 W. 14th St., Kansas City, MO 64105
Prin. Asst. Cond.: Marc Gottlieb
Exec. V. Pres. & Gen. Mgr.: David Kent

Los Angeles Philharmonic Orchestra
135 N. Grand Ave., Los Angeles, CA 90012
Mus. Dir.: Carlo Maria Giulini
Exec. Dir.: Ernest Fleischmann
Gen. Mgr.: Robert Harth

Milwaukee Symphony Orchestra
Performing Arts Center
929 North Water St., Milwaukee, WI 53202
Mus. Dir.: Lukas Foss
Exec. Dir.: Robert Caulfield
Gen. Mgr.: Richard Thomas

Minnesota Orchestra
1111 Nicollet Mall, Minneapolis, MN 55403
Mus. Dir.: Neville Marriner
President: Richard M. Cisek
Gen. Mgr.: Robert C. Jones

Montreal Symphony Orchestra
200 de Maisonneuve Blvd. W.
Montreal, Quebec H2X 1Y9 Canada
Mus. Dir.: Charles Dutoit
Pres. & Mng. Dir.: Roger Larose

National Symphony Orchestra
J F. Kennedy Center for the Performing Arts
Washington, DC 20566
Mus. Dir.: Mstislav Rostropovich
Manager: Robert Noerr

New Jersey Symphony Orchestra
213 Washington St., 16th Floor
Newark, NJ 07101
Mus. Dir.: Thomas Michalak
Exec. Dir.: John L. Hyer

New Orleans Philharmonic Symphony Orchestra
203 Carondelet St., Suite 903
New Orleans, LA 70130
Mus. Adv.: Philippe Entremont
V.P. & Exec. Man.: James D. Hicks

New York Philharmonic Orchestra
Avery Fisher Hall
65th St. and Broadway
New York, NY 10023
Mus. Dir.: Zubin Mehta
Mng. Dir.: Albert K. Webster

North Carolina Symphony Orchestra
Memorial Auditorium, P.O. Box 28026
Raleigh, NC 27611
Art. Dir.: Lawrence Smith
Gen. Mgr.: Hiram Black

Philadelphia Orchestra
1420 Locust St., Philadelphia, PA 19102
Mus. Dir.: Ricardo Muti
Exec. Dir.: Seymour L. Rosen

Pittsburgh Symphony Orchestra
Heinz Hall for the Performing Arts
600 Penn Avenue, Pittsburgh, PA 15222
Mus. Dir.: André Previn
Mng. Dir.: Marshall W. Turkin

Rochester Philharmonic Orchestra
20 Grove Pl., Rochester, NY 14605
Mus. Dir.: David Zinman
Gen. Mgr.: Tony H. Dechario

Saint Louis Symphony Orchestra
718 N. Grand Blvd., St. Louis, MO 63103
Mus. Dir.: Leonard Slatkin
Exec. Dir.: David Hyslop
Manager: Joan Briccetti

San Antonio Symphony Orchestra
109 Lexington Ave., Suite 207
San Antonio, TX 78205
Mus. Dir.: Lawrence Leighton Smith
Mng. Dir.: Nat Greenberg

San Diego Symphony Orchestra
P.O. Box 3175, San Diego, CA 92103
Mus. Dir.: David Atherton
Gen. Mgr.: William L. Denton

San Francisco Symphony Orchestra
Davies Symphony Hall
San Francisco, CA 94102
Mus. Dir.: Edo de Waart
Exec. Dir.: Peter Pastreich

Seattle Symphony Orchestra
305 Harrison St., Seattle, WA 98109
Mus. Dir.: Rainer Miedel
Gen. Mgr.: Lanham Deal

Syracuse Symphony Orchestra
Suite 40, Civic Center, 411 Montgomery St.
Syracuse, NY 13202
Mus. Dir.: Christopher Keene
Gen. Mgr.: Eleanor Shopiro

Toronto Symphony Orchestra
215 Victoria St.
Toronto, Ontario M5B 1V1 Canada
Mus. Dir.: Andrew Davis
Mng. Dir.: Walter Homburger

Utah Symphony Orchestra
123 West South Temple
Salt Lake City, UT 84101
Mus. Dir.: Varujan Kojian
Exec. Dir.: Herold L. Gregory

Vancouver Symphony Orchestra
873 Beatty St.
Vancouver, B.C. V6B 2M6 Canada
Mus. Dir.: Kazuyoshi Akiyama
Gen. Mgr.: Michael Allerton

PROFESSIONAL RESIDENT AND REPERTORY THEATRES

SOURCE: Actors' Equity Association. The following resident and repertory groups are member companies of the League of Resident Theatres or use the L.O.R.T. contract.

ABINGDON (VA): **Barter Theatre;** P.O. Box 250 Abingdon, VA 24210

ALBANY (NY): **The League of Theatre Artists;** P.O. Box 2114, Empire State Plaza, Albany, NY 12203

ALLENTOWN (PA): **Pennsylvania Stage Company;** J.I. Rodale Theatre, 837 Linden St., Allentown, Pa 18101

ANCHORAGE (AK): **Alaska Repertory Theatre;** 523 W. 8th Ave., Suite 110, Anchorage, AK 99501

ANNISTON (AL): **Alabama Shakespeare Festival;** P.O. Box 141, Anniston, AL 36202

ARROW ROCK (MO): **The Lyceum Theatre;** Arrow Rock, MO 63520 (Summer)

ATLANTA (GA): **Alliance Theatre Company;** 1280 Peachtree St., N.E., Atlanta, GA 30309

BALTIMORE (MD): **Center Stage;** 700 N. Calvert St., Baltimore, MD 21202

BROOKLYN (NY): **The Brooklyn Academy of Music;** 30 Lafayette Ave., Brooklyn, NY 11217

BUFFALO (NY): **Studio Arena Theatre;** 710 Main St., Buffalo, NY 14202

CAMBRIDGE (MA): **American Repertory Theatre Company;** 64 Brattle St., Cambridge, MA 02138

CHAPEL HILL (NC): **Playmakers Repertory Company;** 103 South Bldg., U. of N.C., Chapel Hill, NC 27514

CHICAGO (IL): **Goodman Theatre Company;** 200 S. Columbus Dr., Chicago, IL 60603

CINCINNATI (OH): **Cincinnati Playhouse in the Park;** P.O. Box 6537, Cincinnati, OH 45206

CLEVELAND (OH): **Cleveland Playhouse;** 2040 E. 86th St., Cleveland, OH 44106

Great Lakes Shakespeare Festival; P.O. Box 598 Edgewater, Cleveland, OH 44107

COSTA MESA (CA): **South Coast Repertory Theatre;** 655 South Town Center Dr., Costa Mesa, CA 92626

DALLAS (TX): **Theatre 3;** 2800 Routh St., Dallas TX 75201

DENVER (CO): **Denver Center for the Performing Arts;** Denver Center Theatre Co., 1050 13th St., Denver, CO 80204

EAST HADDAM (CT): **Goodspeed Opera House;** East Haddam, CT 06423

EVANSTON (IL): **The North Light Repertory Theatre, Inc,;** 2300 Green Bay Rd., Evanston, IL 60201

FAIRFIELD (CT): **The New Globe Theatre;** 111 Wheeler Park Ave., Fairfield, CT 06432

GAMBIER (OH): **Kenyon Repertory Theatre and Festival, Inc.;** 202 West Brooklyn, Gambier, OH 43022

HARTFORD (CT): **Hartford Stage Company;** 50 Church St., Hartford, CT 06103

HORSE CAVE (KY): **Horse Cave Theatre;** P.O. Box 215, Horse Cave, KY 42749 (Summer)

HOUSTON (TX): **Alley Theatre;** 615 Texas Ave., Houston, TX 77002

HUNTINGTON STATION (NY): **The Performing Arts Foundation;** PAF Playhouse, 185 Second St., Huntington Station, NY 11746

INDIANAPOLIS (IN): **Indiana Repertory Theatre;** 140 W. Washington St., Indianapolis, IN 46204

KANSAS CITY (MO): **Missouri Vanguard Theatre** (Spring); **Missouri Repertory Theatre** (Summer); U. of Missouri at Kansas City, 5100 Rockhill Rd., Kansas City, MO 64110

KNOXVILLE (TN): **The Clarence Brown Theatre Company,** Department of Speech and Theatre; 206 McClung Tower, U. of Tennessee, Knoxville, TN 37916

LAKE PLACID (NY): **Center for Music, Drama, and Art;** Saranac Ave. at Fawn Ridge, Lake Placid, NY 12946

LENOX (MA): **Shakespeare and Company;** The Mount, Plunkett Street, Lenox, MA 01240 (Summer)

LOS ANGELES (CA): **Mark Taper Forum;** Center Theatre Group, 135 N. Grand Ave., Los Angeles, CA 90012

LOUISVILLE (KY): **Actors Theatre of Louisville;** 316-320 W. Main St., Louisville, KY 40202

LOWELL, (MA): **Merrimack Regional Theatre;** P.O. Box 228, Lowell, MA 01853

MADISON (NJ): **New Jersey Shakespeare Festival;** Drew U., Madison, NJ 07940 (Summer & Fall)

MIAMI (FL): **Players State Theatre;** Coconut Grove Playhouse, 3500 Main Hwy., Miami, FL 33133

MIDDLETOWN (VA): **Wayside Theatre;** P.O. Box 260, Middletown, VA 22657

MILWAUKEE (WI): **Milwaukee Repertory Theatre;** Performing Arts Center, 929 N. Water St., Milwaukee, WI 53202

MINNEAPOLIS (MN): **Cricket Theatre;** Hennepin Center for the Arts, 528 Hennepin Avenue, Minneapolis, MN 55403

The Guthrie Theater; 725 Vineland Pl., Minneapolis, MN 55403

MISSOULA (MT): **Montana Repertory Theatre;** U. of Mont., Missoula, MT 59812

NEW BRUNSWICK (NJ): **George Street Playhouse;** 414 George St., New Brunswick, NJ 08901

NEW HAVEN (CT): **Long Wharf Theatre;** 222 Sargent Dr., New Haven, CT 06511

Yale Repertory Theatre; Yale School of Drama, New Haven, CT 06520

NEW YORK (NY): **The Acting Company;** 420 W. 42nd St., 3rd Fl., New York, NY 10036

Chelsea Theatre Center; 407 West 43rd St., New York, NY 10036

The Negro Ensemble Company; 165 W. 46th St., New York, N.Y. 10036

New York Shakespeare Festival; (Delacorte and Mobile Theatres), The Public Theatre, 425 Lafayette St., New York, NY 10003 (Summer)

The Roundabout Theatre Company; 333 W. 23rd St., New York, NY 10011

NORFOLK (VA): **Virginia Stage Co.;** 142 West York St., Suite 902, Norfolk, VA 23510

PARK FOREST (IL): **Illinois Theatre Center;** 400 Lakewood Blvd., Park Forest, IL 60466

PHILADELPHIA (PA): **The Philadelphia Drama Guild;** 220 S. 16th St., Philadelphia, PA 19102

PITTSBURGH (PA): **Pittsburgh Public Theatre;** Suite 230, One Allegheny Square, Pittsburgh, PA 15212

PORTSMOUTH (NH): **Theatre by the Sea;** 125 Bow St., Portsmouth, NH 03801

PRINCETON (NJ): **McCarter Theatre Company, Inc.;** 91 University Place, Princeton U., Princeton, NJ 08540

PROVIDENCE (RI): **Trinity Square Repertory Company;** 201 Washington St., Providence, RI 02903

REDWOOD CITY (CA): **California Actors' Theatre;** P.O. Box 1120, Redwood City, CA 94063

RICHMOND (VA): **Virginia Museum Theatre;** Boulevard & Grove Aves., Richmond, VA 22331 VA 22331

ROCHESTER (MI): **Meadow Brook Theatre;** Oakland U., Rochester, MI 48063

ROCHESTER (NY): **Genesee Valley Arts Foundation (GeVa);** 168 Clinton Ave. South, Rochester, NY 14604

ST. LOUIS (MO): **Loretto Hilton Theatre;** 130 Edgar Rd., St. Louis, MO 63119

ST. PAUL (MN): **Actors Theatre of St. Paul;** 2115 Summit Ave., St. Paul, MN 55105

SAN DIEGO (CA): **Old Globe Theatre;** P.O. Box 2171, San Diego, CA 92112

SAN FRANCISCO (CA): **American Conservatory;** 450 Geary St., San Francisco, CA 94102

SARASOTA (FL): **Asolo Theatre Festival;** P.O. Box Drawer E, Sarasota, FL 33578

SEATTLE (WA): **Seattle Repertory Theatre;** P.O. Box B, Queen Anne Sta., Seattle Center, Seattle, WA 98109

A Contemporary Theatre; 709 First Ave. W., Seattle, WA 98119

Intiman Theatre; Box 4246, Seattle, WA 98119

STAMFORD (CT): **Hartman Theatre Company;** Box 521, Stamford, CT 06901

STRATFORD (CT): **American Shakespeare Theatre;** 1850 Elm Street, Stratford, CT 06497

SYRACUSE (NY): **Syracuse Stage;** University Regent Theatre, 820 E. Genesee St., Syracuse, NY 13210

TUCSON (AZ): **Arizona Theatre Co.;** 120 West Broadway, Tucson, AZ 85701

VISALIA (CA): **California Shakespeare Festival;** 417 North Locust St., Box 590, Visalia, CA 93277

WASHINGTON (DC): **Arena Stage;** Sixth and M Sts. S.W., Washington, DC 20024

Folger Theatre Group; 201 E. Capitol St. S.E., Washington, DC 20003

WATERFORD (CT): **Eugene O'Neill Memorial Theatre Center;** P.O. Box 206, Waterford, CT 06385

WEST SPRINGFIELD (MA): **Stage West;** 1511 Memorial Ave., W. Springfield, MA 01089

ART MUSEUMS

WORLD

AMSTERDAM: Rijksmuseum (1808); *Collections:* 16th/17th-century Dutch paintings and drawings by Rembrandt, Hals, Vermeer, and others.

Stedelijk Museum (1895); *Collections:* Impressionist to modern paintings and sculpture, including works of van Gogh, Chagall, and Dubuffet.

ANTWERP: Koninklijk Museum voor Schone Kunsten (Royal Museum of Fine Arts) (1890); *Collections:* Dutch, Flemish, and French old masters, including Van Eyck, Van der Weyden, Memling, Rubens, Rembrandt, and Hals; 19th/20th-century Belgian art.

BERLIN: National-Galerie (1876); *Collections:* European paintings and sketches from the 18th century to the present.

BRUSSELS: Musée des Beaux-Arts (1892); *Collections:* Old and new masters, drawings, and sculpture.

BUDAPEST: Magyar Nemzeti Museum (Hungarian National Museum) (1802); *Collections:* Archaeological finds; medieval to contemporary art; coins and historical objects.

Szépmüveszéti Museum (Museum of Fine Arts) (1896); *Collections:* Egyptian and Greco-Roman antiquities; Hungarian and foreign old masters; sculpture, drawings, and engravings.

CAIRO: Coptic Museum (1908); *Collections:* Art treasures of early Christian culture in Egypt.

Museum of Islamic Art (1881); *Collections:* Islamic painting, sculpture, ceramics, and applied arts (7th to 19th century).

CALCUTTA: Indian Museum (1814); *Collections:* Indian art from prehistoric to Moslem times; Indian and Persian paintings; and Tibetan banners.

DRESDEN: National Gallery (1846); *Collections:* Italian, Dutch, Flemish, and German old and new masters, including Rembrandt, Correggio, Titian, Rubens, Van Dyck, Veronese, and del Sarto.

FLORENCE: Galleria dell'Accademia (1784); *Collections:* The most complete collection of Michelangelo's statues in Florence, as well as paintings by Tuscan masters of the 13th to 16th centuries.

Galleria degli Uffizi (16th century); *Collections:* The world's finest collection of Italian Renaissance painting.

THE HAGUE: Keninklijk Kabinet van Schilderijen (Mauritshuis) (Royal Picture Gallery) (1820); *Collections:* Dutch and German art; excellent Vermeers and Rembrandts.

ISTANBUL: Museum of the Seraglio of Topkapi (Built mid-15th century); *Collections:* Sultans' treasure; Chinese and Japanese porcelain; enamels, embroidery, miniatures, and precious stones.

JERUSALEM: Museum of Archaeology and Art (1965); *Collections:* Works concerning the Bible and Middle Eastern history; features the Billy Rose Art Garden and the Shrine of the Book.

LENINGRAD: Hermitage (1764); *Collections:* More than 2.5 million objets d'art, including gold artifacts from Helleno-Scythian times, jewelry of the tsars, French impressionist paintings, old and new masters.

State Russian Museum (1898); *Collections:* Exhibits numbering 250,000 of Russian art, sculpture, drawings, coins, and medals.

LONDON: The British Museum; *Collections:* Extensive collections spanning man's art and culture from neolithic age to present, including the Elgin Marbles.

National Gallery (1857); *Collections:* A superb collection from the 12th century to the present.

Tate Gallery (1897); *Collections:* British painting from the 16th century to the present, including works by Blake, Constable, Turner; French impressionists and modern sculpture.

Victoria and Albert Museum (1852); *Collections:* Fine and applied art of all countries, periods, and styles; ceramics, textile, sculpture, woodwork, paintings, prints, and drawings.

MADRID: El Prado (1819); *Collections:* Italian, Flemish, Dutch, and Spanish Renaissance paintings; classical, Renaissance, and baroque sculpture; includes a large collection of Murillo, Goya, El Greco, Rubens, Bosch, Van Dyck, da Vinci, and Tintoretto.

MEXICO CITY: Museo Nacional de Antropologia (1865); *Collections:* Anthropological, ethnological, and archaeological collections relating to Mexico.

MOSCOW: State Tretyakov Gallery (1856); *Collections:* A rich collection of 40,000 Russian icons; Russian and Soviet sculpture, graphics and paintings, dating from the 11th century to the present.

MUNICH: Alte Pinakothek (1836); *Collections:* German, Dutch, Flemish, Italian, Spanish, and French masters.

NEW DELHI: National Museum of India (1949); *Collections:* Indian and Central Asian treasures that date from 3000 B.C. to the present; sculpture, paintings, manuscripts, miniatures, and crafts.

PARIS: Galerie du Jeu de Paume (1920); *Collections:* Including examples by Monet, Cézanne, van Gogh, Renoir, Degas, Pissarro, and Gaugin.

Musée Guimet; *Collections:* The finest European collection of oriental painting, sculpture, and applied arts.

Musée du Louvre (1793); *Collections:* Oriental, Egyptian, Roman, and Greek antiquities; medieval, Renaissance, and modern sculpture and painting.

Musee National d'Art Moderne (1943) **(Centre National d'Art et de Culture Georges Pompidou);** *Collections:* 20th-century paintings and sculpture.

Musée de l'Orangerie (1853); *Collections:* A group of Utrillos, Cézannes, Monets, and others, exhibited in the atmosphere of a collector's apartment.

Musée Rodin (1916); *Collections:* The sculptor's work and collection are displayed in a home and garden.

ROME: Borghese Art Gallery (c. 1616); *Collections:* Classical and baroque sculpture and painting.

ROTTERDAM: Museum Boymans-van Beuningen (1847); *Collections:* European art from the 15th century to the present, including Van Eyck, Breughel the Elder, Hals, Rembrandt, van Ruisdael, Hobbema, Rubens, Titian, Watteau, and Boucher.

SAO PAULO: Museu de Arte Contemporânea (1947); *Collections:* Nearly 1,700 works by such modern masters as Kandinsky, Léger, and the early cubists.

Museu de Arte de São Paulo (1947); *Collections:* A panoramic view of Western art from gothic times to the present; paintings by Hals, Raphael, Renoir, Toulouse-Lautrec, and Rembrandt are included.

TAIPEI: National Palace Museum (1925); *Collections:* Examples of Chinese art from the Shang to the Ch'ing dynasty that were brought to Taipei from the Mainland during the Communist revolution.

TORONTO: Royal Ontario Museum at Toronto (1912); *Collections:* Art and archaeological objects from the Americas, Africa, Polynesia, ancient Egypt, Rome and Greece; Chinese, Japanese, Islamic, and Indian art; European art from all ages.

VIENNA: Kunsthistorisches Museum (Museum of Fine Arts) (1891); *Collections:* Egyptian, Greek, Etruscan, Roman, and Cyprian antiquities; excellent Breughel collection; French, Dutch, Italian, and German Renaissance and baroque art.

UNITED STATES

BALTIMORE: Baltimore Museum of Art (1914); *Collections:* Epstein and Jacobs collections of old masters and sculpture; 19th/20th-century French painting, sculpture, graphics; Toulouse-Lautrec posters; contemporary American art; Oriental art and mosaics.

Walters Art Gallery (1931); *Collections:* More than 25,000 objects, of which the Byzantine and medieval examples are noteworthy; classical art of Greece, Rome, Egypt, medieval to 19th-century European art.

BOSTON: Isabella Steward Gardner Museum (1900); *Collections:* American and European painting and sculpture, from classical times to the 20th century.

Museum of Fine Arts (1870); *Collections:* Exceptionally fine collection of prints, Oriental art, decorative arts; Egyptian, Greek, and Roman art; old masters and 19th-century French paintings.

BUFFALO: Albright-Knox Art Gallery (1862); *Collections:* 18th-century English, 19th-century American and French and contemporary American and European paintings; sculpture (3000 B.C. to the present).

CAMBRIDGE: Harvard University, Fogg Art Museum (1895); *Collections:* Oriental and Western art from ancient times to the present; representative collections of painting, sculpture, prints, and drawings, including Italian primitives and Chinese jades and bronzes.

CHICAGO: Art Institute of Chicago (1879); *Collections:* Major periods of Western art and primitive and Oriental art.

University of Chicago, Oriental Institute Museum (1919); *Collections:* More than 70,000 objects that represent the art, religion, and daily life of ancient Egypt, Nubia, Assyria, Babylonia, Persia, Palestine, Syria, Anatolia, Libya, and Cyprus.

CINCINNATI: Cincinnati Art Museum (1881); *Collections:* Sculpture, painting, and ceramics of Egypt, Greece, Rome; Near Eastern and Far Eastern art; 19th/20th-century European and American art; primitive art from Oceania, Africa, and the Americas.

CLEVELAND: Cleveland Museum of Art (1913); *Collections:* Art from many cultures and periods, including old masters and modern paintings, sculpture, prints, drawings, porcelain, metalwork, and furniture.

COLUMBUS: Columbus Gallery of Fine Arts (1878); *Collections:* Schumacher Collection of old masters; Howald Collection of modern French and American painting; major collection of the art of George Bellows; South Pacific primitives.

DALLAS: Dallas Museum of Fine Arts (1903); *Collections:* Ancient, pre-Columbian, African sculpture, Japanese, European and American art.

DETROIT: Detroit Institute of Arts (1885); *Collections:* Art from many cultures, dating from prehistoric times to the present, including Italian medieval and Renaissance sculpture, 17th-century Dutch paintings, and French-Canadian art.

DISTRICT OF COLUMBIA: Corcoran Gallery of Art (1859); *Collections:* American painting, sculpture, and drawing from the 18th century to the present; Dutch, Flemish, French and English painting.
Hirshhorn Museum and Sculpture Garden (1974); *Collections:* Joseph Hirshhorn's private modern art collection valued at over $1 million.
National Gallery of Art (1937); *Collections:* Mellon, Kress, and Widener collections of old masters; Rosenwald Collection of prints and drawings; Garbisch Collection of American primitive paintings; East Building (1978) contains permanent and changing exhibits of painting and sculpture.
Phillips Collection (1918); *Collections:* Modern art, especially 19th/20th-century American and European works.
Smithsonian Institution, Freer Gallery of Art (1906); *Collections:* Near and Far Eastern art and artifacts, 19th/20th-century American art, including the Peacock Room entirely decorated by Whistler.

FORT WORTH: Amon Carter Museum of Western Art (1961); *Collections:* Western paintings and sculpture, includes Frederic Remington and Charles Russell.
Kimbell Art Museum (1972); *Collections:* masterpieces from ancient times to cubism.
Fort Worth Art Museum (1961); *Collections:* 20th century paintings and sculpture.

HARTFORD: Wadsworth Atheneum (1842); *Collections:* European and American painting from 1400 to the present, including medieval and Renaissance European tapestries; early South and Central American art.

HOUSTON: Museum of Fine Arts of Houston (1900); *Collections:* Paintings, sculpture, and decorative arts covering most periods of history, including Renaissance painting, classical art and sculpture, and American art.

KANSAS CITY (MO.): William Rockhill Nelson Gallery and Atkins Museum of Fine Arts (1926); *Collections:* Oriental art, especially Chinese; classical, European, and American painting, sculpture, and decorative arts.

LOS ANGELES: Los Angeles County Museum of Art (1961); *Collections:* Major periods of European and American art; Oriental art.

MERION STATION (PA.): Barnes Foundation (1922); *Collections:* European Renaissance and 20th-century American painting; African sculpture and Chinese art.

MINNEAPOLIS: Minneapolis Institute of Arts (1914); *Collections:* Oriental and pre-Columbian art; American and European painting and sculpture.
Walker Art Center (1972); *Collections:* 20th century art, changing exhibits.

NEWARK: Newark Museum (1909); *Collections:* American painting and sculpture from all periods; Oriental art, emphasizing the expression of Tibet.

NEW HAVEN: Yale Center for British Art (1977); *Collections:* British paintings, prints and drawings.

NEW ORLEANS: Isaac Delgado Museum of Art (1910); *Collections:* Kress Collection of Renaissance painting; Hyams Collection of the Barbizon school; contemporary European and American painting, sculpture, and drawings; Howard Collection of Greek vases.

NEW YORK CITY: Brooklyn Museum (1893); *Collections:* Egyptian, Near and Far Eastern art; Renaissance and medieval painting; American painting from all periods and 19th/20th-century European art; primitive art and artifacts from Oceania, Africa, the Far East, and South America.
Frick Collection (1935); *Collections:* European painting, sculpture, prints, and drawings from the 14th century to the 1800s that constitute the former personal treasures of Henry Clay Frick; Limoges enamels, French and Chinese porcelains, and period furniture.
Jewish Museum (1904); *Collections:* This largest exhibit of Judaica in the Western Hemisphere is housed in the former Felix Warburg mansion.
Metropolitan Museum of Art (1870); *Collections:* Comprehensive collections that cover 5,000 years of history and represent the arts of Egypt, Babylonia, Assyria, Greece, Rome, Near and Far East, Europe, pre-Columbian culture, and the United States; Robert Lehman collection of European paintings and drawings; includes the Cloisters in Fort Tryon Park.
Museum of Modern Art (1929); *Collections:* One of the foremost collections of 19th/20th-century American and European painting, sculpture, prints, photographs, posters, and films.
Pierpont Morgan Library (1924); *Collections:* Old master drawings, Rembrandt etchings, and manuscripts.
Solomon R. Guggenheim Museum (1937); *Collections:* Impressionist to contemporary painting and sculpture, including the world's largest collection of Kandinsky's work; paintings and sculpture by Picasso, Chagall, Klee, Brancusi, and Modigliani.
Whitney Museum of American Art (1930); *Collections:* American paintings, sculpture, drawings, and prints; the 20th-century American art housed ranges from realism to abstract expressionism.

PASADENA (CALIF.): Norton Simon Museum of Art at Pasadena (1974); *Collections:* European paintings spanning six centuries; modern sculpture garden; Indian and South Asian bronzes and stone figures.

PHILADELPHIA: Philadelphia Museum of Art (1875); *Collections:* Dutch, Flemish, French, American, and Italian masters; cubist and postcubist art; Far Eastern and Near Eastern art; Pennsylvania Dutch folk art; tapestries, silver, china, and period rooms.
University of Pennsylvania, University Museum (1887); *Collections:* Archaeological finds of Near East, Egypt, the Mediterranean, and the Americas; ethnology of Africa, Oceania, and art of China, pre-1000 A.D.

PITTSBURGH: Carnegie Institute, Museum of Art (1896); *Collections:* American and European painting and sculpture, including old masters and impressionists; international collection of modern art.

SAN FRANCISCO: California Palace of the Legion of Honor (1924); *Collections:* European and American painting, sculpture, and decorative arts; Egyptian and Greek antiquities.
M. H. De Young Memorial Museum (1895); *Collections:* European and American art from ancient times to 1850; Oriental and South Pacific art, including the Avery Brundage Collection of Asian art; Kress Collection of European old masters, Flemish tapestries; art of pre-Columbian Central, South, and North American Indians.
San Francisco Museum of Modern Art (1921); *Collections:* Contemporary painting, sculpture, drawings, prints, photography, and decorative arts from Europe, the United States, and Latin America.

SAN MARINO (CALIF.): Henry E. Huntington Library and Art Gallery (1919); *Collections:* Eighteenth-century British portraits and French sculpture; 15th/16th-century Italian and Flemish paintings; 18th/19th-century French and British decorative arts, and Renaissance bronzes.

SEATTLE: Seattle Art Museum (1917); *Collections:* Chinese, Japanese, Indian, and Near Eastern art; Egyptian, Greek, Roman antiquities; European Renaissance painting, sculpture, and porcelain, including the Kress Collection; Northwest Indian and pre-Columbian primitive art.

TOLEDO: Toledo Museum of Art (1901); *Collections:* European art from classical times to the 20th century; American painting and decorative arts.

WORCESTER (MASS.): Worcester Art Museum (1896); *Collections:* American, European, and Oriental art—ancient through contemporary; painting, sculpture, prints, decorative arts; early American and Italian art.

THE REVIEWS: 1980/81
BOOKS

It was an election year again, which perhaps explains the roster of books published between August 1980 and August 1981 that analyzed the office of the President and the men who have filled it over the years. David McCullough took us back to Theodore Roosevelt with *Mornings on Horseback*. Charles L. Mee, Jr., wrote *The Ohio Gang*, a breezy recapitulation of the corrupt Warren G. Harding Administration. A presidential daughter provided both a collection of letters (*Letters from Father: The Truman Family's Personal Correspondence*) and a mystery based upon her Washington, D.C., years (*Murder on Capitol Hill*). The perpetrator of these two books was, of course, Margaret Truman, who had had previous experience with murderous fiction in last year's *Murder in the White House*.

Among the recollections of the Eisenhower years was *Eisenhower The President: Crucial Days 1951-1960*, a warm portrait of Ike by William Bragg Ewald, Jr. There was a full shelf of books probing the death of JFK, including *Kennedy and Lincoln: Medical Ballistic Comparisons of Their Assassinations* by John K. Lattimer and *The Plot to Kill the President*, in which G. Robert Blakey and Richard Billings added more arguments to the theory that organized crime had a hand in the murder. One such book was a bona fide bestseller: *Best Evidence: Deception and Disguise in the Assassination of John F. Kennedy* by David Lifton. Merle Miller's *Lyndon: An Oral Biography* was also a bestseller, but *Making It Perfectly Clear* by Nixon loyalist Herb G. Klein was not. Nor was *Palace Politics: The Presidency of Gerald Ford* by Robert Hartmann.

As to the current resident of the White House, there was a passel of books on him, titles such as *The Real Reagan*, an admiring portrait by Frank van der Linden and *Reagan, The Man, The President* by Hedrick Smith and a quartet of other newsmen. Those amused by fate already know that President Reagan was the subject of one type of book applicable to no other American head of state. It was a picture book compiled by Tony Thomas, and it was called *The Films of Ronald Reagan*.

It has frequently been noted that the mood of the United States tilted to the right with the 1980 election. There were all sorts of reasons, one of which was that the government was too much involved with the lives of its citizens. It was suggested that vast numbers of citizens finally spoke out after years of quiet. One of the spokespeople for this group was affectionately profiled in *The Sweetheart of the Silent Majority*, a biography of Phyllis Schlafly by Carol Felsenthal.

Other writers pointed warningly to the decline of America's stature: *The Present Danger: "Do We Have the Will to Reverse the Decline of American Power?"* by magazine editor Norman Podhoretz and *All Things to All Men: The False Promise of the Modern American Presidency* by Godfrey Hodgson. Gloom piled up everywhere: *Inequality in an Age of Decline* by Paul Blumberg, not to mention *Slowth: The Looming Struggle of Living with Less* by Martin Kupferman and Maurice Levi.

Then good old Richard Curtis had the sense to stare down this contagious malaise and to concoct a humorous survival manual: *How to Prosper in the Coming Apocalypse*. *Great Expectations* by Landon Jones might have seemed to be another optimistic view of what lies ahead, but it was a charting out of the effects of and the disappointments visited upon the 75-million baby boomers who were born between 1946 and 1964. It was tough for these tykes to grow up and discover that much of what they'd been promised faded along with an eternally upward American economy. It took Studs Terkel to interview 100 of his fellow compatriots and to address such reality confrontations with *American Dreams: Lost and Found*.

Part of our frustration was that we couldn't control worldly chaos. Claire Sterling found culprits in a Soviet-orchestrated plot that she described in *The Terror Network: The Secret War of International Terrorism*. A lot of people bought her theory and her book. Even more picked up a copy of *The Fifth Horseman* by Larry Collins and Dominique Lapierre. In that thriller, the novelists showed what could happen if Arab terrorists secreted a hydrogen bomb in New York City.

Still, when matters looked too grim here on Earth, there were always the stars. Carl Sagan's PBS-TV documentary called "Cosmos" was the source of his big book of the same name. Another outsized book on the wonders of outer space was Timothy Ferris's *Galaxies*. But, it was Sagan who created the most headlines, particularly when Simon & Schuster agreed to shell out $2 million for his projected novel. According to reports, it was the most money anyone had ever committed for a novel not yet on paper.

There were other books incredibly beautiful to pore through. One was Eve Arnold's collection of color photographs she took while she was in China. She called the book *In China*. Maurice Sendak's paintings filled one mammoth work about him (*The Art of Maurice Sendak* by Selma G. Lanes) and another by him, the conclusion of the trilogy begun with *Where the Wild Things Are* and *In the Night Kitchen*. The new book was *Outside Over There*, a book reviewed by the critics for adults as much as for children. A fantasy that was a bestseller in England duplicated its success here. *Masquerade* by Kit Williams offered clues to a golden prize buried by the author. No one discovered the secret of the riches, but that didn't keep readers young and old away from the fanciful drawings, each of which had at least one rabbit in it, often deviously disguised.

The look of wonders that warm the stomach as much as the soul could be created with a bestselling cookbook, *Maida Heatter's Book of Great Chocolate Desserts* by (guess who) Maida Heatter. If, after too many calories, one decided to turn over a new leaf, there was *Richard Simmons' Never-Say-Diet Book* by (guess who) Richard Simmons. Simmons outdid Heatter, however, by starring in his own television show and playing himself on the soap opera, "General Hospital." All Heatter had was good taste. This was a commodity much in evidence in one of the most successful books of the year, a paperback edited by Lisa Birnbach entitled *The Official Preppy Handbook*.

A soap opera star terribly unlike Richard Simmons told all in *The Confessions of Phoebe Tyler* by Ruth Warrick with Don Preston. Tyler is the character played by Warrick on ABC-TV's "All My Children," and the book was both about the program and the actress. The actress who was discovered by Otto Preminger for a film based on Joan of Arc was depicted in a saddening biography, *Played Out: The Jean Seberg Story* by David Richards, recounting in particular her life after she was covertly maligned by the FBI. *Swanson on Swanson* by Gloria Swanson was considerably more optimistic. Swanson is after all in her 80s. John Huston was 73 when *An Open Book*, his autobiography, was published. Susan Hayward was the topic of two biographies, as well as a roman à clef, *Flame*, by R.V. Cassill. Actress Fannie Flagg wrote a novel called *Coming Attractions*, and Norman Mailer returned to an actress he'd dealt with before, but this time came a cropper. Accompanying photographs by Milton Greene, Mailer wrote what he imagined Marilyn Monroe's autobiography would have been like had she lived to write it. *Of Women and Their Elegance* attracted few admirers.

More notable fiction of the year included Muriel Spark's *Loitering with Intent, The White Hotel* by D.M. Thomas, John Knowles's sequel to *A Separate Peace* called *Peace Breaks Out*, and Nadine Gordimer's *July's People*. Erica Jong turned out a parody of the 18th-century novel and christened it *Fanny: Being the True History of the Adventures of Fanny Hackabout-Jones*, while Judith Rossner came up with a novel of a young mill woman in 19th-century New England called *Emmeline*. Underground cult writer Tom Robbins was published simultaneously in hardcover and in trade paperback by a paperback house (Bantam) and *Still Life with Woodpecker* became a bestseller.

It was a particularly rich year for short story collectors. To choose from, they had *The Collected Stories of Elizabeth Bowen* (79 of them in that volume), *Fifty Stories* by Kay Boyle, *The Stories of Elizabeth Spencer* (33 tales), *The Collected Stories of Eudora Welty* (41) and *The Stories of Ray Bradbury* (100), among others.

Finally, word must be writ of an uprising of Americans who had had just too much of cats. For years, B. Kliban had charmed the friends of felines with his books and calendars. This year, Skip Morrow had the audacity to illustrate a trade paperback of cartoons called *The Official I Hate Cats Book*. Even worse, Simon Bond proposed *101 Uses for a Dead Cat*. But no matter, Garfield, another favorite of cat people, was back in *Garfield Gains Weight* by Jim Davis. Garfield was pudgy and pushy and hadn't heard of Richard Simmons.

—**Robert Dahlin**

SELECTED BESTSELLERS: 1980-81

FICTION

Title	Author	Publisher
The Covenant	James Michener	Random House
Noble House	James Clavell	Delacorte Press
Gorky Park	Martin Cruz Smith	Random House
Firestarter	Stephen King	Viking
The Key to Rebecca	Ken Follett	Morrow
Free Fall in Crimson	John D. MacDonald	Harper & Row
Answer as a Man	Taylor Caldwell	Putnam
God Emperor of Dune	Frank Herbert	Putnam
Tar Baby	Toni Morrison	Knopf
Reflex	Dick Francis	Putnam
Masquerade	Kit Williams	Schocken
The Fifth Horseman	Larry Collins and Dominique Lapierre	Simon & Schuster
Brain	Robin Cook	Putnam
Come Pour the Wine	Cynthia Freeman	Arbor House
Creation	Gore Vidal	Random House
Unfinished Tales	J.R.R. Tolkien	Houghton Mifflin
The Tenth Commandment	Lawrence Sanders	Putnam
License Renewed	John Gardner	Richard Marek
Loon Lake	E.L. Doctorow	Random House
A Man	Oriana Fallaci	Simon & Schuster
The White Hotel	D.M. Thomas	Viking

NONFICTION

Title	Author	Publisher
Cosmos	Carl Sagan	Random House
Crisis Investing: Opportunities and Profits in the Coming Great Depression	Douglas R. Casey	Stratford Press
The Sky's the Limit	Dr. Wayne Dyer	Simon & Schuster
Richard Simmons' Never-Say-Diet Book	Richard Simmons	Warner Books
The Lord God Made Them All	James Herriot	St. Martin's Press
Wealth and Poverty	George Gilder	Basic Books
The Beverly Hills Diet	Judy Mazel	Macmillan
William E. Donoghue's Complete Money Market Guide	William E. Donoghue with Thomas Tilling	Harper & Row
Paper Money	Adam Smith	Summit Books
Nice Girls Do	Irene Kassorla	Stratford Press
Craig Claiborne's Gourmet Diet	Craig Claiborne	Times Books
Goodbye Darkness: A Memoir of the Pacific War	William Manchester	Little, Brown
Shelly Also Known as Shirley	Shelly Winters	Morrow
The Eagle's Gift	Carlos Castaneda	Simon & Schuster
Maria Callas: The Woman Behind the Legend	Arianna Stassinopoulos	Simon & Schuster
Side Effects	Woody Allen	Random House
American Dreams: Lost and Found	Studs Terkel	Pantheon

THEATRE

In the 1980-1981 season, Broadway shattered box office records with total receipts of $194,-481,091, $50 million more than the previous year. Business was booming, but the quality of the shows, both on- and Off-Broadway, was disappointing. This was a particularly disastrous year for the American musical.

The most important play of the year was Athol Fugard's "A Lesson from Aloes," a searing cry of conscience from South Africa. Featuring three of the year's outstanding performances—by Maria Tucci, Harris Yulin and James Earl Jones—"A Lesson from Aloes" was named Best Play by the New York Drama Critics Circle. The critics also honored Beth Henley's "Crimes of the Heart" as Best American Play. This deeply compassionate story of three eccentric sisters in a small Mississippi town also won the Pulitzer Prize for drama—the first original play by a woman to be so honored since 1945. Miss Henley is one of a number of women beginning to achieve prominence as playwrights.

The Tony award for Best Play was given to Peter Schaffer's "Amadeus," a highly theatrical British import about the rivalry between Mozart and his fellow composer, Salieri. Starring as Salieri was Ian McKellen, named Best Actor by the Tony voters.

Other outstanding plays were Hugh Leonard's "A Life," which continued the story of one of the characters in the playwright's "Da"; Lanford Wilson's "Fifth of July," which first played several seasons ago Off-Broadway, and "A Tale Told," both dramatic chapters in the author's sensitive cycle of plays about the Talley family in Lebanon, Missouri; Mustapha Matura's "Meetings," a comedy about modern Trinidad; Brian Friel's "Translations," about a historic Anglo-Irish conflict; "Cloud 9," Caryl Churchill's send-up of King and Crown; and Dario Fo's comedy of consumerism, "We Won't Pay! We Won't Pay!"

Woody Allen returned to the theatre with "The Floating Lightbulb," a quiet memory play. "Request Concert" was a strange, silent monodrama by the German playwright, Franz Xaver Kroetz. Samuel Beckett was represented by two new short works: "Rockaby," a monologue that marked the American stage debut of the British actress, Billie Whitelaw, and "Texts," an adaptation of his story, "Texts for Nothing," starring Joseph Chaikin. Jane Lapotaire was named Best Actress by the Tony voters for her performance in the title role in Pam Gems' controversial "Piaf."

Musically, Broadway was arid, with Tony prizes going by default to "Woman of the Year," a bland reworking of the Katharine Hepburn movie as a vehicle for Lauren Bacall. "42nd Street" was a rewrite of the movie of the same name, with the year's best choreography by Gower Champion, who died on the day that the show opened. "Sophisticated Ladies" was a stylish collage of Duke Ellington music, featuring Gregory Hines. Off-Broadway, Elizabeth Swados magically reinvented "Alice in Wonderland" as a chamber concert, with Meryl Streep giving a virtuoso performance in the title role. "March of the Falsettos" indicated the musical promise of composer-lyricist William Finn. Both "Brigadoon" and "Can-Can" returned in revivals.

In studying the musical scene, the New York Drama Critics decided that there was no new musical worthy of an award and instead gave special citations to the season's finest musical events, "Lena Horne: the Lady and Her Music" and "The Pirates of Penzance." The first was an evening of unique artistry and performing brilliance. The second was Wilford Leach's New York Shakespeare Festival tuning up of the Gilbert and Sullivan operetta, which won a Tony award as Best Actor in a Musical for Kevin Kline. "Pirates" also featured the theatrical debut of pop star Linda Ronstadt.

It was an active season for revivals. Al Pacino brought back David Mamet's "American Buffalo," stressing the humor in this comedy of friendship and menace. Joe Orton's sexual comedy, "Entertaining Mr. Sloane," was given an excellent production. The C.S.C. presented a three-play cycle of Oedipus plays, featuring a monumental performance by Robert Stattel. On Broadway, Elizabeth Taylor made her stage debut in Lillian Hellman's "The Little Foxes," proving herself to be promising and very popular.

As usual, before the year began, one looked forward to new plays by some of our more established playwrights. Steve Tesich's "Division Street" turned out to be a largely unamusing look at the aftermath of radicalism. Arthur Miller's "The American Clock" could not make up its mind if it was a pastiche of Depression life or a personalized account of the author's family's own hard times. Neil Simon's "Fools" was foolish, and Edward Albee's adaptation of Vladimir Nabokov's "Lolita" was a disservice to both author and adapter. Nikolai Erdman's "The Suicide," a provocative comedy about Russian dissent, was buried under a top-heavy production. Sam Shepard's "True West" was an example of the playwright far below his best.

There were some notable theatrical events. The new Lincoln Center Theatre, under the direction of Richmond Crinkley, re-opened the long-shuttered Vivian Beaumont Theatre with a three-play season of varying quality, beginning with "The Philadelphia Story," starring the lovely Blythe Danner. By the end of the year, the Lincoln Center company had raised enough money to close for a much-needed major overhaul of the stage. The BAM Theatre Company at the Brooklyn Academy of Music had a series of failures in its second season and posted its closing notice. Unfortunately the Chelsea Theatre Center, one of New York's most valuable institutional theatres, was defeated by an economic recession and ended its operation. As usual, there continued to be vitality in theatre outside New York, with this year's Tony award for a regional theatre going to the Trinity Square Repertory Company in Providence, Rhode Island.

Some special place in any summary of the season should be made for "Frankenstein." Not a musical, not much of a play, this was an evening on Broadway—of special effects, scenery, fog and flashes of light in the mad doctor's laboratory. It was a $2.5 million, old-fashioned movie on stage, and, at least for the time being, the last creature feature on Broadway.

—Mel Gussow

MUSIC

The celebration of birthdays and anniversaries stirs special activity in the world of music. During the 1980-81 season in particular, some notable music was heard as a musical personage or institution reached a calendar milestone.

The 100th anniversary of Bela Bartok's birth touched off what *Time* magazine called a "yearlong Bartok festival," with performances nationwide. Major orchestras and artists paid homage to the Hungarian composer, who died in 1945, but none could match for sheer quantity the contribution of Detroit, where its symphony orchestra and other organizations staged a 12-day, 52-artist series of Bartok concerts.

The births of two distinguished 80-year-old composers, Aaron Copland and Ernst Krenek, generated musical observances continued from the previous season. Copland was honored by the Music Society of Lincoln Center in New York, and Krenek composed a new string quartet, his eighth (but his first in 37 years), for performance by the Texas-based Thouvenal String Quartet.

Famed violinists marking their birthdays were Isaac Stern, 60, and Jascha Heifetz, 80. Stern's activities were in marked contrast to the older artist's. Whereas Stern was highly visible in a round of major orchestral and television appearances throughout the season, Heifetz remained aloof from the performing scene, resisting all attempts to lure him from Beverly Hills.

Venerable Carnegie Hall was honored at a concert performed by the New York Philharmonic, conducted by Zubin Mehta, which recreated the hall's opening concert in May 1891. The conductor on that historic occasion was Peter Ilyitch Tchaikovsky.

The Greater Miami Opera marked its 40th season by opening with Verdi's "Nabucco" and a stellar cast, including Rosalind Elias, Sherill Milnes and Jerome Hines. The Chicago Symphony celebrated its 90th season, and director Sir Georg Solti announced a European tour, the fourth in its history, late in 1981. Sir Georg, the CSO's musical director since 1969, said he was determined to remain in the post until the orchestra's centennial.

Critics dusted off the phrase, "Concert of the Century" for a performance by the sensational vocal trio of Joan Sutherland, Marilyn Horne and Luciano Pavarotti before a prime-time nationwide television audience.

The Metropolitan Opera's season saw a number of highly successful productions, including "Tristan und Isolde" under music director James Levine, and a triple French bill with Satie's "Parade," Poulenc's "Les Mamelles de Tiresias" and Ravel's "L'Enfant et les Sortileges," ably led by the 76-year-old conductor, Manuel Rosenthal.

In Dallas, the city's opera presented the American premiere of Vivaldi's "Orlando Furioso," starring the brilliant Miss Horne. Another rarity was Ambroise Thomas' "Hamlet," revived by the Friends of French Opera in a Carnegie Hall stage version.

The operatic novelty of the year was the premiere of the "Sinking of the Titanic" by the young German composer, Wilhelm Dieter Siebert. In this Los Angeles production, the audience participated as second-class passengers on the ill-fated ship (the chorus was steerage and soloists were first-class passengers), exiting from the auditorium amidst smoke, strobe lights and screams. No one was reported missing.

Piano artists took the national spotlight in the televised finals of the Cliburn International Competition in Texas. Andre-Michael Schub won the $15,000 first prize plus a fistful of concert booking guarantees.

Sir Clifford Curzon made one of his infrequent appearances in America, playing a Mozart concerto with the New York Philharmonic. Another veteran, Leon Fleisher, played the Ravel Concerto for Left Hand with the Baltimore Symphony, demonstrating once again that pianism lost a major artist when a debilitating ailment affected his right hand 15 years ago.

Among other pianists who impressed were Ann Shein in a series of Chopin recitals; Daniel Barenboim in an all-Schubert program in Carnegie Hall; Augustin Anievas with his prodigious technique, and such relatively youthful artists as Gregory Allen, Richard Goode, Charles Fisk and Daniel Varsano, the last a French pianist making his American debut.

The debate over what new music should or shouldn't be raged on at a symposium in New York City, where a strong strain surfaced that looked benignly on the use of jazz or rock materials in classical music compositions. Indeed, classical record executives expressed the view during the spring that the popularity of "crossover" artists such as flutist James Galway made them optimistic about the future of classical record sales.

Meanwhile, American orchestras presented numerous premieres which reflected a wide range of forms and styles. Among the leading names was John Williams, the film composer and conductor of the Boston Pops, whose new flute and violin concertos were presented by the Pittsburgh and St. Louis Symphonies, respectively. Alan Hovhaness's "Revelations of St. Paul," the 70-year-old composer's Opus 343, received an enthusiastic reception in a performance by the Music Sacra in New York. Witold Penderecki's "Te Deum" was premiered by the National Symphony, and Pierre Boulez's "Notations" was played by the New York Philharmonic. Ezra Laderman had two premieres: his Violin Concerto No. 2 was played by the Philadelphia Orchestra, and his Concerto for String Quartet was performed by the Pittsburgh Symphony. Significant new works were also introduced by Morton Gould, Robert Starer, Richard Bennett, David del Tredici, Antal Dorati, George Walker, Ralph Shapey, and Robert Moev.

Reaching back into history, a very early Mozart symphony was given its first hearing in New York, and another early symphony by Grieg was premiered in Norway despite the wishes of the composer that it never be performed. A suite for bass voice and orchestra by the late Dimitri Shostakovich was premiered in Cincinnati, and the opera "King Roger" by Karol Szymanowski was given its U.S. premiere by the St. Louis Symphony.

The music world mourned the deaths of composer Samuel Barber, 70, pianist-conductor José Iturbi, 84, and composer-conductor-educator Howard Hanson, 84. **—Henry T. Wallhauser**

TELEVISION

In some distant time of video madness, the television year of 1980–81 may be cited as the bugle call of the revolution.

Technology did not take over the TV scene in 1980–81, but it dominated it, with all signs pointing to more changes in the TV picture than had been seen since the invention of the horizontal hold.

Political wars raged in many American cities over rights to the next video gold mine—cable television franchises. The oracle of commercial TV—the Nielsen ratings—revealed for the first time a significant decline in the share of audience held by the networks. Projections put the network loss of audience at 10 to 15 percent by 1990. The thief: cable and pay TV. Cable profits rose 45 percent for the year; pay TV was up a giddy 85 percent. The surest sign of all that the new technologies were not to be beaten came from the list of those who decided to join 'em: CBS, ABC, RCA, even PBS, all decided to jump into the cable programming business.

The future riches of cable and pay TV were also instrumental in a year of labor upheaval in television. A three-month actors' strike delayed the start of the fall 1980 season—and cost studios millions. A three-month writers' strike put a crimp in the 1981 fall season. The most crippling strike, by directors, was averted with an eleventh-hour settlement. In all three cases, the major issue was dispersal of future windfall profits from the new technologies.

The growing influence of video machinery was also evident in the major events of the year—which paraded across the TV screen like the scenes of a historical drama—only in this case it was all happening live.

A president campaigned, debated, was elected, inaugurated and almost shot to death, all in living color in American living rooms.

Election night brought the most astounding—some said abusive—use thus far of network voter projection techniques, as NBC called the presidential race over by 8:15 p.m. in the East—5:15 p.m. in the West. Outraged reaction came from West Coast voters—and especially losing Democrats—who charged that such early calls swayed elections where the polls were still open. The charge had been heard before, but this time it got as far as a congressional investigation, which decided there was no conclusive evidence that early calls on TV affected western races.

The advanced news-gathering techniques had their finest hours in the event-filled day of January 20, 1981, when one American assumed office at the same time 52 others attained freedom. Television was able to cover all the pomp, pageantry, patriotism and pure emotion of the inauguration of Ronald Reagan and the release of the American hostages from Iran. Network news never had a prouder day.

Much of the same technical wizardry was apparent, but the pride took a beating three months later, when television presented the nation the spectacle of its most prominent citizen being gunned down in the streets of Washington. Like a major sports event, TV offered the assault from endless angles in slow motion, stop-action and freeze-frame replays. Unfortunately, some of the coverage degenerated into emotional displays, and all three networks made the shocking mistake of declaring the presidential press secretary, James Brady, dead. He survived.

Two months later the coverage swung into action again, with an international target this time: Pope John Paul II. The combination of distance from the event and lessons learned from the Reagan shooting lead to a more restrained performance by the news crews.

TV news made its own news, headlined by the retirement of Walter Cronkite from his impregnable position of leadership at the CBS anchor desk. He was succeeded by Dan Rather, who set out to uphold the CBS News tradition of prestige—and success.

At NBC News, Tom Brokaw became the crown prince, parlaying some intense wooing by the rival networks into a co-anchor assignment with Roger Mudd at a wage that made free-agent ballplayers look like pikers.

NBC needed the morale boost of retaining Brokaw because it coincided with the resignation of its corporate president, Fred Silverman. Failing to get the backing of new RCA chairman Thornton Bradshaw, Silverman stepped down after three turbulent years in which his furious manuevering failed to improve substantially the sagging fortunes of NBC. NBC still trailed its rivals in most dayparts, including the crucial prime time, where it was third a sixth year in a row.

Silverman's replacement, Grant Tinker, the highly regarded chief executive of the classy MTM Production Co., buoyed NBC's spirits.

His talents were certain to be tested, especially by a resurgent CBS. That network's return to dominance was highlighted by the stupefying popularity of the soap saga, "Dallas," whose episode resolving the "Who Shot J.R.?" mystery—a mind-boggling national fad—attracted 83 million viewers and the largest rating in TV history.

That popularity did nothing to deter a "moral" brigade bent on reforming TV away from the seamy behavior of the "Dallas" ilk. A threat to boycott sponsors of shows containing undefined examples of immorality gained national headlines—and a measure of success, as advertisers cowered and promised to be more circumspect with their sponsorship, even though the boycott was called off.

This was but one manifestation of a spin in the TV dial to the New Right. The new Administration's philosophy had its greatest television impact in the message sent to public TV: Look elsewhere for funds.

PBS's year was thus more unhappy than usual, with its chronic money problems exacerbated by threatened federal budget cuts. The solutions proposed for PBS all pointed in one direction—toward commercialism.

But most of the inhabitants of the Video Village welcomed the President as one of their own. After all, he was the first chief executive to have been a host on TV's "Death Valley Days" and "GE Theater."

—Bill Carter

FILMS

On the whole, the 1980–81 movie season was one Hollywood would sooner forget. Rising costs of production, advertising and theatre operation and flat or declining attendance squeezed profitability. Protracted actors' and writers' strikes (with a directors' walkout averted at the last minute) left key first-run theatres with revivals of *Airplane!* The long losing streak that began in early 1980 continued well into the new year. Paradoxically but typically, ticket-buying surged to record levels in June with the near simultaneous release of *Superman II, Raiders of the Lost Ark, For Your Eyes Only, Cannonball Run, History of the World—Part I* and *Clash of the Titans,* although the latter three dropped off rapidly in response to negative reviews and word-of-mouth. More words were seemingly written about movies in the financial pages than in the entertainment sections—and the two were increasingly indistinguishable.

In an uncertain financial climate, big-budget productions and whole companies changed hands. M-G-M, out to re-establish itself as the main force in Hollywood, swallowed a battered United Artists (which had been Metro's distribution channel under a 1973 agreement executed when UA was the industry leader and Metro a toothless lion). Cash-rich 20th Century-Fox "went private," acquired by oilman Marvin Davis. Chairman Dennis Stanfill, one of the few top executives to guide one company for more than a decade, resigned; successor Alan Hirschfeld spoke aggressively of dominating the industry with a schedule of 20 to 24 pictures annually.

Other companies were not so bullish. Universal cut back on its own production, relying heavily on an arrangement with Polygram and pickups from Sir Lew Grade's Associated Film Distributors, which later folded. Several of the mini-majors and independents were foundering, retrenching, or unloading expensive projects. Filmways, relying heavily on Brian De Palma's *Blow Out,* sold Milos Forman's *Ragtime* to Paramount. Paramount, having deeply invested in Warren Beatty's costly *Reds,* also rescued Francis Ford Coppola's *One from the Heart* when Coppola's Omni Zöetrope ran out of funds. Undeterred by the trend, CBS established a feature film division with a so-so Sally Field vehicle, *Back Roads,* distributed by Warners. Robert Altman sold his Lion's Gate studios, complaining that there was no interest in his type of film among studios who only wanted *Raiders of the Lost Ark.*

The most successful movies were virtual abstractions of the juvenile film-going experience. *Raiders of the Lost Ark* plundered the netherworld of 1930s serials and "B" pictures like *The Mummy's Hand* and *Tim Tyler's Luck:* the nonstop marathon of fights, chases and escapes suggested a 13-chapter serial seen at one sitting. *Superman II* had the advantage of a more compact story line than the original and suffered from fewer drastic changes in tone and style.

Apart from *Outland,* space wars were out and cheap horror films of the *Prom Night* type were ebbing; psychologically sophisticated horror crossed with science fiction, as in Ken Russell's high-tech trip, *Altered States,* could still turn out the youth audience. David *(Eraserhead)* Lynch had an Oscar contender with his second feature, *The Elephant Man.* John Waters offered suburban sleaze in *Polyester.* George Romero forsook zombies in the somewhat unsuccessful *Knight-riders.* Most notably, John Carpenter's *Escape from New York* offered a vision of the city after a few blackouts and transit strikes too many.

Nine-to-Five appealed to the hunger for broad comedy, aiming genuine stabs at business amid sit-com farce. Mel Brooks' *History of the World* offered sophisticated wit ("Don't be saucy with me, Bernaise!") and too many jokes of the kind found on men's-room walls. *Arthur* came close to recreating 1930s sophisticated comedy.

John Boorman's spectacular but incoherent *Excalibur* (described by one critic as "a medieval *Star Wars*") portended a swords-and-sorcery cycle hopefully forestalled by the apathetic reaction to *Dragonslayer.*

Almost overlooked amid the financial pulse-taking and trend-spotting were films that followed no trends, but built loyal followings. In the Australian *Breaker Morant,* the improbable subject of a Boer War court-martial was made timely by obvious parallels with Vietnam. In Louis Malle's *Atlantic City,* Burt Lancaster excelled as a white-haired small-time semicriminal finally making a big score by accident. (It was a good year for the French: Truffaut's *Last Metro* recalled the lacquer surfaces of '40s studio films like *Casablanca* and *To Be or Not To Be,* Resnais' *Mon Oncle d'Amérique* was an intellectual treat.) John Sayles *Return of the Secaucus Seven,* made for $60,000, succeeded in evoking the tone and style of the antiwar protest era where slick youth films of a decade ago failed.

The Oscars pitted Robert Redford's directorial debut, *Ordinary People,* with its skillful evocation of the ethos of competitiveness and gentility in an upper-middle class suburb, versus Martin Scorsese's *Raging Bull,* a corrective to the *Rocky* fables (from the same producing team). It was no contest. Despite the dead-accurate period atmosphere, stylized fight scenes and uncanny transformation of Robert De Niro into a paunchy strip-club m.c., *Raging Bull's* lack of dramatic development and its unsympathetic protagonist left audiences cold in comparison to the discussion and soul-searching the Redford film provoked.

In a class by itself was Michael Cimino's *Heaven's Gate,* in which the clichés of a 1940s John Wayne-Vera Ralston Republic Western were solemnly intoned as epic. Flourishes worthy of John Ford or King Vidor could not survive the worst continuity of any major film simply on the who's who, what's what level.

The *Heaven's Gate* nightmare gave topicality to Blake Edward's *S.O.B.,* drawn from his own and wife Julie Andrews' box-office poison period in the early 1970s, when Hollywood was shifting from *Dr. Dolittle* to *Myra Breckenridge.* Cimino would have envied the fictional salvage job that turns a G-rated family bomb into a soft-X potboiler which becomes the highest-grossing film of all time, transforming its producer from pariah to (posthumous) hero. But that only happens in the movies.

—**Stephen Handzo**

Prizes

NOBEL PRIZE WINNERS (See page 65 for 1981 awards)

PHYSIOLOGY AND MEDICINE

Year	Winner and Life Dates	Nationality	Achievement
1901	Emil A. von Behring (1854–1917)	German	Serum therapy, especially for work on dipththeria antitoxin.
1902	Ronald Ross (1857–1932)	British	Discovery of the life cycle of the malaria parasite.
1903	Niels R. Finsen (1860–1904)	Danish	Treatment of skin diseases with concentrated light rays, especially lupus vulgaris (skin tuberculosis).
1904	Ivan P. Pavlov (1849–1936)	Russian	Work on the physiology of digestion.
1905	Robert Koch (1843–1910)	German	Work on tuberculosis and the scientific development of bacteriology.
1906	Camillo Golgi (c.1843–1926)	Italian	Their study of the nervous system and of cell distribution.
	Santiago Ramón y Cajal (1852–1934)	Spanish	
1907	Charles L. A. Laveran (1845–1922)	French	Study of protozoa-caused disease.
1908	Paul Ehrlich (1854–1915)	German	Their work on immunology including the introduction of quantitative methods.
	Élie Metchnikoff (1845–1916)	Russian	
1909	E. Theodor Kocher (1841–1917)	Swiss	Work on the physiology, pathology, and surgery of the thyroid gland.
1910	Albrecht Kossel (1853–1927)	German	Contributions to the knowledge of cell chemistry.
1911	Allvar Gullstrand (1862–1930)	Swedish	For his work on ocular dioptrics, the refraction of light through the eye.
1912	Alexis Carrel (1873–1944)	American (b. France)	Development of vascular suture and surgical transplantation of blood vessels and organs.
1913	Charles R. Richet (1850–1935)	French	Work on anaphylaxis.
1914	Robert Bárány (1876–1936)	Austrian	Study of physiology and pathology of the inner ear.
1919	Jules J. P. V. Bordet (1870–1961)	Belgian	Discoveries in the field of immunity.
1920	S. August Krogh (1874–1949)	Danish	Discovering the mechanism that regulates blood-capillary action.
1922	Archibald V. Hill (1886–1977)	English	Discoveries concerning heat produced by muscular activity.
	Otto F. Meyerhof (1884–1951)	American (b. Germany)	Establishing the correlation between oxygen and lactic acid in muscle.
1923	Frederick G. Banting (1891–1941)	Canadian	Their production of insulin and demonstration of its value in combating diabetes.
	John J. R. Macleod (1876–1935)	British	
1924	Willem Einthoven (1860–1927)	Dutch	Invention of the electrocardiograph.
1926	Johannes A. G. Fibiger (1867–1928)	Danish	Experimental work in cancer.
1927	Julius Wagner-Jauregg (1857–1940)	Austrian	Discovery of malarial therapy in paralysis.
1928	Charles J. H. Nicolle (1866–1936)	French	Work on typhus.
1929	Christiaan Eijkman (1858–1930)	Dutch	Discovering vitamin B.
	Frederick G. Hopkins (1861–1947)	English	Discovering vitamin A.
1930	Karl Landsteiner (1868–1943)	American (b. Austria)	Discovery of human blood groups.
1931	Otto H. Warburg (1883–1970)	German	Discovery of the character and action mode of the respiratory enzyme.
1932	Edgar C. Adrian (1889-1977)	English	Studies on the physiology of the nervous system, especially the function of neurons.
	Charles S. Sherrington (1857–1952)	English	
1933	Thomas H. Morgan (1866–1945)	American	Discovering the functions of chromosomes in heredity.
1934	George R. Minot (1885–1950)	American	Their discoveries that administering liver extract increases activity in the bone-marrow where red cells are formed.
	William P. Murphy (1892–)	American	
	George H. Whipple (1878–1976)	American	
1935	Hans Spemann (1869–1941)	German	Discovery of the organizer effect in embryonic development.
1936	Henry H. Dale (1875–1968)	English	Their discoveries of the chemical transmission of nerve impulses.
	Otto Loewi (1873–1961)	American (b. Germany)	
1937	Albert von Szent-Györgyi (1893–)	American (b. Hungary)	Studies of metabolism and the effects of vitamins A and C.
1938	Corneille J. F. Heymans (1892–1968)	Belgian	Discovery of the influence of the carotid sinus on respiration rate.
1939	Gerhard Domagk (1895–1964)	German	Discovering prontosil, the first sulfa drug.
1943	C. P. Henrik Dam (1895–1976)	Danish	Discovering vitamin K.
	Edward A. Doisy (1893–)	American	Discovery of the chemical nature of vitamin K.
1944	E. Joseph Erlanger (1874–1965)	American	Work on the highly differentiated functions of single nerve fibers.
	Herbert S. Gasser (1888–1963)	American	
1945	Alexander Fleming (1881–1955)	British	The discovery of penicillin and its curative properties in infections including those of the heart, syphilis, and certain types of pneumonia.
	Howard W. Florey (1898–1968)	British (b. Australia)	
	Ernst B. Chain (1906–1979)	British (b. Germany)	
1946	Hermann Joseph Muller (1890–1967)	American	Discovering the influence of X rays in genetics.
1947	Carl F. Cori (1896–)	American (b. Czechoslovakia)	Their research on carbohydrate metabolism and enzymes.
	Gerty T. Cori (1896–1957)	American (b. Czechoslovakia)	
	Bernardo A. Houssay (1887–1971)	Argentine	Discovery of the role of the pituitary hormone in sugar metabolism.

Year	Winner and Life Dates	Nationality	Achievement
1948	Paul H. Müller (1899–1965)	Swiss	Discovering the insect-killing properties of DDT.
1949	Walter R. Hess (1881–1973)	Swiss	Discovering how certain parts of the brain control body organs.
	Antonio de Egas Moniz (1874–1955)	Portuguese	Discovery of the therapeutic value in certain psychoses of prefrontal lobotomy.
1950	Philip S. Hench (1896–1965)	American	Their research in hormones including the discovery
	Edward C. Kendall (1886–1972)	American	of cortisone and its antidisease effects.
	Tadeus Reichstein (1897–)	Swiss (b. Poland)	
1951	Max Theiler (1899–1972)	American (b. South Africa)	Developing the yellow-fever vaccine.
1952	Selman A. Waksman (1888–1973)	American (b. Russia)	Work in the discovery of streptomycin and its value in treating tuberculosis.
1953	Fritz A. Lipmann (1899–)	American (b. Germany)	Their biochemical studies on cell metabolism, including the discovery of coenzyme A.
	Hans A. Krebs (1900–)	British (b. Germany)	
1954	John F. Enders (1897–)	American	Their successful growth of polio viruses in cultures
	Thomas H. Weller (1915–)	American	of tissues and discovery of more effective methods
	Frederick C. Robbins (1916–)	American	of polio detection.
1955	A. Hugo T. Theorell (1903–)	Swedish	Discoveries of the nature of oxidation enzymes.
1956	D. W. Richards (1895–1973)	American	Developing a technique of inserting a catheter
	André F. Cournand (1895–)	American (b. France)	through a vein into the heart to chart its interior
	Werner Forssmann (1904–1979)	German	and to diagnose circulatory ailments.
1957	Daniel Bovet (1907–)	Italian (b. Switzerland)	Developing muscle-relaxing drugs used in surgery.
1958	George W. Beadle (1903–)	American	Discovery that genes transmit hereditary traits.
	Edward L. Tatum (1909–1975)	American	
	Joshua Lederberg (1925–)	American	Experiments establishing that sexual recombination of bacteria results in exchange of genetic material.
1959	Severo Ochoa (1905–)	American (b. Spain)	Their synthesis of ribonucleic acid (RNA) and deoxyribonucleic acid (DNA), organic compounds that carry hereditary characteristics, in genetics.
	Arthur Kornberg (1918–)	American	
1960	F. Macfarlane Burnet (1899–)	Australian	Their discovery of acquired immunity, that is, that
	Peter B. Medawar (1915–)	British (b. Brazil)	an animal can be made to accept foreign tissues.
1961	Georg von Békésy (1899–1972)	American (b. Hungary)	Work on the mechanism of the inner ear.
1962	Francis H. C. Crick (1916–)	English	Their determining the molecular structure of deoxy-
	Maurice H. F. Wilkins (1916–)	British	ribonucleic acid (DNA) and its significance for
	James D. Watson (1928–)	American	information transfer in living material.
1963	Alan L. Hodgkin (1914–)	English	Their research on nerve cells and on how electrical
	Andrew F. Huxley (1917–)	English	charges pass through nerve membranes by means
	John C. Eccles (1903–)	Australian	of a sodium-potassium exchange.
1964	Konrad E. Bloch (1912–)	American (b. Germany)	Their discovery of the mechanism and control of
	Feodor Lynen (1911–1979)	German	cholesterol metabolism.
1965	François Jacob (1920–)	French	Their discovery of the regulatory processes in body
	Andre M. Lwoff (1902–)	French	cells that contribute to genetic control of enzymes
	Jacques L. Monod (1910–1976)	French	and virus synthesis.
1966	Charles B. Huggins (1901–)	American (b. Canada)	Discoveries concerning hormonal treatment of prostate-gland cancer.
	Francis P. Rous (1879–1970)	American	Discovery of a cancer virus.
1967	Haldan K. Hartline (1903–)	American	Their discoveries pertaining to the eye's primary
	George Wald (1906–)	American	chemical and physiological processes, including
	Ragnar A. Granit (1900–)	Swedish (b. Finland)	work on color reception.
1968	Robert W. Holley (1922–)	American	Their discovery of the process by which enzymes, con-
	H. Gobind Khorana (c.1922–)	American (b. India)	sisting of a sequence of amino acids, determine a
	Marshall W. Nirenberg (1927–)	American	cell's function in genetic development.
1969	Max Delbrück (1906–1981)	American (b. Germany)	Their discoveries concerning the replication mecha-
	Alfred D. Hershey (1908–)	American	nism and the genetic structure of viruses.
	Salvador E. Luria (1912–)	American (b. Italy)	
1970	Bernard Katz (1911–)	British (b. Germany)	Their discoveries on the nature of the substances
	Ulf von Euler (1905–)	Swedish	found at the end of nerve fibers.
	Julius Axelrod (1912–)	American	
1971	Earl W. Sutherland (1915–1974)	American	Discoveries concerning the mechanisms of the action of hormones.
1972	Gerald M. Edelman (1929–)	American	Research into the chemical structure of antibodies
	Rodney R. Porter (1917–)	English	(Conducted independently).
1973	Konrad Lorenz (1903–)	Austrian	Research into ethology.
	Nikolaas Tinbergen (1906–)	English (b. Netherlands)	
	Karl von Frisch (1886–)	German (b. Austria)	
1974	Albert Claude (1899–)	American	Research which helped create the science of cell
	Christian Rene de Duve (1917–)	Belgian	biology.
	George Emil Palade (1912–)	American	
1975	David Baltimore (1938–)	American	Discoveries concerning the interaction between tumor
	Renato Dulbecco (1914–)	American (b. Italy)	viruses and the genetic material of the cell.
	Howard M. Temin (1935–)	American	
1976	Baruch S. Blumberg (1925–)	American	Discoveries concerning new mechanisms for the origin
	Daniel C. Gajdusek (1923–)	American	and dissemination of infectious diseases.
1977	Rosalyn S. Yalow (1921–)	American	Developed analytic radioimmunoassay technique utilizing isotopes for diagnostic purposes.
	Roger C. L. Guillemin (1924–)	American (b. France)	Their use of radioimmunoassay in pituitary hormone
	Andrew V. Schally (1927–)	American (b. Poland)	research.
1978	Werner Arber (1929–)	Swiss	Discoveries and studies on the restriction enzymes'
	Daniel Nathans (1928–)	American	linkage control of genes on chromosomes.
	Hamilton Smith (1931–)	American	
1979	Allan MacLeod Cormack (1924–)	American (b. S. Africa)	Development of the CAT scan, a three dimensional
	Godfrey Newbold Hounsfield (1919–)	British	X-ray diagnostic technique.
1980	Baruj Benacerraf (1920–)	American (b. Venezuela)	Research in cell immunology and discovery of HLA
	George D. Snell (1903–)	American	antigens, which help fight disease and cause im-
	Jean Dausset (1916–)	French	mune reactions to organ transplants.

CHEMISTRY

Year	Winner and Life Dates	Nationality	Achievement
1901	Jacobus H. van't Hoff (1852–1911)	Dutch	Discovering laws of chemical dynamics and osmotic pressure in solutions.
1902	Emil H. Fischer (1852–1919)	German	Synthesizing sugars and purines.
1903	Svante A. Arrhenius (1859–1927)	Swedish	Originating the theory of ionization.
1904	William Ramsay (1852–1916)	British	Discovering helium, neon, xenon, and krypton.
1905	Adolf von Baeyer (1835–1917)	German	Research in organic dye stuffs, especially hydro-aromatic compounds.
1906	Henri Moissan (1852–1907)	French	Isolation of the element fluorine; development of the electric furnace.
1907	Eduard Buchner (1860–1917)	German	Discovering cell-free fermentation.
1908	Ernest Rutherford (1871–1937)	British	Artificial disintegration of elements; chemistry of radioactive elements.
1909	Wilhelm Ostwald (1853–1932)	German	Work on catalysts, chemical equilibria, and rate of chemical reactions.
1910	Otto Wallach (1847–1931)	German	Pioneer work in the field of alicyclic compounds.
1911	Marie S. Curie (1867–1934)	French (b. Poland)	Discovering radium and polonium.
1912	F. A. Victor Grignard (1871–1935)	French	Discovering the reagent that is named after him.
	Paul Sabatier (1854–1941)	French	Process of hydrogenating organic compounds.
1913	Alfred Werner (1866–1919)	Swiss (b. Germany)	Study of the linkage of atoms in molecules.
1914	Theodore W. Richards (1868–1928)	American	Determining the atomic weights of many elements.
1915	Richard M. Willstätter (1872–1942)	German	Research into plant pigments, especially chlorophyll.
1918	Fritz Haber (1868–1934)	German	Process of synthesizing ammonia from nitrogen and hydrogen.
1920	Walther Nernst (1864–1941)	German	Application of thermodynamics to chemistry.
1921	Frederick Soddy (1877–1956)	British	Research into radioactive substances and isotopes.
1922	Francis W. Aston (1877–1945)	British	Discovering many isotopes by use of the mass spectrograph.
1923	Fritz Pregl (1869–1930)	Austrian	Invention of methods of microanalysis of organic substances.
1925	Richard A. Zsigmondy (1865–1929)	German (b. Austria)	Clarifying the nature of colloid solutions.
1926	Theodor Svedberg (1884–1971)	Swedish	Work on colloids.
1927	Heinrich O. Wieland (1877–1957)	German	Studies of bile acids.
1928	Adolf O. R. Windaus (1876–1959)	German	Work defining a group of sterols (including cholesterol) and their connection to vitamins.
1929	Sir Arthur Harden (1865–1940)	British	Investigations into the fermentation of sugar and fermentative enzymes.
	Hans von Euler-Chelpin (1873–1964)	Swedish (b. Germany)	
1930	Hans Fischer (1881–1945)	German	Research into the constitution of hemin (coloring matter of blood) and chlorophyll.
1931	Carl Bosch (1874–1940)	German	Their invention and development of chemical high pressure methods.
	Friedrich Bergius (1884–1949)	German	
1932	Irving Langmuir (1881–1957)	American	Investigations of the fundamental properties of absorbed films and surface chemistry.
1934	Harold C. Urey (1893–1981)	American	Discovering heavy hydrogen, which he called deuterium.
1935	Frédéric Joliot-Curie (1900–58)	French	Their synthesizing of new radioactive elements, including radioactive nitrogen and phosphorus.
	Irène Joliot-Curie (1897–1956)	French	
1936	Peter J. W. Debye (1884–1966)	American (b. Netherlands)	Studies of the structure of molecules, dipole moments, and the diffraction of electrons and X rays in gases.
1937	Walter N. Haworth (1883–1950)	British	Research into carbohydrates and vitamin C.
	Paul Karrer (1889–1971)	Swiss (b. Russia)	Chemical anlysis of vitamins A and B_2.
1938	Richard Kuhn (1900–67)	Austrian	Work on carotinoids and vitamins.
1939	Adolf F. J. Butenandt (1903–)	German	Studying the chemistry of sex hormones, determining the chemical structure of the female hormone (progestin), and isolating the male hormone (androsterone).
	Leopold Ruzicka (1887–1976)	Swiss (b. Yugoslavia)	Work on polymethylenes and higher terpenes.
1943	Georg von Hevesy (1885–1966)	Hungarian	Using isotopes as tracer elements in chemistry.
1944	Otto Hahn (1879–1968)	German	Discovery of the fission of heavy atomic nuclei.
1945	Artturi I. Virtanen (1895–1973)	Finnish	Work on plant synthesis of nitrogen compounds; development of a new method of making silage.
1946	James B. Sumner (1887–1955)	American	Discovering the crystallizability of enzymes.
	John H. Northrop (1891–)	American	Their preparation of enzymes and virus proteins in pure form.
	Wendell M. Stanley (1904–1971)	American	
1947	Robert Robinson (1886–1975)	British	Research on plant substances, especially alkaloids.
1948	Arne W. K. Tiselius (1902–1971)	Swedish	Devising new methods of separating and detecting colloids and serum proteins.
1949	William F. Giauque (1895–)	American (b. Canada)	Studies of the properties of substances at extremely low temperatures.
1950	Otto P. H. Diels (1876–1954)	German	Developing a method of synthesizing organic compounds of the diene group.
	Kurt Alder (1902–58)	German	
1951	Edwin M. McMillan (1907–)	American	Their work in the field of synthetic transuranium elements.
	Glenn T. Seaborg (1912–)	American	
1952	Archer J. P. Martin (1910–)	British	Advancing the use of paper partition chromatography (a method of separating and identifying chemical substances).
	Richard L. M. Synge (1914–)	British	
1953	Hermann Staudinger (1881–1965)	German	Work in the nature of giant molecules.
1954	Linus C. Pauling (1901–)	American	Studies in molecular structure, especially the nature of the bonding of atoms in molecules.
1955	Vincent du Vigneaud (1901–1978)	American	Work on pituitary hormones and the first synthesis of a polypeptide hormone.
1956	Cyril N. Hinshelwood (1897–1967)	British	Parallel but independent research into the kinetics of certain chemical reactions.
	Nikolai N. Semenov (1896–)	Russian	
1957	Alexander R. Todd (1907–)	British	Studies of the compounds that are the components of nucleic acid.
1958	Frederick Sanger (1918–)	British	Isolating and identifying the amino acid components of the insulin molecule.
1959	Jaroslav Heyrovsky (1890–1967)	Czech	Developing polarography (an electrochemical method of analysis).

Year	Winner and Life Dates	Nationality	Achievement
1960	Willard F. Libby (1908–80)	American	Development of the "atomic time clock" (for determining geological age by measuring the amount of radioactive carbon-14 in organic objects).
1961	Melvin Calvin (1911–)	American	Establishing the chemical reactions that occur during photosynthesis.
1962	Max F. Perutz (1914–)	British (b. Austria)	Discovering the molecular structure of hemoglobin
	John C. Kendrew (1917–)	British	and myoglobin.
1963	Karl Ziegler (1898–1973)	German	Changing simple hydrocarbons into complex molecu-
	Giulio Natta (1903–1979)	Italian	lar substances.
1964	Dorothy C. Hodgkin (1910–)	British	Discovery of the structure of biochemical substances, notably penicillin and vitamin B₁₂.
1965	Robert B. Woodward (1917–1979)	American	Development of fundamental techniques for synthesis of complicated organic compounds, notably chlorophyll and sterols.
1966	Robert S. Mulliken (1896–)	American	Fundamental work on chemical bonds and the electronic structure of molecules by the molecular orbital method.
1967	Manfred Eigen (1927–)	German	Studies of extremely fast chemical reactions effected
	Ronald G. W. Norrish (1897–1978)	English	by disturbing equilibrium by very short energy
	George Porter (1920–)	English	pulsations.
1968	Lars Onsager (1903–76)	American (b. Norway)	Discovery of the reciprocal relations between voltage and temperature that are fundamental for the thermodynamics of irreversible processes, such as those in living cells.
1969	Derek H. R. Barton (1918–)	British	Independent studies of conformation analysis: how
	Odd Hassel (1897–)	Norwegian	certain compounds react when their three-dimensional molecular shape is known.
1970	Luis F. Leloir (1906–)	Argentinian (b. France)	Discovery of sugar nucleotides and their role in the biosynthesis of carbohydrates.
1971	Gerhard Herzberg (1904–)	Canadian (b. Germany)	Study of electronic structure, geometry of molecules.
1972	Dr. Christian Boehmer Anfisen (1916–)	American	Research relating to the chemical structure of a com-
	Dr. Stanford Moore (1913–)	American	plex protein known as ribonuclease.
	Dr. William Howard Stein (1911–80)	American	
1973	Ernst Otto Fischer (1918–)	German	Research into how organic and metallic atoms can
	Geoffrey Wilkinson (1921–)	British	merge.
1974	Paul J. Flory (1910–)	American	For his work in macromolecules.
1975	John W. Cornforth (1917–)	English (b. Australia)	For contributions to stereochemistry — the study of
	Vladimir Prelog (1906–)	Swiss (b. Yugoslavia)	how the properties of a chemical compound are affected by the exact arrangement of their atoms in three-dimension space.
1976	William N. Lipscomb, Jr. (1920–)	American	For studies on the structure and bonding mechanisms of "boranes".
1977	Ilya Prigogine (1917–)	Belgian (b. Russia)	Theoretical work explaining contradictory biological process whereby increased growth and structural complexity on the molecular level are promoted while energy is dissipated.
1978	Peter Mitchell (1920–)	English	Study of energy reception of human cells.
1979	Herbert C. Brown (1912–)	American	Research on the basic molecular structures of boron
	Georg Wittig (1897–)	German	and phosphorus.
1980	Paul Berg (1926–)	American	Development of methods to map in detail the struc-
	Walter Gilbert (1932–)	American	ture and function of DNA.
	Frederick Sanger (1918–)	British	

PHYSICS

1901	Wilhelm C. Roentgen (1845–1923)	German	Discovering X rays.
1902	Hendrik A. Lorentz (1853–1928)	Dutch	Their research into the influence of magnetism upon
	Pieter Zeeman (1865–1943)	Dutch	radiation.
1903	Antoine H. Becquerel (1852–1908)	French	Discovery of spontaneous radioactivity.
	Pierre Curie (1859–1906)	French	Their study of the radiation phenomena that were
	Marie S. Curie (1867–1934)	French (b. Poland)	discovered by Becquerel.
1904	John W. S. Rayleigh (1842–1919)	British	Discovering argon.
1905	Philipp E. A. Lenard (1862–1947)	German (b. Hungary)	Experiments with cathode rays.
1906	Joseph J. Thomson (1856–1940)	British	Investigations on how gases conduct electricity.
1907	Albert A. Michelson (1852–1931)	American (b. Germany)	Developing optical measuring instruments; spectroscopic and meteorological investigations.
1908	Gabriel Lippmann (1845–1921)	French (b. Luxembourg)	Color photography.
1909	Guglielmo Marconi (1874–1937)	Italian	Their separate but parallel development of the wire-
	Karl F. Braun (1850–1918)	German	less telegraph.
1910	Johannes D. van der Waals (1837–1923)	Dutch	Work on an equation relating gases and liquids.
1911	Wilhelm Wien (1864–1928)	German	Discoveries of the laws governing heat radiation.
1912	Nils G. Dalén (1869–1937)	Swedish	Their invention of automatic gas regulators, for turning acetylene buoys, beacons, and railway lights on and off.
1913	Heike Kamerlingh-Onnes (1853–1926)	Dutch	Experiments with the properties of matter at low temperatures, leading to helium liquefaction.
1914	Max von Laue (1879–1960)	German	Employing crystals to diffract X rays.
1915	William H. Bragg (1862–1942)	British	Their use of X rays to determine the structure of
	Lawrence Bragg (1890–1971)	British	crystals.
1917	Charles G. Barkla (1877–1944)	British	Discovery of X-ray radiation of elements.
1918	Max K. E. L. Planck (1858–1947)	German	Formulation of the quantum theory.
1919	Johannes Stark (1874–1957)	German	Discovery of the splitting of spectral lines in an electrical field.
1920	Charles É. Guillaume (1861–1938)	French (b. Switzerland)	Discovering anomalies in nickel-steel alloys.
1921	Albert Einstein (1879–1955)	American (b. Germany)	Contributing to theoretical physics: especially for the discovery of photoelectric-effect law.
1922	Niels H. D. Bohr (1885–1962)	Danish	Studies of the structure of atoms and their radiation.
1923	Robert A. Millikan (1868–1953)	American	Work on electrons and the photoelectric effect.
1924	Karl M. G. Siegbahn (1886–1978)	Swedish	Discoveries in X-ray spectroscopy.
1925	James Franck (1882–1964)	German	Their discovery of the laws governing the impact of
	Gustav Hertz (1887–1975)	German	an electron on an atom.

Year	Winner and Life Dates	Nationality	Achievement
1926	Jean B. Perrin (1870–1942)	French	Work on the discontinuous structure of matter; discovery of sedimentation equilibrium.
1927	Arthur H. Compton (1892–1962)	American	Discovering the Compton effect (the change in wavelength of X rays colliding with electrons).
	Charles T. R. Wilson (1869–1959)	British	Discovery of the cloud chamber method of tracking paths of electrically charged particles.
1928	Owen W. Richardson (1879–1959)	British	Study of electron emission from heated bodies; formulation of the law governing such emission.
1929	Louis-Victor de Broglie (1892–)	French	Discovering the wave nature of electrons.
1930	Chandrasekhara V. Raman (1888–1970)	Indian	Light diffusion research; discovery of Raman effect.
1932	Werner Heisenberg (1901–1976)	German	Creating a quantum mechanics; new discoveries in the study of hydrogen.
1933	Erwin Schrödinger (1887–1961)	Austrian	For their development of new useful forms of atomic theory.
	Paul A. M. Dirac (1902–)	British	
1935	James Chadwick (1891–1974)	British	Discovery of the neutron.
1936	Victor F. Hess (1883–1964)	American (b. Austria)	Discovering cosmic radiation.
	Carl D. Anderson (1905–)	American	Discovery of the positron.
1937	Clinton J. Davisson (1881–1958)	American	Their discovery of the diffraction of electrons by crystals.
	George P. Thomson (1892–1975)	British	
1938	Enrico Fermi (1901–54)	American (b. Italy)	Work on radioactive elements, including artificial ones produced by neutron bombardment.
1939	Ernest O. Lawrence (1901–58)	American	Inventing the cyclotron.
1943	Otto Stern (1888–1969)	American (b. Germany)	Studies related to the magnetic properties of atoms; discovery of the magnetic moment of the proton.
1944	Isidor Isaac Rabi (1898–)	American (b. Austrian)	Discovery of resonance method of recording the magnetic properties of atomic nuclei.
1945	Wolfgang Pauli (1900–58)	American (b. Austrian)	Discovering the exclusion principle governing the quantum state of electrons in an atom.
1946	Percy Williams Bridgman (1882–1961)	American	Work in the field of high-pressure physics.
1947	Edward V. Appleton (1892–1965)	British	Investigations of the physics of the upper atmosphere; discovery of the so-called Appleton layer.
1948	Patrick M. S. Blackett (1897–1974)	British	Improvement of the Wilson cloud chamber method and resulting discoveries in nuclear physics and cosmic rays.
1949	Hideki Yukawa (1907–1981)	Japanese	Theoretical deductions of the existence of mesons.
1950	Cecil F. Powell (1903–69)	British	Photographic method of tracking nuclear particles.
1951	Sir John D. Cockcroft (1897–1967)	British	Their pioneer work in transmuting atomic nuclei with artificially accelerated atomic particles.
	Ernest T. S. Walton (1903–)	Irish	
1952	Felix Bloch (1905–)	American (b. Switzerland)	Developing the nuclear resonance method for precision measurements of atomic nuclei magnetic fields.
	Edward M. Purcell (1912–)	American	
1953	Frits Zernike (1888–1966)	Dutch	Inventing the phase-contrast microscope.
1954	Max Born (1882–1970)	British (b. Germany)	Basic research in quantum mechanics and modern nuclear physics.
	Walther Bothe (1891–1957)	German	Development of the coincidence method for measuring time.
1955	Willis E. Lamb, Jr. (1913–)	American	Discoveries concerning the fine structure of the hydrogen spectrum.
	Polykarp Kusch (1911–)	American (b. Germany)	Precise measurement of the electron's electromagnetic properties.
1956	John Bardeen (1908–)	American	Their work on developing the transistor, a device which replaced electronic tubes in many applications.
	Walter H. Brattain (1902–)	American	
	William B. Shockley (1910–)	American (b. England)	
1957	Tsung-Dao Lee (1926–)	American (b. China)	Their disproving of the law of parity conservation in nuclear physics.
	Chen Ning Yang (1922–)	American (b. China)	
1958	Pavel A. Cherenkov (1904–)	Russian	Discovering the Cherenkov effect (radiated electrons accelerate in water to speeds greater than that of light in the same medium).
	Ilya M. Frank (1908–)	Russian	
	Igor Y. Tamm (1895–1971)	Russian	
1959	Emilio G. Segrè (1905–)	American (b. Italy)	Discovery of the antiproton, a particle of mass identical to the proton but of opposite charge.
	Owen Chamberlain (1920–)	American	
1960	Donald A. Glaser (1926–)	American	Inventing the bubble chamber to study subatomic particles.
1961	Robert Hofstadter (1915–)	American	Investigations of atomic nuclei; discoveries relating to the structure of nucleons.
	Rudolf L. Moessbauer (1929–)	German	The method named for him of producing and measuring recoil-free gamma rays.
1962	Lev D. Landau (1908–68)	Russian	Pioneering studies on condensed gases, especially liquid helium.
1963	Eugene P. Wigner (1902–)	American (b. Hungary)	Contributions to nuclear and theoretical physics.
	Maria Goeppert-Mayer (1906–1972)	American (b. Poland)	Their discoveries regarding atomic nucleus shell structure.
	J. Hans D. Jensen (1907–1973)	German	
1964	Charles H. Townes (1915–)	American	Their fundamental research in quantum electronics that led to development of the maser-laser principle.
	Nikolai G. Basov (1922–)	Russian	
	Aleksander M. Prokhorov (1916–)	Russian	
1965	Richard P. Feynman (1918–)	American	Research in quantum electrodynamics that contributed to the understanding of elementary particles in high-energy physics.
	Julian S. Schwinger (1918–)	American	
	Sin-itiro Tomonaga (1906–1979)	Japanese	
1966	Alfred Kastler (1902–)	French	Discovery and development of optical methods for studying Herzian resonances in atoms.
1967	Hans A. Bethe (1906–)	American (b. Germany)	Contributions to the theory of nuclear reaction; discoveries concerning the energy production of stars.
1968	Luis W. Alvarez (1911–)	American	Contributions to the physics of subatomic particles and techniques for their detection.
1969	Murray Gell-Mann (1929–)	American	Major theoretical insights into the interrelationships of elementary particles, including the theoretical model that he calls "The Eight-fold Way."
1970	Louis Néel (1904–)	French	Discoveries about ferromagnetism and antiferromagnetism; basic work in magneto-hydrodynamics.
	Hannes Alfvén (1908–)	Swedish	

Year	Winner and Life Dates	Nationality	Achievement
1971	Dennis Gabor (1900–1979)	British (b. Hungary)	Inventor of the three-dimensional, lensless system of photography known as holography.
1972	John Bardeen (1908–)	American	Joint development of a theory explaining the phenomenon of superconductivity.
	Leon Cooper (1930–)	American	
	John Robert Schrieffer (1931–)	American	
1973	Leo Esaki (1925–)	Japanese	Research into how electrons tunnel through conductors to become superconductors.
	Ivar Giaever (1929–)	American	
	Brian D. Josephson (1940–)	British	
1974	Sir Martin Ryle (1918–)	British	For their pioneering work in radio astrophysics.
	Anthony Hewish (1924–)	British	
1975	James Rainwater (1918–)	American	Discovery of the connection between collective motion and particle motion in the atomic nucleus and the development of the theory of the structure of the atomic nucleus based on this connection.
	Aage N. Bohr (1922–)	Danish	
	Ben R. Mottelson (1926–)	Danish (b. U.S.)	
1976	Burton Richter (1931–)	American	For independent discovery of a new subatomic particle, known as "psi" or "J".
	Samuel C.C. Ting (1936–)	American	
1977	John H. Van Vleck (1899–1980)	American	For their contributions to the development of modern electronic solid state circuitry and basic theories of magnetism and conduction.
	Philip W. Anderson (1924–)	American	
	Sir Nevill F. Mott (1905–)	British	
1978	Pyotr Kapitsa (1894–)	Russian	Pioneer work in low-temperature physics.
	Arno A. Penzias (1933–)	American (b. Germany)	Discovery of cosmic microwave background radiation, further support for the Big Bang theory.
	Robert W. Wilson (1936–)	American	
1979	Steven Weinberg (1933–)	American	Contributions to unified theory that electromagnetism and the "weak force" in subatomic particles are related phenomena.
	Sheldon L. Glashow (1933–)	American	
	Abdus Salam (1926–)	Pakistani	
1980	James W. Cronin (1931–)	American	Research into the symmetry of subatomic particles.
	Val L. Fitch (1923–)	American	

ECONOMIC SCIENCE

Year	Winner and Life Dates	Nationality	Achievement
1969	Ragnar Frisch (1895–1973)	Norwegian	Their development of econometrics: mathematical models in the analysis of economic processes.
	Jan Tinbergen (1903–)	Dutch	
1970	Paul Anthony Samuelson (1915–)	American	Deriving new theorems; devising new applications.
1971	Simon Kuznets (1901–)	American (b. Russia)	Development of concept of using GNP as measure of national economic growth.
1972	Kenneth J. Arrow (1921–)	American	Contributions to equilibrium theory and welfare theory.
	John R. Hicks (1904–)	English	
1973	Wassily Leontief (1906–)	American (b. Russia)	For the development of "input-output" analysis.
1974	Gunnar Myrdal (1898–)	Swedish	Work on the theory of money and the interdependence of economic, social, and institutional phenomena.
	Friedrich A. von Hayek (1899–)	British (b. Austria)	
1975	Leonid V. Kantorovich (1912–)	Russian	Independent contributions to the theory of optimum allocation of resources.
	Tjalling C. Koopmans (1910–)	American (b. Netherlands)	
1976	Milton Friedman (1912–)	American	For achievements in the fields of consumption analysis, monetary history and theory; demonstration of the complexity of stabilization policy.
1977	Bertil Ohlin (1899–1979)	Swedish	For their contribution to international trade theory.
	James Meade (1907–)	English	
1978	Herbert Simon (1916–)	American	Research in the decision-making process within economic organizations.
1979	Sir Arthur Lewis (1915–)	British (b. West Indies)	For their work on the economic problems of developing nations.
	Theodore W. Schultz (1902–)	American	
1980	Lawrence R. Klein (1920–)	American	For his creation of "econometric" models to forecast economic trends.

LITERATURE

1901	René F. A. Sully-Prudhomme (1839–1907), French	1944	Johannes V. Jensen (1873–1950), Danish
1902	Theodor Mommsen (1817–1903), German	1945	Gabriela Mistral (1889–1957), Chilean
1903	Björnstjerne Björnson (1832–1910), Norwegian	1946	Hermann Hesse (1877–1962), Swiss (b. Germany)
1904	Frédéric Mistral (1830–1914), French	1947	André Gide (1869–1951), French
	José Echegaray (1832–1916), Spanish	1948	T. S. Eliot (1888–1965), British (b. United States)
1905	Henryk Sienkiewicz (1846–1916), Polish	1949	William Faulkner (1897–1962), American
1906	Giosuè Carducci (1835–1907), Italian	1950	Bertrand A. W. Russell (1872–1970), British
1907	Rudyard Kipling (1865–1936), British	1951	Pär F. Lagerkvist (1891–1974), Swedish
1908	Rudolf C. Eucken (1846–1926), German	1952	François Mauriac (1885–1970), French
1909	Selma Lagerlöf (1858–1940), Swedish	1953	Sir Winston Churchill (1874–1965), British
1910	Paul J. L. Heyse (1830–1914), German	1954	Ernest Hemingway (1899–1961), American
1911	Maurice Maeterlinck (1862–1949), Belgian	1955	Halldór K. Laxness (1902–), Icelandic
1912	Gerhart Hauptmann (1862–1946), German	1956	Juan Ramón Jiménez (1881–1958), Spanish
1913	Rabindranath Tagore (1861–1941), Indian	1957	Albert Camus (1913–60), French
1915	Romain Rolland (1866–1944), French	1958	Boris L. Pasternak (1890–1960), Russian
1916	Verner von Heidenstam (1859–1940), Swedish	1959	Salvatore Quasimodo (1901–68), Italian
1917	Karl A. Gjellerup (1857–1919), Danish	1960	Saint-John Perse (1887–1975), French
	Henrik Pontoppidan (1857–1943), Danish	1961	Ivo Andrić (1892–1975), Yugoslav
1919	Carl F. G. Spitteler (1845–1924), Swiss	1962	John Steinbeck (1902–68), American
1920	Knut Hamsun (1859–1952), Norwegian	1963	Giorgos Seferis (1900–71), Greek
1921	Anatole France (1844–1924), French	1964	Jean Paul Sartre (1905–80), French
1922	Jacinto Benavente y Martínez (1866–1954), Spanish	1965	Mikhail A. Sholokov (1905–), Russian
1923	William Butler Yeats (1865–1939), Irish	1966	Samuel Y. Agnon (1888–1970), Israeli (b. Poland)
1924	Wladyslaw S. Reymont (c. 1867–1925), Polish		Nelly Sachs (1891–1970), Swedish (b. Germany)
1925	George Bernard Shaw (1856–1950), British (b. Ireland)	1967	Miguel Angel Asturias (1899–1974), Guatemalan
1926	Grazia Deledda (1875–1936), Italian	1968	Yasunari Kawabata (1899–1972), Japanese
1927	Henri Bergson (1859–1941), French	1969	Samuel Beckett (1906–), Irish (res. France)
1928	Sigrid Undset (1882–1949), Norwegian (b. Denmark)	1970	Aleksandr Solzhenitsyn (1918–), Russian
1929	Thomas Mann (1875–1955), German	1971	Pablo Neruda (1904–1973), Chilean
1930	Sinclair Lewis (1885–1951), American	1972	Heinrich Böll (1917–), German
1931	Erik A. Karlfeldt (1864–1931), Swedish	1973	Patrick White (1912–), Australian
1932	John Galsworthy (1867–1933), English	1974	Eyvind Johnson (1900–76), Swedish
1933	Ivan A. Bunin (1870–1953), Russian		Edmund Martinson (1904–1978), Swedish
1934	Luigi Pirandello (1867–1936), Italian	1975	Eugenio Montale (1896–1981), Italian
1936	Eugene O'Neill (1888–1953), American	1976	Saul Bellow (1915–), American
1937	Roger Martin du Gard (1881–1958), French	1977	Vicente Aleixandre (1898–), Spanish
1938	Pearl S. Buck (1892–1973), American	1978	Isaac Bashevis Singer (1904–), American (b. Poland)
1939	Frans E. Sillanpää (1888–1964), Finnish	1979	Odysseus Elytis (1911–), Greek
		1980	Czeslaw Milosz (1911–), American (b. Poland)

PEACE

1901	Jean H. Dunant (1828–1910), Swiss
	Frédéric Passy (1822–1912), French
1902	Élie Ducommun (1833–1906), Swiss
	Charles A. Gobat (1843–1914), Swiss
1903	William R. Cremer (1828–1908), English
1904	Institute of International Law
1905	Bertha von Suttner (1843–1914), Austrian
1906	Theodore Roosevelt (1858–1919), American
1907	Ernesto T. Moneta (1833–1918), Italian
	Louis Renault (1843–1918), French
1908	Klas P. Arnoldson (1844–1916), Swedish
1909	August M. F. Beernaert (1829–1912), Belgian
	Paul H. Benjamin Estournelles de Constant (1852–1924), French
1910	International Peace Bureau
1911	Tobias M. C. Asser (1838–1913), Dutch
	Alfred H. Fried (1864–1921), Austrian
1912	Elihu Root (1845–1937), American
1913	Henri La Fontaine (1854–1943), Belgian
1917	International Red Cross Committee
1919	Woodrow Wilson (1856–1924), American
1920	Léon Bourgeois (1851–1925), French
1921	Hjalmar Branting (1860–1925), Swedish
	Christian L. Lange (1869–1938), Norwegian
1922	Fridtjof Nansen (1861–1930), Norwegian
1925	Sir J. Austen Chamberlain (1863–1937), British
	Charles G. Dawes (1865–1951), American
1926	Aristide Briand (1862–1932), French
	Gustav Stresemann (1878–1929), German
1927	Ferdinand E. Buisson (1841–1932), French
	Ludwig Quidde (1858–1941), German
1929	Frank B. Kellogg (1856–1937), American
1930	Nathan Söderblom (1866–1931), Swedish
1931	Jane Addams (1860–1935), American
	Nicholas Murray Butler (1862–1947), American
1933	Norman Angell (c. 1872–1967), British
1934	Arthur Henderson (1863–1935), British
1935	Carl von Ossietzky (1889–1938), German
1936	Carlos Saavedra Lamas (1880–1959), Argentine

1937	E. A. R. Cecil (1864–1958), British
1938	Nansen International Office for Refugees
1944	International Red Cross Committee
1945	Cordell Hull (1871–1955), American
1946	John R. Mott (1865–1955), American
	Emily Balch (1867–1961), American
1947	Friends Service Council (British)
	American Friends Service Committee (American)
1949	Sir John Boyd Orr (1880–1971), British
1950	Ralph J. Bunche (1904–71), American
1951	Léon Jouhaux (1879–1954), French
1952	Albert Schweitzer (1875–1965), Alsatian
1953	George C. Marshall (1880–1959), American
1954	Office of the UN High Commissioner for Refugees
1957	Lester B. Pearson (1897–1972), Canadian
1958	Father Georges H. Pire (1910–69), Belgian
1959	Philip J. Noel-Baker (1889–), British
1960	Albert J. Luthuli (1899–1967), South African
1961	Dag Hammarskjöld (1905–61), Swedish
1962	Linus C. Pauling (1901–), American
1963	International Red Cross Committee
	League of Red Cross Societies
1964	Martin Luther King, Jr. (1929–68), American
1965	UNICEF (UN Children's Fund)
1968	René Cassin (1887–1976), French
1969	International Labor Organization
1970	Norman E. Borlaug (1914–), American
1971	Willy Brandt (1913–), German
1973	Henry A. Kissinger (1923–), American
	Le Duc Tho (1910–), Vietnamese
1974	Eisaku Sato (1901–75), Japanese
	Sean McBride (1904–), Irish
1975	Andrei D. Sakharov (1921–), Russian
1976	Mairead Corrigan (1944–), Northern Irish
	Betty Williams (1943–), Northern Irish
1977	Amnesty International
1978	Menachem Begin (1913–), Israeli
	Anwar el-Sadat (1918–), Egyptian
1979	Mother Teresa (1910–), Indian
1980	Adolfo Pérez Esquivel (1932–), Argentine

PULITZER PRIZES

LOCAL INVESTIGATIVE REPORTING

1953 Edward J. Mowery (*New York World-Telegram & Sun*)
1954 Alvin Scott McCoy (*Kansas City* [Mo.] *Star*)
1955 Roland Kenneth Towery (*Cuero* [Tex.] *Record*)
1956 Arthur Daley (*N.Y. Times*)
1957 Wallace Turner and William Lambert (*Portland Oregonian*)
1958 George Beveridge (*Evening Star*, Washington, D.C.)
1959 John Harold Brislin (*Scranton* [Pa.] *Tribune* and *Scrantonian*)
1960 Miriam Ottenberg (*Evening Star*, Washington, D.C.)
1961 Edgar May (*Buffalo* [N.Y.] *Evening News*)
1962 George Bliss (*Chicago* [Ill.] *Tribune*)
1963 Oscar O'Neal Griffin, Jr. (*Pecos* [Tex.] *Enterprise*)
1964 James V. Magee, Albert V. Gaudiosi, and Frederick A. Meyer (*Philadelphia* [Pa.] *Bulletin*)
1965 Gene Goltz (*Houston* [Tex.] *Post*)
1966 John A. Frasca (*Tampa* [Fla.] *Tribune*)
1967 Gene Miller (*Miami* [Fla.] *Herald*)
1968 J. Anthony Lukas (*New York Times*)
1969 Albert L. Delugach Denny Walsh (*St. Louis Globe-Democrat*)

1970 Harold Eugene Martin ([Montgomery] *Alabama Journal*)
1971 William Hugh Jones (*Chicago* [Ill.] *Tribune*)
1972 Richard Cooper and John Machacek (*Rochester* [N.Y.] *Times Union*)
1973 The Sun Newspapers, Omaha, Nebraska
1974 Arthur M. Petacque Hugh F. Hough (*The Chicago Sun-Times*)
1976 *The Chicago* [Ill.] *Tribune*
1977 Acel Moore and Wendell Rawls, Jr. (*The Philadelphia* [Pa.] *Inquirer*)
1978 Anthony R. Dolan (*Stamford* [Conn.] *Advocate*)
1979 Gilbert M. Gaul and Elliot G. Jaspin (*Pottsville* [Pa.] *Republican*)
1980 Stephen A. Kurkjian, Alexander B. Hawes, Jr., Nils J. Bruzelius, Joan Vennochi and Robert Porterfield (*The Boston* [Mass.] *Globe*)
1981 Clark Hallas and Robert B. Lowe (*The Arizona Daily Star*, Tucson, Ariz.)

GENERAL LOCAL REPORTING

1953 Providence (R.I.) *Journal and Evening Bulletin*
1954 Vicksburg (Miss.) *Sunday Post-Herald*
1955 Mrs. Caro Brown (*Alice* [Tex.] *Daily Echo*)
1956 Lee Hills (*Detroit* [Mich.] *Free Press*)
1957 Salt Lake (Utah) *Tribune*
1958 Fargo (N.D.) *Forum*
1959 Mary Lou Werner (*Evening Star*, Washington, D.C.)

1960 Jack Nelson (*Atlanta* [Ga.] *Constitution*)
1961 Sanche de Gramont (*New York Herald Tribune*)
1962 Robert D. Mullins (*Deseret News*, Salt Lake City, Utah)
1963 Sylvan Fox, Anthony Shannon, and William Longgood (*New York World-Telegram & Sun*)
1964 Norman C. Miller, Jr. (*Wall Street Journal*)
1965 Melvin H. Ruder (*Hungry Horse News*, Columbia Falls, Mont.)
1966 *Los Angeles* (Calif.) *Times* staff
1967 Robert V. Cox (*Chambersburg* [Pa.] *Public Opinion*)
1968 *Detroit* (Mich.) *Free Press*
1969 John Fetterman (*Louisville* [Ky.] *Times and Courier-Journal*)
1970 Thomas Fitzpatrick (*Chicago* [Ill.] *Sun-Times*)
1971 *Akron* [Ohio] *Beacon Journal*
1972 Timothy Leland, Gerald M. O'Neill, Stephen A. Kurjan, and Ann Desantis (*Boston Globe*)
1973 *Chicago Tribune*
1974 William Sherman (*New York Daily News*)
1976 Gene Miller (*Miami* [Fla.] *Herald*)
1977 Margo Huston (*The Milwaukee* [Wis.] *Journal*)
1978 Richard Whitt (*Louisville* [Ky.] *Courier-Journal*)
1979 San Diego (Calif.) *Evening Tribune*
1980 Philadelphia (Pa.) *Inquirer*
1981 Longview (Wash.) *Daily News*

NATIONAL REPORTING

1948 Bert Andrews
(New York Herald Tribune)
Nat S. Finney
(Minneapolis [Minn.] Tribune)
1949 C. P. Trussel
(New York Times)
1950 Edwin O. Guthman
(Seattle [Wash.] Times)
1952 Anthony Leviero
(New York Times)
1953 Don Whitehead (AP)
1954 Richard Wilson
(Cowles Newspapers)
1955 Anthony Lewis
(Washington [D.C.] Daily News)
1956 Charles L. Bartlett
(Chattanooga [Tenn.] Times)
1957 James Reston
(New York Times)
1958 Relman Morin (AP)
Clark Mollenhoff
(Des Moines [Iowa] Register & Tribune)
1959 Howard Van Smith
(Miami [Fla.] News)
1960 Vance Trimble
(Scripps-Howard Newspaper Alliance)
1961 Edward R. Cony
(Wall Street Journal)
1962 Nathan G. Caldwell and
Gene S. Graham
(Nashville Tennessean)
1963 Anthony Lewis
(New York Times)
1964 Merriman Smith (UPI)
1965 Louis M. Kohlmeier
(Wall Street Journal)
1966 Haynes Johnson
(Evening Star, Wash., D.C.)
1967 Monroe W. Karmin and
Stanley W. Penn
(Wall Street Journal)
1968 Howard James
(Christian Science Monitor)
Nathan K. Kotz (Des Moines [Iowa] Register)
1969 Robert Cahn
(Christian Science Monitor, Boston, Mass.)
1970 William J. Eaton
(Chicago [Ill.] Daily News)
1971 Lucinda Franks and Thomas Powers (UPI)
1972 Jack Anderson (Columnist)
1973 Robert Boyd and Clark Hoyt (Knight Newspapers)
1974 James R. Polk
(Washington Star News)
Jack White
(Providence Journal-Bulletin)
1975 Donald L. Barlett and
James B. Steele (The Philadelphia Inquirer)
1976 James Risser (Des Moines [Iowa] Register)
1977 Walter Mears (AP)
1978 Gaylord Shaw (Los Angeles [Calif.] Times)
1979 James Risser
(Des Moines [Iowa] Register)
1980 Bette Swenson Orsini and
Charles Stafford
(St. Petersburg [Fla.] Times)
1981 John M. Crewdson (New York Times)

INTERNATIONAL CORRESPONDENCE

1948 Paul W. Ward
(Sun, Baltimore, Md.)

1949 Price Day
(Sun, Baltimore, Md.)
1950 Edmund Stevens
(Christian Science Monitor, Boston, Mass.)
1951 Keyes Beech
(Chicago [Ill.] Daily News)
Homer Bigart
Marguerite Higgins
(New York Herald Tribune)
Relman Morin (AP)
Fred Sparks
(Chicago [Ill.] Daily News)
Don Whitehead (AP)
1952 John M. Hightower (AP)
1953 Austin Wehrwein
(Milwaukee [Wis.] Journal)
1954 Jim G. Lucas
(Scripps-Howard Newspaper Alliance)
1955 Harrison E. Salisbury
(New York Times)
1956 William Randolph Hearst,
Jr., Kingsbury Smith, and
Frank Coniff
(International News Service)
1957 Russell Jones (UPI)
1958 New York Times
1959 Joseph Martin and Philip
Santora (New York Daily News)
1960 A. M. Rosenthal
(New York Times)
1961 Lynn Heinzerling (AP)
1962 Walter Lippmann
(New York Herald Tribune Syndicate)
1963 Hal Hendrix
(Miami [Fla.] News)
1964 Malcolm W. Browne (AP)
David Halberstam
(New York Times)
1965 J. A. Livingston
(Philadelphia Bulletin)
1966 Peter Arnett (AP)
1967 R. John Hughes
(Christian Science Monitor, Boston, Mass.)
1968 Alfred Friendly
(Washington [D.C.] Post)
1969 William Tuohy
(Los Angeles Times)
1970 Seymour M. Hersh
(free-lance reporter)
1971 Jimmie Lee Hoagland
(Washington [D.C.] Post)
1972 Peter R. Kann
(Wall Street Journal)
1973 Max Frankel
(New York Times)
1974 Hedrick Smith
(The New York Times)
1975 William Mullen and
Ovie Carter
(The Chicago Tribune)
1976 Sydney H. Schanberg
(The New York Times)
1978 Henry Kamm (The New York Times)
1979 Richard Ben Cramer
(Philadelphia [Pa.] Inquirer)
1980 Joel Brinkley and Jay Mather
(The Louisville [Ky.] Courier-Journal)
1981 Shirley Christian (The Miami [Fla.] Herald)

EDITORIAL WRITING

1917 New York Tribune
1918 Courier-Journal, Louisville, Ky.

1920 Harvey E. Newbranch
(Evening World-Herald, Omaha, Nebr.)
1922 Frank M. O'Brien
(New York Herald)
1923 William Allen White
(Emporia [Kans.] Gazette)
1924 Boston (Mass.) Herald
Special prize: Frank I. Cobb
(World, New York, N.Y.)
1925 Charleston (S.C.) News and Courier
1926 Edward M. Kingsbury (New York Times)
1927 F. Lauriston Bullard (Boston [Mass.] Herald)
1928 Grover Cleveland Hall
(Montgomery [Ala.] Advertiser)
1929 Louis Isaac Jaffe
(Norfolk Virginian-Pilot)
1931 Charles S. Ryckman
(Fremont [Nebr.] Tribune)
1933 Kansas City (Mo.) Star
1934 E. P. Chase
(Atlantic News Telegraph)
1936 Felix Morley
(Washington [D.C.] Post)
George B. Parker
(Scripps-Howard Newspaper Alliance)
1937 John W. Owens
(Sun, Baltimore, Md.)
1938 W. W. Waymack
(Register and Tribune, Des Moines, Iowa)
1939 Ronald G. Callvert
(Oregonian, Portland, Ore.)
1940 Bart Howard
(St. Louis Post-Dispatch)
1941 Reuben Maury
(Daily News, N.Y.)
1942 Geoffrey Parsons
(New York Herald Tribune)
1943 Forrest W. Seymour
(Register and Tribune, Iowa)
1944 Henry J. Haskell
(Kansas City [Mo.] Star)
1945 George W. Potter
(Providence [R.I.] Journal-Bulletin)
1946 Hodding Carter
(Delta Democrat-Times, Greenville, Miss.)
1947 William H. Grimes
(Wall Street Journal)
1948 Virginius Dabney
(Richmond [Va.] Times-Dispatch)
1949 John H. Crider
(Boston [Mass.] Herald)
Herbert Elliston
(Washington [D.C.] Post)
1950 Carl M. Saunders
(Jackson [Mich.] Citizen Patriot)
1951 William Harry Fitzpatrick
(New Orleans [La.] States)
1952 Louis LaCoss
(St. Louis Globe-Democrat)
1953 Vermont C. Royster
(Wall Street Journal)
1954 Don Murray
(Boston [Mass.] Herald)
1955 Royce Howes
(Detroit [Mich.] Free Press)
1956 Lauren K. Soth
(Des Moines [Iowa] Register and Tribune)
1957 Buford Boone
(Tuscaloosa [Ala.] News)
1958 Harry S. Ashmore
(Arkansas Gazette)

1959 Ralph McGill
      (*Atlanta* [Ga.] *Constitution*)
1960 Lenoir Chambers
      (*Norfolk Virginian-Pilot*)
1961 William J. Dorvillier
      (*San Juan* [P.R.] *Star*)
1962 Thomas M. Storke
      (*Santa Barbara News-Press*)
1963 Ira B. Harkey, Jr.
      (*Pascagoula* [Miss.]
      Chronicle)
1964 Hazel Brannon Smith
      (*Lexington* [Miss.] *Adver-
      tiser*)
1965 John R. Harrison
      (*Gainesville* [Fla.] *Sun*)
1966 Robert Lasch
      (*St. Louis Post-Dispatch*)
1967 Eugene Patterson
      (*Atlanta* [Ga.] *Constitution*)
1968 John S. Knight
      (Knight Newspapers)
1969 Paul Greenberg
      (*Pine Bluff* [Ark.] *Commer-
      cial*)
1970 Philip L. Geyelin
      (*Washington* [D.C.] *Post*)
1971 Horance G. Davis, Jr.
      (*Gainesville* [Fla.] *Sun*)
1972 John Strohmeyer (*Bethlehem*
      [Pa.] *Globe-Times*)
1973 Roger B. Linscott
      (*Berkshire Eagle* [Pittsfield,
      Mass.])
1974 F. Gilman Spencer
      (*Trenton Trentonian*)
1975 John Daniell Maurice
      (*Charleston Daily Mail*)
1976 Philip P. Kerby (*The Los
      Angeles* [Calif.] *Times*)
1977 Warren Lerude, Foster
      Church, Norman F. Cardoza
      (*The Reno* [Nev.] *Evening
      Gazette* and *Nevada State
      Journal*)
1978 Meg Greenfield (*The Wash-
      ington* [D.C.] *Post*)
1979 Edwin M. Yoder, Jr.
      (*The Washington* [D.C.] *Star*)
1980 Robert L. Bartley
      (*The Wall Street Journal*)

CARTOONS

1922 Rollin Kirby
      (*World*, New York, N.Y.)
1924 Jay Norwood Darling
      (*New York Tribune*)
1925 Rollin Kirby
      (*World*, New York, N.Y.)
1926 D. R. Fitzpatrick
      (*St. Louis Post-Dispatch*)
1927 Nelson Harding
      (*Brooklyn* [N.Y.] *Daily
      Eagle*)
1928 Nelson Harding
      (*Brooklyn Daily Eagle*)
1929 Rollin Kirby
      (*World*, New York, N.Y.)
1930 Charles R. Macauley
      (*Brooklyn* [N.Y.] *Daily
      Eagle*)
1931 Edmund Duffy
      (*Sun*, Baltimore, Md.)
1932 John T. McCutcheon
      (*Chicago* [Ill.] *Tribune*)
1933 Harold M. Talburt
      (*Washington* [D.C.] *Daily
      News*)
1934 Edmund Duffy
      (*Sun*, Baltimore, Md.)
1935 Ross A. Lewis
      (*Milwaukee* [Wis.] *Journal*)
1937 Clarence D. Batchelor
      (*Daily News*, New York,
      N.Y.)

1938 Vaughn Shoemaker
      (*Chicago* [Ill.] *Daily News*)
1939 Charles G. Werner
      (*Daily Oklahoman*, Okla-
      homa City, Okla.)
1940 Edmund Duffy
      (*Sun*, Baltimore, Md.)
1941 Jacob Burck
      (*Times*, Chicago, Ill.)
1942 Herbert L. Block
      (NEA Service)
1943 Jay Norwood Darling
      (*New York Herald Tribune*)
1944 Clifford K. Berryman
      (*Evening Star*,
      Washington, D.C.)
1945 William (Bill) Mauldin
      (United Features Syndicate)
1946 Bruce Alexander Russell
      (*Los Angeles* [Calif.] *Times*)
1947 Vaughn Shoemaker
      (*Chicago* [Ill.] *Daily News*)
1948 Reuben L. (Rube) Goldberg
      (*Sun*, New York, N.Y.)
1949 Lute Pease
      (*Newark* [N.J.] *Evening
      News*)
1950 James T. Berryman
      (*Evening Star*,
      Washington, D.C.)
1951 Reginald W. Manning
      (*Arizona Republic*, Phoenix)
1952 Fred L. Packer
      (*New York* [N.Y.] *Mirror*)
1953 Edward D. Kuekes
      (*Cleveland Plain Dealer*)
1954 Herbert L. Block
      (*Washington* [D.C.] *Post &
      Times-Herald*)
1955 Daniel R. Fitzpatrick
      (*St. Louis Post-Dispatch*)
1956 Robert York
      (*Louisville* [Ky.] *Times*)
1957 Tom Little
      (*Nashville Tennessean*)
1958 Bruce M. Shanks
      (*Buffalo Evening News*)
1959 William (Bill) Mauldin
      (*St. Louis Post-Dispatch*)
1961 Carey Orr
      (*Chicago* [Ill.] *Tribune*)
1962 Edmund S. Valtman
      (*Hartford* [Conn.] *Times*)
1963 Frank Miller
      (*Des Moines* [Iowa] *Register*)
1964 Paul Conrad
      (*Denver* [Colo.] *Post*)
1966 Don Wright
      (*Miami* [Fla.] *News*)
1967 Patrick B. Oliphant
      (*Denver* [Colo.] *Post*)
1968 Eugene Gray Payne
      (*Charlotte* [N.C.] *Observer*)
1969 John Fischetti
      (*Chicago* [Ill.] *Daily News*)
1970 Thomas F. Darcy
      (*Newsday*, Garden City, NY)
1971 Paul Conrad
      (*Los Angeles* [Calif.] *Times*)
1972 Jeffrey K. MacNelly (*Rich-
      mond* [Va.] *News Leader*)
1974 Paul Szep
      (*The Boston Globe*)
1975 Garry Trudeau
      (Universal Press Syndicate)
1976 Tony Auth (*The Phila-
      delphia* [Pa.] *Inquirer*)
1977 Paul Szep (*The Boston*
      [Mass.] *Globe*)
1978 Jeffrey K. MacNelly (*Rich-
      mond* [Va.] *News Leader*)
1979 Herbert L. Block
      (*The Washington* [D.C.] *Post*)
1980 Don Wright
      (*The Miami* [Fla.] *News*)

1981 *Mike Peters (Dayton*
      [Ohio] *Daily News*)

PHOTOGRAPHY

1942 Milton Brooks
      (*Detroit* [Mich.] *News*)
1943 Frank Noel (AP)
1944 Frank Filan (AP)
      Earle L. Bunker
      (*World-Herald*, Omaha, Nebr.)
1945 Joe Rosenthal (AP)
1947 Arnold Hardy°
1948 Frank Cushing
      (*Boston* [Mass.] *Traveler*)
1949 Nathaniel Fein
      (*New York Herald Tribune*)
1950 Bill Crouch
      (*Oakland* [Calif.] *Tribune*)
1951 Max Desfor (AP)
1952 John Robinson and Don
      Ultang (*Des Moines* [Iowa]
      Register and Tribune)
1953 William M. Gallagher
      (*Flint* [Mich.] *Journal*)
1954 Mrs. Walter M. Schau°
1955 John L. Gaunt, Jr.
      (*Los Angeles* [Calif.] *Times*)
1956 *Daily News*, New York, N.Y.
1957 Harry A. Trask
      (*Boston* [Mass.] *Traveler*)
1958 William C. Beall
      (*Washington* [D.C.] *Daily
      News*)
1959 William Seaman
      (*Minneapolis* [Minn.] *Star*)
1960 Andrew Lopez (UPI)
1961 Yasushi Nagao
      (*Mainichi Newspapers*,
      Tokyo, Japan)
1962 Paul Vathis (AP)
1963 Hector Rondon
      (*La Republica*, Caracas,
      Venezuela)
1964 Robert H. Jackson
      (*Dallas* [Tex.] *Times Herald*)
1965 Horst Faas (AP)
1966 Kyoichi Sawada (UPI)
1967 Jack R. Thornell (AP)
1968 Rocco Morabito
      (*Jacksonville* [Fla.] *Journal*)
      Toshio Sakai (UPI)
1969 Edward T. Adams (AP)
      Moneta Sleet, Jr. (*Ebony*)
1970 Steve Starr (AP)
      Dallas Kinney
      (*Palm Beach* [Fla.] *Post*)
1971 John Paul Filo (Kent [Ohio]
      State University student)°
      Jack Dykinga
      (*Chicago* [Ill.] *Sun-Times*)
1972 Horst Fass and Michael Lau-
      rent (Associated Press) Dave
      Kenerly (United Press Inter-
      national)
1973 Huynh Cong Ut (AP)
      Brian Lanker (*Topeka*
      [Kans.] *Capital-Journal*)
1974 Slava Veder (AP)
      Anthony K. Roberts (AP)
1975 Gerald H. Gay
      (*The Seattle Times*)
      Matthew Lewis
      (*Washington Post*)
1976 Stanley Forman (*The Boston*
      [Mass.] *Herald-American*);
      Louisville [Ky.] *Courier-
      Journal and Times*
1977 Stanley Forman (*The Bos-
      ton* [Mass.] *Herald-Ameri-
      can*); Neal Ulevich (AP);
      Robin Hood (*The Chatta-
      nooga* [Tenn.] *News-Free
      Press*)
1978 J. Ross Baughman (AP)
      John W. Blair (free-lance,
      UPI Indianapolis [Ind.]
      bureau)

° Amateur photographer.

1979 Thomas J. Kelly 3d (*Pottstown* [Pa.] *Mercury*); the photographic staff of *The Boston* (Mass.) *Herald-American*
1980 Erwin H. Nagler (*The Dallas* [Tex.] *Times Herald*)
1981 Larry C. Price (*Fort Worth* [Tex.] *Star Telegram*); Taro M. Yamasaki (*Detroit* [Mich.] *Free Press*)

MERITORIOUS PUBLIC SERVICE

1918 *New York Times*
1919 *Milwaukee* (Wis.) *Journal*
1921 *Boston* (Mass.) *Post*
1922 *World,* New York, N.Y.
1923 *Memphis* (Tenn.) *Commercial Appeal*
1924 *World* (New York, N.Y.)
1926 *Enquirer Sun* (Columbus, Ga.)
1927 *Canton* (Ohio) *Daily News*
1928 *Indianapolis* (Ind.) *Times*
1929 *Evening World,* New York, N.Y.
1931 *Atlanta* (Ga.) *Constitution*
1932 *Indianapolis* (Ind.) *News*
1933 *New York World-Telegram*
1934 *Medford* (Ore.) *Mail Tribune*
1935 *Sacramento* (Calif.) *Bee*
1936 *Cedar Rapids* (Iowa) *Gazette*
1937 *St. Louis* (Mo.) *Post-Dispatch*
1938 *Bismarck* (N.D.) *Tribune*
1939 *Miami* (Fla.) *Daily News*
1940 *Waterbury* (Conn.) *Republican and American*
1941 *St. Louis* (Mo.) *Post-Dispatch*
1942 *Los Angeles* (Calif.) *Times*
1943 *World-Herald,* Omaha, Nebr.
1944 *New York Times*
1945 *Detroit* (Mich.) *Free Press*
1946 *Scranton* (Pa.) *Times*
1947 *Sun,* Baltimore, Md.
1948 *St. Louis* (Mo.) *Post-Dispatch*
1949 *Nebraska State Journal*
1950 *Chicago* (Ill.) *Daily News* and *St. Louis Post-Dispatch*
1951 *Miami* (Fla.) *Herald* and *Brooklyn* (N.Y.) *Eagle*
1952 *St. Louis* (Mo.) *Post-Dispatch*
1953 *News Reporter* (Whiteville, N.C.) and *Tabor City* (N.C.) *Tribune*
1954 *Newsday,* Garden City, N.Y.
1955 *Columbus* (Ga.) *Ledger* and *Sunday Ledger-Enquirer*
1956 *Watsonville* (Calif.) *Register-Pajaronian*
1957 *Chicago* (Ill.) *Daily News*
1958 *Arkansas Gazette,* Little Rock
1959 *Utica* (N.Y.) *Observer-Dispatch* and *Utica Daily Press*
1960 *Los Angeles* (Calif.) *Times*
1961 *Amarillo* (Tex.) *Globe-Times*
1962 *Panama City* (Fla.) *News-Herald*
1963 *Chicago* (Ill.) *Daily News*
1964 *St. Petersburg* (Fla.) *Times*
1965 *Hutchinson* (Kans.) *News*
1966 *Boston* (Mass.) *Globe*
1967 *Courier Journal* (Louisville, Ky.) and *Milwaukee* (Wis.) *Journal*
1968 *Riverside* (Calif.) *Press-Enterprise*
1969 *Los Angeles* (Calif.) *Times*
1970 *Newsday,* Garden City, N.Y.
1971 *Winston-Salem* [N.C.] *Journal & Sentinel*

1972 *The New York Times*
1973 *The Washington Post*
1974 *Newsday,* Garden City, N.Y.
1975 *Boston* (Mass.) *Globe The Xenia* (Ohio) *Daily Gazette*
1976 *The Anchorage* [Alaska] *Daily News*
1977 *Lufkin* (Tex.) *News*
1978 *Philadelphia* [Pa.] *Inquirer*
1979 *Point Reyes* (Calif.) *Light*
1980 *The Gannett News Service*
1981 *Charlotte* [N.C.] *Observer*

FEATURE WRITING

1979 Jon D. Franklin (*The Baltimore* [Md.] *Evening Sun*)
1980 Madeleine Blais (*The Miami* [Fla.] *Herald*)
1981 Teresa Carpenter, (*The Village Voice,* New York City)

SPECIAL CITATIONS FOR JOURNALISM

1938 Edmonton (Alberta) Journal
1941 New York Times
1944 Byron Price, Director of the Office of Censorship
1944 William Allen White
1945 The cartographers of the American press
1947 Columbia University and the Graduate School of Journalism
1947 *St. Louis Post-Dispatch*
1948 Dr. Frank Diehl Fackenthal
1951 Cyrus L. Sulzberger of the *New York Times*
1952 Max Kase of the *New York Journal-American*
1952 *Kansas City* (Mo.) *Star*
1953 *New York Times* for the "Review of the Week" section
1958 Walter Lippmann
1964 Gannett Newspapers, Rochester, N.Y.
1976 Professor John Hohenberg
1978 Richard L. Strout of *The Christian Science Monitor* and *The New Republic*

BIOGRAPHY OR AUTOBIOGRAPHY

1917 *Julia Ward Howe,* by Laura E. Richards and Maude Howe Elliott, assisted by Florence Howe Hall
1918 *Benjamin Franklin, Self-Revealed,* by William Cabell Bruce
1919 *The Education of Henry Adams,* by Henry Adams
1920 *The Life of John Marshall* by Albert J. Beveridge
1921 *The Americanization of Edward Bok,* by Edward Bok
1922 *A Daughter of the Middle Border,* by Hamlin Garland
1923 *The Life and Letters of Walter H. Page,* by Burton J. Hendrick
1924 *From Immigrant to Inventor,* by Michael Idvorsky Pupin
1925 *Barrett Wendell and His Letters,* by M. A. DeWolfe Howe
1926 *The Life of Sir William Osler,* by Harvey Cushing
1927 *Whitman,* by Emory Holloway
1928 *The American Orchestra and Theodore Thomas,* by Charles Edward Russell

1929 *The Training of an American: The Earlier Life and Letters of Walter H. Page,* by Burton J. Hendrick
1930 *The Raven,* by Marquis James
1931 *Charles W. Eliot,* by Henry James
1932 *Theodore Roosevelt,* by Henry F. Pringle
1933 *Grover Cleveland,* by Allan Nevins
1934 *John Hay,* by Tyler Dennett
1935 *R. E. Lee,* by Douglas S. Freeman
1936 *The Thought and Character of William James,* by Ralph Barton Perry
1937 *Hamilton Fish,* by Allan Nevins
1938 *Pedlar's Progress,* by Odell Shepard, and *Andrew Jackson* (2 volumes), by Marquis James
1939 *Benjamin Franklin,* by Carl Van Doren
1940 *Woodrow Wilson, Life and Letters* (Volumes VII and VIII), by Ray Stannard Baker
1941 *Jonathan Edwards,* by Ola Elizabeth Winslow
1942 *Crusader in Crinoline,* by Forrest Wilson
1943 *Admiral of the Ocean Sea,* by Samuel Eliot Morison
1944 *The American Leonardo: The Life of Samuel F. B. Morse,* by Carleton Mabee
1945 *George Bancroft: Brahmin Rebel,* by Russell Blaine Nye
1946 *Son of the Wilderness,* by Linnie Marsh Wolfe
1947 *The Autobiography of William Allen White*
1948 *Forgotten First Citizen: John Bigelow,* by Margaret Clapp
1949 *Roosevelt and Hopkins,* by Robert E. Sherwood
1950 *John Quincy Adams and the Foundations of American Foreign Policy,* by Samuel Flagg Bemis
1951 *John C. Calhoun: American Portrait,* by Margaret Louise Coit
1952 *Charles Evans Hughes,* by Merlo J. Pusey
1953 *Edmund Pendleton 1721–1803,* by David J. Mays
1954 *The Spirit of St. Louis,* by Charles A. Lindbergh
1955 *The Taft Story,* by William S. White
1956 *Benjamin Henry Latrobe,* by Talbot Faulkner Hamlin
1957 *Profiles in Courage,* by John F. Kennedy
1958 *George Washington* (Volumes I–VI), by Douglas Southall Freeman; Volume VII, by Mary Wells Ashworth and John Alexander Carroll
1959 *Woodrow Wilson, American Prophet,* by Arthur Walworth
1960 *John Paul Jones,* by Samuel Eliot Morison
1961 *Charles Sumner and the Coming of the Civil War,* by David Donald

1963 *Henry James* (Volumes II and III), by Leon Edel

1964 *John Keats,* by Walter Jackson Bate

1965 *Henry Adams* (3 volumes), by Ernest Samuels

1966 *A Thousand Days,* by Arthur M. Schlesinger, Jr.

1967 *Mr. Clemens and Mark Twain,* by Justin Kaplan

1968 *Memoirs (1925–1950),* by George F. Kennan

1969 *The Man from New York: John Quinn and His Friends,* by Benjamin Lawrence Reid

1970 *Huey Long,* by T.H. Williams

1971 *Robert Frost: The Years of Triumph,* by L. R. Thompson

1972 *Eleanor and Franklin,* by Joseph P. Lash

1973 *Luce and His Empire,* by W. A. Swanberg

1974 *O'Neill, Son and Artist,* by Louis Sheaffer

1975 *The Power Broker: Robert Moses and the Fall of New York,* by Robert A. Caro

1976 *Edith Wharton: A Biography,* by R.W.B. Lewis

1977 *A Prince of Our Disorder,* by John E. Mack

1978 *Samuel Johnson,* by Walter Jackson Bate

1979 *Days of Sorrow and Pain: Leo Baeck and the Berlin Jews,* by Leonard Baker

1980 *The Rise of Theodore Roosevelt,* by Edmund Morris

1981 *Peter the Great,* by Robert K. Massie

DRAMA

1918 *Why Marry?,* by Jesse Lynch Williams

1920 *Beyond the Horizon,* by Eugene O'Neill

1921 *Miss Lulu Bett,* by Zona Gale

1922 *Anna Christie,* by Eugene O'Neill

1923 *Icebound,* by Owen Davis

1924 *Hell-Bent for Heaven,* by Hatcher Hughes

1925 *They Knew What They Wanted,* by Sidney Howard

1926 *Craig's Wife,* by G. Kelly

1927 *In Abraham's Bosom,* by Paul Green

1928 *Strange Interlude,* by Eugene O'Neill

1929 *Street Scene,* by Elmer L. Rice

1930 *The Green Pastures,* by Marc Connelly

1931 *Alison's House,* by Susan Glaspell

1932 *Of Thee I Sing,* by George S. Kaufman, Morrie Ryskind, and Ira Gershwin (with music by George Gershwin)

1933 *Both Your Houses,* by Maxwell Anderson

1934 *Men in White,* by Sidney Kingsley

1935 *The Old Maid,* by Zoe Akins

1936 *Idiot's Delight,* by Robert E. Sherwood

1937 *You Can't Take It with You,* by Moss Hart and George S. Kaufman

1938 *Our Town,* by Thornton Wilder

1939 *Abe Lincoln in Illinois,* by Robert E. Sherwood

* Declined.

1940 *The Time of Your Life,* by William Saroyan*

1941 *There Shall Be No Night,* by Robert E. Sherwood

1943 *The Skin of Our Teeth,* by Thornton Wilder

1945 *Harvey,* by Mary Chase

1946 *State of the Union,* by Russel Crouse and Howard Lindsay

1948 *A Streetcar Named Desire,* by Tennessee Williams

1949 *Death of a Salesman,* by Arthur Miller

1950 *South Pacific,* by Richard Rodgers, Oscar Hammerstein II, and Joshua Logan

1952 *The Shrike,* by Joseph Kramm

1953 *Picnic,* by William Inge

1954 *The Teahouse of the August Moon,* by John Patrick

1955 *Cat on a Hot Tin Roof,* by Tennessee Williams

1956 *Diary of Anne Frank,* by Albert Hackett and Frances Goodrich

1957 *Long Day's Journey into Night,* by Eugene O'Neill

1958 *Look Homeward, Angel,* by Ketti Frings

1959 *J. B.,* by Archibald MacLeish

1960 *Fiorello!,* book by Jerome Weidman and George Abbott, music by Jerry Bock, and lyrics by Sheldon Harnick

1961 *All the Way Home,* by Tad Mosel

1962 *How to Succeed in Business Without Really Trying,* by F. Loesser and A. Burrows

1965 *The Subject Was Roses,* by Frank D. Gilroy

1967 *A Delicate Balance,* by Edward Albee

1969 *The Great White Hope,* by Howard Sackler

1970 *No Place to Be Somebody,* by Charles Gordone

1971 *The Effect of Gamma Rays on Man-in-the-Moon Marigolds,* by Paul Zindel

1973 *That Championship Season,* by Jason Miller

1975 *Seascape,* by Edward Albee

1976 *A Chorus Line,* conceived, choreographed and directed by Michael Bennett; book by James Kirkwood & Nicholas Dante; music by Marvin Hamlisch; lyrics by Edward Kleban.

1977 *The Shadow Box,* by Michael Cristofer

1978 *The Gin Game,* by Donald L. Coburn

1979 *Buried Child,* by Sam Shepard

1980 *Talley's Folly,* by Lanford Wilson

1981 *Crimes of the Heart,* by Beth Henley

HISTORY

1917 *With Americans of Past and Present Days,* by His Excellency J. J. Jusserand, Ambassador of France to the U.S.

1918 *A History of the Civil War, 1861–1865,* by James Ford Rhodes

1920 *The War with Mexico* (2 volumes), by Justin H. Smith

1921 *The Victory at Sea,* by William Sowden Sims in collaboration with Burton J. Hendrick

1922 *The Founding of New England,* by James Truslow Adams

1923 *The Supreme Court in United States History,* by Charles Warren

1924 *The American Revolution— A Constitutional Interpretation,* by Charles Howard McIlwain

1925 *A History of the American Frontier,* by F. L. Paxson

1926 *The History of the United States* (Volume VI: *The War for Southern Independence),* by Edward Channing

1927 *Pinckney's Treaty,* by Samuel Flagg Bemis

1928 *Main Currents in American Thought,* 2 volumes, by Vernon Louis Parrington

1929 *The Organization and Administration of the Union Army, 1861–1865,* by Fred Albert Shannon

1930 *The War of Independence,* by Claude H. Van Tyne

1931 *The Coming of the War: 1914,* by Bernadotte E. Schmitt

1932 *My Experiences in the World War,* by John J. Pershing

1933 *The Significance of Sections in American History,* by Frederick J. Turner

1934 *The People's Choice,* by Herbert Agar

1935 *The Colonial Period of American History,* by Charles McLean Andrews

1936 *The Constitutional History of the United States,* by Andrew C. McLaughlin

1937 *The Flowering of New England,* by Van Wyck Brooks

1938 *The Road to Reunion, 1865–1900* by Paul Herman Buck

1939 *A History of American Magazines* by Frank Luther Mott

1940 *Abraham Lincoln: The War Years,* by Carl Sandburg

1941 *The Atlantic Migration, 1607–1860, by Marcus Lee* Hansen

1942 *Reveille in Washington,* by Margaret Leech

1943 *Paul Revere and the World He Lived In,* by Esther Forbes

1944 *The Growth of American Thought,* by Merle Curti

1945 *Unfinished Business,* by Stephen Bonsal

1946 *The Age of Jackson,* by Arthur M. Schlesinger, Jr.

1947 *Scientists Against Time,* by James Phinney Baxter III

1948 *Across the Wide Missouri,* by Bernard DeVoto

1949 *The Disruption of American Democracy,* by Roy Franklin Nichols

1950 *Art and Life in America,* by Oliver W. Larkin

1951 *The Old Northwest: Pioneer Period, 1815–1840,* by R. Carlyle Buley

1952 *The Uprooted,* by Oscar Handlin

1953 *The Era of Good Feelings,* by George Dangerfield

1954 *A Stillness at Appomattox,* by Bruce Catton

1955 *Great River: The Rio Grande in North American History,* by Paul Horgan

1956 *The Age of Reform,* by Richard Hofstadter

1957 *Russia Leaves the War: Soviet-American Relations, 1917–1920,* by George F. Kennan

1958 *Banks and Politics in America—From the Revolution to the Civil War,* by Bray Hammond

1959 *The Republican Era: 1869–1901,* by Leonard D. White, with the assistance of Jean Schneider

1960 *In the Days of McKinley,* by Margaret Leech

1961 *Between War and Peace: The Potsdam Conference,* by Herbert Feis

1962 *The Triumphant Empire: Thunder-Clouds Gather in the West 1763-1766,* by Lawrence H. Gipson

1963 *Washington: Village and Capital, 1800–1878,* by Constance McLaughlin Green

1964 *Puritan Village: The Formation of a New England Town,* by Sumner Chilton Powell

1965 *The Greenback Era,* by Irwin Unger

1966 *Life of the Mind in America From the Revolution to the Civil War,* by Perry Miller

1967 *Exploration and Empire,* by William H. Goetzmann

1968 *The Ideological Origins of the American Revolution,* by Bernard Bailyn

1969 *Origins of the Fifth Amendment,* by Leonard W. Levy

1970 *Present at the Creation: My Years in the State Department,* by Dean Acheson

1971 *Roosevelt: The Soldier of Freedom,* by James MacGregor Burns

1972 *Neither Black Nor White,* by Carl M. Degler

1973 *People of Paradox: An Inquiry Concerning the Origin of American Civilization,* by Michael Kammen

1974 *The Americans,* by Daniel J. Boorstin

1975 *Jefferson and His Time,* by Dumas Malone

1976 *Lamy of Santa Fe,* by Paul Horgan

1977 *The Impending Crisis,* by David M. Potter

1978 *The Invisible Hand: The Managerial Revolution in American Business,* by Alfred D. Chandler

1979 *The Dred Scott Case,* by Don E. Fehrenbacher

1980 *Been in the Storm So Long: The Aftermath of Slavery,* by Leon F. Litwack

1981 *American Education: The National Experience 1783-1876,* Lawrence A. Cremin

PRIZES IN LETTERS

FICTION

1918 *His Family,* by Ernest Poole

1919 *The Magnificent Ambersons,* by Booth Tarkington

1921 *The Age of Innocence,* by Edith Wharton

1922 *Alice Adams,* by B. Tarkington

1923 *One of Ours,* by Willa Cather

1924 *The Able McLaughlins,* by Margaret Wilson

1925 *So Big,* by Edna Ferber

1926 *Arrowsmith,* by S. Lewis

1927 *Early Autumn,* by Louis Bromfield

1928 *The Bridge of San Luis Rey,* by Thornton Wilder

1929 *Scarlet Sister Mary,* by Julia Peterkin

1930 *Laughing Boy,* by Oliver La-Farge

1931 *Years of Grace,* by Margaret Ayer Barnes

1932 *The Good Earth,* by Pearl S. Buck

1933 *The Store,* by T. S. Stribling

1934 *Lamb in His Bosom,* by Caroline Miller

1935 *Now in November,* by Josephine Winslow Johnson

1936 *Honey in the Horn,* by Harold L. Davis

1937 *Gone With the Wind,* by Margaret Mitchell

1938 *The Late George Apley,* by John Phillips Marquand

1939 *The Yearling,* by Marjorie Kinnan Rawlings

1940 *The Grapes of Wrath,* by John Steinbeck

1942 *In This Our Life,* by Ellen Glasgow

1943 *Dragon's Teeth,* by Upton Sinclair

1944 *Journey in the Dark,* by Martin Flavin

1945 *A Bell for Adano,* by John Hersey

1947 *All the King's Men,* by Robert Penn Warren

1948 *Tales of the South Pacific,* by James A. Michener

1949 *Guard of Honor,* by James Gould Cozzens

1950 *The Way West,* by A. B. Guthrie, Jr.

1951 *The Town,* by Conrad Richter

1952 *The Caine Mutiny,* by Herman Wouk

1953 *The Old Man and the Sea,* by Ernest Hemingway

1955 *A Fable,* by Wm. Faulkner

1956 *Andersonville,* by MacKinlay Kantor

1958 *A Death in the Family,* by James Agee

1959 *The Travels of Jaimie McPheeters,* by Robert Lewis Taylor

1960 *Advise and Consent,* by Allen Drury

1961 *To Kill a Mockingbird,* by Harper Lee

1962 *The Edge of Sadness,* by Edwin O'Connor

1963 *The Reivers,* by Wm. Faulkner

1965 *The Keepers of the House,* by Shirley Ann Grau

1966 *Collected Short Stories,* by Katherine Ann Porter

1967 *The Fixer,* by Bernard Malamud

1968 *The Confessions of Nat Turner,* by William Styron

1969 *House Made of Dawn,* by M. Scott Momaday

1970 *Collected Stories,* by Jean Stafford

1972 *Angel of Repose,* by Wallace Stegner

1973 *The Optimist's Daughter,* by Eudora Welty

1975 *The Killer Angels,* by Michael Shaara

1976 *Humboldt's Gift,* by Saul Bellow

1978 *Elbow Room,* by James Allan McPherson

1979 *The Stories of John Cheever*

1980 *The Executioner's Song,* by Norman Mailer

1981 *A Confederacy of Dunces,* by John Kennedy Toole

POETRY

1918 *Love Songs,* by Sara Teasdale

1919 *Old Road to Paradise,* by Margaret Widdemer

1919 *Corn Huskers,* by Carl Sandburg

1922 *Collected Poems,* by Edwin Arlington Robinson

1923 *The Ballad of the Harp-Weaver; A Few Figs from Thistles; eight sonnets in American Poetry, 1922, A Miscellany,* by Edna St. Vincent Millay

1924 *New Hampshire: A Poem with Notes and Grace Notes,* by Robert Frost

1925 *The Man Who Died Twice,* by Edwin Arlington Robinson

1926 *What's O'Clock,* by Amy Lowell

1927 *Fiddler's Farewell,* by Leonora Speyer

1928 *Tristram,* by Edwin Arlington Robinson

1929 *John Brown's Body,* by Stephen Vincent Benét

1930 *Selected Poems,* by Conrad Aiken

1931 *Collected Poems,* by Robert Frost

1932 *The Flowering Stone,* by George Dillon

1933 *Conquistador,* by Archibald MacLeish

1934 *Collected Verse,* by Robert Hillyer

1935 *Bright Ambush,* by Audrey Wurdemann

1936 *Strange Holiness,* by Robert P. Tristram Coffin

1937 *A Further Range,* by Robert Frost

1938 *Cold Morning Sky,* by Marya Zaturenska

1939 *Selected Poems,* by John Gould Fletcher

1940 *Collected Poems,* by Mark Van Doren

1941 *Sunderland Capture,* by Leonard Bacon

1942 *The Dust Which Is God,* by William Rose Benét

1943 *A Witness Tree,* by Robert Frost

1944 *Western Star,* by Stephen Vincent Benét

1945 *V-Letter and Other Poems,* by Karl Shapiro

1947 *Lord Weary's Castle,* by Robert Lowell

1948 *The Age of Anxiety*, by W. H. Auden
1949 *Terror and Decorum*, by Peter Viereck
1950 *Annie Allen*, by Gwendolyn Brooks
1951 *Complete Poems*, by Carl Sandburg
1952 *Collected Poems*, by Marianne Moore
1953 *Collected Poems 1917–1952*, by Archibald MacLeish
1954 *The Waking, Poem 1933-1953*, by Theodore Roethke
1955 *Collected Poems*, by Wallace Stevens
1956 *Poems—North & South*, by Elizabeth Bishop
1957 *Things of This World*, by Richard Wilbur
1958 *Promises: Poems 1954–56*, by Robert Penn Warren
1959 *Selected Poems 1928–1958*, by Stanley Kunitz
1960 *Heart's Needle*, by W. D. Snodgrass
1961 *Times Three: Selected Verse from Three Decades*, by Phyllis McGinley
1962 *Poems*, by Alan Dugan
1963 *Pictures from Breughel*, by William Carlos Williams
1964 *At the End of the Open Road*, by Louis Simpson
1965 *77 Dream Songs*, by John Berryman
1966 *Selected Poems*, by Richard Eberhart
1967 *Live or Die*, by Anne Sexton
1968 *The Hard Hours*, by A. Hecht
1969 *Of Being Numerous*, by George Oppen
1970 *Untitled Subjects*, by Richard Howard
1971 *The Carrier of Ladders*, by William S. Merwin
1972 *Collected Poems*, by James Wright
1973 *Up Country*, by Maxine Winokur Kumin
1974 *The Dolphin*, by R. Lowell
1975 *Turtle Island*, by G. Snyder
1976 *Self-Portrait in a Convex Mirror*, by John Ashbery
1977 *Divine Comedies*, by James Merrill
1978 *Collected Poems*, by Howard Nemerov
1979 *Now and Then*, by Robert Penn Warren
1980 *Selected Poems*, by Donald Rodney Justice
1981 *The Morning of the Poem*, by James Schuyler

GENERAL NONFICTION

1962 *The Making of the President 1960*, by Theodore H. White
1963 *The Guns of August*, by Barbara W. Tuchman
1964 *Anti-intellectualism in American Life*, by R. Hofstadter
1965 *O Strange New World*, by Howard Mumford Jones
1966 *Wandering Through Winter*, by Edwin Way Teale
1967 *The Problem of Slavery in Western Culture*, by David Brion Davis
1968 *The Story of Civilization* (Volume X), by Will and Ariel Durant
1969 *So Human An Animal*, by Rene Jules Dubos
The Armies of the Night, by Norman Mailer

1970 *Gandhi's Truth*, by Erik H. Erikson
1971 *The Rising Sun*, by John Toland
1972 *Stilwell and the American Experience in China, 1911–1945*, by Barbara Tuchman
1973 *Fire in the Lake: The Vietnamese and the Americans in Vietnam*, by Frances Fitz-Gerald, and *Children of Crisis*, by Dr. Robert Coles
1974 *The Denial of Death*, by Ernest Becker
1975 *Pilgrim at Tinker Creek*, by Annie Dillard
1976 *Why Survive? Being Old in America*, by Robert N. Butler
1977 *Beautiful Swimmers: Watermen, Crabs and the Chesapeake Bay*, by William W. Warner
1978 *The Dragons of Eden*, by Carl Sagan
1979 *On Human Nature*, by Edward O. Wilson
1980 *Godel, Escher, Bach: An Eternal Golden Braid*, by Douglas R. Hofstadter
1981 *Fin-de-Siecle Vienna: Politics and Culture*, by Carl E. Schorske

CRITICISM/COMMENTARY

1970 Ada Louise Huxtable of *The New York Times* for distinguished architecture criticism
Marquis Childs of the *St. Louis (Mo.) Post-Dispatch* for distinguished commentary from Washington, D.C.
1971 Harold C. Schonberg, *The New York Times'* senior music critic
William A. Caldwell, *The [Hackensack, N.J.] Record*, for "Simeon Stylites," a column on local affairs, written daily for more than 40 years.
1972 Frank Peters, Jr., *St. Louis (Mo.) Post Dispatch*
1973 Ronald Powers, *Chicago Sun-Times* and David S. Broder, *Washington Post*
1974 Emily Genauer, *Newday*
Edwin A. Roberts, *National Observer*
1975 Mary McGrory, *The Washington Star* and Roger Ebert, *Chicago Sun Times*
1976 Alan M. Kriegsman, *The Washington [D.C.] Post*
Walter W. (Red) Smith, *The New York Times*
1977 William McPherson, *The Washington Post*; George F. Will, Washington Post Writers Group
1978 Walter Kerr, *The New York Times*; William Safire, *The New York Times*
1979 Paul Gapp, *The Chicago Tribune*; Russell Baker, *The New York Times*
1980 William A. Henry III, *The Boston Globe*; Ellen H. Goodman, *The Boston Globe*
1981 Jonathan Yardley, book review editor, *The Washington [D.C.] Star*; Dave Anderson, sports columnist, *The New York Times*

SPECIAL CITATIONS

1944 *Oklahoma!*, by Richard Rodgers and Oscar Hammerstein II

1957 Kenneth Roberts, a special citation for his historical novels which long contributed to the creation of greater interest in early American history
1960 Garrett Mattingly for *The Armada*
1961 *American Heritage Picture History of the Civil War*
1973 *George Washington*, by James Thomas Flexner
1976 Scott Joplin, for his contributions to American music
1977 Alex Haley for *Roots*
1978 E. B. White for his contributions to *The New Yorker* and his general enrichment of the American language

PRIZES IN MUSIC

1943 William Schuman: *Secular Cantata No. 2, A Free Song*
1944 Howard Hanson: *Symphony No. 4, Opus 34*
1945 Aaron Copland: *Appalachian Spring*
1946 Leo Sowerby: *The Canticle of the Sun*
1947 Charles Ives: *Symph. No. 3*
1948 Walter Piston: *Symph. No. 3*
1949 Virgil Thomson: *Louisiana Story*
1950 Gian-Carlo Menotti: *The Consul*
1951 Douglas S. Moore: *Giants in the Earth*
1952 Gail Kubik: *Symphony Concertante*
1954 Quincy Porter: *Concerto for Two Pianos and Orchestra*
1955 Gian-Carlo Menotti: *The Saint of Bleecker Street*
1956 Ernst Toch: *Symphony No. 3*
1957 Norman Dello Joio: *Meditations on Ecclesiastes*
1958 Samuel Barber: the score of *Vanessa*
1959 John La Montaine: *Concerto for Piano and Orchestra*
1960 Elliott Carter: *Second String Quartet*
1961 Walter Piston: *Symph. No. 7*
1962 Robert Ward: *The Crucible*
1963 Samuel Barber: *Piano Concerto No. 1*
1966 Leslie Bassett: *Variations for Orchestra*
1967 Leon Kirchner: *Quartet No. 3*
1968 George Crumb: *Echoes of Time and the River*
1969 Karel Husa: *String Quartet No. 3*
1970 Charles W. Wuorinen: *Time's Encomium*
1971 Mario Davidovsky: *Synchronisms No. 6 for Piano and Electronic Sound*
1972 Jacob Druckman: *Windows*
1973 Elliot Carter: *String Quartet No. 3*
1974 Donald Martino: *Notturno*
1975 Dominick Argento: *From the Diary of Virginia Wolff*
1976 Ned Rorem: *Air Music*
1977 Richard Wernick: *Visions of Terror and Wonder*
1978 Michael Colgrass: *Déja Vu for Percussion Quartet and Orchestra*
1979 Joseph Schwantner: *Aftertones of Infinity*
1980 David Del Tredici: *In Memory of a Summer Day*

OTHER PRIZES AND AWARDS

ACHIEVEMENT

ALL-AMERICA CITIES AWARD PROGRAM (1980-81) for Community Involvement Through Citizen Action, sponsored by the National Municipal League:

Akron, Ohio; Cincinnati, Ohio; Colorado Springs, Colorado; Fergus Falls, Minnesota; Grand Rapids, Michigan; Kotzebue, Alaska; Rochester, New York; Sunnyvale, California; Wichita Falls, Texas; Worcester, Massachusetts.

WOMEN OF THE YEAR AWARDS (1979) for outstanding achievement by women in their fields, presented by *Ladies' Home Journal* magazine:

Women of the Decade (selected by *Journal* readers from past recipients): Marian Anderson; Joan Ganz Cooney; Betty Ford; Helen Hayes; Katherine Hepburn; Barbara Jordan; Elisabeth Kubler-Ross; Sylvia Porter; Beverly Sills; Barbara Walters; Margaret Mead (Posthumous award).

PUBLIC SERVICE

AMERICAN JEWISH COMMITTEE (1981):

Herbert H. Lehman Award in Human Relations: Laurence A. Tisch

MEDALS OF FREEDOM awarded by the President of the United States, for exceptionally meritorious contributions to national security, world peace, or to cultural or other significant public or private endeavors. The most recent recipients are:

Roger Baldwin, founder of the American Civil Liberties Union

Harold Brown, U.S. Secretary of Defense

Zbigniew Brzezinski, White House national security adviser

Warren M. Christopher, Deputy Secretary of State

Walter Cronkite, CBS Television News anchorman

Kirk Douglas, actor

Margaret Craig McNamara, educator and founder of Reading Is Fundamental

Dr. Karl Menninger, noted psychiatrist

Edmund S. Muskie, U.S. Secetary of State

Esther Peterson, special presidential assistant for consumer affairs

Gerald C. Smith, U.S. Ambassador at Large and former director of the Arms Control and Disarmament Agency

Robert S. Strauss, special U.S. trade envoy and past chairman of the Democratic National Committee

Judge Elbert Parr Tuttle, Justice of the U.S. Court of Appeals for the Fifth District

Andrew Young, chief U.S. representative to the United Nations

Earl Warren (dec.), Chief Justice of the U.S. Supreme Court, 1953-1969

TEACHER OF THE YEAR (1981) awarded by the Chief State School Officers, the *Encyclopaedia Britannica*, and *Good Housekeeping* magazine: Mr. Jay Sommer, New Rochelle, New York

SCIENCE

NATIONAL ACADEMY OF SCIENCES AWARDS (1981):

Arctowski Medal: Thomas M. Donahue

John J. Carty Medal: Sing-tung Yau

Arthur L. Day Prize and Lecturship: Gerald J. Wasserburg

Richard Lounsbery Award for Biology and Medicine: Philip Leder

James Murray Luck Award: John S. Chipman

N.A.S. Award in Chemical Sciences: Bruno H. Zimm

N.A.S. Award for Inititatives in Research: Gary D. Patterson

N.A.S. Public Welfare Medal: Russell E. Train

Robertson Memorial Lecture: Stanley Cohen

U.S. Steel Foundation Award in Molecular Biology: Ronald W. Davis and Gerald R. Fink

NATIONAL MEDAL OF SCIENCE, the highest award for outstanding achievement in science and engineering in the United States (1979):

Robert H. Burris, Madison, Wisconsin

Elizabeth Crosby, Ann Arbor, Michigan

Joseph L. Doob, Urbana, Illinois

Richard P. Feynman, Pasadena, California

Donald E. Knuth, Stanford, California

Arthur Kornberg, Stanford, California

Emmett Leith, Ann Arbor, Michigan

Herman F. Mark, Brooklyn, New York

Raymond D. Mindlin, New York, New York

Robert N. Noyce, Santa Clara, California

Severo Ochoa, Nutley, New Jersey

Earl R. Parker, Berkeley, California

Edward M. Purcell, Cambridge, Massachusetts

Simon Ramo, Cleveland, Ohio

John H. Sinfelt, Linden, New Jersey

Lyman Spitzer, Jr., Princeton, New Jersey

Earl R. Stadtman, Bethesda, Maryland

George L. Stebbins, Jr., Davis, California

Paul A. Weiss, New York, New York

Victor F. Weisskopf, Cambridge, Massachusetts

WESTINGHOUSE SCIENCE TALENT SEARCH (1981): high school student scholarship competition conducted by Science Service, Inc., sponsored by Westinghouse Educational Foundation and the Westinghouse Corporation:

$12,000:	Amy Sue Reichel. New York, N.Y.
$10,000:	Douglas Anthony Simons, Vero Beach, Fla.
	Michael Morgan Dowling, Newington, Conn.
$7,500:	Song Tan, Miami, Fla.
	Joel Martin Wein, New York, N.Y.
	Terence David Sanger, New York, N.Y.
$5,000:	Lori Ellen Kaplowitz, Woodmere, N.Y.
	Seth Steven Finkelstein, Bronx, N.Y.
	Mark Lewis Movsesian, Forest Hills, N.Y.
	William I-Wei Chang, Fresh Meadows, N.Y.

JOURNALISM

GEORGE POLK AWARDS (1981) sponsored by Long Island University:

Foreign Reporting: Shirley Christian, *Miami Herald*

National Reporting: Jonathan Neumann and Ted Gup, *Washington Post*

Political Reporting: Bill Moyers, "Bill Moyers' Journal," WNET-TV, New York

Television Reporting—National: Charles Kuralt, CBS News

Television Reporting—Local: Stephen Talbot and Jonathan Dann, KQED-TV, San Francisco, Calif.

NIEMAN FELLOWSHIPS (1981-82) for working Journalists—(Harvard University):

Margot Adler; Christopher Bogan; Peter Brown; Anita Harris; Alexander Jones; Gerald Jordan; Fay Smulevitz Joyce; Johanna Neuman; Steven Oney; Judith Rosenfield; Edward Walsh

SIGMA DELTA CHI AWARDS (1980) for distinguished service in print and broadcast journalism:

Newspapers:

General Reporting: News staff of the Longview, Washington *Daily News*

Editorial Writing: Louis J. Salome, William Hallstrom and Betsy Poller, *The Miami News*

Washington Correspondence: Joseph Albright, Cox Newspapers

Foreign Correspondence: Edward Girardet, *Christian Science Monitor*

News Photography: Giovanni Foggia, The Associated Press

Editorial Cartoon: Paul Conrad, *The Los Angeles Times*

Public Service: The Longbeach, California *Independent, Press-Telegram*

Magazines:

Reporting: Penny Lernoux, *The Nation*

Public Service: *Philadelphia Magazine*

Radio:

Reporting: WHDH Radio News, Boston, Mass.

Public Service: WIND Radio, Chicago, Ill.

Editorializing: Lesley Crosson, WEEI, Boston, Mass.

Television:

Reporting: Bill Blakemore and Greg Dobbs, ABC-TV News

Public Service: KSL, Salt Lake City, Utah

Editorializing: Bill Moyers, WNET, New York, N.Y.

Research About Journalism: John Lofton, St. Louis, Mo.

ARTS

AMERICAN ACADEMY AND INSTITUTE OF ARTS AND LETTERS AWARDS (1981):

Academy-Institute Gold Medals: Malcolm Cowley (Belles Lettres and Criticism), Raphael Soyer (Painting)

ACADEMY-INSTITUTE AWARDS:

In Literature: Louise Glück, Gail Godwin, Howard Frank Mosher, James Salter, Elizabeth Sewell, William Stafford, Hilma Wolitzer, Jay Wright

In Art: John Duff, Friedel Dzubas, Mimi Gross, Leo Manso, Jane Wilson

In Music: Edwin Dugger, Robert Erickson, Meyer Kupferman, Ursula Mamlok

SPECIAL AWARDS:

American Academy in Rome Fellowship in Creative Writing: Edward Field

Arnold W. Brunner Memorial Prize in Architecture: Gunnar Birkerts

Witter Bynner Prize for Poetry: Allen Grossman

Charles Ives Scholarships: Tamar Diesendruck, Allen Gimbel, Thomas Allen LeVines, William Neil, Russell F. Pinkston, Daniel C. Warner

Charles Ives Award: The Charles Ives Society

Sue Kaufman Prize for First Fiction: Tom Lorenz

Goddard Lieberson Fellowship: Chinary Ung

The Loines Award for Poetry: Ben Belitt

The Award of Merit Medal for Drama: John Guare

Richard and Hinda Rosenthal Foundation Awards: Fiction—Jerome Charyn; Painting—Alean Magee

Harold D. Vursell Memorial Award: Edward Hoagland

Marjorie Peabody Waite Award: Norman Lockwood

Morton Dauwen Zabel Award: Guy Davenport

Award for Distinguished Service to the Arts: Joseph Papp

Medal for Spoken Language on the Stage: James Earl Jones

Art

NATIONAL ACADEMY OF DESIGN PRIZES (1981):

Benjamin Altman Prizes: Landscape—Karl Schrag ($3,000); Anne Poor ($1,500); Figure—Lennart Anderson ($3,000); Paul Georges ($1,500)

Emil and Dines Carlsen Award: Alfred Chadbourn ($1,000)

Andrew Carnegie Prize: Francis Speight ($1,000)

Edward Palmer Memorial Prize: James Lechay ($2,000)

Adolph and Clara Obrig Prize: Jack Levine ($600)

Thomas B. Clarke Prize: Mary Beth McKenzie ($500)

Grumbacher Art Award and Gold Medal: Balcomb Greene ($200)

Paul Puzinas Memorial Award: Stephen Greene ($200)

Isaac N. Maynard Prize: May Stevens ($150)

Gladys Emerson Cook Prize: Carl N. Titolo ($100)

S.J. Wallace Truman Prize: Anthony Martino ($850)

Julius Hallgarten Prizes: Gilbert Riou ($400); Charles Pfahl ($300); Phyllis Herfield ($200)

Certificates of Merit: Herman Rose

Sculpture Awards:

Artists Fund Prize: Bruno Lucchesi ($400)

Dessie Greer Prize: Philip Grausman ($100)

N.A.D. Gold Medal: Richard M. Miller

Elizabeth N. Watrous Gold Medal: Anthony Padovano ($350)

Thomas R. Proctor Prize: Robert White ($500)

Ellin P. Speyer Prize: John E. Nordin ($400)

Leslie Gardin Sawyer Prize: Michael Moser ($50)

Certificates of Merit: Calvin Albert; George Segal; Nina Winkel

Graphic Art Awards:

Anonymous Prize: Gerry Hamzik ($100)

Cannon Prize: Bernard Brussel-Smith ($400)

Ralph Fabri Prize: Sigmund Abeles ($200)

William H. Leavin Prize: Olivia Koopalethes ($100)

Helen M. Loggie Prize: Toni Herrick ($50)

Leo Meissner Prize: Robert Kipniss ($200)

Certificates of Merit: Lindsay Barrett; Penny Feder; Lynn Shaler

Watercolor Awards:

Walter Biggs Memorial Award: Virginia Cobb ($200)

Adolph and Clara Obrig Prizes: Serge Hollerbach ($450); Dale Meyers ($300)

William A. Paton Prize: Jeffrey Kronsnoble ($1,000)

Certificates of Merit: Walter Brook; Wes Carlson; Claus Hoie, Walter Du Bois Richards, Lee Weiss

Literature

AMERICAN BOOKSELLERS ASSOCIATION AWARD (1981):

Irita Van Doren Award: The New York Times Book Review

BANCROFT PRIZES (1981) presented by Columbia University for books of exceptional merit and distinction in American history (including biography) and diplomacy:

Ronald Steel, *Walter Lippman and the American Century*

Jean Strouse, *Alice James: A Biography*

THE BOLLINGEN PRIZE IN POETRY (1979-80) an award of $5,000 given by Yale University Library: Howard Nemerov, May Swenson

THE AMERICAN BOOK AWARDS (1981) sponsored by the Association of American Publishers:

General Fiction: *Plains Song,* Wright Morris

General Nonfiction: *China Men,* Maxine Hong Kingston

Biography: *Walt Whitman,* Justin Kaplan

History: *Christianity, Social Tolerance and Homosexuality,* John Boswell

First Novel: *Sister Wolf,* Ann Arensberg

Poetry: *The Need to Hold Still,* Lisa Mueller

Children's Books: *The Night Swimmers,* Betsy Byars (Fiction); *Oh, Boy! Babies,* Alison Craigin Herzig and Jane Lawrence Mali (Nonfiction)

Translation: *The Letters of Gustave Flaubert 1830-1857,* translated by Francis Steelmuller; Arno Schmidt's *Evening Edged in Gold,* translated by John E. Woods

National Medal for Literature: Kenneth Burke

NEWBERY-CALDECOTT MEDALS (1981) presented by the American Library Association for the most distinguished American books in the children's field:

John Newbery Medal: *Jacob Have I Loved,* Katherine Paterson, author

Randolph Caldecott Medal: *Fables,* Arnold Loebel, illustrator

POETRY SOCIETY OF AMERICA PRIZES (1981):

Gordon Barber Memorial Award: Alice Wirth Gray, Grace Morton (shared)

Melville Cane Award: Paul H. Fry, *The Poet's Calling in the English Ode*

Gertrude B. Claytor Memorial Award: Marcia Falk

Gustav Davidson Memorial Award: Gary Miranda

Mary Carolyn Davies Memorial Award: Edmund Pennant

Alice Fay di Castagnola Award: Carolyn Forché

Emily Dickinson Award: Alice Fulton

Consuelo Ford Award: Erika Mumford

Cecil Hemley Memorial Award: Isabel Nathaniel

Elias Lieberman Student Poetry Award: Faith Adielé

John Masefield Memorial Award: R. T. Smith

Alfred Kreymborg Memorial Award: Edmund Pennant

Shelley Memorial Award: Robert Creeley

Celia B. Wagner Award: Gail Mazur, Geneva Emily Nicholson (shared)

William Carlos Williams Award: *Praise,* by Robert Hass

Lucille Medwick Memorial Award: Phyllis Janowitz

Witter Bynner Poetry Translation Prize: Czeslaw Milosz and Lillian Vallee, *Bells in Winter*

Witter Bynner Grant-In-Aid: Stephen Mitchell; Grace Schulman; Clayton Eschelman and Annette J. Smith (shared)

Music

GRAMMY AWARDS (1980) given by the National Academy of Recording Arts and Sciences:

Record of the Year: "Sailing" (Christopher Cross)

Album of the Year: "Sailing" (Christopher Cross)

Song of the Year: "Sailing" (Christopher Cross)

Best New Artist of the Year: Christopher Cross

Best Pop Vocal Performance, Female: "The Rose" (Bette Midler)

Best Pop Vocal Performance, Male: "This Is It" (Kenny Loggins)

Best Pop Vocal Performance, Duo or Group: "Guilty" (Barbra Streisand and Barry Gibb)

Best Pop Instrumental Performance: "One on One" (Bob James and Earl Klugh)

Best Rock Vocal Performance, Female: "Crimes of Passion" (Pat Benatar)

Best Rock Vocal Performance, Male: "Glass Houses" (Billy Joel)

Best Rock Vocal Performance, Group: "Against the Wind" (Bob Seger and the Silver Bullet Band)

Best Rock Instrumental Performance: "Reggatta De Blanc" (Police)

Best Jazz Vocal Performance: Female—"A Perfect Match" (Ella Fitzgerald); Male—"Moody's Mood" (George Benson)

Best Jazz Instrumental Performance, Soloist: "I Will Say Goodbye" (Bill Evans)

Best Jazz Instrumental Performance, Group: "We Will Meet Again" (Bill Evans)

Best Jazz Instrumental Performance, Big Band: "On the Road" (Count Basie)

Best Rhythm & Blues Vocal Performance, Female: "Never Knew Love Like This Before" (Stephanie Mills)

Best Rhythm & Blues Vocal Performance, Male: "Give Me the Night" (George Benson)

Best Rhythm & Blues Instrumental Performance: "Off Broadway" (George Benson)

Best Rhythm & Blues Song: "Never Knew Love Like This Before" (Reggie Lucas and James Mtume, songwriters)

Best Gospel Performance, Contemporary or Inspirational: "The Lord's Prayer" (Reba Rambo, Dony McGuire, B. J. Thomas, Andrae Crouch, The Archers, Walter and Tramaine Hawkins, and Cynthia Clawson)

Best Country Song: "On the Road Again" (Willie Nelson, songwriter)

Best Country Vocal Performance, Female: "Could I Have This Dance" (Anne Murray)

Best Country Vocal Performance, Male: "He Stopped Lovin' Her Today" (George Jones)

Best Country Vocal Performance, Duo or Group: "The Lovin' You Feelin' Again" (Roy Orbison and Emmylou Harris)

Best Country Instrumental Performance: "Orange Blossom Special/Hoedown" ("Urban Cowboy" Band)

Best Recording for Children: "In Harmony/A Sesame Street Record" (Lucy Simon and David Levine, producer)

Best Comedy Recording: "No Respect" (Rodney Dangerfield)

Best Cast Show Album: "Evita—Premier American Recording" (Andrew Lloyd Webber, composer; Tim Rice, lyricist)

Best Classical Album: "Berg: Lulu (complete version)" (Pierre Boulez, conductor; Guenther Breest amd Michael Howarth, producers)

Best Opera Recording: "Berg: Lulu (complete version)" (Pierre Boulez, conductor; Guenther Breest and Michael Howarth, producers)

Televison and Radio

EMMY AWARDS (1980-81): major awards presented by the Academy of Television Arts and Sciences:

Drama Series

Actor: Daniel J. Travanti, "Hill Street Blues"

Actress: Barbara Babcock, "Hill Street Blues"

Supporting actor: Michael Conrad, "Hill Street Blues"

Supporting actress: Nancy Marchand, "Lou Grant"

Directing: Robert Butler, "Hill Street Blues"

Writing: Michael Kozoll and Steven Bochco, "Hill Street Blues"

Best series: "Hill Street Blues"

Comedy Series

Actor: Judd Hirsch, "Taxi"

Actress: Isabel Sanford, "The Jeffersons"

Supporting actor: Danny De Vito, "Taxi"

Supporting actress: Eileen Brennan, "Private Benjamin"

Directing: James Burrows, "Taxi"

Writing: Michael Leeson, "Taxi"

Best series: "Taxi"

Limited Series or Specials

Actor: Anthony Hopkins, "The Bunker"

Actress: Vanessa Redgrave, "Playing for Time"

Supporting actor: David Warner, "Masada"

Supporting actress: Jane Alexander, "Playing for Time"

Best series: "Shogun"

Special (Drama): "Playing for Time"

Special (Comedy or Variety): "Lily: Sold Out," starring Lily Tomlin

1980 GEORGE FOSTER PEABODY BROADCASTING AWARDS

Radio

NBC Radio, New York City: "The Hallelujah Caucus," a Source Report

Minnesota Public Radio, St. Paul: "A Praire Home Companion"

WNCN Radio, New York City: Overall Station Performance, exemplified by "Conversations with Horowitz"

National Public Radio, Washington, D.C.: "Jazz Alive!"

Canadian Broadcasting Corporation: "The Wonderful World of Science"; "Peniel," from the "Hornby Collection" series

San Francisco Opera, San Francisco: San Francisco Opera Radio Broadcasts

Studs Terkel, WFMT Radio, Chicago, Ill.

Television

CBS News, New York City: "Universe"

Mary Nissenson, WTVJ, Miami, Fla.: "Poland: Changing Nation"

CBS Entertainment, New York City: "Gideon's Trumpet"

NBC and Paramount Televison: "Shogun"

Sol Taishoff, Editor, *Broadcasting* magazine

Public Broadcasting Service and Robert Geller, executive producer: "The American Short Story" series

ABC-TV, New York City: "IBM Presents Baryshnikov on Broadway"

Elaine Green, WCPO-TV, Cincinnati, Ohio: "Hoskins Interview"

ABC-TV, New York City: "Amber Waves"

CBS Entertainment, New York City: "Playing for Time"

British Broadcasting Corporation: "All Creatures Great and Small" (James Herriot)

Carroll O'Conner, CBS: for "Edith's Death," an episode of "Archie Bunker's Place"

KCET, Adrian Malone, and Carl Sagan: "Cosmos"

Maryland Instructional Television, Owings Mills: "Terra: Our World"

WQED and the National Geographic Society: National Geographic Specials "Mysteries of the Mind," "The Superliners: Twilight of an Era," and "The Invisible World"

KTEH, Carol Mon Pere and Sandra Nichols: "The Battle of Westlands"

Phil Donohue, host: "The Phil Donohue Show"

KQED-TV, San Francisco: "Broken Arrow: Can A Nuclear Weapons Accident Happen Here?"

KUED-TV, Salt Lake City and WNET-TV, New York City: "The MX Debate," on "Bill Moyers' Journal"

Walter Cronkite, CBS News

ACADEMY AWARD WINNERS

Year	Best Picture	Best Actor	Supporting Actor	Best Actress	Supporting Actress	Best Director
1980	"Ordinary People"	Robert De Niro "Raging Bull"	Timothy Hutton "Ordinary People"	Sissy Spacek "Coal Miner's Daughter"	Mary Steenburgen "Melvin & Howard"	Robert Redford "Ordinary People"
1979	"Kramer vs. Kramer"	Dustin Hoffman "Kramer vs. Kramer"	Melvyn Douglas "Being There"	Sally Field "Norma Rae"	Meryl Streep "Kramer vs. Kramer"	Robert Benton "Kramer vs. Kramer"
1978	"The Deer Hunter"	Jon Voight "Coming Home"	Christopher Walken "The Deer Hunter"	Jane Fonda "Coming Home"	Maggie Smith "California Suite"	Michael Cimino "The Deer Hunter"
1977	"Annie Hall"	Richard Dreyfuss "The Goodbye Girl"	Jason Robards "Julia"	Diane Keaton "Annie Hall"	Vanessa Redgrave "Julia"	Woody Allen "Annie Hall"
1976	"Rocky"	Peter Finch "Network"	Jason Robards "All the President's Men"	Faye Dunaway "Network"	Beatrice Straight "Network"	John G. Avildsen "Rocky"
1975	"One Flew Over the Cuckoo's Nest"	Jack Nicholson "One Flew Over the Cuckoo's Nest"	George Burns "The Sunshine Boys"	Louise Fletcher "One Flew Over the Cuckoo's Nest	Lee Grant "Shampoo"	Milos Forman "One Flew Over the Cuckoo's Nest"
1974	"The Godfather, Part II"	Art Carney "Harry and Tonto"	Robert DeNiro "The Godfather, Part II"	Ellyn Burstyn "Alice Doesn't Live Here Anymore"	Ingrid Bergman "Murder on the Orient Express"	Francis Ford Coppola "The Godfather, Part II"
1973	"The Sting"	Jack Lemmon "Save the Tiger"	John Houseman "The Paper Chase"	Glenda Jackson 'A Touch of Class"	Tatum O'Neal "Paper Moon"	George Roy Hill "The Sting"
1972	"The Godfather"	Marlon Brando "The Godfather"	Joel Grey "Cabaret"	Liza Minnelli "Cabaret"	Eileen Heckart "Butterflies Are Free"	Bob Fosse "Cabaret"
1971	"The French Connection"	Gene Hackman "The French Connection"	Ben Johnson "The Last Picture Show"	Jane Fonda "Klute"	Cloris Leachman "The Last Picture Show"	William Friedkin "The French Connection"
1970	"Patton"	George C. Scott "Patton"	John Mills "Ryan's Daughter"	Glenda Jackson "Women in Love"	Helen Hayes "Airport"	Franklin Schaffner "Patton"
1969	"Midnight Cowboy"	John Wayne "True Grit"	Gig Young "They Shoot Horses, Don't They?"	Maggie Smith "The Prime of Miss Jean Brodie"	Goldie Hawn "Cactus Flower"	John Schlesinger "Midnight Cowboy"
1968	"Oliver!"	Cliff Robertson "Charly"	Jack ALbertson "The Subject Was Roses"	Katharine Hepburn "The Lion in Winter" Barbra Streisand "Funny Girl"	Ruth Gordon "Rosemary's Baby"	Sir Carol Reed "Oliver!"
1967	"In the Heat of the Night"	Rod Steiger "In the Heat of the Night"	George Kennedy "Cool Hand Luke"	Katharine Hepburn "Guess Who's Coming to Dinner?"	Estelle Parsons "Bonnie and Clyde"	Mike Nichols "The Graduate"
1966	"A Man for All Seasons"	Paul Scofield "A Man for All Seasons"	Walter Matthau "The Fortune Cookie"	Elizabeth Taylor "Who's Afraid of Virginia Woolf?"	Sandy Dennis "Who's Afraid of Virginia Woolf?"	Fred Zinnemann "A Man for All Seasons"
1965	"The Sound of Music"	Lee Marvin "Cat Ballou"	Martin Balsam "A Thousand Clowns"	Julie Christie "Darling"	Shelley Winters "A Patch of Blue"	Robert Wise "The Sound of Music"
1964	"My Fair Lady"	Rex Harrison "My Fair Lady"	Peter Ustinov "Topkapi"	Julie Andrews "Mary Poppins"	Lila Kedrova "Zorba the Greek"	George Cukor "My Fair Lady"
1963	"Tom Jones"	Sidney Poitier "Lilies of the Field"	Melvyn Douglas "Hud"	Patricia Neal "Hud"	Margaret Rutherford "The V.I.P.s"	Tony Richardson "Tom Jones"
1962	"Lawrence of Arabia"	Gregory Peck "To Kill a Mockingbird"	Ed Begley "Sweet Bird of Youth"	Anne Bancroft "The Miracle Worker"	Patty Duke "The Miracle Worker"	David Lean "Lawrence of Arabia"
1961	"West Side Story"	Maximilian Schell "Judgment at Nuremberg"	George Chakiris "West Side Story"	Sophia Loren "Two Women"	Rita Moreno "West Side Story"	Jerome Robbins, Robert Wise "West Side Story"
1960	"The Apartment"	Burt Lancaster "Elmer Gantry"	Peter Ustinov "Spartacus"	Elizabeth Taylor "Butterfield 8"	Shirley Jones "Elmer Gantry"	Billy Wilder "The Apartment"
1959	"Ben-Hur"	Charlton Heston "Ben-Hur"	Hugh Griffith "Ben-Hur"	Simone Signoret "Room at the Top"	Shelley Winters "The Diary of Anne Frank"	William Wyler "Ben-Hur"
1958	"Gigi"	David Niven "Separate Tables"	Burl Ives "The Big Country"	Susan Hayward "I Want to Live"	Wendy Hiller "Separate Tables"	Vincente Minnelli "Gigi"
1957	"The Bridge on the River Kwai"	Alec Guiness "The Bridge on the River Kwai"	Red Buttons "Sayonara"	Joanne Woodward "The Three Faces of Eve"	Miyoshi Umeki "Sayonara"	David Lean "The Bridge on the River Kwai"
1956	"Around the World in 80 Days"	Yul Brynner "The King and I"	Anthony Quinn "Lust for Life"	Ingrid Bergman "Anastasia"	Dorothy Malone "Written on the Wind"	George Stevens "Giant"
1955	"Marty"	Ernest Borgnine "Marty"	Jack Lemmon "Mister Roberts"	Anna Magnani "The Rose Tattoo"	Jo Van Fleet "East of Eden"	Delbert Mann "Marty"
1954	"On the Waterfront"	Marlon Brando "On the Waterfront"	Edmond O'Brien "The Barefoot Contessa"	Grace Kelly "The Country Girl"	Eva Marie Saint "On the Waterfront"	Elia Kazan "On the Waterfront"

Year	Best Picture	Best Actor	Supporting Actor	Best Actress	Supporting Actress	Best Director
1953	"From Here to Eternity"	William Holden "Stalag 17"	Frank Sinatra "From Here to Eternity"	Audrey Hepburn "Roman Holiday"	Donna Reed "From Here to Eternity"	Fred Zinnemann "From Here to Eternity"
1952	"The Greatest Show on Earth"	Gary Cooper "High Noon"	Anthony Quinn "Viva Zapata!"	Shirley Booth "Come Back, Little Sheba"	Gloria Grahame "The Bad and The Beautiful"	John Ford "The Quiet Man"
1951	"An American in Paris"	Humphrey Bogart "The African Queen"	Karl Malden "A Streetcar Named Desire"	Vivian Leigh "A Streetcar Named Desire"	Kim Hunter "A Streecar Named Desire"	George Stevens "A Place in the Sun"
1950	"All About Eve"	Jose Ferrer "Cyrano de Bergerac"	George Sanders "All About Eve"	Judy Holliday "Born Yesterday"	Josephine Hull "Harvey"	Joseph L. Mankiewicz "All About Eve"
1949	"All the King's Men"	Broderick Crawford "All the King's Men"	Dean Jagger "Twelve O'Clock High"	Olivia de Havilland "The Heiress"	Mercedes McCambridge "All the King's Men"	Joseph L. Mankiewicz "A Letter to Three Wives"
1948	"Hamlet"	Laurence Olivier "Hamlet"	Walter Huston "The Treasure of the Sierra Madre"	Jane Wyman "Johnny Belinda"	Claire Trevor "Key Largo"	John Huston "The Treasure of the Sierra Madre"
1947	"Gentleman's Agreement"	Ronald Colman "A Double Life"	Edmund Gwenn "Miracle on 34th Street"	Loretta Young "The Farmer's Daughter"	Celeste Holm "Gentleman's Agreement"	Elia Kazan "Gentleman's Agreement"
1946	"The Best Years of Our Lives"	Fredric March "The Best Years of Our Lives"	Harold Russell "The Best Years of Our Lives"	Olivia de Havilland "To Each His Own"	Anne Baxter "The Razor's Edge"	William Wyler "The Best Years of Our Lives"
1945	"The Lost Weekend"	Ray Milland "The Lost Weekend"	James Dunn "A Tree Grows in Brooklyn"	Joan Crawford "Mildred Pierce"	Anne Revere "National Velvet"	Billy Wilder "The Lost Weekend"
1944	"Going My Way"	Bing Crosby "Going My Way"	Barry Fitzgerald "Going My Way"	Ingrid Bergman "Gaslight"	Ethel Barrymore "None But the Lonely Heart"	Leo McCarey "Going My Way"
1943	"Casablanca"	Paul Lukas "Watch on the Rhine"	Charles Coburn "The More the Merrier"	Jennifer Jones "The Song of Bernadette"	Katina Paxinou "For Whom the Bell Tolls"	Michael Curtiz "Casablanca"
1942	"Mrs. Miniver"	James Cagney "Yankee Doodle Dandy"	Van Heflin "Johnny Eager"	Greer Garson "Mrs. Miniver"	Teresa Wright "Mrs. Miniver"	William Wyler "Mrs. Miniver"
1941	"How Green Was My Valley"	Gary Cooper "Sergeant York"	Donald Crisp "How Green Was My Valley"	Joan Fontaine "Suspicion"	Mary Astor "The Great Lie"	John Ford "How Green Was My Valley"
1940	"Rebecca"	James Stewart "The Philadelphia Story"	Walter Brennan "The Westerner"	Ginger Rogers "Kitty Foyle"	Jane Darwell "The Grapes of Wrath"	John Ford "The Grapes of Wrath"
1939	"Gone with the Wind"	Robert Donat "Goodbye, Mr. Chips"	Thomas Mitchell "Stagecoach"	Vivien Leigh "Gone with the Wind"	Hattie McDaniel "Gone with the Wind"	Victor Fleming "Gone with the Wind"
1938	"You Can't Take It with You"	Spencer Tracy "Boys' Town"	Walter Brennan "Kentucky"	Bette Davis "Jezebel"	Fay Bainter "Jezebel"	Frank Capra "You Can't Take It with You"
1937	"The Life of Emile Zola"	Spencer Tracy "Captains Courageous"	Joseph Schildkraut "The Life of Emile Zola"	Luise Rainer "The Good Earth"	Alice Brady "In Old Chicago"	Leo McCarey "The Awful Truth"
1936	"The Great Ziegfeld"	Paul Muni "The Story of Louis Pasteur"	Walter Brennan "Come and Get It"	Luise Rainer "The Great Ziegfeld"	Gale Sondergaard "Anthony Adverse"	Frank Capra "Mr. Deeds Goes to Town"
1935	"Mutiny on the Bounty"	Victor McLaglen "The Informer"	—	Bette Davis "Dangerous"	—	John Ford "The Informer"
1934	"It Happened One Night"	Clark Gable "It Happened One Night"	—	Claudette Colbert "It Happened One Night"	—	Frank Capra "It Happened One Night"
1932-33	"Cavalcade"	Charles Laughton "The Private Life of Henry VIII"	—	Katharine Hepburn "Morning Glory"	—	Frank Lloyd "Cavalcade"
1931-32	"Grand Hotel"	Wallace Beery "The Champ" Fredric March "Dr. Jekyll and Mr. Hyde"	—	Helen Hayes "The Sin of Madelon Claudet"	—	Frank Borzage "Bad Girl"
1930-31	"Cimarron"	Lionel Barrymore "A Free Soul"	—	Marie Dressler "Min and Bill"	—	Norman Taurog "Skippy"
1929-30	"All Quiet on the Western Front"	George Arliss "Disraeli"	—	Norma Shearer "The Divorcee"	—	Lewis Milestone "All Quiet on the Western Front"
1928-29	"Broadway Melody"	Warner Baxter "In Old Arizona"	—	Mary Pickford "Coquette"	—	Frank Lloyd "The Divine Lady"
1927-28	"Wings"	Emil Jannings "The Last Command" "The Way of All Flesh"	—	Janet Gaynor "Seventh Heaven" "Street Angel" "Sunrise"	—	Frank Borzage "Seventh Heaven" Lewis Milestone "Two Arabian Knights"

Theatre

ANTOINETTE PERRY (TONY) AWARDS (1980-81) presented by the League of New York Theatres and Producers and sponsored by the American Theatre Wing:

Best Play: "Amadeus"
Best Musical: "42nd Street"
Best Book of a Musical: Peter Stone, "Woman of the Year"
Best Score: John Kander and Fred Ebb, "Woman of the Year"
Best Actor, Play: Ian McKellen, "Amadeus"
Best Actress, Play: Jane Lapotaire, "Piaf"
Best Actor, Musical: Kevin Kline, "The Pirates of Penzance"
Best Actress, Musical: Lauren Bacall, "Woman of the Year"
Best Featured Actor, Play: Brian Backer, "The Floating Light Bulb"
Best Featured Actress, Play: Swoosie Kurtz, "The Fifth of July"
Best Featured Actor, Musical: Hinton Battle, "Sophisticated Ladies"
Best Featured Actress, Musical: Marilyn Cooper, "Woman of the Year"
Best Director, Play: Peter Hall, "Amadeus"
Best Director, Musical: Wilford Leach, "The Pirates of Penzance"
Best Scenic Designer: John Bury, "Amadeus"
Best Costume Designer: Willa Kim, "Sophisticated Ladies"
Best Lighting Designer: John Bury, "Amadeus"
Best Choreographer: Gower Champion (posthumously), "42nd Street"
Revival of a Play or Musical: "The Pirates of Penzance"
Special Tony Awards: Beth Henley, "Crimes of the Heart"; Trinity Repertory Theater; Daryl Hall; Lena Horne

OBIE (OFF BROADWAY AWARDS) (1980-81):

Best Play: David Henry Hwang, "FOB"
Best Production: Emily Mann, "Still Life"
Sustained Achievement: Negro Ensemble Company
Distinguished Performances: Giancarlo Esposito, "Zooman and the Sign"; Bob Gunton, "How I Got That Story"; Mary Beth Hurt, "Crimes of the Heart"; Kevin Kline, "The Pir-

ates of Penzance"; John Lone, "FOB" and "The Dance and the Railroad"; Mary McDonnel, "Still Life"; Timothy Near, "Still Life"; William Sadler, "Limbo Tales"; Michele Shay, "Meetings"; John Spencer, "Still Life"; Meryl Streep, "Alice in Concert"; Christopher Walken, "The Sea Gull"
Distinguished Direction: Melvin Bernhardt, "Crimes of the Heart"; Wilford Leach, "The Pirates of Penzance"; Toby Robertson, "Pericles"
Playwrighting: Charles Fuller, "Zooman and the Sign"; Amlin Gray, "How I Got That Story"; Len Jenkin, "Limbo Tales" (script and direction)
Design: Bloolips, "Lust in Space" (costumes); Manuel Lutenhorst and Douglas Ball, "Requiem Concert"; Jon Maeda, sustained excellence, set design; Dennis Farichy, sustained excellence, lighting design
Special Citations: JoAnne Akalaitis and Mabou Mines, "Dead End Kids"; Joseph Chaikin and the Winter Project, "Tourists and Refugees"; Bill Irwin, for his inspired clowning; Bruce Myers, "A Dybbuk for Two People"; Repertorio Espanol

Films

CANNES INTERNATIONAL FILM FESTIVAL (1981):

Best Film: "Man of Iron," Andrzej Wajda
Best Actress: Isabelle Adjani, for her roles in "Quartet" and "Possession"
Best Actor: Ugo Tognazzi, "The Tragedy of a Ridiculous Man"

NEW YORK FILM CRITICS CIRCLE AWARD (1980):

Best Film: "Ordinary People"
Best Director: Jonathan Demme, "Melvin and Howard"
Best Actor: Robert De Niro, "Raging Bull"
Best Actress: Sissy Spacek, "Coal Miner's Daughter"
Best Supporting Actor: Joe Pesci, "Raging Bull"
Best Supporting Actress: Mary Steenburgen, "Melvin and Howard"
Best Screenplay: Bo Goldman, "Melvin and Howard"
Best Foreign Film: "Mon Oncle D'Amérique," by Alain Resnais

MISS AMERICA

Year	Winner
1921	Margaret Gorman, Washington, D.C.
1922-23	Mary Campbell, Columbus, Ohio
1924	Ruth Malcolmson, Philadelphia, Pennsylvania
1925	Fay Lamphier, Oakland, California
1926	Norma Smallwood, Tulsa, Oklahoma
1927	Lois Delaner, Joliet, Illinois
1933	Marion Bergeron, West Haven, Connecticut
1935	Henrietta Leaver, Pittsburgh, Pennsylvania
1936	Rose Coyle, Philadelphia, Pennsylvania
1937	Bette Cooper, Bertrand Island, New Jersey
1938	Marilyn Meseke, Marion, Ohio
1939	Patricia Donnelly, Detroit, Michigan
1940	Frances Marie Burke, Philadelphia, Pennsylvania
1941	Rosemary LaPlanche, Los Angeles, California
1942	Jo-Caroll Dennison, Tyler, Texas
1943	Jean Bartel, Los Angeles, California
1944	Venus Ramey, Washington, D.C.
1945	Bess Myerson, New York City, N.Y.
1946	Marilyn Buferd, Los Angeles, California
1947	Barbara Walker, Memphis, Tennessee
1948	BeBe Shopp, Hopkins, Minnesota
1949	Jacque Mercer, Litchfield, Arizona
1951	Yolande Betbeze, Mobile, Alabama
1952	Coleen Kay Hutchins, Salt Lake City, Utah
1953	Neva Jane Langley, Macon, Georgia
1954	Evelyn Margaret Ay, Ephrata, Pennsylvania
1955	Lee Meriwether, San Francisco, Califronia
1956	Sharon Ritchie, Denver, Colorado
1957	Marian McKnight, Manning, South Carolina
1958	Marilyn Van Derbur, Denver, Colorado
1959	Mary Ann Mobley, Brandon, Mississippi
1960	Lynda Lee Mead, Natchez, Mississippi
1961	Nancy Fleming, Montague, Michigan
1962	Maria Fletcher, Asheville, North Carolina
1963	Jacquelyn Mayer, Sandusky, Ohio
1964	Donna Axum, El Dorado, Arkansas
1965	Vonda Kay Van Dyke, Phoenix, Arizona
1966	Deborah Irene Bryant, Overland Park, Kansas
1967	Jane Anne Jayroe, Laverne, Oklahoma
1968	Debra Dene Barnes, Moran, Kansas
1969	Judith Anne Ford, Belvidere, Illinois
1970	Pamela Anne Eldred, Birmingham, Michigan
1971	Phyllis Ann George, Denton, Texas
1972	Laurie Lea Schaefer, Columbus, Ohio
1973	Terry Anne Meeuwsen, DePere, Wisconsin
1974	Rebecca Ann King, Denver, Colorado
1975	Shirley Cothran, Fort Worth, Texas
1976	Tawney Elaine Godin, Yonkers, N.Y.
1977	Dorothy Kathleen Benham, Edina, Minnesota
1978	Susan Perkins, Columbus, Ohio
1979	Kylene Baker, Galax, Virginia
1980	Cheryl Prewitt, Ackerman, Mississippi
1981	Susan Powell, Elk City, Oklahoma
1982	Elizabeth Ward, Russellville, Arkansas

THE DIRECTORY

SOCIETIES AND ASSOCIATIONS

Information abstracted from listings in the *1981* edition of the *Encyclopedia of Associations*, which includes details on more than 14,000 organizations. Used by permission of the publisher, Gale Research Company, Book Tower, Detroit, Michigan 48226

Academy of Applied Science, 65 India Wharf, Boston, MA 02110; **Membership:** 300

Academy of Motion Picture Arts and Science, 8949 Wilshire Blvd., Beverly Hills, CA 90211; **Membership:** 4,225

Academy of Political Science, 619 W. 114th St., Suite 500, New York, NY 10025; **Membership:** 10,000

Actors Equity Association, 165 W. 46th St., New York, NY 10036; **Membership:** 27,000

Adult Education Association of the U.S.A., 810 18th St., NW, Washington, DC 20006; **Membership:** 3,500

Aerospace Industries Association of America, 1725 De Sales St., NW, Washington, DC 20036; **Membership:** 58 companies

African-American Institute, 833 United Nations Plaza, New York, NY 10017

AFS (American Field Service) International Exchange, 313 East 43rd St., New York, NY 10017; **Membership:** 105,500

Air Force Association, 1750 Pennsylvania Ave., NW, Washington, DC 20006; **Membership:** 148,000

Alcoholics Anonymous, 468 Park Ave. S., New York, NY 10016; **Membership:** 1,000,000

Alternatives to Abortion International, Hillcrest Hotel, Suite 511, 16th and Madison Sts., Toledo, OH 43699; **Membership:** 100,000

Amateur Athletic Union of the United States, 3400 West 86th St., Indianapolis, IN 46268; **Membership:** 331,000

America-Mideast Educational and Training Services (AMIDEAST), 1717 Massachusetts Ave., NW, Washington, DC 20036

American Academy of Arts and Letters, 633 West 155th St., New York, NY 10032; **Membership:** 250

American Academy of Arts and Sciences, 165 Allandale St., Boston, MA 02130; **Membership:** 2,300

American Academy of Political and Social Sciences, 3937 Chestnut St., Philadelphia, PA 19104; **Membership:** 12,500

American Alliance for Health, Physical Education, Recreation and Dance, 1900 Association Dr., Reston, VA 22091; **Membership:** 50,000

American Anthropological Association, 1703 New Hampshire Ave., NW, Washington, DC 20009; **Membership:** 10,000

American Antiquarian Society, 185 Salisbury St., Worcester, MA 01609; **Membership:** 350

American Anti-Vivisection Society, Noble Plaza, Suite 204, 801 Old York Rd., Jenkintown, PA 19046

American Arbitration Association, 140 West 51st St., New York, NY 10020

American Association for the Advancement of Science, 1515 Massachusetts Ave., NW, Washington, DC 20005; **Membership:** 133,000

American Association of Advertising Agencies, 200 Park Ave., New York, NY 10017; **Membership:** 490

American Association of Blood Banks, 1828 L St., NW, Washington, DC 20036; **Membership:** 8,000

American Association of Community and Junior Colleges, National Center for Higher Education, 1 Dupont Circle, NW, Washington, DC 20036; **Membership:** 1,305

American Association of Retired Persons, 1909 K St., NW, Washington, DC 20049; **Membership:** 11,500,000

American Association of University Professors, 1 Dupont Circle, NW, Washington, DC 20036; **Membership:** 68,100

American Association of University Women, 2401 Virginia Ave., NW, Washington, DC 20037; **Membership:** 190,600

American Astronomical Society, % Dr. Harry L. Shipman, Physics Dept., Univ. of Delaware, Sharp Labs, Newark, DE 19711; **Membership:** 3,700

American Automobile Association, 8111 Gatehouse Rd., Falls Church, VA 22047; **Membership:** 21,000,000

American Bankers Association, 1120 Connecticut Ave., NW, Washington, DC 20036; **Membership:** 13,588 banks and trust companies

American Bar Association, 1155 East 60th St., Chicago, IL 60637; **Membership:** 263,450

American Bible Society, 1865 Broadway, New York, NY 10023; **Membership:** 328,000

American Camping Association, Bradford Woods, Martinsville,

IN 46151; **Membership:** 6,000

American Cancer Society, 777 Third Ave., New York, NY 10017; **Membership:** 2,500,000 with 58 divisions and 3,000 county units

American Chemical Society, 1155 16th St., NW, Washington, DC 20036; **Membership:** 118,000

American Civil Liberties Union, 22 E. 40th St., New York, NY 10016; **Membership:** 200,000

American Classical League, Miami University, Oxford, OH 45056; **Membership:** 3,000

American College of Hospital Administrators, 840 N. Lake Shore Dr., Chicago, IL 60611; **Membership:** 14,500

American College of Physicians, 4200 Pine St., Philadelphia, PA 19104; **Membership:** 49,000

American College of Surgeons, 55 E. Erie St., Chicago, IL 60611; **Membership:** 42,000

American Contract Bridge League, 2200 Democrat Rd., Memphis, TN 38132; **Membership:** 200,000 in 5,000 clubs

American Council for the Arts, 507 Seventh Ave., New York, NY 10018

American Council on Education, 1 Dupont Circle, NW, Washington, DC 20036; **Membership:** 1,385 and 188 affiliates

American Council for Judaism, 307 Fifth Ave., New York, NY 10016; **Membership:** 20,000

American Council of Learned Societies, 800 Third Ave., New York, NY 10022; **Membership:** 43 organizations

American Council of Life Insurance, 1850 K St., NW, Washington, DC 20006; **Membership:** 480 companies

American Council on Schools and Colleges, P.O. Box 1252, York, PA 17405; **Membership:** 201 institutions

American Council on the Teaching of Foreign Languages, Two Park Ave., New York, NY 10016; **Membership:** 9,000

American Dental Association, 211 E. Chicago Ave., Chicago, IL 60611; **Membership:** 133,000 in 484 societies

American Diabetes Association, 600 Fifth Ave., New York, NY 10020; **Membership:** 150,000 in 68 state organizations

American Dietetic Association, 430 N. Michigan Ave., Chicago, IL 60611; **Membership:** 38,000 in 52 state groups

American Economic Foundation, 51 E. 42nd St., New York, NY 10017; **Membership:** 18,000

American Farm Bureau Federation, 225 Touhy Ave., Park Ridge, IL 60068; **Membership:** 3,198,631

American Federation of Arts, 41 E. 65th St., New York, NY 10021; **Membership:** 2,000

American Federation of Labor and Congress of Industrial Organizations, 815 16th St. NW, Washington, DC 20006; **Membership:** 13,600,000 in 105 organizations

American Federation of Teachers, 11 Dupont Circle, NW, Washington, DC 20036; **Membership:** 555,000

American Federation of Television and Radio Artists, 1350 Ave. of the Americas, New York, NY 10019; **Membership:** 40,000 in 39 locals

American Forestry Association, 1319 18th St., NW, Washington, DC 20036; **Membership:** 79,000

American Friends Service Committee, 1501 Cherry St., Philadelphia, PA 19102; **Membership:** 10 regional Offices

American Geographical Society, Broadway at 156th St., New York, NY 10032; **Membership:** 1,000

American Geological Institute, 5205 Leesburg Pike, Falls Church, VA 22041; **Membership:** 18 societies

American Geophysical Union, 2000 Florida Ave., NW, Washington, DC 20009; **Membership:** 12,000

American Geriatrics Society, 10 Columbus Circle, New York, NY 10019; Membership: 8,000

American Group Psychotherapy Association, 1995 Broadway, 14th Floor, New York, NY 10023; **Membership:** 3,000 in 22 societies

American Heart Association, 7320 Greenville Ave., Dallas, TX 75231; **Membership:** 123,000 in 55 affiliates and 110 chapters

American Historical Association, 400 A St., SE, Washington, DC 20003; **Membership:** 14,500

American Home Economics Association, 2010 Massachusetts Ave., NW, Washington, DC 20036; **Membership:** 45,000 in 52 associations

American Horse Shows Association, 598 Madison Ave., New York, NY 10022; **Membership:** 19,675

American Horticultural Society, Mt. Vernon, VA 22121; **Membership:** 33,000

American Hospital Association, 840 N. Lake Shore Dr., Chicago, IL 60611; **Membership:** 37,392

American Humane Association, 5351 Roslyn, Englewood, CO 80111; **Membership:** 2,000,000 in 2,000 societies

American Institute of Aeronautics and Astronautics, 1290 Ave. of the Americas, New York, NY 10019; **Membership:** 27,000 in 68 sections and 115 student branches

American Institute of Architects, l735 New York Ave., NW, Washington, DC 20006; **Membership:** 34,100

American Institute of Biological Sciences, 1401 Wilson Blvd., Arlington, VA 22209; **Membership:** 9,000

American Institute of Certified Public Accountants, 1211 Ave. of the Americas, New York, NY 10036; **Membership:** 150,000

American Institute of Chemical Engineers, 345 E. 47th St., New York, NY 10017; **Membership:** 47,000

American Institute of Chemists, 7315 Wisconsin Ave., NW, Washington, DC 20014; **Membership:** 5,000 in 25 state groups

American Institute of Nutrition, 9650 Rockville Pike, Bethesda, MD 20014; **Membership:** 1,925

American Institute of Physics, 335 E. 45th St., New York, NY 10017; **Membership:** nine national societies

American Jewish Committee, % Institute of Human Relations, 165 E. 56th St., New York, NY 10022; **Membership:** 45,000 in 80 chapters

American Jewish Congress, 15 E. 84th St., New York, NY 10028; **Membership:** 50,000 in 300 groups

American Kennel Club, 51 Madison Ave., New York, NY 10010; **Membership:** 413 associations

American Law Institute, 4025 Chestnut St., Philadelphia, PA 19104; **Membership:** 2,465

American Legion, 700 N. Pennsylvania St., Indianapolis, IN 46206; **Membership:** 2,630,000 in 58 state departments

American Legion Auxiliary, 777 N. Meridian St., Indianapolis, IN 46204; **Membership:** 1,000,000

American Library Association, 50 E. Huron St., Chicago, IL 60611; **Membership:** 35,000

American Lung Association, 1740 Broadway, New York, NY 10019; **Membership:** 7,500

American Management Associations, 135 W. 50th St., New York, NY 10020; **Membership:** 75,000

American Mathematical Society, P.O. Box 6248, Providence, RI 02940; **Membership:** 19,000

American Medical Association, 535 N. Dearborn St., Chicago, IL 60610; **Membership:** 222,243

American Ministerial Association, P.O. Box 1252, York, PA 17405; **Membership:** 76,000

American National Theatre and Academy, 245 W. 52nd St., New York, NY 10019

American Newspaper Publishers Association, 11600 Sunrise Valley Dr., Reston, VA 22091; **Membership:** 1,364 daily newspapers

American Numismatic Association, P.O. Box 2366, Colorado Springs, CO 80901; **Membership:** 34,000 individuals and 1,000 clubs

American Numismatic Society, 1814 Broadway betw. 155th and 156th St., New York, NY 10032; **Membership:** 1,995

American Nurses' Association, 2420 Pershing Rd., Kansas City, MO 64108; **Membership:** 182,000 in 53 state groups

American Optometric Association, 243 N. Lindbergh Blvd., St. Louis, MO 63141; **Membership:** 20,628

American Ornithologists' Union, National Museum of Natural History, Smithsonian Institution, Washington, DC 20560; **Membership:** 4,000

American Osteopathic Association, 212 E. Ohio St., Chicago, IL 60611; **Membership:** 14,541 in 54 state groups

American Personnel and Guidance Association, 2 Skyline Pl., Suite 400, 5203 Leesburg Pike, Falls Church, VA 22041; **Membership:** 41,000

American Pharmaceutical Association, 2215 Constitution Ave., NW, Washington, DC 20037; **Membership:** 56,000

American Philatelic Society, P.O. Box 800, State College, PA 16801; **Membership:** 50,000

American Philological Association, 617 Hamilton Hall, Columbia University, New York, NY 10027; **Membership:** 2,800

American Philosophical 3ociety, 104 S. Fifth St., Philadelphia, PA 19106; **Membership:** 600

American Physical Society, 335 E. 45th St., New York, NY 10017; **Membership:** 30,000

American Podiatry Association, 20 Chevy Chase Circle, NW, Washington, DC 20015; **Membership:** 7,200 in 52 state groups

American Political Science Association, 1527 New Hampshire Ave., NW, Washington, DC 20036; **Membership:** 15,000

American Power Boat Association, 17640 E. Nine Mile Rd., East Detroit, MI 48021; **Membership:** 6,000 in 300 clubs

American Psychiatric Association, 1700 18th St., NW, Washington, DC 20009; **Membership:** 25,000

American Psychoanalytic Association, 1 E. 57th St., New York, NY 10022; **Membership:** 2,636

American Psychological Association, 1200 17th St., NW, Washington, DC 20036; **Membership:** 50,000

American Public Health Association, 1015 18th St., NW, Washington, DC 20036; **Membership:** 29,423

American Radio Relay League, 225 Main St., Newington, CT 06111; **Membership:** 169,000 in 2,100 clubs

American Red Cross, 17th and D Sts., NW, Washington, DC 20006; **Membership:** 60 divisions and 3,108 chapters

American Social Health Association, 260 Sheridan Ave., Suite 307, Palo Alto, CA 94306; **Membership:** 14,000

American Society for the Prevention of Cruelty to Animals, 141 E. 92nd St., New York, NY 10028; **Membership:** 15,675

American Society of Civil Engineers, 345 E. 47th St., New York, NY 10017; **Membership:** 78,000

American Society of Composers, Authors, and Publishers, 1 Lincoln Plaza, New York, NY 10023; **Membership:** 24,000

American Society of Interior Designers, 730 Fifth Ave., New York, NY 10019; **Membership:** 10,000 in 45 chapters

American Society of Mechanical Engineers, 345 E. 47th St., New York, NY 10017; **Membership:** 95,000 in 177 local groups

American Society of Newspaper Editors, Box 551, 1350 Sullivan Trail, Easton, PA 18042; **Membership:** 800

American Society of Travel Agents, 711 Fifth Ave., New York, NY 10022; **Membership:** 16,000 worldwide

American Sociological Association, 1772 N St., NW, Washington, DC 20036; **Membership:** 14,000

American Speech-Language-Hearing Association, 10801 Rockville Pike, Rockville, MD 20852; **Membership:** 30,000

American Statistical Association, 806 15th St., NW, Suite 640, Washington, DC 20005; **Membership:** 14,000

American Thoracic Society, 1740 Broadway, New York, NY 10019; **Membership:** 8,000

American Trucking Associations, 1616 P St., NW, Washington, DC 20036; **Membership:** 51 organizations

American Veterans Committee, 1346 Connecticut Ave., NW, Washington, DC 20036; **Membership:** 25,000

American Veterinary Medical Association, 930 N. Meacham Rd., Schlumburg, IL 60196; **Membership:** 31,000

American Youth Hostels, Inc., National Campus, Delaplane, VA 22025; **Membership:** 80,000 in 27 local councils

Americans for Democratic Action, 1411 K St., NW, Washington, DC 20005; **Membership:** 65,000 in 20 state groups

Amnesty International, U.S. Affiliate, 304 W. 58th St., New York, NY 10017; **Membership:** 12,000

AMVETS, 1710 Rhode Island Ave., NW, Washington, DC 20036; **Membership:** 150,000

Ancient Order of Hibernians in America, Box 700, Riverdale Station, Bronx, NY 10471; **Membership:** 191,000

Anti-Defamation League of B'nai B'rith, 823 United Nations Plaza, New York, NY 10017

Appalachian Mountain Club, 5 Joy St., Boston, MA 02108; **Membership:** 25,000

Archaeological Institute of America, 53 Park Place, Eighth Fl., New York, NY 10007; **Membership:** 7,500

Army and Navy Union, U.S.A., 1391 Main St., P.O. Box 537, Lakemore, OH 44250; **Membership:** 5,000

Arthritis Foundation, 3400 Peachtree Rd. NE, Atlanta, GA 30326; **Membership:** 71 chapters

Association for the Study of Afro-American Life and History, 1401 14th St., NW, Washington, DC 20005; **Membership:** 30,000

Association of American Colleges, 1818 R St., NW, Washington, DC 20009; **Membership:** 630 institutions

Association on American Indian Affairs, Inc., 432 Park Ave. S., New York, NY 10016

Association of American Railroads, American Railroads Bldg., 1920 L St., NW, Washington, DC 20036; **Membership:** 240

Association of American Universities, 1 Dupont Circle, NW, Suite 730, Washington, DC 20036; **Membership:** 50 university presidents

Association of Chairmen of Departments of Mechanics, % W.E. Jahsman, Dept. of Mechanical Engineering, University of Colorado, Boulder, CO 80302; **Membership:** 98

Association of Computer Programmers and Analysts, 294 Main St., E. Greenwich, RI 02818; **Membership:** 1,000

Association of Governing Boards of Universities and Colleges, 1 Dupont Circle, NW, Suite 720, Washington, DC 20036; **Membership:** 21,000

Association of Junior Leagues, 825 Third Ave., New York, NY 10022; **Membership:** 130,000 in 238 leagues

Audit Bureau of Circulations, 123 N. Wacker Dr., Chicago, IL 60606; **Membership:** 4,800

Authors League of America, 234 W. 44th St., New York, NY 10036; **Membership:** 8,500

Benevolent and Protective Order of Elks, 2750 Lake View Ave., Chicago, IL 60614; **Membership:** 1,650,000 in 2,250 lodges

Big Brothers/Big Sisters of America, 220 Suburban Station Bldg., Philadelphia, PA 19103; **Membership:** 387 local agencies

Blue Cross Association, 840 N. Lake Shore Dr., Chicago, IL 60511; **Membership:** 75 Blue Cross plans

B'nai B'rith International, 1640 Rhode Island Ave., NW, Washington, DC 20036; **Membership:** 500,000 in 3,500 groups

Boys' Clubs of America, 771 First Ave., New York, NY 10017; **Membership:** 1,000,000

Boy Scouts of America, P.O. Box 61030, Dallas . Ft. Worth Airport Sta., Dallas, TX 75261; **Membership:** 4,400,000 scouts and adult leaders

Brand Names Foundation, 470 Park Ave., No. 7D, New York, NY 10022; **Membership:** 400

Brookings Institution, 1775 Massachusetts Ave., NW, Washington, DC 20036

Camp Fire, Inc., 4601 Madison Ave., Kansas City, MO 64112; **Membership:** 750,000

CARE (Cooperative for American Relief Everywhere), 660 First Ave., New York, NY 10016; **Membership:** 27 agencies

Catholic Daughters of America, 10 W. 71st St., New York, NY 10023; **Membership:** 170,000 in 49 state groups

Catholic War Veterans of U.S.A., 2 Massachusetts Ave., NW, Washington, DC 20001; **Membership:** 50,000

CCCO, An Agency for Military and Draft Counseling, 2208 South St., Philadelphia, PA 19146

Chamber of Commerce of the United States, 1615 H St., NW, Washington, DC 20062; **Membership:** 3,900 chambers of commerce and trade associations, 83,000 business firms and individuals

Chautauqua Literary and Scientific Circle, Chautauqua, NY 14722; **Membership:** 1,100

Child Welfare League of America, 67 Irving Pl, New York, NY 10003

College Entrance Examination Board, 888 Seventh Ave., New York, NY 10019; **Membership:** 2,480 colleges, universities, secondary schools, school systems and educational associations

Colonial Dames XVII Century, National Society, 1300 New Hampshire Ave., NW, Washington, DC 20036; **Membership:** 8,500

Committee for Economic Development, 477 Madison Ave., New York, NY 10022; **Membership:** 200 trustees

Common Cause, 2030 M St., NW, Washington, DC 20036; **Membership:** 225,000

The Conference Board, 845 Third Ave., New York, NY 10022; **Membership:** 4,000 organizations

Conference on Jewish Material Claims against Germany, 15 E. 26th St., New York, NY 10010; **Member Organizations:** 22

CORE (Congress of Racial Equality), 1916-38 Park Ave., New York, NY 10037

Cooperative League of the U.S.A., 1828 L St., NW, Washington, DC 20036; **Membership:** 178 organizations

Correspondance Chess League of America, P.O. Box I24, Algonquin, IL 60102; **Membership:** 1,400

Council for the Advancement and Support of Education, 1 Dupont Circle, NW, Washington, DC 20036; **Membership:** 9,000

Council of Better Business Bureaus, 1150 17th St., NW, Washington, DC 20036; **Membership:** 1,000 in 150 member bureaus

Council on Foreign Relations, 58 E. 68th St., New York, NY 10021; **Membership:** 1,940 in 36 local groups

Council of Graduate Schools in the United States, 1 Dupont Circle, NW, Washington, DC 20036; **Membership:** 360

Council on International Educational Exchange, 205 E. 42nd St., New York, NY 10017; **Membership:** 168 North American institutions

Country Music Association, P.O. Box 22299, 7 Music Circle N., Nashville, TN 37203; **Membership:** 5,500

Credit Union National Association, Inc., P.O. Box 431, Madison, WI 53701; **Membership:** 22,069 credit unions

Daughters of the American Revolution, National Society, 1776 D St., NW, Washington, DC 20006; **Membership:** 209,000

Day Care and Child Development Council of America, 520 South-

ern Bldg., 805 15th St., NW, Washington, DC 20005; **Membership:** 6,000

Democratic National Committee, 1625 Massachusetts Ave., NW, Washington, DC 20036; **Membership:** 360

Disabled American Veterans, 3725 Alexandria Pike, Cold Spring, KY 41076; **Membership:** 650,000

Dramatists Guild, 234 W. 44th St., New York, NY 10036

Ecological Society of America, Dept. of Botany and Microbiology, Univ. of Oklahoma, Norman, OK 73019; **Membership:** 6,200

English-Speaking Union of the United States, 16 E. 69th St., New York, NY 10021; **Membership:** 32,000 in 85 branches

Entomological Society of America, 4603 Calvert Rd., College Park, MD 20740; **Membership:** 7,500

Environmental Action, 1346 Connecticut Ave., NW, Suite 731, Washington, DC 20036; **Membership:** 20,000

Epilepsy Foundation of America, 1828 L St., NW, Suite 406, Washington, DC 20036; **Membership:** 161 affiliates in 50 states

Experiment in International Living, United States Headquarters, Brattleboro, VT 05301; **Membership:** national offices in over 60 other countries and 7 regional U.S. offices

Eye-Bank for Sight Restoration, 210 E. 64th St., New York, NY 10021

Federation of American Scientists, 307 Massachusetts Ave., NE, Washington, DC 20002; **Membership:** 5,000

Fellowship of Reconciliation, Box 271, Nyack, NY 10960; **Membership:** 25,238 in 50 groups

Fleet Reserve Association, 1303 New Hampshire Ave., NW, Washington, DC 20036; **Membership:** 148,000

Foreign Policy Association, 205 Lexington Ave., New York, NY 10016

Foster Parents Plan, 155 Plan Way, Warwick, RI 02887

Garden Club of America, 598 Madison Ave., New York, NY 10022; **Membership:** 14,000

General Federation of Women's Clubs, 1734 N St., NW, Washington, DC 20036; **Membership:** 10,000,000 in 34 countries

General Society of Mayflower Descendants, 4 Winslow St., Plymouth, MA 02360; **Membership:** 19,500 in 51 state groups

Gideons International, 2900 Lebanon Road, Nashville, TN 37214; **Membership:** 66,000 in 124 countries

Girl Scouts of the U.S.A., 830 Third Ave., New York, NY 10022; **Membership:** 2,971,000 in 341 local groups

Girls Clubs of America, 205 Lexington Ave., New York, NY 10016; **Membership:** 215,000

Grand Aerie, Fraternal Order of Eagles, 2401 W. Wisconsin Ave., Milwaukee, WI 53233; **Membership:** 750,000 in 50 state groups

Group Health Association of America, 1717 Massachusetts Ave., NW, Washington, DC 20036; **Membership:** 1,000

Guide Dog Foundation for the Blind, Inc., 109-19 72nd Ave., Forest Hills, NY 11375

Hadassah, the Women's Zionist Organization of America, 50 W. 58th St., New York, NY 10019; **Membership:** 370,000 in 1,590 chapters and groups

Health Insurance Institute, 1850 K St., NW, Washington, DC 20006; **Membership:** 324 companies

Helicopter Association of America, 1156 15th St., NW, Suite 610, Washington, DC 20005; **Membership:** 800 firms

Humane Society of the United States, 2100 L St., NW, Washington, DC 20037; **Membership:** 100,000

Imperial Council of the Ancient Arabic Order of Nobles of the Mystic Shrine, 123 N. Michigan Ave., Chicago, IL 60601; **Membership:** 1,000,000

Independent Order of Odd Fellows, 16 W. Chase St., Baltimore, MD 21201; **Membership:** 1,200,000

Indian Rights Association, 1505 Race St., Philadelphia, PA 19102; **Membership:** 2,500

Information Industry Association, 316 Pennsylvania Ave., SE, Suite 502, Washington, DC 20003; **Membership:** 120 companies

Institute of International Education, 809 United Nations Plaza, New York, NY 10017

International Air Transport Association, P.O. Box 550, International Aviation Sq., 1000 Sherbrooke St. W, Montreal, PQ, Canada H3A 2R4; **Membership:** 103 airlines

International College of Surgeons, 1516 Lake Shore Dr., Chicago, IL 60610; **Membership:** 14,000

International Game Fish Association, 3000 E. Las Olas Blvd., Fort Lauderdale, FL 33316; **Membership:** 10,000

International Student Service, 291 Broadway, New York, NY 10007; **Membership:** 190 local groups

Italian-American War Veterans of the U.S., 115 S. Meridian Rd., Youngstown, OH 44509; **Membership:** 8,500 in 110 posts

Izaak Walton League of America, 1800 N. Kent St., Suite 806, Arlington, VA 22209; **Membership:** 53,000

Jewish War Veterans of the U.S.A., 1712 New Hampshire Ave., NW, Washington, DC 20009; **Membership:** 105,000

Junior Achievement, 550 Summer St., Stamford, CT 06901; **Membership:** 245,000

JWB, 15 E. 26th St., New York, NY 10010; **Membership:** 370 Jewish community centers and YM-YWHAs

Kiwanis International, 101 E. Erie St., Chicago, IL 60611; **Membership:** 300,000 in 7,500 clubs

Knights of Columbus, Columbus Plaza, New Haven, CT 06507; **Membership:** 1,314,819

Knights of Pythias, Pythian Bldg., Rm. 201, 47 N. Grant St., Stockton, CA 95202; **Membership:** 200,000 in 55 domains

Knights Templar of the U.S.A., 14 E. Jackson Blvd., Suite 1700, Chicago, IL 60604; **Membership:** 365,000

League of Women Voters of the U.S., 1730 M St., NW, Washington, DC 20036; **Membership:** 125,000 in 1,350 leagues

Leukemia Society of America, Inc., 211 E. 43rd St., New York, NY 10017; **Membership:** 51 local groups

Lions Clubs International, 300 22nd, Oak Brook, IL 60521; **Membership:** 1,282,000

Little League Baseball, Williamsport, PA 17701; **Membership:** 2,500,000

Loyal Order of Moose, Mooseheart, IL 60539; **Membership:** 1,649,661 in 4,169 lodges and chapters

March of Dimes Birth Defects Foundation, 1275 Mamaroneck Ave., White Plains, NY 10605

Marine Corps League, 933 N. Kenmore St., Suite 321, Arlington, VA 22201; **Membership:** 20,000

Masonic Service Association of the U.S., 8120 Fenton St., Silver Spring, MD 20910; **Membership:** 43 grand lodges

Mensa, 1701 W. 3d St., Brooklyn, NY 11223; **Membership:** 40,000 in 200 groups

Mental Health Association, 1800 N. Kent St., Rosslyn, VA 22209; **Membership:** 850 local, 47 state groups

Modern Language Association of America, 62 Fifth Ave., New York, NY 10011; **Membership:** 30,000

Modern Woodmen of America, 1701 First Ave., Rock Island, IL 61201; **Membership:** 510,000 in 1,000 local groups

Motor Vehicle Manufacturers Association of the United States, 300 New Center Bldg., Detroit, MI 48202; **Membership:** 12 manufacturers

Muscular Dystrophy Associations of America, Inc., 810 Seventh Ave., New York, NY 10019; **Membership:** 28,000 in 211 chapters

National Academy of Television Arts and Sciences, 110 W. 57th St., New York, NY 10019; **Membership:** 12,000

National Aeronautic Association, 821 15th St., NW, Washington, DC 20005; **Membership:** 160,000

National Amputation Foundation, 12-45 150th St., Whitestone, NY 11357; **Membership:** 5,200 veterans

National Association for Hearing and Speech Action, 6110 Executive Bldg., Suite 1000, Rockville, MD 20852; **Membership:** 2,000

National Association for Retarded Citizens, 2709 Ave. E East, Arlington, TX 76011; **Membership:** 275,000 in 1,800 local groups

National Association for Stock Car Auto Racing, 1801 Volusia Ave., Daytona Beach, FL 32015; **Membership:** 18,000

National Association for the Advancement of Colored People, 1790 Broadway, New York, NY 10019; **Membership:** 450,673

National Association of Blue Shield Plans, 211 East Chicago Ave., Chicago, IL 60611; **Membership:** 69 medical care plans

National Association of Broadcasters, 1771 N St., NW, Washington, DC 20036; **Membership:** 5,286

National Association of Colored Women's Clubs, 5808 16th St., NW, Washington, DC 20011; **Membership:** 45,000

National Association of Intercollegiate Athletics, 1221 Baltimore, Kansas City, MO 64106; **Membership:** 515 members and 31 groups

National Association of Manufacturers, 1776 F St., NW, Washington, DC 20006; **Membership:** 13,000

National Association of Negro Business and Professional Women's Clubs, 1806 New Hampshire Ave., NW, Washington, DC 20009; **Membership:** 10,000 in 300 groups

National Association of Social Workers, 1425 H St., NW, Washington, DC 20005; **Membership:** 80,000

National Association of State Universities and Land Grant Colleges, 1 Dupont Circle, NW, Suite 710, Washington, DC 20036; **Membership:** 142 colleges and universities

National Association of Theatre Owners, 1500 Broadway, New York, NY 10036; **Membership:** 10,000

National Audubon Society, 950 Third Ave., New York, NY 10022; **Membership:** 400,000 plus 440 affiliated groups

National Automobile Dealers Association, 8400 Westpark Dr., McLean, VA 22101; **Membership:** 21,000

National Board of Review of Motion Pictures, P.O. Box 589, New York, NY 10021; **Membership:** 100

National Braille Association, Inc., 645A Godwin Ave., Midland Park, NJ 07432; **Membership:** 2,700

National Campers and Hikers Association, Inc., 7172 Transit Rd., Buffalo, NY 14221; **Membership:** 200,000

National Catholic Educational Association, 1 Dupont Circle, NW, Suite 350, Washington, DC 20036; **Membership:** 15,000

National Civil Service League, 5530 Wisconsin Ave., NW, Suite 1600, Washington, DC 20015; **Membership:** 3,000

National Collegiate Athletic Association, Nall Ave. At 63rd St., PO Box 1906, Shawnee Mission, KS 66222; **Membership:** 862 colleges and allied organizations

National Conference of Catholic Charities, 1346 Connecticut Ave., NW, Washington, DC 20036; **Membership:** 3,000

National Conference of Christians and Jews, 43 W. 57th St., New York, NY 10019; **Membership:** 70 regional groups

National Conference on Social Welfare, 1730 M St., N.W., Suite 911, Washington, DC 20036; **Membership:** 4,500

National Congress of American Indians, 202 E. St., N.E., Washington, DC 20002; **Membership:** representing 600,000 Indians

National Council of Churches of Christ in the U.S.A., 475 Riverside Dr., New York, NY 10027; **Membership:** 40,191,346 in 32 denominations

National Council of Farmer Cooperatives, 1800 Massachusetts Ave., NW, Washington, DC 20036; **Membership:** 2,500,000 in 161 cooperative associations

National Council of Jewish Women, 15 E. 26th St., New York, NY 10010; **Membership:** 100,000

National Council of Negro Women, 1819 H St., NW, Washington, DC 20006; **Membership:** 4,000,000 in 200 local groups within 27 national affiliated organizations

National Council of State Garden Clubs, 4401 Magnolia Ave., St. Louis, MO 63110; **Membership:** 365,680

National Council of Women of the United States, 345 E. 46th St., New York, NY 10017

National Council on the Aging, 1828 L St., NW, Washington, DC 20036; **Membership:** 3,800

National Council on Crime and Delinquency, Continental Plaza, 411 Hackensack Ave., Hackensack, NJ 07601; **Membership:** 30,000

National Democratic Club, 52 E. 41st St., New York, NY 10017; **Membership:** 1,200

National Easter Seal Society for Crippled Children and Adults, 2023 W. Ogden Ave., Chicago, IL 60612

National Education Association, 1201 16th St., NW, Washington, DC 20036; **Membership:** 1,600,800; 53 state and 10,000 local affiliated groups

National Farmers Union (Farmers Educational and Cooperative Union of America), PO Box 39251, Denver, CO 80251; **Membership:** 300,000 farm families in 3,000 groups

National Federation of the Blind, 1800 Johnson St., Baltimore, MD 21230; **Membership:** 50,000

National Federation of Business and Professional Women's Clubs, Inc., 2012 Massachusetts Ave., NW, Washington, DC 20036; **Membership:** 164,000

National Federation of Music Clubs, 310 S. Michigan Ave., Suite 1936, Chicago, IL 60604; **Membership:** 500,000 in 4,500 clubs

National 4-H Council, 7100 Connecticut Ave., Washington, DC 20015

National Genealogical Society, 1921 Sunderland Pl., NW, Washington, DC 20036; **Membership:** 4,500

National Geographic Society, 17th & M Sts. NW, Washington, DC 20036; **Membership:** 10,700,000

National Grange, 1616 H St., NW, Washington, DC 20006; **Membership:** 475,000 in 5,500 groups

National Hairdressers and Cosmetologists Assoc., Inc., 3510 Olive St., St. Louis, MO 63103; **Membership:** 71,000

National Health Council, Inc., 1740 Broadway, New York, NY 10019; **Membership:** 84 organizations

National Institute of Social Sciences, 150 Amsterdam Ave., New York, NY 10023; **Membership:** 1,000

National League of Cities, 1620 Eye St., NW, Washington, DC 20006; **Membership:** 900 municipal governments in 48 states

National Legal Aid and Defender Association, 1625 K St., NW, Washington, DC 20006; **Membership:** 2,600 offices and organizations

National Medical Association, Inc., 1720 Massachusetts Ave., NW, Washington, DC 20006; **Membership:** 8,000

National Multiple Sclerosis Society, 205 E. 42nd St., New York, NY 10017; **Membership:** 450,000 in 155 chapters

National Municipal League, 47 E. 68th St., New York, NY 10021; **Membership:** 6,500

National Newspaper Publishers Association, 770 National Press Bldg., Washington, DC 20045; **Membership:** 161 publishers

National Organization for Women (NOW), Suite 1048, 425 13th St., NW, Washington, DC 20004; **Membership:** 120,000

National Parks and Conservation Association, 1701 18th St., NW, Washington, DC 20009; **Membership:** 35,000

National Press Club, National Press Bldg., 529 14th St., NW, Room 1380, Washington, DC 20045; **Membership:** 4,734

National PTA, 700 N. Rush St., Chicago, IL 60611; **Membership:** 6,170,141

National Railway Historical Society, P.O. Box 2051, Philadelphia, PA 19103; **Membership:** 10,000

National Rifle Association of America, 1600 Rhode Island Ave., NW, Washington, DC 20036; **Membership:** 1,500,000

National Safety Council, 444 N. Michigan Ave., Chicago, IL 60611; **Membership:** 15,000

National Small Business Association, 1604 K St., NW, Washington, DC 20036; **Membership:** 50,000

National Society for the Prevention of Blindness, 79 Madison Ave., New York, NY 10016; **Membership:** 321

National Tax Association-Tax Institute of America, 21 E. State St., Columbus, OH 43215; **Membership:** 2,100

National Urban League, 500 E. 62nd St., New York, NY 10021; **Membership:** 50,000 in 116 local groups

National Wildlife Federation, 1412 16th St., NW, Washington, DC 20036; **Membership:** 4,100,000

National Woman's Christian Temperance Union, 1730 Chicago Ave., Evanston, IL 60201; **Membership:** 250,000

Newspaper Guild, The, 1125 15th St., NW, Washington, DC 20005; **Membership:** 33,500 in 80 locals

Optimist International, 4494 Lindell Blvd., St. Louis, MO 63108; **Membership:** 125,000

Order of AHEPA (American Hellenic Educational Progressive Association), 1422 K St., NW, Washington, DC 20005; **Membership:** 50,000 in 430 groups

Order of the Eastern Star, General Grand Chapter, 1618 New Hampshire Ave., NW, Washington, DC 20009; **Membership:** 3,000,000

Overseas Press Club of America, 52 E. 41st St., New York, NY 10017; **Membership:** 1,600

Parkinson's Disease Foundation, William Black Medical Research Bldg., Columbia Presbyterian Medical Center, 640 W. 168th St., New York, NY 10032

P.E.N. American Center, 47 Fifth Ave., New York, NY 10003

Photographic Society of America, 2005 Walnut St., Philadelphia, PA 19103; **Membership:** 18,700

Planned Parenthood Federation of America, 810 Seventh Ave., New York, NY 10019; **Membership:** 189 organizations

Polish Legion of American Veterans, U.S.A., 3024 N. Laramie Ave., Chicago, IL 60641; **Membership:** 15,000 in 114 posts

Public Relations Society of America, 845 Third Ave., New York, NY 10022; **Membership:** 9,700 executives

Puppeteers of America, 2311 Connecticut Ave. N.W., Washington, DC 20008; **Membership:** 2,600 in 21 guilds

Republican National Committee, 310 First St., SE, Washington, DC 20003; **Membership:** 162

Rotary International, 1600 Ridge Ave., Evanston, IL 60201; **Membership:** 835,300

Screen Actors Guild, 7750 Sunset Blvd., Hollywood, CA 90046; **Membership:** 39,000

Sierra Club, 530 Bush St., San Francisco, CA 94108; **Membership:** 183,000

Society for the Advancement of Education, 1860 Broadway, New York, NY 10023; **Membership:** 3,000

Society of Automotive Engineers, 400 Commonwealth Dr., Warrendale, PA 15096; **Membership:** 37,000 in 52 groups

Society of the Cincinnati, 2118 Massachusetts Ave., NW, Washington, DC 20008; **Membership:** 2,800 in 14 groups

Sons of the American Revolution, National Society, 1000 S. Fourth St., Louisville, KY 40203; **Membership:** 22,000

Soroptimist International of the Americas, Inc., 1616 Walnut St., Philadelphia, PA 19103; **Membership:** 32,000 in 1,075 groups

Southern Christian Leadership Conference, 334 Auburn Ave. NE, Atlanta, GA 30303; **Membership:** 80 chapters

Speech Communication Association, 5105 E. Backlick Rd., Annandale, VA 22003; **Membership:** 8,000

Sports Car Club of America, 6750 S. Emporia St., Englewood, CO 80112; **Membership:** 24,000

Supreme Council, Ancient Accepted Scottish Rite of Freemasonry, Northern Jurisdiction, 33 Marrett Rd., Lexington, MA 02173; **Membership:** 511,687 in 112 groups

Supreme Council 33°, Ancient Accepted Scottish Rite of Freemasonry, Southern Jurisdiction, 1733 16th St. NW, Washington DC 20009; **Membership:** 665,000

Transportation Association of America, 1100 17th St., NW, Washington, DC 20036; **Membership:** 1,000

UNICEF, 331 E. 38th St., New York, NY 10016; **Membership:** 90

United Cerebral Palsy Associations, 66 E. 34th St., New York, NY 10016; **Membership:** 277 affiliates

United Daughters of the Confederacy, 328 North Blvd., Richmond, VA 23220; **Membership:** 35,000

United Jewish Appeal, Inc., 1290 Ave. of the Americas, New York, NY 10019; **Membership:** 8 regional groups

United Nations Association of the United States of America, 300 E. 42nd St., New York, NY 10017; **Membership:** 26,000 in 200 chapters

United Negro College Fund, 500 E. 62nd St., New York, NY 10021; **Membership:** 39 private accredited four-year colleges; 2 graduate and professional schools

USO (United Service Organizations), 1146 19th St., NW, Washington, DC 20036

United States Catholic Conference, 1312 Massachusetts Ave., NW, Washington, DC 20005

United States Independent Telephone Association, 1801 K St., NW, Washington, DC 20006; **Membership:** 1,600

The United States Jaycees, 4 W. 21st St., P.O. Box 7, Tulsa, OK 74102; **Membership:** 380,000 in 51 state groups

United States Olympic Committee, 1750 E. Boulder St., Colorado Springs, CO 80909; **Membership:** 43

United States Power Squadrons, P.O. Box 30423, Raleigh, NC 27612; **Membership:** 57,000

United States Space Education Association, 746 Turnpike Rd., Elizabethtown, PA 17022; **Membership:** 400

United States Student Association, 1220 G St., SE, Washington, DC 20003; **Membership:** 400 colleges and universities

United Way of America, 801 N. Fairfax St., Alexandria, VA 22314; **Membership:** 1,139

Variety Clubs International, 58 W. 58th St., Suite 23-C, New York, NY 10019; **Membership:** 10,000 in 42 groups

Veterans of Foreign Wars of the U.S.A., V.F.W. Bldg., Kansas City MO 64111; **Membership:** 1,950,000 in 10,000 groups; ladies auxiliary numbers 626,000 in 6,855 groups

Volunteers of America, 340 W. 85th St., New York, NY 10024; **Membership:** 44 state groups

The Wilderness Society, 1901 Pennsylvania Ave., NW, Washington, DC 20006; **Membership:** 55,000

Wildlife Society, 7101 Wisconsin Ave., NW, Suite 611, Washington, DC 20014; **Membership:** 7,500

Women Strike for Peace, 145 S. 13th St., Philadelphia, PA 19107

Women's American ORT (Organization for Rehabilitation through Training), 1250 Broadway, New York, NY 10001; **Membership:** 140,000 in 1,150 chapters

Women's International League for Peace and Freedom, 1213 Race St., Philadelphia, PA 19107; **Membership:** 110 branches

Workmen's Benefit Fund of the U.S.A., 714 Seneca Ave., Brooklyn, NY 11227; **Membership:** 34,000 in 108 groups

Workmen's Circle, 45 E. 33rd St., New York, NY 10016; **Membership:** 60,000 in 310 groups

World Future Society, 4916 St. Elmo Ave., Washington, DC 20014; **Membership:** 50,000 in 60 groups

World Population Society, 1337 Connecticut Ave., NW, Suite 200, Washington, DC 20006; **Membership:** 1,100

Writers Guild of America, East, 555 W. 57th St., New York, NY 10019; **Membership:** 2,500

Writers Guild of America, West, 8955 Beverly Blvd., Los Angeles, CA 90048; **Membership:** 5,100

Young Democrats of America, % Democratic National Committee, 1625 Massachusetts Ave., NW, Washington, DC 20036; **Membership:** 200,000 in 2,000 groups

Young Men's and Young Women's Hebrew Association, 1395 Lexington Ave., New York, NY 10028; **Membership:** 9,000

Young Men's Christian Associations of the U.S.A., National Council, 291 Broadway, New York, NY 10017; **Membership:** 10,000,000 in 1,842 associations

Young Republican National Federation, 310 First St, SE, Washington, DC 20003; **Membership:** 300,000 in 4,000 groups

Young Women's Christian Association of the U.S.A., 600 Lexington Ave., New York, NY 10022; **Membership:** 2,455,000 in 4,850 local groups

Zionist Organization of America, 4 E. 34th St., New York, NY 10016; **Membership:** 150,000 in 600 groups

RELIGION: FAITHS/FOLLOWERS

MAJOR WORLD RELIGIONS

JUDAISM

The religion of the Jewish people is the world's oldest great monotheism and the parent religion of both Christianity and Islam. The name derives from the Latin *Judaeus* and the Hebrew *Yehudhi*, meaning *descendant of Judah*, who was the fourth son of Jacob.

The founder of Judaism was Abraham, who lived about 1500 B.C. and made a covenant with God that he and his descendants, as the Chosen People, would carry the message of one God to the world. The new nation was given structure by Moses, who in the 13th century B.C. led the Israelites out of slavery in Egypt, received the Ten Commandments from God on Mt. Horeb (Sinai), and brought his people to the edge of the land of Canaan, which had been promised to Abraham as part of the covenant.

Once in the Promised Land, the Israelites built a temple, established a priesthood, and began offering sacrifices in accordance with the teachings of Moses—practices that survived the 6th-century Babylonian Exile. But in A.D. 70, when the temple in Jerusalem was destroyed by the Roman army, sacrificial worship was supplanted by study and prayers in synagogues.

Although Judaism has no specific creeds, its sacred writings consist of laws, prophecies, and traditions that reflect 3,500 years of spiritual experience. The principal text is the Torah, or Pentateuch, which consists of the first five books of the Bible. The rest of the Hebrew Bible, known to Christians as the Old Testament, includes the Psalms and writings of the major and minor prophets.

Another authoritative work is the Talmud, a collection of laws that includes the Mishna, a Hebrew compilation of the Oral Law (in Hebrew), and the Gemara, a collection of comments (in Aramaic) on the Mishna by rabbis. There are actually two Talmuds, one that emanated from Palestine in the 5th century and one from Babylonia a century later.

The basis of Judaism is belief in the living God who is transcendent, omnipotent, and just, and who reveals himself to mankind. The faith rests on the words of Deuteronomy 6:4: "Hear, O Israel, the Lord our God, the Lord is One."

For Jews the oneness of God implies the brotherhood of men, and religious knowledge is considered inseparable from the ethical injunction "to do justly, and love mercy, and to walk humbly with thy God." Judaism's elaborate system of laws and rituals, such as dietary regulations, is designed to give sacred meaning to every aspect of daily life.

Jews have an ordained clergy and observe the Sabbath, which runs from sunset Friday to sunset Saturday and is observed with services of prayer and readings in local synagogues. Major festivals include Pesach (Passover, celebrating the Exodus), Shabuoth (Pentecost), Rosh Hashana (New Year), Yom Kippur (Day of Atonement), and Sukkoth (Feast of Tabernacles).

Judaism has generated numerous internal sects and movements, including the Sadduccees and Pharisees during the early Christian era. In the 12th century, Maimonides tried to relate Judaism to Western philosophy, especially that of Aristotle. Modern religious movements developed from Moses Mendelssohn, a rationalist of the 18th-century Enlightenment, and Hasidism, which preaches piety and mysticism.

Present-day American Judaism is divided among three major denominations. The Orthodox stresses strict adherence to the Torah. Reform Jews, in the tradition of Mendelssohn, have repudiated legalism and emphasize the compatibility of Judaism with secular liberal values. Conservative Judaism reflects a middle road—acceptance of the Torah but also a willingness to adapt it to modern conditions. In recent years a Reconstructionist movement, which was originated by Mordecai M. Kaplan and developed out of the Conservative wing, has stressed Judaism as an evolving religious civilization.

Since the destruction of their nation in A.D. 70, Jews have dreamed of once again having their own state. The first Zionist Congress was held (1897) in Basle and, in the wake of the Nazi holocaust that took the lives of six million Jews, the State of Israel came into being in 1948. Although the religious significance of the state's existence is not yet clear, the Six-Day War of 1967 nonetheless made many non-Israeli Jews realize how closely they are involved with Israel both in their cultural and religious lives.

MOSES (c. 1350–1250 B.C.)

According to Biblical accounts, the great lawgiver of Jewish monotheism was born probably in Egypt to slave parents, Amram and Jochebed, of the tribe of Levi. Because of an Egyptian law requiring newborn male Hebrew children to be killed, his mother is said to have hid him in a basket among the reeds of the Nile River. Found by one of Pharaoh's daughters, he was raised by her with Jochebed as his nurse.

As a young man Moses became interested in the cause of his people and had to flee to Midian after slaying an Egyptian whom he had discovered beating a Hebrew. Finding refuge as a shepherd for Jethro, a local priest, Moses married his daughter Zipporah.

While tending sheep one day at Mt. Horeb, Moses had a vision of God in a bush that burned but was not consumed, and he experienced a call to return to Egypt to liberate his people. With the aid of his brother Aaron, he aproached the Pharaoh (probably Ramses II: reigned c. 1292 to 1225 B.C.), who acceded to the Exodus of the Hebrews after a series of 10 plagues, the last of which took the life of his firstborn son. The Pharaoh subsequently changed his mind, pursued the Hebrews, and his army was drowned in the Red Sea, but the Israelites miraculously escaped.

Moses led his people across the Sinai desert to Mt. Horeb (Sinai), where he received the Ten Commandments from God in the form of two tablets, which he smashed on the ground when he discovered his Hebrews worshiping a Golden Calf. Later he prepared two new tablets and placed them in the most sacred section of the Tabernacle, a portable sanctuary that was set up according to divine instructions. He also taught the Hebrews a complete legal code, organized a judicial system, and spelled out sacrificial practices.

Moses spent 40 years leading his people in the wilderness, never entering the promised land of Canaan—a privilege that went to his chosen successor, Joshua. Moses' great achievement, however, was the development of a system of morality and law applicable to all aspects of daily life.

CHRISTIANITY

Christianity developed among first-century Jews out of the conviction that Jesus of Nazareth, who lived from about c. 4 B.C. to A.D. 29, was the long-awaited Hebrew *Messiah*. . . . The name Jesus is Greek for the Hebrew *Joshua*, a name meaning *Savior*, while Christ derives from the Greek *Christos*, meaning *Messiah*, or *Anointed*.

The Christian Bible includes the Hebrew Bible, which is called the Old Testament, and the New Testament, which contains 27 additional books and was formalized by the 4th century. Central are the four Gospels of Matthew, Mark, Luke, and John, which describe the life and teachings of Jesus. Some Christians also accept the 14-book appendix to the Authorized Version of the Old Testament, known as the Apocrypha, as canonical.

The essence of traditional Christian theology is that Jesus was the Son of God who came to save the world, was crucified, resurrected, and will come again to judge mankind. The core of the Christian ethic is the commandment: "Thou shalt love the Lord thy God with all thy heart and thy neighbor as thyself."

A turning point in Christian history occurred at the Council of Jerusalem in A.D. 49 when St. Paul convinced other church leaders to spread the faith to non-Jews. Early Christians endured severe persecution, but in

A.D. 313 Constantine I officially tolerated Christianity in the Roman Empire.

Fundamental theological issues such as the divinity of Jesus Christ were thrashed out at a series of ecumenical councils during the first eight centuries. Doctrinal statements emanated from these councils, such as the Nicene Creed and the teaching of the Trinity, which asserts that God has appeared to man as the Father, the Son, and the Holy Ghost.

In 1054 Christianity was split into a Western or Roman Catholic Church, which acknowledges the pope—the bishop of Rome—as Christ's supreme vicar on earth, and the Eastern Orthodox Churches, which recognize the patriarch of Constantinople as the preeminent ecclesiastical figure. In the 16th century the Roman Catholic Church was further divided by the Protestant Reformation. The ecumenical movement of this century has now shifted momentum toward a quest for unity among Christian churches. An important development was the founding in 1948 of the World Council of Churches, which has more than 220 Protestant and Orthodox churches as members.

ROMAN CATHOLICISM

Roman Catholicism is the form of Christianity practiced by those who recognize the authority of the pope—the bishop of Rome—as the successor of Peter and vicar of Christ on Earth. The great majority of Catholics follow the Western or Latin Rite, but there are also a number of Eastern or Uniate churches, including the Byzantine and Armenian rites, that exercise a considerable degree of autonomy.

The Roman Catholic Church claims to be the "One Holy, Catholic and Apostolic Church." Although it acknowledges the Old and New Testaments and the Apocrypha, it also asserts that teachings disclosed in only seminal form to the Apostles have subsequently germinated and flowered in the Christian Community and have been formulated by General Councils and/or the pope. Recent examples of articles of faith include the doctrines of papal infallibility (1870) and the Assumption of the Virgin Mary (1950).

The basis of the Church's claim to sanctity is its authority to offer the sacrifice of the Mass, the Eucharist, that reenacts and re-presents Christ's sacrifice in behalf of man's sins. There are six other recognized sacraments: baptism, confirmation, confession and penance, matrimony, ordination, and extreme unction.

The key figure in the church hierarchy is the bishop, who has the power to confirm and ordain. The members of the College of Cardinals serve as the pope's privy councillors and also have the responsibility of electing new popes. The central administrative body of the church is the Curia Romana, which is located in Rome and organized around a varying number of sacred "congregations."

Priests are divided into "secular," or diocesan, clergy and "regular" clergy, who belong to religious orders living under a "rule." Since the 12th century, celibacy has been required of both types of clergy.

Following the 16th-century Protestant Reformation, the Church entered a period of retrenchment that was characterized by sharply defined standards of orthodoxy. Since the First Vatican Council, which ended in 1870, the papacy has been exceptionally strong. The Second Vatican Council (1962–65), however, produced significant changes, and the Church is now undergoing a period of uncertainty and flux that is marked by demands for increased power for laymen and priests and serious questioning of such traditions as clerical celibacy and papal authority.

EASTERN ORTHODOXY

The term Eastern Orthodox refers to those churches and their offspring that, for a variety of cultural, political, and theological reasons, split with Rome in A.D. 1054. These churches regard themselves as the true heirs of the early Christian Church and define their theological unity by acceptance of the decrees of the first seven ecumenical (general) councils that were held from A.D. 325 to 787.

The Eastern communion is a fellowship of autonomous churches consisting of the ancient patriarchates of Constantinople, Alexandria, Antioch, and Jerusalem, as well as the Orthodox churches of Cyprus, Russia, Rumania, Yugoslavia, Greece, Bulgaria, Georgia, Albania, Finland, and Czechoslovakia. The leader is the Ecumenical Patriarch of Constantinople, who is regarded as "first among equals" but whose direct authority is limited to the affairs of his own church, whose members are for the most part located in Europe and the Americas.

Eastern Orthodox theology is grounded in Greek philosophy rather than Roman law, and its creeds are important more as acts of worship than as standards of belief. Great reverence is shown for the writings of the church fathers, including Saints Basil the Great, Gregory Nazianzen, and John Chrysostom.

In addition to rejecting the authority of the pope, Eastern Orthodoxy disagrees with the Roman Catholic Church by rejecting all of the Nicene Creed's *Filioque*, which asserts that the Holy Spirit proceeds "from the Son" as well as from the Father. Orthodoxy also has no indulgences and pays honor to Mary as the mother of God but rejects the Roman dogma of Immaculate Conception. It reveres relics and icons but bans all "graven images," except the crucifix.

Orthodox priests may marry before but not after ordination, although monks must remain celibate and bishops are chosen from among the celibate clergy. The liturgy of Eastern Orthodox churches is sung, and great emphasis is placed on fasting. Eastern Orthodox church structures, which are normally square, feature a solid screen that separates the sanctuaries and the edifices' main bodies. They are often elaborately decorated with gilded icons and other works of art.

The fact that a majority of Orthodox believers now live in Communist-controlled areas has cut into the vitality of Orthodoxy, but nonetheless many of its churches—including the Russian one—are active in the World Council of Churches. Relations with Rome have greatly improved, and Ecumenical Patriarch Athenagoras I has had several dramatic meetings with Pope Paul VI, including one on the Mount of Olives in Jerusalem.

PROTESTANTISM

In a broad sense *Protestantism* is a generic term for most Western Christian churches that are not Roman Catholic or Eastern Orthodox. In a narrower connotation, it designates those churches and their heirs that came into being after the 16th-century Protestant Reformation.

The Reformation was sparked by Martin Luther, an Augustinian monk who challenged the papal practice of dispensing indulgences; with the support of German princes, he established a separate church. In addition to the Lutheran, there are at least three other Protestant traditions. The Reformed, or Calvinistic, tradition developed in Switzerland and led to the formation of Presbyterian and related churches. Anglicanism, which is represented in the United States by the Episcopal Church and originated in England, was the parent of Methodism. Numerous "free" or "independent" churches have also developed, including the Baptist and others that exercise a congregational system of government.

The fundamental philosophical characteristics of the reformers were the rejection of the authority of Rome, belief in the Bible as the only source of revelation, recognition of the "priesthood of all believers," and the assertion that salvation is the result of faith rather than good works or the dispensations of a church. Protestantism's characteristic individualism led to the development of religious liberty in many areas, but also contributed to denominational fragmentation.

Protestant churches permit ministers to marry, and even those that have bishops tend to concentrate governing powers in lay boards. Liturgies generally emphasize preaching and Bible reading rather than elaborate ritual; however, some traditions—notably the Anglo-Catholic wing of Anglicanism—are highly liturgical.

The modern ecumenical movement has developed out of Protestantism, and, except for fundamentalist churches (and thereby most Baptist churches), the major Protestant denominations tend to be involved in organizations such as the World Council of Churches. Mergers have been common in recent years, and nine major American denominations are in the process of negotiating a merger that would create a single, 25-million-member church.

JESUS (c. 4 B.C.–A.D. 29)

The founder of Christianity was born in Bethlehem to Mary, the wife of Joseph, who was a carpenter from Nazareth. Little is known about his early life. According to the Gospels, at the age of about 30 he was baptized by his cousin John the Baptist and began to preach, soon gathering a band of 12 disciples.

Jesus, who preached a message of repentance, made repeated attacks on Pharisees and scribes, the rulers of

Judaism. He couched his teachings in parables that could be understood by the masses and reinforced his words with extraordinary deeds that included healing the sick, raising the dead, and changing water into wine at the marriage feast of Cana.

After three years of preaching, Jesus set out for Jerusalem with his disciples for the celebration of Passover. He created a disturbance by throwing the money changers out of the Temple. Meanwhile, the Roman Governor Pontius Pilate, who was sensitive to Jewish nationalist threats, became alarmed. The authorities induced one of the disciples, Judas Iscariot, to betray Jesus. Following a Last Supper with his followers in which the Eucharist, or Lord's Supper, was symbolically enacted, Jesus was arrested in the Garden of Gethsemane.

He was tried for the treasonous charge of calling himself the Messiah and was crucified under a sign reading "Jesus of Nazareth, King of the Jews." The Gospels report, however, that three days later when Mary Magdalene went to the tomb she found it empty. An angel announced that Jesus had been resurrected; according to the Book of Acts, he appeared to his disciples, remained on earth 40 days, and then ascended into heaven.

Orthodox Christian theology asserts that Jesus was God made man and the second Person of the Trinity. The calendar of the Christian Church revolves around the events of his life, beginning with Advent—the preparation for his coming—and concluding with his Resurrection, Ascension, and the reception of the Holy Spirit by the church.

The discovery in 1947 of the Dead Sea Scrolls in a cave above the waters of the northwest Dead Sea in a section known as Qumran provided information about a pacifist and ascetic community generally identified with the Essene Jewish sect.

Some scholars attempted to link Jesus with the "Teacher of Righteousness," an Essene figure who would be "raised up" by God after death. A more general consensus now is that such ties are tenuous and that the scrolls are important primarily for their information about cultural conditions of the early Christian era, especially Palestinian Judaism and the background of John the Baptist.

ISLAM

Islam is the religion founded by the prophet Mohammed (c. A.D. 570–632) in 622 at Yathrib (now Medina) in Arabia. The Arabic word *Islam* means *submission to God*, and followers call themselves Moslems.

Mohammed was a caravan conductor and Mecca shopkeeper of the Koreish tribe who experienced a prophetic call at the age of 40. After founding his religion, he also acted as a governor, general, and judge. Mohammed is regarded as the "Seal of the Prophets"—the last in a series of messengers from God, consisting of Adam, Noah, Abraham, Moses, and Jesus.

The sacred text of Islam is the Koran (*Quran* in Arabic), which means *reading* and contains the revelations of Mohammed over a period of 20 years; it also deals with manners, religious laws, and morals. It has been supplemented by the Sunna, a collection of Traditions (moral sayings and anecdotes), and both are reinforced by the principle of Ijma, which states the belief that a majority of Moslems cannot agree in error. The Koran, the Sunna, and the Ijma are the three foundations of Islam.

Islam is radically theistic, and the essence of its creed is simply stated: "There is no God but Allah, and Mohammed is the messenger [or prophet] of Allah." Mohammed rejected the trinitarianism of Christianity, but he incorporated a number of Judeo-Christian concepts into his system. For example, the creed states: "I believe in God, his Angels, his Books and his Messengers, the Last Day, the Resurrection from the dead, Predestination by God, Good and Evil, the Judgment, the Balance, Paradise and Hell-fire."

There is no professional priesthood in Islam, and followers are expected to refrain from drinking wine. In addition to acceptance and recital of the creed, there are four duties required of the devout: prayer, fasting during the lunar month of Ramadan, giving alms, and a pilgrimage to the holy city of Mecca—if at all possible.

Moslems pray five times a day—at dawn, noon, midafternoon, dusk, and at night. The prayers, which consist primarily of thanksgiving and praise of Allah, are performed facing Mecca and involve traditional physical postures. The principal public service takes place at midday on Friday, usually in a mosque.

Early disputes over the "caliph," or successor of Mohammed, led to sectarian divisions within Islam. The most important were the Sunnites, Shiites, and Khawarij, who differed over matters of ceremony and law. Other modern movements have included the Babis and the Wahabis.

Islam is a missionary religion, though Moslems do not regard Jews and Christians as pagans and have normally permitted them to keep practicing their faiths after conquests. In centuries past, Moslem armies took over large sections of India and once came within 100 miles of Paris.

The principal areas of Islamic influence today are the Middle East, North Africa, and western Asia, and there are substantial communities in the Philippines, Indonesia, and Malaysia. It is currently increasing rapidly in African countries south of the Sahara.

Considerable theological activity has gone on during this century toward discrediting such Islamic practices as polygamy, slavery, and intolerance, thus making Islam more acceptable under modern conditions.

MOHAMMED (c. 570–A.D. 632)

The founder of Islam was born in Mecca in Arabia, the son of a poor merchant from the ruling tribe of Koreish. Both his parents died shortly after his birth, and he was raised by a grandfather and later an uncle. As a youth he was a shepherd and worked as a conductor of trading caravans.

Following his marriage at the age of 24 to the wealthy widow Khadija, who was 15 years his senior, Mohammed settled down in Mecca as a prosperous merchant and began devoting himself to the contemplative life. At the age of 40 in the cave of Mount Hira, north of Mecca, he had a vision, in which he was commanded to preach. This revelation and subsequent ones were recorded in the Koran, the sacred book of the Moslems.

Mohammed's first converts were his wife and children, and he began to collect other followers slowly and secretly, because of his many enemies. He taught belief in only one God, Allah, and preached heaven and hell and divine judgment.

When he began to operate openly, he aroused considerable hostility; some of his followers had to seek sanctuary in Abyssinia because of persecution. In 622 he himself barely escaped assassination and fled to Yathrib, which was later renamed Medina. Moslems regard this flight, the hegira, as the beginning of Islam and the start of their calendar.

Mohammed became the absolute ruler of Yathrib, where he founded his model theocratic state. He built the first mosque, changed the direction of prayers from Jerusalem to Mecca, and instituted the fast month of Ramadan and the practice of tithing. Relations with Christians and Jews deteriorated, but eventually he made treaties granting them freedom of worship in return for taxes. He initiated warfare with the Meccans, eventually gaining control of all of Arabia.

His private life has been the source of much attention, especially his frequent marriages—often politically inspired—and troubles with his harem. He basically led a simple and unpretentious life, however, and in 632 died in the arms of his last favorite wife, Ayesha.

HINDUISM

Known to its followers as *Santana Dharma* (the Eternal Religion), Hinduism is the religion of the majority of Indians today. It has developed gradually over a period of 5,000 years, making it possibly the world's oldest faith.

Hinduism has no ecclesiastical organization, and there are no beliefs or practices universal to all Hindus. It is polytheistic in the extreme, with literally hundreds of thousands of gods and some forms of animal life worshiped. The principal gods are Brahma, the unapproachable creative spirit, and the two popular gods, Siva and Vishnu—both of which have spawned innumerable cults.

Hindus emphasize the divinity of the soul and the harmony of all religions. Life is seen as a series of lives in which a man's position is determined by his *Karma*, or deeds, in previous lives. The social "caste" into which he is born is thus an indication of his spiritual status. The ultimate goal is to be released from the cycle of rebirths in various human and animal forms through absorption by the absolute. Asceticism and the discipline of Yoga are practiced to help achieve this release.

Hinduism has no fixed canon of sacred books. The principal text is the Veda (Vedic word meaning *divine knowledge*), a collection of 1,200 hymns and incantations addressed to various deities, including those of fire and wind. Some of this material is believed to date from the arrival of the Aryans in India c. 1500 B.C. More philosophical works that have also gained wide acceptance include the *Brahamanas*, the *Upanishads*, and the poem "Bhagavad-Gita" (Sanskrit for Song of the Lord).

For the ordinary man, Hinduism involves careful observance of food and marriage rules, pilgrimages to sacred rivers and shrines, participation in festivals, and worship in the temples and shrines that are found in every village. Entry to ultimate truth comes not from the acceptance of certain dogmas but from worship and religious experience.

Over the centuries Hinduism has produced numerous reform movements, including Buddhism and Sikhism. Modern social and cultural conditions are also bringing about modification of the caste system and other changes such as increased social status for women.

BUDDHISM

Buddhism is the way of life based on the teachings of Siddhartha Gautama, an Indian prince who lived in the sixth century B.C. and came to be known as the Buddha (Sanskrit for *enlightened one*).

Dissatisfied with the formalism of the Hinduism of his day and vowing to find an explanation for evil and human suffering, the prince left his family and wandered as a hermit for six years in search of a truth that would liberate mankind. He found it after seven weeks of meditation under a bo (pipal or sacred fig) tree (the tree of enlightenment) and began preaching and sending missionaries forth to spread his discovery.

The Buddha taught that the path beyond sorrow and suffering was the "middle way" between austerity and sensuality. He spoke of "four noble truths": existence involves suffering, suffering results from craving, craving can be destroyed, and such destruction of desire is obtainable by following the "noble eightfold path." The steps of this path are right views, right desires, right speech, right conduct, right livelihood, right endeavor, right mindfulness, and right meditation.

The Buddha did not speak of God, and his teachings constitute, in the ordinary Western sense, more of a philosophy and system of ethics than a religion. Buddhism affirms the law of Karma, by which a person's actions in life determine his status in future incarnations. The object of the Buddhist life is to achieve Nirvana, a condition of enlightenment and detachment from the world by which the cycle of successive rebirths comes to an end.

The simple life of the Buddha and his followers gave way after his death to the creation of monasteries, shrines, and temples; however, Buddhism eventually split into numerous branches. The two major ones today are Mahayana (greater vehicle) Buddhism, which is practiced in China, Korea, and Japan and has an elaborate theology in which the Buddha is regarded as a divine savior, and Hinayana (lesser vehicle) Buddhism, which is concentrated in Southeast Asia and preserves the earlier monastic traditions. Zen Buddhism, a Japanese variation of Mahayana Buddhism, stresses contemplation, while the Lamaism of Tibet represents a mixture of Buddhism with local demonolatry.

BUDDHA (c. 563–483 B.C.)

The founder of Buddhism, known as the Buddha or "Enlightened One," was born into a military caste in Lumbini, near the Himalayas in southern Nepal. Estimates of his precise year range from 624 to 466 B.C.

His original name was Siddhartha Gautama (or Gotama), and legend holds that his father, a rajah, had been warned at his birth that Siddhartha would become either a universal ruler or a universal teacher. Preferring the former course, the father took pains to prevent him from seeing any unpleasant aspects of life that might influence him to renounce the world.

Riding through the royal park one day when he was 29 years old, however, Siddhartha saw human misery for the first time in the form of an old man, a diseased man, a corpse, and a wandering religious mendicant. Resolving to solve the riddle of human suffering, he left his wife and newborn son and spent the next six years as a wandering hermit and ascetic.

His austere living failed to bring illumination, and he became an ordinary mendicant. One day he sat under a

bo tree in the village of Buddh Gaya in northern India and resolved not to rise until he had found enlightenment. He stayed 49 days, resisting temptations by Mara, the Buddhist devil, and was finally rewarded with the "bliss of emancipation," or Nirvana. Suffering, he concluded, was caused by attachment to the world and could only be eliminated through mental discipline and correct living.

Two merchants heard his teachings and became his first lay disciples. Later he preached a sermon to five monks with whom he had shared his ascetic quest, and they were ordained as the first members of the Sangha, the Buddhist monastic order. He returned home briefly and converted his family, thereafter spending the rest of his life teaching among neighboring tribes and organizing monks to spread the message of life lived according to the "middle way" between the extremes of pleasure-seeking and self-mortification.

He died at the age of 80 in the lap of Ananda, his favorite disciple, and his last words were said to have been: "Decay is inherent in all component things. Work out your own salvation with diligence."

SHINTOISM

The ancestral religion of Japan, Shinto developed out of primitive nature and ancestor worship sometime before the sixth century, when written records first appeared. The term *Shinto* is the Chinese equivalent of *the way of the gods*, and came into use at that time to distinguish it from the Buddhism that was then being imported from the Chinese mainland.

Shinto is essentially a set of customs and rituals rather than an ethical or moral system. Followers participate in festivals and pilgrimages, and great emphasis is placed on ceremonial purity and bodily cleanliness. Many Shintoists are also practicing Buddhists.

The religion has a complex pantheon of *kami*, or deities, the most exalted of whom is the sun-goddess known as Ruler of Heaven. Other objects of veneration include deified emperors, guardian family spirits, national heroes, and the divinities of trees, rivers, villages, and water sources.

Shrines ranging from small wayside god-houses to great national sanctuaries have been constructed and dedicated to these deities. Each Shinto home also has a "god-shelf" on which is placed a miniature wooden shrine holding tablets bearing beloved ancestors' names.

TAOISM

The chief rival to Confucianism in influencing Chinese philosophy and culture, Taoism actually consists of two movements: a philosophy (Tao Chia) and a religion (Tao Chiao). Both derive from the philosopher Lao-tze, who, according to tradition, lived in the sixth century B.C.

The term *Tao* has been translated as *way*, *road*, and even *being*. The book *Tao-teh-king*, attributed to Lao-tze, states that "the eternal Tao cannot be put into words, nor can the unchanging name be given a definition."

Philosophical Taoism espoused a radical naturalism that urged the acceptance of "all things in their natural state" and deplored passion, unnecessary invention, artificial ceremonies, and government activities such as war and taxation. Virtue was cast in passive and feminine terms. "There is nothing softer and weaker than water, and yet there is nothing better for attacking hard and strong things," was one of its precepts.

Tao Chia declined by the fourth century, partly because of the excessive assimilation of Buddhism, but its spirit of simplicity and harmony has contributed to such Chinese customs as tea drinking.

Religious Taoism originated in the first century under the leadership of Chang Tao-lin, a popular religious leader who healed the sick and founded large numbers of monasteries, nunneries, and temples. His work was continued in the next four centuries by Wei Po-yang and Ko Hung, both philosophers, and by K'ou Ch'ien-chih, who organized elaborate ceremonies and fixed the names of its multifarious deities.

Taoism has been marked by a proliferation of sects and societies. Since a brief period of state patronage during the T'ang dynasty (618–907), it has been a religion of the semiliterate.

LAO-TZE OR LAO-TZU (b. c. 604 B.C.)

The reputed founder of Taoism is usually said to have been born in 604 B.C. in Honan province, China, though confusion about his historical identity and whether there even was such a person has existed since early times. The name means simply "the old philosopher."

According to Chinese tradition, he was born as Li Erh, lived as a recluse, and became an archivist in the Chou court. He was said to have met his younger contemporary Confucius in 517 and to have rebuked him for his pride and ambition. When he retired in his old age, Lao-tze supposedly journeyed westward and was never heard from again.

Legend says that as he was about to pass out of Honan the gatekeeper asked him to write down his views of the Tao and that in response he created the Tao-teh-king, the text of which became the basis of Taoist philosophy and religion.

Scholars now date the anthology in the mid-third century. It is a remarkable collection that is thought to have been built on Indian legends, especially those about Buddha; however, the work is Chinese in texture and emphasizes ethics and politics.

Living according to Tao (literally Way or Being) involved submission to natural actions and avoidance of all formality and artificiality. It emphasized the virtues of passivity and harmony in an effort to maintain "the original simplicity of human nature." Modern religious Taoism, however, has become highly institutionalized and marked by numerous gods, the use of magic and superstition, and an emphasis on earthly blessings such as wealth and long life.

CONFUCIANISM

More a religious philosophy or ethical system than a religion in the strict sense, Confucianism is known to the Chinese as *Ju Chaio* (teachings of the scholars) and was the dominant force in Chinese thought, education, and government for 2,000 years.

Its founder was Confucius (c. 551–c. 479 B.C.), who was not so much an original thinker as a teacher and compiler of wisdom from the past. His sayings, together with those of Mencius and other disciples, have been collected in the *Wu Ching (Five Classics)*, and the *Shih Shu (Four Books)*, the latter of which includes the *Analects*—the sayings of Confucius.

The central concept of Confucian ethics is *jen*, which originally signified benevolence on the part of rulers but was broadened to encompass the supreme virtue of love and goodness: "that by which a man is a man." Confucianism teaches that man is good and possesses free will and that virtue is its own reward.

There are no churches, clergy, or creeds in Confucianism, and its founder was far more interested in making this world more human than in contemplating the supernatural. Nevertheless, he believed in Heaven—although it

was often interpreted in naturalistic terms—and encouraged the Chinese custom of ancestor-worship as a sign of gratitude and respect. Temples were built for this purpose and sacrificial rites performed in them.

From A.D. 125 to 1905 Confucianism dominated Chinese education, and members of the mandarin class of civil servants were appointed to government posts on the basis of examinations in the Confucian classics. This system had the effect of permitting many individuals from humble backgrounds to rise to prominence, and it placed a premium on the moral basis of the ruler and ruled. At the same time, its emphasis on book learning at the expense of natural science, for example, proved a liability in modern times.

Confucianism went into a period of decline following the elimination of the examination system (1905) and of the sacrificial rites (1911), but its ideas continued to play a part in the thought of some Chinese leaders, including Sun Yat-sen (1866–1925).

CONFUCIUS (551–479 B.C.)

The name of the founder of Confucianism and China's most prominent teacher and philosopher is a Latinized version of the Chinese K'ung Fu-tse.

Little reliable data is available about his life, although it is known that he was born in the feudal province of Lu, now Shantung, probably into an impoverished noble family. His father died when he was three, and he was evidently self-educated and as a young man earned his living keeping accounts.

Confucius became perhaps the most learned man of his day, but he was at heart a reformer rather than a scholar, a pragmatist rather than an intellectual. He was shocked by the constant warfare that went on between various states and by the suffering that aristocratic rulers brought upon the masses. He dedicated his life to relieving this suffering through governmental reforms, including the reduction of taxes, more humane punishments, and a system of statecraft that based on mutual moral responsibilities between the ruler and the ruled.

His lifelong ambition was to occupy a governmental post from which he could implement his reforms, and for a short period he was apparently administrator of justice in his native province. Clashes with the nobility, however, forced him out of office and into voluntary exile.

At the age of 55, Confucius began touring neighboring states speaking to the feudal lords about his ideas. He was received as a scholar, but none of the rulers were willing to put his ideas into practice. He returned home to concentrate on teaching, in which he was successful; some of his students achieved positions of authority that Confucius himself had been unable to reach.

ESTIMATED MEMBERSHIP OF THE PRINCIPAL RELIGIONS OF THE WORLD

SOURCE: Reprinted with permission from the 1980 BRITANNICA BOOK OF THE YEAR, copyright 1980, Encyclopaedia Britannica, Inc., Chicago, Ill.

Religions	No. Amer.[1]	So. Amer.	Europe[2]	Asia[3]	Africa	Oceania[4]	World
Total Christian	235,109,500	177,266,000	342,630,400	95,987,240	129,717,000	18,063,500	998,773,640
Roman Catholic	132,489,000	165,640,000	176,087,300	55,077,000	47,224,500	4,395,500	580,913,300
Eastern Orthodox	4,763,000	517,000	57,035,600	2,428,000	14,306,000[5]	414,000	79,463,600
Protestant[6]	97,857,500	11,109,000	109,507,500	38,482,240	68,186,500[7]	13,254,000	338,396,740
Jewish	6,155,340	635,800	4,061,620	3,212,860	176,400	76,000	14,318,020
Muslim[8]	371,200	251,500	14,145,000	427,266,000	145,214,700	87,000	587,335,400
Zoroastrian	250	2,100	7,000	254,000	650	—	264,000
Shinto[9]	60,000	92,000	—	57,003,000	200	—	57,155,200
Taoist	16,000	10,000	—	31,261,000	—	—	31,287,000
Confucian	97,100	70,150	—	157,887,500	1,500	80,300	158,136,550
Buddhist[10]	171,250	192,300	192,000	264,241,000	14,000	30,000	264,840,550
Hindu[11]	88,500	849,300	350,000	473,073,000	1,079,800	490,000	475,939,600
Totals	242,046,140	179,369,150	361,386,020	1,500,185,600	276,204,250	18,835,800	2,578,049,960

[1] Includes Central America and the West Indies. [2] Includes the U.S.S.R. and other countries with established Marxist ideology where religious adherence is difficult to estimate. [3] Includes areas in which persons have traditionally enrolled in several religions, as well as China with an official Marxist establishment. [4] Includes Australia and New Zealand as well as islands of the South Pacific. [5] Includes Coptic Christians. [6] Protestant statistics usually count "full members," that is adults, rather than all family members or baptized infants and are therefore not comparable with the statistics of ethnic religions or churches counting all constituents of all ages. [7] Including many new sects and cults among African Christians. [8] The chief base of Islam is still ethnic, although some missionary work is now carried on in Europe and America (viz. "Black Muslims"). In countries where Islam is established, minority religions are frequently persecuted and their statistics are hard to come by. [9] A Japanese ethnic religion, Shinto has declined since the Japanese emperor gave up his claim to divinity (1947). Neither does it survive well outside the homeland. [10] Buddhism has produced several modern renewal movements which have gained adherents in Europe and America and other areas not formerly ethnic-Buddhist. In Asia it has made rapid gains in recent years in some areas, and under persecution it has shown greater staying power than Taoism or Confucianism. It transplants better. [11] Hinduism's strength in India has been enhanced by nationalism, a phenomenon also observable in Islam. Modern Hinduism has also developed renewal movements that have won converts in Europe and America.

THE POPES

In the list below, the name of each pope is given, with, if known, his family name and birthplace, and the dates of his pontificate. The dates of the early popes are uncertain.

St. Peter (Simon, son of Jona); Bethsaida in Galilee; c.42–c.67
St. Linus; Tuscany; c.67–c.79
St. Anacletus or St. Cletus; Rome; c.79–c.92
St. Clement I (Clement of Rome); c.92–c.101
St. Evaristus; Asia Minor; c.99–c.107
St. Alexander I; Rome; c.107–c.116
St. Sixtus I; Rome; c.116–c.125
St. Telesphorus; Greece; c.125–c.138
St. Hyginus; Greece; 138–142
St. Pius I; Venetia; 142–155
St. Anicetus; Syria; 155–166
St. Soterus or St. Soter; Campania; c.166–c.174
St. Eleutherius or St. Eleuterius; Greece; c.174–c.189
St. Victor I; Africa; c.189–c.199
St. Zephyrinus; Rome; 199–217
St. Callistus I or St. Calixtus I; Rome; c.217–c.222
St. Urban I; Rome; 222–230
St. Pontianus or St. Pontian; Rome; 230–235
St. Anterus; Greece; c.235
St. Fabian; Rome; 236–250
St. Cornelius; Rome; 251–253
St. Lucius I; Rome; 253–254
St. Stephen I; Rome; 254–257
St. Sixtus II; Greece; 257–258
St. Dionysius; 259–268
St. Felix I; Rome; 269–274
St. Eutychian or St. Eutychianus; Tuscany; 275–283
St. Caius or St. Gaius; Dalmatia; 283–296
St. Marcellinus; Rome; 296–304
St. Marcellus I; Rome; 308–309
St. Eusebius; Greece; c.309–c.310
St. Melchiades or Meltiades or Miltiades; Africa; 311–314
St. Sylvester I; Rome; 314–335
St. Marcus or St. Mark; Rome; 10 months, 336
St. Julius I; Rome; 337–352
Liberius; Rome; 352–366
St. Damasus I; Spain; 366–384
St. Siricius; Rome; 384–399
St. Anastasius I; Rome; 399–401
St. Innocent I; Latium; 401–417
St. Zozimus or St. Zosimus; Greece; 417–418
St. Boniface I; Rome; 418–422
St. Celestine I; Campania; 422–432
St. Sixtus III; Rome; 432–440
St. Leo I (the Great); Tuscany; 440–461
St. Hilary or St. Hilarius; Sardinia; 461–468
St. Simplicius; Latium; 468–483
St. Felix II; Rome; 483–492
St. Gelasius I; Africa; 492–496
Anastasius II; Rome; 496–498
St. Symmacus or St. Symmachus; Sardinia; 498–514
St. Hormisdas; Frosinone; 514–523
St. John I; Tuscany; 523–526
St. Felix III; Rome; 526–530
Boniface II; Rome; 530–532
John II; Rome; 533–535
St. Agapitus or St. Agapetus; Rome; 535–536
St. Silverius; Campania; 536–537
Vigilius; Rome; 537–555
Pelagius I; Rome; 556–561
John III; Rome; 561–574
Benedict I; Rome; 575–579
Pelagius II; Rome; 579–590
St. Gregory I (the Great); Rome; 590–604
Sabinianus or Sabinian; Tuscany; 604–606
Boniface III; Rome; 9 months, 607
St. Boniface IV; 608–615
St. Deusdedit I or St. Adeodatus I; Rome; 615–618
Boniface V; Naples; 619–c.625
Honorius I; Campania; 625–638
Severinus; Rome; 4 months, 640
John IV; Dalmatia; 640–642
Theodore I; Greece?; 642–649
St. Martin I; Umbria?; 649–655
St. Eugene I or St. Eugenius I; Rome; 654–657[a]
St. Vitalian; Latium; 657–672
Adeodatus II or Deusdedit II; Rome; 672–676
Donus I; Rome; 676–678
St. Agatho or St. Agathonus; Sicily; 678–681
St. Leo II; Sicily; 682–683
St. Benedict II; Rome; 684–685
John V; Syria; 685–686
Conon; 686–687
St. Sergius I; Palermo; 687–701
John VI; Greece; 701–705
John VII; Greece; 705–707
Sisinnius; Syria; 2 months, 708

Constantine; Syria; 708–715
St. Gregory II; Rome; 715–731
St. Gregory III; Syria; 731–741
St. Zachary or St. Zacharias; Greece; 741–752
Stephen II; Rome; 752–757
St. Paul I; Rome; 757–767
Stephen III; Sicily; 768–772
Adrian I or Hadrian I; Rome; 772–795
St. Leo III; Rome; 795–816
Stephen IV; Rome; 816–817
St. Paschal I or St. Pascal I; Rome; 817–824
Eugene II or Eugenius II; Rome; 824–827
Valentine; Rome; 2 months, 827
Gregory IV; Rome; 827–844
Sergius II; Rome; 844–847
St. Leo IV; Rome; 847–855
Benedict III; 855–858
St. Nicholas I (the Great); Rome; 858–867
Adrian II; Rome; 867–872
John VIII; Rome; 872–882
Marinus I or Martin II; Rome; 882–884
St. Adrian III; Rome; 884–885
Stephen V; Rome; 885–891
Formosus; Rome; 891–896
Boniface VI; Rome; one month, 896
Stephen VI; Rome; 896–897
Romanus; 4 months, 897
Theodore II; Rome; one month, 897
John IX; Tivoli; 898–900
Benedict IV; Rome; 900–903
Leo V; 3 months, 903
Sergius III; Rome; 904–911
Anastasius III; Rome; 911–913
Lando; Rome; 913–914
John X (John of Tossignano); Emilia-Romagna; 914–928
Leo VI; Rome; 8 months, 928
Stephen VII; Rome; 928–931
John XI; 931–c.935
Leo VII; Rome; 936–939
Stephen VIII; Rome; 939–942
Marinus II or Martin III; Rome; 942–946
Agapitus II or Agapetus II; Rome; 946–955
John XII (Octavian); Latium; 955–964[b]
Leo VIII; Rome; 963–965[b]
Benedict V; Rome; 2 months; 964[b]
John XIII; Rome; 965–972
Benedict VI; Rome; 973–974
Benedict VII; Rome; 974–983
John XIV (Peter Canepanova); 983–984
John XV; Rome; 985–996
Gregory V (Bruno of Carinthia); Germany; 996–999
Sylvester II (Gerbert); France; 999–1003
John XVII (John Sicco); Rome; 7 months, 1003
John XVIII (Fasanus); Rome; 1003–09
Sergius IV (Peter Buccaporci); Rome; 1009–12
Benedict VIII (Theophylactus); 1012–24
John XIX (Romanus); Latium; 1024–c.32
Benedict IX (Theophylactus); 1032–44[c]
Sylvester III (John); Rome; 2 months, 1045
Benedict IX; 2 months, 1045
Gregory VI (John Gratian); Rome; 1045–46
Clement II (Suidger, Lord of Morsleben and Hornburg); Germany; 1046–47
Benedict IX; 1047–48
Damascus II (Poppo); Germany; 2 months, 1048
St. Leo IX (Bruno of Egisheim); Germany; 1048–54
Victor II (Gebhard); Germany; 1055–57
Stephen IX (Frederick); France; 1057–58
Nicholas II (Gerard); France; 1058–61
Alexander II (Anselmo da Baggio); Milan; 1061–73
St. Gregory VII (Hildebrand); Tuscany; 1073–85
Victor III (Dauferius; Desiderius); Campania; 1086–87
Urban II (Odo of Châtillon-sur-Marne); France; 1088–99
Paschal II or Pascal II (Rainerius); Latium; 1099–1118
Gelasius II (John of Gaeta); Latium; 1118–19
Callistus II or Calixtus II (Guido of Burgundy); France; 1119–24
Honorius II (Lambert Scannabecchi); Emilia-Romagna; 1124–30
Innocent II (Gregory Papareschi); Rome; 1130–43
Celestine II (Guido of Castellis); Ancona; 1143–44
Lucius II (Gerardo Caccianemici); Bologna; 1144–45
Eugene III (Bernard); Pisa; 1145–53
Anastasius IV (Conrad de Suburra); Rome; 1153–54
Adrian IV (Nicholas Breakspear); England; 1154–59
Alexander III (Roland Bandinelli); Siena; 1159–81
Lucius III (Ubaldus Allucingolus); Lucca; 1181–85
Urban III (Uberto Crivelli); Milan; 1185–87
Gregory VIII (Alberto de Morra); Benevento; 2 months, 1187
Clement III (Paolo Scolari); Rome; 1187–91
Celestine III (Giacinto Bobo); Rome; 1191–98
Innocent III (Lothar of Segni); Latium; 1198–1216
Honorius III (Cencio Savelli); Rome; 1216–27
Gregory IX (Hugo, Count of Segni); Latium; 1227–41

Celestine IV (Goffredo Castiglioni); Milan; 2 months, 1241
Innocent IV (Sinibaldo Fieschi); Genoa; 1243–54
Alexander IV (Rainaldo, Count of Segni); Latium; 1254–61
Urban IV (Jacques Pantaléon); France; 1261–64
Clement IV (Guy Fulcodi); France; 1265–68
Gregory X (Tedaldo Visconti); Emilia-Romagna; 1271–76
Innocent V (Peter of Tarentaise); Savoy; 5 months, 1276
Adrian V (Ottobono Fieschi); Genoa; 2 months, 1276
John XXI (Petrus Juliani or Petrus Hispanus); Portugal; 1276–77
Nicholas III (Giovanni Gaetano Orsini); Rome; 1277–80
Martin IV (Simon de Brie); France; 1281–85
Honorius IV (Jacobus Savelli); Rome; 1285–87
Nicholas IV (Girolamo Masci); Ascoli; 1288–92
St. Celestine V (Peter of Morrone); Abruzzi e Molise; 5 months, 1294
Boniface VIII (Benedetto Gaetani); Latium; 1294–1303
Benedict XI (Niccolo Boccasini); Venetia; 1303–04
Clement V (Bertrand de Got); France; 1305–14
John XXII (Jacques Duèse); France; 1316–34
Benedict XII (Jacques Fournier); France; 1334–42
Clement VI (Pierre Roger); France; 1342–52
Innocent VI (Étienne Aubert); France; 1352–62
Urban V (Guillaume de Grimoard); France; 1362–70
Gregory XI (Pierre Roger de Beaufort); France; 1370–78
Urban VI (Bartolomeo Prignano); Naples; 1378–89
Boniface IX (Pietro Tomacelli); Naples; 1389–1404
Innocent VII (Cosimo de' Migliorati); Abruzzi e Molise; 1404–06
Gregory XII (Angelo Correr); Venice; 1406–15
Martin V (Oddo Colonna); Abruzzi; 1417–31
Eugene IV (Gabriel Condulmaro); Venice; 1431–47
Nicholas V (Tommaso Parentucelli); Liguria; 1447–55
Callistus III or Calixtus III (Alfonso Borgia); Spain; 1455–58
Pius II (Enea Silvio Piccolomini); Siena; 1458–64
Paul II (Pietro Barbo); Venice; 1464–71
Sixtus IV (Francesco Della Rovere); Liguria; 1471–84
Innocent VIII (Giovanni Battista Cibo); Genoa; 1484–92
Alexander VI (Rodrigo Borgia); Spain; 1492–1503
Pius III (Francesco Todeschini Piccolomini); Siena; 2 months, 1503
Julius II (Giuliano Della Rovere); Liguria; 1503–13
Leo X (Giovanni de' Medici); Florence; 1513–21
Adrian VI (Adrian Florensz Dedal); Utrecht; 1522–23
Clement VII (Giulio de' Medici); Florence; 1523–34
Paul III (Alessandro Farnese); Rome; 1534–49
Julius III (Giovanni Maria Ciocchi del Monte); Rome; 1550–55
Marcellus II (Marcello Cervini); Siena; 2 months, 1555

Paul IV (Gian Pietro Carafa); Avellino; 1555–59
Pius IV (Giovanni Angelo de' Medici); Milan; 1559–65
St. Pius V (Antonio Ghislieri); Alessandria; 1556–72
Gregory XIII (Ugo Boncompagni); Bologna; 1572–85
Sixtus V (Felice Peretti); Astoli-Piceno; 1585–90
Urban VII (Giovanni Battista Castagna); Rome; one month, 1590
Gregory XIV (Niccolo Sfondrati); Milan; 1590–91
Innocent IX (Giovanni Antonio Facchinetti); Bologna; 2 months, 1591
Clement VIII (Ippolito Aldobrandini); Pesaro e Urbino, 1592–1605
Leo XI (Alessandro de' Medici); Florence; one month, 1605
Paul V (Camillo Borghese); Rome; 1605–21
Gregory XV (Alessandro Ludovisi); Bologna; 1621–23
Urban VIII (Maffeo Barberini); Florence; 1623–44
Innocent X (Giovanni Battista Pamphili); Rome; 1644–55
Alexander VII (Fabio Chigi); Siena; 1655–67
Clement IX (Giulio Rospigliosi); Tuscany; 1667–69
Clement X (Emilio Altieri); Rome; 1670–76
Innocent XI (Benedetto Odescalchi); Lombardy; 1676–89
Alexander VIII (Pietro Vito Ottoboni); Venice; 1689–91
Innocent XII (Antonio Pignatelli); Bari; 1691–1700
Clement XI (Giovanni Francesco Albani); Pesaro e Urbino; 1700–1721
Innocent XIII (Michelangelo dei Conti); Rome; 1721–24
Benedict XIII (Pietro Francesco Orsini); Bari; 1724–30
Clement XII (Lorenzo Corsini); Florence; 1730–40
Benedict XIV (Prospero Lambertini); Bologna; 1740–58
Clement XIII (Carlo Rezzonico); Venice; 1758–69
Clement XIV (Giovanni Vincenzo Antonio Ganganelli); Emilia-Romagna; 1769–74
Pius VI (Giovanni Angelo Braschi); Emilia-Romagna; 1775–99
Pius VII (Barnaba Chiaramonti); Emilia-Romagna; 1800–23
Leo XII (Annibale Della Genga); Spoleto; 1823–29
Pius VIII (Francesco Saverio Castiglioni); Ancona; 1829–30
Gregory XVI (Bartolomeo Alberto-Mauro-Cappellari); Venetia; 1831–46
Pius IX (Giovanni M. Mastai Ferretti); Ancona; 1846–78
Leo XIII (Gioacchino Pecci); Latium; 1878–1903
St. Pius X (Giuseppe Melchiorre Sarto); Treviso; 1903–14
Benedict XV (Giacomo Della Chiesa); Genoa; 1914–22
Pius XI (Achille Ratti); Milan; 1922–39
Pius XII (Eugenio Pacelli); Rome; 1939–58
John XXIII (Angelo Giuseppe Roncalli); Lombardy; 1958–63
Paul VI (Giovanni Battista Montini); Lombardy; 1963–1978
John Paul I (Albino Luciani), Venetia; 34 days, 1978
John Paul II (Karol Wojtyla); Wadowice, Poland; 1978–

ª He was elected during the exile of St. Martin I, who had been banished to Crimea for his condemnation of the Monothelite heresy.
ᵇ There is confusion about the legitimacy of claims to the pontificate by Leo VIII and Benedict V. John XII was deposed on Dec. 4, 963. If his deposition was invalid, Leo was an antipope. If it was valid, Leo was the legitimate pope, and Benedict was an antipope.
ᶜ If the triple deposition of Benedict IX (in 1044, in 1046, and again in 1048) was illegitimate, Sylvester III, Gregory VI, and Clement III were antipopes.

CALENDAR OF RELIGIOUS HOLIDAYS: 1981-1982

SOURCE: Yearbook of American and Canadian Churches 1981; © copyright 1981, by the National Council of the Churches of Christ in the United States of America.

1st Sunday in Advent	Nov.	29, 1981	Pentecost (Whitsunday)*	May	30
1st Day of Hanukkah	Dec.	21	Trinity Sunday	Jun.	6
Christmas	Dec.	25	First Day of the Month of Ramadan	Jun.	23
New Year's Eve (Watch Night)	Dec.	31	St. Jean Baptiste Day (Canada)	Jun.	24
New Year's Day	Jan.	1, 1982	Festival of the End of Ramadan	Jul.	21
Twelfth Night: Epiphany Eve	Jan.	5	The Transfiguration	Aug.	6
The Epiphany (Armenian Christmas)	Jan.	6	Labor Sunday	Sep.	5
Mawlid al-Nabi (Prophet Muhammed's Birthday)	Jan.	8	1st Day of Rosh Hashanah	Sep.	18
Week of Prayer for Christian Unity	Jan.	18 to 25	Sacrificial Festival, Pilgrimmage to Mecca	Sep.	27
Presentation of Jesus in the Temple	Feb.	2	Yom Kippur	Sep.	27
Brotherhood Week	Feb.	14 to 21	1st Day of Sukkot	Oct.	2
Last Sunday after the Epiphany	Feb.	21	World Communion Sunday	Oct.	2
Ash Wednesday*	Feb.	24	Shemini Atzeret	Oct.	9
1st Sunday in Lent*	Feb.	28	Simhat Torah	Oct.	10
Purim	Mar.	9	Thanksgiving Day (Canada)	Oct.	11
The Annunciation	Mar.	25	Opening of Muslim liturgical year	Oct.	19
Holy Week*	Apr.	4 to 10	Reformation Day	Oct.	31
Palm Sunday (Passion Sunday)*	Apr.	4	Reformation Sunday	Oct.	31
Maundy Thursday*	Apr.	8	All Saints' Day	Nov.	1
1st Day of Passover	Apr.	8	All Souls' Day	Nov.	2
Good Friday*	Apr.	9	World Community Day	Nov.	5
Easter Eve*	Apr.	10	Stewardship Day	Nov.	14
Easter*	Apr.	11	Bible Sunday	Nov.	21
Easter†	Apr.	18	Thanksgiving Sunday (U.S.)	Nov.	21
National Family Week	May	2 to 9	Thanksgiving Day (U.S.)	Nov.	25
May Fellowship Day	May	7	1st Sunday in Advent	Nov.	28
Rural Life Sunday	May	16	1st Day of Hanukkah	Dec.	11
Ascension Day*	May	20	Christmas	Dec.	25
1st Day of Shavuot	May	28	New Year's Eve (Watch Night)	Dec.	31

*Western Churches. †Eastern Orthodox Churches.

COLLEGE OF CARDINALS

SOURCE: 1982 Catholic Almanac. Data as of June 1, 1981.

The cardinals are bishops chosen by the pope to serve as his principal advisers in the central administration of church affairs; those under the age of 80 are electors of the pope. Collectively, they form the Sacred College of Cardinals.

The college evolved gradually during the first 11 centuries from the synods of Roman clergy. The first cardinals, in about the sixth century, were priests of the leading churches of Rome who assisted the Holy See in directing church affairs.

Name	Office or Dignity	Nationality	Created
Alfrink, Bernard	Former Archbishop of Utrecht	Dutch	1960
Antonelli, Ferdinando		Italian	1973
Aponte Martinez, Luis	Archbishop of San Juan	Puerto Rican	1973
Aramburu, Juan Carlos	Archbishop of Buenos Aires	Argentinian	1976
Arns, Paulo Evaristo	Archbishop of Sao Paolo	Brazilian	1973
Bafile, Corrado	Former Prefect of Sacred Congregation for Causes of Saints	Italian	1976
Baggio, Sebastiano	Prefect of Sacred Congregation for Bishops	Italian	1969
Ballestrero, Anastasio, O.C.D.	Archbishop of Turin	Italian	1979
Baum, William W.	Prefect of the Congregation for Catholic Education	American	1976
Benelli, Giovanni	Archbishop of Florence	Italian	1977
Beras Rojas, Octavio Antonio	Archbishop of Santo Domingo	Dominican	1976
Bertoli, Paolo	Chamberlain of Holy Roman Church	Italian	1969
Brandao Vilela, Avelar	Archbishop of Sao Salvador	Brazilian	1973
Bueno y Monreal, Jose M.	Archbishop of Seville	Spanish	1958
Caprio, Giuseppe	President of Prefecture of Holy See's Economic Affairs	Italian	1979
Carberry, John	Former Archbishop of St. Louis	American	1969
Carpino, Francesco	Referendary of Sacred Congregation of Bishops	Italian	1967
Carter, Gerald Emmett	Archbishop of Toronto	Canadian	1979
Casariego, Mario	Archbishop of Guatemala	Guatamalan	1969
Casaroli, Agostino	Secretary of State	Italian	1979
Cé, Marco	Patriarch of Venice	Italian	1979
Ciappi, Mario Luigi	Pro-Theologian of the Pontifical Household	Italian	1977
Civardi, Ernesto		Italian	1979
Cody, John P.	Archbishop of Chicago	American	1967
Colombo, Giovanni	Former Archbishop of Milan	Italian	1965
Confalonieri, Carlo	Dean of College of Cardinals	Italian	1958
Cooke, Terence	Archbishop of New York	American	1969
Cooray, Thomas B.	Former Archbishop of Colombo	Sri Lankan	1965
Cordeiro, Joseph	Archbishop of Karachi	Pakistani	1973
Corripio Ahumada, Ernesto	Archbishop of Mexico City & Primate of Mexico	Mexican	1979
Darmojuwono, Justin	Archbishop of Semarang	Indonesian	1967
De Araujo Sales, Eugenio	Archbishop of Rio de Janeiro	Brazilian	1969
Dearden, John	Former Archbishop of Detroit	American	1969
de Furstenberg, Maximilien		Dutch	1967
Duval, Leon-Etienne	Archbishop of Algiers	Algerian	1965
Ekandem, Dominic	Bishop of Ikot Ekpene	Nigerian	1976
Enrique y Tarancon, Vicente	Archbishop of Madrid	Spanish	1969
Etchegaray, Roger	Archbishop of Marseilles	French	1979
Felici, Pericle	Prefect Supreme Tribunal of Apostolic Signatura	Italian	1967
Flahiff, George	Archbishop of Winnipeg	Canadian	1969
Florit, Ermenegildo	Former Archbishop of Florence	Italian	1965
Freeman, James Darcy	Archbishop of Sydney	Australian	1973
Gantin, Bernardin	President of Pontifical Commission for Justice and Peace	Beninese	1977
Garrone, Gabriele M.		French	1967
Gonzalez Martin, Marcelo	Archbishop of Toledo	Spanish	1973
Gouyon, Paul	Archbishop of Rennes	French	1969
Gray, Gordon	Archbishop of St. Andrews and Edinburgh	Scottish	1969
Guerri, Sergio	Pro-President of the Pontifical Commission for the Vatican City State	Italian	1969
Guyot, Jean	Former Archbishop of Toulouse	French	1973
Hoeffner, Joseph	Archbishop of Cologne	German	1969
Hume, George Basil, O.S.B.	Archbishop of Westminster	English	1976
Jubany Arnau, Narciso	Archbishop of Barcelona	Spanish	1973
Kim Sou Hwan, Stephan	Archbishop of Seoul	Korean	1969
Knox, James	Prefect of Sacred Congregation for the Sacraments and Divine Worship	Australian	1973
Koenig, Franz	Archbishop of Vienna, President of Secretariat for Non-Believers	Austrian	1958
Krol, John	Archbishop of Philadelphia	American	1967
Landazuri Ricketts, Juan, O.F.M.	Archbishop of Lima	Peruvian	1962
Leger, Paul	Former Archbishop of Montreal	Canadian	1953
Lekai, Laszlo	Archbishop of Esztergom	Hungarian	1976
Lorscheider, Aloisio, O.F.M.	Archbishop of Fortaleza	Brazilian	1976
Macharski, Franciszek	Archbishop of Krakow	Polish	1979
Malula, Joseph	Archbishop of Kinshasa	Zairean	1969

Name	Office or Dignity	Nationality	Created
Manning, Timothy	Archbishop of Los Angeles	American	1973
Marella, Paolo	Sub-Dean of College of Cardinals; Archpriest of Vatican Basilica	Italian	1959
Marty, François	Former Archbishop of Paris	French	1969
Maurer, Jose, C.SS.R.	Archbishop of Sucre	Bolivian	1967
McCann, Owan	Archbishop of Cape Town	South African	1965
Medeiros, Humberto	Archbishop of Boston	American	1973
Miranda y Gomez, Miguel	Former Archbishop of Mexico City	Mexican	1969
Motta, Carlos Carmelo de Vasconcellos	Archbishop of Aparecida	Brazilian	1946
Mozzoni, Umberto	President of Pontifical Commission for Sanctuaries of Pompei, Loreto, and Bari	Italian	1973
Munoz Duque, Anibal	Archbishop of Bogota	Colombian	1973
Munoz Vega, Pablo	Archbishop of Quito	Ecuadorian	
Nasalli Rocca di Corneliano, Mario		Italian	1969
Nsubuga, Emmanuel	Archbishop of Kampala	Ugandan	1976
O'Boyle, Patrick	Former Archbishop of Washington	American	1967
Oddi, Silvio	Prefect of the Sacred Congregation for the Clergy	Italian	1969
O'Fiaich, Tomas	Archbishop of Armagh and Primate of All Ireland	Irish	1979
Otunga, Maurice	Archbishop of Nairobi	Kenyan	1973
Palazzini, Pietro	Prefect of Sacred Congregation for Causes of Saints	Italian	1973
Pappalardo, Salvatore	Archbishop of Palermo	Italian	1973
Parecattil, Joseph	Archbishop of Ernakulam	Indian	1969
Parente, Pietro		Italian	1967
Paupini, Giuseppe	Major Penitentiary	Italian	1969
Pellegrino, Michele	Former Archbishop of Turin	Italian	1967
Philippe, Paul	Former Prefect of Sacred Congregation for Oriental Churches	French	1973
Picachy, Lawrence Trevor, S.J.	Archbishop of Calcutta	Indian	1976
Pironio, Eduardo	Prefect of Sacred Congregation for Religious and Secular Institutes	Argentinian	1976
Poletti, Ugo	Vicar General of Rome	Italian	1973
Poma, Antonio	Archbishop of Bologna	Italian	1969
Primatesta, Raul	Archbishop of Cordoba	Argentinian	1973
Quintero, Jose	Former Archbishop of Caracas	Venezuelan	1961
Ratzinger, Joseph	Archbishop of Munich and Freising	German	1977
Razafimahatrata, Victor, S.J.	Archbishop of Tananarive	Madagascan	1976
Renard, Alexandre	Archbishop of Lyons	French	1967
Ribeiro, Antonio	Patriarch of Lisbon	Portuguese	1973
Righi-Lambertini, Egano		Italian	1979
Rosales, Julio	Archbishop of Cebu	Filipino	1969
Rossi, Agnelo	Prefect of the Sacred Congregation for the Evangelization of Peoples	Brazilian	1965
Rossi, Opilio	President of Pontifical Council for Laity	Italian	1976
Roy, Maurice	Former Archbishop of Québec	Canadian	1965
Rubin, Wladislaw	Prefect of Sacred Congregation for Oriental Churches	Polish	1979
Rugambwa, Laurean	Archbishop of Dar-es-Salaam	Tanzanian	1960
Salazar Lopez, Jose	Archbishop of Guadalajara	Mexican	1973
Samore, Antonio	Librarian and Archivist of Holy Roman Church	Italian	1967
Satowaki, Joseph Asajiro	Archbishop of Nagasaki	Japanese	1979
Scherer, Alfredo	Archbishop of Porto Alegre	Brazilian	1969
Schroffer, Joseph		German	1976
Sensi, Giuseppe M.		Italian	1976
Seper, Franjo	Prefect of Sacred Congregation for Doctrine of Faith	Yugoslavian	1965
Shehan, Lawrence	Former Archbishop of Baltimore	American	1965
Sidarouss, Stephanos, C.M.	Coptic Patriarch of Alexandria	Egyptian	1965
Silva Henriquez, Raul, S.D.B.	Archbishop of Santiago	Chilean	1962
Sin, Jaime L.	Archbishop of Manila	Filipino	1976
Siri, Giuseppe	Archbishop of Genoa	Italian	1953
Slipyj, Josyf	Archbishop of Lwow	Ukrainian	1965
Suenens, Leo	Former Archbishop of Mechelen-Brussels	Belgian	1962
Taofinu'u, Pius	Bishop of Samoa and Tokelau	Samoan	1973
Thiandoum, Hyacinthe	Archbishop of Dakar	Senegalese	1976
Tomasek, Frantisek	Archbishop of Prague	Czech	1976
Trinh-Van-Can, Joseph-Marie	Archbishop of Hanoi	Vietnamese	1979
Ursi, Corrado	Archbishop of Naples	Italian	1973
Volk, Hermann	Bishop of Mainz	German	1973
Willebrands, Johannes	Archbishop of Utrecht, President of the Secretariat for the Union of Churches	Dutch	1969
Zoungrana, Paul	Archbishop of Ouagadougou	Upper Voltese	1965

U.S. RELIGIOUS BODIES

SOURCE: *Yearbook of American and Canadian Churches 1981*, edited by Constant H. Jacquet, Jr. Copyright © 1981, by the National Council of the Churches of Christ in the United States of America.

This directory of American religious denominations includes only those with a membership of 50,000 or more. Membership and other data are for 1979-80 unless otherwise noted.

African Methodist Episcopal Church This church began (1787) in Philadelphia when members of St. George's Methodist Episcopal Church withdrew as a protest against color segregation. In 1816 the denomination was started, led by Rev. Richard Allen. Membership: 1,970,000; Gen. Sec., Dr. Richard A. Chappelle, Sr., P.O. Box 183, St. Louis, MO 63166

African Methodist Episcopal Zion Church The A.M.E. Zion Church is an independent body, having withdrawn (1796) from the John Street Methodist Church of New York City. Membership: 1,125,176; Gen. Sec.-Aud., Earle E. Johnson, P.O. Box 32843, Charlotte, NC 28232

American Baptist Association A fellowship of regular and independent missionary Baptist churches distributed throughout the United States, with their greatest strength in the South. Their national fellowship was formed in 1905. Membership: 1,500,000; Headquarters: 4605 N. State Line Ave., Texarkana, TX 75501

American Baptist Churches in the U.S.A. Formerly known as the Northern Baptist Convention, this body of Baptist churches changed the name to American Baptist Convention at the annual meeting in Boston, May 24, 1950. In 1972 the present name was adopted. Membership: 1,271,688 (1978); Headquarters: Valley Forge, PA 19481

The American Carpatho-Russian Orthodox Greek Catholic Church This body is a self-governing diocese that is in communion with the Ecumenical Patriarchate of Constantinople. In 1938 the late Patriarch Benjamin I canonized the Diocese in the name of the Orthodox Church of Christ. Membership: 100,000 (1976); Headquarters: Johnstown, PA 15906

The American Lutheran Church This body was organized (1960) in Minneapolis. It combined the American Lutheran Church, The Evangelical Lutheran Church, and the United Evangelical Lutheran Church. The union brought together major Lutheran church bodies of different national heritage. In 1963 the Lutheran Free Church merged with The American Lutheran Church. Membership: 2,362,685; National Offices: 422 S. 5th St., Minneapolis, MN 55415

The Antiochian Orthodox Christian Archdiocese of North America was formed (1975) as a result of a merger of The Antiochian Orthodox Christian Archdiocese of NY and All N.A. and the Antiochian Orthodox Archdiocese of Toledo, OH and Dependencies in N.A. It is under the jurisdiction of the Patriarch of Antioch. Membership: 152,000 (1977); Headquarters: 358 Mountain Rd., Englewood, NJ 07631

Apostolic Overcoming Holy Church of God A black body incorporated (1919) in Alabama. It is evangelistic in purpose and emphasizes sanctification, holiness, and divine healing. Membership: 75,000 (1956); Sec., Mrs. Juanita Arrington, 909 Jasper Rd. W., Birmingham, AL 35204

Armenian Apostolic Church of America This church was under the jurisdiction of the Etchmiadzin See (now in Soviet Armenia) from 1887 to 1933, when a division occurred over the church's condition in Soviet Armenia. One group remained independent until 1957 when it came under the jurisdiction of the Holy See of Cilicia in Lebanon. Membership: 125,000 (1972); Headquarters: 138 E. 39th St., New York, NY 10016

Armenian Church of America, Diocese of the (Including Diocese of California) The American branch of the ancient Church of Armenia was established in America in 1889. Diocesan organization is under the jurisdiction of the Holy See of Etchmiadzin, Armenia, USSR. Membership: 450,000; Diocesan offices: St. Vartan Cathedral, 630 Second Ave., New York, NY 10016

Assemblies of God An evangelical missionary fellowship which grew out of the Pentecostal revivals at the turn of this century. Founded (1914) in Hot Springs, Ark., the organization is now composed of self-governing churches which constitute 55 districts and seven foreign language branches. Membership: 1,629,014; Headquarters: 1445 Boonville Ave., Springfield, MO 65802

Baptist General Conference This body has operated as a Conference since 1879; its first church was organized in 1852. It has a ministry through 780 churches and five boards of operation. Membership: 126,800; Headquarters: 2002 S. Arlington Heights Rd., Arlington Heights, IL 60005

Baptist Missionary Association of America A group of regular Baptist churches organized in associational capacity in Little Rock (1950) as North American Baptist Association (present name adopted 1969). In theology these churches are evangelical, missionary, fundamental, and in the main premillennial. Membership: 226,290; Rec. Sec.: Rev. Ralph Cottrell, P.O. Box 2866, Texarkana, AR 75501

Buddhist Churches of America Organized in 1914 as the Buddhist Mission of North America, this body was incorporated in 1942 under the present name and represents the Jodo Shinshu Sect of Buddhism in this country. Membership: 60,000 (1975); Headquarters: 1710 Octavia St., San Francisco, CA 94109

Bulgarian Eastern Orthodox Church (Diocese of N. & S. America and Australia) The Holy Synod of the Bulgarian Eastern Orthodox Church established for its Bulgarian Christians in North and South America and Australia a Bulgarian Orthodox church in 1907, which became (1938) Episcopate and was officially incorporated (1947) in New York State. Membership: 86,000 (1971); Headquarters: NY Diocese, 312 W. 101st St., New York, NY 10025

The Christian and Missionary Alliance An evangelical, evangelistic, and missionary movement, organized (1887) by Rev. A.B. Simpson, in New York. It stresses "the deeper Christian life and consecration to the Lord's service." Membership: 173,986; Headquarters: 350 N. Highland Ave., Nyack, NY 10960

Christian Church (Disciples of Christ) Started on the American frontier in the early 1800s as a movement to unify Christians, this body drew its major inspiration from Thomas and Alexander Campbell in western Pennsylvania and Barton W. Stone in Kentucky. Developing separately, the "Disciples," under Alexander Campbell and the "Christians," led by Stone, merged (1832) in Lexington, Ky. Membership: 1,213,061; Headquarters: 222 S. Downey Ave., Box 1986, Indianapolis, IN 46206

Christian Churches and Churches of Christ The fellowship has its origin in the American movement to "restore the New Testament church in doctrine, ordinances and life" initiated by Thomas and Alexander Campbell, Walter Scott and Barton W. Stone in the early 1800s. Membership: 1,054,266; no general organization.

The Christian Congregation, Inc. Original incorporation, March 10, 1887; revised incorporation, October 29, 1898. The New Commandment, John 13:34-35, is the bond of fellowship in creative ethical activism. Membership: 83,199; Gen. Supt.: Rev. Ora W. Eads, 804 W. Hemlock St., LaFollette, TN 37766

Christian Methodist Episcopal Church In 1870 the General Conference of the M.E. Church, South, approved the request of its colored membership for the formation of a separate ecclesiastical body, which became the Colored Methodist Episcopal Church. The Christian Methodist Episcopal Church became the official name in 1956. Membership: 466,718 (1965); Sec., Rev. N. Charles Thomas, P.O. Box 74, Memphis, TN 38101

Christian Reformed Church in North America A group of Dutch Calvinists that dissented (1857) from the Reformed Church in America and was strengthened by later accessions from the same source and by immigration. Doctrines: the Heidelberg Catechism (1563), the Canons of Dort (1618-19), and the Belgic Confession (1561).

Membership: 212,700; Office Address: 2850 Kalamazoo Ave. SE, Grand Rapids, MI 49560

The Church of Christ, Scientist (Christian Scientists) The Church of Christ, Scientist was founded in 1879 when Mrs. Mary Baker Eddy and 15 students met and voted to "organize a church designed to commemorate the word and works of our Master, which should reinstate primitive Christianity and its lost element of healing." Membership: not given; Headquarters: Christian Science Church Center, Boston, MA 02115

The Church of God This evangelical body was inaugurated by Bishop A.J. Tomlinson, who served (1903-43) as General Overseer, and many groups of the Pentecostal and Holiness Movement stem from it. It is episcopal in administration. Membership: 75,890; Headquarters: 2504 Arrow Wood Drive SE, Huntsville, AL 35803

Church of God (Anderson, IN) This body is one of the largest of the groups that have taken the name "Church of God." It originated about 1880 and emphasizes Christian unity. Membership: 175,113; Headquarters: Box 2420, Anderson, IN 46011

Church of God (Cleveland, TN) America's oldest Pentecostal church began (1886) as an outgrowth of the holiness revival under the name Christian Union. Reorganized (1902) as the Holiness Church, the church adopted (1907) the name Church of God. Its doctrine is fundamental and Pentecostal; it maintains a centralized form of government and a missionary program. Membership: 411,385; Headquarters: Keith St. at 25th NW, Cleveland, TN 37311

The Church of God in Christ was founded in (1906) in Memphis by Charles Harrison Mason, a former Baptist Minister. It is trinitarian in doctrine. Membership: 425,000 (1965); Headquarters: 938 Mason St., Memphis, TN 38126

The Church of God in Christ, International Organized in 1969 in Kansas City, Mo., by 14 bishops of the Church of God in Christ of Memphis, Tenn. The doctrine is the same, but the separation came because of a disagreement over polity and governmental authority. Membership: 501,000 (1971); Headquarters: 170 Adelphi St., Brooklyn, NY 11025

The Church of God of Prophecy Organized (1886) in Monroe Cty., Tenn, and reorganized (1902) at Camp Creek, N.C., this church formally adopted the name Church of God (1907), but since 1952 the name Church of God of Prophecy has been used for secular purposes and in order to avoid confusion with similarly named organizations. Membership: 227,850; Headquarters: Bible Place, Cleveland, TN 37311

The Church of Jesus Christ of Latter-day Saints (The Mormons) was organized (1830) at Fayette, N.Y., by Joseph Smith. Its members consider the Bible, Book of Mormon, Doctrine and Covenants, and the Pearl of Great Price to be the word of God. Their belief is summed up in 13 Articles of Faith written by Joseph Smith. Membership: 2,706,000; Headquarters: 50 East North Temple St., Salt Lake City, UT 84111

Church of the Brethren German pietists-anabaptists founded (1708) under Alexander Mack, Schwarzenau, Germany, entered the colonies in 1719 and settled at Germantown, Pa. They have no creed other than the New Testament, hold to principles of nonviolence, temperance, and voluntarism, and emphasize religion in life. Membership: 172,115; Headquarters: Church of the Brethren General Offices, 1451 Dundee Ave., Elgin, IL 60120

Church of the Nazarene One of the larger holiness bodies, it was organized (1908) in Pilot Point, Tex. It is in general accord with the early doctrines of Methodism and emphasizes entire sanctification as a second definite work of grace. Membership: 474,820; Headquarters: 6401 The Paseo, Kansas City, MO 64131

Churches of Christ This body is made up of a large group of churches, formerly reported with the Disciples of Christ but reported separately since the Religious Census (1906). They are strictly congregational and have no organization larger than the local congregation. Membership: 1,600,000

Community Churches, National Council of This body is a fellowship of locally autonomous, ecumenically minded, congregationally governed, noncreedal Protestant churches. It is the union (1950) of the all-black Biennial Council of Community Churches, and a council of white churches with the same name as the present body. Membership: 190,000; National Office: 89 E. Wilson Bridge Rd., Worthington, OH 43085

Congregational Christian Churches, National Association of Organized (1955) in Detroit by delegates from Congregational Christian Churches committed to continuing the Congregational way of faith and order in church life. It has no doctrinal requirements. Participation by member churches is voluntary. Membership: 100,000; Headquarters: P.O. Box 1620, Oak Creek, WI 53154

Conservative Baptist Association of America Organized (May 17, 1947) at Atlantic City, N.J., the association regards the Old and New Testaments as the divinely inspired Word of God and as infallible and of supreme authority. Each local church is independent and autonomous. Membership: 225,000; Headquarters: Geneva Rd., P.O. Box 66, Wheaton, IL 60187

Coptic Orthodox Church is part of the ancient Coptic Orthodox Church of Egypt, currently headed by His Holiness Pope Shenouda III. Membership: 100,000; Correspondent: Archpriest Fr. Gabriel Abdelsayed, 427 West Side Ave., Jersey City, NJ 07304

Cumberland Presbyterian Church An outgrowth of the Great Revival of 1800, the Cumberland Presbytery was organized on February 4, 1810, in Dickson County, Tenn., by three Presbyterian ministers, Revs. Finis Ewing, Samuel King, and Samuel McAdow. Membership: 94,574; Headquarters: Box 40149, Memphis, TN 38104

The Episcopal Church entered the colonies with the earliest settlers (Jamestown, Va., 1607) as the Church of England. It became autonomous and adopted its present name in 1789. It is an integral part of the Anglican Communion. In 1967 the General Convention adopted "The Episcopal Church" as an alternate name for the Protestant Episcopal Church in the U.S.A. Membership: 2,841,350; Headquarters: 815 Second Ave., New York, NY 10017

ACTIVE EPISCOPAL BISHOPS IN THE U.S.

Note: MB, Missionary Bishop; Address: Right Reverend

Headquarters Staff: Presiding Bishop, John M. Allin; Exec. Vice-Pres., Milton L. Wood; Exec. for Mission and Ministry, Elliott Sorge; Suffragan Bishop for the Armed Forces, Charles L. Burgreen; 815 Second Ave., New York, NY 10017

Alabama: Furman C. Stough, 521 N. 20th St., Birmingham, AL 35203

Alaska: David E. Cochran, Box 441, Fairbanks, AK 99707

Albany: Wilbur E. Hogg, 62 S. Swan St., Albany, NY 12210

Arizona: Joseph T. Heistand, 110 W. Roosevelt St., Phoenix, AZ 85003

Arkansas: Christoph Keller, 300 W. 17th St., P.O. Box 6120, Little Rock, AR 72206

Atlanta: Bennett J. Sims, 2744 Peachtree Rd. NW, Atlanta, GA 30305

Bethlehem: Lloyd E. Gressle, 826 Delaware Ave., Bethlehem, PA 18015

California: William E. Swing, 1055 Taylor St., San Francisco, CA 94108

Central Florida: William H. Folwell, 324 N. Interlachen Ave., Box 790, Winter Park, FL 32789

Central Gulf Coast: George M. Murray, 3800 Old Shell Rd., P.O. Box 8395, Mobile, AL 36608

Central New York: Ned Cole, Jr., 310 Montgomery St., Syracuse, NY 13203

Central Pennsylvania: Dean T. Stevenson, 221 N. Front St., Harrisburg 17101, P.O. Box W, Harrisburg, PA 17108

Chicago: James W. Montgomery, 65 E. Huron St., Chicago, IL 60611

Colorado: William C. Frey, P.O. Box M, Capitol Hill Sta., Denver, CO 80218

Connecticut: Morgan Porteus, 1335 Asylum Ave., Hartford, CT 06105

Dallas: A. Donald Davies, 1630 Garrett St., Dallas, TX 75206

Delaware: William Hawley Clark, 2020 Tatnall St., Wilmington, DE 19802

East Carolina: Hunley A. Elebash, 305 S. 3rd St., Wilmington, NC 28401

Eastern Oregon: Rustin R. Kimsey, 1336 W. Glacier, Redmond, OR 97756

Easton: Moultrie Moore, Box 1027, Easton, MD 21601

Eau Claire: William C. Wantland, 510 S. Farwell St., Eau Claire, WI 54701

El Camino Real: C. Shannon Mallory, % St. Paul's Church, 1071 Pajaro St., Salinas, CA 93901

Erie: Donald J. Davis, 145 W. 6th St., Erie, PA 16501

Florida: Frank S. Cerveny, 325 Market St., Jacksonville, FL 32202

Fond du Lac: William L. Stevens, Box 149, Fond du Lac, WI 54935

Georgia: G. Paul Reeves, 611 E. Bay St., Savannah, GA 31401

Hawaii: Edmond L. Browning, Queen Emma Square, Honolulu, HI 96813

Idaho: Hanford L. King, Box 936, Boise, ID 83701

Indianapolis: Edward W. Jones, 1100 W. 42nd St., Indianapolis, IN 46208

Iowa: Walter C. Righter, 225 37th St., Des Moines, IA 50312

Kansas: Edward C. Turner, Bethany Pl., Topeka, KS 66612

Kentucky: David B. Reed, 421 S. 2nd St., Louisville, KY 40202

Lexington: Addison Hosea, 530 Sayre Ave., Lexington, KY 40508

Long Island: Robert Campbell Witcher, 36 Cathedral Ave., Garden City, NY 11530

Los Angeles: Robert C. Rusack, 1220 W. 4th St., Los Angeles, CA 90017

Louisiana: James Barrow Brown, P.O. Box 15719, New Orleans, LA 70175

Maine: Frederick B. Wolf, 143 State St., Portland, ME 04101

Maryland: David Leighton, Sr., 105 W. Monument St., Baltimore, MD 21230

Massachusetts: John B. Coburn, 1 Joy St., Boston, MA 02108

Michigan: H. Coleman McGehee, Jr., 4800 Woodward Ave., Detroit, MI 48201

Milwaukee: Charles T. Gaskell, 804 E. Juneau Ave., Milwaukee, WI 53202

Minnesota: Robert M. Anderson, 309 Clifton Ave., Minneapolis, MN 55403

Mississippi: Duncan M. Gray, Jr., P.O. Box 1636, Jackson, MS 39205

Missouri: William Augustus Jones, Jr., 1210 Locust St., St. Louis, MO 63103

Montana: Jackson E. Gilliam, 303 Horsky Block, Helena, MT 59601

Navajoland Area Mission: Frederick W. Putnam, P.O. Box 720, Farmington, NM 47401

Nebraska: James Daniel Warner, 200 N. 62nd St., Omaha, NB 68132

Nevada: Wesley Frensdorff, 2930 W. 7th St., Reno, NV 89503

Newark: John Shelby Spong, 24 Rector St., Newark, NJ 07102

New Hampshire: Philip A. Smith, 63 Green St., Concord, NH 03301

New Jersey: Albert W. Van Duzer, 808 W. State St., Trenton, NJ 08618

New York: Paul Moore, Jr., 1047 Amsterdam Ave., New York, NY 10025

North Carolina: Thomas A. Fraser, Jr., 20 St. Alban's, P.O. Box 17025, Raleigh, NC 27609

North Dakota: Harold A. Hopkins, Jr., 809 8th Ave. S., Fargo, ND 58102

Northern California: John L. Thompson III, 1322 27th St., P.O. Box 161268, Sacramento, CA 95816

Northern Indiana: William C.R. Sheridan, 117 N. Lafayette Blvd., South Bend, IN 46601

Northern Michigan: William Arthur Dimmick, 131 E. Ridge St., Marquette, MI 49855

Northwest Texas: —, Texas Commerce Bank Bldg., Ste. 506, 1314 Ave. K, P.O. Box 1067, Lubbock, TX 79408

Ohio: John H. Burt, 2230 Euclid Ave., Cleveland, OH 44115

Oklahoma: Gerald N. McAllister, P.O. Box 1098, Oklahoma City, OK 73101

Olympia: Robert H. Cochrane, 1551 Tenth Ave. E., Seattle, WA 98102

Oregon: Matthew P. Bigliardi, 11800 S.W. Military La., Portland 97219, P.O. Box 467, Portland, OR 97034

Panama: Lemuel B. Shirley (MB), Box R, Balboa, Panama

Pennsylvania: Lyman C. Ogilby, 1700 Market St., Ste. 1600, Philadelphia, PA 19103

Pittsburgh: Robert B. Appleyard, 325 Oliver Ave., Pittsburgh, PA 15222

Puerto Rico: Francisco Reus-Froylán (MB), P.O. Box C, Saint Just, PR 00750

Quincy: Donald J. Parsons, 3601 N. North St., Peoria, IL 61604

Rhode Island: George Hunt, 275 N. Main St., Providence, RI 02903

Rio Grande: Richard M. Trelease, Jr., 120 Vassar S.E., Ste. 1-B, P.O. Box 4130, Albuquerque, NM 87106

Rochester: Robert R. Spears, Jr., 935 East Ave., Rochester, NY 14607

San Diego: Robert M. Wolterstorff, St. Paul's Church, 2728 6th Ave., San Diego, CA 92103

San Joaquin: Victor M. Rivera, 4159 E. Dakota, Fresno, CA 93726

South Carolina: Gray Temple, 1020 King St., Drawer 2127, Charleston, SC 29403

South Dakota: Walter H. Jones, 200 W. 18th St., P.O. Box 517, Sioux Falls, SD 57101

Southeast Florida: Calvin O. Schofield, Jr., 525 NE 15th St., Miami, FL 33132

Southern Ohio: William G. Black, 412 Sycamore St., Cincinnati, OH 45202

Southern Virginia: Claude Charles Vaché, 600 Talbot Hill Rd., Norfolk, VA 23505

Southwest Florida: Emerson Paul Hayes, P.O. Box 20899, St. Petersburg, FL 33742

Southwestern Virginia: A. Heath Light, P.O. Box 2068, Roanoke, VA 24009

Spokane: Leigh Allen Wallace, Jr., 245 E. 13th Ave., Spokane, WA 99202

Springfield: Albert W. Hillestad, 821 S. 2nd St., Springfield, IL 62704

Tennessee: William E. Sanders, Box 3807, Knoxville, TN 37917

Texas: Maurice M. Benitez, 520 San Jacinto St., Houston, TX 77002

Upper South Carolina: William A. Beckham, P.O. Box 1789, Columbia, SC 29202

Utah: E. Otis Charles, 231 E. First St. S., Salt Lake City, UT 84111

Vermont: Robert S. Kerr, Rock Point, Burlington, VT 05401

Virgin Islands: Edward M. Turner (MB), P.O. Box 1589, St. Thomas, U.S. VI 00801

Virginia: Robert B. Hall, 110 W. Franklin St., Richmond, VA 23220

Washington: John T. Walker, Mt. St. Alban, Washington, DC 20016

West Missouri: Arthur Vogel, 415 W. 13th St., P.O. Box 23216, Kansas City, MO 64141

West Texas: Scott Field Bailey, P.O. Box 6885, San Antonio, TX 78209

West Virginia: Robert P. Atkinson, 1608 Virginia St. E., Charleston, WV 25311

Western Kansas: —, 142 S. 8th St., P.O. Box 1383, Salina, KS 67401

Western Louisiana: Willis R. Henton, P.O. Box 4046, Alexandria, LA 71301

Western Massachusetts: Alexander D. Stewart, 37 Chestnut St., Springfield, MA 01103

Western Michigan: Charles E. Bennison, 2600 Vincent Ave., Kalamazoo, MI 49001

Western New York: Harold B. Robinson, 1114 Delaware Ave., Buffalo, NY 14209

Western North Carolina: William G. Weinhauer, P.O. Box 368, Black Mountain, NC 28711

Wyoming: Bob Gordon Jones, 104 S. 4th St., Box 1007, Laramie, WY 82070

The Evangelical Covenant Church of America This church has its roots in historical Christianity. It emerged in the Protestant Reformation, the Biblical instruction of the Lutheran State Church of Sweden, and the spiritual awakenings of the 19th century. The denomination was organized (1885) in Chicago; prior to 1957 it was named the Evangelical Mission Covenant Church of America. Membership: 76,092; Headquarters: 5101 N. Francisco Ave., Chicago, IL 60625

The Evangelical Free Church of America was organized in Boone, Iowa, in the 1880s, as the Swedish Evangelical Free Mission. The Evangelical Free Church Association merged (1950) with this group, and the merged body is known as the Evangelical Free Church of America. Membership: 77,592; Headquarters: 1515 E. 66th St., Minneapolis, MN 55423

Evangelical Lutheran Churches, Association of Organized (1976) in Chicago, the AELC is a church body whose members have joined together to be in mission and ministry. Its congregations are primarily former affiliates of the Missouri Synod, although some are new or previously independent. Membership: 113,942; Headquarters: 12015 Manchester Rd. Ste. 80LL, St. Louis, MO 63131

Free Methodist Church of North America This body grew out of a movement in the Genesee Conference of the Methodist Episcopal Church, about 1850, toward a more original Methodism. It was organized in 1860. Membership: 67,394; Headquarters: 901 College Ave., Winona Lake, IN 46590

Free Will Baptists This evangelical group of Arminian Baptists was organized (1727) by Paul Palmer in N.C. Another movement (teaching the same doctrines of free grace, free salvation and free will) was organized (1780) in N.H. Many northern line churches merged with the Northern Baptist Convention but a remnant of these churches reorganized (1916) into the Cooperative General Association of Free Will Baptists. This Association and the General Conference (churches in the southern line) joined together (1935) to form the National Association of Free Will Baptists. Membership: 231,167; National Offices: 1134 Murfreesboro Rd., Nashville, TN 37217

Friends United Meeting (The Five Years Meeting of Friends) The Friends United Meeting became the name in 1965 for the Five Years Meeting of Friends, a body founded (1902) to facilitate a united Quaker witness in missions, peace education, and Christian education. Additional programs have since been added. There are now fifteen Yearly Meetings with members within and beyond the U.S. Membership: 61,366; Presiding Clerk, Walter Schutt, 101 Quaker Hill Dr., Richmond, IN 47374

Full Gospel Fellowship of Churches and Ministers, International Founded in 1962, the FGFCMI is a fellowship of locally autonomous churches and ministers. All members believe that the Holy Scriptures are the inspired Word of God. Membership: 59,100; Headquarters: FGFCMI General Conference, 1545 W. Mockingbird, Ste. 1012, Lock Box 209, Dallas, TX 75235

General Association of Regular Baptist Churches Founded (1932) in Chicago by a group of churches that had withdrawn from the Northern Baptist Convention (now the American Baptist Churches in the U.S.A.) because of doctrinal differences. It requires all churches to subscribe to the historic New Hampshire Confession of Faith (with a premillennial ending applied to the last article.) Membership: 244,000; Headquarters: 1300 N. Meacham Rd., Schaumburg, IL 60195

General Baptists (General Association of) An Arminian group of Baptists first organized (1607) by John Smyth and Thomas Helwys in England, and transplanted to the colonies in 1714. It died out along the Seaboard, but was revived (1823) in the Midwest by Rev. Benoni Stinson. Membership: 73,046; Exec. Sec., Rev. Glen O. Spence, 100 Stinson Dr., Poplar Bluff, MO 63901

Greek Orthodox Archdiocese of North and South America is under the jurisdiction of the Ecumenical Patriarchate of Constantinople (Istanbul). Chartered in 1922, it has parishes in the U.S., Canada, and Central and South America. Membership: 1,950,000 (1977); Headquarters: 8-10 E. 79th St., New York, NY 10021

Independent Fundamental Churches of America Organized (1930) at Cicero, Ill., by representatives of various independent churches. Membership: 120,446; Headquarters: 1860 Mannheim Rd., P.O. Box 250, Westchester, IL 60153

International Church of the Foursquare Gospel An evangelistic missionary body organized (1927) by Aimee Semple McPherson. The parent church is Angelus Temple in Los Angeles (organized 1923), with mission stations and meeting places in 34 foreign countries. Membership: 89,215 (1963); Headquarters: Angelus Temple, 1100 Glendale Blvd., Los Angeles, CA 90026

Jehovah's Witnesses It is the belief of Jehovah's Witnesses that they adhere to the oldest religion on earth: the worship of Almighty God revealed in his Bible as Jehovah. All of Jehovah's Witnesses are considered to be ministers of the gospel and have no human leader. Their Yearbook shows them active (1979) in 205 countries. Membership: 526,961; Headquarters: 124 Columbia Heights, Brooklyn, NY 11201

Jewish Congregations Jews arrived in the colonies before 1650. The first congregation is recorded (1654) in New York City, the Shearith Israel (Remnant of Israel). Membership of Jewish congregations in the U.S.: 5,860,900

CONGREGATIONAL AND RABBINICAL ORGANIZATIONS

*Union of American Hebrew Congregations (Reform): 838 Fifth Ave., New York, NY 10021; Pres., Rabbi Alexander M. Schindler

*United Synagogue of America (Conservative): 155 Fifth Ave., New York, NY 10010; Pres., Simon Schwartz; Exec. Vice-Pres., Rabbi Benjamin Z. Kreitman

*Union of Orthodox Jewish Congregations of America: 116 E. 27th St., New York, NY 10016; Pres., Julius Berman; Exec. Vice-Pres., Rabbi Pinchas Stolper

*Central Conference of American Rabbis (Reform): 790 Madison Ave., New York, NY 10021; Pres., Rabbi Jerome R. Malino; Exec. Vice-Pres., Rabbi Joseph B. Glaser

Rabbinical Alliance of America (Orthodox): 156 Fifth Ave., New York, NY 10011; Pres., Rabbi David B. Hollander

*The Rabbinical Assembly (Conservative): 3080 Broadway, New York, NY 10027; Pres., Rabbi Saul I. Teplitz; Exec. Vice-Pres., Rabbi Wolfe Kelman

*Rabbinical Council of America, Inc. (Orthodox): 1250 Broadway, New York, NY 10001; Pres., Bernard Rosenweig; Exec. Vice-Pres., Rabbi Israel Klavan

Union of Orthodox Rabbis of the United States and Canada: 235 E. Broadway, New York, NY 10002; Pres., Rabbi Moshe Feinstein, Chpsn., Rabbi Symcha Elberg

*Synagogue Council of America: 432 Park Ave. S., New York, NY 10016; Pres., Rabbi Saul I. Teplitz; Exec. Vice-Pres., Rabbi Bernard Mandelbaum

*Synagogue Council of America is the coordinating body of the organizations starred above

Lutheran Church in America This body was organized (1962) by consolidation of the American Evangelical Lutheran Church (1872); the Augustana Lutheran Church (1860); the Finnish Evangelical Lutheran Church (1891); and the United Lutheran Church in America (1918). Membership: 2,921,090; Headquarters: 231 Madison Ave., New York, NY 10016

The Lutheran Church—Missouri Synod This body (organized 1847) is the second-largest Lutheran church in America. It holds to an unwavering confessionalism coupled with a strong outreach in ministry. Membership: 2,623,181; Headquarters: 500 N. Broadway, St. Louis, MO 63102

Mennonite Church The largest group of the Mennonites who began arriving in the U.S. as early as 1683, settling in Germantown, Pa. They derive their name from Menno Simons, their outstanding leader, b. 1496. Membership: 98,027; General Office: 528 E. Madison St., Lombard, IL 60148

Moravian Church in America (Unitas Fratrum) In 1735 Moravian missionaries of the pre-Reformation faith of John Hus came to Georgia, in 1740 to Pennsylvania, and in 1753 to North Carolina. They established the Moravian Church, which is broadly evangelical, liturgical, with an episcopacy as a spiritual office and in form of government "conferential." NORTHERN PROVINCE: Membership: 32,588; Headquarters: 69 W. Church St., P.O. Box 1245, Bethlehem, PA 18018. SOUTHERN PROVINCE: Membership: 21,058; Headquarters: 459 S. Church St., Winston-Salem, NC 27108

National Baptist Convention of America (organized 1880) is the "unincorporated" body of National Baptists. Membership: 2,668,799 (1956); Corr. Sec., Albert E. Chew, 2823 N. Houston, Ft. Worth, TX 76106

National Baptist Convention, U.S.A., Inc. The older and

parent convention of black Baptists, this body is to be distinguished from the National Baptist Convention of America, usually referred to as the "unincorporated" body. Membership: 5,500,000 (1958); Pres., Rev. J.H. Jackson, 405 E. 31st St., Chicago, IL 60616

National Primitive Baptist Convention, Inc. A group of Baptists having associations, state conventions, and a National Convention (organized 1907). Membership: 250,000 (1975); Headquarters: P.O. Box 2355, Tallahassee, FL 32304

North American Old Roman Catholic Church A body with the doctrine of the Old Catholics in right and succession of Catholic orders. Knott Missal used for Masses. Pontificale used for all Order Rights. Not under Papal jurisdiction. Membership: 69,412; Presiding Archbishop of the Americas and Canada: Most Rev. John E. Schweikert, 4200 N. Kedvale Ave., Chicago, IL 60641

Old Order Amish Church The congregations have no annual conference. They worship in private homes, and adhere to the older forms of worship and attire. This body has bishops, ministers, and deacons. Membership: 80,250; No general organization; Information: Der Neue Amerikanische Calendar, % Raber's Book Store, Baltic, OH 43804

Open Bible Standard Churches, Inc. The merger (1935) of Bible Standard Churches and Open Bible Evangelistic Association, this denomination emphasizes evangelism, missions, and the message of the Open Bible. Membership: 60,000; Headquarters: 2020 Bell Ave., Des Moines, IA 50315

The Orthodox Church in America The Russian Orthodox Greek Catholic Church of America entered Alaska in 1792 before its purchase by the United States in 1867. Its canonical status of independence (autocephaly) was granted (1970) by its Mother Church, the Russian Orthodox Church. Membership: 1,000,000 (1978); Sec. to the Metropolitan: Serge Troubetzkoy, P.O. Box 675, Syosset, NY 11791

Pentecostal Church of God Organized (1919) at Chicago, the first convention was held in October 1953. Membership: 110,870 (1977); Headquarters: Messenger Plaza, 211 Main St., Joplin, MO 64801

Pentecostal Holiness Church, International This body grew out of the holiness movement (1895-1900) in the South and Middle West. It is premillennial in belief, emphasizes Christian perfection as taught by John Wesley, and believes in the Pentecostal baptism with the Holy Spirit, accompanied by glossolalia. Membership: 86,103 (1977); Headquarters: P.O. Box 12609, Oklahoma City, OK 73157

Plymouth Brethren (Christian Brethren) An orthodox and evangelical movement to unite Christians from various denominations which began in the British Isles in the 1820's. In the 1840's the movement divided. The smaller "exclusive" branch stresses the interdependency of congregations. The "open" branch, stressing congregational independence, is greatly involved in evangelism and foreign missions. Membership: 79,000; No general organization.

Polish National Catholic Church of America After a long period of dissatisfaction with Roman Cathoic administration and ideology, accompanied by a strong desire for religious freedom, this body was organized in 1897. Membership: 282,411 (1960); Headquarters: 529 E. Locust St., Scranton, PA 18505

Presbyterian Church in America This body was formed (1973), in Birmingham, Ala., as the result of an act of separation from the Presbyterian Church in the U.S. The PCA has the intent of restoring purity of faith and practice and is committed to the Reformed Faith as set forth in the Westminster Confession and Catechisms. Membership: 86,885; Stated Clk., Rev. Morton H. Smith, P.O. Box 312, Brevard, NC 28712

Presbyterian Church in the United States is a branch of the major American Presbyterian tradition which broke apart during the Civil War. Organized as a separate denomination (1861) in Augusta, Ga., it was constituted as the Presbyterian Church in the U.S. in 1865. Membership: 852,711; Office of the General Assembly: 341 Ponce de Leon Ave. NE, Atlanta, GA 30365

Primitive Baptists A large group of Baptists, located mainly in the South, who are opposed to all centralization and

to modern missionary societies. Membership: 72,000 (1960); Headquarters: Cayce Publ. Co., S. Second St., Thornton, AR 71766

Progressive National Baptist Convention, Inc. This body held its organizational meeting at Cincinnati (1961). The first annual session was held in Philadelphia (1962). Membership: 521,692 (1967); Gen. Sec., Rev. C.J. Malloy, Jr., 601 50th St. NE, Washington, DC 20019

Reformed Church in America This body was established (1628) by the earliest Dutch settlers of New York as the Reformed Protestant Dutch Church. It is the oldest Protestant denomination with a continuous ministry in North America. Membership: 348,417; National Office: 475 Riverside Drive, New York, NY 10115

Reorganized Church of Jesus Christ of Latter Day Saints A division among the Latter-day Saints occurred on the death (1844) of Joseph Smith, Jr. His son, Joseph Smith III, became presiding officer (1860) of this group, which has established headquarters at Independence, Mo. Membership: 188,580; Headquarters: The Auditorium, P.O. Box 1059, Independence, MO 64051

The Roman Catholic Church The largest single body of Christians in the U.S., the Roman Catholic Church is under the spiritual leadership of His Holiness the Pope. Its establishment in America dates back to the priests who accompanied Columbus on his second voyage to the New World. A settlement, later discontinued, was made at St. Augustine, Fla. The continuous history of this Church in the colonies began (1634) at St. Mary's, in Maryland. Membership: 50,449,842. The following information has been furnished by the editor of The Official Catholic Directory for 1981, published by P.J. Kenedy & Sons, P.O. Box 729, New York, NY 10022

VISIBLE HEAD OF THE CHURCH

His Holiness the Pope, Bishop of Rome, Vicar of Jesus Christ, Successor of St. Peter, Prince of the Apostles, Supreme Pontiff of the Universal Church, Patriarch of the West, Primate of Italy, Archbishop and Metropolitan of the Roman Province and Sovereign of Vatican City. ROMAN CATHOLIC HIERARCHY: Supreme Pontiff, His Holiness Pope John Paul II. APOSTOLIC DELEGATE IN THE UNITED STATES: Most Rev. Pio Laghi, 3339 Massachusetts Ave. NW, Washington, DC 20008

BISHOPS AND ARCHBISHOPS

Archdiocese of Anchorage, Alaska–Most Rev. Francis T. Hurley; Diocese of Fairbanks, Alaska–Most Rev. Robert L. Whelan; Diocese of Juneau, Alaska–Most Rev. Michael H. Kenny.

Archdiocese of Atlanta, GA–Most Rev. Thomas A. Donnellan; Diocese of Charlotte, NC–Most Rev. Michael J. Begley; Diocese of Charleston, SC–Most Rev. Ernest L. Unterkoefler; Diocese of Raleigh, NC–Most Rev. F. Joseph Gossman; Diocese of Savannah, GA–Most Rev. Raymond W. Lessard.

Archdiocese of Baltimore, MD–Most Rev. William D. Borders; Diocese of Arlington, VA–Most Rev. Thomas J. Welsh; Diocese of Richmond, VA–Most Rev. Walter F. Sullivan; Diocese of Wheeling-Charleston, WV–Most Rev. Joseph H. Hodges; Diocese of Wilmington, DE–Most Rev. Thomas J. Mardaga.

Archdiocese of Boston, MA–His Eminence Humberto Cardinal Medeiros; Diocese of Burlington, VT–Most Rev. John A. Marshall; Diocese of Fall River, MA–Most Rev. Daniel A. Cronin; Diocese of Manchester, NH–Most Rev. Odore J. Gendron; Diocese of Portland, ME–Most Rev. Edward C. O'Leary; Diocese of Springfield, MA–Most Rev. Joseph F. Maguire; Diocese of Worcester, MA–Most Rev. Bernard J. Flanagan.

Archdiocese of Chicago, IL–His Eminence John Cardinal Cody; Diocese of Belleville, IL–Most Rev. William M. Cosgrove; Diocese of Joliet, IL–Most Rev. Joseph L. Imesch; Diocese of Peoria, IL–Most Rev. Edward W. O'Rourke; Diocese of Rockford, IL–Most Rev. Arthur J. O'Neill; Diocese of Springfield, IL–Most Rev. Joseph A. McNicholas.

Archdiocese of Cincinnati, OH–Most Rev. Joseph L. Bernadin; Diocese of Cleveland, OH–Most Rev. Anthony M. Pilla; Diocese of Columbus, OH–Most Rev. Edward J. Herrmann; Diocese of Steubenville, OH–Most Rev. Albert H. Ottenweller; Diocese of Toledo, OH–Most Rev. James R. Hoffman; Diocese of Youngstown, OH–Most Rev. James W. Malone.

Archdiocese of Denver, CO–Most Rev. James V. Casey; Diocese of Cheyenne, WY–Most Rev. Joseph H. Hart; Diocese of Pueblo, CO–Most Rev. Arthur N. Tafoya.

Archdiocese of Detroit, MI–Vacant; Diocese of Gaylord, MI–Most Rev. Edmund C. Szoka; Diocese of Grand Rapids, MI–Most Rev. Joseph M. Breitenbeck; Diocese of Kalamazoo, MI–Most Rev. Paul V. Donovan; Diocese of Lansing, MI–Most Rev. Kenneth J. Povish; Diocese of Marquette, MI–Most Rev. Mark F. Schmitt; Diocese of Saginaw, MI–Most Rev. Kenneth E. Untener.

Archdiocese of Dubuque, IA–Most Rev. James J. Byrne; Diocese of Davenport, IA–Most Rev. Gerald F. O'Keefe; Diocese of Des Moines, IA–Most Rev. Maurice J. Dingman; Diocese of Sioux City, IA–Most Rev. Frank H. Greteman.

Archdiocese of Hartford, CT–Most Rev. John F. Whealon; Diocese of Bridgeport, CT–Most Rev. Walter W. Curtis; Diocese of Norwich, CT–Most Rev. Daniel P. Reilly; Diocese of Providence, RI–Most Rev. Louis E. Gelineau.

Archdiocese of Indianapolis, IN–Most Rev. Edward T. O'Meara; Diocese of Evansville, IN–Most Rev. Francis R. Shea; Diocese of Fort Wayne-South Bend, IN–Most Rev. William E. McManus; Diocese of Gary, IN–Most Rev. Andrew G. Grutka; Diocese of Lafayette in Indiana, IN––Most Rev. Raymond J. Gallagher.

Archdiocese of Kansas City, KS–Most Rev. Ignatius J. Strecker; Diocese of Dodge City, KS–Most Rev. Eugene J. Gerber; Diocese of Salina, KS–Most Rev. Daniel W. Kucera, O.S.B.; Diocese of Wichita, KS–Most Rev. David M. Maloney.

Archdiocese of Los Angeles, CA–His Eminence Timothy Cardinal Manning; Diocese of Fresno, CA–Most Rev. Joseph J. Madera; Diocese of Monterey, CA–Most Rev. Harry A. Clinch; Diocese of Orange, CA–Most Rev. William R. Johnson; Diocese of San Bernardino, CA–Most Rev. Phillip F. Stralina; Diocese of San Diego, CA–Most Rev. Leo T. Maher.

Archdiocese of Louisville, KY–Most Rev. Thomas J. McDonough; Diocese of Covington, KY–Most Rev. William A. Hughes; Diocese of Memphis, TN–Most Rev. Carroll T. Dozier; Diocese of Nashville, TN–Most Rev. James D. Niedergeses; Diocese of Owensboro, KY–Most Rev. Henry Soenneker.

Archdiocese of Miami, FL–Most Rev. Edward A. McCarthy; Diocese of Orlando, FL–Most Rev. Thomas J. Grady; Diocese of Pensacola-Tallahassee, FL–Most Rev. Rene H. Gracida; Diocese of St. Augustine, FL–Most Rev. John J. Snyder; Diocese of St. Petersburg, FL–Most Rev. W. Thomas Larkin.

Archdiocese of Milwaukee, WI–Most Rev. Rembert G. Weakland, O.S.B.; Diocese of Green Bay, WI–Most Rev. Aloysius J. Wycislo; Diocese of La Crosse, WI–Most Rev. Frederick W. Freking; Diocese of Madison, WI–Most Rev. Cletus F. O'Donnell; Diocese of Superior, WI–Most Rev. George A. Hammes.

Archdiocese of Mobile, AL–Most Rev. Oscar Lipscomb; Diocese of Birmingham, AL–Most Rev. Joseph G. Vath; Diocese of Biloxi, MS–Most Rev. Joseph Lawson Howze; Diocese of Jackson, MS–Most Rev. Joseph B. Brunini.

Archdiocese of Newark, NJ–Most Rev. Peter L. Gerety; Diocese of Camden, NJ–Most Rev. George H. Guilfoyle; Diocese of Paterson, NJ–Most Rev. Frank J. Rodimer; Diocese of Trenton, NJ–Most Rev. John C. Reiss.

Archdiocese of New Orleans, LA–Most Rev. Philip M. Hannan; Diocese of Alexandria-Shreveport, LA–Most Rev. Lawrence P. Graves; Diocese of Baton Rouge, LA–Most Rev. Joseph V. Sullivan; Diocese of Houma-Thibodaux, LA–Most Rev. Warren L. Boudreaux; Diocese of Lafayette, LA–Most Rev. Gerard L. Frey; Diocese of Lake Charles, LA–Most Rev. Jude Speyrer.

Archdiocese of New York, NY–His Eminence Terence Cardinal Cooke; Diocese of Albany, NY–Most Rev. Howard J. Hubbard; Diocese of Brooklyn, NY–Most Rev. Francis J. Mugavero; Diocese of Buffalo, NY–Most Rev. Edward D. Head; Diocese of Ogdensburg, NY–Most Rev. Stanislaus J. Brzana; Diocese of Rochester, NY–Most Rev. Matthew H. Clark Diocese of Rockville Centre, NY–Most Rev. John R. McGann; Diocese of Syracuse, NY–Most Rev. Frank J. Harrison; Military Vicariate–His Eminence Terence Cardinal Cooke.

Archdiocese of Oklahoma City, OK–Most Rev. Charles A. Salatka; Diocese of Little Rock, AR–Most Rev. Andrew J. McDonald; Diocese of Tulsa, OK–Most Rev. Eusebius Beltran.

Archdiocese of Omaha, NB–Most Rev. Daniel E. Sheehan; Diocese of Grand Island, NB–Most Rev. Lawrence J. McNamara; Diocese of Lincoln, NB–Most Rev. Glennon P. Flavin.

Archdiocese of Philadelphia, PA–His Eminence John Cardinal Krol; Diocese of Allentown, PA–Most Rev. Joseph McShea; Diocese of Altoona-Johnstown, PA–Most Rev. James J. Hogan; Diocese of Erie, PA–Most Rev. Alfred M. Watson; Diocese of Greensburg, PA–Most Rev. William G. Connare; Diocese of Harrisburg, PA–Most Rev. Joseph T. Daley; Diocese of Pittsburgh, PA–Most Rev. Vincent M. Leonard; Diocese of Scranton, PA–Most Rev. J. Carroll McCormick.

Archdiocese of Portland, OR–Most Rev. Cornelius M. Power; Diocese of Baker, OR–Most Rev. Thomas J. Connolly; Diocese of Boise, ID–Most Rev. Sylvester W. Treinen; Diocese of Great Falls-Billings, MT–Most Rev. Thomas J. Murphy; Diocese of Helena, MT–Most Rev. Elden F. Curtiss.

Archdiocese of St. Louis, MO–Most Rev. John L. May; Diocese of Jefferson City, MO–Most Rev. Michael F. McAuliffe; Diocese of Kansas City-St. Joseph, MO–Most Rev. John J. Sullivan; Diocese of Springfield-Cape Girardeau, MO–Most Rev. Bernard F. Law.

Archdiocese of St. Paul and Minneapolis, MN–Most Rev. John R. Roach; Diocese of Bismarck, ND–Most Rev. Hilary B. Hacker; Diocese of Crookston, MN–Most Rev. Victor H. Balke; Diocese of Duluth, MN–Most Rev. Paul F. Anderson; Diocese of Fargo, ND–Most Rev. Justin A. Driscoll; Diocese of New Ulm, MN–Most Rev. Raymond A. Lucker; Diocese of Rapid City, SD–Most Rev. Harold J. Dimmerling; Diocese of St. Cloud, MN–Most Rev. George H. Speltz; Diocese of Sioux Falls, SD–Most Rev. Paul V. Dudley; Diocese of Winona, MN–Most Rev. Loras J. Watters.

Archdiocese of San Antonio, TX–Most Rev. Patrick F. Flores; Diocese of Amarillo, TX–Most Rev. Leroy T. Matthiesen; Diocese of Austin, TX–Most Rev. Vincent M. Harris; Diocese of Beaumont, TX–Most Rev. Bernard J. Ganter; Diocese of Brownsville, TX–Most Rev. John J. Fitzpatrick; Diocese of Corpus Christi, TX–Most Rev. Thomas J. Drury; Diocese of Dallas, TX–Most Rev. Thomas Tschoepe; Diocese of Fort Worth, TX–Vacant; Diocese of Galveston-Houston, TX–Most Rev. John L. Morkovsky; Diocese of San Angelo, TX–Most Rev. Joseph A. Fiorenza.

Archdiocese of San Francisco, CA–Most Rev. John R. Quinn; Diocese of Agana, Guam–Most Rev. Felixberto C. Flores; Diocese of Honolulu, HI–Most Rev. John J. Scanlan; Diocese of Oakland, CA–Most Rev. John S. Cummins; Diocese of Reno-Las Vegas, NV–Most Rev. Norman F. McFarland; Diocese of Sacramento, CA–Most Rev. Francis A. Quinn; Diocese of Salt Lake City, UT–Most Rev. William K. Weigand; Diocese of Santa Rosa, CA–Most Rev. Mark J. Hurley; Diocese of Stockton, CA–Most Rev. Roger M. Mahony.

Archdiocese of Santa Fe, NM–Most Rev. Robert F. Sanchez; Diocese of El Paso, TX–Most Rev. Raymundo J. Pena; Diocese of Gallup, NM–Most Rev. Jerome J. Hastrich; Diocese of Phoenix, AZ–Most Rev. James S. Rausch; Diocese of Tucson, AZ–Most Rev. Francis J. Green

Archdiocese of Seattle, WA–Most Rev. Raymond G. Hunthausen; Diocese of Spokane, WA–Most Rev. Lawrence H. Welsh; Diocese of Yakima, WA–Most Rev. William S. Skylstad.

Archdiocese of Washington, DC–Most Rev. James A. Hickey; Diocese of St. Thomas, Virgin Islands–Most Rev. Edward J. Harper, C.S.S.R.

Archeparchy (Byzantine) of Philadelphia, PA–Most Rev. Stephen Sulyk; Eparchy of St. Nicholas in Chicago, IL–Vacant; Diocese of Stamford, CT–Most Rev. Basil H. Losten.

Archdiocese of Pittsburgh, PA–Most Rev. Stephen Kocisko; Eparchy of Parma, OH–Most Rev. Emil Mihalik; Eparchy of Passaic, NJ–Most Rev. Michael J. Dudick.

MARONITES

Diocese of St. Maron, Brooklyn, NY–Most Rev. Francis Zayek.

MELKITES

Exarchy of Newton, MA–Most Rev. Joseph Tawil.

Russian Orthodox Church in the U.S.A., Patriarchal Parishes of the This group of parishes is under the direct jurisdiction of the Patriarch of Moscow and All Russia. Membership: 51,500 (1975); Headquarters: St. Nicholas Patriarchal Cathedral, 15 E. 97th St., New York, NY 10029

The Russian Orthodox Church Outside Russia (Formerly The Russian Orthodox Church Abroad) This body was organized (1920) to unite the missions and parishes of the Russian Orthodox Church outside of Russia. This church emphasizes being true to the old traditions of the Russian Church, but it does not compromise with official church leaders in Moscow. Membership: 55,000 (1955); Headquarters: 75 E. 93rd St., New York, NY 10028

The Salvation Army An international religious & charitable organization with a paramilitary government, founded (1865) by General William Booth in England and introduced (1880) into America. Membership: 414,659; National Headquarters: 120-130 W. 14th St., New York, NY 10011

Serbian Eastern Orthodox Church for the U.S.A. and Canada Membership: 65,000 (1967); Chancery: St. Sava Monastery, P.O. Box 519, Libertyville, IL 60048

Seventh-day Adventists This Protestant body developed out of an interdenominational movement that appeared in the early 19th century, stressing the imminence of the Second Advent of Christ. Seventh-day Adventists were formally organized in 1863. They believe in the personal, imminent, and premillennial return of Christ, and in the observance of the seventh day as the Sabbath. Membership: 553,089; Headquarters: 6840 Eastern Ave. NW, Washington, DC 20012

Southern Baptist Convention was organized (1845) in Augusta, Ga. Its purpose is "to provide a general organization for Baptists in the United States and its territories for the promotion of Christian missions at home and abroad and any other objects...which it may deem proper and advisable for the furtherance of the Kingdom of God." Membership: 13,372,757; Executive Committee Offices: 460 James Robertson Pkwy., Nashville, TN 37219

Triumph the Church and Kingdom of God in Christ (International) The Triumph Church, as this body is more commonly known, was founded in 1902. It was incorporated (1918) in Washington, DC. Membership: 54,307 (1972); National Headquarters: 213 Farrington Ave., Atlanta, GA 30318

Ukrainian Orthodox Church in the U.S.A. was formally organized in the United States in 1919. Archbishop John Theodorovich arrived from Ukraine in 1924. Membership: 87,745 (1966); Headquarters: South Bound Brook, NJ 08880

Unitarian Universalist Association The Unitarian movement arose in Congregationalism in the 18th century and produced (1825) the American Unitarian Association. The philosophy of Universalism originated with the doctrine of universal salvation in the first century, and was brought to America in the 1700s. Universalists were organized in 1793. In 1961 the Unitarian and Universalist bodies were consolidated to become the present noncreedal association. Membership: 139,052; Pres., Dr. O. Eugene Pickett; Headquarters: 25 Beacon St., Boston, MA 02108

United Church of Christ This body results from a union (1957) of the Evangelical and Reformed Church and the Congregational Christian Churches. The union was completed (1961) when the constitution was adopted in Philadelphia. Membership: 1,745,533; Headquarters: 105 Madison Ave., New York, NY 10016

The United Free Will Baptist Church A body that was organized in 1870. Membership: 100,000 (1952); Headquarters: Kinston College, 1000 University St., Kinston, NC 28501

The United Methodist Church The church was formed (1968) in Dallas by the union of The Methodist Church and The Evangelical United Brethren Church. The Methodist movement began in 18th-century England under John Wesley. The organized Methodist Church was founded (1784) in Baltimore. Francis Asbury was elected the first bishop in this country. The Evangelical United Brethren Church was formed (1946) with the merger of the Evangelical Church and the Church of the United Brethren in Christ. Membership: 9,653,711; Sec. of Gen. Conference, Dr. John B. Holt, Perkins School of Theology, Southern Methodist University, Dallas, TX 75222

METHODIST BISHOPS IN U.S.

North Central Jurisdiction: Central Illinois, Leroy C. Hodapp; Detroit, Edsel A. Ammons; East Ohio, James S. Thomas; Iowa, Wayne K. Clymer; Minnesota, Emerson S. Colaw; North Dakota & South Dakota, Edwin C. Boulton; North Indiana, James Armstrong; Northern Illinois, Jesse R. DeWitt; South Indiana, James Armstrong; Southern Illinois, Leroy C. Hodapp; West Michigan, Edsel A. Ammons; West Ohio, Dwight E. Loder; Wisconsin, Marjorie S. Matthews. Northeastern Jurisdiction: Baltimore, D. Frederick Wertz; Central New York, Joseph H. Yeakel; Central Pennsylvania, John B. Warman; Eastern Pennsylvania, F. Herbert Skeete; Maine, George W. Bashore; New Hampshire, George W. Bashore; New York, Roy C. Nichols; Northern New Jersey, Dale White; Northern New York, Joseph H. Yeakel; Peninsula, D. Frederick Wertz; Puerto Rico, F. Herbert Skeete; Southern New England, George W. Bashore; Southern New Jersey, Dale White; Troy, Roy C. Nichols; West Virginia, William B. Grove; Western New York, Joseph H. Yeakel; Western Pennsylvania, James M. Ault; Wyoming, John B. Warman. South Central: Central Texas, John W. Russell; Kansas East, B. R. Oliphint; Kansas West, B. R. Oliphint; Little Rock & North Arkansas, Kenneth W. Hicks; Louisiana, Kenneth W. Shamblin; Missouri East, W.T. Handy, Jr.; Missouri West, W.T. Handy, Jr.; Nebraska, Monk Bryan; New Mexico, L.W. Schowengerdt; North Texas, John W. Russell; Northwest Texas, L.W. Schowengerdt; Oklahoma, John W. Hardt; Oklahoma Indian Missionary, John W. Hardt; Rio Grande, Ernest T. Dixon; Southwest Texas, Ernest T. Dixon; Texas, Finis A. Crutchfield. Southeastern Jurisdiction: Alabama-West Florida, Frank L. Robertson; Florida, Earl G. Hunt, Jr.; Holston, H. Ellis Finger, Jr.; Kentucky, Paul A. Duffey; Louisville, Paul A. Duffey; Memphis, Edward L. Tullis; Mississippi, C.P. Minnick, Jr.; North Alabama, Frank L. Robertson; North Carolina, William R. Cannon; North Georgia, Joel D. McDavid; North Mississippi, C.P. Minnick, Jr.; Red Bird Missionary (KY), Paul A. Duffey; South Carolina, Roy C. Clark; South Georgia, Joel A. McDavid; Tennessee, Edward L. Tullis; Virginia, Robert M. Blackburn; Western North Carolina, L. Scott Allen. Western Jurisdiction: Alaska Missionary, Calvin D. McConnell; California-Nevada, Wilbur W.Y. Choy; Oregon-Idaho, Calvin D. McConnell; Pacific Northwest, Melvin G. Talbert; Pacific and Southwest, Jack M. Tuell; Rocky Mountain, Melvin E. Wheatley, Jr.; Yellowstone, Melvin E. Wheatley, Jr.

United Pentecostal Church International Pentecostal Church, Inc., and Pentecostal Assemblies of Jesus Christ merged (1945) at St. Louis. Membership: 465,000; Headquarters: 8855 Dunn Rd., Hazelwood, MO 63042

The United Presbyterian Church in the United States of America was formed (1958) through a merger of the United Presbyterian Church of N.A. and the Presbyterian Church in the U.S.A. The Presbyterian Church in the U.S.A. dated from 1706 in Philadelphia, while the United Presbyterian Church of N.A. was formed in 1858 when the Associate Reformed Presbyterian Church and the Associate Presbyterian Church united. Membership: 2,477,364; Headquarters: Office of the General Assembly: 475 Riverside Dr., Rm. 1201, New York, NY 10115

The Wesleyan Church This body originated (1968) through the uniting of the Pilgrim Holiness Church (1897) and The Wesleyan Methodist Church of America (1843). It emphasizes scriptural truth concerning the new birth, the entire sanctification of believers, the personal return of Christ, and worldwide holiness evangelism. Membership: 100,925; Headquarters: P.O. Box 2000, Marion, IN 46952

Wisconsin Evangelical Lutheran Synod This body was organized (1850) in Wisconsin and subscribes to the confessional writings of the Lutheran Church. Membership: 404,564; Pres., Rev. Carl H. Mischke, 3512 W. North Ave., Milwaukee, WI 53208

DISASTERS/CATASTROPHES

MAJOR DISASTERS

This list encompasses both natural disasters and such "technological" catastrophes as rail and aircraft crashes (50 or more deaths), shipwrecks (200 or more deaths), and mine accidents (50 or more deaths). Some other calamities that resulted in fewer fatalities are also cited because of their recentness and/or significance. The list is worldwide in scope.

Year	Type of Disaster	Place	Remarks
64 A.D.	Fire	Rome	Fire destroyed most of Rome; Christians were blamed and executed as arsonists
79 A.D.	Volcanic eruption	Pompeii and Herculaneum, Italy	Mount Vesuvius erupted, destroying both cities; more than 2,000 dead
80 A.D.	Epidemic	Rome	Anthrax killed thousands
250–265	Epidemic	Roman Empire	Bubonic plague killed thousands
444	Epidemic	Great Britain	Bubonic plague claimed thousands
526	Earthquake	Antioch, Syria	Shock results killed 250,000 (?)
542	Epidemic	Roman Empire	Bubonic plague killed tens of thousands
558	Epidemic	Europe, Asia, and Africa	Bubonic plague and smallpox pandemic killed millions; 5,000–10,000 died daily in Constantinople
681	Earthquake	Tosa, Japan	Three-square-mile area submerged
740–744	Epidemic	Constantinople	Bubonic plague killed 200,000 (?)
772	Epidemic	Chichester, England	Disease killed 34,000 (?)
856	Earthquake	Corinth, Greece	Disaster killed 45,000 (?)
869	Earthquake	Sanriku coast, Japan	Shock followed by tidal wave; thousands killed
954	Epidemic	Scotland	Bubonic plague killed 40,000 (?)
1038	Earthquake	Shansi, China	Recorded deaths: 23,000
1057	Earthquake	Chihli, China	Earthquake killed 25,000 (?)
1228	Flood	Friesland, Holland	Killed 100,000 (?)
1290	Earthquake	Chihli, China	September 27; 100,000 (?) victims
1293	Earthquake	Kamakura, Japan	May 20; 30,000 (?) lives lost
1340s	Epidemic	Asia and Europe	"The Black Death," bubonic plague pandemic, is said to have killed 25 million
1361	Earthquake	Kotyi, Japan	Thousands killed by quakes
1382–85	Epidemic	Ireland	Bubonic plague claimed thousands
1407	Epidemic	London	Bubonic plague killed 30,000 (?)
1456	Earthquake	Naples	December 5; 30,000–40,000 killed
1491	Fire	Dresden	City almost destroyed
1499–1500	Epidemic	London	Bubonic plague and other scourges killed 30,000 (?)
1528	Epidemic	Italy	July; typhus killed 21,000 (?)
1531	Earthquake	Lisbon	January 26; 30,000 (?) killed
1545	Epidemic	Cuba	Typhus killed 250,000 (?)
1556	Earthquake	Shensi Province, China	January 24; quake killed more than 800,000, the largest number of fatalities from one earthquake in recorded history
1560	Epidemic	Brazil	Smallpox killed several million
1603	Epidemic	London	Bubonic plague killed more than 30,000
1618	Epidemic	Naples	Diphtheria fatal for 8,000 (?)
1624	Fire	Oslo	City destroyed
1625	Epidemic	London	Bubonic plague claimed 35,000
1628	Epidemic	Lyons, France	Typhus killed 60,000 (?)
1631	Volcanic eruption	southern Italy	Mount Vesuvius erupted, followed by earthquake and tidal wave; more than 4,000 dead
1642	Flood	China	Fatalities: 300,000 (?)
1665	Epidemic	London	Bubonic plague killed more than 70,000
1666	Fire	London	September 2–6; "The Great Fire" destroyed about 14,000 buildings, leaving 200,000 homeless
1669	Volcanic eruption	Catania, Italy	Mt. Etna erupted, killing 20,000 (?)
1672	Epidemic	Lyons, France	Bubonic plague killed 60,000 (?)
	Epidemic	Naples	In six months bubonic plague claimed 400,000 (?)
1693	Earthquake	Catania, Italy	January 11; 60,000 died
1694	Fire	Warwick, England	Destroyed more than half of city
1703	Storm	England	November 26–27; "Great Storm" killed 8,000 (?)
	Earthquake	Tokyo	December 30; earthquake killed 200,000 (?)
1711	Epidemic	Germany and Austria	Bubonic plague; more than 500,000 fatalities
	Marine	Egg Island, Labrador	August 23; 8 English transports wrecked; 900 (?) deaths
1716	Earthquake	Algiers	Earthquake killed 20,000 (?)
1720	Epidemic	Marseilles	Bubonic plague killed 50,000–60,000
1728	Fire	Copenhagen	City nearly destroyed
1737	Cyclone	Calcutta	October 7–11; earthquake followed tornado, killing 300,000 (?)
1741	Epidemic	Cadiz, Spain	Yellow fever fatal for 10,000 (?)
1752	Fire	Moscow	Destroyed about 18,000 houses
1755	Earthquake	Lisbon	November 1; quake, fire, and tidal waves killed 60,000 (?)
1759	Earthquake	Baalbek, Lebanon	October 30; death toll: 30,000
1783	Earthquake	southern Italy and Sicily	February 5–March 28; a series of six quakes claimed 50,000 (?)
	Volcanic eruption	Iceland	June 8; Mount Skaptar erupted, killing one fifth of the population
1787	Flood	eastern India	Storm drove seas 20 miles inland; 10,000 (?) fatalities
1792	Earthquake	Hizen, Japan	Earthquake killed 15,000 (?)
	Epidemic	Egypt	Bubonic plague; 800,000 (?) victims
1793	Epidemic	Philadelphia	Yellow fever killed 5,000 (?)
1797	Earthquake	Cuzco, Peru and Quito, Ecuador	February 4; quake killed 40,000 (?)

Year	Type of Disaster	Place	Remarks
1800	Epidemic	Spain	Yellow fever claimed 80,000 (?)
1802	Epidemic	Santo Domingo	Yellow fever killed 29,000 (?) of Napoleon's soldiers
1810	Epidemic	Cadiz and Barcelona, Spain	Yellow fever fatal for 25,000 (?)
1815	Volcanic eruption	Sumbawa Island, Indonesia	April 5; Tamboro erupted, followed by whirlwinds and tidal waves; 12,000 (?) fatalities
1816–19	Epidemic	Ireland	Typhus lessened population by one fourth
1822	Earthquake	Aleppo, Syria	September 5; quake claimed 22,000 (?) victims
1826–37	Epidemic	continental Europe	Cholera pandemic killed millions; 900,000 (?) Europeans died in 1831 alone
1828	Earthquake	Echigo, Japan	December 28; quake killed 30,000 (?)
1831	Marine	off Cape May, New Jersey	July 9; immigrant vessel Lady Sherbrooke sank; 263 dead
1833	Marine	in the Atlantic between England and Quebec	May 11; Lady of the Lake struck iceberg; 215 dead
1834	Fire	London	October 16; Houses of Parliament and part of city burned
1835	Fire	New York City	December 16; 700 buildings destroyed; damage: $20 million
1840–62	Epidemic	worldwide	Cholera pandemic claimed millions
1841	Earthquake	Shinano, Japan	Quake killed 12,000 (?)
1842	Fire	Hamburg, Germany	May 4–7; much of the city destroyed; damage: $35 million
1845–48	Famine	Ireland	Potato crop failure; over 750,000 died of starvation and hundreds of thousands left the country
1846	Fire	Quebec	June 12; theater burned; 200 (?) dead
1847–48	Epidemic	London	Influenza killed 15,000 (?)
1849	Fire	St. Louis	May 17; 15 blocks of the city destroyed; damage: $3.5 million
1850	Marine	off Margate, England	March 29; Royal Adelaide wrecked; 400 (?) lost
1851–55	Epidemic	England	Tuberculosis killed an average of 51,000 a year
1852	Marine	off South Africa	February 26; British troopship Birkenhead wrecked; 454 dead
1853	Marine	off Scotland	September 29; immigrant ship Annie Jane wrecked; 348 dead
1854	Marine	in the Atlantic between London and Philadelphia	March; City of Glasgow vanished; 450 lost
	Marine	in the Atlantic near Grand Banks	September 27; U.S.S. Arctic sank; 350 (?) dead
	Marine	off New Jersey coast	November 13; immigrant ship New Era wrecked; more than 300 dead
1855	Mine	Coalfield, Virginia	Coal mine exploded; 55 dead
1856	Rail	near Philadelphia	July 17; train wrecked; 66 fatalities
	Hurricane	Ile Dernière, Louisiana	August 10–11; tropical storm destroyed the island, killing more than 400
1857	Blizzard	U.S. eastern seaboard	January 17–19; this violent storm caused widespread damage
	Marine	in the Atlantic between New York and Havana	September 12; Central America sank; 400 (?) dead
1858	Marine	in the Atlantic between Hamburg and New York City	September 13; Austria burned; 471 dead
1859	Marine	off Ireland	April 27; Pomona wrecked; 400 (?) lost
	Marine	in the Irish Sea	October 25; Royal Charter wrecked; 450 (?) dead
1860	Marine	on Lake Michigan	September 8; excursion steamer Lady Elgin and lumbership Augusta collided; 300 (?) dead
1863	Epidemic	England	Scarlet fever killed more than 30,000
	Fire	Santiago, Chile	December 8; Church of Campania burned, killing over 2,000
1863–75	Epidemic	worldwide	Cholera pandemic; in 1866 Prussia lost 120,000 (?) and Austria, 110,000
1864	Rail	near St. Hilaire, Canada	June 29; train ran through open switch; 90 (?) dead
	Rail	near Shohola, Pennsylvania	July 15; two-train collision; 65 dead
	Cyclone	Calcutta	October 1; most of city destroyed by storm; 70,000 (?) dead
1865	Marine	Memphis, Tennessee	April 27; river steamer Sultana exploded and sank; 1,400 (?) dead
1866	Fire	Portland, Maine	July 4; city almost destroyed by fire; damage: $10 million
	Fire	Quebec	October 13; about 2,500 buildings destroyed
1867	Mine	Winterpock, Virginia	April 3; coal mines exploded, killing 69
	Marine	St. Thomas, West Indies	October 29; Rhone, Wye, and many small vessels wrecked in storm; 1,000 (?) dead
1868	Earthquake	Peru and Ecuador	August 13–15; quake killed 25,000 (?); damage: $300 million
1869	Mine	Plymouth, Pennsylvania	September 6; coal mine fire killed 110
1870	Marine	off Finistère, France	September 6; English warship Captain foundered; 472 fatalities
1871	Fire	Chicago	October 8–9; 3.5 sq. miles destroyed and 250 (?) dead from "Mrs. O'Leary's cow kicking over lantern"; damage $200 million
	Fire	Michigan and Wisconsin	October 8–14; more than 1 million acres of forest consumed; 1,000 (?) dead, mostly in Peshtigo, Wis.
1872	Fire	Boston	November 9–11; more than 600 buildings burned; damage: $75 million
	Marine	in the Atlantic	About November 25; Nova Scotian Mary Celeste abandoned; 10 lost
1873	Marine	off Nova Scotia	April 1; British steamer Atlantic wrecked; 481 dead
1875	Earthquake	Venezuela and Colombia	May 16; quake killed 16,000 (?)
1876	Cyclone	Bakarganj, India	October 31; storm and subsequent wave killed 200,000 (?)
	Fire	Brooklyn, New York	December 5; Conway's Theater burned; 300 (?) dead
	Rail	Ashtabula River, Ohio	December 29; train derailed as iron bridge collapsed in snowstorm; 91 dead
1877	Fire	St. John, New Brunswick, Canada	June 20; this Canadian fire killed 100; damage: $12.5 million
1878	Epidemic	southern United States	Yellow fever claimed 14,000 (?)
	Marine	on the Thames, London	September 3; British Princess Alice sank; 700 (?) dead
1881	Typhoon	China and Indo-China	October 8; violent storm plus tidal wave killed 300,000 (?)
	Fire	Vienna	December 8; Ring Theater burned; more than 600 dead
1882	Cyclone	Bombay	June 5; storm and subsequent tidal wave killed 100,000 (?)
	Rail	near Tchery, Russia	July 13; train derailed; more than 150 dead
1883	Fire	Berdichev, Russia	January 13; theater fire killed more than 150
	Mine	Braidwood, Illinois	February 16; coal mine flooded; 69 drowned
	Earthquakes	Ischia, Tyrrhenian Sea	July 28 and August 3; these two quakes killed 2,000 (?)

Year	Type of Disaster	Place	Remarks
1883	Volcanic eruption	Sunda Strait, Indonesia	August 26–28; Krakatoa erupted, destroying two thirds of the island; 36,419 dead and many missing after the greatest eruption of modern times.
1883–94	Epidemic	worldwide	Cholera pandemic killed millions
1884	Mine	Crested Butte, Colorado	January 24; coal mine exploded; 59 dead
	Tornado	central United States	February 18–19; series of tornadoes destroyed 10,000 (?) buildings and killed 800 (?)
	Mine	Pocahontas, Virginia	March 13; coal mine explosion killed 112
	Earthquake	Colchester, England	April 22; quake destroyed the city
1886	Blizzard	central United States	January 6–13; Kansas was hardest hit; 70 (?) dead
	Earthquake	Charleston, S.C.	August 31; quake caused severe damage and killed 60
1887	Flood	Honan, China	Yellow River overflowed; more than 900,000 dead
	Fire	Paris	May 25; Opéra Comique burned, killing 200 (?)
	Rail	Chatsworth, Illinois	August 10; train wrecked by collapse of burning bridge; 81 dead
	Fire	Exeter, England	September 4; theater burned; 200 (?) dead
1888	Blizzard	U.S. eastern seaboard	March 11–14; blizzard paralyzed major cities of Northeast, and killed more than 400; damage: several million dollars
	Rail	Mud Run, Pennsylvania	October 10; locomotive hit standing train; more than 50 dead
1889	Flood	Johnstown, Pennsylvania	May 31; this legendary American deluge killed more than 2,000
1889–90	Epidemic	worldwide	Influenza pandemic affected about 40 percent of the globe's population
1891	Mine	Mount Pleasant, Pennsylvania	January 27; coal mine exploded; 109 dead
	Marine	off Gibraltar	March 17; British steamer Utopia sank; 574 dead
	Rail	near Basel, Switzerland	June 14; trains collided; 100 (?) dead
	Earthquake	Mino-Owari, Japan	October 28; quake killed 10,000 (?)
1892	Mine	Krebs, Oklahoma	January 7; coal mine exploded; 100 dead
1893	Hurricane	southern United States and Caribbean	August 23–30; tropical storm devastated Charleston, S.C., and Savannah, Ga.; 1,000 (?) dead
1894	Fire	Hinckley, Minnesota	September 1; more than 160,000 acres of forest burned
1895	Marine	near Gibraltar	March 14; Spanish cruiser Reina Regenta foundered; 400 dead
	Mine	Red Canyon, Wyoming	March 20; coal mine exploded, killing 60
1896	Tornado	St. Louis	May; storm that devastated city killed 306; damage: $13 million
	Earthquake	Sanriku coast, Japan	June; quake and tidal wave killed 27,000 (?)
	Mine	Pittston, Pennsylvania	June 28; coal mine cave-in; 58 dead
	Rail	Atlantic City, New Jersey	July 30; train wrecked; 60 dead
1898	Marine	Havana	February 15; U.S. battleship Maine exploded; more than 260 dead
	Marine	near Sable Island, off Nova Scotia	July 4; French La Bourgogne and British Cromartyshire collided; 560 lost
	Marine	in the Atlantic off U.S. coast	November 26; Portland wrecked during storm; 200 (?) dead
1898–1908	Epidemic	China and India	Bubonic plague killed 3 (?) million
1900	Fire	Hull and Ottawa, Canada	April 26; conflagration damage: $10 million
	Mine	Scofield, Utah	May 1; coal mine exploded; 200 dead
	Fire	Hoboken, New Jersey	June 30; pier burned and 300 died; damage: over $4.6 million
	Hurricane	Texas	August 27–September 15; storm was followed by storm tide that inundated Galveston Island; 6,000 (?) dead
1901	Fire	Jacksonville, Florida	May 3; damage: $10 million
1902	Volcanic eruption	Martinique, West Indies	May 8; Mont Pelée erupted, totally destroying the city of St. Pierre and killing more than 30,000
	Mine	Coal Creek, Tennessee	May 19; coal mine exploded, killing 184
	Mine	Johnstown, Pennsylvania	July 10; coal mine exploded; 112 dead
	Fire	Birmingham, Alabama	September 20; church burned; 115 dead
1903	Flood	Heppner, Oregon	Flood destroyed this town and killed more than 250
	Mine	Hanna, Wyoming	June 30; coal mine explosion and fire killed 169
	Rail	Laurel Run, Pennsylvania	December 23; train crashed into fallen timber; 75 (?) dead
	Fire	Chicago	December 30; Iroquois Theater burned; 600 (?) victims
1904	Mine	Cheswick, Pennsylvania	January 25; coal mine exploded; 179 dead
	Fire	Baltimore	February 7–8; 75 city blocks burned; damage: $85 million
	Fire	Toronto	April 19; damage: $12 million
	Marine	New York City	June 15; steamer General Slocum burned in East River; more than 1,000 dead
	Marine	Rockall Reef, Scotland	June 28; Norge wrecked; more than 600 dead
	Rail	Eden, Colorado	August 7; train wreck killed 96
	Rail	New Market, Tennessee	September 24; train wrecked; 56 dead
1905	Mine	Virginia City, Alabama	February 26; coal mine exploded; 112 dead
1906	Mine	Courrières, France	March 10; explosion fatal for 1,060
	Earthquake	San Francisco	April 18; fire followed famous 'Frisco quake, which together killed 700 (?) and left more than 250,000 homeless; damage: $524 million
	Typhoon	Hong Kong	September 19; tropical cyclone claimed 50,000 (?)
	Rail	Washington, D.C.	December 30; train wrecked; 53 dead
1907	Mine	Stuart, West Virginia	January 29; coal mine exploded; 84 dead
	Mine	Monongah, West Virginia	December 6; coal mine exploded, killing 361
	Mine	Jacobs Creek, Pennsylvania	December 19; coal mine exploded; 239 dead
	Epidemic	India	Bubonic plague killed 1.3 million
1908	Fire	Boyertown, Pennsylvania	January 13; Rhoades Opera House burned; more than 100 dead
	Fire	Collinwood, Ohio	March 4; school burned, killing more than 160
	Mine	Hanna, Wyoming	March 28; coal mine exploded; 59 lost
	Fire	Chelsea, Massachusetts	April 12; city destroyed by fire; damage: $17 million
	Mine	Marianna, Pennsylvania	November 28; coal mines exploded; 154 killed
	Earthquake	southern Italy and Sicily	December 28; quake rendered one million (?) homeless and took lives of 100,000 (?)
	Mine	Switchback, West Virginia	December 29; coal mine exploded; 50 dead
1909	Mine	Switchback, West Virginia	January 12; coal mine exploded; 67 dead
	Fire	Acapulco	February 15; Flores Theater burned; 250 (?) dead
	Hurricane	Louisiana and Mississippi	September 14–21; this tropical storm killed 350
	Mine	Cherry, Illinois	November 13; coal mine fire killed 259
1909–18	Epidemic	China and India	Bubonic plague fatal for 1.5 million (?)
1910	Mine	Primero, Colorado	January 31; coal mine exploded; 75 dead

Year	Type of Disaster	Place	Remarks
	Rail	Wellington, Washington	March 1; avalanche swept two trains into canyon; 96 dead
	Rail	Green Mountain, Iowa	March 21; train wrecked; 55 dead
	Mine	Palos, Alabama	May 5; coal mine exploded; 90 dead
	Mine	Starkville, Colorado	October 8; coal mine exploded; 56 dead
	Mine	Delagua, Colorado	November 8; coal mine explosion and fire killed 79
1910–11	Epidemic	Manchuria	Pneumonic plague killed 60,000 (?)
1911	Flood	China	Yangtze River overflowed; 100,000 (?) dead
	Fire	New York City	March 25; Triangle Shirtwaist Factory holocaust claimed 145
	Mine	Throop, Pennsylvania	April 7; coal mine burned; 72 dead
	Mine	Littleton, Alabama	April 8; coal mine exploded; 128 dead
	Mine	Briceville, Tennessee	December 9; coal mine explosion killed 84
1912	Marine	off Spain	March 5; Spanish Principe de Asturias wrecked; 500 dead
	Mine	McCurtain, Oklahoma	March 20; coal mine exploded; 73 dead
	Mine	Jed, West Virginia	March 26; coal mine exploded; 83 dead
	Marine	in the North Atlantic	April 15; "unsinkable" British Titanic struck an iceberg and sank; 1,500 (?) dead
	Marine	off Japan	September 28; Japanese Kichemaru sank; 1,000 lost
1913	Tornado	Omaha	March 23; storm fatal for 100 (?); damage: $3.5 million
	Flood	Ohio and Indiana	March 25–27; Ohio and Indiana Rivers overflowed; 700 (?) dead
	Mine	Finleyville, Pennsylvania	April 23; coal mine exploded; 96 dead
	Mine	Dawson, New Mexico	October 22; coal mine exploded, killing 263
1914	Mine	Eccles, West Virginia	April 28; coal mines exploded; 183 dead
	Marine	St. Lawrence River	May 29; Canadian Pacific Empress of Ireland collided with collier and sank; 1,024 dead
	Fire	Salem, Massachusetts	June 25–26; conflagration destroyed 1,700 (?) buildings; damage: $14 million
	Mine	Royalton, Illinois	October 27; coal mine exploded; 52 dead
1915	Earthquake	central Italy	January 13; quake killed 30,000 (?)
	Mine	Layland, West Virginia	March 2; coal mine exploded; 112 dead
	Marine	off coast of Ireland	May 7; Lusitania sank after attack by German submarine; 1,198 dead
	Rail	near Gretna, Scotland	May 22; three trains crashed; 227 killed
	Marine	Chicago River, Chicago	July 24; excursion boat Eastland capsized in port; 800–900 dead
	Epidemic	Serbia	Summer; typhus claimed 150,000 (?)
	Hurricane	Texas and Louisiana	August 5–25; tropical storm followed by storm tide; 275 (?) dead
	Hurricane	Gulf Coast	September 22–October 1; in large area of Louisiana, 90 percent of the buildings were destroyed; more than 250 dead
1916	Marine	in the Mediterranean	February 26; French cruiser Provence sank; 3,100 (?) dead
	Fire	Paris, Texas	March 21; fire destroyed 1,440 structures; damage: $11 million
	Tornado	Arkansas	June 5; series of twisters claimed 100 (?)
	Explosion	Jersey City, New Jersey	July 30; German sabotage (explosion and fire) on Black Tom Island killed 4; damage: more than $14 million
	Marine	off China	August 29; Hsin Yu sank; 1,000 (?) dead
1917	Explosion	Chester, Pennsylvania	April 10; munitions-plant blast killed 125
	Mine	Hastings, Colorado	April 27; coal mine exploded; 121 dead
	Mine	Clay, Kentucky	August 4; coal mine exploded; 62 dead
	Fire	Halifax, Nova Scotia	December 6; S.S. Mont Blanc and Belgian relief ship Imo collided and exploded, with resulting fire consuming one square mile of the city; more than 1,400 dead
	Rail	near Modane, France	December 12; troop train derailed near entrance to Mont Cenis tunnel; 550 (?) dead
1917–19	Epidemic	worldwide	Influenza pandemic killed 20–30 million
1917–21	Epidemic	Russia	Typhus killed 2.5–3 million
1918	Marine	Barbados, West Indies	March 4; U.S.S. Cyclops lost at sea; 280 fatalities
	Rail	Ivanhoe, Indiana	June 22; two trains collided; 85 dead
	Rail	near Nashville, Tennessee	July 9; head-on collision killed 100 (?)
	Marine	Tokayama Bay, Japan	July 12; Japanese battleship Kawachi exploded; 500 (?) dead
	Earthquake	Puerto Rico	October 11; sea wave followed quake, causing severe damage; 116 dead
	Fire	Minnesota and Wisconsin	October 13–15; death toll: 1,000 (?); damages from the forest fires: $100 million
	Rail	Brooklyn, New York	November 1; derailment at Malbone St. tunnel; 100 (?) dead
1919	Marine	in the Strait of Messina	January 17; French Chaonia wrecked; 460 dead
	Mine	Wilkes-Barre, Pennsylvania	June 5; coal powder explosion killed 92
	Fire	San Juan, Puerto Rico	June 20; Mayaguez Theater burned, killing 150
	Tornado	Fergus Falls, Minnesota	June 22; storm killed 59; damages: $3.5 million
	Hurricane	Florida, Louisiana, and Texas	September 2–15; cyclone killed 287
1920s	Epidemic	India	Bubonic plague claimed 2 (?) million
1920	Blizzard	New England	March 5–6; this severe snowstorm considered comparable with "Blizzard of '88"
	Earthquake	Kansu, China	December 16; quake destroyed 10 cities and killed 180,000 (?)
1921	Epidemic	India	Cholera claimed 500,000 (?)
	Marine	off Swatow, South China Sea	March 18; Hong Kong wrecked on rocks; 1,000 (?) dead
	Aircraft	near Hull, England	August 24; British dirigible ZR–2 broke in two; 62 dead
	Explosion	Oppau, Germany	September 21; ammonium nitrate blast killed 600 (?)
1922	Fire	Smyrna, Asia Minor	September 13; city almost destroyed; hundreds dead; damage: $100 million
	Mine	Spangler, Pennsylvania	November 6; coal mine exploded; 77 dead
	Mine	Dolomite, Alabama	November 22; coal mine explosion killed 90
1923	Mine	Dawson, New Mexico	February 8; coal mine exploded; 120 dead
	Mine	Kemmerer, Wyoming	August 14; coal mine exploded; 99 dead
	Earthquake	Tokyo and Yokohama	September 1; quake followed by fire destroyed most of both Japanese cities; 200,000 (?) dead
	Fire	Berkeley, California	September 17; fire destroyed more than 600 buildings; damage: $12.5 million
	Aircraft	in the Mediterranean or Sahara Desert	December 21; French dirigible Dixmude disappeared; 50 (?) lost
1924	Epidemic	India	Cholera death toll: 300,000 (?)
	Mine	Castle Gate, Utah	March 8; coal mine exploded; 171 dead

Year	Type of Disaster	Place	Remarks
1924	Mine	Benwood, West Virginia	April 28; coal mine explosion killed 119
	Tornado	Lorain and Sandusky, Ohio	June 28; twister killed 85; damage: $12 million
1925	Mine	Sullivan, Indiana	February 20; coal mine exploded; 52 dead
	Tornado	Missouri, Illinois, and Indiana	March 18; tornado killed 689; damage: $17 million
	Mine	Coal Glen, North Carolina	May 27; coal mine exploded; 53 dead
	Rail	Hackettstown, New Jersey	June 16; train derailed at highway crossing; 50 dead
	Mine	Acemar, Alabama	December 10; coal mine exploded; 53 dead
1926–30	Epidemic	India	Smallpox claimed 423,000 (?)
1926	Mine	Wilburton, Oklahoma	January 13; coal mine explosion killed 91
	Hurricane	Florida and Alabama	September 11–22; 243 dead
1927	Mine	Everettville, West Virginia	April 30; coal mine exploded; 97 dead
	Tornado	Arkansas and Missouri	May 9; 92 dead from storm
	Tornado	St. Louis	September 29; death toll: 90; damage: $40 million
1928	Flood	Santa Paula, California	March 13; St. Francis Dam collapsed; 450 dead
	Mine	Mather, Pennsylvania	May 19; coal mine explosion killed 195
	Flood	southern Florida	September 6–20; hurricane caused Lake Okeechobee to overflow; 1,836 lives lost
	Marine	off the Virginia Capes	November 12; British steamer Vestris sank; 110 (?) dead
1929	Fire	Cleveland	May 15; hospital burned; 125 suffocations from poisonous fumes
	Mine	McAlester, Oklahoma	December 17; coal mine exploded; 61 dead
1930	Fire	Columbus	April 21; Ohio State Penitentiary burned, killing 317 convicts
	Earthquake	Naples	July 23–25; shock results killed 1,883 and injured 10,000 (?)
	Hurricane	Dominican Republic	September 3; storm fatalities: 2,000 (?)
	Aircraft	Beauvais, France	October 5; British dirigible R-101 crashed; 47 dead
	Mine	Millfield, Ohio	November 5; coal mine exploded; 82 dead
1931	Flood	Yangtze River, China	July–August; flood waters of Yangtze leave over 2 million homeless and 140,000 dead
1932	Tornado	southern United States	March 21–22; tornadoes hit five states; at least 362 dead
	Mine	Moweaqua, Illinois	December 23; coal mine exploded; 54 dead
	Earthquake	Kansu, China	December 26; quake killed 70,000 (?)
1933	Earthquake	Sanriku coast, Japan	March 3; quake killed more than 2,500
	Earthquake	Long Beach, California	March 10; quake claimed 115 lives; damage: $40 million
	Aircraft	New Jersey coast	April 4; U.S. dirigible Akron II crashed; 73 dead
1934	Fire	Hakodate, Japan	March 22; fire destroyed city; 1,500 dead (?)
	Marine	off New Jersey	September 8; luxury liner Morro Castle burned; 134 dead
	Typhoon	Honshu, Japan	September 21; storm killed 4,000 (?); damage: $50 million
	Mine	Wrexham, Wales	September 22; coal mine exploded; 265 dead
1935	Epidemic	Uganda	Bubonic plague killed 2,000 (?)
	Earthquake	India and Pakistan	May 31; quake killed more than 50,000
	Hurricane	southern Florida	August 29–September 10; storm killed 408; damage: up to $50 million
	Hurricane	Haiti	October 22; storm and flood fatalities: more than 2,000
1936	Tornado	southern United States	April 5–6; series of twisters, mostly in Mississippi and Georgia, killed 455; damage: $21 million
1937	Fire	Antung, Manchuria	February 13; theater burned, killing 658
	Explosion	New London, Texas	March 19; natural gas explosion destroyed school; more than 400 dead
	Aircraft	Lakehurst, New Jersey	May 6; German zeppelin Hindenburg exploded; 36 dead
	Rail	near Patna, India	July 16; Delhi-Calcutta express derailed; 107 dead
1938	Aircraft	Bogotá, Colombia	July 24; military stunt plane crashed into grandstand, killing 53
	Hurricane	Long Island and lower New England	September 10–22; this storm killed 600; damage: $50–500 million
	Rail	near Kishinev, Rumania	December 25; two-train collision killed 100 (?)
1939	Earthquake	Chile	January 24; quake killed 40,000 (?)
	Marine	off New Hampshire	May 23; U.S. submarine Squalus sank; 26 dead
	Marine	in the Irish Sea	June 1; British submarine Thetis sank; 99 lost
	Marine	off Indochina	June 15; French submarine Phenix sank; 63 dead
	Flood	Tientsin, China	July–August; millions rendered homeless and thousands dead
	Fire	Langunillas, Venezuela	November 14; oil town built over Lake Maracaibo destroyed
	Rail	near Magdeburg, Germany	December 22; two trains collided; 132 dead
	Rail	near Freidrichshafen, Germany	December 22; train wrecked; 99 dead
	Earthquake	Anatolia, Turkey	December 27; series of shocks and subsequent floods devastated about 60,000 square miles; more than 30,000 dead
1940	Mine	Bartley, West Virginia	January 10; coal mine exploded; 91 dead
	Rail	Osaka, Japan	January 29; two trains collided; 200 (?) dead
	Mine	St. Clairsville, Ohio	March 16; coal mine exploded; 72 dead
	Mine	Portage, Pennsylvania	July 15; coal mine explosion killed 63
	Blizzard	U.S. Northeast and Midwest	November 11–12; one of the most destructive snowstorms ever caused 144 deaths; damage: $6 million
1941	Marine	off Maine	June 16; U.S. submarine O-9 sank in test dive; 33 fatalities
1942	Marine	New York City	February 9; French liner Normandie burned at pier; 1 dead
	Tornado	U.S. South and Midwest	March 17; twister killed 111
	Mine	Honkeiko Colliery, Manchuria	April 26; worst mine disaster in history; 1,549 dead
	Mine	Osage, West Virginia	May 12; coal mine exploded; 56 dead
	Marine	off England	October 2; British Curacao rammed and sunk by Queen Mary; more than 330 dead
	Cyclone	Bengal, India	October 16; storm fatalities: 40,000 (?)
	Fire	Boston	November 28; Cocoanut Grove night club burned; 492 dead
1943	Mine	Red Lodge, Montana	February 27; coal mine exploded; 74 dead
	Rail	Philadelphia	September 6; "Congressional Limited" derailed; 80 dead
	Rail	near Lumberton, North Carolina	December 16; two trains collided; 72 dead
1944	Earthquake	San Juan, Argentina	January 15; quake killed 5,000 (?)
	Rail	Leon Province, Spain	January 16; train wrecked inside tunnel; 500–800 dead
	Rail	near Salerno, Italy	March 2; train stalled in tunnel, suffocating 526
	Mine	Belmont, Ohio	July 5; coal mine fire claimed 66
	Fire	Hartford, Connecticut	July 6; circus "big top" burned, killing 168
	Marine	Port Chicago, California	July 18; two ammunition ships exploded; 322 dead
	Aircraft	Freckleton, England	August 23; U.S. bomber crashed into school; more than 70 dead

Year	Type of Disaster	Place	Remarks
	Hurricane	U.S. eastern seaboard	September 9–16; storm killed 46; damage: $50–500 million
	Fire	Cleveland	October 20; liquid gas tanks exploded, setting fire to 50-block area and killing 130; damage: $10 million
	Rail	near Ogden, Utah	December 31; two sections of "Pacific Limited" collided; 50 dead
1945	Marine	off Danzig	January 30; German passengership Wilhelm Gustloff loaded with refugees and hospital ship General Steuben sunk by Soviet submarine; 6,800 lives lost in world's largest marine disaster
	Rail	Cazadero, Mexico	February 1; train struck from rear by freight train; 100 (?) dead
	Marine	Bari, Italy	April 9; U.S.S. Liberty exploded in harbor; 360 dead
	Tornado	Oklahoma and Arkansas	April 12; twister killed 102; damage: $4 million
	Aircraft	New York City	July 28; U.S. bomber crashed into Empire State Building; 13 dead
1946	Rail	near Aracaju, Brazil	March 20; train wreck killed 185
	Earthquake	Dutch Harbor, Alaska	April 1; subterranean quake caused tidal waves that hit Hawaiian Islands, Aleutians, and the West Coast; 173 dead in Hawaii alone and damage there $25 million
	Fire	Atlanta	December 7; Winecoff Hotel burned; 119 dead
	Aircraft	near Shanghai	December 25; three China Air Transport planes crashed, separately, in fog; at least 71 dead
1947	Marine	off Athens	January 19; Greek ship Himera struck mine and sank; 392 lost
	Aircraft	Bogotá, Colombia	February 15; Avianca DC–4 crashed into Mount Tablazo; 53 fatalities
	Mine	Centralia, Illinois	March 25; coal mine exploded; 111 dead
	Tornado	Texas, Oklahoma, and Kansas	April 9; twister killed 167; damage: $10 million
	Explosion	Texas City, Texas	April 16; S.S. Grandcamp blew up, destroying most of city and killing 561; damage: $67 million
	Aircraft	Leesburg, Virginia	June 13; Pennsylvania Central DC–4 crashed; 50 dead
	Explosion	Cadiz, Spain	August 18; dockyard exploded; 147 dead
	Epidemic	Egypt	September–December; cholera killed 10,276
	Hurricane	Florida and Gulf coasts	September 4–21; storm fatalities: 51; damage: $50–500 million
	Typhoon	Honshu, Japan	September 15–19; storm plus floods killed 2,000 (?)
	Aircraft	Bryce Canyon, Utah	October 24; United DC–6 crashed into hillside; 52 dead
	Fire	Bar Harbor, Maine	October 25; forest fire on Mount Desert Island burned large part of famous summer resort; damage: $30 million
1948	Marine	in the Inland Sea, Japan	January 28; freighter Joo Maru struck mine and sank; 250 dead
	Earthquake	Fukui, Japan	June 28; quake destroyed most of city; more than 5,000 dead
	Explosion	Ludwigshafen, Germany	July 28; blast and fire at I. G. Farben chemical works killed more than 200; damage: $6 million
	Aircraft	French West Africa	August 1; Air France plane disappeared on flight from Martinique; 53 lost
	Explosion	Hong Kong	September 22; chemical warehouse blast and fire killed 135
1949	Marine	off southern China	January 27; Chinese Taiping and collier collided and sank; more than 600 dead
	Fire	Effingham, Illinois	April 5; St. Anthony's Hospital burned; 74 dead
	Aircraft	Puerto Rico	June 7; U.S. Strato Freight crashed into water ; 54 dead
	Earthquake	Ecuador	August 5; shock razed 50 towns; 100,000 (?) homeless and 6,000 (?) dead; damage: $20 million
	Marine	Toronto	September 17; Canadian Noronic burned at pier; 130 (?) dead
	Rail	Nowy Dwor, Poland	October 22; Danzig-Warsaw express derailed; 200 (?) dead
	Cyclone	southeastern India	October 27; storm fatalities: 1,000 (?)
	Typhoon	Philippine Islands	October 31–November 2; storm killed 1,000 (?)
	Aircraft	Washington, D.C.	November 1; Bolivian fighter plane and Eastern DC–4 collided over airport; 55 dead
1950	Marine	in the Thames estuary, England	January 12; British submarine Truculent rammed by Swedish tanker; more than 60 dead
	Aircraft	near Cardiff, Wales	March 12; British Avro Tudor V crashed; 80 dead
	Rail	near Tangua, Brazil	April 6; train plunged into Indios River; 108 dead
	Rail	near Jasidih, India	May 7; Punjab mail train crash killed 81
	Fire	Rimouski, Quebec	May 7; blaze left 2,000 homeless; damage: $12 million
	Trolley	Chicago	May 25; trolley and gas truck collided; 34 dead
	Aircraft	in Lake Michigan	June 24; Northwest DC–4 crash claimed 58
	Flood	Anhwei Province, China	August 14; cataclysm inundated more than five million acres, leaving 10 million homeless and killing 500
	Earthquake	Assam, India	August 15; quake killed 1,500 (?) and devastated area of about 30,000 miles
	Aircraft	Cairo	August 31; TWA Constellation crashed; 55 dead
	Hurricane	Florida	October 13–19; Miami struck and four dead; damage: $5–50 million
	Aircraft	Grenoble, France	November 13; Canadian Curtiss-Reid DC–4 crashed; 58 dead
	Rail	Richmond Hill, New York	November 22; commuter train rammed by another; 79 dead
	Blizzard	U.S. Northeast	November 25; this storm killed 100 (?)
1951	Tornado	Comoro Islands	January 4; more than 500 victims
	Rail	Woodbridge, New Jersey	February 6; commuter train plunged through overpass; 84 dead
	Aircraft	in the North Atlantic	March 23; U.S.A.F. plane wreckage found off Ireland; 53 lost
	Marine	off Isle of Wight	April 16; British submarine Affray sank; 75 dead
	Earthquake	Jacuapa, El Salvador	May 6; fatalities numbered more than 1,000
	Mine	Easington, England	May 29; coal mine explosion killed 81
	Rail	Nova Iguaca, Brazil	June 7; train and gasoline truck collided; 54 dead
	Aircraft	Rocky Mountain National Park, Colorado	June 30; United DC–6 crashed; 50 dead
	Flood	Kansas and Missouri	July 2–19; the most severe floods in American history killed 41 and left 200,000 homeless; damage: $1 billion
	Aircraft	near Decoto, California	August 24; United DC–6B crashed; 50 dead
	Flood	Manchuria	August 28; deluge caused extensive damage; 5,000 (?) dead or missing
	Typhoon	Philippine Islands	December 9–10; fatalities: 724
	Aircraft	Elizabeth, New Jersey	December 16; nonscheduled plane plunged into river after take-off from Newark Airport; 56 dead
	Mine	West Frankfort, Illinois	December 21; coal mine exploded; 119 dead

Year	Type of Disaster	Place	Remarks
1952	Rail	near Rio de Janeiro	March 4; two trains crashed; 119 dead
	Tornado	Mississippi Valley	March 21–22; twisters killed 229
	Aircraft	Moscow	March 27; two Soviet planes collided over Tula Airport; 70 dead
	Aircraft	San Juan, Puerto Rico	April 11; Pan Am DC–4 crashed; 52 dead
	Marine	in the Atlantic	April 26; U.S. destroyer-minesweeper **Hobson** and aircraft carrier **Wasp** collided; Hobson sank; 176 dead
	Aircraft	northern Brazil	April 29; Pan Am Stratocruiser crashed in jungle; 50 dead
	Rail	near Rzepin, Poland	July 9; train wrecked; 160 dead
	Earthquake	southern California	July 21; quake killed 14; damage: $60 million
	Bus	near Waco, Texas	August 4; two buses collided; 28 dead
	Rail	Harrow-Wealdstone, England	October 8; two trains collided with a third; 112 dead
	Typhoon	Luzon, Philippine Islands	October 22; this tropical cyclone left 1,000 (?) dead or missing
	Aircraft	near Elmendorf A.F.B., Alaska	November 23; U.S.A.F. plane crashed; 52 dead
	Aircraft	in Moses Lake, Washington	December 20; after takeoff, U.S.A.F. plane crashed and caught fire; 87 dead
1953	Marine	off Pusan, South Korea	January 9; South Korean liner sank in heavy seas; 249 dead
	Flood	northern Europe	January 31–February 1; floods devastated North Sea coastal areas; more than 2,000 dead
	Trolley	Mexico City	February 21; two trolley cars collided; more than 60 dead
	Earthquake	eastern Iran	February 22; town of Trud destroyed; 1,000 dead
	Earthquake	northwestern Turkey	March 18; quake killed 1,200 (?)
	Tornado	Waco, Texas	May 11; series of twisters killed 114
	Tornado	Michigan and Ohio	June 8; tornado series killed 142
	Tornado	central Massachusetts	June 9; storm killed 92; damage: $52 million
	Aircraft	near Tokyo	June 18; U.S.A.F. plane crashed; 129 fatalities
	Aircraft	off Wake Island	July 12; nonscheduled plane crashed in Pacific, killing 58
	Marine	near New Caledonia	August 1; French **Monique** vanished in South Pacific; 120 lost
	Tornado	Vicksburg, Mississippi	December 5; tornado killed 38; damage $25 million
	Rail	near Waiouru, New Zealand	December 24; Wellington-Auckland express plunged into stream; 155 dead
1954	Rail	near Karachi, Pakistan	January 21; mail express wrecked; 60 dead
	Rail	near Seoul, South Korea	January 31; train wreck killed 56
	Marine	off Quonset Point, Rhode Island	May 26; U.S. aircraft carrier **Bennington** exploded and burned; 103 dead
	Flood	Kazvin District, Iran	August 1; flash flood killed 2,000 (?)
	Hurricane	U.S. eastern seaboard	August 25–31; Hurricane Carol left 60 dead; damage: $500 million
	Rail	Negros Island, Philippines	September 2; train wrecked; 55 dead
	Earthquake	Orléansville, Algeria	September 9–12; quake killed 1,600 (?)
	Marine	in Tsugaru Strait, Japan	September 26; Japanese ferry **Toya Maru** sank; 1,172 dead
	Rail	east of Hyderabad, India	September 28; express train plunged from bridge; 137 dead
	Hurricane	Haiti, U.S. eastern seaboard and Canada	October 5–18; Hurricane Hazel took 410 lives in Haiti, 95 in U.S. and 80 in Canada; damage: $400 million
1955	Fire	Yokohama, Japan	February 16–17; home for aged burned, killing 100 (?)
	Aircraft	Honolulu	March 22; U.S. Navy plane hit cliff; 66 dead
	Rail	near Guadalajara, Mexico	April 3; train plunged into canyon; 300 (?) dead
	Tornado	Kansas, Missouri, Oklahoma, and Texas	May 25; series of tornadoes killed 115
	Hurricane	U.S. eastern seaboard	August 7–21; storm and floods, by Hurricane Diane, took 184 lives, caused $1.75 million in damages
	Aircraft	near Edelweiler, West Germany	August 11; two U.S.A.F. planes collided in midair; 66 dead
	Hurricane	Mexico and West Indies	September 22–28; more than 750 lives lost; extensive damage
	Flood	Pakistan and India	October 4; claiming more than 1,700 lives, this deluge devastated about 5.6 million crop acres valued at $63 million
	Aircraft	near Laramie, Wyoming	October 6; United DC–4 crashed in mountains; 66 dead
1956	Aircraft	Malta	February 18; British Lancaster bomber crashed; 50 dead
	Aircraft	near Cairo	February 20; Transport Aeriens Intercontinentaux DC–6B crashed; 52 dead
	Earthquake	northern Afghanistan	June 10–17; series of shocks caused 2,000 (?) deaths
	Aircraft	in the Atlantic, south of New York City	June 20; Venezuelan Super-Constellation crashed; 74 dead
	Aircraft	Grand Canyon, Arizona	June 30; TWA Super Constellation and United DC–7 collided in midair; 128 dead
	Marine	off Massachusetts	July 25; Italian **Andrea Doria** and Swedish **Stockholm** collided in fog, sinking the Doria; 50 (?) dead or missing
	Typhoon	Chekiang, China	August 1; storm and subsequent floods killed more than 2,000
	Explosion	Cali, Colombia	August 7; seven truckloads of dynamite exploded, killing more than 1,200 and destroying town; damage: $40 million
	Mine	Marcinelle, Belgium	August 8; coal mine fire claimed 263
	Rail	near Secunderabad, India	September 21; two trains plunged into river as bridge collapsed; 121 dead
	Aircraft	in the Atlantic, north of the Azores	October 10; U.S.A.F. plane disappeared; 59 lost
	Rail	Marudaiyar River, India	November 23; express train derailed; 143 dead
	Aircraft	near Vancouver, Canada	December 9; Trans-Canada North Star crashed; 62 dead
1957	Fire	Warrenton, Missouri	February 17; home for aged burned; 72 dead
	Aircraft	in the Pacific	March 21; U.S.A.F. transport disappeared; 67 lost
	Blizzard	Midwest	March 22–25; storm claimed 21 lives; damage: $5–6 million
	Tornado	Kansas and Missouri	May 18–21; twister killed 40 (?); damage: over $2 million
	Hurricane	Texas to Alabama	June 25–28; Hurricane Audrey killed 390; damage: $50–500 million
	Earthquake	Caspian Coast, Iran	July 2; quake killed more than 1,500 and rendered more than 10,000 homeless
	Marine	in the Caspian Sea	July 14; USSR **Eshghabad** ran aground in storm; 270 dead
	Aircraft	off Netherlands New Guinea	July 16; KLM Super-Constellation crashed in sea; 57 dead
	Aircraft	Quebec	August 11; Maritime Central DC–4 charter crashed; 79 dead
	Rail	near Kendal, Jamaica	September 1; train plunged into ravine; 175 (?) dead
	Rail	near Montgomery, West Pakistan	September 29; express crashed into standing train; 250 dead

Year	Type of Disaster	Place	Remarks
	Earthquake	Outer Mongolia	December 2; quake fatal for 1,200 (?)
	Rail	near London	December 4; two-train collision killed 92
	Aircraft	near Bolívar, Argentina	December 8; Aerolineas Argentina DC–4 crashed; 62 dead
	Earthquake	western Iran	December 13 and 15–17; quake killed 1,392
1958	Mine	near Asansoi, India	February 19; coal mine exploded; more than 180 dead
	Marine	near Istanbul	March 1; Turkish ferry Uskudar sank; 238 dead
	Rail	Santa Cruz, Brazil	March 7; two trains collided; 67 dead
	Rail	near Rio de Janeiro	May 8; two-train collision killed 128
	Aircraft	Casablanca	May 18; Sabena DC–6B crashed; 65 dead
	Aircraft	in the Atlantic, west of Ireland	August 14; KLM Super-Constellation crashed; 99 dead
	Typhoon	Tokyo	September 21; at least 681 killed
	Typhoon	Honshu, Japan	September 27–28; storm killed 679; many missing
	Aircraft	Kanash, USSR	October 17; Aeroflot TU–104 crashed; 65 dead
	Fire	Chicago	December 1; parochial school burned; 95 dead
	Fire	Bogotá, Colombia	December 16; department store conflagration caused 84 deaths
1959	Aircraft	New York City	February 3; American Electra crashed in the East River; 65 dead
	Rail	Java	May 28; train derailed, spilling into ravine and killing 92
	Rail	São Paulo, Brazil	June 5; two trains collided; 60 (?) dead
	Aircraft	near Milan	June 26; TWA Super-Constellation exploded in storm; 68 dead
	Typhoon	Fukien coast, China	August 20; storm claimed 2,334 lives
	Typhoon	Honshu, Japan	September 26–27; tropical cyclone killed more than 4,400
	Hurricane	Jalisco and Colima, Mexico	October 27–28; storm caused mudslides and floods; 1,400 dead
	Flood	Frejus, France	December 2; Malpasset Dam collapsed; 412 victims
1960	Aircraft	near Wilmington, North Carolina	January 6; National DC–6B "disintegrated" in flight; 34 dead
	Aircraft	near Richmond, Virginia	January 18; Capitol Viscount crashed into ravine; 50 dead
	Mine	Coalbrook, South Africa	January 21; coal mine cave-in and explosion killed over 400
	Aircraft	near La Paz, Bolivia	February 5; Lloyd Aereo Boliviano DC–4 crashed; 56 dead
	Mine	Zwickau, East Germany	February 22; explosion killed 123
	Aircraft	Rio de Janeiro	February 25; U.S. Navy plane and DC–3 collided; 61 dead
	Earthquake	Agadir, Morocco	February 29 and March 1; quakes followed by tidal waves destroyed city; 20,000 (?) dead
	Aircraft	near Tell City, Indiana	March 17; Northwest Electra exploded in flight; 63 dead
	Tornado	Oklahoma and Arkansas	May 5; tornadoes killed 29
	Rail	Leipzig, East Germany	May 15; two trains collided; 59 dead
	Earthquake	Chile, Japan, and Hawaii	May 22–29; series of earthquakes, volcanic eruptions, landslides, and tsunami caused widespread devastation; in Chile, more than 2,000 dead and damage: $550 million; in Hawaii, 61 dead and damage: $22 million; in Japan, 138 dead and damage: $50 million
	Fire	Guatemala City	July 14; hospital burned; 225 (?) dead
	Aircraft	near Dakar, Senegal	August 29; Air France Super-Constellation down at sea; 63 dead
	Hurricane	South and northeast U.S.	September 10; Hurricane Donna killed 50
	Aircraft	Agaña, Guam	September 18–19; World DC–6B exploded; 78 dead
	Aircraft	Boston	October 4; Eastern Electra crashed into harbor; 62 dead
	Cyclone	East Pakistan	October 10 and 31; fatalities from cyclones (6,000) and tidal waves (4,000)
	Fire	Amude, Syria	November 13; movie house burned; 152 deaths
	Rail	Pardubice, Czechoslovakia	November 14; two trains collided; 110 dead
	Aircraft	New York City	December 16; United DC–8 and TWA Super Constellation collided in mid-air over Staten Island, New York; 134 dead
	Fire	Brooklyn Navy Yard	December 19; fire swept aircraft carrier; 50 dead
1961	Aircraft	Berg, Belgium	February 15; Sabena Boeing 707 crashed; 73 dead, including 18 American figure skaters
	Aircraft	Nuremberg, West Germany	March 28; Czechoslovak Ilyushin–18 crashed; 52 dead
	Marine	in the Persian Gulf	April 8; British ship Dara burned; more than 200 dead
	Floods	Midwest United States	Early May; floods caused deaths of 25
	Typhoon	East Pakistan	May 9; cyclone plus tidal waves killed 2,000 (?)
	Aircraft	Ghadames, Libya	May 10; Air France Starliner crashed; 79 dead
	Marine	off Mozambique	July 8; Portuguese Save burned and exploded; 227 dead
	Mine	Dolna Suce, Czechoslovakia	July 8; coal gas explosion killed 108
	Aircraft	Casablanca	July 12; Czechoslovak Ilyushin–18 crashed; 72 dead
	Aircraft	near Chicago	September 1; TWA Constellation crashed in a field; 78 dead
	Aircraft	Shannon, Ireland	September 10; Presidential DC–6 charter crashed; 83 dead
	Hurricane	Southwest and Midwest United States	September 10–14; Hurricane Carla and associated tornadoes and floods caused deaths of 46
	Aircraft	Rabat, Morocco	September 12; Air France Caravelle crashed, killing 77
	Typhoon	Japan	September 16–17; storm killed 185; extensive damage
	Rail	west of Calcutta, India	October 20; express train derailed; more than 50 dead
	Hurricane	Belize, British Honduras	October 31; hurricane devastated city, causing 250 (?) deaths and damage: $150 million
	Aircraft	near Richmond, Virginia	November 8; charter Constellation crashed in woods; 77 dead
	Hurricane	southern Mexico	November 14; hurricane killed at least 330
	Fire	Niteroi, Brazil	December 17; circus tent burned, killing more than 320
	Rail	Catanzaro, Italy	December 23; train fell into gorge; 69 dead
1962	Rail	Woerden, Netherlands	January 8; two trains collided; 91 dead
	Avalanche	Mt. Huscaran, Peru	January 10; Andean avalanche buried more than 3,000
	Mine	Voelklingen, West Germany	February 7; coal mine exploded; 298 dead
	Aircraft	New York City	March 1; American 707 plunged into Jamaica Bay; 95 dead
	Aircraft	near Douala, Cameroon	March 4; British Caledonian DC–7C crashed in jungle; 111 dead
	Hurricane	eastern United States	March 5–7; windstorm and high tides caused 35 deaths
	Aircraft	in the western Pacific	March 16; Flying Tiger charter disappeared; 107 lost
	Rail	Tokyo	May 3; three trains collided; 163 dead
	Rail	Voghera, Italy	May 31; two trains collided; 63 dead
	Aircraft	Paris	June 3; Air France Boeing 707 crashed; 130 killed
	Aircraft	Guadeloupe, West Indies	June 22; Air France Boeing 707 crashed; 113 dead
	Aircraft	Bombay	July 7; Alitalia DC–8 crashed; 94 dead
	Rail	Dumraon, India	July 21; two trains collided; 69 dead

DISASTERS/CATASTROPHES

Year	Type of Disaster	Place	Remarks
	Earthquake	northwestern Iran	September 1; quake killed more than 10,000
	Flood	Barcelona	September 27; flash flood killed more than 470
	Hurricane	Pacific coast of United States	October 12–13; near-hurricane winds and floods killed 40
	Cyclone	Thailand	October 27; hurricane toll: 769 dead and 142 missing
	Aircraft	Lima, Peru	November 27; Varig Boeing 707 crashed; 97 dead
	Aircraft	in the Amazon jungle, Brazil	December 14; Panair Do Brasil Constellation crashed; 50 dead
	Flood	northern Europe	December 31; winter-storm floods caused over 300 deaths
1963	Aircraft	Ankara	February 1; Turkish Air Force plane and Lebanese Viscount collided; 95 dead
	Volcanic eruption	Bali	March 18; Mount Agung erupted, forcing 78,000 to flee homes; 1,584 deaths recorded
	Marine	in the Atlantic, east of Boston	April 10; Thresher, U.S. Navy nuclear submarine, sank; 129 dead in navy's worst peacetime submarine disaster
	Cyclone	Bay of Bengal, East Pakistan	May 28–29; cyclones and tidal waves took lives of 12,000 (?)
	Aircraft	in the Pacific, off Alaska	June 3; Northwest DC-7 charter crashed; 101 dead
	Earthquake	Skopje, Yugoslavia	July 26; quake killed 1,100 (?)
	Aircraft	near Bombay	July 28; wreckage found of United Arab Comet; 62 dead
	Aircraft	Zurich	September 4; Swissair Caravelle crashed; 80 dead
	Hurricane	Caribbean	October 1–9; Hurricane Flora killed 3,500 (?)
	Flood	near Belluno, Italy	October 9; landslides and flooding, near Vaiont Dam, resulted in death for more than 2,000
	Fire	Indianapolis, Indiana	October 31; explosion and fire at Coliseum; 74 dead
	Rail	near Yokohama	November 9; two Japanese trains hurtled into derailed freight train; at least 162 dead
	Mine	Omuta, Japan	November 9; coal mine exploded; 446 dead
	Flood	Haiti	November 14–15; deluges and landslides killed 500 (?)
	Fire	near Norwalk, Ohio	November 23; fire at nursing home for aged; 63 dead
	Aircraft	Montreal	November 29; Trans-Canada DC-8F crashed; 118 dead
	Aircraft	near Elkton, Maryland	December 8; Pan Am Boeing 707 crashed into a field; 81 dead
1964	Rail	Altamirano, Argentina	February 1; two trains collided; 70 dead
	Aircraft	near New Orleans, Louisiana	February 25; Eastern DC-8 crashed into Lake Pontchartrain; 58 dead
	Aircraft	near Innsbruck, Austria	February 29; British turboprop crashed, killing 83
	Aircraft	near Lake Tahoe, California	March 1; nonscheduled carrier plane crashed; 85 dead
	Earthquake	Alaska	March 27; earthquake was responsible for 114 deaths
	Aircraft	Clark A.F.B., Philippines	May 11; U.S. military transport crashed; 75 dead
	Floods	northern Montana	June 8–9; floods were responsible for 36 deaths
	Aircraft	near Fengyuan, Taiwan	June 20; Chinese Civil Air Patrol plane crashed; 57 dead
	Rail	near Oporto, Portugal	July 26; train wreck killed 94
	Bridge	near Caracas, Venezuela	August 23; 50 (?) killed in collapse of bridge over Caroni Falls
	Aircraft	near Granada, Spain	October 2; Union Transports Africains DC-6 crashed; 80 dead
	Floods	western United States	Late December; floods responsible for 45 deaths
1965	Aircraft	in the Andes, Chile	February 6; Chilean Airline DC-6B crashed; 87 dead
	Aircraft	near New York	February 8; Eastern DC-7B crashed in Atlantic; 84 dead
	Earthquake	near Santiago, Chile	March 28; quake killed 400 (?); damage: $200 million
	Aircraft	in the Strait of Gibraltar	March 31; Iberia Convair crashed; 50 dead
	Aircraft	near Damascus	April 10; Royal Jordanian plane crashed; 54 dead
	Tornadoes	Midwest United States	April 11; tornadoes killed 272
	Cyclone	Barisal, East Pakistan	May 12; storm killed 12,000 to 20,000; millions homeless
	Aircraft	near Cairo	May 20; Pakistan International Boeing 707 crashed; 119 dead
	Mine	Bihar State, India	May 28; coal mine accident; more than 400 dead
	Mine	Kyushu, Japan	June 1; accident killed 236
	Mine	Kakanj, Yugoslavia	June 7; gas explosion claimed 108
	Aircraft	near El Toro, California	June 25; military plane hit mountain; 84 dead
	Aircraft	British Columbia	July 8; Canadian Pacific DC-6B crashed; 52 dead
	Explosion	near Searcy, Arkansas	August 9; explosion and fire at missile site killed 53
	Hurricane	Florida and Louisiana	August 27–Sept. 12; Hurricane Betsy killed 75, injured 17,500
	Rail	near Durban, South Africa	October 4; train derailed; 81 dead
	Aircraft	near Cincinnati, Ohio	November 8; American Boeing 727 crashed into hill; 58 dead
	Marine	in the Caribbean	November 13; Panamanian cruise ship Yarmouth Castle caught fire and sank; 89 dead
	Rail	near Toungoo, Burma	December 9; two trains collided, killing 76
	Cyclone	Karachi, Pakistan	December 15; cyclone killed 10,000 (?)
1966	Flood	Rio de Janeiro	January 11–13; deluge and landslides killed more than 300
	Aircraft	in the French Alps	January 24; Air India 707 crashed into Mont Blanc; 117 dead
	Marine	Chandpur Port, East Pakistan	January 30; Pakistani launch and steamer collided; 80 dead
	Marine	near Belawan, Indonesia	February 2; Indonesian oil tanker sank; 89 lost
	Aircraft	Tokyo	February 4; Boeing 727 plunged into Tokyo Bay; 133 dead
	Tornadoes	Mississippi and Alabama	March 3; tornadoes killed 58
	Aircraft	Honshu, Japan	March 5; BOAC Boeing 707 caught fire and crashed into Mount Fujiyama; 124 dead
	Rail	Lumding Junction, India	April 20; train exploded, killing 55
	Aircraft	near Ardmore, Oklahoma	April 22; military charter plane crashed; 83 dead
	Rail	Bombay	June 13; two-train collision claimed 60
	Earthquake	eastern Turkey	August 19; quake killed 2,529, rendering 108,000 (?) homeless
	Aircraft	Belgrade	August 31; British Airways turboprop crashed; 96 dead
	Hurricane	Caribbean and Mexico	September 25–October 1; cyclone fatal for at least 200
	Marine	in the Gulf of Tonkin	October 26; U.S. aircraft carrier Oriskany caught fire; 43 lost
	Marine	in Kosi River, India	October 26; Indian vessel sank; more than 100 dead
	Flood	Arno Valley, Italy	November 3–4; overflow of Arno River, which killed 113, destroyed priceless art treasures in Florence and elsewhere
	Aircraft	Bratislava, Czechoslovakia	November 24; TABSO Bulgarian Ilyushin-18 crashed; 82 dead
	Marine	in the Sea of Crete	December 8; Greek ferry Heraklion sank in storm; 217 dead
	Flood	southern Brazil	January–March; heavy rain floods killed more than 600
	Missile	Cape Kennedy, Florida	January 27; the three-man crew of Apollo 1 die in fire
	Fire	Tasmania	February 7–9; forest fire killed 52; damage: $11.2 million
	Aircraft	Nicosia, Cyprus	April 20; Swiss Globe Britannia turboprop charter crashed while landing; 126 dead
	Tornadoes	northeastern Illinois	April 21; tornadoes killed 55
	Fire	Brussels	May 22; Innovation department store burned; 322 lost their lives

Year	Type of Disaster	Place	Remarks
	Aircraft	in the French Pyrenees	June 3; British Air Ferry Ltd. DC–6 charter crashed into Mont Canigou; 88 dead
	Aircraft	Stockport, England	June 4; British Midland charter DC–4 crashed; 72 dead
	Rail	Langenweddingen, East Germany	June 6; train collided with gasoline truck and exploded; 82 dead
	Aircraft	near Hendersonville, North Carolina	July 19; Piedmont 727 and private plane collided; 82 dead
	Marine	off Vietnam	July 25; U.S. aircraft carrier Forrestal crippled by fire; 134 dead
	Earthquake	Venezuela	July 30–31; quake, ranging from the Andes to Caribbean, killed 277; damage in Caracas alone: $15 million
	Aircraft	southern Turkey	October 12; BEA Comet crashed; 67 dead
	Rail	London	November 5; express train derailed; 53 dead
	Aircraft	near Cincinnati, Ohio	November 20; TWA Convair 880 crashed near airport; 70 dead
	Flood	Lisbon	November 26; fatality toll: 457
1968	Marine	in the eastern Mediterranean	January 26; Israeli submarine Dakar sank; 69 dead
	Marine	in the western Mediterranean	January 27; French submarine Minerve went down; 52 lost
	Aircraft	Guadeloupe, West Indies	March 5; Air France Boeing 707 crashed; 63 dead
	Aircraft	Atlantic Ocean off Wales	March 24; Irish International Viscount crashed; 61 dead
	Marine	Wellington Harbor	April 10; New Zealand ferry Wahine crashed and sank; 51 dead
	Aircraft	Windhoek, South-West Africa	April 20; South African Boeing 707 crashed; 123 dead
	Aircraft	near Dawson, Texas	May 3; Braniff Electra crashed; 85 dead
	Tornadoes	Midwest United States	May 15; tornadoes killed 95
	Marine	Atlantic Ocean, off Azores	May 27; U.S. nuclear submarine Scorpion sank; 99 lost
	Flood	Gujarat, India	August 8–14; floods killed 1,000 (?)
	Earthquake	northeastern Iran	August 31; quake killed 12,000 (?)
	Aircraft	off the French Riviera	September 11; Air France Caravelle crashed; 95 dead
	Mine	Mannington, West Virginia	November 20; coal mine exploded and caught fire; 78 dead
	Aircraft	off Caracas, Venezuela	December 12; Pan Am Boeing 707 crashed; 51 dead
1969	Floods	southern California	January 25–29; floods killed 95
	Aircraft	La Coruba, Venezuela	March 16; VIASA DC–9 crashed near Maracaibo; 154 dead
	Aircraft	Aswan Airport, Egypt	March 20; United Arab IL-18 crashed while landing; 91 dead
	Mine	Barroteran, Mexico	March 31; gas mine exploded; 156 dead
	Cyclone	Dacca, East Pakistan	April 15; storm killed 500 (?)
	Marine	in the South China Sea	June 2; U.S. destroyer Frank E. Evans sliced in two by the Australian carrier Melbourne; 74 assumed dead
	Aircraft	near Monterrey, Mexico	June 4; Mexican Airways Boeing 727 crashed; 79 dead
	Rail	near Benares, India	June 21; train plunged off tracks into river bed; 75 dead
	Rail	Jaipur, India	July 15; freight train rammed standing passenger train; 85 dead
	Hurricane	Mississippi and Louisiana	August 17; Hurricane Camille killed 256; $1.5 billion damage
	Floods	Virginia	August 23; floods killed 100 (?)
	Aircraft	near Indianapolis, Indiana	September 9; small plane and Allegheny DC–9 collided; 83 dead
	Aircraft	near Danang	September 20; Air Vietnam DC–4 crashed; 77 dead
	Aircraft	near La Paz, Bolivia	September 26; Lloyd Aereo Boliviano DC–6 crashed in the Andes; 74 dead
1970	Rail	near Buenos Aires	February 4; commuter train struck by express train; 236 killed
	Avalanche	Val d'Isère, France	February 10; worst snowslide in French history killed 42 at hostel
	Aircraft	in the Caribbean	February 15; Dominican DC–9 crashed, killing 102
	Marine	in the Mediterranean	March 4; French submarine Eurydice exploded, sank; 57 dead
	Earthquake	Kutahya, Turkey	March 28; quake toll: more than 1,000
	Aircraft	Casablanca, Morocco	April 1; Royal Air Maroc Caravelle jetliner crashed; 61 killed
	Explosion	Osaka, Japan	April 8; serial gas-main blasts killed 73; 300 injured
	Avalanche	Saint-Gervais, France	April 16; snowslide hit tuberculosis sanatorium, killing 72
	Flood	Oradea, Rumania	May 11–23; 200 (?) killed; more than 225 towns destroyed
	Earthquake	northern Peru	May 31; quake plus floods and landslides killed 30,000 (?)
	Aircraft	Barcelona	July 4; British charter Comet jet crashed; 112 dead
	Aircraft	Toronto	July 5; Air Canada DC–8 crashed; 108 killed
	Bus	New Delhi	July 22; 25 buses, 5 taxis, and an army vehicle swept into narrow gorge by floods; 600 dead
	Aircraft	near Cuzco, Peru	August 9; Peruvian Electra crashed; 100 dead
	Fire	Saint-Laurent-du-Pont, France	November 1; fire in a dance hall killed 146
	Cyclone	East Pakistan, delta region	November 12; storm and floods killed 200,000 (?)
	Aircraft	Huntington, West Virginia	November 14; Southern Airways DC–9 carrying the Marshall Univ. football team exploded while landing; 75 killed
1971	Aircraft	Moscow	January 1; Aeroflot Il-18 crashed during takeoff; 90 killed
	Earthquake	Los Angeles area	February 9; quake killed 64, of these, 43 were at V.A. hospital
	Tornado	Mississippi and Louisiana	February 21; storm killed 115
	Avalanche	Lima, Peru	February 19; Andean avalanche killed 600 (?)
	Earthquake	Bingol, Turkey	May 23; quake killed 800
	Aircraft	Belgrade	May 23; Yugoslav TU-134A crashed at Rijeka Airport; 78 killed
	Aircraft	Honshu, Japan	July 30; Japanese airliner and fighter plane collide; 162 dead
	Aircraft	Alaska	September 4; Alaska Airlines 727 crashed into a mountain in the Tongass National Forest; all 111 passengers killed
	Fire	Seoul, S. Korea	December 25; explosion and fire at hotel; 163 dead
1972	Flood	Buffalo Creek, W. Virginia	February 26; coal mine waste waters caused a makeshift dam to collapse; 118 dead
	Aircraft	United Arab Emirates	March 14; Danish Sterling Airways charter crashed near Dubai; all 112 passengers killed
	Poisoning	Iraq	March–April; outbreak of mercury poisoning; over 100 dead
	Earthquake	Iran	April 10; 45 villages leveled; over 5,000 dead
	Mine	Kellogg, Idaho	May 2; fire in the Sunshine Silver Mine; 91 miners dead
	Aircraft	Palermo, Italy	May 6; Alitalia DC-8 struck a mountainside in bad weather; all 115 passengers killed
	Fire	Osaka, Japan	May 13; Sennichi department store gutted by flames; 115 killed
	Mine	Northwest Rhodesia	June 6; explosion in Wankie Colliery Co. coal mine; 427 dead
	Flood	Rapid City, S. Dakota	June 10; flash flooding caused over $120 million damage; 226 dead, 124 missing
	Hurricane	Eastern United States	June 10–20; Hurricane Agnes struck Florida, Maryland, Pennsylvania, New York, and Virginia; $1.7 billion damage; 134 dead
	Rail	Soissons, France	June 17; falling rocks in a tunnel cause derailment; 107 dead

Year	Type of Disaster	Place	Remarks
	Aircraft	London	June 18; BEA Trident crashed on takeoff; 118 dead
	Flood	Luzon Island, Philippines	June-August; Typhoon Rita and six weeks of rain caused landslides and burst dams; 427 dead
	Aircraft	East Berlin	August 14; Interflug Ilyushin-62 crashed on takeoff; 156 dead
	Rail	Saltillo, Mexico	October 6; speeding passenger train jumped its tracks; 204 dead
	Aircraft	Krasnaya Polyana, USSR	October 14; Aeroflot Ilyushin-62 crashed; 176 dead
	Aircraft	Canary Islands	December 3; Spanish charter plane exploded; 155 dead
	Earthquake	Managua, Nicaragua	December 23; worst earthquake in Nicaraguan history; leveled 70% of the city; 10,000 dead
	Aircraft	near Miami	December 29; Eastern Airlines Tristar jetliner crashed into Everglades; 98 dead
1973	Aircraft	Kano, Nigeria	January 22; Boeing 707 jet carrying 200 Moslems from a pilgrimage to Mecca crashed in thick fog; 176 dead
	Epidemic	Bangladesh	Reported March 1; smallpox swept country, killing at least 1,000
	Flood	Western Tunisia	March 31; week-long rains flooded Mejerda River; 150 dead
	Aircraft	Basel, Switzerland	April 10; British charter flight crashed; 104 dead
	Marine	Dacca coast	May 5; two riverboats collided; 250 dead
	Storms	Indonesian Islands	Reported June 16; spring storms took 1,650 lives
	Aircraft	Paris	July 11; Brazilian Boeing 707 crashed in an emergency landing at Orly; 122 dead
	Aircraft	Boston	July 31; Delta jetliner crashed in fog; 88 dead
	Earthquake	central Mexico	August 28; earthquake and rains killed 527; 200,000 homeless
	Fire	Kumamoto, Japan	November 29; fire hit department store which had no fire escape chutes; 101 dead; 84 injured
	Marine	Ecuador coast	December 24; overloaded ferryboat capsized, killing 200
1974	Aircraft	Pago Pago, Samoa	January 31; Pan Am jet crashed on landing; 92 dead
	Fire	Sao Paulo, Brazil	February 1; a faulty air conditioner caused a flash fire to sweep a modern bank, killing 189 people in 25 minutes
	Famine	Sahel, West Africa	Reported March 3; 100,000 persons were estimated dead and millions starving due to drought in this sub-Sahara region
			March 3; Turkish DC-10 crashed on takeoff from Orly; 346 dead
	Aircraft	Paris	
	Tornado	central and southern U.S.	April 3–4; tornado series in 11-state area; 336 dead
	Aircraft	Bali, Indonesia	April 22; Pan Am 707 crashed on landing; 107 dead
	Aircraft	Leningrad	April 27; Soviet Ilyushin 18 crashed on takeoff; 108 killed
	Marine	Bangladesh coast	May 1; motor launch capsized; 250 dead
	Rail	Zagreb, Yugoslavia	August 30; express train derailed; 124 dead
	Aircraft	Charlotte, North Carolina	September 11; Eastern jet crashed; 88 dead
	Hurricane	Honduras	September 18–19; Hurricane Fifi killed 5,000 (?)
	Aircraft	near Washington, D.C.	December 1; TWA jet crashed into hill; 92 dead
	Aircraft	Sri Lanka	December 4; jet carrying pilgrims crashed; 191 dead
	Earthquake	northern Pakistan	December 28; quake toll about 5,000
1975	Aircraft	Saigon, South Vietnam	April 4; U.S. Air Force transport jet carrying South Vietnamese orphans to U.S. crashed on takeoff; 155 dead
	Famine	East Africa	Reported May 25; drought since October 1974 in Ethiopia and Somalia; 40,000 dead
	Aircraft	New York	June 24; Eastern Airlines Boeing 727 crashed on landing at Kennedy International Airport; 113 dead
	Flood	northern India	July; month-long monsoon rains caused flooding; 300 dead
	Marine	near Canton, China	August 3; two ferries collided on Hsi River; 500 (?) drowned
	Aircraft	near Agadir, Morocco	August 3; charter Boeing 707 hit mountainside; 188 dead
	Aircraft	Damascus, Syria	August 20; Czechoslovak airliner crashed; 126 dead
	Flood	eastern India	August-September; monsoon rains cause flooding and spread of cholera; 450 (?) dead
	Earthquake	Lice, Turkey	September 6; earthquake leaves 2,312 dead, 3,372 injured
	Mine	near Dhanbad, India	December 27; coal mine explosion caused flooding of mine; 372 believed dead
1976	Aircraft	Saudi Arabia	January 1; Middle East Airlines Boeing 707 crashed; 82 dead
	Earthquake	Guatemala	February 4; earthquake toll estimated 22,419 dead, 74,105 injured and 1 million homeless
	Aircraft	Erivan, USSR	March 5; Soviet Il-18 crashed; 120 dead
	Earthquake	Friuli region of Italy	May 6; earthquake in northeast Italy; more than 1,000 dead
	Earthquake	Indonesia	June 26 and July 14; successive quakes, the first on West New Guinea caused mudslides, which left 443 dead, 3,000 missing; the second quake in Bali left 600 dead, 3,400 injured
	Earthquake	Tangshan area of China	July 28; two major quakes devastated industrial city of Tangshan; casualities estimated to be about 700,000, the second worst disaster in recorded history
	Flood	Big Thompson River, Colo.	July 31; vacationers and campers caught in flash flood in canyon; 138 dead, 5 missing
	Earthquake	southern Philippines	August 17; earthquake hit Mindanao and neighboring islands, 8,000 (?) dead or missing and 175,000 homeless
	Aircraft	near Zagreb, Yugoslavia	September 10; Yugoslav charter jet DC-10 and British Airlines Trident collided in world's worst midair collision; 176 dead
	Aircraft	near Isparta, Turkey	September 19; Turkish Boeing 727 hit mountain; 155 dead
	Flood	La Paz, Mexico	October 1; earthen dam broke after heavy rains; 630 dead
	Aircraft	Santa Cruz, Bolivia	October 15; Boeing 707 cargo plane crashed in downtown Santa Cruz; 100 dead
	Earthquake	Van Province, Turkey	November 24; earthquake; estimated 4,000 dead
1977	Rail	Granville, Australia	January 18; Sydney-bound commuter train derailed; 82 dead
	Earthquake	Bucharest, Romania	March 4; earthquake leaves 1,541 dead, 11,275 injured
	Aircraft	Tenerife, Canary Islands	March 27; Pan American 747 and KLM 747 jumbo jets collide on runway; 579 dead in worst disaster in aviation history
	Tornado	near Dacca, Bangladesh	April 1; tornado struck Madaripur district; about 900 dead
	Aircraft	New Hope, Georgia	April 4; Southern Airways DC-9 emergency landed on highway; 72 dead
	Fire	Southgate, Kentucky	May 28; supper club fire; 161 dead, 129 injured
	Flood	Johnstown, Pennsylvania	July 19-20; nine-inch rainfall caused flash flood; over 70 dead
	Storm	Andhra Pradesh, India	November 19; cyclone caused tidal wave killing 20,000
	Aircraft	Funchal, Madeira	November 19; Portuguese 727 crashed on landing; 130 dead

Year	Type of Disaster	Place	Remarks
	Aircraft	Johore Strait, Malaysia	December 4; Malaysian 737 exploded after hijacking; 100 dead
	Earthquake	Kerman Province, Iran	December 20; earthquake hit rural villages; over 520 dead
1978	Aircraft	near Bombay, India	January 1; Air India 747 exploded and crashed; 213 dead
	Aircraft	near Sofia, Bulgaria	March 16; Bulgarian airliner crashed; 73 dead
	Tornado	Orissa, India	April 16; storm killed 400 to 500 in six villages
	Construction	St. Marys, West Virginia	April 27; scaffolding on cooling tower collapsed; 51 dead
	Explosion	near Tarragona, Spain	July 11; propylene gas truck exploded at tourist camp; 200 dead
	Explosion	Beirut, Lebanon	August 13; blast destroyed building, killing 150 to 200
	Fire	Abadan, Iran	August 20; arsonist-set theater fire killed 430
	Earthquake	Tabas, Iran	September 16; major quake; estmated 25,000 dead
	Aircraft	San Diego, California	September 25; Pacific Southwest 727 jet and private plane collided in midair; 137 aboard the two planes and 7 on ground dead
	Marine	Bay of Bengal	April 4; fleet of cargo boats lost in storm; 1,000 dead
	Mass suicide	Jonestown, Guyana	November 18; mass poisoning and murder in American religious commune; death toll placed at 913
	Aircraft	Leh, India	November 19; Indian Air Force transport crashed; 78 killed
	Storm	Sri Lanka and India	November 23; cyclone leveled 500,000 buildings; over 1,500 dead
	Aircraft	Colombo, Sri Lanka	November 25; charter DC–8 jet crashed; 183 dead
	Aircraft	Tyrrhenian Sea	December 23; Alitalia DC–9 jet ditched at sea; 103 dead
1979	Earthquake	eastern Iran	January 16; quake killed 199
	Flood	southeast Brazil	early February; over 40 days of heavy rain caused severe flooding; over 600 dead, 350,000 homeless
	Volcanic eruption	central Java	February 21; 175 killed, 1,000 others injured by lava flow
	Aircraft	near Moscow	March 17; Tupolev 104 crashed after takeoff; 90 dead
	Poison	near Sverdlovsk, U.S.S.R.	April–May; anthrax epidemic reported, but experts suspect biological weapon mishap; toll put at more than 1,000 dead
	Tornado	Texas and Oklahoma	April 10; twisters struck border area; 60 dead, over 800 injured
	Earthquake	Yugoslavia and Albania	April 15; shocks hit coast; over 120 dead; 1,500 injured
	Cyclones	southeast India	May 12–13; storms killed over 600
	Aircraft	Chicago	May 25; American Airlines DC–10 crashed; 271 on board and 2 on ground dead in worst U.S. air disaster
	Aircraft	Sumatra, Indonesia	July 11; domestic airliner crashed into mountain; 61 dead
	Fire	Saragossa, Spain	July 13; hotel fire; 80 dead
	Bus	Lugezi, Tanzania	July 14; overcrowded bus fell into Lake Victoria; 60 dead
	Tidal wave	Lomblem, Indonesia	July 17; death toll estimated at 539
	Fire	Tuticorin, India	July 29; movie tent fire; 92 dead
	Flood	Morvi, India	August 11; dam collapsed; at least 5,000 dead
	Aircraft	over Ukraine	August 11; two Soviet jet liners collide; 173 dead
	Rail	Bangkok, Thailand	August 21; trains collided; 51 dead
	Hurricane	Caribbean and east coast of U.S.	Aug. 30–Sept. 7; Hurricane David took over 1,100 lives, left 150,000 homeless
	Rail	Stalac, Yugoslavia	Sept. 13; freight and passenger train collided; 80 dead
	Aircraft	Mexico City	October 31; Western Airlines DC–10 crashed on landing; 75 dead
	Marine	near Khulna, Bangladesh	early November; cargo ship and launch collided; 200 dead
	Earthquake	northeastern Iran	November 14; quake took 248 lives
	Marine	Bo Hai Gulf, China	November 25; oil drilling rig collapsed during storm; 70 dead
	Aircraft	Taif, Saudi Arabia	November 26; Boeing 707 jetliner carrying pilgrims from Mecca crashed; 156 dead
	Aircraft	Mt. Erebus, Antarctica	November 28; New Zealand DC–10 hit mountain; 257 dead
	Earthquake	Colombia-Ecuador border	December 12; quake and tidal waves took 200 lives
1980	Aircraft	near Tehran, Iran	January 21; Boeing 707 crashed; 128 dead
	Structural	Sincelejo, Colombia	January 21; bullring collapsed; 222 dead
	Aircraft	near Warsaw	March 14; Polish Ilyushin 62 crashed; 87 dead
	Marine	North Sea	March 27; Oil platform collapsed during storm; 123 dead
	Aircraft	Florianopolis, Brazil	April 12; Boeing 727 crashed; 54 dead
	Aircraft	Canary Islands	April 25; British Boeing 727 crashed; 146 dead
	Volcanic eruption	Mt. St. Helens, Washington	May 18; volcano erupted devastating large area; 60 dead
	Fire	Kingston, Jamaica	May 20; Fire involving arson, in home for elderly; 157 dead
	Aircraft	Tyrrhenian Sea	June 28; Italian DC–9 jet lost; 81 dead
	Aircraft	Alma Ata, U.S.S.R.	July 7; Soviet TU–142 jetliner crashed; 163 dead
	Hurricane	Gulf of Mexico	August 4–11; Hurricane Allen left 273 dead
	Explosion	Bologna, Italy	August 6; bomb exploded in train station; 76 dead
	Flood	Uttar Pradesh, India	August 12; monsoon flooding of Ganges; over 600 dead
	Riot	Moradabad, India	August 13; riot in mosque caused 86 deaths
	Aircraft	Riyadh, Saudi-Arabia	August 19; fire aboard Lockheed L–1011 jet liner; 301 dead
	Rail	near Torun, Poland	August 19; passenger and freight train collided; 69 dead
	Flood	Ibadan, Nigeria	August 31; flooding from rainstorms; 240 dead
	Aircraft	near Medina, Saudi Arabia	Sept. 14; Saudi Air Force transport crashed; 89 killed
	Earthquake	Al Asnam, Algeria	October 10; earthquake toll over 3,000 dead
	Explosion	Ortuella, Spain	October 23; explosion destroyed school; 64 killed
	Fire	Las Vegas, Nevada	November 21; hotel five; 84 dead and 500 injured
	Earthquake	southern Italy	November 23; quake leaves about 3,000 dead, 200,000 homeless
1981	Fire	near Ankara, Turkey	November 24; engagement party fire; 97 dead
	Marine	Amazon River, Brazil	January 6; steamer capsized; 311 (?) dead
	Fire	Keansburg, New Jersey	January 9; fire in home for elderly; 37 dead
	Marine	Java Sea, Indonesia	January 27; ferry burns; 580 (?) dead
	Fire	Dublin, Ireland	February 14; discotheque fire; 44 dead
	Rail	Bihar state, India	June 6; train plunges off bridge; 215 (?) dead
	Earthquake	Kerman Prov., Iran	June 11; earthquake toll over 1,000 dead
	Rail	Georgia, U.S.S.R.	Announced June 28; 2 train collision; 70 dead, 100 injured
	Structural	Kansas City, Missouri	July 17; collapse of hotel aerial walkway; 112 dead
	Flood	Sichuan, China	Late July; flooding of Yangtze; death toll 753, over 800 missing
	Earthquake	Kerman Prov., Iran	July 28; quake toll over 1,500
	Marine	Seram Sea, Indonesia	August 5; overloaded passenger ship sinks; 225 lost at sea
	Aircraft	Sanyi, Taiwan	August 22; passenger jetliner exploded and crashed; 110 dead
	Marine	Obidos, Brazil	September 19; Amazon riverboat sank; over 250 missing

SPORTS

CONTENTS:

	Page
OLYMPICS Summer Games 1980	910–913
Summer Champions	914–918
Winter Games 1980	919
Winter Champions	920–921
1981 NATIONAL SPORTS FESTIVAL	922–923
BASEBALL	924–938
BASKETBALL Professional	939–943
College, Women's	944–945
FOOTBALL Professional	946–952
College	953–957
HOCKEY	958–962
SOCCER	963
GOLF	964–968

	Page
TENNIS	969–972
SULLIVAN TROPHY WINNERS	972
AUTO RACING	973–977
HORSE RACING Thoroughbred	978–980
Harness	981–982
BOXING	983–984
TRACK & FIELD	985–989
SPORTS FIGURES OF THE CENTURY	987
BOWLING	990–991
CHESS	991
SWIMMING AND DIVING	992–993
FISHING RECORDS	994–995
WRESTLING	995
OTHER SPORTS	996–999

THE OLYMPICS

THE SUMMER OLYMPIC GAMES

Sites	Year	Total Events	Total Nations	Total Athletes	Sites	Year	Total Events	Total Nations	Total Athletes
I Athens	1896	42	13	285	XV Helsinki	1952	149	69	5,867
II Paris	1900	60	20	1,066	XVI Melbourne	1956	145	67	3,184
III St. Louis	1904	67	11	496	XVI Stockholm*	1956	3	29	154
IV London	1908	104	22	2,059	XVII Rome	1960	150	84	5,396
V Stockholm	1912	106	28	2,541	XVIII Tokyo	1964	163	94	5,565
VII Antwerp	1920	154	29	2,606	XIX Mexico City	1968	172	109	6,082
VIII Paris	1924	137	44	3,092	XX Munich	1972	194	121	8,500
IX Amsterdam	1928	120	46	3,015	XXI Montreal	1976	198	87	6,512
X Los Angeles	1932	124	37	1,408	XXII Moscow	1980	203	80	5,923
XI Berlin	1936	142	49	4,069	XXIII Los Angeles	1984			
XIV London	1948	138	59	4,468					

* Equestrian Games only.

1980 SUMMER OLYMPIC GAMES Moscow, U.S.S.R., July 19–August 3

Participating Nations

Afghanistan	Cuba	India	Mexico	Sierra Leone
Algeria	Cyprus	Iraq	Mongolia	Spain
Andorra	Czechoslovakia	Ireland	Mozambique	Sri Lanka
Angola	Denmark	Italy	Nepal	Sweden
Australia	Dominican Rep.	Jamaica	Netherlands	Switzerland
Austria	Ecuador	Jordan	New Zealand	Syria
Belgium	Ethiopia	Korea, North	Nicaragua	Tanzania
Benin	Finland	Kuwait	Nigeria	Trinidad & Tobago
Botswana	France	Laos	Peru	Uganda
Brazil	Germany, East	Lebanon	Poland	USSR
Bulgaria	Greece	Lesotho	Portugal	United Kingdom
Burma	Guatemala	Libya	Puerto Rico	Venezuela
Cameroon	Guinea	Luxembourg	Romania	Vietnam
Colombia	Guyana	Madagascar	San Marino	Yugoslavia
Congo	Hungary	Mali	Senegal	Zambia
Costa Rica	Iceland	Malta	Seychelles	Zimbabwe

Non-Participating Nations

Albania	Chile	Iran	Morocco	Sudan
Antigua	China	Israel	Neth. Antilles	Suriname
Argentina	China (Taiwan)	Ivory Coast	Nigeria	Swaziland
Bahamas	Egypt	Japan	Norway	Thailand
Bahrain	El Salvador	Kenya	Pakistan	Togo
Bangladesh	Fiji	Korea, South	Panama	Tunisia
Barbados	Gabon	Liberia	Papua New Guinea	Turkey
Belize	Gambia	Liechtenstein	Paraguay	United Arab Emirates
Bermuda	Germany, West	Malawi	Philippines	United States
Bolivia	Ghana	Malaysia	Qatar	Upper Volta
Canada	Haiti	Mauritania	Saudi Arabia	Uruguay
Cayman Is.	Honduras	Mauritius	Singapore	Virgin Islands
Central African Rep.	Hong Kong	Monaco	Somalia	Zaire
Chad	Indonesia			

1980 SUMMER OLYMPICS MEDAL TABLE

	Gold (1st)	Silver (2nd)	Bronze (3rd)	Total		Gold (1st)	Silver (2nd)	Bronze (3rd)	Total
USSR	80	69	46	195	Switzerland	2	0	0	2
East Germany	47	37	43	127	Spain	1	3	2	6
Bulgaria	8	16	17	41	Austria	1	2	1	4
Cuba	8	7	5	20	Greece	1	0	2	3
Italy	8	3	4	15	Belgium	1	0	0	1
Hungary	7	10	15	32	India	1	0	0	1
Romania	6	6	13	25	Zimbabwe	1	0	0	1
France	6	5	3	14	North Korea	0	3	2	5
Britain	5	7	9	21	Mongolia	0	2	2	4
Poland	3	14	15	32	Mexico	0	1	3	4
Sweden	3	3	6	12	Netherlands	0	1	2	3
Finland	3	1	4	8	Jamaica	0	0	3	3
Czechoslovakia	2	3	8	13	Tanzania	0	2	0	2
Yugoslavia	2	3	4	9	Ireland	0	1	1	2
Australia	2	2	5	9	Venezuela	0	1	0	1
Denmark	2	1	2	5	Uganda	0	1	0	1
Brazil	2	0	2	4	Guyana	0	0	1	1
Ethiopia	2	0	2	4	Lebanon	0	0	1	1

MEDALISTS AT MOSCOW: 1980

1st (gold), 2nd (silver), 3rd (bronze)

ARCHERY

Men—Tomi Poikolainen, Finland
2. USSR, 3. Italy

Women—Keto Losaberidze, USSR
2. USSR, 3. Finland

BASKETBALL

Men—Yugoslavia
2. Italy, 3. USSR

Women—USSR
2. Bulgaria, 3. Yugoslavia

BOXING

106 lb—Shamil Sabyrov, USSR
2. Cuba, 3. Bulgaria, N. Korea

112 lb—Petar Lessov, Bulgaria
2. USSR, 3. Hungary, Ireland

119 lb—Juan Hernandez, Cuba
2. Venezuela, 3. Guyana, Romania

126 lb—Rudi Fink, E. Germany
2. Cuba, 3. Poland, USSR

132 lb—Angel Herrera, Cuba
2. USSR, 3. E. Germany, Poland

140 lb—Patrizio Oliva, Italy
2. USSR, 3. Britain, Cuba

148 lb—Andres Aldama, Cuba
2. Uganda, 3. E. Germany, Poland

157 lb—Armando Martinez, Cuba
2. USSR, 3. Czechoslovakia, E. Germany

165 lb—Jose Gomez, Cuba
2. USSR, 3. Poland, Romania

179 lb—Slobodan Kacar, Yugoslavia
2. Poland, 3. Cuba, E. Germany

hvywt—Teofilo Stevenson, Cuba
2. USSR, 3. E. Germany, Hungary

CANOEING—MEN

Single Canoe
500 m—Sergei Postrekhin, USSR
2. Bulgaria, 3. E. Germany

1000 m—Lubomir Lubenov, Bulgaria
2. USSR, 3. E. Germany

Double Canoe

500 m—Hungary (Foltan, Vaskuti)
2. Romania, 3. Bulgaria

1000 m—Romania (Potzaichin, Simionov)
2. E. Germany, 3. USSR

Single Kayak
500 m—Vladimir Parfenovich, USSR
2. Australia, 3. Romania

1000 m—Rudiger Helm, E. Germany
2. France, 3. Romania

Double Kayak
500 m—USSR (Parfenovich, Chukhrai)
2. Spain, 3. E. Germany

1000 m—USSR (Parfenovich, Chukhrai)
2. Hungary, 3. Spain

Four-Man Kayak
1000 m—East Germany
2. Romania, 3. Bulgaria

CANOEING—WOMEN

Single Kayak
500 m—Birgit Fischer, E. Germany
2. Bulgaria, 3. USSR

Double Kayak
500 m—E. Germany (Genauss, Bischof)
2. USSR, 3. Hungary

CYCLING

100 km Team Road Race—USSR
2. E. Germany, 3. Czechoslovakia

4000 m Team Pursuit—USSR
2. E. Germany, 3. Czechoslovakia

1000 m Time Trial—Lothar Thoms,
E. Germany, 2. USSR, 3. Jamaica

Individual Sprint—Lutz Hesslich,
E. Germany, 2. France, 3. USSR

Individual Pursuit—Robert Dill-Bundi,
Switzerland, 2. France, 3. Denmark

Individual Road Race—Sergei
Sukhoruchenkov, USSR
2. Poland, 3. USSR

DIVING

Springboard
Men—Aleksandr Portnov, USSR
2. Mexico, 3. Italy

Women—Irina Kalinina, USSR
2. E. Germany, 3. E. Germany

Platform
Men—Falk Hoffman, E. Germany
2. USSR, 3. USSR

Women—Martina Jaschke, E. Germany
2. USSR, 3. USSR

EQUESTRIAN

Three-Day Individual—Frederico
Euro Roman, Italy, 2. USSR, 3. USSR

Three-Day Team—USSR
2. Italy, 3. Mexico

Dressage Individual—Elisabeth Theurer,
Austria, 2. USSR, 3. USSR

Dressage Team—USSR
2. Bulgaria, 3. Romania

Jumping Individual—Jan Kowalczyk,
Poland, 2. USSR, 3. Mexico

Jumping Team—USSR
2. Poland, 3. Mexico

FENCING—MEN

Individual Foil—Vladimir Smirnov,
USSR, 2. France, 3. USSR

Team Foil—France
2. USSR, 3. Poland

Individual Epee—Johan Harmenberg,
Sweden, 2. Hungary, 3. France

Team Epee—France
2. Poland, 3. USSR

Individual Sabre—Viktor Krovopuskov,
USSR, 2. USSR, 3. Hungary

Team Sabre—USSR
2. Italy, 3. Hungary

FENCING—WOMEN

Individual Foil—Pascale Trinquet,
France, 2. Hungary, 3. Poland

Team Foil—France
2. USSR, 3. Hungary

FIELD HOCKEY

Men—India
2. Spain, 3. USSR

Women—Zimbabwe
2. Czechoslovakia, 3. USSR

GYMNASTICS—MEN

All-Around—Aleksandr Ditiatin, USSR
2. USSR, 3. Bulgaria

Parallel Bars—Aleksandr Tkachyov,
USSR, 2. USSR, 3. E. Germany

Vault—Nikolai Andrianov, USSR
2. USSR, 3. E. Germany

Pommel Horse—Zoltan Magyar, Hungary
2. USSR, 3. E. Germany

Rings—Aleksandr Ditiatin, USSR
2. USSR, 3. Czechoslovakia

Horizontal Bar—Stoyan Deltchev,
Bulgaria, 2. USSR, 3. USSR

Floor Exercise—Roland Bruckner,
E. Germany, 2. USSR, 3. USSR

Team Competition—USSR
2. E. Germany, 3. Hungary

GYMNASTICS—WOMEN

All-Around—Yelena Davydova, USSR
2. (tie) E. Germany, Romania

Balance Beam—Nadia Comaneci,
Romania, 2. USSR, 3. USSR

Uneven Bars—Maxi Gnauck, E. Germany
2. Romania, 3. (tie) Romania,
E. Germany, USSR

Vault—Natalia Shaposhnikova,
USSR, 2. E. Germany, 3. Romania

Floor Exercise—(tie) Nelli Kim, USSR-
Nadia Comaneci, Romania, 3. (tie)
USSR, E. Germany

Team Competition—USSR
2. Romania, 3. E. Germany

HANDBALL

Men—East Germany
2. USSR, 3. Romania

Women—USSR
2. Yugoslavia, 3. E. Germany

JUDO

132 lb—Thierry Rey, France
2. Cuba, 3. USSR, Hungary

143 lb—Nikolai Solodukhin, USSR
2. Mongolia, 3. Bulgaria, Poland

157 lb—Ezio Gamba, Italy
2. Britain, 3. Mongolia, E. Germany

172 lb—Shota Khabareli, USSR
2. Cuba, 3. E. Germany, France

190 lb—Juerg Roethlisberger, Switzerland
2. Cuba, 3. E. Germany, USSR

209 lb—Robert Van De Walle, Belgium
2. USSR, 3. E. Germany, Netherlands

Over 209 lb—Angelo Parisi, France
2. Bulgaria, 3. Czechoslovakia, Yugoslavia

Open Weight—Dietmar Lorenz, E. Germany
2. France, 3. Hungary, Britain

MODERN PENTATHLON

Individual—Anatoly Starostin, USSR
2. Hungary, 3. USSR

Team—USSR
2. Hungary, 3. Sweden

ROWING—MEN

Single Sculls—Pertti Karppinen,
Finland, 2. USSR, 3. E. Germany

Double Sculls—East Germany (Dreipke-
Kroppelein), 2. Yugoslavia,
3. Czechoslovakia

Pairs w/o Coxswain—E. Germany
(B. Landvoigt-J. Landvoigt)
2. USSR, 3. Britain

Pairs with Coxswain—East Germany
2. USSR, 3. Yugoslavia

Fours w/o Coxswain—East Germany
2. USSR, 3. Britain

Fours with Coxswain—East Germany
2. USSR, 3. Poland

Quadruple Sculls—East Germany
2. USSR, 3. Bulgaria

Eights—East Germany
2. Britain, 3. USSR

ROWING—WOMEN

Single Sculls—Sanda Toma, Romania
2. USSR, 3. E. Germany

Double Sculls—USSR (Khloptseva-
Popova), 2. E. Germany, 3. Romania

Pairs w/o Coxswain—East Germany
(Steindorf-Klier), 2. Poland 3. Bulgaria

Fours with Coxswain—East Germany
2. Bulgaria, 3. USSR

Quadruple Sculls—East Germany
2. USSR, 3. Bulgaria

Eights—East Germany
2. USSR, 3. Romania

SHOOTING

Free Pistol—Aleksandr Melentev,
USSR, 2. E. Germany, 3. Bulgaria

Rapid Fire Pistol—Corneliu Ion,
Romania, 2. E. Germany, 3. Austria

Rifle, Prone—Karoly Varga, Hungary
2. E. Germany, 3. Bulgaria

Rifle, 3-Position—Viktor Vlasov, USSR
2. E. Germany, 3. Sweden

Moving Target—Igor Sokolov, USSR
2. E. Germany, 3. USSR

Skeetshooting—Hans Kjeld Rasmussen,
Denmark, 2. Sweden, 3. Cuba

Trapshooting—Luciano Giovannetti,
Italy, 2. USSR, 3. E. Germany

SOCCER (FOOTBALL)

Team—Czechoslovakia
2. E. Germany, 3. USSR

SWIMMING—MEN

(*Olympic Record)

100 m Freestyle—Jorg Woithe, E. Germany
50.40, 2. Sweden, 3. Sweden

200 m Freestyle—Sergei Kopliakov, USSR
1:49.81*, 2. USSR, 3. Australia

400 m Freestyle—Vladimir Salnikov, USSR
3:51.31*, 2. USSR, 3. USSR

1500 m. Freestyle—Vladimir Salnikov, USSR
14:58.27*, 2. USSR, 3. Australia

100 m Backstroke—Bengt Baron, Sweden
56.53, 2. USSR, 3. USSR

200 m Backstroke—Sandor Wladar,
Hungary 2:01.93, 2. Hungary,
3. Australia

100 m Breaststroke—Duncan Goodhew,
Britain 1:03.34, 2. USSR, 3. Australia

200 m Breaststroke—Robertas Zulpa,
USSR 2:15.85, 2. Hungary, 3. USSR

100 m Butterfly—Par Arvidsson, Sweden
54.92, 2. E. Germany, 3. Spain

200 m Butterfly—Sergei Fesenko, USSR
1:59.76, 2. Britain, 3. E. Germany

400 m Indiv. Medley—Aleksandr
Sidorenko, USSR 4:22.89*, 2. USSR,
3. Hungary

400 m Medley Relay—Australia 3:45.70
2. USSR, 3. Britain

800 m Freestyle Relay—USSR 7:23.50
2. E. Germany, 3. Brazil

SWIMMING—WOMEN

(*Olympic Record)

100 m Freestyle—Barbara Krause,
E. Germany 54.79*, 2. E. Germany,
3. E. Germany

200 m Freestyle—Barbara Krause,
E. Germany 1:58.33*, 2. E. Germany,
3. E. Germany

400 m Freestyle—Ines Diers, E. Germany
4:08.76*, 2. E. Germany,
3. E. Germany

800 m Freestyle—Michelle Ford,
Australia 8:28.90*, 2. E. Germany,
3. E. Germany

100 m Backstroke—Rica Reinisch,
E. Germany 1:00.86*, 2. E. Germany
3. E. Germany

200 m Backstroke—Rica Reinisch,
E. Germany 2:11.77*, 2. E. Germany,
3. E. Germany

100 m Breaststroke—Ute Geweniger,
E. Germany 1:10.11*, 2. USSR,
3. Denmark

200 m Breaststroke—Lina Kachusite, USSR
2:29.54*, 2. USSR, 3. USSR

100 m Butterfly—Caren Metschuck,
E. Germany 1:00.42, 2. E. Germany,
3. E. Germany

200 m Butterfly–Ines Geissler,
E. Germany 2:10.44*, 2. E. Germany,
3. Australia

400 m Indiv. Medley–Petra Schneider,
E. Germany 4:36.29*, 2. Britain,
3. Poland

400 m Medley Relay–East Germany
4:06.67*, 2. Britain, 3. USSR

400 m Freestyle Relay–East Germany
3:42.71*, 2. Sweden, 3. Netherlands

TRACK AND FIELD–MEN
(*Olympic Record)

100 m Dash–Allan Wells, Britain 10.25
2. Cuba, 3. Bulgaria

200 m Dash–Pietro Mennea, Italy
20.19, 2. Britain, 3. Jamaica

400 m Dash–Viktor Markin, USSR 44.60
2. Australia, 3. E. Germany

800 m Run–Steve Ovett, Britain
1:45.4, 2. Britain, 3. USSR

1500 m Run–Sebastian Coe, Britain
3:38.4, 2. E. Germany, 3. Britain

5000 m Run–Miruts Yifter, Ethiopia
13:21.0*, 2. Tanzania, 3. Finland

10,000 m Run–Miruts Yifter, Ethiopia
27:42.7, 2. Finland, 3. Ethiopia

Marathon–Waldemar Cierpinski,
E. Germany 2:11:3, 2. Netherlands,
3. USSR

110 m Hurdles–Thomas Munkelt,
E. Germany 13.39, 2. Cuba, 3. USSR

400 m Hurdles–Volker Beck, E. Germany
48.70, 2. USSR, 3. Britain

3000 m Steeplechase–
Bronislaw Malinowski, Poland 8:09.7,
2. Tanzania, 3. Ethiopia

400 m Relay–USSR 38.26
2. Poland, 3. France

1600 m Relay–USSR 3:01.1
2. E. Germany, 3. Italy

20 km Walk–Maurizio Damilano, Italy
1:23:35.5*, 2. USSR, 3. E. Germany

50 km Walk–Hartwig Gauder, E. Germany
3:49:24.0*, 2. Spain, 3. USSR

Long Jump–Lutz Dombrowski, E. Germany
28' ¼", 2. E. Germany, 3. USSR

Triple Jump–Jaak Uudmae, USSR
56' 11½", 2. USSR, 3. Brazil

High Jump–Gerd Wessig, E. Germany
7' 8¾"*, 2. Poland, 3. E. Germany

Pole Vault–Wladyslaw Kozakiewicz, Poland
18' 11½"*, 2. (tie) USSR, Poland

Shot Put–Vladimir Kiselyov, USSR
70' ½"*, 2. USSR, 3. E. Germany

Discus Throw–Viktor Rashchupkin, USSR
218' 8", 2. Czechoslovakia, 3. Cuba

Javelin Throw–Dainis Kula, USSR
299' 2⅜", 2. USSR, 3. E. Germany

Hammer Throw–Yuri Sedykh, USSR
268' 4½"*, 2. USSR, 3. USSR

Decathlon–Daley Thompson, Britain
8,495 pts., 2. USSR, 3. USSR

TRACK AND FIELD—WOMEN
(*Olympic Record)

100 m Dash–Lyudmila Kondrateva, USSR
11.06, 2. E. Germany, 3. E. Germany

200 m Dash–Barbel Wockel, E. Germany
22.03*, 2. USSR, 3. Jamaica

400 m Dash–Marita Koch, E. Germany
48.88*, 2. Czechoslovakia,
3. E. Germany

800 m Run–Nadezhda Olizarenko, USSR
1:53.5*, 2. USSR, 3. USSR

1500 m Run–Tatyana Kazankina, USSR
3:56.6*, 2. E. Germany, 3. USSR

100 m Hurdles–Vera Komisova, USSR
12.56*, 2. E. Germany, 3. Poland

400 m Relay–East Germany 41.60*
2. USSR, 3. Britain

1600 m Relay–USSR 3:20.2
2. E. Germany, 3. Britain

Long Jump–Tatiana Kolpakova, USSR
23' 2"*, 2. E. Germany, 3. USSR

High Jump–Sara Simeoni, Italy
6' 5½"*, 2. Poland, 3. E. Germany

Shot Put–Ilona Slupianek, E. Germany
73' 6¼"*, 2. USSR, 3. E. Germany

Discus Throw–Evelin Jahl, E. Germany
229' 6½"*, 2. Bulgaria, 3. USSR

Javelin Throw–Maria Colon, Cuba
224' 5"*, 2. USSR, 3. E. Germany

Pentathlon–Nadezhda Tkachenko, USSR
5083 pts.*, 2. USSR, 3. USSR

VOLLEYBALL

Men–USSR
2. Bulgaria, 3. Romania

Women–USSR
2. E. Germany, 3. Bulgaria

WATER POLO

Team–USSR
2. Yugoslavia, 3. Hungary

WEIGHTLIFTING

115 lb–Kanybek Osmanoliev, USSR
2. N. Korea, 3. N. Korea

123 lb–Daniel Nunez, Cuba
2. USSR, 3. Poland

132 lb–Viktor Mazin, USSR
2. Bulgaria, 3. Poland

149 lb–Yanko Roussev, Bulgaria
2. E. Germany, 3. Bulgaria

165 lb–Assen Zlatev, Bulgaria
2. USSR, 3. Bulgaria

182 lb–Yurik Vardanyan, USSR
2. Bulgaria, 3. Czechoslovakia

198 lb–Peter Baczako, Hungary
2. Bulgaria, 3. E. Germany

220 lb–Ota Zaremba, Czechoslovakia
2. USSR, 3. Cuba

242 lb–Leonid Taranenko, USSR
2. Bulgaria, 3. Hungary

Over 242 lb–Sultan Rakhmanov, USSR
2. E. Germany, 3. Poland

WRESTLING, FREESTYLE

106 lb–Claudio Pollio, Italy
2. N. Korea, 3. USSR

115 lb–Anatoly Beloglazov, USSR
2. Poland, 3. Bulgaria

126 lb–Sergei Beloglazov, USSR
2. N. Korea, 3. Mongolia

137 lb–Magomedgasan Abushev, USSR
2. Bulgaria, 3. Greece

149 lb–Saipulla Absaidov, USSR
2. Bulgaria, 3. Yugoslavia

165 lb–Valentin Raitchev, Bulgaria
2. Mongolia, 3. Czechoslovakia

181 lb–Ismail Abilov, Bulgaria
2. USSR, 3. Hungary

198 lb–Sanasar Oganesyan, USSR
2. E. Germany, 3. Poland

220 lb–Ilya Mate, USSR
2. Bulgaria, 3. Czechoslovakia

Over 220 lb–Soisan Andiev, USSR
2. Hungary, 3. Poland

WRESTLING, GRECO-ROMAN

106 lb–Zaksylik Ushkempirov, USSR
2. Romania, 3. Hungary

114 lb–Vakhtang Blagidze, USSR
2. Hungary, 3. Bulgaria

125 lb–Shamil Serikov, USSR
2. Poland, 3. Sweden

136 lb–Stilianos Migiakis, Greece
2. Hungary, 3. USSR

150 lb–Stefan Rusu, Romania
2. Poland, 3. Sweden

165 lb–Ferenc Kocsis, Hungary
2. USSR, 3. Finland

180 lb–Gennady Korban, USSR
2. Poland, 3. Bulgaria

198 lb–Norbert Nottny, Hungary
2. USSR, 3. Romania

220 lb–Gheorghi Raikov, Bulgaria
2. Poland, 3. Romania

Over 220 lb–Aleksandr Kolchinsky, USSR
2. Bulgaria, 3. Lebanon

YACHTING

Tornado Class–Brazil
2. Denmark, 3. Sweden

470 Class–Brazil
2. E. Germany, 3. Finland

Flying Dutchman Class–Spain
2. Ireland, 3. Hungary

Soling Class–Denmark
2. USSR, 3. Greece

Finn Class–Finland
2. Austria, 3. USSR

Star Class–USSR
2. Austria, 3. Italy

SUMMER OLYMPIC CHAMPIONS: SWIMMING AND DIVING, TRACK AND FIELD, TEAM SPORTS

NOTE: An asterisk * denotes Olympic record.

SWIMMING AND DIVING (Men)

Year Champion and Country	Time
100 Meter Free Style	**Min./Sec.**
1896—Alfred Hajos, Hungary	1:22.2
1904—Zoltan de Halmay, Hungary (100 yds.)	1:02.8
1908—Charles Daniels, United States	1:05.6
1912—Duke Kahanamoku, United States	1:03.4
1920—Duke Kahanamoku, United States	1:01.4
1924—John Weissmuller, United States	59.0
1928—John Weissmuller, United States	58.6
1932—Yasuji Miyazaki, Japan	58.2
1936—Ferenc Csik, Hungary	57.6
1948—Walter Ris, United States	57.3
1952—Clarke Scholes, United States	57.4
1956—Jon Hendricks, Australia	55.4
1960—John Devitt, Australia	55.2
1964—Donald A. Schollander, United States	53.4
1968—Michael Wenden, Australia	52.2
1972—Mark Spitz, United States	51.2
1976—Jim Montgomery, United States	49.99*

200 Meter Free Style

1968—Michael Wenden, Australia	1:55.2
1972—Mark Spitz, United States	1:52.8
1976—Bruce Furniss, United States	1:50.29

400 Meter Free Style

1896—Paul Neumann, Austria (500 m.)	8:12.6
1904—Charles Daniels, United States (440 yds.)	6:16.2
1908—Henry Taylor, Great Britain	5:36.8
1912—George Hodgson, Canada	5:24.4
1920—Norman Ross, United States	5:26.8
1924—John Weissmuller, United States	5:04.2
1928—Albert Zorilla, Argentina	5:01.6
1932—Clarence Crabbe, United States	4:48.4
1936—Jack Medica, United States	4:44.5
1948—William Smith, United States	4:41.0
1952—Jean Boiteux, France	4:30.7
1956—Murray Rose, Australia	4:27.3
1960—Murray Rose, Australia	4:18.3
1964—Donald A. Schollander, United States	4:12.2
1968—Michael Burton, United States	4:09.0
1972—Bradford Cooper, Australia	4:00.3
1976—Brian Goodell, United States	3:51.93

1,500 Meter Free Style	**Min./Sec.**
1896—Alfred Hajos, Hungary (1,200 m.)	18:22.2
1900—John Jarvis, Great Britain (1,000 m.)	13:40.2
1904—Emil Rausch, Germany (1,609 m.)	27:18.2
1908—Henry Taylor, Great Britain	22:48.4
1912—George Hodgson, Canada	22:00.0
1920—Norman Ross, United States	22:23.2
1924—Andrew Charlton, Australia	20:06.6
1928—Arne Borg, Sweden	19:51.8
1932—Kusuo Kitamura, Japan	19:12.4
1936—Noboru Terada, Japan	19:13.7
1948—James P. McLane, United States	19:18.5
1952—Ford Konno, United States	18:30.0
1956—Murray Rose, Australia	17:58.9
1960—John Konrads, Australia	17:19.6
1964—Robert Windlo, Australia	17:01.7
1968—Michael Burton, United States	16:38.9
1972—Michael Burton, United States	15:52.6
1976—Brian Goodell, United States	15:02.40

100 Meter Backstroke

1904—Walter Brack, Germany (100 yds.)	1:16.8
1908—Arno Bieberstein, Germany	1:24.6
1912—Harry Hebner, United States	1:21.2
1920—Warren Kealoha, United States	1:15.2
1924—Warren Kealoha, United States	1:13.2
1928—George Kojac, United States	1:08.2
1932—Masaji Kiyokawa, Japan	1:08.6
1936—Adolph Kiefer, United States	1:05.9
1948—Allen Stack, United States	1:06.4
1952—Yoshinobu Oyakawa, United States	1:05.4
1956—David Thiele, Australia	1:02.2
1960—David Thiele, Australia	1:01.9
1964—Not on Program	
1968—Roland Matthes, East Germany	58.7
1972—Roland Matthes, East Germany	56.6
1976—John Naber, United States	55.49*

200 Meter Backstroke

1900—Ernest Hoppenberg, Germany	2:47.0
1964—Jed R. Graef, United States	2:10.3
1968—Roland Matthes, East Germany	2:09.6
1972—Roland Matthes, East Germany	2:02.8
1976—John Naber, United States	1:59.19*

100 Meter Breaststroke

1968—Donald McKenzie, United States	1:07.7
1972—Nobutaka Taguchi, Japan	1:04.9
1976—John Hencken, United States	1:03.11*

200 Meter Breaststroke

1908—Frederick Holman, Great Britain	3:09.2
1912—Walter Bathe, Germany	3:01.8
1920—Haken Malmroth, Sweden	3:04.4
1924—Robert Skelton, United States	2:56.6
1928—Yoshiyuki Tsuruta, Japan	2:48.8
1932—Yoshiyuki Tsuruta, Japan	2:45.4
1936—Tetsuo Hamuro, Japan	2:41.5
1948—Joseph Verdeur, United States	2:39.3
1952—John Davies, Australia	2:34.4
1956—Masura Furukawa, Japan	2:34.7
1960—William Mulliken, United States	2:37.4
1964—Ian O'Brien, Australia	2:27.8
1968—Felipe Muñoz, Mexico	2:28.7
1972—John Hencken, United States	2:21.5
1976—David Wilkie, Great Britain	2:15.11*

100 Meter Butterfly

1968—Douglas Russell, United States	55.9
1972—Mark Spitz, United States	54.3*
1976—Matt Vogel, United States	54.35

200 Meter Butterfly

1956—William Yorzyk, United States	2:19.3
1960—Michael Troy, United States	2:12.8
1964—Kevin Berry, Australia	2:06.6
1968—Carl Robie, United States	2:08.7
1972—Mark Spitz, United States	2:00.7
1976—Michael Bruner, United States	1:59.23*

200 Meter Individual Medley

1968—Charles Hickcox, United States	2:12.0
1972—Gunnar Larsson, Sweden	2:07.2*

400 Meter Individual Medley

1964—Richard W. Roth, United States	4:45.4
1968—Charles Hickcox, United States	4:48.4
1972—Gunnar Larsson, Sweden	4:32.0
1976—Rod Strachan, United States	4:23.68

400 Meter Free Style Relay

1964—United States	3:33.2
1968—United States	3:31.7
1972—United States	3:26.4*

400 Meter Medley Relay

1960—United States	4:05.4
1964—United States	3:58.4
1968—United States	3:54.9
1972—United States	3:48.2
1976—United States	3:42.22*

800 Meter Free Style Relay

1908—Great Britain	10:55.6
1912—Australia	10:11.2
1920—United States	10:04.4
1924—United States	9:53.4
1928—United States	9:36.2
1932—Japan	8:58.2
1936—Japan	8:51.5
1948—United States	8:31.1
1952—United States	8:31.1
1956—Australia	8:23.6
1960—United States	8:10.2
1964—United States	7:52.1
1968—United States	7:52.3
1972—United States	7:38.8
1976—United States	7:23.22*

Springboard Diving	**Points**
1908—Albert Zurner, Germany	85.50
1912—Paul Guenther, Germany	79.23
1920—Louis Kuehn, United States	675.00
1924—Albert C. White, United States	696.40
1928—Pete Desjardins, United States	185.04
1932—Michael Galitzen, United States	161.38
1936—Richard Degener, United States	163.57
1948—Bruce Harlan, United States	163.64
1952—David Browning, United States	205.29
1956—Robert L. Clotworthy, United States	159.56
1960—Gary Tobian, United States	170.00
1964—Kenneth R. Sitzberger, United States	159.90
1968—Bernard Wrightson, United States	170.15
1972—Vladimir Vasin, USSR	594.09
1976—Phil Boggs, United States	619.52

High Diving

1904—Dr. G. E. Sheldon, United States	12.75
1908—Hjalmar Johansson, Sweden	83.75

1912—Erik Adlerz, Sweden	73.94
1920—Clarence Pinkston, United States	100.67
1924—Albert C. White, United States	97.46
1928—Pete Desjardins, United States	98.74
1932—Harold Smith, United States	124.80
1936—Marshall Wayne, United States	113.58
1948—Dr. Samuel Lee, United States	130.05
1952—Dr. Samuel Lee, United States	156.28
1956—Joaquin Capilla, Mexico	152.44
1960—Robert Webster, United States	165.56
1964—Robert Webster, United States	148.58
1968—Klaus DiBiasi, Italy	164.18
1972—Klaus DiBiasi, Italy	504.12
1976—Klaus DiBiasi, Italy	600.51

SWIMMING AND DIVING (Women)

100 Meter Free Style

	Min./Sec.
1912—Fanny Durack, Australia	1:22.2
1920—Ethelda Bleibtrey, United States	1:13.6
1924—Ethel Lackie, United States	1:12.4
1928—Albina Osipowich, United States	1:11.0
1932—Helene Madison, United States	1:06.8
1936—Hendrika Mastenbroek, Netherlands	1:05.9
1948—Greta Andersen, Denmark	1:06.3
1952—Katalin Szoke, Hungary	1:06.8
1956—Dawn Fraser, Australia	1:02.0
1960—Dawn Fraser, Australia	1:01.2
1964—Dawn Fraser, Australia	59.5
1968—Margo Jan Henne, United States	1:00.0
1972—Sandra Neilson, United States	58.6
1976—Kornelia Ender, East Germany	55.65

200 Meter Free Style

1968—Deborah Meyer, United States	2:10.5
1972—Shane Gould, Australia	2:03.6
1976—Kornelia Ender, East Germany	1:59.26

400 Meter Free Style

1920—Ethelda Bleibtrey, United States (300 m.)	4:34.0
1924—Martha Norelius, United States	6:02.2
1928—Martha Norelius, United States	5:42.4
1932—Helene Madison, United States	5:28.5
1936—Hendrika Mastenbroek, Netherlands	5:26.4
1948—Ann Curtis, United States	5:17.8
1952—Valeria Gyenge, Hungary	5:12.1
1956—Lorraine Crapp, Australia	4:54.6
1960—S. Chris Von Saltza, United States	4:50.6
1964—Virginia Duenkel, United States	4:43.3
1968—Deborah Meyer, United States	4:31.8
1972—Shane Gould, Australia	4:19.0
1976—Petra Thuemer, East Germany	4:09.89

800 Meter Free Style

1968—Deborah Meyer, United States	9:24.0
1972—Keena Rothhammer, United States	8:53.7
1976—Petra Thuemer, East Germany	8:37.14

100 Meter Backstroke

1924—Sybil Bauer, United States	1:23.2
1928—Marie Braun, Netherlands	1:22.0
1932—Eleanor Holm, United States	1:19.4
1936—Dina Senff, Netherlands	1:18.9
1948—Karen Harup, Denmark	1:14.4
1952—Joan Harrison, South Africa	1:14.3
1956—Judy Grinham, Great Britain	1:12.9
1960—Lynn Burke, United States	1:09.3
1964—Cathy Ferguson, United States	1:07.7
1968—Kaye Hall, United States	1:06.2
1972—Melissa Belote, United States	1:05.8
1976—Ulrike Richter, East Germany	1:01.83

200 Meter Backstroke

1968—Lillian (Pokey) Watson, United States	2:24.8
1972—Melissa Belote, United States	2:19.2
1976—Ulrike Richter, East Germany	2:13.43

100 Meter Butterfly

1956—Shelley Mann, United States	1:11.0
1960—Carolyn Schuler, United States	1:09.5
1964—Sharon Stouder, United States	1:04.7
1968—Lynn McClements, Australia	1:05.5
1972—Mayumi Aoki, Japan	1:03.3
1976—Kornelia Ender, East Germany	1:00.13*

200 Meter Butterfly

1968—Ada Kok, Netherlands	2:24.7
1972—Karen Moe, United States	2:15.6
1976—Andrea Pollack, East Germany	2:11.41

100 Meter Breaststroke

1968—Djurdjica Bjedov, Yugoslavia	1:15.8
1972—Cathy Carr, United States	1:13.6
1976—Hannelore Anke, East Germany	1:11.16

200 Meter Breaststroke

1924—Lucy Morton, Great Britain	3:33.2
1928—Hilde Schrader, Germany	3:12.6

1932—Clare Dennis, Australia	3:06.3
1936—Hideko Maehata, Japan	3:03.6
1948—Nelly Van Vliet, Netherlands	2:57.2
1952—Eva Szekely, Hungary	2:51.7
1956—Ursula Happe, Germany	2:53.1
1960—Anita Lonsbrough, Great Britain	2:49.5
1964—Galina Prozumenshikova, USSR	2:46.4
1968—Sharon Wichman, United States	2:44.4
1972—Beverly Whitfield, Australia	2:41.7
1976—Marina Koshevaya, USSR	2:33.35

400 Meter Free Style Relay

1912—Great Britain	5:52.8
1920—United States	5:11.6
1924—United States	4:58.8
1928—United States	4:47.6
1932—United States	4:38.0
1936—Netherlands	4:36.0
1948—United States	4:29.2
1952—Hungary	4:24.4
1956—Australia	4:17.1
1960—United States	4:08.9
1964—United States	4:03.8
1968—United States	4:02.5
1972—United States	3:55.2
1976—United States	3:44.82

400 Meter Medley Relay

1960—United States	4:41.1
1964—United States	4:33.9
1968—United States	4:28.3
1972—United States	4:20.7
1976—East Germany	4:07.95

200 Meter Individual Medley

1968—Claudia Kolb, United States	2:24.7
1972—Shane Gould, Australia	2:23.1*

400 Meter Individual Medley

1964—Donna de Varona, United States	5:18.7
1968—Claudia Kolb, United States	5:08.5
1972—Gail Neall, Australia	5:03.0
1976—Ulrike Tauber, East Germany	4:42.77

Springboard Diving

	Points
1920—Aileen Riggin, United States	539.90
1924—Elizabeth Becker, United States	474.50
1928—Helen Meany, United States	78.62
1932—Georgia Coleman, United States	87.52
1936—Marjorie Gestring, United States	89.27
1948—Victoria Draves, United States	108.74
1952—Patricia McCormick, United States	147.30
1956—Patricia McCormick, United States	142.36
1960—Ingrid Kramer, Germany	155.81
1964—Ingrid Engle-Kramer, Germany	145.00
1968—Sue Gossick, United States	150.77
1972—Micki King, United States	450.03
1976—Jennifer Chandler, United States	506.19

High Diving

1912—Greta Johansson, Sweden	39.90
1920—Stefani Fryland-Clausen, Denmark	34.60
1924—Caroline Smith, United States	33.20
1928—Elizabeth Pinkston, United States	31.60
1932—Dorothy Poynton, United States	40.26
1936—Dorothy Poynton Hill, United States	33.93
1948—Victoria Draves, United States	68.87
1952—Patricia McCormick, United States	79.37
1956—Patricia McCormick, United States	84.85
1960—Ingrid Kramer, Germany	91.28
1964—Lesley Bush, United States	99.80
1968—Milena Duchkova, Czechoslovakia	109.59
1972—Ulrike Knape, Sweden	390.00
1976—Yelena Vaitsekhovskaya, USSR	406.49

TRACK AND FIELD (Men)

100 Meter Dash

	Sec.
1896—Thomas E. Burke, United States	12.0
1900—Francis W. Jarvis, United States	10.8
1904—Archie Hahn, United States	11.0
1908—Reginald E. Walker, South Africa	10.8
1912—Ralph C. Craig, United States	10.8
1920—Charles W. Paddock, United States	10.8
1924—Harold M. Abrahams, Great Britain	10.6
1928—Percy Williams, Canada	10.8
1932—Eddie Tolan, United States	10.3
1936—Jesse Owens, United States	10.3
1948—Harrison Dillard, United States	10.3
1952—Lindy J. Remigino, United States	10.4
1956—Bobby J. Morrow, United States	10.5
1960—Armin Hary, Germany	10.2
1964—Robert L. Hayes, United States	10.0
1968—James Hines, United States	9.9*
1972—Valery Borzov, USSR	10.1
1976—Hasely Crawford, Trinidad & Tobago	10.06

200 Meter Dash

1900—John W. B. Tewksbury, United States	22.2
1904—Archie Hahn, United States	21.6
1908—Robert Kerr, Canada	22.6
1912—Ralph C. Craig, United States	21.7
1920—Allan Woodring, United States	22.0
1924—Jackson V. Scholz, United States	21.6
1928—Percy Williams, Canada	21.8
1932—Eddie Tolan, United States	21.2
1936—Jesse Owens, United States	20.7
1948—Melvin Patton, United States	21.1
1952—Andrew W. Stanfield, United States	20.7
1956—Bobby J. Morrow, United States	20.6
1960—Livio Berruti, Italy	20.5
1964—Henry Carr, United States	20.3
1968—Tommie Smith, United States	19.8*
1972—Valery Borzov, USSR	20.0
1976—Donald Quarrie, Jamaica	20.23

400 Meter Dash

1896—Thomas E. Burke, United States	54.2
1900—Maxwell W. Long, United States	49.4
1904—Harry I. Hillman, United States	49.2
1908—Wyndham Halswelle, Great Britain	50.0
1912—Charles D. Reidpath, United States	48.2
1920—Bevil G. D. Rudd, South Africa	49.6
1924—Eric H. Liddel, Great Britain	47.6
1928—Ray Barbuti, United States	47.8
1932—William A. Carr, United States	46.2
1936—Archie Williams, United States	46.5
1948—Arthur Wint, Jamaica	46.2
1952—George Rhoden, Jamaica	45.9
1956—Charles L. Jenkins, United States	46.7
1960—Otis Davis, United States	44.9
1964—Michael D. Larrabee, United States	45.1
1968—Lee Evans, United States	43.8*
1972—Vince Matthews, United States	44.7
1976—Alberto Juantorena, Cuba	44.26

800 Meter Run

	Min./Sec.
1896—Edwin H. Flack, Australia	2:11.0
1900—Alfred E. Tysoe, Great Britain	2:01.4
1904—James D. Lightbody, United States	1:56.0
1908—Melvin W. Sheppard, United States	1:52.8
1912—James E. Meredith, United States	1:51.9
1920—Albert G. Hill, Great Britain	1:53.4
1924—Douglas G. A. Lowe, Great Britain	1:52.4
1928—Douglas G. A. Lowe, Great Britain	1:51.8
1932—Thomas Hampson, Great Britain	1:49.8
1936—John Woodruff, United States	1:52.9
1948—Malvin Whitfield, United States	1:49.2
1952—Malvin Whitfield, United States	1:49.2
1956—Thomas W. Courtney, United States	1:47.7
1960—Peter Snell, New Zealand	1:46.3
1964—Peter Snell, New Zealand	1:45.1
1968—Ralph Doubell, Australia	1:44.3
1972—Dave Wottle, United States	1:45.9
1976—Alberto Juantorena, Cuba	1:43.50*

1,500 Meter Run

1896—Edwin H. Flack, Great Britain	4:33.2
1900—Charles Bennett, Great Britain	4:06.2
1904—James D. Lightbody, United States	4:05.4
1908—Melvin W. Sheppard, United States	4:03.4
1912—Arnold N. S. Jackson, Great Britain	3:56.8
1920—Albert G. Hill, Great Britain	4:01.8
1924—Paavo Nurmi, Finland	3:53.6
1928—Harry E. Larva, Finland	3:53.2
1932—Luigi Beccali, Italy	3:51.2
1936—Jack E. Lovelock, New Zealand	3:47.8
1948—Henry Eriksson, Sweden	3:49.8
1952—Joseph Barthel, Luxembourg	3:45.2
1956—Ronald Delany, Ireland	3:41.2
1960—Herbert Elliott, Australia	3:35.6
1964—Peter Snell, New Zealand	3:38.1
1968—Kipchoge Keino, Kenya	3:34.9*
1972—Pekka Vasala, Finland	3:36.3
1976—John Walker, New Zealand	3:39.17

5,000 Meter Run

1912—Hannes Kolehmainen, Finland	14:36.6
1920—Joseph Guillemot, France	14:55.6
1924—Paavo Nurmi, Finland	14:31.2
1928—Willie Ritola, Finland	14:38.0
1932—Lauri Lehtinen, Finland	14:30.0
1936—Gunnar Hockert, Finland	14:22.2
1948—Gaston Reiff, Belgium	14:17.6
1952—Emil Zatopek, Czechoslovakia	14:06.6
1956—Vladimir Kuts, USSR	13:39.6
1960—Murray Halberg, New Zealand	13:43.4
1964—Robert K. Schul, United States	13:48.8
1968—Mohamed Gammoudi, Tunisia	14:05.0
1972—Lasse Viren, Finland	13:26.4
1976—Lasse Viren, Finland	13:24.76

10,000 Meter Run

1912—Hannes Kolehmainen, Finland	31:20.8
1920—Paavo Nurmi, Finland	31:45.8
1924—Willie Ritola, Finland	30:23.2
1928—Paavo Nurmi, Finland	30:18.8
1932—Janusz Kusocinski, Poland	30:11.4
1936—Ilmari Salminen, Finland	30:15.4
1948—Emil Zatopek, Czechoslovakia	29:59.6
1952—Emil Zatopek, Czechoslovakia	29:17.0
1956—Vladimir Kuts, USSR	28:45.6
1960—Petr Bolotnikov, USSR	28:32.2
1964—William Mills, United States	28:24.4
1968—Naftali Temu, Kenya	29:27.4
1972—Lasse Viren, Finland	27:38.4*
1976—Lasse Viren, Finland	27:40.38

Marathon

	Hr./Min./Sec.
1896—Spyros Loues, Greece	2:58:50.0
1900—Michel Theato, France	2:59:45.0
1904—Thomas J. Hicks, United States	3:28:53.0
1908—John J. Hayes, United States	2:55:18.4
1912—Kenneth McArthur, South Africa	2:36:54.8
1920—Hannes Kolehmainen, Finland	2:32:35.8
1924—Albin Stenroos, Finland	2:41:22.6
1928—A. B. El Ouafi, France	2:32:57.0
1932—Juan Zabala, Argentina	2:31:36.0
1936—Kitei Son, Japan	2:29:19.2
1948—Delfo Cabrera, Argentina	2:34:51.6
1952—Emil Zatopek, Czechoslovakia	2:23:03.2
1956—Alain Mimoun, France	2:25:00.0
1960—Abebe Bikila, Ethiopia	2:15:16.2
1964—Abebe Bikila, Ethiopia	2:12:11.2
1968—Mamo Wolde, Ethiopia	2:20:26.4
1972—Frank Shorter, United States	2:12:19.7
1976—Waldemar Cierpinski, East Germany	2:09:55.0*

110 Meter Hurdles

	Sec.
1896—Thomas P. Curtis, United States	17.6
1900—Alvin E. Kraenzlein, United States	15.4
1904—Frederick W. Schule, United States	16.0
1908—Forrest Smithson, United States	15.0
1912—Frederick W. Kelley, United States	15.1
1920—Earl J. Thomson, Canada	14.8
1924—Daniel C. Kinsey, United States	15.0
1928—Sydney Atkinson, South Africa	14.8
1932—George Saling, United States	14.6
1936—Forrest Towns, United States	14.2
1948—William Porter, United States	13.9
1952—Harrison Dillard, United States	13.7
1956—Lee Q. Calhoun, United States	13.5
1960—Lee Q. Calhoun, United States	13.8
1964—Hayes W. Jones, United States	13.6
1968—Willie Davenport, United States	13.3
1972—Rod Milburn, United States	13.2*
1976—Guy Drut, France	13.30

400 Meter Hurdles

1900—John W. B. Tewksbury, United States	57.6
1904—Harry L. Hillman, United States	53.0
1908—Charles J. Bacon, United States	55.0
1920—Frank F. Loomis, United States	54.0
1924—F. Morgan Taylor, United States	52.6
1928—Lord David Burghley, Great Britain	53.4
1932—Robert Tisdall, Ireland	51.8
1936—Glenn Hardin, United States	52.4
1948—Roy Cochran, United States	51.1
1952—Charles Moore, United States	50.8
1956—Glenn A. Davis, United States	50.1
1960—Glenn A. Davis, United States	49.3
1964—Warren (Rex) Cawley, United States	49.6
1968—David Hemery, Great Britain	48.1
1972—John Akii-Bua, Uganda	47.8
1976—Edwin Moses, United States	47.64*

3,000 Meter Steeplechase

	Min./Sec.
1920—Percy Hodge, Great Britain	10:00.4
1924—Willie Ritola, Finland	9:33.6
1928—Toivo A. Loukola, Finland	9:21.8
1932—Volmari Iso-Hollo, Finland	10:33.4
(3,460 meters—extra lap by official error)	
1936—Volmari Iso-Hollo, Finland	9:03.8
1948—Thore Sjostrand, Sweden	9:04.6
1952—Horace Ashenfelter, United States	8:45.4
1956—Chris Brasher, Great Britain	8:41.2
1960—Zdzislaw Krzyszkowiak, Poland	8:34.2
1964—Gaston Roelants, Belgium	8:30.8
1968—Amos Biwott, Kenya	8:51.0
1972—Kipchoge Keino, Kenya	8:23.6
1976—Anders Gärderud, Sweden	8:08.20*

20,000 Meter Walk

	Hr./Min./Sec.
1956—Leonid Spirine, USSR	1:31:27.4
1960—Vladimir Golubnichy, USSR	1:34:07.2
1964—Kenneth Matthews, Great Britain	1:29:34.0
1968—Vladimir Golubnichy, USSR	1:33:58.4

1972—Peter Frenkel, East Germany	1:26:42.4
1976—Daniel Bautista, Mexico	1:24:40.6

50,000 Meter Walk

1932—Thomas W. Green, Great Britain	4:50:10.0
1936—Harold Whitlock, Great Britain	4:30:41.4
1948—John A. Ljunggren, Sweden	4:41:52.0
1952—Giuseppe Dordoni, Italy	4:28:07.8
1956—Norman Read, New Zealand	4:30:42.8
1960—Donald Thompson, Great Britain	4:25:30.0
1964—Abdon Pamich, Italy	4:11:12.4
1968—Christoph Kohne, East Germany	4:20:13.6
1972—Bernd Kannenberg, West Germany	3:56:11.6

400 Meter Relay — Sec.

1912—Great Britain	42.4
1920—United States	42.2
1924—United States	41.0
1928—United States	41.0
1932—United States	40.0
1936—United States	40.0
1948—United States	40.3
1952—United States	40.1
1956—United States	39.5
1960—Germany	39.5
1964—United States	39.0
1968—United States	38.2
1972—United States	38.2*
1976—United States	38.33

1,600 Meter Relay — Min./Sec.

1908—United States	3:29.4
1912—United States	3:16.6
1920—Great Britain	3:22.2
1924—United States	3:16.0
1928—United States	3:14.2
1932—United States	3:08.2
1936—Great Britain	3:09.0
1948—United States	3:10.4
1952—Jamaica	3:03.9
1956—United States	3:04.8
1960—United States	3:02.2
1964—United States	3:00.7
1968—United States	2:56.1*
1972—Kenya	2:59.8
1976—United States	2:58.65

Pole Vault — Height

1896—William W. Hoyt, United States	10' 9¾"
1900—Irving K. Baxter, United States	10' 9 9/10"
1904—Charles E. Dvorak, United States	11' 6"
1908—Albert C. Gilbert, United States	
Edward T. Cook, Jr., United States	12' 2"
1912—Harry S. Babcock, United States	12' 11½"
1920—Frank K. Foss, United States	12' 5 9/16"
1924—Lee S. Barnes, United States	12' 11½"
1928—Sabin W. Carr, United States	13' 9⅜"
1932—William Miller, United States	14' 1⅞"
1936—Earle Meadows, United States	14' 3¼"
1948—O. Guinn Smith, United States	14' 1¼"
1952—Robert Richards, United States	14' 11¼"
1956—Robert Richards, United States	14' 11½"
1960—Donald Bragg, United States	15' 5⅛"
1964—Fred M. Hansen, United States	16' 8¾"
1968—Robert Seagren, United States	17' 8½"
1972—Wolfgang Nordwig, East Germany	18' ½"
1976—Tadeusz Slusarki, Poland	18' ½"

High Jump

1896—Ellery Clark, United States	5' 11¼"
1900—Irving K. Baxter, United States	6' 2⅘"
1904—Samuel Jones, United States	5' 11"
1908—Harry Porter, United States	6' 3"
1912—Almer Richards, United States	6' 4"
1920—Richmond Landon, United States	6' 4¼"
1924—Harold Osborn, United States	6' 5 15/16"
1928—Robert W. King, United States	6' 4⅜"
1932—Duncan McNaughton, Canada	6' 5⅝"
1936—Cornelius Johnson, United States	6' 7 15/16"
1948—John Winter, Australia	6' 6"
1952—Walter Davis, United States	6' 8¼"
1956—Charles E. Dumas, United States	6' 11¼"
1960—Robert Shavlakadze, USSR	7' 1"
1964—Valery Brumel, USSR	7' 1¾"
1968—Richard Fosbury, United States	7' 4¼"
1972—Juri Tarmak, USSR	7' 3¾"
1976—Jacek Wszola, Poland	7' 4½"

Long Jump — Distance

1896—Ellery Clark, United States	20' 10"
1900—Alvin Kraenzlein, United States	23' 6⅞"
1904—Myer Prinstein, United States	24' 1"
1908—Francis Irons, United States	24' 6½"
1912—Albert Gutterson, United States	24' 11¼"
1920—William Pettersson, Sweden	23' 5½"
1924—DeHart Hubbard, United States	24' 5⅛"
1928—Edward Hamm, United States	25' 4¾"
1932—Edward Gordon, United States	25' ¾"
1936—Jesse Owens, United States	26' 5⅜"
1948—Willie Steel, United States	25' 8"
1952—Jerome Biffle, United States	24' 10"
1956—Gregory C. Bell, United States	25' 8¼"
1960—Ralph H. Boston, United States	26' 7¾"
1964—Lynn Davies, Great Britain	26' 5¾"
1968—Robert Beamon, United States	29' 2½"*
1972—Randy Williams, United States	27' ½"
1976—Arnie Robinson, United States	27' 4¾"

Triple Jump

1896—James B. Connolly, United States	45' 0"
1900—Myer Prinstein, United States	47' 4¼"
1904—Myer Prinstein, United States	47' 0"
1908—Timothy Ahearne, Great Britain	48' 11¼"
1912—Gustaf Lindblom, Sweden	48' 5⅛"
1920—Vilho Tuulos, Finland	47' 6⅞"
1924—Archibald Winter, Australia	50' 11⅛"
1928—Mikio Oda, Japan	49' 10 13/16"
1932—Chuhei Nambu, Japan	51' 7"
1936—Naoto Tajima, Japan	52' 5⅞"
1948—Arne Ahman, Sweden	50' 6¼"
1952—Adhemar Ferreira da Silva, Brazil	53' 2½"
1956—Adhemar Ferreira da Silva, Brazil	53' 7½"
1960—Jozef Schmidt, Poland	55' 1¾"
1964—Jozef Schmidt, Poland	55' 3¼"
1968—Viktor Saneyev, USSR	57' ¾"*
1972—Viktor Saneyev, USSR	56' 11"
1976—Viktor Saneyev, USSR	56' 8¾"

16-Pound Shot Put

1896—Robert Garrett, United States	36' 9¾"
1900—Richard Sheldon, United States	46' 3⅛"
1904—Ralph Rose, United States	48' 7"
1908—Ralph Rose, United States	46' 7½"
1912—Patrick McDonald, United States	50' 4"
1920—Ville Porhola, Finland	48' 7⅛"
1924—Clarence Houser, United States	49' 2½"
1928—John Kuck, United States	52' 13/16"
1932—Leo Sexton, United States	52' 6 3/16"
1936—Hans Woellke, Germany	53' 1¾"
1948—Wilbur Thompson, United States	56' 2"
1952—Wm. Parry O'Brien, Jr., United States	57' 1½"
1956—Wm. Parry O'Brien, Jr., United States	60' 11"
1960—William Nieder, United States	64' 6¾"
1964—Dallas C. Long, United States	66' 8¼"
1968—James Randel Matson, United States	67' 4¾"
1972—Wladyslaw Komar, Poland	69' 6"
1976—Udo Beyer, East Germany	69' 6.7"

Discus Throw

1896—Robert Garrett, United States	95' 7½"
1900—Rudolf Bauer, Hungary	118' 2 9/10"
1904—Martin Sheridan, United States	128' 10½"
1908—Martin Sheridan, United States	134' 2"
1912—Armas Taipale, Finland	145' 9/16"
1920—Elmer Niklander, Finland	146' 7"
1924—Clarence Houser, United States	151' 5¼"
1928—Clarence Houser, United States	155' 2⅝"
1932—John Anderson, United States	162' 4⅞"
1936—Kenneth Carpenter, United States	165' 7½"
1948—Adolfo Consolini, Italy	173' 2"
1952—Sim Iness, United States	180' 6½"
1956—Alfred A. Oerter, United States	184' 10½"
1960—Alfred A. Oerter, United States	194' 2"
1964—Alfred A. Oerter, United States	200' 1½"
1968—Alfred A. Oerter, United States	212' 6½"
1972—Ludwick Danek, Czechoslovakia	211' 3½"
1976—Mac Wilkins, United States	221' 5.4"*

16-Pound Hammer Throw

1900—John Flanagan, United States	167' 4"
1904—John Flanagan, United States	168' 1"
1908—John Flanagan, United States	170' 4¼"
1912—Matthew McGrath, United States	179' 7½"
1920—Patrick Ryan, United States	173' 5⅝"
1924—Frederick Tootell, United States	174' 10¼"
1928—Patrick O'Callaghan, Ireland	168' 7½"
1932—Patrick O'Callaghan, Ireland	176' 11⅛"
1936—Karl Hein, Germany	185' 4¼"
1948—Imre Nemeth, Hungary	183' 11½"
1952—Jozsef Csermak, Hungary	197' 11¾"
1956—Harold V. Connolly, United States	207' 3½"
1960—Vasiliy Rudenkov, USSR	220' 1⅝"
1964—Romuald Klim, USSR	228' 9½"
1968—Gyula Zsivotzky, Hungary	240' 8"
1972—Anatol Bondarchuk, USSR	247' 8"
1976—Yuri Sedykh, USSR	254' 4"

Javelin Throw

1908—Erik Lemming, Sweden	179' 10½"
1912—Erik Lemming, Sweden	198' 11¼"
1920—Jonni Myyra, Finland	215' 9¾"
1924—Jonni Myyra, Finland	206' 6¾"

1928—Erik Lundquist, Sweden	218' 6⅛"
1932—Matti Jarvinen, Finland	238' 7"
1936—Gerhard Stock, Germany	235' 8 5/16"
1948—Tapio Rautavaara, Finland	228' 10½"
1952—Cyrus Young, United States	242' ¾"
1956—Egil Danielson, Norway	281' 2¼"
1960—Viktor Tsibulenko, USSR	277' 8⅜"
1964—Pauli Ne/ala, Finland	271' 2¼"
1968—Janis Lusis, USSR	295' 7¼"
1972—Klaus Wolfermann, West Germany	296' 10"
1976—Miklos Nemeth, Hungary	310' 4½"*

Decathlon   **Points**

1912—Hugo Wieslander, Sweden	7724.49
1920—Helge Lovland, Norway	6804.35
1924—Harold Osborn, United States	7710.77
1928—Paavo Yrjola, Finland	8053.29
1932—James Bausch, United States	8462.23
(Old point system, 1912 through 1932)	
1936—Glenn Morris, United States	7900.00
1948—Robert Mathias, United States	7139.00
1952—Robert Mathias, United States	7887.00
1956—Milton G. Campbell, United States	7937.00
1960—Rafer Johnson, United States	8392.00
(Revised point system, 1936 through 1960)	
1964—Willi Holdorf, Germany	7887.00
(New scoring system)	
1968—William Toomey, United States	8193.00
1972—Nikolai Avilov, USSR	8454.00
1976—Bruce Jenner, United States	8618.00*

TRACK AND FIELD (Women)

100 Meter Dash   **Sec.**

1928—Elizabeth Robinson, United States	12.2
1932—Stanislawa Walasiewicz, Poland	11.9
1936—Helen Stephens, United States	11.5
1948—Francina Blankers-Koen, Netherlands	11.9
1952—Marjorie Jackson, Australia	11.5
1956—Betty Cuthbert, Australia	11.5
1960—Wilma Rudolph, United States	11.0
1964—Wyomia Tyus, United States	11.4
1968—Wyomia Tyus, United States	11.0
1972—Renate Stecher, East Germany	11.1
1976—Annegret Richter, West Germany	11.01*

200 Meter Dash

1948—Francina Blankers-Koen, Netherlands	24.4
1952—Marjorie Jackson, Australia	23.7
1956—Betty Cuthbert, Australia	23.4
1960—Wilma Rudolph, United States	24.0
1964—Edith McGuire, United States	23.0
1968—Irena Kirszenstein Szewinska, Poland	22.5
1972—Renate Stecher, East Germany	22.4
1976—Baerbel Eckert, East Germany	22.37

400 Meter Dash

1964—Betty Cuthbert, Australia	52.0
1968—Colette Besson, France	52.0
1972—Monika Zehrt, East Germany	51.1
1976—Irena Szewinska, Poland	49.29

800 Meter Run   **Min./Sec.**

1928—Linda Radke-Batschauer, Germany	2:16.8
1960—Ljudmila Shevcova-Lysenko, USSR	2:04.3
1964—Ann Packer, Great Britain	2:01.1
1968—Madeline Manning, United States	2:00.9
1972—Hildegard Falck, West Germany	1:58.6
1976—Tatvana Kazankina, USSR	1:54.94

1,500 Meter Run

1972—Ludmila Bragina, USSR	4:01.4
1976—Tatyana Kazankina, USSR	4:05.48

400 Meter Relay   **Sec.**

1928—Canada	48.4
1932—United States	47.0
1936—United States	46.9
1948—Netherlands	47.5
1952—United States	45.9
1956—Australia	44.5
1960—United States	44.5
1964—Poland	43.6
1968—United States	42.8

1972—West Germany	42.8
1976—East Germany	42.55

1,600 Meter Relay   **Min./Sec.**

1972—East Germany	3:23.0
1976—East Germany	3:19.23*

80 Meter Hurdles   **Sec.**

1932—Mildred Didrikson, United States	11.7
1936—Trebisonda Valla, Italy	11.7
1948—Francina Blankers-Koen, Netherlands	11.2
1952—Shirley Strickland de la Hunty, Australia	10.9
1956—Shirley Strickland de la Hunty, Australia	10.7
1960—Irina Press, USSR	10.8
1964—Karin Balzer, Germany	10.5
1968—Maureen Caird, Australia	10.3*

100 Meter Hurdles

1972—Annelie Erhardt, East Germany	12.6
1976—Johanna Schaller, East Germany	12.77

High Jump   **Height**

1928—Ethel Catherwood, Canada	5' 3"
1932—Jean Shiley, United States	5' 5¼"
1936—Ibolya Csak, Hungary	5' 3"
1948—Alice Coachman, United States	5' 6⅛"
1952—Esther Brand, South Africa	5' 5¾"
1956—Mildred McDaniel, United States	5' 9¼"
1960—Iolanda Balas, Rumania	6' ¼"
1964—Iolanda Balas, Rumania	6' 2¾"
1968—Miloslava Rezkova, Czechoslovakia	5' 11¾"
1972—Ulrika Meyfarth, West Germany	6' 3½"
1976—Rosemarie Ackermann, East Germany	6' 4"

Long Jump   **Distance**

1948—Olga Gyarmati, Hungary	18' 8¼"
1952—Yvette Williams, New Zealand	20' 5¾"
1956—Elizbieta Krzeskinska, Poland	20' 9¾"
1960—Vyera Krepkina, USSR	20' 10¾"
1964—Mary Rand, Great Britain	22' 2"
1968—Viorica Viscopoleanu, Rumania	22' 4½"
1972—Heidemarie Rosendahl, West Germany	22' 3"
1976—Angela Voigt, East Germany	22' 2½"

Discus Throw

1928—Helena Konopacka, Poland	129' 11⅞"
1932—Lillian Copeland, Unted States	133' 2"
1936—Gisela Mauermayer, Germany	156' 3 3/16"
1948—Micheline Ostermeyer, France	137' 6½"
1952—Nina Romaschkova, USSR	168' 8½"
1956—Olga Fikotova, Czechoslovakia	176' 1½"
1960—Nina Ponomareva, USSR	180' 8¼"
1964—Tamara Press, USSR	187' 10¾"
1968—Lia Manoliu, Rumania	191' 2½"
1972—Faina Melnik, USSR	218' 7"
1976—Evelin Schlaak, East Germany	226' 4½"

8-Lb./13-Oz. Shot Put

1948—Micheline Ostermeyer, France	45' 1½"
1952—Galina Zybina, USSR	50' 1½"
1956—Tamara Tishkyevich, USSR	54' 5"
1960—Tamara Press, USSR	56' 9¾"
1964—Tamara Press, USSR	59' 6"
1968—Margitta Gummel, East Germany	64' 4"
1972—Nadezhda Chizhova, USSR	69'
1976—Ivanka Khristova, Bulgaria	69' 5"

Javelin Throw

1932—Mildred Didrikson, United States	143' 4"
1936—Tilly Fleischer, Germany	148' 2¾"
1948—Herma Bauma, Austria	149' 6"
1952—Dana Zatopekova, Czechoslovakia	165' 7"
1956—Inessa Janzeme, USSR	176' 8"
1960—Elvira Ozolina, USSR	183' 8"
1964—Mihaela Penes, Rumania	198' 7½"
1968—Angela Nemeth, Hungary	198' ½"
1972—Ruth Fuchs, East Germany	209' 7"
1976—Ruth Fuchs, East Germany	216' 4"

Pentathlon   **Points**

1964—Irina Press, USSR	5,246
1968—Ingrid Becker, West Germany	5,098
1972—Mary Peters, Britain	4,801
1976—Siegrun Siegl, East Germany	4,745

TEAM SPORTS (since 1948)

Field Hockey	Soccer (Football)	Volleyball—Women
1948—India	1948—Sweden	1964—Japan
1952—India	1952—Hungary	1968—USSR
1956—India	1956—USSR	1972—USSR
1960—Pakistan	1960—Yugoslavia	1976—Japan
1964—India	1964—Hungary	**Water Polo**
1968—Pakistan	1968—Hungary	1948—Italy
1972—West Germany	1972—Poland	1952—Hungary
1976—New Zealand	1976—East Germany	1956—Hungary
Handball—Men	**Volleyball—Men**	1960—Italy
1972—Yugoslavia	1964—USSR	1964—Hungary
1976—USSR	1968—USSR	1968—Yugoslavia
Handball—Women	1972—Japan	1972—USSR
1976—USSR	1976—Poland	1976—Hungary

Basketball—Men

1948—United States	
1952—United States	
1956—United States	
1960—United States	
1964—United States	
1968—United States	
1972—USSR	
1976—United States	

Basketball—Women

1976—USSR	

THE WINTER OLYMPIC GAMES

Sites	Year	Sites	Year
I Chamonix, France	1924	VIII Squaw Valley, California	1960
II St. Moritz, Switzerland	1928	IX Innsbruck, Austria	1964
III Lake Placid, New York	1932	X Grenoble, France	1968
IV Garmisch-Partenkirchen, Germany	1936	XI Sapporo, Japan	1972
V St. Moritz, Switzerland	1948	XII Innsbruck, Austria	1976
VI Oslo, Norway	1952	XIII Lake Placid, New York	1980
VII Cortina, Italy	1956	XIV Sarajevo, Yugoslavia	1984

1980 WINTER OLYMPICS MEDAL STANDINGS

	Gold (1st)	Silver (2d)	Bronze (3d)	Total		Gold (1st)	Silver (2d)	Bronze (3d)	Total
East Germany	9	7	7	23	Netherlands	1	2	1	4
U.S.S.R.	10	6	6	22	Italy	0	2	0	2
U.S.A.	6	4	2	12	Canada	0	1	1	2
Norway	1	3	6	10	United Kingdom	1	0	0	1
Finland	1	5	3	9	Hungary	0	1	0	1
Austria	3	2	2	7	Japan	0	1	0	1
Switzerland	1	1	3	5	Bulgaria	0	0	1	1
West Germany	0	2	3	5	Czechoslovakia	0	0	1	1
Sweden	3	0	1	4	France	0	0	1	1
Liechtenstein	2	2	0	4					

LAKE PLACID MEDALISTS: 1980 (*Olympic Record, ** World Record)

ALPINE SKIING (Men)

Downhill
1. Leonhard Stock, Austria
2. Peter Wirnsberger, Austria
3. Steve Podborski, Canada

Giant Slalom
1. Ingemar Stenmark, Sweden
2. Andreas Wenzel, Liechtenstein
3. Hans Enn, Austria

Slalom
1. Ingemar Stenmark, Sweden
2. Phil Mahre, U.S.A.
3. Jacques Luethy, Switzerland

ALPINE SKIING (Women)

Downhill
1. Annemarie Moser-Proell, Austria
2. Hanni Wenzel, Liechtenstein
3. Marie-Theres Nadig, Switzerland

Giant Slalom
1. Hanni Wenzel, Liechtenstein
2. Irene Epple, West Germany
3. Perrine Pelen, France

Slalom
1. Hanni Wenzel, Liechtenstein
2. Christa Kinshofer, West Germany
3. Erika Hess, Switzerland

NORDIC SKIING (Men)

15-kilometer cross-country
1. Thomas Wassberg, Sweden
2. Juha Mieto, Finland
3. Ove Aunli, Norway

30-kilometer cross-country
1. Nikolai Zimyatov, U.S.S.R.
2. Vasili Rochev, U.S.S.R.
3. Ivan Lebanov, Bulgaria

50-kilometer cross-country
1. Nikolai Zimyatov, U.S.S.R.
2. Juha Mieto, Finland
3. Aleksandr Zavjalov, U.S.S.R.

4 x 10-kilometer cross-country relay
1. U.S.S.R. (Rochev, Bazhukov, Beliaev, Zimyatov)
2. Norway
3. Finland

70-meter jump
1. Anton Innauer, Austria
2. (tie) Manfred Deckert, East Germany-Hirokazu Yagi, Japan

90-meter special jump
1. Jouko Tormanen, Finland
2. Hubert Neuper, Austria
3. Jari Puikkonen, Finland

Nordic combined
(jumping and cross-country)
1. Ulrich Wehling, East Germany
2. Jouko Karjalainen, Finland
3. Konrad Winkler, East Germany

NORDIC SKIING (Women)

5-kilometer cross-country
1. Raisa Smetanina, U.S.S.R.
2. Hilkka Riihivuori, Finland
3. Kveta Jeriova, Czechoslovakia

10-kilometer cross-country
1. Barbara Petzold, East Germany
2. Hilkka Riihivuori, Finland
3. Helena Takalo, Finland

4 x 5-kilometer cross-country relay
1. East Germany (Rostock, Anding, Hesse, Petzold)
2. U.S.S.R.
3. Norway

BIATHLON

10-kilometer individual
1. Frank Ullrich, East Germany
2. Vladimir Alikin, U.S.S.R.
3. Anatoli Alabyev, U.S.S.R.

20-kilometer individual
1. Anatoli Alabyev, U.S.S.R.
2. Frank Ullrich, East Germany
3. Eberhard Rosch, East Germany

4 x 7.5-kilometer relay
1. U.S.S.R. (Alikin, Tikhonov, Barnaschov, Alabyev)
2. East Germany
3. West Germany

HOCKEY
1. U.S.A.
2. U.S.S.R.
3. Sweden

BOBSLED

Two-man
1. Switzerland II (Erich Schaerer-Josef Benz)
2. East Germany II
3. East Germany I

Four-man
1. East Germany I (Nehmer, Musiol, Germeshausen, Gerhardt)
2. Switzerland I
3. East Germany II

LUGE

Singles (Men)
1. Bernhard Glass, East Germany
2. Paul Hildgartner, Italy
3. Anton Winkler, East Germany

Doubles (Men)
1. Hans Rinn-Norbert Hahn, East Germany
2. Peter Gschnitzer-Karl Brunner, Italy
3. Georg Fluckinger-Karl Schrott, Austria

Singles (Women)
1. Vera Zozulya, U.S.S.R.
2. Melitta Sollmann, East Germany
3. Ingrida Amantova, U.S.S.R.

FIGURE SKATING

Men
1. Robin Cousins, United Kingdom
2. Jan Hoffmann, East Germany
3. Charles Tickner, U.S.A.

Women
1. Anett Poetzsch, East Germany
2. Linda Fratianne, U.S.A.
3. Dagmar Lurz, West Germany

Pairs
1. Irina Rodnina-Aleksandr Zaitsev, U.S.S.R.
2. Marina Chereskova-Sergei Shakrai, U.S.S.R.
3. Manuela Mager-Uwe Bewersdorf, East Germany

Ice Dancing
1. Natalia Linichuk-Gennadi Karponosov, U.S.S.R.
2. Krisztina Regoczy-Andras Sallay, Hungary
3. Irina Moiseeva-Andrei Minenkov, U.S.S.R.

SPEED SKATING (Men)

500-meter
1. Eric Heiden, U.S.A., 38.03*
2. Evgeni Kulikov, U.S.S.R.
3. Lieuwe DeBoer, Netherlands

1,000-meter
1. Eric Heiden, U.S.A., 1:15.18*
2. Gaetan Boucher, Canada
3. (tie) Frode Roenning, Norway-Vladimir Lobanov, U.S.S.R.

1,500-meter
1. Eric Heiden, U.S.A., 1:55.44*
2. Kai Arne Stenshjemmet, Norway
3. Terje Andersen, Norway

5,000-meter
1. Eric Heiden, U.S.A., 7:2.29*
2. Kai Arne Stenshjemmet, Norway
3. Tom Erik Oxholm, Norway

10,000-meter
1. Eric Heiden, U.S.A. 14:28.13**
2. Piet Kleine, Netherlands
3. Tom Erik Oxholm, Norway

SPEED SKATING (Women)

500-meter
1. Karin Enke, East Germany, 41.78*
2. Leah Poulos Mueller, U.S.A.
3. Natalia Petruseva, U.S.S.R.

1,000-meter
1. Natalia Petruseva, U.S.S.R., 24.1*
2. Leah Poulos Mueller, U.S.A.
3. Silvia Albrecht, East Germany

1,500-meter
1. Annie Borckink, Netherlands, 2:10.95*
2. Ria Visser, Netherlands
3. Sabine Becker, East Germany

3,000-meter
1. Bjoerg Eva Jensen, Norway, 4:32.13*
2. Sabine Becker, East Germany
3. Beth Heiden, U.S.A.

WINTER OLYMPIC CHAMPIONS

ALPINE SKIING (Men)

Downhill
1948—Henri Oreiller, France
1952—Zeno Colo, Italy
1956—Toni Sailer, Austria
1960—Jean Vuarnet, France
1964—Egon Zimmermann, Austria
1968—Jean Claude Killy, France
1972—Bernhard Russi, Switzerland
1976—Franz Klammer, Austria

Giant Slalom
1952—Stein Eriksen, Norway
1956—Toni Sailer, Austria
1960—Roger Staub, Switzerland
1964—Francois Bonlieu, France
1968—Jean Claude Killy, France
1972—Gustavo Thoeni, Italy
1976—Heini Hemmi, Switzerland

Slalom
1948—Edi Reinalter, Switzerland
1952—Othmar Schneider, Austria
1956—Toni Sailer, Austria
1960—Ernst Hinterseer, Austria
1964—Josef Stiegler, Austria
1968—Jean Claude Killy, France
1972—Francisco Fernandez Ochoa, Spain
1976—Piero Gros, Italy

ALPINE SKIING (Women)

Downhill
1948—Hedi Schlunegger, Switzerland
1952—Trude Jochum-Beiser, Austria
1956—Madeleine Berthod, Switzerland
1960—Heidi Biebl, Germany
1964—Christl Haas, Austria
1968—Olga Pall, Austria
1972—Marie-Theres Nadig, Switzerland
1976—Rosi Mittermaier, West Germany

Giant Slalom
1952—Andrea Mead Lawrence, United States
1956—Ossi Reichert, Germany
1960—Yvonne Ruegg, Switzerland
1964—Marielle Goitschel, France
1968—Nancy Greene, Canada
1972—Marie-Theres Nadig, Switzerland
1976—Kathy Kreiner, Canada

Slalom
1948—Gretchen Fraser, United States
1952—Andrea Mead Lawrence, United States
1956—Renee Colliard, Switzerland
1960—Anne Heggtveigt, Canada
1964—Christine Goitschel, France
1968—Marielle Goitschel, France
1972—Barbara Cochran, United States
1976—Rosi Mittermaier, West Germany

NORDIC SKIING AND JUMPING (Men)

15-Kilometer Cross-Country
1924—Thorleif Haug, Norway
1928—Johan Grottumsbraaten, Norway
1932—Sven Utterstrom, Sweden
1936—Erik-August Larsson, Sweden
1948—Martin Lundstrom, Sweden
1952—Hallgeir Brenden, Norway
1956—Hallgeir Brenden, Norway
1960—Hakon Brusveen, Norway
1964—Eero Mantyranta, Finland
1968—Harald Groenningen, Norway
1972—Sven-Ake Lundback, Sweden
1976—Nikolai Bajukov, USSR

30-Kilometer Cross-Country
1956—Veikko Hakulinen, Finland
1960—Sixten Jernberg, Sweden
1964—Eero Mantyranta, Finland
1968—Franco Nones, Italy
1972—Vyacheslav Vedenin, USSR
1976—Sergei Saveliev, USSR

50-Kilometer Cross-Country
1924—Thorleif Haug, Norway
1928—Per Erik Hedlund, Sweden
1932—Veli Saarinen, Finland
1936—Elis Viklund, Sweden
1948—Nils Karlsson, Sweden

1952—Veikko Hakulinen, Finland
1956—Sixten Jernberg, Sweden
1960—Kalevi Hamalainen, Finland
1964—Sixten Jernberg, Sweden
1968—Ole Ellefsaeter, Norway
1972—Paal Tyldum, Norway
1976—Ivar Formo, Norway

4 x 10-Kilometer Cross-Country Relay
1936—Finland	1964—Sweden
1948—Sweden	1968—Norway
1952—Finland	1972—USSR
1956—USSR	1976—Finland
1960—Finland	

70-Meter Special Jump
1964—Veikko Kankkonen, Finland
1968—Jiri Raska, Czechoslovakia
1972—Yukio Kasaya, Japan
1976—Hans-Georg Aschenbach, East Germany

90-Meter Special Jump
1924—Jacob T. Thambs, Norway
1928—Alfred Andersen, Norway
1932—Birger Ruud, Norway
1936—Birger Ruud, Norway
1948—Petter Hugsted, Norway
1952—Arnfinn Bergmann, Norway
1956—Antti Hyvarinen, Finland
1960—Helmut Recknagel, Germany
1964—Toralf Engan, Norway
1968—Vladimir Beloussov, USSR
1972—Wojiech Fortuna, Poland
1976—Karl Schnabl, Austria

Nordic Combined
1924—Thorleif Haug, Norway
1928—Johan Grottumsbraaten, Norway
1932—Johan Grottumsbraaten, Norway
1936—Oddbjorn Hagen, Norway
1948—Heikki Hasu, Finland
1952—Simon Slattvik, Norway
1956—Sverre Stenersen, Norway
1960—Georg Thoma, Germany
1964—Tormod Knutsen, Norway
1968—Franz Keller, West Germany
1972—Ulrich Wehling, East Germany
1976—Ulrich Wehling, East Germany

NORDIC SKIING (Women)

5-Kilometer Cross-Country
1964—Claudia Boyarskikh, USSR
1968—Toini Gustafsson, Sweden
1972—Galina Koulacova, USSR
1976—Helena Takalo, Finland

10-Kilometer Cross-Country
1952—Lydia Wideman, Finland
1956—Lyubov Kozyreva, USSR
1960—Marija Gusakova, USSR
1964—Claudia Boyarskikh, USSR
1968—Toini Gustafsson, Sweden
1972—Galina Koulacova, USSR
1976—Raisa Smetanina, USSR

15-Kilometer Relay
1956—Finland	1968—Norway
1960—Sweden	1972—USSR
1964—USSR	1976 (20 km.)—USSR

BIATHLON

20-Kilometer Individual
1960—Klas Lestander, Sweden
1964—Vladimir Melanin, USSR
1968—Magnar Solberg, Norway
1972—Magnar Solberg, Norway
1976—Nikolai Kruglov, USSR

40-Kilometer Relay
1968—USSR
1972—USSR
1976—USSR

HOCKEY
1920—Canada	1956—USSR
1924—Canada	1960—United States
1928—Canada	1964—USSR
1932—Canada	1968—USSR
1936—Great Britain	1972—USSR
1948—Canada	1976—USSR
1952—Canada	

BOBSLEDDING

Two-Man

1932—United States	1964—Great Britain
1936—United States	1968—Italy
1948—Switzerland	1972—West Germany
1952—Germany	1976—East Germany
1956—Italy	

Four-Man

1924—Switzerland	1956—Switzerland
1928—United States (5-Man)	1964—Canada
1932—United States	1968—Italy
1936—Switzerland	1972—Switzerland
1948—United States	1976—East Germany
1952—Germany	

LUGE

Singles (Men)

1964—Thomas Kohler, Germany
1968—Manfred Schmid, Austria
1972—Wolfgang Scheidel, East Germany
1976—Detlef Guenther, East Germany

Doubles (Men)

1964—Austria
1968—East Germany
1972—Italy, East Germany (tie)
1976—East Germany

Singles (Women)

1964—Ortrun Enderlein, Germany
1968—Erica Lechner, Italy
1972—Anna M. Muller, East Germany
1976—Margit Schumann, East Germany

FIGURE SKATING

Men

1908—Ulrich Salchow, Sweden
1920—Gillis Grafstrom, Sweden
1924—Gillis Grafstrom, Sweden
1928—Gillis Grafstrom, Sweden
1932—Karl Schafer, Austria
1936—Karl Schafer, Austria
1948—Richard Button, United States
1952—Richard Button, United States
1956—Hayes Alan Jenkins, United States
1960—David W. Jenkins, United States
1964—Manfred Schnelldorfer, Germany
1968—Wolfgang Schwartz, Austria
1972—Ondrej Nepela. Czechoslovakia
1976—John Curry, United Kingdom

Women

1908—Madge Syers, Great Britain
1920—Magda Julin-Mauróy, Sweden
1924—Heima von Szabo-Planck, Austria
1928—Sonja Henie, Norway
1932—Sonja Henie, Norway
1936—Sonja Henie, Norway
1948—Barbara Ann Scott, Canada
1952—Jeanette Altwegg, Great Britain
1956—Tenley Albright, United States
1960—Carol Heiss, United States
1964—Sjoukje Dijkstra, Netherlands
1968—Peggy Fleming, United States
1972—Beatrix Schuba, Austria
1976—Dorothy Hamill, United States

Pairs

1908—Germany-Anna Hubler, Heinrich Burger
1920—Finland-Ludovika & Walter Jakobsson
1924—Austria-Helene Engelman, Alfred Berger
1928—France-Andree Joly, Pierre Brunet
1932—France-Andree & Pierre Brunet
1936—Germany-Maxie Herber, Ernst Baier
1948—Belgium-Micheline Lannoy, Pierre Baugniet
1952—Germany-Ria & Paul Falk
1956—Austria-Elisabeth Schwartz, Kurt Oppelt
1960—Canada-Barbara Wagner, Robert Paul
1964—USSR-Ludmila Beloussova, Oleg Protopopov
1968—USSR-Ludmila Beloussova, Oleg Protopopov
1972—USSR-Irina Rodnina, Alexei Ulanov
1976—USSR-Irina Rodnina, Aleksandr Zaitsev

Ice Dancing

1976—USSR-Lyudmila Pakhomova, Aleksandr Gorshkov

SPEED SKATING (Men)

500-Meters

1924—Charles Jewtraw, United States, 44.0
1928—Clas Thunberg, Finland and
    Bernt Evensen, Norway (tie), 43.4
1932—John A. Shea, United States, 43.4
1936—Ivar Ballangrud, Norway, 43.4
1948—Finn Helgesen, Norway, 43.1
1952—Ken Henry, United States, 43.2
1956—Yevgeni Grishin, USSR, 40.2
1960—Yevgeni Grishin, USSR, 40.2
1964—Terry McDermott, United States, 40.1
1968—Erhard Keller, West Germany, 40.3
1972—Erhard Keller, West Germany, 39.4
1976—Evgeni Kulikov, USSR, 39.17

1,000 Meters

1976—Peter Mueller, United States, 1:19.32

1,500-Meters

1924—Clas Thunberg, Finland, 2:20.8
1928—Clas Thunberg, Finland, 2:21.1
1932—John A. Shea, United States, 2:57.5
1936—Charles Mathisen, Norway, 2:19.2
1948—Sverre Farstad, Norway, 2:17.6
1952—Hjalmar Andersen, Norway, 2:20.4
1956—Yevgeni Grishin and Yuri
    Mikhailov, USSR (tie), 2:08.6
1960—Roald Aas, Norway and
    Yevgeni Grishin, USSR (tie), 2:10.4
1964—Ants Anston, USSR, 2:10.3
1968—Cornelis Verkerk, Netherlands, 2:03.4
1972—Ard Schenk, Netherlands, 2:02.9
1976—Jan Egil Storholt, Norway, 1:59.38

5,000-Meters

1924—Clas Thunberg, Finland, 8:39
1928—Ivar Ballangrud, Norway, 8:50.5
1932—Irving Jaffee, United States, 9:40.8
1936—Ivar Ballangrud, Norway, 8:19.6
1948—Reidar Liaklev, Norway, 8:29.4
1952—Hjalmar Andersen, Norway, 8:10.6
1956—Boris Shilkov, USSR, 7:48.7
1960—Viktor Kosichkin, USSR, 7:51.3
1964—Knut Johannesen, Norway, 7:38.4
1968—F. Anton Maier, Norway, 7:22.4*
1972—Ard Schenk, Netherlands, 7:23.6
1976—Sten Stensen, Norway, 7:24.48

10,000-Meters

1924—Julien Skutnabb, Finland, 18:04.8
1928—(ice thawed, event cancelled)
1932—Irving Jaffee, United States, 19:13.6
1936—Ivar Ballangrud, Norway, 17:24.3
1948—Ake Seyffarth, Sweden, 17:26.3
1952—Hjalmar Andersen, Norway, 16:45.8
1956—Sigvard Ericsson, Sweden, 16:35
1960—Knut Johannessen, Norway, 15:46.6
1964—Jonny Nilsson, Sweden, 15:50.1
1968—Johnny Hoeglin, Sweden, 15:23.6
1972—Ard Schenk, Netherlands, 15:01.3
1976—Piet Kleine, Netherlands, 14:50.59

SPEED SKATING (Women)

500-Meters

1960—Helga Haase, Germany, 45.9
1964—Lydia Skoblikova, USSR, 45.0
1968—Ludmila Titova, USSR, 46.1
1972—Anne Henning, United States, 43.3
1976—Sheila Young, United States, 42.76

1,000-Meters

1960—Klara Guseva, USSR, 1:34.1
1964—Lydia Skoblikova, USSR, 1:33.2
1968—Carolina Geijssen, Netherlands, 1:32.6
1972—Monika Pflug, West Germany, 1:31.4
1976—Tatiana Averina, USSR, 1:28.43

1,500-Meters

1960—Lydia Skoblikova, USSR, 2:25.2
1964—Lydia Skoblikova, USSR, 2:22.6
1968—Kaija Mustonen, Finland, 2:22.4
1972—Dianne Holum, United States, 2:20.8
1976—Galina Stepanskaya, USSR, 2:16.58

3,000-Meters

1960—Lydia Skoblikova, USSR, 5:14.3
1964—Lydia Skoblikova, USSR, 5:14.9
1968—Johanna Schut, Netherlands, 4:56.2
1972—Stien Kaiser-Baas, Netherlands, 4:52.1
1976—Tatiana Averina, USSR, 4:45.19

1981 U.S. NATIONAL SPORTS FESTIVAL CHAMPIONS SOURCE: U.S. Olympic Committee

ARCHERY
Men—Darrell Pace, Cincinnati, Ohio
Women—Ruth Rowe, Gaithersburg, Md.

BASEBALL
Team—East

BASKETBALL
Men's Team—West
MVP—Stuart Gray, Sepulveda, Calif.
Women's Team—South
MVP—Janice Lawrence, Lucedale, Miss.

BOXING
106 lb—Jesse Benavides, Corpus Christi,
Tex.
112 lb—Fred Perkins, Ft. Bragg, N.C.
119 lb—Richard Savage, W. Monroe, La.
125 lb—Benji Marquez, Denver, Colo.
132 lb—Vincent Pazienza, Cranston, R.I.
139 lb—Vincent Webb, University City, Mo.
147 lb—Mark Breland, Brooklyn, N.Y.
156 lb—Alfred Mayes, St. Louis, Mo.
165 lb—Randy Smith, Chicago, Ill.
178 lb—Johnny Williams, Chicago, Ill.
Heavyweight—Mark Mahone, Norfolk, Va.

CANOE/KAYAK

CANOE
500 m—Bret Young, Hastings, N.Y.
1000 m—Rod McLain, Gloversville, N.Y.
500 m Doubles—Rod and Rusty McLain,
Gloversville, N.Y.
1000 m Doubles—Tom Smith, Bronx, N.Y.-
Bret Young
500 m Fours—East
1000 m Fours—East

KAYAK
500 m—David Halpern, Seattle, Wash.
Women—Linda Dragan, Washington, D.C.
1000 m—David Halpern
500 m Doubles—Gus Peterson, Agoura,
Calif.-Terry Kent, Rochester, N.Y.
Women—Carol Toeppner, Costa Mesa,
Calif.-Sheila Canover, Hadley, Mass.
1000 m Doubles—Gus Peterson-Terry Kent
500 m Fours—South
Women—West
1000 m Fours—South

CYCLING
Men's 100 km—John Beckman, Beaverton,
Ore.
Women's 50 km—Connie Carpenter,
Madison, Wis.
Criterium—Len Nitz, Flushing, N.Y.
Women—Jacque Bradley, Ames, Iowa
50 km Time Trial—Midwest

DIVING
3-Meter—Dave Burgering, Mission Viejo,
Calif.
Women—Chris Seufert, Ann Arbor, Mich.
Platform—Greg Louganis, Mission Viejo,
Calif.
Women—Chris Seufert

EQUESTRIAN
Dressage—Lendon Gray, Dixmont, Me.
Team—Midwest

Jumping—Katherine Gifford, Elnora, N.Y.
Team—West

FENCING
Epee—Bob Nieman, San Antonio, Tex.
Sabre—Peter Westbrook, New York, N.Y.
Foil—Heik Hambarzumian, San Francisco,
Calif.
Women—Ilona Maskal, Rutherford, N.J.

FIELD HOCKEY
Men's Team—West
Women's Team—Midwest

FIGURE SKATING
Men—Scott Hamilton, Denver, Colo.
Women—Rosalyn Summers, Edmonds,
Wash.
Pairs—Kitty and Peter Carruthers,
Wilmington, Del.
Ice Dancing—Elisa Spitz, Short Hills,
N.J.-Scott Gregory, Skaneateles, N.Y.

GYMNASTICS—MEN
All-Around—Brian Meeker, Edina, Minn.
Floor Exercise—Roy Palassou, Santa
Clara, Calif.
Pommel Horse—Brian Babcock, Enid, Okla.
Rings—Mark Caso, Syracuse, N.Y.
Vault—Ron Galimore, Tallahassee, Fla.
Parallel Bars—Roy Palassou
Horizontal Bar—Tim Daggett, Springfield,
Mass.

GYMNASTICS—WOMEN
All-Around—Beth Pope, Little Rock, Ark.
Floor Exercise—Beth Pope
Beam—Nancy McDonald, Oakland, N.J.
Vault—Patti Rice, Johnstown, Pa.
Uneven Bars—Tammy Smith, Silver Spring,
Md.

ICE HOCKEY
Team—Great Lakes
MVP's—John VanBiesbrock, Detroit,
Mich.-Jeff Johnston, Grosse Pointe,
Mich.

JUDO—MEN
132 lb—Doug Tono, Chicago, Ill.
143 lb—Craig Agena, Aurora, Colo.
156 lb—Mike Swain, Bridgewater, N.J.
172 lb—Brett Barron, San Francisco, Calif.
189 lb—Hector Estivez, Miami, Fla.
209 lb—Miguel Tudela, Alhambra, Calif.
Over 209 lb—Brad Moss, Gilroy, Calif.
Open Div.—Dewey Mitchell, Seven
Springs, Fla.

JUDO—WOMEN
106 lb—Jo Quiring, Littleton, Colo.
114 lb—Robin Tekemori, Alexandria, Va.
123 lb—Ann Maria Burns, Minneapolis,
Minn.
134 lb—Robin Chapman, Cranford, N.J.
145 lb—Christine Penick, San Jose, Calif.
Over 158 lb—Margaret Castro, New York,
N.Y.
Open Class—Barbara Fest, Lynn, Mass.

MODERN PENTATHLON
Blair Driggs, San Antonio, Tex.

RHYTHMIC GYMNASTICS
All-Around—Lydia Crabtree, Redondo
Beach, Calif.
Ribbon—Lydia Crabtree
Rope—Sue Soffe, Agoura, Calif.
Hoop—Michelle Berube, Rochester, Mich.
Clubs—Valerie Zimring, Cheviet Hills,
Calif.

ROLLER SKATING
Figures—Tony St. Jacques, Virginia Beach,
Va.
Women—Anna Conklin, Bakersfield, Calif.
Singles—Tim McGuire, Flint, Mich.
Women—Tina Kneisley, Brighton, Mich.
Mixed Pairs—Tina Kneisley-Paul Price,
Brighton, Mich.
Free Dance—Linda Todd and Charles
Kirchner, Cherry Hill, N.J.
500 m—Donnie Van Patter, Little Rock,
Ark.
Women—Darlene Kessinger, Franklin, Ind.
1000 m—Ray Sharp, N. Little Rock, Ark.
Women—Beverly Calhoun, Hampton, Va.
1500 m—Ray Sharp
Women—Mary Hohl Barriere, Cincinnati,
Ohio
3000 m—Tom Peterson, Tacoma, Wash.
Women—Mary Hohl Barriere
4000 m Relay—West
Women—East
4000 m Mixed Relay—West No. 1

ROWING—MEN
Single Scull—John Bigelow, Bellevue,
Wash.
Single Scull, Petite—Steve Nowinski,
Long Beach, Calif.
Double Scull—Curt Fleming and John
Walker, Costa Mesa, Calif.
Double Scull, Petite—Jerry Suminski
and Brian Benz, Grosse Pointe, Mich.
Four with Coxswain—West
Eight—East

ROWING—WOMEN
Single Scull—Cathleen Thaxton, San Diego,
Calif.
Single Scull, Petite—Karla Drewson,
Philadelphia, Pa.
Double Scull—Nora Nichols, Alexandria,
Va.-Patricia Sweeney, Penn Wynne, Pa.
Double Scull, Petite—Laura Emmons and
Paige Nilles, Seattle, Wash.
Pair without Coxswain—Pat Curnan,
Ridgefield, Conn.-Jean Brown,
Norwich, Conn.
Pair without Coxswain, Petite—Connie
Johnston, Philadelphia, Pa.-Laura
Peck, Waverly, Pa.
Four with Coxswain—South
Four with Coxswain, Petite—West
Eight—West

SHOOTING
Int'l Trap—Dayne Johnson, Ft. Worth, Tex.
Int'l Skeet—Sai Chiang, San Francisco,
Calif.
Men's Free Rifle—Philip Whitworth,
Fairmont, W. Va.
Women's Standard Rifle—Pat Spurgin,
Billings, Mont.

English Match—Kurt Fitz-Randolph, Palm Bay, Fla.
Air Rifle—John Rost, Cincinnati, Ohio
Women—Ethel Ann Alves, New Castle, Del.
Air Pistol—Eric Buljung, Ft. Benning, Ga.
Rapid Fire Pistol—Rojelio Arredondo, Columbus, Ga.
Free Pistol—Eric Buljung
Ladies Small Bore Pistol—Ruby Fox, Parker, Ariz.

SOCCER

Team—East
MVP—Pat McGauley, St. Louis, Mo.

SOFTBALL

Men's Team—Peterbilt (Northwest)
Women's Team—Sun City (Rocky Mountain)

SPEEDSKATING

500 m—Steve Merrifield, Canoga Park, Calif.
Women—Gloria Bogacki, Park Ridge, Ill.
1000 m—Steve Merrifield
Women—Gloria Bogacki
1500 m—Steve Merrifield
Women—Gloria Bogacki
Team 3000 m Relay—Midwest
Women—East

SWIMMING—MEN

100 m Freestyle—Robin Leamy, Palos Verdes, Calif.
200 m Freestyle—Mike Heath, Dallas, Tex.
400 m Freestyle—Doug Towne, Tucson, Ariz.
1500 m Freestyle—Paul Budd, Memphis, Tenn.
100 m Butterfly—Dave Cowell, Belpre, Ohio
200 m Butterfly—John Denucy, Ft. Wayne, Ind.
100 m Breaststroke—Bill Barrett, Alpharetta, Ga.
200 m Breaststroke—John Moffet, Balboa, Calif.
100 m Backstroke—Rick Carey, Mt. Kisco, N.Y.
200 m Backstroke—Rick Carey
200 m Indiv. Medley—Bill Barrett
400 m Indiv. Medley—Roger Von Jouanne, Renton, Wash.
400 m Freestyle Relay—West
800 m Freestyle Relay—West
400 m Medley Relay—West

SWIMMING—WOMEN

100 m Freestyle—Susan Thayer, Barstow, Fla.
200 m Freestyle—Mary Wayte, Mercer Island, Wash.
400 m Freestyle—Sabrina Sagehorn, Martinez, Calif.
100 m Butterfly—Melanie Buddemeyer, Pittsburgh, Pa.
200 m Butterfly—Sara Linke, Walnut Creek, Calif.
100 m Breaststroke—Terri Baxter, Palo Alto, Calif.
200 m Breaststroke—Polly Winde, Ellicott City, Pa.
100 m Backstroke—Theresa Andrews, Annapolis, Md.
200 m Backstroke—Mary Wayte
200 m Indiv. Medley—Patty Gavin, Ardmore, Pa.
400 m Indiv. Medley—Patty Gavin
400 m Freestyle Relay—Midwest
800 m Freestyle Relay—West
400 m Medley Relay—Midwest

SYNCHRONIZED SWIMMING

Solo—Tracie Ruiz, Bothel, Wash.
Duet—Candy Costie, Seattle, Wash.-Tracie Ruiz
Figures—Tracie Ruiz

TABLE TENNIS

Singles—Parry Schwartzburg, Houston, Tex.
Women—Faan Yeen Liu, Arlington Hts., Ill.
Doubles—Sean O'Neill, Vienna, Va.-Randy Seemiller, Pittsburgh, Pa.
Women—Judy Hoarfrost, Beaverton, Ore.-Lisa Gee, San Carlos, Calif.
Mixed Doubles—Michael Lardon, Liberty, Tex.-Cheryl Dadian, Oak Creek, Wis.
Team—East
Women—East

TEAM HANDBALL

Men—East
Women—East

TENNIS

Boys' Singles—Gus Anderson, Salinas, Calif.
Girls' Singles—Robin White, San Jose, Calif.
Boys' Doubles—Randy Vigmostad, Greenlawn, N.Y.-Fred Perrin, Southampton, Pa.
Girls' Doubles—Julie Grummel, Longview, Wash.-Robin White
Mixed Doubles—Andy Winterbauer, Mercer Island, Wash.-Julie Grummel

TRACK AND FIELD—MEN

100 m Dash—James Sanford, Los Angeles, Calif.
200 m Dash—Dwayne Evans, Tempe, Ariz.
400 m Dash—Tony Darden, Norristown, Pa.
800 m Run—James Robinson, Berkeley, Calif.
1500 m Run—Tom Byers, Eugene, Ore.
5000 m Run—Craig Virgin, Lebanon, Ill.
10,000 m Run—Greg Meyer, Holliston, Mass.
Marathon—Pete Pfitzinger, Ithaca, N.Y.
3000 m Steeplechase—Henry Marsh, Eugene, Ore.
20 km Walk—Todd Scully, Blacksburg, Va.
50 km Walk—Vince O'Sullivan, New York, N.Y.
110 m Hurdles—Renaldo Nehemiah, Scotch Plains, N.J.
400 m Hurdles—Andre Phillips, Los Angeles, Calif.
400 m Relay—West
1600 m Relay—East
High Jump—Greg Seay, Oklahoma City, Okla.
Long Jump—Larry Myricks, Clinton, Miss.
Triple Jump—David McFadgen, Petersburg, Va.
Pole Vault—Dave Volz, Bloomington, Ind.
Discus Throw—John Powell, Cupertino, Calif.
Hammer Throw—Dave McKenzie, Sacramento, Calif.
Javelin Throw—Bob Roggy, Eugene, Ore.
Shot Put—Brian Oldfield, Los Angeles, Calif.
Decathlon—Brian Mondschein, Huntington Beach, Calif.

TRACK AND FIELD—WOMEN

100 m Dash—Evelyn Ashford, Los Angeles, Calif.
200 m Dash—Florence Griffith, Los Angeles, Calif.
400 m Dash—Denean Howard, Granada Hills, Calif.
800 m Run—Madeline Manning-Mims, Clarksville, Tenn.
1500 m Run—Cindy Bremser, Madison, Wis.
3000 m Run—Kim Gallagher, Upper Dublin, Pa.
Marathon—Laura DeWald, Arlington, Va.
100 m Hurdles—Stephanie Hightower, Columbus, Ohio
400 m Hurdles—Edna Brown, Philadelphia, Pa.
400 m Relay—West
1600 m Relay—West
High Jump—Pam Spencer, Northridge, Calif.
Long Jump—Kathy McMillan-Ray, Los Angeles, Calif.
Discus Throw—Denise Wood, Montclair, N.J.
Javelin Throw—Patty Kearney, Eugene, Ore.
Shot Put—Denise Wood
Heptathlon—Cindy Greiner, Lebanon, Ore.

VOLLEYBALL

Men's Team—East
Women's Team—West

WATER POLO

Team—East

WEIGHTLIFTING

52 kg—Richard Stoner, Butler, Pa.
56 kg—Brian Miyamoto, Kaneohe, Hawaii
60 kg—Joe Widdel, Waterloo, Iowa
67.5 kg—Don Abrahamson, Winter Park, Fla.
75 kg—Mark Levell, Chicago, Ill.
82.5 kg—Curt White, Charleston, Ill.
90 kg—Kevin Winter, San Jose, Calif.
100 kg—Ken Clark, Pacifica, Calif.
110 kg—Guy Carlton, Colorado Springs, Colo.
Over 110 kg—Mario Martinez, Salinas, Calif.

WRESTLING

FREESTYLE

106 lb—Joe Gallardo, Corona, Calif.
115 lb—Matt Campbell, Havre, Mont.
123 lb—James Jordan, St. Paris, Ohio
132 lb—Marc Sprague, Portland, Ore.
143 lb—Scott Duncan, Marion, Ohio
154 lb—John DeHart, Chesterton, Ind.
165 lb—Howard Lawson, Placentia, Calif.
178 lb—Paul Diekel, Whitehall, N.J.
192 lb—Todd Wyckoff, New London, Ohio
Unlimited—Dave Koplovitz, Schenectady, N.Y.

GRECO-ROMAN

106 lb—Jeff Clark, Voorheesville, N.Y.
115 lb—Gil Sanchez, Cheyenne, Wyo.
123 lb—Kevin Allen, Clarendon, Vt.
132 lb—John Placek, Schenectady, N.Y.
143 lb—William Taylor, Portland, Ore.
154 lb—John Cardi, Ballston Spa, N.Y.
165 lb—Jacob Sabo, Granville, N.Y.
178 lb—Ab Brown, Casper, Wyo.
192 lb—Scott Sabo, Granville, N.Y.
Unlimited—Gary Albright, Billings, Mont.

YACHTING

Team—East

BASEBALL

MAJOR LEAGUE BASEBALL   Office of the Commissioner: 75 Rockefeller Plaza, New York City 10019

Prior to 1920, major league baseball was governed by a three-man commission. However, in that year, following the "Black Sox" scandal of the 1919 World Series, the office of baseball commissioner was created. The first commissioner was Kenesaw M. Landis (1921–44); he was succeeded by Albert B. Chandler (1945–51), Ford C. Frick (1951–65), William D. Eckert (1965–69), and the current commissioner, Bowie Kuhn (1969–).

NATIONAL LEAGUE: One Rockefeller Plaza, Suite 1602, New York City 10020. Organized in 1876.

Eastern Division	Chief Executive	Manager 1981	Western Division	Chief Executive	Manager 1981
Chicago Cubs	William Hagenah, Jr.	Joe Amalfitano	Atlanta Braves	Ted Turner	Bobby Cox
Montreal Expos	John McHale	Jim Fanning	Cincinnati Reds	Richard Wagner	John McNamara
New York Mets	Fred Wilpon	Joe Torre	Houston Astros	Albert Rosen	Bill Virdon
Philadelphia Phillies	R.R.M. Carpenter III	Dallas Green	Los Angeles Dodgers	Peter O'Malley	Tom Lasorda
Pittsburgh Pirates	Daniel Galbreath	Chuck Tanner	San Diego Padres	Ballard Smith	Frank Howard
St. Louis Cardinals	August Busch, Jr.	Whitey Herzog	San Francisco Giants	Robert Lurie	Frank Robinson

AMERICAN LEAGUE: 280 Park Avenue, New York City 10017. Founded in 1900.

Eastern Division	Chief Executive	Manager 1981	Western Division	Chief Executive	Manager 1981
Baltimore Orioles	Jerry Hoffberger	Earl Weaver	California Angels	Gene Autry	Gene Mauch
Boston Red Sox	Jean Yawkey	Ralph Houk	Chicago White Sox	Edward Einhorn	Tony LaRussa
Cleveland Indians	Gabe Paul	Dave Garcia	Kansas City Royals	Ewing Kauffman	Dick Howser
Detroit Tigers	John Fetzer	Sparky Anderson	Minnesota Twins	Calvin Griffith	Billy Gardner
Milwaukee Brewers	Allan Selig	Bob Rodgers	Oakland A's	Roy Eisenhardt	Billy Martin
New York Yankees	George Steinbrenner	Bob Lemon	Seattle Mariners	Daniel O'Brien	Rene Lachemann
Toronto Blue Jays	Peter Bavasi	Bobby Mattick	Texas Rangers	Eddie Chiles	Don Zimmer

MAJOR LEAGUE RECORDS: 1900–1981

BATTING

Highest Batting Average, Lifetime: .367, Ty Cobb (AL), 1905–1928; .358, Rogers Hornsby (NL), 1915–1937.

Highest Batting Average, Season: .424, Rogers Hornsby, St. Louis (NL), 1924; .420, George Sisler, St. Louis (AL), 1922.

Most Years Led League in Batting: 12, Ty Cobb, Detroit (AL), 1907–1915, 1917–1919; 8, Honus Wagner, Pittsburgh (NL), 1900, 1903–1904, 1906–1909, 1911.

Most Years Batting .300 or More: 23, Ty Cobb, Detroit and Philadelphia (AL), 1906–1928; 17, Honus Wagner, Louisville and Pittsburgh (NL), 1897–1913; 17, Stan Musial, St. Louis (NL), 1942–1944, 1946–1958, 1962.

Most Hits: 4,191, Ty Cobb (AL), 1905–1928; 3,697, Pete Rose (NL), 1963–1981.

Most Hits, Season: 257, George Sisler, St. Louis (AL), 1920; 254, Lefty O'Doul, Philadelphia (NL), 1929; 254, Bill Terry, New York (NL), 1930.

Most Consecutive Games Batted Safely: 56, Joe DiMaggio, New York (AL), 1941; 44, Pete Rose, Cincinnati (NL), 1978

Most Consecutive Games Played: 2,130, Lou Gehrig, New York (AL), 1925-39; 1,117, Billy Williams, Chicago (NL), 1963-70.

Most Runs: 2,244, Ty Cobb (AL), 1905–1928; 2,174, Babe Ruth, Boston (AL), New York (AL), Boston (NL), 1914–1935.

Most Runs, Season: 177, Babe Ruth, New York (AL), 1921; 158, Chuck Klein, Philadelphia (NL), 1930.

Most Consecutive Years 100 or More Runs: 13, Lou Gehrig, New York (AL), 1926–1938; 13, Hank Aaron, Milwaukee and Atlanta (NL), 1955–1967.

Most Runs Batted In, Lifetime: 2,297, Hank Aaron, 1954–1976; 2,204, Babe Ruth, 1914–1935.

Most Runs Batted In, Season: 190, Hack Wilson, Chicago (NL), 1930; 184, Lou Gehrig, New York (AL), 1931.

Highest Slugging Percentage, Lifetime: .690, Babe Ruth, Boston and New York (AL), Boston (NL); .634, Ted Williams, Boston (AL).

Most Home Runs, Lifetime: 755, Hank Aaron, Milwaukee and Atlanta (NL), Milwaukee (AL), 1954–1976; 714, Babe Ruth, Boston and New York (AL), Boston (NL).

Most Home Runs, Season: 61, Roger Maris, New York (AL), 1961, 162-game schedule; 60, Babe Ruth, New York (AL), 1927, 154-game schedule.

Most Years League Home-Run Leader: 12, Babe Ruth (AL), 1918–1919, 1920–1921, 1923–1924, 1926–1931; 7, Ralph Kiner, Pittsburgh (NL), 1946–1952.

Most Years 20 or More Home Runs: 19, Henry Aaron (NL); 17, Willie Mays (NL); 16, Babe Ruth (AL).

Most Grand Slam Home Runs, Lifetime: 23, Lou Gehrig, New York (AL); 18, Willie McCovey, San Francisco, San Diego (NL).

Most Grand Slam Home Runs, Season: 5, Ernie Banks, Chicago (NL), 1955; 5, Jim Gentile, Baltimore (AL), 1961.

Most Bases on Balls, Season: 170, Babe Ruth, New York (AL), 1923; 162, Ted Williams, Boston (AL), 1947, 1949.

Fewest Strikeouts, Lifetime (7,000 or More At Bats): 114, Joe Sewell (AL); 173, Lloyd Waner (NL).

Most Consecutive Games without Strikeouts: 98, Nelson Fox, Chicago (AL), 1958; 77, Lloyd Waner (NL), 1941.

Most Pinch Hits, Lifetime: 150, Manny Mota (NL).

Most Stolen Bases, Lifetime: 938, Lou Brock (NL); 892, Ty Cobb (AL).

Most Stolen Bases, Season: 118, Lou Brock, St. Louis (NL), 1974, 162-game schedule; 96, Ty Cobb, Detroit (AL), 1915, 154-game schedule.

PITCHING

Most Games Won, Lifetime: 511, Cy Young (NL–AL); 416, Walter Johnson (AL).

Most Games Won, Season: 41, Jack Chesbro, New York (AL), 1904; 39, Ed Walsh, Chicago (AL), 1908.

Most Years 20-or-More-Game Winner: 16, Cy Young (NL–AL), 1891–1904, 1907–1908; 13, Christy Mathewson (NL), 1901, 1903–1914; 13, Warren Spahn (NL), 1947, 1949–1951, 1953–1954, 1956–1961, 1963; 12, Walter Johnson (AL), 1910–1919, 1924–1925.

Most Consecutive Games Won, Lifetime: 24, Carl Hubbell, New York (NL), 16 in 1936, 8 in 1937; 17, John Allen, Cleveland (AL), 2 in 1936, 15 in 1937; 17, Dave McNally, Baltimore (AL), 2 in 1968, 15 in 1969.

Most Consecutive Games Won, Season: 19, Rube Marquard, New York (NL), 1912; 17, ElRoy Face, Pittsburgh (NL), 1959.

Most Shutout Games, Lifetime: 113, Walter Johnson (AL); 90, Grover Alexander (NL).

Most Shutout Games, Season: 16, Grover Alexander, Philadelphia (NL), 1916; 13, Jack Coombs, Philadelphia (AL), 1910; 13, Bob Gibson, St. Louis, 1968.

Most Consecutive Shutout Games, Season: 6, Don Drysdale, Los Angeles (NL), 1968; 5, Harris White, Chicago (AL), 1904.

Most Consecutive Shutout Innings, Season: 58, Don Drysdale, Los Angeles (NL), 1968; 56, Walter Johnson, Washington (AL), 1913; 46½, Carl Hubbell, New York (NL), 1933.

Lowest Earned Run Average, Season: 1.01, Hubert Leonard, Boston (AL), 1914; 1.04, Three Finger Brown, Chicago (NL), 1906.

Most Consecutive Years Lowest Earned Run Average: 5, Sandy Koufax, Los Angeles (NL), 1962–1966; 4, Lefty Grove, Philadelphia (AL), 1929–1932.

Highest Won-Lost Percentage, Lifetime (100 or More Decisions): .690, Whitey Ford, New York (AL), 1950–1967.

Highest Won-Lost Percentage, Season (15 or More Decisions): .947, ElRoy Face, Pittsburgh (NL), 1959.

Most Strikeouts, Lifetime: 3,508, Walter Johnson (AL); 3,117 Bob Gibson, St. Louis (NL).

Most Strikeouts, Season: 383, Nolan Ryan, California (AL), 1973; 382, Sandy Koufax, Los Angeles (NL), 1965.

Most Strikeouts in 9-Inning Game: 19, Steve Carlton, St. Louis (NL), 1969; 19, Tom Seaver, New York (NL), 1970; 19, Nolan Ryan, California (AL), 1974, 1977.

Most Games Won, Relief Pitcher, Lifetime: 123, Hoyt Wilhelm (NL-AL), 1952-70; 114, Lindy McDaniel (NL-AL), 1955-73.

MAJOR LEAGUE BASEBALL ALL-TIME LEADERS[1]

BATTING

SEASONS		GAMES		BATTING AVERAGE		AT BATS	
James McGuire	26	Hank Aaron	3,298	Ty Cobb	.367	Hank Aaron	12,364
Eddie Collins	25	Carl Yastrzemski	3,058	Rogers Hornsby	.358	Pete Rose	11,910
Bobby Wallace	25	Ty Cobb	3,033	Joe Jackson	.356	Ty Cobb	11,429
Ty Cobb	24	Stan Musial	3,026	Ed Delahanty	.346	Carl Yastrzemski	11,149
Hank Aaron	23	Willie Mays	2,992	Willie Keeler	.345	Stan Musial	10,972
Brooks Robinson	23	Pete Rose	2,937	Ted Williams	.344	Willie Mays	10,881
Rabbit Maranville	23	Brooks Robinson	2,896	Tris Speaker	.344	Brooks Robinson	10,654
Rogers Hornsby	23	Al Kaline	2,834	Billy Hamilton	.344	Honus Wagner	10,427
Stan Musial	22	Eddie Collins	2,826	Dan Brouthers	.342	Lou Brock	10,332
Tris Speaker, Mel Ott	22	Frank Robinson	2,808	Babe Ruth	.342	Luis Aparicio	10,230
Babe Ruth	22	Tris Speaker	2,789	Harry Heilmann	.342	Tris Speaker	10,208
Bill Dahlen	22	Honus Wagner	2,785	Pete Browning	.341	Al Kaline	10,116
Jimmie Dykes	22	Mel Ott	2,730	Bill Terry	.341	Rabbit Maranville	10,078
Cap Anson	22	Rabbit Maranville	2,670	George Sisler	.340	Frank Robinson	10,006
Phil Cavarretta	22	Lou Brock	2,616	Lou Gehrig	.340	Eddie Collins	9,949
Harry Davis	22	Rusty Staub	2,603	Jesse Burkett	.340	Vada Pinson	9,645
Willie Mays, Al Kaline	22	Luis Aparicio	2,599	Nap Lajoie	339	Nap Lajoie	9,589
Harmon Killebrew	22	Willie McCovey	2,588			Sam Crawford	9,579
Willie McCovey	22	Paul Waner	2,549			Jake Beckley	9,476

RUNS		HITS		DOUBLES		TRIPLES	
Ty Cobb	2,244	Ty Cobb	4,191	Tris Speaker	793	Sam Crawford	312
Babe Ruth	2,174	Hank Aaron	3,771	Stan Musial	725	Ty Cobb	297
Hank Aaron	2,174	Pete Rose	3,697	Ty Cobb	724	Honus Wagner	252
Willie Mays	2,062	Stan Musial	3,630	Pete Rose	672	Jake Beckley	246
Stan Musial	1,949	Tris Speaker	3,515	Honus Wagner	651	Roger Connor	227
Pete Rose	1,913	Honus Wagner	3,430	Nap Lajoie	650	Tris Speaker	224
Lou Gehrig	1,888	Eddie Collins	3,311	Hank Aaron	624	Fred Clarke	219
Tris Speaker	1,881	Willie Mays	3,283	Paul Waner	603	Dan Brouthers	212
Mel Ott	1,859	Nap Lajoie	3,251	Carl Yastrzemski	600	Paul Waner	190
Frank Robinson	1,829	Carl Yastrzemski	3,192	Charlie Gehringer	574	Joe Kelley	189
Eddie Collins	1,818	Paul Waner	3,152	Harry Heilmann	542	Bid McPhee	189
Ted Williams	1,798	Cap Anson	3,081	Rogers Hornsby	541	Eddie Collins	186

HOME RUNS		TOTAL BASES		EXTRA BASE HITS		BASES ON BALLS	
Hank Aaron	755	Hank Aaron	6,838	Hank Aaron	1,477	Babe Ruth	2,056
Babe Ruth	714	Stan Musial	6,134	Stan Musial	1,377	Ted Williams	2,018
Willie Mays	660	Willie Mays	6,066	Babe Ruth	1,356	Mickey Mantle	1,734
Frank Robinson	586	Ty Cobb	5,863	Willie Mays	1,323	Mel Ott	1,708
Harmon Killebrew	573	Babe Ruth	5,793	Lou Gehrig	1,190	Carl Yastrzemski	1,683
Mickey Mantle	536	Frank Robinson	5,373	Frank Robinson	1,186	Eddie Yost	1,614
Jimmie Foxx	534	Carl Yastrzemski	5,186	Ty Cobb	1,139	Stan Musial	1,599
Ted Willams	521	Tris Speaker	5,101	Tris Speaker	1,132	Harmon Killebrew	1,559
Willie McCovey	521	Pete Rose	5,078	Jimmie Foxx	1,117	Joe Morgan	1,559
Eddie Mathews	512	Lou Gehrig	5,059	Ted Williams	1,117	Lou Gehrig	1,508
Ernie Banks	512	Mel Ott	5,041	Carl Yastrzemski	1,084	Eddie Collins	1,503
Mel Ott	511	Jimmie Foxx	4,956	Mel Ott	1,071	Willie Mays	1,464
Lou Gehrig	493						
Stan Musial	475						
Willie Stargell	472	STOLEN BASES		RUNS BATTED IN		STRIKEOUTS	
Billy Williams	426	Lou Brock	938	Hank Aaron	2,297	Willie Stargell	1,903
Carl Yastrzemski	426	Ty Cobb	892	Babe Ruth	2,204	Lou Brock	1,730
Reggie Jackson	425	Eddie Collins	743	Lou Gehrig	1,990	Reggie Jackson	1,728
Duke Snider	407	Max Carey	738	Ty Cobb	1,954	Bobby Bonds	1,714
Al Kaline	399	Bert Campaneris	733	Stan Musial	1,951	Mickey Mantle	1,710
Frank Howard	382	Honus Wagner	720	Jimmie Foxx	1,921	Harmon Killebrew	1,699
Orlando Cepeda	379	Joe Morgan	625	Willie Mays	1,903	Dick Allen	1,556
Norm Cash	377	Maury Wills	586	Mel Ott	1,860	Willie McCovey	1,550
Rocky Colavito	374	Luis Aparicio	506	Ted Williams	1,839	Frank Robinson	1,532
Gil Hodges	370	Clyde Milan	494	Al Simmons	1,827	Willie Mays	1,526
Ralph Kiner	369	Cesar Cedeno	487	Frank Robinson	1,812	Eddie Mathews	1,487
		Jimmy Sheckard	460	Honus Wagner	1,732	Frank Howard	1,460

PITCHING

SEASONS		WINS		COMPLETE GAMES		INNINGS PITCHED	
Early Wynn	23	Cy Young	511	Cy Young	751	Cy Young	7,377
Jack Quinn	23	Walter Johnson	416	Pud Galvin	639	Pud Galvin	5,959
Cy Young	22	Christy Mathewson	373	Tim Keefe	554	Walter Johnson	5,924
Sad Sam Jones	22	Grover Alexander	373	Walter Johnson	531	Warren Spahn	5,246
Red Ruffing	22	Warren Spahn	363	Kid Nichols	531	Grover Alexander	5,189
Herb Pennock, Jim Kaat	22	Pud Galvin	361	Mickey Welch	525	Kid Nichols	5,067
Hoyt Wilhelm	21	Kid Nichols	360	John Clarkson	488	Tim Keefe	5,043
Walter Johnson	21	Tim Keefe	343	Old Hoss Radbourn	479	Gaylord Perry	4,949
Warren Spahn	21	John Clarkson	327	Tony Mullane	464	Christy Mathewson	4,781
Eppa Rixey	21	Eddie Plank	327	Jim McCormick	462	Mickey Welch	4,784
Waite Hoyt	21	Mickey Welch	311	Gus Weyhing	448	Robin Roberts	4,689
Ted Lyons	21						

SHUTOUTS		STRIKEOUTS		BASES ON BALLS		EARNED RUN AVERAGE	
Walter Johnson	113	Walter Johnson	3,508	Nolan Ryan	1,812	Ed Walsh	1.82
Grover Alexander	90	Gaylord Perry	3,336	Early Wynn	1,775	Addie Joss	1.88
Christy Mathewson	83	Nolan Ryan	3,249	Bob Feller	1,764	Three Finger Brown	2.06
Cy Young	77	Steve Carlton	3,148	Bobo Newsom	1,732	Monte Ward	2.10
Eddie Plank	64	Bob Gibson	3,117	Amos Rusie	1,637	Christy Mathewson	2.13
Warren Spahn	63	Tom Seaver	3,075	Gus Weyhing	1,569	Rube Waddell	2.16
Ed Walsh	58	Ferguson Jenkins	2,962	Red Ruffing	1,541	Walter Johnson	2.17
Three Finger Brown	58	Jim Bunning	2,855	Bump Hadley	1,442	Orval Overall	2.24
Pud Galvin	57	Cy Young	2,819	Warren Spahn	1,434	Tommy Bond	2.25

[1]At start of 1982 season.

HALL OF FAME

ELECTED FOR MERITORIOUS SERVICE

Barrow, Edward, manager and executive
Bulkeley, Morgan G., first National League president
Cartwright, Alexander J., formulated first baseball rules
Chadwick, Henry, first reporter and keeper of records
Comiskey, Charles A., player, manager, and executive
Conlan, Jocko, National League umpire
Connolly, Thomas, American League umpire
Cummings, William A., early pitcher, said to have invented the curve ball
Evans, William, American League Umpire
Frick, Ford C., National League president and commissioner
Giles, Warren G., general manager and National League pres.
Griffith, Clark C., player, manager, and executive
Harridge, William, American League president
Harris, Stanley (Bucky), player, manager, executive
Hubbard, Robert C. (Cal), American League umpire
Huggins, Miller J., manager
Johnson, Byron Bancroft, first American League president
Klem, William, National League umpire
Landis, Kenesaw M., first commissioner of baseball
Lopez, Alfonso R., manager
Mack, Connie, manager and executive
Mac Phail, Larry, executive
McCarthy, Joseph, manager
McGraw, John J., player and manager
McKechnie, William B., manager
Rickey, W. Branch, manager and executive
Robinson, Wilbert, player and manager
Spalding, Albert G., early pitcher and organizer of the National League
Stengel, Charles D., player and manager
Weiss, George, general manager
Wright, George, early player
Wright, Harry, early player and manager
Yawkey, Tom, executive

PITCHERS

	Years	Won	Lost
Alexander, Grover Cleveland	1911–1930	373	208
Bender, Charles (Chief)	1903–1925	212	128
Brown, Mordecai (Three-Finger)	1903–1916	239	130
Chesbro, John	1899–1909	199	128
Clarkson, John	1882–1894	328	175
Coveleski, Stanley	1912–1928	215	141
Dean, Jerome (Dizzy)	1930–1947	150	83
Faber, Urban (Red)	1914–1933	254	212
Feller, Robert	1936–1956	266	162
Ford, Edward (Whitey)	1950–1967	236	106
Galvin, James (Pud)	1879–1892	361	309
Gibson, Robert	1959–1975	251	174
Gomez, Vernon (Lefty)	1930–1943	189	102
Grimes, Burleigh	1916–1934	270	212
Grove, Robert (Lefty)	1925–1941	300	141
Haines, Jesse	1918–1937	210	158
Hoyt, Waite	1918–1938	237	182
Hubbell, Carl	1928–1943	253	154
Johnson, Walter (Big Train)	1907–1927	416	279
Joss, Adrian (Addie)	1902–1910	160	97
Keefe, Timothy	1880–1893	346	225
Koufax, Sanford	1955–1966	165	87
Lemon, Robert	1941–1958	207	128
Lyons, Theodore	1923–1946	260	230
Marquard, Richard (Rube)	1908–1925	201	177
Mathewson, Christopher	1900–1916	373	188
McGinnity, Joseph (Iron Man)	1899–1908	247	142
Nichols, Charles (Kid)	1890–1906	360	202
Pennock, Herbert	1912–1934	240	162
Plank, Edward	1901–1917	325	190
Radbourne, Charles (Old Hoss)	1880–1891	308	191
Rixey, Eppa	1912–1933	266	251
Roberts, Robin	1948–1966	286	245
Ruffing, Charles (Red)	1924–1947	273	225
Rusie, Amos	1889–1901	246	174
Spahn, Warren	1942–1965	363	245
Vance, Arthur (Dazzy)	1915–1935	197	140
Waddell, George (Rube)	1897–1910	193	140
Walsh, Edward (Big Ed)	1904–1917	195	126
Welch, Mickey	1880–1892	308	209
Wynn, Early	1939–1963	300	244
Young, Denton (Cy)	1890–1911	511	315

ELECTED FROM NEGRO LEAGUES

Bell, James (Cool Page)
Charleston, Oscar
Dihigo, Martin
Foster, Andrew (Rube)
Gibson, Joshua
Irvin, Monte
Johnson, William (Judy)
Leonard, Walter (Buck)
Lloyd, John Henry (Pop)
Paige, Leroy (Satchel)

BATTERS

	Years	Average
Anson, Adrian (Cap)	1876–1897	.339
Appling, Lucius B. (Luke)	1930–1950	.310
Averill, H. Earl	1929–1941	.318
Baker, J. Frank (Home Run)	1908–1922	.307
Bancroft, Dave	1915–1930	.279
Banks, Ernest	1953–1971	.274
Beckley, Jake	1888–1907	.309
Berra, Lawrence (Yogi)	1946–1965	.285
Bottomley, James	1922–1937	.310
Boudreau, Louis	1938–1952	.295
Bresnahan, Roger	1897–1915	.279
Brouthers, Dennis (Dan)	1879–1904	.349
Burkett, Jesse	1890–1905	.342
Campanella, Roy	1948–1957	.276
Carey, Max	1910–1929	.285
Chance, Frank	1898–1914	.297
Clarke, Fred	1894–1915	.315
Clemente, Roberto	1955–1972	.317
Cobb, Tyrus	1905–1928	.367
Cochrane, Gordon (Mickey)	1925–1937	.320
Collins, Edward	1906–1930	.333
Collins, James	1895–1908	.294
Combs, Earle	1924–1935	.325
Connor, Roger	1880–1897	.325
Crawford, Samuel (Wahoo)	1899–1917	.309
Cronin, Joseph	1926–1945	.302
Cuyler, Hazen (Kiki)	1921–1938	.321
Delahanty, Edward	1888–1903	.346
Dickey, William	1928–1946	.313
DiMaggio, Joseph	1936–1951	.325
Duffy, Hugh	1888–1906	.330
Evers, John	1902–1929	.270
Ewing, William (Buck)	1880–1897	.311
Flick, Elmer	1898–1910	.315
Foxx, James	1925–1945	.325
Frisch, Frank	1919–1937	.316
Gehrig, Henry (Lou)	1923–1939	.340
Gehringer, Charles	1924–1942	.320
Goslin, Leon (Goose)	1921–1938	.316
Greenberg, Henry	1930–1947	.313
Hafey, Charles (Chick)	1924–1937	.317
Hamilton, William	1888–1901	.344
Hartnett, Charles (Gabby)	1922–1941	.297
Heilmann, Harry	1914–1932	.342
Herman, William	1931–1947	.304
Hooper, Harry	1909–1925	.281
Hornsby, Rogers (Rajah)	1915–1937	.358
Jennings, Hugh	1891–1918	.314
Kaline, Al	1953–1974	.297
Keeler, William (Wee Willie)	1892–1910	.345
Kelley, Joe	1891–1908	.321
Kelly, George	1915–1932	.297
Kelly, Michael (King)	1878–1893	.313
Kiner, Ralph	1946–1955	.279
Klein, Charles (Chuck)	1928–1944	.320
Lajoie, Napoleon	1896–1916	.339
Lindstrom, Fred	1924–1939	.311
McCarthy, Thomas	1884–1896	.294
Manush, Henry (Heinie)	1923–1939	.330
Mantle, Mickey	1951–1968	.298
Maranville, Walter (Rabbit)	1912–1935	.258
Mathews, Eddie	1952–1968	.271
Mays, Willie	1951–1973	.302
Medwick, Joseph (Ducky)	1932–1948	.324
Mize, Johnny	1936–1953	.312
Musial, Stan	1941–1963	.331
O'Rourke, James	1876–1904	.314
Ott, Melvin	1926–1947	.304
Rice, Edgar (Sam)	1915–1934	.322
Robinson, Jack	1947–1956	.311
Roush, Edd	1913–1931	.323
Ruth, George (Babe)	1914–1935	.342
Schalk, Raymond	1912–1929	.253
Sewell, Joseph	1920–1933	.312
Simmons, Al	1924–1944	.334
Sisler, George	1915–1930	.340
Snider, Edwin (Duke)	1947–1964	.295
Speaker, Tris	1907–1928	.344
Terry, William	1923–1936	.341
Thompson, Samuel L.	1885–1906	.336
Tinker, Joseph	1902–1916	.264
Traynor, Harold (Pie)	1920–1937	.320
Wagner, John (Honus)	1897–1917	.329
Wallace, Roderick (Bobby)	1894–1918	.267
Waner, Lloyd (Little Poison)	1927–1945	.316
Waner, Paul (Big Poison)	1926–1945	.333
Ward, John Montgomery	1878–1894	.283
Wheat, Zachary	1909–1927	.317
Williams, Theodore	1939–1960	.344
Wilson, Hack	1923–1934	.307
Youngs, Ross (Pep)	1917–1926	.322

1981 MAJOR LEAGUE
COMBINED STANDINGS

1—FIRST HALF WINNER; 2—SECOND HALF WINNER

NATIONAL LEAGUE

Eastern Division	W	L	Pct.	GB
St. Louis	59	43	.578	—
2—Montreal	60	48	.556	2
1—Philadelphia	59	48	.551	2½
Pittsburgh	46	56	.451	13
New York	41	62	.398	18½
Chicago	38	65	.369	21½

Western Division	W	L	Pct.	GB
Cincinnati	66	42	.611	—
1—Los Angeles	63	47	.573	4
2—Houston	61	49	.555	6
San Francisco	56	55	.505	11½
Atlanta	50	56	.472	15
San Diego	41	69	.373	26

AMERICAN LEAGUE

Eastern Division	W	L	Pct.	GB
2—Milwaukee	62	47	.569	—
Baltimore	59	46	.562	1
1—New York	59	48	.551	2
Detroit	60	49	.550	2
Boston	59	49	.546	2½
Cleveland	52	51	.505	7
Toronto	37	69	.349	23½

Western Division	W	L	Pct.	GB
1—Oakland	64	45	.587	—
Texas	57	48	.543	5
Chicago	54	52	.509	8½
2—Kansas City	50	53	.485	11
California	51	59	.464	13½
Seattle	44	65	.404	20
Minnesota	41	68	.376	23

1981 ALL-STAR GAME   Cleveland, August 9

NATIONAL LEAGUE

	ab	r	h	bi
Rose, 1b	3	0	1	0
Hooton, p	0	0	0	0
Ruthven, p	0	0	0	0
Guerrero, ph	1	0	0	0
Blue, p	0	0	0	0
Madlock, 3b	3	0	0	0
Concepcion, ss	3	0	0	0
Smith, ss	0	0	0	0
Parker, rf	3	1	1	1
Easler, rf	1	1	0	0
Schmidt, 3b	4	1	2	2
Ryan, p	0	0	0	0
Garner, 2b	0	0	0	0
Foster, lf	2	0	0	0
Baker, lf	2	0	1	0
Raines, lf	0	0	0	0
Dawson, cf	4	0	1	0
Carter, c	3	2	2	2
Benedict, c	1	0	0	0
Lopes, 2b	0	0	0	0
Trillo, 2b	2	0	0	0
Buckner, ph	1	0	0	0
Sutter, p	0	0	0	0
Valenzuela, p	0	0	0	0
Youngblood, ph	1	0	0	0
Seaver, p	0	0	0	0
Knepper, p	0	0	0	0
Kennedy, ph	1	0	0	0
Garvey, 1b	2	0	1	0
Total	35	5	9	5

AMERICAN LEAGUE

	ab	r	h	bi
Carew, 1b	3	0	1	0
Murray, 1b	2	0	0	0
Randolph, 2b	3	0	1	0
Simmons, ph	1	0	1	1
White, 2b	1	0	0	0
Brett, 3b	3	0	0	0
Norris, p	0	0	0	0
Oliver, ph	1	0	0	0
Davis, p	0	0	0	0
Fingers, p	0	0	0	0
Stieb, p	1	0	0	0
Winfield, cf	4	0	0	0
Singleton, lf	3	2	2	1
Burleson, ss	1	0	0	0
Jackson, rf	1	0	0	0
Evans, rf	2	1	1	0
Fisk, c	3	1	1	0
Diaz, c	1	0	0	0
Dent, ss	2	0	2	0
Lynn, ph	1	0	1	1
Armas, lf	1	0	0	0
Morris, p	0	0	0	0
Paciorek, ph	1	0	1	0
Barker, p	0	0	0	0
Thomas, ph	1	0	0	0
Forsch, p	0	0	0	0
Bell, 3b	1	0	0	1
Total	37	4	11	4

National League ..... 0 0 0 0 1 1 1 2 0 — 5
American League ..... 0 1 0 0 0 3 0 0 0 — 4

E—Schmidt, Fingers. LOB—National 7, American 9. 2B—Dent, Schmidt, Garvey. HR—Singleton, Carter 2, Parker, Schmidt. SB—Dawson, Smith. SF—Bell.

	IP	H	R	ER	BB	SO
National—Valenzuela	1	2	0	0	0	0
Seaver	1	3	1	1	0	1
Knepper	2	1	0	0	2	3
Hooton	1⅔	5	3	3	0	1
Ruthven	⅓	0	0	0	0	0
Blue (W)	1	0	1	1	0	1
Ryan	1	0	0	0	0	1
Sutter (S)	1	0	0	0	0	1

	IP	H	R	ER	BB	SO
American—Morris	2	2	0	0	1	2
Barker	2	0	0	0	0	1
Forsch	1	1	1	1	0	0
Norris	1	2	1	1	0	1
Davis	1	1	1	1	0	1
Fingers (L)	⅓	2	2	2	2	0
Stieb	1⅔	1	0	0	1	1

WP—Blue. Time—2:59. Attendance—72,086.

1981 PLAYOFF RESULTS

NATIONAL LEAGUE

Eastern Division—Montreal defeated Philadelphia, 3-1, 3-1, 2-6, 5-6, 3-0
Western Division—Los Angeles defeated Houston, 1-3, 0-1, 6-1, 2-1, 4-0
League Championship—Los Angeles defeated Montreal, 5-1, 0-3, 1-4, 7-1, 2-1

AMERICAN LEAGUE

Eastern Division—New York defeated Milwaukee, 5-3, 3-0, 3-5, 1-7, 7-3
Western Division—Oakland defeated Kansas City, 4-0, 2-1, 4-1
League Championship—New York defeated Oakland, 3-1, 13-3, 4-0

1981 WORLD SERIES BOX SCORES

FIRST GAME: Yankee Stadium, October 20

LOS ANGELES (NL)

	ab	r	h	bi
Lopes, 2b	3	1	0	0
Russell, ss	3	0	0	0
Johnstone, ph	1	0	1	1
Stewart, p	0	0	0	0
Baker, lf	2	0	1	1
Garvey, 1b	4	0	1	0
Cey, 3b	4	0	1	0
Guerrero, rf	3	0	0	0
Monday, rf	4	0	0	0
Yeager, c	3	1	1	1
Landreaux, ph	1	0	0	0
Reuss, p	1	0	0	0
Castillo, p	0	0	0	0
Goltz, p	0	0	0	0
Sax, ph	1	0	0	0
Niedenfuer, p	0	0	0	0
Thomas, ss	0	1	0	0
Total	30	3	5	3

NEW YORK (AL)

	ab	r	h	bi
Randolph, 2b	3	0	0	0
Mumphrey, cf	3	2	2	0
Winfield, lf	3	0	0	1
Piniella, rf	4	1	2	1
Watson, 1b	3	1	2	3
Nettles, 3b	3	0	0	0
Cerone, c	3	0	0	0
Milbourne, ss	4	1	0	0
Guidry, p	2	0	0	0
Davis, p	0	0	0	0
Gossage, p	0	0	0	0
Total	28	5	6	5

Los Angeles .... 0 0 0 1 0 0 2 0 — 3
New York .... 3 0 1 1 0 0 0 x — 5
DP—Los Angeles 1. LOB—Los Angeles 5, New York 6. 2B—Piniella. HR—Watson, Yeager. SB—Mumphrey, Piniella. S—Guidry. SF—Baker.

	IP	H	R	ER	BB	SO
Los Angeles—Reuss (L, 0-1)	2⅔	5	4	4	0	2
Castillo	1	0	1	1	5	0
Goltz	⅓	0	0	0	0	0
Niedenfuer	3	1	0	0	0	0
Stewart	1	0	0	0	1	0
New York—Guidry (W, 1-0)	7	4	1	1	2	6
Davis	0*	0	2	2	2	0
Gossage (S, 1)	2	1	0	0	0	2

* Pitched to two batters in the eighth.
PB—Cerone. Time—2:32. Attendance—56,470.

SECOND GAME: Yankee Stadium, October 21

LOS ANGELES (NL)

	ab	r	h	bi
Lopes, 2b	3	0	0	0
Monday, ph	1	0	0	0
Howe, p	0	0	0	0
Stewart, p	0	0	0	0
Russell, ss	4	0	1	0
Baker, lf	4	0	0	0
Garvey, 1b	3	0	2	0
Cey, 3b	4	0	0	0
Guerrero, rf	4	0	0	0
Landreaux, cf	3	0	0	0
Yeager, c	2	0	0	0
Johnstone, ph	1	0	0	0
Scioscia, c	0	0	0	0
Hooton, p	2	0	0	0
Forster, p	0	0	0	0
Smith, ph	1	0	1	0
Sax, 2b	0	0	0	0
Total	32	0	4	0

NEW YORK (AL)

	ab	r	h	bi
Mumphrey, cf	2	0	0	0
Milbourne, ss	4	0	1	1
Winfield, lf	4	0	0	0
Gamble, rf	2	0	0	0
Piniella, ph	1	0	1	0
Brown, rf	0	1	0	0
Nettles, 3b	4	1	2	0
Watson, 1b	4	0	2	1
Cerone, c	2	0	0	0
Randolph, 2b	2	1	0	1
John, p	1	0	0	0
Murcer, ph	0	0	0	0
Gossage, p	1	0	0	0
Total	27	3	6	3

```
Los Angeles ........... 0 0 0 0 0 0 0 0 0—0
New York ............. 0 0 0 0 1 0 0 2 x—3
```

E—Milbourne, Lopes, Stewart. DP—Los Angeles 1. LOB—Los Angeles 6, New York 9. 2B—Milbourne. S—John, Murcer. SF—Randolph

	IP	H	R	ER	BB	SO
Los Angeles—Hooton (L, 0-1)	6*	3	1	0	4	1
Forster	1	0	0	0	1	0
Howe	1/3	2	2	2	0	0
Stewart	2/3	1	0	0	1	1
New York—John (W, 1-0)	7	3	0	0	0	4
Gossage (S, 2)	2	1	0	0	1	3

* Pitched to two batters in the seventh.
Time—2:29. Attendance—56,505.

THIRD GAME: Dodger Stadium, October 23

NEW YORK (AL)	ab	r	h	bi
Randolph, 2b	2	0	0	0
Mumphrey, cf	5	0	0	0
Winfield, lf	3	0	0	0
Piniella, rf	5	1	1	0
Watson, 1b	4	1	2	1
Cerone, c	4	2	2	2
Rodriguez, 3b	4	0	2	0
Milbourne, ss	2	0	2	1
Righetti, p	1	0	0	0
Frazier, p	1	0	0	0
May, p	0	0	0	0
Murcer, ph	1	0	0	0
Davis, p	0	0	0	0
Total	32	4	9	3

LOS ANGELES (NL)	ab	r	h	bi
Lopes, 2b	4	1	2	0
Russell, ss	5	1	2	0
Baker, lf	4	0	0	0
Garvey, 1b	4	1	2	0
Cey, 3b	2	2	2	3
Guerrero, rf	3	0	1	1
Monday, rf	2	0	1	0
Thomas, rf	1	0	0	0
Yeager, c	1	0	0	0
Scioscia, c	3	0	1	0
Valenzuela, p	3	0	0	0
Total	32	5	11	4

```
New York ........... 0 2 2 0 0 0 0 0 0—4
Los Angeles ........ 3 0 0 0 2 0 0 x—5
```

E—Lopes. DP—New York 2, Los Angeles 3. LOB—New York 9, Los Angeles 9. 2B—Lopes, Cerone, Watson, Guerrero. HR—Cey, Watson, Cerone. S—Righetti, Lopes.

	IP	H	R	ER	BB	SO
New York—Righetti	2*	5	3	3	2	1
Frazier (L, 0-1)	2**	3	2	2	2	1
May	3	2	0	0	0	2
Davis	1	1	0	0	0	1
Los Angeles—Valenzuela	9	9	4	4	7	6

* Pitched to two batters in the third. ** Pitched to four batters in the fifth.
HBP—Guerrero (by Righetti). Time—3:04. Attendance—56,236.

FOURTH GAME: Dodger Stadium, October 24

NEW YORK (AL)	ab	r	h	bi
Randolph, 2b	5	3	2	1
Milbourne, ss	4	1	1	1
Winfield, cf	4	0	0	0
Jackson, rf	3	2	3	1
Gamble, lf	4	1	2	1
Brown, cf	0	0	0	0
Piniella, lf	1	0	0	0
Watson, 1b	3	0	1	2
Cerone, c	5	0	2	1
Robertson, pr	0	0	0	0
Rodriguez, 3b	4	0	2	0
Foote, c	1	0	0	0
Reuschel, p	2	0	0	0
May, p	1	0	0	0
Davis, p	0	0	0	0
Frazier, p	1	0	0	0
John, p	0	0	0	0
Murcer, ph	1	0	0	0
Total	39	7	13	7

LOS ANGELES (NL)	ab	r	h	bi
Lopes, 2b	5	2	2	2
Russell, ss	5	0	1	1
Garvey, 1b	5	1	3	0
Cey, 3b	5	0	2	2
Baker, lf	5	1	1	0
Monday, rf	3	1	1	0
Thomas, cf	1	0	0	0
Guerrero, rf	3	0	2	0
Scioscia, c	1	1	0	0
Yeager, c	0	0	0	1
Welch, p	0	0	0	0
Goltz, p	0	0	0	0
Landreaux, ph	1	1	1	0
Forster, p	0	0	0	0
Smith, ph	1	0	0	0
Niedenfuer, p	0	0	0	0
Johnstone, ph	1	1	1	2
Howe, p	0	0	0	0
Total	36	8	14	8

```
New York ............. 2 1 1 0 0 2 0 1 0—7
Los Angeles .......... 0 0 2 0 1 3 2 0 x—8
```

E—Russell, Jackson, Howe. LOB—New York 12, Los Angeles 10. 2B—Milbourne, Landreaux, Garvey, Monday. 3B—Randolph. HR—Randolph, Johnstone, Jackson. SB—Winfield, Lopes 2. S—Milbourne, Scioscia, Howe. SF—Watson, Yeager.

	IP	H	R	ER	BB	SO
New York—Reuschel	3	6	2	2	1	2
May	1 1/3	2	1	1	0	1
Davis	1	2	3	2	1	2
Frazier (L, 0-2)	2/3	2	2	2	1	0
John	2	2	0	0	0	2
Los Angeles—Welch	0*	3	2	2	1	0
Goltz	3	4	2	2	1	2
Forster	1	1	0	0	2	0
Niedenfuer	2	2	2	0	1	0
Howe (W, 1-0)	3	3	1	1	0	1

* Pitched to four batters in the first.
Time—3:32. Attendance—56,242.

FIFTH GAME: Dodger Stadium, October 25

NEW YORK (AL)	ab	r	h	bi
Randolph, 2b	3	0	0	0
Milbourne, ss	4	0	1	0
Winfield, cf	4	0	1	0
Jackson, rf	4	1	1	0
Gossage, p	0	0	0	0
Watson, 1b	3	0	0	0
Piniella, lf	4	0	2	1
Brown, pr	0	0	0	0
Cerone, c	4	0	0	0
Rodriguez, 3b	3	0	0	0
Guidry, p	3	0	0	0
Mumphrey, cf	0	0	0	0
Total	32	1	5	1

LOS ANGELES (NL)	ab	r	h	bi
Lopes, 2b	3	0	0	0
Russell, ss	4	0	0	0
Garvey, 1b	4	0	0	0
Cey, 3b	2	0	0	0
Landreaux, cf	0	0	0	0
Baker, lf	4	0	0	0
Guerrero, rf	3	1	1	1
Yeager, c	3	1	2	1
Thomas, cf	3	0	0	0
Reuss, p	2	0	0	0
Total	28	2	4	2

```
New York ............. 0 1 0 0 0 0 0 0 0—1
Los Angeles .......... 0 0 0 0 0 0 2 0 x—2
```

E—Lopes 3. DP—Los Angeles 2. LOB—New York 7, Los Angeles 6. 2B—Jackson, Yeager. HR—Guerrero, Yeager. SB—Lopes, Landreaux.

	IP	H	R	ER	BB	SO
New York—Guidry (L, 1-1)	7	4	2	2	2	9
Gossage	1	0	0	1	0	
Los Angeles—Reuss (W, 1-1)	9	5	1	1	3	6

HBP—Cey (by Gossage). Time—2:19. Attendance—56,115.

SIXTH GAME: Yankee Stadium, October 28

LOS ANGELES (NL)	ab	r	h	bi
Lopes, 2b	4	2	1	0
Russell, ss	4	0	2	1
Garvey, 1b	4	1	1	0
Cey, 3b	3	1	2	1
Thomas, 3b	2	1	0	1
Baker, lf	5	2	2	0
Guerrero, cf	5	1	3	5
Monday, rf	3	0	1	0
Landreaux, cf	1	0	0	0
Yeager, c	5	0	1	1
Hooton, p	2	1	0	0
Howe, p	2	0	0	0
Total	40	9	13	9

NEW YORK (AL)	ab	r	h	bi
Randolph, 2b	3	1	2	1
Mumphrey, cf	5	0	1	0
Winfield, lf	4	0	0	0
Jackson, rf	5	0	0	0
Watson, 1b	5	0	0	0
Nettles, 3b	3	0	2	0
Rodriguez, 3b	1	1	1	0
Cerone, c	3	0	0	0
Milbourne, ss	2	0	0	0
John, p	1	0	0	0
Murcer, ph	1	0	0	0
Frazier, p	0	0	0	0
Davis, p	0	0	0	0
Reuschel, p	0	0	0	0
Gamble, ph	1	0	1	1
Piniella, ph	1	0	1	1
May, p	0	0	0	0
Brown, pr	0	0	0	0
LaRoche, p	0	0	0	0
Total	35	2	7	2

```
Los Angeles ........... 0 0 0 1 3 4 0 1 0—9
New York ............. 0 0 1 0 0 1 0 0 0—2
```

E—Milbourne, Nettles, Lopes. LOB—Los Angeles 10, New York 12. 2B—Nettles, Randolph. 3B—Guerrero. HR—Randolph, Guerrero. SB—Randolph, Lopes, Russell. S—Russell.

	IP	H	R	ER	BB	SO
Los Angeles—Hooton (W, 1-1)	5 1/3	5	2	2	5	2
Howe	3 2/3	2	0	0	1	3
New York—John	4	6	1	1	0	2
Frazier (L, 0-3)	1	4	3	3	2	1
Davis	1/3	1	3	2	2	1
Reuschel	2/3	2	1	1	0	0
May	2	1	1	1	1	2
LaRoche	1	0	0	0	0	2

Time—3:09. Attendance—56,513.

1981 CLUB AND INDIVIDUAL RECORDS

NATIONAL LEAGUE

CLUB BATTING

	Avg.	R	H	HR
Philadelphia	.273	491	1,002	69
Cincinnati	.267	464	972	64
St. Louis	.265	464	936	50
Los Angeles	.262	450	984	82
Pittsburgh	.257	407	920	55
Houston	.257	394	948	45
San Diego	.256	382	963	32
San Francisco	.250	427	941	63
New York	.248	348	868	57
Montreal	.246	443	883	81
Atlanta	.243	395	886	64
Chicago	.236	370	838	57

INDIVIDUAL BATTING

	Avg.	R	H	HR
Madlock, Pittsburgh	.341	35	95	6
Rose, Philadelphia	.325	73	140	0
Baker, Los Angeles	.320	48	128	9
Schmidt, Philadelphia	.316	78	112	31
Buckner, Chicago	.311	45	131	10
Griffey, Cincinnati	.311	65	123	2
May, San Francisco	.310	20	98	2
Brooks, New York	.307	34	110	4
Concepcion, Cincinnati	.306	57	129	5
Hernandez, St. Louis	.306	65	115	8

Runs — Schmidt (Phila.) 78, Rose (Phila.) 73, Dawson (Mont.) 71, Hendrick (St. L.) 67

Hits — Rose (Phila.) 140, Buckner (Chi.) 131, Concepcion (Cinc.) 129, Baker (L.A.) 128

Doubles — Buckner (Chi.) 35, Jones (S.D.) 34, Concepcion (Cinc.) 28, Hernandez (St. L.) 27

Triples — Reynolds (Hou.)-Richards (S.D.) 12, Herr (St. L.) 9, 4 tied with 8

Home Runs — Schmidt (Phila.) 31, Dawson (Mont.) 24, Kingman (N.Y.)-Foster (Cinc.) 22

Runs Batted In — Schmidt (Phila.) 91, Foster (Cinc.) 90, Buckner (Chi.) 75, Carter (Mont.) 68

Stolen Bases — Raines (Mont.) 71, Moreno (Pitt.) 39, Scott (Mont.) 30, 3 tied with 26

CLUB PITCHING

	ERA	H	BB	SO
Houston	2.66	842	300	610
Los Angeles	3.01	904	302	603
San Francisco	3.28	970	393	561
Montreal	3.30	902	268	520
Atlanta	3.45	936	330	471
New York	3.55	906	336	490
Pittsburgh	3.56	953	346	492
St. Louis	3.63	902	290	388
San Diego	3.72	1,013	414	492
Cincinnati	3.73	863	393	593
Chicago	4.01	983	388	532
Philadelphia	4.05	967	347	580

INDIVIDUAL PITCHING

	IP	W	L	ERA
Ryan, Houston	149	11	5	1.69
Knepper, Houston	157	9	5	2.18
Hooton, Los Angeles	142	11	6	2.28
Reuss, Los Angeles	153	10	4	2.29
Carlton, Philadelphia	190	13	4	2.42
Blue, San Francisco	125	8	6	2.45
Valenzuela, Los Angeles	192	13	7	2.48
Seaver, Cincinnati	166	14	2	2.55
Sutton, Houston	159	11	9	2.60
Gullickson, Montreal	157	7	9	2.81

Innings Pitched — Valenzuela (L.A.) 192, Carlton (Phila.) 190, Soto (Cinc.) 175, Niekro (Hou.)-Seaver (Cinc.) 166

Complete Games — Valenzuela (L.A.) 11, Carlton (Phila.)-Soto (Cinc.) 10, Reuss (L.A.) 8

Wins — Seaver (Cinc.) 14, Carlton (Phila.)-Valenzuela (L.A.) 13, 3 tied with 12

Shutouts — Valenzuela (L.A.) 8, Knepper (Hou.) 5, Hooton (L.A.) 4, 6 tied with 3

Strikeouts — Valenzuela (L.A.) 180, Carlton (Phila.) 179, Soto (Cinc.) 151, Ryan (Hou.) 140

Saves — Sutter (St. L.) 25, Minton (S.F.) 21, Allen (N.Y.) 18, Camp (Atl.) 17

AMERICAN LEAGUE

CLUB BATTING

	Avg.	R	H	HR
Boston	.275	519	1,052	90
Chicago	.272	476	982	76
Texas	.270	452	968	49
Kansas City	.267	397	952	61
Cleveland	.263	431	922	39
Milwaukee	.257	493	961	96
Detroit	.256	427	922	65
California	.256	476	944	97
New York	.252	421	889	100
Seattle	.251	426	950	89
Baltimore	.251	429	883	88
Oakland	.247	458	910	104
Minnesota	.240	378	884	47
Toronto	.226	329	797	61

INDIVIDUAL BATTING

	Avg.	R	H	HR
Lansford, Boston	.336	61	134	4
Paciorek, Seattle	.326	50	132	14
Cooper, Milwaukee	.320	70	133	12
Henderson, Oakland	.319	89	135	6
Hargrove, Cleveland	.317	43	102	2
Brett, G., Kansas City	.314	42	109	6
Zisk, Seattle	.311	42	111	16
Oliver, Texas	.309	53	130	4
Remy, Boston	.307	55	110	0
Mumphrey, New York	.307	44	98	6

Runs — Henderson (Oak.) 89, Evans (Bost.) 84, Cooper (Milw.) 70, Harrah (Cleve.) 64

Hits — Henderson (Oak.) 135, Lansford (Bost.) 134, Cooper (Milw.)-Wilson (K.C.) 133

Doubles — Cooper (Milw.) 35, Oliver (Tex.) 29, Paciorek (Seat.) 28, Brett (K.C.)-Dauer (Balt.) 27

Triples — Castino (Minn.) 9, Baines (Chi.)-Brett (K.C.)-Wilson (K.C.)-Henderson (Oak.) 7

Home Runs — Murray (Balt.)-Evans (Bost.)-Grich (Calif.)-Armas (Oak.) 22

Runs Batted In — Murray (Balt.) 78, Armas (Oak.) 76, Oglivie (Milw.) 72, Evans (Bost.) 71

Stolen Bases — Henderson (Oak.) 56, Cruz (Seat.) 43, LeFlore (Chi.) 36, Wilson (K.C.) 34

CLUB PITCHING

	ERA	H	BB	SO
New York	2.90	827	287	606
Oakland	3.30	883	370	505
Texas	3.40	851	322	488
Chicago	3.47	891	336	529
Detroit	3.53	840	373	476
Kansas City	3.55	909	273	404
California	3.69	958	323	429
Baltimore	3.70	923	347	489
Boston	3.81	983	354	536
Toronto	3.81	908	377	451
Cleveland	3.88	989	311	569
Milwaukee	3.91	994	352	448
Minnesota	3.98	1,021	376	500
Seattle	4.23	1,039	360	478

INDIVIDUAL PITCHING

	IP	W	L	ERA
McCatty, Oakland	186	14	7	2.32
Stewart, Baltimore	112	4	8	2.33
Lamp, Chicago	127	7	6	2.41
John, New York	140	9	8	2.63
Burns, Chicago	157	10	6	2.64
Gura, Kansas City	172	11	8	2.72
Guidry, New York	127	11	5	2.76
Blyleven, Cleveland	159	11	7	2.88
Forsch, California	153	11	7	2.88
Leonard, Kansas City	201	13	11	2.99

Innings Pitched — Leonard (K.C.) 202, Morris (Det.) 198, Langford (Oak.) 195, McCatty (Oak.) 186

Complete Games — Langford (Oak.) 18, McCatty (Oak.) 16, Morris (Det.) 15, Norris (Oak.) 12

Wins — Vuckovich (Milw.)-Martinez (Balt.)-Morris (Det.)-McCatty (Oak.) 14

Shutouts — Medich (Tex.)-McCatty (Oak.)-Forsch (Calif.)-Dotson (Chi.) 4

Strikeouts — Barker (Cleve.) 127, Burns (Chi.) 108, Blyleven (Cleve.)-Leonard (K.C.) 107

Saves — Fingers (Milw.) 28, Gossage (N.Y.) 20, Quisenberry (K.C.) 18, Corbett (Minn.) 17

ALL-TIME WORLD SERIES RESULTS

Year	Winner	Won	Lost	Loser		Year	Winner	Won	Lost	Loser
1903	.. Boston (AL)	5	.. 3	.. Pittsburgh (NL)		1943	.. New York (AL)	4	.. 1	.. St. Louis (NL)
1905	.. New York (NL)	4	.. 1	.. Philadelphia (AL)		1944	.. St. Louis (NL)	4	.. 2	.. St. Louis (AL)
1906	.. Chicago (AL)	4	.. 2	.. Chicago (NL)		1945	.. Detroit (AL)	4	.. 3	.. Chicago (NL)
1907	.. Chicago (NL)	4	.. 0	.. Detroit (AL)		1946	.. St. Louis (NL)	4	.. 3	.. Boston (AL)
1908	.. Chicago (NL)	4	.. 1	.. Detroit (AL)		1947	.. New York (AL)	4	.. 3	.. Brooklyn (NL)
1909	.. Pittsburgh (NL)	4	.. 3	.. Detroit (AL)		1948	.. Cleveland (AL)	4	.. 2	.. Boston (NL)
1910	.. Philadelphia (AL)	4	.. 1	.. Chicago (NL)		1949	.. New York (AL)	4	.. 1	.. Brooklyn (NL)
1911	.. Philadelphia (AL)	4	.. 2	.. New York (NL)		1950	.. New York (AL)	4	.. 0	.. Philadelphia (NL)
1912	.. Boston (AL)	4	.. 3	.. New York (NL)		1951	.. New York (AL)	4	.. 2	.. New York (NL)
1913	.. Philadelphia (AL)	4	.. 1	.. New York (NL)		1952	.. New York (AL)	4	.. 3	.. Brooklyn (NL)
1914	.. Boston (NL)	4	.. 0	.. Philadelphia (AL)		1953	.. New York (AL)	4	.. 2	.. Brooklyn (NL)
1915	.. Boston (AL)	4	.. 1	.. Philadelphia (NL)		1954	.. New York (NL)	4	.. 0	.. Cleveland (AL)
1916	.. Boston (AL)	4	.. 1	.. Brooklyn (NL)		1955	.. Brooklyn (NL)	4	.. 3	.. New York (AL)
1917	.. Chicago (AL)	4	.. 2	.. New York (NL)		1956	.. New York (AL)	4	.. 3	.. Brooklyn (NL)
1918	.. Boston (AL)	4	.. 2	.. Chicago (NL)		1957	.. Milwaukee (NL)	4	.. 3	.. New York (AL)
1919	.. Cincinnati (NL)	5	.. 3	.. Chicago (AL)		1958	.. New York (AL)	4	.. 3	.. Milwaukee (NL)
1920	.. Cleveland (AL)	5	.. 2	.. Brooklyn (NL)		1959	.. Los Angeles (NL)	4	.. 2	.. Chicago (AL)
1921	.. New York (NL)	5	.. 3	.. New York (AL)		1960	.. Pittsburgh (NL)	4	.. 3	.. New York (AL)
1922	.. New York (NL)	4	.. 0	.. New York (AL)		1961	.. New York (AL)	4	.. 1	.. Cincinnati (NL)
1923	.. New York (AL)	4	.. 2	.. New York (NL)		1962	.. New York (AL)	4	.. 3	.. San Francisco (NL)
1924	.. Washington (AL)	4	.. 3	.. New York (NL)		1963	.. Los Angeles (NL)	4	.. 0	.. New York (AL)
1925	.. Pittsburgh (NL)	4	.. 3	.. Washington (AL)		1964	.. St. Louis (NL)	4	.. 3	.. New York (AL)
1926	.. St. Louis (NL)	4	.. 3	.. New York (AL)		1965	.. Los Angeles (NL)	4	.. 3	.. Minnesota (AL)
1927	.. New York (AL)	4	.. 0	.. Pittsburgh (NL)		1966	.. Baltimore (AL)	4	.. 0	.. Los Angeles (NL)
1928	.. New York (AL)	4	.. 0	.. St. Louis (NL)		1967	.. St. Loius (NL)	4	.. 3	.. Boston (AL)
1929	.. Philadelphia (AL)	4	.. 1	.. Chicago (NL)		1968	.. Detroit (AL)	4	.. 3	.. St. Louis (NL)
1930	.. Philadelphia (AL)	4	.. 2	.. St. Louis (NL)		1969	.. New York (NL)	4	.. 1	.. Baltimore (AL)
1931	.. St. Louis (NL)	4	.. 3	.. Philadelphia (AL)		1970	.. Baltimore (AL)	4	.. 1	.. Cincinnati (NL)
1932	.. New York (AL)	4	.. 0	.. Chicago (NL)		1971	.. Pittsburgh (NL)	4	.. 3	.. Baltimore (AL)
1933	.. New York (NL)	4	.. 1	.. Washington (AL)		1972	.. Oakland (AL)	4	.. 3	.. Cincinnati (NL)
1934	.. St. Louis (NL)	4	.. 3	.. Detroit (AL)		1973	.. Oakland (AL)	4	.. 3	.. New York (NL)
1935	.. Detroit (AL)	4	.. 2	.. Chicago (NL)		1974	.. Oakland (AL)	4	.. 1	.. Los Angeles (NL)
1936	.. New York (AL)	4	.. 2	.. New York (NL)		1975	.. Cincinnati (NL)	4	.. 3	.. Boston (AL)
1937	.. New York (AL)	4	.. 1	.. New York (NL)		1976	.. Cincinnati (NL)	4	.. 0	.. New York (AL)
1938	.. New York (AL)	4	.. 0	.. Chicago (NL)		1977	.. New York (AL)	4	.. 2	.. Los Angeles (NL)
1939	.. New York (AL)	4	.. 0	.. Cincinnati (NL)		1978	.. New York (AL)	4	.. 2	.. Los Angeles (NL)
1940	.. Cincinnati (NL)	4	.. 3	.. Detroit (AL)		1979	.. Pittsburgh (NL)	4	.. 3	.. Baltimore (AL)
1941	.. New York (AL)	4	.. 1	.. Brooklyn (NL)		1980	.. Philadelphia (NL)	4	.. 2	.. Kansas City (AL)
1942	.. St. Louis (NL)	4	.. 1	.. New York (AL)		1981	.. Los Angeles (NL)	4	.. 2	.. New York (AL)

THE ALL-STAR GAMES

Year	Site	Winner	Score		Year	Site	Winner	Score
1933	.. Comiskey Park, Chicago	American	.. 4-2		1960	.. Municipal Stadium, Kansas City	National	... 5-3
1934	.. Polo Grounds, New York	American	.. 9-7			Yankee Stadium, New York	National	.. 6-0
1935	.. Municipal Stadium, Cleveland	American	.. 4-1		1961	.. Candlestick Park, San Francisco	National	.. 5-4
1936	.. Braves Field, Boston	National	.. 4-3			Fenway Park, Boston	Tie	 1-1
1937	.. Griffith Stadium, Washington	American	.. 8-3		1962	.. D.C. Stadium, Washington	National	.. 3-1
1938	.. Crosley Field, Cincinnati	National	.. 4-1			Wrigley Field, Chicago	American	.. 9-4
1939	.. Yankee Stadium, New York	American	.. 3-1		1963	.. Municipal Stadium, Cleveland	National	.. 5-3
1940	.. Sportsman's Park, St. Louis	National	.. 4-0		1964	.. Shea Stadium, New York	National	.. 7-4
1941	.. Briggs Stadium, Detroit	American	.. 7-5		1965	.. Metropolitan Stadium,		
1942	.. Polo Grounds, New York	American	.. 3-1			Bloomington, Minnesota	National	.. 6-5
1943	.. Shibe Park, Philadelphia	American	.. 5-3		1966	.. Busch Stadium, St. Louis	National	.. 2-1
1944	.. Forbes Field, Pittsburgh	National	... 7-1		1967	.. Anaheim Stadium, California	National	.. 2-1
1945	.. Not played	—			1968	.. Houston Astrodome	National	.. 1-0
1946	.. Fenway Park, Boston	American	.. 12-0		1969	.. R. F. Kennedy Stadium, Wash.	National	.. 9-3
1947	.. Wrigley Field, Chicago	American	.. 2-1		1970	.. Riverfront Stadium, Cincinnati	National	.. 5-4
1948	.. Sportsman's Park, St. Louis	American	.. 5-2		1971	.. Tiger Stadium, Detroit	American	.. 6-4
1949	.. Ebbets Field, Brooklyn	American	.. 11-7		1972	.. Atlanta, Georgia	National	.. 4-3
1950	.. Comiskey Park, Chicago	National	.. 4-3		1973	.. Kansas City, Missouri	National	.. 7-1
1951	.. Briggs Stadium, Detroit	National	.. 8-3		1974	.. Pittsburgh, Pennsylvania	National	.. 7-2
1952	.. Shibe Park, Philadelphia	National	.. 3-2		1975	.. Milwaukee, Wis.	National	.. 6-3
1953	.. Crosley Field, Cincinnati	National	.. 5-1		1976	.. Veterans Stadium, Philadelphia	National	.. 7-1
1954	.. Municipal Stadium, Cleveland	American	.. 11-9		1977	.. Yankee Stadium, New York	National	.. 7-5
1955	.. Milwaukee County Stadium	National	.. 6-5		1978	.. San Diego Stadium	National	.. 7-3
1956	.. Griffith Stadium, Washington	National	... 7-3		1979	.. Seattle Kingdome	National	.. 7-6
1957	.. Busch Stadium, St. Louis	American	... 6-5		1980	.. Dodger Stadium, Los Angeles	National	.. 4-2
1958	.. Memorial Stadium, Baltimore	American	.. 4-3		1981	.. Municipal Stadium, Cleveland	National	.. 5-4
1959	.. Forbes Field, Pittsburgh	National	.. 5-4					
	Memorial Coliseum, L.A.	American	.. 5-3					

MODERN FRANCHISE CHANGES IN MAJOR LEAGUES

NATIONAL LEAGUE

Year	New Team	How Created
1953	Milwaukee Braves	Formerly, Boston Braves
1958	Los Angeles Dodgers	Formerly, Brooklyn Dodgers
1958	San Francisco Giants	Formerly, New York Giants
1962	New York Mets	Expansion team
1962	Houston Astros†	Expansion team
1966	Atlanta Braves	Formerly, Milwaukee Braves
1969	Montreal Expos	Expansion team
1969	San Diego Padres	Expansion team

AMERICAN LEAGUE

Year	New Team	How Created
1954	Baltimore Orioles	Formerly, St. Louis Browns
1955	Kansas City Athletics	Formerly, Philadelphia Athletics
1961	Minnesota Twins	Formerly, Washington Senators
1961	Washington Senators*	Expansion team
1961	Los Angeles Angels	Expansion team
1965	California Angels	Formerly, Los Angeles Angels
1968	Oakland Athletics	Formerly, Kansas City Athletics
1969	Kansas City Royals	Expansion team
1969	Seattle Pilots	Expansion team
1970	Milwaukee Brewers	Formerly, Seattle Pilots
1972	Texas Rangers	Formerly, Washington Senators
1977	Seattle Mariners	Expansion team
1977	Toronto Blue Jays	Expansion team

† Originally Colts, then Colt-45's.   * New Washington Senators.

NATIONAL LEAGUE PENNANT WINNERS

Year	Club	Won	Lost	Pct.	Manager	Year	Club	Won	Lost	Pct.	Manager
1901	Pittsburgh	90	49	.647	Fred C. Clarke	1942	St. Louis	106	48	.688	William Southworth
1902	Pittsburgh	103	36	.741	Fred C. Clarke	1943	St. Louis	105	49	.682	William Southworth
1903	Pittsburgh	91	49	.650	Fred Clarke	1944	St. Louis	105	49	.682	William Southworth
1904	New York	106	47	.693	John McGraw	1945	Chicago	98	56	.636	Charles Grimm
1905	New York	105	48	.686	John McGraw	1946	St. Louis	98	58	.628	Edwin Dyer
1906	Chicago	116	36	.763	Frank Chance	1947	Brooklyn	94	60	.610	Burton Shotton
1907	Chicago	107	45	.704	Frank Chance	1948	Boston	91	62	.595	William Southworth
1908	Chicago	99	55	.643	Frank Chance	1949	Brooklyn	97	57	.630	Burton Shotton
1909	Pittsburgh	110	42	.724	Fred Clarke	1950	Philadelphia	91	63	.591	Edwin Sawyer
1910	Chicago	104	50	.675	Frank Chance	1951	New York	98	59	.624	Leo Durocher
1911	New York	99	54	.647	John McGraw	1952	Brooklyn	96	57	.627	Charles Dressen
1912	New York	103	48	.682	John McGraw	1953	Brooklyn	105	49	.682	Charles Dressen
1913	New York	101	51	.664	John McGraw	1954	New York	97	57	.630	Leo Durocher
1914	Boston	94	59	.614	George Stallings	1955	Brooklyn	98	55	.641	Walter Alston
1915	Philadelphia	90	62	.592	Patrick Moran	1956	Brooklyn	93	61	.604	Walter Alston
1916	Brooklyn	94	60	.610	Wilbert Robinson	1957	Milwaukee	95	59	.617	Fred Haney
1917	New York	98	56	.636	John McGraw	1958	Milwaukee	92	62	.597	Fred Haney
1918	Chicago	84	45	.651	Fred Mitchell	1959	Los Angeles	88	68	.564	Walter Alston
1919	Cincinnati	96	44	.686	Patrick Moran	1960	Pittsburgh	95	59	.617	Daniel Murtaugh
1920	Brooklyn	93	61	.604	Wilbert Robinson	1961	Cincinnati	93	61	.604	Fred Hutchinson
1921	New York	94	59	.614	John McGraw	1962	San Francisco	103	62	.624	Alvin Dark
1922	New York	93	61	.604	John McGraw	1963	Los Angeles	99	63	.611	Walter Alston
1923	New York	95	58	.621	John McGraw	1964	St. Louis	93	69	.574	John Keane
1924	New York	93	60	.608	John McGraw	1965	Los Angeles	97	65	.599	Walter Alston
1925	Pittsburgh	95	58	.621	William McKechnie	1966	Los Angeles	95	67	.586	Walter Alston
1926	St. Louis	89	65	.578	Rogers Hornsby	1967	St. Louis	101	60	.627	Albert Schoendienst
1927	Pittsburgh	94	60	.610	Owen Bush	1968	St. Louis	97	65	.599	Albert Schoendienst
1928	St. Louis	95	59	.617	William McKechnie	1969	New York	100	62	.617	Gil Hodges
1929	Chicago	98	54	.645	Joseph McCarthy	1970	Cincinnati	102	60	.630	Sparky Anderson
1930	St. Louis	92	62	.597	Charles Street	1971	Pittsburgh	97	65	.599	Danny Murtaugh
1931	St. Louis	101	53	.656	Charles Street	1972	Cincinnati	95	59	.617	Sparky Anderson
1932	Chicago	90	64	.584	Charles Grimm	1973	New York	82	79	.509	Lawrence Berra
1933	New York	91	61	.599	William Terry	1974	Los Angeles	102	60	.630	Walter Alston
1934	St. Louis	95	58	.621	Frank Frisch	1975	Cincinnati	108	54	.667	Sparky Anderson
1935	Chicago	100	54	.649	Charles Grimm	1976	Cincinnati	102	60	.630	Sparky Anderson
1936	New York	92	62	.597	William Terry	1977	Los Angeles	98	64	.605	Tom Lasorda
1937	New York	95	57	.625	William Terry	1978	Los Angeles	95	67	.586	Tom Lasorda
1938	Chicago	89	63	.586	Charles Hartnett	1979	Pittsburgh	98	64	.605	Chuck Tanner
1939	Cincinnati	97	57	.630	William McKechnie	1980	Philadelphia	91	71	.562	Dallas Green
1940	Cincinnati	100	53	.654	William McKechnie	1981	Los Angeles	63	47	.573	Tom Lasorda
1941	Brooklyn	100	54	.649	Leo Durocher						

AMERICAN LEAGUE PENNANT WINNERS

Year	Club	Won	Lost	Pct.	Manager	Year	Club	Won	Lost	Pct.	Manager
1901	Chicago	83	53	.610	Clark Griffith	1942	New York	103	51	.669	Joseph McCarthy
1902	Philadelphia	83	53	.610	Connie Mack	1943	New York	98	56	.636	Joseph McCarthy
1903	Boston	91	47	.659	James Collins	1944	St. Louis	89	65	.578	James Sewell
1904	Boston	95	59	.617	James Collins	1945	Detroit	88	65	.575	Stephen O'Neill
1905	Philadelphia	92	56	.622	Connie Mack	1946	Boston	104	50	.675	Joseph Cronin
1906	Chicago	93	58	.616	Fielder Jones	1947	New York	97	57	.630	Stanley Harris
1907	Detroit	92	58	.613	Hugh Jennings	1948	Cleveland	97	58	.626	Louis Boudreau
1908	Detroit	90	63	.588	Hugh Jennings	1949	New York	97	57	.630	Charles Stengel
1909	Detroit	98	54	.645	Hugh Jennings	1950	New York	98	56	.636	Charles Stengel
1910	Philadelphia	102	48	.680	Connie Mack	1951	New York	98	56	.636	Charles Stengel
1911	Philadelphia	101	50	.669	Connie Mack	1952	New York	95	59	.617	Charles Stengel
1912	Boston	105	47	.691	J. Garland Stahl	1953	New York	99	52	.656	Charles Stengel
1913	Philadelphia	96	57	.627	Connie Mack	1954	Cleveland	111	43	.721	Alfonso Lopez
1914	Philadelphia	99	53	.651	Connie Mack	1955	New York	96	58	.623	Charles Stengel
1915	Boston	101	50	.669	William Carrigan	1956	New York	97	57	.630	Charles Stengel
1916	Boston	91	63	.591	William Carrigan	1957	New York	98	56	.636	Charles Stengel
1917	Chicago	100	54	.649	Clarence Rowland	1958	New York	92	62	.597	Charles Stengel
1918	Boston	75	51	.595	Edward Barrow	1959	Chicago	94	60	.610	Alfonso Lopez
1919	Chicago	88	52	.629	William Gleason	1960	New York	97	57	.630	Charles Stengel
1920	Cleveland	98	56	.636	Tris Speaker	1961	New York	109	53	.673	Ralph Houk
1921	New York	98	55	.641	Miller Huggins	1962	New York	96	66	.593	Ralph Houk
1922	New York	94	60	.610	Miller Huggins	1963	New York	104	57	.646	Ralph Houk
1923	New York	98	54	.645	Miller Huggins	1964	New York	99	63	.611	Lawrence Berra
1924	Washington	92	62	.597	Stanley Harris	1965	Minnesota	102	60	.630	Sabath Mele
1925	Washington	96	55	.636	Stanley Harris	1966	Baltimore	97	63	.606	Henry Bauer
1926	New York	91	63	.591	Miller Huggins	1967	Boston	92	70	.568	Richard Williams
1927	New York	110	44	.714	Miller Huggins	1968	Detroit	103	59	.636	Mayo Smith
1928	New York	101	53	.656	Miller Huggins	1969	Baltimore	109	53	.673	Earl Weaver
1929	Philadelphia	104	46	.693	Connie Mack	1970	Baltimore	108	54	.667	Earl Weaver
1930	Philadelphia	102	52	.662	Connie Mack	1971	Baltimore	101	57	.639	Earl Weaver
1931	Philadelphia	107	45	.704	Connie Mack	1972	Oakland	93	62	.600	Dick Williams
1932	New York	107	47	.695	Joseph McCarthy	1973	Oakland	94	68	.580	Dick Williams
1933	Washington	99	53	.651	Joseph Cronin	1974	Oakland	90	72	.556	Alvin Dark
1934	Detroit	101	53	.656	Gordon Cochrane	1975	Boston	95	65	.594	Darrell Johnson
1935	Detroit	93	58	.616	Gordon Cochrane	1976	New York	97	62	.610	Billy Martin
1936	New York	102	51	.667	Joseph McCarthy	1977	New York	100	62	.617	Billy Martin
1937	New York	102	52	.662	Joseph McCarthy	1978	New York	100	63	.613	Bob Lemon
1938	New York	99	53	.651	Joseph McCarthy	1979	Baltimore	102	57	.642	Earl Weaver
1939	New York	106	45	.702	Joseph McCarthy	1980	Kansas City	97	65	.599	Jim Frey
1940	Detroit	90	64	.584	Delmar Baker	1981	New York	59	48	.551	Bob Lemon
1941	New York	101	53	.656	Joseph McCarthy						

NATIONAL LEAGUE BATTING CHAMPIONS

Year	Player and Club	Average	Year	Player and Club	Average
1901	Jesse Burkett, St. Louis	.382	1942	Ernie Lombardi, Boston	.330
1902	Clarence Beaumont, Pittsburgh	.357	1943	Stan Musial, St. Louis	.357
1903	Honus Wagner, Pittsburgh	.355	1944	Dixie Walker, Brooklyn	.357
1904	Honus Wagner, Pittsburgh	.349	1945	Phil Cavaretta, Chicago	.355
1905	Cy Seymour, Cincinnati	.377	1946	Stan Musial, St. Louis	.365
1906	Honus Wagner, Pittsburgh	.339	1947	Harry Walker, St. Louis-Philadelphia	.363
1907	Honus Wagner, Pittsburgh	.350	1948	Stan Musial, St. Louis	.376
1908	Honus Wagner, Pittsburgh	.354	1949	Jackie Robinson, Brooklyn	.342
1909	Honus Wagner, Pittsburgh	.339	1950	Stan Musial, St. Louis	.346
1910	Sherwood Magee, Philadelphia	.331	1951	Stan Musial, St. Louis	.355
1911	Honus Wagner, Pittsburgh	.334	1952	Stan Musial, St. Louis	.336
1912	Henry Zimmerman, Chicago	.372	1953	Carl Furillo, Brooklyn	.344
1913	Jake Daubert, Brooklyn	.350	1954	Willie Mays, New York	.345
1914	Jake Daubert, Brooklyn	.329	1955	Richie Ashburn, Philadelphia	.338
1915	Larry Doyle, New York	.320	1956	Hank Aaron, Milwaukee	.328
1916	Hal Chase, Cincinnati	.339	1957	Stan Musial, St. Louis	.351
1917	Edd Roush, Cincinnati	.341	1958	Richie Ashburn, Philadelphia	.350
1918	Zack Wheat, Brooklyn	.335	1959	Hank Aaron, Milwaukee	.355
1919	Edd Roush, Cincinnati	.321	1960	Dick Groat, Pittsburgh	.325
1920	Rogers Hornsby, St. Louis	.370	1961	Roberto Clemente, Pittsburgh	.351
1921	Rogers Hornsby, St. Louis	.397	1962	Tommy Davis, Los Angeles	.346
1922	Rogers Hornsby, St. Louis	.401	1963	Tommy Davis, Los Angeles	.326
1923	Rogers Hornsby, St. Louis	.384	1964	Roberto Clemente, Pittsburgh	.339
1924	Rogers Hornsby, St. Louis	.424	1965	Roberto Clemente, Pittsburgh	.329
1925	Rogers Hornsby, St. Louis	.403	1966	Matty Alou, Pittsburgh	.342
1926	Gene Hargrave, Cincinnati	.353	1967	Roberto Clemente, Pittsburgh	.357
1927	Paul Waner, Pittsburgh	.380	1968	Pete Rose, Cincinnati	.335
1928	Rogers Hornsby, Boston	.387	1969	Pete Rose, Cincinnati	.348
1929	Lefty O'Doul, Philadelphia	.398	1970	Rico Carty, Atlanta	.366
1930	Bill Terry, New York	.401	1971	Joe Torre, St. Louis	.363
1931	Chick Hafey, St. Louis	.349	1972	Billy Williams, Chicago	.333
1932	Lefty O'Doul, Brooklyn	.368	1973	Pete Rose, Cincinnati	.338
1933	Chuck Klein, Philadelphia	.368	1974	Ralph Garr, Atlanta	.353
1934	Paul Waner, Pittsburgh	.362	1975	Bill Madlock, Chicago	.354
1935	Arky Vaughan, Pittsburgh	.385	1976	Bill Madlock, Chicago	.339
1936	Paul Waner, Pittsburgh	.373	1977	Dave Parker, Pittsburgh	.338
1937	Joe Medwick, St. Louis	.374	1978	Dave Parker, Pittsburgh	.334
1938	Ernie Lombardi, Cincinnati	.342	1979	Keith Hernandez, St. Louis	.344
1939	Johnny Mize, St. Louis	.349	1980	Bill Buckner, Chicago	.324
1940	Debs Garms, Pittsburgh	.355	1981	Bill Madlock, Pittsburgh	.341
1941	Pete Reiser, Brooklyn	.343			

NATIONAL LEAGUE HOME RUN CHAMPIONS

Year	Player and Club	Home Runs	Year	Player and Club	Home Runs
1901	Sam Crawford, Cincinnati	16	1937	Mel Ott, New York	31
1902	Tom Leach, Pittsburgh	6		Joe Medwick, St. Louis	31
1903	James Sheckard, Brooklyn	9	1938	Mel Ott, New York	36
1904	Harry Lumley, Brooklyn	9	1939	Johnny Mize, St. Louis	28
1905	Fred Odwell, Cincinnati	9	1940	Johnny Mize, St. Louis	43
1906	Tim Jordan, Brooklyn	12	1941	Dolph Camilli, Brooklyn	34
1907	David Brain, Boston	10	1942	Mell Ott, New York	30
1908	Tim Jordan, Brooklyn	12	1943	Bill Nicholson, Chicago	29
1909	John Murray, New York	7	1944	Bill Nicholson, Chicago	33
1910	Fred Beck, Boston	10	1945	Tommy Holmes, Boston	28
	Frank Schulte, Chicago	10	1946	Ralph Kiner, Pittsburgh	23
1911	Frank Schulte, Chicago	21	1947	Ralph Kiner, Pittsburgh	51
1912	Henry Zimmerman, Chicago	14		Johnny Mize, New York	51
1913	Cliff Cravath, Philadelphia	19	1948	Ralph Kiner, Pittsburgh	40
1914	Cliff Cravath, Philadelphia	19		Johnny Mize, New York	40
1915	Cliff Cravath, Philadelphia	24	1949	Ralph Kiner, Pittsburgh	54
1916	Davis Robertson, New York	12	1950	Ralph Kiner, Pittsburgh	47
	Cy Williams, Chicago	12	1951	Ralph Kiner, Pittsburgh	42
1917	Davis Robertson, New York	12	1952	Ralph Kiner, Pittsburgh	37
	Gavvy Cravath, Philadelphia	12		Hank Sauer, Chicago	37
1918	Gavvy Cravath, Philadelphia	8	1953	Eddie Mathews, Milwaukee	47
1919	Gavvy Cravath, Philadelphia	12	1954	Ted Kluszewski, Cincinnati	49
1920	Cy Williams, Philadelphia	15	1955	Willie Mays, New York	51
1921	George Kelly, New York	23	1956	Duke Snider, Brooklyn	43
1922	Rogers Hornsby, St. Louis	42	1957	Hank Aaron, Milwaukee	44
1923	Cy Williams, Philadelphia	41	1958	Ernie Banks, Chicago	47
1924	Jack Fournier, Brooklyn	27	1959	Eddie Mathews, Milwaukee	46
1925	Rogers Hornsby, St. Louis	39	1960	Ernie Banks, Chicago	41
1926	Hack Wilson, Chicago	21	1961	Orlando Cepeda, San Francisco	46
1927	Hack Wilson, Chicago	30	1962	Willie Mays, San Francisco	49
	Cy Williams, Philadelphia	30	1963	Hank Aaron, Milwaukee	44
1928	Hack Wilson, Chicago	31		Willie McCovey, San Francisco	44
	Jim Bottomley, St. Louis	31	1964	Willie Mays, San Francisco	47
1929	Chuck Klein, Philadelphia	43	1965	Willie Mays, San Francisco	52
1930	Hack Wilson, Chicago	56	1966	Hank Aaron, Atlanta	44
1931	Chuck Klein, Philadelphia	31	1967	Hank Aaron, Atlanta	39
1932	Chuck Klein, Philadelphia	38	1968	Willie McCovey, San Francisco	36
	Mel Ott, New York	38	1969	Willie McCovey, San Francisco	45
1933	Chuck Klein, Philadelphia	28	1970	Johnny Bench, Cincinnati	45
1934	Mel Ott, New York	35	1971	Willie Stargell, Pittsburgh	48
	Rip Collins, St. Louis	35	1972	Johnny Bench, Cincinnati	40
1935	Wally Berger, Boston	34	1973	Willie Stargell, Pittsburgh	44
1936	Mel Ott, New York	33	1974	Mike Schmidt, Philadelphia	36

NATIONAL LEAGUE HOME RUN CHAMPIONS (Cont.)

Year	Player and Club	Home Runs	Year	Player and Club	Home Runs
1975	Mike Schmidt, Philadelphia	38	1979	Dave Kingman, Chicago	48
1976	Mike Schmidt, Philadelphia	38	1980	Mike Schmidt, Philadelphia	48
1977	George Foster, Cincinnati	52	1981	Mike Schmidt, Philadelphia	31
1978	George Foster, Cincinnati	40			

NATIONAL LEAGUE RUNS BATTED IN CHAMPIONS

Year	Player and Club	RBI	Year	Player and Club	RBI
1920	Rogers Hornsby, St. Louis	94	1951	Monte Irvin, New York	121
	George Kelly, New York	94	1952	Hank Sauer, Chicago	121
1921	Rogers Hornsby, St. Louis	126	1953	Roy Campanella, Brooklyn	142
1922	Rogers Hornsby, St. Louis	152	1954	Ted Kluszewski, Cincinnati	141
1923	Irish Meusel, New York	125	1955	Duke Snider, Brooklyn	136
1924	George Kelly, New York	136	1956	Stan Musial, St. Louis	109
1925	Rogers Hornsby, St. Louis	143	1957	Hank Aaron, Milwaukee	132
1926	Jim Bottomley, St. Louis	120	1958	Ernie Banks, Chicago	129
1927	Paul Waner, Pittsburgh	131	1959	Ernie Banks, Chicago	143
1928	Jim Bottomley, St. Louis	136	1960	Hank Aaron, Milwaukee	126
1929	Hack Wilson, Chicago	159	1961	Orlando Cepeda, San Francisco	142
1930	Hack Wilson, Chicago	190	1962	Tommy Davis, Los Angeles	153
1931	Chuck Klein, Philadelphia	121	1963	Hank Aaron, Milwaukee	130
1932	Don Hurst, Philadelphia	143	1964	Ken Boyer, St. Louis	119
1933	Chuck Klein, Philadelphia	120	1965	Deron Johnson, Cincinnati	130
1934	Mel Ott, New York	135	1966	Hank Aaron, Atlanta	127
1935	Wally Berger, Boston	130	1967	Orlando Cepeda, St. Louis	111
1936	Joe Medwick, St. Louis	138	1968	Willie McCovey, San Francisco	105
1937	Joe Medwick, St. Louis	154	1969	Willie McCovey, San Francisco	126
1938	Joe Medwick, St. Louis	122	1970	Johnny Bench, Cincinnati	148
1939	Frank McCormick, Cincinnati	128	1971	Joe Torre, St. Louis	137
1940	Johnny Mize, St. Louis	137	1972	Johnny Bench, Cincinnati	125
1941	Dolf Camilli, Brooklyn	120	1973	Willie Stargell, Pittsburgh	119
1942	Johnny Mize, New York	110	1974	Johnny Bench, Cincinnati	129
1943	Bill Nicholson, Chicago	128	1975	Greg Luzinski, Philadelphia	120
1944	Bill Nicholson, Chicago	122	1976	George Foster, Cincinnati	121
1945	Dixie Walker, Brooklyn	124	1977	George Foster, Cincinnati	149
1946	Enos Slaughter, St. Louis	130	1978	George Foster, Cincinnati	120
1947	Johnny Mize, New York	138	1979	Dave Winfield, San Diego	118
1948	Stan Musial, St. Louis	131	1980	Mike Schmidt, Philadelphia	121
1949	Ralph Kiner, Pittsburgh	127	1981	Mike Schmidt, Philadelphia	91
1950	Del Ennis, Philadelphia	126			

AMERICAN LEAGUE BATTING CHAMPIONS

Year	Player and Club	Average	Year	Player and Club	Average
1901	Nap Lajoie, Phila	.422	1942	Ted Williams, Boston	.356
1902	Ed Delahanty, Wash.	.376	1943	Luke Appling, Chicago	.328
1903	Nap Lajoie, Cleve.	.355	1944	Lou Boudreau, Cleveland	.327
1904	Nap Lajoie, Cleve.	.381	1945	George Stirnweiss, New York	.309
1905	Elmer Flick, Cleve.	.306	1946	Mickey Vernon, Washington	.353
1906	George Stone, St. Louis	.358	1947	Ted Williams, Boston	.343
1907	Ty Cobb, Det.	.350	1948	Ted Williams, Boston	.369
1908	Ty Cobb, Det.	.324	1949	George Kell, Detroit[1]	.343
1909	Ty Cobb, Det.	.377	1950	Billy Goodman, Boston	.354
1910	Ty Cobb, Detroit	.385	1951	Ferris Fain, Philadelphia	.344
1911	Ty Cobb, Detroit	.420	1952	Ferris Fain, Philadelphia	.327
1912	Ty Cobb, Detroit	.410	1953	Mickey Vernon, Washington	.337
1913	Ty Cobb, Detroit	.390	1954	Bobby Avila, Cleveland	.341
1914	Ty Cobb, Detroit	.368	1955	Al Kaline, Detroit	.340
1915	Ty Cobb, Detroit	.369	1956	Mickey Mantle, New York	.353
1916	Tris Speaker, Cleveland	.386	1957	Ted Williams, Boston	.388
1917	Ty Cobb, Detroit	.383	1958	Ted Williams, Boston	.328
1918	Ty Cobb, Detroit	.382	1959	Harvey Kuenn, Detroit	.353
1919	Ty Cobb, Detroit	.384	1960	Pete Runnels, Boston	.320
1920	George Sisler, St. Louis	.407	1961	Norm Cash, Detroit	.361
1921	Harry Heilmann, Detroit	.394	1962	Pete Runnels, Boston	.326
1922	George Sisler, St. Louis	.420	1963	Carl Yastrzemski, Boston	.321
1923	Harry Heilmann, Detroit	.403	1964	Tony Oliva, Minnesota	.323
1924	Babe Ruth, New York	.378	1965	Tony Oliva, Minnesota	.321
1925	Harry Heilmann, Detroit	.393	1966	Frank Robinson, Baltimore	.316
1926	Henry Manush, Detroit	.378	1967	Carl Yastrzemski, Boston	.326
1927	Harry Heilmann, Detroit	.398	1968	Carl Yastrzemski, Boston	.301
1928	Goose Goslin, Washington	.379	1969	Rod Carew, Minnesota	.332
1929	Lew Fonseca, Cleveland	.369	1970	Alex Johnson, California[2]	.329
1930	Al Simmons, Philadelphia	.381	1971	Tony Oliva, Minnesota	.337
1931	Al Simmons, Philadelphia	.390	1972	Rod Carew, Minnesota	.318
1932	Dale Alexander, Detroit-Boston	.367	1973	Rod Carew, Minnesota	.350
1933	Jimmy Foxx, Philadelphia	.356	1974	Rod Carew, Minnesota	.364
1934	Lou Gehrig, New York	.363	1975	Rod Carew, Minnesota	.359
1935	Buddy Myer, Washington	.349	1976	George Brett, Kansas City	.333
1936	Luke Appling, Chicago	.388	1977	Rod Carew, Minnesota	.388
1937	Charley Gehringer, Detroit	.371	1978	Rod Carew, Minnesota	.333
1938	Jimmy Foxx, Boston	.349	1979	Fred Lynn, Boston	.333
1939	Joe DiMaggio, New York	.381	1980	George Brett, Kansas City	.390
1940	Joe DiMaggio, New York	.352	1981	Carney Lansford, Boston	.336
1941	Ted Williams, Boston	.406			

[1] Kell .3429; Ted Williams, Boston .3427. [2] Johnson .3289; Carl Yastrzemski, Boston .3286.

AMERICAN LEAGUE HOME RUN CHAMPIONS

Year	Player and Club	Home Runs	Year	Player and Club	Home Runs
1901	Nap Lajoie, Philadelphia	13	1943	Rudy York, Detroit	34
1902	Ralph Seybold, Philadelphia	16	1944	Nick Etten, New York	22
1903	Buck Freeman, Boston	13	1945	Vern Stephens, St. Louis	24
1904	Harry Davis, Philadelphia	10	1946	Hank Greenberg, Detroit	44
1905	Harry Davis, Philadelphia	8	1947	Ted Williams, Boston	32
1906	Harry Davis, Philadelphia	12	1948	Joe DiMaggio, New York	39
1907	Harry Davis, Philadelphia	8	1949	Ted Williams, Boston	43
1908	Sam Crawford, Detroit	7	1950	Al Rosen, Cleveland	37
1909	Ty Cobb, Detroit	9	1951	Gus Zernial, Chicago-Philadelphia	33
1910	J. Garland Stahl, Boston	10	1952	Larry Doby, Cleveland	32
1911	Franklin Baker, Philadelphia	9	1953	Al Rosen, Cleveland	43
1912	Franklin Baker, Philadelphia	10	1954	Larry Doby, Cleveland	32
1913	Franklin Baker, Philadelphia	12	1955	Mickey Mantle, New York	37
1914	Franklin Baker, Philadelphia	8	1956	Mickey Mantle, New York	52
	Sam Crawford, Detroit	8	1957	Roy Sievers, Washington	42
1915	Robert Roth, Chi.-Cleve.	7	1958	Mickey Mantle, New York	42
1916	Wally Pipp, New York	12	1959	Rocky Colavito, Cleveland	42
1917	Wally Pipp, New York	9		Harmon Killebrew, Washington	42
1918	Clarence Walker, Philadelphia	11	1960	Mickey Mantle, New York	40
	Babe Ruth, Boston	11	1961	Roger Maris, New York	61
1919	Babe Ruth, Boston	29	1962	Harmon Killebrew, Minnesota	48
1920	Babe Ruth, New York	54	1963	Harmon Killebrew, Minnesota	45
1921	Babe Ruth, New York	59	1964	Harmon Killebrew, Minnesota	49
1922	Ken Williams, St. Louis	39	1965	Tony Conigliaro, Boston	32
1923	Babe Ruth, New York	41	1966	Frank Robinson, Baltimore	49
1924	Babe Ruth, New York	46	1967	Harmon Killebrew, Minnesota	44
1925	Bob Meusel, New York	33		Carl Yastrzemski, Boston	44
1926	Babe Ruth, New York	47	1968	Frank Howard, Washington	44
1927	Babe Ruth, New York	60	1969	Harmon Killebrew, Minnesota	49
1928	Babe Ruth, New York	54	1970	Frank Howard, Washington	44
1929	Babe Ruth, New York	46	1971	Bill Melton, Chicago	33
1930	Babe Ruth, New York	49	1972	Dick Allen, Chicago	37
1931	Babe Ruth, New York	46	1973	Reggie Jackson, Oakland	32
	Lou Gehrig, New York	46	1974	Dick Allen, Chicago	32
1932	Jimmy Foxx, Philadelphia	58	1975	Reggie Jackson, Oakland	36
1933	Jimmy Foxx, Philadelphia	48		George Scott, Milwaukee	36
1934	Lou Gehrig, New York	49	1976	Graig Nettles, New York	32
1935	Jimmy Foxx, Philadelphia	36	1977	Jim Rice, Boston	39
	Hank Greenberg, Detroit	36	1978	Jim Rice, Boston	46
1936	Lou Gehrig, New York	49	1979	Gorman Thomas, Milwaukee	45
1937	Joe DiMaggio, New York	46		Ben Oglivie, Milwaukee	41
1938	Hank Greenberg, Detroit	58	1980	Reggie Jackson, New York	41
1939	Jimmy Foxx, Boston	35	1981	Eddie Murray, Baltimore	22
1940	Hank Greenberg, Detroit	41		Dwight Evans, Boston	22
1941	Ted Williams, Boston	37		Bobby Grich, California	22
1942	Ted Williams, Boston	36		Tony Armas, Oakland	22

AMERICAN LEAGUE RUNS BATTED IN CHAMPIONS

Year	Player and Club	RBI	Year	Player and Club	RBI
1920	Babe Ruth, New York	137	1951	Gus Zernial, Chicago-Philadelphia	129
1921	Babe Ruth, New York	171	1952	Al Rosen, Cleveland	105
1922	Ken Williams, St. Louis	155	1953	Al Rosen, Cleveland	145
1923	Babe Ruth, New York	131	1954	Larry Doby, Cleveland	126
1924	Goose Goslin, Washington	129	1955	Ray Boone, Detroit	116
1925	Bob Meusel, New York	138		Jackie Jensen, Boston	116
1926	Babe Ruth, New York	145	1956	Mickey Mantle, New York	130
1927	Lou Gehrig, New York	175	1957	Roy Sievers, Washington	114
1928	Lou Gehrig, New York	142	1958	Jackie Jensen, Boston	122
	Babe Ruth, New York	142	1959	Jackie Jensen, Boston	112
1929	Al Simmons, Philadelphia	157	1960	Roger Maris, New York	112
1930	Lou Gehrig, New York	174	1961	Roger Maris, New York	142
1931	Lou Gehrig, New York	184	1962	Harmon Killebrew, Minnesota	126
1932	Jimmie Foxx, Philadelphia	169	1963	Dick Stuart, Boston	118
1933	Jimmie Foxx, Philadelphia	163	1964	Brooks Robinson, Baltimore	118
1934	Lou Gehrig, New York	165	1965	Rocky Colavito, Cleveland	108
1935	Hank Greenberg, Detroit	170	1966	Frank Robinson, Baltimore	122
1936	Hal Trosky, Cleveland	162	1967	Carl Yastrzemski, Boston	121
1937	Hank Greenberg, Detroit	183	1968	Ken Harrelson, Boston	109
1938	Jimmie Foxx, Boston	175	1969	Harmon Killebrew, Minnesota	140
1939	Ted Williams, Boston	145	1970	Frank Howard, Washington	126
1940	Hank Greenberg, Detroit	150	1971	Harmon Killebrew, Minnesota	119
1941	Joe DiMaggio, New York	125	1972	Richie Allen, Chicago	113
1942	Ted Williams, Boston	137	1973	Reggie Jackson, Oakland	117
1943	Rudy York, Detroit	118	1974	Jeff Burroughs, Texas	118
1944	Vern Stephens, St. Louis	109	1975	George Scott, Boston	109
1945	Nick Etten, New York	111	1976	Lee May, Baltimore	109
1946	Hank Greenberg, Detroit	127	1977	Larry Hisle, Minnesota	119
1947	Ted Williams, Boston	114	1978	Jim Rice, Boston	139
1948	Joe DiMaggio, New York	155	1979	Don Baylor, California	139
1949	Ted Williams, Boston	159	1980	Cecil Cooper, Milwaukee	122
	Vern Stephens, Boston	159	1981	Eddie Murray, Baltimore	78
1950	Vern Stephens, Boston	144			
	Walt Dropo, Boston	144			

PITCHERS WITH BEST WON-AND-LOST PERCENTAGES

NATIONAL LEAGUE				AMERICAN LEAGUE			
Year Pitcher and Club	Won	Lost	Per-cent	Year Pitcher and Club	Won	Lost	Per-cent
1941—Elmer Riddle, Cincinnati	19	4	.826	1941—Lefty Gomez, New York	15	5	.750
1942—Larry French, Brooklyn	15	4	.789	1942—Ernie Bonham, New York	21	5	.808
1943—Mort Cooper, St. Louis	21	8	.724	1943—Spud Chandler, New York	20	4	.833
1944—Ted Wilkes, St. Louis	17	4	.810	1944—Tex Hughson, Boston	18	5	.783
1945—Harry Brecheen, St. Louis	15	4	.789	1945—Hal Newhouser, Detroit	25	9	.735
1946—Murry Dickson, St. Louis	15	6	.714	1946—Dave Ferriss, Boston	25	6	.806
1947—Larry Jansen, New York	21	5	.808	1947—Allie Reynolds, New York	19	8	.704
1948—Harry Brecheen, St. Louis	20	7	.741	1948—Jack Kramer, Boston	18	5	.783
1949—Preacher Roe, Brooklyn	15	6	.714	1949—Ellis Kinder, Boston	23	6	.793
1950—Sal Maglie, New York	18	4	.818	1950—Vic Raschi, New York	21	8	.724
1951—Preacher Roe, Brooklyn	22	3	.880	1951—Bob Feller, Cleveland	22	8	.733
1952—Hoyt Wilhelm, New York	15	3	.833	1952—Bobby Shantz, Philadelphia	24	7	.774
1953—Carl Erskine, Brooklyn	20	6	.769	1953—Ed Lopat, New York	16	4	.800
1954—Antonelli, New York	21	7	.750	1954—Sandy Consuegra, Chicago	16	3	.842
1955—Don Newcombe, Brooklyn	20	5	.800	1955—Tommy Byrne, New York	16	5	.762
1956—Don Newcombe, Brooklyn	27	7	.794	1956—Whitey Ford, New York	19	6	.760
1957—Bob Ruhl, Milwaukee	18	7	.720	1957—Dick Donovan, Chicago	16	6	.727
1958—Warren Spahn, Milwaukee	22	11	.667	Tom Sturdivant, New York	16	6	.727
Lew Burdette, Milwaukee	20	10	.667	1958—Bob Turley, New York	21	7	.750
1959—El Roy Face, Pittsburgh	18	1	.947	1959—Bob Shaw, Chicago	18	6	.750
1960—Ernie Broglio, St. Louis	21	9	.700	1960—Jim Perry, Cleveland	18	10	.643
1961—Johnny Podres, Los Angeles	18	5	.783	1961—Whitey Ford, New York	25	4	.862
1962—Bob Purkey, Cincinnati	23	5	.821	1962—Ray Herbert, Chicago	20	9	.690
1963—Ron Perranoski, Los Angeles	16	3	.842	1963—Whitey Ford, New York	24	7	.774
1964—Sandy Koufax, Los Angeles	19	5	.792	1964—Wally Bunker, Baltimore	19	5	.792
1965—Sandy Koufax, Los Angeles	26	8	.765	1965—Jim Grant, Minnesota	21	7	.750
1966—Juan Marichal, San Francisco	25	6	.806	1966—Sonny Seibert, Cleveland	16	8	.667
1967—Dick Hughes, St. Louis	16	6	.727	1967—Joel Horlen, Chicago	19	7	.731
1968—Steve Blass, Pittsburgh	18	6	.750	1968—Denny McLain, Detroit	31	6	.836
1969—Tom Seaver, New York	25	7	.781	1969—Jim Palmer, Baltimore	16	4	.800
1970—Bob Gibson, St. Louis	23	7	.767	1970—Mike Cuellar, Baltimore	24	8	.750
1971—Tug McGraw, New York	11	4	.733	1971—Daye McNally, Baltimore	21	5	.807
1972—Steve Carlton, Philadelphia	27	10	.730	1972—James Hunter, Oakland	21	7	.750
1973—Tommy John, Los Angeles	16	7	.696	1973—James Hunter, Oakland	21	5	.808
1974—Tommy John, Los Angeles	13	3	.813	1974—Mike Cuellar, Baltimore	22	10	.688
1975—Al Hrabosky, St. Louis	13	3	.813	1975—Roger Moret, Boston	14	3	.824
1976—Steve Carlton, Philadelphia	20	7	.741	1976—Wayne Garland, Baltimore	20	7	.741
1977—John Candelaria, Pittsburgh	20	5	.800	1977—Paul Splittorff, Kansas City	16	6	.727
1978—Gaylord Perry, San Diego	21	6	.778	1978—Ron Guidry, New York	25	3	.893
1979—Tom Seaver, Cincinnati	16	6	.727	1979—Mike Caldwell, Milwaukee	16	6	.727
1980—Jim Bibby, Pittsburgh	19	6	.760	1980—Steve Stone, Baltimore	25	7	.781
1981—Tom Seaver, Cincinnati	14	2	.875	1981—Pete Vuckovich, Milwaukee	14	4	.778

PITCHERS WITH LOWEST-EARNED-RUN AVERAGES

NATIONAL LEAGUE			AMERICAN LEAGUE		
Year Pitcher and Club	Innings Pitched	ERA	Year Pitcher and Club	Innings Pitched	ERA
1945 .... Hank Borowy, Chicago	122	2.14	1945 .... Hal Newhouser, Detroit	313	1.81
1946 .... Howie Pollet, St. Louis	266	2.10	1946 .... Hal Newhouser, Detroit	293	1.94
1947 .... Warren Spahn, Boston	290	2.33	1947 .... Spud Chandler, New York	128	2.46
1948 .... Harry Brecheen, St. Louis	233	2.24	1948 .... Gene Bearden, Cleveland	230	2.43
1949 .... Dave Koslo, New York	212	2.50	1949 .... Mel Parnell, Boston	295	2.78
1950 .... Jim Hearn, St. Louis-New York	134	2.49	1950 .... Early Wynn, Cleveland	214	3.20
1951 .... Chet Nichols, Boston	156	2.88	1951 .... Saul Rogovin, Detroit-Chicago	217	2.78
1952 .... Hoyt Wilhelm, New York	159	2.43	1952 .... Allie Reynolds, New York	244	2.07
1953 .... Warren Spahn, Milwaukee	266	2.10	1953 .... Eddie Lopat, New York	178	2.43
1954 .... John Antonelli, New York	259	2.29	1954 .... Mike Garcia, Cleveland	259	2.64
1955 .... Bob Friend, Pittsburgh	200	2.84	1955 .... Billy Pierce, Chicago	206	1.97
1956 .... Lew Burdette, Milwaukee	256	2.71	1956 .... Whitey Ford, New York	226	2.47
1957 .... John Podres, Brooklyn	196	2.66	1957 .... Bobby Shantz, New York	173	2.45
1958 .... Stu Miller, San Francisco	182	2.47	1958 .... Whitey Ford, New York	219	2.01
1959 .... Sam Jones, San Francisco	271	2.82	1959 .... Hoyt Wilhelm, Baltimore	226	2.19
1960 .... Mike McCormick, San Francisco	253	2.70	1960 .... Frank Baumann, Chicago	185	2.68
1961 .... Warren Spahn, Milwaukee	263	3.01	1961 .... Dick Donovan, Washington	169	2.40
1962 .... Sandy Koufax, Los Angeles	184	2.54	1962 .... Hank Aguirre, Detroit	216	2.21
1963 .... Sandy Koufax, Los Angeles	311	1.88	1963 .... Gary Peters, Chicago	243	2.33
1964 .... Sandy Koufax, Los Angeles	223	1.74	1964 .... Dean Chance, Los Angeles	278	1.65
1965 .... Sandy Koufax, Los Angeles	336	2.04	1965 .... Sam McDowell, Cleveland	273	2.18
1966 .... Sandy Koufax, Los Angeles	323	1.73	1966 .... Gary Peters, Chicago	205	1.98
1967 .... Phil Niekro, Atlanta	207	1.87	1967 .... Joel Horlen, Chicago	258	2.06
1968 .... Bob Gibson, St. Louis	305	1.12	1968 .... Luis Tiant, Cleveland	258	1.60
1969 .... Juan Marichal, San Francisco	300	2.10	1969 .... Dick Bosman, Washington	193	2.19
1970 .... Tom Seaver, New York	291	2.81	1970 .... Diego Segui, Oakland	162	2.56
1971 .... Tom Seaver, New York	286	1.76	1971 .... Vida Blue, Oakland	312	1.82
1972 .... Steve Carlton, Philadelphia	346	1.98	1972 .... Luis Tiant, Boston	179	1.91
1973 .... Tom Seaver, New York	290	2.08	1973 .... Jim Palmer, Baltimore	296	2.40
1974 .... Buzz Capra, Atlanta	217	2.28	1974 .... James Hunter, Oakland	318	2.49
1975 .... Randy Jones, San Diego	288	2.24	1975 .... Jim Palmer, Baltimore	323	2.09
1976 .... John Denny, St. Louis	207	2.52	1976 .... Mark Fidrych, Detroit	250	2.34
1977 .... John Candelaria, Pittsburgh	231	2.34	1977 .... Frank Tanana, California	241	2.54
1978 .... Craig Swan, New York	207	2.43	1978 .... Ron Guidry, New York	274	1.74
1979 .... J. Rodney Richard, Houston	292	2.71	1979 .... Ron Guidry, New York	236	2.78
1980 .... Don Sutton, Los Angeles	212	2.21	1980 .... Rudy May, New York	175	2.47
1981 .... Nolan Ryan, Houston	149	1.69	1981 .... Steve McCatty, Oakland	185	2.33

MOST NO-HITTERS IN A LIFETIME

5, Nolan Ryan, California (AL), 1973, 1973, 1974, 1975;
Houston (NL), 1981
4, Sandy Koufax, Los Angeles (NL), 1962, 1963, 1964, 1965.
3, Cy Young, Boston (NL–AL), 1897, 1904, 1908.
3, Bob Feller, Cleveland (AL), 1940, 1946, 1951.
3, Jim Maloney, Cincinnati (NL), 1965 (2), 1969

NO-HITTERS OF TEN OR MORE INNINGS

Year	Pitcher	Clubs Playing	Score
1884	Samuel Kimber	Brooklyn–Toledo (AA)	0–0
1906	Harry McIntire	Brooklyn–Pittsburgh (NL)	0–1
1908	George Wiltse	New York–Philadelphia (NL)	1–0
1917	Fred Toney	Cincinnati–Chicago (NL)	1–0
1959	Harvey Haddix	Pittsburgh–Milwaukee (NL)*	0–1
1965	Jim Maloney	Cincinnati–New York (NL)	0–1
1965	Jim Maloney	Cincinnati–Chicago (NL)	1–0

* Perfect game for 12 innings. Lost in 13th.

PERFECT GAMES

1880	John Richmond	Worcester–Cleveland (NL)	1–0
1880	John Ward	Providence–Buffalo (NL)	5–0
1904	Cy Young	Boston–Philadelphia (AL)	3–0
1908	Addie Joss	Cleveland–Chicago (AL)	1–0
1917	Ernie Shore*	Boston–Washington (AL)	4–0
1922	Charles Robertson	Chicago–Detroit (AL)	2–0
1956	Don Larsen†	New York (AL)–Brooklyn (NL)	2–0
1964	Jim Bunning	Philadelphia–New York (NL)	6–0
1965	Sandy Koufax	Los Angeles–Chicago (NL)	1–0
1968	Jim Hunter	Oakland–Minnesota (AL)	4–0
1981	Len Barker	Cleveland–Toronto (AL)	3–0

* Babe Ruth, the starting pitcher, was ejected from the game by the umpire after walking the first batter. Ernie Shore relieved him, the base-runner was thrown out trying to steal second base, and Shore retired the next 26 batters to complete a perfect game. † The only World Series perfect game.

CY YOUNG AWARD

Year	Pitcher
BOTH MAJOR LEAGUES	
1956	Don Newcombe, Dodgers (NL)
1957	Warren Spahn, Boston (NL)
1958	Bob Turley, New York (AL)
1959	Early Wynn, Chicago (AL)
1960	Vernon Law, Pittsburgh (NL)
1961	Whitey Ford, New York (AL)
1962	Don Drysdale, Los Angeles (NL)
1963	Sandy Koufax, Los Angeles (NL)
1964	Dean Chance, Los Angeles (AL)
1965	Sandy Koufax, Los Angeles (NL)
1966	Sandy Koufax, Los Angeles (NL)
NATIONAL LEAGUE	
1967	Mike McCormick, San Francisco
1968	Bob Gibson, St. Louis
1969	Tom Seaver, New York
1970	Bob Gibson, St. Louis
1971	Ferguson Jenkins, Chicago
1972	Steve Carlton, Philadelphia
1973	Tom Seaver, New York
1974	Mike Marshall, Los Angeles
1975	Tom Seaver, New York
1976	Randy Jones, San Diego
1977	Steve Carlton, Philadelphia
1978	Gaylord Perry, San Diego
1979	Bruce Sutter, Chicago
1980	Steve Carlton, Philadelphia
AMERICAN LEAGUE	
1967	Jim Lonborg, Boston
1968	Denny McLain, Detroit
1969	Denny McLain, Detroit
	Mike Cuellar, Baltimore
1970	Jim Perry, Minnesota
1971	Vida Blue, Oakland
1972	Gaylord Perry, Cleveland
1973	Jim Palmer, Baltimore
1974	James Hunter, Oakland
1975	Jim Palmer, Baltimore
1976	Jim Palmer, Baltimore
1977	Sparky Lyle, New York
1978	Ron Guidry, New York
1979	Mike Flanagan, Baltimore
1980	Steve Stone, Baltimore

MAJOR LEAGUE NO-HIT GAMES SINCE 1969

Year	Pitcher	Clubs Playing	Score	Year	Pitcher	Clubs Playing	Score
1969	Bill Stoneman	Montreal–Philadelphia (NL)	6–0	1974	Dick Bosman	Cleveland–Oakland (AL)	4–0
1969	Jim Maloney	Cincinnati–Houston (NL)	10–0	1974	Nolan Ryan	California–Minnesota (AL)	4–0
1969	Don Wilson	Houston–Cincinnati (NL)	4–0	1975	Nolan Ryan	California–Baltimore (AL)	1–0
1969	Jim Palmer	Baltimore–Oakland (AL)	8–0	1975	Ed Halicki	San Francisco–New York (NL)	6–0
1969	Ken Holtzman	Chicago–Atlanta (NL)	3–0	1975	Vida Blue, Glenn		
1969	Bob Moose	Pittsburgh–New York (NL)	4–0		Abbott, Paul Lind-		
1970	Dock Ellis	Pittsburgh–San Diego (NL)	2–0		blad, Rollie Fingers	Oakland–California (AL)	5–0
1970	Clyde Wright	California–Oakland (AL)	4–0	1976	Larry Dierker	Houston–Montreal (NL)	6–0
1970	Bill Singer	Los Angeles–Philadelphia (NL)	5–0	1976	John Odom,		
1970	Vida Blue	Oakland–Minnesota (AL)	6–0		Francisco Barrios	Chicago–California (AL)	2–1
1971	Ken Holtzman	Chicago–Cincinnati (NL)	1–0	1976	John Candelaria	Pittsburgh–Los Angeles (NL)	2–0
1971	Rick Wise	Philadelphia–Cincinnati (NL)	4–0	1976	John Montefusco	San Francisco–Atlanta (NL)	9–0
1971	Bob Gibson	St. Louis–Pittsburgh (NL)	11–0	1977	Jim Colborn	Kansas City–Texas (AL)	6–0
1972	Burt Hooton	Chicago–Philadelphia (NL)	4–0	1977	Dennis Eckersley	Cleveland–California (AL)	1–0
1972	Milt Pappas	Chicago–San Diego (NL)	8–0	1977	Bert Blyleven	Texas–California (AL)	6–0
1972	Bill Stoneman	Montreal–New York (NL)	7–0	1978	Bob Forsch	St. Louis–Philadelphia (NL)	5–0
1973	Steve Busby	Kansas City–Detroit (AL)	3–0	1978	Tom Seaver	Cincinnati–St. Louis (NL)	4–0
1973	Nolan Ryan	California–Kansas City (AL)	3–0	1979	Ken Forsch	Houston–Atlanta (NL)	6–0
1973	Nolan Ryan	California–Detroit (AL)	6–0	1980	Jerry Reuss	Los Angeles–San Francisco (NL)	8–0
1973	Jim Bibby	Texas–Oakland (AL)	6–0	1981	Charlie Lea	Montreal-San Francisco (NL)	4–0
1973	Phil Niekro	Atlanta–San Diego (NL)	9–0	1981	Len Barker	Cleveland–Toronto (AL)	3–0
1974	Steve Busby	Kansas City–Milwaukee (AL)	2–0	1981	Nolan Ryan	Houston–Los Angeles (NL)	5–0

LONGEST GAMES IN THE MAJOR LEAGUES

Innings	Teams	Date	Innings	Teams	Date
26	Brooklyn 1, Boston 1, NL	May 1, 1920	24	Houston 1, New York 0, NL	April 15, 1968
25	St. Louis 4, New York 3, NL	Sept. 11, 1974	23	Brooklyn 2, Boston 2, NL	June 27, 1939
24	Philadelphia 4, Boston 1, AL	Sept. 1, 1906	23	San Francisco 8, New York 6, NL	May 31, 1964
24	Detroit 1, Philadelphia 1, AL	July 21, 1945			

MOST-VALUABLE-PLAYER AWARD SOURCE: Baseball Writers' Association of America

NATIONAL LEAGUE

Year	Player	Club
1931	Frank Frisch	St. Louis
1932	Chuck Klein	Philadelphia
1933	Carl Hubbell	New York
1934	Dizzy Dean	St. Louis
1935	Gabby Hartnett	Chicago
1936	Carl Hubbell	New York
1937	Joe Medwick	St. Louis
1938	Ernie Lombardi	Cincinnati
1939	Bucky Walters	Cincinnati
1940	Frank McCormick	Cincinnati
1941	Dolph Camilli	Brooklyn
1942	Mort Cooper	St. Louis
1943	Stan Musial	St. Louis
1944	Marty Marion	St. Louis
1945	Phil Cavarretta	Chicago
1946	Stan Musial	St. Louis
1947	Bob Elliott	Boston
1948	Stan Musial	St. Louis
1949	Jackie Robinson	Brooklyn
1950	Jim Konstanty	Philadelphia
1951	Roy Campanella	Brooklyn
1952	Hank Sauer	Chicago
1953	Roy Campanella	Brooklyn
1954	Willie Mays	New York
1955	Roy Campanella	Brooklyn
1956	Don Newcombe	Brooklyn
1957	Hank Aaron	Milwaukee
1958	Ernie Banks	Chicago
1959	Ernie Banks	Chicago
1960	Dick Groat	Pittsburgh
1961	Frank Robinson	Cincinnati
1962	Maury Wills	Los Angeles
1963	Sandy Koufax	Los Angeles
1964	Ken Boyer	St. Louis
1965	Willie Mays	San Francisco
1966	Roberto Clemente	Pittsburgh
1967	Orlando Cepeda	St. Louis
1968	Bob Gibson	St. Louis
1969	Willie McCovey	San Francisco
1970	Johnny Bench	Cincinnati
1971	Joe Torre	St. Louis
1972	Johnny Bench	Cincinnati
1973	Pete Rose	Cincinnati
1974	Steve Garvey	Los Angeles
1975	Joe Morgan	Cincinnati
1976	Joe Morgan	Cincinnati
1977	George Foster	Cincinnati
1978	Dave Parker	Pittsburgh
1979	Willie Stargell	Pittsburgh
	Keith Hernandez	St. Louis
1980	Mike Schmidt	Philadelphia

AMERICAN LEAGUE

Year	Player	Club
1931	Lefty Grove	Philadelphia
1932	Jimmy Foxx	Philadelphia
1933	Jimmy Foxx	Philadelphia
1934	Mickey Cochrane	Detroit
1935	Hank Greenberg	Detroit
1936	Lou Gehrig	New York
1937	Charley Gehringer	Detroit
1938	Jimmy Foxx	Boston
1939	Joe DiMaggio	New York
1940	Hank Greenberg	Detroit
1941	Joe DiMaggio	New York
1942	Joe Gordon	New York
1943	Spud Chandler	New York
1944	Hal Newhouser	Detroit
1945	Hal Newhouser	Detroit
1946	Ted Williams	Boston
1947	Joe DiMaggio	New York
1948	Lou Boudreau	Cleveland
1949	Ted Williams	Boston
1950	Phil Rizzuto	New York
1951	Yogi Berra	New York
1952	Bobby Shantz	Philadelphia
1953	Al Rosen	Cleveland
1954	Yogi Berra	New York
1955	Yogi Berra	New York
1956	Mickey Mantle	New York
1957	Mickey Mantle	New York
1958	Jackie Jensen	Boston
1959	Nelson Fox	Chicago
1960	Roger Maris	New York
1961	Roger Maris	New York
1962	Mickey Mantle	New York
1963	Elston Howard	New York
1964	Brooks Robinson	Baltimore
1965	Zoilo Versalles	Minnesota
1966	Frank Robinson	Baltimore
1967	Carl Yastrzemski	Boston
1968	Denny McLain	Detroit
1969	Harmon Killebrew	Minnesota
1970	John (Boog) Powell	Baltimore
1971	Vida Blue	Oakland
1972	Dick Allen	Chicago
1973	Reggie Jackson	Oakland
1974	Jeff Burroughs	Texas
1975	Fred Lynn	Boston
1976	Thurman Munson	New York
1977	Rod Carew	Minnesota
1978	Jim Rice	Boston
1979	Don Baylor	California
1980	George Brett	Kansas City

ROOKIE-OF-THE-YEAR AWARD

NATIONAL LEAGUE

Year	Player and Position	Club
1949	Don Newcombe, pitcher	Brooklyn
1950	Sam Jethroe, outfielder	Boston
1951	Willie Mays, outfielder	New York
1952	Joe Black, pitcher	Brooklyn
1953	Jim Gilliam, second baseman	Brooklyn
1954	Wally Moon, outfielder	St. Louis
1955	Bill Virdon, outfielder	St. Louis
1956	Frank Robinson, outfielder	Cincinnati
1957	Jack Sanford, pitcher	Philadelphia
1958	Orlando Cepeda, first baseman	San Francisco
1959	Willie McCovey, first baseman	San Francisco
1960	Frank Howard, outfielder	Los Angeles
1961	Billy Williams, outfielder	Chicago
1962	Ken Hubbs, second baseman	Chicago
1963	Pete Rose, second baseman	Cincinnati
1964	Richie Allen, third baseman	Philadelphia
1965	Jim Lefebvre, second baseman	Los Angeles
1966	Tommy Helms, third baseman	Cincinnati
1967	Tom Seaver, pitcher	New York
1968	Johnny Bench, catcher	Cincinnati
1969	Ted Sizemore, second baseman	Los Angeles
1970	Carl Morton, pitcher	Montreal
1971	Earl Williams, catcher	Atlanta
1972	Jon Matlack, pitcher	New York
1973	Gary Mathews, outfielder	San Francisco
1974	Bake McBride, outfielder	St. Louis
1975	John Montefusco, pitcher	San Francisco
1976	Pat Zachry, pitcher	Cincinnati
	Butch Metzger, pitcher	San Diego
1977	Andre Dawson, outfielder	Montreal
1978	Bob Horner, third baseman	Atlanta
1979	Rick Sutcliffe, pitcher	Los Angeles
1980	Steve Howe, pitcher	Los Angeles

AMERICAN LEAGUE

Year	Player and Position	Club
1949	Roy Sievers, outfielder	St. Louis
1950	Walt Dropo, first baseman	Boston
1951	Gil McDougald, third baseman	New York
1952	Harry Byrd, pitcher	Philadelphia
1953	Harvey Kuenn, shortstop	Detroit
1954	Bob Grim, pitcher	New York
1955	Herb Score, pitcher	Cleveland
1956	Luis Aparicio, shortstop	Chicago
1957	Tony Kubek, infielder-outfielder	New York
1958	Albie Pearson, outfielder	Washington
1959	Bob Allison, outfielder	Washington
1960	Ron Hansen, shortstop	Baltimore
1961	Don Schwall, pitcher	Boston
1962	Tom Tresh, infielder-outfielder	New York
1963	Gary Peters, pitcher	Chicago
1964	Tony Oliva, outfielder	Minnesota
1965	Curt Blefary, outfielder	Baltimore
1966	Tommie Agee, outfielder	Chicago
1967	Rod Carew, second baseman	Minnesota
1968	Stan Bahnsen, pitcher	New York
1969	Lou Piniella, outfielder	Kansas City
1970	Thurman Munson, catcher	New York
1971	Chris Chambliss, infielder	Cleveland
1972	Carlton Fisk, catcher	Boston
1973	Al Bumbry, outfielder	Baltimore
1974	Mike Hargrove, first baseman	Texas
1975	Fred Lynn, outfielder	Boston
1976	Mark Fidrych, pitcher	Detroit
1977	Eddie Murray, first baseman	Baltimore
1978	Lou Whitaker, second baseman	Detroit
1979	John Castino, third baseman	Minnesota
	Alfredo Griffin, shortstop	Toronto
1980	Joe Charboneau, outfielder	Cleveland

ROBERTO CLEMENTE AWARD

Ability, sportsmanship, character, community involvement, humanitarianism, contribution to team and baseball

1971	Willie Mays, San Francisco	1974	Willie Stargell, Pittsburgh	1978	Greg Luzinski, Philadelphia
1972	Brooks Robinson, Baltimore	1975	Lou Brock, St. Louis	1979	Andre Thornton, Cleveland
1973	Al Kaline, Detroit	1976	Pete Rose, Cincinnati	1980	Phil Niekro, Atlanta
		1977	Rod Carew, Minnesota	1981	Steve Garvey, Los Angeles

BASEBALL STADIUMS

AMERICAN LEAGUE

	Seating	Field Distances			Wall Heights		
		LF	CF	RF	LF	CF	RF
Baltimore (Memorial Stadium)	52,860	309'	405'	309'	14'	7'	14'
Boston (Fenway Park)	33,538	315'	390'	302'	37'	17'	3–5'
California (Anaheim Stadium)	67,335	333'	404'	370'	8'	8'	8'
Chicago (Comiskey Park)	44,492	352'	445'	352'	9'	17'	9'
Cleveland (Municipal Stadium)	76,713	320'	400'	320'	9'	8'	9'
Detroit (Tiger Stadium)	52,687	340'	440'	325'	9'	9'	9'
Kansas City (Royals Stadium)	40,760	330'	410'	330'	12'	12'	12'
Milwaukee (County Stadium)	54,192	320'	402'	315'	10'	10'	10'
Minnesota (Metropolitan Stadium)	45,919	343'	402'	330'	12'	8'	8'
New York (Yankee Stadium)	57,545	312'	417'	310'	8'	7'	10'
Oakland (Oakland Coliseum)	50,000	330'	400'	330'	8'	8'	8'
Seattle (Kingdome)	59,438	316'	410'	316'	11½'	11½'	11½'
Texas (Arlington Stadium)	41,097	330'	400'	330'	11'	11'	11'
Toronto (Exhibition Stadium)	43,737	330'	400'	330'	12'	12'	12'

NATIONAL LEAGUE

	Seating	Field Distances			Wall Heights		
		LF	CF	RF	LF	CF	RF
Atlanta (Atlanta Stadium)	52,194	330'	402'	330'	6'	6'	6'
Chicago (Wrigley Field)	37,741	355'	400'	353'	11½'	11½'	11½'
Cincinnati (Riverfront Stadium)	52,392	330'	404'	330'	12'	12'	12'
Houston (Astrodome)	45,000	340'	406'	340'	10'	10'	10'
Los Angeles (Dodger Stadium)	56,000	330'	395'	330'	8'	8'	8'
Montreal (Olympic Stadium)	59,984	325'	404'	325'	12'	12'	12'
New York (Shea Stadium)	55,300	341'	410'	341'	8'	8'	8'
Philadelphia (Veterans Stadium)	65,454	330'	408'	330'	12'	12'	12'
Pittsburgh (Three Rivers Stadium)	54,499	335'	400'	335'	10'	10'	10'
San Diego (San Diego Stadium)	51,362	330'	420'	330'	17'	17'	17'
San Francisco (Candlestick Park)	58,000	335'	410'	335'	12'	12'	12'
St. Louis (Busch Memorial Stadium)	50,222	330'	414'	330'	10½'	10½'	10½'

MINOR LEAGUE BASEBALL AFFILIATIONS: 1981

American League	Class AAA	Class AA	National League	Class AAA	Class AA
Baltimore	Rochester (IL)	Charlotte (SL)	Atlanta	Richmond (IL)	Savannah (SL)
Boston	Pawtucket (IL)	Bristol (EL)	Chicago	Iowa (AA)	Midland (TL)
California	Salt Lake City (PCL)	Holyoke (EL)	Cincinnati	Indianapolis (AA)	Waterbury (EL)
Chicago	Edmonton (PCL)	Glens Falls (EL)	Houston	Tucson (PCL)	Columbus (SL)
Cleveland	Charleston (IL)	Chattanooga (SL)	Los Angeles	Albuquerque (PCL)	San Antonio (TL)
Detroit	Evansville (AA)	Birmingham (SL)	Montreal	Denver (AA)	Memphis (SL)
Kansas City	Omaha (AA)	Jacksonville (SL)	New York	Tidewater (IL)	Jackson (TL)
Milwaukee	Vancouver (PCL)	El Paso (TL)	Philadelphia	Oklahoma City (AA)	Reading (EL)
Minnesota	Toledo (IL)	Orlando (SL)	Pittsburgh	Portland (PCL)	Buffalo (EL)
New York	Columbus (IL)	Nashville (SL)	St. Louis	Springfield (AA)	Arkansas (TL)
Oakland	Tacoma (PCL)	West Haven (EL)	San Diego	Hawaii (PCL)	Amarillo (TL)
Seattle	Spokane (PCL)	Lynn (EL)	San Francisco	Phoenix (PCL)	Shreveport (TL)
Texas	Wichita (AA)	Tulsa (TL)			
Toronto	Syracuse (IL)	Knoxville (SL)			

(AA) American Association, (IL) International League, (PCL) Pacific Coast League, (EL) Eastern League, (SL) Southern League, (TL) Texas League.

COLLEGE BASEBALL CHAMPIONS

	NCAA DIV. I	NCAA DIV. II	NCAA DIV. III	N.A.I.A.	JR. COLLEGES
1974	So. California	Calif.-Irvine	—	Lewis (Ill.)	Ranger (Tex.)
1975	Texas	Florida Southern	—	Lewis (Ill.)	Meramec (Mo.)
1976	Arizona	Cal. Poly-Pomona	Stanislaus St.	Lewis (Ill.)	Central Arizona
1977	Arizona State	Calif.-Riverside	Stanislaus St.	Lipscomb (Tenn.)	Yavapai (Ariz.)
1978	So. California	Florida Southern	Glassboro St.	Emporia St.	Ranger (Tex.)
1979	Cal. St.-Fullerton	Valdosta State	Glassboro St.	Lipscomb (Tenn.)	Middle Georgia
1980	Arizona	Cal. Poly-Pomona	Ithaca	Grand Canyon	Middle Georgia
1981	Arizona State	Florida Southern	Marietta	Grand Canyon	Miami-Dade

BASKETBALL

NATIONAL BASKETBALL ASSOCIATION (NBA)

Olympic Tower, 645 5th Ave., New York City 10022. Commissioner: Lawrence F. O'Brien.

EASTERN CONFERENCE

Atlantic Division	Governor	Coach
Boston Celtics	Harry Mangurian	Bill Fitch
New York Knicks	Michael Burke	Red Holzman
New Jersey Nets	Alan Cohen	Larry Brown
Philadelphia 76ers	F. Eugene Dixon	Billy Cunningham
Washington Bullets	Abe Pollin	Gene Shue

Central Division	Governor	Coach
Atlanta Hawks	Mike Gearon	Kevin Loughery
Chicago Bulls	William Wirtz	Jerry Sloan
Cleveland Cavaliers	Ted Stepien	Don Delaney
Detroit Pistons	William Davidson	Scotty Robertson
Indiana Pacers	Sam Nassi	Jack McKinney
Milwaukee Bucks	James Fitzgerald	Don Nelson

WESTERN CONFERENCE

Midwest Division	Governor	Coach
Dallas Mavericks	Donald Carter	Dick Motta
Denver Nuggets	Carl Scheer	Donnie Walsh
Houston Rockets	Gavin Maloof	Del Harris
Kansas City Kings	Paul Rosenberg	Cotton Fitzsimmons
San Antonio Spurs	Angelo Drossos	Stan Albeck
Utah Jazz	Sam Battistone	Tom Nissalke

Pacific Division	Governor	Coach
Golden State Warriors	Franklin Mieuli	Al Attles
Los Angeles Lakers	Jerry Buss	Paul Westhead
Phoenix Suns	Richard Bloch	John MacLeod
Portland Trail Blazers	Lawrence Weinberg	Jack Ramsay
San Diego Clippers	Irving Levin	Paul Silas
Seattle SuperSonics	Samuel Schulman	Lenny Wilkens

THE NBA CHAMPIONS

Season	Eastern Conference (W–L)	Western Conference (W–L)	Playoff Champions (W–L)
1957/58	Boston Celtics (49–23)	St. Louis Hawks (41–31)	St. Louis Hawks (4–2) over Boston
1958/59	Boston Celtics (52–20)	St. Louis Hawks (49–23)	Boston Celtics (4–0) over Minneapolis
1959/60	Boston Celtics (59–16)	St. Louis Hawks (46–29)	Boston Celtics (4–3) over St. Louis
1960/61	Boston Celtics (57–22)	St. Louis Hawks (51–28)	Boston Celtics (4–1) over St. Louis
1961/62	Boston Celtics (60–20)	Los Angeles Lakers (54–26)	Boston Celtics (4–3) over Los Angeles
1962/63	Boston Celtics (58–22)	Los Angeles Lakers (53–27)	Boston Celtics (4–2) over Los Angeles
1963/64	Boston Celtics (59–21)	San Francisco Warriors (48–32)	Boston Celtics (4–1) over San Francisco
1964/65	Boston Celtics (62–18)	Los Angeles Lakers (49–31)	Boston Celtics (4–1) over Los Angeles
1965/66	Philadelphia 76ers (55–25)	Los Angeles Lakers (45–35)	Boston Celtics (4–3) over Los Angeles
1966/67	Philadelphia 76ers (68–13)	San Francisco Warriors (44–37)	Philadelphia 76ers (4–2) over San Francisco
1967/68	Philadelphia 76ers (62–20)	St. Louis Hawks (56–26)	Boston Celtics (4–2) over Los Angeles
1968/69	Baltimore Bullets (57–25)	Los Angeles Lakers (55–27)	Boston Celtics (4–3) over Los Angeles
1969/70	New York Knickerbockers (60–22)	Los Angeles Lakers (46–36)	New York Knicks (4–3) over Los Angeles
1970/71	Baltimore Bullets (42–40)	Milwaukee Bucks (66–16)	Milwaukee Bucks (4–0) over Baltimore
1971/72	New York Knickerbockers (48–34)	Los Angeles Lakers (69–13)	Los Angeles Lakers (4–1) over New York
1972/73	New York Knickerbockers (57–25)	Los Angeles Lakers (60–22)	New York (4–1) over Los Angeles
1973/74	Boston Celtics (56–26)	Milwaukee Bucks (59–23)	Boston (4–3) over Milwaukee
1974/75	Washington Bullets (60–22)	Golden State Warriors (48–34)	Golden State (4–0) over Washington
1975/76	Boston Celtics (51–28)	Phoenix Suns (42–40)	Boston Celtics (4–2) over Phoenix
1976/77	Philadelphia 76ers (50–32)	Los Angeles Lakers (53–29)	Portland Trail Blazers (4–2) over Phila.
1977/78	Philadelphia 76ers (55–27)	Portland Trail Blazers (58–24)	Washington Bullets (4–3) over Seattle
1978/79	Washington Bullets (54–28)	Seattle SuperSonics (52–30)	Seattle (4–1) over Washington
1979/80	Boston Celtics (61–21)	Los Angeles Lakers (60–22)	Los Angeles (4–2) over Philadelphia
1980/81	Boston Celtics (62-20)	Phoenix Suns (57-25)	Boston (4-2) over Houston

TOP NBA SCORERS

Season	Player and Team	Points	Game Avg.	Season	Player and Team	Points	Game Avg.
1957/58	George Yardley, Detroit	2,001	27.8	1969/70	Jerry West, Los Angeles	2,309	31.2
1958/59	Bob Pettit, St. Louis	2,105	29.2	1970/71	Lew Alcindor, Milwaukee	2,596	31.7
1959/60	Wilt Chamberlain, Philadelphia	2,707	37.6	1971/72	Kareem Abdul-Jabbar, Milwaukee	2,822	34.8
1960/61	Wilt Chamberlain, Philadelphia	3,033	38.4	1972/73	Nate Archibald, Kansas City-Omaha	2,719	34.0
1961/62	Wilt Chamberlain, Philadelphia	4,029	50.4	1973/74	Bob McAdoo, Buffalo	2,261	30.6
1962/63	Wilt Chamberlain, San Francisco	3,586	44.8	1974/75	Bob McAdoo, Buffalo	2,831	34.5
1963/64	Wilt Chamberlain, San Francisco	2,948	36.5	1975/76	Bob McAdoo, Buffalo	2,427	31.1
1964/65	Wilt Chamberlain, Philadelphia	2,534	34.7	1976/77	Pete Maravich, New Orleans	2,273	31.1
1965/66	Wilt Chamberlain, Philadelphia	2,649	33.5	1977/78	George Gervin, San Antonio	2,232	27.2
1966/67	Rick Barry, San Francisco	2,775	35.6	1978/79	George Gervin, San Antonio	2,365	29.6
1967/68	Dave Bing, Detroit	2,142	27.1	1979/80	George Gervin, San Antonio	2,585	33.1
1968/69	Elvin Hayes, San Diego	2,327	28.4	1980/81	Adrian Dantley, Utah	2,452	30.7

TOP NBA FIELD GOAL PERCENTAGE

Season	Pct.	Player and Team	Season	Pct.	Player and Team
1957/58	.452	Jack Twyman, Cincinnati	1969/70	.559	Johnny Green, Cincinnati
1958/59	.490	Ken Sears, New York	1970/71	.587	Johnny Green, Cincinnati
1959/60	.477	Ken Sears, New York	1971/72	.649	Wilt Chamberlain, Los Angeles
1960/61	.509	Wilt Chamberlain, Philadelphia	1972/73	.727	Wilt Chamberlain, Los Angeles
1961/62	.519	Walt Bellamy, Chicago	1973/74	.547	Bob McAdoo, Buffalo
1962/63	.528	Wilt Chamberlain, San Francisco	1974/75	.539	Don Nelson, Boston
1963/64	.527	Jerry Lucas, Cincinnati	1975/76	.561	Wes Unseld, Washington
1964/65	.510	Wilt Chamberlain, Philadelphia	1976/77	.579	Kareem Abdul-Jabbar, Los Angeles
1965/66	.540	Wilt Chamberlain, Philadelphia	1977/78	.578	Bobby Jones, Denver
1966/67	.683	Wilt Chamberlain, Philadelphia	1978/79	.584	Cedric Maxwell, Boston
1967/68	.595	Wilt Chamberlain, Philadelphia	1979/80	.609	Cedric Maxwell, Boston
1968/69	.583	Wilt Chamberlain, Los Angeles	1980/81	.670	Artis Gilmore, Chicago

TOP NBA FREE THROW PERCENTAGE

Season	Pct.	Player and Team	Season	Pct.	Player and Team
1957/58	.904	Dolph Schayes, Syracuse	1969/70	.898	Flynn Robinson, Milwaukee
1958/59	.932	Bill Sharman, Boston	1970/71	.859	Chet Walker, Chicago
1959/60	.892	Dolph Schayes, Syracuse	1971/72	.894	Jack Marin, Baltimore
1960/61	.921	Dolph Schayes, Syracuse	1972/73	.902	Rick Barry, Golden State
1961/62	.896	Bill Sharman, Boston	1973/74	.902	Ernie DiGregorio, Buffalo
1962/63	.881	Larry Costello, Syracuse	1974/75	.904	Rick Barry, Golden State
1963/64	.853	Oscar Robertson, Cincinnati	1975/76	.923	Rick Barry, Golden State
1964/65	.877	Larry Costello, Philadelphia	1976/77	.945	Ernie DiGregorio, Buffalo
1965/66	.881	Larry Siegfried, Boston	1977/78	.924	Rick Barry, Golden State
1966/67	.903	Adrian Smith, Cincinnati	1978/79	.947	Rick Barry, Houston
1967/68	.873	Oscar Robertson, Cincinnati	1979/80	.935	Rick Barry, Houston
1968/69	.864	Larry Siegfried, Boston	1980/81	.958	Calvin Murphy, Houston

NBA REBOUND LEADERS

Season	Rebs.	Player and Team	Season	Rebs.	Player and Team
1957/58	1564	Bill Russell, Boston	1969/70	1386	Elvin Hayes, San Diego
1958/59	1612	Bill Russell, Boston	1970/71	1493	Wilt Chamberlain, Los Angeles
1959/60	1941	Wilt Chamberlain, Philadelphia	1971/72	1572	Wilt Chamberlain, Los Angeles
1960/61	2149	Wilt Chamberlain, Philadelphia	1972/73	1526	Wilt Chamberlain, Los Angeles
1961/62	2052	Wilt Chamberlain, Philadelphia	1973/74	1463	Elvin Hayes, Capital
1962/63	1946	Wilt Chamberlain, San Francisco	1974/75	1077	Wes Unseld, Washington
1963/64	1930	Bill Russell, Boston	1975/76	1383	Kareem Abdul-Jabbar, Los Angeles
1964/65	1878	Bill Russell, Boston	1976/77	1090	Kareem Abdul-Jabbar, Los Angeles
1965/66	1943	Wilt Chamberlain, Philadelphia	1977/78	1288	Truck Robinson, New Orleans
1966/67	1957	Wilt Chamberlain, Philadelphia	1978/79	1444	Moses Malone, Houston
1967/68	1952	Wilt Chamberlain, Philadelphia	1979/80	1216	Swen Nater, San Diego
1968/69	1712	Wilt Chamberlain, Los Angeles	1980/81	1180	Moses Malone, Houston

NBA ASSIST LEADERS

Season	Asst.	Player and Team	Season	Asst.	Player and Team
1957/58	463	Bob Cousy, Boston	1969/70	683	Len Wilkens, Seattle
1958/59	557	Bob Cousy, Boston	1970/71	832	Norm Van Lier, Cincinnati
1959/60	715	Bob Cousy, Boston	1971/72	747	Jerry West, Los Angeles
1960/61	690	Oscar Robertson, Cincinnati	1972/73	910	Nate Archibald, Kansas City-Omaha
1961/62	899	Oscar Robertson, Cincinnati	1973/74	663	Ernie DiGregorio, Buffalo
1962/63	825	Guy Rodgers, San Francisco	1974/75	650	Kevin Porter, Washington
1963/64	868	Oscar Robertson, Cincinnati	1975/76	661	Don Watts, Seattle
1964/65	861	Oscar Robertson, Cincinnati	1976/77	685	Don Buse, Indiana
1965/66	847	Oscar Robertson, Cincinnati	1977/78	837	Kevin Porter, New Jersey
1966/67	908	Guy Rodgers, Chicago	1978/79	1099	Kevin Porter, Detroit
1967/68	702	Wilt Chamberlain, Philadelphia	1979/80	832	Mike Richardson, New York
1968/69	772	Oscar Robertson, Cincinnati	1980/81	734	Kevin Porter, Washington

NBA FINAL STANDINGS: 1980-81

EASTERN CONFERENCE

ATLANTIC DIVISION	Won	Lost	Pct.	G.B.
Boston Celtics	62	20	.756	—
Philadelphia 76ers	62	20	.756	—
New York Knicks	50	32	.610	12
Washington Bullets	39	43	.476	23
New Jersey Nets	24	58	.293	38

WESTERN CONFERENCE

MIDWEST DIVISION	Won	Lost	Pct.	G.B.
San Antonio Spurs	52	30	.634	—
Houston Rockets	40	42	.488	12
Kansas City Kings	40	42	.488	12
Denver Nuggets	37	45	.451	15
Utah Jazz	28	54	.341	24
Dallas Mavericks	15	67	.183	37

CENTRAL DIVISION	Won	Lost	Pct.	G.B.
Milwaukee Bucks	60	22	.732	—
Chicago Bulls	45	37	.549	15
Indiana Pacers	44	38	.537	16
Atlanta Hawks	31	51	.378	29
Cleveland Cavaliers	28	54	.341	32
Detroit Pistons	21	61	.256	39

PACIFIC DIVISION	Won	Lost	Pct.	G.B.
Phoenix Suns	57	25	.695	—
Los Angeles Lakers	54	28	.659	3
Portland Trail Blazers	45	37	.549	12
Golden State Warriors	39	43	.476	18
San Diego Clippers	36	46	.439	21
Seattle SuperSonics	34	48	.415	23

NBA PLAYOFFS: 1981

EASTERN CONFERENCE

FIRST ROUND: Philadelphia over Indiana (2-0)
Chicago over New York (2-0)
SEMIFINALS: Philadelphia over Milwaukee (4-2)
Boston over Chicago (4-0)
FINALS: Boston over Philadelphia (4-3)

WESTERN CONFERENCE

FIRST ROUND: Houston over Los Angeles (2-1)
Kansas City over Portland (2-1)
SEMIFINALS: Houston over San Antonio (4-3)
Kansas City over Phoenix (4-3)
FINALS: Houston over Kansas City (4-1)

CHAMPIONSHIP SERIES

Boston 4   Houston 2

(Most Valuable Player—Cedric Maxwell, Boston)

Game 1 — Boston 98, Houston 95
Game 2 — Houston 92, Boston 90
Game 3 — Boston 94, Houston 71
Game 4 — Houston 91, Boston 86
Game 5 — Boston 109, Houston 80
Game 6 — Boston 102, Houston 91

Scoring Leaders:
Moses Malone, Houston	134 pts.
Cedric Maxwell, Boston	106 pts.
Larry Bird, Boston	92 pts.
Robert Parish, Boston	90 pts.
Robert Reid, Houston	88 pts.

NBA INDIVIDUAL LEADERS: 1980-81

SCORING

Minimum: 70 games played or 1400 points

	Games	FG	FT	Pts.	Avg.		Games	FG	FT	Pts.	Avg.
Dantley, Utah	80	909	632	2452	30.7	Wilkes, L.A.	81	786	254	1827	22.6
Malone, Houston	80	806	609	2222	27.8	King, Golden St.	81	731	307	1771	21.9
Gervin, San Ant.	82	850	512	2221	27.1	Issel, Denver	80	614	519	1749	21.9
Abdul-Jabbar, L.A.	80	836	423	2095	26.2	Drew, Atlanta	67	500	454	1454	21.7
Thompson, Denver	77	734	489	1967	25.5	Newlin, N.J.	79	632	414	1688	21.4
Birdsong, K.C.	71	710	317	1747	24.6	Bird, Boston	82	719	283	1741	21.2
Erving, Phila.	82	794	422	2014	24.6	Griffith, Utah	81	716	229	1671	20.6
Mitchell, Cleve.	82	853	302	2012	24.5	Ma. Johnson, Milw.	76	636	269	1541	20.3
Free, Golden St.	65	516	528	1565	24.1	Cartwright, N.Y.	82	619	408	1646	20.1
English, Denver	81	768	390	1929	23.8	R. Williams, N.Y.	79	616	312	1560	19.7

FIELD GOAL PERCENTAGE

Minimum: 300 FG made

	FG	Attempted	Pct.
Gilmore, Chicago	547	816	.670
Dawkins, Phila.	423	697	.607
Maxwell, Boston	441	750	.588
King, Golden St.	731	1244	.588
Abdul-Jabbar, Los Angeles	836	1457	.574

FREE THROW PERCENTAGE

Minimum: 125 FT made

	FT	Attempted	Pct.
Murphy, Houston	206	215	.958
Sobers, Chicago	231	247	.935
Newlin, New Jersey	414	466	.888
Spanarkel, Dallas	375	423	.887
Bridgeman, Milwaukee	213	241	.884

REBOUNDS

Minimum: 70 games or 800 rebounds

	G	Off.	Def.	Total	Avg.
Malone, Houston	80	474	706	1180	14.8
Nater, San Diego	82	295	722	1017	12.4
Smith, Golden State	82	433	561	994	12.1
Bird, Boston	82	191	704	895	10.9
Sikma, Seattle	82	184	668	852	10.4

ASSISTS

Minimum: 70 games or 400 assists

	G	No.	Avg.
Porter, Washington	81	734	9.1
Nixon, Los Angeles	79	696	8.8
Ford, Kansas City	66	580	8.8
Richardson, New York	79	627	7.9
Archibald, Boston	80	618	7.7

STEALS

Minimum: 70 games or 125 steals

	G	No.	Avg.
Johnson, Los Angeles	37	127	3.43
Richardson, New York	79	232	2.94
Buckner, Milwaukee	82	197	2.40
Cheeks, Philadelphia	81	193	2.38
R. Williams, New York	79	185	2.34

BLOCKED SHOTS

Minimum: 70 games or 100 blocked shots

	G	No.	Avg.
G. Johnson, San Antonio	82	278	3.39
Rollins, Atlanta	40	117	2.93
Abdul-Jabbar, Los Angeles	80	228	2.85
Parish, Boston	82	214	2.61
Gilmore, Chicago	82	198	2.41

NBA ALL-STAR TEAMS: 1980-81

First Team

Player, Club	Position
Julius Erving, Philadelphia	F
Larry Bird, Boston	F
Kareem Abdul-Jabbar, Los Angeles	C
George Gervin, San Antonio	G
Dennis Johnson, Phoenix	G

Second Team

Player, Club	Position
Adrian Dantley, Utah	F
Marques Johnson, Milwaukee	F
Moses Malone, Houston	C
Otis Birdsong, Kansas City	G
Nate Archibald, Boston	G

NBA ALL-ROOKIE TEAM: 1980-81

First Team

Player, Club, Votes

Joe Barry Carroll, Golden State (21)
Darrell Griffith, Utah (19½)
Larry Smith, Golden State (18½)
Kevin McHale, Boston (18)
Kelvin Ransey, Portland (16)

Others Receiving Votes

Player, Club, Votes

Andrew Toney, Philadelphia (11½)
Michael Brooks, San Diego (6½)
Louis Orr, Indiana (3)
Reggie Johnson, San Antonio (1)

NBA ROOKIE OF THE YEAR

Year	Player	Year	Player
1952–53	Don Meineke, Fort Wayne	1967–68	Earl Monroe, Baltimore
1953–54	Ray Felix, Baltimore	1968–69	Wes Unseld, Baltimore
1954–55	Bob Pettit, Milwaukee	1969–70	Lew Alcindor, Milwaukee
1955–56	Maurice Stokes, Rochester	1970–71	Dave Cowens, Boston, and
1956–57	Tom Heinsohn, Boston		Geoff Petrie, Portland
1957–58	Woody Sauldsberry, Philadelphia	1971–72	Sidney Wicks, Portland
1958–59	Elgin Baylor, Minneapolis	1972–73	Bob McAdoo, Buffalo
1959–60	Wilt Chamberlain, Philadelphia	1973–74	Ernie DiGregorio, Buffalo
1960–61	Oscar Robertson, Cincinnati	1974–75	Keith Wilkes, Golden State
1961–62	Walt Bellamy, Chicago	1975–76	Alvan Adams, Phoenix
1962–63	Terry Dischinger, Chicago	1976–77	Adrian Dantley, Buffalo
1963–64	Jerry Lucas, Cincinnati	1977–78	Walter Davis, Phoenix
1964–65	Willis Reed, New York	1978–79	Phil Ford, Kansas City
1965–66	Rick Barry, San Francisco	1979–80	Larry Bird, Boston
1966–67	Dave Bing, Detroit	1980–81	Darrell Griffith, Utah

NBA COACH OF THE YEAR

Year	Coach, Team
1962–63	Harry Gallatin, St. Louis
1963–64	Alex Hannum, San Francisco
1964–65	Red Auerbach, Boston
1965–66	Dolph Schayes, Philadelphia
1966–67	Johnny Kerr, Chicago
1967–68	Richie Guerin, St. Louis
1968–69	Gene Shue, Baltimore
1969–70	Red Holzman, New York
1970–71	Dick Motta, Chicago

Year	Coach, Team
1971–72	Bill Sharman, Los Angeles
1972–73	Tom Heinsohn, Boston
1973–74	Ray Scott, Detroit
1974–75	Phil Johnson, Kansas City–Omaha
1975–76	Bill Fitch, Cleveland
1976–77	Tom Nissalke, Houston
1977–78	Hubie Brown, Atlanta
1978–79	Cotton Fitzsimmons, Kansas City
1979–80	Bill Fitch, Boston
1980–81	Jack McKinney, Indiana

NBA PODOLOFF TROPHY WINNERS (Most Valuable Player)

Year	Player, Team
1959–60	Wilt Chamberlain, Philadelphia
1960–61	Bill Russell, Boston
1961–62	Bill Russell, Boston
1962–63	Bill Russell, Boston
1963–64	Oscar Robertson, Cincinnati
1964–65	Bill Russell, Boston
1965–66	Wilt Chamberlain, Philadelphia
1966–67	Wilt Chamberlain, Philadelphia
1967–68	Wilt Chamberlain, Philadelphia
1968–69	Wes Unseld, Baltimore
1969–70	Willis Reed, New York

Year	Player, Team
1970–71	Lew Alcindor, Milwaukee
1971–72	Kareem Abdul-Jabbar, Milwaukee
1972–73	Dave Cowens, Boston
1973–74	Kareem Abdul-Jabbar, Milwaukee
1974–75	Bob McAdoo, Buffalo
1975–76	Kareem Abdul-Jabbar, Los Angeles
1976–77	Kareem Abdul-Jabbar, Los Angeles
1977–78	Bill Walton, Portland
1978–79	Moses Malone, Houston
1979–80	Kareem Abdul-Jabbar, Los Angeles
1980–81	Julius Erving, Philadelphia

1981 NBA FIRST ROUND COLLEGE DRAFT

	Team	Player	College
1.	Dallas	Mark Aguirre	DePaul
2.	Detroit	Isiah Thomas	Indiana
3.	New Jersey	Buck Williams	Maryland
4.	Atlanta	Al Wood	North Carolina
5.	Seattle	Danny Vranes	Utah
6.	Chicago	Orlando Woolridge	Notre Dame
7.	Kansas City	Steve Johnson	Oregon State
8.	San Diego	Tom Chambers	Utah
9.	Dallas	Rolando Blackman	Kansas State
10.	New Jersey	Albert King	Maryland
11.	Washington	Frank Johnson	Wake Forest
12.	Detroit	Kelly Tripucka	Notre Dame

	Team	Player	College
13.	Utah	Dan Schayes	Syracuse
14.	Indiana	Herb Williams	Ohio State
15.	Portland	Jeff Lamp	Virginia
16.	Portland	Darnell Valentine	Kansas
17.	Kansas City	Kevin Loder	Alabama State
18.	New Jersey	Ray Tolbert	Indiana
19.	Los Angeles	Mike McGee	Michigan
20.	Phoenix	Larry Nance	Clemson
21.	Milwaukee	Alton Lister	Arizona State
22.	Philadelphia	Franklin Edwards	Cleveland State
23.	Boston	Charles Bradley	Wyoming

BASKETBALL HALL OF FAME Springfield, Massachusetts

Player	Year Elected
Paul Arizin	1977
Thomas Barlow	1981
Elgin Baylor	1976
John Beckman	1972
Bennie Borgmann	1961
Joseph Brennan	1974
Wilt Chamberlain	1979
Charles (Tarzan) Cooper	1976
Bob Cousy	1970
Bob Davies	1969
Forrest DeBernardi	1961
H. G. (Dutch) Dehnert	1968
Paul Endacott	1971
Harold (Bud) Foster	1964
Max (Marty) Friedman	1971
Joe Fulks	1977
Lauren (Laddie) Gale	1976
Tom Gola	1975
Robert (Ace) Gruenig	1963
Cliff Hagan	1977
Victor Hanson	1960
Nat Holman	1964
Chuck Hyatt	1959
William Johnson	1976
Edward (Moose) Krause	1975
Bob Kurland	1961
Joe Lapchick	1966
Jerry Lucas	1980
Hank Luisetti	1959
Branch McCracken	1960
Jack McCracken	1962
Ed Macauley	1960
George Mikan	1959
Charles (Stretch) Murphy	1960
H. O. (Pat) Page	1962
Bob Pettit	1970
Andy Phillip	1961
Jim Pollard	1977
Oscar Robertson	1980
Col. John Roosma	1961
John (Honey) Russell	1964
Bill Russell	1974

Player	Year Elected
Dolph Schayes	1972
Ernest Schmidt	1973
John Schommer	1959
Barney Sedran	1962
Bill Sharman	1975
Christian Steinmetz	1961
John (Cat) Thompson	1962
Robert (Fuzzy) Vandivier	1974
Edward Wachter	1961
Jerry West	1980
John Wooden	1960

Coach	Year Elected
A. J. (Red) Auerbach	1968
Sam Barry	1979
Ernest Blood	1960
Howard Cann	1967
Dr. H. Clifford Carlson	1959
Ben Carnevale	1969
Everett Dean	1966
Edgar Diddle	1971
Bruce Drake	1972
Amory (Slats) Gill	1967
Ed Hickey	1979
Howard Hobson	1965
Hank Iba	1968
A. F. (Doggie) Julian	1967
Frank Keaney	1960
George Keogan	1961
Ward Lambert	1960
Harry Litwack	1975
Ken Loeffler	1964
A. C. (Dutch) Lonborg	1972
Arad McCutchan	1981
John McLendon	1979
Frank Meguire	1976
Dr. Walter Meanwell	1959
Ray Meyer	1979
Pete Newell	1979
Adolph Rupp	1968
Leonard Sachs	1961
Everett Shelton	1980
John Wooden	1972

Referee	Year Elected
George Hepbron	1960
George Hoyt	1961
Matthew Kennedy	1959
John Nucatola	1977
Ernest Quigley	1961
J. Dallas Shirley	1980
David Tobey	1961
David Walsh	1961

Contributor	Year Elected
Dr. Forrest (Phog) Allen	1959
Clair Bee	1967
Walter Brown	1965
John Bunn	1964
Bob Douglas	1971
Jim Enright	1979
Harry Fisher	1973
Edward Gottlieb	1971
Dr. Luther Gulick	1959
Les Harrison	1980
Dr. Ferenc Hepp	1981
Edward Hickox	1959
Paul (Tony) Hinkle	1965
Ned Irish	1964
William Jones	1964
Walter Kennedy	1981
Emil Liston	1974
Bill Mokray	1965
Ralph Morgan	1959
Frank Morgenweck	1962
Dr. James Naismith	1959
John O'Brien	1961
Harold Olsen	1959
Maurice Podoloff	1973
H. V. Porter	1960
William Reid	1963
Elmer Ripley	1972
Lynn St. John	1962
Abe Saperstein	1970
Arthur Schabinger	1961
Amos Alonzo Stagg	1959
Chuck Taylor	1968
Oswald Tower	1959
Arthur Trester	1961
Clifford Wells	1971

NBA ALL-STAR GAMES

Year	Result	Site	Year	Result	Site	Year	Result	Site
1952	East 108, West 91	Boston	1962	West 150, East 130	St. Louis	1972	West 112, East 110	Los Angeles
1953	West 79, East 75	Ft. Wayne	1963	West 115, West 108	Los Angeles	1973	East 104, West 84	Chicago
1954	East 98, West 93	New York	1964	East 111, West 107	Boston	1974	West 134, East 123	Seattle
1955	East 100, West 91	New York	1965	East 124, West 123	St. Louis	1975	East 108, West 102	Phoenix
1956	West 108, East 94	Rochester	1966	East 137, West 94	Cincinnati	1976	East 123, West 109	Philadelphia
1957	East 109, West 97	Boston	1967	West 135, East 120	San Francisco	1977	West 125, East 124	Milwaukee
1958	East 130, West 118	St. Louis	1968	East 144, West 124	New York	1978	East 133, West 125	Atlanta
1959	West 124, East 108	Detroit	1969	East 123, West 112	Baltimore	1979	West 134, East 129	Detroit
1960	East 125, West 115	Philadelphia	1970	East 142, West 135	Philadelphia	1980	East 144, West 136	Washington
1961	West 153, East 131	Syracuse	1971	West 108, East 107	San Diego	1981	East 123, West 120	Cleveland

ALL-TIME NBA LEADERS

SOURCE: National Basketball Association

At start of 1981/82 season

Top Scorers

Player	Years	Games	Points	Avg.	Player	Years	Games	Points	Avg.
Wilt Chamberlain	14	1,045	31,419	30.1	Bob Lanier	11	774	16,857	21.8
Oscar Robertson	14	1,040	26,710	25.7	Calvin Murphy	11	874	16,478	18.9
John Havlicek	16	1,270	26,395	20.8	Paul Arizin	10	713	16,266	22.8
Kareem Abdul-Jabbar	12	935	26,270	28.1	Pete Maravich	10	658	15,948	24.2
Jerry West	14	932	25,192	27.0	Jack Twyman	11	823	15,840	19.2
Elvin Hayes	13	1,059	24,547	23.2	Bob McAdoo	9	599	15,792	26.4
Elgin Baylor	14	846	23,149	27.4	Walt Frazier	13	825	15,581	18.9
Hal Greer	15	1,122	21,586	19.2	Bob Dandridge	12	828	15,478	18.7
Walt Bellamy	14	1,043	20,941	20.1	Sam Jones	12	871	15,411	17.7
Bob Pettit	11	792	20,880	26.4	Dick Barnett	14	971	15,358	15.8
Dolph Schayes	16	1,059	19,249	18.2	Dick Van Arsdale	12	921	15,079	16.4
Gail Goodrich	14	1,031	19,181	18.6	Randy Smith	10	814	14,778	18.2
Chet Walker	13	1,032	18,831	18.2	Richie Guerin	13	848	14,676	17.3
Rick Barry	10	794	18,395	23.2	Nate Archibald	12	696	14,588	21.0
Dave Bing	12	901	18,327	20.3	Bill Russell	13	963	14,522	15.1
Lou Hudson	13	890	17,940	20.2	Nate Thurmond	14	964	14,437	15.0
Len Wilkens	15	1,077	17,772	16.5	Jo Jo White	12	837	14,399	17.2
Bailey Howell	12	950	17,770	18.7	Tom Van Arsdale	12	929	14,232	15.3
Earl Monroe	13	926	17,454	18.8	Dave DeBusschere	12	875	14,053	16.1
Bob Cousy	14	924	16,960	18.4	Jerry Lucas	11	829	14,053	17.0

Most Games Played

John Havlicek	1,270
Paul Silas	1,254
Hal Greer	1,122
Len Wilkens	1,077
Elvin Hayes	1,059
Dolph Schayes	1,059
Johnny Green	1,057
Don Nelson	1,053
Leroy Ellis	1,048
Wilt Chamberlain	1,045

Most Field Goals Made

Wilt Chamberlain	12,681
Kareem Abdul-Jabbar	10,815
John Havlicek	10,513
Elvin Hayes	9,875
Oscar Robertson	9,508
Jerry West	9,016
Elgin Baylor	8,693
Hal Greer	8,504
Walt Bellamy	7,914
Gail Goodrich	7,431

Most Field Goals Attempted

John Havlicek	23,900
Wilt Chamberlain	23,497
Elvin Hayes	21,893
Elgin Baylor	20,171
Oscar Robertson	19,620
Kareem Abdul-Jabbar	19,440
Jerry West	19,032
Hal Greer	18,811
Bob Pettit	16,872
Bob Cousy	16,468

Most Assists

Oscar Robertson	9,887
Len Wilkens	7,211
Bob Cousy	6,955
Guy Rodgers	6,917
Jerry West	6,238
John Havlicek	6,114
Dave Bing	5,397
Nate Archibald	5,366
Kevin Porter	5,268
Norm Van Lier	5,217

Highest Scoring Average (400 Games Minimum)

	G	FG	FTM	Pts.	Avg.
Wilt Chamberlain	1,045	12,681	6,057	31,419	30.1
Kareem Abdul-Jabbar	935	10,815	4,640	26,270	28.1
George Gervin	404	4,411	2,435	11,298	28.0
Elgin Baylor	846	8,693	5,763	23,149	27.4
Jerry West	932	9,016	7,160	25,192	27.0
Bob McAdoo	599	6,225	3,339	15,792	26.4
Bob Pettit	792	7,349	6,182	20,880	26.4
Oscar Robertson	1,040	9,508	7,694	26,710	25.7
Pete Maravich	658	6,187	3,564	15,948	24.2
Elvin Hayes	1,059	9,875	4,794	24,547	23.2

Most Minutes Played

Wilt Chamberlain	47,859
John Havlicek	46,471
Oscar Robertson	43,886
Elvin Hayes	43,672
Bill Russell	40,726
Hal Greer	39,789
Walt Bellamy	38,940
Len Wilkens	38,064
Kareem Abdul-Jabbar	37,890
Jerry West	36,571

Highest Field Goal Percentage (2,000 FG Minimum)

	FGA	FGM	Pct.
Artis Gilmore	4,990	2,879	.577
Kareem Abdul-Jabbar	19,440	10,815	.556
Bobby Jones	3,847	2,124	.552
Walter Davis	5,123	2,800	.547
Marques Johnson	5,115	2,773	.542
Adrian Dantley	5,801	3,135	.540
Wilt Chamberlain	23,497	12,681	.540
Swen Nater	4,080	2,201	.539
George Gervin	8,364	4,411	.527
Bernard King	4,405	2,310	.524

Highest Free Throw Percentage (1,200 FTM Minimum)

	FTA	FTM	Pct.
Rick Barry	4,243	3,818	.900
Calvin Murphy	3,389	3,001	.886
Bill Sharman	3,557	3,143	.884
Mike Newlin	3,309	2,879	.870
Fred Brown	1,924	1,650	.858
Rickey Sobers	1,705	1,460	.856
Larry Siegfried	1,945	1,662	.854
Flynn Robinson	1,881	1,597	.849
Brian Winters	1,472	1,247	.847
Dolph Schayes	8,273	6,979	.844

Most Free Throws Made

Oscar Robertson	7,694
Jerry West	7,160
Dolph Schayes	6,979
Bob Pettit	6,182
Wilt Chamberlain	6,057
Elgin Baylor	5,763
Len Wilkens	5,394
John Havlicek	5,369
Walt Bellamy	5,113
Chet Walker	5,079

Most Free Throws Attempted

Wilt Chamberlain	11,862
Oscar Robertson	9,185
Jerry West	8,801
Dolph Schayes	8,273
Bob Pettit	8,119
Walt Bellamy	8,088
Elgin Baylor	7,391
Elvin Hayes	7,158
Len Wilkens	6,973
John Havlicek	6,589

Most Rebounds

Wilt Chamberlain	23,924
Bill Russell	21,620
Elvin Hayes	14,656
Nate Thurmond	14,464
Walt Bellamy	14,241
Wes Unseld	13,769
Kareem Abdul-Jabbar	13,167
Jerry Lucas	12,942
Bob Pettit	12,849
Paul Silas	12,357

Most Personal Fouls

Hal Greer	3,855
Dolph Schayes	3,664
Elvin Hayes	3,551
Walt Bellamy	3,536
Bailey Howell	3,498
Bill Bridges	3,375
Len Wilkens	3,285
John Havlicek	3,281
Sam Lacey	3,125
Paul Silas	3,105

NCAA CONFERENCE CHAMPIONS: 1980-81 (Record of all games shown in parentheses; does not include NCAA and NIT tournaments)

Conference	Champion	CONFERENCE Won	Lost	Conf. Runner Up	Tournament Winner
Atlantic Coast	Virginia (25-3)	13	1	North Carolina (25-7)	North Carolina
Big East	Boston College (21-6)	10	4	Georgetown (20-11)	Syracuse (18-11)
Big Eight	Missouri (22-9)	10	4	Kansas (22-7)	Kansas
				Kansas State (21-8)	
				Nebraska (15-12)	
Big Sky	Idaho (25-3)	12	2	Montana (19-9)	Idaho
				Montana State (16-11)	
Big Ten	Indiana (21-9)	14	4	Iowa (21-6)	Indiana
East Coast (East)	American U (24-5)	11	0	St. Joseph's (22-7)	
				Temple (19-7)	St. Joseph's
East Coast (West)	Lafayette (15-13)	8	8	—	
	Rider (14-14)	8	8		
E.C.A.C. (Metro)	Fordham (19-8)	—	—	St. Peter's (17-9)	Long Island U. (18-10)
E.C.A.C. (North)	Northeastern (23-5)	—	—	Holy Cross (19-9)	Northeastern
E.C.A.C. (South)	James Madison (20-8)	—	—	Old Dominion (18-9)	James Madison
Eastern Eight	Rhode Island (21-7)	10	3		Pittsburgh (18-11)
	Duquesne (20-9)	10	3		
Ivy League	Princeton (18-9)	14	1	Pennsylvania (20-7)	—
Metro	Louisville (21-8)	11	1	Florida State (17-11)	Louisville
Mid-American	Toledo (20-8)	10	6	—	Ball State
	Ball State (20-9)	10	6		
	Northern Illinois (17-12)	10	6		
	Bowling Green (15-12)	10	6		
	Western Michigan (15-12)	10	6		
Mid-Eastern Athletic	North Carolina A & T (21-7)	7	3	Howard (17-11)	Howard
				Florida A & M (16-11)	
Midwestern City	Xavier (Ohio) (12-14)	8	3	Oklahoma City (14-15)	Oklahoma City
				Loyola (Ill.) (13-15)	
Missouri Valley	Wichita State (23-6)	12	4	Tulsa (21-7)	Creighton
				Creighton (21-8)	
Ohio Valley	Western Kentucky (21-6)	12	2	Murray State (17-11)	Western Kentucky
Pacific Coast Athletic	Fresno State (25-3)	12	2	San Jose State (21-8)	Fresno State
Pacific 10	Oregon State (26-1)	17	1	Arizona State (24-3)	Oregon State
Southeastern	Louisiana State (28-3)	17	1	Kentucky (22-5)	Mississippi (16-13)
Southern	Tenn.-Chattanooga (21-8)	11	5	—	Tenn.-Chattanooga
	Appalachian State (20-9)	11	5		
	Davidson (13-13)	11	5		
Southland	Lamar (24-4)	8	2	Texas-Arlington (20-7)	Lamar
				Louisiana Tech (20-10)	
Southwest	Arkansas (22-7)	13	3	Houston (21-8)	Houston
				Baylor (15-12)	
Southwestern Athletic	Southern (17-10)	8	4	—	Southern
	Alcorn State (17-12)	8	4		
Sun Belt	Va. Commonwealth (23-4)	9	3	—	Va. Commonwealth
	South Alabama (23-5)	9	3		
	Alabama-Birmingham (21-8)	9	3		
Trans-America Athletic	Houston Baptist (18-10)	9	3	N.E. Louisiana (14-13)	Mercer (17-11)
West Coast Athletic	San Francisco (24-6)	12	3	Pepperdine (16-12)	—
Western Athletic	Utah (24-4)	13	3	—	—
	Wyoming (23-5)	13	3		

MAJOR INDEPENDENTS (NCAA DIV. I)

Team	Won	Lost	Team	Won	Lost	Team	Won	Lost
DePaul	27	1	Cleveland State	18	9	Penn State	17	10
Notre Dame	22	5	Dayton	17	9	South Carolina	17	10
Southern Mississippi	21	5	Marquette	18	10	Nevada-Las Vegas	16	12
Stetson	18	8	Pan American	18	10			

NATIONAL COLLEGE TOURNAMENT CHAMPIONS

NCAA (Division I)

Year	Champion	Year	Champion
1951	Kentucky	1966	Texas Western
1952	Kansas	1967	UCLA
1953	Indiana	1968	UCLA
1954	LaSalle	1969	UCLA
1955	San Francisco	1970	UCLA
1956	San Francisco	1971	UCLA
1957	North Carolina	1972	UCLA
1958	Kentucky	1973	UCLA
1959	California	1974	N.C. State
1960	Ohio State	1975	UCLA
1961	Cincinnati	1976	Indiana
1962	Cincinnati	1977	Marquette
1963	Loyola (Chicago)	1978	Kentucky
1964	UCLA	1979	Michigan State
1965	UCLA	1980	Louisville
		1981	Indiana

NIT

Year	Champion	Year	Champion
1951	Brigham Young	1966	Brigham Young
1952	LaSalle	1967	Southern Illinois
1953	Seton Hall	1968	Dayton
1954	Holy Cross	1969	Temple
1955	Duquesne	1970	Marquette
1956	Louisville	1971	North Carolina
1957	Bradley	1972	Maryland
1958	Xavier of Ohio	1973	Virginia Tech
1959	St. John's	1974	Purdue
1960	Bradley	1975	Princeton
1961	Providence College	1976	Kentucky
1962	Dayton	1977	St. Bonaventure
1963	Providence College	1978	Texas
1964	Bradley	1979	Indiana
1965	St. John's	1980	Virginia
		1981	Tulsa

NCAA (Division II)

Year	Champion	Year	Champion
1975	Old Dominion	1978	Cheyney St. (Pa.)
1976	Puget Sound	1979	North Alabama
1977	Tenn.-Chattanooga	1980	Virginia Union
		1981	Florida Southern

NCAA (Division III)

Year	Champion	Year	Champion
1975	LeMoyne Owen	1978	North Park (Chicago)
1976	Scranton	1979	North Park (Chicago)
1977	Wittenberg	1980	North Park (Chicago)
		1981	Potsdam St.

1981 NCAA BASKETBALL TOURNAMENT CHAMPIONSHIPS

REGIONALS: Louisiana State 96, Wichita State 85
             Indiana 78, St. Joseph's (Pa.) 46
             North Carolina 82, Kansas State 68
             Virginia 74, Brigham Young 60

SEMIFINALS: Indiana 67, Louisiana State 49
                 North Carolina 78, Virginia 65
THIRD PLACE: Virginia 78, Louisiana State 74
CHAMPIONSHIP: Indiana 63, North Carolina 50

1981 COLLEGE ALL-AMERICA SELECTIONS
Associated Press (AP), United Press (UPI), Sporting News (SN)

Player	Height	School	Class	Selected by	NBA Draft by
Mark Aguirre	6'7"	DePaul	Junior	AP, UPI, SN	Dallas
Danny Ainge	6'5"	Brigham Young	Senior	AP, UPI, SN	Boston
Ralph Sampson	7'4"	Virginia	Sophomore	AP, UPI, SN	—
Isiah Thomas	6'1"	Indiana	Sophomore	AP, UPI, SN	Detroit
Kevin Magee	6'8"	Calif.-Irvine	Junior	AP	—
Kelly Tripucka	6'6"	Notre Dame	Senior	UPI	Detroit
Albert King	6'6"	Maryland	Senior	SN	New Jersey
Rolando Blackman	6'6"	Kansas State	Senior	SN	Dallas

NCAA DIVISION I BASKETBALL RECORDS
Source: N.C.A.A.

INDIVIDUAL

Scoring Average (Career) : 44.2, Maravich, LSU, 1968–70
Scoring Average (Season) : 44.5, Maravich, LSU, 1970
Scoring (Game) : 100 points, Selvy, Furman, 1954
Field Goals Attempted (Season) : 1168, Maravich, LSU, 1970
Field Goal Percentage (Season) : .710, Steve Johnson, Oregon State, 1980
Free Throws Attempted (Season) : 444, Selvy, Furman, 1954
Free Throw Percentage (Season) : .944, Gibson, Marshall, 1978
Rebounds (Season) : 734, Dukes, Seton Hall, 1953
Rebounds Per Game (Season) : 25.6, Slack, Marshall, 1955

TEAM

Points Per Game (Season) : 110.5, Nevada-Las Vegas, 1976
Field Goals Per Game (Season) : 46.3, Nevada-Las Vegas, 1976
Field Goal Percentage (Season) : .572, Missouri, 1980
Free Throw Percentage (Season) : .809, Ohio State, 1970
Least Points Allowed Per Game (Season) : 32.5, Oklahoma State, 1948

WOMEN'S BASKETBALL

WOMEN'S PROFESSIONAL LEAGUE (WBL) — 1980-81 FINAL STANDINGS

COASTAL DIVISION	Won	Lost	Pct.	G.B.
Dallas Diamonds	26	9	.743	—
New Jersey Gems	23	13	.639	3½
New Orleans Pride	18	19	.486	9
San Francisco Pioneers .	14	22	.389	12½
*New England	2	10	.167	12½

*Suspended operations before end of season.

Playoffs: Dallas over New Jersey (2-1)
        Nebraska over Chicago (2-0)

CENTRAL DIVISION	Won	Lost	Pct.	G.B.
Nebraska Wranglers ..	27	9	.750	—
Chicago Hustle	18	18	.500	9
St. Louis Streak	14	20	.412	12
Minnesota Fillies	7	29	.294	20

Championship: Nebraska over Dallas (3-2)

A.I.A.W. COLLEGIATE CHAMPIONS — 1981
Source: Association for Intercollegiate Athletics for Women

DIVISION I
Semifinals: Louisiana Tech 66, Southern California 50;
National Championship: Louisiana Tech 79, Tennessee 59

Tennessee 68, Old Dominion 65
Consolation: Old Dominion 68, Southern California 65

DIVISION II
National Championship: William Penn 64, Charleston 51

DIVISION III
National Championship: Wisconsin-LaCrosse 79, Mt. Mercy 71

OTHER 1981 BASKETBALL CHAMPIONS

N.A.I.A. Tournament: Men—Bethany Nazarene (Oklahoma)
                   Women—Kentucky State

Junior College: Men—Westark Community Coll. (Arkansas)
              Women—Louisburg (North Carolina)

National AAU: Men—Brewster Packing (Washington)

FOOTBALL

NATIONAL FOOTBALL LEAGUE   410 Park Avenue, New York City 10022.   Commissioner: Pete Rozelle.

NATIONAL FOOTBALL CONFERENCE (George Halas, Pres.)

Eastern Division

	Chief Executive	Coach
Dallas Cowboys	Clint W. Murchison, Jr.	Tom Landry
New York Giants	Wellington T. Mara	Ray Perkins
Philadelphia Eagles	Leonard H. Tose	Dick Vermeil
St. Louis Cardinals	William V. Bidwill	Jim Hanifan
Washington Redskins	Jack Kent Cooke	Joe Gibbs

Central Division

Chicago Bears	George Halas, Sr.	Neill Armstrong
Detroit Lions	William Clay Ford	Monte Clark
Green Bay Packers	Dominic Olejniczak	Bart Starr
Minnesota Vikings	Max Winter	Bud Grant
Tampa Bay Buccaneers	Hugh Culverhouse	John McKay

Western Division

Atlanta Falcons	Rankin M. Smith	Leeman Bennett
Los Angeles Rams	Georgia Frontiere	Ray Malavasi
New Orleans Saints	John W. Mecom, Jr.	Bum Phillips
San Francisco 49ers	Edward J. DeBartolo, Jr.	Bill Walsh

AMERICAN FOOTBALL CONFERENCE (Lamar Hunt, Pres.)

Eastern Division

	Chief Executive	Coach
Baltimore Colts	Robert Irsay	Mike McCormack
Buffalo Bills	Ralph C. Wilson, Jr.	Chuck Knox
Miami Dolphins	Joseph Robbie	Don Shula
New England Patriots	William H. Sullivan, Jr.	Ron Erhardt
New York Jets	James Kensil	Walt Michaels

Central Division

Cincinnati Bengals	John Sawyer	Forrest Gregg
Cleveland Browns	Arthur B. Modell	Sam Rutigliano
Houston Oilers	K. S. Adams, Jr.	Ed Biles
Pittsburgh Steelers	Art Rooney	Chuck Noll

Western Division

Denver Broncos	Edgar F. Kaiser, Jr.	Dan Reeves
Kansas City Chiefs	Lamar Hunt	Marv Levy
Oakland Raiders	Al Davis	Tom Flores
San Diego Chargers	Eugene V. Klein	Don Coryell
Seattle Seahawks	Elmer Nordstrom	Jack Patera

PROFESSIONAL FOOTBALL HALL OF FAME (Canton, Ohio)

MEMBERS

Herb Adderly, Defensive Back, Green Bay Packers, 1961–69, Dallas Cowboys, 1970–72.

Lance Alworth, Wide Receiver, San Diego Chargers, 1962–70.

Morris (Red) Badgro, End, New York Yankees, New York Giants, Brooklyn Dodgers, 1927, 1930–36.

Cliff Battles, Back, 1932, Boston Braves; 1933–36, Boston Redskins; 1937, Washington Redskins.

Sammy Baugh, Quarterback, Washington Redskins, 1937–52.

Chuck Bednarik, Center and Linebacker, Philadelphia Eagles, 1949–62.

Bert Bell, Founder, Philadelphia Eagles, 1933, and Head Coach; Commissioner, National Football League, 1946–59.

Raymond Berry, End, Baltimore Colts, 1955–67.

Charles W. Bidwill, Founder, Chicago Cardinals, 1933–47

George Blanda, Quarterback, Kicker, Chicago Bears, Baltimore Colts, Houston Oilers, Oakland Raiders, 1949–75.

Jim Brown, Fullback, Cleveland Browns, 1957–65.

Paul E. Brown, Head Coach, Cleveland Browns, 1946–62; Cincinnati Bengals, 1968–75.

Roosevelt Brown, Tackle, N.Y. Giants, 1953–65.

Dick Butkus, Linebacker, Chicago Bears, 1965–73.

Tony Canadeo, Backfield, Green Bay Packers, 1940–52.

Joe Carr, Founder, Columbus Panhandles, 1904; Organizer, National Football League, 1920; President of League, 1921–39.

Guy Chamberlin, Head Coach, Halfback, End, Canton Bulldogs, Decatur Staleys, Cleveland Bulldogs, Frankford Yellowjackets, Chicago Cardinals, 1918–28.

Jack Christiansen, Defensive Back, Detroit Lions, 1951–58.

Dutch Clark, Quarterback and Head Coach, Portsmouth (O.) Spartans, Detroit Lions, Cleveland Rams, 1931–42.

George Connor, Tackle, Defensive Tackle, Linebacker, Chicago Bears, 1948–55.

Jimmy Conzelman, Head Coach, Halfback, Executive, Decatur Staleys, Rock Island Independents, Milwaukee Badgers, Detroit Panthers, Providence Steam Rollers, Chicago Cardinals, 1920–48.

Willie Davis, Defensive End, Cleveland Browns, Green Bay Packers, 1956–67.

Art Donovan, Tackle, 1950, Baltimore Colts; 1951, New York Yanks; 1952, Dallas Texans; 1953–61, Baltimore Colts.

Paddy Driscoll, Halfback and Head Coach, Chicago Cardinals and Chicago Bears, 1919–31, 1941–68.

Bill Dudley, Halfback, Pittsburgh Steelers, Detroit Lions, Washington Redskins, 1942, 1945–53.

Turk Edwards, Tackle, Washington Redskins, 1932–40.

Weeb Ewbank, Head Coach, 1954–62 Baltimore Colts; 1963–73, New York Jets

Tom Fears, End, Los Angeles Rams, 1948–56.

Ray Flaherty, End and Head Coach, New York Giants, New York Yankees, Boston & Washington Redskins, Chicago Hornets, 1928–49.

Len Ford, Defensive End, Los Angeles Dons, Cleveland Browns, Green Bay Packers, 1948–58.

Daniel J. Fortmann, M.D., Guard, Chicago Bears, 1936–46.

Bill George, Middle Linebacker, Chicago Bears, 1952–65.

Frank Gifford, Halfback, New York Giants, 1952–60, 1962–64.

Otto Graham, Quarterback, Cleveland Browns, 1946–55.

Red Grange, Halfback, Chicago Bears, New York Yankees, 1925–37.

Forrest Gregg, Tackle, 1956, 1958–70, Green Bay Packers; 1971, Dallas Cowboys.

Lou Groza, Tackle, Kicker, Cleveland Browns, 1946–67.

Joe Guyon, Halfback, Canton Bulldogs, Cleveland Indians, Oorang Indians, Rock Island Independents, Kansas City Cowboys, New York Giants, 1919–27.

George Halas, Founder, Head Coach, End, Decatur Staleys (1920) which became the Chicago Bears; retired as Bears' head coach in 1968.

Ed Healey, Tackle, Rock Island Independents, Chicago Bears, 1920–27.

Mel Hein, Center, New York Giants, 1931–45.

Pete Henry, Tackle, Canton Bulldogs, Akron, New York Giants, Pottsville Maroons, Staten Island Stapletons, 1920–30.

Arnie Herber, Halfback, Green Bay Packers, New York Giants, 1930–41, 1944–45.

Bill Hewitt, End, 1932–36, Chicago Bears; 1936–39, Philadelphia Eagles; 1943, Philadelphia-Pittsburgh.

Clarke Hinkle, Fullback, Green Bay Packers, 1932–41.

Elroy Hirsch, End, 1946–48, Chicago Rockets (AAFC); 1949–57, Los Angeles Rams; Rams' club executive, 1960–68.

Cal Hubbard, Tackle, New York Giants, Green Bay Packers, Pittsburgh Pirates, 1927–36.

Lamar Hunt, Founder, American Football League, 1959. Owner, Dallas Texans, 1960–1962, Kansas City Chiefs, 1963 to present.

Don Hutson, End, Green Bay Packers, 1935–45.

Deacon Jones, Defensive End, Los Angeles Rams, 1961–71, San Diego Chargers, 1972–73, Washington Redskins, 1974.

Walt Kiesling, Player-Coach, Duluth Eskimos, Pottsville Maroons, Boston Braves, Chicago Cardinals, Chicago Bears, Green Bay Packers, Pittsburgh Steelers, Philadelphia-Pittsburgh, Chicago-Pittsburgh, 1926–61.

Frank (Bruiser) Kinard, Tackle, 1938–43, Brooklyn Dodgers; 1944, Brooklyn Tigers; 1946–47, New York Yankees.

Curly Lambeau, Founder, Head Coach, Halfback, Green Bay Packers, 1919–49; also Head Coach of Chicago Cardinals and Washington Redskins, 1950–54.

Dick Lane, Defensive Back, Los Angeles Rams, Chicago Cardinals, Detroit Lions, 1952–65.

Yale Lary, Defensive Back, Detroit Lions, 1952–53, 1956–64.

Dante Lavelli, End, Cleveland Browns, 1946–56.

Bobby Layne, Quarterback, Chicago Bears, New York Bulldogs, Detroit Lions, Pittsburgh Steelers, 1948–62.

Alphonse (Tuffy) Leemans, Fullback, New York Giants, 1937–43

Bob Lilly, Defensive Tackle, Dallas Cowboys, 1961–74.

Vince Lombardi, Head Coach, 1959–67, Green Bay Packers; 1969, Washington Redskins.

Sid Luckman, Quarterback, Chicago Bears, 1939–50.

Link Lyman, Tackle, Canton Bulldogs, Cleveland Bulldogs, Chicago Bears, 1922–34.

Tim Mara, Founder, New York Giants, 1925.

Gino Marchetti, Defensive End, Dallas Texans, 1952; Baltimore Colts, 1953–1964–1966.

George P. Marshall, Founder, Washington Redskins (as Boston Braves) in 1932.

Ollie Matson, Halfback, Chicago Cardinals, 1952, 1954–1958, Los Angeles Rams, 1959–1962, Detroit Lions, 1963, Philadelphia Eagles, 1964–1966.

George McAfee, Halfback, Chicago Bears, 1940–41, 1945–50.

Hugh McElhenny, Halfback, San Francisco 49ers, Minnesota Vikings, New York Giants, Detroit Lions, 1952–64.

John Blood McNally, Halfback, Milwaukee Badgers, Duluth Eskimos, Pottsville Maroons, Green Bay Packers, Pittsburgh Steelers, 1925–39.

Mike Michalske, Guard, New York Yankees, Green Bay Packers, 1926–37.

Wayne Millner, End, 1936, Boston Redskins; 1937–41, 1945 Washington Redskins.

Ron Mix, Tackle, Los Angeles-San Diego Chargers, 1960–69, Oakland Raiders, 1971.

Lenny Moore, Running Back, Baltimore Colts, 1956–67.

Marion Motley, Fullback, 1946–53, Cleveland Browns; 1955, Pittsburgh Steelers.

Bronko Nagurski, Fullback and Tackle, Chicago Bears, 1930–37, 1943.

Earl (Greasy) Neale, Head Coach, Philadelphia Eagles, 1941–50.

Ernie Nevers, Fullback and Head Coach, Duluth Eskimos, Chicago Cardinals, 1926–31, 1939.

Ray Nitschke, Linebacker, Green Bay Packers, 1958–72.

Leo Nomellini, Defensive Tackle, San Francisco 49ers, 1950–63.

Jim Otto, Center, Oakland Raiders, 1960–74.

Steve Owen, Player-Coach, Kansas City Cowboys, New York Giants, 1924–53.

Ace Parker, Quarterback, Brooklyn Dodgers, 1937–1941, Boston Yanks, 1945, New York Yankees (AAFC), 1946.

Jim Parker, Tackle, Baltimore Colts, 1957–67.

Joe Perry, Fullback, San Francisco 49ers, Baltimore Colts, 1949–63.

Pete Pihos, End, Philadelphia Eagles, 1947–55.

Hugh (Shorty) Ray, National Football League technical adviser and supervisor of officials, 1938–56.

Dan Reeves, Founder, Cleveland Rams, 1941 (moved to Los Angeles in 1946).

Jim Ringo, Center, Green Bay Packers, Philadelphia Eagles, 1953–67.

Andy Robustelli, Defensive End, 1951–55, Los Angeles Rams; 1956–64, New York Giants.

Art Rooney, Founder, Pittsburgh Steelers, 1933.

Gale Sayers, Running Back, 1965–1971, Chicago Bears.

Joe Schmidt, Linebacker, Detroit Lions, 1953–65.

Bart Starr, Quarterback, Green Bay Packers, 1956–71.

Ernie Stautner, Defensive End, Pittsburgh Steelers, 1950–63.

Ken Strong, Halfback, Staten Island Stapletons, New York Giants, New York Yankees, 1929–37, 1939, 1944–47.

Joe Stydahar, Tackle, Chicago Bears, 1936–42, 1945–46. Head Coach of Los Angeles Rams, 1950–51; Head Coach of Chicago Cardinals, 1953–54.

Jim Taylor, Fullback, Green Bay Packers, New Orleans Saints, 1958–67.

Jim Thorpe, Halfback, Canton Bulldogs, Pine Village (Ind.) A. A., Oorang Indians, Toledo Maroons, Rock Island Independents, New York Giants, 1915–26; President of American Professional Football Association, forerunner of N.F.L., 1920.

Y. A. Tittle, Quarterback, 1948–50, Baltimore Colts; 1951–60, San Francisco 49ers; 1961–64, New York Giants.

George Trafton, Center, Chicago Bears, 1920–32.

Charley Trippi, Halfback-Quarterback, 1947–55, Chicago Cardinals.

Emlen Tunnell, Halfback, New York Giants, Green Bay Packers, 1946–61.

Clyde (Bulldog) Turner, Center, Chicago Bears, 1940–52.

Johnny Unitas, Quarterback, Baltimore Colts, 1956–72, San Diego Chargers, 1973.

Norm Van Brocklin, Quarterback, 1949–57, Los Angeles Rams; 1958–60, Philadelphia Eagles.

Steve Van Buren, Halfback, Philadelphia Eagles, 1944–51.

Bob Waterfield, Quarterback, Cleveland and Los Angeles Rams, 1945–52; Head Coach of Rams, 1960–62.

Bill Willis, Guard, 1946–53, Cleveland Browns.

Larry Wilson, Defensive Back, St. Louis Cardinals, 1960–72

Alex Wojciechowicz, Center and Linebacker, 1938–46, Detroit Lions; 1946–50, Philadelphia Eagles.

NATIONAL FOOTBALL LEAGUE RECORDS Source: Elias Sports Bureau and N.F.L.

Through 1980 season; includes all performances in American Football League (1960–69)

Most Points, Lifetime: 2,002, George Blanda, Chicago Bears, Baltimore, Houston, Oakland

Most Points, Season: 176, Paul Hornung, Green Bay, 1960

Most Points, Game: 40, Ernie Nevers, Chicago Cards vs. Chicago Bears, November 28, 1929

Most Touchdowns, Lifetime: 126, Jim Brown, Cleveland

Most Touchdowns, Season: 23, O. J. Simpson, Buffalo, 1975.

Most Yards Gained Rushing, Lifetime: 12,312, Jim Brown, Cleveland, 1957–65

Most Yards Gained Rushing, Season: 2,003, O. J. Simpson, Buffalo, 1973

Most Yards Gained Rushing, Game: 275, Walter Payton, Chicago vs. Minnesota, Nov. 20, 1977

Highest Average Gain Rushing, Lifetime: 5.22, Jim Brown, Cleveland

Most Touchdowns Rushing, Lifetime: 106, Jim Brown, Cleveland

Most Touchdowns Rushing, Season: 19, Jim Taylor, Green Bay, 1962

Most Passes Completed, Lifetime: 3,686, Fran Tarkenton, Minnesota, New York Giants, Minnesota

Most Passes Completed, Season: 348, Dan Fouts, San Diego, 1980

Most Passes Completed, Game: 42, Richard Todd, N.Y. Jets, 1980

Passing Percent (Attempts-Completions), Season: 70.33, Sammy Baugh, Washington, 1945

Most Yards Gained Passing, Lifetime: 47,003, Fran Tarkenton, Minnesota, New York Giants, Minnesota

Most Yards Gained Passing, Season: 4,715, Dan Fouts, San Diego, 1980

Most Yards Gained Passing, Game: 554, Norm Van Brocklin, Los Angeles, 1951

Most Touchdown Passes, Lifetime: 342, Fran Tarkenton, Minnesota, New York Giants, Minnesota

Receptions, Most Yards Gained, Lifetime: 11,834, Don Maynard, New York Giants, New York Jets, St. Louis

Receptions, Most Yards Gained, Season: 1,746, Charlie Hennigan, Houston, 1961

Receptions, Most Touchdowns, Lifetime: 99, Don Hutson, Green Bay

Receptions, Most Touchdowns, Season: 17, Don Hutson, Green Bay, 1942; 17, Elroy Hirsch, Los Angeles, 1951; 17, Bill Groman, Houston, 1961

Most Receptions, Lifetime: 649, Charley Taylor, Washington

Interceptions, Most Touchdowns from, Lifetime: 9, Ken Houston, Washington

Most Points After Touchdown, Lifetime: 943, George Blanda, Chicago Bears, Baltimore, Houston, Oakland

Most Points After Touchdown, Season: 64, George Blanda, Houston, 1961

Most Consecutive Points After Touchdown: 234, Tommy Davis, San Francisco, 1959–65

Most Field Goals, Lifetime: 335, George Blanda, Chicago Bears, Baltimore, Houston, Oakland

Most Field Goals, Season: 34, Jim Turner, New York Jets, 1968

Most Field Goals, Game: 7, Jim Bakken, St. Louis vs. Pittsburgh, September 24, 1967

Longest Field Goal: 63 yards, Tom Dempsey, New Orleans vs. Detroit, November 8, 1970

Most Consecutive Field Goals: 20, Garo Yepremian, Miami, 1978; New Orleans, 1979

Longest Punt: 98, Steve O'Neal, New York Jets, 1969

Most Punt Returns, Lifetime: 258, Emlen Tunnell, New York Giants and Green Bay

Punt Returns, Most Yardage Gained, Lifetime: 2,651, Rick Upchurch, Denver, 1975–80

Kickoff Returns, Highest Average Yardage Gained, Season: 41.06, Travis Williams, Green Bay, 1967

Most Seasons, Active Player: 26, George Blanda, Chicago Bears, Baltimore, Houston, Oakland

Most Games Played, Lifetime: 340, George Blanda, Chicago Bears, Baltimore, Houston, Oakland

Most Seasons NFL Champion Team: 11, Green Bay, 1929-1931, 1936, 1939, 1944, 1961-1962, 1965-1967.

Team, Most Consecutive Victories, Regular Season: 17, Chicago Bears, 1933-1934

NATIONAL FOOTBALL LEAGUE ALL-TIME LEADERS

Rushing Yardage		Pass Receptions		Points		Interceptions	
12,312	Jim Brown	649	Charley Taylor	2,002	George Blanda	81	Paul Krause
11,236	O. J. Simpson	633	Don Maynard	1,439	Jim Turner	79	Emlen Tunnell
9,352	Franco Harris	631	Raymond Berry	1,380	Jim Bakken	68	Night Train Lane
8,597	Jim Taylor	589	Fred Biletnikoff	1,365	Fred Cox	62	Dick LeBeau
8,386	Walter Payton	567	Lionel Taylor	1,349	Lou Groza	58	Emmitt Thomas

NFL FINAL 1980 STANDINGS

AMERICAN FOOTBALL CONFERENCE

EASTERN DIVISION

	W	L	T	Pct.	Pts.	OP
Buffalo	11	5	0	.688	320	260
New England	10	6	0	.625	441	325
Miami	8	8	0	.500	266	305
Baltimore	7	9	0	.438	355	387
N.Y. Jets	4	12	0	.250	302	395

CENTRAL DIVISION

	W	L	T	Pct.	Pts.	OP
Cleveland	11	5	0	.688	357	310
*Houston	11	5	0	.688	295	251
Pittsburgh	9	7	0	.563	352	313
Cincinnati	6	10	0	.375	244	312

WESTERN DIVISION

	W	L	T	Pct.	Pts.	OP
San Diego	11	5	0	.688	418	327
*Oakland	11	5	0	.688	364	306
Denver	8	8	0	.500	310	323
Kansas City	8	8	0	.500	319	336
Seattle	4	12	0	.250	291	408

*Wild card qualifiers

NATIONAL FOOTBALL CONFERENCE

EASTERN DIVISION

	W	L	T	Pct.	Pts.	OP
Philadelphia	12	4	0	.750	384	222
*Dallas	12	4	0	.750	454	311
Washington	6	10	0	.375	261	293
St. Louis	5	11	0	.313	299	350
N.Y. Giants	4	12	0	.250	249	425

CENTRAL DIVISION

	W	L	T	Pct.	Pts.	OP
Minnesota	9	7	0	.563	317	308
Detroit	9	7	0	.563	334	272
Chicago	7	9	0	.438	304	264
Tampa Bay	5	10	1	.344	271	341
Green Bay	5	10	1	.344	231	371

WESTERN DIVISION

	W	L	T	Pct.	Pts.	OP
Atlanta	12	4	0	.750	405	272
*Los Angeles	11	5	0	.688	424	289
San Francisco	6	10	0	.375	320	415
New Orleans	1	15	0	.063	291	487

POST-SEASON GAMES

	AMERICAN CONFERENCE	NATIONAL CONFERENCE
WILD CARD TEAMS	Oakland 27, Houston 7	Dallas 34, Los Angeles 13
DIVISION PLAYOFFS	San Diego 20, Buffalo 14	Philadelphia 31, Minnesota 16
	Oakland 14, Cleveland 12	Dallas 30, Atlanta 27
CONFERENCE CHAMPIONSHIP	Oakland 34, San Diego 27	Philadelphia 20, Dallas 7

LEAGUE CHAMPIONSHIP (SUPER BOWL)   Oakland 27, Philadelphia 10

1980 INDIVIDUAL LEADERS

RUSHING-AFC	Att.	Yds.	Avg.	Long	TDs.
Campbell, Houston	373	1934	5.2	55	13
Cribbs, Buffalo	306	1185	3.9	48	11
M. Pruitt, Cleveland	249	1034	4.2	56	6
van Eeghan, Oakland	222	838	3.8	34	5
Muncie, San Diego	175	827	4.7	53	6

RUSHING-NFC	Att.	Yds.	Avg.	Long	TDs.
Payton, Chicago	317	1460	4.6	69	6
Anderson, St. Louis	301	1352	4.5	52	9
Andrews, Atlanta	265	1308	4.9	33	4
Sims, Detroit	313	1303	4.2	52	13
Dorsett, Dallas	278	1185	4.3	56	11

PASSING-AFC	Att.	Comp.	Yds.	Int.	TDs.
Sipe, Cleveland	554	340	4132	14	30
Fouts, San Diego	589	348	4715	24	30
Morton, Denver	301	183	2150	13	12
Fuller, Kansas City	320	193	2250	12	10
Jones, Baltimore	446	248	3134	21	23

PASSING-NFC	Att.	Comp.	Yds.	Int.	TDs.
Jaworski, Philadelphia	451	257	3529	12	27
Ferragamo, Los Angeles	404	240	3199	19	30
Bartkowski, Atlanta	463	257	3544	16	31
Montana, San Francisco	273	176	1795	9	15
Danielson, Detroit	417	244	3223	11	13

RECEIVING-AFC	No.	Yds.	Avg.	TDs.
Winslow, San Diego	89	1290	14.5	9
Jefferson, San Diego	82	1340	16.3	13
Joiner, San Diego	71	1132	15.9	4
Largent, Seattle	66	1064	16.1	6
M. Pruitt, Cleveland	63	471	7.5	0

RECEIVING-NFC	No.	Yds.	Avg.	TDs.
Cooper, San Francisco	83	567	6.8	4
Clark, San Francisco	82	991	12.1	8
Lofton, Green Bay	71	1226	17.3	4
Rashad, Minnesota	69	1095	15.9	5
Tilley, St. Louis	68	966	14.2	6

INTERCEPTIONS-AFC	No.	Yds.	Long	TDs.
Hayes, Oakland	13	273	62	1

INTERCEPTIONS-NFC	No.	Yds.	Long	TDs.
Cromwell, Los Angeles	8	140	34	1

PUNTING-AFC	No.	Yds.	Long	Avg.
Prestridge, Denver	70	3075	57	43.9

PUNTING-NFC	No.	Yds.	Long	Avg.
Jennings, New York	94	4211	63	44.8

PUNT RETURNS-AFC	No.	Avg.	Long	TDs.
Smith, Kansas City	40	14.5	75	2

PUNT RETURNS-NFC	No.	Avg.	Long	TDs.
Johnson, Atlanta	23	12.2	56	0

KICKOFF RETURNS-AFC	No.	Avg.	Long	TDs.
Ivory, New England	36	27.6	98	1

KICKOFF RETURNS-NFC	No.	Avg.	Long	TDs.
Mauti, New Orleans	31	25.7	52	0

SCORING/KICKING-AFC	XP	FG	Pts.
Smith, New England	51-51	26-34	129

SCORING/KICKING-NFC	XP	FG	Pts.
Murray, Detroit	35-36	27-42	116

ALL-PRO SELECTIONS (AP) Associated Press, (UPI) United Press International, (SN) Sporting News

Offense

Quarterback	—Brian, Sipe, Cleveland (AP, UPI, SN)
Running backs	—Earl Campbell, Houston (AP, UPI, SN)
	—Walter Payton, Chicago (AP, UPI, SN)
Wide receivers	—John Jefferson, San Diego (AP, UPI, SN)
	—James Lofton, Green Bay (AP, UPI, SN)
	—Charlie Joiner, San Diego (UPI)
Tight end	—Kellen Winslow, San Diego (AP, UPI, SN)
Center	—Mike Webster, Pittsburgh (AP, UPI, SN)
Guards	—John Hannah, New England (AP, UPI, SN)
	—Joe DeLamielleure, Cleveland (AP, SN)
	—Herbert Scott, Dallas (UPI)
Tackles	—Mike Kenn, Atlanta (AP, UPI, SN)
	—Leon Gray, Houston (AP, UPI, SN)
Specialists	
Punter	—Dave Jennings, New York Giants (AP, UPI, SN)
Place kickers	—John Smith, New England (AP)
	—Ed Murray, Detroit (UPI)
	—Fred Steinfort, Denver (SN)

Defense

Ends	—Lee Roy Selmon, Tampa Bay (AP, SN)
	—Art Still, Kansas City (AP, SN)
	—Fred Dean, San Diego (UPI)
	—Lyle Alzado, Cleveland (UPI)
Tackles	—Gary Johnson, San Diego (AP, UPI, SN)
	—Randy White, Dallas (AP, SN)
	—Charlie Johnson, Philadelphia (UPI)
Linebackers	—Ted Hendricks, Oakland (AP, UPI, SN)
	—Jack Lambert, Pittsburgh (AP, UPI, SN)
	—Robert Brazile, Houston (AP, SN)
	—Matt Blair, Minnesota (UPI)
	—Randy Gradishar, Denver (SN)
	—Steve Nelson, New England (SN)
Cornerbacks	—Lester Hayes, Oakland (AP, UPI, SN)
	—Lemar Parrish, Washington (AP, SN)
	—Pat Thomas, Los Angeles (UPI)
Free safety	—Nolan Cromwell, Los Angeles (AP, UPI, SN)
Strong safety	—Donnie Shell, Pittsburgh (AP, UPI, SN)

CHAMPIONSHIP GAMES

NATIONAL FOOTBALL LEAGUE

1933 Dec. Chicago Bears 23, New York Giants 21
1934 Dec. New York Giants 30, Chicago Bears 13
1935 Dec. Detroit Lions 26, New York Giants 7
1936 Dec. Green Bay Packers 21, Boston Redskins 6
1937 Dec. Washington Redskins 28, Chicago Bears 21
1938 Dec. New York Giants 23, Green Bay Packers 17
1939 Dec. Green Bay Packers 27, New York Giants 0
1940 Dec. Chicago Bears 73, Washington Redskins 0
1941 Dec. Chicago Bears 37, New York Giants 9
1942 Dec. Washington Redskins 14, Chicago Bears 6
1943 Dec. Chicago Bears 41, Washington Redskins 21
1944 Dec. Green Bay Packers 14, New York Giants 7
1945 Dec. Cleveland Rams 15, Washington Redskins 14
1946 Dec. Chicago Bears 24, New York Giants 14
1947 Dec. Chicago Cardinals 28, Philadelphia Eagles 21
1948 Dec. Philadelphia Eagles 7, Chicago Cardinals 0
1949 Dec. Philadelphia Eagles 14, Los Angeles Rams 0
1950 Dec. Cleveland Browns 30, Los Angeles Rams 28
1951 Dec. Los Angeles Rams 24, Cleveland Browns 17
1952 Dec. Detroit Lions 17, Cleveland Browns 7
1953 Dec. Detroit Lions 17, Cleveland Browns 16
1954 Dec. Cleveland Browns 56, Detroit Lions 10
1955 Dec. Cleveland Browns 38, Los Angeles Rams 14
1956 Dec. New York Giants 47, Chicago Bears 7
1957 Dec. Detroit Lions 59, Cleveland Browns 14
1958 Dec. Baltimore Colts 23, New York Giants 17
1959 Dec. Baltimore Colts 31, New York Giants 16
1960 Dec. Philadelphia Eagles 17, Green Bay Packers 13
1961 Dec. Green Bay Packers 37, New York Giants 0
1962 Dec. Green Bay Packers 16, New York Giants 7
1963 Dec. Chicago Bears 14, New York Giants 10
1964 Dec. Cleveland Browns 27, Baltimore Colts 0
1966 Jan. Green Bay Packers 23, Cleveland Browns 12
1967 Jan. Green Bay Packers 34, Dallas Cowboys 27
1967 Dec. Green Bay Packers 21, Dallas Cowboys 17
1968 Dec. Baltimore Colts 34, Cleveland Browns 0
1970 Jan. Minnesota Vikings 27, Cleveland Browns 7

NATIONAL FOOTBALL CONFERENCE

1971 Jan. Dallas Cowboys 17, San Francisco 49ers 10
1972 Jan. Dallas Cowboys 14, San Francisco 49ers 3
1972 Dec. Washington Redskins 26, Dallas Cowboys 3
1973 Dec. Minnesota Vikings 27, Dallas Cowboys 10
1974 Dec. Minnesota Vikings 14, Los Angeles Rams 10
1976 Jan. Dallas Cowboys 37, Los Angeles Rams 7
1976 Dec. Minnesota Vikings 24, Los Angeles Rams 13
1978 Jan. Dallas Cowboys 23, Minnesota Vikings 6
1979 Jan. Dallas Cowboys 28, Los Angeles Rams 0
1980 Jan. Los Angeles Rams 9, Tampa Bay Buccaneers 0
1981 Jan. Philadelphia Eagles 20, Dallas Cowboys 7

AMERICAN FOOTBALL LEAGUE

1961 Jan. Houston Oilers 24, San Diego Chargers 16
1961 Dec. Houston Oilers 10, San Diego Chargers 3
1962 Dec. Dallas Texans 20, Houston Oilers 17
1964 Jan. San Diego Chargers 51, Boston Patriots 10
1964 Dec. Buffalo Bills 20, San Diego Chargers 7
1965 Dec. Buffalo Bills 23, San Diego Chargers 0
1967 Jan. Kansas City Chiefs 31, Buffalo Bills 7
1967 Dec. Oakland Raiders 40, Houston Oilers 7
1968 Dec. New York Jets 27, Oakland Raiders 23
1970 Jan. Kansas City Chiefs 17, Oakland Raiders 7

AMERICAN FOOTBALL CONFERENCE

1971 Jan. Baltimore Colts 27, Oakland Raiders 17
1972 Jan. Miami Dolphins 21, Baltimore Colts 0
1972 Dec. Miami Dolphins 21, Pittsburgh Steelers 17
1973 Dec. Miami Dolphins 27, Oakland Raiders 10
1974 Dec. Pittsburgh Steelers 24, Oakland Raiders 13
1976 Jan. Pittsburgh Steelers 16, Oakland Raiders 10
1976 Dec. Oakland Raiders 24, Pittsburgh Steelers 7
1978 Jan. Denver Broncos 20, Oakland Raiders 17
1979 Jan. Pittsburgh Steelers 34, Houston Oilers 5
1980 Jan. Pittsburgh Steelers 27, Houston Oilers 13
1981 Jan. Oakland Raiders 34, San Diego Chargers 27

SUPER BOWL GAMES

I Jan. 15, 1967—Memorial Coliseum, Los Angeles
   Green Bay Packers (NFL) 7   7 14   7 – 35
   Kansas City Chiefs (AFL) . . . . 0 10   0   0 – 10

II Jan. 14, 1968—Orange Bowl, Miami
   Green Bay Packers (NFL) . . . . 3 13 10   7 – 33
   Oakland Raiders (AFL) 0   7   0   7 – 14

III Jan. 12, 1969—Orange Bowl, Miami
   New York Jets (AFL) 0   7   6   3 – 16
   Baltimore Colts (NFL) 0   0   0   7 – 7

IV Jan. 11, 1970—Tulane Stadium, New Orleans
   Kansas City Chiefs (AFL) . . . . 3 13   7   0 – 23
   Minnesota Vikings (NFL) 0   0   7   0 – 7

V Jan. 17, 1971—Orange Bowl, Miami
   Baltimore Colts (AFC) 0   6   0 10 – 16
   Dallas Cowboys (NFC) . . . . 3 10   0   0 – 13

VI Jan. 16, 1972—Tulane Stadium, New Orleans
   Dallas Cowboys (NFC) 3   7   7   7 – 24
   Miami Dolphins (AFC) 0   3   0   0 – 3

VII Jan. 14, 1973—Memorial Coliseum, Los Angeles
   Miami Dolphins (AFC) 7   7   0   0 – 14
   Washington Redskins (NFC) 0   0   0   7 – 7

VIII Jan. 13, 1974—Rice Stadium, Houston
   Miami Dolphins (AFC) 14   3   7   0 – 24
   Minnesota Vikings (NFC) 0   0   0   7 – 7

IX Jan. 12, 1975—Tulane Stadium, New Orleans
   Pittsburgh Steelers (AFC) 0   2   7   7 – 16
   Minnesota Vikings (NFC) 0   0   0   6 – 6

X Jan. 18, 1976—Orange Bowl, Miami
   Pittsburgh Steelers (AFC) 7   0   0 14 – 21
   Dallas Cowboys (NFC) 7   3   0   7 – 17

XI Jan. 9, 1977—Rose Bowl, Pasadena
   Oakland Raiders (AFC) . . . . 0 16   3 13 – 32
   Minnesota Vikings (NFC) 0   0   7   7 – 14

XII Jan. 15, 1978—Superdome, New Orleans
   Dallas Cowboys (NFC) 10   3   7   7 – 27
   Denver Broncos (AFC) 0   0 10   0 – 10

XIII Jan. 21, 1979—Orange Bowl, Miami
   Pittsburgh Steelers (AFC) . . . . 7 14   0 14 – 35
   Dallas Cowboys (NFC) 7   7   3 14 – 31

XIV Jan. 20, 1980—Rose Bowl, Pasadena
   Pittsburgh Steelers (AFC) 3   7   7 14 – 31
   Los Angeles Rams (NFC) 7   6   6   0 – 19

XV Jan. 25, 1981—Superdome, New Orleans
   Oakland Raiders (AFC) 14   0 10   3 – 27
   Philadelphia Eagles (NFC) 0   3   0   7 – 10

   Oak—Branch, 2, pass from Plunkett (Bahr kick)
   Oak—King, 80, pass from Plunkett (Bahr kick)
   Phila—FG, Franklin, 30
   Oak—Branch, 29, pass from Plunkett (Bahr kick)
   Oak—FG, Bahr, 46
   Phila—Krepfle, 8, pass from Jaworski (Franklin kick)
   Oak—FG, Bahr, 35

TEAM DEPARTMENTAL CHAMPIONS

Total Yards Gained		Yards Rushing		Yards Passing		Points Scored	
1980—San Diego (AFC)	6,410	1980—Los Angeles (NFC)	2,799	1980—San Diego (AFC)	4,531	1980—Dallas (NFC)	454
1979—Pittsburgh (AFC)	6,258	1979—New York (AFC)	2,646	1979—San Diego (AFC)	3,915	1979—Pittsburgh (AFC)	416
1978—New England (AFC)	5,965	1978—New England (AFC)	3,165	1978—San Diego (AFC)	3,375	1978—Dallas (NFC)	384
1977—Dallas (NFC)	4,812	1977—Chicago (NFC)	2,811	1977—Buffalo (AFC)	2,530	1977—Oakland (AFC)	351
1976—Baltimore (AFC)	5,236	1976—Pittsburgh (AFC)	2,971	1976—Baltimore (AFC)	2,933	1976—Baltimore (AFC)	417
1975—Buffalo (AFC)	5,467	1975—Buffalo (AFC)	2,974	1975—Cincinnati (AFC)	3,241	1975—Buffalo (AFC)	420
1974—Dallas (NFC)	4,983	1974—Pittsburgh (AFC)	2,417	1974—Washington (NFC)	2,978	1974—Oakland (AFC)	355
1973—Los Angeles (NFC)	4,906	1973—Buffalo (AFC)	3,088	1973—Philadelphia (NFC)	3,236	1973—Dallas (AFC)	388
1972—Miami (AFC)	5,036	1972—Miami (AFC)	2,960	1972—New York Jets (AFC)	2,777	1972—Miami (AFC)	385
1971—Dallas (NFC)	5,035	1971—Miami (AFC)	2,429	1971—San Diego (AFC)	3,134	1971—Dallas (NFC)	406
1970—Oakland (AFC)	4,829	1970—Dallas (NFC)	2,300	1970—San Francisco (NFC)	2,923	1970—San Francisco (NFC)	352
1969—Dallas (NFL)	5,122	1969—Dallas (NFL)	2,276	1969—Oakland (AFL)	3,271	1969—Minnesota (NFL)	379
1968—Oakland (AFL)	5,696	1968—Chicago (NFL)	2,377	1968—San Diego (AFL)	3,623	1968—Oakland (AFL)	453
1967—New York (AFL)	5,152	1967—Cleveland (NFL)	2,139	1967—New York (AFL)	3,845	1967—Oakland (AFL)	468
1966—Dallas (NFL)	5,145	1966—Kansas City (AFL)	2,274	1966—New York (AFL)	3,464	1966—Kansas City (AFL)	448
1965—San Francisco (NFL)	5,270	1965—Cleveland (NFL)	2,331	1965—San Francisco (NFL)	3,487	1965—San Francisco (NFL)	421
1964—Buffalo (AFL)	5,206	1964—Green Bay (NFL)	2,276	1964—Houston (AFL)	3,527	1964—Baltimore (NFL)	428
1963—San Diego (AFL)	5,153	1963—Cleveland (NFL)	2,639	1963—Baltimore (NFL)	3,296	1963—New York (NFL)	448
1962—New York (AFL)	5,005	1962—Buffalo (AFL)	2,480	1962—Denver (AFL)	3,404	1962—Green Bay (NFL)	415
1961—Houston (AFL)	6,288	1961—Green Bay (NFL)	2,350	1961—Houston (AFL)	4,392	1961—Houston (AFL)	513
1960—Houston (AFL)	4,936	1960—St. Louis (NFL)	2,356	1960—Houston (AFL)	3,203	1960—New York (AFL)	382
1959—Baltimore	4,458	1959—Cleveland	2,149	1959—Baltimore	2,753	1959—Baltimore	374
1958—Baltimore	4,539	1958—Cleveland	2,526	1958—Pittsburgh	2,752	1958—Baltimore	381
1957—Los Angeles	4,143	1957—Los Angeles	2,142	1957—Baltimore	2,388	1957—Los Angeles	307
1956—Chicago Bears	4,537	1956—Chicago Bears	2,468	1956—Chicago Bears	2,419	1956—Chicago Bears	363
1955—Chicago Bears	4,316	1955—Chicago Bears	2,388	1955—Philadelphia	2,472	1955—Cleveland	349
1954—Los Angeles	5,187	1954—San Francisco	2,498	1954—Chicago Bears	3,104	1954—Detroit	337
1953—Philadelphia	4,811	1953—San Francisco	2,230	1953—Philadelphia	3,089	1953—San Francisco	372
1952—Cleveland	4,352	1952—San Francisco	1,905	1952—Cleveland	2,566	1952—Los Angeles	349
1951—Los Angeles	5,506	1951—Chicago Bears	2,408	1951—Los Angeles	3,296	1951—Los Angeles	392
1950—Los Angeles	5,420	1950—New York Giants	2,336	1950—Los Angeles	3,709	1950—Los Angeles	466
1949—Chicago Bears	4,873	1949—Philadelphia	2,607	1949—Chicago Bears	3,055	1949—Philadelphia	364
1948—Chicago Cards	4,705	1948—Chicago Cards	2,560	1948—Washington	2,861	1948—Chicago Cards	395
1947—Chicago Bears	5,053	1947—Los Angeles	2,171	1947—Washington	3,336	1947—Chicago Bears	363
1946—Los Angeles	3,793	1946—Green Bay	1,765	1946—Los Angeles	2,080	1946—Chicago Bears	289
1945—Washington	3,549	1945—Cleveland Rams	1,714	1945—Chicago Bears	1,857	1945—Philadelphia	272
1944—Chicago Bears	3,239	1944—Philadelphia	1,661	1944—Washington	2,021	1944—Philadelphia	267
1943—Chicago Bears	4,045	1943—Phil-Pitt	1,730	1943—Chicago Bears	2,310	1943—Chicago Bears	303
1942—Chicago Bears	3,900	1942—Chicago Bears	1,881	1942—Green Bay	2,407	1942—Chicago Bears	376
1941—Chicago Bears	4,265	1941—Chicago Bears	2,263	1941—Chicago Bears	2,002	1941—Chicago Bears	396
1940—Green Bay	3,400	1940—Chicago Bears	1,818	1940—Washington	1,887	1940—Washington	245
1939—Chicago Bears	3,988	1939—Chicago Bears	2,043	1939—Chicago Bears	1,965	1939—Chicago Bears	298
1938—Green Bay	3,037	1938—Detroit	1,893	1938—Washington	1,536	1938—Green Bay	223
1937—Green Bay	3,201	1937—Detroit	2,074	1937—Green Bay	1,398	1937—Green Bay	220
1936—Detroit	3,703	1936—Detroit	2,885	1936—Green Bay	1,629	1936—Green Bay	248
1935—Chicago Bears	3,454	1935—Chicago Bears	2,096	1935—Green Bay	1,449	1935—Chicago Bears	192
1934—Chicago Bears	3,750	1934—Chicago Bears	2,847	1934—Green Bay	1,165	1934—Chicago Bears	286
1933—New York Giants	2,970	1933—Boston Redskins	2,260	1933—New York	1,348	1933—New York Giants	244
1932—Chicago Bears	2,755	1932—Chicago Bears	1,770	1932—Chicago Bears	1,013	1932—Green Bay	152

NATIONAL FOOTBALL LEAGUE STARS: BY YEARS

PASSERS	Passes	Comp	Yards	Tds	Inter.
1980—Brian Sipe, Cleveland (AFC)	554	340	4,132	30	14
1979—Roger Staubach, Dallas (NFC)	461	267	3,586	27	11
1978—Roger Staubach, Dallas (NFC)	413	231	3,190	25	16
1977—Bob Griese, Miami (AFC)	307	180	2,252	22	13
1976—Ken Stabler, Oakland (AFC)	291	194	2,737	27	17
1975—Ken Anderson, Cincinnati (AFC)	377	228	3,169	21	11
1974—Ken Anderson, Cincinnati (AFC)	328	213	2,667	18	10
1973—Roger Staubach, Dallas Cowboys (NFC)	286	179	2,428	23	15
1972—Norm Snead, New York Giants (NFC)	325	196	2,307	17	12
1971—Bob Griese, Miami (AFC)	263	145	2,089	19	9
1970—John Brodie, San Francisco (NFC)	378	223	2,941	24	10
1969—C. A. (Sonny) Jurgensen, Wash. (NFL)	442	274	3,102	22	15
1968—Earl Morrall, Baltimore (NFL)	317	182	2,909	26	17
1967—C. A. (Sonny) Jurgensen, Wash. (NFL)	508	288	3,747	31	16
1966—Len Dawson, Kansas City (AFL)	284	159	2,527	26	10
1965—John Hadl, San Diego (AFL)	348	174	2,798	20	21
1964—Len Dawson, Kansas City (AFL)	354	199	2,879	30	18
1963—Y. A. Tittle, New York (NFL)	367	221	3,145	36	14

PASSERS	Passes	Comp	Yards	Tds	Inter.
1962—Len Dawson, Dallas (AFL)	310	189	2,759	29	17
1961—George Blanda, Houston (AFL)	362	187	3,330	36	22
1960—Jack Kemp, Los Angeles (AFL)	406	211	3,018	20	25
1959—Charles Conerly, N.Y.	194	113	1,706	14	4
1958—Eddie LeBaron, Wash.	145	79	1,365	11	10
1957—Tommy O'Connell, Cleveland	110	63	1,229	9	8
1956—Eddie Brown, Chicago	168	96	1,667	11	12
1955—Otto Graham, Cleveland	185	98	1,721	15	8
1954—Norman Van Brocklin, L.A.	260	139	2,637	13	21
1953—Otto Graham, Clev.	258	167	2,722	11	9
1952—Norman Van Brocklin, L.A.	205	113	1,736	14	17
1951—Bob Waterfield, L.A.	176	88	1,566	13	10
1950—Norman Van Brocklin, L.A.	233	127	2,061	18	14
1949—Sammy Baugh, Wash.	255	145	1,903	18	14
1948—Tommy Thompson, Phila.	246	141	1,965	25	11
1947—Sammy Baugh, Wash.	354	210	2,938	25	15
1946—Bob Waterfield, L.A.	251	127	1,747	18	17
1945—Sid Luckman, Chicago	217	117	1,725	14	10
1944—Frank Filchock, Washington	147	84	1,139	13	9
1943—Sammy Baugh, Wash.	239	133	1,754	23	19
1942—Cecil Isbell, Green Bay	268	146	2,021	24	14
1941—Cecil Isbell, Green Bay	206	117	1,479	15	11
1940—Sammy Baugh, Wash.	177	111	1,367	12	10
1939—Parker Hall, Clev.*	208	106	1,227	9	13
1938—Ed Danowski, N.Y.	129	70	848	8	8
1937—Sammy Baugh, Wash.*	171	81	1,127	7	14

* First year in League

RUSHERS	Yards	Att.	TDs
1980—Earl Campbell, Houston (AFC)..	1,934	373	13
1979—Earl Campbell, Houston (AFC)..	1,697	368	19
1978—Earl Campbell, Houston (AFC)*.	1,450	302	13
1977—Walter Payton, Chicago (NFC)..	1,852	339	14
1976—O. J. Simpson, Buffalo (AFC)..	1,503	290	8
1975—O. J. Simpson, Buffalo (AFC)..	1,817	329	16
1974—Otis Armstrong, Denver (AFC)..	1,407	263	9
1973—O. J. Simpson, Buffalo (AFC)..	2,003	332	12
1972—O. J. Simpson, Buffalo (AFC)..	1,251	292	6
1971—Floyd Little, Denver (AFC)	1,133	284	6
1970—Larry Brown, Washington (NFC)..	1,125	237	5
1969—Gale Sayers, Chicago (NFL)	1,032	236	8
1968—Leroy Kelly, Cleveland (NFL) ...	1,239	248	16
1967—Jim Nance, Boston (AFL)	1,216	269	7
1966—Jim Nance, Boston (AFL)	1,458	299	11
1965—Jim Brown, Cleveland (NFL)	1,544	289	17
1964—Jim Brown, Cleveland (NFL)	1,446	280	7
1963—Jim Brown, Cleveland (NFL)	1,863	291	12
1962—Jim Taylor, Green Bay (NFL)	1,474	272	19
1961—Jim Brown, Cleveland (NFL)	1,408	305	8
1960—Jim Brown, Cleveland (NFL)	1,257	215	9
1959—Jim Brown, Cleveland	1,329	290	14
1958—Jim Brown, Cleveland	1,527	257	17
1957—Jim Brown, Cleveland*	942	202	9
1956—Rick Casares, Chicago Bears	1,126	234	12
1955—Alan Ameche, Baltimore*	961	213	9
1954—Joe Perry, San Francisco	1,049	173	8
1953—Joe Perry, San Francisco	1,018	192	10
1952—Dan Towler, Los Angeles	894	156	10
1951—Eddie Price, New York Giants ..	971	271	7
1950—Marion Motley, Cleveland*	810	140	3
1949—Steve Van Buren, Philadelphia ..	1,146	263	11
1948—Steve Van Buren, Philadelphia ..	945	201	10
1947—Steve Van Buren, Philadelphia ..	1,008	217	13
1946—Bill Dudley, Pittsburgh	604	146	3
1945—Steve Van Buren, Philadelphia ..	832	143	15
1944—Bill Paschal, New York	737	196	9
1943—Bill Paschal, New York*	572	147	10
1942—Bill Dudley, Pittsburgh*	696	162	5
1941—Clarence Manders, Brooklyn	486	111	6
1940—Byron White, Detroit	514	146	5
1939—Bill Osmanski, Chicago Bears* ..	699	121	7
1938—Byron White, Pittsburgh*	567	152	4
1937—Cliff Battles, Washington	874	216	6

RECEIVERS	No.	Yards	TDs
1980—Kellen Winslow, San Diego (AFC) ...	89	1,290	9
1979—Joe Washington, Baltimore (AFC) ...	82	750	3
1978—Rickey Young, Minnesota (NFC)	88	704	5
1977—Lydell Mitchell, Baltimore (AFC) ...	71	620	4
1976—MacArthur Lane, Kansas City (AFC) ...	66	686	1
1975—Chuck Foreman, Minnesota (NFC) ...	73	691	9
1974—Lydell Mitchell, Baltimore (AFC) ...	72	544	2
1973—Harold Carmichael, Philadelphia (NFC)	67	1,116	9
1972—Harold Jackson, Philadelphia (NFC) ..	62	1,048	4
1971—Fred Biletnikoff, Oakland (AFC)	61	929	9
1970—Dick Gordon, Chicago (NFC)	71	1,026	13
1969—Dan Abramowicz, New Orleans (NFL)	73	1,015	7
1968—Lance Alworth, San Diego (AFL)	68	1,312	10
1967—George Sauer, New York (AFL)	75	1,189	6
1966—Lance Alworth, San Diego (AFL)	73	1,383	13
1965—Dave Parks, San Francisco (NFL) ...	80	1,344	12
1964—Charley Hennigan, Houston (AFL) ..	101	1,546	8
1963—Lionel Taylor, Denver (AFL)	78	1,101	10
1962—Bobby Mitchell, Washington (NFL) ..	72	1,384	11
1961—Lionel Taylor, Denver (AFL)	100	1,176	4
1960—Raymond Berry, Baltimore, (NFL) ...	74	1,298	10
1959—Raymond Berry, Baltimore	66	959	14
1958—Raymond Berry, Baltimore	56	794	9
1957—Billy Wilson, San Francisco	52	757	6
1956—Billy Wilson, San Francisco	60	889	5
1955—Pete Pihos, Philadelphia	62	864	7
1954—Pete Pihos, Philadelphia	60	872	10
1953—Pete Pihos, Philadelphia	63	1,049	10
1952—Mac Speedie, Cleveland	62	911	5
1951—Elroy Hirsch, Los Angeles	66	1,495	17
1950—Tom Fears, Los Angeles	84	1,116	7
1949—Tom Fears, Los Angeles	77	1,013	9
1948—Tom Fears, Los Angeles*	51	698	4
1947—Jim Keane, Chicago Bears	64	910	10
1946—Jim Benton, Los Angeles	63	981	6
1945—Don Hutson, Green Bay	47	834	9
1944—Don Hutson, Green Bay	58	866	9
1943—Don Hutson, Green Bay	47	776	11
1942—Don Hutson, Green Bay	74	1,211	17
1941—Don Hutson, Green Bay	58	738	10
1940—Don Looney, Philadelphia*	58	707	4
1939—Don Hutson, Green Bay	34	846	6
1938—Gaynell Tinsley, Chi. Cards	41	516	1
1937—Don Hutson, Green Bay	41	552	7

*First year in League

PUNTERS	Att.	Avg.
1980—Dave Jennings, New York (NFC)	94	44.8
1979—Bob Grupp, Kansas City (AFC)	89	43.6
1978—Pat McInally, Cincinnati (AFC)	91	43.1
1977—Ray Guy, Oakland (AFC)	59	43.3
1976—Marv Bateman, Buffalo (AFC)	86	42.8
1975—Ray Guy, Oakland (AFC)	68	43.8
1974—Ray Guy, Oakland (AFC)	74	42.2
1973—Jerrel Wilson, Kansas City (AFC)	80	45.5
1972—Jerrel Wilson, Kansas City (ACF)	66	44.8
1971—Dave Lewis, Cincinnati (AFC)	72	44.8
1970—Dave Lewis, Cincinnati (AFC)*	79	46.2
1969—David Lee, Baltimore (NFL)	57	45.3
1968—Jerrel Wilson, Kansas City (AFL)	63	45.1
1967—Bob Scarpitto, Denver (AFL)	105	44.9
1966—Bob Scarpitto, Denver (AFL)	76	45.8
1965—Gary Collins, Cleveland (NFL)	65	46.7
1964—Bobby Walden, Minnesota (NFL)	72	46.4
1963—Yale Lary, Detroit (NFL)	35	48.9
1962—Tommy Davis, San Francisco (NFL) ...	48	45.6
1961—Yale Lary, Detroit (NFL)	52	48.4
1960—Jerry Norton, St. Louis (NFL)	39	45.6
1959—Yale Lary, Detroit	45	47.1
1958—Sam Baker, Washington	48	45.4
1957—Don Chandler, New York	60	44.6
1956—Norm Van Brocklin, Los Angeles	48	43.1
1955—Norm Van Brocklin, Los Angeles	60	44.6
1954—Pat Brady, Pittsburgh	66	43.2
1953—Pat Brady, Pittsburgh	80	46.9
1952—Horace Gillom, Cleveland Browns ...	61	45.7
1951—Horace Gillom, Cleveland Browns ...	73	45.5
1950—Fred Morrison, Chicago Bears*	57	43.3
1949—Mike Boyda, N.Y. Bulldogs*	56	44.2
1948—Joe Muha, Philadelphia	57	47.3
1947—Jack Jacobs, Green Bay	57	43.5
1946—Roy McKay, Green Bay	64	42.7
1945—Roy McKay, Green Bay	44	41.2
1944—Frank Sinkwich, Detroit	45	41.0
1943—Sammy Baugh, Washington	50	45.9
1942—Sammy Baugh, Washington	37	48.2
1941—Sammy Baugh, Washington	30	48.7
1940—Sammy Baugh, Washington	35	51.4

TOTAL POINTS	TDs	XP	FG	Points
1980—John Smith, New England (AFC)	0	51	26	129
1979—John Smith, New England (AFC)	0	46	23	115
1978—Frank Corral, Los Angeles (NFC)	0	31	29	118
1977—Errol Mann, Oakland (AFC)	0	39	20	99
1976—Tony Linhart, Baltimore (AFC)	0	49	20	109
1975—O. J. Simpson, Buffalo (AFC)	23	0	0	138
1974—Chester Marcol, Green Bay (NFC) ...	0	19	25	94
1973—David Ray, Los Angeles (NFC)	0	40	30	130
1972—Chester Marcol, Green Bay (NCF)* ..	0	29	33	128
1971—Garo Yepremian, Miami (ACF)	0	33	18	117
1970—Fred Cox, Minnesota (NFC)	0	35	30	125
1969—Jim Turner, New York (AFL)	0	33	32	129
1968—Jim Turner, New York (AFL)	0	43	34	145
1967—Jim Bakken, St. Louis (NFL)	0	36	27	117
1966—Gino Cappelletti, Boston (AFL)	6	35	16	119
1965—Gale Sayers, Chicago (NFL)*	22	0	0	132
—Gino Capelletti, Boston (AFL)	9	27	17	132
1964—Gino Cappelletti, Boston (AFL)	7	36	25	155
1963—Gino Cappelletti, Boston (AFL)	2	35	22	113
1962—Gene Mingo, Denver (AFL)	4	32	27	137
1961—Gino Cappelletti, Boston (AFL)	8	48	17	147
1960—Paul Hornung, Green Bay (NFL)	15	41	15	176
1959—Paul Hornung, Green Bay	7	31	7	94
1958—Jim Brown, Cleveland Browns	18	0	0	108
1957—Sam Baker, Washington	1	29	14	77
—Lou Groza, Cleveland Browns	0	32	15	77
1956—Bobby Layne, Detroit	5	33	12	99
1955—Doak Walker, Detroit	7	27	9	96
1954—Robert Walston, Philadelphia	11	36	4	114
1953—Gordon Soltau, San Francisco	6	48	10	114
1952—Gordon Soltau, San Francisco	7	34	6	94
1951—Elroy Hirsch, Los Angeles	17	0	0	102
1950—Doak Walker, Detroit*	11	38	8	128
1949—Pat Harder, Chicago Cardinals	8	45	3	102
—Gene Roberts, New York Giants	17	0	0	102
1948—Pat Harder, Chicago Cardinals	6	53	7	110
1947—Pat Harder, Chicago Cardinals	7	39	7	102
1946—Ted Fritsch, Green Bay	10	13	9	100
1945—Steve Van Buren, Philadelphia	18	2	0	110
1944—Don Hutson, Green Bay	9	31	0	85
1943—Don Hutson, Green Bay	12	36	3	117
1942—Don Hutson, Green Bay	17	33	1	138
1941—Don Hutson, Green Bay	17	20	1	95
1940—Don Hutson, Green Bay	7	15	0	57
1939—Andy Farkas, Washington	11	2	0	68
1938—Clarke Hinkle, Green Bay	7	7	3	58
1937—Jack Manders, Chicago Bears	5	15	8	69

1980 NFL ALL-ROOKIE TEAM (Selected by United Press International)

Offense

Quarterback	—David Woodley, Miami
Running backs	—Billy Sims, Detroit
	—Joe Cribbs, Buffalo
Wide receivers	—Art Monk, Washington
	—Ray Butler, Baltimore
Tight End	—Junior Miller, Atlanta
Center	—Tommie Ginn, Detroit
Guards	—Ray Snell, Tampa Bay
	—Brent Boyd, Minnesota
Tackles	—Anthony Munoz, Cincinnati
	—Stan Brock, New Orleans
Place kicker	—Ed Murray, Detroit

Defense

Ends	—Marshall Harris, Cleveland
	—Rulon Jones, Denver
Tackle	—Rush Brown, St. Louis
Linebackers	—Al Richardson, Atlanta
	—Bobby Leopold, San Francisco
	—Buddy Curry, Atlanta
	—Matt Millen, Oakland
Cornerbacks	—Roynell Young, Philadelphia
	—Don McNeal, Miami
Free safety	—Darrol Ray, N.Y. Jets
Strong safety	—Johnnie Johnson, Los Angeles
Punter	—Jim Miller, San Francisco

1981 NATIONAL FOOTBALL LEAGUE DRAFT

First Two Choices of Each Team, Position Played, School and Order of Selection

Atlanta	Bobby Butler, db, Florida State (25)
	Lyman White, lb, Louisiana State (54)
Baltimore	Randy McMillan, rb, Pittsburgh (12)
	Donnell Thompson, dt, North Carolina (18)
Buffalo	Booker Moore, rb, Penn State (28)
	Chris Williams, db, Louisiana State (49)
Chicago	Keith Van Horne, ot, USC (11)
	Mike Singletary, lb, Baylor (38)
Cincinnati	David Verser, wr, Kansas (10)
	Chris Collinsworth, wr, Florida (37)
Cleveland	Hanford Dixon, db, Southern Miss. (22)
	Mike Robinson, de, Arizona (92)
Dallas	Howard Richards, ot, Missouri (26)
	Doug Donley, wr, Ohio State (53)
Denver	Dennis Smith, db, USC (15)
	Clay Brown, te, Brigham Young (42)
Detroit	Mark Nichols, wr, San Jose St. (16)
	Curtis Green, de, Alabama State (46)
Green Bay	Rich Campbell, qb, California (6)
	Gary Lewis, te, Texas-Arlington (35)
Houston	Mike Holston, wr, Morgan State (79)
	Nick Eyre, ot, Brigham Young (106)
Kansas City	Willie Scott, te, South Carolina (14)
	Joe Delaney, rb, NW Louisiana (41)
Los Angeles	Mel Owens, lb, Michigan (9)
	Jim Collins, lb, Syracuse (43)
Miami	David Overstreet, rb, Oklahoma (13)
	Andra Franklin, rb, Nebraska (56)
Minnesota	Mardye McDole, wr, Miss. State (39)
	Robin Sendlein, lb, Texas (45)
New England	Brian Holloway, ot, Stanford (19)
	Anthony Collins, rb, East Carolina (47)
New Orleans	George Rogers, rb, South Carolina (1)
	Russell Gary, db, Nebraska (29)
N.Y. Giants	Lawrence Taylor, lb, North Carolina (2)
	Dave Young, te, Purdue (32)
N.Y. Jets	Freeman McNeil, rb, UCLA (3)
	Marion Barber, rb, Minnesota (30)
Oakland	Ted Watts, db, Texas Tech (21)
	Curt Marsh, ot, Washington (23)
Philadelphia	Leonard Mitchell, de, Houston (27)
	Dean Miraldi, og, Utah (55)
Pittsburgh	Keith Gary, de, Oklahoma (17)
	Anthony Washington, db, Fresno State (44)
St. Louis	E. J. Junior, lb, Alabama (5)
	Neil Lomax, qb, Portland State (33)
San Diego	James Brooks, rb, Auburn (24)
	Ervin Phillips, db, Arkansas Tech (77)
San Francisco	Ronnie Lott, db, USC (8)
	John Harty, dt, Iowa (36)
Seattle	Kenny Easley, db, UCLA (4)
	David Hughes, rb, Boise State (31)
Tampa Bay	Hugh Green, lb, Pittsburgh (7)
	James Wilder, rb, Missouri (34)
Washington	Mark May, ot, Pittsburgh (20)
	Russ Grimm, c, Pittsburgh (69)

NATIONAL FOOTBALL LEAGUE STADIUMS

AMERICAN FOOTBALL CONFERENCE

Team	Stadium	Capacity
Baltimore	Memorial Stadium	60,000
Buffalo	Rich Stadium	80,000
Cincinnati	Riverfront Stadium	56,000
Cleveland	Cleveland Stadium	80,000
Denver	Mile High Stadium	75,000
Houston	Astrodome	50,000
Kansas City	Arrowhead Stadium	78,000
Miami	Orange Bowl	75,000
New England	Schaefer Stadium (Foxboro, Mass.)	61,000
N.Y. Jets	Shea Stadium	60,000
Oakland	Oakland-Alameda Co. Coliseum	54,000
Pittsburgh	Three Rivers Stadium	54,000
San Diego	San Diego Stadium	52,000
Seattle	Kingdome	64,000

NATIONAL FOOTBALL CONFERENCE

Team	Stadium	Capacity
Atlanta	Atlanta-Fulton Co. Stadium	60,000
Chicago	Soldier Field	57,000
Dallas	Texas Stadium	65,000
Detroit	Pontiac Silverdome	80,000
Green Bay	Lambeau Field	56,000
	Milwaukee Co. Stadium	55,000
Los Angeles	Anaheim Stadium	69,000
Minnesota	Metropolitan Stadium	48,000
New Orleans	Louisiana Superdome	71,000
N.Y. Giants	Giants Stadium (E. Rutherford, N.J.)	76,000
Philadelphia	Veterans Stadium	71,000
St. Louis	Busch Memorial Stadium	51,000
San Francisco	Candlestick Park	61,000
Tampa Bay	Tampa Stadium	72,000
Washington	Robert F. Kennedy Stadium	55,000

1980 CANADIAN FOOTBALL LEAGUE FINAL STANDINGS

EASTERN CONFERENCE	W	L	T	PF	PA	Pts.
Hamilton Tiger-Cats	8	7	1	332	377	17
Montreal Alouettes	8	8	0	356	375	16
Ottawa Rough Riders	7	9	0	353	393	14
Toronto Argonauts	6	10	0	334	358	12

WESTERN CONFERENCE	W	L	T	PF	PA	Pts.
Edmonton Eskimos	13	3	0	505	281	26
Winnipeg Blue Bombers	10	6	0	394	387	20
Calgary Stampeders	9	7	0	407	355	18
B.C. Lions	8	7	1	381	351	17
Saskatchewan Roughriders	2	14	0	284	469	4

Conference Semifinals: Montreal 25–Ottawa 21, Winnipeg 32–Calgary 14
Conference Finals: Hamilton 24–Montreal 13, Edmonton 34–Winnipeg 24
Championship (Grey Cup): Edmonton 48–Hamilton 10

CANADIAN FOOTBALL LEAGUE CHAMPIONS (GREY CUP)

Year	Champion	Year	Champion	Year	Champion	Year	Champion
1953	Hamilton	1960	Ottawa	1967	Hamilton	1974	Montreal
1954	Edmonton	1961	Winnipeg	1968	Ottawa	1975	Edmonton
1955	Edmonton	1962	Winnipeg	1969	Ottawa	1976	Ottawa
1956	Edmonton	1963	Hamilton	1970	Montreal	1977	Montreal
1957	Hamilton	1964	British Columbia	1971	Calgary	1978	Edmonton
1958	Winnipeg	1965	Hamilton	1972	Hamilton	1979	Edmonton
1959	Winnipeg	1966	Saskatchewan	1973	Ottawa	1980	Edmonton

COLLEGE FOOTBALL

RECORD OF THE MAJOR COLLEGE BOWL GAMES

ROSE BOWL Pasedena, California (January)

Year	Result	Year	Result	Year	Result
1902	Michigan 49, Stanford 0	1937	Pittsburgh 21, Washington 0	1960	Washington 44, Wisconsin 8
1916	Washington State 14, Brown 0	1938	California 13, Alabama 0	1961	Washington 17, Minnesota 7
1917	Oregon 14, Pennsylvania 0	1939	So. California 7, Duke 3	1962	Minnesota 21, UCLA 3
1918	Mare Island Marines 19, Camp Lewis 7	1940	So. California 14, Tennessee 0	1963	So. California 42, Wisconsin 37
1919	Great Lakes 17, Mare Island 0	1941	Stanford 21, Nebraska 13	1964	Illinois 17, Washington 7
1920	Harvard 7, Oregon 6	1942*	Oregon State 20, Duke 16	1965	Michigan 34, Oregon State 7
1921	California 28, Ohio State 0	1943	Georgia 9, UCLA 0	1966	UCLA 14, Michigan State 12
1922	Washington and Jefferson 0, California 0	1944	So. California 29, Washington 0	1967	Purdue 14, So. California 13
1923	So. California 14, Penn State 3	1945	So. California 25, Tennessee 0	1968	So. California 14, Indiana 3
1924	Navy 14, Washington 14	1946	Alabama 34, So. California 14	1969	Ohio State 27, Southern California 16
1925	Notre Dame 27, Stanford 10	1947	Illinois 45, UCLA 14		
1926	Alabama 20, Washington 19	1948	Michigan 49, Southern California 0	1970	So. California 10, Michigan 3
1927	Alabama 7, Stanford 7			1971	Stanford 27, Ohio State 17
1928	Stanford 7, Pittsburgh 6	1949	Northwestern 20, California 14	1972	Stanford 13, Michigan 12
1929	Georgia Tech 8, California 7	1950	Ohio State 17, California 14	1973	So. California 42, Ohio State 17
1930	So. California 47, Pittsburgh 14	1951	Michigan 14, California 6	1974	Ohio State 42, So. California 21
1931	Alabama 24, Washington State 0	1952	Illinois 40, Stanford 7	1975	So. California 18, Ohio State 17
1932	So. California 21, Tulane 12	1953	So. California 7, Wisconsin 0	1976	UCLA 23, Ohio State 10
1933	So. California 35, Pittsburgh 0	1954	Michigan State 28, UCLA 20	1977	So. California 14, Michigan 6
1934	Columbia 7, Stanford 0	1955	Ohio State 20, So. California 7	1978	Washington 27, Michigan 20
1935	Alabama 29, Stanford 13	1956	Michigan State 17, UCLA 14	1979	So. California 17, Michigan 10
1936	Stanford 7, Southern Methodist 0	1957	Iowa 35, Oregon State 19	1980	So. California 17, Ohio State 16
		1958	Ohio State 10, Oregon 7	1981	Michigan 23, Washington 6
		1959	Iowa 38, California 12		

* Played at Durham, North Carolina.

ORANGE BOWL Miami, Florida (January)

Year	Result	Year	Result	Year	Result
1933	Miami (Fla.) 7, Manhattan 0	1948	Georgia Tech 20, Kansas 14	1965	Texas 21, Alabama 17
1934	Duquesne 33, Miami (Fla.) 7	1949	Texas 41, Georgia 28	1966	Alabama 39, Nebraska 28
1935	Bucknell 26, Miami (Fla.) 0	1950	Santa Clara 21, Kentucky 13	1967	Florida 27, Georgia Tech 12
1936	Catholic Univ. 20, Mississippi 19	1951	Clemson 15, Miami (Fla.) 14	1968	Oklahoma 26, Tennessee 24
1937	Duquesne 13, Miss. State 12	1952	Georgia Tech 17, Baylor 14	1969	Penn State 15, Kansas 14
1938	Auburn 6, Michigan State 0	1953	Alabama 61, Syracuse 6	1970	Penn State 10, Missouri 3
1939	Tennessee 17, Oklahoma 0	1954	Oklahoma 7, Maryland 0	1971	Nebraska 17, Louisiana State 12
1940	Georgia Tech 21, Missouri 7	1955	Duke 34, Nebraska 7	1972	Nebraska 38, Alabama 6
1941	Miss. State 14, Georgetown 7	1956	Oklahoma 20, Maryland 6	1973	Nebraska 40, Notre Dame 6
1942	Georgia 40, Texas Christian 26	1957	Colorado 27, Clemson 21	1974	Penn State 16, Louisiana State 9
1943	Alabama 37, Boston College 21	1958	Oklahoma 48, Duke 21	1975	Notre Dame 13, Alabama 11
1944	LSU 19, Texas A&M 14	1959	Oklahoma 21, Syracuse 6	1976	Oklahoma 14, Michigan 6
1945	Tulsa 26, Georgia Tech 12	1960	Georgia 14, Missouri 0	1977	Ohio State 27, Colorado 10
1946	Miami (Fla.) 13, Holy Cross 6	1961	Missouri 21, Navy 14	1978	Arkansas 31, Oklahoma 6
1947	Rice 8, Tennessee 0	1962	Louisiana State 25, Colorado 7	1979	Oklahoma 31, Nebraska 24
		1963	Alabama 17, Oklahoma 0	1980	Oklahoma 24, Florida State 7
		1964	Nebraska 13, Auburn 7	1981	Oklahoma 18, Florida State 17

SUGAR BOWL New Orleans, Louisiana (January)

Year	Result	Year	Result	Year	Result
1935	Tulane 20, Temple 14	1950	Oklahoma 35, Louisiana State 0	1966	Missouri 20, Florida 18
1936	TCU 3, Louisiana State 2	1951	Kentucky 13, Oklahoma 7	1967	Alabama 34, Nebraska 7
1937	Santa Clara 21, LSU 14	1952	Maryland 28, Tennessee 13	1968	Louisiana State 20, Wyoming 13
1938	Santa Clara 6, Louisiana State 0	1953	Georgia Tech 24, Mississippi 7	1969	Arkansas 16, Georgia 2
1939	TCU 15, Carnegie Tech 7	1954	Georgia Tech 42, West Va. 19	1970	Mississippi 27, Arkansas 22
1940	Texas A&M 14, Tulane 13	1955	Navy 21, Mississippi 0	1971	Tennessee 34, Air Force 13
1941	Boston College 19, Tennessee 13	1956	Georgia Tech 7, Pittsburgh 0	1972	Oklahoma 40, Auburn 22
1942	Fordham 2, Missouri 0	1957	Baylor 13, Tennessee 7	1972 (Dec.)	Oklahoma 14, Penn State 0
1943	Tennessee 14, Tulsa 7	1958	Mississippi 39, Texas 7	1973 (Dec.)	Notre Dame 24, Alabama 23
1944	Georgia Tech 20, Tulsa 18	1959	Louisiana State 7, Clemson 0	1974 (Dec.)	Nebraska 13, Florida 10
1945	Duke 29, Alabama 26	1960	Mississippi 21, Louisiana State 0	1975 (Dec.)	Alabama 13, Penn State 6
1946	Oklahoma A & M 33, St. Mary's (Calif.) 13	1961	Mississippi 14, Rice 6	1977	Pittsburgh 27, Georgia 3
1947	Georgia 20, North Carolina 10	1962	Alabama 10, Arkansas 3	1978	Alabama 35, Ohio State 6
1948	Texas 27, Alabama 7	1963	Mississippi 17, Arkansas 13	1979	Alabama 14, Penn State 7
1949	Oklahoma 14, North Carolina 6	1964	Alabama 12, Mississippi 7	1980	Alabama 24, Arkansas 9
		1965	Louisiana State 13, Syracuse 10	1981	Georgia 17, Notre Dame 10

COTTON BOWL Dallas, Texas (January)

Year	Result	Year	Result	Year	Result
1937	Texas Christian 16, Marquette 6	1952	Kentucky 20, Texas Christian 7	1966 (Dec.)	Georgia 24, SMU 9
1938	Rice 28, Colorado 14	1953	Texas 16, Tennessee 0	1968	Texas A&M 20, Alabama 16
1939	St. Mary's 20, Texas Tech 13	1954	Rice 28, Alabama 6	1969	Texas 36, Tennessee 13
1940	Clemson 6, Boston College 3	1955	Georgia Tech 14, Arkansas 6	1970	Texas 21, Notre Dame 17
1941	Texas A&M 13, Fordham 12	1956	Mississippi 14, TCU 13	1971	Notre Dame 24, Texas 11
1942	Alabama 29, Texas A&M 21	1957	Texas Christian 28, Syracuse 27	1972	Penn State 30, Texas 6
1943	Texas 14, Georgia Tech 7	1958	Navy 20, Rice 7	1973	Texas 17, Alabama 13
1944	Randolph Field 7, Texas 7	1959	Air Force 0, Texas Christian 0	1974	Nebraska 19, Texas 3
1945	Oklahoma A & M 34, TCU 0	1960	Syracuse 23, Texas 14	1975	Penn State 41, Baylor 20
1946	Texas 40, Missouri 27	1961	Duke 7, Arkansas 6	1976	Arkansas 31, Georgia 10
1947	Louisiana State 0, Arkansas 0	1962	Texas 12, Mississippi 7	1977	Houston 30, Maryland 21
1948	So. Methodist 13, Penn St. 13	1963	Louisiana State 13, Texas 0	1978	Notre Dame 38, Texas 10
1949	So. Methodist 21, Oregon 13	1964	Texas 28, Navy 6	1979	Notre Dame 35, Houston 34
1950	Rice 27, North Carolina 13	1965	Arkansas 10, Nebraska 7	1980	Houston 17, Nebraska 14
1951	Tennessee 20, Texas 14	1966	Louisiana State 14, Arkansas 7	1981	Alabama 30, Baylor 2

SUN BOWL El Paso, Texas (J=January, D=December)

Year	Result	Year	Result	Year	Result
1936J	H.-Simmons 14, N.M. State 14	1951J	W. Tex. St. 14, Cincinnati 13	1965D	Texas Western 13, TCU 12
1937J	H.-Simmons 34, Tex. Mines 6	1952J	Texas Tech 25, Col. Pacific 14	1966D	Wyoming 28, Florida State 20
1938J	West Virginia 7, Texas Tech 6	1953J	Col. Pacific 26, Miss. Southern 7	1967D	Texas-El Paso 14, Miss. 7
1939J	Utah 26, New Mexico 0	1954J	Tex. Western 37, Miss. So. 14	1968D	Auburn 34, Arizona 10
1940J	Catholic U. 0, Arizona St. 0	1955J	Tex. Western 47, Florida St. 20	1969D	Nebraska 45, Georgia 6
1941J	W. Reserve 26, Arizona St. 13	1956J	Wyoming 21, Texas Tech 14	1970D	Georgia Tech 17, Texas Tech 9
1942J	Tulsa 6, Texas Tech 0	1957J	George Wash. 13, Texas W. 0	1971D	LSU 33, Iowa State 15
1943J	2nd Air Force 13, H.-Simmons 7	1958J	Louisville 34, Drake 20	1972D	N. Carolina 32, Texas Tech 28
1944J	Southwestern 7, New Mexico 0	1958D	Wyoming 14, H.-Simmons 6	1973D	Missouri 34, Auburn 17
1945J	Southwestern 35, U. Mexico 0	1959D	N.M. State 28, N. Tex. State 8	1974D	Miss. State 26, N. Carolina 24
1946J	New Mexico 34, Denver 24	1960D	N.M. State 20, Utah State 13	1975D	Pittsburgh 33, Kansas 19
1947J	Cincinnati 18, Virginia Tech 6	1961D	Villanova 17, Wichita 9	1977J	Texas A & M 37, Florida 14
1948J	Miami (Ohio) 13, Texas Tech 12	1962D	W. Texas St. 15, Ohio U. 14	1977D	Stanford 24, LSU 14
1949J	W. Virginia 21, Texas Mines 12	1963D	Oregon 21, SMU 14	1978D	Texas 42, Maryland 0
1950J	Tex. Western 33, Georgetown 20	1964D	Georgia 7, Texas Tech 0	1979D	Washington 14, Texas 7
				1980D	Nebraska 31, Mississippi St. 17

GATOR BOWL Jacksonville, Florida (J=January, D=December)

Year	Result	Year	Result	Year	Result
1946J	Wake Forest 26, S. Carolina 14	1957D	Tennessee 3, Texas A & M 0	1969D	Florida 14, Tennessee 13
1947J	Oklahoma 34, N.C. State 13	1958D	Mississippi 7, Florida 3	1971J	Auburn 35, Mississippi 28
1948J	Maryland 20, Georgia 20	1960J	Arkansas 14, Georgia Tech 7	1971D	Georgia 7, N. Carolina 3
1949J	Clemson 24, Missouri 23	1960D	Florida 13, Baylor 12	1972D	Auburn 24, Colorado 3
1950J	Maryland 20, Missouri 7	1961D	Penn State 30, Georgia Tech 15	1973D	Texas Tech 28, Tennessee 19
1951J	Wyoming 20, Wash. & Lee 7	1962D	Florida 17, Penn State 7	1974D	Auburn 27, Texas 3
1952J	Miami (Fla.) 14, Clemson 0	1963D	N. Carolina 35, Air Force 0	1975D	Maryland 13, Florida 0
1953J	Florida 14, Tulsa 13	1965J	Florida St. 36, Oklahoma 19	1976D	Notre Dame 20, Penn State 9
1954J	Texas Tech 35, Auburn 13	1965D	Georgia St. 31, Texas Tech 21	1977D	Pittsburgh 34, Clemson 3
1954D	Auburn 33, Baylor 13	1966D	Tennessee 18, Syracuse 12	1978D	Clemson 17, Ohio State 15
1955D	Vanderbilt 25, Auburn 13	1967D	Penn State 17, Florida St. 17	1979D	N. Carolina 17, Michigan 15
1956D	Georgia Tech 21, Pittsburgh 14	1968D	Missouri 35, Alabama 10	1980D	Pittsburgh 37, South Carolina 9

TANGERINE BOWL Orlando, Florida (J=January, D=December)

Year	Result	Year	Result	Year	Result
1947J	Catawba 31, Maryville 6	1958J	E. Texas St. 10, So. Miss. 9	1969D	Toledo 56, Davidson 33
1948J	Catawba 7, Marshall 0	1958D	E. Texas St. 26, Missouri Va. 7	1970D	Toledo 40, William & Mary 12
1949J	Murray St. 21, Sul Ross St. 21	1960J	Middle Tenn. 21, Presbyterian 12	1971D	Toledo 28, Richmond 3
1950J	St. Vincent 7, Emory & Henry 6	1960D	Citadel 27, Tennessee Tech 0	1972D	Tampa 21, Kent State 18
1951J	Mor. Harvey 35, Emory & Henry 14	1961D	Lamar 21, Middle Tennessee 14	1973D	Miami (Ohio) 16, Florida 7
1952J	Stetson 35, Arkansas St. 20	1962D	Houston 49, Miami (Ohio) 21	1974D	Miami (Ohio) 21, Georgia 10
1953J	E. Texas St. 33, Tenn. Tech 0	1963D	W. Kentucky 27, Coast Guard 0	1975D	Miami (Ohio) 20, S. Carolina 7
1954J	E. Texas St. 7, Arkansas St. 7	1964D	E. Carolina 14, Massachusetts 13	1976D	Okla. State 49, Brigham Young 21
1955J	Nebraska (Omaha) 7, E. Ken. 6	1965D	E. Carolina 31, Maine 0	1977D	Florida St. 40, Texas Tech 17
1956J	Juniata 6, Missouri Valley 6	1966D	Morgan St. 14, West Chester 6	1978D	N. Carolina St. 30, Pittsburgh 17
1957J	W. Texas St. 20, So. Miss. 13	1967D	Tenn. (Martin) 25, West Chester 8	1979D	LSU 34, Wake Forest 10
		1968D	Richmond 49, Ohio U. 42	1980D	Florida 35, Maryland 20

BLUEBONNET BOWL Houston, Texas (December)

Year	Result	Year	Result	Year	Result
1959	Clemson 23, TCU 7	1966	Texas 19, Mississippi 0	1973	Houston 47, Tulane 7
1960	Texas 3, Alabama 3	1967	Colorado 31, Miami (Fla.) 21	1974	N.C. State 31, Houston 31
1961	Kansas 33, Rice 0	1968	SMU 28, Oklahoma 27	1975	Texas 38, Colorado 21
1962	Missouri 14, Georgia Tech 10	1969	Houston 36, Auburn 7	1976	Nebraska 27, Texas Tech 24
1963	Baylor 14, LSU 7	1970	Alabama 24, Oklahoma 24	1977	USC 47, Texas A & M 28
1964	Tulsa 14, Mississippi 7	1971	Colorado 29, Houston 17	1978	Stanford 25, Georgia 22
1965	Tennessee 27, Tulsa 6	1972	Tennessee 24, LSU 17	1979	Purdue 27, Tennessee 22
				1980	North Carolina 16, Texas 7

LIBERTY BOWL Memphis, Tennessee* (December)

Year	Result	Year	Result	Year	Result
1959	Penn State 7, Alabama 0	1966	Miami (Fla.) 14, Virginia Tech 7	1973	N.C. State 31, Kansas 18
1960	Penn State 41, Oregon 12	1967	N.C. State 14, Georgia 7	1974	Tennessee 7, Maryland 3
1961	Syracuse 15, Miami (Fla.) 14	1968	Mississippi 34, Virginia Tech 17	1975	USC 20, Texas A & M 0
1962	Oregon St. 6, Villanova 0	1969	Colorado 47, Alabama 33	1976	Alabama 36, UCLA 6
1963	Mississippi St. 16, N.C. State 12	1970	Tulane 17, Colorado 3	1977	Nebraska 21, N. Carolina 17
1964	Utah 32, West Virginia 6	1971	Tennessee 14, Arkansas 13	1978	Missouri 20, LSU 15
1965	Mississippi 13, Auburn 7	1972	Georgia Tech 31, Iowa State 30	1979	Penn State 9, Tulane 6
				1980	Purdue 28, Missouri 25

*Philadelphia 1960-1964, Atlantic City 1965

PEACH BOWL Atlanta, Georgia (December)

Year	Result	Year	Result	Year	Result
1968	LSU 31, Florida State 27	1972	N.C. State 49, W. Virginia 13	1976	Kentucky 21, N. Carolina 0
1969	W. Virginia 14, S. Carolina 3	1973	Georgia 17, Maryland 16	1977	N.C. State 24, Iowa State 14
1970	Arizona St. 48, N. Carolina 26	1974	Vanderbilt 6, Texas Tech 6	1978	Purdue 41, Georgia Tech 21
1971	Mississippi 41, Georgia Tech 18	1975	W. Virginia 13, N.C. State 10	1979	Baylor 24, Clemson 18
				1981	(Jan.) Miami (Fla.) 20, Va. Tech 10

FIESTA BOWL Tempe, Arizona (December)

Year	Result	Year	Result	Year	Result
1971	Arizona St. 45, Florida St. 38	1974	Okla. St. 16, Brigham Young 6	1977	Penn State 42, Arizona St. 30
1972	Arizona St. 49, Missouri 35	1975	Arizona St. 17, Nebraska 14	1978	Arkansas 10, UCLA 10
1973	Arizona St. 28, Pittsburgh 7	1976	Oklahoma 41, Wyoming 7	1979	Pittsburgh 16, Arizona 10
				1980	Penn State 31, Ohio State 19

NATIONAL COLLEGE FOOTBALL CHAMPIONS

The college football team selected each year by The Associated Press poll of sportswriters and the United Press International poll of football coaches is unofficially recognized as national champion. Where the polls disagree, both teams are given.

Year	Champion	Year	Champion	Year	Champion	Year	Champion
1925	Dartmouth	1939	Texas A & M	1953	Maryland	1967	Southern California
1926	Stanford	1940	Minnesota	1954	Ohio State-UCLA	1968	Ohio State
1927	Illinois	1941	Minnesota	1955	Oklahoma	1969	Texas
1928	Southern California	1942	Ohio State	1956	Oklahoma	1970	Texas-Nebraska
1929	Notre Dame	1943	Notre Dame	1957	Auburn-Ohio State	1971	Nebraska
1930	Notre Dame	1944	Army	1958	Louisiana State	1972	Southern California
1931	Southern California	1945	Army	1959	Syracuse	1973	Notre Dame
1932	Michigan	1946	Notre Dame	1960	Minnesota	1974	Oklahoma-USC
1933	Michigan	1947	Notre Dame	1961	Alabama	1975	Oklahoma
1934	Minnesota	1948	Michigan	1962	Southern California	1976	Pittsburgh
1935	Southern Methodist	1949	Notre Dame	1963	Texas	1977	Notre Dame
1936	Minnesota	1950	Oklahoma	1964	Alabama	1978	Alabama-USC
1937	Pittsburgh	1951	Tennessee	1965	Alabama-Mich. St.	1979	Alabama
1938	Texas Christian	1952	Michigan State	1966	Notre Dame	1980	Georgia

COLLEGE FOOTBALL CONFERENCE CHAMPIONS

ATLANTIC COAST		BIG EIGHT		BIG TEN		IVY LEAGUE	
Year	Champion	Year	Champion	Year	Champion	Year	Champion
1963	No. Carolina State	1963	Nebraska	1963	Illinois	1963	Dartmouth-Princeton
1964	No. Carolina State	1964	Nebraska	1964	Michigan	1964	Princeton
1965	Duke	1965	Nebraska	1965	Michigan State	1965	Dartmouth
1966	Clemson	1966	Nebraska	1966	Michigan State	1966	Dartmouth-Harvard-
1967	Clemson	1967	Oklahoma	1967	Indiana-Purdue-		Princeton
1968	No. Carolina State	1968	Kansas-Oklahoma		Minnesota	1967	Yale
1969	South Carolina	1969	Missouri-Nebraska	1968	Ohio State	1968	Yale-Harvard
1970	Wake Forest	1970	Nebraska	1969	Ohio State-Michigan	1969	Princeton-Yale-
1971	North Carolina	1971	Nebraska	1970	Ohio State		Dartmouth
1972	North Carolina	1972	Oklahoma	1971	Michigan	1970	Dartmouth
1973	No. Carolina State	1973	Oklahoma	1972	Ohio State-Michigan	1971	Cornell-Dartmouth
1974	Maryland	1974	Oklahoma	1973	Michigan-Ohio State	1972	Dartmouth
1975	Maryland	1975	Nebraska-	1974	Michigan-Ohio State	1973	Dartmouth
1976	Maryland		Oklahoma	1975	Ohio State	1974	Yale-Harvard
1977	North Carolina	1976	Colorado-	1976	Michigan-Ohio State	1975	Harvard
1978	Clemson		Oklahoma-	1977	Michigan-Ohio State	1976	Yale-Brown
1979	No. Carolina State		Oklahoma State	1978	Michigan St.-Michigan	1977	Yale
1980	North Carolina	1977	Oklahoma	1979	Ohio State	1978	Dartmouth
		1978	Nebraska-Oklahoma	1980	Michigan	1979	Yale
		1979	Oklahoma			1980	Yale
		1980	Oklahoma				

MISSOURI VALLEY		PACIFIC TEN		SOUTHEASTERN		SOUTHERN	
Year	Champion	Year	Champion	Year	Champion	Year	Champion
1963	Cincinnati-Wichita	1963	Washington	1963	Mississippi	1963	Virginia Tech
1964	Cincinnati	1964	Oregon State-	1964	Alabama	1964	West Virginia
1965	Tulsa		Southern California	1965	Alabama	1965	West Virginia
1966	North Texas-Tulsa	1965	UCLA	1966	Georgia-	1966	William & Mary-
1967	North Texas	1966	Southern California		Alabama		East Carolina
1968	Memphis State	1967	Southern California	1967	Tennessee	1967	West Virginia
1969	Memphis State	1968	Southern California	1968	Georgia	1968	Richmond
1970	Louisville	1969	Southern California	1969	Tennessee	1969	Richmond-Davidson
1971	North Texas	1970	Stanford	1970	Louisiana State	1970	William & Mary
1972	Louisville-Drake-	1971	Stanford	1971	Alabama	1971	Richmond
	West Texas	1972	Southern California	1972	Alabama	1972	East Carolina
1973	North Texas-Tulsa	1973	Southern California	1973	Alabama	1973	East Carolina
1974	Tulsa	1974	Southern California	1974	Alabama	1974	VMI
1975	Tulsa	1975	UCLA-California	1975	Alabama	1975	Richmond
1976	Tulsa-N. Mexico State	1976	Southern California	1976	Georgia	1976	East Carolina
1977	West Texas State	1977	Washington	1977	Alabama	1977	VMI-Tenn.-
1978	New Mexico State	1978	Southern California	1978	Alabama		Chattanooga
1979	West Texas State	1979	Southern California	1979	Alabama	1978	Tenn.-Chattanooga-
1980	Wichita St.-Tulsa	1980	Washington	1980	Georgia		Furman
						1979	Tenn.-Chattanooga
						1980	Furman

MID-AMERICAN		SOUTHWEST		WESTERN		PACIFIC COAST	
Year	Champion	Year	Champion	Year	Champion	Year	Champion
1963	Ohio University	1963	Texas	1963	New Mexico	1969	San Diego State
1964	Bowling Green	1964	Arkansas	1964	N. M.-Utah-Arizona	1970	Long Beach State
1965	Miami (Ohio)-	1965	Arkansas	1965	Brigham Young	1971	Long Beach State
	Bowling Green	1966	Southern Methodist	1966	Wyoming	1972	San Diego State
1966	Miami (Ohio)-	1967	Texas A & M	1967	Wyoming	1973	San Diego State
	Western Michigan	1968	Texas-Arkansas	1968	Wyoming	1974	San Diego State
1967	Toledo-Ohio U.	1969	Texas	1969	Arizona State	1975	San Jose State
1968	Ohio University	1970	Texas	1970	Arizona State	1976	San Jose State
1969	Toledo	1971	Texas	1971	Arizona State	1977	Fresno State
1970	Toledo	1972	Texas	1972	Arizona State	1978	Utah State-
1971	Toledo	1973	Texas	1973	Arizona-Ariz. St.		San Jose State
1972	Kent State	1974	Baylor	1974	Brigham Young	1979	Utah State-
1973	Miami (Ohio)	1975	Texas-Texas A & M-	1975	Arizona State		San Jose State
1974	Miami (Ohio)		Arkansas	1976	Wyoming-	1980	Long Beach State
1975	Miami (Ohio)	1976	Houston-Texas Tech		Brigham Young		
1976	Ball State	1977	Texas	1977	Arizona State-		
1977	Miami (Ohio)	1978	Houston		Brigham Young		
1978	Ball State	1979	Arkansas	1978	Brigham Young		
1979	Central Michigan	1980	Baylor	1979	Brigham Young		
1980	Central Michigan			1980	Brigham Young		

1980 REGULAR SEASON RECORDS OF MAJOR COLLEGE FOOTBALL TEAMS

Team	W	L	T	Team	W	L	T	Team	W	L	T
Air Force	2	9	1	Kansas	4	5	2	Richmond	5	6	0
Alabama	9	2	0	Kansas State	3	8	0	Rutgers	7	4	0
Arizona	5	6	0	Kentucky	3	8	0	San Diego State	4	8	0
Arizona State	7	4	0	Louisiana State	7	4	0	San Jose State	7	4	0
Arkansas	6	5	0	Louisville	5	6	0	South Carolina	8	3	0
Army	3	7	0	Maryland	8	3	0	Southern California	8	2	1
Auburn	5	6	0	Memphis State	2	9	0	Southern Methodist	8	3	0
Baylor	10	1	0	Miami (Fla.)	8	3	0	Southern Mississippi	8	3	0
Boston College	7	4	0	Michigan	9	2	0	Stanford	6	5	0
Brigham Young	11	1	0	Michigan State	3	8	0	Syracuse	5	6	0
Brown	6	4	0	Minnesota	5	6	0	Temple	4	7	0
California	3	8	0	Mississippi	3	8	0	Tennessee	5	6	0
Cincinnati	2	9	0	Mississippi State	9	2	0	Texas	7	4	0
Citadel	7	4	0	Missouri	8	3	0	Texas A & M	4	7	0
Clemson	6	5	0	Navy	8	3	0	Texas Christian	1	10	0
Colgate	5	4	1	Nebraska	9	2	0	Texas-El Paso	1	11	0
Colorado	1	10	0	Nevada-Las Vegas	7	4	0	Texas Tech	5	6	0
Colorado State	6	4	1	New Mexico	4	7	0	Tulane	7	4	0
Columbia	1	9	0	New Mexico State	3	7	1	Tulsa	8	3	0
Cornell	5	5	0	North Carolina	10	1	0	UCLA	9	2	0
Dartmouth	4	6	0	North Carolina State	6	5	0	Utah	5	5	1
Duke	2	9	0	North Texas State	6	5	0	Utah State	6	5	0
East Carolina	4	7	0	Northwestern	0	11	0	Vanderbilt	2	9	0
Florida	7	4	0	Notre Dame	9	1	1	Villanova	6	5	0
Florida State	10	1	0	Ohio State	9	2	0	Virginia	4	7	0
Furman	9	1	1	Oklahoma	9	2	0	Virginia Military	3	7	1
Georgia	11	0	0	Oklahoma State	3	7	1	Virginia Tech	8	3	0
Georgia Tech	1	9	1	Oregon	6	3	2	Wake Forest	5	6	0
Harvard	7	3	0	Oregon State	0	11	0	Washington	9	2	0
Hawaii	8	3	0	Pacific	4	8	0	Washington State	4	7	0
Holy Cross	3	8	0	Pennsylvania	1	9	0	West Virginia	6	6	0
Houston	6	5	0	Pennsylvania State	9	2	0	Wichita State	5	5	1
Illinois	3	7	1	Pittsburgh	10	1	0	William & Mary	2	9	0
Indiana	6	5	0	Princeton	6	4	0	Wisconsin	4	7	0
Iowa	4	7	0	Purdue	8	3	0	Wyoming	6	5	0
Iowa State	6	5	0	Rice	5	6	0	Yale	8	2	0

1980 FINAL COLLEGE FOOTBALL RANKINGS

ASSOCIATED PRESS

1. Georgia	11. Southern California
2. Pittsburgh	12. Brigham Young
3. Oklahoma	13. U.C.L.A.
4. Michigan	14. Baylor
5. Florida State	15. Ohio State
6. Alabama	16. Washington
7. Nebraska	17. Purdue
8. Penn State	18. Miami (Fla.)
9. Notre Dame	19. Mississippi State
10. North Carolina	20. Southern Methodist

UNITED PRESS INTERNATIONAL

1. Georgia	11. Brigham Young
2. Pittsburgh	12. Southern California
3. Oklahoma	13. Baylor
4. Michigan	14. U.C.L.A.
5. Florida State	15. Ohio State
6. Alabama	16. Purdue
7. Nebraska	17. Washington
8. Penn State	18. Miami (Fla.)
9. North Carolina	19. Florida
10. Notre Dame	20. Southern Methodist

MAJOR COLLEGE FOOTBALL STADIUMS (43,000 or more seats)

Team (Stadium) Location	Capacity
Air Force (Falcon) A.F. Academy, Colo.	46,600
Alabama (Bryant-Denny) University, Ala.	59,000
Arizona (Arizona) Tucson, Ariz.	57,000
Arizona State (Sun Devil) Tempe, Ariz.	70,300
Auburn (Jordan Hare) Auburn, Ala.	71,800
Baylor (Baylor) Waco, Tex.	48,500
California (Memorial) Berkley, Cal.	76,700
Clemson (Memorial) Clemson, S.C.	53,400
Colorado (Folsom Field) Boulder, Colo.	52,000
Florida (Florida Field) Gainesville, Fla.	62,800
Florida State (Campbell) Tallahassee, Fla.	51,000
Georgia (Sanford) Athens, Ga.	76,000
Georgia Tech (Grant Field) Atlanta, Ga.	58,100
Hawaii (Aloha) Honolulu, Hawaii	50,000
Illinois (Memorial) Champaign, Ill.	71,200
Indiana (Memorial) Bloomington, Ind.	52,300
Iowa (Kinnick) Iowa City, Iowa	60,000
Iowa State (Iowa State) Ames, Iowa	50,000
Jackson State (Miss. Memorial) Jackson, Miss.	61,000
Kansas (Memorial) Lawrence, Kans.	51,500
Kentucky (Commonwealth) Lexington, Ky.	58,000
Long Beach State (Anaheim), Calif.	69,000
Louisiana State (Tiger) Baton Rouge, La.	76,000
Maryland (Byrd) College Park, Md.	45,000
Memphis State (Liberty Bowl) Memphis, Tenn.	50,100
Michigan (Michigan) Ann Arbor, Mich.	101,700
Michigan State (Spartan) East Lansing, Mich.	76,000
Minnesota (Memorial) Minneapolis, Minn.	56,700
Missouri (Faurot Field) Columbia, Mo.	75,000
Nebraska (Memorial) Lincoln, Neb.	73,500
North Carolina (Kenan) Chapel Hill, N.C.	49,500
North Carolina State (Carter-Finley) Raleigh, N.C.	45,600
Northwestern (Dyche) Evanston, Ill.	49,200
Notre Dame (Notre Dame) South Bend, Ind.	59,000
Ohio State (Ohio) Columbus, Ohio	83,100

Team (Stadium) Location	Capacity
Oklahoma (Owen Field) Norman, Okla.	74,700
Oklahoma State (Lewis) Stillwater, Okla.	50,800
Pennsylvania (Franklin Field) Philadelphia, Pa.	60,500
Pennsylvania State (Beaver) University Park, Pa.	83,700
Pittsburgh (Pitt) Pittsburgh, Pa.	56,500
Princeton (Palmer) Princeton, N.J.	45,700
Purdue (Ross-Ade) West Lafayette, Ind.	69,200
Rice (Rice) Houston, Tex.	70,000
San Diego State (San Diego) San Diego, Cal.	53,000
South Carolina (Williams-Brice) Columbia, S.C.	54,400
Stanford (Stanford) Stanford, Cal.	84,800
Tennessee (Neyland) Knoxville, Tenn.	91,200
Texas (Memorial) Austin, Tex.	80,000
Texas A & M (Kyle Field) College Station, Tex.	70,100
Texas Christian (TCU-Amon Carter) Fort Worth, Tex.	46,000
Texas Tech (Jones) Lubbock, Tex.	47,000
Virginia Tech (Lane) Blacksburg, Va.	52,500
Washington (Husky) Seattle, Wash.	59,800
West Virginia (Mountaineer Field) Morgantown, W.Va.	50,000
Wisconsin (Camp Randall) Madison, Wis.	77,200
Yale (Yale Bowl) New Haven, Conn.	70,800

OTHER STADIUMS USED BY MAJOR COLLEGE TEAMS

	Capacity
Astrodome, Houston (Houston, Texas Southern)	50,100
Cotton Bowl, Dallas	72,000
Gator Bowl, Jacksonville, Fla.	72,000
Giants, E. Rutherford, N.J. (Rutgers)	76,500
Legion Field, Birmingham, Ala. (Alabama)	76,000
Los Angeles Memorial Coliseum (USC, UCLA)	92,600
Louisiana Superdome, New Orleans (Tulane)	71,000
Mississippi Memorial, Jackson (Miss., Miss. St.)	61,000
Orange Bowl, Miami (Miami, Fla.)	76,100
Texas Stadium, Irving (Southern Methodist)	65,000
Veterans Stadium, Philadelphia (Temple)	72,000

THE HEISMAN MEMORIAL TROPHY: Awarded annually to the nation's outstanding college football player.

Year	Player and College	Year	Player and College	Year	Player and College
1942	Frank Sinkwich, Georgia	1955	Howard Cassady, Ohio State	1968	O. J. Simpson, USC
1943	Angelo Bertelli, Notre Dame	1956	Paul Hornung, Notre Dame	1969	Steve Owens, Oklahoma
1944	Les Horvath, Ohio State	1957	John Crow, Texas A&M	1970	Jim Plunkett, Stanford
1945	Felix Blanchard, Army	1958	Pete Dawkins, Army	1971	Pat Sullivan, Auburn
1946	Glenn Davis, Army	1959	Billy Cannon, Louisiana State	1972	Johnny Rogers, Nebraska
1947	John Lujack, Notre Dame	1960	Joe Bellino, Navy	1973	John Capelletti, Penn State
1948	Doak Walker, Southern Methodist	1961	Ernie Davis, Syracuse	1974	Archie Griffin, Ohio State
1949	Leon Hart, Notre Dame	1962	Terry Baker, Oregon State	1975	Archie Griffin, Ohio State
1950	Vic Janowicz, Ohio State	1963	Roger Staubach, Navy	1976	Tony Dorsett, Pittsburgh
1951	Dick Kazmaier, Princeton	1964	John Huarte, Notre Dame	1977	Earl Campbell, Texas
1952	Billy Vessels, Oklahoma	1965	Mike Garrett, Southern California	1978	Billy Sims, Oklahoma
1953	John Lattner, Notre Dame	1966	Steve Spurrier, Florida	1979	Charles White, USC
1954	Alan Ameche, Wisconsin	1967	Gary Beban, UCLA	1980	George Rogers, S. Carolina

COLLEGE FOOTBALL COACH OF THE YEAR (American Football Coaches Ass'n)

Year	Coach and College	Year	Coach and College	Year	Coach and College
1946	Earl H. Blaik, Army	1958	Paul Dietzel, Louisiana State	1970	Darrell Royal, Texas
1947	Fritz Crisler, Michigan	1959	Ben Schwartzwalder, Syracuse		Charlie McLendon, La. State
1948	Bennie Oosterbaan, Michigan	1960	Murray Warmath, Minnesota	1971	Paul Bryant, Alabama
1949	Bud Wilkinson, Oklahoma	1961	Paul Bryant, Alabama	1972	John McKay, Southern California
1950	Charlie Caldwell, Princeton	1962	John McKay, Southern California	1973	Paul Bryant, Alabama
1951	Chuck Taylor, Stanford	1963	Darrell Royal, Texas	1974	Grant Teaff, Baylor
1952	Biggie Munn, Michigan State	1964	Ara Parseghian, Notre Dame	1975	Frank Kush, Arizona State
1953	Jim Tatum, Maryland	1965	Tommy Prothro, UCLA	1976	Johnny Majors, Pittsburgh
1954	Red Sanders, UCLA	1966	Tom Cahill, Army	1977	Don James, Washington
1955	Duffy Daugherty, Michigan State	1967	John Pont, Indiana	1978	Joe Paterno, Penn State
1956	Bowden Wyatt, Tennessee	1968	Joe Paterno, Penn State	1979	Earl Bruce, Ohio State
1957	Woody Hayes, Ohio State	1969	Bo Schembechler, Michigan	1980	Vince Dooley, Georgia

OUTLAND AWARDS: Awarded annually to the nation's leading college football lineman.

Year	Player, College, Pos.	Year	Player, College, Pos.	Year	Player, College, Pos.
1946	George Connor, Notre Dame, T	1957	Alex Karras, Iowa, T	1969	Mike Reid, Penn State, DT
1947	Joe Steffy, Army, G	1958	Zeke Smith, Auburn, G	1970	Jim Stillwagon, Ohio State, LB
1948	Bill Fischer, Notre Dame, G	1959	Mike McGee, Duke, T	1971	Larry Jacobson, Nebraska, DT
1949	Ed Bagdon, Michigan St., G	1960	Tom Brown, Minnesota, G	1972	Rich Glover, Nebraska, MG
1950	Bob Gain, Kentucky, T	1961	Merlin Olsen, Utah State, T	1973	John Hicks, Ohio State, T
1951	Jim Weatherall, Oklahoma, T	1962	Bobby Bell, Minnesota, T	1974	Randy White, Maryland, DT
1952	Dick Modzelewski, Maryland, G.	1963	Scott Appleton, Texas, T	1975	Leroy Selmon, Oklahoma, DT
1953	J. D. Roberts, Oklahoma, G	1964	Steve DeLong, Tennessee, T	1976	Ross Browner, Notre Dame, DT
1954	Bill Brooks, Arkansas, G	1965	Tommy Nobis, Texas, G	1977	Brad Shearer, Texas, DT
1955	Calvin Jones, Iowa, G	1966	Lloyd Phillips, Arkansas, T	1978	Greg Roberts, Oklahoma, G
1956	Jim Parker, Ohio State, G	1967	Ron Yary, Southern Cal, T	1979	Jim Richter, N. Carolina St., C
		1968	Bill Stanfill, Georgia, T	1980	Mark May, Pittsburgh, T

1980 COLLEGE ALL-AMERICA SELECTIONS

OFFENSIVE TEAM

Receivers
Dave Young, Purdue (AP) (UPI) (SN) (FW)
Ken Margerum, Stanford (AP) (UPI) (FW)
Anthony Carter, Michigan (AP) (SN)
Mardye McDole, Mississippi State (SN)

Linemen
Mark May, Pittsburgh (AP) (UPI) (SN) (FW)
Keith Van Horne, USC (AP) (UPI) (SN) (FW)
Randy Schleusener, Nebraska (AP) (UPI)
Frank Ditta, Baylor (AP)
Roy Foster, USC (UPI)
Bill Ard, Wake Forest (SN)
Terry Crouch, Oklahoma (SN)
Nick Eyre, Brigham Young (FW)
Louis Oubre, Oklahoma (FW)

Center
John Scully, Notre Dame (AP) (UPI) (SN) (FW)

Quarter-backs
Mark Herrmann, Purdue (AP) (UPI) (FW)
John Elway, Stanford (SN)

Running backs
George Rogers, South Carolina (AP) (UPI) (SN) (FW)
Herschel Walker, Georgia (AP) (UPI) (SN) (FW)
Jarvis Redwine, Nebraska (UPI)
Freeman McNeil, UCLA (FW)

Place-Kickers
Rex Robinson, Georgia (UPI) (FW)
Bill Capece, Florida State (SN)

DEFENSIVE TEAM

Linemen
Hugh Green, Pittsburgh (AP) (UPI) (SN) (FW)
Kenneth Sims, Texas (AP) (UPI) (SN) (FW)
E. L. Junior, Alabama (AP) (UPI) (SN) (FW)
Leonard Mitchell, Houston (AP) (UPI) (SN)
Scott Zettek, Notre Dame (AP)
Ron Simmons, Florida State (UPI)
Derrie Nelson, Nebraska (FW)
Jose Taylor, Houston (FW)

Linebackers
Mike Singletary, Baylor (AP) (UPI) (SN) (FW)
Lawrence Taylor, North Carolina (AP) (UPI) (SN) (FW
David Little, Florida (AP) (FW)
Bob Crable, Notre Dame (UPI) (SN)

Defensive backs
Kenny Easley, UCLA (AP) (UPI) (SN) (FW)
Ronnie Lott, USC (AP) (UPI) (SN) (FW)
John Simmons, SMU (AP) (FW)
Scott Woerner, Georgia (UPI)
Ted Watts, Texas Tech (SN)
Hanford Dixon, Southern Mississippi (SN)

Punter
Rohn Stark, Florida State (UPI) (SN) (FW)

Selections by (AP) Associated Press, (UPI) United Press International, (SN) The Sporting News, (FW) Football Writers Association of America

NATIONAL CHAMPIONSHIP GAMES

Year	NCAA Division I-AA
1978	Florida A&M 35, Massachusetts 28
1979	Eastern Kentucky 30, Lehigh 7
1980	Boise State 31, Eastern Kentucky 29

Year	NCAA Division II
1976	Montana State 24, Akron 13
1977	Lehigh 33, Jacksonville (Ala.) State 0
1978	Eastern Illinois 10, Delaware 9
1979	Delaware 38, Youngstown State 21
1980	Cal Poly-S. L. Obispo 21, Eastern Illinois 13

Year	NCAA Division III
1976	St. Johns (Minn.) 31, Towson State 28
1977	Widener 39, Wabash 36
1978	Baldwin-Wallace 24, Wittenberg 10
1979	Ithaca (N.Y.) 14, Wittenberg 10
1980	Dayton 63, Ithaca 0

Year	NAIA Division I
1976	Texas A & I 26, Central Arkansas 0
1977	Abilene Christian 24, Southwestern Oklahoma State 7
1978	Angelo State (Tex.) 34, Elon (N.C.) 14
1979	Texas A & I 20, Central State Okla. 14
1980	Elon (N.C.) 17, Northeastern Oklahoma 10

Year	NAIA Division II
1976	Westminster (Pa.) 20, Redlands 13
1977	Westminster (Pa.) 17, California Lutheran 9
1978	Concordia (Minn.) 7, Findlay (Ohio) 0
1979	Findlay (Ohio) 51, Northwestern (Iowa) 6
1980	Pacific Lutheran 38, Wilmington (Ohio) 10

HOCKEY

NATIONAL HOCKEY LEAGUE (NHL)

960 Sun Life Building, Montreal, Quebec H3B 2W2, President: John A. Ziegler, Jr. Chairman of the Board: William W. Wirtz. Organized in 1917. The NHL expanded to 21 teams in 1979 with the Edmonton Oilers, Hartford Whalers, Quebec Nordiques and Winnipeg Jets joining the league.

PRINCE OF WALES CONFERENCE

Adams Division	Pres./Owner	Coach
Boston Bruins	Paul A. Mooney	Gerry Cheevers
Buffalo Sabres	Seymour H. Knox III	Scotty Bowman
Hartford Whalers	Howard L. Baldwin	Larry Pleau
Montreal Canadiens	Morgan McCammon	Bob Berry
Quebec Nordiques	Marcel Aubut	Maurice Filion

Patrick Division		
New York Islanders	John O. Pickett, Jr.	Al Arbour
New York Rangers	Jack Krumpe	Herb Brooks
Philadelphia Flyers	Edward M. Snider	Pat Quinn
Pittsburgh Penguins	Vincent J. Bartimo	Ed Johnston
Washington Capitals	Abe Pollin	Gary Green

CLARENCE CAMPBELL CONFERENCE

Norris Division	Pres./Owner	Coach
Chicago Black Hawks	William W. Wirtz	Keith Magnuson
Detroit Red Wings	Bruce A. Norris	Wayne Maxner
Minnesota North Stars	George Gund III	Glen Sonmor
St. Louis Blues	Emile Francis	Red Berenson
Toronto Maple Leafs	Harold E. Ballard	Mike Nykoluk
Winnipeg Jets	Michael Gobuty	Tom Watt

Smythe Division		
Calgary Flames	Nelson Skalbania	Al MacNeil
Colorado Rockies	Armand Pohan	Bert Marshall
Edmonton Oilers	Peter Pocklington	Glen Sather
Los Angeles Kings	Lou Baumeister	Parker MacDonald
Vancouver Canucks	Frank A. Griffiths	Harry Neale

NATIONAL HOCKEY LEAGUE RECORDS   At start of 1981/82 season

Most Goals, Lifetime: 801, Gordie Howe, Detroit Red Wings, Hartford Whalers.

Most Goals, One Season: 76, Phil Esposito, Boston Bruins, 1970/71.

Most Assists, One Season: 109, Wayne Gretzky, Edmonton Oilers, 1980/81.

Most Points, One Season: 164, Wayne Gretzky, Edmonton Oilers, 1980/81.

Most Points, One Game: 10, Darryl Sittler, Toronto Maple Leafs, February 7, 1976.

Most Victories, One Season: 60, Montreal Canadiens, 1976/77.

Longest Winning Streak: 14 games, Boston Bruins, 1929/30.

Most Goals, One Season: 399, Boston Bruins, 1970/71.

Most Shutouts by a Goaltender: 103, Terry Sawchuk, Detroit, Boston, Toronto, Los Angeles, N.Y. Rangers.

Most Penalty Minutes, One Season: 472, Dave Schultz, Philadelphia Flyers, 1974/75.

Most Seasons: 26, Gordie Howe, Detroit Red Wings, 1946/47 through 1970/71, Hartford Whalers, 1979/80.

Most Games, Including Playoffs, Lifetime: 1,924, Gordie Howe, Detroit Red Wings, Hartford Whalers.

Most Goals, Including Playoffs, Lifetime: 869, Gordie Howe, Detroit Red Wings, Hartford Whalers.

Most Assists, Including Playoffs, Lifetime: 1,141, Gordie Howe, Detroit Red Wings, Hartford Whalers.

Most Points, Including Playoffs, Lifetime: 2,010, Gordie Howe, Detroit Red Wings, Hartford Whalers.

Most Penalty Minutes, Including Playoffs, Lifetime: 2,706, Dave Schultz, Philadelphia Flyers, Los Angeles Kings, Pittsburgh Penguins, Buffalo Sabres.

Most Consecutive Games: 914, Garry Unger, Toronto Maple Leafs, Detroit Red Wings, St. Louis Blues, Atlanta Flames, 1967/68–1979/80.

Most Consecutive Complete Games by Goaltender: 502, Glenn Hall, Detroit Red Wings and Chicago Black Hawks, 1955/56 through 1962/63.

Most Shutouts by a Goaltender, One Season: 22, George Hainsworth, Montreal Canadiens, 1928/29.

Longest Shutout Sequence by a Goaltender: 461 Minutes 29 Seconds, Alex Connell, Ottawa Senators, 1927/28.

Most Goals, One Game: 7, Joe Malone, Quebec Bulldogs, January 31, 1920.

Most Assists, One Game: 7, Billy Taylor, Detroit Red Wings, March 16, 1947; Wayne Gretzky, Edmonton Oilers, February 15, 1980.

Most Penalties, One Game: 9, Jim Dorey, Toronto Maple Leafs, October 16, 1968; Dave Schultz, Pittsburgh Penguins, April 6, 1978; Randy Holt, Los Angeles Kings, March 11, 1979; Russ Anderson, Pittsburgh Penguins, January 19, 1980; Kim Clackson, Quebec Nordiques, March 8, 1981.

Most Penalty Minutes, One Game: 67, Randy Holt, Los Angeles Kings, March 11, 1979.

Most Goals in One Period: 4, Harvey (Busher) Jackson, Toronto Maple Leafs, November 20, 1934; Max Bentley, Chicago Black Hawks, January 28, 1943; Clint Smith, Chicago Black Hawks, March 4, 1945; Gordon (Red) Berenson, St. Louis Blues, November 7, 1968; Wayne Gretzky, Edmonton Oilers, February 18, 1981.

Fastest Two Goals: 4 seconds, Nels Stewart, Montreal Maroons, January 3, 1931.

Fastest Three Goals: 21 seconds, Bill Mosienko, Chicago Black Hawks, March 23, 1952.

NHL CHAMPIONS

Season	Regular Season	Stanley Cup
1952/53	Detroit Red Wings	Montreal Canadiens
1953/54	Detroit Red Wings	Detroit Red Wings
1954/55	Detroit Red Wings	Detroit Red Wings
1955/56	Montreal Canadiens	Montreal Canadiens
1956/57	Detroit Red Wings	Montreal Canadiens
1957/58	Montreal Canadiens	Montreal Canadiens
1958/59	Montreal Canadiens	Montreal Canadiens
1959/60	Montreal Canadiens	Montreal Canadiens
1960/61	Montreal Canadiens	Chicago Black Hawks
1961/62	Montreal Canadiens	Toronto Maple Leafs
1962/63	Toronto Maple Leafs	Toronto Maple Leafs
1963/64	Montreal Canadiens	Toronto Maple Leafs
1964/65	Detroit Red Wings	Montreal Canadiens
1965/66	Montreal Canadiens	Montreal Canadiens
1966/67	Chicago Black Hawks	Toronto Maple Leafs
1967/68	Montreal Canadiens* ..... Philadelphia Flyers†	Montreal Canadiens
1968/69	Montreal Canadiens* ..... St. Louis Blues†	Montreal Canadiens
1969/70	Chicago Black Hawks* .... St. Louis Blues†	Boston Bruins
1970/71	Boston Bruins* .... Chicago Black Hawks†	Montreal Canadiens
1971/72	Boston Bruins* .... Chicago Black Hawks†	Boston Bruins
1972/73	Montreal Canadiens* ..... Chicago Black Hawks†	Montreal Canadiens
1973/74	Boston Bruins* .... Philadelphia Flyers†	Philadelphia Flyers
1974/75	Montreal, Buffalo, ... Philadelphia, Vancouver	Philadelphia Flyers
1975/76	Montreal, Boston, ... Philadelphia, Chicago	Montreal Canadiens
1976/77	Montreal, Boston, ... Philadelphia, St. Louis	Montreal Canadiens
1977/78	Montreal, Boston, ... N.Y. Islanders, Chicago	Montreal Canadiens
1978/79	Montreal, Boston, ... N.Y. Islanders, Chicago	Montreal Canadiens
1979/80	Montreal, Buffalo, ... Philadelphia, Chicago	New York Islanders
1980/81	Montreal, Buffalo, ... N.Y. Islanders, St. Louis	New York Islanders

* East Division. † West Division.

NHL FINAL STANDINGS: 1980-81

CAMPBELL CONFERENCE

PATRICK DIVISION	W	L	T	Pts.	GF	GA
NY Islanders	48	18	14	110	355	260
Philadelphia	41	24	15	97	313	249
Calgary	39	27	14	92	329	298
NY Rangers	30	36	14	74	312	317
Washington	26	36	18	70	286	318

SMYTHE DIVISION	W	L	T	Pts.	GF	GA
St. Louis	45	18	17	107	352	281
Chicago	31	33	16	78	304	315
Vancouver	28	32	20	76	289	301
Edmonton	29	35	16	74	328	327
Colorado	22	45	13	57	258	344
Winnipeg	9	57	14	32	246	400

WALES CONFERENCE

ADAMS DIVISION	W	L	T	Pts.	GF	GA
Buffalo	39	20	21	99	327	250
Boston	37	30	13	87	316	272
Minnesota	35	28	17	87	292	263
Quebec	30	32	18	78	314	318
Toronto	28	37	15	71	322	367

NORRIS DIVISION	W	L	T	Pts.	GF	GA
Montreal	45	22	13	103	332	232
Los Angeles	43	24	13	99	337	290
Pittsburgh	30	37	13	73	302	345
Hartford	21	41	18	60	292	372
Detroit	19	43	18	56	252	339

STANLEY CUP PLAYOFFS: 1981 Top 16 Teams (Total Points) Qualify

Preliminary Round (Best-of-five series)
NY Islanders over Toronto: 3-0
St. Louis over Pittsburgh: 3-2
Edmonton over Montreal: 3-0
NY Rangers over Los Angeles: 3-1
Buffalo over Vancouver: 3-0
Philadelphia over Quebec: 3-2
Calgary over Chicago: 3-0
Minnesota over Boston: 3-0

Quarter Finals (Best-of-seven series)
NY Islanders over Edmonton: 4-2
NY Rangers over St. Louis: 4-2
Minnesota over Buffalo: 4-1
Calgary over Philadelphia: 4-3

Semi-Finals (Best-of-seven series)
NY Islanders over NY Rangers: 4-0
Minnesota over Calgary: 4-2

Finals (Best-of-seven series)
1. NY Islanders 6, Minnesota 3
2. NY Islanders 6, Minnesota 3
3. NY Islanders 7, Minnesota 5
4. Minnesota 4, NY Islanders 2
5. NY Islanders 5, Minnesota 1
(NY Islanders win series: 4-1)

STANLEY CUP CHAMPIONS

Season	Champions	Manager
1919-20	Ottawa Senators	Tommy Gorman
1920-21	Ottawa Senators	Tommy Gorman
1921-22	Toronto St. Pats	Charlie Querrie
1922-23	Ottawa Senators	Tommy Gorman
1923-24	Montreal Canadiens	Leo Dandurand
1924-25	Victoria Cougars	Lester Patrick
1925-26	Montreal Maroons	Eddie Gerard
1926-27	Ottawa Senators	Dave Gill
1927-28	New York Rangers	Lester Patrick
1928-29	Boston Bruins	Art Ross
1929-30	Montreal Canadiens	Cecil Hart
1930-31	Montreal Canadiens	Cecil Hart
1931-32	Toronto Maple Leafs	Conn Smythe
1932-33	New York Rangers	Lester Patrick
1933-34	Chicago Black Hawks	Tommy Gorman
1934-35	Montreal Maroons	Tommy Gorman
1935-36	Detroit Red Wings	Jack Adams
1936-37	Detroit Red Wings	Jack Adams
1937-38	Chicago Black Hawks	Bill Stewart
1938-39	Boston Bruins	Art Ross
1939-40	New York Rangers	Lester Patrick
1940-41	Boston Bruins	Art Ross
1941-42	Toronto Maple Leafs	Conn Smythe
1942-43	Detroit Red Wings	Jack Adams
1943-44	Montreal Canadiens	Tommy Gorman
1944-45	Toronto Maple Leafs	Conn Smythe
1945-46	Montreal Canadiens	Tommy Gorman
1946-47	Toronto Maple Leafs	Conn Smythe
1947-48	Toronto Maple Leafs	Conn Smythe
1948-49	Toronto Maple Leafs	Conn Smythe
1949-50	Detroit Red Wings	Jack Adams
1950-51	Toronto Maple Leafs	Conn Smythe
1951-52	Detroit Red Wings	Jack Adams
1952-53	Montreal Canadiens	Frank Selke
1953-54	Detroit Red Wings	Jack Adams
1954-55	Detroit Red Wings	Jack Adams
1955-56	Montreal Canadiens	Frank Selke
1956-57	Montreal Canadiens	Frank Selke
1957-58	Montreal Canadiens	Frank Selke
1958-59	Montreal Canadiens	Frank Selke
1959-60	Montreal Canadiens	Frank Selke
1960-61	Chicago Black Hawks	Tommy Ivan
1961-62	Toronto Maple Leafs	Punch Imlach
1962-63	Toronto Maple Leafs	Punch Imlach
1963-64	Toronto Maple Leafs	Punch Imlach
1964-65	Montreal Canadiens	Sam Pollock
1965-66	Montreal Canadiens	Sam Pollock
1966-67	Toronto Maple Leafs	Punch Imlach
1967-68	Montreal Canadiens	Sam Pollock
1968-69	Montreal Canadiens	Sam Pollock
1969-70	Boston Bruins	Milt Schmidt
1970-71	Montreal Canadiens	Sam Pollock
1971-72	Boston Bruins	Milt Schmidt
1972-73	Montreal Canadiens	Hector Blake
1973-74	Philadelphia Flyers	Keith Allen
1974-75	Philadelphia Flyers	Keith Allen
1975-76	Montreal Canadiens	Sam Pollock
1976-77	Montreal Canadiens	Sam Pollock
1977-78	Montreal Canadiens	Sam Pollock
1978-79	Montreal Canadiens	Irving Grundman
1979-80	New York Islanders	Bill Torrey
1980-81	New York Islanders	Bill Torrey

NHL SCORING LEADERS

Season	Player and Team	Points
1948-49	Roy Conacher, Chicago	68
1949-50	Ted Lindsay, Detroit	78
1950-51	Gordie Howe, Detroit	86
1951-52	Gordie Howe, Detroit	86
1952-53	Gordie Howe, Detroit	95
1953-54	Gordie Howe, Detroit	81
1954-55	Bernie Geoffrion, Montreal	75
1955-56	Jean Beliveau, Montreal	88
1956-57	Gordie Howe, Detroit	89
1957-58	Dickie Moore, Montreal	84
1958-59	Dickie Moore, Montreal	96
1959-60	Bobby Hull, Chicago	81
1960-61	Bernie Geoffrion, Montreal	95
1961-62	Bobby Hull, Chicago	84
1962-63	Gordie Howe, Detroit	86
1963-64	Stan Mikita, Chicago	89
1964-65	Stan Mikita, Chicago	87
1965-66	Bobby Hull, Chicago	97
1966-67	Stan Mikita, Chicago	97
1967-68	Stan Mikita, Chicago	87
1968-69	Phil Esposito, Boston	126
1969-70	Bobby Orr, Boston	120
1970-71	Phil Esposito, Boston	152
1971-72	Phil Esposito, Boston	133
1972-73	Phil Esposito, Boston	130
1973-74	Phil Esposito, Boston	145
1974-75	Bobby Orr, Boston	135
1975-76	Guy Lafleur, Montreal	125
1976-77	Guy Lafleur, Montreal	136
1977-78	Guy Lafleur, Montreal	132
1978-79	Brian Trottier, NY Islanders	134
1979-80	Marcel Dionne, Los Angeles	137
	Wayne Gretzky, Edmonton	137
1980-81	Wayne Gretzky, Edmonton	164

NHL SCORING LEADERS: 1980/81

Player	Team	G	A	Pts.	Player	Team	G	A	Pts.
Wayne Gretzky	Edmonton	55	109	164	Rick Middleton	Boston	44	59	103
Marcel Dionne	Los Angeles	58	77	135	Bryan Trottier	N.Y. Islanders	31	72	103
Kent Nilsson	California	49	82	131	Dennis Maruk	Washington	50	47	97
Mike Bossy	N.Y. Islanders	68	51	119	Wilf Paiement	Toronto	40	57	97
Dave Taylor	Los Angeles	47	65	112	Wayne Babych	St. Louis	54	42	96
Peter Stastny	Quebec	39	70	109	Darryl Sittler	Toronto	43	53	96
Charlie Simmer	Los Angeles	56	49	105	Mike Gartner	Washington	48	46	94
Mike Rogers	Hartford	40	65	105	Bobby Smith	Minnesota	29	64	93
Bernie Federko	St. Louis	31	73	104	Rick Kehoe	Pittsburgh	55	33	88
Jacques Richard	Quebec	52	51	103	Blake Dunlop	St. Louis	20	67	87

NHL ALL-TIME SCORING LEADERS At start of 1981/82 season.

Player (Team)	Seasons	Games	Goals	Assists	Points	Scoring Percentage
Gordie Howe (Detroit, Hartford)	26	1,767	801	1,049	1,850	1.047
Phil Esposito (Chicago, Boston, N.Y. Rangers)	18	1,282	717	873	1,590	1.240
Stan Mikita (Chicago)	22	1,394	541	926	1,467	1.052
Johnny Bucyk (Detroit, Boston)	23	1,540	556	813	1,369	.889
Alex Delvecchio (Detroit)	24	1,549	456	825	1,281	.827
Jean Ratelle (N.Y. Rangers, Boston)	21	1,281	491	776	1,267	.989
Norm Ullman (Detroit, Toronto)	20	1,410	490	739	1,229	.872
Jean Beliveau (Mtl. Canadiens)	20	1,125	507	712	1,219	1.084
Bobby Hull (Chicago, Winnipeg, Hartford)	16	1,063	610	560	1,170	1.100
Frank Mahovlich (Toronto, Detroit, Mtl. Canadiens)	18	1,181	533	570	1,103	.934
Marcel Dionne (Detroit, Los Angeles)	10	779	438	625	1,063	1.364
Henri Richard (Mtl. Canadiens)	20	1,256	358	688	1,046	.833
Rod Gilbert (N.Y. Rangers)	18	1,065	406	615	1,021	.959
Guy Lafleur (Mtl. Canadiens)	10	728	432	579	1,011	1.388
Bobby Clarke (Philadelphia Flyers)	12	929	301	701	1,002	1.078
Andy Bathgate (N.Y. Rangers, Toronto, Detroit, Pittsburgh Penguins)	17	1,069	349	624	973	.910
Dave Keon (Toronto, Hartford)	17	1,218	388	579	967	.793
Maurice Richard (Mtl. Canadiens)	18	978	544	421	965	.987
Gilbert Perreault (Buffalo)	11	809	360	568	928	1.147
Bobby Orr (Boston, Chicago)	12	657	270	645	915	1.393
Darryl Sittler (Toronto)	11	806	371	507	878	1.089
Yvan Cournoyer (Mtl. Canadiens)	16	968	428	435	863	.892
Dean Prentice (N.Y. Rangers, Boston, Detroit, Pittsburgh Penguins, Minnesota)	22	1,378	391	469	860	.624
Ted Lindsay (Detroit, Chicago)	17	1,068	379	472	851	.797
Jacques Lemaire (Montreal Canadiens)	12	853	366	469	835	.979
Red Kelly (Detroit, Toronto)	20	1,316	281	542	823	.625
Bernie Geoffrion (Mtl. Canadiens, N.Y. Rangers)	16	883	393	429	822	.931
Pit Martin (Detroit, Boston, Chicago, Vancouver)	17	1,101	324	485	809	.735
Ken Hodge (Chicago, Boston, N.Y. Rangers)	14	881	328	472	800	.908
Garry Unger (Toronto, Detroit, St. Louis, Atlanta)	14	1,043	404	378	782	.749
Pete Mahovlich (Detroit, Mtl. Canadiens, Pittsburgh Penguins)	16	884	288	486	773	.874
Jean Pronovost (Pittsburgh, Atlanta)	13	988	390	381	771	.780
Wayne Cashman (Boston)	15	898	261	474	735	.818
Butch Goring (Los Angeles, N.Y. Islanders)	12	826	304	426	730	.886
Murray Oliver (Detroit, Boston, Toronto, Minnesota)	17	1,127	274	454	728	.646
Bob Nevin (Toronto, N.Y. Rangers, Minnesota, Los Angeles)	18	1,128	307	419	726	.644
George Armstrong (Toronto)	21	1,187	296	417	713	.601
Vic Hadfield (N.Y. Rangers, Pittsburgh Penguins)	16	1,002	323	389	712	.711
Doug Mohns (Boston, Chicago, Minnesota, Atlanta, Washington)	22	1,390	248	462	710	.511
Bobby Rousseau (Mtl. Canadiens, Minnesota, N.Y. Rangers)	15	942	245	458	703	.736
Brad Park (N.Y. Rangers, Boston)	13	815	171	532	703	.862

NATIONAL HOCKEY LEAGUE TROPHY WINNERS

HART TROPHY For Most Valuable Player

1957/58 Gordie Howe, Detroit	1965/66 Bobby Hull, Chicago	1973/74 Phil Esposito, Boston
1958/59 Andy Bathgate, New York	1966/67 Stan Mikita, Chicago	1974/75 Bobby Clarke, Philadelphia
1959/60 Gordie Howe, Detroit	1967/68 Stan Mikita, Chicago	1975/76 Bobby Clarke, Philadelphia
1960/61 Bernie Geoffrion, Montreal	1968/69 Phil Esposito, Boston	1976/77 Guy Lafleur, Montreal
1961/62 Jacques Plante, Montreal	1969/70 Bobby Orr, Boston	1977/78 Guy Lafleur, Montreal
1962/63 Gordie Howe, Detroit	1970/71 Bobby Orr, Boston	1978/79 Bryan Trottier, N.Y. Islanders
1963/64 Jean Beliveau, Montreal	1971/72 Bobby Orr, Boston	1979/80 Wayne Gretzky, Edmonton
1964/65 Bobby Hull, Chicago	1972/73 Bobby Clarke, Philadelphia	1980/81 Wayne Gretzky, Edmonton

VENZINA TROPHY For Best Goalie Record

1964/65 Terry Sawchuk and Johnny Bower, Toronto	1969/70 Tony Esposito, Chicago	1976/77 Ken Dryden and Michel Larocque, Montreal
1965/66 Lorne Worsley and Charlie Hodge, Montreal	1970/71 Ed Giacomin and Gilles Villemure, New York	1977/78 Ken Dryden and Michel Larocque, Montreal
1966/67 Denis DeJordy and Glenn Hall, Chicago	1971/72 Tony Esposito and Gary Smith, Chicago	1978/79 Ken Dryden and Michel Larocque, Montreal
1967/68 Lorne Worsley and Rogatien Vachon, Montreal	1972/73 Ken Dryden, Montreal	1979/80 Don Edwards and Bob Sauve, Buffalo
1968/69 Glenn Hall and Jacques Plante, St Louis	1973/74 Bernie Parent, Philadelphia and Tony Esposito, Chicago	1980/81 R. Sevigny, D. Herron and M. Larocque, Montreal
	1974/75 Bernie Parent, Philadelphia	
	1975/76 Ken Dryden, Montreal	

JAMES NORRIS TROPHY For Best Defenseman

1956/57 Doug Harvey, Montreal	1964/65 Pierre Pilote, Chicago	1972/73 Bobby Orr, Boston
1957/58 Doug Harvey, Montreal	1965/66 J. Laperriere, Montreal	1973/74 Bobby Orr, Boston
1958/59 Tom Johnson, Montreal	1966/67 Harry Howell, New York	1974/75 Bobby Orr, Boston
1959/60 Doug Harvey, Montreal	1967/68 Bobby Orr, Boston	1975/76 Denis Potvin, N.Y. Islanders
1960/61 Doug Harvey, Montreal	1968/69 Bobby Orr, Boston	1976/77 Larry Robinson, Montreal
1961/62 Doug Harvey, New York	1969/70 Bobby Orr, Boston	1977/78 Denis Potvin, N.Y. Islanders
1962/63 Pierre Pilote, Chicago	1970/71 Bobby Orr, Boston	1978/79 Denis Potvin, N.Y. Islanders
1963/64 Pierre Pilote, Chicago	1971/72 Bobby Orr, Boston	1979/80 Larry Robinson, Montreal
		1980/81 Rudy Carlyle, Pittsburgh

FRANK J. SELKE TROPHY For Best Defensive Forward

1977/78 Bob Gainey, Montreal	1978/79 Bob Gainey, Montreal	1979/80 Bob Gainey, Montreal
		1980/81 Bob Gainey, Montreal

CALDER TROPHY For Best Rookie

1953/54 Camille Henry, New York	1962/63 Kent Douglas, Toronto	1971/72 Ken Dryden, Montreal
1954/55 Ed Litzenberger, Chicago	1963/64 Jacques Laperriere, Montreal	1972/73 Steve Vickers, N. Y. Rangers
1955/56 Glenn Hall, Detroit	1964/65 Roger Crozier, Detroit	1973/74 Denis Potvin, N. Y. Islanders
1956/57 Larry Regan, Boston	1965/66 Brit Selby, Toronto	1974/75 Eric Vail, Atlanta
1957/58 Frank Mahovlich, Toronto	1966/67 Bobby Orr, Boston	1975/76 Bryan Trottier, N.Y. Islanders
1958/59 Ralph Backstrom, Montreal	1967/68 Derek Sanderson, Boston	1976/77 Willie Plett, Atlanta
1959/60 Billy Hay, Chicago	1968/69 Danny Grant, Minnesota	1977/78 Mike Bossy, N. Y. Islanders
1960/61 Dave Keon, Toronto	1969/70 Tony Esposito, Chicago	1978/79 Bobby Smith, Minnesota
1961/62 Bobby Rousseau, Montreal	1970/71 Gil Perreault, Buffalo	1979/80 Ray Bourque, Boston
		1980/81 Peter Stastny, Quebec

LADY BYNG TROPHY For Sportsmanship

1953/54 Red Kelly, Detroit	1962/63 Dave Keon, Toronto	1971/72 Jean Ratelle, New York
1954/55 Sid Smith, Toronto	1963/64 Ken Wharram, Chicago	1972/73 Gil Perreault, Buffalo
1955/56 Earl Reibel, Detroit	1964/65 Bobby Hull, Chicago	1973/74 John Bucyk, Boston
1956/57 Andy Hebenton, New York	1965/66 Alex Delvecchio, Detroit	1974/75 Marcel Dionne, Detroit
1957/58 Camille Henry, New York	1966/67 Stan Mikita, Chicago	1975/76 Jean Ratelle, Boston
1958/59 Alex Delvecchio, Detroit	1967/68 Stan Mikita, Chicago	1976/77 Marcel Dionne, Los Angeles
1959/60 Don McKenney, Boston	1968/69 Alex Delvecchio, Detroit	1977/78 Butch Goring, Los Angeles
1960/61 Red Kelly, Toronto	1969/70 Phil Goyette, St. Louis	1978/79 Bob MacMillan, Atlanta
1961/62 Dave Keon, Toronto	1970/71 Johnny Bucyk, Boston	1979/80 Wayne Gretzky, Edmonton
		1980/81 Rick Kehoe, Pittsburgh

CONN SMYTHE TROPHY For Most Valuable Player in Stanley Cup Playoffs

1965 Jean Beliveau, Montreal	1971 Ken Dryden, Montreal	1976 Reggie Leach, Philadelphia
1966 Roger Crozier, Detroit	1972 Bobby Orr, Boston	1977 Guy Lafleur, Montreal
1967 Dave Keon, Toronto	1973 Yvan Cournoyer, Montreal	1978 Larry Robinson, Montreal
1968 Glenn Hall, St. Louis	1974 Bernie Parent, Philadelphia	1979 Bob Gainey, Montreal
1969 Serge Savard, Montreal	1975 Bernie Parent, Philadelphia	1980 Bryan Trottier, N.Y. Islanders
1970 Bobby Orr, Boston		1981 Butch Goring, N.Y. Islanders

1981 NHL ALL-STARS

Results of voting by members of the Professional Hockey Writers Association

	FIRST TEAM		SECOND TEAM
Goal	Mike Liut, St. Louis	Goal	Mario Lessard, Los Angeles
Defense	Denis Potvin, N.Y. Islanders	Defense	Larry Robinson, Montreal
Defense	Randy Carlyle, Pittsburgh	Defense	Ray Bourgue, Boston
Center	Wayne Gretzky, Edmonton	Center	Marcel Dionne, Los Angeles
Right Wing	Charlie Simmer, Los Angeles	Right Wing	Bill Barber, Philadelphia
Left Wing	Mike Bossy, N.Y. Islanders	Left Wing	Dave Taylor, Los Angeles

NHL ALL-STAR GAME RESULTS

Prior to 1969 the All-Star Game between the chosen team and the holder of the Stanley Cup.

Year	Score	Location	Year	Score	Location
1947	All-Stars 4, Toronto 3	Toronto	1965	All-Stars 5, Montreal 2	Montreal
1948	All-Stars 3, Toronto 1	Chicago	1967	Montreal 3, All-Stars 0	Montreal
1949	All-Stars 3, Toronto 1	Toronto	1968	Toronto 4, All-Stars 3	Toronto
1950	Detroit 7, All-Stars 1	Detroit	1969	East 3, West 3	Montreal
1951	1st Team 2, 2nd Team 2	Toronto	1970	East 4, West 1	St. Louis
1952	1st Team 1, 2nd Team 1	Detroit	1971	West 2, East 1	Boston
1953	All-Stars 3, Montreal 1	Montreal	1972	East 3, West 2	Minnesota
1954	All-Stars 2, Detroit 2	Detroit	1973	East 5, West 4	New York
1955	Detroit 3, All-Stars 1	Detroit	1974	West 6, East 4	Chicago
1956	All-Stars 1, Montreal 1	Montreal	1975	Prince of Wales 7,	
1957	All-Stars 5, Montreal 3	Montreal		Campbell 1	Montreal
1958	Montreal 6, All-Stars 3	Montreal	1976	Wales 7, Campbell 5	Philadelphia
1959	Montreal 6, All-Stars 1	Montreal	1977	Wales 4, Campbell 3	Vancouver
1960	All-Stars 2, Montreal 1	Montreal	1978	Wales 3, Campbell 2	Buffalo
1961	All-Stars 3, Chicago 1	Chicago	1979	no game played	
1962	Toronto 4, All-Stars 1	Toronto	1980	Wales 6, Campbell 3	Detroit
1963	All-Stars 3, Toronto 3	Toronto	1981	Campbell 4, Wales 1	Los Angeles
1964	All-Stars 3, Toronto 2	Toronto			

HOCKEY HALL OF FAME
Source: N.H.L.

Players	Players	Players	Builders
Sidney Abel	Michael Grant	A. Joseph Primeau	Thomas "Frank" Ahearn
John Adams	W. "Shorty" Green	J. R. Marcel Pronovost	John "Bunny" Ahearne
C. J. "Syl" Apps	Silas Griffis	Harvey Pulford	Sir Montague Allen
George Armstrong	George Hainsworth	H. G. "Bill" Quackenbush	John Ashley
I. W. "Ace" Bailey	Glenn Hall	Frank Rankin	Harold Ballard
Donald Bain	Joseph Hall	C. E. "Chuck" Rayner	John Bickell
Hobart Baker	Douglas Harvey	Kenneth Reardon	George Brown
Martin Barry	George Hay	Henri Richard	Walter Brown
Andrew Bathgate	W. M. "Riley" Hern	J. H. Maurice Richard	Frank Buckland
Jean Beliveau	Bryan Hextall	George Richardson	Jack Butterfield
Clinton Benedict	Harry Holmes	Gordon Roberts	Frank Calder
Douglas Bentley	C. Thomas Hooper	Arthur Ross	Angus Campbell
Maxwell Bentley	G. R. "Red" Horner	Blair Russel	Clarence Campbell
Hector "Toe" Blake	M. G. "Tim" Horton	J. D. "Jack" Ruttan	Joseph Cattarinich
Richard Boon	Gordon Howe	Terrance Sawchuk	Joseph "Leo" Dandurand
Emile "Butch" Bouchard	Sydney Howe	Fred Scanlan	Francis Dilio
Frank Boucher	Harry Howell	Milton Schmidt	George Dudley
George "Buck" Boucher	J. B. "Bouse" Hutton	D. "Sweeney" Schriner	James Dunn
John Bower	Harry Hyland	Earl Seibert	Dr. John Gibson
Russell Bowie	J. D. "Dick" Irvin	Oliver Seibert	Thomas Gorman
Francis Brimsek	H. "Busher" Jackson	Edward Shore	Charles Hay
H. L. "Punch" Broadbent	E. "Moose" Johnson	A. C. "Babe" Siebert	James Hendy
W. E. "Turk" Broda	Ivan "Ching" Johnson	Harold Simpson	Foster Hewitt
Johnny Bucyk	Thomas Johnson	Alfred Smith	William Hewitt
Billy Burch	Aurel Joliat	R. "Hooley" Smith	Fred Hume
Harold Cameron	G. "Duke" Keats	Thomas Smith	Thomas Ivan
F. M. "King" Clancy	L. P. "Red" Kelly	Allan Stanley	William Jennings
Aubrey "Dit" Clapper	T. S. "Teeder" Kennedy	R. "Barney" Stanley	Gen. John Kilpatrick
Sprague Cleghorn	Elmer Lach	John Stewart	George Leader
Neil Colville	E. C. "Newsy" Lalonde	Nelson Stewart	Robert LeBel
Charles Conacher	Jean Laviolette	Bruce Stuart	Thomas Lockhart
Alex Connell	Hugh Lehman	Hod Stuart	Paul Loicq
William Cook	Percy LeSeur	F. "Cyclone" Taylor	Maj. Frederic McLaughlin
Arthur Coulter	Robert "Ted" Lindsay	C. R. "Tiny" Thompson	Hon. Hartland Molson
William Cowley	Harry Lumley	Col. Harry J. Trihey	Francis Nelson
S. R. "Rusty" Crawford	D. "Mickey" MacKay	Georges Vezina	Bruce Norris
John Darragh	Frank Mahovlich	John Walker	James Norris, Sr.
A. M. "Scotty" Davidson	Joseph Malone	Martin Walsh	James D. Norris
Clarence "Hap" Day	Sylvio Mantha	Harry Watson	William Northey
Alex Delvecchio	John Marshall	Ralph "Cooney" Weiland	John O'Brien
Cyril Denneny	Fred "Steamer" Maxwell	Harry Westwick	Frank Patrick
Gordon Drillon	Frank McGee	Fred Whitcroft	Allan Pickard
Charles Drinkwater	William McGimsie	Gordon Wilson	Samuel Pollock
Thomas Dunderdale	George McNamara	Lorne "Gump" Worsley	Sen. Donat Raymond
William Durnan	Richard Moore	Roy Worters	John Robertson
M. A. "Red" Dutton	Patrick Moran		Claude Robinson
C. H. "Babe" Dye	Howie Morenz	**Referees**	Philip Ross
Arthur Farrell	William Mosienko	William Chadwick	Frank Selke
Frank Foyston	Frank Nighbor	Chaucer Elliott	Frank Smith
Frank Frederickson	E. Reginald Noble	Robert Hewitson	Conn Smythe
William Gadsby	Harry Oliver	Fred "Mickey" Ion	Lord Stanley of Preston
Charles Gardiner	Bobby Orr	Michael Rodden	Capt. James Sutherland
Herbert Gardiner	Lester Patrick	J. Cooper Smeaton	Anatoli Tarasov
James Gardner	Lynn Patrick	R. A. "Red" Storey	Lloyd Turner
J. A. Bernard Geoffrion	Tommy Phillips	Frank Udvari	William Tutt
Eddie Gerard	J. A. Pierre Pilote		Carl Voss
H. L. "Billy" Gilmour	Didier "Pit" Pitre	**Builders**	Fred Waghorne
F. X. "Moose" Goheen	J. Jacques Plante	Charles Adams	Arthur Wirtz
Ebenezer Goodfellow	Walter "Babe" Pratt	Weston Adams	William Wrltz

NATIONAL COLLEGIATE HOCKEY CHAMPIONSHIPS

DIVISION I

1957	Colorado College 13, Michigan 6
1958	Denver 6, North Dakota 2
1959	North Dakota 4, Michigan State 3
1960	Denver 5, Michigan Tech 3
1961	Denver 12, St. Lawrence 2
1962	Michigan Tech 7, Clarkson 1
1963	North Dakota 6, Denver 5
1964	Michigan 6, Denver 3
1965	Michigan Tech 8, Boston College 2
1966	Michigan State 6, Clarkson 1
1967	Cornell 4, Boston University 1
1968	Denver 4, North Dakota 0
1969	Denver 4, Cornell 3
1970	Cornell 6, Clarkson 4
1971	Boston University 4, Minnesota 2

1972	Boston University 4, Cornell 0
1973	Wisconsin 4, Denver 2
1974	Minnesota 4, Michigan Tech 2
1975	Michigan Tech 6, Minnesota 1
1976	Minnesota 6, Michigan Tech 4
1977	Wisconsin 6, Michigan 5
1978	Boston University 5, Boston College 3
1979	Minnesota 4, North Dakota 3
1980	North Dakota 5, Northern Michigan 2
1981	Wisconsin 6, Minnesota 3

DIVISION II

1978	Merrimack 12, Lake Forest 2
1979	Lowell 6, Mankato State 4
1980	Mankato State 5, Elmira 2
1981	Lowell 5, Plattsburgh State 4

SOCCER

NORTH AMERICAN SOCCER LEAGUE 1133 Avenue of the Americas, New York City 10036

1981 FINAL STANDINGS

Eastern Division	Won	Lost	Pts.	Goals For	Ag'st
New York Cosmos	23	9	200	80	49
Montreal Manic	15	17	141	63	57
Washington Diplomats	15	17	135	59	58
Toronto Blizzard	7	25	77	39	82

Southern Division	Won	Lost	Pts.	Goals For	Ag'st
Atlanta Chiefs	17	15	151	62	60
Ft. Lauderdale Strikers	18	14	144	54	45
Jacksonville Tea Men	18	14	142	51	46
Tampa Bay Rowdies	15	17	139	63	64

Central Division	Won	Lost	Pts.	Goals For	Ag'st
Chicago Sting	23	9	195	84	50
Minnesota Kicks	19	13	163	63	57
Tulsa Roughnecks	17	15	154	60	49
Dallas Tornado	5	27	54	27	69

Western Division	Won	Lost	Pts.	Goals For	Ag'st
San Diego Sockers	21	11	173	68	49
Los Angeles Aztecs	19	13	160	53	55
California Surf	11	21	117	60	77
San Jose Earthquakes	11	21	108	44	78

Northwest Division	Won	Lost	Pts.	Goals For	Ag'st
Vancouver Whitecaps	21	11	186	74	43
Calgary Boomers	17	15	151	59	54
Portland Trail Blazers	17	15	141	52	49
Seattle Sounders	15	17	137	60	62
Edmonton Drillers	12	20	123	59	79

LEADING SCORERS	Games	Goals	Assists	Pts.
Giorgio Chinaglia, New York	32	29	16	74
Karl-Heinz Granitza, Chicago	31	19	17	55
Mike Stojanovic, San Diego	32	23	6	52
Brian Kidd, Atlanta	27	22	8	52
Franz Gerber, Calgary	25	20	10	50
Teofilo Cubillas, Ft. Lauderdale	28	17	10	44

LEADING SCORERS	Games	Goals	Assists	Pts.
Arno Steffenhagen, Chicago	28	17	10	44
Gordon Hill, Montreal	30	16	12	44
Edi Kirschner, Edmonton	31	17	9	43
Duncan McKenzie, Tulsa	31	14	15	43
Roberto Cabanas, New York	22	16	9	41

LEADING GOALKEEPERS	Games	Saves	Goals Ag'st	Avg.
Arnie Mausser, Jacksonville	31	177	39	1.21
Jan van Beveren, Ft. Lauderdale	32	195	43	1.29
Barry Siddall, Vancouver	24	90	33	1.30
Zeljko Bilecki, Tulsa	29	93	39	1.33
Volkmar Gross, San Diego	32	164	45	1.36

LEADING GOALKEEPERS	Games	Saves	Goals Ag'st	Avg.
Hubert Birkenmeier, New York	31	177	45	1.41
Keith MacRae, Portland	20	85	29	1.52
Jim Brown, Washington	31	171	49	1.54
Bob Rigby, Montreal	32	185	52	1.57
Jack Brand, Seattle	23	102	36	1.60

AWARD WINNERS

Most Valuable Player — Giorgio Chinaglia, New York
Most Popular Player — Giorgio Chinaglia, New York
Three Star Player of the Year — Jan van Beveren, Fort Lauderdale
North American Player of the Year — Mike Stojanovic, San Diego
Rookie of the Year — Joe Morrone, Chicago
Goal of the Year — George Best, San Jose

Top Forward — Giorgio Chinaglia, New York
Top Midfielder — Teofilo Cubillas, Fort Lauderdale
Top Defender — Wim Rijsbergen, New York
Top Goalkeeper — Jan van Beveren, Fort Lauderdale
Top Scorer — Giorgio Chinaglia, New York
Most Valuable Player, Soccer Bowl 1981 — Frantz Mathieu, Chicago
Coach of the Year — Willie Roy, Chicago

1981 NASL PLAYOFFS

First Round
New York — bye
Tampa Bay over Vancouver, 4-1, 1-0
Fort Lauderdale over Calgary, 3-1, 2-0
Minnesota over Tulsa, 3-1, 1-0
Chicago over Seattle, 3-2, 0-2, 3-2
Montreal over Los Angeles, 5-3, 2-3, 2-1
San Diego over Portland, 1-2, 5-1, 2-0
Jacksonville over Atlanta, 3-2, 2-1

Second Round
New York over Tampa Bay, 6-3, 2-3, 2-0
Fort Lauderdale over Minnesota, 3-0, 3-0
Chicago over Montreal, 2-3, 4-2, 4-2
San Diego over Jacksonville, 1-2, 2-1, 3-1

Semifinals
New York over Ft. Lauderdale, 4-3, 4-1
Chicago over San Diego, 1-2, 2-1, 1-0

CHAMPIONSHIP GAME (SOCCER BOWL 1981) — Chicago 1, New York 0

NASL ALL-STAR TEAMS: 1981

Position	First Team	Second Team	Honorable Mention
Goalkeeper	Jan van Beveren, Ft. Lauderdale	Hubert Birkenmeier, New York	Volkmar Gross, San Diego
Defender	Wim Rijsbergen, New York	Barry Wallace, Tulsa	Nick Rohmann, San Diego
Defender	Frantz Mathieu, Chicago	Kevin Bond, Seattle	Bob Iarusci, New York
Defender	Peter Nogly, Edmonton	Mihalj Keri, Los Angeles	Dave Huson, Chicago
Defender	John Gorman, Tampa Bay	Pierce O'Leary, Vancouver	Carlos Alberto, California
Midfielder	Teofilo Cubillas, Ft. Lauderdale	Alan Hudson, Seattle	Julie Veee, San Diego
Midfielder	Vladislav Bogicevic, New York	George Best, San Jose	Jomo Sono, Toronto
Midfielder	Arno Steffenhagen, Chicago	Peter Lorimer, Vancouver	Duncan McKenzie, Tulsa
Forward	Giorgio Chinaglia, New York	Karl-Heinz Granitza, Chicago	Mike Stojanovic, San Diego
Forward	Brian Kidd, Atlanta	Roberto Cabanas, New York	Pato Margetic, Chicago
Forward	Gordon Hill, Montreal	Franz Gerber, Calgary	(tie) Alan Green, Jacksonville
			Steve Wegerle, New York

NORTH AMERICAN SOCCER LEAGUE CHAMPIONS: 1968-1981

1968	Atlanta	1972	New York	1976	Toronto	1980	New York
1969	Kansas City	1973	Philadelphia	1977	New York	1981	Chicago
1970	Rochester	1974	Los Angeles	1978	New York		
1971	Dallas	1975	Tampa Bay	1979	Vancouver		

OTHER CHAMPIONSHIPS (1981)

American Soccer League .... Carolina Lightnin'
NASL Indoor .... Edmonton Drillers
Major Indoor League .... New York Arrows
NCAA Division I (1980) .... San Francisco

NCAA Division II (1980) .... Lock Haven State (Pa.)
NCAA Division III (1980) .... Babson (Mass.)
NAIA (1980) .... Quincy (Ill.)
Junior Colleges (1980) .... SUNY (Morrisville)

GOLF

TOTAL MONEY-WINNING LEADERS: 1980 SOURCE: PGA

Official Money shall be awarded to individual prize winners in major tournaments and such other events as the Tournament Policy Board may designate, even if part of the tournament is canceled provided; however, that Official Money shall not be awarded, in any team competition or a pro-am tournament (but Official Money will be awarded in a major tournament for individuals even if held concurrently with a pro-am tournament). The scale of Official Money will be determined from time to time by the Tournament Policy Board.

Rank	Name	Winnings	Rank	Name	Winnings	Rank	Name	Winnings
1.	Tom Watson	$530,808	18.	Don Pooley	$157,973	34.	Tom Purtzer	$118,185
2.	Lee Trevino	385,814	19.	Bob Gilder	152,597	35.	Jay Haas	114,102
3.	Curtis Strange	271,888	20.	Tom Kite	152,490	36.	Dan Halldorson	111,553
4.	Andy Bean	269,033	21.	Jim Colbert	150,411	37.	Jeff Mitchell	111,217
5.	Ben Crenshaw	237,727	22.	Mike Sullivan	147,759	38.	Hale Irwin	109,810
6.	Jerry Pate	222,976	23.	Bill Rogers	146,883	39.	Mark Lye	109,454
7.	George Burns	219,928	24.	Scott Simpson	141,323	40.	Gibby Gilbert	108,603
8.	Craig Stadler	206,291	25.	Leonard Thompson	138,826	41.	Bob Murphy	106,874
9.	Mike Reid	206,097	26.	Peter Jacobsen	138,562	42.	Calvin Peete	105,716
10.	Ray Floyd	192,993	27.	David Graham	137,819	43.	Phil Hancock	105,489
11.	Larry Nelson	182,715	28.	Gil Morgan	135,308	44.	Dan Pohl	105,008
12.	Bill Kratzert	175,771	29.	Lon Hinkle	134,913	45.	Jack Renner	97,501
13.	Jack Nicklaus	172,386	30.	Johnny Miller	127,117	46.	Fuzzy Zoeller	95,531
14.	Howard Twitty	166,190	31.	Dave Eichelberger	122,352	47.	Tom Weiskopf	88,260
15.	John Mahaffey	165,827	32.	Wayne Levi	120,145	48.	Jim Simons	85,527
16.	Bruce Lietzke	163,884	33.	Keith Fergus	119,614	49.	Ed Sneed	83,573
17.	Doug Tewell	161,684				50.	Hubert Green	83,307

THE BRITISH OPEN

Year	Winner	Score	Year	Winner	Score	Year	Winner	Score
1864	Tom Morris	160	1899	Harry Vardon	310	1940–1945 No championships played		
1865	Andrew Strath	162	1900	John H. Taylor	309	1946	Sam Snead	290
1866	Willie Park	169	1901	James Braid	309	1947	Fred Daly	293
1867	Tom Morris	170	1902	Alexander Herd	307	1948	Henry Cotton	294
1868	Tom Morris, Jr.	154	1903	Harry Vardon	300	1949	*Bobby Locke	283 (135)
1869	Tom Morris, Jr.	157	1904	Jack White	296	1950	Bobby Locke	279
1870	Tom Marris, Jr.	149	1905	James Braid	318	1951	Max Faulkner	285
1871	No championship played		1906	James Braid	300	1952	Bobby Locke	287
1872	Tom Morris, Jr.	166	1907	Arnaud Massy	312	1953	Ben Hogan	282
1873	Tom Kipp	179	1908	James Braid	291	1954	Peter Thomson	283
1874	Mungo Park	159	1909	John H. Taylor	295	1955	Peter Thomson	281
1875	Willie Park	166	1910	James Braid	299	1956	Peter Thomson	286
1876	Robert Martin	176	1911	Harry Vardon	303	1957	Bobby Locke	279
1877	Jamie Anderson	160	1912	Edward (Ted) Ray	295	1958	Peter Thomson	278 (139)
1878	Jamie Anderson	157	1913	John H. Taylor	304	1959	Gary Player	284
1879	Jamie Anderson	169	1914	Harry Vardon	306	1960	Kel Nagle	278
1880	Robert Ferguson	162	1915–1919 No championships played		1961	Arnold Palmer	284
1881	Robert Ferguson	170	1920	George Duncan	303	1962	Arnold Palmer	276
1882	Robert Ferguson	171	1921	*Jock Hutchison	296 (150)	1963	*Bob Charles	277
1883	*Willie Fernie	159	1922	Walter Hagen	300	1964	Tony Lema	279
1884	Jack Simpson	160	1923	Arthur G. Havers	295	1965	Peter Thomson	285
1885	Bob Martin	171	1924	Walter Hagen	301	1966	Jack Nicklaus	282
1886	David Brown	157	1925	James M. Barnes	300	1967	Roberto De Vicenzo	278
1887	Willie Park, Jr.	161	1926	Robert T. Jones, Jr.	291	1968	Gary Player	289
1888	Jack Burns	171	1927	Robert T. Jones, Jr.	285	1969	Tony Jacklin	280
1889	*Willie Park, Jr.	155 (158)	1928	Walter Hagen	292	1970	*Jack Nicklaus	283 (72)
1890	John Ball	164	1929	Walter Hagen	292	1971	Lee Trevino	278
1891	Hugh Kirkaldy	166	1930	Robert T. Jones, Jr.	291	1972	Lee Trevino	278
	(Championship extended from		1931	Tommy D. Armour	296	1973	Tom Weiskopf	276
	36 to 72 holes)		1932	Gene Sarazen	283	1974	Gary Player	282
1892	Harold H. Hilton	305	1933	*Denny Shute	292 (149)	1975	*Tom Watson	279 (71)
1893	William Auchterlonie	322	1934	Henry Cotton	283	1976	Johnny Miller	279
1894	John H. Taylor	326	1935	Alfred Perry	283	1977	Tom Watson	268
1895	John H. Taylor	322	1936	Alfred Padgham	287	1978	Jack Nicklaus	281
1896	*Harry Vardon	316 (157)	1937	Henry Cotton	290	1979	Severiano Ballesteros	283
1897	Harold H. Hilton	314	1938	R. A. Whitcombe	295	1980	Tom Watson	271
1898	Harry Vardon	307	1939	Richard Burton	290	1981	Bill Rogers	276

* Winner in playoff, figures in parentheses indicate playoff scores.

THE MASTERS

Year	Winner	Score	Year	Winner	Score	Year	Winner	Score
1934	Horton Smith	284	1952	Sam Snead	286	1967	Gay Brewer	280
1935	Gene Sarazen	282	1953	Ben Hogan	274	1968	Bob Goalby	277
1936	Horton Smith	285	1954	Sam Snead*	289	1969	George Archer	281
1937	Byron Nelson	283	1955	Cary Middlecoff	279	1970	Billy Casper*	279
1938	Henry Picard	285	1956	Jack Burke	289	1971	Charles Coody	279
1939	Ralph Guldahl	279	1957	Doug Ford	283	1972	Jack Nicklaus	286
1940	Jimmy Demaret	280	1958	Arnold Palmer	284	1973	Tommy Aaron	283
1941	Craig Wood	280	1959	Art Wall	284	1974	Gary Player	278
1942	Byron Nelson*	280	1960	Arnold Palmer	282	1975	Jack Nicklaus	276
1946	Herman Keiser	282	1961	Gary Player	280	1976	Ray Floyd	271
1947	Jimmy Demaret	281	1962	Arnold Palmer*	280	1977	Tom Watson	276
1948	Claude Harmon	279	1963	Jack Nicklaus	286	1978	Gary Player	277
1949	Sam Snead	282	1964	Arnold Palmer	276	1979	Fuzzy Zoeller*	280
1950	Jimmy Demaret	283	1965	Jack Nicklaus	271	1980	Severiano Ballesteros	275
1951	Ben Hogan	280	1966	Jack Nicklaus*	288	1981	Tom Watson	280

* Won in playoff.

THE UNITED STATES OPEN
SOURCE: U. S. Golf Association

Year	Site	Winner	Score	Year	Site	Winner	Score
1895	Newport, R.I.	Horace Rawlins	173	1937	Birmingham, Mich.	Ralph Guldahl	281
1896	Southampton, N.Y.	James Foulis	152	1938	Denver, Colo.	Ralph Guldahl	284
1897	Wheaton, Ill.	Joe Lloyd	162	1939	W. Conshohocken, Pa.	Byron Nelson	284*
1898	S. Hamilton, Mass.	Fred Herd	328	1940	Cleveland, Ohio	Lawson Little	287*
1899	Baltimore, Md.	Willie Smith	315	1941	Ft. Worth, Texas	Craig Wood	284
1900	Wheaton, Ill.	Harry Vardon	313	1942–1945	No Competition Held		
1901	S. Hamilton, Mass.	Willie Anderson	331*	1946	Cleveland, Ohio	Lloyd Mangrum	284*
1902	Garden City, N.Y.	Lawrence Auchterlonie	307	1947	Clayton, Mo.	Lew Worsham	282*
1903	Springfield, N.J.	Willie Anderson	307*	1948	Los Angeles, Calif.	Ben Hogan	276
1904	Golf, Ill.	Willie Anderson	303	1949	Medinah, Ill.	Cary Middlecoff	286
1905	S. Hamilton, Mass.	Willie Anderson	314	1950	Ardmore, Pa.	Ben Hogan	287*
1906	Lake Forest, Ill.	Alex Smith	295	1951	Birmingham, Mich.	Ben Hogan	287
1907	Philadelphia, Pa.	Alex Ross	302	1952	Dallas, Texas	Julius Boros	281
1908	S. Hamilton, Mass.	Fred McLeod	322*	1953	Oakmont, Pa.	Ben Hogan	283
1909	Englewood, N.J.	George Sargent	290	1954	Springfield, N.J.	Ed Furgol	284
1910	St. Martins, Pa.	Alex Smith	298*	1955	San Francisco, Calif.	Jack Fleck	287*
1911	Wheaton, Ill.	John J. McDermott	307*	1956	Rochester, N.Y.	Cary Middlecoff	281
1912	Buffalo, N.Y.	John J. McDermott	294	1957	Toledo, Ohio	Dick Mayer	282*
1913	Brookline, Mass.	Walter Hagen	290	1958	Tulsa, Okla.	Tommy Bolt	283
1914	Blue Island, Ill.	Francis Ouimet (A)	304*	1959	Mamaroneck, N.Y.	Bill Casper, Jr.	282
1915	Springfield, N.J.	Jerome D. Travers (A)	297	1960	Englewood, Colo.	Arnold Palmer	280
1916	Minneapolis, Minn.	Charles Evans, Jr. (A)	286	1961	Birmingham, Mich.	Gene Littler	281
1917–1918	No Competion Held			1962	Oakmont, Pa.	Jack Nicklaus	283*
1919	West Newton, Mass.	Water Hagen	301*	1963	Brookline, Mass.	Julius Boros	293*
1920	Toledo, Ohio	Edward Ray	295	1964	Washington, D.C.	Ken Venturi	278
1921	Chevy Chase, Md.	James M. Barnes	289	1965	St. Louis, Mo.	Gary Player	282*
1922	Glencoe, Ill.	Gene Sarazen	288	1966	San Francisco, Calif.	Bill Casper, Jr.	278*
1923	Inwood, N.Y.	Robert T. Jones, Jr. (A)	296*	1967	Springfield, N.J.	Jack Nicklaus	275
1924	Birmingham, Mich.	Cyril Walker	297	1968	Rochester, N.Y.	Lee Trevino	275
1925	Worcester, Mass.	William Macfarlane	291*	1969	Houston, Texas	Orville Moody	281
1926	Columbus, Ohio	Robert T. Jones, Jr. (A)	293	1970	Chaska, Minn.	Tony Jacklin	281
1927	Oakmont, Pa.	Tommy Armour	301*	1971	Ardmore, Pa.	Lee Trevino	280*
1928	Mateson, Ill.	Johnny Farrell	294*	1972	Pebble Beach, Calif.	Jack Nicklaus	290
1929	Mamaroneck, N.Y.	Robert T. Jones, Jr. (A)	294*	1973	Oakmont, Pa.	John Miller	279
1930	Minneapolis, Minn.	Robert T. Jones, Jr. (A)	287	1974	Mamaroneck, N.Y.	Hale Irwin	287
1931	Toledo, Ohio	Billy Burke	292*	1975	Medinah, Ill.	Lou Graham	287*
1932	Flushing, N.Y.	Gene Sarazen	286	1976	Duluth, Ga.	Jerry Pate	277
1933	Glen View, Ill.	John G. Goodman (A)	287	1977	Tulsa, Okla.	Hubert Green	278
1934	Ardmore, Pa.	Olin Dutra	293	1978	Denver, Colo.	Andy North	285
1935	Oakmont, Pa.	Sam Parks, Jr.	299	1979	Toledo, Ohio	Hale Irwin	284
1936	Springfield, N.J.	Tony Manero	282	1980	Springfield, N.J.	Jack Nicklaus	272
				1981	Ardmore, Pa.	Dave Graham	273

(A) Amateur.   *Won Playoff

PGA CHAMPIONSHIP
SOURCE: P.G.A.

Year	Winner	Score	Year	Winner	Score	Year	Winner	Score
1916	James M. Barnes	1 up	1938	Paul Runyan	8 & 7	1960	Jay Hebert	281
1917–1918	No Competition Held		1939	Henry Picard	1 up	1961	Jerry Barber	277*
1919	James M. Barnes	6 & 5	1940	Byron Nelson	1 up	1962	Gary Player	278
1920	Jock Hutchison	1 up	1941	Vic Ghezzi	1 up	1963	Jack Nicklaus	279
1921	Walter Hagen	3 & 2	1942	Sam Snead	2 & 1	1964	Bobby Nichols	271
1922	Gene Sarazen	4 & 3	1943	No Competition Held		1965	Dave Marr	280
1923	Gene Sarazen	1 up	1944	Bob Hamilton	1 up	1966	Al Geiberger	280
1924	Walter Hagen	2 up	1945	Byron Nelson	4 & 3	1967	Don January	281*
1925	Walter Hagen	6 & 5	1946	Ben Hogan	6 & 4	1968	Julius Boros	281
1926	Walter Hagen	5 & 3	1947	Jim Ferrier	2 & 1	1969	Ray Floyd	276
1927	Walter Hagen	1 up	1948	Ben Hogan	7 & 6	1970	Dave Stockton	279
1928	Leo Diegel	6 & 5	1949	Sam Snead	3 & 2	1971	Jack Nicklaus	281
1929	Leo Diegel	6 & 4	1950	Chandler Harper	4 & 3	1972	Gary Player	281
1930	Tommy Armour	1 up	1951	Sam Snead	7 & 6	1973	Jack Nicklaus	277
1931	Tom Creavy	2 & 1	1952	Jim Turnesa	1 up	1974	Lee Trevino	276
1932	Olin Dutra	4 & 3	1953	Walter Burkemo	2 & 1	1975	Jack Nicklaus	276
1933	Gene Sarazen	5 & 4	1954	Chick Harbert	4 & 3	1976	Dave Stockton	281
1934	Paul Runyan	1 up	1955	Doug Ford	4 & 3	1977	Lanny Wadkins	282*
1935	Johnny Revolta	5 & 4	1956	Jack Burke	3 & 2	1978	John Mahaffey	276*
1936	Denny Shute	3 & 2	1957	Lionel Hebert	2 & 1	1979	Dave Graham	272*
1937	Denny Shute	1 up	1958	Dow Finsterwald	276	1980	Jack Nicklaus	274
			1959	Bob Rosburg	277	1981	Larry Nelson	273

*Won Playoff

THE CANADIAN OPEN

Year	Winner	Score	Year	Winner	Score	Year	Winner	Score
1950	Jim Ferrier	271	1960	Art Wall, Jr.	269	1971	Lee Trevino	275*
1951	Jim Ferrier	273	1961	Jacky Cupit	270	1972	Gay Brewer	275
1952	John Palmer	263	1962	Ted Kroll	278	1973	Tom Weiskopf	278
1953	Dave Douglas	273	1963	Doug Ford	280	1974	Bobby Nichols	270
1954	Pat Fletcher	280	1964	Kel Nagle	277	1975	Tom Weiskopf	274*
1955	Arnold Palmer	265	1965	Gene Littler	273	1976	Jerry Pate	267
1956	Doug Sanders (A)	273	1966	Don Massengale	280	1977	Lee Trevino	280
1957	George Bayer	271	1967	Bill Casper	279*	1978	Bruce Lietzke	283
1958	Wesley Ellis, Jr.	267	1968	Bob Charles	274	1979	Lee Trevino	281
1959	Doug Ford	276	1969	Tommy Aaron	275*	1980	Bob Gilder	274
			1970	Kermit Zarley	279	1981	Peter Oosterhuis	280

(A) Amateur.   *Won Playoff

PROFESSIONAL GOLF'S LEADING MONEY WINNERS, 1935–1980

Year	Player	Winnings	Year	Player	Winnings	Year	Player	Winnings
1935	Johnny Revolta	$ 9,543	1950	Sam Snead	$ 35,758	1965	Jack Nicklaus	$140,752
1936	Horton Smith	7,682	1951	Lloyd Mangrum	26,088	1966	Billy Casper	121,944
1937	Harry Cooper	14,138	1952	Julius Boros	37,032	1967	Jack Nicklaus	188,998
1938	Sam Snead	19,534	1953	Lew Worsham	34,002	1968	Billy Casper	205,168
1939	Henry Picard	10,303	1954	Bob Toski	65,819	1969	Frank Beard	175,223
1940	Ben Hogan	10,655	1955	Julius Boros	63,121	1970	Lee Trevino	157,037
1941	Ben Hogan	18,358	1956	Ted Kroll	72,835	1971	Jack Nicklaus	244,490
1942	Ben Hogan	13,143	1957	Dick Mayer	65,835	1972	Jack Nicklaus	320,542
1943	No statistics compiled		1958	Arnold Palmer	42,607	1973	Jack Nicklaus	308,362
1944	Byron Nelson	37,967	1959	Art Wall, Jr.	52,167	1974	Johnny Miller	353,021
1945	Byron Nelson	63,335	1960	Arnold Palmer	75,262	1975	Jack Nicklaus	298,149
1946	Ben Hogan	42,556	1961	Gary Player	64,540	1976	Jack Nicklaus	266,426
1947	Jimmy Demaret	27,936	1962	Arnold Palmer	81,448	1977	Tom Watson	310,653
1948	Ben Hogan	32,112	1963	Arnold Palmer	128,230	1978	Tom Watson	362,429
1949	Sam Snead	31,593	1964	Jack Nicklaus	113,284	1979	Tom Watson	462,636
						1980	Tom Watson	530,808

RYDER CUP MATCHES (Professionals)

Year	Played at	Results	Year	Played at	Results
1927	Worcester C.C., Worcester, Mass.	U.S. 9½–Britain 2½	1959	Eldorado C.C., Palm Desert, Calif.	U.S. 8½–Britain 3½
1929	Moortown, England,	Britain 7 –U.S. 5	1961	Royal Lytham and St. Anne's Golf Club, St. Anne's-On-The-Sea, England	U.S. 14½–Britain 9½
1931	Scioto C.C., Columbus, Ohio	U.S. 9 –Britain 3			
1933	Southport & Ainsdale Courses, England	Britain 6½–U.S. 5½	1963	East Lake C.C., Atlanta, Georgia	U.S. 23 –Britain 9
1935	Ridgewood C.C., Ridgewood, N.J.	U.S. 9 –Britain 3	1965	Royal Birkdale Golf Club, Southport, England	U.S. 19½–Britain 12½
1937	Southport & Ainsdale Courses, England	U.S. 8 –Britain 4	1967	Champions Golf Club, Houston	U.S. 23½–Britain 8½
	Ryder Cup Matches not held during World War II years.		1969	Royal Birkdale Golf Club, Southport, England	U.S. 16–Tie –Britain 16
1947	Portland Golf Club, Portland, Oregon	U.S. 11 –Britain 1	1971	Old Warson Country Club, St. Louis, Mo.	U.S. 18½–Britain 13½
1949	Ganton Golf Course, Scarborough, England	U.S. 7 –Britain 5	1973	Muirfield, Scotland	U.S. 18 –Britain 13
1951	Pinehurst C.C., Pinehurst, N.C.	U.S. 9½–Britain 2½	1975	Laurel Valley Golf Club, Ligonier, Pa.	U.S. 21 –Britain 11
1953	Wentworth, England	U.S. 6½–Britain 5½	1977	Royal Lytham and St. Annes Golf Club, England	U.S. 12½–Britain 7½
1955	Thunderbird Ranch and C.C., Palm Springs, Calif.	U.S. 8 –Britain 4	1979	Greenbrier Hotel Resort, White Sulphur Sprs., W.Va.	U.S. 17 –Europe 11
1957	Lindrick Golf Club, Yorkshire, England	Britain 7½–U.S. 4½	1981	Walton Heath Golf Club, England	U.S. 18½–Europe 9½

PGA HALL OF FAME SOURCE: P.G.A.

Member	Year Elected	Member	Year Elected	Member	Year Elected
Willie Anderson	1940	Johnny Farrell	1961	Byron Nelson	1953
Tommy Armour	1940	Doug Ford	1975	Francis Ouimet	1940
Jim Barnes	1940	Vic Ghezzi	1965	Arnold Palmer	1980
Patty Berg	1978	Ralph Guldahl	1963	Henry Picard	1961
Julius Boros	1974	Walter Hagen	1940	Johnny Revolta	1963
Mike Brady	1960	Chick Harbert	1968	Paul Runyan	1959
Billy Burke	1966	Chandler Harper	1969	Gene Sarazen	1940
Jack Burke, Jr.	1975	Dutch Harrison	1962	Denny Shute	1957
Harry Cooper	1959	Ben Hogan	1953	Alex Smith	1940
Bobby Cruickshank	1967	Jock Hutchison, Sr.	1959	Horton Smith	1958
Jimmy Demaret	1960	Bobby Jones	1940	MacDonald Smith	1954
Roberto De Vicenzo	1978	Lawson Little	1961	Sam Snead	1953
Leo Diegel	1955	Lloyd Mangrum	1964	Jerry Travers	1940
Ed Dudley	1964	John McDermott	1940	Walter Travis	1940
Olin Dutra	1962	Fred McLeod	1960	Craig Wood	1956
Chick Evans	1940	Cary Middlecoff	1974	Babe Zaharias	1976

WORLD AMATEUR TEAM CHAMPIONSHIPS SOURCE: U. S. Golf Association

Year	Men's Champion	Women's Champion	Site
1958	Australia	—	St. Andrews, Scotland
1960	United States	—	Ardmore, Pa.
1962	United States	—	Kanawa, Japan
1964	Great Britain & Ireland	—	Rome, Italy
		France	St. Germain, France
1966	Australia	United States	Mexico City, Mexico
1968	United States	United States	Melbourne, Australia
1970	United States	United States	Madrid, Spain
1972	United States	United States	Buenos Aires, Argentina
1974	United States	United States	LaRomana, Dominican Rep.
1976	Great Britain & Ireland	United States	Algarve, Portugal
1978	United States	Australia	Pacific Harbour, Fiji
1980	United States	United States	Pinehurst, North Carolina

LPGA TOTAL MONEY WINNERS: 1980
SOURCE: L.P.G.A.

Rank	Name	Amount	Rank	Name	Amount	Rank	Name	Amount
1.	Beth Daniel	$231,000	18.	Patty Hayes	$58,145	34.	Jan Stephenson	$41,318
2.	Donna Caponi Young	220,619	19.	Dot Germain	56,823	35.	Debbie Austin	41,302
3.	Amy Alcott	219,887	20.	Pat Meyers	55,625	36.	Kathy Postlewait	41,251
4.	Nancy Lopez-Melton	209,078	21.	Judy Rankin	54,182	37.	Pam Higgins	38,937
5.	JoAnne Carner	185,915	22.	Beth Solomon	51,352	38.	Alice Ritzman	38,024
6.	Pat Bradley	183,377	23.	Shelley Hamlin	50,843	39.	Silvia Bertolaccini	37,674
7.	Sally Little	139,127	24.	Kathy Whitworth	48,392	40.	Kathy McMullen	36,112
8.	Jane Blalock	127,873	25.	Janet Alex	47,613	41.	Carolyn Hill	35,908
9.	Jo Ann Washam	107,063	26.	Barbara Barrow	46,633	42.	Vicki Fergon	34,541
10.	Sandra Post	102,822	27.	Dale Lundquist	45,335	43.	M. J. Smith	33,719
11.	Hollis Stacy	89,913	28.	Bonnie Lauer	44,307	44.	Cathy Morse	31,662
12.	Sandra Palmer	73,598	29.	Sandra Spuzich	43,295	45.	Marlene Floyd	30,858
13.	Donna H. White	70,017	30.	Barbara Moxness	43,287	46.	Judy Clark	30,648
14.	Jerilyn Britz	68,069	31.	Julie Stanger	42,706	47.	Vivian Brownlee	30,245
15.	Debbie Massey	65,239	32.	Penny Pulz	42,061	48.	Peggy Conley	29,503
16.	Lori Garbacz	61,120	33.	Myra Van Hoose	41,396	49.	Mary Dwyer	28,516
17.	Janet Coles	58,377				50.	Betsy King	28,480

LEADING LPGA MONEY WINNERS BY YEAR, 1948–1980

Year	Player	Amount	Year	Player	Amount	Year	Player	Amount
1948	Babe Zaharias	$ 3,400.00*	1959	Betsy Rawls	$26,774.39	1970	Kathy Whitworth	$ 30,235.01
1949	Babe Zaharias	4,650.00*	1960	Louise Suggs	16,892.12	1971	Kathy Whitworth	41,181.75
1950	Babe Zaharias	14,800.00*	1961	Mickey Wright	22,236.21	1972	Kathy Whitworth	65,063.99
1951	Babe Zaharias	15,087.00*	1962	Mickey Wright	21,641.99	1973	Kathy Whitworth	82,864.25
1952	Betsy Rawls	14,505.00	1963	Mickey Wright	31,269.50	1974	JoAnne Carner	87,094.04
1953	Louise Suggs	19,816.25	1964	Mickey Wright	29,800.00	1975	Sandra Palmer	76,374.51
1954	Patty Berg	16,011.00	1965	Kathy Whitworth	28,658.00	1976	Judy Rankin	150,734.28
1955	Patty Berg	16,492.34	1966	Kathy Whitworth	33,517.50	1977	Judy Rankin	122,890.44
1956	Marlene Hagge	20,235.50	1967	Kathy Whitworth	32,937.50	1978	Nancy Lopez	189,813.83
1957	Patty Berg	16,272.00	1968	Kathy Whitworth	48,379.50	1979	Nancy Lopez	197,488.61
1958	Beverly Hanson	12,639.55	1969	Carol Mann	49,152.50	1980	Beth Daniel	231,000.42

* Approximate Figure

WOMEN'S OPEN CHAMPIONSHIP
SOURCE: U.S. Golf Association

Year	Site	Winner	Score	Year	Site	Winner	Score
1946	Spokane, Wash.	Patty Berg	5 & 4	1964	Chula Vista, Calif.	Mickey Wright	290*
1947	Greensboro, N.C.	Betty Jameson	295*	1965	Northfield, N.J.	Carol Mann	290
1948	Northfield, N.J.	Babe Zaharias	300	1966	Minneapolis, Minn.	Sandra Spuzich	297
1949	Landover, Md.	Louise Suggs	291	1967	Hot Springs, Va.	Catherine Lacoste (A)	294
1950	Wichita, Kans.	Mildred Zaharias	291	1968	Fleetwood, Pa.	Susie Berning	289
1951	Atlanta, Ga.	Betsy Rawls	293	1969	Pensacola, Fla.	Donna Caponi	294
1952	Philadelphia, Pa.	Louise Suggs	284	1970	Muskogee, Okla.	Donna Caponi	287
1953	Rochester, N.Y.	Betsy Rawls	302*	1971	Erie, Pa.	JoAnne Carner	288
1954	Peabody, Mass.	Babe Zaharias	291	1972	Mamaroneck, N.Y.	Susie Berning	299
1955	Wichita, Kans.	Fay Crocker	299	1973	Rochester, N.Y.	Susie Berning	290
1956	Duluth, Minn.	Kathy Cornelius	302*	1974	LaGrange, Ill.	Sandra Haynie	295
1957	Mamaroneck, N.Y.	Betsy Rawls	299	1975	Northfield, N.J.	Sandra Palmer	295
1958	Bloomfield Hills, Mich.	Mickey Wright	290	1976	Springfield, Pa.	JoAnne Carner	292*
1959	Pittsburg, Pa.	Mickey Wright	287	1977	Chaska, Minn.	Hollis Stacy	292
1960	Worcester, Mass.	Betsy Rawls	292	1978	Indianapolis, Ind.	Hollis Stacy	289
1961	Springfield, N.J.	Mickey Wright	293	1979	Fairfield, Conn.	Jerilyn Britz	284
1962	Myrtle Beach, S.C.	Murle Lindstrom	301	1980	Nashville, Tenn.	Amy Alcott	280
1963	Cincinnati, Ohio	Mary Mills	289	1981	LaGrange, Ill.	Pat Bradley	279

(A) Amateur.   *Won Playoff

LPGA CHAMPIONSHIP
SOURCE: L.P.G.A.

Year	Winner	Score	Year	Winner	Score	Year	Winner	Score
1955	Beverly Hanson	4 & 3	1964	Mary Mills	278	1973	Mary Mills	288
1956	Marlene Hagge	291*	1965	Sandra Haynie	279	1974	Sandra Haynie	288
1957	Louise Suggs	285	1966	Gloria Ehret	282	1975	Kathy Whitworth	288
1958	Mickey Wright	288	1967	Kathy Whitworth	284	1976	Betty Burfeindt	287
1959	Betsy Rawls	288	1968	Sandra Post	294*	1977	Chako Higuchi	279
1960	Mickey Wright	292	1969	Betsy Rawls	293	1978	Nancy Lopez	275
1961	Mickey Wright	287	1970	Shirley Englehorn	285*	1979	Donna Caponi Young	279
1962	Judy Kimball	282	1971	Kathy Whitworth	288	1980	Sally Little	285
1963	Mickey Wright	294	1972	Kathy Ahern	293	1981	Donna Caponi	280

*Won Playoff

LPGA HALL OF FAME
SOURCE: L.P.G.A.

Member	Year Elected	Member	Year Elected	Member	Year Elected
Patty Berg	1951	Babe Zaharias	1951	Kathy Whitworth	1975
Betty Jameson	1951	Betsy Rawls	1960	Sandra Haynie	1977
Louise Suggs	1951	Mickey Wright	1964	Carol Mann	1977

U.S. AMATEUR CHAMPIONSHIP WINNERS

Source: U.S. Golf Association

1895 Charles B. Macdonald	1915 Robert A. Gardner	1937 John Goodman	1961 Jack Nicklaus
1896 H. J. Whigham	1916 Charles Evans, Jr.	1938 William P. Turnesa	1962 Labron Harris, Jr.
1897 H. J. Whigham	1917–1918 No Competition	1939 Marvin H. Ward	1963 Deane R. Beman
1898 Findlay S. Douglas	1919 S. Davidson Herron	1940 Richard D. Chapman	1964 William C. Campbell
1899 H. M. Harriman	1920 Charles Evans, Jr.	1941 Marvin H. Ward	1965 Robert J. Murphy, Jr.
1900 Walter J. Travis	1921 Jesse P. Guilford	1942–1945 No Competition	1966 Gary Cowan
1901 Walter J. Travis	1922 Jess W. Sweetser	1946 S. E. (Ted) Bishop	1967 Robert B. Dickson
1902 Louis N. James	1923 Max R. Marston	1947 R. H. (Skee) Riegel	1968 Bruce Fleisher
1903 Walter J. Travis	1924 Robert T. Jones, Jr.	1948 William P. Turnesa	1969 Steven Melnyk
1904 H. Chandler Egan	1924 Robert T. Jones, Jr.	1949 Charles R. Coe	1970 Lanny Wadkins
1905 H. Chandler Egan	1926 George Von Elm	1950 Sam Urzetta	1971 Gary Cowan
1906 Eben M. Byers	1927 Robert T. Jones, Jr.	1951 Billy Maxwell	1972 Marvin Giles
1907 Jerome D. Travers	1928 Robert T. Jones, Jr.	1952 Jack Westland	1973 Craig Stadler
1908 Jerome D. Travers	1929 Harrison R. Johnston	1953 Gene Littler	1974 Jerome Pate
1909 Robert A. Gardner	1930 Robert T. Jones, Jr.	1954 Arnold Palmer	1975 Fred Ridley
1910 William C. Fownes, Jr.	1931 Francis Ouimet	1955 E. Harvie Ward, Jr.	1976 Bill Sander
1911 Harold H. Hilton	1932 C. Ross Somerville	1956 E. Harvie Ward, Jr.	1977 John Fought
1912 Jerome D. Travers	1933 George T. Dunlap, Jr.	1957 Hillman Robbins, Jr.	1978 John Cook
1913 Jerome D. Travers	1934 Lawson Little	1958 Charles R. Coe	1979 Mark O'Meara
1914 Francis Ouimet	1935 Lawson Little	1959 Jack Nicklaus	1980 Hal Sutton
	1936 John W. Fischer	1960 Deane R. Beman	1981 Nathaniel Crosby

WOMEN'S AMATEUR CHAMPIONSHIP WINNERS

Source: U.S. Golf Association

1951 Dorothy Kirby	1958 Anne Quast	1966 JoAnne Carner	1974 Cynthia Hill
1952 Jacqueline Pung	1959 Barbara McIntire	1967 Mary Lou Dill	1975 Beth Daniel
1953 Mary Faulk	1960 JoAnne Gunderson	1968 JoAnne Carner	1976 Donna Horton
1954 Barbara Romack	1961 Anne Quast Decker	1969 Catherine Lacoste	1977 Beth Daniel
1955 Patricia Lesser	1962 JoAnne Gunderson	1970 Martha Wilkinson	1978 Cathy Sherk
1956 Marlene Stewart	1963 Anne Quast Welts	1971 Laura Baugh	1979 Carolyn Hill
1957 JoAnne Gunderson	1964 Barbara McIntire	1972 Mary Budke	1980 Juli Inkster
	1965 Jean Ashley	1973 Carol Semple	1981 Juli Inkster

THE WALKER CUP (Men Amateur Golfers)

Source: U.S. Golf Association

Year	Results	Site	Year	Results	Site
1922	U.S. 8, Great Britain 4	Southampton, N.Y.	1955	U.S. 10, Great Britain 2	St. Andrews, Scotland
1923	U.S. 6, Great Britain 5	St. Andrews, Scotland	1957	U.S. 8, Great Britain 3	Minneapolis, Minn.
1924	U.S. 9, Great Britain 3	Garden City, N.Y.	1959	U.S. 9, Great Britain 3	Muirfield, Scotland
1926	U.S. 6, Great Britain 5	St. Andrews, Scotland	1961	U.S. 11, Great Britain 1	Seattle, Wash.
1928	U.S. 11, Great Britain 1	Wheaton, Ill.	1963	U.S. 12, Great Britain 8	Turnberry, Scotland
1930	U.S. 10, Great Britain 2	Sandwich, England	1965	U.S. 11, Great Britain 11	Baltimore, Md.
1932	U.S. 8, Great Britain 1	Brookline, Mass.	1967	U.S. 13, Great Britain 7	Sandwich, England
1934	U.S. 9, Great Britain 2	St. Andrews, Scotland	1969	U.S. 10, Great Britain 8	Milwaukee, Wis.
1936	U.S. 9, Great Britain 0	Clementon, N.J.	1971	Great Britain 13, U.S. 11	St. Andrews, Scotland
1938	Great Britain 7, U.S. 4	St. Andrews, Scotland	1973	U.S. 14, Great Britain 10	Brookline, Mass.
1947	U.S. 8, Great Britain 4	St. Andrews, Scotland	1975	U.S. 15½, Great Britain 8½	St. Andrews, Scotland
1949	U.S. 10, Great Britain 2	Mamaroneck, N.Y.	1977	U.S. 16, Great Britain 8	Southampton, N.Y.
1951	U.S. 6, Great Britain 3	Southport, England	1979	U.S. 15½, Great Britain 8½	Muirfield, Scotland
1953	U.S. 9, Great Britain 3	Marion, Mass.	1981	U.S. 15, Great Britain 9	Pebble Beach, Calif.

THE CURTIS CUP (Women Amateur Golfers)

Source: U.S. Golf Association

Year	Results	Site	Year	Results	Site
1932	U.S. 5½, British Isles 3½	Wentworth, England	1960	U.S. 6½, British Isles 2½	Worksop, England
1934	U.S. 6½, British Isles 7½	Chevy Chase, Md.	1962	U.S. 8, British Isles 1	Colorado Sprs., Colo.
1936	U.S. 4½, British Isles 4½	Gleneagles, Scotland	1964	U.S. 10½, British Isles 7½	Porthcawl, South Wales
1938	U.S. 5½, British Isles 3½	Manchester, Mass.	1966	U.S. 13, British Isles 5	Hot Springs, Va.
1948	U.S. 6½, British Isles 2½	Southport, England	1968	U.S. 10½, British Isles 7½	Newcastle, No. Ireland
1950	U.S. 7½, British Isles 1½	Williamsville, N.Y.	1970	U.S. 11½, British Isles 6½	West Newton, Mass.
1952	British Isles 5, U.S. 4	Muirfield, Scotland	1972	U.S. 10, British Isles 8	Western Gailes, Scotland
1954	U.S. 6, British Isles 3	Ardmore, Pa.	1974	U.S. 13, British Isles 5	San Francisco, Calif.
1956	British Isles 5, U.S. 4	Sandwich Bay, England	1976	U.S. 11½, British Isles 6½	St. Annes-On-Sea, Eng.
1958	British Isles 4½, U.S. 4½	West Newton, Mass.	1978	U.S. 12, British Isles 6	Rye, N.Y.
			1980	U.S. 13, British Isles 5	Chepstow, Wales

OTHER GOLF CHAMPIONS

Year	NCAA Team	NCAA Individual	Women's Intercollegiate
1968	Florida	Grier Jones, Oklahoma State	Gail Sykes, Odessa (Texas)
1969	Houston	Bob Clark, California (L.A.) State	Jane Bastanchury, Arizona State
1970	Houston	John Mahaffey, Houston	Cathy Gaughan, Arizona State
1971	Texas	Ben Crenshaw, Texas	Shelley Hamlin, Stanford
1972	Texas	Ben Crenshaw & Tom Kite, Texas	Ann Laughlin, Miami (Florida)
1973	Florida	Ben Crenshaw, Texas	Bonnie Lauer, Michigan State
1974	Wake Forest	Curtis Strange, Wake Forest	Mary Budke, Oregon State
1975	Wake Forest	Jay Haas, Wake Forest	Barbara Barrow, San Diego State
1976	Oklahoma State	Scott Simpson, Southern California	Nancy Lopez, Tulsa
1977	Houston	Scott Simpson, Southern California	Cathy Morse, Miami (Florida)
1978	Oklahoma State	David Edwards, Oklahoma State	Deborah Petrizzi, Texas-Austin
1979	Ohio State	Gary Hallberg, Wake Forest	Kyle O'Brien, Southern Methodist
1980	Oklahoma State	Jay Don Blake, Utah State	Patty Sheehan, San Jose State
1981	Brigham Young	Ron Commans, Southern California	Terri Moody, Florida State

TENNIS

United States Tennis Association (USTA); 51 East 42nd Street, New York 10017

USTA NATIONAL CHAMPIONS (U.S. Open since 1968)

Men's Singles

1926 Rene Lacoste (France)	1940 Don McNeill (U.S.A.)	1954 Vic Seixas (U.S.A.)	1968 Arthur Ashe (U.S.A.)
1927 Rene Lacoste (France)	1941 Bobby Riggs (U.S.A.)	1955 Tony Trabert (U.S.A.)	1969 Rod Laver (Australia)
1928 Henri Cochet (France)	1942 Ted Schroeder (U.S.A.)	1956 Ken Rosewall (Australia)	1970 Ken Rosewall (Australia)
1929 Bill Tilden (U.S.A.)	1943 Joe Hunt (U.S.A.)	1957 Mal Anderson (Australia)	1971 Stan Smith (U.S.A.)
1930 John Doeg (U.S.A.)	1944 Frank Parker (U.S.A.)	1958 Ashley Cooper (Australia)	1972 Ilie Nastase (Romania)
1931 Ellsworth Vines (U.S.A.)	1945 Frank Parker (U.S.A.)	1959 Neale Fraser (Australia)	1973 John Newcombe (Australia)
1932 Ellsworth Vines (U.S.A.)	1946 Jack Kramer (U.S.A.)	1960 Neale Fraser (Australia)	1974 Jimmy Connors (U.S.A.)
1933 Fred Perry (England)	1947 Jack Kramer (U.S.A.)	1961 Roy Emerson (Australia)	1975 Manuel Orantes (Spain)
1934 Fred Perry (England)	1948 Pancho Gonzales (U.S.)	1962 Rod Laver (Australia)	1976 Jimmy Connors (U.S.A.)
1935 Wilmer Allison (U.S.A.)	1949 Pancho Gonzalez (U.S.A.)	1963 Rafael Osuna (Mexico)	1977 Guillermo Vilas (Argentina)
1936 Fred Perry (England)	1950 Art Larsen (U.S.A.)	1964 Roy Emerson (Australia)	1978 Jimmy Connors (U.S.A.)
1937 Don Budge (U.S.A.)	1951 Frank Sedgman (Australia)	1965 Manuel Santana (Spain)	1979 John McEnroe (U.S.A.)
1938 Don Budge (U.S.A.)	1952 Frank Sedgman (Australia)	1966 Fred Stolle (Australia)	1980 John McEnroe (U.S.A.)
1939 Bobby Riggs (U.S.A.)	1953 Tony Trabert (U.S.A.)	1967 John Newcombe (Australia)	1981 John McEnroe (U.S.A.)

Men's Doubles

1926 Vinnie Richards–R. Norris Williams	1945 Gardnar Mulloy–Bill Talbert	1964 Chuck McKinley–Dennis Ralston
1927 Bill Tilden–Frank Hunter	1946 Gardnar Mulloy–Bill Talbert	1965 Roy Emerson–Fred Stolle
1928 George Lott–John Hennessey	1947 Jack Kramer–Ted Schroeder	1966 Roy Emerson–Fred Stolle
1929 George Lott–John Doeg	1948 Gardnar Mulloy–Bill Talbert	1967 John Newcombe–Tony Roche
1930 George Lott–John Doeg	1949 Jack Bromwich–William Sidwell	1968 Stan Smith–Bob Lutz
1931 Wilmer Allison–John Van Ryn	1950 Jack Bromwich–Frank Sedgman	1969 Ken Rosewall–Fred Stolle
1932 Ellsworth Vines–Keith Gledhill	1951 Frank Sedgman–Ken McGregor	1970 Nikki Pilic–Pierre Barthes
1933 George Lott–Lester Stoefen	1952 Vic Seixas–Mervyn Rose	1971 John Newcombe–Roger Taylor
1934 George Lott–Lester Stoefen	1953 Rex Hartwig–Mervyn Rose	1972 Cliff Drysdale–Roger Taylor
1935 Wilmer Allison–John Van Ryn	1954 Vic Seixas–Tony Trabert	1973 Owen Davidson–John Newcombe
1936 Don Budge–Gene Mako	1955 Kosei Kamo–Atsushi Miyagi	1974 Bob Lutz–Stan Smith
1937 Gottfried von Cramm–Henner Henkel	1956 Lew Hoad–Ken Rosewall	1975 Jimmy Connors–Ilie Nastase
1938 Don Budge–Gene Mako	1957 Ashley Cooper–Neale Fraser	1976 Marty Riessen–Tom Okker
1939 Adrian Quist–Jack Bromwich	1958 Alex Olmedo–Ham Richardson	1977 Bob Hewitt–Frew McMillan
1940 Jack Kramer–Ted Schroeder	1959 Neale Fraser–Roy Emerson	1978 Stan Smith–Bob Lutz
1941 Jack Kramer–Ted Schroeder	1960 Neale Fraser–Roy Emerson	1979 John McEnroe–Peter Fleming
1942 Gardnar Mulloy–Bill Talbert	1961 Chuck McKinley–Dennis Ralston	1980 Stan Smith–Bob Lutz
1943 Jack Kramer–Frank Parker	1962 Rafael Osuna–Antonio Palafox	1981 John McEnroe–Peter Fleming
1944 Don McNeill–Bob Falkenburg	1963 Chuck McKinley–Dennis Ralston	

Women's Singles

1926 Molla Bjurstedt Mallory (U.S.A.)	1945 Sarah Palfrey Cooke (U.S.A.)	1964 Maria Bueno (Brazil)
1927 Helen Wills (U.S.A.)	1946 Pauline Betz (U.S.A.)	1965 Margaret Smith (Australia)
1928 Helen Wills (U.S.A.)	1947 Louise Brough (U.S.A.)	1966 Maria Bueno (Brazil)
1929 Helen Wills (U.S.A.)	1948 Margaret Osborne du Pont (U.S.A.)	1967 Billie Jean King (U.S.A.)
1930 Betty Nuthall (England)	1949 Margaret Osborne du Pont (U.S.A.)	1968 Virginia Wade (England)
1931 Helen Wills Moody (U.S.A.)	1950 Margaret Osborne du Pont (U.S.A.)	1969 Margaret Smith Court (Australia)
1932 Helen Hull Jacobs (U.S.A.)	1951 Maureen Connolly (U.S.A.)	1970 Margaret Court (Australia)
1933 Helen Hull Jacobs (U.S.A.)	1952 Maureen Connolly (U.S.A.)	1971 Billie Jean King (U.S.A.)
1934 Helen Hull Jacobs (U.S.A.)	1953 Maureen Connolly (U.S.A.)	1972 Billie Jean King (U.S.A.)
1935 Helen Hull Jacobs (U.S.A.)	1954 Doris Hart (U.S.A.)	1973 Margaret Court (Australia)
1936 Alice Marble (U.S.A.)	1955 Doris Hart (U.S.A.)	1974 Billie Jean King (U.S.A.)
1937 Anita Lizana (Chile)	1956 Shirley Fry (U.S.A.)	1975 Chris Evert (U.S.A.)
1938 Alice Marble (U.S.A.)	1957 Althea Gibson (U.S.A.)	1976 Chris Evert (U.S.A.)
1939 Alice Marble (U.S.A.)	1958 Althea Gibson (U.S.A.)	1977 Chris Evert (U.S.A.)
1940 Alice Marble (U.S.A.)	1959 Maria Bueno (Brazil)	1978 Chris Evert (U.S.A.)
1941 Sarah Palfrey Cooke (U.S.A.)	1960 Darlene Hard (U.S.A.)	1979 Tracy Austin (U.S.A.)
1942 Pauline Betz (U.S.A.)	1961 Darlene Hard (U.S.A.)	1980 Chris Evert Lloyd (U.S.A.)
1943 Pauline Betz (U.S.A.)	1962 Margaret Smith (Australia)	1981 Tracy Austin (U.S.A.)
1944 Pauline Betz (U.S.A.)	1963 Maria Bueno (Brazil)	

Women's Doubles

1926 Elizabeth Ryan–Eleanor Goss	1954 Shirley Fry–Doris Hart
1927 Mrs. Kathleen McKane Godfree–Ermyntrude Harvey	1955 Louise Brough–Mrs. Margaret Osborne duPont
1928 Mrs. Hazel Wightman–Helen Wills	1956 Louise Brough–Mrs. Margaret Osborne duPont
1929 Mrs. Phoebe Watson–Mrs. L. R. C. Michell	1957 Louise Brough–Mrs. Margaret Osborne duPont
1930 Betty Nuthall–Sarah Palfrey	1958 Jeanne Arth–Darlene Hard
1931 Betty Nuthall–Mrs. Eileen Whittingstall	1959 Jeanne Arth–Darlene Hard
1932 Helen Jacobs–Sarah Palfrey	1960 Maria Bueno–Darlene Hard
1933 Betty Nuthall–Freda James	1961 Darlene Hard–Lesley Turner
1934 Helen Jacobs–Sarah Palfrey	1962 Darlene Hard–Maria Bueno
1935 Helen Jacobs–Mrs. Sarah Palfrey Fabyan	1963 Robyn Ebbern–Margaret Smith
1936 Mrs. Marjorie Van Ryn–Carolin Babcock	1964 Billie Jean Moffitt–Mrs. Karen Susman
1937 Mrs. Sarah Palfrey Fabyan–Alice Marble	1965 Carole Graebner–Nancy Richey
1938 Mrs. Sarah Palfrey Fabyan–Alice Marble	1966 Maria Bueno–Nancy Richey
1939 Mrs. Sarah Palfrey Fabyan–Alice Marble	1967 Mrs. Billie Jean King–Rosemary Casals
1940 Mrs. Sarah Palfrey Fabyan–Alice Marble	1968 Maria Bueno–Margaret Smith Court
1941 Mrs. Sarah Palfrey Cooke–Margaret Osborne	1969 Darlene Hard–Françoise Durr
1942 Louise Brough–Margaret Osborne	1970 Margaret Smith Court–Judy Tegart Dalton
1943 Louise Brough–Margaret Osborne	1971 Rosemary Casals–Judy Tegart Dalton
1944 Louise Brough–Margaret Osborne	1972 Françoise Durr–Betty Stove
1945 Louise Brough–Margaret Osborne	1973 Mrs. Margaret Smith Court–Virginia Wade
1946 Louise Brough–Margaret Osborne	1974 Billie Jean King–Rosemary Casals
1947 Louise Brough–Margaret Osborne	1975 Mrs. Margaret Smith Court–Virginia Wade
1948 Louise Brough–Mrs. Margaret Osborne duPont	1976 Linky Boshoff–Ilana Kloss
1949 Louise Brough–Mrs. Margaret Osborne duPont	1977 Betty Stove–Martina Navratilova
1950 Louise Brough–Mrs. Margaret Osborne duPont	1978 Billie Jean King–Martina Navratilova
1951 Shirley Fry–Doris Hart	1979 Betty Stove–Wendy Turnbull
1952 Shirley Fry–Doris Hart	1980 Billie Jean King–Martina Navratilova
1953 Shirley Fry–Doris Hart	1981 Kathy Jordan–Anne Smith

ALL-ENGLAND CHAMPIONS, WIMBLEDON (Open competition since 1968)

Men's Singles

1930	Bill Tilden (U.S.A.)	1951	Dick Savitt (U.S.A.)	1966	Manuel Santana (Spain)
1931	Sid Wood (U.S.A.)	1952	Frank Sedgman (Australia)	1967	John Newcombe (Australia)
1932	Ellsworth Vines (U.S.A.)	1953	Vic Seixas (U.S.A.)	1968	Rod Laver (Australia)
1933	John Crawford (Australia)	1954	Jaroslav Drobny (Egypt)	1969	Rod Laver (Australia)
1934	Fred Perry (England)	1955	Tony Trabert (U.S.A.)	1970	John Newcombe (Australia)
1935	Fred Perry (England)	1956	Lew Hoad (Australia)	1971	John Newcombe (Australia)
1936	Fred Perry (England)	1957	Lew Hoad (Australia)	1972	Stan Smith (U.S.A.)
1937	Don Budge (U.S.A.)	1958	Ashley Cooper (Australia)	1973	Jan Kodes (Czechoslovakia)
1938	Don Budge (U.S.A.)	1959	Alex Olmedo (U.S.A.)	1974	Jimmy Connors (U.S.A.)
1939	Bobby Riggs (U.S.A.)	1960	Neale Fraser (Australia)	1975	Arthur Ashe (U.S.A.)
1946	Yvon Petra (France)	1961	Rod Laver (Australia)	1976	Bjorn Borg (Sweden)
1947	Jack Kramer (U.S.A.)	1962	Rod Laver (Australia)	1977	Bjorn Borg (Sweden)
1948	Bob Falkenburg (U.S.A.)	1963	Chuck McKinley (U.S.A.)	1978	Bjorn Borg (Sweden)
1949	Ted Schroeder (U.S.A.)	1964	Roy Emerson (Australia)	1979	Bjorn Borg (Sweden)
1950	Budge Patty (U.S.A.)	1965	Roy Emerson (Australia)	1980	Bjorn Borg (Sweden)
				1981	John McEnroe (U.S.A.)

Men's Doubles

1930	Wilmer Allison–John Van Ryn	1951	Ken McGregor–Frank Sedgman	1966	Ken Fletcher–John Newcombe
1931	John Van Ryn–George Lott	1952	Ken McGregor–Frank Sedgman	1967	Bob Hewitt–Frew McMillan
1932	Jean Borotra–Jacques Brugnon	1953	Lew Hoad–Ken Rosewall	1968	John Newcombe–Tony Roche
1933	Jean Borotra–Jacques Brugnon	1954	Rex Hartwig–Mervyn Rose	1969	John Newcombe–Tony Roche
1934	George Lott–Lester Stoefen	1955	Rex Hartwig–Lew Hoad	1970	John Newcombe–Tony Roche
1935	John Crawford–Adrian Quist	1956	Lew Hoad–Ken Rosewall	1971	Rod Laver–Roy Emerson
1936	George Hughes–Charles Tuckey	1957	Gardnar Mulloy–Budge Patty	1972	Bob Hewitt–Frew McMillan
1937	Don Budge–Gene Mako	1958	Sven Davidson–Ulf Schmidt	1973	Jim Connors–Illie Nastase
1938	Don Budge–Gene Mako	1959	Neale Fraser–Roy Emerson	1974	John Newcombe–Tony Roche
1939	Bobby Riggs–Elwood Cooke	1960	Rafael Osuna–Dennis Ralston	1975	Vitas Gerulatis–Sandy Mayer
1946	Jack Kramer–Tom Brown	1961	Neale Fraser–Roy Emerson	1976	Brian Gottfried–Raul Ramirez
1947	Jack Kramer–Bob Falkenburg	1962	Fred Stolle–Bob Hewitt	1977	Ross Case–Geoff Masters
1948	Jack Bromwich–Frank Sedgman	1963	Rafael Osuna–Antonio Palafox	1978	Bob Hewitt–Frew McMillan
1949	Pancho Gonzalez–Frank Parker	1964	Bob Hewitt–Fred Stolle	1979	John McEnroe–Peter Fleming
1950	Jack Bromwich–Adrian Quist	1965	John Newcombe–Tony Roche	1980	Peter McNamara–Paul McNamee
				1981	John McEnroe–Peter Fleming

Women's Singles

1930	Helen Wills Moody (U.S.A.)	1951	Doris Hart (U.S.A.)	1966	Billie Jean King (U.S.A.)
1931	Cecile Aussem (Germany)	1952	Maureen Connolly (U.S.A.)	1967	Billie Jean King (U.S.A.)
1932	Helen Wills Moody (U.S.A.)	1953	Maureen Connolly (U.S.A.)	1968	Billie Jean King (U.S.A.)
1933	Helen Wills Moody (U.S.A.)	1954	Maureen Connolly (U.S.A.)	1969	Ann Haydon Jones (England)
1934	Dorothy Round (England)	1955	Louise Brough (U.S.A.)	1970	Margaret S. Court (Australia)
1935	Helen Wills Moody (U.S.A.)	1956	Shirley Fry (U.S.A.)	1971	Evonne Goolagong (Australia)
1936	Helen Hull Jacobs (U.S.A.)	1957	Althea Gibson (U.S.A.)	1972	Billie Jean King (U.S.A.)
1937	Dorothy Round (England)	1958	Althea Gibson (U.S.A.)	1973	Billie Jean King (U.S.A.)
1938	Helen Wills Moody (U.S.A.)	1959	Maria Bueno (Brazil)	1974	Chris Evert (U.S.A.)
1939	Alice Marble (U.S.A.)	1960	Maria Bueno (Brazil)	1975	Billie Jean King (U.S.A.)
1946	Pauline Betz (U.S.A.)	1961	Angela Mortimer (England)	1976	Chris Evert (U.S.A.)
1947	Margaret Osborne (U.S.A.)	1962	Karen Hantze Susman (U.S.A.)	1977	Virginia Wade (England)
1948	Louise Brough (U.S.A.)	1963	Margaret Smith (Australia)	1978	Martina Navratilova (U.S.A.)
1949	Louise Brough (U.S.A.)	1964	Maria Bueno (Brazil)	1979	Martina Navratilova (U.S.A.)
1950	Louise Brough (U.S.A.)	1965	Margaret Smith (Australia)	1980	Evonne G. Cawley (Australia)
				1981	Chris Evert Lloyd (U.S.A.)

Women's Doubles

1930	Elizabeth Ryan–Helen Wills Moody	1950	Louise Brough–Margaret Osborne duPont	1966	Maria Bueno–Nancy Richey
1931	Mrs. D. C. Shepherd–Baron– Phyllis Mudford King	1951	Shirley Fry–Doris Hart	1967	Billie Jean King–Rosemary Casals
1932	D. Metaxa–J. Sigart	1952	Shirley Fry–Doris Hart	1968	Billie Jean King–Rosemary Casals
1933	Elizabeth Ryan–Rene Mathieu	1953	Shirley Fry–Doris Hart	1969	Margaret S. Court–Judy Tegart
1934	Elizabeth Ryan–Rene Mathieu	1954	Louise Brough–Margaret Osborne duPont	1970	Billie Jean King–Rosemary Casals
1935	Kay Stammers–Freda James	1955	Angela Mortimer–Anne Shilcock	1971	Billie Jean King–Rosemary Casals
1936	Kay Stammers–Freda James	1956	Angela Buxton–Althea Gibson	1972	Billie Jean King–Betty Stove
1937	Rene Mathieu– A. M. Yorke	1957	Althea Gibson–Darlene Hard	1973	Billie Jean King–Rosemary Casals
1938	Alice Marble–Sarah Palfrey Fabyan	1958	Maria Bueno–Althea Gibson	1974	Peggy Michel–Evonne Goolagong
1939	Alice Marble–Sarah Palfrey Fabyan	1959	Jeanne Arth–Darlene Hard	1975	Kazuko Sawamatsu–Ann Kiyomura
1946	Louise Brough–Margaret Osborne	1960	Maria Bueno–Darlene Hard	1976	Chris Evert–Martina Navratilova
1947	Doris Hart–Patricia Canning Todd	1961	Karen Hantze–Billie Jean Moffitt	1977	Helen G. Cawley–Joanne Russell
1948	Louise Brough–Margaret Osborne duPont	1962	Karen Hantze Susman–Billie Jean Moffitt	1978	Wendy Turnbull–Kerry Reid
1949	Louise Brough–Margaret Osborne duPont	1963	Maria Bueno–Darlene Hard	1979	Billie Jean King–Martina Navratilova
		1964	Margaret Smith–Lesley Turner	1980	Kathy Jordan–Anne Smith
		1965	Maria Bueno–Billie Jean Moffitt	1981	Martina Navratilova–Pam Shriver

WIGHTMAN CUP

Year	Result	Year	Result	Year	Result
1931	United States 5, Great Britain 2	1952	United States 7, Great Britain 0	1967	United States 6, Great Britain 1
1932	United States 4, Great Britain 3	1953	United States 7, Great Britain 0	1968	Great Britain 4, United States 3
1933	United States 4, Great Britain 3	1954	United States 6, Great Britain 0	1969	United States 5, Great Britain 2
1934	United States 5, Great Britain 2	1955	United States 6, Great Britain 1	1970	United States 4, Great Britain 3
1935	United States 4, Great Britain 3	1956	United States 5, Great Britain 2	1971	United States 4, Great Britain 3
1936	United States 4, Great Britain 3	1957	United States 6, Great Britain 1	1972	United States 5, Great Britain 2
1937	United States 6, Great Britain 1	1958	Great Britain 4, United States 3	1973	United States 5, Great Britain 2
1938	United States 5, Great Britain 2	1959	United States 4, Great Britain 3	1974	Great Britain 6, United States 1
1939	United States 5, Great Britain 2	1960	Great Britain 4, United States 3	1975	United States 5, Great Britain 2
1946	United Sisters 7, Great Britain 0	1961	United States 6, Great Britain 1	1976	United States 5, Great Britain 2
1947	United States 7, Great Britain 0	1962	United States 4, Great Britain 3	1977	United States 7, Great Britain 0
1948	United States 6, Great Britain 1	1963	United States 6, Great Britain 1	1978	Great Britain 4, United States 3
1949	United States 7, Great Britain 0	1964	United States 5, Great Britain 2	1979	United States 5, Great Britain 2
1950	United States 7, Great Britain 0	1965	United States 5, Great Britain 2	1980	United States 5, Great Britain 2
1951	United States 6, Great Britain 1	1966	United States 4, Great Britain 3	1981	United States 7, Great Britain 0

DAVIS CUP CHALLENGE ROUND (No matches in 1910, 1915–18, and 1940–45)

Year	Result	Year	Result	Year	Result
1906	British Isles 5, United States 0	1933	Great Britain 3, France 2	1961	Australia 5, Italy 0
1907	Australasia 3, British Isles 2	1934	Great Britain 4, United States 1	1962	Australia 5, Mexico 0
1908	Australasia 3, United States 2	1935	Great Britain 5, United States 0	1963	United States 3, Australia 2
1909	Australasia 5, United States 0	1936	Great Britain 3, Australia 2	1964	Australia 3, United States 2
1911	Australasia 5, United States 0	1937	United States 4, Great Britain 1	1965	Australia 4, Spain 1
1912	British Isles 3, Australasia 2	1938	United States 3, Australia 2	1966	Australia 4, India 1
1913	United States 3, British Isles 2	1939	Australia 3, United States 2	1967	Australia 4, Spain 1
1914	Australasia 3, United States 2	1946	United States 5, Australia 0	1968	United States 4, Australia 1
1919	Australasia 4, British Isles 1	1947	United States 4, Australia 1	1969	United States 5, Rumania 0
1920	United States 5, Australasia 0	1948	United States 5, Australia 0	1970	U.S. 5, W. Germany 0
1921	United States 5, Japan 0	1949	United States 4, Australia 1	1971	United States 3, Rumania 2
1922	United States 4, Australasia 1	1950	Australia 4, United States 1	1972	United States 3, Rumania 2
1923	United States 4, Australasia 1	1951	Australia 3, United States 2	1973	Australia 5, United States 0
1924	United States 5, Australia 0	1952	Australia 4, United States 1	1974	South Africa defeated
1925	United States 5, France 0	1953	Australia 3, United States 2		India, by default
1926	United States 4, France 1	1954	United States 3, Australia 2	1975	Sweden 3, Czechoslovakia 2
1927	France 3, United States 2	1955	Australia 5, United States 0	1976	Italy 4, Chile 1
1928	France 4, United States 1	1956	Australia 5, United States 0	1977	Australia 3, Italy 1
1929	France 3, United States 2	1957	Australia 3, United States 2	1978	U.S. 4, Great Britain 1
1930	France 4, United States 1	1958	United States 3, Australia 2	1979	U.S. 5, Italy 0
1931	France 3, Great Britain 2	1959	Australia 3, United States 2	1980	Czechoslovakia 4, Italy 1
1932	France 3, United States 2	1960	Australia 4, Italy 1		

OTHER FOREIGN CHAMPIONSHIPS (Open competition since 1969)

	AUSTRALIAN	CANADIAN	FRENCH	ITALIAN
	Men's Singles	**Men's Singles**	**Men's Singles**	**Men's Singles**
1969	Rod Laver	Cliff Richey	Rod Laver	John Newcombe
1970	Arthur Ashe	Rod Laver	Jan Kodes	Ilie Nastase
1971	Ken Rosewall	John Newcombe	Jan Kodes	Rod Laver
1972	Ken Rosewall	Ilie Nastase	Andres Gimeno	Manuel Orantes
1973	John Newcombe	Tom Okker	Ilie Nastase	Ilie Nastase
1974	Jimmy Connors	Guillermo Vilas	Bjorn Borg	Bjorn Borg
1975	John Newcombe	Manuel Orantes	Bjorn Borg	Raul Ramirez
1976	Mark Edmondson	Guillermo Vilas	Adriano Panatta	Adriano Panatta
1977	Roscoe Tanner	Jeff Borowiak	Guillermo Vilas	Vitas Gerulaitis
1978	Vitas Gerulaitis	Eddie Dibbs	Bjorn Borg	Bjorn Borg
1979	Guillermo Vilas	Bjorn Borg	Bjorn Borg	Vitas Gerulaitis
1980	Guillermo Vilas	Ivan Lendl	Bjorn Borg	Guillermo Vilas
1981	Brian Teacher	Ivan Lendl	Bjorn Borg	Jose-Luis Clerc
	Women's Singles	**Women's Singles**	**Women's Singles**	**Women's Singles**
1969	Margaret Smith Court	Faye Urban	Margaret Smith Court	Julie Heldman
1970	Margaret Smith Court	Margaret Smith Court	Margaret Smith Court	Billie Jean King
1971	Margaret Smith Court	Françoise Durr	Evonne Goolagong	Virginia Wade
1972	Virginia Wade	Evonne Goolagong	Billie Jean King	Linda Tuero
1973	Margaret Court	Evonne Goolagong	Margaret Court	Evonne Goolagong
1974	Evonne Goolagong	Chris Evert	Chris Evert	Chris Evert
1975	Evonne Goolagong	Marcie Louie	Chris Evert	Chris Evert
1976	Evonne Goolagong	Mima Jausovec	Sue Barker	Mima Jausovec
1977	Kerry Reid	Regina Marsikova	Mima Jausovec	Janet Newberry
1978	Evonne Goolagong	Regina Marsikova	Virginia Ruzici	Regina Marsikova
1979	Chris O'Neill	Laura DuPont	Chris Evert Lloyd	Tracy Austin
1980	Barbara Jordan	Chris Evert Lloyd	Chris Evert Lloyd	Chris Evert Lloyd
1981	Hana Mandlikova	Tracy Austin	Hana Mandlikova	Chris Evert Lloyd

THE GRAND SLAM OF TENNIS

Winners of the Australian, French, British and United States Championships in the same season.

Year	Champions	Country	Event
1938	Don Budge	United States	Men's Singles
1951	Frank Sedgman–Ken McGregor	Australia	Men's Doubles
1953	Maureen Connolly	United States	Women's Singles
1960	Maria Bueno	Brazil	Women's Doubles*
1962	Rod Laver	Australia	Men's Singles
1963	Margaret Smith–Ken Fletcher	Australia	Mixed Doubles
1967	Owen Davidson	Australia	Mixed Doubles*
1969	Rod Laver	Australia	Men's Singles
1970	Margaret Smith Court	Australia	Women's Singles

*Won in Australia with a different doubles partner.

COLLEGIATE CHAMPIONS (Division I)

Year	Man	School	Woman	School
1967	Bob Lutz	Southern California	Patsy Rippy	Odessa Jr. College
1968	Stan Smith	Southern California	Emilie Burrer	Trinity
1969	Joaquin Loyo-Mayo	Southern California	Emilie Burrer	Trinity
1970	Jeff Borowiak	U.C.L.A.	Laura DuPont	North Carolina
1971	Jimmy Connors	U.C.L.A.	Pam Richmond	Arizona State
1972	Dick Stockton	Trinity	Janice Metcalf	Redlands
1973	Alex Mayer	Stanford	Janice Metcalf	Redlands
1974	John Whitlinger	Stanford	Carrier Meyer	Marymount
1975	Bill Martin	U.C.L.A.	Stephanie Tolleson	Trinity
1976	Bill Scanlon	Trinity	Barbara Hallquist	Southern California
1977	Matt Mitchell	Stanford	Barbara Hallquist	Southern California
1978	John McEnroe	Stanford	Jeanne DuVall	U.C.L.A.
1979	Kevin Curran	Texas	Kathy Jordan	Stanford
1980	Robert Van't Hof	Southern California	Wendy White	Rollins College
1981	Tim Mayotte	Stanford	Anna Maria Fernandez	Southern California

FEDERATION CUP

Women's International Team Competition

Source: U. S. T. A.

Year	Final Round Results	Year	Final Round Results
1963	United States, 2, Australia 1	1972	South Africa 2, Great Britain 1
1964	Australia 2, United States 1	1973	Australia 3, South Africa 0
1965	Australia 2, United States 1	1974	Australia 2, United States 1
1966	United States 3, West Germany 0	1975	Czechoslovakia 3, Australia 0
1967	United States 2, Great Britain 0	1976	United States 2, Australia 1
1968	Australia 3, Netherlands 0	1977	United States 2, Australia 1
1969	United States 2, Australia 1	1978	United States 2, Australia 1
1970	Australia 3, West Germany 0	1979	United States 3, Australia 0
1971	Australia 3, Great Britain 0	1980	United States 3, Australia 0

1980 TOP MONEY WINNERS

MEN

1.	John McEnroe, United States	$1,026,383
2.	Bjorn Borg, Sweden	723,212
3.	Jimmy Connors, United States	604,641
4.	Ivan Lendl, Czechoslovakia	568,911
5.	Gene Mayer, United States	384,719
6.	Guillermo Vilas, Argentina	378,601
7.	Vitas Gerulaitis, United States	344,666
8.	Wojtek Fibak, Poland	319,887
9.	Brian Gottfried, United States	294,579
10.	Jose Luis Clerc, Argentina	277,234

WOMEN

1.	Tracy Austin, United States	$683,787
2.	Martina Navratilova, United States	674,400
3.	Chris Evert Lloyd, United States	427,705
4.	Hana Mandlikova, Czechoslovakia	376,430
5.	Billie Jean King, United States	321,309
6.	Wendy Turnbull, Australia	315,573
7.	Andrea Jaeger, United States	258,431
8.	Evonne Goolagong Cawley, Australia	210,080
9.	Virginia Ruzici, Romania	194,113
10.	Pam Shriver, United States	182,649

1981 COLLEGIATE TENNIS CHAMPIONS

NCAA DIVISION I
Singles — Tim Mayotte, Stanford
Doubles — David Pate - Karl Richter, TCU
Team — Stanford

NCAA DIVISION II
Singles — Ken Flach, Southern Illinois (Edwardsville)
Doubles — Brian Lusson - Bart Bernstein, Southwest
  Texas State
Team — Southern Illinois (Edwardsville)

NCAA DIVISION III
Singles — Donovan Jones, Claremont-Mudd-Scripps
Doubles — Jim Hearn - Shaun Miller, Gustavus Adolphus
Team — (tie) Swarthmore, Claremont-Mudd-Scripps

AIAW DIVISION I
Singles — Anna Maria Fernandez, Southern California
Doubles — Karen Copeland — Alycia Moulton, Stanford
Team — U.C.L.A.

AIAW DIVISION II
Singles — Barbara Eaton, Northern Colorado
Doubles — Jill Morton - Tracy Wills, Calif. State Poly.-
  Pomona
Team — Calif. State Poly.-Pomona

AIAW DIVISION III
Singles — Kim Schmidt, Drew
Doubles — Becky Donecker - Jenny Haifley, Elizabethtown
Team — California-Davis

NAIA
Men's Singles — Brian Lusson, SW Texas
Team — Southwest Texas
Women's Singles — Pat Smith, Grand Canyon
Team — (tie) Grand Canyon (Ariz.), Guilford (N.C.)

JAMES E. SULLIVAN MEMORIAL TROPHY

Sportsmanship — Outstanding Amateur Athlete

Year	Athlete	Sport	Year	Athlete	Sport
1930	Bobby Jones	Golf	1956	Patricia McCormick	Diving
1931	Bernard Berlinger	Track & Field	1957	Bobby Morrow	Track & Field
1932	James Bausch	Track & Field	1958	Glenn Davis	Track & Field
1933	Glenn Cunningham	Track & Field	1959	Parry O'Brien	Track & Field
1934	Bill Bonthron	Track & Field	1960	Rafer Johnson	Track & Field
1935	Lawson Little	Golf	1961	Wilma Rudolph Ward	Track & Field
1936	Glen Morris	Track & Field	1962	Jim Beatty	Track & Field
1937	Don Budge	Tennis	1963	John Pennel	Track & Field
1938	Donald Lash	Track & Field	1964	Don Schollander	Swimming
1939	Joe Burk	Rowing	1965	Bill Bradley	Basketball
1940	Greg Rice	Track & Field	1966	Jim Ryun	Track & Field
1941	Leslie MacMitchell	Track & Field	1967	Randy Matson	Track & Field
1942	Cornelius Warmerdam	Track & Field	1968	Debbie Meyer	Swimming
1943	Gilbert Dodds	Track & Field	1969	Bill Toomey	Track & Field
1944	Ann Curtis	Swimming	1970	John Kinsella	Swimming
1945	Doc Blanchard	Football	1971	Mark Spitz	Swimming
1946	Arnold Tucker	Football	1972	Frank Shorter	Track & Field
1947	John Kelly, Jr.	Rowing	1973	Bill Walton	Basketball
1948	Robert Mathias	Track & Field	1974	Rick Wohlhuter	Track & Field
1949	Richard Button	Skating	1975	Tim Shaw	Swimming
1950	Fred Wilt	Track & Field	1976	Bruce Jenner	Track & Field
1951	Bob Richards	Track & Field	1977	John Naber	Swimming
1952	Horace Ashenfelter	Track & Field	1978	Tracy Caulkins	Swimming
1953	Sammy Lee	Diving	1979	Kurt Thomas	Gymnastics
1954	Mal Whitfield	Track & Field	1980	Eric Heiden	Skating
1955	Harrison Dillard	Track & Field			

AUTO RACING

THE HISTORY OF THE MILE RECORD

DATE	DRIVER	CAR	AMERICAN TIME	AVG.	WORLD'S TIME	AVG.
12/18/98	Chasseloup-Laubat	Jeantaud			57.000	39.24
1/17/99	Camille Jenatzy	Jamais Contente Jeantzy			54.000	41.42
1/17/99	Chasseloup-Laubat	Jeantaud			51.500	43.69
1/27/99	Camille Jenatzy	Jamais Contente Jeantzy			44.800	49.40
3/4/99	Chasseloup-Laubat	Jeantaud			38.400	58.25
4/29/99	Camille Jenatzy	Jamais Contente Jeantzy			34.400	65.79
4/13/02	Serpollet	Serpollet			29.800	76.06
8/5/02	W. K. Vanderbilt	Mors			29.400	76.08
11/5/02	H. Fournier	Mors			29.200	76.60
11/17/02	Augieres	Mors			29.000	77.13
3/17/03	Rigolly	Gorbron-Brillie			26.800	83.46
11/5/03	A. Duray	Gobron-Brillie			26.400	84.73
1/12/04	Henry Ford	Ford "999"	39.40	91.370		
1/22/04	W. K. Vanderbilt	Mercedes	39.00	92.307		
3/31/04	Rigolly	Gobbron-Brillie			23.600	94.78
5/12/04	De Caters	Mercedes			23.000	97.26
7/21/04	Rigolly	Gobron-Brillie			21.600	103.56
11/13/04	Victor Hemery	Darracq			21.400	104.53
12/30/04	Barras	Darracq			20.400	109.65
1/24/05	Arthur MacDonald	Napier	34.40	104.65		
1/25/05	H. L. Bowden	Mercedes	32.80	109.75		
1/26/06	Fred Marriott	Stanley (Steam)	28.20	127.659		
11/8/09*	Victor Hemery	Benz			17.761	125.914*
3/16/10	Barney Oldfield	Benz	27.33	131.724		
4/23/11	Bob Burman	Benz	25.40	141.732		
6/24/14	L. G. Hornsted	Benz			29.01	124.095
2/12/19	Ralph DePalma	Packard	24.02	149.875		
4/27/20	Tom Milton	Duesenberg	23.07	156.046		
5/17/22	K. Lee Guinness	Sunbeam			27.87	129.171
6/26/24	J. G. Parry-Thomas	Leyland-Thomas			27.75	129.730
7/6/24	Rene Thomas	Delage			25.12	143.312
7/12/24	E. A. D. Eldridge	Fiat			24.675	145.897
9/25/24	Capt. M. Campbell	Sunbeam			24.630	146.163
7/21/25	Capt. M. Campbell	Sunbeam			23.878	150.766
4/27/26	J. G. Parry-Thomas	Thomas Special			21.419	168.075
4/28/26	J. G. Parry-Thomas	Thomas Special			21.099	170.624
2/4/27	Capt. M. Campbell	Napier-Campbell			20.663	174.224
3/29/27	Maj. H. O. D. Seagrave	Sunbeam	17.665	203.790	17.665	203.790
2/19/28	Capt. M. Campbell	Napier-Campbell	17.395	206.956	17.395	206.956
4/22/28	Ray Keech	White Triplex	17.345	207.552	17.345	207.552
3/11/29	Maj. H. O. D. Seagrave	Irving-Napier	15.56	231.446	15.56	231.446
2/5/31	Sir Malcolm Campbell	Napier-Campbell	14.65	245.086	14.65	246.086
2/24/32	Sir Malcolm Campbell	Napier-Campbell	14.175	253.96	14.175	253.96
2/22/33	Sir Malcolm Campbell	Napier-Campbell	13.23	272.109	13.23	272.109
3/7/35	Sir Malcolm Campbell	Bluebird Special	13.01	276.82	13.01	276.82
9/3/35	Sir Malcolm Campbell	Bluebird Special	11.96	301.13	11.96	301.13
11/19/37	Capt. G. E. T. Eyston	Thunderbolt No. 1	11.56	311.42	11.56	311.42
8/27/38	Capt. G. E. T. Eyston	Thunderbolt No. 1	10.42	345.5	10.42	345.5
9/15/38	John Cobb	Railton	10.28	350.2	10.28	350.2
9/16/38	Capt. G. E. T. Eyston	Thunderbolt No. 1	10.07	357.5	10.07	357.5
8/23/39	John Cobb	Railton	9.76	368.9	9.76	368.9
9/16/47	John Cobb	Railton-Mobil Special	9.1325	394.2	9.1325	394.2
8/5/63	Craig Breedlove	Spirit of America	8.6355	407.45	8.8355	407.45
10/2/64	Tom Green	Wingfoot Express	8.7125	413.20	8.7125	413.20
10/5/64	Art Arfons	Art Arfons Green Monster	8.2945	434.02	8.2945	434.02
10/13/64	Craig Breedlove	Spirit of America	7.6805	468.719	7.6805	468.719
10/15/64	Craig Breedlove	Spirit of America	6.8405	526.277	6.8405	526.277
10/27/64	Art Arfons	Art Arfons Green Monster	6.7075	536.71	6.7075	536.71
11/2/65	Craig Breedlove	Spirit of America–Sonic I	6.485	555.127	6.485	555.127
11/7/65	Art Arfons	Art Arfons Green Monster	6.244	576.553	6.244	576.553
11/15/65	Craig Breedlove	Spirit of America–Sonic I	5.994	600.601	5.994	600.601
10/23/70	Gary Gabelich	Blue Flame	5.784	622.407	5.784	622.407
9/9/79**	Stan Barrett	The Budweiser Rocket	5.637	638.637	5.637	638.637

* Records above this point for World's Time were made over the flying kilometer, the recognized distance in the early years.
NOTE: The above records are the average of two runs made in opposite directions within one hour. ** Run made in one direction. Record not officially sanctioned.

FORMULA 1 GRAND PRIX CHAMPIONS Source: Sports Car Club of America

Year	Champion	Car	Country
1950	Giuseppe Farina	Alfa Romeo	Italy
1951	Juan Manuel Fangio	Alfa Romeo	Argentina
1952	Alberto Ascari	Ferrari	Italy
1953	Alberto Ascari	Ferrari	Italy
1954	Juan Manuel Fangio	Mercedes & Maserati	Argentina
1955	Juan Manuel Fangio	Mercedes	Argentina
1956	Juan Manuel Fangio	Lancia	Argentina
1957	Juan Manuel Fangio	Maserati	Argentina
1958	Mike Hawthorn	Ferrari	Great Britain
1959	Jack Brabham	Cooper	Australia
1960	Jack Brabham	Cooper	Australia
1961	Phil Hill	Ferrari	USA
1962	Graham Hill	BRM	Great Britain
1963	Jim Clark	Lotus	Great Britain
1964	John Surtees	Ferrari	Great Britain
1965	Jim Clark	Lotus	Great Britain
1966	Jack Brabham	Brabham	Australia
1967	Denis Hulme	Brabham	New Zealand
1968	Graham Hill	Lotus	Great Britain
1969	Jackie Stewart	Matra	Great Britain
1970	Jochen Rindt	Lotus	Austria
1971	Jackie Stewart	Tyrrell	Great Britain
1972	Emerson Fittipaldi	Lotus	Brazil
1973	Jackie Stewart	Tyrrell	Great Britain
1974	Emerson Fittipaldi	McLaren	Brazil
1975	Niki Lauda	Ferrari	Austria
1976	James Hunt	McLaren	Great Britain
1977	Niki Lauda	Ferrari	Austria
1978	Mario Andretti	Lotus	USA
1979	Jody Scheckter	Ferrari	South Africa
1980	Alan Jones	Williams	Australia
1981	Nelson Piquet	Brabham	Brazil

UNITED STATES GRAND PRIX, WATKINS GLEN, N.Y. Source: Sports Car Club of America

Year	Winner	Car	Year	Winner	Car
1959*	Bruce McLaren	Cooper	1970	Emerson Fittipaldi	Lotus
1960**	Stirling Moss	Lotus	1971	Francois Cevert	Tyrrell
1961	Ines Ireland	Lotus	1972	Jackie Stewart	Tyrrell
1962	Jim Clark	Lotus	1973	Ronnie Peterson	Lotus
1963	Graham Hill	BRM	1974	Carlos Reutemann	Brabham
1964	Graham Hill	BRM	1975	Niki Lauda	Ferrari
1965	Graham Hill	BRM	1976	James Hunt	McLaren
1966	Jim Clark	Lotus	1977	James Hunt	McLaren
1967	Jim Clark	Lotus	1978	Carlos Reutemann	Ferrari
1968	Jackie Stewart	Matra	1979	Gilles Villeneuve	Ferrari
1969	Jochen Rindt	Lotus	1980	Alan Jones	Williams
			1981	(not scheduled)	

* Held at Sebring ** Held at Riverside

UNITED STATES GRAND PRIX WEST, LONG BEACH, CALIF. Source: Sports Car Club of America

Year	Winner	Car	Year	Winner	Car
1976	Clay Regazzoni	Ferrari	1979	Gilles Villeneuve	Ferrari
1977	Mario Andretti	Lotus	1980	Nelson Piquet	Brabham
1978	Carlos Reutemann	Ferrari	1981	Alan Jones	Williams

SPORTS CAR CLUB OF AMERICA SERIES CHAMPIONS Source: Sports Car Club of America

Year	Champion	Car	Year	Champion	Car
Can-Am Challenge			**Trans-Am® Championship**		
1966	John Surtees	Lola	1973	Peter Gregg	Chevrolet
1967	Bruce McLaren	McLaren M6A	1974	Peter Gregg	Porsche
1968	Denis Hulme	McLaren M6A	1975	John Greenwood	Chevrolet
1969	Bruce McLaren	McLaren M8B	1976	George Follmer	Porsche
1970	Denis Hulme	McLaren M8D	1977 Category I	Bob Tullius	Jaguar
1971	Peter Revson	McLaren M8F	Category II	Ludwig Heimrath	Porsche
1972	George Follmer	Porsche 917/10	1978 Category I	Bob Tullius	Jaguar
1974	Mark Donohue	Porsche 917/30	Category II	Greg Pickett	Corvette
1973	Jackie Oliver	Shadow	1979 Category I	Gene Bothello	Corvette
1975–1976	(no series)		Category II	John Paul	Porsche
1977	Patrick Tambay	Lola T-333CS	1980	John Bauer	Porsche
1978	Alan Jones	Lola T-333CS			
1979	Jacky Ickx	Lola T-333CS	**Pro Rally Series**		
1980	Patrick Tambay	Lola T530	1974	Gene Henderson/Ken Pogue	Jeep Cherokee
			1975	John Buffum/Vicki Dykema	Ford Escort
			1976	Hendrik Blok/Erick Hauge	Dodge Colt
Robert Bosch/VW Super Vee (Gold Cup)			1977	John Buffum/"Vicki"	TR-7
1971	Bill Scott	Royale	1978	John Buffum/Doug Shepherd	TR-7
1972	Bill Scott	Royale	1979	John Buffum/Doug Shepherd	TR-8
1973	Bertil Roos	Tui BH3	1980	John Buffum/Doug Shepherd	TR-8
1974	Elliott Forbes-Robinson	Lynn			
1975	Eddie Miller	Lola T-324	**Rabbit/Bilstein Cup**		
1976	Tom Bagley	Zink Z-11	1976	Paul Hacker	Scirocco
1977	Bob Lazier	Lola T-324	1977	Bill Deters	Scirocco
1978	Bill Alsup	Argo	1978	Gary Benson	Rabbit
1979	Geoff Brabham	Ralt RT-1	1979	Gary Benson	Rabbit
1980	Peter Kuhn	Ralt RT-5	1980	Gary Benson	Rabbit

INDIANAPOLIS 500 SOURCE: Jack C. Fox, The Indianapolis 500 (1967), and other sources

Year	Winner	Chassis	Engine	Cylinders	Mph	Gross	Second Place
1920	Gaston Chevrolet	Frontenac	Frontenac	4	88.16	$ 93,550	Rene Thomas
1921	Tommy Milton	Frontenac	Frontenac	8	89.62	$ 86,650	Roscoe Sarles
1922	Jimmy Murphy	Duesenberg	Miller	8	94.48	$ 70,575	Harry Hartz
1923	Tommy Milton	Miller	Miller	8	90.95	$ 83,425	Harry Hartz
1924	L. L. Corum, Joe Boyer	Duesenberg	Duesenberg	8	98.23	$ 86,850	Earl Cooper
1925	Peter DePaolo	Duesenberg	Duesenberg*	8	101.13	$ 87,750	Dave Lewis
1926	Frank Lockhart	Miller	Miller*	8	95.885¹	$ 88,100	Harry Hartz
1927	George Souders	Duesenberg	Duesenberg*	8	97.545	$ 89,850	Earl DeVore
1928	Lou Meyer	Miller	Miller*	8	99.482	$ 90,750	Lou Moore
1929	Ray Keech	Miller	Miller*	8	97.585	$ 95,150	Lou Meyer
1930	Billy Arnold	Summers	Miller†	8	100.448	$ 97,600	Shorty Cantlon
1931	Lou Schneider	Stevens	Miller	8	96.629	$ 81,800	Fred Frame
1932	Fred Frame	Wetteroth	Miller†	8	104.144	$ 93,900	Howdy Wilcox 2d
1933	Lou Meyer	Miller	Miller	8	104.162	$ 54,450	Wilbur Shaw
1934	Bill Cummings	Miller	Miller†	4	104.863	$ 83,775	Mauri Rose
1935	Kelly Petillo	Wetteroth	Offenhauser	4	106.240	$ 78,575	Wilbur Shaw
1936	Lou Meyer	Stevens	Miller	4	109.069	$ 82,525	Ted Horn
1937	Wilbur Shaw	Shaw	Offenhauser	4	113.580	$ 92,135	Ralph Hepburn
1938	Floyd Roberts	Wetteroth	Miller	4	117.200	$ 91,075	Wilbur Shaw
1939	Wilbur Shaw	Maserati	Maserati*	8	115.035	$ 87,050	Jimmy Snyder
1940	Wilbur Shaw	Maserati	Maserati*	8	114.277	$ 85,525	Rex Mays
1941	Floyd Davis, Mauri Rose	Wetteroth	Offenhauser	4	115.117	$ 90,925	Rex Mays
1946	George Robson	Adams	Sparks*	6	114.820	$115,450	Jimmy Jackson
1947	Mauri Rose	Deidt	Offenhauser†	4	116.338	$137,425	Bill Holland
1948	Mauri Rose	Deidt	Offenhauser†	4	119.814	$171,075	Bill Holland
1949	Bill Holland	Deidt	Offenhauser†	4	121.327	$179,050	Johnnie Parsons
1950	Johnnie Parsons	Kurtis Kraft	Offenhauser	4	124.002²	$201,135	Bill Holland
1951	Lee Wallard	Kurtis Kraft	Offenhauser	4	126.244	$207,650	Mike Nazaruk
1952	Troy Ruttman	Kuzma	Offenhauser	4	128.922	$230,100	Jim Rathmann
1953	Bill Vukovich	Kurtis Kraft 500A	Offenhauser	4	128.740	$246,300	Art Cross
1954	Bill Vukovich	Kurtis Kraft 500A	Offenhauser	4	130.840	$269,375	Jimmy Bryan
1955	Bob Sweikert	Kurtis Kraft 500C	Offenhauser	4	128.209	$270,400	Tony Bettenhausen
1956	Pat Flaherty	Watson	Offenhauser	4	128.490	$282,052	Sam Hanks
1957	Sam Hanks	Epperly	Offenhauser	4	135.601	$300,252	Jim Rathmann
1958	Jimmy Bryan	Epperly	Offenhauser	4	133.791	$305,217	George Amick
1959	Rodger Ward	Watson	Offenhauser	4	135.857	$338,100	Jim Rathmann
1960	Jim Rathmann	Watson	Offenhauser	4	138.767	$369,150	Rodger Ward
1961	A. J. Foyt	Watson	Offenhauser	4	139.130	$400,000	Eddie Sachs
1962	Rodger Ward	Watson	Offenhauser	4	140.293	$426,152	Len Sutton
1963	Parnelli Jones	Watson	Offenhauser	4	143.137	$494,031	Jim Clark
1964	A. J. Foyt	Watson	Offenhauser	4	147.350	$506,625	Rodger Ward
1965	Jim Clark	Lotus	Ford‡	8	151.388	$628,399	Parnelli Jones
1966	Graham Hill	Lola	Ford‡	8	144.317	$691,809	Jim Clark
1967	A. J. Foyt	Coyote	Ford‡	8	151.207	$737,109	Al Unser
1968	Bobby Unser	Eagle	Ford‡**	8	152.882	$809,627	Dan Gurney
1969	Mario Andretti	Hawk	Ford‡**	8	156.867	$805,127	Dan Gurney
1970	Al Unser	P. J. Colt	Ford‡**	8	155.749	$1,000,002	Mark Donohue
1971	Al Unser	P. J. Colt	Ford‡**	8	157.735	$1,001,604	Peter Revson
1972	Mark Donohue	McLaren	Offenhauser	8	162.962	$1,011,846	Al Unser
1973	Gordon Johncock	Eagle	Offenhauser	4	159.014	$1,006,105	Billy Vukovich
1974	Johnny Rutherford	McLaren	Offenhauser	4	158.589	$1,015,686	Bobby Unser
1975	Bobby Unser	Eagle	Offenhauser	4	149.213³	$1,001,322	Johnny Rutherford
1976	Johnny Rutherford	McLaren	Drake-Offenhauser	4	148.7⁴	$1,038,776	A. J. Foyt
1977	A. J. Foyt	Coyote	Foyt	8	161.331	$1,116,807	Tom Sneva
1978	Al Unser	Lola	Cosworth	8	161.363	$1,145,255	Tom Sneva
1979	Rick Mears	Penske	Cosworth	8	155.899	$1,271,954	A. J. Foyt
1980	Johnny Rutherford	Chaparral	Cosworth	8	142.862	$1,502,425	Tom Sneva
1981	Bobby Unser	Penske	Cosworth	8	139.084	$1,609,375	Mario Andretti

*Supercharged. **Turbocharged. †Front drive. ‡Rear engine. ¹400 miles. ²345 miles; all other races at 500 miles. ³Race stopped at 435 miles due to rain. ⁴Race stopped at 255 miles due to rain.

NATIONAL RACING CHAMPIONS—USAC*

1902	Harry Harkness	1920	Gaston Chevrolet	1939	Wilbur Shaw	1962	Rodger Ward
1903	Barney Oldfield	1921	Thomas Milton	1940	Rex Mays	1963	A. J. Foyt
1904	George Heath	1922	James Murphy	1941	Rex Mays	1964	A. J. Foyt
1905	Victor Hemery	1923	Eddie Hearne	1946	Ted Horn	1965	Mario Andretti
1906	Joe Tracy	1924	James Murphy	1947	Ted Horn	1966	Mario Andretti
1907	Eddie Bald	1925	Peter DePaolo	1948	Ted Horn	1967	A. J. Foyt
1908	Louis Strang	1926	Harry Hartz	1949	Johnnie Parsons	1968	Bobby Unser
1909	George Robertson	1927	Peter DePaolo	1950	Henry Banks	1969	Mario Andretti
1910	Ray Harroun	1928	Louis Meyer	1951	Tony Bettenhausen	1970	Al Unser
1911	Ralph Mulford	1929	Louis Meyer	1952	Chuck Stevenson	1971	Joe Leonard
1912	Ralph DePalma	1930	Billy Arnold	1953	Sam Hanks	1972	Joe Leonard
1913	Earl Cooper	1931	Louis Schneider	1954	Jimmy Bryan	1973	Roger McCluskey
1914	Ralph DePalma	1932	Bob Carey	1955	Bob Sweikert	1974	Bobby Unser
1915	Earl Cooper	1933	Louis Meyer	1956	Jimmy Bryan	1975	A. J. Foyt
1916	Dario Resta	1934	Bill Cummings	1957	Jimmy Bryan	1976	Gordon Johncock
1917	Earl Cooper	1935	Kelly Petillo	1958	Tony Bettenhausen	1977	Tom Sneva
1918	Ralph Mulford	1936	Mauri Rose	1959	Rodger Ward	1978	Tom Sneva
1919	Howard Wilcox	1937	Wilbur Shaw	1960	A. J. Foyt	1979	A. J. Foyt
		1938	Floyd Roberts	1961	A. J. Foyt	1980	Johnny Rutherford

* USAC founded 1956.

1980 USAC NATIONAL CHAMPIONSHIP SERIES DRIVER STANDINGS

(SOURCE: United States Auto Club)

Pos.	Driver/Hometown	Pts.	Pos.	Driver/Hometown	Pts.
1.	Johnny Rutherford, Ft. Worth, Texas	2,740	17.	Roger Mears, Bakersfield, California	180
2.	Tom Sneva, Spokane, Washington	1,970	18.	Gordon Smiley, Dallas, Texas	170
3.	Bobby Unser, Albuquerque, New Mexico	1,334		Billy Engelhart, Madison, Wisconsin	170
4.	Gordon Johncock, Coldwater, Michigan	1,330	20.	Greg Leffler, Winchester, Indiana	150
5.	Pancho Carter, Brownsburg, Indiana	1,078		Lee Kunzman, Guttenberg, Iowa	150
6.	Bill Alsup, Woodstock, Vermont	990		Vern Schuppan, Whyalla, South Australia	150
7.	Rick Mears, Bakersfield, California	766	23.	Jerry Sneva, Spokane, Washington	120
8.	Gary Bettenhausen, Monrovia, Indiana	726		Tom Gloy, Lafayette, California	120
9.	Sheldon Kinser, Bloomington, Indiana	345	25.	Herm Johnson, Eau Claire, Wisconsin	116
10.	Danny Ongais, Santa Ana, California	330	26.	Dick Ferguson, Glendale, California	105
11.	Howdy Holmes, Ann Arbor, Michigan	266	27.	Roger Rager, Mound, Minnesota	100
12.	Tom Bigelow, Whitewater, Wisconsin	250	28.	Cliff Hucul, Prince George, British Columbia,	
13.	Spike Gehlhausen, Speedway, Indiana	245		Canada	90
14.	Tom Bagley, Centre Hall, Pennsylvania	220	29.	Bill Vukovich, Coarsegold, California	65
15.	Larry Cannon, Danville, Illinois	205	30.	Jan Sneva, Spokane, Washington	60
	Tim Richmond, Ashland, Ohio	205	31.	Rick Muther, Laguna Beach, California	57
			32.	Jerry Karl, Manchester, Pennsylvania	54

1980 USAC TOP MONEY WINNERS

		Total			Total
1.	Johnny Rutherford	$405,077	11.	Bill Alsup	$50,780
2.	Tom Sneva	174,180	12.	Steve Chassey	44,754
3.	Gary Bettenhausen	145,793	13.	Bill Engelhart	44,571
4.	Bobby Unser	134,074	14.	Danny Ongais	44,359
5.	Pancho Carter	93,206	15.	Joe Ruttman	43,948
6.	Gordon Johncock	89,677	16.	Tim Richmond	43,410
7.	Tom Bigelow	74,250	17.	Sheldon Kinser	40,656
8.	Rick Mears	61,531	18.	Rusty Wallace	38,619
9.	Rich Vogler	59,633	19.	Jerry Sneva	37,207
10.	Greg Leffler	54,988	20.	Billy Vukovich	36,989

USAC NATIONAL CHAMPIONSHIP ALL-TIME RACE WINNERS (1956-1980)

Driver	Wins	Driver	Wins	Driver	Wins	Driver	Wins
A. J. Foyt	66	Johnny Rutherford	20	Lloyd Ruby	7	Danny Ongais	6
Al Unser	35	Gordon Johncock	19	Johnny Thomson	6	Jud Larson	5
Mario Andretti	33	Eddie Sachs	8	Parnelli Jones	6	Jim McElreath	5
Bobby Unser	26	Jimmy Bryan	7	Don Branson	6	Wally Dallenbach	5
Rodger Ward	24	Dan Gurney	7	Joe Leonard	6	Roger McCluskey	5

USAC ROOKIE OF THE YEAR

1971	.... George Eaton	1974	.... Duane Carter, Jr.	1977	.... Danny Ongais
1972	.... Mike Hiss	1975	.... Spike Gehlhausen	1978	.... Tom Bagley
1973	.... Tom Sneva	1976	.... Rick Mears	1979	.... Tony Bettenhausen, Jr.
				1980	.... Bill Alsup

1981 DAYTONA-LE MANS 24-HOUR ENDURANCE RACES

	Drivers	Laps	Car	Avg. Speed (Mph)
DAYTONA:	1. Brian Redman, Bobby Rahal and Bob Garretson	708 (2,718.72 mi.)	.... Porsche	113.153
	2. Bob Akin, Derek Bell and Craig Seibert	695	.... Porsche	......
LE MANS:	1. Jacky Ickx (Belgium) and Derek Bell (U.K.)	406 (2,996.95 mi.)	.... Porsche	124.94
	2. Jacky Haran, Jean-Louis Schlesser and and Philippe Streiff (France)	392	.... Rondeau	......

STOCK CAR RACING

SOURCE: The National Association for Stock Car Auto Racing, Inc.

RESULTS OF 1980 WINSTON CUP GRAND NATIONAL SEASON

EVENT-LOCATION	DATE	FIRST	SECOND
WINSTON WESTERN 500 Riverside, Calif.	Jan. 19	Darrell Waltrip Chevrolet	Dale Earnhardt Chevrolet
DAYTONA 500 Daytona Beach, Fla.	Feb. 17	Buddy Baker Oldsmobile	Bobby Allison Mercury
RICHMOND 400 Richmond, Va.	Feb. 24	Darrell Waltrip Chevrolet	Bobby Allison Ford
CAROLINA 500 Rockingham, N.C.	Mar. 9	Cale Yarborough Oldsmobile	Richard Petty Chevrolet
ATLANTA 500 Atlanta, Ga.	Mar. 16	Dale Earnhardt Chevrolet	Rusty Wallace Chevrolet
VALLEYDALE SOUTHEASTERN 500 Bristol, Tn.	Mar. 30	Dale Earnhardt Chevrolet	Darrell Waltrip Chevrolet
CRC CHEMICALS REBEL 500 Darlington, S.C.	Apr. 13	David Pearson Chevrolet	Benny Parsons Chevrolet
NORTHWESTERN BANK 400 North Wilkesboro, N.C.	Apr. 20	Richard Petty Chevrolet	Harry Gant Chevrolet
VIRGINIA 500 Martinsville, Va.	Apr. 27	Darrell Waltrip Chevrolet	Benny Parsons Chevrolet
WINSTON 500 Talladega, Ala.	May 4	Buddy Baker Oldsmobile	Dale Earnhardt Oldsmobile
MUSIC CITY 420 Nashville, Tn.	May 10	Richard Petty Chevrolet	Benny Parsons Chevrolet
MASON-DIXON 500 Dover, Dela.	May 18	Bobby Allison Ford	Richard Petty Chevrolet
WORLD 600 Charlotte, N.C.	May 25	Benny Parsons Chevrolet	Darrell Waltrip Chevrolet
NASCAR 400 College Station, TX	June 1	Cale Yarborough Chevrolet	Richard Petty Chevrolet
WARNER W. HODGDON 400 Riverside, Calif.	June 8	Darrell Waltrip Chevrolet	Neil Bonnett Mercury
GABRIEL 400 Brooklyn, Mi.	June 15	Benny Parsons Chevrolet	Cale Yarborough Chevrolet
FIRECRACKER 400 Daytona Beach, Fl.	July 4	Bobby Allison Mercury	David Pearson Oldsmobile
BUSCH NASHVILLE 420 Nashville, Tn.	July 12	Dale Earnhardt Chevrolet	Cale Yarborough Chevrolet
COCO-COLA 500 Pocono, Pa.	July 27	Neil Bonnett Chevrolet	Buddy Baker Buick
TALLADEGA 500 Talladega, Al.	Aug. 3	Neil Bonnett Mercury	Cale Yarborough Oldsmobile
CHAMPION SPARK PLUG 400 Brooklyn, Mi.	Aug. 17	Cale Yarborough Chevrolet	Neil Bonnett Mercury
BUSCH VOLUNTEER 500 Bristol, Tn.	Aug. 23	Cale Yarborough Chevrolet	Dale Earnhardt Chevrolet
SOUTHERN 500 Darlington, S.C.	Sept. 1	Terry Labonte Chevrolet	David Pearson Chevrolet
CAPITAL CITY 400 Richmond, Va.	Sept. 7	Bobby Allison Ford	Richard Petty Chevrolet
CRC CHEMICALS 500 Dover, De.	Sept. 14	Darrell Waltrip Chevrolet	Harry Gant Chevrolet
HOLLY FARMS 400 North Wilkesboro, N.C.	Sept. 21	Bobby Allison Ford	Darrell Waltrip Chevrolet
OLD DOMINION 500 Martinsville, Va.	Sept. 28	Dale Earnhardt Chevrolet	Buddy Baker Chevrolet
NATIONAL 500 Charlotte, N.C.	Oct. 5	Dale Earnhardt Chevrolet	Cale Yarborough Chevrolet
AMERICAN 500 Rockingham, N.C.	Oct. 19	Cale Yarborough Chevrolet	Harry Gant Chevrolet
ATLANTA JOURNAL 500 Atlanta, Ga.	Nov. 2	Cale Yarborough Chevrolet	Neil Bonnett Mercury
LOS ANGELES TIMES 500 Ontario, Calif.	Nov. 15	Benny Parsons Chevrolet	Neil Bonnett Mercury

WINSTON CUP GRAND NATIONAL CHAMPIONS

1964—Richard Petty, Randleman, N.C. (Plymouth)
1965—Ned Jarrett, Camden, S.C. (Ford)
1966—David Pearson, Spartanburg, S.C. (Dodge)
1967—Richard Petty, Randleman, N.C. (Plymouth)
1968—David Pearson, Spartanburg, S.C. (Ford)
1969—David Pearson, Spartanburg, S.C. (Ford)
1970—Bobby Isaac, Catawba, N.C. (Dodge)
1971—Richard Petty, Randleman, N.C. (Plymouth)
1972—Richard Petty, Randleman, N.C. (Plymouth-Dodge)
1973—Benny Parsons, Ellerbe, N.C. (Chevrolet)
1974—Richard Petty, Randleman, N.C. (Dodge)
1975—Richard Petty, Randleman, N.C. (Dodge)
1976—Cale Yarborough, Timmonsville, S.C. (Chevrolet)
1977—Cale Yarborough, Timmonsville, S.C. (Chevrolet)
1978—Cale Yarborough, Timmonsville, S.C. (Oldsmobile)
1979—Richard Petty, Randleman, N.C. (Chevrolet)
1980—Dale Earnhardt, Kannapolis, N.C. (Chevrolet)

1980 WINSTON CUP GRAND NATIONAL STANDINGS

Pos. Driver	Points	Starts	Wins	Top 5	Top 10	Money Won
1. Dale Earnhardt	4661	31	5	19	24	$588,926
2. Cale Yarborough	4642	31	6	19	22	537,358
3. Benny Parsons	4278	31	3	16	21	385,140
4. Richard Petty	4255	31	2	15	19	374,092
5. Darrell Waltrip	4239	31	5	16	17	382,138
6. Bobby Allison	4019	31	4	12	18	356,050
7. Jody Ridley	3972	31	0	2	18	196,617
8. Terry Labonte	3766	31	1	6	16	215,889
9. Dave Marcis	3745	31	0	4	14	150,165
10. Richard Childress	3742	31	0	0	10	157,420
11. Harry Gant	3703	31	0	9	14	162,190
12. Buddy Arrington	3461	31	0	0	7	120,355
13. James Hylton	3449	31	0	0	4	109,230
14. Ronnie Thomas	3066	30	0	0	4	89,770
15. Cecil Gordon	2993	29	0	0	3	83,300
16. J.D. McDuffie	2968	31	0	0	3	82,402

OTHER NASCAR CHAMPIONS

	WINSTON WEST GRAND NATIONAL	LATE MODEL SPORTSMAN	MODIFIED
1969	Ray Elder, Caruthers, Calif.	Charles (Red) Farmer, Hueytown, Ala.	Carl (Bugs) Stevens, Rehoboth, Mass.
1970	Ray Elder, Caruthers, Calif.	Charles (Red) Farmer, Hueytown, Ala.	Fred De Sarro, Hope Valley, R.I.
1971	Ray Elder, Caruthers, Calif.	Charles (Red) Farmer, Hueytown, Ala.	Jerry Cook, Rome, N.Y.
1972	Ray Elder, Caruthers, Calif.	Jack Ingram, Asheville, N.C.	Jerry Cook, Rome, N.Y.
1973	Jack McCoy, Modesto, Calif.	Jack Ingram, Asheville, N.C.	Richie Evans, Rome, N.Y.
1974	Ray Elder, Caruthers, Calif.	Jack Ingram, Asheville, N.C.	Jerry Cook, Rome, N.Y.
1975	Ray Elder, Caruthers, Calif.	L.D. Ottinger, Newport, Tenn.	Jerry Cook, Rome, N.Y.
1976	Chuck Brown, Portland, Ore.	L.D. Ottinger, Newport, Tenn.	Jerry Cook, Rome, N.Y.
1977	Bill Schmitt, Redding, Calif.	Butch Lindley, Greenville, S.C.	Jerry Cook, Rome, N.Y.
1978	Jim Insolo, Mission Hills, Calif.	Butch Lindley, Greenville, S.C.	Richie Evans, Rome, N.Y.
1979	Bill Schmitt, Redding, Calif.	Gene Glover, Kingsport, Tenn.	Richie Evans, Rome, N.Y.
1980	Roy Smith, Victoria, B.C., Canada	Morgan Shepherd, Conover, N.C.	Richie Evans, Rome, N.Y.

THOROUGHBRED RACING

SOURCE: *American Racing Manual*, 1981 ed. Reproduced with permission of the copyright owner, Daily Racing Form, Inc.

HIGHEST ANNUAL PAYOFF ODDS

Date	Winner	Track	Payoff Odds	Date	Winner	Track	Payoff Odds
1948 Sept. 30	Buddie Bones	Rockingham Park	192–1	1964 Dec. 11	Wilson Hill Doll	Bay Meadows	279–1
1949 Sept. 20	Luxuriant	Narragansett Park	282–1	1965 June 5	Blunt Edge	Cahokia Downs	142–1
1950 Oct. 30	Minnix	Lincoln Downs	253–1	1966 Oct. 7	Dutch Wrackateer	Narragansett Park	186–1
1951 Sept. 27	Royal Marvel	Rockingham Park	183–1	1967 May 26	Mambo Rhythm	Seminole Downs	214–1
1952 Sept. 16	Rock House	Woodbine Park	214–1	1968 June 24	Waverley Steps	Woodbine	396–1
1953 Aug. 28	Can It Yes	Exhibition Park	253–1	1969 Sept. 24	Judes Song	Latonia	241–1
1954 Nov. 10	Ruff Mate	Pimlico Race Course	209–1	1970 May 7	Corpus Delicti	Fort Erie	175–1
1955 May 27	Gold Champ	Suffolk Downs	144–1	1971 Apr. 1	Moonlight City	Portland Meadows	169–1
1956 July 24	Buster Bell	Charles Town	203–1	1972 Nov. 16	Norton	Churchill Downs	190–1
1957 Aug. 27	Miss Profit	Detroit Race Course	172–1	1973 Sept. 28	Cedars Crown	Detroit Race Course	256–1
1958 Mar. 22	Whisk Tru	Bowie Race Course	231–1	1974 Mar. 17	Campus Bright	Yakima Meadows	156–1
1959 June 5	Janie Brown	Thistledown	168–1	1975 Sept. 1	Second Ticking	Narragansett Park	147–1
1960 Nov. 4	Kamal Bey	Laurel Race Course	175–1	1976 Sept. 21	Tiger Red K	Columbus	188–1
1961 Sept. 29	Djebonita	Bay Meadows	259–1	1977 Mar. 10	Black Ticket	Fonner Park	259–1
1962 July 20	Wee Highway	Delaware Park	170–1	1978 Nov. 21	Golden Rubies	Churchill Downs	246–1
1963 Sept. 13	Confiancita	El Comandante	201–1	1979 Mar. 14	Young Migrant	Portland Meadows	228–1
1963 Aug. 12	Ivalinda	Arlington Park	190–1	1980 Nov. 23	Pogong	Sundland Park	220–1

STRAIGHT MUTUEL PAYOFFS RECORD

Tabulation based on a $2 straight mutuel ticket

Horse	Track and Date	Payoff	Horse	Track and Date	Payoff
Wishing Ring, Latonia, June 17, 1912		$1,885.50	Nanamay, Tanforan, April 14, 1932		$602.20
Augeas, Agua Caliente, February 14, 1933		840.00	Zombro, Charles Town, December 5, 1933		590.00
Muzetta W., Lexington, May 7, 1910		830.70	Cadeau, Pimlico, May 7, 1913		577.10
King Jack, Agua Caliente, January 8, 1933		820.00	Escohigh, Tropical Park, December 29, 1937		571.00
Trycook, Hagerstown, May 19, 1934		810.00	Luxuriant, Narragansett Park, September 20, 1949		566.80
Fincastle, Havana, December 19, 1923		702.60	Welga, Douglas Park, May 29, 1916		560.40
Lt. Wm. J. Murray, Havana, February 11, 1923		696.00	Wilson Hill Doll, Bay Meadows, December 11, 1964		559.80
Miss Fountain, Havana, February 9, 1930		685.60	Mad Scramble, Bay Meadows, April 22, 1941		530.80
Playmay, Santa Anita Park, February 4, 1938		673.40	Djebonita, Bay Meadows, September 29, 1961		520.80
Fleetglow, Green Mountain, May 9, 1968		658.80	Black Ticket, Fonner Park, March 10, 1977		520.50
Meadow Money, Lincoln Fields, June 5, 1941		652.40	Cedars Crown, Detroit Race Course, September 28, 1973		514.20
			Minnix, Lincoln Downs, October 30, 1950		508.80

THE TRIPLE CROWN

Only eleven three-year-olds have managed to win the celebrated Triple Crown of American Racing—the Kentucky Derby, the Preakness Stakes, and the Belmont Stakes:

1919—Sir Barton	1943—Count Fleet
1930—Gallant Fox	1946—Assault
1935—Omaha	1948—Citation
1937—War Admiral	1973—Secretariat
1941—Whirlaway	1977—Seattle Slew
	1978—Affirmed

The following horses won two of the three great races: Cloverbrook (1877), Duke of Magenta (1878), Grenada (1880), Saunterer (1881), Belmar (1895), Man o' War (1920), Pillory (1922), Zev (1923), Twenty Grand (1931), Burgoo King (1932), Bold Venture (1936), Johnstown (1939), Bimelech (1940), Shut Out (1942), Pensive (1944), Capot (1949), Middleground (1950), Native Dancer (1953), Nashua (1955), Needles (1956), Tim Tam (1958), Carry Back (1961), Chateaugay (1963), Northern Dancer (1964), Kauai King (1966), Damascus (1967), Forward Pass (1968), Majestic Prince (1969), Canonero II (1971), Riva Ridge (1972), Little Current (1974), Spectacular Bid (1979), Pleasant Colony (1981).

LEADING MONEY-WINNING THOROUGHBRED HORSES

Year	Horse	Age	Starts	1st	2d	3d	Amount Won	Year	Horse	Age	Starts	1st	2d	3d	Amount Won
1925	Pompey	2	10	7	2	0	$121,630	1953	Native Dancer	3	10	9	1	0	$513,425
1926	Crusader	3	15	9	4	0	166,033	1954	Determine	3	15	10	3	2	328,700
1927	Anita Peabody	2	7	6	0	1	111,905	1955	Nashua	3	12	10	1	1	752,550
1928	High Strung	2	6	5	0	0	153,590	1956	Needles	3	8	4	2	0	440,850
1929	Blue Larkspur	3	6	4	1	0	153,450	1957	Round Table	3	22	15	1	3	600,383
1930	Gallant Fox	3	10	9	1	0	308,275	1958	Round Table	4	20	14	4	0	662,780
1931	Top Flight	2	7	7	0	0	219,000	1959	Sword Dancer	3	13	8	4	0	537,004
1932	Gusto	3	16	4	3	2	145,940	1960	Bally Ache	3	15	10	3	1	455,045
1933	Singing Wood	2	9	3	2	2	88,050	1961	Carry Back	3	16	9	1	3	565,349
1934	Cavalcade	3	7	6	1	0	111,235	1962	Never Bend	2	10	7	1	2	402,969
1935	Omaha	3	9	6	1	2	142,255	1963	Candy Spots	3	12	7	2	1	604,481
1936	Granville	3	11	7	3	0	110,295	1964	Gun Bow	4	16	8	4	2	580,100
1937	Seabiscuit	4	15	11	2	2	168,580	1965	Buckpasser	2	11	9	1	0	568,096
1938	Stagehand	3	15	8	2	3	189,710	1966	Buckpasser	3	14	13	1	0	669,078
1939	Challedon	3	15	9	2	3	184,535	1967	Damascus	3	16	12	3	1	817,941
1940	Bimelech	3	7	4	2	1	110,005	1968	Forward Pass	3	13	7	2	0	546,674
1941	Whirlaway	3	20	13	5	2	272,386	1969	Arts and Letters	3	14	8	5	1	555,604
1942	Shut Out	3	12	8	2	0	238,872	1970	Personality	3	18	8	2	1	444,049
1943	Count Fleet	3	6	6	0	0	174,055	1971	Riva Ridge	2	9	7	0	0	503,263
1944	Pavot	2	8	8	0	0	179,040	1972	Droll Role	4	19	7	3	4	471,633
1945	Busher	3	13	10	2	1	273,735	1973	Secretariat	3	12	9	2	1	860,404
1946	Assault	3	15	8	2	3	424,195	1974	Chris Evert	3	8	5	1	2	551,063
1947	Armed	6	17	11	4	1	376,325	1975	Foolish Pleasure	3	11	5	4	1	716,278
1948	Citation	3	20	19	1	0	709,470	1976	Forego	6	8	6	1	1	491,701
1949	Ponder	3	21	9	5	2	321,825	1977	Seattle Slew	3	7	6	0	0	641,370
1950	Noor	5	12	7	4	1	346,940	1978	Affirmed	3	11	8	2	0	901,541
1951	Counterpoint	3	15	7	2	1	250,525	1979	Spectacular Bid	3	12	10	1	1	1,279,334
1952	Crafty Admiral	4	16	9	4	1	277,225	1980	Temperence Hill	3	17	8	3	1	1,130,452

THE KENTUCKY DERBY (THREE-YEAR-OLDS) Distance: 1¼ miles (Churchill Downs, Ky.)

Year	Winner	Jockey	Net to Winner	Time	Second
1939	Johnstown	J. Stout	$ 46,350	2:03¾	Challedon
1940	Gallahadion	C. Bierman	60,150	2:05	Bimelech
1941	Whirlaway	E. Arcaro	61,275	2:01¾	Staretor
1942	Shut Out	W. D. Wright	64,225	2:04⅖	Alsab
1943	Count Fleet	J. Longden	60,275	2:04	Blue Swords
1944	Pensive	C McCreary	64,675	2:04⅕	Broadcloth
1945	Hoop Jr.	E. Arcaro	64,850	2:07	Pot o' Luck
1946	Assault	W. Mehrtens	96,400	2:06⅗	Spy Song
1947	Jet Pilot	E. Guerin	92,160	2:06¾	Phalanx
1948	Citation	E. Arcaro	83,400	2:05⅖	Coaltown
1949	Ponder	S. Brooks	91,600	2:04⅕	Capot
1950	Middleground	W. Boland	92,650	2:01¾	Hill Prince
1951	Count Turf	C. McCreary	98,050	2:02⅗	Royal Mustang
1952	Hill Gail	E. Arcaro	96,300	2:01¾	Sub Fleet
1953	Dark Star	H. Moreno	90,050	2:02	Native Dancer
1954	Determine	R. York	102,050	2:03	Hasty Road
1955	Swaps	W. Shoemaker	108,400	2:01⅘	Nashua
1956	Needles	D. Erb	123,450	2:03⅖	Fabius
1957	Iron Liege	W. Hartack	107,950	2:02⅕	Gallant Man
1958	Tim Tam	I. Valenzuela	116,400	2:05	Lincoln Road
1959	Tomy Lee	W. Shoemaker	119,650	2:02¼	Sword Dancer
1960	Venetian Way	W. Hartack	114,850	2:02⅖	Bally Ache
1961	Carry Back	J. Sellers	120,500	2:04	Crozier
1962	Decidedly	W. Hartack	119,650	2:00⅖	Roman Line
1963	Chateaugay	B. Baeza	108,900	2:01⅗	Never Bend
1964	Northern Dancer	W. Hartack	114,300	2:00	Hill Rise
1965	Lucky Debonair	W. Shoemaker	112,000	2:01⅕	Dapper Dan
1966	Kauai King	D. Brumfield	120,500	2:02	Advocator
1967	Proud Clarion	R. Ussery	119,700	2:00⅗	Barbs Delight
1968	Forward Pass	I. Valenzuela	122,600	2:02⅕	Francie's Hat
1969	Majestic Prince	W. Hartack	113,200	2:01⅘	Arts & Letters
1970	Dust Commander	M. Manganello	127,800	2:03⅖	My Dad George
1971	Canonero II	G. Avila	145,500	2:03⅕	Jim French
1972	Riva Ridge	Ron Turcotte	140,300	2:01.8	No Le Hace
1973	Secretariat	Ron Turcotte	155,050	1:59⅖	Sham
1974	Cannonade	Angel Cordero, Jr.	274,000	2:04	Hudson County
1975	Foolish Pleasure	Jacinto Vasquez	209,600	2:02	Avatar
1976	Bold Forbes	Angel Cordero, Jr.	217,700	2:01⅗	Honest Pleasure
1977	Seattle Slew	Jean Cruguet	214,700	2:02⅕	Run Dusty Run
1978	Affirmed	Steve Cauthen	186,900	2:01⅕	Alydar
1979	Spectacular Bid	Ron Franklin	228,650	2:02⅖	General Assembly
1980	Genuine Risk	Jacinto Vasquez	250,550	2:02	Rumbo
1981	Pleasant Colony	Jorge Velasquez	317,200	2:02	Woodchopper

THE PREAKNESS STAKES (THREE-YEAR-OLDS) Distance 1-3/16 miles (Pimlico, Md.)

Year	Winner	Jockey	Net to Winner	Time	Second
1939	Challedon	G. Seabo	$ 53,710	1:59¾	Gilded Knight
1940	Bimelech	F. A. Smith	53,230	1:58⅘	Mioland
1941	Whirlaway	E. Arcaro	49,365	1:58⅘	King Cole
1942	Alsab	B. James	58,175	1:57	tie
1943	Count Fleet	J. Longden	43,190	1:57⅖	Blue Swords
1944	Pensive	C. McCreary	60,075	1:59⅕	Platter
1945	Polynesian	W. D. Wright	66,170	1:58⅘	Hoop Jr.
1946	Assault	W. Mehrtens	96,620	2:01⅖	Lord Boswell
1947	Faultless	D. Dodson	98,005	1:59	On Trust
1948	Citation	E. Arcaro	91,870	2:02⅖	Vulcan's Forge
1949	Capot	T. Atkinson	79,985	1:56	Palestinian
1950	Hill Prince	E. Arcaro	56,115	1:59⅕	Middleground
1951	Bold	E. Arcaro	83,110	1:56⅖	Counterpoint
1952	Blue Man	C. McCreary	86,135	1:57⅖	Jampol
1953	Native Dancer	E. Guerin	65,200	1:57⅘	Jamie K.
1954	Hasty Road	J. Adams	91,600	1:57⅖	Correlation
1955	Nashua	E. Arcaro	67,550	1:54⅘	Saratoga
1956	Fabius	W. Hartack	84,250	1:58⅕	Needles
1957	Bold Ruler	E. Arcaro	65,250	1:56⅕	Iron Liege
1958	Tim Tam	I. Valenzuela	97,900	1:57⅕	Lincoln Road
1959	Royal Orbit	W. Harmatz	136,200	1:57	Sword Dancer
1960	Bally Ache	R. Ussery	121,000	1:57⅖	Victoria Park
1961	Carry Back	J. Sellers	126,200	1:57⅘	Globemaster
1962	Greek Money	J. L. Rotz	135,800	1:56¼	Ridan
1963	Candy Spots	W. Shoemaker	127,500	1:56⅖	Chateaugay
1964	Northern Dancer	W. Hartack	124,200	1:56⅘	The Scoundrel
1965	Tom Rolfe	R. Turcotte	128,100	1:56⅖	Dapper Dan
1966	Kauai King	D. Brumfield	129,000	1:55⅖	Stupendous
1967	Damascus	W. Shoemaker	141,500	1:55⅕	In Reality
1968	Forward Pass	I. Valenzuela	142,700	1:56⅖	Out of the Way
1969	Majestic Prince	W. Hartack	129,500	1:55⅗	Arts & Letters
1970	Personality	E. Belmonte	151,300	1:56⅕	My Dad George
1971	Canonero II	G. Avila	137,400	1:54	Eastern Fleet
1972	Bee Bee Bee	Eldon Nelson	135,000	1:55.4	No Le Hace
1973	Secretariat	Ron Turcotte	129,900	1:54⅖	Sham
1974	Little Current	Miguel Rivera	156,500	1:54⅗	Neopolitan Way
1975	Master Derby	Darrel McHargue	158,100	1:56⅖	Foolish Pleasure
1976	Elocutionist	John Lively	129,700	1:55	Play the Red
1977	Seattle Slew	Jean Cruguet	138,600	1:54⅖	Iron Constitution
1978	Affirmed	Steve Cauthen	136,200	1:54⅖	Alydar
1979	Spectacular Bid	Ron Franklin	165,300	1:54⅕	Golden Act
1980	Codex	Angel Cordero	180,600	1:54⅕	Genuine Risk
1981	Pleasant Colony	Jorge Velasquez	200,800	1:54⅗	Bold Ego

THE BELMONT STAKES (THREE-YEAR-OLDS)   Distance: 1½ miles. (Elmont, N.Y.)

Year	Winner	Jockey	Net to Winner	Time	Second
1938	Pasteurized	J. Stout	$34,530	2:29⅗	Dauber
1939	Johnstown	J. Stout	37,020	2:29⅗	Belay
1940	Bimelech	F. A. Smith	35,030	2:29⅗	Your Chance
1941	Whirlaway	E. Arcaro	39,770	2:31	Robert Morris
1942	Shut Out	E. Arcaro	44,520	2:29½	Alsab
1943	Count Fleet	J. Longden	35,340	2:28½	Fairy Manhurst
1944	Bounding Home	G. L. Smith	55,000	2:32½	Pensive
1945	Pavot	E. Arcaro	52,675	2:30½	Wildlife
1946	Assault	W. Mehrtens	75,400	2:30⅘	Natchez
1947	Phalanx	R. Donoso	78,900	2:29⅘	Tide Rips
1948	Citation	E. Arcaro	77,700	2:28⅕	Better Self
1949	Capot	T. Atkinson	60,900	2:30½	Ponder
1950	Middleground	W. Boland	61,350	2:28⅘	Lights Up
1951	Counterpoint	D. Gorman	82,000	2:29	Battlefield
1952	One Count	E. Arcaro	82,400	2:30⅕	Blue Man
1953	Native Dancer	E. Guerin	82,500	2:28⅘	Jamie K.
1954	High Gun	E. Guerin	89,000	2:30⅘	Fisherman
1955	Nashua	E. Arcaro	83,700	2:29	Blazing Count
1956	Needles	D. Erb	83,600	2:29⅘	Career Boy
1957	Gallant Man	W. Shoemaker	77,300	2:26⅗	Inside Tract
1958	Cavan	P. Anderson	73,440	2:30½	Tim Tam
1959	Sword Dancer	W. Shoemaker	93,525	2:28⅖	Bagdad
1960	Celtic Ash	W. Hartack	96,785	2:29⅗	Venetian Way
1961	Sherluck	B. Baeza	104,900	2:29½	Globemaster
1962	Jaipur	W. Shoemaker	109,550	2:28⅕	Admiral's Voyage
1963	Chateaugay	B. Baeza	101,700	2:30½	Candy Spots
1964	Quadrangle	M. Ycaza	110,850	2:28⅘	Roman Brother
1965	Hail to All	J. Sellers	104,150	2:28⅖	Tom Rolfe
1966	Amberoid	W. Boland	117,700	2:29⅘	Buffle
1967	Damascus	W. Shoemaker	104,950	2:28⅘	Cool Reception
1968	Stage Door Johnny	H. Gustines	117,700	2:27½	Forward Pass
1969	Arts and Letters	B. Baeza	104,050	2:28⅘	Majestic Prince
1970	High Echelon	J. L. Rotz	115,000	2:34	Needles n Pens
1971	Pass Catcher	W. Blum	97,710	2:30⅖	Jim French
1972	Riva Ridge	Ron Turcotte	93,540	2:28	Ruritania
1973	Secretariat	Ron Turcotte	90,720	2:24	Twice a Prince
1974	Little Current	Miguel Rivera	101,970	2:29½	Jolly Johu
1975	Avatar	W. Shoemaker	116,160	2:28	Foolish Pleasure
1976	Bold Forbes	Angel Cordero, Jr.	117,000	2:29	McKenzie Bridge
1977	Seattle Slew	Jean Cruguet	109,080	2:29⅗	Run Dusty Run
1978	Affirmed	Steve Cauthen	110,580	2:26⅘	Alydar
1979	Coastal	Ruben Hernandez	161,400	2:28⅗	Golden Act
1980	Temperence Hill	Eddie Maple	176,220	2:29⅘	Genuine Risk
1981	Summing	George Martens	170,580	2:29	Highland Blade

WORLD THOROUGHBRED RACING RECORDS

Distance	Horse, age, weight	Track	Date	Time
¼ mi.	Big Racket, 4, 114	Hipodromo de las Americas, Mexico City	Feb. 5, 1945	:20⅘
2½ f.	Tie Score, 5, 115	Hipodromo de las Americas, Mexico City	Feb. 5, 1946	:26⅘
⅜ mi.	Atoka, 6, 105	Butte, Mont.	Sept. 7, 1906	:33½
3½ f.	Tango King, 6, 116	Northlands Park, Canada	April 22, 1978	:38⅘
½ mi.	Norgor, 9, 118	Ruidoso Downs, Ruidoso, N.M.	Aug. 14, 1976	:44¾
4½ f.	Kathryn's Doll, 2, 111	Turf Paradise, Phoenix, Ariz.	April 9, 1967	:50⅘
	Dear Ethel, 2, 114	Miles Park, Louisville, Ky.	July 4, 1967	:50⅘
	Scott's Poppy, 2,118	Turf Paradise, Phoenix, Ariz.	Feb. 22, 1976	:50⅘
⅝ mi.	Zip Pocket, 3, 122	Turf Paradise, Phoenix, Ariz.	April 22, 1967	:55⅘
5½ f.	Zip Pocket, 3, 129	Turf Paradise, Phoenix, Ariz.	Nov. 19, 1967	1:01¾
5¾ f.	Last Freeby, 4, 116	Timonium, Md.	July 20, 1974	1:07⅕
¾ mi	Grey Papa, 6, 112	Longacres, Seattle, Wash.	Sept. 4, 1972	1:07⅕
6½ f.	Best Hitter, 4, 114	Longacres, Seattle, Wash.	Aug. 24, 1973	1:13⅘
⅞ mi.	Rich Cream, 5, 118	Hollywood Park, Inglewood, Calif.	May 28, 1980	1:19⅗
1 mi.	Dr. Fager, 4, 134	Arlington Park, Arlington Heights, Ill.	Aug. 24, 1968	1:32⅕
1 mi. 70 yd.	Aborigine, 6, 119	Penn National, Pa.	Aug. 20, 1978	1:37⅕
1¹⁄₁₆ mi.	Told, 4, 123	Penn National, Pa.	Sept. 14, 1980	1:38
1⅛ mi.	Tentam, 4, 118	Saratoga, Saratoga Springs, N.Y.	Aug. 10, 1973	1:45⅘
	Secretariat, 3, 124	Belmont Park, Elmont, N.Y.	Sept. 15, 1973	1:45⅖
1⅜ mi.	Toonerville, 5, 120	Hialeah Park, Hialeah, Fla.	Feb. 7, 1976	1:51⅗
1¼ mi.	Double Discount, 4, 116	Santa Anita, Arcadia, Calif.	Oct. 9, 1977	1:57⅖
1 5/16 mi.	Roberto, 3, 122	York, England	Aug. 15, 1972	2:07
1⅜ mi.	Cougar II, 6, 126	Hollywood Park, Inglewood, Calif.	April 29, 1972	2:11
1½ mi.	Fiddle Isle, 5, 124	Santa Anita Park, Arcadia, Calif.	Mar. 21, 1970	2:23
	John Henry, 5, 126	Santa Anita, Arcadia, Calif.	Mar. 16, 1980	2:23
1⁹⁄₁₆ mi.	Lone Wolf, 5, 115	Keeneland, Lexington, Ky.	Oct. 31, 1961	2:37¾
1⅝ mi.	Red Reality, 6, 113	Saratoga, Saratoga Springs, N.Y.	Aug. 23, 1972	2:37⅘
	Malwak, 5, 110	Saratoga, Saratoga Springs, N.Y.	Aug. 22, 1973	2:37⅘
1¾ mi.	Noor, 5, 117	Santa Anita Park, Arcadia, Calif.	March 4, 1950	2:52⅘
1⅞ mi.	El Moro, 8, 116	Delaware Park, Wilmington, Del.	July 22, 1963	3:11⅘
2 mi.	Polazel, 3, 142	Salisbury, England	July 8, 1924	3:15
2¹⁄₁₆ mi.	Midafternoon, 4, 126	Jamaica, Jamaica, N.Y.	Nov. 15, 1956	3:29¾
2⅛ mi.	Ceinturion, 5, 119	Newbury, England	Sept. 29, 1923	3:35
2⁹⁄₁₆ mi.	Santiago, 5, 112	Narragansett Park, Pawtucket, R.I.	Sept. 27, 1941	3:51⅕
2¼ mi.	Dakota, 4, 116	Lingfield, England	May 27, 1927	3:37¾
2⅜ mi.	Pamroy, 4, 120	Goodwood Park, Sussex, England	Aug. 1, 1973	4:10⅗
2½ mi.	Miss Grillo, 6, 118	Pimlico, Baltimore, Md.	Nov. 12, 1948	4:14⅘
2⅝ mi.	Girandole, 4, 126	Goodwood Park, Sussex, England	July 31, 1975	4:38⅘
2¾ mi.	Shot Put, 4, 126	Washington Park, Homewood, Ill.	Aug. 14, 1940	4:48⅘
2⅞ mi.	Bosh, 5, 100	Tijuana, Mexico	Mar. 8, 1925	5:23
3 mi.	Farragut, 5, 113	Agua Caliente, Mexico	Mar. 9, 1941	5:15

HARNESS RACING SOURCE: The U.S. Trotting Association
LEADING MONEY-WINNERS

TROTTERS Year	Horse	Amount Won	PACERS Year	Horse	Amount Won
1951	Pronto Don	$ 80,850	1951	Tar Heel	$ 66,629
1952	Sharp Note	101,625	1952	Good Time	110,299
1953	Newport Dream	94,933	1953	Keystoner	59,131
1954	Katie Key	84,867	1954	Red Sails	66,615
1955	Scott Frost	186,101	1955	Adios Harry	98,900
1956	Scott Frost	85,851	1956	Adios Harry	129,912
1957	Hoot Song	114,877	1957	Torpid	113,982
1958	Emily's Pride	118,830	1958	Belle Acton	167,887
1959	Diller Hanover	149,897	1959	Bye Bye Byrd	199,933
1960	Su Mac Lad	159,662	1960	Bye Bye Byrd	187,612
1961	Su Mac Lad	245,750	1961	Adios Butler	180,250
1962	Duke Rodney	206,113	1962	Henry T. Adios	220,302
1963	Speedy Scot	244,403	1963	Overtrick	208,833
1964	Speedy Scot	235,710	1964	Race Time	199,292
1965	Dartmouth	252,348	1965	Bret Hanover	341,784
1966	Noble Victory	210,696	1966	Bret Hanover	407,534
1967	Carlisle	231,243	1967	Romulus Hanover	277,636
1968	Nevele Pride	427,440	1968	Rum Customer	355,618
1969	Lindy's Pride	323,997	1969	Overcall	373,150
1970	Fresh Yankee	359,002	1970	Most Happy Fella	387,239
1971	Fresh Yankee	293,950	1971	Albatross	558,009
1972	Super Bowl	436,258	1972	Albatross	459,921
1973	Spartan Hanover	262,023	1973	Sir Dalrae	307,354
1974	Delmonica Hanover	252,165	1974	Armbro Omaha	357,146
1975	Savoir	351,385	1975	Silk Stockings	336,312
1976	Steve Lobell	357,005	1976	Keystone Ore	539,759
1977	Green Speed	584,405	1977	Governor Skipper	522,148
1978	Speedy Somolli	362,404	1978	Abercrombie	703,260
1979	Chiola Hanover	553,058	1979	Hot Hitter	826,542
1980	Classical Way	350,410	1980	Niatross	1,414,313

HARNESS HORSE OF THE YEAR

Year	Horse	Gait	Year	Horse	Gait
1951	Pronto Don	trotter	1966	Bret Hanover	pacer
1952	Good Time	pacer	1967	Nevele Pride	trotter
1953	Hi-Lo's Forbes	pacer	1968	Nevele Pride	trotter
1954	Stenographer	trotter	1969	Nevele Pride	trotter
1955	Scott Frost	trotter	1970	Fresh Yankee	trotter
1956	Scott Frost	trotter	1971	Albatross	pacer
1957	Torpid	pacer	1972	Albatross	pacer
1958	Emily's Pride	trotter	1973	Sir Dalrae	pacer
1959	Bye Bye Byrd	pacer	1974	Delmonica Hanover	trotter
1960	Adios Butler	pacer	1975	Savoir	trotter
1961	Adios Butler	pacer	1976	Keystone Ore	pacer
1962	Su Mac Lad	trotter	1977	Green Speed	trotter
1963	Speedy Scot	trotter	1978	Abercrombie	pacer
1964	Bret Hanover	pacer	1979	Niatross	pacer
1965	Bret Hanover	pacer	1980	Niatross	pacer

THE HAMBLETONIAN (THREE-YEAR-OLD TROTTERS)

Year	Purse	Winner	Second	Winning Driver	Fastest Heat
1951	$ 95,263	Mainliner	Spennib	Guy Crippen	2:02¾
1952	87,637	Sharp Note	Hit Song	Bion Shively	2:02⅜
1953	117,117	Helicopter	Morse Hanover	Harry M. Harvey	2:01⅜(a)
1954	106,830	Newport Dream	Princess Rodney	Adelbert Cameron	2:02⅘
1955	86,863	Scott Frost	(1)	Joe O'Brien	2:00⅜
1956	100,603	The Intruder	Valiant Rodney	Ned F. Bower	2:01⅘
1957	111,126	Hickory Smoke	Hoot Song	John F. Simpson, Sr.	2:00⅛
1958	106,719	Emily's Pride	Little Rocky	Flave T. Nipe	1:59¼
1959	125,283	Diller Hanover	Tie Silk	Frank Ervin	2:01½
1960	147,481	Blaze Hanover	Quick Song	Joe O'Brien	1:59⅗(b)
1961	131,573	Harlan Dean	Caleb	James W. Arthur	1:58⅖
1962	116,612	A. C.'s Viking	Isaac	Sanders Russell	1:59⅗
1963	115,549	Speedy Scot	Florlis	Ralph N. Baldwin	1:57⅗(c)
1964	115,281	Ayres	Big John	John F. Simpson	1:56⅘(R)
1965	122,245	Egyptian Candor	Armbro Flight	Adelbert Cameron	2:03⅖(d)
1966	122,540	Kerry Way	Polaris	Frank Ervin	1:58⅖
1967	122,650	Speedy Streak	Keystone Pride	Adelbert Cameron	2:00
1968	116,190	Nevele Pride	Keystone Spartan	Stanley Dancer	1:59⅖
1969	124,910	Lindy's Pride	The Prophet	Howard Beissinger	1:57⅗
1970	143,630	Timothy T.	Formal Notice	John F. Simpson, Jr.	1:58⅔(e)
1971	129,770	Speedy Crown	Savoir	Howard Beissinger	1:57⅕
1972	119,090	Super Bowl	Delmonica Hanover	Stanley Dancer	1:56⅗(R)
1973	144,710	Flirth	Florinda	Ralph Baldwin	1:57⅕
1974	160,150	Christopher T.	Nevele Diamond	Wm. Haughton	1:58⅜
1975	232,192	Bonefish	Yankee Bambino	Stanley Dancer	1:59
1976	263,524	Steve Lobell	Zoot Suit	Wm. Haughton	1:56⅔(R)
1977	284,000	Green Speed	Texas	Wm. Haughton	1:55⅗(R)
1978	241,000	Speedy Somolli	Briscoe Hanover	Howard Beissinger	1:55(R)
1979	300,000	Legend Hanover	Chiola Hanover	George Sholty	1:56½
1980	293,570	Burgomeister	Devil Hanover	Wm. Haughton	1:56⅜
1981	419,000	Shiaway St. Pat	Super Juan	Ray Remmen	2:02⅕

(1) Galophone and Leopold Hanover divided second and third monies. (a) By Morse Hanover. (b) By Quick Song and Hoot Frost. (c) By Floris. (d) By Armbro Flight. (e) By Formal Notice. (R) Record.

THE KENTUCKY FUTURITY (THREE-YEAR-OLD TROTTERS)

Year	Purse	Winner	Second	Winning Driver	Fastest Heat
1951	$ 66,659	Ford Hanover	Candy Man	John F. Simpson, Sr.	2:01⅗
1952	66,231	Sharp Note	Duke of Lullwater	Bion Shively	2:00⅘
1953	67,485	Kimberly Kid	Faber Hanover	Thomas S. Berry	2:00⅗
1954	63,121	Harlan	Pronto Boy	Delvin Miller	2:01
1955	62,702	Scott Frost	Home Free	Joe O'Brien	2:00⅗
1956	53,731	Nimble Colby	Barlow Hanover	Ralph N. Baldwin	2:02
1957	50,460	Cassin Hanover	Storm Cloud	Fred Egan	2:02½
1958	53,330	Emily's Pride	Senator Frost	Flave T. Nipe	1:59⅘(a)
1959	53,810	Diller Hanover	Tie Silk	Ralph N. Baldwin	2:01½
1960	64,040	Elaine Rodney	Quick Song	Clint T. Hodgins	1:58⅗
1961	59,330	Duke Rodney	Caleb	Eddie T. Wheeler	1:58⅓(b)
1962	55,230	Safe Mission	Impish	Joe O'Brien	1:59½
1963	61,128	Speedy Scot	Florlis	Ralph N. Baldwin	1:57½
1964	57,096	Ayres	Dashing Rodney	John F. Simpson, Sr.	1:58⅘
1965	65,133	Armbro Flight	Noble Victory	Joe O'Brien	1:59⅗
1966	61,602	Governor Armbro	Gay Sam	Joe O'Brien	2:00⅖
1967	58,642	Speed Model	Rocket Speed	Arthur L. Hult	1:59⅗(c)
1968	57,397	Nevele Pride	Snow Speed	Stanley F. Dancer	1:57 (R)
1969	64,757	Lindy's Pride	Nevele Major	Howard Beissinger	1:59
1970	76,351	Timothy T.	Paris Air	John F. Simpson, Jr.	1:59⅘
1971	63,415	Savoir	Keystone Hilliard	James Arthur	1:58½
1972	56,210	Super Bowl	Spartan Hanover	Stanley Dancer	1:59
1973	64,174	Arnie Almahurst	Knightly Way	Joe O'Brien	1:59½
1974	100,000	Waymaker	Dancing Party	John Simpson, Jr.	1:58½
1975	100,000	Noble Rogue	Exclusive Way	William Herman	1:59 (d)
1976	100,000	Quick Pay	Steve Lobell	Peter Haughton	1:59
1977	100,000	Texas	Cold Comfort	William Herman	1:57⅗
1978	100,000	Doublemint	Way to Gain	Peter Haughton	1:58⅗
1979	100,000	Classical Way	Chiola Hanover	John Simpson, Jr.	1:57⅘
1980	100,000	Final Score	Noble Hustle	Tom Haughton	1:58

(a) By Senator Frost. (b) By Caleb. (c) By Rocket Speed (d) By Exclusive Way. (R) Record.

WORLD HARNESS RACING RECORDS

Age	Record		Horse	Driver	Track	Year
TROTTERS: MILE TRACK						
All Ages	1:54⅘		Nevele Pride	Stanley Dancer	Indianapolis, Ind.	1969
	1:54⅘	(r)	Lindy's Crown	Howard Beissinger	DuQuoin, Ill.	1980
2-year-old	1:57	(r)	Briscoe Hanover	James Miller	Du Quoin, Ill.	1977
3-year-old	1:55	(r)	Speedy Somolli	Howard Beissinger	DuQuoin, Ill.	1978
	1:55	(r)	Florida Pro	George Sholty	DuQuoin, Ill.	1978
4-year-old	1:54⅘	(r)	Lindy's Crown	Howard Beissinger	DuQuoin, Ill.	1980
TROTTERS: FIVE-EIGHTHS MILE						
All Ages	1:57½	(r)	Lindy's Crown	Howard Beissinger	Wilmington, Del.	1980
2-year-old	2:00⅖	(r)	Smokin Yankee	Stanley Dancer	Meadow Lands, Pa.	1980
3-year-old	1:58	(r)	Keystone Sister (f)	Delvin Miller	Meadow Lands, Pa.	1981
4-year-old	1:57½	(r)	Lindy's Crown	Howard Beissinger	Wilmington, Del.	1980
TROTTERS: HALF-MILE TRACK						
All Ages	1:56⅘	(r)	Nevele Pride	Stanley Dancer	Saratoga Springs, N.Y.	1969
2-year-old	2:01½	(r)	Ayres	John Simpson, Sr.	Delaware, Ohio	1963
3-year-old	1:58¾	(r)	Songcan	George Sholty	Delaware, Ohio	1972
4-year-old	1:56⅘	(r)	Nevele Pride	Stanley Dancer	Saratoga Springs, N.Y.	1969
PACERS: MILE TRACK						
All Ages	1:49⅕	(r)	Niatross	Clint Galbraith	Lexington, Ky.	1980
2-year-old	1:54	(r)	French Chef	Stanley Dancer	Indianapolis, Ind.	1980
3-year-old	1:49⅕	(r)	Niatross	Clint Galbraith	Lexington, Ky.	1980
4-year-old	1:52		Steady Star	Joe O'Brien	Lexington, Ky.	1971
PACERS: FIVE-EIGHTHS MILE						
All Ages	1:53⅘	(r)	Storm Damage	Joe O'Brien	Meadow Lands, Pa.	1980
2-year-old	1:56⅕	(r)	French Chef	Stanley Dancer	Columbus, Ohio	1980
3-year-old	1:53⅘	(r)	Storm Damage	Joe O'Brien	Meadow Lands, Pa.	1980
4-year-old	1:54⅖	(r)	Direct Scooter	Warren Cameron	Windsor, Ont.	1980
PACERS: HALF-MILE TRACK						
All Ages	1:54⅘	(r)	Niatross	Clint Galbraith	Delaware, Ohio	1980
2-year-old	1:57⅖	(r)	Slapstick	Jack Parker, Jr.	Louisville, Ky.	1980
3-year-old	1:54⅘		Niatross	Clint Galbraith	Delaware, Ohio	1980
4-year-old	1:55⅗	(r)	Albatross	Stanley Dancer	Delaware, Ohio	1972

(r) Record made in race. Other records were set in time trials. (f) Record made by filly.

HARNESS RACING DOLLAR EARNINGS (through August 21, 1981)

Pacers, All-Time

Rank	Horse	Winnings
1.	Niatross	$2,019,213
2.	Rambling Willie	1,937,602
3.	Albatross	1,201,470
4.	Land Grant	1,094,120
5.	Governor Skipper	1,039,756
6.	Rum Customer	1,001,548
7.	Cardigan Bay	1,000,837
8.	Abercrombie	984,391
9.	Hot Hitter	963,574
10.	McKinzie Almahurst	936,110

Trotters, All-Time

Rank	Horse	Winnings
1.	Bellino II	$1,960,945*
2.	Ideal du Gazeau	1,744,357
3.	Un De Mai	1,660,627*
4.	Eleazar	1,465,454
5.	Savoir	1,365,145
6.	Jorky	1,333,790*
7.	Fresh Yankee	1,294,252
8.	Hadol du Vivier	1,263,121
9.	Keystone Pioneer	1,071,927
10.	Green Speed	953,013

Drivers, All-Time

Rank	Driver	Winnings
1.	Herve Filion	$34,547,002
2.	William Haughton	30,051,369
3.	Carmine Abbatiello	27,678,990
4.	Del Insko	25,056,181
5.	Stanley Dancer	22,410,137
6.	John Chapman	21,350,831
7.	William Gilmour	19,984,031
8.	Joe O'Brien	19,325,192
9.	Ben Webster	18,679,656
10.	Lucien Fontaine	17,870,536

* Compiled by French authorities.

BOXING

AMATEUR BOXING CHAMPIONS

1981 NORTH AMERICAN CHAMPIONS	CLASS	1981 U.S.A. BOXING FEDERATION
Johnny Keys, San Francisco, Calif.	Super Heavyweight (over 201 lbs.)	Tyrone Biggs, Philadelphia, Pa.
Carl Williams, New York, N.Y.	Heavyweight (201 lbs.)	Mark Mahone, U.S. Navy
Johnny Williams, Chicago, Ill.	Light Heavyweight (178 lbs.)	Alex Delucia, Portland, Ore.
Jose Gomez, Cuba	Middleweight (165 lbs.)	Michael Grogan, Atlanta, Ga.
Armando Martinez, Cuba	Light Middleweight (156 lbs.)	James Rayford, U.S. Navy
Louis Howard, St. Louis, Mo.	Welterweight (147 lbs.)	Darryl Robinson, Houston, Tex.
Ricky Anderson, Canada	Light Welterweight (139 lbs.)	James Mitchell, U.S. Army
Angel Herrera, Cuba	Lightweight (132 lbs.)	Joe Manley, U.S. Army
Adolfo Horta, Cuba	Featherweight (125 lbs.)	Guadalupe Suarez, Corpus Christi, Tex.
Richard Savage, W. Monroe, La.	Bantamweight (119 lbs.)	Richard Savage, W. Monroe, La.
Omar Santiesteban, Cuba	Flyweight (112 lbs.)	Fred Perkins, U.S. Army
Hipolito Ramos, Cuba	Light Flyweight (106 lbs.)	Jesse Benavides, Corpus Christi, Tex.

PROFESSIONAL BOXING CHAMPIONS   To October 4, 1981

DIVISION	WORLD BOXING ASSOCIATION (WBA)	WORLD BOXING COUNCIL (WBC)
Heavyweight	Mike Weaver, Los Angeles, Calif.	Larry Holmes, Easton, Pa.
Cruiserweight		Carlos DeLeon, Puerto Rico
Light Heavyweight	Michael Spinks, Philadelphia, Pa.	Matthew Saad Muhammad, Phila., Pa.
Middleweight	Marvin Hagler, Brockton, Mass.	Marvin Hagler
Jr. Middleweight	(Vacant)	Wilfred Benitez, Puerto Rico
Welterweight	Sugar Ray Leonard, Palmer Park, Md.	Sugar Ray Leonard
Jr. Welterweight	Aaron Pryor, Cincinnati, Ohio	Saoul Mamby, New York, N.Y.
Lightweight	Claude Noel, Trinidad	Alexis Arguello, Nicaragua
Jr. Lightweight	Sammy Serrano, Puerto Rico	Rolando Navarrete, Philippines
Featherweight	Eusebio Pedroza, Panama	Salvador Sanchez, Mexico
Jr. Featherweight	Sergio Palma, Argentina	Wilfredo Gomez, Panama
Bantamweight	Jeff Chandler, Philadelphia, Pa.	Lupe Pintor, Mexico
Jr. Bantamweight	Gustavo Ballas, Argentina	Chul Ho-Kim, South Korea
Flyweight	Luis Ibarra, Panama	Antonio Avelar, Mexico
Jr. Flyweight	Kim Hwan-Jin, South Korea	Hilario Zapata, Mexico

HEAVYWEIGHT CHAMPIONSHIP FIGHTS IN WHICH TITLE CHANGED HANDS

Date	Site	Winner	Weight (age)	Citizen	Loser	Weight (age)	Rounds	Referee
July 8, 1889[a]	Richburg, Miss.	John L. Sullivan, 198	(30)	U.S.	Jake Kilrain, 185	(30)	75	John Fitzpatrick
Sept. 7, 1892	New Orleans	James J. Corbett, 178	(26)	U.S.	John L. Sullivan, 212	(33)	21	Prof. John Duffy
Mar. 17, 1897	Carson City, Nev.	Bob Fitzsimmons, 167	(34)	England	James J. Corbett, 183	(30)	KO 14	George Siler
June 9, 1899	Coney Island	[b]James J. Jeffries, 206	(24)	U.S.	Bob Fitzsimmons, 167	(37)	KO 11	George Siler
Feb. 23, 1906	Los Angeles	[c]Tommy Burns, 180	(24)	Canada	Marvin Hart, 188	(29)	20	James J. Jeffries
Dec. 26, 1908	Sydney, Australia	Jack Johnson, 196	(30)	U.S.	Tommy Burns, 176	(27)	KO 14	Hugh McIntosh
April 5, 1915	Havana, Cuba	Jess Willard, 230	(33)	U.S.	Jack Johnson, 205½	(37)	KO 26	Jack Welch
July 4, 1919	Toledo	Jack Dempsey, 187	(24)	U.S.	Jess Willard, 245	(37)	KO 3	Ollie Pecord
Sept. 23, 1926	Philadelphia	[d]Gene Tunney, 189	(28)	U.S.	Jack Dempsey, 190	(31)	10	Pop Reilly
June 12, 1930	New York	[h]Max Schmeling, 188	(24)	Germany	Jack Sharkey, 197	(27)	4	Jim Crowley
June 21, 1932	Long Island City	Jack Sharkey, 205	(29)	U.S.	Max Schmeling, 188	(26)	15	Gunboat Smith
June 29, 1933	Long Island City	Primo Carnera, 260½	(26)	Italy	Jack Sharkey, 201	(30)	KO 6	Arthur Donovan
June 14, 1934	Long Island City	Max Baer, 209½	(25)	U.S.	Primo Carnera, 263¼	(27)	KO 11	Arthur Donovan
June 13, 1935	Long Island City	Jim Braddock, 193¾	(29)	U.S.	Max Baer, 209½	(26)	15	Jack McAvoy
June 22, 1937	Chicago	Joe Louis, 197¼	(23)	U.S.	Jim Braddock, 197	(31)	KO 8	Tommy Thomas
June 22, 1949	Chicago	[e]Ezzard Charles, 181¾	(27)	U.S.	Joe Walcott, 195½	(35)	15	Davey Miller
Sept. 27, 1950	New York	[f]Ezzard Charles, 184½	(29)	U.S.	Joe Louis, 218	(36)	15	Mark Conn
July 18, 1951	Pittsburgh	Joe Walcott, 194	(37)	U.S.	Ezzard Charles, 182	(30)	KO 7	Buck McTiernan
Sept. 23, 1952	Philadelphia	[g]Rocky Marciano, 184	(29)	U.S.	Joe Walcott, 196	(38)	KO 13	Charley Daggert
Nov. 30, 1956	Chicago	Floyd Patterson, 182¼	(21)	U.S.	Archie Moore, 187¾	(42)	KO 5	Frank Sikora
June 26, 1959	New York	Ingemar Johansson, 196	(26)	Sweden	Floyd Patterson, 182	(24)	KO 3	Ruby Goldstein
June 20, 1960	New York	Floyd Patterson, 190	(25)	U.S.	Ingemar Johansson, 193¾	(27)	KO 5	Arthur Mercante
Sept. 25, 1962	Chicago	Sonny Liston, 214	(28)	U.S.	Floyd Patterson, 189	(27)	KO 1	Frank Sikora
Feb. 25, 1964	Miami Beach	Cassius Clay, 210	(22)	U.S.	Sonny Liston, 218	(30)	KO 7	Barney Felix
March 4, 1968	New York	[i]Joe Frazier, 204½	(24)	U.S.	Buster Mathis, 243½	(23)	KO 11	Arthur Mercante
April 27, 1968	Oakland, Calif.	[i]Jimmy Ellis, 197	(28)	U.S.	Jerry Quarry, 195	(22)	15	Elmer Costa
Feb. 16, 1970	New York	[i]Joe Frazier, 205	(26)	U.S.	Jimmy Ellis, 201	(29)	KO 5	Tony Perez
Jan. 22, 1973	Kingston, Jamaica	George Foreman, 217½	(25)	U.S.	Joe Frazier, 214	(29)	TKO 2	Arthur Mercante
Oct. 30, 1974	Zaire, Africa	Muhammad Ali, 216	(32)	U.S.	George Foreman, 220	(25)	KO 8	Zach Clayton
Feb. 15, 1978	Las Vegas	Leon Spinks, 197½	(24)	U.S.	Muhammad Ali, 224½	(36)	15	David Pearl
Sept. 15, 1978	New Orleans	Muhammad Ali, 221	(36)	U.S.	Leon Spinks, 201	(25)	15	Locien Joubert

[a] Last bareknuckle heavyweight title fight. [b] Jim Jeffries retired in March 1905 for lack of opposition. He named Marvin Hart and Jack Root as the leading contenders; they fought on July 3, 1905, and Hart knocked out Root in the 12th round. [c] Burns claimed title after beating Hart. [d] Tunney retired in July 1928. [e] On March 1, 1949, Joe Louis retired; the NBA named Charles champion after he defeated Walcott. [f] Charles became undisputed champion by beating Louis, who had come out of retirement. [g] Marciano retired as champion in April 1956. [h] Won on a foul. [i] Immediately after a Federal Grand Jury had indicted Clay (also known as Muhammad Ali) on May 9, 1967, for refusing to accept induction into the Army, his title was vacated by the World Boxing Association and the New York State Athletic Commission. The WBA then staged an eight-man tournament, won by Ellis, to crown a successor. Frazier eventually earned recognition in New York and several other states and later defeated Ellis.

BOXING CHAMPIONS SOURCE: World Boxing Association

LIGHT HEAVYWEIGHT DIVISION

1903–05	Bob Fitzsimmons
1905–12	"Philadelphia" Jack O'Brien
1912–16	Jack Dillon
1916–20	Battling Levinsky
1920–22	Georges Carpentier
1922–23	Battling Siki
1923–25	Mike McTigue
1925–26	Paul Berlenbach
1926–27	Jack Delaney
1927	Mike McTigue
1927–29	Tommy Loughran
1930	Jimmy Slattery
1930–34	Maxie Rosenbloom
1934–35	Bob Olin
1935–39	John Henry Lewis
1939	Melio Bettina
1939–41	Billy Conn
1941	Anton Christoforidis (NBA)
1941–48	Gus Lesnevich
1948–50	Freddie Mills
1950–52	Joey Maxim
1952–61	Archie Moore
1961–63	Harold Johnson
1963–65	Willie Pastrano
1965–66	Jose Torres
1966–68	Dick Tiger
1968–71	Bob Foster
1971–72	Vicente Rondon
1972–73	Bob Foster
1973–78	Victor Galindez
1978–79	Mike Rossman (WBA)
1979	Victor Galindez (WBA)
1979–80	Marvin Johnson (WBA)
1980–81	Mustafa Muhammad (WBA)
1981–	Michael Spinks (WBA)

MIDDLEWEIGHT DIVISION

1908	Stanley Ketchel
1908	Billy Papke
1908–10	Stanley Ketchel
1913	Frank Klaus
1913–14	George Chip
1914–17	Al McCoy
1917–20	Mike O'Dowd
1920–23	Johnny Wilson
1923–26	Harry Greb
1926	Tiger Flowers
1926–31	Mickey Walker
1931–41	Title in dispute
1941–47	Tony Zale
1947–48	Rocky Graziano
1948	Tony Zale
1948–49	Marcel Cerdan
1949–51	Jake LaMotta
1951	Ray Robinson, Randy Turpin
1951–52	Ray Robinson
1953–55	Bobo Olson
1955–57	Ray Robinson
1957	Gene Fullmer, Ray Robinson
1957–58	Carmen Basilio
1958–60	Ray Robinson
1959–62	Gene Fullmer (NBA)
1960–61	Paul Pender
1961–62	Terry Downes
1962	Paul Pender
1962–63	Dick Tiger
1963–65	Joey Giardello
1965–66	Dick Tiger
1966–67	Emile Griffith
1967	Nino Benvenuti
1967–68	Emile Griffith
1968–70	Nino Benvenuti
1970–77	Carlos Monzon
1977–78	Rodrigo Valdes
1978–79	Hugo Corro
1979–80	Vito Antuofermo
1980	Alan Minter
1980–	Marvin Hagler

WELTERWEIGHT DIVISION

1904–06	Joe Walcott
1906–07	Honey Mollody
1907–15	Mike (Twin) Sullivan
1915–19	Ted Lewis
1919–22	Jack Britton
1922–26	Mickey Walker
1926–27	Pete Latzo
1927–29	Joe Dundee
1929–30	Jackie Fields
1930	Young Jack Thompson
1930–31	Tommy Freeman
1931	Young Jack Thompson
1931–32	Lou Brouillard
1932–33	Jackie Fields
1933	Young Corbett 3d
1933–34	Jimmy McLarnin
1934	Barney Ross
1934–35	Jimmy McLarnin
1935–38	Barney Ross
1938–40	Henry Armstrong
1940–41	Fritzie Zivic
1941–46	Freddie Cochrane
1946	Marty Servo
1946–51	Ray Robinson
1951	Johnny Bratton (NBA)
1951–54	Kid Gavilan
1954–55	Johnny Saxton
1955	Tony DeMarco
1955–56	Carmen Basilio
1956	Johnny Saxton
1956–57	Carmen Basilio
1958	Virgil Akins
1958–60	Don Jordan
1960–61	Benny (Kid) Paret
1961	Emile Griffith
1961–62	Benny (Kid) Paret
1962–63	Emile Griffith
1963	Luis Rodriguez
1963–66	Emile Griffith
1966–69	Curtis Cokes
1969–70	Jose Napoles
1970–71	Billy Backus
1971–72	Jose Napoles
1972–76	Angel Espada
1976–80	Jose Cuevas (WBA)
1980–81	Thomas Hearns (WBA)
1981–	Ray Leonard

LIGHTWEIGHT DIVISION

1901–08	Joe Gans
1908–10	Battling Nelson
1910–12	Ad Wolgast
1912–14	Willie Ritchie
1914–17	Freddie Welsh
1917–25	Benny Leonard
1925	Jimmy Goodrich
1925–26	Rocky Kansas
1926–30	Sammy Mandell
1930	Al Singer
1930–33	Tony Canzoneri
1933–35	Barney Ross
1935–36	Tony Canzoneri
1936–38	Lou Ambers
1938–39	Henry Armstrong
1939–40	Lou Ambers
1940–41	Lew Jenkins
1941–42	Sammy Angott
1943–47	Title holders, according to the N.Y. Commission, were Beau Jack and Bob Montgomery, and according to the NBA, Sammy Angott, Juan Zurita, and Ike Williams.
1947–51	Ike Williams
1951–52	Jimmy Carter
1952	Lauro Salas
1952–54	Jimmy Carter
1954	Paddy DeMarco
1954–55	Jimmy Carter
1955–56	Wallace (Bud) Smith
1956–62	Joe Brown
1962–65	Carlos Ortiz
1965	Ismael Laguna
1965–68	Carlos Ortiz
1968–69	Carlos (Teo) Cruz
1969–70	Mando Ramos
1970	Ismael Laguna
1970–71	Ken Buchanan
1971–72	Mando Ramos
1972–73	Chango Carmona
1973–78	Roberto Duran
1979–80	Ernesto Espana (WBA)
1980–81	Hilmer Kenty (WBA)
1981	Sean O'Grady (WBA)
1981–	Claude Noel (WBA)

FEATHERWEIGHT DIVISION

1912–23	Johnny Kilbane
1923	Eugene Criqui
1923–25	Johnny Dundee
1926–27	Louis (Kid) Kaplan
1927–28	Benny Bass
1928	Tony Canzoneri
1928–29	Andre Routis
1929–32	Battling Battalino
1932	Tommy Paul (NBA)
1932	Kid Chocolate (NY)
1933–36	Freddie Miller
1936–37	Petey Sarron
1937–38	Henry Armstrong
1938–40	Joey Archibald
1940–41	Harry Jeffra
1941	Joey Archibald
1941–42	Chalky Wright
1942–48	Willie Pep
1948–49	Sandy Saddler
1949–50	Willie Pep
1950–57	Sandy Saddler
1957–59	Kid Bassey
1959–63	Davey Moore
1963–64	Sugar Ramos
1964–67	Vicente Saldivar
1968	Raul Rojas
1968	Sho Saijyo
1969	Johnny Famechon
1969–70	Vicente Saldivar
1970–71	Kuniaki Shibata
1971–72	Clemente Sanchez
1972–74	Ernesto Marcell
1974–77	Alexis Arguello
1977	Rafael Ortega
1977–78	Celio Lastra
1978–	Eusebio Pedroza (WBA)

BANTAMWEIGHT DIVISION

1936	Tony Marino
1936–37	Sixto Escobar
1937–38	Harry Jeffra
1938–40	Sixto Escobar
1940–42	Lou Salica
1942–47	Manuel Ortiz
1947	Harold Dade
1947–50	Manuel Ortiz
1950–52	Vic Toweel
1952–54	Jimmy Carruthers
1954–56	Robert Cohen
1956–57	Mario D'Agata
1957–59	Alphonse Halimi
1959–60	Joe Becerra
1961–65	Eder Jofre
1965–68	Masahiko (Fighting) Harada
1968–69	Lionel Rose
1969–70	Ruben Olivares
1970–71	Chucho Castillo
1971–72	Ruben Olivares
1972–73	Enrique Pinder
1973–74	Arnold Taylor
1974–77	Alfonso Zamora
1977–80	Jorge Lujan (WBA)
1980	Julian Solis (WBA)
1980–	Jeff Chandler (WBA)

FLYWEIGHT DIVISION

1938–43	Peter Kane
1943–48	Jackie Paterson
1948–50	Rinty Monaghan
1950	Terry Allen
1950–52	Dado Marino
1952–54	Yoshio Shirai
1954–60	Pascual Perez
1960–62	Pone Kingpetch
1962–63	Masahiko (Fighting) Harada
1963	Pone Kingpetch
1963–64	Hiroyuki Ebihara
1964–65	Pone Kingpetch
1965–66	Salvatore Burruni
1966	Horacio Accavallo
1966	Walter McGowan
1966–69	Chartchai Choinoi
1969	Hiroyuki Ebihara
1969–70	Bernabe Villacampo
1970	Berkrek Chartvanchai
1970–71	Masao Ohba
1971–72	Bertulio Gonzales
1972–73	Masao Ohba
1973–74	Chatchai Chionoi
1974–75	Erbito Salavarria
1976	Alfonso Lopez
1976–78	Gutty Espadas
1978–79	Betulio Gonzalez (WBA)
1979–80	Luis Ibarra (WBA)
1980	Kim Tae-Shik (WBA)
1980–81	Peter Mathebula (WBA)
1981	Santos Laciar (WBA)
1981–	Luis Ibarra (WBA)

TRACK AND FIELD

1981 NCAA INDOOR CHAMPIONS

60-Yard Dash—	Carl Lewis, Houston, 6.16	One-Mile Relay—	Seton Hall, 3:15.91
440-Yard Dash—	Bert Cameron, Texas-El Paso, 48.23	Two-Mile Relay—	Rutgers, 7:30.95
		Distance Medley Relay—	Villanova, 9:47.20
600-Yard Run—	Eugene Sanders, Miss. Valley St., 1:09.84	High Jump—	Leo Williams, Navy, 7′ 5¼″
880-Yard Run—	Sammy Koskei, SMU, 1:52.29	Long Jump—	Carl Lewis, Houston, 27′ 10″
1,000-Yard Run—	Peter Lemashon, Texas-El Paso, 2:12.29	Triple Jump—	Keith Connor, SMU, 56′ 9½″
One-Mile Run—	Suleiman Nyambui, Texas-El Paso, 4:01.85	Pole Vault—	Ed Langford, Purdue, 17′ 9½″
Two-Mile Run—	Doug Padilla, Brigham Young, 8:26.52	35 lb.-Weight Throw—	Robert Weir, SMU, 73′ 7″
Three-Mile Run—	Michael Musyoki, Texas-El Paso, 13:25.03	Shot Put—	Michael Carter, SMU, 69′ 8½″
60-Yard Hurdles—	Terron Wright, Memphis State, 7.14	Team—	Texas-El Paso

1981 AIAW INDOOR CHAMPIONS

60-Meter Dash—	Merlene Ottey, Nebraska, 7.24	3,000-Meter Run—	Patricia Sharples, Idaho, 9:33.96
300-Meter Dash—	Merlene Ottey, Nebraska, 35.83	5,000-Meter Run—	Aileen O'Connor, Virginia, 16:33.6
400-Meter Dash—	Pam Moore, Wisconsin, 53.88	High Jump—	Colleen Reinstra, Arizona State, 6′ 3″
600-Meter Run—	Dalisa Walton, Tennesee, 1:26.56	Long Jump—	Pat Johnson, Wisconsin, 20′ 11¾″
800-Meter Run—	Darlene Beekford, Howard, 2:05.75	Shot Put—	Meg Ritchie, Arizona State, 51′ 10″
1,000-Meter Run—	Josephine White, Richmond, 2:43.33	Pentathlon—	Patsy Walker, Houston, 4215 pts.
1,500-Meter Run—	Jill Haworth, Virginia, 4:25.20	Team—	Virginia

1981 NAIA INDOOR CHAMPIONS

MEN'S EVENTS

		WOMEN'S EVENTS	
60-Yard Dash—	Larry White, Miss. Valley St., 6.22	60-Yard Dash—	Esther Hope, Jackson State, 6.99
440-Yard Dash—	Kevin Jones, Northwood Inst., 47.75	440-Yard Dash—	Yvonne Joseph, Jackson State, 57.96
600-Yard Run—	Eugene Sanders, Miss. Valley St., 1:09.63	600-Yard Run—	Radious Jacobs, Jackson State, 1:27.99
880-Yard Run—	Joel Ngetich, Wayland Baptist, 1:53.04	880-Yard Run—	Donna Bean, Jackson State, 2:16.38
1,000-Yard Run—	Clifton Perry, Texas Southern, 2:13.53	1,000-Yard Run—	Donna Bean, Jackson State, 2:40.36
One-Mile Run—	John Esquibel, Adams State, 4:08.15	One-Mile Run—	Kellie Benzow, Wis.-Parkside, 5:11.63
Two-Mile Run—	Kregg Einspahr, Concordia, 8:50.88	Two-Mile Run—	Wendy Burman, Wis.-Parkside, 10:47.16
Three-Mile Run—	Joel Marchand, Malone, 13:59.86	60-Yard Hurdles—	Linda Weekly, Texas Southern, 7.79
Two-Mile Walk—	Ray Sharp, Wisconsin-Parkside, 12:56.89	One-Mile Relay—	Mississippi Valley State, 3:55.81
60-Yard Hurdles—	Dwayne Allen, Harding, 7.46	Two-Mile Relay—	Jackson State, 9:30.49
One-Mile Relay—	Texas Southern, 3:17.21	High Jump—	Vivian Garner, Jackson State, 5′ 7″
Two-Mile Relay—	Jackson State, 8:05.3	Long Jump—	Lori Risenhoover, Adams State, 18′ 7″
Distance Medley Relay—	Oklahoma Christian, 10:11.23	Shot Put—	Karen Waddell, Prairie View A & M,
High Jump—	Albert Peacock, Ottawa, 7′ 0″		46′ 8½″
Long Jump—	Britt Courville, Texas Southern, 24′ 4¾″	Team—	Jackson State
Triple Jump—	Cary Tyler, Biola, 52′ 2¾″		
Pole Vault—	Brad Pursley, Abilene Christian, 17′ ½″		
Shot Put—	Harold Ledet, Angelo State, 60′ 11¾″		
35 lb.Weight-Throw—	Doug Barnett, Azusa Pacific, 59′ 1¼″		
Team—	Texas Southern		

1981 U.S. INDOOR CHAMPIONS

MEN'S EVENTS

		WOMEN'S EVENTS	
60-Yard Dash—	Stanley Floyd, Houston, Tex., 6.15	60-Yard Dash—	Evelyn Ashford, Los Angeles, 6.63
440-Yard Dash—	Ed Yearwood, L.I. Alliance T.C., 48.12	220-Yard Dash—	Chandra Cheeseborough, Tenn. St., 23.27
600-Yard Run—	Mike Solomon, Phila. Pioneer Club, 1:10.31	440-Yard Dash—	Diane Dixon, Atoms T.C., 55.38
1,000-Yard Run—	Billy Martin, Athletics West, 2:08.37	880-Yard Run—	Delisa Walton, Tennessee, 2:05.1
One-Mile Run—	Steve Scott, Sub.-4 T.C., 3:57.3	One-Mile Run—	Jan Merrill, Age Group A.A., 4:34.03
Three-Mile Run—	Eamonn Coghlan, New York A.C., 12:54.80	Two-Mile Run—	Francie Larrieu, Pacific Coast Club, 9:38.1
60-Yard Hurdles—	Alejandro Casanas, Cuba, 7.14	60-Yard Hurdles—	Benita Fitzgerald, Tennessee, 7.72
One-Mile Relay—	Philadelphia Pioneer Club, 3:12.36	640-Yard Relay—	Tennessee State, 1:08.99
Two-Mile Relay—	Athletic Attic, 7:28.42	One-Mile Relay—	Los Angeles Mercurettes, 3:40.46
Sprint Medley Relay—	Philadelphia Pioneer Club, 2:01.89	Sprint Medley Relay—	Tennessee State, 1:43.25
Two-Mile Walk—	Ray Sharp, Kenosha, Wis., 12:37.65	One-Mile Walk—	Susan Liers-Westerfield, Island T.C., 7:05.0
High Jump—	Jeff Woodard, New Albany, Ind., 7′ 7¾″	High Jump—	Joni Huntley, Pacific Coast Club, 6′
Long Jump—	Larry Myricks, Athletic Attic, 26′ 8¼″		1¼″
Triple Jump—	Mike Marlow, Stars & Stripes T.C., 54′ 6½″	Long Jump—	Ana Alexander, Cuba, 20′ 9¾″
		Shot Put—	Marita Walton, Maryland, 52′ 11″
Pole Vault—	Thierry Vigneron, France, 18′ 4½″		
35 lb.-Weight Throw—	Ed Kania, Pacific Coast Club, 73′ 4″		
Shot Put—	Brian Oldfield, U. of Chicago T.C., 69′ 4″		

1981 NCAA OUTDOOR CHAMPIONS

100-Meter Dash—	Carl Lewis, Houston, 9.99	1,600-Meter Relay—	Tennessee, 3:03.08
200-Meter Dash—	Dwayne Evans, Arizona State, 20.20	High Jump—	Leo Williams, Navy, 7' 4¼"
400-Meter Dash—	Bert Cameron, Texas-El Paso, 44.58	Long Jump—	Carl Lewis, Houston, 27' ¾"
800-Meter Run—	Sammy Koskei, SMU, 1:46.41	Triple Jump—	Steve Hanna, Texas-El Paso, 55' 11"
1,500-Meter Run—	Sydney Maree, Villanova, 3:35.30	Pole Vault—	David Bolz, Indiana, 17' 8¼"
5,000-Meter Run—	Suleiman Nyambui, Texas-El Paso, 13:38.8	Discus Throw—	Scott Crowell, Iowa State, 206' 3"
10,000-Meter Run—	Suleiman Nyambui, Texas-El Paso, 28:34.23	Hammer Throw—	Richard Olsen, SMU, 237'
3,000-Meter Steeplechase—	Solomon Chebor, Fairleigh Dickinson, 8:23.34	Javelin Throw—	Mike Juskus, Glassboro State, 273' 2"
110-Meter Hurdles—	Larry Cowling, California, 13.60	Shot Put—	Michael Carter, SMU, 68' 10¾"
400-Meter Hurdles—	Andre Phillips, UCLA, 49.12	Decathlon—	Tito Steiner, Brigham Young, 8729 pts.
400-Meter Relay—	Northwestern State (La.), 39.32	Team—	Texas-El Paso

1981 AIAW OUTDOOR CHAMPIONS

100-Meter Dash—	Merlene Ottey, Nebraska, 11.20	High Jump—	Colleen Reinstra, Arizona State, 6' 0"
200-Meter Dash—	Merlene Ottey, Nebraska, 22.78	Long Jump—	Donna Thomas, N. Texas State, 20' 9¾"
400-Meter Dash—	Jackie Parsey, Calif. State-Los Angeles, 51.85	Discus Throw—	Ria Stalman, Arizona State, 198' 3"
800-Meter Run—	Leann Warren, Oregon, 2:06.07	Javelin Throw—	Sally Harmon, Oregon, 177' 10"
1,500-Meter Run—	Leann Warren, Oregon, 4:15.00	Shot Put—	Meg Ritchie, Arizona, 57' 1"
3,000-Meter Run—	Regina Joyce, Washington, 9:00.2	Heptathlon—	Patsy Walker, Houston, 5662 pts.
5,000-Meter Run—	Julie Shea, N. Carolina State, 16:11.04	Team—	Tennessee
10,000-Meter Run—	Aileen O'Connor, Virginia, 33:28.20	Div. II Team—	Calif. Poly.-S.L. Obispo
100-Meter Hurdles—	Benita Fitzgerald, Tennessee, 13.12	Div. III Team—	Calif. State-Hayward
400-Meter Hurdles—	Robin Marks, Arizona, 58.41		

1981 NAIA OUTDOOR CHAMPIONS

MEN'S EVENTS		WOMEN'S EVENTS	
100-Meter Dash—	Larry White, Miss. Valley St., 10.63	100-Meter Dash—	Angel Doyle, Southern, 11.855
200-Meter Dash—	Darrell Green, Texas A & I, 21.42	200-Meter Dash—	Angel Doyle, Southern, 23.98
400-Meter Dash—	Eugene Sanders, Miss. Valley St., 45.38	400-Meter Dash—	Loretta Edwards, Prairie View A & M, 54.38
800-Meter Run—	Joel Ngetich, Wayland Baptist, 1:47.76	800-Meter Run—	Cherritta Jackson, Texas Southern, 2:12.05
1,500-Meter Run—	Michael Watson, Jackson State, 3:47.44	1,500-Meter Run—	Mary Danian, Southern Utah, 4:32.35
5,000-Meter Run—	Dave Finnestad, Malone, 14:33.80	5,000-Meter Run—	Wendy Burman, Wisconsin-Parkside, 17:03.77
10,000-Meter Run—	Gordon Sanders, Hillsdale, 29:50.07	Marathon—	Wendy Burman, Wisconsin-Parkside, 2:59:44.10
Marathon—	Karl Niedermeier, Ft. Hays State, 2:29:52.22	3,000-Meter Steeplechase—	Angie Pikschus, Ozarks, 10:11.55
3,000-Meter Steeplechase—	Kregg Einspahr, Concordia, 8:45.69	100-Meter Hurdles—	Linda Weekly, Texas Southern, 13.83
10,000-Meter Walk—	Ray Sharp, Wisconsin-Parkside, 43:31.23	400-Meter Hurdles—	Felicia Durham, Southern, 1:00.47
110-Meter Hurdles—	Steve Parker, Abilene Christian, 13.95	400-Meter Relay—	Texas Southern, 45.41
400-Meter Hurdles—	Ed Brown, Saginaw Valley St., 50.96	1,600-Meter Relay—	Texas Southern, 3:40.24
400-Meter Relay—	Texas Southern, 40.10	3,200-Meter Relay—	Texas Southern, 8:54.34
1,600-Meter Relay—	Mississippi Valley State, 3:05.40	Medley Relay—	Prairie View A & M, 1:40.55
High Jump—	Joe Wise, Arkansas Tech, 7' ¾"	High Jump—	Sybil Reddick, Texas Southern, 5' 10½"
Long Jump—	Britt Courville, Texas Southern, 25' 10¼"	Long Jump—	Cornelia Jackson, Jackson State, 19' 6¾"
Triple Jump—	Cary Tyler, Biola, 54' 8"		
Pole Vault—	Brad Pursley, Abilene Christian, 17' 3"		
Discus Throw—	Martin Guerrero, Abilene Christian, 196' 4"	Discus Throw—	Pam Schmott, Midland Lutheran, 144' 2"
Hammer Throw—	Doug Barnett, Azusa Pacific, 205' 4"	Javelin Throw—	Michaele McCandless, Simon Fraser (Can.), 147' 3"
Javelin Throw—	Mark Barnett, Azusa Pacific, 255' 8"		
Shot Put—	Bob Urey, Malone, 60' 1¼"	Shot Put—	Karen Waddell, Prairie View A & M, 46' 6¼"
Decathlon—	Doug Larson, Whitworth, 7516 pts.		
Team—	Mississippi Valley State	Team—	Texas Southern

1981 U.S. OUTDOOR CHAMPIONS

MEN'S EVENTS		WOMEN'S EVENTS	
100-Meter Dash—	Carl Lewis, Santa Monica T.C., 10.13	100-Meter Dash—	Evelyn Ashford, Medalist T.C., 11.07
200-Meter Dash—	Jeff Phillips, Phila. Pioneer Club, 20.36	200-Meter Dash—	Evelyn Ashford, Medalist T.C., 22.30
400-Meter Dash—	Cliff Wiley, D.C. International, 44.70	400-Meter Dash—	Denean Howard, Shaklee T.C., 51.79
800-Meter Run—	James Robinson, Inner City A.C., 1:45.53	800-Meter Run—	Madeline Manning, Oral Roberts T.C., 1:58.50
1,500-Meter Run—	Sydney Maree, Athletic Attic, 3:35.02	1,500-Meter Run—	Jan Merrill, Age Group A.A., 4:14.62
5,000-Meter Run—	Matt Centrowitz, New York A.C., 13:28.86	3,000-Meter Run—	Brenda Webb, Athletics West, 9:04.54
10,000-Meter Run—	Alberto Salazar, Athletics West, 28:39.33	10,000-Meter Run—	Joan Benoit, Athletics West, 33:37.5
3,000-Meter Steeplechase—	Henry Marsh, Athletics West, 8:30.7	5,000-Meter Walk—	Susan Liers-Westerfield, Island T.C., 24:26.7
5,000-Meter Walk—	Ray Sharp, Athletics Attic, 20:47.52	100-Meter Hurdles—	Stephanie Hightower, L.A. Naturite T.C., 13.09
110-Meter Hurdles—	Gregg Foster, Shaklee T.C., 13.39	400-Meter Hurdles—	Sandy Myers, L.A. Naturite T.C., 56.43
400-Meter Hurdles—	Edwin Moses, unattached, 47.59	400-Meter Relay—	Shaklee T.C., 43.39
High Jump—	Tyke Peacock, Modesto T.C., 7' 4½"	1,600-Meter Relay—	Los Angeles Naturite T.C., 3:27.90
Long Jump—	Carl Lewis, Santa Monica T.C., 28' 3½"	3,200-Meter Relay—	Sports West, 8:36.94
Triple Jump—	Willie Banks, Athletics West, 57' 7½"	800-Meter Medley Relay—	Los Angeles Naturite T.C., 1:37.86
Pole Vault—	Billy Olson, Pacific Coast Club, 18' 2½"	High Jump—	Pam Spencer, L.A. Naturite T.C., 6' 4¾"
Discus Throw—	Ben Plucknett, So. Calif. Striders, 226' 5"	Long Jump—	Jodi Anderson, L.A. Naturite T.C., 22' ¼"
Hammer Throw—	Richard Olsen, New York A.C., 235' 10"	Discus Throw—	Leslie Deniz, Sun Devil Sports, 182' 9"
Javelin Throw—	Bruce Kennedy, Pacific Coast Club, 276' 8"	Javelin Throw—	Karin Smith, Medalist T.C., 208' 2"
Shot Put—	David Laut, Athletics West, 70' 10½"	Shot Put—	Denise Wood, Knoxville T.C., 55' 5¾"

1981 WORLD CUP CHAMPIONS

MEN'S EVENTS

100-Meter Dash—	Allan Wells, Europe (Gr. Br.), 10.20
200-Meter Dash—	Mel Lattany, U.S.A., 20.21
400-Meter Dash—	Cliff Wiley, U.S.A., 44.88
800-Meter Run—	Sebastian Coe, Europe (Gr. Br.), 1:46.16
1,500-Meter Run—	Steve Ovett, Europe (Gr. Br.), 3:34.95
5,000-Meter Run—	Eamonn Coghlan, Europe (Ire.), 14:08.39
10,000-Meter Run—	Werner Schildhauer, E. Germany, 27:38.43
3,000-Meter Steeplechase—	Boguslaw Maminski, Europe (Pol.), 8:19.89
110-Meter Hurdles—	Greg Foster, U.S.A., 13.32
400-Meter Hurdles—	Edwin Moses, U.S.A., 47.37
400-Meter Relay—	Europe, 38.73
1,600-Meter Relay—	U.S.A., 2:59.12
High Jump—	Tyke Peacock, U.S.A., 2.28m (7' 5¾")
Long Jump—	Carl Lewis, U.S.A., 8.15m (26' 8¾")
Triple Jump—	Joao de Oliveira, S. America (Braz.), 17.37m (56' 11¾")
Pole Vault—	Konstantin Volkov, U.S.S.R., 5.70m (18' 8¼")
Discus Throw—	Armin Lemme, E. Germany, 66.38m (217' 9")
Hammer Throw—	Yuri Syedikh, U.S.S.R., 77.42m (254')
Javelin Throw—	Dainis Kula, U.S.S.R., 89.74m (294' 5")
Shot Put—	Udo Beyer, E. Germany, 21.40m (70' 2½")
Final Point Standings—	Europe 147, E. Germany 130, U.S.A. 127, U.S.S.R. 118, S. America 95, Italy 93, Africa 66, Oceania 61, Asia 59

WOMEN'S EVENTS

100-Meter Dash—	Evelyn Ashford, U.S.A., 11.02
200-Meter Dash—	Evelyn Ashford, U.S.A., 22.18
400-Meter Dash—	Jarmila Kratochvilova, Europe (Cz.), 48.61
800-Meter Run—	Lyudmila Veselkova, U.S.S.R., 1:57.48
1,500-Meter Run—	Tamara Sorokina, U.S.S.R., 4:03.33
3,000-Meter Run—	Angelika Zauber, E. Germany, 8:54.89
100-Meter Hurdles—	Tatyana Anisimova, U.S.S.R., 12.58
400-Meter Hurdles—	Ellen Neumann, E. Germany, 54.82
400-Meter Relay—	East Germany, 42.22
1,600-Meter Relay—	East Germany, 3:20.62
High Jump—	Ulrike Meyfarth, Europe (W. Ger.), 1.96m (6' 5")
Long Jump—	Sigrid Ulbricht, E. Germany, 6.80m (22' 3½")
Discus Throw—	Evelin Jahl, E. Germany, 66.70m (218' 9")
Javelin Throw—	Antoaneta Todorova, Europe (Bulg.), 70.08m (229' 11")
Shot Put—	Ilona Slupianek, E. Germany, 20.60m (67' 7")
Final Point Standing—	E. Germany 120.5, Europe 110, U.S.S.R. 98, U.S.A. 89, S. America 72, Italy 68.5, Oceania 58, Asia 32, Africa 26

1981 PACIFIC CONFERENCE GAMES CHAMPIONS

MEN'S EVENTS

100-Meter Dash—	Peter Gandy, Australia, 10.42
200-Meter Dash—	Peter Gandy, Australia, 20.89
400-Meter Dash—	Ed Yearwood, U.S.A., 46.53
800-Meter Run—	Andras Paroczei, Hungary, 1:48.17
1,500-Meter Run—	Michael Hillardt, Australia, 3:41.74
5,000-Meter Run—	Dave-Moorcroft, Gr. Britain, 13:36.79
10,000-Meter Run—	Rod Dixon, New Zealand, 28:35.69
3,000-Meter Steeplechase—	Bronislaw Malinowski, Poland, 8:24.02
110-Meter Hurdles—	Sam Turner, U.S.A., 13.80
400-Meter Hurdles—	Harald Schmid, W. Germany, 50.35
400-Meter Relay—	Canada, 39.6
1,600-Meter Relay—	Australia, 3:07.03
High Jump—	Dean Bauck, Canada, 2.21m (7' 3")
Long Jump—	Mike Marlow, U.S.A., 7.64m (25' ¾")
Triple Jump—	Mike Marlow, U.S.A., 16.49m (54' 1¼")
Pole Vault—	Tomo Takahashi, Japan, 5.25m (17' 2¾")
Discus Throw—	Ben Plucknett, U.S.A., 61.84m (202' 11")
Hammer Throw—	Shigenobu Murofushi, Japan, 69.52m (228' 1")
Javelin Throw—	Miklos Nemeth, Hungary, 84.56m (227' 5")
Shot Put—	Colin Anderson, U.S.A., 19.76m (64' 10")
Decathlon—	John Crist, U.S.A., 7869 pts.

WOMEN'S EVENTS

100-Meter Dash—	Angela Bailey, Canada, 11.46
200-Meter Dash—	Angela Bailey, Canada, 23.37
400-Meter Dash—	Michelle Baumgartner, Australia, 52.85
800-Meter Run—	Leann Warren, U.S.A., 2:03.52
1,500-Meter Run—	Brit McRoberts, Canada, 4:11.87
3,000-Meter Run—	Lorraine Moller, New Zealand, 9:07.86
100-Meter Hurdles—	Grazyna Rabsztyn, Poland, 13.25
400-Meter Hurdles—	Lyn Foreman, Australia, 57.73
400-Meter Relay—	Canada, 44.5
1,600-Meter Relay—	Australia, 3:34.20
High Jump—	Hisayo Fukumitsu, Japan, 1.89m (6' 2½")
Long Jump—	Linda Garden, Australia, 6.53m (21' 5")
Discus Throw—	Gael Mulhall, Australia, 58.10m (190' 7")
Javelin Throw—	Tessa Sanderson, Gr. Britain, 61.56m (202')
Shot Put—	Gael Mulhall, Australia, 17.21m (56' 5½")
Pentathlon—	Karen Page, New Zealand, 4348 pts.

SPORTS FIGURES OF THE CENTURY

Results of a 1980 international poll of twenty leading newspapers of the world.

1. **Pele,** Brazil, soccer
2. **Jesse Owens,** U.S., track and field
3. **Eddy Merckx,** Belgium, cycling
4. **Paavo Nurmi,** Finland, track and field
5. **Bjorn Borg,** Sweden, tennis, and **Mark Spitz,** U.S., swimming
7. **Emil Zatopek,** Czechoslovakia, track and field

8. **Fauto Coppi,** Italy, cycling
9. **Muhammad Ali,** U.S., boxing
10. **Sugar Ray Robinson,** U.S., boxing
11. **Jack Nicklaus,** U.S., golf
12. **Joe Louis,** U.S., boxing
13. **Babe Ruth,** U.S., baseball
14. **Juan Manuel Fangio,** Argentina, auto racing

15. **Jean-Claude Killy,** France, skiing, and **Eric Heiden,** U.S., speed skating
17. **Dawn Fraser,** Australia, swimming, and **Irena Szewinska,** Poland, track and field
19. **Vasily Alexeyev,** USSR, weightlifting, and **Nadia Comaneci,** Romania, gymnastics

AMERICAN TRACK AND FIELD RECORDS

Men's Event	Time/Distance	Name/Site	Date	
100-Meter Dash	9.95 sec.	Jim Hines, Mexico City	Oct.	1968
200-Meter Dash	19.83 sec.	Tommie Smith, Mexico City	Oct.	1968
400-Meter Dash	43.86 sec.	Lee Evans, Mexico City	Oct.	1968
800-Meter Run	1 min., 43.9 sec.	Rick Wohlhuter, Los Angeles, Calif.	June	1974
1,000-Meter Run	2 min., 13.9 sec.	Rick Wohlhuter, Oslo, Norway	July	1974
1,500-Meter Run	3 min., 33.1 sec.	Jim Ryun, Los Angeles, Calif.	July	1967
One-Mile Run	3 min., 49.68 sec.	Steve Scott, Oslo, Norway	July	1981
2,000-Meter Run	5 min., 1.4 sec.	Steve Prefontaine, Coos Bay, Ore.	May	1975
3,000-Meter Run	7 min., 36.69 sec.	Steve Scott, Ingleheim, W. Germany	Sept.	1981
5,000-Meter Run	13 min., 15.1 sec.	Marty Liquori, Dusseldorf, W. Ger.	Sept.	1977
10,000-Meter Run	27 min., 29.16 sec.	Craig Virgin, Paris, France	July	1980
20,000-Meter Run	58 min., 37.46 sec.	Herb Lindsay, Manchester, Vt.	Sept.	1981
25,000-Meter Run	1 hr., 14 min., 12 sec.	Bill Rodgers, Saratoga, Calif.	Feb.	1979
30,000-Meter Run	1 hr., 31 min., 50 sec.	Bill Rodgers, Saratoga, Calif.	Feb.	1979
Marathon	2 hr., 9 min., 27 sec.	Bill Rodgers, Boston, Mass.	Apr.	1979
20-Kilometer Walk	1 hr., 30 min., 10 sec.	Larry Young, Columbia, Mo.	May	1972
30-Kilometer Walk	2 hr., 23 min., 14 sec.	Goetz Klopfer, Seattle, Wash.	Nov.	1970
50-Kilometer Walk	4 hr., 13 min., 36 sec.	Bob Kitchen, San Francisco, Calif	Feb.	1972
110-Meter Hurdles	13.00 sec.	Renaldo Nehemiah, Westwood, Calif.	May	1979
400-Meter Hurdles	47.13 sec.	Edwin Moses, Milan, Italy	July	1980
3000-Meter Steeplechase	8 min., 15.68 sec.	Henry Marsh, Eugene, Ore.	June	1980
4 X 100-Meter Relay	38.03 sec.	World Cup Team, Dusseldorf, W. Ger.	Sept.	1977
4 X 200-Meter Relay	1 min., 20.26 sec.	Southern California, Tempe, Ariz.	May	1978
4 X 400-Meter Relay	2 min., 56.16 sec.	Olympic Team, Mexico City	Oct.	1968
4 X 800-Meter Relay	7 min., 10.4 sec.	Univ. of Chicago T.C., Durham, N.C.	May	1973
4 X 1,500-Meter Relay	14 min., 46.3 sec.	National Team, Bourges, France	June	1979
Sprint Medley Relay (Mile)	3 min., 13.39 sec.	Oklahoma, Des Moines, Iowa	Apr.	1981
Distance Medley Relay (2½ Mi.)	9 min., 24.09 sec.	Georgetown, Philadelphia, Pa.	Apr.	1980
High Jump	2.31 m (7'7'')	Dwight Stones, Nice, France	Aug.	1981
Long Jump	8.90 m (29'2½'')	Bob Beamon, Mexico City	Oct.	1968
Triple Jump	17.56 m (57'7½'')	Willie Banks, Sacramento, Calif.	June	1981
Pole Vault	5.70 m (18'8¼'')	Dave Roberts, Eugene, Ore.	June	1976
Shot Put	22.02 m (72'3'')	Brian Oldfield, Modesto, Calif.	May	1981
Discus Throw	71.19 m (233'7'')	Ben Plucknett, Modesto, Calif.	May	1981
Hammer Throw	72.28 m (237'2'')	David McKenzie, Leningrad, U.S.S.R.	July	1981
Javelin Throw	91.44 m (300')	Mark Murro, Tempe, Ariz.	Mar.	1970
Decathlon	8,617 points	Bruce Jenner, Montreal, Canada	July	1976

Women's Event	Time/Distance	Name/Site	Date	
100-Meter Dash	10.90 sec.	Evelyn Ashford, Colorado Sprs., Colo.	July	1981
200-Meter Dash	21.83 sec.	Evelyn Ashford, Montreal, Canada	Aug.	1979
400-Meter Dash	50.62 sec.	Rosalyn Bryant, Montreal, Canada	July	1976
800-Meter Run	1 min., 57.90 sec.	Madeline Jackson, College Park, Md.	Aug.	1976
1,000-Meter Run	2 min., 37.3 sec.	Madeline Jackson, Montreal, Canada	July	1976
1,500-Meter Run	3 min., 59.43 sec.	Mary Decker, Zurich, Switz.	Aug.	1980
2,000-Meter Run	5 min., 47.5 sec.	Francie Larrieu, Montreal, Canada	July	1976
One-Mile Run	4 min., 21.68 sec.	Mary Decker, Auckland, N.Z.	Jan.	1980
3,000-Meter Run	8 min., 38.73 sec.	Mary Decker, Oslo, Norway	July	1980
5,000-Meter Run	15 min., 30.6 sec.	Jan Merrill, Stanford, Calif.	Mar.	1980
10,000-Meter Run	32 min., 52.5 sec.	Mary Shea, Walnut, Calif.	June	1979
Marathon	2 hr., 27 min., 51 sec.	Patti Lyons-Catalano, Boston, Mass.	Apr.	1981
5-Kilometer Walk	23 min., 19.1 sec.	Sue Brodock, Walnut, Calif.	June	1980
10-Kilometer Walk	50 min., 32.6 sec.	Sue Brodock, Walnut, Calif.	June	1979
100-Meter Hurdles	12.86 sec.	Deby LaPlante, Walnut, Calif.	June	1979
400-Meter Hurdles	56.16 sec.	Esther Mahr, Sittard, Neth.	Aug.	1980
4 X 100-Meter Relay	42.82 sec.	World Cup Team, Rome, Italy	Sept.	1981
4 X 200-Meter Relay	1 min., 32.6 sec.	National Team, Bourges, France	June	1979
4 X 400-Meter Relay	3 min., 22.8 sec.	Olympic Team, Montreal, Canada	July	1976
4 X 800-Meter Relay	8 min., 19.9 sec.	National Team, Bourges, France	June	1979
Sprint Medley Relay	1 min., 37.29 sec.	Los Angeles State, Knoxville, Tenn.	May	1978
High Jump	1.97 m (6'5½'')	Pam Spencer, Wichita, Kans.	May	1981
Long Jump	7.00 m (22'11½'')	Jodi Anderson, Eugene, Ore.	June	1980
Shot Put	19.09 m (62'7¾'')	Maren Seidler, Walnut, Calif.	June	1979
Discus Throw	63.22 m (207'5'')	Lorna Griffin, Long Beach, Calif.	May	1980
Javelin Throw	69.32 m (227'5'')	Kate Schmidt, Fuerth, W. Ger.	Sept.	1977
Pentathlon	4,708 points	Jane Frederick, Gotzis, Austria	May	1979

WORLD TRACK AND FIELD RECORDS

Men's Event	Time/Distance	Name (Country)	Date
100–Meter Dash	9.95 sec.	Jim Hines (United States)	Oct. 1968
200–Meter Dash	19.83 sec.	Tommie Smith (United States)	Oct. 1968
400–Meter Dash	43.86 sec.	Lee Evans (United States)	Oct. 1968
800–Meter Run	1 min., 41.72 sec.	Sebastian Coe (United Kingdom)	June 1981
1,000–Meter Run	2 min., 12.18 sec.	Sebastian Coe (United Kingdom)	July 1981
1,500–Meter Run	3 min., 31.36 sec.	Steve Ovett (United Kingdom)	Aug. 1980
One–Mile Run	3 min., 47.33 sec.	Sebastian Coe (United Kingdom)	Aug. 1981
2,000–Meter Run	4 min., 51.4 sec.	John Walker (New Zealand)	June 1976
3,000–Meter Run	7 min., 32.1 sec.	Henry Rono (Kenya)	June 1978
5,000–Meter Run	13 min., 6.2 sec.	Henry Rono (Kenya)	Sept. 1981
10,000–Meter Run	27 min., 22.4 sec.	Henry Rono (Kenya)	June 1978
20,000–Meter Run	57 min., 24.2 sec.	Jos Hermens (Netherlands)	May 1976
25,000–Meter Run	1 hr., 14 min., 12 sec.	Bill Rodgers (United States)	Feb. 1979
30,000–Meter Run	1 hr., 31 min., 30.4 sec.	Jim Adler (United Kingdom)	Sept. 1970
Marathon	2 hr., 8 min., 34 sec.	Derek Clayton (Australia)	May 1969
One–Hour Run	13 miles, 24 yards	Jos Hermens (Netherlands)	May 1976
20–Kilometer Walk	1 hr., 20 min., 7 sec.	Daniel Bautista (Mexico)	Oct. 1979
30–Kilometer Walk	1 hr., 49 min., 54 sec.	Raul Gonzalez (Mexico)	May 1978
50–Kilometer Walk	3 hr., 52 min., 24 sec.	Raul Gonzalez (Mexico)	May 1978
Two–Hour Walk	16 miles, 1637 yards	Raul Gonzalez (Mexico)	May 1978
110–Meter Hurdles	12.93 sec.	Renaldo Nehemiah (United States)	Aug. 1981
400–Meter Hurdles	47.13 sec.	Edwin Moses (United States)	July 1980
3,000–Meter Steeplechase	8 min., 5.4 sec.	Henry Rono (Kenya)	April 1978
4 X 100–Meter Relay	38.03 sec.	United States	Sept. 1977
4 X 200–Meter Relay	1 min., 20.26 sec.	United States	May 1977
4 X 400–Meter Relay	2 min., 56.16 sec.	United States	Oct. 1968
4 X 800–Meter Relay	7 min., 8.6 sec.	West Germany	Aug. 1966
4 X 1,500–Meter Relay	14 min., 38.8 sec.	West Germany	Aug. 1977
High Jump	2.36m (7'8¾")	Gerd Wessig (East Germany)	Aug. 1980
Long Jump	8.90m (29'2½")	Bob Beamon (United States)	Oct. 1968
Triple Jump	17.89m (58'8¼")	Joao Oliveira (Brazil)	Oct. 1975
Pole Vault	5.81m (19'¾")	Vladimir Polyakov (U.S.S.R.)	June 1981
Shot Put	22.15m (72'8")	Udo Beyer (East Germany)	July 1978
Discus Throw	71.19m (233'7")	Ben Plucknett (United States)	May 1981
Hammer Throw	81.80m (268'4")	Yuri Sedykh (U.S.S.R.)	July 1980
Javelin Throw	96.72m (317'4")	Ferenc Paragi (Hungary)	April 1980
Decathlon	8649 points	Guido Kratschmer (West Germany)	June 1980

Women's Event	Time/Distance	Name (Country)	Date
100–Meter Dash	10.88 sec.	Marlies Gohr (East Germany)	July 1977
200–Meter Dash	21.71 sec.	Marita Koch (East Germany)	June 1979
400–Meter Dash	48.60 sec.	Marita Koch (East Germany)	Aug. 1979
800–Meter Run	1 min., 53.42 sec.	Nadezhde Olizarenko (U.S.S.R.)	July 1980
1,000–Meter Run	2 min., 30.6 sec.	Tatyana Providokhina (U.S.S.R.)	Aug. 1978
1,500–Meter Run	3 min., 52.47 sec.	Tatyana Kazankina (U.S.S.R.)	July 1980
One–Mile Run	4 min., 20.89 sec.	Lyudmila Veselkova (U.S.S.R.)	Sept. 1981
2,000–Meter Run	5 min., 25.5 sec.	Maricica Puica (Romania)	May 1979
3,000–Meter Run	8 min., 27.12 sec.	Lyudmila Bragina (U.S.S.R.)	Aug. 1976
5,000–Meter Run	15 min., 8.8 sec.	Loa Olafsson (Denmark)	May 1978
10,000–Meter Run	31 min., 45.4 sec.	Loa Olafsson (Denmark)	April 1978
Marathon	2 hr., 27 min., 33 sec.	Greta Waitz (Norway)	Oct. 1979
100–Meter Hurdles	12.36 sec.	Grazyna Rabsztyn (Poland)	June 1980
400–Meter Hurdles	54.28 sec	Karin Rossley (East Germany)	May 1980
4 X 100–Meter Relay	41.60 sec.	East Germany	Aug. 1980
4 X 200–Meter Relay	1 min., 28.15 sec.	East Germany	Aug. 1980
4 X 400–Meter Relay	3 min., 19.23 sec.	East Germany	July 1976
4 X 800–Meter Relay	7 min., 52.3 sec.	U.S.S.R.	Aug. 1976
High Jump	2.01m (6'7")	Sara Simeoni (Italy)	Aug. 1978
Long Jump	7.09m (23'3¼")	Vilma Bardauskiene (U.S.S.R.)	Aug. 1978
Shot Put	22.45m (73'8")	Ilona Slupianek (East Germany)	May 1980
Discus Throw	71.80m (235'7")	Maria Vergova-Petkova (Bulgaria)	July 1980
Javelin Throw	71.88m (235'10")	Antoaneta Todorova (Bulgaria)	Aug. 1981
Pentathlon	5083 points	Nadyezhda Tkachenko (U.S.S.R.)	July 1980

BOWLING

1981 LEADING MONEY WINNERS (to Sept. 7)
Source: PBA

	Bowler	Tournaments	Amount		Bowler	Tournaments	Amount
1.	Earl Anthony, Dublin, Calif.	27	$143,135	11.	Bob Handley, Fairway, Kan.	23	$48,230
2.	Marshall Holman, Medford, Ore.	22	119,685	12.	Jay Robinson, Van Nuys, Calif.	27	46,590
3.	Tom Daker, Buffalo, N.Y.	25	100,535	13.	Pete Couture, Windsor Locks, Conn.	28	45,968
4.	Wayne Webb, Tucson, Ariz.	24	80,230	14.	Mal Acosta, Hayward, Calif.	24	45,385
5.	Mark Roth, Spring Lake Heights, N.J.	21	79,130	15.	Bo Bowden, Dallas, Tex.	27	44,248
6.	Mike Durbin, Chagrin Falls, Ohio	26	61,953	16.	Steve Cook, Roseville, Calif.	24	42,570
7.	Steve Martin, Kingsport, Tenn.	22	60,620	17.	Joe Berardi, Brooklyn, N.Y.	21	41,911
8.	Randy Lightfoot, St. Charles, Mo.	23	52,580	18.	Joe Hutchinson, Scranton, Pa.	24	41,390
9.	Gil Sliker, Washington, N.J.	27	51,340	19.	Ernie Schlegel, Vancouver, Wash.	21	41,250
10.	Mike Aulby, Indianapolis, Ind.	27	49,015	20.	George Pappas, Charlotte, N.C.	23	41,220

PBA TOP-MONEY WINNERS, 1959—1980

Year	Bowler	Winnings	Year	Bowler	Winnings
1959	Dick Weber	$ 7,672	1970	Mike McGrath	$ 52,049
1960	Don Carter	22,525	1971	John Petraglia	85,065
1961	Dick Weber	26,280	1972	Don Johnson	56,648
1962	Don Carter	49,972	1973	Don McCune	69,000
1963	Dick Weber	46,333	1974	Earl Anthony	99,585
1964	Bob Strampe	33,592	1975	Earl Anthony	107,585
1965	Dick Weber	47,675	1976	Earl Anthony	110,883
1966	Wayne Zahn	54,720	1977	Mark Roth	105,583
1967	Dave Davis	54,165	1978	Mark Roth	134,500
1968	Jim Stefanich	67,375	1979	Mark Roth	124,517
1969	Billy Hardwick	64,160	1980	Wayne Webb	116,700

BOWLING CHAMPIONS

BPAA U.S. Open (Formerly All-Star)		ABC Masters		PBA National Championship		ABC All-Events	
1962	Dick Weber	1962	Billy Golembiewski	1962	Carmen Salvino	1962	Jack Winters
1963	Dick Weber	1963	Harry Smith	1963	Billy Hardwick	1963	Tom Hennessey
1964	Bob Strampe	1964	Billy Welu	1964	Bob Strampe	1964	Billy Hardwick
1965	Dick Weber	1965	Billy Welu	1965	Dave Davis	1965	Tom Hennessey
1966	Dick Weber	1966	Bob Strampe	1966	Wayne Zahn	1966	Les Schissler
1967	Les Schissler	1967	Lou Scalia	1967	Dave Davis	1967	Bob Strampe
1968	Jim Stefanich	1968	Pete Tountas	1968	Wayne Zahn	1968	Jim Stefanich
1969	Billy Hardwick	1969	Jim Chestney	1969	Mike McGrath	1969	Larry Lichstein
1970	Bobby Cooper	1970	Don Glover	1970	Mike McGrath	1970	Bob Strampe
1971	Mike Lemongello	1971	Jim Godman	1971	Mike Lemongello	1971	Gary Dickinson
1972	Don Johnson	1972	Bill Beach	1972	John Guenther	1972	Teata Semiz
1973	Mike McGrath	1973	Dave Soutar	1973	Earl Anthony	1973	Jimmy Mack
1974	Larry Laub	1974	Paul Colwell	1974	Earl Anthony	1974	Jim Godman
1975	Steve Neff	1975	Ed Ressler	1975	Earl Anthony	1975	Bobby Meadows
1976	Paul Moser	1976	Nelson Burton, Jr.	1976	Paul Colwell	1976	Gary Fust
1977	John Petraglia	1977	Earl Anthony	1977	Tommy Hudson	1977	Dick Ritger
1978	Nelson Burton, Jr.	1978	Frank Ellenburg	1978	Warren Nelson	1978	Bill Beach
1979	Joe Berardi	1979	Doug Myers	1979	Mike Aulby	1979	Nelson Burton, Jr.
1980	Steve Martin	1980	Neil Burton	1980	Johnny Petraglia	1980	Steve Fehr
1981	Marshall Holman	1981	Randy Lightfoot	1981	Earl Anthony	1981	Rod Toft

BOWLER OF THE YEAR
Selected by Bowling Writers Associaton of America

MEN

1956	Bill Lillard, Chicago, Ill.
1957	Don Carter, St. Louis, Mo.
1958	Don Carter, St. Louis, Mo.
1959	Ed Lubanski, Detroit, Mich.
1960	Don Carter, St. Louis, Mo.
1961	Dick Weber, St. Louis, Mo.
1962	Don Carter, St. Louis, Mo.
1963	Dick Weber, St. Louis, Mo.
1964	Billy Hardwick, San Mateo, Calif.
1965	Dick Weber, St. Louis, Mo.
1966	Wayne Zahn, Atlanta, Ga.
1967	Dave Davis, Phoenix, Ariz.
1968	Jim Stefanich, Joliet, Ill.
1969	Billy Hardwick, Louisville, Ky.
1970	Nelson Burton, Jr., St. Louis, Mo.
1971	Don Johnson, Akron, Ohio
1972	Don Johnson, Akron, Ohio
1973	Don McCune, Munster, Ind.
1974	Earl Anthony, Tacoma, Wash.
1975	Earl Anthony, Tacoma, Wash.
1976	Earl Anthony, Tacoma, Wash.
1977	Mark Roth, Staten Island, N.Y.
1978	Mark Roth, N. Arlington, N.J.
1979	Mark Roth, Little Silver, N.J.
1980	Wayne Webb, Tucson, Ariz.

WOMEN

1956	Anita Cantaline, Detroit, Mich.
1957	Marion Ladewig, Grand Rapids, Mich.
1958	Marion Ladewig, Grand Rapids, Mich.
1959	Marion Ladewig, Grand Rapids, Mich.
1960	Sylvia Wene, Philadelphia, Pa.
1961	Shirley Garms, Palatine, Ill.
1962	Shirley Garms, Palatine, Ill.
1963	Marion Ladewig, Grand Rapids, Mich.
1964	LaVerne Carter, St. Louis, Mo.
1965	Betty Kuczynski, Chicago, Ill.
1966	Joy Abel, Chicago, Ill.
1967	Mildred Martorella, Rochester, N.Y.
1968	Dotty Fothergill, N. Attleboro, Mass.
1969	Dotty Fothergill, N. Attleboro, Mass.
1970	Mary Baker, Central Islip, N.Y.
1971	Paula Sperber, Miami, Fla.
1972	Patty Costello, New Carrollton, Md.
1973	Judy Soutar, Kansas City, Mo.
1974	Betty Morris, Stockton, Calif.
1975	Judy Soutar, Kansas City, Mo.
1976	Patty Costello, Scranton, Pa.
1977	Betty Morris, Stockton, Calif.
1978	Donna Adamek, Monrovia, Calif.
1979	Donna Adamek, Duarte, Calif.
1980	Donna Adamek, Duarte, Calif.

1981 LEADING WOMEN'S MONEY WINNERS
Source: Ladies Professional Bowlers Tour (to Sept. 20)

Bowler	Amount	Bowler	Amount
1. Donna Adamek, Duarte, Calif.	$24,520	13. Pat Costello, Dublin, Calif.	$4,335
2. Nikki Gianulias, Vallejo, Calif.	18,595	14. Patty Costello, Scranton, Pa.	3,970
3. Lorrie Nichols, Island Lake, Ill.	12,490	15. Jeanne Maiden, Solon, Ohio	3,957
4. Virginia Norton, South Gate, Calif.	9,845	16. Shirley Hintz, Merritt Island, Fla.	3,785
5. Cindy Coburn, Williamsville, N.Y.	8,950	17. Toni Gillard, Beverly, Ohio	3,725
6. Cindy Mason, La Habra, Calif.	8,665	18. Aleta Rzepecki, Detroit, Mich.	3,600
7. Linda Sherwood, Overland Park, Kans.	6,607	19. Debbie Rainone, South Euclid, Ohio	2,992
8. Pam Buckner, Reno, Nev.	5,515	20. Cheryl Daniels, Detroit, Mich.	2,340
9. Lisa Rathgeber, Palmetto, Fla.	4,850	21. Patty Ann, Arlington Heights, Ill.	2,210
10. Robin Romeo, Beverly Hills, Calif.	4,825	22. Pat Mercatanti, Newtown, Pa.	2,080
11. Betty Morris, Stockton, Calif.	4,515	23. Vesma Grinfelds, San Francisco, Calif.	1,675
12. Cheryl Robinson, Van Nuys, Calif.	4,385	24. Shinobu Saitoh, Japan	1,465

WOMEN'S BOWLING CHAMPIONS

	U.S. Open (Formerly All-Star)	WIBC Queen's Tournament	WPBA National Championship
1961	Phyllis Notaro	Janet Harman	Shirley Garms
1962	Shirley Garms	Dorothy Wilkinson	Stevie Balogh
1963	Marion Ladewig	Irene Monterosso	Janet Harman
1964	LaVerne Carter	D.D. Jacobson	Betty Kuczynski
1965	Ann Slattery	Betty Kuczynski	Helen Duval
1966	Joy Abel	Judy Lee	Judy Lee
1967	Gloria Bouvia	Mildred Martorella	Betty Mivalez
1968	Dotty Fothergill	Phyllis Massey	Dotty Fothergill
1969	Dotty Fothergill	Ann Feigel	Dotty Fothergill
1970	Mary Baker	Mildred Martorella	Bobbe North
1971	Paula Sperber	Mildred Martorella	Patty Costello
1972	Lorrie Koch	Dotty Fothergill	Patty Costello
1973	Mildred Martorella	Dotty Fothergill	Betty Morris
1974	Pat Costello	Judy Soutar	Pat Costello
1975	Paula Sperber	Cindy Powell	Pam Rutherford
1976	Patty Costello	Pam Rutherford	Patty Costello
1977	Betty Morris	Dana Stewart	Vesma Grinfelds
1978	Donna Adamek	Loa Boxberger	Toni Gillard
1979	Diana Silva	Donna Adamek	Cindy Coburn
1980	Pat Costello	Donna Adamek	Donna Adamek
1981	Donna Adamek	Katsuko Sugimoto	

CHESS
Source: U.S. Chess Federation

WORLD CHAMPIONSHIPS

Year	Winner, Country	Year	Winner, Country	Year	Winner, Country
1886	Wilhelm Steinitz, Austria	1921	Jose Capablanca, Cuba	1958	Mikhail Botvinnik, USSR
1889	Wilhelm Steinitz, Austria	1927	Alexander Alekhine, France	1960	Mikhail Tal, USSR
1891	Wilhelm Steinitz, Austria	1929	Alexander Alekhine, France	1961	Mikhail Botvinnik, USSR
1892	Wilhelm Steinitz, Austria	1934	Alexander Alekhine, France	1963	Tigran Petrosian, USSR
1894	Emanuel Lasker, Germany	1935	Max Euwe, Netherlands	1966	Tigran Petrosian, USSR
1897	Emanuel Lasker, Germany	1937	Alexander Alekhine, France	1969	Boris Spassky, USSR
1907	Emanuel Lasker, Germany	1948	Mikhail Botvinnik, USSR	1972	Bobby Fischer, US
1908	Emanuel Lasker, Germany	1951	Mikhail Botvinnik, USSR	1975	Anatoly Karpov, USSR
1909	Emanuel Lasker, Germany	1954	Mikhail Botvinnik, USSR	1978	Anatoly Karpov, USSR
1910*	Emanuel Lasker, Germany	1957	Vassily Smyslov, USSR		

* Two championship matches held in 1910. Lasker won both.

U.S. NATIONAL CHAMPIONSHIPS

UNOFFICIAL CHAMPIONS

1857-71	Paul Morphy	1895	Jackson Showalter	1946	Samuel Reshevsky	1968	Larry Evans
1871-76	George Mackenzie	1896	Jackson Showalter	1948	Herman Steiner	1969	Samuel Reshevsky
1876-80	James Mason	1896	Jackson Showalter	1951	Larry Evans	1972	Robert Byrne
1880-89	George Mackenzie	1897	Harry Pillsbury	1952	Larry Evans	1973	Lubomir Kavalek
1889-90	S. Lipschutz	1898	Harry Pillsbury	1954	Arthur Bisguier		and John Grefe
1890	Jackson Showalter	1909	Frank Marshall	1958	Bobby Fischer	1974	Walter Browne
1890-91	Max Judd	1923	Frank Marshall	1959	Bobby Fischer	1975	Walter Browne
1891	Jackson Showalter	1936	Samuel Reshevsky	1960	Bobby Fischer	1977	Walter Browne
		1938	Samuel Reshevsky	1961	Bobby Fischer	1978	Lubomir Kavalek
CHAMPIONS		1940	Samuel Reshevsky	1962	Larry Evans	1980	Walter Browne
1892	Jackson Showalter	1941	Samuel Reshevsky	1963	Bobby Fischer		Larry Christiansen
1892	S. Lipschutz	1942	Samuel Reshevsky	1964	Bobby Fischer		Larry Evans
1894	Jackson Showalter	1944	Arnold Denker	1965	Bobby Fischer	1981	Walter Browne
1894	Albert Hodges	1946	Arnold Denker	1966	Bobby Fischer		Yasser Seirawan

SWIMMING AND DIVING

1981 NCAA CHAMPIONS

DIVISION I

50 yd. Freestyle	Kris Kirchner, Texas
100 yd. Freestyle	Rowdy Gaines, Auburn
200 yd. Freestyle	Rowdy Gaines, Auburn
500 yd. Freestyle	Doug Towne, Arizona
1,650 yd. Freestyle	Rafael Escalas, UCLA
100 yd. Backstroke	Clay Britt, Texas
200 yd. Backstroke	Wade Flemons, Stanford
100 yd. Breaststroke	Steve Lundquist, SMU
200 yd. Breaststroke	Steve Lundquist, SMU
100 yd. Butterfly	Scott Spann, Texas
200 yd. Butterfly	Craig Beardsley, Florida
200 yd. Indiv. Medley	Bill Barrett, UCLA
400 yd. Indiv. Medley	Jesse Vassallo, Miami (Fla.)
400 yd. Freestyle Relay	Texas
800 yd. Freestyle Relay	Florida
400 yd. Medley Relay	Texas
One Meter Dive	Randal Ableman, Iowa
Three Meter Dive	Robert Bollinger, Indiana
Team	Texas
Division II Team	Northridge State (Calif.)
Division III Team	Kenyon (Ohio)

1981 AIAW CHAMPIONS

DIVISION I

50 yd. Freestyle	Jill Sterkel, Texas
100 yd. Freestyle	Jill Sterkel, Texas
200 yd. Freestyle	Jill Sterkel, Texas
500 yd. Freestyle	Kim Linehan, Texas
1,650 yd. Freestyle	Kim Linehan, Texas
50 yd. Backstroke	Susan Walsh, N. Carolina
100 yd. Backstroke	Susan Walsh, N. Carolina
200 yd. Backstroke	Cheryl Gibson, Arizona State
50 yd. Breaststroke	Kathy Trieble, Florida
100 yd. Breaststroke	Kathy Trieble, Florida
200 yd. Breaststroke	Kathy Trieble, Florida
50 yd. Butterfly	Jill Sterkel, Texas
100 yd. Butterfly	Jill Sterkel, Texas
200 yd. Butterfly	Kim Linehan, Texas
100 yd. Indiv. Medley	Carol Borgmann, Texas
200 yd. Indiv. Medley	Diane Johnson, Arizona
400 yd. Indiv. Medley	Cheryl Gibson, Arizona State
200 yd. Freestyle Relay	Stanford
400 yd. Freestyle Relay	Texas
800 yd. Freestyle Relay	Arizona State
200 yd. Medley Relay	Stanford
400 yd. Medley Relay	Texas
One Meter Dive	Karen Gorham, Arkansas
Three Meter Dive	Chrissy Gentz, Minnesota
Team	Texas
Division II Team	Clarion State (Pa.)
Division III Team	Hamline (Minn.)

1981 NAIA CHAMPIONS

MEN

50 m. Freestyle	Steve Koga, Willamette (Ore.)
100 m. Freestyle	Steve Koga, Willamette (Ore.)
200 m. Freestyle	James Yount, Drury (Mo.)
400 m. Freestyle	James Yount, Drury (Mo.)
1,550 m. Freestyle	Malcolm Crimp, Simon Fraser (Can.)
100 m. Backstroke	Sean Allison, Drury (Mo.)
200 m. Backstroke	Nick Borrelly, Simon Fraser (Can.)
100 m. Breaststroke	Myron Luthringer, Westminster (Pa.)
200 m. Breaststroke	Goran Jern, Denver (Colo.)
100 m. Butterfly	Mark Hartung, Drury (Mo.)
200 m. Butterfly	Paul Eckenroad, Denver (Colo.)
200 m. Indiv. Medley	Steve Boss, Bemidji St. (Minn.)
400 m. Indiv. Medley	Malcolm Crimp, Simon Fraser (Can.)
400 m. Freestyle Relay	Drury (Mo.)
800 m. Freestyle Relay	Drury (Mo.)
400 m. Medley Relay	Drury (Mo.)
One Meter Dive	Mike Lewis, Drury (Mo.)
Three Meter Dive	Jeff Weber, Wisconsin-Eau Claire
Team	Drury (Missouri)

WOMEN

50 m. Freestyle	Beth Carter, Eisenhower (N.Y.)
100 m. Freestyle	Beth Carter, Eisenhower (N.Y.)
200 m. Freestyle	Jill Trotter, Simon Fraser (Can.)
400 m. Freestyle	Judy Baker, Simon Fraser (Can.)
1,500 m. Freestyle	Judy Baker, Simon Fraser (Can.)
100 m. Backstroke	Marcia Konat, Kearney St. (Neb.)
200 m. Backstroke	Karen Workman, Shepherd (W.Va.)
100 m. Breaststroke	Kathy Etzel, Shepherd (W.Va.)
200 m. Breaststroke	Judy Baker, Simon Fraser (Can.)
100 m. Butterfly	Kristy Robertson, Simon Fraser (Can.)
200 m. Butterfly	Kristy Robertson, Simon Fraser (Can.)
200 m. Indiv. Medley	Jill Trotter, Simon Fraser (Can.)
400 m. Indiv. Medley	Judy Baker, Simon Fraser (Can.)
400 m. Freestyle Relay	Shepherd (W.Va.)
200 m. Medley Relay	Shepherd (W.Va.)
400 m. Medley Relay	Simon Fraser (Can.)
One Meter Dive	Kendra Langley, Simon Fraser (Can.)
Three Meter Dive	Kendra Langley, Simon Fraser (Can.)
Team	Simon Fraser (Canada)

1981 U.S. SHORT COURSE CHAMPIONS

MEN

50 yd. Freestyle	Robin Leamy, Mission Viejo
100 yd. Freestyle	Robin Leamy, Mission Viejo
200 yd. Freestyle	David Larson, Florida Aquatic
500 yd. Freestyle	Peter Szmidt, Edmonton Keyano
1,000 yd. Freestyle	Brian Goodell, Mission Viejo
1,650 yd. Freestyle	Dave Sims, Unattached
100 yd. Backstroke	Rick Carey, Badger S.C.
200 yd. Backstroke	Rick Carey, Badger S.C.
100 yd. Breaststroke	Steve Lundquist, Dallas Dr. Pepper
200 yd. Breaststroke	Steve Lundquist, Dallas Dr. Pepper
100 yd. Butterfly	Matt Gribble, Hurricane
200 yd. Butterfly	Craig Beardsley, Florida Aquatic
200 yd. Indiv. Medley	Bill Barrett, Mission Viejo
400 yd. Indiv. Medley	Jesse Vassallo, Mission Viejo
400 yd. Freestyle Relay	Mission Viejo "A"
800 yd. Freestyle Relay	Mission Viejo "A"
400 yd. Medley Relay	Mission Viejo "A"

WOMEN

50 yd. Freestyle	Jill Sterkel, Longhorn Aquatic
100 yd. Freestyle	Jill Sterkel, Longhorn Aquatic
200 yd. Freestyle	Jill Sterkel, Longhorn Aquatic
500 yd. Freestyle	Kim Linehan, Longhorn Aquatic
1,000 yd. Freestyle	Kim Linehan, Longhorn Aquatic
1,650 yd. Freestyle	Kim Linehan, Longhorn Aquatic
100 yd. Backstroke	Susan Walsh, Univ. of N. Carolina
200 yd. Backstroke	Tracy Caulkins, Nashville Aquatic
100 yd. Breaststroke	Tracy Caulkins, Nashville Aquatic
200 yd. Breaststroke	Kim Rhodenbaugh, Cinc. Pepsi Marlins
100 yd. Butterfly	Jill Sterkel, Longhorn Aquatic
200 yd. Butterfly	Mary T. Meagher, Lakeside S.C.
200 yd. Indiv. Medley	Tracy Caulkins, Nashville Aquatic
400 yd. Indiv. Medley	Tracy Caulkins, Nashville Aquatic
400 yd. Freestyle Relay	Mission Viejo "A"
800 yd. Freestyle Relay	Mission Viejo "A"
400 yd. Medley Relay	Nashville Aquatic

1981 U.S. LONG COURSE CHAMPIONS

MEN

50 m. Freestyle	Robin Leamy, Mission Viejo
100 m. Freestyle	Chris Cavanaugh, DeAnza
200 m. Freestyle	David Larson, Florida
400 m. Freestyle	Jeff Float, Arden Hills
800 m. Freestyle	Doug Towne, Tucson Farmer John
1,500 m. Freestyle	Max Metzker, Mission Viejo
100 m. Backstroke	Rick Carey, Badger
200 m. Backstroke	Jesse Vassallo, Mission Viejo
100 m. Breastroke	Nick Nevid, Longhorn
200 m. Breaststroke	Nick Nevid, Longhorn
100 m. Butterfly	Matt Gribble, Hurricane
200 m. Butterfly	Craig Beardsley, Florida
200 m. Indiv. Medley	Bill Barrett, Mission Viejo
400 m. Indiv. Medley	Jesse Vassallo, Mission Viejo
400 m. Freestyle Relay	Mission Viejo "A"
800 m. Freestyle Relay	Florida Aquatic
400 m. Medley Relay	Longhorn Aquatics "A"

WOMEN

50 m. Freestyle	Jill Sterkel, Industry Hills
100 m. Freestyle	Jill Sterkel, Industry Hills
200 m. Freestyle	Marybeth Linzmeier, Mission Viejo
400 m. Freestyle	Tiffany Cohen, Mission Viejo
800 m. Freestyle	Marybeth Linzmeier, Mission Viejo
1,500 m. Freestyle	Marybeth Linzmeier, Mission Viejo
100 m. Backstroke	Theresa Andrews, North Baltimore
200 m. Backstroke	Libby Kinkead, West Chester
100 m. Breastroke	Tracy Caulkins, Nashville
200 m. Breaststroke	Tracy Caulkins, Nashville
100 m. Butterfly	Mary T. Meagher, Lakeside
200 m. Butterfly	Mary T. Meagher, Lakeside
200 m. Indiv. Medley	Tracy Caulkins, Nashville
400 m. Indiv. Medley	Tracy Caulkins, Nashville
400 m. Freestyle Relay	Mission Viejo "A"
800 m. Freestyle Relay	Mission Viejo "A"
400 m. Medley Relay	Mission Viejo "A"

1981 AIAW SYNCHRONIZED SWIMMING CHAMPIONS

Solo Routine	(tie)Tara Cameron, Ohio State
	Pamela Tryon, Arizona
Duet Routine	Julie Olson—Becky Roy, Arizona
Trio Routine	Julie Olson-Becky Roy
	Pamela Tryon, Arizona
Team	Arizona

1981 U.S. DIVING CHAMPIONS

EVENT	INDOOR—MEN	WOMEN	OUTDOOR—MEN	WOMEN
One Meter	Greg Louganis	Diane Dudeck	Greg Louganis	Kelly McCormick
Three Meter	Greg Louganis	Megan Neyer	Greg Louganis	Megan Neyer
Ten Meter	Bruce Kimball	Wendy Wyland	Bruce Kimball	Debbie Rush

WORLD SWIMMING RECORDS (September 1981)

MEN'S EVENTS

Event	Time	Name	Country	Date	
100 meter freestyle	49.36	Rowdy Gaines	United States	April	1981
200 meter freestyle	1:49.16	Rowdy Gaines	United States	April	1980
400 meter freestyle	3:50.49	Peter Szmidt	Canada	July	1980
800 meter freestyle	7:56.49	Vladimir Salnikov	USSR	March	1979
1500 meter freestyle	14:58.27	Vladimir Salnikov	USSR	July	1980
400 meter freestyle relay	3:19.74	Babashoff, Gaines, McCagg, Montgomery	United States	August	1978
800 meter freestyle relay	7:20.82	Furniss, Forrester, Gaines, Hackett	United States	August	1978
100 meter breaststroke	1:02.86	Gerald Morken	West Germany	August	1977
200 meter breaststroke	2:15.11	David Wilkie	United Kingdom	July	1976
100 meter butterfly	53.81	William Paulus	United States	April	1981
200 meter butterfly	1:58.01	Craig Beardsley	United States	August	1981
100 meter backstroke	0:55.49	John Naber	United States	July	1976
200 meter backstroke	1:59.19	John Naber	United States	July	1976
200 meter individual medley	2:02.78	Alex Baumann	Canada	July	1981
400 meter individual medley	4:20.05	Jesse Vassallo	United States	August	1978
400 meter medley relay	3:42.22	Naber, Hencken, Vogel, Montgomery	United States	July	1976

WOMEN'S EVENTS

Event	Time	Name	Country	Date	
100 meter freestyle	54.79	Barbara Krause	East Germany	July	1980
200 meter freestyle	1:58.23	Cynthia Woodhead	United States	Sept.	1979
400 meter freestyle	4:06.28	Tracey Wickham	Australia	August	1978
800 meter freestyle	8:18.77	Cynthia Woodhead	United States	February	1980
1500 meter freestyle	16:04.49	Kim Linehan	United States	August	1979
400 meter freestyle relay	3:42.17	Krause, Metschuck, Diers, Hulsenbeck	East Germany	July	1980
100 meter breaststroke	1:08.60	Ute Geweniger	East Germany	Sept.	1981
200 meter breaststroke	2:28.36	Lina Kachushite	USSR	April	1979
100 meter butterfly	57.93	Mary T. Meagher	United States	August	1981
200 meter butterfly	2:05.96	Mary T. Meagher	United States	August	1981
100 meter backstroke	1:00.86	Rica Reinisch	East Germany	July	1980
200 meter backstroke	2:11.93	Rica Reinisch	East Germany	July	1980
200 meter individual medley	2:11.73	Ute Geweniger	East Germany	July	1981
400 meter individual medley	4:38.44	Petra Schneider	East Germany	May	1980
400 meter medley relay	4:07.95	Richter, Anke, Pollack, Ender	East Germany	July	1976

WORLD FRESHWATER FISHING RECORDS

SOURCE: International Game Fish Association (All tackle records, as of August 31, 1981)

Species	Weight	Where Caught	Date	Angler
Bass, Largemouth	22 lbs. 4 oz.	Montgomery Lake, Ga.	June 2, 1932	George W. Perry
Bass, Redeye	8 lbs. 3 oz.	Flint River, Ga.	Oct. 23, 1977	David A. Hubbard
Bass, Rock	3 lbs.	York River, Ontario	Aug. 1, 1974	Peter Gulgin
Bass, Smallmouth	11 lbs. 15 oz.	Dale Hollow Lake, Ky.	July 9, 1955	David L. Hayes
Bass, Spotted	8 lbs. 15 oz.	Smith Lake, Ala.	Mar. 18, 1978	Philip C. Terry, Jr.
Bass, Striped	59 lbs. 12 oz.	Colorado R., Ariz.	May 26, 1977	Frank W. Smith
Bass, White	5 lbs. 9 oz.	Colorado R., Texas	Mar. 31, 1977	David S. Cordill
Bass, Whiterock	20 lbs. 6 oz.	Savannah R., Ga.	May 28, 1978	Danny Wood
Bass, Yellow	2 lbs. 4 oz.	Lake Monroe, Ind.	Mar. 27, 1977	Donald L. Stalker
Bluegill	4 lbs. 12 oz.	Ketona Lake, Ala.	Apr. 9, 1950	T. S. Hudson
Bowfin	21 lbs. 8 oz.	Florence, S.C.	Jan. 29, 1980	Robert L. Harmon
Buffalo, Bigmouth	70 lbs. 5 oz.	Bussey Brake, La.	Apr. 21, 1980	Delbert Sisk
Buffalo, Smallmouth	51 lbs.	Lawrence, Kansas	May 2, 1979	Scott Butler
Bullhead, Black	8 lbs.	Lake Waccabuc, N.Y.	Aug. 1, 1951	Kani Evans
Carp	55 lbs. 5 oz.	Clearwater Lake, Minn.	July 10, 1952	Frank J. Ledwein
Catfish, Blue	97 lbs.	Missouri River, S.D.	Sept. 16, 1959	Edward B. Elliott
Catfish, Channel	58 lbs.	Santee-Cooper Res., S.C.	July 7, 1964	W. B. Whaley
Catfish, Flathead	79 lbs. 8 oz.	White Riv., Ind.	Aug. 13, 1966	Glenn T. Simpson
Catfish, White	10 lbs. 5 oz.	Raritan R., N.J.	June 23, 1976	Lewis W. Lomerson
Char, Arctic	29 lbs. 11 oz.	Arctic River, N.W.T.	Aug. 21, 1968	Jeanne P. Branson
Crappie, Black	6 lbs.	Seaplane Canal, La.	Nov. 28, 1969	Lettie Robertson
Crappie, White	5 lbs. 3 oz.	Enid Dam, Miss.	July 31, 1957	Fred L. Bright
Dolly Varden	3 lbs. 13 oz.	Unalakleet R., Alaska	Aug. 29, 1980	Ray Lawson
Drum, Freshwater	54 lbs. 8 oz.	Nickajack Lake, Tenn.	Apr. 20, 1972	Benny E. Hull
Gar, Alligator	279 lbs.	Rio Grande, Texas	Dec. 2, 1951	Bill Valverde
Gar, Longnose	50 lbs. 5 oz.	Trinity River, Texas	July 30, 1954	Townsend Miller
Grayling, Arctic	5 lbs. 15 oz.	Katseyedie R., N.W.T.	Aug. 16, 1967	Jeanne P. Branson
Kokanee	6 lbs. 9 oz.	Priest L., Idaho	June 9, 1975	Jerry Verge
Muskellunge	69 lbs. 15 oz.	St. Lawrence R., N.Y.	Sept. 22, 1957	Arthur Lawton
Perch, White	4 lbs. 12 oz.	Messalonskee Lake, Me.	June 4, 1949	Mrs. Earl Small
Perch, Yellow	4 lbs. 3 oz.	Bordentown, N.J.	May 1865	Dr. C. C. Abbot
Pickerel, Chain	9 lbs. 6 oz.	Homerville, Ga.	Feb. 17, 1961	Baxley McQuaig, Jr.
Pike, Northern	62 lbs. 8 oz.	Reuss-Weiher, Switz.	June 15, 1979	Jürg Nötzli
Redhorse, Silver	5 lbs. 14 oz.	Shelbyville, Ind.	Oct. 20, 1980	Ernest Harley, Jr.
Salmon, Atlantic	79 lbs. 2 oz.	Tana River, Norway	1928	Henrik Henriksen
Salmon, Chinook	93 lbs.	Kelp Bay, Alaska	June 24, 1977	Howard C. Rider
Salmon, Chum	27 lbs. 3 oz.	Raymond Cove, Alaska	June 11, 1977	Robert A. Jahnke
Salmon, Coho	31 lbs.	Cowichan Bay, B.C.	Oct. 11, 1947	Mrs. Lee Hallberg
Salmon, Pink	12 lbs. 9 oz.	Moose/Kenai Rivers, Alaska	Aug. 17, 1974	Steven Alan Lee
Sauger	8 lbs. 12 oz.	Lake Sakakawea, N.D.	Oct. 6, 1971	Mike Fischer
Shad, American	9 lbs. 4 oz.	Delaware River, Pa.	Apr. 26, 1979	J. Edward Whitman
	9 lbs. 4 oz.	Connecticut R., Conn.	Apr. 20, 1981	Edward W. Cypus
Sturgeon	407 lbs.	Sacramento R., Calif.	May 10, 1979	Raymond Pittenger
Sunfish, Green	2 lbs. 2 oz.	Stockton Lake, Mo.	June 18, 1971	Paul M. Dilley
Sunfish, Redbreast	1 lb. 8 oz.	Suwanee R., Fla.	Apr. 30, 1977	Tommy D. Cason, Jr.
Sunfish, Redear	4 lbs. 8 oz.	Chase City, Va.	June 19, 1970	Maurice E. Ball
Trout, Brook	14 lbs. 8 oz.	Nipigon River, Ontario	July 1916	Dr. W. J. Cook
Trout, Brown	35 lbs. 15 oz.	Nahuel Huapi, Arg.	Dec. 16, 1952	Eugenio Cavaglia
Trout, Cutthroat	41 lbs.	Pyramid Lake, Nev.	Dec. 1925	John Skimmerhorn
Trout, Golden	11 lbs.	Cook's Lake, Wyo.	Aug. 5, 1948	Chas. S. Reed
Trout, Lake	65 lbs.	Great Bear Lake, N.W.T.	Aug. 8, 1970	Larry Daunis
Trout, Rainbow	42 lbs. 2 oz.	Bell Island, Alaska	June 22, 1970	David R. White
Trout, Tiger	20 lbs. 13 oz.	Lake Michigan, Wis.	Aug. 12, 1978	Pete M. Friedland
Walleye	25 lbs.	Old Hickory L., Tenn.	Aug. 1, 1960	Mabry Harper
Warmouth	2 lbs. 2 oz.	Douglas Swamp, S.C.	May 19, 1973	Willie Singletary
Whitefish, Lake	13 lbs. 1 oz.	Meaford Har., Ont.	Apr. 28, 1978	Denis J. Bouchard
Whitefish, Mountain	5 lbs.	Athabasca R., Alberta	June 3, 1963	Orville Welch

WORLD SALTWATER FISHING RECORDS

SOURCE: International Game Fish Association (All tackle records, as of August 31, 1981)

Species	Weight	Where Caught	Date	Angler
Albacore	88 lbs. 2 oz.	Morgan Port, Canary Islands	11/19/77	Siegfried Dickemann
Amberjack (Greater)	149 lbs.	Bermuda	6/21/64	Peter Simons
Barracuda (Great)	83 lbs.	Lagos, Nigeria	1/13/52	K. J. W. Hackett
Bass (Black Sea)	8 lbs. 12 oz.	Oregon Inlet, N.C.	4/21/79	Joe W. Mizelle, Sr.
Bass (Giant Sea)	563 lbs. 8 oz.	Anacapa Island, Calif.	8/20/68	James D. McAdam, Jr.
Bass (Striped)	72 lbs.	Cuttyhunk, Mass.	10/10/69	Edward J. Kirker
Bluefish	31 lbs. 12 oz.	Hatteras Inlet, N.C.	1/30/72	James M. Hussey
Bonefish	19 lbs.	Zululand, South Africa	5/26/62	Brian W. Batchelor
Bonito (Atlantic)	16 lbs. 12 oz.	Puerto Rico, Canary Is.	12/6/80	Rolf Fedderies
Bonito (Pacific)	23 lbs. 8 oz.	Victoria, Seychelles	2/19/75	Mrs. Anne Cochain
Cobia	110 lbs. 5 oz.	Mombasa, Kenya	9/8/64	Eric Tinworth
Cod	98 lbs. 12 oz.	Isles of Shoals, N.H.	6/8/69	Alphonse J. Bielevich
Dolphin	87 lbs.	Papagayo Gulf, Costa Rica	9/25/76	Manuel Salazar
Drum (Black)	113 lbs. 1 oz.	Lewes, Del.	9/15/75	Gerald M. Townsend
Drum (Red)	90 lbs.	Rodanthe, N.C.	11/7/73	Elvin Hooper
Flounder (Summer)	22 lbs. 7 oz.	Montauk, N.Y.	9/15/75	Charles Nappi
Halibut (California)	38 lbs. 8 oz.	Santa Cruz I., Calif.	5/31/81	Jean S. Hinckley
Jack (Crevalle)	51 lbs.	Lake Worth, Fla.	6/20/78	Stephen V. Schwenk
Jack (Horse-Eye)	22 lbs.	Miami Beach, Fla.	8/26/80	Donald C. Ball
Jewfish	680 lbs.	Fernandina Beach, Fla.	5/20/61	Lynn Joyner
Kawakawa	26 lbs.	Merimbula, N.S.W., Australia	1/26/80	Wally Elfring
Mackerel (King)	90 lbs.	Key West, Fla.	2/16/76	Norton I. Thomton
Marlin (Atlantic Blue)	1282 lbs.	St. Thomas, Virgin Is.	8/6/77	Larry Martin
Marlin (Black)	1560 lbs.	Cabo Blanco, Peru	8/4/53	Alfred C. Glassell, Jr.
Marlin (Pacific Blue)	1153 lbs.	Ritidian Point, Guam	8/21/69	Greg D. Perez
Marlin (Striped)	417 lbs. 8 oz.	Cavalli Is., New Zealand	1/14/77	Phillip Bryers

SALTWATER FISHING RECORDS (Continued)

Species	Weight	Where Caught	Date	Angler
Marlin (White)	181 lbs. 14 oz.	Vitoria, Brazil	12/8/79	Evandro Luiz Coser
Permit	51 lbs. 8 oz.	Lake Worth, Fla.	4/28/78	William M. Kenney
Pollock	46 lbs. 7 oz.	Brielle, N.J.	5/26/75	John Tomes Holton
Pompano (African)	41 lbs. 8 oz.	Fort Lauderdale, Fla.	2/15/78	Wayne Sommers
Roosterfish	114 lbs.	LaPaz, Mexico	6/1/60	Abe Sackheim
Runner (Rainbow)	33 lbs. 10 oz.	Clarion Island, Mexico	3/14/76	Ralph A. Mikkelsen
Sailfish (Atlantic)	128 lbs. 1 oz.	Luanda, Angola	3/27/74	Harm Steyn
Sailfish (Pacific)	221 lbs.	Santa Cruz Island, Galapagos Is.	2/12/47	C. W. Stewart
Seabass (White)	83 lbs. 12 oz.	San Felipe, Mexico	3/31/53	L. C. Baumgardner
Seatrout (Spotted)	16 lbs.	Mason's Beach, Va.	5/28/77	William Katko
Shark (Blue)	437 lbs.	Catherine Bay, Australia	10/2/76	Peter Hyde
Shark (Hammerhead)	717 lbs.	Jacksonville Beach, Fla.	7/27/80	Richard E. Morse
Shark (Mako)	1080 lbs.	Montauk, N.Y.	8/26/79	James L. Melanson
Shark (Porbeagle)	465 lbs.	Padstow, Cornwall, England	7/23/76	Jorge Potier
Shark (Thresher)	802 lbs.	New Zealand	2/8/81	Dianne North
Shark (Tiger)	1780 lbs.	Cherry Grove, S.C.	6/14/64	Walter Maxwell
Shark (White)	2664 lbs.	Ceduna, Australia	4/21/59	Alfred Dean
Skipjack (Black)	14 lbs. 8 oz.	Cabo San Lucas, Mexico	5/24/77	Lorraine Carlton
Snook	53 lbs. 10 oz.	Rio de Parasmina, Costa Rica	10/18/78	Gilbert Ponzi
Spearfish	90 lbs. 13 oz.	Madeira, Port.	6/2/80	Joseph Larkin
Swordfish	1182 lbs.	Iquique, Chile	5/7/53	L. Marron
Tanguigue	85 lbs. 6 oz.	Rottnest I., West Australia	5/5/78	Barry Wrightson
Tarpon	283 lbs.	Lake Maracaibo, Venezuela	3/19/56	M. Salazar
Tautog	21 lbs. 6 oz.	Cape May, New Jersey	6/12/54	R. N. Sheafer
Trevally (Lowly)	116 lbs.	Pago Pago, Amer. Samoa	2/20/78	William G. Foster
Tuna (Atlantic Bigeye)	375 lbs. 8 oz.	Ocean City, Md.	8/26/77	Cecil Browne
Tuna (Blackfin)	42 lbs.	Bermuda	6/2/78	Alan J. Card
Tuna (Bluefin)	1496 lbs.	Aulds Cove, Nova Scotia, Canada	10/26/79	Ken Fraser
Tuna (Dog-tooth)	194 lbs.	Korea	9/27/80	Kim Chul
Tuna (Longtail)	60 lbs.	Bermagui, Australia	3/17/75	N. Noel Webster
Tuna (Pacific Bigeye)	435 lbs.	Cabo Blanco, Peru	4/17/57	Dr. Russel V. A. Lee
Tuna (Skipjack)	40 lbs.	Baie du Tambeau, Mauritius	4/19/71	Joseph R. P. Caboche, Jr.
	39 lbs. 15 oz.	Walker Cay, Bahamas	1/21/52	F. Drowley
Tuna (Southern Bluefin)	348 lbs. 5 oz.	New Zealand	1/16/81	Rex Wood
Tuna (Yellowfin)	388 lbs. 12 oz.	San Benedicto I., Mexico	4/1/77	Curt Wiesenhutter
Tunny (Little)	27 lbs.	Key Largo, Fla.	4/20/76	William E. Allison
Wahoo	149 lbs.	Cat Cay, Bahamas	6/15/62	John Pirovano
Weakfish	17 lbs. 14 oz.	Rye, N.Y.	5/31/80	William N. Herold
Yellowtail (California)	71 lbs. 15 oz.	Alijos Rocks, Mexico	6/24/79	Michael Carpenter
Yellowtail (Southern)	111 lbs.	Bay of Islands, New Zealand	6/11/61	A. F. Plim

WRESTLING

1981 NAT'L AAU FREESTYLE CHAMPIONS
105.5 lbs.—Bill Rosado, Sunkist Kids
114.5 lbs.—Joe Gonzales, Sunkist Kids
125.5 lbs.—John Azevedo, Sunkist Kids
136.5 lbs.—Lee Roy Smith, Cowboy W.C.
149.5 lbs.—Andrew Rein, Wisconsin W.C.
163 lbs.—David Schultz, Oklahoma Underdogs
180.5 lbs.—Dan Zilverberg, Sunkist Kids
198 lbs.—Eric Wais, Oklahoma Underdogs
220 lbs.—Greg Gibson, U.S. Marines
Heavyweight—Jimmy Jackson, Sunkist Kids
Outstanding Wrestler—David Schultz
Team—Sunkist Kids

1981 NCAA CHAMPIONS
DIVISION I
118 lbs.—Gene Mills, Syracuse
126 lbs.—Dan Cuestas, Bakersfield State
134 lbs.—Jim Gibbons, Iowa State
142 lbs.—Andre Metzger, Oklahoma
150 lbs.—Nate Carr, Iowa State
158 lbs.—Rickey Stewart, Oklahoma State

1981 WORLD CUP FREESTYLE CHAMPIONS
105.5 lbs.—Sergei Kornilaev, U.S.S.R.
114.5 lbs.—Gene Mills, U.S.A.
125.5 lbs.—Sergi Beloglasov, U.S.S.R.
136.5 lbs.—M. Abushev, U.S.S.R.
149.5 lbs.—M. Kharachura, U.S.S.R.
163 lbs.—Leroy Kemp, U.S.A.

1981 NAT'L AAU GRECO-ROMAN CHAMPIONS
105.5 lbs.—T.J. Jones, U.S. Navy
114.5 lbs.—Wilfredo Leivia, U.S. Marine Corps
125.5 lbs.—Dan Mello, U.S. Marine Corps
136.5 lbs.—Abdurrahim Kuzu, Nebraska Olympic Club
149.5 lbs.—Doug Yeats, Canada
163 lbs.—David Schultz, Oklahoma Underdogs
180.5 lbs.—Dan Chandler, Twin City W.C.
198 lbs.—Mike Houck, Minnesota W.C.
220 lbs.—Jeff Blatnick, Adirondack 3-Style W.C.
Heavyweight—Ron Carlisle, U.S. Marine Corps
Outstanding Wrestler—Jeff Blatnick
Team—U.S. Marine Corps

167 lbs.—Mark Schultz, Oklahoma
177 lbs.—Ed Banach, Iowa
190 lbs.—Tom Martucci, Trenton State
Heavyweight—Lou Banach, Iowa
Team—Iowa
Division II Team—Bakersfield State
Division III Team—Trenton State

180.5 lbs.—Chris Campbell, U.S.A.
198 lbs.—Sanasar Oganysian, U.S.S.R.
220 lbs.—Ilia Mate, U.S.S.R.
Heavyweight—Soslan Andiev, U.S.S.R.
Teams—1. U.S.S.R., 2. U.S.A., 3. Mongolia, 4. Africa

OTHER SPORTS

ARCHERY (1981)
Nat'l Field Archery Champions
PROFESSIONAL DIVISION
Freestyle—Terry Ragsdale, Illinois
Women—Michelle Ragsdale, Illinois
Freestyle Limited—Frank Gandy, Florida
Women—Thelma Nolan, Ohio
Bowhunter Freestyle—Dennis Hankey, Pennsylvania
Bowhunter Freestyle Limited—Joe Ed Newsome, Texas
ADULT DIVISION
Freestyle—Chris Jensen, New Jersey
Women—Claire Reimer, New Jersey
Freestyle Limited—Jim Atkinson, Florida
Women—Belinda Bayne, California
Barebow—David Hughes, Texas
Women—Gloria Shelley, Connecticut
Bowhunter—Jim Brown, Maryland
Women—Cay McManus, Virginia
Bowhunter Freestyle—Bill Fleet, Kansas
Bowhunter Freestyle Limited—Charles Langston, Texas
Women—Beverly Ann Stone, Texas
U.S. Indoor Target Champions
Men—Rick McKinney, Glendale, Ariz.
Women—Ruth Rowe, Gaithersburg, Md.

BADMINTON (1981)
U.S. National Champions
Men's Singles—Chris Kinard, Pasadena, Calif.
Women's Singles—Utami Kinard, Pasadena, Calif.
Men's Doubles—John Britton, Manhattan Beach, Calif.-Gary Higgins, Alhambra, Calif.
Women's Doubles—Judianne Kelly, Costa Mesa, Calif.-Pam Brady, Grand Blanc, Mich.
Mixed Doubles—Pam Brady-Danny Brady, Grand Blanc, Mich.
AIAW Champions
Singles—Barbara Bidderman, UCLA
Doubles—Claire Allison-Ann French, Wisconsin
Team—Arizona State
World Champions (1980)
Men's Singles—Rudy Hartono, Indonesia
Women's Singles—Wiharjo Verawaty, Indonesia
Men's Doubles—Ade Chandra-Christian Hadinata, Indonesia
Women's Doubles—Nora Perry-Jane Webster, England

BIATHLON
World Cup (1981)—Frank Ullrich, E. Germany
U.S. Nat'l Champions (1980)
(20 km)—Don Nielson, S. Strafford, Vt.
(10 km)—Ken Alligood, Anchorage, Alaska

BILLIARDS (1981)
World Open Champions
Men—Mike Sigel, Towson, Md.
Women—Loree-Jon Ogonowski, Garwood, N.J.
BCA National 8-Ball—Men: Danny Diliberto; Women: Belinda Campos
BCA All-American Team 8-Ball—Men: Tam O'Shanters Baggins, Colorado Springs; Women: Burt's Girls, Colorado Springs

BOBSLEDDING
1981 World 2-Man—East Germany
1981 World 4-Man—East Germany
1980 AAU 2-Man—Brent Rushlaw, Joe Tyler
1980 AAU 4-Man—Bob Hickey, Jeff Jordan, Ron Smith, Jeff Hadley

CANOEING (1981)
U.S. Slalom and Wildwater Champions
Canoe Slalom—David Hearn, Garrett Park, Md.
Canoe Slalom Doubles—Paul Grabow, N. College Park, Md.-David Hearn

Canoe Slalom Mixed Doubles—Linda Harrison, Amherst, Mass.-Paul Grabow
Canoe Wildwater—Chuck Lyda, Olympic Valley, Calif.
Canoe Wildwater Doubles—Bern Collins, Arlington, Va.-Stan Janas, Falls Church, Va.
Canoe Wildwater Mixed Doubles—Michael Hipscher-Elizabeth Johns, Bryson City, N.C.
Kayak Slalom—Tom McGowan, McLean, Va.
Women—Linda Harrison
Kayak Wildwater—Dan Schnurrenberger, Silver Spring, Md.
Women—Carol Fisher, Hanover, N.H.
U.S. Champions — KAYAK
Singles (500m.)—Terry White, Peru, Vt.
Women—Theresa DiMartino, Alexandria, Va.
Singles (1000m.)—Matt Streib, Bristol, Ind.
Women's Singles (5000m.)—Theresa DiMartino
Singles (10,000m.)—Bruce Barton, Homer, Mich.
Tandem (500m.)—Dave Gilman, Berkeley, Calif.-Terry White
Women's Tandem—Roxanne Barton, Homer, Mich.-Lynn Capen, Lansing, Mich.
Tandem (10,000m.)—Dave Gilman-Terry White
Women's Tandem (5000m.)—Margaret Browne, Corona Del Mar, Calif.-Lynn Capen
Tandem (10,000m.)—Dave Gilman-Terry White
U.S. Champions — CANOE
Singles (500m)—Roland Muhlen, Cincinnati, Ohio
Singles (1000m.)—Rod McLain, Gloversville, N.Y.
Singles (10,000m.)—Bruce Merritt, Ridge, Md.
Tandem (500m.)—Barry Merritt, Gaithersburg, Md.-Bruce Merritt
Tandem (1000m.)—Barry Merritt-Bruce Merritt
Tandem (10,000m.)—Barry Merritt-Bruce Merritt
Marathon Champions (16 miles)
Men's Kayak—Steve Geye, W. Dundee, Ill.
Women's Kayak—Leslie Klein, Lexington, Ky.
Men's Canoe—William Reichenstein, Lexington, Ky.

CROSS-COUNTRY (1980)
U.S. National Champions
Men—Jon Sinclair, Frank Shorter, R.I.
Women—Mary Shea, N. Carolina State
Men's Team—Victory Athletic Club
Women's Team—Wisconsin United Track Club
National Collegiate Champions
NCAA Div. I—Suleiman Nyambui, Texas-El Paso
Team—Texas-El Paso
NCAA Div. II—Garry Henry, Pembroke St. (N.C.)
Team—Humboldt State
NCAA Div. III—Jeff Milliman, North Central (Ill.)
Team—Carleton (Minn.)
NAIA—Pat Porter, Adams State (Colo.)
Team—Adams State
Women—Wendy Burman, Wis.-Parkside
Team—Wisconsin-Parkside
AIAW Div. I—Julie Shea, N. Carolina St.
Team—North Carolina State
AIAW Div. II—Patsy Sharples, Idaho
Team—South Dakota State
AIAW Div. III—Terese Kozlowski, Loyola Marymount (Calif.)
Team—California State-Hayward
1981 World Champions
Men—Craig Virgin, Lebanon, Ill.

Team—Ethiopia
Women—Grete Waitz, Norway
Team—U.S.S.R.

CYCLING
1981 World Road Champion (Professional)
Freddy Maertens, Belgium
1981 Tour de France
Bernard Hinault, France
1981 Coors International Classic
Men—Greg LeMond, Washoe Valley, Nev.
Team—U.S.S.R.
1981 World Amateur Champions
Men—Andrei Vedernikov, U.S.S.R.
Women—Ute Enzenhauer, W. Germany
1980 U.S. Champions—ROAD RACING
Men—Dale Stetina, Indianapolis, Ind.
Women—Beth Heiden, Madison, Wis.
1980 World Professional Champions
Sprint—Koichi Nakano, Japan
Pursuit—Tony Doyle, England
Road—Bernard Hinault, France
Points—Stan Tourne, Belgium

DOGS
Best-in-Show Winners
1981 Westminster (N.Y.)—Ch. Dhandy's Favorite Woodchuck (pug); Robert A. Hauslohner, Rosemont, Pa.; 2,920 entries
1981 International (Chicago)—Ch. Dhandy's Favorite Woodchuck (pug); 2,428 entries
1980 Boardwalk (Atlantic City)—Ch. Dhandy's Favorite Woodchuck (pug); 2,541 entries
1981 Westchester (Tarrytown, N.Y.)—Ch. Beaucrest Ruffian (Bouvier des Flandres); Francis-Michel Arbour, Fair Lawn, N.J.; 2,904 entries
1980 Philadelphia—Ch. Thrumpton's Lord Brady (Norwich Terrier), Ruth Cooper, Glenview, Ill.; 2,558 entries

FENCING (1981)
U.S. Champions
Foil—Mark Smith
Epee—Lee Shelley
Sabre—Peter Westbrook, N.Y. Fencers Club
Women's Foil—Jana Angelakis
Women's Epee—Susan Badders
NCAA Champions
Foil—Ernest Simon, Wayne St.
Epee—Gil Pezza, Wayne St.
Sabre—Paul Friedberg, Pennsylvania
Team—Pennsylvania
AIAW Champions
Individual—Jana Angelakis, Penn State
Team—Penn State
Nat'l Intercollegiate Fencing Association Champions — MEN
Foil—Oscar Estell, N.Y.U.
Team—Harvard
Epee—Gregory Pace, Navy
Team—Navy
Sabre—Paul Friedberg, Pennsylvania
Team—Pennsylvania
Overall Team—Pennsylvania
World Team Champions
Foil—U.S.S.R.
Epee—U.S.S.R.
Sabre—Hungary

FIELD HOCKEY (1981)
AIAW Champions
Div. I—Penn State
Div. II—LaSalle
Div. III—Gettysburg
American Cup Champion
Australia

GYMNASTICS (1981)
U.S. National Champions
All Around—Jim Hartung, Omaha, Neb.
Floor Exercise—Jim Hartung
Pommel Horse—Jim Hartung
Rings—Jim Hartung
Vault—Chris Riegel, Reading, Pa.
Parallel Bars—Bart Conner, Oklahoma
Nat'l AAU Champions—MEN
All Around—K. Petit, Tri-County Gym Club

OTHER SPORTS (Cont.)

Floor Exercise—A. Pearce, Nick Wools Academy
Pommel Horse— K. Petit
Rings—A. Pearce
Vault—R. Lane, Nick Wools Academy
Parallel Bars—K. Petit
Horizontal Bar—A. Pearce
Team—Nick Wools Academy, Columbus, Ind.

NAT'I AAU Champions—WOMEN
All Around—L. Cavanaugh, U.S. Academy
Floor Exercise—J. Jackson, U.S. Academy
Vault—M. Gonyias, Gym of Ohio
Balance Beam—L. Cavanaugh
Uneven Parallel Bars—L. Cavanaugh
Team—U.S. Academy

NCAA Champions
Division I
All Around—Jim Hartung, Nebraska
Floor Exercise—James Yuhashi, Oregon
Pommel Horse—Steve Jennings, New Mexico
Rings—Jim Hartung
Vault—Ron Galimore, Iowa State
Parallel Bars—Phil Cahoy, Nebraska
High Bar—Phil Cahoy
Team—Nebraska
Div. II Team—Wisconsin-Oshkosh

AIAW (Women's) Nat'l Champions
Floor Exercise—Heidi Anderson, Penn State
Vault—Sharon Shapiro, U.C.L.A.
Balance Beam—Laurie Carter, Oregon State
Uneven Parallel Bars—Diane Dovas, U.C.L.A.
All Around—Sharon Shapiro
Team—Utah

American Cup
All Around—Bart Conner
Women—Julianne McNamara
NAIA Team—Wisconsin-Oshkosh
Women—Georgia College
World Champions (1980)—Overall
Men—Bogdan Makuts, U.S.S.R.
Women—Stella Zakharova, U.S.S.R.

HANDBALL (1981)
U.S. Handball Ass'n Champions
Singles—Fred Lewis, Tucson, Ariz.
Women—Rosemary Bellini, New York, N.Y.
Doubles—Jack Roberts, Chicago, Ill.-Tom Kopatich, Milwaukee, Wis.
Women—Sue Oakleaf, Texas-Rosemary Bellini

HORSE SHOWS (1981)
National Horse Show Champions
Working Hunter Champion—Super Flash, Mᵣᵣ. Sylvester Johnson
Conformation Hunter Champion—Henry the Hawk, Mrs. Stewart McKinney
Grand Hunter Champion—Super Flash
National Horse Show Equitation Champions
Saddle Seat (Good Hands)—Janice Christensen, Madison, Conn.
ASPCA Trophy (Maclay)—Laura Tidball, Langley, B.C., Canada
The Nations Cup—U.S. Equestrian Team

ICE SKATING (1981)
World Figure Skating Champions
Men—Scott Hamilton, Denver, Colo.
Women—Denise Biellmann, Switzerland
Pairs—Irina Vorobieva-Igor Lisovsky, U.S.S.R.
Dance—Jayne Torvill-Christopher Dean, Great Britain
U.S. Figure Skating Champions
Men—Scott Hamilton, Denver, Colo.
Women—Elaine Zayak, Paramus, N.J.
Pairs—Caitlin and Peter Carruthers, Massachusetts
Dance—Judy Blumberg-Michael Seibert, Colorado Springs, Colo.
World Speed Skating Champions
Men—Amund Sjoebrend, Norway
Women—Natalya Petruseva, USSR

Sprint—Frode Roenning, Norway
Women's Sprint—Karin Enke, E. Germany
U.S. Speed Skating Champions
Outdoor—Tom Grannes, Minneapolis, Minn.
Women—Lisa Merrifield, Butte, Mont.
Indoor—Scott Drebes, Champaign, Ill.
Women—Mary Polaski, Colorado Springs, Colo.
North American Speed Skating Championships
Outdoor—Kevin O'Brien, Pr. Edw. I., Canada
Women—Lisa Merrifield, Butte, Mont.
Indoor—Gaetan Boucher, Quebec, Canada
Women—Margie Burns, Riverside, Ill.

JUDO (1981)
National AAU Champions—MEN
132 Lbs.—Rod Conduragis, Wantagh, N.Y.
143 Lbs.—James A. Martin, Alhambra, Calif.
156 Lbs.—Mike Swain, Bridgewater, N.J.
172 Lbs.—Nick Yonezuka, Watchung, N.J.
189 Lbs.—Robert Berland, Willamette, Ill.
Under 209 Lbs.—Leo White, Ft. Eustis, Va.
Over 209 Lbs.—Doug E. Nelson, Englewood, N.J.
Open Division—Mitch Santa Maria, Roselle Park, N.J.
National AAU Champions—WOMEN
106 Lbs.—Darlene Anaya, Albuquerque, N.M.
114 Lbs.—Robin Takemori, Alexandria, Va.
123 Lbs.—Darlene Hill, Memphis, Tenn.
134 Lbs.—Robin Chapman, Cranford, N.J.
145 Lbs.—Christine Penick, San Jose, Calif.
Under 158 Lbs.—Heidi Bauersaches, New York, N.Y.
Over 158 Lbs.—Juanita Cardwell, Tallahassee, Fla.
Open Division—Karen Mackay, Sioux City, Iowa

JUNIOR COLLEGES (1980-81)
Nat'l J.C. Champions — Men's Div.
Baseball—Miami-Dade C.C. (South)
Basketball—Westark C.C.
Bowling—Sinclair C.C.
Cross-Country—Pima C.C.
Decathlon—Conny Silfer, Ricks Coll.
Football—N.E. Oklahoma A & M
Golf—Chattahoochee Valley St. C.C.
Gymnastics—Odessa College
Ice Hockey—SUNY at Canton
Lacrosse—SUNY at Farmingdale
Marathon—Mark Wazniak, S.W. Michigan Coll.
Skiing (Alpine)—North Country C.C.
Skiing (Nordic)—Paul Smith's College
Skiing (Combined)—Paul Smith's College
Soccer—SUNY at Morrisville
Swimming—Indian River C.C.
Tennis—Central Florida C.C.
Track & Field (Indoor)—Odessa College
Track & Field (Outdoor)—Odessa College
Wrestling—Iowa Central C.C.
Nat'l J.C. Champions—Women's Div.
Basketball—Louisburg College
Bowling—Erie C.C.
Cross-Country—Lane C.C.
Field Hockey—Essex C.C.
Golf—Miami-Dade C.C. (North)
Gymnastics—Spokane C.C.
Skiing (Alpine)—North Country C.C.
Skiing (Nordic)—Vermont Tech. College
Skiing (Combined)—North Country C.C.
Softball (Fast Pitch)—Erie C.C.
Swimming—Daytona Beach C.C.
Tennis—Midland C.C., Schreiner J.C.
Track & Field (Indoor)—E. Oklahoma St. Coll.
Track & Field (Outdoor)—Mt. Hood C.C.
Volleyball—Kellogg C.C.

KARATE
1980 Nat'l AAU Champions
MEN (18-34) KATA
Nov.—Ian Neelan, Ore.
Int.—Neil Eichlebaum, Fla.
Adv.—Domingo Llanos, N.Y.
MEN (18-34) KUMITE
Nov.—Marvin Coleman, Ohio
Int.—Dann Deere, Ohio
Open—Tokey Hill, Ohio
WOMEN (18-34) KATA
Nov.—Sue Gristy, Ill.
Int.—Ann Bouman, N.J.
Adv.—Tilly Garcia, Utah
WOMEN (18-34) KUMITE
Nov.—Elaine Stevens, Ohio
Int.—Ann Bouman, N.J.
Hvwt.—Julia Beal

LACROSSE (1981)
NCAA Div. I—North Carolina
NCAA Div. II—Adelphi
NCAA Div. III—Hobart
AIAW Div. I—Maryland
AIAW Div. II—Delaware
AIAW Div. III—Trenton State

LUGE (1981)
World Champions
Singles—Sergei Danilin, U.S.S.R.
Women—Melitta Sollman, E. Germany
Doubles—Ulrich and Bernd Hahn, E. Germany
U.S. Nat'l Champions
Singles—Frank Masley, Newark, Del.
Women—Donna Burke, Lake Placid, N.Y.
Doubles—Terry Morgan, Saranac Lake, N.Y.-Beau Jamison, Hudson, Ohio

MARATHON
1981 Boston Marathon—Toshikiko Seko, Japan
Women—Allison Roe, New Zealand
1980 N.Y. City Marathon—Alberto Salazar, Eugene, Ore.
Women—Grete Waitz, Norway
1981 London Marathon—(tie) Dick Beardsley, Minneapolis, Minn.-Inge Simonsen, Norway
Women—Joyce Smith, Great Britain
1981 Pro Marathon (Pasadena, Calif.)—
Men—Ron Nabers, San Francisco, Calif.
Women—Cindy Dalrymple, Honolulu, Hawaii

MODERN PENTATHLON
World Champion (1981)—Janusz Peciak, Poland
U.S. Champion (1980)—John Fitzgerald, San Antonio, Tex.
Women (1980)—Kimberly Dunlop, Tallahassee, Fla.

MOTORCYCLING (1981)
AMA National Champions
125 cc Motocross—Mark Barnett, Bridgeview, Ill. (Suzuki)
250 cc Motocross—Ken Howerton, San Antonio, Tex. (Suzuki)
500 cc Motocross—Broc Glover, El Cajon, Calif. (Yamaha)
AMA Supercross (1980)—Mike Bell, Lakewood, Calif. (Yamaha)
U.S. Road Racing—Formula I (750 cc)—Dale Singleton, Dalton, Ga.
Superbike (1980)—Wes Cooley, Santa Ana, Calif.
Lightweight—Eddie Lawson, Ontario, Calif.
Novice—Don Greene, Novato, Calif.
Sidecar—Bruce Lind, Seattle, Wash.
Grand National—Mike Kidd, Boyd, Tex.

PADDLEBALL (1981)
Nat'l Four-Wall Champions
Singles—Steve Wilson, Flint, Mich.
Women—Caprice Behner, St. Charles, Ill.
Doubles—Andy Kasalo-Andy Mitchell, Kalamazoo, Mich.
Women—Grace Louwsma-Judy Shirley, Ann Arbor, Mich.

OTHER SPORTS (Cont.)

PADDLE TENNIS (1981)

U.S. National Champions
Singles—Mark Rifenbark, Los Angeles, Calif.
Doubles—Sol Hauptman-Jeff Fleitman, Brooklyn, N.Y.
Women (1980)—Kathy May, Los Angeles, Calif.
Doubles (1981)—Nena Perez, Venice, Calif.-Kathy May
Mixed Doubles (1980)—Debbie Nuciforo-Brian Lee, Venice, Calif.
U.S. National Beach Champions
Doubles—Sol Hauptman-Jeff Fleitman, Brooklyn, N.Y.
Women—Kim Johns-Mary Ellen Stewart, St. Augustine, Fla.

PARACHUTING (1981)

U.S. Champions
Men's Accuracy—Mark Jones
Men's Style—Maurice Fernandez
Men's Overall—Gene Koehler
Women's Accuracy—Cheryl Stearns
Women's Style—Cheryl Stearns
Women's Combined—Cheryl Stearns
Four-way Relative Work—Golden Knights
Eight-way Relative Work—Mirror Image
Ten-way Relative Work—Magic

PENTATHLON (1981)

U.S. Indoor Champions
Men—Scott Daniels
Women—Marlene Harmon
U.S. Women's Heptathlon Champion—
Jane Frederick, Athletics West

PLATFORM TENNIS (1980-81)

U.S. National Champions
Singles—Doug Russell, New York, N.Y.
Women—Robin Fulton, Norwalk, Conn.
Doubles—Steve Baird, Harrison, N.Y.-Rich Maier, Allendale, N.J.
Women—Yvonne Hackenberg, Kalamazoo, Mich.-Hilary Hilton, Glen Ellyn, Ill.
Mixed—Doug Russell-Hilary Hilton

POLO

1981 Champions
America Cup—Boca Raton
Gold Cup—Boca Raton
Copper Cup—Old Pueblo
Delegate's Cup—Steppenwolf
1980 Champions
U.S. Open—Southern Hills
Silver Cup—Retama
U.S. Handicap—Tulsa
North American Cup—Kingsville
Cup of the Americas—Argentina
Intercollegiate—Calif.-Davis

POWERBOATING

1981 U.S. National Champion—Dean Chenoweth, Tallahassee, Fla.
1981 Championship Boat—Miss Budweiser
1981 U.S. Offshore Champion—Betty Cook, Newport Beach, Calif.
1980 World Offshore Champion—Michael Meynard

QUARTER HORSE RACING (1981)

Race—Winner and Jockey
All American Futurity—Special Effort, W.R. Hunt
All American Derby—Higheasterjet, W.R. Hunt
Rainbow Derby—Higheasterjet, W.R. Hunt
Kansas Futurity—Special Effort, W.R. Hunt
Rainbow Futurity—Special Effort, W.R. Hunt
Kindergarten Futurity—Dash Again, D. Mitchell
Dash For Cash Futurity—Dashingly, J. Nicodemus

RODEO (1980)

World Champions
All Around—Paul Tierney, Rapid City, S.D.

Saddle Bronc Riding—Clint Johnson, Spearfish, S.D.
Bareback Bronc Riding—Bruce Ford, Kersey, Colo.
Bull Riding—Don Gay, Mesquite, Tex.
Steer Wrestling—Butch Myers, Welda, Kans.
Calf Roping—Roy Cooper, Durant, Okla.
Steer Roping—Guy Allen, Santa Anna, Tex.
Team Roping—Tee Woolman, Llano, Tex.
Women's Barrel Racing—Martha Josey, Karnack, Tex.

ROLLER SKATING (1981)

World Champions—Artistic
Singles—Tim McGuire, Flint, Mich.
Women—Tina Kneisley, Marion, Ohio
Dance—Cindy Smith-Mark Howard, Jacksonville, Fla.
Mixed Pairs—Tina Kneisley-Paul Price, Brighton, Mich.
World Champions—Speed
Men—Tom Peterson, Tacoma, Wash.
Women—Sandy Dulaney, Santa Ana, Calif.
U.S. Champions
Singles—Tim McGuire, Flint, Mich.
Women—Tina Kneisley, Marion, Ohio
Figures—Tony St. Jacques, Virginia Beach, Va.
Women—Rita Drogo, Hammonton, N.J.
Dance—Holly Valente-Billy Richardson, Waltham, Mass.
Mixed Pairs—Tina Kneisley-Paul Price, Brighton, Mich.

ROWING (1981)

U.S. Elite Champions
Singles—Jim Dietz, New York A.C.
Quarter Mile Singles—Chris Richard, Detroit
Doubles—New York A.C.
Pairs without Coxswain—Univ. of Pennsylvania
Pairs with Coxswain—Vesper
4s without Coxswain—Vesper
4s with Coxswain—New York A.C.
Quadruple Sculls—New York A.C.
8s—National Lightweight Camp
Intercollegiate Champions
IRA Varsity—Cornell
IRA Freshman—Brown
IRA Junior Varsity—Navy
Women—Washington
Eastern Women's—Yale
Eastern Regional Sprint—Yale
The Boat Race (Cambridge-Oxford)—
Oxford; series: Cam: 68, Oxf: 58, 1 tie
Royal Henley Regatta
Challenge Cup—Oxford & Thames Tradesmen
Ladies Challenge Cup—Washington J.V.
Thames Cup—Charles R. Rowing Assn.

RUGBY

1980 U.S. Nat'l Club Champion—Old Blue R.F.C., Oakland, Calif.
U.S. vs Canada
(1977) Canada 17, U.S.6
(1978) U.S. 12, Canada 7
(1979) Canada 19, U.S. 12
(1980) Canada 16, U.S. 0
(1981) Canada 6, U.S. 3

SHOOTING (1981)

U.S. National Outdoor Champions
Men's Pistol—SFC Joseph Pascarella, Las Cruces, N.M.
Women's Pistol—SP5 Ruby E. Fox, Parker, Ariz.
Smallbore Rifle (Prone)—Mary E. Stidworthy, Prescott, Ariz.
Smallbore Rifle (Position)—Lones W. Wigger, Jr., Ft. Benning, Ga.
High Power Rifle—David I. Boyd II, Triangle, Va.
U.S. National Indoor Champions
Conv. Rifle—Lones W. Wigger, Jr.

Women—Karen E. Monez, Willow Park, Tex.
Int'l Rifle—Lones W. Wigger, Jr.
Women—Karen Monez
Conv. Pistol—Guigno D. Carapellotti, Darby, Pa.
Women—SP5 Ruby E. Fox
Int'l Std. Pistol—Donald L. Hamilton, Kingston, Mass.
Women—Elinor A. Collins, Sanborn, N.Y.
Int'l Free Pistol—Steve F. Reiter, Dale City, Calif.
Women—Patricia A. Graham, Ft. Benning, Ga.
NRA Int'l Clay Pigeon Champions
Men—Terry H. Howard, Scott AFB, Ill.
Women—Audrey Grosch, Eden Prairie, Minn.
NRA Int'l Skeet Champions
Men—Matthew H. Dryke, Ft. Benning, Ga.
Women—Ila Hill, Birmingham, Mich.
NCAA Rifle
Smallbore—Kurt Fitz-Randolph, Tennessee Tech
Air Rifle—John Rost, West Virginia
Team—Tennessee Tech

SKIING

1980-81 World Cup Champions
Overall—Phil Mahre, Yakima, Wash.
Women—Marie-Theres Nadig, Switzerland
Downhill—Harti Weirather, Austria
Women—Marie-Theres Nadig
Slalom—Ingemar Stenmark, Sweden
Women—Erika Hess, Switzerland
Giant Slalom—Ingemar Stenmark
Women—Tamara McKinney, Olympic Valley, Calif.
1981 U.S. Alpine Champions
Downhill—Doug Powell, Chappaqua, N.Y.
Women—Holly Flanders, Deerfield, N.H.
Slalom—Steve Mahre, Yakima, Wash.
Women—Cindy Nelson, Reno, Nev.
Giant Slalom—Phil Mahre, Yakima, Wash.
Women—Tamara McKinney, Olympic Valley, Calif.
1981 U.S. Nordic Champions
Combined—Kerry Lynch, Grand Lake, Colo.
Jumping—Horst Bulau, Canada
Men's Cross-Country
15km.—Bill Koch, Putney, Vt.
30km.—Bill Koch
50km.—Tim Caldwell, Putney, Vt.
Women's Cross-Country
5km.—Alison Owen, Lake Fork, Idaho
10km.—Alison Owen
20km.—Lynn Spencer-Galanes, Newfane, Vt.
1981 NCAA Champions
Slalom—Scott Hoffman, Utah
Giant Slalom—Tor Melander, Vermont
Cross-Country—Bernt Lund, Utah
Cross-Country Relay—Vermont
Team—Utah
1981 AIAW (Women's) Nat'l Champions
Slalom—Becky Simning, Wyoming
Giant Slalom—Becky Simning
Alpine Combined—Becky Simning
Cross-Country (7.5 km.)—Marianne Reid, New Mexico
Team—Vermont

SOFTBALL (1981)

Amateur Softball Ass'n Champions
Men's Fast Pitch—ADM, Decatur, Ill.
Women—Orlando Rebels, Orlando, Fla.
Men's Slow Pitch—Elite Coating, Gordon, Ga.
Men's Super Slow Pitch—Howard's Western Steer, Denver, N.C.
Women—Tifton Tomboys, Tifton, Ga.
Industrial Slow Pitch—Raffield Fisheries, Port St. Joe, Fla.
Women—Provident Vets, Chattanooga, Tenn.
16" Slow Pitch—Budweiser, Harvey, Ill.
Men's Class A Fast Pitch—S. H. Good, Narvon, Pa.

OTHER SPORTS (Cont.)

Women—Montclair 81's, Montclair, N.J.
Men's Class A Slow Pitch—Ray Sears &
  Son, Gambrills, Md.
Women—Orlando Stars, Orlando, Fla.
Men's Class A Industrial Slow Pitch—
  Central Telephone, Hickory, N.C.
Men's Church Slow Pitch—First
  Methodist, Lewisville, Tex.
Women—South Main Baptist, Houston,
  Tex.
Modified Fast Pitch—Clinica, Miami, Fla.
AIAW Div. I—Utah State
  Div.II—Calif. State-Sacramento
  Div. III—E. Connecticut State
  Slow Pitch—Florida State
NAIA—Sam Houston State

SQUASH RACQUETS (1981)

U.S. Association Champions
Men's Singles—Mark Alger, Seattle,
  Wash.
Women's Singles—Barbara Maltby,
  Philadelphia, Pa.
Men's Doubles—Peter Hall, Hamilton,
  Ont.-Victor Harding, Toronto, Ont.
Women's Doubles—Joyce Davenport, King
  of Prussia, Pa.-Carol Thesieres,
  Broomall, Pa.
Mixed Doubles—Ralph Howe, Cold Spring
  Harbor, N.Y.-Joyce Davenport
Intercollegiate—John Nimick, Princeton
North American Open—Sharif Khan,
  Toronto, Ont.
U.S. Pro Singles—Michael Desaulniers,
  Montreal, Que.

TABLE TENNIS

1981 World Champions
Singles—Guo Yuehua, China
Women—Tong Ling, China
Doubles—Li Zhenshi-Cai Zhenhua, China
Women—Zhang Deying-Cao Yanhua,
  China
Mixed Doubles—Xie Saike-Huang Junqun,
  China
Men's Team—China
Women's Team—P.R. China
1980 U.S. National Champions
Singles—Danny Seemiller, Pittsburgh, Pa.
Women—He-Ja Lee, Las Vegas, Nev.
Doubles—Danny and Ricky Seemiller,
  Pittsburgh, Pa.
Women—Angelita Sistrunk, Cardiff,
  Calif.-He-Ja Lee
Mixed Doubles—Cheryl Dadian, Oak
  Creek, Wis.-Ricky Seemiller
1981 U.S. Open Champions
Singles—Xie Saike, China
Women—Tong Ling, China
Doubles—Si Heung-Yoo-Kim Wan,
  South Korea
Women—Hwang Nam Sook-An Hae Sook,
  South Korea
Mixed Doubles—Cai Zhenhua-Zhang
  Deying, China

Men's Team—China
Women's Team—China

VOLLEYBALL (1981)

U.S. Volleyball Ass'n Champions
Men's Open—Nautilus Pacifica, Long
  Beach, Calif.
Women's Open—Utah State, Ogden, Utah
Men's Senior—Legends Restaurant,
  Long Beach, Calif.
Women's Senior—South Bay Spoilers,
  Hermosa Beach, Calif.
Men's Golden Masters—Kansas City
NCAA—UCLA
AIAW Div. I—So. California (1980)
  Div. II—Calif. St.-Northridge (1980)
  Div. III—Calif. St.-Sacramento (1980)
NAIA—Azusa-Pacific (1980)

WATER POLO (1981)

World Cup—USSR
NCAA Champion (1980)—Stanford
Nat'l AAU Outdoor Champions
Men—Industry Hills Aquatic Club (Calif.)
Women—Industry Hills Aquatic Club
Nat'l AAU Indoor Champions
Women—Industry Hills Aquatic Club
Men—(1980) Pepperdine (Calif.)

WATER SKIING (1981)

U.S. Open Champions
Overall—Carl Roberge, Orlando, Fla.
Women—Cyndi Benzel, Newberry Sprs.,
  Calif.
Slalom—Bob La Point, Castro Valley,
  Calif.
Women—Cindy Todd, Pierson, Fla.
Tricks—Cory Pickos, Eagle Lake, Fla.
Women—Barbara Cleveland, Hawthorne,
  Fla.
Jumping—Sammy Duvall, Greenville, S.C.
Women—Linda Giddens, Eastman, Ga.
Masters Tournament
Overall—Mike Hazelwood, London
  England
Women—Judy McClintock, Streetsville,
  Ont.
World Champions
Overall—Sammy Duvall, U.S.A.
Women—Karin Roberge, U.S.A.
Slalom—Andy Mapple, Great Britain
Women—Cindy Todd, U.S.A.
Tricks—Cory Pickos, U.S.A.
Women—Ana Maria Carrasco, Venezuela
Jumping—Mike Hazelwood, Great Britain
Women—Deena Brush, U.S.A.
Team—United States

WEIGHTLIFTING (1981)

World Champions
52 kilos—Osmonaliev, U.S.S.R.
56 kilos—Kodjabashev, Bulgaria
60 kilos—Manolov, Bulgaria
67½ kilos—Kunz, E. Germany
75 kilos—Rusev, Bulgaria
82½ kilos—Vardanian, U.S.S.R.
90 kilos—Blagoev, Bulgaria
100 kilos—Sots, U.S.S.R.
110 kilos—Kravchuk, U.S.S.R.

Over 110 kilos—Pisarenko, U.S.S.R.
Nat'l Champions—MEN
52 kilos—Wren Norvell, Chicago, Ill.
56 kilos—Albert Hood, Los Angeles,
  Calif.
60 kilos—Phil Sanderson, Billings,
  Mont.
67½ kilos—Carl Schake, Butler, Pa.
75 kilos—Fred Lowe, E. Lansing, Mich.
82½ kilos—Val Balison, Superior, Mont.
90 kilos—Kevin Winter, San Jose, Calif.
100 kilos—Ken Clark, Pacifica, Calif.
110 kilos—Guy Carlton, Decatur, Ill.
Over 110 kilos—Jerome Hannan, Colorado
  Springs, Colo.
Nat'l Champions—WOMEN
44 kilos—Joette Weber; Kokomo, Ind.
48 kilos—Quin Burgess, Newman, Ga.
52 kilos—Mary Beth Cervenak,
  Malmstrom A.F.B., Mont.
56 kilos—Lisa Semm, Batavia, Ill.
60 kilos—Kim Besuden, W. Lafayette,
  Ind.
67½ kilos—Judy Glenney, Farmington,
  N.M.
75 kilos—Karyn Bastiansen, New York,
  N.Y.
82½ kilos—Karen Weaver, W. Lafayette,
  Ind.
Over 82½ kilos—Lorna Griffin,
  Huntington Beach, Calif.

YACHTING

1981 U.S. Yacht Racing Union Champions
Mallory Cup—Mark Foster, Corpus
  Christi, Tex.
Adams Trophy—Ann Boyd Sloger,
  Charleston, S.C.
Sears Cup—John Kostecki, Point
  Richmond, Calif.
O'Day Trophy—Steve Lowery, Annapolis,
  Md.
Prince of Wales Bowl—Marvin Beckmann,
  Houston, Tex.
Bemis Trophy—Mike Funsch, St.
  Petersburg, Fla.
Smythe Cup—Louis Verloop, Miami,
  Florida
1981 World Champions
Etchells 22—Dave Curtis, Marblehead,
  Mass.
Flying Jr.—Steve Klotz, Stanford, Calif.
Snipe—Jeff Lenhart, Costa Mesa, Calif.
Soling—Vince Brun, San Diego, Calif.
Sunfish—Dave Chapin, Springfield, Ill.
Tornado—Randy Smyth, Huntington
  Beach, Calif.
1981 World Youth Champions—
  John Shadden and Ron Rosenburg,
  Long Beach, Calif.
1980 America's Cup—US (Freedom;
  Dennis Conner, skipper) over Australia
  (Australia; Jim Hardy, skipper) 4-1
1980 Yachtsman of the Year—Dennis
  Conner, San Diego, Calif.
1980 Yachtswoman of the Year—Lynne
  Jewell, Plymouth, Mass.

POPULARITY OF DOG BREEDS Source: American Kennel Club

1980 Rank	Breed	1980 Registrations	1979 Rank	1980 Rank	Breed	1980 Registrations	1979 Rank
1.	Poodle	95,250	1	16.	Pekingese	18,859	17
2.	Doberman Pinscher	79,908	2	17.	Shih Tzu	17,957	20
3.	Cocker Spaniel	76,113	3	18.	Pomeranian	17,341	19
4.	German Shepherd	58,865	4	19.	Basset Hound	17,151	23
5.	Labrador Retriever	52,398	5	20.	Brittany Spaniel	17,146	18
6.	Golden Retriever	44,100	6	21.	Chihuahua	16,239	21
7.	Beagle	35,091	7	22.	Irish Setter	14,938	14
8.	Miniature Schnauzer	34,962	9	23.	Boxer	14,901	24
9.	Dachshund	33,881	8	24.	Chow Chow	14,589	26
10.	Shetland Sheepdog	28,325	10	25.	Great Dane	14,330	22
11.	Yorkshire Terrier	24,665	12	26.	Boston Terrier	11,636	27
12.	Lhasa Apso	24,477	11	27.	Old English Sheepdog	10,758	25
13.	Collie	21,477	13	28.	German Shorthaired Pointer	10,670	28
14.	English Springer Spaniel	21,370	15	29.	Samoyed	8,430	29
15.	Siberian Husky	20,884	16	30.	Alaskan Malamute	7,642	31

OBITUARIES

Addonizio, Hugh J., 67, Democratic representative from New Jersey and Newark mayor; convicted of extortion (1970) and conspiracy; served five years of 10-year prison sentence, fined $25,000; in Red Bank, N.J., Feb. 2, 1981.

Agar, Herbert, 83, writer, newspaper editor, winner of 1933 Pulitzer Prize for history; resident of England since 1920s; London correspondent for Louisville, Ky., newspapers; wrote *The People's Choice, The Darkest Year: Britain Alone, June 1940 - June 1941* and *A Time for Greatness;* in Sussex, England, Nov. 24, 1980.

Algren, Nelson (born Nelson Algren Abraham), 72, novelist, short story writer, essayist; given first National Book Award (1949) for *The Man With the Golden Arm;* elected to American Academy, Institute of Arts and Letters; in Sag Harbor, N.Y., May 9, 1981.

Alice, Princess, 97, Countess of Athlone and last surviving grandchild of Queen Victoria; daughter of Victoria's fourth son, Prince Leopold, Alice lived through six reigns and made record 20,000 public appearances; in London, Jan. 3, 1981.

Alsop, Mary O'Hara, 95, novelist who wrote *My Friend Flicka*, story about boy and pet colt in Wyoming; novel made into film and television series; among other works, *Thunderhead* and *Green Grass of Wyoming;* in Chevy Chase, Md., Oct. 14, 1980.

Amalrik, Andrei A., 42, Soviet human rights activist and political exile; criticized Soviet society as backward and repressive; first dissident to confer with American correspondents; major works, *Will the Soviet Union Survive Until 1984?* and *Involuntary Journey to Siberia;* killed in automobile accident en route to meeting on human rights; near Guadalajara, Spain, Nov. 11, 1980.

Amerasinghe, Hamilton S., 67, chief delegate to the United Nations from Sri Lanka; leader UN Conference on Law of the Sea (1973-80); in New York City, Dec. 4, 1980.

Andervont, Dr. Howard B., 83, virologist and cancer researcher who directed many studies linking viruses and cancer; former Harvard University epidemiologist; helped create National Cancer Institute in 1930s; in Sarasota, Fla., March 11, 1981.

Arieti, Silvano, 67, Italian-born psychoanalyst and specialist in schizophrenia; National Book Award (1975) for *Interpretation of Schizophrenia;* in New York City, Aug. 7, 1981.

Aronson, Boris, 81, Russian-born Broadway set designer who won six Tony Awards in 50-year career with more than 100 productions; award winners were "The Rose Tattoo," "Zorba," "Pacific Overtures," "Company," "Cabaret," and "Follies"; in Nyack, N.Y., Nov. 16, 1980.

Astaire, Adele, 82, dancer and comedienne who starred with her brother, Fred, in such top musical comedies as "Over the Top," "Funny Face," "Lady Be Good," and "The Band Wagon" from 1917 to 1932; in Phoenix, Ariz., Jan. 25, 1981.

Auchinleck, Gen. Claude John E., 96, British commander-in-chief in Middle East and India during World War II; dismissed by Winston Churchill (1942) for refusing to counterattack German and Italian forces led by Field Marshal Edwin Rommel; instrumental in several important victories of British 8th Army in North Africa; in Marrakech, Morocco, March 23, 1981.

Baker, Crowdus, 75, former mail-order clerk who became president of Sears, Roebuck & Co. (1960-67); vice chairman of board until his retirement in 1969; in Deerfield, Ill., June 6, 1981.

Ball, Edward, 93, chief trustee of Alfred I. du Pont estate; investments increased brother-in-law's fortune from $30 million to $2 billion; controversial leader of "Pork Chop Gang," which controlled Florida politics from 1930s to 1960s; in New Orleans, La., June 24, 1981.

Ballantrae, Baron (born Bernard Edward Ferguson), 69, former British governor-general of New Zealand (1962-67); soldier, poet, and historian; in London, Nov. 28, 1980.

Barber, Samuel, 70, American composer who twice won Pulitzer Prize; considered neo-Romantic and divorced from 20th century avant-garde musical trends ("Adagio," "Vanessa," and "Piano Concerto No. 1"); in New York City, Jan. 23, 1981.

Barnetson, William Denholm, 63, British news executive; chairman (1968-79) of Reuters; chairman of United Newspapers, the *Observer* of London, Thames Television; in London, March 12, 1981.

Barr, Alfred, 79, art scholar who developed New York's Museum of Modern Art into most influential center of its kind in the world; in Salisbury, Conn., Aug. 15, 1981.

Benedictos I (Vassilos Papadopoulos), 88, patriarch of Greek Orthodox church of Jerusalem; spiritual leader (elected 1957) of 10,000 followers in Israel, Jordan, occupied West Bank, Gaza Strip; in Jerusalem, Dec. 10, 1980.

Berman, Emile Zola, 78, trial lawyer best known for defense of Sirhan Sirhan, convicted assassin of Robert F. Kennedy; in New York City, July 3, 1981.

Betancourt, Rómulo, 73, former Venezuelan president who restored democratic rule after years of dictatorship; in New York City, Sept. 28, 1981.

Blackwell, Randolph T., 53, civil rights leader; winner of 1975 Martin Luther King, Jr., Non-Violent Peace Prize; founder (1966) Southern Rural Action, Inc., nonprofit corporation set up to provide jobs and housing for poor; in Atlanta, Ga., May 9, 1981.

Blanke, Henry, 79, German-born film producer who made award-winning adventure films and fictionalized biographies: *The Story of Louis Pasteur, Treasure of the Sierra Madre, The Petrified Forest,* and *The Adventures of Robin Hood;* in Los Angeles, May 28, 1981.

Bliss, Ray C., 73, former Republican National Chairman and quintessential political pragmatist; in Akron, Ohio, Aug. 6, 1981.

Block, Philip D., Jr., 74, chairman of Inland Steel Co. (1967-71); in Chicago, Ill., May 28, 1981.

Boehm, Karl, 86, Austrian conductor; former director Vienna State Opera; leading interpreter of Mozart, Berg, Wagner, and Richard Strauss; in Salzburg, Aug. 14, 1981.

Bondi, Beulah, 92, character actress of stage, screen and television; in Los Angeles, Jan. 12, 1981.

Boone, Richard, 63, actor famed for his portrayal of Western gunman, Paladin, in the television series "Have Gun, Will Travel"; in St. Augustine, Fla., Jan. 10, 1981.

Bordes, François, 61, French archaeologist and noted authority on Neanderthal man; one of first experts to study tools made and used by primitive tribes; in Tucson, Ariz., April 30, 1981.

Bradley, Omar N., 88, last of the U.S. Army's five-star generals; was senior commander of American ground forces in Europe during the later years of World War II, and chairman of the Joint Chiefs of Staff from 1949 to 1953; in New York City, April 18, 1981.

Breuer, Marcel, 79, Hungarian-born architect who brought European modernism to U.S.; taught at Harvard Graduate School of Design; also designed New York Whitney Museum, Paris UNESCO headquarters; in New York City, July 1, 1981.

Brown, Roy, 56, pioneering blues singer whose rock-and-roll style influenced Elvis Presley; height of career (1948-51) saw 12 of his records in top 10; in Los Angeles, May 10, 1981.

Brunschwig, Zelina C., 84, designer and chairman of Brunschwig & Fils Inc.; developed coordinated-swatch system used throughout fabric industry; 40-year career in fabrics and interior design; in New York City, Sept. 10, 1981.

Busignies, Henri Gaston, 76, electronics expert who invented first automatic direction-finder for aircraft; his innovations in aerial navigation and radar aided Allied military effort in World War I; retired chief engineer, International Telephone and Telegraph Corp.; in Antibes, France, June 19, 1981.

Cadieux, Marcel, 65, Canadian ambassador to the United States (1969-75); former ambassador to Europe Economic Community; first French-Canadian appointed ambassador to U.S.; in Pompano Beach, Fla., March 19, 1981.

Caetano, Marcello, 74, premier of Portugal 1968-74) overthrown by military junta, ending almost 50 years of right-wing dictatorship; fled to Brazil after coup ousted him; in Rio de Janeiro, Oct. 6, 1980.

Campora, Hector J., 71, president of Argentina or 49 days (1973) before reinstallation of dictator Juan D. Perón; exiled to Mexico (1979) in Cuernavaca, Mexico, Dec. 19, 1980.

Charney, Jule G., 64, world leader in weather research; pioneer in computerized weather forecasting; former professor of meteorology, Massachusetts Institute of Technology; in Boston, Mass., June 16, 1981.

Chayefsky, Paddy, 58, playwright and three-time Academy Award winner; his play "Marty" is considered one of the classics of the 1950s golden age of television drama; in New York City, Aug. 1, 1981.

Chervenko, Vulko, 80, premier of Bulgaria (1950-56) and Communist Party leader; gained power in 1940s and early 1950s but was ousted from party for Stalinist-type repressions; in Sofia, Bulgaria, Oct. 21, 1980.

Clair, René, 82, French film director, considered one of greatest in French cinema; first film director elected to French Academy solely for film work; some major films, Paris Qui Dort, A Nous la Liberté; in Neuilly, France, March 15, 1981.

Connelly, Marc, 90, Pulitzer Prize-winning author of The Green Pastures, and, with George S. Kaufman, of such Broadway successes as "Dulcy," "Merton of the Movies" and "Beggar on Horseback"; a central figure in the Algonquin Round Table of the 1920s; in New York City, Dec. 21, 1980.

Connelly, Philip Marshall (Slim), 77, first president Los Angeles Newspaper Guild (1936-51); ousted after arrest as Communist leader; convicted (1952) of violating Smith Act prohibiting advocacy of violent overthrow of government; conviction reversed in 1955; in Torrance, Calif., May 20, 1981.

Coon, Carleton S., 76, archaeologist-anthropologist who made major contributions to research into origins of Man; author of The Story of Man, The Seven Caves; in Gloucester, Mass., June 3, 1981.

Craven, Wesley F., 75, professor emeritus of history at Princeton University; authority on Colonial American history; retired (1973); in Princeton, N.J., Feb. 10, 1981.

Cronin, Archibald J., 84, Scottish-born physician who became successful novelist, leaving lucrative London medical practice, in 1931; The Keys of the Kingdom, Shannon's Way, Pocketful of Rye; in Montreux, Switzerland, Jan. 6, 1981.

Crowther, Bosley, 75, New York Times film critic (1940-67); viewed as one of most influential critics in United States; in Mount Kisco, N.Y., March 7, 1981.

Curran, Joseph, 75, former able-bodied seaman who founded National Maritime Union; often accused of encouraging Communist influence in union and of living luxurious life; in Boca Raton, Fla., Aug. 14, 1981.

Daniel, Daniel, 91, often called dean of American baseball writers; covered baseball in New York for more than 50 years; in Pompano Beach, Fla., July 2, 1981.

Darden, Colgate W., Jr., 84, lawyer, educator, and Democratic congressman of Virginia; governor of Virginia (1942-46); helped reform Virginia prisons; battled foes of public school integration; in Norfolk, Va., June 9, 1981.

Day, Dorothy, 83, founder of Catholic Worker Movement (1933); accepted voluntary poverty and opened many homes for poor; nonviolent social activist who stressed importance of individual rather than mass action in improving society; in New York City, Nov. 29, 1980.

Dean, Paul (Daffy), 67, baseball pitcher for St. Louis Cardinals in 1930s; brother of pitching star Jerome (Dizzy) Dean; played for Cardinals, New York Giants, St. Louis Browns; in Springdale, Ark., March 17, 1981.

Dean, William F., 82, heroic U.S. Army general who personally engaged the enemy in combat when he became separated from his division during the early days of the Korean War. He was captured and held prisoner until 1953; in Berkeley, Calif., Aug. 24, 1981.

Delbrück, Max, 74, molecular geneticist, California Institute of Technology professor emeritus; won Nobel Prize (1969) for his research and discoveries; noted for studies of viruses; in Pasadena, Calif., March 9, 1981.

Demichelli, Alberto, 84, president of Uruguay for 80 days in 1976; cooperated with military coup, in 1973, that dissolved Congress; repressed political, union, and news organizations; in Montevideo, Oct. 12, 1980.

De Sola Pool, Tamar, 90, Israeli author and educator; national president of Hadassah, women's Zionist organization (1938-43); in New York City, May 31, 1981.

Dinkeloo, John G., 63, noted architect; helped build Dulles International Airport, the Oakland (Calif.) Museum, and One United Nations Plaza in New York; master plan for new wings of New York Metropolitan Museum of Art; in Fredericksburg, Va., June 15, 1981.

Doenitz, Karl, 89, former German grand admiral who succeeded Hitler; presided over Nazis' unconditional surrender in World War II; served 10 years in Spandau prison as war criminal; near Hamburg, Germany, Dec. 24, 1980.

Donskoi, Mark S., 80, Soviet film director specializing in patriotic films; *The Childhood of Maxim Gorki, On His Own, University of Life;* reported dead in USSR, March 25, 1981.

Douglas, Donald W., 88, founder of Douglas Aircraft (now part of McDonnell Douglas), and master builder of the famed DC-3 passenger plane; in Palm Springs, Calif., Feb. 1, 1981.

Douglas, Melvyn, 80, debonair movie actor who made Greta Garbo laugh in *Ninotchka;* star of Broadway; film Oscars for *Hud* and *Being There;* in New York City, Aug. 4, 1981.

Drew, Richard G., 81, Director of Products Fabrication Laboratory, Minnesota Mining and Manufacturing Co.; created Scotch brand cellophane tape while working as laboratory assistant for 3M Company; in Santa Barbara, Calif., Dec. 7, 1980.

Evans, Madge, 71, screen and stage actress of the 1920s and 1930s who portrayed clean-living heroines throughout her acting career; in Oakland, N.J., April 26, 1981.

Farago, Ladislas, 74, Hungarian-born journalist and author of more than a dozen books on world affairs; his *Patton: Ordeal and Triumph* was made into Academy Award-winning film, *Patton; The Broken Seal* was adapted for movie *Tora! Tora! Tora!;* attracted world notice with 1972 newspaper series contending Hitler's aide, Martin Borman, was alive and living in Argentina; in New York City, Oct. 15, 1980.

Farber, Leslie H., 68, psychoanalyst and leading proponent of existential trend in psychology; denounced impulse to seek final answers to human problems; wrote *The Ways of the Will, Schizophrenia and the Mad Psychiatrist;* in New York City, March 24, 1981.

Farrand, Clair Loring, 85, inventor of radio loudspeaker; helped develop sound, color, and cinematographic technologies for Warner Brothers; his companies held more than 1,000 patents, some used in space programs; in Palm Springs, Calif., Jan. 7, 1981.

Farrell, Edelmiro, 93, Argentine president (1944-45) and Army general; declared war on Japan and Germany toward close of World War II; yielded rule to Juan D. Perón; in Buenos Aires, Oct. 31, 1980.

Fawzi, Mahmoud, 82, Egyptian polylingual diplomat; served as ambassador to many nations during 50-year career; United Nations representative (1946-52) under King Farouk; prime minister to President Sadat (1970-72); one of two vice presidents 'before retirement in 1974; in Cairo, June 12, 1981.

Fisher, Welthy Honsiger, 101, pioneer teacher in India's literacy movement; inspired by Mohandas K. Ghandi to initiate Literacy House; in Southbury, Conn., Dec. 16, 1980.

Fitzsimmons, Frank E., 73, former truck driver who became president of International Brotherhood of Teamsters; took union reins when predecessor James R. Hoffa was sent to prison in 1967; elected to continue as president (1971); in La Jolla, Calif., May 6, 1981.

Fletcher, Harvey, 96, physicist; pioneer of stereophonic sound; helped develop first hearing aids; headed physical research Bell Telephone Laboratories (1933-49); in Provo, Utah, July 23, 1981.

Fox, Carol, 55, co-founder and general manager, for 25 years, of Lyric Opera House of Chicago; in Chicago, July 31, 1981.

Fox, Terry, 22, Canadian hero who made 1980 cross-country run on artificial limb that replaced leg lost to cancer in 1977; raised more than $20 million for cancer research; forced to stop run after four and a half months because of lung infection diagnosed as cancer; in New Westminster, B.C., June 28, 1981.

Fox, Virgil, 68, renowned organist who had played before an estimated six million people throughout the world; in West Palm Beach, Fla., Oct. 25, 1980.

Fraser, Adm. Bruce Austin, 93, British naval officer who won distinction (1943) in naval battle off North Cape, Norway; sank 26,000-ton German cruiser *Scharnhorst;* in London, Feb. 12, 1981.

Frederika, Queen (Louise), 63, former Queen of Greece (1947-64); lived in self-imposed exile following ouster of her son, King Constantine, in 1973; in Madrid, Feb. 6, 1981.

Freidman, Elizabeth S., 88, expert cryptographer who helped crack codes used by foes of U.S. in both world wars; she and her late husband, Col. William Freidman, broke "Purple Code" used by Japanese diplomats before and during World War II; in Plainfield, N.J., Oct. 31, 1980.

Frings, Katherine (Ketti), 61, screenwriter, playwright, and winner of 1958 Pulitzer Prize for stage version of Thomas Wolfe's novel *Look Homeward Angel;* in Los Angeles, Feb. 11, 1981.

Garcia, Sara, 85, known as "grandmother" of Mexican cinema; appeared in 350 films, since 1919, and acted in stage and radio roles; in Mexico City, Nov. 21, 1980.

Gary, Romain, 65, Lithuanian-born French novelist and diplomat; prolific writer especially known for *The Roots of Heaven;* apparent suicide, reportedly without connection to suicide of former wife Jean Seberg; in Paris, Dec. 2, 1980.

George, Chief Dan, 82, Canadian Indian who was spokesman for native rights and who is remembered for his acting role in the movie, *Little Big Man;* in Vancouver, British Columbia, Sept. 23, 1981.

Golden, Harry, 79, editor-publisher of *The Carolina Israelite,* who battled bigotry with humor in his newspaper and books; in Charlotte, N.C., Oct. 2, 1981.

Gopallawa, William, 83, president of Sri Lanka (Ceylon) (1972-78); ambassador to China, U.S., Cuba, and Mexico; in Colombo, Sri Lanka, Jan. 30, 1981.

Gorman, Chester, 43, archaeologist—anthropologist whose excavations in Thailand uncovered bronze artifacts that pushed back earliest date for Bronze Age culture to 3600 B.C.; in Sacramento, Calif., June 7, 1981.

Grassi, Paolo, 62, former director of La Scala Opera House in Milan, and former general manager of Italian broadcast network; in Milan, March 14, 1981.

Grasso, Ella T., 61, Democratic governor of Connecticut (1975-80); first woman elected governor in U.S. in her own right; former U.S. representative (1971-75); resigned as governor during second term because she was stricken with cancer; in Hartford, Conn., Feb. 5, 1981.

Hagerty, James C., 71, respected press secretary to President Eisenhower, 1953-1961; in Bronxville, N.Y., April 11, 1981.

Haley, Bill, 55, guitarist, singer, band leader, and rock-and-roll music pioneer; many hits including "Rock Around the Clock" (1955); considered big influence on Beatles; in Harlingen, Texas, Feb. 9, 1981.

Hanson, Howard, 84, Pulitzer Prize winner, composer-conductor; director of Eastman School of Music (1924-64); "Fourth Symphony" and "Third Symphony" among major works; in Rochester, N.Y., Feb. 26, 1981.

Harburg, Edgar Y., 85, American lyricist best known for 1932 song, "Brother, Can You Spare a Dime?"; collaborated with major American composers on film scores, e.g., for *Finian's Rainbow, Wizard of Oz;* in Los Angeles, March 5, 1981.

Harding, Ann, 79, aristocratically beautiful actress of stage and screen during the 1920s and 1930s; in Sherman Oaks, Calif., Sept. 1, 1981.

Hauge, Gabriel, 67, educator, international banker; chief economic adviser to President Eisenhower; chairman Manufacturers Hanover Trust Co. (1971-79); in New York City, July 24, 1981.

Hayler, Vice Adm. Robert W., 89, one of U.S. Navy's most decorated officers, winner of three Navy crosses; played crucial part in naval battles in Solomon Islands and Surigao Strait; in Carmel, Calif., Nov. 17, 1980.

Healy, George W., Jr., 75, enterprising editor of New Orleans *Times Picayune* for 20 years; president of American Society of Newspaper Editors (1958-59); in New Orleans, La., Nov. 2, 1980.

Hirshhorn, Joseph H., 82, prospector for gold, uranium, and oil; founder and benefactor of Hirshhorn Museum in Washington, D.C.; in Washington, D.C., Sept. 1, 1981.

Howard, Elston, 51, New York Yankees baseball player, who was voted the American League's most valuable player in 1963; he was the first black to play for the Yankees; in New York City, Dec. 14, 1980.

Humes, Helen, 68, noted singer of ballads and blues; vocalist with Count Basie's orchestra for four years; in Santa Monica, Calif., Sept. 13, 1981.

Ichikawa, Fusae, 87, Japanese feminist and former member of Parliament; formed Japan's Women's Suffrage League in 1920s; won right of women to vote (1945); in Tokyo, Feb. 11, 1981.

Ilg, Frances L., 78, pediatrician, co-founder of Gesell Institute in New Haven, Conn., major influence on the rearing of children, 1950s; in Manitowish Waters, Wis., July 26, 1981.

Ireney, Metropolitan, 88, retired primate of Orthodox Church in America (1965-71); leader of church linked to Russian Orthodox Church until it declared autonomy in 1924; in Staten Island, N.Y., March 18, 1981.

Jessel, George, 83, comedian known for patriotism and eulogies; 74-year career included role in original stage production of *The Jazz Singer* (1925); in Los Angeles, May 24, 1981.

Joachim, Sister Ann, 79, first Roman Catholic nun admitted to practice law before U.S. Supreme Court (1936); earned law degree in 1928; in 1971, directed unsuccessful effort to save Wabash Cannonball line of Norfolk & Western Railroad; in Adrian, Mich., Jan. 8, 1981.

Johnson, Pamela Hansford, 69, noted British novelist whose works often mirrored themes similar to those of her late husband, Sir C.P. Snow; wrote 25 novels; some of the more popular, *This Bed Thy Centre, An Impossible Marriage, The Good Husband;* in London, June 18, 1981.

Kardiner, Abram, 89, psychoanalyst and co-founder of New York Psychiatric Institute, first psychoanalytic training school in U.S.; student-patient of Sigmund Freud in 1921; in Easton, Conn., July 20, 1981.

Katona, George, 79, Hungarian-born economist-psychologist, often called dean of behavioral economists; University of Michigan professor (1946-72); wrote *The Mass Consumption Society;* in West Berlin, June 18, 1981.

Kaufman, Joseph W., 81, lawyer and judge who served as prosecutor at Nuremberg war crimes trials after World War II; chief prosecutor in trial of Alfred Krupp and 11 other German armament tycoons; in Washington, D.C., Jan. 30, 1981.

Kelly, Patsy, 71, wise-cracking comedienne who played the trusty friend to many Hollywood leading ladies in films of the 1930s and 1940s; in Woodland Hills, Calif., Sept. 24, 1981.

Kendrick, Pearl L., 90, microbiologist who helped develop whooping cough vaccine (1939); developed standard DPT shot to protect against diptheria, whooping cough, and tetanus; worked with World Health Organization; initiated immunization programs in Mexico, India, Germany, South America, Soviet Union; in Grand Rapids, Mich., Oct. 8, 1980.

Kharitonov, Yevgeny, 40, unpublished Soviet writer whose works circulated privately among Moscow intellectuals; one of seven writers whose attempt, in November 1980, to form literary club provoked arrests; in Moscow, June 29, 1981.

Kintner, Robert E., 71, former president of American Broadcasting Co. and National Broadcasting Co. television and radio networks; greatly expanded news programming; in Washington, D.C., Dec. 20, 1980.

Knight, John S., 87, founder of Knight newspaper publishing empire; battled for journalistic independence; Pulitzer Prize (1968) for "Editor's Notebook" columns; in Akron, Ohio, June 16, 1981.

Kondrashin, Kiril, 67, Soviet symphony conductor who defected to West in December 1978; revitalized Moscow Philharmonic during 1960s; noted for two recordings with American pianist Van Cliburn; in Amsterdam, March 7, 1981.

Kosygin, Aleksey, 76, premier of Soviet Union (1964-77); shared power with Leonid I. Brezhnev; joined Communist party in 1927; supervised evacuation of Leningrad (1941); sought improved trade with Western nations; near Moscow, Dec. 18 or 19, 1980.

Kotelawala, John, 83, prime minister of Sri Lanka (1953-56); third prime minister since Sri Lanka, formerly Ceylon, gained independence from Great Britain; in Colombo, Sri Lanka, Oct. 2, 1980.

Lasker, Edward, 95, five-time winner of U.S. open chess championship (1916, 1917, 1919, 1920, 1921); wrote Chess Strategy; in New York City, March 23, 1981.

Leger, Jules, 67, governor-general of Canada (1974-79); supervised transfer from Britain to Canada of power to declare war, sign peace treaties, and accredit diplomats abroad; in Toronto, Nov. 22, 1980.

Lennon, John, 40, rock star and composer who performed with Paul McCartney, George Harrison and Ringo Starr as The Beatles, the great pop singing group of the sixties, whose music symbolized a generation; shot to death in New York City, Dec. 8, 1980.

Levene, Sam, 75, comic character actor who originated role of Max Kane and made hit as Nathan Detroit in original production of "Guys and Dolls"; in New York City, Dec. 29, 1980.

Levin, Meyer, 75, Zionist, novelist, scriptwriter; novel Compulsion (1956) about 1920s Leopold-Loeb murder case made into successful play; in Jerusalem, July 9, 1981.

Lewis, David, 72, Polish-born founder of Canada's New Democratic party; leader of social causes, proponent of benefits for veterans and elderly; in Ottawa, May 24, 1981.

Lidell, Alvar, 72, British radio news announcer; one of most famous "voices" of British Broadcasting Corp.; he broadcast abdication of King Edward VII, in 1936, and outbreak of World War II in 1939; in London, Jan. 8, 1981.

Lillienthal, David E., 81, first chairman of U.S. Atomic Energy Commission (1946-50) during which time it established civilian control over development of atomic bomb; chairman of Tennessee Valley Authority (1933-46); in New York City, Jan. 15, 1981.

Lindsay, Margaret, 70, Hollywood film actress who appeared in 88 movies between 1931 and 1953; in Los Angeles, May 8, 1981.

Link, Edwin A., 77, inventor of Link flight simulator for training pilots; founder of Link Foundation awarding grants for aeronautic, oceanographic research; 1980 Lindbergh Award for achievement in science and technology; in Binghamton, N.Y., Sept. 7, 1981.

Little, Edward H., 100, former soap salesman who became chairman in 1953 of Colgate-Palmolive Co.; in Memphis, Tenn., July 12, 1981.

Loeb, William, 75, conservative publisher of The Manchester Union Leader and The New Hampshire Sunday News; his scathing editorials denounced liberal Democrats; chairman of Council of Profit-Sharing Industries (1949-1952); in Burlington, Mass., Sept. 13, 1981.

Longo, Luigi, 80, secretary of Italian Communist party (1964-72); one of party founders (1922); imprisoned by Mussolini; fought Germans in World War II as guerrilla leader; in Rome, Oct. 16, 1980.

Loos, Anita, 88, witty novelist and writer of more than 200 film scripts; novel, Gentlemen Prefer Blondes, introduced character, Lorelei Lee; in New York City, Aug. 18, 1981.

Lopokova, Lydia, 88, Russian prima ballerina with Serge Diaghilev's Ballet Russes; married economist John Maynard Keynes, in 1925; in England, June 8, 1981.

Louis, Joe, 66, heavyweight boxing champion who held the world championship title from 1937 to 1949; the "Brown Bomber" was considered by many sports experts to be the best heavyweight fighter of all time; in Las Vegas, Nev., April 12, 1981.

Lundborg, Louis B., 74, retired chairman of BankAmerica Corp.; condemned U.S. role in Vietnam in testimony before U.S. Senate Foreign Relations Committee; in Belvedere, Calif., Jan. 11, 1981.

Mandelstam, Nadezhda, 81, widow of Soviet poet Osip Mandelstam, who died in Siberian concentration camp; established husband's reputation as great poet with her memoirs, Hope Against Hope and Hope Abandoned; in Moscow, Dec. 29, 1980.

Marley, Bob, 36, Jamaican reggae singer known internationally for lively concerts; vigorous disciple of Rastafarianism, a cultish reverence of Haile Selassie, late emperor of Ethiopia; in Miami, May 11, 1981.

Martin, Ross, 61, popular actor best known as character Artemus Gordon on 1960s television series "The Wild, Wild West"; in Ramona, Calif., July 3, 1981.

Massing, Hede, 81, former Viennese actress and confessed Soviet spy who testified against Alger Hiss in 1950; in New York City, March 8, 1981.

Matthias, Bernd T., 62, German-born physicist instrumental in discovery of superconductive niobium-tin alloy for superconducting generators; taught at University of California, San Diego, and worked for Bell Laboratories and Los Alamos Scientific Laboratory in New Mexico; in La Jolla, Calif., Oct. 27, 1980.

McCain, Adm. John S., Jr., 70, commander-in-chief Pacific Forces, Vietnam War; decorated World War II submarine commander; aboard military aircraft, March 22, 1981.

McCormack, John W., 88, Democratic representative from Massachusetts (1928-70) and speaker of the U.S. House of Representatives (1962-70); helped design and pass domestic legislation in most productive congressional era (1960s); in Dedham, Mass., Nov. 22, 1980.

McEwen, John, 80, prime minister of Australia (1967-68); formulated many trade pacts and opposed Britain's entry into the European Community; opened new export markets, including Russia and China; in Melbourne, Australia, Nov. 20, 1980.

McHugh, Frank, 83, veteran supporting actor of the films who played amiable sidekick roles; he was quoted as saying, "I play a dumb cluck"; in Greenwich, Conn., Sept. 11, 1981.

McLuhan, Marshall, 69, noted Canadian communications theorist whose maxim, "the medium is the message," expresses his key concept that the way information is acquired affects the public more than the information content itself; in Toronto, Canada, Dec. 31, 1980.

McQueen, Steve, 50, actor who portrayed tough loner and underdog in many films (The Great Escape, The Cincinnati Kid, Bullitt, and Papillon); underwent controversial diet treatment for cancer in Mexico; in Juarez, Mexico, Nov. 7, 1980.

Montale, Eugenio, 84, Italian poet and literary-music critic for Corriere della Sera newspaper in Milan; 1975 Nobel Prize for literature; major publications included Bones of the Cuttlefish, The Storm and Other Things, Satura; in Milan, Sept. 12, 1981.

Montgomery, Robert, 77, veteran star of screen, stage and television; remembered for his performances in the films Night Must Fall and Here Comes Mr. Jordan, the actor served as presidential television adviser during the Eisenhower administration; in New York City, Sept. 27, 1981.

Moses, Robert, 92, aggressive urban planner who changed the face of New York City and New York state; directed building of 75 state parks, 11 bridges, 481 miles of highway; held 12 positions simultaneously; in West Islip, N.Y., July 29, 1981.

Mosley, Oswald, 84, British fascist leader in 1930s; avowed anti-Semite who led attacks on London Jews; under British detention during World War II; in Orsay, France, Dec. 2, 1980.

Neumann, Emanuel, 87, Latvian-born immigrant who became American Zionist leader; spent most of life helping to establish Israel, building economic and political support in United States for resettlement of Jews in Palestine; in Tel Aviv, Oct. 26, 1980.

Oldfield, Maurice, 65, chief, British Intelligence (1973-78); worked under Kim Philby, Soviet double agent; believed to have inspired creation of spy chief "M" character in Ian Fleming's James Bond books; in London, March 11, 1981.

Olivier, George B., 69, prime minister of Malta (1966-71); responsible for program leading to Malta's independence from Great Britain (1964); major influence in Maltese development for more than 30 years; in Sliema, Malta, Oct. 29, 1980.

O'Neill, Ralph A., 83, World War II flying ace and commercial aviation pioneer; in 1920s, trained Mexican pilots flying against revolutionaries trying to overthrow President Alvaro Obregon; set six-day flight record in 1928, transporting passengers between Miami and Buenos Aires; in Menlo Park, Calif., Oct. 23, 1980.

Palar, Lambertus N., 80, Indonesian diplomat and major advocate of Indonesian independence; delegate to United Nations (1950-53); former ambassador to India, Canada, and United States; in Jakarta, Feb. 12, 1981.

Pauley, Edwin W., 78, petroleum tycoon who advised four Democratic presidents—Roosevelt, Truman, Kennedy, and Johnson; masterminded U.S. petroleum policy in World War II; in Beverly Hills, Calif., July 28, 1981.

Pehrson, Wilfred R., 53, former governor of Penobscot Indan tribe; key negotiator in settlement of 12.5 millon-acre land claim by Penobscot and Passamaquoddy Indians; on Indian Island, Me., Oct. 14, 1980.

Person, Bernard, 86, Dutch-born, print-broadcast journalist; as political exile, delivered daily broadcasts to Nazi-occupied Netherlands in World War II; decorated by Dutch government; helped found Facts on File, news reference publication; in Albuquerque, N.M., March 9, 1981.

Piccard, Rev. Jeannette R., 86, high-altitude balloonist who piloted balloon to record altitude of 57,579 feet, in 1934, with scientist husband Jean Piccard; she defied Episcopal church by entering priesthood in 1974; in Minneapolis, Minn., May 17, 1981.

Pilinsky, Janos, 59, Hungarian poet whose works describe horror of German concentration camps of World War II; in Budapest, May 27, 1981.

Ponselle, Rosa, 84, dramatic soprano considered to be one of America's greatest operatic talents; her career at the Metropolitan Opera lasted from 1918 to 1937; in Baltimore, May 25, 1981.

Presser, William, 74, leader of International Brotherhood of Teamsters for more than 50 years; retired as vice president of union in 1976; served as president of Ohio chapter until his death; twice convicted in 1960s, once for contempt, once for destroying union records; in Lyndhurst, Ohio, July 18, 1981.

Price, Dorothy, 81, U.S. endocrinologist who helped conceptualize sexual hormone "feedback" mechanisms of pituitary gland; work led to development of birth control pill; earned Ph.D. from University of Chicago in 1935; worked there as researcher until 1965 when she became Boerhoave professor at University of Leiden, Netherlands; in Netherlands, Nov. 17, 1980.

Raft, George, 85, film actor known for tough-guy portrayals (Each Dawn I Die, Souls at Sea); convicted of tax evasion, banned (1967) from Britain; in Hollywood, Calif., Nov. 24, 1980.

Rahman, Ziaur, 45, Bangladeshi president and general who took office in 1977; assassinated in Chittagong, Bangladesh, May 30, 1981.

Rausch, Bishop James S., 52, Roman Catholic Church liberal who advocated marriage for priests and ordination of women; former general secretary of National Conference of Catholic Bishops; head of Phoenix diocese since 1977; in Phoenix, Ariz., May 18, 1981.

Rayner, Sydney, 86, tenor at Metropolitan Opera in New York during 1930s; appeared in many roles, including Turiddu in "Cavalleria Rusticana" and title role in Gounod's "Faust"; in East Patchogue, N.Y., Sept. 14, 1981.

Reynolds, Richard S., 72, president and chairman Reynolds Metals Co. (1948-76); eldest son of firm's founder; great nephew of founder of R.J. Reynolds Tobacco Co.; in Richmond, Va., Oct. 5, 1980.

Richter, Karl, 54, German conductor, harpsichordist, and leading interpreter of works of Bach; head-director of Munich Bach Chorus and Orchestra which sparked revival of Bach-Handel music in 1950s and 1960s; in Munich, Feb. 16, 1981.

Roberts, Rachel, 53, Welsh-born actress who played mostly in British films; former wife of actor Rex Harrison; nominated for Oscar for *This Sporting Life;* in Los Angeles, Nov. 26, 1980.

Rudenko, Roman A., 73, Soviet chief prosecutor at Nuremberg war crimes trials (1945-46) against Nazi leaders Rudolph Hess, Herman Goering, and Albert Speer; chief prosecutor in espionage trial of U-2 pilot Francis Gary Powers; in USSR, Jan. 23, 1981.

el-Sadat, Anwar, 62, Egyptian president since 1970; he led Egypt in war against Israel in 1973, but later signed a peace treaty with Israel in 1979, ending 30 years of conflict between the two states; prior to the final signing, Sadat received the 1978 Nobel Peace Prize; assassinated near Cairo, Oct. 6, 1981.

Sanders, Harland (Colonel Sanders), 90, founder of Kentucky Fried Chicken fast-food chain; sold 6,000-outlet worldwide business, in 1964, for $2 million plus $75,000 annual consulting salary; in Shelbyville, Ky., Dec. 16, 1980.

Saroyan, William, 72, author and playwright who published more than 400 short stories; portrayed lives of poor in native city of Fresno and in San Francisco; refused 1939 Pulitzer Prize for play "The Time of Your Life" because he deplored "wealth patronizing art"; in Fresno, Calif., May 18, 1981.

Sayegh, Fayez A., 58, political adviser at Kuwaiti United Nations mission; principal author of U.N. resolution condemning Zionism as "racism" (1975); in New York City, Dec. 9, 1980.

Schanker, Louis, 78, painter, printmaker, sculptor; member in 1930s of "The 10," artists' group defying trend toward realism by using abstract styles; in New York City, May 7, 1981.

Shakow, Dr. David, 80, pioneer psychologist in research on schizophrenia; chief of National Institute of Mental Health clinical psychology laboratory; many awards for contributions to psychology; in Washington, D.C., Feb. 26, 1981.

Sheldon, Charles S., 64, adviser to Congress and noted authority on Soviet space program; former chief of Science Policy Research Division in Library of Congress; in Arlington, Va., Sept. 11, 1981.

Shoumatoff, Elizabeth, 92, artist who did portraits of Presidents Franklin D. Roosevelt and Lyndon B. Johnson; she was painting the former's portrait when he was stricken and died (April 12, 1945); she completed more than 3,000 portraits of wealthy and famous people; in Glen Cove, N.Y., Nov. 30, 1980.

Soong, Ching-ling, 90, Chinese politician and leading stateswoman in Peoples Republic; widow of Sun Yat-sen who led overthrow of Manchu Dynasty, in 1911; she espoused Communism but was not admitted to party until month before her death; named honorary chairman of China; in Peking, May 29, 1981.

Spaak, Fernand, 57, Belgian diplomat and chief of staff to president of European Community Commission; in Ixelles, Belgium, July 18, 1981.

Speer, Albert, 76, Nazi architect and leader who directed forced labor program in Germany during World War II; in London, Sept. 1, 1981.

Stone, Jacob, 86, Wall Street stockbroker and leading figure in finance for 50 years; governor of New York Stock Exchange (1938-40); in Palm Beach, Fla., March 24, 1981.

Sutton, Willie (Willie the Actor), 79, renowned robber and prison escapee; co-authored *I, Willie Sutton* and *Where the Money Was;* in Spring Hill, Fla., Nov. 2, 1980.

Thomas, Lowell, 89, renowned broadcaster, author, and world traveler; career spanned more than 50 years; famous radio network news show started in 1930, continued until 1976; sign-off, "So long until tomorrow," became popular worldwide; during First World War met and lionized Col. T.E. Lawrence (Lawrence of Arabia); in Pawling, N.Y., Aug. 30, 1981.

Tieri, Frank (Funzi), 77, reputed New York Mafia leader and alleged head of "Genovese Family"; first person ever convicted of leading an organized crime "family"; in New York City, March 29, 1981.

Torrijos Herrera, Omar, 52, Panamanian strongman and former chief of government (1972-78), who negotiated the transfer of the Canal Zone from the U.S. to Panama; in plane crash west of Panama City, announced Aug. 1, 1981.

Trifonov, Yuri, 55, Soviet novelist who wrote about Stalinist era (*The Old Man, The Exchange, Taking Stock*); in Moscow, March 28, 1981.

Trippe, Juan, 81, commercial airline pioneer and a founder of Pan American Airways; in New York City, April 3, 1981.

Urey, Harold C., 87, chemist who won Nobel Prize in 1934 for discovering deuterium ("heavy hydrogen"), leading to development of hydrogen bomb; made major contributions to space programs; demonstrated (1953) that lightning may create basic life chemicals; warned that atomic bombs are "evil" and "cannot be used to maintain peace"; in La Jolla, Calif., Jan. 5, 1981.

Urrutia Lleo, Manuel, 79, Cuban judge who became first president of revolutionary Cuba, in 1959; resigned six months later after denouncing Communism; came to U.S., in 1963, after four years house arrest and asylum in Venezuelan and Mexican embassies at Havana; denounced Castro regime in book, *Fidel Castro & Company, Inc.: Communist Tyranny in Cuba;* in New York City, July 4, 1981.

Vagnozzi, Egidio Cardinal, 74, Vatican diplomat who served as apostolic delegate to U.S., from 1959 to 1967; theologically conservative throughout era of Second Vatican Council; in Rome, Dec. 26, 1980.

Van Vleck, John H., 80, "father of modern magnetism" who shared 1977 Nobel Prize in physics for advancing knowledge of behavior of electrons in magnetic, non-crystalline solids; chairman Harvard University Physics Department (1945-49); Harvard's Hollis Professor of Mathematics, oldest endowed chair in U.S. (1951-69); in Cambridge, Mass., Oct. 27, 1980.

Vinson, Carl, 97, Georgia Democrat with record 50-year service in U.S. House of Representatives; known as "Swamp Fox" for canny legislative tactics; aircraft carrier named in his honor (1980); in Milledgeville, Ga., June 1, 1981.

Von Wangenheim, Chris, 39, German-born fashion photographer; work appeared in leading fashion magazines throughout world; on Caribbean island of St. Martin, March 9, 1981.

Wagensteen, Dr. Owen, 82, pioneering heart surgeon who trained generations of distinguished surgeons; credited with saving 100,000 lives through development of abdominal surgery techniques; chief of surgery at University of Minnesota Hospital for 37 years; pioneered open heart surgery in 1950s; in Minneapolis, Jan. 13, 1981.

Wallace, DeWitt, 91, founder of *Reader's Digest* magazine (1922), publication with circulation of 30.5 million, in 163 countries; in Mt. Kisco, N.Y., March 30, 1981.

Wallace, Ilo Browne, 92, widow of Henry A. Wallace, vice president and cabinet officer under U.S. Presidents Franklin D. Roosevelt and Harry S Truman; Iowa-born, she helped promote welfare of small farmer; in South Salem, N.Y., Feb. 22, 1981.

Walsh, James Edward, 90, Roman Catholic missionary of Maryknoll in New York; he spent 12 years in Shanghai prison on charges of spying for Vatican and U.S.; released in 1970; 40 years as missionary in Hong Kong and mainland China; in Ossining, N.Y., July 29, 1981.

Ward, Barbara, 67, British economist-journalist and champion of foreign aid to underdeveloped countries; adviser to many statesmen; foreign editor of *Economist* during World War II; in Lodsworth, England, May 31, 1981.

Weisz, David, 70, last of family of international auctioneers; sold estimated $2 billion in merchandise, including Harland & Wolff Shipyards in Belfast, entire Metro-Goldwyn-Mayer collection of 360,000 props and costumes, and chain of 367 Robert Hall clothing stores; in Beverly Hills, Calif., June 30, 1981.

West, Mae, 87, burlesque queen of 1920s and 1930s who starred in films, stage, and nightclub roles; famous for line "Come up'n see me sometime." Films included *My Little Chickadee* and *I'm No Angel;* in Hollywood, Calif., Nov. 22, 1980.

Whitaker, Roger E.M., 82, editor and writer for the *New Yorker* since 1926; wrote under pseudonyms of "Frimbo", "Old Curmudgeon," "J.W.L.," and "Popsie"; founded and directed magazine's highly accurate fact-checking section; in New York City, May 11, 1981.

Whitehead, Don, 72, reporter-author who twice won Pulitzer Prize for international reporting—on Korean War and some major battles of World War II—as Associated Press war correspondent; authored *The FBI Story,* which was made into a film, and *Attack on Terror,* about FBI probe of Ku Klux Klan in Mississippi; in Knoxville, Tenn., Jan. 12, 1981.

Wilder, Alec, 73, composer of popular songs and classical music; wrote "I'll Be Around" and "It's So Peaceful in the Country" as well as songs for Bing Crosby, Frank Sinatra, and Mildred Bailey; in Gainesville, Fla., Dec. 24, 1980.

Wilkins, Roy, 80, grandson of Mississippi slave, he became skilled politician and statesman; leader of National Association for the Advancement of Colored People (1954-77); passionate, effective crusader for justice and civil rights; led N.A.A.C.P. through turbulent years following 1954 Supreme Court school desegregation decision; in New York City, Sept. 8, 1981.

Williams, Eric, 69, prime minister of Trinidad and Tobago; helped guide country to independence within the British Commonwealth; noted historian, politician; wrote classic *Capitalism and Slavery;* in Port-of-Spain, Trinidad, March 29, 1981.

Williams, Mary Lou, 71, jazz pianist, arranger, and composer who influenced ragtime, Dixieland, swing, be-bop, and sacred jazz music ("Walking but Swingin'," "Froggy Bottom"); in Durham, N.C., May 28, 1981.

Wortman, Sterling, 58, plant geneticist and leader of "green revolution" to fight world famine; developed high-yield grains; served as president and vice president of Rockefeller Foundation; in Greenwich, Conn., May 26, 1981.

Wyler, William, 79, French-born film director whose work during career of more than 50 years won three Academy Awards as best director: *Mrs. Miniver* (1942), *The Best Years of Our Lives* (1946), and *Ben Hur* (1959); in Beverly Hills, Calif., July 27, 1981.

Wyszynski, Stefan Cardinal, 79, Roman Catholic primate of Poland; political prisoner of Communists (1953-56); strengthened Church in Poland by gradual accommodation with Communist rulers; denounced "forced atheization" and led Polish Church for 32 years; in Warsaw, May 28, 1981.

Yukawa, Hideki, 73, Japanese physicist who was awarded the 1949 Nobel Prize for his discovery of the subatomic meson particle; in Kyoto, Japan, Sept. 8, 1981.

Zhao, Dan, 66, Chinese film star and cultural freedom fighter; called "Chinese Clark Gable"; imprisoned (1966-73) by Mao Zedong's wife, who banned his films as decadent; battled Communist party interference in cultural programs; popular films included *Street Angels, Crossroad, The Opium War;* in Peking, Oct. 10, 1980.

Zuckerman, Yitzhak, 66, leader of Polish resistance fighters in World War II; led survivors of Warsaw ghetto massacres through sewers to safety; operated Palestine's Holocaust museum; in Tel Aviv, June 17, 1981.

A

AFL-CIO 71
AID, *see Agency for International Development*
Abortion
debate over 275
Supreme Court rulings 275
Abraham (patriarch) 788
Academy Awards 874-875
Accidental deaths (numbers, rates) 272, 273
automobile 219
(see Disasters/Catastrophes, 898-909)
ACTION (volunteer services) 723
Actors, actresses
past, present 835-842
(see Awards)
Adams, Abigail (Mrs. John) (biog.) . 146
Adams, John
administration 83
ancestry and religion 140
biography 100-101
elections of 1789, 1792, 1796, 1800 153
signer of the Declaration of Independence 73
Adams, John Quincy
administration 85
ancestry and religion 140
biography 104-105
elections of 1820, 1824, 1828 . 154-155
minority president 139
Adams, Louisa (Mrs. John Quincy) (biog.) 147
Administrations (U.S. presidential) 83-98
Address, forms of 765
Advertising
leading TV advertisers............764
volume 763
Afghanistan 504-505
area, population 504
armed forces 735
birth, death rates 504
communications 504
currency 504
economy.........................504
education, health statistics 504
flag.......................504, 513
geographical features 504
government 504
history..........................505
languages, religion..............504
location.........................504
map............................524
transportation statistics 504
weights and measures...........504
Africa
area.............................286
deserts 292
gold production 197
highest and lowest points 286
lakes 292
monarchs (present) 783
mountain peaks 293
rainfall extremes 296
religious membership............886
temperature extremes 296
U.S. aid to 721
volcanoes 295
waterfalls 295
Afro-Mauritian Common Organization (OCAM) 719
Age limits
driving, *see individual state— transportation*
marriage.........................254

voting, *see individual state— government*
Agencies
federal..........................168
United Nations 711-718
Agency for International Development (U.S.) 168
foreign economic assistance 721
Agnew, Spiro T. (biog.).............145
Agriculture in the U.S.
crop production 202
farm payments, state totals 202
farm values, *see specific state*
livestock population 202
Agriculture, U.S. Department of ... 167, 168
Agriculture, world
principal Canadian crops 500
(see individual country, Canada, Canadian province—economy)
Air
composition, temperature 284-285
pollution 276
Air Force, U.S.
satellites, *see Space developments*
strength, *see Armed Forces, U.S.*
Air Force, U.S. Department of . 167, 168
Airlines
passenger service records 238
safety records 239
toll-free telephone numbers ... 223-224
Airmail postal rates 766
Airplanes
commercial passenger 233
warplanes.......................734
Airports, traffic at
major world 238
U.S.............................233
Alabama 352-353
birthrate, health statistics 353
Chamber of Commerce...........353
communications 353
economy........................353
education statistics...............353
finances 353
geographical features 353
government 353
map............................352
marriage, divorce rates 353
population statistics 353
state bird, flag, flower, motto, name origin, nickname, seal, song, tree.....................353
transportation statistics 353
Alaska...................353-355, 357
birthrate, health statistics 357
Chamber of Commerce...........357
communications 357
economy........................357
education statistics...............357
finances 357
geographical features 357
government 355
map............................354
marriage, divorce rates 357
population statistics 357
state bird, flag, flower, motto, name origin, nickname, seal, song, tree.....................355
transportation statistics 357
Albania 505-506
anthem, flag 505, 513
area, population 505
armed forces 735
birth, death rates 505
communications 505
currency 505
economy........................505
education, health statistics 505
geographical features 505
government 505

history..........................506
languages, religion..............505
location.........................505
map............................519
transportation statistics 505
weights and measures...........505
Alberta, Canada 483-484
agriculture 484
area.............................484
birth, death rates 484
communications 484
economy........................484
education statistics...............484
geographical features 484
government 484
health care statistics.............484
location.........................484
map............................483
marriage, divorce rates 484
motor vehicle statistics 484
population statistics 484
revenues and expenditures.......484
Albuquerque, New Mexico.........458
Alcohol import restrictions 232
Aleuts
population (by state) 264
Alexander the Great 578, 790, 809
Algeria 506-507
anthem, flag 506, 513
area, population 506
armed forces 735
birth, death rates 506
communications 506
currency 506
economy........................506
education, health statistics 506
geographical features 506
government 506
history..........................507
languages, religion..............506
location.........................506
map............................520
transportation statistics 506
weights and measures...........506
All-Star baseball games 927, 930
Ambassadors
address, form of 765
foreign (selected) in U.S. 722
foreign heads of missions to UN . . . 718
U.S. ambassadors abroad 723
U.S. Representatives to UN 717
Amendments, Constitutional (U.S.)........................79-82
America, *see North, South America*
America's Cup Race 999
American Indians, *see Indians, American*
American Red Cross, *see Red Cross*
American Revolution, *see Revolutionary War*
American Samoa (U.S. territory) 476
American surnames, common 762
Amin, Dada Idi 683, 809
Amtrak.........................218
Andean Group...................719
Anderson, John
election of 1980 165
Andorra.........................507
anthem, flag 507, 513
area, population 507
birth, death rates 507
communications 507
currency 507
economy........................507
education, health statistics 507
geographical features 507
government 507
history..........................507
languages, religion...............507
location.........................507

map...........519
transportation statistics..........507
weights and measures............507
Angling, *see Fishing*
Angola......................507-508
area, population.................507
armed forces....................735
birth, death rates 508
communications 508
currency.......................507
economy.......................508
education, health statistics........508
flag........................507, 517
geographical features 508
government 508
history.........................508
languages, religion..............507
location........................508
map...........................521
transportation statistics 508
weights and measures............508
Anguilla (British Colony)...........704
Animals
classification of.................289
dogs (breeds) 999
endangered species.............290
gestation, incubation 289
longevity......................288
prehistoric......................287
Anniversary gifts, wedding 782
Antarctica
area..........................286
explorations 808
highest point 286
map...........................710
mountain peaks 293
rainfall extremes 296
temperature extremes 296
volcanoes......................295
Anthems, national, *see specific nation*
Anthony, Susan B.
(suffragist)..................809, 858
Anthropology
fossil man......................288
Antigua (British Associated State) ...705
ANZUS Council....................719
Apollo missions........332, 334-335
first moonwalk (1969) 334
Apothecaries fluid measure and
weight 343
Arab League (AL)................719
Arabia
deserts 292
monarchs (present) 783
Archdioceses (U.S. Roman
Catholic) 895-896
Archery champions...............996
1980 Olympics 911
Architects, noted 822-825
Architecture
major world structures...........297
Arctic explorations.................808
Arctic Ocean
area, depth......................291
Areas
continents......................286
earth 284
major islands...................298
principal lakes 294, 301
measures (units) 340, 343
nations, *see individual nation*
oceans and seas...........284, 291
U.S., *see individual state,*
territory
Argentina 508-510
anthem, flag 508, 513
area, population 508
armed forces....................735
birth, death rates 509
communications 509
currency.......................508

economy.......................509
education, health statistics........509
geographical features 508-509
government 509
history.....................509-510
languages, religion..............508
location.........................508
map...........................525
transportation statistics 509
weights and measures............509
Arithmetic, *see Mathematics*
Arizona 356, 357, 359
birthrate, health statistics 359
Chamber of Commerce...........359
communications 359
economy.......................359
education statistics...............359
finances 359
geographical features 357
government 357
map...........................356
marriage, divorce rates 359
population statistics 359
state bird, flag, flower, motto,
name origin, nickname, seal,
song, tree......................357
transportation statistics 359
Arkansas................358, 359, 361
birthrate, health statistics 361
Chamber of Commerce..........361
communications 361
economy.......................361
education statistics...............361
finances 361
geographical features 361
government 361
map...........................358
marriage, divorce rates 361
population statistics 361
state bird, flag, flower, motto,
name origin, nickname, seal,
song, tree 359, 361
transportation statistics 361
Armament, military
nuclear armament 733
warplanes......................734
(see footnote 733 for glossary
of missiles and armaments)
Armed Forces, U.S.
active military forces........734, 735
blacks in armed forces 735
casualties 728, 731
Joint Chiefs of Staff 731
military cemeteries...............730
National Guard 729
pay scale and grade........729, 730
troop strength by war............728
veterans by war................728
veterans' benefits 732
Armed Forces of the World.......735
Army, U.S.
satellites, *see Space developments*
(see Armed Forces, U.S.—
active military forces)
Army, U.S. Department of 167, 168
Art
awards 872
museums, selected
U.S. (by city) 850-851
world (by city) 850
Artemision at Ephesus
(temple)....................789, 808
Arthur, Chester A.
administration 90
ancestry and religion 140
biography 118-119
election of 1880 158
Arthur, Ellen (Mrs. Chester A.)
(biog.) 149
Articles of Confederation..........67
Artists, noted.................822-825

Ashmore and Cartier Islands
(Australian External Territory)......705
Asia
area..........................286
deserts 292
gold production 197
highest and lowest points 286
lakes 292
monarchs (present) 783-784
mountain peaks 293
rainfall extremes 296
religious membership............886
temperature extremes 296
U.S. aid to 721
volcanoes......................295
waterfalls 295
Asian Americans
employment.....................204
population (by state) 264-265
al-Assad, Hafez (Syrian
president).............673, 674, 809
Assassinations
in the U.S.
Garfield, Pres. James A..........69
Kennedy, Pres. John F......71, 807
Kennedy, Robert F...........71, 807
King, Martin Luther, Jr...71, 268, 807
Lincoln, Pres. Abraham 69
McKinley, Pres. William......69, 806
(see individual nation article
for foreign personages)
Association of Southeast Asian
Nations (ASEAN) 719
Associations
directory of...................877-881
employee 205
Asteroids............................327
Astronauts, astronautics
see Space developments
Astronomical facilities, major. .319-320
Astronomy
asteroids........................327
astronomical instrumentation ..319-320
astronomical phenomena 329
"black holes" 318
celestial events 329
comets 328
constellations..............317-318
eclipses 329
galaxies.................314-315, 319
glossary 315-316
Gum Nebula 318
interstellar molecules............318
meteors 328
moon..........................326
planetary probes 324-325, 331-332
planets................322-324, 327
pulsars 315
quasars........................315
seasons 329
solar system...........322-324, 325
stars 314-315, 316, 317
sun 321
supernovae 318
universe, origin of...............314
(see also Space developments)
Atlanta, Georgia 458
Atlantic Ocean
area, depth......................291
Atomic energy
atomic weights and numbers 337
glossary 344
nuclear power..............208, 216
Attorneys General, U.S. 83-98
Attucks, Crispus (black Revolutionary War hero)............266, 809
Australia 510-511
anthem, flag 510, 513
area, population 510
armed forces....................735
birth, death rates 510

communications 510
currency 510
economy......................... 510
education, health statistics 510
geographical features 510
government 510
history.......................... 511
languages, religion 510
location......................... 510
maps 43, 528
transportation statistics 510
weights and measures........... 510
Australian Antarctic Territory
(Australian External Territory)...... 705
Austria....................... 511-512
anthem, flag 511, 513
area, population 511
armed forces 735
birth, death rates 511
communications 511
currency 511
economy........................ 511
education, health statistics 511
geographical features 511
government 511
history.......................... 512
languages, religion 511
location......................... 511
map............................ 519
transportation statistics 511
weights and measures........... 511
Auto racing 973-977
Daytona-Le Mans............... 976
Formula 1 Grand Prix
champions 974
Indianapolis 500 975
mile record, history.............. 973
NASCAR champions............. 977
SCCA champions............... 974
USAC champions............... 976
Automobiles
deaths by 219, 272
drivers, licensed U.S............. 219
exports, imports, U.S......... 203, 210
inventions, see Inventors and
Inventions, 349
mileage, touring 220
production 203
racing records 973-977
Avalanches, see Disasters/
Catastrophes, 898-909
Aviation
accidents, see Disasters/
Catastrophes, 898-909
airports 233, 238
flying distances.............. 234-235
inventions, see Inventors and
Inventions, 349
mileage tables 221, 234-235
passenger planes, major
commercial 233
passenger service records 238
records, world 236-237
safety record (U.S., world) 239
warplanes...................... 734
Avoirdupois measure 343
Awards
Academy Awards 874-875
achievement awards............ 871
All-America Cities Awards Program 871
American Academy of Arts and
Letters Awards 872
American Book Awards, The 872
American Booksellers Award 872
American Jewish Committee
Awards 871
Antoinette Perry Awards 876
arts awards 872
Bancroft Prizes 872
Bollingen Prize in Poetry......... 872
book awards 863, 867-870, 872

Cannes International Film
Festival awards 876
Emmy Awards................... 873
engineering awards 336
George Foster Peabody Awards ... 873
George Polk Awards 871
journalism awards. .. 864-866, 867, 871
literature awards 872
Medals of Freedom 871
Miss America................... 876
motion picture awards. .. 874-875, 876
music awards................... 873
National Academy of Design
Prizes 872
National Academy of Sciences
Awards 871
National Medal of Science
Awards 871
Newbery-Caldecott Medals........ 872
New York Film Critics Circle
Awards 876
Nieman Fellowships............. 871
Nobel Prizes 858-864
Obie (Off-Broadway Awards) 876
Poetry Society of America
Prizes 872
public service awards............ 871
Pulitzer Prizes 864-870
science awards 871
Sigma Delta Chi Awards 871
sports awards, see Sports
910-999
Teacher of the Year Award 871
television and radio awards 873
theatre awards.................. 876
Westinghouse Science Talent
Search Awards 871
Women of the Year Awards 871

B

Babylon, Hanging Gardens of. 789, 808
Badminton champions 996
Bahamas 512, 529
anthem, flag 512, 513
area, population 512
birth, death rates 512
communications 512
currency 512
economy........................ 512
education, health statistics 512
geographical features 512
government 512
history.......................... 529
languages, religion 512
location......................... 512
map............................ 527
transportation statistics 512
weights and measures........... 512
Bahrain 529
anthem, flag 513, 529
area, population 529
birth, death rates 529
communications 529
currency 529
economy........................ 529
education, health statistics 529
government 529
history.......................... 529
languages, religion 529
location......................... 529
map............................ 524
transportation statistics 529
weights and measures........... 529
Ballet companies, see Dance
Baltic Sea (area, depth)........... 291
Baltimore, Maryland 458-459
Bangladesh 529-530
anthem, flag 513, 529

area, population 529
armed forces 735
communications 530
currency 529
economy........................ 529
education statistics............... 529
geographical features 529
government 529
history.......................... 530
languages, religion 529
location......................... 529
map............................ 523
transportation statistics 529-530
weights and measures........... 530
Banks
central discount rates 198
commercial, largest U.S.......... 200
International Settlements,
Bank for 718
Barbados 530-531
anthem, flag 513, 531
area, population 530
birth, death rates 531
communications 531
currency 531
economy........................ 531
education, health statistics 531
geographical features 531
government 531
history.......................... 531
languages, religion 530-531
location......................... 531
map............................ 527
transportation statistics 531
weights and measures........... 531
Barkley, Alben W. (biog.)......... 145
Baseball 924-938
All-Star Games 927, 930
college 938
Hall of Fame 926
major league records......... 924-925
minor league affiliations........... 938
1981 season 927-929
stadiums....................... 938
World Series............ 927-928, 930
Basketball................... 939-945
College 944-945
Hall of Fame 942
National Basketball
Association 939-943
1980 Olympics 911
Summer Olympic champions...... 918
Women's....................... 945
Begin, Menachem (Israeli prime
minister) 596, 597, 809, 864
Belau, Republic of 478
Belgium.................... 531-532
anthem, flag 513, 531
area, population 531
armed forces 735
birth, death rates 531
communications 532
currency 531
economy........................ 531
education, health statistics 531-532
geographical features 531
government 531
history.......................... 532
languages, religion 531
location......................... 531
map............................ 519
monarch (present)........... 531, 784
transportation statistics 532
weights and measures........... 532
Belize.................... 532-533
area, population 532
birth, death rates 533
communications 533
currency 532
economy.................... 532-533
education, health statistics 533

flag 513, 532
geographical features 532
government 532
history 533
languages, religion 532
location 532
map 527
transportation statistics 533
weights and measures 533
Bell, Alexander Graham 350
Belmont Stakes 980
Ben-Gurion (Israeli leader) 597, 809
Benelux Economic Union 719
Benin 533-534
anthem, flag 513, 533
area, population 533
birth, death rates 533
communications 533
currency 533
economy 533
education, health statistics 533
geographical features 533
government 533
history 534
languages, religion 533
location 533
map 520
transportation statistics 533
weights and measures 533
Bering Sea (area, depth) 291
Bermuda (British Colony) 705
Bhutan 534-535
anthem, flag 513, 534
area, population 534
birth, death rates 534
communications 534
currency 534
economy 534
education, health statistics 534
geographical features 534
government 534
history 535
languages, religion 534
location 534
map 523
monarch (present) 534, 783
transportation statistics 534
weights and measures 534
Biathlon champions 996
Olympics 919, 920
Bicycle racing, see Cycling champions
Billiards champions 996
Binary numbers 341
Biography
artists and architects 822-825
celebrities: past and present . . 835-842
film directors 832-834
men of medicine and
physiology 820-822
notables of the
musical world 829-832
novelists, dramatists and
other writers 825-829
philosophers, theologians and
religionists 819-820
Pulitzer Prizes for 867-868
scientists and mathema-
ticians 818-819
world figures 808-817
**Biological and medical science
review** 269-270
Birds
endangered species 290
official state, see individual state
Birmingham, Alabama 459
Birth statistics
U.S.
illegitimate 251
(see also individual state)
world, see specific nation
Birthstones 782

Bishops
(see under U.S. Religious Bodies,
891-897)
Bismarck, Otto von 575, 801, 809
Black Americans
armed forces participation 735
educational level 737
employment rate 204
equal rights laws 264, 266-268
history 266-268
income and education 738
lynching statistics 268
national convention 268
noted personages, past and
present 266-268
population (by state) 264
population in large cities 266
U.S. armed forces (no. in) 735
"Black holes," stellar 318
Black Sea (area, depth) 291
Blizzards, see Disasters/
Catastrophes, 898-909
Boat racing
America's Cup 999
canoeing 911, 996
powerboat 998
yachting 999
Bobsledding champions 996
Olympics 919, 921
Bolivia 535-536
anthem, flag 513, 535
area, population 535
armed forces 735
birth, death rates 535
communications 535
currency 535
economy 535
education, health statistics 535
geographical features 535
government 535
history 536
languages, religion 535
location 535
map 525
transportation statistics 535
weights and measures 535
Bonaparte, Napoleon 571, 572,
801, 814
Books
awards 872
bestsellers 853
postal rates 766
reference books 758-759
season survey 852-853
Booth, John Wilkes (assassin) . . 69, 809
Bophuthatswana 664
Boston, Massachusetts 459
Botswana 536-537
anthem, flag 513, 536
area, population 536
birth, death rates 536
communications 536
currency 536
economy 536
education, health statistics 536
geographical features 536
government 536
history 537
languages, religion 536
location 536
map 521
transportation statistics 536
weights and measures 536
Bouvet Island (Norwegian
Dependency) 705
Bowl Games, football 953-954
Bowling 990-991
Boxing champions 983-984
1980 Olympics 911
Brazil 537-538
anthem, flag 513, 537

area, population 537
armed forces 735
birth, death rates 537
communications 537
currency 537
economy 537
education, health statistics 537
geographical features 537
government 537
history 538
languages, religion 537
location 537
map 525
transportation statistics 537
weights and measures 537
Breckinridge, John C. (biog.) 143
Brezhnev, Leonid (Soviet
leader) 685, 686, 727, 804, 809
Bridges
collapses, see Disasters/
Catastrophes, 898-909
leading 242-243
longest 243
Britain, see United Kingdom
British Antarctic Territory
(British Colony) 705
British Columbia, Canada 484-486
agriculture 486
area 484
birth, death rates 484
communications 486
economy 486
education statistics 486
geographical features 484
government 484
health care statistics 486
location 484
map 485
marriage, divorce rates 484
motor vehicle statistics 486
population statistics 484
revenues and expenditures 486
British Indian Ocean Territory
(British Colony) 705
British prime ministers 724
British Virgin Islands (British
Crown Colony) 705
Brunei (British Protected State) 705
Buchanan, James
administration 88
ancestry and religion 140
biography 112-113
minority president 139
Buddha (Siddhartha Gautama)
(biog.) 885
Buddhism 885
membership 886
Budget, U.S.
budget dollar 185
federal grants to states 185
1789-1981; 1977-1982 . . . . . . 184, 186
tax dollar expenditure 185
urban family 249
Buffalo, New York 459-460
Buildings, tallest
U.S., world 297
Bulgaria 538-539
anthem, flag 513, 538
area, population 538
armed forces 735
birth, death rates 538
communications 538
currency 538
economy 538-539
education, health statistics 539
geographical features 539
government 538
history 539
languages, religion 538
location 538
map 519

transportation statistics 539
weights and measures........... 539
Burma 539-540
    anthem, flag 513, 539
    area, population 539
    armed forces................... 735
    birth, death rates 539
    communications 539-540
    currency 539
    economy...................... 539
    education, health statistics 539
    geographical features 539
    government 539
    history....................... 540
    languages, religion.............. 539
    location..................... 539
    map....................... 523
    transportation statistics 539
    weights and measures........... 540
Burundi 540-541
    anthem, flag 513, 540
    area, population 540
    armed forces................... 735
    birth, death rates 540
    communications 540
    currency 540
    economy...................... 540
    education, health statistics 540
    geographical features 540
    government 540
    history....................... 541
    languages, religion.............. 540
    location..................... 540
    map....................... 521
    transportation statistics 540
    weights and measures........... 540
Bush, George H. W. (biog.)......... 145
Bus Lines, U.S. intercity 218
Business, *see Advertising, Banks,
    Corporations*
Byrd, Richard E. (explorer) . 70, 808, 810

                        C

CIO, *see Labor unions in U.S.*
COMECON, *see Council for Mutual
    Economic Assistance*
Cabinet members, U.S.
    address, form of 765
    1789-1981 .... 83-98, 167-169
Cabot, John (explorer) 797
Caesar, Julius................ 790, 810
Calendars
    perpetual (1801-2000)...... 310-311
Calhoun, John C. (biog.).......... 142
California 360, 361, 363
    birthrate, health statistics 363
    Chamber of Commerce........... 363
    communications 363
    economy...................... 363
    education statistics.............. 363
    finances 363
    geographical features 363
    government 363
    map......................... 360
    marriage, divorce rates 363
    population statistics 363
    state bird, flag, flower, motto,
        name origin, nickname, seal,
        song, tree................... 363
    transportation statistics 363
Calories
    daily dietary allowances 283
Calvin, John (religionist)....... 798, 819
Cambodia 541-542
    area, population 541
    armed forces................... 735
    communications 541

economy...................... 541
flag................... 513, 541
geographical features 541
government 541
history....................... 542
languages, religion............. 541
location..................... 541
map......................... 523
transportation statistics 541
weights and measures........... 541
Cameroon................... 542-543
    anthem, flag.............. 513, 542
    area, population 542
    armed forces................... 735
    birth, death rates 543
    communications 543
    currency 542
    economy...................... 542-543
    education, health statistics 543
    geographical features 542
    government 542
    history....................... 543
    languages, religion............. 542
    location..................... 542
    map......................... 520
    transportation statistics 543
    weights and measures........... 543
Canada 480-503
    agricultural crops, principal....... 500
    anthem, flag 480, 513
    area......................... 480
    armed forces................... 735
    birth, death rates .:........... 480
    cities, largest................. 503
    communications 480
    currency 480
    economy...................... 480
    education, health statistics 480
    exports (leading commodities)..... 503
    geographical features 480
    government 480
    history 482, 484
    imports (leading commodities)..... 503
    languages, religion.............. 480
    location..................... 480
    maps................. 45, 481, 526
    population 480
        by province 1851-1980 503
    salaries, government officials...... 500
    trade partners, principal 500
    transportation statistics 480
    weights and measures........... 480
    *(see also Alberta, British Columbia,
        Manitoba, New Brunswick, New-
        foundland, Nova Scotia, Ontario,
        Prince Edward Island, Quebec and
        Saskatchewan)*
    *(see also Major World Dance Groups,
        844; Major Symphony Orchestras
        of the U.S.and Canada, 848;
        Art Museums, 850)*
    *Sports: see Baseball, 924-938; Foot-
        ball, 952; Golf, 965; Hockey, 958-
        962; Tennis, 971.*
Canals, major world ship.......... 241
    Panama Canal
        Panama Canal Company 169
        no. of employees 167
Cancer
    death rates 272, 274
    progress against 274
    reference chart 274
    treatment for selected types...... 274
    warning signals 274
**Candidates (U.S. presidential and
    vice-presidential) 1789-1980** . 153-165
Canoeing
    1980 Olympics 911
    U.S. champions 996
Cape Verde 543-544
    anthem, flag................ 517, 543

area, population 543
birth, death rates 543
communications 543
currency 543
economy...................... 543
education statistics.............. 543
geographical features 543
government 543
history....................... 544
languages, religion............. 543
location..................... 543
map......................... 521
transportation statistics ., ... 543
weights and measures........... 543
Capital punishment in U.S. 263
**Cardinals, College of
    (Roman Catholic)** 889-890
Cardiovascular disease,
    see Heart disease
Careers......................... 9-37
**Caribbean Community and Common
    Market (CARICOM)**.............. 719
Caribbean Sea (area, depth)........ 291
Cars, *see Automobiles*
**Car rental toll-free telephone
    numbers** 224
Carter, Bill (television
    survey)....................... 856
**Carter, Eleanor Rosalynn (Mrs.
    Jimmy)** (biog.) 152
Carter, Jimmy
    administration 98
    ancestry and religion 140
    biography 137
    election of 1976 164
    election of 1980 165
Cartoons: Pulitzer Prizes.......... 866
Castro, Fidel
    (Cuban leader)..... 555, 556, 557, 810
Casualties, U.S. war 728, 731
Catastrophes, major world 898-909
Catholic, *see Roman Catholic Church*
Cattle, *see Agriculture*
Cayman Islands (British Crown
    Colony)....................... 705
Celebrities, past, present...... 835-842
Celsius, (centigrade), conversions
    to Fahrenheit 343
Cemeteries
    U.S. military on foreign soil........ 730
Centigrade, *see Celsius*
**Central African Economic and Customs
    Union (UDEAC)**................. 719
Central African Republic 544-545
    anthem, flag................ 517, 544
    area, population 544
    birth, death rates 544
    communications 544
    currency 544
    economy...................... 544
    education, health statistics 544
    geographical features 544
    government 544
    history....................... 544-545
    languages, religion............. 544
    location..................... 544
    map......................... 520
    transportation statistics 544
    weights and measures........... 544
**Central American Common Market
    (CACM)** 719
Ceuta and Melilla (Spanish
    exclaves) 705
Chad....................... 545-546
    anthem, flag................ 513, 545
    area, population 545
    armed forces................... 735
    birth, death rates 545
    communications 545
    currency 545
    economy...................... 545

education, health statistics 545
geographical features 545
government 545
history 545-546
languages, religion 545
location 545
map 520
transportation statistics 545
weights and measures 545
Channel Islands (British
Crown Bailiwicks) 705-706
Charlemagne (Frankish emperor) . . . 793,
810
Charleston, South Carolina 460
Chemistry
atomic weights, numbers 337
discoveries 337, 338-339
glossary 345-346
Nobel Prizes 860-861
periodic table of elements 336
symbols 337
Cheops (Khufu), Pyramid of . . 788, 808
Chess
U.S. champions 991
world champions 991
Chiang Kai-shek (Chinese
leader) 550, 551, 810
Chicago, Illinois 460
Chiefs of Staff, U.S. Joint 731
Chile 546-547
anthem, flag 513, 546
area, population 546
armed forces 735
birth, death rates 546
communications 546
currency 546
economy 546
education, health statistics 546
geographical features 546
government 546
history 546-547
language, religion 546
location 546
map 525
transportation statistics 546
weights and measures 546
Chilean Antarctica (Chilean
Dependency) 706
China (People's Republic) 547-550
anthem, flag 513, 547
area, population 547
armed forces 735
birth, death rates 547
communications 547
currency 547
economy 547
geographical features 547
government 547
history 550
languages, religion 547
location 547
maps 522-523, 548
rulers (past and
present) 547, 549, 550, 727, 785
transportation statistics 547
weights and measures 547
China, Nationalist (Taiwan) 550-551
anthem, flag 513, 550
area, population 550
armed forces 735
birth, death rates 551
communications 551
currency 550
economy 550-551
education, health statistics 551
geographical features 550
government 550
history 551
languages, religion 550
location 550
maps 522-523, 548

transportation statistics 551
weights and measures 551
China Sea (area, depth) 291
Chinese in U.S.
population by state 264
Choreographers, noted 829-832
Chou En-lai see Zhou Enlai
Christianity
description 882-884
Jesus Christ 883-884
(see also specific sect or denomi-
nation under U.S. Religious
Bodies, 891-897)
Christmas Island (Australian
External Territory) 706
Churches
U.S. Religious Bodies 891-897
World Council of Churches 720
(see also Religion)
Churchill, Sir Winston . 70-71, 688, 803,
804, 807, 810
Cincinnati, Ohio 461-462
Cities, U.S.
air distances 221
bridges 242-243
buildings, tall 297
crime in selected cities 262
dance companies 844
family budget 249
family income 248
income taxes 194
latitude and longitude 308
libraries 738, 758
museums 850-851
newspaper circulation 764
opera companies 847
orchestras 848
per capita income 248
population 245, 768-782
black population 266
metropolitan areas 244-245
ports 240
precipitation 304
railway distances 222
road mileage table 220
sales tax rates 194
time differences 307
weather 304-305
zip codes 768-782
(see also pages 458-475)
Cities, world
airline distances 234-235
Canadian, largest 480, 503
cost of living 232
largest (population) 247
museums 850
time differences 241
weather 228-229
Civil rights legislation (1957-1975) . 264
Civil Rights Act (1875) 267
Equal Rights Amendment 266
Executive Order 8802 268
Executive Order 9981 268
Thirteenth Amendment 267
Voting Rights Act 268
Civil War, U.S.
Black American service in 267
casualties, veterans 728
estimated cost in dollars
(Union) 731
numbers in services 728
(see Outline of U.S. History,
66-71)
Cleveland, Frances (Mrs. Grover)
(biog.) 149
Cleveland, Grover
administrations 90, 91
ancestry and religion 140
biography 119-120
elections of 1884, 1888, 1892 . 158-159
minority president 139

Cleveland, Ohio 461
Climate
foreign city weather 228-229
U.S. city weather 304-305
U.S. temperature extremes 302-303
worldwide weather extremes 296
Clinton, George (biog.) 142
Clipperton Island (French
Dependency) 706
Clothing
consumer expenditures 249
exports, imports 210
Clubs, organizations 877-881
Coal
U.S. production 208, 216
world production 210, 211
Coastlines of the U.S. 300
Cocos (Keeling) Islands (Australian
External Territory) 706
Coinage, see Currency
Colfax, Schuyler (biog.) 143
Colleges and universities (U.S.)
control 739-757
expenditures 737
federal aid 737
founding dates 739-757
graduates, number of 736
large libraries 758
religious affiliation 739-757
tuition fees 739-757
Colombia 551-553
anthem, flag 513, 551
area, population 551
armed forces 735
birth, death rates 552
communications 552
currency 551
economy 552
education, health statistics 552
geographical features 551
government 551-552
history 553
languages, religion 551
location 551
map 525
transportation statistics 552
weights and measures 552
Colombo Plan 719
Colonies, see Territories and
dependencies
Colorado 362, 363, 365
birthrate, health statistics 365
Chamber of Commerce 365
communications 365
economy 365
education statistics 365
finances 365
geographical features 365
government 365
map 362
marriage, divorce rates 365
population statistics 365
state bird, flag, flower, motto,
name origin, nickname, seal,
song, tree 365
transportation statistics 365
Colossus of Rhodes (statue) . . 790, 808
Columbus, Christopher
(explorer) 797, 810
Columbus, Ohio 461
Comets 328
Commerce, see Shipping, Trade
Commerce, U.S. Department of 167, 168
Commodities
exports, imports 210
production 211
Common Market, see European
Community
Commonwealth, The 719, 725
Communist China, see China
(People's Republic)

Communist party
Chinese leaders 727
legal status by country 726-727
membership by country. 726-727
Soviet leaders 727
Comoros 553-554
area, population 553
birth, death rates 553
communications 553
currency 553
economy. 553
education, health statistics 553
flag 517, 553
geographical features 553
government 553
history 553-554
languages, religion 553
location 553
map. 523
transportation statistics 553
weights and measures 553
Companies, largest foreign 209
Composers, noted 829-832
Conductors, noted 829-832
Confucianism
description, membership 886
Confucius 886
Congo 554
anthem, flag 513, 554
area, population 554
armed forces 735
birth, death rates 554
communications 554
currency 554
economy. 554
education, health statistics 554
geographical features 554
government 554
history 554
languages, religion 554
location 554
map. 520-521
transportation statistics 554
weights and measures. 554
Congress, United States
address, form of 765
apportionment 173
election results, 1980. 170-172
joint committees and com-
missions 179
officers (97th Congress) 173
party affiliation 174-178
political party breakdown,
Congresses 1-97. . . . 83-98, 173, 177
Presidents Pro-tem (1789-1981) . 83-98
salaries 166
Speakers of the House
(1789-1981) 83-98
standing committees 178-179
votes cast
House of Rep. (1980) 170-172
Senate (1980) 172
Congress of Industrial
Organizations 71
Connecticut 364-366
birthrate, health statistics 366
Chamber of Commerce. 366
communications 366
economy. 366
education statistics 366
finances 366
geographical features 366
government 366
map. 364
marriage, divorce rates 366
population statistics 366
state bird, flag, flower, motto,
name origin, nickname, seal,
tree 366
transportation statistics 366
Conrail 218

Constellations 317-318
Constitution of the United States
amendments 79-82
articles, original 74-78
Bill of Rights 79
preamble. 74
signers of 78-79
Consumer Price Index (U.S.) 250
Consumption in the U.S.
commodity imports. 210
foodstuffs 210
personal expenditures 249
Continental Congress 67
Continents 286
mountain peaks 293
religious membership. 886
volcanoes 295
waterfalls 295-296
Cook Islands (New Zealand
Dependency) 706
Coolidge, Calvin
administrations 93-94
ancestry and religion 140
biography 126-127
elections of 1920, 1924. 160-161
Coolidge, Grace (Mrs. Calvin)
(biog.) 150
Coral Sea Islands Territory
(Australian External Territory). 706
Cornish, Edward 9
Corporations (largest foreign) 209
Corporations (U.S.)
banks, largest commercial 200
companies with most stock-
holders 197
corporate profits (total) 197
financial companies, diversified. . . . 200
industrial corporations, largest 201
life insurance companies,
largest 201
military-industrial complex. 735
retailing companies, largest 201
TV advertising 764
utilities, largest 201
(see Stocks)
Cortés, Hernando 796, 798, 810
Cosmology, theories of 314
Cost of living
medical care 276
U.S. 249, 250
world
cities 232
countries. 249
Costa Rica 554-555
anthem, flag 513, 554
area, population 554
birth, death rates 555
communications 555
currency 554
economy. 555
education, health statistics 555
geographical features 555
government 555
history. 555
languages, religion 554
location. 554-555
map. 527
transportation statistics 555
weights and measures. 555
Council for Mutual Economic
Assistance (COMECON) 719
Council of Europe 719
Countries, world, see Nations of
the World
Courts
International (UN) 713, 717
United States
Court of Appeals. 183
Court of Claims. 183
Court of Customs and
Patent Appeals 183

Customs Court 183
District Courts 183
Judges and Justices . . . 180-182,183
Salaries 166, 183
Supreme Court 180-182, 183
(see also Supreme Court, U.S.)
Crime in the U.S.
by category 262
capital punishment 263
cities (selected). 262
death penalty. 263
drug arrests 260
executions 263
homicides. 273
trend by region 262
trend by years 262
Critics, noted literary 825-828
Crop production in the U.S. 202
Cross-country champions 996
Crusades 794-796
Cuba 555-557
anthem, flag 513, 555
area, population 555
armed forces 735
birth, death rates 556
communications 556
currency 555
economy. 556
education, health statistics 556
geographical features 555
government 555-556
history. 557
languages, religion 555
location. 555
map. 527
transportation statistics 556
weights and measures. 556
Cubes, cube roots (table). 348
Cubic measure 343
Curie, Marie and Pierre 801, 818,
860-861
Currency
monetary terms. 198
U.S.
Bureau of the Mint 195
coinage; history. 195
interest rates 196
paper currency 195
portraits on coins and paper 195
purchasing power of the dollar. . . 250
world
depreciation rates. 198
foreign exchange rates 198
Curtis, Charles (biog.) 144
Customs, U.S.
court 183
duty-free imports 230, 232
duty rates. 232
hints to travelers 230-231
Cycling champions 996
1980 Olympics 911
Cyclones, see Disasters/
Catastrophes, 898-909
Cyprus 557-558
area, population 557
armed forces 735
birth, death rates 557
communications 557
currency 557
economy. 557
education, health statistics 557
flag. 513, 557
geographical features 557
government 557
history. 558
languages, religion 557
location. 557
map. 524
transportation statistics 557
weights and measures. 557

Czechoslovakia 558-559
anthem, flag 513, 558
area, population 558
armed forces 735
birth, death rates 558
communications 558
currency 558
economy. 558
education, health statistics 558
geographical features 558
government 558
history. 559
languages, religion 558
location. 558
map. 519
transportation statistics 558
weights and measures. 559

D

Dahlin, Robert (book survey) . . 852-853
Dallas, George M. (biog.) 143
Dallas, Texas 461-462
Dams, selected major world 294
Dance: major international
companies 844
Darwin, Charles
(naturalist) 339, 801, 818
Davis, Jefferson. 68, 810
Dawes, Charles G. (biog.). 144
Daylight Saving Time 307
Death penalty 263
Deaths
accidental
rate by nation 273
U.S. by type. 272
aircraft. 239
automobile 219
cancer, world rates 274
causes by sex, race (U.S.) 272
homicides (U.S.) 273
infant and neonatal (U.S.). 271
rates (U.S.) 272
suicides (U.S. and world) 273
war casualties (U.S.). 728, 731
(see also individual nation,
Canadian province, Disasters/
Catastrophes, 898-909)
Decathlon records 988-989
Olympics 913, 918
Decatur, Stephen (U.S. naval hero). . . 67
Decimal conversion to fractions . . . 348
Declaration of Independence 72-74
signers 73-74
Defense, U.S. Department of . . 167, 168
creation of 83
employment. 167
expenditures 728
Joint Chiefs of Staff 731
military-industrial complex. 735
de Gaulle, Charles . 571, 572, 804, 811
Delaware 366-369
birthrate, health statistics 367
Chamber of Commerce. 369
communications 369
economy. 368
education statistics 368-369
finances 368
geographical features 368
government 368
map. 367
marriage, divorce rates 368
population statistics 368
state bird, flag, flower, motto,
name origin, nickname, seal,
song, tree. 368
transportation statistics 367

Democratic party
conventions, 1832-1980 155-163,
164, 165
elections, 1828-1980 153-165
1980 election results 165
1976 election results 164
Ninety-seventh Congress—House
and Senate Members 174-178
presidential index 140-141
presidents, U.S. 83-98, 99-138
vice-presidents 142-145
Democratic-Republican party
elections of 1792, 1804, 1808,
1812, 1816, 1820, 1828 153-155
presidents' affiliation 140
Deng Xiaoping (Chinese
leader) 549, 550, 811
Denmark 559-560
anthem, flag 513, 559
area, population 559
armed forces 735
birth, death rates 560
communications 560
currency 559
economy. 559-560
education, health statistics 560
geographical features 559
government 559
history. 560
languages, religion 559
location. 559
map. 519
monarch (present) 559, 784
transportation statistics 560
weights and measures. 560
Denver, Colorado 462
Departments, U.S. Government
employees (no.) 167
heads 168-169
Dependencies, see Territories and
dependencies
Depreciation rates (world money) . . . 198
Deserts, major world. 292
Detroit, Michigan 462
Diet: recommended allowances 283
Diplomats
foreign in U.S. 722
U.S. abroad 723
Directors, noted film 832-834
Disadvantaged, see Poverty in
the U.S.
Disasters, major world 898-909
Discography
classical 846
popular 845
Discount rates (Central Bank) 198
Disease
cancer, see Cancer
death rates 271, 272
definitions 278
heart, see Heart disease
venereal. 270, 273
Distances between cities
airline. 221, 234-235
automobile 220
railroad 222
District Courts (U.S.). 183
District of Columbia 169
(see also Washington, D.C.)
Dividend rates, stock 214
high yield regulars 215
Diving
U.S. champions 993
Olympics. 911, 914-915
Division tables 346
Divorce in the U.S.
grounds, by state 252-253
number, rate 251
status by sex 251
Djibouti 560-561
area, population 560

birth, death rates 560
communications 560
currency 560
economy. 560
education, health statistics 560
flag 517, 560
geographical features 560
government 560
history. 561
languages, religion 560
location. 560
map. 520
transportation statistics 560
weights and measures. 560
Dogs
most popular breeds 999
show winners 996
Dollar (U.S.)
description and history 195
purchasing power 250
Dominica. 561-562
anthem, flag 517, 561
area, population 561
birth, death rates 561
communications 561
currency 561
economy. 561
education, health statistics 561
geographical features 561
government 561
history. 562
languages, religion 561
location. 561
map. 527
transportation statistics 561
weights and measures. 561
Dominican Republic 562-563
anthem, flag 514, 562
area, population 562
armed forces 735
birth, death rates 562
communications 562
currency 562
economy. 562
education, health statistics 562
geographical features 562
government 562
history. 562-563
languages, religion 562
location. 562
map. 527
transportation statistics 562
weights and measures. 562
Douglas, Stephen A. 68, 811
Douglass, Frederick 267, 811
Dow Jones Industrial Average
(description) 213
Drake, Sir Francis 798, 799, 811
Drama, see Theatre
Dramatists, noted 825-829
Drivers, licensed automobile (U.S.) 219
Drugs
drug law enforcement 260
modern drug advances 280-281
pharmaceuticals
uses and abuses 261
Dry measure 343
Dynasties, see Monarchs and dynasties

E

EFTA, see European Free Trade
Association
Earnings (U.S. occupational) . . 205, 206
Earth, the
animal kingdom. 289
life spans 288
gestation periods and litters . . . 289
atmosphere 284-285
climatic extremes 302-303

continental drift theory........... 286
continents....................... 286
dimensions...................... 284
earth's extremes 298
explorations 313
fossil man...................... 288
interior......................... 284
moon, distance from 326
origin of life on 285-286
prehistoric creatures............ 287
rotation of..................... 284
seasons 329
sun, distance from 284, 327, 329
water-covered surface 284
wildlife, endangered 290
Earthquakes, see Disasters/
Catastrophes, 898-909
Easter Island (Chilean
Dependency).................. 706
**Eastern European Mutual Assistance
Treaty (Warsaw Pact)**........... 719
warplanes..................... 734
Eastern Orthodoxy
description 883
individual churches in U.S.,
see U.S Religious Bodies, 891-897
membership.................... 886
Eclipses (sun and moon).......... 329
**Economic and Social Council,
UN** 713, 717
**Economic Community of West
African States (ECOWAS)** 719
Economics
Nobel Prizes 863
U.S.
banks 200
budget, see Budget, U.S.
gross national product (GNP).... 199
income, see Incomes (U.S.)
trade, see Trade
world
economic summary 211
gross national product, per
capita income, see specific
nation—economy; trade, see
Trade, specific nation—economy
Economy, U.S................... 10-13
Ecuador...................... 563-564
anthem, flag 514, 563
area, population 563
armed forces................... 735
birth, death rates 563
communications 563
currency....................... 563
economy....................... 563
education, health statistics 563
geographical features 563
government 563
history........................ 564
languages, religion.............. 563
location....................... 563
map........................... 525
transportation statistics 563
weights and measures........... 563
Edison, Thomas A........... 349, 350
Education
U.S.
colleges and universities
index 739-757
graduates and degrees 736
expenditures on 736, 737
high school graduates.......... 736
levels of education (adult)....... 737
relation to income 736, 738
(see also specific state)
world
number of pupils and schools,
percent of GNP or GDP expended
on education, see specific
nation, Canadian province
Education, U.S. Department of 167, 168
creation of 83

Egypt 564-565
anthem, flag 514, 564
area, population 564
armed forces................... 735
birth, death rates 564
communications 564
currency....................... 564
economy....................... 564
education, health statistics 564
geographical features 564
government 564
history........................ 565
languages, religion.............. 564
location....................... 564
map........................... 520
transportation statistics 564
weights and measures........... 564
Einstein, Albert (physicist) 803, 818, 862
Eisenhower, Dwight D.
administrations 96
ancestry and religion 140
biography.................. 131-132
elections of 1952, 1956.......... 160
Eisenhower, Mamie (Mrs. Dwight)
(biog.)......................... 151
Election results, 1980 .... 165, 170-172
Election returns (U.S. presidential)
by candidate 1789-1972 153-163
1976 election (by state).......... 164
1980 election voter profile........ 246
Electoral votes (U.S.)
1976 election (by state).......... 164
1980 election (by state).......... 165
Electric power
from hydroelectric sources 294
from nuclear sources 208, 216
Elementary schools (U.S.)
expenditures................. 736, 737
federal aid 737
no. of years completed 737
Elements, chemical
discoverers..................... 337
periodic table................... 336
atomic number, weight........... 337
Elevations
average and extreme U.S. state ... 300
mountain peaks, highest
U.S........................ 301
world........................ 293
Elizabeth I (English queen).... 688, 798,
811
Elizabeth II (British queen).... 687, 784
El Salvador.................. 565-566
anthem, flag 514, 565
area, population 565
armed forces................... 735
birth, death rates 566
communications 566
currency 565
economy.................... 565-566
education, health statistics 566
geographical features 565
government 565
history........................ 566
languages, religion.............. 565
location....................... 565
map........................... 527
transportation statistics 566
weights and measures........... 566
Embassies
foreign in U.S. (selected) 722
U.S. abroad................... 723
Emigration, see Immigration (U.S.)
Emmy Awards................. 873
Employment in the U.S.
average annual openings 206
government agencies............. 167
labor force.................... 204
minority groups in labor market..... 204
unemployment rates 204, 265
urban poverty areas.............. 265

Employment, world, see specific
nation—economy
Endangered animal species 290
Energy
consumption per unit of GNP
(selected countries) 208
consumption per capita
(selected countries) 208
dwindling U.S. reserves........... 216
U.S. demand and supply
projections 216
(see also Coal, Fuels, Natural
gas production (U.S.), Nuclear power,
Oil, Petroleum)
Energy, U.S. Department of ... 167, 168
creation of 83
Engineering Awards 336
England, see United Kingdom
Epidemics, see Disasters/
Catastrophes, 898-909
Episcopal Church
(see under U.S. Religious Bodies,
891-897)
Equal Rights Amendment 266
Equatorial Guinea 566-567
anthem, flag 514, 566
area, population 566
armed forces................... 735
birth, death rates 566
communications 566
currency....................... 566
economy....................... 566
education, health statistics 566
geographical features 566
government 566
history........................ 567
languages, religion.............. 566
location....................... 566
map........................... 520
transportation statistics 566-567
weights and measures........... 567
Equestrian champions
1980 Olympics 911
U.S. champions 997
Equivalents (table of weights and
measures) 340-341
Ericsson, Leif (explorer)....... 313, 794
Eskimos, American
population (by state) 264
Ethiopia...................... 567-568
anthem, flag 514, 567
area, population 567
armed forces................... 735
birth, death rates 567
communications 567
currency....................... 567
economy....................... 567
education, health statistics 567
geographical features 567
government 567
history........................ 568
languages, religion.............. 567
location....................... 567
map........................... 520
transportation statistics 567
weights and measures........... 567
Europe
area........................... 286
gold production 197
highest and lowest points 286
lakes 292
monarchs (present) 784
mountain peaks 293
petroleum production 209, 210
rainfall extremes 296
religious membership............. 886
temperature extremes 296
U.S. aid to 721
volcanoes..................... 295
waterfalls 295-296

European Atomic Energy Community
  (EURATOM)..................719
European Coal and Steel Community
  (ECSC)....................719
European Common Market, see
  European Community
European Community (EC)........719
European Free Trade Association
  (EFTA)....................719
Exchange rates, foreign..........198
  (see also specific country—currency)
Executions in the U.S.............263
Executive departments (U.S.
  government)..............166, 167
Exploration, expeditions
  (North, Central and South
  America [1000-1842]).........313
Explosions, see Disasters/
  Catastrophes, 898-909
Exports, imports
  U.S.
    cars.....................203
    commodities..............210
    customs duties (tourist)......232
    duty free (travelers).....230, 232
    geographic areas..........210
    import restrictions.......230-231
    selected merchandise.......210
    tonnage at U.S. ports.......240
    value of.................211
  world
    oil imports...............200
  (see also specific nation—economy)

F

FAO, see Food and Agriculture
  Organization
FCC, see Federal Communications
  Commission
FDIC, See Federal Deposit Insurance
  Corporation
Faeroe Islands (Danish
  Dependency)................706
Fahrenheit, conversion to Centigrade
  (Celsius)..................343
Fairbanks, Charles W. (biog.).....144
Falkland Islands (British Crown
  Colony)...................706
Families (U.S.)
  characteristics; size..........251
  median income: cities, counties...248
  urban family budget..........249
Family history, tracing..........787
Family names (common American) 762
Famous personalities, see Biography
Farms (U.S.)
  average size, value, see specific
    state—economy
  farm payment totals...........202
  leading crops................202
  livestock population..........202
Federal Government
  federal agencies..........168-169
  federal employment...........167
  federal expenditures..........185
  federal grants to states.......185
  federal salaries.............166
  federal taxes, see Taxes
  (see also United States—
    Federal Government)
Federal Republic of Germany, see
  Germany, West
Federalist party
  elections of 1792, 1796, 1800, 1804,
    1808, 1812, 1816......153-154
  presidents' affiliation........140

Fencing champions..............996
  1980 Olympics............911-912
Fermi, Enrico.......339, 806, 818, 862
Field hockey...................996
  1980 Olympics...............912
  Summer Olympic champions.....918
Figure skating, see Ice skating
Fiji.......................568-569
  anthem, flag.............514, 568
  area, population.............568
  birth, death rates...........569
  communications..............569
  currency...................568
  economy.................568-569
  education, health statistics.....569
  geographical features.........568
  government.................568
  history....................569
  languages, religion...........568
  location...................568
  map......................528
  transportation statistics.......569
  weights and measures.........569
Filipinos in U.S.
  population (by state)..........264
Fillmore, Abigail (Mrs. Millard)
  (biog.)....................148
Fillmore, Caroline (Mrs. Millard)
  (biog.)....................148
Fillmore, Millard
  administration.............87
  ancestry and religion.........140
  biography..................111
Film directors, noted.........832-834
Films, see Motion pictures
Finance
  Canada, see specific province
  U.S.
    financial companies, largest....200
    glossary of terms........212-213
    government finances........186
    life insurance companies,
      largest..................201
    (see Banks, Corporations (U.S.),
      Economics, Stocks, individual
      state)
Finland.....................569-570
  anthem, flag.............514, 569
  area, population.............569
  armed forces...............735
  birth, death rates...........569
  communications..............570
  currency...................569
  economy...................569
  education, health statistics.....569
  geographical features.........569
  government.................569
  history....................570
  languages, religion...........569
  location...................569
  map......................519
  transportation statistics.....569-570
  weights and measures.........570
Fires, see Disasters/
  Catastrophes, 898-909
First Ladies (U.S.) (biog.).....146-152
Fish (endangered species).........290
Fishing
  freshwater records...........994
  saltwater records.........994-995
Flags, see specific nation, state
Floods, see Disasters/
  Catastrophes, 898-909
Florida.....................369-371
  birthrate, health statistics......371
  Chamber of Commerce.........371
  communications..............371
  economy................369-370
  education statistics...........371
  finances...................369
  geographical features.........369

government...................369
  map......................370
  marriage, divorce rates........371
  population statistics..........369
  state bird, flag, flower, motto,
    name origin, nickname, seal,
    song, tree................369
  transportation statistics........371
Flowers, official state, see
  individual state
Flowers of the Month............782
Food
  recommended daily quantities.....283
  U.S. consumption..........249, 250
  U.S. exports...............210
  U.S. price indexes............250
  U.S. production.............202
Food and Agriculture Organization,
  UN (FAO)..................714
Football
  American Football League........949
  bowl games.............953-954
  Canadian..................952
  college.................953-957
  National Football League.....946-952
  stadiums...............952, 956
  Super Bowl.................949
Ford, Elizabeth ("Betty") (Mrs.
  Gerald) (biog.)..............152
Ford, Gerald R.
  administration.............98
  ancestry and religion.........140
  biography..................136
  election of 1976.............164
Foreign aid (U.S.)
  by country.................721
  contributions to international
    organizations..............720
Foreign embassies in U.S.........722
Foreign exchange rates..........198
  (see also specific nation—currency)
Foreign government tourist offices 227
Foreign trade, see specific nation—
  economy
Fort Worth, Texas..........462-463
Fractions, decimal equivalents.....348
France.....................570-572
  anthem, flag.............514, 570
  area, population.............570
  armed forces...............735
  birth, death rates...........571
  communications..............571
  currency...................570
  economy.................570-571
  education, health statistics.....571
  geographical features.........570
  government.................570
  history..................571-572
  languages, religion...........570
  location...................570
  map......................519
  monarchs (past).............785
  transportation statistics........571
  weights and measures.........571
Franco, Francisco.....665, 666, 811
Franklin, Benjamin......66, 67, 73, 78,
    100, 101, 349, 430, 811, 818
Fraser, John Malcolm (Australian
  prime minister)........510, 511, 811
French and Indian War......66, 800
French Guiana (French Overseas
  Department)................706
French Polynesia (French Overseas
  Territory)..................706
French Southern and Antarctic
  Territories (French Overseas
  Territory)..................707
Freud, Sigmund (psychiatrist)..277, 821
Fuels
  U.S. exports and imports.......210
  U.S. natural gas reserves......216

U.S. petroleum reserves 216
U.S. production (mineral fuels) 208
(see also Nuclear power)
Future 9-37

G

GATT, *see General Agreement on*
Tariffs and Trade
GNP, *see Gross national product*
Gabon 572-573
  anthem, flag 514, 572
  area, population 572
  birth, death rates 572
  communications 572
  currency 572
  economy. 572
  education, health statistics 572
  geographical features 572
  government 572
  history 573
  languages, religion 572
  location 572
  map. 520-521
  transportation statistics 572
  weights and measures. 572
Galaxies 314-315, 316, 319
  galactic terms 315-316
da Gama, Vasco (explorer). 797, 811
Gambia, The. 573-574
  anthem, flag 514, 573
  area, population 573
  birth, death rates 573
  communications 573
  currency 573
  economy. 573
  education, health statistics 573
  geographical features 573
  government 573
  history 574
  language, religion 573
  location 573
  map. 520
  transportation statistics 574
  weights and measures. 574
Gandhi, Indira (Indian prime
  minister) 587, 588, 589, 811
Gandhi, Mohandas K. 589, 811
Garfield, James A.
  administration 90
  ancestry and religion 140
  biography 118
  election of 1880 158
  uncompleted term. 139
Garfield, Lucretia (Mrs. James)
  (biog.) 149
Garner, John N. (biog.) 144-145
Gaza Strip 564, 565, 596, 597
Gemini space missions (U.S.). 332, 333
Genealogy 787
General Agreement on Tariffs and
  Trade, UN (GATT) 714
General Assembly, UN 711-712
  presidents. 718
Genghis Khan, *see Jenghiz Khan*
Geography
  cities (U.S.), latitude and
    longitude. 308
  coastlines and shorelines (U.S.) . . . 300
  deserts 292
  earth's extremes 298
  elevations (U.S.), average and
    extreme. 300
  extreme points of U.S. 299
  geographic centers of U.S. . . . 244, 299
  glaciers. 292
  islands 298
  lakes 294, 301

mountains 293, 301
oceans, seas 284, 291
rainfall extremes 296
rivers 291, 301
temperature extremes 302
volcanoes. 295
waterfalls 295-296
(see also specific nation, U.S.
state, Canadian province)
Geology
  ancient supercontinents 286
  eras, periods, epochs 284
George III (British king) 785, 800
Georgia 371-373
  birthrate, health statistics 373
  Chamber of Commerce. 373
  communications 373
  economy. 373
  education statistics 373
  finances 371, 373
  geographical features 371
  government 371
  map. 372
  marriage, divorce rates 371
  population statistics 371
  state bird, flag, flower, motto,
    name origin, nickname, seal,
    song, tree. 371
  transportation statistics 373
German Democratic Republic, *see*
  Germany, East
German rulers (past) 786
Germany, East 574-575
  anthem, flag 514, 574
  area, population 574
  armed forces 735
  birth, death rates 574
  communications 574
  currency 574
  economy. 574
  education, health statistics 574
  geographical features 574
  government 574
  history. 575
  languages, religion 574
  location 574
  map. 519
  transportation statistics 574
  weights and measures. 574
Germany, West (Federal
  Republic). 575-576
  anthem, flag 514, 575
  area, population 575
  armed forces 735
  birth, death rates 575
  communications 575
  currency 575
  economy. 575
  education, health statistics 575
  geographical features 575
  government 575
  history 576
  languages, religion 575
  location 575
  map. 519
  transportation statistics 575
  weights and measures. 575
Gerry, Elbridge (biog.) 142
Gettysburg Address 139
Ghana 576-577
  anthem, flag 514, 576
  area, population 576
  armed forces 735
  birth, death rates 576
  communications 576
  currency 576
  economy. 576
  education, health statistics 576
  geographical features 576
  government 576
  history 577

languages, religion 576
location 576
map. 520
transportation statistics 576
weights and measures. 576
Gibraltar (British Colony) 707
Gifts, wedding anniversary 782
Glaciers, major world 292
Gold production (by country). 197
Golf 964-968
  Amateur Championships 966, 968
  British Open. 964
  Canadian Open. 965
  Curtis Cup 968
  Hall of Fame 966-967
  LPGA Champions. 967
  Masters. 964
  money winners 964, 966, 967
  PGA Champions. 965
  Ryder Cup 966
  USGA Women's Open 967
  U.S. Open 965
  Walker Cup 968
Government, *see specific nation,*
  U.S. state or city, Canadian province
Governors
  state, *see individual state*
  territorial, *see U.S. Outlying*
    Areas, 476-478
Grains (U.S. production) 202
Grammy Awards 873
Grant, Julia (Mrs. Ulysses) (biog.) . . 148
Grant, Ulysses S.
  administrations 89
  ancestry and religion 140
  biography 116-117
  elections of 1868, 1872. 157
Great Britain, *see United Kingdom*
Great Pyramid of Khufu
  (Cheops) 788, 808
Greece 577-578
  anthem, flag 514, 577
  area, population 577
  armed forces 735
  birth, death rates 577
  communications 577
  currency 577
  economy. 577
  education, health statistics 577
  geographical features 577
  government 577
  history 578
  languages, religion 577
  location 577
  map. 519
  transportation statistics 577
  weights and measures. 577
Greenland (Danish
  Dependency) 707
Greenwich Mean Time 329
Grenada 578-579
  anthem, flag 517, 578
  area, population 578
  birth, death rates 579
  communications 579
  currency 578
  economy. 578-579
  education, health statistics 579
  geographical features 578
  government 579
  history 579
  languages, religion 578
  location 578
  map. 527
  transportation statistics 579
  weights and measures. 579
Gross national product. 199
  (see also individual nation—
    economy)
Guadeloupe (French Overseas
  Department). 707

Guam (U.S. territory).............476
Guamanians in U.S.
  population (by state) 265
Guatemala 579-580
  anthem, flag 514, 579
  area, population 579
  armed forces 735
  birth, death rates 579
  communications 579
  currency 579
  economy.......................579
  education, health statistics 579
  geographical features 579
  government 579
  history.........................580
  languages, religion 579
  location 579
  map...........................527
  transportation statistics 579
  weights and measures...........579
Guinea......................580-581
  anthem, flag 514, 580
  area, population 580
  armed forces 735
  birth, death rates 580
  communications 580
  currency 580
  economy.......................580
  education, health statistics 580
  geographical features 580
  government 580
  history.........................581
  languages, religion 580
  location 580
  map...........................520
  transportation statistics 580
  weights and measures...........580
Guinea-Bissau.................581
  anthem 581
  area, population 581
  armed forces 735
  birth, death rates 581
  communications 581
  currency 581
  economy.......................581
  education, health statistics 581
  geographical features 581
  government 581
  history.........................581
  languages, religion 581
  location 581
  map...........................520
  transportation statistics 581
  weights and measures...........581
Gussow, Mel (theatre survey) ...854
Gutenberg, Johann..........350, 797
Guyana 581-583
  anthem, flag 514, 581
  area, population 581
  armed forces 735
  birth, death rates 582
  communications 582
  currency 581
  economy.......................582
  education, health statistics 582
  geographical features 582
  government 582
  history.....................582-583
  languages, religion 581
  location 581-582
  map...........................525
  transportation statistics 582
  weights and measures...........582
Gymnastics
  1980 Olympics 912
  U.S. champions 996

H

Haile Selassie 567, 568, 812
Haiti 583-584
  anthem, flag 514, 583
  area, population 583
  armed forces 735
  birth, death rates 583
  communications 583
  currency 583
  economy.......................583
  education, health statistics 583
  geographical features 583
  government 583
  history.....................583-584
  languages, religion 583
  location 583
  map...........................527
  transportation statistics 583
  weights and measures...........583
Hale, Nathan 67, 812
Halicarnassus, Mausoleum at .790, 808
Halls of Fame
  Baseball 926
  Basketball 942
  Football, Professional........946-947
  Golf 966, 967
  Hockey 962
Hambletonian 981
Hamilton, Alexander 67, 78, 812
Hamlin, Hannibal (biog.) 143
Hammarskjöld, Dag..............716
Handball 997
  1980 Olympics 912
  Summer Olympic champions.....918
Handzo, Stephen (film survey)......857
Hanging Gardens of Babylon .789, 808
Hapsburg dynasty 796
Harbors, see Ports
Harding, Florence (Mrs. Warren G.)
  (biog.) 150
Harding, Warren G.
  administration 93
  ancestry and religion 140
  biography..................125-126
  election of 1920 160
  uncompleted term...............139
Harness racing 981-982
  Hambletonian 981
  Horse of the Year 981
  Kentucky Futurity 982
  leading money winners 981
  world records..................982
Harrison, Anna (Mrs. William
  Henry) (biog.) 147
Harrison, Benjamin
  administration 91
  ancestry and religion ....
  biography...................120-121
  elections of 1888, 1892.......158-159
  minority president 139
Harrison, Caroline (Mrs. Benjamin)
  (biog.) 149
Harrison, Mary (Mrs. Benjamin)
  (biog.)..........................149
Harrison, William Henry
  administration 86
  ancestry and religion 140
  biography......................108
  elections of 1836, 1840..........155
  uncompleted term...............139
Hassan II (Moroccan
  king) 629, 630, 783
Hawaii 373-375
  birthrate, health statistics 375
  Chamber of Commerce...........375
  communications 375
  economy.......................375

  education statistics..............375
  finances 373
  geographical features 373
  government 373
  map...........................374
  marriage, divorce rates 373
  population statistics 373
  state bird, flag, flower, motto,
    name origin, nickname, seal,
    song, tree.....................373
  transportation statistics 375
Hawaiians, native
  population (by state) 265
Hayes, Lucy (Mrs. Rutherford)
  (biog.)..........................149
Hayes, Rutherford B.
  administration 89-90
  ancestry and religion 140
  biography..................117-118
  election of 1876 158
  minority president...............139
Heads of state, see individual
  nation
Health and Human Services,
  U.S. Department of........167, 168
  creation of 83
Health care
  costs, U.S......................276
  dietary allowances, daily
    recommended 283
  food quantities, recommended....283
  statistics, see specific nation,
    U.S. state, Canadian province
  travel recommendations 231
  weight, recommended adult 283
Heard and McDonald Islands
  (Australian External Territory)......707
Heart disease
  death rates and ratios 272
Heavyweight boxing champions ...983
Hebrews, see Judaism
Hendricks, Thomas A. (biog.) 143
Henry VIII (English king) 687, 688,
  797-798
High schools (U.S.)
  expenditures................736, 737
  federal aid 737
  graduates 736, 737
  years completed 737, 738
Highest
  buildings and structures 297
  mountains
    U.S...........................301
    world.........................293
  town 298
Highway mileage between
  cities, U.S. 220-221
Hinduism
  description 884-885
  membership....................886
Hirohito (Japanese
  emperor) 600, 602, 783
Hiroshima bombing.......71, 805, 806
History
  outline of U.S. 66-71
  outline of world 788-808
  rulers and dynasties 783-786
  (see specific nation, U.S. state
    or city, Canadian province)
Hitler, Adolf 575, 803, 804, 812
Ho Chi Minh 695, 696, 806, 812
Hobart, Garrett A. (biog.) 144
Hockey
  field hockey, 1980 Olympics.......912
  ice hockey
    college 962
    Hall of Fame 962
    National Hockey League....958-961
    Olympics 919-920
    Stanley Cup..................959
Hohenzollern dynasty 786, 800

Holidays
  legal, public (U.S.) 312
  religious 888
Holland, see Netherlands
Homicides in U.S. 273
Honduras 584-585
  anthem, flag 514, 584
  area, population 584
  armed forces 735
  birth, death rates 584
  communications 584
  currency 584
  economy........................ 584
  education, health statistics 584
  geographical features 584
  government 584
  history..................... 584-585
  languages, religion 584
  location........................ 584
  map........................... 527
  transportation statistics 584
  weights and measures........... 584
Hong Kong (British Colony) 707
Honolulu, Hawaii 463
Hoover, Herbert C.
  administration 94
  ancestry and religion 140
  biography................... 127-128
  elections of 1928, 1932........... 161
Hoover, Lou Henry (Mrs. Herbert C.)
  (biog.) 150-151
Horse racing, see Thoroughbred
  racing, Harness racing
Horse shows 997
Hospital costs (U.S.) 275
  (see also Medical care indexes,
  276, Social Security—Medicaid,
  Medicare programs)
Hotel/Motel toll-free
  telephone numbers 224
House of Representatives, U.S., see
  Congress, U.S.
Housing and Urban Development,
  U.S. Department of 167, 168
  creation of 83
Houston, Texas 463
Howland, Baker, and Jarvis Islands
  (U.S. territory) 476
Hua Guofeng (Kuo-feng) (Chinese
  leader) 549, 550, 812
Humphrey, Hubert H. (biog.) 145
Hungary..................... 585-586
  anthem, flag 514, 585
  area, population 585
  armed forces 735
  birth, death rates 585
  communications 585
  currency 585
  economy........................ 585
  education, health statistics 585
  geographical features 585
  government 585
  history..................... 585-586
  languages, religion 585
  location........................ 585
  map........................... 519
  transportation statistics 585
  weights and measures........... 585
Hurricanes
  names (1982) 306
  (see Disasters/Catastrophes,
  898-909)
Hussein (Jordanian king) .. 602, 603, 783
Hu Yaobang (Chinese
  leader) 547, 550, 727, 812
Hydropower
  dams, man-made lakes; hydroelectric plants, selected world ... 294
  U.S. production 216

I

ICC, see Interstate Commerce
  Commission
ILO, see International Labour
  Organization
IMF, see International Monetary
  Fund
Ice hockey, see Hockey
Ice skating 997
  1980 Olympics.............. 919, 921
Iceland...................... 586-587
  anthem, flag 514, 586
  area, population 586
  birth, death rates 586
  communications 586
  currency 586
  economy........................ 586
  education, health statistics 586
  geographical features 586
  government 586
  history..................... 586-587
  languages, religion 586
  location........................ 586
  map........................... 519
  transportation statistics 586
  weights and measures........... 586
Idaho 375-377
  birthrate, health statistics 377
  Chamber of Commerce........... 377
  communications 377
  economy........................ 377
  education statistics............... 377
  finances 377
  geographical features 375
  government 375
  map........................... 376
  marriage, divorce rates 377
  population statistics 377
  state bird, flag, flower, motto,
    name origin, nickname, seal,
    song, tree...................... 375
  transportation statistics 377
Illinois 377-379
  birthrate, health statistics 379
  Chamber of Commerce........... 379
  communications 379
  economy........................ 379
  education statistics............... 379
  finances 379
  geographical features 377, 379
  government 377
  map........................... 378
  marriage, divorce rates 379
  population statistics 379
  state bird, flag, flower, motto,
    name origin, nickname, seal,
    song, tree...................... 377
  transportation statistics 379
Illiteracy statistics, see individual
  nation—education
Immigration (U.S.) 246
Imports, see Exports, imports
Income taxes, see Taxes
Income Tax Hints 188-189
Incomes (U.S.)
  and education 736, 738
  median family 248
  per capita, by state 186
  per capita, metropolitan areas 248
  (see also individual state—
  finances)
Incomes (world), see individual
  country, Canadian province—
  economy
Independence, Declaration of 72-74
  signers of 73-74
India 587-589
  anthem, flag 514, 587

  area, population 587
  armed forces 735
  birth, death rates 587
  communications 587
  currency 587
  economy........................ 587
  education, health statistics 587
  geographical features 587
  government 587
  history..................... 588-589
  languages, religion 587
  location........................ 587
  map........................... 523
  transportation statistics 587
  weights and measures........... 587
Indian Ocean (area, depth) 291
Indiana 379-381
  birthrate, health statistics......... 381
  Chamber of Commerce........... 381
  communications 381
  economy........................ 381
  education statistics............... 381
  finances 381
  geographical features 381
  government 381
  map........................... 380
  marriage, divorce rates 381
  population statistics 381
  state bird, flag, flower, motto,
    name origin, nickname, seal,
    song, tree...................... 381
  transportation statistics 381
Indianapolis 500 race 975
Indianapolis, Indiana 464
Indians, American
  employment 204
  population (by state) 265
Indians (Asian) in U.S.
  population (by state) 265
Indochina, see Cambodia, Laos,
  Vietnam
Indonesia 589-590
  anthem, flag 514, 589
  area, population 589
  armed forces 735
  birth, death rates 589
  communications 589
  currency 589
  economy........................ 589
  education, health statistics 589
  geographical features 589
  government 589
  history......................... 590
  languages, religion 589
  location........................ 589
  map........................... 523
  transportation statistics 589
  weights and measures........... 589
Industries in U.S.
  industrial corporations,
    largest........................ 201
  metal production 209
  military industries 735
  motor vehicle production 203
  retailing companies, largest 201
  utilities, largest 201
  (see specific state—economy;
  Corporations)
Industries (world), see individual
  nation—economy
Infant and neonatal
  death rates (U.S.) 271
Infant mortality rate, see specific
  nation or state—health statistics
Insurance
  health insurance
    Medicaid...................... 258
    Medicare.................. 257-258
  life insurance
    U.S. companies, largest 201
    veterans' insurance............ 732

Social Security: payments 256
unemployment insurance
benefits...................... 206
Interest rates 196
Inter-Governmental Maritime Consul-
tative Organization, UN (IMCO) .. 714
Interior, U.S. Department of ... 167, 168
National Parks.............. 225-226
Internal Revenue Service
addresses of offices............. 187
taxes 187, 190
International Atomic Energy Agency,
UN (IAEA)...................... 714
International Bank for Reconstruction
and Development, UN (IBRD).... 714
International Civil Aviation
Organization, UN (ICAO) 714
International Committee of the Red
Cross (ICRC), see Red Cross
International Court of Justice,
UN 713, 717
International Criminal Police
Organization (Interpol) 719
International Development Asso-
ciation, UN (IDA)................ 714
International Energy
Agency (IEA) 719-720
International Finance Corporation,
UN (IFC)....................... 714
International Fund for Agricultural
Development, UN (IFAD)......... 714
International Labour Organization,
UN (ILO)....................... 714
International Monetary Fund,
UN (IMF) 714
International organizations, see
Organizations
International system of units, see
Metric system
International Telecommunications
Union, UN (ITU)............. 714-715
Interpol, see International Criminal
Police Organization
Interstellar molecules 318
Inventors and Inventions 349-350
Iowa 381-383
birthrate, health statistics 383
communications 383
economy....................... 383
education statistics.............. 383
finances 383
geographical features 383
government 383
map........................... 382
marriage, divorce rates 383
population statistics 383
state bird, flag, flower, motto,
name origin, nickname, seal,
song, tree..................... 383
transportation statistics 383
Iran 590-593
anthem, flag 514, 590
area, population 590
armed forces 735
birth, death rates 590
communications 591
currency 590
economy................... 590-591
education, health statistics 591
geographical features 590
government 590
history......................... 593
languages, religion.............. 590
location........................ 590
maps 524, 592
transportation statistics 591
weights and measures........... 591
Iraq 592, 593-594
anthem, flag 514, 593
area, population 593
armed forces 735

birth, death rates 592
communications 593
currency 593
economy....................... 593
education, health statistics 593
geographical features 593
government 593
history......................... 594
languages, religion.............. 593
location........................ 593
maps 524, 592
transportation statistics 593
weights and measures........... 593
Ireland 594-595
anthem, flag 514, 594
area, population 594
armed forces 735
birth, death rates 595
communications 595
currency 594
economy................... 594-595
education, health statistics 595
geographical features 594
government 594
history......................... 595
languages, religion.............. 594
location........................ 594
map........................... 519
transportation statistics 594
weights and measures........... 594
Ireland, Northern, see United
Kingdom
Iron production 209
Islam........................... 884
membership.................... 886
Islands (principal world) 298
Isle of Man (British Crown
Fiefdom)...................... 707
Israel 595-597
anthem, flag 514, 596
area, population 595
armed forces 735
birth, death rates 596
communications 596
currency 596
economy....................... 596
education, health statistics 596
geographical features 596
government 596
history......................... 597
languages, religion.............. 596
location........................ 596
map........................... 524
transportation statistics 596
weights and measures........... 596
Italy.......................... 597-598
anthem, flag 514, 597
area, population 597
armed forces 735
birth, death rates 597
communications 597
currency 597
economy....................... 597
education, health statistics 597
geographical features 597
government 597
history......................... 598
languages, religion.............. 597
location........................ 597
map........................... 519
monarchs (past) 786
Roman emperors 786
transportation statistics 597
weights and measures........... 597
Ivory Coast................... 598-599
anthem, flag 514, 598
area, population 598
armed forces 735
birth, death rates 599
communications 599
currency 598

economy....................... 599
education, health statistics 599
geographical features 598
government 599
history......................... 599
languages, religion.............. 598
location........................ 598
map........................... 520
transportation statistics 599
weights and measures........... 599

J

Jackson, Andrew
administrations 85-86
ancestry and religion 140
biography 105-107
birthday (legal holiday) 312
elections of 1824, 1828, 1832 . 154-155
Jackson, Rachel (Mrs. Andrew)
(biog.)......................... 147
Jacksonville, Florida 464
Jamaica 599-600
anthem, flag 514, 599
area, population 599
birth, death rates 600
communications 600
currency 599
economy....................... 600
education, health statistics 600
geographical features 599
government 599-600
history......................... 600
languages, religion.............. 599
location........................ 599
map........................... 527
transportation statistics 600
weights and measures........... 600
Jan Mayen (Norwegian
Dependency).................. 707
Japan 600-602
anthem, flag 514, 600
area, population 600
armed forces 735
birth, death rates 601
communications 601
currency 600
economy....................... 601
education, health statistics 601
geographical features 600
government 600-601
history..................... 601-602
languages, religion.............. 600
location........................ 600
map........................... 522
monarch (present) 600, 783
transportation statistics 601
weights and measures........... 601
Japan Sea (area, depth)........... 291
Japanese in U.S.
population by states............. 264
Jefferson, Martha (Mrs. Thomas)
(biog.)......................... 146
Jefferson, Thomas
administrations 84
ancestry and religion 140
biography 101-102
birthday (legal holiday) 312
elections of 1796, 1800, 1804 153
signer of the Declaration of
Independence 73
Jenghiz Khan 628, 795, 811
Jesus Christ (biog.) 883-884
Jews, see Judaism
Joan of Arc (French martyr) ... 572, 812
Jobs and Careers 9-37
John Paul I, Pope 693, 888
John Paul II, Pope.......... 693, 888

Johnson, Andrew
  administration 89
  ancestry and religion 140
  biography 115-116
  elections of 1864, 1868 157
Johnson, Claudia ("Lady Bird")
  (Mrs. Lyndon) (biog.) 151-152
Johnson, Eliza (Mrs. Andrew)
  (biog.) 148
Johnson, Lyndon B.
  administrations 97
  ancestry and religion 140
  biography 134-135
  birthday (legal holiday) 312
  elections of 1960, 1964 163
Johnson, Richard M. (biog.) . . . 142-143
Johnston Atoll (U.S. territory) 476
Joint Chiefs of Staff, U.S. 731
Jordan 602-603
  anthem, flag 514, 602
  area, population 602
  armed forces 735
  birth, death rates 602
  communications 602
  currency 602
  economy. 602
  education, health statistics 602
  geographical features 602
  government 602
  history 603
  languages, religion 602
  location 602
  map 524
  monarch (present) 602, 783
  transportation statistics 603
  weights and measures 603
Juan Carlos I (Spanish
  king) 665, 666, 784
Juan Fernández (Chilean
  Dependency) 707
Judaism
  description 882
  membership 886
  (see under U.S. Religious Bodies,
    891-897)
Judges, U.S. 183
  Supreme Court 180-182, 183
  salaries 166, 183
Judo
  U.S. champions 997
  1980 Olympics 912
Junior college sports champions . . . 997
Jupiter (planet) 323, 327
  space probes 324-325, 331
Justice, International Court of, UN
  members 713-714, 717
Justice, U.S. Department of . . . 167, 168
  Supreme Court 166, 180-182, 183
  Territorial Judges 183
  U.S. Courts 183

K

Kansas 383-385
  birthrate, health statistics 385
  Chamber of Commerce 385
  communications 385
  economy. 385
  education statistics 385
  finances 385
  geographical features 385
  government 385
  map 384
  marriage, divorce rates 385
  population statistics 385
  state bird, flag, flower, motto,
    name origin, nickname, seal,
    song, tree 385

  transportation statistics 385
Kansas City, Missouri 464
Karamanlis, Constantine (Greek
  president) 577, 578, 812
Karate champions 997
Kaunda, Kenneth (Zambian
  president) 702, 703, 812
Keeling (Cocos) Islands (Australian
  External Territory) 706
Kennedy, Jacqueline (Mrs. John F.)
  (biog.) 151
Kennedy, John F.
  administration 96
  ancestry and religion 140
  biography 133-134
  election of 1960 163
  minority president 139
  uncompleted term 139
Kentucky 385-386, 387
  birthrate, health statistics 386
  Chamber of Commerce 386
  communications 386
  economy 386
  education, health statistics 386
  finances 386
  geographical features 386
  government 386
  map 387
  marriage, divorce rates 386
  population statistics 386
  state bird, flag, flower, motto,
    name origin, nickname, seal,
    song, tree 386
  transportation statistics 386
Kentucky Derby 979
Kenya 603-604
  anthem, flag 514, 603
  area, population 603
  armed forces 735
  birth, death rates 603
  communications 604
  currency 603
  economy 603
  education, health statistics 603
  geographical features 603
  government 603
  history 604
  languages, religion 603
  location 603
  map 520-521
  transportation statistics 603-604
  weights and measures 604
Kenyatta, Jomo 604, 812
Khalid (Saudi Arabian
  king) 656, 657, 783
Khrushchev, Nikita 686, 804, 812
Khomeini, Ayatollah (Iranian religious
  leader) 590, 591, 593, 812
Khufu (Cheops), Pyramid of . . 788, 808
King, Martin Luther,
  Jr. 71, 268, 807, 813, 864
  Martin Luther King Day 312
King, William R. D. (biog.) 143
Kingman Reef (U.S. territory) 476
Kings, see Monarchs and dynasties
Kiribati 604-605
  anthem, flag 517, 604
  area, population 604
  birth, death rates 604
  communications 604
  currency 604
  economy 604
  education, health statistics 604
  geographical features 604
  government 604
  history 605
  languages, religion 604
  location 604
  map 528
  transportation statistics 604
  weights and measures 604

Kissinger, Henry (U.S.
  statesman) 813, 864
Korea, North (Democratic People's
  Republic) 605-606
  anthem, flag 514, 605
  area, population 605
  armed forces 735
  birth, death rates 605
  communications 605
  currency 605
  economy 605
  education, health statistics 605
  geographical features 605
  government 605
  history 606
  languages, religion 605
  location 605
  map 522
  transportation statistics 605
  weights and measures 605
Korea, South (Republic of
  Korea) 606-608
  anthem, flag 514, 606
  area, population 606
  armed forces 735
  birth, death rates 607
  communications 607
  currency 606
  economy 607
  education, health statistics 607
  geographical features 606
  government 607
  history 607-608
  languages, religion 606
  location 606
  map 522
  transportation statistics 607
  weights and measures 607
Koreans in U.S.
  population (by state) 265
Korean War
  estimated cost in dollars 731
  numbers in U.S. services 728
  U.S. casualties, veterans 728
  (see Outline of U.S. History, 66;
    Outline of World History, 806;
    Korea, North; Korea, South)
Kosygin, Aleksey (Soviet
  leader) 686, 727, 804, 813
Kublai Khan 796, 813
Kuwait 608-609
  anthem, flag 515, 608
  area, population 608
  armed forces 735
  birth, death rates 608
  communications 608
  currency 608
  economy 608
  education, health statistics 608
  geographical features 608
  government 608
  history 609
  languages, religion 608
  location 608
  map 524
  monarch (present) 608, 783
  transportation statistics 608
  weights and measures 608

L

Labor
  employment outlook 206
  force (U.S.) 204
  force, world, *see specific nation—*
    economy
  minority groups (U.S.) 204
  unemployment rate (U.S.) 204, 265

Labor, U.S. Department of 167, 168
Labor unions in U.S. 205
Lacrosse champions 997
Lakes
  U.S. 301
  world 292
Landslides, *see Disasters/*
  Catastrophes, 898-909
Lane, Harriet (White House
  hostess for James Buchanan)
  (biog.) 148
Language
  current words, phrases 760-761
  languages of the world 762
  (see also individual nation)
Laos 609-610
  area, population 609
  armed forces 735
  birth, death rates 609
  communications 609
  currency 609
  economy 609
  education, health statistics 609
  flag 515, 609
  geographical features 609
  government 609
  history 610
  languages, religion 609
  location 609
  map 523
  transportation statistics 609
  weights and measures 609
Lao-tze (biog.) 885-886
Latin America, U.S. aid to 721
Latin American Free Trade Asso-
  ciation (LAFTA) 720
Latitude and longitude
  cities, U.S. 308
Lebanon 610-611
  anthem, flag 515, 610
  area, population 610
  birth, death rates 610
  communications 610
  currency 610
  economy 610
  education, health statistics 610
  geographical features 610
  government 610
  history 611
  languages, religion 610
  location 610
  map 524
  transportation statistics 610
  weights and measures 610
Lee, Robert E. 69, 312, 813
Legal holidays (U.S.) 312
Lenin, Vladimir I. 686, 803, 813
Lesotho 611-612
  anthem, flag 515, 611
  area, population 611
  birth, death rates 612
  communications 612
  currency 611
  economy 611-612
  education, health statistics 612
  geographical features 611
  government 611
  history 612
  languages, religion 611
  location 611
  map 521
  monarch (present) 611, 783
  transportation statistics 612
  weights and measures 612
Liberia 612-613
  anthem, flag 515, 612
  area, population 612
  armed forces 735
  birth, death rates 613
  communications 613
  currency 612

  economy 612-613
  education, health statistics 613
  geographical features 612
  government 612
  history 613
  languages, religion 612
  location 612
  map 520
  transportation statistics 613
  weights and measures 613
Libraries
  reference books as nucleus
    for 758-759
  U.S. public 738
  U.S. university 758
Library of Congress
  administrative personnel 169
  employees (no.) 167
Libya 613-614
  anthem, flag 515, 613
  area, population 613
  armed forces 735
  birth, death rates 614
  communications 614
  currency 613
  economy 613-614
  education, health statistics 614
  geographical features 613
  government 613
  history 614
  languages, religion 613
  location 613
  map 520
  transportation statistics 614
  weights and measures 614
Lie Trygve 716
Liechtenstein 614-615
  anthem, flag 515, 614
  area, population 614
  birth, death rates 615
  communications 615
  currency 614
  economy 615
  education, health statistics 615
  geographical features 614
  government 614-615
  history 615
  languages, religion 614
  location 614
  map 519
  monarch (present) 614, 784
  transportation statistics 615
  weights and measures 615
Life expectancy
  U.S. 271
  world, *see specific nation—health*
    statistics
Life insurance
  U.S. companies, largest 201
  U.S. veterans 732
Lincoln, Abraham
  administrations 88
  ancestry and religion 140
  biography 113-114
  birthday (legal holiday) 312
  elections of 1860, 1864 157
  Gettysburg Address 139
  minority president 139
  uncompleted term 139
Lincoln, Mary (Mrs. Abraham)
  (biog.) 148
Linear measure 340, 343
Liquid measure 343
Liquor
  duty free (personal import) 230
  import restrictions 232
Literacy, *see individual nation—*
  education
Literature
  authors, noted 825-829
  Nobel Prizes 863

  other awards 872
  Pulitzer Prizes 869-870
Livestock on U.S. farms and
  ranches, *see Agriculture (U.S.)*
Longest
  bridges (world) 243
  rivers
    U.S. 301
    world 291
  ship canals 241
  tunnels
    railroad (world) 218
    vehicular (U.S.) 217
Longevity, *see Life expectancy*
López Portillo, José (Mexican
  president) 625, 627, 813
Los Angeles, California 464-465
Louis XIV (Sun King) 572, 785, 799
Louis XVI 572, 785, 800
Louisiana 386, 388-390
  birthrate, health statistics 390
  Chamber of Commerce 390
  communications 390
  economy 388
  education statistics 390
  finances 388
  geographical features 388
  government 388
  map 389
  marriage, divorce rates 388
  population statistics 388
  state bird, flag, flower, motto,
    name origin, nickname, seal,
    song, tree 388
  transportation statistics 388, 390
Louisville, Kentucky 465
Luge (sledding)
  champions 997
  Olympics 919, 921
Luther, Martin (biog.) 574, 798, 820,
                                        883
Luxembourg 615-616
  anthem, flag 515, 615
  area, population 615
  birth, death rates 615
  communications 615
  currency 615
  economy 615
  education, health statistics 615
  geographical features 615
  government 615
  history 616
  languages, religion 615
  location 615
  map 519
  monarch (present) 615, 784
  transportation statistics 615
  weights and measures 616

M

Macau (Portuguese Overseas
  Province) 707
MacArthur, Douglas 71, 807, 813
Madagascar 616-617
  anthem, flag 515, 616
  area, population 616
  armed forces 735
  birth, death rates 616
  communications 616
  currency 616
  economy 616
  education, health statistics 616
  geographical features 616
  government 616
  history 617
  languages, religion 616
  location 616

map............................ 521
transportation statistics 616
weights and measures........... 616
Madison, Dolley (Mrs. James)
(biog.)......................... 146
Madison, James
administrations 84-85
ancestry and religion ......:..... 140
biography.................. 102-103
elections of 1808, 1812.......... 154
signer of the Constitution 78
Magazines
advertising volume 763
circulation (U.S.)................. 763
mailing rate 766
Magellan, Ferdinand 313, 798, 813
Maine 390-392
birthrate, health statistics 392
Chamber of Commerce........... 392
communications 392
economy...................... 392
education statistics.............. 392
finances 392
geographical features 390
government 390
map.......................... 391
marriage, divorce rates 392
population statistics 390, 392
state bird, flag, flower, motto,
name origin, nickname, seal,
song, tree.................... 390
transportation statistics 392
Makarios, Archbishop.... 557, 558, 813
Malagasy Republic,
see Madagascar
Malawi 617-618
anthem, flag 515, 617
area, population 617
armed forces.................. 735
birth, death rates 617
communications 617
currency 617
economy..................... 617
education, health statistics 617
geographical features 617
government 617
history....................... 618
languages, religion 617
location...................... 617
map.......................... 521
transportation statistics 617
weights and measures........... 617
Malaysia 618-620
anthem, flag 515, 618
area, population 618
armed forces.................. 735
birth, death rates 618
communications 618
currency 618
economy..................... 618
education, health statistics 618-619
geographical features 618
government 618
history.................... 619-620
languages, religion 618
location...................... 618
map.......................... 523
transportation statistics 619
weights and measures........... 619
Malcolm X 268, 813
Maldives 620-621
anthem, flag 515, 620
area, population 620
birth, death rates 620
communications 620
currency 620
economy..................... 620
education, health statistics 620
geographical features 620
government 620
history.................... 620-621

languages, religion 620
location...................... 620
map.......................... 523
transportation statistics 620
weights and measures........... 620
Mali......................... 621-622
anthem, flag 515, 621
area, population 621
armed forces.................. 735
birth, death rates 621
communications 621
currency 621
economy...................... 621
education, health statistics 621
geographical features 621
government 621
history.................... 621-622
languages, religion 621
location...................... 621
map.......................... 520
transportation statistics 621
weights and measures........... 621
Malta......................... 622
anthem, flag 515, 622
area, population 622
armed forces.................. 735
birth, death rates 622
communications 622
currency 622
economy..................... 622
education, health statistics 622
geographical features 622
government 622
history....................... 622
languages, religion 622
location...................... 622
map.......................... 519
transportation statistics 622
weights and measures........... 622
Man, prehistoric 288
Manitoba, Canada........ 486-487, 489
agriculture 486
area.......................... 486
birth, death rates 486
communications 486
economy..................... 486
education statistics.............. 486
geographical features 486
government 486
health care statistics 486
location...................... 486
map.......................... 487
marriage, divorce rates 486
motor vehicle statistics 486
population statistics 486
revenues and expenditures........ 486
Manpower needs (U.S. future) 206
Manufactures
exports and imports (U.S.) 210
foreign companies, largest 209
metals (U.S.).................. 209
mineral production (world) 210
motor vehicles (world) 203
passenger cars (U.S.) 203
world economic summary........ 211
(see specific Canadian province,
nation, U.S. state—economy)
Mao Zedong (Tse-tung) (Chinese
leader) 549, 550, 805, 806, 814
Marathon champions 997
Olympics 913, 916
Marconi, Guglielmo 350, 801, 861
Marcos, Ferdinand (Philippine
president)........ 647, 648, 814
Marie Antoinette 800, 814
Marine Corps, U.S................ 168
Marine disasters, *see Disasters/*
Catastrophes, 898-909
Mariner space probes (U.S.) . 325, 331
Marriage
adult marital status (U.S.)......... 251

median duration of U.S.
marriages..................... 253
rates in U.S. 251
U.S. laws (by state) 254
Mars (planet)............. 322-323, 327
space probes 324-325, 331-332
Mars space probes (Soviet) ... 324-325
Marshall, Thomas R. (biog.)........ 144
Marshall Islands.................. 478
Martinique (French Overseas
Department).................. 707-708
Marx, Karl................ 801, 814, 820
Mary (Queen of Scots) 798
Maryland.................... 392-394
birthrate, health statistics 394
Chamber of Commerce........... 394
communications 394
economy...................... 394
education statistics.............. 394
finances 394
geographical features 394
government 394
map.......................... 393
marriage, divorce rates 394
population statistics 394
state bird, flag, flower, motto,
name origin, nickname, seal,
song, tree.................. 392, 394
transportation statistics 394
Massachusetts 394-396
birthrate, health statistics 396
Chamber of Commerce........... 396
communications 396
economy...................... 396
education statistics.............. 396
finances 396
geographical features 396
government 396
map.......................... 395
marriage, divorce rates 396
population statistics 396
state bird, flag, flower, motto,
name origin, nickname, seal,
song, tree.................... 396
transportation statistics 396
Mathematicians, noted 818-819
Mathematics
binary numbers................. 341
cubes, cube roots............... 348
division table 346
fractions, decimal equivalents 348
glossary 344-345
multiples and submultiples ......-342
multiplication tables 346
Roman numerals 341
squares, square roots 348
(see Measures, Weights)
Mauritania.................. 622-623
anthem, flag 515, 622
area, population 622
armed forces.................. 735
birth, death rates 623
communications 623
currency 622
economy..................... 622
education, health statistics 623
geographical features 622
government 622
history....................... 623
languages, religion 622
location...................... 622
map.......................... 520
transportation statistics 623
weights and measures........... 623
Mauritius 623, 625
anthem, flag 515, 623
area, population 623
birth, death rates 625
communications 625
currency 623
economy...................... 623

education, health statistics 625
geographical features 623
government 623
history........................ 625
languages, religion 623
location 623
map........................... 523
transportation statistics 625
weights and measures........... 625
Mausoleum at Halicarnassus . 790, 808
Mayors, U.S. cities, see specific city
form of address................. 765
Mayotte (French Territorial
Collectivity) 708
McKinley, Ida (Mrs. William)
(biog.) 149-150
McKinley, William
administrations 91-92
ancestry and religion 140
biography................... 121-122
elections of 1896, 1900........... 159
uncompleted term............... 139
Measures
basis of measurement............ 340
Celsius (Centigrade) scale 343
equivalents, table 340-341
foreign weights and measures 347
metric system 340
temperature conversions......... 343
unit conversions 342
U.S. customary weights and
measures.................... 343
Meats, U.S. exports, imports 210
Medicaid and Medicare....... 257-258
Medicine
current developments........ 269-270
diseases (death rates)........... 272
drugs, recent discoveries 280
glossary................... 278-280
hospital statistics 275
medical care, costs 276
milestones of medicine 277
Nobel Prizes 858-860
noted practitioners 820-822
psychiatric terms............ 281-282
Mediterranean Sea (area, depth).... 291
Memphis, Tennessee............. 465
Mental health
patient care in facilities 282
psychiatric terms............ 281-282
Merchant marine
fleets (by country)............... 240
passenger liners, major.......... 242
Mercury (planet) 322, 327
space probes................... 280
Mercury space missions (U.S.) 332, 333
Metals
U.S. exports, imports............ 210
U.S. production................. 209
Meteorological glossary.......... 306
Meteors....................... 328
Methodist Church, see United
Methodist Church
Metric system
unit conversions 342
weights and measures............ 340
Metropolitan areas
Canadian, see Canada and
individual province
U.S.
largest metropolitan areas 245
per capita income.............. 248
Standard Consolidated
Statistical Areas 244
Mexican War
casualties, veterans 728
estimated cost in dollars 731
numbers in service.............. 728
(see Outline of U.S. History, 68)
Mexico..................... 625-627
anthem, flag 515, 625

area, population 625
armed forces.................... 735
birth, death rates 625
communications 626
currency 625
economy........................ 625
education, health statistics 625
geographical features 625
government 625
history..................... 626-627
languages, religion............... 625
location........................ 625
maps 527, 624
transportation statistics 625
weights and measures........... 626
Mexico, Gulf of (area, depth) 291
Miami, Florida 466
Michigan 396-398
birthrate, health statistics 398
Chamber of Commerce.......... 398
communications 398
economy........................ 398
education statistics.............. 398
finances 398
geographical features 398
government 398
map........................... 397
marriage, divorce rates 398
population statistics 398
state bird, flag, flower, motto,
name origin, nickname, seal,
song, tree.................... 398
transportation statistics 398
Micronesia, Federated States of 478
Midway Islands (U.S. territory)..... 476
Mileage
air 221, 234-235
cities................... 220, 221
Military aid (U.S.) 733
Military cemeteries
U.S. on foreign soil.............. 730
Military pay grades and scales
(U.S.) 729-730
Milwaukee, Wisconsin............ 466
Minerals
exports, imports (U.S.) 210
production, leading U.S. states 457
production, world 210
(see Fuels, Minerals, specific
nation, U.S. state)
Mining disasters, see Disasters/
Catastrophes, 898-909
Ministers, ambassadors
form of address................. 765
(see Ambassadors)
Minneapolis, Minnesota 466-467
Minnesota 398-400
birthrate, health statistics 400
Chamber of Commerce.......... 400
communications 400
economy........................ 400
education statistics.............. 400
finances 400
geographical features 400
government 400
map........................... 399
marriage, divorce rates 400
population statistics 400
state bird, flag, flower, motto,
name origin, nickname, seal,
song, tree.................... 400
transportation statistics 400
Minority groups in the U.S.
blacks, see Black Americans
civil rights legislation 264
employment..................... 204
population (by state) 264-265
unemployment rate 204, 265
Mint, U.S. Bureau of 195
Missiles (U.S. military), see Nuclear
armament

Mississippi.................. 400-402
birthrate, health statistics 402
Chamber of Commerce........... 402
communications 402
economy........................ 402
education statistics.............. 402
finances 402
geographical features 402
government 402
map........................... 401
marriage, divorce rates 402
population statistics 402
state bird, flag, flower, motto,
name origin, nickname, seal,
song, tree.................... 402
transportation statistics 402
Missouri 402-404
birthrate, health statistics 404
Chamber of Commerce........... 404
communications 404
economy........................ 404
education statistics.............. 404
finances 404
geographical features 404
government 404
map........................... 403
marriage, divorce rates 404
population statistics 404
state bird, flag, flower, motto,
name origin, nickname, seal,
song, tree.................... 404
transportation statistics 404
Mitterrand, François
(French president).. 570, 571, 572, 814
Mobutu Sese Seko (Joseph D.)
(Zairian president)........... 701, 702
Modern Dance Companies, see
Dance
Mohammed, Prophet (biog.)........ 884
Mohammedan, see Islam
Monaco 627-628
anthem, flag 515, 627
area, population 627
birth, death rates 627
communications 627
currency 627
economy........................ 627
education, health statistics 627
geographical features 627
government 627
history..................... 627-628
languages, religion............... 627
location........................ 627
map........................... 519
monarch (present)......... 627, 784
transportation statistics 627
weights and measures........... 627
Monarchs and dynasties
present 783-784
past 785-786
Mondale, Walter F. (biog.)......... 145
Monetary, see Currency
Monetary Fund, UN International,
see United Nations
Money, see Currency
Mongolia 628-629
anthem, flag 515, 628
area, population 628
armed forces................... 735
birth, death rates 628
communications 628
currency 628
economy........................ 628
education, health statistics 628
geographical features 628
government 628
history..................... 628-629
languages, religion............... 628
location........................ 628
map........................... 522
transportation statistics 628

weights and measures............628
Monroe, Elizabeth (Mrs. James)
(biog.)......................146-147
Monroe, James
administrations 85
ancestry and religion 140
biography..................103-104
elections of 1816, 1820...........154
Montana.............404, 405, 406
birthrate, health statistics 406
Chamber of Commerce...........406
communications 406
economy.......................406
education statistics..............406
finances 406
geographical features 406
government 406
map...........................405
marriage, divorce rates 406
population statistics 406
state bird, flag, flower, motto,
name origin, nickname, seal,
song, tree....................406
transportation statistics 406
Montserrat (British Crown Colony)...708
Moon
apogee, perigee............326, 329
as earth satellite.................327
configuration with planets.........326
description of...................326
earth, distance from.............326
phases and eclipses 329
space flights 334-335
Morocco 629-630
anthem, flag.................515, 629
area, population 629
armed forces...................735
birth, death rates 629
communications 629
currency 629
economy.......................629
education, health statistics 629
geographical features 629
government 629
history.........................630
languages, religion..............629
location.......................629
map...........................520
monarch (present)...........629, 783
transportation statistics 629
weights and measures...........629
Morse, Samuel F. B..........350, 802
Morton, Levi P. (biog.).........143-144
Moses (biog.)...................882
Moslem, see Islam
Motion pictures
Academy Awards 874-875
actors and actresses, see Celebrities: Past and Present 835-842
biggest moneymakers 843
Cannes film festival 876
directors, noted 832-834
New York Film Critics Circle Awards 876
season survey...................857
Motor vehicles
bus lines, U.S. intercity 218
production 203
(see Automobiles; specific
Canadian province; specific nation, U.S. state—transportation)
Motorcycling champions 997
Mottoes, official state, see
specific state
Mountains
highest U.S. (by state)...........301
highest world (by country) 293
(see also Volcanoes)
Movies, see Motion pictures
Mozambique..................630-631
area, population 630
armed forces...................735

birth, death rates 630
communications 630
currency 630
economy.......................630
education, health statistics 630
flag......................517, 630
geographical features 630
government 630
history.........................631
languages, religion..............630
location.......................630
map...........................521
transportation statistics 630
weights and measures...........630
Multiples and submultiples 342
Multiplication table 346
Murders, see Crime
Museums
selected U.S. (by city) 850-851
selected world..................850
Music
classical discography............846
Grammy Awards................873
popular discography.............845
Pulitzer Prizes...................870
season survey...................855
symphony orchestras, major 848
Musicians, noted 829-832
Mussolini, Benito ...598, 803, 804, 814

N

NASA, see National Aeronautics and
Space Administration
NATO, see North Atlantic Treaty
Organization
Names, common American family . 762
Namibia (South-West Africa)
(disputed territory) 708
Napoleon Bonaparte 572, 785, 801, 814
NASDAQ Composite Index
(description)....................213
Nashville, Tennessee.............467
National anthem, see specific country
**National Basketball
Association** 939-943
National defense, see Defense,
Department of
National Football League......946-952
National Guard, U.S.
units and number of men
by state......................729
National Hockey League 958-961
**National Oceanic and Atmospheric
Administration**..................307
National Park System, U.S......225-226
National Weather Service.........306
Nations of the World
accidental death rate 273
airports, major..................238
armed forces.. (selected nations)..735
bridges, leading, longest......242-243
buildings, tallest 297
canals, major ship 241
capital punishment...............263
car production 203
Communist party strength.....726-727
companies, largest..............209
cost of living 249
dependencies and territories ..704-710
deserts, great world 292
embassies in U.S................722
energy consumption.............208
exchange rates..................198
(see also specific nation)
glaciers, major..................292
gross national product...........199
(see also specific nation)

hydroelectric power 294
islands, principal.................298
lakes, large 292
languages, major 762
largest (by area)................247
merchant fleets (selected) 240
mineral production leaders.......210
mountain peaks, major 293
news events....................49-65
news maps..................38-48
newspapers, largest.............764
nuclear power growth............208
oil production...................209
passenger planes................233
populous, most 247
structures (selected).............297
suicide rates (selected
countries)....................273
tourist offices in New York 227
traffic fatality rates 219
trains, fastest...................239
tunnels, longest.................218
UN, heads of mission to 718
U.S. foreign economic
assistance 721
U.S. military aid 733
volcanoes......................295
waterfalls 295-296
weights and measures...........347
(see specific nation; Outline
of World History, 788-808)
Natural gas production (U.S.)......208
natural gas reserves.............216
Nauru 631-632
area, population 631
birth, death rates 631
communications 631
currency 631
economy.......................631
education, health statistics 631
flag......................515, 631
geographical features 631
government 631
history......................631-632
languages, religion..............631
location.......................631
map...........................528
transportation statistics 631
weights and measures...........631
Navassa Island (U.S. territory)....476
Navy, U.S. Department of 167, 168
Nebraska.............406, 407, 408
birthrate, health statistics 408
Chamber of Commerce..........408
communications 408
economy.......................408
education statistics..............408
finances 408
geographical features 408
government 408
map...........................407
marriage, divorce rates 408
population statistics 408
state bird, flag, flower, motto,
name origin, nickname, seal,
song, tree....................408
transportation statistics 408
Nebulae 318, 319
Negroes, see Black Americans
Nepal 632-633
anthem, flag.................515, 632
area, population 632
armed forces...................735
birth, death rates 632
communications 632
currency 632
economy.......................632
education, health statistics 632
geographical features 632
government 632
history......................632-633

languages, religion 632
location 632
map 523
monarch (present) 632, 783
transportation statistics 632
weights and measures 632
Neptune (planet) 324, 327
Netherlands, The 633-634
anthem, flag 515, 633
area, population 633
armed forces 735
birth, death rates 633
communications 633
currency 633
economy 633
education, health statistics 633
geographical features 633
government 633
history 633-634
languages, religion 633
location 633
map 519
monarch (present) 633, 784
transportation statistics 633
weights and measures 633
Netherlands Antilles (Netherlands
dependency) 708-709
Nevada 408, 409, 410
birthrate, health statistics 410
Chamber of Commerce 410
communications 410
economy 410
education statistics 410
finances 410
geographical features 410
government 410
map 409
marriage, divorce rates 410
population statistics 410
state bird, flag, flower, motto,
name origin, nickname, seal,
song, tree 410
transportation statistics 410
Newark, New Jersey 467
New Brunswick, Canada 488, 489
agriculture 489
area 489
birth, death rates 489
communications 489
economy 489
education statistics 489
geographical features 489
government 489
health care statistics 489
location 489
map 488
marriage, divorce rates 489
motor vehicle statistics 489
population statistics 489
revenues and expenditures 489
New Caledonia (French Overseas
Territory) 709
Newfoundland, Canada 489-491
agriculture 489
area 489
birth, death rates 489
communications 490
economy 490
education statistics 490
geographical features 490
government 490
health care statistics 490
location 490
map 491
marriage, divorce rates 489
motor vehicle statistics 490
population statistics 489
revenues and expenditures 490
New Hampshire 410, 411, 412
birthrate, health statistics 412
Chamber of Commerce 412

communications 412
economy 412
education statistics 412
finances 412
geographical features 412
government 412
map 411
marriage, divorce rates 412
population statistics 412
state bird, flag, flower, motto,
name origin, nickname, seal,
song, tree 412
transportation statistics 412
New Hebrides, see Vanuatu
New Jersey 412-414
birthrate, health statistics 414
Chamber of Commerce 414
communications 414
economy 414
education statistics 414
finances 414
geographical features 414
government 414
map 413
marriage, divorce rates 414
population statistics 414
state bird, flag, flower, motto,
name origin, nickname, seal,
song, tree 414
transportation statistics 414
New Mexico 414-417
birthrate, health statistics 416
Chamber of Commerce 417
communications 417
economy 417
education statistics 416-417
finances 416
geographical features 416
government 416
map 415
marriage, divorce rates 416
population statistics 416
state bird, flag, flower, motto,
name origin, nickname, seal,
song, tree 416
transportation statistics 416
New Orleans, Louisiana 467-468
News events
late-breaking 65
month-by-month 49-65
news maps 38-48
Newspapers
advertising volume 763
largest dailies 764
largest U.S. Sunday 764
mailing rate 766
Pulitzer Prizes 864-866, 867
(see individual nation; U.S.
state or city, Canadian province—
communications)
New World Explorers 313
New York 417-419
birthrate, health statistics 419
Chamber of Commerce 419
communications 419
economy 419
education statistics 419
finances 419
geographical features 417, 419
government 417
map 418
marriage, divorce rates 419
population statistics 419
state bird, flag, flower, motto,
name origin, nickname, seal,
song, tree 417
transportation statistics 419
New York Stock Exchange Common
Stock Index (description) 213
New York, New York 468
New Zealand 634-635

anthem, flag 515, 634
area, population 634
armed forces 735
birth, death rates 634
communications 634
currency 634
economy 634
education, health statistics 634
geographical features 634
government 634
history 635
languages, religion 634
location 634
map 528
transportation statistics 634
weights and measures 634
Nicaragua 635-636
anthem, flag 515, 635
area, population 635
armed forces 735
birth, death rates 635
communications 635
currency 635
economy 635
education, health statistics 635
geographical features 635
government 635
history 636
languages, religion 635
location 635
map 527
transportation statistics 635
weights and measures 635
Nicknames, official state, see
specific state
Niger 636-637
anthem, flag 515, 636
area, population 636
armed forces 735
birth, death rates 636
communications 636
currency 636
economy 636
education, health statistics 636
geographical features 636
government 636
history 637
languages, religion 636
location 636
map 520
transportation statistics 636
weights and measures 636
Nigeria 637-638
anthem, flag 515, 637
area, population 637
armed forces 735
birth, death rates 637
communications 637
currency 637
economy 637
education, health statistics 637
geographical features 637
government 637
history 638
languages, religion 637
location 637
map 520
transportation statistics 637
weights and measures 637
Nimeiry, Jaafar Muhammad al-
(Sudanese president) . . . 667, 668, 814
Niue (New Zealand Territory) 709
Nixon, Richard M.
administrations 97-98
ancestry and religion 140
biography 135-136
elections of 1952, 1956, 1960, 1968,
1972 162-163
minority president 139
uncompleted term 139

Nixon, Thelma ("Pat") (Mrs. Richard) (biog.) 152
Nobel Prizes 858-864
Nordic Council 720
Norfolk, Virginia 468
Norfolk Island (Australian External Territory) 709
North America
area 286
exploration 313
gold production 197
highest and lowest points 286
lakes 292
mountain peaks 293
petroleum production 209
rainfall extremes 296
religious membership 886
temperature extremes 296
volcanoes 295
waterfalls 296
North Atlantic Treaty Organization (NATO) 720
warplanes 734
North Carolina 419-421
birthrate, health statistics 421
Chamber of Commerce 421
communications 421
economy 421
education statistics 421
finances 421
geographical features 421
government 421
map 420
marriage, divorce rates 421
population statistics 421
state bird, flag, flower, motto, name origin, nickname, seal, song, tree 421
transportation statistics 421
North Dakota 421-422, 423
birthrate, health statistics 422
Chamber of Commerce 422
communications 422
economy 422
education statistics 422
finances 422
geographical features 422
government 422
map 423
marriage, divorce rates 422
population statistics 422
state bird, flag, flower, motto, name origin, nickname, seal, song, tree 422
transportation statistics 422
North Sea (area, depth) 291
Northern Ireland, see United Kingdom
Northern Marianas Islands 478
Norway 639-640
anthem, flag 515, 639
area, population 639
armed forces 735
birth, death rates 639
communications 639
currency 639
economy 639
education, health statistics 639
geographical features 639
government 639
history 639-640
languages, religion 639
location 639
map 519
monarch (present) 639, 784
transportation statistics 639
weights and measures 639
Noted personalities, see Biography
Nova Scotia, Canada 490, 492, 494
agriculture 490
area 490

birth, death rates 490
communications 490
economy 490
education statistics 490
geographical features 490
government 490
health care statistics 490
location 490
map 492
marriage, divorce rates 490
motor vehicle statistics 490
population statistics 490
revenues and expenditures 490
Novelists, noted 825-829
Nuclear armaments (U.S. and USSR) 733
description of, see footnotes, 733
Nuclear power 208
Nuclear power plants, U.S. licensed 207
Nutrition, dietary allowances 283
Nyerere, Julius (Tanzanian president) 674, 675, 814

O

OAS, see Organization of American States
OAU, see Organization of African Unity
OECD, see Organization for Economic Cooperation and Development
Obie (Off-Broadway) Awards 876
Obituaries 1000-1007
Observatories, astronomical 319-320
Occupational groups (U.S.) future needs 206
Occupations 9-37
Oceania
gold production 197
monarchs (present) 784
petroleum production 209
rainfall extremes 296
temperature extremes 296
waterfalls 295
Oceans and seas
areas, depths 291
elements in 291
islands 298
Ohio 422, 424, 425
birthrate, health statistics 424
Chamber of Commerce 424
communications 424
economy 424
education statistics 424
finances 424
geographical features 424
government 424
map 425
marriage, divorce rates 424
population statistics 424
state bird, flag, flower, motto, name origin, nickname, seal, song, tree 424
transportation statistics 424
Oil
production 208, 209, 210
U.S. imports 200
U.S. oil reserves 216
Oil Spills in U.S. 276
Oklahoma 424, 426, 427
birthrate, health statistics 426
Chamber of Commerce 426
communications 426
economy 426
education statistics 426
finances 426
geographical features 426

government 426
map 427
marriage, divorce rates 426
population statistics 426
state bird, flag, flower, motto, name origin, nickname, seal, song, tree 426
transportation statistics 426
Oklahoma City, Oklahoma 468-469
Olympian Zeus (statue by Phidias) 789, 808
Olympic Games 910-921
Summer 910-918
1980 Games 910-913
Olympic champions (past) .. 914-918
Winter 919-921
1980 Games 919
Olympic champions (past) .. 920-921
Omaha, Nebraska 469
Oman 640-641
anthem, flag 515, 640
area, population 640
armed forces 735
communications 640
currency 640
economy 640
education, health statistics 640
geographical features 640
government 640
history 640-641
languages, religion 640
location 640
map 524
monarch (present) 640, 783
transportation statistics 640
weights and measures 640
Ontario, Canada 493, 494
agriculture 494
area 494
birth, death rates 494
communications 494
economy 494
education statistics 494
geographical features 494
government 494
health care statistics 494
location 494
map 493
marriage, divorce rates 494
motor vehicle statistics 494
population statistics 494
revenues and expenditures 494
Opera
companies 847
discography, classical 846
Orbits, planetary 327
Orchestras, symphony, see Symphony orchestras
Oregon 426, 428, 429
birthrate, health statistics 428
Chamber of Commerce 428
communications 428
economy 428
education statistics 428
finances 428
geographical features 428
government 428
map 429
marriage, divorce rates 428
population statistics 428
state bird, flag, flower, motto, name origin, nickname, seal, song, tree 428
transportation statistics 428
Organization for Economic Cooperation and Development (OECD) 720
Organization of African Unity (OAU) 720
Organization of American States (OAS) 720

Organization of Petroleum
  Exporting Countries (OPEC)..... 720
Organizations
  directory of associations 877-881
  representative international.... 719-720
  U.S. contributions to 720
Oscars, see Academy Awards
Ottoman dynasty 796
Outlying areas (U.S.) 476-479

P

Pacific Islands (UN trust
  territory) 478
Pacific Ocean
  area, depth..................... 291
  islands 298
Paddleball champions 997
Paddle tennis champions 997
Pahlavi, Mohammed Reza....... 591, 593
Paine, Thomas (author)........... 800
Painters, noted 822-825
Pakistan 641-642
  anthem, flag 515, 641
  area, population 641
  armed forces................... 735
  birth, death rates 641
  communications 641
  currency....................... 641
  economy....................... 641
  education, health statistics 641
  geographical features 641
  government 641
  history........................ 642
  languages, religion............. 641
  location....................... 641
  map........................... 524
  transportation statistics 642
  weights and measures........... 642
Palestine, see Israel, Jordan
Palmyra Island (U.S. territory) 476
Pan American Union, see Organization of American States
Panama...................... 642-643
  anthem, flag 515, 642
  area, population 642
  armed forces................... 735
  birth, death rates 643
  communications 643
  currency....................... 642
  economy....................... 642
  education, health statistics 643
  geographical features 642
  government 642
  history........................ 643
  languages, religion............. 642
  location....................... 642
  map........................... 527
  transportation statistics 643
  weights and measures........... 643
Panama Canal
  cargo traffic 241
  (see also Canals, major world ship)
Papua New Guinea............ 643-644
  anthem, flag 517, 643
  area, population 643
  birth, death rates 644
  communications 644
  currency....................... 643
  economy....................... 644
  education, health statistics 644
  geographical features 644
  government 644
  history........................ 644
  languages, religion............. 643
  location....................... 644
  map........................... 528
  transportation statistics 644

weights and measures........... 644
Parachuting champions 998
Paraguay.................... 644-645
  anthem, flag 515, 644
  area, population 644
  armed forces................... 735
  birth, death rates 645
  communications 645
  currency....................... 644
  economy....................... 645
  education, health statistics 645
  geographical features 644-645
  government 645
  history........................ 645
  languages, religion............. 644
  location....................... 644
  map........................... 525
  transportation statistics 645
  weights and measures........... 645
Parcel post zone rates 767
Park Chung Hee 607, 608, 815
Parks
  U.S. national 225-226
Passport (U.S.)
  issue and renewal............... 227
Pasteur, Louis (scientist) 801, 821
Patent Appeals, U.S. Court of...... 183
Paul VI, Pope 888
Penn, William (colonizer)......... 66
Pennsylvania 428, 430-432
  birthrate, health statistics 432
  Chamber of Commerce.......... 432
  communications 432
  economy....................... 432
  education statistics.............. 432
  finances....................... 430
  geographical features 430
  government 430
  map........................... 431
  marriage, divorce rates 432
  population statistics 430
  state bird, flag, flower, motto,
    name origin, nickname, seal,
    song, tree...................... 430
  transportation statistics 432
Pentathlon 998
Pentathlon, Modern 997
  1980 Olympics 912
Perón, Isabel and Juan... 509, 510, 815
Perry, Matthew C. 68, 802
Personal expenditures (U.S.) 249
Personalities, noted, see Biography
Peru 645-646
  anthem, flag 515, 645
  area, population 645
  armed forces................... 735
  birth, death rates 646
  communications 646
  currency....................... 645
  economy....................... 646
  education, health statistics 646
  geographical features 646
  government 646
  history........................ 646
  languages, religion............. 645
  location..................... 645-646
  map........................... 525
  transportation statistics 646
  weights and measures........... 646
Peter I Island (Norwegian
  Dependency).................... 709
Petroleum
  crude oil production leaders 210
  production by country 209
  U.S. production 208
Pharos at Alexandria, Egypt
  (lighthouse).................. 790, 808
Philadelphia, Pennsylvania 469
Philippines 647-648
  anthem, flag 515, 647
  area, population 647

armed forces..................... 735
birth, death rates 647
communications 647
currency........................ 647
economy........................ 647
education, health statistics 647
geographical features 647
government 647
history.......................... 648
languages, religion............... 647
location......................... 647
map............................ 528
transportation statistics 647
weights and measures............ 647
Philosophers, noted 819-820
Phoenix, Arizona 470
Phonograph records, see Discography
Photography
  noted photographers, see Notables
    of Art and Architecture,
    822-825
  Pulitzer Prizes.................. 866
Phrases, current.............. 760-761
Physics
  glossary....................... 344
  Nobel Prizes 861-863
  (see Astronomy)
Physiology
  Nobel Prizes 858-860
  noted physiologists.......... 820-822
Pianists, noted, see Notables of
  the Musical World, 829-832
Pierce, Franklin
  administration 87-88
  ancestry and religion 140
  biography................... 111-112
  election of 1852 156
Pierce, Jane (Mrs. Franklin)
  (biog.)......................... 148
Pioneer space probes (U.S.) .. 325, 331
Pistol champions 912, 998
Pitcairn Island
  (British Colony) 709
Pittsburgh, Pennsylvania.......... 470
Pius X, Pope.................... 888
Pius XI, Pope................... 888
Pius XII, Pope.................. 888
Pizarro, Francisco . 313, 646, 796, 798,
                      815
Planets
  data........................... 327
  descriptions 322-324
  moon, configurations with........ 329
  planetary probes 324-325, 331-332
  satellites of the solar system 327
Platform tennis 998
Pluto (planet)............... 324, 327
Poetry
  Pulitzer Prizes............... 869-870
  other awards 872
Poets, noted................ 825-829
Poland 648-649
  anthem, flag 515, 648
  area, population 648
  armed forces................... 735
  birth, death rates 648
  communications 648
  currency....................... 648
  economy....................... 648
  education, health statistics 648
  geographical features 648
  government 648
  history........................ 649
  languages, religion............. 648
  location....................... 648
  map........................... 519
  transportation statistics 648
  weights and measures........... 648
Politburo, Communist
  China, People's Rep. of 727
  USSR 727

Polk, James Knox
administration 87
ancestry and religion 140
biography 109-110
election of 1844 156
minority president 139
Polk, Sarah (Mrs. James)
(biog.) 147-148
Pollution, see Air, pollution;
Oil Spills in U.S.
Polo, Marco 795, 796, 815
Polo champions 998
Popes (chronological list) 887-888
Population (U.S.)
and area 244
birthrate, see specific state
center of population, geographic
(1790-1970) 244
cities (by median family
income) 248
cities, towns (1980) 768-782
color and race (by state) 264
counties (by median family
income) (50 largest) 248
death rate 271, 272
divorce rates 251
educational attainment 737
employment 204, 265
family characteristics 251
geographic center of population
(1790-1970) 244
illegitimate births 251
immigration 246
income, per capita 186, 248
labor statistics 204
life expectancy 271
marital status, marriage rates 251
metropolitan areas, largest 245
minority groups 204, 264-265
regions 264
sex ratio 251
Standard Consolidated Statistical
Areas 244
Standard Metropolitan Statistical
Areas 245
state and rank 244
unemployment rate 204
voters, percentages (1980) 246
(see also specific city or state)
Population (world)
annual rate of increase 247
cities and countries, largest 247
growth rate 247
total 247
urban areas, largest 247
urbanization 247
(see also individual nation or
Canadian province)
Portland, Oregon 470-471
Ports
U.S., by cargo tonnage 240
world, see individual country
Portugal 649-650
anthem, flag 515, 649
area, population 649
armed forces 735
birth, death rates 650
communications 649-650
currency 649
economy 649
education, health statistics 649
geographical features 649
government 649
history 650
languages, religion 649
location 649
map 519
transportation statistics 649
weights and measures 650

Possessions, territorial
U.S. 476-479
world 702-710
Postal information
air mail rates 766
book rates 766
C.O.D. rates 766
certified mail 766
first-class rates 766
fourth-class rates 766
insured mail 766
international rates 766
letter packages 766
library rate 766
money order fees 766
parcel post rates 767
postcards 766
priority mail 766
registered mail 766
return receipts 766
second-class rates 766
special delivery rates 766
special handling 766
third-class rates 766
zip codes 768-782
Postal Service, U.S.
creation of 83
employees (no.) 167
Postal Rate Commission 169
Poverty in the U.S.
aid to families with dependent
children 260
disadvantaged: a definition 259
employment in urban poverty
areas 265
facts about the poor 259
rank by state 259
number and percent below
poverty level 259
Powerboating 998
Preakness Stakes 979
Precipitation, see Weather
President of the U.S.
cabinet 167
salary 166
White House staff 166
Presidents (heads of state) see
individual nation
Presidents of the United States
administrations 83-98
ancestry 140
biographies 99-138
birth, death dates 140-141
burial places 141
cabinets 83-98, 167
campaigns 153-165
candidates (1789-1980) 153-165
congresses 83-98
election returns (1789-1980) .. 153-165
inauguration, age at 141
minority 139
native states 140-141
political affiliation 140
religious affiliation 140
uncompleted terms 139
wives, biographies 146-152
Prime ministers
British 724
(see also individual nation—
government)
Prince Edward Island, Canada 494-496
agriculture 496
area 494
birth, death rates 494
communications 496
economy 496
education statistics 496
geographical features 494
government 494, 496
health care statistics 496

location 494
map 495
marriage, divorce rates 494
motor vehicle statistics 496
population statistics 494
revenues and expenditures 496
Prizes, see Awards
Production
automobile (U.S.) 203
farm crops (U.S.) 202
fuels 208, 209
metals (U.S.) 209
minerals (world leaders) 210
motor vehicle (world) 203
(see individual nation, U.S.
state—economy; Canadian
province—economy, motor
vehicles)
Productivity, U.S. 22-24
Protestantism
description 883
in U.S., see individual denomination under U.S. Religious Bodies,
891-897
membership 886
Providence, Rhode Island 471
Prussian rulers 786
Psychiatry
glossary of terms 281-282
Public holidays (U.S.) 312
Public libraries (U.S.) 738
Public schools (U.S.)
elementary and secondary ... 736, 738
federal aid 737
graduates, high school 736, 737
Public service awards
American Jewish Committee 871
Medals of Freedom 871
Pulitzer Prizes 866-867
Teacher of the Year 871
Puerto Rico (U.S. common-
wealth) 476-478
map 477
Pulitzer Prizes 864-870
Pulsars 315
Pyramid of Khufu (Cheops) ... 788, 808

Q

el-Qaddafi, Muammar (Libyan
leader) 613, 614, 815
Qatar 650-651
anthem, flag 516, 650
area, population 650
armed forces 735
communications 651
currency 650
economy 650
education, health statistics 650
geographical features 650
government 650
history 651
languages, religion 650
location 650
map 524
monarch (present) 650, 783
transportation statistics 651
weights and measures 651
Quarter horse racing 998
Quasars 315
Quebec, Canada 496-498
agriculture 496
area 496
birth, death rates 496
communications 496
economy 496
education statistics 496

geographical features 496
government 496
health care statistics 496
location........................496
map...........................497
marriage, divorce rates 496
motor vehicle statistics 496
population statistics 496
revenues and expenditures........496
Queen Maud Land (Norwegian
Dependency)....................709
Queens, see Monarchs and dynasties

R

Race
color and race of U.S. population......................264-265
(see Black Americans; Indians,
American; Spanish Americans)
Racing
airplane records 236-237
automobile, see Auto racing
bicycle.....................911, 996
bobsled.......................996
horse.......................978-982
ice skating 919, 921, 997
powerboat 998
roller skating 998
rowing 998
.... see Swimming
....ack and field
....ching
..................321, 327
..................763
....wards ...873

major world religions 882-886
world membership, est.........886
Popes, list of 887-888
religious holidays 888
U.S. denominations 891-897
Religionists, noted...........819-820
Repertory theatre companies (U.S.) 849
Republican party
conventions, 1856-1980......156-163,
164, 165
elections, 1856-1980 156-165
1980 election..................165
1976 election..................164
Ninety-seventh Congress
House and Senate members 174-178
presidential index 140-141
presidents, U.S. 83-98, 99-138
vice-presidents 142-145
**Resident theatrical companies
(U.S.)** 849
Retailing
largest U.S. companies..........201
retail price indexes 250
Réunion (French Overseas
Department)....................709
Revenues (U.S.)
federal government
expenditures 184, 185, 186
receipts 184, 186
state and local governments
expenditures 186
receipts 186
Revolutionary War
casualties, veterans 728
estimated cost in dollars 731
numbers in services............728
(see Outline of U.S. History, 66-67)
Rhode Island 432-434
birthrate, health statistics 434
Chamber of Commerce..........434
communications 434
economy........................434
education statistics.............434
finances 434
geographical features 432
.overnment 432
.................................433
..orce rates 434
..stics 432
.ver, motto,
.me, seal,
..................432
..................434
..................808

Roman numerals 341
Romania 651-652
anthem, flag...............516, 651
area, population 651
armed forces...................735
birth, death rates 651
communications 651
currency 651
economy.......................651
education, health statistics 651
geographical features 651
government 651
history.........................652
languages, religion 651
location........................651
map...........................519
transportation statistics 652
weights and measures...........652
Romanov, House of 786
Roosevelt, Alice (Mrs. Theodore)
(biog.)........................150
Roosevelt, Edith (Mrs. Theodore)
(biog.).........................150
Roosevelt, Eleanor (Mrs. Franklin D.)
(biog.).........................151
Roosevelt, Franklin D.
administrations 94-95
ancestry and religion 140
biography 129-130
birthday (legal holiday) 312
elections of 1932, 1936, 1940,
1944 161-162
uncompleted term...............139
Roosevelt, Theodore
administrations 92
ancestry and religion 140
biography 122-123
elections of 1900, 1904..........159
Roots (square, cube) (table) 348
Ross Dependency (New Zealand
Territory).......................709
Rowing champions 998
1980 Olympics 912
Royal families (past, present)...783-786
Rugby champions 998
Rulers, see Monarchs and dynasties
Russia, see Union of Soviet
Socialist Republics
Russian rulers (past) 786
Rwanda 652-653
anthem, flag 516, 652
ar.

Saint Lucia 653-654
    area, population 653
    birth, death rates 653
    communications 653
    currency 653
    economy 653
    education, health statistics 653
    flag 517, 653
    geographical features 653
    government 653
    history 653-654
    languages, religion 653
    location 653
    map 527
    transportation statistics 654
    weights and measures 654
Saint Paul, Minnesota 472
Saint Pierre and Miquelon (French
    Overseas Department) 709
**Saint Vincent and the
    Grenadines** 654-655
    anthem, flag 517, 654
    area, population 654
    birth, death rates 654
    communications 654
    currency 654
    economy 654
    education, health statistics 654
    geographical features 654
    government 654
    history 654-655
    languages, religion 654
    location 654
    map 527
    transportation statistics 654
    weights and measures 654
Sala y Gómez Island (Chilean
    Dependency) 709
Salaries (U.S.)
    armed forces 729-730
    federal government officials 166
    Governors, see specific state—
        government
    President 166
    Representatives 166
    Senators 166
    Supreme Court Justices 166, 183
    U.S. Judges 183
    Vice-President 166
Salazar, Antonio 650, 816

São Tomé and Principe 655-656
    anthem, flag 517, 655
    area, population 655
    birth, death rates 656
    communications 656
    currency 655
    economy 656
    education, health statistics 656
    geographical features 655
    government 655-656
    history 656
    languages, religion 655
    location 655
    map 520
    transportation statistics 656
    weights and measures 656
Sarkis, Elias (Lebanese
    president) 610, 611
Saskatchewan, Canada 498-499
    agriculture 498
    area 498
    birth, death rates 498
    communications 498
    economy 498
    education statistics 498
    geographical features 498
    government 498
    health care statistics 498
    location 498
    map 499
    marriage, divorce rates 498
    motor vehicle statistics 498
    population statistics 498
    revenues and expenditures 498
Satellites, solar, see Solar system
Satellites, space, see Space
    developments
Saturn (planet) 323-324, 327
Saudi Arabia 656-657
    anthem, flag 516, 656
    area, population 656
    armed forces 735
    birth, death rates 656
    communications 656
    currency 656
    economy . . . .
    education, health statistics . . . . .
    geographical features . . . . .
    government . . . .
    history . . . .
    languages, religion
    location . . . .
    map . . . . .
    monarch

Seattle, Washington 474-475
Seawater
    elements in 291
Secretariat, UN 713
Security Council, UN 712-713, 717
Senate, U.S., see Congress, U.S.
Senegal 657-658
    anthem, flag 516, 657
    area, population 657
    armed forces 735
    birth, death rates 658
    communications 658
    currency 657
    economy 658
    education, health statistics 658
    geographical features 657
    government 657-658
    history 658
    languages, religion 657
    location 657
    map 520
    transportation statistics 658
    weights and measures 658
**Seven Wonders of the Ancient
    World** 808
Seychelles 658-659
    anthem, flag 516, 658
    area, population 658
    communications 659
    currency 658
    economy 659
    education, health statistics 659
    geographical features 658
    government 658-65
    history . . . .
    languages, religion . . . .
    location . . . .
    map . . . .
    transportation statistics
    weights and measur
Shakespeare, Will
Sherman, Jam
Shintoism

T

Table of equivalents..........340-341
Table tennis champions...........999
Taft, Helen (Mrs. William H.)
  (biog.)..........................150
Taft, William H.
  administration................92-93
  ancestry and religion...........140
  biography..................123-124
  elections of 1908, 1912.........160
Taiwan (Formosa), see China,
  Nationalist
Tampa, Florida................475
Tanzania....................674-675
  anthem, flag.............516, 674
  area, population.............674
  armed forces.................735
  birth, death rates...........674
  communications..............674
  currency......................674
  economy......................674
  education, health statistics....674
  geographical features.........674
  government...................674
  history.......................675
  languages, religion...........674
  location......................674
  map..........................521
  transportation statistics......674
  weights and measures..........674
Taoism
  description...................885
  Lao-tze.................885-886
  membership..................886
Taxes
  selected countries............190
  U.S.
    city
      income taxes.............194
      sales tax rates...........194
    federal
      collections..............190
      expediture of tax dollars....185
      income taxes............187
      income tax hints......188-189
    state
      income, by state.....191-193
      sales and use tax rates....194
Taylor, Margaret (Mrs. Zachary)
  (biog.)........................148
Taylor, Zachary
  administration.................87
  ancestry and religion..........140
  biography..................110-111
  election of 1848...............156
  minority president.............139
  uncompleted term..............139
Telephones
  number, see individual
    nation, U.S. state or city, Canadian
    province—communications
Telescopes, astronomical.....319-320
Television
  advertising leaders............764
  advertising volume............763
  Emmy Awards..................873
  George Foster Peabody Awards...873
  number of receivers or
    stations, see individual nation,
    U.S. city, Canadian province—
    communications
  season survey..................856
Temperature
  cities
    U.S.....................304-305
    world..................228-229
  conversion table..............343
  extremes

U.S. (by state)............302, 303
  world...................296, 298
  wind chill...................303
Tennessee..................438-440
  birthrate, health statistics.....440
  Chamber of Commerce...........440
  communications................440
  economy......................440
  education statistics............440
  finances.....................440
  geographical features.........440
  government...................440
  map..........................439
  marriage, divorce rates........440
  population statistics..........440
  state bird, flag, flower, motto,
    name origin, nickname, seal,
    song, tree..................440
  transportation statistics......440
Tennis.....................971-972
  college champions.......971, 972
  Davis Cup...................971
  Federation Cup..............972
  money winners...............972
  foreign championships.....970-971
  U.S. Open champions..........969
  Wightman Cup................970
  Wimbledon champions.........970
Tennis, Platform—champions......998
Tennis, Table—champions........999
Territorial expansion, U.S.......479
Territorial judges, U.S.........183
Territories and dependencies
  U.S......................476-479
  world...................702-710
Texas.....................440-443
  birthrate, health statistics.....443
  Chamber of Commerce..........443
  communications................443
  economy................441, 443
  education statistics............443
  finances.....................441
  geographical features.........441
  government...................441
  map..........................442
  marriage, divorce rates........443
  population statistics..........441
  state bird, flag, flower, motto,
    name origin, nickname, seal,
    song, tree..................441
  transportation statistics......443
Thailand...................675-676
  anthem, flag.............516, 675
  area, population.............675
  armed forces.................735
  birth, death rates...........675
  communications..............675
  currency......................675
  economy......................675
  education, health statistics....675
  geographical features.........675
  government...................675
  history.......................676
  languages, religion...........675
  location......................675
  map..........................523
  monarch (present)........675, 783
  transportation statistics......675
  weights and measures..........675
Thatcher, Margaret (British prime
  minister)............687, 688, 817
Theatre
  actors, actresses, see Celebrities:
    Past and Present, 835-842
  Broadway runs, longest........844
  dramatists, noted.......825-829, 868
  Obie Awards.................876
  professional resident theatres...849
  Pulitzer Prizes...............868
  repertory theatres............849
  season survey................854

Tony Awards...................876
Theatrical companies (U.S.)......849
Theologians, noted.........819-820
Thoroughbred racing........978-980
  Belmont Stakes...............980
  Kentucky Derby..............979
  leading money winners........978
  Preakness Stakes.............979
  Triple Crown................978
  world records...............980
Tidal waves, see Disasters/
  Catastrophes, 898-909
Time
  conversion from GMT..........329
  Daylight Saving..............307
  difference for cities (world)....241
  Standard Time..........241, 307
  sunrise, sunset table......308-309
  zones
    map........................517
    U.S........................307
    world......................517
Tito, Josip Broz..........700, 817
Tobacco
  U.S. exports, imports.........210
  U.S. production..............202
Togo.......................676-677
  anthem, flag.............516, 676
  area, population.............676
  armed forces.................735
  birth, death rates...........677
  communications..............677
  currency......................676
  economy......................676
  education, health statistics....676
  geographical features.........676
  government...............676-677
  history.......................677
  languages, religion...........676
  location......................676
  map..........................520
  transportation statistics......677
  weights and measures..........677
Tokelau (New Zealand
  Territory)....................710
Toll-free telephone numbers...223-224
Tompkins, Daniel D. (biog.)......142
Tonga......................677-678
  anthem, flag.............516, 677
  area, population.............677
  birth, death rates...........678
  communications..............678
  currency......................677
  economy................677-678
  education, health statistics....678
  geographical features.........677
  government...................677
  history.......................678
  languages, religion...........677
  location......................677
  map..........................528
  monarch (present).......677, 784
  transportation statistics......678
  weights and measures..........678
Tony (Antoinette Perry) Awards....876
Tornadoes, see Disasters/
  Catastrophes, 898-909
Tourist offices, addresses
  (in New York)................227
Track and field
  American records.............988
  1980 Olympics...............913
  Summer Olympic
    champions..............915-918
  U.S. champions..........985-988
  world records...............989
Trade
  Canada..................500, 503
  U.S...............210, 211, 240
  world summary...............211
  (see Exports, imports; specific
    nation—economy)

Traffic
airline 233, 238, 239
auto traffic fatality rates 219
Panama Canal 241
ports, major U.S. 240
railroads, U.S. 217
Trains (fastest) 239
Transkei 664
Transportation, *see Automobiles,*
Aviation, Bus Lines, Railroads,
Shipping, Ships
Transportation, U.S. Department
of 167, 168
creation of 83
Trapshooting champions
1980 Olympics 912
Travel, foreign
customs duty rates 232
customs regulations 230-231
health recommendations 231
passports 227
tourist offices 227
visa requirements 227
Treasury, U.S. Department of . . 167, 168
Trees, official state, *see individual*
U.S. state
Trinidad and Tobago 678-679
anthem, flag 516, 678
area, population 678
birth, death rates 678
communications 678
currency 678
economy 678
education, health statistics 678
geographical features 678
government 678
history 679
languages, religion 678
location 678
map 525
transportation statistics 679
weights and measures 679
Triple Crown (racing) 978
Trophies, *see Sports*
Trotsky, Leon 686, 817
Troy (ancient city) 788
Troy weight (measure) 343
Trudeau, Pierre (Canadian prime
minister) 480, 482, 484, 817
Truman, Elizabeth (Mrs. Harry S)
(biog.) 151
Truman, Harry S
administrations 95-96
ancestry and religion 140
biography 130-131
birthday (legal holiday) 312
elections of 1944, 1948 162
minority president 139
Trust Territory, U.S. 478
Trusteeship Council, UN 713, 717
Tuition (selected colleges) 739-756
Tunisia 679-680
anthem, flag 516, 679
area, population 679
armed forces 735
birth, death rates 679
communications 679
currency 679
economy 679
education, health statistics 679
geographical features 679
government 679
history 680
languages, religion 679
location 679
map 520
transportation statistics 679
weights and measures 679
Tunnels
railroad (world) 218
vehicular (U.S.) 217

Turkey 680-681
anthem, flag 516, 680
area, population 680
armed forces 735
birth, death rates 680
communications 680
currency 680
economy 680
education, health statistics 680
geographical features 680
government 680
history 681
languages, religion 680
location 680
map 524
transportation statistics 680
weights and measures 680
Turks and Caicos Islands (British
Colony) 709-710
Tuvalu 681-682
area, population 681
communications 682
currency 681
economy 682
education, health statistics 682
flag 517, 681
government 682
history 682
languages, religion 681
location 681-682
map 528
transportation statistics 682
weights and measures 682
Tyler, John
administration 86-87
ancestry and religion 140
biography 108-109
elections of 1836, 1840 155
Tyler, Leticia (Mrs. John)
(biog.) 147
Typhoons, *see Disasters/Catas-*
trophes, 898-909

U

UNESCO, *see United Nations Educa-*
tional, Scientific and Cultural
Organization
Uganda 682-683
anthem, flag 516, 682
area, population 682
armed forces 735
birth, death rates 682
communications 683
currency 682
economy 682
education, health statistics 682-683
geographical features 682
government 682
history 683
languages, religion 682
location 682
map 520
transportation statistics 683
weights and measures 683
Ulster (Northern Ireland), *see*
United Kingdom
Unemployment in the U.S.
by sex and color
rate, total 204
insurance and benefits 206
urban poverty areas 265
(see individual Canadian
province—economy)
Union of South Africa, *see South*
Africa, Republic of
Union of Soviet Socialist
Republics 683-686

anthem, flag 516, 683
area, population 683
armaments 733, 734
armed forces 735
birth, death rates 685
communications 685
currency 683
economy 685
education, health statistics 685
government 685
history 686
languages, religion 683
location 683, 685
manned space flights, *see Space*
developments
maps 39, 519, 522, 684
planetary probes, *see Space*
developments
Politburo, Secretariat 727
transportation statistics 685
weights and measures 685
Unions, labor 26, 27, 205
Unit conversions (table) 342
United Arab Emirates 686-687
anthem, flag 516, 686
area, population 686
armed forces 735
communications 686
currency 686
economy 686
education, health statistics 686
geographical features 686
government 686
history 686-687
languages, religion 686
location 686
map 524
transportation statistics 686
weights and measures 686
United Kingdom 687-688
anthem, flag 516, 687
area, population 687
armed forces 735
birth, death rates 687
Commonwealth 725
communications 687
currency 687
economy 687
education, health statistics 687
geographical features 687
government 687
history 688
languages, religion 687
location 687
map 519
monarchs (past,
present) 687, 784, 785
Northern Ireland 687, 688
prime ministers 724
Scotland 687, 688
transportation statistics 687
Wales 687
weights and measures 687
United Methodist Church
see under U.S. Religious Bodies,
891-897
United Nations
Economic and Social Council . 713, 717
Food and Agriculture
Organization (FAO) 714
General Agreement on Tariffs
and Trade (GATT) 714
General Assembly 711-712
presidents 718
heads of missions 718
Inter-Governmental Maritime
Consultative Organization (IMCO) 714
International Atomic Energy
Agency (IAEA) 714
International Bank for
Reconstruction and Development
(IBRD) 714

International Civil Aviation
Organization (ICAO)............714
International Court of
Justice....................713, 717
International Development
Association (IDA)............714
International Finance Corporation
(IFC)........................714
International Fund for Agricultural
Development (IFAD)...........714
International Labour
Organization (ILO) 714
International Monetary Fund
(IMF)......................714
International Telecommunications
Union (ITU)..................714
languages 711
member nations 711
membership, principal organs. 711-714,
717
representative international
organizations...........719-720
Secretariat 713
Secretaries-General............716
Security Council........712-713, 717
specialized agencies 713-715
structure.....................711
35th session 712
Trusteeship Council..........713, 717
United Nations Educational,
Scientific and Cultural Organi-
zation (UNESCO)............715
United Nations Children's Fund
(UNICEF)...................715
United Nations Development
Programme (UNDP)...........715
United Nations Environment
Programme (UNEP)...........715
United Nations Fund for Population
Activities (UNFPA) 715
United Nations High Commissioner
for Refugees (UNHCR) 715
United Nations Industrial
Development Organization
(UNIDO) 715
Universal Postal Union (UPU) 715
U.S. contributions to 720
U.S. Representatives and
Delegates....................717
World Health Organization (WHO) . 715
World Intellectual Property
Organization (WIPO) 715
World Meteorological Organi-
zation (WMO) 715
**United Nations Educational, Scien-
tific and Cultural Organization
(UNESCO)...................715**
**United Nations Children's Fund
(UNICEF).....................715**
**United Nations Development
Programme (UNDP)...............715**
**United Nations Environment
Programme (UNEP)...............715**
**United Nations Fund for Population
Activities (UNFPA)...............715**
**United Nations High Commissioner
for Refugees (UNHCR) 715**
**United Nations Industrial
Development Organization
(UNIDO) 715**
United States
abortion law, debate..............275
advertising volume 763, 764
agricultural porduction, leading
states 457
air distance 221
air pollution 276
airports, major..................233
Amtrak 218
anthem, national................689
area..........................688

armed forces 729, 731, 734, 735
automobile statistics..............219
aviation statistics 233, 239
awards, *see Awards*
birth, death rates 689
(*see individual state—birthrate*)
black Americans, *see Black Americans*
boundaries......................689
bridges: leading, longest......242-243
buildings, tallest 297
bus lines, intercity...............218
canals.........................241
capital punishment...............263
cities: latitudes, longitudes 308
representative cities 458-475
weather..................304-305
coastline (by state)..............300
coinage, *see Currency—U.S.*
colleges, *see Colleges and universities*
Conrail 218
cost of living 249, 250
crime statistics, *see Crime in U.S.*
currency, *see Currency—U.S.*
customary weights and measures. . 343
customs, *see Customs, U.S.*
dams..........................294
death rates (causes) 272
dependencies 476-478
dates of acquisition 479
deserts 292
disasters, *see Disasters/Catas-
trophes, 898-909*
divorce statistics, laws ... 251, 252-253
drugs, uses and abuses 261
economic statistics...........195-215
education, *see Education—U.S.*
elevations, average, extreme 300
employment, *see Employment in
the U.S.*
energy consumption, demand,
reserves...............208, 216
executions in the U.S.............263
exports........................210, 211
extreme points..................299
family budget, urban 249
family population characteristics ...251
film directors, noted 833-834
flag 516, 688-689
foreign embassies in U.S..........722
foreign exchange rates 198
foreign trade..............210, 211
fuels: production, consumption 208, 209, 216
geographic centers 244, 299
geographic features 689
gross national product (GNP) . 199, 689
Hall of Fame 858
health and medicine..........269-283
holidays 312
homicides......................273
hospital costs 275
hydropower................216, 294
illegitimate births...............251
immigration 246
imports 203, 210, 211
income, *see Incomes (U.S.)*
income taxes, city...............194
income taxes, federal 187, 190
income taxes, state 191-193
infant and neonatal mortality
rates 271
labor force 204
labor unions....................205
lakes, large 301
libraries, public 738
life expectancy 271
magazines, leading 763
manpower needs, future 206
maps 46, 351
marriage statistics, laws . 251, 253, 254

mental health care 282
merchant fleet...................240
metals production 209
metropolitan areas, largest 245
mileage between cities 220-222
military cemeteries abroad 730
military forces......729, 731, 734, 735
mineral production, leading
states 457
minority groups, *see Minority
groups, U.S.*
monetary system, *see Currency—U.S.*
mountain peaks, highest..........301
narcotics arrests 260
National Park System 225-226
natural gas production............208
natural gas reserves..............216
news events....................49-65
news maps.................38-48
newspapers, largest..............764
nuclear power..............208, 216
nuclear power plants, licensed......207
oil production 208, 209, 210, 216
oil reserves 216
passenger planes.................233
passports 227
personal expenditures 249
petroleum production.............209
population, *see Population (U.S.)*
postal information 766-767
poverty, *see Poverty in the U.S.*
radio statistics 689, 763
railroads 217, 218, 222, 239
religious groups...............891-897
rivers, principal 301
road mileage table 220
shipping at selected ports........240
Social Security benefits........255-258
societies and associations 877-881
space developments, *see Space
developments*
States, *see States of the U.S.*
structures, selected world 297
suicides 273
sunrise, sunset table 308-309
telescopes, notable 319-320
television statistics 689, 763, 764
temperature extremes 302
territories 476-479
governors, *see U.S. Outlying
Areas, 476-478*
time zones......................307
trade, foreign...........210, 211, 240
travel requirements 227, 230-232
tunnels: railroad, vehicular....217, 218
unemployment insurance 206
unemployment statistics......204, 265
universities 739-757
venereal disease 270, 273
veterans' benefits 732
vital statistics...................689
volcanoes......................295
volunteer services................723
voting requirements, *see specific
state—government*
wars
casualties 728, 731
cost and loans...............731
veterans 728
waterfalls 296
weather....................302-305
weights and measures............343
welfare aid 260
women's rights 266
work and training programs 737
zip codes 768-782
Federal Government
agencies...................168-169
armed forces, *see Armed Forces, U.S.*
budget......................184-186
cabinets, presidential.......83-98, 167

civil rights legislation 264
Congress, see Congress, U.S.
Constitution 79-82
contributions to international
  organizations 720
courts, see Courts—U.S.
customs, see Customs, U.S.
defense expenditures............. 728
departments, federal 167-169
diplomats abroad 723
education, federal aid to 738
employment...................... 167
executive departments........ 166-169
expenditures 184, 185
finances 186
foreign economic aid 721
grants to states................. 185
income taxes 187-194
independent agencies 169
Internal Revenue Service 187
Joint Chiefs of Staff 731
military aid 733
military cemeteries abroad 730
military expenditures 728
military forces, see Armed
  Forces, U.S.
military-industrial complex......... 735
military pay grades.............. 730
military pay scales 729
National Guard 729
National Park System 225-226
National Weather Service 306
nuclear armaments 733
outlying areas 476-479
Presidents, see Presidents of
  the U.S.
Representatives, see Congress, U.S.
representatives and delegates to UN 717
salaries....................... 166
Senators, see Congress, U.S.
Social Security 255-258
Supreme Court Justices. . 180-182, 183
veterans' benefits 732
Vice-presidents (biog.)........ 142-145
warplanes...................... 734
White House staff............... 166
History
  armed forces 728, 731
  black American history 266-268
  Constitution 74-82
  Declaration of Independence 72-74
  disasters, see Disasters/Catas-
    trophes, 898-909
  elections, presidential 153-165
  exploration 313
  news events 49-65
    news maps................. 38-48
  1976 election results 164
  1980 election results 165
  outline of U.S. history.......... 66-71
  Presidents, see Presidents of
    the U.S.
  Vice-presidents (biog.) 142-145
  war casualties, costs......... 728, 731
Universal Postal Union, UN (UPU) . 715
Universe, origin of 314
Universities, see Colleges and
  universities
Upper Volta 689-690
  anthem, flag 516, 689
  area, population 689
  armed forces 735
  birth, death rates 689
  communications 689
  currency 689
  economy.................... 689
  education, health statistics 689
  geographical features 689
  government 689
  history..................... 690
  languages, religion............ 689

location....................... 689
map.......................... 520
transportation statistics 689
weights and measures.......... 690
Uranus (planet)............ 324, 327
Uruguay..................... 690-691
  anthem, flag 516, 690
  area, population 690
  armed forces 735
  birth, death rates 690
  communications 690
  currency 690
  economy.................... 690
  education, health statistics 690
  geographical features 690
  government 690
  history..................... 691
  languages, religion........... 690
  location.................... 690
  map....................... 525
  transportation statistics 690
  weights and measures......... 690
USSR, see Union of Soviet Socialist
  Republics
U Thant 716
Utah 443-445
  birthrate, health statistics 445
  communications 445
  economy.................... 445
  education statistics............ 445
  finances.................... 445
  geographical features 445
  government 443, 445
  map....................... 444
  marriage, divorce rates 445
  population statistics 445
  state bird, flag, flower, motto,
    name origin, nickname, seal,
    song, tree.................. 443
  transportation statistics 445
Utilities
  largest U.S. companies........... 201

V

Vaccinations required for travel,
  see Travel, foreign
Van Buren, Hannah (Mrs. Martin)
  (biog.)..................... 147
Van Buren, Martin
  administration 86
  ancestry and religion 140
  biography.................. 107-108
  elections of 1832, 1836, 1840,
    1848 155-156
Vanuatu...................... 691-692
  area, population 691
  birth, death rates 691
  communications 692
  currency 691
  economy.................... 691
  education, health statistics 691
  flag..................... 517, 691
  geographical features 691
  government 691
  history..................... 692
  languages, religion........... 691
  location.................... 691
  map....................... 528
  transportation statistics 691
  weights and measures.......... 692
Vatican City 692-693
  anthem, flag 516, 692
  area, population 692
  communications 693
  currency 692
  economy.................... 693
  education statistics............ 693
  government 693
  history..................... 693

languages 692
location.................... 692-693
map.......................... 519
transportation statistics 693
weights and measures........... 693
Venda....................... 664
Venera space probes (Soviet). . 324-325
Venereal disease in the U.S. . . 270, 273
Venezuela 693-694
  anthem, flag 516, 693
  area, population 693
  armed forces 735
  birth, death rates 694
  communications 694
  currency 693
  economy.................... 694
  education, health statistics 694
  geographical features 693
  government 693
  history..................... 694
  languages, religion........... 693
  location.................... 693
  map....................... 525
  transportation statistics 694
  weights and measures.......... 694
Venus (planet)............. 322, 327
  space probes 324-325, 331
Vermont.................... 445-447
  birthrate, health statistics 447
  Chamber of Commerce......... 447
  communications 447
  economy.................... 447
  education statistics............ 447
  finances.................... 447
  geographical features 447
  government 445
  map....................... 446
  marriage, divorce rates 447
  population statistics 447
  state bird, flag, flower, motto,
    name origin, nickname, seal,
    song, tree.................. 445
  transportation statistics 447
Veterans (U.S.)
  benefits.................... 732
  by war..................... 728
Vice-Presidents of the U.S.
  accession to presidency 142
  address, form of 765
  administrations 83-98
  biographies 142-145
  candidates (1789-1980) 153-165
  uncompleted terms............ 139
  (see also Presidents of the U.S.—
    biographies, 99-138)
Victoria (British queen) 688, 785, 801, 817
Vietnam 695-696
  anthem, flag 516, 695
  area, population 695
  armed forces 735
  birth, death rates 695
  communications 695
  currency 695
  economy.................... 695
  education, health statistics 695
  geographical features 695
  government 695
  history..................... 696
  languages, religion........... 695
  location.................... 695
  map....................... 523
  transportation statistics 695
  weights and measures.......... 695
Vietnamese in U.S.
  population (by state) 265
Vietnam War
  casualties, veterans 728, 731
  estimated cost in dollars 731
  numbers in U.S. services 728
  (see Outline of World History,
    806; Vietnam)

Viking space probes (U.S.) 323, 325, 332
da Vinci, Leonardo................797
Virgin Islands (British territory) 705
Virgin Islands (U.S. territory) 478
  map...............................477
Virginia 447-449
  birthrate, health statistics 449
  Chamber of Commerce...........449
  communications 449
  economy.........................449
  education statistics..............449
  finances 449
  geographical features 449
  government 449
  map............................448
  marriage, divorce rates 449
  population statistics 449
  state bird, flag, flower, motto,
    name origin, nickname, seal,
    song, tree..................449
  transportation statistics 449
Visas, see Travel, foreign
Volcanoes
  eruptions, see Disasters/Catas-
    trophes, 898-909
  notable 295
Volleyball champions 999
  1980 Olympics 913
  Summer Olympic champions 918
Volume (measure) 340, 341
  (see also Tables of U.S. Customary
    Weights and Measures, 343)
Volunteer services, U.S...........723
Voshkhod space missions (Soviet) 333
Vostok space missions (Soviet)....333
Votes, U.S. (presidential) electoral
  and popular
  1980 election 165, 246
  1976 election 164, 246
  1789-1820 (electoral only) 153-154
  1824-1972 154-163
Voting requirements, state, see
  specific state—government
Voyager space probes (U.S.) ..325, 332

W

WCC, see World Council
  of Churches
WHO, see World Health Organization
WMO, see World Meteorological
  Organization
Wake Island (U.S. territory)........478
Waldheim, Kurt (UN Secretary-
  General) 716, 817
Wallace, Henry A. (biog.) 145
Wallhauser, Henry T. (music
  survey)........................855
Wallis and Futuna (French
  Overseas Territory)..............710
Wall Street
  glossary of financial terms 212-213
  stock indexes (descriptions).......213
War Department, see Defense,
  Department of
War of 1812
  casualties, veterans 728
  estimated cost in dollars 731
  numbers in services..............728
  (see Outline of U.S. History, 67)
Warplanes
  NATO, Warsaw Pact Nations.......734
  U.S. and USSR.................734
Wars
  American casualties, costs,
    loans 728, 731
  see also News events;
    Outline of World History, 788-808;
    specific nation; specific U.S. war

Warsaw Pact, see Eastern European
  Mutual Assistance Treaty
Washington 449-451
  birthrate, health statistics 451
  Chamber of Commerce...........451
  communications 451
  economy........................451
  education statistics..............451
  finances 451
  geographical features 451
  government 451
  map............................450
  marriage, divorce rates 451
  population statistics 451
  state bird, flag, flower, motto,
    name origin, nickname, seal,
    song, tree...................451
  transportation statistics 451
Washington, George
  administrations 83
  ancestry and religion 140
  biography....................99-100
  birthday (legal holiday) 312
  elections of 1789, 1792..........153
  signer of the Constitution 79
Washington, Martha (Mrs. George)
  (biog.)..........................146
Washington, D.C.................475
Water polo champions 999
  1980 Olympics 913
  Summer Olympic champions.....918
Water power, see Hydropower
Water skiing champions..........999
Waterfalls (major world).......295-296
Waterloo (battle) 801
Weather
  cities
    U.S......................304-305
    world....................228-229
  glossary of meteorological
    terms.......................306
  hurricane names (1982) 306
  rainfall extremes.............296, 298
  temperature extremes
    U.S......................302-304
    world....................296, 298
  wind chill 303
  (see Disasters/Catastrophes,
    898-909)
Wedding anniversary gifts........782
Weightlifting
  1980 Olympics 913
  U.S. champions 999
  world champions 999
Weights
  atomic.........................337
  avoirdupois......................343
  conversion tables.............342, 343
  equivalents, table of 340-341
  foreign 347
  masses, weights of..............341
  metric system 340
  multiples, submultiples
    (table).......................342
Weights and measures, customary
  U.S............................343
Welfare in the U.S.
  aid to families with dependent
    children......................260
West African Economic Community
  (CEAO) 720
Western Samoa.............696-697
  anthem, flag 516, 696
  area, population 696
  birth, death rates 697
  communications 697
  currency 696
  economy........................697
  education, health statistics 697
  geographical features 696-697
  government 697

  history...........................697
  languages, religion...............696
  location 696
  map............................528
  transportation statistics 697
  weights and measures...........697
West Germany, see Germany,
  Federal Republic of
West Virginia 451-453
  birthrate, health statistics 453
  Chamber of Commerce...........453
  communications 453
  economy........................453
  education statistics..............453
  finances 453
  geographical features 453
  government 453
  map............................452
  marriage, divorce rates 453
  population statistics 453
  state bird, flag, flower, motto,
    name origin, nickname, seal,
    song, tree...................453
  transportation statistics 453
Wheat
  exports (U.S.) 210
  production (U.S.)................202
Wheeler, William A. (biog.).........143
Whig party (U.S.)
  elections of 1836, 1840, 1844, 1848,
    1852 155-156
  presidential affiliations with.......140
Whirlwinds, see Disasters/Catas-
  trophes, 898-909
White House staff................166
Widows (number of U.S.).........251
Wildfires, see Disasters/Catas-
  trophes, 898-909
Wildlife, endangered 290
William the Conqueror.......688, 794
Wilson, Edith (Mrs. Woodrow)
  (biog.).........................150
Wilson, Ellen (Mrs. Woodrow)
  (biog.).........................150
Wilson, Henry (biog.).............143
Wilson, Woodrow
  administrations 93
  ancestry and religion 140
  biography..................124-125
  elections of 1912, 1916.........160
  minority president................139
Wimbledon tennis champions 970
Wind chill factor, see Weather
Windsor (House of)...........784, 785
Wisconsin....................453-455
  birthrate, health statistics 455
  Chamber of Commerce...........455
  communications 455
  economy........................455
  education statistics..............455
  finances 455
  geographical features 455
  government 455
  map............................454
  marriage, divorce rates 455
  population statistics 455
  state bird, flag, flower, motto,
    name origin, nickname, seal,
    song, tree...................455
  transportation statistics 455
Women
  education and income 738
  height, weight 283
  marriage and divorce statistics 251
  Social Security benefits.......255-258
  unemployment rate..............204
Women's rights (chronology) 266
  Equal Rights Amendment.........266
Wonders of the Ancient World,
  Seven 808
Words, current 760-761

Work ethic 28, 31
Working conditions 22-25, 32-35
World Bank, see International Bank
for Reconstruction and Development
World cities, see Cities, world
World Council of Churches (WCC) . 720
World Court, see International Court
of Justice
World economic summary 211
World figures (biographies) 808-817
World Health Organization, UN
(WHO) 715
World History 788-808
World Meteorological Organization,
UN (WMO) 715
World nations, see Nations of the
World
World Rulers (present) 727, 783-784
(see also individual nation—
government)
World Series (baseball) . . . 927-928, 930
World trade
U.S. 210, 211
(see specific nation—economy)
World War I
estimated cost in dollars 731
numbers in U.S. services 728
U.S. casualties, veterans 728
(see Outline of U.S. History, 70;
Outline of World History, 803)
World War II
estimated cost in dollars 731
numbers in U.S. services 728
U.S. casualties, veterans 728
(see Outline of U.S. History, 70-71;
Outline of World History, 803-
804, 805)
Wrestling
1980 Olympics 913
U.S. champions 995
world champions 995
Writers, noted 825-829
Wyoming 455-457
birthrate, health statistics 457
communications 457
economy 457
education statistics 457
finances 457
geographical features 457
government 457
map 456
marriage, divorce rates 457
population statistics 457
state bird, flag, flower, motto,
name origin, nickname, seal,
song, tree 457
transportation statistics 457

X

Xerxes (Persian king) 789
X-ray (discovery) 801

Y

Yachting
1980 Olympics 913
U.S. champions 999
Yemen (Yemen Arab Republic) . 697-698
anthem, flag 517, 697
area, population 697
armed forces 735
birth, death rates 697
communications 697-698
currency 697
economy 697
education, health statistics 697
geographical features 697
government 697
history 698
languages, religion 697
location 697
map 524
transportation statistics 698
weights and measures 698
Yemen People's Democratic Republic,
see Southern Yemen
Yorktown (battle) 67
Yugoslavia 699-700
anthem, flag 517, 699
area, population 699
armed forces 735
birth, death rates 700
communications 700
currency 699
economy 700
education, health statistics 700
geographical features 699
government 699
history 700
languages, religion 699
location 699
map 519
transportation statistics 700
weights and measures 700

Z

Zaire 701-702
anthem, flag 517, 701

area, population 701
armed forces 735
birth, death rates 701
communications 701
currency 701
economy 701
education, health statistics 701
geographical features 701
government 701
history 702
languages, religion 701
location 701
map 520
transportation statistics 701
weights and measures 701
Zambia 702-703
anthem, flag 517, 702
area, population 702
armed forces 735
birth, death rates 702
communications 702
currency 702
economy 702
education, health statistics 702
geographical features 702
government 702
history 703
languages, religion 702
location 702
map 521
transportation statistics 703
weights and measures 703
Zeus (statue by Phidias) 789, 808
Zhou Enlai (Chinese
leader) 549, 550, 817
Zimbabwe 703-704
anthem, flag 517, 703
area, population 703
armed forces 735
birth, death rates 703
communications 703
currency 703
economy 703
education, health statistics 703
geographical features 703
government 703
history 704
languages, religion 703
location 703
map 521
transportation statistics 704
weights and measures 704
Zip codes, U.S. 768-782
Zond space probes (Soviet) 324